FRISTON ON COSTS

FRISTON ON COSTS

THIRD EDITION

General Editor

DR MARK FRISTON

MA (Cantab), MB BChir, MRCP, FIILPM (Hon), Barrister of the Middle Temple

Contributors

MR RONALD J BAKER *Broadcaster and Founder, VeraSage Institute, California*
MR IMRAN BENSON *Barrister at Hailsham Chambers*
DISTRICT JUDGE IAN BESFORD *Regional Costs Judge, Kingston upon Hull*
MASTER SIMON BROWN *Costs Judge, Senior Courts Costs Office*
DEPUTY MASTER COLIN CAMPBELL *Deputy Costs Judge and Consultant at Kain Knight*
MR JOHN CHISHOLM *John Chisholm Consulting, Victoria*
MR KEVIN DE HAAN QC *Queen's Counsel at Gough Square Chambers*
MR JONATHON DINGLE FRSA *Barrister and Mediator, The Society of Mediators*
PROF PAUL FENN *Emeritus Professor of Insurance Studies, Nottingham University Business School*
PROF MICHAEL FURMSTON *Emeritus Professor of Law, Singapore Management University*
HIS HONOUR JUDGE MARK GOSNELL *Designated Civil Judge, Leeds*
HIS HONOUR JUDGE RICHARD HACON *Presiding Judge, Intellectual Property Enterprise Court*
MS LIZ HARRIS *Director, Ovid Consulting, Victoria*
MASTER PETER HAWORTH *Costs Judge, Senior Courts Costs Office*
MASTER JENNIFER JAMES *Costs Judge, Senior Courts Costs Office*
MR DAVID JUCKES *Barrister at Hailsham Chambers*
MR KEVIN LATHAM *Barrister at Kings Chambers*
MASTER COLUM LEONARD *Costs Judge, Senior Courts Costs Office*
MS LIZ LOVE *Costs Lawyer at Clyde & Co LLP*
DISTRICT JUDGE RICHARD LUMB *Regional Costs Judge, Birmingham*
MR ROCCO PIROZZOLO *Solicitor and Underwriting Director, Quantum Legal Costs Cover Ltd*
MR ROGER QUICK *Solicitor and legal author, Queensland*
MR NICK ROWLES-DAVIES *Chief Executive Officer, Chancery Capital*
MR ANTONY SMITH *Solicitor and Director, Legal Project Management Ltd*
MR MATTHEW SMITH *Barrister at Kings Chambers*
WING WINKY SO *Visiting Professor, Kazan Federal University*
DR JOHN SORABJI *Senior Judicial Institute Fellow, University College London*
MR DAN STACEY *Barrister at Hailsham Chambers*
PROF PAUL SWEETING *Professor of Actuarial Science, University of Kent*
MASTER MARK WHALAN *Costs Judge, Senior Courts Costs Office*
MR JON WILLIAMS *Costs Lawyer, Williams Associates*

UNIVERSITY PRESS

OXFORD
UNIVERSITY PRESS

Great Clarendon Street, Oxford, OX2 6DP,
United Kingdom

Oxford University Press is a department of the University of Oxford. It furthers the University's objective of excellence in research, scholarship, and education by publishing worldwide. Oxford is a registered trade mark of Oxford University Press in the UK and in certain other countries

Third Edition published in 2018
Impression: 2

Published in the United States of America by Oxford University Press
198 Madison Avenue, New York, NY 10016, United States of America

British Library Cataloguing in Publication Data
Data available

Library of Congress Control Number: 2018946422

ISBN 978–0–19–882330–8

Printed in Italy by
L.E.G.O. S.p.A.

In loving memory of
AUDREY AGNES FRISTON
(1937–2017)
and in gratitude to
PROF ROBERT MOOTS BSc (Hons), MB BS (Hons), PhD, FRCP

PREFACE TO THE THIRD EDITION

When I began writing the first edition of this book—then known as *Civil Costs: Law & Practice*—I had no idea that, within a decade, it would grow into a not-insubstantial hardback text published by a leading university press. If I had known, I would have taken up a slightly less demanding and time-consuming hobby.

I am not the only one to have spent my time writing in recent years. All authors of textbooks on costs were placed in a difficult position by the magnitude of the changes that took place in 2013. If they expressed views of their own, they faced criticism for being wrong, yet if they remained silent, they risked being accused of not having tackled the issues. I was spared the worst of this by reason of poor health—now fully resolved—which prevented the planned publication of this book in 2015, but I would like to pay tribute to authors of other textbooks who provided the profession with invaluable guidance at a time when this must have been far from easy.

The editorial philosophy of this book is broadly the same as that of previous editions. In particular, the focus is on describing the law in full, usually with pinpoint references. That said, there are many questions that have yet to be addressed by the higher courts, so, where there are gaps, I have done my best to provide an analysis. I do so reluctantly: I have not gone so far as to add footnotes to explain that I would rather be appearing before the Court of Appeal in my underpants, but the same is implied.

There are a number of changes to the editorial style, as follows.

- After a lively social media discussion on the topic, I have decided to use gender-neutral language; this may grate with some readers, but is the right approach.
- Most chapters have been written with the assistance of at least one other author; this has been necessary because of the complexity and scale of the law of costs.
- Whilst it is not something with which I agree, I recognise that non-binding decisions are now often cited (especially in courts at first instance); as such, this book now refers to County Court decisions and decisions of masters, albeit only sparingly.
- In recognition of the fact that the funding of litigation frequently crosses jurisdictional borders (and also of the fact that this book now has an international readership), this edition has been written with the assistance of experts in jurisdictions beyond England and Wales.
- Given the fact that access to justice now often depends on factors other than the recovery of costs between opposing parties, this book deals with topics that go to the provision of legal services in general, such as legal project management, value-based pricing and litigation funding, among others.

There are too many people to thank. All of the co-authors have been overly generous with their time. I must thank Oxford University Press (OUP) not only for having taken on the task of publishing a book that is more than twice as long as *War and Peace*, but also for having agreed to market it at a price that is only marginally above cost. In particular,

I would like to thank Katie Hooper and Matthew Humphrys of OUP, and Vanessa Plaister (freelance copy-editor). I must thank my partner Liz Love for endless cups of coffee, my teenage children, Emily and George, for having contractually agreed to bear sole responsibility for any errors and omissions, and my teenage stepdaughter, Caitlin, for having explained equitable interference to me. I must also thank Midnight, my cat, for having learned not to walk randomly across my keyboard.

Mark Friston
Temple, 2018

PREFACE TO THE FIRST EDITION

The law of costs is a paradox in that it can be both emotive and outstandingly dull at the same time. It is a difficult area of the law because there are, and will always be, unanswered questions and diametrically competing interests. Perhaps as a result of these things, previous textbooks have been short and have sought to encourage the reader by providing an engaging, and often entertaining, commentary.

There will always remain a place for such textbooks, but there is also a need for a practitioners' text which is focused solely on the law rather than on policy, and which is detailed and fully referenced. This seeks to be such a textbook. Where appropriate, there is analysis and a discussion of the policy behind the law, but the author has taken care to avoid expressing his own views unless they are likely to be uncontentious. Where a point can be argued either way, this is stated and both arguments are set out. Most of the relevant law is included in such a way as to avoid the need to consult reports or other texts; this is in recognition of the fact that not all costs practitioners have access to the full range of law reports. Whilst this book will be of use to any judge or lawyer who finds himself dealing with costs issues, it has been written with the following species of lawyer particularly in mind.

- **Costs practitioners (such as costs lawyers, costs draftspersons, costs counsel, etc)** The chapters are broken down into subchapters dealing with real, practical issues. Subchapters include not only broad topics such 'limitation', 'apportionment', and 'oral retainers', but also day-to-day questions such as 'copying charges' and 'experts' fees'. Authorities are included in a way that makes them easy to find and include points of dispute or replies. Issues ancillary to the practice of costs (such as 'loss of lien', 'security for costs', etc) are also dealt with in sufficient detail to allow the costs practitioner to give sensible and accurate advice without having to consult other texts.
- **Solicitors with management responsibilities** Now more than ever, financial success is dependent on practitioners having a firm grasp of the law of costs: that law pervades legal practice at all levels, and it is no longer sufficient to leave difficult costs issues to the end of the case to be sorted out by the costs practitioners (or, heaven forbid, trial counsel). All practitioners need to know not only how to avoid mantraps, but also how to deal with those traps once they have sprung. This book recognises that mistakes can happen. It provides sensible advice about how to limit the damage that mistakes can cause. This book complements the Solicitors' Code of Conduct 2007, but it also deals with lesser known regulations and rules, such as the Consumer Protection (Distance Selling) Regulations 2000 and the Solicitors' Financial Services (Conduct of Business) Rules 2001.
- **District judges** The law of costs has become so complex that many district judges will not have the time to keep abreast of all recent developments. It can no longer be assumed that even diligent advocates will always be able to unearth all the relevant authorities. This book seeks to describe the relevant law in an even-handed and comprehensive way. Extensive authorities are included (usually in footnotes, and often with paragraph or page numbers). The true law often lies in the actual words used and, for this reason,

authorities are frequently quoted verbatim. Usually, the name of the judge who gave the leading judgment is given, even if he or she is not quoted.

- **Counsel and solicitors with higher rights of audience** In order to avoid snatching defeat from the jaws of victory, advocates need to know which authorities and principles are likely to persuade the court to make the order they seek. This book is designed so that specific questions can be answered relatively quickly, and case examples are given in such a way that the advocate can easily scan a list to find the most appropriate authority. Practical problems (such as 'exaggeration', or 'abandoned issues') are dealt with as discrete topics with cross-referencing where appropriate.

Whilst this book is a practitioners' text rather than a students' text, Parts IV onwards will be of use to students taking the Association of Costs Lawyers' Training Course. It will be of particular use to students seeking to do well in the written assignments of that course.

In addition to thanking the team at Jordan Publishing Ltd [the previous publishers of this book], I would like to thank the following people, some of whom have donated a considerable amount of their time: Mr Justice Kenneth Handley, Professor Paul Sweeting, Master John O'Hare, Master Christopher Wright, District Judge Duerden, Professor Andrew McGee, Mr Stephen Grime QC, Mr Michael Rawlinson QC, Mr Matthew Smith, Mr Andrew Grantham, Mr Paul Hughes, Mr Simon Gibbs, Mr Craig Ralph, Mr Kevin Latham, Mr Para Gorasia, Mr Sam Karim, Mr Carl Dray, Mr Kenneth Brown, Ms Anne Winyard, Mr Murray Heining, Mr Stephen Loxton, Mr Toby Brown, Mr Rocco Pirozzolo, Mr Frank Maher, Mr Nicholas Northrop, Mr Mark Balme, Mr Stephen Averill, Mr Martin Hoyle, Mr Brian Varney, Mr Geoffrey Claughton, and Ms Iram Akhtar. And finally, I thank (with much love) my long-suffering wife and children, Sue, Emily and George.

Mark Friston
Gurnett, 2010

SUMMARY CONTENTS

Table of Cases xxxii
Table of Statutes cxviii
Table of Statutory Instruments cxxx
Table of Rules of Court cxxxviii
Table of Practice Directions and Protocols clii

I HISTORY AND DEVELOPMENT OF COSTS

1. A Brief History of Costs 3

II INTRODUCTION TO THE LAW OF COSTS

2. The Language of Costs 59
3. The Nature of Costs 72
4. The Status of the Rules Governing Costs 103
5. The Courts' Powers Regarding Costs 129

III ORDERS FOR COSTS

6. Orders for Costs (Jurisdiction and Discretion) 141
7. Orders for Costs (Particular Types of Order and Specific Circumstances) 229
8. Orders for Costs (Qualified One-way Costs Shifting) 281
9. Orders for Costs (Non-party Costs Orders and Wasted Costs) 296
10. Orders for Costs (Clarification and Revision of Orders) 352
11. Orders for Costs (Costs-only Proceedings) 360

IV ORDERS REGARDING COSTS

12. Costs Management and Cost Budgeting 371
13. Costs Capping and Related Topics 422
14. Payments on Account of Costs 453
15. Security for Costs 463

V BASES OF COSTS AND PART 36

16. The Bases of Assessment (Indemnity Basis and Standard Basis) 515
17. Part 36 Offers 547

VI POINTS OF LAW REGARDING COSTS

18. The Indemnity Principle 623
19. Plural Liability for and Plural Entitlement to Costs 656
20. Distribution: Apportionment and Division of Costs 665
21. Mutual Liabilities and Set-off 681
22. Agency and Costs 690
23. Finality, Delay and Limitation 697
24. Human Rights and the Law of Costs 729

VII THE OVERRIDING OBJECTIVE, PROPORTIONALITY AND RELIEF FROM SANCTIONS

25. Proportionality and Costs 747
26. The Overriding Objective, Collective Proportionality and Relief from Sanctions 773

VIII AGREEMENTS BETWEEN LEGAL SERVICES PROVIDER AND CLIENT

27. Contracts of Retainer (General Principles) 797
28. Contracts of Retainer, etc (Consumer Issues) 886
29. Contracts of Retainer (Conditional Fee Agreements and Damages-based Agreements) 955
30. Contracts of Retainer (Champerty and Maintenance) 1032
31. Contracts of Retainer (Interpretation and Implied Terms) 1046
32. Contracts of Retainer (Transfer of Contracts of Retainer and the Management of Errors) 1067

IX AGREEMENTS WITH FUNDERS AND INSURERS

33. Litigation Funding 1091
34. Legal Expenses Insurance 1115

X COSTS AS BETWEEN SOLICITOR AND CLIENT

35. Invoices and Bills 1139
36. Solicitor-and-client Assessments 1169
37. The Basis of Assessment between Solicitor and Client 1207
38. Quantum between Solicitor and Client 1217

39. Clients' Rights and Remedies (Alternative Means of Resolving Disputes and Compromise) 1245
40. Solicitors' Rights and Remedies (Proceedings, Lien, Charging Orders and Equitable Interference) 1257

XI PRACTICE ISSUES

41. Legal Project Management 1297
42. Value-based Pricing and Practising without Recording Time 1317

XII ASSESSMENTS, APPEALS AND ALTERNATIVE DISPUTE RESOLUTION BETWEEN OPPOSING PARTIES

43. Detailed Assessments between Opposing Parties 1335
44. Summary Assessments 1440
45. Costs Appeals and Reviews 1452
46. Evidential Issues and Privilege 1477
47. Representation and Rights of Audience 1494
48. Alternative Dispute Resolution of Costs Disputes 1504

XIII QUANTIFICATION OF COSTS BETWEEN OPPOSING PARTIES

49. The Assessment of Costs in General (Including the Assessment of Time) 1533
50. Fixed Costs, Costs on the Small Claims Track and Fast-track Costs 1579
51. Hourly Rates 1698
52. Disbursements and Expenses 1727
53. Counsel's Fees 1760
54. Additional Liabilities 1803
55. Value Added Tax 1864
56. Interest between Opposing Parties 1887
57. Conduct and Misconduct, and the Quantum of Costs 1921
58. Legislative Fetters on the Recovery of Costs 1938

XIV PARTICULAR PERSONS

59. Litigants in Person and Lawyers who Act in their Own Cause 1943
60. Children and Protected Persons 1958
61. Public Bodies and the Crown 1976
62. Costs Against Legally Aided Persons 1982
63. Road Traffic Insurers and Liability for Costs 2002
64. Costs Against the Courts Service 2006

XV PARTICULAR CIRCUMSTANCES

65. Group Litigation, Derivative Claims and Representative Claims 2015
66. Contracts and Trusts 2042
67. Public Law and Judicial Review 2071

XVI MATERIALS

68. Tables 2079

Index 2093

CONTENTS

Table of Cases xxxii
Table of Statutes cxviii
Table of Statutory Instruments cxxx
Table of Rules of Court cxxxviii
Table of Practice Directions and Protocols clii

I HISTORY AND DEVELOPMENT OF COSTS

1. A Brief History of Costs

Terminology 1.02
General Observations 1.03
The Anglo-Saxon Period (500–1066) 1.06
Norman Times (1066–1154) 1.08
Plantagenet Times (1154–1485) 1.11
Tudor Times (1485–1603) 1.32
Stuart Times (1603–1714) 1.45
Georgian Times (1714–1830) 1.61
Victorian Times (1837–1901) 1.73
Edwardian Times (1901–10) 1.106
The First World War and the Interwar Era (1910–39) 1.110
The Second World War and Post-War Times (1939–99) 1.119
The New Millennium 1.157

II INTRODUCTION TO THE LAW OF COSTS

2. The Language of Costs

Costs Terminology in General 2.02
The Citation of Costs Authorities 2.06
Costs Lexicon 2.09

3. The Nature of Costs

The Characteristics of Costs in General 3.03
Contentious and Non-contentious Business 3.21
Costs versus Damages 3.37
The Work of Lawyers in General 3.48
The Work of Lawyers under the Solicitors Act 1974 3.54

The Work of Lawyers under the Courts and Legal Services Act 1990 3.57
The Work of Lawyers under the Legal Services Act 2007 3.76
Work Done by Non-lawyers 3.92

4. The Status of the Rules Governing Costs
The Elements of Costs Law 4.02
Decided Cases and Precedence 4.03
Legislative Interpretation 4.08
The Solicitors' Codes of Conduct 4.14
Other Rules of Professional Conduct 4.29
The Civil Procedure Rules 1998 4.32
The Supreme Court Rules 2009 4.44
The Status of Practice Directions 4.46
Pre-action Protocols 4.56
The Status of Persuasive Informal Guidance 4.63
Parliamentary and Government Papers 4.68

5. The Courts' Powers Regarding Costs
Masters 5.03
The County Court: Common Law and Equity 5.11
Authorised Court Officers (also known as Costs Officers) 5.17
The Court as an Arbiter 5.20
The Province of Parliament 5.22
The Inherent Jurisdiction of the Court 5.24

III ORDERS FOR COSTS

6. Orders for Costs (Jurisdiction and Discretion)
A Forensic Sieve 6.03
Terminology and Terms of Art 6.04
The Jurisdiction to Award Costs 6.09
Factors to be Taken into Account when an Order for Costs is Made 6.16
The Range of Orders Available to the Court 6.29
Success and 'The General Rule' 6.42
Factors Other than the General Rule 6.76
No Order as to Costs 6.262
Interim Costs Orders 6.265

7. Orders for Costs (Particular Types of Order and Specific Circumstances)

More than two parties 7.02
Where Both Parties Claim to be Entitled to Costs 7.34
Circumstances in which the General Rule will not Apply 7.38
Consent Orders and Tomlin Orders 7.65
Forthwith Orders 7.80
Deemed Orders and Default Orders 7.100
Everything agreed Save for Costs 7.141
Where a Party Declines to Pay Costs Prior to the Issue of Proceedings 7.169
Miscellaneous Issues 7.183

8. Orders for Costs (Qualified One-way Costs Shifting)

Terminology and Pronunciation 8.03
Jurisdiction 8.04
The History of and Policies Underpinning QOCS 8.05
The Ambit of QOCS 8.10
Transitional Provisions 8.17
The (Qualified) effect of QOCS 8.22
Exceptions to QOCS 8.27

9. Orders for Costs (Non-party Costs Orders and Wasted Costs)

Non-party Costs Orders (Third-party Costs Orders) 9.02
Wasted Costs 9.93

10. Orders for Costs (Clarification and Revision of Orders)

Terminology: Orders, Judgments and Perfected Orders 10.03
Clarification of Orders for Costs 10.04
Correction of Orders for Costs 10.05
Review of Orders for Costs 10.08
Setting Aside Consent Orders for Costs 10.27

11. Orders for Costs (Costs-only Proceedings)

History and Policy 11.03
Jurisdiction and Application 11.06
Procedure 11.07
The Assessment 11.25

Costs 11.26
The Relevant Wording 11.29

IV ORDERS REGARDING COSTS

12. Costs Management and Cost Budgeting
Introduction 12.02
Terminology 12.03
The History of Costs Management 12.04
Jurisdiction 12.14
Procedural Issues (Other than the Making of Costs Management Orders) 12.20
Costs Management Orders 12.65
The Costs of the Budgeting Exercise 12.130
The Effect of the Budget on the Assessment of Costs 12.137

13. Costs Capping and Related Topics
CPR, Part 3, Section III: Cost Capping in Claims Other than Judicial Review 13.03
CPR, Part 3, Section I: Costs Capping Orders Arising out of the Court's General Case Management Powers 13.43
CPR, Part 46, Section IV, and ss 80 and 89 of the Criminal Justice and Courts Act 2015: Costs Capping Orders in Judicial Review Proceedings 13.46
CPR, Part 45, Section VII: Aarhus Convention Claims 13.78
CPR, Part 52, Section IV: Costs Restriction in Certain Appeals 13.100

14. Payments on Account of Costs
Jurisdiction 14.03
Judicial Roles 14.06
Discretion as to Whether to Make an Award 14.09
Miscellaneous Procedural Points 14.15
Discretion as to the Amount 14.21

15. Security for Costs
Jurisdictions and the Range of Remedies Available 15.02
Principles and Discretion Relating to Security for Costs 15.24
Reapplication for and Variation of Orders for Security for Costs 15.102
Unless Orders and Orders for Security for Costs 15.107

Quantum and Form of Security for Costs 15.110
Procedure and Applications for Security for Costs 15.124

V BASES OF COSTS AND PART 36

16. The Bases of Assessment (Indemnity Basis and Standard Basis)
The Two Bases of Assessment 16.02
The Circumstances in which an Award on the Indemnity Basis Might be Made 16.13
Orders to Pay Costs on the Indemnity Basis Pursuant to CPR, r 44.2 16.15
Case Examples Relating to Costs on the Indemnity Basis 16.31

17. Part 36 Offers
Terminology 17.03
The History of Part 36 17.06
Transitional Provisions 17.18
The Jurisdiction and Legal Framework of Part 36 Offers 17.19
Technical Shortcomings of Part 36 Offers 17.60
The Application and Effect of Part 36 Offers 17.80
Acceptance, Rejection and Withdrawal of Part 36 Offers 17.164

VI POINTS OF LAW REGARDING COSTS

18. The Indemnity Principle
The Indemnity Principle in General 18.02
Evidencing the Indemnity Principle 18.24
The Indemnity Principle in Practice 18.58
The Costs of In-house Staff 18.105
Pro Bono Funding 18.121

19. Plural Liability for and Plural Entitlement to Costs
Terminology and Introduction 19.03
Types of Plural Liability Distinguished 19.05
The Interpretation of Contracts of Retainer with More than One Client 19.10
The Interpretation of Plural Costs Awards 19.11
Joint Liability of Costs Debtors 19.21
Several Liability of Costs Debtors 19.30
Joint and Several Liability of Costs Debtors 19.31
Contributions between Costs Debtors 19.34

20. Distribution: Apportionment and Division of Costs
Terminology 20.03
Types of Distribution 20.05
An Overview of Distribution 20.06
The Relevance of Distribution at the Time of Making a Costs Order 20.11
The Division of Costs 20.13
The Doctrine of Equal Apportionment 20.16
Apportionment as between Legal Services Provider and Two or More Clients 20.34
The Role of Costs Sharing Agreements 20.40
Distribution where there are Reciprocal Entitlements 20.50
Distribution where an Issues Order has been Made 20.64
Special Orders (or Directions) 20.66

21. Mutual Liabilities and Set-off
Overview 21.03
The Jurisdictional Basis of Set-off 21.05
Procedural Issues of Set-off 21.16
Set-off and Discretion 21.21

22. Agency and Costs
An Overview of Agency 22.02
Solicitor Agents 22.06
Non-solicitor agents 22.08
Specific Relationships in which an Issue of Agency May Arise 22.21

23. Finality, Delay and Limitation
Finality and the Law of Costs 23.03
Res Judicata 23.07
Abuse of Process 23.28
Delay and Costs 23.50
Limitation 23.83

24. Human Rights and the Law of Costs
Brexit 24.02
Jurisdiction and Governing Bodies 24.03
Effects, Rights and Remedies 24.13

Determining Incompatibility 24.23

Specific Topics Relevant to the Law of Costs 24.32

VII THE OVERRIDING OBJECTIVE, PROPORTIONALITY AND RELIEF FROM SANCTIONS

25. Proportionality and Costs

The Terminology of Proportionality 25.02

The History of Proportionality 25.04

Individual Proportionality 25.15

26. The Overriding Objective, Collective Proportionality and Relief from Sanctions

The Overriding Objective 26.02

The Approach under the Rules of the Supreme Court and County Court Rules 26.09

The New Approach to Justice under the CPR 26.15

The Overriding Objective: Early Days and Competing Interpretations 26.17

Collective Proportionality 26.26

Relief from Sanctions 26.48

VIII AGREEMENTS BETWEEN LEGAL SERVICES PROVIDER AND CLIENT

27. Contracts of Retainer (General Principles)

Disambiguation 27.03

Miscellaneous Principles Relating to Contracts of Retainer 27.06

Factual Disputes About Retainers 27.92

Private Retainers 27.102

Business Agreements (Non-contentious and Contentious) 27.107

Implied Retainers 27.190

Oral Retainers 27.207

Sham Retainers 27.217

Unlawful Retainers and Statutory Prohibition 27.228

Retainers and Similar Contracts Involving More than One Client 27.302

Retainers with Specific Types of Person 27.319

Terms Commonly Encountered in Contracts of Retainers 27.326

28. Contracts of Retainer, etc (Consumer Issues)

The Legal Services Market and Consumers 28.02
General Consumer Protection Legislation (Present Day) 28.16
General Consumer Protection Legislation (Recently Revoked in Part) 28.149
General Consumer Protection Legislation (Older Revoked Provisions) 28.163
General Protection Legislation for Businesses (Present Day) 28.215

29. Contracts of Retainer (Conditional Fee Agreements and Damages-based Agreements)

The Language of Conditional Fee Agreements 29.02
Types of Conditional Fee Agreement 29.03
Conditional Fee Agreements and the Statutory Law 29.04
The Basic Requirements of all Modern Enforceable Conditional Fee Agreements 29.14
Older Conditional Fee Agreements 29.24
Collective Conditional Fee Agreements 29.111
Retrospectivity and Conditional Fee Agreements 29.132
Damages-based Agreements 29.141
Conditional Fee Agreements, Damages-based Agreements and the Common Law 29.179
The History of Conditional Fee Agreements 29.203
The Relevant Regulations 29.217

30. Contracts of Retainer (Champerty and Maintenance)

Introduction 30.02
Maintenance 30.04
Champerty 30.18
Case Examples Relating to Maintenance and Champerty 30.32

31. Contracts of Retainer (Interpretation and Implied Terms)

Overview of the Interpretation of Contracts of Retainer 31.02
Background Facts and Contractual Interpretation 31.05
The Role of Commercial Common Sense 31.14
The Interpretation of Inconsistent Terms 31.34
The Interpretation of Ambiguous Terms 31.38
The Interpretation of Mistakenly Drafted Contracts 31.41
The Interpretation of Contracts of Retainer in which Terms are Seemingly Missing 31.48

Joinder and Severance in the Context of Interpretation 31.52
Implied Terms 31.57
Specific Implied Terms, Deemed Terms and Presumptions in the Context of Contracts of Retainers 31.69

32. Contracts of Retainer (Transfer of Contracts of Retainer and the Management of Errors)
The Transfer of Contracts of Retainer (Assignment, etc) 32.02
The Management of Defective Contracts of Retainer 32.42

IX AGREEMENTS WITH FUNDERS AND INSURERS

33. Litigation Funding
Introduction 33.03
Public Policy and Relevant History 33.04
Future Developments 33.27
Present Legislative Control 33.32
The Provision of Litigation Funders to Consumers 33.34
Availability and Practice 33.59
Disclosure of Funding 33.85

34. Legal Expenses Insurance
The Nature of Legal Expenses Insurance in General 34.02
Before-the-event Insurance 34.04
After-the-event Insurance 34.21
Top-up Insurance 34.38
Challenges to the After-the-event Premiums 34.41
Formalities Relating to After-the-event Insurance 34.42
Rights Against Legal Expenses Insurers 34.60

X COSTS AS BETWEEN SOLICITOR AND CLIENT

35. Invoices and Bills
The Distinction between Invoices and Statute Bills 35.02
Interim Invoices 35.06
Internal Invoices 35.37
Statute Bills Generally 35.40
The Consequences of Failing to Comply with Solicitors Act 1974, s 69 35.109

How Disbursements are Treated in a Statute Bill 35.116
The Power to Order Delivery of a Bill 35.120

36. Solicitor-and-client Assessments
Assessments on the Application of the Party Chargeable or the Solicitor 36.03
Assessments and Claims for Account on the Application of Third Parties 36.79
The Assessment Hearing and Procedure Leading up to the Assessment Hearing 36.96
Costs Certificates in Solicitor-and-client Assessments and Interim Payments 36.113

37. The Basis of Assessment between Solicitor and Client
The Basis of the Assessment of Costs as between Solicitor and Client 37.02
The Details of Assessment as between Solicitor and Client 37.06
Consumer Protection Issues 37.32

38. Quantum between Solicitor and Client
Non-contentious Costs: Hourly Rates and Value Charges 38.04
Non-contentious Costs: The Limited Role of Authority and Comparators 38.08
Hourly Rates 38.09
The Value Charge 38.15
Shoddy Work 38.35
Inadequate Advice Regarding Funding Options 38.41
Estimates and Assurances on a Solicitor-and-client Basis 38.43
Putative Waiver of Fees 38.80
Assurances About How Services Will be Provided 38.81
Interest between Solicitor and Client 38.86

39. Clients' Rights and Remedies (Alternative Means of Resolving Disputes and Compromise)
Remuneration Certificates (Now Obsolete) 39.02
Non-statutory Assessments (*Turner & Co v Palomo* Quantifications) 39.03
Disputed Compromise 39.08
The Legal Ombudsman and the Solicitors Regulation Authority 39.22

40. Solicitors' Rights and Remedies (Proceedings, Lien, Charging Orders and Equitable Interference)
Suing for Recovery of Fees 40.02
Payments on Account and Interim Payments 40.31

Withdrawal of Services under a Contract of Retainer 40.33
Lien 40.36
Solicitors' Charging Orders 40.89
Solicitors' Security for Costs 40.100
Equitable Interference by the Court 40.106
Statutory Demands and Bankruptcy Proceedings 40.121

XI PRACTICE ISSUES

41. Legal Project Management
Terminology 41.03
History 41.05
The Aims of Legal Project Management 41.07
The Relevance of Legal Project Management to Costs as between Solicitor and Client 41.08
The Relevance of Legal Project Management to Costs as between Parties 41.10
Legal Project Management Distinguished from Other Concepts 41.11
The Phases of Legal Project Management 41.13
Non-traditional Legal Project Management 41.61

42. Value-based Pricing and Practising without Recording Time
Introduction 42.02
Theories of Value 42.04
The State of the Market 42.05
Costs-plus Pricing 42.09
Value-based Pricing 42.16
Chief Value Officers 42.37
Pricing Strategies, Analytics and Reporting 42.39
Practising without Recording Time 42.43

XII ASSESSMENTS, APPEALS AND ALTERNATIVE DISPUTE RESOLUTION BETWEEN OPPOSING PARTIES

43. Detailed Assessments between Opposing Parties
The Venue for Detailed Assessment Proceedings 43.02
Case Management in Detailed Assessment Proceedings 43.25
The Form and Content of Bills of Costs 43.29
Commencement of Detailed Assessment Proceedings 43.51
Points of Dispute 43.108

Default Costs Certificates 43.140
Replies to Points of Dispute 43.166
Requesting an Assessment 43.176
Provisional Assessments 43.196
Agreed Costs and Putative Agreements 43.239
Offers to Settle Detailed Assessment Proceedings 43.252
Detailed Assessment Hearings 43.302
Liability for Costs of Detailed Assessment Proceedings 43.327
Interim Costs Certificates 43.376
Final Costs Certificates and the Conclusion of the Assessment 43.383
Discontinuing Costs Proceedings and Withdrawal 43.394
Enforcement 43.407

44. Summary Assessments
Entitlement to a Summary Assessment 44.03
Discretionary Power to Order that there be No Summary Assessment 44.14
Procedure in General 44.25

45. Costs Appeals and Reviews
Introduction 45.02
Terminology 45.04
Appeals Under CPR, Part 47, Section VIII 45.05
Appeals Under CPR, Part 52 45.14
Judicial Review 45.73

46. Evidential Issues and Privilege
Overview 46.03
Legal Professional Privilege 46.04
Filing Documents at Court 46.28
The Process of Election 46.40
Disclosure in Cases of Fraud 46.75
Disclosure of Non-privileged Material 46.76
Procedure Relating to Evidential Issues 46.77

47. Representation and Rights of Audience
Notification 47.04
Persons who are not Authorised Persons 47.05

Authorised Persons	47.12
Discretion Not to Hear an Authorised Person	47.17
Advocates who Wish to be Heard on their Own Fees	47.18
The Authority of Costs Practitioners	47.23
Bankrupt Persons	47.30
Companies	47.32

48. Alternative Dispute Resolution of Costs Disputes

Costs ADR in General	48.04
Costs Mediation	48.13
Early Neutral Evaluation	48.58
Costs Arbitration	48.65

XIII QUANTIFICATION OF COSTS BETWEEN OPPOSING PARTIES

49. The Assessment of Costs in General (Including the Assessment of Time)

The Assessment Must Not Controvert the Order for Costs	49.03
The Principles of Accounting for Costs	49.06
Time Recording and Estimated Time	49.12
Phases, Tasks and Activities under the CPR	49.20
Activities as Defined in the CPR	49.50
Activities that are not Specifically Defined in the CPR	49.103
Costs Incurred in Particular Circumstances	49.147
The EW-UTBMS Code-set (Otherwise Known as J-Codes)	49.165

50. Fixed Costs, Costs on the Small Claims Track and Fast-track Costs

The Language of Fixed Costs, Predictable Costs, etc	50.04
The History of Fixed Costs	50.07
CPR, Part 45, Section I: Fixed Commencement Costs, Fixed Enforcement Costs, etc	50.48
CPR, Part 45, Section II: Fixed Recoverable Costs	50.67
Pre-April 2013 CPR, Part 45, Sections III, IV and V: Fixed Success Fees	50.102
CPR, Part 45, Section III, and the Related Portal: Portal Costs	50.150
CPR Part 45, Section IIIA: Post-Portal Fixed Costs	50.267
CPR, Part 45, Section IV: Scale Costs for Claims in the Intellectual Property Enterprise Court	50.312
CPR, Part 45, Section V: Fixed Costs—HM Revenue & Customs	50.342

CPR, Part 45, Section VI: Fast-Track Trial Costs 50.345
CPR, Part 45, Section VII: Costs Limits in Aarhus Convention Claims 50.368
Costs on the Small Claims Track 50.369

51. Hourly Rates
The History of Time-based Charging 51.03
The Relevance of Guideline Rates 51.15
Pre-CPR Terminology 51.24
The Relevance of Pre-CPR Law Under the CPR 51.38
The Modern Approach 51.44
The use of Comparators and Precedents 51.84
Composite and Hybrid Rates 51.87

52. Disbursements and Expenses
Introduction and Types of Disbursement 52.02
Expert Witnesses and Advisory Experts 52.10
Fixed-cost Medical Reports and the Medical Reporting Organisation Agreement 52.46
Factual Witnesses 52.47
Medical Records 52.60
Other Types of Personal Records 52.62
Medical Agencies 52.63
Copying Charges 52.73
Couriers, Postage, etc 52.77
Legal Representatives' Hotel Expenses 52.79
Legal Representatives' Travelling Expenses 52.81
Disbursement Funding Loans 52.85
Court Fees 52.87
Foreign Lawyers 52.98
Interpreters 52.100

53. Counsel's Fees
The Nature of Counsel's Right to Payment 53.04
Fee Agreements in Default 53.08
Non-contractual Agreements with Professional Clients 53.09
Contractual Agreements with Professional Clients 53.16
Contractual Agreements with Licensed Access Clients 53.19
Contractual Agreements with Lay Clients 53.24

Liability for Fees as between Counsel and their Instructing Solicitor 53.27
Counsel not in Independent Practice 53.29
Counsel's Fees between Opposing Parties 53.32
The Basis of Charging 53.40
The Scope of Instructions 53.42
Evidencing Counsel's fees 53.45
The Quantum of Counsel's fees 53.51
Delivery, Going Short and Abatement 53.67
The Relevance of Time 53.87
The Use of Comparators 53.91
Other Factors Relevant to Quantum 53.97
Refreshers 53.103
Hourly Charging 53.107
Fees Per Item 53.114
Retainers (or Commitment Fees) 53.116
Booking Fees 53.118
Leading Counsel 53.119
Two Counsel 53.124
Informal Arrangements between Counsel (devilling) 53.130
More than two Counsel 53.131
The New Terms of Work 53.135

54. Additional Liabilities
Jurisdiction 54.04
Points of Principle Regarding Success Fees 54.43
The Assessment of the Amount of Success Fees 54.54
Notice of Funding and Failure to Serve 54.108
Statement of Reasons and Failure to Serve 54.124
The Assessment of the Amount of ATE Premiums 54.127
Miscellaneous Points Regarding ATE Premiums 54.175
Membership Organisations and Notional Premiums 54.179
Alternative Means of Funding 54.191

55. Value Added Tax
Introduction 55.02
Output Tax and Liability for VAT 55.04
Expert Reports and Records 55.22

VAT between Opposing Parties 55.26
Changes of the Rate of VAT 55.33
The Wording of Relevant Provisions 55.45

56. Interest between Opposing Parties
Terminology 56.02
Overview 56.04
Prescribed Rate Interest 56.08
Compensatory Rate Interest 56.55
Enhanced Rate Interest 56.83
Special Situations 56.101
Interest Payable Pursuant to Contract, as Damages, etc 56.116

57. Conduct and Misconduct, and the Quantum of Costs
Conduct as One of the 'Seven Pillars' 57.02
Conduct in General 57.05
Pre-issue Conduct and Pre-action Protocols 57.08
Exaggeration and the Amount of Costs 57.18
Misconduct 57.37

58. Legislative Fetters on the Recovery of Costs
The Slander of Women 58.03
Patent Claims 58.04

XIV PARTICULAR PERSONS

59. Litigants in Person and Lawyers who Act in their Own Cause
Jurisdiction to Allow Costs to Litigants in Person 59.02
Quantum of Costs that may be Allowed to Litigants who Represent Themselves 59.08
Lawyers Acting for Themselves and on Behalf of their Firms 59.38
Corporate Litigants 59.54

60. Children and Protected Persons
Children and Costs 60.03
Protected Persons and Costs 60.49

61. Public Bodies and the Crown
Orders Against the Crown 61.03
Public Bodies Discharging an Administrative Function 61.07

62. Costs Against Legally Aided Persons

Costs Protection 62.04

Transfer from the Legal Services Commission to the Lord Chancellor 62.07

Section 26 of the Legal Aid, Sentencing and Punishment of Offenders Act 2012 62.10

The Wording of the Provisions 62.43

63. Road Traffic Insurers and Liability for Costs

64. Costs Against the Courts Service

The Power to Make Payments 64.03

The Exercise of Discretion 64.09

Quantum 64.15

Procedure 64.18

XV PARTICULAR CIRCUMSTANCES

65. Group Litigation, Derivative Claims and Representative Claims

Group Litigation 65.02

Representative Claims 65.116

Derivative Claims 65.123

66. Contracts and Trusts

Costs Payable Pursuant to Contract or Powers Conferred by Contract 66.02

Costs Relating to Trusts and Trustees 66.35

67. Public Law and Judicial Review

Application for Permission for Judicial Review 67.03

Acknowledgement of Service of Judicial Review Proceedings 67.08

Discretion Relating to the Costs of Judicial Review Proceedings 67.10

Interested Parties and Interveners in Judicial Review Proceedings 67.15

XVI MATERIALS

68. Tables

Index 2093

TABLE OF CASES

1-800 Flowers Inc v Phonenames Ltd [2001] EWCA Civ 712 . . . . 57.32
4 Eng Ltd v Harper [2008] EWHC 915 (Ch) 3.100
7E Communications Ltd v Vertex Antennentechnik GmBH [2007] EWCA Civ 140 . . . . 45.41
9MD Ltd v One Step Beyond [2008] EWHC 3231 (Ch) 9.221

A (a child) (Costs), Re [2013] EWCA Civ 43 . . . . 9.221
A v B [1984] 1 All ER 265 . . . . 40.62
A v B (No 2) [2007] EWHC 54 (Comm), [2007] 1 All ER (Comm) 633 . . . . 16.65
A v BCD (a firm) (1997) 147 NLJ 1422 . . . . 36.72
A v Chief Constable of South Yorkshire [2008] EWHC 1658 (QB) 25.99, 51.64, 51.76, 51.78, 51.79
A v F Co Ltd (unreported), c 1995, QBD 51.65
A v Lancashire County Council [2013] EWHC 851 (Fam) 16.27
A Ltd v B Ltd [1996] 1 WLR 665 . . . . 27.224
A & Anor v Royal Mail Groupat [2015] EW Misc B24 (CC) 60.46
Aaron v Okoye [1998] 2 Costs LR 6 . . . . 35.50, 35.90
Aaron v Shelton [2004] EWHC 1162 (QB) 6.80, 23.06, 23.36, 23.43, 23.46
AB v CD & Ors [2011] EWHC 602 (Ch) 17.31, 17.53, 17.54, 17.58, 17.59, 17.153
AB v British Coal Corpn (Department of Trade and Industry) [2006] EWCA Civ 1357 . . . . . . 65.27
AB v Leeds Teaching Hospitals NHS Trust [2003] EWHC 1034 (QB) 13.11, 13.14, 13.22, 13.26, 13.32, 13.38
AB v Liverpool City Council [2003] EWHC 1539 (QB) 20.37, 65.56, 65.64
AB & Ors v British Coal Corpn [2006] EWCA Civ 987 . . . . 5.21, 53.133, 65.108
AB & Ors v British Coal Corpn [2007] EWHC 1406 (QB) 7.163
AB Bank Ltd v HSBC Bank plc [2016] EWHC 3446 (Comm) 16.57
Abada v Gray and the Motor Insurers Bureau (unreported), 25 June 1997, CA 17.20, 17.161
Abbassi v Secretary of State for the Home Department [1992] Imm AR 349 . . . . 9.170
Abbington Hotel Ltd, In the matter of, sub nom D'angelo v Digrado et al [2010] EWHC 1628 (Ch) 15.47
Abbott, Re (1861) 4 LT 576 . . . . 36.82
Abbott v Long [2011] EWCA Civ 874 . . . . 6.03, 6.50, 6.104, 6.151, 6.153, 6.189, 6.193
ABC (A protected party proceeding by his wife and litigation friend DEF) v Barts Health NHS Trust [2016] EWHC 500 (QB) 17.90, 17.91
ABCI v Banque Franco-Tunisienne & Ors [2003] EWCA Civ 205 . . . . 4.38, 16.53
Abedi v Penningtons [2000] 2 Costs LR 205 . . . . 27.44, 27.58, 27.59, 35.34, 35.35
Abraham v Thompson [1997] 4 All ER 362, CA 15.13
Abrath v North Eastern Rly Co (1883) 11 QBD 440 . . . . 9.131
Abu v MGN [2002] EWHC 2345 (QB) 25.68
AC DG Petrol SRL v Vitol Broking Ltd [2014] EWHC 3900 (Comm) 9.92
Accenuate Ltd v Asigra Inc [2013] EWHC 889 (QB) 51.54
Accident Group Test Cases [2004] EWCA Civ 575 . . . . 2.09
Ackerman v Ackerman [2011] EWHC 2183 (Ch) 15.46, 15.119, 15.121
Ackroyd v Hollely (unreported), 16 January 2013, Leeds County Court 7.44
Acre 1127 Ltd (Formerly known as Castle Galleries Ltd) v De Montfort Fine Art Ltd [2011] EWCA Civ 130 . . . . 17.86
Acres v Royal Devon and Exeter NHS Foundation Trust [2013] EWHC 652 (QB) 51.76
Actavis UK Ltd v Eli Lilly & Co [2015] EWCA Civ 666 . . . . 14.21
Activis Ltd v Merck & Co Inc [2007] EWHC 1625 (Pat) 6.181
Adamastos Shipping Co Ltd v Anglo-Saxon Petroleum [1959] AC 133 . . . . 31.36

Adams v Al Malik [2003] EWHC 3232 (QB) 35.19
Adams v Associated Newspapers Ltd & Ors (1999) EMLR 26 . . . . 19.41
Adams v Ford [2012] EWCA Civ 544 . . . . 9.69
Adams v London Improved Motor Builders Ltd [1921] 1 KB 495. . . . . 18.28, 18.63, 18.65, 27.94, 27.193, 31.69
Adams v MacInnes [2001] EWHC 9014 (Costs) 18.93, 27.206, 31.70, 46.62, 46.66
Adamson v Halifax plc [2002] EWCA Civ 1134 . . . . 45.22
Adegbulugbe v Nursing & Midwifery Council [2014] EWHC 405 (Admin). 9.170
Admiral Management Services Ltd v Para-Protect Europe Ltd [2002] EWHC 233 (Ch) 49.148, 52.17
Adoko v Jemal (1999) The Times, 8 July. 26.43
Adrian Alan Ltd v Fuglers [2002] EWCA Civ 1655 . . . . 38.84
Adris v Royal Bank of Scotland plc & Ors [2010] EWHC 941 (QB), ... 9.50, 9.52
Advanced Technology Structures Ltd v Cray Valley Products Ltd [1993] BCLC 723, CA 30.11
A&E Television Networks LLC v Discovery Communications Europe Ltd [2011] EWHC 1038 (Ch) 13.16
A&E Television Networks LLC v Discovery Communications Europe Ltd [2013] EWHC 276 (Pat). 6.115, 6.246, 16.45, 49.84
AEG v Lewis (1992) The Times, 29 December, CA 40.10
Aegis Group plc v Inland Revenue Commissioners [2005] EWHC 1468 (Ch). 6.106, 7.125
Aehmed v Legal Services Commission [2009] EWCA Civ 572 . . . . 62.13
AEI Rediffusion Music Ltd v Phonographic Performance Ltd [1999] 1 WLR 1507 . . . . . . 6.67, 45.17
Aer Lingus plc v Gildacroft Ltd [2006] EWCA Civ 4. . . . . 23.108
Aerospace Publishing Ltd v Thames Water [2007] EWCA Civ 3 . . . . 3.45, 3.46
AF v BG [2009] EWCA Civ 757 . . . . 17.26, 17.34, 17.37, 52.17
AG's Reference No 82A of 2000 [2002] EWCA Crim 215 . . . . 24.40
A-G v Birmingham Drainage Board (1908) 52 Sol Jo 855 . . . . 52.36
A-G v Brecon Corpn (1878) 10 Ch D 204 . . . . 27.320
A-G v Nethercote (1841) 11 SIM 529. . . . . 56.113
Agassi v Robinson [2005] EWCA Civ 1507 . . . . 3.58, 3.61, 3.63, 3.68, 3.69, 3.74, 3.92, 3.97, 3.98, 22.06, 59.04, 59.30, 59.31
Agents' Mutual Ltd v Gascoigne Halman Ltd [2016] EWHC 2315 (Ch) 15.125
Agricullo Ltd v Yorkshire Housing Ltd (formerly Yorkshire Community Housing Ltd) (2010) EWCA Civ 229. . . . . 66.17
Ahmad v Brent London Borough Council [2011] EWHC 378 (QB) 21.40
Ahmed v Aventis Pharma Ltd (Rev 1) [2009] EWHC 90152 (Costs) 22.16, 22.27, 52.73
Ahmed v Blackburn & Co [2001] EWCA Civ 141 . . . . 15.12, 15.64
Ahmed v Jura [2002] EWCA Civ 210 . . . . 56.72
Ahmed v Powell [2003] EWHC 9011, SCCO, 19 February. 3.88, 29.200, 47.08
Ahmud & Co v MacPherson [2015] EWHC 2240 (QB) 36.05, 36.51, 39.03, 39.07
Aiden Shipping Ltd v Interbulk Ltd [1986] 1 AC 965; [1985] 1 WLR 1222 . . . . 9.03, 9.62, 9.75, 10.13, 49.159, 65.63
Aidiniantz v Sherlock Holmes International Society Ltd [2015] EWHC 2882 (Ch). 15.79
Ainsworth, ex parte The Law Society, In re [1905] 2 KB 103 . . . . 3.65
Ainsworth v Wilding [1900] 2 Ch 315 . . . . 46.09
Ajanaku, Re (unreported), 28 October 1991, QBD 51.54
Akhtar v Bhopal Productions (UK) Ltd [2015] EWHC 154 (IPEC). 50.286, 50.322, 50.325, 50.329, 50.333
Akhtar v Boland (Costs) [2014] EWCA Civ 94 . . . . 45.58, 50.378
Aktas v Adepta [2010] EWCA Civ 1170. . . . . 12.59
Aktieselskabet de Danske Sukkerfabriker v Bajamar Cia Naviera SA, The Torenia [1983] 2 Lloyd's Rep 210 . . . . 52.59
Al-Abbas v As-Dabbagh [2002] EWCA Civ 1962 . . . . 40.91, 40.92
Al-Baho v BGP Global Services Ltd (unreported), 4 July 2017, Ch D. 15.012
AL Barnes v Time Talk (UK) Ltd [2003] EWCA Civ 402 . . . . 6.48, 6.63, 6.67

Al Jaber v Al Ibrahim [2017] EWHC 5092 (Comm) 6.37
Al-Koronky & Anor v Time Life Entertainments Group Ltd [2005] EWHC 1688 (QB) 15.04, 15.38, 15.60, 15.62, 15.73, 15.80, 15.82, 15.89, 15.111, 15.112, 15.115
Al Nehayan v Kent [2016] EWHC 613 (QB) 15.116
Al Nehayan v Kent [2017] EWHC 1347 (Ch) 15.100
Al-Rawas v Pegasus Energy Ltd [2008] EWHC 617 (QB) 3.100
Al Rawi v Security Service [2011] UKSC 34. . . . . 5.28
Al Saud v Apex Global Management Ltd [2014] UKSC 64 . . . . 26.31
Alabaster v Harness [1895] 1 QB 339, CA 30.07, 30.11, 30.34, 30.54
Albemarle Supply Co Ltd v Hind & Co [1928] 1 KB 307. . . . . 40.75, 40.80
Albion Water v Water Services Regulation Authority [2007] CAT 1 . . . . 27.224
Aldi Stores v WSP Group plc [2007] EWCA Civ 1260. . . . . 23.35
Alexander (as representative of the Property118 Action Group) v West Bromwich Mortgage Company Ltd [2016] EWCA Civ 496 . . . . 31.45
Alfred Crompton Amusement Machines Ltd v Commissioners of Customs and Excise (No 2) [1974] AC 405. . . . . 46.25, 46.26
Ali v Channel 5 Broadcast Ltd [2018] EWHC 840 (Ch) 12.57, 12.92, 17.65, 17.66, 17.70, 17.157
Ali v Hudson t/a Hudson Freemen Berg (a firm) [2003] EWCA Civ 1793 . . . . 15.21, 15.97
Ali v Stagecoach [2011] EWCA Civ 1494. . . . . 6.241
Ali Reza-Delta Transport Co v United Arab Shipping Co [2003] EWCA Civ 811 . . . . 17.96
Ali Shipping Corpn v Shipyard Trogir [1999] 1 WLR 314 . . . . 48.85
Alka Arora, sub nom 68b Maud Road, London, E13 0JU [2013] UKUT 362 (LC) 51.81
Allason v Random House UK Ltd [2002] EWHC 1030 (Ch) 14.14, 14.21
Allen v Aldridge; Re Ward (1843) 5 Beav 401. . . . . 3.06
Allen v Bloomsbury Publishing Plc [2011] EWHC 770 (Ch) 15.97, 15.98
Allen v Bone (1841) 4 Beav 493 . . . . 27.96, 27.208
Allen v Colman Coyle LLP [2007] EWHC 90075 (Costs). 36.76
Allen v Yoxall (1844) 1 Car & Kir 315 . . . . 52.44
Allied Carpets Group Plc v MacFarlane [2002] EWHC 1155. . . . . 32.31
Allingham, Re (1886) 32 Ch D 36, CA 36.12
Alliss v Legal Services Commission [2002] EWHC 2079 (Admin) 24.40
Alltrans Express Ltd v CV Holdings Ltd [1984] 1 WLR 394 . . . . 6.44, 6.60
Alpha Rocks Solicitors v Alade [2015] EWCA Civ 685. . . . . 40.23, 40.29
Alsop v Cleydon (1595) 78 ER 718. . . . . 1.38
Alsop Wilkinson (a firm) v Neary [1996] 1 WLR 1220 . . . . 66.41, 66.46, 66.56, 66.62, 66.66
Alternative A5 Alliance's Application, The [2012] NIQB 97. . . . . 13.71
Alternative Investments (Holdings) Ltd & Ors Appellants v Barthelemy [2012] EWCA Civ 843 . . . . 6.212
Altus Group (UK) Ltd v Baker Tilly Tax and Advisory Services LLP [2015] EWHC 411 (Ch) 17.127
Amalgamated General Finance Co Ltd v C E Golding & Co Ltd [1964] 2 Lloyd's Rep 163 . . . . 32.29
Amantilla Ltd v Telefusion plc (1987) 9 Con LR 139 . . . . 23.125
Amber v Stacey [2001] 1 WLR 1225 . . . . 17.11
Amber Construction Services Ltd v London Interspace HG Ltd [2007] EWHC 3042 (TCC), ... 50.54
Amec Process & Energy Ltd v Stork Engineers & Contracts (No 3) [2002] All ER (D) 49.106
Americhem Europe Ltd v Rakem Ltd [2014] EWHC 1881 (TCC) 12.34
Amey LG Ltd v Cumbria County Council [2016] EWHC 2946 (TCC) 6.255
Amin v Amin [2010] EWHC 827 (Ch) 7.37, 21.38
Amin v Amin [2011] EWHC 641 (Ch) 14.15
Amin & Anor v Mullings & Anor [2011] EWHC 278 (QB). 50.109
Amoco (UK) Exploration Co v British American Offshore Ltd [2002] BLR 135 . . . . 16.40, 16.51
Ancell v Slowman (1724) 88 ER 246 . . . . 1.34
Anderson v Bank of British Columbia (1875–76) LR 2 Ch D 644 . . . . 46.10
Anderson v Hills Automobiles (Woodford) Ltd [1965] 1 WLR 745 . . . . 21.14
Anderson v Shetland Island Council [2012] UKSC 7. . . . . 15.06
Andrews v Barnes (1888) [1886–90] All ER Rep 758 . . . . 1.48, 1.64, 1.94, 1.98

Angel Airlines SA v Dean & Dean Solicitors [2006] EWCA Civ 1505 .... 45.51
Angel Airlines (a Romanian company in liquidation) v Dean & Dean [2008] EWHC 1513 (QB) 36.76
Angel Group Ltd v Davey (unreported), 28 March 2017, Ch D 16.48
Anglo-Cyprian Trade Agencies Ltd v Paphos Wine Industries Ltd [1951] 1 All ER 873 ......6.44, 6.60
Anglo-Eastern Trust Ltd & Anor v Kermanshahchi [2002] EWCA Civ 198 ....14.20, 15.78, 15.129, 15.130
Anglo Irish Asset Finance Plc v Flood [2011] EWCA Civ 799 .... 15.65
Anglo Irish Bank Corporation Ltd v Dtz Debenham Tie Leung Ltd [2013] EWHC 596 (Comm) 15.36
Anglo-Moravian Hungarian Junction Rly Co, ex p Watkin, Re (1875) 1 Ch D 130, CA 27.323
Anglo Petroleum Ltd v TFB Mortgages Ltd [2004] EWHC 1177 (Ch) 15.65, 15.70
Angus v Clifford [1891] 2 Ch 449.................... 6.78
Anning v Anning (1907) 4 CLR 1049 .... 32.29
Anon (1732) 2 Barn KB 164.................... 1.82
Anon (1813) 1 Marsh 4 .... 15.96
Ansol Ltd v Taylor Joynson Garrett (a firm) [2002] All ER (D) 44 (Jan).................... 7.130
Antaios Compania Naviera v Salen Rederierna [1985] AC 191 .... 31.22
Anthony v Ellis & Fairburn (a firm) [2000] 2 Costs LR 277....................38.62, 38.78
Antonelli v Allen, The Times, 8 December 2000 .... 6.160, 6.170
Aoun v Bahri [2002] EWHC 29 (Comm) 15.40, 15.41, 15.46, 15.47
AP (UK) Ltd v West Midlands Fire and Civil Defence Authority [2001] EWCA Civ 1917.... 15.122
Apex Global Management v FI Call Ltd [2014] EWHC 779 (Ch) 15.110
Apotex Europe Ltd v SmithKline Beecham plc [2004] EWHC 964 (Ch).................... 6.40
Appah v Monsen [1967] 1 WLR 893 .... 15.33
Appleby v Myers (1867) LR 2 CP 651.................... 27.25
Application in Private [2017] EWHC 3606 (Comm)...............17.141, 17.176, 17.205, 17.211
Aquila Design (GRB) Products Ltd v Cornhill Insurance plc [1988] BCLC 134, CA.... 15.79, 15.84
Arab Monetary Fund v Hashim (unreported), 30 June 2000, Ch D................ 49.11, 49.19
Aramis, The [1989] 1 Lloyd's Rep 213 .... 27.199, 31.65
Aratra Potato Co Ltd v Taylor Joynson-Garrett [1995] 4 All ER 695 ....27.331, 29.180, 29.209, 31.56
Arcadia Group Brands Ltd v Visa Inc [2015] EWCA Civ 883....................16.24, 16.40
Aridila Investments NV v ENRC NV [2015] EWHC 1667 (Comm)............... 15.10, 15.65
Aries Tanker Corpn v Total Transport Ltd [1977] 1 WLR 185, HL 38.36
Arkin v Borchard Lines (unreported), 19 June 2001, QBD.................... 29.132
Arkin v Borchard Lines [2003] EWHC 3088 (Comm) 6.248, 7.06, 7.23, 7.26, 7.28
Arkin v Borchard [2005] EWCA Civ 655............. 9.37, 9.39, 9.41, 15.56, 30.12, 30.48, 33.05, 33.14, 33.15, 33.67, 33.71, 34.30
Armitage v Nurse [2000] 2 Costs LR 231....................47.21, 53.48
Armstrong v Boulton [1990] VR 215 .... 3.16
Arnold v Britton [2015] UKSC 36 .... 31.04, 31.06, 31.09, 31.10, 31.18, 31.19, 31.25, 31.62
Arnold v National Westminster Bank plc [1988] 3 All ER 977.................... 23.17
Arnold v National Westminster Bank plc [1991] 2 AC 93.................... 23.22, 23.23, 23.27
Arnold v Poole Corpn (1842) 4 Man & G 860 .... 27.320
Arrow Nominees Inc v Blackledge [2000] CP Rep 59; [2000] BCLC 167 ....26.41, 40.29
Arrowfield Services Ltd v BP Collins (a firm) [2003] EWHC 830 (Ch); [2005] 2 Costs LR 171.......36.36
Arrowsmith, Ex parte (1806) 13 Ves 124 .... 1.61
Arroyo & Ors v Equion Energia Ltd [2016] EWHC 3348 (TCC) 6.165, 16.35, 16.49
Arthur JS Hall v Simons [2000] 3 All ER 673 .... 23.04
Arts & Antiques Ltd v Richards [2013] EWHC 3361 (Comm) 15.79
Asghar v Bhatti [2017] EWHC 1702 (QB).................... 12.60
Ashendon and Jones v United Kingdom, The Times, 22 September 2011................. 6.113
Ashfield & Anor v Union Pensions Trustees Ltd [2004] All ER (D) 103 (Dec)... 15.03, 15.21, 15.101
Ashia Centur Ltd v Barker Gillette LLP [2011] EWHC 148 (QB) 27.90, 38.80
Ashley-Carter v Hofmann & Mountford Ltd [2010] EWHC 2349 (QB).................. 9.22

Ashmore v Ripley (1617) 79 ER 359 . . . . 1.53, 3.37
Ashworth v Berkeley-Walbrood Ltd (1989) The Independent, 9 October, CA 15.70
Asiansky Television Plc v Bayer-Rosin (a firm) [2001] EWCA Civ 1792, [2002] CPLR 111 . . . 15.100
Asiedu v Dhillon [2012] EWCA Civ 1020 . . . . 45.19
Aspin v Metric Group Ltd [2007] EWCA Civ 922. . . . . .6.03, 6.50, 6.169
Assaubayev v Michael Wilson & Partners Ltd [2014] EWHC 821 (QB). 36.56
Assaubayev & Ors v Michael Wilson & Partners Ltd [2014] EWCA Civ 1491 . . . . 5.28, 5.29, 5.31, 5.32, 5.33
Associated Electric and Gas Insurance Services Ltd v European Reinsurance Co of Zurich [2003] UKPC 11 . . . . 23.15
Associated Leisure v Associated Newspapers [1970] 2 QB 450 . . . . 26.10
Astilleros Canarios SA v 3264741 Nova Scotia Ltd (unreported), 21 July 2017, QBD 16.40
Astilleros Canarios SA v Cape Hatteras Shipping Co SA, The Cape Hatteras [1982] 1 Lloyd's Rep 518 . . . . 27.25
Astley v IRC [1974] STC 367. . . . . 4.07
Aston Cantlow and Wilmcote with Billesley Parochial Church Council v Wallbank [2003] UKHL 37, [2004] 1 AC 546 . . . . 24.10, 24.51
Astonleigh Residential Care Home Ltd v Goldfarb [2014] EWHC 4100 (Ch) 14.04
Astrazeneca UK Ltd v International Business Machines Corpn [2011] EWHC 3373 (TCC). 66.08, 66.09, 66.13, 66.17, 66.19
Atack v Lee [2004] EWCA Civ 1712 . . . . 54.58, 54.60, 54.74, 54.88
Atkins v Johnson Matthey & Co Ltd (unreported), 12 November 1970, QBD. 52.47, 52.57
Atkins (deceased) v Revenue & Customs Commissioners [2011] UKFTT 468 (TC) 6.109
Atkinson v Abbot (1855) 3 Drew 251 . . . . 27.208
Atlantic Bar and Grill Ltd v Posthouse Hotels Ltd [2000] CP Rep 32 . . . . 7.134
Atlas Metal Co v Miller [1898] 2 QB 500. . . . . 20.57
Attorney-General v Corpn of Chester (1851) 14 Beav 338 . . . . 7.06
Attorney General v Ebert [2001] EWHC Admin 695 . . . . 5.27
Attorney General of Belize v Belize Telecom Ltd [2009] UKPC 10 . . . . 31.57
Attorneys & Solicitors Act, Re (1870) 1 Ch D 575 . . . . .39.15
Audergon v La Baguette Ltd [2002] EWCA Civ 10 . . . . 45.16
Aujla v Sanghera [2004] EWCA Civ 121 . . . . 45.33
Austin v Miller Argent (South Wales) Ltd [2013] EWHC 2622 (TCC); [2011] EWCA Civ 928 . . . . 13.57
Austin v Miller Argent (South Wales) Ltd [2014] EWCA Civ 1012 . . . . 13.86
Austin & Ors v Miller Argent (South Wales) Ltd [2011] EWCA Civ 928. . . . . 65.22
Austinsuite Furniture Ltd [1992] BCLC 1047 . . . . 61.09
Australia and New Zealand Banking Group Ltd v Société Générale [2000] 1 All ER (Comm) 682 . . . . 45.61
Automotive Latch Systems Ltd v Honeywell International Inc [2006] EWHC 2340 (Comm). 15.36
Autoneum GB Ltd v Gilbert [2016] EWHC 3016 (QB). 6.274
Autoweld Systems Ltd v Kito Enterprises LLC [2010] EWCA Civ 1469. . . . . 15.10, 15.70, 15.111
Aveling Barford Ltd, Re [1988] 3 All ER 1019 . . . . 40.44
Avonwick Holdings Ltd v Webinvest Ltd [2014] EWCA Civ 1436. . . . . 6.217
Avrahami & Ors v Biran & Ors [2013] EWHC 1776 (Ch). 3.37, 3.39
AW Group Ltd v Taylor Walton [2013] EWHC 2610. . . . . .17.123
Awuah v Secretary of State for the Home Department [2017] UKFTT 555 (IAC) 9.108
Awwad v Geraghty [2001] QB 570. . . . . 4.15, 4.20, 9.49, 18.95, 18.102, 27.228, 27.242, 27.244, 27.264, 28.212, 29.180, 29.212, 31.56
AXA Equity & Law Life Assurance Society plc (No 1) (2001) 2 BCLC 447. . . . . .66.60, 66.66
AXA Sunlife Services plc v Campbell Martin Ltd [2011] EWCA Civ 549 . . . . 6.249
Axel Threlfall v ECD Insight [2013] EWCA Civ 144. . . . . 9.43
Axn & Ors v (1) Worboys [2012] EWHC 1730 (QB) 50.76
Azim v Tradewise Insurance Services Ltd [2016] EWHC B20 (Costs) 32.21
Azure East Midlands Ltd v Manchester Airport Group Property Developers [2014] EWHC 1644 (TCC). 12.57

Azzurrin Communications Ltd v International Telecommunications Equipment Ltd [2013] EWPCC 22 . . . . . 50.330

B v Auckland District Law Society [2003] 2 AC 736 . . . . . 36.107, 36.108, 46.69
B v B (wasted costs) [2001] 3 FCR 724 . . . . . 9.121, 9.161, 9.170, 9.210
B v Pendlebury [2002] EWHC 1797 (QB) 9.178
B (infants) [1965] 2 All ER 651 . . . . . 15.09
B and T (Care Proceedings: Legal Representation), Re [2001] FCR 512 . . . . . 24.41
Babury Ltd v London Industrial plc [1989] NJLR 1596 . . . . . 9.64
Bacal Contracting Ltd v Modern Engineering (Bristol) Ltd [1980] 2 All ER 655 . . . . . 9.03
Bagley v Branch [2007] EWHC 2344 (Ch) 43.159
Baile v Baile (1872) LR 13 Eq 497 . . . . . 23.93, 40.96
Bailes v Bloom (unreported), 23 November 2015, QBD 17.56, 17.145, 17.173
Bailey v GlaxoSmithKline UK Ltd [2017] EWHC 3195 (QB) 15.39, 15.56, 15.85, 15.90, 15.91
Bailey v IBC Vehicles Ltd [1998] 3 All ER 570 . . . . . 18.28, 18.30, 18.31, 18.32, 18.33, 18.34, 18.39, 18.47, 18.48, 18.51, 18.52, 27.94, 27.192, 28.200, 29.44, 29.46, 29.47, 29.49, 31.69, 46.36, 57.58, 57.63, 60.59
Baines v Bromley (1881) 6 QBD 691 . . . . . 6.63, 20.57
Baird v Moule's Patent Earth Closet Co Ltd (1881) LR 17 Ch D 139 . . . . . 7.120
Baird Textiles Holdings Ltd v Marks & Spencer plc [2001] EWCA Civ 274 . . . . . 27.199, 31.65
Bajwa v British Airways [1999] PIQR 152 . . . . . 6.57, 6.67
Bake v French (No 2) [1907] 2 Ch 215 . . . . . 27.119, 27.120, 27.124, 27.126, 27.152
Baker v Barnett [2015] EWHC 1375 (QB) 7.125
Baker v Dening (1838) 8 Ad & E 93 . . . . . 35.80
Baker v Ian McCall International Ltd [2000] CLC 189 . . . . . 23.31
Bal v Singh & Ors [2018] EWHC 119 (Ch) 19.09
Balabel v Air India [1988] Ch 317 . . . . . 46.16
Balch v Symes (1823) 1 Turn & R 87 . . . . . 40.48, 40.84
Baldwyn v Smith [1900] 1 Ch 588 . . . . . 60.61
Balevents Ltd v Sartori [2013] EWHC 2971 (Ch) 15.93
Balme v Paver (1821) Jac Rep 305 . . . . . 1.82, 27.112
Balmoral Group Ltd v Borealis (UK) Ltd [2006] EWHC 2531 (Comm) 16.40, 16.50, 16.61, 16.63
Banchio v Lai [2003] EWHC 9038 (Costs) 11.21, 14.05, 65.112
Bank of Baroda v Panessar [1987] Ch 335 . . . . . 16.50, 66.10
Bank of Baroda v Patel [2008] EWHC 3390 (Ch) 9.83
Bank of Credit and Commerce International SA (in liquidation) v Ali [2001] UKHL 8 . . . . . 31.11, 31.26, 31.29
Bank of Credit and Commerce International SA (in liquidation) v Ali (No 4) [1999] 149 NLJ 1734 . . . . . 6.03, 6.45, 6.160
Bank of Credit and Commerce International SA (in liquidation) v Ali (No 5) [2000] 2 Costs LR 243 . . . . . 20.29, 20.40, 20.44, 20.45, 20.27, 65.57, 65.59, 65.68
Bank of Ireland v Philip Pank Partnership [2014] EWHC 284 (TCC) 12.34
Bank of New South Wales v O'Connor (1889) 14 PC 273 . . . . . 66.27
Bank of Nova Scotia v Hellenic Mutual War Risk Association (Bermuda) Ltd, The Good Luck [1992] 1 AC 233 . . . . . 46.25
Bank of Scotland v Pereira [2011] EWCA Civ 241 . . . . . 6.12
Bank of Scotland v Qutb [2012] EWCA Civ 1661 . . . . . 16.48
Bank of Tokyo-Mitsubishi UFJ Ltd v Baskan Gida Sanayi Ve Pazarlama AS [2009] EWHC 1696 (Ch) 6.108, 16.48, 25.91
Bankamerica Finance Ltd v Nock [1988] AC 1002 . . . . . 7.19, 7.22
Banks v Humphrey & Glasgow [1997] PIQR P464, CA 9.190
Bannai v Erez [2013] EWHC 3204 (Comm) 15.72
Bansal v Cheema [2001] CP Rep 6 . . . . . 26.54
Barber, Re (1845) 14 M&W 720 . . . . . 36.94
Barber v Liverpool City Council (unreported), 16 November 2017, Liverpool County Court . . . 8.41
Barclays plc v Villers [2000] 1 All ER (Comm) 357 . . . . 27.210, 35.55, 35.66, 36.35, 36.36, 39.15, 40.32

Barclays Bank plc v Christie Owen & Davies Ltd (unreported), 24 November 2016, Ch D 6.189, 17.138
Barclays Bank Ltd v Quistclose Investments Ltd [1968] 3 All ER 651, HL 40.53
Barclays Bank plc v Kufner [2008] EWHC Comm 2319 . . . . . 28.172, 28.173
Barhan v Athreya and (2) Barking, Havering & Redbridge NHS Trust (unreported), 16 June 2007, Central London County Court 54.65
Bari v Rosen (t/a RA Rosen & Co Solicitors) [2012] EWHC 1782 (QB). 27.46, 27.52, 27.54, 27.59, 35.20, 35.65, 36.15, 36.33, 36.36
Barker v St Quintin (1844) 12 M & W 441 . . . . . 40.39
Barker v Stonehouse (unreported), 18 August 2015, Chelmsford County Court 50.297
Barkhuysen v Hamilton [2016] EWHC 3371 (QB) 16.49, 16.57, 56.96
Barndeal Ltd v Cherrywalk Properties Ltd [2005] EWHC 1377 (QB). 9.79
Barnes v Stones (a firm) [2007] EWHC 90069 (Costs). 36.36
Barnett v Creggy [2015] EWHC 1316 (Ch) 17.110, 56.47
Barratry, The Case of (30 Eliz 8 Rep 36). 30.04
Barratt, Goff and Tomlinson v Revenue and Customs Commissioners (Law Society intervening) [2011] UKFTT 71 (TC) 55.22, 55.23, 55.24
Barrell Enterprises, Re [1973] 1 WLR 1 . . . . . 10.10
Barr v Biffa Waste Services Ltd [2009] EWHC 1033 (TCC) 54.171, 65.43
Barr v Biffa Waste Services Ltd [2009] EWHC 2444 (TCC) 12.19
Barr v Biffa Waste Services Ltd (Costs) [2011] EWHC 1107 (TCC). 16.36, 16.45
Barret v Nutman (unreported), 20 June 2014, Liverpool County Court. 17.212
Barrett v Anne Robinson [2014] UKUT 322 (LC). 66.17
Barrett v Rutt-Field [2006] TLR 1505 . . . . . 36.94
Barretts & Baird (Wholesale) Ltd v Institute of Professional Civil Servants [1987] IRLR 3 . . . . . 7.112
Barrister (Wasted Costs Order) (No 1 of 1991), Re a [1993] QB 293 . . . . . 9.117, 9.164
Barrister (Wasted Costs Order) (No 4 of 1993), Re a The Times, 21 April 1995 . . . . . 9.193
Barrs v Jackson (1842) 1 Y&C Ch Cas 585. . . . . 23.20
Bartlett v Barclays Bank Trust Co Ltd [1980] Ch 515. . . . . 66.55
Bartletts de Reya v Byrne (1983) 127 Sol Jo 69, CA 35.81
Base Metal Trading Ltd v Shamurin [2003] EWHC 2606 (Comm). 6.183
Bassano v Toft [2014] EWHC 377 (QB) 35.82
Bataillion v Shone [2015] EWHC 3177 (QB). 17.83
Bateman v Joyce [2008] EWHC 90100 (Costs) 7.37
Bateman v Mid-Wales Rly Co (1866) LR 1 CP 499 . . . . . 22.18, 22.19
Baxendale-Walker v Law Society [2006] EWHC 643 (Admin) 61.14
Baxter Healthcare Ltd v Fresenius Kabi Deutschland GmBH [2014] EWHC 3021 (IPEC) 6.106, 50.336
Baylis, In re [1896] 2 Ch 107 . . . . . 27.124, 27.126, 35.45, 36.19
Bayliss v Kelly & Ors [1997] 2 Costs LR 54 . . . . . 20.30, 20.31, 20.37, 27.308, 65.56, 65.57
Bayly's Estate, ex p Humphrey (1860) 12 I Ch R 315 . . . . . 40.46
BCC v Lee [2008] EWCA Civ 891. . . . . 50.380, 50.401, 52.42
BCT Software Solutions Ltd v C Brewer & Sons Ltd [2003] EWCA Civ 939. . . . . 7.147, 45.30
BE Studios v Smith & Williamson Ltd [2005] EWHC 2730 (Ch). 16.40
Beach v Smirnov [2007] EWHC 3499. . . . . 14.21
Beachley Property Ltd v Edgar [1997] PNLR 197 . . . . . 26.40
Beahan v Stoneham (unreported), 19 January 2001, QBD. 6.263
Bean v Wade 2 Times LR 157. . . . . 27.191
Bear v Waxman [1912] VLR 29 . . . . . 27.211
Beasley v Alexander [2012] EWHC 2715 (QB) 17.57
Beattie v Smailes [2011] EWHC 3865 (Ch) 14.30
Beaumont v Senior and Bull [1903] 1 KB 282 . . . . . 1.106, 20.24
Beavan, Davies, Banks & Co v Beavan [1912] 1 Ch 196. . . . . 60.17, 60.62
Becke, Re (1843) 5 Beav 506 . . . . . 36.94
Becket, Purnell v Paine, Re [1918] 2 Ch 72, CA 22.06, 27.37
Beckett Bemrose & Hagan Solicitors v Future Mortgages Ltd [2010] EWHC 1997 (QB) 7.48

Beddoe, Downes v Cottam [1893] 1 Ch 547 . . . . 1.100, 66.32, 66.36, 66.57, 66.59, 66.77
Beecham Peacock Solicitors LLP v Enterprise Insurance Co plc [2014] EWHC 2194 (QB) 34.65
Beety v Nursing & Midwifery Council (unreported), 14 June 2017, QBD 13.57, 13.68, 13.71
Begg v HM Treasury [2016] EWCA Civ 568 . . . . 13.45
Belaney v Ffrench (1872) 8 Ch 918 . . . . 40.71
Belco Trading Ltd v Kordo [2008] EWCA Civ 205 . . . . 15.38, 15.121
Bell v Mahoney (unreported), 17 May 1991, Ch D 43.263, 43.284
Bell's Indenture, Bell v Hickley [1980] 3 All ER 425 . . . . 40.55
Bellamy v Sheffield Teaching Hospitals NHS Trust [2003] EWCA Civ 1124 . . . . 6.228
Bellway Homes Ltd v Seymour (Civil Engineering Contractors) Ltd [2013] EWHC 1890 (TCC) 17.168
Benaim (UK) Ltd v Davies Middleton & Davies Ltd [2004] EWHC 737 (TCC) 29.194, 30.02
Bennett (Viscount), Barclays Bank Ltd, Re [1950] 1 All ER 435 . . . . 53.94
Bensusan v Freedman [2001] EWHC 9001 (Costs), ... 4.67
Bent v Highways and Utilities Construction & Anor [2011] EWCA Civ 1539 . . . . 17.144
Bentinck, Bentinck v Bentinck, Re (1893) 37 Sol Jo 233 . . . . 27.77
Bentine v The Official Solicitor and Wilsons Solicitors LLP [2013] EWHC 3098 (Ch); [2015] EWCA Civ 1168 . . . . 36.76
Bentley v Gaisford [1997] QB 627 . . . . 40.62, 40.80, 40.87
Beoco Ltd v Alfa Laval Co Ltd [1995] 1 QB 137 . . . . 7.12
Berezovsky v Hine [2011] EWCA Civ 1089 . . . . 46.67
Berkeley Administration Inc v McClelland [1990] 2 QB 407, CA 15.73
Berliner Industriebank Aktiengesellschaft v Jost [1971] 1 QB 278 . . . . 23.119, 23.120
Bermuda International Securities Ltd v KPMG [2001] EWCA Civ 269 . . . . 7.48
Berry v British Transport Commission [1961] 3 All ER 65 . . . . 3.38, 3.43, 56.119
Berry v Spousals (unreported), 24 April 2007, Birmingham County Court 29.85
Besterman v British Motor Cab Co Ltd [1914] 3 KB 181 . . . . 7.07
Bestfort Developments LLP v Ras Al Khaimah Investment Authority [2016] EWCA Civ 1099 . . . . 15.73, 15.113
Bethlehem and Bridewell Hospitals, Re (1885) 30 Ch D 542 . . . . 1.103
Betts v Cleaver (1872) 20 WR 732 . . . . 53.134
Bevan Ashford (a firm) v Geoff Yeandle (Contractors) Ltd (in liquidation) [1999] Ch 239 . . . . 29.07, 29.211, 30.17
Beynon v Scadden [1999] IRLR 700 (EAT) 16.55
BFS Investments plc v Manches plc [2007] EWHC 90082 (Costs) 36.36
Bhamjee v Forsdick [2003] EWCA Civ 113 . . . . 5.24
BICC Ltd v Parkman Consulting Engineers (a firm) [2001] EWCA Civ 1621, (2002) BLR 64 . . . . 19.42, 19.43
Biddencare Ltd, Re [1994] 2 BCLC 160 . . . . 66.62
Bidder v Bridges [1887] WN 208 . . . . 59.40, 59.45
Biffa Waste Services Ltd v Maschinenfabrik Ernst Hese GmBH [2008] EWHC 2657 (TCC) 6.152
Biggin & Co Ltd v Permanite Ltd (1951) 2 KB 314, CA 19.44
Bignold, In re (1845) 9 Beav 269 . . . . 36.18
Biguzzi v Rank Leisure plc [1999] EWCA Civ 1972 . . . . 4.38
Bilkus v Stockler Brunton (a firm) [2010] EWCA Civ 101 . . . . 3.21, 3.24, 3.29, 3.36, 27.120, 27.206, 31.70, 35.94, 35.95, 38.27
Billington v Downs Solicitors LLP (unreported), 16 January 2012, SCCO 38.79
Bim Kemi AB v Blackburn Chemicals Ltd [2003] EWCA Civ 889 . . . . 7.184, 45.57, 56.57, 56.66, 56.71, 56.72, 56.77, 56.78, 56.103, 56.105
Bingham v Abru Ltd (unreported), 13 November 2015, Sheffield County Court 17.166
Bird v Acorn Group Ltd [2016] EWCA Civ 1096 . . . . 50.276
Bird v Harris [1881] WN 5, CA 27.207
Bird v Heath (1848) 6 Hare 236 . . . . 40.48
Bird v Meggitt Aerospace (unreported), 22 June 2012, Nottingham County Court 50.139
Birmingham City Council v H (a minor) [1994] 2 WLR 31 . . . . 49.53, 49.54, 53.125
Birmingham City Council v Lee [2008] EWCA Civ 891 . . . . 4.59, 52.25

Bishop, ex p Langley, ex p Smith, Re (1879) 13 Ch D 110, CA 22.06, 27.37
BJ Crabtree v GPT Communication Systems (1990) 59 BLR 43 . . . . 15.10, 15.65, 15.69, 15.70
Black v Arriva North East Ltd [2014] EWCA Civ 1115 . . . . 13.25, 13.38
Black v Davies [2005] EWCA Civ 531 . . . . 56.05, 56.124
Black v Pastouna & Anor [2005] EWCA Civ 1389 . . . . 49.79
Black-Clawson International Ltd v Papierwerke Waldhof-Aschaffenburg AG [1981]
2 Lloyd's Rep 4 . . . . 48.71
Blackham v Entrepose UK [2004] EWCA Civ 1109 . . . . 17.106, 17.107, 17.111
Blackmore, In re (1851) 13 Beav 154 . . . . 35.123, 36.19, 39.11
Bake v French (No 2) [1907] 2 Ch 215 . . . . 39.11
Blake v Hummell (1884) 51 LT 430 . . . . 23.95
Blake v O'Kelly (1874) IR 9 Eq 54 . . . . 23.14, 23.21
Blake, Clutterbuck, Re v Bradford [1945] Ch 61 . . . . 40.91, 40.96
Blakemore v Cummings [2009] EWCA Civ 1276 . . . . 3.100, 14.09, 43.378
Blair & Girling, Re [1906] 2 KB 131 . . . . 22.09, 52.04, 52.08
Blair v Danesh [2009] EWCA Civ 516 . . . . 27.32, 29.58
Blankenstein, The [1985] 1 WLR 435 . . . . 32.36
Blankley v Central Manchester and Manchester Children's University Hospitals NHS Trust
[2014] EWHC 168 (QB); [2015] EWCA Civ 18 . . . . . . 18.28, 18.103, 27.36, 27.80, 60.22, 60.63
Blavo v The Law Society [2017] EWHC 561 (Ch) 40.123
Bligh v Davies (1860) 28 Beav 211 . . . . 40.80
Bloomberg LP v Sandberg (a firm) [2016] EWHC 488 (TCC) 12.93, 12.98, 12.101
Bloomsbury Law v MacPhearson [2016] EWHC 3395 (QB) 35.53, 35.63, 35.125
Bluck v Lovering & Co (1886) 35 WR 232 . . . . 40.60
Blueco Ltd v Bwat Retail Nominee [2014] EWCA Civ 154 . . . . 16.50
Bluewaters Communications Holdings LLC v Ecclestone [2018] EWHC 78 (Comm) 15.57, 15.60,
15.63, 15.91, 15.92, 15.121
Blunt v Heslop (1838) 4 A&E 577 . . . . 36.29, 40.05
Blyth v Fladgate [1891] 1 Ch 337 . . . . 27.323
Blythe v Topham (1607) Cro Jack 158 . . . . 1.38
BMA Special Opportunity Hub Fund Ltd v African Minerals Finance Ltd [2013]
EWCA Civ 416 . . . . 31.20
BNM v MGN Ltd [2017] EWCA Civ 1767 . . . . 2.09, 25.83, 25.84, 52.02
Boake Allen Ltd v Revenue and Customs Commissioners [2007] UKHL 25 . . . . 65.28
Board of Trustees of National Museums & Galleries on Merseyside v AEW Architects &
Designers Ltd [2013] EWHC 3025 (TCC) 12.111, 14.30, 16.33, 16.45
Boardman v Phipps [1967] 2 AC 46 . . . . 27.249
Bobolas v Economist Newspaper Ltd [1987] 3 All ER 121 . . . . 23.21
Bocacina Ltd v Boca Cafes Ltd [2014] EWHC 26 (IPEC) 16.33, 16.34, 50.336
Bock v Gorrissen (1860) 2 De G F & J 434, CA 40.53
Bodo Community, The v Shell Petroleum Development Company of Nigeria Ltd [2014]
EWHC 2170 (TCC) 6.36
Bolden v Nicholay (1857) 3 Jur NS 884 . . . . 27.33, 49.147
Bolivinter Oil SA v Chase Manhattan Bank [1984] 1 Ll R 251 . . . . 40.10
Bolt Burdon Solicitors v Tariq & Ors [2016] EWHC 811 (QB) 4.24, 4.25, 4.27, 4.43, 27.118,
27.131, 27.134, 27.175
Bolton v Liverpool Corpn (1833) 1 My & K 88 . . . . 46.20, 46.25
Bolton Metropolitan District Council v Secretary of State for the Environment [1996]
1 All ER 184 . . . . 67.15
Bonham v Blake Lapthorne Linell and Fishwick [2006] EWHC 2513 (Ch) 66.61
Bonser v Bradshaw (1860) 25 JP 483 . . . . 23.93, 40.96
Booker Belmont Wholesale Ltd v Ashford Developments Ltd [2000] Lexis Citation 1833 . . . . . . 6.15
Boorman & Anor v Godfrey [1981] 2 All ER 1012 . . . . 62.04
Booth v Britannia Hotels Ltd [2002] EWCA Civ 579 . . . . 6.149, 49.11, 57.22
Born, Re [1900] 2 Ch 433 . . . . 40.79, 40.96
Born v Turner [1900] 2 Ch 211 . . . . 1.98

BOS GmbH & Co KG v Cobra UK Automotive Products Division Ltd (in administration) [2012] EW PCC 44 . . . . . 50.336
Bostock v Ransey UDC [1900] 2 QB 616. . . . . 6.78
Boswell v Coaks (1888) 57 LJ Ch 101 . . . . . 56.23
Botham v Khan [2004] EWHC 2602 (QB) 6.218, 18.13, 23.79
Botrill v Thompson (unreported), 27 October 2017, QBD 16.37
Bottin (International) Investments Ltd v Venson Group plc [2005] EWHC 90005 (Costs) 7.87, 7.96, 43.81
Boughton v Knight (1873) LR 3 P & D 64. . . . . 60.57
Bourne v Colodense Ltd (1998) The Times, 4 February; Allen v Francis [1914] 3 KB 1065, CA 30.52
Bourne v Stanbridge [1965] 1 WLR 189, CA 6.22
Bournemouth & Boscombe Athletic Football Club Ltd v Lloyds TSB Bank plc [2004] EWCA Civ 935 . . . . . 9.28
Bourns Inc v Raychem Corpn [1999] 3 All ER 154. . . . . 46.32, 46.69, 46.70
Bovis Homes Ltd v Kendrick Construction Ltd [2009] EWHC 1359 (TCC) 6.109
Bowcott v Walding [2003] EWHC 9042 (Costs). 53.39, 53.82, 53.84
Bowen v Bridgend County Borough Council [2004] EWHC 9010 (Costs) 29.87
Bowman v DPP [1991] RTR 263 . . . . . 50.77
Bowskill v Dawson [1955] 1 QB 13, [1954] 2 All ER 649, CA 34.66
Boxall v Waltham Forest LBC (2001) 4 CCL Rep 258 . . . . . 6.250, 7.25, 7.146, 7.163
Boycott, Re (1885) LR 29 Ch D 571. . . . . 36.36
Boydell v Durmmond (1809) 11 East 142 . . . . . 31.54
Boynton v Willers [2003] EWCA Civ 904 . . . . . 16.33, 21.31, 50.345, 50.397
Bozon v Bolland (1839) 4 My & Cr 354 . . . . . 40.37, 40.40
BP Exploration Co (Libya) Ltd v Hunt (No 2) [1979] 1 WLR 783 . . . . . 27.27
BP Refinery (Westernport) Pty Ltd v President, Councillors and Ratepayers of the Shire of Hastings (1977) 52 ALJR 20 . . . . . 31.60
Brabant, The [1967] 1 QB 588 . . . . . 31.34
Brabners LLP v Commissioners for HM Revenue & Customs [2017] UKFTT 0666 (TC) 55.19, 55.22, 55.24
Bradford and Bingley Building Society v Seddon [1999] 4 All ER 217 . . . . . 23.32
Bradford & Bingley plc v Rashid [2006] UKHL 37 . . . . . 48.44
Bradford Metropolitan District Council v Yorkshire Water Services Ltd [2001] EWHC 803 (Admin) 61.11, 61.13, 61.14
Bradlaugh v Newdegate (1883) 11 QBD 1 . . . . . 30.11, 30.12
Bragg v Crosville Motor Services Ltd [1959] 1 All ER 613 . . . . . 4.07, 169
Brahilika v Allianz Insurance plc (unreported), 30 July 2015, Romford County Court 8.29
Brampton Manor (Leisure) v McLean [2007] EWHC 3340 (Ch) 9.83
Brandao v Barnett (1846) 12 Cl & Fin 787, HL 40.37, 40.53
Brawley v Marczynski (No 1) [2002] EWCA Civ 756 . . . . . 7.142
Brawley v Marczynski & Anor (No 2) [2002] EWCA Civ 1453 . . . . . 16.16
Bray v Stuart A West & Co [1989] NLJR 753. . . . . 23.100
Bray (t/a the Building Company) v Bishop (unreported) 19 June 2009, CA,. 7.125, 7.147
Bray (t/a the Building Company) v Bishop & Anor [2009] EWCA Civ 768 . . . . . 45.30, 45.31
Bray Walker Solicitors (A Firm) v Silvera [2010] EWCA Civ 332; [2008] EWHC 3147 (QB) 29.61, 29.65, 29.79, 29.87, 29.158
Brazier v Camp (1894) 9 R 852, CA. 27.323
Breadner v Granville-Grossman (Costs) [2001] WTLR 377 . . . . . 66.52
Bremer Vulkan Schiffbau und Maschinenfabrik v South India Shipping Corpn Ltd [1981] AC 909 . . . . . 5.32
Brennan v Association Asphalt Ltd [2006] EWHC 90052 (Costs). 29.63
Brennan v Bolt Burdon [2004] EWCA Civ 1017 . . . . . 31.56
Brewer v SCCO [2009] EWHC 986 (QB) 45.75
Bridgewater v Griffiths [2000] 1 WLR 524 . . . . . 18.97, 18.101, 27.203, 27.204
Brierley v Prescott [2006] EWHC 90062 (Costs) 27.32
Briggs v CEF Holdings Ltd [2017] EWCA Civ 2363 . . . . . 17.82, 17.121, 17.131, 17.132, 17.142

Briggs v First Choice Holidays & Flights Ltd [2017] EWHC 2012 (QB). 54.81, 57.34, 65.92, 65.103
Bright v Low 1940 SC 280 . . . . 43.292
Bright v Motor Insurers' Bureau [2014] EWHC 1557 (QB) 54.87
Bright's Trustee v Sellar [1904] 1 Ch 370 . . . . .49.150
Brimko Holdings Ltd v Eastman Kodak Co [2004] EWHC 1343 (Ch). 15.80
Briscoe v Briscoe [1892] 3 Ch 543 . . . . 40.96
Briscoe v Tilt (unreported), 9 February 2012, SCCO. 50.91
Bristol Alliance Ltd v Williams [2012] EWCA Civ 1267 . . . . 63.04
Bristol Corpn v Cox (1884) LR 26 Ch D 678 . . . . .46.20, 46.23
Bristol-Myers Squib Co v Baker Norton Pharmaceuticals Inc (No 2) [2001] RPC 45. . . . . 10.05
Bristol and West Building Society v Evans and Bullock (unreported),
5 February 1996, CA 17.214, 17.215
Bristow v Princess Alexander Hospital NHS Trust [2015] EWHC B22 (Costs) 48.55
Brit Inns Ltd (in liquidation) v BDW Trading Ltd [2012] EWHC 2489 (TCC). 6.113, 6.152, 6.155, 16.36, 16.48, 17.62
British Airways Pension Schemes, Re [2000] Pens LR 311 . . . . .66.60, 66.66
British Cash and Parcel Conveyors Ltd v Lamson Store Service Co Ltd [1908]
1 KB 1006 . . . . .30.07, 30.13, 30.22
British Coal Corpn v Dennis Rye Ltd (No 2) [1988] 1 WLR 1113 . . . . 46.69
British Gas Trading Ltd v Oak Cash and Carry Ltd [2016] EWCA Civ 153. . . . . .26.64, 26.70
British Metal Corpn Ltd v Ludlow Bros [1938] Ch 987 . . . . 53.122
British Racing Drivers' Club Ltd v Hextall Erskine & Co (a firm) [1996] 3 All ER 667 . . . . 3.38, 56.119
British Sky Broadcasting Group PLC v Digital Satellite Warranty Cover Ltd (in liquidation)
[2012] EWHC 3679 (Ch) 16.48
British Waterways Board v Norman (1993) 26 HLR 232 . . . . 27.219, 27.221, 29.180, 29.209
Broad and Broad, Re (1885) 15 QBD 252, DC. 53.131
Broadhurst & Anor v Tan & Anor [2016] EWCA Civ 94. . . . . .4.10, 4.34, 17.163, 43.231, 50.70, 50.287, 50.293, 50.294, 50.295, 50.336
Brockelbank v Brockelbank and Borlase (1911) 27 TLR 569 . . . . 60.04
Brockman, Re [1908–10] All ER Rep 364 . . . . 36.30, 36.31, 40.31
Bromley v Hewson (unreported), 6 September 2012, Medway County Court 50.167
Broni v Ministry of Defence [2015] EWHC 66 (QB) 50.125, 50.126
Brookes v HSBC Bank plc; Jemitus v Bank of Scotland plc [2011]
EWCA Civ 354 . . . . 7.115, 7.120, 7.121, 7.122, 7.126, 7.127, 7.130, 7.133
Brookfield Construction (UK) Ltd v Mott Macdonald Ltd [2010] EWHC 659 (TCC). 48.08
Brooks v AH Brooks & Co (a firm) [2010] EWHC 2720 (Ch) 7.128
Brooks v DC Leisure Management Ltd [2013] EW Misc 17 (CC) 27.32, 27.33, 27.34
Broom v Archer (unreported), 28 March 2018, QBD. 12.104, 12.128
Broomhead, Re (1847) 5 Dow & L 52 . . . . 40.84
Brown, Re (1867) LR 4 Eq 464 . . . . .36.05, 36.82
Brown, In re (1883) 23 Ch D 377. . . . . 20.57
Brown v Bennett [2002] 2 All ER 273 . . . . 9.165
Brown v Bennett (Wasted Costs) (No 1) [2002] 1 WLR 713 . . . . 9.105
Brown v Gould [1972] Ch 53 . . . . 5.21
Brown v Guardian Royal Exchange plc [1994] 2 Lloyd's Rep 325. . . . . 46.67
Brown v KMR Services [1995] 2 Lloyd's Rep 513 . . . . 56.76
Brown v Mcasso Music Production [2005] EWCA Civ 1546 . . . . . .6.207, 6.240, 17.63, 17.65, 17.109
Brown v Rice [2007] EWHC 625 (Ch) 48.26
Brown v Stott [2003] UKHL 21. . . . . 24.08
Brown v Tibbits (1862) 11 CBNS 855 . . . . .35.114
Brown-Quinn & Anor v Equity Syndicate Management Ltd & Anor [2012] EWCA Civ
1633; [2011] EWHC 2661 (Comm). 34.16, 34.17, 34.66, 36.92
Browne v Barber [1913] 2 KB 553. . . . . 2.09, 3.94, 52.02
Browne v Black [1912] 1 KB 316, CA 40.05
Browne v Dunn (1894) 6 R 67 . . . . 8.44
Browne v Gibbons (1702) 91 ER 184 . . . . 1.46

Brownton v Edward Moore Inbucon Ltd [1985] 3 All ER 499 . . . . 30.39
Bruce v Warwick (1815) 6 Taunt 118 . . . . 60.11
Brush v Bower Cotton & Bower [1993] 4 All ER 741; [1993] 1 WLR 1328. . . . . . . 49.17, 49.19, 49.57, 49.63, 49.94, 49.131, 53.43
Bruty v Edmundson [1918] 1 Ch 112, CA 66.79
Bryant, Ex p (1815) 1 Madd 49. . . . . 40.39, 40.107
Bryen & Langley Ltd v Boston [2005] EWCA Civ 973 . . . . 44.24
BSkyB v HP Enterprises [2010] EWHC 862 (TCC) 16.47
Buchanan v Findlay (1829) 9 B & C 738 . . . . 40.53
Buckinghamshire County Council v Moran [1990] Ch 623. . . . . 48.44
Buckland v Watts [1970] 1 QB 27 . . . . 59.02, 59.39, 59.43
Buckton [1907] 2 Ch 406. . . . . 1.106, 66.36, 66.41, 66.46, 66.47, 66.48, 66.49, 66.50, 66.56
Buckwell and Berkeley, Re [1902] 2 Ch 596. . . . . 35.116, 52.04, 52.08
Budana v The Leeds Teaching Hospitals NHS Trust & Anor [2017] EWCA Civ 1980. . . . . 27.72, 27.83, 32.02, 32.06, 32.12, 32.17, 32.18, 32.21, 32.24, 32.25, 32.27, 32.34, 32.39
Budgen v Andrew Gardner Partnership [2002] EWCA Civ 1125. . . . . 6.178, 6.179
Budgens Stores Ltd v Hastings Magistrates Court [2009] EWHC 1646 (Admin) 43.317
Budgett v Budgett [1895] 1 Ch 202 . . . . 23.97, 23.114
Bufton v Hill [2002] EWHC 9024 (Costs) 43.335, 43.364
Buildability Ltd v O'Donnell Developments Ltd [2009] EWHC 3196 (TCC). 54.66
Building Contractors Ltd v Ahmed, The Independent, 23 November 1998 . . . . 6.248, 6.253
Bulkley v Wilford (1834) 2 Cl & Fin 102, H 40.55
Bull v Faulkner (1848) 2 De G & Sm 772 . . . . 40.45
Bullock v London General Omnibus Co and Ors [1907] 1 KB 264 . . . . 1.106, 2.09, 7.05, 7.10, 7.11, 7.17
Burchell v Bullard & Ors [2005] EWCA Civ 358. 6.63, 6.128, 20.03, 20.53
Burchell v Clark (1876) 2 CPD 88 . . . . 31.52
Burford Corpn v Lenthall (1743) 2 Atk 551 . . . . 1.63
Burgess v British Steel plc [2000] PIQR Q240 . . . . 17.55, 17.137
Burgess v Cox [1951] Ch 383 . . . . 31.50
Burke v Greene (1814) 2 Ball & B 517 . . . . 30.12
Burn v Brown (1817) 2 Stark 272 . . . . 40.53
Burridge v Bellew (1875) 32 LT 807. . . . . 20.23, 20.35, 27.310, 27.313
Burridge v Stafford; Khan v Ali [2000] 1 WLR 927. . . . . 62.06, 62.40
Burrows v Vauxhall Motors Ltd [1998] PIQR P48, CA 57.44, 57.52
Burstein v Times Newspapers Ltd [2002] EWCA Civ 1739 . . . . 18.30, 18.35, 18.37, 18.54, 27.223, 27.225, 43.321
Bury v Greenwood (1934) WN 119 . . . . 1.74
Bush, Re (1844) 8 Bear 66 . . . . 35.86
Bush v Bank Mandiri (Europe) Ltd (unreported), 17 January 2014, QBD 15.47, 15.49
Bush v Martin (1863) 2 H & C 311 . . . . 3.06
Bush v Rogers [1915] 1 KB 707. . . . . 1.102
Bushell, ex p Great Western Rly Co, Re (1882) 22 Ch D 470, CA 40.79
Bushwell Properties v Vortex Properties [1975] 2 All ER 214 . . . . 49.112
Business Environment Bow Lane v Deanswater Estates Ltd [2009] EWHC 2014 (Ch) 6.150, 10.12, 49.05, 57.06, 57.34
Butcher v Wolfe [1999] BLR 61 . . . . 7.142
Butler v Hobson (1838) 5 Bing NC 128 . . . . 52.59
Butler's Will, ex p Metropolitan Board of Works, Re (1912) 106 LT 673 . . . . 58.02
Buxton v Baughan (1834) 6 C & P 674 . . . . 40.37
BWE International Ltd v Jones [2003] EWCA Civ 298 . . . . 29.58, 31.49
Byatt v Nash [2002] All ER (D) 353. . . . . 40.125
Byrne v Kunkel & Kunkel [1999] 1 CL 349 . . . . 18.28, 27.194, 27.203
Byrne v Poplar Housing and Regeneration Community Association Ltd [2012] EWCA Civ 832 . . . . 25.13
Byrne v South Sefton Health Authority [2001] EWCA Civ 1904. . . . 7.182, 9.108, 9.111, 9.112, 9.166

C v D [2011] EWCA Civ 646 . . . . .4.81, 17.22, 17.46, 17.67, 17.70, 17.71, 17.73, 17.74, 17.164, 17.166, 17.176, 17.219, 31.27, 31.34
C (a child) (wasted costs), Re [2015] EWHC 3259 (Fam) 9.175
C (a patient acting by her litigation friend Jocelyn Fox) v W [2008] EWCA Civ 1459 . . . . .54.74, 54.85, 54.89, 54.92
Cachia v Hanes (1994) 179 CLR 4030 . . . . 3.16
Caddick v Skidmore (1857) 2 De G&J 52 . . . . 31.48
Cadwallader v Akzo Nobel UK (unreported), 16 June 2014, Liverpool County Court. 43.144
Calderbank v Calderbank [1976] Fam 93. . . . . 6.06, 6.207, 43.253, 43.298
Caldwell v Sumpters [1972] Ch 478, [1971] 3 All ER 892. . . . . .40.80, 40.85
Caley v Caley (1877) 25 WR 528 . . . . 60.05
Caliendo v Mishcon De Reya (a firm) [2014] EWHC 3414 (Ch); [2015] EWCA Civ 1029. . . . 54.119, 54.122, 54.123
Caliendo v Mishcon De Reya (unreported), 18 November 2015, Ch D 12.128
Caliendo v Mischon De Reya [2016] EWHC 150 (Ch) 27.192
Caliendo v Mischon De Reya [2016] EWHC 770 (Ch) 16.48
Callery v Gray [2002] UKHL 28 . . . . 24.44, 24.45, 45.70, 54.137, 54.158, 54.160, 66.04
Callery v Gray [2001] EWCA Civ 1117 . . . . .49.149, 54.60, 54.62, 54.64, 54.65, 57.10
Callery v Gray (No 2) [2001] EWCA Civ 1246 . . . . .4.81, 34.37, 54.143, 54.157, 54.163, 54.166, 54.168, 54.172, 54.125
Callis, Re (1901) 49 WR 316 . . . . 1.112, 36.19, 40.32
Calltel Telecom Ltd & Anor v HM Revenue & Customs [2008] EWHC 2107 (Ch) 15.64, 15.79, 15.80
Cambertown Timber Merchants Ltd v Sidhu [2011] EWCA Civ 1041. . . . . .6.68, 45.25
Camden London Borough Council v Makers UK Ltd [2009] EWHC 605 (TCC) 15.70
Camdex International Ltd v Bank of Zambia (No 1) [1998] QB 22 . . . . .30.10, 30.38
Cameron v Office Depot UK Ltd (unreported), 13 July 2016, Bromley County Court 50.385
Campbell v Campbell [2016] EWHC 2237 (Ch). 12.18
Campbell v Campbell [2017] EWHC 182 (Ch) 3.38
Campbell v Campbell [2018] EWCA Civ 80 . . . . .59.30, 59.35
Campbell v Campbell and Lewis [1941] 1 All ER 274, CA. 40.58, 40.91
Campbell v MGN Ltd [2004] UKHL 22. .24.44, 24.45, 24.46, 24.49–24.53
Campbell v MGN Ltd (No 2) [2005] UKHL 61 . . . . .13.40, 54.203
Cannee v Spanton (1844) 8 Scott NR 714 . . . . 40.76
Cantor Fitzgerald International v Tradition (UK) Ltd [2003] EWHC 1907 (Ch) 53.39
Capita Translation and Interpreting, Re [2015] EWFC 5. . . . . 9.73
Capital Bank Plc v Stickland [2004] EWCA Civ 1677. . . . . .17.176
Capital for Enterprise Fund A LP v Bibby Financial Services Ltd (unreported), 18 November 2015, Ch D (Manchester District Registry) 12.124, 12.125, 14.28
Capital Markets Company (UK) Ltd, The v Tarver [2017] EWHC 2885 Ch 12.62, 12.84, 12.96
Car Giant Ltd v The Mayor and Burgesses of the London Borough of Hammersmith [2017] EWHC 464 (TCC). 12.125, 16.33
Cardshops Ltd v John Lewis Properties Ltd [1983] QB 161 . . . . 29.38
Cardwell, A-G v Day [1912] 1 Ch 779 . . . . 66.45
Carey v HSBC Bank Plc [2009] EWHC 3417 (QB), [2010] Bus LR 114 . . . . 28.193
Carillion JM Ltd v PHI Group Ltd [2011] EWHC 1581 (TCC). 6.258
Carl Zeiss Stiftung v Rayner & Keeler Ltd (No 2) [1965] Ch 596, [1965] 1 All ER 300, CA. . . 53.133
Carl Zeiss Stiftung v Rayner & Keeler Ltd (No 2) [1967] 1 AC 853 . . . . 23.31
Carl Zeiss Stiftung v Rayner & Keeler Ltd (No 3) [1969] 3 All ER 897 . . . . .23.18, 23.24
Carleton v Strutt & Parker (a partnership) [2008] EWHC 424 (QB) 6.128
Carlisle & Cumbria United Independent Supports' Society Ltd v CUFC Holding Ltd [2010] EWCA Civ 463. . . . . .6.132, 66.55
Carlon v Domino's Pizza Group Ltd (unreported), 27 August 2010, Birmingham County Court 50.91
Carlton v Theodore Goddard & Co [1973] 1 WLR 623 . . . . 35.103, 35.105, 35.107, 35.108
Carmichael v National Power plc [1999] 1 WLR 2042. . . . . 50.123

Carnac, ex p Simmonds, In re (1885) 16 QBD 308 . . . . 53.12
Carr v Allen-Bradley Electronics Ltd [1980] ICR 603; [1980] IRLR 263, EAT 9.58
Carroll v Kynaston [2010] EWCA Civ 1404 . . . . 3.38, 3.43, 52.98
Carter, Carter v Carter, Re (1885) 55 LJ Ch 230. . . . . 23.98
Carter-Ruck (a firm) v Mireskandari [2011] EWHC 24 (QB). 4.67, 35.67
Carthew, In re, In re Paull (1884) 27 Ch D 485 . . . . 36.63
Cartwright, Re (1873) LR 16 Eq 469 . . . . 27.59, 35.86, 36.36
Carven, Re (1845) 8 Beav 436 . . . . 35.87
Carver v BAA plc [2008] EWCA Civ 412. . . . . 6.155, 17.15, 17.86, 17.109
Casey's Patents; Stewart v Casey, Re [1892] 1 Ch 104. . . . . 39.20
Cashman v Mid Essex Hospital Services NHS Trust [2015] EWHC 1312 (QB) 17.81, 43.346, 43.349
Casseldine v The Diocese of Llandaff (unreported), 3 July 2015, Cardiff County Court. 8.20
Cassell & Co Ltd v Broome [1972] AC 1027 . . . . 4.06
Castellain v Preston (1883) 11 QBD 380, CA. 18.73, 18.75
Castillejo v Castillejo, The Times, 12 December 1974 . . . . 1.135, 51.09
Catalano v Espley-Tyas Development Group Ltd [2017] EWCA Civ 1132. . . . . 8.19, 8.20
Catalyst Investment Group Ltd v Max Lewisohn, Maximillian and Co (a firm) [2009] EWHC 3501 (Ch) 16.40, 16.44
Catalyst Managerial Services v Libya Africa Investment Portfolio [2017] EWHC 1236 (Comm) 15.38
Catlin, Re (1854) 18 Beav 508 . . . . 35.87, 35.92
Caton v Caton (1867) LR 2 HL 127. . . . . 29.102
Catt v Wood [1908] 2 KB 458, CA. 60.06
Cave v Bulley Davey (a firm) [2013] EWHC 4246 (QB) 17.166, 21.12
Cawdery Kaye Fireman & Taylor v Minkin [2012] EWCA Civ 546. . . . . . . 27.71, 27.89, 38.76, 45.64
Cawley & Whatley, Re (1870) 18 WR 1125 . . . . 1.83, 27.112
Cebora v SIP [1976] 1 Ll R 271 . . . . 40.09
Cecil v Bayat [2011] EWCA Civ 135 . . . . 33.68
Cementation Construction Ltd v Keaveney (1988) The Independent, 12 July 52.20, 52.41
Central Independent Television plc & Ors, Re [1991] 1 All ER 347 . . . . 64.04
Central London Property Trust Ltd v High Trees House Ltd [1947] KB 130 . . . . 39.19
Centrehigh Ltd v Amen [2013] EWHC 625 (Ch) 9.84
Centrehigh Ltd v Amen [2013] EWHC 1448 (Ch) 9.22
Centrehigh Ltd (t/a Shono UK) v Amen (unreported), 18 July 2001, Ch D 10.27
CG v Facebook Ireland Ltd [2015] NIQB 28 . . . . 16.16
CG Group Ltd v Breyer Group plc [2013] EWHC 2959 (TCC). 16.39
CH (a minor) (2000) The Times, 6 June. 57.53
C&H Engineering v F Klucznic & Son Ltd [1992] FSR 667 . . . . 17.55
Chadwell v Bruer (1728) 1 Barn KB 43 . . . . 1.61
Chadwick v Bowman (1885–86) LR 16 QBD 561. . . . . 46.27
Chadwick v Hollingsworth (No 2) [2010] EWHC 2718 . . . . 6.116
Chaffe v Kingsley [2006] EWHC 3412 (QB). 43.322
Chamberlain v Boodle & King [1982] 3 All ER 188; [1982] 1 WLR 1443 . . . . 27.59, 27.130, 27.142, 27.145, 27.148, 27.149, 27.151, 27.162, 27.211, 35.27, 35.86, 36.15, 39.14, 48.09
Chamberlain v DCT (1988) 164 CLR 502. . . . . 23.27
Chandler v Boswell [1936] 3 ARE 179. . . . . 18.99
Chandler v Brown (2001) CP Rep 103 (Ch D). 15.47, 15.48, 15.49
Chanel Ltd v FW Woolworth & Co Ltd [1981] 1 WLR 485. . . . . 10.18
Chantrey Martin (a firm) v Martin [1953] 2 QB 286 . . . . 40.75
Chantrey Vellacott v The Convergence Group plc [2007] EWHC 1774 (Ch) 16.39, 49.133, 49.138
Chaplair Ltd v Kumari [2015] EWCA Civ 798 . . . . 49.164, 66.30
Chaplin v Leslie Frewin (Publishers) Ltd [1966] Ch 71 . . . . 60.19, 60.30
Chapman, Re (1903) 20 TLR 3, CA. 35.124
Chapman v Chapman [1985] 1 WLR 599 . . . . 23.73, 57.56
Chapman v Oakleigh Animal Products Ltd (1970) 8 KIR 1063, CA 27.93

Chappell, ex p Ford (1885) 16 QBD 305, CA 27.191, 27.192, 31.62
Chappell v De Bora's of Exeter (a firm) [2004] EWHC 90020 (Costs) 34.20
Chappell v Mehta [1981] 1 All ER 349 . . . . 35.93
Chapple v Cooper (1844) 13 M & W 252 . . . . 60.16
Chapple v Williams (1999) LTL, 8 December, CA 15.97
Charge Card Services Ltd, Re [1987] Ch 150 . . . . 66.64
Charles v Gillian Radford & Co [2003] EWHC 3180 (Ch) 9.95, 9.113, 9.150, 9.157, 9.166, 9.188
Charles v NTL Group Ltd [2002] EWCA Civ 2004 . . . . 17.28, 17.43
Charles Church Developments Ltd v Stent Foundations Ltd [2007] EWHC 855 (TCC) 6.95
Charlesworth v Relay Road Ltd & Ors [2000] 1 WLR 230 . . . . 26.29, 26.40, 26.41
Charman v Brandon (1900) 82 LT 369 . . . . 53.86
Chartbrook Ltd v Persimmon Homes Ltd [2009] UKHL 38 . . . . 31.04, 31.31, 31.42
Chase v Westmore (1816) 5 M & S 180 . . . . 40.50
Chase Manhattan Bank NA v Israel-British Bank (London) Ltd [1981] Ch 105 . . . . 40.37
Cheater v Cater [1918] 1 KB 247, CA 4.07
Cheese v Keen [1908] 1 Ch 245 . . . . 23.101
Cheeseman, Re [1891] 2 Ch 289, CA 36.38
Chell Engineering Ltd v Unit Tool and Engineering Co Ltd [1950] 1 All ER 378 . . . . 21.10
Chemetall Ltd v Pan European Logistics Ltd (unreported), 12 March 2014, QBD 16.48
Chemistree Homecare Ltd v Roche Products Ltd [2011] EWHC 1579 (Ch) 15.89
Chemistree Homecare Ltd v Teva Pharmaceuticals Ltd [2011] EWHC 2979 (Ch) 15.110
Cherkasov v Olegovich [2017] EWHC 756 (Ch) 15.09
Cherrilow Ltd v Osmond Solicitors and Richard Butler-Creagh [2011] EWHC 3443 (QB) 40.57
Chessels v British Telecommunications plc [2002] Pens LR 141 . . . . . 66.42, 66.56, 66.63, 66.64, 66.66
Chettiar v Chettiar (No 2) [1962] 2 All ER 238 . . . . 66.42
Chief Adjudication Officer v Faulds [2000] 1 WLR 1035 . . . . 4.67
Chief Constable of North Yorkshire v Audsley [2000] Lloyds's Rep PN 675 . . . . 9.120
Chilab v Kings College London [2012] EWCA 1178 . . . . 15.56
Children Act 1989 (Taxation of Costs), Re [1994] 2 FLR 934 . . . . 51.36
China Pacific SA v Food Corpn of India, The Winson [1982] AC 939, HL 40.43
Chinery, Ex p (1884) 12 QBD 342 . . . . 10.03
Chohan v Times Newspapers Ltd (unreported), 7 September 1998, QBD 53.61
Chohan v Times Newspapers Ltd [2001] EWCA Civ 964 . . . . 23.108, 23.119
Chopping v Cowan & Dewey (unreported), 17 April 2013, Ch D 36.84
Christie v Platt [1921] 2 KB 1 . . . . 20.58, 20.60
Chrulew v Borm-Reid & Co [1992] 1 WLR 176 . . . . 43.330
Chuku v Chuku [2017] EWHC 541 (Ch) 15.43
Church Commissioners for England v Ibrahim [1997] 1 EGLR 13 . . . . 66.07, 66.11, 66.14, 66.17, 66.19
Churchill v Boot [2016] EWHC 1322 (QB) 12.117
Churchill Insurance Co Ltd v Fitzgerald & Wilkinson & Ors [2012] EWCA Civ 1166 . . . . 63.04
CIBC Mellon Trust Co v Mora Hotel Corpn NV [2002] EWCA Civ 1688 . . . . 15.21
CIBC Mellon Trust Co v Mora Hotel Corpn NV [2003] EWHC 9037 (Costs) 19.14
CIBC Mellon Trust Co v Stolzenberg [2005] EWCA Civ 628 . . . . 9.31
Cie Générale d'Eaux Minérales et de Bains de Mer, Re [1891] 3 Ch 451 . . . . 15.14
Cinema Press Ltd v Pictures & Pleasures Ltd [1945] KB 356 . . . . 1.118, 6.32, 20.63, 20.64
CIP Properties (AIPT) Ltd v Galliford Try Infrastructure Ltd (unreported), 3 June 2014, QBD (TCC), ... 16.45
CIP Properties (AIPT) Ltd v Galliford Try Infrastructure Ltd [2015] EWHC 481 . . . . 12.19, 12.62, 12.84, 12.85, 12.93
Circuit Systems Ltd (in liquidation) v Zuken-Redac (UK) Ltd [1999] 2 AC 1 . . . . 30.42
Citation Plc v Ellis Whittam Ltd [2012] EWHC 764 (QB) 6.12, 6.107, 49.149, 49.150
City Inn (Jersey) Ltd v Ten Trinity Square Ltd [2008] EWCA Civ 156 . . . . 31.44
Clack v Holland (1854) 19 Beav 262 . . . . 66.36
Claims Direct Test Cases, In the Matter of [2002] EWCA Civ 428 . . . . 45.41
Claims Direct Test Cases [2003] EWCA Civ 136 . . . . 2.09, 4.66, 49.114, 54.60, 54.173, 54.174

Claims Direct Test Cases Tranche 2 [2003] EWHC 9005 (Costs) 3.88, 22.12, 22.13, 47.06, 52.65, 52.66
Clare v Joseph [1907] 2 KB 369 . . . . 1.83, 27.111, 27.140, 27.161, 27.211, 29.204, 39.12
Clark, Re (1851) 13 Beavan 173; (1851) 1 De Gex M & G 43 . . . . 36.66
Clark, ex p Newland, Re (1876) 4 Ch D 515. . . . . 40.52
Clark v Blything Inhabitants (1823) 2 B & C 254 . . . . 18.73
Clark v University of Lincolnshire and Humberside [2000] 3 All ER 752 . . . . 4.07, 50.110
Clark (Inspector of Taxes) v Perks [2001] 1 WLR 17 . . . . 45.41, 45.72
Clarke v Associated Newspapers Ltd (1998) The Times, 28 January. 16.49
Clarke v Maltby (Costs) [2010] EWHC 1856 (QB) 16.52
Clarke v McCullough [2012] NIQB 104 . . . . 28.193, 28.197
Clarke v Meadus [2012] EWHC 3729 (Ch) 7.84
Clarke v Oldham MBC (unreported), 14 April 2008, Oldham County Court. 9.64
Clarke & Chapman v Hart (1868) 6 HLC 633. . . . . 1.90
Clarke's Settlement Fund [1911] WN 39 . . . . 40.38
Clarkson v Gilbert & Ors [2000] EWCA Civ 3018 . . . . 47.06, 47.10
Classic Catering Ltd v Donnington Park Leisure Ltd [2001] 1 BCLC 537 . . . . 15.76
Clearwell v MSN [2012] EWCA 1440. . . . . 44.25
Clearwell International Ltd v (1) MSL Group Holdings Ltd (unreported), 16 November 2012, CA 44.05
Cleveland Bridge UK Ltd v Sarens (UK) Ltd [2018] EWHC 827 (TCC). 14.27, 14.28
Clifford Harris & Co v Solland International Ltd [2004] EWHC 2488 (Ch) 40.77
Clifford Harris & Co v Solland International Ltd [2005] EWHC 141 (Ch). 38.88, 40.84
Cloughton, In the Matter of Tina Jayne (unreported), c 1999, Ch D 49.120
Clutterbuck v A [2017] EWHC 1127 (Ch). 10.15
Clutterbuck v HSBC plc [2015] EWHC 3233 (Ch) 16.52
Clydesdale Bank Plc v Kinleigh Folkard & Hayward Ltd (unreported), 6 February 2014, Ch D 6.12
CM (a protected person by his litigation friend, The Official Solicitor) v Parkdean Holiday Parks Ltd (unreported), 29 March 2017, SCCO. 60.22
CMC Spreadbet plc v Khan [2017] EWHC 2008 (Ch) 16.48
CMCS Common Market Commercial Services AVV v Taylor [2011] EWHC 324 (Ch). 9.168, 9.181
Cobb v Becke (1845) 6 QB 930 . . . . 22.06
Cobbett v Wood [1908] 1 KB 590 . . . . 35.70
Cobbett v Wood [1908] 2 KB 420 . . . . 35.47
Coburn v Colledge [1897] 1 QB 702 . . . . .23.89, 23.91, 23.92
Cockburn v Edwards (1881) 18 Ch D 449 . . . . 1.91, 3.16, 3.39
Cocker v Tempest (1841) 7 M & W 501 . . . . 5.24
Cocks v Bruce Searl & Good (1904) 21 TLR 62. . . . . 52.06
Cody v Murray [2013] EWHC 3448 (Ch) 15.115
Cohen & Cohen, Re [1905] 1 Ch 345 . . . . .37.16
Cohen & Cohen, Re [1905] 2 Ch 137. . . . . 1.111, 36.82, 36.92
Colburt v Beard [1992] 2 Ad R 67 . . . . 6.164
Cole v Booker (1913) 29 TLR 295 . . . . 30.23
Cole v British Telecommunications plc [2000] 2 Costs LR 310 . . . . .18.111
Cole v News Group Newspapers (unreported), 18 October 2006, SCCO 29.50
Colegrave v Manley (1823) Turn & R 400 . . . . 27.83
Colemans-CTTS LLP v O'Keefe [2014] EWHC 4099 (QB). 40.16
Coles & Ravenshear, Re [1907] 1 KB 1. . . . . 26.11, 26.17
Coles v Keklik (unreported), 30 June 2008, Liverpool County Court 50.86
Collen v Wright (1857) 8 E&B 647 . . . . .9.69, 9.70, 27.80
Collier v Gaillard (1776) 2 Black W 1062 . . . . 1.67
Collier v Williams [2006] EWCA Civ 20. . . . . 10.12, 10.18, 43.104
Collins v The Vestry of Paddington (1879-1880) LR 5 QBD 26.10
Collyer Bristow v Robichaux (unreported), 20 July 2001, QBD. 27.73, 35.13
Colour Quest Ltd v Total Downstream UK Plc [2009] EWHC 823 (Comm) 16.39, 17.85, 17.99, 56.39, 65.50

Colquhoun, In re (1854) 5 DM&G 35 . . . . . . 20.21, 20.25, 65.57
Colver v Adams (1881) 6 QBD 622 . . . . . . 40.91
Colwill v European Heritage Ltd [2014] EWCA Civ 238 . . . . . . 6.105
Commerell v Poynton (1818) 1 Swan 1 . . . . . . 40.61
Commission for Equality & Human Rights v Griffin [2011] EWHC 675 (Admin) 14.11, 53.125
Commissioners of Customs & Excise v Vaz [1995] STC 14 . . . . . . 18.86
Commissioners for HMRC v Blue Sphere Global Ltd [2011] EWHC 90217 (Costs) 54.86, 61.11
Compagnie Financiere du Pacifique v Peruvian Guano Co (1882) 11 QBD 55 . . . . . . 26.10
Compagnie Noga D'Importation et D'Exportation SA v Abacha [2003] EWCA Civ 1101 . . . . . . 10.212, 45.35
Company (No 004081 of 1989, Re a) [1995] 2 All ER 155 . . . . . . 49.124, 53.86, 53.123
Company (No 006798 of 1995), Re a [1996] 2 All ER 417 . . . . . . 9.147, 9.180
Condliffe v Hislop [1996] 1 All ER 431; [1996] 1 WLR 753, CA 15.13, 30.11
Conlon v Royal Sun Alliance Insurance plc [2015] EWCA Civ 92 . . . . 45.58, 50.378, 50.391, 50.40§
Connaughton v Imperial College Healthcare NHS Trust [2010] EWHC 90173 (Costs) 7.47
Connecticut Fire Insurance Co v Kavanagh [1892] AC 473 . . . . . . 45.62
Connell v Mutch t/a Southey Building Services [2012] EWCA Civ 1589 . . . . . . 6.33, 7.37
Connelly v DPP [1964] AC 1254 . . . . . . 5.24
Connelly v RTZ Corp Plc (No 2) [1998] AC 584 . . . . . . 65.12
Connolly-Martin v Davies [1999] Lloyd's Rep PN 790 . . . . . . 9.178
Connollys (a firm) v Harrington [2002] All ER (D) 268 (May) 36.46, 39.04
Connor v Birmingham City Council (unreported), 16 March 2005, Birmingham County Court 54.123
Conquer v Boot [1928] 2 KB 336, DC 23.39
Conroy v National Westminster Bank [2009] EWCA Civ 1199 . . . . . . 15.80
Conservative & Unionist Party (Claimant) v Election Commissioner [2010] EWHC 285 (Admin) 6.12
Consolidated Trust Co Ltd v Naylor (1936) 55 CLR 423 . . . . . . 32.29
Constantine Steamship Line Ltd v Imperial Smelting Corpn Ltd [1942] AC 154 . . . . . . 27.226
Continental Assurance Co of London plc (in liquidation), Re [2007] 2 BCLC 287 . . . . . . 16.26
Contractreal Ltd v Davies [2001] EWCA Civ 928 . . . . . . 25.42, 49.156
Conway v George Wimpey & Co Ltd [1951] 1 All ER 56 . . . . . . 15.120
Cook, In re [1960] 1 All ER 689 . . . . . . 35.80
Cook v Gillard (1852) 1 E & B 26 . . . . . . 35.53, 35.55, 35.70
Cook v Imperial Tobacco Co [1922] 2 KB 1.116
Cook v Whellock (1890) 24 QBD 658 . . . . . . 15.44
Cooke v Venulum Property Investments Ltd [2013] EWHC 4288 (Ch) 15.22, 16.57
Cookson, Re (1886) 30 SJ 305 . . . . . . 36.94
Cooper, Ex p (1854) 14 CB 663 . . . . . . 35.114
Cooper v Morgan (unreported), 29 September 2006, Liverpool County Court 29.85
Cooper v P&O Stena Line Ltd [1999] 1 Lloyd's Rep 734 . . . . . . 16.50
Cooper v Tiffin (1789) 100 ER 706 . . . . . . 1.72
Cooper v Whittingham (1880) 15 Ch D 501 . . . . . . 1.100
Cooper v Williams [1963] 2 QB 567 . . . . . . 7.75, 7.78
Co-operative Bank plc v Desmond Victor John Phillips [2014] EWHC 2862 (Ch) 16.58
Co-operative Bank plc v Phillips [2014] EWHC 2862 (Ch) 21.1, 66.11
Co-operative Group Ltd v Birse Development Ltd [2013] EWHC 3352 (TCC) 6.116
Coote v Ford [1895–99] All ER Rep 673 . . . . . . 23.16
Cope v United Dairies (London) Ltd (1968) Costs LR Core vol 23 . . . . . . 49.03
Coral Leisure Group Ltd v Barnett [1981] ICR 503 . . . . . . 4.20, 27.246
Corby Group Litigation [2009] EWHC 2109 (TCC) 6.118
Cordano Building Contractors v Burgess [1988] 1 WLR 890 . . . . . . 15.105
Cormack v Washbourne (formerly t/a Washbourne & Co (a firm)) [2000] Lloyd's Rep PN 459 . . . . . 9.56
Cosedge, Re (1885) 29 SJ 53.109
Cosgrove v Pattison (2001) The Times, 13 February 52.26
Cosslett (Contractors) Ltd) v Bridgend County Borough Council [2001] UKHL 58 . . . . . . 32.66

Costin v Merron [2013] EWCA Civ 380 . . . . .50.90, 50.297, 50.298
Cotterell v Stratton (1872) LR 8 Ch App 295. . . . . 66.11, 66.13
Cotton, Ex p (1846) 9 Beav 107 . . . . 53.11
Council of Civil Service Unions v Minister of State for Civil Service [1985] AC 374. . . . . 64.22
Court v Berlin [1897] 2 QB 396, CA 27.37
Court Line Ltd v Aktiebologet Gotaverken, The Halcyon the Great [1984] 1 Lloyd's Rep 283. . . . 32.29
Courtwell Properties Ltd v Greencore PF (UK) Ltd [2014] EWHC 184 (TCC) 16.17
Coventry v Lawrence (No 3) [2015] UKSC 50 . . . . 24.51
Coward v Phaestos Ltd [2014] EWCA Civ 1256 . . . . .17.25
Cowell v Simpson (1809) 16 Ves 275 . . . . 40.77
Cowell v Taylor (1885) 31 Ch D 34 . . . . 15.96
Cox v MGN Ltd [2006] EWHC 1235 (QB) 25.81, 29.58, 49.131, 51.20, 51.39, 51.44, 51.79, 54.107
Cox v White [1976] RTR 248 . . . . 50.77
Cox v Woodlands Manor Care Home [2015] EWCA Civ 415 . . . . .28.170, 28.182, 28.197
Coyne & Anor v DRC Distribution Ltd [2008] EWCA Civ 488 . . . . .7.153
Coys of Kensington Ltd v Woollcombe Beer Watts (a firm) (unreported), 18 February 1999, QBD 20.16, 20.29, 20.49
Cozens v Graham (1852) 12 CB 398 . . . . 35.71
CR v MZ [2013] EWHC 295 (Fam) 16.48
Crane v Canons Leisure Centre [2007] EWCA Civ 1352. . . .3.88, 22.06, 22.10, 22.13, 22.13, 22.14, 22.17, 22.22, 22.25, 35.116, 47.06, 49.146, 52.06, 52.11, 52.65, 52.98, 53.33, 54.48
Crane v Sky In-home Ltd [2008] EWCA Civ 978 . . . . 45.62
Cranway Ltd v Playtech Ltd [2009] EWHC 823 . . . . 56.40
Credit & Mercantile plc v Kaymuu Ltd [2014] EWHC 1746 (Ch). 66.26
Creggy v Barnett [2016] EWCA Civ 1004. . . . . 23.125
Crema v Cenkos Securities plc [2010] EWCA Civ 1444. . . . . 31.12
Crema v Cenkos Securities plc [2011] EWCA Civ 10 . . . . .14.31, 56.89, 56.96
Cribb v Freyberger [1919] WN 22, CA. 23.25
Cripps v Heritage Distribution Corporation (1999) The Times, 10 November, CA 15.36
Criterion Properties plc v Stratford UK Properties LLC [2004] UKHL 28 . . . . 47.25
Crittenden v Bayliss [2002] All ER (D) 92 . . . . 30.37
CRM Trading Ltd v Chubb Electronic Security Ltd [2013] EWHC 3482 (QB) 12.37, 12.91
Crocuer Enterprises v Giordano Poultry [2013] EWHC 2491 (Ch) 50.330
Cromptons Leisure Machines Ltd [2006] EWHC 3583 (Ch) 4.07
Crook v Birmingham City Council [2007] EWHC 1415 (QB) 29.78, 29.87, 29.90, 29.138, 32.71, 54.46
Crooks v Hendricks Lovell Ltd [2016] EWCA Civ 8 . . . . 17.52, 17.111
Cropper v Smith (1884) 26 Ch D 700 . . . . .26.10, 26.31, 26.41
Crosbie v Munroe [2003] EWCA Civ 350 . . . . .11.28, 43.295, 43.359
Cross v Cross (1880) 43 LT 533 . . . . 40.58
Crossley v Crowther (1851) 9 Hare 384 . . . . 27.96, 27.208
Crouch v King's Healthcare NHS Trust [2004] EWCA Civ 1332 . . . . 6.210
Crowder v Shee (1808) 1 Camp 437. . . . . 35.86
Crown Estate Commissioners v Dorset County Council [1990] Ch 297 . . . . 23.10
Crown & Stafford Stone v Eccleshall Magistrates' Court [1988] 1 All ER 430 . . . . 18.107, 59.18
Crystal Decisions (UK) Ltd v Vedatech Corpn [2007] EWHC 1062 (Ch). 43.67, 43.80
CT Bowring & Co (Insurance) Ltd v Corsi & Partners Ltd [1995] 1 BCLC 148, CA 15.02, 15.09, 15.10, 15.23
Cukurova Finance International Ltd v Alfa Telecom Turkey Ltd [2013] UKPC 20 . . . . 66.04, 66.10, 66.11, 66.13, 66.27, 66.34
Culkin v Wirral Independent Appeals Panel [2011] EWHC 1526 (QB) 27.202
Cumming v Ince (1847) 11 QB 112 . . . . 10.27
Cumper v Pothecary [1941] 2 KB 58 . . . . 17.195, 17.211
Cunliffe-Owen v Teather and Greenwood [1967] 1 WLR 1421 . . . . 27.198, 31.64
Cunningham v AST Express Ltd [2009] EWCA Civ 76. . . . . 17.63, 17.72

Curragh Investments Ltd v Cook [1974] 1 WLR 1559 . . . . 27.239
Curran v Newpark Cinemas Ltd [1951] 1 All ER 295. . . . 32.29
Curran v Revenue and Customs Commissioners [2012] UKFTT 655 (TC). . . . 16.38
Currie & Co v The Law Society [1977] QB 990 . . . . 21.21, 21.30, 35.114
Curtis, David John (2007) VAT Decision 20330 . . . . 55.19
Curtis v Beaney [1911] P 181 . . . . 46.20
Curtis v Pulbrook [2009] EWHC 1370 (Ch) 16.62, 66.53
Curwen v Milburn (1889) 42 Ch D 424, CA 23.96, 23.130
Cusack v Harrow London Borough Council [2013] 1 WLR 2022 . . . . 4.08
Customs & Excise Commissioners v Anchor Foods Ltd (No 3), The Times, 28 September 1999, Ch D 10.14, 10.27
Customs and Excise Commissioners v Ross [1990] 2 All ER 65 . . . . 59.04
Cutcliffe's Estate, Re [1959] P 6 . . . . 7.54
Cuthbert v Gair (unreported), 26 September 2009, SCCO 49.110
Cutter v Eagle Star Insurance Co Ltd [1998] 1 WLR 1647. . . . 50.73, 50.77
Cutter v Powell (1795) 6 Term Rep 320 . . . . 27.09
Cutting v Islam [2014] EWHC 1515 (QB) 6.59, 6.116, 6.188
Cutts v Head [1984] Ch 290 . . . . 6.207, 17.09

D v D [2002] 2 Costs LR 312. . . . 49.110
D v D [2002] EWHC 2511 (Fam) 53.113
D v H (Costs) [2008] EWHC 559 (Fam) 9.168
D Morgan plc v Mace & Jones (a firm) [2011] EWHC 26 (TCC). . . . 16.36, 17.85, 17.99
D Pride & Partners v Institute for Animal Health [2009] EWHC 1617 (QB). . . . 6.196, 17.114, 17.183, 56.39, 56.74, 56.75
D Walter & Co Ltd v Neville Eckley & Co [1997] BCC 331 . . . . 9.138, 9.163
D'Abo v Paget (No 2) (2000) The Times, 10 August 66.54
Daejan Investments Ltd v The Park West Club Ltd [2004] BLR 223 . . . . 6.95
Dahabshiil Transfer Services Ltd v Barclays Bank plc [2013] EWHC 4196 (Ch) 12.74
Dal-Sterling Group plc v WSP South & West Ltd (unreported), 18 July 2001, TCC 30.51
Daley v Diggers Ltd [1951] 1 KB 661 . . . . 18.72
Daley v Environmental Recycling Technologies plc [2009] EWCA Civ 1088 . . . . 15.87
Dallaway (dec'd) [1982] 1 WLR 756 . . . . 66.59
Dallow v Garrold, ex p Adams (1884) 13 QBD 543. . . . 40.94
Dalmar Properties Ltd, sub nom David Norman Kaye v Kingstars Ltd, Re [2008] EWHC 2753 (Ch) 6.80
Dalton v British Telecommunications [2015] EWHC 616 (QB) 4.10, 4.67, 50.136, 50.138
Daly v Hubner [2002] Lloyd's Rep PN 461 (Ch) 9.137
Dammermann v Lanyon Bowdler LLP [2017] EWCA Civ 269 . . . . 50.378, 50.400, 50.401, 50.403
Dane v Mortgage Insurance Corpn [1894] 1 QB 54. . . . 18.73
Daniel v Drew [2005] EWCA 507 . . . . 32.47
Daniels v Commissioner of Police for the Metropolis [2005] EWCA Civ 1312 . . . . 6.233, 6.234
Daniels v Walker [2000] 1 WLR 1382. . . . 52.31
Danilina v Chernukhin [2018] EWHC 39 (Comm) 15.44, 15.74, 15.114
Dar International FEF Co v Aon Ltd [2003] EWCA Civ 1833. . . . 15.08, 15.11, 15.12
Darby v Law Society [2003] EWHC 2270 (Admin). . . . 27.105, 38.50
Dargie, Miller v Thornton-Jones, Re [1954] Ch 16. . . . 66.39
Dartnall, Sawyer v Goddard [1895] 1 Ch 474, CA 66.45
Dashwood v Dashwood [1927] WN 276, 64 LJNC 431. . . . 7.70
Dass v Beggs [2014] EWHC 164 (Ch) 15.46, 15.47, 15.48
Daubney v Phipps (1849) 18 LJQB 337 . . . . 35.86
Davey v Aylesbury Vale DC (2007) EWCA Civ 1166. . . . 67.10, 67.12
Davey v Bentinck [1893] 1 QB 185, CA 5.27
Davey v Durrant (1858) 24 Beav 493 . . . . 52.57
David, Re (1861) 30 Beav 278 . . . . 36.22

Davidsons v Jones-Fenleigh (1980) Costs LR (Core vol) 70; [1980] 124 SJ 204 . . . . . . 23.93, 27.20, 27.58, 35.19, 35.24
Davies, In re [1912] 1 Ch 49 . . . . . . 36.71
Davies v Chatwood (1879) 11 Ch D 244; (1879) 40 LT 187 . . . . . . 20.23, 27.311
Davies v Eli Lilly & Co [1987] 1 WLR 1136 . . . . . . 9.76, 13.08, 20.16, 65.12, 65.63, 65.65, 65.75
Davies v Forrett [2015] EWHC 1761 (QB) 9.09, 26.03
Davies v Gregory (1873) LR 3 P & D 28 . . . . . . 7.59
Davies v Jones [2010] 1 P&CR 22 . . . . . . 32.22
Davies v Taylor (No 2) [1974] AC 225 . . . . . . 18.67, 18.69, 18.75
Davies v Watkins [2012] EWCA Civ 1570 . . . . . . 66.59, 66.67
Davis v Dysart [1855] 25 LJ Ch 122 . . . . . . 35.87
Davis v Hedges (1871) LR 6 QB 687 . . . . . . 21.29
Davis v New England College of Arundel [1977] ICR 6, EAT 50.126
Davison v Leitch [2013] EWHC 3092 (QB) 17.124
Davy-Chiesman v Davy-Chiesman [1984] 1 All ER 321 . . . . . . 9.62, 9.95, 9.161
Dawe v Idg Communications Ltd [2013] EWPCC 33 . . . . . . 49.73, 51.49
Dawnus Sierra Leone Ltd v Timis Mining Corporation Ltd [2016] EWCA Civ 1066 . . . 15.66, 15.70
Dawson v Preston (Law Society, Garnishees) [1955] 1 WLR 1219 . . . . . . 43.414
Day v Day [2006] EWCA Civ 415 . . . . . . 6.52, 6.63, 6.238
Day & Dent Constructions Pty Ltd v North Australian Properties Pty Ltd (1986) 150 CLR 85 . . . . . . 21.05
Days Healthcare UK Ltd v Pihsiang Machinery Manufacturing Co Ltd [2006] EWHC 1444 (QB) 14.19, 36.78, 43.28, 43.382
DB UK Bank Ltd (t/a DB Mortgages) v Jacobs Solicitors [2016] EWHC 1614 (Ch) 17.23
De Beer v Kanaar & Co (a firm) (No 1) [2001] EWCA Civ 1318 . . . . . . 15.31, 15.33, 15.72
De Bry v Fitzgeral [1990] 1 WLR 552 . . . . . . 15.75
De Freitas v Permanent Secretary of Ministry of Agriculture, Fisheries, Lands and Housing [1999] 1 AC 69, PC 24.27
De Seguros Imperio v Heath (REBX) Ltd [2001] 1 WLR 112 . . . . . . 23.87
De Stacpoole v De Stacpoole (1887) 37 Ch D 139 . . . . . . 60.17
Deacon v Morris (1819) 2 B & Ald 393 . . . . . . 1.49, 1.71, 3.37
Deakin, re [1900] 2 QB 489 . . . . . . 40.91
Dean v Allin & Watts [2001] EWCA Civ 758 . . . . . . 27.192
Dean & Dean v Angel Airlines SA [2007] EWHC 399 (QB) 3.36
Deanplan Ltd v Mahmoud [1993] Ch 151 . . . . . . 19.25
Debtor, Re A (1981) The Times, 19 February 21.14
Debtor (No 21 of 1950) (No 1), Re [1951] Ch 313 . . . . . . 21.34
Debtor (No 32 of 1991) (No 2), Re a [1994] BCC 524 . . . . . . 40.123, 40.127
Debtor (No 88 of 1991), In re [1993] Ch 286 . . . . . . 35.113, 40.121, 40.129
Debtor (No 1594 of 1992), Re a (1992) The Times, 8 December 27.130
Debtor (No 833 of 1993 and No 834 of 1993), Re a [1994] NPC 82 . . . . . . 40.124, 40.131
Debtor (No 647-SD-1999), Re (2000) The Times, 10 April 23.121
Dechert LLP v Eurasian Natural Resources Corpn Ltd [2016] EWCA Civ 375 . . . . . . 36.107, 36.109, 36.110, 46.04, 46.69, 46.70
Dee v Telegraph Media Group Ltd [2010] EWHC 1939 (QB) 16.20, 16.40, 16.46
Dee Estates Ltd, Wright v Dee Estates Ltd [1911] 2 Ch 85, CA 40.48
Deg-Deutsche Investitions und Entwicklungsgesellschaft mbH v Koshy & Ors, The Times, 30 March 2000 . . . . . . 6.161
Deg-Deutsche Investitions und Entwicklungsgesellschaft mbH v Koshy [2001] EWCA Civ 79 . . . . . . 10.12, 62.42
Dellow's Will Trusts, Lloyds Bank Ltd v Institute of Cancer Research [1964] 1 All ER 771 . . . 27.226
Deloitte Touche Tohmatsu v JP Morgan Portfolio Services Ltd (2007) 158 FCR 417 . . . . . . 33.19
Demouilpied v Stockport NHS Foundation Trust (unreported), 4 November 2011, Manchester County Court 25.33, 25.87
Dempsey v Johnstone [2003] EWCA Civ 1134 . . . . . . 9.138, 9.151, 9.153

Dempsey v London Borough of Sutton [2013] EWCA Civ 863 . . . . 6.21
Dena Technology (Thailand) Ltd & Anor v Dena Technology Ltd & Anor [2014]
EWHC 616 (Comm) 15.60
Denne & Secretary of State for War, Re (1884) 51 LT 657 . . . . 36.85
Denning v Greenhalgh Financial Services [2017] EWHC 143 (QB) 27.35
Denso Manufacturing UK Ltd v Great Lakes Reinsurance (UK) plc [2017] EWHC 391 (Comm) 34.12
Denton & Ors v TH White Ltd & Ors [2014] EWCA Civ 906 . . . 12.57, 12.167, 16.41, 26.22, 26.25, 26.41, 26.55, 26.60–26.70, 40.30, 43.158, 44.28, 44.30, 54.116, 54.123
Department for Environment, Food and Rural Affairs v Downs [2009] EWCA Civ 257. . . . . . 14.16
Department of Health v Envoy Farmers Ltd [1976] 1 WLR 1018. . . . . .49.158
Department of Trade and Industry v St Christopher Motorists Association Ltd [1974]
1 All ER 395 . . . . 27.283
Derby & Co Ltd v Weldon (No 7) [1990] 1 WLR 1156 . . . . 46.75
Derek Hodd Ltd v Climate Change Capital Ltd [2013] EWHC 1665 (Ch) 29.191
Designers Guild Ltd v Russell Williams (Textiles) Ltd [2000] 1 WLR 2416 , HL 45.64
Designers Guild Ltd v Russell Williams (Textiles) Ltd (t/a Washington DC) (No 2) [2003]
EWHC 9024 (Costs) 54.75
Destra Software Ltd v Comada (UK) LLP [2012] EWPCC Civ 39 . . . . 50.330
Detillin v Gale [1802] 7 Ves 583. . . . . 66.25
Deutsche Bank AG v Sebastian Holdings Inc [2016] EWCA Civ 23 . . . . 8.50, 9.06, 9.12, 9.30, 9.73, 9.79, 9.81, 9.88
Deutsche Bank (Suisse) SA v Khan [2013] EWHC 1020 (Comm) 16.64, 66.17, 66.19
Devenish and Martin (1734) 94 ER 612. . . . . 1.49
Devereux, Re (1902) 46 SJ 320 . . . . 3.06
Devereux v White & Co (1896) 13 TLR 52 . . . . .35.117, 36.65, 52.08
Devine v Franklin [2002] EWHC 1846 (QB) 50.396, 57.21
Devon County Council v Celtic Bioenergy Ltd [2014] EWHC 309 (TCC). 51.54
Dexia Crediop SpA v Comune di Prato [2016] EWHC 252 (Comm). 6.187
Dexter v Vlieland-Boddy [2003] EWCA Civ 14. . . . . 23.35
Dhanoia v Mehmi (unreported), 17 October 2007, Bristol County Court 54.135
Dhillon v Siddiqui & Ors [2010] EWHC 1400 (Ch) 7.167
Diacou v Staden [2000] EWHC 9003 (Costs) 51.79
Diag Human SE v Czech Republic [2013] EWHC 3190 (Comm) 15.115
Diamanttek Ltd v James (unreported), 8 February 2016, Coventry County Court 8.39, 8.41
Diamond v Graham [1968] 1 WLR 1061 . . . . 40.10
Dicas v Stockley (1836) 7 C & P 587 . . . . 40.80
Dickinson v Minister of Pensions [1953] 1 QB 228 . . . . 9.129
Dickinson v Rushmer [2002] 1 Costs LR 128 . . . . . . 18.57, 46.15, 46.16, 46.51, 46.58, 46.64, 46.65
Dibben v Cooke (1734) BRH 8G 2 . . . . 1.90
Digicel (St Lucia) v Cable & Wireless plc [2010] EWHC 774 (Ch) 6.108, 16.48, 16.54
Digicel (St Lucia) Ltd (a company registered under the laws of St Lucia) v Cable &
Wireless plc [2010] EWHC 888 (Ch). 16.27, 16.39
Diptford Parish Lands, Re [1934] Ch 151. . . . . 32.29
Director General of Fair Trading v Proprietary Association of Great Britain [2001]
EWCA Civ 1217 . . . . 24.10
Director General of Fair Trading v Proprietary Association of Great Britain,
In re Medicaments & Related Classes of Goods (No 4) [2002] 1 WLR 269. . . . . 64.04
Dirigo, The [1920] P 425 . . . . 40.92
Dix v Townend & Anor [2008] EWHC 90117 (Costs). 27.237, 30.02
Dixon v Blindley Heath Investments Ltd [2016] EWCA Civ 548 . . . . 7.08, 7.09, 7.17, 7.18, 16.40
DNA Productions (Europe) Ltd v Manoukian [2008] EWHC 2627 (Ch) 9.22, 9.27, 9.28, 9.29
Dockerill v Tullett [2012] EWCA Civ 184. . . . . 50.86, 50.375, 50.397
Dodd's Case (1858) 44 ER 1087 . . . . 1.24
Dolling-Baker v Mettet [1990] 1 WLR 1205 . . . . 48.85
Dolphin Quays Developments Ltd v Mills [2008] 1 WLR 1829 . . . . 9.49

Dominion Brewery v Foster (1897) 77 LT 507 . . . . 15.57
Donald v Suckling (1866) LR 1 QB 585 . . . . 40.44, 40.45
Donald Campbell & Co Ltd v Pollak [1927] AC 732 . . . . 1.100, 6.78, 45.22
Donsland Ltd (a firm) v Van Hoogstraten [2002] EWCA Civ 253 . . . . 27.22, 27.30, 27.78, 47.24
Dooley v Parker [2002] EWCA Civ 1118 . . . . 6.196, 6.200, 6.201
Dorchester Project Management Ltd v BNP Parabas Real State Advisory & Property
Management UK Ltd [2013] EWHC 4555 (Ch) 15.35, 15.91, 15.92, 15.93
Douglas Norman & Co, In re [1898] 1 Ch 199 . . . . 40.77
Douglas v Associated Newspapers (1922) 67 Sol Jo 48 . . . . 53.124
Douglas v Hello! Ltd [2004] EWHC 63 (Ch) 6.175, 56.57, 56.66, 56.68
Douglas v Hello! Ltd [2005] EWCA Civ 595 . . . . 24.25
Downes, Re (1844) 5 Beav 425 . . . . 36.05
Downing v Peterborough & Stamford Hospitals NHS Foundation Trust [2014] EWHC
Civ 4216 (QB) 17.82, 17.129, 17.130, 17.141, 43.349
DPP v Coulman [1993] RTR 230 . . . . 50.77
DR Sheridan v Higgins [2012] EWHC 547 (Ch) 40.57
Drake v Fripp [2011] EWCA Civ 1282 . . . . 54.76
Drew v Josolyne (1888) 4 TLR 717, DC 53.129
Drew v Nunn (1879) 4 QBD 661 . . . . 60.57
Drew v Whitbread [2010] EWCA Civ 53 . . . . 23.36, 23.37, 23.44, 23.46, 23.47, 23.49, 49.05,
50.155, 57.21
Dronsfield v Street (unreported), 25 June 2013, Manchester District Registry 54.81
Dryden v Frost (1838) 3 My & C 670 . . . . 66.25
D'Silva v University College Union [2009] EWCA Civ 1269 . . . . 10.03
DTC (CNC) Ltd v Gary Sergeant & Co (a firm) [1996] 2 All ER 369; [1996] 1 WLR 797 . . . . . 40.38
Dubai Bank Ltd v Galadari [1989] 3 All ER 769, CA 46.27
Dubai Islamic Bank PJSC v PSI Energy Holding Co Bsc & Ors [2011] EWCA Civ 761 . . . . 15.49
Duffet v McEvoy (1885) 10 App Cas 300 . . . . 35.123
Dufoo v Tolaini [2014] EWCA Civ 1536 . . . . 6.28, 6.257, 6.259
Dumrul v Standard Chartered Bank [2010] EWHC 2625 (Comm) 15.70, 15.115
Dungate v Dungate [1965] 1 WLR 1477 . . . . 23.127
Dunhill v Burgin [2014] UKSC 18 . . . . 60.38
Dunhill v Hughmans (a firm) [2017] EWHC 2073 (Ch) 6.107
Dunlop v Higgins (1848) 1 HL Cas 381 . . . . 43.287, 43.289
Dunn v Glass Systems (UK) Ltd [2007] EWHC 1901 (QB) 49.84
Dunn Motor Traction Ltd v National Express Ltd [2017] EWHC 228 (Comm) 15.39
Dunne v Doyle (1860) 10 I Ch R 502 . . . . 23.117
Dunnett v Railtrack plc [2002] EWCA Civ 303 . . . . 6.119
Dunthorne v Bentley (1996) RTR 428, CA 50.75
Dupont Nutrition Biosciences ApS V Novozymes A/S [2013] EWHC 483 (Pat) 56.82
Durham Bros v Robertson [1898] 1 QB 765 . . . . 32.29
Dutton v Minards [2015] EWCA Civ 984 . . . . 17.68, 17.73, 17.76, 17.119, 17.173, 17.174, 17.175
Dweck v Fostater (Defendant) and Rowbury & Ors (Third Parties) [2010] EWHC 1874 (QB) 9.87
Dwyer v Dwyer [1976] 2 All ER 1 . . . . 1.135
Dyke v Stephens (1885) 30 Ch D 189 . . . . 60.03
Dymocks Franchise Systems (NSW) Pty Ltd v Todd [2004] UKPC 39; [2004]
1 WLR 2807 . . . . 9.03, 9.12, 9.13, 9.15, 9.18, 9.23, 9.25, 9.27, 9.28, 9.34, 16.40
Dyson Appliances Ltd v Hoover Ltd [2003] EWHC 624 (Ch) 14.07
Dyson v Leeds City Council [2000] CP Rep 42 . . . . 48.08
Dyson Technology Ltd v Strutt [2007] EWHC 1756 (Ch) 6.36, 7.34, 20.64, 20.66

E (mental health patient), Re [1985] 1 All ER 609 . . . . 60.03
E Ivor Hughes Educational Foundation v Leach [2005] EWHC 1317 (Ch) 25.93, 50.396,
50.398, 57.21
E T Marler v Robertson [1974] ICR 72, NIRC 57.06
Eagleson v Liddell [2001] EWCA Civ 155 . . . . 49.133

Earl v Mawson (1973) 228 Estates Gazette 529; aff'd (1974) 232 Estates Gazette 1315, CA 43.291
Earl of Bristol v Wilsmore (1823) 1 B & C 514 . . . . . 40.81
Earl of Malmesbury, James Carleton Seventh v Strutt and Parker (a partnership) [2008] EWHC 424 (QB) 23.134, 56.49, 56.57
Earl Nelson v Lord Bridport (1845) 8 Beav 527 . . . . . 52.98
Earl of Orford v Churchill (1814) 3 Ves & B 59 . . . . . 60.28
Earl of Portsmouth v Hamilton (2000) The Independent, 27 October 57.55
Earl of Radnor's Will Trust, Re (1890) 45 Ch D 402, CA. 66.42
Earl of Uxbridge, Ex parte (1801) 6 Ves 425 . . . . . 1.61
Earles v Barclays Bank plc [2009] EWHC 2500 (QB) 6.113
Early Red Corpn NV v Glidepath Holdings BV [2005] EWCA Civ 525 . . . . . 45.26
East v Pantiles Plant Hire Ltd [1982] 2 EGLR 111 . . . . . 31.43
East West Corporation v DKBS [2002] All ER (D) 361 . . . . . 17.149
Eastwood, deceased; Lloyds Bank Ltd v Eastwood [1975] Ch 112 . . . . 18.108, 18.109, 27.324, 51.24, 51.26, 51.82, 59.18
Easyair Ltd (t/a Openair) v Opal Telecom Ltd [2009] EWHC 779 (Ch) 16.40, 16.54
Eaton v Caulfield [2013] EWHC 2214 (Ch). 15.03
Eaves v Eaves and Powell [1956] P 154 . . . . . 53.98
Ebert v Birch [2000] Ch 484, CA. 5.26
Economic Life Assurance Society v Usborne [1902] AC 152. . . . . . 56.42
Eden v Rubin [2011] EWHC 3090 (QB) 43.103
Eden Brown v Office of Fair Trading [2011] CAT 29 . . . . . 61.13, 61.14
Edmondson v Copland [1911] 2 Ch 301 . . . . . 66.13
Edray v Canning [2015] EWHC 2744 (Ch) 43.58, 43.156
Edwards v Edwards [1958] 2 All ER 179 . . . . . 9.10, 9.64
Edwards v Worboys [1984] AC 724 . . . . . 49.121
Edwards & Ors v Roche Products Ltd [2003] EWHC 9022 (Costs) 45.56, 53.47
Egan v Kensington Union Guardians (1841) 3 QB 935 . . . . . 53.31
Eicke v Nokes (1829) Mood & M 303 . . . . . 40.131
Eicke v Nokes (1834) 1 M & Rob 359 . . . . . 35.45
Eight Representative Claimants v MGN Ltd [2016] EWHC 855 (Ch). 24.49
Eiles v Southwark London Borough Council [2006] EWHC 2014 (TCC) 17.63, 17.96, 56.67
Ejiofoer (t/a Mitchell and Co Solicitors) v Legal Ombudsman [2016] EWHC 1933 (Admin). 27.91, 29.153, 39.24, 39.29
EI Du Pont De Nemours & Co v ST Dupont [2003] EWCA Civ 1368. . . . . . 4.38
Electrical Trades Union v Tarlo [1964] Ch 720 . . . . . 27.112, 27.211
Electricity Supply Nominees Ltd v Farrell [1997] 2 All ER 498 . . . . . 56.28
Elgindata (No 2), Re [1992] 1 WLR 1207 . . . . . 6.159, 6.160
Eli Lilly & Co Ltd v James [2009] EWHC 198 (QB) 13.30
Eli Lilly & Co Ltd v Neopharma Ltd [2012] EWHC 2297 (Ch) 15.104
Elkamet Kunststofftechnik GmBH v Saint-Gobain Glass France SA [2016] EWHC 3240 (Pat) 16.38
Elkamet Kunststofftechnik GmbH v Saint-Gobain Glass France SA [2016] EWHC 3321 (Pat). 56.48
Ellerbeck Collieries Ltd v Cornhill Insurance Co Ltd [1932] 1 KB 401 . . . . . 18.75
Ellerton v Harris [2004] EWCA Civ 1712 . . . . . 54.66, 54.89
Ellingsen v Det Skandinaviske Compani [1919] 2 KB 567 . . . . . 20.25, 20.27, 65.57
Elliot v Ince (1857) 5 WR 465 . . . . . 15.96
Elliott v Pensions Ombudsman [1998] OPLR 21 . . . . . 9.77
Elliott v Shah [2011] EW Misc 8 . . . . . 17.45, 17.76
Ellis v Torrington [1920] 1 KB 399 . . . . . 30.18
Ellison v Fairclough (unreported), 13 July 2007, Liverpool County Court. 50.99
Elsevier Ltd v Munro [2014] EWHC 2728 (QB) 17.81, 17.158
Elsey v Cox (1858) 26 Beav 95 . . . . . 60.04
Elton John v Price Waterhouse [2002] 1 WLR 953. . . . . . 66.21

Elvanite Full Circle Ltd v AMEC Earth & Environmental (UK) Ltd [2013] EWHC 1643 (TCC) 12.110, 12.124, 12.127, 12.167, 16.38
Elwood v Goodman [2014] Ch 442 . . . . . 32.22
EMI Records Ltd v Wallace [1983] 1 Ch 59 . . . . . 16.03, 66.17, 66.19
Emma Silver Mining Co, Re Turner (1875) 24 WR 54 . . . . . 40.74
Emmanuel v Revenue & Customs [2017] EWHC 1253 (Ch) 26.03
Emmott v Michael Wilson & Partners [2013] EWHC 3690 (Comm) 44.32
EMW Law LLP v Halborg [2017] EWHC 1014 (Ch) 6.218, 22.06, 40.14, 46.11, 46.25, 59.39, 59.43, 59.44, 59.54, 59.55
Endeavour Energy v Hess Ltd [2017] EWHC 1087 (Comm) 15.110, 15.116
Ene 1 Kos Ltd v Petroleo Brasileiro SA [2010] EWCA Civ 772 . . . . . 3.41, 52.98
Energy Venture Partners Ltd v Malabu Oil and Gas Ltd [2014] EWHC 1390 (Comm) 16.48
Enfield, London Borough of v P [1996] 1 FLR 629 . . . . . 23.64, 23.65
Engeham v London & Quadrant Housing Trust [2015] EWCA Civ 1530 . . . . . 27.34, 29.138
English v Emery Reimbold & Strick Ltd [2002] EWCA Civ 605 . . . . . 6.34, 43.317, 45.26
Enron (Thrace) v Clapp [2005] EWCA Civ 1511 . . . . . 10.15, 10.16
Enterprise Managed Services Ltd v McFadden Utilities Ltd [2010] EWHC 1506 (TCC) 6.33, 637
Enviroco Ltd v Farstad Supply A/S, The Far Service [2009] EWCA Civ 1399 . . . . . 31.42
Envis v Thakkar [1997] BPIR 189 . . . . . 15.03, 15.43
Epsom College v Pierse Contracting Southern Ltd (formerly Biseley Construction Ltd) (in liquidation) [2011] EWCA Civ 1449 . . . . . 6.212, 6.240, 16.36, 17.63, 17.71, 17.73, 17.173, 17.205, 17.214, 17.216, 17.219, 56.88
EQ Projects Ltd v Alavi [2006] EWHC 29 (TCC) 16.32
Equitable Life Assurance Society v Hyman [2002] 1 AC 408 . . . . . 31.62
Equitas Ltd v Horace Holman & Co Ltd [2008] EWHC 2287 (Comm) 9.79, 9.83
Equity Solicitors v Javid [2009] EWCA Civ 535 . . . . . 9.191, 9.207
Eron Park Ltd v Secretary of State for Environment [2001] 3 ELR 133 . . . . . 56.76
Ersus v London Borough of Redbridge [2016] EWHC 1025 (QB) 7.130, 7.148
Erven Warnink BV v J Townend & Sons (Hull) Ltd [1979] AC 731 . . . . . 56.24
Esure Services Ltd v Quarcoo [2009] EWCA Civ 595 . . . . . 16.27
Eurasian Natural Resources Corpn Ltd v Dechert LLP [2017] EWHC B4 (Costs) 36.31, 36.36, 40.31
Euro Asian Oil SA v Credit Suisse AG & Ors [2016] EWHC 3340 (Comm) 16.16, 17.137, 66.17
Eurocom Ltd v Siemens plc [2015] EWHC 685 (TCC) 16.47
Eurocross Sales Ltd v Cornhill Insurance plc [1995] 1 WLR 1517 . . . . . 15.53
Euroil Ltd v Cameroon Offshore Petroleum Sarl [2014] EWHC 215 (Comm) 44.18
Europa Holdings Ltd v Circle Industries (UK) plc [1993] BCLC 320, CA 15.82
Europeans Ltd v Commissioners for HM Revenue and Customs [2011] EWHC 948 (Ch) 9.82
Euroption Strategic Fund Ltd v Skandaniaviska Enskilda Banken AB [2012] EWHC 749 (Comm) 6.132, 16.19, 16.27, 16.39
Evans (deceased), Re [1986] 1 WLR 101 . . . . . 13.62, 66.62, 66.63, 66.65
Evans v Arriva Yorkshire Ltd (unreported), 28 November 2013, Leeds County Court 54.189
Evans v Gloucestershire County Council [2008] EWCA Civ 21 . . . . . 29.22
Evans v Royal Wolverhampton Hospitals NHS Foundation Trust [2014] EWHC 3185 (QB) 17.211, 17.213
Evans v Wakefield Metropolitan District Council (unreported), c 2012, Leeds County Court 55.25
Eversheds (a firm) v Osman [2000] 1 Costs LR 54 . . . . . 35.54, 35.65
Eversheds LLP v Cuddy (unreported), 17 December 2009, SCCO 38.54, 38.55
Everton v World Professional Billiards and Snooker Association (Promotions) Ltd [2001] All ER (D) 172 (Dec) 7.129, 7.167
EWA, Re [1901] 2 KB 642, CA 19.25
Eweida v British Airways Plc [2009] EWCA Civ 1025 . . . . . 13.20, 13.101
Ewing v ODPM [2005] All ER (D) 315 . . . . . 67.09
Excalibur Ventures LLC v Texas Keystone Inc [2013] EWHC 2767 (Comm); [2013] EWHC 4278 (Comm) 33.67

Excalibur Ventures LLC v Texas Keystone Inc [2014] EWHC 3436 (Comm); [2016] EWCA Civ 1144; [2016] 1 WLR 2221. . . . . 4.65, 6.03, 6.18, 9.07, 9.15, 9.37, 9.40, 9.42, 9.43, 9.44, 14.10, 14.21, 14.22, 14.23, 14.32, 14.34, 14.36, 15.91, 16.18, 16.28, 16.31, 16.40, 16.46, 16.49, 16.51, 16.57
Excalibur Ventures LLC v Texas Keystone Inc & Ors [2015] EWHC 566 (Comm) 56.32, 56.43, 56.44, 56.54
Excel Securities plc v Masood [2009] EWHC 3912 (Ch) 9.68
Excelerate Technology Ltd v Cumberbatch [2015] EWHC 204 (QB) 16.57
Excelsior Commercial & Industrial Holdings Ltd v Salisbury Hamer Aspden & Johnson (Costs) [2002] EWCA Civ 879 . . . . 16.11, 16.12, 16.19, 16.20, 16.23, 16.25, 16.39, 17.99, 45.26, 56.87
Exchange Securities and Commodities Ltd (No 2), Re [1985] BCLC 392 . . . . 66.64

F v F (Ancillary Relief: Costs) [1995] 2 FLR 702 . . . . 47.19, 53.127
F & C Alternative Investments (Holdings) Ltd & Ors Appellants v Barthelemy [2012] EWCA Civ 843 . . . . 6.212, 16.34, 16.35, 16.36, 17.16, 17.60, 17.61, 17.62, 56.72, 56.73, 56.78, 56.79
Fabio Perini SPA v LPC Group plc [2010] EWCA Civ 525. . . . . 16.44
Fahy's Will Trusts, Re [1962] 1 All ER 73 . . . . 49.147
Fairclough Homes Ltd v Summers [2012] UKSC 26 . . . . 6.151, 6.152, 6.229, 6.232, 17.174
Fairfold Properties Ltd v Exmouth Docks Co Ltd (No 2) [1993] Ch 196 . . . . 40.91, 40.96
Fairview Investments Ltd v Sharma (unreported), 14 October 1999, CA. 16.64, 66.11, 66.17, 66.19
Falmouth House Freehold Co Ltd v Morgan Walker LLP [2010] EWHC 3092 (Ch). 36.33, 36.36, 36.38
Family Housing Association v Hyde [1993] 1 WLR 354 . . . . 6.218
Fanshaw, Re [1905] WN 64. . . . . 35.127
Far Out Productions Inc v Unilever UK & CN Holdings Ltd [2009] EWHC 3484 (Ch). 7.112, 7.121, 7.122
Farag v Commissioner of Police of the Metropolis [2005] EWCA Civ 1814 . . . . 17.216
Farm Assist Ltd (in liquidation) v The Secretary of State for the Environment, Food and Rural Affairs (No 2) [2009] EWHC 1102 (TCC) 48.43
Farman, Re (1883) 18 L Jo 352. . . . . 53.12
Farmer v Moseley (Holdings) Ltd (2001) BCLC 572 . . . . 15.44
Farnworth v Davies (unreported), 4 March 2016, Liverpool County Court 20.62
Farrakhan v Secretary of State for the Home Department [2001] EWHC 781 (Admin). 24.10
Farrell & Anor v Direct Accident Management Services Ltd [2009] EWCA Civ 769 . . . . 9.82
Farrer v Lacy, Hartland & Co (1885) 28 Ch D 482 . . . . 15.79
Fattal v Walbrook Trustees (Jersey) Ltd & Anor [2009] EWHC 1674 (Ch) 38.96, 43.337, 56.31, 56.49, 56.62, 56.81
Fazil-Alizadeh v Nikbin (unreported), 25 February 1993, CA (Civ Div) 6.218
Fearns v Anglo-Dutch Paint & Chemical Co Ltd [2010] EWHC 2366 (Ch) 21.03, 21.34, 21.38
Federal Commerce and Navigation Co Ltd v Molena Alpha Inc [1978] QB 927 . . . . 21.05
Fellows v Barrett (1836) 1 Keen 119. . . . . 15.96
Feltham v Bouskell [2013] EWHC 3086 (Ch D) 17.128, 17.134
Fenton v Holmes [2007] EWHC 2476 (Ch). 29.54, 29.66, 29.100, 29.103, 31.55
Fereidooni v Pettman Smith [2001] EWHC 9007 (Costs) 27.96
Fernandes, In re (1878) WN 57 . . . . 27.162, 35.45, 35.115, 36.26, 40.10
Fernhill Mining Ltd v Kier Construction Ltd (unreported), 27 January 2000, CA 15.57
Feuerheerd v LGO Co [1918] 2 KB 565 . . . . 46.09
FH Brundle v Perry [2014] EWHC 979 (IPEC). 50.333, 50.334
FHR European Ventures LLP v Cedar Capital Partners LLC [2014] UKSC 45 . . . . 40.55
Fidelitas Shipping [1966] QB 630, CA. 23.21, 23.26
Filcross Securities Ltd v Midgeley (unreported), 21 July 1998, CA. 23.96
Filmlab Systems International Ltd & Anor v Pennington [1994] 4 All ER 673. . . . . 9.208
Findcharm Ltd v Churchill Group Ltd [2017] EWHC 1108 (TCC) 12.55

Findon v Parker (1843) 11 M & W 675 . . . . . 30.54
Finglands Coachways Ltd v O'Hare [2014] EWHC 1513 (QB) 25.41, 25.71
Finlay v Mexican Investment Corpn [1897] 1 QB 517 . . . . . 18.74
Finley v Glaxo Laboratories Ltd (1989) 106 Costs LR 106 . . . . . 25.04, 51.29, 51.37, 51.45
Fiona Trust v Privalov [2011] EWHC 1312 (Comm) 56.33
Fiona Trust & Holding Corpn v Privalov [2011] EWHC 664 (Comm) 6.48, 6.194, 16.40, 16.48, 16.52, 16.53
Firle v Datapoint [2001] EWCA Civ 1106 . . . . . 6.67, 17.102
Firstpost Homes Ltd v Johnson [1996] 1 WLR 67 . . . . . 35.84
Fish, Bennett v Bennett, Re [1893] 2 Ch 413, CA. 60.06, 60.21
Fisher v Dudding 9 Dowl 872 . . . . . 56.23
Fisher v Oldham Corpn [1930] 2 KB 364. . . . . . 50.126
Fisher Price Inc & Mattel UK Ltd v RSW Group plc [2004] EWHC 1610 (Ch) 51.71
Fitzhugh Gates (a firm) v Sherman [2003] EWCA Civ 886 . . . . . 9.178
Fitzleet Estates Ltd v Cherry [1977] 1 WLR 1345 . . . . . 4.06
Fitzpatrick Contractors Ltd v Tyco Fire & Integrated Solutions (UK) Ltd [2008] EWHC 1391 (TCC). 16.35, 16.40, 16.58, 17.114
Fitzpatrick Contractors Ltd v Tyco Fire & Integrated Solutions (UK) Ltd [2009] EWHC 274 (TCC). 17.172, 17.183, 50.289
Fitzroy Robinson Ltd v Mentmore Towers Ltd [2010] EWHC 98 (TCC) 6.212, 16.36, 17.62
Fladgate LLP v Harrison [2012] EWHC 67 (AB). 27.202
Flanagan v Liontrust Investment Partners LLP [2016] EWHC 446 (Ch). 6.61
Flatman v Germany [2011] EWHC 2945 (QB) 7.40, 9.71
Flatman v Germany [2013] EWCA Civ 278. . . . . . 9.23, 9.48, 9.49, 9.50, 9.51, 9.52, 9.71, 9.90
Flaxman-Binns v Lincolnshire CC (Practice Note) [2004] EWCA Civ 424. . . . . . 26.22, 26.42
Fleming v The Chief Constable of the Sussex Police Force [2004] EWCA Civ 643. . . . . . 6.72, 6.185
Flemyng v Hector (1836) 2 M & W 172. . . . . . 27.322
Flender Werft AG v Aegean Maritime Ltd [1990] 2 Lloyd's Rep 27 . . . . . 15.86, 15.95
Fletamentos Maritimos v Effjohn International [2003] Lloyd's Rep PN 26 . . . . . 9.178
Fletcher and Dyson, In re [1903] 2 Ch 688. . . . . . 36.68, 52.04
Flitters v Allfrey (1874) LR 10 CP 29 . . . . . 23.25
Floods of Queensferry Ltd v Shand Construction [2002] EWCA Civ 918 . . . . . 9.28, 9.48, 9.49
Floyd & Anor v Legal Services Commission [2010] EWHC 906 (QB). 62.20
Fluflon Ltd v William Frost & Sons Ltd [1965] RPC 574 . . . . . 53.132
Flynn v Scougall [2004] EWCA Civ 873 . . . . . 17.195
FN v Secretary of State for the Home Department [2015] EWHC 3057 (QB) 43.98
Foakes v Beer (1884) 9 App Cas 605 . . . . . 32.54, 39.17, 40.74
Football Association Premier League Ltd v Berry [2014] EWHC 726 . . . . . 14.21
Forbes v Git [1922] 1 AC 256 . . . . . 31.36
Forbes-Smith v Forbes-Smith and Chadwick [1901] P 258, CA 10.13
Force India Formula One Team Ltd v 1 Malaysia Racing Team SDN BHD [2012] EWHC 1726 (Ch). 15.104
Forcelux Ltd v Binnie (Costs) [2009] EWCA Civ 1077 . . . . . 16.35, 66.07, 66.11
Ford, Re (1838) 3 Deac 494, Mont & Ch 97 . . . . . 40.124
Ford v GKR Construction Ltd [2000] 1 WLR 1397 . . . . . 6.238, 17.55, 17.137
Ford v Labrador [2003] UKPC 41 . . . . . 43.159
Forde v Birmingham City Council [2009] EWHC 12 (QB) 18.96, 29.87, 29.132, 29.133, 31.56, 32.46, 32.49, 32.50, 32.52, 32.54, 32.64, 54.44, 54.46
Fore Street Warehouse Co Ltd, The v Durrant & Co (1883) 10 QBD 471 . . . . . 27.80
Formula E Holdings Ltd v CDC Entertainment Ltd [2015] EWHC 2110 (Comm) 15.70, 15.78
Forney v Bushe (1954) 104 L Jo 604. . . . . . 27.83
Foroughi v Foroughi (unreported), 30 July 1993, Fam 50.36
Forshaw, Re (1847) 16 Sim 121 . . . . . 40.48
Forsinard Estate Ltd v Dykes [1971] 1 WLR 232 . . . . . 36.05, 36.22
Forstater v Python (Monty) Pictures Ltd [2013] EWHC 3759 (Ch). 16.56, 54.123
Foster, Re [1920] 3 KB 306 . . . . . 36.18

Forster v Davies (1863) 32 Beav 6, 36.1924, 55 ER 245 . . . . 1.98
Forster v Farquhar [1893] 1 QB 564. . . . . 1.100, 1.102, 6.164
Forster v Friedland (unreported), 10 November 1992, CA (Civ Div) 6.218
Fortune v Roe [2011] EWHC 2953 (QB) 54.61, 65.85
Fosberry & anor v HM Revenue and Customs [2006] EWHC 90061 (Costs) 3.100
Fosberry & anor v HM Revenue and Customs [2007] EWHC 2249 (Ch);
[2008] EWHC 3344 (Ch) 18.55, 29.54, 29.58, 29.63, 29.64, 29.66
Foss, Bilbrough, Plaskitt & Foss, In re [1912] 2 Ch 161 . . . . 36.12, 36.13, 36.18, 36.22
Fosse Motor Engineers Ltd & Ors v Conde Nast and National Magazine Distributors &
Ors [2008] EWHC 2527 (QB). 56.57, 56.81
Foster v Roussel Laboratories (unreported), 29 October 1997, QBD 65.12
Fotedar v St George's Healthcare NHS Trust (No 2) [2005] All ER (D) 33 (QB). 17.153
Fourie v Le Roux & Ors (Rev 1) [2007] UKHL 1. 4.67, 16.26, 20.04, 20.15
Fox v Foundation Piling Ltd [2011] EWCA Civ 790 . . . . 6.61, 6.147, 6.152, 6.155, 6.188, 6.225, 6.238
Fox Gregory Ltd v Hamptons Group Ltd [2006] EWCA Civ 1544 . . . . .7.159
Fozal v Gofur, The Times, 9 July 1993, CA 9.62
FPH Law v Brown [2016] EWHC 1681 (QB) 40.47
Frampton, ex p Frampton, Re (1859) 1 De GF & J 263, CA. 27.37
Francis v Francis and Dickerson [1956] P 87 . . . . 25.55, 49.08, 57.06
Francis v Solomon Taylor & Shaw (a firm) [2013] EWHC 9 (Ch) 40.32
Frankenburg v Famous Lasky Film Service Ltd [1931] 1 Ch 428 . . . . 49.07, 49.147, 52.27
Franklin v Maddison [2014] EWCA Civ 628. . . . . 16.38
Franks v Sinclair (Costs) [2006] EWHC 3656 (Ch). 16.35
Franses (Liquidator of Arab News Network Ltd) v Al Assad [2007] EWHC 2442 (Ch). 16.57
Frape, ex p Perrett, In re [1893] 2 Ch 284. . . . . .27.122, 27.124, 35.73, 36.19
Frape, ex p Perrett (No 2), Re [1894] 2 Ch 290. . . . . 23.42, 49.05
Frascati (unreported), In re 2 December 1981, QBD 49.17, 48.18
Fraser v Buckle [1996] 2 IRLM 34 . . . . 30.09
Fred Perry (Holdings) Ltd v Brands Plaza Trading Ltd [2012] EWCA Civ 224 . . . . .26.28, 26.38, 54.122
Freeport Electronics Ltd v Habib Bank Ltd [2007] EWHC 1149 (QB) 40.50
French v Carter Lemon Camerons LLP [2012] EWCA Civ 1180 . . . . 40.44, 40.60, 40.68
French v Groupama Insurance Co Ltd [2011] EWCA Civ 1119 . . . . 6.207, 6.240, 16.36, 17.18, 17.62, 17.63, 17.76, 17.214
French v Hartman [2014] EWHC 1682 (QB) 32.31
Fresenius Kabi Deutschland GmbH v Carefusion 303 Inc [2011] EWCA Civ 1288. . . . . 7.120
Freudiana Holdings Ltd, Re The Times, 4 December 1995 . . . . 9.200
Fricker v Van Grutten [1896] 2 Ch 662 . . . . 9.64
Friend v Solly (1847) 10 Beav 329. . . . . 53.129
Friswell v King (1846) 15 Sim 191 . . . . 40.48
Fuld (No 4), Re [1968] P 727 . . . . 40.37, 40.39, 40.40, 40.106, 40.107, 40.111, 40.113, 40.114
Fulham Leisure Holdings Ltd v Nicholson Graham & Jones [2006] EWHC 2428 (Ch). 6.57, 6.67, 6.155, 6.176, 6.185, 6.227, 6.238, 17.105, 17.132, 52.28, 52.40
Fulton Motors Ltd v Toyota (GB) Ltd (Costs) [2000] CP Rep 24. 9.30, 16.40
Furlong v Howard (1804) 2 Sch & Lef 115 . . . . 40.71
Furlong v Scallan (1875) IR 9 Eq 202. . . . . 27.312
Fyler v Fyler (1841) 3 Beav 550. . . . . 40.55
Fyson, Re (1846) 9 Beav 117 . . . . 36.85

G, Re (1909) 53 SJ 469. . . . . 36.36
G v G (Minors: Custody Appeal) [1985] 1 WLR 647 . . . . 45.23
G (by her mother and litigation friend M) v Kingston upon Hull City Council (unreported),
18 September 2013, Kingston-upon-Hull County Court. 45.66, 49.161, 51.21, 51.51, 51.78, 51.79
G and C Kreglinger v New Patagonia Meat and Cold Storage Co Ltd [1914] AC 25, HL 4.05
G & Ors (children) (Care Proceedings: Wasted Costs), Re [1999] 4 All ER 371 . . . . 9.104, 9.176

Gabriel v BPE Solicitors [2015] AC 1663 . . . . 54.175
Galland, Re (1885) 31 Ch D 296, CA 27.69, 40.77
Galloway v Corpn of London (1867) LR 4 Eq 90 . . . . 1.83, 27.112
Gamal v Synergy Lifestyle Ltd [2018] EWCA Civ 210 . . . . 17.87
Gamlen Chemical Co (UK) Ltd v Rochem Ltd [1980] 1 WLR 614 . . . . . . 40.60, 40.61, 40.62, 40.63
Gandesha v Nandra (unreported), 21 November 2001, Ch D 9.182
Garbutt v Edwards [2005] EWCA Civ 1206 . . . . 4.15, 4.22, 4.26, 23.114, 27.101, 27.245, 27.248, 27.255, 27.268, 28.98, 28.139, 57.53, 57.54, 60.58
Gardner v Irvin (1878–79) LR 4 Ex D 49 . . . . 46.08
Gardner v M'Mahon (1842) 3 QB 561 . . . . 23.134
Garfield v Fay [1968] P 306 . . . . 46.09
Garnett v Bradley (1878) 3 AC 944 . . . . 1.49, 6.13, 6.14
Garrard v Frankel (1862) 30 Beav 445 . . . . 32.73
Garratt v Saxby [2004] EWCA Civ 341 . . . . 17.59
Garrett v Halton Borough Council [2006] EWCA Civ 1017 . . . . 4.81, 29.29, 29.30, 29.32, 29.54, 29.82, 29.83, 29.84, 29.90, 29.93, 29.95, 29.96, 54.198
Garritt-Critchley v Ronnan [2014] EWHC 1774 (Ch) 6.118, 6.129, 6.136, 6.139, 16.33
Garry v Gwillim [2002] EWCA Civ 1500 . . . . 2.09, 35.53, 35.54, 35.59, 35.61, 35.63
Gatnom v Sanders [2011] EWHC 3716 (Ch) 9.43, 16.48
Gaupen, the [1925] WN 138 . . . . 40.80
Gavaghan v Edwards [1961] 2 QB 220; [1961] 2 All ER 477, CA 47.25
Gavin Edmondson Solicitors Ltd v Haven Insurance Co Ltd [2018] UKSC 21 . . . . 40.39, 40.40, 40.41, 40.42, 40.106, 40.107, 40.108, 40.109, 40.110, 40.114, 40.116, 40.118
Gaynor v Central West London Buses Ltd [2006] EWCA Civ 1120 . . . . 29.11
Gazley v Wade [2004] EWHC 2675 (QB) 51.76, 51.79
GB Gas Holdings Ltd v Accenture (UK) Ltd & Ors [2010] EWCA Civ 912 . . . . 28.162
GB Gas Holdings Ltd v Accenture (UK) Ltd & Ors [2010] EWHC 2928 (Comm) 7.89, 7.94, 43.61, 43.80, 43.82
Gebruder Naf v Ploton (1890) 25 QBD 13, CA 40.48
Gedy, Re (1851) 14 Beav 56 . . . . 35.84
Geilinger v Gibbs [1897] 1 Ch 479 . . . . 9.64
Gempride v Bamrah [2018] EWCA Civ 1367 . . . . 57.38, 57.39, 57.41, 57.42, 57.43, 57.44, 57.45, 57.49, 57.60
General Accident Car and Life Assurance Corpn Ltd v Foster [1972] 3 All ER 877 . . . . 62.19
General of Berne Insurance Co, The v Jardine Reinsurance Management Ltd [1998] 2 All ER 301; [1998] 1 WLR 1231 . . . . 18.11, 18.13, 29.178, 51.44
General Mediterranean Holdings SA v Patel [2000] 1 WLR 272 . . . . 4.37, 9.170, 46.05, 24.56, 57.64
Generics (UK) Ltd v Yeda Research & Development Co Ltd [2012] EWHC 2283 (Ch) 56.39
Geophysical Service Centre Co v Dowell Schlumberger (ME) Inc [2013] EWHC 147 (TCC) 15.38
George v Elston (1835) 1 Bing NC 515 . . . . 1.72
George Holloway & Webb Ltd v Crompton [1916] 2 Ch 436 . . . . 1.118
George Wimpey UK Ltd v Tewkesbury Borough Council [2008] EWCA Civ 12 . . . . 45.04
German Property 50 Sarl v Summers-Inman Construction & Property Consultants LLP [2009] EWHC 2968 (TCC) 14.14, 19.44, 43.378
Gerrards Cross Leisure Services Ltd v Shizentai Health & Exercise Ltd (unreported), 23 January 2017, Oxford County Court 9.36
GFN SA v Bancredit Cayman Ltd (in liquidation) [2009] UKPC 39 . . . . 15.02, 15.03
Ghadami v Lyon Cole Insurance Group Ltd [2010] EWCA Civ 767 . . . . . 18.28, 18.59, 18.68, 27.62, 27.194, 27.202, 27.206, 31.70
Ghaidan v Godin-Mendoza [2004] UKHL 30 . . . . 24.16
Ghannouchi v Houni Ltd & Ors [2004] EWHC 9002 (Costs) 29.66
GHLM Trading v Maroo (unreported) 27 February 2012, Ch D 7.32, 16.40
Giambrone v JMC Holidays Ltd [2002] EWHC 495 (QB) 46.66, 49.74, 49.102, 51.78, 51.79, 65.99,
Giambrone v JMC Holidays Ltd (formerly Sunworld Holidays Ltd) [2002] EWHC 2932 (QB) 7.92, 14.06, 25.41, 25.43, 25.65, 25.68, 25.70, 25.72, 25.82, 25.101, 25.103, 45.50, 65.91, 65.110, 65.111

Gibbon v Manchester City Council [2010] EWCA Civ 726. . . . . . . 17.15, 17.20, 17.22, 17.53, 17.195, 17.202, 17.218
Gibson v May (1853) 4 De GM & G 512 . . . . . . 40.37
Gibson's Settlement Trusts, Re [1981] Ch 179 . . . . . . 3.06, 3.20, 49.06, 49.07, 49.103, 49.128, 49.147
Gil v Baygreen Properties Ltd [2004] EWHC 2029 (Ch). 6.31, 6.108
Gilbert v Endean (1878) 9 Ch D 259, CA. 10.27
Giles v Randall [1915] 1 KB 290. . . . . . 1.111
Giles v Thompson [1994] 1 AC 142; [1993] 3 All ER 321 . . . . . . 9.28, 27.228, 29.197, 30.07, 30.10, 30.11, 30.14, 30.17, 30.19, 30.20, 30.22, 30.28, 33.10
Gilkes v Leonino (1858) 4 CBNS 485 . . . . . . 43.289
Gill v Russell (1673) Freem KB 62 . . . . . . 60.30
Gimex v Chillbag [2012] EW PCC 34. . . . . . 50.330
Girvan v Inverness Farmers Dairy 1998 SC (HL) 1 . . . . . . 45.70
Gittins v Serco Home Affairs [2012] EWHC 651 (Ch). 43.391
Gizmondo Europe Ltd v Fry, In the Matter of [2014] EWHC 4640 (Ch). 16.57
Glasgow Harley (a firm) v McDonald [2001] UKPC 18A 3.16
Glass v Freyssinet Ltd [2016] EWCA Civ 1120 . . . . . . 13.105
Glegg v Bromley [1912] 3 KB 474, CA. 30.38
Glencore Agriculture BV v Vinatex Trading Joint Stock Co HCMC (unreported), 23 May 2018, QBD 16.49
Global Flood Defence Systems Ltd v Johann Van Den Noort Beheer BV [2016] EWHC 189 (IPEC). 50.324, 50.330, 50.335, 50.336, 50.339
Global Marine Drillships Ltd v La Bella [2010] EWHC 2498 (Ch) 51.83, 53.88, 53.99, 53.120
Globe Equities Ltd v Globe Legal Services Ltd [1999] BLR 232. . . . . 9.12, 9.17, 9.62, 9.88, 9.107, 9.140
Gloucestershire County Council v Evans [2008] EWCA Civ 21 . . . . . . 29.130
Glynn v Margetson & Co [1893] AC 351 . . . . . . 31.36, 31.45
GNR v Mossop [1855] 17 CB 130 . . . . . . 10.14, 10.15
Goddard v Nationwide Building Society [1987] 1 QB 670. . . . . . 36.107
Godfrey Morgan Solicitors Ltd v Cobalt Systems Ltd [2011] 6 Costs LR 1006 (EAT) 9.152
Godwin v Swindon Borough Council [2001] EWCA Civ 1478 . . . . . . 4.38, 4.50, 43.267
Golden Eye (International) Ltd v Telefonica UK Ltd [2012] EWHC 723 (Ch) 30.34
Golden Ocean Group Ltd v Salgaocar Mining Industries PVT Ltd [2012] 2 All ER (Comm) 978 . . . . . . 35.79, 35.82
Golding v First Tier Tribunal [2012] EWHC 222 (Admin). 9.48
Goldman v Hesper [1988] 1 WLR 1238. . . . . . 29.47, 46.47, 46.68, 46.69, 46.70
Goldsmith v Russell (1855) 5 De GM & G 547 . . . . . . 7.31
Goldtrail Travel Ltd v Aydin [2017] UKSC 57. . . . . . 15.82, 15.84, 15.86
Gollop v Pryke (unreported), 19 November 2011, Ch D. 14.21
Golubovich v Golubovich [2011] EWCA Civ 528 . . . . . . 15.03, 15.21, 15.82
Gomba Holdings Ltd v Minories Finance Ltd (No 2) [1993] Ch 171 . . . . . . 16.64, 20.46, 56.118, 65.57, 66.04, 66.06, 66.08, 66.10
Goodman v J Eban Ltd [1954] 1 QB 550 . . . . . . 35.80, 35.81
Goodwin v Bennetts UK Ltd [2008] EWCA Civ 1658. . . . . . 6.188
Goodwood Recoveries Ltd v Breen [2005] EWCA Civ 414 . . . . . . 9.12, 9.15, 9.17, 9.26
Gordon v Dalzell (1852) 15 Beav 351 . . . . . . 22.06
Gordon v Gonda [1955] 2 All ER 762. . . . . . 23.14
Gordon v Gordon [2002] EWCA Civ 1884; [2002] All ER (D) 308 (Dec). 40.45
Gore v Harris (1851) 21 LJ Ch 10 . . . . . . 46.09
Gore v Naheed [2017] EWCA Civ 369. . . . . . 6.128
Gosling v Screwfix Direct (unreported), 29 April 2014, Cambridge County Court. 8.35, 8.37, 8.41, 8.45
Gotch v Enelco Ltd [2015] EWHC 1802 (TCC) 6.140
Gould v Davis (1831) 1 Cr & J 415 . . . . . . 40.39
Governing Body of JFS, The [2009] UKSC 1; [2009] 1 WLR 2353 . . . . . . 7.157
Governors & Company of the Bank of Ireland & Anor v Watts Group plc [2017] EWHC 2472 (TCC). 12.168, 16.35

Gower Chemicals Group Litigation [2008] EWHC 735 (QB) 46.46
Graigola Merthyr Co Ltd v Swansea Corpn [1927] WN 30 . . . . 52.27
Grand v Gill [2011] EWCA Civ 902. . . . . 59.26
Grant v Ralls [2016] EWHC 1812 (Ch) 3.100
Grant & Anor v Baker [2016] EWHC 1782 (Ch). 45.17
Grant, Bulcraig & Co, Re [1906] 1 Ch 124 . . . . 35.92
Gray, Re [1901] 1 Ch 239 . . . . .36.83, 36.85
Gray v Going Places Leisure Travel Ltd [2005] EWCA Civ 189 . . . . 9.115, 9.200, 9.206, 9.207, 9.208, 23.44
Gray & Anor v Buss & Merton (a firm) [1999] PNLR 882 . . . . 27.96
Great Future International Ltd & Ors v Sealand Housing Corporation [2003] EWCA Civ 682 . . . . 15.03, 15.21
Great Peace, The [2002] EWCA Civ 14 . . . . 31.45
Great Western Rly Co v Carpalla United China Clay Co Ltd (No 2) [1909] 2 Ch 471 . . . . .52.38, 53.133
Great Western Rly Co v Crouch (1858) 3 H & N 183, Ex Ch. 40.43
Grecoair Inc v Tilling [2009] EWHC 115 . . . . 9.85
Green (as Administratrix of the Estate of Peter Maclean Maitland deceased) v Astor [2013] EWHC 1857 (Ch) 16.50, 66.47, 66.66
Green v Sunset & Vine Productions Ltd (unreported) 4 November 2009, QB 7.14
Greencore (UK) Holdings Plc v Elementis Plc [2005] EWHC 2139 (Comm) 7.94
Greene Wood McLean LLP (in administration) v Templeton Insurance Ltd [2010] EWHC 2679 (Comm) 34.66
Greenwich Millennium Village Ltd v Essex Services Group Plc (Formerly Essex Electrical Group Ltd) [2014] EWHC 1099 (TCC) 17.95, 17.161
Greer v Young (1881–85) All ER Rep 513 . . . . 40.96
Greetham v The Inhabitants of the Hundred of Theale (1765) 97 ER 1066 . . . . 1.53
Gregory v Molesworth (1747) 3 Atk 626 . . . . 23.08
Greig v Lauchlan (unreported), 7 December 2016, Ch D. 12.117
Greig v National Amalgamated Union of Shop Assistants, Warehousemen and Clerks (1906) 22 TLR 274 . . . . .18.66, 30.35, 30.52
Grender v Dresden [2009] EWHC 500 (Ch) 66.53
Grepe v Loam (1887) 37 Ch D 168, CA. 5.26
Gresport Finance Ltd v Battaglia [2015] EWHC 2709 (Ch). 6.128
Greville v Sprake [2001] EWCA Civ 234 . . . . 59.24
Grey, In re [1892] 2 QB 440. . . . . 5.29
Griffin v Hoskyns (1856) 1 H & N 95 . . . . 52.56
Griffin v Smith & Ors [2010] EWHC 3414 (Ch) 7.126
Griffin v Wishbech Phab Club (unreported), 11 July 2011, Norwich County Court 50.76
Griffith, Re (1891) 7 TLR 268 . . . . 35.126
Griffith v Tower Publishing Co [1897] 1 Ch 21 . . . . 32.17
Griffiths v Commissioner of Police for the Metropolis [2003] EWCA Civ 313. . . . . 6.263
Griffiths v Evans [1953] 2 All ER 1364. . . . . 27.48, 27.95
Griffiths v Griffiths (1843) 2 Hare 587 . . . . .27.83, 40.60
Griffiths v Hyde (1809) Dorset Summer Assizes, 2 Selw NP 1320 . . . . 40.37
Griffiths v Solutia (UK) Ltd [2001] EWCA Civ 736. . . . . . . .12.07, 13.10, 18.56, 45.23, 51.63, 51.66, 51.71, 51.73, 51.74, 51.75, 65.91
Griffiths v Williams (1787) 99 ER 1335 . . . . 1.58, 17.07
Griffiths & Ors v British Coal Corpn [2007] EWHC 672 (QB). 65.27
Grimes v Crown Prosecution Service [2003] EWCA Civ 1814. . . . . 61.09, 61.10
Grimthorpe [1958] Ch 615. . . . . 66.36
Grizzly Business Ltd v Stena Drilling Ltd [2017] EWCA Civ 94 . . . . 9.09
Groom v Cheesewright (1885) 1 Ch 730 . . . . 40.96
Group Seven Ltd v Nasir [2016] EWHC 620 (Ch). 12.76, 12.95, 12.101
Group M UK Ltd v Cabinet Office [2014] EWHC 3863 (TCC) 44.25, 44.30
Groupama Insurance Co Ltd v Aon Ltd [2003] EWCA Civ 1846 . . . . .6.20, 6.78, 6.84, 6.109
Grovewood Holdings plc v James Capel & Co Ltd [1995] Ch 80 . . . . .30.43, 33.05

Grupo Torras SA v Sheikh Fahad Mohammed Al-Sabah [1999] CLC 1469, QBD 6.109, 7.49
GSD Law Ltd v Wardman & Ors [2017] EWCA Civ 2144. . . . 18.34, 18.54, 57.49, 57.57, 57.59, 57.62
GSK Project Management Ltd v QPR Holdings Ltd [2015] EWHC 2274 (TCC) 12.62, 12.90, 12.93, 12.94, 12.95, 12.98, 12.101, 12.103
Guerrero & Ors v Monterrico Metals plc [2009] EWHC 2475 (QB) 15.113
Guerrero v Nykoo (unreported), 25 October 2010, Cardiff County Court. 28.193
Guidezone Ltd, In re [2014] EWHC 1165 (Ch) 26.52, 43.134
Guinness Peat Properties Ltd v The Fitzroy Partnership [1987] 1 WLR 1027 . . . . 33.89
Gulati v MGN Ltd [2015] EWHC 1805 (Ch) 16.37, 17.214, 17.215
Gulf Azov Shipping Co Ltd v Idisi [2001] EWCA Civ 505, CA 15.121
Gulf Azov Shipping Co Ltd v Idisi [2004] EWCA Civ 292 .9.32, 9.33, 9.34
Gundry v Sainsbury [1910] 1 KB 645. . . . . .1.83, 18.05, 27.112, 27.211, 29.204
Gupta v Comer [1991] 1 QB 629; [1991] 1 All ER 289 . . . . .9.62, 9.95
Gupta v Union Bank of India [2012] EWHC 4075 (Ch) 10.05
Gustavson v Haviland [1919] 1 Ch 38 . . . . 32.30
Guy v Churchill (1887) 35 Ch D 489. . . . . 40.42, 40.89, 40.96
Guy v Churchill (1888) 40 Ch D 481 . . . . 33.05

H Dakin & Co Ltd v Lee [1916] 1 KB 566, CA 27.24
H Tolputt & Co Ltd v Mole [1911] 1 KB 87 . . . . 3.09, 59.02, 59.39, 59.43
HA Grey [1892] 2 QB 440 . . . . 5.32
Habib Bank Ltd v Ahmed [2004] EWCA Civ 805 . . . . 25.76
Hadley v Baxendale [1843–60] All ER Rep 461 . . . . 56.119
Haederle v Thomas [2017] EWCA Civ 1339 . . . . 15.22
Hahn v NHS England (unreported), 3 August 2015, Liverpool County Court 54.132, 54.164
Haider Kennedy Solicitors v Momson [2017] EWHC 2984 (Ch). 16.49
Haigh, Re (1849) 12 Beav 307 . . . . .36.61, 36.67
Haigh v Brooks (1839) 10 Ad & El 309 . . . . 31.25
Haigh v Ousey (1857) 7 E & B 578 . . . . 1.81, 35.53, 35.59, 35.63
Hair, Re (1847) 10 Beav 187. . . . . 36.11
Hajigeorgeiou v Vasiliou [2005] EWCA Civ 236 . . . . 52.32
Haji-Ioannou v Frangos [2006] EWCA Civ 1663 . . . . 9.101, 23.61, 23.68, 23.69, 23.70, 23.77, 23.78, 23.79, 56.52, 57.39, 57.40, 57.42, 57.48, 57.52
Halabi v Fieldmore Holdings [2006] EWHC 1965 (Ch) 15.97
Hall v Barker, In re (1893) 9 Ch D 538. . . . . .23.93, 27.16, 27.19, 35.22, 35.30
Hall v Hall [1891] P 302, CA 40.58
Hall v Meyrick [1957] 2 QB 455. . . . . .27.311
Hall v Ministry of Defence [2013] EWHC 4092 (QB). 12.59
Hall v Rover Financial Services Ltd (GB) [2002] EWCA Civ 1514. . . . . .6.78, 6.83
Hall v Stone [2007] EWCA Civ 1354. . . . . 6.143, 6.155, 6.199, 6.238, 52.28
Hall (Inspector of Taxes) v Lorimer [1992] 1 WLR 939 (CA). 50.124
Hallam Estates Ltd v Baker [2014] EWCA Civ 661 . . . . 26.03, 26.52, 43.89, 43.92, 43.131, 43.132, 43.134, 43.144, 43.155, 43.158
Hallam-Peel & Co v Southwark LBC [2008] EWCA Civ 1120 . . . . 9.192
Hallet v Mears (1810) 13 East 15 . . . . 52.48
Halloran v Delaney [2003] 1 WLR 28. . . . . .54.48, 54.60
Halsey v Milton Keynes General NHS Trust [2004] EWCA Civ 576. . . . 6.122, 6.123, 6.124, 6.128, 6.129, 6.131, 6.132, 6.133, 6.134, 6.135, 6.136, 6.137, 6.139, 6.220, 48.09, 48.12
Halson, In re [1912] 1 Ch 439 . . . . 66.51
Halvanon Insurance Co Ltd v Central Reinsurance Corpn [1988] 3 All ER 857 . . . . . . .40.52, 40.54
Hamdan v Widodo (No 2) [2010] WASC 6 S. 56.26
Hamer v Giles (1879) 11 Ch D 942 . . . . 7.50
Hamilton v Al Fayed & Ors [2002] EWCA Civ 665 . . . . .9.16, 9.35, 15.77, 30.51
Hamilton v Colhoun [1906] 2 IR 104 . . . . 52.59
Hamlet International plc (in administration), Trident International Ltd, Re v Barlow [1999] 2 BCLC 506. . . . . 40.56

Hammersmatch Properties (Welwyn) Ltd v Saint-Gobain Ceramics & Plastics Ltd [2013] EWHC 2227 (TCC) 6.73, 6.235, 17.102, 17.104
Hammond v Bussey (1888) 20 QBD 1.101, 3.40, 3.43
Hammond Suddard Solicitors v Agrichem International Holdings Ltd [2001] EWCA Civ 2065 . . . . 14.19, 15.12, 43.28, 43.382
Hammonds v Thomas Muckle & Sons [2006] BPIR 704 . . . . 40.79, 40.96
Hanak v Green [1958] 2 QB 9 . . . . 21.05, 21.07, 21.08, 21.14, 21.15, 21.22, 21.37, 38.36
Handley Page Ltd v Customs and Excise Commissioners and Rockwell Machine Tool Co Ltd [1971] 2 Lloyd's Rep 298, CA 22.07, 22.15
Hannaford v Hannaford (1871) 24 LT 86 . . . . 40.60
Hannigan v Hannigan [2000] EWCA Civ 159 . . . . 6.112, 26.20
Hanspaul v Ward [2016] EWHC 1358 (Ch) 7.154, 17.159
Harcus Sinclair v Buttonwood Legal Capital Ltd [2013] EWHC 2974 (Ch) 15.56, 15.96
Harcus Sinclair (a firm) v Buttonwood Legal Capital Ltd [2013] EWHC 1193 (Ch) 33.81
Harding v Harding (1886) 17 QBD 442 . . . . 32.29
Harding v Warrington Borough Council (unreported), 4 November 2014, Burnley County Court 43.232
Harding Evans LLP v Spencer-White [2017] EWCA Civ 434 . . . . 27.10, 27.192, 31.62
Hardingham v Allen (1848) 5 CB 793 . . . . 40.74
Hardy v Sefton Metropolitan Borough Council [2006] EWHC 1928 (Admin) 45.62
Hardy v Sutherland [2001] EWCA Civ 976 . . . . 17.11
Harlequin Property (SVG) Ltd v Cellate Caribbean Ltd (2013) 85 WIR 68 . . . . 45.17
Harlequin Property (SVG) Ltd v Wilkins Kennedy (a firm) [2015] EWHC 1122 (TCC) 15.38
Harley v McDonald, Glasgow Harley (a firm) v McDonald [2001] UKPC 18A 5.31, 9.60, 9.65, 9.71, 9.95, 9.138, 9.150, 9.157, 9.217
Harlow Development Corpn v Kingsgate (Clothing Productions) Ltd (1973) 226 EG 1960 . . . 32.71
Harnett v Vise (1880) 5 Ex D 30 . . . . 6.78
Harold v Smith (1860) 5 Hurlestone & Norman 381 . . . . 1.90, 1.91, 6.12, 18.03, 18.10
Harper v Hussain (unreported), 19 March 2008, Birmingham County Court 17.65
Harpham v Shacklock (1881) 19 Ch D 207, CA 40.55
Harrington v Wakeling [2007] EWHC 1184 (Ch) 18.29, 18.83, 18.87
Harripaul v Lewisham LBC [2012] EWCA Civ 266 . . . . 7.156
Harris v Moat Housing Group South Ltd [2007] EWHC 3092 (QB) 23.39, 43.59
Harris v Quine (1869) LR 4 QB 653 . . . . 23.93
Harris v Wallis [2006] EWHC 630 (Ch) 15.47, 15.48, 15.53
Harris v Yarm [1960] Ch 256 . . . . 36.36
Harrison, Re [1908] 1 Ch 282 53,44
Harrison v Bloom Camillin (a firm) (unreported), 4 February 2000, Ch D 6.160
Harrison v The Cornwall Minerals Railway Co (1884) 53 LJ Ch 596 . . . . 1.98
Harrison v Eversheds LLP [2017] EWHC 2594 (QB) 38.51, 38.58, 38.60, 38.66, 38.75
Harrison v Harrison (1888) 13 PD 180, CA 40.94, 40.111
Harrison v Harrison [2009] EWHC 428 (QB) 9.120, 9.167
Harrison v Hill (1931) SLT 598 . . . . 50.77
Harrison v Leutner (1881) 16 Ch D 559 . . . . 49.125
Harrison v McSheehan (1885) WN 207 . . . . 1.91
Harris v Quite (1969) LR 4 QB 653 . . . . 27.22
Harrison v Tew [1990] 2 AC 523 . . . . 23.100, 36.05, 36.13, 36.21, 39.03
Harrison v Turner (1847) 10 QB 482 . . . . 35.114
Harrison v University Hospitals Coventry & Warwickshire NHS Trust [2017] EWCA Civ 792 . . . . 12.140, 12.144, 12.145, 12.147, 12.151, 14.27, 25.19
Harrods (Buenos Aires) Ltd, Re (unreported) 10 March 1993, CA 7.87, 43.81
Harrods Ltd v Harrods (Buenos Aires) Ltd (1998) The Times, 1 June, CA 27.191, 31.62
Harrods Ltd v Harrods (Buenos Aires) Ltd [2014] 6 Costs LR 975 . . . . 36.16
Hart v Aga Khan Foundation (UK) [1984] 1 WLR 994 . . . . 59.11, 59.17, 59.24, 59.29
Hartland v Murrell (1873) LR 16 Eq 285 . . . . 38.88
Hartley v Bateson (1787) 1 TR 629 . . . . 1.58, 17.07

Harvey v Olliver (1887) WN 149 . . . . . 66.76
Haseldine v Hosken [1933] All ER Rep 1 . . . . . 30.33
Hashem v Shayif [2009] EWHC 864 (Fam) 21.28, 21.37
Hashtroodi v Hancock [2004] EWCA Civ 652 . . . . . 26.02, 26.22, 26.70
Hasker v Wood (1885) 54 LJQB 419, CA 58.02
Havai v Solland [2008] EWHC 2514 (Ch) 15.122
Hawick Jersey International Ltd v Caplan, The Times, 11 March 1988 . . . . . 6.218
Hawkes v Cottrell (1858) 3 H & N 243 . . . . . 27.69
Hawkes, Re; Ackerman v Lockhart [1898] 2 Ch 1, CA 40.44, 40.71
Hawkins v Price [1947] Ch 645 . . . . . 31.50
Hawkins Hill Co v Want (1893) 69 LT 297 . . . . . 15.121
Hawksford Trustees Jersey Ltd (Trustee of The Bald Eagle Trust) v Stella Global UK Ltd [2012] EWCA Civ 987 . . . . . 43.76, 49.157, 54.46, 54.175
Hawley v Luminar Leisure plc [2006] EWCA Civ 30 . . . . . 17.176, 43.292
Hawse v Crowe (1826) Ry & M 414 . . . . . 40.81
Hay v Szterbin [2010] EWHC 1967 (Ch) 20.19, 20.58
Haydon v Strudwick [2010] EWHC 90164 (Costs) 54.123
Haymes v Cooper (1864) 33 Beav 431 . . . . . 40.96
Haynes v Department for Business Innovation and Skills [2014] EWHC 643 (QB) 17.66, 17.169, 20.04, 20.14, 20.15
Hazard v Lane (1817) 3 Mer 285 . . . . . 36.12
Hazel v Manchester College [2013] EWCA Civ 281 . . . . . 13.101
Hazlett v Sefton Metropolitan Borough Council [2000] 4 All ER 887 . . . . . 18.28, 18.35, 18.36, 18.46, 18.55, 23.114, 27.94, 27.192, 31.69
HB (Mother) v (1) PB (Father) (2) OB (A Child by his Guardian) & Croydon London Borough Council (Respondent on issue of costs only) [2013] EWHC 1956 (Fam) 9.73, 13.21
Healy-Upright v Bradley & Anor [2007] EWHC 3161 (Ch) 16.20, 16.40
Hearst Holdings Inc v AVELA Inc [2015] EWCA Civ 470 . . . . . 15.78
Heather, Re (1870) LR 5 Ch App 694 . . . . . 35.87
Heaton & Ors v Axa Equity and Law Life Assurance Society plc & Anor [2000] 4 All ER 673 . . . . 19.11
Hedrich v Standard Bank London Ltd [2008] EWCA Civ 905 . . . . . 9.181
Hegglin v Persons Unknown (1) and Google Inc (2) [2014] EWHC 3793 (QB) 12.78
Heininger & Anor v Bayerische Hypo und Vereinsbank AG [2004] All ER (EC) 1 . . . 28.170, 28.195
Hellas Telecommunications (Luxembourg), Re (unreported), 20 July 2017, Ch D 9.92, 15.56
Hellas Telecommunications (Luxembourg), Re [2017] EWHC 3465 (Ch) 33.88
Helps v Clayton (1864) 17 CB (NS) 553 . . . . . 60.17
Hemming (1879) 28 LT 144, Ex p 36.25
Henderson v All Around the World Recordings Ltd [2013] EWPCC 19 . . . . . 50.330, 50.332, 50.335
Henderson v Henderson (1843) 3 Hare 100 . . . . . 23.28, 23.30, 23.33, 23.34, 23.35, 23.36, 23.38, 23.39, 23.40, 23.41, 23.47
Henderson v Merthyr Tydfil Urban District Council [1900] 1 QB 434 . . . . . 51.80
Henley v Philips (1740) 2 Atk 48 . . . . . 66.39
Henry v British Broadcasting Corporation [2005] EWHC 2503 (QB) 13.30, 54.171
Hepburn v A Tomlinson (Hauliers) Ltd [1966] AC 451; [1966] 1 All ER 418, HL 34.66
Hepburn v Royal Alexandra Hospital NHS Trust (No 3) 2011 SC 20 . . . . . 5.24
Herbert v HH Law Ltd [2018] EWHC 580 (QB) 37.09, 37.11, 37.13, 37.31, 52.05
Heritage, ex p Docker, In re (1878) 3 QBD 726 . . . . . 36.92, 36.94, 39.15
Hermann Loog Ltd, Re (1887) 36 Ch D 502 . . . . . 27.323
Heron v TNT (UK) Ltd [2013] EWCA Civ 469 . . . . . 9.50, 9.52
Hertel & Anor v Saunders & Anor [2015] EWHC 2848 (Ch) 17.64, 17.76
Hertfordshire Investments Ltd v Bubb [2000] All ER (D) 1052 . . . . . 45.60
Hertsmere Primary Care Trust v Rabindra-Anandh [2005] EWHC 320 (Ch) 17.63, 26.03
Heslop v Metcalfe (1837) 3 M & C 183 . . . . . 40.63, 40.87
Hewlett v LCC (1908) 72 JP 136 . . . . . 23.134
Heyting v Dupont [1964] 2 All ER 273 . . . . . 5.20
Hickman v Blake Lapthorn [2006] EWHC 12 (QB); [2006] All ER (D) 67 . . . . . 6.122, 6.135

Hickman v Kent or Romney Marsh Sheepbreeders' Association (1920) 151 LT Jo 5, CA 30.18
Hicks v Russell Jones & Walker [2001] CP Rep 25, CA 7.85, 7.88, 7.95, 21.29
Hicks v Wrench (1821) 6 Madd 93 . . . . 40.52
Hicks, Lindon v Hemery [1893] WN 138 . . . . 60.06
Higgins v Ministry of Defence [2010] EWHC 654 (QB) 51.61, 51.67
Higgins v Scott (1831) 2 B & Ad 413 . . . . 23.98, 40.45, 40.84
Higgs v Camden & Islington Health Authority [2003] EWHC 15 (QB) 45.23, 51.20, 51.31, 51.40, 51.41, 53.53
Higgs v Higgs [1934] 1 P 95 . . . . 40.95
High Commissioner for Pakistan and the United Kingdom v National Westminster Bank Plc [2015] EWHC 55 Ch 8.30, 43.405
Highgate Justices, ex parte Petrou [1954] 1 WLR 485 . . . . 3.16
Highvogue Ltd and Morris v Davies (2007) UKEAT/0093/07 . . . . 9.186
Hill v Archbold [1968] 1 QB 686 . . . . 9.58, 30.13, 30.35, 30.52
Hill v Bailey [2003] EWHC 2835 (Ch) 21.14, 21.29
Hillier v Adams (unreported), 17 March 2015, QBD, Bristol Civil Justice Centre 17.142
Hillingdon London Borough Council v ARC Ltd [1999] Ch 139 . . . . 23.105
Hills v Co-operative Wholesale [1940] 2 KB 435, CA 23.16
Hind v Whitmore (1856) 4 WR 379 . . . . 15.96
Hippisley v Knee Bros [1905] 1 KB 1 . . . . 27.249
Hirst & Capes, In re [1908] 1 AC 416; [1908] 1 KB 982 . . . . 36.33, 36.93
Hitachi Shipbuilding & Engineering Co Ltd v Viafel Compania Navieran SA [1981] 2 Lloyd's Rep 468, CA 15.95
Hitchcock v Stretton [1892] 2 Ch 343 . . . . 36.22, 36.25
HLB Kidsons (a firm) v Lloyds Underwriters subscribing to Lloyds Policy No 621/PKIDOO101 [2007] EWHC 2699 (Comm) 6.165, 16.36
HM Customs & Excise v Chitolie [2000] BPIR 275 (CA) 59.19
Hniadzdzilau v Vajgel [2015] EWHC 1582 (Ch) 15.65, 15.68
Hobart v Butler (1859) 9 ICLR 157 . . . . 53.04, 53.08
Hobbs v Gibson [2011] EWHC 762 (Ch) 16.39
Hobbs v Guy's & St Thomas' NHS Foundation Trust (unreported), 2 November 2015, SCCO 25.45, 25.56
Hobson v Shearwood (1845) 8 Beav 486 . . . . 40.96
Hodgson v Imperial Tobacco Ltd [1998] 1 WLR 1056 . . . . 9.62, 27.75, 29.53
Hodgson v Imperial Tobacco Ltd (No 2) [1998] 2 Costs LR 27 . . . . 20.48
Hodgkinson & Corby Ltd v Wards Mobility Services Ltd [1997] FSR 178 . . . . 6.218
Hoenig v Isaacs [1952] 2 All ER 176 . . . . 27.17, 27.24
Hogan v Hogan (No 2) [1924] 2 IR 14 . . . . 15.95
Hoggins v Gordon (1842) 3 QB 466 . . . . 53.31
Hoist UK Ltd v Reid Lifiting Ltd [2010] EWHC 1922 (Ch) 7.118, 7.134
Holberton's Settlement Trusts, Re [1953] 2 All ER 506 . . . . 53.68, 53.80
Holden v Thompson [1907] 2 KB 489 . . . . 30.12
Holden & Co LLP v Eastbourne Borough Council [2014] EWHC 1322 (QB) 9.175, 9.179
Holding Ltd v Property Trust plc [1989] 1 WLR 1313 . . . . 66.39
Holland v PKF (a firm) [2004] EWHC 9043 (Costs) 25.72
Holliday v EC Realisations Ltd [2008] EWHC 90103 (Costs) 51.42
Hollingsworth v Humphrey, The Independent, 21 December 1987, CA 7.77
Hollington v F Hewthorn & Co Ltd [1943] KB 587 . . . . 9.88, 9.140
Hollins v Russell [2003] EWCA Civ 718 . . . . 1.158, 2.05, 18.49, 18.57, 27.163, 29.28, 29.31, 29.46, 29.47, 29.49, 29.51, 29.52, 29.53, 29.58, 29.63, 29.78, 29.83, 29.85, 29.89, 29.90, 29.109, 31.49, 46.17, 46.26, 46.70, 52.08
Hollis v Claridge (1813) 4 Taunt 807 . . . . 40.38
Holloway v Transport Medical Group (CS) Ltd [2014] EWHC 1641 (QB) 65.36
Holman v Johnson (1775) 1 Cowp 341 . . . . 27.253
Holmes v Alfred McAlpine Homes (Yorkshire) Ltd [2006] EWHC 110 (QB) 29.99, 29.101, 29.135, 29.140

Holsworthy UDC v Holsworthy RDC [1907] 2 Ch 62 . . . . . 10.27
Holt v Heatherfield Trust Ltd [1942] 2 KB 1 . . . . . 32.29, 32.30, 32.31
Holtby v Hodgson (1889) 24 QBD 103 . . . . . 10.09, 43.318
Holton's Settlement Trusts, Holton v Holton (1918) 88 LJ Ch 444. . . . . 66.45
Holyoake v Candy & Anor [2017] EWHC 52 (QB) 15.39
Homes Assured plc, Re [2002] Costs LR 71 . . . . . 23.79
Hong v A&R Brown Ltd [1948] 1 KB 515 . . . . . 7.10, 7.15, 7.30
Hong Kong & Shanghai Banking Corpn v Kloeckner & Co AG [1990] 2 QB 514. . . . . 38.37
Hooker's Settlement, Heron v Public Trustee, Re [1955] Ch 55 . . . . . 5.20
Hooper v Biddle & Co [2006] EWHC 2995 (Ch) 6.57, 6.154, 7.164
Hooper v Gumm (1862) 2 John & H 602. . . . . 46.09
Hope, The (1883) 8 PD 144, CA 40.115
Hoque v Ali [2012] EWCA Civ 274 . . . . . 6.111, 6.260
Horan v Hayhoe [1904] 1 KB 288 . . . . . 50.126
Horizon Technologies International v Lucky Wealth Consultants Ltd [1992] 1 WLR 24. . . . . 6.15, 7.73, 56.10
Horner v Wheelwright (1857) 2 Jur NS 367 . . . . . 66.39
Hornsby v Clarke Kenneth Leventhal (a firm) [2000] 2 Costs LR 295 . . . . . 49.119, 53.54, 53.55, 53.63, 53.93, 53.96, 53.105, 53.114
Horrocks v Ford Motor Co Ltd (1990) The Times, 15 February, CA 65.12
Horsfall, Re (1827) 7 B&C 528 . . . . . 40.75
Horsford v Bird [2006] UKPC 55 . . . . . 43.330, 43.335, 43.338, 43.368, 49.144, 49.145, 52.80
Horth v Thompson [2010] EWHC 1674 (QB) 6.63, 6.256, 7.37
Hosegood v Pedler (1896) 66 LJQB 18. . . . . 66.76
Hosking v Michaelides [2003] EWHC 3029 (Ch) 25.67, 45.49
Hospira UK v Genetech Inc [2014] EWHC 208 (Ch) 16.45
Hospira UK Ltd v Novartis AG [2013] EWHC 886 (Pat) 6.182
Houghton v PB Donoghue (Haulage & Plant Hire Ltd) [2017] EWHC 1738 (Ch) 17.176
Howard v Wigan City Council [2015] EWHC 3643 (Admin). 13.75
Howard de Walden Estates Ltd v Aggio [2008] Ch 26 . . . . . 4.06
Howe v Motor Insurers' Bureau [2017] EWCA Civ 932. . . . . 8.09, 8.11
Howell v Lees-Millais [2011] EWCA Civ 786 . . . . . 6.225, 17.45, 17.76
Howells v Dominion Insurance Co Ltd [2005] EWHC 552 (QB) 9.76, 65.119
Howes Percival LLP v Page [2013] EWHC 4104 (Ch) 18.99, 27.27, 27.28, 27.69, 28.170, 28.183
Howlett v Davies [2017] EWCA Civ 1696 . . . . . 8.37, 8.38, 8.41, 8.43, 8.44
Howlett v Tarte (1861) 10 CBNS 813. . . . . 23.31
HP Bulmer Ltd v J Bollinger SA [1974] Ch 401; [1974] 2 All ER 1226, CA 4.06
HP Davies & Son [1917] 1 Ch 216 . . . . . 36.09
HR Trustees Ltd v German & IMG (UK) Ltd [2010] EWHC 3467 (Ch) 66.42, 66.66
HSS Hire Services Group plc v Builders Merchants Ltd [2005] EWCA Civ 626 . . . . 6.194, 6.209, 15.58
Huck v Robson [2002] EWCA Civ 398 . . . . . 17.120, 17.17.150, 17.151, 17.152
Huddersfield Banking Co Ltd v Henry Lister & Son Ltd [1895] 2 Ch 273, CA 10.27
Huddersfield Police Authority v Watson [1947] KB 842. . . . . 4.06
Hudgell Yeates & Co v Watson [1978] 2 All ER 363. . . . . 3.94
Hudson v New Media Holding Co LLC [2011] EWHC 3068 (QB). 6.46, 6.107, 16.46
Hughes v Biddulph (1827) 4 Russ 190 . . . . . 46.25
Hughes v Hughes [1958] P 224 . . . . . 40.44, 40.49, 40.65, 40.67, 40.85
Hughes v Kingston upon Hull City Council [1999] QB 1193 . . . . . 29.211
Hughes & Ors v London Borough of Newham [2005] EWHC 90019 (Costs). 29.87
Huguenin v Baseley (1807) 14 Ves 273. . . . . 32.45
Hullock v East Riding of Yorkshire County Council [2009] EWCA Civ 1039. . . . . 6.60, 6.147, 6.155, 6.238
Humphreys, ex p Lloyd-George and George, Re [1898] 1 QB 520, CA 40.91
Hunt v RM Douglas (Roofing) Ltd, CAT, 18 November 1987, The Times, 23 November 1987. . . . . 3.07, 3.09, 3.10, 3.11, 3.12, 3.13, 3.15, 49.112, 49.114, 52.85
Hunt v RM Douglas (Roofing) Ltd [1990] 1 AC 398, HL 27.328, 56.25

Hunt (trustee in bankruptcy of Harb) v Harb & Ors [2011] EWCA Civ 1239 . . . . 30.42
Huntley v Simmonds [2009] EWHC 406 (QB). .6.212, 16.36, 17.62, 17.63
Hurley v Makuni (unreported), 28 September 2012, Manchester County Court, Regional Costs. 28.177
Hurst v Denton-Cox [2014] EWHC 3948 (Ch). 7.188, 18.123
Hurst v Leeming [2002] EWHC 1051 (Ch) 6.120, 6.129
Huscroft v P&O Ferries Ltd [2010] EWCA Civ 1483. . . . . 15.03, 15.19, 15.21, 15.97, 15.98
Hussain v Cooke (unreported), 15 February 2010, Ch D (Companies Court) 16.46
Hussain v Seymour (unreported), 13 March 2014, QBD 16.57
Hussain & Ors v Khan (unreported), 19 January 2016, Stoke on Trent County Court. 50.286
Hutchinson v Harris [1978] 10 BLR 19 . . . . 3.41, 3.46
Hutchison Telephone (UK) Ltd v Ultimate Response Ltd [1993] BCLC 307 . . . . 15.67, 15.10, 15.69, 15.70
Hutley v Hutley (1873) LR 8 QB 112 . . . . 30.19, 30.23, 30.45
Hutson v Tata Steel UK Ltd [2017] EWHC 2647 (QB) 65.41
Hutton v Eyre (1815) 6 Taunt 289 . . . . 19.29
Huxley v Wootton (1912) 29 TLR 132. . . . . 60.06
Hyde v Milton Keynes NHS Foundation Trust [2017] EWCA Civ 399 . . . . 18.81
Hyde v Wrench (1840) 3 Beav 334 . . . . 43.290
Hyde Park Residence Ltd v Yelland [1999] RPC 655 . . . . 6.62, 6.69

IBM United Kingdom Pensions Trust Ltd v Metcalfe [2012] EWHC 125 . . . . . . 66.47, 66.60, 66.66
ICS v West Bromwich Building Society [1998] 1 WLR 896, HL 31.42
Ideal Bedding Co Ltd v Holland [1907] 2 Ch 157 . . . . 66.41
Igloo Regeneration (General Partner) Ltd v Powell Williams Partnership (Costs) [2013] EWHC 1859 (TCC) 16.33, 16.35
Ikos Cif Ltd v Hogan Lovells International LLP [2011] EWHC 2724 (Ch) 16.43
Ilahi v Usman (unreported), 29 November 2012, Manchester County Court 50.168, 50.264
Ilangaratne v British Medical Association [2005] EWHC 2096 (Ch) 18.41, 18.42, 18.52, 18.59, 18.68, 25.74
Illumina Inc v Premaitha Health plc [2016] EWHC 1726 (Pat). 6.116
Illumina Inc v Premaitha Health plc [2018] EWHC 180 (Pat) 18.62
Imageview Management Ltd v Jack [2009] EWCA Civ 63. . . . . 27.248
Imperial Loan Co Ltd v Stone [1892] 1 QB 599, CA 60.58
Inca Hall Rolling Mills Co Ltd v Douglas Forge Co (1882) 8 QBD 179. . . . . 21.05
Inchbald v Inchbald, In the Estate of [2017] EWHC 616 (Ch) 16.33
Inchcape, Craigmyle v Inchcape [1942] 2 All ER 157 . . . . 10.05
Inco Europe Ltd v First Choice Distribution [2000] 1 WLR 586. . . . . 4.12, 4.13
Independent Power Tanzania Ltd v Standard Chartered Bank (Hong Kong) Ltd [2016] EWCA Civ 522 . . . . 14.19
Inderwick, Re (1885) 54 LJ Ch 72 . . . . 3.06
Indigo Furniture Ltd v Futurelook Ltd [2011] EWPCC 013 . . . . 50.323, 50.340
Ingle, Re (1855) 25 LJ Ch 169 . . . . 36.22
Ingle v M'Cutchan (1884) 12 QBD 518 . . . . 35.83
Ingle v Wordsworth (1762) 97 ER 835 . . . . 1.90
Ingrams v Sykes (1987) 137 NLJ 1135 . . . . 36.36, 39.15
Inline Logistics Ltd v UCI Logistics Ltd [2002] 2 Costs LR 304 . . . . 4.51
Intellimedia Systems Ltd v Richards (unreported), 1 February 2017, Ch D 12.57
Interactive Technology Corpn Ltd v Ferster [2017] EWHC 1510 (Ch). 6.194, 6.6.269, 17.58
Intergraph (UK) Ltd v Wolfson Microelectronics plc [2012] EWHC 1862 (Ch). 49.53, 49.123, 51.84
International Business Machines Corpn v Phoenix International (Computers) Ltd [1995] 1 All ER 413. . . . . 46.15
International Fina Services AG v Katrina Shipping Ltd, The Fina Samco [1995] 2 Lloyd's Rep 344 . . . . 31.39
Inventors Friend Ltd v Leathes Prior [2011] EWHC 2840 (QB). 15.91, 15.121
Investec Bank (UK) Ltd v Zulman [2010] EWCA Civ 675 . . . . 6.170

Investors Compensation Scheme v West Bromwich Building Society [1998] 1 WLR 896, HL 31.02, 31.13, 31.16, 32.08, 54.88
Involnert Management Inc v Aprilgrange Ltd & Ors [2015] EWHC 2834 (Comm) . . . 56.27, 56.34, 56.35, 56.36, 56.37, 56.61
Ilumina Inc v Premaitha Health plc [2018] EWHC 180 (Pat) 19.08
Ipartner PTE Shipping Ltd v Panacore Resources DMCC [2015] EWHC 1098 (Comm) 15.80
IPC Media v Highbury Leisure Publishing Ltd [2005] EWHC 283 (Ch) 16.39, 16.53, 56.58
I-Remit Inc [2008] EWHC 939 (Ch) 9.31, 9.43
Iran Shipping Lines, Islamic Republic of v Denby [1987] 1 Lloyd's Rep 367 . . . . 40.55
Irish Response Ltd (a company incorporated under the laws of the Republic of Ireland) v (1) Direct Beauty Products Ltd [2011] EWHC 608 (QB) 16.52, 16.58
Irvine v Commissioner of the Police for the Metropolis [2005] EWCA Civ 129 . . . . . . 7.08, 7.11, 7.15, 7.17, 7.18, 7.19, 7.21
Irwin Mitchell v HMRC [2008] EWCA Crim 1741 . . . . 40.44, 40.50, 40.55
IS v Director Legal Aid Casework [2014] EWCA Civ 886 . . . . 13.61
Isaac v Isaac (No 2) [2005] EWHC 435 (Ch) 7.119
Isaacs v Isaacs [1955] 2 All ER 811 . . . . 53.102
Isaacs Partnership (a firm) v Umm Al-Jawaby Oil Service Co Ltd [2003] EWHC 2539 (QB) . . . 9.179
Isaacs & Sons v Salbstein [1916] 2 KB 139 . . . . 23.13, 23.18
Islam v Ali [2003] EWCA Civ 612 . . . . 6.56, 6.67, 6.235, 6.238
Islamic Investment Company of the Gulf (Bahamas) Ltd v Symphony Gems NV & Ors [2014] EWHC 3777 (Comm) 10.22
Ismail v Richards Butler (a firm) [1996] 2 All ER 506 . . . . 40.60, 40.64, 40.69
Ivey (Appellant) v Genting Casinos (UK) Ltd t/a Crockfords [2017] UKSC 67 . . . . 57.57
Ivimey v Marks (1847) 16 M & W 843 . . . . 35.68
Izzo v Philip Ross (2001), The Times, 9 August, Ch D 21.06, 21.22, 21.30, 21.35, 21.40

J v J [2014] EWHC 3654 (Fam) 57.07
J Murphy & Sons Ltd v Johnston Precast Ltd (No 2) [2008] EWHC 3104 (TCC) 6.166, 6.185, 6.186, 56.87
J Rosenthal & Sons Ltd v Esmail [1965] 1 WLR 1117, HL 27.22
Jabang v Wadman & Ors [2017] EWHC 1993 (QB) 7.11, 7.17, 7.18
Jackson, In re [1915] 1 KB 371 . . . . 27.165, 36.22
Jackson v Cambridgeshire County Council (2011) PNLR 32 (EAT) 9.187
Jackson v The Inhabitants of Calesworth (1785) 99 ER 977 . . . . 1.53
Jackson v Lord Chancellor [2003] EWHC 626 (QB) 47.20
Jackson v The Ministry of Defence [2006] EWCA Civ 46 . . . . 6.67, 6.152
Jackson v Smith, ex p Digby (1884) 53 LJ Ch 972 . . . . 40.94
Jackson v Thakrar [2007] EWHC 626 (TCC) 9.36
Jacobs UK Ltd v Skidmore Owings & Merrill LLP [2008] EWHC 2847 (TCC) 15.03, 15.21
Jago v Whitbread Group plc (unreported), 15 October 2016, SCCO 57.60
Jallow v Ministry of Defence [2018] EWHC B7 (Costs) 12.162
Jamadar v Bradford Teaching Hospitals NHS Foundation Trust [2016] EWCA Civ 1001 . . . . . 12.57
James, Ex p (1874) LR 9 Ch 609 . . . . 53.12
James, ex p Quilter, Re (1850) 4 De G & Sm 183 . . . . 36.17
James v James [2018] EWHC 242 (Ch) 17.76
James Bibby Ltd v Woods and Howard [1949] 2 KB 449 . . . . 40.37, 40.40, 40.109
James Buchanan & Co Ltd v Babco Forward and Shipping (UK) Ltd [1977] QB 208 . . . . 4.40
James Carleton Seventh of Malmesbury & Ors v Strutt & Parker [2008] EWHC 424 (QB) . . . 48.46
James Miller & Partners Ltd v Whitworth Street Estates (Manchester) Ltd [1970] AC 583 . . . . 48.71, 48.72
Jarl Trä AB v Convoys Ltd [2003] EWHC 1488 (Comm) 40.76
Jarvis plc v PricewaterhouseCoopers [2000] 2 ECLC 368 . . . . 16.52
Jass v Blackburn [2003] EWHC 2963 (Ch) 7.167
Jaura v Ahmed [2002] EWCA Civ 210 . . . . 56.77
JC and A Solicitors Ltd v Iqbal [2017] EWCA Civ 355 . . . . 50.152, 50.167, 50.173, 50.193

JE (Jamaica) v Secretary of State for the Home Department [2014] EWCA Civ 192 . . . . 13.101, 13.103, 13.107
Jefferson v National Freight Carriers plc [2001] EWCA Civ 2082 . . . . 25.23
Jefferson v Warrington (1840) 7 M&W 137. . . . . 36.12
Jeffery and Katauskas Pty Ltd v Rickard Constructions Pty Ltd (2009) 239 CLR 75. . . . . 33.19
Jeffreys v Commissioner of Police for the Metropolis [2017] EWHC 1505 (QB) 8.11, 8.15, 8.52, 8.53, 8.54, 8.55
Jeffreys v Evans (1845) 14 M&W 210. . . . . 35.115, 40.10
Jemma Trust Co Ltd v Liptrott [2003] EWCA Civ 1476 . . . . 37.29, 38.07, 38.17, 38.20, 38.31
Jemma Trust Co Ltd v Liptrott & Ors (No 2) [2004] EWHC 1404 (Ch). 45.26, 49.14
Jenkins v Young Brothers Transport Ltd [2006] EWHC 151 (QB) 32.06, 32.21, 32.24, 32.29
Jenkyns v Brown (1849) 14 QB 496 . . . . 40.74
Jenner v Morris (1861) 3 De GF & J 45. . . . . 21.29
Jennings v Johnson (1873) LR 8 CP 425. . . . . .27.112, 27.211, 29.204, 30.12
Jennings' Trustee v King [1952] Ch 899. . . . . 27.82
Jerrard v Blyth [2014] EWHC 647 (QB) 16.57
JH Milner & Son v Percy Bilton Ltd [1966] 1 WLR 1582 . . . . 27.69
JH Shannon v Country Casuals Holdings plc (1997) The Times, 16 June 52.51, 52.521
Jirehouse Capital v Beller [2008] EWCA Civ 908 . . . . 15.34, 15.35, 15.50
JMX (a child by his mother and litigation friend, FMX) v Norfolk and Norwich Hospitals NHS Foundation Trust (No 2) [2018] EWHC 675 (QB). 17.81, 17.154
JN Dairies Ltd v Johal Dairies Ltd & Anor [2011] EWHC 90211 (Costs) 54.46
Jockey Club Racecourse Ltd v Willmott Dixon Construction Ltd [2016] EWHC 167 (TCC). 17.154, 17.155
Joel v Barnato (1929) 45 TLR 167 . . . . .2.09, 52.02
John v Central Manchester & Manchester Children's University Hospitals NHS Foundation Trust [2016] EWHC 819 (QB) 16.444
John v John and Goff [1965] P 289. . . . . 4.06
John Bishop (Caterers) Ltd v National Union Bank [1973] 3 All ER 707 . . . . 15.33, 15.71
John Fox v Bannister King & Rigbeys [1988] QB 925 . . . . 5.30
John Morris, In re [1908] 1 KB 473 . . . . 40.84
John Mowlem Construction plc v Neil F Jones & Co [2004] EWCA Civ 768 . . . . 40.55
John Russell & Co Ltd v Cayzer, Irvine & Co Ltd [1916] 2 AC 298, HL 5.02
Johnsey Estates (1990) Ltd v The Secretary of State for the Environment [2001] EWCA Civ 535 . . . . .6.03, 6.26, 6.27, 6.67, 6.192, 6.235, 17.104
Johnson v Cammack (unreported), 12 February 2013, Ch D. 15.101
Johnson v EBS Pensioner Trustees Ltd [2002] EWCA Civ 164 . . . . 32.50
Johnson v Gore Wood & Co [2002] 2 AC 1; [2001] 1 All ER 481. . . . . .23.35, 23.40
Johnson v Raylton, Dixon & Co (1881) 7 QBD 438. . . . . 32.17
Johnson v Reed Corrugated Cases Ltd [1992] 1 All ER 169 . . .49.19, 51.19, 51.30, 51.34, 51.88, 52.74
Johnson v Ribbins [1977] 1 WLR 1458 . . . . 7.25, 7.26
Johnson v Valks (2000) WL 362603, 15 March 2000, CA. 49.119
Jolly v Harsco Infrastructure Services Ltd [2012] EWHC 3086 (QB) .17.178
Jolly v Jay [2002] EWCA Civ 277 . . . . 45.53, 45.72
Jonathan Alexander Ltd v Proctor [1996] 1 WLR 518 . . . . .59.02
Jones, In re [1895] 2 Ch 719. . . . . .27.152
Jones, Re (1886) 54 LT 648 . . . . 35.87
Jones v Associated Newspapers Ltd [2007] EWHC 1489. . . . . .17.109
Jones v Caradon Catnic Ltd [2005] EWCA Civ 1821. . . . . .13.101, 29.21, 29.29, 29.54, 45.52
Jones v Coxeter (1742) 2 Atk 400. . . . . 1.63, 1.65, 7.98
Jones v Curling (1884) 13 QBD 262 . . . . 1.100, 45.70
Jones v D Davies & Sons Ltd [1914] 3 KB 549 . . . . 52.36
Jones v Environcom Ltd & Anor [2009] EWHC 16 (Comm). 15.10, 15.70, 15.118
Jones v Evans (1886) 31 Sol Jo 11 . . . . 15.96
Jones v Harding (unreported), 29 September 2016, Liverpool County Court. 12.155
Jones v Hope [1880] WN 69, CA 27.322

Jones v Lewis [1919] 1 KB 328 . . . . . 23.21
Jones v MBNA International Bank [2000] EWCA Civ 514 . . . . . 45.61
Jones v Reade (1836) 5 A & E 529 . . . . . 1.83, 27.112
Jones v Roberts (1838) 8 Sim 397 . . . . . 36.09
Jones v Roberts (1986) The Times, 2 August 23.64
Jones v Secretary of State for Energy and Climate Change [2012] EWHC 3647 . . . . . 6.165, 65.48, 65.52
Jones v Secretary of State for Energy and Climate Change [2013] EWHC 1023 (QB) 52.85
Jones v Secretary of State for Energy and Climate Change [2014] EWCA Civ 363 . . . . . 52.85, 56.71, 56.72, 56.73, 56.74, 56.79
Jones v Secretary of State for Wales [1997] 1 WLR 1008 . . . . . 51.29, 51.79
Jones v Spire Healthcare Ltd [2016] 3 Costs LO 487 . . . . . 32.15, 32.21
Jones v Twinsectra Ltd [2002] EWCA Civ 668 . . . . . 36.47
Jones v Williams (1841) 8 M & W 349 . . . . . 2.09
Jones v Wrexham Borough Council [2007] EWCA Civ 1356 . . . . 27.04, 27.257, 29.03, 29.13, 29.32, 29.39, 29.40, 29.41, 29.43, 29.85, 29.87, 29.90, 31.29, 31.53, 31.55, 34.26, 38.91
Jones v Wrotham Park Settled Estates [1980] AC 74 . . . . . 4.13
Jones & Everett, Re [1904] 2 Ch 363 . . . . . 36.95
Jones and Saldanha v Gurney [1913] WN 72 . . . . . 15.33, 15.71
Jonesco v Beard [1930] AC 298 . . . . . 10.16
Jopling v Leavesley & Anor [2013] EWCA Civ 1605 . . . . . 17.131, 17.187
Jordan v MGN Ltd [2017] EWHC 1937 (Ch) 7.149, 17.120, 17.159, 17.182
Joseph v Boyd & Hutchinson [2003] EWHC 413 (Ch) 59.16
Joyce v West Bus Coach Services Ltd [2012] EWHC 404 (QB) 17.189
JP Morgan Chase Bank v Springwell Navigation [2008] EWHC 2848 (Comm) 16.48
JSC BTA Bank v Solodchencko (unreported), 23 January 2012, Ch D 6.117
JSC Mezhdunarodniy Promyshlenniy Bank and another v Pugachev and others [2015] EWHC 1694 (Ch) 16.49
JSC Mezhdunarodniy Promyshlenniy Bank and another v Pugachev and others [2017] EWHC 1853 (Ch) 12.117
Juby v LFCDA and Saunders v Essex County Council (unreported), 24 April 1990, QBD 53.120, 53.121, 53.124

K, Re [1990] 2 QB 298 . . . . . 40.50
K v K (Divorce Costs: Interest) (1977) Fam 39 . . . . . 56.24
Kagalovsky v Balmore Investment Ltd [2015] EWHC 1337 (AB) 9.124, 16.49
Kaglovsky v Turevych [2014] EWHC 2697 (QB) 16.49
Kahangi v Nourizadeh [2009] EWHC 2451 (QB) 15.57, 15.60, 15.74, 15.81, 15.86, 15.113
Kai Surrey v Barnet & Chase Farm Hospitals NHS Trust [2016] EWHC 1589 . . . . . 54.147
Kaines (UK) Ltd v Osterreichische Wdrrenhandelsgesellschaft (formerly CGL Handelsgesellschaft mbH) [1993] 2 Lloyd's Rep 1 . . . . . 6.116
Kalma v African Minerals Ltd [2017] EWHC 1471 (QB) 12.54, 12.84, 12.85, 12.98
Kasir v Darlington & Simpson Rolling Mills Ltd [2001] 2 Costs LR 228 . . . . . 43.318, 45.09, 45.34
Kastor Navigation Co Ltd v AXA Global Risks (UK) Ltd [2004] EWCA Civ 277 . . . 6.03, 6.18, 6.20, 6.25, 6.39, 6.48, 6.162, 6.170, 6.174, 6.176, 6.184, 17.89
Kay v Lambeth London Borough Council [2006] UKHL 10 . . . . . 24.12, 24.49
Kazakhstan Investment Fund Ltd v Aims Asset Management (unreported), 22 May 2002, Ch D 15.115
Kazakhstan Kagazy plc v Zhunus [2015] EWHC 404 (Comm) 12.102, 14.16, 14.29
Kazakhstan Kagazy plc v Zhunus [2015] EWHC 996 (Comm) 15.115
Kazakhstan Kagazy plc v Zhunus [2018] EWHC 369 (Comm) 16.48
Kazakhstan, Republic of v Istil Group Inc [2005] EWCA Civ 1468 . . . . . 15.102
Kazakstan Wool Processors (Europe) Ltd v Nederlandsche Credietverzekering Maatschappij [2000] 1 All ER (Comm) 708 . . . . . 31.24
Kazeminy v Siddiqui [2009] EWHC 3207 (Comm) 15.130
KC v MGN Ltd (Costs) [2013] EWCA Civ 3 . . . . . 17.109

Keane v Mount Vernon Colliery Co Ltd [1933] AC 309 . . . . 54.163
Kearns v Kemp [2013] EWHC 4093 (QB) 16.36, 16.40
Kearsley v Klarfeld [2005] EWCA Civ 1510 . . . . 8.43
Keary Developments Ltd v Tarmac Construction Ltd & Anor [1995] 3 All ER 534 . . . . . 15.36, 15.57, 15.60, 15.62, 15.76, 15.78, 15.82, 15.83, 15.84, 15.86, 15.110
Keely v Pashen [2004] EWCA Civ 1491 . . . . 63.04
Keen v Towler (1924) 41 TLR 86 . . . . 20.23, 20.25, 20.33
Keen Phillips v Field [2006] EWCA Civ 1524; [2007] 1 WLR 686 . . . . 43.100
Keene v Ward (1849) 13 QB 513 . . . . 35.68
Kel-Ta Talk Ltd v Revenue & Customs Commissioners [2011] STC 497 . . . . 29.187
Kellar v Williams [2004] UKPC 30 . . . . 29.181, 29.182, 54.46
Kellar v Williams (Appeal No 13 of 2003) [2004] UKPC 30 . . . . . 18.35, 18.93, 29.138, 32.65, 32.73
Kellett (a Protected Party by her Litigation Friend, Alison McMahon) v Wigan & District Community Transport (unreported), 16 September 2015, Manchester County Court 55.25
Kellie v Wheatley & Lloyd Architects Ltd [2014] EWHC 2886 (TCC) (QBD) 12.167, 14.21
Kelly v Black Horse Ltd (unreported), 27 September 2013, SCCO 25.85
Kelly v Cooper [1993] AC 205 . . . . 27.249
Kelly v Hays plc [2015] EWHC 735 (QB) 51.62, 51.65, 51.72, 51.79
Kelly's Directories Ltd v Gavin & Lloyd [1901] 2 Ch 763 . . . . 10.04
Kennedy v Broun (1863) 32 LJ (CP) 137 . . . . 29.197, 39.20
Kennedy v Lyell (1883) LR 23 Ch D 387 . . . . 46.08
Kent v Ward (1894) 70 LT 612 . . . . 3.94
Kesabo & 11 Ors v African Barrick Gold plc [2013] EWHC 4045 (QB) 16.53
Kevan v Hamilton (unreported), 22 March 2013, Liverpool County Court 50.100
Kevorkian v Burney (No 2) [1937] 4 All ER 468 . . . . 15.75
Kevythalli Design v Ice Associates [2010] EWCA Civ 379 . . . . 15.27
Kew v Bettamix Ltd [2006] EWCA Civ 1535 . . . . 6.252
Khaira v Shergill [2017] EWCA Civ 1687 . . . . 7.89, 43.65, 43.66, 43.76, 43.79, 43.82
Khan v Crossland (unreported), 25 November 2011, Ch D 4.67
Khan v Lord Chancellor [2003] EWHC 12 (QB) 59.48, 59.92
Khan v Metainy Maintenance Ltd (unreported), 21 January 2013, Aldershot & Farnham County Court 6.153, 50.397
Khans Solicitor (A Firm) v Chifuntwe & Anor [2013] EWCA Civ 481 . . . . . . 27.329, 40.40, 40.106, 40.107, 40.112, 40.113, 40.114, 40.117, 40.119, 40.120
Khuram v Secretary of State for the Home Department [2015] EWCA Civ 913 . . . . 9.191
Kiam v MGN Ltd (No 2) [2002] EWCA Civ 66 . . . . 6.142, 16.35
Kilby v Gawith [2008] EWCA Civ 812 . . . . 50.113
Kilopress Ltd, In the matter of (unreported), 22 April 2010, Ch D 17.45
Kilroy v Kilroy [1997] PNLR 66 . . . . 9.189
Kim Barker Ltd v Aegon Insurance Co (UK) Ltd (1989) The Times, 9 October, CA 15.36
Kinch v Walcott [1929] AC 482 . . . . 23.15
King v Basildon & Thurrock University Hospitals NHS Foundation Trust (unreported), 20 November 2016, SCCO 25.45
King v Bristow Helicopters Ltd [2002] UKHL 7 . . . . 50.128
King v Rothschild Trust [2002] EWHC 1346 (Ch) 39.04, 39.05
King v Telegraph Group [2005] 1 WLR 2282 . . . . . 9.49, 13.30, 13.32, 13.35, 13.37, 13.38, 13.39, 13.43
King v Telegraph Group Ltd [2005] EWHC 90015 (Costs) 25.70, 25.85, 29.132, 51.77
King v Thipthorp (unreported), 11 February 2016, QBD (TCC) 12.96
King v Victoria Insurance Co [1896] AC 250, PC 23.114, 27.34
King v Zurich Insurance Co [2002] EWCA Civ 598 . . . . 7.04
Kingdon and Wilson [1902] 2 Ch 242 . . . . 52.04
Kings Costs Team 'Costs Law Brief' (2007) 157 NLJ 7278 . . . . 18.87
Kingsley, Re (1978) 122 Sol Jo 457 . . . . 35.67, 49.13
Kingsley v Orban [2014] EWHC 2991 (Ch) 44.28, 44.31
Kingston Solicitors v Reiss Solicitors [2014] EWCA Civ 172 . . . . 35.69, 35.86, 49.159, 53.30
Kirby v Hoff [2010] EWHC 3559 (QB) 9.28

Kirk v Walton [2009] EWHC 703 (QB) 6.146
Kitchen v Burwell Reed & Kinghorn Ltd [2005] EWHC 1771 (QB). 18.06, 18.29, 18.61, 29.115, 29.125, 29.127, 29.182
Klamer v Kyriakides & Braier (a firm) [2005] BPIR, Ch D. 35.113, 40.24, 40.123, 40.124
Kleinwort Benson v De Montenegro [1994] NPC 46 . . . . 9.64, 9.108
Kleinwort Benson Ltd v Lincoln City Council [1999] 2 AC 349. . . . . 40.37
Kleinwort Benson Ltd v South Tyneside Metropolitan Borough Council [1994] 4 All ER 972. . . . 23.129
KMT & Ors (Children) v Kent County Council [2012] EWHC 2088 (QB) 51.19, 51.20, 51.72
Knauer v Ministry of Justice [2016] UKSC 9 . . . . 4.04, 4.06
Knight v Beyond Properties Pty Ltd [2006] EWHC 1242 (Ch) 13.20
Knight v Clifton [1971] 2 All ER 378, [1971] Ch 700 . . . . 3.16, 6.24
Knight v Knight [1925] Ch 835 . . . . 40.54
Knox's Trusts [1895] 2 Ch 483, CA 66.39
Koenigsberg, Public Trustee v Koenigsberg [1949] Ch 348 . . . . 23.21
Kolyada v Yurov [2014] EWHC 2575 (Comm) 15.80
KOO Golden East Mongolia (a body corporate) v Bank of Nova Scotia [2008] EWHC 1120 (QB) 9.167, 9.170
Korner v H Korner & Co Ltd [1951] Ch 11 . . . . 10.04, 20.27
Koshy v Deg-Deutsche Investitions und Entwicklungs Gesellschaft Gmbh [2003] EWCA Civ 1718. . . . . 45.29
Kostic v Chaplin [2007] EWHC 2909 (Ch). 7.52, 7.57, 7.60
KPMG Peat Marwick McLintock v HLT Group Ltd [1995] 2 All ER 180 . . . . 51.77
KR v Bryn Alyn Community (Holdings) Ltd (in liquidation) [2003] EWCA Civ 383 . . . . 17.31
Kralj v Birkbeck Motague (unreported), 18 February 1988, CA. 36.36
Kranidiotes v Paschali [2001] EWCA Civ 357 . . . . 52.43
Kredietbank Antwerp v Midland Bank plc [1998] Lloyd's Rep Bank 173. . . . . 31.26
Krehl v Park (1875) 10 Ch App 334 . . . . 49.151
Kris Motor Spares Ltd v Fox Williams LLP [2009] EWHC 2813 (QB) 27.70, 27.75, 36.33, 36.36, 54.132, 54.140, 54.145, 54.159, 54.170
Kristjansson v R Verney & Co Ltd (unreported) 18 June 1998, CA 15.102
KU v Liverpool City Council [2005] EWCA Civ 475 . . . . 4.52, 45.16, 54.47, 54.58, 54.60, 54.97
Kudos Catering (UK) Ltd v Manchester Central Convention Complex Ltd [2013] EWCA Civ 38 . . . . 28.162
Kuenyehia v International Hospitals Group Ltd [2007] EWCA Civ 274 . . . . 15.84
Kufaan Publishing Elements v Al-Warrack Publishing Ltd [2000] Lexis Citation 2833 . . . . 15.78
Kunaka v Barclays Bank plc [2010] EWCA Civ 1035 . . . . 17.122, 17.161
Kundrath v Henry Kwatia & Gooding [2005] 2 Costs LR 279 . . . . 36.34, 36.36, 36.38
Kupeli v Cyprus Turkish Airlines [2017] EWCA Civ 1037; [2016] EWHC 1125 (QB) 28.180
Kurtz v Spence [1887] LR 36 Ch D 770 . . . . 26.10
Kuwait Airways Corpn v Iraqi Airways Co (No 2) [1995] 1 All ER 790; [2001] 1 WLR 429, HL 10.16, 56.45
Kynaston v Carroll [2011] EWHC 2179 (QB) 3.86, 47.09, 47.16

L v L [1996] 1 FLR 873 . . . . 3.08
L v L [1997] 1 Costs LR 9 . . . . 51.24, 51.31
L (a child) [2013] EWCA Civ 1778 . . . . 26.22
L (a child) (unreported), Re 4 March 2016, Family Court 9.127
L and B (children) (care proceedings: power to revise judgment), Re [2013] UKSC 8. . . . 10.03, 10.10, 10.11, 10.12
L Schuler AG v Wickman Machine Tools Sales Ltd [1974] AC 235 31,22
La Chemise Lacoste SA v Sketchers USA Ltd [2006] EWHC 3642 (Ch) 6.116
Laceward Ltd, Re [1981] 1 WLR 133, ... 40.24, 40.123
Ladd v London Road Car Co [1900] LT 80 . . . . 29.204
Ladd v Marshall [1954] 1 WLR 1489. . . . . 45.60
Ladd v Wright H 43 Eliz 1.38

Ladiaev v Vallen [2008] EWHC 1271 (Ch) 30.31
Lady De la Pole v Dick (1885) 29 Ch D 351, CA 27.85
Lagos v Grunwaldt [1910] 1 KB 41. . . . . 23.125
Lahey v Pirelli Tyres Ltd [2007] EWCA Civ 91; [2007] 1 WLR 998. . . . .6.194, 6.204, 9.101, 10.24, 23.49, 46.79, 49.05, 50.393, 50.397, 57.28, 57.29, 57.35, 57.44, 57.45, 57.47, 65.107
Laing v Chatham (1808) 1 Camp 252 . . . . 21.29
Lake v Hunt Kid Law Firm LLP (in administration) [2011] EWHC 766 (QB). 38.91, 56.49
Lakeheath Investments Ltd v Secretary of State for Communities & Local Government [2014] EWHC 1072 (Admin) 16.48
Lakehouse Contracts Ltd v UPR Services Ltd [2014] EWHC 1223 (Ch). 16.27, 16.57
Laker Vent Engineering Ltd v Templeton Insurance Ltd [2009] EWCA Civ 62. . . . . . . .34.12, 34.20
Lakhani v Mahmud [2017] EWHC 1713 (Ch) 12.57
Lamont v Burton [2007] EWCA Civ 429; [2007] 1WLR 2814 . . . . 50.114, 50.276
Lamont v Hyland [1950] 1 KB 585. . . . . 40.10
Land and Property Trust Co plc (No 4), Re [1994] 1 BCLC 232, CA. 9.79
Landare Investments Ltd v Welsh Development Agency [2004] EWHC 946 (QB) 9.28
Landau & Cohen v Lord Chancellor's Department [1999] 2 Costs LR 5 . . . . 52.76
Landor (a solicitor), Re [1899] 1 Ch 818 . . . . 35.126
Landowners' West of England and South Wales Land Drainage and Inclosure Co v Ashford [1884] 33 WR 41 . . . . 56.23
Langford v Nott (1820) 1 Jac & W 291 . . . . 36.94
Langley v North West Water Authority [1991] 1 WLR 697 . . . . 4.48, 5.25, 5.28
Langsam v Beachcroft LLP & Ors [2011] EWHC 1451 (Ch) 29.99
Langstone Leisure v Willers (unreported), 3 June 2015, Ch D 16.44
Laporte v The Commissioner of Police of the Metropolis [2015] EWHC 371 (QB) 6.128, 16.59
Larner v University Hospital Birmingham NHS Foundation Trust (unreported), 6 May 2015, Worcester County Court 54.155
Latimer Management Consultants Ltd v Ellingham Investments Ltd [2006] EWHC 3662 (Ch) 9.35, 10.12, 10.15
Laurence and Laurence v Singh t/a K & T Investments [1997] 1 Costs LR 58 . . . . 6.59, 45.69
Laurent v Sale & Co (a firm) [1963] 2 All ER 63. . . . . 30.38
Lavelle v Lavelle [2004] EWCA Civ 223 . . . . 6.23
Law v Liverpool City Council (unreported), 10 May 2005, Liverpool County Court. 27.34
Law Debenture Trust Corpn plc v Ukraine [2017] EWHC 1902 (Comm). 66.11, 66.32, 66.33
Law Society v Persaud (1990) Costs LR Core vol 114 . . . . 59.33
Law Society of the United Kingdom v Waterlow Brothers and Layton (1883) 8 App Cas 407 . . . . 3.65, 29.78
Lawal v Northern Spirit (unreported), 19 February 2004, CA (Civ Div) 6.107
Lawler, Re (1878) 4 VLR 8. . . . . 36.90
Lawrence v Campbell (1859) 4 Drew 485. . . . . 46.23
Laws v National Grid Plc [1998] PLR 295 . . . . 66.42
Lawson v Tiger [1953] 1 WLR 503. . . . . 53.106
Lay v Drexler [2007] EWCA Civ 464 . . . . 7.119, 7.160, 45.31
Layard Horsfall Ltd v Legal Ombudsman [2013] EWHC 4137 (QB) 39.24
Lazaris v London & Newcastle (Camden) Ltd [2013] EWHC 97 (TCC). 15.02
LBI HF (Formerly Landsbanki Islands HF) v Stanford [2013] EWHC 2535 (Ch) 6.194
Le Brasseur and Oakley, Re [1896] 2 Ch 487 . . . . 53.04
LE Cattan Ltd v A Michaelides & Co [1958] 1 WLR 717. . . . . 7.27
Leadbitter, In re (1878) 10 Ch D 388 . . . . 36.95
Learoyd v Halifax Banking Co [1893] 1 Ch 686 . . . . 46.26
Ledward Claimants v Kent & Medway Health Authority [2003] EWHC 2551 (QB). . . . 13.11, 13.27, 49.77, 49.78, 49.95, 49.123, 51.76, 51.78, 51.84, 52.82, 52.83
Lee v Birmingham City Council [2008] EWCA Civ 891 . . . . .49.147, 49.149
Leeds City Council v Carr (1999) The Times, 12 November 29.211
Leeds Forge Co Ltd v Deighton's Patent Flue and Tube Co Ltd [1903] 1 Ch 475 . . . . . 52.29, 52.56, 53.110

Leeman v Stocks [1951] Ch 941 . . . . . 35.84
Legal Aid Board v Russell [1991] 2 AC 317 . . . . . 2.09, 7.101, 56.102
Legal Costsmasters Ltd v Insurance & Legal Services UK Ltd (unreported), 30 April 2013, QBD 16.39
Legal Services Commission v F, A & V [2011] EWHC 899 (QB) 20.30, 20.32, 62.38
Legal Services Commission v Henthorn [2011] EWCA Civ 1415 . . . . . 23.119
Legal Services Commission v Rasool [2008] EWCA Civ 154 . . . . . 23.89, 23.91, 23.105
Legg v Sterte Garage Ltd [2016] EWCA Civ 97 . . . . . 9.22, 9.31
Lehman Brothers Finance SA v SAL Oppenheim Jr & Cie KGAA [2014] EWHC 2627 (Comm) 31.33
Leicester Circuits Ltd v Coates Brothers plc (application to lift stay) [2002] EWCA Civ 474 . . . 14.16
Leicestershire County Council v Michael Faraday & Partners Ltd [1941] 2 KB 205 . . . . . 40.75
Leigh v Michelin Tyre plc [2003] EWCA Civ 1766 . . . . . 4.40, 4.53, 12.06, 12.30, 36.36
Leighton's Conveyance, Re [1936] 3 All ER 1033 . . . . . 66.25
Lemprière v Lange (1879) 12 Ch D 675 . . . . . 60.04
Leo Abse & Cohen v Evan G Jones (Builders) Ltd (1984) 128 Sol Jo 317 . . . . . 40.44
Leo Pharma A/S v Sandoz Ltd [2010] EWHC 1911 (Pat) 10.06
Leopold Lazarus Ltd v Secretary of State for Trade and Industry (1976) Costs LR, core vol 62 . . . . . 38.07, 51.24, 51.29
Les Laboratoires Servier v Apotex Inc [2008] EWHC 2563 (Pat) 14.25
Less v Benedict [2005] EWHC 1643 (Ch) 23.71
Leverton Ltd v Crawford Offshore (Exploration) Services Ltd (in liquidation), The Times, 22 November 1996, QBD 9.28
Lewin, Re (1853) 16 Beav 608 . . . . . 36.11
Lewis, ex p Munro, In re (1876) 1 QBD 724 . . . . . 27.151
Lewis v Avery (No 2) [1973] 1 WLR 510 . . . . . 18.69
Lewis v The Royal Shrewsbury Hospital (unreported) 20 May 2005, QBD 43.337, 53.82, 53.84, 53.101
Lewis v Samuel (1846) 8 QB 685 . . . . . 38.37
Leyvand v Barasch [2000] All ER (D) 181 . . . . . 15.75
Lexi Holdings plc v Luqman [2007] EWHC 2410 (Ch) 14.20
Libyan Investment Authority v Goldman Sachs International [2014] EWHC 3364 (Ch) 16.40
LIC Telecommunications SARL v VTB Capital plc (unreported), 14 July 2016, QBD (Comm) 15.85
Lienard v Dresslar (1862) 3 F & F 212 . . . . . 47.29
Lifeline Gloves Ltd v Richardson [2005] EWHC 1524 (Ch) 16.40, 17.129
Light on Line Ltd v Zumtobel Lighting Ltd [2012] EWHC 3376 (QB) 54.125
Lightfoot v Keane (1836) 1 M & W 745 . . . . . 40.44
Lilleyman v Lilleyman [2012] EWHC 1056 (Ch) 7.52, 17.73, 17.136, 17.219
Lillicrap v Nalder & Son [1993] 1 WLR 94 . . . . . 36.107
Linden Gardens Trust Ltd v Lenesta Sludge Disposals Ltd [1994] 1 AC 85 . . . . . 32.08, 32.20, 32.33
Lingfield Properties (Darlington) Ltd v Padgett Lavender Associates [2008] EWHC 2795 (QB) 9.28
Linklaters Business Services v Sir Robert McAlpine Ltd & Ors [2010] EWHC 3123 (TCC) 56.96
Lipkin Gorman v Carpnale Ltd [1989] 1 WLR 1340 . . . . . 6.44, 6.60
Lipscombe v Turner (1846) 4 D & L 125 . . . . . 1.86
Lister v Romford Ice and Cold Storage Co Ltd [1957] AC 555 . . . . . 18.75
Littaur v Steggles Palmer [1986] 1 WLR 287 . . . . . 18.81, 62.04
Little v Courage [1995] CLC 164 . . . . . 29.63
Little Olympian Each-Ways Ltd, Re [1994] 4 All ER 561, Ch D 15.31
Littlestone v MacLeish [2016] EWCA Civ 127 . . . . . 17.87, 66.11, 66.17
Liverpool City Council v Cahvassed Ltd (unreported), 18 August 1999, QBD 6.160
Liverpool City Council v Irwin [1977] AC 239 . . . . . 31.62
Liverpool Freeport Electronics Ltd v Habib Bank Ltd & Legal Services Commission [2009] EWHC 861 (QB) 62.20
Liversidge v Owen Mumford (Costs) [2012] EWPCC 40 . . . . . 50.330
Lloyd v 2 Sisters Poultry Ltd (unreported), 22 May 2018, Caernarfon County Court 50.297

Lloyd v Gough (1894) 70 LT 725 . . . . 40.52
Lloyd v Hathern Station Brick Co Ltd (1901) 85 LT 158 . . . . 15.44
Lloyd v Svenby [2006] EWHC 576 (QB) 6.63, 56.57
Lloyds Bank plc v McBains Cooper [2017] EWHC 30 (TCC) 6.189
Lloyds Investment (Scandinavia) Ltd v Ager-Hanssen [2003] EWHC 1740 (Ch) 10.08
Lloyds TSB Bank Ltd v Cooke-Arkwright (a firm) [2001] All ER (D) 127 (Oct) 23.31
Lloyds TSB Bank Ltd v Crowborough Properties Ltd [2013] EWCA Civ 107 . . . . 7.74
Lloyds TSB Bank plc v Lampert [2003] EWHC 249 (Ch) 25.44
Lloyds TSB Group plc v Allen (unreported), 20 October 2005, Medway County Court 50.68
Load v Green (1846) 15 M & W 216 . . . . 32.73
Lobster Group Ltd v Heidelberg Graphic Equipment Ltd [2008] EWHC 413 (TCC) 15.08, 15.94, 49.137, 57.15
Local Authority v A Mother and Child [2001] 1 Costs LR 136 . . . . 4.50, 4.51
Local Authority v Trimega Laboratories Ltd [2013] EWCC 6 (Fam); [2014] PNLR 7 . . . . 9.73
Locke v Camberwell Health Authority [1991] 2 Med LR 249 . . . . 9.160, 9.161
Lockhard v Hardy (1841) 4 Beav 224 . . . . 36.11
Lockley v National Blood Transfusion Service [1992] 1 WLR 492 . . . . . 21.06, 21.14, 21.23, 21.24, 21.32
Loescher v Dean [1950] 1 Ch 491 . . . . 40.44
Loizou v Gordon & Anor [2012] EWHC 90221 (Costs) 50.109
Lokhova v Longmuir [2017] EWHC 3125 (QB) 16.35
London Borough of Hackney v Campbell [2005] EWCA Civ 613 . . . . 6.34
London Chatham and Dover Rly Co v South Eastern Rly Co (1889) 60 LT 753 . . . . 52.56
London Chatham & Dover Railway Co v South Eastern Railways Co [1893] AC 429 . . . . 56.49, 56.119
London & Quadrant Housing Trust v Prestige Properties Ltd [2012] EWCA Civ 130 . . . . 16.48
London and Regional (St George's Court) Ltd v Ministry of Defence [2008] EWHC 526 (TCC) 30.28, 30.39, 30.54, 33.21, 33.76
London Scottish Benefit Society v Chorley (1884) 12 QBD 452 . . . . 18.116, 51.80, 59.02, 59.15
London Scottish Benefit Society v Chorley (1884) 13 QBD 872 . . . . . 3.06, 3.08, 3.09, 3.14, 49.106, 52.57, 59.39, 59.45, 59.46
London Tara Hotel Ltd v Kensington Close Hotel Ltd [2011] EWHC 29 (Ch) 6.239, 17.45, 17.76, 56.39, 56.45
London Tramways Co Ltd v London County Council [1898] AC 375 . . . . 4.06
London Wharfing Co, In re (1885) 54 LJ Ch 1137 . . . . 56.24
Long, ex p Fuller, Re (1881) 16 Ch D 617 . . . . 40.45
Long v Value Properties Ltd [2014] EWHC 2981 (Ch) 54.124
Longman v Feather & Black (a firm) (unreported), 18 February 2008, Southampton County Court 43.300
Longstaff International Ltd v McKenzie [2004] EWHC 1852 (Ch) 15.36
Lord v Colvin (1859) 4 Drew 366 . . . . 52.98
Lord Chancellor v Rees [2008] EWHC 3168 (QB) 53.93
Lord Chancellor v Wright [1993] 1 WLR 1561 . . . . 53.94
Lord Say and Seals Case (1711) 10 Mod Rep 40 . . . . 31.44
L'Oreal SA v Bellure NV (unreported), 27 July 2010, CA (Civ Div) 6.66
L'Oreal SA v Bellure NV [2010] EWCA Civ 535 . . . . 6.66
Love v Rowtor Steamship Co Ltd [1916] 2 AC 527 . . . . 31.36
Love, Hill v Spurgeon (1885) 29 Ch D 348, CA 66.79
Loveday v Renton (No 2) [1992] 3 All ER 184 . . . . 49.117, 51.29, 51.35, 51.37, 53.44 53.53, 53.58, 53.61, 53.73, 53.78
Lovell and Christmas Ltd v Wall [1911–13] All ER Rep Ext 1630 . . . . 32.68
Loveridge v Botham (1797) 1 Bos & P 49 772 . . . . 35.91
Low v Guthrie [1909] AC 278, HL 27.226
Lowden v Blakey (1889) LR 23 QBD 332 . . . . 46.20
Lowe v W Machell Joinery Ltd [2011] EWCA Civ 794 . . . . 45.62
Lowe v W Machell Joinery Ltd [2011] EWCA Civ 798 . . . . 45.22
Lowin v W Portsmouth & Co [2017] EWCA Civ 2172 . . . . 43.231, 43.233
Lowline (PLS) Ltd v Direct Aviation Ltd (unreported), 8 March 1999, QB (Comm) 9.181

Lownds v Home Office [2002] EWCA Civ 365 . . . . . 16.06, 25.03, 25.04, 25.12, 25.17, 25.23, 25.38, 25.39, 25.43, 25.53, 25.65, 25.66, 26.19, 45.50, 51.75, 66.76
Lowsley v Forbes [1999] AC 329 . . . . . 23.116
LPI (Hotels) Ltd v Technical & General Guarantee Co SA [2010] EWHC 2049 (TCC) 52.12
Lubbe v Cape Plc [2000] 1 WLR 1545 . . . . . 65.12
Lubrizol v Tyndallwoods [1998] All ER (D) 139 . . . . . 9.106
Lucas v Peacock (1844) 8 Beav 1 . . . . . 1.77
Luck v Meyler (1928) 72 Sol Jo 337 . . . . . 27.37
Luke v South Kensington Hotel Co (1879) 11 Ch D 121 . . . . . 27.323
Lumb v Hampsey [2011] EWHC 2808 (QB) 17.161, 17.173, 17.180
Lumsden v The Shipcote Land Co [1906] 2 KB 433 . . . . . 35.90, 35.98
Lumos Skincare Ltd v Sweet Squared Ltd [2012] EWPCC 28 . . . . . 50.341
Lynch v Paul Davidson Taylor (a firm) [2004] EWHC 89 (QB) 37.20
Lynch v Thorne [1956] 1 WLR 303, CA 27.205
Lyster v Spearman (1882) 72 LT Jo 391 . . . . . 53.12
Lythgoe v Vernon (1860) 5 H & N 180 . . . . . 47.29

M v M [2006] All ER (D) 58 (Jun) 52.51
M v Mayor and Burgesses of the London Borough of Croydon [2012] EWCA Civ 595 . . . . . 6.180, 6.251, 7.146, 7.151, 7.153, 7.156, 61.09, 61.12
MA Lloyd & Son Ltd (in administration) v PPC International Ltd [2016] EWHC 1583 (QB) 15.28
MA Lloyd & Son Ltd (in administration) v PPC International Ltd [2016] EWHC 2162 (QB) 9.109, 9.131
Maatschappij voor Fondsenbezit v Shell Transport and Trading Co [1923] 2 KB 166, CA 15.14
Mabb v English (unreported), 6 December 2017, QBD 8.11, 8.30
Mabey & Johnson Ltd v Ecclesiastical Insurance Office plc (Costs) [2000] CLC 1470 . . . . . 14.26
Macaria Investments Ltd v Sanders (unreported), 29 November 2011, Ch D 9.31
MacDonald v Taree Holdings Ltd [2001] 1 Costs LR 147 . . . . . 44.28, 45.65
MacDougall v Boote Edgar Estekin [2001] 1 Costs LR 118 . . . . . 37.09, 37.10, 37.12
Macgregor v Keily (1849) 3 Ex 794 . . . . . 36.86
Machin v National Power [1998] OPLR 187 . . . . . 66.56
MacInnes v Gross [2017] EWHC 127 (QB) 12.145, 12.147
MacKay v Ashwood Enterprises Ltd [2013] EWCA Civ 959 . . . . . 6.12
Mackenzie, Re (1894) 69 LT 751 . . . . . 36.63, 36.64
Mackman v Secretary of State for Communities & Local Government [2013] EWHC 4435 (Admin) 13.68
MacMillan Williams v Range [2004] EWCA Civ 294 . . . . . 29.54
Macro (Ipswich) Ltd, In re [1997] 1 Costs LR 128 . . . . . 45.74
Madej v Maciszyn [2013] Lexis Citation 143 . . . . . 50.83, 52.101, 50.181
Madurasinghe v Penguin Electronics (a firm) [1993] 1 WLR 989 . . . . . 35.100
Maersk Colombo [2001] 2 Lloyd's Rep 275 . . . . . 17.12
Maes Finance Ltd v WG Edwards & Partners [2000] 2 Costs LR 198 . . . . . 18.110
Magill v Weeks [2001] UKHL 67 . . . . . 43.316, 46.39
Mahan Air v Blue Sky One Ltd [2011] EWCA Civ 544 . . . . . 15.78
Ma'har v O'Keefe [2014] EWCA Civ 1684 . . . . . 6.242, 7.50, 7.51
Mahme Trust Reg & Ors v Lloyds TSB Bank plc [2006] EWHC 1782 (Ch) 16.39, 16.46, 53.132, 53.133, 53.134
Mahmood v Elmi [2010] EWHC 1933 (QB) 17.218
Mahmood v Penrose [2002] EWCA Civ 457 . . . . . 44.34
Mahmud v Saddiq (unreported), 23 August 2017, Birmingham County Court 50.286
Mahoney v East Holyford Mining Co (1875) LR 7 HL 869 . . . . . 47.25
Maini v Maini [2009] EWHC 3036 (Ch) 7.127, 7.130, 7.133, 7.134, 16.52
Mainwaring v Goldtech Investments Ltd, [1997] 1 All ER 467, The Times, 19 February 1991, CA 9.102, 18.56, 51.84, 59.14
Mainwaring v Goldtech Investments Ltd (No 2) [1999] 1 WLR 745 . . . . . 19.23, 19.28, 43.58
Malcolm v O'Callaghan (1837) 3 My & Cr 52, CA 66.76

Malik (unreported), re 18 July 2013, QBD 16.57, 16.62
Malik v Wales [2012] EWHC 4281 (QB). 9.108, 9.186
Malkinson v Trim [2002] EWCA Civ 1273. . . . . 3.16, 6.12, 59.15, 59.17, 59.40, 59.41, 59.43, 59.45, 59.46
Maltby v DJ Freeman & Co [1978] 2 All ER 913; [1978] 1 WLR 431. . . . . 38.14, 38.25, 49.19
Manakee v Brattle [1970] 1 WLR 1607 . . . . 3.44
Manches v Trimborn (1946) 174 LT 344 . . . . 60.57
Manches LLP v Green (t/a Green Denman & Co) [2008] EWHC 917 (QB) 38.83, 38.84
Manchester City Council v Manchester Crown Court & Ors [2009] EWHC 1866 (Admin) 61.14
Manchester City Council v Pinnock (No 2) [2011] UKSC 6 . . . . 6.53
Manku v Seehra (1985) 7 Con LR 90 (QBD) 17.211
Manley v The Law Society [1981] 1 WLR 335, CA. 40.114
Manna (a Child and Protected Party) v Central Manchester University Hospitals NHS Foundation Trust [2017] EWCA Civ 12 . . . . 6.208, 16.36, 16.50, 16.52, 16.60
Mannai Investment Co Ltd v Eagle Star Life Assurance Co Ltd [1997] 3 All ER 352 . . . . 31.42
Manning v Kings College Hospital NHS Trust [2011] EWHC 2954 (QB) 31.23, 31.25, 54.72, 54.88, 54.109, 54.113
Manning (Personal Representatives) v King's College Hospital NHS Trust [2011] EWHC 3054 (QB) 43.334
Mannion v Ginty [2012] EWCA Civ 1667. . . . . 25.13
Mansell v Robinson [2007] EWHC 101 (QB) 30.24, 30.50
Mant v Smith (1859) 4 H&N 324 35,86
Manzanilla Ltd v Corton Property and Investments Ltd (No 2) [1997] 3 FCR 389 . . . . . 9.123, 9.219
Mapleson v Masini (1879–80) LR 5 QBD 144. . . . . 15.67, 15.70
Marathon Asset Management LLP v Seddon [2017] EWHC 479 (Comm) 6.62, 6.69
Marcan Shipping (London) Ltd v Kefalas [2007] EWCA Civ 463 . . . . 43.100, 43.192
Marche v Newham London Borough Council [2014] EWHC 1521 (TCC). 50.54
Marcus v Medway Primary Care Trust [2011] EWCA Civ 750 . . . . 6.56, 6.57, 6.60, 6.188
Margetson and Jones, Re [1897] 2 Ch 314 . . . . 40.114
Marie Gartz (No 2) [1920] 1 P 460 . . . . 40.91
Marine Blast Ltd v Targe Towing Ltd [2003] EWCA Civ 1940 . . . . 1.36
Markby, ex p Markby Assignees, Re (1864) 11 LT 250. . . . . 40.48
Markem Corpn v Zipher Ltd [2005] EWCA Civ 267, ... 8.44
Markerstudy Insurance Co Ltd & Ors v Endsleigh Insurance Services Ltd [2010] EWCH 281 (Comm) 28.162
Marks & Spencer plc v Asda Stores Ltd [2016] EWHC 2081 (Pat). 12.93, 12.101
Marks and Spencer plc v BNP Paribas Securities Services Trust Company (Jersey) Ltd & Anor [2015] UKSC 72 . . . . 27.192, 31.57, 31.58, 31.62
Markt & Co Ltd v Knight Steamship Co Ltd [1910] 2 KB 1201. . . . . 9.76, 65.121
Marley v Rawlings [2014] UKSC 14 . . . . 32.68
Marley v Rawlings (No 2) [2014] UKSC 51 . . . . 7.63, 9.57, 9.74
Marren v Dawson Bentley & Co Ltd [1961] 2 QB 135 . . . . 23.89
Mars UK Ltd v Teknowledge Ltd (No 2) [1999] 2 Costs LR 44 . . . . 14.11, 14.21
Marsdens Estate (1889) 40 Ch D 475. . . . . 56.113
Marseilles Extension Rly and Land Co, ex p Evans (1870) LR 11 Eq 151 . . . . 36.17
Marsh and Rainsford's Case (1687) Leon 111. . . . . 53.11
Marsh v Frenchay Healthcare NHS Trust (2001), The Times, 13 March, QBD 17.211
Marsh v Ministry of Justice [2017] EWHC 3185 (QB). 17.143
Marsh v Sofaer and Giffinhoofe & Co (a firm) [2006] EWHC 1217 (Ch) 9.162
Marshalls (a firm) v A Debtor [1993] Ch 286 . . . . 40.121
Martano v Mann (1880) 14 Ch D 419 . . . . 15.96
Martell v Consett Iron Co Ltd [1955] Ch 363 . . . . 30.12, 30.40, 30.53, 33.90
Martin v Andrews (1856) 7 E&B 1 . . . . 52.56
Martin v Gale (1876) 4 Ch D 428 . . . . 60.19
Martin v Holland & Barrett Ltd [2002] 3 Costs LR 530 . . . . 52.37, 53.83
Martin v Kogan [2017] EWHC 3266 (IPEC) 50.330, 50.336

Martin v Pycroft (1852) 2 De GM&G 785 . . . . . 31.50
Martin Boston & Co (a firm) v Levy [1982] 1 WLR 1434 . . . . . 27.126, 27.149, 27.153, 27.162, 35.115, 36.24, 39.14, 40.11
Martindale v Falkner (1846) 2 CB 706 . . . . . 23.93, 35.68
Mason v Brentini (1880) 15 Ch D 287 . . . . . 20.57
Mason v Mason and Cottrell [1933] P 199 . . . . . 40.39, 40.108
Mason v Walton on Thames Charity [2010] EWHC 1688 (Ch) 48.44
Masood v Zahoor [2009] EWCA Civ 650 . . . . . 6.151, 40.29
Massai Aviation Services v Attorney-General [2007] UKPC 12 . . . . . 30.10, 30.21, 30.37
Massey, Re (1865) 34 Beav 463 . . . . . 36.82, 36.90
Massey, Re (1909) 101 LT 517 . . . . . 36.36
Massey and Carey (1884) 26 Ch D 459 . . . . . 38.35
Masson Templier & Co v De Fries (Costs) [1910] 1 KB 535 . . . . . 43.76, 49.157
Master v Miller (1791) 4 Term Rep 320 . . . . . 30.09
Mastercigars Direct Ltd v Withers LLP [2007] EWHC 2733 (Ch) 36.36, 38.54, 38.63, 38.64, 38.65, 38.74, 40.91, 40.96
Mastercigars Direct Ltd v Withers LLP [2009] EWHC 1531 (Ch) 7.37
Mastermailer Stationery Ltd v Sandison (unreported), 20 April 2011, Ch D 15.85
Masterman-Lister v Brutton & Co (No 2) [2003] EWCA Civ 70 . . . . . 62.19
Matadeen v Associated Newspapers (unreported), 17 March 2005, QBD 13.35
Matrix Securities Ltd v Theodore Goddard [1998] PNLR 290 . . . . . 9.160
Matthews v Dorkin [2000] All ER (D) 1584 . . . . . 53.127, 53.128
Matthews (a patient) v Metal Improvements Co Inc [2007] EWCA Civ 215 . . . . . 17.122, 17.132, 17.180
Mawer v Moore [2017] EWHC 1242 (Comp) 54.33
May v Sherwin (1883) 27 Sol Jo 278, CA 27.37
May & Anor v Wavell Group plc & Anor [2016] Lexis Citation 72 . . . . . 4.27
May & Anor v Wavell Group Ltd & Anor [2017] Lexis Citation 462 . . . . . 25.30, 25.33, 25.34, 25.36, 25.55, 25.58a
Mayr v CMS Cameron McKenna LLP (unreported), 21 November 2017, QBD (Comm) 15.39
MB Building Contractors Ltd v Ahmed (1998) The Independent, 23 November 25.74
Mbasogo v Logo Ltd [2006] EWCA Civ 608 . . . . . 15.36
MBI Inc v Riminex Investments Ltd [2002] EWHC 2856 (QB) 6.237, 17.109
McCann v Department for Social Development (unreported), 30 October 2007, Land Tribunal (NI) 52.42
McCarthy v Essex Rivers Healthcare NHS Trust (unreported), 13 November 2009, QBD 54.65, 54.79, 54.85
McCrea v Herefordshire Council (unreported), 18 June 2014, QBD 53.123
McCullie v Butler [1962] 2 QB 309 . . . . . 52.98, 52.99
McDaniel & Co (a firm) v Clarke [2014] EWHC 3826 (QB) 38.41, 54.197
McDonald v Horn [1995] 1 All ER 961 . . . . . 13.08, 66.63, 66.64, 66.66
McE v Prison Service of Northern Ireland [2009] UKHL 15 . . . . . 46.04
McGlinn v Waltham Contractors Ltd [2005] EWHC 698 (TCC) 6.67
McGlinn v Waltham Contractors Ltd [2005] EWHC 1419 (TCC) 4.59, 7.13, 7.181, 49.149, 49.150, 57.17
McGraddie v McGraddie & Anor [2015] UKSC 1 . . . . . 54.11
McGraddie v McGraddie & Anor (Scotland) [2013] UKSC 58 . . . . . 45.64
McGrory v Alderdale Estate Ltd [1918] AC 503 . . . . . 49.03
McIlkenny v Chief Constable of West Midlands Police Force [1980] QB 283 . . . . . 23.27
McIlwraith v McIlwraith [2002] EWHC 1757 (Ch) 36.87
McIlwraith v McIlwraith [2005] EWHC 90010 (Costs) 1.54, 3.04
McInnes v Gross [2017] EWHC 127 (QB) 14.27
McKenzie v McKenzie [1971] P 33 . . . . . 3.100
McKeown v Venton (unreported), 12 June 2017, Liverpool County Court 16.35, 17.182, 17.183, 50.289
McLaughlin, Re (1917) 17 SR (NSW) 392 . . . . . 1.94
McLean v Procurator Fiscal, Fort William [2001] 1 WLR 2425 . . . . . 24.40

McMinn v McMinn [2003] 2 FLR 823 . . . . 6.103
McPhilemy v Times Newspapers Ltd [2001] EWCA Civ 993. . . . . 17.147, 56.45, 56.85, 56.96, 56.97–57.99
McTear v Englehard [2016] EWCA Civ 487 . . . . 26.65
Meadows v La Tasca Restaurants Ltd (unreported), 16 June 2016, Manchester County Court 8.41
Mealey Horgan plc v Horgan [1999] All ER (D). 15.100
Mealing-McLeod v Common Professional Examination Board [2000] 2 Costs LR 223. . . . . . 43.221, 45.24, 45.50, 59.14, 59.24
Mears Ltd v Leeds City Council [2011] EWHC 2694 (TCC) 6.49, 6.175
Medac Gesellschafte fur Klinischespezialpraparate GmbH V Star Pharmaceutical Ltd [2015] EWHC 4063 (Ch) 12.129
Medcalf v Mardell [2002] UKHL 27 . . . . 9.105, 9.121, 9.124, 9.135, 9.145, 9.195, 57.63
Media Cat Ltd v Adams & Ors [2011] EWPCC 010 . . . . 9.51, 9.120
Medical Defence Union Ltd v Department of Trade [1979] 2 All ER 421. . . . . 27.284
Medlicott v Emery (1933) All ER Rep 655 . . . . 35.83, 35.119
Medway Oil and Storage Co Ltd v Continental Contractors Ltd [1929] AC 88 . . . . 7.7.36, 7.37, 15.118, 20.03, 20.12, 20.52, 20.53–20.62
Medway Primary Care Trust v Marcus [2011] EWCA Civ 750 . . . . 6.229, 17.174
Megantic Services Ltd v Dorsey & Whitney [2008] EWHC 2662 (QB) 35.73
Megeurditchian v Lightbound [1917] 2 KB 298, CA 40.38, 40.58
Mehjoo v Harben Barker (a firm) & Anor [2013] EWHC 1669 (QB). 14.21, 14.32, 14.36, 17.139, 17.205, 56.72, 56.76
Mehmi v Pincher (unreported), 10 September 2015, Liverpool County Court. 43.222
Melchior v Vittivel [2002] CP Rep 24 . . . . 9.115
Mellowes Archital Ltd v Bell Properties Ltd (1997) 87 BLR 26, CA. 38.36
Melvin v England Palmer (a firm) [2004] EWHC 90019 (Costs) 53.50
Menary v Darnton (unreported), 13 December 2016, Winchester County Court 8.39, 8.41
Mendes v Hochtief (UK) Construction Ltd [2016] EWHC 976 (QB) 50.276
Mengi v Hermitage [2012] EWHC 2045 (QB) 15.113
Mengiste v Endowment Fund for the Rehabilitation of Tigray [2013] EWCA Civ 1003 . . . . 9.73, 9.200
Mengiste v Endowment Fund for the Rehabilitation of Tigray [2013] EWHC 1087 (Ch). 16.60, 52.98
Merc Property Ltd, Re [1999] 2 BCLC 286 . . . . 9.200
Mercantile Contracts Ltd v Customs and Excise Commissioners (1990) VAT Decisions 4357; [1990] STI 90 . . . . 55.09
Mercedes Daimler Motor Co Ltd v FIAT Motor Cab Co Ltd (1913) 31 RPC 8 . . . . 53.131
Mercer v Graves (1872) LR 7 QB 499. . . . . 21.35, 40.109
Merchantbridge & Co Ltd v Safron General Partner 1 Ltd [2011] EWHC 1524 (Comm) 9.37
Merck KCaA v Merck Sharp & Dohme Corpn [2014] EWHC 3920 (Ch). 6.167
Mercury Model Aircraft Supplies Ltd [1956] 1 WLR 1153. . . . . 53.104
Meretz Investments Ltd v ACP Ltd [2007] EWHC 2635 (Ch). 18.28, 20.26, 20.27, 27.33
Meridian International Services Ltd v Richardson [2008] EWCA Civ 490 . . . . 15.36, 15.113
Merrick v Law Society [2007] EWHC 2997 (Admin) 18.79
Merrix v Heart of England NHS Foundation Trust [2017] EWHC 346 (QB) 12.65, 12.84, 12.143, 12.144, 12.145, 12.146, 12.147, 12.148, 12.154, 12.159, 12.161, 43.272
Messih v McMillan Williams [2010] EWCA Civ 844 . . . . 7.126, 7.130, 7.131, 7.132
Metal Distributors (UK) Ltd [2004] EWHC (Ch). 36.36
Metalloy Supplies Ltd v MA (UK) Ltd [1997] 1 WLR 1613. . . . . 9.22, 9.28, 9.28, 15.96
Metcalfe, Re (1862) 30 Beav 406 . . . . 35.117
Meynell v Surtees (1855) 25 LJ Ch 257. . . . . 43.287
Michael Phillips Architects Ltd v Riklin [2010] EWHC 834 (TCC) 15.38
Michael Wilson & Partners v Sinclair [2013] EWCA Civ 131 . . . . 15.72
Micklefield v SAC Technology Ltd [1990] 1 WLR 1002 . . . . 29.63
Microsoft Corpn v Datel Design and Development Ltd [2011] EWHC 1986 (Ch) 7.41
Midgulf International Ltd v Groupe Chimiche Tunisien (2010) EWCA Civ 66. . . . . 53.111
Mid-Kent Fruit Factory [1896] 1 Ch 567 . . . . 40.52

Midland Bank Trust Co Ltd v Hett, Stubb & Kemp [1979] Ch 384. . . . . 28.07, 40.55
Midleton v Eliot (1847) 15 Sim 531 . . . . 66.13
Milanese v Leyton Orient Football Club Ltd (Costs) [2016] EWHC 1263 (QB) 20.12
Miles v Cain (1989) The Times, 15 December, CA. 27.226
Miles v Elman [1940] AC 282 . . . . 9.95, 9.150
Miles v London Road Veterinary Clinic (unreported), 5 December 2007, Norwich County Court 50.86
Millburn-Snell & Ors v Evans [2011] EWCA Civ 577 . . . . .49.159
Miller v Appleton (1906) 50 Sol Jo 192 . . . . 52.48
Miller v Associated Newspapers Ltd [2016] EWHC 397 (QB). 24.49
Miller v Associated Newspapers Ltd [2017] UKSC 33 . . . . 6.107, 6.261
Miller v Hales [2006] EWHC 1717 . . . . 53.70
Mills v Birchall (sub nom Dolphin Quays Developments v Mills) [2008] EWCA Civ 385. . . . . . 9.03, 9.12, 9.28, 9.29, 15.96
Mills v Cooper [1967] 2 QB 459, [1967] 2 All ER 100 . . . . 23.21
Mills v LCC [1925] 1 KB 213, DC. 4.05
Mills v Revett (1834) 1 A&E 856. . . . . 36.66
Milsom v Ablyazov [2011] EWHC 955 (Ch) 48.85
Milton Keynes Council v Edwards [2004] EWHC 267 (Admin). 61,14
Minkin v Cawdery Kaye Fireman & Taylor [2011] EWHC 177 (QB); [2012] EWCA Civ 546 . . . . .27.65, 27.72, 27.84, 40.33, 40.34, 40.35
Minter v Priest [1930] AC 558 . . . . 46.09
Miom Ltd v Sea Echo ENE (No 2) [2011] EWHC 2715 (Admlty) 6.245
Mireskandari v Law Society [2009] EWHC 2224 (Ch) 7.134
Mireskandari v Solicitors Regulation Authority [2013] EWHC 907 (Admin) 15.87
Mitchell v Gard (1863) 3 Sw & Tr 275 . . . . 7.58
Mitchell v James [2002] EWCA Civ 997 . . . . 43.358
Mitchell v News Group Newspapers Ltd [2013] EWCA Civ 1537 . . . . . . .12.56, 12.57, 26.24, 26.41, 26.50, 26.55, 26.56–26.59, 26.62, 26.70, 43.158
Mitchell v News Group Newspapers Ltd [2013] EWHC 2355 (QB) 26.57
Mitchell v Royal Bank of Scotland plc [2017] EWHC 1771 (Ch). 14.14, 16.53
Mitchell v Younghusband (1744) 94 ER 843 . . . . 1.46
Mitchell & Mitchell v Gard & Kingwell (1863) 3 Sw & Tr 275 . . . . 7.58
MM v Kirk, Re [2017] EWCA Civ 260 . . . . 16.49
Mobiqa Ltd v Trinity Mobile Ltd [2010] EWHC 253 (Pat) 6.113, 6.132, 7.128
Modern Building Wales Ltd v Limmer and Trinidad Co Ltd [1975] 1 WLR 1281, CA 31.36
Moduleco Ltd v Carillon Construction Ltd [2009] EWHC 250 (TCC) 7.48
Mohamadi v Shellpoint Trustees Ltd [2009] EWHC 1098 (Ch) 18.81, 62.06
Mohammed v Alaga & Co [2000] 1 WLR 1815. 4.21, 4.25, 27.235, 27.244
Mohammed v The Home Office [2017] EWHC 3051 (AB) 17.81
Molloy v Shell UK Ltd [2001] EWCA Civ 1272. . . . . 6.67, 6.151
Mölnlycke AB v Proctor & Gamble Ltd (No 6) [1993] FSR 154, Patents Ct. 7.97, 10.05, 43.70
Monarch Energy Ltd v Powergen Retail Ltd [2006] CSOH 102 . . . . 15.39
Mond v Hammond Suddards (No 2) [2000] Ch 40, CA (Civ Div). 9.31
Mondel v Steel (1841) 8 M & W 858 . . . . .21.02, 38.36
Monk v Warbey [1935] 1 KB 75, CA 4.07
Monkton v Tarr (1930) 23 BWCC 504, CA. 37.17
Monsanto Technology LLC v Cargill International SA [2007] EWHC 3113 (Pat). 6.41
Monte Developments Ltd (in administration) of Court Management Consultants Ltd [2010] EWHC 3071 (Ch) 43.414
Montlake & Ors v Lambert Smith Hampton Group Ltd [2004] EWHC 1503 (Comm) 54.123
Moon v Atherton [1972] 2 QB 435. . . . . 9.76
Moon v Garrett [2006] EWCA Civ 1121 . . . . .7.11, 7.17, 7.18
Moon v Hall (1864) 17 CB(NS) 760 . . . . 1.83
Moor v Row (1629) 1 Rep Ch 38 . . . . 53.04

Moorcock, The (1889) 14 PD 64 . . . . 31.59
Moore's (Wallisdown) Ltd v Pensions Ombudsman; Royal and Sun Alliance Life and Pensions Ltd v Pensions Ombudsman [2002] 1 All ER 737 . . . . 6.12, 9.77
Mordecai v Nutting & Ors (1752) 94 ER 848 . . . . 1.72
Morgan v Blyth [1891] 1 Ch 337 . . . . 27.191
Morgan v Spirit Group Ltd [2011] EWCA Civ 58 . . . . 25.77
Morgan v UPS [2008] EWCA Civ 1476. . . . . 6.153
Morgan & Anor v Hinton Organics (Wessex) Ltd [2009] EWCA Civ 107. . . . . 13.41, 52.42
Morley v Boothby (1825) 3 Bing 107 . . . . 32.59
Morley v Hay (1828) 7 LJOSKB 104 . . . . 40.76
Morning Star Co-Operative Society Ltd v Express Newspapers Ltd [1979] FSR 113 . . . . 28.108
Morris, Re (1872) 27 LT 554 . . . . 36.94, 39.15
Morris v Bank of America National Trust (Appeal against Striking out) [2001] 1 All ER 954 . . . . 7.88, 43.76, 43.80
Morris v Browne [2017] EWHC 631 (Ch) 16.48
Morris v Hunt (1819) 1 Chit 544 . . . . 53.34, 53.35
Morris v London Borough of Southwark [2011] EWCA Civ 25 . . . . 27.273, 27.274, 27.275, 27.281, 29.211, 30.14, 30.18, 33.24
Morris v Roberts (HMIT) (wasted costs) [2005] EWHC 1040 (Ch) 9.158
Morris v Sandahtay (unreported), 2 February 2015, Kingston-upon-Hull County Court 43.338, 43.541
Morris v Wentworth-Stanley [1999] 2 WLR 470 . . . . 19.26
Morris v Wiltshire and Woodspring District Council [2002] 1 Costs LR 167 . . . . . . 43.296, 43.354, 43.357, 43.358, 43.365, 43.369, 59.23
Mortgage Agency Number Four Ltd v Alomo Solicitors (a firm) [2011] EWHC B22 (Mercantile). 16.54
Mortgage Corpn v Sandoes (unreported), 26 November 1996, Court of Appeal 26.20
Mortgage Funding Corpn plc v Kashef-Hamadani (unreported), 26 April 1993, CA. 66.11
Morton v Portal Ltd [2010] EWHC 1804 (QB) 6.148, 6.150
Moseley v Victoria Co (1886) 55 LT 482 . . . . 46.08
Mostyn [1928] AC 57, HL 4.07
Mostyn v Mostyn (1870) LR 5 Ch App 457 . . . . 53.11
Mostyn v West Mostyn Coal Co (1876–77) LR 2 CPD 547. . . . . 46.25
Motto & Ors v Trafigura Ltd & Anor [2011] EWCA Civ 1150. . . . 6.201, 6.204, 18.23, 25.41, 25.64, 25.65, 25.75, 25.95, 29.132, 29.134, 29.135, 49.52, 49.113, 49.114, 49.115, 49.116, 51.78, 54.79, 65.100, 65.102
Mouchel Ltd v Van Oord (UK) Ltd (No 2) [2011] EWHC 1516 (TCC). 19.43
Mount Cook Land Ltd v Westminster City Council [2003] EWCA Civ 1346. . . . . 13.77
Mount Eden Land Ltd v Speechly Bircham LLP [2014] EWHC 169 (QB). 36.53, 43.27, 43.113, 43.133
Moxon v Sheppard (1890) 24 QBD 627. . . . . 40.93
MRW Technologies Ltd v Cecil Holdings Ltd & Anor [2001] Lexis Citation 1882 . . . . 17.211
Mulford Holding & Investment Ltd v Greatex Ltd [2010] EWCA Civ 1178 . . . . . 15.03, 15.21, 15.27
Mullarkey v Broad (in the matter of Southill Finance Ltd, in liquidation) [2009] EWCA Civ 2 . . . . 45.62, 45.63
Mullen v Hackney London Borough Council [1997] 1 WLR 1103 . . . . 54.163
Muller v Linsley & Mortimer [1996] 1 PNLR 74 . . . . 40.14
Mulready v JH & W Bell Ltd [1953] 2 All ER 215 . . . . 7.19
Multiple Claimants v Corby District Council (Corby Group Litigation) [2009] EWHC 2109 (TCC) 56.39
Multiplex Constructions (UK) Ltd v Cleveland Bridge UK Ltd [2008] EWHC 2280 (TCC) 6.03, 6.05, 6.26, 6.28, 6.49, 6.62, 6.194, 6.209
Mumbray v Lapper [2005] EWHC 1152 . . . . 65.124
Munir v Jang Publications Ltd [1989] ICR 1 . . . . 23.15
Munkenbeck & Marshall v Harold [2005] EWHC 356 (TCC). 14.30, 29.03, 29.13

Murphy v Rayner [2013] EWHC 3878 (Ch) 4.08, 20.30, 20.32, 62.04, 62.40
Murphy v Young's Brewery [1997] 1 WLR 1592. . . . . 9.54
Murray v Bernard [2015] EWHC 2395 (Ch) 6.118, 6.136
Murray v Neil Dowlman Architecture Ltd [2013] EWHC 872 (TCC) 12.84, 12.127
Murray Construction Ltd v Marino Family Trust Co Ltd [2013] EWHC 3966 (TCC). 15.102
Murray (Edmund) Ltd v BSP International Foundations Ltd (1992) 33 Con LR 1, CA 15.82
Murrell v Clapham (1836) 8 Sim 74. . . . . 15.96
Muscat v Health Professions Council [2009] EWCA Civ 1090 . . . . 45.60
M V Yorke Motors (a firm) v Edwards [1982] 1 All ER 1024. . . . . .15.36, 15.78, 15.80, 15.129
Myatt v National Coal Board [2006] EWCA Civ 1017 . . . . . 4.81, 29.29, 29.30, 29.32, 29.54, 29.82, 29.83, 29.84, 29.90, 29.93, 29.95, 29.96, 54.198
Myatt v National Coal Board (No 2) [2007] EWCA Civ 307. . . . . 9.51, 9.63
Myer Wolff & Manley, Re (unreported), 23 April 1985, CA. 15.40
Myers v Casey (1913) 17 CLR 90 . . . . 23.10
Myers v Defries (1880) 5 Ex D 180. . . . . 6.159
Myers v Elman [1940] AC 282 . . . . 3.16, 5.32, 5.33, 9.65, 9.95
Myler v Williams [2003] EWHC 1587 (QB) 29.58
Mylward v Weldon (1596) Tothill 102, 21 ER 136. . . . . 1.41

NAP Anglia Ltd v Sun-Land Development Co Ltd (No 2) [2012] EWHC 51 (TCC) 51.54
Narich Pty Ltd v Pay-roll Tax Commissioner [1984] ICR 286, PC. 50.126
Naseem t/a SH Builders and Contractors v Kang [2011] EWCA Civ 737. . . . . 6.24, 6.50, 6.196
Nash v Eli Lilly [1993] 4 All ER 383. . . . . 65.04, 65.69
Nash v Inman [1908] 2 KB 1 . . . . 60.11, 60.18
Nash v Ministry of Defence [2018] EW Misc B4 (CC). 12.162
Nasser v United Bank of Kuwait [2001] EWCA Civ 556 . . . . .15.04, 15.39, 15.57, 15.73, 15.74, 15.77, 15.114
National Anti-Vivisection Society Ltd v Duddington (1989) The Times, 23 November. 13.62
National Bank of Kazakhstan v Bank of New York Mellon AS/NV [2018] EWHC 300 (QB). . . . 16.64
National Guild of Removers and Storers Ltd v Milner [2014] EWHC 1117 (IPEC) 50.336
National Justice Compania Naviera SA v Prudential Assurance Co Ltd, The Ikarian Reefer [1993] 2 Lloyd's Rep 68 . . . . 52.14, 52.34
National Provincial Bank of England v Games (1886) LR 31 Ch D 582. . . . . 66.25
National Transit Insurance Co Ltd v Customs and Excise Commissioners [1975] STC 35. . . . . 55.19
National Westminster Bank v Feeny [2006] EWHC 90066 (Costs) 48.50, 49.135
National Westminster Bank v Kotonou [2009] EWHC 3309 (Ch) 49.132
National Westminster Bank Ltd v Stockman [1981] 1 WLR 67 . . . . 40.91
National Westminster Bank plc v Angeli Kotonou [2006] EWHC 1785 (Ch) 6.67
National Westminster Bank plc v Kotonou [2007] EWCA Civ 223. . . . . 6.35
National Westminster Bank plc v Morgan [1985] AC 686 . . . . 32.49
National Westminster Bank plc v Rabobank Nederland [2007] EWHC 1742 (Comm). 16.52
National Westminster Bank plc v Rabobank Nederland [2007] EWHC 3163 (Comm). . . 3.43, 16.65
National Westminster Bank plc and another v Brice Droogleever (a firm) [2003] EWHC 1821 (Ch). 36.10
Nationwide Building Society v Various Solicitors (No 4) (1999) The Independent, 25 October 25 . . . . 65.05, 65.54
Navimpex Centrala Navala v George Moundreas & Co SA (1983) 127 Sol Jo 392, CA 10.06
Ndole Assets Ltd v Designer M&E Services UK Ltd [2017] EWHC 1148 (TCC) 3.78, 3.79
Neafsey v Small (unreported), 9 December 2010, EAT 9.141
Neary v Bedspace Resource Ltd (unreported), 4 December 2015, Chester County Court 50.286
Neave v Neave [2003] EWCA Civ 325. . . . . .17.109
Neck v Taylor [1893] 1 QB 560 . . . . 15.69
Neckles, Re [2003] EWHC 685 (Ch). 21.14
Nederlandse Reassurantie Groep Holding NV v Bacon & Woodrow (No 4) [1998] 2 Costs LR 32. . . . . 18.12
Negus, Re [1895] 1 Ch 73 . . . . 36.85

Neil v Stephenson [2001] EWCA Civ 627 . . . . . 44.23
Nell Gwynn House Maintenance Fund Trustees v C& E Commissioners [1999] STC 79 . . . . . 55.16
Nelson, Son and Hastings, Re (1885) 30 Ch D 1, CA. 23.94, 27.19, 36.36, 53.28
Nelson v Greening & Sykes (Builders) Ltd [2007] EWCA Civ 1358 . . . . . 9.15
Nelson v Nelson [1997] 1 All ER 970 . . . . . 9.65, 9.66, 9.67, 9.70
Nelson's Yard Management Co v Eziefula [2013] EWCA Civ 235 . . . . . 6.113, 7.115, 7.117, 7.120, 7.121, 7.123, 7.124, 7.125, 7.132
Nemetona Trading Ltd v Golding Corpn Ltd [2013] EWHC 4569 (Ch) 16.38, 16.40
Nesham v Sunrick Clothing Ltd (unreported), 22 April 2016, Newcastle upon Tyne County Court 8.41
Nestec SA v Dualit Ltd [2013] EWHC 1577 (Pat) 16.27
Network Rail Infrastructure v Handy [2015] EWHC 1460 (TCC) 16.40
Nevill, ex p White, Re (1871) 6 Ch App 397, CA 22.02
New Brunswick Rly Co v British and French Trust Corpn Ltd [1938] 4 All ER 747 . . . . . 23.12, 23.15
New Victoria Hospital v Ryan [1993] ICR 201, EAT 46.22
Newall v Lewis [2008] EWHC 910 (Ch) 49.148
Newland Shipping & Forwarding Ltd v Toba Trading FZC [2014] EWHC 864 (Comm) 17.31, 17.37
Newman, Re (1861) 30 Beav 196 . . . . . 1.83, 27.112
Newman, Re (1867) 2 Ch App 707 . . . . . 36.92
Newman v Wenden Properties Ltd [2007] EWHC 336 (TCC) 15.60, 15.70
Newton v Grand Junction Railway Co (1846) 153 ER 1133. . . . . 56.23, 56.71
NG Ferguson & Co Ltd v Brown & Tawse (A Firm) 1918 SC (HL) 125. . . . . 9.190
Nicholas v Penny [1950] 2 KB 466. . . . . 4.06
Nicholl v Jones (1865) 2 H & M 588 . . . . . 46.20
Nicholson v Falkiner (1830) 1 Mol 555 . . . . . 66.79
Nightingale v Tildsley [1980] CLY 134, Wolverhampton County Court 40.43
Nittan (UK) Ltd v Solent Steel Fabrications Ltd [1981] 1 Lloyd's Rep 633 . . . . . 31.44
Nizami v Butt [2006] EWHC 159 (QB) 1.162, 18.21, 29.107, 50.81, 50.88, 50.106
NJ Rickard Ltd v Holloway [2015] EWCA Civ 1631 . . . . . 6.139, 17.21, 17.41
N O Turner (t/a Turner Agricultural) v Commissioners of Customs & Excise [1992] STC 621 . . . . . 55.26
Noble, ex p Douglas (1833) 3 Deac & Ch 310 . . . . . 40.76
Nokes v Doncaster Amalgamated Collieries Ltd [1940] AC 1014. . . . . 32.17
Noorani v Calver [2009] EWHC 592 (QB) 16.35, 16.38, 16.57
Nordstern Allgemeine Versicherungs AG v Internav Ltd [1999] 2 Lloyd's Rep 139. . . . . 9.03, 9.04, 9.28, 30.33
Norfolk County Council v Dencare Properties Ltd (unreported), 9 November 2005, CAT. 43.290
Norgeln Ltd v Reeds Rains Prudential Ltd [1999] 2 AC 1. . . . . 30.21
Norjarl K/S A/S v Hyundai Heavy Industries Co Ltd [1991] 3 All ER 211 . . . . . 53.31, 53.78, 53.82, 53.117
Norman, Re (1886) 16 QBD 673. . . . . 36.36
North v Loomes [1919] 1 Ch 378 . . . . . 31.50
North Oxford Golf Club v A2 Dominion Homes Ltd [2013] EWHC 852 (QB) 49.133, 49.135, 49.126
North Shore Ventures Ltd v Anstead Holdings Inc [2010] EWCA Civ 1634 . . . . . 15.88
North West Holdings plc, Re [2001] EWCA Civ 67. . . . . 9.28
North Western Rly Co v M'Michael (1850) 5 Exch 114 . . . . . 60.13, 60.14
Northampton Coal Iron and Waggon Co v Midland Waggon Co (1878) 7 Ch D 500 . . . 15.36, 15.56
Northern and Shell Plc v John Laing Construction Ltd [2002] EWHC 2258 (TCC) 29.132, 29.136
Northop Grumann Mission Systems Ltd v BAE Systems (al Diriyah C41) Ltd [2014] EWHC 3148 (TCC) 6.123, 6.133
Northstar Systems v Fielding [2006] EWCA Civ 1660 . . . . . 6.197, 6.203, 23.44, 57.19
Northumbria, The (1869) LR 3 A&E 6 . . . . . 56.05
Norwich Pharmacal Co & Ors v Customs and Excise Commissioners [1974] AC 133 . . . . . 7.41

Nossen's Patent, Re [1969] 1 All ER 775. . . . . .49.106, 49.108, 52.17, 52.42
Noterise Ltd v Haseltine Lake & Co [1992] BCC 497 . . . . .15.117
Nova (Jersey) Knit Ltd v Kammgarn Spinnerei GmbH [1977] 1 WLR 713, HL. 35.115, 40.09, 40.10
Nova Productions Ltd v Mazooma Games Ltd [2006] EWHC 189 (Ch) 14.13, 56.62
Novoship (UK) Ltd v Mikhaylyuk [2014] EWCA Civ 908 . . . . 56.47
Novus Aviation Ltd v Alubaf Arab International Bank BSC(c) [2016] EWHC 1937 (Comm) 17.110, 17.143
N&R Devine Ltd v McAteer [2013] NEQB 102 . . . . 59.14, 59.18
Nugent v Goss Aviation [2002] EWHC 1281 (QB) 6.197, 6.202
Nulty v Milton Keynes Borough Council [2012] EWHC 730 (QB). 17.176
Nurdin & Peacock plc v DB Ramsden & Co [1999] 1 All ER 941 . . . . 32.73
Nwoko v The Oyo State Government of Nigeria [2014] EWHC 4538 (QB). 9.164, 9.220
Nykredit Mortgage Bank plc v Edward Erdman Group Ltd (No 2) [1997] 1 WLR 1627 . . . . .56.05, 56.10, 56.106

O (Costs: Liability of Legal Aid Board), Re [1997] 1 FLR 465 . . . . .62.21, 62.38
O (a minor) (wasted costs application), Re [1994] 2 FLR 842. . . . . 9.185
O v Ministry of Defence [2006] EWHC 990 (QB) 21.37
Oasis Merchandising Services Ltd, Re [1998] Ch 170 . . . . 30.44
Obrascon Huarte Lain SA v Gibraltar [2014] EWHC 2291 (TCC). 16.40
O'Beirne v Hudson [2010] EWCA 52 . . . . 49.05, 50.51, 50.393, 50.397, 57.21, 57.28, 57.34
O'Brien v Lewis (1863) 32 LT (Ch) 569 . . . . 1.83
O'Brien v Ministry of Justice [2013] 2 All ER 1 . . . . 50.126
O'Brien v Sandown Court Management Co (unreported), 21 July 2011, Liverpool County Court 50.76
O'Brien v Shorrock and MIB [2015] EWHC 1630 (QB) 27.29, 27.31, 29.132, 54.46, 54.58, 54.60, 54.75, 54.77, 54.80, 54.114
Oceanbulk Shipping and Trading SA v TMT Asia Ltd [2010] UKSC 44. . . . . 6.218
Ochwat v Watson Burton (a firm) [1999] All ER (D) 1407. . . . . 65.78
O'Connor v Isaacs [1956] 2 All ER 417 . . . . 23.91
Octoesse LLP v Trak Special Projects Ltd [2016] EWHC 3180 (TCC) 59.31, 59.32
O'Driscoll v Manchester Insurance Committee [1915] 3 KB 499 . . . . 43.414
Office of Fair Trading v Ashbourne Management Services Ltd [2011] EWHC 1237 (Ch) 28.108
Official Receiver v Brunt, sub nom In re Minotaur Data Systems Ltd [1999] 1 WLR 1129. . . . . 59.07, 59.14, 59.18
Ofulue v Bossert [2009] UKHL 16 . . . . .6.214, 40.14
OJSC TNK-BP Holding v Lazurenko [2013] EWCA Civ 137 . . . . 16.45
Okotcha v Voest Alpine Intertrading GmbH [1993] BCLC 474. 15.71, 15.84
Oksuzoglu v Kay [1998] 2 All ER 361 . . . . .6.56, 6.60
Okundu v Secretary of State for the Home Department [2014] UKUT 377 (IAC) 9.181
Olanda, The [1919] 2 KB 728. . . . . 18.94
Olatawura v Abiloye [2002] EWCA Civ 998 . . . . 15.03, 15.19, 15.21, 15.97, 15.99, 15.100
Old Street Homes v Chelsea Bridge Apartments Ltd [2018] EWHC 1162 (Ch) 16.15
Olden v Crown Prosecution Service, In the matter of [2010] EWCA Civ 961 . . . . 6.103
O'Leary v Tunnelcraft Ltd (2011) (unreported), 19 October 2011, SCCO 25.96
Oliver, Re (1867) 36 LJ Ch 261 . . . . 3.06
Oliver v Whipps Cross University NHS Trust [2009] EWHC 1104 (QB) 54.65, 54.78, 54.79, 54.85
Olugbade (a barrister), Re [2008] EWCA Crim 2922. . . . . 9.175
Olympic Airlines SA (in liquidation) V ACG Acquisition XX LLC [2012] EWCA Civ 1659. . . . . 15.03, 15.86
Omar v Worldwide News Inc [1998] IRLR 291 . . . . 6.251
Omatov v Macaria Investment Ltd [2015] EWHC 2799 (Ch) 43.159
OMV Petrom SA v Glencore International AG [2017] EWCA Civ 195 . . . . 17.119, 17.148, 56.92, 56.93, 56.94, 56.95, 56.97
Onay v Brown [2009] EWCA Civ 775. . . . . 6.88, 7.37, 7.161, 17.31, 17.46, 17.67, 17.68, 17.74, 17.219

Ong v Ping [2015] EWHC 3766 (Ch) 14.37
Ontulmus v Collett [2014] EWHC 294 (QB) 15.33
Ontulmus v Collett [2014] EWHC 4117 (QB). 16.43, 17.167, 17.178
OOO Abbott (A company incorporated in the Russian Federation) v Design Display Ltd [2014] EWHC 3234 (IPEC) 17.81
OPM Property Services Ltd v Venner [2004] EWHC 427 (Ch). 47.29
Optical Express v Associated Newspapers (Costs) [2017] EWHC 2707 (QB). 6.59, 16.35, 17.120, 17.121, 17.181
Oraki v Bramston [2016] EWCA Civ 1195 . . . . 14.18
Oram v Hutt [1914] 1 Ch 98, CA. 18.66, 30.35, 30.52
Orange v Taylor (unreported), 21 January 2014, Exeter County Court 50.76
Orb ARL v Ruhan [2015] EWCA Civ 1180 . . . . 14.16
Orchard v South Eastern Electricity Board [1987] QB 565. . . . . 9.62, 9.218
Oriakhel v Vickers [2008] EWCA Civ 748. . . . . 9.14, 9.79
Original Hartlepool Collieries v Moon (1874) 30 LT 193 . . . . 46.08
Orley v Viewpoint Housing Association Ltd (unreported), 7 December 2010, Gateshead County Court 28.193
Ormerod v Tate (1801) 1 East 464 . . . . 40.39, 40.114
Orton v Collins [2007] 1 WLR 2953 . . . . 17.23
Ortwein v Rugby Mansions Ltd [2003] EWHC (Ch) 2077 . . . . .25.44, 25.90, 49.91
Orwin v British Coal Corpn [2003] EWHC 757 (Ch) 53.53, 53.88, 53.94
Osborn and Osborn, Re [1913] 3 KB 862. . . . . 36.69
Osborne, Re (1858) 25 Beav 353. . . . . 3.06
Osborne v Rowlett (1880) 13 Ch D 774 . . . . 4.04
O'Shea v Wood [1891] P 286, CA. 46.08
O'Sullivan v Management Agency & Music Ltd [1985] 1 QB 429 . . . . 32.50
Oswald Hickson Collier & Co v Carter-Ruck [1984] AC 720 . . . . .40.55, 49.121
Otkritie International Investment Management Ltd v Urumov [2014] EWHC 755 (Comm) 14.21, 16.47
Ottway v Jones [1955] 1 WLR 706. . . . . 6.22
OTV Birwelco Ltd v Technical & Guarantee Co Ltd [2002] 4 All ER 668 . . . . 27.320
Ovlas Trading SA v Strand (London) Ltd [2008] EWHC 3236 (Ch) 15.50
Owen v Church (1857) 5 WR 545 . . . . 66.25
Owen v Ord (1828) 3 C & P 349 . . . . 27.207
Owen, ex parte Payton, Re (1885) 52 LT 628 . . . . 1.83, 27.112
Owens v Noble [2010] EWCA Civ 284 . . . . 6.51, 6.53
Owners and/or Bareboat Charterers and/or Sub Bareboat Charterers of Samco Europe v Owners of MSC Prestige [2011] EWHC 1656 (Admlty) 6.207, 17.214, 17.216, 17.217
Owners and/or demise charterers of dredger 'Kamal XXVI' and barge 'Kamal XXIV' v Owners of ship 'Ariela' [2010] EWHC 2531 (Comm) 9.91
Owners, Demise Charters & Time Charterers of 'Western Neptune' [2009] EWHC 1522 (Admlty) 17.102
Oxford Shipping Co Ltd v Nippon Yusen Kaisha [1984] 2 All ER 835 . . . . 48.85
Oyston v The Royal Bank of Scotland plc [2006] EWHC 90053 (Costs). 27.331, 29.66, 29.138, 31.56, 54.46

P (a barrister) (wasted costs order) [2001] EWCA Crim 1728 . . . . 9.213
P & O Nedlloyd BV v Utaniko Ltd [2003] EWCA Civ 174 . . . . 17.31, 17.113
Pablo Star Ltd v Emirates Integrated Telecommunications Co [2009] EWCA Civ 616 . . . . 15.85
Pacey v The Ministry of Defence [2009] EWHC 90138 (Costs). 27.34
Padhiar v Patel [2001] Lloyd's Rep PN 328 . . . . 9.64
Page v Scottish Insurance Corpn Ltd (1929) 140 LT 571, CA. 18.73
Page (No 3), Re (1863) 32 Beav 487 . . . . 52.04
Paine, Re (1912) 28 TLR 201 . . . . 27.96
Painting v University of Oxford [2005] EWCA Civ 161. . . . . 6.03, 6.49, 6.67, 6.141, 6.147, 6.151, 6.153, 6.238

Palermo, The (1883) LR 9 PD 6 . . . 46.20
Palette Shoes Pty Ltd v Krohn (1937) 58 CLR 1 . . . 32.14
Palmer, Re (1890) 45 Ch D 291 . . . 35.124
Palmer v Durnford Ford (a firm) [1992] 2 All ER 122 . . . 23.15
Palmer v Estate of Palmer, Deceased [EWCA] 2008 Civ 46 . . . 9.56
Palmer v Milbrook Beds Ltd (unreported), 23 February 2007, Torquay County Court . . . 43.337
Pamplin v Express Newspapers Ltd [1985] 1 WLR 689 . . . 4.38, 4.54, 18.26, 29.47, 46.01, 46.38, 46.42, 46.46, 46.47, 46.49, 46.50, 46.55, 46.61, 46.74
Pamplin v Fraser (No 2) [1984] 2 All ER 694 . . . 23.64
Pan Ocean Shipping Co Ltd v Creditcorp, The Trident Beauty [1994] 1 All ER 470, [1994] 1 WLR 161 . . . 32.23
Panchaud Frères Établissement Grains [1970] 1 Lloyd's Rep 53 . . . 18.100
Pankhurst v White [2010] EWHC 311 (QB) . . . 17.216, 17.217
Pankhurst v (1) White and (2) Motor Insurers Bureau [2010] EWCA Civ 1445 . . . 17.216, 56.96
Pannone LLP v Aardvark Digital Ltd [2011] EWCA Civ 803 . . . 43.103
Pannone LLP v Aardvark Digital Ltd [2013] EWHC 686 (Ch) . . . 15.70
Pao On v Lau Iu Long [1980] AC 614 . . . 39.21
Papa Johns (GB) Ltd v Doyley [2011] EWHC 2621(QB) . . . 43.92
Papathanassiou v Dutch Communication Co Ltd (unreported), 9 May 1985, QBD . . . 23.73
Papera Traders Co Ltd v Hyundai (Merchant) Marine Co Ltd (No 2) [2002] 2 Lloyd's LR 692 . . . 30.20, 30.28, 30.51, 33.11
Papera Traders Co Ltd & Ors v Hyundai Merchant Marine Co Ltd & Anor [2003] EWHC 9018 (Costs) . . . 49.106
Papera Traders Co Ltd & Ors v Hyundai Merchant Marine Co Ltd, The Keihin Co Ltd [2002] EWHC 2130 (Comm) . . . 52.18
Paragon Finance plc v Freshfields [1999] 1 WLR 1183 . . . 36.107
Paragon Finance plc v Rosling King (unreported), 26 May 2000, Ch D . . . 40.70
Paraguassu Steam Tramroad Co, Re (1872) 8 Ch App 254 . . . 21.35
Parissis v Matthias Gentle Page Hassan Holdings LLP [2017] EWHC 761 (QB) . . . 36.76
Park, Cole v Park, Re (1888) 41 Ch D 326 . . . 36.17
Parker v Butler [2016] EWHC 1251 (QB) . . . 8.15
Parker v Watkins (1859) John 133 . . . 66.25
Parker-Tweedale v Dunbar Bank plc (No 2) [1991] Ch 26 . . . 66.25
Parkes v Martin [2009] EWCA Civ 883 . . . 7.37, 20.61
Parnall v Hurst, The Times, 10 July 2003 . . . 11.11
Parsa v DS Smith plc (unreported), 8 September 2017, Birmingham County Court . . . 50.297
Parvez v Mooney Everett Solicitors Ltd [2018] EWHC 62 (QB) . . . 35.23, 35.37, 35.38, 35.39, 35.69, 35.84, 35.86
Patchett v Sterling Engineering Co Ltd (1953) 71 RPC 61; [1955] AC 534 . . . 23.12, 23.14
Patcroft Ltd v Latif [2018] EWHC 11396 (Ch) . . . 15.51
Patel v Fortis Insurance Ltd (unreported), 23 December 2011, Leicester County Court . . . 50.171
Patel v K & J Restaurants Ltd [2010] EWCA Civ 1211 . . . 66.27
Patel v Secretary of State for the Home Department [2013] UKSC 72 . . . 4.07
Patel v Unite [2012] EWHC 92 (QB) . . . 7.41
Paterson v Glasgow Corpn (1908) 46 SLR 10 . . . 23.134
Paterson v Ogilvy [1957] JC 42 . . . 50.76
Pathology Group v Reynolds (unreported), 28 November 2011, QBD . . . 6.107
Patience v Tanner [2016] EWCA Civ 158 . . . 45.30, 45.31
Patterson v Ministry of Defence [2012] EWHC 2767 (QB) . . . 4.67, 50.120, 50.133, 50.134, 51.76
Paulin v Paulin [2009] EWCA Civ 221 . . . 43.317
Paull, Re (1884) 27 Ch D 485 . . . 36.63
Pauls Agriculture Ltd v Smith (1993) 3 All ER 122 . . . 23.73
Payne, Randle, Re v Payne (1883) 23 Ch D 288 . . . 15.96, 60.28
Payne v Cave (1789) 3 Term Rep 148 . . . 43.286
Payne v Schmidt [1949] 2 All ER 741 . . . 53.101, 53.134
PC Harrington Contractors Ltd v Systech International Ltd [2012] EWCA Civ 1371 . . . 38.85

Peacock v MGN Ltd [2009] EWHC 769 (QB). 13.23, 13.25
Peak Construction (Liverpool) Ltd v McKinney Foundation (1970) 1 Build LR 111 . . . . 3.41, 56.119
Peak Hotels & Resorts Ltd v Tarek Investments Ltd [2015] EWHC 2886 (Ch) 15.106
Peak Hotels & Resorts Ltd v Tarek Investments Ltd & Ors [2015] EWHC 386 (Ch). 15.70
Peakman v Linbrooke Services Ltd [2008] EWCA Civ 1239 . . . . 6.68, 50.397, 57.21
Pearce v Gardener [1897] 1 QB 688 . . . . 31.53
Pearce v Secretary of State for Energy and Climate Change [2015] EWHC 3775 (QB) 65.35, 65.36
Pearse v Lord [2015] EWHC 3046 (Ch). 6.107
Pearse v Pearse (1846) 1 De G & S 12. . . . . 46.20
Pearson v Naydler [1977] 3 All ER 531 . . . . 15.76
Peet v Mid Kent Healthcare NHS Trust [2001] EWCA Civ 1703 . . . . 52.31
Pell v Daubeny (1850) 5 Exch 955 . . . . 52.48
Pell Frischmann Consultants Ltd v Prabhu [2013] EWHC 2203 (Ch). 66.51
Pelly v Wathen (1849) 7 Hare 351 . . . . 40.48
Pendle Metalwares Ltd v Walter Page (Safeway's) Ltd [2014] EWHC 1144 (Ch) 6.114
Penley v Anstruther (1883) (1) 52 L J (Ch) 367 . . . . 35.82, 35.83
Penn v Bristol & West Building Society [1997] 1 WLR 1356. . . . . 16.64
Pennington v Reliance Motor Works Ltd [1923] 1 KB 127. . . . . 40.80
Penningtons (a firm) v Brown (unreported), 30 April 1998, CA. 35.102, 35.104, 35.105, 35.106, 35.107, 40.22
Pentecost v John [2015] EWHC 1970 (QB) 29.21, 29.132
Pepin v Watts [2002] EWCA Civ 958 . . . . 18.37, 18.71
Pepper v Hart [1992] UKHL 3. . . . . .4.38, 4.55, 4.75
Peppy, The [1997] 2 Lloyd's Rep 722 . . . . 27.249
Percival v Dunn (1885) 29 Ch D 128 . . . . 32.31
Percy v Anderson-Young [2017] EWHC 2712 (QB). 54.140, 54.147, 54.156, 56.157, 54.170
Perloff v Gordon Dadds & Co (1989) The Independent, 20 November 53.126
Perotti v Collyer-Bristow (a firm) [2003] EWCA Civ 1521 . . . . 24.40
Perriam Ltd v Wayne [2011] EWHC 403 (QB) 6.48, 6.194, 6.209
Perry v London General Omnibus Co [1916] 2 KB 335 . . . . .1.116
Perry v Lord Chancellor (1994) The Times, 26 May, QBD. 49.119
Perry & Co Ltd v Hessin & Co (1913) 108 LT 332. . . . . 53.134
Persaud v Persaud [2003] EWCA Civ 394 . . . . 9.144, 9.149, 9.150, 9.156
Persimmon Homes Ltd v Great Lakes Reinsurance (UK) Plc [2010] EWHC 1705 (Comm) 15.38, 34.32, 34.64
Peterborough v Stamford Hospitals NHS Trust [2017] EWCA 1941 (Civ) 25.84, 54.130, 54.137, 54.138, 54.139
Petroleo Brasileiro SA v Petromec Inc [2005] EWHC 2430 (Comm). 9.46
Petromec Inc v Petroleo Brasileiro [2006] EWCA Civ 1038. . . . . .9.04, 9.30, 9.43
Petromec Inc v Petroleo Brasileiro [2006] EWHC 3518 (Comm) 14.08
Petromin SA v Secnav Marine Ltd [1995] 1 Lloyd's Rep 603, QBD 15.70, 15.118
Petrotrade Inc v Texaco Ltd [2001] 4 All ER 853 . . . . 3.100, 17.147
Petrotrade Inc v Texaco Ltd (Note) [2002] 1 WLR 947 . . . . .17.93, 17.182
PGF II SA v OMFS Co [2012] EWHC 83 (TCC) 48.08
PGF II SA v OMFS Co 1 Ltd [2013] EWCA Civ 1288. . . . . .6.126, 6.127, 6.128, 6.132, 6.136, 6.139
Phaestos Ltd v Ho [2012] EWHC 668 (TCC) 16.33
Phelps v Stewards (a firm) [2007] EWHC 1561 (Ch) 27.03
PHI Group Ltd v Robert West Consulting Ltd [2012] EWCA Civ 588 . . . . 17.46, 17.62, 17.74, 17.76, 17.78
Philby v Hazle (1860) 8 CB (NS) 647. . . . . 1.83, 27.111, 35.47, 39.16
Philips Electronique Grand Public SA v British Sky Broadcasting Ltd [1995] EMLR 472 . . . . . 31.61
Phillips v Alhambra Palace Co [1901] 1 KB 59 . . . . 32.17
Phillips v Broadley (1846) 9 QB 744 . . . . .23.94, 23.95
Phillips v Evershed [2002] EWCA Civ 486 . . . . 15.35, 15.36
Phillips v Phillips (1879) 5 QBD 60 . . . . 7.81
Phillips v Symes [2004] EWHC 2330 (Ch) 9.73

Phillips v Willis [2016] EWCA Civ 401 . . . . 50.151, 50.167, 50.172, 50.240
Phillips & Co (a firm) v Bath Housing Co-operative Ltd [2012] EWCA Civ 1591 . . . . 23.125, 23.126, 23.127, 39.04, 40.123
Phoenix Finance Ltd v Federation Internationale de l'Automobile [2002] EWHC 1028 (Ch). 6.106, 16.30
Phoenix Life Assurance Co, Howard and Dolman's Case, Re (1863) 1 Hem & M 433. . . . . 40.48
Phonographic Performance Ltd v AEI Rediffusion Music Ltd [1999] 1 WLR 1507 . . . . 1.156, 6.43, 6.159, 17.163
Phonographic Performance Ltd v Hagan [2016] EWHC 3076 (IPEC) 50.336
Photo Production Ltd v Securicor Transport Ltd [1980] AC 827 . . . . 28.162
Picasso v Maryport Harbour Trustees (1884) WN 85 . . . . 52.39, 52.56
Pickering (t/a City Agents) v Sogex Services (UK) Ltd [1982] 1 EGLR 42 . . . . .29.200, 30.46
Pickford v Ewington (1835) 4 Dowl 453. . . . . 27.37
Picnic at Ascot v Karlus Derigs [2001] FSR 2 . . . . 6.274
Picton Jones & Co v Arcadia Developments Ltd [1989] 1 EGLR 43. . . . . .29.200, 30.46
Picton, Picton v Picton [1931] WN 254 . . . . 60.05
Piglowska v Piglowski [1999] 1 WLR 1360 . . . . 45.25
Pilbrow v Pearless de Rougement & Co [1999] 3 All ER 355 . . . . 38.83
Pilford's, Robert case (1613) 10 CO Rep, 2 Inst 269. . . . . .1.24, 1.71, 3.37
Pilgrim v Hirschfeld (1863) 3 New Rep 36. . . . . 35.51
Pindell Ltd & Anor v Airasia Berhad (formerly known as Airasia SDN BHD) [2010] EWHC 3238 (Comm). 6.53, 6.63, 6.165, 6.186
Pine v DAS Legal Expenses Insurance Co Ltd [2011] EWHC 658 (QB). 34.16
Pine v Law Society [2002] EWCA Civ 175. . . . . 36.91, 36.92
Pine v Law Society (unreported), 26 October 2004, QBD 36.36
Pine v Solicitors' Disciplinary Tribunal [2001] EWCA Crim 1574. . . . . 24.41
Pink Floyd Music Ltd & Anor v EMI Records Ltd [2010] EWCA Civ 1429. . . . . 31.30, 31.31
Pinkerton v Easton (1873) LR 16 Eq 490 . . . . 40.92
Pinnel's Case (1602) 5 Co Rep 117a 39.17
Pinnock v Harrison (1838) 3 M & W 532 . . . . 40.50
PIP Breast Implant Litigation, Re [2013] EWHC 3643 (QB). 65.42
Piper Double Glazing Ltd v DC Contracts [1994] 1 WLR 777 . . . . 2.09, 3.68, 3.72
Pirie v Ayling [2003] EWHC 9006 (Costs) 25.88, 30.02, 30.48
Pirta v Shahi (unreported), 2 July 2015, Birmingham County Court 29.21
Pittalis v Grant [1989] QB 605. . . . . 45.62
Pittman v Prudential Deposit Bank Ltd (1896) 13 TLR 110 . . . . 29.205
Planche v Colburn (1831) 8 Bing 14 . . . . 18.99
Plant v Bourne [1897] 2 Ch 281 . . . . 31.48
Plant dec'd, Re [1926] P 139 . . . . .7.55
Plant Health Care (UK) Ltd v Holohan [2017] EWHC 1119 (QB) 16.49
Plating Co Ltd v Farquharson (1881) 17 Ch D 49. . . . . 1.98
Platt v GKN Kwikform Ltd [1992] 1 WLR 465 . . . . 43.259, 43.282, 43.360
Plevin v Paragon Personal Finance Ltd [2017] UKSC 23; [2017] 1 WLR 1249. . . . 8.20, 32.16, 32.18, 32.39, 32.40, 32.54, 34.38, 49.157, 50.190, 54.175, 54.176
Plunkett v Barclays Bank Ltd [1936] 2 KB 107. . . . . 40.55
Pochin Construction Ltd v Liberty Property (GP) Ltd [2014] EWHC 2919 (TCC) 16.39
Pocklington Steel Structures Ltd v Cordell Group Ltd (unreported) 9 December 2010, TCC, Manchester District Registry. 7.153
Polak v Machioness of Winchester [1956] 2 All ER 660 . . . . 35.92, 35.93, 35.100
Pole v Leask (1863) 33 LJ Ch 155 . . . . 22.02
Police Federation v Ryder (1990) The Times, 30 July 19.40
Pomeroy & Tanner, Re [1897] 1 Ch 284 . . . . .3.92, 22.06, 35.116
Pomiechowski v District Court of Legnica, Poland [2012] UKSC 20. . . . . 36.05
Pontifex v Farnham (1892) 41 WR 238 . . . . .27.152
Pool v Pool (1889) 61 LT 401 . . . . 27.77
Popat v Edwin Coe LLP [2013] EWHC 4524 (Ch) 18.62

Porter Amphlett and Jones, Re [1912] 2 Ch 98 . . . . 52.04
Porzelack KG v Porzelack (UK) Ltd [1987] 1 All ER 1074 . . . . 15.60, 15.61, 15.63
Potter v Duffield (1874) LR 18 Eq 4 . . . . 31.48
Potter v Sally Montague Hair and Spa (unreported), 7 October 2016, Nottingham County Court 43.266
Potts, ex p Établissements Callot and De Schrijver v Leonard Tubbs & Co and Official Receiver [1934] Ch 356 . . . . 40.131
Pounset v Humphreys (1837) Coop Pr Cas 142 . . . . 40.58
Pourghazi v Kamyab (unreported), 3 December 2015, Ch D 16,49
Powell v Brodhurst [1901] 2 Ch 160 . . . . 19.23
Powell v Ely (unreported), 19 May 1980, Divisional Court 3.70
Powell v Herefordshire Health Authority [2002] EWCA Civ 1786 . . . . 56.110
Powles v Reeves [2016] EWCA Civ 1375 . . . . 7.145, 7.147, 7.153, 7.162, 45.30
PR Records v Vinyl 2000 [2008] EWHC 192 (Ch) 9.36
Practice Guidance (McKenzie Friends: Civil and Family Courts) [2010] 1 WLR 1881 . . . . 47.10
Pratt v Bull; Hollins v Russell [2003] EWCA Civ 718 . . . . 29.83
Praxis Capital Ltd v Burgess [2015] EWHC 1801 (Ch) 6.166
Preece v Caerphilly County Borough Council (unreported), 15 August 2007, Cardiff County Court 29.54, 29.103
Premier Motorauctions v PWC LLP [2016] EWHC 2610 . . . . 34.30
Premier Motorauctions Ltd v Pricewaterhousecoopers LLP [2017] EWCA Civ 1872 . . . . 15.35, 15.37, 15.38, 15.39, 15.56
Premium Nafta Products Ltd (20th Defendant) & Ors v Fili Shipping Co Ltd & Ors [2007] UKHL 40 . . . . 48.74
Prestney v Colchester Corpn (1883) 24 Ch D 376, CA 10.17
Preston Banking Co v William Allsup & Sons [1895] 1 Ch 141, CA 10.05
Preston's Estate, Re [1951] 1 Ch 878 . . . . 66.40, 66.52
Price v Carter [2010] EWHC 1737 (TCC) 49.64, 49.73, 49.86
Price v Egbert H Taylor & Co Ltd (unreported), 16 June 2016, Birmingham County Court 8.21
Primus Telecommunications Netherlands BV v Pan European Ltd [2005] EWCA Civ 273 . . . . 43.92
Princo v Phillips [2003] EWHC 2589 (Ch) 9.35
Pringle v Secretary of State of India (1888) 40 Ch D 288 . . . . 9.64
Prior v Silverline International Ltd (unreported), 8 July 2015, Liverpool County Court 25.97
Pritchard and Riccio v Ford Motor Co Ltd [1997] 1 Costs LR 39 . . . . 49.143
Procon (Great Britain) Ltd v Provincial Building Co Ltd [1984] 1 WLR 557; [1984] 2 All ER 368, CA 15.110, 15.111, 15.119
Procter & Gamble Co v Svenska Cellulosa Aktiebolaget SCA [2012] EWHC 2839 (Ch) 17.34, 17.37, 17.41, 17.68, 17.161
Professional Information Technology Consultants Ltd v Jones [2001] EWCA Civ 2103 . . . . . . 6.116
Promar International Ltd v Clarke [2006] EWCA Civ 332 . . . . 7.165
Property and Reversionary Investment Corpn Ltd v Secretary of State for the Environment [1975] 2 All ER 436; [1975] 1 WLR 1504 . . . . 38.07, 38.26, 49.92
Protank Shipping Inc v Total Transport Corpn, The Protank Orinoco [1997] 2 Lloyd's Rep 42 . . . . 31.44
Prothero v Thomas (1815) 6 Tuant 196 . . . . 35.116, 52.04
Providence Capitol Trustees Ltd v Ayres [1996] 4 All ER 760, Ch D9.77
Prudential Insurance Co v IRC [1904] 2 KB 658 . . . . 2.09, 27.280
Puddephatt v Leith (No 2) [1916] 2 Ch 168 . . . . 21.30, 21.41
Pure Spirit Company v Fowler (1890) 25 QBD 235 . . . . 15.36
Purrunsing v A'Court & Co and House Owners Conveyancers Ltd (Costs) [2016] EWHC 1528 (Ch) 16.34, 17.106
Purser v Hibbs [2015] EWHC 1792 (QB) 12.165, 13.133
Pyman & Co v Burt, Boulton & Anor [1884] WN 100 . . . . 56.23

Q v J [2003] EWHC 251 (Fam) 23.80
Q v Q (Family Division: Costs; Summary Assessment) [2002] 2 FLR 668 . . . . 44.10

Qader v Esure Services Ltd [2016] EWCA Civ 1109 . . . . .4.12, 50.170, 50.270
Quarcoo v Esure Services Ltd [2009] EWCA Civ 595 . . . . 16.47
Quarmby Construction Co Ltd v Office of Fair Trading [2012] EWCA Civ 1552 . . . .6.03, 6.51, 6.68
Quartz Hill Consolidated Gold Mining Co v Eyre (1883) 11 QBD 674. . . . . 1.74, 3.43
QBE Management Services (UK) Ltd v Dymoke [2012] EWHC 116 (QB) 16.48
Quinn v Ministry of Defence [1998] PIQR 387 . . . . 50.126
Quorum v Schramm (No 2) [2002] 2 Lloyd's Rep 72. . . . . 6.235

R v A [2001] UKHL 25 . . . . 24.19
R v Archbishop of Canterbury [1903] 1 KB 289. . . . . 18.64
R v Aziz [2014] EWCA Crim 1387 . . . . .9.174
R v Barnett London Borough Council, ex p Shah [1983] 2 AC 309, HL. 15.31
R v Bassettlaw DC, ex parte Aldergate Estates Ltd [2000] Lexis Citation 5478, QBD . . . 7.130, 7.131
R v Boswell; R v Halliwell [1987] 2 All ER 513. . . . . 18.107, 59.18
R v Bow Street Metropolitan Stipendiary Magistrate, ex p Mirror Group Newspapers Ltd [1992] 2 All ER 638 (QBD) 64.04
R v Camden London Borough Council, ex parte Martin [1997] 1 WLR 359 . . . . 9.106
R v Cardiff City Council, ex p Brown (unreported), 11 August 1999, QBD 44.20
R v Common Professional Examination Board, ex p Mealing-McCleod (2000) The Times, 2 May, CA 15.105
R v Cripps, ex parte Muldoon [1984] 2 All ER 705. . . . . 10.05
R v Derby Magistrates' Court, ex p B [1996] AC 487 . . . . 46.04, 46.05, 46.43
R v Dimsey [2001] UKHL 46 . . . . 24.27
R v Doutre (1884) 9 App Cas 745, PC 53.04
R v Dudley Magistrates' Court, ex p Power City Stores Ltd (1990) 154 JP 654. . . . . .53.119
R v Findlay and MacGregor [2002] 2 Costs LR 322. . . . . 55.17
R v Forbes, ex parte Bevan (1972) 127 CLR 1. . . . . 9.69
R v Ghosh [1982] EWCA Crim 2. . . . . .57.57
R v Greenwich LBC, ex p Lovelace (No 2) [1992] QB 155 . . . . 62.21
R v His Honour Judge Sir Donald Hurst, ex p Smith [1960] 2 All ER 385 . . . . 45.74
R v Holderness Borough Council, ex parte James Robert Developments [1993] 1 PLR 108 . . . . .7.153
R v Horsham District Council & Anor, ex parte Wenman & Ors [1995] 1 WLR 680 . . . . 9.183
R v Industrial Disputes Tribunal, ex p American Express Co Inc [1954] 2 All ER 764 . . . . .67.15
R v Inhabitants of Calesworth (1785) 1 TR 71, 99 ER 977. . . . . 1.71
R v Islington London Borough Council, ex p Hooper [1995] COD 76. . . . . 67.06
R v Kensington and Chelsea Royal London Borough Council, ex p Ghebregiogis [1994] COD 502 . . . . 67.06
R v Legal Aid Board, ex p Bruce [1992] 3 All ER 321; [1991] 1 WLR 1231 . . . . 22.15, 49.118
R v Legal Aid Board, ex p Duncan [2000] COD 159 . . . . 34.20
R v Legal Aid Board, ex p Eccleston [1998] 1 WLR 1279. . . . . 3.17, 52.57
R v Legal Services Commission, ex p Wulfsohn [2002] EWCA Civ 250 . . . . .59.24, 59.26
R v Liverpool City Council, ex p Newman & Ors [1993] 5 Admin LR 669 . . . . . . 7.130, 7.148, 7.162
R v London Borough of Hammersmith and Fulham, ex p CPRE [2000] ENVLR 544 . . . . 13.67
R v Lord Chancellor, ex p Child Poverty Action Group [1998] 2 All ER 755 . . . . . 13.47, 13.60, 61.09
R v Lord Mayor of London, ex p Boaler [1893] 2 QB 146, DC 27.82
R v Manchester Crown Court, ex p Rogers [1999] 1 WLR 832 . . . . 46.17
R v Mason [2002] EWCA Crim 385 . . . . 24.25
R v Miller (Raymond) [1983] 1 WLR 1056. . . . .18.28, 18.47, 18.70, 18.194, 27.94, 27.192, 31.69, 53.35
R v Mills and Morris [1997] 1 Costs LR 49. . . . . 53.99
R v National Anti-Vivisection Society Ltd v Duddington (1989) The Times, 23 November. . . . 66.66
R v North & West Devon Health Authority & Ors, ex p Bowhay & Ors [2001] 60 BMLR 228 . . . . 7.130, 7.162
R v Oldham Metropolitan Borough Council, ex p G [1993] 1 FLR 645 . . . . 60.16
R v Onuigbo (aka Okoronkwo) [2014] EWCA Crim 65. . . . . 40.69
R v Oxfordshire County Council [1987] NLJ Rep 542 QBD. 9.160
R v Panel on Take-overs and Mergers, ex p Datafin plc [1987] QB 815 . . . . .67.15

R v Prime Minister, ex p CND [2002] EWHC 2712 (Admin) 13.60
R v Sandhu (1984) 29 November, SCTO, reported in Senior Courts Taxing Office (SCTO) 49.70, 49.72, 49.73, 49.75
R v SCTO, ex p John Singh & Co (1997) 1 Costs LR 49 . . . . 25.04, 45.74, 45.75
R v Secretary of State, ex p Factortame (unreported) 18 October 2000, QBD 17.137
R v Secretary of State for the Environment, ex p Spath Holme Ltd [2001] 2 AC 349 . . . . . . 4.09, 4.10
R v Secretary of State for the Home Department, ex p Gunn [2001] EWCA Civ 891 . . . . . . 62.13, 62.15, 62.17, 62.20, 62.21, 62.38
R v Secretary of State for the Home Department, ex p Osman [1993] COD 204 . . . . 9.39, 33.86
R v Secretary of State for Transport, ex p Factortame [2002] EWCA Civ 932. . . . . 2.09, 27.243, 27.275, 29.197, 29.198, 30.18, 30.22, 30.25, 30.26, 30.49, 30.51
R v Sharpe (unreported), 10 November 1995, QBD 59.02
R v Slessor (1984) Taxing Masters Compendium, App 7 . . . . 52.84
R v Slessor [1997] Costs LR (Core Vol) 438 . . . . 49.80
R v Soneji [2006] 1 AC 340 . . . . 35.73
R v Stafford, Stone and Eccleshall Justices, ex p Robinson [1988] 1 WLR 369 . . . . 59.40, 59.45
R v Supreme Court Taxing Office ex p John Singh and Co [1997] 1 Costs LR 49 . . . . 25.53
R v Taxing Officer, ex p Bee-Line Roadways International Ltd (1982) The Times, 11 February 45.74
R v Thakrar [2001] EWCA Crim 1096 . . . . 24.40
R v Tottenham Justices, ex parte Joshi [1982] 2 All ER 507 . . . . 3.16
R v Warley Justices, ex p Callis [1994] COD 240 . . . . 67.06
R v Westminster City Council, ex p Chorion plc [2002] EWCA Civ 1126 . . . . 7.130
R v Wilkinson [1980] 1 WLR 396 . . . . 1.136, 51.10, 51.24, 51.29
R (ex p Medical Justice) v Secretary of State for the Home Department [2011] EWCA Civ 269 . . . . . . 45.52
R (a child) (disclosure), Re [2004] EWHC 2085 (Fam) 7.48
R (on the application of Action against Medical Accidents) v General Medical Council [2009] EWHC 2522 (Admin) 13.59
R (on the application of AK & Ors) v Secretary of State for the Home Department & Ors [2011] EWCA Civ 895 . . . . 61.09
R (on the application of Akram) v Secretary of State for the Home Department [2015] EWHC 1359 (Admin) 38.85
R (on the application of Allbutt) v Ministry of Defence [2009] EWHC 3351 (Admin) 7.122
R (on the application of Amin Sino) v Secretary of State for The Home Department [2016] EWHC 803 (Admin) 6.03, 6.45
R (on the application of Association of Personal Injury Lawyers v Secretary of State for Justice) [2013] EWHC 1358 (Admin) 50.35
R (on the application of) Bahta & Ors v Secretary of State for the Home Department & Ors [2011] EWCA Civ 895 . . . . 6.106, 7.146, 61.04, 61.09, 61.12, 61.14
R (on the application of Bakhtiyar) v Secretary of State for the Home Department [2015] UKUT 519 (IAC) 18.114, 51.82
R (on the application of Brewer) v Supreme Court Costs Office [2006] EWHC 1955 (Admin) 45.75, 49.10
R (on the application of Botley Parish Action Group) v Eastleigh Borough Council [2014] EWHC 4388 (Admin) 13.92
R (on the application of Bullmore) v West Hertfordshire Hospitals NHS Trust [2007] EWHC 1350 (Admin) 13.57, 13.61
R (on the application of Burkett) v Hammersmith and Fulham London Borough Council [2004] EWCA Civ 1342 . . . . 21.06, 21.14, 21.23, 21.25, 21.26, 21.29
R (on the application of Cart) v Upper Tribunal; R (on the application of MR (Pakistan)) v Upper Tribunal (Immigration and Asylum Chamber) & Anor [2011] UKSC 28 . . . . 45.76
R (on the application of Compton) v Wiltshire Primary Care Trust [2008] EWCA Civ 749 . . . . . 5.22, 13.54, 13.57, 13.60, 13.69, 13.71, 13.72, 13.73
R (on the application of Corner House Research) v Secretary of State for Trade and Industry [2005] EWCA Civ 192 . . . . 13.08, 13.53, 13.71, 13.73, 16.40
R (on the application of CPW) v Harrow Crown Court [2014] EWHC 2061 (Admin) 16.57

R (on the application of Crawford) v Newcastle upon Tyne University [2014] EWHC 1197 (Admin). 6.133
R (on the application of D) v Life Sentence Review Commissioners [2008] UKHL 33 . . . . . 9.102, 27.226
R (on the application of Daniel Baxter) v Lincolnshire County Council [2015] EWCA Civ 1290 . . . . . 7.130
R (on the application of Davies) v Birmingham Deputy Coroner [2004] EWCA Civ 207 . . . . . .67.13
R (on the application of Davies) v Royal College of Veterinary Surgeons [2015] EWHC 3707 (Admin) 6.237
R (on the application of Dempsey) v Sutton BC [2013] EWCA Civ 863. . . . . .7.162
R (on the application of E) v Governing Body of JFS and the Admissions Appeal Panel of JFS [2009] UKSC 1 . . . . .6.250, 13.68
R (on the application of Edwards & Anor) v Environment Agency (Cemex UK Cement Ltd, intervening) [2010] UKSC 57 . . . . 13.76, 13.81, 13.94, 13.96, 57.36
R (on the application of Factortame) v Secretary of State for Transport (No 2) [2002] EWCA Civ 932 . . . . 52.18
R (on the application of G) v Worcestershire County Council [2005] EWHC 2332 (Admin) 7.143
R (on the application of Gassama) v Secretary of State for the Home Department [2012] EWHC 3049 (Admin). 9.175, 16.57, 16.62
R (on the application of Goodson) v Bedfordshire & Luton Coroner [2005] EWCA Civ 1172. . . . . 13.52, 13,61
R (on the application of Gorlov) v Institute of Chartered Accountants in England and Wales [2001] EWHC 220 (Admin) 61.14
R (on the application of (1) Gransian Ltd (2) Xon Yong Zhou) v Home Department [2008] EWHC 3431 (Admin). 9.101, 9.170
R (on the application of Grimshaw) v Southward LBC (unreported), 17 July 2013, QBD (Admin) 9.175
R (on the application of Grimshaw) v Southwark London Borough Council [2013] EWHC 4504 (Admin). 16.57, 16.62
R (on the application of Hide) v Staffordshire CC [2007] EWHC 2441 (Admin) 9.126
R (on the application of HS2 Action Alliance Ltd) v Secretary of State for Transport [2015] EWCA Civ 203. . . . . 13.90, 13.93
R (on the Application of Idira) v The Secretary of State for the Home Department [2015] EWCA Civ 1187 . . . . 16.42
R (on the application of J) v Hackney London Borough Council [2010] EWHC 3021 (Admin). 7.162
R (on the application of JBOL LTD) v City of Westminster Magistrates' Court [2013] EWHC 1010 (Admin) 59.12
R (on the application of Kamau) v Secretary of State for the Home Department [2007] All ER (D) 111 (Apr) 9.184
R (on the application of Kuzeva & Anor) v Southwark London Borough Council [2002] EWCQ Civ 781 . . . . 6.250
R (on the application of Latchman) v Home Department [2004] EWHC 2795 (Admin) 9.177, 9.187
R (on application of Lewis) v DPP [2004] EWHC 3081 Admin. 50.77
R (on the application of Litvinenko) v Secretary of State for the Home Department [2013] EWHC 3135 (Admin) 13.61, 13.67
R (on the application of Loucif) v Secretary of State for the Home Department [2011] EWHC 3640 (Admin). 67.03
R (on the application of Matthias Rath BV) v the Advertising Standards Authority Ltd [2001] EMLR 22 . . . . 24.25
R (on the application of Morgan Grenfell & Co Ltd) v Special Commissioners of Income Tax [2002] UKHL 21 . . . . 24.56
R (on the application of Mount Cook Land Ltd) v Westminster City Council [2003] EWCA Civ 1346 . . . . 67.02, 67.04, 67.05, 67.08
R (on the application of MVN) v London Borough of Greenwich [2015] EWHC 2663 (Admin) 17.149, 17.156
R (on application of the National Council for Civil Liberties) v Secretary of State for the Home Department [2018] EWHC 976 (Admin) 16.49

R (on the application of Naureen) v Salford City Council [2012] EWCA Civ 1795 ......7.157, 7.166
R (on the application of Perinpanathan) v City of Westminster Magistrates' Court & Anor [2010] EWCA Civ 40.. 61.13, 61.14
R (on the application of Plantagenet Alliance Ltd) v (1) Secretary of State for Justice [2013] EWHC 3164 (Admin).. 13.70
R (on the application of (1) Prudential Plc) v Special Commissioner of Income Tax [2010] EWCA Civ 1094; aff'd at [2013] UKSC 1 .... 46.22
R (on the application of Rawlinson & Hunter Trustees SA & Ors) v Serious Fraud Office [2012] EWHC 3218 (Admin) 16.27, 16.57, 16.63
R (on the application of Rottman) v Metropolitan Police Commissioner [2002] UKHL 20 ....24.24, 24.25
R (on the application of Roudham & Larling Parish Council) v Breckland Council [2008] EWCA Civ 714.. 49.83
R (on the application of Rusbridger) v Attorney General [2003] UKHL 38 .... 24.11
R (on the application of Sager House (Chelsea) Ltd) v First Secretary of State & Anor [2006] EWHC 1251 (Admin) 16.46
R (on the application of Santur) v Home Department [2007] EWHC 741 (Admin).......... 9.173
R (on the application of Schwartz) v Highbury Corner Magistrates Court [2009] EWHC 1397 Admin 49.76
R (on the application of Scott) v London Borough of Hackney [2009] EWCA Civ 217....6.250, 7.148
R (on the application of Scott Halborg, trading under the style of Halborg & Co, Solicitors) v Law Society [2010] EWHC 38 (Admin) 27.54, 27.59
R (on the application of Simmons) v Bolton Metropolitan Borough Council [2011] EWHC 2729 (Admin) 13.74
R (on the application of Sivanandan) v Disciplinary Tribunal of the Council of the Inns of Court [2014] EWHC 1570 (Admin) 59.02, 59.40, 59.49
R (on the application of Sivasubramaniam) v Wandsworth County Court [2002] EWCA Civ 1738 .... 45.54, 45.74
R (on the application of Srinivasans Solicitors v Croydon County Court) [2013] EWCA Civ 249; [2011] EWHC 3615 (Admin)...................6.195, 36.44, 40.19, 45.74, 67.10
R (on the application of Strickson) v Preston County Court & Ors [2007] EWCA Civ 1132 .... 45.74, 45.75
R (on the application of Tallington Lakes Ltd) v Grantham Magistrates' Court (unreported), 24 February 2011, QBD.. 9.22
R (on the application of Telford and Wrekin Borough Council) v Crown Court at Shrewsbury [2003] EWHC 230 (Admin) 61.13
R (on the application of Thurman) v Lewisham LBC (unreported), 1 January 2007, QBD (Admin)...67.10
R (on the application of Touche) v Inner London North Coroner [2001] 2 All ER 752......... 9.77
R (on the application of Tull) v Camberwell Green Magistrates' Court [2004] EWHC 2780 (Admin) 67.13
R (on the application of Varma) v Redbridge Magistrates' Court [2009] EWHC 836 (Admin)...... 67.13
R (on the application of Valentines Homes & Construction Ltd) v Revenue and Customs Commissioners [2010] EWCA Civ 345 ....67.10
R (on the application of Whistl UK Ltd (formerly TNT Post UK Ltd)) v Revenue and Customs Commissioners [2014] EWHC 4118 (Admin)...........................67.10
R (on the application of Whitston) (Asbestos Victims Support Groups Forum UK) v Secretary of State for Justice [2014] EWHC 3044 (Admin) 54.29
R (on the application of Young) v Oxford City Council [2012] EWCA Civ 46......... 13.61, 13.86
R (Adesina & Ors) v The Nursing & Midwifery Council [2013] EWCA Civ 818............ 36.06
R (Alconbury Developments Ltd) v Secretary of State for the Environment, Transport and the Regions [2001] UKHL 23 .... 24.12
R (Buglife) v Thurrock Gateway Development Corp & Anor [2008] EWCA Civ 1209 .... 13.61
R (Cowl) v Plymouth City Council [2001] EWCA Civ 1935 .... 48.10
R (Ecclestone) v Legal Aid Board [2001] EWHC 9008 (Costs) 18.53

R (England) v Tower Hamlets LBC [2006] EWCA Civ 1742. . . . . 13.61
R (Factortame Ltd and others) v Secretary of State for Transport, Local Government and Regions (No 8) [2002] EWCA Civ 932; [2003] QB 381 . . . . .3.69, 30.24, 33.13
R (Farrakhan) v Secretary of State for the Home Department [2002] EWCA Civ 606. . . . . 24.27
R (Jarrett) v Legal Services Commission [2001] EWHC 389 (Admin). 24.40
R (Latchman) v Secretary of State for the Home Department [2004] EWHC 2795 (Admin) . . 9.154
R (Leach) v Commissioner for Local Administration [2001] EWHC 455 (Admin) 67.08
R (McCormick) v Liverpool Justices [2001] 2 All ER 705 . . . . 18.06
R (Morgan Grenfell & Co Ltd) v Special Commissioner of Income Tax [2003] 1 AC 563 . . . . . 46.04
R (Public and Commercial Services Union) v Minister for the Civil Service [2010] ICR 1198 . . . 4.10
R (RJM (FC)) v Secretary of State for Work and Pensions [2008] UKHL 63 . . . . 24.12
R (Roudham & Larling Parish Council) v Breckland Council [2008] EWCA Civ 714. . . . . .67.11
R (UNISON) v Lord Chancellor [2017] UKSC 51 . . . . 26.09
R & T Thew v Reeves [1982] QB 1285-6 . . . . 5.32
R+V Versicherung AG v Risk Insurance and Reinsurance Solutions SA (No 3) [2006] EWHC 42 (Comm). 52.17
Rabin v Mendoza & Co [1954] 1 WLR 271 . . . . 40.14
Rabiu v Marlbray Ltd [2016] EWCA Civ 476 . . . . 19.33
Racecourse Association v The Respondent et al [2006] CAT 1. . . . . 61.02, 61.09
Radcliffe, In re [2004] EWHC 90039 (Costs) 49.66, 49.70, 49.75, 49.101
Radford & Anor v Frade & Ors [2018] EWCA Civ 119; [2016] EWHC 1600 (QB). . . . 18.28, 18.56, 18.98, 27.76, 31.28, 31.40, 31.55, 32.65
Radstock Co-operative and Industrial Society v Norton-Radstock UDC [1967] Ch 1094. . . . . 32.23
Radu v Houston [2006] EWCA Civ 1575 . . . . 15.84, 15.107
Raftopoulou v Revenue & Customs Commissioners [2015] UKUT 630 (TCC) 18.123
Rahimian v Allan Janes LLP [2016] EWHC B18 (Costs). 35.54
Rahman v Ary Network Ltd [2016] EWHC 3570 (QB). 16.48
Railways Commissioner v O'Rourke [1896] AC 594 . . . . .52.42, 52.52, 52.79
Rainbow v Kittoe [1916] 1 Ch 313 . . . . 15.96
Rainy Sky SA v Kookmin Bank [2011] UKSC 50; [2011] 1 WLR 2900 . . . . 4.08, 31.06, 31.08, 31.17
Rajvel Construction Ltd v Bestville Properties Ltd [2012] EWCA Civ 587 . . . . .15.78, 15.104, 15.122, 15.129
Rallison v North West London Hospitals NHS Trust [2015] EWCA 3255 (QB) 14.29
Rama Corpn Ltd v Proved Tin and General Investments Ltd [1952] 2 QB 147. . . . . 47.25
Rambus Inc v Hynx Semiconductor UK Ltd [2004] EWHC 2313 (Pat) 7.161
Ramos v Oxford University NHS Trust [2016] EWHC B4 (Costs) 54.204
Ramsey v Hartley [1977] 2 All ER 673; [1977] 1 WLR 686 . . . . 15.33, 33.05
Ramsgate Victoria Hotel Co Ltd v Montefiore (1866) LR 1 Exch 109 . . . . 43.287
Randolph v Tuck [1961] 1 All ER 814. . . . . 23.14
Rasbora Ltd v JCL Marine Ltd [1977] 1 Lloyd's Rep 645 . . . . .32.36, 32.37
Ratcliffe v Eden & Ors (1776) 98 ER 1200 . . . . 1.24
Rattan v UBS AG London Branch [2014] EWHC 665 (Comm) 16.46, 16.57
Rawlinson, decd, In re [2010] EWHC 1789 (Ch). 7.52
Rawlinson v Moss (1861) 30 LJ Ch 797 . . . . 27.83
Rawlinson & Hunter Trustees SA v ITG Ltd & Ors [2015] EWHC 1924 (Ch) 7.85, 7.95, 7.99, 14.12, 14.14, 16.54
Rawnsley v Weatherall Green & Smith North Ltd [2009] EWHC 2482 (Ch) 33.05
Rawson v Samuel (1841) Cr & Ph 161 . . . . 221.05
Ray v Newton [1913] 1 KB 249 . . . . .27.126, 36.24, 40.11
Raybould v Raybould [1968] 1 All ER 608. . . . . 53.98
RBG Resources plc (in liquidation) v Rastogi and ors [2005] EWHC 994 (Ch). 6.128, 7.125, 7.152
RBIL v Ryhurst [2011] EWHC 2209; [2011] BLR 721 . . . . 15.93
RBS Rights Issue Litigation [2016] EWHC 3161 (Ch). 46.24
RBS Rights Issue Litigation, Re [2017] EWHC 463 (Ch) 9.92, 15.56
RBS Rights Issue Litigation (No 2), Re [2017] EWHC 1217 (Ch) 15.55, 15.56, 15.90, 65.42
Read v Dupper (1795) 6 Term Rep 361 . . . . 40.39, 40.116

Read v Edmed [2004] EWHC 3274 (QB) 17.92
Ready-Mixed Concrete (South East) Ltd v Minister of Pensions and National Insurance [1968] 2 QB 497. . . . . 50.122
Reardon Smith v Cayzer Irvine (1929) Com Cas 270 . . . . 23.16
Reaveley v Safeway Stores plc [1998] PNLR 526. . . . . 9.160
Recovery Partners GB Ltd v Rukhadze [2018] EWHC 95 (Comm). 15.38, 15.39, 15.121, 15.122, 15.123
Redbridge London Borough Council v Mustafa [2010] EWHC 1105 (Ch) 9.178
Redbus LMDS Ltd v Jeffrey Green & Russell (a firm) [2006] EWHC 2938 (Ch) 3.43
Redwing Construction Ltd v Wishart [2011] EWHC 19 (TCC) 25.85, 54.123, 54.135, 54.156, 54.170
Reed Executive plc v Reed Business Information Ltd [2004] EWCA Civ 887 . . . . .6.207, 6.210, 6.220, 46.73
Rees v De Bernardy [1896] 2 Ch 437 . . . . 30.16, 30.19
Rees v Gateley Wareing (a firm) & Ors [2014] EWCA Civ 1351. . . . . 29.12, 29.188
Rees v Williams (1875) LR 10 Exch 200. . . . . .27.170
Reeve v Gibson [1891] 1 QB 652 . . . . 1.91, 58.02
Reeves v Butler (1726) Gilb Rep 195 . . . . .1.66, 25.06
Reeves v Sprecher [2007] EWHC 3226 (Ch) 9.92, 15.129, 46.19
Redfern v Corby Borough Council [2014] EWHC 4526 (QB). 12.85
Redfern & Son v Rosenthall Bros (1902) 86 LT 855, CA 40.91
Reflo Ltd (in liquidation) v Varsani [2012] EWHC 3848 (Ch). 9.83
Regent Leisuretime Ltd v Skerrett [2006] EWCA Civ 1032. . . . . 9.199
Rehill v Rider Holdings Ltd [2014] EWCA Civ 42 . . . . .17.161
Reid v Buckinghamshire Healthcare NHS Trust [2015] EWHC B21 (Costs) 48.54
Reid v The Capita Group Plc (unreported) 17 October 2005, Ch D 7.119
Reid v Capita Group plc [2005] EWHC 2448 (Ch) 7.128
Reid v Cupper [1915] 2 KB 147 . . . . 21.06
Reid v Langlois (1849) 1 Mac & G 627 . . . . 46.09
Reid Hewitt & Co v Joseph [1918] AC 717. . . . . 1.102
Reid Minty (a firm) v Taylor [2001] EWCA Civ 1723 . . . . 6.142, 16.15, 16.18, 16.22, 16.24, 16.26, 16.32, 16.33
Reigate v Union Manufacturing Co (Ramsbottom) Ltd [1918] 1 KB 592. . . . . 31.59
Relational LLC v Hodges [2011] EWCA Civ 774. . . . . .15.115
Relfo Ltd v Varsani [2012] EWHC 3848 . . . . 16.48
Remnant, Re (1849) 11 Beav 603 . . . . 35.116, 52.04, 52.08, 52.11
Renewable Power & Light plc v Renewable Power & Light Services Inc [2008] EWHC 3584 (QB) 14.15, 66.32
Republic of Djibouti v Boreh [2016] EWHC 1035 (Comm) 15.91
Research in Motion UK Ltd v Visto Corpn [2008] EWHC 819 (Pat). 56.73
Revenue & Customs Commissioners v Talentcore Ltd (unreported), 19 November 2011, UT (Tax) 4.33, 4.53
Revenue & Customs Commissioners v Xicom Systems Ltd [2008] EWHC 1945 (Ch). 21.34
Reynolds v Llanelly Associated Tinplate Co Ltd [1948] 1 All ER 140, CA 54.163
Reynolds v Meston (unreported), 24 February 1986, QBD 52.37
Reynolds v Stone Rowe Brewer (a firm) [2008] EWHC 497. . . . . .38.62, 38.74
Rezvi v Brown Cooper (a firm) [1997] Costs LR 109 . . . . 35.87, 35.91
RH Tomlinssons (Trowbridge) Ltd v Secretary of State for the Environment, Transport and the Regions [2000] BCC 576. . . . . 12.18
Rhodes v Sugden (1885) 29 Ch D 517 . . . . 40.93
Rhodes v Swithenbank (1889) 22 QBD 577, CA 60.03
Rhodes, Rhodes v Rhodes (1890) 44 Ch D 94 . . . . 60.62
Rhom & Haas Co v Collag Ltd (2002) IPD 25007 . . . . 40.96
Rhone v Stephens [1994] 2 AC 310. . . . . .32.22, 32.24
Richard v The British Broadcasting Corporation [2017] EWHC 1666 (Ch) 12.85
Richard Buxton (a firm) v Mills-Owens [2008] EWHC 1831 (QB); [2010] EWCA Civ 122 . . . . .27.23, 27.70, 27.84

Richard West & Partners (Inverness) Ltd v Dick [1969] 2 Ch 424 . . . . 4.05
Richards, Re [1912] 1 Ch 49. . . . . 36.69, 36.76
Richards v Platel (1841) 10 LJ Ch 375 . . . . 40.82
Richards & Wallington (Plant Hire) Ltd v Monk & Co (1984) Costs LR Core vol 79 . . . . 49.106, 52.17
Richardson v Richardson [1875] P 276 . . . . 1.90
Richardson v Wakefield Council (unreported), 9 June 2017, Wakefield County Court. . . . 17.183, 50.289
Richardson Roofing Co Ltd (Claimant) v Ballast plc (dissolved) (unreported), 13 February 2009, CA (Civ Div) 6.15
Richco International Ltd v Alfred C Toepfer GmbH [1991] 1 Lloyd's Rep 136. . . . . 29.63
Richmond Pharmacology Ltd v Chester Overseas Ltd [2014] EWHC 3418 (Ch). 16.35
Riddell, Public Trustee, Re v Riddell [1936] 2 All ER 1600 . . . . 40.51
Ridehalgh v Horsefield [1994] Ch 205 . . . . 9.10, 9.62, 9.65, 9.95, 9.103, 9.104, 9.110, 9.117, 9.120, 9.125, 9.127, 9.130, 9.131, 9.134, 9.137, 9.138, 9.139, 9.141, 9.143, 9.146, 9.149, 9.150, 9.154, 9.155, 9.157, 9.160, 9.161, 9.164, 9.174, 9.198, 9.209, 9.213, 9.218, 57.45, 57.63
Rigge v Burbidge (1846) 15 M & W 598 . . . . 23.16
Riley v Dibb Lupton Alsop, sub nom A v BCD (a firm) (1997) 147 NLJ 1422 . . . . . 36.33, 36.36, 36.72
Ring Sights Holding Co Ltd & Anor v Lawrence Graham (unreported), 8 October 2001, Ch D 35.60
Riniker v University College London [2001] 1 Costs LR 20. . . . . 45.54, 45.72
Rio Properties Inc v Gibson Dunn & Crutcher [2005] EWCA Civ 534 .17.55
Ritter v Godfrey [1920] 2 KB 47 . . . . 1.100, 6.110, 17.136
Riva Bella SA v Tamsen Yachts GmBH [2011] EWHC 2338 (Comm). 10.05, 10.06
RNB v London Borough of Newham (unreported), 4 August 2017, SCCO 12.162
Roach v Home Office [2009] EWHC 312 (QB). 47.07, 49.147, 49.155
Roache v Newsgroup Newspapers Ltd [1998] EMLR 161 . . . . . . 6.03, 6.58, 6.60, 6.67, 17.109, 45.22
Robbins v Fennell (1847) 11 QB 248 . . . . 22.06
Robert v Momentum Services Ltd [2003] EWCA Civ 299. . . . . .26.52, 43.89, 43.134
Roberts v Gray [1913] 1 KB 520. . . . . 60.19
Robertson v French (1803) 4 East 130 . . . . 31.36
Robertson v Swift ([2014] UKSC 50; [2012] EWCA Civ 1794. . . . . 28.169, 28.183
Robertson Research International Ltd v ABG Exploration BV, The Times, 3 November 1999, QBD (Pat Ct) 9.84, 9.9.91
Robins v Bridge (1837) 3 M & W 114 . . . . 52.49
Robins v Goldingham (1872) LR 13 Eq 440 . . . . 40.60
Robinson, Re (1867) LR 3 Ex 4 . . . . 36.36
Robinson v Price (1886) 2 TLR 242. . . . . 27.320
Roburn Construction Ltd v William Irwin (South) & Co Ltd [1991] BCC 726 . . . . .15.110
Rocco Guiseppe & Figli v Tradex Export SA [1984] 1 WLR 742 . . . . 56.42
Rodger v Normad [1995] SLT 411 . . . . 50.77
Rofa Sport Management AG v DHL International (UK) Ltd [1989] 1 WLR 902. . . . . 7.76
Rogers v Merthyr Tydfil County Borough Council [2006] EWCA Civ 1134. . . . 25.86, 29.96, 45.16, 54.148, 54.152, 54.155, 54.159, 54.164, 54.166, 54.170
Rogers v Wood (1831) 2 B & Ad 245 . . . . 23.15
Rohm Haas Co v Collag Ltd [2002] IPD 25007 . . . . 21.41
Rolf v de Guerin [2011] EWCA Civ 78. . . . . .6.128, 6.169, 6.235
Romer & Haslam, Re [1893] 2 QB 286 . . . . 27.18, 27.59, 27.65, 35.15, 35.27, 35.31, 35.52, 36.24
Rondel v Worsley [1969] 1 AC 191 . . . . 9.154
Ropac Ltd v Inntrepreneur Pub Co (CPC) Ltd [2001] CP Rep 31; [2001] L&TR 10 . . . . 26.16, 43.91
Roper v Auckland Risk Advisors Ltd (unreported), 5 September 2011, QBD. 6.107
Rosario v Nadell Patisserie Ltd [2010] EWHC 1886 (QB) 17.22
Rose v CMS Operations Ltd [2002] EWHC 59 (Ch); [2002] All ER (D) 20 (Jan) 40.81
Rosengrens Ltd v Safe Deposit Centres Ltd [1984] 1 WLR 1334 . . . . .15.121
Rosling King v Rothschild Trust [2002] EWHC 1346 (Ch) 43.323
Ross v Bowbelle (Owners) [1997] 1 WLR 1159 . . . . 43.372, 56.114

Ross v Buxton (1889) 42 Ch D 190 . . . . 40.47, 40.108, 40.110, 40.117, 40.119
Ross v Laughton (1813) 1 Ves & B 349. . . . . 40.71
Ross v Owners of the Bowbelle (Review of Taxation under Ord 62 r 35) (1997) 2 Lloyd's Rep 196 (Note) QBD (Admlty) 49.07, 49.128, 49.129, 65.100
Ross v Stonewood Securities Ltd [2004] EWHC 2235 (Ch). 25.68, 25.70, 45.61, 51.78, 51.84, 51.86, 53.48
Ross v York Newcastle & Berwick Railway Co (1849) 18 LJR 199 . . . . 1.90
Ross River Ltd v Waverly Commercial Ltd [2012] EWHC 3006 (Ch) 16.27, 16.54
Rossiter v Miller (1878) 3 App Cas 1124. . . . . 31.48
Rothery v Munnings (1830) 1 B & Ad 15 . . . . 23.94
Rothewel v Pewer (1431) YB 9 Hen 6 . . . . 30.12
Roult v North West Strategic Health Authority [2010] EWCA Civ 444. . . . . 10.14, 10.27
Roundstone Nurseries Ltd v Stephenson Holdings Ltd [2009] EWHC 1431 (TCC) 6.112, 49.133, 49.149
Rourke v Robinson [1911] 1 Ch 480 . . . . 66.13
Rovi Solutions Corpn v Virgin Media Ltd [2014] EWHC 2449. . . . . 14.21
Rowbury v Official Receiver sub nom Re Mark Forstater (Keystone Law LLP) [2015] EWHC 2951 (Ch) 40.132
Rowe & Maw v Customs and Excise Commissioners [1975] STC 340 . . . . 55.19
Rowles-Davies v Call 24-7 Ltd [2010] EWHC 1695 (Ch) 6.219
Royal Bank of Canada v Secretary of State for Defence [2003] EWHC 1841 (Ch). 6.129
Royal Bank of Scotland v Etridge (No 2) [2002] 2 AC 773. . . . . .32.46, 32.49
Royal Bank of Scotland v Hicks [2012] EWCA Civ 1665. . . . . 15.03, 15.21, 15.113
Royal Bank of Scotland PLC v Highlands Financial Partners LP [2013] EWCA Civ 472. . . . . . 16.48
Royal British Bank v Turquand (1856) 6 E&B 327 . . . . 47.25
Royal Devon & Exeter NHS Foundation Trust v Acres [2013] EWHC 652 (QB) 51,76
Royal Society for the Protection of Birds Friends of the Earth Ltd & Anor v Secretary of State for Justice the Lord Chancellor [2017] EWHC 2309 (Admin). 13.96, 13.98, 13.99
RSA Pursuit Test Cases, Re [2005] EWHC 90003 (Costs) 25.85, 25.88, 54.140
RTZ Pension Property Trust Ltd v ARC Property Developments Ltd [1999] 1 All ER 532 . . . . 7.122, 7.125
Ruddock's Case (1599) 6 Co Rep 25a. 19.25
Rudow v Great Britain Mutual Life Assurance Society (1879) 17 Ch Div 600 . . . . 7.06
Rubin v Cobalt Pictures Ltd & Ors [2010] EWHC 3223 (Ch). 9.31
Rush & Tompkins Ltd v Greater London Council [1989] AC 1280 . . . . 6.207, 6.214, 6.215, 6.217, 40.14
Rushforth v Hadfield (1805) 6 East 519 . . . . 40.37
Russell-Cooke Trust Co v Prentis [2002] EWHC 1435 (Ch) 10.23
Russell Son & Scott, In re [1885] 30 Ch D 114. . . . . 27.113, 27.162, 27.211, 36.36
Russell Young & Co v Brown & Ors [2007] EWCA Civ 43 . . . . 65.59, 65.84
Russian Commercial and Industrial Bank v Comptoir d'Escompte de Mulhouse [1923] 2 KB 630; [1925] AC 112, HL 6.12
Rust v McNaught (1917) 144 LT Jo 76 (on appeal (1918) 144 LT Jo 440, CA) 40.80
Rutter v Sheridan-Young [1958] 1 WLR 444 . . . . 35.124
Ruttle Plant Hire Ltd v DEFRA [2007] EWHC 1633 (QB). 3.18
Ryan v Dolan (1872) 7 Ir (Eq) 92. . . . . .1.111
Ryan v Tretol Group Ltd [2002] All ER (D) 156 . . . . .51.76
Rybak & Ors v Langbar International Ltd [2010] EWHC 2015 (Ch). 43.103
Rybak v Langbar International Ltd [2011] EWHC 451 (Ch) 9.180
Rybak v Langbar International Ltd [2011] EWHC 452 (Ch) 16.40
Ryder v Wombwell (1868) LR 4 Exch 32 . . . . 60.17
Ryder plc v Beever [2012] EWCA Civ 1737 . . . . .43.101, 43.102, 43.104
Rye v The Liquidator of Ashfield Nominees Ltd [2005] EWHC 1189 (Ch) 43.314
RXDA v Northampton Borough Council [2015] EWHC 2936 (QB) .17.124

S (Care Order: Implementation of Care Plan), Re [2002] UKHL 10 . . . . 24.14, 24.17
S v F Co Ltd (1996) SCTO Digest 13. . . . . 51.65

S v M [1998] 3 FCR 665 . . . . . 9.214
St John v Earl of Bessborough (1819) 1 Hog 41 . . . . . 15.96
St John Shipping Corpn v Joseph Rank Ltd [1957] 1 QB 267 . . . . . 27.231, 27.240
Saab v Saudi American Bank [1999] 1 WLR 1861 . . . . . 7.88, 7.94
Saad v Griffin [1908] 2 KB 510, CA 35.87
Sabah Flour and Feed Mills Sdn Bhd v Comfez Ltd [1988] 2 Lloyd's Rep 18 . . . . . 31.36
Sadd v Griffin [1908] 2 KB 510 . . . . . 35.118
Safa Ltd v Banque du Caire [2000] All ER (D) 1010 . . . . . 35.115, 40.10
Safety Explosives Ltd, Re [1904] 1 Ch 226 . . . . . 40.83
Safeway v Twigger [2010] EWCA Civ 1472 . . . . . 6.270, 6.271, 45.29
Sagheera, The [1997] 1 Lloyd's Rep 160 . . . . . 46.16
Saheid v Revenue & Customs Commissioners [2013] UKFTT 38 (TC) 55.26
Sahota v Sohi [2006] EWHC 344 Ch 7.50
Saigol v Thorney Ltd [2014] EWCA Civ 556 . . . . . 17.219
Sainsbury plc v Broadway Malyan [1998] 61 Con LR 31 . . . . . 19.40
Salaman, In re [1894] 2 Ch 201 . . . . . 36.10, 65.109
Salat v Barutis [2013] EWCA Civ 1499 . . . . . 28.165
Salekipour v Parmar [2013] EWCA Civ 1376 . . . . . 43.164
Salt v Corris Developments Ltd [2011] EWHC 3822 (Ch) 16.28, 16.48
Sampla v Rushmoor Borough Council [2008] EWHC 2616 (TCC) 17.176, 17.195
Sampson v John Buddy Timber Ltd, The Independent, 17 May 1995 . . . . . 9.149
Samsung Electronics (UK) Ltd v Apple Inc [2012] EWCA Civ 1430 . . . . . 16.49
Samuel v Swansea City & County Council (unreported), 15 July 2008, Swansea County Court 9.55
Samuel J Cohl Co v Eastern Mediterranean Maritime Ltd ('The Silver Fir') [1980] 1 Lloyd's Rep 371 . . . . . 15.10, 15.69, 15.70
Sandback v Thomas (1816) 1 Stark 306; 171 ER 481 . . . . . 1.74
Sanders v Isaacs [1971] 1 WLR 240 . . . . . 36.34, 36.36
Sanderson v Blyth Theatre Co [1903] 2 KB 533, CA 1.106, 2.09, 7.05, 7.10, 7.11, 7.17
Sandiford (No 2), re [1935] Ch 681 . . . . . 53.04
Sandvik Intellectual Property AB v Kennametal UK Ltd [2012] EWHC 245 (Pat) 54.203
Saner v Bilton (1879) 11 Ch D 416 . . . . . 20.57
Sanguineti v Stuckey's Banking Co (No 2) [1896] 1 Ch 502 . . . . . 23.45
Sarah C Getty Trust, Re Getty v Getty [1985] 3 WLR 302 . . . . . 46.09
Sargeant (by her mother and litigation friend, Kearns) v Fellows (unreported), 12 October 2012, Dudley County Court 50.91
SARPD Oil International Ltd v Addax Energy SA [2016] EWCA Civ 120 . . . . . 12.84, 12.145, 15.35, 15.36, 15.116, 15.117
Sarwar v Alam [2001] EWCA Civ 1401 . . . . . 29.84, 34.19, 34.20, 54.198, 54.199, 54.200, 54.201
Satellite (2003) Ltd (unreported), Re 17 November 2003, Ch D 16.57
Saunderson v Glass (1742) 2 Atk 296 . . . . . 1.83, 27.111
Savile, In the matter of the Administration of the Estate of Jimmy [2014] EWHC 1683 (Ch) 16.57, 66.52
Savings Advice Ltd v EDF Energy Customers Ltd [2017] EWHC B1 (Costs) 48.45
Savings & Investment Bank Ltd v Fincken [2003] EWCA Civ 1630 . . . . . 26.41
Saxon v Bayliss (unreported), 20 March 2013, Ch D 9.73
Sayer v Wagstaff (1844) 14 LJ Ch 116 . . . . . 36.24
Sayers v Clarke-Walker [2002] EWCA Civ 645 . . . . . 26.20, 43.89
Sayers v Merck SmithKline Beecham plc; X v Schering Healthcare Ltd; Afrika v Cape plc [2001] EWCA Civ 2017 . . . . . 20.37, 65.12, 65.64, 65.72, 65.73, 65.85, 65.88
Saville Bros Ltd v Langman (1898) 79 LT 44, CA 30.15
Savoye and Savoye Ltd v Spicers Ltd [2015] EWHC 33 (TCC) . . . 25.33, 25.73, 25.92, 25.96, 25.100
Scammell v Dicker [2001] 1 WLR 631 . . . . . 17.195
Scarf v Jardine (1882) 7 App Cas 345 . . . . . 32.20, 32.36
Scarfe v Morgan (1838) 4 M & W 270 . . . . . 40.43
Scarth v Rutland (1866) LR 1 CP 642 . . . . . 27.112
SCF Finance Co Ltd v Masri (No 3) [1987] QB 1028, CA 23.15

Scrace v Whittington (1823) 2 B & C 11 . . . . 22.06
Scheider v Door2Door PTS Ltd [2011] EWHC 90210 (Costs). 50.75, 50.76
Scherer & Anor v Counting Instruments Ltd [1986] 2 All ER 529. . . . . 6.03, 6.19, 6.267, 6.268
Schlumberger Holdings Ltd v Electromagnetic Geoservices AS [2009] EWHC 773 (Pat). 18.14, 56.40, 56.42, 56.45
Schmitt v Depuy International Ltd [2016] EWHC 638 (QB) 65.16
Schneider v Norris (1814) 2 M&S 286 . . . . 35.80
Scholes Windows v Magnet (No 2) [2000] ECDR 266 . . . . 6.44
Scholey v Peck [1893] 1 Ch 709 . . . . 40.96
Schoole v Noble, Lett, and Byrne (1788) 126 ER 15 . . . . 1.72
Schroder v Clough (1877) 35 LT 850 . . . . 56.23, 56.24
Schumann v Veale Wasbrough [2013] EWHC 4070 (QB) 56.63
Scott v Bradley [1971] Ch 850 . . . . 31.50
Scott v Conwy County Borough Council as Conwy Harbour Authority (unreported), 16 February 2018, QBD (Admlty) 15.49
Scott v Duncan [2012] EWHC 1792 (QB). 54.123
Scott v Fenning (1845) 15 LJ Ch 88 . . . . 27.83
Scott v National Society for Prevention of Cruelty to Children and Parr (1909) 25 TLR 789 . . . 30.36
Scott v Transport for London (unreported), 23 December 2009, Hastings County Court. 27.32, 27.33, 27.36
Scottish Metropolitan Assurance Co v P Samuel & Co [1923] 1 KB 348 . . . . 40.37
Scougall v Campbell (1826) 3 Russ 545 . . . . 1.82, 27.112
SCT Finance v Bolton [2002] EWCA Civ 56. . . . . 6.31, 6.81, 7.26, 25.102, 45.18
Seabrook v British Transport Commission [1959] 1 WLR 509. . . . . 46.22
Seaga v Harper [2009] UKPC 26 (Jamaica). 54.11
Seal, ex p Crickett (1893) 37 Sol Jo 842, CA. 35.117, 52.08, 53.08
Sears Tooth (a firm) v Payne Hick Beach (a firm) & Ors [1997] 2 FLR 116. . . . . 30.47
Seavision Investment SA v Norman Thomas Evennett, The Tiburon [1992] 2 Lloyd's Rep 26. . . . 3.38, 52.98, 56.119
SEB Trygg Liv Holding Aktiebolag v Manches [2005] EWCA Civ 1237 . . . . 9.65, 9.66
Secretary of State for Business, Innovation and Skills v PLT Anti-Marketing Ltd [2015] EWCA Civ 76 . . . . 28.109, 28.110
Secretary of State for Communities and Local Government v Venn [2014] EWCA Civ 1539 . . . . 13.81
Secretary of State for Home Department v Rehman [2001] UKHL 47. . . . . 24.31
Secretary of State for Trade and Industry v Aurum Marketing [2000] EWCA Civ 224 . . . . 16.31
Secretary of State for Trade and Industry v Backhouse [2001] EWCA Civ 67 . . . . 9.28
Secretary of State for Trade and Industry v Gee (2006) BCC 384 . . . . 16.52
Secretary of State for Trade and Industry v Lewis [2001] 2 BCLC 597 . . . . 45.16
Seear v Lawson [1880] 15 Ch D 426. . . . . 33.05
Seechurn v Ace Insurance Sa-Nv [2002] EWCA Civ 67. . . . . 23.134
Seeff v Ho [2011] EWCA Civ 186 . . . . 6.129
Seeff v Ho [2011] EWCA Civ 401 . . . . 17.70
Seele Austria GmbH Co v Tokio Marine Europe Insurance Ltd [2009] EWHC 255 (TCC). 23.33, 23.35
Segbedzi v Glah (1989) New LJ 1303, CA 40.48
Select Car Rentals (North West) Ltd v Esure Services Ltd [2017] EWHC 1434 (QB) 8.49, 8.50, 8.51, 9.73
Self v Self [1954] 2 All ER 550 . . . . 53.98, 53.101
Sellers v Buyer [2014] EWHC 596 (Ch). 6.194
Semler v Murphy [1968] 1 Ch 183; [1967] 2 All ER 185 . . . . 15.03, 15.44
Sempra Metals Ltd (formerly Metallgesellschaft Ltd) v Inland Revenue Commissioners & Anor [2007] UKHL 34 . . . . 56.124, 56.127
Seray-Wurie v London Borough of Hackney [2002] EWCA Civ 909. . . . . 43.159, 43.160, 43.163
Serious Organised Crime Agency v Agidi [2011] EWCA Civ 1350. . . . . 15.121, 16.55
Serpes v Revenue & Customs Commissioners (unreported), 22 December 2008. . . . . 59.02
Service v Flateau (1900) 16 WN (NSW) 248 . . . . 6.13

SES Contracting Ltd v UK Coal plc [2007] EWCA Civ 791 . . . . 7.42, 7.43, 7.45
Seymour v Seymour (1989) The Times, 16 February 32.70
SG v Hewitt [2012] EWCA Civ 1053. . . . 17.20, 17.122, 17.126, 17.129, 17.132, 17.142, 17.161, 17.180
Shackleton & Associates Ltd v Shamsi [2017] EWHC 304 (Comm) 16.39
Shah v Breed [2013] EWHC 232 (QB). 43.341, 49.88
Shah v Elliot [2011] EW Misc 8 . . . . 17.39
Shalaby v London North West Healthcare NHS Trust [2018] EWCA Civ 1323 . . . . 17.99
Shalson v DF Keane Ltd [2003] EWHC 599 (Ch) 40.121
Shania Investment Corpn v Standard Bank London Ltd (unreported), 2 November 2001 . . . . . 16.38
Sharif v The Law Society [2005] EWHC 90018 (Costs) 36.36, 36.37
Shark AG (a company incorporated in Austria) v Monster Energy Co (unreported),
6 September 2013, Ch D (Patents Court) 15.92
Sharland v Sharland [2015] UKSC 60 . . . . 10.16
Sharma & Anor v Hunters [2011] EWHC 2546 (COP) 9.116, 9.136, 9.207
Sharp v Blank [2015] EWHC 2685 (Ch) 12.80, 12.100, 12.120
Sharp v Leeds City Council [2017] EWCA 33 . . . . 50.271
Sharp v Southern [1905] VLR 223 . . . . 3.06
Sharpe, In the Matter of an application of Timothy (unreported), 20 November
1995, QBD 59.39, 59.43
Sharratt v London Bus Co Ltd (The Accident Group Test Cases) [2003] EWCA 718 . . . . 3.87
Sharratt v London Central Bus Co (No 2) [2004] EWCA Civ 575. . . . . 45.42, 54.129, 54.146,
54.163, 54.164, 54.167, 54.172, 54.174
Sharp v Blank [2017] EWHC 141 (Ch) 12.45
Shaw v Groom [1970] 2 QB 504. . . . . 27.241
Shaw v Medtronic Corevalve LLC & Ors [2017] EWHC 1397 (QB) 8.11, 8.30, 8.31, 8.52, 8.53, 8.55
Shaw v Merthyr Tydfil County Borough [2014] EWCA Civ 1678 . . . . 17.22, 17.61,
17.69, 17.73, 17.75, 17.76
Shaw v Neale (1858) 6 HL Cas 581 . . . . 40.38, 40.58
Shaw-Lloyd v ASM Shipping [2006] EWHC 1958 (QB) 15.70
Shepard v Hughes (unreported), 28 January 2015, Mold County Court. 43.277
Shepherd v Robinson [1919] 1 KB 474, CA 10.27
Shepherds Investments Ltd v Walters [2007] EWCA Civ 29 . . . . 6.194
Sherlock Holmes International Society Ltd, Re [2016] EWHC 1392 (Ch). 9.64, 9.68
Sherman v Perkins [2002] WTLR 603. . . . . 9.211
Sherred v Carpenter (unreported), 5 March 2009, Taunton County Court 50.86
Shiloh Spinners Ltd v Harding [1973] AC 691 and Harrison v Tew [1989] QB 307, HL. 5.28
Shirlaw v Southern Foundries (1926) Ltd [1939] 2 KB 206 . . . . 31.59
Shirley v Caswell [2001] 1 Costs LR 1 . . . . 6.196, 6.198, 6.199, 6.201, 57.29
Shlaimoun & Anor v Mining Technologies International Inc [2012] EWCA
Civ 772 . . . . 15.03, 15.21, 15.98
Shoe Machinery Co v Cutlan [1896] 1 Ch 667. . . . . 23.25
Shore v Sedgewick Financial Services Ltd [2007] EWHC 3054 (QB) 6.185
Short v Ridge (1876) WN 47 . . . . 7.31
Shovelar v Lane [2011] EWCA Civ 802 . . . . 6.212, 6.240, 6.254, 7.61, 14.36, 17.25, 17.122,
17.123, 17.131, 17.140
Shrapnel v Laing (1888) 20 QBD 334 . . . . 20.57
Shuttleworth & Co v Commissioners of Customs and Excise (LON/94/986A) 55.19
Sibley & Co v Reachbyte Ltd [2008] EWHC 2665 (Ch) . . . 27.96, 45.26, 52.28, 53.42, 53.79, 53.106
Sibthorpe v Southwark BL [2011] 1 WLR 2111 . . . . 9.49
Sidhu v Sandhu [2008] EWHC 90108 (Costs). 2.09, 29.02
Sidhu v Sandhu (unreported), 5 May 2009, QBD 29.63
Siegel v Pummell [2015] EWHC 195 (QB) 16.19, 16.49, 16.60
Silver Valley Mines (Winding Up), Re (1882) LR 21 Ch D 381, CA. 9.31
Simaan General Contracting Co v Pilkington Glass Ltd [1987] 1 All ER 345, CA. 15.128
Simcoe v Jacuzzi UK Group Plc [2012] EWCA Civ 137. . . . . 56.10, 56.16, 56.22, 56.26, 56.30,
56.31, 56.65, 56.85

Simmonds v Great Eastern Rly Co (1868) 3 Ch App 797 . . . . 40.71
Simmons & Politzer, In re [1954] 2 QB 296 . . . . 27.169, 27.178, 39.11, 40.32
Simmons v Castle [2012] EWCA Civ 1039 . . . . .32.57, 54.195, 54.204
Simmons & Simmons LLP v Hickox [2013] EWHC 2141 (QB) 16.19, 16.39, 16.40, 16.57
Simms v Law Society [2005] EWCA Civ 849. . . . . 16.54, 25.48
Simpkin v The Berkeley Group Holdings plc [2016] EWHC 1619 (QB) 12.82
Simpkin Marshall Ltd, Re [1959] Ch 229. . . . . .2.09, 3.26, 3.28, 3.29
SimplySure Ltd & Anor v Personal Touch Financial Services Ltd [2016] EWCA Civ 461 . . . . . 31.22
Simpson v British Industries Trust Ltd (1923) 39 TLR 286 . . . . 3.43
Simpson v MGN Ltd [2015] EWHC 126 (QB) 6.114, 44.31
Simpson (as assignee of Catchpole) v Norfolk & Norwich University Hospital NHS Trust [2011] EWCA Civ 1149 . . . . .30.08, 30.10, 30.22, 30.38
Simpsons Motor Sales (London) v Hendon Borough Council [1965] 1 WLR 112 . . . . . 53.52, 53.87, 53.92
Sinclair v Great Eastern Railway Co (1870) 21 LT 752. . . . . 53.31
Sinclair-Jones v Kay [1988] 2 All ER 611; [1989] 1 WLR 114 CA 9.95, 9.102
Singapore Airlines Ltd & Anor v Buck Consultants Ltd [2011] EWCA Civ 1542. . . . . 66.47
Singh v Aja (unreported), 27 September 2016, Bristol County Court. 50.167, 50.270
Singh v Aqua Descaling Ltd (unreported), 12 June 2008, Walsall County Court. 50.397
Singh v Bhasin [2000] WTLR 275. . . . . 66.61
Singh v Observer Ltd [1989] 3 All ER 777 . . . . 18.85, 27.224
Singh v Singh [2014] EWHC 1770 (Ch) 16.39
Sinochem v Mobil [2000] 1 All ER (Comm) 474 . . . . 31.39
Sir Lindsay Parkinson & Co Ltd v Triplan Ltd [1973] QB 609. . . . . . 15.57, 15.58, 15.63, 15.79, 15.96
Sisu Capital Fund Ltd & Ors v Tucker [2005] EWHC 2321 (Ch) 49.106, 49.110, 59.27
Sitapuria v Khan (unreported), 10 December 2007, Liverpool County Court 50.109
Skinner, Cooper v Skinner [1904] 1 Ch 289. . . . . 66.45
Skuse v Granada Television Ltd [1994] 1 WLR 1156 . . . . 23.42, 46.75, 49.05
Skylight Maritime SA v Ascot Underwriting Ltd & Ors [2005] EWHC 15 (Comm) 9.70
Skyscape Cloud Services Ltd v Sky plc [2016] EWHC 1340 (IPEC) 50.332, 50.334
Skywell (UK) Ltd v Revenue & Customs Commissioners [2012] UKFTT 611 (TC). 30.38
Slack & Partners Ltd v Slack [2010] EWCA Civ 204 . . . . 45.63
Slade & Company Solicitors v Boodia [2017] EWHC 2699 (QB) 35.49, 35.117, 36.15
Slater Ellison v Law Society [2002] All ER (D) 335 (Feb). 7.163
Slator v Brady (1863) 14 ICLR 61 . . . . 60.19
Slatter v Ronaldsons [2002] 2 Costs LR 267. . . . . 18.84, 27.90, 38.80, 40.69, 40.72, 40.84
Slaughter v Talbott (1739) Willes 190. . . . . 60.06
Slazengers Ltd v Seaspeed Ferries International Ltd [1987] 3 All ER 967, CA. 15.33, 15.71
Slick Seating Systems v Adams [2013] EWHC 1642 (QB) 16.54
Slingsby v Attorney-General [1918] P 236 . . . . .35.64, 52.98
Sloggett and Perry v Stroud [2000] Lexis Citation 2052, CA 32.68
Slot v Isaac [2002] EWCA Civ 481. . . . . 45.50
Smails v McNally [2012] EWHC 3793 (Ch) 16.49, 16.57
Smales v Lea [2011] EWCA Civ 1325. . . . . 27.22
Small v Cohen, The Times, 7 September 1992, CA 7.97
Smart v East Cheshire NHS Trust [2003] EWHC 2806 .13.17, 13.22, 13.26
Smart Currency Exchange v Martell [2014] EWHC 1507 (QB). 16.39
Smart-Tel (UK) plc, In the matter of sub nom OR v Doshi [2007] BCC 896. . . . . . . 7.122, 7.125, 7.152
Smith, Re (1841) 4 Beav 309 . . . . 27.69
Smith, Re (1861) 9 WR 396 . . . . 27.83
Smith v Barker (1864) 2 H & M 498 . . . . 26.11
Smith v Betty [1903] 2 KB 317, CA 23.96
Smith v Buller (1875) LR 19 Eq 473. . . . . 49.122, 52.35
Smith v Croft [1986] 1 WLR 580, CA 65.124
Smith v Daniel (1874) 18 LR Eq 649 . . . . 46.21
Smith v Edwardes (1888) 22 QBD 103 . . . . .36.05, 36.51
Smith v Howes [1922] 1 KB 592 . . . . .35.118

Smith v Interlink Express Parcels Ltd [2007] EWHC 90095 (Costs). . . . 34.20, 54.143, 54.149, 54.152
Smith v Royce Properties Ltd [2001] EWCA 949. . . . . 31.36
Smith v Smith [1906] VLR 78 . . . . 1.111
Smith v Trafford Housing Trust [2012] EWHC 3320 . . . . 17.121, 17.130
Smith v UIC Insurance Co Ltd [2001] BCC 11 . . . . 15.36
Smith Graham v Lord Chancellor's Department [1999] 2 Costs LR 1 . . . . 22.11, 52.06, 52.98
Smiths Dock Ltd v Edwards [2004] EWHC 116 (QB). 54.93
Smith's Mortgage, In re (1931) 2 Ch 168 . . . . 66.25
Smith's Trusts (1890) 25 LR Ir 439 . . . . 60.14
Smolen v Solon Co-operative Housing Services Ltd [2005] EWCA Civ 1567. . . . . 43.159
Smout v Ilbery (1842) 10 M & W 1 . . . . 27.78
Snook v London & West Riding Investments Ltd [1967] 2 QB 786 . . . . 27.217
Snowden v Ministry of Defence [2001] EWCA Civ 1524. . . . . 36.104
Soames v Spencer (1822) 1 Dow & Ry KB 32. . . . . 47.29
Societa Finanziaria Industrie Turistiche SpA v Manfredi Lefebvre D'Ovidio De Clunieres Di Balsorano & Anor [2006] EWHC 90068 (Costs). 52.98
Société Anonyme Pêcheries Ostendaises v Merchants Marine Insurance Co [1928] 1 KB 750. . . . 49.07, 49.125, 49.147, 49.153
Société Générale, London Branch v Geys [2012] UKSC 63 . . . . 27.72, 31.58, 31.62
Société Générale SA v Saad Trading, Contracting & Financial Services Co [2012] EWCA Civ 695 . . . . 15.12, 15.72, 15.87
Société Internationale de Téléommunications Aéronautiques SC v Wyatt Co (UK) Ltd [2002] EWHC 2401 (Ch) 6.121
Software Solutions Ltd v C Brewer & Sons Ltd [2003] EWCA Civ 939 . . . . 7.143, 7.144
Solicitor, ex p Incorporated Law Society, Re a (1894) 63 LJQB 397, DC. 53.12
Solicitor, ex p Law Society, A [1912] 1 KB 302 . . . . 29.205
Solicitor, In re a [1955] 2 QB 252 . . . . 1.128, 3.27
Solicitor, In re a [1956] 1 QB 157 . . . . 27.121, 27.211, 29.190, 39.14
Solicitor, In re a; In re Taxation of Costs [1947] Ch 274 . . . . 35.124
Solicitor, In re; In re a Taxation of Costs [1953] Ch 480 . . . . 35.123
Solicitor, Re A (1909) 54 Sol Jo 67 . . . . 35.120
Solicitor, Re A [1952] Ch 328. . . . . 40.55
Solicitor, Re A [1955] 2 All ER 283. . . . . 35.58
Solicitor, Re A [1956] 3 All ER 305 . . . . 1.83
Solicitor, Re a [1961] Ch 491 . . . . 36.36
Solicitor, Re A (unreported), 10 October 1994, QBD. 35.60
Solicitor, Re a: In re a Taxation of Costs [1955] 2 QB 252. . . . . 35.57
Solicitor (No 2), Re a [1956] 1 QB 155 . . . . 27.112, 27.211
Solicitor (wasted costs order) [1993] 2 FLR 959 . . . . 9.175
Solicitors, Re (1934) 50 TLR 327. . . . . 36.36
Solicitors, Re [1982] 2 All ER 683 . . . . 57.46
Solicitors, Re Firm of, ex p D'Aragon (1887) 3 TLR 815. . . . . 35.84, 36.20
Solicitors Indemnity Fund Ltd v Hewitson & Harker [2010] EWCA Civ 147 . . . . 35.86, 36.46
Solley v Wood (1852) 16 Beav 370 . . . . 22.06, 27.37
Solly v Forbes (1820) 2 Brod & Bing 38 . . . . 31.25
Solo Industries v Canara Bank [2001] All ER (D) 34 (Jul) 40.10
Solomon v Cromwell Group Plc (unreported) 2 August 2010, Manchester County Court. 17.27
Solomon v Cromwell Group Plc [2011] EWCA Civ 1584. . . . . 7.109, 7.173, 11.14, 50.70
Somatra Ltd v Sinclair Roche & Temperley [2002] EWHC 1627 (Comm) 16.49
Somerset-Leeke & Anor v Kay Trustees [2003] EWHC 1243 (Ch) 15.73, 15.127
Somes v British Empire Shipping Co (1860) 8 HL Cas 338 . . . . 40.43
Sonmez v Kebabery Wholesale Ltd [2009] EWCA Civ 1386 . . . . 6.86, 6.190, 7.37
Sony/ATV Music Publishing LLC v WPMC Ltd (in liquidation) [2017] EWHC 465 (Ch) 17.81, 43.346
Sony Communications International AB v SSH Communications Security Corporation [2016] EWHC 2985 (Pat) 12.150, 12.158, 12.160, 12.164, 44.11, 44.18

Sorsbie v Park (1843) 12 M & W 146 . . . 19.16
Sousa v Waltham Forest LBC [2011] EWCA Civ 194. . . 5.04, 18.76, 24.49, 24.50, 24.51
South Durham Iron Co, Smith's Case, Re (1879) 11 Ch D 579, CA. . . 4.06
South Coast Shipping Co Ltd v Havant Borough Council [2002] 3 All ER 779. . . 46.43, 46.52, 46.54, 46.56, 46.57
Southbourne Sheet Metal Co Ltd [1993] 1 WLR 244 . . . 61.08, 61.09
Southern Counties Fresh Foods v RWM Purchasers Ltd [2011] EWHC 1370 (Ch) . . . 6.65
Southern Counties Fresh Foods Ltd, Cobden Investments Ltd, Re v Romford Wholesale Meats Ltd [2011] EWHC 1370 (Ch) . . . 56.64, 56.80
Southern & District Finance Plc v Turner [2003] EWCA Civ 1574 . . . 25.13
Southern Livestock Producers Ltd [1963] 3 All ER 801 . . . 40.37, 40.50
Southwark LBC v IBM UK Ltd (Costs) [2011] EWHC 653 (TCC) . . . 16.35, 16.36
Southwark Water Co v Quick (1878) 3 QBD 315. . . 46.20
Southway Ltd v Wolff [1991] 57 BLR 33. . . 32.25, 32.26
SP Bass v Hickford (1738) 95 ER 441 . . . 1.46
Sparrow v Johns (1838) 3 M & W 600, 150 ER 1284 . . . 35.126
Spath Holmes Ltd v Chairman of the Greater Manchester and Lancashire Rent Assessment Committee [1998] 1 Costs LR 40 . . . 53.14, 53.15, 53.75
Spears v Hartly (1800) 3 Esp 81 . . . 23.98
Speciality Produce Ltd v Secretary of State for Environment, Food & Rural Affairs [2014] EWCA Civ 225 . . . 7.147, 7.168
Specsavers International Healthcare Ltd v Asda Stores Ltd (Costs) [2012] EWCA Civ 494 . . . 17.109
Spectrum Plus Ltd (In liquidation) [2005] 2 AC 680 . . . 4.06
Spencer v Fielder [2014] EWHC 2768 (Ch). . . 66.66
Spencer v Hemmerde [1922] 2 AC 507. . . 23.127
Spencer v Wood [2004] EWCA Civ 352 . . . 29.63, 29.108
Sperling, In re (1863) 3 Sw & Tr 272 . . . 35.80
Spier v Barnard (1863) 8 LT 396 . . . 35.86
Spiers v English [1907] P 122. . . 7.56, 7.58
Springer v University of Leicester NHS Trust [2018] EWCA Civ 436 . . . 54.109, 54.112, 54.123
Spy Academy Ltd v Sahar International Inc [2009] EWCA Civ 481. . . 15.88
Spyre v Porter (1856) 7 E & B 58 . . . 30.45
Square Mile Partnership Ltd v Fitzmaurice McCall Ltd [2006] EWHC 236 (Ch) . . . 6.68, 7.37
Squirrel v Squirrel (1792) 2 Dick 765 . . . 15.96
Stabilad Ltd v Stephens & Carter Ltd [1999] 1 WLR 1201. . . 15.11
Stables v York City Council (unreported), 13 October 2008, Leeds County Court . . . 46.17, 46.76
Stagecoach Group plc v Wilson (unreported), 21 December 2016, Manchester County Court . . . 50.78
Standard Chartered Bank v Ceylon Petroleum Corpn [2011] EWHC 2094 (Comm) . . . 56.39, 56.46
Staniar v Evans, Evans v Staniar (1886) 34 Ch D 470. . . 27.323
Stanley v Jones (1831) 7 Bing 369. . . 30.45
Starbucks Ltd v British Sky Broadcasting Group plc [2012] EWHC 4085 (Ch) . . . 14.21
Starkey v Railway Executive [1951] 2 All ER 902 . . . 18.72
Starlight Shipping Co v Allianz Marine & Aviation Versicherungs AG [2014] EWCA Civ 1010. . . 3.38, 52.98
Starsin, The [2004] 1 AC 715, HL . . . 31.22
Starving v Cousins (1835) 1 Gale 159. . . 27.313
Static Control Components (Europe) Ltd v Egan [2004] EWCA Civ 392 . . . 31.47
Steadman v Hockley (1846) 15 M & W 553. . . 40.38
Stedman v Collett (1854) 17 Beav 608 . . . 1.83, 39.12
Steeden v Walden [1910] 2 Ch 393 . . . 60.06
Steel & Morris v UK [2005] EMLR 15. . . 24.36
Steele Ford & Newton v Crown Prosecution Service [1994] 1 AC 22 . . . 64.04
Stein v Blake [1996] AC 243. . . 21.05
Stein v Blake (2000) 97(43) LSG 38. . . 46.16
Steinberg v Scala (Leeds) Ltd [1923] 2 Ch 452, CA . . . 60.15
Stena Rederi Aktiebolag [2003] EWCA Civ 214 . . . 6.162, 6.183

Stephens v Lord Newborough (1848) 11 Beav 403 . . . . 53.65
Sterling, Ex p (1809) 16 Ves 258. . . . . 40.53, 40.54
Sterling Publications Ltd v Burroughs [2000] 2 Costs LR 155 . . . . 45.26
Stevens v Bell (Costs) [2001] OPLR 123. . . . . 66.66
Stevensdrake Ltd v Hunt [2016] EWHC 342 (Ch) 27.198, 31.13, 31.63, 31.65, 31.66, 32.48
Stevenson v Yorke (1790) 4 TR 10 . . . . 1.58, 17.07
Stocker v Stocker [2015] EWHC 1634 (QB) 12.95
Stockinger v Highdorn Co Ltd [2001] All ER (D) 62 (Apr) (QBD) 49.109, 59.16, 59.23
Stocznia Gdanska SA v Latvian Shipping Co [2001] BCC 174; The Times, 8 May 2001 . . . . . . 6.162, 30.34, 33.11
Stogdon, In re (1887) 56 LJ (Ch) 420 . . . . 36.19, 36.22
Stogdon, ex p Baker, Re (1887) 51 JP 565. . . . . 39.11
Stokes Pension Fund Trustees v Western Power Distribution (South West) Plc [2005] EWCA Civ 854 . . . . 6.225, 17.14, 17.18, 17.216
Stokors SA & Ors v Ig Markets Ltd [2012] EWCA Civ 1706 . . . . 15.90
Stokors SA & Ors v Ig Markets Ltd [2012] EWHC 1684 (Comm). 15.103
Stone v Hitch [2001] EWCA Civ 63. . . . . 27.220
Stone Rowe Brewer LLP v Just Costs Ltd [2015] EWCA Civ 1168 . . . . 36.33, 36.37, 36.65, 36.72, 36.73, 36.74, 36.75, 36.76
Storer v British Gas plc [2000] 2 All ER 440 . . . . 45.16
Storer & Co v Johnson (1890) 15 App Cas 203, HL. 39.04
Strachey v Ramage [2008] EWCA Civ 804 . . . . 6.128
Straker v Tudor Rose (a firm) [2007] EWCA 368. . . . . 6.20, 6.141, 6.212, 6.240, 7.152, 17.102, 17.103, 45.21, 50.99
Stratford-on-Avon District Borough Council v Clarke [2015] EWHC 1539 (Ch) 49.160
Street, Re (1870) LR 10 Eq 165 . . . . 36.15, 36.19, 36.25
Streetmap.EU Ltd v Google Inc (unreported), 24 May 2016 . . . . 14.17
Stretchline Intellectual Property Ltd v H&M Hennes & Mauritz (UK) Ltd [2016] EWHC 163 (Pat). 6.173
Stringer v Copley (unreported), 17 May 2002, Kingston on Thames County Court 22.12, 52.65, 52.67
Stuart, ex p Cathcart, In Re [1893] 2 QB 201 . . . . 27.134, 27.169, 27.175
Stuart, Johnson v Williams, Re [1940] 4 All ER 80 . . . . 66.42
Stubblefield v Kemp [2001] 1 Costs LR 30. . . . . 18.107, 51.80, 59.20
Stubbs v Board of Governors of the Royal National Orthopaedic Hospital [1997] Costs LR (Core Vol) 117, QBD 51.29
Stumm v Dixon & Co & Knight (1889) 22 QBD 529 . . . . 6.257, 19.13
Sturmey Motors Ltd, Rattray v Sturmey Motors Ltd [1913] 1 Ch 16 . . . . 21.29
Sudarshan Chemical Industries Ltd v Clariant Produkte (Deutschland) GMBH [2012] EWHC 2941 (Pat). 16.60
Suffield v Watts, ex parte Brown (1888) 20 QBD 693. . . . . 10.27
Sugar Hut Group Ltd v AJ Insurance Service (a partnership) [2016] EWCA Civ 46 . . . . 6.73, 6.179, 6.243
Suisse Security Bank & Trust Ltd v Julian Francis [2006] UKPC 41 . . . . 9.31
Sullivan v Co-operative Insurance Society Ltd [1999] 2 Costs LR 51.63, 51.68, 51.69, 51.70,
Sullivan v Pearson, ex p Morrison (1868) LR 4 QB 153 . . . . 40.42, 40.58
Sullivan v Rollingsons Solicitors (unreported), 21 March 2014, Liverpool County Court 43.169
Summers v Bundy [2016] EWCA Civ 126. . . . . 54.204
Summers v Fairclough Homes Ltd [2012] UKSC 26 . . . . 17.133, 40.29
Summit Navigation Ltd v Generali Romania Asigurare Reasigurare Sa (2) Ardaf Sa Insurance & Reinsurance Co [2014] EWHC 398 (Comm) 15.109
Summit Property Ltd v Pitmans [2002] EWCA Civ 2020 . . . . 6.67, 6.162, 6.172, 6.180, 6.192
Sumpter v Hedges [1898] 1 QB 673, CA 27.08, 27.25
Sunnucks v Smith [1950] 1 All ER 550. . . . . 53.96
Super Group Plc v Just Enough [2014] EWHC 3260 (Comm). 17.189
Supperstone v Hurst [2008] EWHC 735 (Ch) 54.123

Surrey v Barnet & Chase Farm Hospitals NHS Trust & Ors [2018] EWCA Civ 451 . . . . 54.194, 54.195, 54.196, 54.204
Sutherland v Turnbull [2010] EWHC 2699 (QB) 6.205, 17.186
Sutradhar v Natural Environment Research Council [2006] 4 All ER 490 . . . . 26.34
Sutton, Ex p (1805) 11 Ves 163. . . . . 40.131
Sutton & Elliot, In re (1883) 11 QBD 337 . . . . .35.84, 36.20
Sutton v Selwyns Travel (unreported), 8 August 2008, Birkenhead County Court (Regional Costs) 52.72, 55.30
Sutton v Sears [1959] 3 All ER 545. . . . . 39.04
Swain v Hillman [2001] All ER 91 . . . . 45.50
Swain v The Law Society [1983] 1 AC 598; [1982] 2 All ER 827 . . . . 4.15, 4.23, 4.25, 27.255
Swain-Mason & Others v Mills & Reeve LLP [2011] EWCA Civ 14 . . . . 26.41
Swale Borough Council v Boulter [2002] All ER (D) 378 (Oct) 61.14
Swedac Ltd v Magnet and Southern plc [1989] FSR 243 QBD 9.159
Sweetman v Nathan [2003] EWCA Civ 1115. . . . . 23.31
Swift & Co v Board of Trade [1926] 2 KB 131 . . . . 61.03
SwissMarine Corpn Ltd v O W Supply & Trading A/S [2015] EWHC 1571 (Comm) 31.32
Sycamore Bidco Ltd v Breslin [2013] EWHC 583 (Ch) 17.94, 56.33, 56.69, 56.72, 56.73, 56.76
Sykes v Wright (unreported), 13 February 2017, EAT 9.115
Symbol Park Lane Ltd v Steggles Palmer [1985] 1 WLR 668, CA. 5.28
Symphony Group plc v Hodgson [1994] QB 179 . . . . 9.11, 9.14, 9.20, 9.62, 9.79, 9.81
Syngenta Ltd v Chemsource Ltd [2012] EWHC 1507 (Pat) 13.18
Systemcare (UK) Ltd v Services Design Technology Ltd [2011] EWCA Civ 546 . . . . . 9.05, 9.07, 9.15
Szekeres v Alan Smeath & Co [2005] EWHC 1733 (Ch) 36.30, 36.40
Szfranski v Twyfords Ltd (unreported), 2 October 2008, Stoke-on-Trent County Court 54.126

T v Cardiff City and County Council [2007] EWHC 2568 (Admin) 67.13
T (formerly H) v Nugent Care Society (formerly Catholic Social Services) [2004] EWCA Civ 51 . . . . 65.36
Tabram v Horne (1827) 1 Man & Ry 228. . . . . 1.83, 27.112
Tag World Services Ltd, In the matter of [2008] EWHC Ch 1866. . . . . 28.179
Tailby v Official Receiver (1888) 13 App Cas 523. . . . . 32.14
Taly v Terra Nova Insurance Co [1985] 1 WLR 1359 . . . . .15.117
Tam Wing Chuen v Bank of Credit and Commerce Hong Kong Ltd [1996] 2 BCLC 69 . . . . . . 31.40
Tanfern Ltd v Cameron-MacDonald [2000] 2 All ER 801 . . . . 45.16, 45.17
Tankard v John Fredricks Plastics Ltd [2008] EWCA Civ 1375 . . . . 1.158, 29.28, 29.30, 29.54, 29.88, 29.90, 29.91, 29.93, 29.95, 29.96, 29.166, 60.39
Tappenden (t/a English and American Autos) v Artus [1964] 2 QB 185 . . . . 40.45
Tarbuck v Avon Insurance plc [2001] 2 All ER 503 . . . . .34.64, 34.65
Tasleem v Beverly [2013] EWCA Civ 1805 . . . . 11.05, 11.08, 11.27, 43.148
Tate v Hart [1999] PNLR 787 . . . . 9.152, 9.190
Taxation of Costs, Re [1936] 1 KB 523 . . . . 35.118, 36.66, 36.76, 53.35
Taxation of Costs; In re Solicitors, In re [1943] KB 69 . . . . .35.88, 35.100
Taylor, Stileman and Underwood, Re [1891] 1 Ch 590. . . . . 40.51, 40.78
Taylor v Pace Developments Ltd [1991] BCC 406 . . . . 9.28
Tchenguiz v Serious Fraud Office [2014] EWCA Civ 1471. . . . . 16.57
Tearle & Co (a firm) v Sherring (unreported), 29 October 1993, QBD. 35.95, 35.96
Teasdale v HSBC Bank plc; Brookes v HSBC Bank plc [2010] EWHC 612 (QB) 7.115, 7.121, 7.122, 7.123, 7.127, 7.130
Technical Fibre Products & Anor v David Walton Bell & Ors [2010] EWPCC 011 . . . . 50.330
Ted Baker plc v AXA Insurance UK plc [2012] EWHC 1779 (Comm) 6.194, 17.58, 17.59
Ted Baker plc v AXA Insurance UK plc [2014] EWHC 4178 (Comm) 17.121, 17.123, 17.125, 17.146
Tees Conservancy Comrs v James [1935] Ch 544. . . . . 4.05
Teheran-Europe Co Ltd v ST Belton (Tractors) Ltd [1971] 2 QB 491 . . . . 6.270
Tel-Ka Talk Ltd v Revenue & Customs Commissioners [2010] EWHC 90175 (Costs) 3.33, 3.34, 3.35, 3.36, 27.164
Templeton and Cox, Re (1909) 101 LT 144, CA. 27.177

Templeton Insurance Ltd v Penningtons Solicitors LLP [2006] EWHC 685 (Ch) 40.53
Terrell v Hutton (1854) 4 HL Cas 1091 . . . . 27.37
Teva UK v Leo Pharma [2014] EWHC 3522 . . . . 14.21, 14.28
Texuna International Ltd v Cairn Energy plc [2004] EWHC 1102 (Comm) 15.31, 15.50, 15.111, 15.115
TGA Chapman Ltd v Christopher and Sun Alliance [1998] 2 All ER 873 . . . . 9.11, 9.56
Thai Airways International Public Co Ltd v KI Holdings Co Ltd (formerly known as Koito Industries Ltd) [2015] EWHC 1476 (Comm). 17.81, 17.138
Thai Trading Co (a firm) v Taylor [1998] 3 All ER 65 . . . . 27.224, 29.180, 29.181, 29.182, 29.210, 28.211, 30.11, 30.14, 30.23, 30.25
Thakkar v Patel [2017] EWCA Civ 117 . . . . 6.128, 6.136, 6.138, 6.207
Thames Chambers Solicitors v Miah [2013] EWHC 1245 (QB). 9.165, 9.185, 9.186
Thamesmead Town Ltd v Allotey (1998) 20 HLR 1052 . . . . 32.24
Thenga v Quinn [2009] EWCA Civ 151. . . . . 50.110
Thinc Group Ltd v Kingdom [2013] EWCA Civ 1306 . . . . 17.124, 17.132, 17.135, 17.139, 17.147, 17.161
Thistle Hotels Ltd v Gamma Four Ltd [2004] EWHC 322 (Ch) 15.36, 15.69
Thoday v Thoday [1964] P 181 . . . . 23.19
Thomas v Bunn [1991] AC 362. . . . . 49.03, 56.23, 56.26, 56.42
Thomas v Cross (1864) 29 JP 4. . . . . .35.115
Thomas v Cunard Whitestar Line [1950] 2 All ER 1157. . . . . 49.151, 49.162
Thomas v Palin (1882) 21 Ch D 360 . . . . 6.111
Thomas v Parry (1880) WN 184. . . . . 52.100
Thomas Bates v Wyndham's (Lingerie) Ltd [1981] l WLR 505 . . . . 32.72
Thomas Johnson Ciker v Barkkand Clearing Co (1999) The Times, 6 December, CA 52.31
Thomas Pink Ltd v Victoria's Secret UK Ltd [2014] EWHC 3258 (Ch) 12,73
Thomas Watts & Co (a firm) v Smith [1998] 2 Costs LR 59 . . . . 39.04, 39.05, 39.17
Thompson v Go North East Ltd (unreported), 30 August 2016, Sunderland County Court. 7.135, 8.41, 9.182, 16.38
Thompson v Percival (1834) 5 B & Ad 925. . . . . 19.27
Thompson v Reeve (unreported), 20 March 2017, QBD. 17.24, 17.43
Thompson (a minor) & Ors v Bruce [2011] EWHC 2228 (QB) 6.106, 17.27
Thompson ex p Baylis, In Re [1894] 1 QB 462 . . . . 27.126, 27.151, 36.22, 36.25, 39.11
Thompson, Re (1885) 30 Ch D 441 . . . . 35.86, 35.87, 35.90, 35.92
Thomson v Berkhampsted Collegiate School [2009] EWHC 2374 (QB) 9.22, 9.36, 9.89
Thoni GmbH v RTP [1979] 2 Ll R 282, CA. 40.10
Thornbury v Bevill (1842) 1 Y & C Ch Cas 554 . . . . 43.290
Thorne v Smith (1851) 10 CB 659. . . . . 19.25
Thornhill v Nationwide Metal Recycling Ltd [2011] EWCA Civ 919. . . . . 6.95
Thornley v Lang [2003] EWCA Civ 1484 . . . . 18.06, 18.61, 29.55, 29.111, 29.114, 29.115, 29.116, 29.128
Thornley (a child) v MoD [2010] EWHC 2584 (QB) 29.52, 29.85, 51.76, 54.58
Three Rivers District Council v Governor and Company of the Bank of England [2004] UKHL 48 . . . . 46.04, 46.09, 46.10
Three Rivers District Council & Ors v Bank of England [2006] EWHC 816 (Comm) 16.39, 16.53, 16.54, 16.63, 23.46
Three Rivers District Council & Ors v The Governor and Company of the Bank of England (No 3) [2003] 2 AC 1 . . . . 26.02
Three Rivers District Council & Ors v The Governor and Company of the Bank of England (No 5) [2003] EWCA Civ 474 . . . . 46.24
Thynne v Thynne [1955] P 272, CA 10.05
Tibbles v SIG Plc (t/a Asphaltic Roofing Supplies) [2012] EWCA Civ 518 . . . . 10.19, 26.50
Tibbs v Dick [1999] 2 FCR 322, CA 10.27
Tichband v Hurdman [2003] EWCA Civ 718; [2003] 1 WLR 2487 . . . . 29.63, 31.29
Tidal Energy Ltd v Bank of Scotland Plc [2014] EWCA Civ 847 . . . . 13.04, 13.19, 13.20, 13.25, 13.29, 13.103

Tierney v News Group Newspapers Ltd [2006] EWHC 3275 (QB). 13.30, 13.31, 13.33, 13.34, 13.37, 13.38, 13.40, 13.42
Tildesley v Harper (1878) 10 Ch D 393 . . . . 26.10, 26.17
Till, ex p Parsons (1871) 19 WR 325. . . . . 40.80
Tim Martin Interiors Ltd v Akin Gump LLP [2011] EWCA Civ 1574 . . . . .36.82, 36.83, 36.84, 36.85, 36.112, 66.34
Times Newspapers v Flood [2017] UKSC 33 . . . . 24.53
Times Newspapers Ltd v Burstein [2002] EWCA Civ 1739 . . . . 29.27
Timmins v Moreland Street Property Ltd [1958] Ch 110 . . . . 31.54
Tinseltime Ltd v Roberts [2012] EWHC 2628 (TCC). 9.49
Titmus v General Motors UK Ltd [2016] EWHC 2021 (QB) 17.24, 17.166
Tito v Waddell (No 2) [1977] 1 Ch 106 . . . . .32.22, 32.23
Tiuta Plc v Rawlinson & Hunter (a firm) [2016] EWHC 3480 (QB) 6.59, 17.82, 17.120, 17.181
Tiverton Estates Ltd v Wearwell Ltd [1975] Ch 146. . . . . .27.149
TJ Brent Ltd v Black & Veatch Consulting Ltd [2008] EWHC 1497 (TCC). 4.60, 6.94
Toghill v Grant, Re Boord (1840) 2 Beav 261 . . . . 36.09
Tolhurst v Associated Portland Cement Manufacturers (1900) Ltd [1902] 2 KB 660 . . . .32.09, 32.17, 32.20, 32.25
Tolstoy-Miloslavsky v Lord Aldington [1996] 2 All ER 556; [1996] 1 WLR 736, CA 9.48, 9.62, 9.63, 9.161, 9.172
Tolstoy v Aldington (1993) The Times, 16 December, CA 19.25
Tombstone Ltd v Raja [2008] EWCA Civ 1444 . . . . .5.27, 9.62, 45.75, 53.111
Tomlin v Standard Telephones and Cables Ltd [1969] 1 WLR 1378. . . . . 6.218
Tomlinson v Broadsmith [1896] 1 QB 386, CA 27.37
Tomlinson v Land and Finance Corporation Ltd (1884) 14 QBD 539, CA 15.14
Toni, The [1974] 1 Lloyd's Reports 489 . . . . 6.219, 17.214
Toprak Enerji Sanayi AS v Sale Tilney Technology Plc [1994] 1 WLR 840 . . . . .17.171
Torkington v Magee [1902] 2 KB 427 . . . . 32.08
Total Spares & Supplies Ltd v Antares SRL [2006] EWHC 1537 (Ch). 9.18, 9.84
Town Investments Limited and Ors v Department of the Environment [1978] AC 359 . . . . . . .18.114
Townsend v Stone Toms and Partners [1981] 1 WLR 1153, CA 19.07
Trade Storage Ltd v Papanicola [2011] EWHC 598 (Ch) 15.78, 15.129
Trademark Licensing Co Ltd v Leofelis SA [2010] EWHC 969 (Ch) 15.130
Tramountana Armadora SA v Atlantic Shipping Co SA, The Vorros [1978] 2 All ER 870 (Comm) 36.76
Transformers and Rectifiers Ltd v Needs Ltd [2015] EWHC 1687 (TCC). 44.35, 44.36
Transocean Drilling UK Ltd v Providence Resources plc [2016] EWHC 2611 (Comm). 17.97, 17.160
Trant v Stokes (unreported), 3 December 2014, CA (Civ Div) 6.155
Travel-Vac SL v Antelm Sanchís [1999] All ER (EC) 656 . . . . .28.170, 28.180, 28.189
Travelers Casualty and Surety Co of Canada v Sun Life Assurance Co of Canada (UK) Ltd [2006] EWHC 2885 (Comm) 6.03, 6.16, 6.22, 6.179, 6.229, 16.35, 16.57, 16.65, 17.174
Travellers Insurance Co Ltd v Advani (unreported), 10 May 2013, QBD 43.414
Treasury Solicitor v Regester & Anor [1978] 1 WLR 446. . . . . .1.135, 38.07, 38.08, 38.19, 38.20, 38.23, 38.26, 51.09
Trehan v Liverpool Victoria Insurance Company Ltd (unreported), 3 October 2017, Nottingham County Court 9.74, 9.186
Trendtex Trading Corpn v Crédit Suisse [1982] AC 629. . . . . 30.28, 30.34, 30.38, 30.40, 30.41
Trepca Mines Ltd (No 2), Re [1963] Ch 199. . . . . .30.08, 30.15, 30.18, 30.22, 30.29
Trident International Freight Services Ltd v Manchester Ship Canal Co [1990] BCLC 263, CA 15.84
Trill v Sacher (No 2) [1992] 40 LS Gaz R 32, CA 9.189
Trimax Trading Int Ltd v HMRC [2014] UKFTT 733 (TC). 16.57
Triple Point Technology Inc v PTT Public Co Ltd [2018] EWHC (TCC) 56.47
Triplerose Ltd [2016] EKUT 77 (LC) 18.06, 18.35
Trollope & Colls Ltd v Atomic Power Constructions Ltd [1963] 1 WLR 333. . . . . 29.132, 29.136
Trollope & Colls Ltd v North West Metropolitan Regional Hospital Board [1973] 1 WLR 601. . . . 31.62

Troy Foods v Manton [2013] EWCA Civ 615. . . . . 12.161
Truex v Toll [2009] EWHC 369 (Ch) 35.113, 36.46, 39.04, 39.11, 39.19, 40.24, 40.123, 40.124, 40.125, 40.126, 40.128
Truscott v Truscott; Wraith v Sheffield Forgemasters Ltd [1998] 1 WLR 132. . . . . . . 51.56, 51.57–51. 51.62, 51.68, 51.77
Trustee Corpn Ltd v Nadir (2001) The Independent, 29 . . . . .66.63, 66.66
Trustees for the Greater World Association Trust v Customs and Excise Commissioners [1989] VATTR 91 . . . . 55.09
Trustees of Olympic Airlines SA Pension & Life Assurance Scheme v Olympic Airlines SA [2013] EWCA Civ 218 . . . . 15.86
Trustees of the Redeemed Christian Church of God v Grestar Ltd [2016] EWCA Civ 134 . . . . .9.174
Trustees of Stokes Pension Fund v Western Power Distribution (Southwest) Plc [2005] EWCA (Civ) 854 . . . . 6.207
Trytel, The [1952] 2 TLR 32. . . . . 32.13
Tubridy v Sarwar [2012] EWCA Civ 184 . . . . 50.86
Tucker v Hampshire Hospitals NHS Foundation Trust [2017] EWHC 3650 (QB) 54.77
Tudor Furnishers Ltd v Montague & Co and Finer Production Co Ltd [1950] Ch 113. . . . . .15.14
TUI UK Ltd v Tickell [2016] EWHC 2741 (QB) 25.98, 45.23, 49.67, 49.87
Tullett Prebon plc v BGC Brokeers LP [2010] EWHC 989 (QB) 6.194, 6.209
Turner, Re [1907] 2 Ch 126 . . . . 40.93
Turner v Hand (1859) 27 Beav 561. . . . . 39.11
Turner v Plasplugs Ltd [1996] 2 All ER 939 . . . . 18.81, 62.04
Turner v Tennant (1846) 10 Jur 429 . . . . 1.83, 27.112
Turner v Turner (1726) 2 Stra 708 . . . . 60.04
Turner v Willis [1905] 1 KB 468 . . . . 35.115, 40.10
Turner & Co v O Palomo [2000] 1 WLR 37, CA. 23.125, 39.01, 39.03, 39.04, 39.17, 40.125
Turner Page Music v Torres Design Associates Ltd, The Times, 3 August 1998, CA. 9.124, 9.124
Tuson v Murphy (unreported), 6 April 2016, Oxford County Court .17.133
Tweedie, Re [1909] WN 110 . . . . 36.36
Twigg Farnell v Wildblood, (unreported) CA, 26 September 1997; (1998) PNLR 211 . . . . 56.19
Twin Benefits Ltd v Barker [2017] EWHC 1882 (Ch) 10.15
Twinsectra Ltd v Yardley [2002] UKHL 12 . . . . 40.53, 40.55
Twynam v Porter (1870) LR 11 Eq 181. . . . . 40.93
Tyndall v Battersea Dogs Home [2005] EWHC 90011 (Costs) 54,155
Tyrrell v Bank of London (1862) 10 HLC 26 . . . . 1.83, 39.12
Tyte v Globe (1797) 7 TR 267 . . . . 1.72

U v Liverpool County Council [2005] EWCA Civ 475 . . . . . .4.52, 45.16, 54.47, 54.58, 54.60, 54.97
UCB Corporate Services Ltd (formerly UCB Bank Plc) v Halifax (SW) Ltd [1999] CPLR 691. . . . . 26.41
Udall v Capri Lighting Ltd [1988] 1 QB 907 . . . . 40.88
Uddington Business Ltd v Browne (unreported), 9 December 2011, Ch D. 15.100
Udogaranya v Nwagw [2010] EWHC 90186 (Costs). 12.135, 50.91
UK Exploration Co v British American Offshore Ltd [2002] BLR 135. . . . . 56.60
Ul-Haq v Shah [2009] EWCA Civ 542 . . . . .6.151
Ultimate Products Ltd v Woolley [2014] EWHC 1919 (Ch). 40.16
Ultimate Utilities Ltd v McNicholas Construction Services Ltd (unreported), 9 April 2014, QBD (TCC). 15.70,1 15.80, 15.84, 15.118
Ultraframe (UK) Ltd v Eurocell Building Plastics Ltd & Anor [2006] EWHC 90069 (Costs) 18.112
Ultraframe (UK) Ltd v Fielding [2006] EWCA Civ 1660 . . . . 25.91
U&M Mining Zambia Ltd v Konkola Copper Mines plc [2014] EWHC 3250 (Comm) 16.57
Underwood, Son & Piper v Lewis [1894] 2 QB 306 . . . . .23.93, 27.13, 27.14, 27.71, 27.78, 35.14
Unilever plc v Procter & Gamble Co [2000] 1 WLR 2436. . . . . 6.207, 6.215, 6.218, 48.44
Union Discount Co Ltd v Zoller (Costs) [2001] EWCA Civ 1755 . . . . .3.38, 3.43, 56.119
Unisoft Group Ltd (No 2) [1993] BCLC 532 . . . . 15.35, 15.36, 15.50
Unison v Kelly [2012] EWCA Civ 1148 . . . . 13.101
United Airlines Inc v United Airways Ltd (2011) EWHC 2411 (Ch) 14.21

United Building and Plumbing Contractors v Malkit Singh Kajila [2002] EWCA Civ 628 . . . . . 3.97, 59.30, 59.33
United Engineering Workers' Union v Devanayagam [1968] AC 356 . . . . 5.02
United Marine Aggregates Ltd v G M Welding & Engineering Ltd [2013] EWCA Civ 516 . . . . 6.254, 17.131
United States v Motor Trucks Ltd [1924] AC 196. . . . . 32.69
Universal Cycles v Grangebriar Ltd (unreported), 8 February 2000, CA 6.161
Universal Thermosensors Ltd v Hibben (unreported), 6 March 1992, Ch D 18.13
University of Cambridge v Murray [1993] ICR 460, EAT 40.05
University of Nottingham v Eyett (No 2) [1999] 2 All ER 445 . . . . 9.77
Unwired Planet International Ltd v Huawei Technologies Co Ltd [2015] EWHC 3837 (Ch) . . . 6.62
Unwired Planet International Ltd v Huawei Technologies Co Ltd [2016] EWHC 410 (Pat) 50.50.336
US Bank Trustees Ltd v Titan Europe 2007-1 (NHP) Ltd [2014] EWHC 1189 (Ch). . . . 31.12, 31.25
Utting v McBain [2007] EWHC 90085 (Costs) 2.09, 29.02
Utting v McBain [2007] EWHC 3293 (QB) 27.04, 29.13, 29.63, 31.55
Uwug Ltd (in liquidation) v Ball [2015] EWHC 74 (IPEC) 17.216

Vald Nielsen Holding A/S v Baldorino [2017] EWHC 1033 (Comm) 15.102, 15.104
Valentine v Allen [2003] EWCA Civ 1274. . . . . 6.133
Vallee v Birchwook [2013] EWHC 1449 (Ch) 66.66
Van Aken v London Borough of Camden [2002] EWCA Civ 1724 . . . . 4.38, 4.55, 43.267
Van Laun, ex p Chatterton, In re [1907] 1 KB 155 . . . . .35.124, 36.27, 39.12
Van Lynn Developments Ltd v Pelias Construction Co Ltd [1969] 1 QB 607. . . . . 32.29
Van Oord Ltd v Allseas UK Ltd [2015] EWHC 3385 (TCC). 17.35, 17.36, 17.38
Various Claimants v Corby Borough Council [2008] EWHC 619 (TCC) 65.95
Various Claimants v Gower Chemicals Ltd (unreported), 28 February 2007, Swansea County Court 29.124, 29.125
Various Claimants v Gower Chemicals Ltd (unreported), 12 March 2008, SCCO 29.125
Various Claimants v Gower Chemicals Ltd (unreported), 27 August 2010, Cardiff County Court 6.117
Various Claimants v MGN Ltd [2016] EWHC 1894 (Ch). 12.29, 12.33, 43.275, 54.49, 54.178
Various Claimants v Mirror Group Newspapers Ltd (unreported), 4 October 2016, SCCO. . . . 48.57
Various Claimants v TUI UK Ltd (unreported), 11 August 2005, SCCO 49.131
Vaughan v (1) Jones & (2) Fowler [2006] EWHC 2123 (Ch) 9.53, 9.79
Vaughan v Vanderstegen (1854) 2 Drew 408 . . . . 40.51
Vector v JD Williams [2009] EWHC 3601 (TCC) 6.147, 7.153
Vedatech Corporation v Crystal Decisions (UK) Ltd [2002] EWCA Civ 356 . . . . 15.88, 15.92
Vellacott v The Convergance Group plc [2007] EWHC 17874 (Ch) 9.28
Venture Finance Plc v Mead & Anor [2005] EWCA Civ 325 . . . . .7.147, 45.30, 45.31, 66.08, 66.09, 66.10
Venture Investment Placement Ltd v Hall [2005] EWHC 1227 (Ch) 48.27, 48.43
Venus Asset Management Ltd v Matthews & Goodman LLP [2015] EWHC 2896 (Ch) 12.120, 12.121, 12.122
Vera Cruz, The (No 2) (1884) 9 PD 96, CA 4.06
Vernon v Spoudeas [2010] EWCA Civ 666 . . . . 43.104
Vernon & Co (Pulp Products) Ltd's Patent, Re [1976] RPC 625 . . . . 3.16
Verslot Dredging BV v Hdi Gerling Versicherung AG [2013] EWHC 658 (Comm) 15.121
Vestergaard Frandsen A/S v Bestnet Europe Ltd [2014] EWHC 4371 (Ch) 6.154, 6.238, 16.48
Victor Kiam v MGN Ltd [2002] EWCA Civ 66. . . . . 16.24
Vigers v Cook [1919] 2 KB 475, CA 27.07
Vigneron-Dahl Ltd v Pettit [1925] WN 177. . . . . 46.20
Villa Agencies Spf Ltd v Kestrel Travel Consultancy Ltd (unreported), 17 January 2012, CA (Civ Div) 6.64
Vimbos Ltd, Re [1900] 1 Ch 470 . . . . 47.29
Vinayak & Anor (t/a Doctors Chambers) v Lovegrove & Eliot (a firm) [2007] EWHC 90096. . . . .29.49

Vincent v Slaymaker (1810) 12 East 372 . . . . . 35.86
Vinos v Marks & Spencer plc [2001] 3 All ER 784 . . . . . 4.37, 26.42
Virani v Manuel Revert y Cia Sa [2003] EWCA Civ 1651 . . . . . 6.133, 16.33
Virany v Warne (1801–04) 4 Esp 47 . . . . . 53.31
Virdi v RK Joinery Ltd [2016] EWCA Civ 539 . . . . . 9.22
Virgin Atlantic Airways Ltd v Jet Airways (India) Ltd [2012] EWHC 3318 (Pat) 17.59
Virgin Atlantic Airways Ltd v Zodiac Seats UK Ltd (formerly Contour Aerospace Ltd) [2013] UKSC 46 . . . . . 23.07, 23.08, 23.19, 23.34
Viridor Waste Management Ltd v Veolia ES Ltd [2015] EWHC 2321 (Comm) 16.41
Vitol Bahrain EC v Nasdec General Trading LLC (2013) 163 (7584) NLJ 20 . . . . . 25.80
Viva! Campaigns Ltd v Scott [2013] EWHC 3639 (Ch) 7.52
Vivian v Kennelly (1890) 63 LT 778 . . . . . 60.04
Vlamaki v Sookias & Sookias [2015] EWHC 3334 (QB) 27.46, 27.49, 27.51, 27.52, 27.53, 27.54, 31.11, 31.40, 35.12, 35.19, 35.25
Voice and Script International Ltd v Ashraf Alghafar [2003] EWCA Civ 736 . . . . . 50.393
VTB Bank v Skurikhin [2014] EWHC 3522 . . . . . 14.21

W v Veolia Environmental Services (UK) plc [2011] EWHC 2020 (QB) 28.181
W Savory Ltd v World of Golf Ltd [1914] 2 Ch 566 . . . . . 1.100
Wadsworth, Rhodes, Re v Sugden (1885) 29 Ch D 517 . . . . . 15.121
Wadsworth, Rhodes v Sugden, In re (1886) 34 Ch D 155 . . . . . 40.96
Wagemaar v Weekend Travel Ltd [2014] EWCA Civ 1105 . . . . . 4.35, 8.04, 8.14, 8.16
Waggett v Warchalowski (unreported), 15 September 2015, Blackpool County Court 8.41
Wagstaff v Colls [2003] EWCA Civ 469 . . . . . 9.112, 9.115, 9.116, 9.122, 9.212, 9.216
Wain v Gloucester County Council [2014] EWHC 1274 (TCC) 12.57
Waites Construction Ltd v HGP Greentree Alchurch Evans Ltd [2005] EWHC 2174 (TCC) 16.33, 16.39
Wakefield v Brown (1874) LR 9 CP 410 . . . . . 53.64
Wakefield (t/a Wills Probate and Trusts of Weybridge) v Ford [2009] EWHC 122 (QB) 43.287, 43.358
Walbrook Properties Ltd v Severn Trent Water Ltd & Ors [2002] EWHC 9016 (Costs) 51.55
Wale, Re [1956] 1 WLR 1346 . . . . . 32.31
Wales, Public Service Ombudsman for v Heesom [2015] EWHC 3306 (QB) 43.02, 43.03
Walker v Birch (1795) 6 Term Rep 258 . . . . . 40.53
Walker v Burton [2013] EWHC 811 (Ch) 20.48
Walker v Robinson (1745) 1 Wils KB 94 . . . . . 1.67
Walker v Royal College of Veterinary Surgeons [2007] UKPC 20 . . . . . 61.14
Walker v Wilsher (1889) 23 QBD 335 . . . . . 6.213, 6.218
Walker Construction (UK) Ltd v Quayside Homes Ltd [2014] EWCA Civ 93 . . . . . 6.230, 17.96, 25.94, 57.20
Walker, Meredith, Re v Walker (1893) 68 LT 517 . . . . . 40.51
Walker Residential Ltd v Davis & Anor [2005] EWHC 3483 (Ch) 10.24
Walker Wingsail Systems plc, In re [2005] EWCA Civ 247 . . . . . 7.112, 7.120, 7.121, 7.123, 7.127, 7.130
Wall v Lefever [1998] 1 FCR 605 . . . . . 9.120, 16.40
Wall v Royal Bank of Scotland Plc [2016] EWHC 2460 (Comm) 9.92, 33.88, 65.42
Wallace v Brian Gale & Associates [1998] 2 Costs LR 53 . . . . . 3.46, 49.151
Wallace v Kelsall (1840) 7 M & W 264 . . . . . 19.26
Wallace LLP v Yates [2010] EWHC 1098 (Ch) 40.123
Waller v Lacey (1840) 133 ER 245 . . . . . 46.14
Wallersteiner v Moir (No 2) [1975] QB 373; [1975] 1 All ER 849 . . . . . 29.179, 29.204, 29.205, 29.207, 29.212, 65.124, 66.60, 66.66
Wallis v Duke of Portland (1797) 3 Ves 494 . . . . . 30.07.30.22
Walsh v Julius (1927) The Times, 13 July 27.37
Walsh v Missledine [2000] CP Rep 74 . . . . . 26.20
Walsh v Shanahan [2013] EWCA Civ 675 . . . . . 17.131

Walsh v Singh (aka Buddha and Walsh) [2011] EWHC Civ 80 . . . . .6.104, 6.151, 6.193, 17.127, 17.132, 17.134
Walsham v Stainton (1863) 2 H & M 1 . . . . 46.20
Walter Lilly & Co Ltd v Mackay [2012] EWHC 1972 (TCC) 16.40
Walters, Re (1845) 9 Beav 299 . . . . 35.90
Walton v Egan [1982] QB 1232 . . . . .27.108, 27.127, 38.87, 38.90
Walton v Scottish Ministers [2012] UKSC 44 . . . . 13.84
Ward v Guinness Mahon plc [1996] 1 WLR 894 . . . . 20.12, 65.12, 65.75, 65.77
Ward v Lawson (1890) 43 Ch D 353, CA. 22.06
Ward v Snell (1788) 126 ER 7 . . . . 1.24
Warmingtons v McMurray [1937] 1 All ER 562. . . . . 27.22, 36.15
Warner v Barnes [2012] EWHC 4223 (Ch) 16.49
Warner v Merriman White [2008] EWHC 1129 (Ch) 9.65
Warren v Marsden [2014] EWHC 4410 (Comm) 15.49, 15.93, 15.113
Warkworth, The (1885) 1 TLR 659, CA. 53.101
Watchorn v Jupiter Industries Ltd [2014] EWHC 3003 (Ch) 17.81, 17.82
Waterson Hicks v Eliopoulos (1995) Costs LR (Core Vol) 363 . . . . 3.88, 47.27
Wates Construction Ltd v HGP Greentree Allchurch Evans Ltd [2006] BLR 45 . . . . 16.38
Watson, Re (1884) 53 LJ Ch 305 . . . . 40.44
Watson v Gray (unreported), 8 February 2005, Liverpool County Court. 50.110
Watson v HM Courts & Tribunals Service National Taxing Team [2012] EWHC 2865 (Admin) 51.84
Watson v Lyon (1855) 7 de GM & C288 . . . . 40.80
Watson, ex p Phillips, Re (1887) 19 QBD 234, CA 27.33, 49.147
Watt v Assets Co; Bain v Assets Co [1905] AC 317, HL 10.27
Watters (1881) 7 LR Ir 531 . . . . 40.44
Watters v Smith (1831) 2 B & Ad 889. . . . . 19.26
Watts v Official Solicitor [1936] 1 All ER 249, CA. 49.121
Waugh v HB Clifford & Sons Ltd [1982] Ch 374 . . . . 47.26
Waveney District Council v Lowestoft (North East Suffolk) Magistrates' Court [2008] EWHC 3295 (Admin) 61.14
Way v Latilla [1937] 3 All ER 759, ... 18.93
Wealcan Enterprises Inc v Banque Algerienne Du Commerce Exterieur SA [2012] EWHC 4151 (Comm) 66.11
Webb v Bromley London Borough Council (unreported), 18 February 2016, SCCO. 32.21
Webb v Crosse [1912] 1 Ch 323 . . . . 66.13
Webb v Environment Agency (unreported) 5 April 2011, QBD 7.125
Webb (by her litigation friend Perkins) v Liverpool Women's NHS Foundation Trust [2016] EWCA Civ 365. . . . . 17.25, 17.90
Webb Resolutions Ltd v Countrywide Surveyors Ltd (unreported), 4 May 2016, Ch D. . . . 6.12, 17.137
Webster v Le Hunt (1861) 9 WR 804 . . . . 40.60
Webster v Ridgeway School [2010] EWHC 318. 14.33, 14.35, 16.29. 16.39
Wedstock Realisations Ltd [1988] BCLC 354 . . . . .66.63, 66.64
Wei v Cambridge Power and Light (unreported), 10 September 2010, Cambridge County Court 28.197
Weill v Mean Fiddler Holding Ltd [2003] EWCA Civ 1058 . . . . 6.62
Weir v Secretary of State for Transport (unreported), 20 April 2005, Ch D 13.32
Wells v Barnsley Metropolitan Borough Council (1999) The Times, 12 November, QBD. 27.222, 29.204
Wells v Wells [1914] 1 P 157 . . . . 53.04
Welsh v Hole (1779) 1 Dougl KB 238 . . . . 40.39, 40.114, 40.116
Werner v Humphreys (1841) 2 Man & G 853. . . . . 27.77
Wes Futures Ltd v Allen Wilson Construction Ltd [2016] EWHC 2893 (TCC) 17.73, 17.167
West Ham Union Guardians v Churchwardens of St Matthew, Bethnal Green [1896] AC 6.14
West, King & Adam, ex p Clough, In re [1892] 2 QB 102 . . . . 35.123, 36.18, 36.22, 39.14

West London Pipeline & Storage Ltd v Total UK Ltd [2008] EWHC 1296 (Comm). 54.171
Westacott v Bevan [1891] 1 QB 774, DC 40.92
Westdeutsche Landesbank Girozentrale v Islington London Borough Council
[1996] AC 669 . . . . 56.04, 56.124
Westdock Realisations Ltd, In re [1988] BCLC 354 . . . . 65.72, 66.59
Westerton, Re [1919] 2 Ch 104. . . . . 32.29
Westland Helicopters Ltd v Al-Hejailan [2004] EWHC 1625 (Comm). 3.100, 22.19
Weston v Weston [2006] EWCA Civ 1554. . . . . 23.79
Westwood v Knight [2011] EWPCC 011 . . . . 50.323, 50.327, 50.330, 50.338, 50.340
Wetherall v Harrison [1976] QB 773 . . . . 54.163
Wethered Estate Ltd v Davis [2005] EWHC 1903 (Ch). 6.132
W H Payne & Co (1995) VAT Decision 13668 . . . . 55.12
Whaleys (Bradford) Led v Bennett & Anor [2017] EWCA Civ 2143 . . . . 16.19, 16.27,
16.47, 16.49, 50 54
Whalley v Halley (1829) 8 LJOSKB 6 . . . . 40.80
Wharton v Bancroft [2012] EWHC 91 (Ch) 7.52, 7.56, 7.58, 7.62, 17.150
Wheeler v The Chief Constable of Gloucestershire Constabulary [2013] EWCA Civ 1791 . . . . 44.28
Wheeler v Le Marchant (1881) 17 Ch D 675, at 679; Macfarlan v Rolt (1872) LR
14 Eq 580. . . . . 46.07, 46.09, 46.10, 46.21
Whitaker v Ford & Warren (a firm) (unreported), 25 November 2015, QBD (Leeds DR) 6.12
Whitcombe, re (1844) 8 Beav 140 . . . . 1.83, 27.111. 39.14
White v Butt [1909] 1 KB 50 . . . . 15.43
White v Hyde [1933] P 105 . . . . 40.93
White v Milner (1794) 2 H Bl 357 . . . . 36.66
White v PSM Residential Finance Ltd [2017] EWHC 3500 (TCC). 16.50
White v Revell [2006] EWHC 90054 (Costs) 29.85
White v Smith (1744) CB Paschæ 17G 2 . . . . 1.66
White v Tyndall (1888) 13 App Cas 263 . . . . 19.17, 19.19
White v White [2001] UKHL 9; [2001] 2 All ER 43 . . . . 31.09
Whitecap Leisure Ltd v John H Rundle Ltd [2008] EWCA Civ 1026 . . . . 6.63
Whitehead v Lord (1852) 7 Exch 691 . . . . 27.78
Whitehead, David McLeish v Barrie Searle, Hibbert Downall and Newton (a firm) [2007]
EWHC 2046 (QB) 7.17
Whitehouse v Jordan [1981] 1 WLR 246 . . . . 52.14
Whitehouse & Co (1878) Ch D 595. . . . . 21.05, 21.35
Whiteley Exerciser Ltd v Gamage [1898] 2 Ch 405 . . . . .49.153
Wickens v Townshend (1830) 1 Russ & M 361 . . . . 40.37
Wicks v MoD (unreported), 30 July 2003, SCCO 51.61
Widlake v BAA Ltd [2009] EWHC Civ 1256 . . . . .6.104, 6.146, 6.151, 6.152, 6.193
Wiggins v Peppin (1839) 2 Beav 403 . . . . 27.207
Wild v Simpson [1918–19] All ER Rep 682 . . . . 18.95, 27.88
Wild v Simpson [1919] 2 KB 544 . . . . 27.08, 27.23, 30.29, 30.33, 32.54
Wildbore v Bryan, ex p Wildbore (1820) 8 Price 677 . . . . 22.06
Wilde (a solicitor, IN RE) [1910] 1 Ch 100. . . . . 36.09
Wilden Pump Engineering Co v Fusfeld (1985) FSR 159, CA (Civ Div). 46,09
Wilkinson v Allott (1777) M 16 G 3 BR. 1.53
Wilkinson v Byers (1834) 1 Ad & El 106 . . . . 39.17
Wilkinson v Kerdene [2013] EWCA Civ 44. . . . . 32.22
Wilkinson v London Strategic Health Authority [2012] EWPCC 55. . . . . 16.34, 50.336
Wilkinson v Smart (1875) 24 WR 42. . . . . 23.95, 35.47, 39.16
Willcox v Kettell [1937] 1 All ER 222 . . . . 20.66
Willers v Joyce [2016] UKSC 44 . . . . .4.03, 4.06
William Brandt's & Sons v Dunlop Rubber Co Ltd [1905] AC 454 . . . . 32.31
Williams v Boag [1941] 1 KB 1, CA 17.57
Williams v Crosling (1847) 3 CB 957. . . . . .15.14

Williams v Hull [2009] EWHC 2844 (Ch) 48.44
Williams v Jevis [2009] EWHC 1837 (QB) 16.60
Williams v Jones (1886) 34 Ch D 120 . . . . . 66.50
Williams v Moor (1843) 11 M & W 256 . . . . . 60.14
Williams v Redcard Ltd [2011] EWCA Civ 466. . . . . 27.320
Williams v Roffey Bros & Nicholls (Contractors) Ltd [1991] 1 QB 1 . . . . . 32.54, 39.17
Williams v Secretary of State for Business, Energy & Industrial Strategy [2018] EWCA Civ 852 . . . . . 50.70, 50.136, 50.165, 50.50.255, 50.260
Williams, Williams v Williams [1912] 1 Ch 399 . . . . . 66.39
Willis v MRJ Rundell & Associates Ltd [2013] EWHC 2923 (TCC). 12.30, 12.41, 12.76, 12.85
Willis v Nicolson [2007] EWCA Civ 199. . . . . 5.23, 13.11, 26.19
Willis v Redbridge Health Authority [1996] 1 WLR 1228. . . . . 16.16
Willmott v Barber [1880] 15 Ch D 96 . . . . . 1.118, 6.32
Willmott v Barber (1881) WN 107. . . . . 1.90, 3.16
Wills v Crown Estate Commissioners [2003] EWHC 1718 (Ch) 7.73, 43.283, 56.112, 56.113
Wilson v First County Trust Ltd (No 2) [2003] UKHL 40, [2004] 1 AC 816. . . . . 29.29
Wilson v River Dun Navigation Co (1839) 5 M & W 90, 151 ER 39 . . . . . 1.49
Wilson v The Spectre Partnership [2007] EWHC 133 (Ch) 27.145, 27.148, 27.149, 27.155
Wilson v Wallani (1880) 5 Ex D 155 . . . . . 32.29
Wilson v William Sturges & Co [2006] EWHC 792 (QB) 27.87
Wilson v Wilson (1854) 5 HL Cas 40. . . . . 31.44
Wilson Lovatt & Sons Ltd, Re [1977] 1 All ER 274 . . . . . 15.96
Wilsons Solicitors (in a matter of wasted costs) v Johnson, 9 February 2011 . . . . . 9.205
Wilsons Solicitors LLP v Bentine [2015] EWCA Civ 1168 . . . . . 36.58, 36.60, 36.66, 36.71
Wiltshire Iron Co, ex p Pearson (1868) 3 Ch App 443 . . . . . 40.79
Wiltshire Police Authority v Wynn [1980] ICR 649, [1981] QB 95, CA 50.126
Wimbourne v Fine [1952] 2 All ER 681 . . . . . 40.93
Winchester Commodities Group Ltd v RD Black & Cl [2000] BCC 310. . . . . 36.36
Wingfields, Halse and Trustram, Jonesco, In re an undertaking v Evening Standard Co [1932] 2 KB 340. . . . . 27.127, 27.165, 40.40.104
Winter v Winter [2000] All ER (D) 1791 . . . . . 6.37
Winterthur Swiss Insurance Co v AG (Manchester) Ltd (in liquidation) [2006] EWHC 839 (Comm). 34.32, 46.67
Wiseman Lee (a firm) (wasted costs order) (No 5 of 2000), Re [2001] EWCA Crim 707 . . . . . 9.204
Witham v Hill & Ors (1759) 95 ER 703. . . . . 1.24
Withers LLP v Langbar International Ltd [2011] EWCA Civ 1419. . . . . 40.53
Wobben Properties GmbH [2015] EWHC 2863 (Pat) 6.182
Wokingham Borough Council v Dunn (unreported), 3 June 2015, QBD, per Judge Seymour QC 6.253
Wong v Vizards [1997] 2 Costs LR 46 . . . . . 27.73, 35.14, 38.58, 38.62, 38.63
Wood v Capita Insurance Services Ltd [2017] UKSC 24 . . . . . 31.06, 31.18
Wood v Worthing & Southlands Hospitals NHS Trust (unreported), 18 October 2004, QBD 31.37
Woodard, Re (1869) 18 WR 37 . . . . . 36.23, 40.32
Woodburn v Thomas (unreported), 11 August 2017, Senior Courts Costs Office. 12.24, 12.30, 12.132
Woodford v AIG Europe Ltd [2018] EWHC 358 (QB) 16.64
Woodhouse v Consignia Plc [2002] EWCA Civ 275 . . . . . 10.18
Woodhouse AC Israel Cocoa Ltd SA v Nigerian Produce Marketing Co [1972] AC 741. . . . . 31.02
Woollam v Cleanaway Ltd (unreported), 26 July 2004, Chester County Court 29.45, 29.48
Woollard & Anor v Fowler [2005] EWHC 90051 (Costs) 52.69
Woolwich Equitable Building Society v IRC (No 2) [1993] AC 70, HL 40.37
Worcester Works Finance Ltd v Cooden Engineering Co Ltd [1972] 1 QB 210 . . . . . 4.06
Workmeister v Healy (1876) IR 10 CL 450. . . . . 15.14
Worrell v Nicholls (unreported), 17 August 2017, Preston County Court. 17.78

Wraith v Sheffield Forgemasters Ltd [1998] 1 WLR 133 . . . . 54.194
Wright v Bennett [1947] KB 828 . . . . 53.106
Wright v Bennett [1948] 1 QB 601 . . . . 49.157
Wright v HSBC Bank plc [2006] EWHC 1473 (Admin) 6.110
Wright v Rowland [2016] EWHC 2206 (Comm) 12.78
Wright, Blizard v Lockhart [1954] Ch 347; [1954] 2 All ER 98 . . . . 23.21
Wu v Hellard (unreported), 25 November 2013, Ch D 15.02, 15.36, 15.96
Wyatt v Portsmouth Hospitals NHS Trust [2006] EWCA Civ 529 . . . . 62.16, 62.19, 62.25, 62.26, 62.27, 62.29, 62.32, 62.35
Wyld v Silver (No 2) [1962] 2 All ER 809, CA 15.120
Wylde v Culver [2006] EWHC 1313 (Ch) 7.125

X v Dartford and Gravesham NHS Trust [2015] EWCA Civ 96 . . . . 36.109
Xhosa Office Rentals Ltd v Multi High Tech PCB Ltd [2014] EWHC 1286 (QB) 9.83, 15.121
XYZ v Schering Health Care: Oral Contraceptive Litigation [2004] All ER (D) 577 (Mar) 53.60, 53.88, 53.109
XYZ v Travelers Insurance Co Ltd [2017] EWHC 287 (QB) 9.22, 9.31
XYZ v Various (Including Transform Medical Group (CS) Ltd and Spire Healthcare Ltd) & Ors [2014] EWHC 4056 (QB) 65.42

Yarnworth's Case (1823) 2 Dow & Ry KB 423 . . . . 15.96
Yat Tung Investment Co Ltd v Dao Heng Bank Ltd [1975] AC 581 . . . . 23.34
Yentob v MGN Ltd [2015] EWCA Civ 1292 . . . . 17.119, 17.120
Yeo v Times Newspapers Ltd [2015] EWHC 209 (QB) 12.38, 12.85, 12.96, 12.99, 12.117, 12.121, 12.122
Yonge v Toynbee [1910] 1 KB 215 . . . . 9.65, 9.67, 9.69, 27.80
York Glass Co Ltd v Jubb (1925) 134 LT 36, CA 60.58
Youdjeu v Home Office [2011] EWHC 2002 (QB) 16.56
Young v Bristol Aeroplane Co Ltd [1944] KB 718 . . . . 4.06
Young v JR Smart (Builders) Ltd [2004] EWHC 103 . . . . 25.103
Young v Leighton (unreported), c 1969, QBD 52.15
Young v Walker (1847) 16 M&W 446 . . . . 35.84
Young v Young and Kohler [1955] 1 All ER 796 . . . . 53.98
Young and Woods Ltd v West [1980] IRLR 201, CA 50.126
Your Response Ltd v Datateam Business Media Ltd [2014] EWCA Civ 281; [2014] All ER (D) 156 (Mar) 40.49

Zapello v Chief Constable of Sussex Police [2010] EWCA Civ 1417 . . . . 6.109
Zappia Middle East Construction Co Ltd v Clifford Chance (a firm) [2001] EWCA Civ 946 . . 21.37
Zimi v London Central Bus Co Ltd (unreported), 18 January 2015, Central London County Court 8.39
Zissis v Lukomski [2006] EWCA Civ 341 . . . . 16.40, 16.66
Zoan v Rouamba [2000] 2 All ER 620 . . . . 31.09, 31.11
Zoya Ltd v Ahmed [2016] EWHC 2249 (Ch) 9.68
Zuliani v Veira [1994] 1 WLR 1149 PC 35.73, 35.92, 35.93, 35.96
Zurich Insurance plc v Bain (unreported), 4 June 2015, Newcastle upon Tyne County Court 8.40, 8.41

INTERNATIONAL COURTS

European Court of Human Rights

Airey v Ireland, App No 6289/73 (1978–80) 2 EHRR 305 . . . . 1.141, 24.35, 24.38, 24.39
Aït-Mouhoub v France, App No 22924/93 [1998] ECHR 97 . . . . 15.112
Apostol v Georgia, App No 40765/02 28 November 2006, ECtHR 24.42
Ashendon and Jones v United Kingdom, The Times, 22 September 2011 . . . . 3.16

Ashingdane v United Kingdom (1985) 7 EHRR 528 . . . . . 24.34, 24.37
B v United Kingdom, No 10615/83, 38, EComHR 9.97
Buckley v United Kingdom (1996) 23 EHRR 101 . . . . . 24.27, 24.28
Chapman v United Kingdom (2001) 33 EHRR 399 . . . . . 24.27
Delcourt v Belgium (1970) 1 EHRR 355 . . . . . 24.34
Dombo Beheer v The Netherlands (1994) 18 EHRR 213 . . . . . 24.36
Faulkner v United Kingdom (2000) The Times, 11 January, ECtHR. 24.40
Fayed v United Kingdom (1994) 18 EHRR 393. . . . . 24.26, 24.35
Golder v United Kingdom (1975) 1 EHRR 524 . . . . . 24.34, 24.35
Handyside v United Kingdom (1976) 1 EHRR 737. . . . . 24.27, 24.29
Hakansson and Sturesson v Sweden (1990) 13 EHRR 1. . . . . 24.28
James & Ors v United Kingdom, App No 8793/79 (1986) 8 EHRR 123 . . . . . 24.30, 24.36
Jedamski and Jedamska v Poland (2007) 45 EHRR 47 . . . . . 24.39
MGN Ltd v United Kingdom, App No 39401/04 [2011] ECHR 66. . . . . 24.47, 24.49–24.53
Robins v United Kingdom, App no 22410/93 (1997) 26 EHRR 527 . . . . . 44.17
Sporrong and Lönnroth v Sweden, App Nos 7151/75, 7152/75 (1982) 5 EHRR 35 . . . . . 24.15, 24.29
Stankov v Bulgaria (2009) 49 EHRR 7; [2007] ECHR 582 . . . . . 24.39
Steel and Morris v United Kingdom, App No 68416/01 (2005) 41 EHRR 403 24,40
Sunday Times v United Kingdom [1979] ECHR 1. . . . . 24.34
Sunday Times v United Kingdom, App No 6538/74 (1979) 2 EHRR 245 . . . . . 24.35
Tolstoy Miloslavsky v United Kingdom, App No 18139/91 (1995) 20 EHRR 442 . . . . . 36.05
Tudor-Comert v Moldova, App No 27888/04 4 November 2008, ECtHR 24.39
Velikovi & Ors v Bulgaria (2009) 48 EHRR 27 . . . . . 24.30
Weissman v Romania, App No 63945/00 [2011] ECHR 2204. . . . . 24.39
X v Germany, No 7544/76, 14, EComHR. 9.97
Young, James and Webster v United Kingdom (1981) 4 EHRR 38. . . . . 24.48

European Court of Justice

Case 152/85 Misset v EC Council [1987] ECR 223 . . . . . 40.05
C-222/84 Johnston v Chief Constable of the Royal Ulster Constabulary [1986] 3 All ER 135. . . . . 28.170
C-740/93 Verein gegen Unwesen in Handel und Gewerbe Köln v Mars GmbH [1995] ECR I-1923 . . . . . 28.108
C-45/96 Bayerische Hypothetken v Dietzinger [1998] 1 WLR 1035 . . . . . 28.172
C-210/96 Gut Springenheide GmbH and Rudolf Tusky v Oberkreisdirektor des Kreises Steinfurt—Amt für Lebensmittelüberwachung [1998] ECR I-46571 . . . . . 28.108
C-203/99 Veedfald v Århus Amtskommune [2001] ECR I-3569 . . . . . 28.170
C-307/01 Peter d'Ambrumenil and Dispute Resolution Services Ltd v Commissioners of Customs & Excise [2003] EWECJ 55.23
C-412/06 Annelore Hamilton v Volksbank Filder eG [2008] ECR I-2383. . . . . 28.195
C-199/08 Eschig v UNIQA Sachversicherung AG [2009] ECR 1-08295 . . . . . 34.16, 34.17
C-215/08 E Friz GmbH v Carsten von der Heyden, Opinion of AG Trstenjak, 8 September 2009 (unreported) 28.172
C-122/10 Konsumentombudsmannen v Ving Sverige AB [2011] WLR (D) 181. . . . . 28.121
C-293/10 Stark v DAS Oesterreiche Algemeine Rechtsschutzversicherung AG [2011] ECR I-04711 . . . . . 34.17
C-260/11, R (on the application of Edwards) v Environment Agency [2013] 1 WLR 2914 . . . . . 13.94, 24.36
C-530/11, European Commission v United Kingdom of Great Britain and Northern Ireland ECLI:EU:C:2014:67 . . . . . 13.81
C-442/12 Sneller v DAS Nederlandse Rechtsbijstand Verzekeringsmaatschappij NV [2014] Lloyds' Rep IR 238 . . . . . 34.16, 34.17
De Danske Bilimportører v Skatteministeriet, Told-og Skattestyrelsen [2006] ECR I-4945 . . . . . 54.18, 54.24
International Chemical Corpn v Amministrazione delle Finanze dello Stato [1981] ECR 1191 . . . . 4.06

NATIONAL COURTS

Australia

Aon Risk Services Australia Ltd v Australian National University [2009] HCA 27; (2009) 258 ALR 14 . . . . . 26.22, 26.38, 26.46
Avonbank Dairy Co Pty Ltd, Re [1962] Tas SR 121 . . . . . 9.664
Brookfield Multiplex Ltd v International Litigation Funding Partners Pte Ltd (2009) 256 ALR 427 . . . . . 33.23
Brown v Bank of Australasia [1915] VLR 453. . . . . 32.29
Campbells Cash and Carry Pty Ltd v Fostif Pty Ltd (2006) 229 CLR 386. . . . . 33.16, 33.17, 33.19
Carey v Korda [2012] WASCA 228 (Western Australia) 66.04
Clairs Keeley (a firm) v Treacy & Ors (2003) 28 WAR 139 . . . . . 33.13
D'Alessandro & D'Angelo v Cooper (unreported), 21 June 1996, WASC, Full Ct 27.211, 39.20
Darcey v Pre-Term Foundation Clinic [1983] 2 NSWLR 497 . . . . . 9.69
Douglas, In the Will of (1951) 51 SR (NSW) 282. . . . . 3.6
Elders Trustee & Executor Co Ltd v EG Reeves Pty Ltd (1988) 20 FCR 164 (Federal Court of Australia) 65.04
Fostif Pty Ltd v Campbells Cash & Carry Pty Ltd (2005) 63 NSWLR 203 . . . . . 33.16
Government Insurance Office of New South Wales v R J Green & Lloyd Pty Ltd (1966) 114 CLR 437 . . . . . 50.75
Grey v Australian Motorists & General Insurance Co Pty Ltd [1976] 1 NSWLR 669 . . . . . 32.29
Hartley Poynton Ltd v Ali [2005] VSCA 53. . . . . 56.42
Hermann v Charny [1976] 1 NSWLR 261. . . . . 3.16
Hughes v Western Australian Cricket Assn (Inc) (1986) ATPR 40-748 . . . . . 6.42
International Litigation Partners Pte Ltd v Chameleon Mining NL [2011] NSWCA 50 . . . . . 33.24
Isaacs v Ocean Accident (1957) 58 SRNSW 69 . . . . . 23.15
Jeffery & Katauskas Pty Ltd v SST Consulting Pty Ltd; Jeffery & Katauskas Pty Ltd v Rickard Constructions Pty Ltd [2009] HCA 43 . . . . . 9.38, 9.39, 9.42
Knight v FP Special Assets Ltd (1992) 174 CLR 178. . . . . 9.52
Macquarie International Health Clinic Pty Ltd v Sydney South West Area Health Service (No 2) [2011] NSWCA 171 (New South Wales). 66.04
Marston v Statewide Independent Wholesalers Ltd [2003] NSWSC 816. . . . . 33.13
Mobil Oil Australia Pty Ltd v Trendlen Pty Ltd [2006] HCA 42. . . . . 33.16, 33.19
Norman v Federal Comr of Taxation (1963) 109 CLR 9 . . . . . 32.08, 32.13, 32.14, 32.31
Patel v Sica [1982] VR 273 . . . . . 35.58
Purton, In the Estate of (1935) 53 WN (NSW) 148 . . . . . 3.06
QIW Retailers Ltd v Felview [1989] 2 Qd R 245 . . . . . 3.40
QPSX Ltd v Ericsson Australia Pty Ltd (No 3) (2005) 219 ALR 1 . . . . . 33.16
Queanbeyan Leagues Club Ltd v Poldune Pty Ltd [2000] NSWSC 1100. . . . . 3.40
Queensland Fish Board v Bunney, ex parte Queensland Fish Board [1979] Qd R 301 . . . . . 6.6.13
Sanderson, Re [1927] VLR 394 . . . . . 3.52
Schlieskev Overseas Construction Co Pty Ltd [1960] VR 195 . . . . . 9.68
Vered v Inscorp Holdings Ltd (1993) 31 NSWLR 290, NSW SC. 40.45
Vilensky v Banning (unreported), 20 June 1996, WA Sup Ct. 35.118
Wentworth v de Montfort (1988) 15 NSWLR 348. . . . . 40.75
Wentworth v Lloyd (No 2) (1865) 34 Beav 455 . . . . . 52.98, 52.99
Woolf v Trebilco [1933] VLR 180. . . . . 36.26

Canada

Barrick v Clark [1951] SCR 177, [1950] 4 DLR 529, Supreme Court of Canada 43.288
Bergel & Edson v Wolf (2000) 50 OR (3d) 777 (SCJ) 29.197
Gough v Toronto & York Radial Railway Co (1918) 42 OntLR 415. . . . . 18.74
Underwood v Cox (1912) 4 DLR 66. . . . . 6.218
Marcotte v Longueil(ville) [2009] 3 RCS 65. . . . . 26.46
McIntyre Estate v Ontario (Attorney-General) [2001] OJ 713 (SCJ) 29.197

Hong Kong

Abani Trading Pte Ltd v BNP Paribas [2014] SGHC 111 . . . . . 66.34
Heung Kong (Holdings) Ltd v Chan Wai Yip [2002] HKCFI 631 (Hong Kong) 18.35

Ireland

A & L Goodbody Solicitors v Colthurst (unreported) 5 November 2003, High Court of Ireland 27.268
Aikin's Estate, Re [1894] 1 IR 225 . . . . . 40.75
Boyne v Dublin Bus [2006] IEHC 209 . . . . . 27.251, 27.268
Crean v M'Millan [1922] 2 IR 105 . . . . . 20.58
Curran v Finn [2002] IEHC 124 (Republic of Ireland) 18.35
Dawson v Irish Brokers Association [2002] IESC 36 . . . . . 1.54, 3.04, 18.116
Fraser v Buckle [1996] 2 IRLM 34 . . . . . 30.45
Galdan Properties Ltd (in liquidation), In the Matter of [1988] IR 213 . . . . . 40.37, 40.52, 40.85
Greenclean Waste Management Ltd v Leahy (No 2) [2014] IEHC 314; [2015] IECA 97 . . . . . 30.25, 30.48
Henehan v Allied Irish Banks plc (unreported), 19 October 1984, IEHC 18.116
Landers v Judge Patwell & Anor [2006] IEHC 248 . . . . . 4.67
Persona Digital Telephony Ltd & Sigma Wireless Networks Ltd v The Minister for Public Enterprise [2017] IESC 27 . . . . . 30.25, 33.03
Red Sail Frozen Foods Ltd (in receivership), Re [2007] 2 IR 361 . . . . . 66.04, 66.25
Sheehan v Corr [2016] IECA 168 . . . . . 42.50
Superquinn Ltd v Bray EDC [2001] 1 IR 459 . . . . . 5.04
Thema International Fund PLC v HSBC Institutional Trust Services (Ireland) Ltd [2011] IEHC 357 . . . . . 30.25, 30.48, 33.03

Isle of Man

Tomlinson v Thane Investments Ltd (unreported), 2 March 2006, Chancery Division of the High Court in the Isle of Man 33.87

New Zealand

Arklow Investments Ltd v MacLean (unreported), 19 May 2000, High Court of New Zealand 9.38
Bunting v Buchanan [2013] NZHC 1921 . . . . . 66.04
Longreach Oil Ltd v Southern Cross Exploration NL 1988 NSW Lexis 9762 . . . . . 27.310
Moevao v Department of Labour [1980] 1 NZLR 464 . . . . . 26.40
Saunders v Houghton [2009] NZCA 610 . . . . . 9.39
Waterhouse v Contractors Bonding Ltd [2013] NZSC 89 . . . . . 33.87, 33.89

Singapore

Law Society of Singapore v Kurubalan s/o Manickam Rengaraju [2013] SGHC 135 . . . . . 29.180, 29.181

United States

Del Webb Communities, Inc v Partington, 652 F3d 1145, 1156 (9th Cir 2011) 33.87
Johnson v Georgia Highway Express 488 F 2d 714, 717–19 (5th Cir, 1974) 37.25
Trust for the Certificate Holders of the Merrill Lynch Mortgage Investors, Inc v Love Funding Corpn, 13 NY3d 190 (NY 2009) 33.87
Trust for the Certificate Holders of the Merrill Lynch Mortgage Investors, Inc v Love Funding Corpn, 591 F3d 116 (2d Cir 2010) 33.87

TABLE OF STATUTES

Access to Health Records Act 1990 . . . . . .55.24
Access to Justice Act 1999 . . . . . 29.214, 54.138
Pt I. 1.164, 2.09
s 9(6) 1.166
s 10(1) 18.80, 54.195
s 11. . . . . 6.250, 62.03
s 11(1). 62.20, 62.22
s 22(2) 18.80, 54.195
s 27(1) 29.186
s 29 . . . . 1.157, 2.09, 54.175
s 30 . . . . . 2.09, 9.59, 43.185, 50.143, 54.181, 54.183, 54.184, 54.188
s 30(1) 54.182
s 30(3) 54.188
s 31. . . . . .1.160, 18.19
s 54(4) 45.54
s 57. . . . . .45.41
s 57(1)(a). 45.41
Access to Justice Act 2000 . . . . .50.19
Access to Medical Reports Act 1988. . . . . .55.24
Act for abolishing certain offices of the High Court of Chancery in England, 5 & 6 Vict c 103 . . . . .43.12
Act for the Better Regulation of Attornies and Solicitors 1728 (2 Geo II, c 23) . . . 1.61
s 23 . . . . .1.61
Administration of Justice Act 1696 (8 & 9 Will 3, c 11). 1.60
s 1 . . . . .1.60
s 2 . . . . .1.60
Administration of Justice Act 1841 . . . . . . .1.73
Administration of Justice Act 1970
s 44 . . . . 56.43
s 44A 56.42, 56.46
Administration of Justice Act 1985
s 9 . . . . . 2.09, 3.49, 3.67, 34.47, 59.05, 59.50
s 9A 34.47
s 32A 3.49
Sch 2, para 29. . . . . .35.73
Administration of Justice (Miscellaneous Provisions) Act 1933
s 7 . . . . .61.03
Adoption and Children Act 2002. . . . . . . .29.18
Anti-social Behaviour Crime and Policing Act 2014
s 180. . . . . .1.187
Arbitration Act 1996 . . . . 48.69, 48.77
s 1 . . . . .48.73
s 4(1) 48.75
s 4(2) 48.75
s 5(1) 48.77
s 5(2) 48.77
s 6(1) 48.76
s 14(1). 48.79
s 14(4) 48.79
s 34 . . . . .48.78
s 34(2) 48.84
s 35. . . . . .48.81
s 44 . . . . .40.98
ss 46–58. . . . . .48.93
s 47. . . . . .48.93
s 49. . . . . .56.125
s 59(1) 48.81, 48.97
s 59(2) 48.97
s 60 . . . . .48.98
s 61(1). 48.99
s 61(2) 48.100
s 63(1) 48.101
s 63(3) 48.101
s 63(4) 48.76, 48.102
s 63(5) 48.101
s 63(7) 48.96
s 64(1) 48.103
s 64(2) 48.103
s 64(4) 48.103
s 65. . . . . .13.10
s 65(1). 48.104
s 65(2) 48.104
s 66(1) 48.94
Sch 1 . . . . .48.75
Attorneys Act 1605 (3 James I, c 7). 1.50
Attorneys' and Solicitors' Act 1870 . . . . . . 1.82, 1.84, 27.169, 27.211
s 2 . . . . .27.116
s 4 . . . . 27.139, 27.140, 27.213, 50.12
s 5 . . . . .18.04
s 8 . . . . .27.116, 27.134
s 9 . . . . .27.113, 27.134
Bills of Exchange Act 1882
s 27(3) 40.37
Champerty Act 1275 (3 Edw I, c 25) 1.21, 30.05, 30.19
Charging Orders Act 1979. . . . . . . 40.01, 40.99
s 1(1). 40.99
Charitable Trusts Act 1853
s 20 . . . . .66.45

Charities Act 1993
s 50 . . . . 27.3139
s 60 . . . . 27.319
Charities Act 2006
s 75(1) 27.319
Sch 8
para 96. . . . . 27.319
para 143. 27.319
Charities Act 2011
s 127 . . . . 18.136
s 251. . . . . 27.319
s 260 . . . . 27.319
s 261. . . . . 27.319
Children Act 1989 . . . . .60.03
Pt 1 . . . . 29.18
Pt II 29.18
Pt IV 29.18
Civil Evidence Act 1995
s 2(1) 43.325
Civil Liability (Contribution) Act 1978. . . . 19.43, 23.107, 34.66
s 1 . . . . 19.34, 19.40
s 1(4) 19.41
s 2 . . . . 19.35, 19.40, 19.42
s 3 . . . . 19.28
s 6(1) 19.37, 19.42
Civil Partnership Act 2004
Pt 2, Ch 2. . . . . 29.18
Sch 5 . . . . 29.18
Sch 6 . . . . 29.18
Sch 7 . . . . 29.18
Civil Procedure Act 1997 (CPA 1997) 4.48
s 1 . . . . 18.20
s 1(1). 4.33
s 2 . . . . 4.34
s 3(1)(b) 4.34
s 3(2) 4.34
s 4(1) 4.36
s 4(2) 4.36
s 4(5) 4.36
s 5 . . . . 4.50
s 5(2) 4.48
s 6 . . . . 4.36
s 9(20. . . . . 4.41
Sch 1
para 4. . . . . 4.43
para 5. 4.42, 4.48
para 6. . . . . 4.41
para 9(2) 4.46
Commissioners for Revenue and Customs Act 2005
s 2 . . . . 50.342
Commonhold and Leasehold Reform Act 2002 . . . . 18.06
Common Law Procedure Act 1860, (23 & 24 Vict, c. 126)
s 28 . . . . 40.89, 40.96
Companies Act 1985 . . . . .32.61
s 1 . . . . 27.320
s 726(1) 15.07, 15.35
s 1295. . . . . 15.07
Companies Act 2006
s 39. . . . . 27.319
s 40 . . . . 27.319
s 42 . . . . 27.319
s 43 . . . . 27.320
s 44 . . . . 27.320
s 44(1) 27.320
s 44(5) 27.320
s 45. . . . . 27.320
s 46 . . . . 27.320
s 260(3) 65.123
s 261. . . . . 65.125
s 262 . . . . 65.125
s 264 . . . . 65.125
Compensation Act 2006 . . . . .33.33
Part 2. . . . . 29.144, 29.201
s 2 . . . . 26.144
Competition Act 1998
s 47C(8) 29.146
Constitutional Reform Act 2005
s 5(5) 4.48
s 5(6) 4.48
s 40(5) 6.09
s 41(2) 6.09
s 45. . . . . 4.44
Sch 1 . . . . 4.33, 4.34
para 4(1)(b) 4.36
para 4(2) 4.36
Sch 2 . . . . 4.48
para 2(1). 4.47
Sch 14
Pt 4 . . . . 5.03
Consumer Credit Act 1974 . . . . . .33.32, 33.34, 33.51–33.58, 52.86
s 65(1). 33.56, 33.57
s 127 . . . . 33.57
s 135. . . . . 33.57
s 136 57
Consumer Credit Act 2000 . . . . .33.32
Consumer Credit Act 2006 . . . . 52.86
Consumer Insurance (Disclosure and Representations) Act 2012 . . . . .63.04
Consumer Protection Act 1987
Pt III 38.57
ss 20–21. . . . . 38.57
Consumer Protection Act 1997
Pt I, ss 1–9 . . . . 28.18
Consumer Rights Act 2015 . . . . . .28.01, 28.23, 28.24, 28.41, 28.158, 31.68
Pt 1 . . . . . .28.01, 28.06, 28.07, 28.29–28.39
Pt 1, Ch 2. . . . . 28.156, 31.73

Consumer Rights Act 2015 (*cont.*)
Pt 2 . . . . 27.130, 28.01, 28.06, 28.07, 28.40–28.44, 28.149, 28.159
Pt 3 . . . . .28.104
s 2(2) 28.26
s 2(3) 28.25
s 49. . . . . 28.07
s 49(1) 28.157
s 49(2) 28.35
s 50 . . . . .27.55, 27.195, 27.213, 28.07, 28.30, 31.72, 37.33, 38.68
s 50(1) 31
s 50(2) 28.31, 38.71
s 50(2)(b) 38.70
s 50(3) 28.31
s 50(4) 28.34, 38.70
s 51. . . . . 27.195, 28.07, 28.37, 28.157
s 52. . . . . 28.07, 28.38, 28.157, 31.72
s 53(1) 28.28
s 53(2) 28.28
s 54 . . . . 28.134, 28.143
s 55. . . . . 28.35, 28.134, 28.145
s 56 . . . . .28.35, 28.134, 28.146
s 57. . . . . 28.36
s 62(1) 28.42, 37.34
s 62(2) 28.42, 37.35
s 62(3) 28.42, 37.34, 37.35
s 62(4) 28.41, 37.34
s 62(5) 28.41
s 62(6) .28.41, 37.35
s 63(1) 28.43
s 63(2) 28.43
Sch 1
para 3. . . . . .28.105
paras 37–52 . . . . 28.156, 31.73
Sch 2
paras 114–115 . . . . .28.105
Pt 1 . . . . 28.43
Pt 1, para 6. . . . . 28.44
Pt 1, para 8. . . . . 28.44
Sch 4
paras 2–27 . . . . .28.159
Sch 8 . . . . .29.143
para 37. . . . . .29.146
Consumers, Estate Agents and Redress Act 2007
s 59. . . . . 28.21, 28.164, 28.168
s 62(3) 28.21
s 62(3)(f) 28.21, 28.164
Contracts (Rights of Third Parties) Act 1999 . . . . .34.65
s 1(1). 34.65
s 1(2) 34.65
s 1(3) 34.65
Copyright, Designs and Patents Act 1988
s 290 . . . . 58.04
Coroners and Justice Act 2009
s 154. . . . . .29.141, 29.145, 29.168
Corporate Bodies' Contracts Act 1960
s 1 . . . . .27.320
Costs Act 1531, 23 Hen 8, c 15 (sub nom An Act that the Defendant shall recover Costs against the Plaintiff, if the Plaintiff be nonsuited, or if the Verdict pass against him) . . . 1.35, 1.36, 1.39
s 2 . . . . .1.35
Costs 1606 (4 James I, c 3) 1.52
Costs Act 1607. . . . . .8.05
County Courts Act 1235 . . . . 1.17
County Courts Act 1846 . . . . .1.68
s 129. . . . . .1.86
County Courts Act 1867
s 5 . . . . .1.89
County Courts Act 1984 . . . . .21.05
s 18. . . . . .5.13, 5.15
s 23 . . . . .5.12
s 23(g) 5.12
s 24 . . . . .5.13, 5.15
s 42 . . . . 36.44, 36.48
s 63 . . . . .45.67
s 69(1) 38.92, 56.118, 56.120, 56.121
s 74. . . . . 43.194, 56.05, 56.14
s 74(1). 56.15, 56.16, 56.43
s 74A(2) 4.48
s 74(5A) 56.42, 56.46
s 76. . . . . 5.26
Court of Chancery Act 1842 (5 & 6 Victoriae, c 103) 1.73
Courts and Legal Services Act 1990 (CLSA 1990) . . . 3.49, 3.52, 3.56, 3.57, 3.61, 3.74, 3.89, 3.94, 5.13, 5.15, 29.132
s 4 . . . . 9.03, 9.96, 9.108
s 7(2) 45.70
s 11. . . . . .3.100
s 17. . . . . .3.58
s 27 . . . . 2.09, 3.60
s 27(2)(a)(i). 2.09
s 27(2)(b) 3.100
s 27(2)(c) 3.100
s 27(9) 2.09
s 27(1) 3.57
s 27(2)(b) 47.10
s 28 . . . . 3.60, 53.19
s 28(2)(c) 47.10
s 28(5) 3.60
s 28(6) 3.58, 3.60
s 57 . . . .27.127, 29.186, 29.187, 29.188, 29.190
s 57(1). 27.125, 27.126, 27.259
s 57(2) 27.123

s 57(3) 27.119, 27.120, 27.122
s 57(4) 27.128
s 57(5) 27.128, 27.129
s 57(6) 27.128, 27.129
s 57(7) 27.119
s 58 . . . . . 1.143, 27.230, 29.04, 29.07, 29.23, 29.53, 29.194, 29.209
s 58(1) 4.19, 27.214, 27.215, 29.14, 29.25, 29.54, 29.78, 29.106,29.107, 29.123, 29.181, 29.184, 29.187, 29.190, 29.194, 29.198, 54.44
s 58(2) 2.09
s 58(2)(a) 2.09, 29.04, 29.13, 29.33
s 58(2)(b) 2.09, 29.19
s 58(2)(c) 54.55
s 58(3) 2.09, 29.15, 29.16, 29.20
s 58(3)(a) 27.36, 27.214
s 58(3)(c) 29.25
s 58(4) 29.20, 54.06
s 58(5) 27.118, 27.215, 29.106, 29.184, 29.186, 29.190
s 58A 29.04, 29.07, 29.181, 33.27
s 58A(1) 29.18, 29.145
s 58A(1)(a) 54.10
s 58A(2) 29.18, 29.145
s 58A(2)(b) 29.02
s 58A(3)(a) 29.78
s 58A(4) 29.07, 29.11
s 58A(6) 29.19, 54.07
s 58AA 29.143, 29.144, 29.181
s 58AA(1) 29.145, 29.147
s 58AA(2) 29.145, 29.147, 29.190
s 58AA(4) 29.145
s 58AA(4)(b) 29.168
s 58AA(7) 29.144, 29.168
s 58AA(9) 27.118, 29.145, 29.147, 29.187, 29.190
s 58AA(11) 29.146
s 58B 2.09, 33.27
s 58B(2) 2.09
s 58B(8) 33.06, 33.27
s 58C 54.38
s 58C(1) 54.12
s 61 . . . . 53.04, 53.08
s 61(1) 27.128
s 70 . . . . 3.62, 3.63
s 70(1) 3.63
s 70(3) 3.63
s 98 . . . . 27.117, 27.123
s 98(5) 51.11
s 111 . . . . 9.62
s 112 . . . . 9.62
s 119 . . . . 3.34, 29.06, 29.07
s 119(1) 2.09, 3.54, 3.73, 3.75, 9.108, 9.111, 29.11
s 124(3) 58.04
s 125(7) 45.70, 58.04
s 154 . . . . 29.03
Sch 20 . . . . 45.70, 58.04
Creating Frivolous Suits Act 1601 (43 Eliz, c 6) 1.43
s 2 . . . . 1.43
Crime and Courts Act 2013
s 17 . . . . 36.47, 45.74
s 17(5) 5.15, 27.167
s 61(3) 5.15
s 101 . . . . 18.136
Sch 9
Pt 3, para 52(1)(b) 5.15, 27.167
Pt 3, para 52(2) 5.15, 27.167
Criminal Justice and Court Services Act 2000
s 15 . . . . 53.19
Criminal Justice and Courts Act 2015 . . . . 8.38, 13.69
s 36 . . . . 9.96
s 57 . . . . 6.89, 6.90, 8.34, 57.04
s 57(9) 6.89
s 80 . . . . 13.01
s 87 . . . . 67.17
s 88 . . . . 13.52, 13.56, 13.58, 13.60, 13.61, 13.62, 13.67, 13.70, 13.74
s 88(1) 13.46, 13.50
s 88(2) 13.48, 13.51
s 88(3) 13.51
s 88(4) 13.51
s 88(5) 13.51
s 88(6)–(8) 13.82
s 88(6) 13.58
s 88(6)(a) 13.53
s 88(6)(b) 13.53, 13.58
s 88(6)(c) 13.53
s 88(7)(a) 13.54
s 88(7)(b) 13.54
s 88(7)(c) 13.54
s 88(8)(a) 13.55
s 88(8)(b) 13.55
s 88(8)(c) 13.55
s 88(12) 13.46, 13.48, 13.52
s 88(13) 13.48, 13.52
s 89 . . . . . . 13.01, 13.52, 13.53, 13.58, 13.60, 13.61, 13.62, 13.67, 13.70, 13.74
s 89(1) 13.70, 13.72
s 89(1)(a) 13.64, 13.66
s 89(1)(b) 13.61, 13.64
s 89(1)(c) 13.64
s 89(1)(d) 13.64
s 89(1)(e) 13.64
s 89(2) 13.63, 13.71
s 89(6) 13.48
s 90 . . . . 13.83

Criminal Law Act 1967
s 13(1) 30.05
s 14(1) 30.05
s 14(2) 1.132, 29.206, 30.05
Crown Debts Act 1541 (33 Hen 8, c 39)
s 54 . . . . . 1.39
Crown Proceedings Act 1947 . . . . . 61.03
s 23(1) 61.03
s 23(2) 61.03
s 23(3) 61.03
s 24 . . . . . 56.19
s 24(2) 61.05
s 25(1) 61.06
s 38(4) 61.03
Damages Act 1996
s 2(4) 17.49
s 7(1) 52.62
Dangerous Dogs Act 1871 . . . . . 61.14
Data Protection Act 1998 . . . . . 52.60, 55.24
Defamation Act 2013
s 14(1) 58.03
Domestic Proceedings and Magistrates' Courts Act 1978 . . . . . 29.18
Duties on Law Proceedings Act 1670 (22 & 23 Cha 2, c 9) 25.06
Annex IX 1.58
Electronic Communications Act 2000
s 7(2) 35.76
Employers' Liability (Compulsory Insurance) Act 1969 . . . . . 50.125
s 2(1) 50.121, 50.140
Environmental Protection Act 1990
s 80 . . . . . 61.14
s 82 . . . . . 29.18, 29.20
Equality Act 2010
s 83(2)(a) 50.126
European Communities Act 1972 . . . . . 24.02
s 2(2) 28.62, 28.164, 34.34.14
Family Law Act 1996
Pt IV 29.18
Family Law Reform Act 1969
s 1(1) 60.03
Fatal Accidents Act 1976 . . . 8.52, 17.176, 27.34
s 1(3) 8.48, 8.51
Female Genital Mutilation Act 2003
Sch 2, Pt 1 . . . . . 29.18
Financial Services and Markets Act 2000 . . . . . 27.277, 27.288, 27.289, 33.34, 33.36–33.50
Part XX 33.48, 33.49, 34.46, 34.47
s 19 . . . . . 33.37, 34.43
s 20 . . . . . 33.50
s 22 . . . . . 33.38
s 23 . . . . . 33.50, 34.43, 34.47
s 26 . . . . . 27.278, 27.279, 33.50, 34.50
s 27 . . . . . 34.50
s 28 . . . . . 27.237, 27.285
s 28(4) 27.285
s 38 . . . . . 34.50
s 327 . . . . . 27.289, 33.47, 34.45
s 327(3) 27.296
Sch 2 . . . . . 33.39
Sch 2, Pt 1
para 2 . . . . . 33.39
para 3 . . . . . 33.39
para 6 . . . . . 33.39
First Statute of Westminster 1275 . . . . . 1.21
Foreign Limitation Periods Act 1984 . . . . . 23.83
Frivolous Suits Act 1601, 43 Eliz I, c 6 . . . . 25.06
Frivolous Suits Act 1698 (11 & 12 W 3, c 9)
s 1 . . . . . 1.45
Great Charter 1225 . . . . . 1.15
Human Rights Act 1998 . . . . 9.79, 15.77, 15.82, 24.02, 24.09, 64.04
s 2 . . . . . 24.12
s 2(1)(a) 4.06
s 2(1)(b) 4.06
s 3 . . . . . 24.15, 24.17
s 3(1) 24.14, 24.16, 24.17
s 3(2)(b) 24.19
s 4 . . . . . 5.09, 24.20
s 6 . . . . . 24.09, 24.11
s 6(1) 24.21
s 6(3)(a) 24.09
s 6(6) 24.23
s 7 . . . . . 24.10
s 7(1) 64.04
s 8 . . . . . 24.22
Sch 1 . . . . . 46.44
Insolvency Act 1986
s 123(1)(a) 43.414
s 222(1)(a) 43.414
s 267(2)(b) 35.113
s 268 . . . . . 40.122
s 283(1) 27.82, 32.04
s 287 . . . . . 47.30
s 303 . . . . . 47.31
s 306 . . . . . 32.04
s 311 . . . . . 47.31
s 312 . . . . . 47.31
s 322 . . . . . 27.82
s 436 . . . . . 32.04
Interpretation Act 1978 . . . . . 3.34
s 21(1) 4.37, 4.50
Sch 1 . . . . . 2.09, 36.29, 40.05

Judgments Act 1838 . . . . 56.35
s 17 . . . . 43.194, 56.05, 56.12, 56.15, 56.55, 56.70
s 17(1) 56.42
Judicature Act 1873
s 49 . . . . 45.70
Judicature Act 1875
Sch 66.36
Judicature Act 1881
s 25 . . . . 1.92
Judicature Acts 66.36
Land Registration Act 2002
Sch 2, para 5 . . . . 2.09
Late Payment of Commercial Debts
(Interest) Act 1998 . . . . 38.97–38.102,
56.118, 56.122
s 2(1) 56.122
s 2(5) 38.98
s 2(7) 38.98
s 3(2) 38.98, 38.101, 56.122
s 3(3) 38.98, 38.101, 56.122
s 3A 38.99
s 3B 38.99
s 3C 38.100
s 4 . . . . 38.98
s 5A 38.102
s 5A(2A) 38.102
s 5A(4) 38.100
Law Reform (Frustrated Contracts)
Act 1943 . . . . 27.27
s 1 . . . . 27.78
Law Reform (Miscellaneous Provisions)
Act 1934
s 3 . . . . 56.118
Law of Property Act 1925
s 74A 32.62
s 136 . . . . 32.14, 32.29, 32.31
s 146 . . . . 66.17
s 146(3) 66.17
Law of Property (Miscellaneous Provisions)
Act 1989
s 1(1) 32.60
s 36A 32.61
Law Reform (Miscellaneous Provisions)
Act 1934 . . . . 17.176, 27.34
s 1(1) 8.52
Leases Act 1845 . . . . 1.172
s 3 . . . . 1.81
Legal Aid Act 1974
s 8 . . . . 18.80, 18.81
Legal Aid Act 1988
s 3 . . . . 1.140
Legal Aid and Advice Act 1949 . . . . 1.122, 8.06
Legal Aid, Sentencing and Punishment
of Offenders Act 2012 . . . . 1.174, 62.03, 62.07
Pt 1 . . . . 2.09, 43.99, 44.12
s 1 . . . . 62.07
s 2 . . . . 62.07
s 4 . . . . 2.09
s 5(2) 62.08, 62.12
s 8 . . . . 62.07
s 26 . . . . . . 62.01, 62.10–62.12, 62.16, 62.43
s 26(1) 62.19, 62.20, 62.22, 62.31, 62.34
s 26(3)–(5) 62.08, 62.12
s 26(6)(a)–(g) 62.08, 62.12
s 26(7) 62.08, 62.12
s 26(9) 62.08, 62.12
s 38(1) 62.08
s 44 . . . . 32.40
s 44(4) 54.07
s 44(6) 29.23, 32.39, 54.08, 54.34
s 45 . . . . 29.145
s 45(4) 29.19
s 45(10) 29.03
s 45(13) 29.141
s 46 . . . . 54.12
s 46(1) 54.38
s 46(3) 54.13, 54.34, 54.176, 54.177
s 47(1) 54.184
s 47(2) 54.184
s 48 . . . . 54.22, 54.28
s 51 . . . . 62.03
s 61 . . . . 18.123, 18.136
s 61(2) 18.123
Sch 1
Pt 1 . . . . 44.12
Pt 2 . . . . 44.12
Sch 4
para 7(1) 62.09
para 7(3) 62.09
para 7(5) 62.09
Sch 5
para 51 . . . . 62.08
para 68 . . . . 18.136
Legal Services Act 2007 (LSA 2007) 1.170,
2.09, 3.52, 3.53, 3.55, 3.56, 3.67,
3.74, 3.76, 3.89, 3.94, 9.108,
29.06, 36.81, 47.02, 59.50
Pt 3 . . . . 3.77
Pt 5 . . . . 2.09
s 1 . . . . 3.49
s 1(1) 3.76
s 12 . . . . 3.49
s 12(1) 2.09, 3.49, 3.50, 47.02
s 12(3) 2.09
s 12(4) 2.09
s 13 . . . . 3.77
s 13(1) 3.49, 47.02
s 13(2) 3.49, 3.77, 47.02, 47.03
s 13(2)(a) 3.48
s 13(2)(b) 3.48

Legal Services Act 2007 (LSA 2007) (*cont.*)
s 14 . . . 3.51
s 14(1) . . . 3.51, 3.77, 47.03
s 15(4) . . . 3.84
s 15(6) . . . 3.84
s 16(2) . . . 3.90
s 16(4) . . . 3.90
s 18 . . . 2.09
s 18(1)(a) . . . 47.03
s 19 . . . 3.100, 47.10
s 21 . . . 2.09
s 69(4) . . . 3.49
s 83 . . . 34.47
s 126 . . . 39.24
s 128(4) . . . 39.24
s 128(5)(b) . . . 39.24
s 131 . . . 39.24
s 133 . . . 39.27
s 133(3)(e) . . . 39.27
s 133(3)(h) . . . 39.33
s 133(3)(i) . . . 39.33
s 133(4) . . . 39.24, 39.27
s 133(5) . . . 39.27
s 133(6) . . . 39.33
s 136 . . . 39.26
s 137 . . . 39.28, 39.29
s 137(2) . . . 39.31
s 138 . . . 39.32
s 139 . . . 39.34
s 140(4) . . . 39.34
s 140(11) . . . 39.24, 40.08
s 141 . . . 39.34
s 157 . . . 39.22
s 177 . . . 3.54, 3.55, 3.70, 35.43, 35.72, 35.85, 35.99, 38.40, 40.06
s 190(6) . . . 2.09
s 192 . . . 47.17
s 192(2) . . . 47.12
s 194 . . . 2.09, 13.65, 13.71, 18.01, 18.123, 18.125, 18.129, 18.136, 43.165
s 194(1)(a) . . . 18.123
s 194(2) . . . 18.123
s 194(3) . . . 6.262, 18.124, 18.131, 18.132, 18.135, 43.165, 43.330, 43.381, 43.387, 55.14
s 194(4) . . . 18.126
s 194(5) . . . 18.130
s 194(8) . . . 18.124
s 194(10) . . . 2.09, 18.123
s 194(11) . . . 18.123
s 207 . . . 3.49
s 207(1) . . . 3.54
s 210 . . . 3.55, 3.70, 38.40
Sch 1
para 2(3)–(5) . . . 3.49
Sch 2 . . . 3.77
para 2 . . . 3.80
para 3 . . . 2.09, 3.78
para 4 . . . 2.09
para 5 . . . 3.55, 3.81
Sch 3
para 1(2) . . . 3.100, 47.05, 47.07, 47.10, 47.16
para 1(3) . . . 3.80
para 1(6) . . . 3.80
para 1(7) . . . 3.86, 47.10
para 2(2) . . . 3.79
para 2(4) . . . 3.79
para 3 . . . 3.82
para 3(9) . . . 3.82
Sch 4, para 19 . . . 33.49, 34.47
Sch 15
para 2(3) . . . 3.49
Sch 16
Pt 1, para 1 . . . 3.54, 3.55, 3.70, 35.43, 35.72, 35.85, 35.99, 38.40, 40.06
Pt 1, para 25 . . . 3.54
Pt 1, para 26(a) . . . 3.55, 3.70
Pt 1, para 39 . . . 38.40
Pt 1, para 60 . . . 35.99, 40.06
Pt 1, para 64(1) . . . 35.43, 35.72, 35.85
Pt 1, para 64(3) . . . 35.43, 35.72, 35.85
Sch 22 . . . 3.57, 3.76, 3.77
para 2(6) . . . 3.49
para 2(7)(b) . . . 3.49
para 14 . . . 35.43, 35.72, 35.85
Sch 23 . . . 3.55, 38.40
Limitation Act 1623 (21 James I, c 16) . . . 25.06
s 6 . . . 1.45
Limitation Act 1980 . . . 23.83
s 5 . . . 23.85, 23.86
s 10(1) . . . 23.107
s 21(3) . . . 23.87
s 24 . . . 23.117
s 29 . . . 23.124, 39.04
s 29(5) . . . 23.123, 23.125, 40.125
s 29(7) . . . 23.123
s 30 . . . 23.126
s 32(1) . . . 23.135
s 35(1)(b) . . . 21.39
s 35(2) . . . 21.39
s 38 . . . 23.100
Limitation of Actions and Costs Act 1842 . . . 1.85, 1.86, 18.03
s 1 . . . 1.85
s 2 . . . 1.85
Limitation (Enemies and War Prisoners) Act 1945 . . . 23.83
s 1(1) . . . 59.02
s 1(2) . . . 59.03
Limited Liability Partnerships Act 2000
s 1(3) . . . 27.321
s 6 . . . 27.321

Litigants in Person (Costs and Expenses) Act 1975. . . . . 3.09, 59.04
s 1(1). 18.16
Maintenance Act 1275 (Edw I, c 28) 1.21
Marshalsea, exportation of corn, safe-conducts, sub-poenas, attaints, etc 1436 (15 Henry 4, c 4) 1.30
Matrimonial Causes Act 1973 . . . . 29.18
Matrimonial and Family Proceedings Act 1984
Pt III 29.18
Mental Capacity Act 2005 . . . . . . 27.181, 60.01, 60.50, 60.51, 60.52–60.56
s 1 . . . . 60.54
s 2 . . . . 60.55
s 2(1) 60.52
s 2(2) 60.55
s 2(3) 60.55
s 3 . . . . 60.56
s 7 . . . . 60.62, 60.63
s 16. . . . . 60.66
s 42 . . . . 60.52
s 43 . . . . 60.52
s 67(1). 27.181
Sch 6
para 22(1). 27.181
para 22(3) 27.181
Partnership Act 1890 . . . . 19.18
s 9 . . . . 19.18
Patents Act 1977
s 104(2) 53.19
Pollock's Act of 1842 (5 & 6 Victoriæ, c 97). 1.85
Poor Persons Act 1495 (11 Henry 7, c 12). 1.33
Poor Prisoners Defence Act 1903 . . . . 1.109
Prosecution of Offences Act 1985. . . . . . . 52.52, 59.39, 59.43
Recital of Intention 1670
s 136 . . . . 1.59
Recovery of Damages and Costs Act 1278 . . . . 1.21, 1.22, 1.23
Representation of the People Act 1983
s 156. . . . . 6.12
Road Traffic Act 1988
s 143. . . . . 63.04
s 145. . . . . 63.04
s 145(3)(a). 50.75
s 148(5) 63.04
s 151 . . . . 34.66, 63.04
s 151(4). 63.04
s 152(1)(a). 63.04
s 152. . . . . 63.04
s 152(2) 63.04
Road Traffic Acts 50.77
Sale of Goods Act 1954
s 3 . . . . 60.62
Senior Courts Act 1981
s 1 . . . . 4.33
s 9(1) 45.39
s 15(1). 5.25
s 1891)(f) 45.70
s 19(1). 5.25
s 32(4) 14.02, 43.377
s 32(5) 14.03, 43.377
s 33. . . . . 50.271
s 35A 38.88, 38.92
s 35A(1) 56.118, 56.120, 56.121
s 49(2) 21.05
s 51. . . . . . 3.30, 6.09, 6.12, 6.13, 7.186, 9.03, 9.10, 9.96, 9.99, 18.75, 21.06, 49.154, 49.155, 56.85, 57.17, 64.04, 64.05, 66.06, 66.17, 66.22, 67.02
s 51(a). 49.147
s 51(1). 7.177, 9.47, 9.107, 9.115
s 51(2) 18.19, 18.21, 18.22, 29.68
s 51(3) 4.35, 8.04, 9.03, 9.47, 9.61, 9.62, 9.63, 9.107, 13.14, 66.56
s 51(6) 9.62, 9.93, 9.95, 9.98, 9.101, 9.107, 9.108, 9.111, 9.115
s 51(7) 9.61, 9.62, 9.93, 9.95, 9.98, 9.106, 9.107, 9.111, 9.115, 66.11
s 51(13). 9.108
s 57. . . . . 8.40, 8.43
s 72 . . . . 21.19
s 75. . . . . 21.19
s 89(1) 5.03
s 89(3)(c) 5.03
s 91. . . . . 5.07
s 128 . . . . 2.09, 3.23
Slander of Women Act 1891 (54 & 55 Vict, c 51) 1.44, 58.03
Small Debts (London City) Act 1605 (3 Jas 1, c 15)
s 2(1) 1.50
Small Debts, Southwark, etc Act 1748 (22 G 2, c 47). 1.68
Social Security (Recovery of Benefits) Act 1997 . . . . 17.51
ss 1–3. . . . . 17.51
s 1(4)(b) 17.52
s 1A(5)(b). 17.52
ss 4–5. . . . . 17.51
s 6 . . . . 17.51
s 8 . . . . 17.51
Solicitors Act 1870
s 4 . . . . 50.12
Solicitors Act 1843 (6 & 7 Vict c 73) . . . 1.81, 36.21
s 2 . . . . 3.65
s 41. . . . . 36.20

Solicitors Act 1932 . . . . 1.112, 35.81
s 57. . . . . 27.213
s 60 . . . . 27.178
s 81(1). 3.26
Solicitors Act 1957 . . . . 3.27, 27.198
s 50(2) 9.95
Solicitors Act 1974 (SA 1974). . . 1.81, 1.112, 3.34, 3.54, 3.57, 3.61, 27.70, 27.110, 27.154, 28.28, 35.53, 35.98, 36.13, 36.21, 36.46, 36.56, 39.15, 39.19, 40.01, 40.07, 40.11
Pt III 40.15
s 1 . . . . 2.09, 3.54
s 1B 3.54
s 9 . . . . 33.49
s 9A 33.49
s 15(1). 27.83
s 20 . . . . 3.54, 3.69
s 22 . . . . 3.55, 3.70, 3.71
s 25. . . . . 3.51, 3.52, 3.100, 22.19
s 25(1) 3.56
s 31. . . . . 4.15, 27.244, 34.47
s 37A 38.40
s 50 . . . . 5.29
s 50(2) 5.26
s 57. . . . . 2.09, 27.117, 27.213, 27.214, 27.215, 29.106, 29.145, 29.147
s 57(1). 27.215
s 57(5) 27.133, 36.43, 39.12, 39.15
ss 59–63. . . . . 27.136, 27.138
s 59. . . . . 27.139, 27.142, 27.143, 27.148, 27.213, 29;195
s 59(1) 27.142, 27.144, 27.145, 32.64
s 59(2) 27.164
s 60 . . . . 27.158, 27.178
s 60(1) 27.114, 27.156, 27.159, 40.18
s 60(2) 27.159
s 60(3) 18.04, 27.159, 27.324
s 60(4) 27.159
s 60(5) 27.159
s 60(6) 27.159
s 61. . . . . 27.167, 27.168
s 61(1). 27.168, 27.170, 27.172, 27.186, 27.187, 36.43
s 61(2) 27.157, 27.172
s 61(2)(b) 27.155, 27.170
s 61(3) 27.168, 27.172
s 61(4) 27.157, 27.168, 27.170, 27.172, 27.173, 39.12, 39.15
s 61(4A) 27.157, 27.168, 27.174
s 61(4B) 27.157, 27.168, 27.174
s 61(5) 27.168, 27.185, 36.43
s 61(6) 36.43, 36.44
s 62 . . . . 27.179, 36.43, 60.37, 60.67
s 62(4)(c) 27.181
s 62(4)(d) 27.181
s 63 . . . . 27.26, 27.182, 27.188
s 63(3) 27.184, 38.35, 38.38
s 64 . . . . 35.58, 35.99
s 64(1) 2.09
s 64(2) 35.87, 35.88, 35.97, 35.100, 35.101, 35.102, 35.103, 35.103, 35.107
s 64(4) 2.09, 35.89, 35.101, 36.99
s 65. . . . . 35.80
s 65(1). 28.190, 35.10, 40.100
s 65(2) 23.86, 27.21, 27.39, 27.40, 27.73, 35.11
s 67. . . . . 35.116
s 68 . . . . 35.120, 35.123
s 68(1) 35.11
s 68(2) 36.50
s 68(3) 35.83
s 69. . . . . 35.01, 35.42, 35.43, 35.44, 35/109, 35.112, 35.114
s 69(1) 23.91, 27.156, 35.115, 40.06, 40.129
s 69(2) 35.03, 35.06, 35.45, 36.20
s 69(5) 35.76
s 69(2)(a) 35.72
s 69(2)(b) 35.85
s 69(2A) 35.72
s 69(2B) 35.76
s 69(2C) 35.85, 40.04
s 69(2D) 35.85, 40.04
s 69(2E) 35.44, 35.48, 35.54
s 69(3) 5.15, 36.47, 36.50, 40.19
s 70 . . . . 17.31, 27.46, 27.60, 35.20, 36.03, 36.04, 36.17, 36.18, 36.20, 36.22, 36.23, 36.57, 36.77, 36.83, 36.86, 36.87, 36.99, 39.03, 39.04, 40.24
s 70(1) 36.30,36.72, 36.74, 40.07
s 70(2) 35.19, 36.31, 40.08
s 70(2)(b) 36.98
s 70(3) 40.08
s 70(3)(a)–(c) 36,32
s 70(4) 5.28, 36.05, 36.86
s 70(5) 36.54
s 70(6) 36.54, 36.113
s 70(8) 36.78, 36.111, 36.115
s 70(9) 36.58, 36.74
s 70(9)(a) 36.78
s 70(12) 36.55
s 71. . . . . . .36.35, 36.69, 36.79, 36.81, 36.82, 36.83, 36.84, 36.85, 39.03, 60.10
s 71(1). 36.79, 36.86, 36.89, 36.90, 36.91, 36.94
s 71(2) 36.35

s 71(3) 36.13, 36.79, 36.86, 36.87, 36.88, 36.89, 36.90, 36.95
s 71(4) 36.87
s 71(4)(a) 36.87
s 71(4)(b) 36.88
s 71(6) 36.89
s 72(4) .36.51, 36.116
s 73. . . . . .23.99, 40.89–40.98
s 73(1)9a) 40.96
s 73(2) 23.99
s 74(3) 37.19, 37.20, 37.22, 37.23
s 79 . . . . .34.47
s 80 . . . . .34.47
s 87 . . . . .2.09, 3.25, 3.27, 3.54
s 87(1) 3.03, 3.24
Solicitors Remuneration Act 1881 . . . . .1.99
s 8(1) 27.213
Statute of Gloucester (1278) (6 Edw 1, c 1). . . . 1.10, 1.14, 1.19, 1.21, 1.22, 1.24, 8.05
Statute of Marlborough 1267. . . . . . . 1.19, 8.05
Statute of Merton. .1.17
Suing in forma pauperis 1495. . . . . .1.33
Supply of Goods and Services Act 1982 . . . 28.01, 28.09, 28.12, 28.13, 28.23, 28.32, 28.156–28.158, 28.215
s 12. . . . . 28.156, 31.73
s 12(1) 28.156, 31.73
s 13. . . . . 28.156, 31.73
s 14(1). 28.156, 31.73
s 15. . . . . .27.195
s 15(1). 27.196, 28.156, 31.73
Supreme Court Act 1981
s 152(4) 1.39
Sch 7 . . . . .1.39
Supreme Court of Judicature Act 1873 (36 & 37 Vict, c 66) 21.05
s 3 . . . . .1.92
s 4 . . . . .1.92
Supreme Court of Judicature Act 1875 (38 & 39 Vict, c 77) 1.92, 56.23
Tenures Abolition Act 1660 (12 Car 2, c 24) 1.20
Terrorist Asset-Freezing etc Act 2010 . . . . .13.44
Third Parties (Rights against Insurers) Act 1930. . . . . 34.64
s 1(1). 34.64
Third Parties (Rights against Insurers) Act 2010 . . . . 34.62
s 1(2) 34.63
s 1(3) 34.63
s 1(4) 34.63
s 2(2) 34.63
s 2(4) 34.63
s 4(1) 34.63
s 6(1) 34.63
s 6(2) 34.63
s 8 . . . . 34.63
s 10. . . . . 34.63
Sch 3, para 3. 34.64
Third Parties (Rights against Insurers) Acts 15.38
Tribunals, Courts and Enforcement Act 2007 . . . . 3.33, 9.108
s 3(3) 3.31, 3.31
s 3(5) 3.36
s 57. . . . . .5.07
Sch 7 . . . . 2.09
Sch 8, para 15. 3.34
Tribunals and Inquiries Act 1992
s 16(1) 2.09
Sch 1 . . . . .3.35
Trustee Act 2000
s 31(1). 66.36
s 32(1) 66.36
Unfair Contract Terms Act 1977 . . . . 28.01, 28.09, 28.12, 28.13, 28.23, 28,159–28.162, 28.215
s 3 . . . . .28.162
s 9(1) 28.162
s 9(2) 28.162
s 11(1). 28.161
s 11(3). 28.162
s 11(4) 28.162
s 12(1) 28.162
s 14. . . . . .28.162
s 26 . . . . .28.162
s 27(2) 28.162
Untrue Suggestions in Chancery (7 Ric II, c 6) .1.29
Vagabonds and Beggars Act 1494. . . . . .1.33
Value Added Tax Act 1994
s 3(1) 55.04
s 4(1) 55.12
s 6(3) 55.06, 55.07
s 6(4)–(14) 55.07
s 6(4) 55.37
s 6(5) 55.37
s 6(6) 55.37
s 6(10) 55.37
s 9 . . . . .55.12
s 9(5)(a) 55.12
s 9(5)(b) 55.12
s 24(1) 55.04
s 24(2) 55.04
s 47(3) 55.15
s 88 . . . . .55.36

Vexatious Arrests and Delays at Law Act 1661 (13 Car 2, st 2, c 2) 1.57
Wardship Act 1267 . . . . 1.20, 1.22
s 3 . . . . 1.19
Workmen's Compensation Acts 54.163

TABLE OF EU LAW

Directives

Council Directive 85/577/EEC of 20 December 1985 to protect the consumer in respect of contracts negotiated away from business premises, OJ L 372/31, 31 December 1985 (the Doorstep Selling Directive) 28.10, 28.20, 28.21, 28.24, 28.164, 28.170, 28.172, 28.195
Art 2 . . . . 28.168
Council Directive 93/13/EEC of 5 April 1993 on unfair terms in consumer contracts, OJ L 95/29, 21 April 1993 (the Unfair Terms in Consumer Contracts Directive) 28.10
Directive 97/7/EC of the European Parliament and of the Council of 20 May 1997 on the protection of consumers in respect of distance contracts, OJ L 144/19, 4 June 1997 . . . . 28.10, 28.201
Directive 1999/93/EC of the European Parliament and of the Council of 13 December 1999 on a Community framework for electronic signatures, OJ L 13/12, 19 January 2000 . . . . 35.76
Directive 2000/31/EC of the European Parliament and of the Council of 8 June 2000 on certain legal aspects of information society services, in particular electronic commerce, in the Internal Market, OJ L 178/1, 17 July 2000 (the E-Commerce Directive) 28.10
Directive 2000/35/EC of the European Parliament and of the Council of 29 June 2000 on combating late payment in commercial transactions, OJ L 200/35, 8 August 2000 . . . . 38.97
Directive 2005/29/EC of the European Parliament and of the Council of 11 May 2005 concerning unfair business-to-consumer commercial practices in the internal market, OJ L 149/22, 11 June 2005 (the Unfair Commercial Practices Directive) 28.06, 28.20, 28.104
Directive 2006/112/EC of 28 November 2006 on the common system of value added tax, OJ L 347/1, 11 December 2006 (Principal VAT Directive) 55.02
Art 73 . . . . 55.15
Art 79 . . . . 55.15
Art 79(c) 55.15
Art 226 . . . . 35.13
Directive 2006/123/EC of the European Parliament and of the Council of 12 December 2006 on services in the internal market, OJ/L 376/36, 27 December 2006 (Services in the Internal Market Directive) 28.45
Directive 2009/103/EC of the European Parliament and of the Council of 16 September 2009 relating to insurance against civil liability in respect of the use of motor vehicles, and the enforcement of the obligation to insure against such liability, OJ L 263/11, 7 October 2009 . . . . 63.02
Directive 2009/138/EC of the European Parliament and of the Council of 25 November 2009 on the taking-up and pursuit of the business of Insurance and Reinsurance, OJ L 335/1, 17 December 2009 (the Solvency II Directive) 34.14, 34.17
Art 6 . . . . 34.14
Directive 2011/7/EU of the European Parliament and of the Council of 16 February 2011 on combating late payment in commercial transactions (recast), OJ L 48/1, 23 February 2011 . . . . 38.97
Directive 2011/83/EU of the European Parliament and of the Council of 25 October 2011 on consumer rights, OJ L 304/64, 22 November 2011 (the Consumer Rights Directive) . . . 28.06, 28.24, 28.25, 28.59
Directive 2013/11/EU of the European Parliament and of the Council of 21 May 2013 on alternative dispute resolution for consumer disputes, OJ L 165/63, 18 June 2013 (Directive on Consumer ADR) 28.63

Regulations

Regulation (EU) 2016/679 of the European Parliament and of the Council of 27 April

2016 on the protection of natural persons with regard to the processing of personal data and on the free movement of such data, OJ L 119/1, 4 May 2016 (General Data Protection Regulation (GDPR)) 52.61, 55.24

Treaties

Treaty on the Functioning of the European Union (TFEU)
Art 169.1 . . . . .28.17
Art 169.4 . . . . .28.21
Art 288 . . . . .28.18

NATIONAL LEGISLATION

Isle of Man

Administration of Justice Act 2008 (Statutes of the Isle of Man 2008 c 14) 43.198

TABLE OF INTERNATIONAL INSTRUMENTS

Brussels Convention 1968 . . . . 15.114
Carriage of Goods by Rail (Berne) 1952
Art 55. . . . . .15.05
Carriage of Passengers by Rail (Berne) 1961
Art 56 . . . . .15.05
Carriage of Goods by Road (Geneva) 1956
Art 31. . . . . .15.05
Carriage of Passengers by Road Convention 1973
Art 41. . . . . .15.05
Convention for the Unification of Certain Rules Relating to International Carriage by Air, signed at Warsaw on 12 October 1929
Art 17. . . . . .50.128
European Convention on Human Rights 1950 . . . . .1.125, 15.04, 24.03, 24.08, 24.13, 24.20, 46.44
Art 1 . . . . 24.52, 28.165
Art 6 . . . . 1.141, 6.113, 15.82, 24.08, 24.32, 24.34, 24.38, 24.40, 24.52, 36.53, 36.110, 43.27
Art 6(1) 9.97, 24.35, 36.05, 36.06, 44.17, 64.04
Art 6(11). 15.112
Art 8 . . . . 24.08, 24.32, 24.50, 24.56
Art 10. . . . . 24.08, 24.32, 24.46, 24.48, 24.53
Art 14. . . . . .15.73
Art 34 . . . . .24.10
Protocol 1, Art 1. . . . . .9.97, 24.53
Protocol 14. . . . . 24.04
Lugano Convention 1988 . . . . 15.114
Third Party Liability in the Field of Nuclear Energy (Paris) 1960
Art 14 (as amended) 15.05
Treaty of Lisbon 2009 . . . . .24.05
UNECE Convention on Access to Information, Public Participation in Decision-Making and Access to Justice in Environmental Matters, made in Aarhus, Denmark, on 25 June 1998 (Aarhus Convention) 13.01, 13.78, 13.79, 13.84–13.99, 16.67, 50.368
Art 9(1) 13.86
Art 9(2) 13.86
Art 9(3) 13.86
Art 9(4) 13.85

TABLE OF STATUTORY INSTRUMENTS

Access to Justice Act 1999 (Commencement No 3, Transitional Provisions and Savings) Order 2000 (SI 2000/774)
art 8(3) . . . 62.11
Access to Justice Act 1999 (Commencement No 10) Order 2003 (SI 2003/1241)
art 2 . . . 18.19
Access to Justice Act 1999 (Destination of Appeals) Order 2000 (SI 2000/1071) . . . 45.03, 45.39
art 5(a) . . . 45.05, 45.70
Access to Justice Act 1999 (Destination of Appeals) Order 2016 (SI 2016/917) . . . 45.27, 45.39
art 6 . . . 45,40
art 7 . . . 45.03, 45.39
art 8 . . . 45.39
Access to Justice Act 1999 (Transitional Provisions) Order 2000 (SI 2000/900) . . . 29.35
Access to Justice (Membership Organisations) Regulations 2000 (SI 2000/693) . . . 54.182
Access to Justice (Membership Organisation) Regulations 2005 (SI 2005/2306) . . . 54.182
reg 2(2) . . . 54.182
reg 5 . . . 54.188
Alternative Dispute Resolution for Consumer Disputes (Competent Authorities and Information) Regulations 2015 (SI 2015/542) . . . 27.337, 28.01, 28.06, 28.07, 28.53
reg 1 . . . 28.53
reg 3 . . . 28.54
reg 19 . . . 28.54
Association of Law Costs Draftsmen Order 2006 (SI 2006/3333) . . . 47.03
Business Protection from Misleading Marketing Regulations 2008 (SI 2008/1276) . . . 28.01, 28.12, 28.216
Cancellation of Contracts Made in a Consumer's Home or Place of Work etc Regulations 2008 (SI 2008/1816) (Doorstep Selling Regulations) . . . 28.01, 28.10, 28.18, 28.21, 28.24, 28.58, 28.64, 28.163–28.200
reg 2 . . . 28.171
reg 5 . . . 28.166
reg 5 . . . 28.178
reg 5(a) . . . 28.180
reg 5(c) . . . 28.180
reg 6 . . . 28.176
reg 6(d) . . . 28.184
reg 7(1) . . . 28.186
reg 7(2) . . . 28.186, 28.192
reg 7(3) . . . 28.192
reg 7(4) . . . 29.193
reg 7(5) . . . 29.193
reg 7(6) . . . 29.195
reg 8 . . . 28.187
reg 9 . . . 28.188
reg 9(2) . . . 28.188
reg 10 . . . 28.190
reg 11(1) . . . 28.191
reg 12 . . . 28.191
reg 15 . . . 28.185
Sch 3, para 6 . . . 28.176
Sch 4 . . . 28.192
Civil Legal Aid (Assessment of Resources) (Amendment) Regulations 1993 (SI 1993/788) . . . 1.151
Civil Legal Aid (Costs) Regulations 2013 (SI 2013/611) . . . 62.08, 62.112
reg 2 . . . 62.04
reg 3 . . . 9.127
reg 3(a) . . . 62.24
reg 3(b) . . . 62.24
reg 5 . . . 62.04
reg 6 . . . 62.05
reg 8(1) . . . 62.04
reg 8(2)(a) . . . 62.05
reg 8(2)(b) . . . 62.05
reg 9(1) . . . 62.44
reg 10 . . . 62.44
reg 10(1) . . . 62.19
reg 10(3)(b)(i) . . . 62.20
reg 10(3)(b)(ii) . . . 62.15, 62.20
reg 10(3)(c) . . . 62.39
reg 10(4) . . . 62.35, 62.40
reg 10(5) . . . 62.37
reg 10(6) . . . 62.36
reg 10(7) . . . 62.36
reg 10(8) . . . 62.36
reg 10(9) . . . 62.15
reg 10(10) . . . 62.15
reg 11 . . . 62.44
reg 13 . . . 62.44

reg 13(1) . . . 62.33
reg 13(2) . . . 62.33
reg 13(3) . . . 62.33
reg 13(4) . . . 62.33
reg 13(5) . . . 62.34
reg 14 . . . 62.44
reg 15 . . . 62.44
reg 15(1) . . . 62.14, 62.23
reg 15(2) . . . 62.14
reg 15(3) . . . 62.14
reg 15(4) . . . 62.14
reg 15(7) . . . 62.14
reg 16 . . . 62.44
reg 16(2)–(7) . . . 62.29
reg 16(2) . . . 62.15, 62.20, 62.29
reg 16(2)(b) . . . 62.29
reg 16(3) . . . 62.29
reg 16(3)(a) . . . 62.15
reg 16(3)(b) . . . 62.15, 62.29
reg 16(3)(c) . . . 62.15
reg 16(4) . . . 62.15, 62.29
reg 16(5) . . . 62.15, 62.29
reg 16(5)(a) . . . 62.15
reg 16(6) . . . 62.15, 62.29
reg 16(7) . . . 62.15, 62.29
reg 16(8) . . . 62.15
reg 17 . . . 62.29, 62.44
reg 18 . . . 62.44
reg 19 . . . 62.41, 62.44
reg 19(4)(b) . . . 62.15, 62.20
reg 19(5) . . . 62.41
reg 21 . . . 7.25, 18.17
Civil Legal Aid (General) Regulations 1989 (SI 1989/339)
reg 82(2) . . . 9.190
reg 107 . . . 16.16
reg 107B(1) . . . 18.17
reg 107B(3)(b) . . . 18.17
reg 112 . . . 43.35
reg 113(2) . . . 45.56
reg 119 . . . 43.35
reg 121 . . . 43.35
Civil Procedure (Amendment) Rules 2002 (SI 2002/2058)
r 19 . . . 59.19
Civil Procedure (Amendment) Rules 2008 (SI 2008/2178) . . . 7.106
Civil Procedure (Amendment) Rules 2010 (SI 2010/621)
r 1(2) . . . 50.26
Civil Procedure (Amendment) Rules 2013 (SI 2013/262) . . . 6.169, 7.106, 11.05, 25.21, 26.55, 57.37
r 2 . . . 43.201
r 15 . . . 54.17
r 16 . . . 43.201
r 22 . . . 43.201
r 22(1) . . . 17.31
r 22(9) . . . 43.318, 45.34
r 22(10) . . . 43.253, 43.254, 43.280
r 22(11) . . . 43.372
Civil Procedure (Amendment) Rules 2016 (SI 2016/234)
r 23 . . . 12.51
Civil Procedure (Amendment) Rules 2017 (SI 2017/95) . . . 7.106, 12.84, 12.140, 13.88
r 8 . . . 13.80, 13.82, 50.170, 50.270, 50.275, 50.280, 50.281
r 13(3) . . . 13.80
Civil Procedure (Amendment No 2) Rules 2002 (SI 2002/3219) . . . 15.31
Civil Procedure (Amendment No 2) Rules 2003 (SI 2003/1242) . . . 7.106
r 6 . . . 18.87, 29.38
Civil Procedure (Amendment No 2) Rules 2011 (SI 2011/1979) . . . 17.15, 17.101
Civil Procedure (Amendment No 2) Rules 2012 (SI 2012/2208) . . . 45.14
Civil Procedure (Amendment No 2) Rules 2013 (SI 2013/515) . . . 25.49
Civil Procedure (Amendment No 2) Rules 2015 (SI 2015/670)
r 11 . . . 60.40
Civil Procedure (Amendment No 2) Rules 2016 (SI 2016/707) . . . 13.13
r 6 . . . 13.49
Civil Procedure (Amendment No 3) Rules 2000 (SI 2000/1317) . . . 24.56
r 17 . . . 11.03
Civil Procedure (Amendment No 3) Rules 2006 (SI 2006/3435) . . . 17.14, 17.18, 17.25
r 7(2) . . . 1.18
Civil Procedure (Amendment No 3) Rules 2008 (SI 2008/3327)
r 9 . . . 13.12
Civil Procedure (Amendment No 3) Rules 2016 (SI 2016/788) . . . 45.02, 45.05
art 8 . . . 45.03
r 16 . . . 45.04
Civil Procedure (Amendment No 4) Rules 2000 (SI 2000/2092) . . . 7.106
Civil Procedure (Amendment No 4) Rules 2014 (SI 2014/867)
para 4 . . . 12.18
Civil Procedure (Amendment No 4) Rules 2015 (SI 2015/1569)
r 8 . . . 43.52
Civil Procedure (Amendment No 6) Rules 2013 (SI 2013/1695) . . . 50.27
r 6 . . . 50.287
r 10 . . . 50 68, 50.69, 50.166, 50.170, 50.273

Civil Procedure (Amendment No 6) Rules 2014 (SI 2014/2044)
r 14 . . . . . 50.184, 50.206, 52.71
Civil Procedure (Amendment No 7) Rules 2013 (SI 2013/1974) . . . 7.106, 50.313
r 2 . . . . . 43.201
r 30 . . . . . 50.313
r 30(b) 50.313
r 30(c) 50.313
Civil Procedure (Amendment No 8) Rules 2014 (SI 2014/3299)
r 5 . . . . . 60.40
r 18 . . . . . 50.166, 50.274
r 18(2) 17.57, 17.58, 17.164, 17.166, 17.176, 17.188
Sch 1 . . . . . 17.18
Civil Proceedings and Family Proceedings Fees (Amendment) Order 2015 (SI 2015/576) 1.187, 43.187
art 1 . . . . . 52.87
art 2 . . . . . 52.87
Civil Proceedings Fees Order 2004 (SI 2004/3121) 52.97
Sch 1, para 2.3 . . . . . 52.89
Civil Proceedings Fees Order 2008 (SI 2008/1053) 1.187
art 1(1) 43.187
Sch 1 . . . . . 43.188, 43.189
Sch 1, para 1.1 . . . . . 52.87, 52.88, 52.93
Sch 1, para 2.2 . . . . . 52.94
Sch 1, para 2.3 . . . . . 52.90
Sch 1, para 5.1 . . . . . 52.95
Sch 1, para 5.2 . . . . . 52.95
Sch 1, para 5.3 . . . . . 52.96
Sch 1, para 5.5 . . . . . 52.96
Civil Proceedings Fees (Amendment) Order 2014 (SI 2014/874) 1.187, 52.93, 52.94
Sch 1 . . . . . 1.187, 43.187
para 2 . . . . . 1.187
Civil Proceedings Fees (Amendment) Order 2016 (SI 2016/1191)
art 2 . . . . . 52.90
Civil Proceedings Fees (Amendment No 2) Order 2013 (SI 2013/1410) 52.88
Civil Proceedings, First-tier Tribunal, Upper Tribunal and Employment Tribunals Fees (Amendment) Order 2016 (SI 2016/807) 43.187, 52.94
Collective Conditional Fee Agreements Regulations 2000 (SI 2000/2988) (CCFA Regulations 2000) 29.02, 29.03, 29.111, 29.113, 29.114, 29.116, 29.117–29.120, 29.121–29.128, 29.129, 29.218
reg 1(2) 2.09
reg 3(1) 29.112
reg 3(1)(b) 2.09
reg 3(2) 29.112
reg 3A 29.03
reg 4 . . . . . 29.02, 29.117, 29.118
reg 4(1A) 29.117
reg 5 . . . . . 29.02, 29.113, 29.119
reg 5(2)(b) 29.120, 54.51
reg 5(2)(c) 29.120, 54.51
reg 5(3) 29.02
reg 5(4) 29.120
reg 5(5) 29.113
reg 5(6) 29.113
reg 5(7) 29.113
Community Legal Service (Cost Protection) Regulations 2000 (SI 2000/824) 62.08, 62.12
reg 7(2) 6.250
Community Legal Service (Cost Protection) (Amendment No 2) Regulations 2001 (SI 2001/3812) 62.20
Community Legal Services (Costs) Regulations 2000 (SI 2000/441) . . . 62.08, 62.12, 62.20
reg 3 . . . . . 6.250
reg 9 . . . . . 62.29
reg 15(1) 6.250
reg 15(2) 6.250
Companies Act 2006 (Commencement No 8, Transitional Provisions and Savings) Order (SI 2008/2860)
art 4 . . . . . 15.07
art 5 . . . . . 15.07
Sch 1, Pt 1 . . . . . 15.07
Sch 2, para 1 (as amended) 15.07
Compensation (Claims Management Services) Regulations 2006 (SI 2006/3322) 29.201
Conditional Fee Agreements (Miscellaneous Amendments) Regulations 2003 (SI 2003/1240) 1.160, 29.113, 29.216
reg 2 . . . . . 29.37
Conditional Fee Agreements (Miscellaneous Amendments) (No 2) Regulations 2003 (SI 2003/3344) 29.113, 29.218
Conditional Fee Agreements Order 1995 (SI 1995/1674) 1.155, 29.209
Conditional Fee Agreements Order 1998 (SI 1998/1860) 1.155
Conditional Fee Agreements Order 2000 (SI 2000/823) 1.157
Conditional Fee Agreements Order 2013 (SI 2013/689)
art 2 . . . . . 29.20, 54.10

art 3 . . . . 29.20
art 5 . . . . 29.23
para 6(2)(a) 54.26
Conditional Fee Agreements Regulations 1995 (SI 1995/1675) 1.155, 29.209
Conditional Fee Agreements Regulations 2000 (SI 2000/692) (CFA Regulations 2000) 1.157, 18.39, 29.02, 29.10, 29.25, 29.26, 29.27, 29.30, 29.34, 29.36, 29.37, 29.46, 29.49, 29.55, 29.106, 29.162, 29.215, 29.217, 31.29, 31.55
reg 2 . . . . . . 29.45, 29.68, 29.70, 29.71, 29.74, 29.104, 29.105
reg 2(1) 29.56, 29.57, 29.58
reg 2(2) 29.59, 29.78
reg 3 . . . . 29.45, 29.68, 29.70, 29.71, 29.74, 29.104, 29.105
reg 3a 18.86
reg 3(1) 29.104
reg 3(1)(a) 29.61, 43.185
reg 3(1)(b) 29.02, 29.62, 54.101
reg 3(2) 29.65, 29.66
reg 3(2)(b) 54.51
reg 3(2)(c) 54.51
reg 3(4) 29.74
reg 3(6) 29.74
reg 3A 29.38, 29.45, 29.67, 29.68, 29.70, 29.76, 29.104, 29.105
reg 3A(1) 29.39, 29.72
reg 3A(3) 29.97
reg 3A(4) 29.74
reg 3A(5) 29.73
reg 3A(5A) 29.73
reg 3A(6) 29.74
reg 4 . . . . 29.52, 29.59, 29.68, 29.70, 29.71, 29.74, 29.77, 29.78, 29.90, 29.104, 29.105
reg 4(1)–(6) 29.45
reg 4(1) 29.79, 29.81, 29.86
reg 4(2) 29.77, 29.78, 29.87, 29.89, 29.98
reg 4(2)(a) 29.79
reg 4(2)(b) 29.80, 29.83
reg 4(2)(c) 29.78, 29.81, 29.84, 29.85
reg 4(2)(d) 29.86, 29.87
reg 4(2)(e) 29.54, 29.88, 29.89, 29.90, 29.91, 29.93
reg 4(2)(e)(ii) 29.90
reg 4(3) 29.97, 29.98, 29.100
reg 4(4) 29.78
reg 4(5) 29.79, 29.80, 29.81, 29.86, 29.97
reg 4(6) 29.97
reg 5 . . . . 29.39, 29.45, 29.102, 29.153
reg 5(1)(c) 43.185
reg 5(2) 29.102
reg 5A(1) 29.39
reg 6 . . . . 29.104
reg 8 . . . . 29.111, 29.114
Conditional Fee Agreements (Revocation) Regulations 2005 (SI 2005/2305) 1.161, 29.216, 54.124
reg 1 . . . . 29.34
reg 2 . . . . 29.34
reg 3(1) 29.34
Consumer Contracts (Information, Cancellation and Additional Charges) Regulations 2013 (SI 2013/3134) 28.01, 28.07, 28.24, 28.25, 28.31, 28.32, 28.58–28.100, 28.163, 28.201, 35.21, 38.58, 38.67, 38.69, 38.70, 53.26
Pt 2 . . . . 28.67
reg 1(2) 28.64
reg 2 . . . . 28.64, 28.163, 28.201
reg 4 . . . . 28.63
reg 5 . . . . 28.65, 28.69
reg 6 . . . . 28.64
reg 7 . . . . 28.67
reg 7(4) 28.67
reg 8 . . . . 28.67
reg 9 . . . . 28.31, 28.34, 28.69, 28.97
reg 9(1) 27.65
reg 9(3) 27.55, 28.73, 38.67
regs 10–16 . . . . 28.100
reg 10 . . . . 28.31, 28.34, 28.76, 28.97
reg 10(1) 27.55
reg 10(2) 28.78, 28.82
reg 10(5) 28.80
reg 12(1) 28,79
reg 12(2) 28.79
reg 12(3) 28.79
reg 12(4) 28.79
reg 13 . . . . 28.31, 28.34, 28.81, 28.97
reg 13(1) 27.55
reg 13(1)(a) 28.82
reg 13(3) 28.82
reg 13(4) 28.82
reg 13(6) 28.80
reg 14 . . . . 28.83
reg 14(2) 28.84
reg 14(3) 28.84
reg 14(4) 28.84
reg 14(5) 28.85, 28.97
reg 15 . . . . 28.86
reg 16 . . . . 28.87
reg 16(1) 28.88
reg 16(2) 28.88
reg 16(4) 28.88
reg 16(5) 28.88
reg 17(1) 28.100
reg 17(2) 28.100
reg 18 . . . . 28.99

Consumer Contracts (Information, Cancellation and Additional Charges) Regulations 2013 (SI 2013/3134) (*cont.*)
reg 19 . . . . . 28.97
reg 20 . . . . . 28.97
reg 26 . . . . . 28.100
reg 29(1) 28.91
reg 29(1)(d) 28.91
reg 30(1) 28.89
reg 30(2) 28.89
reg 30(2)–(6) 28.89
reg 31(2) 28.89
reg 31(3) 28.89, 28.97
reg 32(1) 28.92
reg 32(2) 28.92
reg 32(3) 28.92
reg 32(5) 28.92
reg 32(6) 28.100
reg 33 . . . . . 28.93
reg 34(6) 28.93
reg 34(7) 28.93
reg 34(8) 28.93
reg 34(13) 28.93
reg 36(1) 28.90, 28.95, 28.96, 28.97
reg 36(4) 28.91, 28.96
reg 36(5) 28.96
reg 36(6)(a) 28.96
reg 36(6)(b) 28.90, 28.96, 28.97
reg 38 . . . . . 28.94
reg 38(3) 28.94
Sch 1 . . . . . 27.55, 28.71, 38.58
Sch 2 . . . . . 27.55, 28.76, 28.77, 28.82, 28.84
Sch 2, para (f) 38.58
Consumer Protection (Amendment) Regulations 2014 (SI 2014/870) 28.06, 28.134, 28.136, 28.137, 28.140
para 2(3) 28.107
para 2(6) 28.106
para 2(7) 28.107
Consumer Protection (Cancellation of Contracts Concluded Away from Business Premises) Regulations 1987 (SI 1987/2117) 28.01, 28.10, 28.20, 28.163, 28.174, 28.214
Consumer Protection (Distance Selling) Regulations 2000 (SI 2000/2334) 28.01, 28.10, 28.24, 28.58, 28.64, 28.201–28.212
reg 3(1) 28.201
reg 4 . . . . . 28.203
reg 7(1)(a) 28.204
reg 7(2) 28.204
reg 7(3) 28.204
reg 7(4) 28.204
reg 8 . . . . . 28.205, 28.206
reg 8(2)(c) 28.204
reg 8(2)(e) 28.204
reg 8(3) 28.206
reg 10 . . . . . 28.209
reg 10(4) 28.209
reg 12 . . . . . 28.206, 28.208
reg 12(1) 28.208
reg 12(2) 28.208
reg 12(3)(a) 28.208
reg 13 . . . . . 28.206
reg 13(1)(a) 28.206, 28.208
reg 14 . . . . . 28.210
reg 15 . . . . . 28.210
reg 19 . . . . . 28.207
reg 25 . . . . . 28.206
Sch 1 . . . . . 28.203
Consumer Protection from Unfair Trading Regulations 2008 (SI 2008/1277) 28.01, 28.06, 28.101–28.148, 28.217
reg 1.1 . . . . . 28.120
reg 1(3) 28.133, 28.135
reg 2(1) 28.106, 28.112
reg 2(2) 28.115
reg 2(4) 28.115
reg 2(5) 28.115
reg 3(1) 28.103, 38.72
reg 3(3)(a) 28.111
reg 3(3)(b) 28.111
reg 5 . . . . . 28.138
reg 5(2) 28.114
reg 5(3)(a) 28.116
reg 5(3)(b) 28.117
reg 5(4) 28.115
reg 5(6) 28.115
reg 6(1) 28.119
reg 6(2) 28.119
reg 6(4) 28.120
reg 6(4)(f) 28.120
reg 7 . . . . . 28.136
reg 7(1) 28.124
reg 7(2) 28.124, 28.126
reg 7(3)(b) 28.124, 28.125
regs 8–16 . . . . . 28.131, 38.72
reg 17 . . . . . 28.131
reg 27A 28.134, 28.135
reg 27B 28.134, 28.135
reg 27E 28.134, 28.137
reg 27F 28.134, 28.137
reg 27I 28.140
reg 27J 28.134
reg 29 . . . . . 28.102, 28.132
Sch 1, para 26 . . . . . 28.128

Consumer Rights Act 2015 (Commencement No 3, Transitional Provisions, Savings and Consequential Amendments) Order 2015 (SI 2015/1630)
art 3 . . . . 28.156, 28.159, 31.73
art 6(1) 28.29
art 6(4) 27.130, 28.37, 28.40, 28.149
Consumer Rights (Payment Surcharges) Regulations 2012 (SI 2012/3110) 28.61
Copyright, Designs and Patents Act 1988 (Commencement No 1) Order 1989 (SI 1989/816)
art 2 . . . . 58.04
Costs in Criminal Cases (General) Regulations 1986 (SI 1986/1335) (as amended) 52.52, 59.39, 59.43
County Courts (Interest on Judgment Debts) Order 1991 (SI 1991/1184) 56.15, 56.16, 56.18
art 2(1) 56.18
art 2(2) 38.93
art 4(1) 56.20
art 4(3) 56.21
art 5 . . . . 56.15, 56.42
art 5(2) 56.46
County Courts (Interest on Judgment Debts) (Amendment) Order 1996 (SI 1996/2516) 56.15, 56.16, 56.18
Crime and Courts Act 2013 (Commencement No 10 and Transitional Provisions) Order 2014 (SI 2014/954) 36.47
Criminal Justice and Courts Act 2015 (Commencement No 1, Saving and Transitional Provisions) Order 2015 (SI 2015/778)
art 3 . . . . 6.89
Sch 1, para 47 . . . . 6.89
Sch 2, para 66 . . . . 7.15
Criminal Justice and Courts Act 2015 (Commencement No 4 and Transitional Provisions) Order 2016 . . . . 13.49
Criminal Justice and Courts Act 2015 (Disapplication of Sections 88 and 89) Regulations 2017 (SI 2007/100) 13.50, 13.83, 13.86
Crown Prosecution Service (Witnesses' etc Allowances) Regulations 1988 (SI 1988/1862) (as amended) 52.52
Damages-Based Agreements Regulations 2010 (SI 2010/1206) 29.219
Damages-Based Agreements Regulations 2013 (SI 2013/609) 2.09, 27.118, 29.145, 29.152, 29.175, 29.176, 29.219
reg 1(2) 29.153, 29.155, 29.156, 29.164, 29.173
reg 3 . . . . 29.149
reg 3(a) 29.149
reg 3(b) 29.149
reg 3(c) 29.149
reg 4 . . . . 29.150, 29.151
reg 4(1)(a) 29.150
reg 5 . . . . 29.153
reg 5(1) 29.153, 29.155,29.164
reg 5(2)(a) 29.155, 29.158
reg 5(2)(b) 29.159
reg 5(2)(c) 29.161
reg 5(2)(d) 29.164
reg 5(2)(e) 29.166
reg 6 . . . . 29.167
reg 7 . . . . 29.168
reg 8 . . . . 29.171, 29.172
Data Protection (Subject Access) (Fees and Miscellaneous Provisions) Regulations 2000 (SI 2000/191) (as amended)
reg 3 . . . . 52.62
reg 6(2) 52.61
Sch 52.61
Defamation Act 2013 (Commencement) (England and Wales) Order 2013 (SI 2013/3027)
art 2 . . . . 58.03
Electronic Commerce (EC Directive) Regulations 2002 (SI 2002/2013) 28.01, 28.10, 28.213
Electronic Signature Regulations 2002 (SI 2002/318)
reg 2 . . . . 35.77
Employment Appeal Tribunal Rules 1993 (SI 1993/2854)
r 34B(1)(c) 5.05
European Communities (Services of Lawyers) Order 1978 (SI 1978/1910) 2.09
Financial Services and Markets Act 2000 (Regulated Activities) Order 2001 (SI 2001/544) 27.277, 27.293, 33.43, 33.46, 33.55, 34.44
art 3(1) 34.02, 34.42
arts 60B–60M 33.55
art 60B 33.40
art 60C 33.41
art 60L(1) 33.44, 33.52
Ch 14A 33.43
Sch 1, Pt 1, para 17 . . . . 34.02, 34.42
Financial Services and Markets Act 2000 (Regulated Activities) (Amendment) Order 2004 (SI 2004/1610) 27.277

High Court and County Courts Jurisdiction Order 1991 (SI 1991/724) 1.142, 5.12
art 2(5) 58.04
art 2(7) 5.15, 36.47, 36.50, 40.19
art 2(8) 5.15, 36.47, 36.50, 40.19
Sch, Pt I 5.15, 36.47, 36.50, 40.19
Insurance Companies (Legal Expenses Insurance) Regulations 1990 (SI 1990/1159) 34.14
reg 3 .... 34.14
reg 4 .... 34.15
reg 4(a) 34.15
reg 4(b) 34.15
reg 5 .... 34.15
reg 7 .... 34.14
reg 8 .... 34.15
Judgment Debts (Rate of Interest) Order 1985 (SI 1985/437) 56.43
Judgment Debts (Rate of Interest) Order 1993 (SI 1993/564) 56.02, 56.43
Late Payment of Commercial Debts (Rate of Interest) (No 3) Order 2002 (SI 2002/1675)
art 4 .... 38.102
Late Payment of Commercial Debts Regulations 2013 (SI 2013/395) 56.118
reg 1 .... 38.97
Lay Representatives (Rights of Audience) Order 1999 (SI 1999/1225)
art 2 .... 3.100
Legal Advice and Assistance Regulations 1993 (SI 1993/790) 1.151
Legal Aid Board (Abolition) Order 2001 (SI 2001/779) 1.164
Legal Aid (General) Regulations 1980 (SI 1980/1894)
reg 65 .... 18.81
Legal Aid (General) Regulations 1989 (SI 1989/339)
reg 64 .... 18.80
Legal Aid, Sentencing and Punishment of Offenders Act 2012 (Commencement No 5 and Saving Provisions) Order 2013 (SI 2013/77)
art 3(c) 54.32, 54.35
art 4 .... 54.32, 54.35
art 4(a) 54.22
Legal Aid, Sentencing and Punishment of Offenders Act 2012 (Commencement No 12) Order 2016 (SI 2016/345) 54.32
Legal Services Act 2007 (Alteration of Limit) Order 2012 (SI 2012/3091) 39.32
Legal Services Act 2007 (Commencement No 1 and Transitory Provisions) Order 2008 (SI 2008/222) 3.49
Legal Services Act 2007 (Commencement No 4, Transitory and Transitional Provisions and Appointed Day) Order 2009 (SI 2009/503) 3.49
Legal Services Act 2007 (Commencement No 5, Transitory and Transitional Provisions) Order 2009 (SI 2009/1365) 2.09, 3.54
Legal Services Act 2007 (Commencement No 6, Transitory, Transitional and Saving Provisions) Order 2009 (SI 2009/3250) 3.49
art 2(f)(ii) 3.54, 3.55
Legal Services Act 2007 (Prescribed Charity) Order 2008 (SI 2008/2680)
art 2 .... 18.124
Limited Liability Partnerships (Application of Companies Act 2006) Regulations 2009 (SI 2009/1804)
reg 4 .... 27.321
Matrimonial Causes (Costs) Rules 1988 (SI 1988/1328)
r 13(iii) 49.141
Mental Capacity Act 2005 (Transitional and Consequential Provisions) Order 2007 (SI 2007/1898) 60.52
Provision of Services Regulations 2009 (SI 2009/2999) 27.338, 28.01, 28.06, 28.07, 28.12, 28.13, 28.45, 28.46, 28.67, 28.215, 53.06
reg 2 .... 28.46
reg 4 .... 28.46
reg 5(3) 28.46
reg 5(4) 28.46
reg 7 .... 28.50
reg 8(2) 28.48
reg 9 .... 28.52
reg 10 .... 27.337, 28.51
reg 11 .... 28.49
Recovery of Costs Insurance Premiums in Clinical Negligence Proceedings Regulations 2013 (SI 2013/92) ... 25.84, 54.39
Recovery of Costs Insurance Premiums in Clinical Negligence Proceedings (No 2) Regulations 2013 (SI 2013/739)
reg 3 .... 54.39
reg 3(2) 54.40
Regulatory Reform (Execution of Deeds and Documents) Order 2005 (SI 2005/1906) 27.320, 27.321
Rules of the Court of Judicature (Northern Ireland) 1980 (SR 1080/346) 52.98
Rules of the Supreme Court (Solicitors' Remuneration) Rules 1920 (SI 1920/683) 1.112
Solicitors' (Non-Contentious Business) Remuneration Order 1994 (SI 1994/2616) 2.09, 37.25, 38.17
art 14 .... 38.91, 38.95

Solicitors' (Non-Contentious Business) Remuneration Order 2009 (SI 2009/1931) 1.150, 27.117, 35.58, 36.36, 37.01, 37.04, 37.25, 38.17, 38.22, 38.27, 38.89, 38.90, 40.101
art 2 . . . . .36.78
art 3 . . . . .37.24
art 3(f) 38.05, 38.15
art 3(h). 38.23
art 5 . . . . 38.89
art 5(2) 38.90
Solicitors' (Non-Contentious Business) Remuneration (Amendment) Order 2010 (SI 2010/2262) 38.89, 39.31
Solicitors' Remuneration (Gross Sum) Order 1934 . . . . 1.112
Solicitors' Remuneration Order 1953 (SI 1953/117) .1.126
Solicitors' Remuneration Order 1972 (SI 1972/1139) 37.25
Supply of Services (Exclusion of Implied Terms) Order 1982 (SI 1982/1771)
reg 2. . . . . .28.158
Transfer of Functions (Minister for the Civil Service and Treasury) Order 1981 (SI 1981/1670). 5.03
Tribunal Procedure (First-tier Tribunal) (Property Chamber) Rules 2013 (SI 2013/1169)
r 13(8) 4.33
Unfair Terms in Consumer Contracts Regulations 1999 (SI 1999/2083). . . 28.01, 28.09, 28.23, 28.149–28.155, 28.173, 31.40, 32.52
reg 3(1). 28.150
reg 4(1). 28.149
reg 5. . . . . .28.151
reg 5(1). 28.152
reg 6. . . . . .28.153
reg 7. . . . . .27.130
reg 8(1). 28.154
reg 8(2). 28.154
Sch 2
para 1(g). 28.152
para 1(i) 28.152
para 1(q). 27.337, 28.152
Unfair Trading Regulations 2008 (SI 2008/1277) 28.20
Unregistered Companies Regulations 2009 (SI 2009/2436) 27.319
Value Added Tax Regulations 1995 (SI 1995/2518)
reg 29. . . . . .55.04
reg 92. . . . . .55.08
Value Added Tax (Health and Welfare) Order 2007 (SI 2007/206) 55.23
Value Added Tax (Place of Supply of Services) Order 1992 (SI 1992/3121)
art 7(11) 55.12

NATIONAL COURTS

Isle of Man

Rules of the High Court of Justice 2009 (SD 352/09) .52.98

Scotland

Act of Sederunt (Rules of the Court of Session 1994) 1994 (SI 1994/1443) . . . 52.98

TABLE OF RULES OF COURT

Civil Procedure Rules 1998 (SI 1998/3132 as amended) (CPR) 1.174, 2.03, 3.03, 3.65, 3.66, 3.68, 3.70, 3.72, 3.87, 4.01, 4.02, 4.32, 4.33, 4.34, 4.37, 4.65, 6.70, 6.103, 6.158, 6.159, 6.160, 6.161, 6.164, 7.98, 9.62, 9.77, 9.134, 9.203, 10.03, 10.08, 12.03, 12.06, 15.82, 15.84, 15.96, 16.21, 21.18, 23.05, 23.16, 23.61, 23.62, 23.64, 23.09, 24.29, 24.48, 24.52, 25.12, 25.13, 26.01, 26.02, 26.05, 26.15–26.16, 26.18, 26.20, 26.38, 26.41, 27.202, 29.08, 29.68, 36.38, 36.97, 36.115, 37.20, 39.04, 42.10, 43.35, 43.310, 43.330, 43.332, 45.04, 46.32, 46.33, 46.36, 48.04, 48.06, 48.08, 49.21, 49.23, 49.50, 49.63, 49.91, 49.106, 50.04, 51.22, 51.23, 51.38, 51.40, 53.43, 53.94, 53.106, 53.108, 54.17

Pt 1 . . . . 17.32, 65.09

r 1.1 . . . 25.12, 25.21, 26.02, 26.04, 26.08, 26.34, 26.46, 49.79

r 1.1(1) 52.02

r 1.1(2) 25.20, 26.33, 48.08

r 1.1(2)(a)–(d) 25.20

r 1.1(2)(c) 34.20

r 1.1(2)(d) 45.19

r 1.1(2)(e) 16.40, 26.29, 26.32, 26.48

r 1.1(2)(f) 26.48

r 1.2 . . . . 4.39

r.1.3 . . . . 26.06, 49.79

r 1.4 . . . . 26.07

r 1.4(2)(a) 48.08

r 1.4(2)(e) 48.08

Pt 2

r 2.3 . . . . 29.153, 50.72

r 2.3(1) 2.09, 3.66, 3.67, 12.34

r 2.4 . . . . 43.13

r 2.4(a) 5.09

r 2.8 . . . . 43.128

r 2.8(3) 43.283

r 2.8(4) 17.47, 43.129, 44.283

r 2.8(5) 43.129

r 2.10 . . . . 43.87

r 2.11 . . . . 43.89, 43.91, 43.130, 43.131

Pt 3 . . . . . . 5.27, 12.14, 12.143, 13.13, 15.01, 15.02, 15.15, 17.24, 43.89, 65.09

Section I 13.01, 13.43–13.45

Section II 12.15, 12.17, 12.18, 12.76, 12.79, 12.84, 12.110, 12.119, 12.148, 12.168, 13.13, 13.15, 13.18, 13.21, 26.56

Section III 13.01, 13.03–13.42, 13.43

r 3.1 . . . . 12.10, 12.19, 15.15, 15.19, 15.98, 26.03, 43.386, 62.20

r 3.1(f) 48.08

r 3.1(1) 14.19, 43.28

r 3.1(2)(a) 43.89, 43.90, 43.130, 45.50

r 3.1(2)(f) 49.152

r 3.1(2)(m) 4.40, 5.21, 10.08, 13.43, 15.21, 35.96, 43.210, 65.42, 66.56

r 3.1(3) 15.03, 15.19, 15.20, 15.97, 43.161

r 3.1(4) 6.96

r 3.1(5) 15.03, 15.19, 15.20, 15.97, 15.100, 15.101

r 3.1(6) 6.96, 15.03, 15.19

r 3.1(6A) 15.03, 15.20

r 3.1(7) 10.08, 10.18, 10.19, 10.20, 10.27, 15.102, 26.50

r 3.2 . . . . 43.24

r 3.4 . . . . 40.27

r 3.7 . . . . 7.106

r 3.7(4)(b)(ii) 10.24

r 3.7(7) 7.106

r 3.7A 7.107

r 3.7B 7.108

r 3.8(1) 26.48

r 3.8(2) 26.51

r 3.8(3) 43.92, 43.131

r 3.8(4) 43.92, 43.131

r 3.9 . . . . 26.48, 26.50, 26.51, 26.53, 26.56, 26.62, 26.68, 26.70, 43.89, 43.158, 54.116, 54.117, 54.123

r 3.9(1) 26.60, 26.66

r 3.9(1)(a) 54.123

r 3.9(1)(b) 43.159

r 3.9(2) 43.153, 54.121

r 3.10 . . . . 17.24

r 3.12 . . . . 12.15, 66.44

r 3.12(1) 12.18, 12.71

r 3.12(1)(e) 12.18, 12.69, 12.74

r 3.12(1A) 12.19, 12.69

r 3.12(2) 12.02

r 3.13 . . . . 12.18, 12.43, 16.57

r 3.13(1) 12.44, 12.51

r 3.13(2) 2.09, 12.51

r 3.14 . . . . 6.114, 12.56, 12.58, 17.115, 17.117, 26.56

r 3.15 . . . . 12.70

r 3.15(1) 2.09, 12.66

r 3.15(2) 2.09, 12.03, 12.67, 12.74, 12.75, 12.76, 12.100

r 3.15(4) 12.139,

r 3.16(1) 12.03, 12.61
r 3.16(2) 12.61
r 3.17 . . . . 12.63
r 3.18 . . . . 12.129, 12.140, 12.147, 12.159, 12.163, 12.166, 17.117
r 3.18(b) 12.123, 12.152
r 3.18(c) 12.139
r 3.19 . . . . 13.25
r 3.19(1)(a) 2.09
r 3.19(2) 13.46
r 3.19(4) 13.16
r 3.19(5) 13.16, 13.17
r 3.19(5)(a) 13.17
r 3.19(5)(b) 13.17
r 3.19(5)(c) 13.17, 13.19, 13.20, 13.21, 13.22
r 3.19(6)(a)–(d) 13.24
r 3.19(7) 13.03, 13.31, 13.41
r 3.20(1) 13.27
r 3.20(2) 13.27
r 3.20(3)(c) 13.35
r 3.21 . . . . 13.41
Pt 5
r 5.4 . . . . 66.71
Pt 6 . . . . 17.28, 43.278
Section IV 43.127
r 6.2 . . . . 50.289, 50.290
r 6.20 . . . . 17.29
r 6.20(1)(a) 17.43, 43.136
r 6.20(1)(b) 17.43, 43.136
r 6.20(1)(c) 17.43, 43.136
r 6.20(1)(d) 17.43, 43.137, 43.138
r 6.20(1)(e) 17.43, 43.136
r 6.20(2) 17.44, 43.136
r 6.20(3) 17.44, 43.136
r 6.22 . . . . 17.43
r 6.23 . . . . 17.43
r 6.26 . . . . 17.29
r 6.28 . . . . 17.43
Pt 7 . . . . . . 7.170, 11.12, 12.18, 40.15, 40.26, 50.239, 50.252, 50.258
r 7.2(1) 6.12, 25.19
r 7.2(2) 25.19
Pt 8 . . . . 7.170, 11.07, 11.09, 12.18, 17.32, 27.188, 27.189, 36.39, 40.24, 40.97, 50.151, 54.48, 64.18, 6.44
r 8 . . . . 50.232
r 8.1(3) 50.241
r 8.2 . . . . 11.09
r 8.2(b)(ii) 11.10
r 8.2(d) 11.10
r 8.2(e) 11.10
r 8.4(2) 40.25
r 8.5 . . . . 11.09
r 8.5(3) 11.18
r 8.9 . . . . 11.20
r 8.9(a)(ii) 11.09
r 8.9(c) 11.28, 50.386
Pt 11 . . . . 7.174
Pt 12 . . . . 50.349
r 12.1 . . . . 40.24
r 12.2(b) 40.24
r 12.3(1) 40.24
r 12.3(3) 40.26
r 12.4(1) 40.24
r 12.7(2) 40.26
Pt 16
r 16.6 . . . . 21.09, 21.16
Pt 18 . . . . 28.199, 46.37
Pt 19
Section II 65.117
Section III 65.04, 65.09, 65.11, 65.14
r 19.6(1) 65.117
r 19.6(4) 9.76, 65.118
r 19.7(2) 66.60
r 19.8A 65.122
r 19.9(1) 65.123
r 19.9E 65.124
r 19.10 . . . . 65.04, 65.10, 65.16
r 19.11 . . . . 65.16, 65.17
r 19.11(2)(a) 65.04
r 19.11(2)(b) 65.106
r 19.11(2)(c) 65.04
r 19.11(3)(b) 65.97
r 19.12 . . . . 65.26
r 19.12(1) 65.37
r 19.12(4) 65.113
r 19.13 . . . . 65.38
r 19.13(c) 65.41, 65.100
r 19.13(e) 65.97
r 19.14 . . . . 65.32, 65.105
Pt 20 . . . . 6.248, 7.26, 7.28, 15.11, 15.117, 20.62, 25.102, 50.345
r 20.2 . . . . 17.31
r 20.3 . . . . 15.11, 17.31
r 20.3(1) 17.33
Pt 21 . . . . 50.83, 50.182, 60.31
r 21.1 . . . . 50.269, 50.349
r 21.1(2) 50.165
r 21.1(2)(d) 60.49
r 21.2 . . . . 60.03
r 21.2(3) 60.03
r 21.4(3)(c) 60.06, 60.21, 60.28
r 21.9(6) 60.08
r 21.10 . . . . 60.38
r 21.10(2) 50.376
r 21.10(3) 60.35, 60.36
r 21.12 . . . . 27.36, 60.21, 60.42, 60.69
r 21.12(1A) 60.40, 60.69
r 21.12(1A)(b) 44.12, 60.41, 60.68
r 21.12(3) 60.43

Civil Procedure Rules 1998 (SI 1998/3132 as amended) (CPR) (*cont.*)
r 21.12(4) 60.44
r 21.12(5) 60.44
Pt 22
r 22.12(6) 60.21, 60.45
r 22.12(7) 60.45
Pt 23 . . . . . 13.27, 13.41, 13.72, 13.74, 17.193, 17.213, 35.128, 43.379, 65.20
r 23.3(2)(b) 13.72
Pt 24 . . . . . 15.01, 15.02, 15.15, 50.349
r 24.2(a)(i) 40.23
r 24.2(a)(ii) 40.20
r 24.5(1)–(5) 40.21
r 24.6 . . . . . 15.03, 15.16, 15.97, 15.130
Pt 25
Section II 15.01, 15.06, 15.07, 15.15, 15.21, 15.98
r 25.1(1)(c)(ii) 40.58, 40.59
r 25.1(1)(k) 36.113
r 25.1(1)(m) 40.69, 40.70
r 25.2(c) 15.05
r 25.12 . . . . . 15.21, 15.30, 15.98, 15.124
r 25.12(1) 15.06, 15.09, 15.11
r 25.13 . . . . . 15.21, 15.98
r 25.13(a) 15.116
r 25.13(1) 15.24
r 25.13(1)(a) 15.57
r 25.13(2) 15.26, 15.98
r 25.13(2)(a) 15.30, 15.78
r 25.13(2)(b) 15.26
r 25.13(2)(c) 15.34, 15.36
r 25.13(2)(d) 15.03, 15.40
r 25.13(2)(e) 15.03, 15.42
r 25.13(2)(f) 15.03, 15.43
r 25.13(2)(g) 15.03, 15.46, 15.47, 15.48
r 25.14 . . . . . 15.28
r 25.14(2) 15.03, 15.13
r 25.14(2)(a) 15.03, 15.52
r 25.14(2)(b) 15.03, 15.54, 15.56, 33.88
r 25.15 . . . . . 15.12, 15.50
r 25.15(1) 15.26
r 25.15(2) 15.03, 15.27, 15.50
Pt 26
r 26.6 . . . . . 50.69
r 26.6(4) 50.345
r 26.6(5) 50.345
r 26.7 . . . . . 50.345
r 26.7(1) 50.345
r 26.7(3) 12.63, 50.346, 50.381
r 26.8 . . . . . 50.371
r 26.8(1) 50.345
r 26.8(1)(b) 50.345
r 26.8(1)(c) 50.345
r 26.8(1)(d) 50.345
r 26.8(1)(e) 50.345
r 26.8(1)(f) 50.345
r 26.8(1)(g) 50.345
r 26.8(1)(h) 50.345
r 26.8(1)(i) 50.345
r 26.8(2) 50.68, 50.345
Pt 27 . . . . . 50.390
r 27.2(1)(g) 50.401
r 27.14 . . . . . 50.377
r 27.14(1) 50.381
r 27.14(1)(g) 7.136
r 27.14(2) 45.58, 50.369, 50.378
r 27.14(2)(b) 50.370
r 27.14(2)(e) 52.49, 52.57
r 27.14(2)(g) 50.400
r 27.14(2)(i) 50.378
r 27.14(2A) 43.364
r 27.14(3) 6.221, 50.401
r 27.14(4) 3.100, 50.369
Pt 30 . . . . . 50.314
r 30.1(2)(c) 5.16
r 30.2 . . . . . 43.08
r 30.3 . . . . . 43.09
r 30.3(2)(h) 61.06
Pt 31
r 31.22 . . . . . 16.57
Pt 32
r 32.6(1) 43.320
r 32.10 . . . . . 43.92
Pt 33
r 33.3 . . . . . 43.325
Pt 34
r 34.7 . . . . . 52.49
r 34.7(a) 52.49
r 34.7(b) 52.49
Pt 35
r 35.1 . . . . . 52.22, 52.27, 52.30
r 35.4 . . . . . 52.22, 52.23
r 35.4(1) 52.30
r 35.4(2) 52.12
r 35.4(3A) 52.24
r 35.4(3B) 52.46
r 35.4(4) 52.12
r 35.6 . . . . . 52.22
r 35.6(4) 52.12, 52.45
r 35.7 . . . . . 52.22, 52.31, 52.43
r 35.8(3)(a) 52.43
r 35.8(4)(a) 52.16, 52.43
r 35.8(5) 52.43
r 35.12 . . . . . 52.22
r 35.15 . . . . . 45.66, 52.22
Pt 36 . . . 6.06, 6.17, 6.76, 6.176, 6.207, 6.210, 6.212, 6.221, 6.225, 6.232, 6.236, 6.237, 6.254, 7.01, 7.08, 7.13, 7.19, 7.26, 7.109, 7.149, 7.173, 8.25, 11.28, 16.24, 16.36, 17.01, 17.06, 17.08, 17.11, 17.12, 1.15, 1.16, 1.17, 17.18, 17.19, 17.20–17.22,

17.24, 17.25, 17.26, 17.31, 17.33, 17.34, 17.42, 17.52, 17.62, 17.66, 17.67, 17.71, 17.73, 17.76, 17.77, 17.78, 17.89, 17.90, 17.106, 17.118, 17.120, 17.131, 17.136, 17.141, 17.149, 17.161, 17.162, 17.181, 17.202, 17.214, 17.216, 23.16, 39.07, 40.231, 43.255, 43.256, 43.284. 50.287, 55.42
Section I. . . 6.03, 6.06, 6.244, 17.01, 17.32, 17.40, 17.49, 17.50, 17.52, 36.77
Section II 17.01, 17.32
r 36.1 . . . . 6.06, 17.69, 17.78
r 36.1(1) 17.20
r 36.1(3) 17.32
r 36.2 . . . . 17.31, 17.34
r 36.2(1) 17.32
r 36.2(2) 17.49, 17.50, 17.52, 17.61
r 36.2(3) 17.30, 17.31
r 36.2(3)(a) 17.30
r 36.2(3)(b) 17.30
r 36.2(4)(a) 17.26
r 36.3 . . . . 17.03
r 36.3(a) 17.03
r 36.3(b) 17.03
r 36.3(c) 17.03, 56.88
r 36.3(d) 17.03, 17.176, 17.205
r 36.3(e) 17.03
r 36.3(f) 17.03
r 36.3(g) 17.47
r 36.3(1) 17.11
r 36.3(2)(b) 17.31
r 36.3(4) 17.113
r 36.3m(e) 17.188
r 36.4(1) 17.31, 17.113
r 36.4(2) 17.31, 17.33
r 36.5 . . . . 6.03, 6.06, 6.240, 17.24, 17.78, 43.253, 43.255, 50.221
r 36.5(d) 17.30, 17.31
r 36.5(1) 43.266
r 36.5(1)(c) 17.03, 17.46
r 36.5(1)(a) 17.40
r 36.5(1)(b) 17.40
r 36.5(1)(c) 17.40
r 36.5(1)(d) 43.265, 43.266, 43, 267
r 36.5(1)(e) 17.40
r 36.5(1)(e) 17.33
r 36.5(2) 17.40, 17.106, 43.256
r 36.5(3) 17.49, 17.50, 17.52, 43.266
r 36.5(4) 43.266, 43.267
r 36,6 43,256
r 36.6(1) 17.31, 17.42
r 36.6(2) 17.31, 17.42, 17.45, 43.270
r 36.7 . . . . 17.28, 17.28
r 36.7(1) 17.26, 43.282, 43.351
r 36.7(2) 17.28, 43.258, 43.259
r 36.8 . . . . 17.85
r 36.8(1) 17.55, 43.355
r 36.8(2) 17.55
r 36.8(3) 17.55
r 36.9(1) 17.198, 17.201
r 36.9(2) 17.164, 17.166, 17.198, 17.202, 17.206, 17.207
r 36.9(3) 17.198, 17.203, 17.206
r 36.9(3)(d) 17.176
r 36.9(4) 17.201, 17.207, 17.220
r 36.9(4)(a) 17.205, 17.207
r 36.9(4)(b) 17.73, 17.206, 17.219
r 36.9(5) 17.200, 17.202, 17.205
r 36.9(5)(a) 17.202
r 36.9(5)(b) 17.202
r 36.10 . . . . . 17.197, 17.198, 17.201, 17.208
r 36.10(1) 17.201
r 36.10(2) 17.205, 17.208, 17.210
r 36.10(2)(a) 17.205, 17.209, 17.210
r 36.10(2)(b) 17.209, 17.210
r 36.10(3) 17.203, 17.211
r 36.10(5) 17.119, 17.173, 17.180
r 36.11(1) 17.192
r 36.11(2) 17.164, 17.166
r 36.11(3) 17.176
r 36.11(3)(b) 17.176
r 36.11(3)(c) 17.176
r 36.11(3)(d) 17.176, 17.205, 43.277
r 36.11(4) 17.193
r 36.12 . . . . 17.164
r 36.12(1) 17.188
r 36.12(2) 17.188
r 36.12(3) 17.188
r 36.13 . . . . 7.109, 17.40, 17.46, 17.57, 17.117, 17.172, 36.289, 56.102
r 36.13(1) 7.109, 7.110, 17.27, 17.167, 17.170, 17.173, 17.178, 20.62
r 36.13(2) 7.110, 17.176, 17.185
r 36.13(3) 17.167, 17.168, 17.172
r 36.13(4) 17.176
r 36.13(4)(a) 17.176, 17.184
r 36.13(4)(b) 17.176, 17.177
r 36.13(4)(c) 17.176, 17.185
r 36.13(5) 17.173, 17.174, 17.178, 17.179, 17.180, 17.181, 17.182, 17.184, 50.289
r 36.13(5)(b) 17.117
r 36.13(6) 17.130, 17.173, 17.180
r 36.13(7) 17.190
r 36.14 . . . . 16.21, 17.57, 17.98
r 36.14(1)(a) 17.98
r 36.14(1)(b) 6.142
r 36.14(2) 6.240
r 36.14(3) 6.240, 17.98, 17.185, 43.346, 56.83
r 36.15(3)(a) 56.91
r 36.14(3)(b) 6.176
r 36.14(3)(c) . . . 56.02, 56.06, 56.88, 56.91

Civil Procedure Rules 1998 (SI 1998/3132 as amended) (CPR) (*cont.*)
r 36.14(3)(d) 43.345
r 36.14(4) 56.89
r 36.14(5) 56.91
r 36.14(6) 17.166, 21.12
r 36.15(2) 17.176
r 36.15(3)(b) 56.88
r 36.15(3)(c) 56.88
r 36.15(4) 17.176
r 36.16(1) 17.57
r 36.16(2) 17.57, 43.315
r 36.16(3) 17.57
r 36.16(4) 17.58
r 36.17 . . . . . 17.89, 17.90, 17.118, 17.175, 17.205, 17.214, 50.290
r 36.17(1)(b) 17.94
r 36.17(2) 17.86, 17.101, 17.109, 43.345, 43.350
r 36.17(3) . . . 17.118, 17.163, 17.178, 17.177, 43.260, 43.273, 43.343, 43.352, 50.290, 50.292
r 36.17(3)(a) 17.117
r 36.17(4) 17.81, 17.117, 17.177, 17.178, 43.260, 43.352, 50.336
r 36.17(4)(a) 17.81, 43.345, 50.236
r 36.17(4)(b) 17.81, 17.117, 43.345
r 36.17(4)(c) 17.81, 43.345
r 36.17(4)(d) 17.81, 43.260, 43.345, 43.352
r 36.17(4)(d)(ii) 17.30, 17.31
r 36.17(5) 17.55, 17.129, 17.130, 17.131, 43.344, 43.348
r 36.17(5)(b) 43.260, 43.351, 43.352
r 36.17(5)(c) 43.351
r 36.17(5)(e) 17.149
r 36.17(6) 43.345
r 36.17(7) 17.99, 17.118, 17.198, 17.214, 17.219, 43.343, 43.345, 43.353
r 36.17(8) 17.99
r 36.18 . . . . . 17.31
r 36.18(2) 17.30, 17.49, 17.50
r 36.18(4) 17.49
r 36.19 . . . . . 17.30, 17.31
r 36.19(1) 17.50
r 36.19(2) 17.50
r 36.20 . . . . . 17.32, 17.40, 17.46, 50.170, 50.289, 50.304, 56.102
r 36.20(2) 50.287
r 36.20(3) 17.185, 50.288
r 36.20(4) 50.289
r 36.20(5) 50.289
r 36.20(6) 50.289
r 36.20(7) 50.289
r 36.20(9) 50.289
r 36.20(10) 50.288, 50.289
r 36.20(11) 50.289
r 36.20(12) 50.289
r 36.20(13) 50.287, 50.289
r 36.21 . . . . . 17.32, 17.163, 50.292, 50.293, 50.304, 56.102
r 36.21(1) 50.290
r 36.21(2) 50.290
r 36.21(3)(a)–(b) 50.290
r 36.21(3)(c) 50.290
r 36.21(4) 50.290
r 36.21(5) 50.290
r 36.21(6) 50.290
r 36.21(7) 50.290
r 36.21(9) 50.290
r 36.21(10) 50.290
r 36.22 . . . . . 17.52
r 36.22(2) 17.52
r 36.22(3) 17.52, 17.111
r 36.22(3)(b) 17.176
r 36.22(6) 17.52, 17.112
r 36.22(8) 17.111, 17.112
r 36.23 . . . . . 17.116, 17.117
r 36.24 . . . . . 17.32
r 36.25 . . . . . 50.289, 50.290
r 36.26 . . . 50.221, 50.236, 50.289, 50.290
r 36.28(1)–(2) 50.221, 50.236
r 36.29 . . . . . 50.244, 50.245, 50.246
r 36.29(2)(a) 50.236
r 36.29(2)(b) 50.236
r 36.29(3) 50.236
r 36.29(4) 50.236
r 36.49(4) 56.06
r 36.49(a) 56.115
r 36.49(c) 56.115
Pt 38 . . . . . 43.395, 43.398, 43.403
r 38.2(b) 43.403
r 38.2(c) 43.403
r 38.2(1) 43.397, 43.403
r 38.2(3) 43.404
r 38.2(4) 43.405
r 38.3 . . . . . 43.399
r 38.3(1) 7.119
r 38.4 . . . . . 8.30
r 38.4(1) 7.135
r 38.5 . . . . . 7.118
r 38.6 . . . . . 7.114, 7.117, 7.138, 43.403
r 38.6(1) 7.120, 10.24, 65.89
r 38.6(2) 7.119
r 38.6(3) 7.136
r 38.7 . . . . . 43.401, 43.406
r 38.8 . . . . . 7.140
r 38.8(2) 7.135
Pt 39
r 39.2 . . . . . 43.306
r 39.2(1) 36.109
r 39.2(3) 36.109

r 39.2(3)(c) 13.95
r 39.6 . . . . 12.18, 47.32
r 39n.11(3) 17.176
Pt 40
r 40.2 . . . . 10.03
r 40.3(1)(d) 7.65
r 40.6 . . . . 7.68, 11.19, 43.244
r 40.6(1) 7.65
r 40.6(2) 7.65
r 40.6(3) 7.65
r 40.6(3)(b)(vii) 7.65
r 40.6(5) 7.66
r 40.6(6) 7.66
r 40.6(7) 7.67
r 40.8 . . . . 56.16, 56.22
r 40.8(2) 56.06, 56.29
r 40.9 . . . . 10.26
r 40.12(1) 10.05
r 40.13 . . . . 21.03, 21.31
r 40.13(3) 21.31
Pt 41
r 41.3A 17.176
Pts 43–48 . . . . 4.32, 12.34
Pt 43
r 43.2(1) 29.02
r 43.2(1)(a) 3.03
r 43.2(1)(k) 50.189
r 43.2(3) 18.20, 18.88, 18.89, 29.68, 29.109
r 43.2(4) 6.145, 29.08
r 43.3 . . . . 2.09
Pts 44–Part 47 . . . . 18.122, 18.132, 45.14
Pt 44 . . . . 6.254, 7.149, 14.02, 16.24, 17.25, 17.131, 50.336
Pt 44
Section II 8.04, 8.11, 8.12, 8.13, 8.14, 8.15, 8.16, 8.17, 8.19, 8.20, 8.22, 8.23, 8.32, 8.47, 8.52, 8.53, 9.08, 52.98
r 44 . . . . 43.391
r 44.1 . . . . 44.02, 50.04
r 44n.1 . . . . 55.26
r 44.1(1) 2.09, 3.03, 5.17, 5.18, 43.11, 43.13
r 44.1(2)(a) 6.03, 61.02
r 44.1(2)(a)(i) 48.99, 48.102
r 44.2. . . . 6.03, 6.09, 6.16, 6.17, 6.73, 6.110, 6.113, 6.210, 6.244, 6.257, 6.259, 7.07, 7.08, 7.21, 7.40, 7.50, 7.117, 7.124, 7.147, 9.09, 9.221, 11.27, 15.03, 16.01, 16.13, 16.15–16.30, 16.43, 17.86, 17.89, 17.90, 17.96, 17.102, 17.122, 17.127, 17.132, 17.173, 17.205, 23.37, 39.07, 43.296, 50.331, 50.342, 50.397, 61.15, 62.25, 66.08, 66.09, 66.10
r 44.2(a) 16.06, 25.48
r 44.2(1)(b) 16.15
r 44.2(2) 7.57
r 44.2(2)(a) 6.42, 6.124, 7.16, 7.38, 7.39, 7.142, 7.143
r 44.2(2)(b) 6.50, 7.143
r 44.2(2)(c) 17.205
r 44.2(3) 17.72
r 44.2(3)(b) 7.64
r 44.2(4) 6.03, 6.76, 6.155, 6.162, 16.18, 17.123, 17.127
r 44.2(4)(a) 6.77, 6.93, 6.155
r 44.2(4)(b) 6.162, 6.163, 6.169
r 44.2(4)(c) 2.09, 6.03, 6.207, 6.210, 6.212, 17.25, 17.60, 17.85, 17.98, 17.102, 43.296
r 44.2(5) 6.77, 6.162, 6.163, 16.18
r 44.2(5)(a) 4.58, 6.93, 50.255
r 44.2(5)(b) 6.170, 7.21, 65.50, 65.51
r 44.2(5)(c) 6.03, 6.170
r 44.2(5)(d) 6.03, 6.145
r 44.2(6) 6.01, 6.03, 6.29, 6.30, 6.31, 6.163, 21.10
r 44.2(6)(a) 6.32, 6.34, 7.37
r 44.2(6)(e) 6.30
r 44.2(6)(f) 6.03, 6.30, 6.34, 6.37
r 44.2(6)(g) 56.06, 56.29, 56.55, 56.56, 56.70, 56.72, 56.85, 56.106, 56.109, 56.110
r 44.2(7) 6.03, 6.29, 6.30, 6.33, 6.34, 21.10
r 44.2(8) 2.09, 6.03, 6.29, 14.02, 14.03, 14.07, 14.09, 43.161
r 44.2(9) 7.37
r 44.3. . . 12.163, 16.02, 16.04, 16.09, 23.44, 23.47, 37.27, 44.42, 56.62, 61.03
r 44.3(1) 16.10
r 44.3(2) . . 16.05, 25.25, 25.33, 25.49, 57.29
r 44.3(2)(a) 12.77
r 44.3(2)(b) 25.43
r 44.3(3) 51.33
r 44.3(a) 16.03
r 44.3(b) 16.03
r 44.3(3) 37.02, 37.03, 37.24, 51.44
r 44.3(4) 16.02, 16.15
r 44.3(4)(c) 43.298
r 44.3(5) 6.99, 12.99, 12.101, 16.06, 25.27, 25.29, 25.31, 25.32, 25.33, 25.34, 25.36, 25.37, 25.39, 25.51, 25.55, 25.56, 25.57, 25.59, 25.77, 57.07
r 44.3(5)(a) 6.96, 25.58, 25.75
r 44.3(5)(b) 25.58, 25.81, 25.95
r 44.3(5)(c) 25.58, 25.78, 25.95
r 44.3(5)(d) 25.91
r 44.3(5)(e) 25.31, 25.33, 25.58, 25.73, 25.100
r 44.3(6) 16.02

Civil Procedure Rules 1998 (SI 1998/3132 as amended) (CPR) (*cont.*)
r 44.3(7) 16.05, 16.06, 16.07, 25.17, 25.63
r 44.3(8) 14.03, 14.04
r 44.3A 44.39
r 44.3B 54.109, 54.110
r 44.3B(1) 54.123, 54.125
r 44.3B(1)(a) 54.102
r 44.3B(1)(c) 54.125
r 44.3B(1)(e) 54.130
r 44.3C 18.132
r 44.4 . . . . 13.37, 16.05, 23.37, 25.33, 25.49, 50.342, 54.129, 54.133
r 44.4(1) 18.09
r 44.4(3) 25.26, 25.32, 25.33, 37.24, 37.25, 51.50, 51.78, 52.42
r 44.4(3)(a) 57.03
r 44.4(3)(h) 12.142, 25.26
r 44.4(5) 25.35, 25.36
r 44.4(5)(a) 25.35
r 44.4(5)(c) 25.35
r 44.5 . . . . 13.37, 23.44, 23.47, 57.48, 66.09, 66.17, 66.18, 66.19, 66.31, 66.34, 66.36, 66.58
r 44.5(1) 66.18, 66.20
r 44.5(2) 66.18, 66.20
r 44.5(3) 1.127, 25.53, 64.15
r 44.6(1) 44.03
r 44.7 . . . . 23.56
r 44.8(3) 23.57
r 44.9 . . . . 7.103
r 44.9(1) 7.109, 7.110
r 44.9(1)(b) 17.17.167, 56.102
r 44.9(2) 7.109, 7.173, 17.27, 17.167, 56.101
r 44.9(3) 43.330
r 44.9(4) 56.06, 56.102
r 44.10 . . . . 6.264
r 44.10(1)(a) 6.262, 66.80
r 44.10(1)(b) 66.80
r 44.10(2) 7.102, 7.185, 45.57
r 44.10(4) 7.184, 45.57
r 44.10(5) 7.187
r 44.11 . . . . 6.108, 6.146, 9.100, 9.101, 9.102, 9.148, 9.175, 9.202, 9.215, 12.149, 23.54, 23.59, 23.66, 23.67, 23.68, 23.71, 23.74, 23.77, 23.81, 23.119, 57.25, 57.37, 57.41, 57.52, 57.53, 57.57
r 44n.11 . . . . 57.44
r 44.11(1) 9.101
r 44.11(1)(a) 9.101, 57.37, 57.38, 57.42, 57.49
r 44.11(1)(b) 57.16, 57.37, 57.38, 57.41, 57.42, 57.44, 57.48, 57.49
r 44.11(2) 23.82, 57.61, 57.64
r 44.11(3) 23.82, 57.64
r 44.12 . . . . 7.37, 21.17
r 44.12(a) 50.324
r 44.12(1) 21.09
r 44.12(1)(a) 50.324
r 44.12(1)(b) 7.173
r 44.12B 54.130, 54.139
r 44.13 . . . . 2.09, 8.10, 8.12
r 44.13(1) 8.52
r 44.13(1)(c) 8.11
r 44.13(2) 8.14
r 44.14 . . . . 8.23, 11.29, 23.70
r 44.14(1) 8.24, 8.26
r 44.14(2) 8.24
r 44.15 . . . . 8.28, 8.30, 50.304, 54.110
r 44.15(1) 54.45
r 44.15(1)(a) 8.31
r 44.15(1)(c)(i) 8.29
r 44.15(2) 54.45
r 44.16 . . . . 8.32, 8.33, 8.50, 50.304
r 44.16(1) 8.35, 8.37, 16.48
r 44.16(2) 8.46, 8.47
r 44.16(2)(a) 8.48, 8.50, 8.51, 9.73
r 44.16(2)(b) 8.52, 8.54, 8.55
r 44.16(3) 8.46, 8.47
r 44.17 . . . . 8.17
r 44.18 . . . . 29.176, 29.177
r 44.18(2)(a) 29.178
r 44.20(4) 17.26
r 44.26(1) 8.37
r 44.40(5) 19.20
Pt 45 . . . . 4.10, 4.67, 12.135, 17.01, 17.162, 22.05, 29.107, 29.150, 42.23, 42.43, 50.76, 50.77, 50.314, 54.58
Section I 2.09, 11.15, 50.01, 50.02, 50.14, 50.48–50.66
Section II 1.168, 11.10, 11.14, 11.23. 44.05, 50.01, 50.02, 50.67–50.101, 60.35, 60.36
Section III 1.168, 50.01, 50.02, 50.150–50.266, 60.35, 60.36
Section IIIA 7.110, 17.32, 17.84, 17.163, 17.185, 50.01, 50.02, 50.27, 50.68, 50.121, 50.267–50.311, 60.36
Section IV 1.169, 17.163, 50.01, 50.02, 50.312–50.341
Section V 1.169, 50.01, 50.02, 54.26
Section VI 50.01, 50.02
Section VII 13.01, 13.78–13.83, 13.88, 13.89, 13.90, 13.93, 50.01, 50.02, 50.368–50.403
r 45 . . . . 11.31
r 45.1(1) 50.52
r 45.1(2) 50.50, 50.52
r 45.1(2)(c) 50.51
r 45.1(2)(f) 50.51
r 45.1(3) 50.57

r 45.1(4) 50.52
r 45.1(5) 50.51
r 45.2 . . . . 50.57, 50.307
r 45.3(1) 50.53
r 45.4 . . . . .50.63
r 45.6 . . . . .50.65
r 45.7 . . . . .50.61
r 45.8 . . . . 50.53, 50.54, 50.66
r 45.9 . . . . .50.76
r 45.9(1)–(3). 50.68
r 45.9(1)(a) 11.14
r 45.9(2)(a) 50.68
r 45.9(2)(b). 50.68
r 45.9(2)(c) 50.68, 50.69
r 45.9(3)(a) 50.68
r 45.9(3)(b). 50.68
r 45.9(4) 50.119
r 45.9(4)(a) 50.72
r 45.9(4)(b). 50.72
r 45.9(4)(c) 50.73
r 49.10 . . . . .50.79
r 45.11 . . . . .2.09, 50.79, 50.80
r 45.11(2) 4.49
r 45.11(3) 50.81
r 45.12 . . . . 50.79, 50.83, 50.86, 50.90
r 45.12(b) 50.84
r 45.12(2)(b)(i) 50.86
r 45.12(2)(c) 11.10, 11.15, 50.83, 50.86, 52.101
r 45.13 . . . . 50.90, 50.298
r 45.13(2) 50.93
r 45.13(3) 50.93
r 45.14 . . . . .50.90
r 45.16(1) 50.155, 50.227, 50.264
r 45.16(2) 50.254
r 45.17 . . . . .50.173
r 45.18 . . . . . 2.09, 50.144, 50.172, 50.173, 50.174, 50.176, 50.177
r 45.18(1) 50.174
r 45.18(2) 50.174
r 45.18(4) 50.175
r 45.18(5) 50.176, 50.177
r 45.18(6) 50.174
r 45.19 . . . . 50.175, 50.176, 50.177, 50.186, 50.190, 50.220, 50.236, 50.251, 50.263, 50.278
r 45.19(1) 50.181
r 45.19(2)(a)(i) 50.182
r 45.19(2)(a)(ii) 50.182
r 45.19(2)(a)(ii)(aa) 50.182
r 45.19(2)(a)(ii)(bb). 50.182
r 45.19(2)(b) 50.182
r 45.19(2)(c) 50.182
r 45.19(2)(d) 50.182
r 45.19(2)(e) 50.181
r 45.19(2A). 50.184, 50.206, 52.71
r 45.19(2A)(a). 50.184
r 45.19(2A)(b) 50.184
r 45.19(2A)(c). 50.184
r 45.19(2A)(d) 50.184
r 45.19(2A)(e). 50.184
r 45.19(2B). 50.188, 52.38
r 45.19(2C). 50.184, 50.187
r 45.19(2D) 50.184
r 45.19(2E). 50.188
r 45.19(3) 50.185
r 45.19(3)(1)(a) 50.182, 50.277
r 45.20 . . . . 50.236, 50.245
r 45.20(2)(a)(i) 50.133
r 45.20(2)(a)(iv) 50.133
r 45.21(1) 50.220
r 45.21(2) 50.220
r 45.21(3) 50.220
r 45.21(4)–(6). 50.220
r 45.22(1) .50.251
r 45.22(2). .50.251
r 45.22(3). .50.251
r 45.22(4). .50.251
r 45.22(5). .50.251
r 45.22(6). .50.251
r 45.22(7). .50.251
r 45.23 . . . . .50.251
r 45.23A. 50.173, 50.179, 50.229
r 45.23B 50.173, 50.180
r 45.24 . . . . 50.202, 50.234, 50.254, 50.256, 50.257, 50.258, 50.259, 50.263, 50.265, 50.300
r 45.24(b)(ii). 50.168
r 45.24(1) 50.258
r 45.24(2) 50.175, 50.198, 50.258, 50.261, 50.264
r 45.24(2)(a) 50.261
r 45.24(2)(b). 50.258
r 45.24(2)(c) 50.268, 50.260
r 45.24(2A) 50.198, 50.262
r 45.24(3) 50.211
r 45.25(2) 50.248
r 45.25(3) 50.248
r 45.25(4) 50.248
r 45.26 . . . . 50.244
r 45.27 . . . . 50.242
r 45.27C(1). 50.275
r 45.27C(2) 50.275
r 45.27E(2). 50.306
r 45.27I 50307
r 45.28 . . . . .50.275
r 45.29 . . . . 11.07, 11.14
r 45.29(1)–(2). 50.248
r 45.29(1)(c) 50.303
r 45.29(3) 50.248, 50.303
r 45.29(4) 50.249
r 45.29(4)(a) 50.276

Civil Procedure Rules 1998 (SI 1998/3132 as amended) (CPR) (*cont.*)
r 45.29A(1) 50.170
r 45.29A(1)(a) 50.269
r 45.29A(1)(b) 50.269
r 45.29A(2) 50.170, 50.259, 50.269
r 45.29A(3) 50.259, 50.265, 50.300
r 45.29B 50.170, 50.286, 29.292, 50.293, 50.307
r 45.29B(a) 50.275
r 45.29B(b) 50.275
r 45.29C 50.307
r 45.29C(1) 50.275
r 45.29C(2)(b) 50.309
r 45.29C(2)(c) 50.309
r 45.29C(3) 50.275
r 45.29C(4)(b)–(c) 50.275
r 45.29D(a) 50.279
r 45.29D(b) 50.279
r 45.29E(1) 50.279
r 45.29E(2) 50.282
r 45.29E(3) 50.279
r 45.29E(4)(a) 50.283
r 45.29E(4)(b) 50.283
r 45.29E(4)(c) 50.283
r 45.29F 50.304
r 45.29F(1)(a) 50.304
r 45.29F(1)(b) 50.304
r 45.29F(2) 50.301
r 45.29F(3) 50.303, 50.305
r 45.29F(4)(a) 50.306
r 45.29F(4)(b) 50.306
r 45.29F(4)(c) 50.306
r 45.29F(8) 50.304
r 45.29F(9) 50.304
r 45.29F(10) 50.304
r 45.29G(1) 50.307
r 45.29G(2) 50.308
r 45.29H(1) 50.301, 50.311
r 45.29H(2) 50.301, 50.311
r 45.29H(3) 50.301, 50.311
r 45.29H(4) 50.301, 50.311
rr 45.29I–45.29L 50.307
r 45.29I 50.275, 50.289, 50.290, 50.301, 50.303, 50.308, 50.311
r 45.29I(1) 50.277, 50.284
r 45.29I(2)(a) 50.284
r 45.29I(2)(a)(i) 50.277
r 45.29I(2)(a)(ii) 50.277
r 45.29I(2)(a)(ii)(aa) 50.277
r 45.29I(2)(a)(ii)(bb) 50.277
r 45.29I(2)(b) 50.284
r 45.29I(2)(c) 50.284
r 45.29I(2)(d) 50.284
r 45.29I(2)(e) 50.277
r 45.29I(2)(f) 50.277
r 45.29I(2)(g) 50.284
r 45.29I(2)(h) 50.284
rr 25.29I(2B)–(2E) 50.278, 50.285
r 25.29I(2B) 52.38
r 45.29I(3) 50.278, 50.285
r 45.29I(3)(b)(i) 50.277
r 45.29I(3)(b)(ii) 50.277
r 45.29J(1) 50.297
r 45.29J(2) 50.297
r 45.29J(3) 50.297
r 45.29K(1) 50.297
r 45.29L 50.229
r 45.30 . . . . . 50.317
r 45.30(2)(a) 50.331
r 45.30(3) 44.05, 50.336, 50.337, 50.338
r 45.30(4) 50.322
r 45.31 . . . . . 50.04, 50.324, 50.329
r 45.31(1) 50.326
r 45.31(1)(a) 50.330
r 45.31(2) 50.330, 50.336
r 45.31(4) 50.326
r 45.31(4A) 50.330
r 45.31(5) 50.330
r 45.32 . . . . . 50.331
r 45.33(1) 50.342
r 45.33(2) 50.342
r 45.33(3) 50.342
r 45.33(5) 50.343
r 45.33(6) 50.343
r 45.34 . . . . . 50.343
r 45.35 . . . . . 50.344
r 45.36 . . . . . 50.344
r 45.37 . . . . . 2.09
r 45.37(1) 50.345
r 45.37(2) 50.174, 50.347, 50.348
r 45.38 . . . . . 2.09, 50.236
r 45.38(1) 50.350
r 45.38(2) 50.356
r 45.38(3) 50.352
r 45.38(3)(a) 50.352
r 45.38(3)(b)(i) 50.352
r 45.38(3)(b)(ii) 50.352
r 45.38(3)(b)(iii) 50.352
r 45.38(4) 50.352
r 45.38(5) 50.352
r 45.38(6) 50.355
r 45.39(3) 50.359
r 45.39(4) 50.359
r 45.39(5) 50.350, 50.352, 59.02, 59.19
r 45.39(6) 50.360
r 45.39(7) 50.357
r 45.39(8) 50.358
r 45.40 . . . . . 50.286
r 45.40(1) 50.367
r 45.40(3) 50.362
r 45.40(4) 50.362, 50.367

r 45.40(5) 50.367
r 45.41 . . . . 13.86
r 45.42 . . . . 13.87
r 45.43 . . . . 13.91, 13.95, 50.329
r 45.43(3)(b) 13.96
r 45.44 . . . . 13.88
r 45.44(3)(b) 16.67
r 45.95I(2E) 50.206
Pt 46 . . . . 11.05, 60.31
Section IV 13.01, 13.47, 13.51
r 46.1 . . . . 7.39, 9.78, 9.79
r 46.1(2) 7.41, 7.42, 7.49
r 46.1(2) 11.06, 11.07
r 46.2 . . . . 8.48, 9.78
r 46.2(1)(a) 9.79
r 46.2(1)(b) 9.79
r 46.2(2)(a)(ii) 9.79
r 46.2(2)(b) 9.79
r 46.3(3) 16.14
r 46.4 . . . . 5.19, 60.33
r 46.4(2)(a) 60.68
r 46.4(5)(b) 44.12
r 46.5 . . . . .2.09, 11.24, 59.02, 59.10, 59.19
r 46.5(3) 3.95, 59.21
r 46.5(3)(a) 59.25, 59.28
r 46.5(3)(a)(ii) 3.97, 59.30
r 46.5(3)(b) 3.92, 59.04, 59.30, 59.35
r 46.5(3)(c) 59.04, 59.36
r 46.5(4) 59.11, 59.19
r 46.5(4)(b) 59.22
r 46.5(5) 59.34
r 46.5(5)(b) 60.41
r 46.5(6) 59.06, 59.43, 59.49, 59.54
r 46.5(6)(b)(v) 59.55
r 46.6 . . . . 9.76
r 46.6(b)(ii) 27.308
r 46.6(2) 65.04
r 46.6(2)(i) 65.04
r 46.6(2)(ii) 65.04
r 46.6(2)(iii) 65.04
r 46.6(3) 65.74
r 46.6(4) 20.37, 65.56, 65.58, 65.66
r 46.6(4)(b) 65.57
r 46.6(5) 65.45, 65.114
r 46.6(6) 59.40, 59.43, 59.44, 65.60, 65.66, 65.79
r 46.6(7) 65.61, 65.66, 65.87
r 46.7(1) 18.121, 18.125, 18.126, 18.131
r 46.7(1)(a) 18.131
r 46.7(1)(b) 18.131
r 46.7(2) 18.121, 18.125
r 46.7(3) 18.125
r 46.7(4)(a) 18.126
r 46.8 . . . . .9.78, 9.99, 9.100, 9.101, 9.102, 18.117
r 46.8(1) 9.93
r 46.9 . . . . 36.77, 36.82, 37.06, 37.26, 37.27, 37.31
r 46.9(2) 37.18, 37.23
r 46.9(2)(a)–(b) 27.147
r 46.9(2)(b) 36.83
r 46.9(3) 16.10, 16.14, 28.154, 37.02, 38.12, 66.17
r 46.9(3)(b) 38.11
r 46.9(3)(c) 27.327
r 46.9(4) 37.30
r 46.10 . . . . 36.96, 36.97
r 46.10(2) 35.89, 35.101, 36.99
r 46.10(5)(b) 36.102
r 46.11 . . . . 50.382
r 46.11(2) 50.383
r 46.12(1) 50.353
r 46.12(2) 50.353
r 46.13 . . . . 50.391
r 46.13(1) 50.382, 50.386
r 46.13(2) 50.388
r 46.13(3) 50.394
r 46.14 . . . . 11.02
r 46.14(1) 11.06, 11.07, 50.68
r 46.14(3) 11.05, 11.09
r 46.14(4) 11.09
r 46.14(5) 11.14, 11.21
r 46.14(6) 11.28
r 46.14(7) 11.24
r 46.15 . . . . 67.16
r 46.16(1)(a) 13.48
r 46.16(2) 13.46
r 46.17(1)(a) 13.72
r 46.17(1)(b) 13.72
r 46.17(2) 13.72
r 46.17(3) 13.72
r 46.17(4) 13.72
r 46.18 . . . . 13.72
r 46.19(1) 13.74
r 46.19(2) 13.74
r 46.19(3) 13.74
r 46.56(4) 59.24
Pt 47 . . . . .11.28, 12.143, 14.02, 17.31, 33.11, 43.149, 43.283, 43.284, 43.319, 43.367
Section VIII 45.01, 45.02, 45.06, 45.08, 45.09
r 47.1 . . . .2.09, 6.272, 7.81, 23.108, 43.60, 43.71, 43.79, 43.80, 48.52
r 47.2 . . . . 7.90, 43.75, 45.37
r 47.3 . . . . 5.19, 43.22, 43.205, 43.206
r 47.3(1)(b)(i) 23.81
r 47.4 . . . . 43.02
r 47.4(2) 43.04, 43.06, 45.43
r 47.4(3) 43.06
r 47.4(4) 43.02
r 47.6(1) 43.51, 43.87
r 47.6(1)(a) 43.51

Civil Procedure Rules 1998 (SI 1998/3132 as amended) (CPR) (*cont.*)
r 47.6(1)(b) 43.51
r 47.6(1)(c) 43.52
r 47.6(2) 43.51
r 47.6(3) 43.56
r 47.7 . . . . 23.58, 43.85, 43.177
r 47.8 . . . . 23.68, 23.77
r 47.8(1) 23.67, 43.96, 43.97
r 47.8(2) 23.62, 43.97, 43.102
r 47.8(3) 23.67, 23.74, 23.119, 43.88, 43.92, 43.105, 56.06, 56.50, 56.51
r 47.8(4) 43.99
r 47.9 . . . . 43.126, 43.143, 43.312
r 47.9(2) 43.127, 43.155
r 47.9(3) 43.139
r 47.9(4) 43.139, 43.155
r 47.9(5) 43.144
r 47.10 . . . . 43.243
r 47.11(3) 43.165
r 47.12 . . . . .43.151, 43.152
r 47.12(1) 43.155
r 47.12(3) 43.165
r 47.13(1) 43.166, 43.168
r 47.13(2) 43.168
r 47.14 . . . . .43.212
r 47.14(1) . . 43.177, 43.178, 43.214, 43.216
r 47.14(2) 23.58, 43.97, 43.190, 43.195, 43.204, 43.223
r 47.14(3) 43.97, 43.191
r 47.14(4) 23.57, 23.67, 43.193, 43.194, 56.06, 56.51
r 47.14(5) 43.312
r 47.14(6) 43.205, 43.314
r 47.14(7) 43.205, 43.318, 45.09, 45.34
r 47.15 . . . . 14.02, 43.201
r 47.15(1) 43.200, 43.201
r 47.15(2) 43.202
r 47.15(3) 43.207
r 47.15(4) 23.119, 43.207
r 47.15(5) 43.230, 43.231
r 47.15(6) 43.211, 43.212
r 47.15(7)–(9) 43.226
r 47.15(7) 43.178, 43.224
r 47.15(8)(a) 43.220
r 47.15(10) 43.235, 43.237, 43.238
r 47.16 . . . . .2.09, 43.377, 43.379
r 47.16(1) 43.377, 43.379
r 47.16(2) 43.379
r 47.16(3) 43.379
r 47.16(4) 43.381
r 47.17 . . . . .43.392
r 47.17(1) 43.385
r 47.17(2) 43.384
r 47.17(4) 43.389
r 47.17(5) 43.388
r 47.17(6) 43.387
r 47.18 . . . . .36.113, 43.205, 43.254, 43.280, 43.366
r 47.19 . . . . 4.41, 43.205, 43.253, 43.254, 43.280, 66.81
r 47.19(1) 43.281
r 47.20 . . . . 43.253, 45.07
r 47.20(1) 18.135, 43.330, 43.374
r 47.20(2) 18.135, 43.330
r 47.20(3) 43.331
r 47.20(3)(a) 43.334
r 47.20(3)(b) 43.336
r 47.20(3)(c) 43.339
r 47.20(4) 17.30, 17.31, 17.33, 36.77, 43.255
r 47.20(4)(d) 43.279
r 47.20(4)(e) 43.343, 43.345
r 47.20(5) 43.373
r 47.20(6) 43.370, 43.372, 56.06
r 47.20(7) 11.28, 43.278, 43.342
r 47.21 . . . . 43.206, 45.06
r 47.24(a) 45.06
rr 47.22–47.24 . . . . 43.205
r 47.22 . . . . .45.06
r 47.23 . . . . 45.07, 45.08
r 47.23(1) 45.09
r 47.23(2) 45.09
Pt 48 . . . . .4.32
r 48.1 . . . . .7.91, 43.55, 50.83, 50.105, 50.118, 50.119, 50.131, 50.132, 50.189, 54.17
r 48.1(1) 44.37
r 48.1(1)(a)(i) 54.18
r 48.1(1)(a)(i)(bb) 50.190
r 48.1(1)(a)(iii) 50.190
r 48.1(2) 7.45
r 48.1(2)(b) 7.49
r 48.2 . . . . 8.17, 44.37, 50.79, 50.88, 50.105, 54.33, 54.37
r 48.2(1) 8.18, 54.37, 54.54
r 48.2(1)(a)(iii) 54.185
r 48.2(1)(b) 54.23
r 48.2(2) 54.23
r 48.3 . . . . .66.18
r 48.6 . . . . .59.43
r 48.6(3)(c) 47.11
r 48.6(6)(b) 59.47, 59.50
r 48.7(3) 24.56, 46.06
r 48.8(2) 53.131
r 48.10(2) 35.108
r 48n.1 . . . . .29.68
Pt 51
r 51.2 . . . . 4.49, 43.202
Pt 52 . . . . . .13.80, 15.02, 15.12, 15.15, 15.18, 45.01, 45.02, 45.03, 45.09, 45.16, 45.27, 45.32–45.56

Section IV 13.01
r 52.1(2) 45.05
r 52.1(3)(a) 45.04
r 52.1(3)(b) 45.04
r 52.1(3)(c) 45.04
r 52.1(3)(d) 45.04
r 52.1(3)(e) 45.04
r 52.1(3)(f) 45.04
r 52.6(1) 45.33
r 52.7 . . . . . 45.71
r 52.8–5.11 . . . . . 45.04, 45.33
r 52.9 . . . . . 15.97, 45.52
r 52.9(1) 15.03, 15.11
r 52.9(2) 15.03, 15.11
r 52.9A 13.102, 45.58, 45.59
r 52.10(1) 56.103
r 52.10(2)(d) 56.06, 56.103
r 52.11(1)–(3) 43.220
r 52.11(2)(b) 45.60
r 52.12(1) 45.33
r 52.12(2) 43.318, 45.33, 45.44
r 52.12(2)(a) 45.33
r 52.12(2)(b) 45.33
r 52.12(3) 45.36
r 52.13(1) 45.04
r 52.13(2) 45.04, 45.45
r 52.13(3) 45.04
r 52.14 . . . . . 50.378
r 52.15(1) 45.35
r 52.16 . . . . . 14.16, 45.37, 45.38
r 52.19 . . . . . 13.102, 13.103, 13.104, 13.105, 13.107
r 52.19(2) 105
r 52.19(3) 13.106
r 52.19(4) 13.107
r 52.19A 13.108
r 52.20(2)(e) 7.184
r 52.21(1)(b) 45.16
r 52.21(3) 45.16, 45.46
r 52.23(1) 45.41
Pt 54 . . . . . 67.02
r 54.9(2) 67.09
Pt 57
r 57.7(5) 7.56, 7.57, 7.58
Pt 59
r 59.9(2) 15.97
r 52.9A 50.378
Pt 61
r 61.4 . . . . . 6.244
r 61.4(11) 6.03
Pt 63 . . . . . 50.314
r 63.1 . . . . . 50.320
r 63.26 . . . . . 44.05
r 63.26(1) 50.330, 50.339
r 63.26(2) 50.329, 50.330, 50.331
r 63.26(3) 50.315, 50.316, 50.330
r 63.28(2) 50.316, 50.330
Pt 64
r 64.2 . . . . . 66.68
r 64.2(a) 66.31, 66.35
r 64.3 . . . . . 66.68
Pt 65
r 65.1(1)(g) 50.313
Pt 66 . . . . . 61.03
r 66.1(2) 61.03
r 66.2 . . . . . 61.03
r 66.6(3) 61.06
Pt 67
r 67.2(1) 35.121
r 67.2(1)(a) 35.126
r 67.2(2) 35.128
r 67.2(3) 35.122
r 67.3 . . . . . 36.39
r 67.3(1) 5.14, 40.13, 40.17
r 67.3(1)(a) 36.50, 40.19
r 67.3(1)(b) 36.50, 40.17
r 67.3(2) 27.188, 27.189, 36.39, 36.43, 36.45, 40.15, 40.24, 40.97
r 67.3(3)(c) 36.50
r 67.3(3)(c)(ii) 36.47
r 67.17A 50.319
r 67.17A(3) 50.321
Pt 69 . . . . . 43.413
Pt 70
r 70.1(2)(a) 43.391, 43.408
r 70.1(2)(b) 43.391, 43.408
r 70.1(2)(d) 43.391, 43.408
r 70.3 . . . . . 56.19
Pt 72 . . . . . 43.413
Pt 73 . . . . . 43.413
Pt 83 . . . . . 43.413
Pt 84 . . . . . 43.413
Pt 85 . . . . . 15.14
r 85.11 . . . . . 15.14
Pt 86 . . . . . 15.14
r 86.1(2)(a) 15.14
r 86.1(2)(b) 15.14
r 86.4 . . . . . 15.14
Civil Procedure Rules pre-2013
Pt 3
r 3.9 . . . . . 54.123
Pt 43
r 43.2(1)(a) 2.09
r 43.2(1)(l) 54.55
r 43.2(k) 2.09
r 43.2(l) 2.09
r 43.2(m) 2.09
r 43.2(o) 2.09, 29.02
r 43.3(h) 2.09
Pt 44
r 44.3 . . . . . 16.05, 16.07, 44.02

Civil Procedure Rules pre-2013 (*cont.*)
r 44.12A 11.07
r 44.12A(4)(a) 11.21
r 44.12A(4)(b) 11.04, 11.05, 11.21
r 44.16 . . . . . 54.51
Pt 45
Section III 50.102–50.117
Section IV 50.118–50.130
Section V 50.119–50.120, 50.128, 50.131–50.149
Section VII 13.81
r 45.7(4)9a) 50.119
r 45.10 . . . . . 50.83
r 45.11 . . . . . 50.79
r 45.12(2) 50.105
r 45.15(2) 50.105
r 45.15(3) 50.105
r 45.15(4)(a) 50.105
r 45.15(4)(b) 50.105
r 45.15(4)(c) 50.105
r 45.15(6) 50.109
r 45.15(6)(d) 50.116
r 45.16 . . . . . 50.107
r 45.17(2)–(5) 50.149
r 45.17(5) 50.149
r 45.18 . . . . . 50.192
r 45.18(2) 50.111
r 45.18(3) 50.111, 50.144
r 45.18(4) 50.145
r 45.19 . . . . . 50.112
r 45.20(1) 50.119
r 45.20(1)(a) 50.119
r 45.20(1)(b) 50.119
r 45.20(2) 50.119
r 45.20(2)(a) 50.120
r 45.20(2)(a)(i) 50.119
r 45.20(2)(a)(ii) 50.119
r 45.20(2)(a)(iii) 50.119
r 45.20(2)(a)(iv) 50.119
r 45.20(2)(b)(i) 50.119
r 45.20(3) 50.121
r 45.20(3)(a) 50.140
r 45.21 . . . . . 50.129
r 45.22 . . . . . 50.130
r 45.23(1) 50.132
r 45.23(2) 50.132
r 45.23(2)(a) 50.140
r 45.23(3) 50.141
r 45.23(3)(c) 50.128, 50.134
r 45.23(3)(d)(i) 50.128, 50.134
r 45.23(3)(d)(ii) 50.134
r 45.24 . . . . . 50.143
r 45.25(1)(a) 50.147
r 45.25(2)(a) 50.147
r 45.25(3) 50.149
r 45.26 . . . . . 50.144
r 45.31 . . . . . 50.189
r 45.31(4) 50.189
r 45.32(6) 50.189
Pt 47 . . . . . 55.32
r 47.12.(2) 43.149
r 47.19 . . . . . 43.253, 43.333, 43.364
Pt 48
r 48.8 . . . . . 9.134
r 48.8(2) 16.14
r 48.8(7) 9.134
Civil Procedure Rules pre-2015
Pt 36 . . . . . 17.58, 17.60, 17.63, 17.176
r 36.2(2)(b) 17.40
r 36.2(2)(c) 17.40
r 36.2(2)(d) 17.40
r 36.2(2)(e) 17.40
r 36.9(5) 17.176
Civil Procedure Rules pre-2017
Part 45, Section VII 13.95
County Court Rules (SI 1981/1687) (CCR 1981) 1.1.137, 4.42, 10.03, 26.01, 26.02, 26.08, 26.09–26.14, 26.21, 26.41
Ord 25 . . . . . 23.116
Ord 26 . . . . . 23.116
Ord 27 43,413
Ord 33 . . . . . 15.14
Ord 38 . . . . . 50.49, 50.58
r 3(3) 1.137
r 4(1) 1.138
r 4(6) 1.138
r 5 . . . . . 1.139
r 9 . . . . . 1.138
r 9(5) 1.138
r 12(1) 1.139
r 19(3) 1.144
r 20 . . . . . 1.137
r 24 . . . . . 1.137

General Orders

Ord April 1596 . . . . . 1.49
Ord 14 January 1617–18 . . . . . 1.49
Ord 29 January 1618–19 . . . . . 1.49
Ord 17 November 1631 . . . . . 1.49
Ord 22 August 1654 . . . . . 1.49
Ord 25 June 1658 . . . . . 1.49
Ord 29 October 1683 . . . . . 1.49
Ord 29 October 1692 . . . . . 1.49
RSC (Revision) 1962 (SI 1962/2145) 1.131
RSC (Revision) 1965 (SI 1965/1776) 1.131
Rules of the Supreme Court 1883 . . . . . 1.94, 1.131, 50.12
Ord LXV, r 8 . . . . . 50.12
Ord LXV, r 11 . . . . . 50.12
Ord LXV, r 27(29) 37.16

Ord 70
r 1 . . . . .25.08
App N 1.95
Rules of the Supreme Court 1950
Ord 62, r 28(2). 25.10, 25.38
Rules of the Supreme Court 1965. . . 1.131, 4.42
Rules of the Supreme Court (RSC)
(SI 1776/1965) 7.101, 13.08, 16.21, 17.55, 17.214, 23.16, 23.61, 23.62, 23.63, 23.64, 23.116, 25.08, 25.12, 26.01, 26.02, 26.08, 26.09–26.14, 26.21, 26.41, 39.04, 46.32, 46.36, 49.19, 49.91
Ord 1, r 4(1) 36.51
Ord 1, r 4(2) 36.51
Ord 15, r 4 . . . . .65.12
Ord 16
Ord 17 . . . . 15.14
Ord 18, r 7 . . . . .26.10
Ord 20, r 8 . . . . .26.10
Ord 23
r 1(3) 15.14
rr 23–31D 1.110
Ord 46, r 8 . . . . .23.116
Ord 62
r 11(1). 9.95
r 28(2) 1.129
App 2, para 2 . . . . .35.50
Ord 62 . . . . 23.64
Ord 62, r 3 (2) .16.64
Ord 62, r 14 . . . . .66.76
Ord 62, r 15 . . . . .37.06
Ord 62, r 28(4). 23.66
Ord 62, r 29(3). 23.62
Ord 62, r 29(7)(c)(iii) 49.141
Ord 62, r 32 . . . . .43.198
Ord 65
r 1 . . . . .1.100, 6.110
r 10(1) 57.44, 57.52
r 27(48) 53.106
r 28 . . . . .57.46
r 28(1) 57.52
r 29 . . . . 1.95, 1.97, 25.04
Ord 106, r 5A. 36.46
Rules of the Supreme Court (Amendment No 3) 1986 (SI 1986/2289) 1.144
Supreme Court Rules 2009 (SCR)
(SI 2009/1603). . . . 4.01, 4.44–4.45, 10.03
pt 7. . . . . 4.44, 5.01
r 2 . . . . .4.45
r 36 . . . . .15.125
r 36(1) 15.06

NATIONAL COURTS

Canada

Rules of Civil Procedure
r 1.04 . . . . 26.46
Rules of the High Court of Justice 2008
O62, r 21B. 43.219

Isle of Man

Administration of Justice Act 2008
(Statutes of the Isle of Man 2008 c 14) 43.198
Rules of the High Court of Justice 2009
O48A, r 28(1) 43.198, 43.219, 43.220

Ireland

Rules of the Superior Courts 1986
(SI 1986/15). 52.98

United States

Federal Rules of Civil Procedure
r 1 . . . . .26.16

TABLE OF PRACTICE DIRECTIONS AND PROTOCOLS

PRACTICE DIRECTIONS

Costs Practice Direction (CPD)
revoked. 4.46, 4.50, 6.18, 9.196, 9.201, 9.202, 12.08, 24.48, 24.52, 27.202, 38.56, 49.149, 50.118, 54.17, 54.71
art 2.2 . . . . 29.02
art 3.1. . . . . 44.42
art 4.2 . . . . 18.132
art 4.5 . . . . 43.35
art 4.6(7) 49.89, 49.149
art 4.16(2) 49.82, 49.99
art 4.17. . . . . 43.35
art 4.17(1). 43.42
art 5.21 . . . . 18.132
art 6 . . . . 12.171
art 6.2 . . . . 18.132
art 6.4(2) 27.202, 38.56
art 8.3(2) 6.11
art 8.4 . . . . 6.18
art 10 . . . . 54.115
art 10.2 . . . . 43.305, 43.306
art 10A.1 . . . . 18.131, 18.132
art 10A.2 . . . . 18.132
art 11.1. . . . . 25.77
art 11.2. . . . . 25.78
art 11.3. . . . . 53.89
art 11.5. . . . . 25.85
art 11.7. . . . . 54.73
art 11.8(1). 54.71, 54.105
art 11.8(2) 54.47
art 11.9. . . . . 25.83
art 11.10 . . . . 34.37, 54.144
art 11.10(1). 54.146
art 11.10(5). 54.154
art 11.11 . . . . 54.188, 54.189
art 13.2 . . . . 43.183, 44.15, 44.40
art 14.1. . . . . 44.41
art 14.2 . . . . 44.41
art 14.5. . . . . 7.91
art 14.9. . . . . 44.37
art 17.3(5) 11.23, 16.03
art 17.9(1)(a). 11.17
art 17.11 . . . . 11.05
art 18.3 . . . . 57.16
art 19.1(1). 54.111
art 19.3(2)(a) 54.113
art 19.4(1). 54.111
art 19.4(2) 54.111
art 19.4(3) 54.130
art 19.4(3)(c) 43.175
art 19.5. . . . . 65.44
art 20.3 . . . . 54.51
art 20.4 . . . . 43.174, 54.53
art 20.5 . . . . 43.305, 54.51
art 20.6 . . . . 54.41
art 20.7 . . . . 54.53
art 20.7(1) 43.305, 54.52, 54.53
art 20.8 . . . . 54.52
art 20.8(1) 43.326
art 20.8(2) 43.326
art 20.8(2) 43.326
art 22.3 . . . . 62.11
art 23.2 . . . . 62.15
art 23.2A 62.15
art 23A.3 . . . . 13.21
art 23A.4 . . . . 13.21
art 25B.1 . . . . 50.131, 50.142
art 28.1(4)(a)–(b) 43.67
art 32.4 . . . . 43.55, 54.124
arts 32.5–32.7 . . . . 43.55
art 32.5 . . . . 43.185
art 32.5(1) 54.124
art 32.5(1)(d) 29.49
art 32.5(2) 54.130, 54.169
art 32.5(3) 54.188
art 32.6 . . . . 54.188
art 32.7 . . . . 54.124
art 35.3(3) 43.116
art 35.4(2) 43.127
art 35.6 . . . . 43.110
art 35.7. . . . . 43.123
art 36.2 . . . . 11.04
art 39.2 . . . . 43.175
art 39.1(2) 43.167
art 40.10. . . . . 35.98
art 40.12 . . . . 46.29
art 40.14. . . . . 4.38, 24.57
art 45.3. . . . . 43.309
art 45.5(3) 43.372
art 46.1 . . . . 43.283, 43.285, 43.367
art 46.2 . . . . 43.263, 43.284, 43.357, 55.32
art 46.4 . . . . 43.364
art 48.3 . . . . 45.11
art 50.1 . . . . 66.20

art 50A.1 . . . . 66.36
art 52.1. . . . . 47.11
art 52.5. . . . . .59.40
art 53.4. . . . . .9.201
art 53.6 . . . . .9.202
art 53.7. . . . . .9.202
art 53.10. . . . . .9.196
art 54.2(1) 16.14
art 56.6(2) 9.201
art 56.9 . . . . .36.101
art 56.17. . . . . .36.113
art 56.19. . . . . .36.112
art 57.9(3). 54.45
Section VI 12.08
Judicial Committee of the Privy Council PD 8 (Costs)
para 14. . . . . .43.198
PD 2B 66.74
para 1.2 . . . . .5.08
para 2.2 . . . . .5.09
para 2.3 . . . . .5.09
para 2.3(c) 5.09
para 2.3(d) 5.09
para 2.4 . . . . .5.09
para 5.1 . . . . .5.09
para 6.2 . . . . .5.08
para 7B.2(c) .66.74
PD 2.8 . . . . .11.31
PD 2.9 . . . . .11.31
PD 3
para 6A 2.09
PD 3E 12.17
para 1. 12.16, 13.30
para 2(a). 12.82
para 2(b) 12.79
para 3. . . . . .13.28
para 4. . . . . .12.73
para 5. . . . . .12.83
para 5(f). 12.81
para 6. . . . . .12.21, 12.24, 12.34
para 6(a). 12.22, 12.29
para 6(b) 12.24
para 6(c). 12.18, 12.28
para 6A 12.52, 12.53
para 7.1 . . . . .12.70
paras 7.2–7.10 . . . . .12.70
para 7.2 . . . . .12.130
para 7.3 . . 12.48, 12.84, 12.89, 12.92, 12.161
para 7.4 . . . . 12.39, 12.84, 12.85, 12.92, 12.99, 12.119, 12.121, 12.139
para 7.5 . . . . .12.106
para 7.6 . . . . . 12.36, 12.108, 12.112, 12.114, 12.116, 12.121
para 7.7 . . . . 12.92, 12.104
para 7.8 . . . . .12.18
para 7.9 . . . 12.32, 12.39, 12.83, 12.106, 12.122
para 7.10. . . . . 12.95, 12.97, 12.98
Precedent H. 12.22, 12.23, 12.24, 12.25, 12,25, 12.26, 12,27, 12.28, 12.30, 12.31, 12.38, 12.96, 12.131, 12.133, 12.134, 13.28
PD 3F
para 1. . . . . .13.30
para 1.1 . . . . 13.07, 13.22
para 1.2 . . . . .13.24
para 2. . . . . .13.28
para 4. . . . . .13.36
para 5. . . . . 66.43
PD 6A 17.43, 43.136
para 4.1 . . . . .17.43, 43.138
para 4.1(1) 43.137
para 4.1(2)(a) 43.138
para 4.1(2)(b) 43.137
para 4.2 . . . . .17.43, 43.137
para 4.3 . . . . .43.137, 43.138
PD 6B 17.44
PD 7
paras 2.1–2.4 .40.13
PD 8B 17.32, 50.150, 50.151, 50.155, 50.173, 50.228, 50.230, 50.252
para 1.1 . . . . 50.230
para 1.2 . . . . .50.252
para 2.1 . . . . .50.252
para 2.2 . . . . .50.252
para 5.1 . . . . 50.230
para 5.2 . . . . 50.230
para 6.1 . . . . 50.231, 50.252
para 6.1(2) 50.235
para 6.1A(1) 50.206
para 6.1A(2) 50.206
para 6.2 . . . . .50.232
para 6.5 . . . . .50.250
para 7.2 . . . . .50.239
para 7.3 . . . . .50.239
para 8.1 . . . . .50.233
para 8.3 . . . . .50.233
para 8.4 . . . . .50.233
para 9.1 . . . . 50.234
para 10.1 . . . . 50.172, 50.237
para 11.1 . . . . 50.243
para 11.2 . . . . 50.243
para 11.4 . . . . 50.243
para 12.2 . . . . 50.220
para 12.3 . . . . 50.220
para 12.4 . . . . 50.220
para 12.5 . . . . 50.172, 50.220
para 13.2 . . . . .50.251
para 13.3 . . . . .50.251
para 14.1 . . . . 50.242
paras 16.1–16.6 . . . . .50.252
para 16.1 . . . . .50.252

PD 8B (*cont.*)
para 16.2 . . . . 50.252
para 16.4 . . . . 50.252
para 16.7 . . . . 50.252
para 17.1. . . . . 50.238
PD 12
para 1.1 . . . . 40.24
PD 16
para 13.1 . . . . 23.96
PD 16B
para 1. . . . . 65.09
PD 18
para 1.2 . . . . 43.124
para 1.6 . . . . 43.124
PD 19B 65.04, 65.09, 65.11, 65.53, 65.107
para 2.2 . . . . 65.41
para 3.1 . . . . 65.20
para 3.2 . . . . 65.20
para 3.3 . . . . 65.18
para 3.5 . . . . 65.21
para 3.6 . . . . 65.21
para 3.7 . . . . 65.21
para 3.8 . . . . 65.22
para 4. . . . . 65.19
para 6.1 . . . . 65.28
para 6.1A 65.28
para 6.2 . . . . 65.28
para 6.3 . . . . 65.29
para 6.4 . . . . 65.30
para 6.5 . . . . 65.04, 65.31
para 7.1 . . . . 65.94
para 8. . . . . 65.04, 65.39, 65.40, 65.109
para 12.1 . . . . 65.38
para 12.2 . . . . 65.25
para 12.3 . . . . 65.33, 65.109
para 12.4 . . . . 65.62, 65.115
para 13. . . . . 65.35, 65.97
para 15.2 . . . . 65.101
para 16. . . . . 65.45
para 16.2 . . . . 65.107, 65.114
PD 19C
para 2(2). 65.124
para 5. . . . . 65.125
PD 21. . . . . 60.07
para 2.2(e) 60.07, 60.21, 60.28
para 3.3(4) 60.07, 60.21, 60.28
para 11 . . . . 44.12, 60.41, 60.47
para 11.3 . . . . 60.48
PD 22
para 2.2A. 12.34
PD 24 . . . . 15.17
para 1.3 . . . . 40.21
para 2. . . . . 40.21
para 4. . . . . 15.03, 15.97
para 5. . . . . 15.03
PD 26
para 2.2 . . . . 12.46
para 7.1 . . . . 50.345
para 7.7 . . . . 50.345, 50.374
para 9.1 . . . . 60.345
para 9.1(3)(c) 50.345
para 9.2 . . . . 50.345
para 9.2(3)(a) 50.345
para 12. . . . . 50.276
para 12.8 . . . . 50.346
PD 27 . . . . 52.49, 52.57
para 7. . . . . 50.372
para 7.3 . . . . 50.372, 52.49, 52.57
para 7.3(1) 50.370
para 7.3(2) 50.370, 52.24
para 7.4 . . . . 50.372
PD 30
para 9.1 . . . . 50.320
PD 32
para 18.2(2) 43.325
PD 34A 52.49
para 3.1 . . . . 52.47
para 3.3 . . . . 52.39, 52.58
PD 35
para 3. . . . . 52.50
para 6.2 . . . . 52.45
para 7. . . . . 52.22
para 7.1 . . . . 45.68
para 7.2 . . . . 45.68
PD 36
para 1.1 . . . . 1.39, 17.192
para 1.2 . . . . 17.33, 17.192, 17.203, 17.206
para 2.2(1) 17.213
para 2.2(2) 17.213
para 3.1 . . . . 17.192
para 3.2 . . . . 17.193
para 3.3 . . . . 17.193, 17.194
para 3.3(1) 17.176
para 3.3(2) 17.176
PD 39A
para 1.2 . . . . 43.306
para 1.14 . . . . 3.86
para 5. . . . . 47.32
para 5.1 . . . . 47.04
PD 40
para 4.2 . . . . 10.07
para 4.4 . . . . 10.07
PD 40B 10.04
para 3. . . . . 7.69
para 3.3 . . . . 7.66
para 3.3(2) 7.67
para 3.4 . . . . 7.67
para 3.5(2) 7.73
para 4.5 . . . . 10.04
PDs 44–48. . . . . 4.46, 4.54

PD 44 . . . . 6.18, 8.36, 15.108, 44.12, 44.15, 55.14, 55.17, 55.40
para 1.2 . . . . 44.25
para 2. . . . . 55.45
para 2.3–2.9. . . . . 55.26
para 2.7 . . . . 55.35
para 2.8 . . . . 55.29, 55.35
para 2.9 . . . . 55.40
para 2.10 . . . . 55.40, 55.44
para 2.11 . . . . 55.15
para 2.11(1) 55.15
para 2.11(2) 55.19
para 2.11(4) 55.15
para 2.11(5) 55.19
para 2.11(6) 55.19
para 2.12 . . . . 55.15
para 2.13 . . . . 55.14
para 2.14 . . . . 55.14
para 3. . . . . 12.169
para 3.3 . . . . 43.120
para 4.1 . . . . 6.11
para 4.2 . . . . 6.07, 6.266, 6.273
para 5.6 . . . . 55.13
para 6.1 . . . . 16.10
para 6.2 . . . . 16.10
para 7.1 . . . . 66.34
para 7.2 . . . . 66.23
para 7.3 . . . . 66.24
para 8.1 . . . . 44.03
para 9.1 . . . . 44.08
para 9.2 . . . . 44.12, 44.14, 44.19
para 9.2(a) 44.06
para 9.2(b) 44.06, 44.07
para 9.3 . . . . 44.12
para 9.4 . . . . 7.65, 44.13
para 9.5 . . . . 43.309, 44.27
para 9.5(1) 44.25
para 9.5(2) 44.31
para 9.5(4) 44.30, 44.31, 44.32
para 9.5(4)9a). 50.296
para 9.6 . . . . 44.29
para 9.7 . . . . 44.33, 44.35
para 9.8 . . . . 44.12
para 9.9 . . . . 44.14
para 9.9(1) 44.12, 60.36
para 9.9(2) 44.12, 60.36
para 11.1 . . . . 43.305, 57.61
para 11.2 . . . . 9.148, 57.16, 57.51
para 11.3 . . . . 23.75, 23.82, 57.64
para 12. . . . . 8.04
para 12.2 . . . . 8.51
para 12.3 . . . . 8.51
para 12.4 . . . . 8.42
para 12.5(a) 8.48
para 12.5(b) 8.51
para 12.6 . . . . 8.33
para 12.7 . . . . 8.22
PD 45 . . . . 13.93, 16.67, 50.58, 50.65, 50.327, 50.328
para 2.1 . . . . 50.68
para 2.2 . . . . 50.68
para 2.3 . . . . 50.68, 50.82
para 2.4 . . . . 50.68
para 2.5 . . . . 50.80
para 2.6 . . . . 50.81, 50.176, 50.177, 50.275, 50.306
para 2.8 . . . . 11.10, 11.15, 50.92, 50.95, 50.298
para 2.9 . . . . 11.10, 11.15, 50.96
para 2.10 . . . . 50.96
para 2A.1 . . . . 50.277, 50.284
para 4.1 . . . . 50 345
para 4.2 . . . . 50.345, 50.346, 50.397
para 4.3 . . . . 50.346
PD 46 . . . . . . 9.196, 11.17, 36.97, 36.101, 66.36
para 1.1 . . . . 16.14, 66.36, 66.77
para 1.2 . . . . 66.77
para 2.1 . . . . 60.34
para 2.6 . . . . 50.282
para 3.1 . . . . 3.96, 59.37
para 3.4 . . . . 59.23
para 4.1 . . . . 18.133, 18.134
para 5. . . . . 9.215
para 5.1 . . . . 2.09, 9.93
para 5.4 . . . . 9.199
para 6.1 . . . . 37.15
para 6.2 . . . . 16.14, 37.02, 37.08, 37.09
para 6.3 . . . . 6.39, 36.97
para 6.4 . . . . 36.40
para 6.5 . . . . 36.51
para 6.6(b) 36.99
para 6.7 . . . . 36.100
para 6.8 . . . . 36.115, 43.141
para 6.9 . . . . 36.102
para 6.10 . . . . 36.102
para 6.11 . . . . 36.102
para 6.12 . . . . 36.103
para 6.14 . . . . 36.104
para 6.18 . . . . 36.114
para 6.19 . . . . 36.51, 36.111
para 7.1(2) 50.383
para 7.1(3) 50.384
para 8.1 . . . . 50.390
para 8.2 . . . . 50.395
para 9. . . . . 11.02, 11.13, 11.30, 44.03
para 9.2 . . . . 11.10, 11.13, 44.04
para 9.3 . . . . 11.10
para 9.3(a) 11.10
para 9.3(b) 11.10
para 9.3(c) 11.10
para 9.4 . . . . 11.23, 16.03

PD 46 (*cont.*)
para 9.5 . . . . 11.08, 11.09
para 9.6 .11.21, 11.22
para 9.7 . . . . 11.16
para 9.8 . . . . 11.19
para 9.9 . . . . 11.25, 44.04
para 9.10 . . . . 11.17
para 9.11 . . . . 11.20, 11.28
para 9.12 . . . . .11.05, 11.12
para 10.1 . . . . .13.72
para 10.2 . . . . .13.72
para 18.3(c) .60.32
para 29. . . . . 44.04
PD 47. . . . . .18.134, 22.24, 23.81, 36.40, 36.99, 43.51, 43.153, 43.242, 43.373, 46.35, 49.82, 49.100, 49.150, 56.111
para 1.1 . . . . 43.69, 43.71, 43.75
paras 1.2–1.4 .43.63
para 1.2 . . . . 43.64, 43.72
para 1.3 . . . . .7.174, 43.62, 43.64, 43.67
para 1.4 . . . . 7.174, 43.62, 43.64
para 2. . . . . 7.90, 43.77, 45.37, 45.38
para 3.1 . . . . .5.18
para 3.2 . . . . 43.20
para 3.3 . . . . 43.20
para 4.1 . . . . .43.03
para 4.2 . . . . .43.03
para 4.2(c) 45.43
para 4.2(2)(b). 43.142, 43.154
para 4.3(2) 43.04
para 3. . . . . .43.21
para 3.2 . . . . .5.18
para 5.1 . . . . 43.30, 43.48
para 5.2 . . . . 9.205, 43.183
para 5.2(a) 43.51
para 5.2(b) 43.51
para 5.2(c) 43.51
para 5.2(d) 43.51
para 5.2(e) 43.51
para 5.2(f) 43.52
para 5.3 . . . . .43.54
para 5.4 . . . . 43.57, 43.127
para 5.5 . . . . .43.51
para 5.6 . . . . 9.198, 43.34
para 5.7 . . . . .9.201, 9.202, 43.33
para 5.8 . . . . 43.36
para 5.8(2) 18.127, 18.134
para 5.8(6) 56.111
para 5.8(7) 25.18
para 5.9 . . . . .9.213
para 5.10 . . . . .43.35
para 5.11 . . . . .43.35
para 5.11(3) 32.64
para 5.12 . . . . .43.39
para 5.12(1) .49.151
para 5.12(3) 52.11
para 5.12(8) 49.132
para 5.12(7) 49.82, 49.149
para 5.12(10) 49.90
para 5.13 . . . . 43.41, 43.42
para 5.13(1) 49.96
para 5.14 . . . . .49.97
para 5.15 . . . . 43.42
para 5.17 . . . . .43.35
para 5.18 . . . . .49.98
para 5.19 . . . . . . .43.35, 43.42, 49.140, 52.95
para 5.20 . . . . 43.35, 43.37
para 5.21 . . . . .43.35, 49.141
para 5.22(1) 49.97, 49.100
para 5.22(2) 49.96, 49.98, 49.99
para 5.22(3) 49.76, 52.07, 52.81
para 5.22(4) 52.07, 52.77
para 5.22(5) 52.07
para 5.22(6) 22.07, 22.24, 43.40
para 5.A1 . . . . 43.44
para 5.A2. . . . . 43.33, 43.45
para 5.A3. . . . . 43.46
para 5.A4 . . . . .43.32
para 6.1 . . . . 43.89, 43.91
para 7.1(1). 50.379
para 8.1 . . . . 43.130, 43.131
para 8.2 . . . . 43.109, 43.111, 43.113, 43.115, 32.119, 50.379
para 8.3 . . . . .43.118, 43.182, 43.185, 43.258, 43.301
para 9.1 . . . . 7.66, 43.240
para 9.2 . . . . .7.175, 43.251
para 9.3 . . . . 43.244
para 9.4 . . . . 43.241, 43.395
para 9.4(1) 43.403
para 9.4(2) 43.247, 43.249, 43.403
para 9.4(3) 43.247, 43.403
para 9.4(4) 43.249, 43.406
para 9.9 . . . . .11.25
para 9.10 .11.05, 11.18
para 9.12 . . . . 7.172
para 10.1 . . . . .43.142
para 10.1(1) .43.147
para 10.1(2) .43.147
para 10.4 . . . . .43.141
para 10.5 . . . . .43.412
para 10.6 . . . . 43.408
para 10.7 . . . . .43.148
para 10.7 . . . . .43.148
para 11.1 . . . . .43.139, 43.150
para 11.2 . . . . .23.81
para 11.2(1) .43.153
para 11.2(2) .43.159
para 11.2(3) 43.153, 43.159
para 11.3 . . . . .9.215, 43.161
para 12.1 . . . . .43.171

para 12.2 . . . . 43.167
para 13.1 . . . . 43.177
para 13.1(1) 43.168
para 13.2 . . . . 43.167, 43.179, 43.182
para 13.2(a) 43.183
para 13.2(b) 43.183
para 13.2(c) 43.183
para 13.2(d) 43.183
para 13.2(e) 43.183
para 13.2(f) 43.183
para 13.2(g) 43.183
para 13.2(h) 43.183
para 13.2(i). 18.41, 28.198, 43.180, 46.35, 46.66
para 13.2(i)(iv) 43.35
para 13.2(j) 43.183
para 13.2(l) 43.183
para 13.2(v) 43.183
para 13.3 . . . . 43.35, 43.183
para 13.4 . . . . 43.302
para 13.5 . . . . 43.302
para 13.6 . . . . 43.305
para 13.8(1)(b) 43.306
para 13.8(1)(c) 43.306
para 13.8(2) 43.240
para 13.8(3) 43.306
para 13.8(4) 43.306
para 13.9 . . . . 43.204
para 13.10 . . . . 35.98, 43.125
para 13.10(1) 35.98
para 13.11 . . . . 43.307, 46.28, 46.31, 46.33, 46.34
para 13.12 . . . . .43.308, 46.29, 46.33
para 13.13 . . . . 24.57, 46.42
para 14. . . . . 43.206
para 14.1 . . . . 43.200, 43.202
para 14.2 . . . . 43.204
para 14.3 . . . . 43.2008
para 14.3(b) 43.183, 43.185
para 14.3(c) 43.185
para 14.3(d) 43.185
para 14.3(e) 43.185
para 14.4(2) 43.223
para 14.5 . . . . 43.237
para 14.6 . . . . 43.234
para 15 . . . . 43.379
para 16. . . . . 43.393
para 16.1 . . . . 43.319, 43.385
para 16.2 . . . . 43.319, 43.385
para 16.3 . . . . 43.384
para 16.4 . . . . 43.384
para 16.5 . . . . 43.389
para 16.6 . . . . 43.386
para 16.7 . . . . 43.390
para 16.9 . . . . 43.388
para 16.10 . . . . 43.380
para 16.11 . . . . 43.380, 43.391, 43.412
para 16.12 . . . . 43.380, 43.408, 43.411
para 17. . . . . 43.183
para 17.(1) 66.83
para 18. . . . . 66.82
para 19. . . . .43.262, 43.264, 43.267, 43.269, 43.275, 43.284, 43.350, 43.357, 43.361, 43.363, 43.364, 43.375, 54.32
para 20.2 . . . . 45.06, 45.11, 45.12, 45.13
para 20.3 . . . . 45.08
para 20.4 . . . . 45.06
para 20.5 . . . . 45.10
para 20.5(a) 45.10
para 20.5(b) 45.10
para 20.6 . . . . 45.08
para 47.15(7) 43.224
para 47.20 . . . . 45.02
para 51.1 . . . . 9.202
PD 48 . . . . 4.32
para 1.4(b) 54.110
para 2. . . . . 54.25, 54.26
para 3. . . . . 54.36
para 4.2 . . . . 25.84
para 4. . . . . 54.41
PD 51D 12.10
para 1.1 . . . . 12.10
para 1.2 . . . . 12.10
PD 51E 43.202
para 8(1). 43.238
para 8(2) 43.238
para 8(3). 43.238
PD 51G
para 1.1 . . . . 12.10
para 1.2 . . . . 12.03
para 1.4 . . . . 12.10
PD 51O 43.310
PD 52. 44.05, 45.14
para 3.2 45,44
para 4.2 . . . . 45.04
para 14 . . . . 53.58
PDs 52A–52C 45.55
PDs 52A–52E 45.02, 45.14
PD 52A 45.14, 53.112
para 2.2(b) 45.05
para 3.5 . . . . 45.05
paras 3.6–3.8 . . . . 45.39
para 4.3 . . . . 45.39
para 4.4(a) 45.39
para 4.4(b) 45.39
para 4.5 . . . . 45.39
para 4.6 . . . . 45.28
para 4.7 . . . . 45.40, 45.45.70
para 5.1 . . . . 45.47
para 5.1(5)(a) 53.112
para 5.1(5)(b) 53.112

PD 52A (*cont.*)
para 5.2 . . . . 45.47
para 5.3 . . . . 44.27, 53.61, 53.111
PD 52B 45.14, 45.35, 45.47
para 4.2 . . . . 45.44
para 4.2(d) 45.44
para 6.2 . . . . 45.55
para 6.4 . . . . 45.55
para 8.1 . . . . 45.53
para 8.2 . . . . 45.53
Section VIII 45.47
PD 52C 45.14
para 3 . . . . 45.44
para 5 . . . . 45.44
para 5A 45,71
para 16(2) 45.53
para 20 . . . . 45.53
para 31 . . . . 45.48
PD 52D 45.04, 45.14, 45.33
PD 52E 45.14
PD 54A 67.05
para 8.5 . . . . 67.04
para 8.6 . . . . 67.04
PD 64A 13.02, 66.68
para 6.2 . . . . 66.31, 66.58
para 6.3 . . . . 66.31, 66.56, 66.58
para 6.4 . . . . 66.58
para 6.5 . . . . 66.72
para 6.6 . . . . 66.72
para 6.8 . . . . 66.68
PD 64B 66.68
para 2 . . . . 66.71
para 6.1 . . . . 66.73
para 6.2 . . . . 66.73
para 7.1 . . . . 66.69
para 7.2 . . . . 66.69, 66.70
para 7.3 . . . . 66.71
para 7.5 . . . . 66.70
PD 67
paras 1–4 . . . . 36.39
paras 1(1)–(5) 36.43
para 1(2)–(5) 27.188
para 1(2) 36.43
para 1(3) 36.43
para 1(5) 27.189, 36.45
para 1(6) 27.188, 36.43
para 2.1 . . . . 27.188, 36.43, 36.48
para 2.1(1) 27.189, 36.43, 36.45
para 2.1(2) 35.128
para 2.2 . . . . 36.43, 36.48
para 2.2A 34.61
para 4 . . . . 36.41
para 4.2 . . . . 36.48
PD 70
para 2 . . . . 56.19

Practice Direction pre-2013
PD 52, para 14 . . . . 44.05, 44.06
Practice Direction of 9 May (Barrister: Fees) [1989] 1 WLR 605 . . . . 53.58
Practice Direction (Children and Protected Parties)
para 2.2(e) 60.21, 60.28
para 3.3(4) 60.21, 60.28
Practice Direction (Citation of Authorities) [2012] 1 WLR 780 . . . . 2.08, 4.06
Practice Direction (Costs: Taxation: Procedure) (No 2 of 1992) [1993] 1 All ER 263 . . . . 52.49
Practice Direction 13 (Costs)
para 1.4 . . . . 4.33
Practice Direction (Counsel's Fees) [1957] 1 WLR 839 . . . . 53.108
Practice Direction (Judgments: Form and Citation) [2001] 1 WLR 194 . . . . 2.06
Practice Direction (Pre-Action Conduct) . . . 2.09, 4.56, 6.03, 6.93, 6.96, 49.149
para 2.2 . . . . 66.70
para 3 . . . . 6.97
para 4 . . . . 6.99
para 4.3(1) 6.94
para 4.5 . . . . 50.98
para 5 . . . . 6.99
para 11 . . . . 6.128
para 13 . . . . 6.94, 6.96
para 14 . . . . 6.96
para 15 . . . . 6.96
Annex A
para 6.1 . . . . 57.13
para 6.2 . . . . 57.15
Practice Direction (Pre-action Protocols)
para 9.3 . . . . 54.112
Practice Direction (Protocols) 6.96
art 2.3(2) 16.56
para 2.4 . . . . 50.97
para 4.A 54.45
Practice Direction (Refresher Fees to Counsel) [1959] 1 WLR 350 . . . . . . 53.126
Practice Direction (Supreme Court Taxing Office) No 1 of 1986 (unreported), February 1986, SCTO 49.12
Practice Direction (Taxation: Indemnity Principle) [1998] 1 WLR 1674 . . . . . . 18.02
Practice Directions Applicable to Judicial Taxations in the House of Lords (26 March 2007)
para 26.7 . . . . 53.48
Practice Note [1942] WN 89, PC 4.07
Practice Note (Barrister: Fees) [1994] 1 WLR 74 . . . . 53.58, 53.62
Practice Note: Brief Fees [1989] 1 WLR 605, CA 53.62

Practice Statement (Judicial Precedent) [1966] 1 WLR 1234. . . . . 4.06
Practice Statement (Judicial Review: Costs) The Times, 20 May 2004, QBD. 7.185
Practice Statement (Judicial Review: Costs) [2004] 1 WLR 1760. . . . . 67.03
Senior Courts Taxing Office (SCTO) Practice Direction No 2 of 1992 (unreported), c September 1992
para 1.8 . . . . 49.66
Supreme Court Practice Direction 4.7.1 . . . 15.06
UKSC Practice Direction 7 . . . . . . 4.46, 15.125
UKSC Practice Direction 13 . . . 4.44, 4.46, 5.01
para 14 . . . . 43.198

PROTOCOLS

Civil Justice Council, Protocol for the Instruction of Experts to give Evidence in Civil Claims (June 2005, amended October 2009)
para 7.6 . . . . 52.18
para 7.7 . . . . 52.19
Pre-action Protocols. 4.57–4.62
Pre-action Protocol for Construction and Engineering disputes 4.61, 6.100
Pre-Action Protocol for Defamation 57.11
para 3.7 . . . . 7.11
Pre-Action Protocol for Disease and Illness Claims
para 2A.1 . . . . 57.12
para 4.5 . . . . 57.14
Pre-Action Protocol for Judicial Review
para 3.1 . . . . 57.12
Pre-Action Protocol for Low Value Personal Injury (Employers' Liability and Public Liability) Claims (the EL/PL Protocol). 17.32, 50.27, 50.121, 50.122, 50.150, 50.153, 50.167, 50.170, 50.182, 50.192, 50.269, 50.286, 52.38, 52.46, 60.35
para 1.1(1) 50.172
para 1.1(13) 50.121
para 1.1(14)(a) 50.127
para 2.1 . . . . 50.255
para 4.1(1)(a) 50.162
para 4.1(2) 50.162
para 4.1(3) 50.162
para 4.1(4) 50.162
para 4.2 . . . . 50.168, 50.172
para 4.3(1) 50.165
para 4.3(2) 50.165
para 4.3(3) 50.165
para 4.3(4) 50.165
para 4.3(5) 50.165
para 4.3(6) 50.165
para 4.3(7) 50.165
para 4.3(8) 50.165
para 4.3(9) 50.165
para 4.3(10) 50.165
para 4.3(11) 50.161, 50.165
para 4.4 . . . . 50.169
para 5.9 . . . . 50.167
para 5.11 . . . . 50.165, 50.172
para 6.1 . . . . 50.194
para 6.1(b) 50.194
para 6.7 . . . . 50.172, 50.198
para 6.9 . . . . 50.172, 50.197
para 6.11 . . . . 50.197
para 6.11(a) 50.197
para 6.11(b) 50.197
para 6.13 . . . . 50.167, 50.199
para 6.13(1) 50.172
para 6.13(4)(b) 50.167, 50.172
para 6.14 . . . . 50.172, 50.199
para 6.16 . . . . 50.201
para 6.17 . . . . 50.172
para 7.1 . . . . 50.204
para 7.2 . . . . 50.204
para 7.3 . . . . 50.204
para 7.6 . . . . 50.204
para 7.7 . . . . 50.172, 50.204, 50.206, 50.208, 50.277, 50.284
para 7.11. . . . . 50.209
para 7.12. . . . . 50.211
para 7.15. . . . . 50.211
para 7.17. . . . . 50.211
para 7.17(2) 50.263
para 7.17(3) 50.263
para 7.18. . . . . 50.211
para 7.18(2) 50.263
para 7.18(3) 50.263
paras 7.24–7.25 . . . . 50.211
para 7.24 . . . . 50.250
paras 7.26–7.28 . . . . 50.211
para 7.26 . . . . 50.263
para 7.28 . . . . 50.172
para 7.29 . . . . 50.207, 50.209, 50.213
para 7.31. . . . . 50.212
para 7.32 . . . . 50.214
para 7.33 . . . . 50.214, 50.215
para 7.34 . . . . 50.216
para 7.35 . . . . 50.212
para 7.36(a) 50.172, 50.212
para 7.36(b) 50.172
para 7.38 . . . . 50.216
para 7.40 . . . . 50.217
para 7.43 . . . . 50.172, 50.218
para 7.44 . . . . 50.219, 50.250
paras 7.46–7.47 . . . . 50.219
para 7.48 . . . . 50.223
para 7.49 . . . . 50.223

Pre-Action Protocol for Low Value Personal Injury (Employers' Liability and Public Liability) Claims (the EL/PL Protocol) (*cont.*)
para 7.53. . . . . .50.225
para 7.54 . . . . .50.225
para 7.55. . . . . 50.226
paras 7.56–7.58 . . . . .50.172
para 7.58 . . . . 50.172, 50.226
para 7.59. . . . . 50.172, 50.192
para 7.61. . . . . .50.192
para 8.1 . . . . 50.230
Pre-Action Protocol for Low Value Personal Injury Claims in Road Traffic Accidents (the RTA Protocol) 17.32, 50.26, 50.27, 50.31, 50.40, 50.68, 50.69, 50.150, 50.153, 50.156, 50.158, 50.166, 50.167, 50.168, 50.176, 50.182, 50.184, 50.185, 50.196, 50.273, 50.285, 50.307, 52.38, 52.46, 60.35
Preamble, para 2.1 . . . . .50.255
para 1.1(1) 50.172
para 1.1(1A) .50.188
para 1.1(6) 50.286
para 1.1(10A) 50.188, 50.289, 50.290
para 1.1(16) 50.127, 50.156
para 1.1(16A) 50.206, 50.289, 50.290
para 1.1(18) 50.160
para 1.2 . . . . .50.157
para 4.1 . . . . .50.156
para 4.2(2) .50.156
para 4.3 . . . . 50.168, 50.172
para 4.4 . . . . .50.160
para 4.5(1) .50.158
para 4.5(2) .50.158
para 4.5(3) .50.158
para 4.5(4) .50.158
para 4.5(5) .50.158
para 4.5(6) .50.158
para 4.6 . . . . .50.159, 50.169
para 4.7 . . . . 50.206
para 5.9 . . . . .50.167
para 5.11 . . . . .50.158, 50.172
para 6.1 . . . . .50.194
para 6.1(b) .50.194
para 6.3A(1) 50.195
para 6.3A(2). 50.198, 50.262
para 6.3A(3) 50.198
para 6.4 . . . . 50.160, 50.196
para 6.4(1) .50.196
para 6.4(2) .50.196
para 6.8 . . . . .50.172
para 6.8(1) .50.198
para 6.8(2) .50.198
para 6.10 . . . . .50.197
para 6.11 . . . . .50.197
para 6.13 . . . . .50.197
para 6.14 . . . . .50.197
para 6.15 . . . . .50.167, 50.199
para 6.15(1) 50.172
para 6.15(2) 50.172
para 6.15(3) 50.172
para 6.15(4)(b) 50.167, 50.172
para 6.16 . . . . .50.199
para 6.18 . . . . 50.172, 50.201
para 6.18(2) 50.201
para 6.19 . . . . 50.172, 50.202
para 7.1 . . . . 50.204
para 7.2 . . . . 50.204
para 7.3 . . . . 50.204
para 7.3(a) 50.277
para 7.5 . . . . 50.205
para 7.8 . . . . 50.204
para 7.8A(1) 50.206
para 7.8B(1) 50.206
para 7.8B(2) 50.206
para 7.8B(3) 50.206
para 7.9 . . . . .50.208, 50.277, 50.284
para 7.10. . . . . 50.208
para 7.12. . . . . 50.204, 50.206, 50.209
para 7.13. . . . . .50.211
para 7.14(2) 50.263
para 7.14(3) 50.263
para 7.16. . . . . .50.211
para 7.18. . . . . .50.211
para 7.19. . . . . .50.211
para 7.19(2) 50.263
para 7.19(3) 50.263
paras 7.26–7.27 . . . . .50.211
para 7.26 . . . . 50.240
paras 7.28–7.30 . . . . .50.211
para 7.28 . . . . 50.263
para 7.30 . . . . .50.172
para 7.31. . . . . 50.207, 50.209, 50.213
para 7.33 . . . . .50.212
para 7.35 . . . . .50.214
para 7.36 . . . . .50.214
para 7.37 . . . . .50.216
para 7.38 . . . . 50.214, 50.215
para 7.39(a) 50.172, 50.212
para 7.39(b) 50.172
para 7.40 . . . . .50.172
para 7.41 . . . . .50.216
para 7.43 . . . . .50.217
para 7.46 . . . . 50.172, 50.218
para 7.47 . . . . .50.119, 50.150
paras 7.51–7.54. . . . . 50.222
para 7.58 . . . . .50.192
para 7.64 . . . . 50.223
para 7.66 . . . . 50.223
para 7.67 . . . . 50.224
para 7.70 . . . . .50.225

paras 7.72–7.74 . . . . . 50.172
para 7.72 . . . . . 50.226
paras 7.73–7.74 . . . . . 50.219
para 7.75 . . . . . 50.172, 50.226
para 7.76 . . . . . 50.172, 50.192
para 8.1 . . . . . 50.230
Pre-action Protocol for Personal Injury Claims 50.100, 50.171
para 2.16 . . . . . 57.12
para 3.2 . . . . . 54.112
para 5.1 . . . . . 50.200
para 6.3 . . . . . 50.167, 50.200
Pre-Action Protocol for Professional Negligence
para B1.6 . . . . . 57.12
Pre-action Protocol for the Resolution of Clinical Disputes
para 3.12 . . . . . 4.61, 6.100, 57.14
para 5.1 . . . . . 57.12
Pre-Action Protocol for the Resolution of Package Travel Claims (Travel Protocol) 50.267
para 2.2 . . . . . 57.14
para 4.1 . . . . . 50.269
para 4.3 . . . . . 50.269
para 5.2 . . . . . 50.172
para 6.3 . . . . . 50.269
para 14.3 . . . . . 57.12

CODES OF CONDUCT ETC

ACL Code of Conduct 2011
art 6.8 . . . . . 47.28
Association of Litigation Funders (ALF) Code of Conduct 15.56
Code of Conduct of Litigation Funders 2018 . . . . . 33.07, 33.27, 33.28, 33.72, 33.73, 3.77, 33.78, 33.82, 33.83
para 9.1 . . . . . 33.28, 33.72
para 9.2 . . . . . 33.28
para 9.3 . . . . . 33.28, 33.73
para 9.4 . . . . . 33.28
para 9.5 . . . . . 33.28
para 10 . . . . . 33.28, 33.84
para 11 . . . . . 33.29, 33.79
para 11.1 . . . . . 33.78
para 11.2 . . . . . 33.80
para 12 . . . . . 33.29, 33.80
para 13 . . . . . 33.29, 33.80
para 13.2 . . . . . 33.83
CLSB Code of Conduct: Costs Lawyers 2014 . . . . . 47.13, 47.14, 47.15
EU Code of Conduct for Mediators 48.17
para 4 . . . . . 48.43
Financial Services (Conduct of Business) Rules 2001 . . . . . 4.29, 4.30
Legal Services Commission (LSC) Funding Code 4.02
Paralegal Practitioners' Code of Conduct 28.52
Personal Injury Multi-Track Code 18.06
para 5.1 . . . . . 18.06
para 5.2 . . . . . 18.06
Rules of the Association of Litigation Funders
r 3.15 . . . . . 33.28
Solicitors' Accounts Rules 1998 . . . . . 40.50
Solicitors' Accounts Rules 2011 . . . . . 4.29
Solicitors' Code of Conduct 2007 . . . 2.09, 4.17, 4.21, 4.31, 18.59, 27.62, 27.70, 27.74, 27.97, 27.104, 27.154, 27.214, 27.261, 27.264, 27.268, 27.296, 29.03, 38.47, 40.72
r 2 . . . . . 1.161
r 2.02(2) 38.81
r 2.03(1) 27.62, 27.98, 38.47
r 2.03(2) 27.62, 27.100
r 2.03(5) 27.62, 27.97, 38.47
r 2.03(6) 38.48
r 2.04 . . . . . 27.261, 27.262
r 2.06 . . . . . 27.296
r 9.01(4)–(6) 33.33
r 11 . . . . . 49.52
r 12 . . . . . 2.09, 3.54
r 15.02 . . . . . 27.262
r 24 . . . . . 27.261
Solicitors' Code of Conduct 2011 (SRA Code of Conduct) . . . 4.02, 4.14, 4.16, 4.17, 4.18, 4.19, 4.21, 4.24, 4.25, 4.26, 4.27, 4.28, 4.29, 4.31, 27.63, 27.70, 27.74, 27.99, 27.104, 27.154, 27.260, 27.266, 27.268, 27.269, 27.295, 28.52, 28.113, 29.03, 33.33, 38.49, 38.52, 38.57, 39.22, 40.12, 42.21, 49.115, 54.200, 60.64
Ch 15 . . . . . 4.17
IB(1.13)–(1.21) 27.99
IB(1.16) 34.19, 54.200
IB(1.19) 27.63
IB(1.21) 35.10
IB(1.26) 27.70, 27.99
IB(1.27) 27.99, 27.266
IB(8.7) 38.57
IB(8.9) 38.57
O(1.1) 27.99
O(1.6) 42.21
O(1.9) 27.63
O(1.10) 27.63
O(1.12) 27.99
O(1.13) 27.99, 38.51
O(1.14) 27.99
O(1.15) 27.99, 35.52
O(8.1) 38.57
OP(1.1) 27.295

Solicitors' Code of Conduct 2011 (SRA Code of Conduct) (*cont.*)
OP(1.3) 27.266
r 5.01(1)(c) 4.29
r 8(1)(g) 27.338
r 8(1)(n) 27.338
r 9(1)(d) 27.338
r 10(1) 27.338
Solicitors' Costs Information and Client Care Code 1999 . . . . 38.46
para 3(a)–(c). 38.46
para 3(3). 27.98
para 4(1). 38.46
Solicitors' Financial Services (Scope) Rules 2001 . . . . 4.29, 4.30, 27.291
Solicitors Practice Rules 1990 . . . . 27.105, 27.255, 27.260, 27.264
r 20.04 . . . . 49.52
Solicitors Regulation Authority (Accounts Rules) 2011 . . . . 35.12, 35.37, 36.22
r 12.2(c) 35.12
r 12.2(e) 35.12
r 13 . . . . 40.55
r 14,1 35,12
r 17. . . . . 35.12
r 17.2 . . . . 35.12, 35.13, 35.23, 35.45
r 17.3 . . . . 35.12
r 17.4 . . . . 35.12
r 17.7 . . . . 35.12, 35.112
r 18. 35,12
Solicitors Regulation Authority Disciplinary Rules 2011 . . . . 27.269
SRA Financial Services (Conduct of Business) Rules 2001 . . . . . 27.291, 27.297, 27.298, 29.90, 34.51–34.59
para 3. . . . . 34.52
para 3(3). 34.52
para 5. . . . . 34.53
para 6. . . . . 34.53
para 8A 34.54
para 9. . . . . 34.53
r 3.3 . . . . 27.298
r 4 . . . . 27.299
r 5 . . . . 27.299
r 8A 27.300
r 9 . . . . 27.299
App 1 . . . . 27.300
App, para 1. . . . . 34.55
App, para 1(2) 34.55
App, para 1(3) 34.55
App, para 1(4) 34.57
App, para 2. . . . . 34.58
App, para 3. . . . . 34.59
SRA Financial Services (Scope) Rules 2001 . . . . 27.291, 27.292, 34.47–34.50
para 2.1(p) 33.49
para 2.1(q) 33.49

NATIONAL COURTS

Australia

Supreme Court of Western Australia Consolidated Practice Direction (2009)
para 4.7.2 . . . . 43.198

United States

American Bar Association Model Rules of Professional Conduct (2004)
r 1:5 . . . . 29.197

‘I was never ruined but twice:
once when I lost a lawsuit,
and once when I won one.’

(Voltaire, 1694–1778)

Part I

HISTORY AND DEVELOPMENT OF COSTS

1

A BRIEF HISTORY OF COSTS

This chapter deals with the following topics: 1.01

- terminology (1.02);
- general observations (1.03);
- the Anglo-Saxon period (1.06);
- Norman times (1.08);
- Plantagenet times (1.11):
  - the Angevin kings (1.12);
  - the Plantagenets (main line) (1.15);
  - the House of Lancaster (1.30);
  - the House of York (1.31);
- Tudor times:
  - Henry VII (1.32);
  - Henry VIII (1.35);
  - Elizabeth I (1.40);
- Stuart times:
  - Stuart times in general (1.45);
  - the Jacobean period (1.50);
  - the Carolean period (1.54);
  - the Restoration (1.57);
  - the Glorious Revolution (1.60);
- Georgian times:
  - George II (1.61);
  - George III (1.69);
- Victorian times:
  - before the Judicature Acts (1.73);
  - after the Judicature Acts (1.92);
- Edwardian times (1.106);
- the First World War and the interwar era:
  - the First World War (1.110);
  - the interwar era (1.112);
- the Second World War and post-war times (1939–99):
  - the Second World War and its immediate aftermath (1.119);
  - the 1950s (1.126);
  - the 1960s (1.131);
  - the 1970s (1.133);

- the 1980s (1.136);
- the 1990s (1.145);
- the new millennium:
  - the first decade (1.157);
  - modern times (1.171); and
  - old wine in new bottles? (1.190)

Terminology

1.02 This book uses modern terminology (including modern names for parties and for ancient legislation); purists will be able to find the original names, including regnal years and chapters, in the footnotes.

General Observations

1.03 It has been said that if one waits long enough, every costs regime will come full circle as old ideas are given new form.[1] This is true, but only to a limited extent. Certain policies do appear to go around in circles—especially those of whether costs should be fixed and of what should happen to the costs of modest claims—but, on the whole, the history of the law of costs is one of progression rather than circularity. There is, however, a general observation that seems to be almost axiomatically true. Professor Zuckerman (an Emeritus Oxford academic) made it in the following way: 'As … the history of procedural reform shows, any attempt at rendering procedure more affordable can and will be defeated by those with an economic interest in doing so.'[2] This, of course, does not mean that procedural reforms will always fail, but it does mean that reforms tend to persist only to the extent that they are economically viable for all concerned. If they are not, they tend to be replaced by later reforms—or at least partially reversed. Put otherwise, successful policies and practices tend to arise by evolution rather than by revolution, although reforms—including radical reforms—are a part of that process.

1.04 Another general observation is that reforms that are intended to reduce costs almost always have unintended consequences of a type that have the potential to lead to costs inflation. This means that it is almost impossible to design a perfect system of costs. This is another reason why the history of costs is best thought of as being an evolutionary process rather than a process of striving towards a perfectly designed system of adjectival law.

1.05 Generalities aside, the main benefit that accrues from a knowledge of the history of costs is the ability to put matters into context. This is because the law of costs, like the law of taxation or of criminal sentencing, is very much a creature of its own time. It would be dangerous to try to discern the *ratio* of older authorities without having a firm understanding of the historical circumstances in which they were decided. This is why this chapter is so detailed and why it is set out in a broadly chronological fashion.

[1] See, eg, Hurst, P, 'Going Round in Circles' (2006) 25 CJQ 546.
[2] Zuckerman, A, 'Lord Woolf's Access to Justice: Plus ça Change …' (1996) 59 MLR 773, at 781.

The Anglo-Saxon Period (500–1066)

The early Anglo-Saxons were organised into small kingdoms. Over time, several levels of court came into existence. The highest was the *witenagemot*; an assembly of ecclesiastical and secular rulers known as *witans* whose ultimate jurisprudential function was to advise the king on issues as diverse as taxation and security.[3] Below the *witenagemot* were the Shire Courts; below those, the Hundred Courts.[4] **1.06**

Most persons who appeared before a *witenagemot* would have been represented by a person of stature and this, no doubt, would have come at a price. Such expenditure would, however, have been necessary because it was regarded as self-evident that a person would need influential supporters if he—and it always was a 'he'—was to have any chance of succeeding.[5] There is evidence to suggest that limited allowances for costs may have been made under in the *witenagemot* of Ine (who was King of Wessex from 688 to 726).[6] If so, then Ine's *witenagemot* may have been the first court in England to have made an award of costs.[7] That said, in the absence of a recognisable legal profession, the 'costs' would have been very different from costs of today; in particular, they would probably have been the costs of *keeping* court rather than the costs of *attending* court. Even if it is right to say that Ine's *witenagemot* had the power to award costs, that practice seems not to have been widespread. There is no reliable evidence of Shire Courts or Hundred Courts making such awards. **1.07**

Norman Times (1066–1154)

The Normans brought with them the *Curia Regis* (the King's Court), which replaced the *witenagemots*.[8] In time, the Anglo-Saxons' codes gave way to the customary law of the Duchy of Normandy.[9] This would ultimately give rise to what has been called the 'great structure'[10] that would be the forerunner of the common law.[11] The Shire Courts and the Hundred Courts continued to exist, albeit under the new law. **1.08**

---

[3] Hodgkin, T, *The History of England from the Earliest Times to the Norman Conquest* (New York, 1906; repr. New York, 1969), p 232.

[4] Milsom, SF, *Historical Foundations of the Common Law* (2nd edn, London: Butterworths, 1981), pp 1–23.

[5] See Musson, A, *Crime and the Compensation Culture in Medieval England* (London: Museum of London, 2009). Indeed, it was this reliance on influence in the Middle Ages that would ultimately lead to the law of champerty (see 30.19), because there were fears that unscrupulous persons of stature were lending—or even selling—their names to bolster the credibility of doubtful and fraudulent claims: see Winfield, PH, 'The History of Maintenance and Champerty' (1919) 35 LQR 50.

[6] See the Laws of Ine, 42, referred to in Plucknett, T, *A Concise History of the Common Law* (5th edn, Indianapolis, IN: Liberty Fund Inc, 2010).

[7] It has to be stressed, however, that the evidence for any such award ever having been made is rather thin.

[8] Gordley, J, *An Introduction to the Comparative Study of Private Law: Readings, Cases, Materials* (Cambridge: Cambridge University Press, 2006), p 3.

[9] See Renaud, J, 'The Duchy of Normandy', in *The Viking World* (London: Routledge, 2008), pp 453–7.

[10] This being the phrase used by John Dawson (a US legal academic) in *The Oracles of the Law* (Ann Arbor, MI: University of Michigan School of Law, 1968) at pp 1–6, 228 and 229.

[11] Plucknett, T, *A Concise History of the Common Law* (5th edn, Indianapolis, IN: Liberty Fund Inc, 2010).

1.09 The *Curia Regis* followed the king—that is, it moved from place to place[12]—and this meant that litigants had to incur the expense of travelling and staying away from home.[13] Again, such expenditure would have been the costs of keeping court rather than the costs of attending before a court, but there is good evidence of such costs being substantial.[14] Whilst the supporting evidence is somewhat thin, it would seem that the 12th-century custumal of Preston[15] contains a record of an award being made that included such monies. If this is right, then the *Curia Regis* made awards of costs more than a century before statutory provision was made for such in civil courts (see 1.19). That said, such awards—if they were made—were not commonly made.

1.10 There is, however, no doubt that an unsuccessful Norman claimant could be amerced (that is, fined) for having wrongly brought an action.[16] Amercements differed from awards of costs in that they would have been for the benefit of the king or the lord rather than the party who had wrongly been brought before the court. Sir John Hullock had this to say on the topic:

> 'Before the statute of Gloucester [(1278) (6 Edw 1 cl s 127)] no person was entitled to recover any costs of suit either in plea real, personal, or mixed; but by the Common Law, if the plaintiff failed in his action, he was amersed (by the coroner and his jury) *pro falso clamore*,[[17]] if he succeeded, the defendant was in *misericordia* for his unjust detention of the plaintiff's rights.'[18]

Plantagenet Times (1154–1485)

1.11 From about 1150, a small, but increasing, number of people became experts in canon law (albeit in furtherance of other professional goals, such as serving the Roman Catholic Church as priests).[19] By no later than 1230 (and possibly well before then), there had been a sea change in attitudes in that people began to practise canon law as a profession in its own right.[20] Thus, by the time of the main line of Plantagenet kings (see 1.15), a legal profession had come into being; this created conditions in which there was a greater need for awards of costs. From the very early days of the legal profession, there was a natural division of labour between the *advocatus* ('forespeaker') and the *attornatus* ('representative').[21]

---

12 See Holdsworth, WS, *A History of English Law* (Boston, MA: Little, Brown, & Co, 1922), vol 1, at p 33. The very high cost that this generated was one of the reasons why Ch 17 of Magna Carta specifically made provision that 'common pleas shall not follow [the monarch's] court but should be held in some fixed place'.

13 A very detailed contemporaneous record of the costs of a claim that ran from 1158 to 1163 can be found in *EXT 6/143: Account of Richard de Anesty of all his expenses in prosecuting his suit for the lands of his uncle William de Sackville*, held by the National Archives, Kew. For a summary, see Stephen, JF, *A History of the Criminal Law of England, 1829–1894* (London: MacMillan, 1883), p 88.

14 *Ibid.*

15 A custumal was a survey that included details of the rents, services and customs by which tenants held their land.

16 *Wharton's Law Lexicon* (14th edn, London: Stevens & Sons, 1946), p 59; see also *Quick on Costs* (Thomson Reuters, online), para 2.30.

17 A nominal amercement of a claimant for his false claim.

18 Hullock, J, *Costs in Civil Actions and Criminal Proceedings* (2nd edn, London: W Clarke & Sons, 1810), p 2.

19 Brundage, JA, 'The Rise of the Professional Jurist in the Thirteenth Century' (1994) 20 Syracuse J Int'l L & Com 186.

20 *Ibid*, at 186.

21 Baker, JH, *An Introduction to English Legal History* (4th edn, Oxford: Oxford University Press, 2007).

The Angevin kings (1154–1216)

1.12 By the middle of the 12th century, there were several legal codes and a collection of ecclesiastical and civil courts, often with overlapping jurisdictions.[22] Many courts were inefficient, and in particular there were complaints that the Shire Courts and the Hundred Courts were unable to dispense justice properly.[23] Henry II introduced legislation that was intended to tackle these problems.[24] In particular, in about 1176, he created the General Eyre, which involved dispatching itinerant royal justices to the counties in England.[25] On their return to London, these justices would record their decisions and discuss them with other judges; in time, this led to a record of decisions and the development of the doctrine of precedent (or *stare decisis*). It was in this way that the common law came into being ('common' meaning that it was uniform throughout the realm).[26]

Early powers to make costs awards

1.13 Whilst there is a lack of documentary evidence on the point, Georgian and Victorian writers have recorded the fact that the common law had 'always' tolerated the inclusion of costs within awards of damages, the implication being that the power to award costs came into being during early Plantagenet times. Those writers include Sir Jeffrey Gilbert (writing in about 1740),[27] Sir William Blackstone (writing in 1765),[28] Sir John Hullock (writing in 1810),[29] and Sir Frederick Pollock and Frederic William Maitland (writing in 1895).[30] If what they say is correct, then it is possible that the power to award costs grew out of the old practices of the *Curia Regis* (see 1.09); an alternative view (which is supported by the absence of any reliable pre-Georgian evidence on the point) is that they were merely relying on what other Georgian scholars had said and that the power to award costs under the common law did not exist.

1.14 Be that as it may, there is no doubt that awards of costs could be made in ecclesiastical courts. In 1175, the Synod of Winchester decreed that 'in actions between clerks for the recovery of money, the party who should be the loser should be condemned to pay the costs'. This applied only in ecclesiastical courts, but given the decree's application in cases often involving purely temporal interests—such as land disputes involving the church[31]—it

[22] Including Mercian law, the Danelaw and the law of Wessex.

[23] White, GJ, *Restoration and Reform 1153–1165: Recovery from Civil War in England* (Cambridge: Cambridge University Press, 2000), at p 166.

[24] *Ibid*, at pp 177–9.

[25] Brand, P, *Henry II and the Creation of the English Common Law* (Rochester, NY: Boydell Press, 2007), pp 216–32.

[26] *Black's Law Dictionary* (10th edn, Eagen, MN: Thomson West, 2014): '3. General law common to a country as a whole, as opposed to special law that has only local application.'

[27] In his *History of the Court of Common Pleas*, for example, Lord Chief Baron Gilbert describes in detail the fact that from a time that pre-dates the Status of Gloucester, the Justices in Eyre used to assess costs 'unbended with damages': Gilb HCP 266.

[28] See Blackstone, W, *Commentaries on the Laws of England* (Oxford: Clarendon Press, 1765), vol 3, at p 399: '[In] reality costs were always considered and included in that quantum of damages, in such actions where damages are given; and, even now, costs for the plaintiff are always entered on the roll as increase of damages by the court.'

[29] Hullock, J, *Costs in Civil Actions and Criminal Proceedings* (2nd edn, London: W Clarke & Sons, 1810), p 3.

[30] Pollock, F, and Maitland, FW, *History of English Law* (2nd edn, Cambridge: Cambridge University Press, 1911), vol 2, at p 597.

[31] Bigelow, MM, *History of Procedure in England from the Norman Conquest* (Boston, MA: Little, Brown & Co, 1880), p 26.

is, perhaps, the earliest example of an enactment governing costs. The ecclesiastical costs system was surprisingly nuanced, for example containing rules on costs on appeals,[32] and costs-shifting rules for different procedural and interlocutory stages.[33] It has to be stressed, however, that these powers did not apply in courts of common law.

The Plantagenets (main line) (1216–1399)

1.15 As every student of history knows, King John placed his seal on Magna Carta in 1215. This marked the start of a process that continued under Henry III, pursuant to which justice and administration would become separate. Almost immediately after it was made, Magna Carta was superseded by the Great Charters of 1216 and 1217. The Great Charter of 1225 largely confirmed those of 1216 and 1217.[34] None of the Great Charters made any mention of costs, but they had a role to play in the *history* of costs; this is because they created (or, at least, increased) the need for legal services.

The rise of the legal profession

1.16 At the beginning of the 13th century, there were two types of lawyer: attorneys and *narratores*. Attorneys had the power to bind their masters, so their existence and role is well documented. *Narratores*, in contrast, did not have the power to bind their masters, so less is known about them; it was said that they were responsible for reciting the *narratio*, which essentially was an early form of pleadings.[35]

1.17 The County Courts Act 1235 provided that 'every Freeman, which oweth Suit … may freely make his Attorney to do those Suits for him'.[36] Thus anyone (or, more accurately, any freeman) was permitted to instruct an attorney. Indeed, this was compulsory in certain circumstances.[37] The 1230s also saw the emergence of regulation of the legal profession in the form of a papal requirement that certain lawyers had to swear an oath of admission.[38]

1.18 Towards the end of the 13th century, a third type of lawyer came into existence—namely, the serjeant-at-law.[39] As is explained at 1.27, they would become the most senior and revered members of the legal professions.

Statutory powers to make awards of costs

1.19 It is often said that the first statutory power to award costs was created by the Statute of Gloucester 1278. This is not correct—not only for the reasons referred to in 1.14, but also

32 Alberigo, G, et al (eds), trans NP Tanner, *Decrees of the Ecumenical Councils* (Washington, DC: Georgetown University Press, 1990), p 214; see also *Glos ord to X 1.33.17 v in expensis*, cited in Brundage, JA, 'Taxation of Costs in Medieval Canonical Courts', in *The Medieval Origins of the Legal Profession: Canonists, Civilians and Courts* (Chicago, IL: University of Chicago Press, 2008), p 567.

33 Brundage, JA, *Medieval Canon Law* (London: Routledge, 1995), p 142.

34 Despite the fact that it was made by Henry III, it was put on the statute roll no earlier 1279 during than the reign of Edward I; as such, it is cited as the statute *Confirmatio Cartarum* of 25 Edward I.

35 See, eg, the list prefixed to Pulling, A, *The Order of the Coif* (first published London: W Clowes & Sons, 1884; republished Charleston, SC: Nabu Press, 2010).

36 This being c 10 of the *Provisiones de Merton*, 20 Hen 3 (part of the Statute of Merton).

37 *Liber de Antiquis Legibus*, 42–3.

38 See Brundage, JA, 'The Rise of the Professional Jurist in the Thirteenth Century' (1994) 20 Syracuse J Int'l L & Com 188. That requirement was created in 1237.

39 For a general overview of this historical branch of the legal profession, see Baker, JH, *The Order of Serjeants at Law, 1383–1875* (London Seldon Society, 1984).

because a power to award costs was contained in the Statute of Marlborough, which was made in 1267. In particular, s 3 of the Wardship Act 1267[40] read as follows (in translation):

> 'And if any chief Lords do maliciously implead such Feoffees, faining this Case, namely, where the Feoffments were made lawful, and in good faith, then the Feoffees shall have their Damages awarded, and their Costs which they have sustained by occasion of the foresaid Plea, and the Plaintiffs shall be grievously punished by Amerciament.'

There are two reasons why this provision is of interest: first, it created a power for the benefit of defendants rather than claimants; and secondly, it made reference to 'costs' by that name (albeit in Latin). These things may be of interest, but the powers to award costs under the Wardship Act 1267 were intended to deal with a specific mischief (namely, fraudulent feoffments), so they cannot properly be regarded as being a significant milestone in the history of costs. Indeed, they were little more than a sideshow and were eventually rendered obsolete by the abolition of ancient tenures in 1660.[41] **1.20**

Of much greater importance were the reforms that Edward I made in the 1270s in an attempt to restore order and royal authority following his father's reign,[42] including the following. **1.21**

- **The First Statute of Westminster 1275** This included the Champerty Act 1275,[43] which dealt with the mischief of unwelcome meddling in litigation by people of influence, and the Maintenance Act 1275,[44] that being an Act which provided that 'clerks shall not commit Maintenance'.
- **The Statute of Gloucester 1278** This included the Recovery of Damages and Costs Act 1278[45] (see 1.22) and also revived the system of General Eyres (whereby royal justices go on tour throughout the land—see 1.12).

The Recovery of Damages and Costs Act 1278[46]—part of the Statute of Gloucester—not only gave the court the power to compensate a party for the expenses of litigation (albeit initially limited to the cost of the writ),[47] but it did so by referring to those monies as 'costs'.[48] This seems to have been the first time that such terminology had been used since the Wardship Act 1267. The relevant provisions read as follows (in translation): **1.22**

> 'The demandant in assise of novel disseisin, in writs of mort d'ancestor, cosinage, aiel and be sail, shall have damages. And the demandant shall have the costs of the writ purchased, together with damages, and this act shall hold place in all cases where the party recovers damages, and every person shall render damages where land is recovered against him upon his own intrusion, or his own act.'

---

40 52 Hen 3, c 6.

41 See The Tenures Abolition Act 1660 (12 Car 2, c 24).

42 See Plucknett, TFT, *The Legislation of Edward I* (Oxford: Oxford University Press, 1949).

43 The Champerty Act 1275 (3 Edw I, c 25).

44 Maintenance Act 1275 (3 Edw I, c 28).

45 Otherwise known as the Statute of Gloucester (6 Edw I, c 1).

46 Otherwise known as the Statute of Gloucester (6 Edw I, c 1).

47 Birks, M, *Gentlemen of the Law* (Stevens & Sons, 1960), p 221. See also, Pound, R, and Plucknett, T, *Readings on the History of the Common Law* (3rd edn, Rochester: Lawyers Co-operative, 1927), p 441.

48 Notwithstanding the fact the monies were referred to as 'costs', the notion of costs as being distinct from damages had yet to be made and, as such, the costs were regarded being costs *de incremento* (meaning costs 'of increase'): see Bacon, M, *A New Abridgement of the Law* (7th edn, London: J & WT Clarke, 1832), vol 2, at pp 288–9.

1.23 The historical importance of the Recovery of Damages and Costs Act 1278 cannot be overstated: it was one of the most important milestones in the history of the law of costs. Over time, its ambit (and that of related legislation) grew to embrace the whole of the costs of the claim[49] rather than merely the costs of the writ.[50] There remained an important limitation, however, in that where the successful party was the defendant, he was (in general) without remedy;[51] thus, to use modern terminology, costs shifting was generally simplex (that is, one-way) costs rather than duplex.

1.24 Costs were recoverable only in certain categories of claim and only then when damages were also recovered.[52] Whilst it took centuries to clarify the law,[53] it was eventually determined that if damages would not have been recoverable prior to the Statute of Gloucester, then a successful claimant would not be entitled to costs (unless, of course, a subsequent Act made specific provision to the contrary),[54] but if damages would have been recoverable at common law, costs too would be recoverable.[55] Costs were also generally recoverable in statutory claims for debt.[56]

Early judicial assessment of costs

1.25 Prior to the reign of Edward I, costs were generally awarded by juries rather than judges. During that reign (or possibly earlier), judges began to exercise a power by which they would 'correct' what they regarded to be an inadequate or overgenerous assessment by a jury.[57] This can be seen as being the beginnings of the judicial assessment of costs.

Development of the legal profession

1.26 During the reign of Henry III, the legal profession had become sufficiently substantial to require a degree of regulation (see 1.17). This trend continued. In 1280, for example, the mayor's court of the City of London made regulations that included a requirement that lawyers swear an oath of admission.[58] In 1292, a royal writ was sent to Meetingham CJ that

---

49 See Christian, EBV, *A Short History of Solicitors* (Cambridge: FB Rothman, 1896), p 25; see also *Reeves v Butler* [1726] Gilb Rep 195, 25 ER 136. See also Hullock's comments on the way in which the Act was 'liberally interpreted': see Hullock, J, *Costs in Civil Actions and Criminal Proceedings* (2nd edn, London: W Clarke & Sons, 1810), p 5.

50 'Readings and Moots at the Inns of Court in the Fifteenth Century' (1954) 71 Selden Society 153, at 154. Hullock (writing in Georgian times) records that, by 'liberal interpretation', this was extended to the claimant's costs of the claim (but not to include any 'monies expended on account of himself, or for the loss of his own time'): see Hullock, J, *Costs in Civil Actions and Criminal Proceedings* (2nd edn, London: W Clarke & Sons, 1810), at p 5.

51 For a discussion of this, see *ibid*, at p 3.

52 Holdsworth, WS, *A History of English Law* (London: Methuen, 1971), vol 4, at p 537 (instancing proceedings in error).This principle continued to have an influence up until the 19th century, as demonstrated by *Dodd's Case* (1858) 44 ER 1087 (concerning *habeus corpus*).

53 For a description of the way in which the law developed, see Hullock, J, *Costs in Civil Actions and Criminal Proceedings* (2nd edn, London: W Clarke & Sons, 1810), pp 6–12.

54 *Robert Pilford's case* (1613) 10 CO Rep, 2 Inst 269. That said, some commentators have said that that rule eventually fell by the wayside: see, eg, Gray, J, *A Treatise on the Law of Costs in Action and Other Proceedings in the Courts of Common Law at Westminster* (London: E Lumley, 1853), pp 4 and 5.

55 *Witham v Hill & Ors* (1759) 95 ER 703. Also see *Ratcliffe v Eden & Ors* (1776) 98 ER 1200.

56 See, eg, *Ward v Snell* (1788) 126 ER 7; also see Hullock, J, *Costs in Civil Actions and Criminal Proceedings* (2nd edn, London: W Clarke & Sons, 1810), p 17.

57 Washington, GT, 'Damages in Contract at Common Law' (1931) 47 LQR 354. Printed records show judges doing this as early as Edward I: Sayles, GO, *King's Bench* (London: Selden Society, 1971), vol 2, at p cxi.

58 See Hamilton Baker, J, *An Introduction to British Legal History* (3rd edn, London: Butterworths, 1990), p 179.

enjoined him to 'provide and ordain ... a certain number, from every county, of the better, worthier and more promising students and no others' to be trained as lawyers.[59] The principle of offering successful students a monopoly on practice meant that being an attorney[60] became a closed profession[61]—as confirmed by the fact that entrance into the profession was controlled by the court. This was the origin of what would become the court's inherent jurisdiction over solicitors.

By the end of the 13th century, some attorneys—or possibly *narratores*—had specialised so as to become serjeants-at-law. Serjeants-at-law were seen as being in competition with the permanent clerical staff in the courts of equity,[62] so, in 1292, Edward II directed that they be excluded from those courts.[63] They were, however, granted exclusive rights of audience in the Court of Common Pleas. **1.27**

Fees charged by serjeants were said to be very high: indeed, this was so well known as to be mentioned by Chaucer.[64] This, however, is not wholly surprising given the extraordinary overheads they had to bear. Plucknett (an Oxford academic) had this to say on the point: **1.28**

> '[T]hey ranked as knights and surrounded themselves with elaborate and costly ceremonial. The creation of a serjeant obliged him to provide a feast comparable to a king's coronation, to distribute liveries and gold rings in profusion, and to maintain the proceedings for seven days.'[65]

Another factor that would have justified high fees was the fact that serjeants were few in number; indeed, their numbers were so small that every serjeant had his own pillar in St Paul's Cathedral, which served him as office and consultation room.[66]

In 1393, the power to award costs in the Court of Chancery was put on a statutory footing.[67] For the reasons set out in 1.30, 1.48 and 1.49, this seems to have made very little difference to the way in which that court dealt with costs, however. **1.29**

---

[59] Rot Parl, i 84; long afterwards (in 1402), substantially the same provisions were imposed by statute—namely, 4 Henry 4, c 18.

[60] Unpaid attorneys were commonplace, for example clerks of the courts often acting as attorneys for members of the public: see Sayles, GO, *King's Bench* (London: Selden Society, 1971), vol 1, at p xcviii.

[61] See, eg, Richardson, HG, *Transactions of the Royal Historical Society* (Cambridge: Cambridge University Press, 1932), pp 66–8. The profession was closed in the sense that it was open only to those who had been educated to it and admitted to it. As a result of Edward I's decision not to restrict senior legal positions to persons of high birth, it was not closed in the sense that it was impossible for an otherwise obscure person to practise: see Stubbs, W, *Constitutional History* (Oxford: Clarendon Press, 1875), vol 2, at pp 189–90.

[62] See Richardson, HG, *Transactions of the Royal Historical Society* (Cambridge: Cambridge University Press, 1932), pp 66–8.

[63] See Sayles, GO, *King's Bench* (London: Selden Society, 1971), vol I, at p cv, n 3.

[64] See Chaucer, G, *The Riches of Chaucer: In which His Impurities Have Been Expunged ...*, vol 1, p 68, at l-310.

[65] See Plucknett, T, *A Concise History of the Common Law* (5th edn, Indianapolis, IN: Liberty Fund Inc, 2010), in which Plucknett refers to *Sed quære*: Cohen, H, *A History of the English Bar* (London: Sweet & Maxwell, 1929), p 490.

[66] See Plucknett, T, *A Concise History of the Common Law* (5th edn, Indianapolis, IN: Liberty Fund Inc, 2010).

[67] This statute was Untrue Suggestions in Chancery (7 Ric II, c 6), which was made in 1393. Moreover, in due course, 15 Henry VI, c 4 would confirm this power and add a power to take security for costs.

The House of Lancaster

1.30 In 1436, it was confirmed that, in the Court of Chancery, costs were payable as part of the damages.[68] As that jurisdiction developed, the extent to which the Court of Chancery relied on statute for its powers to award costs (see 1.29) lessened.[69] In due course, this would lead to the Court exercising what would now be called its 'inherent jurisdiction' to award costs, being a power that is encountered even today (albeit only rarely—see 9.60 and 9.64–9.69). This was also broad enough not only to cover the award of costs by the Chancellor, but also to cover the provision of security for costs.[70] As is set out in 1.49, this led to the Court of Chancery making awards that, to modern eyes, were based on powers so unstructured as to be almost invented on the spot.

The House of York

1.31 By 1483—this being towards the end of Richard III's reign—the Court of Requests (latterly known as the Court of Request or Conscience) was created as an offshoot of the King's Council.[71] It was a court of equity that was intended to provide easy access to justice for poor persons.[72] Its cheap and simple procedure attracted many claimants, not all of them poor, but, for the first time, a significant number of whom were women. As is set out at 1.51 and 1.68, it was a success, in broad terms, and was reinvented or reinvigorated on more than one occasion.

Tudor Times (1485–1603)

Henry VII (1485–1509)

*Access to justice and justice for the poor (*in forma pauperis*)*

1.32 The aftermath of the War of the Roses meant that Henry VII had to restore royal authority. He is well known for having made effective use of the Star Chamber (which focused on serious disputes involving the use of personal power or on matters that threatened royal authority), but his efforts to ensure that ordinary subjects had access to justice were, arguably, just as important. Henry VII used justices of the peace on a nationwide scale as an efficient way of providing justice as they were expected to carry out their duties not for remuneration, but for the local influence and prestige that the office afforded.[73]

---

[68] This statute was made in 1436; it was called *Marshalsea, exportation of corn, safe-conducts, sub-poenas, attaints, etc*, and its citation is 15 Henry 4, c 4.

[69] See Blackstone, W, *Commentaries on the Laws of England* (a facsimile of the first edition of 1765–69, reprinted Chicago, IL: University of Chicago Press, 1979), vol 3, at pp 451–2; *Andrews v Barnes* (1888) [1886–90] All ER Rep 758, at 761, *per* Fry LJ.

[70] Holdsworth, WS, *A History of English Law* (London: Methuen, 1956), vol 1, at p 403.

[71] Kleineke, H, 'Richard III and the Origins of the Court of Requests' (2007) 17 The Ricardian 22. It is possible that it was created earlier—possibly during the reign of Richard II: see Spence, G, *An Inquiry into the Origin of the Laws and Political Institutions of Modern Europe, particularly those of England* (London: John Murray, 1826), p 350.

[72] Kleineke, H, 'Richard III and the Origins of the Court of Requests' (2007) 17 The Ricardian 22. It was established when the Chancery official responsible for sorting petitions from the poor became clerk of the Council of Requests.

[73] MacCulloch, D, 'The Consolidation of England 1485–1603', in *The Oxford Illustrated History of Tudor and Stuart Britain* (Oxford: Oxford University Press, 1996), pp 39–42.

In 1495, Henry VII made statutory provision for claims to be brought *in forma pauperis*. Where a potential claimant was able to show that they had a meritorious claim but were too poor to bring it, they would be relieved of paying court fees; moreover, the claimant's case would be allocated to a lawyer who would give advice for no fee.[74] The relevant statute read as follows: **1.33**

> 'Every poor person or persons which have or hereafter shall have cause of action against any person within this realm, shall have by the discretion of the Chancellor of this realm, for the time being, writ or writs original, and subpoenas, according to the nature of the causes, therefore nothing paying to your Highness for the seals of the same, nor to any person the writing of the said writs to be hereinafter sued; and that said Chancellor shall assign clerks to write the same writs ready to be sealed and also learned counsel and attorneys for the same, without any reward taken therefore and if the said write or writs be returned before the king in his bench, the justices shall assign to the same poor person or persons, counsel learned, buy their discretions, which shall give their counsel, nothing taking for the same, and the justices shall, likewise appoint attorney for such poor person or persons, and all other officers requisite and necessary to be had for the speed of the said suits, which shall do their duties without any reward counsels, help, and business in the same, and the same law shall be observed of all such suits to be made before the king's justices of his Common place, and barons of his Exchequer, and all other justices in the courts or records any suit shall be.'[75]

Surprisingly, a person who was a pauper at the time the costs were incurred would not have been required to pay if they were subsequently to cease to be a pauper.[76] In the event that a pauper was awarded more than £5, however, court fees would be payable regardless of their financial situation.[77] **1.34**

Henry VIII (1509–47)

The *in forma pauperis* procedure was controversial, not least because it was feared that persons with unmeritorious claims would abuse it for mischievous purposes. This, no doubt, was the reason why an Act was passed in 1531 that allowed the courts to impose punishment on unsuccessful claimants,[78] the punishment most commonly imposed being whipping or, at the election of the poor person, payment of the costs.[79] That said, this practice of whipping seemed to mainly merely exist on paper and was rarely seen in practice.[80] **1.35**

---

[74] The Poor Persons Act 1495 (11 Henry 7, c 12), also sometimes referenced as the Vagabonds and Beggars Act 1494 or Suing *in forma pauperis* 1495.

[75] *Ibid.*

[76] See *Ancell v Slowman* (1724) 88 ER 246.

[77] Hullock, J, *Costs in Civil Actions and Criminal Proceedings* (2nd edn, London: W Clarke & Sons, 1810), p 212.

[78] This being the Costs Act 1531, 23 Hen 8, c 15, sub nom *An Act that the Defendant shall recover Costs against the Plaintiff, if the Plaintiff be nonsuited, or if the Verdict pass against him.*

[79] See s 2 of the Costs Act 1531, 23 Hen 8, c 15; also see Finlayson, WF, *Reeves' History of the English Law* (London: Reeves & Turner, 1869), p 300, and Hullock, J, *Costs in Civil Actions and Criminal Proceedings* (2nd edn, London: W Clarke & Sons, 1810), p 212.

[80] It was said in an anonymous case that 'a pauper shall not pay costs, unless he be nonsuit; but then he shall pay costs, or be whipped'. Upon a motion for such whipping to be done, Holt CJ denied it and said that 'he had no officer for [the purpose of whipping a pauper for non-payment of costs upon a nonsuit] and never knew it done': (1697) 2 Salk 506. This is also the view shared by various leading authors: *Blackstone's Commentaries of the Laws of England* (Chicago, IL: Chicago University Press, 1979), vol 3, at p 400; Baker, J, *The Oxford History of the Laws of England* (Oxford: Oxford University Press, 2002), vol 6, at p 379; Holdsworth, WS, *A History of English Law* (7th edn, London: Methuen, 1956), vol 6, at p 538.

Early defendant costs orders

1.36 The Costs Act 1531 made the following provision for defendants' costs:

> 'If,—in any action, bill or plaint, of trespass upon the statute of King Richard the Second, for entries into lands and tenements where no entry is given by law,—or of debt or covenant, upon any specialty made to the plaintiff or plaintiffs, or upon any contract supposed to be made between the plaintiff or plaintiffs, and another person or persons, or of detinue or any goods or chattels on a supposed right of property, or of account charging the defendant as bailiff or receiver, or upon the case, or upon any statute of any offence or wrong personal immediately supposed to be done to the plaintiff,—the plaintiff, after appearance of the defendant, be nonsuited, or that any verdict happen to pass, by lawful trial, against the plaintiff, the defendant, in every such action, bill or plaint, to be assessed and taxed at the discretion of the Court, and shall have such process and execution for the recovery and having his costs against the plaintiff, as the plaintiff should or might have had against the defendant, in case the judgement had been given for the plaintiff.'[81]

1.37 This was not full reciprocal (duplex) costs shifting, as that would not come until 1607 (see 1.52), but it was very much a step in that direction.

1.38 The requirement that the defendant should have 'his costs against the plaintiff as the plaintiff should or might have had against the [him]' did not prevent recovery of costs from a claimant whose claim was so lacking in merit as obviously to fail to amount to a cause of action.[82] Where such a claim had been made, the justification for awarding costs to the defendant was that they were 'given for the vexation'.[83] The conduct of the parties was a relevant factor; if a claimant, upon realising that they had made a mistake, took steps to stop costs running by admitting the error, it was open to the court to not condemn the claimant in costs.[84]

The Crown's costs

1.39 At about the same time, an Act was made that said that the Crown should neither pay nor receive costs.[85] In view of the fact that it was the Crown's prerogative not to pay costs, it was thought that it would be beneath its dignity to receive them.[86] Henry VIII seems to have had second thoughts on this point: a decade later, a further Act was passed that expressly permitted the Crown to recover costs 'as common persons do in their suits'.[87]

Elizabeth I (1558–1603)

Attorneys' fees

1.40 The methods of assessing costs payable between attorney and client were far from perfect. In particular, there was a tendency for lawyers to be paid according to the length of the

---

[81] This being the Costs Act 1531, s 1 (23 Hen 8, c 15), also known as *An Act that the Defendant shall recover Costs against the Plaintiff, if the Plaintiff be nonsuited, or if the Verdict pass against him*. See also Bacon, M, *A New Abridgement of the Law* (7th edn, London: J & WT Clarke, 1832), p 302.

[82] See *Alsop v Cleydon* (1595) 78 ER 718.

[83] See, eg, *Ladd v Wright* H 43 Eliz. See also, eg, 2 Ro Rep 213, at 327, in which it was held that that it would be unjust to deprive a defendant of his costs merely because the action brought against him was erroneous, as well as wrongful.

[84] See, eg, *Blythe v Topham* (1607) Cro Jack 158.

[85] Costs Act 1531 (24 Hen 8, c 8).

[86] Hullock, J, *Costs in Civil Actions and Criminal Proceedings* (2nd edn, London: W Clarke & Sons, 1810), p 5.

[87] See s 54 of the Crown Debts Act 1541 (33 Hen 8, c 39). That Act remained in force until it was repealed by s 152(4) of, and Sched 7 to, the Supreme Court Act 1981.

documents they produced: the longer the document, the greater the fee.[88] This resulted in lawyers having a direct financial interest in producing documents of undue length.[89] In time, these concerns would lead to the court having greater control over lawyers' fees (see 1.61).

That said, 16th-century judges developed some gratifyingly robust methods for discouraging such practices. In 1596, for example, a lawyer who had drafted a pleading that ran to 120 pages had to parade around court 'bareheaded and barefaced', with his head poking through a hole that had been cut in the offending documents.[90] He was then sent to prison. **1.41**

Queen's Counsel

In 1596, Francis Bacon persuaded Elizabeth I to appoint him Queen's Counsel (or, more accurately, 'Queen's Counsel Extraordinary'), this being a new rank that was in competition with that of the serjeants-at-law.[91] As Bacon had predicted, Queen's Counsel proved to be more cost-effective[92] than serjeants-at-law and, as a result, the latter role gradually fell into decline.[93] Queen's Counsel were (and still are) barristers; their origin was that they assisted serjeants-at-law to present easier cases and, as a result, they came to be known as outer (or 'utter') barristers, this being because they were confined to the outer bar of the court.[94] **1.42**

The 40-shilling rule

During the reign of Elizabeth I, it became apparent that local courts were being underused because litigants had a preference for bringing claims in Westminster—even though many of the claims brought in Westminster were for modest amounts. The Creating Frivolous Suits Act 1601[95] was intended to deal with this.[96] It stipulated that, in certain personal actions for less than 40*s*, the recoverable costs would be limited to the recoverable damages: **1.43**

> 'If upon any action personal to be brought in any her [*sic*] majesty's courts at Westminster, not being for any title or interest of lands, nor concerning the freehold or inheritance of any lands,

[88] It seems that this dubious practice began with notaries (*tabelliones*) of the late Roman Empire. They were responsible for drafting wills, conveyances and contracts. They were widely considered to be 'barely literate hacks who wrapped the simplest transactions in mountains of legal jargon, since they were paid by the line': see Jones, AHM, *The Later Roman Empire, 284–602: A Social, Economic, and Administrative Survey* (Norman, OK: University of Oklahoma Press, 1964), vol 1, at p 516. In fact, this practice persisted in England for conveyancing fees until as late as 1845: Holdsworth, WS, *A History of English Law* (London: Methuen, 1956), vol 15, at p 227.

[89] Indeed, some commentators say that the practice of adding 'recitals' to contracts and agreements arose not out of a desire to enhance the clarity of legal writing, but out of a need to increase the size of the document and hence the fee: Butt, P, and Castle, R, *Modern Legal Drafting: A Guide to Using Clearer Language* (2nd edn, Cambridge: Cambridge University Press, 2006), p 27.

[90] *Mylward v Weldon* (1596) Tothill 102, 21 ER 136.

[91] Megarry, R, *Inns Ancient and Modern* (London: Selden Society, 1972), p 19.

[92] And possibly more hardworking, as Thomas Middleton would have us believe: Taylor, G, and Lavaghino, J (eds), *Thomas Middleton: The Collected Works* (Oxford: Oxford University Press, 2007), p 339.

[93] The process of decline was protracted, however: the last serjeant-at-law was Baron Lindley, who died in the early 20th century.

[94] Von Kynell, K, *Saxon and Medieval Antecedents of the English Common Law* (New York: Edwin Mellen Press, 2000), p 92.

[95] The Creating Frivolous Suits Act 1601 (43 Eliz, c 6).

[96] See Plucknett, T, *A Concise History of the Common Law* (5th edn, Indianapolis, IN: Liberty Fund Inc, 2010), under 'Tudors and the Local Courts'.

nor for any battery, it shall appear to the judges for the same court or set down by the justices before whom the same shall be tried, that the debt or damages to be recovered therein, in the same court, shall not amount to the same of forty shillings or above, that in every such case the judges and justices before whom any such action shall be pursued, shall not award to the plaintiff any greater or more costs than the sum of the debt or damages so recovered shall amount until, but less at their discretions.'[97]

1.44 This rule was remarkably long-lived; indeed, it continued to survive (albeit in an attenuated and obscure form) until as recently as 2014.[98] This may have been so, but the reality is that it was a failure; the long and sorry story continues at 1.45, at 1.59 and at 1.66.

Stuart Times (1603–1714)

Stuart times in general

The thwarting of the 40-shilling rule

1.45 Subsequent Acts made during the Stuart period sought to expand the ambit of the 40-shilling rule (see 1.43). In 1623, it was extended to cover claims in slander;[99] in 1698, its geographical ambit would be enlarged so as to apply to courts in the principality of Wales and in the counties palatine.[100] This was in addition to a 'Recital of Intention' made in 1670 during the reign of Charles II (see 1.59).

1.46 This keenness for enlarging the ambit of the 40-shilling rule was curious given the fact that the judiciary consistently and effectively thwarted it. The first method the judiciary used was the simple expedient of refusing to certify that the damages were less than 40*s* (this being something that they were able to do regardless of whether the amount was actually awarded).[101] When the law was changed so as to prevent this, judges of the Courts of the King's Bench and Common Pleas simply concluded that whilst *their* hands were tied, the juries hearing certain cases[102] had free reign and, as such, they were at liberty to 'give ten pounds costs, where they give but ten-pence damages'.[103] As if that were not inventive enough, ever-finer distinctions were discovered that—miraculously—always seemed to have the effect of defeating the operation of the rule.[104]

1.47 For all of these reasons, the 40-shilling rule was virtually ignored during the early Stuart period. The story of that rule continues at 1.59.

---

97 Section 2 of Creating Frivolous Suits Act 1601 (43 Eliz, c 6).

98 When the Slander of Women Act 1891 (54 & 55 Vict, c 51) was repealed.

99 See s 6 of the Limitation Act 1623 (21 James I, c 16).

100 See s 1 of the Frivolous Suits Act 1698 (11 & 12 W 3, c 9).

101 For a discussion of this, see Hullock, J, *Costs in Civil Actions and Criminal Proceedings* (2nd edn, London: W Clarke & Sons, 1810), p 23. Also see Bacon, M, *A New Abridgement of the Law* (7th edn, London: J & WT Clarke, 1832), Costs B; Holdsworth, WS, *A History of English Law* (London: Methuen, 1903), vol 1, p 74, n 7.

102 In particular, slander cases.

103 See Salk 207, quoted in Hullock, J, *Costs in Civil Actions and Criminal Proceedings* (2nd edn, London: W Clarke & Sons, 1810), p 32.

104 See *Browne v Gibbons* (1702) 91 ER 184, *SP Bass v Hickford* (1738) 95 ER 441 and *Mitchell v Younghusband* (1744) 94 ER 843. As a contrary example, however, see *Denny v Wigg* (1736) 125 ER 1008. In so far as slander was concerned, for example, and action for words was distinguished from an action for special damages occasioned by their publication; the latter, apparently, was not affected by the 40-shilling rule.

Awards in the Court of Chancery

It will be recalled from 1.30 that the Court of Chancery regarded itself as having an inherent power to award costs. Those powers were reflected in General Orders, which were the Stuart equivalent of modern-day rules of court. Such orders were not made under any statutory authority, but instead were made under the general and inherent authority of the Lord Chancellor.[105] **1.48**

During Stuart times, these General Orders used varied language to express different measures that the Court of Chancery would use when awarding costs. They included: 'good costs',[106] 'very good costs',[107] 'utmost costs',[108] 'full costs',[109] 'such costs as the court shall think reasonable'[110] and 'such costs as their Lordships shall think fit to inflict'.[111] They also included 'double costs',[112] 'treble costs'[113] and even 'quadruple costs'.[114] These awards of multiple costs,[115] which were undoubtedly penal in nature[116]—and which probably arose under the influence of Roman law[117]—complemented a similar system of awarding multiple damages.[118] As is explained at 1.64 and 1.98, it would seem that some of these measures can properly be regarded as being early ancestors of the modern-day indemnity basis of assessment. **1.49**

The Jacobean period (1603–25)

The right to a bill and to challenge it in court

By the time that James I inherited the realm of Elizabeth I in 1603, there was a perception that attorneys and solicitors were abusing the system for personal financial gain.[119] Indeed, **1.50**

105 See the historical notes made by Fry LJ in *Andrews v Barnes* (1888) [1886–90] All ER Rep 758, at 760.

106 Ord 14 January 1617–18, at p 219.

107 Ord 17 November 1631, at p 66; Ord 25 June 1658, at p 280.

108 Ord 29 January 1618–19, at p 116. Indeed, references to 'utmost costs' go back as far as Tudor times: see Ord April 1596, at p 69.

109 Ord 22 August 1654, at p 262.

110 Ord 29 October 1683, at p 359.

111 Ord 29 October 1692, at p 397.

112 Ord 17 November 1635, p 182.

113 Ord 29 January 1618–19, at p 117. The mode of taxing treble costs is explained in *Wilson v River Dun Navigation Co* (1839) 5 M & W 90, 151 ER 39.

114 Ord 29 January 1618–19, at p 117.

115 There were two kinds of multiple costs: those that gave multiple damages and were therefore deemed to give multiple costs (see *Deacon v Morris* (1819) 2 B & Ald 393); and those that expressly gave multiple costs (see Williams, J, *The Institutes of Justinian Illustrated by English Law*, 2nd edn, London: Clowes, 1863, at p 266). There is also a general jurisdiction to grant punitive costs under Roman law: C. 7. 51. 4.

116 If there was any doubt about this, it was dispelled by Lord Hatherley in *Garnett v Bradley* (1878) 3 AC 944, at 957.

117 Roman law classified actions as '*actiones in simplum*', '*in duplum*', '*in triplum*' or '*in quadrupulum*'. In the *actio in simplum*, the claimant sought to recover the value of what he claimed, but in other actions the defendant might be condemned to pay double (*duplum*), treble (*triplum*) or four times (*quadruplum*) the value: see Moyle, JB, *Imperatoris Iustiniani Institutiones* (2nd edn, Oxford: Clarendon Press, 1890), Bk 4, at p 554.

118 This is discussed in *Deacon v Morris* (1819) 2 B & Ald 393. The costs were awarded independently of the damages (see Sayer, J, *The Law of Costs*, London: J & WT Clarke, 1768, at p 195), but if statute provided that double or treble damages were payable in a case in which single damages were recoverable at common law, the costs also—as parcel of the damages—would be doubled or trebled: see See Gilb CP 268, P Aston J Cowp 368, Dy 159 b Carth 279; see also Hullock, J, *Costs in Civil Actions and Criminal Proceedings* (2nd edn, London: W Clarke & Sons, 1810), p 19. There was reciprocity in the awards of double and treble costs in that a claimant who would have been entitled to such costs had he succeeded may have to pay such costs upon being non-suited or upon discontinuing: see, eg, *Devenish and Martin* (1734) 94 ER 612.

119 See Brooks, CW, *Pettyfoggers and Vipers of the Commonwealth* (Cambridge: Cambridge University Press, 1986), pp 106, 138–40.

the behaviour of some was such that Parliament had to impose state regulation,[120] this being in the form of the Attorneys Act 1605 (or, in the more expressive language of the day, an Act to 'reform the Multitudes and Misdemeanors of Attornies at Law and to Avoid Unnecesary Suits and Charges in Law').[121] The mischief that Parliament wished to regulate was identified in this way:

> 'For that through the abuse of sundry attornies and solicitors by charging their clients with excessive fees and other unnecessary demands, such as were not, nor ought by them to have been employed or demanded, whereby the subjects grow to be overmuch burdened.'

That Act provided that attorneys and solicitors should obtain a 'ticket' (that is, a receipt) for any fees paid to specified third parties and that they must render a 'true bill' to their clients. Thus the modern practice of delivering bills supported by vouchers was born. Shortly thereafter, the practice of 'chancering' bills came into being; this involved the assessment of fees as an exercise of discretion and, as such, could be said to have been a predecessor of modern-day assessments.

Access to justice

1.51 In 1606, an enactment was made that provided as follows:

> '[Every] citizen and freeman of the city of London, and every other person inhabiting ... the said city ... which now, or hereafter, shall have any debt owing unto him, not amounting to forty shillings, ... may summon such debtor to the Court of Requests or Conscience, in London, which court shall have power to determine such cases.'[122]

In line with the '40-shilling rule' that (theoretically) applied in Westminster (see 1.45–1.47), penalties were visited upon claimants who failed appropriately to bring claims in a Court of Requests or Conscience. Indeed, a claimant who sued in the wrong court was at risk of being condemned in costs even if their claim were successful.[123] Perhaps partly because of that rule, the Courts of Requests or Conscience were a considerable success.

Duplex costs shifting

1.52 It will be recalled that whilst provision had been made for defendants' costs orders as early as 1531 (see 1.36), they were limited in their scope. In 1607, general reciprocal provisions for defendants were created[124]—in particular, s 2 of the Costs Act 1607 enacting the following rule:

> 'If any person shall sue in any court any action whatsoever, wherein the plaintiff might have costs, in case judgement should be given for him, the defendant shall have judgment to recover costs against the plaintiff, if he be nonsuited, or a verdict pass against him.'

---

120 See Holdsworth, WS, *A History of English Law* (3rd edn, London: Methuen, 1923), vol 3, at p 392.

121 The Act was *Attorneys* (3 James I, c 7), made in about 1605.

122 The Small Debts (London City) Act 1605 (3 Jas 1, c. 15), s 2(1).

123 See s 4 of the Small Debts (London City) Act 1605.

124 See Costs 1606 (4 James I, c 3; often also written as 4 Jac 1, c 3). Those provisions were reciprocal in the sense that the defendant was able to recover costs only in those cases in which the claimant would also, had he won, have been able to recover costs: see Sayer, J, *The Law of Costs* (London: J & WT Clarke, 1768), p 68.

That said, there were two exceptions to the availability of defendants' costs after this reform: it did not apply where the party was a corporation; and it did not apply in certain actions—most notably, that of trespass (which, at the time, was a class of action that would encompass claims that today would include most personal injury claims). Some modern-day commentators have pointed out that the Jackson reforms (see 1.174) have, in many ways, restored the law to how it was in the start of the 17th century.[125]

The rule seems to have been regarded as being fair and appropriate. Speaking of this rule in 1642, no less a commentator than Sir Edward Coke (speaking extrajudicially) said that 'where costs are given the winner ought to be ordered to pay the loser's costs'.[126] Similarly, in the 1760s, Sir William Blackstone (again speaking extrajudicially) summed it up in the following way: 'Thus much for judgments; to which costs are a necessary appendage; it being now as well the maxim of ours as of the civil law, that "*victus victori in expensis condemnandus est*".'[127] Once that system was in place—that is, the principle that the loser pays, whomsoever they should be—it became a rule so ingrained in English law that it was said to typify it.[128] It is worth noting, however, that costs continued to be regarded (at least in some circumstances) as being very much a species of damages.[129] **1.53**

The Carolean period (1625–49)

Costs distinguished from expenses

In the early days of the reign of Charles I (and probably before this), judges began to distinguish between recoverable 'costs' and 'expenses', the latter being merely an incident of litigation. In 1628, for example, Sir Edward Coke (speaking extrajudicially) dealt with the distinction in this way: **1.54**

> 'Here [the Statute of Gloucester] is express mention made but of the costs of his writ, but it extendeth to all the legal cost of the suit, but not to the costs and expenses of his travel and loss of time, and therefore "costages" cometh of the verb "conster", and that again of the verb "constare", for these "costages" must "constare" to the court to be legal costs and expenses.'[130]

---

125 See further, So, W, 'A Brief History of the Law of Costs: Lessons for the Jackson Reforms and Beyond' (2013) 32 CJQ 333.

126 Coke, E, *The Second Part of the Institutes of the Laws of England; Containing the Exposition of Many Ancient and Other Statutes* (London: E & R Brooke, 1797), p 289.

127 Blackstone, W, *Commentaries on the Laws of England* (a facsimile of the first edition of 1765–69, reprinted Chicago, IL: University of Chicago Press, 1979), vol 3, at p 399. Yet this is somewhat inaccurate because the civilian sense of *condemnandus* is truly punitive: 'Distribution of Legal Expenses among Litigants' (1940) 49 Yale LJ 699, at 704. Furthermore, under the civil law *in expensis* included only the court fees and not those of the legal representatives: Engelmann, A, et al (eds), *A History of Continental Civil Procedure* (Boston, MA: Little, Brown & Co, 1927), p 403.

128 See, eg, *Greetham v The Inhabitants of the Hundred of Theale* (1765) 97 ER 1066 (in which the principle of reciprocity was found to apply despite the fact that post-Gloucester legislation created a right to claim damages for firesetting from the relevant Hundred rather than only from the firesetter himself) and *Jackson v The Inhabitants of Calesworth* (1785) 99 ER 977. That said, see also *Wilkinson v Allott* (1777) M 16 G 3 BR, in which *Greetham* was doubted. See also Quick, R, 'The English Rule', in *Quick on Costs* (Thomson Reuters, online), paras 2.30 *et seq*.

129 See, eg, *Ashmore v Ripley* (1617) 79 ER 359.

130 *Institutes of the Laws of England; Containing the Exposition of Many Ancient and Other Statutes* (2 Inst 288).

This distinction remains relevant today (see 3.03–3.05); indeed, Coke's words are still occasionally cited.[131] Similarly, reference is also often made to the absence of any principle that the expenditure of the costs of litigation should be recoverable in full.[132]

Expansion of the cases in which costs were awarded

1.55 By the Carolean period, the rule in *Pilford's case* began to be questioned (that rule being that if damages would not have been recoverable prior to the Statute of Gloucester, then a successful claimant would not be entitled to costs—see 1.24). In particular, Coke commented that the Act gave costs in all cases in which damages had been given and, in this regard, he said (in translation), 'where costs are given the winner ought to be ordered to pay the loser costs'.[133]

The legal profession

1.56 By the 17th century, serjeants-at-law had largely given way to barristers-at-law. In about 1629, the Bar adopted an affectation that has caused subsequent generations of barristers no end of trouble. Plucknett describes it in this way:

> 'The barrister asserted a social superiority by declining to sue for his fees (the rule appears in 1629–1630), although attorneys continued to do so. In the meanwhile, many students of the Inns of Court specialised in pleading and conveyancing, and practised as members of new sub-divisions of the legal profession as "pleaders", "equity draftsmen" and "conveyancers". There was no need for such men to be called to the bar, and as a rule they were not. They were therefore described as "practitioners".'[134]

This incomprehensible rule continued to apply until as recently as 2013 (see 53.05).

The Restoration (1660–88)

Costs upon discontinuance

1.57 In 1661, statutory provision was made for claimants who had failed to prosecute their claims to be condemned in costs;[135] in essence, that provision was the forerunner of the modern-day rules regarding discontinuance. That said, costs would not be payable if the discontinuance were to arise after demurrer or as a result of the operation of the law.[136]

Payments into court

1.58 In about 1665, Kelynge LCJ allowed a practice to develop whereby payments were made into court.[137] Hullock records that the system was:

> '... introduced for the purposes of avoiding the hazard of pleading a tender, and with a view of enabling a party, who had had no opportunity of making a tender, or at least had omitted

[131] See, eg, *McIlwraith v McIlwraith* [2005] EWHC 90010 (Costs) and the Irish case of *Dawson v Irish Brokers Association* [2002] IESC 36.

[132] See Sir Rupert Jackson's comments about the relatively recent 'myth' that clients are entitled to full costs recovery: Jackson, R, 'Legal Aid and the Costs Review Reforms', Talk delivered to the Cambridge Law Faculty, 5 September 2011, at p 5.

[133] *Institutes of the Laws of England; Containing the Exposition of Many Ancient and Other Statutes* (2 Inst 289).

[134] See Plucknett, T, *A Concise History of the Common Law* (5th edn, Indianapolis, IN: Liberty Fund Inc, 2010), ch 12.

[135] Vexatious Arrests and Delays at Law Act 1661 (13 Car 2, st 2, c 2).

[136] See Comb, 323, and Hold, 156.

[137] There would seem to be no contemporary record of this, but it is recorded as a historical note in more recent reports, such as White and Woodhouse (1727) 94 ER 17.

> to do so, to satisfy the debt, for which the action was commenced, without incurring any further expence.'[138]

It would be more than a century before the court would treat payments in as providing the type of costs protection that is now afforded by Part 36 offers (see 17.08),[139] but Kelynge LCJ's innovative system was a step in that direction.

An attempt to revive the 40-shilling rule

It will be recalled that, during early Stuart times, the 40-shilling rule was so disliked by the judiciary that it was consistently thwarted (see 1.45). In an attempt to revive that rule, a statutory 'Recital of Intention' was made in 1670, which restated it as follows: **1.59**

> '[And for prevention of triviall and vexatious Suites in Law, whereby many good Subjects of this Realme have beene and are dayly undone contrary to the intention of [the 40-shilling rule] for avoiding of infinite numbers of small and trifling Suites commenced in the Courts at Westminster Bee it further enacted for makeing the said Law effectuall That ... the Plaintiffe in such Action in case the Jury shall finde the Dammage to be under the value of forty shillings shall not recover or obtaine more Costs of Suite, then the Dammages soe found shall amount unto, And if any more Costs in any such Action shall be awarded, the Judgement shall be void, and the Defendant is hereby acquitted of, and from the same, and may have his Action against the Plaintiffe for such vexatious Suite, and recover his Damages and Costs of such his Suite in any of the said Courts of Record.'[140]

Unsurprisingly, given the history of the matter, this 'Recital of Intention' was largely disregarded (not least because it was interpreted as applying only to trespass and assault and battery).[141] As such, the 40-shilling rule continued to be ignored. The story of the 40-shilling rule continues at 1.66.

The Glorious Revolution (1688–1714)

The Glorious Revolution resulted in James II yielding his throne to the co-revenants William III and Mary II of England. From a legal standpoint, their reign is best remembered for the Bill of Rights 1689. Whilst of far less historical significance, advances were also made in costs jurisprudence. **1.60**

- **Hopeless cases** The courts continued to be troubled by frivolous and vexatious suits,[142] so, in 1696, legislation was made that tackled that mischief. In particular, if judgment

[138] Hullock, J, *Costs in Civil Actions and Criminal Proceedings* (2nd edn, London: W Clarke & Sons, 1810), p 212.

[139] The earliest instance that the authors have been able to find of the court making such an award is *Griffiths v Williams* (1787) 99 ER 1335—although part of the reasoning in that case was doubted in *Stevenson v Yorke* (1790) 4 TR 10. That said, in *Hartley v Bateson* (1787) 1 TR 629, the following note appears (which suggests that the practice of awarding costs to a defendant who had 'beaten' a payment in was already well established by 1787): 'On inquiring of the Master, it appears to be the constant and regular practice that the plaintiff is entitled to have his costs to the time of paying money into Court, and the defendant all his subsequent costs.'

[140] See s 136 (also referred to as Annex IX) of the Duties on Law Proceedings Act 1670 (22 & 23 Cha 2, c 9).

[141] See Gilb HCP 264. Hullock was not impressed by this analysis, noting that the contrary analysis (that the 1670 Act applied to all personal actions) was 'obvious, if we avert to the object, which the legislature had in view': see Hullock, J, *Costs in Civil Actions and Criminal Proceedings* (2nd edn, London: W Clarke & Sons, 1810), p 43.

[142] Indeed, the original title of the Administration of Justice Act 1696 (8 & 9 Will 3, c 11) was 'An Act for the better preventing of frivolous and vexatious Suits'.

had been entered for the defendant upon a demurrer (that is, if judgment had been entered because the pleaded case was shown to be irrelevant or simply wrong in law), the defendant would be entitled to costs.[143]

- **'Amicable defendants'** In a similar vein, where a claimant had sued many defendants, but had succeeded against only one, the courts were given discretionary power[144] to order the claimant to pay the costs of the defendants against whom their claim had failed.[145] This power was required to deal with the problem caused by 'amicable defendants', who were defendants in league with the claimant such that they permitted judgment in default to be entered against them, this having the effect of precluding the court from condemning the claimant to pay the costs of any other defendant.[146]

Georgian Times (1714–1830)

George II (1727–60)

Statutory provisions for bills, and solicitor and client assessments

1.61 Since long before statute intervened, the court had exercised an inherent jurisdiction over solicitors as officers of the court,[147] but the first statute containing provision for the taxation (that is, assessment) of solicitors' bills was enacted in the early 18th century.[148] The solicitor was required to deliver a bill:

> '... written in a common legible hand and in the English tongue (except law terms and names of writs) and in words at length [ie not abbreviated] (except times and sums) which bill shall be subscribed with the proper hand of such attorney or solicitor respectively.'[149]

The bill would be assessed by the Chancery Office of the Six Clerks. The statutory right to an assessment was a significant improvement in terms of consumer protection, not least because, under the court's inherent jurisdiction, the client was required to bring the amount of the disputed bill into court, this being a requirement that did not apply to a statutory assessment.[150]

1.62 Provision was also made for preventing a solicitor from bringing an action for fees until after the expiration of one month or more from the delivery of his bill,[151] which provision has been repeated in subsequent Solicitors Acts and survives even today.

---

143 See s 2 of the Administration of Justice Act 1696 (8 & 9 Will 3, c 11). It is worth noting that some contemporary textbooks record that there were instances of the court making such an order under 23 H 8, 15: see Hard 153 arg, Jenk 161 and Cro Car 533.

144 The test in s 1 of the Administration of Justice Act 1696 was whether or not there was a 'reasonable cause for the making such person or persons a defendant or defendants'.

145 See s 1 of the Administration of Justice Act 1696 (8 & 9 Will 3, c 11). The Act extended to trespass, assault, false imprisonment and ejectment.

146 See Hullock, J, *Costs in Civil Actions and Criminal Proceedings* (2nd edn, London: W Clarke & Sons, 1810), p 143, who quotes the following authorities: Moore, 770, and Noy, 101.

147 See the judgments of Lord Eldon LC in *Ex parte Earl of Uxbridge* (1801) 6 Ves 425 and of Lord Erskine LC in *Ex parte Arrowsmith* (1806) 13 Ves 124; see also *Chadwell v Bruer* (1728) 1 Barn KB 43.

148 An Act for the Better Regulation of Attornies and Solicitors 1728 (2 Geo II, c 23).

149 *Ibid*, s 23.

150 *Ibid.*

151 *Ibid.*

Costs in the Court of Chancery

It will be recalled that, during Stuart times, the Court of Chancery had developed a dizzying array of bases upon which costs could be awarded (see 1.49). This was challenged from time to time, but such challenges tended to fail. In 1742, for example, Lord Hardwicke had this to say: 'The giving of costs in equity is entirely discretionary, and is not at all conformable to the rule of law.'[152] And the following year, in a different case, he said this: **1.63**

> '[C]ourts of equity have in all cases done it [ie dealt with costs], not from any authority [ie as we understand, from any statutory or delegated authority], but from conscience, and *arbitrio boni viri*, as to the satisfaction on one side or other on account of vexation.'[153]

Whilst it is hard to be precise as to the chronology, it would be fair to say that some of the more generous awards made by the Court of Chancery were very similar to awards of costs on the modern-day indemnity basis.[154] It is not known exactly when that power came into being, but it was certainly well before 1875 (when the Judicature Acts fully came into force).[155] This, however, was only in the courts of equity; it would be more than a century before common-law courts would be able to make such awards (see 1.98). **1.64**

Interim awards of costs

Interim costs orders also came into existence, the first being made when the Lord Chancellor exercised his discretion to make such an award for the purposes of allowing an impecunious litigant to carry on with their claim.[156] **1.65**

The 40-shilling rule

It will be recalled that the 40-shilling rule—which had originally been introduced during the reign of Elizabeth I (see 1.45), but had been virtually ignored by the Stuart-era judiciary (see 1.46 and 1.47)—had been 'restated' in legislation enacted during the reign of Charles II (see 1.59). It seems that, during early Georgian times, the rule continued to be all but ignored. Gilbert B said that the rule was 'pretty darkly penn'd and therefore … had very little or no effect'.[157] Whilst this editor's own research suggests that Gilbert B was only partly correct,[158] it would seem that Hullock believed that 'no instance of a certificate … is to be met with the books earlier than about the middle of reign of King George the Second'.[159] **1.66**

[152] *Jones v Coxeter* (1742) 2 Atk 400.

[153] *Burford Corpn v Lenthall* (1743) 2 Atk 551.

[154] Indeed, Fry LJ's analysis of the relevant history is very much in keeping with such a view: see *Andrews v Barnes* (1888) [1886–90] All ER Rep 758, at 761.

[155] *Ibid.*

[156] *Jones v Coxeter* (1742) 2 Atk 400.

[157] *Reeves v Butler* (1726) Gilb Rep 195. See also Sayer, J, *The Law of Costs* (London: J & WT Clarke, 1768), p 12, and *Quick on Costs* (Thomson Reuters, online).

[158] The editor's (necessarily limited) research has shown that the earliest reported instance of the 40-shilling rule being applied by a judge was in a case heard by Willes LCJ in 1744—*White v Smith* (1744) CB Paschæ 17G 2, in which modest damages had been awarded against a party who had taken sand and gravel from a heath—but it would seem that there were earlier occasions on which the rule was applied by officers of the court: see, eg, *Claxton and Laws* (1673) 84 ER 702.

[159] See Hullock, J, *Costs in Civil Actions and Criminal Proceedings* (2nd edn, London: W Clarke & Sons, 1810), p 24, where Hullock cites the following authorities: V d Gilb Eq Rep 196 and 3 Wils 325. (It should be noted that, by then, the rules regarding certificates had changed such that a certificate would be required to *dis*apply the 40-shilling rule rather than to apply it, but—whilst the contrary is possible—it seems unlikely that Hullock was referring to certificates of the former kind.)

That said, this does not detract from the general point that Hullock makes, which is that the rule was largely ignored.

1.67 Subsequent to the mid-1740s, however, it seems that the 40-shilling rule was applied with more enthusiasm (if that is the right word),[160] at least in so far as cases not concerning slander were concerned.[161] A cynic would say that, by this point in time, it had become an almost academic matter, as the real value of 40*s* was so much less than when the rule was first made, so it applied only to relatively modest cases.

Courts of Requests

1.68 The Courts of Requests or Conscience, as reinvented by James I (see 1.49), had fallen victim to their own success, this being because of a perception on the part of the common-law courts that the former was taking work from the latter. This created a feud that ultimately led to the original Court of Requests ceasing to exist.[162] Be that as it may, new Courts of Requests were created in 1748.[163] These too were a success, as was made clear by the Victorian historian James Grant:

> 'Courts of Conscience, or Requests, as they are now generally termed, are very important institutions in the estimation of the lower classes, though known only by name to those in affluent or easy circumstances. ... They are Courts for the recovery of small debts by an easier, more summary, and cheaper process than exists in the ordinary courts of law.'[164]

The new Courts of Requests survived until they were replaced by county courts in 1847.[165]

George III (1760–1820)

Costs as a specialist subject

1.69 The realisation that the law of costs was a legal topic in its own right started to take hold in the 18th century. The first major textbook on the topic (*Sayer's Law of Costs*) was published in 1768, but this was the first of many. In 1790, a little-known man called Thomas Jefferson advised an aspiring lawyer that *Sayer's* was essential reading[166]—the same Thomas Jefferson who, 11 years later, would go on to become the third President of the United States.

1.70 In 1792, Sir John Hullock published his *Law of Costs*. By 1796, this had grown to be the *Law of Costs in Civil Actions and Criminal Proceedings*. This (in this editor's view) was a masterly work that, even now, rewards careful study. Time and again, this editor has found

---

160 In a case concerning the right to charge a toll, for example, Dennison J found that the quantum of damages was not so much the matter in controversy as the prescription and right to the toll (which meant that the principle of the matter was of more importance than the relatively trivial sums that were claimed): *Walker v Robinson* (1745) 1 Wils KB 94. Notwithstanding this, the court applied the 40-shilling rule: For a large number of other examples, see Hullock, J, *Costs in Civil Actions and Criminal Proceedings* (2nd edn, London: W Clarke & Sons, 1810), pp 9, 24–31.

161 See *Collier v Gaillard* (1776) 2 Black W 1062.

162 Carter, AT, *A History of English Legal Institutions* (London: Butterworths, 1910), p 167.

163 See Small Debts, Southwark, etc. Act 1748 (22 G 2, c. 47).

164 Grant, J, *Sketches in London* (London: WS Orr & Co, 1838), ch 10, at p 322.

165 County Court Act 1846.

166 Mews, H, *Reader Instruction in Colleges and Universities: Teaching the Use of the Library* (Hamden, CT: Linnet Books, 1972).

that where Hullock and other authors appear not to agree, primary source material has shown Hullock to have been accurate.

Judicial broadening of the power to award costs

It continued to be the case that costs were recoverable only in certain types of claim. There was, however, a gradual broadening of the array of cases in which costs were recoverable, this being as a result of judge-made law. In particular, the rule in *Pilford's case* (see 1.24) continued to come under attack (that rule being that if damages would not have been recoverable prior to the Statute of Gloucester, then a successful claimant would not be entitled to costs).[167] That said, even as late as 1819, costs (or, at least, multiple costs) were very much regarded as being a species of damages.[168] **1.71**

Examples of the court's new-found powers included the following. **1.72**

- **Competing orders as to costs** Whilst previous attempts to persuade the court to make cross-orders as to costs had failed on the basis that such orders were without precedent,[169] in 1788 the Court of Common Pleas made orders that permitted a claimant, in essence, to deduct costs that were payable to a successful defendant from costs that were recoverable from the unsuccessful defendants.[170]
- **Defendants' costs following *nolle prosequi*** In 1789, defendants benefited in the sense that it was determined that a claimant may be liable to pay costs if they were to enter a *nolle prosequi*.[171]
- ***Tyte v Globe*** In 1797, it was the turn of claimants to benefit, in that it was decided that a successful claimant should be entitled to costs even in the absence of a specific statutory provision to that effect.[172]

Victorian Times (1837–1901)

Before the Judicature Acts

Taxing masters

The new emphasis on costs created a need for judges who had the time and the ability to carry out taxations (that is, assessments). That need was addressed by the Court of Chancery Act 1842,[173] which abolished the Chancery Office of the Six Clerks and created the posts of taxing masters (now more commonly referred to as costs judges). At about the same time, there was a change of emphasis in the Exchequer of Pleas in that it became a **1.73**

[167] In particular, that case was questioned in *R v Inhabitants of Calesworth* (1785) 1 TR 71, 99 ER 977. Indeed, the doctrine itself appears to have ceased to have any significance by the 19th century: see Gray, J, *A Treatise on the Law of Costs in Action and other proceedings in the Courts of Common Law at Westminster* (London: Edward Lumley, 1853), pp 4 and 5.

[168] See, eg, *Deacon v Morris* (1819) 2 B & Ald 393; see also *Phillips v Bacon* (1808) 9 East 298, at 304.

[169] See, eg, *Mordecai v Nutting & Ors* (1752) 94 ER 848.

[170] *Schoole v Noble, Lett, and Byrne* (1788) 126 ER 15. It should be noted that this was an unusual case in that it would appear that the two unsuccessful defendants had committed trespass whilst acting under the authority of the successful defendant. See also *George v Elston* (1835) 1 Bing NC 515.

[171] See *Cooper v Tiffin* (1789) 100 ER 706.

[172] *Tyte v Globe* (1797) 7 TR 267.

[173] 5 & 6 Victoriae, c 103.

common-law court. The 1842 Act was one of the first of a series of Acts that had as their aim the fusing of courts of common law and courts of equity (see 1.92).[174]

Concerns about the amounts of costs

1.74 By the early 19th century, there were concerns that litigation costs were getting out of control. This prompted Jeremy Bentham (an English philosopher) to describe costs as 'the grand instrument of mischief in English practice'.[175] Sir Thomas Erskine May (a constitutional theorist) had this to say on the point:

> 'Heart-breaking delays and ruinous costs were the lot of suitors. Justice was dilatory, expensive, uncertain, and remote. To the rich it was a costly lottery: to the poor a denial of right, or certain ruin. The class who profited most by its dark mysteries were the lawyers themselves.'[176]

It is implicit in what Erskine May said that there was a distinction between costs as between opposing parties and costs as between solicitor and client; the courts recognised that distinction, but the phrase 'solicitor and client costs' had yet to come into common usage; instead, the phrase 'extra costs' was used.[177]

1.75 In 1828, Bentham's concerns prompted Lord Brougham (a parliamentarian) to give a famously long speech—six hours!—which was based on the premise that costs could be controlled by regulating lawyers' charges rather than restricting the recovery of costs:

> '... How much nobler will be the Sovereign's [George IV] boast when he shall have it to say that he found law dear and left it cheap; found it a sealed book, left it a living letter; found it the patrimony of the rich, left it the inheritance of the poor; found it the two edged sword of craft and oppression, left it the staff of honesty and the shield of innocence.'[178]

1.76 It was said that the scale of fees used in this time were out of date and extremely low. The result was that attorneys and solicitors were forced to undertake services that were completely unnecessary to make up for the poor levels of remuneration. Lord Brougham had had this to say on the point:

> '... the necessary consequence of not suffering an attorney to be paid what he ought to receive for certain things, is that he is driven to do a number of needless things which he knows are allowed as a matter of course.'[179]

1.77 These concerns were illustrated by *Lucas v Peacock*,[180] which concerned the administration of an estate in which a solicitor represented a claimant *and* two of the defendants at the same time. In the capacity of the claimant's solicitor, he took out more than 200 warrants in the Masters' Office, all of which were served on himself in the capacity as the representative of the defendants. The taxing master took a hard line and taxed off most of these

---

174 See the Administration of Justice Act 1841.

175 Bentham, T, *Principles of Judicial Procedure* (1820–27), as reprinted in Bowring, J (ed), *The Works of Jeremy Bentham* (Edinburgh: W Tait, 1938–43), vol 7, at p 111.

176 Sir Thomas Erskine May, *Constitutional History* (1863), vol 2, at p 384, cited in Plucknett, T, *A Concise History of the Common Law* (5th edn, Indianapolis, IN: Liberty Fund Inc, 2010).

177 See, eg, *Sandback v Thomas* (1816) 1 Stark 306, at 307, 171 ER 481, at 481. See also *Quartz Hill Consolidated Gold Mining Co v Eyre* (1883) 11 QBD 674, at 682, and (as a much later example) *Bury v Greenwood* (1934) WN 119.

178 Brougham, Hansard (NS), House of Commons, 7 February 1828, vol 18.

179 Parliamentary Papers 1828, vol 13, p 296.

180 *Lucas v Peacock* (1844) 8 Beav 1, 50 ER 1.

costs—yet, on appeal, Lord Longdale expressed much sympathy to the solicitor: 'I shall be slow to admit that he is to be deprived of any lawful fees which the established practice of the Court warrants, on the notion that the business charged for might have been of no practical benefit.'[181] The appeal was successful. The 'grand instrument of mischief' continued unabated.

Concerns about the inefficiency of the law

In 1852, Charles Dickens published his serialised novel *Bleak House*, which introduced the world to *Jarndyce v Jarndyce*, a fictional Chancery case that was said to have dragged on for so long that the original dispute had long since been forgotten and the lawyers—like 'maggots in nuts'—fed upon the ongoing wreckage of the costs.[182] **1.78**

One would have hoped that Dickens had overstated the malaise in the English legal system, but his comments in the Preface to *Bleak House* suggest otherwise: **1.79**

> 'At the present moment (August, 1853) there is a suit before the court which was commenced nearly twenty years ago, in which from thirty to forty counsel have been known to appear at one time, in which costs have been incurred to the amount of seventy thousand pounds, which is A FRIENDLY SUIT, and which is (I am assured) no nearer to its termination now than when it was begun.[183] There is another well-known suit in Chancery, not yet decided, which was commenced before the close of the last century and in which more than double the amount of seventy thousand pounds has been swallowed up in costs.[184]'

Notwithstanding the fact that the cases Dickens referred to are identifiable by name and were contemporary, the received academic view is that Dickens was 25 years out of date in his criticisms. This is because the problems with the Court of Chancery had been highlighted by a report published in 1826[185] and had, supposedly, been addressed by the time Dickens wrote *Bleak House*.[186] Regardless of whether the received view is correct, *Bleak House*[187] certainly raised public awareness of the problems caused by inefficient legal practices and it may well have prompted the debate that ultimately would lead to the making of the Judicature Acts (see 1.92). **1.80**

Refinements to solicitor and client assessments

The Solicitors Act 1843 imposed a limit on the period of time during which a client may apply for an assessment of his costs, this being similar to the corresponding provisions in the modern-day Solicitors Act 1974. It also introduced the one-fifth rule (or, as it was when first introduced, the one-sixth rule). In a decision that remains good law even today, in 1857 it was decided that a bill ought to be drawn with a narrative sufficient to allow the client to know **1.81**

---

181 *Ibid*, at 5–6.

182 Dickens, C, *Bleak House* (1852–53), ch 10.

183 Based on information in a letter by Dickens, this case is generally thought to have been about a dispute over the will of one Mr Charles Day: see Dunstan, W, 'The Real Jarndyce and Jarndyce' (1997) 93 The Dickensian 24, at 27. Proceedings were issued in 1837 and concluded in 1854.

184 This was almost certainly *Jennens v Jennens*, which commenced in 1798 and was eventually abandoned in 1915 because, after 117 years of arguing, the lawyers' fees had eaten through the entirety of the estate.

185 See First Chancery Commission of 1826, Parliamentary Papers, vol 15 (1826).

186 See Holdsworth, WS, *Dickens as a Legal Historian* (New Haven, CT: Yale University Press, 1923), p 81.

187 One might note the interesting point that Dickens wrote one book on the Common Pleas (*The Pickwick Papers*, 1837), one book on the Chancery (*Bleak House*) and one book for the Ecclesiastical Courts (*David Copperfield*, 1850): Wiener, FB, 'A Cosey, Dosey, Old-Fashioned, Time-Forgotten, Sleepyheaded Little Family Party' (1979) 39 Louisiana L Rev 1035, at 1035.

whether it was fair, to allow a solicitor to advise upon it and the court to know the fairness of the items contained therein.[188] The age-old suspicion (see 1.40) that lawyers were enhancing their fees by drafting overly long documents lingered on. In an attempt to deal with this problem, Parliament enacted various statutes (such as the Leases Act 1845), which provided[189] that fees should be based on 'not the Length of [the document in question], but only the Skill and Labour employed, and Responsibility incurred in the Preparation thereof'.

Restrictions on agreements between solicitors and client

1.82 Prior to the coming into force of the Attorneys' and Solicitors' Act 1870 (see 1.84), agreements between solicitors and clients were governed by two common-law principles: the first was that it was contrary to public policy for a solicitor to recover by agreement more than would be awarded on taxation; the second was that the fiduciary relationship between solicitor and client made it necessary for the solicitor to show that any agreement had not been unduly affected. Despite initial doubts during Georgian times,[190] it soon became settled law that a solicitor could not contract out of taxation.[191] Any such agreement would be at risk of being set aside (this being independently of statute).[192]

1.83 That said, fees already incurred could be settled for a gross sum without delivery of a bill, but only if the solicitor could show that the agreement had been made fairly and with proper knowledge on both sides[193]—the burden of proving which proved a heavy one, because the relationship with the client was a fiduciary relationship.[194] This meant that any such agreement would be viewed with 'great jealousy' and suspicion.[195] A binding agreement that precluded taxation in respect of costs yet to be incurred had to be favourable to the client to avoid being set aside.[196] Examples of such agreements included those to limit the amount of costs,[197] to take less than ordinary fees,[198] to take nothing in the event of the client losing[199] or to act only for out-of-pocket expenses.[200]

Business agreements

1.84 The Attorneys' and Solicitors' Act 1870 introduced the concept of agreements in writing (which were precursors of contentious and non-contentious business agreements). This provision permitted solicitors to agree terms of remuneration with their clients in such a

---

188 *Haigh v Ousey* (1857) 7 E & B 578.

189 At s 3.

190 See, eg, Anon (1732) 2 Barn KB 164.

191 See, eg, *Balme v Paver* (1821) Jac Rep 305; also see *Scougall v Campbell* (1826) 3 Russ 545.

192 See *Saunderson v Glass* (1742) 2 Atk 296, at 298; *Philby v Hazle* (1860) 8 CB (NS) 647, at 652; *O'Brien v Lewis* (1863) 32 LT (Ch) 569.

193 See *Stedman v Collett* (1854) 17 Beav 608, at 615, and, more recently, *Clare v Joseph* [1907] 2 KB 369, at 376.

194 *Tyrrell v Bank of London* (1862) 10 HLC 26, at 44.

195 See *Re Whitcombe* (1844) 8 Beav 140, at 144, and, more recently, *Clare v Joseph* [1907] 2 KB 369, at 376.

196 See *Philby v Hazle* (1860) 8 CB (NS) 647, *Re Newman* (1861) 30 Beav 196 and *Re Cawley & Whatley* (1870) 18 WR 1125.

197 *Moon v Hall* (1864) 17 CB(NS) 760; *Re Owen, ex parte Payton* (1885) 52 LT 628.

198 Whilst relatively modern cases, see *Clare v Joseph* [1907] 2 KB 369 and *Re A Solicitor* [1956] 3 All ER 305.

199 *Tabram v Horne* (1827) 1 Man & Ry 228; *Turner v Tennant* (1846) 10 Jur 429 (n); *Galloway v Corpn of London* (1867) LR 4 Eq 90, at 97. See also, more recently, *Gundry v Sainsbury* [1910] 1 KB 645.

200 *Jones v Reade* (1836) 5 A & E 529.

way as to avoid the costs being assessed, and such agreements were (and still are) subject to the scrutiny of the court. This had a significant bearing on the way in which solicitors were able to interact with their clients (and see 1.82 for the pre-existing law).

Compensatory costs

Lord Brougham's suggestions (see 1.75) were not adopted by Parliament, but instead provision was made for assessing costs between opposing parties on a compensatory basis. In particular, the Limitation of Actions and Costs Act 1842[201] repealed provisions that allowed for payment of double, treble and quadruple costs, and of costs as if they had been allowed between solicitor and client (see 1.49). In claims based on personal or local Acts, the 1842 Act made provision for party and party costs,[202] and in claims based on public Acts, it made provision for 'a full and reasonable indemnity as to all costs, charges and expenses incurred in and about any action, suit or other legal proceeding, as shall be taxed by the proper officer in that behalf.'[203] The new emphasis on costs as compensation would ultimately give rise to the modern-day indemnity principle (see 1.91). **1.85**

As is explained in 1.98, certain courts continued to have the power to make awards of costs that were, in effect, on the indemnity basis, this being pursuant to their equitable jurisdiction rather than pursuant to their jurisdiction as a court of common law. In particular, the Court of Chancery often made orders that costs be allowed as between solicitor and client.[204] In addition, certain instances of double and treble costs and other unusual types of order lingered, notwithstanding the 1842 Act.[205] **1.86**

County courts

By the beginning of the 19th century, there was widespread dissatisfaction among litigants who wished to pursue claims for debt.[206] There was a perception that the rules governing pleading and practice were so complex that legal representation was essential, even in simple claims.[207] Shire Courts and Hundred Courts continued to exist, but most of these ceased to be active by 1820 (not least because their jurisdictions were limited to cases for 40*s* or less).[208] Courts of Request were better regarded, but they lacked effective jurisdiction over persons not residing in their limited catchment areas,[209] which made it difficult for traders operating on a national scale to bring claims.[210] Moreover, they were not available in every town. Lord Brougham asked the Common Law Commissioners to look into the **1.87**

201 Otherwise known as Pollock's Act of 1842 (5 & 6 Victoriæ, c 97).

202 Limitation of Actions and Costs Act 1842, s 1.

203 *Ibid*, s 2.

204 See, eg, *Lipscombe v Turner* (1846) 4 D & L 125, at 129.

205 This is because the 1842 Act did not deal with those cases in which such were payable as a result of express statutory provision to that effect. The most significant example of this was s 129 of the County Courts Act 1846, which provided that where a claimant failed in an action in a superior court that should have been brought in the newly constituted county courts, the defendant should be entitled to costs as between attorney and client unless the judge certified that the action was one fit for the superior court.

206 See, eg, the preface of the More Easy Recovery of Small Debts 1782.

207 Cornish, WR, and Clarke, G, *Law and Society in England 1750–1950* (London: Sweet & Maxwell, 1989), p 25.

208 Polden, P, *A History of the County Court, 1846–1971* (Cambridge: Cambridge University Press, 1999), p 17.

209 Winder, WH, 'The Courts of Request' (1936) 207 LQR 369, at 391.

210 Polden, P, *A History of the County Court, 1846–1971* (Cambridge: Cambridge University Press, 1999), p 12.

matter.[211] He introduced a Bill to Parliament in 1830 to establish a national system of county courts, but it failed because of opposition from the legal profession in London, who wanted to protect their litigation practices,[212] and also because of pressure from provincial solicitors, who wanted to protect their conveyancing practices.[213]

1.88 Eventually, the county court system was created by the County Courts Act 1846, which received royal assent on 28 August 1846 and was brought into force on 15 March 1847. This replaced the Courts of Request, the Shire Courts and the Hundreds Courts. With the exception of the City of London, the country was divided into 60 circuits, with a total of 491 county courts within these circuits.[214] The theory was that everyone would be within 7 miles of a court. One county court judge was appointed to each circuit, assisted by one or more registrars.[215]

1.89 From 1867 onwards, a rule would apply that was intended to discourage smaller claims being brought in the High Court. It was the Victorian equivalent of the rule referred to in 1.51: if a High Court claimant recovered no more than £20 in a case based on contract or £10 in a case based on tort, then unless they were able to justify their choice of venue, the claimant would recover no costs at all.[216]

Costs confirmed as not being punitive in nature

1.90 In about 1860[217] (see 3.16), it was realised that an order condemning a party in costs was not penal in nature; prior to that, the question of whether costs were compensatory or punitive (or both) had yet to be settled.[218]

The indemnity principle

1.91 Unsurprisingly given the matters set out in 1.85, in the 1860s the law developed in such a way as to confirm that costs between opposing parties must be assessed in accordance with the indemnity principle.[219] It was known that an award of reasonable costs was not

---

[211] This resulted in the publication of the First Report of the Common Law Commissioners, Parliamentary Papers 1829 (46).

[212] See Abel-Smith, B, *Lawyers and the Courts: A Sociological Study of the English Legal System* (London: Heinemann Press, 1967), p 33.

[213] See Kirk, H, *Portrait of a Profession: A History of Solicitors' Profession, 1100 to the Present Day* (London: Oyez Longman, 1976), p 155.

[214] Polden, P, *A History of the County Court, 1846–1971* (Cambridge: Cambridge University Press, 1999), p 38.

[215] *Ibid.*

[216] See s 5 of the County Courts Act 1867.

[217] See *Harold v Smith* (1860) 5 Hurlestone & Norman 381, at 385. See also *Willmott v Barber* (1881) WN 107, at 108, and *Ross v York Newcastle & Berwick Railway Co* (1849) 18 LJR 199, at 200. Finally, see also *Clarke & Chapman v Hart* (1868) 6 HLC 633, in which Cranworth LC said that costs are not a penalty, but a necessary consequence of instituting litigation that has failed.

[218] In 1734, for example, Lord Hardwicke had said that 'Acts giving costs have always been looked on as penal Acts not to be extended by equity', the implication being that a party should be condemned in costs only if a strict interpretation would permit such a step: see *Dibben v Cooke* (1734) BRH 8G 2. In a similar vein, in 1762, Lord Mansfield had said that 'all act [*sic*] that give costs, are to be construed strictly': *Ingle v Wordsworth* (1762) 97 ER 835. And in 1798, Sayer said that 'every statute under which costs may be recovered is to be construed strictly; costs being a kind of penalty': Sayer, *The Law of Costs* (London: J & WT Clarke, 1768), p 68. At times, this worked in a sensible way that avoided injustice. In *Richardson v Richardson* [1875] P 276, for example, the receiving party was a pauper and, under the laws of the day, this would have led to non-recovery of costs as compensation; the court avoided that restriction by awarding costs as a penalty.

[219] *Harold v Smith* (1865) H & N 381.

a penalty (see 1.90), but there continued to be a dispute about whether costs were an 'indemnity' or whether they were just 'costs'. That dispute rumbled on until 1890, when Halsbury LC resolved it by the elegant finding that they were both—that is, that an award of costs was an indemnity as to costs.[220] At about the same time, it was also—eventually—determined that costs were not a species of damages.[221]

After the Judicature Acts

The Judicature Acts and the creation of the Rules of the Supreme Court 1883

In a process that began in the 1870s and was competed in the 1880s, the Judicature Acts of 1873 and 1875[222] merged the previously separate English courts of common law and equity into the new Supreme Court of Judicature. By ss 3 and 4 of the 1873 Act, the Court of Chancery, the Court of Queen's Bench, the Court of Common Pleas, the Court of Exchequer, the High Court of Admiralty, the Court of Probate, and the Court of Divorce and Matrimonial Causes were consolidated into the Supreme Court of Judicature. This was subdivided into two courts: the High Court of Justice and the Court of Appeal. There were originally three common-law divisions of the High Court corresponding with the three former courts of common law, but, in due course, the High Court came to consist of the Chancery Division, the Queen's Bench Division, and the Probate, Divorce and Admiralty Division.[223] **1.92**

The Court of Appeal had jurisdiction to hear costs appeals on discretionary issues only if the court below had granted permission.[224] **1.93**

Prior to the creation of the new courts, adjectival law had been either judge-made or made in General Orders of the court. In particular, the General Orders in the Court of Chancery had not been made under any statutory authority, but instead had been made under the general and inherent authority of the Lord Chancellor.[225] As such, the rules differed from court to court. This meant that new rules of court were needed, these—eventually—being the Rules of the Supreme Court 1883 (RSC). Those new rules would contain what would become the iconic 'Order 65', which would govern the law of costs for more than a century. That said, it is worth noting that many of the pre-existing rules were highly regarded, especially in so far as the law of costs was concerned.[226] **1.94**

---

220 *Reeve v Gibson* [1891] 1 QB 652, at 660.

221 See *Cockburn v Edwards* (1881) 18 Ch D 449, at 462 and 463; see also *Harrison v McSheehan* (1885) WN 207.

222 Supreme Court of Judicature Act 1873 (36 & 37 Vict, c 66) and the Supreme Court of Judicature Act 1875 (38 & 39 Vict, c 77).

223 These changes were made after the deaths of Kelly LCB (on 17 September 1880) and Cockburn LCJ (on 10 November 1880). The Common Pleas and Exchequer Divisions were combined with the Queen's Bench Division into a single division, under the presidency of the Lord Chief Justice of England, to whom all of the statutory jurisdiction of the Chief Baron and the Chief Justice of the Common Pleas was transferred: see the Judicature Act 1881, s 25.

224 See s 49 of the 1873 Act. The scope of this restriction was cut back, the Court of Appeal taking a narrow view as to what was 'discretionary': *Jones v Curling* (1884) 13 QBD 262, at 267 and 271.

225 See the historical notes made by Fry LJ in *Andrews v Barnes* (1888) [1886–90] All ER Rep 758, at 760.

226 This was largely because one of the Masters, Thomas Dax, wrote a number of directions and books concerning costs. It has been suggested that his books influenced the scale costs (ie Appendix N) and the provisions for taxation in the 1883 Rules of the Supreme Court: see Grayson, E, 'More about Costs and the Solicitor' 73 LSG 77; see also *In Re McLaughlin* (1917) 17 SR (NSW) 392, at 396.

Scale costs

1.95 Appendix N of the Rules of the Supreme Court 1883[227] introduced a scale of charges for certain types of work. Scale costs could be allowed on 'the lower scale' or 'the higher scale'.[228] Costs on the higher scale were allowed only if '[o]n special grounds arising out of the nature and importance or the difficulty or urgency of the case the Judge … so ordered'.

1.96 One consequence of the merger of common law and equity was the fact that costs would now generally be in the discretion of the court; prior to that merger, statutory costs were often allowed as of right in common-law courts.[229]

Party and party basis

1.97 Where costs were to be assessed rather than fixed by reference to a scale (see 1.95), RSC Order 65, r 29 provided that the appropriate measure was what was 'necessary and proper for the attainment of justice':

> 'On every taxation the Taxing Master shall allow all such costs, charges and expenses as shall appear to him to have been necessary or proper for the attainment of justice or for defending the rights of any party, but save as against the party who incurred the same no costs shall be allowed which appear to the Taxing Master to have been incurred or increased through over caution, negligence or mistake or by payment of special fees to counsel or special charges or expenses to witnesses or other persons, or by other unusual expenses.'

This basis of assessment became known as the party-and-party basis. It would survive for over a century.

The indemnity basis and 'solicitor and client costs'

1.98 It will be recalled that, during Stuart times (see 1.49), the Court of Chancery had developed a jurisdiction that allowed it to make awards of costs that were very similar to modern-day awards on the indemnity basis. It will also be recalled that this power was confirmed during the Georgian era (see 1.64). One could be forgiven for having assumed that such a jurisdiction would have fallen by the wayside following the Judicature Acts, but this was not so. In 1888, Fry LJ confirmed that a general and discretionary equitable power to award costs 'as between solicitor and client to a successful party, as and when the justice of the case might so require' continued to exist.[230] Indeed, such orders seemed to have been relatively commonplace, at least in so far as claimants were concerned.[231] Moreover, the phrase 'extra costs' (see 1.74) was replaced by the more modern phrase 'solicitor and client costs'.[232]

---

227 One of the most well-known treatises on this would be King, *Costs on the High Court Scale—being Appendix N to the Rules of the Supreme Court 1883 with Practical Notes, an Analytical Index and an Extended Table of Cases* (London: Stevens & Sons, 1901).

228 RSC Ord 65, r 29.

229 Orkin, M, *The Law of Costs* (2nd edn, looseleaf, Aurora, ON: Canada Law Books, 1987), para 1-1.

230 See *Andrews v Barnes* (1888) [1886–90] All ER Rep 758, at 761. Also see Blackstone, W, *Commentaries on the Laws of England* (a facsimile of the first edition of 1765–69, reprinted Chicago, IL: University of Chicago Press, 1979), vol 3, at pp 451 and 452.

231 See, eg, *Plating Co Ltd v Farquharson* (1881) 17 Ch D 49, at 57; *Harrison v The Cornwall Minerals Railway Co* (1884) 53 LJ Ch 596, at 597; *Forster v Davies* (1863) 32 Beav 624, at 627, 55 ER 245, at 246; *Born v Turner* [1900] 2 Ch 211, at 217.

232 Saddington, AG, *Taxation of Costs between Parties* (Sydney: Law Book Co of Australasia, 1919), pp 16, 17 and 31, suggests that the origin of the term might lie in the wording to the proviso to s 5 of the Attorneys' and Solicitors' Act 1870: '… provided always, that the client who has entered into such agreement shall not

The distinction between contentious and non-contentious business

In 1883, the Solicitors Remuneration Act 1881 impliedly brought about a statutory distinction between contentious and non-contentious work. This distinction was made because the Act related only to the following types of work, which were classified as being non-contentious: **1.99**

> '... business connected with sales, purchases, leases, mortgages, settlements, and other matters of conveyancing, and in respect of other business not being business in any action, or transacted in any court, or in the chambers of any judge or master, and not being otherwise contentious business.'

The 1870 Act continued to govern contentious work.

'Good cause', an early form of third-party costs, and issues-based costs orders

By the late 19th century, it had become generally accepted that a successful claimant should be deprived of costs only if there were 'good cause'[233] to do so (which usually meant misconduct, omission or neglect on the claimant's part).[234] In so far as some types of litigation were concerned, that approach continued into the 20th century.[235] **1.100**

Whilst not quite the same as a modern-day third-party costs order, in 1888 it was also determined that a claimant who had been ordered to pay damages and costs to a third party was able, in subsequent proceedings, to recover party and party costs as damages.[236] **1.101**

Again, whilst not quite the same as its modern equivalent, in 1893 Bowen LJ opened the door to issues-based costs orders.[237] **1.102**

The quality of costs advocacy

Despite being a relatively new branch of the judiciary (see 1.73), taxing masters must have performed their duties well, because the dramatist Herman Charles Merivale singled them out as being an 'exquisite and rational product of British law'.[238] It would seem, however, **1.103**

---

be entitled to recover from any other person under any order for the payment of any costs which are the subject of such agreement more than the amount payable by the client to his own attorney or solicitor under the same.'

233 This phrase was inserted into RSC Ord 65, r 1, by the 1883 revision. Its purpose was directed to place a check on the Chancery practice of awarding a trustee costs out of a fund as a matter of course and without considering whether, as a matter of discretion, he should have them: see *Re Beddoe, Downes v Cottam* [1893] 1 Ch 547, at 554.

234 See *Jones v Curling* (1884) 13 QBD 262, at 265, and *Cooper v Whittingham* (1880) 15 Ch D 501, at 504; cf *Forster v Farquhar* [1893] 1 QB 564.

235 In 1927, it was finally realised that the 'good cause' rule applied only to jury trials: see *Donald Campbell & Co Ltd v Pollak* [1927] AC 732, at 766. Prior to this, there was a line of cases, beginning with *Cooper v Whittingham* (1880) 15 Ch D 501 and culminating in *Ritter v Godfrey* [1920] 2 KB 47, which assimilated the entitlement in jury and non-jury cases. In so far as copyright cases are concerned, see *W Savory Ltd v World of Golf Ltd* [1914] 2 Ch 566, at 571; more generally, see RSC Ord 65, r 1, up until the 1929 revision.

236 See *Hammond v Bussey* (1888) 20 QBD, at 79.

237 See *Forster v Farquhar* [1893] 1 QB 564, at 569 and 570. The claimant claimed as special damage the cost of repairing a drain and medical expenses alleged to have been caused by the defective drain. He succeeded in general, but not on the medical aspects of the claim. The trial judge directed that he should pay the defendants' costs of the items of special damage upon which he had failed. Bowen LJ was of the opinion that the question created by the various claims of damage upon which the claimant had failed was an 'issue'. See also *Bush v Rogers* [1915] 1 KB 707 and *Reid Hewitt & Co v Joseph* [1918] AC 717.

238 Merivale, HC, *Faucit of Balliol* (1882), II.i.xvii.22.

that costs practitioners of the time did not have such high standards, as is made apparent by the following observations of Chitty J:

> 'Very often neither counsel nor solicitors attend on the summons, but gentlemen come before me, subordinate clerks, who are not very competent to transact the business, and after a question or two as to the matters entrusted to them are found to be perfectly at sea, without rudder or compass.'[239]

The cost of litigation

1.104 One would have thought that the effect of all of the above (and, in particular, the effect of the changes made by the Judicature Acts) would have been to improve the lot of the court user. This was true in many regards, but not in so far as the expense of litigation was concerned. In this regard, in 1886, Lord Bowen (speaking extrajudicially) had this to say:

> 'The Judicature Acts ... placed within the reach of every litigant a very complete weapon, but one far too elaborate and precise for the necessities of every case. The first result was to increase by something like twenty per cent the ordinary expenses of a common law action.'[240]

1.105 Indeed, Sir Mackenzie Chambers (writing in 1880) said much the same thing.[241] It would seem that one of the reasons that costs increased was because of the mandatory requirement to give disclosure.[242]

Edwardian Times (1901–10)

Edwardian times in general

1.106 The Supreme Court Taxing Office was founded in 1902.[243] The Edwardian era saw the court begin to tackle more modern issues, such as apportionment (20.24)[244] and *Sanderson* and *Bullock* orders (7.04 and Figure 7.1).[245] There was also progress in so far as the costs of trustees were concerned (66.46).[246]

Access to justice

1.107 At the start of the Edwardian era, there was precious little support for poor litigants. The Poor Man's Lawyers movement attempted to ease the plight of such people; this was a charitable body established at the end of the 19th century at Mansfield House and Toynbee Hall in East London.[247] This and other such charities tended to provide *pro bono* legal advice, but they stopped short of providing representation.[248] Even the founders of

---

239 *Re Bethlehem and Bridewell Hospitals* (1885) 30 Ch D 542.

240 Bowen, C, 'Law Courts under the Judicature Acts' (1886) 2 LQR 1.

241 Quoted by Mullins, C, *In Quest of Justice* (London: John Murray, 1931), pp 201–2.

242 See Bowen, C, 'Law Courts under the Judicature Acts' (1886) 2 LQR 1 and Rosenbaum, S, 'Studies in English Procedure' (1915) 63 U Pa L Rev 273.

243 HM Courts & Tribunals Services, *Senior Courts Costs Office Guide* (London: HMSO, 2018), para 1.1.

244 See *Beaumont v Senior and Bull* [1903] 1 KB 282.

245 See *Sanderson v Blyth Theatre Co* [1903] 2 KB 533, CA, and *Bullock v London General Omnibus Co and Ors* [1907] 1 KB 264.

246 *Re Buckton* [1907] 2 Ch 406.

247 In London, from 1929 onwards, most of the centres were run by the Bentham Committee, which was an organisation formed for the purposes of providing assistance to poor litigants in the county courts.

248 See Brooke, H, 'The History of Legal Aid 1945 to 2010', 16 July 2016, available at https://sirhenrybrooke.me/2016/07/16/the-history-of-legal-aid-1945-to-2010

one such charity had doubts as to the effectiveness of such schemes, saying that the lack of funding for legal representation made the rule of law 'an anaemic attenuated make-believe which we flash in the eyes of the poor as justice.'[249]

It is worth noting that such charities seem to have had a fairly cavalier attitude towards the indemnity principle—in particular, permitting lawyers to seek costs from losing opponents (often on the basis that some or all of the monies received would be paid to the charity). Indeed, one of the most prominent charities, the Bentham Committee, actually demanded recovery of such costs.[250] **1.108**

Edwardian times were marked by a growing political awareness of the working class, this being reflected in the rise of the unions, the Labour movement and various charitable bodies (see 1.107). The Poor Prisoners Defence Act 1903 provided legal assistance for some poor defendants in the magistrates' courts, but there was no such help with civil litigation. This was especially unfortunate because workers had made great progress in securing for themselves legal rights in the events of illness or accidents; as such, demand for legal services was high.[251] **1.109**

The First World War and the Interwar Era (1910–39)

The First World War (1914–18)

For the reasons set out in 1.107–1.109, something more needed to be done to enhance access to justice for poor persons. In 1914, Rules of Court were made that permitted a person to apply to be 'admitted as a poor person'.[252] There was a means test[253] and a merits test,[254] but if those hurdles where cleared, the applicant would be protected both from having to pay fees to their own lawyers and from having to pay costs to their opponents.[255] In keeping with the spirit of the time, the framers of the scheme hoped that lawyers would be paid out of a charitable fund, but the outbreak of the First World War eight months later put paid to that idea.[256] Notwithstanding the conspicuous lack of funding, however, the system operated with some success during the war. This story continues at 1.114. **1.110**

In 1914, the Court of Appeal determined that an agreement that a party pay 'costs as between solicitor and client to be taxed (if necessary)' was not to be regarded as being a full indemnity.[257] This illustrated the fact that, by that stage, there was a recognition that costs as between opposing parties were not the same as costs as between solicitor and client.[258] **1.111**

[249] See Gurney Chapman, FCG, *Justice and the Poor in England* (London: Routledge, 1926), p 21.

[250] See *Report of the Committee on Legal Aid and Legal Advice in England and Wales*, Cmd 6641 (London: HMSO, 1945), paras 85 and 86.

[251] Regan, F, *The Transformation of Legal Aid: Comparative and Historical Studies* (Oxford: Oxford University Press, 1999), pp 89–90, 114.

[252] See RSC Order 16, rr 22–31D, which are more fully described in the *Report of the Committee on Legal Aid and Legal Advice in England and Wales*, Cmd 6641 (London: HMSO, 1945), at para 8.

[253] The applicant had to show that he had assets of less than a certain amount (originally £50): see *ibid*, at para 8(a).

[254] See *ibid*, at para 8(c). A court-appointed solicitor would prepare a report on the merits.

[255] See *ibid*, at para 8(e).

[256] See *ibid*, at para 9.

[257] *Giles v Randall* [1915] 1 KB 290.

[258] For the cases that ultimately led to that realisation, see *Ryan v Dolan* (1872) 7 Ir (Eq) 92, at 94, *Smith v Smith* [1906] VLR 78, at 80 and 81, and *Re Cohen & Cohen* [1905] 2 Ch 137.

The interwar era (1918–39)

Gross sum bills and Solicitors Acts

1.112 In 1920, secondary legislation was made that sought to simplify matters by giving solicitors the option of rendering gross sum statute bills.[259] Prior to this, gross sum *invoices* were permitted, but they were not regarded as being statute bills.[260] The new provision protected clients by giving them the power to ask for the gross sum bill to be replaced with a bill containing detailed items of charges (see 35.99–35.108). The Solicitors Act 1932 was a consolidating Act (which was, in many ways, very similar to the modern 1974 Act). The Solicitors' Remuneration (Gross Sum) Order 1934 repeated the option for the solicitor to charge by a gross sum in lieu of a bill containing detailed charges.

Docketing comes and goes

1.113 It will be recalled that, in the late 1800s, there was general disappointment at the fact that the Judicature Acts had, if anything, increased the expense of litigation (see 1.104). Things did not improve, so, in 1931, Claud Mullins (a prominent legal commentator) published *In Quest of Justice*, in which he expressed concern about the complexity and length of litigation and its excessive cost.[261] Those feelings were shared widely, and this led to an attempt to make the courts more efficient. In particular, a system not unlike modern-day docketing was introduced, which meant that claims were allotted to named judges, who were then required to give all of the necessary directions for trial and who were ultimately supposed to hear the trial.[262] Neither judges nor lawyers liked this procedure and, by 1939, it had fallen into disuse.[263]

The Lawrence Committee and access to justice

1.114 As has been mentioned in 1.110, Edwardian times saw the RSC being amended so as to create a scheme for the provision of legal services to 'poor persons'; given the fact that there was no obvious source of funding for the scheme, it worked remarkably well. Following the First World War, however, there was a fear that people were falling through the net; this is because many people were unable to afford the out-of-pocket expenses that were needed to obtain an order that they were poor persons[264]—at least in part because solicitors were charging 'office expenses' to make up for lost profit costs.[265]

1.115 In 1919, a Committee chaired by Sir Geoffrey Lawrence recommended that the RSC be amended so as to prevent solicitors from levying such charges.[266] This recommendation

---

[259] Rules of the Supreme Court (Solicitors' Remuneration) Rules 1920 (SI 1920/683).

[260] *Re Callis* (1901) 49 WR 316.

[261] Mullins, C, *In Quest of Justice* (London: J Murray, 1931).

[262] This followed the *Report of the Royal Commission on the Dispatch of Business at Common Law, 1934–36*, Cmd 5065 (London: HMSO, 1936).

[263] See the long letter written by Sir Frederick Lawton published in *The Times*, 28 June 1995.

[264] It seems that, for civil cases in the High Court, only about 25 per cent of applications were successful: see *Report of the Committee on Legal Aid and Legal Advice in England and Wales*, Cmd 6641 (London: HMSO, 1945), para 10. It was thought that many applications fell by the wayside because of problems with funding.

[265] See Lord Chancellor's Department, *The Poor Persons Rules Committee*, Cmd 430 (London: HMSO, 1919).

[266] *Report of the Committee on Legal Aid and Legal Advice in England and Wales*, Cmd 6641 (London: HMSO, 1945), paras 12–15.

was implemented, but it did not improve matters, not least because of difficulties in finding lawyers who were prepared to work for the meagre remuneration that was then on offer. The same Committee revisited the issue in 1925, when it recommended that the whole of the burden of representing poorer litigants be placed directly on the shoulders of the legal profession, who would be expected to provide representation free of charge, with the Law Society and every provincial law society given the task of organising this.[267] Public funds were to be made available, but only for administration costs.[268]

Unsurprisingly, the law societies did not find it easy to find solicitors who were prepared to work for free. Moreover, there was no comparable system for civil cases in the county courts.[269] For a period of time, the county courts followed the procedure that applied in the High Court,[270] but in 1922 the Court of Appeal explained that this was unlawful.[271] For this and other reasons (see 1.121), the scheme was not a success. **1.116**

The Hanworth Reports and the Peel Report

Other attempts at procedural reform in this period could be seen in the Hanworth Reports of 1933[272] and the Peel Report of 1936,[273] which made some streamlining changes to the different courts' jurisdictions and structure. **1.117**

Issues-based orders and fractional orders

After 1930, there was a different approach to the way in which the court dealt with the costs of issues. First, only the increased costs of the issue were to be taken into account where the order gave a party the costs of the action except in so far as these related to issues on which that party had failed.[274] Secondly, there was an increasing judicial use of fractional orders to avoid the complicated, unpredictable and expensive taxations occasioned by orders as to costs requiring the taxation of costs of issues.[275] **1.118**

---

[267] See Lord Chancellor's Department, *The Poor Persons Rules Committee*, Cmd 2358 (London: HMSO, 1925).

[268] *Report of the Committee on Legal Aid and Legal Advice in England and Wales*, Cmd 6641 (London: HMSO, 1945), at para 20.

[269] *Ibid*, para 32, recorded the fact that '[n]o system has ever existed in the County Court for the assistance of Poor Persons engaged in litigation in that court'.

[270] In this regard, they were following *Chinn v Bullen* (1849) 13 JP 780, at 782.

[271] See *Cook v Imperial Tobacco Co* [1922] 2 KB 158. There was an earlier case that came to much the same conclusions (*Perry v London General Omnibus Co* [1916] 2 KB 335), but contemporary textbooks say that it was not until 1922 that practices changed: see, eg, Egerton, R, *Legal Aid* (London: Trench, Trubner & Co, 1945), p 23.

[272] *First Interim Report of the Royal Commission on the Business of the Courts Committee*, Cmd 4265 (London: HMSO, 1933); *Second Interim Report of the Royal Commission on the Business of the Courts Committee*, Cmd 4471 (London: HMSO, 1933); *Third and Final Report of the Royal Commission on the Business of the Courts Committee*, Cmd 5066 (London: HMSO, 1936).

[273] *Report of the Royal Commission on the Dispatch of Business at Common Law, 1934–36*, Cmd 5065 (London: HMSO, 1936)

[274] This was under the principle laid down in *George Holloway & Webb Ltd v Crompton* [1916] 2 Ch 436.

[275] An early example of such an order was *Willmott v Barber* [1880] 15 Ch D 96, at 105. A later example is *Cinema Press Ltd v Pictures & Pleasures Ltd* [1945] KB 356, at 361.

The Second World War and Post-War Times (1939–99)

The Second World War and its immediate aftermath (1939–50)

The Rushcliffe Report, the post-war settlement and legal aid

1.119 As is often the case, war proved to be the catalyst for societal change. The changes that were planned for after the First World War were profound. Whilst not as celebrated as the 1942 Beveridge Report or the Education Act 1944, the 1945 Rushcliffe Report[276] was a remarkable product of a remarkable time. The remit of the Rushcliffe Committee was:

> '... to enquire what facilities at present exist in England and Wales for giving legal advice and assistance to poor persons, and to make such recommendations as appear to be desirable for the purpose of securing that poor persons in need of legal advice may have such facilities at their disposal, and for modifying and improving, so far as seems expedient, the existing system whereby legal aid is available to poor persons in the conduct of litigation in which they are concerned, whether in civil or criminal courts'.[277]

1.120 One reason why the report was notable was because it was written whilst 'buzz bombs were wreaking terrific havoc, [and whilst] the civilian was silently suffering extreme deprivation of physical wants'[278]—put otherwise, whilst this country was still at war with Germany. Another reason why it was extraordinary is because it cost the then nearly bankrupt nation a mere £453 (of which £81 was the cost of printing).[279]

1.121 One of the problems the Committee found was that, during the Second World War, the number of practising solicitors had fallen from 17,000 to 7,000; as a result, there was insufficient capacity within the profession to carry out charitable work.[280] Moreover, there was a need to ensure that servicemen (who, on the whole, were not poor enough to pass the means test but were too poor to be able to afford private legal assistance) were treated fairly.[281] The Law Society had set up a department that provided legal advice to servicemen who were getting divorced, but the scope of that scheme was very limited.

1.122 The Rushcliffe Committee's recommendations led to legal aid being introduced in 1949.[282] It was, at that stage, run and managed by the Law Society. It should be noted, however, that legal aid was *not* one of the pillars of the new welfare state (those being the National Health Service, or NHS, universal housing, state security in the form of benefits and universal education). Perhaps this was for the reason given by Mr Justice Finlay (acting extra-judicially as the chair of a committee), who, when responding to a suggestion that there should be a 'legal hospital system' analogous to the NHS, expressed the view that whilst it

[276] *Report of the Committee on Legal Aid and Legal Advice in England and Wales*, Cmd 6641 (London: HMSO, 1945), which committee was chaired by Lord Rushcliffe.

[277] See *ibid*, at para 1.

[278] Elson, A, 'The Rushcliffe Report' (1946) 13 U Chic L Rev 131, at 132.

[279] See Cross, M, 'Legal Aid's Founding Text Turns 70', *Law Society Gazette*, 28 May 2013. This compares with the cost of Sir Rupert Jackson's civil costs review, which (according to an answer given in response to a freedom of information request made by the editor) was £11,915, exclusive of the cost of Sir Rupert's time.

[280] See *Report of the Committee on Legal Aid and Legal Advice in England and Wales*, Cmd 6641 (London: HMSO, 1945), at para 23.

[281] See *ibid*, at paras 24–26.

[282] See the Legal Aid and Advice Act 1949.

was in the state's interests for people to be healthy, it was not necessarily in its interest for them to be litigious.[283]

Notwithstanding this, legal aid was to be available in all courts and tribunals in which lawyers normally appeared for private clients (although, at first, it was targeted almost exclusively at family cases). Eligibility would be extended to those of 'small or moderate means', but there would be a sliding scale of contributions for those who could afford it. **1.123**

Professor Zuckerman has pointed out that when legal aid was introduced, hardly any consideration was given to the effect that the injection of a massive amount of money into the legal services' marketplace would have. He suggested that, in time, the increased funds acted in concert with existing inflationary factors to produce a tremendous upward pressure on lawyers' fees, which, he says, led to significant costs inflation.[284] **1.124**

The European Convention on Human Rights

Drafted in 1950, the European Convention on Human Rights came into force in 1953. The UK was a founding member of the Convention and was influential in its design; indeed, it was amongst the first states to ratify the treaty. **1.125**

The post-war period: the 1950s

Remuneration certificates and 'fair and reasonable' basis of assessment

The 1920 Rules and 1934 Orders (see 1.112) were revoked by the Solicitors Remuneration Order 1953,[285] which introduced two new concepts: the remuneration certificate (or, rather, its 1950s' equivalent); and a requirement to inform the client of the right to such a certificate. The 1953 Order also introduced the 'fair and reasonable' basis for assessing costs of non-contentious work as between solicitor and client. In particular, on any solicitor and client assessment of non-contentious costs, it was the duty of the solicitor to satisfy the costs judge as to the fairness and reasonableness of his charges. **1.126**

The Seven Pillars of Wisdom

The 1953 Order also provided that costs should be assessed with reference to certain prescribed factors, which, with biblical overtones,[286] became known as the seven pillars of wisdom. To deal with the perennial problem of overly long documents, express provision was made that non-contentious costs should be assessed by 'the number and importance of the documents prepared or perused, *without regard to length*' (emphasis added). **1.127**

Non-contentious and contentious business

In 1955, Denning LJ observed that the distinction between contentious and non-contentious costs was in need of clarification.[287] Parliament duly responded by enacting the Solicitors (Amendment) Act 1956; this provided a statutory definition (albeit a somewhat circular one) that, by and large, is the same as that which is still in use today (see 3.21–3.36). **1.128**

---

[283] See Brooke, H, 'The History of Legal Aid 1945 to 2010', 16 July 2016, available at https://sirhenrybrooke.me/2016/07/16/the-history-of-legal-aid-1945-to-2010

[284] See Zuckerman, AAS, 'A Reform of Civil Procedure, Rationing Justice Rather than Access to Justice' (1995) 22 J L & Soc 155, at 158.

[285] SI 1953/117.

[286] See Proverbs 9:1; the modern versions of the seven pillars are found in CPR, r 44.5(3).

[287] *In re a Solicitor* [1955] 2 QB 252, at 269.

The Evershed Report

1.129 In 1953, the Committee on Supreme Court Practice and Procedure, chaired by Lord Evershed, published its report.[288] The aim of the report was said to be to move towards a 'new approach towards less costly litigation'.[289] That report stated the principle that 'extravagant' costs should not be recoverable between opposing parties; it is now thought that Lord Evershed's concept of what was and what was not extravagant was, perhaps, the forerunner of modern proportionality.[290] In any event, changes were made in 1959 to the party and party basis of assessment. The test of what was 'necessary and proper' was retained, but the test was qualified as 'all such costs as were necessary or proper for the attainment of justice or for enforcing or defending the rights of the party whose costs are being taxed'.[291] Scale costs were also retained for certain types of case.

1.130 Another innovation that followed the Evershed Report was the introduction of a procedure known as the robust summons—but it was not a success. The idea was that the parties would give disclosure at an early stage, following which a named judge would give directions for trial that the judge would then hear. Within about two years, the robust summons procedure had become memory,[292] one commentator even going so far as to say that the attempt 'bordered on the cute'.[293] Sir Frederick Lawton blamed this on the fact that the procedure 'had been rendered naught largely by the legal profession's dislike of, and resistance to, change ... Effecting a change of attitude in the lawyers is likely to be more difficult than changing the rules of court.'[294] Zuckerman's axiom (see 1.03) comes to mind.

The post-war period: the 1960s

Rules of the Supreme Court 1965

1.131 By the middle of the 20th century, the Rules of the Supreme Court 1883 had been amended so often that they were made up of 144 separate Orders and Rules and nine Acts;[295] this was why the Evershed Report (see 1.129) recommended that 'a complete revision of the Rules be immediately put in hand'.[296] The new rules—the Rules of the Supreme Court 1965—took over a decade to write.[297] They came into force on 1 October 1966.

Maintenance, champerty and conditional fee agreements

1.132 In 1966, the Law Commission proposed that maintenance and champerty should be decriminalised; this was achieved in 1967.[298] At that stage, the Law Commission continued

288 *Final Report of the Committee on Supreme Court Practice and Procedure*, Cmnd 8878 (London: HMSO, 1953).

289 *Ibid*, at p 37.

290 See Jackson, R, *Review of Civil Litigation Costs: Final Report* (London: HMSO, 2009), para 3.1.

291 RSC Ord 62, r 28(2).

292 See the long letter written by Sir Frederick Lawton published in *The Times*, 28 June 1995. Also see Gower, LC, 'The Cost of Litigation' (1954) 17 MLR 1.

293 Clark, 'The Evershed Report and Civil Procedural Reform' (1954) 29 NYU L Rev 1046, n 1.

294 See the long letter written by Sir Frederick Lawton published in *The Times*, 28 June 1995.

295 The Supreme Court Practice 1967, vol 1, Preface to the first edition.

296 *Evershed Committee on Supreme Court Practice and Procedure Second: Second Interim Report*, Cmd 8176 (London: HMSO, 1951), para 117.

297 Work started shortly after Evershed's final report in 1953. Around half of the rules were revised and introduced on 1 January 1964—see RSC (Revision) 1962 (SI 1962/2145)—with the remaining rules being revised by RSC (Revision) 1965 (SI 1965/1776).

298 See Criminal Law Act 1967, s 14(2).

to refuse to recommend making conditional fee agreements lawful,[299] but this had, at least, become a topic for discussion.

The post-war period: the 1970s

Access to justice

In response to calls for the wider availability of affordable legal advice,[300] the first publicly funded law centre was opened in 1970. In 1973, a scheme was introduced by the Law Society known as the 'green form' scheme. This scheme allowed a person to receive advice and assistance from a solicitor on any matter of English law on the basis of a simplified test of income and expenditure. It has been suggested that the scheme was in response to the perceived threat that law centres posed to traditional solicitors' practices.[301] **1.133**

The Association of Law Costs Draftsmen

The Association of Costs Lawyers—then known as the Association of Law Costs Draftsmen (ALCD)—was established in 1977. At this stage, neither it nor its members were regulated. **1.134**

The emerging use of hourly rates

As far as this editor's research has revealed (see 51.03–51.11), routine use of hourly rates began to emerge in the late 1960s, perhaps as a result of cross-pollination from secondary legislation relating to family law and legal aid.[302] By the mid-1970s, charging by time was established in matrimonial cases (although hourly rates sat alongside scale costs, rather than replaced them).[303] By the late 1970s, hourly rates began to appear in civil cases (see 51.09), but they were not even remotely regarded as being 'the' way in which costs were assessed. In *Treasury Solicitor v Regester & Anor*,[304] for example, Donaldson J commented that hourly rates were 'only one of a number of cross-checks on the fairness and reasonableness of the final figure'. **1.135**

The post-war period: the 1980s

The rise of the use of hourly rates

Donaldson J returned to the topic of hourly rates in *R v Wilkinson*,[305] a criminal case. The solicitor relied on the 'Expense of Time' calculation (see 51.27) in preparing his bill; Donaldson J made a number of comments about that calculation that led, in 1988, to the Law Society revising its guidance and to that guidance becoming more commonly used. It would seem that the hegemony of hourly rates took off from there, despite the fact that it was expressly stated in *The Expense of Time* that the publication was intended to be a tool for management purposes rather than for the ascertainment of costs (see 51.10). **1.136**

---

299 *Proposals for Reform of the Law Relating to Champerty and Maintenance*, Law Com No 7 (London: HMSO, 1966), para 19, and *Sixth Annual Report 1970–1971*, Law Com No 47 (London: HMSO, 1971), pp 7–8, paras 33–35.

300 Lord Chancellor's Advisory Committee on Legal Aid 1970.

301 See Pickup, D, 'Green Forms and Fixed Fees', *Law Society Gazette*, 4 April 2012. This, however, may not be correct: in 1979, the Law Society told the Royal Commission on Legal Services that law centres were not a threat. Indeed, they generated work for private practices: see Brooke, H, 'The History of Legal Aid 1945 to 2010', 16 July 2016, available at https://sirhenrybrooke.me/2016/07/16/the-history-of-legal-aid-1945-to-2010

302 Such as the Matrimonial Causes (Costs) Rates 1968.

303 See, eg, *Castillejo v Castillejo*, The Times, 12 December 1974; see also *Dwyer v Dwyer* [1976] 2 All ER 1.

304 *Treasury Solicitor v Regester & Anor* [1978] 1 WLR 446.

305 *R v Wilkinson* [1980] 1 WLR 396.

The County Court Rules 1981

1.137 On 1 September 1982, the County Court Rules 1981[306] came into force, replacing the County Court Rules 1936. The rules relating to the costs (that is, Order 38) were stated more simply and concisely than previously.[307] The time for lodging a bill of costs was extended from 14 days to three months after the making of the order for costs; the registrar was given the option of either fixing an appointment or carrying out a provisional taxation (that is, a provisional assessment in the absence of the parties).[308] The time limits for 'bringing in objections' (this being the equivalent of contemporary points of dispute) and thereafter applying for a review of taxation were also extended. That said, objections were considered without a hearing.[309] There were three appendices (A, B and C), which dealt with Higher Scales of Costs, Fixed Costs and the Assessment of Costs, respectively. Costs were payable according to four scales of costs—namely, a lower scale and three higher scales, as set out in Appendix A.[310]

1.138 If the person receiving costs was the claimant, the value of the claim was determined by the amount recovered, but if that person was the defendant, then the value was determined by the amount claimed.[311] If, however, the judge certified that a difficult question of law or a question of fact of exceptional complexity had been involved, the judge was entitled to award costs on any scale.[312] Moreover, where, in any proceedings in which the costs were to be assessed, and where the judge was satisfied from the nature of the case or the conduct of the proceedings that costs which may be allowed on assessment may be inadequate in the circumstances, the judge was able to issue a certificate that permitted such larger sum as may be appropriate.[313] This power could be exercised either by the judge who made the order for costs or by the judge who carried out the assessment.[314]

1.139 The scales themselves were flexible; rather than stating a single set figure, they would often merely state a range of figures or a cap and, where this was so, the court exercised its discretion within the stated limits.[315] Costs that were not in the scale would either be assessed solely on the grounds of reasonableness or would be assessed by reference to scale costs of a similar nature.[316]

---

306 SI 1981/1687.

307 See the Explanatory Note to SI 1981/1687, at para 29.

308 CCR 1981, Ord 38, r 20.

309 CCR 1981, Ord 38, r 24.

310 CCR 1981, Ord 38, r 3(3). In relation to a claim for money only, the scales were: exceeding £25, but not exceeding £100 (lower scale); exceeding £100, but not exceeding £500 (scale 1); exceeding £500, but not exceeding £3,000 (scale 2); and exceeding £3,000 (scale 3). In very general terms, costs on scale 3 were either assessed without prescribed limit or were subject to a fairly generous cap. The Higher Scales of Costs were in five parts: Part I included fees for institution of proceedings, interlocutory proceedings, documentary work and copying; Part II was the 'Block Allowance'; Part III was for preparation for trial; Part IV was for attendances (such as lodging papers, attending counsel, interlocutory attendances, examinations and attendances at trial); and Part V was counsel's fees. The Block Allowance (ie Part II) applied in any action for damages for personal injuries, or for the cost of repairs to collision-damaged vehicles, and in any other action or matter as the party entitled to receive the costs may elect. It was an allowance that was intended to cover all of the work that would otherwise have been covered by Part I.

311 CCR 1981, Ord 38, r 4(1).

312 CCR 1981, Ord 38, r 4(6).

313 CCR 1981, Ord 38, r 9. This did not apply to a part of the costs, known as a block allowance.

314 CCR 1981, Ord 38, r 9(5).

315 See CCR 1981, Ord 38, r 5.

316 See CCR 1981, Ord 38, r 12(1).

The creation of the Legal Aid Board

In 1988, the responsibility for the administration of legal aid was transferred from the Law Society to the Legal Aid Board.[317] This was to resolve the anomalous position of the Law Society being both the paymaster and representative of the profession receiving funds.[318] To avoid allegations of conflict, the new body was created as a non-departmental public body (that is, independently of what is now the Ministry of Justice). **1.140**

Public funding and access to justice

Legal aid always had its imperfections (the most notable of which was the fact that successful defendants could not recover their costs, meaning that they were exposed to pressures to settle unmeritorious claims). Those systemic imperfections grew as legal aid became more and more restricted to those of more limited means. By the 1980s, it had become clear that—unless they were supported by a funder, such as a union or insurer—only the poor or the wealthy could afford to litigate. Indeed, the situation was perceived as being so concerning that the UK's compliance with Article 6 of the European Convention on Human Rights (that is, the obligation to provide effective access to the civil courts) was being put at risk.[319] **1.141**

The Hodgson Review

The cost and delay involved in civil litigation continued to be a source of concern. A civil justice review (which was chaired by Lord Hodgson) was carried out in 1988,[320] but its recommendations were largely rejected.[321] It recommended that High Court litigation should be confined to public law cases, specialist cases (such as commercial litigation and Admiralty) and cases involving important, complex or substantial claims; in the event, the only change of note that was made was the fact that county courts' jurisdiction was extended.[322] **1.142**

Conditional fee agreements

Another recommendation of the Hodgson Review was that the law of conditional fee agreements ought to be re-evaluated.[323] This recommendation was made because attitudes towards such agreements were beginning to change and, in 1989, the political mood began to shift in their favour.[324] The relevant statutory provisions were swiftly made,[325] although it was some years before the requisite delegated legislation was made (see 1.155). **1.143**

---

[317] By the Legal Aid Act 1988, s 3.

[318] See Lord Chancellor's Department, *Legal Aid Efficiency Scrutiny* (London: HMSO, 1986) and Lord Chancellor's Department, *Legal Aid, England and Wales: A New Framework*, Cm 118 (London: HMSO, 1987).

[319] See, eg, *Airey v Ireland* (1978–80) 2 EHRR 305.

[320] *Civil Justice Review: Report of the Review Body on Civil Justice*, Cm 394 (London: HMSO, 1988).

[321] See the 30-page note in *Civil Justice Quarterly* (1988), at 281–312; see also Thomas, R, 'Civil Justice Review: Treating Litigants as Consumers' (1990) 6 CJQ 51.

[322] The High Court and County Courts Jurisdiction Order 1991 (SI 1991/724). See Andrews, N, *Principles of Civil Procedure* (London: Sweet & Maxwell, 1994), p 68.

[323] *Civil Justice Review: Report of the Review Body on Civil Justice*, Cm 394 (London: HMSO, 1988), paras 384–389.

[324] See the Lord Chancellor's Green Paper, *Contingency Fees*, Cm 571 (London: HMSO, 1989), and the White Paper, *Legal Services: A Framework for the Future*, Cm 740 (London: HMSO, 1990).

[325] See s 58 of the Courts and Legal Services Act 1990, as originally enacted.

Standard and indemnity bases of assessment

1.144 The party and party basis of assessment (see 1.97 and 1.129) remained until 28 April 1986, when it was replaced by the standard basis of assessment.[326] This allowed recovery of 'a reasonable amount in respect of all costs reasonably incurred'. Orders could also be made for costs on the indemnity basis. The reason for the change was the perception that costs on the party and party basis were too limited to compensate the receiving party properly for costs reasonably incurred. Scale charges were retained for several types of county court work,[327] but a fundamental change was that all costs which were not fixed were discretionary and were to be amenable to assessment.

The post-war period: the 1990s

The Woolf Review

1.145 In the early 1990s, there was unease about the health of the civil litigation system in general (and costs in particular).[328] In 1994, the Lord Chancellor asked Lord Woolf, then Master of the Rolls, to carry out a review of civil justice. In his Interim Report, Lord Woolf highlighted the problems of 'excessive and unaffordable costs' and of 'disproportionate costs', commenting that 'the problem of costs is the most serious problem besetting our litigation system'.[329] He went on to say (of the state of the civil justice system):

> 'Without effective control ... the adversarial process is likely to encourage an adversarial cultural and to degenerate into an environment in which the litigation process is too often seen as a battlefield where no rules apply. In this environment, question of expense, delay, compromise and fairness have only a low priority. The consequence is that the expense is often excessive, disproportionate and unpredictable; and delay is frequently unreasonable.'[330]

1.146 Lord Woolf made a number of observations that, whilst counter-intuitive, support Zuckerman's axiom (see 1.03). In particular, he noted that whilst the rules concerning the exchange of witness statements may have lowered trial costs (which was their intended purpose), this was at the expense of higher costs in general.[331]

1.147 In his Final Report (published in 1996), Lord Woolf identified a number of objectives, including that parties should be encouraged to explore alternative methods of dispute resolution, that there should be a single set of rules governing proceedings in the High Court and the county courts, that there should be a shortening of the time it took for cases to reach trial, that there should be protocols to govern the case management of certain types of claim and that there should be more case management by judges.[332]

---

326 See Rules of the Supreme Court (Amendment No 3) 1986 (SI 1986/2289).

327 CCR, Ord 38, r 19(3).

328 See, eg, *Report of the General Council of the Bar and the Law Society of the United Kingdom: Civil Justice on Trial—The Case for Change* (London: Law Society, 1993).

329 *Access to Justice: Interim Report to the Lord Chancellor on the Civil Justice System in England and Wales* (London: HMSO, 1995), at ch 3, paras 13–28.

330 *Ibid*, Introduction, at p 3.

331 See Glasser, C, 'Solving the Litigation Crisis' (1994) 1 The Litigator 14; also see Zuckerman, AAS, 'A Reform of Civil Procedure: Rationing Justice Rather than Access to Justice' (1995) 22 J L & Soc 155, at 158.

332 *Access to Justice: Final Report to the Lord Chancellor on the Civil Justice System in England and Wales* (London: HMSO, 1996), ch 7. Also see Zuckerman, A, 'Lord Woolf's Access to Justice: Plus ça Change ...' (1996) 59 MLR 773, at 8.

The Middleton Review

Not everyone applauded Lord Woolf's proposals. In particular, Professor Zander (who, at the time, held a chair at the London School of Economics) argued that the problem was the very nature of the task of going to court in an adversarial system of law; he was concerned by the fact that the recommendations seemed not to be based on any research as to what, if anything, was wrong with the existing adjectival law.[333] By that stage, there had been a change of government and the new government thought it prudent to ask for a review—which was carried out by Sir Peter Middleton, a former permanent secretary to the Treasury. In September 1997, Middleton published a review that largely endorsed Woolf's recommendations.[334] Middleton expressed the view that conditional fee agreements could be used to replace legal aid in civil money claims. In due course, a White Paper on the topic was published.[335] This ultimately led to the changes discussed in 1.157. **1.148**

The indemnity principle revived

In 1993, the Divisional Court upheld a challenge by a losing party to a claim for costs based on an agreement under which the winner's solicitor was entirely dependent for payment on winning the case and recovering costs from her opponent.[336] This case reminded costs practitioners of the existence and utility of the indemnity principle; as a result, disputes concerning the indemnity principle gained traction.[337] This, it has been said, was one of the factors that ultimately led to the 'costs war' (see 1.58).[338] **1.149**

Solicitors' remuneration

The modern regime of solicitor and client assessments was ushered in by the Solicitors' (Non-Contentious Business) Remuneration Order 1994, which was—and, in its modern guise,[339] still is—similar to the 1953 Order, in that it provided that solicitors' costs were to be such sum as might be fair and reasonable to both solicitor and client. The client retained the right (now revoked[340]) to a certificate, which was then known as a remuneration certificate; the solicitor retained the duty to inform the client of their rights to seek to obtain a remuneration certificate and to have the bill taxed. **1.150**

Legal aid

In 1993, the government lowered the financial eligibility limits for civil legal aid and increased the levels of contributions payable.[341] In addition, it limited the availability of 'green form' advice and assistance.[342] **1.151**

---

333 See, eg, Zander, M, 'The Government's Plans on Legal Aid and Conditional Fees' (1998) 61 MLR 538.

334 Sir Peter Middleton GCB, *Report to the Lord Chancellor on the Review of Civil Justice and Legal Aid* (London: HMSO, 1997).

335 Lord Chancellor's Department, *Modernising Justice: The Government's Plans for Reforming Legal Services and the Courts*, Cm 4155 (London: HMSO, 1998).

336 *British Waterways Board v Norman* (1994) 26 HLR 232.

337 See Jackson, R, *Review of Civil Litigation Costs: Preliminary Report* (London: HMSO, 2009), ch 3, para 5.4.

338 *Ibid.*

339 Solicitors (Non-Contentious Business) Remuneration Order 2009, as amended.

340 *Ibid.*

341 Civil Legal Aid (Assessment of Resources)(Amendment) Regulations 1993 (SI 1993/788).

342 Legal Advice and Assistance Regulations 1993 (SI 1993/790).

1.152 In July 1995, the Lord Chancellor responded to pressure from the Treasury by publishing a Green Paper[343] in which he outlined radical proposals for altering the existing legal aid scheme. By far the most important proposal was that legal aid expenditure should be capped or subject to a ceiling. Fierce criticism followed, but this did not prevent the Lord Chancellor from publishing a White Paper[344] that included suggestions that:

- the legal aid budget as a whole should be capped;
- all providers should be franchised and should bid for resources from within these budgets;
- legal aid should be available from a range of service providers, including, but not limited to, lawyers in private practice; and
- a new range of contributions should become payable.

That White Paper ultimately led to the changes referred to in 1.163.

Consumer surveys

1.153 In 1995, a survey was carried out by the National Consumer Council,[345] which found that three out of four people who had been involved in serious legal disputes were dissatisfied with the civil justice system. It found that, of the 1,019 respondents, 77 per cent believed that the system was too slow, 74 per cent stated that the system was too complicated, and 73 per cent said that it was unwelcoming and outdated.[346]

1.154 In the 1990s, the liberal professions (in general) were moving away from reliance on tradition and opinion, towards evidence-based practices.[347] In line with this, it was thought that empirical research (that is, observable research) was needed if any decision were to be made about the way in which consumers use legal services. The first such survey was the Paths to Justice Survey in 1997.[348] This was followed in successive decades by the Civil and Social Justice Survey, which was carried out in 2001, 2004, 2006–09, 2010 and 2012.[349] Those surveys were large-scale, nationally representative household surveys that provided detailed information on the prevalence of issues regarding legal services.[350] They provided an insight into ordinary people's experience of legal issues and their strategies for dealing with them.[351]

---

[343] Lord Chancellor's Department, *Legal Aid: Targeting Need—The Future of Publicly Funded Help in Solving Legal Problems and Disputes in England and Wales*, Cm 2854 (London: HMSO, 1995).

[344] Lord Chancellor's Department, *Striking the Balance: The Future of Legal Aid in England and Wales*, Cm 3305 (London: HMSO, 1996).

[345] National Consumer Council, *Seeking Civil Justice: A Survey of People's Needs and Experiences* (London: NCC, 1995).

[346] Slapper, G, 'The Civil Process', in Slapper, G, and Kelly, D (eds), *The English Legal System* (9th edn, London: Routledge, 2008), ch 9, at p 334.

[347] In medicine, for example, the concept of evidence-based medicine was introduced in 1992; in due course, this became evidence-based practice (EBP).

[348] Genn, H, *Paths to Justice: What People Do and Think about Going to Law* (Oxford: Hart, 1999).

[349] For example, Pleasence, P, and Balmer, NJ, *Civil Justice in England and Wales: Report of the 2006–09 English and Welsh Civil and Social Justice Survey* (London: Legal Services Commission, 2010); also see Pleasence, P, et al, *Civil Justice in England and Wales 2010: Report of the First Wave of the English and Welsh Civil and Social Justice Panel Survey* (London: Legal Services Commission, 2011).

[350] These comments were made by Ames, A, Dawes, W, and Cooke, A, *Online Survey of Individuals' Handling of Legal Issues in England and Wales 2015* (London: Ipsos Mori, 2016), para 2.2.

[351] *Ibid.* It is therefore somewhat surprising that there seems to have been little liaison between the researchers and costs practitioners. Not only have most costs practitioners never heard of the surveys, but also

Conditional fee agreements

Conditional fee agreements became a practical reality in 1995 when the necessary delegated legislation was made.[352] With certain limited exceptions, they were permitted only in personal injury work, in cases of insolvency and in cases before the European Commission of Human Rights.[353] In 1997, Lord Woolf's report (see 1.145) was followed by a review of legal aid by Sir Peter Middleton (see 1.148), whose review recommended the wider implementation of conditional funding.[354] In 1998, legislation was enacted that effectively extended conditional funding to include all civil claims (but not family cases).[355] At that stage, there was no provision for the recovery of a success fee from an unsuccessful opponent. **1.155**

The Civil Procedure Rules 1998

Lord Woolf's recommendations resulted in the introduction of the Civil Procedure Rules 1998 (CPR), which became effective on 26 April 1999. The new Rules of Court were a 'new procedural code'[356] (see 26.02) that introduced the notion of the 'overriding objective' (see 26.04). The CPR retained the standard basis of assessment, but altered the way in which the costs were to be assessed—in particular, subjecting costs to a test of 'proportionality'. The courts soon interpreted the CPR as encouraging a more liberal approach to the incidence of costs than had existed previously. Judges were encouraged not to automatically award the winner the entirety of their costs, but to make separate orders that reflected the outcome of different issues.[357] **1.156**

The New Millennium

The first decade (1999–2009)

Additional liabilities became recoverable

In April 2000, the statutory provisions relating to conditional fee agreements were amended to permit the recovery of success fees from unsuccessful opponents;[358] similar provisions were made for the recovery of after-the-event insurance premiums.[359] At about the same time—as is explained below—legal aid was, for all practical purposes, withdrawn for personal injury work (except clinical negligence), fatal accidents and a whole swathe of other types of claim. This heralded a shift from public funding to conditional funding. **1.157**

---

the surveys themselves present their findings in a way that makes little sense to costs practitioners (the prime example of this being the fact that next to no distinction is made between contentious business and non-contentious business).

352 See the Conditional Fee Agreements Regulations 1995 (SI 1995/1675) and the Conditional Fee Agreements Order 1995 (SI 1995/1674).

353 Conditional Fee Agreements Order 1995 (SI 1995/1674), art 2(1).

354 Sir Peter Middleton GCB, *Report to the Lord Chancellor on the Review of Civil Justice and Legal Aid* (London: HMSO, 1997), Executive Summary, at para 10.

355 Conditional Fee Agreements Order 1998 (SI 1998/1860).

356 CPR, r 1.1(1) (SI 3132/1998). For an extended discussion, see Sorabji, J, *English Civil Justice after the Woolf and Jackson Reforms: A Critical Analysis* (Cambridge: Cambridge University Press, 2014).

357 See *Phonographic Performance Ltd v AEI Rediffusion Music Ltd* [1999] 1 WLR 1507, at 1522.

358 See the Conditional Fee Agreements Regulations 2000 (SI 2000/692) and the Conditional Fee Agreements Order 2000 (SI 2000/823).

359 See the Access to Justice Act 1999, s 29.

The costs war

1.158 The regulations governing conditional fee agreements led to a surge in satellite litigation concerning costs. The result was the 'costs war' of the early 2000s.[360] It is now the received view that the costs war had two phases, the first being up to the decision of the Court of Appeal in *Hollins v Russell*,[361] (May 2003) and the second following that decision.[362]

1.159 Speaking extrajudicially, Sir Rupert Jackson identified the following trends as being some of the factors that led to that war:

- the renewed interest that costs draftpersons had for the indemnity principle (see 1.149);
- the rise of the 'costs negotiator'[363] (especially where such people were working on a basis whereby their remuneration was linked to performance); and
- the increased financial pressure placed upon liability insurers as a result of credit-hire claims.[364]

1.160 In an attempt to bring that 'war' to an early end, simplified regulations were introduced for certain types of conditional fee agreement (that is, 'CFAs Lite').[365] At the same time, the government brought into force s 31 of the Access to Justice Act 1999, which enabled the Rules Committee to disapply the indemnity principle—which was done, but only for cases in which CFAs Lite were used.

1.161 The CFA Lite provisions were made without consultation and did not have the impact that was intended. In November 2005, the regulations relating to conditional fee agreements were revoked entirely.[366] Two years later, changes were made to the professional rules that govern solicitors, which changes made consumer protection in conditional funding a professional, rather than a regulatory, matter.[367]

1.162 Whilst many practitioners would disagree, there are those who believe that the costs war lingered until 2008.[368] It has been said that a factor that played a large part in ending the war was the fact that fixed recoverable costs (see 1.168) took the wind out of the belligerents' sails[369] (especially given the fact that, in 2006, the Court of Appeal confirmed that the indemnity principle does not apply to fixed recoverable costs[370]).

---

360 The phrase 'costs war' was used by the Civil Justice Council in its press release, 'Further Success for the Civil Justice Council: Helping to Bring an End to the "Costs War" ', October 2003; see also *Tankard v John Fredricks Plastics Ltd* [2008] EWCA Civ 1375, at [2]. For a more detailed account, see Kalish, SE, 'The English Costs War, 2002–2003, and a Moment of Repose' (2004) 83 Nebraska L Rev 114.

361 *Hollins v Russell* [2003] EWCA Civ 718.

362 Jackson, R, *Review of Civil Litigation Costs: Preliminary Report* (London: HMSO, 2009), ch 3, at paras 5.16 and 5.32.

363 These were costs specialists, sometimes costs draftpersons and sometimes not, employed by liability insurers to secure a reduction in the costs that the insurer had to pay successful claimants.

364 Jackson, R, *Review of Civil Litigation Costs: Preliminary Report* (London: HMSO, 2009), ch 3, at paras 5.2–5.8.

365 Conditional Fee Agreements (Miscellaneous Amendments) Regulations 2003 (SI 2003/1240).

366 See the Conditional Fee Agreements (Revocation) Regulations 2005 (SI 2005/2305).

367 See Solicitors' Code of Conduct 2007, r 2.

368 See, eg, Pawlowski, M, 'Beneficial Ownership and Detriment' (2008) 152 Solicitors Journal 16, at 18–19.

369 See Jackson, R, *Review of Civil Litigation Costs: Preliminary Report* (London: HMSO, 2009), ch 3, at para 5.29.

370 *Nizami v Butt* [2006] EWHC 159 (QB).

Legal aid

Whilst the Legal Aid Board was, in many ways, a success, there were concerns about its cost and effectiveness. There was a strong feeling that funding was not necessarily being directed at the right cases—in particular, that civil certificates were dominated by the funding of mainstream personal injury claims.[371] There were concerns that the scheme was not proactive and that the Legal Aid Board was essentially a passive funder making decisions on the applications that it received.[372] Moreover, the Middleton Review (see 1.148) had concluded that conditional fee agreements should replace legal aid in most civil money claims. **1.163**

The Access to Justice Act 1999 changed a great deal.[373] On 2 April 2001, the Legal Aid Board was abolished and replaced with an independent government agency, the Legal Services Commission.[374] This was tasked with developing and maintaining the Community Legal Service. Lord Irvine (then Lord Chancellor) had this to say about the role that organisation would play: **1.164**

> 'The CLS is the first attempt ever by government to deliver legal services in a joined up way. It will provide a framework for comprehensive local networks of good quality legal advice services supported by co-ordinated funding, and based on the needs of local people.'[375]

In 2000, legal aid ceased to be routinely available in personal injury claims (other than those for clinical negligence), claims brought by business, boundary disputes, and claims arising out of company and trust law. These changes had a dramatic effect on expenditure on non-family civil cases in that expenditure would fall from about £400m in 1997 to about £200m in 2005.[376] **1.165**

A Funding Code was created, as a set of rules drawn up by the Legal Services Commission, but approved by ministers. Any amendments to the Code involving substantive, rather than procedural, change would require approval of both Houses of Parliament.[377] **1.166**

On 2 March 2005, the government announced a package of measures to reform civil legal aid.[378] This followed the Consultation Paper.[379] The main theme of the paper was to refocus the civil legal aid scheme to encourage early resolution in civil dispute cases and the use of alternative dispute resolution (ADR) measures, such as negotiation or mediation, and to direct it away from contested litigation. This led to certain changes (known as the New Focus) being implemented in April 2005. The New Focus consultation confirmed that clinical negligence was not (at that time) an appropriate area for conditional fee agreements.[380] **1.167**

---

[371] According to Sir Rupert Jackson, in the mid-1990s the Legal Aid Board issued more than 100,000 certificates per year for personal injury claims: see Jackson, R, *Review of Civil Litigation Costs: Preliminary Report* (London: HMSO, 2009), ch 12, at para 1.6.

[372] *Ibid.*

[373] See the Access to Justice Act 1999, Pt I.

[374] See the Legal Aid Board (Abolition) Order 2001 (SI 2001/779).

[375] See the speech given by Lord Irvine at the Law Society's conference in Cardiff in October 1997.

[376] See the graph on p 26 of Sir Ian Magee, *Review of Legal Aid Delivery and Governance* (London: HMSO, 2010).

[377] See s 9(6) of the Access to Justice Act 1999.

[378] See *A Fairer Deal for Legal Aid*, Cm 6591 (London: HMSO, 2005), Pt 6, 'Delivering a Fairer Deal: Helping Vulnerable and Disadvantaged People to Solve Their Disputes Faster', at para 6.12.

[379] Legal Services Commission, *A New Focus for Civil Legal Aid: Encouraging Early Resolution; Discouraging Unnecessary Litigation* (London: LSC, 2004).

[380] See *A Fairer Deal for Legal Aid*, Cm 6591 (London: HMSO, 2005), Pt 6, 'Delivering a Fairer Deal: Helping Vulnerable and Disadvantaged People to Solve Their Disputes Faster', at para 6.15.

Fixed fees

1.168 In December 2002, the Civil Justice Council organised an industry-wide quasi-mediation to agree a solution to the problems that were being experienced, particularly in the low-value bulk road traffic accident (RTA) market.[381] A measure of agreement was reached and there was a broad consensus on the shape of a scheme to fix costs in this area. This ultimately gave rise to CPR, Part 45, Section II (that is, the scheme for 'fixed recoverable costs' in RTA cases settled for no more than £10,000). The scheme applied to RTAs occurring after 5 October 2003.[382]

1.169 Similar provisions were introduced in 2004 in relation to employers' liability claims and industrial disease claims.[383] It is worth noting that the number of consumers who take advantage of fixed fees has steadily increased such that, in 2015, it was said to be as high as 46 per cent.[384]

The Clementi Review

1.170 The Office of Fair Trading (OFT) carried out a review of the way in which legal services were provided[385] and, in 2004, this gave rise to a major review of the legal services regulatory framework by Sir David Clementi. That report ultimately gave rise to the changes made by the Legal Services Act 2007.

Modern times (2009–15)

The Jackson Review

1.171 In January 2009, Master of the Rolls Sir Anthony Clarke appointed Sir Rupert Jackson to carry out a review of the rules and principles governing the costs of civil litigation. The still-evolving reforms resulting from the Jackson Review (sometimes known as the Civil Costs Review) are generally referred to as 'the Jackson reforms' (see 1.174). The Review had three phases, as follows.

Phase 1 (January–April 2009) Fact-finding, preliminary consultation and preparation of the Preliminary Report[386]
Phase 2 (May–July 2009) Consultation
Phase 3 (September–December 2009) An analysis of material received and preparation of the Final Report[387]

1.172 In addition to these formal phases, there were pilot exercises, such as the pilots relating to costs budgeting (see 12.10) and to provisional assessments (see 43.198–43.199). The Jackson Review differed from previous reviews in that it was not merely about court procedure and how to minimise costs, but also about how much was being received by lawyers—in particular, a concern that there was 'too much money swirling around in the system' (to use Sir Rupert

381 Jackson, R, *Review of Civil Litigation Costs: Preliminary Report* (London: HMSO, 2009), ch 3, at para 5.26.
382 See CPR, Pt 45 III.
383 See CPR, Pt 45 IV and V.
384 See Competition and Markets Authority, *Legal Services Market Study: Interim Report* (London: CMA, 2016), n 11.
385 See Office of Fair Trading, *Competition in Professions*, OFT328 (London: OFT, 2001).
386 Jackson, R, *Review of Civil Litigation Costs: Preliminary Report* (London: HMSO, 2009).
387 Jackson, R, *Review of Civil Litigation Costs: Final Report* (London: HMSO, 2010).

Jackson's words).[388] This focus on profits, as opposed to costs, was new and, unless one goes back to Bentham's observation that costs are 'the grand instrument of mischief in English practice' (see 1.74) and the Leases Act 1845 (see 1.81), the Jackson Review was qualitatively different from previous reviews.

The Final Report of the Jackson Review was published on time in December 2009.[389] The incoming government (which did not initiate the Jackson Review, but subsequently elected to adopt it) began its own consultation in November 2010. In March 2011, it published its response,[390] in which Secretary of State (Kenneth Clarke) had this to say: **1.173**

> '[I]n recent years, the system has got out of kilter, fuelled to a significant extent by the way that 'no win, no fee' conditional fee agreements (CFAs) now work. They have played an important role in extending access to justice but they also enable claims to be pursued with no real risk to claimants and the threat of excessive costs to defendants. It cannot be right that, regardless of the extreme weakness of a claim, the sensible thing for the defendant to do is to settle, and get out before the legal costs start running up.'

Thus the political will to implement the reforms was there. This led to the Jackson reforms.

The Jackson reforms

The Jackson reforms mostly came into force on 1 April 2013. Prior to that, the senior judiciary had been keeping the public up to date by giving a series of implementation lectures.[391] There were three methods by which the proposed reforms were implemented, as follows. **1.174**

- **Primary legislation** Parts of the reforms were effected by primary legislation. The necessary Act—the Legal Aid, Sentencing and Punishment of Offenders Act 2012—received royal assent on 1 May 2012.
- **Secondary legislation and rule changes** (in particular, changes to the CPR)
- **Judicial supervision** A Judicial Steering Group (JSG) was created, chaired by the Master of the Rolls.

The reforms abrogated duplex costs shifting in many personal injury claims, created budgeting and costs management, expanded the ambit of fixed fees, and abrogated the recoverability of most success fees and after-the-event premiums. **1.175**

Contrary to Sir Rupert's recommendations, legal aid for civil claims was cut back so far that, for all practical purposes, it almost ceased to exist (see 1.183). This was unfortunate, because it meant that whilst many of the changes that had originally been made in 2000 were reversed, this did not extend to the reinstatement of public funding; the effect was to leave a considerable hiatus in the availability of funding. **1.176**

The Young Report

It will be recalled that, in 2011, then Secretary of State Kenneth Clarke said that access to justice had got 'out of kilter' in that defendants were finding it commercially difficult **1.177**

---

[388] Jackson, R, 'Legal Aid and the Costs Review Reforms', Talk delivered to the Cambridge Law Faculty, 5 September 2011, at p 4.

[389] *Ibid.*

[390] *Reforming Civil Litigation Funding and Costs in England and Wales: Implementation of Lord Justice Jackson's Recommendations—The Government Response*, Cm 8041 (London: HMSO, 2011).

[391] Those lectures can be found online at https://www.judiciary.gov.uk/publications/review-of-civil-litigation-costs-lectures/

to defend claims (see 1.173). Those comments were made shortly after his government had published *Common Sense, Common Safety*, a report written by Lord Young on what is commonly described as the 'compensation culture'. The general tone of that controversial report can be gleaned from the following passage:

> 'It may seem unusual to commence a review of health and safety with the state of litigation in the country but I believe that a "compensation culture" driven by litigation is at the heart of the problems that so beset health and safety today. Last year over 800,000 compensation claims were made in the UK while stories of individuals suing their employers for disproportionately large sums of money for personal injury claims, often for the most trivial of reasons, are a regular feature in our newspapers.'[392]

1.178 It is not only politicians who have raised such concerns. Sir Rupert Jackson has had some fairly forthright things to say about the compensation industry too:

> 'In the context of personal injury litigation, one consequence of the recoverability regime [ie the recoverability of additional liabilities] is that there is now far too much money swirling around in the system. This has led to a progressive escalation of the referral fees which lawyers pay to get a share of the business. Thus the beneficiaries are not the accident victims, but usually the referrers and (when no referral fee is paid) the lawyers. The referrers who benefit from this state of affairs are claims management companies, BTE insurers, trades unions and others. At the moment market forces compel personal injury solicitors to hand over a large part of the costs which they receive to claims management companies, BTE insurers etc in the form of referral fees. In other words, these middlemen who add no value to the process are the true beneficiaries of competition. In low value cases more than half the costs received sometimes go out in referral fees. In high value cases referral fees may be £10,000 or more. In my view such referral fees should be banned, as they were up until March 2004.'[393]

1.179 These comments focused attention on a particularly controversial aspect of the compensation industry—namely, the profits being made by middlemen (and, in particular, claims referrers). Such issues are beyond the scope of this book, but it is clear that there was a political will to bring about radical changes.

1.180 The reports and lectures referred to in the foregoing paragraphs have caused some commentators to complain that the political pendulum is swinging too far towards defendants. One can understand why such fears are being expressed,[394] but an analysis based on that single axis (that is, claimant–defendant) is overly simplistic in the context of the present-day legal marketplace. In particular, it is entirely credible that the true political motivation has little to do with that axis, but is to reduce legal fees generally and to encourage greater competition in the legal marketplace.[395] The Jackson reforms could be seen as an attempt to encourage competition by shifting the focus of funding away from opponents to clients, whilst at the same time encouraging innovation in the marketplace.

---

[392] Young, D, *Common Sense, Common Safety* (London: HMSO, 2010), p 11.

[393] Jackson, R, 'Legal Aid and the Costs Review Reforms', Talk delivered to the Cambridge Law Faculty, 5 September 2011, p 4.

[394] Sir Rupert Jackson himself commented that '[n]o procedural code can achieve in every case the twin objectives of perfect justice and certainty of outcome': see Jackson, R, 'Technical Aspects of Implementation: Third Lecture in the Implementation Programme', 31 October 2011, at para 1.3.

[395] Indeed, this has been expressly stated as being an intended aim: see Jackson, R, 'Legal Aid and the Costs Review Reforms', Talk delivered to the Cambridge Law Faculty, 5 September 2011, at p 4.

The relevance of this is that there are certain aspects of the consumer legal services that have, by reason of their understandable desire for new business, become undesirable in a societal context; the political will exists to reduce the profits made by that sector. Whilst this is almost diametrically opposite to the concerns that were being expressed in previous decades (see 1.141) and whilst it is entirely possible that the pendulum will swing back again at some point, it should be borne in mind that the pendulum's cycle is measured in decades rather than years. Perhaps more importantly, the following comments made by Lord Neuberger MR in May 2012 ought to be borne in mind: 'One day in the future, it may be that the call to adopt the US costs rule or the German fixed costs regime will become too great to resist. However, we are not there yet ...'[396] **1.181**

This is a clear warning that (unlike in the past) the current reforms will be audited for effectiveness. Indeed, Sir Rupert Jackson has repeatedly commented on the need for audit (although he has not referred to it by that name).[397] **1.182**

Legal aid

The relationship between the Legal Services Commission and the Ministry of Justice came under increasing strain in the late 2000s. Indeed, in 2009, the former was severely criticised when it was forced to qualify its 2008–09 accounts.[398] In October 2009, the then Justice Secretary asked Sir Ian Magee to carry out an independent review of the Legal Services Commission. Sir Ian's report was published in 2010,[399] and recommended fundamental changes to the governance, structure and financial management of the Legal Services Commission. Notwithstanding the fact that precisely the opposite policy had been adopted in 1988 (see 1.140), one of the recommendations was that legal aid should be administered by an executive agency of the Ministry of Justice.[400] **1.183**

In the event, radical changes were made. The scope of legal aid for civil cases was severely restricted. The Legal Aid, Sentencing and Punishment of Offenders Act 2012 made provision for the abolition of the Legal Services Commission; thus, on 1 April 2013, it was replaced by the Legal Aid Agency, an executive agency of the Ministry of Justice. The office of Director of Legal Aid Casework was created, the incumbent of which would have independence from the Lord Chancellor for the purpose of individual funding decisions. **1.184**

The Association of Costs Lawyers

In January 2011, the Association of Law Costs Draftsmen (see 1.134) changed its name to the Association of Costs Lawyers. Regulated costs lawyers came into existence. **1.185**

[396] 'Keynote Address: Fourteenth Lecture in the Implementation Programme', Delivered to the Association of Costs Lawyers' Annual Conference 2012, 11 May 2012, at para 20.

[397] See Jackson, R, *Review of Civil Litigation Costs: Final Report* (London: HMSO, 2010), ch 6, at para 2.4; see also Jackson, R, 'Assessment of Costs in the Brave New World: Eighth Lecture in the Implementation Programme', Delivered at KPMG Forensic's [*sic*] Leeds Law Lecture 2012, 25 January 2012, at para 2.3, where Sir Rupert comments on the need for a costs council.

[398] See Ministry of Justice, *Legal Services Commission move to Agency Status: Business Case (Version 2)* (London: HMSO, 2012), para 1.4.

[399] Sir Ian Magee, *Review of Legal Aid Delivery and Governance* (London: HMSO, 2010).

[400] This is discussed in detail in Ministry of Justice, *Legal Services Commission move to Agency Status: Business Case (Version 2)* (London: HMSO, 2012).

The Legal Services Market Study

1.186 In 2013, the OFT commissioned a report looking at 'the impact of the regulatory restrictions in the legal services sector'.[401] This prompted its successor, the Competition and Markets Authority, to express concern about what it calls 'unmet demand':

> 'Our current work was prompted by a range of concerns raised by interested parties that the legal services sector may not be working as well as it should be, including concerns related to the affordably of legal services, the high proportion of consumers that were not seeking to purchase legal services when they had legal needs ("unmet demand") and the possibility that regulation might be dampening competition.'[402]

Court fees

1.187 Court fees used to be regarded as being a peripheral issue: a minor addition to the bill, at most. Now, in contrast, they are a major part of the expenditure of litigation (see 52.87). This is as a result of a series of changes[403] to the tariffs that were first made in 2013.[404] The early fee reforms came into force on 22 April 2014, designed to ensure that the fees charged in the civil courts were set at a level[405] that covered the full cost of the court.[406] This was said to reflect the fact that governmental policy, in general, was to charge the full amount for services provided.[407] The increases that took effect on 9 March 2015, however, went further than this: some of the fees that were created were 'enhanced fees',[408] which exceeded cost, and it was said that these were intended to generate income to be used for court infrastructure. Put otherwise, the cost was moved away from the public purse and towards the court

---

[401] See Office of Fair Trading, *Competition in Professions*, OFT328 (London: OFT, 2001).

[402] See Competition and Markets Authority, *Legal Services Market Study: Interim Report* (London: CMA, 2016), para 1.7.

[403] All of the Orders worked by amending the Civil Proceedings Fees Order 2008 (SI 2008/1053) under powers conferred by s 92 of the Courts Act 2003. That said, in anticipation of a jurisdictional challenge, the Explanatory Memorandum that dealt with the changes made in 2015 also referred to the power to set enhanced fees conferred by s 180 of the Anti-social Behaviour Crime and Policing Act 2014.

[404] The first increases were made by the Civil Proceedings Fees (Amendment) Order 2014 (SI 2014/874); these came into force on 22 April 2014. That Order increased fees payable in civil proceedings (see Sched 1 to the Order), but it also abrogated the need to pay a fee when filing a directions questionnaire, receiving a notice of allocation or filing a pre-trial checklist (see Sched 1, para 2). Then came the Civil Proceedings and Family Proceedings Fees (Amendment) Order 2015 (SI 2015/576).

[405] The method that was used to calculate the fee was set out in para 3(7) of the Explanatory Memorandum to the Civil Proceedings Fees (Amendment) Order 2014 (SI 2014/874): 'Many fees have increased to ensure that the fee charged reflects the full cost of the type of proceedings to which it relates. The cost is calculated by adding the actual cost of the staff and judicial time to process this type of application, and a portion of the costs of the overheads (e.g. IT and estates) of the civil court system.'

[406] The Explanatory Memorandum to the Civil Proceedings Fees (Amendment) Order 2014 (SI 2014/874) had this to say on the point (at para 3(2)): '[The intention is] to recover close to the full cost of the civil court system through fees, transferring more of the cost to the user and reducing the cost to the general taxpayer. It also sought to continue to simplify and rationalise the fees charged across the courts, so that similar processes attracted similar fees, making the fee system easier for users of the courts, and for court staff, to understand.'

[407] This policy is explained in the Explanatory Memorandum to the Civil Proceedings and Family Proceedings Fees (Amendment) Order 2015 (SI 2015/576), paras 7.3–7.6. See also HM Treasury, *Managing Public Money* (London: HMSO, 2013, rev'd 2015).

[408] The Civil Proceedings and Family Proceedings Fees (Amendment) Order 2015 (SI 2015/576) created a new fee for money claims with a value of £10,000 or more. The fee to start proceedings became 5 per cent of the value of the claim, albeit with a maximum fee of £10,000. The percentage in respect of claims of £10,000 or more filed electronically via the County Court Business Centre or Money Claim OnLine became 4.5 per cent. The fees for a claim with a value of less than £10,000 remain unchanged.

user.[409] The government has said that this may generate an extra £120m per year.[410] It has been widely criticised, not least by senior members of the judiciary.[411]

Ongoing matters

The process of change is ongoing, and there are those who believe that the current funding regime imperils rights and safeguards that had taken centuries to secure. One commentator had this to say on the point: **1.188**

> 'Many lawyers will, or will soon, be gaining practical experience of the hard cases that will now ensue as parties are unable to litigate. It is a salutary thought that some 799 years after the first promulgation of Magna Carta, the undertaking that "to no one will we sell, to no one deny or delay right or justice" may be one too radical for governments of any political complexion to consider honouring in "the current funding climate".'[412]

These concerns may be justified, but so are the concerns of those who point to the unacceptably high cost of litigation. In June 2014, Lord Neuberger (speaking extrajudicially) called for lawyers to cut their fees to increase access to justice, arguing that there is a 'long-standing and justified concern about the level of cost of litigation' and suggesting that one solution might be the German system of fixed costs, in which lawyers' fees are set according to the value of the case.[413] Whether Parliament will ultimately choose to take such a drastic step remains to be seen. **1.189**

Old wine in new bottles?

As was almost inevitable, given the long history of costs, many of Sir Rupert's recommendations bear a resemblance to provisions that had gone before, but the overall regime is novel. Most of Sir Rupert's recommendations have historical pedigrees, some of which are remarkable for their antiquity. One-way costs shifting,[414] for example, was the default position from about 1267 until 1606 (see 1.26), whilst qualified one-way costs shifting was commonplace under the various legal aid regimes, the first of which was first introduced in 1949 (see 1.107). A test of global proportionality[415] existed for several decades from 1670 (albeit in only limited circumstances—see 1.46) and has cropped up from time to time in a number of different guises (some of which were rather curious, such as under the Slander of Women Act 1891).[416] Fixed costs[417] are the modern counterpart of scale charges, those having been first introduced in 1883 (albeit initially for non-contentious work).[418] Finally, success fees became irrecoverable between opposing parties;[419] that was the position between 1995 and 2000 (see 1.175). **1.190**

---

[409] See the Explanatory Memorandum to the Civil Proceedings and Family Proceedings Fees (Amendment) Order 2015 (SI 2015/576).

[410] See para 10 of the Explanatory Memorandum to the Civil Proceedings and Family Proceedings Fees (Amendment) Order 2015 (SI 2015/576).

[411] See, eg, Lord Thomas's letter to the Ministry of Justice, dated 19 December 2014 and headed 'Response to consultation on Court Fees: Enhanced Charging'.

[412] Smith, JB, 'The Costs of Complexity: A Practical View from the Bar', *Practical Law*, 3 October 2014.

[413] See *The Times*, 24 June 2014 (online edition).

[414] Jackson, R, *Review of Civil Litigation Costs: Final Report* (London: HMSO, 2010), at para 9.6.11.

[415] *Ibid*, at para 3.6.1.

[416] See Chapter 58.

[417] Jackson, R, *Review of Civil Litigation Costs: Final Report* (London: HMSO, 2010), para 15.7.1.

[418] Albeit only in the county courts: see 1.87.

[419] Jackson, R, *Review of Civil Litigation Costs: Final Report* (London: HMSO, 2010), para 10.6.1.

Part II

INTRODUCTION TO THE LAW OF COSTS

2

THE LANGUAGE OF COSTS

This chapter deals with the following topics: **2.01**

- costs terminology in general (2.02);
- the citation of costs authorities (2.06); and
- the language of costs (costs lexicon) (2.09).

Costs Terminology in General

In the same way as costs regimes have a habit of reinventing themselves (see 1.03), the language of costs has repeatedly undergone stylistic changes: time after time, old wine has been decanted into new bottles bearing elegant new labels. Whilst the use of obsolete terminology is to be discouraged, echoes of expired terminology linger on, and the result is that it is often necessary to know both the old and new terms. **2.02**

Whilst purists will object, modern nomenclature is used throughout this book regardless of whether the authorities referred to pre-date the Civil Procedure Rules (CPR). Where appropriate, the expired terminology is also given (usually in the footnotes); this is particularly the case where the old terminology is still frequently in use. **2.03**

For obvious reasons, it is preferable to use modern terminology where it exists. Occasionally, however, a supposedly expired term will have no modern counterpart, an example being the vocabulary used to describe the anatomy of a bill of costs (such as 'the chronology'). Where no modern equivalent exists, the otherwise-expired term is used. **2.04**

Some phrases mean more than the sum total of their words and are best regarded as being terms of art. Examples include the phrases 'genuine issue'[1] (see 18.35) and 'material breach'[2] (see 29.53). Other phrases draw upon the name of the case that was seminal in the relevant area of the law, such as 'the *Bailey* presumption' (see 18.30) and 'the *Pamplin* procedure' (see 46.42). Such phrases are best described in context, so they are, on the whole, addressed in the main text rather than in this chapter. **2.05**

---

[1] This being a phrase that is often used as shorthand for the standard of evidence required to rebut a certain presumption concerning the weight that can be afforded to the certificate to a bill: see *Hazlett v Sefton Metropolitan Borough Council* [2000] 4 All ER 887.

[2] This is a phrase that refers to a process whereby breaches of certain regulations that do not matter are distinguished from those that do matter: see *Hollins v Russell* [2003] EWCA Civ 718, at [221], *per* Brooke LJ.

The Citation of Costs Authorities

Neutral citation

2.06 A topic that often causes confusion is the neutral citation of costs reports in the Senior Courts Costs Office. The official neutral citation system was introduced in January 2001,[3] and operates for judgments of the Supreme Court, Privy Council, Court of Appeal and all divisions of the High Court.

2.07 Costs judgments of costs judges in the Senior Courts Costs Office are often afforded a similar citation (such as [2006] EWHC 90052 (Costs)). This citation is not official, but is used by respected sources such as the British and Irish Legal Information Institute (BAILII). The fact that a case citation includes the abbreviation 'EWHC' does not mean that the case has been heard by a High Court judge nor does it mean that a case has been heard on appeal.

2.08 On a related note, it should not be forgotten that where cases are to be cited in court, neutral citation should not be used in preference to reported citation. In this regard, the requirements of the Practice Direction (Citation of Authorities)[4] apply just as much to costs litigation as they do to other legal disciplines. The relevant directions are set out in the footnotes.[5] The fact that this book generally uses neutral citation should not detract from those directions.

Costs Lexicon

2.09 The following is a lexicon of words, phrases and acronyms commonly encountered in practice.

Act as a solicitor, to / *v. phr.* To perform those acts that only a solicitor may perform.[6]

---

3 *Practice Direction (Judgments: Form and Citation)* [2001] 1 WLR 194, issued on 11 January 2001.

4 *Practice Direction (Citation of Authorities)* [2012] 1 WLR 780, revoking *Practice Notes on Citation of Authorities (Court of Appeal) (Civil Division)* [1995] 1 WLR 1096 and [1996] 1 WLR 854.

5 '6. Where a judgment is reported in the Official Law Reports (AC, QB, Ch, Fam) published by the Incorporated Council of Law Reporting for England and Wales, that report must be cited. These are the most authoritative reports; they contain a summary of the argument. Other series of reports and official transcripts of judgment may only be used when a case is not reported in the Official Law Reports. 7. If a judgment is not (or not yet) reported in the Official Law Reports but it is reported in the Weekly Law Reports (WLR) or the All England Law Reports (All ER) that report should be cited. If the case is reported in both the WLR and the All ER either report may properly be cited. 8. If a judgment is not reported in the Official Law Reports, the WLR, or the All ER, but it is reported in any of the authoritative specialist series of reports which contain a headnote and are made by individuals holding a Senior Courts qualification (for the purposes of s 115 of the Courts and Legal Services Act 1990), the specialist report should be cited. 9. Where a judgment is not reported in any of the reports referred to in paragraphs [6] to [8] above, but is reported in other reports, they may be cited. 10. Where a judgment has not been reported, reference may be made to the official transcript if that is available, not the handed-down text of the judgment, as this may have been subject to late revision after the text was handed down. Official transcripts may be obtained from, for instance, BAILII (http://www.bailii.org/). An unreported case should not usually be cited unless it contains a relevant statement of legal principle not found in reported authority.'

6 *Piper Double Glazing Ltd v DC Contracts* [1994] 1 WLR 777, at 786, which analysis was approved by Phillips MR in *R v Secretary of State for Transport, ex parte Factortame* [2002] EWCA Civ 932, at [26].

Additional liability / *n. phr.* The success fee, the insurance premium or the additional amount in respect of provision made by a membership organisation, as the case may be.[7]

Admissible offer / *n. phr.* An offer to settle that is not an offer to which costs consequences under Part 36 apply and which is capable of being drawn to the court's attention.[8]

ADR / *abv.* Abbreviation for alternative dispute resolution.

Advocacy services / *n. phr.* Any services that it would be reasonable to expect a person who is exercising, or contemplating exercising, a right of audience in relation to any proceedings, or contemplated proceedings, to provide.[9]

After-the-event insurance / *n. phr.* Legal expenses insurance (a form of general insurance) incepted after the event giving rise to the claim to which the insurance relates, usually specific to a single claim.[10]

After-the-event premium / *n. phr.* A premium payable for after-the-event insurance.

Alternative dispute resolution / *n. phr.* Collective description of methods of resolving disputes otherwise than through the normal trial process.[11]

Appropriate authorised body / *n. phr.* † In relation to any person claiming to be entitled to any right of audience by virtue of s 27(2)(a)(i) of the Courts and Legal Services Act 1990 (as originally enacted), the authorised body (a) granting that right and (b) of which that person is a member.[12]

Assisted person / *n. phr.* † **1.** A person who is in receipt of legal aid—to be distinguished from a client funded by the Legal Services Commission (LSC; *var.* 'funded client'), who is a person in receipt of Community Legal Service (CLS) funding. † **2.** A person within the statutory provisions relating to legal aid.[13]

Authorised advocate / *n. phr.* † Any person (including a barrister or solicitor) who had a right of audience granted by an authorised body in accordance with the provisions of the Courts and Legal Services Act 1990 (as enacted);[14] now superseded by the term 'authorised person'.

Authorised body / *n. phr.* † (a) The General Council of the Bar, (b) the Law Society or (c) any professional or other body that has been designated by Order in Council as an authorised body for the purposes of s 27 of the Courts and Legal Services Act 1990 (as enacted);[15] now superseded by the term 'relevant approved regulator'.

Authorised court officer / *n. phr.* Any officer of (a) the County Court and its hearing centres, (b) a district registry, (c) the Principal Registry of the Family Division or

† = obsolete or archaic; *adj.* = adjective; *abv.* = abbreviation; *n.* = noun; *n. phr.* = noun phrase; *prop. n. phr.* = proper noun phrase; *v.* = verb

---

[7] See the pre-2013 CPR, r 43.2(o).

[8] See CPR, r 44.2(4)(c).

[9] See s 190(6) of the Legal Services Act 2007, as amended, and, previously, s 119(1) of the Courts and Legal Services Act 1990, as amended.

[10] Prior to 1 April 2013, s 29 of the Access to Justice Act 1999 read: 'Where in any proceedings a costs order is made in favour of any party who has taken out an insurance policy against the risk of incurring a liability in those proceedings, the costs payable to him may ... include costs in respect of the premium of the policy.'

[11] This being the definition given in the CPR Glossary.

[12] See s 27(9) of the Courts and Legal Services Act 1990 (as originally enacted).

[13] See pre-2013 CPR, r 43.3(h).

[14] See s 119(1) of the Courts and Legal Services Act 1990.

[15] See *ibid.*

(d) the Costs Office, whom the Lord Chancellor has authorised to assess costs;[16] often colloquially referred to as a 'costs officer'.

Authorised litigator / *n. phr.* † Any person (including a solicitor) who has a right to conduct litigation granted by an authorised body in accordance with the provisions of the Courts and Legal Services Act 1990 (as enacted);[17] now superseded by the term 'authorised person'. Whilst not an exhaustive list, authorised litigators included: solicitors; Fellows of the Institute of Legal Executives; barristers; costs lawyers; trade mark attorneys; and officers of the Children and Family Court Advisory and Support Service.

Authorised person / *n. phr.* (For the purposes of the Legal Services Act 2007 and in relation to an activity—the relevant activity—which is a reserved legal activity) **1.** A person who is authorised to carry on the relevant activity by a relevant approved regulator in relation to the relevant activity (other than by virtue of a licence under Part 5 of the 2007 Act). **2.** A licensable body that, by virtue of such a licence, is authorised to carry on the relevant activity by a licensing authority in relation to the reserved legal activity.[18]

Base costs / *n. phr.* Costs other than the amount of any additional liability.[19]

Base rate / *n. phr.* The interest rate set by the Bank of England, which is used as the basis for other banks' rates.[20]

Before-the-event insurance / *n. phr.* Legal expenses insurance that is incepted before the event giving rise to any claim.

Budget / *n.* An estimate of the reasonable and proportionate costs (including disbursements) that a party intends to incur in the proceeding.[21]

Budget, to / *v.* To prepare a budget.

Budget discussion report / *n. phr.* A document based on Precedent R that is prepared for the court and which contains a record of (a) those figures that are agreed for each phase, (b) those figures that are not agreed for each phase and (c) a brief summary of the grounds of dispute.[22]

***Bullock* order** / *n. phr.* A co-defendant order whereby the claimant is to pay the successful defendant's costs, but is permitted to add those costs to the costs to be recovered from an unsuccessful defendant.[23]

CCFA / *abv.* Abbreviation for collective conditional fee agreement.

Central funds / *n. phr.* Used in enactments to refer to money provided by Parliament (usually in the context of criminal costs).[24]

CFA / *abv.* Abbreviation for conditional fee agreement.

CFA Lite / *n. phr.* A colloquial phrase used to refer to a conditional fee agreement whereby the monies paid to the legal services provider are (often within certain constraints) limited to those costs that are recovered from an opponent.

† = obsolete or archaic; *adj.* = adjective; *abv.* = abbreviation; *n.* = noun; *n. phr.* = noun phrase; *prop. n. phr.* = proper noun phrase; *v.* = verb

---

16 See CPR, r 44.1(1).
17 See s 119(1) of the Courts and Legal Services Act 1990.
18 See s 18 of the Legal Services Act 2007.
19 See CPD, art 2.2, now revoked.
20 This being the definition given in the CPR Glossary.
21 This being the definition given in the CPR Glossary.
22 See CPR, r 3.13(2), and PD 3, para 6A.
23 *Bullock v London General Omnibus Co* [1907] 1 KB 264.
24 See Sched 1 to the Interpretation Act 1978.

Collective conditional fee agreement / *n. phr.* **1.** A template contract for services that may be applied to individual cases to form conditional-fee-agreement-like arrangements, either for the benefit of the counterparties or other persons. † **2.** Formerly formally defined as:

> '... an agreement which—(a) disregarding section 58(3)(c) of the Courts and Legal Services Act 1990, would be a conditional fee agreement, and (b) does not refer to specific proceedings, but provides for fees to be payable on a common basis in relation to a class of proceedings, or, if it refers to more than one class of proceedings, on a common basis in relation to each class.'[25]

Conditional fee agreement / *n. phr.* **1.** An agreement enforceable under s 58 of the Courts and Legal Services Act 1990.[26] **2.** An agreement with a person providing advocacy or litigation services that provides for that person's fees and expenses, or any part of them, to be payable only in specified circumstances.[27]

Contentious business / *n. phr.* **1.** 'Business done, whether as solicitor or advocate in or for the purpose of proceedings begun before a court or before an arbitrator ... not being business which falls within the definition of non-contentious or common form probate business contained in section 128 of the Senior Courts Act 1981.'[28] **2.** 'All business is now to be regarded as contentious which is done before proceedings are begun provided that the business is done with a view to the proceedings being begun, and they are in fact begun, and also all business done in the course of the proceedings. All other business is non-contentious.'[29]

Contentious business agreement / *n. phr.* A contract of retainer that is compliant with the requirements of s 59 of the Solicitors Act 1974 and which, subject to certain safeguards, will allow the solicitor to recover their fees for contentious work as if those fees were an ordinary debt.

Contingency fee agreement / *n. phr.* **1.** A contract of retainer under which the legal representative's fee, usually in relation to non-contentious business, is calculated by reference to the amount of money that is recovered for the client.[30] **2.** Generic (somewhat indistinct) term used to mean any conditional fee agreement of any sort.[31]

Contract of retainer / *n. phr.* A contract for services pursuant to which a legal services provider agrees to provide legal services for valuable consideration.

Costs / *n.* Includes fees, charges, disbursements, expenses, remuneration, reimbursement allowed to a litigant in person under CPR, r 46.5, and any fee or reward charged by a lay representative for acting on behalf of a party in proceedings allocated to the small claims track.[32] Where appropriate, any additional liability

† = obsolete or archaic; *adj.* = adjective; *abv.* = abbreviation; *n.* = noun; *n. phr.* = noun phrase; *prop. n. phr.* = proper noun phrase; *v.* = verb

[25] See the now-revoked Collective Conditional Fee Agreements Regulations 2000 (SI 2000/2988).
[26] See CPR, r 44.1(1).
[27] See s 58(2)(a) of the Courts and Legal Services Act 1990, as amended.
[28] Section 87 of the Solicitors Act 1974.
[29] *In re Simpkin Marshall Ltd* [1959] Ch 229, at 235, *per* Wynn-Parry J.
[30] See, eg, 'Criminal Solicitors Gear up for Mile-High Club' (2002) 99 LSG 11, at 41.
[31] See, eg, the Solicitors' Code of Conduct 2007, which defined a contingency fee as 'defined in rule 24 (Interpretation) as any sum (whether fixed, or calculated either as a percentage of the proceeds or otherwise) payable only in the event of success'; see also the SRA Code of Conduct 2011.
[32] See CPR, r 44.1(1).

incurred under a funding arrangement may be included, but this would be under the pre-2013 CPR, r 43.2(1)(a) rather than the present-day equivalent.[33]

Costs capping order / *n. phr.* An order limiting the amount of future costs (including disbursements) that a party may recover pursuant to an order for costs subsequently made.[34]

Costs judge / *n. phr.* **1.** A 'taxing master of the Senior Court'.[35] **2.** Colloquially also used to refer to regional costs judges.

Costs management / *n. phr.* The ability of the court to manage the costs to be incurred by the parties to litigation by making costs management orders.[36]

Costs management order / *n. phr.* An order that will (a) record the extent to which the budgeted costs are agreed between the parties, (b) in respect of the budgeted costs that are not agreed, record the court's approval after making appropriate revisions, and (c) record the extent (if any) to which incurred costs are agreed.[37]

Costs Office / *prop. n. phr.* The Senior Courts Costs Office (formerly known as the Supreme Court Costs Office and, prior to 1999, as the Supreme Court Taxing Office).

Costs officer / *n. phr.* Collective term for a costs judge, a district judge or an authorised court officer.[38]

Court / *n.* Includes: (a) a tribunal that is (to any extent) a listed tribunal for, or for any of, the purposes of Sched 7 to the Tribunals, Courts and Enforcement Act 2007 ('Functions etc of Administrative Justice and Tribunals Council'); (b) a court-martial; (c) a statutory inquiry within the meaning of s 16(1) of the Tribunals and Inquiries Act 1992; (d) an ecclesiastical court (including the Court of Faculties).[39]

Damages-based agreement / *n. phr.* An agreement that complies with the provisions of the Damages-Based Agreements Regulations 2013 (SI 2013/609).[40]

DBA / *abv.* Abbreviation for damages-based agreement.

Deemed order / *n. phr.* An order that is deemed to be made on the happening of a specified event, generally where (a) a party allows court fees to remain unpaid after having been given notice to pay by the court, (b) a party accepts a Part 36 offer or (c) a party discontinues a claim.

Default costs certificate / *n. phr.* A costs certificate that is issued in default of a paying party not serving points of dispute.

Detailed assessment / *n. phr.* The procedure by which the amount of costs is decided by a costs officer in accordance with Part 47.[41]

Detailed bill / *n. phr.* A statute bill (rendered to a client) that contains detailed items[42] and is therefore not a gross sum bill.

† = obsolete or archaic; *adj.* = adjective; *abv.* = abbreviation; *n.* = noun; *n. phr.* = noun phrase; *prop. n. phr.* = proper noun phrase; *v.* = verb

33 See *BNM v MGN Ltd* [2017] EWCA Civ 1767.
34 See CPR, r 3.19(1)(a).
35 See CPR, r 44.1(1).
36 See CPR, r 3.15(1).
37 See CPR, r 3.15(2).
38 See CPR, r 44.1(1).
39 See the Legal Services Act 2007.
40 SI 2013/609. This being the definition given in the CPR Glossary.
41 See CPR, r 44.1(1).
42 See s 64(1) of the Solicitors Act 1974.

Detailed breakdown / *n. phr.* A document, often in a similar format to a bill of costs, which contains particulars of the costs that have already been claimed in a gross sum bill.[43]

Director / *n.* (In the context of legal aid) The person designated as the Director of Legal Aid Casework pursuant to s 4 of the Legal Aid, Sentencing and Punishment of Offenders Act 2012, or a person entitled to exercise the functions of the director.[44]

Disburse, to / *v.* To pay monies (usually disbursements).

Disbursement / *n.* **1.** Money paid on behalf of the client.[45] **2.** As between solicitor and client, those monies that are not profit costs or taxes, but which can properly be included within a statute bill.[46] **3.** As between opposing parties, recoverable monies paid by the client to persons other than their legal services provider.

Discounted conditional fee agreement / *n. phr.* A type of conditional fee agreement whereby reduced (discounted) costs are payable in the event of the case not ultimately being successful.

Final costs certificate / *n. phr.* A document that states the amount of costs which have been assessed and, unless the court orders otherwise, will include an order to pay the costs to which it relates.[47]

Fixed costs / *n. phr.* Costs, the amounts of which are fixed by the CPR, whether or not the court has a discretion to allow some other or no amount, and which include: (a) the amounts that are to be allowed in respect of legal representatives' charges in the circumstances set out in Section I of Part 45; (b) fixed recoverable costs calculated in accordance with CPR, r 45.11; c) the additional costs allowed by r 45.18; (d) fixed costs determined under CPR, r 45.21; and (e) costs fixed by CPR, rr 45.37 and 45.38.[48]

Fixed price agreement / *n. phr.* A contract of retainer that provides for remuneration of a legal services provider on a predetermined, fixed basis.

Forthwith order / *n. phr.* An order made prior to the conclusion of proceedings for the purposes of allowing a party's costs to be assessed notwithstanding the general rule (in CPR, r 47.1) that the costs of any proceedings are not to be assessed by the detailed procedure until the conclusion of the proceedings.

FPA // *abv.* Abbreviation for a fixed price agreement.

Free of charge / *n. phr.* Otherwise than for, or in expectation of, fee, gain or reward.[49]

Fund / *n.* **1.** Includes any estate or property held for the benefit of any person or class of person and any fund to which a trustee or personal representative is entitled in their capacity.[50] **2.** Colloquial term used to refer to the Legal Aid Fund or the CLS Fund.

Funder / *n.* **1.** A third party who has funded litigation. **2.** '[A] person ("the funder") agrees to fund (in whole or in part) the provision of advocacy or litigation services (by someone other than the funder) to another person ("the litigant").'[51] **3.** The party to

† = obsolete or archaic; *adj.* = adjective; *abv.* = abbreviation; *n.* = noun; *n. phr.* = noun phrase; *prop. n. phr.* = proper noun phrase; *v.* = verb

43 See s 64(4) of the Solicitors Act 1974.
44 See CPR, r 44.1(1).
45 *Browne v Barber* [1913] 2 KB 553, at 573, *per* Vaughan Williams LJ.
46 *Joel v Barnato* (1929) 45 TLR 167.
47 See CPR, r 47.17(5).
48 See CPR, r 44.1(1).
49 See *ibid.*
50 See *ibid.*
51 Section 58B of the Courts and Legal Services Act 1990, as amended.

a collective conditional fee agreement who, under that agreement, is liable to pay the legal representative's fees.[52]

Funding arrangement / *n. phr.* An arrangement whereby a person has (a) entered into a conditional fee agreement or a collective conditional fee agreement that provides for a success fee within the meaning of s 58(2) of the Courts and Legal Services Act 1990, (b) taken out an insurance policy to which s 29 of the Access to Justice Act 1999 ('Recovery of insurance premiums by way of costs') applies or (c) made an agreement with a membership organisation to meet the person's legal costs.[53]

Future costs / *n. phr.* 1. Costs incurred in respect of work done after the date of a costs capping order, but excluding the amount of any additional liability.[54] 2. Informal term for any costs yet to be incurred.

General retainer / *n. phr.* A contract of retainer (usually of either indeterminate length or for a period of time) pursuant to which a legal services provider provides services generally rather than in respect of a specific claim or matter.

Gross sum bill / *n. phr.* A statute bill that lacks detailed items;[55] used only in relation to contentious business.

Indemnity / *n.* A right to recover from a third party the whole amount that the recoverer is liable to pay.[56]

Indemnity basis / *n. phr.* A basis of assessment whereby the court will resolve any doubt as to whether the costs were reasonably incurred or were reasonable in amount in favour of the receiving party; under the CPR, the costs would not be subjected to a test of proportionality.[57]

Insurance / *n.* **1.** The payment of one or more sums of money, commonly called 'premiums', by one party ('the policyholder'), in return for which the other party ('the insurer') undertakes to pay a sum of money on the happening of a specified event, which event must be one that is adverse to the interests of the policyholder.[58] **2.** After-the-event insurance.

Insurance premium / *n. phr.* **1.** The consideration required of the assured in return for which the insurer undertakes its obligation under the contract of insurance.[59] **2.** (In the context of after-the-event insurance) A sum of money paid or payable for insurance against the risk of incurring a costs liability in the proceedings, taken out after the event that is the subject matter of the claim.[60]

Interim costs certificate / *n. phr.* A certificate containing an order for an interim payment of costs made after the receiving party has filed a request for a detailed assessment hearing.[61]

† = obsolete or archaic; *adj.* = adjective; *abv.* = abbreviation; *n.* = noun; *n. phr.* = noun phrase; *prop. n. phr.* = proper noun phrase; *v.* = verb

52 See the now-revoked Collective Conditional Fee Agreements Regulations 2000 (SI 2000/2988), reg 1(2).

53 See pre-1 April 2013 CPR, r 43.2(k).

54 See CPR, r 3.19(1)(a).

55 See s 64(1) of the Solicitors Act 1974.

56 This being the definition given in the CPR Glossary.

57 *Claims Direct Test Cases* [2003] EWCA Civ 136.

58 *Prudential Insurance Co v IRC* [1904] 2 KB 658, *per* Channell J.

59 *MacGillivray on Insurance Law* (9th edn, London: Sweet & Maxwell, 1997), approved of in *Claims Direct Litigation* [2003] EWCA Civ 136, at [25], and *The Accident Group Test Cases* [2004] EWCA Civ 575, at [17].

60 See pre-2013 CPR, r 43.2(l) and (m).

61 See CPR, r 47.16.

Interim statute bill / *n. phr.* A statute bill (that is, not a request for a payment on account) that is rendered by a solicitor to a client prior to the determination of the relevant retainer.

Joint liability / *n. phr.* A single liability shared jointly between parties; each party can be held liable for the whole of it.[62]

Legal activities / *n. phr.* (For the purposes of the Legal Service Act 2007) (a) An activity that is a reserved legal activity within the meaning of that Act (as enacted) and (b) any other activity that consists of one or both of: (i) the provision of legal advice or assistance in connection with the application of the law or with any form of resolution of legal disputes; (ii) the provision of representation in connection with any matter concerning the application of the law or any form of resolution of legal disputes.[63] The definition does not include any activity of a judicial or quasi-judicial nature (including acting as a mediator).[64]

Legal aid / *n. phr.* (In the context of civil law) Civil legal services made available under arrangements made for the purposes of Part 1 of the Legal Aid, Sentencing and Punishment of Offenders Act 2012.[65]

Legal representative / *n. phr.* **1.** (For the purposes of the CPR) A (a) barrister, (b) solicitor, (c) solicitor's employee, (d) manager of a body recognised under s 9 of the Administration of Justice Act 1985 or (e) person who, for the purposes of the Legal Services Act 2007, is an authorised person in relation to an activity that constitutes the conduct of litigation (within the meaning of that Act), who has been instructed to act for a party in relation to proceedings.[66] **2.** (For the purposes of s 194 of the Legal Services Act 2007, ie *pro bono* representation) A person exercising a right of audience or conducting litigation on a party's behalf.[67]

Litigation funding agreement / *n. phr.* **1.** (Informally and generally) An agreement between a party in litigation and a third party whereby the latter, in return for valuable consideration, provides commercial funding for the purposes of funding the former's involvement in the litigation. **2.** (For the purposes of s 58B of the Courts and Legal Services Act 1990, which is not yet in force at time of writing) An agreement under which (a) a person ('the funder') agrees to fund (in whole or in part) the provision of advocacy or litigation services (by someone other than the funder) to another person ('the litigant') and (b) the litigant agrees to pay a sum to the funder in specified circumstances.[68]

Litigation services / *n. phr.* Any services that it would be reasonable to expect a person who is exercising, or contemplating exercising, a right to conduct litigation in relation to any proceedings, or contemplated proceedings, to provide.[69]

† = obsolete or archaic; *adj.* = adjective; *abv.* = abbreviation; *n.* = noun; *n. phr.* = noun phrase; *prop. n. phr.* = proper noun phrase; *v.* = verb

---

62 This being the definition given in the CPR Glossary.
63 See s 12(3) and (4) of the Legal Services Act 2007.
64 See s 12(4) of the Legal Services Act 2007.
65 See CPR, r 44.1(1).
66 See CPR, r 2.3(1).
67 See s 194(10) of the Legal Services Act 2007.
68 See s 58B(2) of the Courts and Legal Services Act 1990.
69 See s 190(6) of the Legal Services Act 2007, as amended, and, previously s 119(1) of the Courts and Legal Services Act 1990, as amended.

LSC-funded client / *n. phr.* An individual who receives services funded by the Legal Services Commission as part of the Community Legal Service within the meaning of Part I of the Access to Justice Act 1999.[70]

Membership organisation / *n. phr.* A body prescribed for the purposes of s 30 of the Access to Justice Act 1999 (recovery where body undertakes to meet costs liabilities).[71]

Non-contentious business / *n. phr.* Any business done as a solicitor that is not contentious business.[72]

Non-contentious business agreement / *n. phr.* A contract of retainer that is compliant with the requirements of s 57 of the Solicitors Act 1974 and which, subject to certain safeguards, will allow the solicitor to recover their fees for non-contentious work as if those fees were an ordinary debt.

Non-party costs order / *n. phr.* An order against a person who is not a party to the litigation, but who is in some way connected to it.

Notional premium / *n. phr.* (Informal) An additional amount payable to a membership organisation pursuant to s 30 of the Access to Justice Act 1999.

Paying party / *n. phr.* A party liable to pay costs.[73]

Payment on account / *n. phr.* **1.** (Between opposing parties) A payment made pursuant to an order made under CPR, r 44.2(8). **2.** (Between solicitor and client) A payment made on account of costs (either generally or in respect of specific items) that is not made in satisfaction of a statute bill.

Percentage increase / *n. phr.* The percentage by which the amount of a legal representative's fee can be increased in accordance with a conditional fee agreement that provides for a success fee.[74]

Porrect, to / *v.* † To put forward or submit a bill for examination or correction.[75]

Postponement charge / *n. phr.* That part of the percentage increase, if any, which relates to the cost to the legal representative of the postponement of the payment of their fees and expenses;[76] also known as postponement element[77] or a charge for postponement.[78]

Practice form / *n. phr.* Form to be used for a particular purpose in proceedings, the form and purpose being specified by a practice direction.[79]

Pre-action protocol / *n. phr.* Statements of best practice about pre-action conduct that have been approved by the Head of Civil Justice and are listed in *Practice Direction (Pre-Action Conduct)*.[80]

† = obsolete or archaic; *adj.* = adjective; *abv.* = abbreviation; *n.* = noun; *n. phr.* = noun phrase; *prop. n. phr.* = proper noun phrase; *v.* = verb

---

70 See pre-2013 CPR, r 43.3(h).

71 See CPR, r 43.3(n).

72 See s 87 of the Solicitors Act 1974; Ward LJ described the definition as a 'fairly useless circular definition' in *Garry v Gwillim* [2002] EWCA Civ 1500, at [14].

73 See CPR, r 44.1(1).

74 See the pre-2013 CPR, r 43.2(l) and (m).

75 *Oxford English Dictionary* (3rd edn). See also *Wharton's Law Lexicon* (5th edn, London: Stevens & Sons, 1872): 'Porrecting, producing for examination or taxation, as porrecting a [bill of costs], by a proctor.'

76 See the now-revoked Conditional Fee Agreement Regulations 2000 (SI 2000/2988), reg 3(1)(b).

77 See *Sidhu v Sandhu* [2008] EWHC 90108 (Costs), at [19].

78 See *Utting v McBain* [2007] EWHC 90085 (Costs), at [23].

79 This being the definition given in the CPR Glossary.

80 This being the definition given in the CPR Glossary.

Privilege / *n. phr.* The right of a party to refuse to disclose a document or to produce a document or to refuse to answer questions on the ground of some special interest recognised by law.[81]

***Pro bono* representation** / *n. phr.* 1. Legal representation provided free of charge.[82] 2. Representation provided in accordance with s 194 of the Legal Service Act 2007.

Profit costs / *n. phr.* The fees (that are not disbursements) charged by a solicitor for the legal services they have provided.

QOCS /*pron.* 'kwɒks / *abv.* (Also spelt QOWCS) Abbreviation for qualified one-way costs shifting.

Qualified one-way costs shifting / *n. phr.* A procedural fetter on the recovery of costs in certain personal injury and fatal accident cases such that (unless the claimant has been fundamentally dishonest), only the claimant may recover the costs of the claim.[83]

Receiving party / *n. phr.* A party entitled to be paid costs.[84]

Regional costs judge / *n. phr.* A specialist district judge who has been appointed to hear certain higher-value or complex detailed assessments.

Regulated person / *n. phr.* (For the purposes of the Legal Services Act 2007) 'Any class of persons which consists of or includes—(a) persons who are authorised by the body to carry on an activity which is a reserved legal activity; (b) persons who are not so authorised, but are employees of a person who is so authorised.'[85]

Relevant lawyer / *n. phr.* (For the purposes of the Legal Services Act 2007) An individual who is (a) a solicitor, (b) a barrister, (c) a solicitor in Scotland, (d) an advocate in Scotland, (e) a solicitor of the Court of Judicature of Northern Ireland, (f) a member of the Bar of Northern Ireland, (g) a registered foreign lawyer (within the meaning of s 89 of the Courts and Legal Services Act 1990), (h) an individual not within (a)–(g) who is an authorised person in relation to an activity that is a reserved legal activity or (i) a European lawyer (within the meaning of the European Communities (Services of Lawyers) Order 1978).[86]

Remuneration certificate / *n. phr.* † A certificate that used to be afforded to clients of solicitor pursuant a now-obsolete procedure governed by the Solicitors' (Non-Contentious Business) Remuneration Order 1994[87] by which the Law Society (via a department known as the Legal Complaints Service) would state the amount that a client was to pay.

Request for payment on account / *n. phr.* An invoice (other than a statute bill) rendered by a solicitor to a client requesting a payment on account of costs.

Reserved instrument activities / *n. phr.* (For the purposes of the Legal Services Act 2007) Collective phrase for the act of (a) preparing any instrument of transfer or charge for the purposes of the Land Registration Act 2002, (b) making an application or lodging a document for registration under that Act, (c) preparing any other

† = obsolete or archaic; *adj.* = adjective; *abv.* = abbreviation; *n.* = noun; *n. phr.* = noun phrase; *prop. n. phr.* = proper noun phrase; *v.* = verb

[81] This being the definition given in the CPR Glossary.
[82] See CPR, r 44.1(1).
[83] See CPR, r 44.13.
[84] See CPR, r 44.1(1).
[85] Section 21 of the Legal Services Act 2007.
[86] SI 1978/1910. See s 190 of the Legal Services Act 2007, as amended.
[87] SI 1994/2616.

instrument relating to real or personal estate for the purposes of the law of England and Wales or instrument relating to court proceedings in England and Wales—but which does not include the preparation of an instrument relating to any particular court proceedings if, immediately before the appointed day, no restriction was placed on the persons entitled to carry on that activity.[88]

Reserved legal activity / *n. phr.* (For the purposes of the Legal Services Act 2007) Activity including (a) the exercise of a right of audience, (b) the conduct of litigation, (c) reserved instrument activities, (d) probate activities, (e) notarial activities and (f) the administration of oaths.[89]

Retainer / *n.* **1.** A contract of retainer. **2.** The professional relationship between a legal services provider and client consequent upon the given and acceptance of the client's instruction. **3.** The client's authority for a legal services provider to act. **4.** A fee paid to a legal services provider to secure its services in a particular case. † **5.** A fee paid to counsel to secure their services in the future.

Right of audience / *n. phr.* The right to exercise any of the functions of appearing before and addressing a court, including the calling and examining of witnesses.[90]

Right to conduct litigation / *n. phr.* **1.** (For the purposes of Legal Services Act 2007) (a) The issuing of proceedings before any court in England and Wales, (b) the commencement, prosecution and defence of such proceedings, and (c) the performance of any ancillary functions in relation to such proceedings (such as entering appearances to actions).[91] † **2.** (For the purposes of the Courts and Legal Services Act 1990 prior to 2010) The right (a) to exercise all or any of the functions of issuing a writ or otherwise commencing proceedings before any court and (b) to perform any ancillary functions in relation to proceedings (such as entering appearances to actions).[92]

Rules of Court / *n. phr.* **1.** (For present-day purposes relating to the law of civil costs) The Civil Procedure Rules 1998. **2.** Rules made by the authority having power to make rules or orders regulating the practice and procedure of the court.[93] † **3.** Rulings of the court in individual cases.[94]

***Sanderson* order** / *n. phr.* A co-defendant order whereby an unsuccessful defendant is ordered directly to pay the successful defendant's costs.[95]

Service / *n.* Steps required by rules of court to bring documents used in court proceedings to a person's attention.[96]

† = obsolete or archaic; *adj.* = adjective; *abv.* = abbreviation; *n.* = noun; *n. phr.* = noun phrase; *prop. n. phr.* = proper noun phrase; *v.* = verb

88 See Sched 2, para 5, to the Land Registration Act 2002.
89 See s 12(1) of the Legal Services Act 2007.
90 See 119(1) of the Courts and Legal Services Act 1990 before 2010 and Sched 2, paras 3 and 4, to the Legal Services Act 2007, as amended, thereafter.
91 See Sched 2, paras 3 and 4, to the Legal Services Act 2007, as amended.
92 See s 119(1) of the Courts and Legal Services Act 1990.
93 See Sched 1 to the Interpretation Act 1978.
94 *Jones v Williams* (1841) 8 M & W 349, at 538, *per* Parke B; see also *Legal Aid Board v Russell* [1991] 2 AC 317, at 819, *per* Lord Ackner.
95 *Sanderson v Blyth Theatre Co* [1903] 2 KB 533.
96 This being the definition given in the CPR Glossary.

Several liability / *n. phr.* Liability whereby a person may remain liable for the whole claim even where judgment has been obtained against the others with whom they share liability.[97]

Standard basis / *n. phr.* A basis of assessment whereby the court will resolve any doubt as to whether the costs were reasonably incurred or were reasonable in amount in favour of the paying party; under the CPR, the costs would be subjected to a test of proportionality.[98]

Statute bill / *n. phr.* An invoice rendered by a solicitor to a client that is *bona fide* compliant with the requirements of s 69 of the Solicitors Act 1974.

Success fee / *n. phr.* **1.** A type of additional liability that is the product of a percentage increase and the base costs to which, pursuant to a conditional fee agreement, it applies. **2.** A colloquial term for a percentage increase. **3.** A conditional fee agreement provides for a success fee if it provides for the amount of any fees to which it applies to be increased, in specified circumstances, above the amount that would be payable if it were not payable only in specified circumstances.[99]

Third-party costs order / *n. phr.* A non-party costs order.

Unqualified person / *n. phr.* (For the purposes of the Solicitors Act 1974) A person who has not been admitted as a solicitor and who does not hold a current practising certificate.[100]

Wasted costs / *n. phr.* Costs, other than costs ordered pursuant to the court's inherent jurisdiction, which are ordered against a legal representative (or which are disallowed, as the case may be) as a result of that person's negligent, unreasonable or improper behaviour.

Wasted costs order / *n. phr.* An order (a) that the legal representative pay a specified sum in respect of costs to a party or (b) for costs relating to a specified sum or items of work to be disallowed.[101]

Without prejudice / *adj.* **1.** Without loss of any rights. **2.** Restriction on the circumstances in which the content of negotiations conducted with a view to settlement may be revealed to the court.[102]

† = obsolete or archaic; *adj.* = adjective; *abv.* = abbreviation; *n.* = noun; *n. phr.* = noun phrase; *prop. n. phr.* = proper noun phrase; *v.* = verb

[97] This being the definition given in the CPR Glossary.

[98] See CPR, r 44.3(3).

[99] See s 58(2)(b) of the Courts and Legal Services Act 1990, as amended.

[100] See ss 1 and 87 of the Solicitors Act 1974. Since 31 March 2009, the person must also be 'recognised' (or employed by a person who is recognised, or otherwise satisfying the requirements for in-house solicitors): see r 12 of the Solicitors Code of Conduct 2007 and (from 1 July 2009) s 1B of the Solicitors Act 1974, as amended by the Legal Services Act 2007 and the Legal Services Act 2007 (Commencement No 5, Transitory and Transitional Provisions) Order 2009 (SI 2009/1365).

[101] See PD 46, para 5.1.

[102] This being the definition given in the CPR Glossary.

3

THE NATURE OF COSTS

3.01 This chapter deals with the following topics:

- the characteristics of costs in general (3.03):
  - costs arise from litigation or professional work (3.06);
  - costs are not the same as charges (3.07);
  - costs must have been actually incurred (3.09);
  - costs must be calculable (3.10);
  - no such thing as 'loss of opportunity' costs (3.12);
  - costs must not merely be the costs of being a litigant (3.13);
  - costs are not subject to a test of remoteness (3.15);
  - costs are not a punishment or a reward (3.16);
  - policy considerations relating to costs (3.17);
- contentious and non-contentious business (3.21):
  - the distinction between contentious and non-contentious business (3.23);
  - examples of contentious business (3.31);
  - examples of non-contentious business (3.32);
  - the meaning of the word 'court' (3.34);
- costs versus damages (3.37):
  - the fees of professional advisers (3.42);
  - the consequences of misclassification (3.44);
- the work of lawyers in general (3.48);
- the work of lawyers under the Solicitors Act 1974 (3.54);
- the work of lawyers under the Courts and Legal Services Act 1990 (3.57):
  - 'acting as a solicitor' (3.65);
  - 'conducting litigation' (3.73);
  - 'rights of audience' (3.75);
- the work of lawyers under the Legal Services Act 2007 (3.76):
  - 'conduct of litigation' (3.78);
  - 'rights of audience' (3.80);
  - 'reserved instrument activities' (3.81);
  - agents, employers and employees (3.83);
- work done by non-lawyers (3.92):
  - expert assistance for litigants in person in costs litigation (3.95);
  - restriction on disbursements incurred by litigation in person (3.97); and
  - specific situations in which work is done by persons other than a properly instructed lawyer (3.100).

As can be seen from the above list, this chapter discusses those identifying features that, first, allow monies to be recognised as costs (as opposed to damages or other monies) and, secondly, allow costs to be characterised as arising from contentious or non-contentious business. It then examines the nature of lawyers' work, explaining why the professional exertions of lawyers tend to give rise to monetary losses of a type that can be said to be 'costs' and why the same cannot generally be said of the monetary losses arising from the exertions of others. **3.02**

The Characteristics of Costs in General

Section 87(1) of the Solicitors Act 1974 defines costs as 'fees, charges, disbursements, expenses and remuneration'. Similarly, prior to 1 April 2013, the Civil Procedure Rules (CPR) provided the following definition: **3.03**

> ' "Costs" includes fees, charges, disbursements, expenses, remuneration, reimbursement allowed to a litigant in person under rule 48.6, any additional liability incurred under a funding arrangement and any fee or reward charged by a lay representative for acting on behalf of a party in proceedings allocated to the small claims track.'[1]

The present definition is the same other than that it omits the reference to additional liability.[2] None of these definitions is fully inclusive in the sense that it will be determinative of the issue of what may be categorised as *not* being costs; it is therefore necessary to look to case law for assistance.

Not all monies occasioned by a person's involvement in litigation can be said to be costs. This was realised many centuries ago (see 1.54). There is, for example, a passage in Lord Coke's writings of 1642 that acknowledges this distinction: **3.04**

> 'Here [the Statute of Gloucester] is express mention made but of the costs of his writ, but it extendeth to all the legal cost of the suit, but not to the costs and expenses of his travel and loss of time, and therefore "costages" cometh of the verb "conster", and that again of the verb "constare", for these "costages" must "constare" to the court to be legal costs and expenses.'[3]

The fact that there is a distinction between monies that are and monies that are not 'costs' remains relevant today; indeed, Lord Coke's analysis is still occasionally cited.[4]

There is no single test that will determine whether monies can be said to be costs, but the factors described at 3.06–3.17 may, in an appropriate case, be relevant. Some of the factors relate to the nature of the monies in question, whereas others go to policy or to the way in which the court quantifies costs. Different factors may be relevant in different circumstances; a summary can be found at 3.19. **3.05**

---

[1] CPR, r 43.2(1)(a), as it then was.

[2] See CPR, r 44.1(1). This was intentional and significant: see *BNM v MGN Ltd* [2017] EWCA Civ 1767, at [81], *per* Sir Terence Etherton MR.

[3] Lord Coke, 'The Second Part of the Institutes of the Laws of England; Containing the Exposition of Many Ancient and Other Statutes' (1797) 2 Inst 288.

[4] See, eg, *McIlwraith v McIlwraith* [2005] EWHC 90010 (Costs) and the Irish case of *Dawson v Irish Brokers Association* [2002] IESC 36.

Costs arise from litigation or professional work

3.06 In so far as litigation is concerned, costs must arise from the litigation in question. Bowen LJ said: 'Only legal costs which the Court can measure are to be allowed, and that such legal costs are to be treated as expenses necessarily arising from the litigation and necessarily caused by the course which it takes.'[5] The test of whether the monies in question have arisen from the litigation is only the starting point, however. Monies failing to satisfy that test will not be costs, but where that test is satisfied, the monies may or may not be costs depending on the factors set out below. Additionally, solicitors' fees must relate to the professional work of providing legal services. This means that the following will not generate costs because they do not involve the provision of legal services: finding a business partner;[6] securing a loan;[7] collecting rent;[8] distributing monies in the context of winding up an estate;[9] dealing with administrative issues in the context of probate;[10] acting as a town clerk;[11] acting as an election agent;[12] and acting as a court official.[13] Disbursements are addressed at 52.02–52.09, 52.10 and at Figure 52.1. Counsel is addressed at 53.31.

Costs are not the same as charges

3.07 The court assesses costs rather than charges. Put another way, it would be wrong to say that all fees and charges arising out of the litigation are costs. The identification of what monies are recoverable as costs and what are not is a matter for the court—that is, the issue is not a mere function of the losses borne by the receiving party. In this regard, Purchas LJ made the following observations: 'An award of costs has always ... ultimately been a matter of discretion in the court rather than the recognition by the court of a right possessed by a successful litigant.'[14]

3.08 Brett MR had this to say on the topic:

> 'I should have thought that the person wrongfully brought into litigation ought to be indemnified against the expenses to which he is unjustly put; but there cannot be a perfect indemnity, because it is impossible to determine how much of the costs is incurred through his own over-anxiety.'[15]

The theme could be further developed by saying that costs are an assessment of what it is reasonable for the paying party to pay rather than what the receiving party might have incurred.[16]

---

5 *London Scottish Benefit Society v Chorley* (1884) 13 QBD 872, at 877. See also the comments of Megarry V-C in *Re Gibson's Settlement Trusts* [1981] Ch 179, at 185.

6 *Sharp v Southern* [1905] VLR 223.

7 *Re Inderwick* (1885) 54 LJ Ch 72.

8 *Re Devereux* (1902) 46 SJ 320 and *In the Estate of Purton* (1935) 53 WN (NSW) 148; that said, see *Re Shilson Coode & Co* [1904] 1 Ch 837.

9 See the Australian case of *In the Estate of Purton* (1935) 53 WN (NSW) 148. (The writer is grateful to Roger Quick for assistance in finding the Australian cases.)

10 See the Australian case of *In the Will of Douglas* (1951) 51 SR (NSW) 282.

11 *Bush v Martin* (1863) 2 H & C 311.

12 *Re Oliver* (1867) 36 LJ Ch 261, but only where that does not involve giving legal advice (see *Re Osborne* (1858) 25 Beav 353).

13 *Allen v Aldridge; Re Ward* (1843) 5 Beav 401.

14 *Hunt v RM Douglas (Roofing) Ltd*, CAT, 18 November 1987, The Times, 23 November 1987, at p 21 of the official transcript.

15 *London Scottish Benefit Society v Chorley* (1884) 13 QBD 872, at 875.

16 *L v L* [1996] 1 FLR 873, at 885, *per* Neill LJ.

Costs must have been actually incurred

With one or two minor exceptions,[17] costs are limited to compensation for losses actually incurred. Put another way, most costs are limited to real rather than notional losses (see 59.29). Nourse LJ has commented that this is a 'cardinal requirement'.[18] The requirement that costs be actually incurred would not ordinarily prevent the court from assessing costs on the basis of a notional *management* (such as on the basis that counsel's advice ought to have been taken in writing rather than in conference); this, presumably, is permissible because the costs were actually incurred notwithstanding the notional management (see 57.32). There is a limit to which the court can do this, however; there is no authority for the proposition that the court can effectively rewrite the bill of costs (see 57.31–57.32). **3.09**

Costs must be calculable

This factor turns on whether losses can be computed, in the sense that they can be expressed as a calculable sum. Purchas LJ rejected the notion that this was the only factor relevant for the purposes of deciding what are and are not costs.[19] The need for costs to be in a specifiable amount was another factor that Nourse LJ said was a 'cardinal requirement': 'The job of a taxing master is difficult enough without his having to worry his head over an item as foggy and suppositional as [an unquantified claim].'[20] **3.10**

In a similar vein, Bowen LJ had this to say: 'Professional skill and labour are recognised and can be measured by the law; private expenditure of labour and trouble by laymen cannot be measured. It depends on the zeal, assiduity, or the nervousness of the individual.'[21] **3.11**

No such thing as 'loss of opportunity' costs

Loss-of-opportunity costs are monies that, but for the litigation, the receiving party (as distinct from their lawyers) would have made or earned. They are similar to economic losses in the law of tort. Unless there is provision to the contrary, they are not recoverable as legal costs.[22] **3.12**

Costs must not merely be the costs of being a litigant

The costs must arise from the litigation and not merely be costs of *being* a litigant (see, for example, 49.106). In this regard, Purchas LJ has this to say: **3.13**

> 'Certain costs incurred by a litigant in person have never been considered as falling within the category of "legal costs". These are immediately discernible, eg the litigant's personal expenses of travel to court, his loss of time at court and his loss of earning or profit in whatever capacity he may operate. He has never been allowed to claim in a Bill of Costs these items where they arise solely from the occurrence of the litigation.'[23]

---

[17] The Litigants in Person (Costs and Expenses) Act 1975, for example, permits recovery of notional monies and even before that Act came into force it was held that a solicitor litigant in person was able to recover monies that would have been incurred had the litigant instructed solicitors (see *H Tolputt & Co Ltd v Mole* [1911] 1 KB 87 and *London Scottish Benefit Society v Chorley* (1884) 13 QBD 872).

[18] *Hunt v RM Douglas (Roofing) Ltd*, CAT, 18 November 1987, The Times, 23 November 1987, at p 24 of the official transcript.

[19] *Ibid*, at p 21 of the official transcript.

[20] *Ibid*, at p 24 of the official transcript.

[21] *London Scottish Benefit Society v Chorley* (1884) 13 QBD 872, at 877.

[22] *Hunt v RM Douglas (Roofing) Ltd*, CAT, 18 November 1987, The Times, 23 November 1987, at p 23 of the official transcript, *per* Purchas LJ.

[23] *Ibid*, at p 17 of the official transcript.

3.14 In a slightly different context (that is, the nature of the costs that a solicitor litigant in person is able to recover), Brett MR had this to say: 'The unsuccessful adversary ... cannot be charged for what does not exist, he cannot be charged for the solicitor consulting himself, or instructing himself, or attending upon himself.'[24] The context in which these comments were made was such that Brett MR intended no allowance to be made in lieu of these matters: the implication is that the costs of being a litigant are not recoverable (see 59.46).

Costs are not subject to a test of remoteness

3.15 There is no test of remoteness in relation to legal costs.[25] Very remote costs are likely to have been unreasonably incurred, but would still, in principle, be costs.

Costs are not a punishment or a reward

3.16 Costs are neither punishment nor reward, but instead are an imperfect indemnity.[26] Bramwell B put it in this way:

> 'Costs as between party and party are given by the law as an indemnity to the person entitled to them: they are not imposed as a punishment on the party who pays them, nor given as a bonus to the party who receives them.'[27]

Likewise, Jessel MR said that the court had no power to order by way of a penalty that a party is to pay 'costs beyond the costs of the suit' (see 1.90).[28] This is the case even if the costs are described as being damages.[29] With one unimportant exception,[30] costs are not capable of being awarded specifically as a punishment.[31] Older decisions (from before about 1850[32]) that imply the contrary are no longer good law (see 1.49). That said, some commentators have noted that procedural abuses and defaults are often met with orders that have a flavour of penalty about them.[33]

---

24 *London Scottish Benefit Society v Chorley* (1884) 13 QBD 872, at 876.

25 *Hunt v RM Douglas (Roofing) Ltd*, CAT, 18 November 1987, The Times, 23 November 1987, at p 18 of the official transcript, *per* Purchas LJ.

26 *Malkinson v Trim* [2002] EWCA Civ 1273, at [11], *per* Chadwick LJ.

27 *Harold v Smith* (1860) 5 Hurlestone & Norman 381, at 385.

28 *Willmott v Barber* (1881) WN 107, at 108. See also *Ross v York Newcastle & Berwick Railway Co* (1849) 18 LJR 199, at 200, and *Clarke & Chapman v Hart* (1868) 6 HLC 633, in which Cranworth LC said that costs are not a penalty, but a necessary consequence of instituting litigation that has failed.

29 *Willmott v Barber* (1881) 17 Ch D 772, CA; *Re Vernon & Co (Pulp Products) Ltd's Patent* [1976] RPC 625; *Cockburn v Edwards* (1881) 18 Ch D 449, at 459.

30 There is one minor exception to this rule and even that is debatable under the CPR, ie where a non-party costs order is made against a legal representative pursuant to the court's inherent jurisdiction, in which case the order can be seen as having a punitive element: see *Glasgow Harley (a firm) v McDonald* [2001] UKPC 18A and *Myers v Elman* [1940] AC 282.

31 See *Highgate Justices, ex parte Petrou* [1954] 1 WLR 485; *Knight v Clifton* [1971] 1 Ch 700; *R v Tottenham Justices, ex parte Joshi* [1982] 2 All ER 507. This rule holds good in other common-law jurisdictions too: see, eg, *Armstrong v Boulton* [1990] VR 215, at 221, and *Cachia v Hanes* (1994) 179 CLR 4030. Whilst dealing with a criminal matter, the European Court of Human Rights has held that the fact that a litigant had elected to exercise his right to silence was something that could be taken into account as being a relevant factor without imposing a penalty: *Ashendon and Jones v United Kingdom*, The Times, 22 September 2011.

32 This is around the period that the efforts to move away from 'double' and 'treble' costs began to be recognised by the courts in the way that they analysed costs generally: see 1.85; see also Quick, R, *Quick on Costs* (Thomson Reuters, online), para 2.130.

33 Mause, PJ, 'Winner Takes All: A Re-examination of the Indemnity System' (1969) 55 Iowa LR 26, at 37. See also the New South Wales case in which it was said that '[o]rders for costs are one of the ways, possibly one of the most effective ways, of a court controlling the standards of the profession and the efficiency of litigation': *Hermann v Charny* [1976] 1 NSWLR 261, at 268.

Policy considerations relating to costs

The rationale underlying decisions as to what are and are not costs may often turn on policy rather than legal principles. In this regard, Sedley J made the following comments about the recoverability of certain travelling expenses (see 52.57): **3.17**

> '[The restriction on the recovery of certain expenses was rather] regarded as a policy limitation than as a legal distinction. Certainly both in and after Coke's time, local courts were in chronic decline and the cost of coming to Westminster for justice was widely regarded as a scandal which was aggravated by the irrecoverability of the expenses: see Veall[34] ... where it is said that Coke himself estimated that litigants were spending a million pounds a year in coming to London for justice in the first quarter of the 17th Century. But the anomaly, if that is what it is, has become enshrined in the law.'[35]

Finally, it is worth mentioning that the mere fact that monies cannot be characterised as being legal costs does not mean that the parties cannot agree that they will be treated as being recoverable as if they were costs: if a consent order specifically provides that certain monies will be recoverable, they will be recoverable even though they would not normally be thought of as being legal costs.[36] **3.18**

Summary

In summary, there is no single test that can be applied to determine what are and are not costs, but the following generalisations can be made. **3.19**

- Costs will generally arise from the litigation.
- Costs will not be the mere expenses of being a litigant.
- Costs must be calculable.
- Costs must have been actually incurred.

These factors help to determine whether monies can be said to be costs; further considerations may need to be taken into account in deciding whether monies that are putatively costs are, in principle, recoverable as such.[37] Those considerations will usually depend on the nature of the monies in question. Examples of the types of question that may need to be asked can be found at 49.104–49.136 and 49.147–49.164. **3.20**

Contentious and Non-contentious Business

Whilst it is true to say that there are differences between contentious and non-contentious costs, that distinction is far less significant than one might expect. The law has developed with such little regard to that distinction that the present-day position is that those differences are, in general, limited to the following. **3.21**

- Non-contentious costs may not be assessed in the County Court and its hearing centres (see 5.14).

[34] Veall, D, *The Popular Movement for Law Reform 1640–1660* (Oxford: Clarendon Press, 1970), pp 36–9.

[35] *R v Legal Aid Board, ex parte Eccleston* [1998] 1 WLR 1279, at 1282.

[36] See, eg, *Ruttle Plant Hire Ltd v DEFRA* [2007] EWHC 1633 (QB). This, presumably, would be subject to any affirmative restriction imposed by legislation.

[37] In *Re Gibson's Settlement Trusts* [1981] Ch 179, at 185, Megarry V-C identified three strands of reasoning that the court will take into account when gauging whether costs are *recoverable* in principle, but that is a slightly different topic that is dealt with at 49.07.

- Contentious costs and non-contentious costs are assessed on different bases.[38]
- Unwritten agreements between solicitor and client may be dealt with differently (see 27.210–27.213).
- Conditional fee agreements (including contingency fee agreements) are unlawful at common law if and in so far as they relate to work that is contentious.

3.22 The relevance of the final distinction has been significantly curtailed by statute (see 29.04, 29.203–29.216 and Chapter 29 generally). For most practical purposes, the distinction remains relevant only to the extent that it has a bearing on whether damages-based agreements and other such agreements are lawful (see 29.176–29.197), and on whether unwritten agreements as to costs between solicitor and client can be enforced (see 27.210–27.213).

The distinction between contentious and non-contentious business

3.23 Whether costs are contentious or non-contentious depends on the type of business from which they arose. Broadly speaking, the distinction between contentious and non-contentious business is that:

- all business that is done in proceedings is contentious, as is all business done before proceedings are begun, provided that the business is done with a view to the proceedings being begun *and* provided that they are, in fact, begun; and
- all other business is non-contentious, as is common-form probate work.[39]

3.24 Stanley Burnton LJ has explained[40] that the distinction does not depend on the nature of the work in hand, but on whether it was done 'in or for the purposes of proceedings begun before a court or before an arbitrator'.[41] Therefore, even if the work relates to a highly disputatious matter, it cannot be regarded as being intrinsically contentious for that reason alone.

3.25 Taken in isolation, the legislative definitions are somewhat circular. Part of the definition of contentious business includes a reference to non-contentious business (see 3.26 below), but non-contentious business is defined as '[a]ny business done as a solicitor which is not contentious business as defined by this subsection'.[42] The definitions of contentious and non-contentious business are, therefore, interdependent at the very least.

3.26 Prior to 1957, contentious business was defined as being '[a]ny business done by a solicitor in any court, whether as a solicitor or as an advocate'.[43] Thus the definition of contentious business was a narrow definition that, for example, would not have included work ancillary to proceedings in court (such as conveyancing business done for the purposes of a claim).[44]

---

[38] This can be significant, albeit rarely: see, eg, *Bilkus v Stockler Brunton (a firm)* [2010] EWCA Civ 101, in which a finding that certain work was contentious deprived a solicitor of a £50,000 value element.

[39] Common-form probate business of the type contained in s 128 of the Senior Courts Act 1981 relates to obtaining probate and administration where there is no contention as to the rights to probate.

[40] *Bilkus v Stockler Brunton (a firm)* [2010] EWCA Civ 101 (Ch).

[41] This being the wording of s 87(1) of the Solicitors Act 1974.

[42] See Solicitors Act 1974, s 87. Ward LJ described the definition as a 'fairly useless circular definition' in *Garry v Gwillim* [2002] EWCA 1500, at [14].

[43] See Solicitors Act 1932, s 81(1). Also see 1.99 and 1.128.

[44] See *In re Simpkin Marshall Ltd* [1959] Ch 229, at 235.

Since 1957,[45] however, contentious business has been defined as: **3.27**

> 'Business done, whether as solicitor or advocate in or for the purpose of proceedings begun before a court or before an arbitrator ... , not being business which falls within the definition of non-contentious or common form probate business contained in section 128 of the Senior Courts Act 1981.'[46]

This definition has been carried through to modern-day legislation.[47] It is wider than the previous definition in that it includes work done for the purpose of proceedings, which would include work such as conveyancing done for the purposes of a claim. In this regard, Wynn-Parry J had this to say: **3.28**

> 'There is now a clear and, I should have thought, logical division between contentious and non-contentious business. All business is now to be regarded as contentious which is done before proceedings are begun provided that the business is done with a view to the proceedings being begun, and they are in fact begun, and also all business done in the course of the proceedings. All other business is non-contentious.'[48]

This oft-quoted passage does not convey the difficulty that Wynn-Parry J had in formulating his judgment. He candidly admitted that he found the question to be 'a really difficult one'[49] and he specifically commented that 'a different view could well be entertained'.[50] Stanley Burnton LJ has found that the phrase 'in or for the purposes of proceedings' must be read as a composite whole and that it is permissible to look at the circumstances in which the work was being carried out—finding, in the case before him, that work carried out for the purpose of valuing shares was contentious work in the context of it being carried out for litigation and under the direction of the court.[51] **3.29**

Whilst not part of the definition, it is worth noting that s 51 of the Senior Courts Act 1981 reads as follows: 'Subject to the provisions of this or any other enactment and to rules of court, the costs of and incidental to all proceedings ... shall be in the discretion of the court.' This provision is in keeping with Wynn-Parry J's analysis. **3.30**

Examples of contentious business

The following are conventionally given[52] as examples of contentious business: **3.31**

- proceedings that have been begun in any court of record (not including a coroner's court);

---

[45] See the Solicitors Act 1957, which was probably in response to the following comments made by Denning LJ in *In re a Solicitor* [1955] 2 QB 252, at 269: 'Sir Hartley Shawcross asked us to draw a clear line for the guidance of the profession. We should have liked to accede to his request if we could. It seems to me that if a clear line is to be drawn there is only one possible place for it, namely, the issue of the writ or other originating process in the courts of law. All business before that date could be said to be non-contentious, and all business afterwards to be contentious. It would be very convenient if we could draw that line, but I do not think that we are at liberty to do so, for the simple reason that it is not the line drawn by Parliament'.

[46] Solicitors Act 1974, s 87.

[47] See *ibid.*

[48] *In re Simpkin Marshall Ltd* [1959] Ch 229, at 235.

[49] *Ibid*, at 236.

[50] *Ibid*, at 239.

[51] *Bilkus v Stockler Brunton (a firm)* [2010] EWCA Civ 101 (Ch), at [44].

[52] This list is based on, but not identical to, the list published by the Law Society in the booklet *Non-Contentious Costs* (London: Practice Advice Service, 2010).

- proceedings that have been begun before an arbitrator;
- proceedings that have been begun before the Lands Tribunal (more correctly known as the Lands Chamber of the Upper Tribunal);[53]
- proceedings that have been begun before the Employment Appeals Tribunal (but not in an employment tribunal itself);
- proceedings that have been begun in the Upper Tribunal;[54]
- proceedings that have been begun which relate to contentious probate;
- proceedings that have been begun in the magistrates' court relating to licensing; and
- any work that was done in anticipation of the above (but only where proceedings have actually been commenced).

Examples of non-contentious business

3.32 Likewise, the following are conventionally given as being examples of non-contentious work:

- business done where no proceedings have been issued;
- business done where proceedings have been issued, but in a foreign court;
- non-contentious or common-form probate work;
- proceedings before the Criminal Injuries Compensation Authority;
- proceedings in inquiries (including planning) or tribunals other than the Lands Tribunal, the Employment Appeals Tribunal or a statutory inquiry;
- business done in respect of licensing relating to where the body to whom representations are made is the local authority; and
- proceedings before a coroner's court (unless that work is for the purposes of a claim, which is subsequently brought).[55]

3.33 Whilst not binding, Master Hurst has found that this conventional view has become so well established that the aggregate consequences of adopting a different view would be worse than the aggregate consequences of allowing it to continue.[56] Specifically, he has rejected the submission that proceedings in tribunals constituted before the coming into force of the Tribunals, Courts and Enforcement Act 2007 should be regarded as being contentious, whilst leaving open the issue of whether proceedings in the First-tier Tribunal should be regarded as contentious or non-contentious.[57]

The meaning of the word 'court'

3.34 There is no definition of the word 'court' in the Solicitors Act 1974 or in the Interpretation Act 1978. Whilst not binding, Master Hurst has found that the word 'court' means 'court of record',[58] which guidance has been adopted by the Law

---

53 It is likely that, at first instance, this tribunal will, in due course, be assimilated into a body that will be known as the Land, Property and Housing Chamber First-tier Tribunal.

54 This is a recent addition to this list, but it would seem to be a correct one given the fact that s 3(3) of the Tribunals, Courts and Enforcement Act 2007 provides that the Upper Tribunal is a superior court of record.

55 This list is based on, but not identical to, the list published by the Law Society in the booklet *Non-Contentious Costs* (London: Practice Advice Service, 2010), but it should be noted that the editor has had difficulty in finding confirmative authority for many of the items.

56 *Tel-Ka Talk Ltd v Revenue & Customs Commissioners* [2010] EWHC 90175 (Costs), at [145]. The master did not specifically address the lists set out above (which are based on guidance issued by the Law Society), but his conclusion was compatible with those lists being broadly correct.

57 *Ibid*, at [136].

58 *Ibid*, at [145].

Society.[59] It is, perhaps, instructive that s 119 of the Courts and Legal Services Act 1990 (as amended[60]) refers to the following definition in the Legal Services Act 2007 (at para 207):

> ' "Court" includes—
> (a) a tribunal that is (to any extent) a listed tribunal for, or for any of, the purposes of Schedule 7 to the Tribunals, Courts and Enforcement Act 2007 (functions etc of Administrative Justice and Tribunals Council);
> (b) a court-martial;
> (c) a statutory inquiry within the meaning of section 16(1) of the Tribunals and Inquiries Act 1992 (c 53); [and]
> (d) an ecclesiastical court (including the Court of Faculties).'

If this definition does apply, then it is possible that proceedings in the First-tier Tribunal would be regarded as being contentious.[61] The importance of this is that work which was formerly regarded as being non-contentious may become (and may already now be) contentious; this may have the effect of rendering unenforceable retainers that hitherto have been regarded as being not only permissible, but also the norm.[62] This would be a significant change in so far as litigation funding is concerned and there is much force in the suggestion that it would be so inconvenient a change in the law that it ought to be rejected unless expressly provided for in legislation. This was one of the many reasons Master Hurst mentioned when he rejected an argument that a First-tier Tribunal was a 'court'. Whilst persuasive rather than binding, he found that a narrow interpretation should be preferred because 'the aggregate consequences on the parties and ... for the law generally, of a broader construction [would be] significantly worse than the aggregate consequences of a narrow construction'.[63] **3.35**

Master Hurst also found that the fact that a claim is subject to assessment under the CPR (or by analogy with the CPR) is not, of itself, reason to find that it is to be regarded as the subject of contentious work.[64] In a similar vein, Stanley Burnton LJ came to much the same conclusion in respect of work done after proceedings have concluded where such work was done not for the purpose of the proceedings, but in consequence thereof.[65] Given the fact that s 3(5) of the Tribunals, Courts and Enforcement Act 2007 specifically designates the Upper Tribunal as a superior court of record, it is likely that work in that tribunal would be regarded as being contentious.[66] **3.36**

---

[59] See Law Society, *Non-Contentious Costs* (London: Practice Advice Service, 2010).

[60] In particular, as amended by Sched 8, para 15, to the Tribunals, Courts and Enforcement Act 2007.

[61] The list of supervised tribunals was previously set out in Sched 1 to the Tribunals and Inquiries Act 1992.

[62] In brief, damages-based agreements (which are usually referred to simply as 'contingency fee agreements') that might have been enforceable in proceedings before tribunals that were not under the aegis of the Council on Tribunals may well not be enforceable if and when that tribunal comes under the supervision of the Administrative Justice and Tribunals Council (unless, of course, the agreement complies with the relevant statutory provisions).

[63] *Tel-Ka Talk Ltd v Revenue & Customs Commissioners* [2010] EWHC 90175 (Costs), at [145].

[64] In *ibid*, at [137]–[142]; see also *Dean & Dean v Angel Airlines SA* [2007] EWHC 399 (QB), at [16] *et seq*, *per* McKay J.

[65] *Bilkus v Stockler Brunton (a firm)* [2010] EWCA Civ 101, at [44]–[46].

[66] Master Hurst indicated that this was probably the case, but he declined to make a finding on the point: *Tel-Ka Talk Ltd v Revenue & Customs Commissioners* [2010] EWHC 90175 (Costs), at [136].

Costs versus Damages

3.37 As a general rule, expenses incurred in connection with litigation will be recoverable, if at all, pursuant to a costs order rather than by way of damages.[67] The distinction between costs and damages is not always easy to make.[68] Indeed, up until the mid-19th century, costs were often regarded as being included as part of the damages.[69] This, however, was largely as a consequence of a now-obsolete system by which 'double' or 'treble' damages were accompanied by 'double' or 'treble' costs (see 1.49),[70] the relevance of which is that authorities decided before about 1850 ought to be treated with considerable caution.

3.38 As explained at 3.05–3.19, not all fees and expenses that arise during a claim will be costs. Where they have arisen as *part of* the claim or counterclaim (rather than *in consequence of* its prosecution or defence), they may best be categorised as being damages rather than costs[71]—and this will be the case even where the monies were spent purchasing legal services. An example would be the costs of proceedings in other jurisdictions[72] or fees paid for purchasing other non-contentious legal services.[73] Where the monies are properly and unambiguously regarded as being costs, then they would not be recoverable as damages.[74] Thus a party cannot claim costs-like monies from a party if, in truth, those monies would be or have been disallowed as costs against the same party.[75] Ward LJ approved the following extract from *McGregor on Damages* on this point:

> 'It would make nonsense of the rules about costs if the successful party in an action who has been awarded costs could claim in a further action by way of damages the amount by which the costs awarded him fell short of the costs actually incurred by him. This has naturally never been allowed, and it is hardly surprising that there is a dearth of authority on the point. *Cockburn v Edwards* (1881) 18 Ch D 449 is probably the only case in which such a claim was attempted but without success ...'[76]

3.39 One would have thought that the editors of *McGregor* would have been on safe ground in suggesting that no one would be audacious enough to try to have two bites at the

---

67 *Avrahami & Ors v Biran & Ors* [2013] EWHC 1776 (Ch), at [294], *per* Newey J.

68 Counter-intuitive examples exist. Thus a 'costs' order made against a solicitor under the inherent jurisdiction of the court is a summary procedure that is in lieu of the claim that could be brought for damages against the errant solicitor: see Chapter 7 and, in particular, *Collen v Wright* (1857) 8 E&B 647.

69 See *Pilford's Case* (1613) 10 Co Rep 115b, 77 ER 110 (Co Rep) 2, at 116b; see also *Ashmore v Ripley* (1617) 79 ER 359 and Sayer, J, *The Law of Costs* (London: J & WT Clarke, 1768), p 271.

70 See *Deacon v Morris* (1819) 2 B & Ald 393; *Phillips v Bacon* (1808) 103 ER 587, at 590 (ER).

71 This description of the law (which first appeared in the second edition of this book) was cited with approval by MH Rosen QC (sitting as a deputy High Court judge) in *Campbell v Campbell* [2017] EWHC 182 (Ch), at [178].

72 See, eg, *Starlight Shipping Co v Allianz Marine & Aviation Versicherungs AG* [2014] EWCA Civ 1010, at [21], *per* Longmore LJ, in which insurers obtained damages for costs incurred by reason of proceedings commenced in Greece by shipowners in breach of English jurisdiction and settlement agreements. Also see *Seavision Investment SA v Norman Thomas Evennett, The 'Tiburon'* [1992] 2 Lloyd's Rep 26.

73 See, eg, *Berry v British Transport Commission* [1961] 3 All ER 65, *British Racing Drivers' Club Ltd v Hextall Erskine & Co (a firm)* [1996] 3 All ER 667 and *Union Discount Co Ltd v Zoller (Costs)* [2001] EWCA Civ 1755.

74 See *Carroll v Kynaston* [2010] EWCA Civ 1404, at [23], *per* Ward LJ.

75 Whilst an Australian case (and therefore only persuasive), see *Coleman v Buckinghams Ltd* [1963] SR (NSW) 171, in which it was held that an action for malicious prosecution would lie where the damage alleged was costs incurred in defending proceedings in a court that had no jurisdiction to award costs.

76 *McGregor on Damages* (18th edn, London: Sweet & Maxwell, 2009), para 17-003, quoted with approval in *Carroll v Kynaston* [2010] EWCA Civ 1404, at [23].

cherry, but in fact there are have been several occasions on which this has happened (always without success).[77] Brett LJ had this to say on the topic:

> '[T]he damages in an action of tort must have been incurred when the action is brought, except in some cases where they include everything up to the time of trial, and they cannot include any expenses incurred in the action itself. The law considers the extra costs which are disallowed on taxation between party and party as a luxury for which the other party ought in no case to be liable, and they cannot be allowed by way of damages.'[78]

Whilst an Australian case and therefore only persuasive, Hamilton J refused to allow a party to claim monies as damages where there had been an attempt to recover those monies from another party as costs and he had this to say: '[T]he best conclusion is that the rule should be that all costs of all parties in multi-party proceedings should be dealt with by costs orders made in exercise of the court's discretionary power to make such orders'.[79] The fact that costs have been disallowed as between parties, however, will not necessarily prevent those monies from being recovered as damages where they are properly recoverable as such from a third party.[80] **3.40**

The distinction between costs and damages is often resolved by considering whether the losses or liabilities arose as a natural consequence of the defendant's actions.[81] If they did, then the monies will usually be damages. Misclassification is troublesome because if costs are wrongly claimed as damages or vice versa, they may be disallowed entirely.[82] Sometimes, the distinction between costs and damages is extremely narrow, as Sir Mark Waller, for example, acknowledged when he explained that expenses incurred by an owner of an arrested ship for the purposes of obtaining bail are damages, but the expenses of putting up a guarantee to avoid an arrest can properly be said to be costs.[83] **3.41**

The fees of professional advisers

The issue of whether monies are costs or damages often arises where the monies in question are fees for professional advisers who were engaged for the purposes of dealing with the after-effects of whichever wrong it was that led to the claim. An example might be the fees of a quantum surveyor who was instructed to advise on the costs of rebuilding a property destroyed by a defendant's carelessness: on one analysis, the surveyor's fees could be thought of as being the expenses of rebuilding the property, but a competing analysis would be that their fees are expert fees of preparing a **3.42**

---

[77] See *Cockburn v Edwards* (1881) 18 Ch D 449, at 462–3, *Harrison v McSheehan* (1885) WN 207 and *Ross v Caunters* [1979] 3 All ER 580, at 600–1, *per* Megarry VC. Also see the dictum of Hanworth MR in *Pêcheries Ostendaises (SA) v Merchants' Marine Insurance Co* [1928] All ER Rep at 176 and *Bevan v Blackhall & Struthers (No 2)* [1973] 2 NZLR 45, at 74–5 and 84 (preliminary costs not recoverable as damages).

[78] *Cockburn v Edwards* (1881) 18 Ch D 449, at 462, cited with approval in *Avrahami & Ors v Biran & Ors* [2013] EWHC 1776 (Ch), at [294], *per* Newey J.

[79] *Queanbeyan Leagues Club Ltd v Poldune Pty Ltd* [2000] NSWSC 1100, at [14]; also see *QIW Retailers Ltd v Felview* [1989] 2 Qd R 245.

[80] *Hammond v Bussey* (1888) 20 QBD 79.

[81] See *Peak Construction (Liverpool) Ltd v McKinney Foundation* (1970) 1 Build LR 111; *Hutchinson v Harris* [1978] 10 BLR 19, at 39.

[82] An example is where damages have wrongly been claimed as costs, but which, had they been claimed as damages, would have been subject to a test of causation or remoteness.

[83] *Ene 1 Kos Ltd v Petroleo Brasileiro SA* [2010] EWCA Civ 772, at [39]–[57].

report on quantum. If, for example, only 50 per cent of the damages were recoverable as a result of contributory negligence, a dispute as to the nature of those fees would be more than merely academic.

3.43 Where the claimant seeks to recover such fees as damages, there would usually be no objection in principle (or if there were to be an objection, it would usually be resolved by consent). This is because even if an objection were to be made and upheld, it would usually do nothing more than to move the fees from the claimant's schedule of special damages to their bill of costs (see 3.44–3.45). Any difficulties are further diminished by the fact that, in certain circumstances, the court is able to treat the monies as costs notwithstanding the fact that they are claimed damages.[84] This, of course, assumes that there are no other factors at play. There is, for example, a general rule that a person may not bring an action for 'damages' where those monies are in truth costs that the person has failed to recover in a previous claim against the same party.[85] Likewise, a person may not claim costs as 'damages' if the reason they are doing so is because those costs would be, or have been, disallowed if claimed as costs (see 3.38). The mere fact that monies have been or would be disallowed as costs between parties will not, however, necessarily prevent them from being recovered from a third party.[86] Moreover, these principles will not apply where the claim is a claim for a contractual indemnity.[87] Issues such as these seldom arise in the context of the law of costs; as such, further details are relegated to the footnotes.[88]

The consequences of misclassification

3.44 A finding that 'damages' ought to have been claimed as costs is commonly of little consequence because it will often be possible to transfer those monies to a bill of costs at the conclusion of the litigation. The more difficult situation, however, is where monies are claimed as 'costs' when they ought to have been claimed as damages; this is more problematic because it would often be too late to claim those monies as damages. Mocatta J had the following points to make about that topic:

> 'The question has been raised whether the fees of a witness, which included expenditure that could have been claimed as damages in an action but were not included in the damages claimed, can be claimed instead as costs. I can see no reason why they should not be,

[84] That is, the court is able to delegate the task of ascertaining quantum to a costs judge who would 'assess' the monies on the standard basis: *Redbus LMDS Ltd v Jeffrey Green & Russell (a firm)* [2006] EWHC 2938 (Ch). Delegation to a costs judge would be particularly appropriate where the fees were those of a legal adviser and where those fees were extensive.

[85] The seminal case on the point is *Quartz Hill Gold Mining Co v Eyre* (1883) 11 QBD 674, at 690, *per* Bowen LJ: 'If the judge refuses to give him costs, it is because he does not deserve them: if he deserves them, he will get them in the original action ...' As a more modern example, see *Carroll v Kynaston* [2010] EWCA Civ 1404. See also *The 'Tiburon'* [1992] 2 Ll L Rep 26.

[86] *Hammond v Bussey* (1888) 20 QBD 79.

[87] The indemnity will apply only to the costs claimed, not to the costs of bringing the claim for the indemnity: *Simpson v British Industries Trust Ltd* (1923) 39 TLR 286.

[88] The principle stated above (that costs may not be claimed as damages where, in truth, they are unrecovered costs) will usually apply, but not always. For example, there is no rule of law that costs incurred in foreign proceedings are irrecoverable as damages in an English action between the same parties where a separate cause of action existed in relation to those costs: *Union Discount Co Ltd v Zoller (Costs)* [2001] EWCA Civ 1755; *National Westminster Bank Plc v Rabobank Nederland* [2007] EWHC 3163 (Comm). Likewise, the rule does not apply where costs have been or could have been recovered in criminal proceedings and are now sought in a claim based on criminal conduct: see *Berry v British Transport Commission* [1962] 1 QB 306, in which the subsequent (ie, civil) claim was for malicious prosecution, false imprisonment and conspiracy.

provided that they were not recovered in the judgment by way of damages, provided that they are a proper item, and can be justified as to quantum.'[89]

Thus there is no reason in principle why monies that are capable of being claimed as damages cannot be claimed as costs. This, however, is only where they are 'a proper item'; Mocatta J did not expand upon what he meant by a 'proper item', but a paying party would have good grounds for arguing that an item is not a proper item where that party can show prejudice arising from the decision not to claim the monies as damages. It could, for example, be said that a fee cannot properly be claimed as costs if it would have been subject to reduction for contributory negligence as damages. Where—as is often the case—the fees are for professional advice concerning the damage sustained, it may be worth examining the nature of the evidence that has been adduced for the purposes of proving the claim;[90] that will usually reveal whether the monies were a natural consequence of the defendant's actions or a necessary part of proving the claim. **3.45**

A professional's fees may be damages at one stage in the claim and costs at another. An example might be where the quantum surveyor mentioned above (see 3.42) supervised the purchase of materials (in which case, their fees would normally be damages), but then prepared an expert report on the costs of repair (in which case, their fees would normally be costs). Whilst speaking in the context of an attempt to claim monies as damages rather than costs, Longmore LJ has said that where a party seeks to claim monies in different categories, that party must prove that this is appropriate on clear evidence.[91] There are examples of the court making a distinction between costs and damages in respect of monies claimed in the same case.[92] **3.46**

In summary, the question of whether monies are costs or damages is usually determined by considering whether they were incurred as a natural consequence of the defendant's actions. Where the distinction cannot fairly be made in this way, then the court will look at the issue of prejudice and decide whether it is fair that monies are claimed in the form that the receiving party wishes to claim them. **3.47**

The Work of Lawyers in General

Other than in the occasional anomalous case, the greater part of any bill of costs will be the fees charged by the lawyers. In the present context, the work of lawyers is relevant because there are categories of work that can be done *only* by 'authorised persons'[93] or 'exempt persons'.[94] Where such work has been carried out by someone else, it will usually be the case that no fees are recoverable. Most readers will not need to trouble themselves with the detail of the remainder of this section (3.49–3.91); this is because the conclusion that is reached (see 3.91) is easily stated (this being in contrast to the tortuous route by which it **3.48**

89 *Manakee v Brattle* [1970] 1 WLR 1607, at 1608.

90 See, eg, *Aerospace Publishing Ltd v Thames Water* [2007] EWCA Civ 3, at [86], which deals with the costs of employees diverted from their usual duties by the litigation.

91 *Ibid*, at [75].

92 *Wallace v Brian Gale & Associates* [1998] 2 Costs LR 53, at 56. See also the commentary in *Hutchinson v Harris* [1978] 10 BLR 19, at 23 and at 38–40.

93 See s 13(2)(a) of the Legal Services Act 2007.

94 See s 13(2)(b) of the Legal Services Act 2007.

is reached). That conclusion is that there is only a narrow class of work that can be carried out only by an authorised or exempt person, and where work has been carried out that does not fall within that category, costs will not be irrecoverable by reason of that work having been carried out by someone who was not an authorised or exempt person.

3.49 As of 1 January 2010,[95] the question of whether a person is entitled to carry on an activity that is a reserved legal activity is to be determined solely in accordance with the provisions of the Legal Services Act 2007 (as amended) (LSA 2007).[96] That Act defines two categories of work, the wider of which wholly includes the narrower. The narrower category is that of 'reserved legal activities', which are defined in the following way in s 12(1):

> '(1) In this Act [the Legal Services Act 2007] "reserved legal activity" means—
> (a) the exercise of a right of audience;
> (b) the conduct of litigation;
> (c) reserved instrument activities;
> (d) probate activities;
> (e) notarial activities;
> (f) the administration of oaths.'

These categories of work are those that *only* authorised or exempt persons are permitted to do.[97]

3.50 The wider category is that of 'legal activity', which is defined in s 12(1) of the 2007 Act in this way:

> '(3) In this Act "legal activity" means—
> (a) an activity which is a reserved legal activity within the meaning of this Act as originally enacted, and
> (b) any other activity which consists of one or both of the following—
> (i) the provision of legal advice or assistance in connection with the application of the law or with any form of resolution of legal disputes;
> (ii) the provision of representation in connection with any matter concerning the application of the law or any form of resolution of legal disputes.
> (4) But "legal activity" does not include any activity of a judicial or quasi-judicial nature (including acting as a mediator).'

Whilst it is highly relevant for the purposes of regulation, this wider category is of little relevance to the law of costs and it is mentioned only for the sake of completeness. In particular, unlike reserved legal activities, the fact that a legal activity may have been carried out by a person who was neither authorised nor exempt would, of itself, have little bearing on the recoverability of the fees for that work.

---

95 Before this date, the issues were governed by the Courts and Legal Services Act 1990, as amended. The relevant provisions were introduced in a staged way: the majority of the provisions came into force on 1 January 2010—see the Legal Services Act 2007 (Commencement No 6, Transitory, Transitional and Saving Provisions) Order 2009 (SI 2009/3250); in so far as s 12 of the Act defines the term 'reserved legal activity' for the purposes of ss 1, 207, 69(4), Sched 1, para 2(3)–(5), Sched 15, para 2(3), (4), and Sched 22, para 2(6), (7)(b), the relevant date was 7 March 2008—see Legal Services Act 2007 (Commencement No 1 and Transitory Provisions) Order 2008 (SI 2008/222); in so far as s 12 defines that term for the purposes of the Administration of Justice Act 1985, ss 9, 32A, the relevant date was 31 March 2009—see Legal Services Act 2007 (Commencement No 4, Transitory and Transitional Provisions and Appointed Day) Order 2009 (SI 2009/503).

96 See s 13(1) of the Legal Services Act 2007.

97 See s 13(2) of the Legal Services Act 2007.

There are two questions that must be addressed when considering whether the costs of an activity are irrecoverable by reason of the status of the person who carried it out. The first is whether the work in question—which is referred to as 'the relevant activity'[98]—was a reserved legal activity; the second is whether the person who carried it out was an authorised or an exempt person. There are three outcomes that need to be considered, as follows. **3.51**

- **Authorised or exempt person** The first outcome is where the relevant activity was carried out by a person acting as an exempt or an authorised person. In those circumstances, the costs of performing the activity would not be irrecoverable by reason of the status of the person who carried it out—and this would be the case regardless of whether the relevant activity was or was not a reserved legal activity.
- **Reserved legal activity and person not authorised or exempt** The second outcome is where the relevant activity was a reserved legal activity and it was carried out by a person who was neither an authorised nor an exempt person in respect of that activity. In those circumstances, the performance of the activity would have been an offence[99] and—by reason of the doctrine of implied statutory prohibition[100] (and, in some circumstances, also by reason of an express statutory prohibition[101])—no costs would be recoverable in respect of that activity.
- **Not a reserved legal activity** The third outcome is where the relevant activity was not a reserved legal activity and it was carried out by a person who was neither an authorised nor an exempt person. In those circumstances, the costs of carrying out the task would not be irrecoverable by reason of the status of the person who carried out the work, but other factors may apply (see 3.92–3.100).

The rest of this section deals with the detail of the law, but—for the reasons set out above—most readers will not need to trouble themselves with the minutiae. There is an overview at 3.91.

In a broad sense, costs—or, rather, profit costs, counsel's fees, costs lawyers' fees, etc—are the fees charged by lawyers for carrying out lawyers' work. What constitutes lawyers' work used to be governed by diverse and sundry sources of law, but since 1990 it has been a subject governed by statute. The first of the governing statutes was the Courts and Legal Services Act 1990 (as amended) (CLSA 1990); on 1 January 2010, this was replaced by the LSA 2007.[102] Transitional provisions apply.[103] In the present context, the relevance of these Acts is that if work has been carried out lawfully, then a professional fee may be raised and costs may thereby be created, but if the work has been carried out unlawfully, then no fee may be raised and no costs will be created.[104] The issue is more complex than simply determining whether the work that has been done was work that would normally **3.52**

[98] See, eg, s 14(1) of the Legal Services Act 2007.
[99] See s 14 of the LSA 2007.
[100] The reason for this would be 'implied statutory prohibition'.
[101] See Solicitors Act 1974, s 25.
[102] The introduction of this Act was staggered.
[103] See fn 95 for an explanation of the staged introduction; transitional provisions are found at Sched 22 to the LSA 2007.
[104] If authority were needed for this assertion, it can be found (albeit only in relation to unqualified persons acting as a solicitor) in the SA 1974, s 25.

be done by lawyers: in some jurisdictions, the test is, on occasion, as simple as that, but[105] in England and Wales, a much more restrictive test applies.

3.53 Notwithstanding the fact that the present regime is now governed by LSA 2007, it is necessary to know about the old regime, this being because costs incurred under that regime will continue to be encountered for some years to come. As such, both regimes are described. In any event, because both the CLSA 1990 and the LSA 2007 make frequent reference to the Solicitors Act 1974 (SA 1974), it is convenient to deal with that Act first. It should be stressed, however, that, in the present context, that Act's relevance under the new regime (that is, under LSA 2007) is not particularly great.

The Work of Lawyers under the Solicitors Act 1974

3.54 The 1974 Act is concerned with solicitors rather than other categories of legal representative—that is, it does not define the entire range of persons who are authorised litigators.[106] The starting point is that s 20 of the SA 1974 prohibits any unqualified person from acting as a solicitor.[107] The Act defines an 'unqualified person' as being a person who has not been admitted as a solicitor and does not have in force a practising certificate.[108] Since 31 March 2009, the person must, if a corporation, also be 'recognised', or employed by a person who is recognised, or must otherwise satisfy the requirements concerning recognition.[109]

3.55 Prior to 1 January 2010,[110] s 22 of the SA 1974 provided as follows:

> '(1) Subject to subsections (2) and (2A), any unqualified person who directly or indirectly—
> (a) draws or prepares any instrument of transfer or charge for the purposes of the Land Registration Act 2002, or makes any application or lodges any document for registration under that Act at the registry, or
> (b) draws or prepares any other instrument relating to real or personal estate, or any legal proceeding shall, unless he proves that the act was not done for or in the expectation of any fee, gain or reward, be guilty of an offence ...'

This section was repealed on that date, however,[111] and the function of classifying instruments of this nature now falls to the LSA 2007 itself (see 3.76–3.91).[112]

---

[105] See, eg, the Australian case of *In re Sanderson* [1927] VLR 394, in which the following test was promulgated: 'What I do decide is that if a person does a thing usually done by a solicitor and does it in such a way as to lead to the reasonable inference that he is a solicitor—if he combines professing to be a solicitor with actions usually taken by a solicitor—I think he then acts as a solicitor.'

[106] See LSA 2007, s 207(1); prior to 1 January 2010, see CLSA 1990, s 119(1).

[107] This section was substituted by the LSA 2007, s 177 and Sched 16, Pt 1, paras 1, 25: see the Legal Services Act 2007 (Commencement No 6, Transitory, Transitional and Saving Provisions) Order 2009 (SI 2009/3250), art 2(f)(ii).

[108] See SA 1974, ss 1 and 87.

[109] See r 12 of the Solicitors' Code of Conduct 2007 and (from 1 July 2009) SA 1974, s 1B, as amended by the LSA 2007 and the Legal Services Act 2007 (Commencement No 5, Transitory and Transitional Provisions) Order 2009 (SI 2009/1365).

[110] See the Legal Services Act 2007 (Commencement No 6, Transitory, Transitional and Saving Provisions) Order 2009 (SI 2009/3250), art 2(f)(ii).

[111] See LSA 2007, ss 177, 210, Sched 16, Pt 1, paras 1, 26(a), and Sched 23.

[112] See LSA 2007, Sched 2, para 5.

Section 25(1) of the SA 1974 provides: 'No costs in respect of anything done by any unqualified person acting as a solicitor shall be recoverable by him, or by any other person, in any action, suit or matter.' Thus there is an express statutory prohibition against the recovery of fees charged by an unqualified person acting as a solicitor. Whether that prohibition will apply will be determined by the nature of the work done. The 1974 Act created several classes of work for which costs could be recovered only if and to the extent that the work had been carried out by a practising solicitor, but the position was significantly altered by the CLSA 1990, which afforded other categories of legal representative the facility to charge a fee for providing certain legal services. Moreover, from 1 January 2010 onwards, the LSA 2007 has applied and the extent to which that Act refers back to the SA 1974 is limited. In any event, the practical effect of the express statutory probation mentioned above would be eclipsed by the implied statutory prohibition mentioned below (see 3.63), so, in practical terms, the SA 1974 is of only passing relevance to the issue of whether the status of the person who carried out the work has a bearing on the recoverability of the costs relating to that work. **3.56**

The Work of Lawyers under the Courts and Legal Services Act 1990

What is set out below applies only to work done before 1 January 2010; transitional provisions apply.[113] Before that date, legal services were governed by the CLSA 1990, which is an Act that can be thought of as acting in concert with the SA 1974 to widen the category of persons who were able to claim fees for providing legal services. It achieved this in two stages: first, it defined categories of persons who were able to conduct litigation or who had rights of audience (or both); secondly, it disapplied the prohibition in the SA 1974 against recovery of those persons' fees (see 3.54). In particular, the CLSA 1990 provided that a person who is able to conduct litigation or who has rights of audience will not be an 'unqualified person' for the purposes of the 1974 Act;[114] instead, such a person would be an 'authorised litigator'. **3.57**

Section 17 of the CLSA 1990 introduced the twin concepts of 'the statutory objective' and 'the general principle': **3.58**

> '(1) The general objective of this Part is the development of legal services in England and Wales ... by making provision for new or better ways of providing such services and a wider choice of persons providing them, while maintaining the proper and efficient administration of justice.
>
> (2) In this Act that objective is referred to as "the statutory objective".
>
> (3) As a general principle the question whether a person should be granted a right of audience, or be granted a right to conduct litigation in relation to any court or proceedings, should be determined only by reference to—
> (a) whether he is qualified in accordance with the educational and training requirements appropriate to the court or proceedings;
> (b) whether he is a member of a professional or other body which—
> (i) has rules of conduct (however described) governing the conduct of its members;

[113] See fn 95 for an explanation of the staged introduction; transitional provisions are found at Sched 22 to the Legal Services Act 2007.

[114] See CLSA 1990, ss 27(10) and 28(6), and *Agassi v Robinson* [2005] EWCA Civ 1507, at [57].

(ii) has an effective mechanism for enforcing the rules of conduct; and
(iii) is likely to enforce them;

[...]

(d) whether the rules of conduct are, in relation to the court or proceedings, appropriate in the interests of the proper and efficient administration of justice; and

(4) In this Act that principle is referred to as "the general principle".'

3.59 Thus the CLSA 1990 created the 'general principle' that the issue of whether a person is able to conduct litigation or has rights of audience would be decided on the basis of:

- the person's qualifications;
- whether that person was a member of a professional or other body; and
- whether that body's own rules of conduct were in the interests of the administration of justice.

3.60 Section 28 of the 1990 Act dealt with the right to conduct litigation (see 3.73). For persons entitled to conduct litigation, s 28(6) disapplied the prohibition against the recovery of fees created by the SA 1974. The persons who were able to conduct litigation (that is, 'authorised litigators') were defined in s 28(5) of the CLSA 1990, that being a section that widened that category of persons. Section 27 of the CLSA 1990 made similar provisions relating to rights of audience (see 3.75).

3.61 Thus there was considerable interplay between the CLSA 1990 and the SA 1974. Dyson LJ (giving the judgment of the court) summarised that interplay in the following way:

> 'An authorised litigator is not an unqualified person within the meaning of the 1974 Act: section 28(6) of the 1990 Act. A person who is not an authorised litigator may not exercise the right to conduct litigation within the meaning of the 1990 Act and may not act as a solicitor within the meaning of section 20(1) of the 1974 Act and may not draw or prepare an instrument contrary to section 22(1) of the 1974 Act. If he purports to do any of these things, he will not be entitled to recover his costs for doing so. A person who does not have a current practising certificate and who is not an authorised litigator within the meaning of the 1990 Act acts as a solicitor in breach of section 20(1) of the 1974 Act at least if he (a) issues proceedings; (b) performs any ancillary functions in relation to proceedings or (c) draws or prepares an instrument relating to legal proceedings contrary to section 22(1) of the 1974 Act.'[115]

3.62 For the reasons set out above (see 3.54), there was (subject to the provisions in the CLSA 1990) an express statutory prohibition against the recovery of fees by a person acting as a solicitor where that person was not entitled so to do. The topic of what was meant by 'acting as a solicitor' will be dealt with below (see 3.65), but there is another mechanism whereby a fee may be negated by the operation of the law—namely, by means of the implied statutory prohibition arising out of s 70 of the 1990 Act.

3.63 That mechanism turns not on whether a person was 'acting as a solicitor', but on whether they were 'conducting litigation' (or, for that matter, on whether the person was carrying out any activity that they were prohibited from carrying out). Section 70 of the CLSA 1990 defined criminal offences, providing in particular that:

- a person not entitled to conduct litigation was guilty of an offence if they did any act in purported exercise of a right to conduct litigation in relation to any proceedings or contemplated proceedings (s 70(1)); and

[115] *Agassi v Robinson* [2005] EWCA Civ 1507, at [57].

- a person was guilty of an offence if they wilfully pretended to be entitled to exercise any right to conduct litigation (s 70(3)).

These were relevant because, in addition to the express statutory prohibition mentioned above (see 3.58), there was an implied statutory prohibition that arose out of the fact that a person would have committed an offence if they were to carry out work that they were not permitted to do. The doctrine of implied statutory prohibition is a consequence of the fact that the court will not allow itself to be used for the purpose of enforcing unlawful bargains. Whilst there is no express authority on this point, Dyson LJ has implied that this principle applies.[116]

Two questions arise: the first is what is meant by 'acting as a solicitor'; and the second is what is meant by 'conducting litigation'? These topics are dealt with in turn. There is a degree of overlap. **3.64**

'Acting as a solicitor'

What is set out in the next few paragraphs applies to work done both before and after 1 January 2010, albeit in the context of different statutory regimes (see 3.48–3.53). That said, its practical effect after 1 January 2010 is not marked. The House of Lords has explained that if a step in proceedings is, by legislation, required to be done by the party or the party's solicitor and if that step is taken by an unqualified person other than the party themselves, that person would necessarily be acting as a solicitor.[117] The CPR have the force of statute: the relevance of this is that where the CPR require that an act be done by a person or the person's solicitor, it is an act that, if carried out by someone other than the party themselves, would be an act carried out as a solicitor. **3.65**

Thus it may be relevant if the CPR refer to an act being carried by 'a solicitor'—but the CPR usually refer to 'legal representatives' rather than 'solicitors'. The term 'legal representative' was, prior to 1 October 2008, defined by CPR, r 2.3(1), to mean '[a] barrister or a solicitor, solicitor's employee or other authorised litigator (as defined in the Courts and Legal Services Act 1990) who has been instructed to act for a party in relation to a claim'. **3.66**

After that date,[118] CPR, r 2.3(1), read (and still does read) as follows: **3.67**

> ' "[L]egal representative" means a—
> (a) barrister;
> (b) solicitor;
> (c) solicitor's employee;
> (d) manager of a body recognised under section 9 of the Administration of Justice Act 1985; or

[116] *Ibid*, at [28].

[117] *The Law Society of the United Kingdom v Waterlow Brothers and Layton* (1883) 8 App Cas 407. This case related to a predecessor Act to the SA 1974, but on this specific point the principles are likely to be the same (cf 3.68). An example would be in *In re Ainsworth, ex parte The Law Society* [1905] 2 KB 103, in which it was held that an unqualified person who gives notice of appearance is thereby acting in contravention of s 2 of the Solicitors Act 1843. In reaching this conclusion, Lord Alverstone CJ was influenced by the fact that the relevant rule of court required a notice of appearance to be given either by the defendant himself or by his solicitor.

[118] See the 47th Update to the CPR.

(e) person who, for the purposes of the Legal Services Act 2007, is an authorised person in relation to an activity which constitutes the conduct of litigation (within the meaning of that Act),

who has been instructed to act for a party in relation to proceedings.'

Thus, where the CPR require that an act be done by a party or the party's legal representative (as opposed to a 'solicitor'), it cannot be said as a matter of textural interpretation that only a solicitor could carry out that act. For the reasons set out below, it is unlikely that carrying out an act that is required to be carried out by a 'legal representative' would be interpreted as 'acting as a solicitor'.

3.68 Nonetheless, it is possible to say that where the CPR say that an act must be performed by a solicitor, the performance of that act will be to act as a solicitor. Whilst helpful, however, this does not provide a complete definition of what is meant by 'acting as a solicitor', because there may be other acts not specified in the CPR that also fall within the category of acting as a solicitor. There are old authorities that pointed to a plethora of such acts, but Dyson LJ has made it clear that those authorities have been superseded.[119] Instead, he preferred the following analysis of Potter J:

> 'So far as I am aware, the claim consultants [in this case, representing the receiving party] have not at any stage held themselves out as solicitors, but have at all times acted specifically as "claims consultants" in relation to their representation of the claimant. Section 25 of the Solicitors Act 1974 is linked and, in my view, falls to be construed with the sections which precede it. Those sections are penal in nature and relate to unqualified persons acting as solicitors (section 20), pretending to be solicitors (section 21), drawing or preparing instruments of transfer or charge etc, the drawing of which is limited to solicitors and certain other exempted professions (section 22) and preparing papers for probate, etc: section 23. By section 24 of the Act of 1974 those penal provisions are applied to bodies corporate. In these circumstances, it seems clear to me that the words "acting as a solicitor" are limited to the doing of acts which only a solicitor may perform and/or the doing of acts by a person pretending or holding himself out to be a solicitor. Such acts are not to be confused with the doing of acts of a kind commonly done by solicitors, but which involve no representation that the actor is acting as such. On that basis it seems plain to me that the claims consultants did not "act as a solicitor" in conducting the arbitration on behalf of the claimant. Accordingly, on the basis of the facts existing in this case, I answer the first preliminary issue in the affirmative.'[120]

3.69 This means that the phrase 'acting as a solicitor' should be read as being limited to 'the doing of acts which only a solicitor may perform'.[121] This definition invites the obvious question of how the phrase 'acts which only a solicitor may perform' is to be construed. In *Agassi v Robinson*,[122] the Court of Appeal was presented with a list of activities that counsel described as 'administrative support' and hence not acts that only a solicitor may perform. The Court did not comment on the accuracy or otherwise of that list, but Dyson LJ did say that—because of the penal nature of s 20 of the SA 1974—the definition of 'acting as

[119] He has criticised them as containing little analysis of what is meant by the phrase 'acting as a solicitor': *Agassi v Robinson* [2005] EWCA Civ 1507, at [35] and [42].

[120] *Piper Double Glazing Ltd v DC Contracts* [1994] 1 WLR 777, at 786. This analysis was approved by Phillips MR in *R v Secretary of State for Transport, ex parte Factortame* [2002] EWCA Civ 932, at [26].

[121] This view was also implicitly approved by Phillips MR (giving the judgment of the court) in another case: *R (Factortame Ltd and others) v Secretary of State for Transport, Local Government and Regions (No 8)* [2002] EWCA Civ 932, [2003] QB 381.

[122] [2005] EWCA Civ 1507.

a solicitor' should be read restrictively. In particular, he concluded that the act of merely giving legal advice would not fall within that definition.

Whilst there remains room for argument on the finer details, it seems that the definition of what amounts to 'acting as a solicitor' is closely aligned with those acts that are required by legislation to be done by a solicitor or by the party themselves. For obvious reasons, the CPR—being the relevant rules of procedure—contain most of the applicable provisions, but there are one or two further provisions that can be found elsewhere. In particular, prior to 1 January 2010,[123] s 22 of the SA 1974, prohibited drawing an instrument for any legal proceedings in expectation of a fee (see 3.55). In this regard, Waller LJ cited the following passage with approval: **3.70**

> 'In this context, "instrument" means any formal document. It would therefore be an offence for an unqualified person for or in expectation of a fee or reward, to settle a writ, statement of claim or defence or any other document of a similar character on behalf of another person.'[124]

Thus, prior to 1 January 2010, the act of drawing of an instrument for a fee by an unqualified person would have been unlawful pursuant to the 1974 Act—and this would have been so regardless of what the CPR had to say on the matter. The function performed by s 22 of the SA 1974 is now performed by the LSA 2007 (see 3.76–3.91). **3.71**

Finally, the test of what is 'acting as a solicitor' does not vary from tribunal to tribunal (although the effect of that test may vary), which means that where the tribunal in question is a tribunal to which neither the CPR nor any similar rules apply, there may be no acts that would amount to 'acting as a solicitor'. Indeed, Potter J found that this was true of arbitrations and that therefore no part of the arbitral process could be said to involve acts that were 'acting as a solicitor'.[125] It could well be the case that the same is true of certain other tribunals. **3.72**

'Conducting litigation'

What is set out in the next few paragraphs applies only to work carried out before 1 January 2010.[126] Section 119(1) of the CLSA 1990 defined the right to conduct litigation as the right '(a) to issue proceedings before any court; and (b) to perform any ancillary functions in relation to proceedings (such as entering appearances to actions)'. This means that there were two parts to the definition of 'conducting litigation': first, the act of issuing proceedings before any court; and secondly, the act of performing any ancillary functions in relation to proceedings. **3.73**

The concept of issuing proceedings presents no conceptual difficulties.[127] What amounted to the performance of ancillary functions is, however, not so obvious. The issue turns on what is meant by the phrase 'ancillary functions'. There are factors that pull in different directions: on the one hand, the need to protect the public from unqualified lawyers demands **3.74**

[123] This was repealed by the LSA 2007, ss 177, 210, Sched 16, Pt 1, paras 1 and 26(a), and Sched 23.
[124] *Powell v Ely* (unreported), 19 May 1980, Divisional Court.
[125] *Piper Double Glazing Ltd v DC Contracts* [1994] 1 WLR 777, at 786, as commented on by Dyson LJ in *Agassi v Robinson* [2005] EWCA Civ 1507, at [41] and [42].
[126] See 3.57.
[127] It includes ancillary applications and appeals in the course of litigation: *Agassi v Robinson* [2005] EWCA Civ 1507, at [53].

a wide interpretation; on the other hand, the punitive nature of the legislation calls for a narrow interpretation. Dyson LJ was more influenced by the latter:

> 'The word "ancillary" indicates that it is not all functions in relation to proceedings that are comprised in the "right to conduct litigation". The usual meaning of "ancillary" is "subordinate". A clue to what was intended lies in the words in brackets "(such as entering appearances to actions)". These words show that it must have been intended that the ancillary functions would be formal steps required in the conduct of litigation. These would include drawing or preparing instruments within the meaning of section 22 of the 1974 Act and other formal steps. It is not necessary for the purposes of this case to decide the precise parameters of the definition of "the right to conduct litigation". It is unfortunate that this important definition is so unclear. But because there are potential penal implications, its very obscurity means that the words should be construed narrowly. Suffice it to say that we do not see how the giving of legal advice in connection with court proceedings can come within the definition.'[128]

So the definition of what is and is not 'conducting litigation' for the purposes of work carried out before 1 January 2010 is not precisely defined in the CLSA 1990 nor has it been precisely defined by case law. Given the fact that very similar wording appears in the LSA 2007, the same remains true in the present day.

'Rights of audience'

3.75 In so far as work carried out before 1 January 2010 is concerned, the approach is similar to that set out immediately above. Section 119(1) of the CLSA 1990 defined 'right of audience' as 'the right to exercise any of the functions of appearing before and addressing a court including the calling and examining of witnesses'. The position after that date is addressed below.

The Work of Lawyers under the Legal Services Act 2007

3.76 What is set out below applies to work carried out on or after 1 January 2010; transitional provisions apply.[129] As of that date, the matters discussed in this section were governed by the LSA 2007, s 1(1) of which Act included the following as being its objectives: protecting and promoting the public interest; protecting and promoting the interests of consumers; and improving access to justice. There is interplay with the SA 1974, but it is of no great practical relevance.

3.77 A person is entitled to carry on a reserved legal activity where they are an authorised or exempt person in relation to that activity.[130] It is an offence for a person to carry on such an activity without being entitled to do so,[131] the relevance of which is that fees so incurred are almost certainly unenforceable (see, by analogy, 3.63). Part 3 of the LSA 2007 concerns 'reserved legal activities', which have been defined in general terms above (see 3.49). Those activities are categorised as being rights of audience, conduct of litigation, reserved

---

128 *Ibid*, at [56].

129 See fn 95 for an explanation of the staged introduction; transitional provisions are found at Sched 22 to the Legal Services Act 2007.

130 See LSA 2007, s 13(2).

131 See LSA 2007, s 14(1).

instrument activities, probate activities, notarial activities and administration of oaths.[132] The precise provisions are qualified by transitional provisions.[133] What is set out below is limited to a simplified summary of the first three reserved legal activities.

'Conduct of litigation'

Schedule 2, para 3, to the LSA 2007 defines 'conduct of litigation' in the following way: **3.78**

> '(1) The "conduct of litigation" means—
> (a) the issuing of proceedings before any court in England and Wales,
> (b) the commencement, prosecution and defence of such proceedings, and
> (c) the performance of any ancillary functions in relation to such proceedings (such as entering appearances to actions).
>
> (2) But the "conduct of litigation" does not include any activity within paragraphs (a) to (c) of sub-paragraph (1), in relation to any particular court or in relation to any particular proceedings, if immediately before the appointed day no restriction was placed on the persons entitled to carry on that activity.'

Coulson J has found that serving proceedings falls within the ambit of 'prosecution of proceedings'.[134]

Authorised persons will be able to conduct litigation to the extent of their authority, but **3.79** a person who is not authorised may have the right conferred upon them by the court.[135] A litigant is an exempt person[136] and, when acting in person, may have the right to delegate certain tasks, such as service of proceedings.[137] There is also a degree of overlap with 'reserved instrument activities' (see 3.81).

'Rights of audience'

Schedule 2, para 2, to the LSA 2007 defines 'rights of audience' in the following way: **3.80**

> '(1) A "right of audience" means the right to appear before and address a court, including the right to call and examine witnesses.
>
> (2) But a "right of audience" does not include a right to appear before or address a court, or to call or examine witnesses, in relation to any particular court or in relation to particular proceedings, if immediately before the appointed day no restriction was placed on the persons entitled to exercise that right.'

Authorised persons have rights of audience either in all courts (for example barristers) or only in some courts (or relating only to particular aspects of litigation). This is dealt with in detail in Chapter 47 (albeit in the context of cost litigation). A person may become an exempt person for the purposes of appearing in proceedings if they are granted a right of audience by the relevant court.[138] Employees may be exempt persons (see 3.85). A litigant is an exempt person.[139]

---

[132] See LSA 2007, Sched 2.
[133] See LSA 2007, Scheds 2 and 22, and s 13.
[134] *Ndole Assets Ltd v Designer M&E Services UK Ltd* [2017] EWHC 1148 (TCC), at [25]–[28] and [31], *per* Coulson J.
[135] See LSA 2007, Sched 3, para 2(2).
[136] See LSA 2007, Sched 3, para 2(4).
[137] *Ndole Assets Ltd v Designer M&E Services UK Ltd* [2017] EWHC 1148 (TCC), at [34]–[36] and [39], *per* Coulson J.
[138] See LSA 2007, Sched 3, para 1(3).
[139] See LSA 2007, Sched 3, para 1(6).

'Reserved instrument activities'

3.81 In so far as it is likely to be relevant to the law of costs, Sched 2, para 5, to the LSA 2007 defines 'reserved instrument activities' in the following way:

> '(1) "Reserved instrument activities" means—
> [...]
> (c) preparing any ... instrument relating to court proceedings in England and Wales.
>
> (2) But "reserved instrument activities" does not include the preparation of an instrument relating to any particular court proceedings if, immediately before the appointed day, no restriction was placed on the persons entitled to carry on that activity.'

3.82 There are other provisions, such as those concerning instruments for the sale of land. As can be seen, however, the act of preparing an instrument relating to court proceedings is a 'reserved instrument activity'. Authorised persons will be able to carry out a reserved instrument activity to the extent of their authority. Lengthy provisions govern who is and who is not an exempt person,[140] but, in essence, a person is exempt if they are employed by and supervised by a suitably authorised person.[141] A person is exempt if they are employed merely to engross the instrument or application.[142]

Agents, employers and employees

3.83 The issue that is addressed in the next few paragraphs is what should be made of the situation in which a person engages an assistant to carry out a reserved legal activity, but only one of those persons is authorised to carry out the activity in question. This usually arises in the context of those persons being employee and employer, but it may also arise in the context of principal and independent agent. What follows deals with the topic in only a very general sense; the topic of whether costs can be recovered in respect of agent or employee is dealt with in Chapter 22 and the topic of rights of audience is addressed in Chapter 47.

Unauthorised employer

3.84 Where an employee is authorised to carry out the relevant activity, but their employer is not, then unless the provision of services is directly to the public (or a section of the public)[143] or unless it is part of the employer's business, the former will not carry on a reserved legal activity by virtue of the latter performing it in their capacity as employee.[144] This may be relevant if the fees in question are putatively payable to the employer.

Unauthorised employee (such as an in-house costs draftsperson)

3.85 In so far as the law of costs is concerned, the reverse situation is more commonly encountered—namely, where the person who carries out the work is not authorised, but the person who gives the instructions is authorised. This situation commonly arises in the context of unauthorised costs draftspersons seeking to be heard in court.

---

[140] See LSA 2007, Sched 3, para 3.
[141] *Ibid.*
[142] See LSA 2007, Sched 3, para 3(9).
[143] In general, this does not include the membership of a trade union: see LSA 2007, s 15(5). Lengthy provisions apply: see LSA 2007, s 15(6).
[144] See LSA 2007, s 15(4).

The starting point is that where a person is authorised to conduct litigation and where the person assisting is under that person's supervision, then the assistant will be an exempt person for those purposes. It is by this mechanism that employees of authorised persons (such as in-house costs draftspersons) derive their right of audience. Indeed, Burnett J has commented (albeit only in the context of an application for permission to appeal) that this would be the case where the employer is a costs lawyer.[145] A right of audience will exist, however, only if the proceedings are being heard in chambers and are not reserved family proceedings.[146] The word 'chambers' is not defined in the LSA 2007. Moreover, the CPR refer to 'in private' and 'in public' rather than 'in chambers' and 'in court'. As such, there is uncertainty as to what is meant by 'chambers'. Whilst not a source of law, Practice Direction (PD) 39A, para 1.14, may be an aid to interpretation of the word 'chambers': **3.86**

> 'References to hearings being in public or private or in a judge's room contained in the Civil Procedure Rules (including the Rules of the Supreme Court and the County Court Rules scheduled to Part 50) and the practice directions which supplement them do not restrict any existing rights of audience or confer any new rights of audience in respect of applications or proceedings which under the rules previously in force would have been heard in court or in chambers respectively.'

Thus, whilst there is no authority on the point and whilst the contrary is easily arguable, it would seem that the CPR preserve the distinction between 'chambers' and 'in court' in such a way as to preserve (but not enlarge) the rights of audience that used to exist before the introduction of the CPR. It is by that mechanism that an employee of an authorised person may claim the right to be heard in court. In this regard, it is relevant that solicitors have long been able to delegate certain tasks to unqualified staff.[147] **3.87**

Unauthorised independent agent (such as an independent costs draftspersons)

The situation with independent agents (such as an independent costs draftsperson or process server) is less clear (see 47.07–47.08). It has long been the case that an independent costs draftsperson may be regarded as being temporarily employed for the purposes of the hearing in respect of which they were instructed.[148] Whilst writing extrajudicially, District Judge Hill (a former regional costs judge) had this to say on the topic: **3.88**

> 'For many years persons employed by solicitors have been entitled to appear before the court when the court is sitting in chambers. This is recognised by long usage and it was not the purpose of the 1990 Act, nor is it of the 2007 Act, to restrict these long-established rights. But as I have already said, a disciplinary process is integral to a right of audience ... With a self-employed agent there is no employer or disciplinary body to which he can be reported if he were to behave in an inappropriate way.'[149]

---

[145] *Kynaston v Carroll* [2011] EWHC 2179 (QB), at [6]–[8].

[146] See LSA 2007, Sched 3, para 1(7).

[147] If authority were needed on the point, the fact that certain work can be delegated to unadmitted staff was confirmed in *Sharratt v London Bus Co Ltd (The Accident Group Test Cases)* [2003] EWCA 718, at [196] and [212].

[148] The authority that is usually given in this regard is *Waterson Hicks v Eliopoulos* (1995) Costs LR (Core Vol) 363, at 373, *per* Evans LJ, but that case actually deals with authority as an agent rather than rights of audience. Other cases that deal with the point are *Claims Direct Test Cases Tranche 2* [2003] EWHC 9005 (Costs), at [115], and *Crane v Canons Leisure Centre* [2007] EWCA Civ 1352, at [12], *per* May LJ. Contrary examples exist: see *Ahmed v Powell* [2003] EWHC 9011, SCCO, 19 February.

[149] Hill, R, 'In Practice: Benchmarks—Rights of Audience', Law Society Gazette, 23 September 2010, at p 20.

3.89 This highlights the distinction between an employed assistant and an independent agent. Whilst it is not binding on any court and is not a source of law, District Judge Hill's analysis has been cited in support of the proposition that a more cautious approach is required under the LSA 2007 than under the CLSA 1990.[150] The effect of this is that it is now not unheard of for the court to decline to hear from unqualified independent agents.[151]

3.90 Whilst a defence of due diligence may be available,[152] an employer who unlawfully carries on a reserved legal activity through an employee would be guilty of an offence.[153]

Summary

3.91 To summarise, the following statements are *generally* correct.

- In so far as the law of costs is concerned, the relevance of what is and is not lawyers' work—that is, what is and is not a 'legal activity'—is that if the work in question ('the relevant activity') has been carried out unlawfully, then the doctrine of implied statutory prohibition will prevent recovery of fees.
- Where the relevant activity was a 'reserved legal activity', the fees will be recoverable only if that person who carried out the work was an authorised or exempt person in relation to that activity.
- For practical purposes, the three most important reserved legal activities are conducting litigation, exercising a right of audience and reserved instrument activities.

This means that reserved legal activities comprise only a narrow class of work and work that does not fall within that category will not be irrecoverable by reason of it having been carried out by someone who was not an authorised or exempt person.

Work Done by Non-lawyers

3.92 This section deals with the recoverability of fees levied by persons who represent others, but who lack the status of being authorised persons, this being a class of person that should be distinguished from:

- persons who have been properly instructed by authorised persons, which persons are, as a result of their instruction, agents, meaning that their fees are recoverable *qua* agency[154] (an issue dealt with 22.08–22.20);
- experts other than experts on the law of costs within the meaning of CPR, r 46.5(3)(b) (which persons are dealt with at 52.10–52.45); and
- employees of litigants (which issue is dealt with briefly at 18.115–18.120).

---

150 It is also in keeping with the concerns expressed in courts that deal in matters other than costs: see, eg, Madge-Wyld, S, 'Who May Exercise a Right of Audience in Claims for Possession in the County Court?' (2011) 14 JHL 16. See also 47.07.

151 If costs are retrospectively claimed for such a person, it may be necessary to determine whether the assistant should be regarded as being an exempt person by implication (ie by reason of the court not having declined to hear them). That would be an arguable point to take, but there is a very powerful argument to the contrary, not least because there is no mention in the LSA 2007 of any such rights being conferred by implication.

152 See LSA 2007, s 16(4).

153 See LSA 2007, s 16(2).

154 See *In re Pomeroy & Tanner* [1897] 1 Ch 284 and the discussion in *Agassi v Robinson* [2005] EWCA Civ 1507, at [74] *et seq.*

The topics covered in this section will, with one unimportant exception,[155] relate exclusively to work done on behalf of persons who are litigants in person. This is because the person who seeks to represent the litigant would have no formal status and this would mean that the litigant would be classed as being unrepresented. Where, in this section, reference is made to costs of litigants in person, this is a reference to fees for work done *for* a litigant in person (such as fees charged by a *McKenzie* friend) rather than costs for work done *by* a litigant in person. **3.93**

Where a person who is not an authorised litigator conducts litigation, purports to exercise a right of audience or draws a reserved instrument, the fees for that work are not recoverable for the reasons set out above (see 3.76–3.91). Whilst there is no authority specifically relating to the LSA 2007, if that Act is to be interpreted in the same way as the CLSA 1990, then these categories are to be construed narrowly (see 3.74). This would mean that, in the ordinary run of things, fees for most of the work carried out by a non-lawyer would not be irrecoverable by reason of the effect of the LSA 2007 (but, as is explained in 3.97, they are often irrecoverable for other reasons). Where an unauthorised person incurs disbursements with the client's express authority, those monies remain recoverable,[156] but this will, in general, not be the case in the absence of express authority (this being because an unauthorised person will, in general, not have any implied authority).[157] Furthermore, the fact that a partnership has as one of its members an unauthorised person will not prevent the remaining partners from recovering the fees for work done by them.[158] **3.94**

Expert assistance for litigants in person in costs litigation

What is set out above, however, is only the starting point. The CPR make a number of provisions that either affirm or qualify the law. Most of those qualifications arise out of the fact that where a person appears in court with a representative who is not a lawyer, that person will be a litigant in person. If small claims are disregarded for the moment (see 3.100),[159] CPR, r 46.5(3), provides that a litigant in person may recover: **3.95**

- payments reasonably made by that litigant in person for certain legal services relating to the conduct of the proceedings (see 59.30 and 59.35); and
- the costs of obtaining expert assistance in assessing the costs claim (see 59.36–59.37).

The costs of a solicitor, a Fellow of the Institute of Legal Executives (FILEx),[160] etc will be recoverable, but so are the fees of:[161] **3.96**

- Fellows of the Association of Costs Lawyers;[162]

[155] The only exception to this is where the litigant is represented by an authorised litigator, but separately instructs a person who is not an authorised litigator without the authorised litigator's involvement. For obvious reasons, those circumstances will very rarely arise.

[156] *Hudgell Yeates & Co v Watson* [1978] 2 All ER 363, at 367.

[157] *Kent v Ward* (1894) 70 LT 612, at 613; *Re Browne v Barber* [1913] 2 KB 553, at 573, 574 and 576.

[158] *Hudgell Yeates & Co v Watson* [1978] 2 All ER 363.

[159] Special provisions apply to costs on the small claims track (which is the arena in which the issues addressed in these paragraphs will most often arise). Those provisions are dealt with below, but will usually overshadow the other factors.

[160] This is the phrase used in PD 46, para 3.1, but it is almost certainly intended to refer to a Fellow of the Chartered Institute of Legal Executives, ie a Fellow of CILEx.

[161] See PD 46, para 3.1.

[162] This is a rather curious description because there is no such thing as a Fellow of the Association of Costs Lawyers. It is almost certainly intended to refer to costs lawyers.

- costs draftspersons who are members of the Academy of Experts; and
- costs draftspersons who are members of the Expert Witness Institute.

These persons may or may not be authorised litigators, but their fees will be recoverable in principle regardless of their status.

Restriction on disbursements incurred by litigation in person

3.97 The next provision also arises out of status as a litigant in person, but is restrictive rather than affirmative. The issue is whether the fees of a person who does not fall within any of the categories mentioned immediately above can be recovered as a general disbursement under CPR, r 46.5(3)(a)(ii). This provision restricts recovery to those disbursements that would have been allowed had the disbursements been made by a legal representative on the litigant in person's behalf. That restriction is important in that it often precludes recovery of the non-lawyer's fees; this is because those fees will not be recoverable if they related to work that a legal representative would normally have done. This is the conclusion that both Tuckey LJ[163] and Dyson LJ[164] came to in different cases. Dyson LJ explained his reasoning in this way:

> 'It is true that the rule refers to costs which would have been allowed as a disbursement if the disbursement had been made by a legal representative. But this does not require the court to make a fanciful hypothesis as to what disbursements a legal representative might have made. The rule contemplates allowing as costs only those categories of disbursements which would normally have been made by a legal representative. If the expenditure is for work which a legal representative would normally have done himself, it is not a disbursement within the language of [what is now CPR, r 46.5(3)(a)(ii)].'[165]

3.98 Dyson LJ went on to explain that the services of some non-lawyers may, where appropriate, be characterised as being expert in nature (but, obviously, only where those services were not the type of work normally done by authorised persons):

> 'It does not necessarily follow that [the receiving party] is not entitled to recover costs in respect of the ancillary assistance provided by [the non-lawyer] in these appeals. [The non-lawyer] is an accountant who has expertise in tax matters ... It may be appropriate to allow the appellant at least part of [the non-lawyer's] fees as a disbursement. It may be possible to argue that the cost of discussing the issues with counsel, assisting with the preparation of the skeleton argument etc is allowable as a disbursement, because the provision of this kind of assistance in a specialist esoteric area is not the kind of work that would normally be done by the solicitor instructed to conduct the appeals. Another way of making the same point is that it may be possible to characterise these specialist services as those of an expert, and to say for that reason that the fees for these services are in principle recoverable as a disbursement.'[166]

3.99 It is worth pausing here to summarise the position. Where, in appropriate circumstances, the representative falls within one of the categories mentioned at 3.96, their reasonable fees would—in the ordinary run of things and provided that they are not carrying out reserved activities—be recoverable. Where the representative does not fall within one of those categories, their fees would be recoverable in theory, but in practice their client is

---

163 *United Building and Plumbing Contractors v Malkit Singh Kajila* [2002] EWCA Civ 628.
164 *Agassi v Robinson* [2005] EWCA Civ 1507.
165 *Ibid*, at [73].
166 *Ibid*, at [76].

likely to be a litigant in person, in which case the fees would be disallowed to the extent that they related to work that a solicitor would normally have carried out. This would normally preclude recovery of all of the representative's fees (see 3.97), but there is scope for fees to be recovered where the work relates to 'esoteric' matters and work that would not normally be done by solicitors (see 3.98 and 59.31–59.32).

Specific situations in which work is done by persons other than a properly instructed lawyer

The following miscellaneous points can be made about certain specific circumstances, including where the representative was granted a right to be heard, where counsel was instructed by a person not entitled to conduct litigation and where the claim is consigned to the small claims track. **3.100**

- ***McKenzie* friends** Where a person appears in a court as a lay representative (often called a *McKenzie* friend[167]), that person may be granted rights of audience or the right to conduct litigation for the purposes of that claim pursuant to s 19 of, and Sched 3, para 1(2), to the LSA 2007 (or, before 1 January 2010, pursuant to ss 27(2)(b) and 28(2)(c), respectively, of the CLSA 1990[168]). The issue of whether such a person should be granted rights of audience is addressed at 47.10. Whilst his decision is not binding on any court, Master Wright has found that where the court has exercised its discretion in this way, the fees of the *McKenzie* friend are, in principle, recoverable.[169]
- **Managerial time** Jack J has explained that management time spent on preparing a claim for damages is not recoverable as damages or as costs[170]—although a different approach may be taken where the work was needed for the purposes of investigating fraud, which may be recoverable as damages.[171] (See also 'The costs of marshalling the facts' at 49.104.)
- **Improperly instructed counsel** Where counsel has been instructed by a person who was not entitled to conduct litigation, counsel's fees are not recoverable in that litigation. This is because the prohibition created by s 25 of the SA 1974 relates not only to the unentitled person's own fees, but also to those of counsel whom the unentitled person has instructed.[172]
- **Small claims track** As mentioned above, particular provisions apply to cases allocated to the small claims track. Section 11 of the Courts and Legal Services Act 1990 provides that the Lord Chancellor may make an order granting lay representatives rights of audience in the County Court and its hearing centres. The relevant Order[173] reads as follows:

  '(1) Subject to paragraph (2), any person may exercise rights of audience in proceedings dealt with as a small claim in accordance with rules of court.

---

167 After *McKenzie v McKenzie* [1971] P 33.

168 An example is *Blakemore v Cummings* [2009] EWCA Civ 1276, in which Dyson LJ granted rights to a law costs draftsperson to represent a litigant in the Court of Appeal.

169 *Fosberry & anor v HM Revenue and Customs* [2006] EWHC 90061 (Costs).

170 *Al-Rawas v Pegasus Energy Ltd* [2008] EWHC 617 (QB), at [24]. For the position as between liquidators and directors of an insolvent company, see *Grant v Ralls* [2016] EWHC 1812 (Ch), at [20]. Whilst *obiter*, see also *Petrotrade Inc v Texaco Ltd* [2001] 4 All ER 853, at [63], *per* Woolf MR.

171 *4 Eng Ltd v Harper* [2008] EWHC 915 (Ch), at [29], *per* David Richards J.

172 *Westland Helicopters Ltd v Al-Hejailan* [2004] EWHC 1625 (Comm).

173 The Lay Representatives (Rights of Audience) Order 1999 (SI 1999/1225), art 2.

(2) A lay representative may not exercise any right of audience—
(a) where his client does not attend the hearing;
(b) at any stage after judgment; or
(c) on any appeal brought against any decision made by the district judge in the proceedings.'

Thus there is no reason in principle why a *McKenzie* friend should not recover costs in a small claim. This, of course, is subject to the small claims costs regime, which is an issue that is dealt with in more detail at 50.369–50.403. In particular, however, CPR, r 27.14(4), reads as follows:

> 'The limits on costs imposed by this rule also apply to any fee or reward for acting on behalf of a party to the proceedings charged by a person exercising a right of audience by virtue of an order under section 11 of the Courts and Legal Services Act 1990 (a lay representative).'

4

THE STATUS OF THE RULES GOVERNING COSTS

This chapter deals with the following topics: 4.01

- the elements of costs law (4.02);
- decided cases and precedence (4.03);
- aids to interpretation (4.10);
- the Solicitors' Codes of Conduct (4.14);
- other rules of professional conduct (4.29);
- the Civil Procedure Rules 1998 (CPR) (4.32);
- the Supreme Court Rules 2009 (SCR) (4.44);
- practice directions (4.46);
- pre-action protocols (4.56);
- persuasive informal guidance (4.63); and
- parliamentary and government papers (4.68).

The Elements of Costs Law

As is often the case with adjectival law, the law of costs is an admixture of many elements. Whilst some of the items may be encountered only rarely, the sources of costs law include: 4.02

- domestic primary legislation (that is, Acts of the UK Parliament);
- secondary legislation (also known as delegated legislation) made by statutory instruments (that is, orders or regulations);
- European legislation (regulations, directives and decisions) and other instruments (recommendations, opinions, etc);
- rules of court (the present iteration of which are the Civil Procedure Rules 1998, or CPR);
- practice directions;
- pre-action protocols;
- reported and unreported domestic cases (that is, decisions of courts in England and Wales);
- reported and unreported cases from other jurisdictions;
- decisions of the Court of Justice of the European Union (CJEU) and of the European Court of Human Rights (ECtHR);
- codes of conduct, such as the Solicitors Regulation Authority (SRA) Code of Conduct 2011;
- other codes, such as the Funding Code published by the Legal Services Commission (LSC);
- persuasive informal guidance, such as the Supreme Court Costs Office Guide;

- parliamentary materials, such as bills, Command papers, Hansard, etc;
- consultation papers; and
- textbooks, articles and online publications.

Decided Cases and Precedence

Ratio, obiter and persuasiveness

4.03 Judges are required to follow decisions that are binding upon them (this being the principle of *stare decisis*[1]). In recent years, the Supreme Court has been at pains to emphasise this point. Lord Neuberger, for example, had this to say:

> 'In a common law system, where the law is in some areas made, and the law is in virtually all areas developed, by judges, the doctrine of precedent, or as it is sometimes known *stare decisis*, is fundamental. Decisions on points of law by more senior courts have to be accepted by more junior courts. Otherwise, the law becomes anarchic, and it loses coherence clarity and predictability.'[2]

4.04 In a different case, Lord Neuberger and Lady Hale jointly had this to say:

> '[It] is important not to undermine the role of precedent in the common law. Even though it appears clear that both the reasoning and conclusion [of a certain case is] flawed ... it is important that litigants and their advisers know, as surely as possible, what the law is. Particularly at a time when the cost of litigating can be very substantial, certainty and consistency are very precious commodities in the law. If it is too easy for lower courts to depart from the reasoning of more senior courts, then certainty of outcome and consistency of treatment will be diminished, which would be detrimental to the rule of law.'[3]

Not everything that a senior judge may say will be binding, however. Only the *ratio decidendi* of the decision will bind lower courts, that being the 'principle underlying and determining' the issue that was before the court.[4] *Obiter dicta*, in contrast, are not binding.[5]

4.05 Whilst not binding, *obiter dicta* may be persuasive.[6] Moreover, there are degrees of persuasiveness: where a sufficiently senior judge seizes an opportunity to give general guidance on a point of principle, then their comments may be regarded as being 'highly persuasive'.[7] The term 'judicial *dicta*' may be used to refer to comments that have been promoted in this way. Similarly, if a sufficiently senior judge is known to have had an interest in a topic, then their comments on that topic are likely to be followed—and the same is true where all members of a court concur on a point,[8] or where a judge sets out what they believe to be the *ratio* of an unreported case.[9]

---

1 This derives from the Latin maxim *stare decisis et non quieta movere*, meaning 'to stand by decisions and not disturb the undisturbed'.

2 See *Willers v Joyce* [2016] UKSC 44, at [4].

3 *Knauer v Ministry of Justice* [2016] UKSC 9, at [21]–[23].

4 This is the definition given in the *Oxford English Dictionary* (3rd edn).

5 *Osborne v Rowlett* (1880) 13 Ch D 774, at 785.

6 See *Tees Conservancy Comrs v James* [1935] Ch 544.

7 *G and C Kreglinger v New Patagonia Meat and Cold Storage Co Ltd* [1914] AC 25, HL.

8 See *Mills v LCC* [1925] 1 KB 213, DC.

9 *Richard West & Partners (Inverness) Ltd v Dick* [1969] 2 Ch 424, at 431.

Precedence

Precedence depends on a pecking order that operates in the following way. 4.06

- **Supreme Court and House of Lords** A decision of the Supreme Court (or of its predecessor, the House of Lords) is binding on all lower courts.[10] The Supreme Court has the power to depart from its own decisions,[11] but it should be 'very circumspect before accepting an invitation to invoke [that] power'.[12]
- **Privy Council** The Judicial Committee of the Privy Council (JCPC) is generally concerned with foreign law, which means that its decisions are generally incapable of binding any judge in England or Wales.[13] This, however, is subject to a recently discovered power whereby the JCPC may expressly direct that a decision *is* to bind courts in England and Wales.[14] Be that as it may, Lord Neuberger has explained that where there is no conflict with English authority, decisions of the JCPC should normally be regarded 'as being of great weight and persuasive value'.[15]
- **Court of Justice of the European Union** A decision of the CJEU is, strictly speaking, binding only on the court from which the referral arose,[16] but the Court has held that where the issue is the interpretation of a European Union (EU) instrument, its decisions ought generally to be followed.[17]
- **European Court of Human Rights** Where a domestic court decides a matter that relates to a guaranteed right, it must take into account any relevant decision of the ECtHR.[18]
- **Court of Appeal** A decision in the Court of Appeal will bind itself and all courts below.[19] There are exceptions, however, in that:

---

[10] See *Willers v Joyce* [2016] UKSC 44, at [4]. Moreover, the Court of Appeal is not permitted to advise judges to disregard such decisions on the grounds that they are unworkable or wrong: *Cassell & Co Ltd v Broome* [1972] AC 1027.

[11] Until the middle of the last century, the House of Lords was thought to be bound by its previous decisions: see, eg, *London Tramways Co Ltd v London County Council* [1898] AC 375. That changed in 1966 following *Practice Statement (Judicial Precedent)* [1966] 1 WLR 1234, which emphasised that whilst the Law Lords would regard their earlier decisions as 'normally binding', they would depart from them 'when it appears right to do so'. That said, the importance of consistency in the law was emphasised by Lord Wilberforce in *Fitzleet Estates Ltd v Cherry* [1977] 1 WLR 1345, at 1349, when he explained that the Practice Statement should not be invoked to depart from an earlier decision merely because a subsequent committee of Law Lords take a different view of the law; there has to be something more.

[12] See *Knauer v Ministry of Justice* [2016] UKSC 9, at [21]–[23]. Lord Neuberger and Lady Hale were giving joint judgment on the point; they emphasised the importance of precedence, and the need for certainty and consistency in the law.

[13] See *In re Spectrum Plus Ltd (In liquidation)* [2005] 2 AC 680, at [93], *per* Lord Scott. More recently, see *Willers v Joyce* [2016] UKSC 44, at [15].

[14] Where a decision of the Supreme Court, House of Lords or Court of Appeal is at odds with a decision of the JCPC, the former will prevail, but Lord Neuberger has recently explained that this is subject to the JCPC exercising a power expressly to direct that its decision is to be binding on the English courts: see *Willers v Joyce* [2016] UKSC 44, at [12] and [19]–[21].

[15] See *Willers v Joyce* [2016] UKSC 44, at [13]–[18]; see also *Worcester Works Finance Ltd v Cooden Engineering Co Ltd* [1972] 1 QB 210.

[16] *HP Bulmer Ltd v J Bollinger SA* [1974] Ch 401, [1974] 2 All ER 1226, CA.

[17] *International Chemical Corpn v Amministrazione delle Finanze dello Stato* [1981] ECR 1191.

[18] Human Rights Act 1998, s 2(1)(a) and (b).

[19] The principles were set out by the Court of Appeal in a passage from *Young v Bristol Aeroplane Co Ltd* [1944] KB 718, at 729–30, which was approved by the House of Lords in *Davis v Johnson* [1979] AC 264 and, more recently, by the Supreme Court in *Willers v Joyce* [2016] UKSC 44, at [8]. See also *Re South Durham Iron Co, Smith's Case* (1879) 11 Ch D 579, CA.

(1) the Court of Appeal is entitled and bound to decide which of two conflicting decisions of its own it will follow;[20]
(2) it is bound to refuse to follow a decision of its own that, although not expressly overruled, cannot, in its opinion, stand with a decision of the House of Lords[21] or the Supreme Court;[22] and
(3) it is not bound to follow a decision of its own if it is satisfied that the decision was given *per incuriam* (such as where a decision was made in ignorance of legislation).[23]

- **Divisional Court** A decision in the Divisional Court is binding upon itself[24] and upon judges deciding cases at first instance.[25]
- **High Court** A decision of a puisne judge (that is, a High Court judge) will bind masters and all judges in the County Court.[26] Technically speaking, puisne judges do not bind each other,[27] but in practice they will regard appropriate first-instance decisions at the same level as being persuasive (this being as a matter of judicial comity).[28] Indeed, Lord Neuberger has recently explained that they should generally follow a decision of a court of coordinate jurisdiction unless there is 'a powerful reason for not doing so'.[29]
- **Circuit judges, masters and district judges** Traditional teaching is that decisions at these judicial levels will bind no court and that such decisions ought not to be cited unless they have been reported or unless they contain a relevant statement of legal principle not found in reported authority.[30] As a matter of practice, however, such decisions are increasingly being cited in detailed assessments and in costs litigation generally. In previous editions of this book, the editor has resisted this trend, but it seems that he may have been wrong to do so because Lord Neuberger has recently said that circuit judges should adopt much the same approach to decisions of other circuit judges as puisne judges do to decisions of other puisne judges.[31] That comment was certainly *obiter* and it was phrased in such a way as to make it easy to dismiss it as a mere puff—but, in the context of the very strong emphasis that the Supreme Court now places on the need for predictability and certainty in the law (see 4.03), one could easily argue that the law has moved on from the traditional teaching.

---

[20] See *Willers v Joyce* [2016] UKSC 44, at [8]; see also *Re South Durham Iron Co, Smith's Case* (1879) 11 Ch D 579, CA.

[21] See, eg, *Huddersfield Police Authority v Watson* [1947] KB 842. Mere misinterpretation of a decision in the House of Lords would not be sufficient, however: see *Williams v Glasbrook Bros Ltd* [1947] 2 All ER 884, CA.

[22] See *Willers v Joyce* [2016] UKSC 44, at [8].

[23] See, eg, *Young v Bristol Aeroplane Co Ltd* [1944] KB 718, [1944] 2 All ER 293, CA.

[24] *Huddersfield Police Authority v Watson* [1947] KB 842, [1947] 2 All ER 193, DC. The exceptions in the Court of Appeal apply: *Nicholas v Penny* [1950] 2 KB 466.

[25] *John v John and Goff* [1965] P 289.

[26] This was recently clarified by Lord Neuberger PSC in *Willers v Joyce* [2016] UKSC 44, at [5], in which he referred to a 'note' at the end of *Howard de Walden Estates Ltd v Aggio* [2008] Ch 26.

[27] *The Vera Cruz (No 2)* (1884) 9 PD 96, CA.

[28] *Russian and English Bank v Baring Bros & Co Ltd* [1935] Ch 120, CA.

[29] See *Willers v Joyce* [2016] UKSC 44, at [9].

[30] *Practice Direction (Citation of Authorities)* [2012] 1 WLR 780, at [10].

[31] See *Willers v Joyce* [2016] UKSC 44, at [9].

Miscellaneous points about decided cases

The following miscellaneous points can be made about decided cases (the first of which is particularly relevant to the law of costs). **4.07**

- **Discretionary decisions and evaluative judgments** Of especial importance in the context of the law of costs is the often-overlooked principle that the exercise of discretion in one case is not to be taken as being a guide to the exercise of discretion in another case. Hodson LJ had this to say:

  > 'It is dangerous in the exercise of discretion to take a reported case as a guide for that exercise in another case. This is specially true when the judgment on costs is taken apart from its context of the findings of fact which are contained in the same judgment.'[32]

The fact that this book contains numerous case examples should not be regarded as being a tacit invitation to derogate from this principle (which also applies to evaluative judgments); examples are provided merely to illustrate the way in which the law is applied and to help the reader with further legal research.

- **Unclear *ratio*** If the *ratio* is not clear, then there is no duty upon the court to seek to spell the *ratio* out to apply it.[33] Likewise, *ratio* from lengthy judgments should not be taken out of context.[34]
- **Conflicting decisions at the same judicial level** As a matter of general principle, where there are conflicting decisions from judges of coordinate jurisdiction, then, in the absence of cogent reasons to the contrary, the second of those decisions should be followed.[35] In particular, the most recent decision will be preferred if it has been arrived at after full consideration of the earlier decision.[36]
- **Long-standing decisions** Where a non-binding decision has stood the test of time and has been frequently cited, it will usually be regarded as being highly persuasive.[37]
- **Decisions on applications for permission to appeal** Judgments given on applications for permission to appeal are not binding authorities; the court does not encourage reference to be made thereto.[38]
- **Judicial interjections** Interjections during argument are not binding.[39]
- **Multiple reasoning** In general, where the court has given more than one reason for arriving at the decision reached, each will be capable of being *ratio*.[40]
- **Citation of authorities** This is addressed at 2.06.

---

32 *Bragg v Crosville Motor Services Ltd* [1959] 1 All ER 613, at 615.
33 *The Mostyn* [1928] AC 57, HL.
34 *Monk v Warbey* [1935] 1 KB 75, CA.
35 See *Patel v Secretary of State for the Home Department* [2013] UKSC 72, at [59].
36 *Re Cromptons Leisure Machines Ltd* [2006] EWHC 3583 (Ch).
37 See, eg, *Astley v IRC* [1974] STC 367.
38 *Clark v University of Lincolnshire and Humberside* [2000] 3 All ER 752, at 762f, *per* Lord Woolf MR.
39 *Practice Note* [1942] WN 89, PC, *per* Viscount Simon C.
40 *Cheater v Cater* [1918] 1 KB 247, CA.

Legislative Interpretation

4.08 Where legislation is ambiguous or its putative effect is difficult to understand or justify, the court may have to determine its true legislative meaning, this being a process of identifying the intention of Parliament. Nowadays, the courts seek to do more than merely identify the mischief the legislation is intended to cure. Lord Neuberger PSC had this to say on the issue of interpretation generally:

> 'Interpretation of any document ultimately involves identifying the intention of Parliament, the drafter, or the parties. That intention must be determined by reference to the precise words used, their particular documentary and factual context, and, where identifiable, their aim or purpose.'[41]

Starting with the precise words used: where they admit of only one meaning in the relevant context, that is the end of the matter; if not, a court is entitled to prefer that construction which makes the better sense, even if less consistent with the language.[42]

4.09 In adopting a purposive approach to the interpretation of statutory language, courts must, where appropriate, seek to identify and give effect to the purpose of the legislation. Whilst there is a constitutional consideration that there ought to be certainty in legislation, this does not mean that the courts are confined to looking solely at the language in question in its context within the legislation. Lord Nicholls has said that that would impose much too restrictive an approach and that no legislation is enacted in a vacuum.[43]

Aids to interpretation

4.10 The documents that the court may take into account are referred to as 'aids to interpretation'. They may be 'intrinsic aids' or 'extrinsic aids'.[44]

- **Intrinsic aids to interpretation** Other provisions in the same legislation may shed light on the meaning of the words under consideration.
- **Extrinsic aids to interpretation** Aids may be external to the legislation, such as its background setting and its legislative history.[45] This may include legislative antecedents, reports of Royal Commissions and advisory committees,[46] and reports of the Law Commission and the Civil Justice Council.[47] It may also include explanatory

---

41 *Cusack v Harrow London Borough Council* [2013] 1 WLR 2022, at [58].

42 See *Rainy Sky SA v Kookmin Bank* [2011] 1 WLR 2900, at [21], [40], *per* Lord Clarke, which was in the context of a contract case, but is equally applicable to legislation: see *Murphy v Rayner* [2013] EWHC 3878 (Ch), at [81], *per* Nicholas Strauss QC (sitting as a deputy High Court judge).

43 *R v Secretary of State for the Environment, ex parte Spath Holme Ltd* [2001] 2 AC 349, at 397C–398D.

44 *Ibid*, *per* Lord Nicholls.

45 As an example of the court taking into account the legislative history, see *Dalton v British Telecommunications* [2015] EWHC 616 (QB), in which Phillips J interpreted a provision in CPR, Part 45, by reference to legislation that was made in 1906.

46 See, eg, *R (Public and Commercial Services Union) v Minister for the Civil Service* [2010] ICR 1198, in which Sales J considered a report of the Joint Superannuation Committee of the national Whitely Council; see also *Dalton v British Telecommunications* [2015] EWHC 616 (QB), at [59].

47 See, eg, *Dalton v British Telecommunications* [2015] EWHC 616 (QB), at [58], *per* Phillips J.

memoranda.[48] Lord Nicholls has cautioned that external aids to interpretation should be used only with circumspection.[49]

Regard may also be had to extraneous circumstances, such as the setting in which the legislation was enacted. This is a matter of everyday occurrence, but Lord Nichols has said that the court should be slow to permit external aids to displace meanings that are otherwise clear.[50] **4.11**

Obvious drafting errors

It may be that, having taken into account all of the relevant circumstances, the court is satisfied that the legislation in question suffers from an obvious drafting mistake; this being so, the court has an exceptional jurisdiction to give effect to the true meaning of the legislation.[51] Lord Nicholls had this to say on the topic: **4.12**

> 'It has long been established that the role of the courts in construing legislation is not confined to resolving ambiguities in statutory language. The court must be able to correct obvious drafting errors. In suitable cases, in discharging its interpretative function the court will add words, or omit words or substitute words. Some notable instances are given in Professor Sir Rupert Cross's admirable opuscule, *Statutory Interpretation*, 3rd ed. (1995), pp. 93–105. He comments, at p. 103:
>
> > "In omitting or inserting words the judge is not really engaged in a hypothetical reconstruction of the intentions of the drafter or the legislature, but is simply making as much sense as he can of the text of the statutory provision read in its appropriate context and within the limits of the judicial role."
>
> This power is confined to plain cases of drafting mistakes. The courts are ever mindful that their constitutional role in this field is interpretative. They must abstain from any course which might have the appearance of judicial legislation. A statute is expressed in language approved and enacted by the legislature. So the courts exercise considerable caution before adding or omitting or substituting words.'[52]

Lord Nicholls went on to make the following comments: **4.13**

> 'Before interpreting a statute in this way the court must be abundantly sure of three matters: (1) the intended purpose of the statute or provision in question; (2) that by inadvertence the draftsman and Parliament failed to give effect to that purpose in the provision in question; and (3) the substance of the provision Parliament would have made, although not necessarily the precise words Parliament would have used, had the error in the Bill been noticed. The third of these conditions is of crucial importance. Otherwise any attempt to determine the meaning of the enactment would cross the boundary between construction and legislation: see *per* Lord Diplock in *Jones v Wrotham Park Settled Estates* [1980] AC 74, 105–106.'[53]

---

[48] See, eg, *Broadhurst & Anor v Tan & Anor* [2016] EWCA Civ 94, at [15] and [33], *per* Dyson MR. Where this is so, the three conditions specified by Lord Browne-Wilkinson in *Pepper v Hart* [1993] AC 593 should be taken into account: see *Broadhurst & Anor v Tan & Anor* [2016] EWCA Civ 94, at [33].

[49] *R v Secretary of State for the Environment, ex parte Spath Holme Ltd* [2001] 2 AC 349, at 397C–398D.

[50] *Ibid.*

[51] As an example of a costs case in which the court exercised this exceptional jurisdiction, see *Qader v Esure Services Ltd* [2016] EWCA Civ 1109, at [35(d)], *per* Briggs LJ.

[52] *Inco Europe Ltd v First Choice Distribution* [2000] 1 WLR 586, at 592.

[53] *Ibid.*

The Solicitors' Codes of Conduct

4.14 The present incarnation of the code regulating solicitors[54] is the SRA Code of Conduct 2011. Prior to 6 October 2011, it was the Solicitors' Code of Conduct 2007; prior to 1 July 2007, it was the Solicitors' Practice Rules 1990 (SPR). This chapter refers to a number of cases that related to the older provisions,[55] so caution must be exercised in this regard because there are differences in the style and content of the two codes.

Jurisdiction and *vires*

4.15 The power of the SRA (and, before it, the Law Society[56]) to make codes of conduct derive from s 31 of the Solicitors Act 1974,[57] which provision enables the SRA to make rules that have the force of statute. This was explained by Lord Brightman in the following way: 'The rules [in that case, the SPR] have the force of a statute . . . just as much as if [they] were set out in a Schedule to the Act.'[58] The principle that the relevant provisions must be interpreted and applied as if they were set out in a Schedule to an Act was affirmed by Schiemann LJ in 1999,[59] then again by Arden LJ in 2005.[60] It is a principle that remains good law under the CPR[61] (not least because it is substantive law).

'Outcomes', 'indicative behaviours' and 'outcomes-focused regulation'

4.16 Whilst it is safe to say that the 2011 Code of Conduct has the force of statute (see 4.15), there is some uncertainty as to how this will apply in practice. This is because the 2011 Code is a move away from the traditional prescriptive method of regulating solicitors. It is based on 'outcomes-focused regulation' (OFR), and rather than containing prescriptive rules and guidance, the new Code focuses on mandatory 'outcomes' and non-mandatory 'indicative behaviours'.[62]

- **Outcomes** These describe what solicitors are expected to achieve to comply with the Principles in specific contexts and they are mandatory.

---

[54] It is worth noting that the 2011 Code of Conduct regulates not only solicitors in traditional firms and in-house practice, but also any person who chooses to be regulated by the SRA, and this may include other species of lawyer, as well as new entrants to the legal services market, such as non-lawyer managers of alternative business structures.

[55] Generally speaking, what is said in this chapter about the 2007 and 2011 Codes of Conduct is also true of the SPR and vice versa.

[56] The SRA was established in January 2007 and was previously called the Law Society Regulation Board. It is part of the Law Society, but acts independently of it.

[57] Which provides: '[The] Council [of the Law Society] may, if they think fit, make rules, with the concurrence of the Master of the Rolls, for regulating in respect of any matter the professional practice, conduct and discipline of solicitors and for empowering the Society to take such action as may be appropriate to enable the Society to ascertain whether or not the provisions of rules made, or of any code or guidance issued, by the Council are being complied with.'

[58] *Swain v The Law Society* [1983] 1 AC 598, at 621.

[59] In *Awwad v Geraghty* [2001] QB 570, at 583–584.

[60] *Garbutt v Edwards* [2005] EWCA Civ 1206, at [31].

[61] *Ibid.* Arden LJ explained that the SPR were there to protect the legitimate interests of the client and the administration of justice.

[62] See *Outcomes-Focused Regulation at a Glance: Your Quick Guide to Getting Started with OFR and the New Handbook* (London: Law Society, 2011), para 3.

- **Indicative behaviours** These provide examples of the type of behaviours that may establish whether the relevant outcomes have been achieved and whether there has been compliance with the Principles. They are not mandatory

Outcomes-focused regulation is not something that is achieved by the 2011 Code of Conduct in isolation; rather, it is achieved by that Code working in concert with certain other provisions, which are set out in the SRA Handbook. From the point of view of the law of costs, the relevant parts are: **4.17**

- ten high-level Principles;[63]
- the 2011 Code of Conduct itself; and
- the Accounts Rules and rules dealing with financial services (see 4.29).[64]

Transitional provisions exist.[65]

The effect of a breach of the 2011 Code of Conduct

The fact that the 2011 Code of Conduct has force as though it were set out in a Schedule to an Act (see 4.15) is only the starting point. Its effect is often mediated through the common law and, in particular, through the common law's interpretation of public policy. Broadly speaking, where something is done in breach of the 2011 Code, that breach will fall into one or both of two categories: **4.18**

(1) it may be a failure in the performance of an obligation; and/or
(2) it may be something that is prohibited.

An example of (1) would be a failure to provide a client with a proper estimate; an example of (2) would be entering into a prohibited retainer (such as an unlawful contingency fee agreement). For the reasons set out below, the law takes more notice of breaches of type (2) than of type (1).

Implied statutory prohibition

Whilst the starting point is to determine the meaning of the 2011 Code of Conduct by a process of legislative interpretation, the legal mechanism by which a breach gives rise to private law rights will vary from case to case. Those mechanisms may be placed in the categories of express and implied statutory prohibition (a detailed description of the mechanisms of statutory prohibition is given at 27.228–27.301). In this context, the word 'prohibition' is used to include failing to do that which ought to have been done. Express statutory prohibition is—in the context of contracts of retainer, for example—where a statute not only states what is or is not permissible, but also prescribes that, in the event of a breach of the relevant requirement, any associated contract or entitlement to costs will be prohibited. Implied statutory prohibition is where a prohibition exists, but is implied rather than expressly stated. In the context of costs law, express statutory prohibition is uncommon,[66] especially in so far as the 2011 Code is concerned. **4.19**

[63] These are similar to the core principles in the 2007 Code of Conduct.
[64] Large parts of the Solicitors Accounts Rules 1998 have been retained. Nevertheless, some operational flexibility has been introduced, eg in relation to the payment of interest and signing on client account.
[65] See Chapter 15 of the 2011 Code of Conduct.
[66] A notable exception to this is s 58(1) of the Courts and Legal Services Act 1990, as amended.

4.20 A prohibited contract or entitlement to costs may be such that the court's processes will not be used to enforce it (hence the term 'unenforceable'), but this will not always be the outcome. In the context of general litigation rather than costs, Browne-Wilkinson J had this to say:

> 'The fact that a party has in the course of performing a contract committed an unlawful or immoral act will not by itself prevent him from further enforcing that contract unless the contract was entered into with the purpose of doing that unlawful or immoral act or the contract itself (as opposed to the mode of his performance) is prohibited by law.'[67]

4.21 Where a breach of the 2011 Code of Conduct contains an implied statutory prohibition against a thing done or made, its effect is usually mediated via the common-law concept of public policy. This can be illustrated by reference to the example of a contingency fee agreement under the 2007 Code of Conduct. A contingency fee agreement was not made unenforceable as a direct result of a provision in that Code, but instead it was made unenforceable by reason of it being contrary to public policy, as reflected in that Code (see 4.25 for authorities on this point).[68] As a matter of public policy, the court's processes would not be used to enforce it. Whilst in a different league of culpability, an analogy may be drawn with a contract to commit a crime: a contract to rob a bank is unenforceable not because there is a statute that says that it unenforceable (that is, express statutory prohibition), but because the common law will not allow the court to be used to enforce such an obnoxious contract (that is, there is an implied statutory prohibition arising out of public policy).

The role of discretion

4.22 Where the prohibition is implied, it is usually the case that the court has a degree of discretion. The court will determine what is and what is not contrary to public policy, and the consequences of the breach will then be in the discretion of the court (guided, of course, by precedent). At one extreme, the court may ignore the breach entirely;[69] at the other, it may find that the breach is so egregious that the entire solicitor–client relationship has been tainted with illegality.

4.23 The fact that the court has discretion was explained by Lord Diplock in the following way:

> 'The Council in exercising its powers under the Act to make rules and regulations and the Society in discharging functions vested in it by the Act or by such rules or regulations are acting in a public capacity and what they do in that capacity is governed by public law; and although the legal consequences of doing it may result in creating rights enforceable in private law, those rights are not necessarily the same as those that would flow in private law from doing a similar act otherwise than in the exercise of statutory powers.'[70]

Timing

4.24 Whilst an obvious point, it is worth noting that the court will tend not to apply hindsight. An example of this is a case in which a businessman had entered into a contingency fee agreement; the outcome of his claim was so good that his solicitors were able to claim a handsome sum indeed. He complained that this was as a result of him not being treated

[67] *Coral Leisure Group Ltd v Barnett* [1981] ICR 503, at 509.

[68] See *Mohammed v Alaga & Co* [2000] 1 WLR 1815, at 1823, for an analogous situation involving a prohibited contract other than a retainer; see also *Awwad v Geraghty* [2001] QB 570, at 587.

[69] See Arden LJ's analysis in *Garbutt v Edwards* [2005] EWCA Civ 1206, at [31].

[70] *Swain v The Law Society* [1983] 1 AC 598, at 608.

'fairly', as required by Outcome 1.1 of the 2011 Code of Conduct. Spencer J rejected that argument and, in doing so, he was careful to look at the facts as they were at the time that the agreement was made and to ensure that he did not allow himself to be bowled over by the actual outcome of the case.[71]

The relevance of public policy

In view of the fact that the effect of a breach of the 2011 Code of Conduct may be dependent on public policy, it is worth saying a word about the nature of public policy itself. Bingham CJ had this to say: **4.25**

> 'When making such subordinate legislation [ie the 2007 Code of Conduct or the SPR], the Law Society is acting in the public interest and not (should there be any conflict) in the narrower interests of the solicitors' profession: see *Swain v The Law Society* [1983] 1 AC 598. The concurrence of the Master of the Rolls is required as a guarantee that the interests of the public are fully safeguarded.'[72]

Thus public policy is reflected in the relevant provisions (at time of writing, the 2011 Code of Conduct). Put another way, the 2011 Code ought to be regarded as an indicator of the public interest rather than an indicator of what is in the interests of the solicitors' profession. The 2011 Code does not, however, *define* what is in the public interest because the court may take other factors into account.[73]

Other factors

In addition to taking into account the nature of the breach of the 2011 Code of Conduct, the court may also consider the motives of the person seeking to rely on that breach. For obvious reasons, the court would be more likely to give more credence to a complaint made by the client than it would be to that made by a stranger (such as a paying party seeking to rely on a technical argument). In this regard, Arden LJ said: **4.26**

> 'In making these Rules, the Council of the Law Society is acting in the public interest . . . The inference I would draw is that the Code is there to protect the legitimate interests of the client, and the administration of justice, rather than to relieve paying parties of their obligations to pay costs which have been reasonably incurred.'[74]

Thus the court will tend to look unfavourably upon complaints raised by paying parties. This is not to say that the court will always rush to the aid of a client who seeks to rely on a putative breach of the 2011 Code of Conduct. This is because each case will turn on its own facts. An example of this is the case referred to in 4.24 in which a former client complained about having to pay a very large contingency fee—so large, he contended, as to be in breach of the obligation in the 2011 Code of Conduct to treat clients fairly. Spencer J rejected that argument and, in doing so, he gave great weight to the fact that the client was a 'very experienced businessman' who had taken an active part in negotiating the supposedly unfair contract of retainer.[75] Spencer J also placed emphasis on the fact that it would have **4.27**

[71] *Bolt Burdon Solicitors v Tariq & Ors* [2016] EWHC 811 (QB), at [163].

[72] *Mohammed v Alaga & Co* [2000] 1 WLR 1815, at 1823.

[73] An example of this is *Bolt Burdon Solicitors v Tariq & Ors* [2016] EWHC 811 (QB), at [158]–[171], in which Spencer J took into account a whole range of factors when deciding whether a firm of solicitors had discharged its duty under Outcome 1.1 to treat their clients 'fairly'.

[74] *Garbutt v Edwards* [2005] EWCA Civ 1206, at [36].

[75] See *Bolt Burdon Solicitors v Tariq & Ors* [2016] EWHC 811 (QB), esp at [157] and [158]. Indeed, it would seem that the former client had actually suggested the level of the fee: see *ibid*, [162].

been difficult to fund the former client's claim in any way other than that which had been negotiated.[76]

4.28 Thus the effect and authority of the 2011 Code of Conduct will, in the absence of express statutory prohibition, depend on the facts of the case. It would be wrong simply to say that it has the force of statute and to assume that this is the answer to all issues; whilst there is still a lack of authority on the issue, it is likely that the approach of the court will continue to be far more nuanced than that.

Other Rules of Professional Conduct

Financial and accounting rules

4.29 There are rules that are not within the 2011 Code of Conduct itself, but which are afforded a similar status. Examples include:

- the Solicitors' Accounts Rules 2011;
- the Solicitors' Financial Services (Scope) Rules 2001; and
- the Financial Services (Conduct of Business) Rules 2001.

Indeed, the 2011 Code of Conduct may itself require compliance with these other rules.[77]

4.30 There are some aspects of the Solicitors' Financial Services (Scope) Rules 2001 and the Financial Services (Conduct of Business) Rules 2001 that are examples of express statutory prohibition. This issue is beyond the scope of this chapter, but is dealt with in detail at 34.42.

Guidance Notes to the 2011 Code of Conduct

4.31 The Guidance Notes that used to accompany the 2007 Code of Conduct were not made by statutory instrument and are therefore not afforded the same status as the Code. The guidance that accompanies the 2011 Code is, however, much more integrated within that Code, to the extent that it is difficult to see how the Code could be placed in context without taking that guidance into account. That said, at the time of writing, there was no authority on the status of the guidance.

The Civil Procedure Rules 1998

4.32 The CPR are particularly relevant to costs law because it is, on the whole, an adjectival discipline.[78] Indeed, many disputes are about the CPR and nothing else. On 1 April 2013,

---

[76] See *ibid*, esp [157]. Similarly, in a case in which no estimate of overall cost had been given to the client, Master Rowley dismissed any complaint by referring to the fact that it was a foregone conclusion that any such estimate would not have made any difference: see *May & Anor v Wavell Group plc & Anor* [2016] Lexis Citation 72, at [41]. It should be noted, however, that this was not a case in which the Master thought that there was an obligation to provide such an estimate. This case was successfully appealed, but on a different point: see [2017] Lexis Citation 462.

[77] An example being r 5.01(1)(c), in respect of which the Guidance Notes make it clear that the Solicitors' Accounts Rules 1998 should be complied with in certain circumstances.

[78] This is why Blackstone's writings on costs in *Commentaries on the Laws of England* (Oxford: Clarendon Press, 1765–69) are contained in a chapter bearing the title 'Of Pleading' (see Book Three, ch 20).

the CPR were updated in such a way as to radically change those Parts that governed costs (which used to be CPR Parts 43–48, but are now limited to Parts 44–48). Many of the provisions have been retained (or retained with only slight modifications), but with different numbering. Transitional provisions apply in such a way as to make the 'old' provision potentially relevant for many years to come.[79]

Jurisdiction and the procedure of making the CPR

The CPR are made pursuant to s 1(1) of the Civil Procedure Act 1997 (CPA 1997).[80] They apply in the civil division of the Court of Appeal, the High Court, and the County Court and its hearing centres. In so far as the law of costs is concerned, the CPR may also apply by analogy in other courts, such as the Supreme Court,[81] and in tribunals.[82] Where this is the case, the CPR will generally apply only to the extent that they do not conflict with rules specific to the tribunal or court in question. **4.33**

The CPA 1997 makes provisions about how the CPR are to be made.[83] Section 2 provides that proposed rules are formulated by the Civil Procedure Rule Committee (often loosely referred to as 'the Rules Committee') and that they may then be either allowed or disallowed by the Secretary of State for Justice (previously the Lord Chancellor). If the Secretary of State allows the proposed rules, s 3(1)(b) of the CPA 1997 provides that they are to be made by statutory instrument. Section 3(2) provides that they are subject to annulment by negative resolution of either House of Parliament—which means that they will be made unless one or other of the Houses objects. It should be noted that the negative resolution procedure does not permit Parliament to amend any draft put before it; it may only annul any draft of which it disapproves.[84] **4.34**

It has been argued that the fact that s 51(3) of the Senior Courts Act 1981 (as amended) provides that 'the court shall have full power to determine by whom and to what extent the costs are to be paid' means that primary legislation is required to limit any such power. If that argument is right, then the CPR would be *ultra vires* to the extent that they tried impose a fetter (such as qualified one-way costs shifting or the small claims track costs restrictions). This argument rarely succeeds: Vos LJ, for example, rejected that contention.[85] **4.35**

Henry VIII clauses

The Secretary of State for Justice receives advice from the Civil Justice Council.[86] He has significant powers to make or negate enactments in consequence of the CPR, which power arises out of a provision that is often referred to as a 'Henry VIII clause'. In particular, s 4(1) of the CPA 1997 allows the Secretary of State to amend, repeal or revoke any **4.36**

---

[79] See, eg, CPR, Pt 48, and PD 48.

[80] The power is also governed by the Constitutional Reform Act 2005 and, in particular, by Sched 1 to that Act.

[81] See para 1.4 of the Supreme Court, *Practice Direction 13 (Costs)*; see also Senior Courts Act 1981, s 1.

[82] See, eg, *Revenue & Customs Commissioners v Talentcore Ltd* (unreported), 19 November 2011, UT (Tax), *per* Roth J. Indeed, some rules expressly incorporate the CPR: see, eg, the Tribunal Procedure (First-tier Tribunal) (Property Chamber) Rules 2013 (SI 2013/1169), r 13(8).

[83] See also the Constitutional Reform Act 2005 and, in particular, Sched 1 to that Act.

[84] This was made clear by Dyson MR in *Broadhurst & Anor v Tan & Anor* [2016] EWCA Civ 94, at [33].

[85] See *Wagemaar v Weekend Travel Ltd* [2014] EWCA Civ 1105, at [22]–[27].

[86] See Civil Procedure Act 1997, s 6.

enactment to the extent that it is desirable in consequence of the CPR. If the Secretary of States wishes to do this, they must make the change by statutory instrument,[87] which may be subject to annulment by negative resolution of either House.[88] If the Secretary of State wishes, they may also amend, repeal or revoke relevant enactments made before the CPR came into force, but if they intend to do that, affirmative approval of both of the Houses of Parliament must be obtained.[89]

Interpretation of the CPR

4.37 Although they are usually referred to as being 'rules', the CPR as a whole not only are made by statutory instrument, but also *are* a statutory instrument[90]—that is, they are subordinate legislation.[91] This means that the interpretation of the CPR is a process of legislative interpretation that—where appropriate—requires the application of ordinary canons of construction.[92] It also means that the court does not have the power to override the CPR (unless, of course, there is some contrary statutory provision, such as a provision under the Human Rights Act 1998).[93]

4.38 The intention of the original framers of the CPR was that they were to be provisions that spoke for themselves, so that there would be no need to refer to an ever-increasing body of authority to apply them.[94] Reference to pre-CPR case law is generally to be discouraged for the purposes of interpreting the CPR,[95] but there may be circumstances in which it is instructive.[96] Some provisions are codifications of pre-existing judge-made procedures and, in those circumstances, reference to pre-CPR authorities may be helpful.[97] Where two competing interpretations of a provision in the CPR are possible, it would be legitimate to take practice directions into account as an extrinsic aid to interpretation,[98] but May LJ has commented that they are 'at best a weak aid'.[99]

4.39 When interpreting the CPR, the court must seek to give effect to the overriding objective.[100] The fact that the overriding objective was amended on 1 April 2013 so as to place greater emphasis on the importance of proportionality is likely to become increasingly relevant. This topic is addressed in detail in Chapter 26.

---

87 See Constitutional Reform Act 2005, Sched 1, para 4(1)(b).

88 See Constitutional Reform Act 2005, Sched 1, para 4(2).

89 CPA 1997, s 4(2) and (5).

90 See the Civil Procedure Rules 1998 (SI 1998/3132), which gave rise to the first version of the CPR. All subsequent amendments have been made by statutory instrument.

91 See Interpretation Act 1978, s 21(1), which provides that ' "subordinate legislation" means Orders in Council, orders, rules, regulations, schemes, warrants, byelaws and other instruments made by or under any Act'.

92 *Vinos v Marks & Spencer plc* [2001] 3 All ER 784.

93 *General Mediterranean Holdings SA v Patel* [2000] 1 WLR 272.

94 *ABCI v Banque Franco-Tunisienne & Ors* [2003] EWCA Civ 205, at [68].

95 *Biguzzi v Rank Leisure plc* [1999] EWCA Civ 1972.

96 *EI Du Pont De Nemours & Co v ST Dupont* [2003] EWCA Civ 1368, at [86].

97 An example being the procedure as described in *Pamplin v Express Newspapers Ltd* [1985] 1 WLR 689, which is codified at CPD, art 40.14.

98 *Van Aken v London Borough of Camden* [2002] EWCA Civ 1724, at [36]. In some circumstances, it may be possible to take Hansard into account: *Pepper v Hart* [1992] UKHL 3.

99 *Godwin v Swindon Borough Council* [2001] EWCA Civ 1478, at [11].

100 CPR, r 1.2.

The court has a wide discretion to regulate its own procedure. Such regulation must be within the constraints imposed by the CPR, but in view of the fact that CPR, r 3.1(2)(m), expressly confers the power to take any 'step or make any ... order for the purpose of managing the case and furthering the overriding objective', the ambit of that discretion is wide. Dyson LJ has noted that, in many respects, the CPR is 'open-textured' and that the court may 'fill in gaps left by those rules', which further widens the ambit of that discretion.[101] **4.40**

Provisions made by directions

Schedule 1, para 6, to the CPA 1997 provides that 'Civil Procedure Rules may refer to provisions made by directions'. Section 9(2) defines 'practice directions' as 'directions as to the practice and procedure of any court within the scope of the Civil Procedure Rules', so the CPR will, if they are so worded, incorporate provisions made in practice directions.[102] This does not mean that practice directions are ordinarily to be afforded the same status as the CPR; indeed, the opposite is generally true (see 4.46–4.55). **4.41**

The County Court Rules, Rules of the Supreme Court, etc

It is occasionally the case that the CPR may still refer to rules that they replaced—namely, the Rules of the Supreme Court 1965 and the County Court Rules 1981. Where this is the case, the CPR may apply those rules to any extent, with or without modification.[103] **4.42**

Rules of evidence

Whilst it will rarely be relevant to the law of costs, the CPR may modify the rules of evidence as they apply to proceedings in any court within the scope of the Rules.[104] **4.43**

The Supreme Court Rules 2009

Whilst this book does not deal with costs in the Supreme Court, it is worth saying in passing that that Court has its own equivalent of the CPR—namely, the Supreme Court Rules 2009 (SCR).[105] Those Rules are made by the Senior Lord of Appeal in Ordinary in exercise of the power conferred by s 45 of the Constitutional Reform Act 2005. Those Rules relate to all appeals, civil or otherwise, including cases decided under Scottish law and cases decided in Northern Ireland. This is undoubtedly why they appear to be less prescriptive than the CPR. **4.44**

---

[101] *Leigh v Michelin Tyre plc* [2003] EWCA Civ 1766, at [21]. Whilst in a different context (ie purposive construction in a more general sense), Denning MR explained that that court 'will fill in gaps, quite unashamedly, without hesitation': *James Buchanan & Co Ltd v Babco Forward and Shipping (UK) Ltd* [1977] QB 208. An analogy could be drawn with rules of court.

[102] An example is the last sentence of CPR, r 47.19, which defers to the CPD.

[103] CPA 1997, Sched 1, para 5.

[104] CPA 1997, Sched 1, para 4. An example of a flexible approach of this nature is *Bolt Burdon Solicitors v Tariq & Ors* [2016] EWHC 811 (QB), at [141], in which Spencer J found it to be a case in which the court itself should undertake an enquiry into certain facts.

[105] SI 2009/1603, esp Part 7; see also UKSC Practice Direction 13. Both deal with costs.

4.45 The aim and objective of the Supreme Court is wholly different from that under the CPR, this presumably being as a result of its particular role of it being a law-making court. The relevant provisions, in SCR, r 2, read as follows:

> '2.–(1) These Rules apply to civil and criminal appeals to the Court and to appeals and references under the Court's devolution jurisdiction.
> (2) The overriding objective of these Rules is to secure that the Court is accessible, fair and efficient.
> (3) The Court must interpret and apply these Rules with a view to securing that the Court is accessible, fair and efficient and that unnecessary disputes over procedural matters are discouraged.'

The Status of Practice Directions

4.46 Practice directions may be said to be directions as to the practice and procedure of any court within the scope of rules to which they apply.[106] This book discusses only those practice directions that relate to the CPR—namely, Practice Directions (PDs) 44–48 and their predecessor, the Costs Practice Direction—but it should not be forgotten that other practice directions exist in the Supreme Court.[107] For the reasons set out below, however, less weight should be given to practice directions than to the CPR themselves.

The power to make practice directions

4.47 It is for the Lord Chief Justice, or a judicial office holder nominated by the Lord Chief Justice with the agreement of the Secretary of State for Justice, to make or give practice directions.[108] That power may be delegated to the Vice-Chancellor, as Head of Civil Justice, and subsequently to the Deputy Head of Civil Justice.[109] Thus practice directions are usually made by the Lord Chief Justice, the Master of the Rolls (in so far as they affect civil appeals), the Vice-Chancellor, or the Head or Deputy Head of Civil Justice.

Bar against local practice directions

4.48 It used to be common for county courts to issue local practice directions.[110] They used to be able to do this because, prior to the CPA 1997, they had an inherent power to regulate their own practices and procedures.[111] Whilst its demise was mourned by some,[112] that power has now been restricted such that it now exists only to the extent that the directions in question have been approved by or on behalf of the Secretary of State for Justice or the

---

106 CPA 1997, Sched 1, para 9(2).

107 See UKSC Practice Directions 7 and 13.

108 See Constitutional Reform Act 2005, Sched 2, para 2(1).

109 This is pursuant to the powers conferred by s 19 of the Constitutional Reform Act 2005.

110 An example of this was described in 'Litigation Focus', Law Society Gazette, 18 March 1992, at 89, in which it was said that failure to adhere to local practice directions could result in wasted costs.

111 *Langley v North West Water Authority* [1991] 1 WLR 697.

112 In 'One Fixed Place or Several', Birkenhead Lecture, 21 October 2013, Grays Inn, at para 34, Lord Thomas said that 'judges in [local courts used] to devise their own solutions' and that it had 'not been easy to persuade some that local practices are no longer necessary or lawful', going on to say that this was because judges 'have a tendency to think that the solution we have devised is the best'.

Lord Chief Justice.[113] Speaking extrajudicially, Thomas LCJ had this to say about the importance of this change:

> '[P]rocedural uniformity is essential for a number of reasons. First, we are one jurisdiction in England and Wales; local practices are not consistent with the uniform application of the law. Second, local practices are a barrier to competition; there is no easier way of making it difficult for a practitioner from another city or from another area of the law to act in a case than by creating local practices. Third, digitalisation is only practicable and affordable if practices are uniform.'[114]

The status of practice directions

The following discussion assumes that the provisions under scrutiny are not provisions that have been incorporated into the CPR themselves by express wording (see 4.41). Where express incorporation has taken place, then the relevant provisions in a practice direction must be afforded the same status as the CPR. The need to consign a provision to a practice direction usually arises where there is too much detail to be set out in the rules themselves or where there are details that may be subject to frequent change. An example is CPR, r 45.11(2), which relegates lists of certain geographical details to PD 45. The need to incorporate may also arise where the practice direction relates to temporary measures, such as transitional provisions and pilot schemes (see, for example, CPR, r 51.2, and the associated practice directions). **4.49**

Not a source of law Practice directions are made pursuant to s 5 of the CPA 1997. They may provide for any matter that may be provided for by the CPR. The fact that practice directions are made pursuant to a statutory power does not afford them the status of being subordinate legislation; in particular, practice directions do not meet the standard statutory definition of subordinate legislation.[115] In this regard, Hale LJ commented: '[Practice directions] are probably not "made under" any Act at all: the fact that the CPR "may refer" to them does not mean that they are "made under" the [Civil Procedure Act] 1997.'[116] Consequently, practice directions—including the now-revoked Costs Practice Direction (CPD)—are not able to override the CPR or any other form of subordinate legislation.[117] **4.50**

Poorly drafted and *ultra vires* practice directions Practice directions are not made by the Civil Procedure Rule Committee and are not laid before Parliament. Judges have been known to criticise the provisions in practice directions as being poorly constructed.[118] Hale LJ had the following to say on the topic: **4.51**

> 'They [practice directions] go through no democratic process at all, although if approved by the Lord Chancellor he will bear ministerial responsibility for them to Parliament. But

[113] See s 5(2) of the Civil Procedure Act 1987, as amended by the Constitutional Reform Act 2005, Sched 2. Prior to 3 April 2006, see s 74A(2) of the County Courts Act 1984, as amended by CPA 1997, Sched 1, para 5. There are limited exceptions to the bar against local practice directions: see s 5(5) and (6) of the Constitutional Reform Act 2005.

[114] See Lord Thomas, 'One Fixed Place or Several', Birkenhead Lecture, 21 October 2013, Grays Inn, at paras 34 and 35.

[115] See Interpretation Act 1978, s 21(1).

[116] *A Local Authority v A Mother and Child* [2001] 1 Costs LR 136, at 144.

[117] See May LJ's comments in *Godwin v Swindon Borough Council* [2001] EWCA Civ 1478, at [11].

[118] *Inline Logistics Ltd v UCI Logistics Ltd* [2002] 2 Costs LR 304.

> there is a difference in principle between delegated legislation which may be scrutinised by Parliament and ministerial executive action. There is no ministerial responsibility for Practice Directions made for the Supreme Court by the Heads of Division. As Professor Jolowicz says … "It is right that the court should retain its power to regulate its own procedure within the limits set by statutory rules, and to fill in gaps left by those rules; it is wrong that it should have power actually to legislate." '[119]

4.52 In a different case but a similar vein, Brooke LJ developed the theme in this way:

> 'It is sufficient for present purposes to say that a practice direction has no legislative force. Practice directions provide invaluable guidance to matters of practice in the civil courts, but in so far as they contain statements of the law which are wrong they carry no authority at all.'[120]

By reason of the fact that they carry no authority, the court has the power to override a practice direction.[121]

Application of practice directions

4.53 Notwithstanding the above, practice directions should not be disregarded: the analysis merely means that they are not a source of law. As mentioned at 4.40, the court may need to fill in gaps left by the CPR. Where this is done by a practice direction, it will not necessarily create a clash between that practice direction and the rule it supplements.[122] In a similar vein, tribunals that apply the CPR by analogy may also apply the relevant practice directions by analogy.[123]

4.54 It is noticeable that Practice Directions 44–48 largely reflect what is set out in the CPR themselves, but where this is not the case, is usually because a practice direction is addressing administrative issues (which are not issues of law) or because it is describing—some may say codifying—the common law[124] (and therefore merely reflecting the law). Whilst an obvious point, the court may take non-compliance with practice directions into account when deciding the incidence or quantum of costs—and for this reason alone it would be foolhardy to disregard practice directions without good reason. In this regard, it is not unlikely that the court would treat practice directions dealing with administrative steps as being similar to an order of the court.

4.55 In summary, practice directions are not a source of law and, at best, are an extrinsic aid to interpretation,[125] but they may fill in gaps in the CPR and they are an important source of administrative guidance. Of particular importance in the context of costs is the fact that unjustified non-compliance with a practice direction may be a factor that the court takes into account when deciding either the incidence or quantum of costs.

---

[119] *A Local Authority v A Mother and Child* [2001] 1 Costs LR 136, at [26].
[120] *U v Liverpool City Council* [2005] EWCA Civ 475, at [47].
[121] See, eg, *ibid.*
[122] *Leigh v Michelin Tyre plc* [2003] EWCA Civ 1766, at [21].
[123] See *Revenue & Customs Commissioners v Talentcore Ltd (t/a Team Spirits)* (unreported), 19 November 2011, UT (Tax), *per* Roth J.
[124] An example being the procedure as described in *Pamplin v Express Newspapers Ltd* [1985] 1 WLR 689, which is codified at PD 47, para 13.13.
[125] *Van Aken v London Borough of Camden* [2002] EWCA Civ 1724, at [36]. In some circumstances, it may be possible to take Hansard into account: *Pepper v Hart* [1992] UKHL 3.

Pre-action Protocols

A pre-action protocol may be defined as a statement of best practice about pre-action conduct.[126] To qualify as a pre-action protocol under the CPR, that statement must have been approved by the Head of Civil Justice and must be listed in Practice Direction (Pre-Action Conduct).[127] **4.56**

There are a number of pre-action protocols. At the time of writing, they were as listed in Table 4.1. **4.57**

Relevance as to expectations of disputants

Whilst there are exceptions,[128] in the context of the law of costs, the pre-action protocols and the practice direction that accompanies them will rarely be relevant as being a source of law. They are nonetheless relevant in that they create obligations and expectations that, if ignored or thwarted, may be reflected in either the incidence or quantum of costs. In this regard, CPR, r 44.2(5)(a), defines relevant conduct for the purposes of deciding the incidence of costs as including the extent to which the parties followed any relevant pre-action protocol. This issue is discussed in detail at 6.93–6.100, 6.106, 7.41 and 7.125. **4.58**

Table 4.1 Pre-action protocols

Protocol	Came into force
Personal Injury	26 April 1999
Clinical Disputes	26 April 1999
Construction and Engineering	2 October 2000
Defamation	2 October 2000
Professional Negligence	16 July 2001
Judicial Review	4 March 2002
Disease and Illness	8 December 2003
Housing Disrepair	8 December 2003
Possession Claims Based on Rent Arrears	2 October 2006
Possession Claims Based on Mortgage Arrears, etc	19 November 2008
Low Value Personal Injury Claims in Road Traffic Accidents	30 April 2010
Claims for Damages in Relation to the Physical State of Commercial Property at Termination of a Tenancy ('Dilapidations Protocol')	1 January 2012
Low Value Personal Injury (Employers; Liability and Public Liability) Claims	31 July 2013
Possession Claims by Social Landlords	30 January 2017
Debt Claims	1 October 2017
Pre-Action Protocol for Resolution of Package Travel Claims	7 May 2018

In addition to these specific protocols, there is a general Practice Direction (Pre-Action Conduct), which is often afforded a status similar to a protocol.

126 See the Glossary to the CPR.

127 *Ibid.*

128 An example being the requirements to give information about funding arrangements in practice directions and protocols.

4.59 Pre-action protocols may also be relevant in the sense that the court may take a protocol into account when deciding what should be done generally for the purposes of better managing the class of claim to which the protocol relates. This may be an issue of deciding how best to make the protocol 'work' or of ensuring that the protocol is not used by a party as a reason to visit unfairness on an opponent.[129] In a similar vein, the court might take a pre-action protocol into account in such a way as to ensure that costs are dealt with in accordance with the protocol's broad objectives.[130]

Substance over semantics

4.60 When taking pre-action protocols into account, the court tends to look at their substance and gist of what is written, rather than focusing on the protocols' technical or semantic aspects. In this regard, Akenhead J said: 'The Court should be slow to allow the rules to be used in those circumstances for one party to obtain a tactical or costs advantage where in substance the principles of the Protocol have been complied with.'[131]

Specific costs provisions

4.61 Some pre-action protocols themselves contain specific provisions and costs sanctions for non-compliance. For example, the Pre-action Protocol for Construction and Engineering Disputes suggests that a failure by a defendant to say at an early stage that it is the 'wrong' defendant may be taken into account when deciding the incidence of costs. Another example is that a defendant in a clinical negligence claim may face sanctions for not supplying clinical records in a timely fashion.[132] This is a topic that is addressed more fully at 6.10.

4.62 In summary, whilst pre-action protocols would rarely be a source of law in the context of costs, they are often taken into account when the law is applied and, in particular, they may have a significant bearing on the incidence of costs.

The Status of Persuasive Informal Guidance

4.63 There are many sources of informal guidance (such as guides, books and journals), but, in so far as the law of costs is concerned, they will usually be regarded as being instructive rather than authoritative. Such materials are often referred to as being 'secondary sources' of the law. This is in comparison with 'primary sources', which are themselves authoritative statements of the law. The authority of a secondary source has to be determined.

Court guides

4.64 The Senior Courts Costs Office publishes a lengthy court guide that is often referred to in court on matters of procedure. That guide, like most court guides, is a narrative document

[129] An example is *Birmingham City Council v Lee* [2008] EWCA Civ 891, in which the Court found that a particular type of order was necessary if the protocol in question was not to operate as a means of preventing recovery of reasonably incurred legal costs.

[130] See, eg, *McGlinn v Waltham Contractors Ltd* [2005] EWHC 1419 (TCC), in which it was held that it would be wrong to make an award that would effectively penalise a claimant for having done what a pre-action protocol required—namely, to narrow the issues.

[131] *TJ Brent Ltd v Black & Veatch Consulting Ltd* [2008] EWHC 1497 (TCC), at [45].

[132] Pre-Action Protocol for the Resolution of Clinical Disputes, para 3.12.

written or approved of by specialist judges acting in an extrajudicial capacity. Court guides provide a narrative to the CPR or other primary sources of the law, often explaining how they are to be applied in practice; however, court guides are not sources of law and cannot override any provision in the CPR. Whilst there is no authority on the point, some commentators have said that where ambiguity exists in primary sources of the law, court guides may be used as an extrinsic aid to interpretation.[133] There is, however, no authority to support that proposition.

Learned journals

Learned journals may be peer-reviewed or not peer-reviewed; for obvious reasons, the former will carry greater weight. Examples of peer-reviewed journals are the *Cambridge Law Review*, the *Oxford Journal of Legal Studies*, the *Law Quarterly Review* and the *Modern Law Review*. It is not common for articles on costs to appear in these journals; instead, articles on costs normally appear in the *New Law Journal*, the *Law Gazette* and the *Solicitors Journal*. None of these are peer-reviewed and they should be regarded as being nothing more than an aid to research. That said, such publications are occasionally relied upon by the court.[134] **4.65**

Books and dictionaries

Other than rare exceptions that, for present purposes, can be disregarded,[135] textbooks and dictionaries ought never to be regarded as being primary sources of law. Even where textbooks are properly cited as being persuasive,[136] they can never be binding (unless, of course, an extract is subsequently adopted by the court).[137] **4.66**

The following points can be made. **4.67**

- **Peer-reviewed textbooks** Costs disputes will often turn on the law of contract and, in those circumstances, it is commonly the case that established peer-reviewed books such as *Chitty on Contracts* are cited. Their value, however, derives from the fact that they can be trusted to record and describe the law accurately rather than from any intrinsic authority.
- **Textbooks on costs** It is not unknown for the court to cite textbooks on costs (such as *Cook on Costs*,[138] *Butterworths Costs Service*[139] and *Greenslade on Costs*[140]), but whilst such books are often trusted to state the law correctly, they are not themselves sources of law.

---

133 See, eg, *Civil Procedure* (London: Sweet & Maxwell, 2009), vol 1, para 2.3.6.

134 See, eg, *Excalibur Ventures LLC v Texas Keystone Inc & Ors* [2016] EWCA Civ 1144, at [27].

135 Whilst now rarely relied upon, there are about two dozen early textbooks, collectively known as the books of authority, which are regarded as being intrinsically authoritative on the grounds that they are evidence of judicial decisions that are not otherwise recorded (ie medieval and early modern decisions): see Blackstone, M, *Commentaries on the Laws of England* (Oxford: Clarendon Press, 1765–69), Book I, at pp 72–3.

136 Books such as *The White Book, Chitty on Contracts* and other such esteemed works.

137 See, eg, *Claims Direct Test Cases* [2003] EWCA Civ 136, in which Brooke LJ adopted the 'ready reckoner' in Middleton, S, and Rowley, J, *Cook on Costs* (London: LexisNexis, 2003) as being a useful tool for the purposes of assessing success fees.

138 See, eg, *Fourie v Le Roux & Ors (Rev 1)* [2007] UKHL 1, *per* Lord Carswell.

139 See, eg, *Bensusan v Freedman* [2001] EWHC 9001 (Costs), *per* Master Hurst.

140 See, eg, the Irish case of *Landers v Judge Patwell & Anor* [2006] IEHC 248, *per* Smyth J.

- **Ancient and foreign textbooks** Whilst it would rarely be relevant in the context of costs law, where a textbook is the only record of the law as at the time in question, it will usually be afforded some weight. In this regard, modern readers may be surprised to learn that costs textbooks have been in existence for centuries.[141] Similarly, provided that it is only for the purposes of illustration, textbooks on the law in other common-law jurisdictions may be taken into account.
- **Non-legal textbooks and works of fiction** Where appropriate, the court may take medical or other textbooks into account, an example being where the court had to decide what 'disease' means for the purposes of CPR, Part 45.[142] Whilst they could never be regarded as a correct statement of the law, it is occasionally the case that the court will illustrate its findings by reference to fiction. Where the court wishes to emphasise absurdity, for example, references to *Jarndyce v Jarndyce* (see 1.78) are not uncommon.[143]
- **Dictionaries** Dictionaries may be used as an extrinsic aid to interpretation, but the weight to which the court affords them is usually limited.[144]

As with any publication that is not a primary source of law, some caution ought to be exercised when citing textbooks because, no matter how careful the author may be, textbooks not only may contain errors, but also may even propagate errors in other textbooks.[145] As such, where the circumstances permit, it is always good practice to cite the primary source of law.

Parliamentary and Government Papers

4.68 Lawyers who specialise in the law of costs need to have a working knowledge of parliamentary papers. This is because such papers often contain useful information about the discourse, data and dogma that have fashioned the law. They also need to know about Command papers, which are documents that the government has made available to Parliament.

4.69 The term 'parliamentary papers' includes:

- the working papers of Parliament (such as Bills, Lords Hansard, Commons Hansard, business papers, etc);
- other papers produced by Parliament and its committees; and
- papers presented to Parliament by outside bodies (such as responses to consultation) or by government.

---

[141] These include: Sayer, J, *The Law of Costs* (London: J & WT Clarke, 1768); Hullock, J, *Costs in Civil Actions and Criminal Proceedings* (first published 1796; 2nd edn, London: W Clarke & Sons, 1810); Tidd, W, *The Law of Costs in Civil Actions* (London: A Strahan & W Woodfall, 1793); Beames, J, *A Summary of Doctrine of Courts of Equity with Respect to Costs, Deduced from Leading Cases* (London: Pheney & Sweet, 1822); Gray, J, *A Treatise on the Law of Costs in Actions and Other Proceedings in the Courts of Common Law at Westminster* (London: Lumley, 1853); Dax, ET, *New Book of Costs in the Superior Courts of Common Law* (London: O Richards, 1847). Some of these are difficult to obtain, but the author may be able to assist in this regard.

[142] See *Dalton v British Telecommunications* [2015] EWHC 616 (QB), at [12], *per* Phillips J.

[143] See, eg, *Khan v Crossland* (unreported), 25 November 2011, Ch D, *per* Judge Behrens.

[144] See, eg, Lord Clyde's comments in *Chief Adjudication Officer v Faulds* [2000] 1 WLR 1035, at 1051H. See also *Patterson v Ministry of Defence* [2012] EWHC 2767 (QB), at [34], *per* Males J.

[145] See, eg, *Carter-Ruck (a firm) v Mireskandari* [2011] EWHC 24 (QB), at [80], in which the court discovered an error that appeared in more than one textbook.

Parliamentary business papers

Both the House of Lords and the House of Commons publish documents that arise both from their own work and the work of their committees. Much of what is published is of no relevance to the law of costs (such as registers of interests), but the following may be of interest from time to time: **4.70**

- Votes and Proceedings (Commons) and the Minute (Lords) (these being the formal, authoritative record of the decisions taken by each House); and
- Select Committee reports and evidence.

The current and future business of Parliament is set out in a collection of daily documents. In the House of Commons, these papers are called the 'Vote Bundle';[146] in the House of Lords, they are known as House of Lords Business.[147] Documents are divided into those that relate to the coming day and those that look further ahead. **4.71**

- **The coming day** A brief overview of the coming day's business in the Commons is set out in the 'Summary Agenda'. A more detailed agenda is contained in the 'Order of Business'. Together, the Summary Agenda and Order of Business are the 'Order Paper'.
- **Further ahead in the future** Future business in the House of Commons is set out in the Future Business papers.[148] Questions to be answered in the Commons on future days are contained in Part 2 of Questions for Oral or Written Answer (also known as the Questions Book). In the House of Lords, future business is set out in Notices and Orders of the Day, along with questions for written answer, forthcoming committee meetings and Bills in progress.

House of Commons (HC) papers and House of Lords (HL) papers have separate numbering sequences, starting at 1 in every session. Papers are referred to in the format: 'HC 507 200–01' or 'HL Paper 17 200–05'. Numbers are allocated to HC papers by the Journal Office and to HL papers by the Table Office. **4.72**

Hansard

Hansard is the traditional name of the transcripts of parliamentary debates.[149] They are a substantially verbatim report of what is said in Parliament.[150] Members' words are recorded, then edited to remove repetitions and obvious mistakes, albeit without detracting **4.73**

---

[146] In the House of Commons, a publication called Votes and Proceedings formally records what the House did the previous day. It includes decisions, amendments to Bills, and a list of publications and other documents laid before the House. It does not include what is said in the House; this is recorded in Hansard.

[147] In the House of Lords, the previous day's business, including judicial decisions, is formally recorded in the Minutes of Proceedings publication. It does not include what is said in the House; this is recorded in Hansard.

[148] This is made up of eight parts: (1) the provisional business for the following week; (2) backbench business; (3) remaining Orders and Notices (formally set down for today, but not expected to be taken today); (4) business for Westminster Hall; (5) other future business (usually ten-minute rule Bills and private members' Bills); (6) business to be taken in European committees; (7) notices of public petitions; and (8) notices of written ministerial statements.

[149] It is named after Thomas Curson Hansard (1776–1833), a London printer and publisher, who was the first official printer to the Parliament at Westminster.

[150] I Church Official Report [HANSARD] Centenary Volume (2009), p xvi.

from the meaning. Hansard also sets out details of divisions and reports decisions taken during a sitting.

4.74 A 'rolling' version of Hansard is published online in instalments during sitting days, with the printed record (daily part) of a day's sitting becoming available the next morning alongside an online version. Each House of Parliament has separate publications. Commons Hansard includes proceedings in the Commons Chamber and Westminster Hall, as well as written ministerial statements, petitions and ministerial corrections, whilst Lords Hansard details proceedings in the Lords Chamber and Grand Committee. Separate reports are produced of proceedings in Commons General and public Bill committees.

The admissibility of Hansard

4.75 It may be that a party wishes to refer to Hansard for the purposes of interpreting legislation. The court may permit such a thing, but only if certain criteria are met. Lord Browne-Wilkinson had the following to say on the point:

> '[R]eference to Parliamentary material should be permitted as an aid to the construction of legislation which is ambiguous or obscure or the literal meaning of which leads to an absurdity. Even in such cases references in court to Parliamentary material should only be permitted where such material clearly discloses the mischief aimed at or the legislative intention lying behind the ambiguous or obscure words. In the case of statements made in Parliament, as at present advised I cannot foresee that any statement other than the statement of the Minister or other promoter of the Bill is likely to meet these criteria.'[151]

4.76 Thus the following conditions must be met if the court is to have regard to Hansard for the purposes of statutory interpretation.

- The legislative provision in question must be ambiguous or obscure, or its literal meaning must lead to an absurdity.
- The material to be relied upon must consist of statements by a minister or other promoter of the Bill that lead to the enactment of the legislation (together, if necessary, with such other parliamentary material as was necessary to understand such statements and their effect).
- Those statements must be clear.

Papers presented to Parliament

4.77 Many documents are presented to Parliament by bodies outside Parliament, including government departments; some of these are then published or republished under Parliament's authority. Many are presented by bodies that are required to present documents from time to time.[152] Others are presented because the government has decided to provide the information to Parliament, which documents are Command papers (see below).

---

[151] *Pepper v Hart* [1993] AC 593, at 634.

[152] These may include: (1) annual reports of government departments or other bodies and agencies; (2) periodic reports of certain activities or programmes (eg reports of Her Majesty's Inspector of Prisons); (3) reports by the National Audit Office; (4) estimates, accounts and other government financial papers, such as the Budget; and (5) reports of inquiries into particular events.

Command papers

Government publications presented to Parliament are known as Command papers. The term 'Command' is in the formula carried on the papers: 'Presented to Parliament by the Secretary of State for ... by Command of Her Majesty'. Command papers may include the following. **4.78**

- **White Papers** White Papers relate to government policy initiatives and proposals for legislation—that is, they are policy documents produced by the government that set out its proposals for future legislation. As such, they very often touch on issues relating to the law of costs. White papers may include a draft version of a Bill that is being planned. This provides a basis for further consultation and discussion with interested or affected groups, and allows final changes to be made before a Bill is formally presented to Parliament.
- **Green Papers** Green Papers are consultation documents produced by the government. They are created so as to allow people from both inside and outside Parliament to give feedback on the legislative proposals. Again, it is commonplace for such documents to deal with issues that relate to the law of costs.
- **State papers** State papers include treaties and international agreements. They will rarely touch on the law of costs.
- **Reports** Command papers may include reports of royal commissions or other committees of inquiry. These will rarely touch on issues of costs law.

Most, but not all, Command papers are published in a numbered series. Unlike HC Papers (see 4.72), the numbering of Command papers does not begin afresh each session; instead, they are allocated a prefix, which is an abbreviation of the word 'command', and a running number. A new series begins when the numbering approaches 10,000. **4.79**

The first series began in 1833 without a prefix; the current series (the sixth, at time of writing) began in 1986 and uses the prefix Cm. The full set of series is as displayed in Table 4.2. **4.80**

The use of consultation papers in court

It may happen that a party wishes to draw the court's attention to consultation papers (such as a White Paper or other type of Command paper) that have been drafted in such a way as to describe the background to, and history of, some legislative provision or **4.81**

Table 4.2 Command paper series

Abbreviation	Period
—	1833–69
C.	1870–99
Cd.	1900–18
Cmd.	1919–56
Cmnd.	1956–86
Cm.	1986–

another. Whilst there are examples of the court doing this without comment,[153] is a moot point whether the court is able to take consultation papers into account as an extrinsic aid to interpretation.[154] That said, they are often useful in other ways, such as identifying the law that was changed by the legislation in question or chronicling the history of the legislation in question.

153 See, eg, *C v D* [2011] EWCA Civ 646, at [31].

154 Examples do exist of the court taking consultation papers into account. In a costs context, see *Garrett v Halton Borough Council; Myatt v National Coal Board* [2006] EWCA Civ 1017, at [91] and [95]. However, Phillips MR has indicated that they are not admissible, although this seems to have been for want of authority on the point: see *Callery v Gray (No 2)* [2001] EWCA Civ 1246, at [50].

5

THE COURTS' POWERS REGARDING COSTS

This chapter deals with the following topics:[1] 5.01

- the functions and powers of masters (5.03);
- the functions and powers of costs judges in the County Court (5.11);
- the functions and powers of authorised court officers (colloquially known as costs officers) (5.17);
- the court as an arbiter (5.20);
- the province of Parliament (5.22);
- the inherent jurisdiction of the court (5.24).

All judges stand in the place of the Crown and conduct proceedings in its name.[2] 5.02
Whilst their powers ultimately derive from that same source,[3] not all judges have the same range of functions and powers. Where the words 'costs judge' are used in this chapter, it is a reference to any judge who deals with matters relating to the assessement of costs. The topic of allocation of cases within the judiciary is dealt with at 43.10.

Masters

Masters (also known as costs judges) are appointed by the Lord Chancellor with the 5.03
concurrence of the Treasury,[4] upon the recommendation of the Judicial Appointments Commission (JAC).[5] The most senior (known as the senior costs judge[6]) is appointed in a similar manner.[7] Full-time masters (but not deputy masters) are barred from legal practice.[8]

Masters are expert in matters concerning costs. Ward LJ, for example, had this to say: '[T]his 5.04
judgment is written by a mere mortal Lord Justice; divine judgment is delivered by costs

[1] This chapter deals only with jurisdictional issues that are likely to arise in the context of cost litigation. It does not deal with costs in the Supreme Court because that court has its own practice and procedural rules: see the Supreme Court Rules 2009 (SI 2009/1603), Pt 7, and UKSC Practice Direction 13.

[2] *John Russell & Co Ltd v Cayzer, Irvine & Co Ltd* [1916] 2 AC 298, HL, at 302.

[3] *United Engineering Workers' Union v Devanayagam* [1968] AC 356, at 382–3, *per* Lord Guest.

[4] See the Senior Courts Act 1981, s 89(1); this should be read in conjunction with the Transfer of Functions (Minister for the Civil Service and Treasury) Order 1981 (SI 1981/1670), which clarifies that the reference to the minister is a reference to the Treasury.

[5] See Pt 4 of, and Sched 14 to, the Constitutional Reform Act 2005.

[6] Also known as the chief taxing master.

[7] See Senior Courts Act 1981, s 89(3)(c).

[8] Courts and Legal Services Act 1990, s 75 and Sched 11.

judges and the Supreme Court only.'[9] This, as far as the editor is aware, is the only source of authority for the proposition that masters are infallible.

Range of jurisdiction

5.05 Masters and deputies are able to assess costs arising out of proceedings in the following courts and tribunals: the Court of Appeal (Civil Division); the High Court; the Administrative Court; the Admiralty Registrar;[10] the Commercial Court; the Companies Court; the Technology and Construction Court, and the Court of Protection; the Employment Appeal Tribunal;[11] the Principal Registry of the Family Division; and bankruptcy proceedings under the Insolvency Rules.

5.06 All masters and deputies have been appointed deputy district judges of the County Court and district registries for the purpose of assessment of costs.[12] Where a costs judge sits as a deputy district judge in a County Court hearing centre, the comments made at 5.11–5.13 would apply, and this would be so regardless of the fact that the costs judge may also sit as a master.

5.07 In addition, some deputy costs judges will also sit as costs judges of the First-Tier and Upper Tier Tribunals.[13]

Allocation

5.08 The senior costs judge will make arrangements for proceedings to be assigned to individual masters.[14] The fact that a case has been assigned to a particular master does not prevent another master from dealing with that case if circumstances require.[15] Masters are not obliged to hear everything that comes before them; in particular, they have the power to refer matters to a High Court judge.[16] Deputies are assigned cases too, but as a matter of practice they do not hear solicitor-and-client assessments under the Solicitors Act 1974 nor do they hear assessments that are likely to last more than two days.[17]

Restrictions on the powers of masters

5.09 Where the Civil Procedure Rules (CPR) provide for the court to perform any act, then, except where an enactment, rule or practice direction provides otherwise, it may be

---

9 *Sousa v Waltham Forest LBC* [2011] EWCA Civ 194, at [4]. See also the Irish case of *Superquinn Ltd v Bray EDC* [2001] 1 IR 459.

10 The Master of the Administrative Court and the Admiralty Registrar both have powers to assess costs incurred in their respective courts, but since well before the introduction of the CPR, they have requested the masters to assess those costs on their behalf.

11 See Employment Appeal Tribunal Rules 1993 (SI 1993/2854), r 34B(1)(c).

12 See *Notes for New Deputy Masters*, January 2013, p 4.

13 See s 91 of the Senior Courts Act 1981, as amended by s 57 of the Tribunals, Courts and Enforcement Act 2007.

14 PD 2B, para 6.2.

15 *Ibid*. The fact that a case has been assigned to a particular master does not prevent another master from dealing with that case if circumstances require, whether at the request of the assigned master or otherwise.

16 PD 2B, para 1.2. This is almost never done, however. Modern-day masters have no difficulty in conducting lengthy trials; if a matter is particularly weighty, provision may be made for the trial to take place in a room with a bench and bar, but this would almost never be by a High Court judge.

17 *Notes for New Deputy Masters*, January 2013, p 4.

performed by a master.[18] There are restrictions on what a master can do,[19] but those restrictions are not commonly of relevance. That said, the following restrictions may arise from time to time.

- Masters are precluded from making orders or granting interim remedies relating to appeals from masters or district judges.[20]
- Masters are precluded from making orders or granting interim remedies relating to appeals against costs assessments[21] (unless, of course, it is an appeal from the decision of an authorised court officer).
- With certain exceptions,[22] masters may not grant injunctions or make orders that relate to injunctions.[23]
- In proceedings in the Chancery Division, there is a restriction on dealing with the following without the consent of the Chancellor of the High Court:[24]
  - approving compromises:
    - on behalf of a person under disability where that person's interest in a fund, or if there is no fund, the maximum amount of the claim, exceeds £100,000; and
    - on behalf of absent, unborn and unascertained persons;
  - making declarations, except in plain cases;
  - the proceedings are brought by a Part 8 claim form, seeking determination of any question of law or as to the construction of a document that is raised by the claim form;
  - giving permission to executors, administrators and trustees to bring or defend proceedings, or to continue the prosecution or defence of proceedings, and granting an indemnity for costs out of the trust estate, except in plain cases;
  - granting an indemnity for costs out of the assets of a company on the application of minority shareholders bringing a derivative action, except in plain cases; and
  - making an order for rectification.
- There is a restriction on masters hearing applications for declarations of incompatibility in accordance with s 4 of the Human Rights Act 1998.[25]

In practice, the only restrictions that are encountered as anything but a rarity are those **5.10** concerning the powers of a master to make declarations or to make orders for rectification. If a master finds that they lack the power to make the appropriate order, then they can either refer the matter to a High Court judge[26] or seek approval from the Chancellor of the High Court.[27]

---

[18] CPR, r 2.4(a).
[19] They are summarised in PD 2B.
[20] See PD 2B, para 2.3(d).
[21] See PD 2B, para 2.3(e). Master Hurst often hears such appeals, but this is because he sits as a recorder.
[22] Such as where the parties consent: see PD 2B, paras 2.3 and 2.4.
[23] PD 2B, para 2.2. This would include an order for specific performance where such an order would involve an injunction.
[24] See PD 2B, para 5.1.
[25] See PD 2B, para 7A.
[26] See PD 2B, para 1.2.
[27] See PD 2B, para 5.1.

The County Court: Common Law and Equity

5.11 As they were created wholly by statute, the County Court and its hearing centres have only those powers that are conferred upon them by legislation. In proceedings dealing with the common law, there is no limit to those powers, but this is not true of proceedings in which equitable remedies are sought.

Jurisdiction and 'the County Court limit'

5.12 Whilst uncommon in the context of costs litigation, it may be necessary for the court to grant an equitable remedy (such as rectification of a contract of retainer). Section 23 of the County Courts Act 1984 confers an equitable jurisdiction on the County Court, but that jurisdiction is restricted in the following way: 'Proceedings for relief against fraud or mistake, where the damage sustained or the estate or fund in respect of which relief is sought does not exceed in amount or value the county court limit.'[28] This means that a County Court hearing centre has an equitable jurisdiction only in those cases in which the relief sought does not exceed the 'County Court limit'. That limit is currently £30,000.[29] (This should not be confused with the limit that applies to solicitor-and-client assessments: see 5.15.) There is no reason to believe that this restriction will not apply when a costs judge sits as either a deputy district judge or a recorder of the County Court.

5.13 Notwithstanding these restrictions, the parties may agree that the County Court should excercise an equitable jurisdiction. Any such agreement must be recorded in a memorandum signed by the parties or by their respective agents or legal representatives.[30]

County Court: solicitor and client

5.14 The County Court has no jurisdiction to hear assessments in relation to non-contentious business.[31]

5.15 As to contentious business, s 69(3) of the Solicitors Act 1974 (as amended[32]) makes the following provisions:

> 'Where a bill of costs relates wholly or partly to contentious business done in [the County Court[33]] and the amount of the bill does not exceed £5,000, the powers and duties of the High Court under this section and sections 70 and 71 in relation to that bill may be exercised and performed by [the County Court[34]] in which any part of the business was done.'

Therefore the County Court does not have jurisdiction to assess bills relating to contentious business exceeding £5,000. The parties may, however, extend jurisdiction by consent,

---

[28] See s 23(g) of the County Courts Act 1984.

[29] The High Court and County Courts Jurisdiction Order 1991 (SI 1991/724).

[30] See s 24 of the County Courts Act 1984, as amended by Courts and Legal Services Act 1990; see also s 18.

[31] CPR, r 67.3(1).

[32] By the High Court and County Courts Jurisdiction Order 1991 (SI 1991/724), art 2(7) and (8), and Sched, Pt I.

[33] At the time of writing, this amendment had yet to come into force generally: see the Crime and Courts Act 2013, s 17(5), Sched 9, Pt 3, para 52(1)(b) and (2), and (as to date of commencement) s 61(3).

[34] *Ibid.*

but only if they sign a memorandum to that effect.[35] That said, it is the editor's experience that very few parties actually bother to do this: it is almost always the case that the limit is simply disregarded (perhaps because of ignorance of its existence).

An application made in the wrong court can be transferred (such as from the County Court to the High Court or vice versa).[36] **5.16**

Authorised Court Officers (also known as Costs Officers)

An authorised court officer is a civil servant who hears certain lower-value cases. Authorised court officers are informally referred to as 'costs officers', but use of that phrase ought to be avoided because it is a generic term that also embraces judges[37] (see 2.09). **5.17**

Rule 44.1(1) of the CPR reads as follows: **5.18**

> ' "Authorised court officer" means any officer of—
> (i) a county court;
> (ii) a district registry;
> (iii) the Principal Registry of the Family Division; or
> (iv) the Costs Office, whom the Lord Chancellor has authorised to assess costs.'

The powers of an authorised court officer are significantly more limited than the powers of a master or a district judge. An authorised court officer does not have jurisdiction to hear claims for costs for more than £110,000 (inclusive of additional liability, but exclusive of value added tax, or VAT) or £35,000 in the case of a senior executive officer.[38] The parties have the power to agree that the assessment should not be heard by an authorised court officer.[39]

The powers of an authorised court officer are set out in CPR, r 47.3: **5.19**

> '(1) An authorised court officer has all the powers of the court when making a detailed assessment, except—
> (a) power to make a wasted costs order as defined in rule 48.7;
> (b) power to make an order under—
>   (i) rule 44.11 (powers in relation to misconduct);
>   (ii) rule 47.8 (sanction for delay in commencing detailed assessment proceedings);
>   (iii) paragraph (2) (objection to detailed assessment by authorised court officer); and
> (c) power to make a detailed assessment of costs payable to a solicitor by his client, unless the costs are being assessed under rule 46.4 (costs where money is payable to a child or protected party).
>
> (2) Where a party objects to the detailed assessment of costs being made by an authorised court officer, the court may order it to be made by a costs judge or a district judge.'

Thus an authorised court officer does not have penal powers nor (for all practical purposes) are they able to hear a solicitor-and-client assessment under CPR, r 46.49.

---

35 See s 24 of the County Courts Act 1984, as amended by Courts and Legal Services Act 1990; see also s 18. There are restrictions in family cases, Chancery cases and Admiralty cases.
36 CPR, r 30.1(2)(c).
37 See CPR, r 44.1(1).
38 PD 47, para 3.1.
39 See PD 47, para 3.2.

The Court as an Arbiter

5.20 It occasionally happens that the parties are before the court not because the court has an express power to hear the matter, but because the parties agree that the court should act as arbiter. This can be done only to the extent that it is not prohibited by statute or rules of court.[40] In general litigation, examples are very few and far between, but this is not true of costs litigation. Examples include consensual compensation schemes and the quantification of *ex gratia* payments made to persons who are required to give evidence to non-statutory enquiries.[41] The court's involvement in those circumstances will usually be wholly as a result of the parties' consent. It is also done with the consent of the court: it is not possible for a person to impose on a judge the jurisdiction or duty to adjudicate on a matter where no statutory or common-law right to an adjudication exists.[42]

5.21 For obvious reasons, where the parties are before the court consensually, it will rarely be the case that they will dispute the court's powers. Where they do, the dispute will usually not be about the court's general power to hear the matter, but about whether the court is able to decide a particular issue. This will be an issue of contractual interpretation (that is, interpretation of the agreement that has led the parties to be before the court), but the court will often be reluctant to give up jurisdiction in circumstances in which the intervention would further the overriding objective. In a consensual compensation scheme involving a mammoth number of claimants, Pill LJ found that the court had the power to impose sanctions on the basis that some of the claims (a very small percentage) had been issued and stayed. In the same case, Arden LJ commented that CPR, r 3.1(2)(m), confers very wide powers on the court.[43] This seems to be in keeping with the way in which comparable matters are dealt with in litigation other than costs; in particular, Megarry J has found that where the agreed machinery for resolving a dispute had broken down, the court was not precluded from making an adjudication.[44]

The Province of Parliament

5.22 The court may, in appropriate circumstances, decline jurisdiction on the basis that an issue should properly be decided by Parliament. Whilst a dissenting judgment and therefore only illustrative of the type of issues that are capable of being beyond the proper jurisdiction of the court, Buxton LJ made the following observations (in the context of protective costs orders, or PCOs):

> 'One of the criteria for making a PCO is effectively that the claimant is not eligible for Community Legal Service funding. The limits on such funding are very controversial, but that controversy is about decisions taken by Parliament or under its authority. The court should in my view be very cautious in taking steps that extend support from public funds beyond that chosen by Parliament ...'[45]

---

[40] See, in a non-costs context, *Heyting v Dupont* [1964] 2 All ER 273.
[41] Such as the Stephen Lawrence Inquiry.
[42] *Re Hooker's Settlement, Heron v Public Trustee* [1955] Ch 55.
[43] *AB & Ors v British Coal Corpn* [2006] EWCA Civ 987.
[44] *Brown v Gould* [1972] Ch 53.
[45] *R (Compton) v Wiltshire Primary Care Trust* [2008] EWCA Civ 749, at [70].

Thus the extent of public funding is an area in which the court will be cautious about intruding on the province of Parliament.

Another example of a court declining jurisdiction is *Willis v Nicolson*,[46] in which the Court of Appeal refused to issue guidance on costs capping. This was on the basis that the issues were best dealt with by the Civil Procedure Rule Committee following consultation. Where the Civil Procedure Rule Committee proposes rules, the proposed draft must be approved by the Lord Chancellor. Whilst it is not necessary for Parliament to positively affirm the proposed rules, they must be laid before the Houses and can be rejected by negative resolution of either House (see 4.34). The Court of Appeal's decision to decline jurisdiction in *Willis* had the effect of requiring any appropriate guidance on the issue to be laid before Parliament. **5.23**

The Inherent Jurisdiction of the Court

The notion of a court's inherent jurisdiction refers to the panoply of implied, but somewhat amorphous, powers[47] by which courts ensure that they properly and effectively fulfil their role as courts of law.[48] It is a power that goes to the regulation of curial processes.[49] It is an aspect of procedural law[50] rather than substantive law.[51] Alderson B explained the need for such a jurisdiction in this way: **5.24**

> '[T]he power of each court over its own processes is unlimited; it is a power incident to all courts, inferior as well as superior; were it not so, the court would be obliged to sit still and see its own process abused for the purpose of injustice.'[52]

This introduces the concept of 'superior' and 'inferior' courts, the essence of which is as follows. **5.25**

- **Superior court** A superior court of record is a court that has unrestricted powers (or is of 'general competence') within its jurisdictional limits.[53] Examples include the High Court[54] and the Court of Appeal.[55]

---

[46] [2007] EWCA Civ 199.

[47] One respected commentator has said that it is 'so amorphous and ubiquitous and so pervasive in its operation that it seems to defy the challenge to determine its quality and to establish its limits': Jacob, I, 'The Inherent Jurisdiction of the Court' (1970) 23 CLP 23.

[48] See *Connelly v DPP* [1964] AC 1254.

[49] Donnelly, J, 'Inherent Jurisdiction and Inherent Powers' [2009] 2 JSIJ 211, at 211.

[50] See *Bhamjee v Forsdick* [2003] EWCA Civ 113.

[51] See Jacob, I, 'The Inherent Jurisdiction of the Court' (1970) 23 CLP 23, at 24 and 25. Substantive law stands in contrast to procedural law, which is the machinery for enforcing those rights and duties. Procedural law comprises the rules by which a court hears and determines what happens in proceedings, as well as the method and means by which substantive law is made and administered.

[52] *Cocker v Tempest* (1841) 7 M & W 501, at 503–4, cited with approval in *Hepburn v Royal Alexandra Hospital NHS Trust (No 3)* 2011 SC 20, at [5], *per* Lord Hamilton.

[53] In particular, a senior court is a court that exercises the full range of judicial power in all matters concerning the general administration of justice within its jurisdictional limits, and enjoys unrestricted and unlimited powers in all matters of substantive law except in so far as that has been taken away in unequivocal terms by statutory enactment: see *Langley v North West Water Authority* [1991] 1 WLR 697, CA.

[54] See the Senior Courts Act 1981, s 15(1).

[55] See the Senior Courts Act 1981, s 19(1).

- **Inferior court** An inferior (or lower) court is a court of limited jurisdiction (either in terms of value of case or type of case). Examples include the County Court and its hearing centres, and specialist tribunals.

5.26 In common-law jurisdictions, any court that is a superior court of record will have an inherent jurisdiction to create processes that govern its practices.[56] Inferior courts created by statute (such as the County Court) will generally have their own jurisdiction to regulate their own procedures[57] and, as such, can be said to have their own inherent jurisdictions. That said, the fact that the County Court is able to adopt and apply the principles and practices in the High Court[58] means that those jurisdictions are, in many ways, not dissimilar.

Inherent jurisdiction and other adjectival rules

5.27 There are those who say that the term 'inherent jurisdiction' should not be used to distinguish similar powers conferred under common law, statute or rules of court,[59] arguing that if procedural rules are compatible with the steps that the court would have taken under its inherent jurisdiction, then those rules can be said to bolster the inherent jurisdiction rather than to replace it.[60] This, presumably, is why some judges refer to CPR, Part 3, as being synonymous with the inherent jurisdiction. There is little to be gained by doing this: regardless of whether the court has an overlapping inherent jurisdiction, where the matter in hand falls within the ambit of the CPR, it should be dealt with in accordance with those Rules.[61] In view of this, it is usually clearer to make the distinction between rules of court and the inherent jurisdiction.

Limits

5.28 There are limits to the extent to which the court may exercise its inherent jurisdiction.

- The inherent jurisdiction of the court should be invoked only to avoid a clear injustice.[62]
- The court is not able to regulate its own procedures in such a way as to deny parties their fundamental right to participate in the proceedings in accordance with the common-law principles of natural justice and open justice.[63]

---

56 This fact is confirmed by s 50(2) of the Solicitors Act 1974, which provides: '[The] High Court ... and the Court of Appeal respectively, or any division or judge of those courts, may exercise the same jurisdiction in respect of solicitors as any one of the superior courts of law or equity from which the Senior Courts were constituted might have exercised immediately before the passing of the Supreme Court of Judicature Act 1873 in respect of any solicitor, attorney or proctor admitted to practise there.'

57 In so far as the County Court is concerned, see *Langley v North West Water Authority* [1991] 3 All ER 610, [1991] 1 WLR 697, CA.

58 Section 76 of the County Courts Act 1984 provides that, other than where legislation provides otherwise, the general principles of practice in the High Court may be adopted and applied to proceedings in the County Court; see also s 38 (as amended), which provides that, in any proceedings in the County Court and its hearing centres, the court may make any order that could be made by the High Court if the proceedings were in the High Court. Section 76 has been held to allow a County Court judge to exercise the same inherent power as the High Court: see *Ebert v Birch* [2000] Ch 484, CA, *per* Lord Woolf; also see *Grepe v Loam* (1887) 37 Ch D 168, CA.

59 *Davey v Bentinck* [1893] 1 QB 185, CA.

60 In another case, it was said that the CPR serve to bolster the principle that, in the exercise of its inherent jurisdiction, the court has power to restrain litigants from disturbing the orderly conduct of court processes: see, eg, *Attorney General v Ebert* [2001] EWHC Admin 695.

61 See *Tombstone Ltd v Raja* [2008] EWCA Civ 1444, at [78].

62 *Symbol Park Lane Ltd v Steggles Palmer* [1985] 1 WLR 668, CA.

63 *Al Rawi v Security Service* [2011] UKSC 34.

- The court's inherent jurisdiction may not be used in a way that is inconsistent with the legislation that created or that governs that court.[64] Where the legislature has stepped in by making provisions regarding wasted costs, then, within that particular area, the existing inherent jurisdiction will be ousted or curtailed, at least to the extent that the legislation is negative in character.[65] An example of this is the fact that the inherent jurisdiction of the High Court could be said to extend to ordering an assessment of a solicitor's bills of costs, but the fact that there is a statutory time limit of 12 months after delivery of a bill[66] displaces the court's inherent jurisdiction in this respect such that an application for assessment must be made within that time limit.[67]

Officers of the court

In so far as the law of costs is concerned, one of the most important aspects of the court's inherent jurisdiction is the High Court's power to regulate solicitors as officers of the court (see 9.60–9.71).[68] Christopher Clarke LJ has explained that the court has a supervisory power over officers of the court.[69] Lord Esher had this to say on the topic: **5.29**

> '[T]he Court has a punitive and disciplinary jurisdiction over solicitors, as being officers of the Court, which is exercised not for the purpose of enforcing legal rights, but for the purpose of enforcing honourable conduct on the part of the Court's own officers ... the Court has a right to see that its own officer does not act contrary to his duty.'[70]

In a similar vein, Donaldson MR has said that the inherent jurisdiction to regulate officers of the court is: **5.30**

> '... indeed extraordinary, being based upon the right of the court to see that a high standard of conduct is maintained by its officers acting as such ... It is, in a sense, a domestic jurisdiction to which solicitors are only amenable because of their special relationship with the court and it is designed to impose higher standards than the law applies generally.'[71]

The inherent jurisdiction to regulate officers of the court extends only to solicitors, so it does not cover barristers, costs lawyers or other regulated lawyers.[72] Christopher Clarke LJ had this to say on the point: **5.31**

> 'Those who appear before the Court but who are not, and do not purport, to be, solicitors or recognised bodies, do not come within the jurisdiction. The most obvious example is barristers. They owe duties to the Court but are not subject to the jurisdiction of the Court over its officers, which they are not. All those who appear before the Court, whether lawyers, litigants, witnesses or watchers of proceedings may, of course, face the sanction of contempt if they misbehave. Their misbehaviour may, if sufficiently serious, amount to a criminal

[64] See *Langley v North West Water Authority* [1991] 3 All ER 610, [1991] 1 WLR 697, CA.

[65] See *Shiloh Spinners Ltd v Harding* [1973] AC 691 and *Harrison v Tew* [1989] QB 307, HL.

[66] See s 70(4) of the Solicitors Act 1974.

[67] *Assaubayev & Ors v Michael Wilson & Partners Ltd* [2014] EWCA Civ 1491, at [29], *per* Christopher Clarke LJ.

[68] See s 50 of the Solicitors Act 1974.

[69] *Assaubayev & Ors v Michael Wilson & Partners Ltd* [2014] EWCA Civ 1491, at [28], *per* Christopher Clarke LJ.

[70] See *In Re Grey* [1892] 2 QB 440, at 443.

[71] *John Fox v Bannister King & Rigbeys* [1988] QB 925, at 931.

[72] *Assaubayev & Ors v Michael Wilson & Partners Ltd* [2014] EWCA Civ 1491, at [32], *per* Christopher Clarke LJ. A discussion of this topic can be found in the Privy Council decision in the New Zealand case *Harley v McDonald, Glasgow Harley (a firm) v McDonald* [2001] UKPC 18A, at [41]–[47].

offence (such as perjury or attempting to pervert the course of justice). But neither contempt nor criminal conduct of itself brings them within the supervisory jurisdiction.'[73]

Christopher Clarke LJ went on to say that corporate bodies who are not themselves solicitors do not come within the jurisdiction.[74]

Remedies

5.32 Whilst the jurisdiction has punitive origins,[75] its purpose is to avoid injustice[76] and, in that regard, it can also be said to be compensatory (see 9.69).[77] Christopher Clarke LJ has said that the court has discretion as to the relief to be granted.[78]

Procedure

5.33 As to procedure, it is for the court to decide whether, when and how to exercise its inherent jurisdiction. The court may, and often does, act summarily, but it may adopt whatever procedure it thinks fit and decide what evidence it will receive and in what form.[79] Although the court will often wish to act immediately, it may decide to adjourn any consideration of whether or not to exercise the jurisdiction pending other developments.[80]

---

[73] *Assaubayev & Ors v Michael Wilson & Partners Ltd* [2014] EWCA Civ 1491, at [32].

[74] See *ibid*, at [47].

[75] *In re HA Grey* [1892] 2 QB 440, at 443, *per* Lord Esher MR.

[76] See *Bremer Vulkan Schiffbau und Maschinenfabrik v South India Shipping Corpn Ltd* [1981] AC 909, at 977, in which Lord Diplock described the court's inherent jurisdiction as a general power to control its own procedure so as to prevent its being used to achieve injustice.

[77] *Myers v Elman* [1940] AC 282, at 317, *per* Lord Wright. Also see *Udall v Capri Lighting Ltd* [1987] 1 QB 907.

[78] *Assaubayev & Ors v Michael Wilson & Partners Ltd* [2014] EWCA Civ 1491, at [29]. Similar observations may also be found in *R & T Thew v Reeves* [1982] QB 1285–6 and in *Harrison v Tew* [1990] 2 AC 523, at 529.

[79] See *Myers v Elman* [1940] AC 282, at 318, and *Brendon v Spiro* [1936] I KB 176, at 192 and 195.

[80] *Assaubayev & Ors v Michael Wilson & Partners Ltd* [2014] EWCA Civ 1491, at [31], *per* Christopher Clarke LJ.

Part III

ORDERS FOR COSTS

6

ORDERS FOR COSTS (JURISDICTION AND DISCRETION)

This chapter deals with the following topics: 6.01

- a forensic sieve (6.03);
- terminology and terms of art:
  - terminology used in this chapter (6.05);
  - terms of art and orders for costs (6.07);
- the jurisdiction to award costs:
  - statutory powers to award costs (6.09);
  - non-statutory powers to award costs (6.13);
  - formalities in respect of orders for cost (6.15);
- factors to be taken into account when an order for costs is made (6.16):
  - miscellaneous points regarding the power to award costs (6.18);
  - judge-made checklists regarding the power to award costs (6.26);
- the range of orders available to the court:
  - types of order listed in CPR, r 44.2(6) (6.29);
  - types of order other than those listed in CPR, r 44.2(6) (6.31);
  - percentage orders (6.32);
- success and 'the general rule' (6.42):
  - the meaning of success for the purposes of general rule (6.45);
  - the measure of success for the purposes of general rule (6.46);
  - partial success (6.74);
- factors other than the general rule (6.76):
  - conduct and the incidence of costs: general points (6.77);
  - conduct relating to procedural matters (6.93);
  - conduct and the incidence of costs: refusal to engage in ADR (6.118);
  - conduct and the incidence of costs: overly aggressive insistence on engaging in ADR (6.140);
  - conduct and the incidence of costs: failure to respond to an offer (6.141);
  - conduct and the incidence of costs: exaggeration and the incidence of costs (6.144);
  - issues and the incidence of costs (6.156);
  - admissible offers and the incidence of costs (6.207);
  - the relevance of changes in the law (6.246);
  - irrelevant and barely relevant factors (6.247);
- no order as to costs (6.262); and
- interim orders as to costs (6.265).

6.02 This chapter examines the principles that govern the question of who pays costs, this being known as the incidence of costs. Certain specific situations are additionally discussed in Chapter 7.

A Forensic Sieve

6.03 The following forensic sieve may be used as a brief summary of the law in outline and for the purposes of finding the relevant paragraphs.

- **Part 36** If the costs consequences of Part 36, Section I,[1] of the Civil Procedure Rules (CPR) apply, then the provisions that govern those consequences ought to be applied rather than CPR, r 44.2 (see 17.25 and Chapter 17 in general).
- **'The whole battlefield'** The aim is to 'make an order that reflects the overall justice of the case'.[2] In doing so, all of the relevant circumstances—or, in the words of Buckley LJ, the 'whole battlefield'[3]—are to be taken into account (see 6.19).[4]
- **Interim orders** If it is not appropriate to make a final determination as to the incidence of the costs, then it may be appropriate to make an interim order, such as an order that costs be reserved (see 6.265–6.274).
- **The 'general rule'** Unless the 'general rule' in CPR, r44.2(1)(a), does not apply (see 6.42–6.73), the starting point is that the unsuccessful party will be ordered to pay the costs of the successful party.
- **The successful party** Success must be real, rather than technical or Pyrrhic[5] (see 6.45). The relevant question is 'who, as a matter of substance and reality, has won?'[6] The following may apply.
  - Where prompt concessions or admissible offers have been made, they may be relevant to the issue of who has won (see 6.55–6.65), but where this is not so, it would be wrong to say that a party has lost simply on the basis that they obtained less than they sought[7] (see 6.50–6.51 and 6.154–6.155).
  - In commercial litigation in which each party has claims and asserts that a balance is owing in its own favour, the party that receives payment should generally be characterised as the successful party (see 6.63–6.67).
  - It would be wrong to confuse success on an issue—even an important issue that took up a great deal of time—with success in a more general sense (see 6.49). That said,

[1] Or, in admiralty claims, those of CPR, r 61.4(11).

[2] *Travelers Casualty and Surety Co of Canada v Sun Life Assurance Co of Canada (UK) Ltd* [2006] EWHC 2885 (Comm), at [11], *per* Christopher Clarke J.

[3] *Scherer & Anor v Counting Instruments Ltd* [1986] 2 All ER 529, at 533.

[4] See, eg, *Excalibur Ventures LLC Claimant v Texas Keystone Inc* [2016] EWCA Civ 1144, at [21], *per* Tomlinson LJ, and *Kastor Navigation Co Ltd v AXA Global Risks (UK) Ltd* [2004] EWCA Civ 277, at [153], *per* Rix LJ.

[5] *Bank of Credit and Commerce International SA (in liquidation) v Ali (No 4)* [1999] 149 NLJ 1734. See also *R (on the application of Amin Sino) v Secretary of State for The Home Department* [2016] EWHC 803 (Admin), at [21], *per* Hayden J.

[6] *Roache v Newsgroup Newspapers Ltd* [1998] EMLR 161, at 168, *per* Bingham MR. See also *Johnsey Estates (1990) Ltd v The Secretary of State for the Environment* [2001] EWCA Civ 535; *Painting v University of Oxford* [2005] EWCA Civ 161; *Roache v Newsgroup Newspapers Ltd* [1998] EMLR 161.

[7] *Aspin v Metric Group Ltd* [2007] EWCA Civ 922, at [25]. Where, however, the conduct of the claimant was such that they can be said to have exaggerated their claim, this may justify depriving them of their costs: see, eg, *Abbott v Long* [2011] EWCA Civ 874.

success on an issue that has allowed a party to prevail may carry with it the costs of the claim (see 6.49).
  - It may not always be possible for the court to say, when considering the action as a whole, that one party should be regarded as the overall winner[8] (see 6.68). In particular, if a party has suffered such significant losses on individual issues that it cannot fairly be said to be the winner, it would be open to the court to make no order for costs[9] (see 6.51).
- **Departure from the general rule** Having determined who is the successful party, consideration will then be given to what departures, if any, are required from the general rule (see CPR, r 44.2(4)).
- **Conduct** Where appropriate, the following ought to be taken into account, along with any other relevant conduct:
  - the manner in which a party has pursued or defended its case (see CPR, r 44.2(5)(c) and 6.77 *et seq*);
  - whether any admissible offers to settle have been made (see 6.207–6.243), which does not include any offers to which the cost consequences under Part 36 apply (see CPR, r 44.2(4)(c)), but may include Part 36 offers that have not been accepted or 'beaten', as well as those that have been withdrawn or which have failed to comply with the requirements of CPR, r 36.5;
  - the conduct of the parties before, as well as during, the proceedings (see 6.77–6.92), which, in particular, will include the extent to which the parties followed the Practice Direction (Pre-action Conduct) or any relevant pre-action protocol (see 6.96–6.101);
  - whether the successful party has unreasonably refused to engage in alternative dispute resolution (ADR) or has acted unreasonably in relation to ADR in any other way (see 6.118–6.140);
  - whether a party has unreasonably failed to respond to an offer (see 6.141); and
  - whether a claimant who has succeeded in the claim, in whole or in part, advanced an exaggerated claim (see CPR, r 44.2(5)(d)) (see 6.144–6.155).
- Where appropriate, consideration may be given to making an award on the indemnity basis (see Chapter 16).
- **Issue-aware approach** Where the circumstances of the case require an issue-aware costs order, that is what the court should make. In particular, the court will:
  - take into account whether a party succeeded on part of its case, even if the party has not been wholly successful (see 6.156–6.194); and
  - consider whether it was reasonable for a party to raise, pursue or contest a particular issue and the manner in which that party did so.
- **Formulation of the award** The range of orders set out in CPR, r 44.2(6), should be taken into account (see 6.29). The following should then be borne in mind.
  - The order can and, where appropriate, should reflect the relative success of the parties on different issues.[10]

[8] *Roache v Newsgroup Newspapers Ltd* [1998] EMLR 161.

[9] An example of this is *Quarmby Construction Co Ltd v Office of Fair Trading* [2012] EWCA Civ 1552, in which the Court found that the appellant should not be regarded as being the winner, despite the fact that they succeeded in having a penalty significantly reduced, because it lost on (among other things) its appeal to have the penalty quashed entirely.

[10] *Multiplex Constructions (UK) Ltd v Cleveland Bridge UK Ltd* [2008] EWHC 2280 (TCC), at [72].

- Before the court considers making an issue-based award (that is, an award under CPR, r 44.2(6)(f)), it will consider whether it is practicable to make a percentage award or an award of costs from or until a certain date only (see CPR, r 44.2(7) and 6.32).
- Where it is appropriate to make a percentage order, the award should first be formulated, but the court should then stand back and ask itself if the proposed result is the right result (see 6.39–6.41).

• **Payment on account** Where the court orders a party to pay costs subject to detailed assessment, it will order that party to pay a reasonable sum on account of costs, unless there is good reason not to do so (see CPR, r 44.2(8)) (see Chapter 14).

Terminology and Terms of Art

6.04 Most of the language of the incidence of costs is self-explanatory, but the following topics merit particular attention:

- terminology relating to issue-aware orders (6.05);
- terminology relating to offers (6.06); and
- terms of art as used in orders for costs (6.07).

Terminology used in this chapter

Terminology relating to issue-aware orders

6.05 The terminology in reported cases has never been used consistently and, in any event, it has evolved over recent years;[11] hence it is necessary to define certain terminology for the purposes of describing the law. The following definitions are as good as any.

- **Issue-aware approach** This is any method of determining the incidence of costs that takes account of issues.
- **Issue-aware order** This is an order that has been made by an issue-aware approach; it is not the same as an issue-based order.
- **Issue-based order** This is an order that allows or disallows the costs of specific issues; it is a type of issue-aware order.
- **Successful issues** These are issues upon which the party in question has succeeded.
- **Unsuccessful issues** These are issues upon which the party in question has not succeeded.
- **Abandoned issues** These are a species of unsuccessful issue in which the party pursuing or defending the issue in question has abandoned it, either entirely or in substance.

Terminology used in respect of offers

6.06 In this chapter, the following words have the following meanings.

[11] It should be noted that the terminology as used in this book is different from that used in previous editions. In particular, in previous editions, the phrase 'issue-based' was used to mean what is now referred to as 'issue-aware' and the phrase 'issue order' was used to mean what is now referred to as an 'issue-aware order'. This change has been made to reflect the way in which the term 'issue-based order' is used in oft-quoted authorities such as *Multiplex Constructions (UK) Ltd v Cleveland Bridge UK Ltd* [2008] EWHC 2280 (TCC), at [72].

- **Admissible offer** This means any offer to settle that is evidentially admissible, but which is not an offer to which costs consequences under Part 36 apply; this may include a 'failed' Part 36 offer (that is, an offer that was intended to comply with the requirements of CPR, r 36.6(5), but which failed to do so), Part 36 offers that have been withdrawn or Part 36 offers in which the costs consequences of Part 36 have not been engaged.
- **Part 36 offer** This means any offer that has been made pursuant to CPR, Part 36, Section I;[12] depending on the context, it may or may not mean an offer that is compliant with the procedural requirements of CPR, r 36.5.
- ***Calderbank* offer** This is an offer named after *Calderbank v Calderbank*[13] and is a contractual offer to settle some or part of the claim that is made without prejudice other than as to costs. It is a form of admissible offer.
- **Offeror** This is the party making the offer in question.
- **Offeree** This is the party to whom the offer is made.
- **Beaten** This means that the party in question has achieved a result that is at least as advantageous to it as the terms of the offer.

In the context of Part 36, some of these phrases have technical meanings that go beyond what is set out above; these are addressed at 17.03.

Terms of art and orders for costs

The words that are employed in costs orders are often terms of art. Practice Direction (PD) 44, para 4.2, gives guidance as to what those terms mean. That guidance is stated to be in respect of orders made in proceedings before trial, but it is clear from the context in which it is given that it is of general applicability. **6.07**

The guidance is as follows: **6.08**

> '4.2 There are certain costs orders which the court will commonly make in proceedings before trial. The following table sets out the general effect of these orders. The table is not an exhaustive list of the orders which the court may make.

Term	Effect
Costs Costs in any event	The party in whose favour the order is made is entitled to that party's costs in respect of the part of the proceedings to which the order relates, whatever other costs orders are made in the proceedings.
Costs in the case Costs in the application	The party in whose favour the court makes an order for costs at the end of the proceedings is entitled to that party's costs of the part of the proceedings to which the order relates.
Costs reserved	The decision about costs is deferred to a later occasion, but if no later order is made the costs will be costs in the case.
Claimant's/Defendant's costs in case/application	If the party in whose favour the costs order is made is awarded costs at the end the proceedings, that party is entitled to that party's costs of the part of the proceedings to which the order relates. If any other party is awarded costs at the end of the proceedings, the party in whose favour the final costs order is made is not liable to pay the costs of any other party in respect of the part of the proceedings to which the order relates.

[12] See CPR, r 36.1.
[13] [1976] Fam 93.

Costs thrown away	Where, for example, a judgment or order is set aside, the party in whose favour the costs order is made is entitled to the costs which have been incurred as a consequence. This includes the costs of— – preparing for and attending any hearing at which the judgment or order which has been set aside was made; – preparing for and attending any hearing to set aside the judgment or order in question; – preparing for and attending any hearing at which the court orders the proceedings or the part in question to be adjourned; – any steps taken to enforce a judgment or order which has subsequently been set aside.
Costs of and caused by	Where, for example, the court makes this order on an application to amend a statement of case, the party in whose favour the costs order is made is entitled to the costs of preparing for and attending the application and the costs of any consequential amendment to his own statement of case.
Costs here and below	The party in whose favour the costs order is made is entitled not only to that party's costs in respect of the proceedings in which the court makes the order but also to that party's costs of the proceedings in any lower court. In the case of an appeal from a Divisional Court the party is not entitled to any costs incurred in any court below the Divisional Court.
No order as to costs Each party to pay own costs	Each party is to bear that party's own costs of the part of the proceedings to which the order relates whatever costs order the court makes at the end of the proceedings.'

The Jurisdiction to Award Costs

Statutory powers to award costs

6.09 With only limited exceptions (see 6.13–6.14), the power to make orders for costs derives from the Senior Courts Act 1981 (as amended), s 51 of which provides as follows:

> '51 **Costs in civil division of Court of Appeal, High Court and county courts**
>
> (1) Subject to the provisions of this or any other enactment and to rules of court, the costs of and incidental to all proceedings in—
> (a) the civil division of the Court of Appeal;
> (b) the High Court;
> (ba) the family court; and
> (c) the county court,
>
> shall be in the discretion of the court.
>
> (2) Without prejudice to any general power to make rules of court, such rules may make provision for regulating matters relating to the costs of those proceedings including, in particular, prescribing scales of costs to be paid to legal or other representatives or for securing that the amount awarded to a party in respect of the costs to be paid by him to such representatives is not limited to what would have been payable by him to them if he had not been awarded costs.
>
> (3) The court shall have full power to determine by whom and to what extent the costs are to be paid.
>
> (4) In subsections (1) and (2) "proceedings" includes the administration of estates and trusts.
>
> (5) Nothing in subsection (1) shall alter the practice in any criminal cause, or in bankruptcy.'

Whilst this section expressly applies to the civil division of the Court of Appeal, the High Court, and the County Court and its hearing centres, it also applies in the Supreme Court, albeit only by analogy.[14]

The power to make an order for costs is subject to rules of court and, in particular, to CPR, r 44.2: **6.10**

> '(1) The court has discretion as to—
> (a) whether costs are payable by one party to another;
> (b) the amount of those costs ...'

Whilst not a source of law, PD 44, para 4.1, adds that '[t]he court may make an order about costs at any stage in a case'.[15] **6.11**

Limits of the court's power to make a costs order

The power to make a costs order is broad, extending even so far as to permit the court to make orders against a person who is not a party (see 9.03) or a person who has volunteered to become a party (see 9.106).[16] The courts' powers are not wholly without fetter, however; in particular, the following limits will apply. **6.12**

- **Powers are subject to other legislation** The powers conferred by s 51 of the Senior Courts Act 1981 are expressly stated to be subject to other legislation.[17]
- **Proceedings must have commenced** The court must be seised of the matter. The power to award costs arises not upon service of proceedings, but upon issue.[18] For the avoidance of doubt, where proceedings have been issued, the court has the power to award costs that arose prior to issue (see 49.147).
- **Parties must exist** The persons to whom and against whom costs are awarded must exist.[19] That said, the parties do not need to be present at the time the order is made.[20]

---

[14] The Supreme Court has power to determine any question necessary to be determined for the purposes of doing justice in an appeal to it under any enactment and its decisions are to be regarded as the decision of a court from which the appeal is heard: see ss 40(5) and 41(2) of the Constitutional Reform Act 2005.

[15] The now-revoked Costs Practice Direction used to contain a provision that expressly stated that the court may make an order about costs when it deals with any application (see CPD, art 8.3(2)), but this has been omitted from PD 44, presumably because it was such an obvious point that it would be implied within the meaning of PD 44, para 4.1.

[16] See, eg, *Moore's (Wallisdown) Ltd v Pensions Ombudsman; Royal and Sun Alliance Life and Pensions Ltd v Pensions Ombudsman* [2002] 1 All ER 737. The fact that the party volunteered to become a party may, however, be taken into account when deciding whether an order should be made.

[17] See, eg, *Conservative & Unionist Party (Claimant) v Election Commissioner* [2010] EWHC 285 (Admin), in which Keith J confirmed that s 156 of the Representation of the People Act 1983 restricted the court's powers to make an order for costs against a non-party.

[18] This is because CPR, r 7.2(1), provides that 'proceedings are started when the court issues a claim form at the request of the claimant': *Citation Plc v Ellis Whittam Ltd* [2012] EWHC 764 (QB), at [16], *per* Tugendhat J. Whilst not binding, see *Clydesdale Bank Plc v Kinleigh Folkard & Hayward Ltd* (unreported), 6 February 2014, Ch D (Master Bragge); *Whitaker v Ford & Warren (a firm)* (unreported), 25 November 2015, QBD (Leeds DR) (District Judge Geddes); *Webb Resolutions Ltd v Countrywide Surveyors Ltd* (unreported), 4 May 2016, Ch D (Deputy Master Nurse).

[19] There are limits, however. A non-existent person cannot be ordered to pay costs or to receive them: *Russian Commercial and Industrial Bank v Comptoir d'Escompte de Mulhouse* [1923] 2 KB 630 (reversed on appeal, but on factual bases: [1925] AC 112, HL).

[20] In particular, the court has the power to make a costs order against a party even if that party is not present by reason of it being before the court by reason of an application having been made without notice: see *MacKay v Ashwood Enterprises Ltd* [2013] EWCA Civ 959, at [49], *per* Lloyd LJ. However, the party

- **Costs must exist** The court may make an award of costs only where costs exist; costs may not be created as a punishment or reward.[21] Bramwell B made that point in the following way:

> 'Costs as between party and party are given by the law as an indemnity to the person entitled to them: they are not imposed as a punishment on the party who pays them, nor given as a bonus to the party who receives them.'[22]

The court has no power to make an award in respect of monies that cannot be said to be costs; this is dealt with in more detail in Chapter 3.

Non-statutory powers to award costs

6.13 Whilst, in ancient times, there may have been such a power (see 1.13), there is now no general common-law power to award costs.[23] This means that (other than the exceptions set out immediately below) the power to award costs must be expressly provided for by statute[24] or must be a statutory power that arises by necessary implication.[25] This presents few problems in modern-day civil litigation because s 51 of the Senior Courts Act 1981 confers an almost boundless jurisdiction; thus there is rarely any need for the court to rely on other powers.

6.14 Other powers do (arguably) exist, but they are rarely encountered in modern-day practice.

- **The court's inherent jurisdiction** Non-party costs awards against solicitors—which are not the same as wasted costs—may be made pursuant to the court's inherent jurisdiction, this being an ancient power[26] (see 9.60–9.71) that should not be confused with the common law.
- **The court's equitable jurisdiction** There used to be a free-standing equitable jurisdiction to award costs, but it is questionable whether it survived the Judicature Acts,[27] and even if it did, it has now been eclipsed by statute and is of no practical relevance.

Formalities in respect of orders for cost

6.15 Other than for consent orders and Tomlin orders (see 7.65–7.79), there are no formalities concerning the form of orders for costs, but any order must be tolerably clear and must 'stand alone'—that is, it must not be intelligible only by referring back to the judgment that preceded it.[28] The words that give rise to the entitlement must be in the order itself; a

affected by the making of a costs order could apply to the court that made it to reconsider the merits at first instance: *Bank of Scotland v Pereira* [2011] EWCA Civ 241.

[21] *Malkinson v Trim* [2002] EWCA Civ 1273, at [11].

[22] *Harold v Smith* (1860) 5 Hurlestone & Norman 381, at 385.

[23] *Garnett v Bradley* [1878] 3 AC 944, at 958, *per* Lord O'Hagan.

[24] This does not cause any difficulties in England and Wales because of the wide ambit of s 51 of the Senior Courts Act 1981, as amended, but the point does arise in other common-law jurisdictions: see, eg, *Service v Flateau* (1900) 16 WN (NSW) 248. See Quick, R, *Quick on Costs* (Thomson Reuters, online) for a full discussion of the topic.

[25] Whilst not binding, see *Queensland Fish Board v Bunney, ex parte Queensland Fish Board* [1979] Qd R 301.

[26] The fact that the House of Lords' power to make an award of costs derived from its inherent jurisdiction rather than from statute is now of only historical relevance: see *West Ham Union Guardians v Churchwardens of St Matthew, Bethnal Green* [1896] AC for a discussion about the origin of the House of Lords' powers.

[27] *Garnett v Bradley* [1878] 3 AC 944, at 958, *per* Lord O'Hagan.

[28] *Richardson Roofing Co Ltd (Claimant) v Ballast plc (dissolved)* (unreported), 13 February 2009, CA (Civ Div) (Jacob, Aiken and Sullivan LJJ).

provision contained within the schedule of a *Tomlin* order would not be an order for costs and (in the absence of a further order) would not give rise to a right to an assessment.[29] The topic of *Tomlin* orders is addressed in more detail at 7.70–7.79.

Factors to be Taken into Account when an Order for Costs is Made

Whilst a trite point, each order for costs will be decided on the facts of the case in hand and in accordance with the relevant general principles set out in CPR, r 44.2. The aim always is to 'make an order that reflects the overall justice of the case'.[30] **6.16**

CPR, r 44.2, reads as follows: **6.17**

> '(1) The court has discretion as to—
> (a) whether costs are payable by one party to another;
> (b) the amount of those costs; and
> (c) when they are to be paid.
>
> (2) If the court decides to make an order about costs—
> (a) the general rule is that the unsuccessful party will be ordered to pay the costs of the successful party; but
> (b) the court may make a different order.
>
> (3) The general rule does not apply to the following proceedings—
> (a) proceedings in the Court of Appeal on an application or appeal made in connection with proceedings in the Family Division; or
> (b) proceedings in the Court of Appeal from a judgment, direction, decision or order given or made in probate proceedings or family proceedings.
>
> (4) In deciding what order (if any) to make about costs, the court will have regard to all the circumstances, including—
> (a) the conduct of all the parties;
> (b) whether a party has succeeded on part of its case, even if that party has not been wholly successful; and
> (c) any admissible offer to settle made by a party which is drawn to the court's attention, and which is not an offer to which costs consequences under Part 36 apply.
>
> (5) The conduct of the parties includes—
> (a) conduct before, as well as during, the proceedings and in particular the extent to which the parties followed the Practice Direction–Pre-action Conduct or any relevant pre-action protocol;
> (b) whether it was reasonable for a party to raise, pursue or contest a particular allegation or issue;
> (c) the manner in which a party has pursued or defended its case or a particular allegation or issue; and
> (d) whether a claimant who has succeeded in the claim, in whole or in part, exaggerated its claim.

[29] See, by analogy, *Horizon Technologies International v Lucky Wealth Consultants Ltd* [1992] 1 WLR 24. The fact that a *Tomlin* order has been made does not deprive the court of the jurisdiction to make an award of costs (unless, of course, it contains conclusive terms as to that issue): see *Booker Belmont Wholesale Ltd v Ashford Developments Ltd* [2000] Lexis Citation 1833, at [13], *per* Waller LJ.

[30] *Travelers Casualty and Surety Co of Canada v Sun Life Assurance Co of Canada (UK) Ltd* [2006] EWHC 2885 (Comm), at [11], *per* Christopher Clarke J.

(6) The orders which the court may make under this rule include an order that a party must pay—
(a) a proportion of another party's costs;
(b) a stated amount in respect of another party's costs;
(c) costs from or until a certain date only;
(d) costs incurred before proceedings have begun;
(e) costs relating to particular steps taken in the proceedings;
(f) costs relating only to a distinct part of the proceedings; and
(g) interest on costs from or until a certain date, including a date before judgment.

(7) Before the court considers making an order under paragraph (6)(f), it will consider whether it is practicable to make an order under paragraph (6)(a) or (c) instead.

(8) Where the court orders a party to pay costs subject to detailed assessment, it will order that party to pay a reasonable sum on account of costs, unless there is good reason not to do so.'

Miscellaneous points regarding the power to award cost

All circumstances are to be taken into account

6.18 Decided cases are littered with exhortations to take all of the relevant circumstances into account.[31] The now-revoked Costs Practice Direction even went so far as to state this guidance in express terms.[32] It is likely that this guidance was omitted from PD 44 because it is obvious and therefore otiose; there is no reason to believe that its omission has in any way changed the law.

6.19 Although a pre-CPR decision, Buckley LJ focused on the fact that litigation has battle-like qualities and that, as such, there is a need to scan the 'whole battlefield':

> 'We have been referred to [authorities] for the proposition that we must have regard to all circumstances relevant to the issues in the action and the history of the action hitherto and the matters leading to the action. Those were both cases in which the orders for costs there under consideration were orders made at the trial of the actions. In such cases no doubt the relevant field to be scanned is the whole battlefield of the action and the whole of the conduct of the parties in relation to the matter in dispute may be relevant.'[33]

It is all but certain that these comments remain good law.

The need to focus on the CPR rather than on case law and to avoid an overly technical approach

6.20 When making an order for costs, the court should generally look to the rules of court rather than to decided cases. Brooke LJ described those rules as 'the essential working tool'.[34] Waller LJ cautioned that in so far as the incidence of costs is concerned—in which regard

[31] See, eg, *Excalibur Ventures LLC Claimant v Texas Keystone Inc* [2016] EWCA Civ 1144, at [21], *per* Tomlinson LJ; *Kastor Navigation Co Ltd v AXA Global Risks (UK) Ltd* [2004] EWCA Civ 277, at [153], *per* Rix LJ.

[32] CPD, art 8.4, reads as follows: 'In deciding what order to make about costs the court is required to have regard to all the circumstances including any payment into court or admissible offer to settle made by a party which is drawn to the court's attention, and which is not an offer to which costs consequences under Part 36 apply.'

[33] *Scherer & Anor v Counting Instruments Ltd* [1986] 2 All ER 529, at 533.

[34] *Groupama Insurance Co Ltd v Aon Ltd* [2003] EWCA Civ 1846, at [27].

all cases are different and fact-specific—authorities that do not lay down clear principles are of little assistance.[35] Rix LJ had the following to say on the topic:

> 'It is trite to state but important to bear in mind that the rules prescribe the way in which the court's discretion as to costs should be exercised rather than any decision of this court on the facts of any particular case.'[36]

This is perhaps an expression of the general, but often overlooked, principle that the exercise of discretion in one case is not to be taken as being a guide to how discretion should be exercised in another (see 4.07).

In a similar vein, Pill LJ had this to say about the dangers of overly technical approaches towards awards of costs: **6.21**

> 'There is a danger in taking an over-technical view of this question of costs ... One has to take an overall view of the situation and, applying good sense, decide on the reasonableness of the conduct of the parties including the conduct of the party seeking costs.'[37]

Indeed, whilst no more than the editor's own thoughts, one could extend Buckley LJ's battlefield analogy (see 6.19) by saying that 'war is a matter of improvisation; organisation is the enemy of improvisation'.[38]

Awards of costs must be reasoned and judicial

There needs to a degree of organisation, however. Discretion should be exercised judicially to make an award that meets the justice of the situation. Whilst it is a point that has already been made (see 6.16), the aim is always to make 'an order that reflects the overall justice of the case'.[39] Discretion cannot be exercised arbitrarily; it must be based on principles dictated by reason and justice.[40] **6.22**

The court should strive to give reasons for its orders as to costs. Phillips MR had the following to say on this topic: **6.23**

> 'We understand that the costs were dealt with at the end of a long day and that the reasons were perfunctory. Costs are important, particularly where, as I fear in this case, they are disproportionate to what is at stake. Judges must be sure that their reasons for costs' orders are clear; they should not be left to inference, albeit that it is often possible to infer the reasons.'[41]

No extraneous factors are to be taken into account

The factors to be taken into account are the factors in the claim and not extraneous to it, such as unresolved suspicions or other unproven matters.[42] The oft-cited example of a court wrongly taking extraneous factors into account is a case in which the costs of a **6.24**

---

[35] *Straker v Tudor Rose (a firm)* [2007] EWCA 368, at [10]. Waller LJ went on to say that it is to the CPR that one should go and that it is by reference to the CPR that an appeal court should test whether a judge has gone wrong in any particular instance.

[36] *Kastor Navigation Co Ltd v AXA Global Risks (UK) Ltd* [2004] EWCA Civ 277, at [143].

[37] *Dempsey v London Borough of Sutton* [2013] EWCA Civ 863, at [24].

[38] Quote attributable to politician Max Beaverbrook, during the Second World War.

[39] *Travelers Casualty and Surety Co of Canada v Sun Life Assurance Co of Canada (UK) Ltd* [2006] EWHC 2885 (Comm), at [11], *per* Christopher Clarke J.

[40] *Ottway v Jones* [1955] 1 WLR 706, CA; *Bourne v Stanbridge* [1965] 1 WLR 189, CA.

[41] *Lavelle v Lavelle* [2004] EWCA Civ 223, at [52].

[42] See, eg, *Naseem t/a SH Builders and Contractors v Kang* [2011] EWCA Civ 737, at [40].

motion for committal for contempt of an injunction were awarded against the alleged contemnor based on his conduct, even though the court had found the allegations to be not proven.[43]

The approach to awarding costs is not a mathematical exercise

6.25 When making an order for costs that takes competing factors into account, the approach is not a mathematical approach, but one that does justice between the parties. It is necessary to stand back and look at the effect of the proposed order. In this regard, Rix LJ (giving judgment of the Court of Appeal) had the following to say:

> 'The rules required [the judge] to have regard to all the circumstances of the case ... He should have stood back from the mathematical result and asked himself whether in all the circumstances, including the other factors to which we have referred, it was the right result.'[44]

The topic of standing back and looking at percentage orders is addressed at 6.39.

Judge-made checklists regarding the power to award cost

6.26 There are two judge-made checklists that are often cited:

- Chadwick LJ's checklist in *Johnsey Estates (1990) Ltd v The Secretary of State for the Environment*;[45] and
- Jackson J's list in *Multiplex Constructions (UK) Ltd v Cleveland Bridge UK Ltd*.[46]

Chadwick LJ's guidance in Johnsey Estates

6.27 Chadwick LJ has given the following guidance as to the general approach to making a costs order (with particular emphasis on cases involving more than one litigated issue):

> 'The principles applicable in the present case may, I think, be summarised as follows:
> (i) Costs cannot be recovered except under an order of the court;
> (ii) the question whether to make any order as to costs—and, if so, what order—is a matter entrusted to the discretion of the trial judge;
> (iii) the starting point for the exercise of discretion is that costs should follow the event; nevertheless,
> (iv) the judge may make different orders for costs in relation to discrete issues—and, in particular, should consider doing so where a party has been successful on one issue but unsuccessful on another issue and, in that event, may make an order for costs against the party who has been generally successful in the litigation; and
> (v) the judge may deprive a party of costs on an issue on which he has been successful if satisfied that the party has acted unreasonably in relation to that issue;
> (vi) an appellate court should not interfere with a judge's exercise of discretion merely because it takes the view that it would have exercised that discretion differently.'[47]

---

[43] *Knight v Clifton* [1971] 2 All ER 378, [1971] Ch 700. In a similar vein, Sir James Munby has explained that although the contemnor's conduct in the underlying litigation may plainly be relevant, a contemnor who ought not to have been committed is not to be deprived of the costs of a successful appeal that they could otherwise expect to be awarded merely because of their previous litigation conduct or even because they were, in fact, guilty of the alleged contempt: see *Re MM v Kirk* [2017] EWCA Civ 260, at [9], *per* Sir James Munby P.

[44] *Kastor Navigation Co Ltd v AXA Global Risks (UK) Ltd* [2004] EWCA Civ 277, at [153].

[45] [2001] EWCA Civ 535.

[46] [2008] EWHC 2280 (TCC).

[47] *Johnsey Estates (1990) Ltd v The Secretary of State for the Environment* [2001] EWCA Civ 535, at [21].

Jackson J's guidance in Multiplex

Jackson J offered the following guidance—which was originally formulated for the purposes of making issue-aware orders in commercial litigation, but which has, in recent years, been applied far more broadly than that: **6.28**

> 'From this review of authority I derive the following eight principles.
>
> (i) In commercial litigation where each party has claims and asserts that a balance is owing in its own favour, the party which ends up receiving payment should generally be characterised as the overall winner of the entire action.
> (ii) In considering how to exercise its discretion the court should take as its starting point the general rule that the successful party is entitled to an order for costs.
> (iii) The judge must then consider what departures are required from that starting point, having regard to all the circumstances of the case.
> (iv) Where the circumstances of the case require an issue-based costs order, that is what the judge should make. However, the judge should hesitate before doing so, because of the practical difficulties which this causes and because of the steer given by rule 44.3(7).
> (v) In many cases the judge can and should reflect the relative success of the parties on different issues by making a proportionate costs order.
> (vi) In considering the circumstances of the case the judge will have regard not only to any Part 36 offers made but also to each party's approach to negotiations (insofar as admissible) and general conduct of the litigation.
> [... [48]]
> (viii) In assessing a proportionate costs order the judge should consider what costs are referable to each issue and what costs are common to several issues. It will often be reasonable for the overall winner to recover not only the costs specific to the issues which he has won but also the common costs.'[49]

The Range of Orders Available to the Court

Types of order listed in CPR, r 44.2(6)

A range of orders that the court may make are listed in CPR, r 44.2: **6.29**

> '(6) The orders which the court may make under this rule include an order that a party must pay—
> (a) a proportion of another party's costs;
> (b) a stated amount in respect of another party's costs;
> (c) costs from or until a certain date only;
> (d) costs incurred before proceedings have begun;
> (e) costs relating to particular steps taken in the proceedings;
> (f) costs relating only to a distinct part of the proceedings; and
> (g) interest on costs from or until a certain date, including a date before judgment.
>
> (7) Before the court considers making an order under paragraph (6)(f), it will consider whether it is practicable to make an order under paragraph (6)(a) or (c) instead.
>
> (8) Where the court orders a party to pay costs subject to detailed assessment, it will order that party to pay a reasonable sum on account of costs, unless there is good reason not to do so.'

[48] Point (vii)—which related to the combination of a 'near miss' and a refusal to negotiate—has been omitted because it is no longer good law: see *Dufoo v Tolaini* [2014] EWCA Civ 1536, at [39], *per* Jackson LJ.

[49] *Multiplex Constructions (UK) Ltd v Cleveland Bridge UK Ltd* [2008] EWHC 2280 (TCC), at [72].

The relative desirability of the orders in range as set out in CPR, r 44.2(6)

6.30 It has been said that the range of orders set out in CPR, r 44.2(6), is in decreasing order of desirability in that the judges should seek to make orders higher up the list in preference to orders lower down.[50] There probably is some truth in this—as implied by r 44.2(7), which encourages the court to choose orders from the upper reaches of the list—but it is axiomatic that each case will have to be decided on its own facts. It would, for example, make little sense for a party to be awarded 5 per cent of its costs (that is, as per category (a) of the list) as opposed to its costs in respect of a particular part of the proceedings (as per category (f)). It should be borne in mind, however, that orders relating to specific steps or that relate only to distinct parts of the proceedings (that is, categories (e) and (f)) are prone to lead to disagreements as to both their precise meaning and effect. It is perhaps for this reason that the Judicial Studies Board (JSB) recommends that a costs order in accordance with r 44.2(6)(e) or (f) should be made only exceptionally.[51]

Types of order other than those listed in CPR, r 44.2(6)

6.31 CPR, r 44.2(6), provides a list of available orders (see 6.29), but it is not an exhaustive list; other orders can be made, where appropriate. Examples might include where a party is awarded its costs less a fixed sum[52] or where costs are capped at a certain level.[53] The court has considerable freedom in this regard, but unconventional orders should be made only where they can be justified on principled grounds.[54]

Percentage orders

6.32 Percentage orders (also known as fractional orders or proportional orders) are orders by which the receiving party is entitled to only a proportion of the costs incurred (see CPR, r 44.2(6)(a)). Neither they[55] nor the notion that they are to be preferred to issue-based orders are anything new.[56]

Percentage orders (or similar) are preferred

6.33 As has already been said (see 6.30), if the court is minded to award a party costs, but the intended award relates to only a distinct part of the proceedings, CPR, r 44.2(7), urges the court to make an order either that that party receives a proportion of its costs (that is, a percentage award) or that the award is for costs from a certain date only.[57] The circumstances in which this guidance would generally become relevant would be where a predominantly successful party has had more success on a number of issues than on others (see 6.156). The effect of r 44.2(7) is to discourage issue-based awards—but, for the reasons set out elsewhere in this chapter, an issue-*aware* approach to making awards is not discouraged; indeed, it is actively encouraged.

---

[50] See, eg, The Civil Bench Book, para 8.14.

[51] See *ibid.*

[52] See, eg, *Gil v Baygreen Properties Ltd* [2004] EWHC 2029 (Ch); see also *Wright v HSBC Bank plc* [2006] EWHC 1473 (Admin).

[53] See, eg, *SCT Finance v Bolton* [2002] EWCA Civ 56.

[54] *Ibid.*

[55] The earliest example the editor has been able to find is *Willmott v Barber* [1880] 15 Ch D 96, at 105, where Fry J made an issue-aware percentage order.

[56] See, eg, *Cinema Press Ltd v Pictures & Pleasures Ltd* [1945] KB 356 at 361.

[57] See also *Enterprise Managed Services Ltd v McFadden Utilities Ltd* [2010] EWHC 1506 (TCC), at [8], *per* Akenhead J.

6.34 The Court of Appeal has emphasised that percentage orders are to be made, where practicable.[58] Lord Phillips MR had the following to say on this matter:

> 'We would emphasise that the CPR requires that an order which allows or disallows costs by reference to certain issues should be made only if other forms of order cannot be made which sufficiently reflect the justice of the case (see [CPR, r 44.2(7)]). In our view there are good reasons for this rule. An order which allows or disallows costs of certain issues creates difficulties at the stage of the assessment of costs because the Costs Judge will have to master the issue in detail to understand what costs were properly incurred in dealing with it and then analyse the work done by the receiving party's legal advisers to determine whether or not it was attributable to the issue the costs of which had been disallowed. All this adds to the costs of assessment and to the amount of time absorbed in dealing with costs on this basis. The costs incurred on assessment may thus be disproportionate to the benefit gained. In all the circumstances, contrary to what might be thought to be the case, a "percentage" order (under [CPR, r 44.2(6)(a)]) made by the Judge who heard the application will often produce a fairer result than an "issues based" order under [CPR, r 44.2(6)(f)]. Moreover such an order is consistent with the overriding objective of the CPR.'[59]

6.35 The benefit of making percentage awards in preference to issue-based orders was explained by Chadwick LJ:

> 'That [a percentage order] would obviate the need for a detailed assessment of the separate costs of each issue. That, as it seems to me, is not only a proper approach: it is the approach which is positively required by the Rules.'[60]

6.36 In a similar vein, Patten J had the following to say:

> '[T]he implementation of [issues orders] or indeed for any kind of division of costs in relation to specific issues can involve the parties and the costs judge in extensive further litigation in the course of the detailed assessment, during which the whole history of the action is scrutinised in order to determine which part of any expenditure related to which issue. … These matters need, I think, to be borne firmly in mind by a trial judge who is asked to make a complicated order for costs. There is much to be said for the application of the general rule that costs should follow the event and for keeping to the simple formula of orders for a stated proportion of the costs or a stated amount of costs in cases where recognition of a limited degree of success by one or other party is called for.'[61]

Not always inappropriate to prefer an issues-based order over a percentage order

6.37 The fact that percentage orders are to be preferred to orders for the cost of a distinct part of the proceedings does not mean that CPR, r 44.2(6)(f)—namely, issues-based orders—should be disregarded entirely. Brooke LJ, for example, has commented that the ability to make an order that deals with only a part of the proceedings might enable a court to do greater justice if the successful party had caused costs to be incurred on an issue that, in the event, was abandoned.[62] There may be other reasons for making an issues-based order. Sir Michael Burton, for example, made an issues order in a case in which certain discrete issues had been

[58] See *London Borough of Hackney v Campbell* [2005] EWCA Civ 613.
[59] *English v Emery Reimbold & Strick Ltd* [2002] EWCA Civ 605, at [115].
[60] *National Westminster Bank plc v Kotonou* [2007] EWCA Civ 223, at [23].
[61] *Dyson Technology Ltd v Strutt* [2007] EWHC 1756 (Ch), at [6]. Akenhead J has also made similar comments: see *The Bodo Community v Shell Petroleum Development Company of Nigeria Ltd* [2014] EWHC 2170 (TCC), at [8].
[62] *Winter v Winter* [2000] All ER (D) 1791.

identified, but quantification of the costs associated with them would require further work.[63] Whilst *obiter*, Akenhead J has commented that an issues-based order under CPR, r 44.2(6)(f), may be appropriate where it is not possible to determine who has won overall.[64]

6.38 **Reciprocal orders vs percentage awards** It may be that both sides have had such a degree of success such that—as a starting point, at least—would justify them both being awarded costs. The issue of reciprocal orders (otherwise known as cross-orders) is addressed in detail at 7.34–7.37. For the reasons set out therein, such orders are problematic, but it would not necessarily be wrong for the court to make such an order in an appropriate case. In a case in which the trial judge felt that it would be better for a costs judge to gauge the amounts payable (and in which he gave extensive guidance to assist the costs judge), Tomlinson LJ found that whilst a percentage order would have been preferable, reciprocal orders were within the range of available awards.[65]

The method by which percentage orders are made: formulation and standing back

6.39 When making a percentage order, the approach is to identify the relevant factors, and then to make an order that takes them into account and that meets the justice of the situation. This is not a mathematical exercise (see 6.169 and 6.25). If the factors pull in different directions, the task is to see whether one set of factors pulls more strongly than the other and then to take that into account by adjusting the percentage within the appropriate range.[66] Rix LJ, giving judgment in 2004, recognised that this approach, unlike a rigorously mathematical approach, might lead to uncertainty, but he explained that justice was to be preferred over certainty:

> '[We] think it was an error of approach by the judge simply to visit the mathematical outcome of the issue by issue approach on the owners. This took no account of the other factors to which we have referred. The rules required him to have regard to all the circumstances of the case and it does not seem to us that he did so, at least not in the way the rules required. He should have stood back from the mathematical result and asked himself whether in all the circumstances, including the other factors to which we have referred, it was the right result.'[67]

6.40 At about the same time, Pumfrey J gave similar guidance, and in doing so he drew on his experience of patent claims (which have long been the subject of issue-aware orders).[68] His guidance can be summarised in the following way.

- The court should decide whether, notwithstanding its overall success, the successful party should be deprived of some part of its costs.
- If the successful party is to be deprived of some part of its costs, the court should determine the matters to which those parts relate.
- The court should decide whether, in relation to those matters, it should not also pay the costs of the unsuccessful party.
- The court must then convert the conclusion into an award of costs based upon a percentage.

---

63 See *Al Jaber v Al Ibrahim* [2017] EWHC 5092 (Comm), at [13].

64 See also *Enterprise Managed Services Ltd v McFadden Utilities Ltd* [2010] EWHC 1506 (TCC), at [10(a)], *per* Akenhead J.

65 *Connell v Mutch t/a Southey Building Services* [2012] EWCA Civ 1589, at [25], *per* Tomlinson LJ.

66 *Kastor Navigation Co Ltd v AXA Global Risks (UK) Ltd* [2004] EWCA Civ 277, at [156].

67 *Ibid*, at [153].

68 *Apotex Europe Ltd v SmithKline Beecham plc* [2004] EWHC 964 (Ch), at [9]–[13].

- This should be done only if it is clearly understood that the process being undertaken is not that of detailed assessment.
- All costs are notionally allocated to the issues; the successful party is assumed to recover all its reasonable costs of the action and the percentage deduction is made from that overall sum.

Pumfrey J made no mention of Rix LJ's guidance about standing back and asking whether the result was the right result (see 6.39); indeed, it is entirely possible that Pumfrey J was not aware of Rix LJ's guidance as Rix LJ had given his judgment only a few weeks beforehand. There is no reason to believe that Pumfrey J intended that there should not be a stage of standing back to look at the result.

In a different case—in which his analysis had echoes of the Welamson doctrine (see 6.75)—Pumfrey J explained that it is often convenient to treat both parties' costs of an issue as being equal in amount and to double the deduction, with the result that if a party fails to recover costs of an issue amounting to, say, 15 per cent of its total costs, 30 per cent of those costs will be deducted if the court concludes that the party should also pay the costs of that issue to the other.[69] These comments were made in the context of a patents claim; it is possible that this approach would be less useful in other types of claim in which the court might not be so sure that the parties' costs of the issues in question are likely to be similar in amount. **6.41**

Success and 'The General Rule'

CPR, r 44.2(2)(a), introduces 'the general rule'[70]—namely, that the loser pays. That rule has been a feature of litigation in England and Wales for centuries[71] (see 1.14 and 1.53). It is so fundamental to the operation of common-law legal systems that, in an Australian case, it was found to be an implied statutory provision.[72] The general rule does not apply in all circumstances; this topic is discussed at 7.38–7.64. **6.42**

Prior to the coming into force of the CPR, a party who had enjoyed substantial success could reasonably expect to be awarded the entirety of its costs. That state of affairs changed with the introduction of the CPR. Even before the printers' ink was dry, Lord Woolf MR took to promoting the fact that a 'winner takes all' ethos was a practice to be consigned to history: **6.43**

> 'I draw attention to the new rules because, while they make clear that the general rule remains that the successful party will normally be entitled to costs, they at the same time indicate the wide range of considerations which will result in the court making different orders as to costs. From 26 April 1999 the "follow the event principle" will still play a significant role, but it will be a starting point from which a court can readily depart. This is also the

---

69 *Monsanto Technology LLC v Cargill International SA* [2007] EWHC 3113 (Pat).

70 This rule is also often referred to as costs 'following the event', although that phrase should be used with caution because it can also mean other things.

71 In about 1765, Blackstone recorded the maxim as '*victus victori in expensis condemnandus est*': Blackstone, W, *Commentaries on the Laws of England* (a facsimile of the first edition of 1765–69, reprinted Chicago, IL: University of Chicago Press, 1979), vol 3, at p 399. See Quick, R, *Quick on Costs* (Thomson Reuters, online), para 2.30, for a full discussion of the topic.

72 See, eg, *Hughes v Western Australian Cricket Assn (Inc)* (1986) ATPR 40-748, at 48 and 136.

> position prior to the new rules coming into force. The most significant change of emphasis of the new rules is to require courts to be more ready to make separate orders which reflect the outcome of different issues. In doing this the new rules are reflecting a change of practice which has already started. It is now clear that a too robust application of the "follow the event principle" encourages litigants to increase the costs of litigation, since it discourages litigants from being selective as to the points they take. If you recover all your costs as long as you win, you are encouraged to leave no stone unturned in your effort to do so.'[73]

6.44 Thus, under the CPR, the court is to take a more nuanced approach to the incidence of costs than merely looking at who had won. It should not be forgotten, however, that even before the introduction of the CPR, a claimant who recovered next to nothing would have been lucky to have been awarded costs.[74] It is also worth noting that, even in the early days of the CPR, it was recognised that it was necessary to give 'real weight' to the overall success of the winning party.[75]

The meaning of success for the purposes of general rule

6.45 Success must be real rather than technical or Pyrrhic (also see 6.68). This was explained by Lightman J in the following way: 'For the purposes of the CPR, success [is not] a technical term but a result in real life, and the question as to who succeeded is a matter for the exercise of common sense.'[76] The difficulty, in general, lies not in knowing, in conceptual terms, what success is, but in measuring it. This is addressed next.

The measure of success for the purposes of general rule

6.46 In most cases, it will be obvious who has won, but the following issues may arise:

- cases in which there is more than one issue (6.47);
- starting points and finishing points for gauging success (6.54);
- gauging success where there will be more than one trial (6.62);
- gauging success in commercial litigation (6.63);
- the effect of costs on success and vice versa (6.71); and
- the relevance of partial success (6.74).

Whilst the court is not always bound to accept the correctness of a resolution upon which it has not ruled,[77] it is possible for a party to succeed by way of compromise; this is addressed at 7.141–7.168.

The approach to gauging success in cases with more than one issue

6.47 In cases in which the court has ruled on more than one issue, it may not always be obvious who has won. Whilst there may be a degree of overlap, for descriptive purposes it is possible to discern the following types of case:

---

73 *Phonographic Performance Ltd v AEI Rediffusion Music Ltd* [1999] 1 WLR 1507, at 1522.

74 See, eg, *Anglo-Cyprian Trade Agencies Ltd v Paphos Wine Industries Ltd* [1951] 1 All ER 873; *Alltrans Express Ltd v CV Holdings Ltd* [1984] 1 WLR 394; *Lipkin Gorman v Carpnale Ltd* [1989] 1 WLR 1340.

75 *Scholes Windows v Magnet (No 2)* [2000] ECDR 266, at 268.

76 *Bank of Credit and Commerce International SA (in liquidation) v Ali (No 4)* [1999] 149 NLJ 1734, at the seventh paragraph. See also *R (on the application of Amin Sino) v Secretary of State for The Home Department* [2016] EWHC 803 (Admin), at [21], *per* Hayden J.

77 An example of this is *Hudson v New Media Holding Co LLC* [2011] EWHC 3068 (QB), at [24], *per* Eady J, in which the court declined to accept that a finding of a US court was determinative of the issue of whether the application in question had merit.

- cases in which there is one predominant issue (6.48);
- cases in which there are many issues (6.50);
- cases in which there is a primary case and a secondary case (6.52); and
- cases in which a point of principle has arisen (6.53).

Each is addressed in turn.

Gauging success where there has been one predominant issue It would be wrong to confuse success on an issue—even an important one that took up a great deal of time—with success in a more general sense. All of the facts need to be taken into account (see 6.18) and this includes issues that have been pursued without success. The court needs to gauge matters in the appropriate context; this may mean, for example, that it would be wrong to make an immediate order following a preliminary issues hearing without knowing the final result.[78] The court needs to survey the 'whole battlefield' (see 6.19)—which is why Longmore LJ has commented that it would generally not be right to segregate a large element of the costs and thereafter decide who is the successful party.[79] **6.48**

That said, where a single issue has dominated the claim, that issue may be highly relevant, as is illustrated by the following. **6.49**

- **Where success on one issue is sufficient to afford the remedy sought** Ramsey J has said (on the facts of the case before him) that where a party has succeeded on an issue and has thereby obtained the relief sought thereby, this will carry with it not only the costs of that issue, but also the common costs incurred in pursuit of the proceedings.[80] In this regard, Ramsey J seems to have gone further than Jackson J, who commented only that it would be *open* to the court to deal with a case in that way.[81] This seems to illustrate that each case will turn on its own facts.
- **Where success on one issue impacts on other issues** Success on one issue may impact on others. A common example is where the court finds that there has been exaggeration—a finding that often results in the exaggerator's credibility being annihilated. In this regard, Maurice Kay LJ (with whom Longmore LJ agreed) said:

> 'To the question: who was the real winner in this litigation? there is, in my judgment, only one answer. The two-day hearing was concerned overwhelmingly with the issue of exaggeration, and the [defendant] won on that issue. [The claimant's] submission that that was only one issue, the other issue being the quantification of the claim, is not persuasive. Quite simply, that second issue was hardly an issue at all once the Recorder had found the exaggeration ...'[82]

Unsurprisingly, the claimant in that case was ordered to pay the defendant's costs.

[78] *Perriam Ltd v Wayne* [2011] EWHC 403 (QB), at [58], *per* Coulson J; cf *Fiona Trust & Holding Corpn v Privalov* [2011] EWHC 664 (Comm), at [14], in which Andrew Smith J explained that the application of the general rule requires consideration of the overall relative success of the parties in respect of the relevant hearing(s) or stage(s) in the litigation, ie generally those in respect of which an award of costs is being considered, and the court is not concerned, for this purpose, about which party has won on individual issues.

[79] *AL Barnes v Time Talk (UK) Ltd* [2003] EWCA Civ 402, at [28], cited with approval in *Kastor Navigation Co Ltd v Axa Global Risks (UK) Ltd* [2004] EWCA Civ 277, at [146].

[80] *Mears Ltd v Leeds City Council* [2011] EWHC 2694 (TCC), at [28].

[81] *Multiplex Constructions (UK) Ltd v Cleveland Bridge UK Ltd* [2008] EWHC 2280 (TCC), at [72(viii)].

[82] *Painting v University of Oxford* [2005] EWCA Civ 161, at [21].

6.50 **Gauging success where there have been many issues** Where the outcome is one in which a party has succeed on a number of discrete issues, but lost on others, the court will, in accordance with CPR, r 44.2(4)(b), consider whether an issue-aware approach should be taken. This is a very common situation. Issues should not be confused with the amounts awarded: Chadwick LJ has said that it would be wrong to deprive the successful party of its costs on the basis that that party had obtained less than it had sought.[83] Whilst each case will turn on its own facts, Jackson LJ came to much the same conclusion in a case in which the successful party had lost on a number of significant issues.[84]

6.51 If a putatively successful party has suffered such significant losses on individual issues that it cannot fairly be said to be the winner or the loser overall, the court may make no order for costs.[85] Likewise, in a case in which a party won on the facts, but lost on a point of procedure that was said to be the 'main issue', Smith LJ said that no order for costs may be appropriate.[86] More is said on this topic at 6.56, in the context of comparing the sums claimed with the amounts allowed.

6.52 **Gauging success where there have been both primary and secondary cases** If a party advances a primary case and a secondary case, then that party may still be the successful party if it wins on only one of those cases (especially if they were in the alternative). A more challenging situation, however, is where both parties are unsuccessful in their primary cases (such as where they both say there is a point of law that will decide the matter); where this happens, the court should look at who has won on their secondary cases as being the measure of success generally. It would generally be wrong in those circumstances to say that there has been a draw as a result of both parties having failed on their primary cases.[87]

6.53 **Gauging success in cases in which a point of principle has arisen** Where a point of general importance arises, Lord Neuberger MR has implied that there is a difference between hearings at first instance (where he dealt with the issue of success on the basis of who had achieved the result that they were seeking) and hearings on appeal (where he distinguished between success on the facts and success on the point of principle).[88] This compares with the approach taken by Tomlinson LJ (sitting in a case at first instance) in which he said that whilst an 'enthusiastic lawyer' might have believed that the case before him was about a point of law, ultimately it was about money.[89] This difference of approach merely highlights the fact that each case will be decided on its own facts.

---

[83] *Aspin v Metric Group Ltd* [2007] EWCA Civ 922, at [25]. Where, however, the conduct of the claimant was such that they can be said to have exaggerated their claim, this may justify depriving them of their costs: see, eg, *Abbott v Long* [2011] EWCA Civ 874.

[84] See *Naseem t/a SH Builders and Contractors v Kang* [2011] EWCA Civ 737, at [40].

[85] An example of this is *Quarmby Construction Co Ltd v Office of Fair Trading* [2012] EWCA Civ 1552, in which the Court found that the appellant should not be regarded as being the winner, despite the fact that it succeeded in having a penalty significantly reduced, because it lost on (among other things) its appeal to have the penalty quashed entirely.

[86] *Owens v Noble* [2010] EWCA Civ 284, at [8].

[87] *Day v Day* [2006] EWCA Civ 415.

[88] *Manchester City Council v Pinnock (No 2)* [2011] UKSC 6, at [18]. See also *Owens v Noble* [2010] EWCA Civ 284, at [8].

[89] *Pindell Ltd & Anor v Airasia Berhad (formerly known as Airasia SDN BHD)* [2010] EWHC 3238 (Comm), at [4].

Gauging success: starting points and offers

In addition to taking into account its own findings, the court may wish to take into account what the parties themselves had to say during the litigation. In this regard, the parties' starting points and their offers (see 6.56) may be relevant, as may be any offers that the parties have made and the nature of the case. What is said below assumes that there has been no culpable exaggeration; if there has been such, then different considerations will apply (see 6.149). **6.54**

Gauging success: starting points and offers in specific circumstances It may be necessary to focus on the stances the parties took to assess how far their opponent's costs expenditure caused them to yield, be that by consent or by adjudication. **6.55**

Starting points with regards to quantum Where the parties have advanced competing views as to the value of the claim, it may be appropriate to take those views into account. In an appeal from a trial in which a claimant had recovered just under a tenth of the sums that were claimed, but still more than the defendant had offered, Auld LJ had this to say: **6.56**

> 'In my view, the reality of this case is that [the defendant] was the winner. She was facing a claim substantially greater than the amount finally awarded. There were, as I have said, competing claims and offers, not only as to the manner of calculation of the amount due but as to the amount … The sum ordered was arguably as limited a loss as it was a gain. And it emerged as a result, not only of [the claimant] losing the case on principle on the main issues in the case, but also as to the true amount due out of a very much larger claim. The disparity between what [the claimant] sought, including what he put [the defendant] through to get it, and what he received was so large as to put the relatively small amount finally awarded in the balance between two rival contentions into relative insignificance.'[90]

Auld LJ went on to say that the defendant had won the case in principle, or as near as could be, given the large competing sums being canvassed between the parties and the wide issue between them as to the proper basis of the claim. The appropriate order was that there be no order for costs. Thus, in line with cases discussed in 6.59, a modest 'win' may, in truth, not be sufficient to get the putatively successful claimant entirely past the post.

Mummery LJ—who was hearing the same appeal—referred to 'special circumstances' in that case, but it is not the only instance in which a modest 'win' by a claimant was regarded as being something else. In a clinical negligence case in which the claimant recovered £2,000 out of a claim for £525,000, May and Tomlinson LJJ (Jackson LJ dissenting[91]) found that this constituted a win on the part of the defendant.[92] In a different case, Mann J found that a defendant who was ordered to pay £6,750 in a claim for more than £7 million was the successful party (although ultimately, he found that other factors prevailed).[93] Other case examples exist.[94] **6.57**

---

[90] *Islam v Ali* [2003] EWCA Civ 612, at [23].

[91] This was primarily on the basis that the defendant ought to have made a Part 36 offer, which is what they would have done had they followed the pre-CPR authority of *Oksuzoglu v Kay* [1998] 2 All ER 361: see *Marcus v Medway Primary Care Trust* [2011] EWCA Civ 750, at [21].

[92] *Marcus v Medway Primary Care Trust* [2011] EWCA Civ 750.

[93] *Fulham Leisure Holdings Ltd v Nicholson Graham & Jones* [2006] EWHC 2428 (Ch).

[94] *Bajwa v British Airways* [1999] PIQR 152, at [38]; for an example of the court making no order for costs, see *Hooper v Biddle & Co* [2006] EWHC 2995 (Ch), *per* Susan Prevezer QC.

6.58 In a similar vein, Lord Bingham MR made the following observations:

> 'The judge must look closely at the facts of the particular case before him and ask: who, as a matter of substance and reality, has won? Has the plaintiff won anything of value which he could not have won without fighting the action through to a finish? Has the defendant substantially denied the plaintiff the prize which the plaintiff fought the action to win?'[95]

Lord Bingham's comments were made in the context of offers made without prejudice save as to costs, but there is no reason to believe that they would not also apply where the parties' positions are openly stated.

6.59 It is open to the court to find that there has been only a degree of success. In a somewhat extreme example regarding a personal injury claim, Patterson J found that a claimant who had been awarded 3 per cent of her claim was the winner.[96] At first blush, this might seem like a surprising conclusion, but Patterson J clarified her decision by saying this:

> '[One needs to take into account] the overall commercial realities of the case. For the claimant to receive 100% of her costs for recovering 3% of her claim does not, in the circumstances of this case, seem to me to be justified.'[97]

Thus the claimant had won, but ought not be entitled to all of her costs. There is nothing new about such an approach.[98] Warby J, however, took a different approach (in a commercial case in which the claimant had recovered only 5.93 per cent of the monies it claimed), finding that it may be appropriate to leave the issue of reducing costs to a costs judge on assessment.[99]

6.60 *Starting points where the defendant has not made any offers* Where a defendant is faced with a claim they believe to be significantly overvalued, it will not always be necessary to make an offer to avoid being condemned in costs; rather, the defendant might seek to rely on the notion that, at the end of the day, the court will ask itself, 'who, as a matter of substance and reality, has won?'[100] Whilst that may be appropriate where the defendant believes that it is likely that the claimant will be found to be guilty of culpable exaggeration,[101] it would be a risk-laden tactic in most claims. Likewise, whilst every defendant is aware of the need to keep offers under review (especially in cases involving expert evidence[102]), a failure in this regard will not inescapably result in an adverse order for costs. Where, for example, a low,

---

[95] *Roache v Newsgroup Newspapers Ltd* [1998] EMLR 161, at 168–9.

[96] This was, first, because the defendant had not made any effective offers, and secondly, because the claimant had to go to trial to get general damages: *Cutting v Islam* [2014] EWHC 1515 (QB), at [72], *per* Patterson J.

[97] *Ibid*, at [83].

[98] Whilst it is a pre-CPR decision relating to scale costs, see *Laurence and Laurence v Singh t/a K & T Investments* [1997] 1 Costs LR 58, at 62, *per* Leggatt LJ.

[99] See *Optical Express v Associated Newspapers (Costs)* [2017] EWHC 2707 (QB), at [39], *per* Warby J. It should be noted, however, that this was a case to which the provisions in CPR Part 36 applied. In a similar vein, see *Tiuta Plc v Rawlinson & Hunter (a firm)* [2016] EWHC 3480 (QB), *per* Andrew Baker J—also a case decided under the Part 36 regime, but in which no reduction was made for the fact that the claimant accepted £100,000 as against its claim for £45m.

[100] See *Marcus v Medway Primary Care Trust* [2011] EWCA Civ 750, at [46], *per* Tomlinson LJ, who cited *Roache v Newsgroup Newspapers Ltd* [1998] EMLR 161. See also *Hullock v East Riding of Yorkshire County Council* [2009] EWCA Civ 1039, at [32], *per* Patten LJ.

[101] See, eg, *Hullock v East Riding of Yorkshire County Council* [2009] EWCA Civ 1039, at [32], *per* Patten LJ.

[102] Whilst a pre-CPR case, see *Oksuzoglu v Kay* [1998] 2 All ER 361.

but protective offer could have been made, but would certainly not have been accepted, the act of making an offer may be thought of as being a mere matter of ritual; whilst such an approach is supported by authority,[103] not all judges agree that it is correct.[104]

Starting points where both parties have made offers A not uncommon scenario is that both parties turn out to have been overly optimistic in their Part 36 offers in that the claimant recovers more than the defendant had offered, but less than the claimant had offered to accept. Jackson LJ has explained that, in such a case, the claimant should normally be regarded as 'the successful party' because the claimant will have been forced to bring proceedings to recover the sum awarded.[105] **6.61**

Gauging success where there is (or will be) more than one trial

It may be that a party succeeds at a trial that is not the final trial. Where this is so and where it would be uncertain until the conclusion of the final trial who has won, then it would be proper for the court to defer making a decision as to the incidence of costs until the conclusion of the final trial. This may, for example, be appropriate if there is uncertainty as to whether the putatively successful claimant will recover more than merely nominal damages[106] (which would generally count as defeat[107]) or because an offer may need to be taken into account.[108] If, on the other hand, a subsequent trial would not have a bearing on the issues or on the degree of success already achieved by one or other party, then it may be appropriate to make an order without waiting for the final outcome.[109] As to issue-aware orders and split trials, see 6.194 and 6.209. **6.62**

Gauging success in commercial litigation

Commercial claims are often complex, not only in the sense that there is often a claim and a counterclaim, but also in the sense that there may be several components to each. Whilst very much the exception in commercial litigation (but not in other types of litigation[110]), circumstances may exist in which the claim and counterclaim may need to be considered separately for the purposes of determining who is the successful party,[111] but in general the measure of who has won is often who has been ordered to pay money to the other. Longmore LJ had this to say on the point: 'The most important thing is to identify **6.63**

---

[103] See *Anglo-Cyprian Trade Agencies Ltd v Paphos Wine Industries Ltd* [1951] 1 All ER 873, *per* Devlin J, cited with approval by Tomlinson LJ in *Marcus v Medway Primary Care Trust* [2011] EWCA Civ 750, at [51]. See also *Alltrans Express Ltd v CVA Holdings Ltd* [1983] 1 WLR 394, at 402, *per* Stephenson LJ, and at 404, *per* Griffiths LJ.

[104] See *Marcus v Medway Primary Care Trust* [2011] EWCA Civ 750, at [21], *per* Jackson LJ.

[105] *Fox v Foundation Piling Ltd* [2011] EWCA Civ 790, at [46]. In a similar vein, see *Flanagan v Liontrust Investment Partners LLP* [2016] EWHC 446 (Ch), in which Henderson J found that a claimant who had claimed £8 million, but recovered only £214,383, was still the winner in the context of the claimant having made an offer to accept £800,000 and the defendant having made an offer of only £50,000. That said, the claimant suffered heavy losses in his costs by virtue of having raised a number of unsuccessful issues.

[106] See, eg, *Weill v Mean Fiddler Holding Ltd* [2003] EWCA Civ 1058.

[107] See *Hyde Park Residence Ltd v Yelland* [1999] RPC 655, at 670, *per* Jacob J; *Marathon Asset Management LLP v Seddon* [2017] EWHC 479 (Comm), at [3], *per* Leggatt J.

[108] See, eg, *Multiplex Constructions (UK) Ltd v Cleveland Bridge (UK) Ltd* [2007] EWHC 659 (TCC), at [26].

[109] See, eg, *Unwired Planet International Ltd v Huawei Technologies Co Ltd* [2015] EWHC 3837 (Ch).

[110] See, eg, *Horth v Thompson* [2010] EWHC 1674 (QB).

[111] See, eg, *Lloyd v Svenby* [2002] EWHC 576 (QB), at [5], *per* Stanley Burnton J. The circumstances in that case that justified that approach were that the costs of the counterclaim were negligible.

the party who is to pay money to the other. That is the surest indication of success and failure.'[112]

6.64 Similarly, in a property claim concerning maintenance in which there was a claim and a counterclaim, Maurice Kay LJ confirmed that it would be wrong to say that the claim was 'all about the counterclaim'; rather, there was one dispute—namely, whether one party owed money to the other.[113]

6.65 Warren J has commented that the putatively unsuccessful party does not bear the burden of showing that the adoption of the general rule would be unjust: instead, it is for the court to consider all of the circumstances of the case and to make an order accordingly.[114]

6.66 **Gauging success in commercial claims that are not solely about damages** The approach as set out in 6.63 may not be appropriate where the claim is not for damages for past wrongs (such as a trademark dispute where the question is one of principle or a claim for an injunction), but even where this is so, it is usually possible to decide who has achieved the most advantageous commercial benefit.[115]

6.67 **Judge Coulson QC's guidance in *McGlinn* about gauging success in commercial cases** Judge Coulson QC (sitting as a deputy High Court judge) provided the following summary of the authorities relating to who has won and who has lost in commercial litigation:

> '[...]
> (a) The starting point for the exercise of the court's discretion is that costs follow the event[[116]] ... To work out who is the successful party, the court has to ask: "Who, as a matter of substance and reality, has won?"[[117]] ...
> (b) In a commercial case, it is important to identify which party is to pay money to the other[[118]] ... Where there has been a payment into court, it is important to see whether or not that payment into court has been beaten[[119]] ...
> (c) A defendant's failure to beat a payment into court will usually mean that he is treated by the court as the losing party, particularly if the case is not appropriate for an issue-based costs order[[120]] ... However, such failure may not always be regarded as decisive[[121]] ...
> (d) Depending on the facts, the court may treat a defendant who has failed to beat the payment into court as the successful party, or make no order as to costs; although it is

112 *AL Barnes Ltd v Time Talk (UK) Ltd* [2003] EWCA Civ 402, at [28]; see also *Pindell Ltd & Anor v Airasia Berhad (formerly known as Airasia SDN BHD)* [2010] EWHC 3238 (Comm), at [4]; *Burchell v Bullard & Ors* [2005] EWCA Civ 358, at [33]; *Day v Day* [2006] EWCA Civ 415 (which was not a commercial claim, but which was a claim about money); *Whitecap Leisure Ltd v John H Rundle Ltd* [2008] EWCA Civ 1026. The concept is not a new one: see, eg, *Baines v Bromley* (1881) 6 QBD 691.

113 *Villa Agencies Spf Ltd v Kestrel Travel Consultancy Ltd* (unreported), 17 January 2012, CA (Civ Div).

114 See *Southern Counties Fresh Foods v RWM Purchasers Ltd* [2011] EWHC 1370 (Ch), at [12].

115 *L'Oreal SA v Bellure NV* (unreported), 27 July 2010, CA (Civ Div) (Jacob LJ and Sir David Keene); the substantive case was *L'Oreal SA v Bellure NV* [2010] EWCA Civ 535.

116 *Johnsey Estates (1990) Ltd v The Secretary of State for the Environment* [2001] EWCA Civ 535.

117 *Roache v Newsgroup Newspapers Ltd* [1998] EMLR 161; *Painting v University of Oxford* [2005] EWCA Civ 161.

118 *AL Barnes v Time Talk (UK) Ltd* [2003] EWCA Civ 402.

119 *Johnsey Estates (1990) Ltd v The Secretary of State for the Environment* [2001] EWCA Civ 535.

120 *Johnsey Estates (1990) Ltd v The Secretary of State for the Environment* [2001] EWCA Civ 535; *Firle v Datapoint* [2001] EWCA Civ 1106; *Jackson v The Ministry of Defence* [2006] EWCA Civ 46.

121 *Bajwa v British Airways* [1999] PIQR 152.

not possible to list all the circumstances in which this may be appropriate, they might include the situation where the claimant has only just beaten the payment into court; where the payment into court reflected much more closely the amount eventually recovered, as compared to the amount claimed; where the claimant's conduct made it difficult or even impossible to make an effective payment in; and where the trial was largely devoted to the failure of the claimant's exaggerated case[[122]] ...

(e) It may not always be possible for the court to say, when considering the action as a whole, that one party should be regarded as the overall winner[[123]] ... Indeed, even if it is possible to identify one party as the successful party, it may still be appropriate, depending on the circumstances, to make an issue-based costs order, so as to give effect to the substance of the result and to move away from too rigid an application of the "follow the event principle".[[124]] ...

[...]'[125]

As can be seen from this analysis, it is necessary to take many factors into account when the issue of success is decided in commercial cases.

Broadly equal degrees of success In some cases, it can be said that both parties have benefited (or not) in equal measure and that the outcome is a draw. Where this is so, this would normally result in an order that there be no order for costs.[126] The points made at 6.56 and 6.59 may be relevant in that regard. Ward LJ has commented that, where there has been broadly equal success on both sides and both sides have conducted themselves badly, the court would be fully entitled to visit a plague on both their houses and cast them away with no order for costs.[127] **6.68**

Gauging success in cases in which nominal damages are awarded In a commercial case, a judgment for only nominal damages is generally regarded as being a defeat. The position was trenchantly put by Jacob J in the following way (albeit in a pre-CPR case): **6.69**

> 'It seems to me that the whole question of nominal damages is at the end of this century far too legalistic. A plaintiff who recovers only nominal damages has in reality lost and in reality the defendant has established a complete defence.'[128]

Leggatt J has confirmed that the position is the same under the CPR, going on to say that if a claimant were to pursue a claim seeking only nominal damages, the claim could properly be struck out as an abuse of process on the ground that dealing with it would be a waste of court time and resources.[129] **6.70**

---

[122] *Bajwa v British Airways* [1999] PIQR 152; *Molloy v Shell UK Ltd* [2001] EWCA Civ 1272; *Islam v Ali* [2003] EWCA Civ 612; *Painting v University of Oxford* [2005] EWCA Civ 161.

[123] *Roache v Newsgroup Newspapers Ltd* [1998] EMLR 161.

[124] *AEI Rediffusion Music Ltd v Phonographic Performance Ltd* [1999] 1 WLR 1507; *Summit Property Ltd v Pitmans* [2002] EWCA Civ 2020; *Fulham Leisure Holdings Ltd v Nicholson Graham & Jones* [2006] EWHC 2428 (Ch); *National Westminster Bank plc v Angeli Kotonou* [2006] EWHC 1785 (Ch).

[125] *McGlinn v Waltham Contractors Ltd* [2005] EWHC 698 (TCC), at [89].

[126] See, eg, *Square Mile Partnership Ltd v Fitzmaurice McCall Ltd* [2006] EWHC 236 (Ch); see also the *obiter* comments of Mummery LJ in *Peakman v Linbrooke Services Ltd* [2008] EWCA Civ 1239. Whilst not a commercial case, see *Quarmby Construction Co Ltd v Office of Fair Trading* [2012] EWCA Civ 1552.

[127] *Cambertown Timber Merchants Ltd v Sidhu* [2011] EWCA Civ 1041, at [35].

[128] *Hyde Park Residence Ltd v Yelland* [1999] RPC 655, at 670; see also *Marathon Asset Management LLP v Seddon* [2017] EWHC 479 (Comm), at [3], *per* Leggatt J.

[129] *Ibid.*

The effect of costs on success and vice versa

6.71 A party's putative success may be diminished or negated by the fact that it has to pay costs (either to the other side or to its own lawyers). Two issues arise: first, whether the court should try to preserve a party's success by not condemning it in costs (see 6.72); and secondly, whether a party's liability for costs should be taken into account when deciding who has won (see 6.73). The short answer to both is 'no'.

6.72 **Putative preservation of a party's success** The application of the general rule will usually mean that a party who has been awarded damages will also be awarded costs. This means that the issue of diminution of damages by an award of costs will arise only where there is a proposed departure from the general rule, perhaps as a result of the otherwise successful party having lost on one or more issues. It would, generally speaking,[130] be wrong for the court to decline to make an issue-aware award on the supposed basis that doing so would diminish the otherwise successful party's damages. In this regard, Potter LJ found that a trial judge had been wrong to take into account the possibility that the claimant—who, in the case before him, had been awarded aggravated damages—might not get the full benefit of their award if an issue-aware award were made.[131]

6.73 **The effect of costs on success and 'near misses'** In some circumstances, the court may be asked to take into account the fact that a successful litigant has had to incur costs that are not recovered from a paying party; in particular, it may be said that if those costs are taken into account, the putatively successful party is not the real victor. Such an argument would almost always fail, other than as a background fact or makeweight point. In so far as Part 36 offers are concerned, this is for the reasons given at 17.86. In so far as other admissible offers are concerned, Ramsey J had this to say:

> 'I am doubtful that, on analysis, a "near miss" offer can generally add anything to what otherwise would be conduct in the form of unreasonable refusal to negotiate. To do so would ... seek to base an exercise in discretion on offers which neither party made at the time but which, with the benefit of hindsight, one party should have made and the other party should have accepted.'[132]

Ramsey J went on to make it clear that if there were an unreasonable failure to negotiate, that would be a factor that could be taken into account under CPR, r 44.2, as a general background fact.[133]

Partial success

6.74 'Partial success' is a phrase that will mean that one or both of the following is the case:

- a claimant has recovered much less than was claimed, or a defendant must pay an amount only modestly more than had been conceded; or
- a party has succeeded generally, but lost on a number of issues.

---

130 In family cases, however, decisions of the court as to financial matters as between the parties (including cost) should take into account the incidence of an order of costs and the effect upon the parties' means.

131 *Fleming v The Chief Constable of the Sussex Police Force* [2004] EWCA Civ 643.

132 *Hammersmatch Properties (Welwyn) Ltd v Saint-Gobain Ceramics & Plastics Ltd* [2013] EWHC 2227 (TCC), at [36], for reasons explained at [30]–[35]. See also *Sugar Hut Group Ltd v AJ Insurance Service (a partnership)* [2016] EWCA Civ 46, at [31], *per* Tomlinson LJ.

133 *Hammersmatch Properties (Welwyn) Ltd v Saint-Gobain Ceramics & Plastics Ltd* [2013] EWHC 2227 (TCC), at [36].

The first of these topics has already been addressed at 6.54–6.68; it is discussed further (in the context of exaggeration) at 6.144–6.155. The second topic is considered at 6.156–6.205.

Welamson doctrine

It is worth noting that, in some jurisdictions, a method known as the Welamson doctrine applies.[134] Greatly simplified, this means that if a party recovers half of that which was in dispute, that should be regarded as being half a loss and half a win, and, as such, the appropriate order should be no order for costs. Likewise, if the party recovers three-quarters of that which was in dispute, that should be regarded as being a quarter loss and three-quarters win, and, as such, that party should receive half of its costs. The Welamson doctrine is mentioned because other jurisdictions (including arbitral jurisdictions) have shown an interest in it.[135] It is possible that, at some stage, English courts will take an interest in it; one could argue that this would be an approach that would have resonance with the overriding objective, not least because (if offers and concessions were taken into account) it would be an added incentive for parties to narrow the gap, especially in commercial claims. **6.75**

Factors Other than the General Rule

CPR, r 44.2(4), imposes a mandatory requirement that the court should take into account factors other than the general rule. Those factors are: **6.76**

- conduct—that is, the conduct of all the parties (see 6.77);
- partial success and issues—that is, whether a party has succeeded on part of its case, even if it has not been wholly successful (see 6.74 and, in respect of issues, 6.156–6.205); and
- admissible offers—that is, any admissible offer to settle[136] made by a party that is drawn to the court's attention and which is not an offer to which cost consequences under Part 36 apply (see 6.207–6.243).

Conduct and the incidence of costs: general points

CPR, r 44.2(4)(a), provides that, in deciding what order (if any) to make about costs, the court will have regard to all of the circumstances, including the conduct of all of the parties (see 6.17). CPR, r 44.2(5), points to the following as being particularly relevant: **6.77**

- conduct before, as well as during, the proceedings and in particular the extent to which the parties followed the Practice Direction (Pre-action Conduct) or any relevant pre-action protocol;
- whether it was reasonable for a party to raise, pursue or contest a particular allegation or issue;
- the manner in which a party has pursued or defended its case or a particular allegation or issue; and
- whether a claimant who has succeeded in their claim, in whole or in part, exaggerated that claim.

---

134 See Welamson, L, 'Principer om rattegangskostnader under debatt' [1964] Festskrift Till Olivecrona 684; Gotanda, J, 'Awarding Costs and Attorneys' Fees in International Commercial Arbitrations' (1999) 21 Mich J Int'l L 1.

135 See, eg, Quick, R, *Quick on Costs* (Thomson Reuters, online), para 10.2361.

136 Prior to 1 April 2003, the CPR also expressly included any payment into court.

Conduct in general

6.78 It has long been established that, for the purposes of costs, the court is entitled to take into account the conduct of the parties, including pre-proceedings conduct (or 'anterior conduct', as it is sometimes known).[137] The CPR have not changed this.[138] Indeed, the emphasis on 'front loading' and on pre-action protocols has, if anything, heightened the importance of such issues, as has the 2013 amendment to the overriding objective (see Chapter 26).

6.79 The matter is best analysed by drawing a distinction between procedural and non-procedural conduct. There is no doubt that the former can be taken into account in all courts, but in so far as the latter is concerned, there seems to be a divergence between practice in the Commercial Court—a subdivision of the Queen's Bench Division—and the practices in other courts. Each of those types of case is considered in turn.

How conduct should be taken into account: order or assessment?

6.80 It is open to a trial judge to make an order that the costs judge is to determine issues relating to conduct; this may be appropriate where those issues are particularly numerous and detailed.[139] Nonetheless, whilst it used to be thought that a failure to raise such issues at the time the order was made would preclude those issues being raised during the detailed assessment,[140] it is now known that this is not correct. This is dealt with at 23.43–23.48. Notwithstanding this better understanding of the law, good practice requires that the trial judge is given opportunity to give directions that might assist the costs judge, and common sense dictates that this means that issues concerning conduct ought to be raised sooner rather than later.

6.81 Where a judge believes that costs are disproportionate, but nonetheless wishes to award that party only proportionate costs, it would be wrong in principle to make an order that costs be assessed subject to a cap, because such an order might deprive that party of costs proportionately incurred.[141] This topic is also addressed at 6.255.

Non-procedural conduct

6.82 The focus in this section is on pre-proceedings conduct. Whilst it may be an oversimplification to say that the Commercial Court tends to give less weight to the circumstances that led to the claim than do other courts, a complaint that a party brought litigation upon itself is less likely to find favour in that court than it would in other courts.

6.83 **Commercial Court** Longmore LJ (with whom Tuckey LJ agreed) said this:

> 'The relevant conduct must be conduct in the proceedings themselves ... It is not, in my view, proper to disallow a successful party her costs simply because of anterior dishonest conduct

[137] *Hall v Rover Financial Services Ltd (GB)* [2002] EWCA Civ 1514, at [18]. It was originally believed that there needed to be a 'good cause' for pre-proceedings conduct to displace the rule that costs follow the event (*Angus v Clifford* [1891] 2 Ch 449; *Harnett v Vise* (1880) 5 Ex D 30; *Bostock v Ransey UDC* [1900] 2 QB 616), but as long ago as the 1920s the House of Lords clarified that the court's discretion was unfettered in this respect (*Donald Campbell & Co Ltd v Pollak* [1927] AC 732).

[138] *Groupama Insurance Co Ltd v Aon Ltd* [2003] EWCA Civ 1846.

[139] See, eg, *Re Dalmar Properties Ltd*, sub nom *David Norman Kaye v Kingstars Ltd* [2008] EWHC 2753 (Ch).

[140] See *Aaron v Shelton* [2004] EWHC 1162 (QB), which is now known not to be good law.

[141] *SCT Finance v Bolton* [2002] EWCA Civ 56, at [36].

which, while it may have been a part of the transaction which gives rise to the proceedings, cannot be characterised as misconduct in relation to the proceedings themselves.'[142]

Commenting in a later case, Brooke LJ (with whom Latham and Butler-Sloss LJJ agreed) expressed doubt as to whether all of the relevant authorities had been drawn to Longmore LJ's attention. Brooke LJ did not go so far as to cast doubt on the correctness of what Longmore and Tuckey LJJ had said, preferring instead to distinguish the practice in the Commercial Court from the practices in other courts: **6.84**

> 'Longmore and Tuckey LJJ both have immense experience of practice in the Commercial Court, where issues of this kind arise very frequently, and in this passage Longmore LJ should be interpreted as doing no more than describing the contemporary practice of the judges of that court. In commercial transactions business people not infrequently do not follow the Queensberry Rules in their dealings with each other, but this in itself is not seen to be sufficient to deprive one of them, if successful in the ensuing litigation, of his costs of the litigation.'[143]

Other courts Brook LJ explained the practices in courts other than the Commercial Court in this way: **6.85**

> 'The philosophy of the Woolf Reforms is that the parties should lay their cards on the table as fully as possible and as early as possible, so that they can assess the desirability of a negotiated settlement (as against the risks of contested litigation) in a well-informed way. If they then decide to litigate (and to burden other parties with the costs of litigation), and to pursue the litigation to trial they must expect, as a general rule, to have to pay the costs of parties necessarily joined to the litigation if they lose.'[144]

Case examples are given at 6.102–6.107 (although they should not be given much weight for the reasons given at 6.20).

Is contributory negligence a relevant form of conduct? It could be argued that contributory negligence is a type of pre-proceedings conduct. The Civil Bench Book has the following to say on the topic: **6.86**

> 'As has always been the case, it is probable a proportion [of costs] only will be awarded in an accident claim where a claimant has been held to be partly responsible for what occurred, the starting point being a reduction equal to the percentage or proportion of the contributory negligence as found.'[145]

This guidance is rarely followed and may indeed be wrong (see 6.189).[146]

Fundamental dishonesty in personal injury claims The provisions that are discussed in the following paragraphs are in addition to those that govern fundamental dishonesty in the context of qualified one-way costs shifting (see 8.34–8.45). **6.87**

---

142 *Hall v Rover Financial Services Ltd (GB)* [2002] EWCA Civ 1514, at [18]. This was a case in which the claimant had been guilty of 'moral blindness' in the transaction that led to the claim.

143 *Groupama Insurance Co Ltd v Aon Ltd* [2003] EWCA Civ 1846, at [39].

144 *Ibid.*

145 The Civil Bench Book, para 8.14.

146 In support of the proposition that the guidance is wrong, see *Sonmez v Kebabery Wholesale Ltd* [2009] EWCA Civ 1386, at [22], *per* Ward LJ; *Onay v Brown* [2009] EWCA Civ 775, at [29], *per* Goldring LJ.

6.88 Fraud in the context of personal injury claims is anything but rare—especially in the context of low-velocity road traffic accidents (RTAs). The editors of Butterworths Personal Injury Litigation Service have this to say on the point:

> 'Typical frauds in road traffic accidents are: fabricated accidents, where there was never an accident; staged accidents, where a car slams on its brakes to engineer a rear-end shunt; phantom passengers, where there was an accident but the particular claimant was not present. Other variations include someone other than the driver later claiming to be the driver either in court or for the purposes of the medical report. The issue is made more difficult as a typical whiplash injury may well be diagnosed on self-reporting or the medical report may be prepared after recovery.'[147]

6.89 Section 57 of the Criminal Justice and Courts Act 2015 was enacted in an attempt to deal with these issues and has been in force since 13 April 2015.[148] The provision applies to proceedings started on or after that date[149] and reads as follows (limited to those provision that are relevant to the law of costs):

> '57 **Personal injury claims: cases of fundamental dishonesty**
>
> (1) This section applies where, in proceedings on a claim for damages in respect of personal injury ("the primary claim")—
> (a) the court finds that the claimant is entitled to damages in respect of the claim, but
> (b) on an application by the defendant for the dismissal of the claim under this section, the court is satisfied on the balance of probabilities that the claimant has been fundamentally dishonest in relation to the primary claim or a related claim.
>
> (2) The court must dismiss the primary claim, unless it is satisfied that the claimant would suffer substantial injustice if the claim were dismissed.
>
> (3) The duty under subsection (2) includes the dismissal of any element of the primary claim in respect of which the claimant has not been dishonest.
>
> (4) The court's order dismissing the claim must record the amount of damages that the court would have awarded to the claimant in respect of the primary claim but for the dismissal of the claim.
>
> (5) When assessing costs in the proceedings, a court which dismisses a claim under this section must deduct the amount recorded in accordance with subsection (4) from the amount which it would otherwise order the claimant to pay in respect of costs incurred by the defendant.'

6.90 Thus, if a claim falls within the ambit of this section, then, subject to a test of substantial injustice, the primary claim will be dismissed (including those parts of the claim that are not tainted by dishonesty) and costs putatively payable to the claimant will be reduced by the amount of damages that the court would have allowed had it not dismissed the primary claim. For obvious reasons, this means that s 57 will, in general, have teeth only in those cases in which only part of the claim (as opposed to the whole of the claim) was fraudulent; as a result, it will tend to be relevant only in cases of culpable exaggeration. That said, it is possible that it will also apply in other circumstances, such as where a driver's honest claim is tainted by the dishonesty of fraudulent claim brought by a passenger.

---

[147] Butterworths Personal Injury Litigation Service, ch 13, para 306.
[148] SI 2015/778, art 3, Sched 1, para 47.
[149] See Criminal Justice and Courts Act 2015, s 57(9).

There is no guidance in the legislation as to what is meant by 'fundamental dishonesty'— no doubt for the reasons given at 6.34 in the analogous situation of qualified one-way costs shifting. At the time of writing, there were no reported cases dealing specifically with fundamental dishonesty in the context of s 57, but the cases referred to at 8.34–8.45 dealing with qualified one-way costs shifting may apply by analogy. **6.91**

There were, at the time of writing, no decided cases of the test of substantial injustice, but it will no doubt be a high hurdle to clear. It is possible that dishonesty on the part of litigation friends who act on behalf of honest children or persons who lack capacity may suffice. **6.92**

Conduct relating to procedural matters

In contrast to non-procedural conduct, all courts are readily inclined to reflect procedural failings in their orders for costs. This, no doubt, will be no less common following the revision to the overriding objective in 2013 (see Chapter 26). The willingness to take procedural default into account relates both to pre-proceedings conduct and to conduct during the claim; indeed, the CPR specifically refer to the court taking into account conduct before the proceedings, including the extent to which the parties followed the Practice Direction (Pre-action Conduct) and any applicable pre-action protocol (see 6.77).[150] **6.93**

The court tends to look at the substance of the guidance given in the applicable protocol or direction, rather than its technical or semantic aspects. Akenhead J had the following to say on the topic: 'The Court should be slow to allow the rules to be used ... for one party to obtain a tactical or costs advantage where in substance the principles of the Protocol have been complied with.'[151] Paragraph 13 of the Practice Direction (Pre-action Conduct) now expressly refers to a similar test (see 6.96) and adds that the court is especially likely not be concerned about minor or technical infringements where the matter was urgent (for example an application for an injunction). **6.94**

Need to avoid double jeopardy

Where there has been a breach of a pre-action protocol, it is often appropriate to deal with that breach at an early stage in the litigation, thereby putting the parties back into the positions they would have been in had there not been a breach.[152] This would militate against the court reserving such issues until the conclusion of the litigation. Sir Henry Brooke has cautioned against double jeopardy; where a breach of a pre-action protocol has been put right and has been reflected in an interim costs order, the court should avoid reflecting the same breach in the final costs award.[153] **6.95**

The Practice Direction (Pre-action Conduct)

The Practice Direction (Pre-action Conduct) gives the following guidance (which has been edited to include only those provisions that relate to costs[154]): **6.96**

---

[150] See CPR, r 44.2(4)(a) and (5)(a).

[151] *TJ Brent Ltd v Black & Veatch Consulting Ltd* [2008] EWHC 1497 (TCC), at [45] (pre-*Denton*, but likely to remain good law). See also Practice Direction (Pre-Action Conduct), para 4.3(1).

[152] *Charles Church Developments Ltd v Stent Foundations Ltd* [2007] EWHC 855 (TCC), *per* Ramsey J; see also *Daejan Investments Ltd v The Park West Club Ltd* [2004] BLR 223.

[153] *Thornhill v Nationwide Metal Recycling Ltd* [2011] EWCA Civ 919, at [47].

[154] Before 9 April 2009, similar, but not identical, guidance was given in the Practice Direction (Protocols); if the conduct under consideration occurred before that date, it may be appropriate to refer to the contemporaneous requirements, where appropriate. There are, however, no transitional provisions in this regard.

'**Compliance with this Practice Direction and the Protocols**

13. If a dispute proceeds to litigation, the court will expect the parties to have complied with a relevant pre-action protocol or this Practice Direction. The court will take into account non-compliance when giving directions for the management of proceedings (see CPR 3.1(4) to (6)) and when making orders for costs (see CPR 44.3(5)(a)). The court will consider whether all parties have complied in substance with the terms of the relevant pre-action protocol or this Practice Direction and is not likely to be concerned with minor or technical infringements, especially when the matter is urgent (for example an application for an injunction).

14. The court may decide that there has been a failure of compliance when a party has—
(a) not provided sufficient information to enable the objectives in paragraph 3 to be met;
(b) not acted within a time limit set out in a relevant protocol, or within a reasonable period; or
(c) unreasonably refused to use a form of ADR, or failed to respond at all to an invitation to do so.

15. Where there has been non-compliance with a pre-action protocol or this Practice Direction, the court may order that
(a) the parties are relieved of the obligation to comply or further comply with the pre-action protocol or this Practice Direction;
(b) the proceedings are stayed while particular steps are taken to comply with the pre-action protocol or this Practice Direction;
(c) sanctions are to be applied.

16. The court will consider the effect of any non-compliance when deciding whether to impose any sanctions which may include—
(a) an order that the party at fault pays the costs of the proceedings, or part of the costs of the other party or parties;
(b) an order that the party at fault pay those costs on an indemnity basis;
[...]'

6.97 The reference to para 3 is to the following:

'3. Before commencing proceedings, the court will expect the parties to have exchanged sufficient information to—
(a) understand each other's position;
(b) make decisions about how to proceed;
(c) try to settle the issues without proceedings;
(d) consider a form of Alternative Dispute Resolution (ADR) to assist with settlement;
(e) support the efficient management of those proceedings; and
(f) reduce the costs of resolving the dispute.'

6.98 Thus the court may ask a non-compliant party to explain its conduct. The court will look at the effect of the non-compliance, but will not be overly concerned about minor or technical shortcomings.

6.99 The precursor to the current Practice Direction–Pre-action Conduct used to provide that proportionality may be taken into account. The current Practice Direction now contains the following, more expansive, guidance:

'**Proportionality**

4. A pre-action protocol or this Practice Direction must not be used by a party as a tactical device to secure an unfair advantage over another party. Only reasonable and proportionate

steps should be taken by the parties to identify, narrow and resolve the legal, factual or expert issues.

5. The costs incurred in complying with a pre-action protocol or this Practice Direction should be proportionate (CPR 44.3(5)). Where parties incur disproportionate costs in complying with any pre-action protocol or this Practice Direction, those costs will not be recoverable as part of the costs of the proceedings.'

Where there is a pre-action protocol

A list of pre-action protocols may be found at 4.58. A number specifically provide that non-compliance may lead to costs sanctions being imposed. The Pre-action Protocol for Construction and Engineering Disputes, for example, says that a failure by a defendant to clarify at an early stage that it is the 'wrong' defendant may be taken into account. Another example is that a defendant in a clinical negligence claim may face sanctions for not supplying clinical records in a timely fashion.[155] **6.100**

Where there is no pre-action protocol

There are general provisions relating to claims not covered by specific pre-action protocols; in so far as those provisions mention costs at all, they do so by cautioning against excessive costs (see 6.97 and 6.99). **6.101**

Case examples relating to conduct The following are case examples of conduct being reflected in the incidence of costs (both pre-proceedings and during proceedings). Some relate to procedural default and others relate to non-procedural conduct. They are nothing more than examples and should not be regarded as setting any form of precedent. In particular, the editor has intentionally selected cases that are unusual or out of the norm because such cases illustrate the bounds of the court's reaction to certain wrongdoings. If any of the following paragraphs are cited to any court, this fact ought to be drawn to the court's attention. It cannot be overemphasised that each case has to be decided on its own facts and that decisions in other cases are of only limited assistance (see 6.20). Moreover, many of the examples pre-date the changes made in 2013 to the overriding objective and this ought to be borne in mind. **6.102**

Criminality **6.103**

- **Murder** Whilst an extreme example, where a husband succeeded in his claim in respect of property jointly owned with his wife, he was deprived of his costs by reason of the fact that he had murdered her.[156]
- **Fraud** In a similar vein, a defendant in a criminal matter was denied an individual costs award (which is a matter to which the CPR apply) because he had engaged in the systemic dishonest abuse of various persons—this being despite the fact that he was acquitted of the actual offences of which he was charged.[157] (For a discussion of fraud in the context of qualified one-way costs shifting, see 8.34–8.45; see also 6.87 for a discussion of fraud in personal injury cases.)

---

[155] Pre-Action Protocol for the Resolution of Clinical Disputes, para 3.12.

[156] *McMinn v McMinn* [2003] 2 FLR 823.

[157] *In the matter of Olden v Crown Prosecution Service* [2010] EWCA Civ 961.

6.104 *Reprehensible conduct*

- **Reckless attitude to the mitigation of costs** A systemic or reckless attitude to mitigation of costs is conduct that is capable of being conduct that is taken into account.[158]

6.105 *Collateral purposes*

- **Prolonging litigation for collateral purposes** If litigation is prolonged for collateral purposes, this may sound in costs; thus, in an appeal that was pursued all the way to a hearing before the Court of Appeal despite the fact that the respondent had conceded the matter, Davis LJ condemned the appellant in costs to reflect the fact that the litigation had been prolonged in an attempt to obtain certain documentation that was irrelevant to the appeal.[159]

6.106 *Failure to send letter of claim, to respond to letter of claim (and delay)*

- **No letter of claim** In a case in which no letter of claim had been sent, Morritt V-C ordered the 'successful' claimants—if that is the correct word—not only to pay the defendant's costs, but also to do so on the indemnity basis.[160] That was an exceptional case on its facts, but Judge Hacon has explained that it is virtually always appropriate for a claimant to write a letter before action even if there is no reasonable expectation that there will be any sensible response.[161]
- **Late response to letter of claim** In a case concerning a well-resourced defendant (that is, the state), Park J discounted its costs by 15 per cent to take account of the fact that the response to a letter had been issued about six weeks later than it should have been according to the applicable pre-action protocol.[162] Being late in providing a response will usually sound in the amount of costs rather than the incidence of costs in principle, this being a reflection of the fact that the claimant will have to read into the matter again if a long period of time is allowed to lapse before they receive a response.[163]
- **The relevance of overwork** The fact that a person may be overworked and was putatively not able to respond to correspondence tends not to be a factor that can properly be taken into account.[164]

6.107 *Prematurity and aggression*

- **Aggressive correspondence** Aggressive conduct on the part of a party who goes on to lose may be reflected in a costs order, and may contribute to an award on the indemnity

[158] See, eg, *Abbott v Long* [2011] EWCA Civ 874, at [15] and [17], in which Arden LJ said that a reckless attitude to mitigation of costs (such as where a serial litigant repeatedly incurs expenses without taking any steps to minimise their expenditure) may be relevant in that it may justify the court making a reduction to the costs that is not necessarily limited to the increase in costs that that conduct had caused. In this regard, Arden LJ referred to *Widlake v BAA* [2009] EWHC Civ 1256, at [41], *per* Ward LJ; *Walsh v Singh* [2011] EWHC Civ 80, at [25], *per* Arden LJ.

[159] See *Colwill v European Heritage Ltd* [2014] EWCA Civ 238, at [23]–[25], *per* Davis LJ.

[160] *Phoenix Finance Ltd v Federation Internationale de l'Automobile* [2002] EWHC 1028 (Ch).

[161] *Baxter Healthcare Ltd v Fresenius Kabi Deutschland GmBH* [2014] EWHC 3021 (IPEC), at [23], *per* Judge Hacon.

[162] *Aegis Group plc v Inland Revenue Commissioners* [2005] EWHC 1468 (Ch).

[163] *Thompson (a minor) & Ors v Bruce* [2011] EWHC 2228 (QB), at [58], *per* John Leighton Williams QC (sitting as a deputy judge of the High Court).

[164] *R (on the application of) Bahta & Ors v Secretary of State for the Home Department & Ors* [2011] EWCA Civ 895, at [60], *per* Pill LJ.

basis (see 16.49). Whilst each case will be decided on its own facts, Longmore LJ found that it was permissible for a successful litigant to be deprived of her costs solely by reason of the fact that she had engaged in correspondence that was deplorable in its tone and worthy of condemnation.[165] However, Lord Neuberger has urged restraint in that regard.[166]

- **Aggressive prematurity** Aggression and prematurity on the part of the successful party may result in an adjustment to the incidence of costs,[167] but it is the conduct of both sides that is relevant, including the reaction of an opponent. Thus if a defendant's reaction to supposedly premature issue of a claim is not to react straight away, but to wait and then to deny liability, the putative prematurity would be irrelevant.[168] (For premature issue in the context of fixed costs, see 50.97–50.100.)
- **Aggressive pursuance of costs** An overly aggressive attitude towards the recovery of costs can backfire and is capable of contributing to an adverse costs award, or even an adverse costs award on the indemnity basis.[169]
- **Abusive proceedings** In a case in which the claimant had brought an abusive claim, Tugdenhat J ruled the defendant should not have its costs pre-issue because it would not have been able to seek an order for those costs if the abusive claim had not been brought.[170] This somewhat at odds with the way in which such costs are treated on an assessment (see 49.147–49.150) and, as such, is perhaps best regarded as being an illustration of the fact that each case must be determined on its own facts.
- **Unreasonable issuance of a statutory demand** In a case in which a firm of solicitors had caused costs to be incurred by issuing a statutory demand against a former client in circumstances in which they ought to have known that she was pursuing an appeal that may have negated their entitlement to the monies sought, Barling J found that the solicitors' actions had been unreasonable and ordered them to pay costs accordingly.[171]
- **Obstructive or oppressive conduct** If a party acts oppressively in relation to practical arrangements (such as venues[172]), then that may sound in costs.

Fabricating evidence and dishonest cases **6.108**

- **Fabricated evidence** In a case in which a successful claimant had fabricated evidence, Mr Nicholas Davidson QC (sitting as a deputy judge of the Chancery Division) deducted £20,000 from her costs to take account of that behaviour (and to take account of the fact that she had failed to take advantage of a sensible opportunity to negotiate).[173] Whilst rarely invoked in practice, there is also the possibility of sanctions relating to misconduct under CPR, r 44.11.

---

165 *Lawal v Northern Spirit* (unreported), 19 February 2004, CA (Civ Div) (Longmore, Laws and Peter Gibson LJJ).

166 *Miller v Associated Newspapers Ltd* [2017] UKSC 33, at [70].

167 See, eg, *Pathology Group v Reynolds* (unreported), 28 November 2011, QBD, *per* HHJ Seymour QC (sitting as a judge of the High Court).

168 See *Roper v Auckland Risk Advisors Ltd* (unreported), 5 September 2011, QBD, *per* Eder J.

169 *Hudson v New Media Holding Co LLC* [2011] EWHC 3068 (QB), at [30], *per* Eady J.

170 *Citation Plc v Ellis Whittam Ltd* [2012] EWHC 764 (QB), at [28].

171 *Dunhill v Hughmans (a firm)* [2017] EWHC 2073 (Ch).

172 See, eg, *Pearse v Lord* [2015] EWHC 3046 (Ch), *per* Barling J, in which a modest reduction was made to reflect the 'marginally oppressive conduct' in relation to venues.

173 *Gil v Baygreen Properties Ltd* [2004] EWHC 2029 (Ch).

- **Knowingly advancing an exaggerated claim** A party who might otherwise have been awarded costs on the indemnity basis may lose that benefit if found guilty of knowingly advancing a false case.[174] (See also 'culpable exaggeration' at 6.149–6.153.)

6.109 *Departing from industry practice and from guidelines*

- **Departure from industry norms** Brooke LJ penalised a litigant for having altered a fax contrary to acceptable market practice.[175]
- **Directors' poor conduct** Breach of a director's duty and dishonest assistance may be taken into account when making a costs order.[176]
- **Failure to raise the possibility of arbitration** Where a party wrongly failed to raise the possibility of arbitration in a case in which that would have been expected and required, Coulson J found that that was a factor that the court was able to take into account.[177]
- **Departure from own guidelines** If an organisation departs from its own guidelines, that may result in an adverse costs order.[178]
- **Failure to apply complaints procedure** A failure on the part of a defendant police force to keep up to date with a complaint that had been made by the claimant was found to be a factor that could be taken into account.[179]

6.110 *Allowing an opponent to proceed on an incorrect footing*

- **Defendant's failure to correct an opponent** A well-resourced defendant had allowed a litigant in person to proceed on a mistaken understanding as to which regulations applied. The defendant succeeded, but Jack J ordered that its costs be discounted by a fixed sum (£5,000) to take account of that conduct.[180] Whilst now a very old authority decided under a regime other than CPR, r 44.2,[181] Lord Sterndale MR has commented that because a defendant is brought into litigation against its will and therefore has less control over matters than a claimant, less weight should be attributed to such conduct on the part of a defendant.[182]

6.111 *Refusal to pay costs properly incurred*

- A refusal to pay costs properly incurred may itself be justification for an award of costs,[183] but the failure to pay needs to be relevant to the matter in hand and, as such, it would be

---

[174] See, eg, *Bank of Tokyo-Mitsubishi UFJ Ltd v Baskan Gida Sanayi Ve Pazarlama AS* [2009] EWHC 1696 (Ch), *per* Briggs J; see also *Digicel (St Lucia) v Cable & Wireless plc* [2010] EWHC 774 (Ch), *per* Morgan J.

[175] *Groupama Insurance Co Ltd v Aon Ltd* [2003] EWCA Civ 1846.

[176] *Grupo Torras SA v Sheikh Fahad Mohammed Al-Sabah* [1999] CLC 1469, QBD.

[177] *Bovis Homes Ltd v Kendrick Construction Ltd* [2009] EWHC 1359 (TCC).

[178] See, eg, *Atkins (deceased) v Revenue & Customs Commissioners* [2011] UKFTT 468 (TC), in which HHJ N Nowlan awarded costs against HM Revenue & Customs on the basis that it had failed to follow its own guidelines, thereby incurring expense unnecessarily.

[179] *Zapello v Chief Constable of Sussex Police* [2010] EWCA Civ 1417.

[180] *Wright v HSBC Bank plc* [2006] EWHC 1473 (Admin).

[181] Specifically, the regime (RSC Ord 65, r 1, in its pre-1929 guise) involved a test of whether there was 'good cause' to deprive the successful party of its costs.

[182] *Ritter v Godfrey* [1920] 2 KB 47, at 52.

[183] Although a very old case, *Thomas v Palin* (1882) 21 Ch D 360 illustrates this fact that, in an appropriate case, it may be reasonable to issue proceedings solely for the purposes of asking the court to rule on the recoverability of disputed costs.

in only exceptional circumstances that an award would reflect the late payment of costs in another application.[184]

6.112 *Pouncing on oversights*

- Taking advantage of an opponent by pouncing on a procedural mishap may result in an adverse costs award.[185] In this regard, it is relevant that procedural mishaps can often be remedied by consent and with the party not at fault being awarded its costs,[186] although the way in which the post-2013 overriding objective is interpreted may limit this in future.

6.113 *Failure to give disclosure and failure to give evidence*

- **Failing to give disclosure** A failure to give disclosure at an appropriate stage is capable of giving rise to adverse costs orders: Judge Simon Brown QC (sitting as a deputy judge of the High Court) halved a successful party's costs to take account of such conduct.[187] Contrary examples exist, however: whilst in a context other than the exercise of discretion under CPR, r 44.2,[188] Floyd J commented that a party may escape criticism for not having accelerated its disclosure if resolution of the factual dispute between the parties would not have disposed of the claim generally.[189]
- **Exercise of a right to silence** Whilst a criminal case, the European Court of Human Rights has ruled that it would not be a breach of Art 6 of the European Convention on Human Rights (ECHR) for the court to take into account the fact that a defendant had exercised a right of silence.[190] There is no reason to believe that it would be a breach of Art 6 if the court were to take into account the fact that a party has chosen not to give evidence. Similarly, it is, in principle, open to a party to claim that the reason they did not make a suitable Part 36 offer is because their opponent did not provide certain requisite information (see immediately below).[191]
- **Refusal to give information** If a party unreasonably refuses to give information, then this may be a factor that the court can take into account.[192]

6.114 *Procedural failures*

- **Wrong court** Judge Purle QC (sitting as a judge of the High Court) has said that the fact that a case should have been started in or transferred to some other court

[184] *Hoque v Ali* [2012] EWCA Civ 274.

[185] Whilst it did not relate to pre-proceedings conduct, Coulson J took a dim view of a party who had sought judgment in default when it was known that an extension was being sought: see *Roundstone Nurseries Ltd v Stephenson Holdings Ltd* [2009] EWHC 1431 (TCC).

[186] See, eg, *Hannigan v Hannigan* [2000] EWCA Civ 159.

[187] *Earles v Barclays Bank plc* [2009] EWHC 2500 (QB), *per* HHJ Simon Brown QC.

[188] The context was whether to depart from the default position that a person who has discontinued should pay costs: see 7.112 *et seq*.

[189] See *Mobiqa Ltd v Trinity Mobile Ltd* [2010] EWHC 253 (Pat), at [25]. It was clear that there were other factors at play in that case and, in particular, the defendant had explained its case with great clarity.

[190] *Ashendon and Jones v United Kingdom*, The Times, 22 September 2011. The Court was careful to point out that the findings of the trial court were phrased in such a way as to make it clear that the costs award did not imply a suspicion that the defendant might have committed the offence.

[191] See *Brit Inns Ltd (in liquidation) v BDW Trading Ltd* [2012] EWHC 2489 (TCC), at [49], *per* Coulson J.

[192] See, eg, *Nelsons Yard Management Co v Eziefula* [2013] EWCA Civ 235.

having a no or low costs regime can have a very decisive effect on the costs order made.[193]

- **Failing to deal with budgets correctly** A failure to serve or file a costs budget may sound in costs.[194] Specific restrictions may apply (see CPR, r 3.14).

6.115 *Prolixity*

- **Grandstanding** Whilst it was only one of many factors he took into account, Peter Smith J has explained that where a party uses its witness statements as being a platform for arguing its case (rather than merely as a platform for presenting its evidence), that is a factor that can be taken into account:

> 'The purpose of my criticism is to put down a marker for all of the legal profession to take on board, that witness statements are supposed to be live evidence of witnesses. Drafting long witness statements with craggy submissions and masses of documents and then, in effect, throwing those witnesses to the wolves without preparing them is one of the many failings of the use of witness statements.'[195]

- **Overly elaborate evidence** Whilst not a source of law, the Chancery Guide gives the following guidance:

> 'It is incumbent on solicitors and counsel not to allow the costs of preparation of witness statements to be unnecessarily increased by over-elaboration of the statements. Any unnecessary elaboration may be the subject of a special order as to costs.'[196]

6.116 *Amendments, late amendment and repeated amendments*

- **Amendments generally** The party who is seeking an amendment will usually be ordered to pay costs of and occasioned by the amendment, but this is not always the case. In particular, if a party unreasonably opposes an amendment, they may be penalised in costs.[197] Whilst each case must be decided on its own facts, Rix LJ has explained that the amendment will, in general, be a factor to the issue of who pays costs only if (a) the amendment 'substantially alter[ed] the case the defendant ha[d] to meet' and (b) without the amendment 'the action [would have] fail[ed]'.[198] Even where those conditions are met, there may be reasons for not adjusting the costs.[199] Where appropriate, it would be open to the court to make a percentage order,[200] and that is a not an uncommon outcome where there has been significant overlap between the work the defendant has done and the work they will have to do to meet the amended case.[201]

---

193 See *Pendle Metalwares Ltd v Walter Page (Safeway's) Ltd* [2014] EWHC 1144 (Ch), at [6].

194 See, eg, *Simpson v MGN Ltd* [2015] EWHC 126 (QB).

195 *A&E Television Networks LLC v Discovery Communications Europe Ltd* [2013] EWHC 276 (Pat), at [18].

196 The Chancery Guide 2017, appx 9, para 19.7 (at p 81).

197 *La Chemise Lacoste SA v Sketchers USA Ltd* [2006] EWHC 3642 (Ch).

198 *Chadwick v Hollingsworth (No 2)* [2010] EWHC 2718, at [26].

199 An example of this is to be found in *Kaines (UK) Ltd v Osterreichische Wdrrenhandelsgesellschaft (formerly CGL Handelsgesellschaft mbH)* [1993] 2 Lloyds Rep 1, at 9, in which the judge was satisfied that even if the amendment had been made earlier, the action would have been vigorously resisted.

200 *Professional Information Technology Consultants Ltd v Jones* [2001] EWCA Civ 2103.

201 See, eg, *Cutting v Islam* [2014] EWHC 1515 (QB), at [69]–[74], [82] and [84], *per* Patterson J.

- **Failure to state case** In particular, a party's failure properly to state their case is capable of leading to that party being deprived of costs (in addition to the costs of the amendment), or may even lead to that party having to pay costs.[202]
- **Late amendments** Timing may be important. As a general rule, where a claimant makes a late amendment, the defendant is entitled to the costs of the claim down to the date of the amendment;[203] very late amendments may sound in costs to a significant degree.[204] It may be inappropriate to make an order at the time that permission is given for the amendment because the court may not be able to take offers into account; the better solution may be to reserve costs.[205] Indeed, this may be appropriate even where there are no offers.[206]
- **Numerous amendments** The number of amendments may be a relevant factor. Whilst he was concerned with the summary assessment of costs, Akenhead J has made it clear that re-amendments, particularly involving appeals and particularly involving repeat re-amendments, can have a very substantial effect on costs.[207] There is no reason to believe that the court could not take such matters into account at the stage of deciding the incidence of costs.

Putatively good conduct and cooperation 6.117

- **A high degree of cooperation** Where the parties cooperate to a high degree, it is possible that their conduct could give rise to a tacit understanding that there will be no order for costs in respect of the issues over which they are cooperating.[208]
- **Good conduct** Whilst not binding, Judge Graham Jones has found that an assertion that good conduct should be reflected in the incidence of costs was novel and unsupported by authority.[209]

Conduct and the incidence of costs: refusal to engage in ADR

The present state of the law has been pithily summed up by Akenhead J thus: '[T]he real question is did [the party in question] act unreasonably in refusing ADR?'[210] If the answer to that question is in the affirmative, then the party at fault may suffer adverse costs consequences (including, in cases in which aggravating circumstances exist, being condemned to pay costs on the indemnity basis).[211] Issues concerning the basis of costs are dealt with in Chapter 16. 6.118

---

[202] See, eg, *Gold v Mincoff Science & Gold* [2004] EWHC 2036 (Ch).

[203] See *Chadwick v Hollingsworth (No 2)* [2010] EWHC 2718, at [25], in which Rix LJ quoted Stuart-Smith LJ's analysis in *Beoco Ltd v Alfa Laval Co Ltd* [1995] QB 137, at 154 and 156, with approval. For examples of this principle being considered under the CPR, see *Magical Marking Ltd v Ware & Kay LLP* [2013] EWHC 636, at [14], and *Cutting v Islam* [2014] EWHC 1515 (QB), at [61], *per* Patterson J.

[204] See, eg, *Cooper v Thameside Construction Co Ltd* [2016] EWHC 1694 (TCC), *per* Carr J.

[205] *Chadwick v Hollingsworth (No 2)* [2010] EWHC 2718 (QB), at [30], *per* Rix LJ (sitting in the QBD).

[206] See, eg, *Illumina Inc v Premaitha Health plc* [2016] EWHC 1726 (Pat).

[207] *Co-operative Group Ltd v Birse Development Ltd* [2013] EWHC 3352 (TCC), at [9], *per* Akenhead.

[208] See, eg, *JSC BTA Bank v Solodchencko* (unreported), 23 January 2012, Ch D, *per* Henderson J.

[209] See *Various Claimants v Gower Chemicals Ltd* (unreported), 27 August 2010, Cardiff County Court, at [29], *per* HHJ Graham Jones.

[210] *Corby Group Litigation* [2009] EWHC 2109 (TCC), at [23].

[211] See, eg, *Garritt-Critchley v Ronnan* [2014] EWHC 1774 (Ch), *per* Judge Waksman QC (sitting as a judge of the High Court), in which the party who refused had accepted a Part 36 at a very late stage. As a contrasting case, see *Murray v Bernard* [2015] EWHC 2395 (Ch), *per* Mann J.

Early cases under the CPR

6.119 An indication that a refusal to engage in ADR could have adverse costs consequences was given by the Court of Appeal as early as 2002.[212] Whilst detailed guidance was not given, Brooke LJ made the following comments that forewarned of what was to come:

> 'It is to be hoped that any publicity given to this part of the judgment of the court will draw the attention of lawyers to their duties to further the overriding objective in the way that is set out in Part 1 of the Rules and to the possibility that, if they turn down out of hand the chance of alternative dispute resolution when suggested by the court, as happened on this occasion, they may have to face uncomfortable costs consequence.'[213]

Brooke LJ was right to say that his comments would attract publicity: for a period of time, there was widespread anxiety that a refusal to mediate would generally result in adverse costs consequences, with some commentators even going so far as to say that a refusal to mediate would give rise to a formal presumption in that regard.[214] It soon became apparent, however, that there was no such presumption.

6.120 What there was, however, was a realisation that an unprincipled or unreasonable refusal to mediate was a high-risk strategy. Lightman J—also speaking in 2002—was the first to articulate this:

> 'If mediation can have no real prospect of success a party may, with impunity, refuse to proceed to mediation on this ground. But refusal is a high risk course to take, for if the court finds that there was a real prospect, the party refusing to proceed to mediation may ... be severely penalised. Further, the hurdle in the way of a party refusing to proceed to mediation on this ground is high, for in making this objective assessment of the prospects of mediation, the starting point must surely be the fact that the mediation process itself can and does often bring about a more sensible and more conciliatory attitude ...'[215]

On the facts of the case before him, which he said were 'quite exceptional', Lightman J found that the defendant had acted reasonably in refusing mediation.

6.121 At about the same time, Park J noted that an 'offer' to mediate could be little more than a tactical step. He had this to say on the point:

> 'In my judgment it would be a grave injustice to [the party who seeks costs] to deprive them of any part of their costs on the ground that they declined [the other party's] self-serving invitations (demands would be a more accurate word) to participate in the mediation.'[216]

There followed several cases in which the court declined to visit adverse costs consequences on a party who refused to mediate.

The guidance in Halsey v Milton Keynes General NHS Trust

6.122 In 2004, things changed. This is because Dyson LJ (giving judgment of a court comprising Ward and Laws LJJ) gave guidance on the topic in the seminal case of *Halsey v Milton Keynes General NHS Trust*.[217] In essence, the touchstone was a test of reasonableness, pursuant to

---

212 *Dunnett v Railtrack plc* [2002] EWCA Civ 303.

213 *Ibid*, at [18].

214 See, eg, 'The CPR Regime Five Years on' (2004) 154 NLJ 7126, at 644–5.

215 *Hurst v Leeming* [2002] EWHC 1051 (Ch), at [15].

216 *Société Internationale de Télécommunications Aéronautiques SC v Wyatt Co (UK) Ltd* [2002] EWHC 2401 (Ch), at [16].

217 [2004] EWCA Civ 576.

which the unsuccessful party would bear the burden of showing that the successful party's refusal to mediate was unreasonable. The guidance in *Halsey* has been summarised by Jack J in the following way:

> '(a) A party cannot be ordered to submit to mediation as that would be contrary to Article 6 of the European Convention on Human Rights ...
> (b) The burden is on the unsuccessful party to show why the general rule of costs following the event should not apply, and it must be shown that the successful party acted unreasonably in refusing to agree to mediation ...
> (c) A party's reasonable belief that he has a strong case is relevant to the reasonableness of his refusal, for otherwise the fear of cost sanctions may be used to extract unmerited settlements ...
> (d) Where a case is evenly balanced ... a party's belief that he would win should be given little or no weight in considering whether a refusal was reasonable ... his belief must be unreasonable ...
> (e) The cost of mediation is a relevant factor ...
> (f) Whether the mediation had a reasonable prospect of success is relevant to the reasonableness of a refusal to agree to mediation ...
> (g) In considering whether the refusal to agree to mediation was unreasonable it is for the unsuccessful party to show that there was a reasonable prospect that the mediation would have been successful ...
> (h) Where a party refuses to take part in mediation despite encouragement from the court to do so, that is a factor to be taken into account ...
> (i) Public bodies are not in a special position ...'[218]

The Court of Appeal identified certain factors that have now achieved something akin to 'checklist' status,[219] albeit not an exhaustive one.[220] Those factors are: **6.123**

- the nature of the dispute (see 6.129);
- the merits of the case (see 6.130);
- the extent to which other settlement methods had been attempted (see 6.133);
- whether the costs of ADR were disproportionately high (see 6.134);
- delay and associated matters (see 6.136); and
- whether ADR had a reasonable prospect of success (see 6.137).

Putative presumptions and the burden of proof

There is no presumption operating against a party who refuses mediation;[221] indeed, the burden is on the unsuccessful party to show why there should be a departure from the general rule in CPR, r 44.2(2)(a). Dyson LJ had this to say on the topic: '[T]he fundamental principle is that such departure is not justified unless it is shown (the burden being on the unsuccessful party) that the successful party acted unreasonably in refusing to agree to ADR.'[222] **6.124**

It seems reasonable to conclude that, to an extent, the tables would be turned if the party who had refused mediation were the unsuccessful party. Put otherwise, if an unsuccessful **6.125**

---

[218] *Hickman v Blake Lapthorn* [2006] EWHC 12 (QB), [2006] All ER (D) 67, at [21].

[219] See, eg, *Northop Grumann Mission Systems Ltd v BAE Systems (al Diriyah C41) Ltd* [2014] EWHC 3148 (TCC), at [5], *per* Ramsey J.

[220] *Halsey v Milton Keynes General NHS Trust* [2004] EWCA Civ 576, at [16], *per* Dyson LJ.

[221] *Ibid*, at [19], *per* Dyson LJ.

[222] *Ibid*, at [13].

party were to seek to depart from the general rule for some reason, the fact that they had refused mediation would probably be a factor that would militate against that argument unless they were able to prove that the refusal was reasonable. It is likely, however, that the question would still be whether the refusal was unreasonable and that, whilst an unsuccessful party would be arguing from a position of weakness, the burden of proof would lie with the party who alleged unreasonable conduct.

The relevance of a party's response to an offer of mediation

6.126 The way in which a party responds to an offer of mediation may be relevant. Briggs LJ made the following comments about what a party should do if it believes that there are reasonable grounds for refusing to mediate:

> 'The ADR Handbook [[223]] ... sets out at length the steps which a party faced with a request to engage in ADR, but which believes that it has reasonable grounds for refusing to participate at that stage, should consider in order to avoid a costs sanction. The advice includes: (a) not ignoring an offer to engage in ADR; (b) responding promptly in writing giving clear and full reasons why ADR is not appropriate at the stage based if possible on the Halsey guidelines; (c) raising with the opposing party any shortage of information or evidence believed to be an obstacle to successful ADR together with consideration of how that shortage might be overcome; (d) not closing off ADR of any kind and for all time in case some other method than that proposed or ADR at some later date might prove to be worth pursuing. That advice may fairly be summarised as calling for constructive engagement in ADR rather than flat rejection, or silence. It is apparent from the footnotes that the authors drew heavily on the first instance decision in the present case ...'[224]

6.127 Briggs LJ dismissed the appeal in respect of a costs order that was adverse to a party who had declined mediation and went on to say:

> 'As is recognised by the weight placed on the judge's decision in the passage in the ADR Handbook to which I have referred, this case sends out an important message to civil litigants, requiring them to engage with a serious invitation to participate in ADR, even if they have reasons which might justify a refusal, or the undertaking of some other form of ADR, or ADR at some other time in the litigation. To allow the present appeal would, as it seems to me, blunt that message. The court's task in encouraging the more proportionate conduct of civil litigation is so important in current economic circumstances that it is appropriate to emphasise that message by a sanction which, even if a little more vigorous than I would have preferred, none the less operates pour encourager les autres ...'[225]

6.128 The following miscellaneous points may be made about the way in which parties may react to an invitation to mediate.

- **Simple refusal to mediate** Ward LJ (with whom Rix LJ agreed) had the following to say about how the court would deal with a party who shrugged aside a reasonable invitation to mediate:

  > 'The court has given its stamp of approval to mediation and it is now the legal profession which must become fully aware of and acknowledge its value. The profession can no longer

[223] Blake, S, *The Jackson ADR Handbook* (2nd edn, Oxford: Oxford University Press, 2016).
[224] *PGF II SA v OMFS Co 1 Ltd* [2013] EWCA Civ 1288, at [30].
[225] *Ibid*, at [56].

with impunity shrug aside reasonable requests to mediate ... [litigants] can expect little sympathy if they blithely battle on regardless of the alternatives.'[226]

- That said, Patten LJ (in a more recent case) had this to say:

  'Speaking for myself, I have some difficulty in accepting that the desire of a party to have his rights determined by a court of law in preference to mediation can be said to be unreasonable conduct particularly when, as here, those rights are ultimately vindicated. But ... a failure to engage, even if unreasonable, does not automatically result in a costs penalty. It is simply a factor to be taken into account by the judge when exercising his costs discretion.'[227]

- **Failing to respond to an invitation to mediate** Silence in the face of an offer to mediate would, as a general rule, be unreasonable conduct meriting a costs sanction—and it would be so even if an outright refusal to mediate might have been justified.[228] Whilst not a source of law, Practice Direction—Pre-action Conduct, para 11, provides that:

  'If proceedings are issued, the parties may be required by the court to provide evidence that ADR has been considered. A party's silence in response to an invitation to participate or a refusal to participate in ADR might be considered unreasonable by the court and could lead to the court ordering that party to pay additional court costs.'

- **Holding out for unrealistic demands** Whilst he was dealing with informal negotiations rather than a formal mediation, Lightman J imposed a percentage reduction on a successful defendant to take account of the fact that he refused to enter into productive negotiations and instead insisted on a term of settlement that he knew, or ought to have known, was unrealistic.[229] Likewise, if a person fails to settle a case because they unreasonably hold out for their costs, that is a factor that may be reflected in an adverse costs award.[230]
- **Putative preconditions** The court is generally cautious about the notion of regarding an assertion by one or other of the parties as being an unreasonable precondition or refusal to mediate. Turner J had the following to say on the topic:

  'It is always likely that those representing any given party to a dispute will seek to lower the expectations of the other side in preparation for ADR. Simply because one side makes a prediction of what it might take to reach a settlement does not entitle the other side to treat such a prediction, without more, as a formal pre-condition. Tactical positioning should not too readily be labelled as intransigence.'[231]

- **Lip service and failure to attend** A party who agreed to mediation, but then took an unreasonable position in the mediation, would, in general, be in the same position as a party who unreasonably refused to mediate.[232] However, it will usually be the case that events of the mediation are entirely without prejudice, in which case the evidence of

[226] *Burchell v Bullard* [2005] EWCA Civ 358, at [43].
[227] *Gore v Naheed* [2017] EWCA Civ 369, at [49].
[228] See *Thakkar v Patel* [2017] EWCA Civ 117, at [27], *per* Jackson LJ; *PGF II SA v OMFS Co 1 Ltd* [2013] EWCA (Civ) 1288, at [34]–[40], *per* Briggs LJ.
[229] *RBG Resources plc (in liquidation) v Rastogi and ors* [2005] EWHC 994 (Ch).
[230] See, eg, *Strachey v Ramage* [2008] EWCA Civ 804.
[231] *Laporte v The Commissioner of Police of the Metropolis* [2015] EWHC 371 (QB), at [55(iii)].
[232] *Carleton v Strutt & Parker (a partnership)* [2008] EWHC 424 (QB).

what happened during the mediation would be inadmissible.[233] Failure to attend a mediation would be a very serious matter.[234]

- **Refusal to mediate by a claimant** Whilst there is no authority on the point, a claimant who refused to mediate would find it more difficult to justify their position than a defendant. This is because a defendant who offers mediation is presumably willing to negotiate and a willingness to negotiate implies a willingness to settle. Thus a claimant who refuses mediation would be giving up a chance to achieve the very thing that they had chosen to seek.
- **Parties who want their day in court** At the risk of stating the obvious, if a party refuses mediation because it wants its day in court, that might sound in costs.[235]

The nature of the dispute

6.129 Even the most ardent supporters of ADR acknowledge that the subject matter of some disputes render them intrinsically unsuitable for ADR.[236] Whether a dispute is of a nature that is suitable for mediation is a question to be determined on the facts of each case, but the following points may be made.

- **Points of law, construction or principle** Where the parties wish the court to determine issues of law or construction that may be essential to the future trading relations of the parties, such as under an ongoing long-term contract or where the issues are generally important for those participating in a particular trade or market, then the case may not be suitable for mediation.[237]
- **Disputes over binary issues** It may be that one of the parties believes that mediation would not be appropriate because the dispute is over a binary issue (such as a point of law). Judge Waksman QC (sitting as a judge of the High Court) had this to say on the point:

  > 'To consider that mediation is not worth it because the sides are opposed on a binary issue, I'm afraid seems to me to be misconceived. The points on the nature of the dispute raised in *Halsey* indicate that the sort of case where exceptionally its nature might rule out mediation will be where the party wishes to resolve a point of law, considers a binding precedent would be useful, or in cases where injunctive or other relief is essential to protect the parties. But paragraph 17 concludes, "In our view most cases are not by their very nature unsuitable for ADR".'[238]

- **Allegations of fraud or misconduct** Issues that involve allegations of fraud or other commercially disreputable conduct against an individual or group may not be suitable for mediation.[239]

---

[233] *Halsey v Milton Keynes General NHS Trust* [2004] EWCA Civ 576, at [14], *per* Dyson LJ.

[234] Whilst it did not concern the incidence of costs, see, eg, *Gresport Finance Ltd v Battaglia* [2015] EWHC 2709 (Ch), *per* Chief Master Marsh.

[235] As an example of this in practice, see *Rolf v de Guerin* [2011] EWCA Civ 78. The refusal to mediate was just one factor amongst many in that case.

[236] *Halsey v Milton Keynes General NHS Trust* [2004] EWCA Civ 576, at [17], *per* Dyson LJ.

[237] See the Commercial Court Working Party on ADR (1999), cited in *Halsey v Milton Keynes General NHS Trust* [2004] EWCA Civ 576, at [17], *per* Dyson LJ.

[238] *Garritt-Critchley v Ronnan* [2014] EWHC 1774 (Ch), at [14] and [15].

[239] See the Commercial Court Working Party on ADR (1999), cited in *Halsey v Milton Keynes General NHS Trust* [2004] EWCA Civ 576, at [17], *per* Dyson LJ.

- **Professional negligence** Lightman J has found that the fact that a claim was a professional negligence claim would not, of itself, make it inappropriate for mediation.[240]
- **Where injunctive relief is required** Cases in which injunctive or other relief is essential to protect the position of a party may not be suitable for mediation.[241]
- **Dispute between neighbours** Disputes between neighbours are notoriously expensive. In a dispute about a garage roof, Thomas LJ commented (*obiter*) that if the order in the court below had not reflected a refusal to mediate, that would have been an error.[242] Whilst he did not expressly refer to the fact, it is likely that Thomas LJ took that view because disputes between neighbours are of a type in which mediation can be particularly effective.
- **Disputes involving government departments** In 2001, the Lord Chancellor's Department made a formal pledge on behalf of government departments that 'Alternative Dispute Resolution will be considered and used in all suitable cases wherever the other party accepts it'.[243] In a case in which a government department refused to mediate, Lewison J said that pledge was something to which he ought to attach 'great weight'.[244] Dyson LJ did not agree:

> 'In our judgment, the judge was wrong to attach such weight to the ADR pledge. The pledge was no more than an undertaking that ADR would be considered and used in all suitable cases. If a case is suitable for ADR, then it is likely that a party refusing to agree to it will be acting unreasonably, whether or not it is a public body to which the ADR pledge applies. If the case is not suitable for ADR, then a refusal to agree to ADR does not breach the pledge. It is, therefore, difficult to see in what circumstances it would be right to give great weight to the ADR pledge.'[245]

The merits of the case

The fact that a party reasonably believes that it has a strong case is relevant to the question of whether that party has acted reasonably in refusing ADR. There is some overlap with the issue of whether the use of ADR was likely to be successful (see 6.137). **6.130**

Dyson LJ had this to say on the topic of merits: **6.131**

> 'If the position were otherwise, there would be considerable scope for a claimant to use the threat of costs sanctions to extract a settlement from the defendant even where the claim is without merit. Courts should be particularly astute to this danger. Large organisations ... are vulnerable to pressure from claimants who, having weak cases, invite mediation as a tactical ploy. They calculate that such a defendant may at least make a nuisance-value offer to buy off the cost of a mediation and the risk of being penalised in costs for refusing a mediation even if ultimately successful.'[246]

The following miscellaneous points may be made about the relevant of the merits of the case. **6.132**

- **Objectively very strong cases** If a party were to have an objectively very strong case, then a refusal to mediate may be regarded as being reasonable. The example that Dyson LJ gave

240 *Hurst v Leeming* [2002] EWHC 1051 (Ch).
241 *Halsey v Milton Keynes General NHS Trust* [2004] EWCA Civ 576, at [17], *per* Dyson LJ.
242 *Seeff v Ho* [2011] EWCA Civ 186, at [49] and [50].
243 Office of Government Compliance, *Dispute Resolution Guidance* (London: HMSO, 2002), para 2.1.
244 *Royal Bank of Canada v Secretary of State for Defence* [2003] EWHC 1841 (Ch), at [12].
245 *Halsey v Milton Keynes General NHS Trust* [2004] EWCA Civ 576, at [35].
246 *Ibid*, at [18].

was where a party would have succeeded in an application for summary judgment had such an application been made.[247]

- **Objectively very weak opponent cases** In a similar vein (or perhaps the same scenario put in a different way), if a party had refused to mediate because it reasonably saw no merit in its opponent's case, then if the court were subsequently to find that that optimism was correct, that party would, in general, not be penalised for having refused to mediate.[248]
- **Borderline cases** Borderline cases are likely to be suitable for ADR unless there are significant countervailing factors that tip the scales the other way.[249]
- **Subjective belief of the merits** Subjective belief may be relevant,[250] but it is generally a factor that is given little or no weight.[251] Unsurprisingly, the fact that a party unreasonably believed that its case was watertight would be no justification for refusing mediation, but the fact that a party reasonably believed that it had a watertight case may well be sufficient justification for a refusal to mediate.[252]
- **Opponent's case waning** In a case in which the claimant's negotiating position had progressed steadily downwards as the case had progressed, Floyd J found (albeit in a context other than the exercise of discretion under CPR, r 44.2[253]) that it was reasonable for the defendant to decline to mediate, this being on the basis (amongst others—see 6.120) that, given time, the claimant's case would collapse.[254]
- **Awaiting clarification of case** A party may escape being penalised for refusing to mediate until after the issue of proceedings if that refusal were on the basis that it was necessary to know the full details of the parties' cases before seeking to settle the matter.[255]
- **Awaiting evidence** Whilst in a context other than the exercise of discretion under CPR, r 44.2,[256] Floyd J has commented that a party may escape criticism if the putative refusal was, in reality, a reasonable request to await exchange of expert evidence—and that this would be especially true if that party were reasonably to believe that, given time, the other side's case would collapse.[257]
- **Cases procedurally close to settlement** In a case in which a compromise had nearly been reached, but there were some procedural issues that remained, Arden LJ has explained that the court may fall into error if it were to impose its own view as to what would have been required to bring the matter to a close.[258]

---

[247] *Ibid*, at [19], *per* Dyson LJ.

[248] See, eg, *Euroption Strategic Fund Ltd v Skandaniaviska Enskilda Banken AB* [2012] EWHC 749 (Comm), *per* Gloster J.

[249] *Halsey v Milton Keynes General NHS Trust* [2004] EWCA Civ 576, at [19], *per* Dyson LJ.

[250] See *PGF II SA v OMFS Co 1 Ltd* [2013] EWCA (Civ) 1288, at [36], *per* Briggs LJ.

[251] *Halsey v Milton Keynes General NHS Trust* [2004] EWCA Civ 576, at [19], *per* Dyson LJ; see also *Hurst v Leeming* [2002] EWHC 1051 (Ch).

[252] *Halsey v Milton Keynes General NHS Trust* [2004] EWCA Civ 576, at [19], *per* Dyson LJ.

[253] The context was whether to depart from the default position that a person who has discontinued should pay costs: see 7.112 *et seq*.

[254] *Mobiqa Ltd v Trinity Mobile Ltd* [2010] EWHC 253 (Pat), at [27] and [28].

[255] See, eg, *Wethered Estate Ltd v Davis* [2005] EWHC 1903 (Ch), *per* Clive Freedman QC.

[256] The context was whether to depart from the default position that a person who has discontinued should pay costs: see 7.112 *et seq*.

[257] *Mobiqa Ltd v Trinity Mobile Ltd* [2010] EWHC 253 (Pat), at [27] and [28].

[258] *Carlisle & Cumbria United Independent Supports' Society Ltd v CUFC Holding Ltd* [2010] EWCA Civ 463, at [13].

The extent to which other settlement methods had been attempted

The extent to which other settlement methods have been thought about or tried will depend on the facts, but the following points may be made. 6.133

- **Settlement offers in general** Dyson LJ had the following to say about settlement offers:

> 'The fact that settlement offers have already been made, but rejected, is a relevant factor. It may show that one party is making efforts to settle, and that the other party has unrealistic views of the merits of the case. But it is also right to point out that mediation often succeeds where previous attempts to settle have failed. Although the fact that settlement offers have already been made is potentially relevant to the question whether a refusal to mediate is unreasonable, on analysis it is in truth no more than an aspect of factor.'[259]

- **Interaction between refusal to mediate and admissible offers** The effects of a party's refusal to mediate may be mitigated or negated by its opponent's failure to accept a reasonable offer.[260]
- **Attempts at other methods of ADR** In a case in which the successful party had refused mediation, but had engaged in other forms of dispute resolution (such as making generous offers), Peter Gibson LJ found that that party had acted reasonably.[261] Similarly, in a dispute between a university and one of its students, the former was found to have acted reasonably in refusing to mediate because it had already agreed to adjudication, which itself was a form of ADR.[262]
- **Court-sanctioned schemes** Where a refusal is in respect of a court-sanctioned scheme and where that refusal was unreasonable, it would be open to the court to condemn the refusing party in costs on the indemnity basis.[263]

Whether the costs of ADR would have been disproportionately high

Mediation can be an expensive process; as such, the costs of mediation may be a relevant factor (especially in smaller cases). Indeed, Dyson LJ has said that: 6.134

> 'Since the prospects of a successful mediation cannot be predicted with confidence ... the possibility of the ultimately successful party being required to incur the costs of an abortive mediation is a relevant factor that may be taken into account in deciding whether the successful party acted unreasonably in refusing to agree to ADR.'[264]

The following related points may be made. 6.135

- **Smaller claims** Dyson LJ had the following to say about the costs of mediation in the context of smaller claims:

> 'This is a factor of particular importance where, on a realistic assessment, the sums at stake in the litigation are comparatively small. A mediation can sometimes be at least

[259] *Halsey v Milton Keynes General NHS Trust* [2004] EWCA Civ 576, at [20].

[260] See, eg, *Northrop Grumman Mission Systems Europe Ltd v BAE Systems (AL Diriyah C41) Ltd* [2014] EWHC 3148 (TCC), at [73]–[76], *per* Ramsey J.

[261] *Valentine v Allen* [2003] EWCA Civ 1274.

[262] *R (on the application of Crawford) v Newcastle upon Tyne University* [2014] EWHC 1197 (Admin), *per* Mr Andrew Grubb (sitting as a deputy judge of the High Court).

[263] *Virani v Manuel Revert y Cia Sa* [2003] EWCA Civ 1651.

[264] *Halsey v Milton Keynes General NHS Trust* [2004] EWCA Civ 576, at [21].

as expensive as a day in court. The parties will often have legal representation before the mediator, and the mediator's fees will usually be borne equally by the parties regardless of the outcome . . .'[265]

- **The relevance of the costs of the litigation** Whilst a slight digression from the *Halsey* checklist, a factor that may seem, at first blush, to be highly relevant is the amount of costs that mediation would have avoided. Jack J has found that whilst this is a factor to be taken into account, it should not be afforded such significance that a defendant is put in the position of being required to settle a claim for more than it is worth solely for the purposes of avoiding an adverse costs order.[266]

Delay and associated matters

6.136 The following related points may be made about delay and associated matters.

- **Late proposal** If the proposal to mediate is made late in the day, acceptance of it may have the effect of delaying the trial of the action. This may be a relevant factor.[267]
- **Foot dragging** If, when faced with an offer of mediation, a party drags its feet to such an extent that its opponent loses interest, that may sound in costs, even though that may, in the words of Jackson LJ, be a 'tough order'.[268]
- **Changes of heart** If a party initially refuses to mediate, the fact that it changes its mind (even if, by that stage, its opponent has also changed its mind) may mitigate against the effect of the initial refusal to mediate.[269]
- **The relevance of a prompt response** Compliance with the advice given in the *Jackson ADR Handbook* (see 6.124) would certainly be a factor to be taken into account, but Judge Waksman QC (sitting as a judge of the High Court) has made it clear that the mere fact of responding promptly would not be sufficient to protect a party who refused mediation if the reasons it gave were misconceived.[270]

Whether ADR had a reasonable prospect of success

6.137 The issue of whether a case was suitable for mediation will be a question of fact to be decided on the basis of the case in hand. Dyson LJ has explained that it would not be appropriate for the court to confine itself to a consideration of whether, viewed objectively, a mediation would have had a reasonable prospect of success. That would be an unduly narrow approach because it would focus on the nature of the dispute, and would leave out of account the parties' willingness to compromise and the reasonableness of their attitudes.[271] It should be noted that there is some overlap between the matters discussed below and the topic of the merits of the case (see 6.130).

---

[265] *Ibid.*

[266] *Hickman v Blake Lapthorn* [2006] EWHC 12 (QB), [2006] All ER (D) 67, at [21].

[267] *Halsey v Milton Keynes General NHS Trust* [2004] EWCA Civ 576, at [22], *per* Dyson LJ.

[268] See *Thakkar v Patel* [2017] EWCA Civ 117, at [29], referring to *PGF II SA v OMFS Co 1 Ltd* [2013] EWCA (Civ) 1288.

[269] See, eg, *Murray v Bernard* [2015] EWHC 2395 (Ch), *per* Mann J.

[270] *Garritt-Critchley v Ronnan* [2014] EWHC 1774 (Ch), at [28], *per* Judge Waksman QC (sitting as a judge of the High Court).

[271] *Halsey v Milton Keynes General NHS Trust* [2004] EWCA Civ 576, at [26].

In a commercial dispute, Jackson LJ identified the following factors (here paraphrased) as confirming that the case before him was suitable for mediation[272]—that is, the facts: **6.138**

- that the dispute was a commercial one and it was 'purely about money';
- that the defendants were willing to pay a sum of money and that the claimants were willing, or became willing, to accept a sum that was in the same ballpark (these being the editor's words);
- that the costs of litigation were vastly greater than the sum in issue;
- that bilateral negotiations between the parties had been unsuccessful; and
- that:

> 'Any mediator would have had both parties in the room with him. He would have let them have their say. He would then have pointed out (a) the small gap between their respective positions, and (b) the huge future costs of the litigation.'[273]

These factors are reproduced here because they describe a set of circumstances that is common, if not quotidian, in the context of commercial litigation. Jackson LJ went on to say that, in those circumstances, he would have been 'astonished if a skilled mediator [had] failed to bring the parties to a sensible settlement'.[274]

The following miscellaneous points regarding the prospects of success may be made. **6.139**

- **Intransigence on the part of a party** Dyson LJ has said (in 2004) that where a party has adopted a position of intransigence, that party's opponent may reasonably take the view that a mediation has no reasonable prospect of success and that this would be a proper basis for concluding that a mediation would have no reasonable prospect of success.[275] This no doubt would remain true where such facts can be shown to exist, but a party who sought to rely on such an argument today would—for the reasons set out immediately below—find it difficult to prove that the fault lay with their opponent (especially where the invitation to mediate came from that quarter).
- **Supposedly intractable disputes** As to the relevance of the fact that a dispute may be said to be intractable, Vos LJ said that 'if one were to say to any accredited mediator that any dispute was too intractable to be successfully mediated, he or she would roll their eyes. No dispute is too intractable to be mediated ...'[276] In a similar vein, Judge Waksman QC (sitting as a judge of the High Court) had this to say:

> '[I]t is precisely where there may be distrust or emotion between the parties, which it might be thought is pushing them down the road to an expensive trial, where the skills of a mediator come in most usefully. They are well trained to diffuse emotion, feelings of distrust and other matters in order that the parties can see their way to a commercial settlement.'[277]

---

[272] *Thakkar v Patel* [2017] EWCA Civ 117, at [27].
[273] *Ibid.*
[274] *Ibid.*
[275] *Halsey v Milton Keynes General NHS Trust* [2004] EWCA Civ 576, at [25].
[276] *NJ Rickard Ltd v Holloway* [2015] EWCA Civ 1631, at [34]. Vos LJ went on to cite *PGF II SA v OMFS Co 1 Ltd* [2013] EWCA Civ 1288, at [34], in which Briggs LJ expressed a similar sentiment.
[277] *Garritt-Critchley v Ronnan* [2014] EWHC 1774 (Ch), at [18].

- **Parties supposedly very far apart** It may be that one or both parties believe that mediation is not worthwhile because they are too far apart. Judge Waksman QC (sitting as a judge of the High Court) had this to say on the point:

  'Parties don't know whether in truth they are too far apart unless they sit down and explore settlement. If they are irreconcilably too far apart, then the mediator will say as much within the first hour of mediation. That happens very rarely in my experience.'[278]

- **Ignoring the guidance of the court** It is often the case that judges say that a case is suitable for mediation and encourage the parties to go down that road. Dyson LJ had this to say on the topic:

  'Where a successful party refuses to agree to ADR despite the court's encouragement, that is a factor which the court will take into account when deciding whether his refusal was unreasonable. The court's encouragement may take different forms. The stronger the encouragement, the easier it will be for the unsuccessful party to discharge the burden of showing that the successful party's refusal was unreasonable.'[279]

  If the court makes an ADR order, then a failure to comply with that order may, for that reason alone, result in adverse costs consequences for the party who was in default.[280]

Conduct and the incidence of costs: overly aggressive insistence on engaging in ADR

6.140 It may be that a party is so intent on pursuing ADR that they cross a line in that their conduct becomes inappropriate. In a case in which a party aggressively pursued its opponents in an attempt to force their hand into agreeing to arbitration, Edwards-Stuart J visited adverse costs consequences upon that party, branding its behaviour 'a negotiating tactic'.[281]

Conduct and the incidence of costs: failure to respond to an offer

6.141 Failing to respond to an offer (including an offer of mediation—see 6.128) is conduct that can be taken into account for the purposes of determining the incidence of costs. An oft-cited example is *Painting v University of Oxford*,[282] in which the failure to respond was one factor that resulted in adverse costs consequences being visited upon the claimant, but it would be wrong to regard *Painting* as laying down a point of principle, not least because the claimant's conduct was 'extreme with a vastly exaggerated case supported by untruthful evidence'.[283]

6.142 Unless CPR, r 36.14(1)(b), applies, a failure to respond to an offer would rarely merit an award of costs on the indemnity basis,[284] but again the failure may be a factor to be taken into account. Kay LJ made the following remarks, which have resonance in this specific context notwithstanding the fact that they were made in a more general context:

---

278 *Ibid*, at [22].
279 *Halsey v Milton Keynes General NHS Trust* [2004] EWCA Civ 576, at [29].
280 *Ibid*.
281 *Gotch v Enelco Ltd* [2015] EWHC 1802 (TCC), at [60].
282 [2005] EWCA Civ 161.
283 *Straker v Tudor Rose (a firm)* [2007] EWCA Civ 368.
284 *Kiam v MGN Ltd (No 2)* [2002] EWCA Civ 66.

'The approach of the CPR is a relatively simple one: namely, if one party has made a real effort to find a reasonable solution to the proceedings and the other party has resisted that sensible approach, then the latter puts himself at risk that the order for costs may be on an indemnity basis.'[285]

In a similar vein, Smith LJ had this to say: **6.143**

'... In these days where both sides are expected to conduct themselves in a reasonable way and to seek agreement where possible, it may be right to penalise a party to some degree for failing to accept a reasonable offer or for failing to come back with a counter offer.'[286]

Conduct and the incidence of costs: exaggeration and the incidence of costs

This section deals with exaggeration and the incidence of costs. The issue of exaggeration in the context of the assessment of costs is dealt with at 57.18–57.36 and exaggeration in the context of qualified one-way costs shifting is addressed at 8.34–8.41. Issues regarding the basis upon which costs may be payable are addressed in Chapter 16. It should be noted that, in cases of fundamental dishonesty in a personal injuries claim, special provisions may apply (see 6.87–6.92). **6.144**

Jurisdictional matters

Where a person has advanced an exaggerated claim, the court is able to reflect that fact in the incidence of costs. Indeed, when CPR, r 43.2(4), is read in conjunction with CPR, r 44.2(5)(d), it can be seen that the court 'will' take into account whether a claimant 'who has succeeded in the claim, in whole or in part, exaggerated its claim'. **6.145**

The court is not limited to exercising its ordinary discretion as to costs under CPR, r 44.2; instead, in egregious cases, the court is able to invoke its powers in relation to misconduct.[287] In even more extreme cases, committal for contempt of court may be an option.[288] **6.146**

Terminology of exaggeration

The word 'exaggeration' carries two meanings. No one would dispute that a claim that had been improperly or dishonestly inflated should be said to have been exaggerated, but it is often not realised that an honest and proper claim that ultimately was allowed at a sum very much lower than it was originally put may also be said to have been exaggerated. These two interpretations are referred to as 'culpable exaggeration' (see 6.149–6.153) and 'innocent exaggeration' (see 6.154–6.155), respectively,[289] and **6.147**

---

285 *Reid Minty (a firm) v Taylor* [2001] EWCA Civ 1723, at [37].

286 *Hall v Stone* [2007] EWCA Civ 1354, at [82].

287 See CPR, r 44.11, and Ward LJ's comments in *Widlake v BAA Ltd* [2009] EWCA Civ 1256, at [41]. It is not a jurisdiction that is commonly invoked outwith a detailed assessment, not least because there is no need: a trial judge would not need to rely on that jurisdiction to make an order against an exaggerator.

288 See, eg, Kirk *v Walton* [2009] EWHC 703 (QB).

289 In *Hullock v East Riding of Yorkshire County Council* [2009] EWCA Civ 1039, Patten LJ draws a distinction between cases in which there was no culpable exaggeration and cases like *Painting v Oxford University* [2005] EWCA Civ 161. Patten LJ had this to say about the differences between culpable and non-culpable (in *Hullock v East Riding of Yorkshire County Council* [2009] EWCA Civ 1039, at [31]): '[There is] a clear and justifiable distinction between a case where the Claimant fails to make out the full measure of the claim and one where the outcome of the proceedings largely turns on a particular issue or issues on which the Defendant [NB should be Claimant] is clearly the loser.'

Jackson LJ has confirmed that different considerations may arise depending upon this distinction.[290]

6.148 The phrases 'intentional exaggeration' and 'unintentional exaggeration' are also often used. Walker J has used the word 'concoction' to describe culpable exaggeration.[291]

6.149 **Culpable exaggeration** Culpable exaggeration may be taken into account either at the time that the costs order is made or at the time that costs are assessed,[292] or (provided that the order permits such an approach) both.

6.150 *Identifying culpable exaggeration* The following points can be made about identifying cases in which there has been culpable exaggeration.

- **The ingredients of culpable exaggeration** Culpable exaggeration connotes at least an element of dishonesty in advancing an inflated claim. Walker J has made it clear that the mere fact that a claim has settled for a figure that was considerably less than that which had been claimed would not, of itself, be sufficient to justify a finding of culpable exaggeration and this would be so even where it was known that the claimant had lied.[293]
- **Evidence of exaggeration** Walker J has explained that where exaggeration is alleged, but not admitted, and where the court has not heard evidence, then considerable caution must be exercised before reaching—on a broad-brush examination of documents alone—any conclusion adverse to the alleged exaggerator. Indeed, Walker J had this to say:

  > 'Lies are told in litigation every day up and down the country and quite rightly do not lead to a penalty being imposed in respect of them. There is a considerable difference between a concocted claim and an exaggerated claim and judges must be astute to measure how reprehensible the conduct is.'[294]

- **Use of hindsight** Mann J has made it clear that particular care needs to be taken to avoid applying hindsight,[295] although this would not normally be a concern where the exaggeration was culpable.

6.151 *The general approach in cases of culpable exaggeration* The following points can be made about the court's approach to culpable exaggeration in general.

- **Each case is to be decided on its own facts** Ward LJ has said that, in so far as damages are concerned, there is no rule of law that a genuine claim which had been exaggerated should be dismissed;[296] as such, it would be wrong to believe that such a rule existed

---

290 *Fox v Foundation Piling Ltd* [2011] EWCA Civ 790, at [48]–[63]. See also *Painting v University of Oxford* [2005] EWCA Civ 161, at [26], *per* Longmore LJ, and *Vector v JD Williams* [2009] EWHC 3601 (TCC), at [75], *per* Ramsey J.

291 *Morton v Portal Ltd* [2010] EWHC 1804 (QB), at [41].

292 See, eg, *Booth v Britannia Hotels Ltd* [2002] EWCA Civ 579.

293 *Morton v Portal Ltd* [2010] EWHC 1804 (QB), at [48]–[54].

294 *Ibid*, at [41].

295 *Business Environment Bow Lane v Deanswater Estates Ltd* [2009] EWHC 2014 (Ch).

296 The case to which Ward LJ referred was *Ul-Haq v Shah* [2009] EWCA Civ 542, at [43]–[46], in which Smith LJ said that the inclusion of a false claim with a genuine claim does not of itself turn a genuine claim into a false one or justify the striking out of the genuine claim or claims and that to do so would be to deprive a claimant of their substantive rights as a mark of disapproval, which the court has no power to do. That said, Lord Clarke has explained that he prefers the approach in *Masood v Zahoor* [2009] EWCA Civ 650 and that,

for costs.[297] Put otherwise, it is not the case that a claimant who has culpably exaggerated a claim will necessarily be condemned to pay the whole of the costs of the claim. Ward LJ explained that the court should exercise its discretion, that being a process of determining who has won and of regarding any putative exaggeration as being just one aspect of the parties' conduct.[298]

- **Approach to costs occasioned by exaggeration** Lord Clarke has explained that, in the ordinary run of things, the court would penalise a dishonest and fraudulent claimant in costs.[299] He went on to say that it is entirely appropriate in a case of culpable exaggeration to order the exaggerator to pay the costs on an indemnity basis of any part of the process that has been caused by the exaggerator's fraud or dishonesty.[300] There have been cases in which culpable exaggeration has led to the claimant being condemned to pay the whole of the defendant's costs,[301] but such cases tend to be exceptional.[302]
- **Culpable exaggeration and issues** Whilst exaggeration is a topic that is often articulated in terms of conduct in general, it is also a topic that may lend itself to being dealt with on an issue-aware basis. This is because exaggeration is often reflected in the costs of a well-defined and easily identifiable issue or set of issues (such as the costs of obtaining evidence as to quantum or the costs of preparing certain pleadings). It may be appropriate to disallow the exaggerator's costs in pursuing the exaggerated aspects of the claim and to make an allowance for the corresponding costs incurred by their opponent.[303]
- **Where culpable exaggeration is the dominant issue** In some cases, exaggeration will be seen as being the only relevant issue, because where it exists, exaggeration tends to become dominant. In *Painting*,[304] Maurice Kay LJ had this to say:

> 'To the question: who was the real winner in this litigation? There is, in my judgment, only one answer. The two-day hearing was concerned overwhelmingly with the issue of exaggeration, and the [defendant] won on that issue. [The claimant's] submission that that was only one issue, the other issue being the quantification of the claim, is not persuasive.

as such, the court has the power to strike out a claim at any stage on the ground that it is an abuse of process of the court, but it will do so at the end of a trial only in very exceptional circumstances: *Fairclough Homes Ltd v Summers* [2012] UKSC 26, at [36], [41] and [42].

[297] Law LJ's comments suggesting the contrary in *Molloy v Shell (UK) Ltd* [2001] EWCA Civ 1272, at [18], should now be treated with caution: see *Widlake v BAA Ltd* [2009] EWCA Civ 1256, at [34], *per* Ward LJ.

[298] See *ibid.* See also *Abbott v Long* [2011] EWCA Civ 874, at [15] and [17], *per* Arden LJ, and *Walsh v Singh* [2011] EWHC Civ 80, at [25], *per* Arden LJ.

[299] See *Fairclough Homes Ltd v Summers* [2012] UKSC 26, at [53] and [61].

[300] See *ibid*, at [53].

[301] In *Painting v University of Oxford* [2005] EWCA Civ 161, for example, the claimant in a personal injury claim was awarded £25,331 out of about £400,000 that had been sought. Maurice Kay LJ ordered costs against the claimant and commented that, on the facts of the case before him, the following factors were significant: (i) when viewed objectively, the judgment was overwhelmingly favourable to the defendant, who was, in real terms, the winner; (ii) had there been no exaggeration, the claim would probably have been compromised at an early stage and with only modest costs; and (iii) the claimant had failed to demonstrate any willingness to negotiate or to put forward a proposal to accept a reasonable sum.

[302] Facts such as those in *Painting* will not present themselves every day; a differently constituted Court of Appeal described *Painting* as being 'extreme [and] vastly exaggerated case supported by untruthful evidence': *Straker v Tudor Rose (a firm)* [2007] EWCA Civ 368, at [9].

[303] *Widlake v BAA Ltd* [2009] EWCA Civ 1256, at [34] *et seq*. As another example of this (this time, in the context of a credit hire case in which the exaggerated claim was six times the amount recovered and the claimant's conduct was 'reprehensible'), see *Abbott v Long* [2011] EWCA Civ 874.

[304] See fn 301 for the facts.

Quite simply, that second issue was hardly an issue at all once the Recorder had found the exaggeration . . .'[305]

- Thus where the culpable exaggeration is the only (or the overwhelmingly dominant) issue, then it may be the factor that determines who is the victor.
- **Exaggeration involving fundamental dishonesty in personal injury claims** This is addressed at 6.87.

6.152 *The relevance of offers in cases of culpable exaggeration* The absence or presence of offers may have a significant bearing on the incidence of costs in cases of culpable exaggeration. The following points may be made.

- **Where the defendant has made no offer at all** If a defendant fails to make an adequate offer to protect themselves, that may be a factor to be taken into account.[306] In a case in which a defendant had not moved from its position of denying liability and had not engaged in making or considering offers, Ramsey J found that the general rule that costs follow the event was not displaced.[307] There have been other cases in which the court has awarded significant costs to the claimant on the basis that the defendant could have protected itself by making an offer.[308]
- **Where the defendant has made no Part 36 offers** When faced with an exaggerated claim, the defendant might elect not to make or accept a Part 36 offer, because if it were to be accepted, the claimant would be entitled to the whole of the costs of the claim, including those that went to the dishonest or exaggerated aspects (see 6.232). There is no doubt that the court can—and usually does—take such matters into account, but it may also be relevant that there are alternatives to making or accepting a Part 36 offer, as follows.
  - As Lord Clarke has explained, a defendant who finds itself in that position would be able to make a *Calderbank* offer (that being an 'admissible offer' under the CPR) that made appropriate provision for costs (see 6.232).[309]
  - Again, as Lord Clarke has explained, it may be appropriate for a defendant to seek permission to commence contempt proceedings against the claimant.[310]
  - If the defendant has received a Part 36, it would be open to them to invoke the 'just-out-of-time' jurisdiction (although this is not without its problems—see 17.173–17.175).

  In the ordinary run of things, the court tends to focus on whether an 'admissible offer' had been made.
- **Offers and the absence of information** It is, in principle, open to a party to claim that the reason why it did not make a suitable Part 36 offer is because its opponent

---

305 *Painting v University of Oxford* [2005] EWCA Civ 161, at [21].

306 See, eg, *Widlake v BAA Ltd* [2009] EWCA Civ 1256, at [39]. See also *Fox v Foundation Piling Ltd* [2011] EWCA Civ 790, at [48].

307 *Biffa Waste Services Ltd v Maschinenfabrik Ernst Hese GmBH* [2008] EWHC 2657 (TCC); see also *Widlake v BAA Ltd* [2009] EWCA Civ 1256, at [39].

308 See, eg, *Jackson v The Ministry of Defence* [2006] EWCA Civ 46, in which about £1 million had been claimed, but only £155,000 awarded. Tuckey LJ refused to disturb the trial judge's award of 75 per cent of the claimant's costs on the basis that 'the defendant was perfectly able to protect itself against the fact that it faced an exaggerated claim': *ibid*, at [15].

309 *Fairclough Homes Ltd v Summers* [2012] UKSC 26, at [14].

310 *Ibid*, at [61].

did not provide certain requisite information.[311] Where this is so, the court will look at whether the evidence supports the contention that the timeous supply of the information would have made a difference.[312] A degree of specificity is required in this regard: the court is likely to be unimpressed by nebulous complaints of inadequate particularisation or scanty disclosure.[313] Moreover, Coulson J has pointed out that if the difficulties really were so great that a party could not properly protect itself by making an offer, then it may be relevant that an application could have been made for specific disclosure.[314]

- **Where the exaggerator has made no offers** This is addressed immediately below.

Miscellaneous points regarding culpable exaggeration The following miscellaneous points may be made about culpable exaggeration. **6.153**

- **Incorrect allocation as a result of culpable exaggeration** The topic of misallocation as a result of culpable exaggeration is addressed at 57.21. It should be noted that where there has been exaggeration that has resulted in misallocation, it does not necessarily follow that the exaggerator will be awarded the costs that would have been allowed had it been correctly allocated. In particular, if the defendant is able to show that, in the absence of exaggeration, the claim would not have been settled on commercial grounds, the claimant may be condemned in costs.[315]
- **Failure by the exaggerator to negotiate** The willingness of the exaggerator to negotiate may be a relevant factor. In particular, if an exaggerator has made no offers to accept a reasonable sum, that might be a factor that would count against that party even if its opponent had failed to beat their own offers.[316] In this regard, Maurice Kay LJ said the following:

  'At no stage did [the exaggerator] manifest any willingness to negotiate or to put forward a counter-proposal to the Part 36 payment. No-one can compel a claimant to take such steps. However to contest and lose an issue of exaggeration without having made ever a counter-proposal is a matter of some significance in this kind of litigation. It must not be assumed that beating a Part 36 payment is conclusive. It is a factor and will often be conclusive, but one has to have regard to all the circumstances of the case.'[317]

- Longmore LJ added his own comments:

  '[The claimant] herself made no attempt to negotiate, made no offer of her own and made no response to the offers of the University. That would not have mattered in pre-CPR days but, to my mind, that now matters very much.'[318]

---

[311] See *Brit Inns Ltd (in liquidation) v BDW Trading Ltd* [2012] EWHC 2489 (TCC), at [49], *per* Coulson J.
[312] *Ibid*, at [46] and [47], *per* Coulson J.
[313] See, eg, *ibid*, at [47], *per* Coulson J.
[314] *Ibid*, at [48].
[315] Whilst not binding, an oft-cited example of this is *Khan v Metainy Maintenance Ltd* (unreported), 21 January 2013, Aldershot & Farnham County Court, in which Judge Iain Hughes QC ordered a claimant to pay 80 per cent of the defendant's costs on the grounds that if the claim had been made without exaggeration, it would have been for such a small sum (£150) that it would certainly have settled on commercial grounds.
[316] See, eg, *Abbott v Long* [2011] EWCA Civ 874, at [8] *et seq*, per Arden LJ.
[317] *Painting v University of Oxford* [2005] EWCA Civ 161, at [22].
[318] *Ibid*, at [27].

- **Admissions that a claim is exaggerated** If an exaggerator accepts evidence of exaggeration and alters their position accordingly, then that can be a factor capable of mitigating the effect of the original exaggeration.[319]

6.154 **Innocent exaggeration** Whilst there have been exceptions,[320] in general the mere fact that a party has recovered less than it claimed is not a reason for disapplying the general rule.[321] That party may find that its own costs are reduced on an issue-aware basis, but as a matter of general principle the general rule will apply. In particular, the Welamson doctrine (see 6.75) seems not—or not yet—to have become a feature of the law in this jurisdiction, even in commercial cases.

6.155 The following points may be made about innocent exaggeration.

- **Innocent exaggeration and the issue of who has won** As to what may be sufficient to disapply the general rule, Smith LJ said this (*obiter*):

  'I would accept that exaggeration by a claimant may be taken into account as "conduct" under [what is now CPR 44.2(4)(a)]. However, for a defendant to regard himself as a winner or even partial winner on an issue of exaggeration, the exaggeration must be an important feature of the claim with costs consequences.'[322]

  Jackson LJ came to a very similar conclusion in a subsequent case.[323] As is explained below, other than in extreme cases, much will turn on whether the defendant has protected themselves by making an offer.
- **The relevance of offers** As to the relevance of offers, Smith LJ (Waller LJ dissenting) had the following to say:

  'It seems to me that [what is now CPR, r 44.2(4)] is designed to allow the judge to take into account on costs the fact that the losing party actually won on one (or more than one) issue in the case. I do not think it means that the judge can cut down the costs of the successful party merely because he has not done quite as well as he had hoped. But if the claimant's exaggeration was no more than to put his case rather high, it does not seem to me that a defendant who has not made an effective and admissible offer can be regarded as the victor.'[324]

  Thus a defendant who has failed to make an offer will, in general, not be regarded as being the victor. As is explained below, however, they may be able to rely on their success on discrete issues.
- **Innocent exaggeration and concessions** If a defendant admits a certain part of a claim, it would be wrong (in the absence of some other admissible offer) to attach

[319] *Morgan v UPS* [2008] EWCA Civ 1476.

[320] There have been cases in which innocent exaggeration has displaced the general rule merely by reason of the amounts claimed. *Hooper v Biddle & Co* [2006] EWHC 2995 (Ch), *per* Susan Prevezer QC, for example, was a commercial case in which a successful claimant was deprived of costs by reason of having recovered less than was claimed. He had claimed £3.75 million, but had recovered only £38,000.

[321] As an example of this, see *Vestergaard Frandsen A/S v Bestnet Europe Ltd* [2014] EWHC 4371 (Ch), *per* Rose J.

[322] *Hall v Stone* [2007] EWCA Civ 1354, at [72]–[73].

[323] *Fox v Foundation Piling Ltd* [2011] EWCA Civ 790, at [63].

[324] *Hall v Stone* [2007] EWCA Civ 1354, at [72]–[73].

excessive weight to the fact that they achieve a result that is no worse than what had been admitted.[325]

- **Innocent exaggeration and issues** Patten LJ had this to say on the distinction between innocent exaggeration and issues:

  '[There is] a clear and justifiable distinction between a case where the Claimant fails to make out the full measure of the claim and one where the outcome of the proceedings largely turns on a particular issue or issues on which the defendant [NB should be claimant] is clearly the loser'.[326]

  Thus where the claimant has recovered less than they hoped because they have failed on a number of issues, then the issue-aware approach to the incidence of costs (see 6.156–6.243) may be the appropriate way to proceed. If a defendant had failed to make a protective offer, then this would generally be means by which the exaggeration would be reflected in the incidence of costs.
- **Innocent exaggeration and the issue of who has won in extreme cases** If the difference between the parties is so great as to render the chances of the defendant's offer being accepted close to nil, then the act of making an offer may be thought of as being 'a mere matter of ritual'. In those circumstances, the claimant may be found to be the loser even though they have not received any offers (see 6.60 for details). It has to be stressed, however, that there is significant divergence of judicial opinion on that point (see 6.60) and that as such it would be a risky strategy to elect to rely on that argument in preference to making an offer.
- **Paying the defendant's costs** Where—in the absence of culpable exaggeration—a claimant is awarded far less than they claimed, one or both of the following would, in general, have to be present for that party to be condemned to pay the defendant's costs:
  - a near-total failure on the issues that went to trial;[327] or
  - a failure to accept a reasonable offer.[328]
- **The relevance of who was at fault (lawyer, expert or client)** Where exaggeration is a factor that ought to be reflected in the costs order, this will tend to happen regardless of which individual (that is, lawyer, expert or client) was to blame. Ward LJ has said that a claim may still be categorised as being an exaggerated claim even though the fault lay with the professionals advising the claimant rather than the claimant themselves.[329]

Issues and the incidence of costs

The following discussion focuses on how the court deals with the costs of identifiable, discrete issues (that is, separate contentions and arguments) that a party has advanced or defended. If the context in which the topic arises is in group litigation, the points made at 65.45–65.52 also ought to be taken into account. **6.156**

[325] See *Trant v Stokes* (unreported), 3 December 2014, CA (Civ Div), *per* Pitchford LJ, Burnett LJ and Sir Timothy Lloyd.

[326] *Hullock v East Riding of Yorkshire County Council* [2009] EWCA Civ 1039, at [31].

[327] See, eg, *ibid, per* Patten LJ; see also *Brit Inns (in liquidation) v BDW Trading Ltd* [2012] EWHC 2489 (TCC), *per* Coulson J.

[328] See, eg, *Fulham Leisure Holdings Ltd v Nicholson Graham & Jones* [2006] EWHC 2428 (Ch), *per* Mann J; see also *Brit Inns (in liquidation) v BDW Trading Ltd* [2012] EWHC 2489 (TCC), *per* Coulson J.

[329] *Carver v BAA plc* [2008] EWCA Civ 412, at [35].

Terminology relating to issue-aware orders

6.157 This is addressed at 6.05. It should be noted that the terminology used in reported cases is not consistent. In particular, the phrases 'issues order' and 'issues-based order' are often used to mean different things.

A necessary historical perspective

6.158 Authorities decided during the first two years of the CPR (1999–2001) are still encountered from time to time. For the reasons set out below, they must be put into historical context.

6.159 As explained at 6.42, the pre-CPR ethos was—in general terms—that the 'winner takes all'. The fact that the winner may have raised issues that ultimately failed would not have debarred them from having the whole of their costs.[330] This philosophy meant that issue-aware costs orders were a rarity (although, historically, they were less of a rarity than some of the authorities referred to below seem to acknowledge[331]). The CPR brought about significant changes. Speaking shortly before its introduction, Lord Woolf MR explained the new ethos:

> 'The most significant change of emphasis of the new rules is to require courts to be more ready to make separate orders which reflect the outcome of different issues. In doing this, the new rules are reflecting a change of practice which has already started. It is now clear that a too robust application of the "follow the event principle" encourages litigants to increase the costs of litigation, since it discourages litigants from being selective as to the points they take. If you recover all your costs as long as you win, you are encouraged to leave no stone unturned in your effort to do so.'[332]

6.160 Shortly thereafter, Lightman J said similarly that '[t]he straight jacket imposed on the Court by [*Elgindata*[333]] … is gone, and the search for justice is untrammelled by constraints beyond those laid down by the new code itself'.[334] Neuberger J echoed these comments, saying that whilst *Elgindata* should not be overlooked, it could not be said that it represented the law under the CPR.[335]

6.161 **Caution required with cases decided shortly after the coming into force of the CPR** Not all judges agreed that the introduction of the CPR had effected such a radical change in the law. In 2000, Rimer J said that the court had always had the power to disallow costs of issues that had been unreasonably advanced and that the CPR merely spelt out more specifically those factors which the court was able to take into account.[336] At about the same time, Hale LJ said that some of the reasoning in *Elgindata* was capable of applying under the CPR.[337]

6.162 This meant that, in the early days of the CPR, there were two schools of thought: both accepted that the costs of unsuccessful issues could be disallowed, but one believed that this

330 See *Re Elgindata (No 2)* [1992] 1 WLR 1207.

331 Early examples included *Myers v Defries* (1880) 5 Ex D 180, at 187, and *Reid Hewitt & Co v Joseph* [1918] AC 717, at 723. Porter, AW, and Wortham, FG, *A Guide to Costs* (19th edn, London: Waterlow & Sons, 1932), p 683, appears to record issue-aware awards as being unremarkable and ordinary events.

332 *Phonographic Performance Ltd v AEI Rediffusion Music Ltd* [1999] 1 WLR 1507, at 1522.

333 *Re Elgindata (No 2)* [1992] 1 WLR 1207.

334 *Bank of Credit and Commerce International SA (in liquidation) v Ali (No 4)* [1999] 149 NLJ 1734, at the seventh paragraph.

335 *Harrison v Bloom Camillin (a firm)* (unreported), 4 February 2000, Ch D; see also *Antonelli v Allen*, The Times, 8 December 2000, in which Neuberger J made an issue-aware costs order shortly thereafter. See also *Liverpool City Council v Cahvassed Ltd* (unreported), 18 August 1999, QBD.

336 *Deg-Deutsche Investitions und Entwicklungsgesellschaft mbH v Koshy & Ors*, The Times, 30 March 2000.

337 *Universal Cycles v Grangebriar Ltd* (unreported), 8 February 2000, CA.

was the case only if those issues had been unreasonably raised or presented in an unreasonable way. In the event, the latter school of thought was shown to be wrong.[338] Thomas J had the following to say on the topic:

> 'Under [CPR r 44.2(4)] the court is bound to have regard to all the circumstances of the case, including two specific matters: (a) the conduct of all the parties, and (b) whether a party succeeded on part of this case. The conduct of the parties is defined under [CPR, r 44.2(5)]. Under paragraph (5), the definition includes the reasonableness of raising, pursuing and contesting a particular allegation or issues. However, it seems to me clear that under subparagraph (b) of [CPR r 44.2(4)] the reasonableness of the party taking a particular point . . . is not necessarily relevant; that subparagraph is quite distinct from conduct of the parties and therefore the reasonableness of raising an issue does not necessarily have to be taken into account. Quite apart from the language of the CPR, it seems to me this construction gives effect to the particular purpose of encouraging litigants to be selective as to the points they take and thus decreasing costs of litigation.'[339]

In view of the above, caution ought to be exercised when considering authorities that were decided in 2000 and 2001 (and possibly as late as early 2002).

The approach to issue-aware orders

The approach to making an issue-aware may be summarised in the following way. **6.163**

- **Examine the issues and determine who has won** CPR, r 44.2(4)(b), specifically requires the court to have regard to whether a party has succeeded on part of its case, even if the party has not been wholly successful.
- **Consider whether any issues were unreasonably argued** CPR, r 44.2(5), requires the court to consider whether it was reasonable for a party to raise, pursue or contest a particular issue and the manner in which that party has pursued or defended that issue.
- **Consider the available range of orders** CPR, r 44.2(6), sets out a range of orders that might be suitable for an issue-aware approach (see 6.29).

What is meant by 'an issue'? A point that has not been addressed in any great detail under the CPR is what constitutes 'an issue'. Whilst it is guidance that was considered under a very different regime to the CPR, it is perhaps worth noting that Bowen LJ referred to issues as being 'heads of controversy'.[340] Thomas J (giving judgment in a pre-CPR case) has referred to an issue as being 'identified parts of the litigation in respect of which the party's costs may be taxed'.[341] **6.164**

For an issue-aware order to be made, it would generally be the case that the issue is a discrete matter in the sense that costs may be attributed to it.[342] Stuart-Smith LJ had this to say on the topic: **6.165**

> 'I would . . . not be prepared to say that the Court could never make an order depriving a party of part of its costs without being able to identify that there were (or would have

[338] See *Summit Property Ltd v Pitmans* [2002] EWCA Civ 2020; *Stena Rederi Aktiebolag* [2003] EWCA Civ 214; *Kastor Navigation Co Ltd & Anor v AXA Global Risks (UK) Ltd & Ors* [2004] EWCA Civ 277.

[339] *Stocznia Gdanska SA v Latvian Shipping Co*, The Times, 8 May 2001.

[340] *Foster v Farquhar* [1893] 1 QB 564.

[341] *Colburt v Beard* [1992] 2 Ad R 67, at 69.

[342] See, eg, *HLB Kidsons (a firm) v Lloyds Underwriters* [2007] EWHC 2699 (Comm), at [12], *per* Gloster J; see also *Pindell v Airasia Berhad* [2010] EWHC 3238 (Comm), at [12], [13] and [16], *per* Tomlinson LJ; *Jones v SS for Energy and Climate Change* [2012] EWHC 3647 (QB), at [61], *per* Swift J; *Arroyo & Ors v Equion Energia Ltd* [2016] EWHC 3348 (TCC), at [15]–[17], *per* Stuart-Smith J.

been) costs discretely attributable to the circumstances on which the unsuccessful party relies. However, in general, it is unlikely to be just to deprive a successful party of part of his costs (still less to make an order which effectively requires him to pay part of the unsuccessful party's costs) by reference to an issue or other circumstances which have not affected the overall level of costs that have been incurred. Even when what is being considered is conduct, rather than the loss of one or more issues, it will generally not be just to deprive a successful party of part of its costs because of conduct which has had no adverse impact on the incidence of costs. Put another way, if what is complained about has had no impact on costs, it will require cogent reasons to justify depriving a successful party of part of its costs on the basis of the complaint.'[343]

6.166 In a similar vein, Coulson J had this to say:

> 'If a defendant took 10 points, and was successful on 7 of them, such that the claim against him failed, it seems to me that the claimant should only be entitled to an issue-based costs order if the three points on which the defendant was unsuccessful made a material difference to the length of the trial, and therefore the costs incurred on both sides.'[344]

Judge Hodge QC (sitting as a judge of the Chancery Division) has said that this means that the costs of evidence which would have been adduced in any event cannot be regarded as being the costs of discreet issues.[345]

6.167 It would be a mistake to equate issues with the mere facts of the arguments that may have been put; in this regard Nugee J had the following to say:

> 'I accept that in some cases the court can take the view that a party that has succeeded overall should not recover all its costs if it has lost on some sub-issues. But there is a limit to which this principle can be taken. I do not regard it as appropriate ... to drill down below [the substantial issues in the case] ... Any issue of any complexity is likely to involve sub-issues and sub-sub-issues on which one side or other has the better of the argument: this is not by itself a reason for departing from the general rule.'[346]

6.168 Whilst it is no more than the editor's own thoughts, an issue may be said to be an identifiable aspect of the litigation that is sufficiently discrete and substantial to allow costs, other than insignificant costs, specifically to be attributed to it.

6.169 **The need to consider an issue-aware approach** Circumstances may arise in which the court would be required to consider making an issue-aware order. This tends particularly to be so in cases in which the issues are distinct. By way of illustration, Chadwick LJ made the following comments in a case in which the trial judge had (wrongly) failed to analyse the matter in an issue-aware way:

> 'This was a case in which, as it seems to me, the judge was required to consider whether to make an issue-based costs order; he had to consider that question if he were to comply with the guidance given in [the then equivalent of CPR 44.2 rule (4)(b)] ... [Certain claims] clearly did raise quite separate issues: perhaps distinct from each other and clearly distinct from the [other] issues. The matters for consideration, and the evidence in relation to those

343 *Arroyo & Ors v Equion Energia Ltd* [2016] EWHC 3348 (TCC), at [17].
344 *J Murphy & Sons Ltd v Johnston Precast Ltd (No 2)* [2008] EWHC 3104 (TCC), at [11].
345 *Praxis Capital Ltd v Burgess* [2015] EWHC 1801 (Ch), at [18].
346 *Merck KCaA v Merck Sharp & Dohme Corpn* [2014] EWHC 3920 (Ch), at [6].

> two claims were, as it seems to me, quite distinct from the matters which had to be considered in relation to [those other issues].'[347]

In this regard, it is worth noting that that CPR, r 44.2(4)(b), now says that the court 'will' have regard to whether a party has succeeded on part of its case, even if the party has not been wholly successful. Prior to 1 April 2013, the then-equivalent rule used to say 'must';[348] it is a moot point whether this minor change of wording has changed the law.

The exercise of discretion When considering whether an issue-aware approach is appropriate, Neuberger J has suggested that the following factors might be relevant: **6.170**

- the reasonableness of the successful party taking the point on which the party was unsuccessful in that connection (CPR, r 44.2(5)(b));
- the manner in which the successful party took the point and conducted its case generally (CPR, r 44.2(5)(c));
- the reasonableness of the point—that is, whether it was reasonable for the successful party to have taken the point in the circumstances;
- the extra costs in terms of preparing for the trial and preparing witness statements, documents and so on;
- the extra time taken in court over the particular issues raised by the point;[349]
- the extent to which the point was interrelated in terms of evidence and argument with the points on which the successful party was successful; and
- standing back and looking at the matter globally, the extent to which it is just in all of the circumstances to deprive the successful party of all or any of its costs because of the fact that it was unsuccessful on one or more issues.[350]

This list of factors (which was formulated in 2000) is very much in keeping with the guidance that Rix LJ would give four years later,[351] so the concerns mentioned at 6.158–6.162 probably do not apply. Put otherwise, there is no reason to believe that Neuberger J's comments do not remain good law.

Determination of the correct order Regardless of the eventual form of the order, the making of an issue-aware order is a two-stage process. The first may be called the 'formulation' stage (6.172–6.173), and the second, the 'adjustment' stage (6.174–6.175). **6.171**

The formulation stage The first stage involves identifying the appropriate competing issues and formulating the approach to be taken. Chadwick LJ described the process in this way: **6.172**

> 'An issue based approach requires a judge to consider, issue by issue in relation to those issues to which that approach is to be applied, where the costs on each distinct or discrete issue should fall. If, in relation to any issue in the case before it the court considers that it should adopt an issue based approach to costs, the court must ask itself which party has been successful on that issue. Then, if the costs are to follow the event on that issue, the party who has

[347] *Aspin v Metric Group Ltd* [2007] EWCA Civ 922, at [23]. See also *Rolf v de Guerin* [2011] EWCA Civ 78.

[348] See The Civil Procedure (Amendment) Rules 2013 (SI 2013/262).

[349] Where an issue arises only during the course of argument, it may be open to the court to find that it was too bound up with the rest of the issues to justify an issue-aware award: see *Investec Bank (UK) Ltd v Zulman* [2010] EWCA Civ 675, at [5], *per* Longmore LJ.

[350] *Antonelli v Allen*, The Times, 8 December 2000.

[351] *Kastor Navigation Co Ltd v AXA Global Risks (UK) Ltd* [2004] EWCA Civ 277.

> been unsuccessful on that issue must expect to pay the costs of that issue to the party who has succeeded on that issue. That is the effect of applying the general principle on an issue by issue based approach to costs.'[352]

6.173 Where an issues-based order is sought, Henry Carr J has commented that it may be helpful if the court is provided with a document akin to a *Scott* schedule that gives an indication as to the amounts of costs involved in respect of each issue.[353]

6.174 *The adjustment stage* The second stage involves standing back and looking at the effect of the proposed order. Rix LJ (giving judgment of the court) had this to say on the subject:

> 'The rules required [the judge] to have regard to all the circumstances of the case ... He should have stood back from the mathematical result and asked himself whether in all the circumstances, including the other factors to which we have referred, it was the right result.'[354]

6.175 For obvious reasons, there will be a significant amount of overlap between the two stages. Rix LJ cautioned against an overly rigorous and mathematical approach to the formulation of orders (see 6.25).[355] In a similar vein, Ramsey J has commented (in the context of a percentage order) that there is no simple formula for establishing the award based on the number of issues, pages of evidence or paragraphs of submissions or judgments; he said that the decision must, to some extent, be impressionistic based on knowledge of the case.[356]

6.176 **Issue-aware orders and Part 36 offers** Under the original wording of Part 36, Rix LJ found that the phrase 'his costs' in what was the then equivalent of CPR, r 36.14(3)(b), should not be read as if it said 'all his costs'; therefore, if the court wished to deprive an otherwise successful litigant of costs of an unsuccessful issue, then the fact that that claimant had beaten a Part 36 offer did not prevent the court from giving effect to its wishes.[357] This is no longer good law: although the jurisdiction to make such an order exists, where a party's entitlement to costs has arisen by reason of that party having beaten a Part 36 offer, the court would have to be persuaded that there was something unjust in applying the normal rule.[358] This is addressed in more detail at 17.88–17.91 and Chapter 17 generally.

6.177 **Depriving a successful party of the costs of an unsuccessful issue** For the reasons set out above (see 6.162), a party may be deprived of the costs of unsuccessful issues regardless of whether they were reasonably or unreasonably argued. This does not necessarily mean that the costs of an unsuccessful issue will be awarded against a party, however (see 6.178–6.189). For obvious reasons, a party is more likely to be deprived of the

---

352 *Summit Property Ltd v Pitmans* [2002] EWCA Civ 2020, at [27].

353 See *Stretchline Intellectual Property Ltd v H&M Hennes & Mauritz (UK) Ltd* [2016] EWHC 163 (Pat).

354 *Kastor Navigation Co Ltd v AXA Global Risks (UK) Ltd* [2004] EWCA Civ 277, at [153].

355 See also *Douglas v Hello! Ltd* [2004] EWHC 63 (Ch), in which it was held that an overly rigorous issue-aware approach would not properly reflect the amount of time taken up by the fact that so many issues were unnecessarily taken.

356 *Mears Ltd v Leeds City Council* [2011] EWHC 2694 (TCC), at [28].

357 *Kastor Navigation Co Ltd v AXA Global Risks (UK) Ltd* [2004] EWCA Civ 277, at [135]–[139].

358 *Fulham Leisure Holdings Ltd v Nicholson Graham & Jones* [2006] EWHC 2428 (Ch).

costs of an unsuccessful issue—or even condemned to pay those costs—if it was argued unreasonably (see below).

Requiring a successful party to pay the costs of an unsuccessful issue

Where an unsuccessful issue was argued unreasonably Where an unsuccessful issue was argued unreasonably, then there are good reasons why the party at fault may be condemned to pay the costs of that issue. Simon Brown LJ explained it in this way: **6.178**

> 'For my part I have no doubt whatever that judges nowadays should be altogether readier than in times past to make costs orders which reflect not merely the overall outcome of proceedings but also the loss of particular issues. If, moreover, the "winning" party has not merely lost on an issue but has pursued an issue when clearly he should not have done, then there are two good reasons why that should be reflected in the costs order: first, as a sanction to deter such conduct in future; secondly, to relieve the "losing" party of at least part of his costs liability. It is one thing for the losing party to have to pay the costs of issues properly before the court, another that he should have to pay also for fighting issues which were hopeless and ought never to have been pursued.'[359]

Where an unsuccessful issue was argued reasonably As has already been mentioned, a party who reasonably argued an unsuccessful issue may be deprived of the costs of that issue (see 6.165 and 6.177). A related, but distinct, topic is whether the costs of an unsuccessful issue can be awarded against a party who reasonably pursued the point in question. Christopher Clarke J—having made the observation that 'it is a fortunate litigant who wins on every point'—went on to say that if a successful claimant had lost on a number of issues, then unless those issues were argued unreasonably, it would normally be inappropriate to condemn the claimant in the costs of those issues.[360] In a similar vein, Simon Brown LJ said that 'the court can properly have regard to the fact that in almost every case even the winner is likely to fail on some issues'.[361] **6.179**

That said, such a forgiving approach will not be appropriate in every case. Indeed, Longmore LJ has found that an adverse award of costs of lost issues may be made even in the absence of unreasonable conduct.[362] Longmore LJ went on to introduce the notion that a case must be 'exceptional': **6.180**

> 'It is thus a matter of ordinary common sense that if it is appropriate to consider costs on an issue basis at all, it may be appropriate, in a suitably exceptional case, to make an order which not only deprives a successful party of his costs of a particular issue but also an order which requires him to pay the otherwise unsuccessful party's costs of that issue, without it being necessary for the court to decide that allegations have been made improperly or unreasonably.'[363]

In a similar vein, Lord Neuberger MR said (*obiter*) that, in 'an extreme case, he [the generally successful party] may even have to pay some of the unsuccessful party's costs'.[364]

---

359 *Budgen v Andrew Gardner Partnership* [2002] EWCA Civ 1125, at [26].

360 *Travelers Casualty and Surety Co of Canada v Sun Life Assurance Co of Canada (UK) Ltd* [2006] EWHC 2885 (Comm), at [12].

361 *Budgen v Andrew Gardner Partnership* [2002] EWCA Civ 1125, at [35]. See also *Sugar Hut Group Ltd v AJ Insurance Service (a partnership)* [2016] EWCA Civ 46, at [14], *per* Tomlinson LJ.

362 *Summit Property Ltd v Pitmans* [2002] EWCA Civ 2020.

363 *Ibid*, at [17].

364 *M v Mayor and Burgesses of the London Borough of Croydon* [2012] EWCA Civ 595, at [45].

6.181 Longmore LJ did not expand upon what might amount to an exceptional case, but, in a subsequent case, Warren J had this to say:

> 'I note there the words "in a suitably exceptional case". I do not read those words "suitably exceptional case" as meaning that one goes back to *Elgindata* and has to find unreasonable or improper conduct or, because we know that that is not what we have to find, something pretty close to it; but it does mean something out of the ordinary in some sort of relevant way.'[365]

Warren J went on to say this:

> 'The task is to identify those cases where the loss on an issue carries the costs sanction ranging from deprivation of costs to an order against the losing party on that issue. The test ... is that one no longer has to find improper or unreasonable conduct. Instead, as Longmore LJ puts it [in *Summit*], one has to find a suitably exceptional case so far as concerns making adverse orders.'[366]

6.182 The topic of what amounts to an exceptional case is addressed at 6.185. It should be noted, however, that both Arnold J[367] and Birss J[368] have said—in patent cases—that Longmore LJ's mention of the phrase 'suitably exceptional' is not a criterion that was intended to impose a specific requirement of exceptionality; as such, it appears that there is a range of judicial opinion as to what the appropriate test is, at least in patent cases.

6.183 *Two spurious arguments* It has been argued that if the court were to order parties to pay costs of issues that were unsuccessfully, but reasonably, argued, then the court's armoury would be left understocked for those cases in which there had been improper conduct. That argument did not find favour with Aldous, Chadwick or Munby LJJ.[369] Indeed, Tomlinson J has commented on the positive benefits that issue-aware awards would bring in encouraging parties to be selective about the points that they take.[370]

6.184 It has also been argued that awarding costs against a party who had won the litigation, but who had lost on an issue, might do injustice by 'redefining who has won'. Rix LJ (giving judgment to which Tuckey and Neuberger LJJ had contributed) rejected that submission.[371]

6.185 *What amounts to an exceptional case?* Warren J was able to find exceptionality in the fact that an issue was discrete and significant.[372] In a similar vein, Mann J said that had it not been for the fact that one of the parties had made an offer, he would have found that the fact that a party had chosen, albeit reasonably, to defend its position without any affirmative supporting evidence would have made the case exceptional.[373] It seems, therefore, that the requirement of exceptionality is not a significant fetter upon the court's discretion.

---

365 *Activis Ltd v Merck & Co Inc* [2007] EWHC 1625 (Pat), at [15].

366 *Ibid*, at [26] and [30].

367 See *Hospira UK Ltd v Novartis AG* [2013] EWHC 886 (Pat), at [4], *per* Arnold J.

368 See *Wobben Properties GmbH* [2015] EWHC 2863 (Pat), at [8], *per* Birss J.

369 *Stena Rederi Aktiebolag* [2003] EWCA Civ 214.

370 *Base Metal Trading Ltd v Shamurin* [2003] EWHC 2606 (Comm).

371 *Kastor Navigation Co Ltd & Anor v AXA Global Risks (UK) Ltd & Ors* [2004] EWCA Civ 277, at [143].

372 Coulson J rejected the submission that *Fleming v Chief Constable of Sussex Police Force* [2004] EWCA Civ 643 was authority for the proposition that an issue-aware order was required where any discrete issue added significantly to the length of the trial: *J Murphy & Sons Ltd v Johnston Precast Ltd (Formerly Johnston Pipes Ltd) (No 2 Costs)* [2008] EWHC 3104 (TCC), at [9]; cf *Shore v Sedgewick Financial Services Ltd* [2007] EWHC 3054 (QB).

373 *Fulham Leisure Holdings Ltd v Nicholson Graham & Jones* [2006] EWHC 2428 (Ch), at [10].

This should come as no surprise because the art of making orders for costs is not a matter of applying mechanistic rules, but a matter of making an order that best suits the facts of the case in hand.

The court will not focus on every small issue that may have been lost and adjust the costs accordingly. In this regard, Coulson J had this to say in the context of a commercial claim: **6.186**

> 'In civil litigation it is almost inevitable that there will have been some point or argument, raised by the otherwise successful party but rejected by the judge, which will have added to the length of the trial. In my view, the mere fact that the successful party was not successful on every last issue cannot, of itself, justify an issue-based costs order.'[374]

At the other end of the spectrum, if a party has taken a 'kitchen sink approach', that party may find that the court will make very significant adjustments, even to the extent of making no order as to costs.[375] **6.187**

The costs of reasonably argued unsuccessful issues in personal injury cases In the context of a personal injuries case, Jackson LJ came to much the same conclusion that Coulson J had reached in a commercial claim (see 6.186).[376] In a different case, Jackson LJ appeared to draw a distinction between personal injury cases and other types of case: **6.188**

> 'In a personal injury action the fact that the claimant has won on some issues and lost on other issues along the way is not normally a reason for depriving the claimant of part of his costs ... Indeed the fact that the claimant has deliberately exaggerated his claim may in certain instances not be a good reason for depriving him of part of his costs ... Nevertheless in other cases ... the fact that the successful party has failed on certain issues may constitute a good reason for modifying the costs order in his favour.'[377]

In a similar vein, Patterson J has commented that, in a personal injury action, the fact that the claimant has won on some issues and lost on others is not unusual.[378]

Unsuccessful issues in the context of contributory negligence Contributory negligence merits particular attention (also see 6.86). In comments that resonate with those of Stuart-Smith LJ regarding the fact that the costs of issues must be discrete and discernible (see 6.164), Arden LJ has said that it is permissible to proceed on the basis that an issue of contributory negligence caused no distinct costs and that any reduction on account of contributory negligence would have been of the most minimal kind.[379] That said, she stressed the fact that there is no general rule that there can be no reduction in any circumstances in which there **6.189**

---

[374] *J Murphy & Sons Ltd v Johnson Precast Ltd (No 2) (Costs)* [2008] EWHC 3104 (TCC), at [10]. See also *Pindell Ltd & Anor v Airasia Berhad (formerly known as Airasia SDN BHD)* [2010] EWHC 3238 (Comm), at [12] and [19], *per* Tomlinson LJ (sitting in the Commercial Court).

[375] See, eg, *Dexia Crediop SpA v Comune di Prato* [2016] EWHC 252 (Comm), *per* Walker J.

[376] *Goodwin v Bennetts UK Ltd* [2008] EWCA Civ 1658, at [21]; see also *Fox v Foundation Piling Ltd* [2011] EWCA Civ 790, at [47]. Gloster LJ approved of that analysis: *Walker Construction (UK) Ltd v Quayside Homes Ltd* [2014] EWCA Civ 93, at [88].

[377] *Fox v Foundation Piling Ltd* [2011] EWCA Civ 790, at [48]. Whilst a dissenting judgment, see also *Marcus v Medway Primary Care Trust* [2011] EWCA Civ 750, at [30], *per* Jackson LJ.

[378] *Cutting v Islam* [2014] EWHC 1515 (QB), at [72].

[379] *Abbott v Long* [2011] EWCA Civ 874, at [13]. See also *Barclays Bank plc v Christie Owen & Davies Ltd* (unreported), 24 November 2016, Ch D, at [6]–[12], *per* Mr Richard Spearman QC.

has been a claim for contributory negligence; indeed, there have been instances in which the court has taken contributory negligence into account for the purposes of making an issue-aware order.[380]

6.190 In practice, the court will regard an allegation of contributory negligence as being part of the trial on liability—and this is so even if that issue is heard as a preliminary issue. Where the parties have treated liability and contributory negligence as being separate topics for the purposes of negotiation, that is something that may be taken into account as being part of the parties' conduct.[381]

6.191 **Successful issues argued unreasonably and 'costs building'** It sounds oxymoronic to speak of successful issues that were argued unreasonably, but in practice it is relatively common for parties to incur inappropriate costs expenditure in dealing with issues that simply did not justify it. At its most extreme, such practices may be categorised as 'costs building'.

6.192 It is therefore relevant that the issue-aware approach is not limited to unsuccessful issues. Chadwick LJ had this to say on the topic:

> 'There will be cases ... where, on an issue by issue approach, a party who has been successful on an issue may still be denied his costs of that issue because, in the view of the court, he has pursued it unreasonably.'[382]

Likewise, in a different case, Chadwick LJ remarked that the 'judge may deprive a party of costs on an issue on which he has been successful if satisfied that the party has acted unreasonably in relation to that issue'.[383]

6.193 A systemic or reckless attitude to mitigation of costs may be relevant.[384] For the avoidance of doubt, the court may disallow the costs of a successful issue where either there was no need to litigate the point at all, because it was not a necessary ingredient of a party's case, or where the issue was not likely to be contentious and did not need to be proved. The court may also disallow costs to the extent that a party has incurred excessive costs in proving a point, but that is something that would generally best be addressed at the time costs are assessed.

6.194 **Issues and preliminary issues hearings** The court may order—often at the request of the parties—that certain issues be decided at a preliminary issues hearing or preliminary trial of the issues. Where this is so, the following points may arise.

---

[380] See, eg, *Lloyds Bank plc v McBains Cooper* [2017] EWHC 30 (TCC), at [92]–[95], *per* Sir Antony Edwards-Stuart.

[381] See *Sonmez v Kebabery Wholesale Ltd* [2009] EWCA Civ 1386, at [22], *per* Ward LJ; *Onay v Brown* [2009] EWCA Civ 775, at [29], *per* Goldring LJ.

[382] *Summit Property Ltd v Pitmans* [2002] EWCA Civ 2020, at [27].

[383] *Johnsey Estates (1990) Ltd v Secretary of State for the Environment* [2001] EWCA Civ 535, at [21].

[384] See, eg, *Abbott v Long* [2011] EWCA Civ 874, at [15] and [17], in which Arden LJ said that a reckless attitude to mitigation of costs (such as where a serial litigant repeatedly incurs expenses without taking any steps to minimise his expenditure) may be relevant in that it may justify the court making a reduction to the costs that is not necessarily limited to the increase in costs that that conduct had caused. In this regard, she referred to *Widlake v BAA* [2009] EWHC Civ 1256, at [41], *per* Ward LJ, and *Walsh v Singh* [2011] EWHC Civ 80, at [25], *per* Arden LJ.

- **Success on an issue generally** Whilst it may, from time to time, be appropriate to make an order at the end of a preliminary issues hearing, it would be wrong to confuse success on an issue (even an important one that took up a great deal of time) with success in the litigation as a whole.[385] Coulson J had this to say on the point:

  'The mere fact that a party has won a preliminary issue does not, of itself, entitle that party to its costs of that issue. Before knowing the overall outcome of the trial, it is always dangerous to give one party its costs of an issue merely because, through a sensible case management decision, one aspect of the substantive dispute was dealt with in advance of the others.'[386]

  Similarly, Jack J said that it would be only in the most exceptional case that the determination of costs should take place prior to the conclusion of the proceedings.[387] Somewhat at odds with Coulson J's comment are the following comments of Nugee J:

  'It is in general a salutary principle that those who lose discrete aspects of complex litigation should pay for the discrete applications or hearings which they lose, and should do so when they lose them rather than leaving the costs to be swept up at trial.'[388]

  That said, Nugee J was dealing with a preliminary issues hearing in which the 'main' issues for trial would be dependent on the outcome of the hearing and had not yet been pleaded. The apparent difference between Nugee J's approach and that of Coulson J is merely a reflection of the fact that each case must be decided on its own facts.
- **Success on an issue in relation to an offer** In a similar vein, Jackson J has explained that where a party raises the issue of an offer prior to the conclusion of proceedings, the normal response would be to reserve costs.[389] The topic of offers and preliminary issues is addressed in detail at 17.58.
- **Group litigation** The topic of preliminary issues in the context of group litigation is addressed at 65.107.
- **Change of mind** Where the court orders that a preliminary issues hearing should take place, it will state those issues,[390] usually in the form of an order. Where a party changes its mind about the usefulness of a preliminary issues hearing, that party may be ordered to pay the costs thrown away.[391]

---

[385] *Perriam Ltd v Wayne* [2011] EWHC 403 (QB), at [58]; cf *Fiona Trust & Holding Corpn v Privalov* [2011] EWHC 664 (Comm), at [14], in which Andrew Smith J explained that the application of the general rule requires consideration of the overall relative success of the parties in respect of the relevant hearing(s) or stage(s) in the litigation, ie generally those in respect of which an award of costs is being considered, and the court is not concerned, for this purpose, about which party has won on individual issues.

[386] *Perriam Ltd v Wayne* [2011] EWHC 403 (QB), at [53].

[387] *Tullett Prebon plc v BGC Brokers LP* [2010] EWHC 989 (QB), at [6]; see also *HSS Hire Services Group plc v Builders Merchants Ltd* [2005] EWCA Civ 626; *Shepherds Investments Ltd v Walters* [2007] EWCA Civ 29; *Multiplex Constructions (UK) Ltd v Cleveland Bridge (UK) Ltd* [2007] EWHC 659 (TCC), at [26].

[388] *Merck KCaA v Merck Sharp & Dohme Corpn* [2014] EWHC 3920 (Ch), at [6].

[389] *Multiplex Constructions (UK) Ltd v Cleveland Bridge (UK) Ltd* [2007] EWHC 659 (TCC), at [26]. See also *Ted Baker plc v AXA Insurance UK Plc* [2012] EWHC 1779 (Comm); *Sellers v Buyer* [2014] EWHC 596 (Ch), at [16], *per* Morgan J; *Interactive Technology Corpn Ltd v Ferster* [2017] EWHC 1510 (Ch), *per* Morgan J.

[390] *Lahey v Pirelli Tyres Ltd* [2007] EWCA Civ 91, at [4].

[391] *LBI HF (Formerly Landsbanki Islands HF) v Stanford* [2013] EWHC 2535 (Ch), *per* Mann J.

Issues that were abandoned or barely pursued

6.195 The costs of issues that have been abandoned or barely pursued merit special attention. There is no doubt that the court can take such issues into account, even if they are abandoned before they ever come before the court.[392]

6.196 Whilst they are now both quite old, two cases are relevant. The first, *Shirley v Caswell*,[393] was clarified by the second, *Dooley v Parker*.[394] Before those cases are addressed, it is worth saying—at the risk of stating the obvious—that the fact that an issue has not been pursued will not always mean that adverse costs consequences will be visited upon the party who raised it. By way of example, Tugendhat J has said that the court should be careful not to discourage parties from keeping all of their arguments under review and from sensibly deciding not to argue a point.[395] Again at the risk of stating the obvious, it should be noted that only those issues that were part of the claim should be taken into account; it would not be appropriate to take into account issues that were in dispute, but which were not part of the claim.[396]

6.197 **The need to avoid double jeopardy** The net effect of *Shirley* and *Dooley* is that the court should be careful not to penalise a receiving party twice for the same decision—that is, a costs judge should not normally disallow costs because an issue was not pursued if the costs of that issue have already been taken into account when the costs order was made.[397] *Shirley* and *Dooley* are relevant not only to how the order should be framed, but also to how the assessment should be conducted.

6.198 ***Shirley v Caswell*** *Shirley* was a claim in professional negligence against a barrister. After a lengthy trial, the claimants won, but they had abandoned—or had barely pursued—a number of the pleaded issues. The trial judge took the view that these issues should be reflected in the costs order, so he made a reciprocal order for costs in that he ordered the defendant to pay 60 per cent of claimants' costs and the claimants to pay 40 per cent of defendant's costs. The claimants appealed that decision.

6.199 Chadwick LJ (with whom Buxton and Aldous LJJ agreed) found that there was no basis for disturbing the order that the claimants pay 40 per cent of the defendant's costs, the order being justified as taking into account 'costs thrown away'. However, Chadwick LJ found that the trial judge's order in relation to the claimants' costs should not stand:

> 'The costs of issues abandoned, or not pursued at trial, ought, *prima facie*, to be disallowed against the party incurring them on an assessment of the costs of that party by the costs judge because, again *prima facie*, they are costs which have been unnecessarily incurred in the litigation. To take them into account in making a special costs order

392 If authority were needed on the point, see *R (on the application of Srinivasans Solicitors v Croydon County Court* [2013] EWCA Civ 249, at [13], *per* Mummery LJ.

393 *Shirley v Caswell* [2001] 1 Costs LR 1.

394 *Dooley v Parker* [2002] EWCA Civ 1118.

395 *D Pride & Partners v Institute for Animal Health* [2009] EWHC 1617 (QB).

396 See, eg, *Naseem t/a SH Builders and Contractors v Kang* [2011] EWCA Civ 737, at [40].

397 This must be distinguished from circumstances in which costs have been unreasonably or improperly incurred in pursuing an issue—such as where the issue was dishonestly advanced—in which case the court may take that conduct into account both at the time of making the order and when assessing the costs: *Northstar Systems v Fielding* [2006] EWCA Civ 1660; *Nugent v Goss Aviation* [2002] EWHC 1281 (QB), at [50].

> carries the risk that the claimants will be doubly penalised. They will be deprived of costs under the order, and again deprived of the same costs on an assessment or taxation.'[398]

Chadwick LJ indicated that the appropriate way of dealing with the costs of abandoned issues was to leave those costs for assessment, where they could be disallowed as being unreasonably incurred. In a different case, Waller LJ came to a similar conclusion concerning the costs of medical reports that had been left unused.[399]

Dooley v Parker In *Dooley*, which was heard about a year after *Shirley*, Dyson LJ clarified Chadwick LJ's comments. *Dooley* concerned a dispute over certain rights over land; the claimant had raised a number of issues, two of which had been abandoned. The court was troubled to hear that *Shirley* was being perceived as laying down a principle that where a party had been successful generally, but had raised and then abandoned certain issues, the court was prevented from awarding that party only a proportion of its costs. Dyson LJ strongly disagreed with that interpretation of *Shirley*. After having set out the relevant part of Chadwick LJ's judgment, he made these comments: **6.200**

> 'I do not read this passage as laying down any broad statement of principle other than the obvious one that an order should not penalise a party twice over. It is plain ... that there is jurisdiction to order the paying party to pay only a proportion of the receiving party's costs. That will commonly be appropriate where the receiving party has failed on one or more issues in the case having succeeded on others. Of course, if an order is made disallowing part of a receiving party's costs, then the costs judge must take account of that fact when making the assessment of costs and take great care to make sure that a double penalty is not imposed. There should be no difficulty about this, since the costs judge should know from the terms of the judgment of the trial judge ordering payment of a proportion of a party's costs, that that is what the trial judge did and the reasons why he or she did it.'[400]

Some commentators have said that *Dooley* has confined *Shirley* to its own facts. Whilst it is only his opinion, the editor does not agree.[401] The better analysis, in his view, is that the question of whether abandoned issues are reflected in the order for costs will depend on the facts of each case—that is, that the court is free to do what most adequately meets the justice of the situation. Where, as in *Shirley*, the task of disentangling and quantifying the costs of abandoned issues is likely to be a one that, if relegated to the assessment, would result in the requisite reductions being made on the grounds of reasonableness, then it may well be appropriate for the trial judge to award the successful party costs without deduction. Where, on the other hand, it is not clear whether the costs would be disallowed on the assessment or where there is a risk that significant costs would be incurred in resolving that topic, then it may be appropriate for abandoned issues to be reflected in the order for costs. **6.201**

The role of the costs judge in relation to the costs of abandoned issues Whilst the court should be cautious not to penalise a party twice over, it should not be forgotten that the costs judge's ordinary function is to disallow costs that have been unreasonably incurred. This was explained by Burton J: **6.202**

> 'On an assessment the costs judge, who will *prima facie* disallow costs in respect of issues abandoned or not pursued, as the Court of Appeal has directed to do in

398 *Shirley v Caswell* [2001] 1 Costs LR 1, at [18].
399 *Hall & Ors v Stone* [2007] EWCA Civ 1354, at [79].
400 *Dooley v Parker* [2002] EWCA Civ 1118, at [32].
401 Not least because Neuberger MR made no adverse comment about *Shirley* in *Motto & Ors v Trafigura Ltd & Anor* [2011] EWCA Civ 1150, at [79].

Shirley v Caswell, will in any event disallow the costs of any claims which were positively struck out.'[402]

When Burton J's judgment is read in the light of *Dooley*, it is clear that the costs judge's role is not immutable, but will turn on the correct interpretation of the costs order. A corollary to this is that the costs judge's ordinary function ought to be borne in mind when the order is made.

6.203 In particular, it should be borne in mind that a costs judge will ordinarily disallow costs unreasonably or disproportionately incurred and that this may be in addition to the costs affirmatively struck out by way of the costs order. Whilst not relating specifically to the costs of abandoned issues, Waller LJ has made it clear that—if the circumstances so require, such as where the receiving party has been dishonest—there is no reason in principle why the costs of an issue should not be taken into account both at the time the order was made and at the time of the assessment:

> 'Clearly there is no problem if the judge's order makes "no order as to costs", but if the judge orders a reduction by say 20% without more, what would be the natural construction of that order? My view is that the natural construction of such an order, unless the contrary is expressly stated, is that the party guilty of dishonesty should not be entitled to say on assessment, "my costs incurred in seeking to make a dishonest case can be taken as reasonably incurred because the judge has made a reduction". If the dishonest party was entitled to succeed on such an argument, he will hardly suffer any penalty at all.'[403]

Thus the court is, in appropriate circumstances, able to make disallowances both in the costs order and upon assessment (although care must be taken not to inflict double jeopardy).

6.204 Whilst a slight digression, it is worth noting that Neuberger MR had this to say about the role of a costs judge in relation to the costs of abandoned issues in a case in which no relevant issue-aware order had been made:

> 'Having said that the trial judge could "deprive [a successful claimant] of costs on issues on which they failed", Chadwick LJ [in *Shirley* at [60]] clearly proceeded on the basis that, on an assessment the costs judge could deprive the claimant of such costs even if there was a full costs order in his favour—unless the trial judge had clearly held that the claimant should recover such costs.'[404]

Thus, unless prevented from doing so in accordance with *Dooley*, a costs judge has free rein. Again, this fact ought to be borne in mind at the time the costs order is made.

6.205 **Issues supposedly abandoned and offers** It will not always be obvious whether a party has abandoned an issue. In a case in which the defendant had made an offer putatively in respect of only one aspect of the claimant's injuries (this being on the basis that the other injuries had allegedly been caused by someone else), Stadlen J found that the offer was capable of being accepted in respect of the whole claim and that the claimant was entitled to her costs accordingly.[405]

---

402 *Nugent v Goss Aviation* [2002] EWHC 1281 (QB), at [50].

403 *Northstar Systems v Fielding* [2006] EWCA Civ 1660, at [33].

404 *Motto & Ors v Trafigura Ltd & Anor* [2011] EWCA Civ 1150, at [79]. Neuberger MR additionally cited *Lahey v Pirelli Tyres Ltd* [2007] EWCA Civ 91, at [23], on this point.

405 *Sutherland v Turnbull* [2010] EWHC 2699 (QB), at [29]–[32].

Abandoned issues and group litigation The topic of abandoned issues in the context of group litigation is addressed at 65.50. **6.206**

Admissible offers and the incidence of costs

Negotiations or offers that have taken place on a 'without prejudice, save as to costs' basis are admissible on the question of entitlement to costs.[406] Where such an offer is admissible and where it is not an offer to which the costs consequences under Part 36 apply, it is referred to as an 'admissible offer'.[407] Withdrawn Part 36 offers are a species of admissible offer,[408] as are offers that have fallen short of being Part 36 offers for technical reasons (these being so-called failed Part 36 offers).[409] For present purposes, an admissible offer differs from a *Calderbank* offer[410] only in name, but there may be differences in that it is possible that some admissible offers may not be capable of acceptance if there is a dispute as to their status (see 17.77–17.78). Extant Part 36 offers are dealt with at 17.80–17.163. Part 36 offers that have been withdrawn and withdrawn offers generally are addressed at 6.240. Special provisions apply to admiralty claims (see 6.244–6.245). **6.207**

The relevance of negotiations generally (as opposed to offers per se)

The reasonableness of offers (and responses thereto) should be distinguished from the reasonableness of a party's conduct in negotiations in general. Whilst this may be a factor, in general, the court will be slow to consider the latter (although see 6.118 in relation to ADR and 6.141 in relation to a failure to respond to offers). Tomlinson LJ had this to say on the topic: **6.208**

> 'A judge should in my view be very slow to entertain a discussion as to whether parties to litigation have negotiated in a reasonable manner. Such an enquiry opens up the prospect of undesirable and wasteful satellite litigation, as the reasonableness of a negotiating stance may and almost certainly usually will depend upon a careful evaluation of the respective states of knowledge of the parties. The Part 36 regime is designed precisely to obviate this kind of enquiry.'[411]

The point in time at which to consider admissible offers

A party may make an offer and then have such a degree of success prior to conclusion of the proceedings that it is nearly inevitable that they will beat the offer, such as where there has been a trial on a preliminary issue. Where those are the circumstances, it does not follow that the court should determine the relevant costs at that stage. This is not only because it will be only upon conclusion that the court could be sure that the offeror had truly beaten the offer, but also because their putative entitlement to costs may be influenced by factors **6.209**

---

406 See *Reed Executive plc v Reed Business Information Ltd* [2004] EWCA Civ 887, at [20], which confirmed that *Calderbank v Calderbank* [1976] Fam 93 and *Cutts v Head* [1984] Ch 290 remained good law under the CPR. See also *Rush & Tompkins Ltd v Greater London Council* [1989] AC 1280 and *Unilever plc v Procter & Gamble Co* [2000] 1 WLR 2436, at 2445.

407 See CPR, r 44.2(4)(c).

408 See, eg, *Thakkar v Patel* [2017] EWCA Civ 117, at [22]–[26], in which Jackson LJ makes reference to *Trustees of Stokes Pension Fund v Western Power Distribution (Southwest) Plc* [2005] EWCA (Civ) 854 and *Owners and/or Bareboat Charterers and/or Sub Bareboat Charterers of Samco Europe v Owners of MSC Prestige* [2011] EWHC 1656 (Admlty).

409 See, eg, *French v Groupama Insurance Co Ltd* [2011] EWCA Civ 1119, at [41] *et seq*, per Rix LJ; *Brown v Mcasso Music Production* [2005] EWCA Civ 1546, *per* Neuberger LJ.

410 Named after *Calderbank v Calderbank* [1976] Fam 93.

411 *Manna v Central Manchester University Hospitals NHS Foundation Trust* [2017] EWCA Civ 12, at [40].

such as set-off, the costs of issues, etc. It was for reasons such as these that Jack J said that it would be in only the most exceptional case that the determination of costs should take place prior to the conclusion of the proceedings.[412] Jackson J commented that where a party raises the issue of an offer prior to the conclusion of a trial on a preliminary issue, the normal order would be to reserve costs.[413]

Admissibility of offers in principle

6.210 CPR, r 44.2(4)(c), provides that, in deciding what order, if any, to make about costs, the court must have regard to all of the circumstances, including any admissible offer that is drawn to the court's attention.[414] It is implicit in CPR, r 44.2(4)(c), that not all offers to settle are admissible; otherwise, the phrase 'admissible offer' would not have been used. This invites the question of when an offer ought to be regarded as being an admissible offer. There is nothing within r 44.2 that purports to regulate the existing law relating to without prejudice negotiations.[415] In particular, the reference to 'all the circumstances' should be read as meaning 'all the admissible circumstances'.[416]

6.211 The following issues arise:

- the special status of Part 36 offers (6.212);
- without-prejudice offers (6.213);
- withdrawn offers and failed attempts to accept offers (6.219);
- the admissibility of offers to mediate (6.220); and
- admissibility on the small claims track (6.221).

6.212 **The special status of Part 36 offers** CPR, r 44.2(4)(c), specifically excludes 'offers to which costs consequences under Part 36 apply' from the ambit of admissible offers, and Ward LJ has confirmed that such an offer cannot be taken into account under CPR Part 44, in which regard he said that 'Part 36 trumps Pt 44'.[417] If, however, the offer falls short of complying with the procedural requirements of CPR, r 36.5 (that is, if it is a 'failed' Part 36 offer), or if it ceased to be a Part 36 offer by reason of it having been withdrawn, then it will be (or will become) an admissible offer (see 17.60–17.63 and 17.214–17.217). This would also be true of an offer that has not been beaten (not least because that would not be an offer to which the consequences under Part 36 would apply), in which case it may be taken into account under CPR, r 44.2, as being a relevant background fact.[418] Whilst a

---

412 *Tullett Prebon plc v BGC Brokers LP* [2010] EWHC 989 (QB), at [6]. See also *HSS Hire Services Group plc v Builders Merchants Ltd* [2005] EWCA Civ 626; *Shepherds Investments Ltd v Walters* [2007] EWCA Civ 29; *Multiplex Constructions (UK) Ltd v Cleveland Bridge (UK) Ltd* [2007] EWHC 659 (TCC), at [26].

413 *Multiplex Constructions (UK) Ltd v Cleveland Bridge (UK) Ltd* [2007] EWHC 659 (TCC), at [26]. In a similar vein, Coulson J had this to say about preliminary points generally: 'The mere fact that a party has won a preliminary issue does not, of itself, entitle that party to its costs of that issue. Before knowing the overall outcome of the trial, it is always dangerous to give one party its costs of an issue merely because, through a sensible case management decision, one aspect of the substantive dispute was dealt with in advance of the others' (*Perriam Ltd v Wayne* [2011] EWHC 403 (QB), at [53]).

414 See also *Crouch v King's Healthcare NHS Trust* [2004] EWCA Civ 1332, which has been superseded by changes in CPR, Part 36, but remains good law in so far as it confirms that *Calderbank* offers are admissible in money claims.

415 *Reed Executive plc v Reed Business Information Ltd* [2004] EWCA Civ 887, at [12].

416 *Ibid*, at [31].

417 *Shovelar v Lane* [2011] EWCA Civ 802, at [52].

418 See, eg, *Straker v Tudor Rose (a firm)* [2007] EWCA Civ 368, at [3] (although it should be noted that this case was decided under a differently worded iteration of Part 36 from that which presently exists).

claimant's offer that had unreasonably been rejected may sound in indemnity basis costs, no admissible offer[419] could ever mechanistically give rise to the benefits of Part 36.[420]

Admissibility of without-prejudice offers Negotiations or offers that have taken place on a basis that was without prejudice (as opposed to without prejudice save as to costs) are not admissible on the question of entitlement to costs. This rule (which can be analysed as being a rule of evidence, a rule relating to privilege or a rule of law) was laid down in *Walker v Wilsher*,[421] in which Bowen LJ reasoned the matter in this way: **6.213**

> '... [It] would be a bad thing and lead to serious consequences if the Courts allowed the action of litigants, on letters written to them "without prejudice", to be given in evidence against them or to be used as material for depriving them of costs. It is most important that the door should not be shut against compromises, as would certainly be the case if letters written "without prejudice" and suggesting methods of compromise were liable to be read when a question of costs arose.'[422]

Lord Griffiths had this to say on the point: 'The rule applies to exclude all negotiations genuinely aimed at settlement whether oral or in writing from being given in evidence.'[423] When made for the purposes of without prejudice negotiations, there is no distinction between an acknowledgement and an admission: both will be treated as being inadmissible.[424] **6.214**

Without-prejudice negotiations are not admissible in part Without-prejudice negotiations will normally be inadmissible in their entirety. In this regard, Robert Walker LJ had this to say: **6.215**

> 'But to dissect out identifiable admissions and withhold protection from the rest of without prejudice communications (except for a special reason) would not only create huge practical difficulties but would be contrary to the underlying objective of giving protection to the parties, in the words of Lord Griffiths in the *Rush & Tompkins case* [1989] A.C. 1280, 1300: "to speak freely about all issues in the litigation both factual and legal when seeking compromise and, for the purpose of establishing a basis of compromise, admitting certain facts." Parties cannot speak freely at a without prejudice meeting if they must constantly monitor every sentence, with lawyers or patent agents sitting at their shoulders as minders.'[425]

Without-prejudice negotiations following compromise The without-prejudice rule can continue to apply even after a compromise has been agreed. Lord Griffiths said that 'as a **6.216**

---

[419] See *Epsom College v Pierse Contracting Southern Ltd* [2011] EWCA Civ 1449, at [71] and [72], *per* Rix LJ; *F & C Alternative Investments (Holdings) Ltd & Ors Appellants v Barthelemy* [2012] EWCA Civ 843, at [70], *per* Davies LJ.

[420] See *Fitzroy Robinson Ltd v Mentmore Towers Ltd* [2010] EWHC 98 (TCC), at [25]; *F & C Alternative Investments (Holdings) Ltd & Ors Appellants v Barthelemy* [2012] EWCA Civ 843, at [63], in which Davies LJ said (*obiter*) that 'perhaps there can be de minimis errors or obvious slips which mislead no one: but the general rule, in my opinion, is that for an offer to be a Part 36 offer it must strictly comply with the requirements'. Davies LJ said—contrary to Underhill J's analysis in *Huntley v Simmonds* [2009] EWHC 406 (QB)—that it was 'not permissible wholly to discount a number of failures to comply with the requirements of Part 36 as the merest technicality'. In a similar vein, Davies LJ said that, in *Fitzroy Robinson Ltd v Mentmore Towers Ltd* [2010] EWHC 98 (TCC), at [25], Coulson J went too far in awarding indemnity costs on the grounds that if '[those] offers [had] been made as Part 36 offers, then indemnity costs would have been payable as a matter of course'.

[421] (1889) 23 QBD 335.

[422] *Ibid*, at 339.

[423] *Rush & Tompkins Ltd v GLC* [1989] 1 AC 1280, at 1299.

[424] *Ofulue v Bossert* [2009] UKHL 16.

[425] *Unilever plc v Procter & Gamble Co* [2000] 1 WLR 2436, at 2448–9.

general rule the "without prejudice" rule renders inadmissible in any subsequent litigation connected with the same subject matter proof of any admissions made in a genuine attempt to reach a settlement'.[426]

6.217 Lewison LJ (with whom Sharp and Burnett LJJ agreed) had this to say: 'The general rule however is still that stated in *Rush & Tompkins Ltd v Greater London Council & Another* . . ., namely that without prejudice negotiations once privileged remain privileged even after settlement'.[427]

6.218 *Exceptions to the inadmissibility of without-prejudice negotiations* There are exceptions to the without-prejudice rule.[428] In the context of civil proceedings (and costs in particular), those exceptions are where:

- an offer was expressly stated to be without prejudice save as to costs (see 6.207);
- all[429] relevant parties waive privilege;[430]
- the court is required to decide whether the negotiations have led to a concluded compromise;[431]
- in cases in which facts were identified during without-prejudice negotiations that lead to a settlement, those facts are admissible in evidence to ascertain the true construction of the agreement as part of its factual matrix or surrounding circumstances;[432]
- the court is required to decide whether an apparent agreement should be set aside on the grounds of misrepresentation, fraud or undue influence;[433]
- the court is required to decide whether the negotiations have led to an estoppel;[434]
- the exclusion of the evidence would act as a cloak for perjury, blackmail or unambiguous impropriety;[435] and
- the court is required to rule on the effect of delay or apparent acquiescence (such as when an application is made to strike out for want of prosecution) and evidence of the negotiations is required to explain that delay or apparent acquiescence[436] (in which case, the

---

426 *Rush & Tompkins Ltd v GLC* [1989] 1 AC 1280, at 1301.

427 *Avonwick Holdings Ltd v Webinvest Ltd* [2014] EWCA Civ 1436, at [22].

428 Many of these have been listed in *Unilever plc v Procter & Gamble Co* [2000] 1 WLR 2436, at 2444–5, *per* Robert Walker LJ.

429 See *Avonwick Holdings Ltd v Webinvest Ltd* [2014] EWCA Civ 1436, at [21], *per* Lewison LJ; see also *EMW Law LLP v Halborg* [2017] EWHC 1014 (Ch), at [39], *per* Newey J.

430 An example being *Botham v Khan* [2004] EWHC 2602 (QB), in which the parties waived privilege to allow the court to deal with an application pursuant to CPR, r 44.14.

431 See, eg, *Tomlin v Standard Telephones and Cables Ltd* [1969] 1 WLR 1378, at 1382, *per* Danckwerts J.

432 See *Oceanbulk Shipping and Trading SA v TMT Asia Ltd* [2010] UKSC 44, at [45] and [46], *per* Lord Clarke.

433 See, eg, the Ontario case of *Underwood v Cox* (1912) 4 DLR 66.

434 See *Hodgkinson & Corby Ltd v Wards Mobility Services Ltd* [1997] FSR 178 (a decision that was not disapproved on appeal).

435 See, eg, *Hawick Jersey International Ltd v Caplan*, The Times, 11 March 1988. The phrase 'unambiguous impropriety' was used by Hoffmann LJ in *Forster v Friedland* (unreported), 10 November 1992, CA (Civ Div), Transcript No 1052 of 1992. In *Forster v Friedland* and *Fazil-Alizadeh v Nikbin* (unreported), 25 February 1993, CA (Civ Div), Transcript No 205 of 1993, Simon Brown LJ (with whom Peter Gibson and Balcombe LJJ agreed) warned that the exception should be applied only in the clearest cases of abuse of a privileged occasion.

436 In *Walker v Wilsher* (1889) 23 QBD 335, at 338, Lindley LJ regarded this exception as limited to 'the fact that such letters have been written and the dates at which they were written', but in *Unilever plc v Procter & Gamble Co* [2000] 1 WLR 2436, at 2445, Robert Walker LJ said (*obiter*) that 'fuller evidence [may be] needed in order to give the court a fair picture of the rights and wrongs of the delay'.

court will usually order that the without-prejudice material is to be admitted only for the purpose of deciding the limited issue before the court).[437]

Admissibility of withdrawn offers and failed attempts to accept offers It is now settled law (contrary to some older authorities[438]) that if an admissible offer is withdrawn, it may be taken into account as being part of the background facts; indeed, such an offer may be given considerable weight. This is addressed in detail at 17.214–17.217. It may be that a party seeks to accept an offer made by an opponent, but, for whatever reason, is not able to do this. Bernard Livesey QC (sitting as a deputy judge of the Chancery Division) has found that this is capable of being a form of admissible offer.[439] **6.219**

Admissibility of offers to mediate One type of offer that cannot be in the form of a Part 36 offer is an offer to mediate. As such, if such an offer were to be taken into account, it could be only as an admissible offer. The effect of offers to mediate is dealt with in more detail at 6.118.[440] In so far as admissibility is concerned, Jacob LJ (with whom Rix and Auld LJJ agreed) has said that an offer to mediate may be taken into account if it is made without prejudice save as to costs, but it may not be taken into account if it is made on a merely 'without prejudice' basis, Jacob LJ explaining this in the following way: **6.220**

> 'I therefore conclude that the rule in *Walker v Wilsher* remains good law and that the court cannot order disclosure of "without prejudice" negotiations against the wishes of one of the parties to those negotiations. This may (indeed does) mean in some cases the court when it comes to the question of costs cannot decide whether one side or the other was unreasonable in refusing mediation.
>
> I do not regard such a conclusion as disastrous or damaging from the point of view of encouraging ADR. Far from it. Everyone knows the *Calderbank* Rules. It is open to either side to make open or *Calderbank* offers of ADR. These days there is no shame or sign of weakness in so doing. The opposite party can respond to such matters, either openly or in *Calderbank* form. If it does so and gives good reason(s) why it thinks ADR will not serve a useful purpose, then that is one thing. If it fails to do so, then that is a matter the court may consider relevant (not decisive, of course) in exercising its discretion as to costs. The reasonableness or otherwise of going to ADR may be fairly and squarely debated between the parties and under the *Calderbank* procedure made available to the court but only when it comes to consider costs.'[441]

The effect of this is that a party may, if it so wishes, make an offer to mediate on a wholly without-prejudice basis, in which case it will not be admissible for the purposes of deciding the incidence of costs.

Admissibility of offers on the small claims track A further type of offer that can be taken into account only as an admissible offer is an offer made in a claim that has been allocated to the small claims track. This is because CPR Part 36 does not apply to such claims. For reasons set out at 50.369–50.370, unless a party has acted unreasonably, only very limited costs are allowed on that track. In this regard, CPR, r 27.14(3), gives the following guidance: **6.221**

> 'A party's rejection of an offer in settlement will not of itself constitute unreasonable behaviour under paragraph (2)(g) but the court may take it into consideration when it is applying the unreasonableness test.'

---

437 See, eg, *Family Housing Association v Hyde* [1993] 1 WLR 354.

438 See, eg, *The Toni* [1974] 1 Lloyd's Reports 489, at 496–7, *per* Megaw LJ.

439 *Rowles-Davies v Call 24-7 Ltd* [2010] EWHC 1695 (Ch), at [27].

440 See the line of cases beginning with *Halsey v Milton Keynes General NHS Trust* [2004] 3 Costs LR 393.

441 *Reed Executive plc v Reed Business Information Ltd* [2004] EWCA Civ 887, at [34]–[35].

6.222 Where they wish to persuade the court that their opponent has acted unreasonably, an offeror will therefore not be able to rely on an admissible offer in isolation, although it may be taken into account alongside other factors. This restriction will apply only if the offeror seeks more than limited costs; if the argument is that an opponent should be deprived of costs, then there is no requirement of unreasonable behaviour.

The effect of a refusal to waive privilege relating to an offer

6.223 If a party refuses to waive privilege in substantive litigation, it would be wrong to regard that refusal as giving rise to an adverse inference to be drawn against the refusing party.[442] In theory, there is no reason to believe that this principle does not apply to costs litigation (including decisions as to the incidence of costs) with just as much force as it does to substantive litigation. In practice, however, a party who refuses to waive privilege may encounter a degree of judicial antagonism if the offer related to issues that have ceased to be in dispute and there is no rational basis for refusing to be candid with the court.

The effect of admissible offers on the incidence of costs

6.224 Whether the existence of an admissible offer will have a bearing on the incidence of costs will depend on the facts of the case in question. Generally speaking, the offeror will hope to rely on the offer for one or more of the following purposes:

- to demonstrate a willingness to narrow the issues and further the overriding objective;
- to demonstrate a willingness to enter into negotiations or to dispel any allegation to the contrary;
- to highlight an opponent's reluctance to enter into negotiations; and
- to obtain an outcome that is at least as advantageous as the offer (for the purposes of obtaining either a favourable costs order or an award of costs on the indemnity basis).

6.225 The effect of an admissible offer may fall anywhere from having no effect on the incidence of costs to having an effect similar to a Part 36 offer.[443] Jackson LJ has explained that the court's discretion is wider where an admissible offer has been beaten than where a Part 36 offer has been beaten.[444] In the latter instance, the court's discretion is dictated by the provisions of Part 36; in the former, no such restraint exists. Unlike under CPR Part 36, there are no prescribed rules as to the effect of an admissible offer; rather, the presence (or, occasionally, absence) of an offer will merely be one factor amongst others to be taken into account. Thus each case will turn on its own facts. One factor that might be relevant is the status the parties afforded the offer; thus if the parties were to believe that an offer was a Part 36 offer and act as if this were the case, then that would be a factor to be borne in mind even though they may have been mistaken.[445]

6.226 There are 11 scenarios that merit particular attention:

- 'drop hands' offers (6.227);
- all-inclusive offers and offers with restraints as to costs (6.229);
- offers in cases of suspected fraud (6.232);

---

[442] *Ibid*, at [36].

[443] As an example of the latter, see *Stokes Pension Fund Trustees v Western Power Distribution (South West) Plc* [2005] EWCA Civ 854; see also *Fox v Foundation Piling Ltd* [2011] EWCA Civ 790, at [45].

[444] *Fox v Foundation Piling Ltd* [2011] EWCA Civ 790, at [44] and [45].

[445] *Howell v Lees-Millais* [2011] EWCA Civ 786, at [24]–[28].

- a defendant's refusal to come to a commercial settlement (6.233);
- unrealistic offers and offers that are markedly different from the amounts claimed (6.235);
- non-monetary offers (6.237);
- absence of offers (6.238);
- very late offers (6.239);
- withdrawn or defective Part 36 offers and withdrawn offers generally (6.240);
- conditional offers (6.241); and
- Part 61 offers (which are percentage offers in admiralty collision claims) (6.244).

The effect of 'drop hands' offers A 'drop hands' offer is an offer to leave the claim where it lies, with each party bearing its own costs (or taking only those monies that have already been paid). If, for example, no monies have been paid in the claim to date, such an offer will be that the claim (and, if there is one, the counterclaim) be abandoned without either party having to pay costs. Mann J has explained that where a party has made a drop-hands offer that has not been accepted, the correct approach is to consider what the appropriate costs order would have been in the absence of that offer and then to compare that hypothetical position with the actual offer made.[446] **6.227**

Where an admissible drop-hands offer has been made and the court decides not to take it into account, reasons should be given. Chadwick LJ (with whom Rix and Thorpe LJJ agreed) had this to say on the point: **6.228**

> 'If the judge was to deny the party who had been successful overall the costs, or any part of the costs, of his success, then he had to explain why the other party, who had refused to accept the "drop hands" proposal ... was entitled to ignore that proposal and run up further costs.'[447]

This means that whilst drop-hands offers cannot be ignored for no reason at all, they are capable of being disregarded for principled reasons.

All-inclusive offers and offers with restraints as to costs It may be that a defendant wishes to make an offer to settle the whole claim, but is concerned about the risk of having to bear all of the claimant's costs if that offer were to be accepted, including the costs of issues that were unreasonably pursued or which related to an exaggerated claim (see 6.232). Where this is so, whilst one option would be to make a Part 36 offer that was narrow in its scope (that is, applying to only a part of the claim), it would often be better for the defendant to make a *Calderbank* offer. Provided that the defendant was right to have concerns, the court would probably regard the defendant's decision not to make a Part 36 offer as being reasonable (see 6.232).[448] **6.229**

---

446 *Fulham Leisure Holdings Ltd v Nicholson Graham & Jones* [2006] EWHC 2428 (Ch).

447 *Bellamy v Sheffield Teaching Hospitals NHS Trust* [2003] EWCA Civ 1124, at [36].

448 There are several authorities that say that if a defendant is justified in refusing to accept a Part 36 offer because it would be inappropriate for them to be condemned to pay the costs of the whole proceedings, this is a factor that the court can take into account: see, eg, *Fairclough Homes Ltd v Summers* [2012] UKSC 26, at [53]–[54], *per* Lord Clarke; *Medway Primary Care Trust v Marcus* [2011] EWCA Civ 750, at [51] and [52], *per* Tomlinson LJ; *Travelers Casualty and Surety Co of Canada v Sun Life Assurance Co of Canada (UK) Ltd*

6.230 There are two types of offer that are restricted as to costs: the first is the all-inclusive offer; the second is where the offer states which costs will and will not be payable. Ordinarily, the court regards such offers as of little consequence, but if the defendant is able to justify the decision not to make a Part 36 offer, then the court may give weight to such an offer. In this regard, Gloster LJ had this to say:

> '[The] judge should ... have asked himself whether the allowance of about £19,000 for costs, in [the defendant's] *Calderbank* offer, given [the claimant's] ultimate recovery of about £11,000, represented a reasonable offer on costs. I accept [the] submission that such an offer was indeed a reasonable and proportionate one. The judge was entitled to look at the matter with the benefit of hindsight ...'[449]

6.231 Gloster LJ went on to explain that, when considering the adequacy of an all-inclusive offer, the judge is entitled to look at the matter with the benefit of hindsight and in the knowledge of the amounts ultimately awarded.[450] Whilst there is no authority on the point, it is likely that the same would apply to an offer to pay only restricted costs.

6.232 **Offers in cases of suspected fraud** In a similar vein to the above, it may be that a defendant believes that the claim is partly fraudulent. If this is so, then the ability to make Part 36 offers would afford little protection because no such defendant would be happy to make an offer to pay the costs of the seemingly fraudulent aspect of the claim. The Supreme Court has accepted that Part 36 may be of little assistance in protecting defendants in these circumstances. Lord Clarke suggested that a defendant in such circumstances could make an admissible offer to settle the genuine part of the claim on terms that the claimant pay the defendant's costs incurred in respect of the remainder, but this being on the basis that if the offer were to be accepted, the costs of the exaggerated aspect of the claim are to be paid by the claimant on the indemnity basis.[451] That would certainly be an option, but it would be a bold offer to make because, to rely on the offer, the defendant would have to prove that it was reasonable to include the requirement that costs be paid on the indemnity basis. In practical terms, such offers should be reserved only for those instances in which the defendant either believes that the offer is likely to be accepted or that there would be little chance that the court doubt the claimant's fraudulent intent. Where appropriate, a safer strategy would be to make an offer in respect of the genuine aspect of the claim only (that is, without making any demands in so far as the rest of the claim is concerned). For the avoidance of doubt, it would be a risky strategy for a defendant to elect not to make any offer at all, this being because, whilst not determinative of matter, the existence of an offer is a factor to be taken into account.[452] This is addressed in more detail at 6.152 and 6.238.

6.233 **The effect of a defendant's refusal to come to a commercial settlement** The fact that a successful defendant may have rejected a claimant's offer would not, in the ordinary run of things, lead to the defendant being penalised for not having previously agreed to compromise that claim on commercial grounds. Dyson LJ had this to say on the point:

[2006] EWHC 2885 (Comm), at [86], *per* Christopher Clarke J. There was no mention of the 'just out of time' jurisdiction in any of those cases.

[449] *Walker Construction (UK) Ltd v Quayside Homes Ltd* [2014] EWCA Civ 93, at [91]; see also [89]–[95].
[450] *Ibid*, at [91].
[451] See *Summers v Fairclough Homes Ltd* [2012] UKSC 26.
[452] *Ibid*, at [53], *per* Lord Clarke.

'If defendants ... wish to take a stand and contest [unfounded claims] rather than make payments (even nuisance value payments) to buy them off, then the court should be slow to characterise such conduct as unreasonable so as to deprive defendants of their costs, if they are ultimately successful.'[453]

Ward LJ—giving judgment in the same case—added the following: **6.234**

'If the parties reasonably believe that they have a real prospect of success each is entitled fully and properly to advance his or her case or defence, but neither can then complain that the fight is taken to the bitter end of a judgment of the court. Each will have to accept that those who live by the sword must risk dying by the sword as well. That is the inevitable risk of litigation.'[454]

The effect of unrealistic offers and offers markedly different from the amounts claimed An offeror will usually hope to benefit from having made an offer, but where an admissible offer is redolent on unrealistic expectations, it may be capable of working against the offeror.[455] This might happen where an unrealistic offer is regarded as evidence of expectations that were out of reach and unrealistic. In general, nonetheless, a party should not be penalised for pitching an offer too high (or too low, in the case of a defendant); Ramsey J has emphasised that the court should avoid getting drawn into an exercise of making an adjudication as to the reasonableness of offers.[456] **6.235**

The fact that a party has made an offer that is markedly different from the amounts claimed (or openly offered) may lead to an opponent saying that the offer is indicative of the unreasonableness of the offeror's open position. Each case will turn on its own facts, but such an argument would generally fail (other than as a makeweight). In particular, there is nothing in CPR Part 36 which states that an offeror is to be prejudiced as to costs because they have expressed a willingness to accept less or pay more than their open position; indeed, Rix LJ commented that that would make the procedure a most dangerous one to use.[457] **6.236**

The effect of non-monetary offers Where a non-monetary offer is made—such as an offer to extend a lease or to set a boundary in a certain position—it may be taken into account as being an admissible offer.[458] It may be appropriate to assess the effect of the offer by examining whether the offeror has 'secured broadly' a result which was better for them than that which they had offered.[459] There is a further discussion of non-monetary offers at 17.109, in the context of CPR Part 36: most of what is said in that context also has resonance in the context of admissible offers. **6.237**

The effect of the absence of offers The absence of an offer (be it a Part 36 offer or admissible offer) may be relevant in the following situations. **6.238**

[453] *Daniels v Commissioner of Police for the Metropolis* [2005] EWCA Civ 1312, at [31].
[454] *Ibid*, at [36].
[455] See, eg, *Islam v Ali* [2003] EWCA Civ 612, at [18].
[456] *Hammersmatch Properties (Welwyn) Ltd v Saint-Gobain Ceramics & Plastics Ltd* [2013] EWHC 2227 (TCC), at [36], citing *Johnsey Estates (1990) Ltd v The Secretary of State for the Environment* [2001] EWCA Civ 535. See also *Rolf v De Guerin* [2011] EWCA Civ 78 and *Quorum v Schramm (No 2)* [2002] 2 Lloyd's Rep 72.
[457] *Rolf v De Guerin* [2011] EWCA Civ 78, at [34].
[458] See, eg, *R (on the application of Davies) v Royal College of Veterinary Surgeons* [2015] EWHC 3707 (Admin).
[459] *MBI Inc v Riminex Investments Ltd* [2002] EWHC 2856 (QB).

- **Non-culpable exaggeration** Where a claim has been exaggerated, but this was not as a result of a deliberate attempt to deceive or of other culpable conduct, the absence of a claimant's offer would normally not necessarily leave the defendant exposed to the risk of an adverse costs award, but it would be a factor that would militate against the claimant being awarded all of their costs.[460] This is commensurate with the general principle that whilst a non-culpably exaggerated claim may, in some circumstances, result in a claimant being deprived of costs,[461] it would usually be only where the exaggeration was culpable that the claimant would be ordered to pay costs. For the avoidance of doubt, this means that a defendant faced with a claim that was non-culpably exaggerated would be well advised to make an offer.
- **Culpable exaggeration** Where there has been culpable exaggeration of a claim, this would put the claimant at risk of being ordered to pay costs[462] or even to pay costs on the indemnity basis,[463] and (in some circumstances[464]) this would be so regardless of whether an offer had been made.[465] Patten LJ has explained that the fact that the defendant had failed to make an effective offer would not prevent the court from finding costs that were attributable to the exaggerated aspects of the claim.[466] As such, where a party defends itself from an exaggerated claim, it would not necessarily have to make an offer to provide costs protection. That said, a defendant would do well to take note of the points made at 6.232.
- **Alternative cases** Where a party advances a primary case, but also advances a secondary case in the alternative, thought ought to be given to making a protective offer based on that alternative case. Ward LJ has explained that the absence of such of an offer may result in the defendant being condemned in costs.[467]

6.239 **Very late offers** An offer made very late in the proceedings may be given little or no weight.[468]

6.240 **Would-be, quasi and withdrawn Part 36 offers** Whilst offers to which the costs consequences in Part 36 apply are not themselves admissible offers,[469] withdrawn Part 36 offers

[460] See *Hall v Stone* [2007] EWCA Civ 1354, at [72]–[73], *per* Smith LJ. Jackson LJ came to a similar conclusion in a subsequent case: see *Fox v Foundation Piling Ltd* [2011] EWCA Civ 790, at [63]. See also *Vestergaard Frandsen A/S v Bestnet Europe Ltd* [2014] EWHC 4371 (Ch), *per* Rose J.

[461] See, eg, *Islam v Ali* [2003] EWCA Civ 612, followed in *Fulham Leisure Holdings Ltd v Nicholson Graham & Jones (Costs)* [2006] EWHC 2428 (Ch).

[462] *Ford v GKR Construction Ltd* [2000] 1 WLR 1397.

[463] See, eg, *Painting v Oxford University* [2005] EWCA Civ 161.

[464] An award on the indemnity basis may, for example, be appropriate where the exaggeration was the only, or nearly the only, issue to be tried, or where the claimant's conduct was poor in other ways.

[465] *Hullock v East Riding of Yorkshire County Council* [2009] EWCA Civ 1039, at [32], *per* Patten LJ. In a similar vein, see *Marcus v Medway Primary Care Trust* [2011] EWCA Civ 750, at [46], *per* Tomlinson LJ.

[466] *Hullock v East Riding of Yorkshire County Council* [2009] EWCA Civ 1039, at [32].

[467] *Day v Day* [2006] EWCA Civ 415, at [20], in which Ward LJ said this: 'In my judgment the valuable use of payments into court and Part 36 offers to settle place an onus, in the first place, on the defendant. He had the ability to pay his fallback position into court and he could, if he took the view, have done so, confident that his greedy mother backed by his horrible brother would not have taken that money but would have fought him to the bitter end for the whole of the proceeds of sale, but that was his means of protecting his position. He failed to avail it, and it seems to me that that loses him the protection of the rules.'

[468] *London Tara Hotel Ltd v Kensington Close Hotel Ltd* [2011] EWHC 29 (Ch), at [30], *per* Roth J. See also *Rees v IBC Vehicles Ltd* [1999] Lexis Citation 3877.

[469] *Shovelar v Lane* [2011] EWCA Civ 802, at [52], *per* Ward LJ.

are,[470] as are offers that have fallen short of being Part 36 offers for want of compliance with CPR, r 36.5 (that is, so-called failed Part 36 offers).[471] Such an admissible offer would not have the same mechanistic effect as a Part 36 offer. In this regard, Rix LJ had this to say:

> 'The question remains not merely whether the withdrawn offer be taken into account but whether Part 36 consequences should ordinarily flow where a Part 36 offer has been withdrawn ... [It] has become hard to ignore the rules which state that the Part 36 costs consequences (*viz* the consequences of amended rule 36.14(2) and (3)) "do not apply" to even a Part 36 offer that has been withdrawn ... After all, if a mechanistic rule that an offer which beats the judgment should result in all costs being switched to the offeree is to make sense, there needs to be sufficient formality about the making and maintenance of the offer. That formality is provided by the rules, and it is not altogether obvious to see why the mechanistic rule should *prima facie* survive when the formalities are not observed.'[472]

Part 36 offers that have been withdrawn and withdrawn offers generally are addressed at 17.214–17.217.

Conditional offers A conditional offer to pay a sum of money on account pending adjudication (as opposed to an offer to pay a sum of money that, if accepted, would dispose of the dispute or part of the dispute) is not an offer to which much weight is generally given. That said, Longmore LJ has confirmed that such an offer is admissible in principle notwithstanding the fact that it would be afforded only limited weight.[473] On the facts of the case before him (in which the claim was probably exaggerated), he regarded it as being a factor that justified an order that there be no order as to costs. **6.241**

An offer may be conditional in the sense that some future event may need to take place before it can be accepted (such as the agreement of a third party)—that is, an offer may be made that is technically incapable of acceptance at the time it is made. Lewison LJ has held that such offers may still be taken into account as admissible offers as being evidence of a reasonable conduct and a desire to settle.[474] Lewison LJ went on to say that the weight that the court attaches to such an offer is a matter for the court. **6.242**

A mere statement by an opponent as to what a claim or part of a claim may be worth is not an offer and will not give rise to any presumption of unreasonable conduct if a party then pursues a more advantageous outcome. Tomlinson LJ said that 'it cannot be misconduct, or unreasonable conduct, simply to pursue a claim in an amount greater than that at which it is valued by the opponent party. Something more is required to render pursuit of the claim unreasonable.'[475] **6.243**

---

[470] *Epsom College v Pierse Contracting Southern Ltd (formerly Biseley Construction Ltd) (in liquidation)* [2011] EWCA Civ 1449, at [54] *et seq*, per Rix LJ. Presumably the same is true of a Part 36 offer to which the costs consequences in Part 36 do not apply, such as where an offer has not been 'beaten': see *Straker v Tudor Rose (a firm)* [2007] EWCA Civ 368, at [3].

[471] See, eg, *French v Groupama Insurance Co Ltd* [2011] EWCA Civ 1119, at [41] *et seq*, per Rix LJ; *Brown v Mcasso Music Production* [2005] EWCA Civ 1546, *per* Neuberger LJ.

[472] *French v Groupama Insurance Co Ltd* [2011] EWCA Civ 1119, at [41]. See also *Epsom College v Pierse Contracting Southern Ltd (formerly Biseley Construction Ltd) (in liquidation)* [2011] EWCA Civ 1449, at [54] *et seq*, per Rix LJ.

[473] *Ali v Stagecoach* [2011] EWCA Civ 1494, at [8] and [9].

[474] *Ma'har v O'Keefe* [2014] EWCA Civ 1684, at [31], *per* Lewison LJ.

[475] *Sugar Hut Group Ltd v AJ Insurance Service (a partnership)* [2016] EWCA Civ 46, at [24].

6.244 **Admiralty claims ('Part 61 offers')** Special rules apply to percentage offers made in collision claims. The relevant parts of CPR, r 61.4, read as follows:

> '(10) The consequences set out in paragraph (11) apply where a party to a claim to establish liability for a collision claim (other than a claim for loss of life or personal injury)—
> (a) makes an offer to settle in the form set out in paragraph (12) not less than 21 days before the start of the trial;
> (b) that offer is not accepted; and
> (c) the maker of the offer obtains at trial an apportionment equal to or more favourable than his offer.
>
> (11) Where paragraph (10) applies the parties will, unless the court considers it unjust, be entitled to the following costs—
> (a) the maker of the offer will be entitled to—
> (i) all his costs from 21 days after the offer was made; and
> (ii) his costs before then in the percentage to which he would have been entitled had the offer been accepted; and
> (b) all other parties to whom the offer was made—
> (i) will be entitled to their costs up to 21 days after the offer was made in the percentage to which they would have been entitled had the offer been accepted; but
> (ii) will not be entitled to their costs thereafter.
>
> (12) An offer under paragraph (10) must be in writing and must contain—
> (a) an offer to settle liability at stated percentages;
> (b) an offer to pay costs in accordance with the same percentages;
> (c) a term that the offer remain open for 21 days after the date it is made; and
> (d) a term that, unless the court orders otherwise, on expiry of that period the offer remains open on the same terms except that the offeree should pay all the costs from that date until acceptance.'

Whilst there is no authority on the point, it is likely that those provision take precedence over the provisions in CPR, r 44.2, in the same way that those in Part 36, Section I, also take precedence.

6.245 Teare J has found that the approach to interpreting putatively defective Part 61 offers is similar to that which is taken with Part 36 offers[476] (see 17.67–17.76).

The relevance of changes in the law

6.246 If the law changes (as a result of a decision in another case, for example), then the parties may need to carry out work in response. In a case in which that additional work had been carried out at the request of the court, Peter Smith J held that the correct order should be no order for the costs of that work,[477] despite the fact that the general conduct of one of the parties in that case justified an award of costs against it on the indemnity basis. Peter Smith J qualified his comments by saying that he did not find the decision to be an easy one[478] and he made no attempt to lay down any point of principle. This highlights that each case should be determined on its own facts.

---

[476] See *Miom Ltd v Sea Echo ENE (No 2)* [2011] EWHC 2715 (Admlty).
[477] *A&E Television Networks LLC v Discovery Communications Europe Ltd* [2013] EWHC 276 (Pat), at [21]–[31].
[478] *Ibid*, at [21] and then again at [31].

Irrelevant and barely relevant factors

Almost any admissible factor can be taken into account for the purposes of determining the incidence of costs, but a number of factors are usually regarded as being irrelevant, barely relevant or inadmissible. These include, but are not limited to, the following. **6.247**

Impecuniosity

A party's impecuniosity is usually[479] regarded as being irrelevant[480] (although it may be a factor that has a bearing on other factors, such as a party's perception of the value of a claim). In the context of a commercial claim, Colman J refused to make an order against a Part 20 defendant where one of the principal reasons for asking for that order was the fact that the unsuccessful claimant was unable to pay.[481] **6.248**

Financial inequality

In so far as the incidence of costs in private law claims is concerned, the fact that one party is financially stronger than another will not be a factor to which much weight will be given (although it may be a factor to which considerable weight may have been given in the management of the claim pursuant to the overriding objective). In this regard, Stanley Burnton LJ said this: **6.249**

> 'The claims between the parties arise out of their commercial relations. This context is very different from the public law cases in which a substantial defendant may be required to bear all parties' costs, or be deprived of its own costs on the issues on which it succeeds. The fact that the Appellant is a larger organisation than the Respondents does not in our view affect the costs issues.'[482]

The availability of public funding

The fact that a party has the benefit of public funding is, by the operation of statute, a factor that of itself is affirmatively irrelevant.[483] Likewise, the fact that the court has the option to make an order against the Legal Services Commission (LSC) in respect of the costs incurred in a funded claim is largely irrelevant.[484] That said, the fact that a party may have public funding may, in some circumstances, be a relevant background fact in public law cases: the Supreme Court has held that, when deciding what, if any, costs order to make in a public law case, the consequences for solicitors who do publicly funded work is a factor that may be taken into account. Their Lordships found that the court should be very slow **6.250**

---

479 The most common exception to this is where a non-party costs order is sought against a director who has litigated for their own purposes through a worthless company: see 9.21–9.31. Another exception is where the court takes the parties' solvency into account when determining the correct type of co-defendant order to make: see 7.23.

480 Whilst a pre-CPR case, see *Building Contractors Ltd v Ahmed*, The Independent, 23 November 1998, *per* Hirst LJ and Cazalet J.

481 *Arkin v Borchard* [2003] EWHC 3088 (Comm).

482 *AXA Sunlife Services plc v Campbell Martin Ltd* [2011] EWCA Civ 549, at [2].

483 See regs 3, 15(1) and (2) of the Community Legal Services (Costs) Regulations 2000 (SI 2000/441), and s 11 of the Access to Justice Act 1999. See also *Boxall v Waltham Forest LBC* (2001) 4 CCL Rep 258, *per* Scott Baker J; *R (on the application of Kuzeva & Anor) v Southwark London Borough Council* [2002] EWCQ Civ 781, *per* Schiemann, Sedley and Hale LJJ; *R (on the application of Scott) v London Borough of Hackney* [2009] EWCA Civ 217, *per* Sir Andrew Morritt C, Richards, Hallett LJJ.

484 See reg 7(2) of the Community Legal Service (Cost Protection) Regulations 2000 (SI 2000/824), which provides as follows: 'Nothing in these Regulations shall be construed, in relation to proceedings where one of more parties are receiving, or have received, funded services, as: (a) requiring a court to make a costs order where it would not otherwise have made a costs order; or (b) affecting the court's power to make a wasted costs order against a legal representative.'

to impose an order that each side must be liable for its own costs in a high-cost case in which either or both sides are publicly funded.[485]

The availability of funding other than public funding

6.251 The fact that a party may be backed by a well-financed funder, such as a union, would normally be regarded as an irrelevant factor[486] (unless, of course, the issue was whether a non-party costs order should be made). Indeed, Lord Neuberger MR has had this to say on the topic:

> 'The … basis upon which the successful party's lawyers are funded, whether privately in the traditional way, under a "no win no fee" basis, by the Community Legal Service, by a Law Centre, or on a *pro bono* arrangement, will rarely, if ever, make any difference to that party's right to recover costs.'[487]

The possible concerns of legal expenses insurers

6.252 Leveson LJ has explained that it would not be a reason to avoid making an issue-aware costs order merely because the funding criteria of after-the-event (ATE) insurers required that certain points be taken, and that if costs were to be awarded on an issues-aware basis, this would discourage ATE insurers from providing insurance and impair access to justice.[488] Presumably, the same would apply to costs orders other than issue-aware orders.

Litigants in person

6.253 The fact that a party acts in person is, by and large, not of itself regarded as being relevant to the incidence of costs,[489] but it may be a factor that has a bearing on other issues, such as conduct. In particular, in practice, a litigant in person will usually be afforded more leeway than a person who was represented. Moreover, if an opponent has failed to give reasonable assistance to a litigant in person, that may sound in costs.[490]

The amount of costs claimed

6.254 Where the court believes that the costs claimed by a party are excessive, the correct approach is to leave the issue of the amount of costs to the costs judge and to assume that the costs will, once assessed, be reasonable and proportionate.[491] If appropriate, the court is able to make its concerns known to the costs judge. Tomlinson LJ had this to say about a case in which the court below had attempted to adjust the costs order to take into account the fact that the costs as claimed were excessive:

> '… [It] is plain that the judge erred in principle in reflecting his concern as to the level of costs incurred by [the receiving party] by making a reduction in the proportion of those costs which would be recoverable. That was a matter for assessment. The judge could of course have made clear his concerns for the benefit of the costs judge.'[492]

---

485 *R (on the application of E) v Governing Body of JFS and the Admissions Appeal Panel of JFS* [2009] UKSC 1.

486 Whilst a case in the employment tribunal rather than the civil courts, *Omar v Worldwide News Inc* [1998] IRLR 291 illustrates this principle.

487 *M v Mayor and Burgesses of the London Borough of Croydon* [2012] EWCA Civ 595, at [46].

488 *Kew v Bettamix Ltd* [2006] EWCA Civ 1535.

489 See *Building Contractors Ltd v Ahmed*, The Independent, 23 November 1998, *per* Hirst LJ and Cazalet J.

490 See, eg, *Wokingham Borough Council v Dunn* (unreported), 3 June 2015, QBD, *per* Judge Seymour QC (sitting as a judge of the High Court).

491 *Shovelar v Lane* [2011] EWCA Civ 802, at [54].

492 Whilst he was dealing with a matter to which Part 36 applied rather than Part 44, Ward LJ has confirmed that the court must assume that the sums claimed will be assessed and that, as such, the fact that a seemingly excessive amount is not to be given weight, this being because the 'assessment will produce the

Proportionality

In a similar vein, proportionality is a factor for assessment rather than for the judge exercising their discretion as to the incidence of costs. This, not least, is because of the risk of double jeopardy.[493] **6.255**

Additional liabilities

Where they are payable, additional liabilities do not impinge on the issue of the incidence of costs.[494] **6.256**

Contributions

Whilst he was at pains to point out that it should not be regarded as being a legal principle, Jackson LJ has said that where more than one party unsuccessfully advances the same case against a common adversary, the normal starting point for a court considering costs under CPR, r 44.2, is that they should all contribute to the recoverable costs of the successful party.[495] **6.257**

Akenhead J has found that when deciding the incidence of costs in a case in which a contribution was sought between defendants, the court is not limited by the contribution made (or not made) between the defendants nor by any apportionment relating thereto.[496] **6.258**

It may be that two or more parties come to a settlement that does not involve all of the parties, but which settles the issue of costs as between the parties to the settlement. Where this is so, the settlement will not bind the court in so far as any party who was not a party thereto; instead, the settlement is merely a fact to be taken into account. Jackson LJ had this to say on the topic: **6.259**

> 'That agreement did not and could not preclude [a party who was a party to the settlement] from claiming his costs as against [a party who was not]. I have, with some regret, come to the conclusion that the settlement agreement … is not an answer to [the] contribution claim. It is merely part of the circumstances of the case which the judge, exercising his discretion under CPR 44.2, should take into account.'[497]

Late payment of prior costs orders

Neuberger MR has said that it would be only in exceptional circumstances that it would be appropriate for an award of costs to reflect the late payment of costs in another application.[498] Presumably, this would not be the case where the late payment directly led to the application in question. **6.260**

The right to freedom of expression

Lord Neuberger has explained that the fact that a person (such a publisher) unsuccessfully resisted a claim on the basis of a putative right to freedom of expression would, other than **6.261**

right figure … [and the paying party] will be properly condemned in that sum and no greater sum': *Shovelar v Lane* [2011] EWCA Civ 802, at [53], *per* Ward LJ. In a similar vein, see *United Marine Aggregates Ltd v G M Welding & Engineering Ltd* [2013] EWCA Civ 516, at [37], *per* Tomlinson LJ.

493 See *Amey LG Ltd v Cumbria County Council* [2016] EWHC 2946 (TCC), at [20]–[30], *per* Judge Steven Davies (sitting as a judge of the High Court).

494 See, eg, *Horth v Thompson* [2010] EWHC 1674 (QB), at [17], *per* Rafferty J.

495 *Dufoo v Tolaini* [2014] EWCA Civ 1536, at [58]. In this regard, Jackson LJ drew upon *Stumm v Dixon & Co and Knight* (1889) 22 QBD 529 (see 19.13) as being an illustration of that proposition.

496 *Carillion JM Ltd v PHI Group Ltd* [2011] EWHC 1581 (TCC).

497 *Dufoo v Tolaini* [2014] EWCA Civ 1536, at [55].

498 *Hoque v Ali* [2012] EWCA Civ 274, at [21].

in exceptional circumstances, not be a factor that should disturb the position under the general rule.[499]

No Order as to Costs

6.262 With one or two exceptions (see 7.102), where the court makes no order for costs, that will mean that no party is entitled to costs or required to pay costs.[500] That said, the fact that the court has not made an order for costs at the end of a hearing does not always mean that neither party will be entitled to costs at the conclusion of the claim. In particular, if the hearing were adjourned part-heard (such as on the first day of a trial lasting more than one day), then the court would generally deal with the costs of that day upon conclusion of the trial.

6.263 Where, on the other hand, the court turns its mind to the issue of costs, but makes no order, that will, in general, be a disposal of that issue on the basis that neither party is entitled to costs. This would prevent the court from making a subsequent order for costs in respect of the same matter (unless, of course, that were to be as a result of a successful appeal).[501] Where no order for costs is made in respect of a hearing and the court makes no order relating to consequential costs (such as costs thrown away by an adjournment), that may be interpreted as disentitling the parties from those consequential costs.[502]

6.264 The wording of the relevant provision—namely, CPR, r 44.10—is as follows:

> '(1) Where the court makes an order which does not mention costs—
> (a) subject to paragraphs (1A) and (1B), the general rule is that no party is entitled—
> (i) to costs; or
> (ii) to seek an order under section 194(3) of the Legal Services Act 2007,
> in relation to that order; but
> (b) this does not affect any entitlement of a party to recover costs out of a fund held by that party as trustee or personal representative, or pursuant to any lease, mortgage or other security.
>
> (2) Where the court makes—
> (a) an order granting permission to appeal;
> (b) an order granting permission to apply for judicial review; or
> (c) any other order or direction sought by a party on an application without notice,
> and its order does not mention costs, it will be deemed to include an order for applicant's costs in the case.
>
> (3) Any party affected by a deemed order for costs under paragraph (2) may apply at any time to vary the order.'

Interim Costs Orders

6.265 In this context, interim costs orders are orders that are made during proceedings and which either reserve costs to some later stage or award costs conditionally upon the happening of some future event.

---

499 *Miller v Associated Newspapers Ltd* [2017] UKSC 33, at [68].
500 CPR, r 44.10(1)(a). No party will be entitled to an order under s 194(3) of the Legal Services Act 2007 either.
501 *Griffiths v Commissioner of Police for the Metropolis* [2003] EWCA Civ 313, at [6]–[11].
502 *Beahan v Stoneham* (unreported), 19 January 2001, QBD, *per* Buckley J.

Available orders

There are no restrictions on the orders that are available to the court when making an order at an interim stage, but the following orders may be particularly relevant.[503] 6.266

- **Costs reserved** The decision about costs is deferred to a later occasion, but if no later order is made the costs will be costs in the case.
- **Claimant's/defendant's costs in case/application** If the party in whose favour the costs order is made is awarded costs at the end the proceedings, that party is entitled to its costs of the part of the proceedings to which the order relates. If any other party is awarded costs at the end of the proceedings, the party in whose favour the final costs order is made is not liable to pay the costs of any other party in respect of the part of the proceedings to which the order relates.

Discretion

The exercise of the court's discretion at an interim stage is much the same as at any other stage. There are, however, some differences. In a pre-CPR case, Buckley LJ explained those differences in the following way: 6.267

> '[H]ere we are concerned with the costs of an interlocutory application. Conduct which might be relevant to how the costs of the action should ultimately be borne may be quite irrelevant to whether a party was justified in making a particular interlocutory application. In such a context one naturally starts from a basis of considering whether the defendants were justified in launching their [interlocutory applications].'[504]

Having set the scene, Buckley LJ went on to say this: 6.268

> 'When [the court is concerned with] an interlocutory step in an action, the circumstances may be such that it is not then possible to see on which side justice requires that the decision who should bear the costs of that step should ultimately fall. This may depend on how the issues in the action are eventually decided. Consequently, costs in interlocutory matters are often made costs in the cause or reserved.'[505]

Therefore the interests of justice may require the court to defer making an order in respect of some interim step until the conclusion of the claim. An example of this would be where an interim injunction has been made (see 6.273).

Where a Part 36 offer has been made, it may be appropriate to postpone the determination of the costs generally until such time as the outcome of the claim has been determined (see 17.58).[506] 6.269

The effect of interim costs orders

There is authority (albeit pre-CPR[507]) for the proposition that a final costs order does not negate the effect of earlier costs orders. By way of example, if a defendant has been awarded the costs of a hearing, the fact that the claimant is subsequently awarded the costs of the claim in general would not change the defendant's entitlement to the costs of that hearing. It is possible that there is an exception to principle, however, in that Pill LJ had this to say of an appeal in which the claimant had discontinued a claim after having been awarded the costs of a strike out application: 6.270

---

503 See the table at PD 44, para 4.2.
504 *Scherer & Anor v Counting Instruments Ltd* [1986] 2 All ER 529, at 533.
505 *Ibid*, at 536.
506 See, eg, *Interactive Technology Corpn Ltd v Ferster* [2017] EWHC 1510 (Ch), *per* Morgan J.
507 *Teheran-Europe Co Ltd v ST Belton (Tractors) Ltd* [1971] 2 QB 491, at 493, *per* Widgery LJ.

'[B]y discontinuing their claim, [the Claimant] accepted that it is not a valid claim against the Defendant. The position should be, and in my view the wording of the rule provides, that in those circumstances the Claimant is on the face of it liable for the ... Defendant's costs. That would have the effect of reversing the order for costs below. The Claimant should not normally have the luxury of bringing a claim now accepted as invalid and not meeting costs incurred along the way.'[508]

6.271 Thus the act of discontinuing is capable of giving rise to a reversal of interim costs orders previously made in the discontinuer's favour. Pill LJ's comments were made in the context of the interim order in question being the subject of an appeal; it is therefore possible that he intended his comments to be limited to situations in which the interim order had come back before the court by reason of it being appealed. That is certainly an arguable reading of his judgment, but the fact that Pill LJ went on to say that the effect of the discontinuance ought to have been the same even if the appeal had been dismissed rather suggests that his comments were intended to be of wider application.[509]

6.272 Unless the court makes a 'forthwith order', the beneficiary of an interim costs order will not be able to commence detailed assessment proceedings until the conclusion of the proceedings.[510] This issue is discussed in detail at 7.80–7.99.

6.273 It is implicit from the table in PD 44, para 4.2 (see 6.266), that where costs are reserved, but where no subsequent order is expressly made, the reserved costs will be in the case (or in the application, as the case may be).

Interim injunctions

6.274 The way in which Neuberger J dealt with the issue of costs following an application for an interim injunction may be paraphrased in the following way.[511]

- Other than where there are special factors at play, where a claimant has obtained an interim injunction on the basis of 'balance of convenience', the court would normally reserve costs.
- In general, a defendant who consented to an interim injunction before the hearing should not, for that reason alone, be in a worse position than if they had fought and lost.
- The court may depart from these principles in appropriate circumstances (such as where the outcome of the hearing was so plain that the court could conclude that one of the parties had wasted court time). It might also be appropriate to depart from the general approach where the court formed a realistic view that the case was not likely to go to trial and the substantive merits were very plain.
- Where a claimant had obtained an interim injunction, it was useful to ask whether it would be unfair for the claimant to have their costs of the application even if they lost at trial and whether the opposition to the application was justified.

More recently, Martin Chamberlain QC (sitting as a deputy judge of the High Court) has confirmed these principles.[512] The parties had agreed terms on the day of the hearing; Martin Chamberlain QC found that the respondents' delay had caused the claimant to incur the costs of the hearing, so he awarded those costs, but reserved the balance of the costs.

508 *Safeway v Twigger* [2010] EWCA Civ 1472, at [58].
509 *Ibid*, at [60].
510 See CPR, r 47.1.
511 See *Picnic at Ascot v Karlus Derigs* [2001] FSR 2.
512 See *Autoneum GB Ltd v Gilbert* [2016] EWHC 3016 (QB), at [5] and [6].

7

ORDERS FOR COSTS (PARTICULAR TYPES OF ORDER AND SPECIFIC CIRCUMSTANCES)

This chapter deals with the following topics: 7.01

- where there are more than two parties (7.02):
  - co-defendant orders (*Bullock* and *Sanderson* orders) (7.04);
  - additional party orders (7.26);
  - joint and joint and several orders (7.32);
- where both parties claim to be entitled to costs (7.34);
- circumstances in which the general rule will not apply (7.38):
  - pre-action disclosure and applications for disclosure against non-parties (7.39);
  - dissolution of accounts between partners (7.50);
  - proving probate claims and litigation concerning wills (7.52);
- consent orders and Tomlin orders (7.65);
- forthwith orders (7.80);
- deemed orders and default orders (7.100):
  - default orders (7.102);
  - general points about deemed orders (7.103);
  - non-payment of court fees (7.105);
  - dishonouring a cheque in relation to court fees (7.108);
  - CPR, Part 36 (7.109);
  - discontinuance (7.112);
- everything agreed save for costs (7.141);
- where a party declines to pay costs prior to the issue of proceedings (7.169);
- miscellaneous issues (7.183):
  - costs of appeals (7.184);
  - commencing proceedings in the wrong venue (7.186);
  - costs following transfer between courts (7.187); and
  - where a judge recuses himself or herself (7.188).

More than two parties

Where there are more than two parties, issues may arise as to how the costs of the successful 7.02
parties (who may include claimants, defendants or additional parties) are to be borne. The distinction between the types of order referred to below may have some importance if one of the parties is insolvent.

7.03 The following types of order may be encountered.

- **Co-defendant orders** These are orders that may, in some circumstances, be made where a claimant has brought a claim against two or more defendants. There are two types—namely, *Sanderson* orders and *Bullock* orders (see 7.04–7.25). The difference between them is illustrated in Figure 7.1.
- **Additional party orders** These are orders that may be made where a defendant has brought into the proceedings an additional party. Again, there are two types—namely, passing-up-the-line orders and cut-through orders (see 7.26–7.31). The difference between them is illustrated by Figure 7.2.
- **Joint and joint and several orders** These are orders whereby the liability for costs is, in some way, borne jointly by the losing parties (see 7.32–7.33).

Co-defendant orders (*Bullock* and *Sanderson*)

7.04 Co-defendant orders are typically available when a claimant sues two defendants and is successful against only one of them. The effect of these orders is to make the unsuccessful defendant bear the successful defendant's costs. Keene LJ explained the policy behind these orders in this way: '[W]here a plaintiff had behaved reasonably in suing both defendants

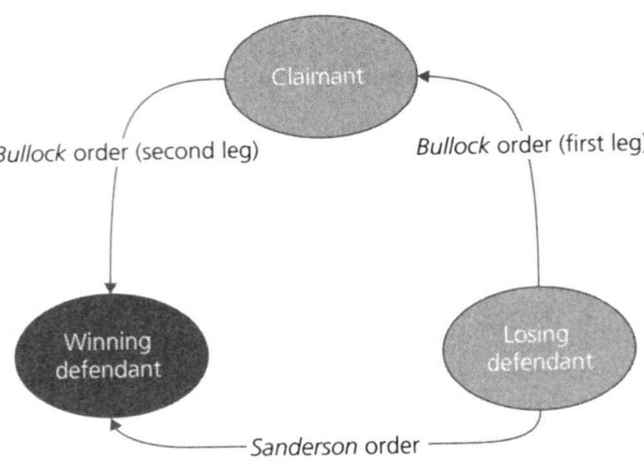

Figure 7.1 Co-defendant orders

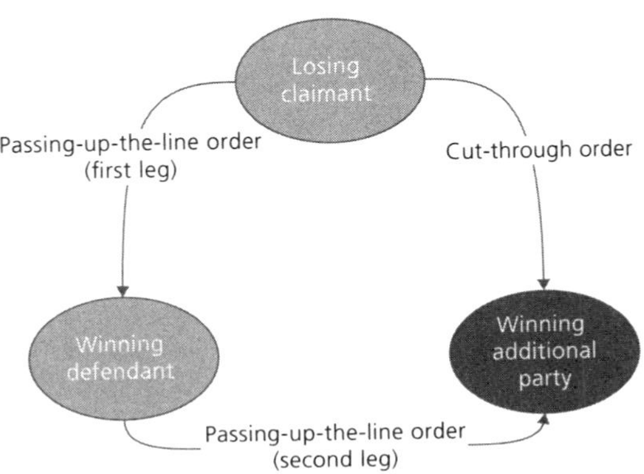

Figure 7.2 Additional party orders

he should not normally end up paying costs to either party even though he succeeded only against one of the defendants.'[1] This type of situation is different from when a claimant sues two defendants and loses against both of them. This situation is addressed at 7.12–7.14.

Types of order

The difference between the two types of co-defendant order is that one (*Sanderson*[2]) achieves the aim of making the unsuccessful defendant bear the successful defendant's costs by direct means, whereas the other (*Bullock*[3]) does so indirectly. This is illustrated by Figure 7.1. In particular: **7.05**

- with the direct (*Sanderson*) order, the unsuccessful defendant pays the successful defendant's costs; and
- with the indirect (*Bullock*) order, the claimant pays the successful defendant's costs, but the claimant is permitted to add those costs to those to be recovered from the unsuccessful defendant.

The explanation for the development of these two types of order is now a matter of historical interest only;[4] in particular, the distinction arose out of a now obsolete rule. It has been suggested that there is no ongoing need for these two variants; that may be so, but the distinction may make a significant difference in practical terms if the claimant is insolvent or incapable of having a costs order enforced against them. In particular, a *Sanderson* order has the advantage of bypassing the claimant and therefore may be preferable where, for example, the claimant is insolvent.[5] It also has the advantage of avoiding the possibility of the successful defendant's costs being assessed twice. **7.06**

Discretion

The usual circumstances in which a co-defendant order would be appropriate are where a claimant has a claim—classically arising out of a road traffic accident[6]—in which one of two or more persons are potentially at fault, but it is not clear which. The factors set out in the Civil Procedure Rules (CPR), r 44.2 (see 6.17), are just as relevant to the exercise of the court's discretion as they are to other types of order for costs order, but the following general points may be made. **7.07**

- A co-defendant order is a 'strong order' that should be made only after careful consideration (see 7.08–7.09). In particular, there is no rule of law that makes a co-defendant order mandatory in any given circumstances (see 7.10–7.11).
- For a co-defendant order to be appropriate, the claimant must generally have succeeded against one of the defendants or, if there are two or more defendants, against one or more of them (see 7.12–7.14).

---

1 *King v Zurich Insurance Co* [2002] EWCA Civ 598, at [33].

2 After *Sanderson v Blyth Theatre Co* [1903] 2 KB 533.

3 After *Bullock v London General Omnibus Co* [1907] 1 KB 264.

4 The indirect order developed as a result of a now obsolete, but mandatory, rule in jury trials that costs had to follow the event and the direct order arose out of the need to do justice in cases against the Attorney-General, who, in the 19th century, was effectively immune against costs: *Attorney-General v Corpn of Chester* (1851) 14 Beav 338. See also *Rudow v Great Britain Mutual Life Assurance Society* (1879) 17 Ch Div 600, which extended the application of the direct order following the Judicature Acts.

5 See the discussion of this topic by Colman J in *Arkin v Borchard Lines Ltd* (unreported) 16 December 2003, Ch D, at [11]–[15].

6 *Besterman v British Motor Cab Co Ltd* [1914] 3 KB 181.

- The claims against the defendants will generally be connected (see 7.15–7.16) and will typically have been 'in the alternative' (see 7.17–7.20).
- Ultimately, the question is one of reasonableness and, in this regard, the claimant's conduct may be relevant—especially in the sense of whether it was reasonable of the claimant to bring proceedings against more than one defendant (see 7.21).
- In deciding what type of order to make, the court will have regard to the real effect of the order and, in this regard, the 'balance of hardship' may be relevant (see 7.22–7.23).

7.08 **The need for careful consideration** That the power to make a co-defendant order has survived the introduction of the CPR was confirmed by Peter Gibson LJ, who went on to say that a co-defendant order is a 'strong order' that is capable of working injustice to the defendant against whom the claim has succeeded:

> 'There is no doubt that the jurisdiction to make a *Bullock* or *Sanderson* order has survived the introduction of the CPR, though the exercise of discretion to make such an order must be guided by the overriding objective and the specific provisions of [what is now CPR, r 44.2]. The jurisdiction is a useful one. It is designed to avoid the injustice that when a claimant does not know which of two or more defendants should be sued for a wrong done to the claimant, he can join those whom it is reasonable to join and avoid having what he recovers in damages from the unsuccessful defendant eroded or eliminated by the order for costs against the claimant in respect of his action against the successful defendant or defendants. However, it must also be recognised that it is a strong order, capable of working injustice to the defendant against whom the claim has succeeded, to be made liable not only for the claimant's costs of the action against that defendant, but also the costs of the other defendants whom the claimant has chosen to join but against whom the claimant has failed.'[7]

7.09 This is undoubtedly still good law, but Hildyard J (delivering judgment of a court that included Longmore and Jackson LJJ) has explained that the need to avoid injustice means that there is a need for careful application of co-defendant orders as opposed to a need excessively to restrict the making of such orders.[8]

7.10 **Not mandatory** The rationale behind *Bullock* and *Sanderson* is entirely adjectival and does not create any principle of law; therefore each case must be decided on its own facts. In particular, there is no rule of law compelling the court to make a *Bullock* or *Sanderson* order.[9]

7.11 Waller LJ has stressed that there are 'no hard and fast rules as to when it is appropriate to make a *Bullock* or *Sanderson* order'.[10] Ultimately, the question is one of reasonableness, as Waller LJ has emphasised:

> 'The court takes into account the fact that, if a claimant has behaved reasonably in suing two defendants, it will be harsh if he ends up paying the costs of the defendant against whom he has not succeeded. Equally, if it was not reasonable to join one defendant because the cause of action was practically unsustainable, it would be unjust to make a co-defendant pay those

---

7 *Irvine v Commissioner of the Police for the Metropolis* [2005] EWCA Civ 129, at [22]. More recently, see *Dixon v Blindley Heath Investments Ltd* [2016] EWCA Civ 548, at [59], *per* Hildyard J.

8 See *Dixon v Blindley Heath Investments Ltd* [2016] EWCA Civ 548, at [79], *per* Hildyard J.

9 Whilst a pre-CPR case, *Hong v A&R Brown Ltd* [1948] 1 KB 515 is still informative in this regard.

10 See *Moon v Garrett* [2006] EWCA Civ 1121, at [38] and [39].

defendant's costs. Those costs should be paid by a claimant. It will always be a factor whether one defendant has sought to blame another.'[11]

The requirement for success against at least one defendant Prior to the introduction of the CPR, neither type of co-defendant order would have been available where the claimant had failed against both or all defendants. In this regard, Stuart Smith LJ (with whom Gibson and Balcombe LJJ agreed) had the following to say: **7.12**

> 'The fallacy of [counsel's] argument is this: while an unsuccessful defendant, A, will normally be held liable to pay the costs of a successful defendant, B, whether directly or indirectly, whom he had blamed, that does not apply where the plaintiff fails against both. In such circumstances A is not ordered to pay the costs of B, even though he may have blamed him.'[12]

It has been argued that this analysis is no longer good law under the CPR, which require a more flexible approach to costs. Judge Coulson QC (sitting as a judge of the High Court) rejected that contention: **7.13**

> 'It seems to me that it could only be in truly exceptional circumstances that a claimant, who has lost against both defendants, might recover the costs of pursuing one defendant against the other defendant. In my judgment, if the claimant has been unsuccessful against both defendants, the justification for a *Bullock/Sanderson* order simply does not arise. Thus I consider that this principle, succinctly explained by Stuart-Smith LJ in *Beoco*, remains good law, notwithstanding the greater flexibility of the CPR.'[13]

It therefore remains the case that neither *Bullock* nor *Sanderson* orders are normally available in circumstances in which the claimant has lost against both or all of the defendants. If, however, the defendants litigated issues as between themselves, then it may be appropriate to make an order as between them and, in some circumstances, this may relieve the unsuccessful claimant of the burden of paying the whole of the defendants' costs.[14] **7.14**

The requirement that there is a nexus between claims Whilst they should not be elevated to being points of law, certain factors can be identified that are relevant to the issue of whether the court should make a co-defendant order, perhaps the most important of which is whether the claims against the defendants are connected. In this regard, Lord Goddard had this to say (albeit in a pre-CPR case): **7.15**

> 'It does not appear to us that it [ie a *Bullock* order] is an appropriate order to make where a plaintiff is alleging perfectly independent causes of action against two defendants where the breaches of duty alleged are in no way connected the one with the other.'[15]

Thus, where the claims are unconnected, it will not ordinarily be appropriate to make a co-defendant order. The rationale behind this is that where a claimant pursues two unconnected claims, the general rule in CPR, r 44.2(2)(a)—that an unsuccessful party should pay the costs of the successful party—would suggest that the claimant should pay the costs **7.16**

---

[11] See *ibid*, at [38]. See also *Irvine v Commissioner of the Police for the Metropolis* [2005] EWCA Civ 129, at [30]; *Jabang v Wadman & Ors* [2017] EWHC 1993 (QB), at [14], *per* Nichol J.

[12] *Beoco Ltd v Alfa Laval Co Ltd* [1995] 1 QB 137, at 157.

[13] *McGlinn v Waltham Contractors Ltd* [2005] EWHC 1419 (TCC), at [21].

[14] See, eg, *Green v Sunset & Vine Productions Ltd* (unreported) 4 November 2009, QBD, at [7]–[9], *per* Ouseley J.

[15] *Hong v A&R Brown Ltd* [1948] 1 KB 515, cited with approval post-CPR in *Irvine v Commissioner of the Police for the Metropolis* [2005] EWCA Civ 129, at [27].

of the unsuccessful claim. Moreover, it might be unjust to visit the costs of the successful defence on the unsuccessful defendant in circumstances in which the latter had no connection with the former's successful defence.

7.17 **The requirement that claims are 'in the alternative'** Another relevant—or, more accurately, related—factor is whether the defendants have been sued 'in the alternative'. Whilst not a requirement that should be elevated to being a point of principle,[16] *Bullock* and *Sanderson* orders tend to be made in circumstances in which those circumstances exist.[17] Waller LJ had this to say on the point:

> 'The fact that cases are in the alternative so far as they are made against two defendants will be material, but the fact that claims are not truly alternative does not mean that the court does not have the power to order one defendant to pay the costs of another.'[18]

Thus the fact that the defendants were sued in the alternative will be a material factor, but should not be regarded as being a condition precedent to the making of co-defendant order.

7.18 The stances taken by the defendants will generally be relevant in this regard. Whilst the paradigm type of case in which a co-defendant order will be made is that in which the defendants will have each blamed one another other,[19] the existence of such circumstances would merely be a relevant factor rather than a requirement. Hildyard J had this to say on the point:

> 'It [is not] necessary that one of two or more defendants sued should have blamed the other. As Peter Gibson LJ acknowledged [in *Irvine v Commissioner of the Police for the Metropolis* [2005] EWCA Civ 129, at [29]], that is a relevant consideration but it is not determinative.'[20]

Hildyard J went on to say that the fact that a claimant may have advanced inconsistent cases against defendants would not be a bar to a co-defendant order being made.

7.19 It is usually said that 'in the alternative' means that the claimant was expected to succeed against one defendant, but not both. This notion seems to have arisen out of contract cases in which apportionment of liability would not normally be a realistic option.[21] This, of course, is different from claims in tort, in which the court may find that both defendants are liable (albeit only to limited extents). Modern practice is not to regard the possibility of such a finding as being a bar to a co-defendant order. Indeed, whilst he was speaking prior to the introduction of the CPR, Lord Goddard seems to have regarded this as being the most common instance in which such an order would be appropriate:

> 'A *Bullock* order is appropriate where a plaintiff is in doubt as to which of two persons is responsible for the act or acts of negligence which caused his injury, the most common

---

16 See *Dixon v Blindley Heath Investments Ltd* [2016] EWCA Civ 548, at [75], *per* Hildyard J. See also *Moon v Garrett* [2006] EWCA Civ 1121, at [38] and [39], *per* Waller LJ. To the extent that *Whitehead, David McLeish v Barrie Searle, Hibbert Downall and Newton (a firm)* [2007] EWHC 2046 (QB), at [24], *per* Griffith Williams J, suggests otherwise, it is likely to be wrong: see *Jabang v Wadman & Ors* [2017] EWHC 1993 (QB), at [13], *per* Nichol J.

17 See *Irvine v Commissioner of the Police for the Metropolis* [2005] EWCA Civ 129, at [26].

18 See *Moon v Garrett* [2006] EWCA Civ 1121, at [39].

19 See *ibid*, at [38] and [39], *per* Waller LJ.

20 See *Dixon v Blindley Heath Investments Ltd* [2016] EWCA Civ 548, at [76]. See also *Jabang v Wadman & Ors* [2017] EWHC 1993 (QB), at [14(v)], *per* Nichol J.

21 See *Bankamerica Finance Ltd v Nock* [1988] AC 1002, at 1011; see also *Irvine v Commissioner of the Police for the Metropolis* [2005] EWCA Civ 129.

> instance being, of course, where a third person is injured in a collision between two vehicles and where the accident is, therefore, caused by the negligence of one or the other, *or both*.'[22]

Whilst there is no authority on the point, a plausible analysis is that the issue is not whether the claim could have succeeded against one defendant, but not both, but whether it was within the power of the unsuccessful defendant to dispose of the entirety of the matter by making an appropriate admission or offer. If this is correct, a claim should be regarded as having been brought 'in the alternative' if full settlement of one claim would have disposed of the other. **7.20**

Relevance of claimant's conduct As with all orders for costs made under CPR, r 44.2, conduct will be a relevant factor. A particularly relevant consideration is CPR, r 44.2(5)(b),[23] which, in the present context, would include the reasonableness of the claimant's conduct in joining and pursuing a claim against a defendant against whom the claimant did not succeed.[24] The conduct of the other parties may also be relevant. **7.21**

Whether to make a *Bullock* or a *Sanderson* order and the 'balance of hardship' The next issue is whether an order should be a *Sanderson* order or a *Bullock* order. There are no rules of law in this regard, but the real effect of the order will be a relevant factor. The court will consider those effects in what Lord Brandon called the 'balance of hardship', when he offered the following guidance: **7.22**

> 'The judge must have been aware of these matters. Having regard to them it seems to me impossible to say that the judge could not, in the judicial exercise of his discretion, have made a *Sanderson* order but was bound to make a *Bullock* order. On the contrary the balance of hardship seems to me, not to require the judge to make a *Sanderson* order than a *Bullock* order, but at least to provide a legitimate ground for him, in the judicial exercise of his discretion, to do so.'[25]

Thus, contrary to the general principle that the court will regard impecuniosity as irrelevant to the incidence of costs (see 6.248), the court may enquire as to the solvency of the claimant and the losing defendant before deciding the form of the order to make. Colman J has commented that whilst the balance of hardship might be the determining factor, it is open to the court to take into account other factors when deciding the form of the order.[26] **7.23**

Where more than one party is sued because of doubt about the law Whilst there is no binding authority on the point, first-instance decisions suggest that co-defendant orders are not ordinarily available where two defendants have been sued as a result of doubt as to the true law. That may or may not be so, but one could easily argue that the touchstone will always be reasonableness. **7.24**

Legal aid The fact that a person is legally aided is not a factor that should be taken into account,[27] although such a person will often be impecunious and hence, to that extent, **7.25**

---

22 *Mulready v JH & W Bell Ltd* [1953] 2 All ER 215, at 219, emphasis added.
23 'Whether it was reasonable for a party to raise, pursue or contest a particular allegation or issue.'
24 See *Irvine v Commissioner of the Police for the Metropolis* [2005] EWCA Civ 129, at [30].
25 *Bankamerica Finance Ltd v Nock* [1988] AC 1002, at 1012.
26 *Arkin v Borchard Lines Ltd* [2003] EWHC 3088 (Comm), at [18].
27 *Johnson v Ribbins* [1977] 1 WLR 1458, at 1463–4; see also Civil Legal Aid (Costs) Regulations 2013 (SI 2013/611), reg 21 (although this, on one reading, relates only to the amount of costs rather than to the amount allowable when making an order for costs).

their financial status may be relevant (see 7.23). In this regard, Goff LJ had the following to say (albeit in the context of a passing-up-the-line order):

> 'It cannot be right to deprive a third party of an order for costs to which he is otherwise entitled against the defendant, because the defendant when looking to the plaintiff for reimbursement finds a person not worth powder and shot.'[28]

Additional party orders

Passing-up-the-line orders

7.26 The costs of successful parties brought in under what is now Part 20 of the CPR may pass up the line (see Figure 7.2). In a pre-CPR case, Goff LJ had this to say:

> 'In the exercise of that discretion ... in our judgment, the court should be guided by the principle that normally costs follow the event as is expressly provided by RSC Ord 62, r 3(2) and should, therefore, normally order the defendant, though successful in the action, to pay the costs of the third party if he also be successful. Then if in the circumstances of the case these costs ought fairly to be borne by the plaintiff the court will further order that they be added to the defendants' costs of the action as against the plaintiffs.'[29]

The applicability of this line of thinking under the CPR has been confirmed.[30]

7.27 Similar logic applies to 'strings of contracts'. In a pre-CPR case concerning arbitrations, Diplock J had the following to say:

> 'I think that I should make these observations about the way in which costs should be dealt with where third, fourth, fifth or sixth parties have been brought in these string contract cases which are very common ... In the ordinary way, however, where damages are claimed for breach of contract on one contract in a string of contracts, and the seller brings in his immediate seller as a third party, and the third party brings in his immediate seller as a fourth party, then, provided that the contracts are the same or substantially the same so that the issue whether the goods comply with a description is the same, the defendant (in this case it was the plaintiffs, because it was a counterclaim), if successful, should recover against the plaintiffs not only his costs but any costs of the third party which he has been ordered to pay: the third party in like manner should recover from the defendant his own costs and any costs of the fourth party which he has been compelled to pay, and so on down the string. That is the normal way in which costs should be dealt with in this kind of action where there is a string of contracts in substantially the same terms. In saying that, I am not excluding the possibility that there may be special reasons for departing from that normal practice. Whether it was reasonable for the defendant to bring in a third party at all is always a question to be considered, and that is a matter on which a lot of facts may be relevant.'[31]

Cut-through orders

7.28 No difficulty arises if the parties are solvent, but where the claimant is insolvent, the difficult question arises of whether the successful Part 20 defendant should share, with the successful defendant, the burden of the unsuccessful claimant's impecuniosity. That would

---

[28] *Johnson v Ribbins* [1977] 1 WLR 1458, at 1464; on the effect of legal aid on the incidence of costs generally, see *Boxall v Waltham Forest LBC* (2001) 4 CCL Rep 258.

[29] *Johnson v Ribbins* [1977] 1 WLR 1458, at 1463–4.

[30] *SCT Finance v Bolton* [2002] EWCA Civ 56, at [23]; *Arkin v Borchard Lines Ltd* [2003] EWHC 3088 (Comm), at [22].

[31] *LE Cattan Ltd v A Michaelides & Co* [1958] 1 WLR 717, at 719.

be achieved by making a 'cut-through order', which is an order that the successful Part 20 defendant would recover their costs directly from the claimant—essentially treating the defendant and the Part 20 defendant as if they were co-defendants (see Figure 7.2). Colman J had the following to say on the topic:

> 'The fact that it is the policy of the law to give effect to access to justice permitting an impecunious claimant to sue and so to expose an ultimately successful defendant to shoulder the burden of his own costs see *Hamilton v Al Fayed (No 2)* [2002] 3 All ER 641, *per* Simon Brown LJ at 658–659, raises the question whether, if that defendant, with knowledge of the claimant's lack of resources, then chooses to protect his position by joining a third party Part 20 defendant, it is in the interests of justice that the third party should be placed in a similar position as to the recovery of his costs, if successful, to that of the defendant who has chosen to join him. It is indeed hard to see why the apparent injustice to the defendant by reason of his inability to recover his costs from the impecunious claimant should ordinarily be spread to the third party who has been sued involuntarily by a sufficiently resourced defendant. If, as it is ultimately decided, he has been wrongly sued and is under no liability to the defendant, to expose him by a costs order to the impecuniosity of the claimant would normally not only be unnecessary to do justice to the defendant but would do serious injustice to the third party. This, as I see it, represents a quite different position from that which arises where there are co-defendants both of whom have been sued by the same impecunious claimant. In such a case there is often a far stronger character of injustice if the successful defendant is deprived of his costs which can in appropriate cases be cured by a cut-through or *Sanderson* order causing them to be paid by the unsuccessful defendant.'[32]

Coleman J went on to comment on the 'separability principle', which is the term he gave to the principle that a Part 20 claim is something separate from the original claim. He emphasised that this distinguished cut-through orders from co-defendant orders, where claims would conventionally have been brought against the co-defendants in the alternative (see 7.17–7.20).[33] He found that it was only in exceptional cases that there should be departure from the separability principle. **7.29**

In any event, the court must consider whether it would work injustice on an unsuccessful defendant to make them liable for the costs of another defendant against whom the claimant had failed.[34] Again, this highlights that each case will be decided on its own facts. **7.30**

Although the authorities on the point are now very old, it is generally thought that the principles set out above will apply even where one or more of the litigants is a child.[35] **7.31**

Joint and joint and several orders

Where a party has succeeded against more than one other party, then the types of order that could be made are several, joint, and joint and several. The effect of those types of order is discussed in detail at 19.05–19.33. In general, joint (or joint and several) orders will be made against two or more losing parties only if the claims or defences that they ran were linked in such a way as to make it just that they each be liable for the winning party's costs, which generally means that they had made common cause in the litigation. Thus, in a case in which three defendants had interests that were intimately related and on which **7.32**

[32] *Arkin v Borchard Lines Ltd* [2003] EWHC 3088 (Comm), at [32].
[33] This is not always the case, however: see 7.19.
[34] *Hong v A&R Brown Ltd* [1948] 1 KB 515.
[35] *Short v Ridge* (1876) WN 47, at 48; *Goldsmith v Russell* (1855) 5 De GM & G 547, at 556.

they made common cause, Newrey J found that they could not sensibly be differentiated because their approach had been to act together and indivisibly; as such, all three defendants were held liable to pay all of the relevant costs.[36]

7.33 Where such circumstances exist, the provisions of a costs-sharing agreement may have a bearing on the incidence of costs[37] (especially in group litigation—see 65.46 *et seq*). Thus if the court were minded to make a joint order against two defendants who had agreed to bear the burden of any costs ordered against them equally, then it would be open to the court to exercise its discretion so as to give effect to that agreement, either by ordering each defendant to pay half of the costs (a several order) or by making a joint and several order.

Where Both Parties Claim to be Entitled to Costs

7.34 It will often be the case that both parties have a legitimate claim to costs. In many cases, such a situation would best be addressed by making an issues-aware order (see 6.156–6.205), such as a percentage order, but circumstances will arise in which it would be appropriate to make a reciprocal costs order (otherwise known as a cross-order), which means that both parties would pay and receive costs. Such orders are notoriously troublesome and wasteful of resources—especially for costs judges. Patten J had this to say on the point:

> 'The implementation of orders of this kind [ie reciprocal orders as to costs of issues] or indeed for any kind of division of costs in relation to specific issues can involve the parties and the costs judge in extensive further litigation in the course of the detailed assessment, during which the whole history of the action is scrutinised in order to determine which part of any expenditure related to which issue. In the present case, [the costs judge] was sensibly asked by the parties to make certain preliminary rulings as to the principles on which the division of the common costs should be approached. But I am told that this process has so far generated tens of thousands of pounds in additional costs and that the hearing of the detailed assessment has been allocated a further four days of court time. There is therefore every prospect that the length of time taken in the assessment of costs will exceed the length of the trial itself and add vastly to the costs of the litigation in general. These matters need, I think, to be borne firmly in mind by a trial judge who is asked to make a complicated order for costs. There is much to be said for the application of the general rule that costs should follow the event and for keeping to the simple formula of orders for a stated proportion of the costs or a stated amount of costs in cases where recognition of a limited degree of success by one or other party is called for.'[38]

7.35 A reciprocal costs order will not always be problematic, however. Where the competing claims relate to entirely separate subject matters, no conceptual difficulty will arise: each entitlement will be assessed by a costs judge in the ordinary way and there will be little scope for disagreement about whether any of the costs should be ascribed to one competing claim or the other. Likewise, other than considering whether to make an order for set-off, the judge making the costs order will not need to spend much time considering

36 See *GHLM Trading v Maroo* (unreported) 27 February 2012, Ch D, *per* Newey J.

37 It may be, for example, that the co-defendants have agreed that any order should be made against one of them only, this being on the basis that they have agreed to some other dispute-resolution procedure to resolve the issue of how much the other co-defendant should pay. Costs-sharing agreements are particularly common in the context of clinical negligence claims against more than one medical services provider.

38 *Dyson Technology Ltd v Strutt* [2007] EWHC 1756 (Ch), at [6].

how the two entitlements interact. Whilst it would be open to the court to make a percentage order instead (see 6.39–6.41), a reciprocal costs order in such circumstances will rarely cause difficulties (other than the fact that such orders tend to lead to two, rather than one, detailed assessments).

The same is not true where the competing claims touch upon similar subject matters (such as where disputed factual evidence went to both a claim and a counterclaim). This is because there will be costs that are common to each claim and, where this is so, the *Medway Oil* principle[39] will apply (see 50.51–50.63). Where this is so, a reciprocal order for costs will almost certainly cause practical and conceptual difficulties upon assessment. This is not only because it can lead to unfair and unexpected results, but also because the costs of assessment are often far in excess of the net payment that one party is ordered to make to the other. Whilst each case must be decided on its own facts, one could make out a strong case for saying that reciprocal orders that engage the *Medway Oil* principle ought to be orders of last resort. **7.36**

The following miscellaneous points may be made. **7.37**

- ***Medway Oil*** In a case in which there are likely to be costs common to both a claim and a counterclaim, the *Medway Oil* principle (see 20.51–20.63) ought to be borne in mind. For the reasons given in Chapter 20, orders that invoke that principle are problematic and ought to be avoided, where possible. Indeed, in a case that had no conspicuously remarkable features, Ward LJ commented that it would be wrong for the court not to consider making other orders, such as a percentage order under what is now CPR, r 44.2(6)(a).[40]
- **Disapplication of *Medway Oil*** 'Special orders' ought to be borne in mind: the order may, for example, provide for reciprocal entitlements, but also provide that the principle in *Medway Oil* should not apply and that costs may be apportioned by the costs judge.[41]
- **Set-off** The issue of set-off is addressed in Chapter 21. If the court is minded to make an order that costs be set-off, but if it is not possible to know, in broad terms, the amounts of the competing claims, it may be appropriate to wait until the relevant figures are available and then, at that stage, to take a view as to whether set-off would be appropriate.[42] The powers referred to at 21.09–21.10 (regarding CPR, r 44.12) ought to be noted.
- **Broadly balancing entitlements** Morgan J has indicated that where each party has unsuccessfully raised issues on an application, and where those issues were similar in terms of complexity and degree of involvement, it would be appropriate to make no order for costs rather than to order that there be cross-assessments.[43]

39 After *Medway Oil and Storage Co Ltd v Continental Contractors Ltd* [1929] AC 88.
40 *Burchell v Bullard* [2005] EWCA Civ 358, at [29]–[30].
41 Whilst not binding, an example of the court finding that the principles in *Medway Oil* did not apply is *Bateman v Joyce* [2008] EWHC 90100 (Costs), in which Master Campbell found that the parties did not have the principles in *Medway Oil* in mind at the time they agreed the order.
42 Whilst he did not mention CPR, r 44.2(9), by that name, see *Amin v Amin* [2010] EWHC 827 (Ch), at [51], *per* Warren J.
43 *Mastercigars Direct Ltd v Withers LLP* [2009] EWHC 1531 (Ch). In a similar vein, see, eg, *Square Mile Partnership Ltd v Fitzmaurice McCall Ltd* [2006] EWHC 236 (Ch).

- **Where the court is not easily able to gauge the amounts** In a case in which the trial judge felt that it would be better for a cost judge to gauge the amounts payable (and in which he gave extensive guidance to assist the costs judge), Tomlinson LJ found that whilst a percentage order would have been preferable, reciprocal orders were within the range of available awards.[44]
- **Counterclaim does not necessarily have to have been pleaded** It is not always necessary for a defendant to bring a formal counterclaim to have the court take its existence into account. Thus, in a case in which the parties had agreed that the issue of liability would dispose of both the claim and the counterclaim, and that there was no need to formally plead a counterclaim, Smith LJ found that it was open to the court to take the unpleaded counterclaim into account.[45]
- **Contributory negligence** The fact that contributory negligence has been argued is not generally regarded as a discrete issue separate from the general issue of liability (see 6.189–6.190). This means that reciprocal orders as to costs would rarely be appropriate in respect of primary liability and contributory negligence.[46]
- **The relevance of success fees** It would seem that the court is entitled to disregard the effect of success fees when considering whether to set off at the stage of making the costs order—and that has led to curious results. In a claim in which a claimant and a defendant were found to be 65 per cent and 35 per cent responsible for a road traffic accident, for example, Rafferty J declined to interfere with an order that each party must pay the other side's costs; because the defendant claimed a success fee and the claimant did not, the effect of this was that the net result was in the defendant's favour.[47]

Circumstances in which the General Rule will not Apply

7.38 There are circumstances in which the general rule in CPR, r 42.2(2)(a), will not apply. Some (such as family cases) are beyond the scope of this book. The following, however, merit attention:

- pre-action disclosure and applications for disclosure against non-parties (7.39);
- dissolution of accounts between partners (7.50); and
- proving probate claims and litigation concerning wills (7.52).

Special rules also apply in cases concerning trusts; these are addressed in Chapter 66.

Pre-action disclosure and applications for disclosure against non-parties

7.39 CPR, r 46.1, creates a general rule that is different from that in CPR, r 44.2(2)(a):

> '(1) This paragraph applies where a person applies—
> (a) for an order under—
> (i) section 33 of the Senior Courts Act 1981; or
> (ii) section 52 of the County Courts Act 1984,
> (which give the court powers exercisable before commencement of proceedings); or

44 *Connell v Mutch t/a Southey Building Services* [2012] EWCA Civ 1589, at [25].
45 *Parkes v Martin* [2009] EWCA Civ 883, *per* Smith and Rimer LJJ.
46 See *Sonmez v Kebabery Wholesale Ltd* [2009] EWCA Civ 1386, at [22], *per* Ward LJ; *Onay v Brown* [2009] EWCA Civ 775, at [29], *per* Goldring LJ.
47 *Horth v Thompson* [2010] EWHC 1674 (QB), at [19].

(b) for an order under—
(i) section 34 of the Senior Courts Act 1981; or
(ii) section 53 of the County Courts Act 1984,
(which give the court power to make an order against a non-party for disclosure of documents, inspection of property etc).

(2) The general rule is that the court will award the person against whom the order is sought his costs—
(a) of the application; and
(b) of complying with any order made on the application.

(3) The court may however make a different order, having regard to all the circumstances, including—
(a) the extent to which it was reasonable for the person against whom the order was sought to oppose the application; and
(b) whether the parties to the application have complied with any relevant pre-action protocol.'

There is therefore a general rule—namely, that the respondent will be awarded their costs not only of the application, but also of the task of complying with any order that is made—which is different from the general rule in CPR, r 44.2. This rule usually applies to orders for disclosure against non-parties,[48] including those that are based on the *Norwich Pharmacal* principle.[49] **7.40**

In considering whether it should depart from the general rule in CPR, r 46.1(2), the court may take into account the parties' conduct, including whether it was reasonable to oppose the application and whether there has been compliance with the relevant pre-action protocol. There is no requirement that the court should decide the issue of costs at the same time as the order regarding disclosure is made; where appropriate, for example, the costs may be reserved pending the conclusion of the proceedings.[50] **7.41**

Deviation from the general rule in CPR, r 46.1(2)

Moore-Bick LJ has explained that the general rule in CPR, r 46.1(2), is a starting point and that the onus will be on the applicant to persuade the court that some other order is appropriate: **7.42**

> 'By laying down a general rule that the respondent will be awarded his costs, therefore, I think that the Rules implicitly recognise that it will not usually be unreasonable for him to require the applicant to satisfy the court that he ought to be granted the relief which he seeks. The reason for that (if it be necessary to find one) lies, I think, in a recognition that a private person who is not a party to existing litigation which brings with it an obligation of disclosure is entitled to maintain the privacy of his papers unless sufficient grounds can be shown for overriding it and that it is for the person seeking to invade that privacy to justify doing so. At all events, the rule is clear in its terms and provides the point of departure for a judge dealing with the costs of an application of this kind.'[51]

[48] There is a further type of order that may be sought against non-parties against whom a non-party costs order was sought: *Flatman v Germany* [2011] EWHC 2945 (QB). This is addressed in more detail at 9.71.
[49] After *Norwich Pharmacal Co & Ors v Customs and Excise Commissioners* [1974] AC 133. See, eg, *Patel v Unite* [2012] EWHC 92 (QB), *per* HHJ Parkes QC (sitting as judge of the High Court).
[50] See, eg, *Microsoft Corpn v Datel Design and Development Ltd* [2011] EWHC 1986 (Ch).
[51] *SES Contracting Ltd v UK Coal plc* [2007] EWCA Civ 791, at [17].

7.43 After having dismissed the suggestion that applications for pre-action disclosure are such an ingrained aspect of litigation that opposition would, in general, be unreasonable, Moore-Bick LJ went on to pose the question that the court should ask itself:

> 'The real question which arises in this case, therefore, is whether it was unreasonable for [the respondent] to oppose the application at all, and if not, whether its conduct in relation to the application was capable of justifying [an order which departed from the general rule mentioned above].'[52]

7.44 Whilst not binding, Judge Gosnell has commented that there are two types of unreasonable opposition: the first is where there has been an unreasonable opposition from the outset; the second is where the continuing opposition either becomes unreasonable or is effected in unreasonable fashion.[53]

7.45 Amongst other factors, Moore-Bick LJ took into account the nature of the claim, the fact that the application was not routine, the reasons given for opposing the application and the manner of the opposition. He explained that the court should make use of the range of orders available to it. Moore-Bick LJ then went on to confirm that the respondent should not ordinarily be ordered to pay costs, which he explained was true even where the respondent's conduct could be criticised:

> 'The fact is that, short of ordering [the respondent] to pay the costs of [the applicant] on the indemnity basis, the judge's order was the strongest available to him. If one is starting from the position set out in rule 48.1(2) one would expect an order of this kind to be made only in a case where it was clearly unreasonable for the respondent to oppose the application or where the manner of his opposition was so unreasonable as to make it appropriate to require him to bear the whole of both parties' costs.'[54]

7.46 These comments were made in the context of the court below having ordered the respondent to bear the whole of the costs of the application. It would seem that such a strong order would be expected only where the opposition to the application was 'clearly unreasonable' or where the manner of the opposition would justify such an order. On the facts of the case before Moore-Bick LJ, the order against the respondent was substituted with no order for costs.

The indemnity principle and applications for pre-action disclosure

7.47 It has been argued that where the party who is funded by way of a conditional fee agreement is awarded costs of the application, no costs would be payable unless and until the case is 'won'. Whilst not binding, Master Haworth rejected that argument; he identified the issue as matter of contractual interpretation and found that the ambit of the (entirely standard[55]) contractual clause dealing with interim hearings was wide enough to encompass applications for disclosure.[56] The success fee, however, would become payable (if it is payable at all) only if the claim were 'won'. That may be so, but it would have no bearing on the court's decision as to what order to make.

---

52 *Ibid*, at [18].

53 *Ackroyd v Hollely* (unreported) 16 January 2013, Leeds County Court, at [13].

54 *SES Contracting Ltd v UK Coal plc* [2007] EWCA Civ 791, at [24].

55 The agreement that was before Master Haworth was, in essence, a standard Law Society conditional fee agreement. It read as follows: 'If on the way to winning or losing you are awarded any costs ... then we are entitled to payment of those costs together with a success fee on those charges if you win overall.'

56 See *Connaughton v Imperial College Healthcare NHS Trust* [2010] EWHC 90173 (Costs), at [32].

Case examples concerning applications for pre-action disclosure

Akenhead J found that it could be reasonable for a respondent to carefully consider its response to an application for disclosure.[57] Similarly, in a family matter in which a respondent National Health Service (NHS) trust had concerns about disclosing a child's records, Sumner J commented that the respondent was entitled to present a proper argument to the court raising legitimate concerns and to ask the court to consider whether, in the exercise of its discretion, those concerns were or were not to prevail.[58] In a commercial claim, Waller LJ refused to interfere with an order condemning a respondent in costs in a case in which it had acted unreasonably in resisting an application 'root and branch'.[59] In an application in which electronic data had been destroyed because it was more than six years old, Judge Seymour (sitting as a judge of the High Court) found that the court below was wrong to deprive a solicitor of his costs merely because he had asserted privilege concerning the reasons as to why the file had been destroyed; Judge Seymour found that the solicitor's only obligation when he was asked for a file was to tell the truth.[60] **7.48**

The costs of compliance with orders for pre-action disclosure

The general rule in CPR, r 46.1(2), is that the court will award the person against whom the order is sought their costs of complying with any order made on the application.[61] If the respondent has already scanned the documents into digital form, Mance J has confirmed that it is open to the court to find that the costs of copying are limited to the costs of providing the data as opposed to the original fee for scanning.[62] This may be relevant if the court intends to assess the costs by way of summary assessment. **7.49**

The dissolution of accounts between partners

In the case of the taking of a dissolution account between partners, the starting point is no order as to costs (that is, the general rule in CPR, r 44.2, will not apply).[63] Park J had this to say on the point: **7.50**

> 'If and to the extent that the principle applies to costs incurred in connection with a partnership action the effect strictly depends on whether in the first instance costs are met out of the partnership funds or are met by the separate partners individually. If they are met out of the partnership funds they are simply left to lie where they fall, and reduce the fund falling to be divided between the partners. The effect is much the same as "No order as to costs". If costs have been met by the partners separately but are fairly to be regarded as going to the sorts of matters covered by *Hamer v Giles*, each partner should strictly be required to contribute to an aliquot share of the costs incurred by the other partners.'[64]

After having reminded himself what Park J had said, Lewison LJ added that litigation concerning dissolution of accounts was different from the more familiar adversarial litigation because it was not so easy to see who was the winner and who was the loser.[65] Lewison LJ **7.51**

---

57 *Moduleco Ltd v Carillon Construction Ltd* [2009] EWHC 250 (TCC).
58 *Re R (a child) (disclosure)* [2004] EWHC 2085 (Fam), at [71].
59 *Bermuda International Securities Ltd v KPMG* [2001] EWCA Civ 269.
60 *Beckett Bemrose & Hagan Solicitors v Future Mortgages Ltd* [2010] EWHC 1997 (QB), at [63].
61 CPR, r 48.1(2)(b).
62 *Grupo Torras SA v Al-Sabah* [1997] CLC 1553.
63 See *Hamer v Giles* (1879) 11 Ch D 942, *per* Sir George Jessel MR, cited with approval by Lewison LJ in *Ma'har v O'Keefe* [2014] EWCA Civ 1684, at [15].
64 *Sahota v Sohi* [2006] EWHC 344 (Ch), at [16].
65 *Ma'har v O'Keefe* [2014] EWCA Civ 1684, at [17].

went on to find, however, that it was open to the court to exercise its discretion as to cost in an appropriate case.

Proving probate claims and litigation concerning wills

7.52 In general, costs tend to follow the event;[66] to that extent, litigation concerning wills is the same as other litigation.[67] Two circumstances have long been recognised in which this tends not to be the case, however. Whilst remembering that costs are always in the discretion of the court, those circumstances are as follows.[68]

- **Where the testator or the beneficiaries have been at fault** If the cause of the litigation has its origin in the fault of the testator or of those interested in residue, then the costs may properly be paid out of the estate (see 7.53–7.55).[69]
- **Where there were reasonable grounds for questioning the will** Where there were reasonable grounds for questioning the execution of the will or where there were reasonable grounds for questioning the testator's capacity, the court may make no order for costs, this being pursuant to what is known as the probate rule (see 7.56–7.62).

Departure from these principles is permitted; in an appropriate case, a hybrid order may be required.[70]

Where the testator or the beneficiaries are at fault

7.53 Where a testator has themselves caused litigation, then it is only fair that the cost of that litigation is paid from their estate; similarly, where beneficiaries have been the cause, it also may be appropriate to order that costs are paid out of the estate. If, however, it is neither the testator nor those who benefit under the will who are at fault, then it may not be easy to attribute the litigation to any party, in which case the court will generally exercise its discretion to make whatever order is appropriate.

7.54 The testator being at fault means, for example, their testamentary papers being surrounded with confusion or uncertainty in law or fact. The mere fact that a testator made comments that were inconsistent with their will would not generally amount to such a state of affairs.[71]

7.55 Whilst the context in which he was speaking was not precisely on point, Scrutton LJ had this to say:

> 'I should be reluctant to do anything to create the idea that unsuccessful litigants might get their costs out of the estate, without making a very strong case on [their] facts. The lure of "costs out of the estate" is responsible for much unnecessary litigation.'[72]

---

[66] See *In re Rawlinson, decd* [2010] EWHC 1789 (Ch), and *Kostic v Chaplin* [2007] EWHC 2909 (Ch). See also Learmonth, A, Ford, C, Clark, J, and Martyn, JR (eds), *Williams, Mortimer & Sunnucks: Executors, Administrators and Probate* (20th edn, London: Sweet & Maxwell, 2013), ch 39, para 39-01.

[67] In this regard, a person challenging a will is participating in a commercial transaction and must accept the risks of litigation. This was demonstrated in the case of *Lilleyman v Lilleyman* [2012] EWHC 1056 (Ch), at [21], in which Briggs J stated that a party challenging a will had 'engaged in a high risk venture in which she played for high stakes and, in substance, lost'.

[68] See, eg, *Viva! Campaigns Ltd v Scott* [2013] EWHC 3639 (Ch), at [32], *per* Judge Simon Barker QC (sitting as a judge of the High Court).

[69] See, eg, *Wharton v Bancroft* [2012] EWHC 91 (Ch), at [3], *per* Norris J.

[70] *Viva! Campaigns Ltd v Scott* [2013] EWHC 3639 (Ch), at [32], *per* Judge Simon Barker QC (sitting as a judge of the High Court).

[71] *Re Cutcliffe's Estate* [1959] P 6, at 19, *per* Hodson LJ.

[72] *Re Plant dec'd* [1926] P 139, at 152.

Where 'the probate rule' applies

7.56 The probate rule derives from two sources, as follows.[73]

- **The probate rule in CPR, r 57.7(5)** A party who says that there is a reasonable cause for inquiry and who merely invites the court to undertake an inquiry can obtain costs protection under CPR, r 57.7(5) (see 7.57).
- **The probate rule in common law** A party who has run an active case, but has failed, may seek protection under the common-law probate rule (and, in particular, under the principle of *Spiers v English*[74]) (see 7.58–7.62).

7.57 **The probate rule in CPR, r 57.7(5)** CPR, r 57.7(5), reads as follows:

> '(a) A defendant may give notice in his defence that he does not raise any positive case, but insists on the will being proved in solemn form and, for that purpose, will cross-examine the witnesses who attested the will.
> (b) If a defendant gives such a notice, the court will not make an order for costs against him unless it considers that there was no reasonable ground for opposing the will.'

Thus the general rule in CPR, r 44.2(2), will not apply in cases concerning probate that fall within the ambit of CPR, r 57.7(5);[75] instead, the probate rule will protect a defendant from being condemned in costs.

7.58 **The probate rule in common law** Historically, the function of the court has been 'to investigate the execution of a will and the capacity of the maker and having done so, to ascertain and declare what is the will of the testator'.[76] This led to the creation of the common-law principle that where a defendant has given notice by which they request a will to be proved in solemn form, costs would not follow the event if the circumstances had reasonably led to the defendant's request.[77] Norris J has confirmed that the common-law probate rule continues to apply alongside CPR, r 57.7(5),[78] and in particular that it applies in circumstances in which the defendant has taken a more active role than that envisaged by CPR, r 57.7(5).

7.59 According to Sir James Hannen, 'where the facts show that neither the testator nor the persons interested in the residue have been to blame'—that is, where the principle referred to in 7.58 does not apply—but the common law probate rule will apply 'where the opponents of the will have been led reasonably to the *bona fide* belief that there was good ground for impeaching the will'.[79] Sir James went on to say that the opponents must have taken:

> '... all proper steps to inform themselves as to the facts of the case, but if, having done so, they *bona fide* believe in the existence of a state of things which, if it did exist, would justify

[73] See *Wharton v Bancroft* [2012] EWHC 91 (Ch), at [13], *per* Norris J.
[74] *Spiers v English* [1907] P 122.
[75] See also *Kostic v Chaplin & Ors* [2007] EWHC 2909 (Ch), which deals with conduct in contentious probate.
[76] *Mitchell v Gard* (1863) 3 Sw & Tr 275, at 277-8, *per* Sir James Wilde.
[77] *Spiers v English* [1907] P 122, at 126, *per* Sir Gorrell Barnes, involving the principle first articulated by Sir JP Wilde in *Mitchell & Mitchell v Gard & Kingwell* (1863) 3 Sw & Tr 275, at 278. See also *Twist v Tye* [1902] P 92 and *Re Cutliffe's Estate* [1959] P 6.
[78] See *Wharton v Bancroft* [2012] EWHC 91 (Ch), at [13].
[79] See *Davies v Gregory* (1873) LR 3 P & D 28, at 33, cited in *Kostic v Chaplin* [2007] EWHC 2909 (Ch), at [12].

litigation, then although no blame should attach to the testator or the executors and persons interested in the residue, each party must bear his own costs.'[80]

7.60 The common-law probate rule is applied less frequently in modern litigation than it was in the past. Henderson J had this to say on the point:

> '... [I]t is I think fair to say that the trend of the more recent authorities has been to encourage a very careful scrutiny of any case in which the first exception is said to apply, and to narrow rather than extend the circumstances in which it will be held to be engaged. There are at least two factors which have in my judgment contributed to this change of emphasis. First, less importance is attached today than it was in Victorian times to the independent duty of the court to investigate the circumstances in which a will was executed and to satisfy itself as to its validity. Secondly, the courts are increasingly alert to the dangers of encouraging litigation, and discouraging settlement of doubtful claims at an early stage, if costs are allowed out of the estate to the unsuccessful party.'[81]

7.61 The probate rule does not apply in all circumstances; different considerations apply to cases having different jurisdictional origins. The probate rule will apply in the type of case that used to be heard in the Ecclesiastical Courts and the Probate Division.[82] The probate rule will not apply in a Chancery action for a declaration of constructive trust. Ward LJ had this to say on that topic:

> 'The probate rule is rooted in the inquisitorial exercise that was conducted by the Ecclesiastical Courts and the Probate Division where the court had to be satisfied of the validity of the will before it could pronounce for the will and admit it to probate. The effect of mutual wills upon the distribution of the estate under a later will which is admitted to probate is a matter for the Chancery Division applying the law of trusts; it is not a matter of probate law and practice. The nature of that litigation is not inquisitorial: it is adversarial and, not infrequently, very adversarial as the two families disunited by death battle for their perceived true inheritance.'[83]

7.62 Norris J has explained that 'an assertion of undue influence which cannot be struck out as having no real prospect of success' or even 'an arguable case of undue influence' would not fall within the ambit of the probate rule.[84]

Wills and third parties

7.63 In cases regarding wills in general, the involvement of third parties may be a factor to be taken into account. Where a solicitor had caused a will to be incorrectly executed and where this led to litigation between potential beneficiaries, the Supreme Court has said that it would be unfair to order that both parties' costs be paid out of the estate, because this would have extinguished the estate. The court noted that it was by no means unusual to make an order for costs against a party who had caused the need for the litigation and, in view of this, the solicitor was ordered to pay the costs of one of the parties (see 9.74).[85]

---

80 See *Davies v Gregory* (1873) LR 3 P & D 28, at 33.
81 *Kostic v Chaplin* [2007] EWHC 2909 (Ch), at [21].
82 *Shovelar v Lane* [2011] EWCA Civ 802, at [44].
83 *Ibid.*
84 See *Wharton v Bancroft* [2012] EWHC 91 (Ch), at [13].
85 *Marley v Rawlings (No 2)* [2014] UKSC 51, at [7]–[13].

Probate cases in the Court of Appeal

Special provisions apply in the Court of Appeal.[86] **7.64**

Consent Orders and Tomlin Orders

Consent orders (of which Tomlin orders are a specific type) may make provision as to costs. **7.65** The CPR permit the parties to place a draft consent order before the court so that the court may make it in the agreed terms.[87] Indeed, where the costs relate to an application that has otherwise gone by consent, the CPR positively encourage the parties to agree the incidence of costs in the form of a consent order.[88] Where a costs order is made, it will usually (but not always) be possible to ask a court officer to enter and seal the order.[89] The notable exceptions are:

- where one or more of the parties is a litigant in person;
- where one or more of the parties is a child; and
- where one or more of the parties is a patient.[90]

Where any of these circumstances exist, the order must be made by a judge upon application; that application may be heard in the absence of the parties.[91] Where the agreement relates to a detailed assessment, the parties should apply for a final costs certificate; there is express provision for the certificate to be issued by a court officer.[92] **7.66**

Formalities relating to consent orders in general

Certain formalities apply to consent orders (see 7.68 and 7.69). The order must be expressed as being 'by consent' and it must be signed by the legal representative acting for each of the parties, or by the party themselves if a litigant in person.[93] This is counter-intuitive, because it is the party's legal representative who must sign (if there is one), not the party. Where the order is to go before a judge, a space must be left to allow the judge's name and judicial title to be inserted.[94] **7.67**

The provisions relating to consent orders in CPR, r 40.6

The wording of CPR, r 40.6, is as follows: **7.68**

> '(1) This rule applies where all the parties agree the terms in which a judgment should be given or an order should be made.

---

[86] CPR, r 44.2(3)(b), provides that: 'the general rule does not apply in the following proceedings: proceedings in the Court of Appeal from a judgment, direction, decision or order given or made in probate proceedings'.

[87] CPR, rr 40.3(1)(d) and 40.6(1).

[88] See PD 44, para 9.4: 'Where an application has been made and the parties to the application agree an order by consent without any party attending, the parties should seek to agree a figure for costs to be inserted in the consent order or agree that there should be no order for costs.'

[89] See CPR, r 40.6(3)(b)(vii).

[90] See CPR, r 40.6(2) and (3).

[91] See CPR, r 40.6(5) and (6), and PD 40B, para 3.3.

[92] PD 47, para 9.1, reads as follows: 'Where the parties have agreed terms as to the issue of a costs certificate (either interim or final) they should apply under rule 40.6 (Consent judgments and orders) for an order that a certificate be issued in the terms set out in the application. Such an application may be dealt with by a court officer, who may issue the certificate.'

[93] CPR, r 40.6(7), and PD 40B, para 3.4.

[94] PD 40B, para 3.3(2).

(2) A court officer may enter and seal an agreed judgment or order if—
(a) the judgment or order is listed in paragraph (3);
(b) none of the parties is a litigant in person; and
(c) the approval of the court is not required by these Rules, a practice direction or any enactment before an agreed order can be made.

(3) The judgments and orders referred to in paragraph (2) are—
(a) a judgment or order for—
(i) the payment of an amount of money (including a judgment or order for damages or the value of goods to be decided by the court); or
(ii) the delivery up of goods with or without the option of paying the value of the goods or the agreed value.
(b) an order for—
(i) the dismissal of any proceedings, wholly or in part;
(ii) the stay of proceedings on agreed terms, disposing of the proceedings, whether those terms are recorded in a schedule to the order or elsewhere;
(iii) the stay of enforcement of a judgment, either unconditionally or on condition that the money due under the judgment is paid by instalments specified in the order;
(iv) the setting aside under Part 13 of a default judgment which has not been satisfied;
(v) the payment out of money which has been paid into court;
(vi) the discharge from liability of any party;
(vii) the payment, assessment or waiver of costs, or such other provision for costs as may be agreed.

(4) Rule 40.3 (drawing up and filing of judgments and orders) applies to judgments and orders entered and sealed by a court officer under paragraph (2) as it applies to other judgments and orders.

(5) Where paragraph (2) does not apply, any party may apply for a judgment or order in the terms agreed.

(6) The court may deal with an application under paragraph (5) without a hearing.

(7) Where this rule applies—
(a) the order which is agreed by the parties must be drawn up in the terms agreed;
(b) it must be expressed as being "By Consent";
(c) it must be signed by the legal representative acting for each of the parties to whom the order relates or, where paragraph (5) applies, by the party if he is a litigant in person.'

7.69 Practice Direction (PD) 40B, para 3, provides as follows:

'3.1 Rule 40.6(3) sets out the types of consent judgments and orders which may be entered and sealed by a court officer. The court officer may do so in those cases provided that:
(1) none of the parties is a litigant in person, and
(2) the approval of the court is not required by the Rules, a practice direction or any enactment.

3.2 If a consent order filed for sealing appears to be unclear or incorrect the court officer may refer it to a judge for consideration.

3.3 Where a consent judgment or order does not come within the provisions of rule 40.6(2):
(1) an application notice requesting a judgment or order in the agreed terms should be filed with the draft judgment or order to be entered or sealed, and
(2) the draft judgment or order must be drawn so that the judge's name and judicial title can be inserted.

3.4 A consent judgment or order must:
(1) be drawn up in the terms agreed,
(2) bear on it the words "By Consent", and
(3) be signed by
 (a) solicitors or counsel acting for each of the parties to the order, or
 (b) where a party is a litigant in person, the litigant.

3.5 Where the parties draw up a consent order in the form of a stay of proceedings on agreed terms, disposing of the proceedings, and where the terms are recorded in a schedule to the order, any direction for:
(1) payment of money out of court, or
(2) payment and assessment of costs

should be contained in the body of the order and not in the schedule.'

Tomlin orders

Tomlin orders (which are named after Tomlin J rather than a case[95]) are a type of bipartite consent order comprising a body and an attached schedule; the schedule will usually contain the terms of the compromise and the body will contain the procedural provisions (including the costs order). In some circumstances, the schedule may be kept confidential even from the court. As of July 2015, provisions have applied in the Chancery Division that say that the confidential schedules are to be held by the parties' solicitors rather than lodged at court.[96] **7.70**

The form of a Tomlin order in so far as it relates to costs

The wording of a Tomlin order is usually as follows: **7.71**

> 'IT IS ORDERED BY CONSENT THAT UPON the parties having agreed the terms set out in the attached schedule, all further proceedings in this claim be stayed except for the purpose of carrying such terms into effect AND for that purpose the parties have permission to apply.'

As of July 2015, where the claim is solely about money and is in the Chancery Division, the following certificate should appear in the body of the order: **7.72**

> 'We certify that the only relief sought in this claim/counterclaim is the payment of money including any interest and costs, and that no ancillary relief has been sought at any stage.'[97]

The purpose of this certificate is to assist the court by allowing the order to be sealed by a clerk rather than a master.

An agreement to pay costs that is contained within the schedule of a Tomlin order rather than in the order itself is not an order for costs; this means that, without further order, it will not give rise to a right to an assessment.[98] Likewise, a provision for costs in the schedule of a Tomlin order will not attract judgment debt interest on those costs.[99] It is for these **7.73**

---

95 The judge was Tomlin J and the phrase comes from his ruling in *Dashwood v Dashwood* [1927] WN 276, 64 LJNC 431.
96 See Chancery Note, issued in July 2015, para 22.11.
97 See *ibid.*
98 See, by analogy, *Horizon Technologies International v Lucky Wealth Consultants Ltd* [1992] 1 WLR 24.
99 *Wills v Crown Estate Commissioners* [2003] EWHC 1718 (Ch), at [20].

reasons that PD 40B, para 3.5(2), stipulates that any order for the payment or assessment of costs is to be contained in the body of the order and not in the schedule.

7.74 If a mistake is made in recording the terms of the agreement in the schedule, an application for rectification may be made.[100]

The effect of a Tomlin order

7.75 It is worth saying a word or two about the effect of a Tomlin order, because it is relevant to the issue of what a party can do if another party fails to abide by the terms of the agreement as set out in the schedule. The making of a Tomlin order leaves the underlying claim extant. Denning MR had this to say on the point:

> '... I am of the opinion that the effect of a stay is that it is not equivalent to a discontinuance, or to a judgment for the plaintiff or the defendant. It is a stay which can be and may be removed if proper grounds are shown.'[101]

7.76 Likewise, Neill LJ made the following points:

> 'In my judgment, for the sake of clarity and certainty the word "stay" in an order should not be treated as a possible equivalent of a dismissal or a discontinuance. There may well, of course, be cases, however, where the person who wishes to have the stay removed will face great difficulties. An action which has been stayed by consent following a compromise provides an obvious example. But, as it seems to me, the action following a stay remains technically in being. The action cannot proceed or resume its active life without an order of the court, but I do not consider that it can properly be regarded as dead in the same way as an action which has been dismissed or discontinued by order.'[102]

7.77 The importance of this is that if a party fails to perform its obligations under the terms of the agreement as set out in the schedule, it is open to the court to lift the stay and to continue with the claim. This does not mean that the court will readily entertain such an application. This was made clear by Fox LJ in the following way:

> 'The first question, it seems to me, is the meaning of the agreement reached between the parties. That agreement, I think, consists not only of the schedule terms of the compromise but includes the provision for a stay itself which is an integral part of the compromise. The wording of the order is that "all further proceedings in this action except for the purpose of carrying the said terms into effect be stayed". As between the parties, therefore, it seems to me that, while the action is not continued or dismissed, the bargain was that the action would not be resorted to thereafter save for the purpose of enforcing the terms. That is the plain meaning of the language used. Moreover, it seems to me that there is no reason why the parties should have intended anything else.'[103]

7.78 Fox LJ went on to say that the test was whether 'proper grounds had been shown' and added: 'In deciding whether "proper grounds are shown" (or "good cause" is shown) for lifting the stay it is necessary to consider all the circumstances of the case.'[104]

---

[100] *Lloyds TSB Bank Ltd v Crowborough Properties Ltd* [2013] EWCA Civ 107.
[101] *Cooper v Williams* [1963] 2 QB 567, at 580.
[102] *Rofa Sport Management AG v DHL International (UK) Ltd* [1989] 1 WLR 902, at 911.
[103] *Hollingsworth v Humphrey*, The Independent, 21 December 1987, CA.
[104] *Cooper v Williams* [1963] 2 QB 567, at 580.

Where a party is aggrieved by another party's refusal to comply with the terms of the compromise and where the court does not lift the stay, that party's remedy is to sue upon the compromise or apply for specific performance. **7.79**

Forthwith Orders

Generally speaking, detailed assessment proceedings may not be commenced unless the court so orders or until the claim has been concluded (see 43.60–43.82). If circumstances permit, a party who has been awarded costs to be assessed by detailed assessment may ask for an order that their costs be assessed immediately; this is known as a forthwith order. **7.80**

The relevant law used to be judge-made law,[105] but it is now contained in CPR, r 47.1: **7.81**

> 'The general rule is that the costs of any proceedings or any part of the proceedings are not to be assessed by the detailed procedure until the conclusion of the proceedings but the court may order them to be assessed immediately.'

This general rule stems from the recommendations made in 1983 by the then equivalent of the senior costs judge.[106] Those recommendations were intended to ensure that costs were assessed in their entirety at the conclusion of the proceedings rather than in a piecemeal way; given the way in which the test of proportionality is now applied, that reasoning is even more persuasive today. That said, in practical terms, that commendable objective is often thwarted under the CPR because costs are now—at least in part—frequently subjected to summary assessment.

When a forthwith order may be appropriate

The question of whether a forthwith order should be made usually arises in the context of split trials; less commonly, it may arise in protracted proceedings in which the costs of an interlocutory step are substantial. That said, there are no fetters on when a forthwith order may be made, so an application may be made at any time in long-running proceedings (such as group litigation). **7.82**

Whilst there is no authority dealing with the point directly, there appears to be no presumption that a forthwith order will be made. It would seem that the court's discretion is unfettered, although the policy referred to at 7.81 is a factor that the court would no doubt bear in mind. **7.83**

A request for a forthwith order may be refused if it would cause prejudice to the paying party. Warren J has explained that the overall aim is to achieve justice.[107] Whilst he stressed that it was not an exhaustive list, he said that the court would take into account: **7.84**

- the paying party's ability to pay and the effect that paying would have on the paying party's ability to conduct litigation;

---

[105] This was in accordance with the maxim *unica directio fiat damnorum*, ie there should be only one certification of the damages, which rule arose at a time when damages were considered to include costs: see *Phillips v Phillips* (1879) 5 QBD 60.

[106] See para 30 of the report of a working party on Order 62 chaired by Master Horne, dated 25 January 1983.

[107] *Clarke v Meadus* [2012] EWHC 3729 (Ch), at [23], *per* Warren J.

- the effect the payment would have on the receiving party;
- any potential problem of recovery if the paying party were eventually to succeed and whether an assessment would be required at all if that were to happen; and
- what factual issues the assessment would involve and if there were overlap with the issues that would be determined in the litigation itself.[108]

Forthwith orders in the context of legal aid

7.85 If the receiving party is a legally aided party and if the costs might be subject to set-off in the event of a subsequent costs order being made against that party, it would usually not be appropriate that a forthwith order is made.[109]

Forthwith orders and costs judges

7.86 The issue of whether a costs judge is able to make a forthwith order is dealt with at 43.62–43.68.

Appeals and forthwith orders (and stays)

7.87 Appeals may present problems of their own. As is discussed at 43.74–43.82, the issue is surprisingly complex. In view of this, the following pre-CPR guidance still has resonance: 'When there is doubt as to whether or not an order results in the "conclusion or the cause or matter" the wise course is to ask the court ... for consent to proceed to taxation forthwith.'[110]

7.88 Where an appeal on a discrete point has resulted in a costs order being made and where that appeal will not dispose of the claim as a whole, the appeal court will often order that the costs of the appeal be assessed forthwith with immediate payment thereafter.[111] There have also been instances of the court ordering that the costs be assessed forthwith without payment immediately thereafter,[112] but it is not clear whether this is still something that should still happen.[113]

7.89 It may be that an appeal court has made an order for costs that does not contain a forthwith order and that the matter then proceeds in the court below (or some other court). Where this is so, Hamblen J has said that the court in which the matter proceeds would have jurisdiction to order that the costs in the appeal court be assessed forthwith.[114]

---

[108] *Ibid*, at [24] *et seq*. Warren J commented that if there were substantial overlap between the issues to be decided on the assessment and the issues to be decided at trial, that would be a factor in favour of not making an unless order.

[109] See, eg, *Hicks v Russell Jones & Walker* [2001] CP Rep 25, CA. As to set-off, see *Rawlinson & Hunter Trustees SA v ITG Ltd & Ors* [2015] EWHC 1924 (Ch), at [13]–[24], *per* Morgan J.

[110] *Harrods (Buenos Aires) Ltd* (unreported) 10 March 1993, CA, *per* Sir Mervyn Davies. This case is not reported, but it is cited in *Bottin (International) Investments Ltd v Venson Group plc* [2005] EWHC 90005 (Costs), at [45].

[111] See, eg, *Morris v Bank of America National Trust (Appeal against Striking out)* [2001] 1 All ER 954.

[112] See, eg, *Saab v Saudi American Bank* [1999] 1 WLR 1861.

[113] In *Saab v Saudi American Bank* [1999] 1 WLR 1861, the Court of Appeal was dealing with a discrete matter (namely, an appeal as to jurisdiction). It found it had the power to make an order for detailed assessment forthwith, but with the question of payment of the assessed amount deferred to another time. It is not clear whether that power continues to exist under the CPR: The White Book 2017, para 47.1.1, refers to it as being extant, but Robert Walker LJ has said that such an order 'would not be an economic use of resources': *Hicks v Russell Jones & Walker* [2001] CP Rep 25, CA, at [12]. If the jurisdiction still exists, it is rarely invoked.

[114] See *GB Gas Holdings Ltd v Accenture (UK) Ltd & Ors* [2010] EWHC 2928 (Comm), at [28], *per* Hamblen J.

David Richards LJ, however, has explained that this is not correct because the powers of the High Court do not extend to dealing with orders made by the Court of Appeal.[115]

It will often be the case that a party wishes to bring an appeal that, if successful, might alter the incidence of costs. Where a party has permission to bring such an appeal, it does not follow that the assessment proceedings will automatically be stayed, as is made clear by CPR, r 47.2: 'Detailed assessment is not stayed pending an appeal unless the court so orders.' Therefore, in the absence of an order to the contrary, the (for now) receiving party would not have to wait until the conclusion of the appeal to bring detailed assessment proceedings. If a party would like a stay, it would generally be best to seek this from the appeal court. That said, an application for a stay may be made either to the court whose order is being appealed or to that court which will hear the appeal.[116] **7.90**

Additional liabilities

Success fees may present problems because a receiving party would usually be reluctant to disclose the risk assessment until the conclusion of the case. This issue continues to be governed by now-revoked Costs Practice Direction (CPD), art 14.5,[117] which provides that: 'Where there has been a trial of one or more issues separately from other issues, the court will not normally order detailed assessment of the additional liability until all issues have been tried unless the parties agree.' This provision permits the receiving party to keep its risk assessment close to its chest until the appropriate stage has been reached. **7.91**

Group litigation

Group litigation can create its own difficulties because it is a type of litigation that is especially prone to tie up resources for many years. This will not, however, generally be a reason to make a forthwith order. Whilst he was dealing with an appeal from a decision of a costs judge rather than an application for an 'unless order', Morland J had the following to say on the topic: **7.92**

> 'In … almost all group litigation cases there should be no need for any detailed assessment of costs until the conclusion of the group litigation. Solicitors engaged in group litigation will be specialists and experienced in the field. Solicitors for claimants are fully entitled to an adequate cash flow from the defendants once the general issue of liability has been admitted or determined in the claimants' favour, similarly on determination of generic issues in the claimants' favour and on the assessment or settlement of awards of damages to individual or batches of claimants.'[118]

Thus, whilst it is true to say that it would usually not be desirable for a forthwith order to be made prior to the conclusion of group litigation,[119] it would not be unusual for a paying party to be ordered to make an interim payment. It should also be noted that Morland J's comments were made in the pre-budgeting era (and at a time when the *Lownds* test still applied); it is arguable that his comments should, accordingly, now be given less weight. **7.93**

---

[115] See *Khaira v Shergill* [2017] EWCA Civ 1687, at [58]–[61].
[116] PD 47, para 2.
[117] See CPR, r 48.1.
[118] *Giambrone v JMC Holidays Ltd (formerly Sunworld Holidays Ltd)* [2002] EWHC 2932 (QB), at [10].
[119] Contrary examples are easy to find, however, especially where the litigation is very long-running. See, eg, the British Coal Respiratory Disease Litigation, in which forthwith orders were repeatedly made over the best part of an entire decade.

Case examples

7.94 **Where there are discrete issues** The fact that the costs in question relate to discrete issues (discrete in the sense that the costs incurred have little connection with the costs of the remainder of the claim) is a factor that will, to an extent, favour the making of a forthwith order. Thus, in a case in which an appeal turned on a discrete issue as to jurisdiction, an order may be made.[120] The same is true of costs that relate to the trial of a preliminary issue in which discrete issues were addressed.[121]

7.95 **Where there may be set-off** Where a paying party's liability for costs may be diminished as a result of set-off, this may be a factor to be taken into account when deciding whether it is appropriate to make a forthwith order.[122]

7.96 **Where both parties are entitled to costs** Where both parties are entitled to costs, the court may take into account the fact that only one party seeks a forthwith order in deciding whether it is right to make such an order.[123]

7.97 **Outstanding issues** Although a pre-CPR case, where accounts remained outstanding in a partnership dispute, the Court of Appeal found that the proceedings had not yet concluded.[124] A contrary example (also pre-CPR) is a case in which a claimant had obtained an order for an enquiry as to damages: the Patents Court ruled that the proceedings could be treated as being concluded.[125]

7.98 **Poverty and access to justice** Whilst it was in an ancient case decided under a jurisdiction entirely different from the CPR,[126] Hardwick LC ruled that a claimant should have her costs if, by reason of her poverty, she would otherwise not have been able to continue the litigation.[127]

7.99 **Insolvency** Morgan J declined to make an order for the immediate assessment of the defendants' costs of an application because there was concern as to the defendants' solvency and there was a possibility that the claimant may obtain future costs orders in its favour.[128]

Deemed Orders and Default Orders

7.100 Default orders are orders that (in the absence of a contrary order) will arise as the automatic consequences of some other order being made. They arise where the court makes no other order regarding costs following a limited range of applications (see 7.102).

---

[120] See, eg, *Saab v Saudi American Bank* [1999] 1 WLR 1861.

[121] See, eg, *Greencore (UK) Holdings Plc v Elementis Plc* [2005] EWHC 2139 (Comm); cf *Gb Gas Holdings Ltd v Accenture (UK) Ltd* [2010] EWHC 2928 (Comm), in which Hamblen J declined to make a forthwith order because it would fail to save expense and would detract from preparations for trial.

[122] See, eg, *Hicks v Russell Jones & Walker* [2001] CP Rep 25, CA. More recently, see *Rawlinson & Hunter Trustees SA v ITG Ltd & Ors* [2015] EWHC 1924 (Ch), at [13]–[24], *per* Morgan J.

[123] See *Bottin (International) Investments Ltd v Venson Group plc* [2005] EWHC 90005 (Costs), *per* Master Campbell.

[124] *Small v Cohen*, The Times, 7 September 1992, CA.

[125] *Mölnlycke AB v Proctor & Gamble Ltd (No 6)* [1993] FSR 154, Patents Ct, at 156.

[126] That jurisdiction was the inherent jurisdiction of the Courts of Chancery.

[127] *Jones v Coxeter* (1742) 2 Atk 400.

[128] *Rawlinson & Hunter Trustees SA v ITG Ltd* [2015] EWHC 1924 (Ch).

Deemed orders are similar, but they are orders that are automatically made on the occurrence of some event, without the intervention or further intervention of the court. They are orders for costs, rather than mere procedural entitlements to costs.[129] They will arise where: 7.101

- a party allows court fees to remain unpaid after having been given notice to pay by the court (see 7.105);
- a party dishonours a cheque in relation to court fees (see 7.108);
- a party accepts a Part 36 offer (see 7.109); and
- a party discontinues a claim (see 7.112).

The court may or may not have discretion to disapply a deemed order (see 7.120).

Default orders

Generally speaking, where the court makes no order for costs, no party will be entitled to costs (see 6.262–6.264). There are exceptions, however, in that default orders will, where the court is silent on the issue of costs, arise where: 7.102

- the court makes an order granting permission to appeal;
- the court makes an order granting permission to apply for judicial review; and
- the court makes any order or direction sought by a party on an application without notice.[130]

In all of those circumstances, where the court takes no active steps to make an order for costs, an order for the applicant's costs in the case will be made by default.

Deemed orders

The starting point for deemed orders is CPR, r 44.9, which reads as follows: 7.103

> '(1) Subject to paragraph (2), where a right to costs arises under—
> (a) rule 3.7 or 3.7A1 (defendant's right to costs where claim is struck out for non-payment of fees);
> (a1) rule 3.7B (sanctions for dishonouring cheque);
> (b) rule 36.10(1) or (2) (claimant's entitlement to costs where a Part 36 offer is accepted); or
> (c) rule 38.6 (defendant's right to costs where claimant discontinues),
>
> a costs order will be deemed to have been made on the standard basis.
>
> (2) Paragraph 1(b) does not apply where a Part 36 offer is accepted before the commencement of proceedings.
>
> (3) Where such an order is deemed to be made in favour of a party with *pro bono* representation, that party may apply for an order under section 194(3) of the [Legal Services Act 2007].

[129] This may be relevant in so far as interest is concerned. The need for deemed orders was noted by Lord Ackner in *Legal Aid Board v Russell* [1991] 2 AC 317, in which the entitlement to costs arose out of a provision that fell short of creating an actual order for costs (and therefore failed to come within the ambit of ss 17 and 18 of the Judgments Act 1838). This led to the Rules of the Supreme Court (RSC) being changed in October 1991 in such a way as to elevate the entitlement to the status of being a deemed order and to affirm the right to interest.

[130] See CPR, r 44.10(2).

(4) Interest payable under section 17 of the Judgments Act 1838 or section 74 of the County Courts Act 1984 on the costs deemed to have been ordered under paragraph (1) will begin to run from the date on which the event which gave rise to the entitlement to costs occurred.'

7.104 It can be seen that deemed orders are on the standard basis. They give rise to an entitlement to judgment-debt interest in exactly the same way as they would if made by a judge.

Deemed orders and non-payment of court fees

7.105 There is a mechanism by which the court may give notice to a party that court fees need to be paid.[131] If that notice goes unheeded, then the claim will be automatically struck out and the defaulting party will become liable for costs.

7.106 The relevant provisions are in CPR, r 3.7 (as amended[132]), which, in so far as it is relevant, provides as follows:

> (1) Except where rule 3.7A1 applies, this rule applies to fees payable by the claimant where—
> [...]
> (d) the court has made an order giving permission to proceed with a claim for judicial review; or
> (e) the fee payable for a hearing specified by the Civil Proceedings Fees Order 2008 (Fees Order 2008) is not paid.
>
> (Rule 54.12 provides for the service of the order giving permission to proceed with a claim for judicial review)
>
> (2) The court will serve a notice on the claimant requiring payment of the fee specified in the Fees Order 2008 if, at the time the fee is due, the claimant has not paid it or made an application for full or part remission.
> (3) The notice will specify the date by which the claimant must pay the fee.
> (4) If the claimant does not—
> (a) pay the fee; or
> (b) make an application for full or part remission of the fee, by the date specified in the notice—
> (i) the claim will automatically be struck out without further order of the court; and
> (ii) the claimant will be liable for the costs which the defendant has incurred unless the court orders otherwise.
>
> (Rule 44.9 provides for the basis of assessment where a right to costs arises under this rule and contains provisions about when a costs order is deemed to have been made and applying for an order under section 194(3) of the Legal Services Act 2007.)
>
> (5) Where an application for—
> (a) full or part remission of a fee is refused, the court will serve notice on the claimant requiring payment of the full fee by the date specified in the notice; or

[131] It used to be that reminders were sent out, but this is frequently no longer the case (especially in relation to hearing fees).

[132] Amended by the Civil Procedure (Amendment No 4) Rules 2000 (SI 2000/2092), the Civil Procedure (Amendment) Rules 2002 (SI 2002/2058), the Civil Procedure (Amendment No 2) Rules 2003 (SI 2003/1242), the Civil Procedure (Amendment) Rules 2008 (SI 2008/2178), the Civil Procedure (Amendment) Rules 2013 (SI 2013/262), the Civil Procedure (Amendment No 7) Rules 2013 (SI 2013/1974) and the Civil Procedure (Amendment) Rules 2017 (SI 2017/95).

(b) part remission of a fee is granted, the court will serve notice on the claimant requiring payment of the balance of the fee by the date specified in the notice; and

(6) If the claimant does not pay the fee by the date specified in the notice—
(a) the claim will automatically be struck out without further order of the court; and
(b) the claimant will be liable for the costs which the defendant has incurred unless the court orders otherwise.
[...]'

CPR, r 3.7(7), goes on to provide a mechanism by which a defaulting party may apply for relief. Those details are not set out here.

CPR, r 3.7A1, provides as follows: **7.107**

(1) In this rule and in rule 3.7AA—
(a) "Fees Order 2008" means the Civil Proceedings Fees Order 2008;
(b) "fee notice" means a notice of—
  (i) the amount of a trial fee;
  (ii) the trial fee payment date; and
  (iii) the consequences of non-payment of the trial fee;
(c) "trial date" means the date of the trial in relation to which the trial fee is payable, and if the trial in relation to which the trial fee is payable is scheduled to commence during the course of a specified period, "trial date" means the date of the Monday of the first week of that specified period;
(d) "trial fee" means fee 2.1 set out in the Table in Schedule 1 to the Fees Order 2008 and payable for the trial of a case on the multi-track, fast track or small claims track;
(e) "trial fee payment date" means the date by which the trial fee must be paid, calculated in accordance with the Fees Order 2008;
(f) "revised trial fee payment date" means, if an application for fee remission is denied in whole or part, the revised date by which the fee or part of it is to be paid, calculated in accordance with the Fees Order 2008.

(2) This rule applies in relation to trial fees where that fee is to be paid by the claimant and the court notifies the parties in writing of the trial date.

(3) When the court notifies the parties in writing of the trial date, the court must also send a fee notice to the claimant.

(4) The fee notice may be contained in the same document as the notice of trial date, or may be a separate document.

(5) Where an application for full or part remission of a trial fee is refused, when the court sends written notice to the claimant of the refusal, the court must also notify the claimant in writing—
(a) that the claimant is required to pay the full trial fee by the revised trial fee payment date; and
(b) of the consequences of non-payment of the trial fee.

(6) Where part remission of a fee is granted, when the court sends written notice to the claimant of the part remission, the court must also notify the claimant in writing—
(a) that the claimant is required to pay the balance of the trial fee by the revised trial fee payment date; and
(b) of the consequences of non-payment of the balance of the trial fee.

(7) If—
(a) the claimant has had notice in accordance with this rule to pay the trial fee;
(b) the claimant has not applied to have the trial fee remitted in whole or part; and
(c) the trial fee has not been paid on or before the trial fee payment date,

the claim will automatically be struck out without further order of the court, and unless the court orders otherwise, the claimant will be liable for the costs which the defendant has incurred.

(8) If—

(a) the claimant has had notice in accordance with this rule to pay the trial fee;
(b) the claimant has applied to have the trial fee remitted in whole or part;
(c) remission is refused or only part remission of the trial fee is granted;
(d) following the decision on remission, the claimant has had notice in accordance with this rule to pay the full trial fee or balance of it; and
(e) the full trial fee or balance of it (as appropriate) has not been paid on or before the revised trial fee payment date,

the claim will automatically be struck out without further order of the court, and, unless the court orders otherwise, the claimant will be liable for the costs which the defendant has incurred.

(Rule 44.9 provides for the basis of assessment where a right to costs arises under this rule and contains provisions about when a costs order is deemed to have been made and applying for an order under section 194(3) of the Legal Services Act 2007.)

(9) If—

(a) a claimant applies to have the claim reinstated; and
(b) the court grants relief,

the relief must be conditional on the claimant either paying the trial fee or filing evidence of full or part remission of that fee within the period specified in paragraph (10).

(10) The period referred to in paragraph (9) is—

(a) if the order granting relief is made at a hearing at which the claimant is present or represented, 2 days from the date of the order;
(b) in any other case, 7 days from the date of service of the order on the claimant.

(11) If a fee is not paid for a claim where there is also a counterclaim, the counterclaim will still stand.'

Deemed orders on dishonouring a cheque in relation to court fees

7.108 CPR, r 3.7B, reads as follows:

'(1) This rule applies where any fee is paid by cheque and that cheque is subsequently dishonoured.

(2) The court will serve a notice on the paying party requiring payment of the fee which will specify the date by which the fee must be paid.

(3) If the fee is not paid by the date specified in the notice—

(a) where the fee is payable by the claimant, the claim will automatically be struck out without further order of the court;
(b) where the fee is payable by the defendant, the defence will automatically be struck out without further order of the court,

and the paying party shall be liable for the costs which any other party has incurred unless the court orders otherwise.

(Rule 44.9 provides for the basis of assessment where a right to costs arises under this rule.)

(4) If—

(a) the paying party applies to have the claim or defence reinstated; and
(b) the court grants relief,

the relief shall be conditional on that party paying the fee within the period specified in paragraph (5).

(5) The period referred to in paragraph (4) is—
(a) if the order granting relief is made at a hearing at which the paying party is present or represented, 2 days from the date of the order;
(b) in any other case, 7 days from the date of service of the order on the paying party.

(6) For the purposes of this rule, "claimant" includes a Part 20 claimant and "claim form" includes a Part 20 claim.'

Deemed orders and CPR, Part 36

Where a claimant accepts a Part 36 offer, that act creates a deemed order that the defendant will pay the claimant's costs on the standard basis.[133] This means that the claimant is granted not a mere contractual right to costs, but an enforceable order for costs. This will not be the case, however, if the Part 36 offer is accepted before the commencement of proceedings; if those are the circumstances, then whilst the claimant will have a contractual right to costs arising out of the operation of CPR, r 36.13(1), they will have to bring costs-only proceedings if an order is required.[134] The relevant part of CPR, r 36.13, is discussed further at 17.167. **7.109**

Different rules apply where Section IIIA of Part 45 applies; the relevant provisions are discussed at 50.287–50.289. It is a moot point whether acceptance of a Part 36 offer that falls within the ambit of Section IIIA of Part 45 would give rise to a deemed order to costs or to a mere contractual entitlement;[135] the point is arguable either way. **7.110**

The court has no jurisdiction to disapply a deemed order that arises from acceptance of a Part 36 offer. If an offeror does not wish acceptance of the offer to give rise to a deemed order, they should make their offer as a *Calderbank* offer (see 6.207 and 6.229–6.232) or as a commercial offer (for example '£X,000 with no order for costs'). If it is the offeree who wishes to escape the effect of a deemed order (perhaps because they believe that they are entitled to costs on the indemnity basis rather than on the standard basis), the offeree could wait until the expiry of the 21-day relevant period and then immediately accept the offer. That would have the effect of placing the costs at large and within the court's jurisdiction. This topic—known as the just-out-of-time jurisdiction—is discussed at 17.173–17.175. As can be seen from that discussion, it is a jurisdiction that is not without its problems. **7.111**

Deemed orders and discontinuance

Unless the court orders otherwise, discontinuance of a claim will result in the discontinuer being deemed to be liable for costs. This is the default position and, as such, does not need to be justified on a case-by-case basis,[136] but the justification of the **7.112**

---

[133] See CPR, r 44.9(1).

[134] See CPR, r 44.9(2). This change to the CPR was made as a result of Moore-Bick LJ confirming that costs orders cannot exist in a vacuum: see *Solomon v Cromwell Group Plc* [2011] EWCA Civ 1584, at [16].

[135] This is because CPR, r 44.9(1), refers to deemed orders being made where an entitlement to costs arises as a result of CPR, r 36.13(1) or (2), but it makes no mention of CPR, Section II, which is the section that applies where Section IIIA of Part 45 applies.

[136] If there ever were a rule that the claimant would be required only to pay a defendant's costs on discontinuance if the claimant was, in effect, surrendering and acknowledging defeat, that rule no longer applies under the CPR: *In re Walker Wingsail Systems plc* [2005] EWCA Civ 247, overturning *Barretts & Baird (Wholesale) Ltd v Institute of Professional Civil Servants* [1987] IRLR 3.

policy itself is thought to be that the effect of discontinuance is to deprive the defendant of the opportunity of vindicating himself.[137] The court has the power to depart from the default position, but for the reasons set out at 7.120 a discontinuing claimant would face a notoriously daunting challenge in making such an application. Unless able to show a change of circumstance that has arisen by reason of unreasonable conduct on the part of the defendant (see 7.83), a claimant who may be contemplating discontinuing and making such an application would usually be well advised to consider other courses of action.

7.113 Some discontinuing claimants will be fortunate enough to have the benefit of qualified one-way costs shifting, which topic is addressed at 8.30.

Jurisdiction

7.114 CPR, r 38.6, provides as follows:

> '(1) Unless the court orders otherwise, a claimant who discontinues is liable for the costs which a defendant against whom he discontinues incurred on or before the date on which notice of discontinuance was served on him.
> (2) If proceedings are only partly discontinued—
> (a) the claimant is liable under paragraph (1) for costs relating only to the part of the proceedings which he is discontinuing; and
> (b) unless the court orders otherwise, the costs which the claimant is liable to pay must not be assessed until the conclusion of the rest of the proceedings.
>
> (3) This rule does not apply to claims allocated to the small claims track.
> (Rule 44.12 provides for the basis of assessment where the right to costs arises on discontinuance and contains provisions about when a costs order is deemed to have been made and applying for an order under section 194(3) of the Legal Services Act 2007.)'

Moore-Bick LJ's summary

7.115 Before the topic is addressed in detail, the following summary (which had its origins in a judgment of Judge Waksman QC[138] and was adapted by Moore-Bick LJ) is a useful guide:

> '(1) [W]hen a claimant discontinues the proceedings, there is a presumption by reason of CPR 38.6 that the defendant should recover his costs; the burden is on the claimant to show a good reason for departing from that position;
> (2) the fact that the claimant would or might well have succeeded at trial is not itself a sufficient reason for doing so;
> (3) however, if it is plain that the claim would have failed, that is an additional factor in favour of applying the presumption;
> (4) the mere fact that the claimant's decision to discontinue may have been motivated by practical, pragmatic or financial reasons as opposed to a lack of confidence in the merits of the case will not suffice to displace the presumption;
> (5) if the claimant is to succeed in displacing the presumption he will usually need to show a change of circumstances to which he has not himself contributed;

---

[137] *Far Out Productions Inc v Unilever UK & CN Holdings Ltd* [2009] EWHC 3484 (Ch), at [4], *per* Mr N Strauss QC (sitting as a deputy judge of the High Court).

[138] See *Teasdale v HSBC Bank plc; Brookes v HSBC Bank plc* [2010] EWHC 612 (QB).

(6) however, no change in circumstances is likely to suffice unless it has been brought about by some form of unreasonable conduct on the part of the defendant which in all the circumstances provides a good reason for departing from the rule.'[139]

Thus the claimant must show 'good reason' why the default provisions should not apply; merely pointing to the fact that the claim would or might have succeeded would not be sufficient. It would usually be necessary to be able to demonstrate that unreasonable conduct on the part of the defendant has caused a change in circumstances to which the claimant has not contributed. **7.116**

Having cited Moore-Bick LJ's summary, Beatson LJ added the following (which was one of the points originally made by Judge Waksman QC in his summary of the law): '[T]he context for the Court's mandatory consideration of all the circumstances under [what is now CPR, r 44.2] is the determination of whether there is a good reason to depart from the presumption imposed by CPR 38.6.'[140] Put otherwise, the factors outlined in CPR, r 44.2, are relevant. **7.117**

Points of principle

Service of a notice of discontinuance brings an end to the claim, but issues concerning costs remain extant to the extent that they need to be determined (see CPR, r 38.5). The date of the deemed order is the date of service of the notice; the court may take into account any delay between that date and the application that the court should 'order otherwise'.[141] **7.118**

Whether a claim has been discontinued will depend on the facts. Where the entire claim has been brought to an end, there will usually be no potential for dispute because CPR, r 38.3(1), provides that, to discontinue a claim, a claimant must file and serve a notice of discontinuance. Therefore the issue will usually be a straightforward matter of whether a notice of discontinuance had been served. The issue can prove more troublesome if only parts of the claim have been brought to an end or if a claim is abandoned without notice being served. The following points may be made. **7.119**

- **Where part of the claim has been discontinued** Where only a part of the claim has been discontinued, there may be a dispute as to whether CPR, r 38.6(2), should apply to the abandoned part of the claim (either directly or by analogy). The matter may be analysed in terms of constructive discontinuance. An example is where claimants amended their pleadings in such a way as to abandon their claim for damages; Park J found that this was capable of amounting to discontinuance.[142]

[139] *Brookes v HSBC Bank plc; Jemitus v Bank of Scotland plc* [2011] EWCA Civ 354, at [6], *per* Moore-Bick LJ, cited with approval in *Nelson's Yard Management Co v Eziefula* [2013] EWCA Civ 235, at [14], *per* Beatson LJ.

[140] *Nelson's Yard Management Co v Eziefula* [2013] EWCA Civ 235, at [15].

[141] See, eg, *Hoist UK Ltd v Reid Lifting Ltd* [2010] EWHC 1922 (Ch), at [10], *per* Mr Roger Wyand QC (sitting as a deputy High Court judge). In that case, the court did not give much weight to the fact that there had been delay (of about a month), this being because the discontinuer had given notice of the intention to make the application.

[142] *Isaac v Isaac (No 2)* [2005] EWHC 435 (Ch). See also *Lay v Drexler* [2007] EWCA Civ 464 (in which the defendants, who had effectively started their own claim, abandoned it) and *Reid v The Capita Group Plc* (unreported) 17 October 2005, Ch D (in which the proceedings had been issued prematurely and there was insufficient notice of proceedings to defendant).

- **Constructive discontinuance** There is such a thing as constructive discontinuance of the entire claim. That would occur where the court finds that the claimant has effectively abandoned the whole of the claim and is dealt with in detail at 7.159.

Discretion

7.120 Where a discontinuer makes an application to depart from the default position, the burden will be on them to prove that there is 'good reason' why the court should accede to such a request.[143] Chadwick LJ had this to say on the point:

> 'The form in which that Rule is expressed ... makes it clear that the normal order on discontinuance is that the claimant bears the Defendants' costs up to the date on which notice of discontinuance is served. [CPR, r 38.6(1)] makes it clear that the court may order otherwise; but the burden is on the party who seeks to persuade the court that some other consequence should follow; and the task of the court is to consider whether there is some good reason to depart from the normal order.'[144]

Lewison LJ has explained that this is the case in all courts.[145]

7.121 As has been said above (see 7.115), the discontinuer would generally have to show that unreasonable conduct on the part of the defendant had caused a change in circumstances to which the claimant had not contributed; merely pointing to the fact that the claim would or might have succeeded would not be sufficient.[146] Likewise, a mere change of heart on the part of the claimant or a re-evaluation of the worth of the litigation would not be sufficient.[147] Indeed, such a factor would tend to work against the claimant. Chadwick LJ had the following to say on the topic:

> '... [J]ustice will normally lead to the conclusion that a defendant who defends himself at substantial expense against a [claimant] who changes his mind in the middle of the action for no good reason—other than that he has re-evaluated the factors that have remained unchanged—should be compensated for his costs.'[148]

7.122 If the claimant seeks to rely on the fact that there was new evidence or disclosure, the court may decline to make an order in the claimant's favour if that evidence or disclosure lacked causal significance (or, in the words of Pitchford J, if it was not a 'discrete clinching piece of evidence'[149]). Similarly, it may be relevant that the claimant could have clarified

---

143 *In re Walker Wingsail Systems plc* [2005] EWCA Civ 247, at [24], *per* Chadwick LJ. More recently, see *Brookes v HSBC Bank plc; Jemitus v Bank of Scotland plc* [2011] EWCA Civ 354, at [6], *per* Moore-Bick LJ; *Nelson's Yard Management Co v Eziefula* [2013] EWCA Civ 235, at [14], *per* Beatson LJ.

144 *In re Walker Wingsail Systems plc* [2005] EWCA Civ 247, at [24].

145 *Fresenius Kabi Deutschland GmbH v Carefusion 303 Inc* [2011] EWCA Civ 1288, at [12] *et seq*. This arose in the context of a practice that had arisen in patent cases of making '*Earth Closet* orders', a practice that the court ruled should now stop, overruling *Baird v Moule's Patent Earth Closet Co Ltd* (1881) LR 17 Ch D 139.

146 See *Brookes v HSBC Bank plc; Jemitus v Bank of Scotland plc* [2011] EWCA Civ 354, at [6], *per* Moore-Bick LJ; *Nelson's Yard Management Co v Eziefula* [2013] EWCA Civ 235, at [14], *per* Beatson LJ. See also *Far Out Productions Inc v Unilever UK & CN Holdings Ltd* [2009] EWHC 3484 (Ch), at [2], *per* Mr N Strauss QC (sitting as a deputy judge of the High Court).

147 See *Brookes v HSBC Bank plc; Jemitus v Bank of Scotland plc* [2011] EWCA Civ 354. See also *Teasdale v HSBC Bank plc; Brookes v HSBC Bank plc* [2010] EWHC 612 (QB), at [7], *per* HHJ Waksman QC (sitting as a deputy High Court judge), upheld on appeal as *Brookes v HSBC Bank plc; Jemitus v Bank of Scotland plc* [2011] EWCA Civ 354.

148 *In re Walker Wingsail Systems plc* [2005] EWCA Civ 247, at [36].

149 *R (on the application of Allbutt) v Ministry of Defence* [2009] EWHC 3351 (Admin), at [30].

the position in pre-action correspondence[150] or that the claimant has failed to clarify the position in the context of delay in the claim generally.[151] At the other end of the spectrum, if the defendant can be shown to have perversely encouraged a claimant by concealing the existence of a defence, then the defendant will be at risk.[152]

Once a case has been discontinued, it is not the function of the court to decide whether or not the claim would have succeeded.[153] It is, however, the function of the court to consider whether the unreasonableness of a defendant's conduct provides a good reason for departing from the default rule.[154] **7.123**

Beatson LJ has noted that the factors listed in CPR, r 44.2, ought to be taken into account.[155] This means that the court ought to take into account all of the circumstances, including the conduct of the parties (including pre-issue conduct and the manner in which a party has pursued or defended its case or a particular allegation or issue) and any admissible offers.[156] **7.124**

Conduct

Defendant's conduct The court may, in its discretion, reduce or negate (or even reverse) a defendant's entitlement to costs to take account of that party's conduct. Case examples are given below, but caution ought to be exercised with some of them because they pre-date the guidance referred to in 7.115. They are, however, useful in illustrating the type of conduct that the court will regard as being sufficiently unreasonable: **7.125**

- a defendant having an unreasonable attitude to negotiations[157] or a perverse attitude towards disclosing their defence[158] (although it would be wrong to place too much weight on supposed failures to engage in negotiations[159]);
- a defendant failing to discharge duties that they could be expected to discharge;[160]

---

150 *Ibid.*

151 *Far Out Productions Inc v Unilever UK & CN Holdings Ltd* [2009] EWHC 3484 (Ch), at [5], *per* Mr N Strauss QC (sitting as a deputy judge of the High Court). Delay during the claim will, of itself, usually have only a very limited influence on the final order: whilst not binding, see *In the matter of Smart-Tel (UK) plc*, sub nom *OR v Doshi* [2007] BCC 896, Companies Ct, at [38], *per* Mr Registrar Baister.

152 The *obiter* comments of Potter LJ in *RTZ Pension Property Trust Ltd v ARC Property Developments Ltd* [1999] 1 All ER 532, at 541, have been cited under the CPR as remaining good law: see *Teasdale v HSBC Bank plc; Brookes v HSBC Bank plc* [2010] EWHC 612 (QB), at [7(6)], *per* HHJ Waksman QC (sitting as a deputy High Court judge), upheld on appeal as *Brookes v HSBC Bank plc; Jemitus v Bank of Scotland plc* [2011] EWCA Civ 354.

153 See *Nelson's Yard Management Co v Eziefula* [2013] EWCA Civ 235, at [32], *per* Beatson LJ, citing *In re Walker Wingsail Systems plc* [2005] EWCA Civ 247, at [12], *per* Chadwick LJ and HHJ Waksman's second principle in *Teasdale v HSBC Bank plc; Brookes v HSBC Bank plc* [2010] EWHC 612 (QB), at [7(2)].

154 See *Nelson's Yard Management Co v Eziefula* [2013] EWCA Civ 235, at [32], *per* Beatson LJ.

155 *Ibid*, at [15].

156 *Ibid*, at [16] and [17].

157 *RBG Resources plc (in liquidation) v Rastogi and ors* [2005] EWHC 994 (Ch).

158 *RTZ Pension Property Trust Ltd v ARC Property Developments Ltd* [1999] 1 All ER 532, at 541 (see the footnotes above).

159 See, eg, *Bray (t/a the Building Company) v Bishop* (unreported) 19 June 2009, CA, *per* Longmore and Lloyd LJJ.

160 Whilst not binding, see *In the matter of Smart-Tel (UK) plc* sub nom *OR v Doshi* [2007] BCC 896, Companies Ct, at [42], in which Mr Registrar Baister reduced a defendant's entitlement to costs on the basis that he created difficulties by not fully discharging his duties as an accountant.

- a defendant significantly changing their case such that the proceedings had to be discontinued in favour of proceedings in a different forum;[161]
- a failure on the part of a defendant to comply with pre-action protocol[162] or to provide information;[163] and
- an absence of evidence to support a defendant's contention that the claimant's challenge to a will was unreasonable.[164]

7.126 The fact that discontinuance has resulted in a saving of costs and time would not, of itself, justify a departure from the default position.[165] Whilst *obiter*, Moore-Bick LJ has said that whilst there may be cases in which a defendant may have brought the litigation on themselves, even that would be unlikely to justify a departure from the rule if the claimant were to discontinue in circumstances that amounted to a failure of the claim.[166]

7.127 Where the supposed supervening event is, in reality, nothing more than the claimant becoming alive to the commercial wisdom of continuing with the claim and where that realisation was based on factors that were, or could have been, known at the outset of the claim, there would be no reason for the court to relieve the discontinuer of the burden of paying costs.[167] Likewise, a decision to discontinue motivated by practical, pragmatic or financial reasons as opposed to a lack of confidence in the merits of the case will not, without more, assist the discontinuer.[168]

7.128 *Premature issue* Where a discontinuer has brought a claim unreasonably early and without having given adequate notice to the defendant, the discontinuer's application not to pay the costs is likely to fail.[169] Likewise, if the defendant has given a clear account of its case that went beyond that which it was required to give under the relevant rules, directions or protocol, that may be a factor that the court will take into account.[170] Where the need for discontinuance arises by reason of carelessness, it is likely that the court would be unsympathetic to the discontinuer; an example might be where a claimant intends to bring proceedings against a natural person, but inadvertently sues the partnership of which that person is a member.[171]

7.129 **Supervening events** Where a claimant has to discontinue because of some supervening event beyond their control (such as an opponent becoming bankrupt for reasons unrelated

---

161 *Webb v Environment Agency* (unreported) 5 April 2011, QBD, *per* Sweeney J.

162 *Aegis Group plc v Inland Revenue* [2005] EWHC 1468 (Ch).

163 See, eg, *Nelson's Yard Management Co v Eziefula* [2013] EWCA Civ 235, *per* Beatson LJ, and *Baker v Barnett* [2015] EWHC 1375 (QB), *per* Lang J.

164 *Wylde v Culver* [2006] EWHC 1313 (Ch), *per* G Bompas QC.

165 *Messih v McMillan Williams* [2010] EWCA Civ 844, at [31], *per* Patten LJ; see also *Griffin v Smith & Ors* [2010] EWHC 3414 (Ch), at [19], *per* David Richards J.

166 *Brookes v HSBC Bank plc; Jemitus v Bank of Scotland plc* [2011] EWCA Civ 354, at [10].

167 *In re Walker Wingsail Systems plc* [2005] EWCA Civ 247; see also *Teasdale v HSBC Bank plc; Brookes v HSBC Bank plc* [2010] EWHC 612 (QB), at [7], *per* HHJ Waksman QC (sitting as a deputy High Court judge).

168 *Maini v Maini* [2009] EWHC 3036 (Ch), at [11]; see also *Teasdale v HSBC Bank plc; Brookes v HSBC Bank plc* [2010] EWHC 612 (QB), at [7(4)], *per* HHJ Waksman QC (sitting as a deputy High Court judge), upheld on appeal as *Brookes v HSBC Bank plc; Jemitus v Bank of Scotland plc* [2011] EWCA Civ 354.

169 *Reid v Capita Group plc* [2005] EWHC 2448 (Ch).

170 See, eg, *Mobiqa Ltd v Trinity Mobile Ltd* [2010] EWHC 253 (Pat), at [25]–[28], *per* Floyd J.

171 See, eg, *Brooks v AH Brooks & Co (a firm)* [2010] EWHC 2720 (Ch), *per* HHJ Cooke (sitting as a judge of the High Court).

to the claim), then the interests of justice may justify departure from a deemed order.[172] In these circumstances, the court will usually have to decide the incidence of costs without having made any finding as to the substantive issues; this is a topic that is dealt with in detail at 7.141.

The following is a summary of the approach the court will take. **7.130**

- The default position is not that there shall be no order as to costs, but that the discontinuing party will bear the costs.
- The supervening event must generally be independent in the sense that it must not have resulted from the very fact of the claim.[173]
- The burden of persuading the court to depart from the deemed order will lie with the claimant.[174] The test is not a threshold test, but is a matter of identifying all of the relevant factors and weighing them.[175]
- Where the discontinuer wishes to claim costs on the basis that the supervening event amounts to success in their claim, they will bear the burden of proving the requisite causal link between the supervening event and the putative success.[176]
- Where the claim has been discontinued as a result of a supervening event that was within the control of the defendant and which was, in reality, a capitulation on the part of the defendant, the appropriate order would usually be an award to the claimant.[177]
- Similarly, where a claimant has effectively achieved their aim by reason of interlocutory relief being afforded, the court may relieve the claimant of the burden of paying costs if the court finds that there was reasonable justification for bringing the claim.[178]
- Where an independent supervening event has made it unnecessary to continue with the claim and where it is not possible to know who would have won or what would have happened had the supervening event not occurred, an order that there be no order to costs may be appropriate.[179]
- Where the putative supervening event is, in reality, nothing more than the claimant becoming alive to the commercial wisdom of the matter and where that realisation was based on factors that were, or could have been, known at the outset of the claim, the burden of costs will generally lie with the claimant.[180]

---

[172] See, eg, *Everton v World Professional Billiards and Snooker Association (Promotions) Ltd* [2001] All ER (D) 172 (Dec), *per* Gray J.

[173] An example would be where the defendant had run out of money by defending the claim: *Teasdale v HSBC Bank plc; Brookes v HSBC Bank plc* [2010] EWHC 612 (QB), at [7(5)], *per* HHJ Waksman QC (sitting as a deputy High Court judge), upheld on appeal as *Brookes v HSBC Bank plc; Jemitus v Bank of Scotland plc* [2011] EWCA Civ 354.

[174] *In re Walker Wingsail Systems plc* [2005] EWCA Civ 247, at [24]. See 7.170.

[175] *Messih v McMillan Williams & Ors* [2010] EWCA Civ 844, at [27], *per* Patten LJ.

[176] See *Ersus v London Borough of Redbridge* [2016] EWHC 1025 (QB), at [23], *per* Supperstone J. See also *R (on the application of Daniel Baxter) v Lincolnshire County Council* [2015] EWCA Civ 1290, at [44], *per* Simon LJ.

[177] As an example, see *R v North & West Devon Health Authority & Ors, ex p Bowhay & Ors* [2001] 60 BMLR 228. See also *R v Bassettlaw DC, ex parte Aldergate Estates Ltd* [2000] Lexis Citation 5478, QBD, *per* Jackson J.

[178] *Ansol Ltd v Taylor Joynson Garrett (a firm)* [2002] All ER (D) 44 (Jan).

[179] Although a pre-CPR case, *R v Liverpool City Council, ex p Newman & Ors* [1993] 5 Admin LR 669 is an example of this.

[180] *In re Walker Wingsail Systems plc* [2005] EWCA Civ 247; see also *Teasdale v HSBC Bank plc; Brookes v HSBC Bank plc* [2010] EWHC 612 (QB), at [7], *per* HHJ Waksman QC (sitting as a deputy High

- Likewise, where the decision to discontinue was motivated by practical, pragmatic or financial reasons as opposed to a lack of confidence in the merits of the case, the burden of costs will also usually lie with the claimant.[181]
- The court should consider taking an issues-aware approach in suitable cases.[182]

7.131 Events that lack independence from the litigation will rarely be given weight (unless, of course, the event is capitulation on the part of a defendant).[183] If, for example, there are two defendants and if the claimant discontinues against one of them because the claimant has achieved what amounts to the satisfaction of their whole claim against the other, that would not usually justify a departure from the ordinary rule that, on discontinuance, a claimant should pay the costs of the defendant against whom they have discontinued.[184]

7.132 The mere fact that a claimant has got all—or almost all—that they could reasonably hope to achieve from the proceedings has been said not to justify a claimant from relying on the avoidance of a trial that would be solely about liability to recover costs as justifying a departure from the default rule.[185] The extent to which this remains true under the post-2013 overriding objective is a moot point, but it would be a risky strategy for a claimant to try to argue that point rather than, for example, applying for summary judgment. In this regard, it is worth noting that, a mere fortnight before the new overriding objective came into being, Beatson LJ said this:

> 'Is the claimant obliged, absent an agreement as to costs, to proceed to a trial which in reality would be solely about liability to recover costs? Where the defendant's position is one deserving argument at trial, the general answer must be "yes".'[186]

7.133 *A word of caution* If a claimant is considering whether to discontinue, the points made at 7.148–7.150 may be relevant. Proudman J has explained that the role of the court is limited and that the court cannot, as if by magic, look into the hearts and minds of the parties to determine the ultimate truth behind the dispute:

> 'A party who brings a claim takes the risks of the litigation ... The court decides a case on the evidence at trial. It is a misunderstanding of the role of the court to think that the judge can simply look into the parties' hearts and minds to determine the ultimate truth behind the dispute. If for whatever reason a Claimant cannot make good his case on the evidence at trial he must take the consequences of the litigation risk he assumed. It is unjust for the Defendant to bear the costs of an action which the Claimant cannot, for whatever reason ... prove at trial.'[187]

This passage was paraphrased and approved by Moore-Bick LJ.[188]

Court judge), upheld on appeal as *Brookes v HSBC Bank plc; Jemitus v Bank of Scotland plc* [2011] EWCA Civ 354.

[181] *Maini v Maini* [2009] EWHC 3036 (Ch), at [11]; see also *Teasdale v HSBC Bank plc; Brookes v HSBC Bank plc* [2010] EWHC 612 (QB), at [7(4)], *per* HHJ Waksman QC (sitting as a deputy High Court judge).

[182] *R v Westminster City Council, ex p Chorion plc* [2002] EWCA Civ 1126.

[183] For an example of capitulation, see *R v Bassettlaw DC, ex parte Aldergate Estates Ltd* [2000] Lexis Citation 5478, QBD, *per* Jackson J.

[184] *Messih v McMillan Williams & Ors* [2010] EWCA Civ 844, at [28], *per* Patten LJ.

[185] See *Nelson's Yard Management Co v Eziefula* [2013] EWCA Civ 235, at [31], *per* Beatson LJ, citing Patten LJ in *Messih v MacMillan Williams* [2010] EWCA Civ 844, at [28], [30] and [31].

[186] See *Nelson's Yard Management Co v Eziefula* [2013] EWCA Civ 235, at [33].

[187] *Maini v Maini* [2009] EWHC 3036 (Ch), at [11].

[188] *Brookes v HSBC Bank plc; Jemitus v Bank of Scotland plc* [2011] EWCA Civ 354, at [10].

The basis of costs

A deemed order is on the standard basis, but there is no reason in principle why the court should not order that costs be payable on the indemnity basis.[189] The court has the power to make such an order regardless of the purpose of the application; it is for this reason that Proudman J has warned that an application made by the claimant may inadvertently afford the defendant a forum in which to seek indemnity basis costs.[190] In any event, case examples in which indemnity basis costs were sought are as follows. **7.134**

- In a case in which he had found that the discontinuer had deliberately sought to delay the trial of the matter before discontinuing, Blackburn J made an award of costs on the indemnity basis.[191]
- In a case in which the discontinuer served notice of discontinuance on the second day of the trial in circumstances in which it had previously conceded that it was unlikely to succeed, Rattee J made an award of costs on the indemnity basis.[192]
- In a case in which the discontinuer had advanced a hopeless claim, Henderson J made an order against him on the indemnity basis.[193]

A defendant has a right to apply to have the notice of discontinuance set aside (see CPR, r 38.4(1)), which right must be exercised within 28 days after the notice of discontinuance was served (CPR, r 38.8(2)). This may be appropriate if, for example, the defendant wishes to make an application for wasted costs.[194] **7.135**

Small claims

Discontinuance of a claim on the small claims track will not result in a deemed costs order being made (see CPR, r 38.6(3)), but, where the discontinuer has behaved unreasonably, the court may make an award as a matter of discretion (see CPR, r 27.14(1)(g)). **7.136**

Group litigation

Discontinuance in group litigation is often viewed in a different light from discontinuance in other claims because there are many legitimate reasons why a claimant in those circumstances might choose to discontinue a claim other than the claim being flawed. Each order must therefore be decided on its own merits. **7.137**

It is often the case that there is a provision in the group litigation order that disapplies CPR, r 38.6, for cases on the group litigation register. This issue is dealt with in more detail at 65.87–65.89. **7.138**

Qualified one-way costs shifting

It may be the case that the discontinuing claimant has the benefit of qualified one-way costs shifting. Where this is so, then the entitlement to costs will be determined according the principles that would apply to any other discontinued claim, but the defendant's ability **7.139**

---

189 For a discussion of this, see *Hoist UK Ltd v Reid Lifting Ltd* [2010] EWHC 1922 (Ch), at [6]–[9], *per* Mr Roger Wyand QC (sitting as a deputy High Court judge).

190 *Maini v Maini* [2009] EWHC 3036 (Ch), at [7].

191 *Naskaris v ANS plc* [2002] EWHC 1782 (Ch).

192 *Atlantic Bar and Grill Ltd v Posthouse Hotels Ltd* [2000] CP Rep 32.

193 *Mireskandari v Law Society* [2009] EWHC 2224 (Ch), esp at [73].

194 See, eg, *Thompson v Go North East Ltd* (unreported), 30 August 2016, Sunderland County Court, *per* Judge Charnock-Neal.

to enforce a costs order will (subject to certain safeguards) be curtailed. This topic is addressed in Chapter 8—see, in particular, 8.23.

Enforcement

7.140 It may happen that a claimant discontinues part of the claim, but fails to pay their opponent's costs. If these are the facts, the CPR provide a mechanism by which the claimant may be prevented from continuing with the remainder of the claim unless they pay what is due. CPR, r 38.8, reads as follows:

> '(1) This rule applies where—
> (a) proceedings are partly discontinued;
> (b) a claimant is liable to pay costs under rule 38.6; and
> (c) the claimant fails to pay those costs within 14 days of—
> (i) the date on which the parties agreed the sum payable by the claimant; or
> (ii) the date on which the court ordered the costs to be paid.
>
> (2) Where this rule applies, the court may stay the remainder of the proceedings until the claimant pays the whole of the costs which he is liable to pay under rule 38.6.'

Everything agreed Save for Costs

7.141 This section deals with the topic of how a court should dispose of a dispute as to the incidence of costs where costs are the only issue that the court is asked to determine. If the claim has come to an end by way of discontinuance, then the matters discussed at 7.112–7.140 will be relevant.

Jurisdiction and discretion

7.142 The fact that all substantive issues—that is, the issues other than the incidence and basis of costs—have been settled does deprive the court of the jurisdiction to adjudicate upon and make a costs order.[195] In this regard, the court's discretion is unfettered; in particular, there is no tradition that, in those circumstances, the court will make no order for costs.[196] As is set out below, the starting point is that if a winner can be identified on a proper basis of agreed or determined facts, the 'general rule' in CPR, r 44.2(2)(a), will apply.

Whether to make an order

7.143 The fact that the court has the power to award costs without having adjudicated upon the substantive dispute does not mean that the court is obliged to exercise that power. Indeed, very often, it will decline to do so. This is because the court will be reluctant to make an award unless there is a proper basis of agreed or determined facts upon which the court can decide who has won.[197] Chadwick LJ had the following to say on the topic:

> 'The first question for the court—in every case—is whether it is satisfied that it is in a position to make an order about costs at all ... In addressing that question the court must

[195] *Brawley v Marczynski (No 1)* [2002] EWCA Civ 756; although pre-CPR, see also *Butcher v Wolfe* [1999] BLR 61.

[196] *Brawley v Marczynski (No 1)* [2002] EWCA Civ 756.

[197] As an example of a case in which the court declined to exercise its jurisdiction, see *R (on the application of G) v Worcestershire County Council* [2005] EWHC 2332 (Admin). Everything had settled at mediation save for the costs; Collins J found that it was impossible to say that it was obvious that either party would have won.

have regard to the need (if an order about costs is to be made) to have a proper basis of agreed or determined facts upon which to decide, in the light of the principles set out under the other provisions in CPR 44, what order should be made. The general rule, if the court decides to make an order about costs, is that the unsuccessful party will be ordered to pay the costs of the successful party—[CPR, r 44.2(2)(a)]. But the court may make a different order—[CPR, r 44.2(2)(b)]. Unless the court is satisfied that it has a proper basis of agreed or determined facts upon which to decide whether the case is one in which it should give effect to "the general rule"—or should make "a different order" (and, if so, what order)—it must accept that it is not in a position to make an order about costs at all. That is not an abdication of the court's function in relation to costs. It is a proper recognition that the course which the parties have adopted in the litigation has led to the position in which the right way in which to discharge that function is to decide not to make an order about costs.'[198]

General approach

Chadwick LJ went on to give further guidance, which may be summarised as follows.[199] **7.144**

- The court should be slow to embark on a determination of disputed facts solely to put itself in a position to make a decision about costs.
- The court is entitled to say to the parties that if they have not reached an agreement on costs, they have not settled the dispute.
- If the court is unable to decide who is the winner or loser without effectively trying the action, it should make no order as to costs.
- There is no tradition of making no order for costs.
- There is likely to be difficulty in deciding who is the winner and loser in more complex cases without embarking on a trial, for example, of cases involving a number of issues and claims for discretionary equitable relief.
- In straightforward cases, it will be reasonably clear from the terms of settlement which party has won or lost, but it will often be the case that neither side has won or lost.

David Richards LJ has explained that where the court is deprived of the compass normally provided by the outcome of the case, the court instead has to look for other factors to determine the appropriate order for costs, prominent amongst which will be the result of the settlement, the conduct of the parties in the course of the litigation, any reasonable offers of settlement that may have been made and—in any case in which it is tolerably clear—which party would have succeeded at trial.[200] Where appropriate, the court is entitled to take into account the terms as recorded in a Tomlin order.[201] **7.145**

Scott Baker J gave similar guidance for public law cases;[202] Lord Neuberger MR has confirmed that the principles in public law cases are the same as in private law **7.146**

---

198 *BCT Software Solutions Ltd v C Brewer & Sons Ltd* [2003] EWCA Civ 939, at [22].

199 *Ibid.*

200 *Powles v Reeves* [2016] EWCA Civ 1375, at [19], *per* David Richards LJ.

201 *Ibid*, at [32] and [33], *per* David Richards LJ.

202 *Boxall v Waltham Forest LBC* (2001) 4 CCL Rep 258, at [22], cited with approval by Pill LJ in *R (on the application of Bahta & Ors) v Secretary of State for the Home Department & Ors* [2011] EWCA Civ 895, at [7], and by Lord Neuberger MR in *M v Mayor and Burgesses of the London Borough of Croydon* [2012] EWCA Civ 595, at [34]: 'Having considered the authorities, the principles I deduced to be applicable are as follows: (i) the court has power to make a costs order when the substantive proceedings have been resolved without a trial but the parties have not agreed about costs; (ii) it will ordinarily be

cases.[203] Thus, in both private and public law cases, much will turn on the ease with which the court can determine the facts about the claim and who has won.

7.147 Notwithstanding the relatively detailed guidance that has been given, Patten LJ has confirmed that judicial guidance on the exercise of the discretion is not a restatement of the rules in CPR, r 44.2.[204] Parties should be careful about how they put their arguments at first instance because the court will usually allow the appeal only if the decision of the court below was 'manifestly unjust'.[205] This is discussed in more detail at 45.30–45.31.

The need to avoid litigation solely about costs

7.148 As to the desirability of litigation solely about costs, Simon Brown J had this to say (in the context of discontinuance):

> 'It would seldom be the case that on discontinuance this court would think it necessary or appropriate to investigate in depth the substantive merits of what had by then become an academic challenge. That ordinarily would be a gross misuse of this court's time and further burden its already over-full list.'[206]

7.149 Whilst he was dealing with the matter in the context of Part 36 rather than Part 44, Mann J had this to say on the topic (this being in circumstances in which the claimant ultimately accepted a relatively low offer on the eve of trial):

> '... [I]t would have been quite wrong and an abuse of the process to use court resources and have a 4–5-day trial involving all matters in issue on the pleadings when in fact the dispute was (on the facts) just about costs. ... The over-riding objective required that; the need to deal with matters proportionately meant that a trial was inappropriate. ... What would have been proportionate would have been for the defendant to accept that damages were agreed ... and agree that the court should determine the only outstanding issue of costs.'[207]

---

irrelevant that the Claimant is legally aided; (iii) the overriding objective is to do justice between the parties without incurring unnecessary court time and consequently additional cost; (iv) at each end of the spectrum there will be cases where it is obvious which side would have won had the substantive issues been fought to a conclusion. In between, the position will, in differing degrees, be less clear. How far the court will be prepared to look into the previously unresolved substantive issues will depend on the circumstances of the particular case, not least the amount of costs at stake and the conduct of the parties; (v) in the absence of a good reason to make any other order the fall back is to make no order as to costs; (vi) the court should take care to ensure that it does not discourage parties from settling judicial review proceedings for example by a local authority making a concession at an early stage.' Pill LJ has clarified that (vi) will not allow a party to avoid the consequences of non-compliance with a pre-action protocol: *R (on the application of Bahta & Ors) v Secretary of State for the Home Department & Ors* [2011] EWCA Civ 895, at [64].

203 *M v Mayor and Burgesses of the London Borough of Croydon* [2012] EWCA Civ 595, at [52]–[58].

204 *Speciality Produce Ltd v Secretary of State for Environment, Food & Rural Affairs* [2014] EWCA Civ 225, at [30].

205 *BCT Software Solutions Ltd v C Brewer & Sons Ltd* [2003] EWCA Civ 939. See also *Powles v Reeves* [2016] EWCA Civ 1375, at [21]–[24], *per* David Richards LJ. For examples in which the result was found to be manifestly unjust, see *Venture Finance Plc v Mead & Anor* [2005] EWCA Civ 325 and *Bray (t/a the Building Company) v Bishop & Anor* [2009] EWCA Civ 768.

206 *R v Liverpool City Council, ex p Newman & Ors* [1993] 5 Admin LR 669, at 671, cited with approval in *Ersus v London Borough of Redbridge* [2016] EWHC 1025 (QB), at [10], *per* Supperstone J. See also similar comments in *R (on the application of Scott) v London Borough of Hackney* [2009] EWCA Civ 217, at [44], *per* Hallett LJ.

207 *Jordan v MGN Ltd* [2017] EWHC 1937 (Ch), at [45], citing *Hanspaul v Ward* [2016] EWHC 1358 (Ch).

These comments of Simon Brown J and Mann J are highly relevant, but the matters discussed at 7.131 and 7.133 mean that if there are unresolved issues deserving of determination at trial, a claimant would be well advised to manage the situation without discontinuing the claim. Indeed, one could argue that discontinuance ought to be a step of last resort. **7.150**

Stanley Burnton LJ has commented that no order for costs will be the default order when the judge cannot, without disproportionate expenditure of judicial time, if at all, fairly and sensibly make an order in favour of either party without disproportionate expenditure of judicial time.[208] **7.151**

Fact-finding and adjudication as to who has won

The fact that the court has not determined the substantive issues does not deprive the court of the ability to reflect the parties' conduct in the incidence of costs,[209] but if the court is to disapply the general rule,[210] clear findings or agreed facts are necessary.[211] **7.152**

Evidence Stanley Burnton LJ has said that it is important that the costs of preparing the parties' submissions on costs ought to be proportionate to the amount at stake.[212] In a different case, Rimer LJ explained that if a factual enquiry is required, no party has the right to insist on oral evidence being heard.[213] He explained that the court is entitled to deal with such a matter summarily;[214] it is normally sufficient, he said, that the court reads the evidence and hears the parties' arguments. Whilst his guidance implied that the court would always have the freedom to deal with such issues in a summary way, Rimer LJ went on to say that, in an exceptional case (such as where the costs in question are very considerable), it may be consistent with the overriding objective for the court to hear oral evidence.[215] In deciding whether to do this, the fact that the parties have not proceeded to a trial of the substantive issues is often afforded some weight.[216] Ramsey J cited the following pre-CPR judgment of Simon Browne LJ—who, it should be noted, was giving a dissenting judgment—in a case in which the substantive issues had been appealed solely for the purposes of dealing with costs: **7.153**

> '[Where the only outstanding issues are those relating to costs] an altogether broader approach should be adopted. One which enables the court in a comparatively short time to decide, and decide, moreover, without giving a fully-reasoned judgment, into which general category of discontinuance the case falls. Can it really be an appropriate use of court time (not to mention the parties' ever escalating costs) to resolve in a series of decisions (including

---

208 *M v Mayor and Burgesses of the London Borough of Croydon* [2012] EWCA Civ 595, at [77].

209 As examples of this, see *RBG Resources plc (in liquidation) v Rastogi and ors* [2005] EWHC 994 (Ch); *In the matter of Smart-Tel (UK) plc*, sub nom *OR v Doshi* [2007] BCC 896, Companies Ct.

210 See 6.42 *et seq.*

211 *Straker v Tudor Rose (a firm)* [2007] EWCA 368, at [13].

212 *M v Mayor and Burgesses of the London Borough of Croydon* [2012] EWCA Civ 595, at [77]. See also *Powles v Reeves* [2016] EWCA Civ 1375, at [19], *per* David Richards LJ.

213 *Coyne & Anor v DRC Distribution Ltd* [2008] EWCA Civ 488, at [68] and [69].

214 *Ibid.*

215 *Ibid*, at [69] *et seq.*

216 By way of example, HHJ Stephen Davies (sitting as a High Court judge) gave some weight to the fact that a party who alleged poor conduct had chosen not to withdraw a Part 36 offer upon becoming aware of the facts that led to the allegation. This was one of the factors that persuaded him to deal with allegations summarily: *Pocklington Steel Structures Ltd v Cordell Group Ltd* (unreported) 9 December 2010, TCC, Manchester District Registry.

perhaps the House of Lords hereafter?) what, in all other respects, is a purely academic question, even if an important one, just so as to deal fairly and properly with the costs incurred by the parties before that question became academic? I would hold not. I would suggest instead that the costs can and properly should be dealt with once only, and even then generally on a broad-brush approach.'[217]

7.154 **'Trial lite'** Procedurally, Chief Master Marsh has mooted the idea of a 'trial lite' in appropriate cases, pointing out that it is open to the court to call for further disclosure on the question of costs.[218] This would enable the court to take into account the respective positions adopted by the parties and the causes of the litigation.

Discontinuance

7.155 A situation in which the court is often asked to decide the incidence of costs is where a claimant has discontinued a claim or otherwise abandoned a claim. Where the claim has been discontinued, there is a presumption that the discontinuer will pay costs, but the court has the power to make a different order. This topic is addressed in detail at 7.112–7.140. As is explained, this may work very substantially against a discontinuer who seeks to avoid paying costs. The topic of discontinuance by reason of some supervening event is dealt with at 7.129.

Concessions and compromises

7.156 At the other end of the scale from discontinuance is where the claimant secures concessions that make adjudication superfluous; in between those two extremes are compromises. The approach of the court will depend on the extent to which the claimant can be said to be the victor.[219] Whilst a lengthy extract, the following comments of Neuberger MR bear close scrutiny:

> '[There is] a sharp difference between (i) a case where a Claimant has been wholly successful whether following a contested hearing or pursuant to a settlement, and (ii) a case where he has only succeeded in part following a contested hearing, or pursuant to a settlement, and (iii) a case where there has been some compromise which does not actually reflect the Claimant's claims. While in every case, the allocation of costs will depend on the specific facts, there are some points which can be made about these different types of case.
>
> In case (i), it is hard to see why the Claimant should not recover all his costs, unless there is some good reason to the contrary. Whether pursuant to judgment following a contested hearing, or by virtue of a settlement, the Claimant can, at least absent special circumstances, say that he has been vindicated, and, as the successful party, that he should recover his costs. In the latter case, the Defendants can no doubt say that they were realistic in settling, and should not be penalised in costs, but the answer to that point is that the Defendants should, on that basis, have settled before the proceedings were issued ...
>
> In case (ii), when deciding how to allocate liability for costs after a trial, the court will normally determine questions such as how reasonable the Claimant was in pursuing the

[217] *Vector Investments v JD Williams* [2009] EWHC 3601 (TCC), at [25], citing *R v Holderness Borough Council, ex parte James Robert Developments* [1993] 1 PLR 108, at 115–19, *per* Simon Browne LJ.

[218] See *Hanspaul v Ward* [2016] EWHC 1358 (Ch).

[219] See *Harripaul v Lewisham LBC* [2012] EWCA Civ 266, at [10], in which a concession resulted in judgment being entered for the appellant. Rimer LJ confirmed that the appellant was to be regarded as the successful party and that the starting point was that she should be entitled to her costs; he went on to say that the making by the respondent of the concession is a factor that must be brought into consideration.

unsuccessful claim, how important it was compared with the successful claim, and how much the costs were increased as a result of the Claimant pursuing the unsuccessful claim. Given that there will have been a hearing, the court will be in a reasonably good position to make findings on such questions. However, where there has been a settlement, the court will, at least normally, be in a significantly worse position to make findings on such issues than where the case has been fought out. In many such cases, the court will be able to form a view as to the appropriate costs order based on such issues; in other cases, it will be much more difficult. I would accept the argument that, where the parties have settled the Claimant's substantive claims on the basis that he succeeds in part, but only in part, there is often much to be said for concluding that there is no order for costs. ... However, where there is not a clear winner, so much would depend on the particular facts. In some such cases, it may help to consider who would have won if the matter had proceeded to trial, as, if it is tolerably clear, it may, for instance support or undermine the contention that one of the two claims was stronger than the other ...

In case (iii), the court is often unable to gauge whether there is a successful party in any respect, and, if so, who it is. In such cases, therefore, there is an even more powerful argument that the default position should be no order for costs. However, in some such cases, it may well be sensible to look at the underlying claims and inquire whether it was tolerably clear who would have won if the matter had not settled. If it is, then that may well strongly support the contention that the party who would have won did better out of the settlement, and therefore did win.'[220]

After having paraphrased Neuberger MR's guidance, Jackson LJ drew attention to the following comments made by Lord Hope: **7.157**

'It is one thing for solicitors who do a substantial amount of publicly funded work, and who have to fund the substantial overheads that sustaining a legal practice involves, to take the risk of being paid at lower rates if a publicly funded case turns out to be unsuccessful. It is quite another for them to be unable to recover remuneration at *inter partes* rates in the event that their case is successful. If that were to become the practice, their businesses would very soon become financially unsustainable. The system of public funding would be gravely disadvantaged in its turn, as it depends upon there being a pool of reputable solicitors who are willing to undertake this work.'[221]

Examples of cases in which everything has been agreed other than costs

Case examples may be divided into two groups: **7.158**

- those in which there is a clear winner (see 7.159)—that is, the first of Lord Neuberger MR's categories in the extract cited at 7.156; and
- those in which it is not clear who has won (see 7.165)—that is, the second and third of those categories.

Each is dealt with in turn. It should be borne in mind that (unless otherwise stated) what is said below applies only where the litigation has come to an end by reason of concessions and compromise; whilst there is room for a degree of overlap, if the topic is discontinuance, those examples listed at 7.125 and 7.130 ought to be taken into account instead.

[220] *M v Mayor and Burgesses of the London Borough of Croydon* [2012] EWCA Civ 595, at [60]–[63].

[221] *R (on the application of Naureen) v Salford City Council* [2012] EWCA Civ 1795, at [34], quoting from *The Governing Body of JFS* [2009] UKSC 1, [2009] 1 WLR 2353, at [25].

Case examples of cases in which there was a clear winner or loser

7.159 **Examples of a clear winner: interim relief and undertakings** The first example is *Fox Gregory Ltd v Hamptons Group Ltd.*[222] The claimant used to employ a third party who, after leaving the claimant's employment, took up employment with the defendant. The employee had removed confidential property before leaving the claimant's employment. The claimant asked for an undertaking for delivery of the property. This request was initially ignored, but, after a time, the defendant indicated that it was looking into the matter. The claimant issued a claim for injunctive relief. The defendant then voluntarily gave the undertakings sought; the claim was dismissed by consent. The only outstanding issue was the costs. The judge at first instance found that the defendant had won. Arden LJ disagreed:

> 'The next question is whether it would be possible to say who was the winner and who was the loser. The only issue, in my judgment, was whether interim relief in the form of the undertakings would have been given if the undertakings had not been given. That, as I see it, is the substance of the issue before the court on 29 November. As I have explained, no significant costs were incurred on the other matters. In my judgment, if one looks at that issue then it is clear that the winner was Fox Gregory, rather than Hamptons, because Hamptons had to give those undertakings, and for this reason I would take the view that the judge was wrong in principle to say that Hamptons was substantially the winner.'[223]

7.160 **Grant of lease** The next example is *Lay v Drexler.*[224] The claimant brought a claim for the grant of a new tenancy; the dispute was not about the grant of a proposed new lease, but about its terms. About a year after issue of proceedings, the claimant indicated that it no longer wanted a new lease. The claim was dismissed by consent. The judge at first instance made no order for costs on the basis that the claim had been settled; he believed that there was insufficient material before him to allow him to exercise his discretion one way or the other. Evans-Lombe J (sitting in the Court of Appeal) disagreed. He found that the situation was analogous to discontinuance and that the claimant should therefore bear the costs.

7.161 **Split on liability** In *Onay v Brown*,[225] Goldring LJ found that a trial judge had erred in not giving adequate weight to the fact that acceptance of an offer to settle liability in a 75/25 split in the claimant's favour was a win; to describe it as anything else would be 'wholly artificial'.[226] In a different case, Mann J acknowledged the jurisdiction to make an issues-aware costs order, but he declined to do so on the facts of the case before him.[227]

7.162 **Non-financial goals** Where a supervening event has made it unnecessary to continue with a claim and where it is not possible to know who would have won or what would have happened had the supervening event not occurred, an order that there be no order to costs might be appropriate.[228] Where, however, the claim has been discontinued as a result of a supervening event that was within the control of the defendant and which was, in reality,

---

222 *Fox Gregory Ltd v Hamptons Group Ltd* [2006] EWCA Civ 1544.
223 *Ibid*, at [28].
224 *Lay v Drexler* [2007] EWCA Civ 464.
225 *Onay v Brown* [2009] EWCA Civ 775.
226 *Ibid*, at [29(5)].
227 *Rambus Inc v Hynx Semiconductor UK Ltd* [2004] EWHC 2313 (Pat).
228 Although a pre-CPR case, *R v Liverpool City Council, ex parte Newman & Ors* [1993] 5 Admin LR 669 is an example of this.

a capitulation in the face of the claimant's strong case, the appropriate order would usually be an award to the claimant. An example would be where a claimant pursued a claim with the aim of keeping a building open: after the issue of proceedings, the defendant took steps that ensured exactly that which the claimant wanted; Crane J ordered the defendant to pay the claimant's costs.[229] Another example would be where the claimant successfully sought a particular type of nursing care and accommodation.[230] A further example is a case in which a defendant in a boundary dispute sold the property to a purchaser without any reservations regarding the boundary; the purchaser then promptly agreed the boundary as per the claimant's assertions.[231]

Concessions on appeal A concession made on an appeal after permission has been given may also amount to success,[232] as may a concession in judicial review proceedings.[233] Where, in judicial review proceedings, the concession has been made for commercial reasons unconnected with those proceedings, the claimant may find themselves going without their costs.[234] **7.163**

Compromise for far less than was claimed Acceptance of an offer that was very significantly less than the amount claimed can amount to a sufficient absence of a win to displace the general rule that the successful party will be awarded costs.[235] **7.164**

Examples of cases in which there was no clear winner or loser

Undertakings and damages *Promar International Ltd v Clarke*[236] is an example of a case in which there was no clear winner or loser. The claimant (who was the defendant's former employer) brought proceedings for an injunction and damages for breach of a restrictive covenant. The claim was disputed, but the covenant was accepted. An interim injunction was granted; this was soon replaced by undertaking until trial or further order. By the time the trial took place, the restrictive covenant had all but expired. The claimant sought damages of £133,000. During the course of opening submissions, the defendant made an unconditional offer to give an undertaking. This satisfied the claimant, who then abandoned the claim for damages. The only issue that the parties were unable to resolve was the costs. The judge made no order for costs (on the basis that the claimant had secured something of value, yet had not proceeded with the rest of the claim). The claimant appealed, but lost that appeal. Hallett LJ said: **7.165**

> 'The only message that this case may send out is to reiterate and reinforce the warnings given by this court in *BCT Software and Venture Finance* of the dangers of trial judges being persuaded to decide issues of costs when all issues, save costs, have been settled or resolved without the necessity for a judgment.'[237]

---

229 *R v North & West Devon Health Authority & Ors, ex parte Bowhay & Ors* [2001] 60 BMLR 228. In a similar vein, see *R (on the application of J) v Hackney London Borough Council* [2010] EWHC 3021 (Admin), *per* McKenna J. Another example is *Thomas Brown Estates Ltd v Hunters Partners* [2012] EWHC 30 (QB), in which Eder J awarded a claimant its costs after it became unnecessary for it to continue its claim for declarations because the defendant had abandoned its case concerning the claimant's use of a trading name.

230 *R (on the application of Dempsey) v Sutton BC* [2013] EWCA Civ 863.

231 See *Powles v Reeves* [2016] EWCA Civ 1375, at [28], *per* David Richards LJ.

232 *AB & Ors v British Coal Corpn* [2007] EWHC 1406 (QB).

233 *Boxall v Waltham Forest LBC* (2001) 4 CCL Rep 258, *per* Scott Baker J.

234 *Slater Ellison v Law Society* [2002] All ER (D) 335 (Feb).

235 *Hooper v Biddle* [2006] EWHC 2995 (Ch).

236 *Promar International Ltd v Clarke* [2006] EWCA Civ 332.

237 *Ibid*, at [40].

7.166 Another example is a case in which a married couple from Pakistan sought a judicial review of a local authority's decision not to provide them with accommodation and support, the need for which litigation fell away when the Secretary of State (a third party) granted exceptional leave to remain. Jackson LJ found that the trial judge had been entitled to find that it was not possible to say who would have won and that, as such, the order that there be no order as to costs should stand.[238]

7.167 **Supervening insolvency** A claim may be discontinued not as a result of one or other party succeeding, but because some independent supervening event has made the outcome of the claim irrelevant (see 7.129–7.135). This was the case in *Everton v World Professional Billiards and Snooker Association (Promotions) Ltd*,[239] when the claimant became bankrupt: Gray J ordered that there be no order for costs. Where a claim was brought against several defendants, but was discontinued because the insolvency of the main defendants made it uneconomic to continue, Lewison J declined to relieve the claimant of the obligation to pay costs on the basis that the claimant had elected not to proceed against the remaining defendant.[240] Similarly, Norris J ordered a claimant to pay costs in a case in which a case had been maintained against a secondary defendant; he found that the court should not 'do anything to encourage litigants to pursue multiple parties to cater for remote contingencies'.[241]

7.168 **Concurrent and supervening adjudication** A claim may come to an end because the remedy that was sought was obtained in other proceedings (such as arbitration proceedings or a statutory appeals process). Patten LJ has commented that, for this to count as success for the claimant, the link between the claim and the relief obtained needs to be so clear that the claimant could properly be treated as the successful party for the purpose of an award of costs.[242] For that link to be established, the court was usually required to be satisfied that the claimant was likely to have won and that the claim had to be causative of the relief obtained; where (as in the case before him) the claim and the concurrent proceedings were based on self-contained and separate grounds, it would be difficult to say that the claim caused the remedy to be obtained in the concurrent proceedings.[243]

Where a Party Declines to Pay Costs Prior to the Issue of Proceedings

7.169 This section deals with the topic of whether a party can obtain an order for costs where proceedings have not been issued. As to the situation in which proceedings have been issued, but not served, see 6.12.

Where defendants refuse to pay costs pre-proceedings

7.170 Where a defendant declines to pay costs of a claim that has, in some way, concluded without proceedings being issued, then if costs are sought, the claimant must issue proceedings.

238 *R (on the application of Naureen) v Salford City Council* [2012] EWCA Civ 1795.
239 *Everton v World Professional Billiards and Snooker Association (Promotions) Ltd* [2001] All ER (D) 172 (Dec).
240 *Jass v Blackburn* [2003] EWHC 2963 (Ch).
241 *Dhillon v Siddiqui & Ors* [2010] EWHC 1400 (Ch), at [36].
242 *Speciality Produce Ltd v Secretary of State for Environment, Food & Rural Affairs* [2014] EWCA Civ 225.
243 *Ibid*, at [29] and [30].

If there is accord as to the incidence of costs, but not the amount, then costs-only proceedings should be issued (see Chapter 11). Where there is no such accord, the claimant may have to bring either a Part 7 or a Part 8 claim, depending upon the facts and the cause of action.

Where claimants claim cost pre-proceedings

Types of claim If it has not been compromised, then it may be appropriate to bring a claim on the original cause of action. Where there has been a compromise, it may be appropriate to sue upon the compromise, depending on its terms. **7.171**

The existence of costs-only proceedings does not detract from the availability of other means of bringing the matter before the court. PD 47, para 9.12, makes the following provisions: **7.172**

> 'Where there are other issues nothing in rule 46.14 prevents a person from issuing a claim form under Part 7 or Part 8 to sue on an agreement made in settlement of a dispute where that agreement makes provision for costs, nor from claiming in that case an order for costs or a specified sum in respect of costs but the "costs only" procedure in rule 46.14 must be used where the sole issue is the amount of costs.'

Acceptance of Part 36 offers If a claim settles pre-issue by way of a Part 36 offer being accepted, it is not possible to rely on that acceptance as giving rise to a free-standing right to assessment. Moore-Bick LJ had this to say on the point: **7.173**

> 'An order for costs cannot exist in a vacuum divorced from any substantive proceedings and accordingly an order for costs cannot be deemed to have been made under rule 44.12(1)(b) if a Part 36 offer is made and accepted before any proceedings have been commenced.'[244]

This has now been codified by an amendment to the CPR, which reads as follows: 'Paragraph 1(b) [the provision that gives rise to a deemed costs order] does not apply where a Part 36 offer is accepted before the commencement of proceedings.'[245] As such, costs-only proceedings must be brought to obtain an order, regardless of whether the pre-issue compromise was or was not in accordance with the procedure in Part 36. Costs-only proceedings are addressed in Chapter 11.

Detailed assessment proceedings If the person who is served with notice of commencement wishes to contend that the claimant was not entitled to costs, that person could make an application pursuant to PD 47, para 1.3 and 1.4, the wording of which is as follows: **7.174**

> '1.3 A party who is served with a notice of commencement ... may apply to a costs judge or a district judge to determine whether the party who served it is entitled to commence detailed assessment proceedings. On hearing such an application the orders which the court may make include: an order allowing the detailed assessment proceedings to continue, or an order setting aside the notice of commencement.
>
> 1.4 A costs judge or a district judge may make an order allowing detailed assessment proceedings to be commenced where there is no realistic prospect of the claim continuing.'

Alternatively, an application could be made pursuant to CPR, Part 11 (this being the procedure to dispute the court's jurisdiction), but only where the circumstances made such a course of action appropriate.

---

244 *Solomon v Cromwell Group Plc* [2011] EWCA Civ 1584, at [16].
245 See CPR, r 44.9(2).

7.175 Occasionally, a claimant will wish to argue that not only has the incidence of costs been agreed, but also so has the amount; where this is so, then a claim ought to be brought on the compromise. It would not be appropriate in those circumstances to make an application pursuant to PD 47, para 9.2 (which is a procedure for dealing with disputes as to compromise of costs—see 43.250–43.251); this is because that provision is limited to purported agreement made 'in the course of proceedings'.

Where claimants refuse to pay costs pre-proceedings

Where defendants claim cost pre-proceedings

7.176 **Abandoned claims** If a defendant has successfully defeated a claim such that the claimant decides not to issue proceedings, it would be procedurally difficult for that defendant to obtain an order for their costs. This is because a defendant, unlike a claimant, would not normally be able to issue proceedings based on the original cause of action.

7.177 The difficulty that such a defendant would face is highlighted by the way in which s 51(1) of the Senior Courts Act 1981 is worded. That section makes provision for the court to make orders for the costs 'of and incidental to proceedings'; if there are no proceedings, that power will not exist. For the reasons set out below, a defendant would face almost insuperable procedural problems in securing an award of costs.

7.178 If there has been a compromise that the claimant will pay costs notwithstanding the fact that no proceedings have been issued, then the defendant could sue upon that compromise, but it would be a rare event for a claimant to agree to such a compromise.

7.179 **The successful defendant's conundrum** In theory, a defendant could themselves initiate proceedings—perhaps in the guise of a claim for costs payable as damages or just an unabashed claim for costs—but a defendant who wished to do that (or defendant-turned-claimant as they would have become by that stage) would face arguments about such a claim being an abuse of process.

7.180 Even if the defendant-turned-claimant were able to avoid having their claim struck out as being an abuse of process, they would still face difficulties in proving that the court has the power to make an award. This is because the pre-action costs would generally not be 'of or incidental' to the proceedings; rather, they will be of or incidental to some other claim, that being a claim which was never brought.

7.181 This jurisdictional conundrum would not be the only difficulty a defendant-turned-claimant would face. Even if they were able to show that the court had jurisdiction to make an award of costs, a defendant-turned-claimant would have difficulties in persuading the court to exercise its discretion in their favour. Whilst not binding, Judge Coulson QC considered a similar issue in a claim in which the claimant had abandoned a significant part of its claim as a result of liaison with the defendant in accordance with a pre-action protocol; the abandoned issues were so significant that they amounted to a separate claim. The issue was whether the defendant could recover the costs of the claim that was never brought. The judge found that the defendant could not recover those costs:

> 'It would be wrong in principle to penalise the Claimant for abandoning claims which the Defendants had demonstrated were not going to succeed, because to do so would

be to penalise the Claimant for doing the very thing which the Protocol is designed to achieve.'[246]

In other words, the purpose of the pre-action period is to allow the parties to try to settle the matter (by not proceeding, if appropriate) and it would not be right to penalise a claimant for having taken a sensible decision not to issue proceedings. Judge Coulson QC went on to say that an order would be appropriate only where there were exceptional circumstances, such as unreasonable conduct.

The wasted costs jurisdiction does not apply to cases in which proceedings have not been issued.[247] The combined effect of these things is that a defendant who has successfully defeated a claim prior to the issue of proceedings would find it almost impossible to get an order for costs. It is perhaps because of this that it is not unknown for defendants to encourage claimants to issue proceedings before putting all of their cards on the table; for obvious reasons, such a practice would be contrary to the overriding objective and is therefore not to be encouraged. **7.182**

Miscellaneous Issues

The following miscellaneous issues are here considered in turn: **7.183**

- costs of appeals (7.184);
- where a claimant commences proceedings in the wrong venue (7.186);
- costs following transfer between courts (7.187); and
- where a judge recuses themselves (7.188).

Costs of appeals

The appeal court has the power to make orders about costs.[248] The court hearing an appeal may, unless it dismisses the appeal, make orders about the costs of the proceedings giving rise to the appeal, as well as the costs of the appeal (see 45.57–45.59).[249] Where an appeal results in a reversal of a costs order and where costs have already been paid under that order, the court may order the party who has to repay costs also to pay interest on those costs.[250] This topic is addressed in more detail at 56.103–56.107. **7.184**

Where the court makes an order granting permission to appeal, the order will be deemed to include an order for the applicant's costs in the case.[251] **7.185**

Commencing proceedings in the wrong venue

Section 51 of the Senior Courts Act 1981 provides: **7.186**

'(8) Where—

(a) a person has commenced proceedings in the High Court; but

[246] *McGlinn v Waltham Contractors Ltd* [2005] EWHC 1419 (TCC), at [14].
[247] *Byrne v South Sefton Health Authority* [2001] EWCA Civ 1904.
[248] CPR, r 52.20(2)(e).
[249] See CPR, r 44.10(4).
[250] *Bim Kemi AB and Blackburn Chemicals Ltd* [2003] EWCA Civ 889.
[251] CPR, r 44.10(2); see also *A Practice Statement (Judicial Review: costs)* The Times, 20 May 2004, QBD.

(b) those proceedings should, in the opinion of the court, have been commenced in a county court in accordance with any provision made under section 1 of the Courts and Legal Services Act 1990 or by or under any other enactment,

the person responsible for determining the amount which is to be awarded to that person by way of costs shall have regard to those circumstances.

(9) Where, in complying with subsection (8), the responsible person reduces the amount which would otherwise be awarded to the person in question—

(a) the amount of that reduction shall not exceed 25 per cent; and
(b) on any taxation of the costs payable by that person to his legal representative, regard shall be had to the amount of the reduction.'

So if a person commences proceedings in the High Court that ought to have been commenced in the County Court, that person's costs may be reduced, but that reduction will be limited to 25 per cent.

Costs following transfer between courts

7.187 Subject to any order made by the transferring court, where proceedings are transferred from one court to another, the court to which they are transferred may deal with all of the costs, including the costs incurred prior to the transfer.[252]

Where a judge recuses themselves

7.188 It may be that a particular judge has to recuse themselves, thereby causing costs to be thrown away. If so, then whilst each case will be determined on its own facts, it would generally not be appropriate to condemn one or other parties to pay for the costs thrown away[253] (unless, of course, the reason for the recusal was one of the parties' fault).

---

252 See CPR, r 44.10(5).
253 See, eg, *Hurst v Denton-Cox* [2014] EWHC 3948 (Ch), *per* Nugee J.

8

ORDERS FOR COSTS (QUALIFIED ONE-WAY COSTS SHIFTING)

This chapter deals with the following topics: **8.01**

- terminology and pronunciation (8.03);
- jurisdiction (8.04);
- the history of and policies underpinning qualified one-way costs shifting (QOCS) (8.05);
- the ambit of QOCS (8.10);
- transitional provisions (8.17);
- the effect of QOCS (8.22); and
- exceptions to QOCS (8.27).

Qualified one-way costs shifting (QOCS) is the implementation of a recommendation that was intended to lessen the impact of the abrogation of the recoverability of after-the-event (ATE) insurance premiums. It applies only to personal injury claims (including clinical negligence claims). It is a means by which claimants who bring such claims are afforded a degree of protection from having to pay costs, that protection arising out of a qualified bar against enforcement of any costs order that may be made against them. Qualified one-way costs shifting has no bearing on whether a costs order should be made; it goes only to enforcement. **8.02**

Terminology and Pronunciation

The acronym QOCS is pronounced 'kwɒks' rather than 'kɒks'. That pronunciation does not imply that the acronym may be spelt QWOCS; the acronym QOWCS is, however, encountered occasionally. **8.03**

Jurisdiction

Qualified one-way costs shifting is governed by the Civil Procedures Rules (CPR), Part 44, Section II, as supplemented by Practice Direction (PD) 44, para 12. Vos LJ has noted that CPR, Part 44, Section II, is not *ultra vires* for being in conflict with s 51(3) of the Senior Courts Act 1981 (as amended), that section providing that 'the court shall have full power to determine by whom and to what extent the costs are to be paid'.[1] **8.04**

[1] See *Wagenaar v Weekend Travel Ltd* [2014] EWCA Civ 1105, at [22]–[27].

The History of and Policies Underpinning QOCS

8.05 One-way costs shifting is as old as the law of costs itself. The first non-ecclesiastical statutory power to award costs (under the Statute of Marlborough 1267—see 1.19) was available only for the benefit of one side (in that instance, defendants who had successfully resisted fraudulent feoffments). Shortly thereafter, the Statute of Gloucester introduced a type of one-way costs shifting that benefited only claimants (see 12.21–12.24). Indeed, duplex costs shifting did not come into being until the coming into force of the Costs Act 1607, more than three centuries later (see 1.52).

8.06 In more modern times, one-way costs shifting came into being on the recommendation of the Rushcliffe Committee when the Legal Aid and Advice Act 1949 came into force (see 1.119–1.124). The vast majority of personal injury claims proceeded under the legal aid shield until 2000, when the system of recoverable ATE insurance premiums was created (see 1.157). When that system was mostly abrogated in 2013 (see 1.175), something was required in its place. This point was addressed by Sir Rupert Jackson in his review of 2008–09.

8.07 In his Final Report, Sir Rupert Jackson noted that, in 2008–09, 73 per cent of all households had savings of less than £10,000; he contrasted this with the high costs incurred by defendants in fully contested litigation and the fact that defendants in personal injury claims were, in general, either insured or self-insured.[2] Sir Rupert went on to identify the following factors that he said pointed towards a need for QOCS:

> '(i) Claimants are successful in the majority of personal injury claims. Defendants seldom recover costs, so they derive little benefit from two way costs shifting.
> (ii) Personal injuries litigation is the paradigm instance of litigation in which the parties are in an asymmetric relationship ...
> (iii) The principal objective of recoverable ATE insurance premiums is to protect claimants against adverse costs orders. One way costs shifting would be a less expensive method of achieving the same objective.
> (iv) One way costs shifting is not a novel concept in personal injuries litigation.'[3]

Sir Rupert went on to note that the position with clinical negligence claims was not quite the same, but was broadly similar.

8.08 Another point that Sir Rupert noted was that the Association of British Insurers and an unnamed insurer—intriguingly referred to as 'insurer X'—believed that QOCS would be cheaper than the then applicable regime of recoverable ATE premiums.[4] Sir Rupert went on to conclude that 'the overall effect of substituting one way costs shifting for recoverability of ATE insurance premiums [would be] bound to be one of costs saving'.[5]

8.09 Sir Rupert went on to reach the following conclusions:

> '4.1 In my view, the regime of recoverable ATE insurance premiums is indefensible ... On the other hand, most claimants in personal injury cases have for many years enjoyed qualified

[2] Jackson, R, *Review of Civil Litigation Costs: Final Report* (London: HMSO, 2010), at para 19.1.2.
[3] *Ibid*, at para 19.1.3.
[4] *Ibid*, at paras 19.2.1–19.2.3.
[5] *Ibid*, at para 19.2.4.

protection against liability for adverse costs and there are sound policy reasons to continue such protection. The only practicable way that I can see to achieve this result is by qualified one way costs shifting.'[6]

Although the broad thrust of Sir Rupert's recommendations was accepted, the eventual scheme embodied in CPR, Part 44, Section II, did not follow the legal aid model. Lewison LJ has noted that it is much more prescriptive than the broader, more discretionary, approach that Sir Rupert had envisaged.[7]

The Ambit of QOCS

CPR, r 44.13, defines the ambit of QOCS in the following way: **8.10**

'(1) This Section applies to proceedings which include a claim for damages—
(a) for personal injuries;
(b) under the Fatal Accidents Act 1976; or
(c) which arises out of death or personal injury and survives for the benefit of an estate by virtue of section 1(1) of the Law Reform (Miscellaneous Provisions) Act 1934,

but does not apply to applications pursuant to section 33 of the Senior Courts Act 1981 or section 52 of the County Courts Act 1984 (applications for pre-action disclosure), or where rule 44.17 applies.

(2) In this Section, "claimant" means a person bringing a claim to which this Section applies or an estate on behalf of which such a claim is brought, and includes a person making a counterclaim or an additional claim.'

Types of proceeding

As can be seen from the rule set out above, CPR, Part 44, Section II, applies only to personal injury claims and fatal accident claims. In his Final Report, however, Sir Rupert Jackson said that QOCS should be treated as a 'broad concept'[8] and, in practice, that is how it has been applied. For example, CPR, Part 44, Section II, embraces claims in which the claimant's injuries were caused by clinical negligence[9] or by putatively defective products,[10] and it will apply regardless of whether the claim is brought on behalf of an estate,[11] or against the Motor Insurer's Bureau,[12] or against a defendant outside the jurisdiction.[13] Claims for aggravated, exemplary and restitutionary damages may be included,[14] but it would seem that this will depend on the circumstances.[15] **8.11**

---

[6] *Ibid*, at para 19.4.1.

[7] See *Howe v Motor Insurers' Bureau* [2017] EWCA Civ 932, at [11], *per* Lewison LJ.

[8] Whilst not a source of law, see Jackson, R, *Review of Civil Litigation Costs: Final Report* (London: HMSO, 2010), para 19.1.1. See also *Howe v Motor Insurers' Bureau* [2017] EWCA Civ 932, at [11], *per* Lewison LJ.

[9] Whilst not a source of law, see Jackson, R, *Review of Civil Litigation Costs: Final Report* (London: HMSO, 2010), para 19.1.1. As an example of a clinical negligence claim in which QOCS applies, see *Mabb v English* (unreported), 6 December 2017, QBD, *per* May J.

[10] See, eg, *Shaw v Medtronic Corevalve LLC & Ors* [2017] EWHC 1397 (QB).

[11] See CPR, r 44.13(1)(c).

[12] See *Howe v Motor Insurers' Bureau* [2017] EWCA Civ 932, at [39], *per* Lewison LJ.

[13] See, eg, *Shaw v Medtronic Corevalve LLC & Ors* [2017] EWHC 1397 (QB).

[14] See, eg, *ibid*, at [46], *per* Lavender J.

[15] See, eg, *Jeffreys v Commissioner of Police for the Metropolis* [2017] EWHC 1505 (QB), at [42], in which Morris J found on the facts of that case that the fact that no proof of damage was required to pursue these claims pointed to them not being claims for personal injury, etc.

Mixed claims

8.12 The wording of CPR, r 44.13, is that CPR, Part 44, Section II, will apply to proceedings that 'include' a claim for damages for personal injury claims and fatal accident claims; this implies that QOCS will apply to the whole of proceedings that includes any such claim, rather than only to those specific aspects of any such claim.[16] This may be so, but it is only the starting point, because a mixed claim would be subject to the exceptions described below and, in particular, to those set out in 8.46.

Pre-action disclosure

8.13 CPR, Part 44, Section II, will not apply to applications for pre-action disclosure (presumably because such a claim is a free-standing claim that is not a claim for personal injury).

Counterclaims and additional claims

8.14 CPR, Part 44, Section II, applies regardless of whether the claim was brought as a claim, a counterclaim or an additional claim.[17] That said, it would be wrong to believe that the mere fact that part of the proceedings falls within the ambit of CPR, Part 44, Section II, means that QOCS will apply umbrella-like to all counterclaims and additional claims that may be before the court. In this regard, Vos LJ had this to say:

> 'It is true ... that the word "proceedings" in CPR Rule 44.13 is a wide word which could, in theory, include the entire umbrella of the litigation in which commercial parties dispute responsibility for the payment of personal injury damages. I do not think that would be an appropriate construction. Instead, I think the word "proceedings" in CPR Part 44.13 was used because the QOCS regime is intended to catch claims for damages for personal injuries, where other claims are made in addition by the same claimant. There may, for example, in the ordinary road traffic claim, be claims for damaged property in addition to the claim for personal injury damages, and the draftsman would plainly not have wished to allow such additional matters to take the claim outside the QOCS regime. Thus, in my judgment, CPR Rule 44.13 is applying QOCS to a single claim against a defendant or defendants, which includes a claim for damages for personal injuries or the other claims specified in CPR Rule 44.13(1)(b) and (c), but may also have other claims brought by the same claimant within that single claim.'[18]

Thus QOCS would not, for example, apply to a dispute between a defendant and a third party where that dispute was merely about who should bear responsibility for paying the claimant's damages.

Appeals

8.15 CPR, Part 44, Section II, applies to appeals, as well as proceedings at first instance.[19] This is so regardless of any power in CPR, Part 52, to order that the recoverable costs of an appeal be limited.[20] CPR, Part 44, Section II, will apply even where the appeal is in relation

[16] See *ibid*, at [34], *per* Morris J.

[17] See CPR, r 44.13(2).

[18] See *Wagenaar v Weekend Travel Ltd* [2014] EWCA Civ 1105, at [39] and [40].

[19] See *Parker v Butler* [2016] EWHC 1251 (QB), at [16]–[19], *per* Edis J. See also *Howe v Motor Insurers' Bureau* [2017] EWCA Civ 932, at [3], *per* Lewison LJ.

[20] See *Parker v Butler* [2016] EWHC 1251 (QB), at [19], *per* Edis J.

to something other than the substance of the underlying litigation (such as an appeal in respect of costs).[21]

Retrospective effect

Whilst there are transitional provision (see 8.17–8.21), CPR, Part 44, Section II, is retrospective in the sense that it will apply to all cases in which no pre-commencement funding arrangement was made, regardless of whether the decision not to create such an arrangement was taken before or after CPR, Part 44, Section II, came into force. Vos LJ had this to say on the point: **8.16**

> 'It is well established that the presumption against retrospection does not apply to legislation concerned with matters of procedure, and that provisions of that nature are to be construed as retrospective unless there is a clear indication that that was not the legislature's intention ... There is nothing in CPR Rules 44.13 to 44.17 to indicate that they were not intended to be retrospective. Indeed, they show clearly that they were.'[22]

The fact that a defendant may have entered into a pre-commencement funding arrangement does not have any bearing on the matter.[23]

Transitional Provisions

Where the claimant has the benefit of a pre-commencement funding arrangement (see 8.18), CPR, Part 44, Section II, will be of no effect. This is made clear by CPR, r 44.17, which reads: 'This Section does not apply to proceedings where the claimant has entered into a pre-commencement funding arrangement (as defined in rule 48.2).' Thus if the claimant has entered into a pre-commencement funding arrangement, QOCS will not apply. **8.17**

CPR, r 48.2(1), has the following to say about what is meant by a pre-commencement funding arrangement: **8.18**

> '(1) A pre-commencement funding arrangement is—
> (a) in relation to proceedings other than insolvency-related proceedings, publication and privacy proceedings or a mesothelioma claim—
> (i) a funding arrangement as defined by rule 43.2(1)(k)(i) where—
> (aa) the agreement was entered into before 1 April 2013 specifically for the purposes of the provision to the person by whom the success fee is payable of advocacy or litigation services in relation to the matter that is the subject of the proceedings in which the costs order is to be made; or
> (bb) the agreement was entered into before 1 April 2013 and advocacy or litigation services were provided to that person under the agreement in connection with that matter before 1 April 2013;

[21] See the costs judgment following *Jeffreys v Commissioner of Police for the Metropolis* [2017] EWHC 1505 (QB), *per* Morris J.

[22] See *Wagenaar v Weekend Travel Ltd* [2014] EWCA Civ 1105, at [30].

[23] See *ibid*, at [31]–[33], *per* Vos LJ.

(ii) a funding arrangement as defined by rule 43.2(1)(k)(ii) where the party seeking to recover the insurance premium took out the insurance policy in relation to the proceedings before 1 April 2013;

(iii) a funding arrangement as defined by rule 43.2(1)(k)(iii) where the agreement with the membership organisation to meet the costs was made before 1 April 2013 specifically in respect of the costs of other parties to proceedings relating to the matter which is the subject of the proceedings in which the costs order is to be made ...'

8.19 It may be that a claimant has or had a pre-commencement funding arrangement, but that, for one reason or another, it is said not to relate to the proceedings in question. Such a claimant may try to rely on this for the purposes of benefiting from the provisions of CPR, Part 44, Section II, but such an argument will generally fail. Longmore LJ has confirmed that the concept of a pre-commencement funding arrangement is 'remarkably wide': it is not limited to situations in which legal services were in fact provided under such an arrangement before 1 April 2013, but also to an arrangement made before that date for the provision of such services in the future.[24] The fact that an arrangement may have been terminated does not result in the engagement of CPR, Part 44, Section II.[25] Longmore LJ expressed no view as to whether it would be possible for CPR, Part 44, Section II, to apply where no work whatsoever had been carried out under a pre-commencement funding arrangement, but he did say that such circumstances would be relatively rare.[26]

8.20 It is worth noting that District Judge Phillips found, in a case in which a pre-commencement funding arrangement had been terminated such that no additional liabilities were recoverable by the claimant, that CPR, Part 44, Section II, would be engaged.[27] Longmore LJ cast doubt on that decision, but he did say (*obiter*) that it may be possible for CPR, Part 44, Section II, to be engaged if the pre-commencement funding arrangement had been completely and retrospectively replaced by some other contract of retainer.[28]

8.21 Whilst not binding, Judge Lopez has held that where a defendant relies on an incorrect representation that a claimant had a pre-commencement funding agreement, the claimant will be estopped from denying the existence of that agreement for the purposes of the aforesaid transitional provisions.[29]

The (Qualified) effect of QOCS

8.22 CPR, Part 44, Section II, does not prevent the court from making an order for costs; indeed, PD 44 expressly provides that where costs are ordered against a claimant, this may be on a standard or indemnity basis and may be subject to a summary or detailed assessment.[30]

---

[24] See *Catalano v Espley-Tyas Development Group Ltd* [2017] EWCA Civ 1132, at [21].

[25] See *ibid*, at [23], *per* Longmore LJ.

[26] See *ibid*, at [29].

[27] *Casseldine v The Diocese of Llandaff* (unreported), 3 July 2015, Cardiff County Court.

[28] See *Catalano v Espley-Tyas Development Group Ltd* [2017] EWCA Civ 1132, at [29], *per* Longmore LJ, who made reference to *Plevin v Paragon Personal Finance Ltd* [2017] 1 WLR 1249, at [13].

[29] See *Price v Egbert H Taylor & Co Ltd* (unreported), 16 June 2016, Birmingham County Court, at [48]–[51], and [78]–[80], *per* Judge Lopez.

[30] See PD 44, para 12.7.

The implication is that the fact that a claimant may be entitled to the benefit of CPR, Part 44, Section II, has no bearing on the incidence of costs.

Rather than going to the incidence of costs, CPR, Part 44, Section II, restricts the extent to which an order against a claimant may be enforced. In particular, CPR, r 44.14, has the following to say: **8.23**

> '(1) Subject to rules 44.15 and 44.16, orders for costs made against a claimant may be enforced without the permission of the court but only to the extent that the aggregate amount in money terms of such orders does not exceed the aggregate amount in money terms of any orders for damages and interest made in favour of the claimant.
>
> (2) Orders for costs made against a claimant may only be enforced after the proceedings have been concluded and the costs have been assessed or agreed.
>
> (3) An order for costs which is enforced only to the extent permitted by paragraph (1) shall not be treated as an unsatisfied or outstanding judgment for the purposes of any court record.'

Thus, unless the court orders otherwise, an order against a claimant may be 'enforced' (or, more accurately, set off) only if and to the extent that the total costs do not exceed the aggregate of the damages and interest awarded to the claimant.[31] Even then, orders may be enforced only after proceedings have been concluded and the costs have been assessed or agreed.[32] **8.24**

It is likely that the policy that underpins this qualification is that there is a need to ensure that Part 36 continues to have teeth. In particular, if Part 36 is to have any effect on claimants in personal injury claims, there must be *some* risk to a claimant in respect of CPR, Part 36, however attenuated that risk may be. **8.25**

It should also be noted that the costs that may be enforced pursuant to CPR, r 44.14(1), are the 'aggregate amount in money terms of such orders [ie orders for costs]', the relevance of which is that this will include costs incurred at interim hearings. Presumably, the policy that underpins this is similar to the point made above—namely, that claimants who make unmeritorious interim applications or who wrongly defend such interim applications are placed at a degree of risk, even if that risk is attenuated. **8.26**

Exceptions to QOCS

Qualified one-way costs shifting, by definition, is qualified: in addition to the qualification referred to above (8.24), there are three exceptions, two of which are dependent on the court granting permission (8.32) and one of which is not (8.28). **8.27**

Exceptions to QOCS where permission not required

CPR, r 44.15, reads as follows: **8.28**

> '(1) Orders for costs made against the claimant may be enforced to the full extent of such orders without the permission of the court where the proceedings have been struck out on the grounds that—

[31] CPR, r 44.14(1).
[32] CPR, r 44.14(2).

(a) the claimant has disclosed no reasonable grounds for bringing the proceedings;
(b) the proceedings are an abuse of the court's process; or
(c) the conduct of—
  (i) the claimant; or
  (ii) a person acting on the claimant's behalf and with the claimant's knowledge of such conduct,

is likely to obstruct the just disposal of the proceedings.'

8.29 Thus an adverse costs order may be enforced without permission if the claim has been struck out on the basis that it disclosed no reasonable grounds, that it was an abusive claim or that the conduct of the claimant (or a person acting on the claimant's behalf and of whose conduct the claimant has knowledge) was likely to obstruct the just disposal of proceedings.[33] The policy that underpins these provisions is obvious—namely, to deter poor conduct. It is, at first blush, somewhat curious that these provisions are described as giving rise to exceptions that may be enforced without the court's permission because it is a prerequisite for each of them that the court must make an adverse (if not damning) finding against the claimant, but presumably this has been done to ensure that the court gives effect to the underlying policy.

8.30 It may be that a claimant sees the writing on the wall and discontinues an ill-conceived claim before it is struck out. If that were to happen, the court would have the power to set aside the notice of discontinuance and then to strike out the claim, thereby invoking CPR, r 44.15.[34] Whilst he recognised the existence of such a power, Lavender J declined an application to set aside a notice of discontinuance; instead, he preferred to give the discontinuing claimant the benefit of the doubt in view of the fact that there was 'a possibility that the Claimant [had] simply recognised … that the claim [would] not stand'.[35] He found that this did not amount to an 'abuse of process or anything sufficient to justify setting aside the notice of discontinuance'.[36] In a similar vein, May J declined to set aside a notice of discontinuance in a clinical negligence claim in which the court had drawn the claimant's attention to the weakness of her case on causation.[37]

8.31 It may be that the appropriate relief to grant a defendant is to set aside service of the claim form rather than to strike the claim out. An example would be where the claim form was served outside the jurisdiction without permission: where this is so, the court would have no power under CPR, r 44.15, to allow enforcement of costs as against the claimant. Lavender J has commented on this fact and has called upon the Civil Procedure Rule Committee to reconsider the scope of CPR, r 44.15(1)(a).[38]

---

[33] Whilst not binding on any court, in a case in which the claimant failed to attend court to be cross-examined, District Judge Dodsworth invoked CPR, r 44.15(1)(c)(i), on the basis that the 'just disposal of the proceedings' included enabling the defendant to have the opportunity to test the claimant's evidence and determine if there had been fundamental dishonesty: see *Brahilika v Allianz Insurance plc* (unreported), 30 July 2015, Romford County Court.

[34] See CPR, r 38.4. As to the principles to be applied when exercising that power, see *Gillam v Browning* [1998] 2 All ER 68. See also *High Commissioner for Pakistan and the United Kingdom v National Westminster Bank Plc* [2015] EWHC 55 Ch, in which Henderson J stated that whilst abuse was a persuasive factor in favour of setting aside a notice of discontinuance, the reason for discontinuance was the key question.

[35] *Shaw v Medtronic Corevalve LLC & Ors* [2017] EWHC 1397 (QB), at [58].

[36] *Ibid*, at [58].

[37] See *Mabb v English* (unreported), 6 December 2017, QBD, *per* May J.

[38] *Shaw v Medtronic Corevalve LLC & Ors* [2017] EWHC 1397 (QB), at [51], *per* Lavender J.

Exceptions to QOCS where permission required

There are two exceptions where permission to enforce is required, both of which are governed by CPR, r 44.16. The first is where there has been fundamental dishonesty (see 8.34); the second, where the claim is made for the benefit of persons other than the claimant or for the benefit of a claimant to whom CPR, Part 44, Section II, does not apply (see 8.46). **8.32**

Where the court gives permission to enforce a costs order against a claimant pursuant to CPR, r 44.16, it will normally order the claimant (or the person for whose benefit a claim was made, as the case may be) to pay costs notwithstanding that the aggregate amount in money terms of such orders exceeds the aggregate amount in money terms of any orders for damages, interest and costs made in favour of the claimant.[39] Put otherwise, enforcement will generally be full in its extent rather than limited to mere set-off. **8.33**

Fundamental dishonesty

The following provisions apply in addition to those in s 57 of the Criminal Justice and Courts Act 2015 (see 6.87–6.92). If a claim has been exaggerated, then, where appropriate, it would generally be prudent to consider whether an order should be made under that section. **8.34**

CPR, r 44.16(1), reads as follows: 'Orders for costs made against the claimant may be enforced to the full extent of such orders with the permission of the court where the claim is found on the balance of probabilities to be fundamentally dishonest.' Thus an adverse costs order may be enforced in full with the court's permission where the claim is found, on the balance of probabilities, to have been fundamentally dishonest. The reference to 'the balance of probabilities' in CPR, r 44.16(1), makes it clear that there is no special intermediate standard of proof required (that is, a standard between the civil standard and the criminal standard)[40]—although, in practice, many judges will make a finding of fundamental dishonesty only if the evidence points strongly in that direction. **8.35**

There is no guidance in PD 44 as to what amounts to fundamental dishonesty. This is deliberate, as Sir Rupert Jackson explained: **8.36**

> 'I do not believe that either litigants or the court will be assisted by a practice direction which gives guidance on borderline cases. Any such guidance is likely to generate increased satellite litigation ... There is a whole Costs Bar out there just waiting to sink its teeth into the new provisions.'[41]

In a judgment that was subsequently approved by Newey LJ,[42] Judge Maloney QC had the following to say about how the test is to be applied: **8.37**

> '["Fundamentally dishonest"] has to be interpreted purposively and contextually in the light of the context. This is, of course, the determination of whether the claimant is "deserving" ... of the protection (from the costs liability that would otherwise fall on him) extended, for reasons of social policy, by the QOCS rules. It appears to me that when one

[39] See PD 44, para 12.6.
[40] Whilst not binding, see *Gosling v Screwfix Direct* (unreported), 29 April 2014, Cambridge County Court, at [58], *per* Judge Malone QC.
[41] See Jackson, R, 'Technical Aspects of Implementation: Third Lecture in the Implementation Programme', 31 October 2011, at para 4.2.
[42] See *Howlett v Davies* [2017] EWCA Civ 1696, at [16] and [17], *per* Newey LJ.

> looks at the matter in that way, one sees that what the rules are doing is distinguishing between two levels of dishonesty: dishonesty in relation to the claim which is not fundamental so as to expose such a claimant to costs liability, and dishonesty which is fundamental, so as to give rise to costs liability.'[43]

It is worth pausing here to note that whilst Judge Maloney QC was no doubt entitled to interpret CPR, r 44.26(1), purposively, it should not be forgotten that the phrase 'fundamentally dishonest' also appears in s 57 of the Criminal Justice and Courts Act 2015. It would be a curious state of affairs if that phrase were, by reason of a purposive construction, to be given a different meaning depending on whether that section or CPR, r 44.16(1), was being interpreted.

8.38 That said, Judge Maloney QC went on to say this (which, it would appear, is entirely compatible with the use of the similar language in the 2015 Act):

> 'The corollary term to "fundamental" would be a word with some such meaning as "incidental" or "collateral". Thus, a claimant should not be exposed to costs liability merely because he is shown to have been dishonest as to some collateral matter or perhaps as to some minor, self-contained head of damage. If, on the other hand, the dishonesty went to the root of either the whole of his claim or a substantial part of his claim, then it appears to me that it would be a fundamentally dishonest claim: a claim which depended as to a substantial or important part of itself upon dishonesty.'[44]

On the facts of the case before him, Judge Maloney QC found that the fact that the claimant had exaggerated the extent of his claim for damages by a factor of about two justified the loss of costs protection.

8.39 In a similar vein, District Judge Madge had the following to say: 'I assume that the word, fundamental, means something going to the base, something going to the core of the claim, something of central importance and something which is crucial.'[45] Whilst not binding, Judge Gregory cited these comments with approval.[46] Judge Gregory went on to allow an appeal in which the court below had failed to find fundamental dishonesty on the mistaken basis that the test was whether the claimant was fundamentally dishonest, as opposed to the claim being fundamentally dishonest[47] (although, of course, in many circumstances the two will be much the same).

8.40 Whilst he ultimately allowed the appeal on the basis that the claim had been fundamentally dishonest, Judge Freedman had the following to say (*obiter*): '[W]hat does fundamentally dishonest mean? It does not, in my judgment, cover situations where there is simply exaggeration or embellishment.'[48] To the extent that Judge Freedman meant minor exaggeration, he was undoubtedly right, but if and to the extent that he meant that exaggeration could never amount to fundamental dishonesty, the editor respectfully disagrees. This is because the same wording is used in s 57 of the Criminal Justice and Courts Act

---

43 *Gosling v Screwfix Direct* (unreported), 29 April 2014, Cambridge County Court, at [44].

44 *Ibid*, at [45]. Again, Newey LJ approved of Judge Maloney's words: see *Howlett v Davies* [2017] EWCA Civ 1696, at [16] and [17], *per* Newey LJ.

45 See *Zimi v London Central Bus Co Ltd* (unreported), 18 January 2015, Central London County Court.

46 See *Diamanttek Ltd v James* (unreported), 8 February 2016, Coventry County Court, at [10] and [11].

47 Judge Iain Hughes QC came to much the same conclusion in *Menary v Darnton* (unreported), 13 December 2016, Winchester County Court.

48 See *Zurich Insurance plc v Bain* (unreported), 4 June 2015, Newcastle upon Tyne County Court, at [11].

2015 and, for the reasons set out in 6.90, the prime (if not sole) focus of that section is on exaggerated claims. Moreover, as is set out below, there have been instances of the court making a finding of fundamental dishonesty as a result of exaggeration.

Case examples Whilst each case must be decided on its own facts, the following examples may assist. 8.41

- **Claims arising out of accidents that did not happen** Judge Iain Hughes QC found that fundamental dishonesty had been made out in a case in which the alleged road traffic accident was missing a crucial ingredient—namely, a collision.[49]
- **Cumulative evidence of dishonesty** In the case of a road traffic accident in which there was a catalogue of concerns about the evidence of a counterclaimant, Deputy District Judge Oldroyd found that the cumulative effect of those concerns amounted to fundamental dishonesty.[50] In a claim in which the claimant's evidence was riddled with inconsistencies about his prior medical condition and about the way in which the accident occurred, Judge Charnock-Neal made a finding of fundamental dishonesty (together with a wasted costs order against the claimant's solicitors).[51]
- **Exaggerated claim** Mr Recorder Knifton found fundamental dishonesty in a case in which the claimant, whilst having brought a claim that was *bona fide* in principle, had significantly exaggerated his loss of earnings.[52]
- **Noise-induced hearing loss** Judge Gregory found fundamental dishonesty in a claim in which the claimant had lied about not being afforded ear protection in his workplace.[53]
- **Failure to declare pre-existing condition** Whilst it was only one factor at play, Judge Freeman found fundamental dishonesty in a claim in which the claimant, after being 'cold-called' by a claim handler, claimed to have suffered a back injury, but failed to tell the medical expert that he had suffered back pain prior to the index accident.[54]
- **Mere rejection of a claimant's evidence** In a case in which the claimant had advanced two entirely inconsistent accounts of how the accident had occurred, Judge Freedman refused to grant permission to appeal the decision of the court below not to find that there had been fundamental dishonesty.[55]

Procedural issues As to procedure, PD 44, para 12.4, gives the following guidance: 8.42

> 'In a case to which rule 44.16(1) applies (fundamentally dishonest claims)—
> (a) the court will normally direct that issues arising out of an allegation that the claim is fundamentally dishonest be determined at the trial;

---

[49] See *Menary v Darnton* (unreported), 13 December 2016, Winchester County Court.

[50] See *Waggett v Warchalowski* (unreported), 15 September 2015, Blackpool County Court.

[51] See *Thompson v Go North East Ltd* (unreported), 30 August 2016, Sunderland County Court.

[52] See *Barber v Liverpool City Council* (unreported), 16 November 2017, Liverpool County Court. See also *Gosling v Screwfix Direct* (unreported), 29 April 2014, Cambridge County Court.

[53] See *Diamanttek Ltd v James* (unreported), 8 February 2016, Coventry County Court.

[54] See *Zurich Insurance plc v Bain* (unreported), 4 June 2015, Newcastle upon Tyne County Court.

[55] See *Nesham v Sunrick Clothing Ltd* (unreported), 22 April 2016, Newcastle upon Tyne County Court. It should be noted that the court at first instance did not find the claimant to have been dishonest at all. In a similar vein, see *Meadows v La Tasca Restaurants Ltd* (unreported), 16 June 2016, Manchester County Court, in which Judge Hodge QC refused to find fundamental dishonesty arising out of mere inconsistences in the claimant's evidence; cf *Howlett v Davies* [2017] EWCA Civ 1696, in which the inconsistencies contributed to a finding of fundamental dishonesty.

(b) where the proceedings have been settled, the court will not, save in exceptional circumstances, order that issues arising out of an allegation that the claim was fundamentally dishonest be determined in those proceedings;
(c) where the claimant has served a notice of discontinuance, the court may direct that issues arising out of an allegation that the claim was fundamentally dishonest be determined notwithstanding that the notice has not been set aside pursuant to rule 38.4;
(d) the court may, as it thinks fair and just, determine the costs attributable to the claim having been found to be fundamentally dishonest.'

8.43 It should be noted that, in contrast to s 57 of the Criminal Justice and Courts Act 2015, there is no requirement that the defendant makes an application alleging fundamental dishonesty (see 6.89). The fact that fraud has not been pleaded will not prevent the court from making such a finding, because the provisions relating to QOCS do not impose any pleading requirement.[56] The same can be said of the fact that fundamental dishonesty may not have been pleaded.[57] Newey LJ has explained that the key question would be whether the claimant had been given adequate warning of, and a proper opportunity to deal with, the possibility of a finding of fundamental dishonesty and the matters leading the judge to it rather than whether the defendant had positively alleged fraud in its defence.[58]

8.44 It is trite law that if the court is to be asked to disbelieve a witness, the witness should be cross-examined on that point.[59] In the context of fundamental dishonesty, Newey LJ had this to say on the topic:

> 'First, where a witness' honesty is to be challenged, it will always be best if that is explicitly put to the witness. There can then be no doubt that honesty is in issue. But what ultimately matters is that the witness has had fair notice of a challenge to his or her honesty and an opportunity to deal with it. It may be that in a particular context a cross-examination which does not use the words "dishonest" or "lying" will give a witness fair warning. That will be a matter for the trial judge to decide. Secondly, the fact that a party has not alleged fraud in his pleading may not preclude him from suggesting to a witness in cross-examination that he is lying. That must, in fact, be a common occurrence.'[60]

8.45 There have been instances of the court making a finding of fundamental dishonesty without cross-examination specifically on that topic. Whilst not binding, Judge Maloney QC has explained that, where possible, any consideration of the issue of whether there has been fundamental dishonesty ought to be by way of an 'efficient and summary approach'.[61] He declined to hold an oral hearing solely to determine the issue of whether the claimant had lied about the circumstances of the accident.[62] He was, however, prepared to determine the issue of whether there had been fundamental dishonesty in relation to quantum, this being

---

56 See *Howlett v Davies* [2017] EWCA Civ 1696, at [30] and [31], *per* Newey LJ. It should be noted that, in low-velocity road traffic accidents, it is commonplace—following certain guidance given by Brooke LJ in *Kearsley v Klarfeld* [2005] EWCA Civ 1510, at [41]–[48]—for fraud not to be pleaded.

57 See *Howlett v Davies* [2017] EWCA Civ 1696 at [32], *per* Newey LJ.

58 See *ibid*, at [31]. Newey LJ went on to say that the facts that the defendant had pleaded that the accident did not occur as alleged or at all, that the claimant was put to strict proof and that the accident was 'staged/contrived' were sufficient to put the claimant on notice: see *ibid*, at [33].

59 See, eg, *Browne v Dunn* (1894) 6 R 67, as cited in *Markem Corpn v Zipher Ltd* [2005] EWCA Civ 267, at [58].

60 See *Howlett v Davies* [2017] EWCA Civ 1696, at [39].

61 *Gosling v Screwfix Direct* (unreported), 29 April 2014, Cambridge County Court, at [24].

62 *Ibid*, at [33].

in the context of the existence of a 'frankly devastating surveillance video'.[63] Judge Maloney QC rejected the submission that he was obliged to hear oral evidence from the claimant before determining the issue.[64] Given the guidance given by Newey LJ (see 8.44), it is moot point whether it would be the correct way to proceed (although it has to be said that the facts of the case before Judge Maloney QC were remarkably compelling).

Claims for the benefit of people other than the claimant

CPR, r 44.16(2) and (3), reads as follows: **8.46**

> '(2) Orders for costs made against the claimant may be enforced up to the full extent of such orders with the permission of the court, and to the extent that it considers just, where—
> (a) the proceedings include a claim which is made for the financial benefit of a person other than the claimant or a dependant within the meaning of section 1(3) of the Fatal Accidents Act 1976 (other than a claim in respect of the gratuitous provision of care, earnings paid by an employer or medical expenses); or
> (b) a claim is made for the benefit of the claimant other than a claim to which this Section applies.
>
> (3) Where paragraph (2)(a) applies, the court may, subject to rule 46.2, make an order for costs against a person, other than the claimant, for whose financial benefit the whole or part of the claim was made.'

Thus the court may give permission for an adverse order to be enforced where the claim includes a claim that is made (i) for the 'financial benefit of a person other than the claimant or a dependant within the meaning of section 1(3) of the Fatal Accidents Act 1976' (see 8.48), or (ii) for the benefit of the claimant other than a claim to which CPR, Part 44, Section II, applies (see 8.52), this being the type of mixed claim referred to in 8.12 above. The extent to which an order may be enforced is at the discretion of the court, but is limited to that which the court considers just.[65] **8.47**

Where the proceedings include a claim for the financial benefit of another person CPR, r 44.16(2)(a), may apply where the proceedings include a claim that is made for the financial benefit of a person other than the claimant or a dependant within the meaning of s 1(3) of the Fatal Accidents Act 1976. Where this is so, the court may—subject to CPR, r 46.2 (see 9.78–9.90)—make an order for costs against the person for whose financial benefit that claim was made.[66] The court will usually order that person to pay the costs of that aspect of the claim, but exceptionally it may make such an order permitting enforcement against the claimant.[67] **8.48**

Turner J has explained that the aforesaid provisions do not operate in a way that is distinct from older case law governing non-party costs orders. In the context of proceedings that included a claim for credit hire, he had this to say: **8.49**

> 'The suggestion that [CPR, r 44.16] has effectively created a new category of discretion to be exercised in a conceptually different way is unattractive. [The defendants] argue that there should be a different and broader discretion to award costs in the context of credit hirers

[63] *Ibid*, at [34]–[49].
[64] *Ibid*, at [52]–[58].
[65] See CPR, r 44.16(2).
[66] See CPR, r 44.16(3).
[67] See PD 44, para 12.5(a).

operating behind the protecting veil of the QOCS regime. It may well be that, as is often the case, where a credit hire company promotes litigation for its own financial benefit, knowing that the party in whose name the claim is brought will enjoy some level of protection under the QOCS regime or will probably not be able to satisfy any adverse costs order in any event, then this is a factor which the court may take into account when considering whether it is just for the credit hire company to pay costs. ... Thus the CPR 44.16 does not change the nature of the discretion but merely operates in circumstances in which factors in favour of the exercise of that discretion may well come into play.'[68]

8.50 Turner J added this:

> 'I am further satisfied that there is nothing in the wording of CPR 44.16 which is inconsistent with the case law as it has evolved over the last thirty years. The test of what is just under the Rule is entirely consistent with the central observation of the Court of Appeal in [*Deutsche Bank AG v Sebastian Holdings Inc* [2016] EWCA Civ 23] that "the only immutable principle is that the discretion must be exercised justly".'[69]

He went on to explain that a finding of financial benefit (see CPR, r 44.16(2)(a)) is a necessary, but not sufficient, condition of exposure to liability to an adverse costs order in this context, making it clear that the making of an order is a matter firmly within the discretion of the court.[70]

8.51 The following points can be made about CPR, r 44.16(2)(a), and PD 44, para 12.

- **'... a person other than ...'** Examples of claims made for the financial benefit of 'a person other than the claimant or a dependant within the meaning of section 1(3) of the Fatal Accidents Act 1976' are subrogated claims and claims for credit hire.[71] Presumably, this is to ensure that QOCS is made available only to those persons to whom the concerns referred to in 8.07 apply.
- **' ... financial benefit ...'** Turner J has explained that the party making the claim for costs against the person other than the claimant or dependant does not have to prove that that person stands to make a profit; instead, the financial benefit is made out because it is to the financial benefit of that person to recover the monies due through the process of the claimant's litigation. Turner J summed this up by saying that '[s]ome money is better than no money'.[72]
- **Gratuitous provision of care** CPR, r 44.16(2)(a), will not apply to the provision of personal services rendered gratuitously by persons such as relatives and friends for things such as personal care, domestic assistance, childminding, home maintenance and decorating, gardening and chauffeuring.[73]
- **Earnings paid by an employer or medical expenses** CPR, r 44.16(2)(a), will not apply to claims brought in respect of earnings paid by an employer or medical expenses.[74]
- **Attribution** The court may, as it thinks fair and just, determine the costs attributable to claims for the financial benefit of persons other than the claimant.[75]

---

68 *Select Car Rentals (North West) Ltd v Esure Services Ltd* [2017] EWHC 1434 (QB), at [29].
69 *Ibid*, at [31].
70 *Ibid*, at [38].
71 See PD 44, para 12.2.
72 *Select Car Rentals (North West) Ltd v Esure Services Ltd* [2017] EWHC 1434 (QB), at [32].
73 See CPR, r 44.16(2), and PD 44, para 12.3.
74 See CPR, r 44.16(2)(a).
75 See PD 44, para 12.5(b).

Where the proceedings comprise mixed claims CPR, r 44.16(2)(b), may apply where a claim is made 'for the benefit of the claimant other than a claim to which this Section applies'. Morris J has commented on the fact that this provision is not clearly expressed, not least because CPR, Part 44, Section II, does not apply to claims, but to proceedings.[76] He was, however, able to conclude that it meant 'where the proceedings include a claim other than a personal injury claim'[77] (by which, presumably, he meant to include a claim under the Fatal Accidents Act 1976 or s 1(1) of the Law Reform (Miscellaneous Provisions) Act 1934). Morris J adopted the observations of Langstaff J, who had the following to say when given permission to appeal: **8.52**

> 'In order to give [meaning to CPR, r 44.16(2)(b)], I suspect a court should hold that it is intended to cover a situation in which a claim is made which, if it stood in proceedings on its own, would not attract Qualified One-Way Costs Shifting. If so, then in any proceedings which include both a claim and a separate claim for personal injuries, it is open to the court to permit an exception to Qualified One-Way Costs Shifting to the extent it thinks just.'[78]

In a similar vein, Lavender J has explained that CPR, r 44.16(2)(b), will apply if the claim form and particulars of claim include a claim that falls outside the scope of CPR, r 44.12.[79]

Examples of claims that will cause proceedings to be mixed include: claims for misrepresentation, deceit or unjust enrichment;[80] claims for false imprisonment, malicious prosecution and misfeasance in public office;[81] and claims for loss of liberty and distress, humiliation, fear and upset.[82] The fact that a claim may be actionable per se (that is, without proof of damage) points in the direction of it not falling within the ambit of CPR, Part 44, Section II.[83] **8.53**

Where a claim is a mixed claim, then there is no requirement that for CPR, r 44.16(2)(b), to apply, the personal injury claim and the non-personal injury claim must be 'divisible'. Morris J pointed out that there is nothing in the wording of the CPR to support this nor was he able to identify any reason in principle why there should be such a requirement.[84] He went on to say that if the two claims are inextricably linked or otherwise very closely related, then that relationship can be reflected in the exercise of discretion (in the claimant's favour) that arises once CPR, r 44.16(2)(b), has been found to apply.[85] **8.54**

Lavender J has made it clear that if CPR, r 44.16(2)(b), is to apply, any such claim must actually be pursued; it is not sufficient that it is merely mentioned in the claim form.[86] Morris J has confirmed that the court is able to exercise its discretion under CPR, r 44.16(2)(b), where the claim has been dismissed in its entirety.[87] **8.55**

---

[76] See CPR, r 44.13(1), and *Jeffreys v Commissioner of Police for the Metropolis* [2017] EWHC 1505 (QB), at [36].
[77] See *ibid*, at [35] and [36], *per* Morris J.
[78] *Ibid*, at [36], *per* Morris J, citing Langstaff J's order giving permission to appeal.
[79] *Shaw v Medtronic Corevalve LLC & Ors* [2017] EWHC 1397 (QB), at [60], *per* Lavender J.
[80] *Ibid.*
[81] See *Jeffreys v Commissioner of Police for the Metropolis* [2017] EWHC 1505 (QB), at [41], *per* Morris J.
[82] *Ibid*, at [42].
[83] *Ibid.*
[84] *Ibid*, at [44].
[85] *Ibid.*
[86] *Shaw v Medtronic Corevalve LLC & Ors* [2017] EWHC 1397 (QB), at [60].
[87] See *Jeffreys v Commissioner of Police for the Metropolis* [2017] EWHC 1505 (QB), at [55]–[57].

9

ORDERS FOR COSTS (NON-PARTY COSTS ORDERS AND WASTED COSTS)

9.01 This chapter deals with the following topics:

- non-party costs orders (9.02):
  - – jurisdiction (9.03);
  - – exceptionality and causation (9.11);
  - – categories of order (9.20);
  - – procedure (9.78);
  - – evidence (9.84);
  - – privilege and disclosure (9.89);
- wasted costs (9.93):
  - – jurisdiction (9.95);
  - – discretion (9.117);
  - – evidential issues (9.128);
  - – impropriety, unreasonableness and negligence (9.141);
  - – causation (9.164);
  - – case examples (9.169);
  - – quantum (9.194); and
  - – procedure (9.197).

Non-party Costs Orders (Third-party Costs Orders)

9.02 Non-party costs orders (also known as third-party costs orders) are orders against persons who are not parties to the litigation, but are in some way connected to it. An archetypal example is where an order is made against a non-party director who has used a company (a party) for their own purposes. Broadly speaking, to obtain a non-party costs order, the court must be satisfied that such an 'exceptional' order is justified—although the test of exceptionality is a low hurdle to clear—and that the conduct of the non-party has caused the costs in question to be incurred. Different considerations apply to some types of non-party costs order, however, as will be explained below.

Jurisdiction

Statutory powers and the basic principles involved

9.03 The power to make a non-party costs order most commonly arises out of s 51 of the Senior Courts Act 1981 (as amended) (SCA 1981). The relevant part of s 51 reads as follows: '(3) The court shall have full power to determine by whom and to what extent the costs are to be paid.' The House of Lords has clarified that this subsection provides a sufficiently wide discretion to permit the court to make costs orders against a person who, at the material time, was not a party to the litigation.[1] The Act was amended in 1990,[2] but those amendments did not diminish the ambit of the court's powers,[3] and there is no reason to believe that subsequent amendments brought about any changes in this respect. Non-party costs orders made under the aforesaid provisions are discretionary and so the ultimate question is always whether, in all of the circumstances, it would be just to make the order.[4] The court must take into account all of the facts of the case, including the conduct of the proceedings.[5] As is explained below (see 9.11–9.14 and 9.15–9.19), there is both an 'exceptionality' requirement and a causation requirement, but both of these tend to be applied in a flexible way.

The jurisdiction is statutory and is independent of the common law. In particular, it is not a jurisdiction that has arisen out of the presence of champertous maintenance; if the relationship between a party and a non-party is champertous, then that will be merely a factor to be taken into account.[6] Indeed, it is worth emphasising that the jurisdiction is a simple matter of the exercise of a discretionary power to order a party to pay costs. Laws LJ had this to say on that point: **9.04**

> '[It would not be desirable if] the exercise of this jurisdiction becomes over-complicated by reference to authority. Indeed I think it has become overburdened. Section 51 confers a discretion not confined by specific limitations. While the learning is, with respect, important in indicating the kind of considerations upon which the court will focus, it must not be treated as a rule-book.'[7]

Lewison LJ approved of those comments, but felt obliged to refer to the sizeable body of learning on the topic.[8] In the same case, however, Lloyd LJ went on to say this: **9.05**

> 'This jurisdiction risks becoming over-elaborate in its exercise, with too much reference to authority, over-literal reliance on descriptive reasoning in previous cases as if it laid down a formal classification of possible cases under the section, too many incidental applications, and too many appeals.'[9]

In a similar vein, Moore-Bick LJ had this to say: **9.06**

> 'We think it important to emphasise that the only immutable principle is that the discretion must be exercised justly. It should also be recognised that, since the decision involves an exercise of discretion, limited assistance is likely to be gained from the citation of other decisions at first instance in which judges have or have not granted an order of this kind.'[10]

---

1 *Aiden Shipping Ltd v Interbulk Ltd* [1986] 1 AC 965. Early examples exist of the court exercising the jurisdiction: see *Bacal Contracting Ltd v Modern Engineering (Bristol) Ltd* [1980] 2 All ER 655.
2 Courts and Legal Services Act 1990, s 4.
3 *Nordstern Allgemeine Versicherungs AG v Internav Ltd* [1999] 2 Lloyd's Rep 139.
4 See, eg, *Dymocks Franchise Systems (NSW) Pty Ltd v Todd* [2004] UKPC 39, at [25]; *Mills v Birchall & Anor* [2008] EWCA Civ 385, at [30] and [74].
5 *DNA Productions (Europe) Ltd v Manoukian* [2008] EWHC 2627, at [6(ii)].
6 *Nordstern Allgemeine Versicherungs AG v Internav Ltd* [1999] 2 Lloyd's Rep 139.
7 *Petromec Inc v Petroleo Brasileiro* [2006] EWCA Civ 1038, at [19].
8 See *Systemcare (UK) Ltd v Services Design Technology Ltd* [2011] EWCA Civ 546, at [21], *per* Lewison LJ.
9 See *ibid*, at [64].
10 *Deutsche Bank AG v Sebastian Holdings Inc* [2016] EWCA Civ 23, at [62].

9.07 There is no comprehensive checklist of necessary (or sufficient) factors that would justify an award being made; the underlying question that the court is weighing is the injustice caused to the winning party by not having any great chance of recovering its costs from its impecunious opponent against the harm or injustice to the non-party by making that person liable to pay those costs.[11] There is, as will be seen, a great deal of authority on that topic, but it is important to not lose sight of this simple question.

Qualified one-way costs shifting

9.08 It may be that the application for a non-party costs order is made in the context of a personal injury claim to which Civil Procedure Rules (CPR), Part 44, Section II, applies. This topic is addressed at 8.46–8.51.

Orders made against parties that are analogous to non-party costs orders

9.09 It may be that a party to the proceedings acted in such a way that it would have been appropriate to make a non-party costs order against that party had it not been such. Where this is so, there is no reason why an order may not be made pursuant to CPR, r 44.2, that is analogous to a non-party costs order. Thus, in a case in which one defendant had successfully resisted a claim made against it, but had funded and controlled another defendant who had been found liable, but who was close to being insolvent, it was open to the court to make an order against the first defendant that was analogous to a non-party costs order.[12]

Non-statutory powers

9.10 Powers other than those under SCA 1981, s 51, exist, such as the power to make awards against solicitors arising out of the inherent jurisdiction of the court.[13] Such powers are addressed below (see 9.60–9.71), but are far less frequently encountered than the powers referred to above.

Exceptionality and causation

Exceptionality

9.11 In the early days of the development of the jurisdiction to make non-party costs orders, Balcombe LJ said that such an order would always be 'exceptional' and that any application for such an order should be treated with 'considerable caution'.[14] The jurisdiction has now matured: the need for the case to be exceptional is now known to be little more than expression of the fact that the circumstances of the case must be beyond ordinary. Phillips LJ had this to say on the point: 'The test is whether they [ie the factors that are said to make the case exceptional] are extraordinary in the context of the entire range of litigation that comes to the courts.'[15] This affirmed the existence of the test, but made it clear that the test was whether the matter was extraordinary in the context of everything that the court

[11] *Excalibur Ventures LLC v Texas Keystone Inc* [2014] EWHC 3436 (Comm), at [64], *per* Christopher Clarke LJ, who referred to *Systemcare (UK) Ltd v Services Design Technology Ltd* [2011] EWCA Civ 546, at [26] and [64].

[12] See *Grizzly Business Ltd v Stena Drilling Ltd* [2017] EWCA Civ 94, at [58]–[68]. See also *Davies v Forrett* [2015] EWHC 1761 (QB).

[13] For a description of this, see *Ridehalgh v Horsefield* [1994] Ch 205, at 228; as an example of that jurisdiction in action, see *Edwards v Edwards* [1958] 2 All ER 179.

[14] *Symphony Group plc v Hodgson* [1994] QB 179.

[15] *TGA Chapman Ltd v Christopher and Sun Alliance* [1998] 2 All ER 873, at [20].

sees rather than extraordinary in the context of the particular class of claim that is before the court.

The present understanding of the law seems to be that there continues to be an exceptionality test,[16] but that it does not confine the court in any undesirable way. This is because it is merely a test of whether the case is out of the ordinary run of things.[17] Lord Brown, giving the judgment of their Lordships in a Privy Council matter, had this to say: **9.12**

> 'Although costs orders against non-parties are to be regarded as "exceptional", exceptional in this context means no more than outside the ordinary run of cases where parties pursue or defend claims for their own benefit and at their own expense. The ultimate question in any such "exceptional" case is whether in all the circumstances it is just to make the order. It must be recognised that this is inevitably to some extent a fact-specific jurisdiction and that there will often be a number of different considerations in play, some militating in favour of an order, some against.'[18]

Lord Brown's comments were not binding, but they were soon taken up by the Court of Appeal[19] and are therefore binding on most courts.

In practice, the test of exceptionality will often be satisfied merely by the situation that exists. In those circumstances, the court's attention will be focused on the other factors, such as whether it would be just to make the order sought. Indeed, there are circumstances—such as where a director has funded and controlled a claim for their own benefit—where the making of a non-party order would be the 'ordinary' consequence of the state of affairs in hand since the director is the 'real party'.[20] **9.13**

It remains the case that it will be genuinely exceptional for an order for the payment of costs to be made against a non-party where the applicant had a cause of action against the non-party and could have joined that person as a party to the original proceedings. This is because joinder as a party to the proceedings gives the person concerned all of the protection conferred by the rules.[21] **9.14**

Causation

The involvement of the non-party must have caused costs to be incurred. Lewison LJ had this to say on the point: '[A] non-party costs order should not be made where the relevant costs would have been incurred anyway without the involvement of the non-party.'[22] Similarly, Lawrence Collins LJ has called proof of causation 'a necessary pre-condition of **9.15**

---

[16] See below; cf *Globe Equities Ltd v Globe Legal Services Ltd* [1999] BLR 232, in which it was said that the test of exceptionality should not be elevated into a precondition to the exercise of the power to make a costs order against a non-party.

[17] *Mills v Birchall (*sub nom *Dolphin Quays Developments v Mills)* [2008] EWCA Civ 385, at [74], *per* Collins LJ.

[18] *Dymocks Franchise Systems (NSW) Pty Ltd v Todd* [2004] UKPC 39, at [25(i)].

[19] *Goodwood Recoveries Ltd v Breen* [2005] EWCA Civ 414. More recently, see *Deutsche Bank AG v Sebastian Holdings Inc* [2016] EWCA Civ 23, at [19] and [62], *per* Moore-Bick LJ.

[20] See, eg, *Dymocks Franchise Systems (NSW) Pty Ltd v Todd* [2004] UKPC 39, at [25], *per* Lord Brown.

[21] *Oriakhel v Vickers* [2008] EWCA Civ 748, at [31], *per* Jacob LJ, citing with approval *Symphony Group plc v Hodgson* [1994] QB 179.

[22] *Systemcare (UK) Ltd v Services Design Technology Ltd* [2011] EWCA Civ 546, at [23]. Lewison LJ referred to *Dymocks Franchise Systems (NSW) Pty Ltd v Todd* [2004] UKPC 19, at [18]–[20], *Goodwood Recoveries Ltd v Breen* [2005] EWCA Civ 414, at [74], and *Nelson v Greening & Sykes (Builders) Ltd* [2007] EWCA Civ 1358, at [61].

an order against a non-party'.[23] This is certainly true of the law as it is classically described, but over recent years the need for the court to find a direct causative link between conduct and costs has progressively diminished.[24] Whilst, in many cases, a test of 'but for' causation may be satisfied, in some circumstances an 'effective cause' may be sufficient.[25]

9.16 When the jurisdiction was first discovered, conventional teaching was that there must be a direct causal link. Simon Brown LJ spoke of it being a 'necessary precondition': 'Proof of causation is a necessary pre-condition of the making of a section 51 order against a non-party, as to which there is ample authority and, as I understand it, no dispute.'[26]

9.17 Even in those early days, the court rejected the notion that 'exceptional circumstances' must have caused costs to be incurred. In this regard, Morritt LJ had the following to say:

> '[Counsel for the non-party] submitted that the proper question was "but for the exceptional circumstances would the costs sought have been incurred". I do not accept that submission. I accept that the costs claimed must have been caused to some extent by the non-party against whom the order is sought for otherwise it is hard to envisage any circumstance in which it could be just to order the non-party to pay them. But I do not see why they must be caused by all the factors which render the case exceptional. For example, one of the factors likely to be present in most, if not all, cases where an order is made is that the litigation was for the benefit of the non-party; but that is no reason to require that the costs were all incurred in obtaining that benefit.'[27]

9.18 Richards J explained that circumstances might exist in which a causative link between conduct and costs would not be an essential ingredient at all. His view was based on an analysis of the authorities. In particular, he noted the following extract from *Dymocks Franchise System (NSW) Pty Ltd v Todd*:[28]

> 'Although the position may well be different when a number of non-parties act in concert, their Lordships are content to assume for the purposes of this application that a non-party could not *ordinarily* be made liable for costs if those costs would in any event have been incurred even without such non-party's involvement in the proceedings.'[29]

Richards J went on to draw the following conclusion:

> 'It cannot in my judgment any longer be said that causation is a necessary pre-condition to an order for costs against a non-party. Causation will often be a vital factor but there may be cases where, in accordance with principle, it is just to make an order for costs against a non-party who cannot be said to have caused the costs in question.'[30]

9.19 Thus it is not necessary to have a direct causal link, although it would be a mistake to believe that causation is no longer relevant: indeed, in many cases it will go to the very heart

---

23 *Nelson v Greening & Sykes (Builders) Ltd* [2007] EWCA Civ 1358, at [61].

24 For a discussion on this point, see Gearon, P, 'Third Parties Beware' (2006) 156 NLJ 7238, at 1312–13.

25 For a discussion of this point, see *Excalibur Ventures LLC Claimant v Texas Keystone Inc* [2014] EWHC 3436 (Comm), at [139]–[148], *per* Christopher Clarke LJ (sitting as a judge of the High Court); not doubted (or even challenged) on appeal at [2016] EWCA Civ 1144, [2016] 1 WLR 2221.

26 *Hamilton v Al Fayed & Ors* [2002] EWCA Civ 665, at [54].

27 *Globe Equities Ltd v Globe Legal Services Ltd* [1999] BLR 232, at [28]; see also *Goodwood Recoveries Ltd v Breen* [2005] EWCA Civ 414, at [65].

28 [2004] 1 WLR 2807, at [20].

29 As quoted in *Total Spares & Supplies Ltd v Antares SRL* [2006] EWHC 1537 (Ch), at [52], emphasis added by Richards J.

30 *Total Spares & Supplies Ltd v Antares SRL* [2006] EWHC 1537 (Ch), at [54].

of the exercise of the court's discretion. It should be remembered that the factual situation that led Richards J to come to the conclusion that a causative link was not required was, on any analysis, unusual.[31]

Categories of order

There is a categorisation of non-party costs orders known as the *Symphony Group* categories.[32] The categories contained therein are very far from being either exhaustive or mutually exclusive; indeed, the law has moved on so much since those categories were first formulated that one could argue that they no longer define the law. That may be so, but they remain a useful framework for describing the law and, as such, are used in this book. They are as follows. **9.20**

- **Category one: controllers** Where the non-party has had a hand in controlling the proceedings; this category will include directors and shadow directors, liquidators and receivers, 'active' shareholders and office holders (see 9.21–9.31).
- **Category two: funders** Where the non-party has maintained or financed the proceedings; this category will include pure funders, commercial funders, insurers and unions (see 9.32–9.59).
- **Category three: legal representatives** Where the non-party is a legal representative of a party (see 9.60–9.71).
- **Category four: causative persons** Where the non-party has caused the proceedings (see 9.72–9.75).
- **Category five: related persons** Where the non-party is a party to related proceedings that were heard at the same time as the index proceedings, but which were not consolidated with them (see 9.75).
- **Category six: group litigation** Where the non-party has an interest in the proceedings by reason of the claim being a test claim in group litigation or representative proceedings (see 9.76).

Some commentators would add a seventh category—namely, tribunals (see 9.77).

Category one (controllers)

Where a non-party directs and manages a claim or a defence, that person would place themselves at risk of being ordered to pay costs. Very often, a controller would also fall within one of the other categories; in particular, many funders are also controllers. **9.21**

The types of non-party who classically fall into this category include directors, receivers, liquidators, etc, but they may include 'active' shareholders, family members,[33] local authorities[34] or even insurers.[35] This diversity illustrates the fact that it is not the status of **9.22**

[31] The conduct of the non-party was unrelated to control or funding of the proceedings; instead, he had moved assets away from one of the parties in such a way as to make it 'judgment proof'. That conduct could not in any sense be said to be causative of the costs of the litigation, but was clearly germane in a wider sense.

[32] See *Symphony Group plc v Hodgson* [1994] QB 179, at 197.

[33] See, eg, *Thomson v Berkhampsted Collegiate School* [2009] EWHC 2374 (QB), *per* Blake J; the family interference in the claim also stretched to funding. See also *Virdi v RK Joinery Ltd* [2016] EWCA Civ 539.

[34] See, eg, *R (on the application of Tallington Lakes Ltd) v Grantham Magistrates' Court* (unreported), 24 February 2011, QBD, *per* Stephen Morris QC (sitting as a deputy judge of the High Court), in which a local authority sought to use the magistrates' court for the purposes of enforcing a claim from rates.

[35] See, eg, *XYZ v Travelers Insurance Co Ltd* [2017] EWHC 287 (QB), *per* Thirwall LJ; *Legg v Sterte Garage Ltd* [2016] EWCA Civ 97.

the person that is determinative of the matter, but what that person does in the claim and what role they choose to play; thus the mere fact that an insolvent party is held by a holding company will not, without more, justify an order being made against the holding company.[36] Instead, the non-party must be the 'real party' (otherwise known as the real party interested,[37] or the real litigant).[38] Evans-Lombe J had this to say on the topic (this being in the context of a director):

> 'The fundamental contrast is between a director who *bona fide* pursues unsuccessful litigation in the name of the company for the benefit of the company, but where the company cannot pay the order for costs against it, for the benefit of its creditors, and where the director in question is the real litigant in the sense that the court can be satisfied that without his initiative and finance the litigation would not have been pursued by the company, and who stood, albeit with others including creditors, to benefit materially from its success.'[39]

9.23 In a similar vein, Lord Brown said a real party was a person who was: 'not so much facilitating access to justice by the party funded as himself gaining access to justice for his own purposes', going on to explain that the real party need not be the only party with an interest in the matter.[40] It is often the case that the court's first task is to decide whether the non-party in question was, in truth, the real party (or, more accurately, a real party).[41] It is instructive to examine this issue by focusing on company directors, but the principles are the same for other types of non-party.

9.24 The ability to identify a real-party director and to make a costs order against that person is a method by which the corporate veil may be lifted. The existence of that ability does not snatch the veil away entirely, however, because directors who do nothing more than the performance of their ordinary functions will not be at risk. If, for example, a director causes costs to be incurred knowing that the company would not be able to meet its costs liabilities in the event that the claim is unsuccessful, then that director would not be at risk if they had acted for the company's benefit rather than in their own interests; if, on the other hand, a director—perhaps *qua* shareholder—stands to personally gain or if they have been advised that the company does not have a case, then they would be at risk.

9.25 Lord Brown has said that where a person has funded and controlled litigation and has sought to benefit from it, justice will 'ordinarily require' that they should pay the successful party's costs if that person ultimately fails.[42] He went on to say this:

> '[Their] Lordships would hold that, generally speaking, where a non-party promotes and funds proceedings by an insolvent company solely or substantially for his own financial benefit, he should be liable for the costs if his claim or defence or appeal fails. As explained in the cases, however, that is not to say that orders will invariably be made in such cases, particularly, say, where the non-party is himself a director or liquidator who can realistically be

---

[36] *Centrehigh Ltd v Amen* [2013] EWHC 1448 (Ch), *per* Jonathon Gaunt QC.

[37] *Metalloy Supplies Ltd v MA (UK) Ltd* [1997] 1 WLR 1613, at 1620, *per* Millett LJ.

[38] *DNA Productions (Europe) Ltd v Manoukian* [2008] EWHC 2627 (Ch), at [6(i)], *per* Evans-Lombe J.

[39] *Ibid.* Indeed, there may be more than one 'real party' and where this is so, an order may be made against them that is joint and several: see, eg, *Ashley-Carter v Hofmann & Mountford Ltd* [2010] EWHC 2349 (QB), *per* HHJ Thornton QC (sitting as a judge of the High Court).

[40] *Dymocks Franchise Systems (NSW) Pty Ltd v Todd* [2004] UKPC 39, at [25(3)]. As an example of the court finding that there was more than one real party, see *Myatt v National Coal Board (No 2)* [2007] EWCA Civ 307.

[41] See *Flatman v Germany* [2013] EWCA Civ 278, at [28], *per* Leveson LJ.

[42] *Dymocks Franchise Systems (NSW) Pty Ltd v Todd* [2004] UKPC 39, at [25(3)].

regarded as acting in the interests of the company (and more especially its shareholders and creditors) than in his own interests.'[43]

This analysis was duly adopted by Rix LJ, although Rix LJ placed emphasis on the fact that each case will turn on its own facts: **9.26**

'Where a non-party director can be described as the "real party", seeking his own benefit, controlling and/or funding the litigation, then even where he has acted in good faith or without any impropriety, justice may well demand that he be liable in costs on a fact-sensitive and objective assessment of the circumstances.'[44]

Any fact may be relevant—indeed, the court must take into account all of the relevant circumstances[45]—but there are certain issues upon which the court tends to focus, as are addressed below. Whilst some of those issues (such as the non-party's conduct) are almost always taken into account, none of them should be regarded as having been elevated to conditions prerequisite to the making of a non-party costs order. **9.27**

Conduct Traditional teaching is that non-party costs orders against directors are 'necessarily rare' and are made only in cases in which the director has failed to act in good faith in the interest of the company.[46] The ambit of that category of case has gradually increased over the last 15 years or so. It was soon discovered that impropriety would suffice and the court also allowed itself to look at what the non-party had expected to gain.[47] As the concept of the 'real party' became more widely received, the court began to look not merely at *bona fide* belief, but also at whether the director, *qua* alter ego, was litigating for their own interests or the company's interests.[48] Over time, the law developed such that Lord Brown was able to say this: 'The authorities establish that, whilst any impropriety or the pursuit of speculative litigation may of itself support the making of an order against a non-party, its absence does not preclude the making of such an order.'[49] Thus the presence of impropriety or unreasonableness will count against the non-party,[50] but its absence will not preclude the making of an order.[51] The same is true **9.28**

---

43 *Ibid*, at [29].

44 *Goodwood Recoveries Ltd v Breen* [2005] EWCA Civ 414, at [59].

45 *DNA Productions (Europe) Ltd v Manoukian* [2008] EWHC 2627, at [6(ii)]; *Dymocks Franchise Systems (NSW) Pty Ltd v Todd* [2004] UKPC 39, at [25(1)].

46 The cases that are usually cited on this point are *Taylor v Pace Developments Ltd* [1991] BCC 406, at 409, *per* Lloyd J, and *Metalloy Supplies Ltd v MA (UK) Ltd* [1997] 1 WLR 1613, at 1620, *per* Millett LJ. For a more recent authority, see *Landare Investments Ltd v Welsh Development Agency* [2004] EWHC 946 (QB), at [61] and [62], *per* McKinnon J. See also *Floods of Queensferry Ltd v Shand Construction* [2002] EWCA Civ 918, in which the principles in *Taylor* were reaffirmed as representing the law. As an example of a case in which an order was made, see *Secretary of State for Trade and Industry v Backhouse* [2001] EWCA Civ 67, in which the director treated the company's money as his own. See also *Leverton Ltd v Crawford Offshore (Exploration) Services Ltd (in liquidation)*, The Times, 22 November 1996, QBD, in which the director forged documents, manufactured and suppressed evidence, and eventually ended up controlling and financing the proceedings.

47 *Metalloy Supplies Ltd v MA (UK) Ltd* [1997] 1 WLR 1613, at 1620, *per* Millett LJ.

48 *Re North West Holdings plc* [2001] EWCA Civ 67. As an example of a case in which the court found that the putative funder was not the 'real party', see *Lingfield Properties (Darlington) Ltd v Padgett Lavender Associates* [2008] EWHC 2795 (QB).

49 *Dymocks Franchise Systems (NSW) Pty Ltd v Todd* [2004] UKPC 39, at [33].

50 An example is *Bournemouth & Boscombe Athletic Football Club Ltd v Lloyds TSB Bank plc* [2004] EWCA Civ 935, in which a director of an impecunious football club persisted in bringing pointless claims against its bank.

51 See also *Mills v Birchall* (sub nom *Dolphin Quays Developments v Mills)* [2008] EWCA Civ 385, at [69]; *DNA Productions (Europe) Ltd v Manoukian* [2008] EWHC 2627, at [6(iii)].

of bad faith.[52] Whilst it is not necessary that any of the requirements of champerty are present, 'wanton and officious intermeddling' in a dispute would be a factor relevant.[53] Where poor conduct exists, it will have the same capacity to sound in a non-party costs order as it would in any other type of costs order. In particular, where the conduct is sufficiently culpable, there is no reason why the award cannot be made on the indemnity basis.[54] The fact that an award has been made on the indemnity basis against the funded party is not generally a relevant factor.[55]

9.29 **Availability of alternative securities or remedies** One factor that may be particularly relevant is whether the applicant (that is, the person seeking the order) could have taken steps to protect their position during the course of the proceedings. This usually means considering the availability of an order for security for costs.[56] That said, the court would not be precluded from making a non-party costs order solely because the applicant had failed to apply for security for costs.[57]

9.30 **The relevance of funding** The issue of funding per se is dealt with in the second *Symphony Group* category (see 9.32–9.59), but for many years it was believed that it was a prerequisite for a third-party costs order against a director that they should have funded the litigation.[58] This is no longer the case. Whilst *obiter*, Longmore LJ had this to say on the topic:

> 'Although funding took place in most of the reported cases, it is not, in my view, essential, in the sense of being a jurisdictional pre-requisite to the exercise of the court's discretion. If the evidence is that a respondent (whether director or shareholder or controller of a relevant company) has effectively controlled the proceedings and has sought to derive potential benefit from them, that will be enough to establish the jurisdiction. Whether such jurisdiction should be exercised is, of course, another matter entirely and the extent to which a respondent has, in fact, funded any proceedings may be very relevant to the exercise of discretion.'[59]

Obviously, if there has been funding, this will be a factor that may be taken into account.[60] Leaving funds in a company where they could have been taken out may amount to funding.[61] Where a director has funded proceedings, but only from a certain point

[52] See, eg, *Kirby v Hoff* [2010] EWHC 3559 (QB), in which Davis J found that an order against a controlling non-party could be upheld notwithstanding the fact that the court below had made an error in finding that she had acted in bad faith.

[53] *Nordstern Allgemeine Versicherungs AG v Internav Ltd* [1999] 2 Lloyd's Rep 139, at 152, relying on *Giles v Thompson* (1994) 1 AC 142.

[54] See, eg, *Vellacott v The Convergance Group plc* [2007] EWHC 17874 (Ch), in which Rimer J made an order against a director who had controlled a 'hopeless' Part 20 claim solely for his personal benefit.

[55] See *Landare Investments Ltd v Welsh Development Agency* [2004] EWHC 946 (QB), at [55], *per* McKinnon J.

[56] *DNA Productions (Europe) Ltd v Manoukian* [2008] EWHC 2627, at [6(iv)].

[57] *Mills v Birchall (*sub nom *Dolphin Quays Developments v Mills)* [2008] EWCA Civ 385, at [62], *per* Collins LJ.

[58] By way of illustration, see *Fulton Motors Ltd v Toyota (GB) Ltd (Costs)* [2000] CP Rep 24, in which Peter Gibson LJ made non-party orders against certain directors, but he limited their liability to that period after which they had started to fund the matter.

[59] *Petromec Inc v Petroleo Brasileiro* [2006] EWCA Civ 1038, at [10]. See also *Deutsche Bank AG v Sebastian Holdings Inc* [2016] EWCA Civ 23, at [47], *per* Moore-Bick LJ.

[60] *Deutsche Bank AG v Sebastian Holdings Inc* [2016] EWCA Civ 23, at [47], *per* Moore-Bick LJ.

[61] See, eg, *Petromec Inc v Petroleo Brasileiro* [2006] EWCA Civ 1038.

onwards, it is open to the court to restrict that director's liability to costs incurred from that point in time onwards.[62]

Active shareholders Most of the comments made above relate to directors. There are other classes of controllers that merit a mention, however, as follows. **9.31**

- **Active shareholders** Where the court is considering the extent to which the non-party has controlled the litigation, it will take into account the extent to which that person could be expected to control the litigation by reason of their status. A sole director, for example, would have no choice but to be in control; shareholders, on the other hand, would have a choice whether to do so, and this is the principal reason why 'active' shareholders often fare badly in so far as non-party costs orders are concerned. This was explained by Chadwick LJ thus:

  > '[A] shareholder is not under any duty to the company in relation to the conduct of litigation. He is not required to decide whether it is, or is not, in the interests and for the benefit of the company to bring or defend proceedings. He does not require the protection of the company's separate corporate personality to enable him to fulfil his role as shareholder in relation to the litigation. If he chooses to involve himself in the company's litigation—thereby usurping the role of the directors—he does so at his own risk.'[63]

  If confirmation of the correctness of these comments were needed, it may be found in the many examples that exist of the court making orders against 'active' shareholders.[64] For the avoidance of doubt, the fact that the company may be insolvent would not prevent an order being made.[65]
- **Receivers, secured creditors and administrators** As to receivers of insolvent companies and similar office holders, Lawrence Collins LJ has concluded that a non-party costs order could be made against a receiver or against the secured creditor, especially where the non-party was the real party. His analysis demonstrated that the court would give weight to the actions (or lack thereof) taken in respect of security for costs. He also made it clear that there must something about the case that lifts it out of the ordinary run of things.[66] Where an order is made against an administrator, the court has the power to issue an order preventing the administrator from recouping expenses from the company's assets.[67]
- **Insurers** In general, the issue of non-party costs orders against insurers as controllers will not arise because the insurer will be controlling litigation in respect of which it is obliged to provide an indemnity; as such, there is no need to invoke the jurisdiction to make non-party costs orders as an order because the insurer would generally be required to provide an indemnity that would ensure that any order made against its insured

[62] *Fulton Motors Ltd v Toyota (GB) Ltd (Costs)* [2000] CP Rep 24, *per* Peter Gibson LJ (but see the comments made in the footnotes above—it is possible that this case would now be decided differently).

[63] *CIBC Mellon Trust Co v Stolzenberg* [2005] EWCA Civ 628, at [24].

[64] See, eg, *I-Remit Inc* [2008] EWHC 939 (Ch), *per* David Richards J; *Suisse Security Bank & Trust Ltd v Julian Francis* [2006] UKPC 41.

[65] See, eg, *Macaria Investments Ltd v Sanders* (unreported), 29 November 2011, Ch D, *per* Newey J.

[66] *Mills v Birchall (*sub nom *Dolphin Quays Developments v Mills)* [2008] EWCA Civ 385, at [29] *et seq*, per Collins LJ.

[67] *Rubin v Cobalt Pictures Ltd & Ors* [2010] EWHC 3223 (Ch), at [100]–[104]; see also *Re Silver Valley Mines (Winding Up)* (1882) LR 21 Ch D 381, CA, and *Mond v Hammond Suddards (No 2)* [2000] Ch 40, CA (Civ Div).

would be met. This will not always be the case, however: in group litigation in which only some of the claims were covered by the insurance in question but the insurer took an active role in defending all of them, Thirwall LJ made a non-party costs order against the insurer in respect of the non-insured claims.[68] In any event, if an insurer controls litigation in its own interests (as opposed to merely that of its insured), this may lead to an order being made (see also 9.56–9.57).[69]

Category two (funders)

9.32 Funders are persons who fund litigation; this may include litigation funders (see Chapter 33), but is by no means confined to such entities. The provision of funds is potentially in the public interest because it enhances access to justice. This means that there is a need to balance the desirable (that is, encouraging access to justice) against the undesirable (that is, the possibility that the opponent incurs irrecoverable costs that, without the funding, they would not have incurred). Over the last 15 years or so, there has been a change in public perceptions of what is and is not to be encouraged,[70] and this has led to the recognition that there are two categories of funder:

- **pure funders**—that is, the person who provides assistance for non-commercial or altruistic reasons (see 9.34–9.36); and
- **commercial funders**—that is, the person who has a commercial interest in the funded litigation (see 9.37–9.44), which category would include litigation funders, but is not limited to such persons.

There are other types of funder that merit a brief mention because they do not easily fall within the two categories above—that is, liability insurers (see 9.56–9.57), and unions and membership organisations (see 9.58–9.59).

9.33 As is explained below, the law treats pure funders and commercial funders very differently. It is worth noting, however, that the distinction between pure funders and commercial funders is not a hard-and-fast distinction that separates those who are at risk of having orders made against them from those who are not. In this regard, Phillips MR commented:

> 'We are not sure that the adjective "pure" assists in the analysis. It is, we believe, designed to draw a distinction between those who assist a litigant without ulterior motive and those who do so because they have a personal interest in the outcome of the litigation. Public policy now recognises that it is desirable, in order to facilitate access to justice, that third parties should provide assistance designed to ensure that those who are involved in litigation have the benefit of legal representation. Intervention to this end will not normally render the intervener liable to pay costs. If the intervener has agreed, or anticipates, some reward for his intervention, this will not necessarily expose him to liability for costs. Whether it does will depend upon what is just, having regard to the facts of the individual case. If the intervention is in bad faith, or for some ulterior motive, then the intervener will be at risk in relation to costs occasioned as a consequence of his intervention.'[71]

---

68 See *XYZ v Travelers Insurance Co Ltd* [2017] EWHC 287 (QB), *per* Thirwall LJ.
69 See, eg, *Legg v Sterte Garage Ltd* [2016] EWCA Civ 97; *Palmer v Palmer* [2008] EWCA Civ 46.
70 See the discussion in *Gulf Azov Shipping Co Ltd v Idisi* [2004] EWCA Civ 292, at [35], *per* Phillips MR.
71 *Ibid*, at [54].

Pure funders It is generally true to say that pure funders are unlikely to be at risk of having non-party costs orders made against them. Simply providing funds without more involvement in the matter would not, in general, expose the funder to the risk of an order being made.[72] Lord Brown had this to say on the topic: 9.34

> 'Generally speaking the discretion will not be exercised against "pure funders" ... as those with no personal interest in the litigation, who do not stand to benefit from it, are not funding it as a matter of business, and in no way seek to control its course. In their case the court's normal approach is to give priority to the public interest in the funded party getting access to justice over that of the successful unfunded party recovering his costs and so not having to bear the expense of vindicating his rights.'[73]

Notwithstanding this, each case will turn on its own facts and the fact that a non-party does not have a direct financial interest in the litigation will not prevent an order being made in appropriate cases. The archetypal example is a non-party funder whose interests have more to do with a personal acrimony than with money.[74] Unnecessary meddling in the litigation is another situation in which an order can be made, as is the 'pure' funder who is exposed as having an indirect commercial interest.[75] 9.35

That said, the fact that a non-party has a financial interest in the litigation will not necessarily prevent that party from being classified as being a pure funder, not least because the funder may be acting out of other motives. Judge Coulson QC found that a wife of a bankrupt had provided funding for his counsel out of natural love and affection rather than out of some interest of her own—this despite the fact that there was an indirect financial link between the bankrupt and his non-party wife.[76] Similarly, where a charity provided funding to a claimant in respect of which it had an indirect financial interest, Judge Harris QC found that it was not appropriate to make an order because the charity's motivation had merely been to assist the claimant.[77] It should be noted, however, that these cases were decided on the basis of the conduct and motivation of the non-parties, not their status. In particular, the court will not always regard funding within a marriage as being pure funding; where there is a commercial interest, that can result in the non-party spouse being regarded as a commercial funder.[78] Likewise, the fact that the funder is a close family member will by no means provide protection against an order being made, especially if the funder meddled in the matter.[79] 9.36

Commercial funders In very general terms, commercial funders fall into two groups: litigation funders of the sort discussed in Chapter 33 (otherwise known as professional funders or third-party funders) and other commercial funders. As is explained below (see 9.38–9.44), litigation funders tend to benefit from a cap on the amounts that they may be ordered to pay, known as the *Arkin* cap.[80] There is no reason in principle why the *Arkin* cap 9.37

---

[72] *Ibid.*

[73] *Dymocks Franchise Systems (NSW) Pty Ltd v Todd* [2004] UKPC 39, at [25].

[74] See, eg, *Latimer Management Consultants Ltd v Ellingham Investments Ltd* [2006] EWHC 3662 (Ch); cf *Hamilton v Al-Fayed (No 2)* [2002] EWCA Civ 665.

[75] See, eg, *Princo v Phillips* [2003] EWHC 2589 (Ch), *per* Pumfrey J.

[76] *Jackson v Thakrar* [2007] EWHC 626 (TCC).

[77] See *Gerrards Cross Leisure Services Ltd v Shizentai Health & Exercise Ltd* (unreported), 23 January 2017, Oxford County Court, *per* Judge Harris QC.

[78] *PR Records v Vinyl 2000* [2008] EWHC 192 (Ch).

[79] See, eg, *Thomson v Berkhampsted Collegiate School* [2009] EWHC 2374 (QB), *per* Blake J.

[80] After *Arkin v Borchard* [2005] EWCA Civ 655.

should not apply to other commercial funders, but in practice this tends not to happen. In particular, if the funder was not in the business of providing litigation funding,[81] if the extent of the funding was difficult to quantify or if the funder became the 'real person interested', then the cap would not apply. Moreover, whilst *obiter*, Christopher Clarke LJ has said that if a litigation funder behaved dishonestly or improperly, or if the funding agreement fell foul of the policy considerations that render an agreement champertous (for example if the funder has taken control over the litigation), it may be that there should be no cap at all.[82]

9.38 *Litigation funders and the* Arkin *cap* Statute has intervened,[83] but the provisions are not yet in force, so issues concerning litigation funding arrangements fall to be decided under the common law. At common law, both in England and Wales and abroad,[84] litigation funders can be found to be liable for the costs of the litigation that they have funded. There are two competing policies at play:

- **access to justice**—that is, the need not to discourage funders by exposing them to an unlimited liability for costs; and
- **'costs shifting'**—that is, the need to compensate opponents for costs that have been incurred as a result of the funding.

9.39 Whilst there are older authorities that touch upon the issue,[85] the seminal case of *Arkin v Borchard*[86] sought to strike a balance between these two policies. Phillips MR had the following to say (although note that he used the term 'professional funder' rather than 'litigation funder'):

> '[The] existence of this rule [that costs should normally follow the event), and the reasons given to justify its existence, render it unjust that a funder who purchases a stake in an action for a commercial motive should be protected from all liability for the costs of the opposing

[81] See, eg, *Merchantbridge & Co Ltd v Safron General Partner 1 Ltd* [2011] EWHC 1524 (Comm), at [46], in which Judge Mackie (sitting as a judge of the High Court) had this to say: '[It has been] submitted that it would be unfair, if an order were made, for his clients to have to pay to the Claimants an amount greater then [*sic*] they had paid towards the cost of the defence. That submission derives from the decision of the Court of Appeal in *Arkin* and [counsel] says that it would be unfair for his clients to be put in a worse position than a professional litigation funder. I do not agree ... That approach [in *Arkin*] makes it possible for people without money to obtain professional funding for part of their costs of conducting a case. The situation is very different from that in this case and is driven by more obvious policy considerations that do not apply here, except to the limited extent to which access to justice has been relied on.'

[82] *Excalibur Ventures LLC v Texas Keystone Inc* [2014] EWHC 3436 (Comm), at [72], *per* Christopher Clarke LJ (sitting as a judge of the High Court); upheld on appeal at [2016] EWCA 1144, in which hearing Tomlinson LJ made no comment on the *Arkin* cap.

[83] Whilst it is not yet in force, s 58B of the Courts and Legal Services Act 1990 (as amended) provides a formal structure for commercial funding arrangements.

[84] See, eg, New Zealand, *Arklow Investments Ltd v MacLean* (unreported), 19 May 2000, High Court of New Zealand, *per* Fisher J: '[T]he overall rationale [is] that it is wrong to allow someone to fund litigation in the hope of gaining a benefit without a corresponding risk that that person will share in the costs of the proceedings if they ultimately fail ...' See, however, *Jeffery & Katauskas Pty Ltd v SST Consulting Pty Ltd; Jeffery & Katauskas Pty Ltd v Rickard Constructions Pty Ltd* [2009] HCA 43, in which the Australian High Court found that it was not appropriate to make an order against a funder.

[85] See, eg, *R v SSHD, ex p Osman* [1993] COD 204.

[86] [2005] EWCA Civ 655. Not all common-law jurisdictions approach this matter in the same way: see, eg, *Jeffery & Katauskas Pty Ltd v SST Consulting Pty Ltd; Jeffery & Katauskas Pty Ltd v Rickard Constructions Pty Ltd* [2009] HCA 43 (Australia), in which it was held that there must be an element of abuse of process before an order could be made. See also *Saunders v Houghton* [2009] NZCA 610.

party if the funded party fails in the action. Somehow or other a just solution must be devised whereby on the one hand a successful opponent is not denied all his costs while on the other hand commercial funders who provide help to those seeking access to justice which they could not otherwise afford are not deterred by the fear of disproportionate costs consequences if the litigation they are supporting does not succeed.

> If a professional funder contemplating funding a discrete part of an action were potentially liable for the entirety of the opponent's costs should the claim fail, no professional funder would be likely to take that risk. However there was a practicable solution which would reconcile the desirability of access to justice with the rule that costs generally follow the event.
>
> A professional funder who finances part of a litigant's costs of litigation should be potentially liable for the costs of the opposing party to the extent of the funding provided.'[87]

Thus a litigation funder will be at risk of a non-party costs order, but its potential liability would ordinarily be limited to the extent of its funding; the upper limit of liability (that is, the *Arkin* cap) is calculated by reference to the monies invested for funding the costs of the litigation plus any monies invested for the purpose of security for costs.[88] **9.40**

Phillips MR commented that the *Arkin* cap would have the following effects.[89] **9.41**

- Funders are likely to cap the funds that they provide to limit their exposure to a reasonable amount.
- This should have a salutary effect in keeping costs proportionate.
- Funders will also have to consider with even greater care whether the prospects of the litigation are sufficiently good to justify the support that they are asked to give.

There are those who believe that *Arkin* was overly indulgent of litigation funders. Jackson LJ (speaking extrajudicially) had these points to make on the topic: **9.42**

> 'It is perfectly possible for litigation funders to have business models which encompass full liability for adverse costs. This will remain the case, even if [after-the-event] ATE insurance premiums (in those cases where ATE insurance is taken out) cease to be recoverable under costs orders ... In my view, it is wrong in principle that a litigation funder, which stands to recover a share of damages in the event of success, should be able to escape part of the liability for costs in the event of defeat.'[90]

That may be so, but the *Arkin* cap is now well established and forms a settled part of the business models that are used by litigation funders. Although Tomlinson LJ has said this was a 'debate for another day',[91] it may well be the case that this is an issue that could now be addressed only by legislation. In any event, it is worth mentioning that some common-law jurisdictions have found that litigation funders should not suffer any exposure to adverse costs,[92] so there is scope for funders to resist any shift away from *Arkin*.

---

[87] *Arkin v Borchard* [2005] EWCA Civ 655, at [38]–[40].

[88] *Excalibur Ventures LLC Claimant v Texas Keystone Inc* [2014] EWHC 3436 (Comm), at [133]–[138], *per* Christopher Clarke LJ (sitting as a judge of the High Court). This case went on appeal and was upheld, but on a different point: [2016] EWCA Civ 1144.

[89] *Arkin v Borchard* [2005] EWCA Civ 655, at [42].

[90] Jackson, R, *Review of Civil Litigation Costs: Final Report* (London: HMSO, 2010), ch 11, para 4.5.

[91] *Excalibur Ventures LLC v Texas Keystone Inc* [2016] EWCA Civ 1144, at [28].

[92] In *Jeffery & Katauskas Pty Ltd v SST Consulting Pty Ltd* [2009] HCA 43, the High Court of Australia found that the funder should not be liable to pay adverse costs.

9.43 If, as is commonly the case, several litigation funders have contributed to the funding, then it would be reasonable to hold them liable for costs incurred from the date on which they provided funding.[93] Where funding has been provided by a holding or parent company, it is open to the court to make an award against that company notwithstanding the fact that the funding agreement was with a subsidiary company.[94] On the facts of the case before him, Christopher Clarke LJ commented that 'parent and subsidiary should … stand together'.[95] The fact that the funded party would have no rights against the holding or parent company was largely irrelevant, this being because the making of a non-party costs order is a matter of discretion rather than rights.[96]

9.44 Any funding by way of a contribution to security for costs counts towards the level of the cap.[97] If, for example, a funder were to contribute £100 to costs and £100 to security for costs, the *Arkin* cap would be £200. If the receiving party obtains an indemnity basis costs order in its favour against its opponent, its opponent's funder will, in general, be bound by an order on the same basis—which topic is addressed at 16.28.

9.45 **Persons who are to be distinguished from commercial funders** There are many people who, as a result of their professional or trade activities, may provide funding. Some may have a financial interest in the litigation in the sense that they may not get paid if the litigation goes against the party they have assisted. As is explained below, the mere fact that they provided funding or financial assistance would not necessarily mean that they should be characterised as being commercial funders. The following categories of person merit mention:

- lenders (see 9.46);
- legal representatives (see 9.47–9.52);
- peripherally interested persons (see 9.53); and
- legal expenses insurers (see 9.54–9.55).

9.46 *Lenders* Whilst an obvious point, a lender who has no involvement or interest in the proceedings cannot be categorised as being a commercial funder.[98]

9.47 *Legal representatives* The general topic of non-party costs orders against legal representatives is dealt with at 9.60–9.71, which addresses the issue of whether a legal representative can be said to be a commercial funder. If an order is to be made against a legal representative

---

93 *Excalibur Ventures LLC v Texas Keystone Inc* [2014] EWHC 3436 (Comm), at [139]–[151], *per* Christopher Clarke LJ (sitting as a judge of the High Court); upheld on appeal at [2016] EWCA 1144.

94 See *Excalibur Ventures LLC v Texas Keystone Inc* [2014] EWHC 3436 (Comm), at [153]–[170]; upheld on appeal at [2016] EWCA 1144. See also *Petromec Inc v Petroleo Braisleiro Petrobas* [2006] EWCA Civ 1038, *per* Moore-Bick J; *I-Remit Inc v Far East Express Remittance Ltd* [2008] EWHC 939 (Ch), at [14], *per* David Richards J; *Gatnom v Sanders* [2011] EWHC 3716 (Ch), at [13], *per* Newey J.

95 *Excalibur Ventures LLC v Texas Keystone Inc* [2014] EWHC 3436 (Comm), at [157]; upheld on appeal at [2016] EWCA 1144.

96 See *ibid*, at [153]–[170], in which Christopher Clarke LJ (sitting as a judge of the High Court) approved of the following judgment of Lewison LJ in *Axel Threlfall v ECD Insight* [2013] EWCA Civ 144, at [13]: '[T]he separate personality of a corporation, even a single-member corporation, is deeply embedded in our law. But its purpose is to deal with legal rights and obligations. By contrast, the exercise of discretion to make a non-party costs order leaves rights and obligations where they are. The very fact that the making of such an order is discretionary demonstrates that the question is not one of rights and obligations of a non-party, for no obligations exist unless and until the court exercises its discretion.'

97 *Excalibur Ventures LLC v Texas Keystone Inc* [2016] EWCA Civ 1144, at [39]–[51].

98 *Petroleo Brasileiro SA v Petromec Inc* [2005] EWHC 2430 (Comm), at [32].

acting in that capacity, then s 51(1) and (3) of the Senior Courts Act 1981 has no application (see 9.60). This section deals with solicitors who are said to have stepped outside the role of being legal representative and to have become funders as a result. In this context, funding may mean the provision of legal services on financially favourable terms.

A legal representative will not become a commercial funder solely by reason of extending credit to their client[99] or providing their legal services *pro bono*. On this point, Rose LJ had this to say: **9.48**

> 'There is in my judgment no jurisdiction to make an order for costs against a solicitor solely on the ground that he acted without fee. It is in the public interest and it has always been recognised that it is proper for counsel and solicitors to act without fee. The access to justice which this can provide, for example in cases outside the scope of legal aid, confers a benefit on the public.'[100]

Similarly, a legal representative who acts for a client who may not be able to pay the other side's costs if they lose will not become a funder merely because the client does not have legal expenses insurance. In this regard, Leveson LJ had this to say: **9.49**

> 'As for the policy imperative argued by [counsel], after the event insurance is not a pre-requisite of bringing a claim on a CFA. That much is also clear from the fact that solicitors are entitled to act on a normal fee or conditional fee for an impecunious client whom they know or suspect will not be able to pay own (or other side's costs) if unsuccessful.'[101]

Unless (arguably) it is demonstrably provable that the costs would not otherwise have been incurred,[102] the fact that the legal representative has negligently failed to obtain after-the-event (ATE) insurance (as opposed to not being able to obtain such insurance) is of no causative relevance.[103] Leveson LJ went on to say that the act of extending credit for the purposes of paying disbursements would not of itself result in a potential liability for costs: **9.50**

> '[T]he legislation [relating to conditional fee agreements] does visualise the possibility that a solicitor might fund disbursements and, in that event, it would not be right to conclude that such a solicitor was "the real party" or even "a real party" to the litigation ... [P]ayment of disbursements, without more, does not incur any potential liability to an adverse costs order.'[104]

Notwithstanding the above, the provision of legal services is capable of amounting to funding (although such cases tend to turn on other issues, such as whether the legal representative was the 'real party' and whether they were controlling the litigation). In a case **9.51**

---

[99] See *Floods of Queensferry Ltd v Shand Construction Ltd & Ors* [2002] EWCA Civ 918, at [81], *per* Hale LJ; see also *Flatman v Germany* [2013] EWCA Civ 278, at [30], *per* Leveson LJ.

[100] *Tolstoy-Miloslavsky v Lord Aldington* [1996] 2 All ER 556, at 565. See also *Golding v First Tier Tribunal* [2012] EWHC 222 (Admin), in which a tax adviser who was acting *pro bono* was found not to fall within the category of a funder.

[101] *Flatman v Germany* [2013] EWCA Civ 278, at [45] and [46]; see also *Tinseltime Ltd v Roberts* [2012] EWHC 2628 (TCC), *per* Judge Stephen Davies. Leveson LJ referred to *King v Telegraph Group* [2005] 1 WLR 2282, at [100], *Floods of Queensferry Ltd v Shand Construction Ltd & Ors* [2002] EWCA Civ 918, at [37], *Sibthorpe v Southwark BL* [2011] 1 WLR 2111, at [50], *Awwad v Geraghty* [2001] QB 570, at 588, and *Dolphin Quays Developments Ltd v Mills* [2008] 1 WLR 1829, at [75].

[102] As happened in *Adris v Royal Bank of Scotland plc & Ors* [2010] EWHC 941 (QB), *per* HHJ Waksman QC (sitting as judge of the High Court). This case ought to be viewed with some caution following *Flatman v Germany* [2013] EWCA Civ 278, however.

[103] *Heron v TNT (UK) Ltd* [2013] EWCA Civ 469, at [37], *per* Leveson LJ.

[104] *Flatman v Germany* [2013] EWCA Civ 278, at [45] and [47].

in which the solicitors had been acting in a dual role—partly for themselves and partly for their client—Lloyd LJ found that the provision of legal services for no fee was something that went to fund the claim.[105] Whilst *obiter*, Leveson LJ has commented that if solicitors have pressed on with litigation without ATE insurance, contrary to their client's express instructions and in circumstances in which they stood to recover substantial fees if they were to win, those solicitors would be at risk of being found to have taken over the litigation.[106] Whilst not binding, Judge Birse QC found that if services were provided for the solicitors' benefit as well as those of the client, the solicitors may have a dual role even if instructed under a conditional fee agreement (albeit a damages-based agreement of sorts); he impliedly found that it is not a condition precedent to such a finding that the agreement is shown to be a sham.[107]

9.52 On the whole, however, the provision of legal services tends to be only a contributory factor. The fact that costs have been incurred as a consequence of a gross breach of duty to obtain ATE insurance may contribute to a finding that the legal representative was a funder,[108] but for the reasons set out above this would not of itself be sufficient to justify a non-party order being made. Likewise, if the client is insolvent or a man of straw, whilst that will not of itself be sufficient to justify a finding that the legal representative was a 'real party', it is a factor that the court may take into account.[109]

9.53 *Peripherally interested persons* Even if the funder has a commercial motive, a non-party would not generally be condemned in costs if the litigation were merely ancillary to the purpose for which that non-party provided funds to the litigant.[110]

9.54 *Legal expenses insurers* There is a distinction to be drawn between legal expenses insurers and insurers who conduct litigation as a result of being subrogated to their insured's rights (see 9.56). Generally speaking, a legal expenses insurer would not be required to pay more than the limit of the cover provided for in the policy. As a result, a legal expenses insurer can be expected to indemnify its client up to the limit of cover, but the court would generally not make a non-party costs order against it for anything beyond that limit.[111] In a case in which the insurer had taken an ordinary passive role in the litigation, Phillips LJ explained his conclusion by referring to the facts that:

- the legal expenses insurer had no interest in the result of the litigation, other than in so far as it affected its liability to pay costs;

[105] *Myatt v National Coal Board (No 2)* [2007] EWCA Civ 307, at [25].

[106] *Flatman v Germany* [2013] EWCA Civ 278, at [52].

[107] *Media Cat Ltd v Adams & Ors* [2011] EWPCC 010, at [96] and [97]. The agreement in that case was a damages-based agreement of sorts whereby the solicitor was entitled to 65 per cent of the monies recovered.

[108] Whilst they should be viewed with some caution following *Flatman v Germany* [2013] EWCA Civ 278, examples of the court finding that the absence of ATE was significant include *Adris v Royal Bank of Scotland plc & Ors* [2010] EWHC 941 (QB), *per* HHJ Waksman QC (sitting as judge of the High Court), and *Clarke v Oldham MBC* (unreported), 14 April 2008, Oldham County Court, *per* HHJ Armitage QC. *Adris* was commented upon by Leveson LJ in *Heron v TNT (UK) Ltd* [2013] EWCA Civ 469, at [37].

[109] See the Australian case of *Knight v FP Special Assets Ltd* (1992) 174 CLR 178, which was cited with approval by Leveson LJ in *Flatman v Germany* [2013] EWCA Civ 278, at [26].

[110] See, eg, *Vaughan v Jones* [2006] EWHC 2123 (Ch), in which David Richards J declined to make an order against a 'funder' who had provided money to the litigant for the purposes of annulling the litigant's bankruptcy.

[111] *Murphy v Young's Brewery* [1997] 1 WLR 1592.

- the legal expenses insurer had not initiated the litigation;
- the legal expenses insurer exercised no control over the conduct of the litigation; and
- the legal expenses insurer could not have been accused of 'wanton and officious intermeddling' in the dispute.[112]

It can be seen that Phillips LJ's decision was based on the facts, but in most cases in which a party had the benefit of legal expenses insurance, the facts would be such that his analysis would apply. By way of example, Judge Vosper QC declined to make an order against an ATE insurer who had cancelled a claimant's policy on the basis that the insurer had no more control of the litigation than an insurer ordinarily would have.[113] That said, it is not difficult to envisage circumstances in which an unusually proactive legal expenses insurer might find that it is at risk of a non-party costs order being made that exceeds the limit of cover. 9.55

Liability insurers Liability insurers are in a different position from legal expenses insurers. This is because they will usually fund litigation not in the interests of their client, but in their own interests. As a result, a liability insurer may be ordered to pay more than the limit of cover.[114] It would rarely be the case that an opponent would need to go to the trouble of seeking a formal non-party costs order where the limit of cover has not been reached, however, because the insurer would be contractually bound to provide an indemnity. Non-party costs orders might be sought, however, where there is a coverage issue (pending the resolution of which insurers defend the claim), or it is a term of the insurance that defence costs are met notwithstanding that (perhaps for aggregation reasons) there are no funds available to meet the damages (as is often the case in certain professional indemnity policies). There are other examples.[115] Indeed, if the insurer litigates in such a way as to place its interests concerning the limit ahead of its client's interests, then that may of itself be a factor that the court is entitled to take into account.[116] 9.56

Whilst it is not always easy to identify the precise jurisdiction under which such an order has been made, where an insured would otherwise be ordered to pay costs, there have been instances in which that person's insurers have instead been ordered to pay costs directly to whoever it is who is entitled to them.[117] 9.57

Unions and membership organisations Whilst it is a point that is almost never litigated, unless the proceedings are in the Employment Appeals Tribunal (EAT),[118] unions and membership organisations who support their members are particularly at risk of non-party costs orders being made against them (or, more accurately, if they were not already almost universally in the habit of meeting their members' obligations, they would be at risk of 9.58

[112] *Ibid*, at 1602.
[113] *Samuel v Swansea City & County Council* (unreported), 15 July 2008, Swansea County Court.
[114] *TGA Chapman Ltd v Christopher and Sun Alliance* [1998] 2 All ER 873.
[115] See, eg, *Palmer v Estate of Palmer, Deceased* [2008] EWCA Civ 46.
[116] *Cormack v Washbourne (formerly t/a Washbourne & Co (a firm))* [2000] Lloyd's Rep PN 459.
[117] See, eg, *Marley v Rawlings (No 2)* [2014] UKSC 51, at [7]–[13].
[118] See *Carr v Allen-Bradley Electronics Ltd* [1980] ICR 603, [1980] IRLR 263, EAT, in which it was decided that, given the special nature of the EAT, it would not be appropriate to follow the practice in the High Court.

non-party costs orders being made against them). Denning MR had the following to say on the point:

> 'Most of the actions in our courts are supported by some association or other, or by the state itself. Comparatively few litigants bring suits, or defend them, at their own expense. Most claims by workmen against their employers are paid for by a trade union. Most defences of motorists are paid for by insurance companies. This is perfectly justifiable and is accepted by everyone as lawful, provided always that the one who supports the litigation, if it fails, pays the costs of the other side.'[119]

9.59 Prior to 1 April 2013, s 30 of the Access to Justice Act 1999 provided a formal mechanism whereby unions and membership organisations could recover their costs of bearing the risk of having to pay an adverse costs order. This issue is dealt with elsewhere in this book (see 54.179–54.190).

Category three (legal representatives)

9.60 The jurisdiction that is discussed below is a special—and rarely encountered—jurisdiction to make non-party costs awards against legal representatives (or, more accurately, solicitors).[120] It is entirely different both from the jurisdiction under the wasted costs regime (see 9.94) and that which arises where a legal representative becomes a funder or a controller (see 9.47 and 9.61). Instead, the jurisdiction arises under the 'inherent jurisdiction' of the court (see 5.24–5.33) and, as such, is almost unique in the sense that it is a jurisdiction to make an award of costs that is not based on statutory powers.

9.61 **Three mutually exclusive jurisdictions** If they were to be particularly misfortunate, a solicitor may suffer orders made under no fewer than three entirely separate jurisdictions (although this could never happen in respect of costs incurred at the same time). If, at the material time, the solicitor was representing a client in that capacity and if that solicitor was acting in no other capacity, the only jurisdiction that may arise would be the wasted costs regime under SCA 1981, s 51(7) (see 9.93–9.221). If they were acting as a solicitor, but without authority, then they may be at risk of a non-party order made under the inherent jurisdiction of the court. If they were acting as a funder or a controller (as may happen entirely properly if, for example, the dispute becomes a dispute solely about costs), then the jurisdiction under SCA 1981, s 51(3), may arise (see 9.47).

9.62 Subject to what is said below about 'dual roles' (see 9.63), the three jurisdictions are, for practical purposes, mutually exclusive.[121] The non-party costs jurisdictions (that is, the second two jurisdictions mentioned above) are incapable of arising where a legal representative is acting exclusively in that capacity on behalf of a client;[122] where this is so, the

---

119 *Hill v Archbold* [1968] 1 QB 686, at 494.

120 It is a moot point whether the court's inherent jurisdiction applies to barristers. For a discussion of this topic in the context of New Zealand law, see *Harley v McDonald, Glasgow Harley (a firm) v McDonald* [2001] UKPC 18A, at [41]–[47].

121 There is an example of the court making orders under two of these jurisdictions at the same time, but it is not clear whether the court was asked to consider the issue of jurisdiction in any detail: see *Globe Equities Ltd v Kotrie* [1999] BLR 232, in which the Court of Appeal made no comment when it heard that an order had been made under both s 51(3) and s 51(6) and (7) against the same person acting in the same case.

122 In *Tolstoy-Miloslavsky v Lord Aldington* [1996] 1 WLR 736, CA, at 743, Rose LJ explained that there are six reasons why the court has no jurisdiction under SCA 1981, s 51(3), to make a costs order against a legal representative acting in that capacity. (1) It is inconceivable that Parliament would have introduced the wasted costs regime if the court's powers under SCA 1981, s 51(3), were already sufficiently wide to enable

only jurisdiction that could be invoked is the wasted costs regime.[123] The court's inherent jurisdiction cannot be invoked in such a way as to do something that is inconsistent with the CPR;[124] this means that the jurisdiction to make a non-party costs order against a legal representative may not be used to make an award that would be precluded by the wasted costs regime.

Dual role of representatives The jurisdiction to make an order against a legal representative acting as a funder or controller is the same as that which has been described in the sections on 'controllers' and 'funders' above. Ward LJ has confirmed that if a legal representative goes beyond conducting proceedings as a legal representative and behaves as a quasi-party, they will not be immune from a costs order under SCA 1981, s 51(3), merely because they are a barrister or a solicitor.[125] This may be particularly relevant in the context of costs litigation because such litigation is often for the benefit of the legal representative rather than the client.[126] A legal representative may find themselves acting in more than one capacity at the same time—that is, it is possible for a legal representative to represent both themselves *and* a client in circumstances in which the legal representative's interests can be regarded as being significant. Where this is so, then it is open to the court to find that the legal representative had a 'dual role', in which case the court may make an order that reflects that situation (such as a percentage order).[127] Case examples are given at 9.47–9.52. **9.63**

Inherent jurisdiction It is the court's inherent jurisdiction that is the focus of these remaining few paragraphs. The usual circumstances in which the non-party costs jurisdiction is exercised are when a solicitor commences or pursues proceedings without the authority of their client,[128] where there has been a misunderstanding as to what the client's instructions were,[129] where a solicitor acts on behalf of a client who lacks capacity[130] or **9.64**

it to make orders against solicitors. (2) Even prior to the introduction of the wasted costs regime, there was no authority that s 51(3) conferred jurisdiction to award costs against legal representatives; indeed, there were *obiter* observations to the contrary (see *Gupta v Comer* [1991] 1 All ER 289, at 293). (3) The provisions that introduced the wasted costs regime were not retrospective (see *Fozal v Gofur*, The Times, 9 July 1993, CA, and *Ridehalgh v Horsefield* [1994] Ch 205, at 250), and there was no jurisdiction to make orders against a barrister prior to that amendment (*Fozal v Gofur*, The Times, 9 July 1993, CA; *Davy-Chiesman v Davy-Chiesman* [1984] 1 All ER 321, at 328; *Orchard v South Eastern Electricity Board* [1987] QB 565, at 571–81, *per* Donaldson MR and Dillon LJ). (4) The provisions that were introduced in the civil courts were mirrored by similar statutory provisions introduced in the criminal courts (see Courts and Legal Services Act 1990, ss 111 and 112), which suggests that Parliament intended all legal representatives to be treated alike. (5) Balcombe LJ's analysis in *Symphony Group* did not suggest that *Aiden Shipping* has any application to legal representatives. (6) The origins of the wasted cost regime lay in the provisions of procedural rules of court, which reflected the court's inherent jurisdiction in relation to solicitors, but there is no such suggestion in relation to s 51(3) (see *Ridehalgh v Horsefield* [1994] Ch 205, at 226–31).

[123] *Hodgson v Imperial Tobacco Ltd* [1998] 1 WLR 1056, at 1066, *per* Woolf LJ.

[124] *Tombstone Ltd v Raja* [2008] EWCA Civ 1444.

[125] *Tolstoy-Miloslavsky v Lord Aldington* [1996] 2 All ER 556, at 570, *per* Ward LJ.

[126] See, eg, *Myatt v National Coal Board (No 2)* [2007] EWCA Civ 307.

[127] See *Myatt v National Coal Board (No 2)* [2007] EWCA Civ 307, at [27], distinguishing *Tolstoy-Miloslavsky v Lord Aldington* [1996] 2 All ER 556. Whilst not binding on any court, HHJ Armitage QC has made an award based on a 'dual role' in a case in which solicitors had failed to take out ATE insurance and used their own money to fund a claim, partly for the purposes of recovering profit costs: *Clarke v Oldham MBC* (unreported), 14 April 2008, Oldham County Court.

[128] *Fricker v Van Grutten* [1896] 2 Ch 662.

[129] See, eg, *Edwards v Edwards* [1958] 2 All ER 179, in which Sachs J made an order against solicitors who had allowed proceedings to continue in circumstances in which if they had taken account of certain items of disclosure, they would have realised that the proceedings were based on a misunderstanding.

[130] *Geilinger v Gibbs* [1897] 1 Ch 479, *per* Kekewitch J.

authority[131] to give instructions, or where a solicitor acts on behalf of a 'client' who does not exist.[132] In other jurisdictions, awards have been made where a solicitor has invoked a jurisdiction that does not exist.[133]

9.65 The conceptual basis for such an order is as breach of an implied contract or warranty given by the solicitor that they were authorised so to act by their client.[134] In modern terminology, the type of contract would be a collateral contract.[135] This has certain consequences that are discussed below. Lord Bingham MR has explained that the court's inherent jurisdiction has regulatory origins;[136] whilst that may be so, the regulatory aspects of the court's inherent jurisdiction tend to be reflected only in the fact that the order is made against a solicitor personally.[137] Waller LJ has said that a relevant factor is whether there was a client against whom the court could make an order and he clarified that the jurisdiction can be exercised without any fault on the part of the solicitor other than the fact that the solicitor lacked authority to act.[138] Put otherwise, to that extent, the solicitor's liability is strict.[139]

9.66 One of the consequences of the contractual basis for the jurisdiction is that the solicitor's potential liability will be defined by the extent of the warranty that they give (either expressly or by implication). McCowan LJ has explained that any such implied warranty has its limits:

> 'I see nothing ... to contradict the contention ... that a solicitor who lends his name to the commencement of proceedings is saying: (1) that he has a client; (2) that the client bears the name of the party to the proceedings; and (3) that that client has authorised the proceedings. He does not represent that the client has a good cause of action.'[140]

Whilst McCowan LJ did not go so far as to say that this was the appropriate test or threshold criterion, he did allow the appeal that was before him on the basis that the solicitor could not have been criticised for not having done more. It may be that other considerations will be appropriate in other cases, but at the very least McCowan LJ's three duties give an indication as to how the court should exercise its discretion.

9.67 Whilst *obiter*, McCowan LJ went on to say the following about how the court should exercise its discretion:

> 'I should finally make clear two things. First, because even in the want of authority case the court is exercising its inherent jurisdiction, it must be right to say that the court ultimately

131 See the discussion of this topic in *Re Sherlock Holmes International Society Ltd* [2016] EWHC 1392 (Ch).

132 As a modern example, see *Padhiar v Patel* [2001] Lloyd's Rep PN 328; see also *Babury Ltd v London Industrial plc* [1989] NJLR 1596, *per* Steyn J. See also *Kleinwort Benson v De Montenegro* [1994] NPC 46, *per* Aldous J.

133 See *Pringle v Secretary of State of India* (1888) 40 Ch D 288; *Re Avonbank Dairy Co Pty Ltd* [1962] Tas SR 121.

134 *Yonge v Toynbee* [1910] 1 KB 215; see also *Nelson v Nelson* [1997] 1 All ER 970 and *Warner v Merriman White* [2008] EWHC 1129 (Ch).

135 *SEB Trygg Liv Holding Aktiebolag v Manches* [2005] EWCA Civ 1237, at 57, *per* Buxton LJ.

136 *Ridehalgh v Horsefield* [1994] Ch 205, at 211.

137 See, eg, the way in which Lord Hope described the jurisdiction in *Harley v McDonald, Glasgow Harley (a firm) v McDonald* [2001] UKPC 18A, at [49]. See also the comments of Lord Wright in *Myers v Elman* [1940] AC 282, at 319.

138 *Nelson v Nelson* [1997] 1 All ER 970, at 977; see also *SEB Trygg Liv Holding Aktiebolag v Manches* [2005] EWCA Civ 1237.

139 See also *Yonge v Toynbee* [1910] 1 KB 215, at 255 and 226, *per* Buckley LJ.

140 *Nelson v Nelson* [1997] 1 All ER 970, at 973. See also *SEB Trygg Liv Holding Aktiebolag v Manches* [2005] EWCA Civ 1237, at [66] and [67], *per* Buxton LJ.

> has a discretion. But second, it is of such importance that solicitors do not commence proceedings without authority leaving the opposing party without even a person or entity against whom an order for costs can be obtained, that it is difficult to contemplate circumstances where, if the lack of authority leads to that result, the discretion would be exercised in favour of the solicitors.'[141]

Another consequence of the contractual basis for the jurisdiction is that the implied contract may be excluded or modified by the facts of a particular case. In this regard, Buckley LJ had the following to say: **9.68**

> 'If for instance, the agent proved that at the relevant time he told the party with whom he was contracting that he did not know whether the warrant of attorney under which he was acting was genuine or not, and would not warrant its validity, or that his principal was abroad and he did not know whether he was still living, there will have been no representation upon which the implied contract will arise.'[142]

In a similar vein, William Trower QC (sitting as a deputy judge of the High Court) has said that some form of reliance has to be shown to justify the relief sought.[143] Thus if the person who seeks costs was aware of the fact that the solicitors did not have (or may not have had) authority, there may be no reliance.[144]

The nature of the remedy is a claim for damages and the measure of damages is the costs thrown away by the opposite party (see 5.32).[145] Other common-law jurisdictions have described the power as being a means to remedy a misuse of the court's process.[146] **9.69**

Disclosure, factual disputes, etc In a straightforward case, the remedy is exercised summarily under the court's inherent jurisdiction over its officers (see 5.33),[147] although if there are substantial points of law or fact to be resolved, it may be appropriate to leave the issue to be resolved through the commencement of separate proceedings.[148] **9.70**

There have been instances of the court ordering disclosure against solicitors against whom an order was sought.[149] Leveson LJ approved of a summary of factors to be considered **9.71**

---

141 *Nelson v Nelson* [1997] 1 All ER 970, at 978.

142 *Yonge v Toynbee* [1910] 1 KB 215, at 227.

143 *Zoya Ltd v Ahmed* [2016] EWHC 2249 (Ch), at [36] and [39], citing *Excel Securities plc v Masood* [2009] EWHC 3912 (Ch), at [54] and [55], in which the warranty was given outside the context of litigation, and *Padhiar v Patel* [2001] Lloyd's Rep PN 328 and *Re Sherlock Holmes International Society Ltd* [2016] EWHC 1392 (Ch), in which the warranties were said to have been given when purporting to act for the claimant in legal proceedings. See also *Schlieskev Overseas Construction Co Pty Ltd* [1960] VR 195.

144 For a discussion of this point, see *Zoya Ltd v Ahmed* [2016] EWHC 2249 (Ch). No warranty of authority would arise in circumstances in which the litigation is about the very issue alleged to have been warranted: *Re Sherlock Holmes International Society Ltd* [2016] EWHC 1392 (Ch).

145 See *Yonge v Toynbee* [1910] 1 KB 215, at 229, and *Adams v Ford* [2012] EWCA Civ 544, at [31], *per* Toulson LJ. The court's inherent jurisdiction is usually exercised summarily, without the need for fresh proceedings to be brought by the 'opponent' against the solicitor; the summary process will be in lieu of the claim that could be brought pursuant to *Collen v Wright* (1857) 8 E&B 647.

146 *R v Forbes, ex parte Bevan* (1972) 127 CLR 1, at 8; see also *Darcey v Pre-Term Foundation Clinic* [1983] 2 NSWLR 497, at 504.

147 *Nelson v Nelson* [1997] 1 All ER 970 at 976, per Waller LJ and *Collen v Wright* (1857) 8 E&B 647.

148 *Skylight Maritime SA v Ascot Underwriting Ltd & Ors* [2005] EWHC 15 (Comm), at [6]–[14], *per* Colman J.

149 See, eg, *Flatman v Germany* [2011] EWHC 2945 (QB), at [28] and [29]. It should be noted, however, that whilst the appeal from this decision was dismissed, Eady J's reasoning (that, by providing credit for

when assessing whether disclosure is necessary for the fair determination of an application for a non-party costs order (see 9.90). Leveson LJ commented that the fact that a solicitor has acted in a certain way in one case is capable of influencing the decision of the court in respect of a difference case if it can be said that the facts are similar.[150] If the court concludes that—given the summary nature of the jurisdiction—further investigation is not appropriate, that should not be seen as a surrender by the court of its responsibilities, because it would be done in the knowledge of the client having other remedies, such as a complaint to the Law Society or a claim in negligence.[151]

Category four (causative persons)

9.72 A non-party who causes costs to be incurred may find that they have to pay those costs. There are two ways in which this state of affairs may arise: first, the non-party may have caused costs to be thrown away in existing proceedings; and secondly, the non-party may be the cause of the entire dispute between the parties.

9.73 The following are examples of the non-party causing costs to be thrown away in litigation that already existed.

- **Local authority causes wastage of costs** In a case in which hearings were vacated because of a local authority's failure to properly prepare a report in private law family proceedings, Cobb J found that an order should be made against the authority as it was sufficiently 'closely connected' with the litigation to justify such an outcome.[152]
- **Private company** A private company's failure to provide interpreters under contract with HM Courts & Tribunal Service had to pay the costs thrown away by the fact that this failure led to a hearing being vacated.[153]
- **Expert witness causes wastage of costs** In a case in which an expert, by his evidence, had caused significant expense to be incurred—in flagrant and reckless disregard of his duties to the court—Peter Smith J ordered the expert to pay the costs that were thrown away as a result.[154] It seems that this power may not be confined to cases in which the expert has acted in flagrant and reckless disregard of their duties, but may also extend to cases in which there has been a breach of the expert's duties, and additional costs and delay have been caused as a result.[155] However, merely being a witness and turning up to robustly do battle would not justify an order being made.[156]
- **Factual witnesses** If a witness gives false evidence that causes costs to be incurred, they would be at risk of an order being made, but this would be rare. In this regard, Moore-Bick LJ has said that whilst witness immunity does not apply as a matter of law,

disbursements, the solicitors had stepped outside the normal role of a solicitor) was found to be incorrect: see [2013] EWCA Civ 278, at [50], *per* Leveson LJ.

[150] *Germany v Flatman* [2013] EWCA Civ 278, at [52], *per* Leveson LJ.

[151] *Harley v McDonald, Glasgow Harley (a firm) v McDonald* [2001] UKPC 18A, at [54].

[152] *HB (Mother) v (1) PB (Father) (2) OB (A Child by his Guardian) & Croydon London Borough Council (Respondent on issue of costs only)* [2013] EWHC 1956 (Fam), at [59].

[153] *Re Capita Translation and Interpreting* [2015] EWFC 5.

[154] *Phillips v Symes* [2004] EWHC 2330 (Ch); cited with apparent approval by Arden LJ in *Mengiste v Endowment Fund for the Rehabilitation of Tigray* [2013] EWCA Civ 1003, at [7].

[155] *A Local Authority v Trimega Laboratories Ltd* [2013] EWCC 6 (Fam), [2014] PNLR 7, albeit that the order was made with the offending respondent's agreement.

[156] *Saxon v Bayliss* (unreported), 20 March 2013, Ch D, *per* John Baldwin QC.

it is important to have regard to the principles that underlie that doctrine. He had the following to say on the topic:

> '[T]here may be cases in which it will be just to make an order for costs (not necessarily the whole costs of the action) against a witness and we do not think that the possibility should be excluded. The power to make such an order should, however, be exercised with considerable care. To make an order for costs against a witness simply because he has given false evidence might well infringe the principles of witness immunity, but to make such an order on the grounds that he had conspired with others to pursue a claim that was entirely fabricated would not, even if in order to support it he had given false evidence.'[157]

- **Credit hire companies** Turner J upheld an order made against a credit company that had been responsible for a large part of a claim that had been brought by a person who had failed to prove that she had been injured in a road traffic accident.[158] This was in a case in which the exception to qualified one-way costs shifting (QOCS) at CPR, r 44.16(2)(a), applied, as is discussed at 8.48–8.51.

The following are examples of the non-party being the cause of the dispute. **9.74**

- **Litigation caused by professional negligence** Generally speaking, lawyers' fees incurred as a result of the negligence of a professional person will be recoverable only as damages rather than costs (see 3.42–3.43), but this will not always be the case. In a case in which a solicitor's failings over the execution of a will had caused litigation between intended beneficiaries and alleged beneficiaries in intestacy, Neuberger PSC commented that it would have been appropriate to order the solicitors to pay the costs of those proceedings.[159] In the event, the order was made directly against the solicitor's professional indemnity insurers,[160] but this did not in any way detract from Neuberger PSC's reasoning vis-à-vis the solicitor.
- **Litigation caused by the error of a tribunal** Incorrect decisions taken by tribunals may lead to litigation that otherwise would have been avoided, especially if the tribunal resists any attempt to correct its decision. Special rules apply that are tribunal-specific; other than what is said at 9.77, such issues are beyond the scope of this book.
- **Litigation caused by claims management companies** Whilst he did not refer to it as being a category four matter, Judge Godsmark QC made a non-party costs order against the director of claims management company that had caused a claim to be brought by forging documents so as to give the impression that its client had given instructions.[161]

Category five (related claims)

An example of where the non-party is a party to related proceedings that were heard at the same time as the index proceedings, but which were not consolidated with them, would be the case of *Aiden Shipping Co Ltd v Interbulk Ltd.*[162] **9.75**

---

[157] *Deutsche Bank AG v Sebastian Holdings Inc* [2016] EWCA Civ 23, at [44].

[158] *Select Car Rentals (North West) Ltd v Esure Services Ltd* [2017] EWHC 1434 (QB).

[159] See *Marley v Rawlings (No 2)* [2014] UKSC 51, at [7]–[13]. In the event, the Supreme Court ordered the solicitor's professional negligence insurers to pay the cost of the proceedings directly.

[160] See *ibid.*

[161] See *Trehan v Liverpool Victoria Insurance Company Ltd* (unreported), 3 October 2017, Nottingham County Court, *per* Judge Godsmark QC.

[162] [1986] AC 965.

Category six (group actions and representative claims)

9.76 The common-law position was established in *Davies v Eli Lilly & Co.*[163] CPR, r 46.6, is the result of an attempt to codify *Davies* and subsequent authorities; it is addressed in detail at 65.36. Whether there has been agreement as to costs between the co-litigants will be a relevant factor; the court will regard the persons whom the party represents as being beneficiaries of the litigation in the sense that they will be bound by its outcome.[164] This common-law position remains good law under the CPR[165] and is reflected in r 19.6(4), which provides:

> '(4) Unless the court otherwise directs any judgment or order given in a claim in which a party is acting as a representative under this rule—
> (a) is binding on all persons represented in the claim; but
> (b) may only be enforced by or against a person who is not a party to the claim with the permission of the court.'

Whilst these things are factors to be taken into account, they will not result in a costs order against the representative party being enforceable against the persons whom that party represents. If the receiving party wishes to enforce against the persons whom the party represents (such as where the party was a member of an unincorporated association and the receiving party wishes to pursue the other members), then that is something that must be addressed in the order.[166]

Tribunals

9.77 If a tribunal represents itself on an appeal from or review of its own decision, the court has the power to make an order against it.[167] Such orders may or may not be non-party costs orders depending on whether the tribunal was made a party (other than solely for the purposes of costs). To the extent that such orders can be said to be non-party costs orders, they are treated very differently from other types of non-party costs order. Ferris J has found that where a tribunal makes itself a party to the litigation, it puts the tribunal at risk as to costs, but whether such an order would actually be made was a matter of discretion to be exercised in accordance with the principles set out in the CPR, including the general rule that the unsuccessful party would be ordered to pay the costs of the successful party.[168] Ferris J declined to follow the pre-CPR rule that the tribunal would be liable only for those costs that have been occasioned by its involvement.[169]

Procedure

9.78 The relevant procedure is contained in CPR, r 46.2, and has been developed in the case law. The rule reads as follows:

---

163 [1987] 1 WLR 1136.

164 *Markt & Co Ltd v Knight Steamship Co Ltd* [1910] 2 KB 1201, at 1039; see also *Moon v Atherton* [1972] 2 QB 435.

165 *Howells v Dominion Insurance Co Ltd* [2005] EWHC 552 (QB).

166 *Ibid.*

167 *Providence Capitol Trustees Ltd v Ayres* [1996] 4 All ER 760, Ch D. As an example, see *R (on the application of Touche) v Inner London North Coroner* [2001] 2 All ER 752.

168 *Moore's (Wallisdown) Ltd v Pensions Ombudsman* [2002] 1 All ER 737, at [25].

169 *Ibid*, at [38], in which Ferris J refused to follow *Elliott v Pensions Ombudsman* [1998] OPLR 21 and *University of Nottingham v Eyett (No 2)* [1999] 2 All ER 445.

'(1) Where the court is considering whether to exercise its power under section 51 of the Senior Courts Act 1981 (costs are in the discretion of the court) to make a costs order in favour of or against a person who is not a party to proceedings, that person must—
(a) be added as a party to the proceedings for the purposes of costs only; and
(b) be given a reasonable opportunity to attend a hearing at which the court will consider the matter further.

(2) This rule does not apply—
(a) where the court is considering whether to—
   (i) make an order against the Lord Chancellor in proceedings in which the Lord Chancellor has provided legal aid to a party to the proceedings;
   (ii) make a wasted costs order (as defined in rule 46.8); and
(b) in proceedings to which rule 46.1 applies (pre-commencement disclosure and orders for disclosure against a person who is not a party).'

Whilst there are no immutable rules as to the 'right' procedure,[170] the following comments may be made. **9.79**

- With certain exceptions[171] and whilst the precise procedure will turn on the facts of each case,[172] a non-party should be added as a party to the proceedings for the purposes of addressing the issue of costs.[173] Where appropriate, that non-party must be given a reasonable opportunity to attend a hearing at which the court will consider the matter further.[174]
- A failure to comply with those requirements may amount to a denial of the non-party's fundamental rights[175] and that is capable of being a reason for the court refusing to hear the application.[176]
- It is desirable that there should be a concise statement of the grounds and essential allegations of fact relied on by the applicant. If the need were to arise, that statement could be amended or supplemented.[177]
- The application should normally be determined by the trial judge.[178] Where the non-party has had a close connection with the trial, the procedure to be adopted should be summary in nature, in the sense that the judge would make an order based on the

[170] *Deutsche Bank AG v Sebastian Holdings Inc* [2016] EWCA Civ 23, at [21], *per* Moore-Bick LJ.

[171] These are: where the court is considering whether to make an order against the Lord Chancellor in proceedings in which the Lord Chancellor has provided legal aid to a party to the proceedings (CPR, r 46.2(2)(a)(ii)); where the court is considering whether to make a wasted costs order (CPR, r 46.2(2)(a)(ii)); and in proceedings to which r 46.1 applies (pre-commencement disclosure and orders for disclosure against a person who is not a party) (CPR, r 46.2(2)(b)).

[172] *Deutsche Bank AG v Sebastian Holdings Inc* [2016] EWCA Civ 23, at [18], *per* Moore-Bick LJ.

[173] CPR, r 46.2(1)(a). This does not mean, however, that the non-party should be joined for the purposes of the substantive proceedings where there is not cause of action against that party: see *Deutsche Bank AG v Sebastian Holdings Inc* [2016] EWCA Civ 23, at [40] and [41], *per* Moore-Bick LJ. That said, where there is a cause of action against the non-party, they ought generally to be joined: see *Oriakhel v Vickers* [2008] EWCA Civ 748, at [31], *per* Jacob LJ.

[174] CPR, r 46.2(1)(b).

[175] As a pre-Human Rights Act 1998 example of this, see *Re Land and Property Trust Co plc (No 4)* [1994] 1 BCLC 232, CA.

[176] See, eg, *Barndeal Ltd v Cherrywalk Properties Ltd* [2005] EWHC 1377 (QB), *per* Newman J.

[177] *Vaughan v (1) Jones & (2) Fowler* [2006] EWHC 2123 (Ch), *per* Richards J.

[178] *Equitas Ltd v Horace Holman & Co Ltd* [2008] EWHC 2287 (Comm), *per* Andrew Smith J; see also *Symphony Group plc v Hodgson* [1994] QB 179.

evidence given and the facts found at trial, together with their assessment of the behaviour of those involved in the proceedings.[179]

9.80 It is implicit in what has been said above that the appropriate procedure is likely to turn on the extent to which the non-party has been involved with the substantive litigation. In particular, if the non-party were a 'real party' (in the sense of a controller), it would generally be the case that they would already have knowledge of what happened during the litigation, and in these circumstances it may be appropriate to tailor the proceedings accordingly.

Procedure and non-party costs orders: notice and warnings

9.81 Whilst not a formal procedural requirement, Balcombe LJ has commented that the applicant should, at the earliest opportunity, notify the non-party of the possibility that the applicant may seek to apply for costs against it.[180] However, Balcombe LJ's guidance was made in the context of the non-party having had a fairly tenuous connection with the substantive proceedings, and Moore-Bick LJ has explained that that guidance was not directed at the situation in which costs are sought against a third party who can properly be regarded as a 'real party' to the litigation.[181] Moore-Bick LJ went on to say this:

> 'The importance of a warning will vary from case to case and may depend on the extent to which it would have affected the course of the proceedings ... If the third party against whom an order for costs is sought is the real party to the litigation, the absence of a warning may be of little consequence. We should make it clear that we do not accept [counsel's] submission that the [party seeking the order] was under an obligation to explain why it had not warned [non-party] of the risk he faced. The fact that he had not been warned was all that was relevant and the judge duly took it into account.'[182]

Thus, where the non-party is a 'real party', whether notice was given is merely a factor to be taken into account. For obvious reasons, a party who seeks a non-party costs order would be in a better position if notice had been given and, as such, it would generally be sensible to err on the side of caution and give notice, wherever possible.

9.82 In a similar vein, Proudman J has explained that early warning is not a stand-alone requirement that will operate conclusively against the non-party; rather, it is no more than a material consideration—albeit a highly material consideration.[183] Similarly, Sir Andrew Morritt C has confirmed that the giving of prompt notice of a possible claim for a non-party costs order is not a condition of an order, but a 'material consideration in determining whether to make one and, if so, to what extent'.[184]

9.83 Lewison J has held that it may be appropriate to restrict entitlement to such reasonable period of time after the notification was given to allow the non-party to reflect upon its position.[185] Likewise, whilst there were other factors at play, Sales J reversed a non-party costs order on the basis that the non-party had not been given proper notice that an order

---

179 *Deutsche Bank AG v Sebastian Holdings Inc* [2016] EWCA Civ 23, at [17], *per* Moore-Bick LJ. See also *Symphony Group plc v Hodgson* [1994] QB 179, at 193.

180 *Symphony Group plc v Hodgson* [1994] QB 179, at 193.

181 *Deutsche Bank AG v Sebastian Holdings Inc* [2016] EWCA Civ 23, at [31], *per* Moore-Bick LJ.

182 *Ibid*, at [32].

183 *Europeans Ltd v Commissioners for HM Revenue and Customs* [2011] EWHC 948 (Ch), at [30].

184 *Farrell & Anor v Direct Accident Management Services Ltd* [2009] EWCA Civ 769, at [11].

185 *Brampton Manor (Leisure) v McLean* [2007] EWHC 3340 (Ch).

might be sought against him.[186] In a different case, however, Sales J found that the applicants could not have given an early warning because the facts that led to the application became apparent only when the non-parties gave evidence at trial.[187] In any event, where the facts support such a conclusion, it is open to the court to find that the non-party had constructive notice.[188]

Evidence

Notwithstanding its unusual nature, an application for a non-party costs order is still an application for costs and therefore there is a limit to the extent to which the court is able proportionately to determine contested issues of fact. Morgan J has commented that—as a matter of policy—applications for non-party costs orders are to be kept within proper bounds and the court is to do the best justice it can 'without having the full procedures pre-trial and at the trial'.[189] This general principle does not stretch so far as to preclude the determination of contested issues of fact; rather, the procedure is comparable to that on a summary judgment application or on a contested winding-up petition.[190] Unlike the jurisdiction to make a wasted costs order, there is no requirement that the issues must be capable of being dealt with summarily.[191] **9.84**

Burton J has said that there may be exceptional cases in which, in the interests of fairness, the procedure can be adapted to allow evidence to be given orally and for witnesses to be cross-examined: **9.85**

> 'If I were to say ... that there can never be in a s 51 application an order for evidence to be given orally, in chief or cross examination ... then that would be, in my judgment, a licence for people to be able to give evidence in writing which they knew could never be tested. On the other hand, if this is the first time that an order is made and as a result orders will be sought on other occasions, that does not open too wide a floodgate, because I accompany it, and I am sure any other judge would accompany it, with a substantial reminder that the procedure is ordinarily summary, and that the procedure is ordinarily intended to reflect all the caveats which the s 51 jurisprudence and the reported cases have set up for us to bear in mind. One, these are ancillary proceedings, and should not grow out of control into satellite litigation. Two, proportionality must always be considered. Three, it must always be borne in mind that the ordinary process is a summary process.'[192]

Thus Burton J identified three safeguards governing oral evidence: **9.86**

- that it must be borne in mind that the proceedings are ancillary proceedings and that they should not grow out of control into satellite litigation;
- that proportionality must always be considered; and
- that it must always be borne in mind that the ordinary process is a summary process.

---

[186] *Bank of Baroda v Patel* [2008] EWHC 3390 (Ch). See also *Equitas Ltd v Horace Holman & Co Ltd* [2008] EWHC 2287 (Comm), in which Andrews J declined to make an order for want of notice in a claim in which the non-party could not have been said to have been the 'real party'.

[187] *Reflo Ltd (in liquidation) v Varsani* [2012] EWHC 3848 (Ch), at [37], *per* Sales J.

[188] See, eg, *Xhosa Office Rentals Ltd v Multi High Tech Pcb Ltd* [2014] EWHC 1286 (QB), at [16], *per* Sir David Eady.

[189] *Centrehigh Ltd v Amen* [2013] EWHC 625 (Ch), at [47].

[190] *Total Spares & Supplies Ltd v Antares SRL* [2006] EWHC 1537 (Ch), *per* Richards J.

[191] *Robertson Research International Ltd v ABG Exploration BV*, The Times, 3 November 1999, QBD (Pat Ct), *per* Laddie J.

[192] *Grecoair Inc v Tilling* [2009] EWHC 115, at [42].

9.87 That said, circumstances will arise in which cross-examination is mandatory. For example, in a case in which the court below had made adverse findings as to a non-party's motives on the basis of statements alone, Judge Anthony Thornton QC (sitting as a judge of the High Court) found that those findings were flawed because the non-parties had not been given opportunity to answer the criticisms in cross-examination.[193]

9.88 Where they were made in proceedings not involving the same parties, judicial findings are generally inadmissible as evidence of the facts (not being matters of record) upon which they were based.[194] This has the potential to cause difficulties in respect of findings made before the non-party was added as a party; in practice, however, such problems rarely arise.[195] On a related point, Moore-Bick LJ had the following to say:

> '[T]here is a clear distinction to be drawn between the process by which the court makes an order for costs at the conclusion of a trial, whether that order involves the parties alone or one or more persons who are not parties, and separate proceedings against a third party consequent upon the outcome of the trial. In the former case, the ordinary rules of evidence do not apply, precisely because the person against whom an order for costs is sought has had a sufficiently close connection with the proceedings to justify the court's treating him as if he were a party.'[196]

Moore-Bick LJ went on to say that a strict approach to issues of evidence may be inappropriate where the non-party was a 'real party'.

Privilege and disclosure

9.89 In general, there will be no disclosure for the purposes of deciding whether to make a non-party costs order, but this will not always be the case. Blake J had this to say on the topic:

> 'If the court decides that it is necessary and in the interests of justice to make a disclosure order, it may proceed to give a detailed order within its general powers under the CPR to remove outstanding issues that may be the source of delay and further expense if unaddressed. Such an order may include inspection of documents by the court where there is a clear issue as to whether privilege attaches to them.'[197]

9.90 Leveson LJ approved of the following summary of factors to be considered when assessing whether disclosure is necessary for the fair determination of an application for a non-party costs order:

> '(i) The strength of the application as it now appears unassisted by disclosure;
> (ii) The potential value to the fair determination of the application of the documents of which the claimant seeks disclosure and whether they are likely to elucidate considerations highly probative of the exercise of the court's discretion, or threaten to drag the application into a side alley of satellite litigation with diminishing returns for the overall issue;
> (iii) Whether on a summary assessment it is obvious that the documents for which disclosure is sought will be the subject of proper legal professional privilege;

193 *Dweck v Fostater (Defendant) and Rowbury & Ors (Third Parties)* [2010] EWHC 1874 (QB).
194 *Hollington v F Hewthorn & Co Ltd* [1943] KB 587.
195 If the factual findings at trial are relevant, then the non-party tends to be closely connected to the proceedings and so tends to be content to accept those findings. An unconstrained approach to admitting evidence from the trial can be justified where the non-party was sufficiently close to the original proceedings that they would be kept from injustice: see *Globe Equities Ltd v Kotrie* [1999] BLR 232, at [18(6)].
196 *Deutsche Bank AG v Sebastian Holdings Inc* [2016] EWCA Civ 23, at [22].
197 *Thomson v Berkhampsted Collegiate School* [2009] EWHC 2374 (QB), at [16].

(iv) Whether the likely effect of any order the court might be minded to make will be proportionate and just in all the circumstances.'[198]

Drawing upon Laddie J's comments that the court should exercise its considerable administrative powers to ensure that an application for a non-party costs order should be dealt with as speedily and inexpensively as possible,[199] Burton J approached the issue of disclosure by identifying the live issues and by limiting disclosure to those issues.[200] Burton J went on to conclude that communications passing between a legal representative and his client were not covered by legal professional privilege if the client acted for some criminal purpose, and he found that this was the case regardless of whether it was the client himself who had the criminal intention or whether some other person was using the client as his innocent tool.[201] **9.91**

Sir Donald Rattee has confirmed that the court has the inherent power to order a funded party to disclose the identity and address of its commercial funder, and that the court has the power to order that party to say whether funding has been provided in return for a share in the money or property recovered.[202] That power has also been said to be implicit within the CPR's power to make security for costs orders against funders.[203] Orders requiring disclosure may be made against a party's solicitors.[204] **9.92**

Wasted Costs

Wasted costs are costs that are ordered against a legal representative (or, where costs would otherwise be payable, where they are disallowed).[205] It is a jurisdiction that arises where a legal representative has been acting in that capacity and where there has been an improper, unreasonable or negligent act or omission on the part of that person or their employee.[206] Practice Direction (PD) 46, para 5.1, gives the following definition: **9.93**

'A wasted costs order is an order—
(1) that the legal representative pay a specified sum in respect of costs to a party; or
(2) for costs relating to a specified sum or items of work to be disallowed.'

---

198 *Germany v Flatman* [2013] EWCA Civ 278, at [49].

199 *Robertson Research International Ltd v ABG Exploration BV*, The Times, 3 November 1999, QBD (Pat Ct), at [40]. Laddie J's comments were made in a context other than disclosure.

200 *Owners and/or demise charterers of dredger 'Kamal XXVI' and barge 'Kamal XXIV' v Owners of ship 'Ariela'* [2010] EWHC 2531 (Comm), at [10]–[12].

201 *Ibid*, at [25].

202 *Reeves v Sprecher* [2007] EWHC 3226 (Ch). In the case before him (ie prior to the issue of an application for security for costs), Sir Donald Rattee refused to order disclosure of the funding agreement itself, but he did not rule out disclosure in other circumstances. See also *Re RBS Rights Issue Litigation* [2017] EWHC 463 (Ch); *Wall v Royal Bank of Scotland Plc* [2016] EWHC 2460 (Comm); *Re Hellas Telecommunications (Luxembourg)* (unreported), 20 July 2017, Ch D, *per* Snowden J.

203 *Wall v RBS* [2016] EWHC 2460 (Comm), *per* Andrew Baker QC (sitting as a deputy High Court judge); *Re Hellas Telecommunications (Luxembourg)* (unreported), 20 July 2017, Ch D, *per* Snowden J.

204 See, eg, *AC DG Petrol SRL v Vitol Broking Ltd* [2014] EWHC 3900 (Comm).

205 Whilst neither the relevant primary legislation nor the CPR make any express mention of it, the term 'wasted costs' is also used to refer to a costs indemnity that a legal representative may be ordered to provide for the benefit of one or more of the parties (ie an indemnity in respect of costs ordered against one or more of the parties where those costs arose by reason of the legal representative's improper, unreasonable or negligent act or omission).

206 See Senior Courts Act 1981, s 51(6) and (7); CPR, r 46.8(1).

9.94 In some circumstances (such as where the legal representative has acted as a quasi-party or where they were acting without authority), the jurisdiction to make non-party costs orders might be relevant (as described at 9.47). Non-party costs orders against lawyers are not wasted costs awards, however (see 9.60).

Jurisdiction

9.95 The jurisdiction to make a wasted costs order has its origins in the court's role in supervising officers of the court,[207] but it now arises[208] from SCA 1981, s 51(6) and (7) (as amended[209]):

> '(6) In any proceedings mentioned in subsection (1), the court may disallow, or (as the case may be) order the legal or other representative concerned to meet, the whole of any wasted costs or such part of them as may be determined in accordance with rules of court.
>
> (7) In subsection (6), "wasted costs" means any costs incurred by a party—
>
> (a) as a result of any improper, unreasonable or negligent act or omission on the part of any legal or other representative or any employee of such a representative; or
>
> (b) which, in the light of any such act or omission occurring after they were incurred, the court considers it is unreasonable to expect that party to pay.'

9.96 As of 1 April 2013, s 51 has been amended[210] to include the following subsection:

> '(7A) Where the court exercises a power under subsection (6) in relation to costs incurred by a party, it must inform such of the following as it considers appropriate—
>
> (a) an approved regulator;
>
> (b) the Director of Legal Aid Casework.'

Whilst the need for these new provisions arose out of perceived problems relating to judicial review proceedings, there is nothing to suggest that they should not apply to other types of civil proceeding.[211]

9.97 The jurisdiction to make wasted costs orders is consistent with the European Convention on Human Rights.[212]

Relationship with other powers

9.98 It is possible for the court to make orders against legal representatives other than those made under SCA 1981, s 51(6) and (7), but this will usually be the case only where the court exercises its inherent power to control officers of the court or where the

---

207 See *Charles v Gillian Radford & Co* [2003] EWHC 3180 (Ch), at [22], in which Neuberger J referred to *Harley v McDonald, Glasgow Harley (a firm) v McDonald* [2001] UKPC 18, *Ridehalgh v Horsefield* [1994] Ch 205, at 232, and *Miles v Elman* [1940] AC 282.

208 The history and development of the jurisdiction can be traced through the following (in chronological order): *Myers v Elman* [1940] AC 282; Solicitors Act 1957, s 50(2); *Davy-Chiesman v Davy-Chiesman* [1984] Fam 48; RSC Ord 62, r 11(1); *Sinclair-Jones v Kay* [1989] 1 WLR 114; *Gupta v Comer* [1991] 1 QB 629.

209 By Courts and Legal Services Act 1990, s 4.

210 See Criminal Justice and Courts Act 2015, at s 36.

211 This was certainly the Ministry of Justice's view: see Ministry of Justice, *Judicial Review: Proposals for Further Reform—The Government's Response* (London: HMSO, 2014).

212 Wasted costs orders do not breach ECHR, Protocol 1, Art 1 (*X v Germany*, No 7544/76, 14, EComHR), nor do they raise issues under ECHR, Art 6(1) (*B v United Kingdom*, No 10615/83, 38, EComHR).

legal representative is not acting in that capacity. These topics are dealt with in detail at 9.60–9.71.

Rules of court: substantive litigation

As with all powers originating under SCA 1981, s 51, the powers are regulated by rules of court. In particular, CPR, r 46.8, reads as follows. **9.99**

> '(1) This rule applies where the court is considering whether to make an order under section 51(6) of the Senior Courts Act 1981 (court's power to disallow or (as the case may be) order a legal representative to meet, "wasted costs").
>
> (2) The court will give the legal representative a reasonable opportunity to make written submissions or, if the legal representative prefers, to attend a hearing before it makes such an order.
>
> (3) When the court makes a wasted costs order, it will—
> (a) specify the amount to be disallowed or paid; or
> (b) direct a costs judge or a district judge to decide the amount of costs to be disallowed or paid.
>
> (4) The court may direct that notice must be given to the legal representative's client, in such manner as the court may direct—
> (a) of any proceedings under this rule; or
> (b) of any order made under it against his legal representative.'

The effect of these rules is that the power to make an award against a legal representative may be exercised only after the court has given the representative reasonable opportunity to show cause why such an order should not be made—as is dealt with in detail at 9.197.

Rules of court: detailed assessments

In addition to the provisions in CPR, r 46.8, there are the lesser-known provisions in CPR, r 44.11, which are generally called into play where there has been a shortcoming on the part of a legal representative during costs proceedings (as opposed to substantive proceedings), although this is not always the case. The relevant provisions are as follows: **9.100**

> '(1) The court may make an order under this rule where—
> (a) a party or that party's legal representative, in connection with a summary or detailed assessment, fails to comply with a rule, practice direction or court order; or
> (b) it appears to the court that the conduct of a party or that party's legal representative, before or during the proceedings or in the assessment proceedings, was unreasonable or improper.
>
> (2) Where paragraph (1) applies, the court may—
> (a) disallow all or part of the costs which are being assessed; or
> (b) order the party at fault or that party's legal representative to pay costs which that party or legal representative has caused any other party to incur.'

CPR, r 44.11(1)(a), will apply only to detailed assessment proceedings, but there have been instances of the court making an order under CPR, r 44.11, in substantive proceedings.[213] **9.101**

[213] See, eg, *R (on the application of (1) Gransian Ltd (2) Xon Yong Zhou) v Home Department* [2008] EWHC 3431 (Admin).

Even though that jurisdiction exists, there is usually little point in the court preferring that jurisdiction over the general wasted costs jurisdiction, this being because CPR, r 46.8, affords the court wider powers. Furthermore, Dyson LJ has given extensive *obiter* guidance that the word 'unreasonable' in CPR, r 44.11(1), is to be interpreted in a narrow way that is commensurate with the interpretation of the same word in SCA 1981, s 51(6).[214] The effect of this is that where they both apply, CPR, r 44.11(1), adds almost nothing to the powers under the general wasted costs provisions. Other than to say that its only real function is (arguably) to allow costs judges to deal with unreasonable or improper behaviour that comes to light only upon assessment, CPR, r 44.11, seems not to have any useful separate function; it is therefore not addressed in any detail here (but it is addressed in detail at 57.37–57.64).

9.102 Whilst there is no authority directly on the point, where the court is minded to make a wasted costs order against a legal representative in costs proceedings, there is no reason to believe that the existence of the powers in CPR, r 44.11, releases the court from the need to afford the legal representative those procedural safeguards embodied in CPR, r 46.8. Furthermore, case law under the pre-CPR equivalent of CPR, r 44.11 (if of any continuing relevance) demonstrates that a finding against a legal representative should be made only in limited circumstances.[215] In particular, the following conditions would normally need to be met:

- that the legal representative had wasted costs by their failure to conduct the proceedings with reasonable competence and expedition;
- that the costs claimed were caused by that failure; and
- that (given that a finding against a solicitor would affect their reputation) the evidence amounts to a high standard of proof against the legal representative.[216]

Initiation of the inquiry

9.103 It will usually be a party who will initiate an inquiry into whether a wasted costs order should be made, but in some circumstances the court may act of its own volition.[217] PD 46, para 5.3, makes the following provision: 'The court may make a wasted costs order against a legal representative on its own initiative.'

9.104 Lord Bingham MR has said that the court should be slow to initiate an enquiry because such a course of action may lead to difficult and often embarrassing issues concerning the costs of the enquiry.[218] Where, however, the proceedings are such that costs would not normally be sought in an adversarial fashion (as in some family proceedings) and where public funds are under consideration, it may be appropriate for the court to initiate an enquiry.[219]

---

[214] See *Lahey v Pirelli Tyres Ltd* [2007] EWCA Civ 91, at [28], which cites with approval the comments of Park J in *Haji-Ioannou v Frangos* [2006] EWCA Civ 1663, at [10].

[215] *Mainwaring v Goldtech Investments Ltd*, The Times, 19 February 1991, CA, which relied in part on *Sinclair-Jones v Kay* [1988] 2 All ER 611, CA.

[216] Lord Carswell has now clarified that the standard itself is 'finite and invariable; but that where fraud or impropriety is alleged, the court will look more critically or more anxiously than in other [cases before it] can be satisfied to the requisite standard: *R (on the application of D) v Life Sentence Review Commissioners* [2008] UKHL 33, at [28].

[217] *Ridehalgh v Horsefield* [1994] Ch 205.

[218] *Ibid*, at 228.

[219] *Re G & Ors (children) (Care Proceedings: Wasted Costs)* [1999] 4 All ER 371, at 379–81.

Miscellaneous points about when the wasted costs jurisdiction will be available

No need for legal representative to be an opponent There is nothing to prevent a party from applying for a wasted costs order against its own legal representative.[220] 9.105

The need for the applicant for wasted costs to be a party For a person to be made an award pursuant to SCA 1981, s 51(7), that person must be a 'party'; not every person who has an interest in the proceedings will be a party. For example, Sedley J has found that a person who voluntarily appears at a without-notice hearing as a prospective respondent to a judicial review is not entitled to wasted costs because such a person could not be said to be a party.[221] Carnwath J, on the other hand, has interpreted the word 'party' in a more matter-of-fact way, finding that a respondent to a claim for interim relief must necessarily be a party 'in some sense' and that the jurisdiction to make a wasted costs order therefore did arise.[222] 9.106

Where a lawyer is not acting for a party (and therefore not acting as a legal representative), the jurisdiction to make a wasted costs order pursuant to SCA 1981, s 51(6) and (7), will not arise,[223] but in those circumstances the court may make a non-party costs order, where appropriate.[224] This is covered in more detail at 9.61. 9.107

The status of the person against whom the order is sought SCA 1981, s 51(6) refers to orders being made against a 'legal or other representative', whereas CPR, r 46.8, refers only to 'legal representative'. This invites the question of whether the court has jurisdiction to make a wasted costs order against a person who does not fall within the definition of 'legal representative' in CPR, r 2.3(1). The answer is almost certainly in the negative because SCA 1981, s 51(13), defines 'legal or other representative' as 'any person exercising a right of audience or right to conduct litigation on his behalf'. This definition was introduced by s 4 of the Courts and Legal Services Act 1990 and—as Chadwick LJ has explained—takes its meaning from s 119(1) of the 1990 Act; as such, it is linked to both the 'right of audience' and the 'right to conduct litigation',[225] which are rights that (under present-day legislation) only persons authorised or exempt under the Legal Services Act 2007 would have. Moreover, based on very similar wording in the Tribunals, Courts and Enforcement Act 2007, McCloskey J found that the power to make a wasted costs order did not apply to an unregulated person (in that case, a Home Office presenting officer).[226] That said, Judge Mackie QC (sitting as a judge of the High Court) made a wasted costs order against a claims management company in the context of him having found it to have been conducting litigation despite it being neither an authorised nor an exempt person for the purposes of the Legal Services Act 2007.[227] It would seem, however, that Judge Mackie QC did not hear much argument on the point. 9.108

---

220 *Medcalf v Mardell* [2002] UKHL 27; see also *Brown v Bennett (Wasted Costs) (No 1)* [2002] 1 WLR 713.

221 *R v Camden London Borough Council, ex parte Martin* [1997] 1 WLR 359.

222 *Lubrizol v Tyndallwoods* [1998] All ER (D) 139.

223 *Globe Equities Ltd v Kotrie* [1999] BLR 232. The Court of Appeal made no comment when it heard that an order had been made under both s 51(1) and (3), and s 51(6) and (7), against the same person acting in the same case; it seems, however, as if the Court was not asked to consider this apparent incongruity.

224 See, eg, *Kleinwort Benson v De Montenegro* [1994] NPC 46, *per* Aldous J.

225 *Byrne v South Sefton (Merseyside) Health Authority* [2001] EWCA Civ 1904, at [28].

226 See *Awuah v Secretary of State for the Home Department* [2017] UKFTT 555 (IAC).

227 *Malik v Wales* [2012] EWHC 4281 (QB), at [41].

9.109 In a case in which it was strikingly unclear in what capacity an organisation that purported to represent a litigant had been acting, Judge Seys-Llewellyn QC (sitting as a judge of the High Court) found that a solicitor who had been associated with that organisation had been engaged in the conduct of the litigation as a supervising solicitor; as a result, he found that the court had the power to make a wasted costs order against that solicitor in person.[228] It is therefore not the case that the power to make an award is restricted only to those who are on the record for a party.

9.110 For the avoidance of doubt, advocates are not immune from wasted costs orders being made against them[229] (but see 9.125).

9.111 **The need for proceedings to have been issued** Chadwick LJ has found that the definitions[230] in s 119(1) of the Courts and Legal Services Act 1990 apply to SCA 1981, s 51(6) and (7), and that therefore there is no jurisdiction to make a wasted costs order against a legal representative in a case in which no proceedings were ever issued.[231]

9.112 **Pre-proceedings work** Where, at the time of the act or omission complained of, proceedings had not been issued, but where proceedings are subsequently issued and the legal representative then carries out work, Ward LJ has found that the jurisdiction to make a wasted costs order will exist.[232]

9.113 Where, however, the acts or omissions occurred prior to the issue of proceedings, Neuberger J has drawn a distinction between cases in which the legal representative did and did not carry out work after the issue of proceedings. He found that where the legal representative did not go on to carry out work post-issue, a wasted costs order may not be made in respect of those acts and omissions unless there are 'special circumstances':

> '[A] solicitor can be liable for wasted costs as a result of some action on his part which was "immediately relevant" to the exercise of "the right to conduct litigation" prior to the actual issue of proceedings. However, as I see it, in light of authorities referred to, that does not detract from the requirement that the conduct must not only be "improper, unreasonable or negligent," but it must also amount in some way to "a breach of duty to the court".'[233]

9.114 As is explained under 'causation' (see 9.164–9.168), for most practical purposes the jurisdiction will not exist where the legal representative had ceased to act prior to the issue of proceedings. This, however, is not a jurisdictional restriction; it is merely an almost unavoidable consequence of the facts.

9.115 **Effect of an award under SCA 1981, s 51(1)** The power to make an order under SCA 1981, s 51(6) and (7), is an additional power to that exercisable under s 51(1). Thus, where an original costs order has been made between the parties in the substantive claim, this

---

[228] *MA Lloyd & Son Ltd (in administration) v PPC International Ltd* [2016] EWHC 2162 (QB).

[229] *Ridehalgh v Horsefield* [1994] Ch 205; *Brown v Bennett* [2002] 2 All ER 273, at 291.

[230] The right to conduct litigation is defined by s 119(1) of the Courts and Legal Services Act 1990 as the right to issue proceedings and to perform ancillary functions in relation to proceedings.

[231] *Byrne v South Sefton Health Authority* [2001] EWCA Civ 1904.

[232] *Wagstaff v Colls* [2003] EWCA Civ 469, at [73]–[75], distinguishing *Byrne v South Sefton Health Authority* [2001] EWCA Civ 1904.

[233] *Charles v Gillian Radford & Co* [2003] EWHC 3180 (Ch), at [20], [33] and [41]–[44].

will not preclude a wasted costs order being made against a legal representative at a later stage.[234] An application for a wasted costs order may be made after the general costs order in the substantive claim has been perfected.[235]

Compromised proceedings Where proceedings have been stayed by way of a Tomlin order, those proceedings will remain extant, so a wasted costs application could be made without having to lift the stay.[236] Where, however, proceedings have been brought to an end in such a way as to totally extinguish the possibility of any further steps being taken (such as by the whole proceedings being absorbed within the terms of a compromise), then there will be no jurisdiction.[237] **9.116**

Discretion

The court applies a three-stage test, as follows.[238] **9.117**

(1) Has the legal representative of whom complaint is made acted improperly, unreasonably or negligently?
(2) If so, did such conduct cause the applicant to incur unnecessary costs?
(3) If so, is it just in all of the circumstances to order the legal representative to compensate the applicant for the whole or any part of the relevant costs?

(PD 46, para 5.5, sets out these three stages in such a way as to reflect the common law.)

The first of these issues is dealt with in detail at 9.141 and the second, at 9.164. The third, more general, issue is discussed below. It should be borne in mind that these three issues are dealt with in two arenas: first, the court will decide whether the respondent legal representative must show cause as to why they should not pay costs; then, where appropriate, the court will finally determine that issue. Therefore, whilst the test is a three-stage test, the first question the court must ask itself is usually whether it should exercise its discretion to allow an enquiry to take place. **9.118**

Discretion generally

Four aspects of the issue of discretion merit particular attention, some of which relate to whether the legal representative should be required to show cause and some of which relate to the final exercise of discretion. Those issues are: **9.119**

- proportionality (9.120);
- the summary nature of the jurisdiction (9.123);
- the status of the persons involved (9.125); and
- the relevance of public funding (9.127).

Each of these is considered in turn.

---

[234] *Melchior v Vittivel* [2002] CP Rep 24; see also *Gray v Going Places Leisure Travel Ltd* [2005] EWCA Civ 189, at [16]. Whilst it related to the EAT, also see *Sykes v Wright* (unreported), 13 February 2017, EAT, *per* Singh J.
[235] *Wagstaff v Colls* [2003] EWCA Civ 469, at [49].
[236] *Ibid.*
[237] *Sharma & Anor v Hunters* [2011] EWHC 2546 (COP), at [28].
[238] This test was first formulated in *In re a Barrister (Wasted Costs Order) (No 1 of 1991)* [1993] QB 293 and approved by Bingham MR (giving the judgment of the court) in *Ridehalgh v Horsefield* [1994] Ch 205.

9.120 **Proportionality and the requirement to show cause** The court will always take into account the costs of the proposed enquiry.[239] As to the need to avoid disproportionate satellite litigation, Lord Woolf MR had this to say:

> 'The wasted costs jurisdiction is salutary as long as it is not allowed to be a vehicle which generates substantial additional costs to the parties. It should not be used to create subordinate or satellite litigation, which is as expensive and as complex as the original litigation. It must be used as a remedy in cases where the need for a wasted costs order is reasonably obvious. It is a summary remedy which is to be used in circumstances where there is a clear picture which indicates that a professional adviser has been negligent etc.'[240]

9.121 Wall J, on the other hand, has commented that it cannot be right for a respondent to seek to prevent an otherwise wholly meritorious application for wasted costs proceeding merely because the costs incurred in defending it will be substantial.[241] Likewise, a legal representative cannot escape the consequences of the wasted costs jurisdiction by the mere fact that the litigation in which their conduct is challenged is complex.[242]

9.122 The issue of proportionality may turn on the nature of the allegations that are made. The more serious the allegations, the greater the risk that the court will exercise its discretion against the applicant on the grounds that the application is disproportionate.[243]

9.123 **The summary nature of the jurisdiction** Both the House of Lords and the Court of Appeal have repeatedly stressed the summary nature of wasted costs applications. Lord Woolf MR commented on the extent to which the court can consider disputed issues of fact:

> 'The ability of the court to make a wasted costs order can have advantages, but it will be of no advantage if it is going to result in complex proceedings which involve detailed investigation of facts. If a situation involves detailed investigation of facts, and indeed actions of dishonesty, then it may well be that the wasted costs procedure is largely inappropriate to cover the situation, except in what would be an exceptional case.'[244]

9.124 Whilst *obiter*, Roch LJ has commented that if the situation involved allegations of breach of professional duty to the solicitor's client, that too may make the application one that is not suited to a summary procedure.[245]

---

239 *Ridehalgh v Horsefield* [1994] Ch 205. See, eg, *Chief Constable of North Yorkshire v Audsley* [2000] Lloyd's Rep PN 675, in which Keene J refused to entertain an application where the costs of the application (estimated at £130,000) were not a great deal less than the sums claimed (£169,000); see also *Harrison v Harrison* [2009] EWHC 428 (QB).

240 *Wall v Lefever* [1998] 1 FCR 605, at 614; see also *Chief Constable of North Yorkshire v Audley* [2000] Lloyd's Rep PN 675; *White v White* [2002] All ER (D) 454 (Mar) (in which an application was dismissed at the first stage because, amongst other things, the disposition of the issues would have required a further trial); *Media Cat Ltd v Adams & Ors* [2011] EWPCC 010, at [9], [15], [29] and [31] (in which HHJ Peter Birse QC restricted the number of allegations that would be allowed to proceed to the second stage on the grounds that it would be too costly to investigate the entirety of the legal representative's behaviour).

241 *B v B (wasted costs)* [2001] 3 FCR 724, at [35].

242 See Peter Gibson LJ's comments in *Medcalf v Mardell* [2001] LLR (PN) 146, at 159, which Ward LJ has confirmed remains good guidance notwithstanding the fact that the House of Lords allowed the subsequent appeal: *Wagstaff v Colls* [2003] EWCA Civ 469, at [59].

243 *Wagstaff v Colls* [2003] EWCA Civ 469, at [81].

244 *Manzanilla Ltd v Corton Property and Investments Ltd (No 2)* [1997] 3 FCR 389, at p 2E of the transcript, cited by Roch LJ in *Turner Page Music v Torres Design Associates Ltd*, The Times, 3 August 1998, CA.

245 *Turner Page Music v Torres Design Associates Ltd*, The Times, 3 August 1998, CA. See also *Kagalovsky v Balmore Investment Ltd* [2015] EWHC 1337 (AB), at [9], [12], [30] and [31], in which Turner J found that

The status of the person against whom costs are sought Whilst advocate immunity is not itself relevant to the issue of wasted costs (see 9.110), the policy underlying it should be borne in mind for the purposes of discretion. Lord Bingham MR gave the following guidance: **9.125**

> 'Any judge who is invited to make or contemplates making an order arising out of an advocate's conduct of court proceedings must make full allowance for the fact that an advocate in court, like a commander in battle, often has to make decisions quickly and under pressure, in the fog of war and ignorant of developments on the other side of the hill. Mistakes will inevitably be made, things done which the outcome shows to have been unwise. But advocacy is more an art than a science. It cannot be conducted according to formulae. Individuals differ in their style and approach. It is only when, with all allowances made, an advocate's conduct of court proceedings is quite plainly unjustifiable that it can be appropriate to make a wasted costs order against him.'[246]

When exercising its discretion, the court may take into account the effect that a wasted costs order would have on the legal representative. In a case in which he found that an order would lead to bankruptcy of the person involved (a solicitor advocate), Wyn Williams J decided that such would be a disproportionate consequence of her unreasonable conduct and that the order therefore should not be made.[247] There have been calls for the court to take the size of firm into account because—it has been said—an order against a small firm may cause real difficulties to the firm in question.[248] As far as the editor is aware, however, no such consideration has ever persuaded a court not to make a wasted cost order. **9.126**

The relevance of public funding The fact that a party has the benefit of cost protection as a result of being publicly funded is not a factor to be taken into account. Lord Bingham MR has commented that it would subvert the benevolent purposes of public funding if legal representatives were subject to any unusual personal risk.[249] Moreover, there is nothing within the regime governing costs orders against the Lord Chancellor—previously the Legal Services Commission (LSC)—which affects the court's power to make a wasted costs order against a legal representative.[250] There have been calls for the court to be able to take into account the strictures that are imposed by public funding,[251] but at the time of writing there is no authority on that point. **9.127**

Evidential issues

The points made above about the summary nature of the jurisdiction are repeated (see 9.123): the court will not carry out in-depth analyses of the facts. **9.128**

The burden of proof

As with any civil application, the legal burden lies with the party who seeks to persuade the court to take action.[252] **9.129**

---

the issues raised were too complex for summary determination, relying on *Medcalf v Mardell* [2003] 1 AC 120, at [24].

246 *Ridehalgh v Horsefield* [1994] Ch 205, at 236; see also *Brown v Bennett* [2002] 2 All ER 273.
247 *R (on the application of Hide) v Staffordshire CC* [2007] EWHC 2441 (Admin).
248 Cottam, H, 'Wasted Costs' (2010) 96 Fam LJ 22.
249 *Ridehalgh v Horsefield* [1994] Ch 205.
250 The Civil Legal Aid (Costs) Regulations 2013 (SI 2013/611), reg 3.
251 See, eg, *Re L (a child)* (unreported), 4 March 2016, Family Court, *per* Judge Clifford Bellamy.
252 *Dickinson v Minister of Pensions* [1953] 1 QB 228.

9.130 The fact that a respondent legal representative may be required to 'show cause' does not mean that the burden is on that party to exculpate itself; rather, it is for the applicant to prove that the order should be made (or, where the enquiry has been initiated by the court, it is for the court to satisfy itself that the order should be made).[253]

9.131 However, as with any civil application, the evidential burden may shift as the evidence unfolds.[254] A respondent legal representative will not be called upon to show cause unless an apparently strong *prima facie* case has been made out and Bingham MR noted that the language of the then-applicable rule of court (which is not dissimilar to the present rule) recognised a shift in the evidential burden.[255] Thus Lord Bingham MR seems to have recognised that whilst the legal burden will rest with the applicant at all times, the evidential burden may, as the application proceeds, shift towards the respondent legal representative. Certainly, if a respondent legal representative fails to adduce evidence of matters only they could know about, that will count—possibly heavily—against them.[256]

Privilege and inferences

9.132 Legal professional privilege belongs to the client, not the legal representative; only the client can waive privilege. Issues of privilege may arise in two ways: the applicant's privilege and the respondent's privilege.

9.133 **Privilege claimed by the applicant** The applicant's privilege may be relevant to the issue of what the application would or would not have done had the respondent legal representative not acted in the manner complained of. If an applicant declines to waive privilege in relation to material relevant to that issue, then there is a gap in the evidence for the applicant. In practice, however, difficulties do not usually arise because the applicant and their lawyers generally act as one.

9.134 **Privilege claimed by the respondent** A respondent (that is, the legal representative) is in a different position because they may wish to rely on material that their client wishes to remain privileged. This can give rise to tensions between the rights of the legal representative and the rights of the client (because privilege is not the legal representative's to waive).[257] It used to be the case that, in some instances, the potential for injustice could be mitigated by referring the matter to a costs judge,[258] but Lord Bingham MR has commented that only in a small minority of cases would this procedure be appropriate. Indeed, the CPR no longer contain any express facility for such a step to be taken.[259]

9.135 If the respondent legal representative is prevented from referring to the advice and guidance that they gave to the client, there would be potential for injustice. Lord Bingham MR had this to say:

---

253 *Ridehalgh v Horsefield* [1994] Ch 205.

254 *Abrath v North Eastern Rly Co* (1883) 11 QBD 440.

255 *Ridehalgh v Horsefield* [1994] Ch 205, at 228.

256 See, eg, *MA Lloyd & Son Ltd (in administration) v PPC International Ltd* [2016] EWHC 2162 (QB).

257 *Ridehalgh v Horsefield* [1994] Ch 205.

258 This used to be possible under the pre-1 April 2013 CPR, r 48.8(7), but those provisions no longer exist in the CPR.

259 The old CPR, r 48.8, used to contain the following provisions: '(6) Before making a wasted costs order, the court may direct a costs judge or a district judge to inquire into the matter and report to the court. (7) The court may refer the question of wasted costs to a costs judge or a district judge, instead of making a wasted costs order.' Those provisions no longer appear in the current edition of the CPR.

> 'Where a wasted costs order is sought against a practitioner precluded by legal professional privilege from giving his full answer to the application, the court should not make an order unless, proceeding with extreme care, it is (a) satisfied that there is nothing the practitioner could say, if unconstrained, to resist the order and (b) that it is in all the circumstances fair to make the order.'[260]

Henderson J added the following emphasis: **9.136**

> 'The court should make an order only if, proceeding "with extreme care", it is satisfied that there is *nothing* (my emphasis) the practitioner could say to resist the order, had privilege been waived, and, in addition, that it is in all the circumstances fair to make the order.'[261]

Lord Bingham has explained that a full allowance ought to be made for the inability of a respondent legal representative to tell the whole story. Where there is room for doubt, the respondents are entitled to the benefit of that doubt.[262] The court may make assumptions in favour of a respondent where it is fairly possible to do so.[263] It is only when—with all allowances made—a legal representative's conduct of proceedings is quite plainly unjustifiable that it would be appropriate to make a wasted costs order.[264] **9.137**

The following are examples of the court giving the respondent legal representative the benefit of the doubt. **9.138**

- Latham LJ found that it would not be proper to infer from the fact that public funding was granted that counsel had advised that the case had merit; rather, the court would need to see counsel's advice (or, presumably, some other direct evidence) before it could come to that conclusion.[265]
- In the same case, Latham LJ gave another example: where a concession was made shortly after an authority was drawn to the respondent legal representative's attention, it would not be proper to infer that the legal representative was unaware of that authority.[266]
- In a New Zealand case before the Privy Council, Lord Hope explained that it would almost always be unwise for the court to regard the pursuit of hopeless cases as a demonstration of incompetence.[267]

Fact finding

Formal processes of disclosure are inappropriate in the context of wasted costs applications.[268] Interrogation of a respondent legal representative is not generally permitted.[269] **9.139**

The admissibility of judicial findings Whilst judicial findings are generally inadmissible as evidence of the facts upon which they were based,[270] given that legal representatives **9.140**

---

260 *Medcalf v Mardell* [2002] UKHL 27, at [23].
261 *Sharma & Anor v Hunters* [2011] EWHC 2546 (COP), at [20].
262 *Ridehalgh v Horsefield* [1994] Ch 205; see also *Daly v Hubner* [2002] Lloyd's Rep PN 461 (Ch).
263 *Daly v Hubner* [2002] Lloyd's Rep PN 461 (Ch), at [27].
264 *Ridehalgh v Horsefield* [1994] Ch 205.
265 *Dempsey v Johnstone* [2003] EWCA Civ 1134, at [32]; see also *D Walter & Co Ltd v Neville Eckley & Co* [1997] BCC 331, in which Scott V-C said much the same.
266 *Dempsey v Johnstone* [2003] EWCA Civ 1134, at [33].
267 *Harley v McDonald, Glasgow Harley (a firm) v McDonald* [2001] UKPC 18.
268 *Ridehalgh v Horsefield* [1994] Ch 205, at 238H.
269 *Ibid.*
270 *Hollington v F Hewthorn & Co Ltd* [1943] KB 587.

will usually be closely connected to the relevant proceedings, this limitation does not apply.[271]

Impropriety, unreasonableness and negligence

9.141 For a wasted costs order to be made, the legal representative must have acted improperly, unreasonably or negligently. Lord Bingham MR explained that there is a good deal of overlap between these three categories:

> 'We were invited to give the three adjectives (improper, unreasonable and negligent) specific, self-contained meanings, so as to avoid overlap between the three. We do not read these very familiar expressions in that way. Conduct which is unreasonable may also be improper, and conduct which is negligent will very frequently be (if it is not by definition) unreasonable. We do not think any sharp differentiation between these expressions is useful or necessary or intended.'[272]

Where the court finds that the standard of conduct is deficient, the court must give reasons.[273]

9.142 Each of the three types of failing is dealt with in turn. Two further topics are then considered: pursuing a hopeless case (9.153–9.158) and sheltering behind counsel (9.159–9.161).

Impropriety

9.143 Lord Bingham MR explained the meaning of the word 'improper' in this way:

> ' "[I]mproper" . . . covers, but is not confined to, conduct which would ordinarily be held to justify disbarment, striking off, suspension from practice or other serious professional penalty. It covers any significant breach of a substantial duty imposed by a relevant code of professional conduct. But it is not in our judgment limited to that. Conduct which would be regarded as improper according to the consensus of professional (including judicial) opinion can be fairly stigmatised as such whether or not it violates the letter of a professional code.'[274]

9.144 Peter Gibson LJ has made it clear that any impropriety has to be 'very serious'—that is, there has to be something more than negligence; there has to be something akin to an abuse of process.[275]

9.145 Where it is said that the legal representative should not have pleaded fraud, it will not be for the legal representative to show that they had admissible evidence of fraud, but only that material existed which allowed the allegations to be based.[276]

Unreasonableness

9.146 Lord Bingham MR explained the meaning of the word 'unreasonable' in this way:

> ' "Unreasonable" . . . aptly describes conduct which is vexatious, designed to harass the other side rather than advance the resolution of the case, and it makes no difference that the conduct is the product of excessive zeal and not improper motive. But conduct cannot be

---

271 *Globe Equities Ltd v Kotrie* [1999] BLR 232, at [18(6)].
272 *Ridehalgh v Horsefield* [1994] Ch 205, at 233.
273 Whilst an EAT matter, the general reasoning of Underhill J in *Neafsey v Small* (unreported), 9 December 2010, EAT, at [26] *et seq*, applies.
274 *Ridehalgh v Horsefield* [1994] Ch 205, at 232.
275 *Persaud v Persaud* [2003] EWCA Civ 394, at [23].
276 *Medcalf v Mardell* [2002] UKHL 27.

> described as unreasonable simply because it leads in the event to an unsuccessful result or because other more cautious legal representatives would have acted differently. The acid test is whether the conduct permits of a reasonable explanation. If so, the course adopted may be regarded as optimistic and as reflecting on a practitioner's judgment, but it is not unreasonable.'[277]

In so far as acting on instructions is concerned, there is a distinction to be drawn between allowing a client to take a bad point and making representations to the court that the point is a good point. On this point, Chadwick J said: **9.147**

> 'I do not hold that a solicitor who, on his client's express instructions, presents a petition in those circumstances [knowing the petition will fail] must, necessarily, be said to have acted unreasonably or improperly. I do hold that a solicitor who, in swearing an affidavit ... to support [the] petition, asserts on his oath a belief that [he believes the case to be sound], acts improperly if he does not have that belief; and acts unreasonably if there are no grounds upon which a competent solicitor could reach that view on the material available to him.'[278]

Where unreasonable conduct is calculated to prevent or inhibit the court from furthering the overriding objective, it would be proper to consider making an order under CPR, r 44.11.[279] For the reasons set out above (see 9.101), however, this jurisdiction would normally be exercised only in respect of (or during the course of) costs proceedings. **9.148**

Negligence

Lord Bingham MR explained the meaning of the word 'negligent' thus: **9.149**

> ' "[N]egligent" should be understood in an untechnical way to denote failure to act with the competence reasonably to be expected of ordinary members of the profession. In adopting an untechnical approach to the meaning of negligence in this context, we would however wish firmly to discountenance any suggestion that an applicant for a wasted costs order under this head need prove anything less than he would have to prove in an action for negligence: "advice, acts or omissions in the course of their professional work which no member of the profession who was reasonably well-informed and competent would have given or done or omitted to do"; an error "such as no reasonably well-informed and competent member of that profession could have made".'[280]

One of the most important differences between 'negligence' in the use of that word for the purposes of wasted costs and 'negligence' in the sense of a tort is that the former is based on a duty to the court, whereas the latter is not. Neuberger J has commented that a bare finding of negligence in the latter sense would not be sufficient to found a wasted costs order: there must also be a breach of duty to the court.[281] For example, merely advancing a hopeless case will not of itself normally justify a wasted costs order (see 9.153).[282] **9.150**

---

[277] *Ridehalgh v Horsefield* [1994] Ch 205, at 232.

[278] *Re a Company (No 006798 of 1995)* [1996] 2 All ER 417, at 432.

[279] See PD 44, para 11.2, which reads as follows: 'Conduct which is unreasonable or improper includes steps which are calculated to prevent or inhibit the court from furthering the overriding objective.'

[280] *Ridehalgh v Horsefield* [1994] Ch 205, at 233. See also *Persaud v Persaud* [2003] EWCA Civ 394, at [19]–[23], *per* Gibson LJ, in which the Court declined to modify the test; *Sampson v John Buddy Timber Ltd*, The Independent, 17 May 1995.

[281] *Charles v Gillian Radford & Co* [2003] EWHC 3180 (Ch), at [22], in which Neuberger J referred to *Harley v McDonald, Glasgow Harley (a firm) v McDonald* [2001] UKPC 18, *Ridehalgh v Horsefield* [1994] Ch 205, at 232, and *Miles v Elman* [1940] AC 282.

[282] *Persaud v Persaud* [2003] EWCA Civ 394.

9.151 Where the court is examining the quality of advice given (such as where counsel has advised that a case qualifies for public funding), the test is whether no reasonably competent legal representative would have continued with the action.[283]

9.152 Where an allegation is based on a putative breach of requirement set out in a detailed statutory code (such as those relating to public funding), the court should be slow to supplement the statutory or regulatory duties so as to require a legal representative to meet some higher standard than that set out.[284] Where the requirement is a failure to comply with some procedural requirement, the fact that an opponent is a litigant in person may be of relevance.[285]

9.153 **Hopeless cases** An oft-encountered aspect of allegedly negligent conduct is where it is said that a legal representative has pursued a hopeless case. If a hopeless case has been advanced on the recommendation of the legal representative, then, for obvious reasons, that would put the representative at risk; if, for example, a legal representative had failed to appreciate that there was a binding authority that was fatal to their client's case, that would be capable of being negligence of a type that would justify the making of a wasted costs order.[286]

9.154 In contrast, a legal representative should not be held to have acted improperly, unreasonably or negligently simply because they have acted for a party who pursued a case that was plainly doomed to fail;[287] something more is required, such as advancing a case that is so poor as to be an abuse of process (see 9.156). Whilst they cite no authority for the proposition, the editors of the White Book say that it would rarely, if ever, be safe for a court to assume that a hopeless case was being litigated on the advice of the lawyers involved; the lawyers were there to present the case, and it was for the judge and not the lawyers to judge it.[288] The court is able to take account of the fact that the lawyers may have difficulty in getting instructions.[289]

9.155 After having noted the 'cab rank' rule that binds barristers and the commendable tendency of solicitors to act in a similar way, Lord Bingham MR made it clear that a legal representative is not to be held to have acted improperly, unreasonably or negligently simply because they act for a party who pursues a claim or a defence that is plainly doomed to fail.[290] This does not permit a legal representative to advance proceedings that are an abuse of the court (whether this is on instructions or not), as Bingham MR indicated:

> 'A legal representative is not entitled to use litigious procedures for purposes for which they were not intended, as by issuing or pursuing proceedings for reasons unconnected with

---

283 *Dempsey v Johnstone* [2003] EWCA Civ 1134, at [28].

284 *Tate v Hart* [1999] PNLR 787.

285 *Godfrey Morgan Solicitors Ltd v Cobalt Systems Ltd* [2011] 6 Costs LR 1006 (EAT), at [21], *per* Underhill J.

286 *Dempsey v Johnstone* [2003] EWCA Civ 1134.

287 *Ridehalgh v Horsefield* [1994] Ch 205, relying on observations in *Rondel v Worsley* [1969] 1 AC 191, at 275.

288 See para 48.7.5 of vol 1 of the White Book 2017.

289 See, eg, *R (Latchman) v Secretary of State for the Home Department* [2004] EWHC 2795 (Admin), in which the claimant had advanced a case notwithstanding the fact that it had become academic. Bennett J accepted that the claimant's solicitors had attempted to contact the claimant on a number of occasions without success and that, in those circumstances, the solicitors' conduct had not been unreasonable.

290 *Ridehalgh v Horsefield* [1994] Ch 205, relying on observations in *Rondel v Worsley* [1969] 1 AC 191, at 275.

success in the litigation or pursuing a case known to be dishonest, nor is he entitled to evade rules intended to safeguard the interests of justice, as by knowingly failing to make full disclosure on *ex parte* application or knowingly conniving at incomplete disclosure of documents.'[291]

As indicated above, some cases may be so poor that they can be regarded as being an abuse of process. A clear distinction has to be drawn between a hopeless case being presented and the lending of assistance to a case that amounted to an abuse of process.[292] The editors of the White Book say that it is not easy to distinguish, by definition, between a hopeless case and a case that amounted to an abuse of the process, but in practice it was not hard to say which was which; to the extent that there is doubt in this regard, they say that the legal representative is entitled to its benefit.[293] **9.156**

Whilst he was dealing with a slightly different topic,[294] Lord Hope (sitting in the Privy Council) explained that errors of judgement do not, of themselves, attract the exercise of the jurisdiction to make a wasted costs order as they are not errors that go to the duty owed to the court.[295] This would be a relevant consideration where a case can be said to have such poor chances of success that it was an abuse of process to advance it. **9.157**

Where the conduct admits of no reasonable explanation, it will be no answer to an allegation of pursuing a case that is an abuse of process to rely on the lay client's refusal to waive privilege.[296] **9.158**

Sheltering behind counsel Where a solicitor instructs counsel and counsel gives advice that is incorrect, the solicitor may, in appropriate circumstances, be able to avoid a wasted costs order on the basis that they were following counsel's advice.[297] **9.159**

However, a solicitor does not abdicate their professional responsibility by taking counsel's advice.[298] A solicitor has to apply their 'own expert professional mind to the substance of the advice received'.[299] In a case in which a solicitor had applied his own mind to the matter and had doubts about it, and where, as a result of those doubts, the solicitor had taken counsel's advice and acted upon that advice, Aldous LJ held that it would not be appropriate to find that the solicitor had acted negligently.[300] **9.160**

---

291 *Ridehalgh v Horsefield* [1994] Ch 205, at 232.

292 *Persaud v Persaud* [2003] EWCA Civ 394.

293 See para 48.7.5 of vol 1 of the White Book 2017.

294 That being a non-English legal point that is more akin to non-party costs orders than wasted costs orders.

295 *Harley v McDonald, Glasgow Harley (a firm) v McDonald* [2001] UKPC 18, at [57]. Wasted costs orders in New Zealand cases are technically made under the court's inherent powers and, as such, are not wasted costs orders, but Lord Hope made the comment on *Ridehalgh v Horsefield* [1994] Ch 205 and therefore nothing seems to turn on this jurisdictional distinction. Neuberger J commented that *Harley* was of assistance in this regard in *Charles v Gillian Radford & Co* [2003] EWHC 3180 (Ch), at [24].

296 *Morris v Roberts (HMIT) (wasted costs)* [2005] EWHC 1040 (Ch).

297 See, eg, *Swedac Ltd v Magnet and Southern plc* [1989] FSR 243 QBD.

298 *Locke v Camberwell Health Authority* [1991] 2 Med LR 249, approved of in *Ridehalgh v Horsefield* [1994] Ch 205; see also *Matrix Securities Ltd v Theodore Goddard* [1998] PNLR 290, at 322, in which the specialist was a tax counsel.

299 *Ridehalgh v Horsefield* [1994] Ch 205, at 228.

300 *Reaveley v Safeway Stores plc* [1998] PNLR 526, at 532; see also *R v Oxfordshire County Council* [1987] NLJ Rep 542 QBD.

9.161 The more specialist the nature of the advice, the more reasonable is it likely to be for a solicitor to accept it and to act upon it.[301] Common sense dictates that the same can be said of advice obtained from very experienced counsel, but examples do exist of solicitors being criticised for failing to scrutinise work carried out even by senior leading counsel.[302] Moreover, a solicitor will find it difficult to shelter behind counsel in circumstances in which counsel has given incorrect advice as a result of being inadequately instructed.[303]

9.162 **Reliance on experts** In addition to relying on counsel, a solicitor may also be able to rely on experts. In a case in which the applicant complained that no reasonable solicitor would have advanced the case, David Richards J refused to make a wasted costs order on the basis that there was supportive expert evidence.[304]

9.163 **Failure to take advice** Examples exist of the court making an order against solicitors for having failed to take counsel's advice in circumstances in which counsel's advice was required.[305]

Causation

9.164 The court has jurisdiction to make a wasted costs order only if and to the extent that the conduct complained of has caused costs to be wasted.[306] Eder J has explained that it is incumbent upon the party seeking costs to place proper evidence before the court that allows it to identify what costs have been caused by the allegedly deficient conduct.[307]

9.165 The issue of causation should be dealt with on the balance of probabilities rather than on a loss-of-chance basis.[308] Speculative causation defences—such as a suggestion that a bankrupt client would have brought the claim regardless of whether the consent of the trustee in bankruptcy had been obtained[309]—will generally fail.

9.166 Chadwick LJ has commented that the causation requirement will not often be met where the legal representative had ceased to act by the time that the proceedings were brought.[310] Although *obiter*, Neuberger J has qualified this by saying that it was not an inflexible rule, giving the example that it would be curious if solicitors were able to avoid a wasted costs order merely by causing their client to instruct someone else for the purposes of issuing proceedings.[311]

---

[301] *B v B (wasted costs)* [2001] 3 FCR 724, at 737; *Davy-Chiesman v Davy-Chiesman* [1984] 1 All ER 321; *Locke v Camberwell Health Authority* [1991] 2 Med LR 249, at 254; also approved of in *Ridehalgh v Horsefield* [1994] [1994] Ch 205.

[302] See, eg, *Tolstoy-Miloslavsky v Lord Aldington* [1996] 1 WLR 736, CA.

[303] See *Locke v Camberwell Health Authority* [1991] 2 Med LR 249, in which solicitors were criticised for not having given certain material (medical notes) to counsel. The decision to make an order for that reason was later reversed on the facts.

[304] *Marsh v Sofaer and Giffinhoofe & Co (a firm)* [2006] EWHC 1217 (Ch).

[305] See, eg, *D Walter & Co Ltd v Neville Eckley & Co* [1997] BCC 331.

[306] *In re a Barrister (Wasted Costs Order) (No 1 of 1991)* [1993] QB 293, approved by Bingham MR (giving the judgment of the court) in *Ridehalgh v Horsefield* [1994] Ch 205.

[307] *Nwoko v The Oyo State Government of Nigeria* [2014] EWHC 4538 (QB), at [8], *per* Eder J.

[308] *Brown v Bennett* [2002] 2 All ER 273, at 291.

[309] *Thames Chambers Solicitors v Miah* [2013] EWHC 1245 (QB), at [49], *per* Tugendhat J.

[310] *Byrne v South Sefton Health Authority* [2001] EWCA Civ 1904, at [31].

[311] *Charles v Gillian Radford & Co* [2003] EWHC 3180 (Ch), at [47].

An application may fail for want of causation where the court is satisfied that the costs will be paid by the respondent legal representative's lay client. Silber J, for example, refused to find that a causative link had been made out in a case in which a lay client had historically discharged its costs liabilities.[312] Mackay J came to a similar conclusion in an application for wasted costs against a barrister in a case in which only a relatively modest amount remained outstanding under the substantive costs order and was, in any event, likely to be paid.[313] **9.167**

Where a person has waived the right to recover the costs from a third party, the legal representative's conduct cannot be said to be causative of the costs thrown away; indeed, there would be a risk of double recovery in such circumstances.[314] Where the opponent could have taken steps to prevent costs being wasted, but chose not to do so, it will be open to the court to find an absence of causative influence.[315] **9.168**

Case examples

A number of case examples are given below, but each case must be decided on its own facts and it should be remembered that it is 'dangerous in the exercise of discretion to take a reported case as a guide for that exercise in another case'.[316] In particular, unless the contrary is stated, none of the examples given below establishes any principle or rule of law. **9.169**

Abusive proceedings

Where an appeal contained elements that rendered it incapable of succeeding, it was an abuse of the appellate process to bring an appeal; a legal representative who advised such a course of action would be acting both unreasonably and improperly.[317] In a case in which solicitors had had a hand in setting up a device designed to frustrate the proper operation of immigration law, Blake J made an order that those solicitors pay wasted costs.[318] In a case in which fraud was alleged, a wasted costs order was made against solicitors who knew that fraud had been admitted in other proceedings, but who had failed to disclose that fact.[319] Where a claimant had a weak case on the law (because of the effect of state immunity), Silber J declined to find negligence because the law could not be said to have been so straightforward that the claimant could be criticised for pursuing the claim.[320] Where solicitors pursued an appeal notwithstanding the fact that their lateness in submitting the notice of appeal had deprived the court of jurisdiction, Andrews J found that there had been an abuse of process and made an order (based on negligence) for wasted costs accordingly.[321] **9.170**

---

[312] *KOO Golden East Mongolia (a body corporate) v Bank of Nova Scotia* [2008] EWHC 1120 (QB), at [72].
[313] *Harrison v Harrison* [2009] EWHC 428 (QB).
[314] *D v H (Costs)* [2008] EWHC 559 (Fam).
[315] An example being where a party could have applied to strike out: *CMCS Common Market Commercial Services AVV v Taylor* [2011] EWHC 324 (Ch), at [65]–[75], *per* Briggs J.
[316] *Bragg v Crosville Motor Services Ltd* [1959] 1 All ER 613, at 615, *per* Hodson LJ.
[317] *B v B (wasted costs)* [2001] 3 FCR 724.
[318] *R (on the application of (1) Gransian Ltd (2) Xon Yong Zhou) v Home Department* [2008] EWHC 3431 (Admin).
[319] *General Mediterranean Holdings SA v Patel* [2000] 1 WLR 272.
[320] *KOO Golden East Mongolia v Bank of Nova Scotia* [2008] EWHC 1120 (QB), *per* Silber J.
[321] *Adegbulugbe v Nursing & Midwifery Council* [2014] EWHC 405 (Admin), *per* Andrews J.

Frivolous proceedings

9.171 Where a misguided appeal had been begun and then frivolously pursued despite the fact that the tribunal had made it clear it was ill-advised, counsel and his instructing solicitors were ordered to pay the costs.[322]

Vexatious proceedings

9.172 A wasted costs order was made in a case that heaped 'fraud and perjury upon the vicious calumny of the allegation of being a war criminal', this being in circumstances in which the court had accepted the legal representatives' belief in the good faith of their client.[323]

Pointless proceedings

9.173 A hopeless application to remove an order that itself had been put in place to manage the possibility of hopeless applications being made may result in an order being made.[324]

Failure to prepare

9.174 Where counsel had had insufficient time to prepare for a hearing, the court should give weight to the fact that counsel's hands may be tied by the 'cab rank' rule in such a way that there is little that counsel can do about the situation.[325] Whilst it related to criminal costs, Elias J criticised a solicitor for having taken a case on when he may have had insufficient time to prepare it, but he did not find that this justified the making of a wasted costs order.[326] A failure to provide a bundle for a hearing in sufficient time to allow an opponent to deal with it may lead to an order being made.[327]

Failure to liaise with court

9.175 Although in a criminal case, Hooper LJ has found that a failure by counsel to inform the court of a new time estimate for trial may result in a wasted costs order if that was as a result of an error that no reasonably well-informed member of the bar would have made.[328] Leggatt J made an order against a firm of solicitors who (in addition to pursuing a spurious claim for damages) had failed to tell the court that its client had already obtained the relief sought in judicial review proceedings.[329] In a case in which a solicitor had informed the court of the need for an adjournment only a day before a hearing, the particular facts of the case—in which there were administrative difficulties with public funding—led the Court of Appeal to find that there had been only an error of judgement and that it would not be appropriate to make an order.[330] In a case in which a solicitor had failed to liaise with the

---

322 *Abbassi v Secretary of State for the Home Department* [1992] Imm AR 349.

323 *Tolstoy-Miloslavsky v Lord Aldington* [1996] 1 WLR 736, CA.

324 *R (on the application of Santur) v Home Department* [2007] EWHC 741 (Admin).

325 *Antonelle v Wade Grey Farr (a firm)*, which was one of the appeals heard at the same time as *Ridehalgh v Horsefield* [1994] Ch 205.

326 See *R v Aziz* [2014] EWCA Crim 1387.

327 See, eg, *The Trustees of the Redeemed Christian Church of God v Grestar Ltd* [2016] EWCA Civ 134, *per* Dyson MR.

328 *Re Olugbade (a barrister)* [2008] EWCA Crim 2922. In a similar vein, see *Re C (a child) (wasted costs)* [2015] EWHC 3259 (Fam).

329 *R (on the application of Grimshaw) v Southward LBC* (unreported), 17 July 2013, QBD (Admin), *per* Leggatt J. In a similar vein, see *R (on the application of Gassama) v Secretary of State for the Home Department* [2012] EWHC 3049 (Admin), in which Haddon-Cave J made an order against a firm that had 'sat on its hands' after a judicial review had been rendered academic. It seems that the case was decided under what is now CPR, r 44.11; this was probably an error because the case did not relate to the assessment of costs.

330 *Re a Solicitor (wasted costs order)* [1993] 2 FLR 959.

court regarding an adjournment, Jay J upheld an order for wasted costs and, in doing so, rejected the submission that the solicitors were unable to take any steps because an embargo had been placed on their client's legal aid certificate.[331]

Failure to liaise with experts

In a family case, Wall J found counsel to have been guilty of unreasonable conduct in failing to properly liaise with his client's expert to ensure that the expert was apprised of all of the relevant issues in the case.[332] **9.176**

Failure to liaise with opponents

In an administrative case, Bennett J refused to make an award against solicitors who had failed to keep an opponent abreast of the difficulties that the solicitors were having in obtaining instructions.[333] **9.177**

Failure to assist an opponent

Whilst cooperation between parties is to be commended, a legal representative's duty is to their lay client, not to their opponent,[334] so a failure to inform an opponent of a court order or to assist an opponent would not lead to an order being made. However, an obstructive attitude or a personal vendetta against an opponent might be a factor that would justify an order.[335] Sir Andrew Morritt has found that where a person had obtained a bankruptcy order against another person, but later discovered that there was no debt, he was not under a duty to contact the trustee in bankruptcy to prevent costs being incurred.[336] **9.178**

Failure to heed issues drawn to a party's attention

Gross J upheld a wasted costs order in a case in which the respondent solicitors had failed to apply the correct legal test, which had been drawn to their attention by their opponents.[337] **9.179**

Advancing incorrect evidence

Chadwick J found that it was improper for a solicitor to swear an affidavit saying that he believed that a company was insolvent if he did not hold that belief; he found that it was unreasonable to swear such an affidavit if no reasonable solicitor would have held that belief.[338] **9.180**

Failure to disclose

Where a solicitor failed to give full and frank disclosure when drafting an affidavit for use in an *ex parte* application, Rix J found that it was appropriate to make a wasted costs order **9.181**

---

331 *Holden & Co LLP v Eastbourne Borough Council* [2014] EWHC 1322 (QB), *per* Jay J, applying *Re a Solicitor (wasted costs order)* [1993] 2 FLR 959.

332 *Re G & Ors (children) (care proceedings: wasted costs)* [1999] 4 All ER 371.

333 *R (on the application of Latchman) v Home Department* [2004] EWHC 2795 (Admin).

334 *Fitzhugh Gates (a firm) v Sherman* [2003] EWCA Civ 886, at [64]; *Connolly-Martin v Davies* [1999] Lloyd's Rep PN 790, at 795. See also *B v Pendlebury* [2002] EWHC 1797 (QB).

335 *Fletamentos Maritimos v Effjohn International* [2003] Lloyd's Rep PN 26.

336 *Redbridge London Borough Council v Mustafa* [2010] EWHC 1105 (Ch).

337 *The Isaacs Partnership (a firm) v Umm Al-Jawaby Oil Service Co Ltd* [2003] EWHC 2539 (QB). See also *Holden & Co LLP v Eastbourne Borough Council* [2014] EWHC 1322 (QB), *per* Jay J, in which an order was made where a solicitor failed to take heed of comments made by an opponent about the absence of jurisdiction to hear an appeal.

338 *Re a Company (No 006798 of 1995)* [1996] 2 All ER 417; cf *Rybak v Langbar International Ltd* [2011] EWHC 451 (Ch), in which the solicitor was found not to be at fault for not ensuring that the evidence that his clients were giving was correct.

regardless of whether the solicitor appreciated the significance of a non-disclosed fact.[339] Failure to give full and frank disclosure in other circumstances may also justify an award.[340] Ward LJ found that the duty to give disclosure does not, for the purposes of wasted costs, extend to requiring legal representatives actually to inspect his client's documents (in that case, a CD-ROM) to verify his client's word.[341] A failure to supervise redaction may, however, fall below the requisite standard.[342]

Incredible witnesses

9.182 Where the claim turns on credibility, it would not be appropriate to make a wasted costs order against a legal representative for failing to realise that their witnesses would not do well under cross-examination.[343] That said, there are limits to this approach: in a case in which the claim was fundamentally dishonest, Judge Charnock-Neal made a wasted costs order against a firm of solicitors that had failed to properly analyse the evidence.[344]

Specialist proceedings

9.183 Although *obiter*, Brooke J has indicated that a lack of familiarity with specialist proceedings would put a legal representative at risk of a wasted costs order if he had held himself out as being competent in that specialist arena.[345]

Wrong proceedings

9.184 In an application in which the legal representatives had wrongly applied for a judicial review rather than a statutory review of a decision of an immigration judge, Collins J ordered those legal representatives to pay costs.[346]

Failure to realise client is a patient or is a bankrupt

9.185 In a family case in which a solicitor had failed to realise that the client was a patient, Cornell J commented that he would have considered making a wasted costs order only if the solicitor had ignored the need to consider the client's mental capacity, the implication being that—within reason—an incorrect conclusion would not of itself be sufficient.[347] Accepting instructions from a bankrupt and conducting litigation on their behalf without the consent of the trustee in bankruptcy would be capable of being sufficient, and may even amount to conduct that was unreasonable, negligent and improper.[348]

Absence of instructions, instructions from the wrong person and no right to conduct litigation

9.186 In an EAT case in which a legal representative made an accusation of bias without instructions, that was found to be capable of being grounds for a wasted costs order;[349] where the

---

339 *Lowline (PLS) Ltd v Direct Aviation Ltd* (unreported), 8 March 1999, QB (Comm), *per* Rix J.

340 Whilst it was a tax case, see, eg, *Okundu v Secretary of State for the Home Department* [2014] UKUT 377 (IAC), *per* Green J.

341 *Hedrich v Standard Bank London Ltd* [2008] EWCA Civ 905.

342 See *CMCS Common Market Commercial Services AVV v Taylor* [2011] EWHC 324 (Ch), at [60] *et seq*, per Briggs J.

343 *Gandesha v Nandra* (unreported), 21 November 2001, Ch D, *per* Jacob J.

344 *Thompson v Go North East Ltd* (unreported), 30 August 2016, Sunderland County Court, *per* Judge Charnock-Neal.

345 *R v Horsham District Council & Anor, ex parte Wenman & Ors* [1995] 1 WLR 680.

346 *R (on the application of Kamau) v Secretary of State for the Home Department* [2007] All ER (D) 111 (Apr).

347 *Re O (a minor) (wasted costs application)* [1994] 2 FLR 842, at 847.

348 See, eg, *Thames Chambers v Miah* [2013] EWHC 1245 (QB), *per* Tugendhat J.

349 *Highvogue Ltd and Morris v Davies* (2007) UKEAT/0093/07, *per* Beatson J.

legal representative is acting completely without instructions, this would be grounds for the court making an order under its inherent jurisdiction (see 9.65). Tugendhat J made an order against a firm of solicitors that, despite having been told that its client was bankrupt, brought a claim without the consent of the trustee in bankruptcy.[350] Judge Godsmark QC made an order against a firm of solicitors that had failed to carry out any effective identity checks and had failed to take proper instructions from its client, thereby failing to realise that the documents that had been provided by a claims management company had been forged.[351] Judge Mackie QC (sitting as a judge of the High Court) made a wasted costs order against a claims management company that had illegally conducted litigation despite not being an authorised or exempt person in respect of the activities it was carrying out[352] (although the points made in 9.108 should be noted).

Inability to obtain instructions and pro bono

Where solicitors had been aware for a period of about two months that a claim (an application for judicial review) had been rendered academic and where the claim was withdrawn only four days before the hearing, Bennett J declined to make a wasted costs order because the solicitors had tried, but failed, to obtain instructions.[353] The fact that the lawyer is acting *pro bono* probably is a factor that may be taken into account.[354] **9.187**

Failure to observe time limits

Although *obiter*, Neuberger J commented on his decision not to make a wasted costs order in the case before him: **9.188**

> 'It should be emphasised that I am not suggesting that by failing to miss any time limit, so that he is in breach of his duty to his client, a solicitor could not be liable for a wasted costs order. Indeed there will be many occasions where such an order would be appropriate. For example, where a solicitor fails to serve a document on another party within a time limit laid down by a court order or by the CPR, through an oversight. In such a case, there would be a very strong case for saying that a solicitor should pay the costs of all parties to an application to extend time, or for relief from sanctions, which was necessary as a result of the oversight.'[355]

Given the fact that the overriding objective has been amended in such a way as to focus on compliance with the rules of court, it is possible that orders against legal representatives who fail to comply with time limits will become more common.

Unacceptable delay

Unexplained and unacceptable delay may lead to an order being made.[356] Where an acceptable reason for the delay is advanced (such as funding difficulties), it would not be appropriate to make an order.[357] **9.189**

[350] *Thames Chambers Solicitors v Miah* [2013] EWHC 1245 (QB).

[351] See *Trehan v Liverpool Victoria Insurance Company Ltd* (unreported), 3 October 2017, Nottingham County Court, *per* Judge Godsmark QC.

[352] *Malik v Wales* [2012] EWHC 4281 (QB).

[353] *R (on the application of Latchman) v Home Department* [2004] EWHC 2795 (Admin).

[354] Whilst based on rules specific to the EAT, see *Jackson v Cambridgeshire County Council* (2011) PNLR 32 (EAT).

[355] *Charles v Gillian Radford & Co* [2003] EWHC 3180 (Ch), at [30].

[356] *Kilroy v Kilroy* [1997] PNLR 66.

[357] *Trill v Sacher (No 2)* [1992] 40 LS Gaz R 32, CA.

Failure to serve notices

9.190 There are many instances of the court making wasted costs orders against solicitors who failed to serve notices of revocation or discharge of public funding.[358] In this regard, it is worth noting that a legally aided person's solicitor was under a duty to serve notice of revocation or discharge of legal aid on all other parties to the proceedings;[359] any failings in this regard could amount to unreasonable behaviour.

Failure to attend a hearing

9.191 Failing to attend a hearing may give rise to a wasted costs order,[360] but if the solicitor reasonably relied on an assurance given by another solicitor that the latter would go on the record and attend, then that might amount to a defence even if the first solicitor were to remain on the record throughout.[361]

Raising new points at a late stage

9.192 The fact that a new point is raised at a late stage will not necessarily result in a finding of unreasonable conduct; failing to realise that some act may result in new avenues of argument being opened up will also not normally qualify as a shortcoming that is unreasonable.[362]

Trial overrunning

9.193 Where counsel had to seek an adjournment of a trial because another trial in which he was briefed had begun late, the Court of Appeal found that no order should be made; the court reminded itself of the need to bear in mind the demands of practice.[363]

Quantum

9.194 Quantum is assessed in the usual way (often by summary assessment).

9.195 The legal representative's liability is not limited only to those costs incurred whilst exercising rights of audience.[364]

9.196 Where an additional liability is claimed, it is likely that the court would follow the now-revoked Costs Practice Direction (CPD), in which case it would defer the assessment of any additional liability payable by the respondent legal representative until the conclusion of the proceedings.[365] Whilst there is no authority on the point, a party seeking a success fee against a legal representative would probably have an uphill battle unless they had given notice of the fact that a success fee would be claimed from the legal representative.

---

358 See, eg, *Banks v Humphrey & Glasgow* [1997] PIQR P464, CA; cf *Tate v Hart* [1999] PNLR 787. See also *NG Ferguson & Co Ltd v Brown & Tawse (A Firm)* 1918 SC (HL) 125.

359 See Civil Legal Aid (General) Regulations 1989 (SI 1989/339), reg 82(2).

360 Whilst no wasted costs order was made (because no costs has been incurred), Gloster LJ found that the requisite threshold had been met in a case in which a solicitor failed to attend a hearing and then gave misleading information regarding the need for an adjournment: see *Khuram v Secretary of State for the Home Department* [2015] EWCA Civ 913.

361 See, eg, *Equity Solicitors v Javid* [2009] EWCA Civ 535, at [24], *per* Holman J.

362 *Hallam-Peel & Co v Southwark LBC* [2008] EWCA Civ 1120.

363 *Re a Barrister (Wasted Costs Order) (No 4 of 1993)*, The Times, 21 April 1995.

364 *Medcalf v Mardell* [2002] UKHL 27.

365 See the now-revoked CPF—in particular, CPD, art 53.10, which has no counterpart in PD 46.

Procedure

The following topics are now discussed in turn: procedure generally, the two stages, timing, particulars, ancillary proceedings, notice, the court's duty to report and settled applications. **9.197**

Procedure generally

The procedure will be tailored to suit the needs of the case.[366] PD 47, para 5.6, provides that: 'The court will give directions about the procedure that will be followed in each case in order to ensure that the issues are dealt with in a way which is fair and as simple and summary as the circumstances permit.' **9.198**

PD 46, para 5.4, stipulates the mechanisms by which an application may be made: **9.199**

> 'A party may apply for a wasted costs order—
> (1) by filing an application notice in accordance with Part 23; or
> (2) by making an application orally in the course of any hearing.'

Oral applications for a wasted costs order should be heard only if the basis of the costs sought to be recovered was narrow and clear; where this is not the case, the court should require the applicant to make a written application, supported by evidence, if so advised.[367]

The application ought to be heard by the judge who heard the proceedings to which the application relates.[368] Where possible, this ought to be so even if that judge's judgment on the substantive issues contained criticisms of the respondent legal representatives.[369] There is a limit to the extent to which a judge can criticise a legal representative, however; where their findings are extreme and unbalanced, then the trial judge may have to recuse themselves from any application for wasted costs.[370] **9.200**

The two stages

As a general rule, the court considers the issue in two stages, as explained by PD 47, para 5.7: **9.201**

> 'As a general rule the court will consider whether to make a wasted costs order in two stages—
> (a) at the first stage the court must be satisfied—
> (i) that it has before it evidence or other material which, if unanswered, would be likely to lead to a wasted costs order being made; and
> (ii) the wasted costs proceedings are justified notwithstanding the likely costs involved;

366 Although a pre-CPR case, this was explained in *Ridehalgh v Horsefield* [1994] Ch 205, at 238G.

367 *Regent Leisuretime Ltd v Skerrett* [2006] EWCA Civ 1032.

368 *Re Merc Property Ltd* [1999] 2 BCLC 286; *Gray v Going Places Leisure Travel Ltd* [2005] EWCA Civ 189. See also Arden LJ's comments in *Mengiste v Endowment Fund for the Rehabilitation of Tigray* [2013] EWCA Civ 1003, at [1]–[7].

369 *In re Freudiana Holdings Ltd*, The Times, 4 December 1995.

370 *Mengiste v Endowment Fund for the Rehabilitation of Tigray* [2013] EWCA Civ 1003, at [7]. This was a case in which the judge strongly criticised a party's solicitors for supposedly having failed to advise an expert in Ethiopian law about the duties of being an expert witness. Arden LJ found that those criticisms left no room for manoeuvre and that, in those circumstances, the judge ought to have recused himself in order to avoid any appearance of bias. Arden LJ made no comment about what should happen when a different judge hears the application for wasted costs; in particular, there was no mention of what weight (if any) the new judge should give to the findings of the trial judge.

(b) at the second stage, the court will consider, after giving the legal representative an opportunity to make representations in writing or at a hearing, whether it is appropriate to make a wasted costs order in accordance with paragraph 5.5 above.'

The equivalent guidance in the now-revoked CPD used to have additional words that emphasised the need to proceed with the second stage even where the court is satisfied on the first stage that an order should be made.[371] Whilst there is no authority on the point, the removal of those words is almost certainly of no significance.

9.202 It is not always necessary for there to be an adjournment between the two stages, as PD 47, para 5.7, provides: 'The court may proceed to the second stage described in paragraph 5.7 without first adjourning the hearing if it is satisfied that the legal representative has already had a reasonable opportunity to make representations.' This guidance differs from the guidance that used to be given under the now-revoked CPD in that (it seems) the court can proceed directly to the second stage in any case; under the CPD, this was permissible only if the application had been made under Part 23.[372] If the court is dealing with the matter under CPR, r 44.11, the similar provisions apply.[373]

9.203 There is pre-CPR authority to suggest that there is a degree of flexibility in the need for a two-stage procedure. In a case in which counsel acting on behalf of the respondent solicitors had made concessions that justified a wasted costs order against those solicitors, and where those solicitors were present in court and did not object to counsel's concessions or ask for an adjournment, the Court of Appeal found that that was sufficient opportunity to show cause; the Court was not obliged to insist on a full investigation of the solicitors' conduct.[374] Whether this would remain the case under the CPR (and after the coming into force of the Human Rights Act 1998) is a moot point.

9.204 By analogy with criminal procedure, the court should not make a wasted costs order on the basis that the respondent legal representative has permission to apply to set it aside; the legal representative must be given an opportunity to make representations before the order is made, not after.[375]

Timing and applications

9.205 Unless the proceedings are wholly extinguished, the jurisdiction to make a wasted costs order may be made at any stage of the proceedings, not least because it is a matter of case management.[376] PD 47, para 5.2, provides as follows:

---

371 CPD, art 56.5(2), used to read 'at the second stage (even if the court is satisfied under paragraph (1)) the court will consider, after giving the legal representative an opportunity to give reasons why the court should not make a wasted costs order, whether it is appropriate to make a wasted costs order in accordance with paragraph 53.4 above'.

372 CPD, para 53.7, used to read: 'On an application for a wasted costs order under Part 23 the court may proceed to the second stage described in paragraph 53.6 without first adjourning the hearing if it is satisfied that the legal representative has already had a reasonable opportunity to give reasons why the court should not make a wasted costs order. In other cases the court will adjourn the hearing before proceeding to the second stage.'

373 PD 47, para 51.1, provides as follows: 'Before making an order under rule 44.11 the court must give the party or legal representative in question a reasonable opportunity to attend a hearing to give reasons why it should not make such an order.'

374 *Woolwich Building Society v Finberg* [1998] PNLR 216, CA.

375 *Re Wiseman Lee (a firm) (wasted costs order) (No 5 of 2000)* [2001] EWCA Crim 707.

376 Whilst it was in the EAT and therefore not binding, see *Wilsons Solicitors (in a matter of wasted costs) v Johnson*, 9 February 2011, at [34], *per* Underhill J.

'Rule 48.7 deals with wasted costs orders against legal representatives. Such orders can be made at any stage in the proceedings up to and including the proceedings relating to the detailed assessment of costs. In general, applications for wasted costs are best left until after the end of the trial.'

Neuberger LJ (with whom Latham and Brooke LJJ agreed) gave the following guidance about the timing of applications for wasted costs.[377] **9.206**

- The making of an order as to who should bear the costs and on what part terms are part of the overall order made by the court at the conclusion of the trial.
- In the absence of at least a good reason to the contrary, the costs of proceedings should be dealt with by the tribunal that determines the issue which disposes of the case immediately after the judgment in disposing of the case.
- In principle, there is no difference in this connection between a costs order against a party and a costs order against a non-party: orders for wasted costs are all part of the costs allocation exercise that is to be implemented by the judge hearing the trial in relation to the costs of the action.
- Where a wasted costs order is sought in respect of an interlocutory matter before trial, it is often better for the application for wasted costs to be made only after the trial.
- It is, however, not mandatory that the application for wasted costs is made at the end of the trial. In many cases, a party considering an application for a wasted costs order will ask the judge for time to consider whether to make such an application and, even if such an application is made, the normal course is for the court to give directions in relation to the disposal of the application rather than to deal with it straight away.
- The application for a wasted costs order can be made after the order in relation to the proceedings has been drawn up—although the court entertaining the application late will not necessarily grant it if there is no good reason for the delay.

Holman J has noted that applications are often made in a hasty and insufficiently considered manner, and has warned that adverse costs consequences would often result from this.[378] Henderson J, however, has commented on the need for applications to be made promptly.[379] **9.207**

Aldous J had the following to say: **9.208**

'Although the right to seek and obtain wasted costs orders is not limited under the statute, I envisage that it would rarely be wise or right to seek to obtain such an order until after trial. Further, I do not envisage that the right to seek and obtain such an order could or should be affected by waiting until after trial before making a claim; although on rare occasions it might be desirable to inform the legal representative that such an order might be sought.'[380]

Lord Bingham MR agreed with the thrust of what Aldous J had to say, but he went on to add that it is impossible to lay down rules of universal application and that circumstances may exist in which an interlocutory battle resolves the real dispute between the parties.[381] **9.209**

---

[377] *Gray v Going Places Leisure Travel Ltd* [2005] EWCA Civ 189, at [11]–[16].

[378] *Equity Solicitors v Javid* [2009] EWCA Civ 535, at [26], *per* Holman J.

[379] *Sharma & Anor v Hunters* [2011] EWHC 2546 (COP), at [21], *per* Henderson J, citing *Gray v Going Places Leisure Travel Ltd* [2005] EWCA Civ 189, at [14]–[15].

[380] *Filmlab Systems International Ltd & Anor v Pennington* [1994] 4 All ER 673, at 679; *Gray v Going Places Leisure Travel Ltd* [2005] EWCA Civ 189.

[381] *Ridehalgh v Horsefield* [1994] Ch 205, at 228.

9.210 Wall J has commented that, in certain proceedings, it may be appropriate to hear an application before the conclusion of the case.[382] It would be a rare case that would fall into that category, however.

9.211 In appropriate circumstances, a wasted costs order may be heard as late as on an appeal.[383]

9.212 The fact that the substantive proceedings may have been stayed will not prevent the court from hearing the application.[384]

Particulars

9.213 Fairness requires that the respondent legal representative is told clearly what it is alleged they have done wrong and what is claimed.[385] It is for this reason that PD 47, para 5.9, stipulates the following:

> 'On an application for a wasted costs order under Part 23 the application notice and any evidence in support must identify—
> (1) what the legal representative is alleged to have done or failed to do; and
> (2) the costs that he may be ordered to pay or which are sought against him.'

9.214 Pumfrey J commented on the topic:

> 'It seems to me that it is wrong in principle to make an order to "show cause" in the absence of a clear statement of what the respondent lawyer is said to have done wrong. Only then is it possible for the court to decide whether a sufficiently strong *prima facie* case exists to justify the order.'[386]

9.215 The procedure under CPR, r 44.11 (that is, misconduct), does not contain any express provision that the legal representative must be given particulars,[387] but in light of what Pumfrey J has said it is likely that there is an implied requirement that particulars are given. Moreover, PD 47, para 11.3, reads as follows:

> 'Although rule 44.11(3) does not specify any sanction for breach of the obligation imposed by the rule the court may, either in the order under rule 44.11(2) or in a subsequent order, require the legal representative to produce to the court evidence that the legal representative took reasonable steps to comply with the obligation.'

It is a necessary implication that if the court seeks evidence of steps to comply with an obligation, that obligation will need to be specified.

9.216 Where fraud is alleged, this must be made clear.[388]

Ancillary proceedings

9.217 Where the court finds that a wasted costs order should be made, it would not normally be appropriate for the court to express a view as to whether the legal representative's conduct was a breach of professional rules of conduct or whether their lay client had a civil claim

---

[382] *B v B (wasted costs order)* [2001] 3 FCR 724.
[383] *Sherman v Perkins* [2002] WTLR 603, *per* David Mackie QC.
[384] *Wagstaff v Colls* [2003] EWCA Civ 469.
[385] See, by way of analogy with criminal procedure, *Re P (a barrister) (wasted costs order)* [2001] EWCA Crim 1728; see also *Ridehalgh v Horsefield* [1994] Ch 205, at 238.
[386] *S v M* [1998] 3 FCR 665, at 673.
[387] See PD 46, para 5.
[388] *Wagstaff v Colls* [2003] EWCA Civ 469, at [79].

against the representative. Those were issues to be dealt with in the appropriate forums in a focused way, with the legal representative being given a proper opportunity to deal with any contested issue of fact or law.[389]

Giving notice

No potential applicant should threaten an opponent with a wasted costs application or use the spectre of an application as a means of intimidation.[390] There is nothing objectionable about alerting an opponent to the possibility, where appropriate.[391] **9.218**

Settled applications

Where an application is settled, a now relatively old case states that the parties should prepare a short and succinct written note explaining what happened as far as the lawyers were concerned. That note should inform the court of those matters that are relevant to the reputation of the lawyers, which, as a result of the settlement that has been achieved, would otherwise not be brought to the court's attention. Lord Woolf MR explained that the purpose of such a note would be to avoid the need for further hearings after the parties had come to terms.[392] **9.219**

Details of costs claimed

Eder J has explained that it is incumbent on the party applying for wasted costs to provide the court with sufficient detail regarding the costs to allow the court to know which costs have been caused by the allegedly deficient conduct.[393] This would, in general, mean that a costs schedule of costs ought to be drawn up that reflects the potential findings that the court may make regarding causation. **9.220**

Costs of the application

The costs of the application will be determined according to the usual principle in CPR, r 44.2. Where an applicant had failed on causation, but had succeeded in showing that the respondent's conduct fell woefully short of that required, McFarlane LJ said that it would be wrong in principle to award the applicant its costs where it had failed to achieve the substantive order for which it had applied.[394] In a case in which the court had refused an application for wasted costs on the basis that the application was disproportionate and frivolous, Evans-Lombe J found that the court below had erred in failing to award the costs of the application to the respondent.[395] **9.221**

389 *Harley v McDonald, Glasgow Harley (a firm) v McDonald* [2001] UKPC 18, at [51].
390 *Orchard v South Eastern Electricity Board* [1987] QB 565.
391 *Ridehalgh v Horsefield* [1994] Ch 205.
392 *Manzanilla Ltd v Corton Property and Investments Ltd* [1997] 3 FCR 389, at [39].
393 *Nwoko v The Oyo State Government of Nigeria* [2014] EWHC 4538 (QB), at [8], *per* Eder J.
394 *Re A (a child) (Costs)* [2013] EWCA Civ 43, at [43].
395 *9MD Ltd v One Step Beyond* [2008] EWHC 3231 (Ch).

10

ORDERS FOR COSTS (CLARIFICATION AND REVISION OF ORDERS)

10.01 This chapter deals with the following topics:

- relevant terminology—orders, judgments and perfected orders (10.03);
- clarification of orders for costs (10.04);
- correction of orders for costs (10.05);
- review of orders for costs (10.08); and
- setting aside consent orders for costs (10.27).

10.02 It may be that one or more of the parties wishes to return to the judge who made an award of costs for the purposes of clarifying the order, correcting it or asking the court to make a different order. Each of these scenarios is dealt with in turn, followed by a short discussion of setting aside orders made by consent.

Terminology: Orders, Judgments and Perfected Orders

10.03 Prior to the introduction of the Civil Procedure Rules (CPR), the words 'order' and 'judgment' were both used to refer to enforceable final decisions of the court.[1] Under the CPR, however, whilst the older usage is still encountered from time to time,[2] the word 'judgment' tends to be used to refer to the reasoning underlying the order. Ward LJ put it this way: 'Orders reflect the judgment. The reasons for the orders are to be contained in the judgment, not in the order'.[3] With certain exceptions, every judgment or order should be sealed, should bear the name of the person who made it and should bear the date on which it was made.[4]

---

1 Under the Supreme Court Rules 2009 (SI 2009/1603) and the County Court Rules (CCR), civil proceedings could be either an 'action' or a 'matter'; a 'judgment' was a final decision obtained in an action and every other decision, whether obtained in an action or a matter, was an 'order': *Ex parte Chinery* (1884) 12 QBD 342. Different enforcement provisions applied to 'orders' and 'judgments': see the White Book at para 40.1.1.

2 It is still common to see the word 'judgment' being used to refer to a final decision of the court in a claim and the word 'order' to any other decision.

3 *D'Silva v University College Union* [2009] EWCA Civ 1269, at [16].

4 See CPR, r 40.2, which reads as follows: '(1) Every judgment or order must state the name and judicial title of the person who made it, unless it is—(a) default judgment entered under rule 12.4(1) (entry of default judgment where judgment is entered by a court officer) or a default costs certificate obtained under rule 47.11; (b) judgment entered under rules 14.4, 14.5, 14.6, 14.7 and 14.9 (entry of judgment on admission where judgment is entered by a court officer); (c) a consent order under rule 40.6(2) (consent orders made by court officers); (d) an order made by a court officer under rule 70.5 (orders to enforce awards as if payable

An order that has been sealed by the court in this way is known as a perfected order.[5]

Clarification of Orders for Costs

10.04 There used to be an ancient rule of practice that once a costs order had been drawn up, there could be no further reference to the judge who made it.[6] In the 1950s, Singleton LJ made it clear that this rule was not in the public interest; he said that where difficulty has arisen over the interpretation of an order, trouble and expense would be saved if the parties were able to go back to the judge even after the order had been drawn up.[7] Those comments were made prior to the introduction of the CPR, but, if anything, the CPR have made his remarks even more apposite. In any event, the court has an inherent power—which is expressly preserved in Practice Direction (PD) 40B—to vary its own orders to make the meaning and intention of the court clear.[8]

Correction of Orders for Costs

10.05 The court may correct an accidental slip or omission in an order under what is colloquially known as the slip rule.[9] The slip rule is limited to correcting clerical and administrative mistakes, and cannot be used to vary the substance of the order[10] or to resolve a misunderstanding as to the effect of an order.[11]

10.06 It is often the case that the court will ask the parties to draw up an order. Where this happens, it does not matter that the error may have originated under counsel's hand[12] nor does it matter if the error arose under the hand of one of the parties,[13] but an order may not admit an alteration if it was by consent and if it correctly recorded the intentions of the parties at the time it was sealed.[14]

10.07 Where the slip rule is invoked, the application notice (which may be an informal document such as a letter) should describe the error and set out the correction required. Such

---

under a court order); or (e) an order made by a court officer under rule 71.2 (orders to obtain information from judgment debtors). (2) Every judgment or order must—(a) bear the date on which it is given or made; and (b) be sealed by the court.'

[5] *Re L and B (children) (care proceedings: power to revise judgment)* [2013] UKSC 8, at [19], *per* Lady Hale SCJ.

[6] *Kelly's Directories Ltd v Gavin & Lloyd* [1901] 2 Ch 763.

[7] *Korner v H Korner & Co Ltd* [1951] Ch 11.

[8] PD 40B, para 4.5.

[9] CPR, r 40.12(1)—a right that also exists under the common law: see *Re Inchcape, Craigmyle v Inchcape* [1942] 2 All ER 157; *Thynne v Thynne* [1955] P 272, CA; *Bristol-Myers Squib Co v Baker Norton Pharmaceuticals Inc (No 2)* [2001] RPC 45, at [25], *per* Aldous LJ.

[10] *Preston Banking Co v William Allsup & Sons* [1895] 1 Ch 141, CA. Whilst *obiter*, see *Riva Bella SA v Tamsen Yachts GmBH* [2011] EWHC 2338 (Comm), at [22], *per* Elder J; see also *R v Cripps, ex parte Muldoon* [1984] 2 All ER 705. For an example relating to the quantum of costs, see *Gupta v Union Bank of India* [2012] EWHC 4075 (Ch), *per* David Donaldson QC.

[11] *Mölnlycke AB v Procter & Gamble Ltd (No 6)* [1993] FSR 154, Ch D.

[12] *Riva Bella SA v Tamsen Yachts GmBH* [2011] EWHC 2338 (Comm), *per* Elder J.

[13] Whilst a pre-CPR case in a slightly different context to the present context, see *Navimpex Centrala Navala v George Moundreas & Co SA* (1983) 127 Sol Jo 392, CA.

[14] *Leo Pharma A/S v Sandoz Ltd* [2010] EWHC 1911 (Pat).

an application may be dealt with without a hearing where the applicant so requests, or with the consent of the parties, or where the court does not consider that a hearing would be appropriate.[15] If the application is opposed, it should, if practicable, be listed for hearing before the judge who gave the judgment or made the order in question.[16]

Review of Orders for Costs

10.08 The CPR make express provision for orders to be set aside or varied.[17] The CPR do not expressly distinguish between final and interim orders, but they are treated differently. Indeed, there are six situations that merit discussion:

- review of a draft order before it is sealed (10.09);
- revocation or variation of a final order for costs (10.13);
- revocation or variation of an interim order relating to costs (10.17);
- orders that contain a provision that there be liberty to apply (10.23);
- deemed orders (10.24); and
- cases of real injustice in the Court of Appeal (10.25).

Review of a draft order or judgment before it is sealed

10.09 What follows relates to draft orders before they have been sealed and to references made to orders for costs in draft judgements. Put otherwise, what follows does not apply to perfected orders. In this regard, it should be borne in mind that a costs order takes effect from the time when the judge pronounces it and the subsequent entry of it is in obedience to the rules of court.[18] As such, in the context of costs, what follows has only limited application. It will generally apply where the court has stated an intention to make a certain order for costs in a draft judgment.

10.10 It used to be the case (as described in the first edition of this book) that the jurisdiction to review an order or to reverse a decision prior to a perfected order being made could be exercised only if there were 'exceptional circumstances' or 'strong reasons'.[19] Lady Hale SCJ has now explained that the true law is less restrictive than this:

> '[There] is jurisdiction to change one's mind up until the order is drawn up and perfected. ... [The] overriding objective must be to deal with the case justly. A relevant factor must be whether any party has acted upon the decision to his detriment, especially in a case where it is expected that they may do so before the order is formally drawn up ... A carefully considered change of mind can be sufficient. Every case is going to depend upon its particular circumstances.'[20]

Thus the test is to deal with the case justly and in accordance with the overriding objective.

---

[15] PD 40, para 4.2.
[16] PD 40, para 4.4.
[17] See CPR, r 3.1(7). The power also probably exists by virtue of r 3.1(2)(m): see *Lloyds Investment (Scandinavia) Ltd v Ager-Hanssen* [2003] EWHC 1740 (Ch).
[18] *Holtby v Hodgson* (1889) 24 QBD 103.
[19] This jurisdiction used to be known as the *Barrell* jurisdiction after *Re Barrell Enterprises* [1973] 1 WLR 1.
[20] *Re L and B (children) (care proceedings: power to revise judgment)* [2013] UKSC 8, at [19]–[27].

Lady Hale SCJ went on to say that a judge lacks jurisdiction to change their mind after the order has been sealed unless the court has an express power to vary its own previous order[21] (in which case the matters referred to in 10.13–10.23 will become relevant). **10.11**

Lady Hale SCJ commented with apparent approval on the following examples of circumstances in which the jurisdiction might be exercised: **10.12**

- where the judge has changed their mind after careful consideration;
- where there has been a plain mistake by the court;
- where the parties have failed to draw the court's attention to a plainly relevant fact or point of law; and
- where new facts have been discovered after judgment has been given.[22]

This is by no means an exhaustive list. Whilst they were decided by reference to an overly stringent test, some of the older case examples[23] are still informative as to the types of circumstance that would justify the court changing a decision or reviewing an order.

Final orders (including orders for costs)

For present purposes, a final order—be it an order for costs or an order relating to costs—is an order that determines issues that are the subject matter of the litigation, which order would generally give rise to a cause of action or issue estoppel (see 23.08–23.27). To the extent that it remains relevant under the CPR, there is pre-CPR authority to show that an order for costs is a final order.[24] Certainly, perfected orders for costs are generally treated as being final. **10.13**

The grounds on which a final order may, in theory,[25] be varied or revoked fall into two categories: **10.14**

- the original order was made on the basis of erroneous information (whether given accidentally or not); or
- subsequent events, which were unforeseen at the time it was made, have destroyed the basis on which the original order was made.[26]

---

[21] *Ibid*, at [19].

[22] *Ibid*, at [25].

[23] Even under the old test, an order may be revised if the order was made on a false basis: whilst *obiter*, see Mann J's comments in *Business Environment Bow Lane v Deanwater Estates Ltd* [2009] EWHC 2014 (Ch), at [40]. See, in a context other than costs, *Lloyds Investments (Scandinavia) Ltd v Ager-Hanssen* [2003] EWHC 1740 and *Collier v Williams* [2006] EWCA Civ 20). Bernard Livesey QC varied an order after learning that the court had been misled as to the financial positions of the parties and as to who was benefiting from the litigation: *Latimer Management Consultants Ltd v Ellingham Investments Ltd* [2006] EWHC 3662 (Ch). Another example is where a legally aided party's financial circumstances changed in such a way as to make it appropriate to vary the order so as to remove a prohibition against immediate enforcement: *Deg-Deutsche Investitions und Entwicklungsgesellschaft mbH v Koshy* [2001] EWCA Civ 79.

[24] As to the finality of the order, see *Forbes-Smith v Forbes-Smith and Chadwick* [1901] P 258, CA; disapproved in *Aiden Shipping Co Ltd v Interbulk Ltd* [1986] 2 All ER 409, at 412, but on a point that was different from the issue in hand—namely, whether a costs order can be regarded as being final.

[25] The editors of the White Book say that the power exists—see The White Book 2017, at para 3.1.12—but for the reasons set out below it is doubtful if that power exists in relation to orders for costs.

[26] The editors of the White Book quote *Roult v North West Strategic Health Authority* [2010] EWCA Civ 444 as authority for the proposition stated.

Even where such facts are established, it is doubtful that they would afford the court the power to vary or revoke a final costs order (other than in cases of fraud—see 10.16). In particular, there are powerful public policy reasons that favour notions of finality[27] and, in any event, a judge may not hear an appeal from themselves.[28]

10.15 Whilst it is fair to record the fact that there have been cases in which the court has varied a final costs order[29] or has proceeded on the basis that such a power exists,[30] this has usually been in circumstances in which the court has heard little argument on the point. In contrast, Mr M H Rosen QC (sitting as a deputy judge of the High Court) said—after having reviewed a large number of authorities—that CPR, r 3.1(7), does not give the court the power to revoke or vary a final costs order:

> 'Left to myself, were it necessary for me to decide the question of jurisdiction, I would hold as a matter of law that CPR 3.1(7) is not applicable in the case of final orders. The position in principle and practice prior to CPR 3.1(7)—and with continuing currency and emphasis thereafter—is that the only way in which final orders can be challenged, the court itself being *functus officio* once it has made final orders, save in exceptional circumstances where it has retained jurisdiction and power over the performance of those final orders, is, notwithstanding allegations of fraud, by way of an appeal or by way of separate fresh proceeding seeking to set aside an order or final orders and judgments as induced by reason of false representations, which would require, of course, pleadings and Part 7 processes—disclosure, witness statements and trial involving cross-examination and the like.'[31]

Technically, Mr Rosen's comments were *obiter*, but even if he were wrong, other than in cases of fraud, it would be difficult to envisage circumstances in which it would be appropriate to seek to vary or revoke a final costs order rather than to appeal.

10.16 In cases of orders obtained by fraud, the court may set aside the order,[32] but it would generally be necessary to fully particularise the allegations of fraud in new proceedings.[33]

Interim orders regarding costs and relating to costs

10.17 Not all orders that have a bearing on costs are final orders. In particular, orders that do not finally decide any substantive issues between the parties will be interim orders.[34] For example, orders for payment of costs on account or orders regarding allocation to track would be interim orders.

10.18 The mere fact that an order is an interim order does not mean that a party who is dissatisfied with it may have a second bite at the cherry. Estoppel may operate to prevent this

---

27 See, eg, *GNR v Mossop* [1855] 17 CB 130.

28 *Roult v North West Strategic Health Authority* [2009] EWCA Civ 444; see also *Customs & Excise Commissioners v Anchor Foods Ltd (No 3)*, The Times, 28 September 1999, Ch D, in which Neuberger J rejected the notion that the court should go behind its own costs order and act as an appellant court.

29 See, eg, *Latimer v Ellingham Investments & Anor* [2007] 1 WLR 2569.

30 See, eg, *Twin Benefits Ltd v Barker* [2017] EWHC 1882 (Ch), at [32].

31 See *Clutterbuck v A* [2017] EWHC 1127 (Ch), at [61]; Mr Rosen QC cited *GNR v Mossop* [1855] 17 CB 130 and *Enron (Thrace) v Clapp* [2005] EWCA Civ 1511.

32 Whilst on a topic other than costs orders, see *Sharland v Sharland* [2015] UKSC 60, in which the Supreme Court restated the principle that 'fraud unravels all'.

33 See *Jonesco v Beard* [1930] AC 298. See also *Kuwait Airways Corpn v Iraqi Airways Co (No 2)* [2001] 1 WLR 429, HL; *Jonesco v Beard* [1930] AC 298; *Enron (Thrace) v Clapp* [2005] EWCA Civ 1511.

34 *Prestney v Colchester Corpn* (1883) 24 Ch D 376, CA, at 384.

(see 23.26), but even where this is not the case there must be good grounds for making an application to vary or revoke.[35] In particular, the power under CPR, r 3.1(7), may not be used as an alternative means by which an order may, in effect, be appealed.[36]

Rix LJ—having reviewed the authorities—gave the following guidance: **10.19**

> '(i) Despite occasional references to a possible distinction between jurisdiction and discretion in the operation of CPR 3.1(7), there is in all probability no line to be drawn between the two. The rule is apparently broad and unfettered, but considerations of finality, the undesirability of allowing litigants to have two bites at the cherry, and the need to avoid undermining the concept of appeal, all push towards a principled curtailment of an otherwise apparently open discretion. ...
>
> (ii) ... [T]he jurisprudence has laid down firm guidance as to the primary circumstances in which the discretion may, as a matter of principle, be appropriately exercised, namely normally only (a) where there has been a material change of circumstances since the order was made, or (b) where the facts on which the original decision was made were (innocently or otherwise) misstated.
>
> [...]
>
> (iv) [T]here is room for debate in any particular case as to whether and to what extent, in the context of principle (b) in (ii) above, misstatement may include omission as well as positive misstatement, or concern argument as distinct from facts. In my judgment, this debate is likely ultimately to be a matter for the exercise of discretion in the circumstances of each case.
>
> (v) Similarly, questions may arise as to whether the misstatement (or omission) is conscious or unconscious; and whether the facts (or arguments) were known or unknown, knowable or unknowable. These, as it seems to me, are also factors going to discretion: but where the facts or arguments are known or ought to have been known as at the time of the original order, it is unlikely that the order can be revisited, and that must be still more strongly the case where the decision not to mention them is conscious or deliberate.
>
> [...]
>
> (vii) The cases considered above suggest that the successful invocation of the rule is rare. Exceptional is a dangerous and sometimes misleading word: however, such is the interest of justice in the finality of a court's orders that it ought normally to take something out of the ordinary to lead to variation or revocation of an order, especially in the absence of a change of circumstances in an interlocutory situation.'[37]

Thus there is no doubt that considerations of finality militate against an unrestrained exercise of the power under CPR, r 3.1(7). The applicant would generally need to be able to show either that: **10.20**

- there has been a material change of circumstances since the order was made; or
- the facts on which the original decision was made were (innocently or otherwise) misstated.

Rix LJ went on to make it clear that if an application needs to be made, delay may count against the applicant.

---

[35] See *Chanel Ltd v FW Woolworth & Co Ltd* [1981] 1 WLR 485; *Woodhouse v Consignia Plc* [2002] EWCA Civ 275.

[36] *Collier v Williams* [2006] EWCA Civ 20, at [120].

[37] *Tibbles v SIG Plc (t/a Asphaltic Roofing Supplies)* [2012] EWCA Civ 518, at [39].

10.21 Whilst there is no binding authority on the point, it probably remains the case that it would be wrong to review interim orders retrospectively on the basis of the outcome of the claim.[38]

10.22 For the avoidance of doubt, if the order were obtained by fraud, it would generally be permissible for an interim order to be varied or revoked.[39]

Orders that contain a provision that there be liberty to apply

10.23 Whilst rare, costs orders may be made that contain a provision that there be liberty to apply. Where this happens, the court making the order will continue to be siesed of the matter.[40]

Deemed orders for costs

10.24 Unless the CPR provide otherwise, the court has no power to set aside or vary an order that has been deemed to be made by the operation of the Rules.[41] The CPR provide otherwise where the deemed order arises out of discontinuance[42] or non-payment of court fees,[43] so the bar against revocation and variation of a deemed order applies only to orders deemed to be made as a result of acceptance of a CPR Part 36 offer.

The Court of Appeal in cases of real injustice

10.25 In cases of real injustice, the Court of Appeal has a residual jurisdiction to review an order,[44] but that jurisdiction is exercised only very rarely and has never been exercised solely in relation to costs.

Procedural issues

10.26 The parties may apply to set aside or vary an order, as may a non-party (such as a funder) who is directly affected by the order.[45]

Setting Aside Consent Orders for Costs

10.27 Where an order has been made by consent, it may be set aside on any ground that would undermine a compromise itself. CPR, r 3.1(7), is applicable to case management decisions and therefore does not apply where the order was based upon a final settlement agreed between the parties.[46] Whilst most do not relate to orders for costs, there are case examples of orders being set aside by reason of them being obtained by misrepresentation,[47] duress[48]

38 *Compagnie Noga D'Importation et D'Exportation SA v Abacha* [2003] EWCA Civ 1101.
39 Whilst not an example relating to costs, see *Islamic Investment Company of the Gulf (Bahamas) Ltd v Symphony Gems NV & Ors* [2014] EWHC 3777 (Comm).
40 *Russell-Cooke Trust Co v Prentis* [2002] EWHC 1435 (Ch).
41 See *Lahey v Pirelli Tyres Ltd* [2007] EWCA Civ 91, at [18], in which Dyson LJ approved the comments of Park J in *Walker Residential Ltd v Davis & Anor* [2005] EWHC 3483 (Ch), at [49].
42 See CPR, r 38.6(1).
43 See CPR, r 3.7(4)(b)(ii).
44 *Taylor v Lawrence* [2002] EWCA Civ 90.
45 See CPR, r 40.9.
46 *Roult v North West Strategic Health Authority* [2009] EWCA Civ 444.
47 *Gilbert v Endean* (1878) 9 Ch D 259, CA.
48 *Cumming v Ince* (1847) 11 QB 112.

and mutual mistake of fact.[49] Neuberger J has confirmed that, in so far as costs are concerned, the jurisdiction may be exercised only in exceptional circumstances.[50] Orders may also be set aside where they have been obtained without authority;[51] the fact that authority may have been given as a result of negligent legal advice would not be a ground for setting aside a consent order.[52] Likewise, a compromise based on a mistake of law would not usually be set aside for that reason.[53] A factor that the court will take into account when deciding whether to set a consent order aside is whether the application to set aside has been made promptly.[54] Another relevant factor is whether the order has been sealed:[55] once the order has been perfected, the judge making the order is *functus officio*[56] and should play no further role in respect of that order.[57]

[49] *Huddersfield Banking Co Ltd v Henry Lister & Son Ltd* [1895] 2 Ch 273, CA.

[50] *Centrehigh Ltd (t/a Shono UK) v Amen* (unreported), 18 July 2001, Ch D; see also *Customs and Excise Commissioners v Anchor Foods Ltd (No 3)*, The Times, 28 September 1999, Ch D.

[51] See, eg, *Shepherd v Robinson* [1919] 1 KB 474, CA.

[52] *Tibbs v Dick* [1999] 2 FCR 322, CA.

[53] *Holsworthy UDC v Holsworthy RDC* [1907] 2 Ch 62.

[54] *Watt v Assets Co; Bain v Assets Co* [1905] AC 317, HL.

[55] *Huddersfield Banking Co Ltd v Henry Lister & Son Ltd* [1895] 2 Ch 273, CA.

[56] This means that the judge has 'performed their office', in which case the judge has no ongoing legal authority because their duties have been performed.

[57] *Re Suffield v Watts, ex parte Brown* (1888) 20 QBD 693, as considered in *Centrehigh Ltd (t/a Shono UK) v Amen* (unreported), 18 July 2001, Ch D.

11

ORDERS FOR COSTS (COSTS-ONLY PROCEEDINGS)

11.01 This chapter deals with the following topics:

- history and policy (11.03);
- jurisdiction and application (11.06);
- procedure (11.07);
- the assessment (11.25);
- costs of costs-only proceedings (11.26); and
- the wording of the provisions that govern costs-only proceedings (11.29).

11.02 Costs-only proceedings are a mechanism, governed by Civil Procedure Rules (CPR), r 46.14, and Practice Direction (PD) 46, para 9, by which parties may obtain an order for costs to be assessed without the need to issue proceedings in the substantive claim. The procedure allows the recovery of those costs that would have been recoverable in the proceedings, had they been issued.[1]

History and Policy

11.03 The facility to bring costs-only proceedings was created on 3 July 2000.[2] Prior to this, a claimant would have been faced with the prospect of issuing a Part 7 claim (either on the original claim or on a compromise) solely for the purposes of obtaining a costs order. This, for obvious reasons, was undesirable and wasteful of resources.

11.04 Almost as soon as the facility came into being, problems arose. In December 2000, Senior Master Hurst (writing extrajudicially) said that both sides were misusing the new procedure: receiving parties were too eager to use the new procedure, whilst paying parties were defensively qualifying all of their offers as being 'for the purpose of negotiation only'.[3] These problems were, however, short-lived. Between the early 2000s and 2013, the only major problem with the costs-only procedure was that it had to be consensual[4] and this afforded the opportunity for some defendants to act in an obstructive manner.

---

[1] *Callery v Gray* [2001] EWCA Civ 1117, at [54], *per* Woolf CJ.

[2] See the Civil Procedure (Amendment No 3) Rules 2000 (SI 2000/13), r 17.

[3] See Hurst, P, 'Guiding Light Shines Down on Costs', *Law Society Gazette*, 18 December 2000.

[4] CPR, r 44.12A(4)(b) (as it was before 1 April 2013). The Costs Practice Direction (CPD), art 36.2, has no applicability because it relates to putative compromises of the costs that are claimed, as opposed to putative compromises leading to an entitlement to costs.

On 1 April 2013, the costs-only provisions were amended.[5] In addition to being moved from CPR, Part 44, into CPR, Part 46, certain other changes were made, the second of which addressed the problem referred to above. **11.05**

- **Costs-only proceedings became mandatory** In its original form, the facility to bring costs-only proceedings was not mandatory in the sense that there was nothing to stop a receiving party from bringing a Part 7 claim either for the damages originally sought or for an agreed amount of costs.[6] Since 1 April 2013, however, where the parties have reached an agreement on all issues save for the amount of costs payable, the costs-only procedure *must* be used (see 11.06).[7]
- **Loss of right to veto costs-only proceedings** The need for costs-only proceedings to be consensual was removed, this being achieved by the right of a defendant to veto the procedure being abrogated.[8] Where an application is contested, the court is now able to adjudicate on the matter and give directions (see 11.18).
- **Loss of explicit provision that either party could bring costs-only proceedings** There used to be a rule that expressly provided that either party could bring costs-only proceedings.[9] This is no longer so, but—whilst the contrary is arguable (see 11.08)—it is doubtful if this has deprived defendants of the ability to bring costs-only proceedings.[10]

Jurisdiction and Application

The costs-only procedure applies where—in the absence of proceedings having already been commenced—the parties to a dispute have reached an agreement on all issues (including which party is to pay the costs) that is made or confirmed in writing, but have failed to agree the amount of those costs.[11] Where these conditions are met, the use of the costs-only procedure is the only procedure that may be used to bring the matter before the court for an assessment.[12] **11.06**

Procedure

Costs-only proceedings are brought using the Part 8 procedure.[13] Separate provisions relate to low-value road traffic accident claims.[14] **11.07**

---

[5] The Civil Procedure (Amendment) Rules 2013 (SI 2013/262).

[6] See the now-revoked CPD, art 17.11.

[7] See CPR, r 46.14(3); PD 46, para 9.12.

[8] PD 47, para 9.10.

[9] See the pre-1 April 2013 version of CPR, r 44.12A(2).

[10] Support for this can be obtained from the fact that Sharp LJ made no mention of this in *Tasleem v Beverly* [2013] EWCA Civ 1805, at [14].

[11] See CPR, r 46.14(1).

[12] See CPR, r 46.14(2).

[13] CPR, r 46.14(1) and (2).

[14] CPR, r 45.29, reads as follows: '(1) This rule sets out the procedure where a) the parties to a dispute have reached an agreement on all issues (including which party is to pay the costs) which is made or confirmed in writing; but (b) they have failed to agree the amount of those costs; and (c) proceedings have been started under Part 8 in accordance with Practice Direction 8B. (2) Either party may make an application for the court to determine the costs. (3) Where an application is made under this rule the court will assess the costs in accordance with rule 45.22 or rule 45.25. (4) Rule 44.5 (amount of costs where costs are payable pursuant to a contract) does not apply to an application under this rule.'

Who can bring a claim?

11.08 As mentioned above (see 11.05), there used to be an express rule that made it clear that either party could bring costs-only proceedings.[15] This is no longer so. It has been suggested that only receiving parties are now permitted to bring costs-only proceedings; this—it is said—is because PD 46, para 9.5, refers to the need 'to prove the defendant's agreement to *pay* costs' (emphasis added), which implies that defendants will be paying parties.[16] Paying parties may have just as much reason as receiving parties to have costs assessed, so perhaps the better analysis is that PD 46, para 9.5, is referring to the defendant in the original dispute. In any event, whilst no more than persuasive, Sharp LJ made no mention of such a restriction when she commented on the differences between the old and the new regimes.[17]

Claim form

11.09 As with any Part 8 claim, formal pleadings are not required.[18] The claim form must contain or be accompanied by the agreement that entitles the receiving party to costs;[19] this includes copies of the documents on which the claimant relies to prove the defendant's agreement to pay costs.[20]

11.10 The claim form ought to contain the following information.[21]

- **Remedy** It should state the remedy sought (that is, that the Part 8 claimant seeks an order for costs to be assessed) and the legal basis for the claim to that remedy.[22]
- **Dispute** It should identify the claim or dispute to which the agreement to pay costs relates.[23]
- **Agreement** It should state the date and terms of the agreement on which the claimant relies.[24]
- **Draft order** It should set out or have attached to it a draft of the order that the claimant seeks.[25]
- **Amount** It should state the amount of the costs claimed.[26]
- **Fixed costs** Where CPR, Part 45, Section II, applies, it should state details of any disbursements or success fee that the receiving party wishes to claim[27]—including any details of the particular feature of the dispute that necessitated a claim under CPR, r 45.12(2)(c).[28] If the receiving party seeks costs that exceed fixed costs, the claim form

---

[15] See the pre-1 April 2013 version of CPR, r 44.12A(2).
[16] See Underwood, K, 'Commencing Costs Only Proceedings', https://kerryunderwood.wordpress.com/ (accessed 15 August 2018). It has been suggested that this reflects the fact that the number of paying parties who wish to bring costs-only proceedings is very small.
[17] See *Tasleem v Beverly* [2013] EWCA Civ 1805, at [14].
[18] CPR, r 8.9(a)(ii).
[19] CPR, r 46.14(4).
[20] PD 46, para 9.5; CPR, r 8.5.
[21] PD 46, para 9.3; CPR, rr 8.2 46.14(3).
[22] See CPR, r 8.2(b)(ii); see also PD 46, para 9.3, which expressly draws attention to CPR, r 8.2(b)(ii).
[23] PD 46, para 9.3(a).
[24] PD 46, para 9.3(b).
[25] PD 46, para 9.3(c).
[26] PD 46, para 9.3(a).
[27] PD 46, para 9.2.
[28] PD 45, para 2.9.

should state details of the exceptional circumstances that the receiving party considers justifies the additional costs.[29]

- **Representative claims** If the claimant is claiming (or the defendant is sued) in a representative capacity, it should state what that capacity is.[30]

Whilst there is no authority directly on the point, by analogy with litigation other than costs procedural errors will not necessarily lead to the claim being struck out.[31] **11.11**

Alternatives

As has been said in 11.06, where the costs-only procedure applies, its use is mandatory. The key point is that where the only outstanding issue is the amount of costs, that procedure must be used. If, however, a claimant needs to sue on the other aspects of the claim, they may do so. Moreover, if the claimant wishes to sue for an agreed amount of costs, or if there has been no agreement to pay costs and the claimant seeks a discretionary order for costs, they may bring a claim. Any such claim may be brought either by the Part 7 procedure or by the Part 8 procedure.[32] **11.12**

Venue

The claim form should not be issued in the High Court unless the dispute to which the agreement relates was of such a value or type that, had proceedings been begun, they would have been commenced in the High Court.[33] If the claim form needs to be issued in the Royal Courts of Justice (RCJ), it should be issued in the Senior Courts Costs Office (SCCO).[34] **11.13**

Fixed costs

Whilst the costs that are the subject of costs-only proceedings are to be assessed, that assessment may reflect provisions for fixed costs. In particular, it is not possible to avoid the operation of CPR, Part 45, Section II, by issuing costs-only proceedings in the hope that the court will assess the costs on the basis of what is reasonable rather than on the basis of fixed costs because the court is expressly given the power to make an order that fixed costs are paid, where this is appropriate.[35] **11.14**

The fixed costs regimes under Part 45 are tightly integrated with the costs-only provisions.[36] Where the claimant is claiming an amount of costs that exceeds the amount of the fixed recoverable costs, they must state details of the exceptional circumstances that are said to justify the additional costs.[37] That party must also include details of any relevant disbursements or success fees.[38] If the disbursements fall within the ambit of CPR, r 45.12(2)(c) **11.15**

---

29 PD 45, para 2.8.
30 CPR, r 8.2(d) and (e).
31 See, eg, *Parnall v Hurst*, The Times, 10 July 2003, in which HHJ Peter Langan QC declined to strike out a Part 8 claim where the evidence in support had not been served along with the claim form.
32 PD 46, para 9.12.
33 PD 46, para 9.1.
34 PD 46, para 9.2.
35 CPR, r 46.14(5). See also *Solomon v Cromwell Group Plc* [2011] EWCA Civ 1584.
36 See, eg, CPR, rr 45.9(1)(a) and 45.29.
37 PD 45, para 2.8.
38 *Ibid.*

(that is, disbursements that have arisen due to a particular feature of the dispute), the claimant must give details of the particular feature of the dispute and must explain why the expenditure was necessary.[39] Further details may be found at 50.83 and 50.96.

Uncontested claims

11.16 When the time for filing the acknowledgement of service has expired, the claimant may ask the court to make an order in the terms of the claim.[40] This is often done by way of a letter. The claimant may not make such a request if the defendant has filed an acknowledgement of service stating that they intend to contest the claim or to seek a different order.[41]

Contested claims

11.17 A claim will be treated as opposed if the defendant files an acknowledgement of service stating that they intend to contest the making of an order for costs or to seek a different remedy.[42] It will not be treated as opposed, however, if the defendant files an acknowledgement of service stating merely that they dispute the amount claimed.[43]

11.18 If a costs-only claim is opposed, the defendant must file a witness statement in accordance with CPR, r 8.5(3), explaining what their case is.[44] The court will then give directions including, if appropriate, a direction that the claim shall continue as if it were a Part 7 claim.

Consent orders

11.19 If, as is often the case, the parties agree the draft order, the terms of that draft need not be the same as those sought in the claim itself. Where the costs-only proceedings are dealt with by consent, the provisions in CPR, r 40.6, apply (see 7.68).[45]

Allocation (or absence thereof) and smaller claims

11.20 Costs-only claims will not generally be allocated to a track; in particular, they will not be deemed to be allocated to the multitrack.[46]

Disposal

11.21 The court may make an order for the payment of costs to be determined by assessment or, where appropriate, for the payment of fixed costs.[47] The old rule that the court must dismiss the claim if it is opposed[48] no longer applies (although the court still has the power to dismiss a claim, should that be appropriate).[49] It is not clear whether the court has a

---

39 PD 45, para 2.9.

40 PD 46, para 9.7.

41 *Ibid.*

42 This used to be made clear by CPD, art 17.9(1)(a); PD 46 does not expressly refer to this point, but there is no reason why the court would deal with the matter any differently as a result.

43 PD 46, para 9.10.

44 PD 47, para 9.10.

45 PD 46, para 9.8.

46 See PD 46, para 9.11, which disapplies CPR, r 8.9.

47 See CPR, r 46.14(5).

48 See the old CPR, r 44.12A(4)(a) and (4)(b).

49 PD 46, para 9.6.

jurisdiction to make an order—other than by consent—that a payment on account of the costs to be assessed is made in costs-only proceedings.[50]

For the avoidance of doubt, a costs judge or district judge has jurisdiction to hear and decide any issue that may arise in a claim issued under CPR, r 46.14, irrespective of the amount of the costs claimed or of the value of the claim to which the agreement to pay costs relates.[51] **11.22**

Basis upon which costs are payable

There used to be a requirement that the Part 8 claim form had to state whether the costs were claimed on the standard or indemnity basis;[52] this is no longer the case, presumably because it would almost never be the case that a party would agree to pay costs on the indemnity basis. That said, PD 46, para 9.4, provides that unless the court orders otherwise or unless CPR, Part 45, Section II, applies, the costs will be treated as being claimed on the standard basis.[53] If this provision is there to take account of the possibility that a party would agree to pay costs on the indemnity basis, then it is unobjectionable, but if—as could well be the case—it is intended to imply that the court has the *discretion* to make such an award, it is likely to be *ultra vires* because a practice direction is not a source of law and would not be able to confer the power to contradict the terms of the agreement to pay costs. **11.23**

For the avoidance of doubt, the fact that there has been agreement as to the incidence of costs does not mean that costs are payable under contract in the sense that CPR, r 46.5, applies.[54] Therefore there is no basis for saying that costs are automatically payable pursuant to contract on indemnity basis. **11.24**

The Assessment

Where costs are ordered to be assessed, the general rule is that this should be by detailed assessment.[55] It used to be the case that the only type of assessment that a claimant could ask for was a detailed assessment. This is no longer held to be so because PD 47, para 9.9, provides that where an order for costs is made following a hearing and where the court is in a position to do so, it should assess costs summarily. Given the fact that most costs-only proceedings are disposed on the papers, this provision is of limited practical benefit. If a claimant were to want a summary assessment, they would be well advised to mention this in the claim form. **11.25**

Costs

The costs of the assessment will be dealt with as per the costs of any other assessment. What follows relates to the costs of the costs-only proceedings rather than to the costs of the assessment. **11.26**

---

[50] *Banchio v Lai* [2003] EWHC 9038 (Costs).
[51] See PD 46, para 9.6.
[52] See CPD, art 17.3(5).
[53] PD 46, para 9.4.
[54] CPR, r 46.14(7).
[55] PD 46, para 9.9.

11.27 Costs-only proceedings are distinct from detailed assessment proceedings and, as such, they are to be dealt with separately and in accordance with CPR, r 44.2.[56] In view of this, Sharp LJ has said that care should be taken to ensure that matters properly encompassed within the detailed assessment and default regime are not claimed as part of the costs-only proceedings.[57]

11.28 The following miscellaneous points may be made.

- **Provisional assessments** It has been suggested that where costs-only proceedings lead to provisional assessment, the costs of the costs-only proceedings are included within the cap on costs that applies to such assessments. Whilst it is no more than the editor's opinion, that argument seems to be misguided—for the simple reason that the costs-only proceedings are not part of the detailed assessment proceedings.[58]
- **Default costs certificates** The fact that costs-only proceedings have ultimately resulted in a default costs certificate being issued does not deprive the court of the jurisdiction to award costs of those proceedings.[59]
- **Small claims** The small claims provisions do not apply to costs-only proceedings because the claim is treated as if it had not been allocated.[60]
- **Part 47 offers** Where a Part 47 offer is for the costs of a claim that settled without the need for the issue of proceedings, it will not by default be taken to include the costs of any subsequent cost-only proceedings.[61]
- **Part 36 offers** Where a Part 36 offer is accepted, CPR, r 47.20(7), expressly provides that the detailed assessment proceedings are to be regarded as being an independent claim. As such, it must follow that any such offer will not include the costs of the costs-only proceedings and that the court has the power to deal with these under the provisions of Part 36.
- **Failure to comply with the costs-only procedure** Where a party fails to follow the mandatory costs-only procedure, CPR, r 46.14(6), provides that the party will not be allowed costs greater than those that would have been allowed to that party had the procedure been followed. The rule goes on to say that the court may award the other party the costs of the proceedings up to the point at which an order for the payment of costs is made.

The Relevant Wording

11.29 CPR, r 46.14, reads as follows:

> '14(1) This rule applies where—
> (a) the parties to a dispute have reached an agreement on all issues (including which party is to pay the costs) which is made or confirmed in writing; but

56 There is no fixed costs regime relating to cost-only proceedings. Sharp LJ has noted this and suggested that this is a matter that may merit examination by the Civil Procedure Rules Committee: see *Tasleem v Beverly* [2013] EWCA Civ 1805, at [23].

57 *Ibid.*

58 Whilst on a slightly different point, see *ibid*, at [18], *per* Sharp LJ.

59 See *ibid.*

60 PD 46, para 9.11, which overrides CPR, r 8.9(c).

61 *Crosbie v Munroe* [2003] EWCA Civ 350.

(b) they have failed to agree the amount of those costs; and
(c) no proceedings have been started.

(2) Where this rule applies, the procedure set out in this rule must be followed.

(3) Proceedings under this rule are commenced by issuing a claim form in accordance with Part 8.

(4) The claim form must contain or be accompanied by the agreement or confirmation.

(5) In proceedings to which this rule applies the court may make an order for the payment of costs the amount of which is to be determined by assessment and/or, where appropriate, for the payment of fixed costs.

(6) Where this rule applies but the procedure set out in this rule has not been followed by a party—
(a) that party will not be allowed costs greater than those that would have been allowed to that party had the procedure been followed; and
(b) the court may award the other party the costs of the proceedings up to the point where an order for the payment of costs is made.

(7) Rule 44.5 (amount of costs where costs are payable pursuant to a contract) does not apply to claims started under the procedure in this rule.'

PD 46, para 9, provides as follows: **11.30**

'9.1 A claim form under rule 46.14 should not be issued in the High Court unless the dispute to which the agreement relates was of such a value or type that proceedings would have been commenced in the High Court.

9.2 A claim form which is to be issued in the High Court at the Royal Courts of Justice will be issued in the Costs Office.

9.3 Attention is drawn to rule 8.2 (in particular to paragraph (b)(ii)) and to rule 46.14(3). The claim form must—
(a) identify the claim or dispute to which the agreement relates;
(b) state the date and terms of the agreement on which the claimant relies;
(c) set out or attach a draft of the order which the claimant seeks;
(d) state the amount of the costs claimed.

9.4 Unless the court orders otherwise or Section II of Part 45 applies the costs will be treated as being claimed on the standard basis.

9.5 The evidence required under rule 8.5 includes copies of the documents on which the claimant relies to prove the defendant's agreement to pay costs.

9.6 A costs judge has jurisdiction to hear and decide any issue which may arise in a claim issued under this rule irrespective of the amount of the costs claimed or of the value of the claim to which the agreement to pay costs relates. The court may make an order by consent under paragraph 9.8, or an order dismissing a claim under paragraph 9.10 below.

9.7 When the time for filing the defendant's acknowledgement of service has expired, the claimant may request in writing that the court make an order in the terms of the claim, unless the defendant has filed an acknowledgement of service stating the intention to contest the claim or to seek a different order.

9.8 Rule 40.6 applies where an order is to be made by consent. An order may be made by consent in terms which differ from those set out in the claim form.

9.9 Where costs are ordered to be assessed, the general rule is that this should be by detailed assessment. However when an order is made under this rule following a hearing and the court is in a position to summarily assess costs it should generally do so.

9.10 If the defendant opposes the claim the defendant must file a witness statement in accordance with rule 8.5(3). The court will then give directions including, if appropriate, a direction that the claim shall continue as if it were a Part 7 claim. A claim is not treated as opposed merely because the defendant disputes the amount of the claim for costs.

9.11 A claim issued under this rule may be dealt with without being allocated to a track. Rule 8.9 does not apply to claims issued under this rule.

9.12 Where there are other issues nothing in rule 46.14 prevents a person from issuing a claim form under Part 7 or Part 8 to sue on an agreement made in settlement of a dispute where that agreement makes provision for costs, nor from claiming in that case an order for costs or a specified sum in respect of costs but the "costs only" procedure in rule 46.14 must be used where the sole issue is the amount of costs.'

11.31 CPR, r 45, PDs 2.8 and 2.9 (which apply to fixed costs), provide:

'2.8 Costs-only proceedings are commenced using the procedure set out in rule 46.14. A claim form should be issued in accordance with Part 8. Where the claimant is claiming an amount of costs which exceed the amount of the fixed recoverable costs he must include on the claim form details of the exceptional circumstances which he considers justifies the additional costs.

2.9 The claimant must also include on the claim form details of any disbursements or success fee he wishes to claim. The disbursements that may be claimed are set out in rule 45.12(1). If the disbursement falls within 45.12(2)(c) (disbursements that have arisen due to a particular feature of the dispute) the claimant must give details of the particular feature of the dispute and why he considers the disbursement to be necessary.'

PART IV

ORDERS REGARDING COSTS

12

COSTS MANAGEMENT AND COST BUDGETING

This chapter deals with the following topics: **12.01**

- introduction (12.02);
- terminology (12.03);
- the history of costs management (12.04);
- jurisdiction (12.14):
  - prescribed jurisdiction (12.15);
  - discretionary jurisdiction (12.19);
- procedural issues (other than the making of costs management orders) (12.20):
  - Precedent H and its completion (12.21);
  - filing and exchanging budgets (12.43);
  - agreed budgets (12.48);
  - replying to budgets and budget discussion reports (12.51);
  - failure to file a budget (12.56);
  - costs management hearings (12.61);
  - the interaction between the budget and case management (12.63);
- costs management orders (12.65):
  - whether to make a costs management order (12.69);
  - the treatment of costs already incurred (12.84);
  - the exercise of discretion as to the level of the budget (12.87);
  - procedure after approval (12.104);
  - the treatment of interim applications (12.106);
  - amendments, revisions, etc (12.107);
- the costs of the budgeting exercise (12.130):
- the effect of the budget on the assessment of costs (12.137):
  - where a costs management order has been made and the incurred costs fall to be assessed (12.138);
  - where a costs management order has been made and costs are payable on the standard basis (12.140);
  - assessment on the indemnity basis and the relevance of the budget (12.166); and
  - where no costs management order has been made (12.169).

Introduction

12.02 Costs management—or costs budgeting as it is otherwise called—is the process of managing and ascertaining (but not assessing in advance) the reasonable and proportionate costs that are likely to be incurred in pursuing or defending a claim. Civil Procedure Rules (CPR), r 3.12(2), has this to say on the topic: 'The purpose of costs management is that the court should manage both the steps to be taken and the costs to be incurred by the parties to any proceedings so as to further the overriding objective.' Thus costs management is not a quantification that is carried out *in vacuo*; instead, it runs side by side with case management.

Terminology

12.03 The following points may be made about the relevant terminology (both defined and colloquial).

- **The meaning of 'budget'** The CPR defines the noun 'budget' as '[a]n estimate of the reasonable and proportionate costs (including disbursements) which a party intends to incur in the proceedings'.[1]
- **The meaning of 'budgeting'** The verb to 'budget' does not appear in the CPR, but it is used colloquially to refer to the judicial process of approving the budget.[2]
- **The meaning of 'costs management'** Costs management is the process of adjusting and approving costs yet to be incurred, this being distinguishable from assessment, which goes to the ascertainment of costs that have already been incurred.
- **The meaning of 'approval'** Approval and assessment are similar, but they are not the same. Assessment is the retrospective quantification of costs, whereas approval is a prospective exercise.
- **'Costs management order' (CMO)** A CMO is an order approving a costs budget (either as claimed or as adjusted).[3] It will (a) record the extent to which the budgeted costs are agreed between the parties, (b) in respect of those budgeted costs that are not agreed, record the court's approval after making appropriate revisions and (c) record the extent (if any) to which incurred costs are agreed.[4]
- **Types of hearing** Where a hearing is convened solely for the purpose of costs management (for example to approve a revised budget), it is referred to as a 'costs management conference'.[5] Where case management takes place at the same time, the hearing is referred to as a 'costs and case management hearing'.

---

[1] See the Glossary to the CPR.

[2] In Jackson, R, *Review of Civil Litigation Costs: Preliminary Report* (London: HMSO, 2009), ch 48, Sir Rupert Jackson said this: '3.5 What is costs budgeting? Costs budgeting is not a term found in the CPR. It is a term that has been derived from consultation papers and reviews that have taken place over the past decade. The essence of costs budgeting is that the costs of litigation are planned in advance; the litigation is then managed and conducted in such a way as to keep the costs within the budget.'

[3] CPR, r 3.15, echoing a similar provision in the Mercantile Pilot (PD 51G, para 1.2).

[4] See CPR, r 3.15(2).

[5] CPR, r 3.16(1).

The History of Costs Management

The Woolf reforms

Despite the fact that controlling costs was intended to be its central feature,[6] it is often said that the Woolf reforms (see 1.145) were a noticeable failure in so far as costs were concerned.[7] The main thrust of those reforms related to costs management via case management (that is, keeping costs under control by controlling the case itself).[8] Even before Lord Woolf had written his Final Report, however, it was recognised that there was a risk that this would not work. Writing in 1999, Professor Zuckerman (an Oxford academic) had this to say on the topic: **12.04**

> 'The new approach to the conduct of litigation [under the CPR], therefore, imposes a heavy burden on the parties' lawyers. They are expected to clear the ground of the dispute from ambiguities and marshall [*sic*] their evidence and arguments clearly and succinctly so that the field may be ready for judicial examination. However, this process of preparing the ground may be just as expensive, if not more expensive, than the present less exacting approach.'[9]

The Woolf Inquiry Team considered a number of suggested methods of dealing with this problem,[10] one of which was a process similar to modern-day costs management—namely, 'prospective budget setting'.[11] Lord Woolf rejected the 'radical proposal' of prospective budgeting[12] and instead focused on retrospective methods of controlling costs, such as a greater emphasis on conduct-based and issues-based costs orders[13] and the introduction of a test of proportionality for the purposes of assessment.[14] Other than case management, the only noticeable method of prospective costs control was a somewhat ineffective requirement to file estimates of costs.[15] **12.05**

---

[6] Indeed, in *Access to Justice: Final Report* (London: HMSO, 1996), ch 7, at para 5, Lord Woolf (speaking extrajudicially) said: 'Virtually all my recommendations are designed at least in part to tackle the problems of costs.'

[7] See, eg, Morgan QC, J, 'Costs Management: The Policy Background and the Law', Paper presented at a seminar on costs management, Royal College of Surgeons, 23 November 2010.

[8] Case management was 'a fundamental shift in the responsibility for the management of civil litigation in this country from litigants and their legal advisers to the courts': see Woolf, Access to Justice, Interim Report to the Lord Chancellor on the civil justice system in England and Wales (June 1995), ch 5, para 2.

[9] Zuckerman, AAD, 'Devices for Controlling the Cost of Litigation through Costs Taxation' (1996) 1 JILT, at para 3.

[10] These included fixed litigation costs relating to value, fixed fees relating to procedural activity and constraints on costs via professional obligations: *ibid*, at para 21 *et seq*.

[11] The inquiry team even went so far as to consider whether budget setting should apply between solicitor and client, as well as between opposing parties: *ibid*, at para 20.

[12] Lord Woolf did consider costs budgeting, but he ultimately rejected it for the following reasons: 'The paper occasioned a general outcry from the legal profession. Prospective budget-setting was seen as unworkable, unfair and likely to be abused by the creation of inflated budgets. The ability of judges to be involved in the hard detail of matters such as cost was generally doubted. The imposition of fixed fees, even relating only to *inter partes* costs, was seen as unrealistic and as interference with parties' rights to decide how to instruct their own lawyers.' (See Lord Woolf, *Access to Justice: Final Report* (London: HMSO, 1996), paras 16 and 17.)

[13] See, eg, *ibid*, ch 7, para 5; see also Lord Woolf, *Access to Justice: Interim Report to the Lord Chancellor on the Civil Justice System in England and Wales* (London: HMSO, 1995), ch 25, under 'Recommendations'.

[14] *Lownds v Home Office* [2002] EWCA 365.

[15] This was both between opposing parties via the CPR and between solicitor and client via professional obligations: Lord Woolf, *Access to Justice: Final Report* (London: HMSO, 1996), ch 7, at paras 7 and 28. Estimates between opposing parties were intended for purposes that were very different from budgeting: 'Estimates need not go into detail ... They would fall short of the radical proposals set out by Adrian Zuckerman in the issues paper. The estimates would be an indication to help the procedural judge decide the best course of action, rather than budgets which limited what parties could recover.'

The early days of the CPR

12.06 Almost immediately after the introduction of the CPR, estimates came to be regarded as being a toothless means of controlling costs.[16] This led, in 2003, to Dyson LJ (speaking judicially) inviting the Civil Procedure Rule Committee to revisit the issue of costs management:

> 'It seems to us that the prospective fixing of costs budgets is likely to achieve that objective [of controlling costs] far more effectively. The question of costs budgets was raised before the Civil Procedure Rule Committee in June 2001. It is contentious and important. The committee decided to explore the issue, but has not reached any conclusion about it. We invite the committee to re-examine the provisions relating to costs estimates to see whether they should be amended to make them more effective in the control of costs; and also to reach a conclusion on the issue of cost budgets.'[17]

12.07 Dyson LJ was not alone in holding this view: his remarks echoed *obiter* comments made by Latham LJ[18] as well as remarks made by the academic community.[19] The courts experimented with costs capping, but little came of that.

12.08 In about 2005, the Costs Practice Direction (CPD) was revised so as to strengthen the provisions relating to estimates,[20] but even then the practical effect of estimates on the costs of litigation was peripheral at best. Jeremy Morgan QC (one of the first barristers to specialise in the law of costs) had this say on the topic:

> '[The use of estimates] was watered down in practice ... In the writer's experience even the mandatory requirements have very often been ignored: on numerous occasions when consulted on a costs claim at the end of a case he has asked for the estimates produced ... only to be told that one side, or both sides, did not produce one at all. Similarly the discretionary power to call for estimates at any stage has not been greatly used ... In the author's view the tightening up of the CPD has had little practical effect on the allowance on assessment.'[21]

Sir Rupert Jackson's Preliminary Report

12.09 It was not until the end of the next decade that the issue of costs management started to move up the agenda. Sir Rupert Jackson was asked by the Master of the Rolls to carry out a review to 'promote access to justice at proportionate cost'[22] (see 1.171). Perhaps because of his experiences as a judge in the Technology and Construction Court, Jackson was attracted by the notion of 'project management'—that is, an analysis that had previously

---

16 See the views of the circuit judge as recorded in *Leigh v Michelin Tyre plc* [2003] EWCA Civ 1766.

17 *Ibid*, at [34].

18 See *Griffiths v Solutia (UK) Ltd* [2001] EWCA Civ 736, at [29].

19 See, eg, *Zuckerman on Civil Procedure* (2nd edn, London: Sweet & Maxwell, 2006), ch 26; Zuckerman, AAD, 'Editorial Note' (2007) 26 CJQ 271; Peysner, J, 'Predictability and Budgeting' (2004) 23 CJQ 15.

20 The 40th update to the CPR came into force on 1 October 2005. It amended Section VI of the CPD. The court was given an express power to seek an explanation as to why costs had increased by 20 per cent or more from a prior estimate and if the receiving party was not able to provide an explanation or if the paying party was able to demonstrate reliance on the prior estimate, then the court was able to rely on the prior estimate as evidence that the costs incurred were either unreasonable or disproportionate.

21 Morgan QC, J, 'Costs Management: The Policy Background and the Law', Paper presented at a seminar on costs management, Royal College of Surgeons, 23 November 2010.

22 Jackson, R, *Review of Civil Litigation Costs: Preliminary Report* (London: HMSO, 2009), ch 1, at para 2.1.

been advocated by Professor Peysner (then an academic at Nottingham Trent University).[23] Jackson defined costs management in the following terms: 'The essence of costs management is that the costs of litigation are planned in advance; the litigation is then managed and conducted in such a way as to keep the costs within the budget.'[24]

Jackson's Preliminary Report was published in 2009 (see 1.173), following which the concept of costs management was put out for consultation. In particular, the legal professions were asked to consider the question of whether a budget should effectively constitute a cap in certain forms of litigation. Numerous meetings with stakeholders took place, as did a number of organised semi-public meetings.[25] In addition to this, there were two pilots, the Mercantile Pilot and the Defamation Pilot.[26] There were teething problems,[27] but most commentators agree that the Mercantile Pilot was a considerable success (not least because of the enthusiasm of Judge Simon Brown QC, a circuit judge in Birmingham).[28] This may have been because that pilot was not mandatory and lawyers who practised in the Mercantile Court were already well equipped to deal with costs management. The **12.10**

[23] *Ibid*, ch 48, at para 3.5, referring to Peysner, J, 'Predictability and Budgeting' (2004) 23 CJQ 15.

[24] Jackson, R, *Review of Civil Litigation Costs: Preliminary Report* (London: HMSO, 2009), ch 48, at para 3.5.

[25] Morgan QC, J, 'Costs Management: The Policy Background and the Law', Paper presented at a seminar on costs management, Royal College of Surgeons, 23 November 2010.

[26] The first pilot, the Mercantile Pilot (formally known as the Costs Management in Mercantile Courts and Technology and Construction Courts Scheme), ran in all mercantile courts and technology and construction courts. It applied to cases in which the first case management conference was heard on or after 1 October 2011 (PD 51G, para 1.1). The Mercantile Pilot began as a voluntary scheme on 1 June 2009 and was due to run until 30 September 2012, but in fact ran much longer than that (see Jackson, R, *Review of Civil Litigation Costs: Final Report*, London: HMSO, 2010, ch 40, at para 21). The pilot was expressly stated to be without prejudice to the court's general management powers under CPR, r 3.1 (PD 51G, para 1.4). Those litigants who took part in the Mercantile Pilot were required to complete an estimate of costs that was much more detailed than CPR Precedent H. At each hearing the judge would—either by agreement between the parties or after argument—record approval or disapproval of each side's budget for each step in the litigation. Initial take-up was slow, but by 2010 (ie when Sir Rupert Jackson published his Final Report), 11 cases had been included within the pilot, the value of which cases ranged from £50,000 to £450,000, with costs budgets in those cases ranging from £20,000 to £158,000 on the claimants' side and £18,000 to £121,000 on the defendants' side.

The Defamation Pilot, formally known as the Defamation Proceedings Costs Management Scheme, was run in the Royal Courts of Justice and the Manchester District Registry. It applied to cases in which there were allegations of libel, slander and/or malicious falsehood (PD 51D, paras 1.1 and 1.2), but only where the claim was started on or after 1 October 2009 (PD 51D, para 1.1). It too was due to run until 30 September 2012 (PD 51D, para 1.1), but was extended. It started on 1 October 2009, but, unlike the Mercantile Pilot, it was mandatory from the start (see Jackson, R, *Review of Civil Litigation Costs: Final Report*, London: HMSO, 2010, ch 40, at para 3.1). The way in which the Defamation Pilot operated has been described as 'the more draconian' of the two because (in contrast to the Mercantile Pilot) unless there were exceptional circumstances, the court would not approve as reasonable and proportionate any costs claimed that did not fall within the budget.

For a summary of the procedure, see Morgan QC, J, 'Costs Management: The Policy Background and the Law', Paper presented at a seminar on costs management, Royal College of Surgeons, 23 November 2010.

[27] Many solicitors did not like filling in the budget form because it took them, on average, about two-and-a-half hours. That said, some solicitors commented that they found it a useful exercise because it gave them better insight into the issue of costs: Jackson, R, *Review of Civil Litigation Costs: Final Report* (London: HMSO, 2010), ch 40.

[28] Jackson, R, *Review of Civil Litigation Costs: Final Report* (London: HMSO, 2010), ch 40, at para 2.9, records Judge Simon Brown QC as a strong supporter of costs budgeting, commenting that budgets are 'wonderful tools for both Costs and Case proper management—indeed essential'. In particular, he commented favourably on the impact on clients of knowing their own and their opponents' costs.

Defamation Pilot was more controversial, possibly because it was mandatory.[29] Judges gave a mixed response in that whilst they found costs management to be a useful aid to case management, they also noted that costs management made hearings longer by a (surprisingly conservative) 15 to 30 minutes.[30]

12.11 Construction lawyer Nicholas Gould was asked to head a team to monitor the Mercantile Pilot. He and his team reported in early 2012, when he noted broadly supportive views among participants.[31]

Sir Rupert Jackson's Final Report

12.12 Neither of the pilots had been completed by the time Sir Rupert Jackson published his Final Report. That said, the issue of costs management was actively being addressed by a judicial steering group and this reduced the need for further consultation.[32] This did not stop the professions from expressing their views, however, not all of which were entirely in favour of costs management.[33]

12.13 It was against this background that Sir Rupert Jackson, writing in his Final Report, described the 'essence' of costs management as comprising four parts:

> '1. The parties prepare and exchange litigation budgets or (as the case proceeds) amended budgets.
> 2. The court states the extent to which those budgets are approved.
> 3. So far as possible, the court manages the case so that it proceeds within the approved budgets.
> 4. At the end of the litigation, the recoverable costs of the winning party are assessed in accordance with the approved budget.'[34]

Sir Rupert Jackson made a number of recommendations,[35] most of which have now been implemented.

Jurisdiction

12.14 The jurisdiction to make a costs management order derives from CPR, Part 3. There is a prescribed jurisdiction (see 12.15–12.18) and a discretionary jurisdiction (see 12.19); both, however, are discretionary in the sense that the court has the power to disapply the prescribed jurisdiction (see 12.74–12.83).

---

29 See *Cook on Costs 2014* (LexisNexis, online), para 15.3.

30 Gould, N, King, C, Lockwood, C, and Hutchison, T, *Costs Management Pilot: Interim Report* (London: King's College, 2012), p 10; see also Jackson, R, *Review of Civil Litigation Costs: Final Report* (London: HMSO, 2010), ch 40.

31 They comment that there were significant concerns about the time spent completing Form HB (that being the equivalent of Precedent H), but participants seemed to acknowledge that Form HB would become easier to deal with once familiarity with it had increased. They commented that the budgeting exercise helped them to better understand their potential liabilities (including the potential liability to the other party if they did not win) and that it could also assist with settlement: Gould, N, King, C, Lockwood, C, and Hutchison, T, *Costs Management Pilot: Interim Report* (London: King's College, 2012).

32 Ministry of Justice, *Proposals for Reform of Civil Litigation Funding and Costs in England and Wales*, Cm 7947 (London: HMSO, 2010), para 264.

33 See Jackson, R, *Review of Civil Litigation Costs: Final Report* (London: HMSO, 2010), ch 40, at para 6.2.

34 *Ibid*, at para 1.4.

35 *Ibid*, at paras 7 and 8.

Prescribed jurisdiction

The prescribed jurisdiction came into existence on 1 April 2013 when the 60th and 61st updates to the CPR were implemented. The power to manage costs is expressly set out in CPR, Part 3, Section II ('Costs Management'). In particular, CPR, r 3.12 (as it now reads), provides as follows: **12.15**

> '3.12 (1) This Section and Practice Direction 3E apply to all Part 7 multi-track cases, except—
> (a) where the claim is commenced on or after 22nd April 2014 and the amount of money claimed as stated on the claim form is £10 million or more; or
> (b) where the claim is commenced on or after 22nd April 2014 and is for a monetary claim which is not quantified or not fully quantified or is for a non-monetary claim and in any such case the claim form contains a statement that the claim is valued at £10 million or more; or
> (c) where in proceedings commenced on or after 6th April 2016 a claim is made by or on behalf of a person under the age of 18 (a child) (and on a child reaching majority this exception will continue to apply unless the court otherwise orders); or
> (d) where the proceeding are the subject of fixed costs or scale costs; or
> (e) the court otherwise orders.
>
> (1A) This Section and Practice Direction 3E will apply to any other proceedings (including applications) where the court so orders.
>
> (2) The purpose of costs management is that the court should manage both the steps to be taken and the costs to be incurred by the parties to any proceedings so as to further the overriding objective.'

In a similar vein, Practice Direction (PD) 3E, para 1, provides as follows: 'The Rules require the parties in Part 7 multi-track claims with a value of less than £10 million to file and exchange costs budgets: see rules 3.12 and 3.13.' The reference to CPR, r 3.13, is to the rules that govern the stage at which budgets are to be exchanged and filed (see 12.43). **12.16**

Thus, unless the court orders otherwise (see 12.69), the provisions of CPR, Part 3, Section II, and PD 3E apply to all Part 7 multitrack cases, except: **12.17**

- those that were commenced on or after 22 April 2014 and which have a value (monetary or otherwise) of £10 million or more;
- certain claims by or on behalf of children (but not persons who lack mental capacity);[36] and
- those to which fixed costs or scale costs apply.

The following additional points can be made. **12.18**

- **Part 8 claims and applications** The prescribed jurisdiction applies only to Part 7 claims[37]—although the court is encouraged to make cost management orders under the discretionary jurisdiction in more demanding Part 8 claims and applications (see 12.83).
- **Smaller claims and 'costs management Lite'** The prescribed jurisdiction applies only to multitrack claims and, as such, it will not apply to fast-track claims or to those

[36] The editors of the White Book explain that this exception was limited to children because cases involving children often take many years to conclude, this not being a feature of litigation involving those who lack capacity: see The White Book 2017, para 3.12.1.

[37] See CPR, r 3.12(1).

allocated to the small claims track. In smaller cases (that is, cases in which a party's budgeted costs do not exceed £25,000 or in which the value of the claim as stated on the claim form is less than £50,000), the parties will be required to complete only the first page of Precedent H.[38] That type of budgeting (which may also be adopted as a matter of discretion under the discretionary jurisdiction) has been referred to as 'costs management Lite'.

- **Older cases** The rules as originally made provided that unless the court ordered otherwise, CPR, Part 3, Section II, would apply only to those cases that were commenced on or after 1 April 2013.[39] As of 22 April 2014, this has no longer been the case.[40] There are now no transitional provisions, so it would seem that costs management applies to all Part 7 multitrack claims, regardless of whether budgeting used to apply when CPR, Part 3, Section II, first came into force. Presumably, the protection against those provisions being applied inappropriately (such as in a case that is too far advanced for budgeting to make sense) lies in the fact that the court can disapply those provisions pursuant to CPR, r 3.12(1)(e).
- **Litigants in person** Whilst the court has discretion to order otherwise,[41] a litigant in person[42] is not required to prepare and file a budget,[43] the implication being that a litigant in person's costs will generally not be costs managed (although, of course, their opponent's costs generally would be[44]). There is nothing in the rules or practice directions to cover the possibility of a litigant in person subsequently choosing to instruct legal representatives; presumably, this would trigger an application for a cost management order, either by the (former) litigant in person or by their opponent.
- **Claimants with limited life expectancy** There is a rebuttable presumption against CPR, Part 3, Section II, applying to claimants with limited life expectancy (see 12.79).
- **Local practices** It used to be the case that judges in certain courts indicated in advance that certain cases would not be subject to costs management,[45] but those practices were only transient and no longer exist.

---

38 See PD 3E, para 6(c).

39 See CPR, r 3.12(1), as it was originally made. Ramsay J (speaking extrajudicially) has said that the approach was not to usher in routine costs management in cases issued before 1 April 2013, which point he made in answer to questions from the audience during the annual general meeting of the Association of Costs Lawyers on 11 May 2013.

40 See the Civil Procedure (Amendment No 4) Rules 2014 (SI 2014/867), para 4.

41 Whilst not binding, Chief Master Marsh has found that the court has the power to order a litigant in person to produce a budget and to make a costs management order in respect of that person, should the circumstances so require: see *Campbell v Campbell* [2016] EWHC 2237 (Ch).

42 It is not clear whether a body corporate that wishes to act in person will always be a litigant in person for the purposes of costs budgeting. CPR, r 46.5(6)(a), explicitly states (in relation to costs) that a corporate body may be a litigant in person; this implies that a corporate body may act without a legal representative: see *RH Tomlinssons (Trowbridge) Ltd v Secretary of State for the Environment, Transport and the Regions* [2000] BCC 576. That said, since a corporate body requires permission before it can be represented at trial by someone other than a person with rights of audience (see CPR, r 39.6), it is not entirely clear whether such a litigant is entitled to be treated as a litigant in person prior to the first hearing at which the issue of permission is addressed.

43 See CPR, r 3.13; see also PD 3E, para 7.8.

44 A litigant in person is entitled to be served with an opponent's budget: see PD 3E, para 7.8.

45 In mid-2013, it was said by many commentators that the masters in the Royal Court of Justice dealing with clinical negligence cases would defer budgeting until about October 2013.

Discretionary jurisdiction

Whilst there is very little authority on the point,[46] the power to make a cost management order has probably always existed under the court's general case management powers.[47] That general jurisdiction possibly continues to exist, but it has now been rendered otiose because CPR, r 3.12(1A), provides that '[that] Section and Practice Direction 3E will apply to any other proceedings (including applications) where the court so orders'. As such, the court has an express jurisdiction to make a cost management order in any case it sees fit.[48] 12.19

Procedural Issues (Other than the Making of Costs Management Orders)

The following topics are addressed under this heading: 12.20

- Precedent H and its completion (12.21);
- filing and exchanging budgets (12.43);
- what happens when budgets are agreed (12.48);
- replying to budgets—budget discussion reports (12.51);
- the consequences of failing to file a budget (12.56);
- costs management hearings (12.61); and
- the interaction between budgets and case management (12.63).

Precedent H and its completion

As to the format of the budget, PD 3E, para 6, provides as follows: 12.21

> '6. (a) Unless the court otherwise orders, a budget must be in the form of Precedent H annexed to this Practice Direction. It must be in landscape format with an easily legible typeface. In substantial cases, the court may direct that budgets be limited initially to part only of the proceedings and subsequently extended to cover the whole proceedings. A budget must be dated and verified by a statement of truth signed by a senior legal representative of the party.
> (b) Parties must follow the Precedent H Guidance Note in all respects.
> (c) In cases where a party's budgeted costs do not exceed £25,000 or the value of the claim as stated on the claim form is less than £50,000, the parties must only use the first page of Precedent H.
>
> (The wording for a statement of truth verifying a budget is set out in Practice Direction 22.)'

---

[46] It is implicit that some of the relevant powers existed, because otherwise it would not have been necessary for the Mercantile Pilot to specifically state that it was without prejudice to the court's general powers under CPR, r 3.1: see Jackson, R, *Review of Civil Litigation Costs: Final Report* (London: HMSO, 2009), para 7.5. Sir Rupert Jackson also commented that Coulson J—a judge known for his interest in costs made a form of costs management order as long ago as 2009, in *Barr v Biffa Waste Services Ltd* [2009] EWHC 2444 (TCC), at [53]–[60]. Whilst he was speaking extrajudicially, Sir Rupert obviously approved of that approach.

[47] Speaking of the law as it used to be before 1 April 2013, Sir Rupert Jackson summarised the position in this way (again, speaking extrajudicially): 'Although not spelt out in terms within the CPR, the jurisdiction for costs management already exists. Within the CPR judges are given an armoury of powers which collectively enable cases to be managed not only by reference to the steps that may be taken in the given proceedings, but also by reference to the level of costs to be incurred' (Jackson, R, *Review of Civil Litigation Costs: Preliminary Report*, London: HMSO, 2009, ch 48, para 2.1).

[48] See, eg, *CIP Properties (AIPT) Ltd v Galliford Try Infrastructure Ltd* [2015] EWHC 481, in which Coulson J made a costs management order in a claim with a stated value of more than £10 million.

12.22 Thus a budget must be in the form of Precedent H annexed to PD 3E and the Guidance Notes to that Precedent must be followed 'in all respects' (see 12.24). A budget must be dated and verified by a statement of truth, signed by a senior legal representative of the party (see 12.34). It must be in landscape format, in an easily legible typeface, and it must be dated.[49]

Precedent H

12.23 A template budget (Precedent H, otherwise known as Form H) is published as an .xls file on the Ministry of Justice's website at the foot of PD 3E.[50] It was revised on 1 October 2013,[51] on 22 April 2014[52] and then again on 6 April 2016. It can be edited in Microsoft Excel,[53] Google Spreadsheets and other such programs. The discussion that follows is based on editing in Microsoft Excel 2016.

12.24 There is no guidance within the CPR themselves about the completion of a budget; instead, all such matters are relegated to the PD 3E, para 6 (see 12.21). In addition to the practice direction, there is a .pdf document called 'Guidance Notes for Precedent H', which can also be found at the end of PD 3E. The Guidance used not to be a part of the Practice Direction, but it is now expressly incorporated by PD 3E, para 6(b) (see 12.22). Whilst not binding, Master McCloud (sitting as a deputy costs judge) has confirmed that it is mandatory and must be followed 'in all respects'.[54]

12.25 Precedent H is capable of calculating totals automatically; in the event that it fails to do so, left-clicking on Data | Refresh All will allow manual calculation. In general, data is entered in the yellow and grey cells only; the white cells contain formulas that the user does not need to edit. It is in landscape layout, but—somewhat counter-intuitively—the pages run transversely rather than horizontally. This means that the user cannot depress PgUp and PgDn to move through the document page by page; instead, they must use Alt+PgUp and Alt+PgDn to do so.

12.26 Unless the case is a smaller case (see 12.28), the worksheet 'Precedent H FULL' should be used. Page 1 of the worksheet contains space for the party in question to enter (a) the parties' details, (b) estimates for the ten fixed categories (known as phases—see Table 12.1),[55] and (c) a description of and the figures for optional contingent categories (if any—see 12.36–12.41). There is also a summary of the approved budget. A statement of truth must

[49] See PD 3E, para 6(a).

[50] The file is 56KB in size. It opens in most recent versions of Excel without a need for conversion. It is on the same page as PD 3E.

[51] This amendment was necessary because Precedent H originally stated that court fees were to be excluded and this was at odds with those parts of the Precedent that required court fees to be set out.

[52] This was necessary so that it could include the new 'Statement of Truth'.

[53] On most computers, it is necessary to click 'enable editing' first; the relevant box will usually appear under the toolbars.

[54] See *Woodburn v Thomas* (unreported), 11 August 2017, Senior Courts Costs Office, at [4].

[55] The fixed categories are: pre-action costs; issue/statements of case; case management conference; disclosure; witness statements; expert reports; pre-trial review; trial preparation; trial and settlement/alternative dispute resolution (ADR). The use of the word 'phase' should not be regarded as being a direct reference to phases as used in e-billing and coding. In particular, there seems to be only a loose relationship between the phases in Precedent H and phase codes as used in Legal Electronic Data Exchange Standards (LEDES) or the Uniform-Task Based Management System (UTBMS).

be made (see 12.30); this no longer needs to be inserted into the template, because it is already included by default, but it does need to be signed.

Pages 2–7 of the worksheet 'Precedent H FULL' contain the fixed phases and contingent categories of costs. For each phase or contingent category, there is a space on page 1 to record any phase/category-specific assumptions (such as the extent of disclosure or the number of witnesses—see 12.35). On pages 2–7, there is space for entering the fee earners' details, the hourly rates, the costs already incurred, the estimated number of hours likely to be incurred, experts' fees and expenses,[56] counsel's fees, court fees and other disbursements (together with an explanation of the details thereof). The hourly rates entered in cells I9–I13 on page 2 will be carried over automatically to pages 3–7. If the user wishes to provide a detailed breakdown of the time spent, they can do this easily by adding a new worksheet for each phase, summating the time spent using AutoSum, and then replicating the relevant summated cell in the relevant phase. Unless the case is a smaller case (see 12.28), the user may disregard (or even delete) worksheet 'Precedent H (page one only)'. **12.27**

Smaller cases

In smaller cases (that is, those in which the budgeted costs do not exceed £25,000 and the value of the claim, as stated on the claim form, is less than £50,000), only the first page of Precedent H should be completed.[57] This can be found as a separate worksheet in Precedent H, that worksheet bearing the name 'Precedent H (page one only)'. **12.28**

Large cases and group litigation

In substantial cases, the court may direct that budgets be limited initially to only part of the proceedings and subsequently extended to cover the whole proceedings.[58] In group litigation, 'template budgets' have been used—that is, standardised budgets that are intended to be representative of some or all of the costs claimed in so far as individual costs are concerned.[59] **12.29**

General points regarding form and content

The following miscellaneous points can be made about the form and content of budgets. **12.30**

- **What to include** In addition to the phase-specific comments (see Table 12.1), the Guidance states that 'in so far as they are required by the circumstances of the case, [items of work] should be included'.[60] Whilst there is no authority on the point, Dyson LJ's guidance relating to old-style estimates remains relevant—namely, that the drafter should assume that the case will not settle (that is, that the budget should not merely be an estimate of future costs up to some unspecified date on which it is thought that the case is likely to, or might, settle).[61]
- **Attendances** The Guidance says that '[a]llowance must be made in each phase for advising the client, taking instructions and corresponding with the other party/parties and

56 Those expenses are referred to as 'disbursements'.
57 See PD 3E, para 6(c).
58 See PD 3E, para 6(a).
59 See, eg, *Various Claimants v MGN Ltd* [2016] EWHC 1894 (Ch), at [3], *per* Mann J.
60 See Guidance Notes on Precedent H, para 4.
61 *Leigh v Michelin Tyre plc* [2003] EWCA Civ 1766, at [37].

the court in respect of matters falling within that phase'.[62] This means that attendances must be included in the relevant phase.

- **Expert reports and costs of instructing experts** It is not the case that all of the costs associated with experts go into the 'Expert reports' phase. Where, for example, an expert is instructed to attend a trial, those costs would instead go in the 'Trial preparation' phase.[63] In contrast to what has previously happened with experts' fees at assessment (where they were generally allowed with, at most, only modest discounts), it is common to see significant reductions in experts' fees on the basis that the sums claimed are disproportionate or unreasonable.[64] As such, if the fees are conspicuously high, a short explanation would usually assist the court.
- **Duplicated costs and misclassified costs** Costs should not be duplicated or misclassified—in particular, costs should not be said to have been both incurred and estimated. If this happens, the court may refuse to approve the budget on the grounds that it cannot make an order without including costs that have already been incurred.[65]
- **Oppressive conduct by opponents** The Guidance states that '[a]ny party may apply to the court if it considers that another party is behaving oppressively in seeking to cause the applicant to spend money disproportionately on costs and the court will grant such relief as may be appropriate.'[66] Presumably, this means that it is permissible to prepare a budget that is based on the premise that an opponent's oppressive conduct will continue and to ask the court to approve the budget on that basis.
- **Costs of preparing the budget** Other than as set out in Table 12.1, the costs of preparing the budget and associated material must not be claimed under any phase. This is because the permitted figure will be inserted once the final budget figure has been approved by the court.[67]
- **Costs of revising and reviewing budgets** Whilst the Guidance is not entirely clear on the point, Master McCloud (sitting as a deputy costs judge) has explained that the costs of reviewing an opponent's budget and the costs of correspondence with opponent to agree budgets are to be included in the relevant case management conference (CMC) phase, and the costs of preparing an updated costs budgets or of reviewing an opponent's updated budget are to be included in the relevant pre-trial review (PTR) phase.[68]

Contents of phases

12.31 The Guidance gives advice about which costs to include in which phases (see Table 12.1).[69]

Costs that are excluded from the budget

12.32 PD 3E, para 7.9, provides that: '[i]f interim applications are made which, reasonably, were not included in a budget, then the costs of such interim applications shall be treated as additional to the approved budgets' (see 12.106). The effect of this is that the drafter of the budget does not need to be concerned about the costs of interim applications of a type

62 See Guidance Notes on Precedent H, para 5.
63 Whilst only persuasive, see O'Hare, J, 'Drafting Matters' (2013) 163(7576) NLJ 15.
64 See, eg, *Willis v MRJ Rundell & Associates Ltd* [2013] EWHC 2923 (TCC), at [20], *per* Coulson J.
65 *Ibid*, at [19], *per* Coulson J.
66 See Guidance Notes on Precedent H, para 7.
67 See Guidance Notes on Precedent H, para 9.
68 See *Woodburn v Thomas* (unreported), 11 August 2017, Senior Courts Costs Office, at [21].
69 See Guidance Notes on Precedent H, para 4.

Table 12.1 What to include in each phase

Phase	Includes	Does not include
Pre-action	Pre-Action Protocol correspondence Investigating the merits of the claim and advising client Considering alternative dispute resolution (ADR), including advising on settlement and Part 36 offers All other steps taken and advice given pre-action	Any work already incurred in relation to any other phase of the budget
Statements of case	Preparation of claim form Issue and service of proceedings Preparation of particulars of claim, defence, reply, including taking instructions, instructing counsel and any necessary investigation Considering opposing statements of case and advising client Part 18 requests (request and answer) Any conferences with counsel primarily relating to statements of case Updating schedules and counter-schedules of loss	Amendments to statements of case (see below)
CMC	Completion of directions questionnaires Arranging a CMC Reviewing opponent's budget Correspondence with opponent to agree directions and budgets, where possible Preparation for, and attendance at, the CMC Finalising the order	Subsequent CMCs Preparation of costs budget for first CMC (which will be inserted in the approved budget)
Disclosure	Obtaining documents from client and advising on disclosure obligations Reviewing documents for disclosure, and preparing disclosure report or questionnaire response and list Inspection Reviewing opponent's list and documents, undertaking any appropriate investigations Correspondence between parties about the scope of disclosure and queries arising Consulting counsel, so far as appropriate, in relation to disclosure	Applications for specific disclosure Applications and requests for third-party disclosure
Witness statements	Identifying witnesses Obtaining statements Preparing witness summaries Consulting counsel, so far as appropriate, about witness statements Reviewing opponent's statements and undertaking any appropriate investigations Applications for witness summaries	Arranging for witnesses to attend trial (include in trial preparation)

(continued)

Table 12.1 Continued

Phase	Includes	Does not include
Expert reports	Identifying and engaging suitable expert(s) Reviewing draft and approving report(s) Dealing with follow-up questions of experts Considering opposing experts' reports Any conferences with counsel primarily relating to expert evidence Meetings of experts (preparing agenda, etc)	Obtaining permission to adduce expert evidence (include in CMC or as separate application) Arranging for experts to attend trial (include in trial preparation)
PTR	Bundle Preparation of updated costs budgets and reviewing opponent's budget Preparing and agreeing chronology, case summary and *dramatis personae* (if ordered and not already prepared earlier in case) Completing and filing pre-trial checklists Correspondence with opponents to agree directions and costs budgets, if possible Preparation for and attendance at the PTR	Assembling and/or copying the bundle (which is not fee earners' work)
Trial preparation	Trial bundles Witness summonses and arranging for witnesses to attend trial Any final factual investigations Supplemental disclosure and statements (if required) Agreeing brief fee Any pre-trial conferences and advice from counsel Pre-trial liaison with witnesses	Assembling and/or copying the trial bundle (which is not fee earners' work) Counsel's brief fee and any refreshers
Trial	Solicitors' attendance at trial All conferences and other activity outside court hours during the trial Attendance on witnesses during the trial Counsel's brief fee and any refreshers Dealing with draft judgment and related applications	Preparation for trial Agreeing brief fee
Settlement	Any conferences and advice from counsel in relation to settlement Settlement negotiations, including Part 36 and other offers, and advising the client Drafting settlement agreement or Tomlin order Advice to the client on settlement (excluding advice included in the pre-action phase)	Mediation (should be included as a contingency)

that are not reasonably foreseeable (such as applications for orders arising out of non-compliance with the court's directions). Moreover, it would appear from the wording of the paragraph that there would be no need to apply to amend the budget to take account of an interim application.

Precedent H also specifies that certain costs are excluded from the budget entirely. Where applicable, these are value added tax (VAT), success fees, after-the-event (ATE) insurance premiums,[70] the costs of detailed assessment, the costs of any appeals and the costs of enforcing any judgment. **12.33**

Verification of budgets

Budgets must be verified with a statement of truth. The following points may be made about this. **12.34**

- **Form of verification** Whilst minor errors may be tolerated,[71] a budget should be verified with a statement of truth in the following terms: 'This budget is a fair and accurate statement of incurred and estimated costs which it would be reasonable and proportionate for my client to incur in this litigation.'[72] The statement of truth goes only to the fact that the costs claimed are believed to be reasonable and proportionate.[73] This contrasts with the wording as it was before 22 April 2014, when it required a statement of truth to confirm that there had been no breach of the indemnity principle in relation to costs already incurred.[74]
- **Persons allowed to verify** Whilst minor departures from what is required may still be substantially compliant,[75] a budget should be dated and verified by a 'senior legal representative' of the party in question.[76] There is no definition of 'senior legal representative' in the CPR, but 'legal representative' is defined.[77] There is uncertainty as to whether a costs lawyer would qualify if they were to be instructed directly by the client in that capacity.[78] In any event, Stuart-Smith J has found that the representative must be *representing* the party and that this is not what is being done when the person's only

[70] Mann J has confirmed that additional liabilities are not to be included: see *Various Claimants v MGN Ltd* [2016] EWHC 1894 (Ch), at [17] and [18].

[71] See, eg, *Bank of Ireland v Philip Pank Partnership* [2014] EWHC 284 (TCC), in which Stuart-Smith J found that where a solicitor had failed to notice, when signing a budget, that the words 'statement of truth' appeared next to his signature without the actual statement of truth being present, this error did not render the budget a nullity.

[72] See PD 3E, para 6; PD 22, para 2.2A.

[73] See *Bank of Ireland v Philip Pank Partnership* [2014] EWHC 284 (TCC), at [11].

[74] See PD 22, para 2.2A, as it then was.

[75] See, eg, *Americhem Europe Ltd v Rakem Ltd* [2014] EWHC 1881 (TCC), at [12], in which Stuart-Smith J found that the fact that the budget had been signed by a costs draftsperson did not, of itself, invalidate the budget.

[76] See PD 3E, para 6.

[77] CPR, r 2.3(1), provides the following definition of 'legal representative': '(a) barrister; (b) solicitor; (c) solicitor's employee; (d) manager of a body recognised under section 9 of the Administration of Justice Act 1985; or (e) person who, for the purposes of the Legal Services Act 2007, is an authorised person in relation to an activity which constitutes the conduct of litigation (within the meaning of that Act), who has been instructed to act for a party in relation to proceedings.'

[78] A costs lawyer is, by virtue of the powers stipulated in the Statement of Rights Granted to Fellows Holding a Current ALCD Practising Certificate (2007), permitted to conduct litigation in 'all proceedings under Parts 43–48 of the CPR and under Part 52 of those rules with regard to appeals from detailed assessment to the listed before a High Court Judge or a Circuit Judge'. This does not include Part 3, Section II.

involvement is to prepare the budget.[79] He went on to say that the verification must be made by someone having conduct of the action and who is in a position to gauge what resources are likely to be required to prosecute the action to its conclusion.[80] A costs lawyer or costs draftsperson would rarely fall within that category, even if instructed by a professional client.

Assumptions

12.35 Written assumptions are not normally required by the court in cases in which the parties are required to lodge only the first page.[81] The assumptions that are reflected in the Guidance are implied and are not to be rehearsed in the budget.[82] The Guidance goes on to say the following:

> 'Include only those assumptions that significantly impact on the level of costs claimed such as the duration of the proceedings, the number of experts and witnesses or the number of interlocutory applications envisaged. Brief details only are required in the box beneath each phase. Additional documents are not encouraged and, where they are disregarded by the court, the cost of preparation may be disallowed, and additional documents should be included only where necessary.'[83]

It is worth noting that this is markedly different from the practice of legal project management (where assumptions are generally set out in full—see 41.18). It is also worth noting that experienced commentators have recommended that assumptions are very fully recorded.[84]

Contingencies

12.36 The Guidance has the following to say about contingency costs:

> 'The "contingent cost" sections … should be used for *anticipated costs* which do not fall within the main categories set out in this form [ie the phases]. Examples might be the trial of preliminary issues, a mediation, applications to amend, applications for disclosure against third parties or (in libel cases) applications re meaning. Only include costs which are more likely than not to be incurred. *Costs which are not anticipated* but which become necessary later are dealt with in paragraph 7.6 of PD3E.'[85]

The reference to PD 3E, para 7.6, is to the power to amend budgets (see 12.108). Thus there is a need to distinguish between anticipated costs—that is, those that are more likely than not to be incurred—and costs that do not meet the threshold of anticipation. As is explained below (see 12.39–12.40), only the former will qualify as contingent costs.

12.37 The court has the power to classify costs as being contingent even where they were not claimed as such.[86]

---

79 See *Americhem Europe Ltd v Rakem Ltd* [2014] EWHC 1881 (TCC), at [10].
80 See *ibid*, at [11].
81 See Guidance Notes on Precedent H, para 8.b.
82 See Guidance Notes on Precedent H, para 8.a.
83 See Guidance Notes on Precedent H, para 8.a.
84 See, eg, Latham, K, '*Harrison*: A Budgeting Score Draw?' (2017) 110 Litigation Funding 8.
85 Guidance Notes on Precedent H, para 6, emphasis original.
86 See, eg, *CRM Trading Ltd v Chubb Electronic Security Ltd* [2013] EWHC 3482 (QB), at [5], in which Judge Mackie QC said: '[T]he prospect of some formal ADR are minimal and therefore [only a modest amount is allowed]. If, of course, the parties unexpectedly take up a much more elaborate ADR process, then of course there can be an agreement or if necessary a discussion in court about revising the budget further.'

Warby J had the following to say about contingent costs: 12.38

> 'The first point to make about contingencies is that they must involve work that does not fall within the main categories on Precedent H. Secondly, in order for work to qualify as a contingency it must be possible to identify to the opposite party and the court what that work would be. Otherwise it would be impossible to determine whether the work falls within or outside a specified category, and it is hard to see how any assessment could be made of what its cost would be. Thirdly, there is the important issue of how likely it needs to be that the work will be required, before it can properly be included as a contingency.'[87]

Thus contingent costs need to be identifiable as such and must not be costs that would ordinarily fall within one of the main categories in Precedent H. Having made those points, Warby J went on to say this about the threshold of anticipation: 12.39

> 'In my judgment work should be included as a contingency only if it is foreseen as more likely than not to be required. This seems to me a clear criterion that provides a practical solution, consistent with PD3E 7.4 and 7.9. If work that falls outside one of the main categories is not thought probable, it can reasonably and should be excluded from the budget. The time and costs involved in estimating how much work would cost are not easily justified if the work is no more than a possibility or is unlikely. If work identified as a contingency is included in a budget but not considered probable by the court no budget for it should be approved. If the improbable occurs, in the form of an unexpected interim application, the costs will be added to the budget pursuant to PD3E 7.9, unless the matter involves a "significant development" within para 7.4 in which case, if time permits, a revised budget should be prepared and agreed or approved.'[88]

Thus the test that distinguishes contingency costs from costs that are too remote to justify inclusion within the budget is whether they are more likely to be incurred than not. Again, it is worth noting that this is a different approach from that used in legal project management, where contingency planning tends to take into account remote—or even very remote—possible expenditure (see 41.22). 12.40

Contingent costs should not be presented as unexplained lump sums, but ought to be explained and, where appropriate, broken down into their constituent parts.[89] 12.41

The client and the budget

Surprisingly, there is nothing in either the Rules or the Practice Direction that requires that the budget is to be shown to the client (that is, the party whose budget it is). Notwithstanding this (or perhaps *because* of this), many judges will ask whether the client has approved the budget. Indeed, some judges will go so far as to require the parties (that is, the parties themselves) to attend. The authors of *Cook on Costs* give the following sage advice on the point: 12.42

> 'From a practical perspective discussions must be undertaken with the client prior to completion of the budget. The client may well have a very different idea as to what budget he will require to pursue, or defend a case and this must be addressed at the outset. An explanation should be provided as to the costs that will need to be incurred; incurred costs should already have been discussed. It is also essential to explain that the costs budget will provide the basis for determining the recoverable costs at the end of the proceedings.'[90]

---

87 See *Yeo v Times Newspapers Ltd* [2015] EWHC 209 (QB), at [70].

88 See *ibid*, at [71].

89 *Willis v MRJ Rundell & Associates Ltd* [2013] EWHC 2923 (TCC), at [21] and [22], *per* Coulson J.

90 See *Cook on Costs 2017* (LexisNexis, online), para 15.21.

Filing and exchanging budgets

12.43 Draft or agreed budgets must be filed in accordance with CPR, r 3.13, which reads as follows:

> '3.13 (1) Unless the court otherwise orders, all parties except litigants in person must file and exchange budgets—
> (a) where the stated value of the claim on the claim form is less than £50,000, with their directions questionnaires; or
> (b) in any other case, not later than 21 days before the first case management conference.'

Thus, unless the court orders otherwise, in all cases other than those in which the value of the claim is stated to be less than £50,000, budgets must be exchanged and filed no later than 21 days before the first CMC. Where the claim is for less than £50,000, budgets must be filed and exchanged with the parties' directions questionnaires.

12.44 As can be seen from CPR, r 3.13(1), the requirement does not apply to litigants in person (unless, of course, the court so orders). PD 3E, para 7.8, makes it clear that whilst such litigants are not required to file and exchange budgets, they are entitled to receive them: 'A litigant in person, even though not required to prepare a budget, shall nevertheless be provided with a copy of the budget of any other party.'

Additional information

12.45 The Guidance provides as follows: 'Save in exceptional circumstances, the parties are not expected to lodge any documents other than Precedent H and the budget discussion report.'[91] Thus, other than in exceptional circumstances, additional information is not something that the court would expect to see. Nonetheless, it is commonly the case that the parties seek to rely on extra documentation. In particular, it is often the case that reliance is placed on one or more witness statements from either the solicitor with conduct of the claim or the costs lawyer or costs draftsperson who drafted the budget. Indeed, in a complex matter, the documentation may be surprisingly voluminous.[92]

12.46 To the extent that that information relates to *case* management, PD 26, para 2.2, may apply if the hearing is a case and costs management conference. In so far as it is relevant, those provisions read as follows:

> **'Provision of Extra Information**
>
> (1) If a party wishes to give the court further information which is believed to be relevant to allocation or case management it shall be given when the party files the directions questionnaire and copied to all other parties.
>
> (2) The general rule is that the court will not take such information into account unless the document containing it either:
> (a) confirms that all parties have agreed that the information is correct and that it should be put before the court, or
> (b) confirms that the party who has sent the document to the court has delivered a copy to all the other parties.

[91] Guidance Notes on Precedent H, para 2.

[92] By way of example, during submissions in *Sharp v Blank* [2017] EWHC 141 (Ch), Chief Master Marsh commented that the court had been assisted by the lengthy witness statements that the parties had filed and the exhibits, which ran to six lever arch files.

(3) The following are examples of information which will be likely to help the court:
[...]
(c) the steps the parties have taken in the preparation of evidence (in particular expert evidence), the steps they intend to take and whether those steps are to be taken in co-operation with any other party,
(d) the directions the party believes will be appropriate to be given for the management of the case ...'

In the editor's experience, the court rarely excludes evidence on the basis that there has been non-compliance with those provisions. Presumably this is because they relate to case management rather than costs management. **12.47**

Agreed budgets

Budgets may be, and often are, agreed. Where this is so, PD 3E, para 7.3, provides as follows: 'If the budgeted costs or incurred costs are agreed between all parties, the court will record the extent of such agreement. ...' Thus, if the budgeted costs or incurred costs are agreed between all the parties, the court will record the extent of such agreement. This will then stand as a costs management order. **12.48**

The generally received view is that the court lacks the power to interfere with a budget or part thereof where it has been agreed; thus, where the whole budget has been agreed, there is little that the court can do in terms of costs management. That said, that received view is correct only to an extent: as the editors of The White Book point out, 'where parties have agreed a budget which is clearly disproportionate the court may choose not to make a costs management order'.[93] This is a topic that is addressed in more detail at 12.77. In any event, there would be nothing to prevent the court from imposing its own view for the purposes of *case* management. If, for example, the parties had agreed a budget for experts on each side in a case in which the court believed that one jointly instructed expert would be sufficient, the fact that the parties' budget reflected a prodigal option would not prevent the court from giving more frugal directions. **12.49**

Where only a part of the budget has been agreed, then—whilst there is no authority directly on the point—it can safely be assumed that the court would take those costs into account for the purposes of considering the reasonableness and proportionality of remaining costs. Moreover, there would be nothing to prevent a judge from commenting on the agreed costs. Many judges are alive to the possibility that there is a risk that the parties' lawyers may collude to inflate the budgets; adversely commenting on the budget would be an effective way of combating such behaviour. **12.50**

Replying to budgets and budget discussion reports

There used to be no specific provision that allowed or required a party served with a budget to respond, but CPR, r 3.13(2), now provides as follows: **12.51**

'(2) In the event that a party files and exchanges a budget under paragraph (1), all other parties, not being litigants in person, must file an agreed budget discussion report no later than 7 days before the first case management conference.'

[93] See The White Book 2017, para 3.15.1.

Thus, in the event that a party files and exchanges a budget under CPR, r 3.13(1), all parties (other than litigants in person) must file an agreed budget discussion report no later than seven days before the first CMC. This rule does not apply to cases commenced before 6 April 2016.[94] Moreover, the editors of The White Book point out that if the court gives case management directions without a case management hearing, there will be no need for budget discussion reports; they go on to say this:

> 'Rule 3.13(2) does not require the filing of budget discussion reports before any hearing after the first case management hearing. Nevertheless, it may sometimes be appropriate to adopt such a procedure in respect of a subsequent hearing where substantial revisions to a costs budget are proposed and disputed'.[95]

12.52 As to the content of budget discussion reports, PD 3E, para 6A, imposes the following mandatory requirements:

> '6A. The budget discussion report required by rule 3.13(2) must set out—
> (a) those figures which are agreed for each phase;
> (b) those figures which are not agreed for each phase; and
> (c) a brief summary of the grounds of dispute.
>
> The parties are encouraged to use the Precedent R Budget Discussion Report annexed to this Practice Direction.'

12.53 Thus the budget discussion report *must* set out:

- those figures that are agreed for each phase;
- those figures that are not agreed for each phase; and
- a brief summary of the grounds of dispute.

PD 3E, para 6A, goes on to say that the parties are encouraged to use the Precedent R budget discussion report annexed to that Practice Direction. That document is in the form of a spreadsheet. It expressly states that only budgeted costs should be included.

12.54 In complex matters, the parties may wish to supplement their Precedent R budget discussion reports with statements (often made by a costs lawyer or a costs draftsperson); this is not standard practice, but it is not an uncommon occurrence.[96] Such statements frequently express an opinion as to the amounts of costs that should be approved and, given the fact that the same points could be made by way of submissions, it is—in the editor's experience—rarely the case that the court declines to take such evidence into account.

12.55 The court will be astute to the possibility that parties may try to distort the court's appraisal of the budgets by submitting inappropriately low offers in their Precedent Rs. Coulson J had this to say on the point:

> '[E]ven now, some parties seem to treat cost budgeting as a form of game, in which they can seek to exploit the cost budgeting rules in the hope of obtaining a tactical advantage over the other side. In extreme cases, this can lead one side to offer very low figures in their Precedent R, in the hope that the court may be tempted to calculate its own amount, somewhere between the wildly different sets of figures put forward by the parties.'[97]

---

[94] Civil Procedure (Amendment) Rules 2016 (SI 2016/234), r 23.
[95] See The White Book 2017, para 3.13.3.
[96] See, eg, *Kalma v African Minerals Ltd* [2017] EWHC 1471 (QB), at [2], *per* Senior Master Fontaine.
[97] *Findcharm Ltd v Churchill Group Ltd* [2017] EWHC 1108 (TCC), at [3].

Unsurprisingly, Coulson J went on to deprecate such practices and, in doing so, he singled out the costs practitioners who prepared the offending Precedent R.

Failure to file a budget

If a party fails to file a budget on time,[98] draconian consequences may follow. This is because CPR, r 3.14, reads as follows: 'Unless the court otherwise orders, any party which fails to file a budget despite being required to do so will be treated as having filed a budget comprising only the applicable court fees.' **12.56**

Subject to what is said below, the effect of this will be that a party who has failed to file a budget on time will have to litigate in the knowledge that the recovery of nearly all of their future costs is likely to be dependent on being able to persuade the court to 'order otherwise'—which it is difficult to do.[99] Arnold J has found that the sanction applies from the date on which the budget should have been filed rather than the date of the costs management hearing.[100] The court may award relief from sanctions, but there have been (in)famous instances of the court declining to do so.[101] Following *Denton*,[102] however, it is less likely than before that relief will be refused (although it can still happen[103]). The topic of relief from sanctions is addressed at 26.48 *et seq*. On the whole, it is commonly the case that the court will overlook minor failings. If a budget were served a day or two late, for example, that would generally be seen as being a minor matter that is worthy of relief.[104] It would generally not be appropriate for the court to grant partial relief.[105] **12.57**

The harsh consequences of CPR, r 3.14, may be ameliorated by the effect of CPR, r 36.23, which reads as follows: **12.58**

> '(1) This rule applies in any case where the offeror is treated as having filed a costs budget limited to applicable court fees, or is otherwise limited in their recovery of costs to such fees.
>
> (Rule 3.14 provides that a litigant may be treated as having filed a budget limited to court fees for failure to file a budget.)
>
> (2) "Costs" in rules 36.13(5)(b), 36.17(3)(a) and 36.17(4)(b) shall mean—
> (a) in respect of those costs subject to any such limitation, 50% of the costs assessed without reference to the limitation; together with
> (b) any other recoverable costs.'

Thus, if a party is caught by CPR, r 3.14, and has been unable to obtain relief from sanctions, one option would be to make a realistic Part 36 offer.

[98] As opposed to at all: *Mitchell v News Group Newspapers Ltd* [2013] EWCA Civ 1537, at [30], *per* Dyson MR.

[99] The test that would be applied would effectively be the same test as would apply on relief from sanctions: see *Mitchell v News Group Newspapers Ltd* [2013] EWCA Civ 1537, at [32], *per* Dyson MR.

[100] See *Ali v Channel 5 Broadcast Ltd* [2018] EWHC 840 (Ch), at [55], *per* Arnold J.

[101] Most famously, see *Mitchell v News Group Newspapers Ltd* [2013] EWCA Civ 1537.

[102] *Denton & Ors v TH White Ltd & Ors* [2014] EWCA Civ 906.

[103] See, eg, *Jamadar v Bradford Teaching Hospitals NHS Foundation Trust* [2016] EWCA Civ 1001; *Lakhani v Mahmud* [2017] EWHC 1713 (Ch).

[104] See *Wain v Gloucester County Council* [2014] EWHC 1274 (TCC). See also *Azure East Midlands Ltd v Manchester Airport Group Property Developers* [2014] EWHC 1644 (TCC). For a more extreme example, see *Mott v Long* [2017] EWHC 2130 (TCC), *per* Judge Grant, in which the budget was ten days late because of problems with the solicitors' IT system. See also *Intellimedia Systems Ltd v Richards* (unreported), 1 February 2017, Ch D, *per* Warren J.

[105] See *Mitchell v News Group Newspapers Ltd* [2013] EWCA Civ 1537, at [58], *per* Dyson MR.

12.59 Another option, if the defaulting party were a claimant, would be to discontinue to the existing claim and bring a new one. This would mean that the claimant would have to pay the defendant's costs, but those costs are likely to be less than the costs that would otherwise be forfeited. It would seem that such a course of action would not necessarily lead to the new claim being struck out as being an abuse of process,[106] but the editors of The White Book express their doubts about that.[107]

12.60 Where a party has been limited to court fees only and where there have been significant developments that would justify a revision of the budget, it is open to the court to make a cost management order that allows for the costs attributable to those significant developments. In the absence of relief from sanctions, any such order should be limited to those costs; it would be an error in principle to allow more.[108]

Costs management hearings

12.61 Many costs management orders will be made at the same time as the court decides issues of case management, in which case the hearing will be a case and costs management hearing; where the court deals only with the topic of costs management, the hearing will be referred to as a costs management hearing.[109] Such hearings will, where practicable, be conducted either in writing or by telephone.[110]

12.62 Whilst there is no prescribed forensic method for conducting a costs management hearing, many judges have followed the lead of Coulson J in adopting the following forensic sieve.[111]

1. Consider the issue of proportionality.
2. Consider the issue of reasonableness.
3. Identify the options available to the court.
4. Decide which options are appropriate.

Stuart-Smith J has explained that this approach is 'a guide rather than a straightjacket'.[112] Indeed, where appropriate, the court may affirmatively find that it will *not* deal with the hearing in this way.[113]

The interaction between the budget and case management

12.63 CPR, r 3.17, provides as follows:

> '(1) When making any case management decision, the court will have regard to any available budgets of the parties and will take into account the costs involved in each procedural step.
>
> (2) Paragraph (1) applies whether or not the court has made a costs management order.'

---

106 See, by analogy, *Aktas v Adepta* [2010] EWCA Civ 1170; *Hall v Ministry of Defence* [2013] EWHC 4092 (QB).

107 See The White Book 2017, para 3.14.3.

108 See *Asghar v Bhatti* [2017] EWHC 1702 (QB), *per* Lewis J.

109 This is as a result of CPR, r 3.16(1), which provides as follows: 'Any hearing which is convened solely for the purpose of costs management (for example, to approve a revised budget) is referred to as a "costs management conference".'

110 This is as a result of CPR, r 3.16(2), which provides that '[w]here practicable, costs management conferences should be conducted by telephone or in writing'.

111 *CIP Properties (AIPT) Ltd v Galliford Try Infrastructure Ltd* [2015] EWHC 481 (TCC).

112 *GSK Project Management Ltd v QPR Holdings Ltd* [2015] EWHC 2274 (TCC), at [10].

113 See, eg, *The Capital Markets Company (UK) Ltd v Tarver* [2017] EWHC 2885 Ch, at [3], *per* Mr Michael Furness QC (sitting as a deputy judge of the High Court).

In so far as the first of these decisions is concerned (that is, whether to allocate the claim to the small claims track or the fast track), it should be borne in mind that, for claims issued on or before 31 March 2013, the consent of the parties will be needed.[114]

The interaction between costs management and case management is not expressly set out in the CPR, but it is obvious that the court will take into account the budget when considering case management directions and vice versa. The authors of *Cook on Costs* sensibly have this to say on the interaction: **12.64**

> '[T]he requirement for the parties to provide information as to their estimated costs, as well as costs already incurred, will enable the court to consider these estimates alongside the directions to be given for the case management of the proceedings. Where a court considers the estimated costs to be disproportionate, it will tailor the directions to bring the costs down to a reasonable and proportionate level; this is particularly likely to affect those phases of the litigation where costs have traditionally been disproportionate such as disclosure, experts' reports and trial.'[115]

Costs Management Orders

Carr J has described costs management orders in the following way: **12.65**

> 'A costs management order is a recording of the extent to which budgets are agreed between the parties or in respect of budgets or parts of budgets which are not agreed, a record of the court's approval after making appropriate revisions.'[116]

CPR, r 3.15(1), creates—or confirms, depending on your point of view—the power to manage costs. It reads as follows: 'In addition to exercising its other powers, the court may manage the costs to be incurred (the budgeted costs) by any party in any proceedings.' **12.66**

The way in which the jurisdiction is exercised is governed by CPR, r 3.15(2): **12.67**

> '(2) The court may at any time make a "costs management order". Where costs budgets have been filed and exchanged the court will make a costs management order unless it is satisfied that the litigation can be conducted justly and at proportionate cost in accordance with the overriding objective without such an order being made. By a costs management order the court will—
> (a) record the extent to which the budgeted costs are agreed between the parties;
> (b) in respect of the budgeted costs which are not agreed, record the court's approval after making appropriate revisions;
> (c) record the extent (if any) to which incurred costs are agreed.
>
> (3) If a costs management order has been made, the court will thereafter control the parties' budgets in respect of recoverable costs.
>
> (4) Whether or not the court makes a costs management order, it may record on the face of any case management order any comments it has about the incurred costs which are to be taken into account in any subsequent assessment proceedings.'

The following topics are addressed: **12.68**

- whether to make a costs management order (12.69);
- costs already incurred (12.84);

[114] See CPR, r 26.7(3), as it was prior to 31 March 2014 (ie before it was deleted entirely).
[115] See *Cook on Costs 2017* (LexisNexis, online), para 15.2.
[116] *Merrix v Heart of England NHS Foundation Trust* [2017] EWHC 346 (QB), at [19].

- the exercise of discretion as to the level of the budget (12.87);
- procedure after approval (12.104);
- the treatment of interim applications (12.106); and
- amendments, revisions, etc (12.107).

Whether to make a costs management order

12.69 Circumstances will exist in which the court will exercise a discretion as to whether or not to make a costs management order. This issue may arise when considering whether to disapply the prescribed jurisdiction (see CPR, r 3.12(1)(e), and 12.15) or to make an order under the discretionary jurisdiction (see CPR, r 3.12(1A), and 12.19).

12.70 There is a rebuttable presumption that where budgets are filed and exchanged, the court will make a costs management order. This is made clear by PD 3E, para 7.1, which reads: 'Where costs budgets are filed and exchanged, the court will generally make a costs management order under rule 3.15. If the court makes a costs management order under rule 3.15, the following paragraphs shall apply.' The reference to 'the following paragraphs applying' are to PD 3E, paras 7.2–7.10 (the provisions that govern budgeting).

12.71 In a similar vein, whilst he was speaking extrajudicially before the directions set out above had been made, Ramsey J said that 'as costs management is a necessary adjunct to proper case management and to the furtherance of the overriding objective there will, in most cases, be a presumption in favour of making a costs management order'.[117] He also suggested that 'the courts are likely to make costs management orders both in the cases which are defined in CPR, r 3.12(1) and in other proceedings outside the defined class'.[118]

Obligation on the parties to consider whether a costs management order should be made

12.72 The parties are under an obligation to consider the issue of whether a costs management order should be made and, where practicable, to discuss that topic. This is made clear by PD 3E, para 3, which reads: 'At an early stage in the litigation the parties should consider and, where practicable, discuss whether to apply for an order for the provision of costs budgets, with a view to a costs management order being made.'

12.73 Where those discussions lead to agreement that an order for provision of costs budgets should be made, the court will, other than in exceptional circumstances, make such an order. This is made clear by PD 3E, para 4, which reads: 'If all parties consent to an application for an order for provision of costs budgets, the court will (other than in exceptional cases) make such an order.' Birss J has expressed the view (albeit *obiter*) that where budgets have been agreed, the court ought to make a costs management order.[119] In practice, this is what tends to happen.

[117] Ramsey, J, 'Costs Management: A Necessary Part of the Management of Litigation—16th Lecture in the Implementation Programme', 29 May 2012, at para 19.

[118] *Ibid.*

[119] *Thomas Pink Ltd v Victoria's Secret UK Ltd* [2014] EWHC 3258 (Ch), at [43].

Disapplication of the prescribed jurisdiction

Where costs budgeting would otherwise apply by default, the court has the power under CPR, r 3.12(1)(e), to order that it should not apply (see 12.15). CPR, r 3.15(2), imposes the following rebuttable presumption: '[T]he court will make a costs management order unless it is satisfied that the litigation can be conducted justly and at proportionate cost in accordance with the overriding objective without such an order being made.' Notwithstanding this, the court is not obliged to make a costs management order at the *first* costs management hearing. An example is a case in which the discrepancy between the parties' budgets was very marked: Carr J refused to approve the budgets; instead, he ordered that the budgets be revised and resubmitted for later consideration.[120] **12.74**

Disapplication because no costs management order is required It is implicit from the wording of CPR, r 3.15(2) (see 12.67), that the court is entitled not make a costs management order if it is satisfied that the litigation could be conducted justly and at proportionate cost in accordance with the overriding objective without such an order being made. That power not to make a costs management order certainly exists, but (except as set out in the following paragraphs) it is difficult to envisage circumstances in which it would be appropriate to exercise that power. **12.75**

Disapplication because of disapproval of an unagreed budget It may be that the court believes that the budgets are so far removed from what is reasonable and proportionate that it would not be appropriate to make a costs management order. In particular, the court may conclude that the parties should be encouraged to revise their budgets.[121] The power to deal with the matter in that way continues to exist under the present incarnation of CPR, Part 3, Section II, but it should be borne in mind that, since 22 April 2014, the court '*will* make a costs management order unless it is satisfied that the litigation can be conducted justly and at proportionate cost in accordance with the overriding objective without such an order being made' (emphasis added—see CPR, r 3.15(2), and 12.67). As such, whilst it may be appropriate to make such an order for the purposes of having the parties revise their budgets, it would probably not be appropriate to decline to make an order without the intention of revisiting the matter at a later stage. **12.76**

Disapplication because of disapproval of an agreed budget It may be that the court is not impressed with an agreed budget. The authors of *Cook on Costs* have this to say on the point: **12.77**

> 'Experience suggests that there is a situation where the court may wish not to make a costs management order. This is where the parties agree budgets that the court regards as disproportionate, but those budgets are predicated on proportionate directions (and so the court cannot use the imposition of proportionate directions to revisit the budgets). While there is an argument that even a costs management order recording an agreed budget on this basis is better than leaving costs at large, another approach, and one that one of us has adopted, is to record that the court is not making a costs management order because, while it accepts the directions are proportionate, the sums agreed by way of budgets are not, record what

[120] *Dahabshiil Transfer Services Ltd v Barclays Bank plc* [2013] EWHC 4196 (Ch).

[121] See, eg, *Willis v MRJ Rundell & Associates Ltd* [2013] EWHC 2923 (TCC) (a case decided under a pilot scheme); see also *Group Seven Ltd v Nasir* [2016] EWHC 620 (Ch), in which Morgan J encouraged the parties to revise their budgets in accordance with certain findings he had made.

the court thinks is the proportionate overall sum and reserve any subsequent "between the parties" assessment to the case managing judge (ie to the one making these recitals) and recite a reminder to the parties of the terms of CPR 44.3(2)(a)—namely that proportionality trumps reasonableness. The clear message is that the court does not want to be limited to the "incurred costs" only at a subsequent assessment (assuming that these, too, are not agreed), so that, instead, the CPR 44.3(2)(a) proportionality cross check applies to all costs.'[122]

12.78 **Disapplication in part** If the court makes a costs management order, it does not necessarily follow that the order is obliged to encompass all of the costs placed before the court in the draft budget. In particular, if the court believes that certain aspects of the costs would be better addressed by a costs judge at a detailed assessment—such as if there were a point of principle involved—it would be open to the court to make an order that did not encompass those costs.[123] Similarly, if the court does not approve of certain items, the court may exclude those items from the budget[124]—on the basis that the parties are encouraged to revise those aspects of the budgets.

12.79 **Where the claimant has a limited life expectancy** There is a rebuttable presumption that CPR, Part 3, Section II, will not apply where the claimant has a limited life expectancy. This is made clear by PD 3E, para 2(b), which reads: 'In cases where the Claimant has a limited or severely impaired life expectation (5 years or less remaining) the court will ordinarily disapply cost management under Section II of Part 3.' This provision is particularly important in mesothelioma cases in which the claimant is still alive because the avoidance of delay in such cases is of especial importance.[125]

12.80 **Group litigation** In group litigation, it may be that the amounts stated on each claim form are for the individual claim rather than amounts claimed collectively; either that, or no amount may be stated at all. On a strict reading of the rules, either of these situations would engage the prescribed jurisdiction. In a case in which the total claimed in the litigation significantly exceeded £10 million, Nugee J explained that the court is able to take the collective total into account for the purposes of exercising its discretion as to whether to make a costs management order.[126]

12.81 **Personal injury cases** Some commentators have suggested that costs management may be unnecessary for defendants in those claims subject to the qualified one-way costs shifting (QOCS) regime (which is addressed in Chapter 8); others say that budgeting is required even where QOCS applies because (a) the defendant might be able to recover costs by way of set-off and (b) the court needs to know about the costs for the purpose of managing the case proportionately.[127] It seems that the latter view tends to prevail. Moreover, support for that view can be gleaned from PD 3E, para 5(f) (see 12.83).

Application of the discretionary jurisdiction

12.82 PD 3E, para 2(a), gives the following guidance about the discretionary jurisdiction (which is outlined at 12.19):

> 'In any case where the parties are not required by rules 3.12 and 3.13 to file and exchange costs budgets, the court has a discretion to make an order requiring them to do so. That

122 See *Cook on Costs 2017* (LexisNexis, online), para 15.7.
123 See, eg, *Wright v Rowland* [2016] EWHC 2206 (Comm), at [12], *per* Flaux J.
124 See, eg, *Hegglin v Persons Unknown (1) and Google Inc (2)* [2014] EWHC 3793 (QB), *per* Edis J.
125 See The White Book 2017, para 3.12.1.
126 See *Sharp v Blank* [2015] EWHC 2685 (Ch).
127 See *Cook on Costs 2017* (LexisNexis, online), para 15.4.

power may be exercised by the court on its own initiative or on the application of a party. Where costs budgets are filed and exchanged, the court will be in a position to consider making a costs management order: see Section D below. In all cases the court will have regard to the need for litigation to be conducted justly and at proportionate cost in accordance with the overriding objective.'

As can be seen, the court has the power to order the parties to exchange and file costs budgets to enable the court to decide whether to make a costs management order. In all cases, the court will have regard to the need for litigation to be conducted justly and at proportionate cost in accordance with the overriding objective. If, for example, there is significant disparity between the financial resources of the parties, discretionary costs management may be appropriate in an effort to ensure a level playing field.[128]

There are certain circumstances in which a discretionary order for the provision of costs budgets would be particularly appropriate. These are set out in PD 3E, para 5: **12.83**

'5. An order for the provision of costs budgets with a view to a costs management order being made may be particularly appropriate in the following cases:
(a) unfair prejudice petitions under section 994 of the Companies Act 2006;
(b) disqualification proceedings pursuant to the Company Directors Disqualification Act 1986;
(c) applications under the Trusts of Land and Appointment of Trustees Act 1996;
(d) claims pursuant to the Inheritance (Provision for Family and Dependants) Act 1975;
(e) any Part 8 or other claims or applications involving a substantial dispute of fact and/or likely to require oral evidence and/or extensive disclosure; and
(f) personal injury and clinical negligence cases where the value of the claim is £10 million or more.'

It should be noted that substantial applications may fall into this category. As such, if the court were concerned about the costs of an interim application, it would—as an alternative to relying on PD 3E, para 7.9 (see 12.106)—be open to the court to make a costs management order that applied specifically to that application.

The treatment of costs already incurred

In general terms, the court lacks the power to approve costs that have already been incurred (that is, 'incurred costs').[129] This is made clear by PD 3E, para 7.4, which reads as follows: **12.84**

'As part of the costs management process the court may not approve costs incurred before the date of any costs management hearing. The court may, however, record its comments on those costs and will take those costs into account when considering the reasonableness and proportionality of all budgeted costs.'

---

[128] See, eg, *Simpkin v The Berkeley Group Holdings plc* [2016] EWHC 1619 (QB).

[129] Any suggestion to the contrary made in *SARPD Oil International Ltd v Addax Energy SA* [2016] EWCA Civ 120 is no longer good law because PD 3E was amended on 6 April 2017 in response to that case: see the Explanatory Note to The Civil Procedure (Amendment) Rules 2017 (SI 2017/95). Moreover, authorities decided in 2012 and 2013 suggesting that there can be retrospective approval of budgets should be approached with some caution: see, eg, *Murray v Neil Dowlman Architecture Ltd* [2013] EWHC 872 (TCC). This is because they related to one of the two pilot schemes, both of which had provisions relating to past costs that are different from those in CPR, Part 3, Section II.

Thus incurred costs[130] will not form part of the budgeted costs, but they will—not may[131]—be taken into account for the purposes of making a costs management order.[132]

12.85 Where the incurred costs are already unreasonable or disproportionate, the following options are potentially available to the court.

- **Disallowance or substantial abatement of the budgeted costs** If the incurred costs are sufficiently high, the court may disallow or significantly restrict any allowance for costs yet to be incurred (that is, the budgeted costs). There have been instances of the court dealing with such circumstances in this way,[133] but Coulson J has pointed out that this would expose the party whose budget it is to the risk of double jeopardy in the sense that the party could not only be deprived of an allowance in respect of budgeted costs, but also could suffer significant reductions to the incurred costs on assessment.[134]
- **Ordinary allowance of budgeted costs** In contrast to disallowing or significantly restricting budgeted costs, the court may consider making an ordinary allowance for budgeted costs on the premise that the incurred costs will be reduced to a reasonable and proportionate level on assessment.[135] Coulson J commented that such an approach may be workable, but would result in an overall figure in the budget that would be in excess of what the court considers reasonable and proportionate, and 'would have the effect of allowing [the party whose budget it is] to ride roughshod over the costs management process'.[136]
- **Modified approach** Coulson J has commented that, in preference to the two approaches referred to above, the court could make an allowance for budgeted costs, but in the context of the court ordering that the incurred costs for each phase are to be restricted to a certain amount.[137] This method assumes, however, that the court is in a position to determine a reasonable and proportionate allowance for the incurred costs; where this is not practicable, it may not be a workable solution.[138]
- **Task-based approach** Michael Furness QC (sitting as a deputy judge of the High Court) has said that where the incurred costs are high, it may be open to the court to

---

130 Carr J has commented that the costs of the case management conference are to be treated as costs already incurred: *Merrix v Heart of England NHS Foundation Trust* [2017] EWHC 346 (QB), at [16].

131 PD 3E, para 7.3, was amended from 'shall' to 'will'. Coulson J has explained that this now means that this is a mandatory requirement: see *CIP Properties (AIPT) Ltd v Galliford Try Infrastructure Ltd* [2015] EWHC 481, at [7]. There have been instances of the court declining to do this—see, eg, *Kalma v African Minerals Ltd* [2017] EWHC 1471 (QB), at [20(iii)], *per* Senior Master Fontaine—but they appear to have been decided without any detailed argument on the issue. See also *The Capital Markets Company (UK) Ltd v Tarver* [2017] EWHC 2885 Ch.

132 See, eg, *Yeo v Times Newspapers Ltd* [2015] EWHC 209 (QB), at [60], *per* Warby J; *Redfern v Corby Borough Council* [2014] EWHC 4526 (QB), at [32], *per* Judge Seymour QC; *CIP Properties (AIPT) Ltd v Galliford Try Infrastructure Ltd* [2015] EWHC 481 (TCC).

133 Whilst the court dealt with the matter in only a broad-brush way, see *Redfern v Corby Borough Council* [2014] EWHC 4526 (QB), at [32] and [33], *per* Judge Seymour QC (sitting as a deputy judge of the High Court).

134 See *CIP Properties (AIPT) Ltd v Galliford Try Infrastructure Ltd* [2015] EWHC 481, at [92] and [95].

135 As an example of a very similar approach, see *Kalma v African Minerals Ltd* [2017] EWHC 1471 (QB), at [20(iii)], *per* Senior Master Fontaine.

136 See *CIP Properties (AIPT) Ltd v Galliford Try Infrastructure Ltd* [2015] EWHC 481, at [90], [91] and [96].

137 See *ibid*, at [96] and [97].

138 See, eg, *The Capital Markets Company (UK) Ltd v Tarver* [2017] EWHC 2885 Ch, at [6], *per* Mr Michael Furness QC (sitting as a deputy judge of the High Court).

find that sufficient time has already been allowed for certain tasks, in which case no further allowance needs to be made.[139]

- **Indication for assessment** Whilst the court lacks the power to approve incurred costs, it is able to comment on them[140] for the purposes of assisting any costs judge who may subsequently assess those costs. The court may be reluctant to make such comments if the court believes that the costs judge would be better placed to take a view as to what should be allowed.[141] Anecdotally, the court is more inclined to comment on specific items of principle (such as use of leading counsel) than general allegations going to quantum (such as excessive use of counsel).[142] For obvious reasons, where an adverse comment is made, it may substantially influence the outcome of any detailed assessment.
- **Decline to approve the budget** Finally, it would, in theory, be open to the court to decline to approve the budget entirely. Whilst such an approach may be appropriate in some circumstances,[143] Coulson J has commented that this would simply store up problems for the future and that, in general, it would not assist the parties.[144]

Respected commentators have referred to the fact that incurred costs are not subject to approval as being 'a failing in the scheme'.[145] This is certainly a cogent point to make given the fact that some claimants 'front-load' their claims so as to have already carried out most of the work that was required before the first budget is drafted. **12.86**

The exercise of discretion as to the level of the budget

When making a costs management order, the court's task is to adjust and approve the relevant costs. CPR, r 3.12(2), provides the following rather anodyne guidance: 'The purpose of costs management is that the court should manage both the steps to be taken and the costs to be incurred by the parties to any proceedings so as to further the overriding objective.' **12.87**

PD 3E, para 7.3, provides more detail: **12.88**

> 'In so far as the budgeted costs are not agreed, the court will review them and, after making any appropriate revisions, record its approval of those budgeted costs. The court's approval will relate only to the total figures for budgeted costs of each phase of the proceedings, although in the course of its review the court may have regard to the constituent elements of each total figure. When reviewing budgeted costs, the court will not undertake a detailed assessment in advance, but rather will consider whether the budgeted costs fall within the range of reasonable and proportionate costs.'

Thus, to the extent that the budgeted costs are not agreed, the court will review them and—after having made any appropriate revisions—record its approval.

---

139 See *ibid*, at [17].

140 See PD 3E, para 7.4. For an example of such comments being made in practice, see *Yeo v Times Newspapers Ltd* [2015] EWHC 209 (QB).

141 See, eg, *Richard v The British Broadcasting Corporation* [2017] EWHC 1666 (Ch), at [6], *per* Chief Master Marsh.

142 See Denis-Smith, J, 'Costs Budgeting: Completion and Challenges', *Westlaw Insight*, 13 November 2017, at para 19.

143 See, eg, *Willis v MRJ Rundell & Associates Ltd & Anor* [2013] EWHC 2923 (TCC).

144 *CIP Properties (AIPT) Ltd v Galliford Try Infrastructure Ltd* [2015] EWHC 481, at [87]–[89].

145 See *Cook on Costs 2017* (LexisNexis, online), para 15.8.

12.89 It should be noted that:

- the court's approval will relate only to the total figures for budgeted costs of each phase of the proceedings—although, in the course of its review, the court may have regard to the constituent elements of each total figure; and
- when reviewing budgeted costs, the court will not undertake a detailed assessment in advance, but rather will consider whether the budgeted costs fall within the range of reasonable and proportionate costs.[146]

12.90 Thus the process of reviewing and approving a budget is fundamentally different from a detailed assessment. In this regard, Stuart-Smith J had this to say:

> 'Experience in the [Technology and Construction Court] has shown most cost budgeting reviews can and should be carried out quickly and with the application of a fairly broad brush. Only exceptionally, will it be appropriate or necessary to go through a Precedent H with a fine tooth-comb [*sic*], analysing the makeup of figures in detail.'[147]

12.91 If the costs are reasonable, then approval may be given without any revision of the amount claimed. This used to happen commonly, because many judges adopted a 'light touch' in relation to such matters. Indeed, in the early days of budgeting, some judges went so far as to suggest that the court ought to be cautious about altering budgets at all.[148] Now that judges have gained more experience and confidence, however, it is considerably less common for contested budgets to be approved as claimed.

Timing of futurity

12.92 There can be no doubt that budgeting is a prospective exercise, but the wording of PD 3E, para 7.4, is that 'the court may not approve costs incurred before the date of any costs management hearing'. This implies that the court is unable to approve costs that were yet to be incurred at the time the draft budget was prepared, but which had been incurred by the time of the hearing (or at least the time of the first costs management hearing). Indeed, there is some support for this view in the authorities.[149] This may be so, but, in practice and in the absence of a reason to do otherwise, most judges will work pragmatically on the basis that the draft budget states the costs at the time of the hearing. One could argue that drafters of budgets ought to attempt to keep the provision of PD 3E, para 7.4, in mind.

Comparison of budgets

12.93 For obvious reasons, when considering the amounts claimed in a party's budget, the court may have regard to the amounts claimed in the opponent's budget. That said, both Stuart-Smith J[150] and Judge Hacon[151] have explained that it would not be appropriate to take the

---

[146] See PD 3E, para 7.3.

[147] *GSK Project Management Ltd v QRP Holdings Ltd* [2015] EWHC 2274 (TCC), at [9].

[148] See *CRM Trading Ltd v Chubb Electronic Security Ltd* [2013] EWHC 3482 (QB), at [3], *per* Judge Mackie QC.

[149] See, eg, *Ali v Channel 5 Broadcast Ltd* [2018] EWHC 840 (Ch), at [55], *per* Arnold J. See also *Merrix v Heart of England NHS Foundation Trust* [2017] EWHC 346 (QB), at [16], *per* Carr J: 'They [PD 3E, paras 7.3, 7.4, and 7.7] confirm that when setting a costs budget, a court is dealing only with prospective costs. There is an ability, but no requirement, to comment on costs already incurred. Additionally, costs of the case management conference are to be treated as costs already incurred.'

[150] See *GSK Project Management Ltd v QRP Holdings Ltd* [2015] EWHC 2274 (TCC) at [14].

[151] See *Marks & Spencer plc v Asda Stores Ltd* [2016] EWHC 2081 (Pat), at [7]. Judge Hacon went on to say: '[W]hile of course it is true to say that the burden on one party in any litigation may be greater than that on the other party, and therefore one party's cost are no necessary guide to the costs liable to be incurred by

other party's costs budget as a starting point, this being because different parties to litigation have different roles and responsibilities.[152] Moreover, the court often accepts that firms who work for insured clients often charge a lower hourly rate.[153]

12.94 The court tends to be alive to the fact that some parties may be tempted to depress their budgets artificially in an attempt to cajole the court into reducing the amounts that the court approves for their opponent's budget. It will often be obvious when a party has succumbed to such a temptation. Nonetheless, Stuart-Smith J has said that if a party wishes to impugn an opponent's certificate that the budget is a fair and accurate statement of incurred and estimated costs that it would be reasonable and proportionate for that party to incur (see 12.34), such an assertion needs to be properly substantiated and, in general, evidence will be required.[154] The evidence of the costs lawyer or a costs draftsperson may be helpful in that regard.

Hourly rates

12.95 As to hourly rates, PD 3E, para 7.10, provides as follows:

> 'The making of a costs management order under rule 3.15 concerns the totals allowed for each phase of the budget. It is not the role of the court in the cost management hearing to fix or approve the hourly rates claimed in the budget. The underlying detail in the budget for each phase used by the party to calculate the totals claimed is provided for reference purposes only to assist the court in fixing a budget.'

Thus the court will not fix or approve hourly rates. There have been instances of the court approving specific hourly rates,[155] but those cases tend to have been decided before the paragraph cited above came into being.

12.96 That said, the court will not ignore the hourly rates. The reality must be that the court is, at the very least, entitled to take them into account when considering the costs claimed in each phase. In this regard, Warby J had this to say:

> 'Precedent H allows the court to review hourly rates and estimated hours by requiring these to be stated on the form. It seems to me that whilst the question of whether the totals are reasonable and proportionate will always be the overall criterion, the court may need to consider rates and estimated hours. The approach will need to be tailored to the case before the court.'[156]

In a similar vein, Stephen Furst QC (sitting in the Technology and Construction Court) noted that the fact the overall budget figures were not disproportionate did not preclude the court from going on to look at the objections raised in relation to individual items

---

the other party, it is still legitimate to make a comparison, and then having done so to consider whether good reasons have been advanced to explain any difference, particularly where the difference in costs projected are quite dramatic.'

[152] That said, the court will bear in mind the fact that both sides need to 'be on top of all the relevant material': see *CIP Properties (AIPT) Ltd v Galliford Try Infrastructure Ltd* [2015] EWHC 481 (TCC), at [49], *per* Coulson J.

[153] See, eg, *Bloomberg LP v Sandberg (a firm)* [2016] EWHC 488 (TCC), at [18], *per* Mr Acton Davis QC (sitting as a deputy judge of the High Court).

[154] *GSK Project Management Ltd v QRP Holdings Ltd* [2015] EWHC 2274 (TCC), at [15].

[155] See, eg, *Stocker v Stocker* [2015] EWHC 1634 (QB); *GSK Project management Ltd v QPR* [2015] EWHC 2274 (TCC); *Group Seven Ltd v Nasir* [2016] EWHC 620 (Ch), at [40]–[45], *per* Morgan J.

[156] *Yeo v Times Newspapers Ltd* [2015] EWHC 2132 (QB), at [66].

claimed in those budgets.[157] Similarly, Michael Furness QC (sitting as a deputy judge of the High Court) specifically commented on the hourly rates as being a factor that led him to find that the costs claimed were excessive.[158]

12.97 The fact that the court will not fix or approve hourly rates has generated a certain degree of debate. Matthew Harman (a highly respected costs lawyer) has said that hourly rates must at least have 'some impact on budgets' and that it would be difficult to 'square not looking at hourly rates when dealing with the budget'.[159] Given the fact that the court will not, in general, examine the hourly rate at assessment (see 12.161), one can understand why those concerns exist. Indeed, whilst it is only his opinion and whilst he could be wrong, the editor believes that PD 3E, para 7.10, should be interpreted as meaning that the court may, if it so chooses, have regard to the rates that are claimed and will, if appropriate, set a figure for each phase that is based on lower (or possibly higher) hourly rates, but that the court will stop short of fixing or approving the rates and that any working views that the court may have expressed will not be part of the approved budget. In particular, if the court has expressed a working view on the rates, the party whose budget it is may, if it so chooses upon being awarded costs, be free to claim whatever rates it believes appropriate.

12.98 In any event, it would seem that the court is able to *comment* on hourly rates even if it does not fix them. Where there is a significant disparity in the hourly rates claimed by the parties and where the court wishes to compare the parties' budgets, it is open to the court to focus on the hours claimed.[160] As an example of the way in which the court will approve a budget, it is instructive to look at what Senior Master Fontaine had to say with regards to a multimillion-pound budget in group litigation:

> 'In accordance with PD 3E, paragraph 7.10, I have neither approved hourly rates nor set particular hours. Consideration of the underlying detail in the budgets has assisted me in arriving at the appropriate figures for estimated costs for each phase. However I have taken account in my determination of the reasonable and proportionate amount of profit costs that I consider that the hourly rates charged by the Claimants are too high for the claims in this case.'[161]

Proportionality

12.99 For the purposes of applying the new proportionality test,[162] the court will take into account the whole of the costs claimed (including costs already incurred).[163] The court will stand back and consider whether the total sums on each side are proportionate in accordance with CPR, r 44.3(5).[164] The topic of proportionality in general is addressed in

---

[157] See *King v Thipthorp* (unreported), 11 February 2016, QBD (TCC).

[158] See *The Capital Markets Company (UK) Ltd v Tarver* [2017] EWHC 2885 Ch, at [15] and [16].

[159] See Rose, N, 'Master More than Halves £1m Budget', *Litigation Futures*, 12 September 2013.

[160] See, eg, *GSK Project Management Ltd v QRP Holdings Ltd* [2015] EWHC 2274 (TCC), at [8], *per* Stuart-Smith J; cf *Bloomberg LP v Sandberg (a firm)* [2016] EWHC 488 (TCC), at [25], *per* Mr Acton Davis QC (sitting as a deputy judge of the High Court).

[161] *Kalma v African Minerals Ltd* [2017] EWHC 1471 (QB), at [20(iv)].

[162] See Lord Neuberger of Abbotsbury, MR, 'Proportionate Costs: 15th Lecture in the Implementation Programme', 29 May 2012, at para 3 *et seq.*

[163] See PD 3E, para 7.4 (emphasis added): 'The court may ... record its comments on those costs and *will* take those costs into account when considering the reasonableness and proportionality of all subsequent costs.'

[164] See *Yeo v Times Newspapers Ltd* [2015] EWHC 209 (QB), at [66], *per* Warby J. As an example of the court taking CPR, r 44.3(5), into account, see *Kalma v African Minerals Ltd* [2017] EWHC 1471 (QB), at [6], *per* Senior Master Fontaine. See also Ramsay J, 'Costs Management: A Necessary Part of the Management

Chapter 25. As can be seen from what is said in that chapter, the court ought to take into account all of the relevant circumstances, but it ought to base its evaluative judgment of the proportionate allowance on the factors listed in CPR, r 44.3(5).

Nugee J has explained that, when interpreting CPR, r 3.15(2), it would be a mistake to take an overly narrow view of proportionality: **12.100**

> 'It does seem to me that this application should be determined on whether the making of a costs management order would be something that is likely overall to save expense and thereby enable the court to deal with the case more justly and more in accordance with the overriding objective or whether it would really be a waste of money and not achieve anything that was worth the money that had to be spent on it.'[165]

Morgan J has explained that the rules do not prescribe any particular mathematical relationship between the costs and the sums in issue, saying that 'it would obviously be inappropriate to do so'.[166] That said, certain rules of thumb (arguably) are developing—although it ought to be borne in mind that all of the relevant facts ought to be taken into account and value is only one of the factors listed in CPR, r 44.3(5). Certainly, where costs are in excess of the damages in dispute, the court will be concerned about proportionality.[167] Moreover, Judge Hacon (sitting as a judge of the High Court) had this to say: **12.101**

> '[O]ne approach to assessing proportionality, by way of a very rough rule of thumb, is to consider whether the costs budget exceeds half the value of the claim. I think all that was being suggested by Morgan J is that as a starting point, if the court comes to the view that the costs budget in question significantly exceeds half the value of the claim, then this may raise a rebuttable indication that those costs are not proportionate. It is not difficult to think of circumstances that would rebut that indication; for example, that there may be litigation which is extremely important to a particular party such that the outcome will determine whether that party can continue to trade or not. Alternatively, the issues may be very complex. However, the comparison between the costs budget and the value of the claim provides some sort of a starting point and therefore I must consider it.'[168]

Where appropriate, the court may take into account its own knowledge of the amount of costs that are typically incurred in the type of case in question.[169]

Leggatt J had the following to say about proportionality in high-value cases: **12.102**

> 'In a case such as this where very large amounts of money are at stake, it may be entirely reasonable from the point of view of a party incurring costs, to spare no expense that might possibly help to influence the risk of the proceedings. It does not follow, however, that such expense should be guarded as reasonably or proportionately incurred or reasonable and proportionate in amount when it comes to determining what costs are recoverable from

of Litigation—16th Lecture in the Implementation Programme', 29 May 2012, at para 16: '[The] judge carrying out costs management will not only scrutinise the reasonableness of each party's budget, but also stand back and consider whether the total sums on each side are "proportionate" in accordance with the new definition.' Ramsay J's comments were based almost word for word on Jackson, R, *Review of Civil Litigation Costs: Final Report* (London: HMSO, 2010), ch 40, at para 7.23.

165 *Sharp v Blank* [2017] EWHC 141 (Ch), at [8].

166 See *Group Seven Ltd v Nasir* [2016] EWHC 620 (Ch), at [22].

167 See, eg, *GSK Project Management Ltd v QRP Holdings Ltd* [2015] EWHC 2274 (TCC), at [12], *per* Stuart-Smith J. See also *Bloomberg LP v Sandberg (a firm)* [2016] EWHC 488 (TCC).

168 *Marks & Spencer plc v ADSA Stores Ltd* [2016] EWHC 2081 (Pat), at [11].

169 See, eg, *ibid*, at [25].

> the other party. What is reasonable and proportionate in that context must be judged objectively. The touchstone is not the amount of costs which it was in a party's best interests to incur but the lowest amount which it could reasonably have been expected to spend in order to have its case conducted and presented proficiently, having regard to all the relevant circumstances. Expenditure over and above this level should be for a party's own account and not recoverable from the other party ...'[170]

Thus proportionality applies to such cases.

Grossly excessive budgets

12.103 As to grossly excessive budgets, Stuart-Smith J had this to say:

> 'It is hard to imagine anything more sterile than arguing about a grossly excessive costs estimate. It does not go to the issues, it is wasteful of Court and the parties' time, and it offends against the obligation to keep costs to the reasonable minimum (both in the fact of the estimate and the need to whittle it down).'[171]

Procedure after approval

12.104 Once the budgeted costs have been approved (or agreed), then PD 3E, para 7.7, will apply. It reads as follows: 'After its budgeted costs have been approved or agreed, each party shall re-file and re-serve the budget in the form approved or agreed with re-cast figures, annexed to the order approving the budgeted costs or recording the parties' agreement.' This means that, following approval or agreement, parties must recast the budget with the approved or agreed figures, and then refile and re-serve that document in the form of an annex to the costs management order. Fraser J has said that it would not be right to depart from this requirement by simply recording the relevant figures in the draft costs management order, not least because this may lead to errors being made.[172] Where the budget has been approved on the basis of assumptions that are different from those in the initial budget, it would be wise to revise those assumptions accordingly.[173]

12.105 Many courts now deal with budgets electronically, which (subject to the court's wishes) may obviate the need for the parties to refile and re-serve the approved budgets.

The treatment of interim applications

12.106 In so far as interim applications are concerned, PD 3E, para 7.9, provides as follows: 'If interim applications are made which, reasonably, were not included in a budget, then the costs of such interim applications shall be treated as additional to the approved budgets.' Whilst there is no authority on the point, it is implicit in this rule that such costs, if not agreed, would be assessed without reference to the budget (either by way of summary or detailed assessment). As such, there would be no need to apply to amend the budget to take them into account; indeed, one could argue that the court would, in general, have no power to allow such an amendment because such costs would generally be incurred as a matter of urgency and therefore would already have been incurred by the time that any such application had been made.

---

170 *Kazakhstan Kagazy Plc v Zhunas* [2015] EWHC 404 (Comm), at [13].

171 *GSK Project Management Ltd v QRP Holdings Ltd* [2015] EWHC 2274 (TCC), at [62].

172 See *Broom v Archer* (unreported), 28 March 2018, QBD, *per* Fraser J.

173 This is the advice of the editors of *Cook on Costs 2017*, both of whom are experienced judges: see *Cook on Costs 2017* (LexisNexis, online), para 15.7.

Amendments, revisions, etc

Budgeting may be a difficult exercise and, as such, it may be foreseeable that a review will be necessary. In this regard, PD 3E, para 7.5, provides as follows: 'The court may set a timetable or give other directions for future reviews of budgets.' Thus, where appropriate, it is possible to plan to review budgets. **12.107**

In addition to planned reviews, reviews may be necessary as a result of significant developments in the litigation. In this regard, PD 3E, para 7.6, provides as follows: **12.108**

> 'Each party shall revise its budget in respect of future costs upwards or downwards, if significant developments in the litigation warrant such revisions. Such amended budgets shall be submitted to the other parties for agreement. In default of agreement, the amended budgets shall be submitted to the court, together with a note of (a) the changes made and the reasons for those changes and (b) the objections of any other party. The court may approve, vary or disapprove the revisions, having regard to any significant developments which have occurred since the date when the previous budget was approved or agreed.'

It should be noted that budgets may need to be revised either upwards *or* downwards—although the latter is rarely encountered in practice (see 12.129).

As can be seen from 12.108, parties are under a duty to revise their budgets in respect of 'future costs' if significant developments in the litigation warrant such revisions. Revised budgets ought to be submitted to the other parties for agreement. If no agreement can be reached, then they ought to be submitted to the court together with a note of: **12.109**

- the changes made and the reasons for those changes; and
- the objections of any other party.

The court may then approve, vary or disapprove the revisions, having regard to any significant developments that have occurred since the date on which the previous budget was approved or agreed. In practice, 'notes' are often in the form of witness statements.

The need to apply promptly and the influence of delay

Whilst he was talking about a case being managed under the Mercantile Pilot rather than CPR, Part 3, Section II, Coulson J had the following to say about when an application should be made: 'When should an application to revise/amend a costs management order be made? In my judgement, it ought to be made immediately it becomes apparent that the original budget costs have been exceeded by more than a minimal amount.'[174] It would seem that a relevant factor in deciding whether to allow an application for an amendment is the prejudice to the other side caused by any delay in making the application. If, for example, the failure to apply timeously has led to the opponent having insufficient ATE insurance, then that would be a factor that could be taken into account.[175] It is possible that the same could be said of litigation funding. **12.110**

Applications may be made right up to and including—but not after (see 12.124)—trial, although very late applications are unlikely to find favour, not least because, by that **12.111**

[174] See *Elvanite Full Circle Ltd v AMEC Earth & Environmental (UK) Ltd* [2013] EWHC 1643 (TCC), at [37].

[175] See, eg, *ibid*, at [41].

stage, it may have become appropriate simply to leave matters in the hands of a costs judge.[176]

The need to attempt to agree amended budgets

12.112 PD 3E, para 7.6, expressly provides that amended budgets shall be submitted to the other parties for agreement. If this is not done, the application may be refused on that ground alone.

12.113 It should be noted that it is possible that budgets that have been amended by consent may still have to be founded on 'significant developments' in the sense that the court may decline to approve an amended budget (or a costs judge may find good reason to depart from it) if the reality of the situation is that the parties have consensually agreed to 'repair' a defective budget.

12.114 It has been suggested that the wording of PD 3E, para 7.6, is such that a budget that has been amended by agreement does not need to be filed at court.[177] This may be so, but perhaps the better interpretation is that the provisions as set out in 12.108 apply to such budgets in just the same way as they apply to other budgets. In any event, it is difficult to envisage circumstances in which any benefit would derive from not filing such documents.

The applicable test

12.115 Whilst PD 3E, para 7.6, does not expressly state the applicable test, it is implicit that that test is whether there have been significant developments that have occurred since the date on which the previous budget was approved or agreed that warrants the revision that is sought. This—arguably—is a higher threshold than showing 'good reason' at an assessment, but it should be noted that if such developments exist, the parties appear (according to the first sentence of PD 3E, para 7.6) to be under a duty to submit revised budgets. As such, a receiving party may find it difficult to persuade a costs judge that a 'good reason' exists if that party elected not to submit a revised budget when that would have been an appropriate course of action. Each case would, no doubt, be decided on its own facts.

12.116 Picken J has explained that putative developments that were foreseeable at the time of the most recent approved or agreed budget may not suffice,[178] but it ought to be borne in mind that the test for including contingencies is whether those costs are more likely than not to be incurred (see 12.36–12.41). One could argue that the test of whether the costs were foreseeable should have regard to that standard.

12.117 As to what may constitute a 'significant development', see the footnotes.[179] Whilst an obvious point, the court will tend to reflect the case management decisions taken during the course of a case and the costs management hearing in the costs management order.

---

[176] Whilst now an old case, see *Board of Trustees of National Museums & Galleries on Merseyside v AEW Architects & Designers Ltd* [2013] EWHC 3025 (TCC), at [40].

[177] See, eg, The White Book 2017, para 3.15.1.

[178] See *Churchill v Boot* [2016] EWHC 1322 (QB), at [10] and [14].

[179] An increase in the size of the claim does not necessarily mean that the costs of the claim will rise: see *ibid*, at [10]. The mere fact that a trial has been adjourned will not necessarily amount to a significant development (see *ibid*, at [11]), but an increase in the length of the trial may (see *JSC Mezhdunarodniy Promyshlenniy Bank and another v Pugachev and others* [2017] EWHC 1853 (Ch), *per* Birss J, and *Sharp v Blank* [2017] EWHC 3390 (Ch), *per* Chief Master Marsh). A change of counsel would not, of itself, generally amount to a significant development: see *Greig v Lauchlan* (unreported), 7 December 2016, Ch D, *per* Richard Millett QC. A change in the

Retrospective amendments and judicial comments on costs incurred since the date of the last approved or agreed budget

It may be that a party seeks to revise a budget that includes costs which have already been incurred. There is some doubt about how such costs are to be treated. **12.118**

In 2017, the editors of The White Book have pointed out that the amendments made to CPR, Part 3, Section II, now make it clear that there is a distinction between 'incurred costs' and 'budgeted costs'.[180] They said that: **12.119**

> 'Practice Direction 3E, para.7.4 (amended by CPR Update 88, again with effect from 6 April 2017), provides that the court may not approve costs incurred before the date of any case management hearing but may take those costs [ie the incurred costs] into account when considering the reasonableness and proportionality of all budgeted costs.'[181]

They went on to say that '[t]his paragraph makes little sense unless the words "those costs" are construed as costs previously placed in the incurred costs columns', explaining as follows:

> 'For example, a party's budget may have been reasonably drawn on the assumption that no formal mediation would take place. Consequently, none of the budgeted costs relate to mediation. If, later in the proceedings, a real possibility of mediation arises, the parties need not seek prior approval in respect of it before incurring any expense. Of course, the parties should not delay in seeking the agreement of other parties or, failing that, the approval of the court. Also, any costs incurred on mediation before agreement or approval is obtained are at risk that such agreement or approval might never be obtained.'[182]

This guidance—which no longer appears in The White Book—has been interpreted as meaning that costs that have been incurred in the interval between the last agreed or approved budget and the date on which the court considers an application to revise that budget are to be treated as being costs that potentially will be placed into the 'budgeted costs' category.[183] Put otherwise, this has been interpreted as meaning that the court is able to allow those costs retrospectively as being included in the budget. Indeed, whilst his decision is not binding, Chief Master Marsh has gone so far as to allow costs to be retrospectively added to the budget that pre-dated the last agreed budget.[184] **12.120**

There are powerful arguments against such an approach (not least among which is the fact that the current edition of The White Book no longer contains these passages). It could be said that it would run counter to the whole ethos of budgeting to include costs already incurred as if they were budgeted costs, which, by its very nature, is a prospective exercise (see 12.92). Moreover, PD 3E, para 7.6, refers—in terms—to 'future costs'. Furthermore, Warby J has explained (albeit under the pre-April 2017 rules) that the power to amend a **12.121**

---

law will not necessarily amount to a significant development (not least because it would not necessarily be a development in the litigation): see *Yeo v Times Newspapers Ltd* [2015] EWHC 2132 (QB), at [50] and [51], *per* Warby J.

[180] See The White Book 2017, para 3.12.3.

[181] See *ibid.*

[182] See *ibid.*

[183] Whilst not binding, see *Sharp v Blank* [2017] EWHC 3390 (Ch), *per* Chief Master Marsh.

[184] See *ibid*; cf *Venus Asset Management Ltd v Matthews & Goodman LLP* [2015] EWHC 2896 (Ch), at [48], also *per* Chief Master Marsh. In *Sharp v Blank* [2017] EWHC 3390 (Ch), at [30], Chief Master Marsh sought to distinguish *Venus* on the basis that 'it was not a case based upon significant developments'.

budget is 'not an apt vehicle for obtaining the court's approval for costs incurred before the budget',[185] and it is not entirely clear why the fact that the rules now make an express distinction between the incurred costs and budgeted costs should change this. Furthermore, the rules now expressly provide that the court lacks the power to approve 'costs incurred before the date of *any* costs management hearing' (see PD 3E, para 7.4, emphasis added), which arguably confirms that this restriction is not limited to cost incurred before the first costs management hearing.

12.122 As such, it would seem—at the very least—arguable that the power of the court is limited to making revisions to costs yet to be incurred at the time of the costs management hearing (or possibly, and pragmatically, some earlier date, such as that on which the application to amend was made). This interpretation would be consistent with the fact that (a) genuinely urgent matters will usually lead to interim applications, the costs of which are treated as being additional to the approved budgets (see PD 3E, para 7.9), and (b) there is a fall-back provision in the sense that a costs judge would have the power to depart from the budget for 'good reason'.[186]

12.123 If it is right to say that the court lacks the power to approve costs incurred since the last approved or agreed budget, then if the amount of those costs in any phase exceed the relevant costs in that budget, they would, if appropriate, fall to be considered by a costs judge under the 'good reason' provisions (see 12.151–12.153). It this is right, then those costs ought not to feature at all in the budget (either as incurred costs or budgeted costs); instead, they should be claimed in the bill of costs in the relevant phase, whereupon the costs judge will consider whether they should be allowed pursuant to CPR, r 3.18(b). That said, the contrary is arguable (not least on the grounds of pragmatism). It is far from clear what the correct procedure is.

12.124 What is beyond doubt, however, is that the court lacks the power to amend a budget after trial.[187] Whilst he was talking about a case being managed under the Mercantile Pilot, Coulson J had the following to say about an application to amend the budget that was made after the trial:

> '[I]n my judgment, an application to amend an approved costs budget after judgment is a contradiction in terms. First, it would mean that the exercise would no longer be a budgeting exercise, and would instead be based on the actual costs that have been incurred. Secondly, it would encourage parties to "wait and see"; only applying to increase the budget costs if it was in their interests. Thirdly, it would make a nonsense of the costs management regime if, at the end of the trial, a party could apply to double the amount of its costs budget. The certainty provided by the new rules would be lost entirely if the parties thought that, after the trial, the successful party could seek

---

185 *Yeo v Times Newspapers Ltd* [2015] EWHC 2132 (QB), at [47]. See also *Venus Asset Management Ltd v Matthews & Goodman LLP* [2015] EWHC 2896 (Ch), *per* Chief Master Marsh.

186 In this regard, see *Venus Asset Management Ltd v Matthews & Goodman LLP* [2015] EWHC 2896 (Ch), at [48], *per* Chief Master Marsh; see also *Yeo v Times Newspapers Ltd* [2015] EWHC 2132 (QB), at [48], *per* Warby J.

187 See *Elvanite Full Circle Ltd v AMEC Earth & Environmental (UK) Ltd* [2013] EWHC 1643 (TCC), at [39], *per* Coulson J; see also *Capital for Enterprise Fund A LP v Bibby Financial Services Ltd* (unreported), 18 November 2015, Ch D (Manchester District Registry), at [3], *per* Judge Pelling QC (sitting as a judge of the High Court).

retrospective approval for costs incurred far beyond the level approved in the costs management order.'[188]

It may be that a judge, after trial, is asked to pass comment on costs incurred since the last agreed or approved budget. Judge Pelling (sitting as a judge of the High Court) has doubted the existence of any such power.[189] Whilst other judges have taken a different view, they tend to discourage such a practice. Mr Stephen Furst QC (sitting as a deputy High Court judge) had this to say on the point: **12.125**

'I can understand that there might be cases where the trial judge has a particular view of costs or on an aspect of costs, having conducted the trial or where he has had to decide an issue which is directly relevant to the assessment of costs. Absent such circumstances it would seem to me that a court should not seek to trammel the Costs Judge's jurisdiction, particularly where the Costs Judge has much greater experience of such matters than I have.'[190]

Errors and omissions

A party who makes a mistake when preparing a budget may find themselves being forced to live with the consequences. The editors of The White Book say this on the point: **12.126**

'The court expects parties to prepare budgets carefully and requires them to certify their accuracy. Rule 1.1 (definition of the overriding objective) and r3.9 (relief from sanctions), as amended, indicate that the courts should now take a tougher, no-nonsense approach to rule-compliance.'[191]

In a similar vein, Coulson J had this to say (albeit in the context of the Mercantile Pilot rather that CPR, Part 3, Section II): **12.127**

'In my view, in an ordinary case, it will be extremely difficult to persuade a court that inadequacies or mistakes in the preparation of a costs budget, which is then approved by the court, should be subsequently revised or rectified, ... The courts will expect parties to undertake the costs management exercise properly first time around, and will be slow to revise approved budgets merely because, after the event, it is said that particular items had been omitted or under-valued. I also agree that any other approach could make a nonsense of the whole costs management regime.'[192]

Indeed, PD 3E appears not to contain any express provision that allows the court to approve retrospectively an amendment of this nature (not least because it would not arise as a result of a significant development in the litigation).

Whilst an obvious point, errors in the costs management order itself may readily be remedied.[193] Mathematical errors may be met with a degree of judicial criticism.[194] **12.128**

---

[188] See *Elvanite Full Circle Ltd v AMEC Earth & Environmental (UK) Ltd* [2013] EWHC 1643 (TCC), at [39].

[189] *Capital for Enterprise Fund A LP v Bibby Financial Services Ltd* (unreported), 18 November 2015, Ch D (Manchester District Registry), at [5]–[7].

[190] *Car Giant Ltd v The Mayor and Burgesses of the London Borough of Hammersmith* [2017] EWHC 464 (TCC), at [34].

[191] See The White Book 2018, para 3.15.4.

[192] *Murray & Anor v Neil Dowlman Architecture Ltd* [2013] EWHC 872 (TCC), at [17]; see also *Elvanite Full Circle Ltd v AMEC Earth & Environmental (UK) Ltd* [2013) EWHC 1643 (TCC), at [49], *per* Coulson J.

[193] See, eg, *Caliendo v Mishcon De Reya* (unreported), 18 November 2015, Ch D, *per* Rose J.

[194] See *Broom v Archer* (unreported), 28 March 2018, QBD, *per* Fraser J.

Early settlement and narrowing of the issues

12.129 It is surprising that there have been very few instances of applications being made to revise budgets downwards. If the parties have narrowed the issues, then this would be a paradigm case for such an application to be made. Moreover, whilst there is no authority on the point, if a matter settles at a stage at which the costs judge may not find it easy to know the extent to which the costs under any given phase ought to have been spent at the point of settlement, one could argue that rather than relying on the 'good reason' provisions in CPR, r 3.18 (see 12.157), it may be more appropriate to apply to vary the budget. Whether this would be appropriate would depend on the facts, but there have been instances of the court exercising its discretion following discontinuance, so it seems as if the jurisdiction does exist.[195]

The Costs of the Budgeting Exercise

12.130 As to the costs of the budgeting exercise, PD 3E, para 7.2, reads as follows:

> 'Save in exceptional circumstances—
> (a) the recoverable costs of initially completing Precedent H shall not exceed the higher of £1,000 or 1% of the total of the incurred costs (as agreed or allowed on assessment) and the budgeted costs (agreed or approved); and
> (b) all other recoverable costs of the budgeting and costs management process shall not exceed 2% of the total of the incurred costs (as agreed or allowed on assessment) and the budgeted (agreed or approved) costs.'

12.131 Thus there are two components to the allowable costs: first, there is an allowance for the costs of initially completing Precedent H, which will not exceed the higher of £1,000 or 1 per cent of the total of the incurred costs (as agreed or allowed on assessment) and the budgeted costs (agreed or approved); and second, there is an addition allowance for all other recoverable costs, which will not exceed 2 per cent of those amounts. These limits may be disapplied in exceptional circumstances, but, where they apply, they will—in combination—limit the total costs of the budgeting exercise to 3 per cent of the approved or agreed budget. These provisions changed on 22 November 2017, the effect of which changes is that the amounts allowable may not be determined until after the incurred costs have been assessed or agreed.

12.132 It will be recalled that the Guidance stipulates that certain costs relating to budgeting[196] are to be included within the relevant case management conference (CMC) or pre-trial review (PTR) phase of the budget (see 12.30). This, presumably, means that those costs would be subject to the restrictions of any costs management order that was made in respect of those phases; what is less clear is whether those costs would also be included in the percentage caps referred to above. Master McCloud (sitting as a deputy costs judge) has commented on this issue, but did not decide it; indeed, she said that it would be helpful if the Civil Procedure Rule Committee could clarify this point.[197] On the basis of the Guidance as it

[195] *Medac Gesellschafte fur Klinischespezialpraparate GmbH V Star Pharmaceutical Ltd* [2015] EWHC 4063 (Ch).

[196] Namely, the costs of reviewing the opponent's budget, of correspondence with the opponent to agree budgets, of preparing updated costs budgets and of reviewing the opponent's revised budgets.

[197] See *Woodburn v Thomas* (unreported), 11 August 2017, Senior Courts Costs Office, at [23].

presently stands, there is a strong argument for saying that those monies should not be subject to the percentage cap, because otherwise cases may arise in which there would be uncertainty as to whether the budgeted CMC and PTR phases ought to be adjusted to take into account the fact that part of the costs were subject to the percentage cap. A contrary interpretation is arguable, however.

Whilst there is no authority on the point, it is likely that the percentage limits are exclusive of VAT. This is because Precedent H is designed in such a way as to discourage VAT being recorded therein,[198] so it would seem odd if the costs were payable on a VAT-inclusive basis. Moreover, if it were not a VAT-exclusive limit, then a VAT-registered litigant would have the advantage over a non-VAT-registered litigant—and that would be a curious state of affairs. **12.133**

Some commentators have pointed out that these allowances are likely to be well below the true costs involved.[199] The allowance of 1 per cent for initially completing Precedent H, for example, seems low when compared to the costs of drawing a bill of costs (which, anecdotally, are between 4 per cent and 6 per cent of the base costs as claimed). There will be cases in which the amount recoverable will not be sufficient to cover the costs, but it should not be forgotten that there is a great deal of overlap between the work that is done for the purposes of budgeting and the work that needs to be done in any event for the purposes of client care. Respected commentator Michael Cook has this to say on the point (in the context of the Defamation Pilot): **12.134**

> 'Although the scheme is mandatory, the costs estimates required are less detailed than those needed for a costs capping order and should not require much more than the level of information that solicitors are already obliged to provide their clients.'[200]

In this context, the allowable maxima do not seem as inadequate as they may at first appear.

There is no authority as to what amounts to 'exceptional circumstances', but if cases relating to similar provisions in CPR, Part 45, are anything to go by, then poor conduct on the part of an opponent of the party in question could well meet the relevant threshold, especially where that conduct has led to a wastage of costs (such as a need to repeatedly amend the budget).[201] That said, some commentators have noted that even where the threshold is met, it will not automatically follow that the court would wish to set the limits aside, because other types of order (especially interim costs orders) would often be a better and more immediate way of dealing with poor conduct.[202] **12.135**

It is not known how the court would apply the cap where the work of costs management was carried out at the same time as case management (such as a hearing that covered both).[203] Presumably, some sort of apportioning exercise would be required. **12.136**

---

198 In particular, there is a draft statement on the first page that reads: 'This estimate excludes VAT (if applicable) …'

199 See, eg, Gibbs, S, 'More Costs, Less Control: Is This Proportionality?' (2014) 158(1) SJ 27.

200 *Cook on Costs 2012* (LexisNexis, online), para 10.22.

201 See, eg, *Udogaranya v Nwagw* [2010] EWHC 90186 (Costs), at [23], *per* Master Haworth.

202 See, eg, *Cook on Costs 2017* (LexisNexis, online), para 15.10.

203 This was a point that was raised in Gibbs, S, 'More Costs, Less Control: Is This Proportionality?' (2014) 158(1) SJ 27.

The Effect of the Budget on the Assessment of Costs

12.137 A budget may be relevant to the assessment of costs in the following circumstances:

- where a costs management order has been made and the incurred costs fall to be assessed (see 12.138);
- where a costs management order has been made and the budgeted costs are to be assessed on the standard basis (12.140);
- where a costs management order has been made and the budgeted costs are to be assessed on the indemnity basis (12.166); and
- where no costs management order has been made (12.169).

Where a costs management order has been made and the incurred costs fall to be assessed

12.138 Where a costs management order has been made, incurred costs will be recorded in the budget, but will not have been subject to judicial scrutiny in the sense of having been budgeted (see 12.84). They are therefore not part of the budgeted costs and, as such, they will be assessed in the usual way. The issue of whether there is a good reason simply will not arise and this is so regardless of whether the judge who made the costs management order took them into account for the purposes of making that order.[204]

12.139 The judge who made the costs management order may, however, have made comments regarding those costs on the face of the order pursuant to CPR, r 3.15(4), or PD 3E, para 7.4 (see 12.84). Where this is so, CPR, r 3.18(c), provides that the costs judge will take those comments into account.

Where a costs management order has been made and costs are payable on the standard basis

12.140 Where a costs management order has been made and where costs are payable on the standard basis, then CPR, r 3.18,[205] will apply, which reads as follows:

> '**Assessing costs on the standard basis where a costs management order has been made**
>
> 3.18 In any case where a costs management order has been made, when assessing costs on the standard basis, the court will—
> (a) have regard to the receiving party's last approved or agreed budgeted costs for each phase of the proceedings;
> (b) not depart from such approved or agreed budgeted costs unless satisfied that there is good reason to do so; and
> (c) take into account any comments made pursuant to rule 3.15(4) or paragraph 7.4 of Practice Direction 3E and recorded on the face of the order.
>
> (Attention is drawn to rules 44.3(2)(a) and 44.3(5), which concern proportionality of costs.)'

204 *Harrison v University Hospitals Coventry & Warwickshire NHS Trust* [2017] EWCA Civ 792, at [45]–[54], *per* Davis LJ.

205 This provision was amended by the Civil Procedure (Amendment) Rules 2017 (SI 2017/95) to deal with the confusion engendered by *SARPD Oil International Ltd v Addax Energy SA & Anot* [2016] EWCA Civ 120, which caused there to be a belief that incurred costs fell within those costs that had been fixed by the budget.

Thus, on a standard-basis assessment, an assessment of budgeted costs should be by reference to each of the budgeted phases (as opposed to the total budgeted costs). The court will be able to use Precedent Q (see 43.52) for the purposes of comparing the costs that are claimed with those that were budgeted for each phase. The court will not depart from the amounts in each phase in the most recent approved or agreed budget unless there is 'good reason' to do so. **12.141**

Is it only the receiving party who has to show 'good reason' to depart from the budget?

It has never been in doubt that if a receiving party wishes to recover an amount that is, for any phase, greater than the budgeted costs, they will have to show that there is a 'good reason' to do so (assuming, of course, that the costs are payable on the standard basis). It has, however, been argued that the same is not true where a paying party contends for an amount that is less than the relevant budgeted costs. In particular, it has been argued that the existence of a costs management order does not in any way prevent the court, upon detailed assessment from reducing costs in accordance with the ordinary principles of assessment and that, in this regard, the budget would be merely a factor to be taken into account. In this respect, reliance has been placed on CPR, r 44.4(3)(h), which lists 'the last agreed or approved budget' as a factor that the court will take into account. **12.142**

This issue arose in an appeal before Carr J. She posed the question that she had to answer in the following way: 'To what extent, if at all, does the costs budgeting regime under CPR Part 3 fetter the powers and discretion of the costs judge at a detailed assessment of costs under CPR Part 47?'[206] Carr J went on to expand upon that question: **12.143**

> '[The receiving party] contended that where a receiving party claims costs at or less than the budgeted figure, his or her costs should be assessed as claimed, unless the paying party establishes a good reason to depart from the budgeted figure. [The paying party], by contrast, contended that the paying party is entitled to benefit from a full detailed assessment *de novo*, with the costs budget being but one factor in determining reasonable and proportionate costs on detailed assessment. The costs judge is not fettered in that assessment by the costs budget. Thus the Respondent's position was (and remains) that a paying party does not need good reason to persuade a court to depart from an approved or agreed budget downwards, but a receiving party needs a good reason to persuade a court to depart from an approved or agreed budget upwards.'[207]

In the court at first instance, District Judge Lumb had found for the paying party (albeit in a nuanced way). In particular, he had found that the budget, although not binding, was a 'strong guide' to what ought to be allowed on a detailed assessment, but that there was no need for the paying party to point to a good reason why the costs should be allowed at a lesser figure.

Carr J's conclusion—which was subsequently cited with approval by the Court of Appeal in a different case[208]—was as follows: **12.144**

> '[W]here a costs management order has been made, when assessing costs on the standard basis, the costs judge will not depart from the receiving party's last approved or agreed

[206] See *Merrix v Heart of England NHS Foundation Trust* [2017] EWHC 346 (QB), at [3].
[207] See *ibid*, at [4].
[208] See *Harrison v University Hospitals Coventry & Warwickshire NHS Trust* [2017] EWCA Civ 792, at [28], *per* Davis LJ.

budget unless satisfied that there is good reason to do so. This applies as much where the receiving party claims a sum equal to or less than the sums budgeted as where the receiving party seeks to recover more than the sums budgeted.'[209]

12.145 Carr J also said:

> 'The words [of CPR, r 3.18] are clear. The court will not—the words are mandatory—depart from the budget, absent good reason. On a detailed assessment on a standard basis, the costs judge is bound by the agreed or approved costs budget, unless there is good reason to depart from it. No distinction is made between the situation where it is claimed that budgeted figures are or are not to be exceeded. It is not possible to square the words of CPR 3.18 with the suggestion that the assessing costs judge may nevertheless depart from the budget without good reason and carry out a line by line assessment, merely using the budget as a guide or factor to be taken into account in the subsequent detailed assessment exercise. The obvious intention of CPR 3.18 was to reduce the scope of and need for detailed assessment. The Respondent's approach would defeat that object.'[210]

Thus the need to show good reason will apply to both paying and receiving parties. Davis LJ subsequently had this to say on the topic:

> 'The appellant's argument [to the contrary] has this initial, and unattractive, oddity. If it is right, it involves a most unappealing lack of reciprocity. It means that a receiving party may only seek to recover more than the approved or agreed budgeted amount if good reason is shown; whereas the paying party may seek to pay less than the approved or agreed budgeted amount without good reason being required to be shown. It is difficult to see the sense or fairness in that. Nor does this argument show much appreciation for the position of the actual parties to the litigation—not just the prospective paying party but also the prospective receiving party—who need at an early stage in the litigation to know, as best they can, where they stand.'[211]

12.146 Returning to Carr J's judgment, she went on to add this:

> 'It is important to remember at the outset (and also in the context of the debate as to the meaning of the word "budget" addressed below) precisely what a judge is doing at the cost-budgeting stage. He/she is not identifying what is the maximum amount by way of future costs considered to be reasonable and proportionate. He/she is identifying what future costs are reasonable and proportionate.'[212]

12.147 Carr J went on to say that 'the significance of the rule in CPR 3.18 cannot be overstated' and that 'the setting of a costs budget is an exercise of fundamental importance'.[213] She added this:

> 'It is fair to ask the question that, if it be right that an agreed or approved costs budget is no more than a guide at detailed assessment, even if a strong one, what point there can be in the parties and the court spending so much time on the cost budgeting exercise. The Respondent counters that it will still have value in that it can be a strong

---

209 See *Merrix v Heart of England NHS Foundation Trust* [2017] EWHC 346 (QB), at [92].

210 See *ibid*, at [67]. In this regard, Carr J placed reliance on *SARPD Oil International Ltd v Addax Energy SA* [2016] EWCA Civ 120, at [41], [43], [47], [49] and [52], and *MacInnes v Gross* [2017] EWHC 127 (QB), at [25].

211 See *Harrison v University Hospitals Coventry & Warwickshire NHS Trust* [2017] EWCA Civ 792, at [36].

212 See *Merrix v Heart of England NHS Foundation Trust* [2017] EWHC 346 (QB), at [68].

213 See *ibid*, at [71], drawing upon comments made by Coulson J in *MacInnes v Gross* [2017] EWHC 127 (QB), at [25].

guide and so be likely to deter some detailed assessments altogether. But it is still difficult to see why so much time and money would be invested at the costs management stage if the budget were to be no more than a guide in any case where there is an underspend.'[214]

Davis LJ subsequently made similar comments.[215]

As to the suggestion that the above approach might replace detailed assessment, Carr J had this to say: **12.148**

> 'It is of course right to say that costs budgeting under section II of CPR 3 does not "replace" detailed assessment. It is common ground that ... Precedent Q is not an advanced assessment of the recoverable costs. It informs the court, in a readily accessible format, what has been spent compared with the budget. But the Appellant is not contending that there should be no detailed assessment. On the contrary, the question is how that assessment should be conducted. Further and on any analysis, there remains room for detailed assessment outside the budget—for example in relation to pre-incurred costs not the subject of the costs budget; costs of interim applications which were reasonably not included in a budget; where costs are being assessed on an indemnity basis; where the costs judge finds there to be a good reason for departing from the costs budget.'[216]

Carr J went on to say that 'the scope and cost of detailed assessment of costs on a standard basis will indeed be reduced materially'.[217]

Where the amounts claimed are lower in certain phases than the budgeted costs

If the sums claimed for any phase are lower than the budgeted amount, then by operation of the indemnity principle (see 12.154–12.156), the amount that may be allowed for that phase will be restricted to that lower amount, albeit on a generous basis (see 12.155). In an appropriate case, it may be open to a receiving party to argue that savings in one phase may amount to 'good reason' for allowing a greater amount in another phase, such as where savings were made on disclosure, but this resulted in more work being required on witness statements. This does not mean, however, that it would ever be appropriate to move costs between phases in an unprincipled way in an attempt to make the costs claimed match the amounts budgeted in each phase. If there has been an element of 'robbing Peter to pay Paul', the editor is firmly of the view that this always ought to be brought to the court's attention in the context of it being a putative good reason to depart from the budget. Indeed, surreptitiously doing otherwise would probably amount to misconduct within the meaning of CPR, r 44.11. **12.149**

Whilst he was dealing with a summary assessment rather than a detailed assessment, Roger Wyand QC (sitting as a deputy judge of the High Court) accepted that where there had been overspend in some phases and underspend in others, it was legitimate to have regard to the fact that the total budget had not been overtopped.[218] **12.150**

---

214 See *Merrix v Heart of England NHS Foundation Trust* [2017] EWHC 346 (QB), at [71].
215 See *Harrison v University Hospitals Coventry & Warwickshire NHS Trust* [2017] EWCA Civ 792, at [32].
216 See *Merrix v Heart of England NHS Foundation Trust* [2017] EWHC 346 (QB), at [78].
217 See *ibid*, at [83].
218 See *Sony Communications International AB v SSH Communications Security Corporation* [2016] EWHC 2985 (Pat), at [15(iii)] and [17].

Good reason and points of assessment in general

12.151 As is set out above, a good reason is required to depart from the budgeted costs in any given phase. As to the standard of reason required, Davis LJ had this to say:

> '[The requirement that there be a good reason] is a significant fetter on the court having an unrestricted discretion: it is deliberately designed to be so. Costs judges should therefore be expected not to adopt a lax or over-indulgent approach to the need to find "good reason": if only because to do so would tend to subvert one of the principal purposes of costs budgeting and thence the overriding objective.'[219]

Thus costs judges ought to be careful not to adopt a lax or overindulgent approach to the need to find 'good reason'.

12.152 Davis LJ added this:

> '[W]hile the context and the wording of CPR 3.18 (b) is different from that of CPR 3.9 relating to relief from sanctions, the robustness and relative rigour of approach to be expected in that context (see *Denton v TH White Limited* [2014] EWCA Civ 906 ...) can properly find at least some degree of reflection in the present context.'[220]

Thus the question of whether there is 'good reason' is a question that bears some resemblance, in terms of the requisite robustness and rigorousness, to the question of whether relief from sanctions ought to be granted.

12.153 That said, Davis LJ went on to say this:

> 'Nevertheless, all that said, the existence of the "good reason" provision gives a valuable and important safeguard in order to prevent a real risk of injustice; and, as I see it, it goes a considerable way to meeting [the paying party's] doom-laden predictions of detailed assessments becoming mere rubber stamps of CMOs and of injustice for paying parties if the approach is to be that adopted in this present case. As to what will constitute "good reason" in any given case I think it much better not to seek to proffer any further, necessarily generalised, guidance or examples. The matter can safely be left to the individual appraisal and evaluation of costs judges by reference to the circumstances of each individual case.'[221]

Thus, at the end of day, it will be for the costs judge to decide what amounts to a 'good reason' and the ability of costs judges to do so is an important safeguard against injustice.

12.154 **The indemnity principle** It seems beyond doubt that the operation of the indemnity principle will, where applicable, amount to an unassailable 'good reason' to depart from the budget. Thus, where the receiving party has incurred less than the amounts in the approved or agreed budget, that would amount to a 'good reason' for restricting the allowable costs accordingly. It could not be any other way, because there is nothing in the legislation governing budgets that in any way abrogates the indemnity principle. Carr J had this to say on the topic:

> '[C]learly, if the receiving party has spent less than was agreed or approved in the budget, the need to comply with the indemnity principle would require departure from the budget. There is no question of a party receiving more by way of costs than was actually spent.'[222]

---

219 See *Harrison v University Hospitals Coventry & Warwickshire NHS Trust* [2017] EWCA Civ 792, at [44].
220 See *ibid.*
221 *Ibid.*
222 See *Merrix v Heart of England NHS Foundation Trust* [2017] EWHC 346 (QB), at [74].

This does not mean, however, that where the indemnity principle applies in such a way as to restrict the costs, the court will then assess the costs unfettered by the budget; indeed, quite the opposite is true. In this regard, Carr J approved of the following comments of District Judge Baldwin sitting as a regional costs judge: **12.155**

> '[B]ut, in my judgment, the presumption must then be that the lower figure is even more reasonable and proportionate than the approved amount, and therefore a high burden would remain upon the paying party to show a good reason to award less than the lower figure. The raising of such an argument would only exceptionally, in my view, be a proportionate or appropriate use of scarce court resources.'[223]

Thus, where the costs incurred are lower than the relevant amount in the relevant phase of the approved or agreed budget, the receiving party will be bound by the operation of the indemnity principle, but—all else being equal—the paying party will have a steep uphill struggle to persuade the court that there is 'good reason' to allow an amount that is less than the amount claimed. **12.156**

Early settlement Whilst, surprisingly, there is no binding authority on the point, it seems generally to be accepted that where a case settles such that the receiving party has not used the budgeted costs for any given phase, that will amount to a 'good reason' to depart from the budget. There is, however, no agreed method as to *how* the court should deal with such a situation. One option would be to try to apportion the costs of that phase, but very often this would lead to more problems than simply assessing the relevant costs. Presumably, each case will turn on its own facts. **12.157**

Failure to revise the budget As is explained at 12.109, the parties are under a duty to apply for a revision of the budget if there have been significant developments since the last agreed or approved budget. Whilst he was dealing with a summary assessment rather than a detailed assessment, Roger Wyand QC (sitting as a deputy judge of the High Court) noted that this was a factor that court could take into account when considering whether there was 'good reason' to depart from the budget.[224] **12.158**

Proportionality As to proportionality, Carr J had this to say: **12.159**

> 'This approach [of only departing from the budget if there is good reason] does not make it impossible to apply the proportionality test . . . The proportionality test can be applied at the time of fixing the budget. If there is good reason to depart from that decision, the judge on detailed assessment can do so. Additionally, as the notes to CPR 3.18 in the *White Book* suggest, once pre-incurred costs have been assessed on the basis of reasonableness and added to the budgeted costs, the total figure is then subject to an overall assessment of proportionality. So, unless there is good reason to depart from the budget, the overall figure can never be less than the budget, but it can be less than the total of the budget sum plus the reasonably incurred and reasonable in amount non-budgeted sum.'[225]

Thus it is open to a costs judge to consider the issue of proportionality afresh if there is a good reason to do so, but even if this is not the case, a costs judge is permitted to reduce the total of the budgeted costs and incurred costs to a proportionate level. If, however, that

---

[223] See *ibid*, citing *Jones v Harding* (unreported), 29 September 2016, Liverpool County Court.

[224] See *Sony Communications International AB v SSH Communications Security Corporation* [2016] EWHC 2985 (Pat), at [14(iv)], [16(ii)] and [17].

[225] See *Merrix v Heart of England NHS Foundation Trust* [2017] EWHC 346 (QB), at [82].

total is to fall below the amount of the budgeted costs, the costs judge must be satisfied that this is for a good reason.

12.160 **Very large cases** Roger Wyand QC (sitting as a deputy judge of the High Court and in the context of a summary assessment rather than a detailed assessment) accepted that, in very large cases, the court may be more indulgent with regards to errors in estimating the costs than in smaller cases.[226]

12.161 **Hourly rates** As to the fact that hourly rates are not fixed or approved at the time of making a costs management order (see 12.95), Carr J had this to say:

> 'Nothing in paragraph 7.3 of Practice Direction 3E, where it is stated that when reviewing budgets the court will not carry out a detailed assessment "in advance", impinges on this approach [ie that the budget will be departed from only for 'good reason']. The Practice Direction is there setting out the nature of the assessment exercise at the costs budgeting stage. The court will not carry out a detailed assessment at that stage; rather it will consider whether the budgeted costs fall within the range of reasonable and proportionate costs. It is not stating that, whatever costs budget is approved or agreed, there will be an unfettered detailed assessment in due course. The fact that hourly rates are not fixed at the costs budgeting stage is no obstacle to such a conclusion. As the notes to CPR 3.18 in the *White Book* reflect, the fact that hourly rates at the detailed assessment stage may be different to those used for the budget may be a good reason for allowing less, or more, than some of the phase totals in the budget.'[227]

Thus the court may reduce (or may even increase) the hourly rates on assessment, but only for 'good reason'.[228]

12.162 There have been differing approaches to this issue in practice. Some judges, upon assessing the hourly rate applicable to incurred costs as being lower than that applicable to the budgeted costs, have regarded that as being a 'good reason' to carry forward the assessed rate into the budgeted costs,[229] whilst others have not.[230] There was, at the time of writing, no binding authority on this issue, but one could argue that it is wrong in principle to routinely dissect components of the budgeted costs in this way without having made a prior finding that there was 'good reason' to depart from the budget as a whole for the phase in question. Put otherwise, one could argue that whilst it would be open to a costs judge to find that that there was 'good reason' to depart from the budget and *then* to look at rates, it would be wrong in principle to impugn the budget mechanistically on the basis of rates alone. If this is right, then the distinction between these two approaches may be a fine one where the costs judge believed that the overall budget was excessive *because* of the rates, such as where a costs judge, with the benefit of the papers, believes that much of the work ought to have been carried out by lower-grade fee earners. That, however, would be very different from

226 See *Sony Communications International AB v SSH Communications Security Corporation* [2016] EWHC 2985 (Pat), at [15(i)] and [17].

227 See *Merrix v Heart of England NHS Foundation Trust* [2017] EWHC 346 (QB), at [73].

228 To the extent that it was ever applicable, *Troy Foods v Manton* [2013] EWCA Civ 615 is no longer good law on this point.

229 See, eg, *RNB v London Borough of Newham* (unreported), 4 August 2017, SCCO, *per* Deputy Master Campbell (subject to appeal at the time of writing).

230 See, eg, *Jallow v Ministry of Defence* [2018] EWHC B7 (Costs), *per* Master Rowley; *Nash v Ministry of Defence* [2018] EW Misc B4 (CC), *per* Master Nangalingam.

routinely applying a wholesale revision of the hourly rates as per the ordinary principles of assessment.

Whilst no more than the editor's own view (which could be wrong), regardless of what was recorded in an approved or agreed budget it would be open to a costs judge to reduce hourly rates that were *un*reasonable and this would be so even if the sums claimed in the phase in question were within the amount allowed in the budget. Indeed, the editor believes that the court would have a duty to do this in an appropriate case, for the simple reason that CPR, r 44.3, provides that the court will not allow costs that are unreasonable in amount (a fundamental principle of costs). There is nothing in CPR, r 3.18, which disapplies CPR, r 44.3; indeed, the signpost at the end of CPR, r 3.18, draws attention to the parts of the latter. **12.163**

Developments at trial Roger Wyand QC (sitting as a deputy judge of the High Court) accepted that the way in which the trial unfolded may be a relevant factor.[231] **12.164**

Surveillance evidence A party (usually a defendant) may have very good reason for not including within their draft budget any mention of the fact that their opponent is under surveillance. There have been indications that a reasonable decision to omit such costs from a budget would amount to a 'good reason' for allowing those costs in assessment.[232] **12.165**

Assessment on the indemnity basis and the relevance of the budget

There is uncertainty as to what extent, if any, a receiving party's most recent budget will play in role in an indemnity basis assessment of that party's costs. The generally received view is that CPR, r 3.18, does nothing to constrain the recipient of indemnity basis costs to the party's budget; indeed, many commentators say that because budgets are a creation of proportionality, they are not even *relevant* to an assessment on the indemnity basis.[233] **12.166**

Any discussion of this topic must begin with Coulson J's comments, made in 2013 under a pilot scheme, that the last approved or agreed budget is not only relevant to an assessment on the indemnity basis, but also is the 'starting point'. He went on to imply that a receiving party would have to show 'good reason' to depart from their last approved or agreed budget.[234] The authors of *Cook on Costs* disagreed with that analysis,[235] as did Judge Keyser QC (sitting as a judge of the High Court).[236] There can be no doubt **12.167**

---

231 See *Sony Communications International AB v SSH Communications Security Corporation* [2016] EWHC 2985 (Pat), at [28].

232 See, eg, *Purser v Hibbs* [2015] EWHC 1792 (QB), *per* Judge Moloney.

233 See, eg, Rose, N, 'Judges at Odds over Relationship between Budgeting and Indemnity Costs', *Litigation Futures*, 1 September 2014, and *Cook on Costs 2017* (LexisNexis, online), paras 15.12 and 24.5.

234 In *Elvanite Full Circle Ltd v AMEC Earth & Environmental (UK) Ltd* [2013] EWHC 1643 (TCC), at [28], Coulson J had this to say on the point: '[The most recent approved or agreed budget would be] the starting point of an assessment of costs on an indemnity basis, even if the "good reasons" to depart from it are likely to be more numerous and extensive if the indemnity basis is applied.'

235 *Cook on Costs 2014* (LexisNexis, online), para 24.5.

236 This was when deciding the costs of *Kellie v Wheatley & Lloyd Architects Ltd* [2014] EWHC 2886 (TCC) (QBD), of which there is no transcript, but only a summary by Rose, N, 'Judges at Odds over Relationship between Budgeting and Indemnity Costs', *Litigation Futures*, 1 September 2014. It is reported there that Judge Keyser QC made the following points: '(1) Budgets are designed to set out the probable limits of the costs that will be proportionately incurred. It is for that reason that rule 3.18 refers specifically to standard assessment and not to indemnity assessment; there is "no logical analysis [that] requires importing the approach in rule 3.18 into assessment on the indemnity basis". (2) Coulson J was concerned that if an

that, to an extent, they were right, because (whilst *obiter*) in 2014 Dyson MR had the following to say:

> 'If the offending party ultimately loses, then its conduct may be a good reason to order it to pay indemnity costs. Such an order would free the winning party from the operation of CPR rule 3.18 in relation to its costs budget.'[237]

Thus there can be no question of a receiving party who is entitled to costs on the indemnity basis being formally constrained by the budget.

12.168 That said, Coulson J (giving judgment in 2017 and therefore in respect of a case governed by CPR, Part 3, Section II) had this to say:

> 'But I repeat what I said at paragraphs 27–30 of my judgment in *Elvanite*: it seems to me that there are great difficulties in arguing that, because the successful party is entitled to indemnity costs, the approved costs budget figure becomes irrelevant and no longer acts as a cap. I think the approved figure should be the starting point for an assessment of costs on an indemnity basis, as well as for an assessment on the standard basis.'[238]

These comments were *obiter*, but they are very clear. It should be noted, however, that there is some controversy as to whether what Coulson J said was correct.

Where no costs management order has been made

12.169 Whilst it is likely that they will be encountered only infrequently, there will be cases in which budgets have been filed and exchanged, but no costs management order has been made. Where this is so, the budget will be regarded as being an estimate.[239] This is made clear by PD 44, para 3, which reads as follows:

> '3.1 In any case where the parties have filed budgets in accordance with Practice Direction 3E but the court has not made a costs management order under rule 3.15, the provisions of this subsection shall apply.
>
> 3.2 If there is a difference of 20% or more between the costs claimed by a receiving party on detailed assessment and the costs shown in a budget filed by that party, the receiving party must provide a statement of the reasons for the difference with the bill of costs.
>
> 3.3 If a paying party—
> (a) claims to have reasonably relied on a budget filed by a receiving party; or
> (b) wishes to rely upon the costs shown in the budget in order to dispute the reasonableness or proportionality of the costs claimed,
>
> the paying party must serve a statement setting out the case in this regard in that party's points of dispute.
>
> 3.4 On an assessment of the costs of a party, the court will have regard to the last approved or agreed budget, and may have regard to any other budget previously filed by that party, or by any other party in the same proceedings. Such other budgets may be taken into account when assessing the reasonableness and proportionality of any costs claimed.

order for indemnity costs allowed a receiving party to ignore the budget, that would encourage successful parties to argue for indemnity costs every time; Judge Keyser QC said that the answer to that was "by ensuring that applications for indemnity costs are carefully scrutinised and ... by the proper application of the well understood criteria of assessment in rule 44.3(3) to the facts of the particular case".'

237 *Denton & Ors v TH White Ltd & Ors* [2014] EWCA Civ 906, at [43].

238 *Governors & Company of the Bank of Ireland & Anor v Watts Group plc* [2017] EWHC 2472 (TCC), at [16].

239 See PD 44, para 3.

> 3.5 Subject to paragraph 3.4, paragraphs 3.6 and 3.7 apply where there is a difference of 20% or more between the costs claimed by a receiving party and the costs shown in a budget filed by that party.
>
> 3.6 Where it appears to the court that the paying party reasonably relied on the budget, the court may restrict the recoverable costs to such sum as is reasonable for the paying party to pay in the light of that reliance, notwithstanding that such sum is less than the amount of costs reasonably and proportionately incurred by the receiving party.
>
> 3.7 Where it appears to the court that the receiving party has not provided a satisfactory explanation for that difference, the court may regard the difference between the costs claimed and the costs shown in the budget as evidence that the costs claimed are unreasonable or disproportionate.'

Thus, if there is a difference of 20 per cent or more between the costs claimed and the amount shown on the budget, the receiving party must provide a statement of reasons for the difference with the bill of costs. If a paying party then claims to have reasonably relied on a budget or wishes to rely upon the costs shown in the budget to dispute the reasonableness or proportionality of the costs claimed, the paying party must serve a statement setting out the case in this regard in that party's points of dispute. The budgets of all of the parties (and presumably the statements made about the budgets, where appropriate) may be taken into account for the purposes of the assessment. **12.170**

These provisions are almost the same as those that were contained in the old CPD, para 6. Those provisions were hardly ever used to any significant effect (see 12.06–12.08) and there is no reason to believe that the provision set out above will be any different.[240] **12.171**

[240] For more detail on the law, see the second edition of this book, at paras 34.52–34.67.

13

COSTS CAPPING AND RELATED TOPICS

13.01 This chapter deals with the following topics:

- Part 3, Section III—costs capping in claims other than judicial review (13.03);
- Part 3, Section I—costs capping orders arising out of the court's general case management powers (13.43);
- Part 46, Section IV, and ss 80 and 89 of the Criminal Justice and Courts Act 2015—costs capping in judicial review proceedings (13.46);
- Part 45, Section VII—costs capping and restriction in Aarhus Convention claims (13.78);
- Part 52, Section IV—costs restriction in appeals from no-cost or low-cost tribunals (13.100):
  - non-Aarhus Convention claims (13.101); and
  - Aarhus Convention claims (13.108).

13.02 The following related topics are dealt with elsewhere in this book:

- costs management and budgeting (see Chapter 12); and
- PD 64A, para 6—*Beddoe* orders (see 66.56–66.74).

CPR, Part 3, Section III: Cost Capping in Claims Other than Judicial Review

13.03 Costs capping orders under Part 3, Section III, of the Civil Procedure Rules (CPR) are orders that pre-emptively restrict the amount of costs that a party can recover in litigation (other than judicial review proceedings). Once a costs capping order has been made, then, unless it is varied, it will limit the costs recoverable by the party to whom it relates to the amount stated in the order.[1]

13.04 Costs management has done for CPR, Part 3, Section III, what video did for the radio star. Indeed, even before costs management became commonplace, CPR, Part 3, Section III, was an almost entirely impotent jurisdiction. Arden LJ has recently suggested that it has some continuing utility in the sense that an order may be appropriate where a costs judge would find it difficult to distinguish adequately between costs reasonably incurred and costs unreasonably incurred,[2] but it is difficult—even hypothetically—to envisage a case in which that would be so.

---

[1] CPR, r 3.19(7).
[2] *Tidal Energy Ltd v Bank of Scotland Plc* [2014] EWCA Civ 847, at [14].

In view of the above, the editor wholeheartedly agrees with other commentators that CPR, Part 3, Section III, ought to be repealed.[3] Its continued inclusion in the CPR simply adds to the already unbearable complexity of the law of costs, and (with one insignificant exception: see 65.94) practitioners would do well to disregard CPR, Part 3, Section III, entirely. **13.05**

Terminology

CPR, r 3.19(1)(a) and (b), gives the following definitions: **13.06**

> '(a) "costs capping order" means an order limiting the amount of future costs (including disbursements) which a party may recover pursuant to an order for costs subsequently made; and
> (b) "future costs" means costs incurred in respect of work done after the date of the costs capping order but excluding the amount of any additional liability.'

The history of the jurisdiction

Although costs capping orders in claims other than judicial review proceedings are now regulated by CPR, Part 3, Section III, those provisions describe a regime that (with one possible exception[4]) is noticeably similar to the judge-made regime that preceded it. This means that older authorities may still be relevant. It should be noted, however, that the apparent judicial enthusiasm for costs capping orders in the mid-2000s quickly waned; as such, authorities from that period ought to be treated with caution. **13.07**

From as far back as just prior to the introduction of the CPR, the courts articulated a jurisdiction to make pre-emptive orders limiting a party's liability to pay costs—albeit only in certain public law cases (see 13.47). Despite the fact that pre-emptive costs orders were not unknown under the Rules of the Supreme Court (RSC),[5] in the private-law setting costs capping was not perceived as being available.[6] To a large extent, this was as a result of the court giving precedence to the principle that the winner should be compensated in costs.[7] **13.08**

The landscape changed with the introduction of the CPR, but the CPR, as they originally were lacked express provision for costs capping orders. This was despite the fact that the concept of costs management—which, at that stage, meant something other than modern-day budgeting—had widely been canvassed in consultation; as is explained below, this was largely because the concept of *case* management was believed to be preferable to *costs* management (see 12.04). **13.09**

This omission contrasted with the legislation governing arbitral proceedings, in which forum specific statutory provision for costs capping had existed since 1996.[8] Given the fact that those had been formulated at roughly the same time as the CPR, it was thought by some that the absence of an express power to cap costs in civil litigation was a deliberate omission indicating that the court did not have that power. A series of decisions, both at **13.10**

---

[3] See, eg, *Cook on Costs 2017* (LexisNexis, online), para 17.1.

[4] There is one potential exception, in that PD 3F, para 1.1, seems to have introduced a test of exceptionality.

[5] See, as probably the first example, *Davies v Eli Lilly & Co* [1987] 1 WLR 1136 at 1141.

[6] In *McDonald v Horn* [1995] 1 All ER 961, at 969, for example, Hoffman LJ commented: 'It is difficult to imagine a case falling within the general principle in which it would be possible for the court properly to exercise its discretion in advance of the substantive decision.'

[7] For a detailed exposition of the history of costs in this regard, see *R (on the application of Corner House Research) v Secretary of State for Trade and Industry* [2005] EWCA Civ 192, at [6]–[23].

[8] Arbitration Act 1996, s 65.

first instance and on appeal, proved this view to be incorrect. In so far as proceedings other than judicial review proceedings were concerned, the first reported case to deal with costs capping—albeit only as an *obiter* comment—was *Griffiths v Solutia UK Ltd* in 2001, in which Sir Christopher Staughton had this to say: '[Surely] case management powers will allow a judge in the future to exercise the power of limiting costs, either indirectly or even directly, so that they are proportionate to the amount involved.'[9]

13.11 In 2003, in a group action for clinical negligence, Gage J—whom many regarded as the architect of the then-new judge-made powers—held that the court's general powers of case management were sufficiently wide to encompass the making of a costs capping order.[10] Shortly thereafter, Hallett J came to the same conclusion.[11] In mid-2000, a number of costs capping orders were made (many by consent); in 2007, the Court of Appeal was presented with a case in which it had an opportunity to clarify the law. Buxton LJ explained, however, that whilst the Court of Appeal had drafted a 'comprehensive set of principles', it had decided not to include them in its judgment and that any further development of the law was a matter for the Civil Procedure Rule Committee.[12] With hindsight, that was the point at which the jurisdiction ceased to have any real potency.

13.12 At about the same time, the Civil Procedure Rule Committee set up a subcommittee whose remit was to examine all aspects of the matter other than protective costs orders. A Consultation Paper was published in 2008,[13] which was followed by responses in early 2009. On 6 April 2009, provisions that are now contained in CPR, Part 3, Section III, came into force.[14] Whilst those provisions were not expressed as being such, they were, in essence, a codification of the pre-existing judge-made law—but those new powers were almost never exercised, largely because of the *Catch-22* provision that is discussed at 13.18–13.21.

13.13 On 1 April 2013, those new rules were moved from Part 44 to Part 3, largely without change. In 2015, the Civil Procedure Rules Committee suggested that the costs capping jurisdiction was to be rescinded, but, in the event, it was granted a reprieve. Indeed, in 2016, CPR, Part 3, Section III, was amended[15] (albeit largely only to make reference to the new procedure for judicial review claims that is discussed at 13.46–13.99).

The source of the jurisdiction

13.14 As with almost all modern costs orders, the power by which costs capping orders are made ultimately derives from s 51(3) of the Senior Courts Act 1981, which provides that a court shall have 'full power to determine by whom and to what extent costs are to be paid'. There is nothing within that Act which limits the court to exercising this power only retrospectively.[16]

---

[9] *Griffiths v Solutia UK Ltd* [2001] EWCA Civ 736, at [29].

[10] *AB v Leeds Teaching Hospitals NHS Trust* [2003] EWHC 1034 (QB).

[11] *Ledward Claimants v Kent & Medway Health Authority* [2003] EWHC 2551 (QB).

[12] *Willis v Nicolson* [2007] EWCA Civ 199, at [24]. This conclusion was reached after discussion with the Master of Rolls and the Deputy Head of Civil Justice.

[13] Ministry of Justice, *Civil Procedure Rules: Costs Capping Orders* (London: HMSO, 2008).

[14] Civil Procedure (Amendment No 3) Rules 2008 (SI 2008/3327), r 9.

[15] Civil Procedure (Amendment No 2) Rules 2016 (SI 2016/707).

[16] *AB v Leeds Teaching Hospitals NHS Trust* [2003] EWHC 1034 (QB).

The power to make a pre-emptive costs order (such as a costs capping order) is subject to the prevailing rules of court. Although more general power seems still to exist (see 13.43), specific provision for costs capping orders is now made in CPR, Part 3, Section III, and it is that Section that governs what is set out below. **13.15**

The ambit of Part 3, Section III

The following points may be made. **13.16**

- **Ambit** A costs capping order may pertain to the whole litigation or any issues that are ordered to be tried separately.[17]
- **Parties** The court may make a costs capping order against any or all of the parties and an order against all the parties is often referred to as a 'mutual capping order'.
- **Stage** A costs capping order may be made at any stage of proceedings[18]—although, in practice, a late application is likely to fail for that reason alone (see 13.30).

Conditions requisite to making an order

CPR, r 3.19(5), provides that a costs capping order may be made only where the following conditions are met:[19] **13.17**

- that it is in the interests of justice to make such an order;[20]
- that there is a substantial risk that, without such an order, costs will be disproportionately incurred;[21] and
- that the court is not satisfied that that risk can be adequately controlled by:
  - case management directions or orders made under Part 3; or
  - detailed assessment of costs.[22]

For the reasons set out immediately below, it is almost impossible to satisfy the third of these conditions.

'The court is not satisfied that that risk can be adequately controlled'

The third of the conditions referred to above has created a *Catch-22* situation that has deprived CPR, Part 3, Section III, of all utility. This is because a party will apply for a costs capping order only if they fear that the costs may ultimately be disproportionately excessive, but if the party succeeds in proving that, this will simply demonstrate that the costs will be reduced—and therefore adequately controlled—on assessment.[23] **13.18**

---

17 CPR, r 3.19(4). See *A&E Television Networks LLC v Discovery Communications Europe Ltd* [2011] EWHC 1038 (Ch), at [17], in which Mann J made a costs capping order limiting the costs of certain work that a solicitor wished to do in-house to no more than would have been incurred had it been done by an outside agency.

18 CPR, r 3.19(5).

19 These conditions reflect those first articulated in *Smart v East Cheshire NHS Trust* [2003] EWHC 2806, at [22], *per* Gage J.

20 See CPR, r 3.19(5)(a).

21 See CPR, r 3.19(5)(b).

22 See CPR, r 3.19(5)(c).

23 As a typical example, see *Syngenta Ltd v Chemsource Ltd* [2012] EWHC 1507 (Pat), in which Daniel Alexander QC found that it was not in the interests of justice to make a costs capping order in a modest claim alleging patent and trade mark infringement, because any disproportionate costs could be more effectively controlled post-trial at assessment.

13.19 Arden LJ had this to say about the requirement in CPR, r 3.19(5)(c):

> 'In my judgment, it is clear that a mechanism may constitute adequate control if it neutralises or satisfactorily manages the risk. It may not be possible to eliminate a risk but only to manage it. But, to my mind, that must be the interpretation of the rule because otherwise a detailed assessment of costs could never or scarcely ever be a mechanism of control within 5(c). Moreover, as I see it that would reflect a policy decision which the drafter of 3.19 may reasonably have taken, namely that the court should not be troubled by satellite litigation, constituted by cost cap litigation if the long-standing system of assessing costs would provide an adequate mechanism.'[24]

As such, the test is not whether the risk can be negated, but merely whether it can be managed.

13.20 Arden LJ went on to say this and, in doing so, coined the terms '*ex ante* mechanism' and '*a posteriori* mechanism' for managing costs:

> '[The] risk can be managed either in advance or after the event or, as I put it in argument, apologising for using Latin the mechanism in 5(c)(i) is an *ex-ante* mechanism and that in 5(c)(ii) *a posteriori* mechanism after the event to limit costs.'[25]

Thus, if an adequate *a posteriori* mechanism for managing the risk exists, the condition in CPR, r 3.19(5)(c), will not be satisfied. Detailed assessment is just such a mechanism, which is why it is almost impossible to satisfy that condition. In this regard, the following observations of Mann J—about what he called 'the normal role of the costs judge'—are relevant:

> 'It is the normal role of the costs judge to filter out the sort of extravagant costs which have in fact, in some cases, led to the making of a costs-capping order. One should continue to expect them to be able to do that ... [One] would have thought that the exercise of doing that retrospectively (the costs judge's job) would be easier than doing it prospectively (the function of the costs-capping judge).'[26]

13.21 Edis J had this to say on the topic:

> 'It is obvious from the terms of CPR r. 3.19(5)(c) that I must do what I can by way of case management directions or orders at this hearing in order to ensure (among other things) that costs between now and the end of the trial are not disproportionately incurred. Only once I have done that can I assess whether these measures do not adequately control the risk that this will happen and properly decide whether to make a cost capping order (if I also consider that the risk will not be adequately controlled by a detailed assessment of costs by the court after the event). The inadequacy of case management measures before trial, and detailed assessment of costs after trial, is a precondition to a valid exercise of the discretion to make a costs capping order.'[27]

Thus the court will turn its thoughts to controlling costs by *case* management and the condition in CPR, r 3.19(5)(c), must be addressed with this in mind. This is another reason—namely, Arden LJ's *ex ante* mechanism—why that condition is almost never met. In this

---

[24] *Tidal Energy Ltd v Bank of Scotland Plc* [2014] EWCA Civ 847, at [10]. See similar comments at *Eweida v British Airways Plc* [2009] EWCA Civ 1025, at [31], *per* Lloyd LJ.

[25] *Tidal Energy Ltd v Bank of Scotland Plc* [2014] EWCA Civ 847, at [10].

[26] *Knight v Beyond Properties Pty Ltd* [2006] EWHC 1242 (Ch), at [15].

[27] See *Hegglin v Google Inc* [2014] EWHC 3793 (QB), at [7].

regard, it should be borne in mind that CPR, Part 3, Section II, makes provision for the court to have significant case management powers and to be provided with the requisite estimates, schedules, etc, to enable it to exercise those powers,[28] so the *ex ante* mechanism is anything but ineffective.

The requirement of exceptionality

Practice Direction (PD) 3F, para 1.1, states that a costs capping order will be made only in 'exceptional circumstances'. This is the one area in the regime in CPR, Part 3, Section III, that differs from the original judge-made law.[29] It is moot point whether this provision changes matters, however, because if a case were to satisfy the requirement in CPR, r 3.19(5)(c), it would have to be a truly exceptional case in any event. **13.22**

That said, there have been cases in which the court has focused on the topic of exceptionality. In particular, Eady J regarded the requirement as being a significant fetter upon his discretion. Whilst he began his judgment (in a case he had described as being a 'ding dong' dispute) on the footing that the need for exceptional circumstances was merely an expression of the fact that suitable cases for costs capping will be rare, his analysis led him to the conclusion that it was, in truth, a more restrictive principle: **13.23**

> 'If I had a free hand ... I should be strongly inclined to impose a costs cap and to refer the matter to a costs judge to address hourly rates ... [but] consistency in these matters is important and I do not have a free hand. I am inhibited both by the "exceptionality" principle and by the fact that I am satisfied that the risk of disproportionality could be adequately controlled by a costs judge at the stage of detailed assessment.'[30]

In what circumstances should a costs capping order be made?

In considering whether to exercise its discretion under CPR, Part 3, Section III, the court will consider all of the circumstances of the case,[31] including: **13.24**

- whether there is a substantial imbalance between the financial position of the parties;
- whether the costs of determining the amount of the cap are likely to be proportionate to the overall costs of the litigation;
- the stage that the proceedings have reached;[32] and
- the costs that have been incurred to date and the future costs.

Of course, the *Catch-22* situation referred to earlier (see 13.18) generally prevents the court from considering these factors in any meaningful way.

Whilst they are of almost no practical relevance, the following miscellaneous points may be made about the circumstances in which a costs capping order may be made. **13.25**

---

[28] See CPR, r 3.13. See also PD 3F, para 2: 'The budget required by rule 3.20 must be in the form of Precedent H annexed to this Practice Direction.' Prior to 1 April 2013, see CPD, arts 23A.3 and 23A.4.

[29] This is because Gage J—who many would regard as being the architect of judge-made costs capping orders—has, on more than one occasion, emphasised that exceptional circumstances are not a condition for making a costs capping order: see, eg, *Smart v East Cheshire NHS Trust* [2003] EWHC 2806, at [22]; *AB v Leeds Teaching Hospitals NHS Trust* [2003] EWHC 1034 (QB), at [19].

[30] *Peacock v MGN Ltd* [2009] EWHC 769 (QB), at [22].

[31] CPR, r 3.19(6)(a)–(d).

[32] See also PD 3F, para 1.2.

- **The relevance of access to justice** It is not the function of costs capping to remedy the problems of access to finance for litigation.[33]
- **The risk of satellite litigation** As to the risk of satellite litigation arising out of applications under CPR, r 3.19, Arden LJ had this to say:

> 'It has been submitted in the appeal court the dangers of inappropriate satellite litigation are not as great as they are at first instance. With respect I do not consider that that is so. This case has been allocated a hearing time of 1 day and this application of itself has taken over an hour to hear. It would increase the sitting time of the court considerably if there were a large number of costs capping applications and in addition that would result in other litigants who want to have their appeals heard being put back.'[34]

- **Arms race** One argument that has been advanced is that a detailed assessment will not stop an 'arms race'. If, for example, a claimant instructs a particularly costly counsel, then so will the defendant; these costs—so the argument goes—might be entirely avoidable, but it is unlikely that they would be disallowed on assessment. That argument rarely succeeds.[35]

Group litigation

13.26 Group litigation can be particularly expensive. Indeed, the Woolf report specifically identified group litigation as an area in which costs management would be appropriate.[36] Against this background, it is hardly surprising that group litigation was one of the first types of claim to be subject to costs capping orders. Prior to the introduction of what is now CPR, Part 3, Section III, the notion of making costs capping orders in group litigation had become unremarkable practice.[37] It should be noted, however, that even in the mid-2000s most such orders were, in effect, made by consent.[38] There were calls for specific provisions relating to group litigation,[39] but it seems as though that suggestion was rejected. The result is that group litigation cases are now subject to the same threshold criteria as other cases.

Procedure

13.27 An application for a costs capping order under CPR, Part 3, Section III, must be made on notice in accordance with Part 23.[40] The following mandatory requirements apply:

> 'The application notice must—
> (a) set out—
> (i) whether the costs capping order is in respect of the whole of the litigation or a particular issue which is ordered to be tried separately; and
> (ii) why a costs capping order should be made; and

[33] See *Black v Arriva North East Ltd* [2014] EWCA Civ 1115, at [11]–[26].
[34] *Tidal Energy Ltd v Bank of Scotland Plc* [2014] EWCA Civ 847, at [12].
[35] See, eg, *Peacock v MGN Ltd* [2009] EWHC 769 (QB), at [22].
[36] Lord Woolf MR, *Access to Justice: Final Report* (London: HMSO, 1996), ch 7, at para 39.
[37] The rationale behind this was explained (*obiter*) by Gage J in *Smart v East Cheshire NHS Trust* [2003] EWHC 2806 (QB), at [23].
[38] See, eg, *AB v Leeds Teaching Hospitals NHS Trust* [2003] EWHC 1034 (QB), at [19]; *Ledward Claimants v Kent & Medway Health Authority and East Kent Hospitals NHS Trust* [2003] EWHC 2551 (QB).
[39] See Ministry of Justice, *Civil Procedure Rules: Costs Capping Orders—Summary of Responses* (London: HMSO, 2009), p 8.
[40] CPR, r 3.20(1).

(b) be accompanied by a budget setting out—
 (i) the costs (and disbursements) incurred by the applicant to date; and
 (ii) the costs (and disbursements) which the applicant is likely to incur in the future conduct of the proceedings.'[41]

The estimate must be in the form of Precedent H.[42] PD 3F, para 3, gives the following additional guidance: **13.28**

> 'The schedule of costs referred to in rule 3.20(3)—
> (a) must set out—
> (i) each sub-heading as it appears in the applicant's budget (column 1);
> (ii) alongside each sub-heading, the amount claimed by the applicant in the applicant's budget (column 2); and
> (iii) alongside the figures referred to in subparagraph (ii) the amount that the respondent proposes should be allowed under each sub-heading (column 3); and
> (b) must be supported by a statement of truth.'

Whilst not a requirement in the rules, Arden LJ has suggested that if an application is to succeed because of some feature of the case that would make it difficult for a costs judge to assess the costs (see 13.04), the evidence of a costs lawyer or costs draftsperson may be required.[43] **13.29**

The stage at which to exercise the jurisdiction

PD3 F, para 1, offers the following guidance: **13.30**

> 'An application for a costs capping order must be made as soon as possible, preferably before or at the first case management hearing or shortly afterwards. The stage which the proceedings have reached at the time of the application will be one of the factors the court will consider when deciding whether to make a costs capping order.'

Thus applications ought to be made at an early stage. In so far as the judge-made law remains relevant, that too stipulated that applications should be timeous.[44] An application for a costs capping order made very late in the day might be rejected for that reason.[45] However, it is possible to make an application too early: Dobbs J, for example, allowed an appeal against an order that had been made at a stage when the court was not in a position to examine all of the appropriate case management options.[46]

The scope and effect of the order

CPR, r 3.19(7), describes the effect of a costs capping order thus: 'A costs capping order, once made, will limit the costs recoverable by the party subject to the order unless a party successfully applies to vary the order.' A costs capping order does not limit the expenditure of the capped party; it merely limits the amount that can be recovered from the other side in the event of success.[47] **13.31**

---

41 CPR, r 3.20(2).
42 See PD 3F, para 2.
43 *Tidal Energy Ltd v Bank of Scotland Plc* [2014] EWCA Civ 847, at [13].
44 *King v Telegraph Group Ltd* [2005] 1 WLR 2282, at [80], *per* Brooke LJ, as emphasised by Eady J in *Tierney v News Group Newspapers Ltd* [2006] EWHC 3275 (QB), at [2].
45 *Henry v British Broadcasting Corporation* [2005] EWHC 2503 (QB), at [39].
46 *Eli Lilly & Co Ltd v James* [2009] EWHC 198 (QB).
47 *Tierney v News Group Newspapers Ltd* [2006] EWHC 3275 (QB), at [16].

13.32 Generally speaking, costs capping orders operate prospectively and not retrospectively.[48] That said, retrospective orders have been made, usually with the consent of the parties.[49]

13.33 Although it is not unheard of for restrictions to be imposed on only one party, where a costs capping order is made it is often the case that they cap all or both of the parties. Eady J has commented that there is something to be said for the latter approach, because it is capable of imposing effective discipline.[50]

13.34 Whilst each case will turn on its own facts, it would not ordinarily be appropriate for separate provision to be made for the costs of interim applications.[51]

The quantum of the cap

13.35 Prior to the introduction of what is now CPR, Part 3, Section III, the task of setting the level of a cap was generally a matter that was carried out by a costs judge,[52] but the new regime makes specific provision for the court to sit with an assessor,[53] so it will not always be the case that the involvement of a costs judge would result in a separate hearing.

13.36 As to the factors to be taken into account, PD 3F, para 4, makes these provisions:

> 'When assessing the quantum of a costs cap, the court will take into account the factors detailed in rule 44.5 and the relevant provisions supporting that rule in the Practice Direction supplementing Part 44. When considering a party's budget of the costs they are likely to incur in the future conduct of the proceedings, the court may also take into account a reasonable allowance on costs for contingencies.'

13.37 (The reference to CPR, r 44.5, is almost certainly a mistake, because it is a provision that deals with costs payable under contract. It is almost certain that the reference intended was to CPR, r 44.4.) Those factors are relevant both to the costs that have already been incurred (which may be taken into account in some circumstances) and the costs yet to be incurred.[54] The base costs and additional liability must be assessed separately.[55] That said, the court should prescribe a total amount of recoverable costs, which will be inclusive, where relevant, of any additional liability.[56]

13.38 Whilst they are of almost no practical relevance, the following miscellaneous points can be made about the assessment of the amount of the cap.

- **Value of the claim** The value of the claim is a relevant factor, but it is only one factor amongst others.[57] Non-monetary factors may be taken into account, but the monetary value of the claim would usually be the starting point for estimating the claim's worth.[58]

48 See *King v Telegraph Group Ltd* [2005] 1 WLR 2282, at [80], *per* Brooke LJ; *Weir v Secretary of State for Transport* (unreported), 20 April 2005, Ch D, at [28], *per* Lindsay J.
49 See, eg, *AB v Leeds Teaching Hospitals NHS Trust* [2003] EWHC 1034 (QB).
50 See *Tierney v News Group Newspapers Ltd* [2006] EWHC 3275 (QB), at [3].
51 See *ibid*, at [39].
52 *King v Telegraph Group Ltd* [2005] 1 WLR 2282, at [94].
53 See CPR, r 3.20(3)(c); see also *Matadeen v Associated Newspapers* (unreported), 17 March 2005, QBD, *per* Master Eyre (not binding).
54 *Tierney v News Group Newspapers Ltd* [2006] EWHC 3275 (QB), at [17].
55 *Ibid*, at [18].
56 *King v Telegraph Group Ltd* [2005] 1 WLR 2282, at [101].
57 See *Tierney v News Group Newspapers Ltd* [2006] EWHC 3275 (QB), at [10].
58 *King v Telegraph Group Ltd* [2005] 1 WLR 2282, at [95].

- **Conduct and access to justice** In a case in which an appellant was not able to fund her appeal because the April 2013 changes had left her without access to adequate after-the-event (ATE) insurance, Christopher Clarke LJ commented that it was not the function of costs capping to remedy the problems of access to finance for litigation.[59] On a different topic, the conduct of the other side may be relevant—in particular, if it leads to disproportionate expenditure or expenditure on irrelevant matters.[60]
- **Comparators** In gauging the reasonableness of the costs proposed, the costs to be incurred by the other side may provide a guide—in some respects, a good guide.[61]
- **Success fees** Whilst recoverable success fees will now rarely be encountered in the context of costs capping, it is likely that art 11.9 of the Costs Practice Direction (CPD) will continue to be relevant, in that a percentage increase will not be reduced simply on the ground that, when added to base costs that are reasonable and (where relevant) proportionate, the total appears disproportionate.[62] Different considerations may apply to defamation claims (see 13.39–13.40).
- **Postponement of payment** It has been held that, in circumstances in which the risk assessment has not been disclosed, it would be wrong to restrict the level of the success fee to take account of that part of the success fee which is attributable to the postponement of payment of fees and expenses.[63] (This is relevant because that part of the success fee is not recoverable between opposing parties.) This is not to say, however, that a costs judge could not take this factor into account if the relevant information were available.
- **Costs of the application** The costs of the costs capping application itself should not have any impact on the capped figure, but should be treated separately.[64]

Defamation claims One or two points need to be made about defamation claims, which are in a class of their own because the costs can be high—especially when compared to the likely award of damages. It is also relevant that very high costs may have a 'chilling effect on press freedom'.[65] The court has a desire to cut down costs that have such a tendency. That desire does not sit easily with the principle that the court will not reduce a success fee solely on the basis that, when added to the base costs, the total appears disproportionate. Brooke LJ has commented that these conflicting principles give rise to a need 'to square the circle' and his view is that there is a need to apply the regime of conditional funding in such a way as to minimise the chilling effect: **13.39**

> 'If the introduction of this novel costs-capping regime means that a claimant's lawyers may be reluctant to accept instructions on a [conditional fee agreement] basis unless they assess the chances of success as significantly greater than evens (so that the size of the success fee will be to that extent reduced), this in my judgment will be a small price to pay in contrast to the price that is potentially to be paid if the present state of affairs is allowed to continue.'[66]

---

59 See *Black v Arriva North East Ltd* [2014] EWCA Civ 1115, at [11]–[26].

60 See the example in *Tierney v News Group Newspapers Ltd* [2006] EWHC 3275 (QB), at [35], where the defendant failed to admit that a photograph was that of the claimant, thus putting the claimant to the expense of proving this fact.

61 *AB v Leeds Teaching Hospitals NHS Trust* [2003] EWHC 1034 (QB), *per* Gage J.

62 *Tierney v News Group Newspapers Ltd* [2006] EWHC 3275 (QB), at [17].

63 *Ibid*, at [42].

64 See Master Hurst's view, as echoed by Eady J in *ibid*, at [14].

65 *King v Telegraph Group Ltd* [2005] 1 WLR 2282, at [101], *per* Brooke LJ.

66 *Ibid*, at [102].

13.40 It has been argued that this is wrong, because to treat defamation claims differently would be to make a rule that could only properly be made by Parliament.[67] There is authority to support this view,[68] but it seems to be well established that there is a need for a 'palliative' (to use Lord Hoffmann's terminology). In particular, Lord Hoffmann has expressed a view that Brooke LJ's guidance ought to be followed.[69]

Variation of the order

13.41 A costs capping order may be varied, but only if the application is made in accordance with CPR, Part 23.[70] A variation will be permitted only where:

- there has been a material and substantial change of circumstances since the date on which the order was made; or
- there is some other compelling reason why a variation should be made.[71]

The costs of the capping exercise

13.42 The costs of the costs capping exercise will be dealt with by the court in the usual way. It is within the court's power to make a forthwith order in respect of those costs.[72]

CPR, Part 3, Section I: Costs Capping Orders Arising out of the Court's General Case Management Powers

13.43 Whilst very much a footnote, it seems that the court has a residual power to make a costs capping order (often called a protective costs order) under CPR, r 3.1(2)(m).[73] That power would not exist in judicial review proceedings (see 13.50), but there appears to be nothing in CPR, Part 3, Section III, to disapply that power in other types of claim. This means that if the interests of justice call for a costs capping order in a case that does not sit well within the regime created by CPR, Part 3, Section III, the court is able to make such an order. The editor has to qualify this statement, however, by saying that in the only recent case in which that power seems to have been exercised (see 13.45), there was not much discussion about the precise *vires* under which the proposed order was sought.

Closed-material cases

13.44 In certain matters relating to terrorism—particularly under the Terrorist Asset-Freezing etc Act 2010—evidence may be 'closed material' in the sense that disclosure is prohibited on national security grounds. This may make it difficult for the party in question to know the case against them and may create a special category of case in which it may be appropriate to make a protective cost order that is not governed by the principles referred to above.

67 For an analysis of the competing arguments, see *Tierney v News Group Newspapers Ltd* [2006] EWHC 3275 (QB), at [21]–[25].

68 See Lord Hoffmann's speech in *Campbell v MGN Ltd (No 2)* [2005] UKHL 61, where he concluded: 'In the end, therefore, it may be that a legislative solution will be needed to comply with Article 10.'

69 *Ibid*, at [34].

70 See CPR, r 3.21.

71 CPR, r 3.19(7).

72 *Tierney v News Group Newspapers Ltd* [2006] EWHC 3275 (QB), at [45]–[46].

73 See, eg, *King v Telegraph Group Ltd* [2005] 1 WLR 2282, at [82].

In just such a case (which was not a judicial review proceeding), Dyson MR approved of Cranston J's analysis of when it may be appropriate to make a protective costs order: **13.45**

> 'First, the case must be of real benefit to the individual bringing it. Secondly, the individual must not be able to assess the prospects of success in the ordinary way. In other words, it must appear from the open material that the case is such that a reasonable person would litigate, but because of the closed material on which the defendant relies, reputable and competent legal representatives cannot advise whether the prospects are, in fact, good. Thirdly, having regard to the financial resources of the individual and to the amount of costs likely to be involved it is fair and just to make the order. Fourthly, if the order is not made the applicant will probably discontinue the proceedings and will be acting reasonably in doing so. Finally, the individual should not benefit from the order if his conduct is later judged to be unreasonable or abusive.'[74]

CPR, Part 46, Section IV, and ss 80 and 89 of the Criminal Justice and Courts Act 2015: Costs Capping Orders in Judicial Review Proceedings

This section deals with costs capping orders in judicial review proceedings; the law that governs other types of claim does not apply to judicial reviews and vice versa.[75] As can be seen, in contrast to CPR, Part 3, Section III, costs capping in judicial review proceedings is a vibrant jurisdiction. **13.46**

The history of judicial review costs capping orders

Prior to the coming into force of the provisions referred to at 13.48–13.77, judge-made law existed that allowed the court to make protective costs orders (PCOs) in public law claims.[76] Details may be found in the second edition of the book. In the early 2010s, concerns were raised that the use of PCOs had gone too far and that they imposed an excessive burden on the public purse. In response, on 6 September 2013, the Justice Secretary launched a consultation entitled *Judicial Review: Proposals for Further Reform*. This resulted in ss 80 and 89 of the Criminal Justice and Courts Act 2015 being made. CPR, Part 46, Section IV, was created when those provisions came into force on 8 August 2016. **13.47**

Terminology

The following terminology applies. **13.48**

- **'Costs capping order'** For the purpose of the 2015 Act, this means an order limiting or removing the liability of a party to judicial review proceedings to pay another party's costs in connection with any stage of the proceedings.[77]
- **'Judicial review costs capping order'** This is the phrase used in the CPR (and this book) and, in essence, it is the same as a costs capping order.[78]
- **'The court'** This means the High Court or the Court of Appeal.

---

[74] *Begg v HM Treasury* [2016] EWCA Civ 568, at [15] and [26].
[75] See CPR, r 46.16(2), CPR, r 3.19(2), and Criminal Justice and Courts Act 2015, s 88(1) and (12).
[76] A public law challenge was defined in *R v Lord Chancellor, ex p Child Poverty Action Group* [1998] 2 All ER 755, at 756, thus: 'The essential characteristics of a public law challenge are that it raises public law issues which are of general importance, where the applicant has no private interest in the outcome of the case.'
[77] See Criminal Justice and Courts Act 2015, s 88(2) and (12).
[78] See CPR, r 46.16(1)(a).

- **'Judicial review proceedings'** This means: (a) proceedings on an application for leave to apply for judicial review; (b) proceedings on an application for judicial review; (c) any proceedings on an application for leave to appeal from a decision in proceedings described in (a) or (b); and (d) proceedings on an appeal from such a decision.[79]
- **'Stages'** This means stages (a)–(d) above.[80]
- **'Applicant for judicial review'** This means the person who is or was the applicant in the proceedings on the application for judicial review.[81]
- **'Public interest proceedings'** This has the meaning discussed in 13.54–13.57.
- **'Free of charge'** This means otherwise than for or in expectation of a fee, gain or reward.[82]

Transitional provisions

13.49 What follows applies to judicial review claims made on or after 8 August 2016.[83] In the event that the reader wishes to know about the law prior to that date (namely, the law of PCOs in public interest claims), the second edition of the book ought to be consulted.

Origin of powers and ambit

13.50 The judge-made law relating to PCOs in public law claims no longer applies. This is because s 88(1) of the 2015 Act provides that costs capping orders may not be made by the High Court or the Court of Appeal in connection with judicial review proceedings except in accordance with ss 88 and 89. Those sections do not apply to Aarhus Convention claims.[84]

13.51 A judicial review costs capping order may be made in respect of any 'stage' (see 13.48) of judicial review proceedings[85]. That said, the court may make a costs capping order only if leave to apply for judicial review has been granted.[86] Moreover, the court may make a costs capping order only on application for such an order by the applicant for judicial review in accordance with rules of court,[87] which means that there must be compliance with the provisions of CPR, Part 46, Section IV.

---

[79] See Criminal Justice and Courts Act 2015, s 88(12).

[80] See Criminal Justice and Courts Act 2015, s 88(12).

[81] See Criminal Justice and Courts Act 2015, s 88(13). References to relief being granted to the applicant for judicial review include the upholding on appeal of a decision to grant such relief at an earlier stage of the proceedings.

[82] See Criminal Justice and Courts Act 2015, s 89(6).

[83] See Civil Procedure (Amendment No 2) Rules 2016 (SI 2016/707), r 6, and Criminal Justice and Courts Act 2015 (Commencement No 4 and Transitional Provisions) Order 2016.

[84] See The Criminal Justice and Courts Act 2015 (Disapplication of Sections 88 and 89) Regulations 2017 (SI 2007/100).

[85] See Criminal Justice and Courts Act 2015, s 88(2).

[86] See Criminal Justice and Courts Act 2015, s 88(3).

[87] See Criminal Justice and Courts Act 2015, s 88(4). Subsection (5) provides: 'Rules of court may, in particular, specify information that must be contained in the application, including—(a) information about the source, nature and extent of financial resources available, or likely to be available, to the applicant to meet liabilities arising in connection with the application, and (b) if the applicant is a body corporate that is unable to demonstrate that it is likely to have financial resources available to meet such liabilities, information about its members and about their ability to provide financial support for the purposes of the application.'

Echoing the law that existed before the coming into force of ss 88 and 89 of the 2015 Act,[88] the new provisions expressly provide that the order may relate to appeals—because an appeal is one of the 'stages' of judicial review proceedings (see 13.48).[89] Indeed, s 88(13) of the 2015 Act goes so far as to stipulate that the jurisdiction will include the upholding on appeal of a decision to grant an order at an earlier stage of the proceedings. **13.52**

Conditions for making an order

The court may make a judicial review costs capping order only if it is satisfied that the following conditions are met:[90] **13.53**

- the proceedings are public interest proceedings (see 13.54–13.57);[91] and
- in the absence of the order, the applicant for judicial review would withdraw the application for judicial review or cease to participate in the proceedings[92] and it would be reasonable for the applicant for judicial review to do so (see 13.58–13.59).[93]

'Public interest proceedings'

The requirement that the proceedings be 'public interest proceedings' has a number of sub-requirements, as follows. **13.54**

- An issue that is the subject of the proceedings must be of general public importance.[94]
- The public interest must require the issue to be resolved.[95]
- The proceedings must be likely to provide an appropriate means of resolving that issue.[96]

Waller LJ has commented that the tests of 'general public importance' and 'public interest' in the issue being resolved may be difficult to separate;[97] indeed, there is certainly the potential for overlap on the issues.

The matters to which the court must have regard when determining whether proceedings are public interest proceedings include: **13.55**

- the number of people likely to be directly affected if relief is granted to the applicant for judicial review;[98]
- how significant the effect on those people is likely to be;[99] and
- whether the proceedings involve consideration of a point of law of general public importance.[100]

---

88 *R (on the application of Goodson) v Bedfordshire & Luton Coroner* [2005] EWCA Civ 1172, at [15], *per* Moore-Bick LJ.

89 See Criminal Justice and Courts Act 2015, s 88(12).

90 What is set out in this section is not markedly dissimilar to the factors set out in *R (on the application of Corner House Research) v Secretary of State for Trade and Industry* [2005] EWCA Civ 192, at [74], *per* Phillips MR, which was the seminal case relating to PCOs.

91 See Criminal Justice and Courts Act 2015, s 88(6)(a).

92 See Criminal Justice and Courts Act 2015, s 88(6)(b).

93 See Criminal Justice and Courts Act 2015, s 88(6)(c).

94 See Criminal Justice and Courts Act 2015, s 88(7)(a).

95 See Criminal Justice and Courts Act 2015, s 88(7)(b).

96 See Criminal Justice and Courts Act 2015, s 88(7)(c).

97 *R (Compton) v Wiltshire Primary Care Trust* [2008] EWCA Civ 749, at [21].

98 See Criminal Justice and Courts Act 2015, s 88(8)(a).

99 See Criminal Justice and Courts Act 2015, s 88(8)(b).

100 See Criminal Justice and Courts Act 2015, s 88(8)(c).

13.56 The phrases 'public interest' and 'general public importance' are the same as those that were used under the judge-made regime that existed prior to the coming into force of ss 88 and 89 of the 2015 Act. It would therefore seem that—on those points at least—guidance can still be obtained from older authorities.

13.57 The following miscellaneous points can be made.

- **No absolute standard** Smith LJ had the following observations to make:

  'First, there is no absolute standard by which to define what amounts to an issue of general public importance. Second, there are degrees to which the requirement may be satisfied; some issues may be of the first rank of general public importance, others of lesser rank although still of general public importance. Third, making the judgment is an exercise in which two judges might legitimately reach a different view without either being wrong.'[101]

- **Not a test of whether the matter is of national importance** The need to show that an issue is of general public importance does not mean that it needs to be of *national* importance.[102] Waller LJ had this to say on the point:

  'I do not read the word "general" as meaning that it must be of interest to all the public nationally. On the other hand I would accept that a local group may be so small that issues in which they alone might be interested would not be issues of "general public importance". It is a question of degree ...'[103]

- **Parochial issues** Where an issue can be shown to be parochial, in the sense that it is important to only some members of the community (such as a focus group), the requisite standard may not be met. For example, the Court of Appeal did not express any adverse comment on a case in which Lloyd Jones J declined to make an order under the old regime on the basis that the application represented a particular interest of a focus group rather than the interest of the community at large; the court did say, however, that such circumstances would not necessarily preclude an order.[104]
- **Number of people affected** The mere fact that only a relatively small number of people may be affected will not preclude the making of an order. In a case involving services provided by midwives, Oueseley J made an order notwithstanding the fact that the numbers involved were small, but not insubstantial.[105]

'Withdraw the application for judicial review'

13.58 The condition that, in the absence of the order, the applicant for judicial review would withdraw the application for judicial review or cease to participate in the proceedings[106] is similar to the test that existed prior to the coming into force of ss 88 and 89 of the 2015

---

[101] *R (Compton) v Wiltshire Primary Care Trust* [2008] EWCA Civ 749, at [75], *per* Smith LJ.

[102] *R (Compton) v Wiltshire Primary Care Trust* [2008] EWCA Civ 749, at [77].

[103] *Ibid*, at [24].

[104] *R (on the application of Bullmore) v West Hertfordshire Hospitals NHS Trust* [2007] EWHC 1350 (Admin), considered in *R (Compton) v Wiltshire Primary Care Trust* [2008] EWCA Civ 749. Similarly, see *Austin v Miller Argent (South Wales) Ltd* [2013] EWHC 2622 (TCC), a case concerning alleged noise nuisance in which Judge Milwyn-Jarman QC declined to make a PCO, largely because any remedy was likely to be directed to the precise conditions prevailing at the applicant's home and might well be implemented in practice without any significant change in general. This decision was upheld on appeal ([2011] EWCA Civ 928).

[105] See *Beety v Nursing & Midwifery Council* (unreported), 14 June 2017, QBD.

[106] See Criminal Justice and Courts Act 2015, s 88(6)(b).

Act. To that extent, guidance from older authorities may still be of assistance. It should be noted, however, that there is now an express requirement that the court consider whether it would be reasonable for the applicant to cease to take part in the proceedings if denied an order.[107]

Under the judge-made regime, when looking at whether the applicant would discontinue, it was permissible to look at whether a person other than the applicant would continue the litigation if the applicant were to discontinue by reason of not obtaining an order. Thus, in a case in which he was satisfied that if the applicant charity were to discontinue, a private individual would continue the litigation, Mann J found that he was justified in not making an order.[108] **13.59**

Exceptionality

It should be noted that there is no express requirement that the matter be exceptional. This is in line with the judge-made law that existed before ss 88 and 89 of the 2015 Act came into force. Whilst—in the early days of the development of the judge-made law—it was said that the jurisdiction 'should be exercised only in the most exceptional circumstances',[109] in practice the need for 'exceptionality' came not to regarded as being an additional criterion, but as merely a prediction as to the effect of applying the other criteria relating to such orders.[110] **13.60**

Private interest

There is now no requirement that the applicant has to prove the absence of a private interest in the matter. Even under the old regime, that requirement had been the subject of adverse comment.[111] Whilst early cases indicated a restrictive approach to private interests (as advocated by Moore-Bick LJ[112] and Buxton LJ[113]), more recent decisions paved **13.61**

---

[107] See Criminal Justice and Courts Act 2015, s 88(6).

[108] *R (on the application of Action against Medical Accidents) v General Medical Council* [2009] EWHC 2522 (Admin).

[109] *R v Prime Minister, ex p CND* [2002] EWHC 2712 (Admin), at [3], *per* Simon Brown LJ; *R v Lord Chancellor, ex p Child Poverty Action Group* [1998] 2 All ER 755, at 757.

[110] *R (Compton) v Wiltshire Primary Care Trust* [2008] EWCA Civ 749, at [24], *per* Waller and Smith LJJ (Buxton LJ dissenting). See also *R (on the application of Corner House Research) v Secretary of State for Trade and Industry* [2005] EWCA Civ 192, at [72].

[111] As a working group convened by Liberty and chaired by Maurice Kay LJ pointed out—see *Litigating the Public Interest: Report of the Working Group on Facilitating Public Interest Litigation* (London: Liberty, 2006), para 80—no individual could simultaneously allege that they were the victim of a human rights violation and that they also lacked a private interest in the claim they had brought. See also *Ensuring Access to Environment Justice in England and Wales: Report of the Working Group on Access to Environmental Justice* (London: World Wildlife Fund, 2008), this being the report of a committee chaired by Sullivan J. Both of those reports have received favourable judicial comment and have undoubtedly had a role in shaping the current law: see *R (England) v Tower Hamlets LBC* [2006] EWCA Civ 1742, at [14], where Carnwath LJ (with the agreement of Neuberger LJ) commented that the Kay Report was a 'valuable discussion'. Although this was in the context of an application for permission to appeal, the Court took the view that their comments were of wider significance and, as such, took the exceptional step of authorising reference to their judgment where relevant in other proceedings: see *ibid*, at [17].

[112] Moore-Bick LJ said that the requirement is an unqualified requirement (ie there must be no private interest and it is not sufficient that the public interest transcends or wholly outweighs the private interest): *R (on the application of Goodson) v Bedfordshire & Luton Coroner* [2005] EWCA Civ 1172, at [27].

[113] See 13.11.

the way to a more flexible approach.[114] Indeed, immediately prior to the coming into force of ss 88 and 89 of the 2015 Act, the test had become a matter of degree rather than a matter of absolutes.[115] In any event, it seems that that requirement has gone—although the court is required to take a private interest into account for the purposes of exercising its discretion[116] (see 13.64).

Discretion

13.62 As with all pre-emptive or protective costs orders, each case will turn on its own facts.[117]

No discretion to impose a unilateral cap

13.63 The court now has no power to make an order that caps only one side's costs. This is because s 89(2) of the 2015 Act provides that:

> 'A costs capping order that limits or removes the liability of the applicant for judicial review to pay the costs of another party to the proceedings if relief is not granted to the applicant for judicial review must also limit or remove the liability of the other party to pay the applicant's costs if it is.'

The factors to be taken into account

13.64 The matters to which the court must have regard when considering whether to make an order (and what the terms of such an order should be) include:

- the financial resources of the parties to the proceedings, including the financial resources of any person who provides, or may provide, financial support to the parties;[118]
- the extent to which the applicant for the order is likely to benefit if relief is granted to the applicant for judicial review;[119]
- the extent to which any person who has provided, or may provide, the applicant with financial support is likely to benefit if relief is granted to the applicant for judicial review;[120]
- whether legal representatives for the applicant for the order are acting free of charge;[121] and
- whether the applicant for the order is an appropriate person to represent the interests of other persons or the public interest generally.[122]

---

[114] *Morgan & Anor v Hinton Organics (Wessex) Ltd* [2009] EWCA Civ 107, at [38] and [39], *per* Carnwath LJ, citing with apparent approval the comments of Lloyd Jones J in *R (Bullmore) v West Hertfordshire Hospitals NHS Trust* [2007] EWHC 1350 (Admin). See also *R (Buglife) v Thurrock Gateway Development Corp & Anor* [2008] EWCA Civ 1209. See *R (on the application of Young) v Oxford City Council* [2012] EWCA Civ 46, at [9] and [11]–[17], in which the applicant's primary ground for bringing the proceedings was the impact of noise on houses adjoining his home and in which Richards LJ found that that interest was not fatal to his application, but was a factor to be taken into account. See also *R (on the application of Litvinenko) v Secretary of State for the Home Department* [2013] EWHC 3135 (Admin), at [27]–[33], in which, similarly, Goldring LJ found that an applicant's private interest in her challenge of a decision not to hold a public inquiry into the death of her husband was 'a factor to take into account when balancing the other Corner House criteria', rather than a factor that 'would prevent [the court] making an order'.

[115] See, eg, *IS v Director Legal Aid Casework* [2014] EWCA Civ 886.

[116] See Criminal Justice and Courts Act 2015, s 89(1)(b).

[117] Whilst it preceded the coming into force of ss 88 and 89 of the 2015 Act, see *Re Evans (deceased)* [1986] 1 WLR 101; see also *National Anti-Vivisection Society Ltd v Duddington* (1989) The Times, 23 November, *per* Mummery J, which confirms that the discretion must be exercised judicially.

[118] See Criminal Justice and Courts Act 2015, s 89(1)(a).

[119] See Criminal Justice and Courts Act 2015, s 89(1)(b).

[120] See Criminal Justice and Courts Act 2015, s 89(1)(c).

[121] See Criminal Justice and Courts Act 2015, s 89(1)(d).

[122] See Criminal Justice and Courts Act 2015, s 89(1)(e).

Other than the penultimate item, this list of factors is not dissimilar to the list that could have been drawn up describing the factors that were commonly taken into account under the judge-made law. The only real difference is the penultimate item, because it is arguable that there is a difference between acting *pro bono* and acting free of charge (see 18.121). That argument would be based on the premise that it would be curious if a respondent could be held liable for a significant award under s 194 of the Legal Services Act 2007 whilst at the same time being entitled to the benefit of a reciprocal costs capping order. It should also be noted that the issue of private interest is now expressly a factor to take into account (as opposed to a condition). **13.65**

Financial resources The court must take into account the financial resources of the parties to the proceedings, including the financial resources of any person who provides, or may provide, financial support to the parties.[123] The court is entitled to expect significant disclosure in this regard (see 13.72). **13.66**

Whilst they pre-dated the coming into force of ss 88 and 89 of the 2015 Act, the following comments of Richards J still have resonance: **13.67**

> '[The court should] seek to give effect to the overriding objective and should have particular regard to the need, so far as practicable, to ensure that the parties are on an equal footing and that the case is dealt with in a way which is proportionate to the financial position of each party.'[124]

Under the judge-made regime, an applicant could have been refused an order if their financial position were such that it would not be just to make such an order[125] and presumably the same applies under the new provisions.

The following miscellaneous points regarding financial resources may be made. **13.68**

- **Crowdfunding** Monies raised by crowdfunding may be taken into account.[126]
- **No need to show impecuniosity** The applicant does not need to show that they are impecunious.[127]
- **Conditions imposed by the Legal Services Commission** The Supreme Court (albeit under the old regime) has ruled that if the Legal Services Commission had decided to fund a litigant, that decision ordinarily had to be seen to carry with it something close to an assurance that it would continue to support that party in any subsequent appeal by the unsuccessful party.[128] Their Lordships found that it was unlawful for the Commission to stipulate that an order must be made as a condition of funding and they declared that the Commission must continue to provide public funding for the purposes of an appeal brought by its client's opponent.

---

123 See Criminal Justice and Courts Act 2015, s 89(1)(a).

124 *R v London Borough of Hammersmith and Fulham, ex p CPRE* [2000] ENVLR 544, at 544–5.

125 See, eg, *R (on the application of Litvinenko) v Secretary of State for the Home Department* [2013] EWHC 3135 (Admin).

126 See *Beety v Nursing & Midwifery Council* (unreported), 14 June 2017, QBD, *per* Ouseley J.

127 See, eg, *Mackman v Secretary of State for Communities & Local Government* [2013] EWHC 4435 (Admin), at [23], in which Lang J (who made a PCO) found that the applicant was not wealthy, but he was not impecunious.

128 *R (on the application of E) v Governing Body of JFS and the Admissions Appeal Panel of JFS* [2009] UKSC 1.

Appeals

13.69 Under the judge-made regime, where an application was made for an order on appeal, it was for that court to determine whether such an order should be made and, if so, the level of the cap.[129] The way in which the court dealt with such matters turned on whether the applicant was the appellant or the respondent:

- where the application was made by the party who sought to appeal to the Court of Appeal, the issue of an order was considered afresh by the Court of Appeal upon its merits; and
- where the beneficiary of an order had succeeded in the court at first instance, it was ordinarily the case that the order would continue to apply in the Court of Appeal.[130]

There is no particular reason to believe that things are any different under the 2015 Act, but there is no authority on that point. Moreover, given the facts (a) that judicial review costs capping orders are now necessarily reciprocal (see 13.63) and (b) that the 'stage' of proceedings now expressly include appeals (see 13.48), it may be that stand-alone applications in the Court of Appeal become less common.

The amount of the cap

13.70 Haddon-Cave J has explained that the fairness of an order can be properly calibrated by an appropriate 'cap' that has taken all of the circumstances of the case into account.[131] This undoubtedly remains true under ss 88 and 89 of the 2015 Act because the list of factors in s 89(1) is not an exhaustive list.

13.71 In what follows, the editor has attempted to adapt guidance given by Phillips MR in 2005[132] to take into account subsequent cases and modern methods of funding, and to apply that guidance to the regime under the 2015 Act. What follows has not been approved by any court, however, and should therefore be treated with caution.

- Pursuant to s 89(2) of the 2015 Act (see 13.63), the court must impose a reciprocal cap[133]—although this does not mean that the amount of the cap has to be same for each side.[134]
- An order that caps—rather than negates—potential liability for costs is likely to be required in all cases except where the party's lawyers are acting free of charge (as opposed to *pro bono* within the meaning of s 194 of the Legal Services Act 2007).
- Other than where no costs will be payable by the party in question, the form of any cap should state the total amount of the costs potentially payable, either inclusive or exclusive of value added tax (VAT).

---

129 *R (Compton) v Wiltshire Primary Care Trust* [2008] EWCA Civ 749, at [28].

130 *Ibid*, at [47].

131 See *R (on the application of Plantagenet Alliance Ltd) v (1) Secretary of State for Justice* [2013] EWHC 3164 (Admin), at [49].

132 *R (on the application of Corner House Research) v Secretary of State for Trade and Industry* [2005] EWCA Civ 192, at [76].

133 This means that the comments of Smith LJ about 'heads you win, tails I lose' in *R (on the application of Compton) v Wiltshire Primary Care Trust* [2008] EWCA Civ 749, at [86], are no longer good law.

134 See, eg, *Beety v Nursing & Midwifery Council* (unreported), 14 June 2017, QBD, *per* Ouseley J.

- The purpose of the order will be to limit or negate the liability of whichever party it is who loses, and whilst the figures for each party's cap do not need to match, they should both be reasonably modest.
- The overriding purpose of setting the level of the cap is to enable each party to present its case with a reasonably competent advocate and without being exposed to such serious financial risks as would deter the party from advancing its case. In setting the amount, the court may take into account the financial means of the parties.[135]
- As such, it would generally be appropriate to restrict the costs to reasonable profit costs, disbursements and a fee for a single advocate of junior counsel status,[136] and the amounts that will be allowed for these purposes will be modest.

Procedure on applying for judicial review costs capping orders

The following procedural points may be made about applications for judicial review costs capping orders. **13.72**

- **Form of application** An application must be made on notice and (subject to what is said below) in accordance with CPR, Part 23.[137] This suggests that a stand-alone application should be made, but PD 46, para 10.2, provides that when the application is in the High Court, it must normally be contained in, or accompany, the claim form. This does not cause any problems, however, because such an application would still fall within the ambit of Part 23 by reason of CPR, r 23.3(2)(b). There are no express requirements relating to appeals, but it would be sensible to make the application at the same time as making the application for permission to appeal.[138]
- **Evidence** An application must be supported by evidence setting out:
  - (a) why a judicial review costs capping order should be made, having regard, in particular, to the matters listed in ss 88(6)–(8) and 89(1) of the 2015 Act (see 13.53–13.55 and 13.64);
  - (b) a summary of the applicant's financial resources, which (unless the court directs otherwise) must include a summary of the details of:
    - (i) the applicant's significant assets, liabilities, income and expenditure; and
    - (ii) in relation to any financial support that any person has provided, or is likely to provide, to the applicant, the aggregate amount that has been, or is likely to be, provided;[139]
  - (c) the costs (and disbursements) that the applicant considers the parties are likely to incur in the future conduct of the proceedings; and
  - (d) if the applicant is a body corporate, whether it is able to demonstrate that it is likely to have financial resources available to meet liabilities arising in connection with the proceedings.[140]

---

135 *R (Compton) v Wiltshire Primary Care Trust* [2008] EWCA Civ 749, at [27]. As an example of this happening in practice, see Northern Ireland case *The Alternative A5 Alliance's Application* [2012] NIQB 97, at [6], in which Horner J set a £20,000 limit, this being about £150 per member of the Alliance: a figure he did not regard as being 'prohibitively expensive'.

136 *R (Compton) v Wiltshire Primary Care Trust* [2008] EWCA Civ 749, at [86], *per* Smith LJ.

137 See CPR, r 46.17(1)(a).

138 Support for this approach may be found in *R (on the application of Compton) v Wiltshire Primary Care Trust* [2008] EWCA Civ 749.

139 PD 46, para 10.1.

140 See CPR, r 46.17(1)(b).

- **Service** The applicant must serve a copy of the application notice and copies of the supporting documents on every other party.[141] That said, on application by the applicant, the court may dispense with the need for the applicant to serve the evidence setting out a summary of the applicant's financial resources on one or more of the parties.[142]
- **Additional evidence** The court may direct the applicant to provide additional information or evidence to support its application.[143]
- **Court to consider making directions** If the applicant is a body corporate and if the evidence supporting its application in accordance with the above suggests that it is unable to demonstrate that it is likely to have financial resources available to meet liabilities arising in connection with the proceedings, the court must consider giving directions for the provision of information about the applicant's members and their ability to provide financial support for the purposes of the proceedings.[144]

Variation

13.73 It is often the case that applications are decided on paper without the attendance of the parties. Such decisions may be reviewed on oral application, but—to the extent that the judge-made law still applies—the decision will be overturned only if the person seeking to vary the order is able to show 'compelling reasons' why that should be so.[145] It was often said that the way in which the test was applied favoured respondents to the judicial review in that an applicant to the judicial review who was refused an order had the right to renew the application at an oral hearing without constraint, but a respondent who had had an order made against them had to establish compelling reasons.[146] It is not known whether this continues to be the case, but, given that orders are reciprocal, any such concerns are likely to prove less divisive.

13.74 **Procedure on applications to vary** The following procedural points may be made about applications to vary judicial review costs capping orders.

- **Form** Echoing the practice prior to the coming into force of ss 88 and 89 of the 2015 Act,[147] CPR, r 46.19(1), now expressly provides that an application to vary a judicial review costs capping order must be made on notice and, subject to r 46.19(2) and (3), in accordance with CPR, Part 23.[148]
- **Service** The applicant must serve a copy of the application notice and copies of any supporting documents on every other party.[149] That said, if the application to vary is

141 See CPR, r 46.17(2).

142 See CPR, r 46.17(3).

143 See CPR, r 46.17(4).

144 CPR, r 46.18.

145 *R (on the application of Corner House Research) v Secretary of State for Trade and Industry* [2005] EWCA Civ 192, at [79].

146 *R (Compton) v Wiltshire Primary Care Trust* [2008] EWCA Civ 749, at [42]. This has been justified on the basis that the claimant, who may have been refused a PCO, should have more latitude, because without a PCO no proceedings will be brought at all, whereas the existence of a PCO will not prevent a defendant from defending the merits of the case if the PCO is set aside. Smith LJ has explained that a further justification is that there is a need to impose a procedure that would avoid drawn-out preliminary skirmishes: see *ibid*, at [90].

147 See *R (on the application of Simmons) v Bolton Metropolitan Borough Council* [2011] EWHC 2729 (Admin), *per* Judge Pelling QC.

148 CPR, r 46.19(1).

149 CPR, r 46.19(2).

supported by evidence setting out a summary of the applicant's financial resources, the court may, on application by the applicant, dispense with the need for the applicant to serve such evidence on one or more of the parties.[150]

Reservation of right to vary Supperstone J has found that it is permissible for the court to make an order that permits a party to apply retrospectively to disapply a cap (albeit under the judge-made regime).[151] **13.75**

Putative 'variation' at a detailed assessment Whilst their Lordships were dealing with the rules that govern their court rather than the CPR, the Supreme Court has ruled that where applications to reduce or cap a party's liability had been made and rejected by the court, it was not open to a costs officer subsequently to achieve that same result through the detailed assessment process.[152] **13.76**

Costs of applications

If the defendant successfully resists the application, then it is likely still to be the case that that they will be awarded costs, but only in a modest amount.[153] **13.77**

CPR, Part 45, Section VII: Aarhus Convention Claims

The topic of the Aarhus Convention[154] may arise either in the context of the claimant applying for a protective costs order or in the context of an assessment. It is convenient to consider those two aspects of the matter together because, for all practical purposes, they are both governed by CPR, Part 45, Section VII. What follows is different from the other provisions in this chapter because certain limits apply by default—which, presumably, is why the relevant provisions are in Part 45 (which is that Part which deals with fixed costs). **13.78**

Environmental claims

Environmental cases tend to be in a different class from other claims. This is because of a treaty known as the Aarhus Convention, which imposes an obligation on public authorities to ensure that certain claims—known as Aarhus Convention claims—are not 'prohibitively expensive'. If a claim falls within that category, then the parties may be entitled to the benefit of the relatively restrictive limits on costs contained in CPR, Part 45, Section VII. **13.79**

CPR, Part 45, Section VII, makes express provision for a special costs protection. As is explained below, on 28 February 2017,[155] that Section was replaced with a new Section VII—together with new provision in Part 52 covering appeals (see 13.100–13.108).[156] **13.80**

---

150 CPR, r 46.19(3).

151 *Howard v Wigan City Council* [2015] EWHC 3643 (Admin).

152 *R (on the application of Edwards & Anor) v Environment Agency (Cemex UK Cement Ltd, intervening)* [2010] UKSC 57.

153 Whilst it was decided prior to the coming into force of ss 88 and 89 of the 2015 Act, see *Mount Cook Land Ltd v Westminster City Council* [2003] EWCA Civ 1346, at [76(1)].

154 The UNECE Convention on Access to Information, Public Participation in Decision-Making and Access to Justice in Environmental Matters, made in Aarhus, Denmark, on 25 June 1998.

155 See Civil Procedure (Amendment) Rules 2017 (SI 2017/95), r 13(3).

156 See Civil Procedure (Amendment) Rules 2017 (SI 2017/95), r 8.

This was, amongst other things, to take account of guidance given in two cases in the Court of Justice of the European Union (CJEU) (see the footnotes to 13.81).

The old CPR, Part 45, Section VII

13.81 It is now known that CPR, Part 45, Section VII (as it was prior to 28 February 2017), was not compliant with the UK's obligations under the Aarhus Convention.[157] The cumulative effect of those concerns was that there was a need for the Section to be revised.

The new CPR, Part 45, Section VII, and other provisions

13.82 The new provisions,[158] like those they replaced, have as their starting point a default cap on the liability of an unsuccessful Aarhus claimant to pay the defendant's costs of £5,000 (or £10,000, if the claimant is not an individual), together with a reciprocal cross-cap on an unsuccessful defendant's liability to pay the claimant's costs of £35,000. That said, the new provisions differ in the following respects.[159]

- They extend beyond judicial reviews to include statutory reviews (in particular, planning challenges).
- They allow the court to increase or lower the cap and cross-cap, provided always that any change does not render the cost of proceedings prohibitively expensive for the claimant.
- They require the court, when assessing whether proceedings would be prohibitively expensive if the change were or were not made, to take into account a list of factors that mirrors those set out by the CJEU.[160]
- They make specific provision requiring the court to apply the same principles on appeal as at first instance.

13.83 Section 90 of the Criminal Justice and Courts Act 2015 provides a framework that permits the Lord Chancellor to make secondary legislation regarding costs in environmental cases.[161] Other than the provisions in CPR, Part 45, Section VII, no such secondary legislation has been made. Section 88 and 89 do not apply to Aarhus Convention claims.[162]

---

[157] In 2010, the Supreme Court referred a matter to the CJEU for an explanation of what was meant by the expression 'not prohibitively expensive' (see *R (on the application of Edwards & Anor) v Environment Agency & Ors* [2010] UKSC 57, at [42]). The CJEU responded by saying that the test is not purely subjective; the cost of proceedings must not exceed the financial resources of the person concerned nor must they 'appear to be objectively unreasonable'. Furthermore—said the CJEU—the court was entitled to take into account the merits of the claim. When the case returned to the Supreme Court, Lord Carnwath interpreted that guidance as meaning that the certain factors ought to be taken into account when considering the issue of costs relating to Aarhus Convention claims: *R (on the application of Edwards & Anor) v Environment Agency & Ors (No 2)* [2013] UKSC 78, at [28]. They are discussed at 13.92. Much of what Lord Carnwath had to say has now been incorporated into CPR, Part 45, Section VII. In the second case, the CJEU found that there was a lack of predictability under the CPR: see Case C 530/11, *European Commission v United Kingdom of Great Britain and Northern Ireland* ECLI:EU:C:2014:67, at [58]. In addition to the above, Sullivan LJ noted that the provisions in the old CPR, Part 45, Section VII, were deliberately limited to judicial review claims; this meant that they did not extend to statutory appeals or applications: see *The Secretary of State for Communities and Local Government v Venn* [2014] EWCA Civ 1539, at [33] and [34]. This, Sullivan LJ said, meant that the UK was in breach of its obligations under the Aarhus Convention.

[158] See Civil Procedure (Amendment) Rules 2017 (SI 2017/95), r 8.

[159] See Civil Procedure (Amendment) Rules 2017 (SI 2017/95), Explanatory Note.

[160] See fn 158.

[161] See Criminal Justice and Courts Act 2015, s 90.

[162] See The Criminal Justice and Courts Act 2015 (Disapplication of Sections 88 and 89) Regulations 2017 (SI 1017/100).

The Aarhus Convention

The Aarhus Convention is a treaty made by the United Nations Economic Commission for Europe (UNECE). By providing for access to information, public participation and access to justice in environmental matters, it aims to encourage members of the public to participate in decision-making processes that affect the environment. The Aarhus Convention is not part of domestic law, except where incorporated through European directives.[163] **13.84**

In so far as the law of costs is concerned, the significant provisions of the Aarhus Convention are as follows: **13.85**

> '9.4 ... [T]he procedures referred to ... above shall provide adequate and effective remedies, including injunctive relief as appropriate, and be fair, equitable, timely and not prohibitively expensive. Decisions under this article shall be given or recorded in writing. Decisions of courts, and whenever possible of other bodies, shall be publicly accessible.'

Thus member states must ensure that proceedings to which the Aarhus Convention applies must not be 'prohibitively expensive'. What follows is a discussion of the way in this is achieved in this jurisdiction.

Aarhus Convention claims

In so far as the CPR are concerned, an Aarhus Convention claim is a claim brought by one or more members of the public: **13.86**

- by judicial review or review under statute that challenges the legality of any decision, act or omission of a body exercising public functions and which is within the scope of Article 9(1) or (2) of the Aarhus Convention; or
- by judicial review that challenges the legality of any such decision, act or omission and which is within the scope of Article 9(3) of the Aarhus Convention.[164]

Not all cases relating to the environment are Aarhus Convention claims.[165]

Opting out and disputes regarding status

The claimant may, as of right, opt out of a claim being an Aarhus Convention claim. This is provided for by CPR, r 45.42: **13.87**

> '(1) Subject to paragraph (2), rules 45.43 to 45.45 apply where a claimant who is a member of the public has—
> (a) stated in the claim form that the claim is an Aarhus Convention claim; and
> (b) filed and served with the claim form a schedule of the claimant's financial resources which takes into account any financial support which any person has provided or is likely to provide to the claimant and which is verified by a statement of truth.

163 *Walton v Scottish Ministers* [2012] UKSC 44, at [100].

164 See CPR, r 45.41 (as amended by The Criminal Justice and Courts Act 2015 (Disapplication of Sections 88 and 89) Regulations 2017, SI 2017/95).

165 See, eg, *R (on the application of Young) v Oxford City Council* [2012] EWCA Civ 46, at [9] and [11]–[17], in which Richards LJ found that the Aarhus Convention did not engage in a judicial review of the local authority's decision to grant planning permission for the redevelopment of a university campus. In contrast, in *Austin v Miller Argent (South Wales) Ltd* [2014] EWCA Civ 1012, at [17], [21]–[22] and [24], Elias LJ said that complaints about noise nuisance could, in principle, be Aarhus claims.

(2) Subject to paragraph (3), rules 45.43 to 45.45 do not apply where the claimant has stated in the claim form that although the claim is an Aarhus Convention claim, the claimant does not wish those rules to apply.

(3) If there is more than one claimant, rules 45.43 to 45.45 do not apply in relation to the costs payable by or to any claimant who has not acted as set out in paragraph (1), or who has acted as set out in paragraph (2), or who is not a member of the public.'

13.88 A defendant does not have any such right, but if they dispute the fact that a claim is an Aarhus Convention claim, then (for claims commenced on or after 28 February 2017[166]) CPR, r 45.44,[167] will apply:

'(1) Where a claimant has complied with rule 45.42(1), and subject to rule 45.42(2) and (3), rule 45.43 will apply unless—
(a) the defendant has in the acknowledgment of service—
 (i) denied that the claim is an Aarhus Convention claim; and
 (ii) set out the defendant's grounds for such denial; and
(b) the court has determined that the claim is not an Aarhus Convention claim.

(2) Where the defendant denies that the claim is an Aarhus Convention claim, the court must determine that issue at the earliest opportunity.
(3) In any proceedings to determine whether the claim is an Aarhus Convention claim—
(a) if the court holds that the claim is not an Aarhus Convention claim, it will normally make no order for costs in relation to those proceedings;
(b) if the court holds that the claim is an Aarhus Convention claim, it will normally order the defendant to pay the claimant's costs of those proceedings to be assessed on the standard basis, and that order may be enforced even if this would increase the costs payable by the defendant beyond the amount stated in rule 45.43(3) or any variation of that amount.'

13.89 Thus, in essence, where a defendant successfully challenges the status of the claim, there will be a rebuttable presumption that the defendant will bear their own costs. If, however, a defendant fails in such a challenge, then they would normally be condemned in pay costs—and this would be so regardless of the protection of CPR, Part 45, Section VII. Contrary to the provisions as they were prior to 28 February 2017, there is no presumption that those costs would be payable on the indemnity basis.

13.90 Any type of person (natural or corporate) may benefit from CPR, Part 45, Section VII. The fact that a party is a local authority does not prevent it from enjoying the protection that Section VII affords.[168]

The limits on the amounts payable in Aarhus Convention claims

13.91 CPR, r 45.43, provides that a party to an Aarhus Convention claim may not be ordered to pay costs exceeding the following amounts:

'**Limit on costs recoverable from a party in an Aarhus Convention claim: Rule 45.43**

(1) Subject to rules 45.42 and 45.45, a claimant or defendant in an Aarhus Convention claim may not be ordered to pay costs exceeding the amounts in paragraph (2) or (3) or as varied in accordance with rule 45.44.

---

166 Different provisions (ie a now-deleted CPR, r 45.42(2)) applied to claims commenced before 28 February 2017; details may be found in the second edition of this book.

167 This provision was inserted by the Civil Procedure (Amendment) Rules 2017 (SI 2017/95).

168 *R (on the application of HS2 Action Alliance Ltd) v Secretary of State for Transport* [2015] EWCA Civ 203.

(2) For a claimant the amount is—
(a) £5,000 where the claimant is claiming only as an individual and not as, or on behalf of, a business or other legal person;
(b) £10,000 in all other cases.

(3) For a defendant the amount is £35,000.

(4) In an Aarhus Convention claim with multiple claimants or multiple defendants, the amounts in paragraphs (2) and (3) (subject to any direction of the court under rule 45.44) apply in relation to each such claimant or defendant individually and may not be exceeded, irrespective of the number of receiving parties.'

Whilst his decision related to the pre-2017 provisions, Collins J has explained that where there is more than one claimant, the cap has to be considered separately in respect of each claimant, and he applied a cap of £15,000 accordingly to a case in which the first claimant was an unincorporated association (attracting a £5,000 cap) and the second claimant was a parish council (attracting a £10,000 cap).[169] **13.92**

In the unlikely event that the court had to assess the costs rather than merely apply the aforesaid limits, it is likely that the assessment would be exactly the same as would any other assessment. This—as Sullivan LJ has explained—is because once it has been established that a claim is an Aarhus Convention claim and that the claimant wishes it to be treated as such, CPR, Part 45, Section VII, and PD 45 apply, without further reference to the Aarhus Convention.[170] **13.93**

Variation of the limit

There may be a need to vary the cap. If so, then the court will need to tackle the issue of whether costs are 'prohibitively expensive'. As has already been mentioned,[171] this is a question that so vexed the Supreme Court that it made a referral to the CJEU.[172] The guidance that the CJEU gave (which is similar to the guidance now given in the CPR) can be summarised in the following way.[173] **13.94**

1. Where a court needs to determine whether proceedings would be prohibitively expensive for a claimant, it should not act solely on the basis of that claimant's financial situation, but should carry out an objective analysis of the amount of the costs.
2. The court could also take into account:
   - the situation of the parties concerned;
   - whether the claimant had a reasonable prospect of success;
   - the importance of what was at stake for the claimant and for the protection of the environment;

[169] *R (on the application of Botley Parish Action Group) v Eastleigh Borough Council* [2014] EWHC 4388 (Admin), at [124].
[170] See *R (on the application of HS2 Action Alliance Ltd) v Secretary of State for Transport* [2015] EWCA Civ 203, at [12].
[171] See fn 158.
[172] *R (on the application of Edwards & Anor) v Environment Agency (Cemex UK Cement Ltd, intervening)* [2010] UKSC 57, at [36].
[173] Case C-260/11, *R (on the application of Edwards) v Environment Agency* [2013] 1 WLR 2914, at [37]–[48]. See also Lord Carnwath's commentary in *R (on the application of Edwards & Anor) v Environment Agency (Cemex UK Cement Ltd, intervening) (No 2)* [2013] UKSC 78, at [23].

– the complexity of the relevant law and procedure;
– the potentially frivolous nature of the claim at its various stages; and
– the existence of a national legal aid scheme or a costs protection regime.

3. The fact that a claimant had not been deterred, in practice, from asserting their claim was not of itself sufficient to establish that the proceedings were not prohibitively expensive.

13.95 As of 28 February 2017, most of this guidance is now expressly set out in the CPR:

> '**Varying the limit on costs recoverable from a party in an Aarhus Convention claim**
>
> 45.43. (1) The court may vary the amounts in rule 45.43 or may remove altogether the limits on the maximum costs liability of any party in an Aarhus Convention claim.
>
> (2) The court may vary such an amount or remove such a limit only if satisfied that—
> (a) to do so would not make the costs of the proceedings prohibitively expensive for the claimant; and
> (b) in the case of a variation which would reduce a claimant's maximum costs liability or increase that of a defendant, without the variation the costs of the proceedings would be prohibitively expensive for the claimant.
>
> (3) Proceedings are to be considered prohibitively expensive for the purpose of this rule if their likely costs (including any court fees which are payable by the claimant) either—
> (a) exceed the financial resources of the claimant; or
> (b) are objectively unreasonable having regard to—
> (i) the situation of the parties;
> (ii) whether the claimant has a reasonable prospect of success;
> (iii) the importance of what is at stake for the claimant;
> (iv) the importance of what is at stake for the environment;
> (v) the complexity of the relevant law and procedure; and
> (vi) whether the claim is frivolous.
>
> (4) When the court considers the financial resources of the claimant for the purposes of this rule, it must have regard to any financial support which any person has provided or is likely to provide to the claimant.
>
> (Rule 39.2(3)(c) makes provision for a hearing (or any part of it) to be in private if it involves confidential information (including information relating to personal financial matters) and publicity would damage that confidentiality.)'

Thus the test is what is objectively reasonable and there is provision for the court to receive evidence as to the financial status of the claimant.[174]

13.96 It is worth noting that, when the matter came back before the Supreme Court, Lord Carnwath deliberated upon the relevant factors and, in doing so, put some meat on the bones of what are now the factors in CPR, r 45.43.(3)(b):

> 'Taking the points in turn I would suggest the following:
> i) *A reasonable prospect of success* Lack of a reasonable prospect of success in the claim may, it seems, be a reason for allowing the respondents to recover a higher proportion of their costs. The fact that "frivolity" is mentioned separately (see below), suggests that

[174] Whilst it relates to the pre-2017 version of CPR, Part 45, Section VII, it seems that evidence of the risk of prohibitive expense is required: *Austin v Miller Argent (South Wales) Ltd* [2011] EWCA Civ 928, at [65].

something more demanding is envisaged than, for example, the threshold test of reasonable arguability.

ii) *The importance of what is at stake for the claimant* As indicated by Advocate General Kokott, this is likely to be a factor increasing the proportion of costs fairly recoverable. As she said, a person with "extensive individual economic interests" at stake in the proceedings may reasonably be expected to bear higher risks in terms of costs.

iii) *The importance of what is at stake for the protection of the environment* Conversely, and again following the Advocate General's approach, this is likely to be a factor reducing the proportion of costs recoverable, or eliminating recovery altogether. As she said, the environment cannot defend itself, but needs to be represented by concerned citizens or organisations acting in the public interest.

iv) *The complexity of the relevant law and procedure* This factor is not further explained. Its relevance seems to be that a complex case is likely to require higher expenditure by the respondents, and thus, objectively, to justify a higher award of costs. Although mention is only made of complexity of law or procedure, the same presumably should apply to technical or factual complexity.

v) *The potentially frivolous nature of the claim at its various stages* The respondents should not have to bear the costs of meeting a frivolous claim.'[175]

The claimant's own costs may be taken into account when considering whether to vary the cap and in setting that cap.[176]

As to the stage at which an application to vary the cap should be made, Dove J had the following to say: **13.97**

'[A]ny application to vary the default costs caps should ... be included within the acknowledgement of service, nevertheless as a matter of practice reading the [Aarhus Convention] as a whole, if a defendant proposes to contend that the default costs caps should be varied they need to do so (and as a matter of proper procedure bearing in mind the overriding objective must do so) in their acknowledgement of service.'[177]

Thus applications (on the part of defendants) should be made in the acknowledgement of service.

If an application was not made at that time, then the following comments of Dove J would apply: **13.98**

'If the application was made because the defendant had failed for whatever reason to engage with the question of whether or not the default levels of the costs caps were appropriate at the permission stage, then it would be too late for that issue to be raised subsequently in the absence of good reason. Such an application would not have been brought as soon as it became apparent that it was necessary or desirable to make it. It would additionally, in principle, be in breach of the EU principles which have been set out above.'[178]

Thus a late application to vary the cap could be made only for good reason. Dove J went on to say that if the claimant had provided false or misleading information in the

175 See *R (on the application of Edwards & Anor) v Environment Agency (Cemex UK Cement Ltd, intervening) (No 2)* [2013] UKSC 78, at [28].

176 *The Royal Society for the Protection of Birds Friends of the Earth Ltd & Anor v Secretary of State for Justice the Lord Chancellor* [2017] EWHC 2309 (Admin), at [58], *per* Dove J.

177 *Ibid*, at [38].

178 *Ibid*, at [39].

schedule of financial resources, or if there had been a material change in the claimant's financial resources that justified a re-examination of the issue, that might amount to good reason.

13.99 In practice, applications to vary are normally dealt on the papers, but if a dispute in relation to the appropriate level of costs caps were to proceed to a hearing, then that hearing should be held in private in the first instance.[179]

CPR, Part 52, Section IV: Costs Restriction in Certain Appeals

13.100 What follows is a discussion of certain specific provisions that apply when an appeal is heard from a 'no costs' or 'low costs' tribunal (see 13.101), or in an Aarhus Convention claim (see 13.108). In all other circumstances, costs capping on appeals is governed by the other provisions referred to in this chapter.

Costs restriction in appeals (non-Aarhus Convention claims)

13.101 It has long been the case that the Court of Appeal has had the power to make pre-emptive orders that restrict or negate the ability of one or both of the parties to recover costs, often of its own volition.[180] Whilst there were cases in which such an order was made,[181] there was a lacuna in the rules in that such orders were not readily available when the case moved from a 'low costs' or 'no costs' tribunal to an appeal court where no such protections existed.[182] This lacuna was capable of giving rise to injustice.[183] This resulted in Sir Rupert Jackson making a number of recommendations in his Final Report,[184] which ultimately led to the introduction of the rules set out below. The first incarnation of those rules came into force on 1 April 2013.

13.102 In so far as those provisions relate to claims that are not Aarhus Convention claims (see 13.108), they are to be found at CPR, r 52.19:

> '(1) Subject to rule 52.19A [this being a reference to Aarhus Convention claims], in any proceedings in which costs recovery is normally limited or excluded at first instance, an appeal court may make an order that the recoverable costs of an appeal will be limited to the extent which the court specifies.
>
> (2) In making such an order the court will have regard to—
> (a) the means of both parties;
> (b) all the circumstances of the case; and
> (c) the need to facilitate access to justice.
>
> (3) If the appeal raises an issue of principle or practice upon which substantial sums may turn, it may not be appropriate to make an order under paragraph (1).

---

179 *Ibid*, at [57].

180 This is what happened in *Jones v Caradon Catnic Ltd* [2005] EWCA Civ 1821, for example.

181 See, eg, *Unison v Kelly* [2012] EWCA Civ 1148. See also *Hazel v Manchester College* [2013] EWCA Civ 281, at [29]–[35], where Jackson LJ explains the need for such a rule.

182 See *Eweida v British Airways PLC* [2009] EWCA Civ 1025.

183 See, eg, the comments of Jackson LJ in *Hazel v Manchester College* [2013] EWCA Civ 281, at [30].

184 See *JE (Jamaica) v Secretary of State for the Home Department* [2014] EWCA Civ 192, at [7], where Jackson LJ refers to Jackson, R, *Review of Civil Litigation Costs: Final Report* (London: HMSO, 2010), pp 340 and 341.

(4) An application for such an order must be made as soon as practicable and will be determined without a hearing unless the court orders otherwise.'

As can be seen, any appeal court is now able to afford the parties a degree of costs protection in an appeal from a 'no costs' or 'low costs' tribunal. More specifically, where costs recovery at first instance was limited or excluded, an appeal court may make an order that the recoverable costs of an appeal will be limited to the extent that the court specifies.[185]

Ambit

Both Jackson LJ[186] and Arden LJ[187] have explained that the provisions in CPR, r 52.19, will not apply in proceedings to which costs recovery are not normally limited or excluded at first instance. Moreover, Jackson LJ has made it clear that the rule does not contemplate an order in favour of only one party, win or lose.[188] **13.103**

CPR, r 52.19, does not remove costs protection that is conferred by other provisions. Put otherwise, if the CPR provide that the costs of an appeal should be restricted in principle, CPR, r 52.19, does not give the appeal court the discretion to *dis*apply those provisions. In so far as claims on the small claims track are concerned, see 50.378; in so far as qualified one-way costs shifting (QOCS) is concerned, see 8.15. **13.104**

Discretion

The appeal court will have regard to: **13.105**

- the means of both parties;
- all of the circumstances of the case; and
- the need to facilitate access to justice.[189]

As to the first of these factors, the fact that a party has been granted a costs indulgence in the court below does not imply that the party will be regarded as being financially deserving of an order pursuant to CPR, r 52.19.[190]

Unsurprisingly, the rules provide that if the appeal raises an issue of principle or practice upon which substantial sums may turn, it may not be appropriate to make an order.[191] **13.106**

Procedure

The following miscellaneous points may be made. **13.107**

- **Form** Whilst not mandatory, Jackson LJ has explained that if the appellant seeks an order under CPR, r 52.19, it may be convenient and economic to include such an application in the appellant's notice.[192]
- **Timing** An application for such an order must be made as soon as practicable.[193] Jackson LJ has explained that if a party wishes to make an application, that party

[185] See CPR, r 52.9A.
[186] *JE (Jamaica) v Secretary of State for the Home Department* [2014] EWCA Civ 192, at [8].
[187] *Tidal Energy Ltd v Bank of Scotland Plc* [2014] EWCA Civ 847, at [1].
[188] *JE (Jamaica) v Secretary of State for the Home Department* [2014] EWCA Civ 192, at [8].
[189] CPR, r 52.19(2).
[190] *Glass v Freyssinet Ltd* [2016] EWCA Civ 1120, at [14], *per* Floyd LJ.
[191] CPR, r 52.19(3).
[192] *JE (Jamaica) v Secretary of State for the Home Department* [2014] EWCA Civ 192, at [12].
[193] See CPR, r 52.19(4).

must give prompt consideration to the matter—which, he said, 'does not mean immediately, [but] it envisages that both parties will require a reasonable time in which to consider their position'.[194] He went on to say that whilst he could see force in the submission that an application ought to be made no later than two weeks after permission has been granted, it was not the function of the court to rewrite the rules and each case must be decided on its own facts. On the facts of the case before him—in which the application was made on the eve of the appeal—he found that the request had been made 'far too late'.[195]

- **Disposal** Applications under CPR, r 52.19, are normally dealt with on the papers, but the court may order otherwise.[196]

Costs restriction in appeals (Aarhus Convention claims)

13.108 Different provisions apply in Aarhus Convention claims. CPR, r 52.19A, reads as follows:

> '(1) In this rule, "Aarhus Convention claim" and "prohibitively expensive" have the same meanings as in Section VII of Part 45, and "claimant" means a claimant to whom rules 45.43 to 45.45 apply.
>
> (2) In an appeal against a decision made in an Aarhus Convention claim to which rules 45.43 to 45.45 apply, the court must—
> (a) consider whether the costs of the proceedings will be prohibitively expensive for a party who was a claimant; and
> (b) if they will be, make an order limiting the recoverable costs to the extent necessary to prevent this.
>
> (3) When the court considers the financial resources of a party for the purposes of this rule, it must have regard to any financial support which any person has provided or is likely to provide to that party.'

---

194 *JE (Jamaica) v Secretary of State for the Home Department* [2014] EWCA Civ 192, at [11].

195 *Ibid*, at [14].

196 See CPR, r 52.19(4); *JE (Jamaica) v Secretary of State for the Home Department* [2014] EWCA Civ 192, at [4] and [13], *per* Jackson LJ.

14

PAYMENTS ON ACCOUNT OF COSTS

This chapter deals with the following topics: 14.01

- jurisdiction (14.03);
- judicial roles (14.06);
- discretion as to whether to make an award (14.09);
- miscellaneous procedural points (14.15); and
- discretion as to the amount (14.21).

It should be noted that a payment on account of costs is not the same as a payment made in compliance with interim costs certificate (see 43.376). An order for a payment on account of costs is made in the litigation itself under Civil Procedure Rules (CPR), Part 44, whereas an interim costs certificate is issued in assessment proceedings under CPR, Part 47. The terms are often used inconsistently in the authorities, as is the term 'interim payment'; in this chapter, the phrase 'payment on account of costs' is used to mean a payment made pursuant to CPR, r 44.2(8), and the term 'interim costs certificate' is used to mean a certificate awarded pursuant to CPR, r 47.15. 14.02

Jurisdiction

The power[1] to make an order for a payment on account of costs is governed by CPR, r 44.2(8), which reads: 'Where the court orders a party to pay costs subject to detailed assessment, it will order that party to pay a reasonable sum on account of costs, unless there is good reason not to do so.' This differs from the test as it was before 1 April 2013, which was that the court '*may* order' (emphasis added) an amount to be paid on account before the costs are assessed.[2] In view of this, authorities decided before this date ought to be treated with caution (see 14.21–14.24). 14.03

Prerequisites

A payment on account may be made only if an order for costs has been made in favour of the party who would receive that payment.[3] A written statement of costs is not a prerequisite to making an order under this rule.[4] 14.04

[1] Section 32(5) of the Senior Courts Act 1981 (which prevents the court from making certain interim payments) is disapplied for the purposes of costs proceedings by s 32(4) of that Act.

[2] See CPR, r 44.3(8), as it was pre-1 April 2013.

[3] There is no express judicial authority on this point, but it is implied by the wording of CPR, r 44.3(8). There have been instances of parties who have not been awarded costs requesting payments on account for 'cash flow purposes'; in the editor's view, the court now has power to accede to such a request.

[4] *Astonleigh Residential Care Home Ltd v Goldfarb* [2014] EWHC 4100 (Ch), *per* Asplin J.

Costs-only proceedings

14.05 It has been suggested that the court lacks jurisdiction to make an order that a payment on account be made in costs-only proceedings.[5] There is no binding authority on this point, however.

Judicial Roles

Trial judges

14.06 The trial judge will generally be in the best position to deal with the issue of payments on account. Morland J has indicated that (in group litigation, at least) applications should be made to the trial judge, where possible (see 65.111).[6]

Judges other than trial judges

14.07 A judge who has made an award of costs following trial will generally be willing to make an order for a payment on account (especially under the post-1 April 2013 regime), but the same may not be true of a judge who has had a lesser involvement in the case. Whilst he was dealing with the pre-1 April 2013 provisions, Laddie J had this to say on the topic:

> 'It seems to me that whatever the normal rule should be where there has been a full trial, different considerations may apply where there has not been a full trial. As is apparent in this case, there is a world of difference between a judge's ability to make a fair and rational assessment of costs for payment under the provisions of [CPR, r 44.2(8)] when he has heard the whole trial, or the whole inquiry as to damages, compared with his ability to do that when he has heard virtually nothing.'[7]

Costs judges

14.08 Laddie J has noted the powers of a costs judge to issue an interim costs certificate (see 43.376–43.383) and commented on the fact that a costs judge may have an advantage over other judges because the costs judge would have more material upon which to base an interim assessment.[8] This may be so in some respects (namely, the fact that a costs judge would generally have the benefit of a bill of costs, points of dispute and replies), but it should be borne in mind that a costs judge would rarely be able to read the papers in detail for the purposes of an application for an interim costs certificate. Perhaps this is why Gloster J—in a case in which she had heard extensive evidence concerning allegations of fraud—said that it would be 'unreal' to expect a costs judge to be in a better position to take a view on the quantum of a payment on account.[9] Whilst no more than the editor's own opinion, a costs judge would be in a better position to deal with issues relating to quantum only where there were technical issues relating to costs and in other such circumstances in which the court would be assisted by having sight of a bill of costs, points of dispute, etc. Even where such circumstances existed, it would

---

[5] See, eg, *Banchio v Lai* [2003] EWHC 9038 (Costs).
[6] *Giambrone v JMC Holidays Ltd (formerly Sunworld Holidays Ltd)* [2002] EWHC 2932 (QB), at [11]–[12].
[7] *Dyson Appliances Ltd v Hoover Ltd* [2003] EWHC 624 (Ch), at [15].
[8] *Ibid.*
[9] *Petromec Inc v Petroleo Brasileiro* [2006] EWHC 3518 (Comm).

rarely be the case under the post-1 April 2013 test that no payment on account of costs be made at all.

Discretion as to Whether to Make an Award

Discretion and payments on account

Presumptions

It used to be said that the notion that the receiving party should not be kept out of their money should not be afforded the status of being a presumption.[10] The new wording of CPR, r 44.2(8), appears to have changed this.[11] Thus a payment on account will be made unless there is 'good reason' to do otherwise (see 14.03). **14.09**

Factors to be taken into account

The court must take into account all of the relevant circumstances. Christopher Clarke LJ (sitting in the Commercial Court) had this to say: **14.10**

> 'In determining whether to order any payment and its amount, account needs to be taken of all relevant factors including the likelihood (if it can be assessed) of the claimants being awarded the costs that they seek or a lesser and if so what proportion of them; the difficulty, if any, that may be faced in recovering those costs; the likelihood of a successful appeal; the means of the parties; the imminence of any assessment; any relevant delay and whether the paying party will have any difficulty in recovery in the case of any overpayment.'[12]

In a similar vein, Jacob J has commented that relevant factors might include the fact that a party wishes to appeal, the conduct of the parties, their financial positions, etc.[13] The fact that the entitlement has been diminished by set-off may be relevant (see 14.12).[14] **14.11**

The relevance of set-off If there is a real prospect of a party's entitlement to costs being negated or diminished at some point in the future by reason of set-off, then this may be a factor that militates against an order being made for a payment on account.[15] **14.12**

Payments by instalment If a paying party would have difficulty in making payments, it is open to the court to order that payments be made in instalments.[16] **14.13**

The relevance of financial resources and insolvency Factors relevant to the exercise of discretion may also include the financial resources of the parties.[17] The resources of the paying party may be relevant: in a case in which there was a possibility that the paying party would not be able to satisfy its liability for costs, Laddie J regarded as relevant the fact that an order for a payment on account of costs may encourage settlement and may **14.14**

---

[10] *Blakemore v Cummings* [2009] EWCA Civ 1276.
[11] See CPR, r 44.2(8).
[12] *Excalibur Ventures LLC v Texas Keystone Inc & Ors* [2015] EWHC 566 (Comm), at [24].
[13] *Mars UK Ltd v Teknowledge Ltd (No 2)* [1999] 2 Costs LR 44, at 46.
[14] See *Commission for Equality & Human Rights v Griffin* [2011] EWHC 675 (Admin), at [16], *per* Moore-Bick LJ.
[15] See *Rawlinson & Hunter Trustees SA v ITG Ltd & Ors* [2015] EWHC 1924 (Ch), at [25], *per* Morgan J.
[16] *Nova Productions Ltd v Mazooma Games Ltd* [2006] EWHC 189 (Ch).
[17] See *German Property 50 Sarl v Summers-Inman Construction & Property Consultants LLP* [2009] EWHC 2968 (TCC), at [11], *per* Coulson J.

relieve the parties of the financial burden of having to prepare for a detailed assessment.[18] Morgan J, on the other hand, declined to make an order for a payment on account of the defendants' costs of an application because there was concern as to the defendants' solvency and there was a possibility that the claimant may obtain future costs orders in its favour.[19]

Miscellaneous Procedural Points

Stays of payments on account

14.15 Where circumstances merit such a step, there is no reason why an order for a payment on account of costs cannot be stayed.[20] Stays may be conditional. In this regard, Warren J has confirmed that it is not a contradiction in terms to grant a stay pending the outcome of some event.[21]

14.16 After having made reference to what is now CPR, r 52.16,[22] Leggatt J refused to grant a stay of a payment on account pending an appeal on the basis that 'solid grounds are required to justify a stay pending an appeal such as that, absent a stay, the appeal would be stifled'.[23] This, perhaps, was a reference to a similar test that is often applied in cases relating to non-costs appeals.[24] It is not wholly clear whether such a stringent test would always apply. In this regard, it is worth noting that Longmore LJ has explained (albeit in a non-costs case) that whilst the general rule is that a stay of judgment will not be granted, (a) the court has an unfettered discretion, (b) no authority can lay down rules for its exercise, (c) the proper approach is to make the order that best accords with the interests of justice, (d) the court has to balance the alternatives to decide which is less likely to cause injustice and (e) where the justice of letting the general rule take effect is in doubt, the answer may well depend on the perceived strength of the appeal.[25] It may be relevant that one option would be to order that the monies be paid into court pending the appeal.[26] The fact that the party ordered to make a payment on account made that payment before making an application for a stay would be a factor that would militate against ordering that there should be a stay.[27]

14.17 It may be that a paying party has insurance that will cover part of the payment on account; where this is so, then where appropriate, it is open to the court to order that payment of the amount not covered by the insurance is to be stayed.[28]

---

[18] *Allason v Random House UK Ltd* [2002] EWHC 1030 (Ch), at [12]. See also *Mitchell v The Royal Bank of Scotland plc* [2017] EWHC 1771 (Ch), at [50], *per* Judge Davis-White QC (sitting as a judge of the Chancery Division).

[19] *Rawlinson & Hunter Trustees SA v ITG Ltd* [2015] EWHC 1924 (Ch).

[20] See, eg, *Renewable Power & Light plc v Renewable Power & Light Services Inc* [2008] EWHC 3584 (QB).

[21] *Amin v Amin* [2011] EWHC 641 (Ch), at [18].

[22] A rule that says that, subject to certain exceptions, an appeal shall not operate as a stay of any order or decision of the lower court.

[23] See *Kazakhstan Kagazy PLC v Zhunus* [2015] EWHC 404 (Comm), at [9].

[24] See, eg, *Department for Environment, Food and Rural Affairs v Downs* [2009] EWCA Civ 257.

[25] See *Leicester Circuits Ltd v Coates Brothers plc (application to lift stay)* [2002] EWCA Civ 474, at [12] and [13].

[26] See, eg, *Orb ARL v Ruhan* [2015] EWCA Civ 1180, at [15], *per* Floyd LJ.

[27] See, eg, *ibid*, at [28]–[30], per Floyd LJ.

[28] See, eg, *Streetmap.EU Ltd v Google Inc* (unreported), 24 May 2016, Ch D, *per* Roth J.

If a party seeks to rely on impecuniosity as being a reason to ask for a stay, that party can be expected to provide solid evidence in support of that contention.[29] **14.18**

Where there has been a failure to make a payment on account

Langley J has confirmed that if a paying party fails to meet its obligations under an order for payments on account of costs, the court is able to exercise its inherent jurisdiction, as preserved by CPR, r 3.1(1), to debar a paying party from taking any further part in the detailed assessment pending compliance with the order.[30] Langley J went on to say that such an order could also be justified as being the exercise of the general power of the court to debar a party in contempt.[31] Similarly, if a party who wishes to appeal has failed to abide by an order to make a payment on account, conditions may be imposed.[32] **14.19**

'Unless orders' may be made in respect of orders that a payment on account be made. Whilst there is no authority directly on the point, it is likely that the general principles relating to unless orders apply (see 43.100) and that, in particular, no such order should require a payment so large that there is no prospect of it being paid.[33] The fact that there are doubts about the honesty and *bona fides* of the paying party will generally not, of itself, be sufficient justification for making an unless order.[34] **14.20**

Discretion as to the Amount

Amount of payments on account: general principles

Non-budgeted costs

Background history As to the amount of the payment on account of costs prior to the introduction of budgeting, there used to be two schools of thought—although, for the reasons set out below, it is now known that the second prevails. **14.21**

- **'Irreducible minimum'** Many—indeed, in the past, most—judges allowed the bare minimum amount to which the receiving party was likely to be entitled. Jacob J, for example, allowed the monies that the receiving party would 'almost certainly collect',[35] Laddie J allowed 'the absolute bare minimum'[36] and Arnold J allowed the 'irreducible minimum'.[37] These cases pre-date April 2013 (see 14.03); other judges have applied a

[29] See, eg, *Oraki v Bramston* [2016] EWCA Civ 1195, at [20], *per* Gloster LJ.

[30] *Days Healthcare UK Ltd v Pihsiang Machinery Manufacturing Co Ltd* [2006] EWHC 1444 (QB), at [18]–[20], [23] and [25]–[27]. See also *Hammond Suddard Solicitors v Agrichem International Holdings Ltd* [2001] EWCA Civ 2065, at [48], *per* Clarke LJ.

[31] *Days Healthcare UK Ltd v Pihsiang Machinery Manufacturing Co Ltd* [2006] EWHC 1444 (QB), at [23].

[32] See, eg, *Independent Power Tanzania Ltd v Standard Chartered Bank (Hong Kong) Ltd* [2016] EWCA Civ 522, at [60], *per* Lloyd Jones LJ.

[33] See, by way of analogy, *Anglo-Eastern Trust Ltd & Anor v Kermanshahchi* [2002] EWCA Civ 198, at [22], *per* Park J.

[34] See, by way of analogy, *Lexi Holdings plc v Luqman* [2007] EWHC 2410 (Ch), at [44], *per* Briggs J.

[35] *Mars UK Ltd v Teknowledge Ltd (No 2)* [1999] 2 Costs LR 44, at 46; see also *Shovelar v Lane* [2011] EWCA Civ 802, at [58].

[36] *Allason v Random House UK Ltd* [2002] EWHC 1030 (Ch), at [14].

[37] See *Starbucks Ltd v British Sky Broadcasting Group plc* [2012] EWHC 4085 (Ch), at [4]. The transcript says 'reducible minimum', but that is clearly a typographical error. See also *Beach v Smirnov* [2007] EWHC 3499, at [13].

similar test since that date,[38] but at least one of them seems not to have had all of the relevant law brought to his attention.[39] Whilst nothing more than a very general observation, awards based on this 'irreducible minimum' test were typically between 35 per cent and 60 per cent of the amount claimed.

- **'Reasonable sum'** Followers of the second school of thought allowed a reasonable sum, this generally (at least as a starting point) being an approximation of the most likely amount that the receiving party would receive. Vos J, for example, expressed a preference for using an estimate of the amount most likely to be allowed,[40] whilst Eder J seems to have accepted that The White Book was right to refer to this measure.[41] The approach taken by Vos J was followed by Warren J,[42] whose approach was in turn accepted in principle by Silber J,[43] by Judge Keyser QC (sitting as a judge of the High Court)[44] and by others.[45] The 'reasonable sum' method typically resulted in higher interim payments than did the 'irreducible minimum' approach: allowances of 70 per cent and even 85 per cent of the monies claimed were not unknown.[46] That said, Floyd LJ has said that payments on account should be 'cautious'.[47]

14.22 **The modern approach** Whilst, at the time, he was sitting in the Commercial Court rather than the Court of Appeal, Christopher Clarke LJ has carried out an analysis of the authorities and concluded that the 'reasonable sum' test is the correct test given the changes to the relevant rule in April 2013. He had this to say on the point:

> 'It is clear that the question, at any rate now, is what is a "reasonable sum on account of costs"? It may be that in any given case the only amount that it is reasonable to award is the irreducible minimum. I do not, however, accept that that means that "irreducible minimum" is the test. That would be to introduce a criterion (a) for which the rules do not provide: (b) which is not the same as the criterion for which they do provide; and (c) which has potential drawbacks of its own, not least because it begs the question whether it means

[38] See, eg, *Rovi Solutions Corpn v Virgin Media Ltd* [2014] EWHC 2449, in which Mann J applied the test in *Mars UK Ltd v Teknowledge Ltd (No 2)* [1999] 2 Costs LR 44. In *Hospira UK Ltd v Genentech Inc* [2014] EWHC 1688, Birss J also held that the test in *Mars UK* should apply, but in the subsequent case of *Teva UK v Leo Pharma* [2014] EWHC 3522, he made reference to 'a fair irreducible minimum', yet went on to allow a figure that was 'not too much below' the likely level of a detailed assessment. It should be noted that Christopher Clarke LJ has said that he did not agree with Birss J's analysis in *Hospira*: see *Excalibur Ventures LLC v Texas Keystone Inc & Ors* [2015] EWHC 566 (Comm), at [22].

[39] In *VTB Bank v Skurikhin* [2014] EWHC 3522, Simon J referred to *Mars UK Ltd v Teknowledge Ltd (No 2)* [1999] 2 Costs LR 44 and to the change in the rules (although his citation of the new rule was that it provided for a payment to be made on account of costs unless there was good reason not to do so, ie he did not refer to the words 'a reasonable sum') and awarded an amount that he thought reflected an irreducible amount of what would be recovered. *United Airlines Inc v United Airways Ltd* (2011) EWHC 2411 (Ch) does not appear to have been cited.

[40] See *United Airlines Inc v United Airways Ltd* [2011] EWHC 2411 (Ch) (in the post-hearing discussion not recorded in any report, but recorded in the official transcript).

[41] *Otkritie International Investment Management Ltd v Urumov* [2014] EWHC 755 (Comm), at [20].

[42] *Gollop v Pryke* (unreported), 19 November 2011, Ch D.

[43] *Mehjoo v Harben Barker (a firm) & Anor* [2013] EWHC 1669 (QB), at [88], but not what was said at [89] and [90], where the judge departed from the 'most likely' test because of a paucity of information in support of the costs.

[44] *Kellie & Anor v Wheatley & Lloyd Architects Ltd* [2014] EWHC 2886 (TCC).

[45] See, eg, *Football Association Premier League Ltd v Berry* [2014] EWHC 726.

[46] See *Gollop v Pryke* (unreported), 19 November 2011, Ch D; *Otkritie International Investment Management Ltd v Urumov* [2014] EWHC 755 (Comm). It should be noted that, in *Otkritie*, Eder J then went on to further reduce the 85 per cent allowance, but that reduction is not relevant to the matter in hand.

[47] *Actavis UK Ltd v Eli Lilly & Co* [2015] EWCA Civ 666, at [10].

those costs which could not realistically be challenged as to item or amount or some more generous test. On one approach it admits of every objection to costs, which cannot be treated as fanciful.'[48]

Thus the test is one of what is a 'reasonable sum on account of costs', but this may mean, in an appropriate case, that only an 'irreducible minimum' will be allowed (although that would not be the test itself). Christopher Clarke LJ went on to say this: **14.23**

'What is a reasonable amount will depend on the circumstances, the chief of which is that there will, by definition, have been no detailed assessment and thus an element of uncertainty, the extent of which may differ widely from case to case as to what will be allowed on detailed assessment. Any sum will have to be an estimate. A reasonable sum would often be one that was an estimate of the likely level of recovery subject, as the costs claimants accept, to an appropriate margin to allow for error in the estimation. This can be done by taking the lowest figure in a likely range or making a deduction from a single estimated figure or perhaps from the lowest figure in the range if the range itself is not very broad.'[49]

It would seem, therefore, that a reasonable sum would often be Vos J's 'most likely' amount (see 14.21), but this may be tempered by the fact that there will inevitably be an error in the estimation. The amount that Christopher Clarke LJ allowed in the particular application before him was based on a recovery of 80 per cent (although the claim was exceptional in many ways and the costs were payable on the indemnity basis). In the editor's experience, awards in respect of non-budgeted costs generally tend to be lower than this (although, of course, each case will turn on its own facts). **14.24**

Other approaches Other judicial methods are occasionally encountered, usually in specialist courts. In view of what Christopher Clarke LJ has said, it would be wrong for the court to apply any test other than the 'reasonable amount' test, but (whilst there is no authority on the point) this would not prevent the court from taking into account factors specific to the court or case in question. Norris J, for example (hearing a patents matter that pre-dated April 2013), said that the court may seek to allow a figure that would discourage the prosecution of an assessment.[50] This approach has so far failed to gain any traction, but given the fact that, in many cases, costs will have been budgeted (see 14.27–14.28), it may be that this will change. It should be borne in mind, however, that an overly generous payment on account would be just as likely to lead to a detailed assessment as an overly frugal one. **14.25**

There are examples of the court ordering a relatively generous payment on account of costs (effectively, a summary assessment), which could be followed by a detailed assessment if the receiving party were to believe that more was payable.[51] Those examples are, however, limited to the early days of the CPR and it is not an approach that has found general favour. **14.26**

Budgeted costs

It is only to be expected that, in a case that has been subject to costs managements, the court will regard the receiving party's budget as a factor to take into account. Indeed, it may be a very important factor—but only in so far as the budgeted costs are concerned; non-budgeted costs in a budgeted case will be dealt with according to the principles set out at **14.27**

48 *Excalibur Ventures LLC v Texas Keystone Inc & Ors* [2015] EWHC 566 (Comm), at [22].
49 *Ibid*, at [23].
50 *Les Laboratoires Servier v Apotex Inc* [2008] EWHC 2563 (Pat), at [7].
51 *Mabey & Johnson Ltd v Ecclesiastical Insurance Office plc (Costs)* [2000] CLC 1470.

14.22–14.24.[52] Coulson J had the following to say on the topic: 'In my view, the ... [most recent approved or agreed] costs budget is the appropriate starting point for the calculation of any interim payment on account of costs.'[53] If certain case-specific matters are disregarded, Coulson J went on to allow 90 per cent of the figure in the most recent approved or agreed budget because the reduction of 10 per cent was 'the maximum deduction that is appropriate in a case where there is an approved costs budget'.[54]

14.28 Other judges have taken different approaches. Judge Pelling QC (sitting as a judge of the High Court) took as his starting point an allowance of 70 per cent of the budgeted costs.[55] In a case in which the receiving party claimed significantly more that the budgeted costs, Morgan J allowed 50 per cent of the amount claimed.[56] That may be so, but, at the time of writing, it seemed as if Coulson J's method was in the process of becoming the preferred approach.[57]

Amount of payments on account: specific circumstances and factors

Proportionality

14.29 Where the costs claimed are disproportionate, this will not be a factor that will prevent the court from ordering a payment on account. As to the amount, Leggatt J had this to say: 'If costs claimed by a party are disproportionate, there is no reason why that should affect (either upwards or downwards) the sum which it is reasonable to order the other party to pay on account.'[58] It would seem that what Leggatt J meant by this was that (where the costs fall to be assessed on the standard basis) the court will allow a proportionate and reasonable amount and no more, and that this will be so regardless of what is claimed. Other judges have expressly taken proportionality into account: Garnham J, for example, gave considerable weight to possible arguments regarding proportionality when determining the appropriate amount.[59]

Contracts of retainer

14.30 Where the receiving party's recovery of costs is at risk by reason of a credible challenge as to the enforceability of the retainer, then the amount ordered should be moderated accordingly.[60] Likewise, the court may take into account the fact that there

---

[52] See *Cleveland Bridge UK Ltd v Sarens (UK) Ltd* [2018] EWHC 827 (TCC), at [9]–[31], *per* Miss Joanna Smith QC (sitting as a deputy judge of the High Court).

[53] *McInnes v Gross* [2017] EWHC 127 (QB), at [25]. This approach was approved of by Davis LJ in *Harrison v University Hospitals Coventry & Warwickshire NHS Trust* [2017] EWCA Civ 792, at [40].

[54] *McInnes v Gross* [2017] EWHC 127 (QB), at [28].

[55] See *Capital for Enterprise Fund A LP v Bibby Financial Services Ltd* (unreported), 18 November 2015, QBD (Manchester District Registry).

[56] *Teva UK Ltd v Boehringer Ingelheim Pharma GmbH & Co KG* [2015] EWHC 3771 (Pat).

[57] See, eg, *Cleveland Bridge UK Ltd v Sarens (UK) Ltd* [2018] EWHC 827 (TCC), at [20], *per* Miss Joanna Smith QC (sitting as a deputy judge of the High Court).

[58] See *Kazakhstan Kagazy PLC v Zhunus* [2015] EWHC 404 (Comm), at [10].

[59] See *Rallison v North West London Hospitals NHS Trust* [2015] EWCA 3255 (QB).

[60] See, eg, *Board of Trustees of National Museums & Galleries on Merseyside v AEW Architects & Designers Ltd* [2013] EWHC 3025 (TCC), at [48] and [49], where Akenhead J said that whilst he believed the conditional fee agreement to be likely to be 'broadly enforceable', it was appropriate to order that a payment on account is made on the assumption that the receiving party would succeed on this issue. See also *Munkenbeck & Marshall v Harold* [2005] EWHC 356 (TCC), at [31], *per* Richard Harvey QC (sitting as a deputy judge of the High Court).

is doubt as to what the contractual terms of the retainer are and what effect they will have.[61]

Additional liabilities

Whilst he did not deal with the issue in any detail, when formulating the amount of a payment on account Aikens LJ appears to have taken into consideration the fact that a very substantial success fee was sought.[62] **14.31**

Paucity of information

Whilst it would not ordinarily be the case that the court would expect evidence in support of the costs that are claimed, where costs are unusually high, a prudent receiving party may elect to adduce evidence (such as a witness statement from the conducting fee earner, or even a report from an independent costs lawyer or costs draftsperson[63]). In a case in which he found that such evidence would have been helpful, but was noticeably absent, Judge Keyser QC (sitting as a judge of the High Court) declined to be as generous as to apply the 'most likely' test.[64] This pre-dated the guidance given by Christopher Clarke LJ (see 14.22), but is still indicative of the fact that the court is able to take such matters into account. **14.32**

The absence of information will rarely cause the court to decline to make an award in its entirety. In a case in which the court had only a crude estimate of the relieving party's costs, for example, Nichol J found that he was 'confident that [the] recoverable costs will be very substantial' and allowed a third of that which had been estimated (see also 14.04).[65] **14.33**

Solvency of receiving party

Whilst it is rarely more than a factor that merits a brief mention, the fact that a paying party would not have difficulty in recovering any overpayment may be something that the court will take into account,[66] this being a finding that the court is particularly likely to make if the receiving party has the benefit of a funder or insurer. **14.34**

The court's own observations

The court is permitted to take into account what it has seen of the way in which the proceedings were conducted. In a case that culminated in a six-week trial with both leading and junior counsel, for example, Nichol J found that the costs would be 'very substantial' and made an award of £250,000.[67] **14.35**

Comparators

The amount of costs that would have been claimed by the paying party had it been awarded costs is not an appropriate measure,[68] but it may be a factor to be taken into **14.36**

---

[61] See, eg, *Beattie v Smailes* [2011] EWHC 3865 (Ch), in which Norris J took into account the fact that there was doubt as to what effect a conditional fee agreement would have in relation to costs incurred before it was made.

[62] See *Crema v Cenkos Securities plc* [2011] EWCA Civ 10, at [12]–[14]. See also *John v Central Manchester & Manchester Children's Hospitals NHS Foundation Trust* [2016] EWHC 819 (QB), *per* Picken J.

[63] As an example of the court taking a costs draftsperson's report into account, see *Excalibur Ventures LLC v Texas Keystone Inc & Ors* [2015] EWHC 566 (Comm), at [26].

[64] *Mehjoo v Harben Barker (a firm) & Anor* [2013] EWHC 1669 (QB), at [89] and [90].

[65] *Webster v Ridgeway School* [2010] EWHC 318, at [17].

[66] As an example of the court taking a costs draftsperson's report into account, see *Excalibur Ventures LLC v Texas Keystone Inc & Ors* [2015] EWHC 566 (Comm), at [28].

[67] *Webster v Ridgeway School* [2010] EWHC 318, at [17].

[68] *Shovelar v Lane* [2011] EWCA Civ 802, at [59].

account,[69] and the fact that there is an unexplained disparity between the receiving party's costs and those of its opponents may be a relevant factor.[70] Where the cost are *prima facie* higher than one would expect, the fact that no explanation has been offered may be relevant—especially where details about the costs would have been readily to hand.[71]

Where there are multiple receiving parties

14.37 If there are several receiving parties, Morgan J has said that it may be appropriate to bear in mind the fact that there may have been duplication of costs[72]—a fact that may justify a lower payment on account than might otherwise have been the case.

69 See, eg, *Excalibur Ventures LLC v Texas Keystone Inc & Ors* [2015] EWHC 566 (Comm), at [27], *per* Christopher Clarke LJ.

70 See, eg, *Mehjoo v Harben Barker (a firm)* [2013] EWHC 1669 (QB), at [85], *per* Silber J.

71 See *ibid*, at [86] and [87], *per* Silber J.

72 See *Ong v Ping* [2015] EWHC 3766 (Ch).

15

SECURITY FOR COSTS

Security for costs is a discretionary interim remedy by which a litigant (usually a claimant) may be ordered to provide security as a condition for continuing to pursue its case. This chapter deals with the following topics: **15.01**

- jurisdiction and the range of remedies available (15.02):
  - the range of remedies available (15.03);
  - international jurisdiction (15.04);
  - primary jurisdiction (that is, under CPR, Part 25, Section II) (15.06);
  - secondary jurisdictions (that is, under CPR, Parts 3, 24 and 52) (15.15);
  - cases that are not suitable for security for costs (15.22);
  - detailed assessments (15.23);
- principles and the exercise of discretion (15.24):
  - the conditions and factors relating to the primary jurisdiction (15.26);
  - the exercise of discretion under the primary jurisdiction (15.57);
  - the exercise of discretion under the secondary jurisdictions (15.97);
- reapplication and variation (15.102);
- unless orders (15.107);
- quantum and the form of security (15.110):
  - the amount for which security is to be given (15.111);
  - the forms in which security is to be given (15.121);
- procedure (15.124); and
- evidence and disclosure (15.127).

Jurisdictions and the Range of Remedies Available

The court's powers regarding security for costs are to be found, first, in CPR, Part 25, Section II, and, secondly, in CPR, Parts 3, 24 and 52, these being referred to in this chapter as 'the primary jurisdiction' and 'the secondary jurisdictions' respectively. There is a degree of overlap between the primary jurisdiction and the secondary jurisdictions.[1] The power to order that there be security for costs originally derived from the court's inherent jurisdiction,[2] but that power is residual and is now of only academic interest.[3] **15.02**

---

[1] In *Lazaris v London & Newcastle (Camden) Ltd* [2013] EWHC 97 (TCC), at [26]–[36], for example, Akenhead J found that, in the case before him, one jurisdiction informed the other.

[2] See, eg, *GFN SA v Bancredit Cayman Ltd (in liquidation)* [2009] UKPC 39.

[3] The exercise of that jurisdiction is circumscribed by the CPR such that the court has to limit itself to exercising jurisdiction in cases that fall within the scope of the CPR: see *Wu v Hellard* (unreported),

Range of remedies available

15.03 There are many circumstances in which the court has the power to order a party to give security for costs. Table 15.1 is a summary, in which 'the applicant' means the person who applies for security and 'the respondent' means the person against whom the order is sought. In most instances, the applicant will be the defendant and the respondent will be the claimant, but this is far from always the case. A section on 'alternatives to security for costs' has been included to draw attention to the fact there are other ways in which an applicant may deal with perceived enforcement difficulties.[4]

International conventions and human rights

15.04 Provided that persons resident in other contracting states are not unlawfully burdened with orders that could not be made against persons within this jurisdiction and provided that discretion is exercised on objectively justifiable grounds, then the jurisdiction to make orders for security for costs is compatible with the European Convention on Human Rights (ECHR).[5]

15.05 There are some specialist types of claim (mostly involving travel) in which the jurisdiction is excluded by international convention—exclusions well known to those who practise in these areas of the law and hence not set out here.[6] There are also specific rules relating to arbitrations.[7]

Primary jurisdiction regarding security for costs

15.06 The primary jurisdiction (that is, the jurisdiction under CPR, Part 25, Section II) is a creation of delegated legislation (that is, the CPR). In particular, CPR, r 25.12(1),[8] provides as follows:

> '(1) A defendant to any claim may apply under this Section of this Part for security for his costs of the proceedings.

---

25 November 2013, Ch D, *per* Judge Dight. One of the last occasions on which the inherent jurisdiction was mentioned was in *CT Bowring & Co (Insurance) Ltd v Corsi & Partners Ltd* [1995] 1 BCLC 148, CA, in which Dillon LJ commented that it would be difficult to envisage the court creating a new category of case in which a party could be required to give security without leaving that to the Rule Committee or Parliament. See also *GFN SA v Bancredit Cayman Ltd (in liquidation)* [2009] UKPC 39.

4 See, as an example, *Eaton v Caulfield* [2013] EWHC 2214 (Ch), in which, in unfair prejudice proceedings, the court contemplated the making of an order that a party would not be entitled to receive any interim costs.

5 *Nasser v United Bank of Kuwait* [2001] EWCA Civ 556, at [56]–[61], *per* Mance LJ; see also *Al-Koronky & Anor v Time Life Entertainments Group Ltd* [2005] EWHC 1688 (QB), at [21]–[28], *per* Eady J.

6 Whilst not yet in force in the UK, the following conventions have been ratified and do exclude an order for security for costs: Carriage of Goods by Rail (Berne) 1952, see Art 55; Carriage of Goods by Road (Geneva) 1956, Art 31; Third Party Liability in the Field of Nuclear Energy (Paris) 1960, Art 14 (as amended); Carriage of Passengers by Rail (Berne) 1961, Art 56; and Carriage of Passengers by Road Convention 1973, Art 41.

7 There are specific rules for security for costs applications in arbitrations in which (for example) the CIA International Arbitration Practice Guideline for Applications for Security for Costs apply. Although the English common-law cases are usually treated as providing at the least significant guidance, there are certain differences of approach, eg reasonable grounds for concluding that there is a 'serious risk' that the defendant/respondent may not be able to enforce a costs award in its favour because the claimant will not have the funds to pay the costs awarded (cf 'reason to believe will be unable to pay defendant's costs' in CPR 25(2)(c)).

8 In the Supreme Court, the relevant rule is that the making of an order for security for costs is at the discretion of the court: see Supreme Court Rules 2009 (SI 2009/1603), r 36(1). The old default rule in the House of Lords was that the appellant was required to make a payment as security for costs; that rule no longer applies because it was thought that it would be an obstacle to justice: see *Anderson v Shetland Island Council* [2012] UKSC 7, at [10]. Indeed, the position now is that orders for security will be made only sparingly: see Supreme Court Practice Direction 4.7.1.

Table 15.1 Security for costs and the powers available to the court

Reason for making order	Status of persons against whom an order may be made	Types of legal entity against whom an order may be made	Details of the power available to the court and of the orders that may be made	Notes and the source of the power to make the order
Primary jurisdiction The court will make an order under the primary jurisdiction only if it is satisfied, having regard to all of the circumstances of the case, that it is just to make such an order[9]				
Where there is a concern about enforcing an order against a foreign company[10]	Claimants or appellants (including Part 20 claimants[11] and respondents who appeal[12])	There are no restrictions.	An order may be made where the respondent is (a) resident out of the jurisdiction, but (b) not resident in a contracting state (see **15.30**). Whilst more generous orders may be made, the order will typically be for security for the additional costs of enforcement[13] (and possibly execution[14]) that arise by reason of the party's place of residence (see **15.114**).	CPR, r 25.13(2)(a)
Where there is concern that a party may be unable to pay costs if ordered to do so	Claimants or appellants (including Part 20 claimants and respondents who appeal)	The respondent must be a 'company or other body (whether incorporated inside or outside Great Britain)'.[15] This includes unlimited companies.[16]	An order may be made where there is reason to believe that the respondent, being a company or other body, will be unable to pay the applicant's costs if ordered to do so (see **15.34**). The order would usually be an order for security for costs of the claim or appeal.	CPR, r 25.13(2)(c)

(continued)

[9] See CPR, r 25.13(1).

[10] A contracting state is a Brussels contracting state, a Lugano contracting state or a regulation state, as defined in s 1(3) of the Civil Jurisdiction and Judgments Act 1982: see CPR, r 25.13(2)(a)(ii). Contracting states are as follows: Austria; Belgium; Denmark; Finland; France; Germany; Greece; Iceland; Ireland; Italy; Luxemburg; Netherlands; Norway; Poland; Portugal; Spain; Sweden; Switzerland; and the United Kingdom. The Isle of Man is not a contracting state: *Greenwich Ltd v National Westminster Bank plc* [1999] 2 Lloyd's Rep 308.

[11] There is a marginal note in the Civil Procedure Rules 1998 (SI 1998/3132) (as originally made in print) that confirms that an application may be made by persons served with Part 20 claims.

[12] See CPR, r 25.15(1)(b).

[13] See *Nasser v United Bank of Kuwait* [2001] EWCA Civ 556, at [61].

[14] In *Dumrul v Standard Chartered Bank* [2010] EWHC 2625 (Comm), at [23], Hamblen J found that security could not be ordered for the costs of execution, but in *Cody v Murray* [2013] EWHC 3448 (Ch), at [10]–[12], David Donaldson QC (sitting as a deputy High Court judge) said that *Dunrul* was wrongly decided on this point and that costs of execution may be included.

[15] CPR, r 25.13(2)(c).

[16] See *Jirehouse Capital v Beller* [2008] EWCA Civ 908, at [17]–[19], *per* Arden LJ.

Table 15.1 Continued

Reason for making order	Status of persons against whom an order may be made	Types of legal entity against whom an order may be made	Details of the power available to the court and of the orders that may be made	Notes and the source of the power to make the order
	Appellants (including respondents who appeal[17])	The party must be a limited company.	An order may be made where there is reason to believe that the respondent will be unable to pay the costs of the other parties to the appeal should its appeal be unsuccessful (see **15.50**). Where this is so, the respondent would generally be ordered to give security for the costs of the appeal.	CPR, r 25.15(2)
	Nominal claimants or appellants (including respondents who appeal)	There are no restrictions.	An order may be made where the respondent is acting as a nominal claimant (other than as a representative claimant under CPR, Part 19) and there is reason to believe that they will be unable to pay the defendant's costs if ordered to do so (see **15.43**). Pre-CPR authority suggests that there would have to be an element of duplicity or window-dressing before a claimant could be labelled nominal (see **15.43**).[18]	CPR, r 25.13(2)(f)
Where there is concern about the address given by a claimant or appellant	Claimants or appellants (including Part 20 claimants and respondents who appeal)	There are no restrictions.	An order may be made against a respondent who has failed to give their address in the claim form or who has given an incorrect address (see **15.42**), or against a claimant who has changed their address with a view to evading the consequences of the litigation (see **15.40**).	CPR, r 25.13(2)(d) and (e)
Where steps have been taken to make it difficult to enforce an award of costs	Claimants or appellants (including Part 20 claimants and respondents who appeal)	There are no restrictions.	An order may be made against a claimant or an appellant who has taken steps in relation to their assets that would make it difficult to enforce an order for costs against them (see **15.46**).	CPR, r 25.13(2)(g)
	Persons other than the claimant	There are no restrictions other than that the person must be a person against whom a costs order can be made.[19]	An order may be made against a person who has assigned the right to the claim to the claimant with a view to avoiding the possibility of a costs order being made against them (see **15.52**).	CPR, r 25.14(2)(a)

[17] See CPR, r 25.15(2).

[18] *Envis v Thakkar* [1997] BPIR 189; see also *Semler v Murphy* [1968] 1 Ch 183, in which an order was made notwithstanding the fact that a narrow test was applied. In days gone by, a test of whether the claimant was 'a mere shadow of another *per*son' was applied (see 1885 Law Times Rep LIII 484/2).

[19] See CPR, r 25.14(2).

Where the claim is being funded	Persons other than the claimant	There are no restrictions other than that the person must be a person against whom a costs order can be made.[20]	An order may be made against a party who has contributed or agreed to contribute to the claimant's funding in return for a share of any money or property that the claimant may recover in the proceedings (see **15.54**).	CPR, r 25.14(2)(b)
Secondary jurisdictions *The secondary jurisdictions may be used where the primary jurisdiction is not available (such as where there is an application for permission to appeal,[21] an application for summary judgment,[22] an application to strike out[23]). The monies paid in shall be security for any sum payable by that party to any other party in the proceedings.[24]*				
Where there has been poor compliance with rules, practice directions or pre-action protocols	Any party to the proceedings	There are no restrictions.	An order to pay monies into court may be made against a party who, without good reason, has failed to comply with a rule, practice direction or a relevant pre-action protocol. The court must have regard to (a) the amount in dispute and (b) the costs that the parties have incurred or which they may incur (see **15.15** and **15.97**).	CPR, r 3.1(5), (6) and (6A)
Where there is a need to control the future conduct of a party	Any party to the proceedings	There are no restrictions.	When the court makes an order, it may (a) make it subject to conditions, including a condition to pay a sum of money into court, and (b) specify the consequence of failure to comply with the order or a condition (see **15.15** and **15.97**). Such an order is parasitic upon some other order being made and, as such, may not be used to make a free-standing order for security for costs (see **15.15**).[25]	CPR, r 3.1(3) and (6A)

(continued)

20 See CPR, r 25.14(2).

21 See *Shlaimoun & Anor v Mining Technologies International Inc* [2012] EWCA Civ 772, at [12]–[16], *per* Neuberger MR. See also *Royal Bank of Scotland v Hicks* [2012] EWCA Civ 1665; *Mulford Holding & Investment Ltd v Greatex Ltd* [2010] EWCA Civ 1178, *per* Lloyd LJ; *Great Future International Ltd & Ors v Sealand Housing Corporation* [2003] EWCA Civ 682; in a family setting, *Golubovich v Golubovich* [2011] EWCA Civ 528.

22 *Jacobs UK Ltd v Skidmore Owings & Merrill LLP* [2008] EWHC 2847 (TCC).

23 *Ashfield & Anor v Union Pensions Trustees Ltd* [2004] All ER (D) 103 (Dec).

24 CPR, r 3.1(6A).

25 *Huscroft v P&O Ferries Ltd* [2010] EWCA Civ 1483, at [18].

Table 15.1 Continued

Reason for making order	Status of persons against whom an order may be made	Types of legal entity against whom an order may be made	Details of the power available to the court and of the orders that may be made	Notes and the source of the power to make the order
Where, in the context of an application for summary judgment, the court has concerns about the merits of a claim or defence	Any party to the proceedings	There are no restrictions.	An order for security may be made where, on an application for summary judgment, it appears to the court that it is possible that a claim or defence may succeed, but improbable that it will do so (see **15.15** and **15.97**).[26]	CPR, r 24.6; PD 24, paras 4 and 5
Where, in the context of an appeal, there are concerns about whether the appellant would pay costs if it were to lose	Appellants only (regardless of whether they were claimants or defendants in the court below)	There are no restrictions.	If there are compelling reasons for it doing so,[27] an appeal court may grant permission to appeal that is conditional on security for costs being given (see **15.15** and **15.97**).[28]	CPR, r 52.9(1) and (2)
Alternatives to security for costs	*The following are included in this table as alternative remedies to security for costs.*			
Where there is a concern about an opponent's ability to pay costs	Any party to the proceedings who, if they are successful overall, is likely to be both entitled to costs and liable to pay costs	There are no restrictions.	An order restricting that party's right to costs may be made (such as where the party will not be entitled to receive any interim costs[29]) so as to leave those monies available for set-off upon conclusion of the claim.	CPR, r 44.2
	Any party to the proceedings	There are no restrictions.	If they agree, the party whose ability to pay is in doubt could agree to pay monies into an escrow account—and this would not necessarily have to be drawn to the court's attention.	Not applicable

26 See *Olatawura v Abiloye* [2002] EWCA Civ 998.
27 See CPR, r 52.9(2).
28 See CPR, r 52.9(1). See also, eg, *Olympic Airlines SA (in liquidation) V ACG Acquisition XX LLC* [2012] EWCA Civ 1659.
29 See, eg, *Eaton v Caulfield* [2013] EWHC 2214 (Ch).

(Part 3 provides for the court to order payment of sums into court in other circumstances. Rule 20.3 provides for this Section of this Part to apply to Part 20 claims.)

(2) An application for security for costs must be supported by written evidence.

(3) Where the court makes an order for security for costs, it will—

(a) determine the amount of security; and

(b) direct—

(i) the manner in which; and

(ii) the time within which the security must be given.'

There used to be a statutory jurisdiction regarding security for costs arising under s 726(1) of the Companies Act 1985, but that section was repealed on 1 October 2009,[30] with no replacement being enacted. This was because the 1985 provisions were believed to be otiose given the existence of the powers under CPR, Part 25, Section II. It should be noted that the wording of that statutory jurisdiction was similar to the primary jurisdiction and that, as such, cases decided under the older jurisdiction may still be instructive. **15.07**

For the primary jurisdiction to arise, the costs over which security is sought must be litigation costs.[31] That said, security may include the costs of complying with any relevant pre-action protocol.[32] In theory, there is no jurisdictional limit that prevents the court from ordering that security be given for costs that have already been incurred (such as where an order is made by an appeal court for the costs in the court below[33]), but, in practice, such an order would be unusual.[34] **15.08**

Claimants and the primary jurisdiction regarding security for costs

The primary jurisdiction is, in general, not available to claimants—unless, of course, they are subject to a counterclaim (see 15.10). It is a moot point whether a claimant in a claim can stand in the place of a defendant by virtue of the fact that an interim application has been made against them. If pre-CPR authority is any guide, then the answer is in the negative, because the jurisdiction will arise only where the applicant is a defendant 'to a claim' and that phrase has been read as meaning proceedings arising out of a cause of action.[35] That said, there have been instances of the court regarding applications of substance that are independent of the claim as being a 'claim' for the purposes of CPR, r 25.12(1).[36] **15.09**

---

[30] It was repealed in 2009: see Companies Act 2006, s 1295 and Sch 16; Companies Act 2006 (Commencement No 8, Transitional Provisions and Savings) Order (SI 2008/2860), arts 4 and 5, Sch 1, Pt 1, and Sch 2, para 1 (as amended).

[31] Coulson J, for example, found that, on the facts of the case before him, he lacked the power to make an order in respect of costs of a failed pre-issue mediation: *Lobster Group Ltd v Heidelberg Graphic Equipment Ltd* [2008] EWHC 413 (TCC), at [15] *et seq*.

[32] See The White Book, at para 25.12.7.

[33] See, eg, *Dar International FEF Co v Aon Ltd* [2003] EWCA Civ 1833.

[34] In *ibid*, at [17], for example, Mance LJ called an application for just such an order an 'oddity'.

[35] *Re B (infants)* [1965] 2 All ER 651, at 652, *per* Pennycuick J.

[36] See *Cherkasov v Olegovich* [2017] EWHC 756 (Ch), at [44]–[57], *per* Rose J, relying on *GFN SA & Ors v The Liquidators of Bancredit Cayman Ltd (in official liquidation)* [2009] UKPC 39. A distinction may be drawn between applications that are in substance independent of the issues in dispute in the parent action and other applications. As a counter-example, see *Bowring (CT) & Co (Insurance) Ltd v Corsi & Partners Ltd* [1994] 2 Lloyd's Rep 567 (no jurisdiction where the defendant's application is for an enquiry as to damages).

Counterclaimants and the primary jurisdiction to make a security for costs order

15.10 Where a counterclaim can be said to have an 'independent vitality of its own'[37] that goes beyond it being a defence to the claim, then the power to make an order against the counterclaimant (that is, the defendant) under the primary jurisdiction may arise.[38] If, however, the counterclaim is merely an 'automatic counterpart of the defence',[39] then that jurisdiction would generally not arise.[40] Whilst there is a degree of overlap, the topics can probably best be regarded as going to the issue of discretion rather than jurisdiction and, as such, are addressed at 15.65–15.70.

Other Part 20 claims and the primary jurisdiction to make a security for costs order

15.11 The primary jurisdiction applies to Part 20 claims other than counterclaims in which a Part 20 defendant is able to seek an order against a Part 20 claimant.[41] As to the position of a defendant who wishes to include the costs of a Part 20 claim within an order against the claimant, see 15.117.

Appeals and the primary jurisdiction to make a security for costs order

15.12 The following points can be made about appeals.

- **Defendant will remain a defendant** A defendant will not cease to be a defendant merely because judgment has been entered against them. This means that if a defendant were to appeal, they would still be able to ask for security for the costs.[42]
- **Powers regarding appellants** An order may be made against an appellant (or a respondent who also brings an appeal).[43] The CPR contain express provision to this effect, this presumably being necessary for the purposes of allowing an order to be made against a defendant who appeals.
- **Conditional permission (any party)** Where there is compelling reason to do so, an order may be made under the provision in Part 52 that states that the appeal court may impose conditions upon which an appeal may be brought (see 15.06).[44]
- **Conditional permission (defendants)** In the Court of Appeal, an order for security for costs may be accompanied by an order that, as a condition of being granted

[37] To use the words of Bingham LJ in *Hutchinson Telephone (UK) Ltd v Ultimate Response Ltd* [1993] BCLC 307, at 317D.

[38] *Jones v Environcom Ltd & Anor* [2009] EWHC 16 (Comm), at [24]–[26]; see also the discussion in *Hutchison Telephone (UK) Ltd v Ultimate Response Ltd* [1993] BCLC 307, at 316, *per* Dillon LJ, where the issue of equitable set-off is addressed. Likewise, see *C T Bowring & Co (Insurance) Ltd v Corsi & Partners Ltd* [1995] 1 BCLC 148, at 153, *per* Dillon LJ, and *Autoweld Systems Ltd v Kito Enterprises LLC* [2010] EWCA Civ 1469, at [31], [32] and [35], *per* Black LJ. See also *BJ Crabtree v GPT Communication Systems* (1990) 59 BLR 43; *Apex Global Management v FI Call Ltd* [2014] EWHC 779 (Ch), at [26], [27] and esp [39]; *Samuel J Cohl Co v Eastern Mediterranean Maritime Ltd ('The Silver Fir')* [1980] 1 Lloyd's Rep 371, *per* Lawton LJ; *Aridila Investments NV v ENRC NV* [2015] EWHC 1667 (Comm), at [67]–[69], *per* Simon J.

[39] *Hutchison Telephone (UK) Ltd v Ultimate Response Ltd* [1993] BCLC 307, at 316, *per* Dillon LJ.

[40] *Samuel J Cohl Co v Eastern Mediterranean Maritime Ltd ('The Silver Fir')* [1980] 1 Lloyd's Rep 371; see also *Hutchison Telephone (UK) Ltd v Ultimate Response Ltd* [1993] BCLC 307, at 317.

[41] See CPR, rr 25.12(1) and 20.3.

[42] *Dar International FEF Co v Aon Ltd* [2003] EWCA Civ 1833, at [12], *per* Mance LJ, but the comments, at [17], also ought to be noted (namely, that it would be an 'oddity' if a successful claimant were to be ordered to give security for costs to which it was already entitled). In a similar vein, if a claimant is successful, but the defendant brings an appeal, the court may, pending the appeal, stay the payment out of monies previously paid in as security: *Stabilad Ltd v Stephens & Carter Ltd* [1999] 1 WLR 1201.

[43] See CPR, r 25.15; see also *Antonelli v Allen* [2001] EWCA Civ 1563.

[44] See CPR, r 52.9(1) and (2).

permission, a defendant who appeals must pay some or all of the judgment debt into court.[45]

- **Costs of applications for permission to appeal** An order for security may be made where a party seeks permission to appeal, but this would be under the secondary jurisdictions (see 15.15–15.22 and, in particular, 15.21).
- **Claimants' costs in the court below** There seem to be conflicting authorities on the question of whether the court has jurisdiction to make an award in respect of a claimant's costs in the court below.[46] According to May LJ, however, the issue of jurisdiction is largely academic, because it would be an 'oddity' to require a successful claimant to give security for costs to which it was already entitled.[47]

Third parties and the primary jurisdiction to make a security for costs order

An order for security may be made against a person who has assigned the right to the claim to the claimant for the purposes of avoiding the possibility of a costs order being made against them.[48] Similarly, an order may be made against a person who has contributed or agreed to contribute to the claimant's costs in return for a share of any money or property that the claimant may recover in the proceedings.[49] A claimant may be required to provide certain details regarding the person who had provided funding (see 15.129).[50] **15.13**

Interpleaders and security for costs order

Interpleader is a procedure that allows a party ('the stakeholder'[51]) to bring a claim ('the stakeholder application'[52]) for the purposes of compelling two or more other persons ('the parties to the issue') to litigate a dispute in the context of a 'trial of the issue'.[53] Such proceedings are often used to resolve disputes arising under insurance policies. Since 6 April 2014,[54] such matters have been governed by CPR, Part 86. CPR, Part 85, creates a similar mechanism for dealing with claims for controlled or executed goods. The ordinary rules relating to security for costs will apply.[55] For the purposes of ascertaining whether a party is liable to give security for costs, the court will have to determine which of the parties is, in substance, the claimant in the trial of the issue. In this regard, the court will seek to determine the substantive statuses of the parties (that is, as the claimant or defendant to the issue[56]), **15.14**

[45] See *Hammond Suddards, Solicitors v Agrichem International Holdings Ltd* [2001] EWCA Civ 2065, in which Clarke LJ confirmed that the Court of Appeal had jurisdiction to grant permission to appeal subject to the applicant paying either a part or the whole of the judgment debt into court. By CPR, r 52.9(2), such an order would be made only if there were a compelling reason. See also, eg, *Société Générale SA v Saad Trading, Contracting & Financial Services Co* [2012] EWCA Civ 695.

[46] In *Ahmed v Blackburn & Co* [2001] EWCA Civ 141, at [8], May LJ found that that jurisdiction did not exist, but in *Dar International FEF Co v Aon Ltd* [2003] EWCA Civ 1833, at [12], Mance LJ came to the opposite conclusion.

[47] *Dar International FEF Co v Aon Ltd* [2003] EWCA Civ 1833, at [17].

[48] CPR, r 25.14(2).

[49] CPR, r 25.14(2). For the history of the jurisdiction, see *Abraham v Thompson* [1997] 4 All ER 362, CA, and *Condliffe v Hislop* [1996] 1 All ER 431, CA.

[50] See also the related topic of nominal claimants at 15.43.

[51] See CPR, r 86.1(2)(a).

[52] See CPR, r 86.1(2)(b).

[53] See CPR, rr 85.11 and 86.4.

[54] Prior to that date, the county courts used to apply RSC Order 17 and CCR Order 33.

[55] Whilst a pre-CPR case, see *Tudor Furnishers Ltd v Montague & Co and Finer Production Co Ltd* [1950] Ch 113. Whilst it dealt with interpleader only as an analogy, see *Maatschappij voor Fondsenbezit v Shell Transport and Trading Co* [1923] 2 KB 166, CA.

[56] Whilst a pre-CPR case, see *Tudor Furnishers Ltd v Montague & Co and Finer Production Co Ltd* [1950] Ch 113; *Rhodes v Dawson* (1886) 16 QBD 548, CA; *Tomlinson v Land and Finance Corporation*

which may be different from their nominal statuses in the stakeholder application.[57] This means that the 'defendant' may, in substance, be the claimant to the issue[58] and vice versa.[59] Such issues are not always clear-cut and, in this regard, the court has a wide discretion to make whatever order is appropriate.[60]

Secondary jurisdictions

15.15 The secondary jurisdictions are creations of the CPR, but they arise under the general powers in CPR, Parts 3, 24 and 52, rather than under the specific powers in CPR, Part 25, Section II. The relevant provisions in CPR, r 3.1, are as follows:

> '(2) Except where these Rules provide otherwise, the court may—
> [...]
> (m) take any other step or make any other order for the purpose of managing the case and furthering the overriding objective.
>
> (3) When the court makes an order, it may—
> (a) make it subject to conditions, including a condition to pay a sum of money into court; and
> (b) specify the consequence of failure to comply with the order or a condition.
>
> (4) Where the court gives directions it will take into account whether or not a party has complied with the Practice Direction (Pre-Action Conduct) and any relevant pre-action protocol.
>
> (5) The court may order a party to pay a sum of money into court if that party has, without good reason, failed to comply with a rule, practice direction or a relevant pre-action protocol.
>
> (6) When exercising its power under paragraph (5) the court must have regard to—
> (a) the amount in dispute; and
> (b) the costs which the parties have incurred or which they may incur.
>
> (6A) Where a party pays money into court following an order under paragraph (3) or (5), the money shall be security for any sum payable by that party to any other party in the proceedings.'

15.16 The relevant powers in CPR, r 24.6 (which apply only if an application for summary judgment has been made), are as follows:

> 'When the court determines a summary judgment application it may—
> (a) give directions as to the filing and service of a defence;
> (b) give further directions about the management of the case.
>
> (Rule 3.1(3) provides that the court may attach conditions when it makes an order.)'

15.17 Practice Direction (PD) 24 supplements these provisions in the following way:

> '4 Where it appears to the court possible that a claim or defence may succeed but improbable that it will do so, the court may make a conditional order, as described below.

Ltd (1884) 14 QBD 539, CA; *Maatschappij voor Fondsenbezit v Shell Transport and Trading Co* [1923] 2 KB 166, CA.

[57] Indeed, RSC Ord 23, r 1(3), used to provide that 'references ... to a plaintiff and a defendant shall be construed as references to the person (howsoever described on the record) who is in the position of plaintiff or defendant, as the case may be ...'

[58] See, eg, *Williams v Crosling* (1847) 3 CB 957; *Tomlinson v Land and Finance Corporation Ltd* (1884) 14 QBD 539, CA.

[59] See, eg, *Tudor Furnishers Ltd v Montague & Co and Finer Production Co Ltd* [1950] Ch 113, [1950] 1 All ER 65; *Re Cie Générale d'Eaux Minérales et de Bains de Mer* [1891] 3 Ch 451.

[60] As an example of this, see *Re Cie Générale d'Eaux Minérales et de Bains de Mer* [1891] 3 Ch 451, in which mutual security was ordered; cf *Workmeister v Healy* (1876) IR 10 CL 450, in which the competing claims for security led to no order being made.

[...]

5.2 A conditional order is an order which requires a party:
(1) to pay a sum of money into court, or
(2) to take a specified step in relation to his claim or defence, as the case may be, and provides that that party's claim will be dismissed or his statement of case will be struck out if he does not comply.'

The relevant powers in CPR, Part 52, are as follows (under the heading '... imposing conditions on permission to appeal'): **15.18**

'52.9 (1) The appeal court may—
[...]
(c) impose or vary conditions upon which an appeal may be brought.

(2) The court will only exercise its powers under paragraph (1) where there is a compelling reason for doing so.'

Moore-Bick LJ has emphasised that CPR, r 3.1, gives rise to two distinct jurisdictions, as follows.[61] **15.19**

- **CPR, r 3.1(3)** This jurisdiction is designed to control the future conduct of the party on whom it is imposed.[62] Moore-Bick LJ has explained that when the rule speaks of the court making an order, it is referring to a direction that a party act in a certain way or that a certain state of affairs should exist;[63] hence it is not a jurisdiction that allows free-standing orders for security for costs to be made. This means that it is a parasitic jurisdiction in that when the court makes an order, an order made under CPR, r 3.1(3), may operate upon it to make that order subject to conditions, including a condition to pay a sum of money into court.[64]
- **CPR, r 3.1(5)** This is a jurisdiction that is intended to give the court power to manage a party whose past conduct has been found wanting.[65] Unlike the jurisdiction under CPR, r 3.1(3), the court is able to make a free-standing order for security for costs. Where a party has, without good reason, failed to comply with a rule, practice direction or a relevant pre-action protocol, then that party may be ordered to pay money into court.[66] Dyson LJ had this to say about that jurisdiction:

  'Rule 3(3) in terms allows the court to make any order conditional on (amongst other things) the payment of money into court. Yet more specifically rule 3(5) empowers the court to order a non-compliant party to pay money into court and rule 3(6) requires the court in exercising that power to have regard to the costs incurred or to be incurred.'[67]

  The court must have regard to the amount in dispute and the costs that the parties have incurred or which they may incur.[68]

---

[61] *Huscroft v P&O Ferries Ltd* [2010] EWCA Civ 1483 at [18].
[62] *Ibid*, at [17].
[63] *Ibid*, at [18].
[64] CPR, r 3.1(3). Akenhead J has found that it would not be appropriate to make such an order where there was no continuing non-compliance or order for the court to make to which a payment into court would be ancillary: *Lazaris v London & Newcastle (Camden) Ltd* [2013] EWHC 97 (TCC), at [22]–[25].
[65] *Huscroft v P&O Ferries Ltd* [2010] EWCA Civ 1483, at [17].
[66] CPR, r 3.1(5).
[67] *Olatawura v Abiloye* [2002] EWCA Civ 998, at [20].
[68] CPR, r 3.1(6).

15.20 Where a party pays money into court following an order under CPR, r 3.1(3) or (5), the money will stand as security for any sum payable by that party to any other party in the proceedings.[69]

15.21 The secondary jurisdictions come into their own where, procedurally, the powers under the primary jurisdiction are unavailable.[70] Moore-Bick LJ has cautioned that it would be wrong to regard the secondary jurisdictions as a convenient means of circumventing the requirements of the primary jurisdiction, thereby providing a less demanding route by which security for costs may be obtained:

> 'In my view, when the court is asked to consider making an order under r 31(3) or 3.1(5) which is or amounts to an order for security for costs or when it considers doing so of its own motion, it should bear in mind the principles underlying rules 25.12 and 25.13.'[71]

That said, secondary jurisdictions are capable of plugging gaps in a wide range of circumstances.[72] Examples include an application for permission to appeal,[73] an application for summary judgment,[74] an application to strike out[75] and when giving directions.[76] This is by no means an exhaustive list. The secondary jurisdictions should be distinguished from the power to stay the claim pending payment of existing liabilities (such as existing costs orders): an application dependent on orders that have already been made will turn on different bases from those that govern applications for security for costs.[77]

Cases that are not suitable for security for costs

15.22 The court has no jurisdiction to afford a party security for costs by imposing a freezing order on the opponent.[78] Moreover, it would not be appropriate to make an order in committal proceedings, because such proceedings go to the liberty.[79]

Detailed assessments and orders for security for costs

15.23 It is not clear whether the primary jurisdiction would empower the court to make an order for security for costs in respect of a detailed assessment. An analogous situation would be where a defendant seeks an enquiry as to damages: under a comparable jurisdiction in a

---

69 CPR, r 3.1(6A).

70 See *Great Future Ltd v Sealand Housing Corporation* [2003] EWCA Civ 682 (CPR, Part 25, Section II did not apply at the material time because permission to appeal had not been granted).

71 *Huscroft v P&O Ferries Ltd* [2010] EWCA Civ 1483, at [14].

72 Whilst there are no reported examples of the power being used in isolation, Simon Brown LJ has implied that there is a power under CPR, r 3.1(2)(m) that, if it exists as a discrete *vires*, would be a widely applicable power: see *Olatawura v Abiloye* [2002] EWCA Civ 998, at [25]. See also *Great Future Ltd v Sealand Housing Corporation* [2003] EWCA Civ 682.

73 See *Shlaimoun & Anor v Mining Technologies International Inc* [2012] EWCA Civ 772, at [12]–[16], *per* Neuberger MR. See also *Royal Bank of Scotland v Hicks* [2012] EWCA Civ 1665; *Mulford Holding & Investment Ltd v Greatex Ltd* [2010] EWCA Civ 1178, *per* Lloyd LJ; *Great Future International Ltd & Ors v Sealand Housing Corporation* [2003] EWCA Civ 682; in a family setting, *Golubovich v Golubovich* [2011] EWCA Civ 528.

74 *Jacobs UK Ltd v Skidmore Owings & Merrill LLP* [2008] EWHC 2847 (TCC).

75 *Ashfield & Anor v Union Pensions Trustees Ltd* [2004] All ER (D) 103 (Dec).

76 *Ali v Hudson t/a Hudson Freemen Berg (a firm)* [2003] EWCA Civ 1793.

77 This is an issue that goes beyond the scope of this book, but it is discussed in *CIBC Mellon Trust Co v Mora Hotel Corpn NV* [2002] EWCA Civ 1688.

78 See *Cooke v Venulum Property Investments Ltd* [2013] EWHC 4288 (Ch), at [11]–[18], *per* Morgan J.

79 See *Haederle v Thomas* [2017] EWCA Civ 1339.

pre-CPR case, Dillon LJ found that the power to make an order would not arise in those circumstances, primarily on the basis that the assessment was made at the behest of the defendant, who could not be said to be in the position of a claimant for the purposes of the assessment.[80] It is possible that the same applies to detailed assessments. In any event, there is no obvious reason why an order could not be made under the court's secondary jurisdictions.

Principles and Discretion Relating to Security for Costs

Whether an order for security for costs is made is a matter of discretion. In so far as the primary jurisdiction is concerned, an order will be made only if it is just to make such an order and if certain conditions have been satisfied. In this regard, CPR, r 25.13(1), provides as follows: **15.24**

'(1) The court may make an order for security for costs under rule 25.12 if—
(a) it is satisfied, having regard to all the circumstances of the case, that it is just to make such an order; and
(b) [...]
(i) one or more of the conditions in paragraph (2) applies, or
(ii) an enactment permits the court to require security for costs.'

The secondary jurisdictions are less well structured. They are addressed at 15.97–15.101. **15.25**

Conditions and factors (primary jurisdiction)

The conditions that are most frequently relied upon are set out in CPR, r 25.13(2),[81] and they apply to both claimants and appellants (and to respondents who bring a cross-appeal[82]): **15.26**

'(2) The conditions are—
(a) the claimant is—
(i) resident out of the jurisdiction; but
(ii) not resident in a Brussels Contracting State, a State bound by the Lugano Convention or a Regulation State, as defined in section 1(3) of the Civil Jurisdiction and Judgments Act 1982;
[...]
(c) the claimant is a company or other body (whether incorporated inside or outside Great Britain) and there is reason to believe that it will be unable to pay the defendant's costs if ordered to do so;
(d) the claimant has changed his address since the claim was commenced with a view to evading the consequences of the litigation;
(e) the claimant failed to give his address in the claim form, or gave an incorrect address in that form;
(f) the claimant is acting as a nominal claimant, other than as a representative claimant under Part 19, and there is reason to believe that he will be unable to pay the defendant's costs if ordered to do so;

[80] *CT Bowring & Co (Insurance) Ltd v Corsi & Partners Ltd* [1995] 1 BCLC 148, CA (the jurisdiction arose under the now-revoked s 726(1) of the Companies Act 1985).
[81] CPR, r 25.13(2)(b), has been repealed and not replaced.
[82] CPR, r 25.15(1), which reads: 'The court may order security for costs of an appeal against—(a) an appellant; (b) a respondent who also appeals, on the same grounds as it may order security for costs against a claimant under this Part.'

(g) the claimant has taken steps in relation to his assets that would make it difficult to enforce an order for costs against him.

(Rule 3.4 allows the court to strike out a statement of case and Part 24 for it to give summary judgment.)'

15.27 In addition, there are further provisions—set out in CPR, r 25.15(2)—that relate only to appellants (and respondents who also appeal, but not to persons who only seek permission to appeal[83]):

'(2) The court may also make an order under [the primary jurisdiction] where the appellant, or the respondent who also appeals, is a limited company and there is reason to believe it will be unable to pay the costs of the other parties to the appeal should its appeal be unsuccessful.'

15.28 It is possible for a defendant to seek an order against a person other than a claimant.[84] CPR, r 25.14, makes the requisite provisions:

'(1) The defendant may seek an order against someone other than the claimant, and the court may make an order for security for costs against that person if—
(a) it is satisfied, having regard to all the circumstances of the case, that it is just to make such an order; and
(b) one or more of the conditions in paragraph (2) applies.

(2) The conditions are that the person—
(a) has assigned the right to the claim to the claimant with a view to avoiding the possibility of a costs order being made against him; or
(b) has contributed or agreed to contribute to the claimant's costs in return for a share of any money or property which the claimant may recover in the proceedings; and

is a person against whom a costs order may be made.'

15.29 Thus the primary jurisdiction is available where any of the conditions listed at 15.26–15.28 is met. Each of those conditions is addressed in turn.

Residence and conditions regarding security for costs: CPR, r 25.13(2)(a)

15.30 The question here is whether the claimant is resident in a contracting state[85] (CPR, r 25.13(2)(a)). If the answer to that question is in the negative, an order under CPR, r 25.12, may be made—but only if there is reason to do so (see 15.72–15.73).

15.31 This condition will turn on the interpretation of the word 'resident'. The comparable words 'ordinarily resident' are, in other contexts, usually given their ordinary and natural meaning,[86] and there is no reason to believe that the word 'resident' in this context should be treated differently.[87] Where the person is a corporation, its residency will

[83] *Kevythalli Design v Ice Associates* [2010] EWCA Civ 379, at [3], *per* Aikens LJ. Where the application is wrongly made under the primary jurisdiction, it is open to the court to allow the application notice to be amended to substitute the correct (ie secondary) jurisdiction: see, eg, *Mulford Holding & Investment Ltd v Greatex Ltd* [2010] EWCA Civ 1178, *per* Lloyd LJ.

[84] Whilst not binding, Master Kay QC has found that the power does not apply to a solicitor who was being pursued for wasted costs, but he did not refer to CPR, r 25.14, presumably because it was thought not to apply: see *MA Lloyd & Son Ltd (in administration) v PPC International Ltd* [2016] EWHC 1583 (QB).

[85] See fn 10 for a list of contracting states.

[86] See, eg, *R v Barnett London Borough Council, ex p Shah* [1983] 2 AC 309, HL.

[87] As originally worded, CPR, Part 25, Section II, used the words 'ordinarily resident': see Civil Procedure (Amendment No 2) Rules 2002 (SI 2002/3219). Whilst the contrary is arguable, it is generally accepted that

depend on where its central management and control lies.[88] The fact that a company may not have paid corporation tax in the UK is a factor relevant to the issue of whether it is resident outside the jurisdiction[89] and, presumably, the same applies to other contracting states.

For the reasons set out more fully at 15.72–15.73, the mere fact that the claimant is resident outside a contracting state would not, without more, be sufficient to justify the court exercising its discretion in favour of the defendant. In particular, the defendant must show, on objectively justified grounds, that there was a real risk that it would not be in a position to enforce an order for costs against the claimant and that, in all of the circumstances, it was just to make an order for security. Human rights issues also arise (see 15.73). **15.32**

It is actual residence that is relevant, not planned residence.[90] There is no requirement to prove residence at any particular address.[91] The fact that a person may have other residences in places other than a contracting state will not prevent the court from finding that the person is resident within a contracting state.[92] Voluntary visits to a contracting state may be sufficient to prove that the person making those visits is resident in that state.[93] A person resident outside a contracting state is not able to evade the jurisdiction by the expedient of moving assets into a contracting state.[94] The fact that a claimant has a co-claimant who is resident in the jurisdiction will not, of itself, preclude an order being made.[95] **15.33**

Ability of company to pay and conditions regarding security for costs: CPR, r 25.13(2)(c)

The main questions that arise under CPR, r 25.13(2)(c), are (a) whether the claimant is 'a company or other body', and (b) whether there is reason to believe that the claimant will be unable to pay the defendant's costs if ordered to do so. Other issues may arise and, in this regard, 15.43–15.45 and 15.52–15.53 may (with appropriate modifications) be relevant. As to (a), the phrase 'a company or other body' includes unlimited, as well as limited, companies.[96] Presumably, it also applies to limited liability partnerships. **15.34**

As to (b), the phrase 'reason to believe that [the party in question] will be unable to pay' is almost identical to that used in s 726(1) of the Companies Act 1985, so some assistance **15.35**

---

the loss of the word 'ordinarily' was only stylistic, because the Explanatory Notes to the amendment state that it was made for other reasons—namely, to comply with the guidance given in *De Beer v Kanaar & Co (a firm) (No 1)* [2001] EWCA Civ 1318.

[88] *Re Little Olympian Each-Ways Ltd* [1994] 4 All ER 561, Ch D.

[89] *Texuna International Ltd v Cairn Energy plc* [2004] EWHC 1102 (Comm), at [8], *per* Gross J. See also *Re Little Olympian Each-Ways Ltd (No 2)* [1995] 1 BCLC 48.

[90] See *Appah v Monsen* [1967] 1 WLR 893, in which the court found that a person will not be regarded as being resident in a country merely because they have made a decision to move there.

[91] See *Ontulmus v Collett* [2014] EWHC 294 (QB), at [33]–[35], *per* Tugendhat J.

[92] See *Somerset-Leeke & Anor v Kay Trustees* [2003] EWHC 1243 (Ch), at [1], *per* Jacob J. Authorities decided before 2001 ought to be viewed with care, because the wording of the rules changed on this point in that year.

[93] See, eg, *Ontulmus v Collett* [2014] EWHC 294 (QB), at [14]–[32], *per* Tugendhat J.

[94] *De Beer v Kanaar & Co (a firm) (No 1)* [2001] EWCA Civ 1318.

[95] *Slazengers Ltd v Seaspeed Ferries International Ltd* [1987] 3 All ER 967, CA. This will be particularly so where the person within a contracting state has been added solely for the purposes of defeating an application for security for costs: whilst on a slightly different point, see *Jones and Saldanha v Gurney* [1913] WN 72, *per* Swinfen Eady J. See also *John Bishop (Caterers) Ltd v National Union Bank* [1973] 3 All ER 707.

[96] See *Jirehouse Capital v Beller* [2008] EWCA Civ 908, at [17]–[19], *per* Arden LJ.

can be gained by looking at the authorities relating to that section.[97] After having reviewed those authorities, Arden LJ had this to say:

> 'In my judgment, there is a critical difference between a conclusion that there is "reason to believe" that the company will not be able to pay costs ordered against it and a conclusion that it has been proved that the company will not be able to pay costs ordered against it. In the former case, there is no need to reach a final conclusion as to what will probably happen. In the latter case, a conclusion has to be reached on the balance of probabilities.'[98]

Arden LJ went on to say that the correct approach was not that there must be a finding that, on the balance of probabilities, the company would not be able to pay; rather, the threshold was much lower—namely, that there was reason to believe (that is, a factor that gave rise to a risk) that the company would not be able to pay. She went on to discourage the practice of substituting the statutory words[99] with a test of whether there was a 'significant danger' that the company would not be able to pay—a practice that had arisen under s 726(1) of the Companies Act 1985.[100] Put otherwise, the test should not be paraphrased.

15.36 The following comments may be made about ability to pay in the context of CPR, r 25.13(2)(c).

- **Liquidation** Whilst it seems not to have been elevated to the status of a presumption of fact, the fact that a company is in liquidation is capable of being *prima facie* evidence of the fact it would be unable to meet a costs order.[101] Burton J has explained that it would not automatically be the case that an insolvent company would be regarded as being unable to pay costs, because the applicant would, in an appropriate case, have to establish doubt as to the ability of the liquidator to use the company's assets to pay out in priority the costs to which the applicant would be entitled if it were ultimately successful.[102]
- **Balance-book insolvency** The fact that a company is balance-book insolvent would generally be sufficient to prove an inability to pay, but this would not always be the case.[103]
- **Timing and future developments** Timing may be important in two regards: first, if the claimant's financial position is likely to change, that may be taken into account;[104] and

---

[97] See, eg, *ibid*, at [2], and *Dorchester Project Management Ltd v BNP Parabas Real Estate Advisory & Property Management UK Ltd* [2013] EWHC 4555 (Ch), at [42], *per* Proudman J.

[98] *Jirehouse Capital v Beller* [2008] EWCA Civ 908, at [26], where Arden LJ cited Sir Donald Nicholls VC's judgment in *Re Unisoft Group Ltd* [1993] BCLC 532, at 534 e-I, at length.

[99] The need not to paraphrase the relevant words of the rule was repeated by Sales LJ in *SARPD Oil International Ltd v Addax Energy SA & Anor* [2016] EWCA Civ 120, at [13], and by Longmore LJ in *Premier Motorauctions Ltd v Pricewaterhousecoopers LLP* [2017] EWCA Civ 1872, at [7].

[100] This practice arose out of a misunderstanding as to what Buxton LJ had said in *Phillips v Evershed* [2002] EWCA Civ 486: see *Jirehouse Capital v Beller* [2008] EWCA Civ 908, at [30]–[33].

[101] See, eg, *Northampton Coal Iron and Waggon Co v Midland Waggon Co* (1878) 7 Ch.D 500; *Pure Spirit Company v Fowler* (1890) 25 QBD 235. See also *Smith v UIC Insurance Co Ltd* [2001] BCC 11.

[102] See *Anglo Irish Bank Corporation Ltd v Dtz Debenham Tie Leung Ltd* [2013] EWHC 596 (Comm).

[103] See, eg, *Kim Barker Ltd v Aegon Insurance Co (UK) Ltd* (1989) The Times, 9 October, CA, in which the Court found that the cash flow would be sufficient to allow a seemingly insolvent company to meet any liability for the defendant's costs.

[104] By way of example, Kennedy LJ refused to interfere with a decision not to make an order in circumstances in which the claimant was likely to be awarded a substantial sum in another action before

secondly, the court will look at the question of whether the claimant will be able to pay when ordered to do so. This raises questions concerning liquidity (see below).

- **Liquidity** Park J has approved of the following pre-CPR comments of Nicholls V-C: '[T]he question is, will the company be able to meet the costs order at the time when the order is made and requires to be met?'[105] Thus, regardless of whether the claimant's assets would be sufficient to discharge any relevant costs debt, an order may be made against a claimant where those assets are illiquid to such an extent that they could not be realised in time to pay. (In practice, however, many claimants prefer to borrow against the assets or to obtain a bank guarantee rather than have an order made against them.)
- **Contributions** The court may have regard to the finances of persons who are sufficiently close to the claimant to be expected to make a contribution towards any costs debt. In this regard, Rimer LJ had this to say: 'Nowadays the court has to have regard not just to whether the corporate appellant can itself provide security, but whether those behind it can put it in funds to do so.'[106]
- **Methods of funding** The fact that a party has entered into a conditional fee agreement is not evidence of the fact that it is impecunious.[107] Whilst it would now rarely be relevant, the fact that a defendant is legally aided—even with a nil contribution—would not necessarily lead to the conclusion that they could not find monies for the purposes of paying costs.[108]
- **After-the-event (ATE) insurance** This is addressed in detail below (see 15.37).
- **Refusal to provide information** Sales LJ has explained that if a claimant has been given the opportunity to adduce evidence that it can pay a defendant's costs and deliberately refuses to do so, there would be every reason to believe that if and when it is required to pay a defendant's costs, it would be unable to do so.[109]

The existence of ATE insurance may be a relevant factor. Longmore LJ has explained that since, in an appropriate case, it will in any event be inevitable that the question of whether ATE insurance gives sufficient protection to the defendant has to be decided at the discretionary stage, it will not perhaps be too troubling to have to determine the question at the jurisdiction stage.[110] It is therefore addressed here, but it ought to be borne in mind that what follows would also be relevant both to discretionary issues and to issues of quantum. **15.37**

The fact that a claimant has ATE insurance may be relevant because this may provide a source from which a costs order can be met.[111] Whilst there have been instances of ATE **15.38**

---

any enforcement proceedings would be likely to be required on behalf of the defendant: *Cripps v Heritage Distribution Corporation* (1999) The Times, 10 November, CA. See also *Automotive Latch Systems Ltd v Honeywell International Inc* [2006] EWHC 2340 (Comm).

105 *Longstaff International Ltd v McKenzie* [2004] EWHC 1852 (Ch), at [18], quoting from *Re Unisoft Group Ltd (No 2)* [1993] BCLC 532, at 534. See also the comment of Sonia Proudman QC (sitting as a High Court judge) in *Thistle Hotels Ltd v Gamma Four Ltd* [2004] EWHC 322 (Ch), at [11].

106 *Meridian International Services Ltd v Richardson* [2008] EWCA Civ 490, at [16]. See also *Keary Developments Ltd v Tarmac Construction Ltd & Anor* [1995] 3 All ER 534, at 540, *per* Peter Gibson LJ.

107 See *Wu v Hellard* (unreported), 25 November 2013, Ch D, *per* Judge Dight.

108 *M V Yorke Motors (a firm) v Edwards* [1982] 1 All ER 1024.

109 *SARPD Oil International Ltd v Addax Energy SA & Anor* [2016] EWCA Civ 120, at [17], *per* Sales LJ. See also *Mbasogo v Logo Ltd* [2006] EWCA Civ 608; *Marine Blast Ltd v Targe Towing Ltd* [2003] EWCA Civ 1940; *Phillips v Eversheds* [2002] EWCA Civ 486.

110 *Premier Motorauctions Ltd v PricewaterhouseCoopers LLP* [2017] EWCA Civ 1872, at [23].

111 See, eg, *ibid*, at [22], *per* Longmore LJ.

insurers avoiding their liabilities,[112] in the absence of evidence to the contrary (and subject to what is said in 15.39 about anti-avoidance clauses), the court's starting position is that a properly drafted ATE policy that has been provided by a substantial and reputable insurer should be regarded as being a reliable source of funding.[113] The court's tasks would be to establish the meaning of the ATE policy, how readily it might be legitimately avoided and the likelihood of circumstances arising that would enable it to be legitimately avoided.[114] To amount to a valid objection that an ATE policy does not provide appropriate security, the defendant's concern must be realistic, not theoretical or fanciful.[115] A close examination of the nature and terms of the insurance may well be required. If, for example, the whole case were to turn on whether the claimant is telling the truth, a policy that precludes indemnity in circumstances in which the insured has lied would not afford any real comfort to the defendant.[116] Likewise, the court may find that a policy that can be cancelled at any time for no reason or a wide variety of reasons should not be regarded as affording any protection to the defendant.[117] Other considerations may apply.[118]

15.39 The following further points may be made about ATE policies.

- **Anti-avoidance clauses** It is becoming increasingly common for ATE policies to contain 'anti-avoidance clauses', pursuant to which insurers promise not to avoid their liabilities or promise only to rely on any non-disclosure or misrepresentation if it is made fraudulently (see 34.31). For obvious reasons, such a clause may be relevant in so far as the adequacy of insurance may be concerned.[119] The absence of such a clause may be relevant and this may be so even where the ATE was incepted on the basis of diligent professional advice. In a case in which there was no anti-avoidance clause, Longmore LJ had this to say:

  'The judge felt he could rely on the fact that the proposals to insurers were made by Joint Liquidators who are independent professional insolvency office-holders, and who investigated the claims with the assistance of experienced solicitors and counsel providing a high

---

112 See, eg, *Persimmon Homes Ltd v Great Lakes Reinsurance (UK) Plc* [2010] EWHC 1705 (Comm), in which a successful defendant was unable to recover its costs from ATE insurers.

113 See *Geophysical Service Centre Co v Dowell Schlumberger (ME) Inc* [2013] EWHC 147 (TCC), at [15], *per* Stuart Smith J. See also *Harlequin Property (SVG) Ltd v Wilkins Kennedy (a firm)* [2015] EWHC 1122 (TCC), at [26], *per* Coulson J.

114 See *Geophysical Service Centre Co v Dowell Schlumberger (ME) Inc* [2013] EWHC 147 (TCC), at [19], *per* Stuart Smith J.

115 See *Harlequin Property (SVG) Ltd v Wilkins Kennedy (a firm)* [2015] EWHC 1122 (TCC), at [21], *per* Coulson J; see also *Recovery Partners GB Ltd v Rukhadze* [2018] EWHC 95 (Comm), at [18] and [29], *per* Nicholas Vineall QC (sitting as a deputy judge of the High Court).

116 See, eg, *Al-Koronky & Anor v Time Life Entertainments Group Ltd* [2005] EWHC 1688 (QB); see also *Belco Trading Ltd v Kordo* [2008] EWCA Civ 205.

117 See, eg, *Michael Phillips Architects Ltd v Riklin* [2010] EWHC 834 (TCC), at [29], *per* Akenhead J.

118 The Third Parties (Rights against Insurers) Acts may not apply in all jurisdictions, which may be a factor in the absence of a direct indemnity: see *Harlequin Property (SVG) Ltd v Wilkins Kennedy (a firm)* [2015] EWHC 1122 (TCC), at [29], [31]–[33] and [37], *per* Coulson J; *Catalyst Managerial Services v Libya Africa Investment Portfolio* [2017] EWHC 1236 (Comm), *per* Teare J. The conduct of the insured party may be relevant: Teare J, for example, was concerned about the fact that new solicitors had been instructed and that the court could not be confident that the insurers had been told everything that they should have been told.

119 See the *obiter* comments of Mance LJ in *Nasser v United Bank of Kuwait* [2001] EWCA Civ 556, at [60], cited by Longmore LJ in *Premier Motorauctions Ltd v PricewaterhouseCoopers LLP* [2017] EWCA Civ 1872, at [20]. The existence of an anti-avoidance clause would not necessarily mean, however, that the security afforded was adequate: see, by analogy, *Holyoake v Candy & Anor* [2017] EWHC 52 (QB).

level of objective professional scrutiny. All this is, of course, true but the best professional advice cannot cater for cases of non-disclosure of matters which the professionals do not know. Neither the defendants nor the court have been provided with the placing information put before the insurers but, even if that had been provided, it is unlikely that the court could be satisfied that the prospect of avoidance is illusory. Even at the jurisdictional stage of considering security for costs, the defendants must, as Mance LJ said in Nasser, "be entitled to some assurance that [the insurance] was not liable to be avoided for misrepresentation or non-disclosure".'[120]

Longmore LJ went on to say that whilst it may not be a particularly difficult exercise for a judge to assess the likelihood of avoidance if the right to avoid is confined to fraud, where there is no anti-avoidance clause of any kind, the exercise is very much more difficult.[121]

- **Direct deeds of indemnity** It may be that an ATE insurer (or, for that matter, some other person[122]) provides a 'deed of indemnity' by which the insurer (or other person) gives up their rights to avoid an indemnity. This practice has become more common over recent years and may be a way of increasing the security afforded by ATE insurance, especially where there are concerns about the possible effect of insolvency.[123] Whilst such deed may be regarded as affording sufficient security,[124] Longmore LJ has explained that the court would need to examine the terms of any such deed before knowing what bearing it may have on the matter.[125]
- **Conduct generally and ATE insurance** The court may disregard the policy if there is a high risk that there was material non-disclosure of the relevant facts.[126] In a case in which he expressed concern about the way in which the lawyers representing the claimants had presented and valued their case, Foskett J found that it was not possible to discount as illusory the prospect of the avoidance of the ATE insurance cover at some stage (in the context of the ATE policy not containing any provisions that would, of themselves, lead to that conclusion).[127]

Change of address and conditions regarding security for costs: CPR, r 25.13(2)(d)

The question here is whether the claimant changed their address with a view to evading the consequences of the litigation (CPR, r 25.13(2)(d)). This is a question of fact and degree. To satisfy this condition, there is a need to show a subjective intention to evade the consequences of the litigation and Moore-Bick J has explained that 'the consequences of the litigation' are not confined solely to the debt or damages sought.[128] **15.40**

120 *Premier Motorauctions Ltd v PricewaterhouseCoopers LLP* [2017] EWCA Civ 1872, at [28] and [29].

121 *Ibid*, at [31].

122 Indemnities provided by persons other than insurers may not be given as much weight, however: see, eg, *Dunn Motor Traction Ltd v National Express Ltd* [2017] EWHC 228 (Comm).

123 See, eg, *Harlequin Property (SVG) Ltd v Wilkins Kennedy (a firm)* [2015] EWHC 1122 (TCC), at [29], [31]–[33] and [37], *per* Coulson J.

124 See, eg, *Mayr v CMS Cameron McKenna LLP* (unreported), 21 November 2017, QBD (Comm), *per* Andrew Baker J; see also *Recovery Partners GB Ltd v Rukhadze* [2018] EWHC 95 (Comm), at [29]–[30], *per* Nicholas Vineall QC (sitting as a deputy judge of the High Court).

125 *Premier Motorauctions Ltd v PricewaterhouseCoopers LLP* [2017] EWCA Civ 1872, at [33], *per* Longmore LJ.

126 Whilst a Scottish case, see *Monarch Energy Ltd v Powergen Retail Ltd* [2006] CSOH 102.

127 See *Bailey v GlaxoSmithKline UK Ltd* [2017] EWHC 3195 (QB), at [70].

128 *Aoun v Bahri* [2002] EWHC 29 (Comm), at [18]; cf *Re Myer Wolff & Manley* (unreported), 23 April 1985, CA, in which a person's return to the jurisdiction was found to be *bona fide*.

15.41 Where a natural person changes address for *bona fide* personal reasons, that may be sufficient explanation to avoid an order being made.[129] Presumably, the same is true if a company changes its addresses for *bona fide* business reasons unrelated to the litigation.

Failure to give correct address and conditions regarding security for costs: CPR, r 25.13(2)(e)

15.42 This condition will be met if the claimant has failed to give their correct address in the claim form (CPR, r 25.13(2)(e)). Whether this condition is satisfied is likely to be a matter of fact and degree. Whilst the rule does mention intention, it is likely that, in the exercise of its discretion, the court would take into account factors such as whether the incorrect address was given by reason of mistake, who made the mistake, whether it was done for tactical purposes, etc.

Nominal claimants and conditions regarding security for costs: CPR, r 25.13(2)(f)

15.43 This condition will be met if the claimant is acting as a nominal claimant and there is reason to believe that they will be unable to pay the defendant's costs if ordered to do so (CPR, r 25.13(2)(f)). Whether the claimant is acting as a nominal claimant will be a matter of fact, degree and law. Kennedy LJ has confirmed that the concept of a 'nominal claimant' should be narrowly interpreted and restricted to cases in which there was an element of duplicity or window-dressing.[130] In a similar vein, Buckley LJ said:

> 'It is a rule that a plaintiff ... cannot be called on to give security for costs merely because he is poor, it being deemed right and expedient that a court of justice should be open to every one. An exception, however, from that rule is that, if a plaintiff is what has been called a "nominal plaintiff" or what, by way of alternative expression, I will call a "fictitious plaintiff", and is without means, security for costs will be ordered. An example of the kind of case in which that expression "nominal plaintiff" is applicable is where a person in whom a cause of action was vested, not being minded to bring an action himself, has assigned that cause of action to another, whom he puts forward for the purpose of suing, but who has no beneficial interest in the subject-matter of the litigation.'[131]

15.44 Decisions concerning nominal claimants are highly fact-sensitive, but case examples are illustrative of the court's approach. A claimant who had assigned the benefit of the claim to a third party without retaining any interest in the matter himself was, for example, found to be a nominal claimant;[132] a bankrupt to whom the trustee had assigned the right to claim damages, however, was not (largely because the trustee retained a third interest in the benefit of the claim).[133] The court came to a similar conclusion in the context of corporate insolvency, in which case the liquidator retained a 50 per cent interest in the benefit of a claim.[134]

---

[129] *Aoun v Bahri* [2002] EWHC 29 (Comm), at [27].

[130] *Envis v Thakkar* [1997] BPIR 189; see also *Semler v Murphy* [1968] 1 Ch 183, in which an order was made notwithstanding the fact that a narrow test was applied. In days gone by, a test of whether the claimant was 'a mere shadow of another person' was applied: see 1885 Law Times Rep LIII 484/2. See also *Chuku v Chuku* [2017] EWHC 541 (Ch), at [26]–[28], *per* Newey J.

[131] *White v Butt* [1909] 1 KB 50, at 55.

[132] See, eg, *Lloyd v Hathern Station Brick Co Ltd* (1901) 85 LT 158; *Semler v Murphy* [1967] 2 All ER 185; cf *Cook v Whellock* (1890) 24 QBD 658. As a contrary example, see *Danilina v Chernukhin* [2018] EWHC 39 (Comm), in which the so-called nominal claimant had an interest in the matter arising out of the option agreement.

[133] See *Ramsey v Hartley* [1977] 1 WLR 686.

[134] *Farmer v Moseley (Holdings) Ltd* (2001) BCLC 572, *per* Neuberger J.

The topic of whether a claimant would be unable to pay the defendant's costs if ordered to do so is covered at 15.50–15.51. Whilst a different topic, the matters set out at 15.13 (concerning third parties) may also be relevant. **15.45**

Asset sequestration and conditions regarding security for costs: CPR, r 25.13(2)(g)

This condition would be met if the claimant were to take steps in relation to their assets that would make it difficult to enforce an order for costs (CPR, r 25.13(2)(g)). This is a matter of fact and degree,[135] and is often described as being a question that has two distinct parts: first, the question of whether the 'gateway condition' has been satisfied (see 15.47); and secondly, if that condition has been satisfied, the question of whether, in all of the circumstances, it would be just to make an order.[136] Applying this two-stage method gives rise to all manner of issues, but, fortunately, Roth J has formulated the following forensic sieve: **15.46**

> 'The general principles that govern the making of an order for security and the application of CPR 25.13(2)(g) are well-recognised. They include the following:
>
> (i) The requirement is that the claimant has taken in relation to his assets steps which, if he loses the case and a costs order is made against him, will make that order difficult to enforce. It is not sufficient that the claimant has engaged in other conduct that may be dishonest or reprehensible: *Chandler v Brown* [2001] CP Rep 103 at [19]–[20];
> (ii) The test in that regard is objective: it is not concerned with the claimant's motivation but with the effect of steps which he has taken in relation to his assets: *Aoun v Bahri* [2002] EWHC 29 (Comm) ... [25]–[26];
> (iii) If it is reasonable to infer on all the evidence that a claimant has undisclosed assets, then his failure to disclose them could itself, although it might not necessarily, lead to the inference that he had put them out of reach of his creditors, including a potential creditor for costs: *Dubai Islamic Bank v PSI Energy Holding Co* [2011] EWCA Civ 761 at [26];
> (iv) There is no temporal limitation as to when the steps were taken: they may have been taken before proceedings had been commenced or were in contemplation: *Harris v Wallis* [2006] EWHC 630 (Ch) at [24]–[25];
> (v) However, motive, intention and the time when steps were taken are all relevant to the exercise of the court's discretion: *Aoun v Bahri, ibid; Harris v Wallis, ibid.*
> (vi) In the exercise of its discretion, the court may take into account whether the claimant's want of means has been brought about by any conduct of the defendant: *Sir Lindsay Parkinson & Co v Triplan* [1973] QB 609 *per* Lord Denning MR at 626; *Spy Academy Ltd v Sakar International Inc* [2009] EWCA Civ 985 at [14].
> (vii) Impecuniosity is not a ground for ordering security; on the contrary, security should not be ordered where the court is satisfied that, in all the circumstances, this would probably have the effect of stifling a genuine claim: *Keary Developments Ltd v Tarmac Construction* [1995] 3 All ER 534 at 540, para 6. Thus the court must not order security in a sum which it knows the claimant cannot afford: *Al-Koronky v Time-Life Entertainment* [2006] CP Rep 47 at [25]–[26] (where this was referred to as "the principle of affordability");
> (viii) The court can order any amount (other than a simply nominal amount) by way of security up to the full amount claimed: it is not bound to order a substantial amount: *Keary* at 540, para 5.

[135] Roth J has summarised the relevant law in *Ackerman v Ackerman* [2011] EWHC (Ch), at [16].

[136] *Dass v Beggs* [2014] EWHC 164 (Ch), at [12], *per* David Donaldson QC (sitting as a deputy High Court judge).

(ix) The burden is on the claimant to show that he is unable to provide security not only from his own resources but by way of raising the amount needed from others who could assist him in pursuing his claim, such as relatives and friends: *Keary* at 540, para 6. However, the court should evaluate the evidence as regards third party funders with recognition of the difficulty for the claimant in proving a negative: *Brimko Holdings Ltd v Eastman Kodak Co* [2004] EWHC 1343 (Ch) at [12].

(x) When a party seeks to ensure that any security that may be required is within his resources, he must be full and candid as to his means: the court should scrutinise what it is told with a critical eye and may draw adverse inferences from any unexplained gaps in the evidence: *Al-Koronky* at [27].'[137]

15.47 It is worth saying a little more about the gateway condition. The motivation of the claimant is irrelevant.[138] This means that a claimant might, for example, fall into the ambit of CPR, r 25.13(2)(g), completely innocently (such as by converting easily available assets into a loan to a struggling business).[139] That said, it is unlikely that the court would exercise its discretion against a party who had taken steps to which no realistic objection could be taken, such as paying their own costs of the litigation.[140] In a similar vein, it would be in only the rarest of circumstances that the court would exercise its discretion to make an order for security solely because there had been an assignment of rights under a loan agreement.[141]

15.48 For the reasons set out above, CPR, r 25.13(2)(g), is capable of being engaged by commonplace business activities. It has been argued that, in view of this, the gateway condition can be satisfied only by recent events. Ferris J rejected that argument and explained that there is no basis for overlaying some temporal limitation on the steps that are required to satisfy the gateway condition; thus, if a person had taken steps to avoid enforcement of a costs order, those steps may be taken into account regardless of the fact that they were taken many years ago.[142] Indeed, there is no requirement that the steps were taken at a time when the proceedings were in contemplation.[143] That said, there must be some link between the steps and the putative enforcement difficulties, and in this regard the effluxion of time may be relevant in the sense that it may lead to the causal effect being spent.[144] Moreover, the effluxion of time would be relevant to the way in which the court exercises its discretion.

15.49 A refusal on the part of the claimant to give details about their finances may result in the court drawing adverse inferences about the way in which they have dealt with their assets.[145] A history of dishonesty on the part of the claimant would not, of itself, be reason to

[137] *Ackerman v Ackerman* [2011] EWHC 2183 (Ch), at [16].

[138] *Aoun v Bahri* [2002] EWHC 29 (Comm), at [26], *per* Moore-Bick J; *Harris v Wallis* [2006] EWHC 630 (Ch), at [22]. See also *Dass v Beggs* [2014] EWHC 164 (Ch), at [6].

[139] See *Bush v Bank Mandiri (Europe) Ltd* (unreported), 17 January 2014, QBD, at [23], *per* N Strauss QC; *Aoun v Bahri* [2002] EWHC 29 (Comm), at [25].

[140] *Chandler v Brown* (2001) CP Rep 103 (Ch D), at [23], *per* Park J.

[141] *In the Matter of Abbington Hotel Ltd, sub nom D'angelo v Digrado et al* [2010] EWHC 1628 (Ch), at [12], *per* Judge Pelling QC (sitting as a judge of the High Court).

[142] *Harris v Wallis* [2006] EWHC 630 (Ch), at [22].

[143] *Dass v Beggs* [2014] EWHC 164 (Ch), at [7], *per* David Donaldson QC (sitting as a deputy High Court judge); *Harris v Wallis* [2006] EWHC 630 (Ch), at [24] and [25].

[144] *Dass v Beggs* [2014] EWHC 164 (Ch), at [7], *per* David Donaldson QC (sitting as a deputy High Court judge); *Chandler v Brown* [2001] CP Rep 103, at [20].

[145] See, eg, *Dubai Islamic Bank PJSC v PSI Energy Holding Co Bsc & Ors* [2011] EWCA Civ 761, in which the claimant asserted that his seemingly substantial income was mostly loans from 'family, family-affiliated companies and third parties'; in those circumstances, it was possible to infer that there were

find that the requisite threshold had been met.[146] The fact that a claimant is able to point to the existence of a dispute about their assets would not prevent the court from making an order.[147] Creating or (putatively) putting assets into trusts for no explicable reason may lead to an order being made.[148]

Appeals and inability to bear costs and conditions regarding security for costs: CPR r 25.15(2)

The question here—which applies only to appellants and respondents who also appeal—is whether the appellant (or appealing respondent) would be unable to pay the costs of the other parties to the appeal should its appeal be unsuccessful (CPR, r 25.15(2)). If the answer to that question is in the affirmative, the court is able to make an order pursuant to CPR, r 25.15. This condition is atypical in that it applies only to appeals rather than to claims and appeals—although a very similar test may be relevant in the context of corporate claimants and nominal claimants who bring claims (see 15.34 and 15.43–15.45 respectively). Arden LJ has confirmed that the court must take into account all of the relevant facts: **15.50**

> 'The phrase "the company will be unable to pay" requires more than simply that there is doubt whether the company will pay. Otherwise the second limb would have to say "the company may be unable to pay the costs". Secondly ... the court must have regard to conflicting evidence. The court must reach its conclusion as to whether the conditions in the statute are satisfied by reference to the totality of the evidence.'[149]

These comments were not made under the CPR,[150] but Rattee J has confirmed that they continue to apply by analogy.[151]

The issue of whether the claimant will be able to meet an adverse costs order is a matter of fact and degree, and expert evidence may be required. The points made at 15.36 will apply. Fancourt J has found that a failure to satisfy orders for costs previously made may, in the absence of evidence to the contrary, give rise to an inference that there is reason to believe the company in question will be unable to pay.[152] **15.51**

Assignment with a view of evasion and conditions regarding security for costs: CPR, 25.14(2)(a)

The question here is whether a person has assigned the right to the claim to the claimant with a view to avoiding the possibility of a costs order being enforced (CPR, r 24.14(2)(a)). If the answer to that question is in the affirmative, the court will be able to order that person to give security for costs. The issue of whether there has been an assignment will be largely a question of law. There is no authority addressing unsuccessful attempts to assign, **15.52**

undisclosed assets. See also *Bush v Bank Mandiri (Europe) Ltd* (unreported), 17 January 2014, QBD, *per* N Strauss QC.

146 *Chandler v Brown* (2001) CP Rep 103 (Ch D), at [20]–[23], *per* Park J.

147 *Warren v Marsden* [2014] EWHC 4410 (Comm), at [13], *per* Teare J.

148 See, eg, *Scott v Conwy County Borough Council as Conwy Harbour Authority* (unreported), 16 February 2018, QBD (Admlty), *per* Teare J.

149 *Jirehouse Capital v Beller* [2008] EWCA Civ 908, at [24]. See also *Unisoft Group Ltd (No 2)* [1993] BCLC 532; *Texuna International Ltd v Cairn Energy plc* [2004] EWHC 1102 (Comm), at [13], *per* Gross J.

150 They were made under the now-revoked provisions mentioned at 15.07.

151 *Ovlas Trading SA v Strand (London) Ltd* [2008] EWHC 3236 (Ch), at [9].

152 See *Patcroft Ltd v Latif* [2018] EWHC 11396 (Ch), at [11].

but where those were the facts, it may be that the court would consider invoking the secondary jurisdictions.

15.53 To invoke the primary jurisdiction, the court must, in addition to finding that there has been an assignment, be satisfied that there was a subjective intention on the part of the claimant to avoid the possibility of a costs order being enforced against them.[153] That will be a question of fact and degree.

Third parties (funders) and conditions regarding security for costs: CPR, r 25.14(2)(b)

15.54 Whilst CPR, r 25.14(2)(b), may apply to other persons, the prime focus of that rule is on litigation funders. The issue here is whether any person has contributed (or has agreed to contribute) to the claimant's costs in return for a share of the proceeds (CPR, r 25.14(2)(b)); whether there is an agreement to contribute in return for a share of the proceeds of the claim will be a matter of fact.

15.55 For obvious reasons, a third party ought to be ordered to give security only if and to the extent that it is at risk of being ordered to pay costs. In this regard, the points made in Chapter 9 will be relevant. Hildyard J had the following to say on the topic:

> 'Of particular relevance in assessing whether an interlocutory order against a non-party under CPR 25.14(2)(b) to secure a contingent liability pursuant to Section 51 is appropriate and just will be
> (1) Whether it is sufficiently clear that the non-party is to be treated as having in effect become in all but name a real party motivated to participate by its commercial interest in the litigation;
> (2) Whether there is a real risk of non-payment such that security against the contingent liability should be granted;
> (3) Whether there is a sufficient link between the funding and the costs for which recovery is sought to make it just for an order to be made;
> (4) Whether a risk of liability for costs has sufficiently been brought home to the non-party, either by express warning, or by reference to what a person in its position should be taken to appreciate as to the inherent risks;
> (5) Whether there are factors, including for example, delay in the making of an application for security or likely adverse effects such as to tip the overall balance against making an order.'[154]

15.56 The following miscellaneous points may be made about cases involving funders.

- **Disclosure** The court has the power to order disclosure in so far as the identity of funders and details of the funding arrangements are concerned.[155] This topic is addressed in more detail at 33.85–33.90.
- **Status of funder** The fact that the person in question may have been joined as a party will not necessarily change that person's status for the purposes of CPR, r 25.14(2)(b).[156]

---

153 *Eurocross Sales Ltd v Cornhill Insurance plc* [1995] 1 WLR 1517; see also Ferris J's *obiter* comments in *Harris v Wallis* [2006] EWHC 630 (Ch), at [22].

154 *The RBS Rights Issue Litigation (No 2)* [2017] EWHC 1217 (Ch), at [19].

155 See *In the matter of Hellas Telecommunications (Luxemburg)* (unreported), 20 July 2017, Ch D, *per* Snowden J. See also *Wall v Royal Bank of Scotland Plc* [2016] EWHC 2460 (Comm); *Re RBS Rights Issue Litigation* [2017] EWHC 463 (Ch).

156 See, eg, *Harcus Sinclair v Buttonwood Legal Capital Ltd* [2013] EWHC 2974 (Ch), in which David Donaldson QC found that a party who was a defendant in respect of the proceedings, but was not a party to the issue in question (that being an interpleader issue), was to be treated as a third party in relation to that issue.

- **Solvency and risk of non-payment** Whilst a member of the Association of Litigation Funders (ALF) will, when compliant with its Code of Conduct, '[maintain] at all times access to adequate financial resources to meet the obligations of the Funder',[157] it does not follow that all litigation funders will be in this position. Foskett J, for example, found on evidence that a funder who was not a member was balance-book insolvent and that such a funder would 'be an almost inevitable target for a security for costs application'.[158]
- **The relevance of the *Arkin* cap** As is explained at 9.37–9.44, in general the liability of a funder to pay costs by way of a non-party costs order is limited to the amount of funding, known as the *Arkin* cap.[159] Foskett J has explained that this cap is, at least arguably, not an absolute cap and that it therefore does not act as an absolute limit on the amount of security that a litigation funder may be ordered to pay.[160] He went on to say that the *Arkin* cap is a factor to be taken into account, but that (in an appropriate case) it may be exceeded for the purposes of ordering security.[161]
- **Group litigation** Hildyard J has commented that the fact that, in group litigation, a group of claimants has a group litigation order that affords them the benefit of having only several, rather than joint, liability for costs may be a factor to take into account.[162]
- **Non-commercial funders** Where the putative funder is the spouse of one of the parties, it would not follow that funding provided by that person must have been in return for a share of any money or property that the claimant may recover; rather, the natural inference would be the opposite—namely, that the funding was given for reasons of natural love and affection.[163]
- **Applications to stay** It used to be the case that applications against third parties were commonly accompanied by applications to stay the proceedings on the grounds of champertous maintenance, but this is less common now that the law of champerty has been put in its highly fact-sensitive modern context (see 30.13–30.16 and 30.25–30.28).

Discretion under the primary jurisdiction to make orders for security for costs

The court's task is to make an order that is just.[164] The test is whether the court is satisfied, having regard to all the circumstances of the case, that it is just to make an order for security for costs.[165] The court will not exercise its discretion to order security merely on the **15.57**

---

[157] See the ALF Code of Conduct.

[158] See *Bailey v GlaxoSmithKline UK Ltd* [2017] EWHC 3195 (QB), at [25]–[34]. See also *Northampton Coal Iron and Waggon Co v Midland Waggon Co* (1878) 7 Ch D 500, as followed by *Pure Spirit Company v Fowler* (1890) 25 QBD 235, both of which were cited by Longmore LJ in *Premier Motorauctions Ltd v PricewaterhouseCoopers LLP* [2017] EWCA Civ 1872, at [37].

[159] After *Arkin v Borchard Lines Ltd* [2005] EWCA Civ 655.

[160] See *Bailey v GlaxoSmithKline UK Ltd* [2017] EWHC 3195 (QB), at [59].

[161] See *ibid*, at [61].

[162] *The RBS Rights Issue Litigation (No 2)* [2017] EWHC 1217 (Ch), at [16].

[163] See *Chilab v Kings College London* [2012] EWCA 1178, at [7]–[10], *per* Hughes LJ.

[164] *Fernhill Mining Ltd v Kier Construction Ltd* (unreported), 27 January 2000, CA, at [52], *per* Evans LJ. Popplewell J has explained that the aim is to avoid injustice to a claimant who has a meritorious claim and who may be prevented from bringing the claim or for whom such an order would represent a major hurdle in the path that the claimant must follow to obtain justice: see *Bluewaters Communications Holdings LLC v Ecclestone* [2018] EWHC 78 (Comm), at [27]. He went on to say that evidence would be required in this regard.

[165] CPR, r 25.13(1)(a).

basis that one of the preconditions mentioned above has been satisfied.[166] Whilst the court has repeatedly reminded itself that it has the freedom to take into account any admissible circumstances that it deems to be relevant,[167] the power should not be used to discriminate against persons on grounds unrelated to enforcement.[168]

15.58 Whilst it was formulated pre-CPR, the following forensic sieve formulated by counsel in a case before Denning MR is still regarded as being of general assistance:

> '[T]he matters which the court should take into account in considering whether anything tells in favour of the impecunious company and against making an order are: (1) whether the plaintiff's case is bona fide and not a sham; (2) whether the plaintiff has a reasonably good prospect of success on his part of the claim; (3) whether there has been an admission, formal or informal, in the course of the proceedings, of some part of the plaintiff's claim; (4) whether there has been a payment into court, or its equivalent in arbitration proceedings, of a substantial sum which indicates that the plaintiff's claim is not merely a nuisance value claim; (5) whether there are any grounds for thinking that the defendants are using the application to prevent the plaintiff's case from coming before an adjudicating tribunal; (6) whether an order for security might enable a defendant to, defeat a claim on the ground of the plaintiff's impecuniosity which the defendant himself has caused; and (7) whether the defendant applicant for security has been guilty of delay in making the application.'[169]

Merits of the claim and discretion regarding security for costs (first instance)

15.59 The Commercial Court Guide has the following to say on the topic (which, for the reasons given below, is of general application in so far as claims at first instances are concerned):

> 'Investigation of the merits of the case on an application for security is strongly discouraged. It is usually only in those cases where it can be shown without detailed investigation of evidence or law that the claim is certain or almost certain to succeed or fail will the merits be taken into consideration.'[170]

15.60 If the strengths and weaknesses of the claim at first instance can be discerned without prolonged examination of voluminous evidence, it is open to the court to take the merits of the case into account.[171] Where the claimant seeks to rely on the strength of its case, this will be a relevant factor only where it can be shown that the claim is 'highly likely to succeed'.[172] If that is the case, then the court will, in general, either make no order for

---

166 See *Nasser v United Bank of Kuwait* [2002] EWCA Civ 556, at [56]–[61]; see also *Kahangi v Nourizadeh* [2009] EWHC 2451 (QB), at [11], *per* Eady J.

167 Whilst pre-CPR cases, *Sir Lindsay Parkinson & Co Ltd v Triplan Ltd* [1973] QB 609, at 623, and *Keary Developments Ltd v Tarmac Construction Ltd* [1995] 3 All ER 534, at 539, are both frequently cited on this point. See also *Dominion Brewery v Foster* (1897) 77 LT 507.

168 *Nasser v United Bank of Kuwait* [2002] EWCA Civ 556, at [56]–[61].

169 *Sir Lindsay Parkinson & Co Ltd v Triplan Ltd* [1973] QB 609, at 623.

170 *Commercial Court Guide*, 10th edn, Appendix 10.

171 *Porzelack KG v Porzelack (UK) Ltd* [1987] 1 All ER 1074; see also *Dena Technology (Thailand) Ltd & Anor v Dena Technology Ltd & Anor* [2014] EWHC 616 (Comm), at [7], *per* Leggatt J.

172 This is a long-established principle: see *Porzelack KG v Porzelack (UK) Ltd* [1987] 1 All ER 1074, at 1077, *per* Browne-Wilkinson V-C; *Keary Developments Ltd v Tarmac Construction Ltd* [1995] 3 All ER 534, at 540, *per* Peter Gibson LJ. More recently, see *Bluewaters Communications Holdings LLC v Ecclestone* [2018] EWHC 78 (Comm), at [6]–[9] and [12], in which Popplewell J declined to find that admissions made in other proceedings were sufficient to meet the threshold (although he did describe them as 'weighty considerations').

security for costs[173] or it will make an order for an amount that is less than would otherwise have been ordered.[174] The fact that a claim is highly likely to fail may also be a relevant factor in certain circumstances.[175]

Browne-Wilkinson V-C had this to say about the extent to which the court should examine the merits of a claim at first instance: **15.61**

> 'Undoubtedly, if it can clearly be demonstrated that the plaintiff is likely to succeed, in the sense that there is a very high probability of success, then that is a matter that can properly be weighed in the balance. Similarly, if it can be shown that there is a very high probability that the defendant will succeed, that is a matter that can be weighed. But for myself I deplore the attempt to go into the merits of the case unless it can be clearly demonstrated one way or another that there is a high degree of probability of success or failure.'[176]

A similar point was made by Eady J: **15.62**

> 'A vitally important principle for me to have in mind in the instant case ... is that the court should not, upon such an application, enter into the merits of the case in any detail, save in the exceptional case where one party or the other can demonstrate a high degree of probability of success.'[177]

Where a case will turn on oral evidence rather than documentary evidence, it will generally not be the case that the court will find that a case is 'highly likely' to succeed.[178] Browne-Wilkinson V-C has confirmed that the court may take into account any open offer,[179] this being potentially indicative of the parties' belief in the strength of their respective cases. For obvious reasons, the court will not take into account inadmissible offers (see 15.125). When it chooses to take an offer into account, the court will bear in mind that the offer may have been made for commercial reasons as opposed to for reasons that reflect the advice the parties have received.[180] **15.63**

Merits of the claim and discretion regarding security for costs (appeals)

Appeals are not generally treated in the same way as described at 15.61–15.63. This is because the court will already know a great deal about the claim. In this regard, Briggs J had this to say: **15.64**

> 'The starting point is not that the court simply has no idea [about the merits] ... I bear in mind that there is an appeal which is not suggested to be fanciful or lacking any real prospect

---

[173] See, eg, *Al-Koronky & Anor v Time Life Entertainments Group Ltd* [2005] EWHC 1688 (QB), at [33]; see also *Keary Developments Ltd v Tarmac Construction Ltd* [1995] 3 All ER 534, at 539 and 540; *Kahangi v Nourizadeh* [2009] EWHC 2451 (QB), at [8], *per* Eady J; cf *Northampton Regional Livestock Centre Co v Cowling* [2013] EWHC 1720 (QB), in which the court found that the claimant was merely likely to succeed and therefore that this was not a reason not to make an order.

[174] See, eg, *Dena Technology (Thailand Ltd) v Dena Technology Ltd* [2014] EWHC 616 (Comm), in which Leggatt J reduced the amount of security by 50 per cent to take account of the fact that the claimants had a high prospect of success.

[175] See, eg, *Newman v Wenden Properties Ltd* [2007] EWHC 336 (TCC).

[176] *Porzelack KG v Porzelack (UK) Ltd* [1987] 1 All ER 1074, at 1077.

[177] *Al-Koronky & Anor v Time Life Entertainments Group Ltd* [2005] EWHC 1688 (QB), at [33]; see also *Keary Developments Ltd v Tarmac Construction Ltd* [1995] 3 All ER 534, at 539 and 540.

[178] See, eg, *Bluewaters Communications Holdings LLC v Ecclestone* [2018] EWHC 78 (Comm), at [10], *per* Popplewell J.

[179] See *Porzelack KG v Porzelack (UK) Ltd* [1987] 1 WLR 420, at 423.

[180] *Ibid*. See also *Sir Lindsay Parkinson & Co Ltd v Triplan Ltd* [1973] QB 609, at 623, *per* Denning MR.

of success. Against those conclusions the court does not, as it usually does in a first instance security case, start with there having been no investigation of the merits by any tribunal at any level at all.'[181]

The relevance of counterclaims to applications for security for costs and the Crabtree *principle*

15.65 Where a defendant seeks (or where both parties seek) security for costs, the fact that there is a counterclaim may be relevant. Security will usually not be ordered where, if it were to be ordered, but unpaid, and the claim were to be struck out, the issues would be litigated anyway on the counterclaim[182]—colloquially known as the *Crabtree* principle.[183] This principle is intended to avoid the creation of one-sided litigation. In any event, it would normally not be appropriate to make an order for security of costs in favour of either party if to do so would, for practical purposes, give that party security for the costs of its own claim or counterclaim.[184] The same is broadly true where security is sought by a claimant in respect of a counterclaim that raises issues which are largely the same as those raised by the claim.[185]

15.66 As is explained below, much will turn on whether the counterclaim can be said to have 'independent vitality'. If it does not have independent vitality (that is, if the counterclaim can be said to be, in substance, a mere defence to the claim), then an order may be made against the claimant; if it does have independent vitality, the appropriate order will ordinarily be that both parties provide security (where this is appropriate) or that neither party does so.[186]

15.67 Hamblen LJ has explained that the essential question to be considered is whether, in substance, the defendant was doing more than simply defending themselves in that they were launching a counterclaim with an 'independent vitality' of their own.[187] This test drew upon the following formulation, with which Bingham LJ clarified that the test is one of substance rather than form: 'So the question may arise, as a question of substance, not formality or pleading: is the defendant simply defending himself, or is he going beyond mere self-defence and launching a cross-claim with an independent vitality of its own?'[188]

15.68 Richard Millett QC (sitting as a deputy judge of the High Court) had this to say about the independent vitality test:

> 'The whole point about the independent vitality test is that you can say that even if the claimant had not sued, the defendant could and would have made his own claim, such that it can continue if the claim is dismissed or falls away.'[189]

---

[181] *Calltel Telecom Ltd & Anor v HM Revenue & Customs* [2008] EWHC 2107 (Ch), at [17]; see also *Ahmed v Blackburn & Co* [2001] EWCA Civ 141, at [10], where May LJ took into account that the judge who gave permission to appeal did not give 'undue encouragement' to the appellant.

[182] *BJ Crabtree (Insulation) Ltd v GPT Communication Systems Ltd* (1990) 59 BLR 43.

[183] See, eg, the use of the phrase in *Ardila Investments NV v ENRC NV* [2015] EWHC 1667 (Comm), at [60], *per* Simon J; *Hniadzdzilau v Vajgel* [2015] EWHC 1582 (Ch), at [7] and [10], *per* Mr Richard Millett QC (sitting as a deputy judge of the High Court).

[184] See *Anglo Irish Asset Finance Plc v Flood* [2011] EWCA Civ 799.

[185] See *Anglo Petroleum Ltd v TFB Mortgages Ltd* [2004] EWHC 1177 (Ch).

[186] *Dawnus Sierra Leone Ltd v Timis Mining Corporation Ltd* [2016] EWCA Civ 1066, at [30], *per* Hamblen LJ.

[187] *Ibid*, at [23].

[188] *Hutchison Telephone (UK) Ltd v Ultimate Response Ltd* [1993] BCLC 307, at 317. See also *Mapleson v Masini* (1879) 5 QBD 144, at 147, *per* Field J: 'The substantial position of the parties must always be looked at.'

[189] *Hniazdzilau v Vajgel* [2015] EWHC 1582 (Ch), at [17].

In commercial litigation, the question of whether a party is a claimant or a defendant is frequently a matter of who won the race to issue proceedings. In recognition of this, the court may exercise its discretion against making an order for security if the effect of such an order would be to give one of the parties an undeserved advantage. In this regard, Bingham LJ had this to say: 15.69

> '[Making an order for security] would have the effect . . . of preventing the plaintiffs pursuing their claim. It would, however, leave the defendants free to pursue their counterclaim. The plaintiffs could then defend themselves against the counterclaim although their own claim was stayed. ... [In the] course of defending the counterclaim all the same matters would be canvassed as [they] would be canvassed if the plaintiffs were to pursue their claim, but on that basis they would defend the claim and advance their own in a somewhat hobbled manner, and would be conducting the litigation (to change the metaphor) with one hand tied behind their back. I have to say that that does not appeal to me on the facts of this case as a just or attractive way to oblige a party to conduct its litigation.'[190]

In a similar vein, Lawton LJ has explained that where both parties claim to be entitled to damages and where it was mere chance that one started the claim before the other could get in a claim, both should be treated alike.[191] As has been mentioned above, this may mean that security is ordered against neither or both.

The following miscellaneous points may be made. 15.70

- **Overlap of costs** Whilst it should not be regarded as being a simple rule of thumb,[192] the court will generally not make an order for security of costs of a claim if the costs incurred in defending the claim would also be incurred in prosecuting the counterclaim.[193]
- **Overlap of the facts relied upon** The fact that a counterclaim is based on the same facts as the claim is a factor in favour of it being a counterpart of the defence.[194] This, however, would not be determinative of the issue.[195]
- **Significant disparity between claim and counterclaim** The fact that a counterclaim is for a significantly greater amount that the claim may indicate that it has independent

[190] See *BJ Crabtree (Insulation) Ltd v GPT Communications Systems Ltd* (1990) 59 BLR 43, at 49. On a similar point, see *Anglo Petroleum v TFB* [2003] EWHC 1177.

[191] *Samuel J Cohl Co v Eastern Mediterranean Maritime Ltd ('The Silver Fir')* [1980] 1 Lloyd's Rep 371, at 374. See also *Hutchison Telephone (UK) Ltd v Ultimate Response Ltd* [1993] BCLC 307, at 317, *per* Bingham LJ, confirming *Neck v Taylor* [1893] 1 QB 560, at 562, *per* Esher MR; *Thistle Hotels Ltd v Gamma Four Ltd* [2004] EWHC 322 (Ch), at [30], *per* Sonia Proudman QC (sitting as a High Court judge).

[192] See Morgan J's comments on this in *Pannone LLP v Aardvark Digital Ltd* [2013] EWHC 686 (Ch), at [19]. See also *BJ Crabtree (Insulation) Ltd v GPT Communication Systems Ltd* (1990) 59 BLR 43, at 49, in which Bingham LJ said that there could be 'no rule of thumb as to the grant or refusal of an order for security in the circumstances'. Similarly, see *Peak Hotels & Resorts Ltd v Tarek Investments Ltd & Ors* [2015] EWHC 386 (Ch), at [71], *per* Henderson J.

[193] *Dumrul v Standard Chartered Bank* [2010] EWHC 2625 (Comm), at [5] *per* Hamblen J. See also *Mapleson v Masini* (1879–80) LR 5 QBD 144; *Anglo Irish Asset Finance Plc v Flood* [2011] EWCA Civ 799. In *Anglo Petroleum v TFB* [2003] EWHC 1177, at [32], Park J said: 'In general, the courts recognise that, where there are cross-proceedings, the position is as I have described, and the courts do not order a person in the position of A to provide security for the costs of the claim he is making himself.'

[194] Whilst a pre-CPR case, see *Ashworth v Berkeley-Walbrood Ltd* (1989) The Independent, 9 October, CA.

[195] See *Samuel J Cohl Co v Eastern Mediterranean Maritime Ltd ('The Silver Fir')* [1980] 1 Lloyd's Rep 371; *Hutchison Telephone (UK) Ltd v Ultimate Response Ltd* [1993] BCLC 307, at 317. See also *Eminent Energy Ltd v Berkley Energy Services Ltd* [2016] EWHC 2585 (Comm), at [38] and [39], *per* Richard Salter QC (sitting as a deputy judge of the High Court).

vitality.[196] In particular, the fact that a counterclaim may overtop the claim is a factor that points towards the counterclaim being more than a counterpart of the defence, but, again, it is not determinative of the issue.[197]

- **Relevance of a link to the same transaction** The fact that a counterclaim arises out of the same transaction as the claim does not mean that it is the counterpart of the defence.[198]
- **Partial overlap** Where the claim raises factual inquiries that are not the subject of the counterclaim (that is, where the overlap between the claim and the counterclaim is only partial), an order for security for costs may be appropriate notwithstanding the fact that the claim provides a defence to the counterclaim.[199] Such an order would normally be limited to the costs of addressing additional issues raised solely by the claim,[200] but this would not be mandatory.[201] There is no requirement that the court should vex itself with any rule similar to that in *Medway Oil*.[202]
- **Competing claims for an order for security** Where both parties carry on business outside the jurisdiction, and where each claims against the other as parties who have been badly treated and who have suffered damage, then it is permissible to treat them both alike and to make orders against both of them.[203] That said, cross-orders for security usually arise in the context of arbitration;[204] where the proceedings are solely conducted in a court, it would generally (but not always) be appropriate to make no order rather than to make cross-orders for security.[205]
- ***Dumrul* undertakings** It may be that a defendant wishes to say, in an attempt to persuade the court that their claim does not have independent vitality, that their counterclaim will not be pursued if the claim is not pursued. This is referred to as a *Dumrul* undertaking,[206] being an undertaking to give up the counterclaim if the claimant was ordered to, but failed to put up security so that their claim was dismissed. Where such an

196 See, eg, *L/M International Construction Inc v Circle Partnership Ltd* [1995] CLY 4010, CA.

197 *Hutchison Telephone (UK) Ltd v Ultimate Response Ltd* [1993] BCLC 307, at 317, *per* Bingham LJ. See also *Newman v Wenden Properties Ltd* [2007] EWHC 336 (TCC).

198 *Hutchison Telephone (UK) Ltd v Ultimate Response Ltd* [1993] BCLC 307, at 317; see also *Samuel J Cohl Co v Eastern Mediterranean Maritime Ltd ('The Silver Fir')* [1980] 1 Lloyd's Rep 371, CA.

199 See, eg, *Shaw-Lloyd v ASM Shipping* [2006] EWHC 1958 (QB); *Newman v Wenden Properties Ltd* [2007] EWHC 336 (TCC).

200 *Dumrul v Standard Chartered Bank* [2010] EWHC 2625 (Comm), at [8]. For an example of how costs may be apportioned, see *Ultimate Utilities Ltd v McNicholas Construction Services Ltd* (unreported), 9 April 2014, QBD (TCC), in which Ramsey J found that a third of the costs related to the claim, another third related to the counterclaim and the remaining third related to both, then made an order that gave security for only the third that related to the claim. Similarly, see *Peak Hotels & Resorts Ltd v Tarek Investments Ltd & Ors* [2015] EWHC 386 (Ch), at [71], *per* Henderson J. See also *Formula E Holdings Ltd v CDC Entertainment Ltd* [2015] EWHC 2110 (Comm), at [34], *per* Flaux J.

201 See, eg, *Jones v Environcom Ltd & Anor* [2009] EWHC 16 (Comm), at [24]–[26]; see also *Petromin SA v Secnav Marine Ltd* [1995] 1 Lloyd's Rep 603, QBD.

202 *Medway Oil and Storage Co Ltd v Continental Contractors Ltd* [1929] AC 88.

203 *Samuel J Cohl Co v Eastern Mediterranean Maritime Ltd ('The Silver Fir')* [1980] 1 Lloyd's Rep 371, *per* Lawton LJ.

204 In *Autoweld Systems Ltd v Kito Enterprises LLC* [2010] EWCA Civ 1469, at [43], Black LJ said of *The Silver Fir*: 'It is of note that this was an arbitration between two foreign corporations and the Court of Appeal were fortified in their conclusion by the way in which matters were dealt with in commercial arbitrations elsewhere in Europe.'

205 *Apex Global Management Ltd (sub nom in the matter of Fi Call Ltd) v FI Call Ltd* [2014] EWHC 779 (Ch), at [43], *per* Newey J.

206 After *Dumrul v Standard Chartered Bank* [2010] EWHC 2625 (Comm), at [13(ff)].

undertaking is offered, this is a factor that the court is able to take into account.[207] That said, Hamblen LJ has explained that this would not be a consideration of particular significance in addressing the question of whether a counterclaim has independent vitality, the answer to which question will primarily depend on an analysis of the substance of the claims being made and the inferences to be drawn therefrom.[208]

- **Merits** Where the claim has no reasonable prospects of success, this may be a factor that would pull in the direction of an order being made against a claimant notwithstanding the matters set out above.[209]
- **Need for review** The status of a counterclaim is capable of review—in particular, of the nature and size of a counterclaim, which may change as the claim progresses.[210]

Plural litigants and discretion regarding security for costs

The fact that a claimant has a co-claimant who is resident in the jurisdiction will not, of itself, preclude an order being made.[211] The fact that a co-claimant would be able to proceed with the claim even if an order were to be made against another co-claimant would not be a reason for not making an order.[212] **15.71**

Residency, conduct and discretion regarding security for costs

Conduct may play a part in the decision to make an order. A refusal to provide full disclosure, for example, may lead to an order;[213] a history of not complying with orders to pay costs (either in this jurisdiction or elsewhere) may be another factor,[214] as may a lack of probity.[215] However, past compliance may not be sufficient to avoid being ordered to pay security. In a case with a tortuous procedural history, Rix LJ found that whilst payments had been made 'in the circumstances which arose in the past, [when] it was in the interests of [the appellant] not to be put into deliberate and longstanding contempt of court', he could not be sure that those circumstances would exist in the future.[216] **15.72**

The mere fact that a person is resident outside a contracting state would be not sufficient to justify an order for security being made.[217] Such an approach would be discriminatory **15.73**

---

[207] Whilst *obiter*, see *Hniazdzilau v Vajgel* [2015] EWHC 1582 (Ch), at [22].

[208] *Dawnus Sierra Leone Ltd v Timis Mining Corporation Ltd* [2016] EWCA Civ 1066, at [28].

[209] See, eg, *Newman v Wenden Properties Ltd* [2007] EWHC 336 (TCC).

[210] *Camden London Borough Council v Makers UK Ltd* [2009] EWHC 605 (TCC), at [47], *per* Akenhead J.

[211] *Slazengers Ltd v Seaspeed Ferries International Ltd* [1987] 3 All ER 967, CA. This will be particularly so where the person within a contracting state has been added solely for the purposes of defeating an application for security for costs: whilst on a slightly different point, see *Jones and Saldanha v Gurney* [1913] WN 72, *per* Swinfen Eady J. See also *John Bishop (Caterers) Ltd v National Union Bank* [1973] 3 All ER 707.

[212] *Okotcha v Voest Alpine Intertrading GmbH* [1993] BCLC 474.

[213] See, eg, *Société Générale SA v Saad Trading, Contracting & Financial Services Co* [2013] EWCA Civ 1020.

[214] See, eg, *Bannai v Erez* [2013] EWHC 3204 (Comm), in which Burton J made an order against a party who, in addition to having no assets in this country, had failed to pay orders for costs made against it in Egypt.

[215] See, eg, *De Beer v Kanaar & Co (a firm) (No 1)* [2001] EWCA Civ 1318, at [73] and [89]–[91], *per* Jonathan Parker LJ (giving judgment of the Court), in which it was said that where there had been a lack of probity on the part of the claimant and there was a 'risk' that an order for costs would be difficult or impossible to enforce, then it may be appropriate to award security representing the entirety of the defendant's costs.

[216] *Michael Wilson & Partners v Sinclair* [2013] EWCA Civ 131, at [8].

[217] See *Al-Koronky & Anor v Time Life Entertainments Group Ltd* [2005] EWHC 1688 (QB), at [23], *per* Eady J, referring to *Nasser v United Bank of Kuwait* [2001] EWCA Civ 556. See also *Berkeley Administration Inc v McClelland* [1990] 2 QB 407, CA; *Somerset-Leeke & Anor v Kay Trustees* [2003] EWHC 1243 (Ch), at [9]–[12], *per* Jacob J.

and contrary to Art 14 ECHR.[218] The court adopts a more flexible approach in that discretion should be exercised on objectively justified grounds relating to obstacles to, or the burden of, enforcement in the context of the particular country concerned.[219] Gloster LJ has explained that the test is not whether there is a likelihood (that is, on the balance of probabilities) of substantial obstacles to enforcement, but merely that there is a real risk of such obstacles.[220] She went on to say that:

> '[It] is sufficient for an applicant for security for costs simply to adduce evidence to show that "on objectively justified grounds relating to obstacles to or the burden of enforcement", there is a real risk that it will not be in a position to enforce an order for costs against the claimant/appellant and that, in all the circumstances, it is just to make an order for security. Obviously there must be "a proper basis for considering that such obstacles may exist or that enforcement may be encumbered by some extra burden" but whether the evidence is sufficient in any particular case to satisfy the judge that there is a real risk of serious obstacles to enforcement, will depend on the circumstances of the case.'[221]

15.74 Mance LJ has explained that the mere absence of reciprocal arrangements or legislation providing for enforcement of foreign judgments could not of itself justify an inference that enforcement would not be possible.[222] There is no need to adduce evidence of the obvious: he noted that there are parts of the world in which the natural assumption would be not only that there would be substantial obstacles to enforcement, but also that enforcement may be impossible, and that there are other areas in which enforcement would be difficult and would involve an additional burden of costs or delay.[223] Mance LJ seems to have implied that these issues could be addressed by way of judicial notice without inquiry. This may be an important point because it may, on occasion, be difficult to find a witness (such as a local lawyer) who is willing to give evidence about the relevant legal system. Eady J appeared to accept that this was a factor that may be taken into account when evaluating the evidence.[224] Documents published by international commentators, courts and trade journals may be relevant in this regard.[225]

The influence of assets within a contracting state on whether an order security for costs should be made

15.75 Where a claimant is resident outside a contracting state, but has assets within a contracting state, then the court will take into account the integrity of the claimant. If that is not in

---

[218] In this regard, Gloster LJ has commented that CPR, r 25.13(2)(a), is inherently potentially discriminatory: see *Bestfort Developments LLP v Ras Al Khaimah Investment Authority* [2016] EWCA Civ 1099, at [53]–[56].

[219] *Nasser v United Bank of Kuwait* [2002] EWCA Civ 556, at [56]–[61].

[220] *Bestfort Developments LLP v Ras Al Khaimah Investment Authority* [2016] EWCA Civ 1099, at [74].

[221] *Ibid*, at [77].

[222] *Nasser v United Bank of Kuwait* [2001] EWCA Civ 556, at [65].

[223] *Ibid*, at [64]. More recently, Cockerill J has noted that '[w]hilst there must be some proper basis for considering that such problems [with enforcement] exist, the court will take note of obvious realities': *Danilina v Chernukhin* [2018] EWHC 39 (Com), at [20].

[224] *Kahangi v Nourizadeh* [2009] EWHC 2451 (QB), at [13]–[20] (taking into account evidence from a local lawyer, who was anonymous).

[225] For an example of the type of material that may be relied upon, see *ibid*, at [14] *et seq*.

doubt, the court will, in general, not conclude that there is a risk that steps will be taken to put the assets beyond reach. If, however, the claimant's integrity is in doubt, then the court will examine the nature of the assets to form a view as to how easily they may be put beyond reach.[226] The court may consider making an order that the assets are not to be removed from the contracting state without the consent of the defendant or an order of the court.[227]

The financial position of the parties and its relevance to the exercise of discretion

In so far as impecuniosity is concerned, there are two competing factors at play:[228] first (and subject to what is said below), the court will seek to prevent an impecunious claimant using their inability to pay as a weapon in the litigation;[229] but secondly, the court will seek not to make an order that will stifle the claim. To strike a balance, the court will take into account the relative financial strengths of the parties.[230] **15.76**

The risk of stifling the claim is discussed in detail at 15.83–15.89. The extent to which the court is able to give effect to the first of these factors has been diminished by the Human Rights Act 1998 (HRA 1998) and by modern attitudes towards access to justice.[231] Mance LJ has explained that the modern emphasis on access to justice means that the court will not make an order based only on the bare fact that a claimant would be unable to meet a costs order made against it.[232] **15.77**

Evidence of the financial status of the claimant and of the role of the defendant Where a claimant seeks to resist an order for security on the grounds of their own impecuniosity, the onus would be on them to prove that assertion. In so doing, the claimant would be expected to make full and frank disclosure,[233] and this may include evidence to show that there will be no funds forthcoming from any outside source, such as creditors or shareholders.[234] That requirement is not incompatible with Art 6 ECHR.[235] If the claimant chooses not to disclose up-to-date accounts, then they may fail to prove sufficient liquidity to discharge an order.[236] If the claimant fails to give full disclosure, then an application may be renewed once the true facts come to light.[237] **15.78**

---

226 *Leyvand v Barasch* [2000] All ER (D) 181, at [6], *per* Lightman J.

227 See, eg, *De Bry v Fitzgeral* [1990] 1 WLR 552; *Kevorkian v Burney (No 2)* [1937] 4 All ER 468.

228 *Keary Developments Ltd v Tarmac Construction Ltd* [1995] 3 All ER 534, at 540.

229 This is a long-established principle: see *Pearson v Naydler* [1977] 3 All ER 531, at 537; *Keary Developments Ltd v Tarmac Construction Ltd* [1995] 3 All ER 534, at 540.

230 *Classic Catering Ltd v Donnington Park Leisure Ltd* [2001] 1 BCLC 537, *per* Judge Weeks (sitting as a judge of the High Court).

231 For a general discussion of a related topic, see *Hamilton v Al Fayed & Ors* [2002] EWCA Civ 665, at [40]–[43], *per* Simon Brown LJ.

232 *Nasser v United Bank of Kuwait* [2001] EWCA Civ 556, at [34].

233 *M V Yorke Motors (a firm) v Edwards* [1982] 1 All ER 1024, at 1027, *per* Lord Diplock; affirmed post-CPR in *Anglo-Eastern Trust Ltd & Anor v Kermanshahchi* [2002] EWCA Civ 198.

234 See *Kufaan Publishing Elements v Al-Warrack Publishing Ltd* [2000] Lexis Citation 2833, at [34], *per* Potter LJ; *Hearst Holdings Inc v AVELA Inc* [2015] EWCA Civ 470, at [25], *per* Sir Colin Rimer. See also *Formula E Holdings Ltd v CDC Entertainment Ltd* [2015] EWHC 2110 (Comm), at [37], *per* Flaux J.

235 *Mahan Air v Blue Sky One Ltd* [2011] EWCA Civ 544, at [38], *per* Stanley Burnton LJ.

236 *Trade Storage Ltd v Papanicola* [2011] EWHC 598 (Ch).

237 See, eg, *Rajvel Construction Ltd v Bestville Properties Ltd* [2012] EWCA Civ 587.

15.79 Where the defendant has caused or contributed to the claimant's impecuniosity, that is a factor that the court is able to take into account.[238] Whilst in a pre-CPR case, Bowen LJ highlighted the injustice of allowing a defendant to benefit from having wrongly caused the claimant to become impecunious:

> 'Suppose the Plaintiff in that case had been right on the point of law, his insolvency would have arisen from the wrongful act complained of in the action. To have required a security for costs on the ground of an insolvency which (if the Plaintiff was right) the Defendant had wrongly caused might have been a denial of justice.'[239]

The court is not always so accommodating towards the claimant, however, especially where the court does not have sufficient evidence before it to test the claimant's claim that its lack of funds arose out of the negligence of another party.[240]

15.80 **The relevance of access to funding** The fact that a party does not have capital does not mean that funds could not be raised.[241] In considering whether the claimant would be able to provide security, the court is able to take into account the resources of third parties who could reasonably be expected to assist, which may, in the case of a corporate claimant, include shareholders[242] or associated companies; in the case of an individual claimant, this may include friends and relatives.[243] Briggs J has commented that a factor to be taken into account is the likelihood that the third party in question would be likely to make the payment voluntarily if an adverse costs order were to be made.[244] Where appropriate, the court may also expect the claimant to explain why it would not be possible to obtain litigation funding to allow the claim to continue.[245]

15.81 **Wealth and whether an order for security for costs should be made** In the same way as impecuniosity will not be determinative of whether an order for security should be made, even significant wealth on the part of the claimant will not be a complete answer to an application where other enforcement problems are raised.[246]

---

238 See *Aidiniantz v Sherlock Holmes International Society Ltd* [2015] EWHC 2882 (Ch), at [64] and [67]–[72], *per* Henderson J. Whilst a pre-CPR case, see *Farrer v Lacy, Hartland & Co* (1885) 28 Ch D 482, at 485, *per* Bowen LJ. See also *Aquila Design (GRB) Products Ltd v Cornhill Insurance plc* [1988] BCLC 134, CA, at 137, *per* Fox LJ; *Keary Developments Ltd v Tarmac Construction Ltd* [1995] 3 All ER 534, at 540.

239 *Farrer v Lacy, Hartland & Co* (1885) 28 Ch D 482, at 485. See also *Calltel Telecom Ltd & Anor v HM Revenue & Customs* [2008] EWHC 2107 (Ch), at [16], *per* Briggs J; *Keary Developments Ltd v Tarmac Construction Ltd* [1995] 3 All ER 534, at 540, *per* Peter Gibson LJ (it might not be ordered 'particularly where the failure to meet the claim might in itself have been a material cause of the plaintiff's impecuniosity'). See also *Sir Lindsay Parkinson v Triplan* [1973] QB 609, at 626H, *per* Lord Denning MR (the court 'will also consider whether the company's want of means has been brought about by any conduct of the defendant, such as delay in payment or delay in doing their part of the work').

240 In *Arts & Antiques Ltd v Richards* [2013] EWHC 3361 (Comm), at [62], *per* Hamblen J.

241 See *Ultimate Utilities Ltd v McNicholas Construction Services Ltd* (unreported), 9 April 2014, QBD (TCC), in which Ramsey J applied *M V Yorke Motors (a firm) v Edwards* [1982] 1 All ER 1024.

242 As a contrary example, see *Ipartner PTE Shipping Ltd v Panacore Resources DMCC* [2015] EWHC 1098 (Comm), in which Blair J accepted that there was evidence that shareholders would not be willing to fund the litigation.

243 Whilst *obiter*, see the comments of Rimer LJ in *Conroy v National Westminster Bank* [2009] EWCA Civ 1199, at [31]. See also *Brimko Holdings Ltd v Eastman Kodak Co* [2004] EWHC 1343 (Ch), *per* Park J; *Al-Koronky & Anor v Time Life Entertainments Group Ltd* [2005] EWHC 1688 (QB), at [32].

244 *Calltel Telecom Ltd & Anor v HM Revenue & Customs* [2008] EWHC 2107 (Ch), at [23].

245 See, eg, *Kolyada v Yurov* [2014] EWHC 2575 (Comm), at [30], *per* Mr S Rainey QC (sitting as a judge of the High Court).

246 *Kahangi v Nourizadeh* [2009] EWHC 2451 (QB), at [12], *per* Eady J.

The possibility of stifling the claim As explained at 15.76–15.77, the court will strive not make an order that will stifle the claim.[247] Peter Gibson LJ had this to say about the possibility of oppression (albeit prior to the introduction of the HRA 1998 and the CPR): 15.82

> 'The court must carry out a balancing exercise. On the one hand it must weigh the injustice to the plaintiff if prevented from pursuing a proper claim by an order for security. Against that, it must weigh the injustice to the defendant if no security is ordered and at the trial the plaintiff's claim fails and the defendant finds himself unable to recover from the plaintiff the costs which have been incurred by him in his defence of the claim.'[248]

Gibson LJ went on to say this: 15.83

> 'The court will properly be concerned not to allow the power to order security to be used as an instrument of oppression, such as by stifling a genuine claim by an indigent company against a more prosperous company, particularly when the failure to meet that claim might in itself have been a material cause of the plaintiff's impecuniosity ... But it will also be concerned not to be so reluctant to order security that it becomes a weapon whereby the impecunious company can use its inability to pay costs as a means of putting unfair pressure on the more prosperous company.'[249]

Where the claimant seeks to avoid an order on the grounds that it would stifle the claim, the onus is on the claimant to prove that assertion.[250] They do not need to show with certainty that the claim will be stifled; it would be sufficient to show that this was more likely than not.[251] Merely showing that there would be a risk of the claim being stifled, however, would not be sufficient;[252] the claimant would have to show something more than a mere discouraging effect, for it has been established since well before the introduction of the CPR that the possibility or probability that the claimant will be deterred from pursuing its claim by an order for security is not, without more, a sufficient reason for not ordering security.[253] 15.84

Rix LJ has confirmed that the court may take into account not only the financial position of the claimant, but also the relative positions of the parties and the conduct of the defendant; if the defendant has sought, by its conduct, to the stifle the claim, then that too may be a factor to take into account.[254] That said, Foskett J has explained that the fact that 15.85

---

[247] *Goldtrail Travel Ltd v Aydin* [2017] UKSC 57, at [16]. See, eg, *Europa Holdings Ltd v Circle Industries (UK) plc* [1993] BCLC 320, CA; *Murray (Edmund) Ltd v BSP International Foundations Ltd* (1992) 33 Con LR 1, CA.

[248] *Keary Developments Ltd v Tarmac Construction Ltd* [1995] 3 All ER 534, at 540. This was a pre-CPR case, but it was cited with approval by Eady J in *Al-Koronky & Anor v Time Life Entertainments Group Ltd* [2005] EWHC 1688 (QB), at [28]. For a post-HRA 1998 example of the court not making an order because of concern about ECHR Art 6, see *Golubovich v Golubovich* [2011] EWCA Civ 528.

[249] *Keary Developments Ltd v Tarmac Construction Ltd* [1995] 3 All ER 534, at 540.

[250] *Goldtrail Travel Ltd v Aydin* [2017] UKSC 57, at [15]; *Kuenyehia v International Hospitals Group Ltd* [2007] EWCA Civ 274, at [26]–[27], *per* Tuckey LJ. See also *Radu v Houston* [2006] EWCA Civ 1575, at [19]; *Keary Developments Ltd v Tarmac Construction Ltd* [1995] 3 All ER 534, at 540–1; *Aquila Design (GRB) Products Ltd v Cornhill Insurance plc* [1988] BCLC 134, CA.

[251] *Trident International Freight Services Ltd v Manchester Ship Canal Co* [1990] BCLC 263, CA.

[252] See, eg, *Ultimate Utilities Ltd v McNicholas Construction Services Ltd* (unreported), 9 April 2014, QBD (TCC), *per* Ramsey J.

[253] See *Okotcha v Voest Alpine Intertrading GmbH* [1993] BCLC 474, at 479, *per* Bingham LJ; *Keary Developments Ltd v Tarmac Construction Ltd* [1995] 3 All ER 534, at 540, *per* Gibson LJ.

[254] *Pablo Star Ltd v Emirates Integrated Telecommunications Co* [2009] EWCA Civ 616, at [29]. As an example of this, see *Mastermailer Stationery Ltd v Sandison* (unreported), 20 April 2011, Ch D, in which Vos J found that the application for security had been geared to defeat the claim.

the defendant may be well funded and well able to afford to finance the litigation would not preclude the making of an order.[255]

15.86 The court is permitted to take into account financial support that directors, shareholders or other backers may be able to provide.[256] Because these are things that are peculiarly within the respondent's knowledge, the respondent will bear the burden of proving matters in that regard.[257] Where the party is backed by the government of a state, that too can be taken into account.[258]

15.87 The court will often be ready to draw inferences concerning a person's wealth. Thus considerable wealth in the recent past may be evidence (in an appropriate case) of the fact that a person continues to have control over assets.[259] Similarly, the fact that a supposedly impecunious person repeatedly appears by leading counsel may be a factor to be taken into account.[260] The fact that a company is continuing to raise finance for the purposes of trading may be relevant. Moore-Bick LJ, for example, was persuaded that, despite a claimant's finances being in a parlous state, the fact that it was still trading was evidence that an order would not stifle the claim.[261]

15.88 Longmore LJ has explained that because a stay immediately before a trial is similar in effect to an unless order, the court will be more inclined to accept that a claim is likely to be stifled if that assertion is made in the context of an application shortly before trial.[262] If the application is made in the context of an extant appeal where the judgment below is stayed pending the appeal and if lifting the stay on that judgment would stifle the appeal, it is an option to modify the stay so as to grant the respondent a degree of security for costs.[263]

15.89 As to the nature of evidence required, Eady J had this to say: 'There needs to be full, frank, clear and unequivocal evidence before I should draw any conclusion that a particular order will have the effect of stifling. The test is whether it is more likely than not.'[264] It is not uncommon to see expert reports analysing the claimant's financial situation.[265]

15.90 **Cross-undertakings as to damages** An order that a claimant gives security may, if that part is ultimately not ordered to pay costs, lead to that party suffering losses. Where this is

---

[255] See *Bailey v GlaxoSmithKline UK Ltd* [2017] EWHC 3195 (QB), at [76]. See also *LIC Telecommunications SARL v VTB Capital plc* (unreported), 14 July 2016, QBD (Comm), *per* Judge Waksman QC.

[256] *Goldtrail Travel Ltd v Aydin* [2017] UKSC 57, at [23].

[257] This is a principle that precedes the CPR: see *Flender Werft AG v Aegean Maritime Ltd* [1990] 2 Lloyd's Rep 27, *per* Saville J; *Keary Developments Ltd v Tarmac Construction Ltd* [1995] 3 All ER 534, at 541. Whilst *obiter*, see also *Kahangi v Nourizadeh* [2009] EWHC 2451 (QB), at [9], *per* Eady J.

[258] See, eg, *Trustees of Olympic Airlines SA Pension & Life Assurance Scheme v Olympic Airlines SA* [2013] EWCA Civ 218; *Olympic Airlines SA (in liquidation) v ACG Acquisition XX LLC* [2012] EWCA Civ 1659.

[259] See, eg, *Société Générale SA v Saad Trading, Contracting & Financial Services Co* [2012] EWCA Civ 695, at [44].

[260] See, eg, *Mireskandari v Solicitors Regulation Authority* [2013] EWHC 907 (Admin).

[261] *Daley v Environmental Recycling Technologies plc* [2009] EWCA Civ 1088, at [21]–[22].

[262] *Vedatech Corporation v Crystal Decisions (UK) Ltd* [2002] EWCA Civ 356, at [25]. See also *Spy Academy Ltd v Sahar International Inc* [2009] EWCA Civ 481.

[263] *North Shore Ventures Ltd v Anstead Holdings Inc* [2010] EWCA Civ 1634.

[264] *Al-Koronky & Anor v Time Life Entertainments Group Ltd* [2005] EWHC 1688 (QB), at [31].

[265] As an example of this, see *Chemistree Homecare Ltd v Roche Products Ltd* [2011] EWHC 1579 (Ch).

a risk, it is open to the court to order the applicant to give a cross-undertaking as to damages.[266] In this regard, the Commercial Courts Guide has the following to say:

> 'In appropriate cases an order for security for costs may only be made on terms that the applicant gives an undertaking to comply with any order that the Court may make if the court later finds that the order for security for costs has caused loss to the claimant and that the claimant should be compensated for such loss. Such undertakings are intended to compensate claimants in cases where no order for costs is ultimately made in favour of the applicant.'[267]

Late applications for security for costs

15.91 The Commercial Court Guide says that first applications for security for costs should be made no later than the case management conference and that, in any event, any application should not be left until close to the trial date (see 15.126).[268] That may be so, but applications may be made at any time (even post-judgment[269]). Where an application is made very late (for example shortly before trial), that is a factor that the court is able to take into account[270]—especially if the court finds that this has been done for tactical reasons.[271] One way in which late applications have been disposed of in the past (albeit only by consent) has been for security to be given in a form that can be given immediately—namely, a personal guarantee.[272] The result might be that the party making the application has to bear the risk as to the worthlessness of the personal guarantee, but that would be fair only if that party were responsible for the fact that the application was made so late.

15.92 Where a party seeks to defend an application on the basis that it had been made late, the mere fact that it could have been made earlier would not afford a defence; there would have to be disadvantage arising out of the delay before a defence could be successful.[273] Applications may be delayed for entirely proper reasons. It may, for example, be entirely proper to take time before issuing the application to seek the agreement of the party against whom the order is sought[274] or to wait until the claim has been fully pleaded.[275] That said, the fact that an application has been made late can be a significant factor against the applicant (not least because the fact that an application had been made late will usually mean

---

[266] See, eg, *Bailey v GlaxoSmithKline UK Ltd* [2017] EWHC 3195 (QB), at [82], *per* Foskett J. See also *The RBS Rights Issue Litigation (No 2)* [2017] EWHC 1217 (Ch), at [150], *per* Hildyard J; *Stokors SA & Ors v Ig Markets Ltd* [2012] EWCA Civ 1706, at [35].

[267] See *The Commercial Court Guide (incorporating The Admiralty Court Guide)* (10th edn, London: HMSO, 2017), Appx 10, para 5.

[268] *Ibid*, para 1.

[269] See *Republic of Djibouti v Boreh* [2016] EWHC 1035 (Comm), *per* Fluax J. See also *Excalibur Ventures LLC v Gulf Keystone Inc* [2013] EWHC 4278 (Comm).

[270] See, eg, *Dorchester Project Management Ltd v BNP Parabas Real Estate Advisory and Property Management UK Ltd* [2013] EWHC 4555 (Ch), at [54], *per* Proudman J.

[271] Whilst *obiter*, see *Bailey v GlaxoSmithKline UK Ltd* [2017] EWHC 3195 (QB), at [81], *per* Foskett J. As a contrary example, see *Bluewaters Communications Holdings LLC v Ecclestone* [2018] EWHC 78 (Comm), at [24], where Popplewell J found that it was 'perfectly reasonable for the defendants to wait until the Particulars of Claim had been served and to conduct the bulk of the work on preparing the defences before raising the question of security and seeking to identify the amount in which security would be sought'.

[272] *Inventors Friend Ltd v Leathes Prior* [2011] EWHC 2840 (QB).

[273] See *Balevents Ltd v Sartori* [2013] EWHC 2971 (Ch), at [24], *per* Morgan J.

[274] See, eg, *Shark AG (a company incorporated in Austria) v Monster Energy Co* (unreported), 6 September 2013, Ch D (Patents Court), *per* Master Bragge.

[275] *Bluewaters Communications Holdings LLC v Ecclestone* [2018] EWHC 78 (Comm), at [24], *per* Popplewell J.

that substantial costs have already been incurred).[276] Ward LJ had the following to say on the topic:

> 'I am satisfied that, when the judge came to exercise his discretion, he did not bear in mind what seems to me to be the crucial distinguishing fact in this case, that is the judge gave his judgment three weeks before a 20-day trial was listed for hearing. The claimant had already put up security in actual money, and was to be deemed to have put up further security through the operation of the Part 36 offers. That is one point. Secondly, because the trial is three weeks away, the order of security could not sensibly be made on the usual terms that the trial of the action be stayed.'[277]

15.93 Ward LJ went on to say that, in many cases, it would be oppressive to require a party to find large amounts of money immediately before trial.[278] Where the court does make an order for security for costs, the amount of that order may be reduced to take account of any difficulties that the tardiness of the application may have caused.[279] Teare J, for example, restricted the award to future costs only.[280]

The nature of the costs for which security is sought

15.94 The court has the power to make an order in respect of pre-action costs, but Coulson J has explained that the court should be slow to do so, expressing concern that if the pre-issue phase of the litigation were lengthy, the costs might be high, and that an order for security for costs may become penal in nature.[281] He also explained that particular caution ought to be exercised where the costs in respect of which the security is sought were incurred long before the proceedings were commenced, primarily because he believed that such costs were more likely to be disputed.

Cross liabilities, etc, and orders for security for costs

15.95 The fact that the defendant may already have an order in their favour (such as an order made in other proceedings) will not diminish the court's jurisdiction to make an order for security.[282] Where, however, the effect of a pre-existing freezing order is to provide sufficient security, this may be reason to decline to make an order.[283] Likewise, if the defendant has made admissions that equal or exceed the appropriate amount of security, it would be open to the court to decline to make an order on the basis that the defendant is, in effect, providing their own security.[284]

---

[276] See, eg, *Dorchester Project Management Ltd v BNP Parabas Real Estate Advisory and Property Management UK Ltd* [2013] EWHC 4555 (Ch), at [49], *per* Proudman J.

[277] *Vedatech Corporation v Crystal Decisions (UK) Ltd & Anor* [2002] EWCA Civ 356, at [20].

[278] *Ibid.* See also *Dorchester Project Management Ltd v BNP Parabas Real Estate Advisory and Property Management UK Ltd* [2013] EWHC 4555 (Ch), at [53], *per* Proudman J.

[279] See, eg, *RBIL v Ryhurst* [2011] EWHC 2209, [2011] BLR 721, in which the amount was discounted to take account of certain trading difficulties that had been caused by the lateness of the application.

[280] *Warren v Marsden* [2014] EWHC 4410 (Comm), at [21], where Teare J approved of the guidance given in The White Book 2014, para 25.12.6.

[281] *Lobster Group Ltd v Heidelberg Graphic Equipment Ltd* [2008] EWHC 413 (TCC), at [11]–[12].

[282] Whilst a pre-CPR case, see *Flender Werft AG v Aegean Maritime Ltd* [1990] 2 Lloyd's Rep 27, QBD, in which it was held that the fact that a defendant had an arbitral award against the claimant did not prevent the court from making an order for security for costs.

[283] *Hitachi Shipbuilding & Engineering Co Ltd v Viafel Compania Navieran SA* [1981] 2 Lloyd's Rep 468, CA.

[284] *Hogan v Hogan (No 2)* [1924] 2 IR 14. Whilst this is a pre-CPR case, there is no reason to believe that the principle does not apply under the CPR. See also *Sir Lindsay Parkinson & Co Ltd v Triplan Ltd* [1973] QB 609, at 623.

Specific types of claimant and applications for security for costs

15.96 It is worth focusing on four specific types of litigant: liquidator and receivers; children; litigation friends; and solicitors. As will be seen, ancient rules and practices may have had their day.

- **Liquidators, receivers, administrators, etc** It is well established that a liquidator who had brought an action in their personal capacity would not have a security for costs order made against them.[285] A liquidator does not have a duty to ensure that the company can meet the defendant's costs order and Lawrence Collins LJ has explained that a defendant's protection would lie in making an application against the company rather than against the liquidator or receiver personally.[286] Similarly, the court will not require security for costs to be given by a claimant trustee, even where they are in insolvent circumstances.[287] The same can be said of an administrator, even though the letters of administration were granted to them only as the attorney of a person who is abroad.[288]
- **Children** There is ancient authority that security for costs ought not to be ordered against children, even where the litigation friend is insolvent.[289] It is not known whether that thinking survives under the CPR, but one of the principles underlying it is still relevant today—namely, that a child usually has no voice in the litigation, which is usually brought on his behalf by others.[290] It is for this reason, amongst others, that the law focuses on the litigation friend rather than the child (see below).
- **Litigation friends** There is an ancient rule in Chancery that it would be dangerous to displace a litigation friend for poverty.[291] This developed into a rule against requiring security for costs from the litigation friend of a child.[292] Towards the end of the nineteenth century, that rule began to be eroded;[293] even before this, it was often circumvented.[294] Under the CPR, there is no mention of litigation friends in the context of orders for security for costs. It is probably the case that the court is now unencumbered by the ancient rule mentioned above and that it will simply decide each case on its own facts.[295]

---

[285] *Re Wilson Lovatt & Sons Ltd* [1977] 1 All ER 274; see also *Wu v Hellard* (unreported), 25 November 2013, Ch D, *per* Judge Dight.

[286] *Mills v Birchall* [2008] EWCA Civ 385, at [84]–[88]; see also *Metalloy Supplies Ltd v MA (UK) Ltd* [1997] 1 WLR 1613, at 1718, *per* Waller LJ.

[287] *Cowell v Taylor* (1885) 31 Ch D 34.

[288] *Rainbow v Kittoe* [1916] 1 Ch 313.

[289] *Yarnworth's Case* (1823) 2 Dow & Ry KB 423; *Anon* (1813) 1 Marsh 4.

[290] *Re Payne, Randle v Payne* (1883) 23 Ch D 288, at 289, *per* Cotton LJ.

[291] See *Squirrel v Squirrel* (1792) 2 Dick 765.

[292] See, eg, *Fellows v Barrett* (1836) 1 Keen 119; *St John v Earl of Bessborough* (1819) 1 Hog 41.

[293] See, eg, *Martano v Mann* (1880) 14 Ch D 419; *Jones v Evans* (1886) 31 Sol Jo 11.

[294] Where, for example, a litigation friend was in poverty, it was open to the court to stay the claim until a litigation friend with means was appointed: see *Hind v Whitmore* (1856) 4 WR 379; *Elliot v Ince* (1857) 5 WR 465.

[295] In support of this proposition, it is noticeable that the law distinguished between different types of litigation friend even when the aforesaid rule was still observed. Where, for example, a woman sued through one litigation friend and then brought a fresh action through another litigation friend without having discharged the costs debt outstanding from the first proceedings, Cotton LJ found that the woman had sufficient say in the litigation to make it fair to order that the second proceedings should be stayed pending payment of that debt. He commented that the situation would have been different if the litigant had been a child because the child would have lacked sufficient voice in the litigation to influence the litigation: see *Re Payne, Randle v Payne* (1883) 23 Ch D 288, at 289. As an example of the court refusing to make an order in the case of a child, see *Murrell v Clapham* (1836) 8 Sim 74.

- **Legal representatives** Although he was dealing with the matter in the context of the solicitor being a third party, David Donaldson QC (sitting as a deputy judge of the High Court) found that when an application was made against a firm that represented one of the parties, it was necessary to look at funding, control and benefit, and how the court's discretion should be applied in light of those factors.[296] He noted that it was in only a small number of cases that a solicitor would not provide at least some element of financing. He went on to say, however, that the existence of funding by a solicitor could not in itself be a sufficient basis for finding that the solicitor was vulnerable to a non-party order for costs. The potential benefit if victory enabled the client to pay the solicitor was not a factor that could properly open the door to an order against the solicitor.

Discretion (secondary jurisdictions) to make orders for security for costs

15.97 As has been explained above (see 15.19), each of the secondary jurisdictions needs to be considered separately because their purposes differ.

- **CPR, r 3.1(3)** Moore-Bick LJ has explained that the power under CPR, r 3.1(3), should not be exercised solely on the grounds that the party in question is not conducting the litigation in good faith nor should it be exercised on the sole grounds that there is a history of repeated failures to comply with orders of the court;[297] instead, before exercising the power given by that rule, the court should identify the purpose of imposing a condition and satisfy itself that the condition it has in mind represents a proportionate and effective means of achieving that purpose, having regard to the order to which it is to be attached.[298]
- **CPR, r 3.1(5)** Clarke LJ gave the following guidance (which related primarily to CPR, r 3.1(5), but may be of wider application):

  'The correct general approach may be summarised as follows:
  i) it would only be in an exceptional case (if ever) that a court would order security for costs if the order would stifle a claim or an appeal;
  ii) in any event,
     a) an order should not ordinarily be made unless the party concerned can be shown to be regularly flouting proper court procedures or otherwise to be demonstrating a want of good faith; good faith being understood to consist ... of a will to litigate a genuine claim or defence (or appeal) as economically and expeditiously as reasonably possible in accordance with the overriding objective; and
     b) an order will not be appropriate in every case where a party has a weak case. The weakness of a party's case will ordinarily be relevant only where he has no real prospect of succeeding.'[299]

- **CPR, r 24.6** This applies where an application has been made for summary judgment. An order under CPR, r 24.6, to provide security for costs may be appropriate where it is possible, but improbable, that a claim or defence may succeed.[300] It would, however, be wrong to order that security be given merely because the claim or defence is weak; some

---

296 *Harcus Sinclair v Buttonwood Legal Capital Ltd* [2013] EWHC 2974 (Ch).

297 *Huscroft v P&O Ferries Ltd* [2010] EWCA Civ 1483, at [18], overruling *Halabi v Fieldmore Holdings* [2006] EWHC 1965 (Ch), *per* Rimer J.

298 *Huscroft v P&O Ferries Ltd* [2010] EWCA Civ 1483, at [18].

299 *Ali v Hudson t/a Hudson Freemen Berg (a firm)* [2003] EWCA Civ 1793, at [40].

300 See CPR, r 24.6; PD 24, para 4.

other factor must be present so as to give rise to a suspicion that the claim or defence may not be *bona fide*.[301] Alternatively, an order may also be made if an order would have been made under the primary jurisdiction.[302] The order must be a condition that is capable of being complied with and, as such, a party should not be ordered to pay into court a sum of money that they are unlikely to be able to raise.[303]

- **CPR, r 52.9** This applies where a party seeks permission to appeal. It would be appropriate to make an order that security for costs be given only if there were a 'compelling reason' why that should be done.[304]

There are also principles that apply to both of the secondary jurisdictions under CPR, r 3.1. Moore-Bick LJ has explained that when the court is asked to consider making an order under either of the secondary jurisdictions, it should bear in mind the principles underlying CPR, r 25.12 and 25.13.[305] Indeed, whilst he does not seem to have heard a great deal of argument on the point, Neuberger MR found the same test to apply and that, as such, it would be necessary for one or more of the conditions under CPR, r 25.13(2), to be satisfied.[306] Clarke LJ's guidance about not stifling the claim (see 15.97) is almost certainly applicable under both of the secondary jurisdictions. **15.98**

Simon Brown LJ has explained that the court should be alert and sensitive to the risk that, by making an order for security, it might be denying the party concerned the right to access to justice—in which regard, he commented that this was true regardless of the jurisdiction.[307] He explained that relevant considerations included the ability of the person concerned to pay, their conduct during the proceedings (including, in particular, their compliance or otherwise with any applicable rule, practice direction or protocol) and the apparent strength of their case (whether claim or defence).[308] **15.99**

Notwithstanding the broad range of circumstances in which the secondary jurisdictions may arise, it seems that they are jurisdictions that will be invoked only infrequently. Sir Andrew Morritt has commented that it is a remedy of last resort.[309] Simon Brown LJ had this to say (in respect of CPR, r 3.1(5)): **15.100**

> 'A party only becomes amenable to an adverse order for security under r 3.1(5) (or perhaps r 3.1(2)(m)) once he can be seen either to be regularly flouting proper court procedures (which must inevitably inflate the costs of the proceedings) or otherwise to be demonstrating a want

[301] See *Olatawura v Abiloye* [2002] EWCA Civ 998; *Ali v Hudson* [2003] EWCA Civ 1793.

[302] *Allen v Bloomsbury Publishing Plc* [2011] EWHC 770 (Ch).

[303] *Chapple v Williams* (1999) LTL, 8 December, CA. That said, the ability to raise funds when needed (such as from directors' loans) may be taken into account: see *Foot & Bowden v Anglo Europe Corporation Ltd* (unreported), 17 February 2000, CA.

[304] See CPR, r 59.9(2).

[305] *Huscroft v P&O Ferries Ltd* [2010] EWCA Civ 1483, at [14]. As an example of the principles in CPR, Part 25, Section II, being applied by analogy, see *Allen v Bloomsbury Publishing plc* [2011] EWHC 770 (Ch) (upheld on appeal).

[306] *Shlaimoun & Anor v Mining Technologies International Inc* [2012] EWCA Civ 772, at [14].

[307] *Olatawura v Abiloye* [2002] EWCA Civ 998, at [22].

[308] *Ibid*, at [24].

[309] *Uddington Business Ltd v Browne* (unreported), 9 December 2011, Ch D, in which *Asiansky Television Plc v Bayer-Rosin (a firm)* [2001] EWCA Civ 1792, [2002] CPLR 111, was followed. See also *Al Nehayan v Kent* [2017] EWHC 1347 (Ch), in which Christopher Hancock QC found that the fact that many of the failings had either already been cured or, where already subject to sanctions, counted against the making of an order.

> of good faith—good faith for this purpose consisting of a will to litigate a genuine claim or defence as economically and expeditiously as reasonably possible in according with the overriding objective.'[310]

He went on to explain that it is not to be thought that an order for security for costs will be appropriate in every case in which a party appears to have a somewhat weak claim or defence.[311]

15.101 As to conduct, Patten J found that a failure to comply with an order concerning disclosure was not enough to amount to regular flouting of court procedures.[312] Whilst he did not expressly refer to CPR, r 3.1(5), Briggs J found that a repeated failure to pay past orders for costs did merit an order being made.[313]

Reapplication for and Variation of Orders for Security for Costs

15.102 An order for security for costs may be varied or revoked pursuant to CPR, r 3.1(7). In general,[314] the grounds for doing so fall into one of two categories:

- where the original order was made on the basis of erroneous information, whether erroneously or accidentally given; and
- where subsequent events had destroyed the basis on which it was made.[315]

Clarke MR had this to say about orders for further security consequent upon a material change of circumstances:

> 'The correct approach ... is that where the court has awarded security in respect of, say, the whole of an action or application, it will not make a further order in the absence of a material change of circumstances. However, it will or may do so if there has been a material change of circumstances ... That principle applies where a court makes an order for security for costs and is asked to make a further order. Moreover, it applies whether the first order is made with or without the consent of the parties. Thus it applies, for example, where the parties consent to an order. Subject to the express terms of the agreement it also applies where the parties agree that security will be provided and security is provided pursuant to an agreement without an order.'[316]

15.103 In a similar vein, Popplewell J had these comments to make on the topic:

> '[W]here a security for costs up to a particular stage of proceedings has already been provided, a defendant who applies to increase the amount of security for the costs of that same

---

[310] *Olatawura v Abiloye* [2002] EWCA Civ 998, at [25]; see also Buckley J's judgment in *Mealey Horgan plc v Horgan* [1999] All ER (D), which Simon Brown LJ quoted with approval.

[311] *Olatawura v Abiloye* [2002] EWCA Civ 998, at [26].

[312] *Ashfield & Anor v Union Pensions Trustees Ltd* [2004] All ER (D) 103 (Dec).

[313] See *Johnson v Cammack* (unreported), 12 February 2013, Ch D.

[314] Barling J has said that a more flexible approach may be taken where liberty to apply was granted at the time the order was made: see *Al-Baho v BGP Global Services Ltd* (unreported), 4 July 2017, Ch D, *per* Barling J.

[315] *Murray Construction Ltd v Marino Family Trust Co Ltd* [2013] EWHC 3966 (TCC), in which Ramsey J quoted *Roult v North West SHA* [2009] EWCA Civ 444.

[316] *Republic of Kazakhstan v Istil Group Inc* [2005] EWCA Civ 1468, at [32]. See also the comments of Beldam LJ in *Kristjansson v R Verney & Co Ltd* (unreported) 18 June 1998, CA, at 12 of the official transcript; *Vald Nielsen Holding A/S v Baldorino* [2017] EWHC 1033 (Comm), at [34], *per* Mr Robin Dicker QC (sitting as a deputy High Court judge).

> stage in proceedings will generally have to justify a further order by reference to circumstances which did not exist or were not apparent at the time the order was made. For it to be just to order further security, a defendant will generally have to show a material change of circumstances from those which pertained or were envisaged when the matter was before the court making the order. Otherwise the court is simply being asked to reconsider a decision made on the basis of arguments which were made or could have been made at the time.'[317]

Examples include where it is discovered that full and frank disclosure was not given[318] and where the disclosure proved to be much more expensive than was originally thought.[319] A change of circumstance may be easily shown if the original order gave security up to a specified stage in the proceedings and that stage had now been reached.[320] Where costs have been awarded against a party who had been ordered to provide security for costs and where part of the security is used to pay those orders, then it would be prudent to consider whether the remaining monies continue to provide adequate security.[321] Amendments to the claim as pleaded may suffice.[322] **15.104**

If the circumstances change such that security is no longer required, an application may be made for the order to be varied or set aside.[323] Where the security was financed by a loan on terms that gave rise to a resulting trust in favour of the lender, then the court will strive to give effect to that trust and will seek not to make orders that could defeat it.[324] **15.105**

Extensions of time may be granted in appropriate circumstances. Where an application was made prior to the expiry of the time to pay, *Denton* would not apply.[325] **15.106**

Unless Orders and Orders for Security for Costs

Waller LJ explained that if an unless order is made at the time the order for security is made, then either it ought not to be made as a first order or the claimant ought to be granted a generous period of time for compliance: **15.107**

> 'The obtaining of an order for security for costs is a rather special form of order. It is intended ... to give a claimant a choice as to whether he puts up security and continues with his action or withdraws his claim. That choice is meant to be a proper choice ... The making of an order for security is not intended to be a weapon by which a defendant can obtain a speedy summary judgment without a trial.'[326]

Practices vary from court to court. In the Commercial Court, it is unusual for an unless order to be made (at least when the order for security is first made); in other courts, an unless order may be the usual order, this reflecting the wording of the standard court form.[327] **15.108**

---

317 *Stokors SA v IG Markets Ltd* [2012] EWHC 1684 (Comm), at [13], *per* Popplewell J.
318 See, eg, *Rajvel Construction Ltd v Bestville Properties Ltd* [2012] EWCA Civ 587.
319 See, eg, *Stokors SA & Ors v Ig Markets Ltd* [2012] EWHC 1684 (Comm).
320 *Eli Lilly & Co Ltd v Neopharma Ltd* [2012] EWHC 2297 (Ch).
321 See *Force India Formula One Team Ltd v 1 Malaysia Racing Team SDN BHD* [2012] EWHC 1726 (Ch).
322 See, eg, *Vald Nielsen Holding A/S v Baldorino* [2017] EWHC 1033 (Comm), at [34]–[43], *per* Mr Robin Dicker QC (sitting as a deputy High Court judge).
323 Whilst pre-CPR, see *Cordano Building Contractors v Burgess* [1988] 1 WLR 890.
324 *R v Common Professional Examination Board, ex p Mealing-McCleod* (2000) The Times, 2 May, CA.
325 *Peak Hotels & Resorts Ltd v Tarek Investments Ltd* [2015] EWHC 2886 (Ch), *per* Hildyard J.
326 *Radu v Houston* [2006] EWCA Civ 1575, at [18].
327 PD 44.

15.109 Where an unless order is triggered, relief may be granted.[328] In any event, it is often the case that the order giving rise to the stay can be construed as giving rise to a temporary stay. Clear and express words would be needed, however, before any such stay could be said to be self-lifting upon payment of the security.[329]

Quantum and Form of Security for Costs

15.110 The court has freedom to make an award in any amount that is justified (other than a purely nominal amount); there is no presumption that the amount will be substantial.[330] Whilst in a pre-CPR case, McCowan LJ has held that sufficient security for costs does not mean complete security, but security of a sufficiency in all of the circumstances of the case as to be just.[331] It is often the case that security is payable in tranches rather than as a single sum, which may be to take account of the fact that the claim may settle.[332] An alternative way of dealing with the possibility of settlement is to discount the amount allowed for future costs.[333] Similarly, if the amount of security is particularly large, then the court may order that it is payable in stages, for the purposes of allowing the respondent time to raise the funds in an orderly fashion.[334]

The amount for which security is to be given

15.111 Broadly speaking, there are two measures that may be used to set the amount of the security, depending on the circumstances: the first is the amount of costs over which the security is reasonably sought (usually the likely costs of the case or relevant part thereof); the second is the reasonable monetary value of the extra burden of enforcement outside the zone of contracting states.[335] (It used to be the case that a rule of thumb was used by means of which the court awarded a fixed proportion of the costs likely to be incurred up to the relevant stage of the litigation, but that is no longer recommended practice.[336]) In any event, fixing the appropriate figure for security is not an exact science and will, of necessity, be something that may need to be approached robustly.[337]

15.112 The first of these measures is a matter of assessment (for the judge making the order) based on the sums claimed. The only fetter is that an order that the claimant lacks the means to pay may amount to a breach of Art 6(11) ECHR.[338] Where, however, the court

---

[328] See, eg, *Summit Navigation Ltd v Generali Romania Asigurare Reasigurare Sa (2) Ardaf Sa Insurance & Reinsurance Co* [2014] EWHC 398 (Comm).

[329] *Ibid*, at [21]–[22], *per* Leggatt J.

[330] Whilst pre-CPR authorities, see *Roburn Construction Ltd v William Irwin (South) & Co Ltd* [1991] BCC 726 and *Keary Developments Ltd v Tarmac Construction Ltd* [1995] 3 All ER 534, at 540.

[331] *Innovare Displays plc v Corporate Broking Services Ltd* [1991] BCC 174, CA.

[332] See The White Book, at para 25.12.7.

[333] See, eg, *Procon (Great Britain) Ltd v Provincial Building Co Ltd* [1984] 1 WLR 557.

[334] See, eg, *Chemistree Homecare Ltd v Teva Pharmaceuticals Ltd* [2011] EWHC 2979 (Ch). Indeed, this is common practice in the Commercial Court: see *Endeavour Energy v Hess Ltd* [2017] EWHC 1087(Comm), at [10], *per* Males J.

[335] *Texuna International Ltd v Cairn Energy plc* [2004] EWHC 1102 (Comm), at [29]–[32], *per* Gross J.

[336] *Al-Koronky & Anor v Time Life Entertainments Group Ltd* [2005] EWHC 1688 (QB), at [26]–[27], *per* Eady J; see also *Procon (GB) Ltd v Provincial Building Co Ltd* [1984] 2 All ER 368, CA.

[337] *Autoweld Systems Ltd v Kito Enterprises LLC* [2010] EWCA Civ 1469, at [64], *per* Black LJ.

[338] *Aït-Mouhoub v France*, App no 22924/93, [1998] ECHR 97.

is not persuaded that it has been given a full account of the claimant's resources, it has a discretion to set an amount according to its best estimate of what the claimant can afford.[339]

It will often be the case that the court will estimate the monies that are likely to be allowed on a detailed assessment on the standard basis.[340] Although they would now rarely be encountered, additional liabilities may or may not form part of that estimate.[341] If value added tax (VAT) would normally be disallowed on an assessment, then it should be disregarded.[342] Whilst an obvious point, if the costs of the application are going to be been summarily assessed at the end of the hearing, they should not be included in the estimate.[343] **15.113**

The second of these measures (the costs of enforcement) is a question of fact and discretion. The measure will usually be the additional burden of enforcing in the claimant's country of residence—that is, in essence, security is available only in respect of additional obstacles to, and burdens of enforcement in, the foreign jurisdiction as compared with those in a state that was party to the Brussels Convention 1968 or the Lugano Convention 1988.[344] If enforcement is possible, but there is a real risk that it will take longer or cost more, security will generally be ordered to cover that risk only.[345] Where the evidence indicates that there is a real risk of non-enforcement, then the court may order security to cover the full likely recoverable amount of costs to date and then later to trial. Cockerill J has said that cases may fall between these two extremes;[346] she took a risk-based approach to quantum.[347] **15.114**

There are conflicting decisions on whether security can be given for the additional costs of execution arising out of the need to pursue a person in a foreign country.[348] Set-off by a foreign court will not normally be regarded as an additional burden,[349] although the extent to which the applicant may be liable to the respondent in monies other than costs may be a **15.115**

339 *Al-Koronky v Time-Life Entertainment Group Ltd* [2006] EWCA Civ 1123.

340 See, eg, *Royal Bank of Scotland v Hicks* [2012] EWCA Civ 1665, at [15]–[18], where Lewison LJ made an allowance of 70 per cent of the monies claimed.

341 Although they would now rarely apply, it is generally the case that success fees are taken into account for the purposes of deciding quantum: see *Mengi v Hermitage* [2012] EWHC 2045 (QB) *per* Tugendhat J; *Kahangi v Nourizadeh* [2009] EWHC 2451 (QB), at [26], *per* Eady J. Rimer LJ, however, has found that it may be unjust to do so in circumstances in which the applicant has not disclosed their conditional fee agreement: *Meridian International Services Ltd v Richardson* [2008] EWCA Civ 490, at [16]. Similarly, in the context of an application for a freezing injunction, Gloster J found that it would be unfair to take into account the full amount of an ATE premium because this would shift the preponderance of risk onto the party giving security and, in effect, would be to require that party to give security for its own costs: *Guerrero & Ors v Monterrico Metals plc* [2009] EWHC 2475 (QB), at [40].

342 *Warren v Marsden* [2014] EWHC 4410 (Comm), at [22], *per* Teare J.

343 *Ibid.*

344 *Nasser v United Bank of Kuwait* [2001] EWCA Civ 556, at [61], *per* Mance LJ.

345 *Ibid*, at [64]. See also *Bestfort Developments LLP v Ras Al Khaimah Investment Authority* [2016] EWCA Civ 1099, at [85], *per* Gloster LJ; *Danilina v Chernukhin* [2018] EWHC 39 (Comm), at [62], *per* Cockerill J.

346 See *Danilina v Chernukhin* [2018] EWHC 39 (Comm), at [65], *per* Cockerill J.

347 *Ibid*, at [66]–[77].

348 In *Dumrul v Standard Chartered Bank* [2010] EWHC 2625 (Comm), at [23], Hamblen J found that security could not be ordered for the costs of execution, but in *Cody v Murray* [2013] EWHC 3448 (Ch), at [10]–[12], David Donaldson QC (sitting as a deputy High Court judge) said that *Dunrul* was wrongly decided on this point and that costs of execution may be included.

349 *Relational LLC v Hodges* [2011] EWCA Civ 774, at [17] *et seq.*

factor that can be taken into account.[350] Where the claimant's assets are in a country that is different from their place of residence, then the court will take into account the additional burden of enforcing in the country in which the assets lie, rather than in the country of residency.[351] Gross J has confirmed that where it is effectively impossible to enforce an order for payment of costs, then this situation would provide 'an objective justification for the court exercising its discretion to make an order for payment of the full amount of the costs likely to be ordered against a claimant if unsuccessful in the litigation'.[352]

15.116 Where the relevant costs are subject to a costs management order, the relevant starting point may be taken from the last approved or agreed budget (or part thereof).[353] That said, it should be borne in mind that incurred costs will not have been subject to the court's approval or agreed by the parties.[354] It would, in any event, be a mistake to believe that the court should simply allow the amount in the budget (or the relevant part thereof); this is for many reasons, including (among many others) the fact that the court will not wish to make an order that stifles the claim, the fact that—where CPR, r 25.13(a), applies—the court may be focusing only on the additional costs of enforcement out of the jurisdiction.[355] Notwithstanding these points, however, it is likely that existence of a costs management order would make the court's task far easier than it otherwise would have been.

Quantification of security where there is a Part 20 claim

15.117 It may be that a defendant has brought a Part 20 claim in circumstances in which, if successful in its defence, it would obtain a passing-up-the-line order such that whilst it would be ordered to pay the Part 20 defendant's costs, it would be able to recover those costs from the claimant (see 7.26). Where this is so, the Part 20 defendant would not be able to seek security for costs directly against the Part 20 claimant,[356] but the defendant (that is, the Part 20 claimant) would be able to seek security for those costs (and its own costs of the Part 20 claim) from the claimant (that is, the Part 20 defendant).[357]

Quantification of security where both parties seek security

15.118 It may be that the court has to determine the quantum of orders for both sides' costs. Where this is so, the court need not vex itself with any rule similar to that in *Medway Oil*[358] (see 20.59). Where a counterclaim is founded on the same body of facts as the claim itself

[350] See, eg, *Diag Human SE v Czech Republic* [2013] EWHC 3190 (Comm), in which Burton J refused to make an order for security for costs in an application to set aside an arbitral award enforcement order because the amount of the award and interest would far extinguish the costs of the enforcement of the award.

[351] *Kazakhstan Investment Fund Ltd v Aims Asset Management* (unreported), 22 May 2002, Ch D, *per* Mr Gabriel Moss QC (sitting as a deputy judge of the High Court). See also *Kazakhstan Kagazy plc v Zhunis* [2015] EWHC 996 (Comm), at [205], *per* Walker J.

[352] *Texuna International Ltd v Cairn Energy plc* [2004] EWHC 1102 (Comm), at [23(vi)]; see also *Al-Koronky & Anor v Time Life Entertainments Group Ltd* [2005] EWHC 1688 (QB), at [25], *per* Eady J.

[353] Whilst the comments regarding incurred costs are no longer good law, see *SARPD Oil International Ltd v Addax Energy SA & Anor* [2016] EWCA Civ 120, at [31]–[53].

[354] See *Endeavour Energy v Hess Ltd* [2017] EWHC 1087(Comm), at [13], *per* Males J.

[355] See, eg, *Al Nehayan v Kent* [2016] EWHC 613 (QB).

[356] See *Taly v Terra Nova Insurance Co* [1985] 1 WLR 1359, cited by Sales LJ in *SARPD Oil International Ltd v Addax Energy SA & Anor* [2016] EWCA Civ 120, at [27].

[357] *SARPD Oil International Ltd v Addax Energy SA & Anor* [2016] EWCA Civ 120, at [27]–[30], *per* Sales LJ. See also *Noterise Ltd v Haseltine Lake & Co* [1992] BCC 497, at 501 and 502.

[358] *Medway Oil and Storage Co Ltd v Continental Contractors Ltd* [1929] AC 88.

and where it is appropriate to make an order, there is no requirement to limit the security to those exclusively referable to the counterclaim; instead, where appropriate, the entirety of the costs of the counterclaim may be included, regardless of whether they were common to both the claim and the counterclaim.[359] That said, where the court wishes to order security for the claim, but not the counterclaim, it is open to the court to exclude the costs of the latter even if this would mean that no security would be offered for the costs that are common to both the claim and the counterclaim.[360]

Quantification where there is a lack of information

Whilst in a pre-CPR case, Griffiths LJ has commented that if there is a paucity of information that is put before the court to allow it to estimate costs, then it will be reasonable to make a large discount—particularly when it is borne in mind that if the security proves inadequate as litigation progresses, it is always possible for a further application to be made for more security.[361] Roth J has impliedly confirmed that the court may take a broad-brush approach to quantum if it finds that the costs are disproportionate.[362] **15.119**

Quantification of security when there is public funding

Denning MR has held that where a person is in receipt of public funding, the amount they can be ordered to pay in security must not exceed the amount that they would be required to pay if they were to lose.[363] Put another way, the costs protection afforded by the public funding must be taken into account. **15.120**

The form of the security

There are many forms that security can take. Indeed, the court has the power to order that more than one type of security may be given.[364] The usual method is payment into court,[365] but alternatives include: **15.121**

- ATE insurance[366]—the existence of which may also be a reason for not making an order (see 15.38);[367]
- monies held to order by the claimant's solicitors;
- security by way of undertaking to pay costs;[368]

---

[359] *Jones v Environcom Ltd & Anor* [2009] EWHC 16 (Comm), at [24]–[26]; see also *Petromin SA v Secnav Marine Ltd* [1995] 1 Lloyd's Rep 603, QBD.

[360] See, eg, *Ultimate Utilities Ltd v McNicholas Construction Services Ltd* (unreported), 9 April 2014, QBD (TCC), in which Ramsey J found that a third of the costs related to the claim, another third related to the counterclaim and the remaining third related to both, then made an order that gave security for only the third that related to the claim.

[361] *Procon (GB) Ltd v Provincial Building Co Ltd* [1984] 2 All ER 368, at 379.

[362] *Ackerman v Ackerman* [2011] EWHC (Ch), at [32].

[363] *Wyld v Silver (No 2)* [1962] 2 All ER 809, CA. It used to be the case that no order at all would be made against a publicly funded client (see *Conway v George Wimpey & Co Ltd* [1951] 1 All ER 56), but Denning MR confirmed that the fact of public funding is only a factor to be taken into account.

[364] See, eg, *Belco Trading Ltd v Kordo* [2008] EWCA Civ 205.

[365] If monies are paid into court, they should not be viewed as being property recovered or preserved for the purposes of a solicitors' charging order: *Re Wadsworth, Rhodes v Sugden* (1885) 29 Ch D 517. See 40.93.

[366] See, eg, *Bluewaters Communications Holdings LLC v Ecclestone* [2018] EWHC 78 (Comm), at [38].

[367] See, eg, *Belco Trading Ltd v Kordo* [2008] EWCA Civ 205.

[368] *Hawkins Hill Co v Want* (1893) 69 LT 297. As a more recent example, see the undertaking described in *Recovery Partners GB Ltd v Rukhadze* [2018] EWHC 95 (Comm), at [8], *per* Nicholas Vineall QC (sitting as a deputy High Court judge).

- security by way of a personal guarantee;[369]
- security by way of a deed of indemnity from a creditworthy insurance company;[370]
- security by way of mortgage or charge over land (but see 15.122);[371] and
- security by way of a guarantee given by a bank[372] (often phrased as being a guarantee from 'a first-class London bank').

15.122 The final item on this list (the bank guarantee) is usually preferred over a charge or mortgage, the rationale being that if the property in issue has real value, a guarantee ought to be reasonably easy to obtain.[373] This would not prevent the court from accepting a charge where that was appropriate, however, and factors the court may take into account in that regard are the value of the property (and whether that value is likely to remain sufficient[374]) and the ease with which its value could be realised.[375] If two different forms of security would provide protection, the court should, all else being equal, order that form which is least onerous to the party that is providing the security.[376]

15.123 It may be that a party who has already provided security in one form wishes to provide it in another. In the context of a party seeking to be released from an undertaking giving by a London solicitor on the grounds that it had secured ATE insurance (backed by a deed of indemnity), Nicholas Vineall QC (sitting as a deputy judge of the High Court) had this to say:

> 'In my view, and remembering that the burden is on the party seeking release from an undertaking, the factors which might be material on an application of the present type, and which do arise and are material in this case, include the following: (a) how long the old security has been in place and whether the costs which it secured have already been incurred; (b) the extent of the difference (if any) between the quality of the old security and the quality of the new security; (c) the strength of the explanation given for the Claimant's change of position; (d) in particular, whether or not, and if so to what extent, declining to permit the change would cause hardship or prejudice to the Claimant or inhibit its ability to pursue its claim.'[377]

There is no reason to believe that any different approach would be required if other forms of security were involved.

---

[369] See, eg, *Inventors Friend Ltd v Leathes Prior* [2011] EWHC 2840 (QB), *per* Simon L. This was ordered because there was insufficient time before trial to allow a more orthodox type of security to be obtained.

[370] See *Verslot Dredging BV v Hdi Gerling Versicherung AG* [2013] EWHC 658 (Comm), in which Christopher Clarke J found that such security was at least as good as a bank guarantee.

[371] See, eg, *Ackerman v Ackerman* [2011] EWHC 2183 (Ch); *Serious Organised Crime Agency v Agidi* [2011] EWCA Civ 1350; *Xhosa Office Rentals Ltd v Multi High Tec PCB Ltd* [2012] EWHC 3673 (QB).

[372] See, eg, *Rosengrens Ltd v Safe Deposit Centres Ltd* [1984] 1 WLR 1334; *Gulf Azov Shipping Co Ltd v Idisi* [2001] EWCA Civ 505, CA.

[373] *AP (UK) Ltd v West Midlands Fire and Civil Defence Authority* [2001] EWCA Civ 1917.

[374] This is not simply a matter of looking at the rising costs in the claim; it may also be a matter of reviewing the security itself. An example of this is *Rajvel Construction Ltd v Bestville Properties Ltd* [2011] EWHC 2669 (TCC), in which the claimant tried to diminish the security in the charge by granting another company a competing interest in the land.

[375] *Havai v Solland* [2008] EWHC 2514 (Ch).

[376] See, eg, *Recovery Partners GB Ltd v Rukhadze* [2018] EWHC 95 (Comm), at [17], *per* Nicholas Vineall QC (sitting as a deputy High Court judge).

[377] *Recovery Partners GB Ltd v Rukhadze* [2018] EWHC 95 (Comm), at [42], *per* Nicholas Vineall QC (sitting as a deputy High Court judge).

Procedure and Applications for Security for Costs

CPR, r 25.12, reads as follows: **15.124**

'(1) A defendant to any claim may apply under this Section of this Part for security for his costs of the proceedings.

(Part 3 provides for the court to order payment of sums into court in other circumstances. Rule 20.3 provides for this Section of this Part to apply to Part 20 claims.)

(2) An application for security for costs must be supported by written evidence.

(3) Where the court makes an order for security for costs, it will—

(a) determine the amount of security; and

(b) direct—

(i) the manner in which; and

(ii) the time within which the security must be given.'

Surprisingly, there is no practice direction relating to applications for security for costs. Respected commentators advise that a skeleton bill of the costs ought to be appended to the application.[378] This would certainly seem sensible and would be 'best practice', but, in the editor's experience, it is often sufficient to rely on a schedule in the form of Precedent H, but with additional detail in appended schedules where appropriate. Roth J had the following to say: **15.125**

'In support of its application for security for costs a defendant is, of course, not obliged to present a costs budget in the precise form of Precedent H, but it can be expected … to prepare a full schedule showing how the sub-totals under the various specified heads were arrived at, including the rates being charged and hours estimated.'[379]

Whilst the relevant provisions are very similar,[380] the above rules do not apply in the Supreme Court.

The Commercial Court Guide gives the following guidance about application for security for costs (which can sensibly be regarded as providing guidance in other courts): **15.126**

'First applications for security for costs should not be made later than at the Case Management Conference and in any event any application should not be left until close to the trial date. Delay to the prejudice of the other party or the administration of justice might well cause the application to fail, as will any use of the application to harass the other party. Where it is intended to make an application for security at the Case Management Conference the procedure, and timetable for evidence, for an ordinary application must be followed (see section F5 of the Guide).

Successive applications

Successive applications for security can be granted where the circumstances warrant. If a claimant wishes to seek to preclude any further application it is incumbent on the claimant to make that clear.'[381]

---

378 See, eg, *Cook on Costs 2017* (Butterworths LexisNexis, online), para 13.30.

379 *Agents' Mutual Ltd v Gascoigne Halman Ltd* [2016] EWHC 2315 (Ch), at [27].

380 See the Supreme Court Rules 2009 (SI 2009/1603), r 36, and UKSC Practice Direction 7.

381 See *Commercial Court Guide*, 10th edn, Appendix 10.

Evidence and disclosure

15.127 Applications are made on notice, supported by evidence. Jacob J has said that where more than one ground is relied upon, the application and evidence should make clear which points of evidence are relied on in support of each ground.[382]

15.128 Whilst an obvious point, without-prejudice negotiations should not be taken into account without the consent of those concerned.[383]

15.129 Where a claimant seeks to resist an order on the basis of their own impecuniosity, the onus is on the claimant to prove that fact and, in so doing, they would be expected to make full and frank disclosure.[384] If the claimant chooses not to disclose up-to-date accounts, then they may fail to prove sufficient liquidity to discharge an order as and when it fell due.[385] If the claimant fails to give full disclosure, then an application may be renewed once the true facts come to light.[386] Where it is said that a claim is being funded by a third party and where that is admitted or proved, the court has the power to order the claimant to disclose the name of the funder.[387]

15.130 Where a party seeks an order for security for costs under CPR, r 24.6, as an alternative to summary judgment, proper notice ought to be given.[388] Where this has not been done, the court will not, as a general rule, order payment of a sum that may be beyond that party's ability to pay.[389] In any event, where the court intends to make an order for a significant amount, the court may allow the respondent a short period in which to adduce evidence as to its means.[390]

---

382 *Somerset-Leeke & Anor v Kay Trustees* [2003] EWHC 1243 (Ch), at [5].
383 *Simaan General Contracting Co v Pilkington Glass Ltd* [1987] 1 All ER 345, CA.
384 *M V Yorke Motors (a firm) v Edwards* [1982] 1 All ER 1024, at 1027, *per* Lord Diplock; affirmed post-CPR in *Anglo-Eastern Trust Ltd & Anor v Kermanshahchi* [2002] EWCA Civ 198.
385 *Trade Storage Ltd v Papanicola* [2011] EWHC 598 (Ch).
386 See, eg, *Rajvel Construction Ltd v Bestville Properties Ltd* [2012] EWCA Civ 587.
387 *Reeves v Sprecher* [2007] EWHC 3226 (Ch), *per* Rattee J.
388 See *Anglo-Eastern Trust Ltd & Anor v Kermanshahchi* [2002] EWCA Civ 198.
389 See *ibid.*
390 See, eg, *Kazeminy v Siddiqui* [2009] EWHC 3207 (Comm); *Trademark Licensing Co Ltd v Leofelis SA* [2010] EWHC 969 (Ch).

Part V

BASES OF COSTS AND PART 36

16

THE BASES OF ASSESSMENT (INDEMNITY BASIS AND STANDARD BASIS)

This chapter examines the two bases on which the court ascertains the quantum of costs between opposing parties: the standard basis and the indemnity basis. It deals with the following topics: **16.01**

- the two bases of assessment (16.02);
- the circumstances in which an award on the indemnity basis might be made (16.13);
- orders to pay costs on the indemnity basis pursuant to CPR, r 44.2:
  - the origin and extent of the jurisdiction (16.15);
  - proportionality and applications for costs on the indemnity basis (16.17);
  - the circumstances in which the jurisdiction will be exercised (16.18);
- case examples relating to costs on the indemnity basis (16.31):
  - failure to cooperate with a view to resolving the dispute (16.32);
  - offers in general (16.34);
  - weak cases (claims or defences) (16.38);
  - relief from sanctions and extensions of time (16.41);
  - abandonment of a case or of issues (16.43);
  - overenthusiastic pursuance of a case (including the pursuance of costs) (16.46);
  - dishonest, improper or misleading conduct (16.47);
  - inflammatory behaviour, contempt of court, etc (16.49);
  - unjustified allegations of dishonesty, fraud and exaggeration (16.50);
  - changing the case to fit the circumstances (16.53);
  - where there is a real issue over proportionality (16.54);
  - failure to make reasonable enquiries (16.55);
  - failure to comply with a pre-action protocol (16.56);
  - unreasonable conduct and failure to comply with procedural requirements (16.57);
  - expert evidence and failures on the part of experts (16.60);
  - breach of fiduciary duty, breach of duty to the court and failures to abide by orders (16.62);
  - courting publicity (16.63);
  - contractual and collateral entitlements (16.64);
  - anti-suit provisions, arbitration provisions and jurisdiction clauses (16.65);
  - litigation solely about costs (16.66); and
  - Aarhus Convention claims (16.67).

Unlike in previous editions of this book, the topic of claimants' Part 36 offers is now in Chapter 17, rather than in this chapter.

The Two Bases of Assessment

16.02 Under the Civil Procedure Rules 1998 (CPR), costs may be assessed on only the standard basis or the indemnity basis.[1] The former is by far the more common.

The default position under the CPR

16.03 CPR, r 44.3(4), reads as follows:

> '(4) Where—
> (a) the court makes an order about costs without indicating the basis on which the costs are to be assessed; or
> (b) the court makes an order for costs to be assessed on a basis other than the standard basis or the indemnity basis, the costs will be assessed on the standard basis.'

Thus, should the court make an order for costs to be assessed on a basis that is other than one of these two bases, the costs will be assessed on the standard basis by default.[2] It is generally the case that cost orders are silent on the issue of which basis is to apply; where this is so, the costs will be assessed on the standard basis.[3] Likewise, if costs-only proceedings fail to specify the basis of the order that is sought, the costs will be treated as having been claimed on the standard basis.[4]

The test to be applied on assessment

No costs to be allowed that were unreasonably incurred or which are unreasonable in amount

16.04 The provisions in CPR, r 44.3, apply to both the standard and the indemnity bases:

> '(1) Where the court is to assess the amount of costs (whether by summary or detailed assessment) it will assess those costs—
> (a) on the standard basis; or
> (b) on the indemnity basis,
>
> but the court will not in either case allow costs which have been unreasonably incurred or are unreasonable in amount.'

Thus, regardless of the basis on which the costs are assessed, the court will not allow costs that have been unreasonably incurred or are unreasonable in amount.

The test to be applied on assessment: standard basis

16.05 In so far as the standard basis is concerned, CPR, r 44.3(2), reads as follows:

> '(2) Where the amount of costs is to be assessed on the standard basis, the court will—

---

[1] See CPR, r 44.3(4). This provision does not apply to a solicitor's remuneration in respect of non-contentious business regulated by any general orders made under the Solicitors Act 1974 (see CPR, r 44.3(6)). Costs payable under a contract are in a special category, which (unless the contract provides otherwise) is similar to the indemnity basis, although it is not referred to as such in the CPR (see CPR, rr 44.3 and 46.9).

[2] See CPR, r 44.3(4)(b), negating the decision in *EMI Records Ltd v Wallace* [1983] 1 Ch 59. This provision probably does not oust the court's power to decide, as a matter of construction, whether the court making the costs order intended costs to be assessed on the indemnity basis.

[3] CPR, r 44.3(4)(a).

[4] PD 46, para 9.4 (previously CPD, art 17.3(5)).

(a) only allow costs which are proportionate to the matters in issue. Costs which are disproportionate in amount may be disallowed or reduced even if they were reasonably or necessarily incurred;[[5]] and
(b) resolve any doubt which it may have as to whether costs were reasonably and proportionately incurred or were reasonable and proportionate in amount in favour of the paying party.

(Factors which the court may take into account are set out in rule 44.4.[[6]])'

Thus, where costs are assessed on the standard basis, the court will resolve any doubt that it may have as to whether costs were reasonably and proportionately incurred, or were reasonable and proportionate in amount in favour of the paying party. Moreover, it will allow only costs that are proportionate to the matters in issue. The factors the court will take into account are addressed at 25.26.

Provisions regarding proportionality These provisions changed on 1 April 2013, in that the court's power to ablate disproportionate expenditure was bolstered (see 25.29).[7] Transitional provisions apply.[8] Where the old provisions continue to apply, the *Lownds* test will continue to govern the test of proportionality.[9] **16.06**

Under the new provisions, the CPR expressly provide that costs that are disproportionate in amount may be disallowed or reduced even if they were reasonably or necessarily incurred (see 16.05).[10] Moreover, if costs are assessed on the standard basis, the court will additionally disallow any costs that it considers to have been disproportionately incurred or to be disproportionate in amount.[11] Some commentators regard the inclusion of an express power to disallow costs on the grounds of proportionality as a change 'of quite extraordinary potency',[12] because it seemingly affords the court the power to make larger reductions than previously. This topic is discussed in Chapter 25. The effect of these amendments is not only to augment the court's powers to disallow disproportionate costs, but also to widen the gap between the sums recoverable on the standard basis and on the indemnity basis. **16.07**

The irrelevance of the issue of doubt to the resolution of factual issues The issue of doubt has no part to play in the court's determination of points of fact. If, for example, the issue is whether the conducting fee earner was (as a matter of fact) a Grade A fee earner or **16.08**

---

[5] This sentence will not apply if the case was commenced before 1 April 2013 or if the costs were incurred in respect of work done before that date (see CPR, r 44.3(7)). Prior to that date, CPR, r 44.3, would apply, but those provisions were the same as the new provisions.

[6] This is a reference to what used to be called the 'Seven Pillars of Wisdom', but which now includes an eighth factor—namely, the receiving party's last approved or agreed budget.

[7] It achieves this by way of now including the words (which apply only on the standard basis) 'costs which are disproportionate in amount may be disallowed or reduced even if they were reasonably or necessarily incurred'.

[8] Where the work was done before 1 April 2013 or where the case was commenced before 1 April 2013, the new words in CPR, r 44.2(a) (and the new provisions in CPR, r 44.3(5)), will not apply. CPR, r 44.3(7), reads as follows: 'Paragraphs (2)(a) and (5) do not apply in relation to—(a) cases commenced before 1st April 2013; or (b) costs incurred in respect of work done before 1st April 2013, and in relation to such cases or costs, rule 44.4.(2)(a) as it was in force immediately before 1st April 2013 will apply instead.'

[9] That is, the test articulated by Woolf MR in *Lownds v Home Office* [2002] EWCA Civ 365 (see 25.38).

[10] This sentence will not apply if the case was commenced before 1 April 2013 or if the costs were incurred in respect of work done before that date (see CPR, r 44.3(7)). Prior to that date, CPR, r 44.3, would apply, but those provisions were the same as the new provisions.

[11] See PD 44, para 6.2.

[12] See *Cook on Costs 2017* (LexisNexis, online), para 24.4.

a Grade B fee earner, this issue should be determined by the court sitting as a tribunal of fact and in accordance with the evidence: the evidence would either discharge the burden of proof or it would not. The issue of doubt would not arise and would have no part to play. This would be an entirely different exercise from asking whether it was *reasonable* to allocate the matter to a Grade A or a Grade B fee earner: where that is the question, the issue of doubt might have a considerable part to play.

The test to be applied on assessment: indemnity basis

16.09 In so far as the indemnity basis is concerned, CPR, r 44.3(3), reads as follows:

> '(3) Where the amount of costs is to be assessed on the indemnity basis, the court will resolve any doubt which it may have as to whether costs were reasonably incurred or were reasonable in amount in favour of the receiving party.'

Thus, on the indemnity basis, the court will resolve any doubt that it may have as to whether costs were reasonably incurred or were reasonable in amount in favour of the receiving party. Moreover, proportionality will not apply and the receiving party will not be constrained by any costs management order (see 12.166–12.171).

The differences between the two bases of assessment

16.10 Whilst each basis embraces a number of variations on its theme,[13] the two bases of assessment may be distinguished in the following ways.[14]

- **Benefit of doubt** On the indemnity basis, where there is a need to resolve doubt as to whether costs were reasonably incurred or reasonable in amount, it is the receiving party who gets the benefit of that doubt; on the standard basis, the beneficiary is the paying party (see 16.05, 16.09 and 16.11).
- **Proportionality** On the standard basis, the receiving party will bear the burden of proving that the costs are proportionate; on the indemnity basis, that burden will not exist. The topic of proportionality is dealt with in Chapter 25.
- **Budgets** On the standard basis, the court will depart from the last approved or agreed budget only if satisfied that there is 'good reason' to do so (see 12.140–12.165); on the indemnity basis, this restriction does not exist (see 12.166–12.171).

The differences between the two bases of assessment: doubt and reasonableness

16.11 As to the way in which the two bases of assessment differ in their treatment of the issue of reasonableness, Woolf CJ had this to say:

> 'The differences are two-fold. First, the differences are as to the onus which is on a party to establish that the costs were reasonable. In the case of a standard order, the onus is on the party in whose favour the order has been made. In the case of an indemnity order, the onus of showing the costs are not reasonable is on the party against whom the order has been made.'[15]

[13] For example, the way in which the court deals with proportionality when carrying out an assessment under the standard basis will vary depending on when the case was commenced and when the work was done (see 25.17 *et seq*). Likewise, costs on the indemnity basis may, in some circumstances, be subject to certain presumptions, some of which may have a substantial bearing on the outcome of the assessment (see, eg, CPR, r 46.9(3)).

[14] CPR, r 44.3(1); see also PD 44, paras 6.1 and 6.2.

[15] *Excelsior Commercial & Industrial Holdings Ltd v Salisbury Hamer Aspden & Johnson (Costs)* [2002] EWCA Civ 879, at [15].

The differences between the two bases of assessment: proportionality

Woolf CJ had the following to say about the rule that proportionality plays in distinguishing the two bases of assessment: **16.12**

> 'The other important distinction between a standard order and an indemnity order is the fact that, whereas in the case of a standard order the court will only allow costs which are proportionate to the matters in issue, this requirement of proportionality does not exist in relation to an order which is made on the indemnity basis. This is a matter of real significance. On the one hand, it means that an indemnity order is one which does not have the important requirement of proportionality which is intended to reduce the amount of costs which are payable in consequence of litigation. On the other hand, an indemnity order means that a party who has such an order made in their favour is more likely to recover a sum which reflects the actual costs in the proceedings.'[16]

These observations were made before implementation of the changes referred to in 16.06, but they remain apposite.

The Circumstances in which an Award on the Indemnity Basis Might be Made

Broadly speaking, there are two circumstances in which a party engaged in litigation may be ordered to pay their opponent's costs on the indemnity basis. The first is as a result of the court exercising its discretion under CPR, r 44.2; the second is as a result of a defendant failing to beat a claimant's extant Part 36 offer. The latter is dealt with in Chapter 17 (see, in particular, 17.81). **16.13**

This chapter focuses primarily on costs between opposing parties. The indemnity basis will also apply in certain other circumstances, such as where the costs are payable by a client to their own solicitor[17] (see 37.02), where the costs of a trustee or personal representative are to be paid out of the relevant trust fund or estate[18] (see 66.36) or where costs are payable on the indemnity basis pursuant to contract (see 66.18). **16.14**

Orders to Pay Costs on the Indemnity Basis Pursuant to CPR, r 44.2

The origin and extent of the jurisdiction

The jurisdiction to make an award on the indemnity basis arises from the CPR. The CPR do not confer that power by express terms, but, when read in conjunction with CPR, rr 44.1 and 44.3(4), CPR, r 44.2(1)(b), confers the power by implication.[19] The court lacks the power to delegate the task of deciding the basis upon which costs are to be assessed to a costs judge.[20] **16.15**

[16] *Ibid.*

[17] See CPR, r 46.9(3); PD 46, para 6.2 (previously CPR, r 48.8(2)); CPD, art 54.2(1)).

[18] See CPR, r 46.3(3); PD 46, para 1.1 (previously CPR, r 48.4(3)).

[19] If authority is needed on the point, see *Reid Minty (a firm) v Taylor* [2001] EWCA Civ 1723, at [27].

[20] *Old Street Homes v Chelsea Bridge Apartments Ltd* [2018] EWHC 1162 (Ch), at [31], *per* Kramer J.

The (extremely rare) circumstances in which an award on the indemnity basis cannot be made

16.16 The jurisdiction to make an award on the indemnity basis is subject to certain restrictions arising out of the indemnity principle, but they are so rarely encountered that they can safely be disregarded in most circumstances.

- **Restriction in the retainer** If, as occasionally happens,[21] the retainer expressly provides that costs will be assessed on the standard basis, then, by operation of the indemnity principle, costs will be recoverable only to that extent. It should be noted that litigation funding agreements often contain provisions that costs will be funded only to the extent that they would be allowable on a standard basis; if (as sometimes happens) that agreement becomes part of, or qualifies, the contract of retainer, it is easily arguable that this would preclude an award of costs on the indemnity basis.
- **Legally aided costs incurred under a certificate issued in other jurisdictions or before 1994** Costs may not be recovered on the indemnity basis if the receiving party is a legally aided party whose legal aid certificate was granted before February 1994.[22] The same may be true if legal aid has been granted in certain other jurisdictions, such as Northern Ireland.[23]

Proportionality and applications for costs on the indemnity basis

16.17 As with any other aspect of litigation, applications for costs on the indemnity basis are themselves subject to the restraint of proportionality. Akenhead J had this to say on the topic:

> 'In cases where the parties have settled through the Part 36 procedure or otherwise but leave the Judge to decide costs, particularly where indemnity costs are claimed, parties must act in a proportionate way. There can be few if any cases in which there should in effect be a trial of all or some of the settled issues in the case. Where the indemnity costs application depends on evidence which is likely to involve material conflicts of evidence the applicant party needs to think long and hard about whether it is appropriate to pursue the application.'[24]

Thus, where a proposed application depends on evidence that is likely to involve material conflicts of evidence, the applicant must think long and hard about whether it will be appropriate to go down that road.

The circumstances in which the jurisdiction will be exercised

16.18 The discretion to make an award on the indemnity basis is to be exercised judicially and having regard to the matters referred to in CPR, r 44.2(4) and (5).[25] Tomlinson LJ has

[21] Such restrictions are (generally) found only in standard agreements between liability insurers and their solicitors, and even then only rarely. As an example of a case in which such a restriction was a factor, see *Euro Asian Oil SA v Credit Suisse AG & Ors* [2016] EWHC 3340 (Comm), *per* Cranston J.

[22] See *Willis v Redbridge Health Authority* [1996] 1 WLR 1228; *Brawley v Marczynski & Anor (No 2)* [2002] EWCA Civ 1453, at [17]. This is because the indemnity principle would apply and the costs of such a legally aided litigant's solicitor could be assessed on only a standard basis: see Civil Legal Aid (General) Regulations 1989 (SI 1989/339) (in its original form), reg 107. For the avoidance of doubt, the restriction does not apply to publicly funded litigants whose certificates were issued after February 1994: see *Brawley v Marczynski & Anor (No 2)* [2002] EWCA Civ 1453.

[23] Whilst not binding, see, eg, *CG v Facebook Ireland Ltd* [2015] NIQB 28.

[24] *Courtwell Properties Ltd v Greencore PF (UK) Ltd* [2014] EWHC 184 (TCC), at [42].

[25] *Reid Minty (a firm) v Taylor* [2001] EWCA Civ 1723, at [27].

made it clear that 'the discretion [to award costs on the indemnity basis] is to be exercised in the light of *all* the circumstances of the case'.[26]

The general forensic method

Neither the CPR nor their associated practice directions provide any express guidance as to the forensic method that should apply when the court is deciding whether to make an award on the indemnity basis. Waller LJ, however, formulated the following question: 'The question will always be: is there something in the conduct of the action or the circumstances of the case which takes the case out of the norm in a way which justifies an order for indemnity costs?'[27] Whilst this is the test that is often cited by practitioners,[28] it is a test of limited practical use because it is circular—in particular, it is not a test of whether the circumstances are simply out of the norm, but whether the circumstances are out of the norm *in a way that justifies an order for indemnity costs.* That said, it is often cited as being shorthand for the more extensive guidance that is discussed at 16.21–16.27. The phrase 'exceptional' is also often used as shorthand for 'out of the norm': Newey LJ has explained that the mere fact that a judge uses that terminology does not mean that the wrong test has been applied,[29] but both he and David Richards LJ have said that it would be preferable to use the correct terminology.[30] **16.19**

As with most matters relating to costs, hindsight should be avoided.[31] Beyond this, it is neither necessary nor desirable to be prescriptive about the factors that may be taken into account or the circumstances in which an indemnity basis costs order might be appropriate. Indeed, in response to an invitation to give general guidance, Woolf CJ declined in the following way: **16.20**

> 'In my judgment it is dangerous for the court to try and add to the requirements of the CPR which are not spelt out in the relevant parts of the CPR. This court can do no more than draw attention to the width of the discretion of the trial judge and re-emphasise the point that has already been made that, before an indemnity order can be made, there must be some conduct or some circumstance which takes the case out of the norm. That is the critical requirement.'[32]

This does not mean that the law is incapable of being summarised, however; judicial summaries of the law may, if the claim is comparable, be of assistance. Moreover, case examples may assist to a limited extent (see 16.31–16.67).

---

[26] See *Excalibur Ventures LLC Claimant v Texas Keystone Inc* [2016] EWCA Civ 1144, at [21], emphasis original.

[27] *Excelsior Commercial & Industrial Holdings Ltd v Salisbury Hamer Aspden & Johnson (Costs)* [2002] EWCA Civ 879, at [39].

[28] See, eg, *Siegel v Pummell* [2015] EWHC 195 (QB), at [11], *per* Wilkie J; *Euroption Strategic Fund Ltd v Skandaniaviska Enskilda Banken AB* [2012] EWHC 749 (Comm), at [25], *per* Gloster J; see also *Simmons & Simmons LLP v Hickox* [2013] EWHC 2141 (QB), at [14], *per* Coulson J.

[29] *Whaleys (Bradford) Led v Bennett& Anor* [2017] EWCA Civ 2143, at [21], *per* Newey LJ.

[30] *Ibid*, at [28], *per* David Richards LJ: 'Whatever the precise linguistic analysis, "exceptional" is apt as a matter of ordinary usage to suggest a stricter test and is best avoided.'

[31] *Healy-Upright v Bradley & Anor* [2007] EWHC 3161 (Ch), *per* Jonathan Gaunt QC (sitting as a deputy judge of the High Court); see also *Dee v Telegraph Media Group Ltd* [2010] EWHC 1939 (QB), at [3], *per* Sharpe J.

[32] *Excelsior Commercial & Industrial Holdings Ltd v Salisbury Hamer Aspden & Johnson (Costs)* [2002] EWCA Civ 879, at [32].

Culpability

16.21 Under the CPR, in contrast to the position under the Rules of the Supreme Court (RSC), an award of costs on the indemnity basis would not necessarily imply a degree of culpability on the part of the party against whom the award was made. This much would generally be obvious where the award is made under CPR, r 36.14 (see 17.81), but—as the Court of Appeal has often stressed and as is set out below—it would also be the case where an award is made under CPR, r 44.2. Nonetheless, for the reasons set out below, in *practice* it is rare for an award of costs on the indemnity basis to be made pursuant to CPR, r 44.2, unless there has been an element of unreasonable conduct on the part of the person against whom the order is made.

16.22 One of the first cases to deal with the issue of culpability was *Reid Minty*.[33] Having previously made an offer that the claim be discontinued with costs, the defendant went on to successfully defend the claim. The trial judge declined to make an award of costs on the indemnity basis, commenting that 'costs should only be awarded on an indemnity basis if there has been some sort of moral lack of probity or conduct deserving of moral condemnation on the part of the paying party'.[34]

16.23 In another case, May LJ held that the trial judge had misdirected himself:

> 'Under the CPR, it is not ... correct that costs are only awarded on an indemnity basis if there has been some sort of moral lack of probity or conduct deserving moral condemnation on the part of the paying party. The court has a wide discretion under Rule 44.3 which is not constrained ... by authorities decided under the rules which preceded the introduction of the CPR.'[35]

16.24 A few months later, in *Victor Kiam*,[36] a differently constituted Court of Appeal sought to clarify what had been said in *Reid Minty*. Simon Browne LJ said:

> 'I for my part, understand the Court [in *Reid Minty*] to have been deciding no more than that conduct, albeit falling short of misconduct deserving of moral condemnation, can be so unreasonable as to justify an order for indemnity costs. With that I respectfully agree. To my mind, however, such conduct would need to be unreasonable to a high degree; unreasonable in this context certainly does not mean merely wrong or misguided in hindsight. An indemnity costs order made under Rule 44 (unlike one made under Rule 36) does, I think, carry at least some stigma. It is of its nature penal rather than exhortatory.'[37]

16.25 In a further subsequent case before the Court of Appeal, both Waller LJ and Woolf CJ were keen to emphasise that there would still be cases in which an award of costs on the indemnity basis would be made even where there was no unreasonable conduct on the part of the party condemned in costs. In particular, Waller LJ said that Simon Browne LJ's language was not apposite to all circumstances.[38] Although Woolf CJ declined to give general

---

33 *Reid Minty (a firm) v Taylor* [2001] EWCA Civ 1723.

34 *Ibid*, at [9], *per* May LJ (citing the trial judge).

35 *Excelsior Commercial & Industrial Holdings Ltd v Salisbury Hamer Aspden & Johnson (Costs)* [2002] EWCA Civ 879, at [27], *per* May LJ (with whom Kay and Ward LJJ agreed).

36 *Victor Kiam v MGN Ltd* [2002] EWCA Civ 66.

37 *Ibid*, at [12]. See also *Arcadia Group Brands Ltd v Visa Inc* [2015] EWCA Civ 883, at [83], in which Sir Terence Etherton C referred to awards on the indemnity basis as being 'in its nature penal'.

38 *Excelsior Commercial & Industrial Holdings Ltd v Salisbury Hamer Aspden & Johnson (Costs)* [2002] EWCA Civ 879, at [38].

guidance (see 16.20), he did give the following illustrative examples of when an award may be made without culpable conduct:

> 'I give as an example a situation where a party is involved in proceedings as a test case although, so far as that party is concerned, he has no other interest than the issue that arises in that case, but is drawn into expensive litigation. If he is successful, a court may well say that an indemnity order was appropriate, although it could not be suggested that anyone's conduct in the case had been unreasonable. Equally there may be situations where the nature of the litigation means that the parties could not be expected to conduct the litigation in a proportionate manner. Again the conduct would not be unreasonable and it seems to me that the court would be entitled to take into account that sort of situation in deciding that an indemnity order was appropriate.'[39]

These examples are helpful, but largely because they illustrate how rare it would be for the court to make a discretionary award of costs on the indemnity basis where there has been no unreasonable conduct.[40] Indeed, a number of senior judges have expressed concern about the thought that a party could be condemned in indemnity costs in the absence of unreasonable conduct on that party's behalf.[41] **16.26**

It is fair to say that, in practice, most judges regard an award of costs on the indemnity basis as implying at least degree of moral condemnation[42] and, as such, there is often a degree of judicial resistance to applications for such costs. As a general practical rule, a 'significant level of unreasonableness or otherwise inappropriate conduct in its wider sense' is required.[43] The fact that unreasonable conduct may be commonly encountered in practice does not mean that it should be regarded as the benchmark: Newey LJ has explained that the word 'norm' is not intended to reflect whether what occurred was something that happened often, so that in one sense it might be seen as 'normal', but was intended to reflect something outside the ordinary and reasonable conduct of proceedings.[44] In addition to looking at conduct, many judges also ask themselves whether any injustice would arise if they were to deny the paying party the benefit of an assessment that is subject to a **16.27**

---

[39] *Ibid*, at [31].

[40] Indeed, the editor has found it a difficult task to identify case examples in which a purely discretionary award of costs on the indemnity basis has been made in the absence of some form of culpable conduct. It is possible, however, to point to the transcript (dated 13 June 2001) of a decision of Park J following his own decision in *Re Continental Assurance Co of London plc (in liquidation)* [2007] 2 BCLC 287, in which he made an award against liquidators who had—quite reasonably and properly—increased costs by taking certain points.

[41] It is worth noting that, whilst *obiter*, both Lord Roger and Lord Carswell have expressed concern about awards of costs on the indemnity basis where there has been no unreasonable conduct (*Fourie v Le Roux* [2007] UKHL 1, at [46] and [49]). Although his was a dissenting speech, Lord Hope (at [10]) went so far as to interpret the judgment in *Reid Minty* as showing that an 'award of costs on [the indemnity] basis will not be justified unless the conduct of the paying party can be said in some respect to have been unreasonable'. It would be wrong to read too much into these comments (not least because their Lordships were at pains to emphasise that the responsibility for overseeing costs awards lay with the Court of Appeal rather than with them), but these comments do illustrate the fact that the jurisdiction under CPR, r 44.2, to make an award on the indemnity basis in the absence of unreasonable conduct is one that rarely arises.

[42] See, eg, *A v Lancashire County Council* [2013] EWHC 851 (Fam), at [24], in which Peter Jackson J declined to make an indemnity basis award against a local authority because he believed that their conduct did not 'merit the additional penalty or stigma of an award on the indemnity basis'.

[43] *R (on the application of Rawlinson & Hunter Trustees SA & Ors) v Serious Fraud Office* [2012] EWHC 3218 (Admin), at [6(c)], *per* Silber J.

[44] *Whaleys (Bradford) Led v Bennett & Anor* [2017] EWCA Civ 2143, at [22], citing comments made by Waller LJ in *Esure Services Ltd v Quarcoo* [2009] EWCA Civ 595, at [25].

'proportionate' limitation.[45] Other judges will—in some way—avoid making an award on the indemnity basis by taking into account facts that dilute any adverse findings that they may have made regarding the behaviour of the party who is to pay costs, such as where the other party had failed on certain issues[46] or had itself acted unreasonably.[47]

16.28 **The distinction between the party putatively at fault and their advisers** It may be that the person who is being ordered to pay cost on the indemnity basis is not the same person as that who was guilty of culpable conduct. Each case will turn on its own facts, but it is open to the court to regard the putatively guilty side as being tarred with the same brush. In this regards, Tomlinson LJ had this to say (in the context of whether a litigation funder should pay costs on the indemnity basis):

> 'Where conduct comes into consideration in this context, the successful party is afforded a more generous basis for assessing which of his costs should be paid by his opponent because of the way in which the latter, or *those in his camp*, have acted. Thus ... a litigant may find himself liable to pay indemnity costs on account of the conduct of those whom he has chosen to engage—e.g. lawyers, or experts, which experts may themselves have been chosen by the lawyers, or the conduct of those whom he has chosen to enlist, e.g. witnesses, even though he is not personally responsible for it. ... [The] analysis here is not dependent upon rules of agency—expert and factual witnesses are not agents of the party on whose behalf they give evidence any more than they are agents of the funder. The principle is a broader principle of justice. Deployment of lawyers, experts and other witnesses is a necessary part of bringing the claim to a successful conclusion for the benefit of the litigant, and it is equally a necessary part of bringing it to a successful conclusion for the benefit of the funder.'[48]

That said, it is worth bearing in mind that there have been instances of the court deciding not to award costs on the indemnity basis on the grounds that it was not the paying party who was personally at fault.[49]

The costs of issues

16.29 An award on the indemnity basis does not need to relate to the whole of the costs in question; where practicable, an award on the indemnity basis may be made in respect of only certain issues.[50]

Causation

16.30 There is no requirement that the behaviour or circumstances that took the case out of the norm caused an increase in the costs claimed[51]—although, no doubt, if this can be shown, it would be a factor that could be taken into account.

---

[45] See, eg, *Euroption Strategic Fund Ltd v Skandaniaviska Enskilda Banken AB* [2012] EWHC 749 (Comm), at [18], *per* Gloster J. See also *Ross River Ltd v Waverly Commercial Ltd* [2012] EWHC 3006 (Ch), at [41]–[44], *per* Morgan J; *Digicel (St Lucia) Ltd (a company registered under the laws of St Lucia) v Cable & Wireless plc* [2010] EWHC 888 (Ch), at [13], [16], [18] and [19], *per* Morgan J.

[46] See, eg, *Nestec SA v Dualit Ltd* [2013] EWHC 1577 (Pat), in which Arnold J found that the paying parties' conduct had been unreasonable to such a degree that it would have been appropriate to order assessment upon the indemnity basis, but a fair reflection of the overall position (considering that the other side had been unsuccessful on two aspects) was to order that they pay costs on the standard basis.

[47] See, eg, *Lakehouse Contracts Ltd v UPR Services Ltd* [2014] EWHC 1223 (Ch).

[48] *Excalibur Ventures LLC v Texas Keystone Inc & Ors* [2016] EWCA Civ 1144, at [24].

[49] See, eg, *Salt v Corris Developments Ltd* [2011] EWHC 3822 (Ch), at [25].

[50] See *Webster v Ridgeway Foundation School* [2010] EWHC 318 (QB), at [7], *per* Nichol J.

[51] See *Phoenix Finance Ltd v Federation International de l'Automobile* [2002] EWHC 1028 (Ch).

Case Examples Relating to Costs on the Indemnity Basis

Whilst each case will turn on its own facts, the following examples (16.32–16.67) are illustrative of the types of case in which orders for indemnity basis costs may be made. It should not be forgotten that general guidance purporting to place a gloss on the CPR is generally unhelpful (see 16.20). Moreover, Mummery LJ's cautionary guidance on this point should be borne in mind—namely, that what may be sufficient to justify the exercise of the discretion in one case should not be treated as a necessary factor for its exercise in another.[52] **16.31**

Failure to cooperate with a view to resolving the dispute

A refusal to consider options other than squaring up for a fight will put an unregenerate party at risk. Kay LJ had this to say on the topic: **16.32**

> 'The approach of the CPR is a relatively simple one: namely, if one party has made a real effort to find a reasonable solution to the proceedings and the other party has resisted that sensible approach, then the latter puts himself at risk that the order for costs may be on an indemnity basis.'[53]

The following circumstances merit particular mention. **16.33**

- **Mediation** Unreasonably refusing an offer of mediation is capable of leading to an award of costs on the indemnity basis,[54] especially where the offer was in respect of a court-sanctioned scheme.[55] That said, the mere fact that there was a disagreement as to the timing of mediation would not generally justify an award of costs on the indemnity basis.[56] A refusal to mediate may also count against a party if that party is seeking costs on the indemnity basis.[57]
- **Failure to act on judicial encouragement** A refusal to respond to judicial encouragement to settle may lead to an award of costs on the indemnity basis—although Potter LJ expressed some doubt about the notion of the court giving weight to such issues.[58]

---

52 *Secretary of State for Trade and Industry v Aurum Marketing* [2000] EWCA Civ 224, at [4]; see also *Excalibur Ventures LLC Claimant v Texas Keystone Inc* [2014] EWHC 3436 (Comm), at [116], *per* Christopher Clarke LJ (sitting as a judge of the High Court), aff'd [2016] EWCA Civ 1144.

53 *Reid Minty (a firm) v Taylor* [2001] EWCA Civ 1723, at [37]; as a case example, see also *EQ Projects Ltd v Alavi* [2006] EWHC 29 (TCC).

54 See, eg, *Garritt-Critchley v Ronnan* [2014] EWHC 1774 (Ch), in which Judge Waksman QC made an order on the indemnity basis against a party who, in addition to having refused an offer of mediation, had unreasonably failed to engage in negotiation throughout.

55 *Virani v Manuel Revert y Cia Sa* [2003] EWCA Civ 1651.

56 See *Car Giant Ltd v Hammersmith LBC* [2017] EWHC 464 (TCC), at [24] and [27], *per* Stephen Furst QC.

57 See, eg, *In Re The Estate of Inchbald v Inchbald* [2017] EWHC 616 (Ch).

58 *Boynton v Willers* [2003] EWCA Civ 904, at [44]. See also *Board of Trustees of National Museums & Galleries on Merseyside v AEW Architects & Designers Ltd* [2013] EWHC 3025 (TCC), [22], [26] and [31–[32], where the court said that the defendant's conduct supported a case for indemnity costs, but once the claimant's procedural failings were taking into account, it would not be appropriate to make such an award. If, in a claim a judge says is weak, the defendant chooses not to take any steps to try to settle the matter, an award on the standard basis may be appropriate: see, eg, *Bocacina Ltd v Boca Cafes Ltd* [2014] EWHC 26 (IPEC), at [38], *per* Daniel Alexander QC.

- **Unrealistic attempts to resolve the dispute** If an attempt to resolve the dispute 'was close to an invitation by a defendant to the claimant to throw his hand in', it is likely that it would not be given much weight.[59]
- **Wasting the court's resources** The fact that a party's failure to cooperate has led to the court's resources being wasted may be relevant.[60] In view of the matters set out at 26.04, this may well be a factor to which more weight will be attached in the future.

Offers in general

16.34 Any admissible offer may be taken into account, including an offer made at a very early stage in proceedings that was not accompanied by an offer to pay the claimant's costs.[61] The decision whether to make an award on the indemnity basis has to be made according to the facts of the case in hand. The reasonableness of an offeree's failure to accept an offer must be gauged by reference to the facts as they were at the time; it would be wrong to say that just because an offeror has done better than their offer, the offeree acted unreasonably in not accepting it.[62]

16.35 The following circumstances merit particular mention.

- **Claimant's offers** A failure to accept a claimant's offer may be a relevant factor, but it would not give rise to a presumption that the defendant should pay costs on the indemnity basis,[63] because, in general, a claimant would have to show that the offeree had acted unreasonably.[64] (See also 16.36 and 16.37.)
- **Defendant's offers** The act of rejecting a defendant's offer to settle will not of itself ordinarily result in an award of costs on the indemnity basis,[65] even where the offer was a

---

[59] *Reid Minty (a firm) v Taylor* [2001] EWCA Civ 1723, at [30], *per* May LJ; as an example of this happening in practice, see *Waites Construction Ltd v HGP Greentree Alchurch Evans Ltd* [2005] EWHC 2174 (TCC).

[60] See, eg, *Igloo Regeneration (General Partner) Ltd v Powell Williams Partnership (Costs)* [2013] EWHC 1859 (TCC), at [32], *per* Akenhead J. Whilst it related to an application rather than a total claim, see *Phaestos Ltd v Ho* [2012] EWHC 668 (TCC) (changing solicitors at a time when the parties ought to have been engaged in resolving the issues in the application, in respect of which the paying party ultimately said virtually nothing).

[61] Whilst the court did not make an award on the indemnity basis, see *Bocacina Ltd v Boca Cafes Ltd* [2014] EWHC 26 (IPEC), at [15], *per* Daniel Alexander QC. See also *Wilkinson v London Strategic Health Authority* [2012] EWPCC 55, *per* Birss J.

[62] See *F & C Alternative Investments (Holdings) Ltd & Ors Appellants v Barthelemy* [2012] EWCA Civ 843, at [69], *per* Davis LJ. See also, on a related point, *Purrunsing v A'Court & Co and House Owners Conveyancers Ltd (Costs)* [2016] EWHC 1528 (Ch), at [27], *per* Judge Pelling QC (sitting as a judge of the High Court).

[63] *Fitzpatrick Contractors Ltd v Tyco Fire & Integrated Solutions (UK) Ltd* [2008] EWHC 1391 (TCC), at [37], which was in the context of a late acceptance of a claimant's Part 36 offer, but the issue that was being addressed was whether the defendant had acted reasonably. See also *Travelers Casualty and Surety Co of Canada v Sun Life Assurance Co of Canada (UK) Ltd* [2006] EWHC 2885 (Comm), at [8] and [9], *per* Christopher Clarke J. Whilst not binding, see also *McKeown v Venton* (unreported), 12 June 2017, Liverpool County Court, at [43]–[49], *per* Judge Graham Wood QC. See also *Car Giant Ltd v Hammersmith LBC* [2017] EWHC 464 (TCC), at [28] and [29], *per* Stephen Furst QC.

[64] See *F & C Alternative Investments (Holdings) Ltd & Ors Appellants v Barthelemy* [2012] EWCA Civ 843, at [70], *per* Davis LJ. Indeed, in *Travelers Casualty and Surety Co of Canada v Sun Life Assurance Co of Canada (UK) Ltd* [2006] EWHC 2885 (Comm), at [8], Christopher Clarke J referred to *Kiam v MGN Ltd (No 2)* [2002] EWCA Civ 66 and found that an award on the indemnity basis 'requires unreasonableness to a high degree'. See also *Governors and Company of the Bank of Ireland v Watts Group plc* [2017] EWHC 2472 (TCC), *per* Coulson J.

[65] This will be the case even where a defendant has put forward other reasonable offers: see *Epsom College v Pierse Contracting Southern Ltd (formerly Biseley Construction Ltd) (in liquidation)* [2011] EWCA Civ 1449, at [72], *per* Rix LJ.

'drop hands' offer that the offeror subsequently 'beat'[66] (see also 16.36). Simon Brown LJ had the following to say on the point:

> '[It] will be a rare case indeed where the refusal of a settlement offer will attract under Rule 44 not merely an adverse order for costs, but an order on an indemnity rather than standard basis. Take this very case. No encouragement in the way of an expectation of indemnity costs was required ... [The offer's] object was to protect the respondent against a standard costs order were the Court, say, to reduce the damages to that level.'[67]

Where the refusal is coupled with other factors, an award on the indemnity basis may be justified.[68]

- **Withdrawn Part 36 offers** See 16.37.
- **Late acceptance of offers** The same applies to late acceptance of an offer, especially if the amount claimed had changed in such a way as to make the offer more attractive to the offeree.[69] Accepting an offer late without explanation may result in an award on the indemnity basis.[70]
- **Unreasonable conduct and offers** Circumstances in which an order on the indemnity basis may be made include where the offeree's rejection was combined with unreasonable conduct in general,[71] or where a claimant has rejected two reasonable offers made by the defendant (this, nonetheless, being by no means an invariable rule).[72] Another example would be where significant costs had been incurred as a result of a claimant's unwillingness to accept an amount, offered by the defendant, at which they had been prepared to settle only a few days earlier.[73]

As can be seen from the first two points above, a party who makes an offer should not expect to be awarded costs on the indemnity basis merely because they subsequently 'beat' it (unless, of course, it is an extant claimant's Part 36 offer). If the offeror is a claimant, then the offer will be taken into account and may give rise to such an award,[74] but this would **16.36**

---

66 *Forcelux Ltd v Binnie (Costs)* [2009] EWCA Civ 1077, at [18], *per* Warren J.

67 *Victor Kiam v MGN Ltd* [2002] EWCA Civ 66, at [13].

68 See *Richmond Pharmacology Ltd v Chester Overseas Ltd* [2014] EWHC 3418 (Ch), at [4(i)], *per* Mr Stephen Jourdan QC (sitting as a deputy High Court judge); see also *Arroyo & Ors v Equion Energia Ltd* [2016] EWHC 3348 (TCC), at [65], *per* Stuart-Smith J.

69 *Fitzpatrick Contractors Ltd v Tyco Fire & Integrated Solutions (UK) Ltd* [2008] EWHC 1391 (TCC), at [37] and [38], in the context of a late acceptance of a claimant's Part 36 offer, but the issue that was being addressed was whether the defendant had acted reasonably. Late acceptance of a defendant's offer may give rise to an award on the indemnity basis: see, eg, *Lokhova v Longmuir* [2017] EWHC 3125 (QB), *per* Warby J (although there were factors other than the late acceptance at play).

70 See, eg, *Optical Express v Associated Newspapers (Costs)* [2017] EWHC 2707 (QB), at [50]–[53], *per* Warby J.

71 See *Noorani v Calver* [2009] EWHC 592 (QB), at [12], *per* Coulson J; *Southwark LBC v IBM UK Ltd (Costs)* [2011] EWHC 653 (TCC), at [4(h)], *per* Akenhead J.

72 *Southwark LBC v IBM UK Ltd (Costs)* [2011] EWHC 653 (TCC), at [4(i)], *per* Akenhead J. *Franks v Sinclair (Costs)* [2006] EWHC 3656 (Ch), *per* David Richards J, is often cited as being authority for the proposition that a refusal of two reasonable offers will justify an award of costs on the indemnity basis, but Rix LJ explained that this was only one factor amongst others (the implication being that it was not of itself sufficient to justify an award on the indemnity basis).

73 See, eg, *Igloo Regeneration (General Partner) Ltd v Powell Williams Partnership (Costs)* [2013] EWHC 1859 (TCC), at [32], *per* Akenhead J.

74 See *F & C Alternative Investments (Holdings) Ltd & Ors Appellants v Barthelemy* [2012] EWCA Civ 843, at [63], in which Davies LJ said (*obiter*) that 'perhaps there can be *de minimis* errors or obvious slips which mislead no one: but the general rule, in my opinion, is that for an offer to be a Part 36 offer it must strictly

not be as a result of a mechanistic entitlement as per Part 36[75]—and this would particularly be so if the offer were made just before trial or at a time when evidence was still being disclosed.[76] If the offeror is a defendant, they would generally not be entitled to such an award because it would usually be sufficient that the offer afforded protection against an adverse costs order.[77] That said, if the court finds—as it occasionally will—that it was unreasonable of the claimant (or appellant or applicant) to fail to accept the offer, then the court may be persuaded to make an award on the indemnity basis.[78]

16.37 In a case in which two claimants had made 'admissible offers', one of which was a withdrawn Part 36 offer and the other of which was a *Calderbank* offer, Mann J found of the former that it 'could play a part in a general assessment of the reasonableness or unreasonableness of the [offeree's] conduct, but it cannot be elevated to a position comparable to a living Part 36 offer merely because it has been beaten'.[79] On the facts of the case before him (in which the offer was being relied upon for the purposes of trying to obtain costs in the indemnity basis), Mann J said that it '[added] little'.[80] As to the *Calderbank* offer, he said that it was 'no stronger, and if anything [was] weaker by never having been a Part 36 offer'.[81] That said, there have been instances of the court awarding indemnity basis costs as a result of a failure to accept a withdrawn Part 36 offer in cases in which the facts would permit such a finding on the grounds of conduct.[82]

Weak cases (claims or defences)

16.38 Provided that it was at least arguable, the pursuit of a weak case—be it a fragile claim or a brass-necked defence—will not of itself be sufficient to justify an order for costs on the indemnity basis.[83] Where, however, the insubstantiality of the case was such that it was

---

comply with the requirements'. Davies LJ said that—contrary to Underhill J's analysis in *Huntley v Simmonds* [2009] EWHC 406 (QB)—it was 'not permissible wholly to discount a number of failures to comply with the requirements of Part 36 as the merest technicality'. In a similar vein, Davies LJ said that, in *Fitzroy Robinson Ltd v Mentmore Towers Ltd* [2010] EWHC 98 (TCC), at [25], Coulson J went too far in awarding indemnity costs on the grounds that if '[those] offers [had] been made as Part 36 offers, then indemnity costs would have been payable as a matter of course'.

[75] See *F & C Alternative Investments (Holdings) Ltd & Ors Appellants v Barthelemy* [2012] EWCA Civ 843, at [64], *per* Davies LJ. See also *Brit Inns Ltd (in liquidation) v BDW Trading Ltd* [2012] EWHC 2489 (TCC), at [34], *per* Coulson J; *French v Groupama Insurance Co Ltd* [2011] EWCA Civ 1119, at [41]; *Epsom College v Pierse Contracting Southern Ltd (formerly Biseley Construction Ltd) (in liquidation)* [2011] EWCA Civ 1449, at [54] *et seq*, *per* Rix LJ.

[76] See *Manna (a Child and Protected Party) v Central Manchester University Hospitals NHS Foundation Trust* [2017] EWCA Civ 12, at [40], *per* Tomlinson LJ.

[77] See also *HLB Kidsons (a firm) v Lloyds Underwriters subscribing to Lloyd's Policy No 621/PKIDOO101* [2007] EWHC 2699 (Comm). See also *Société Internationale de Télécommunications Aéronautiques SC v Wyatt Co (UK) Ltd* [2002] EWHC 2401 (Ch).

[78] See, eg, *Kearns v Kemp* [2013] EWHC 4093 (QB), at [15], *per* Nichol J; *D Morgan plc v Mace & Jones (a firm)* [2011] EWHC 26 (TCC), *per* Coulson J. In a similar vein, see *Southwark LBC v IBM UK Ltd (Costs)* [2011] EWHC 653 (TCC), *per* Akenhead J; *Barr v Biffa Waste Services Ltd (Costs)* [2011] EWHC 1107 (TCC), *per* Coulson J, both cited with apparent approval by Rix LJ in *Epsom College v Pierse Contracting Southern Ltd (formerly Biseley Construction Ltd) (in liquidation)* [2011] EWCA Civ 1449, at [72].

[79] See *Gulati v MGN Ltd* [2015] EWHC 1805 (Ch), at [22].

[80] See *ibid*, at [23].

[81] *Ibid*, at [25].

[82] See, eg, *Botrill v Thompson* (unreported), 27 October 2017, QBD, *per* Judge Waksman QC (sitting as a judge of the High Court), in which case the offer was said to have been very generous.

[83] *Shania Investment Corpn v Standard Bank London Ltd* (unreported), 2 November 2001.

hopeless[84] or doomed to failure,[85] then that may well lead to such an award. Where the frailty of the case is not so great, it may still be the factor that tips the balance when other factors are taken into account. When deciding the merits of a case or of a part thereof, it is permissible to look at the whole of the case rather than at each part individually.[86]

In addition to the specific points made at 16.40, the following more general points can be made about weak claims and poor defences. **16.39**

- **Claimants and applicants** Whilst losing a case is not to be equated with unreasonable conduct, there does come a point at which a claim is so hopeless that its pursuit can properly be said to be unreasonable.[87] Reasonableness would appear to be the touchstone: advancing a 'hopeless' claim or application,[88] an 'unarguable' claim,[89] a 'far-fetched and speculative' claim,[90] or a claim that is 'speculative, grossly exaggerated and opportunistic'[91] would put the claimant at risk. Advancing a claim that was arguable, but weak, would generally not pose such a risk,[92] but there are exceptions (especially where there were other factors at play).[93] Panglossian optimism may prove dangerous and, in this regard, Laddie J has observed that pursuing a claim that is 'Macawber-ish in the hope that something might turn up' is a high-risk strategy.[94]

[84] See *Elvanite Full Circle Ltd v Amec Earth & Environmental UK Ltd* [2013] EWHC 1643 (TCC), at [16], *per* Coulson J. See also *Franklin v Maddison* [2014] EWCA Civ 628. If the case is an abuse of process, that can result in an award on the indemnity basis: see the brief discussion of this topic by Morgan J in *Nemetona Trading Ltd v Golding Corpn Ltd* [2013] EWHC 4569 (Ch), at [22].

[85] '[T]o maintain a claim that you know, or ought to know, is doomed to fail on the facts and on the law, is conduct that is so unreasonable as to justify an order for indemnity costs': *Wates Construction Ltd v HGP Greentree Allchurch Evans Ltd* [2006] BLR 45, at [27], *per* Judge Coulson QC. In a similar vein, see *Noorani v Calver* [2009] EWHC 592 (QB), at [9], *per* Coulson J. More recently, see *Elkamet Kunststofftechnik GmBH v Saint-Gobain Glass France SA* [2016] EWHC 3240 (Pat), at [37] and [38], *per* Arnold J (defendant ultimately forced to accept that the patent was not infringed in circumstances in which that conclusion was more or less inevitable).

[86] Whilst only persuasive rather than binding, see *Curran v Revenue and Customs Commissioners* [2012] UKFTT 655 (TC), at [7]–[8], [13], [17], [19]–[20] and [24]–[26], *per* Judge Roger Berner.

[87] *Webster v The Ridgeway Foundation School* [2010] EWHC 318 (QB), at [7].

[88] See, eg, *Legal Costsmasters Ltd v Insurance & Legal Services UK Ltd* (unreported), 30 April 2013, QBD, *per* Judge Seymour QC. See also *Simmons & Simmons LLP v Hickox* [2013] EWHC 2141 (QB), at [15], *per* Coulson J: '[The] application was (and should have been seen to have been) hopeless.' See also *Waites Construction Ltd v HGP Greentree Alchurch Evans Ltd* [2006] BLR 45.

[89] *Mahme Trust Reg & Ors v Lloyds TSB Bank plc* [2006] EWHC 1782 (Ch), at [1] and [13], *per* Evans-Lombe J.

[90] See, eg, *Singh v Singh* [2014] EWHC 1770 (Ch), at [8], in which Sir William Blackburne made an award against a claimant who, amongst other things, had brought a claim that 'overall was far-fetched, speculative and irreconcilable with a whole raft of documents'.

[91] See, eg, *Euroption Strategic Fund Ltd v Skandaniaviska Enskilda Banken AB* [2012] EWHC 749 (Comm), at [18], *per* Gloster J. See also *Smart Currency Exchange v Martell* [2014] EWHC 1507 (QB), in which Judge Seymour QC made an order on the indemnity basis against a defendant who had sought certain injunctions that were misconceived and speculative, and who discontinued those claims the day before the hearing.

[92] See, eg, *CG Group Ltd v Breyer Group plc* [2013] EWHC 2959 (TCC), in which Akenhead J found that whilst the losing party's case was weak, it had 'some merit'.

[93] See, eg, *Three Rivers District Council & Ors v Bank of England* [2006] EWHC 816 (Comm), at [25], *per* Tomlinson J. See also *Excelsior Commercial & Industrial Holdings Ltd v Salisbury Hamer Aspden & Johnson (Costs)* [2002] EWCA Civ 879; as an example in practice, see *Waites Construction Ltd v HGP Greentree Alchurch Evans Ltd* [2005] EWHC 2174 (TCC).

[94] *IPC Media v Highbury Leisure Publishing Ltd* [2005] EWHC 283 (Ch), at [24]. See also *Digicel (St Lucia) Ltd (a company registered under the laws of St Lucia) v Cable & Wireless plc* [2010] EWHC 888 (Ch), at [13], [16], [18] and [19], in which Morgan J was unimpressed by the scattergun approach of the claimant.

- **Defendants, counterclaimants and respondents** Similar principles to those set out above will apply where the case is a counterclaim[95] or, with appropriate modifications, a defence.[96] Where the court makes an award on the indemnity basis against a defendant, it is not uncommon for it to relate to only part of the case. In a case in which he found that the denial of liability was 'unreasonable to a marked extent', for example, David Steel J found that it was appropriate to make an award of costs on the indemnity basis, but only up to the date on which an admission was tardily made.[97]

16.40 Whilst nothing that is set out below amounts to a rule or principle, the following observations may be of assistance.

- **Use of the court's resources** It is worth noting that (after 1 April 2013, in particular[98]) the court is able take into account the drain which unmeritorious litigation can impose on it resources.[99]
- **Hindsight** As with most issues relating to costs, hindsight should be avoided—in particular, it would be wrong to label a claim has being hopeless if that conclusion is made only with the benefit of hindsight.[100]
- **Resounding success (by an opponent)** In a similar vein, the fact of success, no matter how resounding, will not of itself generally be sufficient to justify an award of costs on the indemnity basis.[101] Where a party has been so successful that it is possible to say that the other side's case was an abuse of process or was unarguable, however, then an award on the indemnity basis would often follow.[102]
- **Summary judgment** Hopeless cases are, of course, the norm in respect of successful applications for summary judgment. As such, it would generally not be appropriate to order costs on the indemnity basis solely on the ground that the losing side's case had been found to have no real prospect of success.[103] Making an unjustified application for

[95] *Chantrey Vellacott v The Convergence Group plc* [2007] EWHC 1774 (Ch), *per* Rimer J. See also *Shackleton & Associates Ltd v Shamsi* [2017] EWHC 304 (Comm), at [28]–[36], *per* Teare J.

[96] See, eg, *Hobbs v Gibson* [2011] EWHC 762 (Ch), *per* Judge Purle QC (defendant liquidators had maintained an untenable position throughout); *Pochin Construction Ltd v Liberty Property (GP) Ltd* [2014] EWHC 2919 (TCC), *per* Akenhead (a complete absence of a defence to enforcement of an adjudication award and no justifiable reason for the refusal to pay).

[97] *Colour Quest Ltd v Total Downstream UK Plc* [2009] EWHC 823 (Comm).

[98] See CPR, r 1.1(2)(e).

[99] See, eg, *Excalibur Ventures LLC Claimant v Texas Keystone Inc* [2013] EWHC 4278 (Comm), at [63], *per* Christopher Clarke LJ (sitting in the High Court), aff'd [2016] EWCA Civ 1144.

[100] *Healy-Upright v Bradley & Anor* [2007] EWHC 3161 (Ch), *per* Jonathan Gaunt QC (sitting as a deputy judge of the High Court); see also *Dee v Telegraph Media Group Ltd* [2010] EWHC 1939 (QB), at [3], *per* Sharpe J. See also *Obrascon Huarte Lain SA v Gibraltar* [2014] EWHC 2291 (TCC); *Amoco (UK) Exploration Co v British American Offshore Ltd* [2002] BLR 135; *Balmoral Group Ltd v Borealis (UK) Ltd* [2006] EWHC 2531 (Comm).

[101] See *Obrascon Huarte Lain SA v Gibraltar* [2014] EWHC 2291 (TCC), aff'd on appeal at [2015] EWCA Civ 712; *Amoco (UK) Exploration Co v British American Offshore Ltd* [2002] BLR 135. See also *Balmoral Group Ltd v Borealis (UK) Ltd* [2006] EWHC 2531 (Comm). In a similar vein, Lewison J has found that there is nothing out of the ordinary about making an order for summary judgment in a case in which that was the very application before the court: *Easyair Ltd (t/a Openair) v Opal Telecom Ltd* [2009] EWHC 779 (Ch).

[102] See the brief discussion of this topic by Morgan J in *Nemetona Trading Ltd v Golding Corpn Ltd* [2013] EWHC 4569 (Ch), at [22].

[103] See *Astilleros Canarios SA v 3264741 Nova Scotia Ltd* (unreported), 21 July 2017, QBD (Comm), *per* David Foxton QC.

summary judgment may attract an award on the indemnity basis,[104] as may capitulating the claim after having opposed an application.[105]

- **Large claims** The fact that a claimant loses a massive claim and does so badly is not of itself a reason for ordering indemnity costs; cases involving very large sums that founder on craggy juridical rocks are not automatically outside of the norm.[106] That said, if that litigation resulted in a resounding defeat on a party's factual case with the rejection of most of their evidence, that party will be at risk.[107] Similarly, if a claimant brought large-scale and expensive litigation that was calculated to exert commercial pressure on an opponent, that party too may be at risk.[108]
- **Abandoned issues** If a party abandons arguments relating to discrete issues, then whilst it is possible that they may have to pay costs on the indemnity basis, this would not generally be the case.[109] This is addressed more fully at 16.43.
- **Parts of claims and applications** It does not have to be the whole claim that was misconceived: making a baseless application (such as an application for wasted costs[110]) may result in an award on the indemnity basis. Similarly, in cases concerning public law, an unmeritorious application will often result in an award of costs on the indemnity basis.[111]
- **Weak legal arguments** Sir Terence Etherton C has explained that weakness of a legal argument is not, without more, justification for an indemnity basis of costs.[112]
- **Poor judgement and poor legal advice** Misjudging the merits of a case may lead to an award on the indemnity basis.[113] There is no general principle that a litigant would be immune from such an award if they were able to show that they had acted only on legal advice,[114] but there will be occasions on which this will be factor that will weigh against such an order.[115] The way in which a claim is presented may be a factor: if a weak case has 'all the hallmarks of a lawyer's artefact',[116] the party who argues that case (or possibly their legal representatives) will be at risk.

---

[104] See, eg, *Libyan Investment Authority v Goldman Sachs International* [2014] EWHC 3364 (Ch), *per* Rose J. See also *Simmons & Simmons v Charles Hickox* [2013] EWHC 2141 (QB).

[105] See, eg, *Lifeline Gloves Ltd v Richardson* [2005] EWHC 1524 (Ch).

[106] *Excalibur Ventures LLC Claimant v Texas Keystone Inc* [2013] EWHC 4278 (Comm), at [7], *per* Christopher Clarke LJ (sitting in the High Court), aff'd [2016] EWCA Civ 1144.

[107] *Walter Lilly & Co Ltd v Mackay* [2012] EWHC 1972 (TCC), at [15], *per* Akenhead J.

[108] *Fiona Trust & Holding Corpn v Privalov* [2011] EWHC 664 (Comm), at [61(8)(g)], *per* Andrew Smith J.

[109] See, eg, at *Catalyst Investment Group Ltd v Max Lewisohn, Maximillian and Co (a firm)* [2009] EWHC 3501 (Ch), at [44] and [48], *per* Barling J.

[110] See, eg, *Rybak v Langbar International Ltd* [2011] EWHC 452 (Ch).

[111] *R (on the application of Corner House Research) v Secretary of State for Trade and Industry* [2005] EWCA Civ 192, at [79]. This was a misguided application to set aside a protective costs order.

[112] *Arcadia Group Brands Ltd v Visa Inc* [2015] EWCA Civ 883, at [83].

[113] *Wall v Lefever* [1998] 1 FCR 605, at 614, in which Lord Woolf MR made an order just before the introduction of the CPR.

[114] The seminal case that is usually referred to on this point is *Dymocks Franchise Systems (NSW) Ltd v Todd* [2004] 1 WLR 2807, at [33], in which the Privy Council regarded the existence of encouraging advice from leading counsel as no ground for not making a non-party costs order. For more recent authorities, see *Kearns v Kemp* [2013] EWHC 4093 (QB), at [15], *per* Nichol J; *Excalibur Ventures LLC Claimant v Texas Keystone Inc* [2014] EWHC 3436 (Comm), at [94] and [118], *per* Christopher Clarke LJ (sitting as a judge of the High Court), aff'd [2016] EWCA Civ 1144. See also *BE Studios v Smith & Williamson Ltd* [2005] EWHC 2730 (Ch), at [19], *per* Evans-Lombe J, which was referred to by Christopher Clarke LJ in *Excalibur*, at [122].

[115] See *Zissis v Lukomski* [2006] EWCA Civ 341, at [51], *per* Sir Peter Gibson.

[116] *Excalibur Ventures LLC Claimant v Texas Keystone Inc* [2013] EWHC 4278 (Comm), at [42], *per* Christopher Clarke LJ (sitting as a judge of the High Court), aff'd [2016] EWCA Civ 1144.

- **Litigants in person** In a similar vein, the fact that a party is or has been a litigant in person is a factor that may weigh against an order on the indemnity basis if the absence of legal guidance has contributed to conduct that would otherwise have been unreasonable.[117]
- **Weak claims brought against parties in the alternative** An order for costs on the indemnity basis may be made against a party who brings a weak case, even where it was brought as a claim in the alternative in circumstances in which it would have been unclear to the claimant whom to sue.[118]
- **Weak claims funded by litigation funders** Where a claim funded by a litigation funder is objectively hopeless, and where it required much time, labour and expense to refute, that would itself be a ground for indemnity costs both against the litigant *and* the funder.[119] In this regard, Tomlinson LJ had this to say:

  '[T]he derivative nature of a commercial funder's involvement should ordinarily lead to his being required to contribute to the costs on the basis upon which they have been assessed against those whom he chose to fund. That is not to say that there is an irrebuttable presumption that that will be the outcome, but rather that that is the outcome which will ordinarily, in the nature of things, be just and equitable.'[120]

  The fact that such an order may deter litigation funders from offering to provide funding, thereby making access to justice that much harder, is not a reason for not making such an award.[121] There is no general principle that a funder would be immune from such an award by reason of the fact that it acted on legal advice.[122]
- **Evidence** Losing as a result of a party's evidence deteriorating under cross-examination will not, of itself, lead to an award on the indemnity basis.[123] The issue of expert evidence is addressed at 16.60.

Relief from sanctions and extensions of time

16.41 If a party seeks relief from sanctions, it is possible—depending on the facts—that they will be condemned to pay the costs of the application (or any costs thrown away) on the indemnity basis (see 16.42). That said, it should be borne in mind that Dyson MR and Vos LJ said (in a judgment to which they both contributed) that the parties should not 'adopt an uncooperative attitude in unreasonably refusing to agree extensions of time and

117 See, eg, *GHLM Trading v Maroo* (unreported), 27 February 2012, Ch D, *per* Newey J.

118 See *Dixon v Blindley Heath Investments Ltd* [2016] EWCA Civ 548, at [20]–[53], *per* Hildyard J.

119 *Excalibur Ventures LLC Claimant v Texas Keystone Inc* [2014] EWHC 3436 (Comm), at [97], *per* Christopher Clarke LJ (sitting as a judge of the High Court), aff'd [2016] EWCA Civ 1144 (see esp [23]–[28]).

120 *Excalibur Ventures LLC Claimant v Texas Keystone Inc* [2016] EWCA Civ 1144, at [27].

121 *Excalibur Ventures LLC Claimant v Texas Keystone Inc* [2014] EWHC 3436 (Comm), at [129], *per* Christopher Clarke LJ (sitting as a judge of the High Court), aff'd [2016] EWCA Civ 1144.

122 See *Excalibur Ventures LLC Claimant v Texas Keystone Inc* [2014] EWHC 3436 (Comm), at [119], *per* Christopher Clarke LJ (sitting as a judge of the High Court), aff'd [2016] EWCA Civ 1144 (esp at [24]). This was partly a decision taken on pragmatic grounds—namely, that 'such an inquiry [as to the funder's knowledge and role] would ... be difficult in circumstances where the true position is in large measure known only to the funder and his agents and where many of the relevant communications may be privileged (either in favour of the funder or the person funded)': *ibid*, at [119], *per* Christopher Clarke LJ. See also *Fulton Motors Ltd v Toyota (GB) Ltd* [2000] CP Rep 24 (indemnity costs of an appeal ordered against directors with a personal stake in the litigation financing an appeal that could not 'on any realistic assessment' be said to have a good prospect of success).

123 *Fitzpatrick Contractors Ltd v Tyco Fire & Integrated Solutions (UK) Ltd* [2008] EWHC 1391 (TCC). More recently, see *Network Rail Infrastructure v Handy* [2015] EWHC 1460 (TCC), at [5]–[7], *per* Akenhead.

in unreasonably opposing applications for relief from sanctions', going on to say that it would be 'unacceptable for a party to try to take advantage of a minor inadvertent error'.[124] It should therefore come as no surprise that if a party unreasonably seeks to take advantage of their opponent's default, that party may be condemned to pay costs on the indemnity basis.[125]

That said, where the default was a matter of substance, it will be the applicant who will be at risk. In a case in which he refused to disturb an award on the indemnity basis, Dyson MR had this to say: **16.42**

> 'I would emphasise the words "unreasonably" and "minor inadvertent". A party is not required to agree to an extension of time in every case where the extension will not disrupt the time-table for the appeal or will not cause him to suffer prejudice. If the position were otherwise, the court would lose control of the management of the litigation.'[126]

Dyson MR went on find that the default in the instant case was 'substantial and unjustified'. For obvious reasons, the matters set out in 26.04–26.08 may be relevant to the court's thinking in that regard.

Abandonment of a case or of issues

If a party abandons their whole case or part thereof (or accepts an offer that amounts to capitulation[127]), then whilst there will be no presumption that they will pay costs on the indemnity basis, the party may well be ordered to do so if the court concludes that the case was unarguable.[128] The topic of weak cases is discussed in 16.38–16.40. **16.43**

If a party abandons arguments relating to discrete issues, they may have to pay costs on the indemnity basis either of the whole claim or (more commonly) of those abandoned issues—but this would be rare, because mere abandonment would not generally justify such an award[129] (especially where the issue was raised and then abandoned on expert advice[130]). Likewise, where a party abandons a point because, upon reviewing the evidence, **16.44**

[124] See *Denton & Ors v TH White Ltd & Ors* [2014] EWCA Civ 906, at [43].

[125] See, eg, *Viridor Waste Management Ltd v Veolia ES Ltd* [2015] EWHC 2321 (Comm), *per* Poppelwell J.

[126] *R (on the Application of Idira) v The Secretary of State for the Home Department* [2015] EWCA Civ 1187, at [80].

[127] See, eg, *Ontulmus v Collett* [2014] EWHC 4117 (QB), at [57] and [58], *per* Warby J (accepted an offer of £500 that suggested that there was nothing of substantial value in its claim except certain modest special damages). It should be noted that the 'compromise' came about as a result of the claimant accepting a Part 36; this is therefore an example of the court departing from the usual consequences of CPR, r 36.13, by exercising its discretion under CRR, r 44.2. The court is able to do this because the issue was the basis (as opposed to incidence) of costs and, as a result, the injustice test did not apply.

[128] See, eg, *Ikos Cif Ltd v Hogan Lovells International LLP* [2011] EWHC 2724 (Ch), in which the abandoned application to strike out was not one that could be said to have been hopeless or improper and Mann J found that the mere fact that a litigant had abandoned its application was not reason to order costs against it on the indemnity basis.

[129] See, eg, *Catalyst Investment Group Ltd v Max Lewisohn, Maximillian and Co (a firm)* [2009] EWHC 3501 (Ch), at [44] and [48]. See also *Langstone Leisure v Willers* (unreported), 3 June 2015, Ch D, *per* Birss J (withdrawn appeal against an interim payment, but to award such costs would take away the incentive to make the interim payment).

[130] See, eg, *John v Central Manchester & Manchester Children's University Hospitals NHS Foundation Trust* [2016] EWHC 819 (QB), *per* Picken J (ophthalmic claim pursued at a time when it had been supported by expert evidence, but was then dropped when the expert evidence ceased to support it).

they realise it is a bad point, it does not necessarily follow that an award on the indemnity basis will be made.[131]

16.45 Where an award on the indemnity basis is appropriate (which will generally be where there are other factors at play), then it is not only the costs relating to the abandoned issues that are put at risk; in particular, if a claim is so undermined by the other side's case that part of it needs to be abandoned, the residuum may also be deemed to be misjudged notwithstanding the fact that the claim, as originally brought, was satisfactory.[132] Timing can be important: if a party abandons issues or their case and delays doing so until a late stage, they may be found liable to pay costs on the indemnity basis,[133] but this will not always be the case, especially where their opponent's conduct was itself guilty of delay.[134]

Overenthusiastic pursuance of a case (including the pursuance of costs)

16.46 Whilst nothing that is set out below should be regarded as establishing any rule or principle, the following observations can be made about overenthusiastic litigants and awards on the indemnity basis.

- **Overenthusiastic arguments** Overburdening the court with an excessive number of documents[135] and chasing every conceivable point is capable of resulting in an award of costs on the indemnity basis.[136]
- **Machiavellian conduct** Unscrupulously opportunistic behaviour will put a party at significant risk. In what Males J called a 'misguided piece of opportunism', the claimant was ordered to pay costs on the indemnity basis for having argued against a time limit for filing budgets that he had previously agreed.[137]
- **Disclosure** Extravagant demands for disclosure may count against a party.[138]
- **Collateral purposes** Likewise, pursing a weak case for a collateral purpose will put the pursuer at risk.[139]

---

[131] *Fabio Perini SPA v LPC Group plc* [2010] EWCA Civ 525, at [122], *per* Lord Neuberger MR.

[132] *Barr v Biffa Waste Services Ltd* [2011] EWHC 1107 (TCC), at [40], in which Coulsen said that the residuum claims in group litigation 'could not sustain the increased weight that they inevitably would have to bear'. See also *A&E Television Networks LLC v Discovery Communications Europe Ltd* [2013] EWHC 276 (Pat), in which Peter Smith J identified the point in time at which the claimant ought to have known that its case was hopeless.

[133] An example of this is *OJSC TNK-BP Holding v Lazurenko* [2013] EWCA Civ 137, in which an appellant withdrew an application for permission to appeal only two days before the hearing. See also *Board of Trustees of National Museums & Galleries on Merseyside v AEW Architects & Designers Ltd* [2013] EWHC 3025 (TCC), at [22], [26], [31] and [32], in which Akenhead J said that the fact that the defendant had made concessions only shortly before trial was a factor that could have contributed to an award on the indemnity basis. See also *Hospira UK v Genetech Inc* [2014] EWHC 208 (Ch), in which Birss J made an order against a claimant surrendered one of its patents in suit at a late stage.

[134] See, eg, *CIP Properties (AIPT) Ltd v Galliford Try Infrastructure Ltd* (unreported), 3 June 2014, QBD (TCC), *per* Ramsey J.

[135] See, eg, *Excalibur Ventures LLC Claimant v Texas Keystone Inc* [2013] EWHC 4278 (Comm), at [60], *per* Christopher Clarke LJ (sitting as a judge in the High Court), aff'd [2016] EWCA Civ 1144. See also *R (on the application of Sager House (Chelsea) Ltd) v First Secretary of State & Anor* [2006] EWHC 1251 (Admin).

[136] This was one factor amongst others in *R (on the application of Sager House (Chelsea) Ltd) v First Secretary of State & Anor* [2006] EWHC 1251 (Admin).

[137] *Rattan v UBS AG London Branch* [2014] EWHC 665 (Comm), at [10]–[13].

[138] See, eg, *Excalibur Ventures LLC Claimant v Texas Keystone Inc* [2013] EWHC 4278 (Comm), at [52], *per* Christopher Clarke LJ (sitting as a judge of the High Court), aff'd [2016] EWCA Civ 1144.

[139] As an example of this, see *Mahme Trust Reg & Ors v Lloyds TSB Bank plc* [2006] EWHC 1782 (Ch), at [15] *et seq*, *per* Evans-Lombe J.

- **Aggression** Pursuing 'highly aggressive tactics in the conduct of the litigation' may contribute to the making of such an order.[140]
- **Conditional fee agreements** Whilst she did not elaborate on the point, Sharpe J has indicated that a certain amount of leeway should be afforded to parties who are represented under conditional fee agreements because these can result in 'costs pressure' (as she put it).[141] Presumably, this means that the fact that the lawyers had an interest in the matter is a factor to be taken into account—although whether this is correct is a moot point.
- **Costs arguments** An overly aggressive attitude towards the recovery of costs can backfire and contribute to an award on the indemnity basis.[142]

Dishonest, improper or misleading conduct

Where dishonesty is alleged and proven,[143] it may—unsurprisingly—be taken into account.[144] Where the claim is *based* on a party's dishonesty, an award on the indemnity basis would not be unlikely.[145] Waller LJ had this to say on that topic: **16.47**

> 'The best method by which a court can mark its disapproval [of dishonest conduct on the part of the paying party] when, as here, the Claimant would be the paying party, is by making an order for indemnity costs. I for my part have no hesitation in saying that, where insurers establish that a claim has been brought dishonestly, they should on the whole be entitled to an order for indemnity costs not just because of the extra cost they may incur in defending such a claim—though that is considerable—but so that others are discouraged. It is both in the interests of insurers and indeed any Defendants, and in the interests of the court, that persons should be discouraged from bringing dishonest claims and from supporting dishonest claims by lies.'[146]

Dishonesty and impropriety manifest themselves in myriad ways, so it is impossible to deal with all potential circumstances. That said, the following points can usefully be made. **16.48**

- **Lying** Lying may contribute to an award of costs on the indemnity basis[147] and this may be so even where a person has lied by the concealment of facts.[148] That said, each

[140] See *Hussain v Cooke* (unreported), 15 February 2010, Ch D (Companies Court), *per* David Donaldson QC (sitting as a deputy High Court judge).

[141] *Dee v Telegraph Media Group Ltd* [2010] EWHC 1939 (QB), at [3], *per* Sharpe J.

[142] *Hudson v New Media Holding Co LLC* [2011] EWHC 3068 (QB), at [30], *per* Eady.

[143] A strong *prima facie* case of fraud may be sufficient in some circumstances, although not necessarily on its own: see *Eurocom Ltd v Siemens plc* [2015] EWHC 685 (TCC), at [8] and [9], *per* Sir Vivian Ramsey. As Sir Vivian went on to find, the absence of an explanation in such circumstances may be sufficient to justify an award.

[144] If authority were needed on the point, see *BSkyB v HP Enterprises* [2010] EWHC 862 (TCC), at [37]–[40], *per* Ramsay J; *Eurocom Ltd v Siemens plc* [2015] EWHC 685 (TCC), at [7], *per* Sir Vivian Ramsey.

[145] See, eg, *Otkritie International Investment Management Ltd v Urumov* [2014] EWHC 755 (Comm), at [16], in which Eder J made an award against persons who had committed a fraud against the claimant.

[146] *Quarcoo v Esure Services Ltd* [2009] EWCA Civ 595, at [27]. See also *Whaleys (Bradford) Led v Bennett & Anor* [2017] EWCA Civ 2143, at [20]–[21], *per* Newey LJ.

[147] See, eg, *London & Quadrant Housing Trust v Prestige Properties Ltd* [2012] EWCA Civ 130, in which (in the court at first instance) it was noted that the paying parties had been 'brazen in their dishonesty and had told preposterous lies'. See also *Lakeheath Investments Ltd v Secretary of State for Communities & Local Government* [2014] EWHC 1072 (Admin), in which Burnett J made an award against a property investment company that had relied on a statement of truth that was untrue and which the company knew to be untrue. See also *CMC Spreadbet plc v Khan* [2017] EWHC 2008 (Ch) (claimant's dishonesty in claiming that he did not have experience of spread betting).

[148] See, eg, *Royal Bank of Scotland PLC v Highlands Financial Partners LP* [2013] EWCA Civ 472, in which (on appeal) it transpired that the claimant had obtained judgment on liability by fraud through the

case must be decided on its own facts and this means that such an award will not always be made, which is especially true where there is no other dishonest or improper conduct,[149] or where the fault lay with someone other than the party itself[150] (although see 16.28).

- **Obfuscation or evasiveness** Obfuscation[151] or evasiveness[152] may give rise to an award on the indemnity basis.
- **Sham documents and forgeries** Relying on sham documents may lead to an award on the indemnity basis.[153]
- **Attempts to disregard relevant documents** If a party unsuccessfully sought to disregard a long-standing contract in an attempt to construct an elaborate claim based on what they alleged was the true relationship between the parties, that party may be required to pay costs on an indemnity basis.[154] Similarly, in a case in which the court revoked letters of administration where the deceased had not in fact died intestate, but had made a valid will, the court was sufficiently troubled by the fact that the defendants ought to have been aware of the fact that a will had been made to condemn them to pay costs on the indemnity basis.[155]
- **Collateral purposes** Where a party seeks improperly to use the litigation for a collateral purpose (such as an attempt to take over a competitor's business),[156] they will be at risk of an award on the indemnity basis. Similarly, in a case in which he found that the defendant 'persisted out of... "bloody-mindedness" or a desire simply to be difficult', Sir David Eady made an order on the indemnity basis.[157]
- **Dishonestly trying to shift the blame** Similarly, where a party dishonestly tries to implicate an innocent third party, they will be at risk of paying costs on the indemnity basis.[158]
- **'Fundamental dishonesty' within the meaning of CPR, r 44.16(1)** For obvious reasons, where the court finds that a claimant in a personal injuries claim has been guilty

mis-statement and concealment of facts by its key witness. See also *Energy Venture Partners Ltd v Malabu Oil and Gas Ltd* [2014] EWHC 1390 (Comm), at [54], in which it is recorded that Gloster J made an award against a party whose main witness had been 'deliberately dishonest', and 'argumentative and extravagant', whilst giving evidence.

149 In a case in which a senior employee of a company had lied in evidence, Ramsey J declined to make an award of costs on the indemnity basis, because there was no evidence of systemic fraud: see *QBE Management Services (UK) Ltd v Dymoke* [2012] EWHC 116 (QB).

150 In a case in which the court had been misled about the parties' profitability, for example, Mr Bernard Livesey QC declined to award indemnity costs, because it was not the parties themselves who were at fault, but their solicitors, who had submitted only partial evidence: see *Salt v Corris Developments Ltd* [2011] EWHC 3822 (Ch), at [25].

151 See, eg, *American Science & Engineering Inc v Rapiscan Systems Ltd* [2016] EWHC 1384 (Pat), at [9], [10], [14], [15] and [20], *per* Arnold (defendant found to have been guilty of obfuscation and to have failed to face up to what it ought to have known from its own internal documentation).

152 See fn 174.

153 See, eg, *CR v MZ* [2013] EWHC 295 (Fam).

154 *JP Morgan Chase Bank v Springwell Navigation* [2008] EWHC 2848 (Comm), at [13(ix)], *per* Gloster J. See also *Angel Group Ltd v Davey* (unreported), 28 March 2017, Ch D, *per* Andrew Hochhauser QC.

155 *Morris v Browne* [2017] EWHC 631 (Ch), at [25], *per* Barling J.

156 See *QBE Management Services (UK) Ltd v Dymoke* [2012] EWHC 116 (QB).

157 *Rahman v Ary Network Ltd* [2016] EWHC 3570 (QB), at [5].

158 See, eg, *British Sky Broadcasting Group PLC v Digital Satellite Warranty Cover Ltd (in liquidation)* [2012] EWHC 3679 (Ch), *per* Sir William Blackburne.

of 'fundamental dishonesty' within the meaning of CPR, r 44.16(1) (see 8.34–8.47), an award of costs on the indemnity basis may (and usually will) follow.[159]

- **Fundamentally false basis for case** Advancing a case on a factual premise that was fundamentally false and which was known to be false would be sufficient alone to take the case out of the norm.[160]
- **Exaggeration** Where a claimant culpably exaggerates their case, they may be at risk of an award on the indemnity basis,[161] but merely recovering very much less than was claimed would not be sufficient to merit such an award.[162]
- **Improper conduct by agents** Where an agent knowingly acts beyond the limits of their authority, this may result in an award of indemnity basis costs being made against that agent.[163]
- **Dishonesty by the successful party** The dishonest party is not always the losing party. Where the winning party has been found to be dishonest and where they would otherwise have been entitled to costs on the indemnity basis, the dishonest conduct can be reflected in the loss of that benefit.[164]
- **Prompt admission** If a party has lied or otherwise been dishonest, then they can mitigate the consequences of that improbity by making a prompt admission.[165]
- **Complicity in funding** Where a person who provides funds is complicit in advancing a dishonest case and where a non-party costs order is made against the funder, both may be condemned to pay costs on the indemnity basis[166] (although, for the reasons set out in 16.28, this may happen anyway).
- **Controlling persons** Where a person, such as a director, controls a party who advanced a dishonest case and where a non-party costs order is made against that person, both the party and the controller may be condemned to pay costs in the indemnity basis.[167]

Inflammatory behaviour, contempt of court, etc

The following points may be made about inflammatory and disrespectful behaviour. **16.49**

- **Aggression** Whilst mere forensic aggression will rarely justify an award on the indemnity basis,[168] launching an unjustified attack on an opponent's integrity could well lead

---

[159] See, eg, *Thompson v Go North East Ltd* (unreported), 30 August 2016, Sunderland County Court, *per* District Judge Charnock-Neal.

[160] If authority is needed on that point, see *Caliendo v Mischon De Reya* [2016] EWHC 770 (Ch), *per* Arnold J. See also *Kazakhstan Kagazy plc v Zhunus* [2018] EWHC 369 (Comm), at [143]–[157], *per* Piken J (a dishonest defence).

[161] In a case in which the exaggeration was not culpable, Coulson J declined to make an award on the indemnity basis: *Brit Inns Ltd (in liquidation) v BDW Trading Ltd* [2012] EWHC 2489 (TCC), *per* Coulson J.

[162] *Vestergaard Frandsen A/S v Bestnet Europe Ltd* [2014] EWHC 4371 (Ch), *per* Rose J.

[163] See, eg, *Bank of Scotland v Qutb* [2012] EWCA Civ 1661, in which a paying party had acted in breach of a warrant of authority in conducting litigation brought against a bank.

[164] See, eg, *Fiona Trust & Holding Corpn v Privalov* [2011] EWHC 664 (Comm), at [64], *per* Andrew Smith J; *Bank of Tokyo-Mitsubishi UFJ Ltd v Baskan Gida Sanayi Ve Pazarlama AS* [2009] EWHC 1696 (Ch), *per* Briggs J. See also *Digicel (St Lucia) v Cable & Wireless plc* [2010] EWHC 774 (Ch), *per* Morgan J.

[165] See, eg, *Chemetall Ltd v Pan European Logistics Ltd* (unreported), 12 March 2014, QBD, *per* Slade J.

[166] See, eg, *Relfo Ltd v Varsani* [2012] EWHC 3848, in which financial assistance was given to the defendant by the defendant's father. Between them, they controlled the dishonest defence of the action, from which they stood to benefit.

[167] See, eg, *Gatnom v Sanders* [2011] EWHC 3716 (Ch), in which the controlling director was the company's ultimate beneficial owner and the guiding force behind its dishonest defence.

[168] See *Kaglovsky v Turevych* [2014] EWHC 2697 (QB), *per* Patterson J.

to such an award.[169] In one of the more memorable cases cited in this book, Warby J condemned a defendant to pay costs on the indemnity basis where she had bellicosely maintained—all the way to trial—a false allegation that the claimant had had sex with one of her pigs.[170] On an altogether more prosaic level, Lightman J found that the making of a gratuitous personal attack on a witness during cross-examination justified such an award.[171] The same may apply to experts (see 16.60).

- **Attempts to cause a forensic distraction** If a party caries out a hostile forensic assault in an attempt to muddy the waters, then they will be at risk of award on the indemnity basis. This will particularly be so where the assault went to collateral matters and did not engage with the real issues in the case.[172]
- **Correspondence** Whilst belligerent correspondence is capable of contributing to such an award,[173] the mere fact that a party had departed from the principles of cooperation and reasonable discussion would not ordinarily result in an award being made on the indemnity basis.[174]
- **Contempt of court** Whilst an obvious point, where a party has been guilty of contempt of court, this may lead to an award on the indemnity basis.[175] That said, where, on appeal, it is found that a contemnor ought not in principle to have been committed in the first place, it would be wrong to condemn that person to pay costs on the indemnity basis merely because of their previous litigation conduct.[176]
- **Disregarding orders of the court** If a party knowingly chooses to disregard a mandatory order of the court, they will be at risk of an award on the indemnity basis.[177] Similarly, if a party is guilty of a series of relatively minor errors, the totality may take the case out of the norm.[178]
- **Frustrating proceedings** Similarly, if a party seeks to frustrate proceedings, the case may fall outside the norm.[179]

---

[169] *Somatra Ltd v Sinclair Roche & Temperley* [2002] EWHC 1627 (Comm). See also *Siegel v Pummell* [2015] EWHC 195 (QB) (personal attack on opponent's expert).

[170] See *Barkhuysen v Hamilton* [2016] EWHC 3371 (QB), at [3]–[6], [11], [12] and [20]–[22], *per* Warby J.

[171] Although a pre-CPR case, see *Clarke v Associated Newspapers Ltd* (1998) The Times, 28 January, *per* Lightman J.

[172] See, eg, *Kagalovsky v Balmore Invest Ltd* [2014] EWHC 161 (Comm).

[173] Christopher Clarke LJ (sitting as a judge of the High Court) has explained that whilst the question of whether a party should pay costs on the indemnity basis is not to be determined by one letter or even more than one, the manner in which the case was promoted (of which correspondence is a part) is one of the factors to be taken into account: *Excalibur Ventures LLC Claimant v Texas Keystone Inc* [2013] EWHC 4278 (Comm), at [9], [48]–[53] and [54], aff'd [2016] EWCA Civ 1144.

[174] See, eg, *Smails v McNally* [2012] EWHC 3793 (Ch).

[175] See, eg, *Warner v Barnes* [2012] EWHC 4223 (Ch); *Plant Health Care (UK) Ltd v Holohan* [2017] EWHC 1119 (QB), *per* Jay J. See also *Glencore Agriculture BV v Vinatex Trading Joint Stock Co HCMC* (unreported), 23 May 2018, QBD, *per* Robin Knowles J.

[176] See *Re MM v Kirk* [2017] EWCA Civ 260, at [9], *per* Sir James Munby P.

[177] See, eg, *Samsung Electronics (UK) Ltd v Apple Inc* [2012] EWCA Civ 1430. See also *Haider Kennedy Solicitors v Momson* [2017] EWHC 2984 (Ch); *R (on application of the National Council for Civil Liberties) v Secretary of State for the Home Department* [2018] EWHC 976 (Admin), *per* Singh LJ (failure to serve a skeleton argument in accordance with a court-specified deadline).

[178] See, eg, *Arroyo & Ors v Equion Energia Ltd* [2016] EWHC 3348 (TCC), in which the claimants were guilty of inadequacies in the preparation and construction of their schedules of loss, the service of a defective body of expert evidence and a breach of an order limiting the scope of additional expert reports. See also *Whaleys (Bradford) Led v Bennett & Anor* [2017] EWCA Civ 2143.

[179] See, eg, *Pourghazi v Kamyab* (unreported), 3 December 2015, Ch D, *per* Master Matthews (defendant's attempt to delay, defeat and frustrate enforcement proceedings by repeatedly not attending oral examinations);

Unjustified allegations of dishonesty, fraud and exaggeration

It is commonly the case that a failure to prove dishonesty or fraud will result in an award of costs on the indemnity basis if the allegations are found to have been unreasonably made.[180] Given the fact that, where allegations of fraud are made out, the party accused will often be condemned to pay costs on the indemnity basis (see 16.47), it is no surprise that Tomlinson LJ made the point that 'what is sauce for the goose should be sauce for the gander'.[181] **16.50**

There is no requirement that the allegations were made improperly. Christopher Clarke LJ (sitting in the High Court) had this to say on that topic: **16.51**

> '[One] of the risks of making an unsuccessful allegation of dishonesty is that (even if the allegation is not improperly made) it may well attract indemnity costs, as some imperfect recompense to the Defendants for what they have had to endure.'[182]

The following points may be made. **16.52**

- **Scandalous allegations** Allegations that are scandalous (in the legal sense of that word[183]) will put the party who made the allegations at risk.[184] The risk will continue even if the allegations are withdrawn rather than disproved.[185]
- **Allegations of tampering with evidence** Unfounded allegations of improperly tampering with electronic data may lead to an award on the indemnity basis.[186]
- **Unsupported allegations of exaggeration** Allegations of exaggeration that were unsupported or contradicted by the evidence may lead to such an award, especially if those allegations are enthusiastically—or even courteously[187]—pursued all the way to cross-examination.[188]

---

cf *JSC Mezhdunarodniy Promyshlenniy Bank and another v Pugachev and others* [2015] EWHC 1694 (Ch), in which Hildyard J declined to make an order on the indemnity basis on the ground that the defendant had tried to avoid engaging in cross-examination out of a fear of exposing his assets to further unlawful expropriation by the Russian state.

[180] Although both pre-CPR, the cases that are usually cited in this regard are *Bank of Baroda v Panessar* [1987] Ch 335 and, in a personal injury setting, *Cooper v P&O Stena Line Ltd* [1999] 1 Lloyd's Rep 734. Post-CPR examples are *Blueco Ltd v Bwat Retail Nominee* [2014] EWCA Civ 154 and *White v PSM Residential Finance Ltd* [2017] EWHC 3500 (TCC). As a counter-example (ie in which no award on the indemnity basis was made), see *Green (as Administratrix of the Estate of Peter Maclean Maitland deceased) v Astor* [2013] EWHC 1857 (Ch), at [54]–[58], *per* Roth J. Christopher Clarke J referred to 'the making of allegations of dishonesty that turn out to be misconceived', but it is doubtful if he meant to include allegations that were reasonably made at the time, but which were shown to be wrong: *Balmoral v Borealis UK Ltd* [2006] EWHC 2531, at [1].

[181] See *Manna (a Child and Protected Party) v Central Manchester University Hospitals NHS Foundation Trust* [2017] EWCA Civ 12, at [42].

[182] *Excalibur Ventures LLC Claimant v Texas Keystone Inc* [2013] EWHC 4278 (Comm), at [42]–[47] and [127], aff'd [2016] EWCA Civ 1144. See also *Amoco (UK) Exploration Company v British American Offshore Ltd* [2002] BLR 135, at [7], *per* Langley J.

[183] Legal lexicographer Bryan Garner defines scandal thus: 'Scandal consists in the allegation of anything [that] is unbecoming the dignity of the court to hear, or is contrary to decency or good manners, or which charges some person with a crime not necessary to be shown in the cause ... and [which] is also irrelevant to the case' (Garner, BA (ed), *Black's Law Dictionary*, 9th edn, St. Paul, MN: West, 2009, at p 1462).

[184] *Maini v Maini* [2009] EWHC 3036 (Ch), at [14], *per* Proudman J.

[185] See, eg, *Secretary of State for Trade and Industry v Gee* (2006) BCC 384.

[186] *Fiona Trust & Holding Corpn v Privalov* [2011] EWHC 664 (Comm), at [68(iii)], *per* Andrew Smith J.

[187] See, eg, *Manna (a Child and Protected Party) v Central Manchester University Hospitals NHS Foundation Trust* [2017] EWCA Civ 12, at [41], in which an award was made notwithstanding that Tomlinson LJ commented on the fact that counsel had acted 'in a fair and courteous manner a case which proved unsustainable'.

[188] *Clarke v Maltby (Costs)* [2010] EWHC 1856 (QB), *per* Owen J, in which the allegations were particularly distressing because the claimant was a solicitor, so the allegation would have serious consequences for her if found to be true.

- **Unfounded allegations of inactivity in the face of corruption** Groundless allegations of tacit acceptance of corruption may lead to an award on the indemnity basis.[189]
- **Abandonment of allegations of fraud** Allegations of fraud made by a claimant will, in general, justify an award on the indemnity basis where the claimant serves notice of discontinuance.[190]
- **Failure to 'load test' allegations** A failure properly to 'load test' (as Sir Anthony Coleman put it) an allegation of dishonesty by considering motive may lead to an award on the indemnity basis.[191]
- **Tactical allegations** Allegations made for tactical reasons (that is, with a view to influencing behaviour rather than resolving the dispute) will put the party making the allegations at particular risk.[192]

Changing the case to fit the circumstances

16.53 Whilst amendments to the pleadings for legitimate reasons (such as making them clearer[193]) will not put the party making those amendments at risk, a shifting case in which opportunistic changes are made to suit the circumstances will create such a risk.[194] This is especially true where the case itself is weak[195] or where it was large-scale litigation calculated to put commercial pressure on the defendant.[196]

Where there is a real issue over proportionality

16.54 The following two circumstances may arise from time to time.

- **Where it is said that disproportionate costs were incurred for good reason** The fact that proportionality trumps all (see 16.07) means that it is possible to have costs that were incurred for good reason, but which are nonetheless disproportionate. In the past, a receiving party would, on the whole, typically be content to take their chances before a costs judge at an assessment, because it would have been unlikely that, under the *Lownds* test, they would have suffered significant reductions. Since 1 April 2013, however, the risks are higher (for the reasons set out in 16.10) and, in view of this, it may be that a litigant who seeks to recover such costs would prefer to argue their case before the judge making the costs order, in the hope that the court would make an award on the indemnity basis. There was, at the time of writing, no authority

---

189 *Ibid.*

190 See *Jarvis plc v PricewaterhouseCoopers* [2000] 2 ECLC 368, *per* Lightman J, and, more recently, *Clutterbuck v HSBC plc* [2015] EWHC 3233 (Ch), at [20], *per* David Richards J.

191 *National Westminster Bank Plc v Rabobank Nederland* [2007] EWHC 1742 (Comm), at [44].

192 *Irish Response Ltd (a company incorporated under the laws of the Republic of Ireland) v (1) Direct Beauty Products Ltd* [2011] EWHC 608 (QB), at [37] *et seq*, *per* HHJ Richard Seymour QC (sitting as judge of the High Court).

193 See *Kesabo & 11 Ors v African Barrick Gold plc* [2013] EWHC 4045 (QB). That said, if a case is unclear because it was badly pleaded, that may be a factor against the party whose case it is.

194 *Three Rivers District Council v Bank of England* [2006] EWHC 816 (Comm); *ABCI v Banque Franco-Tunisienne & Ors* [2003] EWCA Civ 205. See also *Mitchell v Royal Bank of Scotland* [2017] EWHC 1771 (Ch), *per* Judge Davis-White QC.

195 See, eg, *IPC Media v Highbury Leisure Publishing Ltd* [2005] EWHC 283 (Ch), at [24], *per* Laddie J.

196 *Fiona Trust & Holding Corpn v Privalov* [2011] EWHC 664 (Comm), at [61(8)(g)], *per* Andrew Smith J.

on the point,[197] but anecdotally the editor understands that the number of applications for costs on the indemnity basis have risen substantially since 1 April 2013.

- **Where it would be unfair to require the paying party to pay disproportionate costs** This is the reverse of the above scenario in that the party likely to be condemned in costs wishes to argue that the costs claimed are disproportionate. If the court feels that it would be unfair to deprive the paying party of the benefit of proportionality an assessment,[198] it would not be appropriate to make an order on the indemnity basis, because such an order would preclude subsequent considerations of proportionality.[199] Thus, for example, in the context of an application that was anything but demanding, Morgan J declined to award costs on the indemnity basis because the receiving party was under an obligation to respond 'in a proportionate way and [as a result] their costs should be subject to the restriction of proportionality'.[200] That said, if a party has shown no interest in proportionality, but instead has cast their case widely in the expectation that their opponent will have to meet it, it would be open to the court to make such an award.[201] If so minded, the court may make an observation about proportionality to assist the costs judge.[202] It should also be noted that Lewison J has said that the requirement of proportionality is a useful brake on the escalation of costs[203] (the implication being that it is a brake that should not be released for no reason).

Failing to make reasonable enquiries

Where a party trusts to fortune and potters along without properly testing their case and making proper enquiries, they will be at risk of being condemned in indemnity basis costs. Lindsay J had this to say on the point: **16.55**

> 'A party who, despite having had an apparently conclusive opposition to his case made plain to him, persists with the case down to the hearing in the "Micawberish" hope that something might turn up and yet who does not even take such steps open to him to see whether anything is likely to turn up, runs a risk, when nothing does turn up, that he will be regarded as having been at least unreasonable in the conduct of his litigation.'[204]

A failure to ask the other side to clarify their case is capable of resulting in an indemnity costs order being made, but this is not a foregone conclusion.[205]

---

197 The nearest was *Mortgage Agency Number Four Ltd v Alomo Solicitors (a firm)* [2011] EWHC B22 (Mercantile), in which Judge Simon Brown QC made some adverse comments about a paying party's conduct, and went on to say that it would be appropriate that the paying party should be able to dispute the costs on basis of reasonableness alone rather than reasonableness and proportionality. Compare this, however, with *Easyair Ltd (t/a Openair) v Opal Telecom Ltd* [2009] EWHC 779 (Ch), at [7], in which Lewison J noted that proportionality was an important brake on the escalation on costs.

198 See *Ross River Ltd v Waverly Commercial Ltd* [2012] EWHC 3006 (Ch), at [41]–[44], *per* Morgan J.

199 *Simms v Law Society* [2005] EWCA Civ 849, at [28].

200 See *Rawlinson & Hunder Trustees SA v ITG Ltd* [2015] EWHC 1924 (Ch), at [11].

201 See *Digicel (St Lucia) v Cable & Wireless plc* [2010] EWHC 774 (Ch), at [68], *per* Morgan J.

202 Indeed, the trial judge has a duty to assist the costs judge in the assessment of costs, which duty should not be vanquished by a party offering to pay costs on an indemnity basis whilst reserving the right to argue that the costs are extravagant: *Three Rivers District Council v Bank of England* [2006] EWHC 816 (Comm).

203 *Easyair Ltd (t/a Openair) v Opal Telecom Ltd* [2009] EWHC 779 (Ch), at [7].

204 *Beynon v Scadden* [1999] IRLR 700 (EAT), at 703. Lindsay J was dealing with incidence of costs in an employment tribunal rather than the basis of costs in the civil court, but the test he was applying was not dissimilar to that which applies under the CPR.

205 For example, in a strike-out application in which that error had been made, Ouseley J rejected an application for costs on the indemnity basis, because the expenditure of costs would have been much the same

Failure to comply with a pre-action protocol

16.56 If non-compliance with a pre-action protocol has led to costs being incurred that might otherwise have been avoided (including the costs of the whole claim), the orders the court may make include an order that the party at fault pay those costs on an indemnity basis.[206] In a case in which the defendant (the Home Office) was said to be in the habit of not engaging in negotiations until the day before trial, Cox J made such an order; she was not persuaded that such an order would discourage late compromises.[207]

Unreasonable conduct and failure to comply with procedural requirements

16.57 The following is a non-exhaustive list of shortcomings that may cause or contribute to the errant party being condemned in costs on the indemnity basis:

- failing to engage in the litigation process;[208]
- taking futile and time-wasting points;[209]
- unreasonably challenging the court's jurisdiction;[210]
- intentional obstreperousness (such as withholding arguments until the very last minute);[211]
- engaging in delay tactics;[212]
- conducting in litigation for collateral purposes,[213] such as serving further and better particulars for inappropriate purposes[214] or waging a vendetta against an opponent;[215]

---

even if proper enquiries had been made: see *Serious Organised Crime Agency v A* [2011] EWHC 520 (Admin), at [23]–[29].

206 Practice Direction (Protocols), art 2.3(2). As an example of the court making an award because of non-compliance with pre-action protocols, see *Forstater v Python (Monty) Pictures Ltd* [2013] EWHC 3759 (Ch).

207 *Youdjeu v Home Office* [2011] EWHC 2002 (QB), at [19].

208 See, eg, *Slick Seating Systems v Adams* [2013] EWHC 1642 (QB), at [11], in which Judge Simon Brown QC found that the paying party should have made a decision whether to participate in the proceedings or not, and that 'dropping out of the litigation while occasionally sending e-mails' involved the court and the other parties in additional work.

209 See, eg, *Rattan v UBS AG London Branch* [2014] EWHC 665 (Comm), in which Male J made an award against a party who, having agreed that costs budgets should be filed on a certain date, filed his budget early and then argued that his opponent's budget was out of time because the agreed date was not seven days before the management hearing, as required by CPR, r 3.13. See also *Thoratec Europe Ltd v Ais GmBH Aachen Innovative Solutions* (unreported), 25 January 2017, Ch D, *per* Arnold J (a comparison between Dutch and English law came to no ultimate purpose and was a waste of money).

210 See, eg, *Travelers Casualty and Surety Co of Canada v Sun Life Assurance Co of Canada (UK) Ltd* [2006] EWHC 2885 (Comm), at [36] and [37], in which Christopher Clarke J found that an attempt to play one court off against another was 'an exercise in litigious hardball to the fullest extent'.

211 See, eg, *In the Matter of the Administration of the Estate of Jimmy Savile* [2014] EWHC 1683 (Ch), in which Sales J made an order against a residual beneficiary who, amongst other things, unreasonably left it until the hearing before disclosing its opposition to a proposed scheme.

212 See, eg, *Simmons & Simmons LLP v Hickox* [2013] EWHC 2141 (QB), at [15], *per* Coulson J.

213 This may be entirely overt, such as where an application is made under CPR, r 31.22, to use documents in other proceedings: see, eg, *Tchenguiz v Serious Fraud Office* [2014] EWCA Civ 1471. Vos LJ made it clear, however, that there was no presumption that a party who made such an application would be ordered to pay costs on the indemnity basis: *ibid*, at [7].

214 See, eg, *Trimax Trading Int Ltd v HMRC* [2014] UKFTT 733 (TC), at [53], in which Judge Mosedale found (amongst other things) that the appellant had used further and better particulars for the purpose of forestalling arguments and points that did not exist.

215 See, eg, *Noorani v Calver (No 2)* [2009] EWHC 592 (QB), at [19] *et seq*, in which, whilst there were many other factors that contributed to the award, Coulson J ordered indemnity basis costs against a claimant who pursued a 'bizarre vendetta' against its opponent. See also *Barkhuysen v Hamilton* [2016] EWHC 3371 (QB), at [3]–[6], [11], [12] and [20]–[22], *per* Warby J.

- failing to clarify whether a claim is being pursued;[216]
- making an application on a without-notice basis when it should have been made with notice;[217]
- failing to make full-and-frank disclosure when applying without notice;[218]
- failing to give proper disclosure of documents[219] (including electronic data[220]);
- presenting a winding-up petition when the petitioner knew that the petition debt was genuinely disputed;[221]
- acting in dereliction of a party's duty to the court;[222]
- contumaciously flouting an order[223] or an undertaking;[224] and
- bringing abusive proceedings.[225]

The failings on the following list (which, again, is not exhaustive) would, in general, not cause or significantly contribute towards an award on the indemnity basis: **16.58**

- failing to prepare bundles properly;[226]
- bringing a claim for possession of property for the purposes of putting pressure on the owner to repay a debt secured on the property;[227] and

216 See *Jerrard v Blyth* [2014] EWHC 647 (QB), in which Sir David Eady made an award against a claimant who had failed to serve a claim form on a defendant and then who failed to clarify whether the claim was being pursued when asked.

217 See *Franses (Liquidator of Arab News Network Ltd) v Al Assad* [2007] EWHC 2442 (Ch). See also *Cooke v Venulum Property Investments Ltd* [2013] EWHC 4288 (Ch), at [11]–[18], in which Morgan J criticised a claimant for having made a novel and (ultimately) misguided application on a without-notice basis.

218 See, eg, *AB Bank Ltd v HSBC Bank plc* [2016] EWHC 3446 (Comm), *per* Teare J (material non-disclosure on a without-notice application for a *Norwich Pharmacal* order). See also *R (on the application of CPW) v Harrow Crown Court* [2014] EWHC 2061 (Admin), at [11], in which Andrews J found that it was a 'paradigm case for the award of indemnity costs'; *Hussain v Seymour* (unreported), 13 March 2014, QBD, in which Andrews J made an order against the claimants (a firm of solicitors) who had applied for a freezing injunction, but had not told the court that their client had already offered adequate security; *U&M Mining Zambia Ltd v Konkola Copper Mines plc* [2014] EWHC 3250 (Comm), *per* Teare.

219 See *R (on the application of Rawlinson & Hunter Trustees SA & Ors) v Serious Fraud Office* [2012] EWHC 3218 (Admin), at [12], *per* Silber J. See also *Excalibur Ventures LLC Claimant v Texas Keystone Inc* [2013] EWHC 4278 (Comm), at [55], *per* Christopher Clarke LJ (sitting as a judge of the High Court), aff'd [2016] EWCA Civ 1144. As an example of a case in which indemnity basis costs were not ordered notwithstanding the fact that one of the parties had acted in almost complete ignorance of the details of an extra disclosure exercise they were undertaking, see *Smails v McNally* [2012] EWHC 3793 (Ch). For an example of a case in which a failure to comply with an ongoing duty to give disclosure contributed to an award on the indemnity basis, see *In the Matter of Gizmondo Europe Ltd v Fry* [2014] EWHC 4640 (Ch), *per* Richard Millett QC.

220 See, eg, *Excelerate Technology Ltd v Cumberbatch* [2015] EWHC 204 (QB).

221 See, eg, *Lakehouse Contracts Ltd v UPR Services Ltd* [2014] EWHC 1223 (Ch); see also *Re Satellite (2003) Ltd* (unreported), 17 November 2003, Ch D.

222 *R (on the application of Gassama) v Secretary of State for the Home Department* [2012] EWHC 3049 (Admin), *per* Haddon-Cave J. See also *R (on the application of Grimshaw) v Southwark London Borough Council* [2013] EWHC 4504 (Admin).

223 Whilst it arose out of a criminal case, see, eg, *Re Malik* (unreported), 18 July 2013, QBD (Admin), *per* Stuart-Smith J.

224 See, eg, *Flogas Britain Ltd v Cylinder Gas Co Ltd* (unreported), 24 March 2014, QBD, *per* McKenna J.

225 See, eg, *Re Satellite (2003) Ltd* (unreported), 17 November 2003, Ch D, in which the claimant had abusively used winding-up proceedings for debt collection purposes.

226 See *Fitzpatrick Contractors Ltd v Tyco Fire & Integrated Solutions (UK) Ltd* [2009] EWHC 274 (TCC), at [48] and [49], *per* Barling J.

227 See, eg, *Co-operative Bank plc v Desmond Victor John Phillips* [2014] EWHC 2862 (Ch), at [54]–[56] and [65]–[71], *per* Morgan J.

- mishaps of a technical nature, such as typographical errors in the pleadings.[228]

16.59 Good compliance with procedural requirements may militate against an award of costs on the indemnity basis.[229]

Expert evidence and failures on the part of experts

16.60 The following points may be made about the errant experts.

- **Experts from the wrong discipline** Peter Smith J has found that a failure to instruct an appropriate expert may lead to the legal representatives who instructed him being required to show why they should not pay the costs thrown away.[230] If they were to fail to show such cause, then it would be open to the court to require them to pay those costs on the indemnity basis.
- **Unacceptable conduct on the part of experts** In a case in which an expert behavioural neurologist behaved abnormally, both by being combative and dismissive of other medical professionals and by giving such poor oral evidence that Wilkie J had to ask him for a written clarification, his client was condemned to pay certain costs on the indemnity basis.[231]
- **Expert failing to discharge duties** Whilst it was only one of several factors that gave rise to his findings, Tomlinson LJ refused to disturb an award that a defendant pay the costs of a quantum trial to be assessed on the indemnity basis in a case in which one expert's evidence was 'extraordinary and ... wholly out of kilter with awards made in this area' and another's was 'illogical' and 'unrealistic'.[232] Similarly, Roderick Evans J made an award on the indemnity basis in a case in which a party's experts had been severely criticised for not having addressed their responsibilities and not having conducted themselves in the manner that is expected of expert witnesses.[233] In a case in which a defendant had unreasonably tried to pick holes in the claimant's evidence, Mr John Baldwin QC condemned the defendant to pay costs on the indemnity basis.[234]

16.61 Where the expert evidence merits such a step, it is possible for the court to order that only the costs of the expert are to be paid on the indemnity basis, with the rest of the costs being on the standard basis.[235]

---

228 *Irish Response Ltd (a company incorporated under the laws of the Republic of Ireland) v (1) Direct Beauty Products Ltd* [2011] EWHC 608 (QB), at [47] *et seq*, *per* HHJ Richard Seymour QC (sitting as judge of the High Court)—although the judge awarded indemnity basis costs for other reasons, however (see 16.52).

229 See, eg, *Laporte v The Commissioner of Police of the Metropolis* [2015] EWHC 371 (QB), at [66], *per* Turner J.

230 See, eg, *Mengiste v Endowment Fund for the Rehabilitation of Tigray* [2013] EWHC 1087 (Ch), in which Peter Smith J found that the first stage in the procedure to grant a wasted costs order had been satisfied where a firm of solicitors had allowed a purported expert witness on the Ethiopian legal code to serve reports and give oral evidence although the court had found that his evidence had been tendentious and inappropriate.

231 *Siegel v Pummell* [2015] EWHC 195 (QB), at [13]–[20] and [37]–[39], *per* Wilkie J.

232 See *Manna (a Child and Protected Party) v Central Manchester University Hospitals NHS Foundation Trust* [2017] EWCA Civ 12, at [41].

233 *Williams v Jevis* [2009] EWHC 1837 (QB).

234 *Sudarshan Chemical Industries Ltd v Clariant Produkte (Deutschland) GMBH* [2012] EWHC 2941 (Pat).

235 See, eg, *Balmoral Group Ltd v Borealis (UK) Ltd* [2006] EWHC 2531 (Comm).

Breach of fiduciary duty, breach of duty to the court and failures to abide by orders

Where a trustee wrongly applied money owned by a person to whom he owed a fiduciary duty, Richard Sheldon QC (sitting as a deputy judge of the High Court) found that it was appropriate to make an order against him on the indemnity basis.[236] In a case in which a party's solicitors had acted in dereliction of their duty to the court, Haddon-Cave J made an award of costs on the indemnity basis.[237] Whilst it arose out of a criminal case, Stuart-Smith J made an award on the indemnity basis against the Crown Prosecution Service (CPS) where it had failed completely to comply with an order without a satisfactory explanation.[238] **16.62**

Courting publicity

Where a party actively seeks to court publicity in support of its serious allegations and where those allegations prove to be unfounded, an award on the indemnity basis may be appropriate;[239] likewise the conduct of an extensive publicity campaign designed to drive an opponent to settlement.[240] **16.63**

Contractual and collateral entitlements

Where a contractual right to costs exists (arising, for example, out of a mortgage or lease), the court's discretion should ordinarily be exercised so as to reflect that contractual right (see 66.04–66.17).[241] Thus, where the contract provides for costs on the indemnity basis, this will ordinarily result in an award of costs on the indemnity basis, as will a provision that 'all' costs will be paid.[242] This, however, will not always be the case.[243] As to the collateral rights of auditors to recover from the assets, see 66.22. **16.64**

---

236 *Curtis v Pulbrook* [2009] EWHC 1370 (Ch).

237 *R (on the application of Gassama) v Secretary of State for the Home Department* [2012] EWHC 3049 (Admin). See also *R (on the application of Grimshaw) v Southwark London Borough Council* [2013] EWHC 4504 (Admin).

238 *Re Malik* (unreported), 18 July 2013, QBD (Admin), *per* Stuart-Smith J.

239 *Three Rivers District Council v Bank of England* [2006] EWHC 816 (Comm), at [25], *per* Tomlinson J. In a similar vein, but in the context of proceedings brought by the state, see *R (on the application of Rawlinson & Hunter Trustees SA & Ors) v Serious Fraud Office* [2012] EWHC 3218 (Admin), at [15] *per* Silber J.

240 Whilst it was only an *obiter* comment, see *Balmoral v Borealis UK Ltd* [2006] EWHC 2531, at [1], *per* Christopher Clarke LJ.

241 *Gomba Holdings Ltd v Minories Finance Ltd (No 2)* [1993] Ch 171. More recently, see *National Bank of Kazakhstan v Bank of New York Mellon AS/NV* [2018] EWHC 300 (QB), at [3], *per* Popplewell J; *Woodford v AIG Europe Ltd* [2018] EWHC 358 (QB), at [133]–[137] and [150]–[153], *per* Moulder J.

242 See *Deutsche Bank (Suisse) SA v Khan* [2013] EWHC 1020 (Comm), at [19]–[24], *per* Hamblen J. See *also Fairview Investments Ltd v Sharma* (unreported), 14 October 1999, CA.

243 Whilst a pre-CPR, case, in *Penn v Bristol & West Building Society* [1997] 1 WLR 1356, Waller LJ had to consider whether a mortgagee was entitled to costs on the indemnity basis in a case in which it and the mortgagor were brought into litigation by a third party. He found that, in view of the fact that Ord 62, r 3(2), was to prevent costs being included in an award of damages in third-party and other proceedings in the same action, the fact that the costs would have been recoverable as damages if separate proceedings had been brought was not by itself a ground for awarding indemnity costs; rather, there had to be some additional factor of the nature that normally gave rise to such an order. It is arguable that this case is no longer good law in view of its reliance on Ord 62, r 3(2).

Anti-suit provisions, arbitration provisions and jurisdiction clauses

16.65 In a case in which a losing party had brought a claim in defiance of an anti-suit provision, Coleman J found that an award on the indemnity basis was appropriate for the purpose of restoring the parties to the position in which they would have been had that provision not been breached.[244] Christopher Clarke LJ found that an award on the indemnity basis was appropriate in a case in which the paying party had sought to dispute jurisdiction in 'an exercise in litigious hardball to the fullest extent', this being so even where that party had done nothing that was in breach of the relevant rules of court.[245] Coleman J commented that the same logic would apply to breaches of jurisdiction clauses and arbitration clauses.[246]

Litigation solely about costs

16.66 There is no sound reason why parties litigating on issues of costs should be more vulnerable to an order for costs on the indemnity basis than other litigants.[247]

Aarhus Convention claims

16.67 It may be that, in an environmental claim, the defendant wishes to argue that the claim is not an Aarhus Convention claim. CPR, r 45.44(3)(b), provides that if the court subsequently holds that the claim is an Aarhus Convention claim, it will normally order the defendant to pay the claimant's costs of those proceedings on the indemnity basis and that order may be enforced notwithstanding that this would increase the costs payable by the defendant beyond the amount prescribed in Practice Direction (PD) 45.

---

244 *National Westminster Bank plc v Rabobank Nederland* [2007] EWHC 3163 (Comm), *per* Colman J.

245 *Travelers Casualty and Surety Co of Canada v Sun Life Assurance Co of Canada (UK) Ltd* [2006] EWHC 2885 (Comm), at [36] and [37].

246 *A v B (No 2)* [2007] EWHC 54 (Comm), [2007] 1 All ER (Comm) 633.

247 *Zissis v Lukomski* [2006] EWCA Civ 341, at [52].

17

PART 36 OFFERS

17.01 This chapter deals with the following topics:

- terminology (17.03);
- the history of Part 36 offers (17.06);
- transitional provisions (17.18);
- the jurisdiction and legal framework of Part 36 offers:
  - the interpretation and nature of Part 36 (17.20);
  - the time at which offers are made (17.26);
  - types of claim and status of parties (17.30);
  - the format and service of offers (17.39);
  - the 'relevant period' (17.46);
  - personal injury claims (17.48);
  - clarity and adequacy of information (17.53);
  - disclosure of Part 36 offers to the court (17.57);
- technical shortcomings of Part 36 offers:
  - discretion, substantial compliance, waiver and estoppel (17.62);
  - interpretation (17.67);
  - the status of offers that do not comply (17.77);
- the application and effect of Part 36 offers:
  - where offers are not accepted (17.80);
  - where a claimant beats the offer (17.81);
  - where a defendant beats the offer (17.98);
  - measuring success—gauging the value of Part 36 offers (17.106);
  - discretion and Part 36—when the benefit of Part 36 would be 'unjust' (17.118);
  - interaction between Part 36 and Part 45 (17.162);
- the acceptance, rejection and withdrawal of Part 36 offers:
  - acceptance (17.164);
  - rejection (17.195); and
  - withdrawal or change (17.197).

17.02 This chapter deals with offers made under Section I of Part 36 of the Civil Procedure Rules (CPR). CPR, Part 36, Section II—that is, offers in respect of low-value road traffic accident (RTA) claims—is addressed in Chapter 50 (see, in particular, 50.70, 50.114, 50.287–50.296, 50.304 and 50.336).

Terminology

17.03 CPR, r 36.3, provides the following definitions.

- **'offeror'** The party who makes the offer in question[1]
- **'offeree'** The party to whom the offer in question is made[2]
- **'the relevant period'**[3]
  - In the case of an offer made not less than 21 days before a trial, the period specified under CPR, r 36.5(1)(c), or such longer period as the parties agree
  - Otherwise, the period up to the end of such trial
- **'trial'** Any trial in a case, whether it is a trial of all issues or a trial of liability, quantum or some other issue in the case[4]
- **'in progress'** The status of a trial between the time when it starts and the time when judgment is given or handed down[5]
- **'decided'** The status of a case when all issues in the case have been determined, whether at one or more trials[6]
- **'trial judge'** Among others,[7] the judge (if any) allocated in advance to conduct a trial[8]

17.04 Whilst the words 'beaten' and 'bettered' are often heard in practice and are universally understood, the CPR themselves do not define a word to refer to the situation in which either (a) a defendant obtains a result at least as advantageous to them as their Part 36 offer, or (b) a claimant obtains a result that is at least as advantageous to them as the proposals contained in their Part 36 offer. The word 'beaten' will be used in this book. In general, that word will be used to refer to a result that has come about by adjudication, but where the context so requires, it may also be used to refer to results reached by way of settlement.

17.05 As to the phrases 'present-day Part 36', 'pre-2015 Part 36' and 'original Part 36', see 17.18.

The History of Part 36

17.06 The history of Part 36 is a meandering tale. Notwithstanding this, it is generally regarded as being a success story, even by those who were otherwise critical of the Woolf reforms.[9]

Early history (pre-1995)

17.07 Around 1665, Kelynge LCJ allowed a practice to develop whereby payments were made into court (see 1.58).[10] Hullock records that the system was:

> '... introduced for the purposes of avoiding the hazard of pleading a tender, and with a view of enabling a party, who had had no opportunity of making a tender, or at least had omitted

[1] CPR, r 36.3(a).
[2] CPR, r 36.3(b).
[3] CPR, r 36.3(g).
[4] CPR, r 36.3(c).
[5] CPR, r 36.3(d).
[6] CPR, r 36.3(e).
[7] This is the word used in the CPR (as opposed to 'means').
[8] CPR, r 36.3(f).
[9] Jackson, R, *Review of Civil Litigation Costs: Final Report* (London: HMSO, 2010), ch 6, at para 1.2.
[10] The editor has not been able to find a contemporary record of this, but it is recorded as a historical note in reports such as White and Woodhouse (1727) 94 ER 17.

> to do so, to satisfy the debt, for which the action was commenced, without incurring any further expence.'[11]

It would be more than a century before the court would treat payments in as providing the type of costs protection that is now afforded by Part 36 offers,[12] but Kelynge LCJ's innovative system was a step in that direction.

References to something similar to Part 36 can be found in Blackstone's writings in the middle of the 18th century.[13] He records that offers made by defendants were regarded as being 'a species of confession' that operated in the following way: **17.08**

> 'By paying into the hands of the proper officer of the court as much as the defendant acknowledges to be due, together with the costs hitherto incurred, in order to prevent the expense of any farther proceedings ... If, after the money paid in, the plaintiff proceeds in his suit, it is at his own peril: for, if he does not prove more due than is so paid into court, he shall be nonsuited and pay the defendant costs; but he shall still have the money so paid in, for that the defendant has acknowledged to be his due.'[14]

Thus a defendant could garner a degree of costs protection by making a confession, but to do so he had to make a payment into court.[15] As can be seen (see 17.10–17.13), the notion of making a payment into court persisted until as recently as the mid-2000s.

Over time, defendants' proposals came to be regarded as being offers rather than confessions. As to the need to make a payment into court, in 1984 Oliver LJ had this to say: **17.09**

> 'In the case of the simple money claim, a defendant who wishes to avail himself of the protection afforded by an offer must, in the ordinary way, back his offer with cash by making a payment in and speaking for myself, I should not, as at present advised, be disposed in such a case to treat a *Calderbank* offer as carrying the same consequences as payment in.'[16]

The Woolf reforms (1995–99)

The seeds of change were sown in 1995 when, in his Interim Report, Lord Woolf proposed a system under which defendants' offers could be made without monies being paid into court.[17] In addition, Lord Woolf proposed rules that would allow claimants to make offers. Those proposals were met with opposition, not least by the Law Society.[18] Lord Woolf stuck to his guns, however, and in 1996, in his Final Report, he had the following to say: **17.10**

> '[I recommend] in respect of defendants' offers, that the making of the offer itself should be the critical step, while the backing of a payment in will be secondary and optional. This

[11] Hullock, J, *Costs in Civil Actions and Criminal Proceedings* (2nd edn, London: W Clarke & Sons, 1810), at p 212.

[12] The earliest instance that the editor has been able to find of the court making such an award is *Griffiths v Williams* (1787) 99 ER 1335—although part of the reasoning in that case was doubted in *Stevenson v Yorke* (1790) 4 TR 10. That said, in *Hartley v Bateson* (1787) 1 TR 629, the following note appears, which suggests that the practice of awarding costs to a defendant who had 'beaten' a payment in was already well established by 1787: 'On inquiring of the Master, it appears to be the constant and regular practice that the plaintiff is entitled to have his costs to the time of paying money into Court, and the defendant all his subsequent costs.'

[13] See Blackstone, W, *Commentaries on the Laws of England (1765–1769), Book Three*, ch 20.

[14] *Ibid.*

[15] *Ibid.* Apparently there was a similar procedure under French law: the reference that Gladstone cites in this regard is Sp L, b 6, c 4.

[16] *Cutts v Head* [1984] Ch 290, at 312.

[17] Lord Woolf, *Access to Justice: Interim Report* (London: HMSO, 1995), ch 24.

[18] The Law Society, for example, pointed to the fact that a payment into court was a useful way of allowing the offeree to satisfy themselves of the genuineness of the offeror's intent and of the substance of the offer.

means that [the common law rule] which prevents the making of a *Calderbank* offer where a payment into court can be made, will no longer apply under the [CPR].'[19]

Lord Woolf did make one concession, however: he accepted that payments in should not be abolished altogether.

The CPR as it was originally made (1999–early-2000s)

17.11 Broadly speaking, Lord Woolf's revised recommendations were accepted and incorporated into the nascent CPR, but his concession regarding payments into court (see 17.10) deprived Part 36 of some of its potency—more so given the fact that the CPR were silent on the weight to be afforded to defendants' offers that were not accompanied by a payment into court.[20] The effect was that judges often disregarded such offers. In 2001, for example, Sir Anthony Evans held that it was wrong to afford a defendants' Part 36 offer the same status as a Part 36 payment and (in the same case) Simon Brown LJ approvingly cited several reasons given by the Law Society why payments into court had their advantages.[21]

17.12 Later that year, Clarke LJ made similar comments in a different case, but he also reminded himself of the need to take into account all of the circumstances.[22] Having done this, he refused to disturb an order in which a trial judge had given effect to a Part 36 offer that had not been backed up by a Part 36 payment.[23] This marked the beginning of a gradual move towards Part 36 offers not needing to be bolstered by Part 36 payments into court of the sum offered.

A move away from payments into court (early 2000s–2008)

17.13 It was not until the mid-2000s that attitudes began to change in any significant way, however. That change came about partly as a result of influential organisations—most notably, the National Health Service Litigation Authority (NHSLA)—habitually making Part 36 offers that were not backed by corresponding payments into court. Its argument was concise, yet compelling: the NHS was good for the money, and the funds were put to better use treating patients than languishing in court.

17.14 In 2005, Dyson LJ looked at the matter afresh. He concluded that the court was at liberty to give effect to a Part 36 offer regardless of whether a payment into court had also been made.[24] This prompted a consultation by the Department of Constitutional Affairs,[25] the result of which was the effective abolition of Part 36 payments into court in 2007 (this being the 44th update of the CPR).[26]

---

[19] Lord Woolf, *Access to Justice: Interim Report* (London: HMSO, 1995), ch 11, at para 4.

[20] In particular, CPR, r 36.3(1), as it was originally, provided that: 'Subject to rules 36.2A(2), 36.5(5) and 36.23, an offer by a defendant to settle a money claim will not have the consequences set out in this Part unless it is made by way of a Part 36 payment.'

[21] *Amber v Stacey* [2001] 1 WLR 1225; see also *Hardy v Sutherland* [2001] EWCA Civ 976.

[22] *The Maersk Colombo* [2001] 2 Lloyd's Rep 275. Even in the early days of the CPR, the court had a discretion to take into account offers that were not Part 36 payments (or, for that matter, offers that did not comply with Part 36 at all). The court's power to do so arose from the provisions in what used to be CPR, r 44.3(4), but which are now found at CPR, r 44.2(4)(c).

[23] *The Maersk Colombo* [2001] 2 Lloyd's Rep 275, in which, for the sake of accuracy, it should be recorded that a payment had been made, but it was late.

[24] *Stokes Pension Fund v Western Power Distribution (South West) plc* [2005] EWCA Civ 854.

[25] Department of Constitutional Affairs, *Civil Procedure Rules Part 36: Offers to Settle and Payments into Court*, CP 02/06 (London: HMSO, 2006).

[26] See the Civil Procedure (Amendment No 3) Rules 2006 (SI 2006/3435).

The rise and fall of flexibility under Part 36 (2008–10)

In 2008, the Court of Appeal dallied with the notion of being flexible when considering whether a Part 36 offer had been beaten in the sense that it was suggested that the court ought to take into account factors that were not related directly to the subject matter of the offer.[27] This led to arguments about whether the difference between what had been offered and what had been awarded was worth the effort. For the next year or so, the courts were frequently burdened with unprepossessing arguments about whether the game had been worth the candle. In 2010, however, a differently constituted Court of Appeal explained that that was not the correct way in which to deal with Part 36 offers.[28] In time,[29] this led to an amendment to the CPR (on 1 October 2011) that made it clear that 'more advantageous' meant better in monetary terms by any amount, however small.[30] **17.15**

Refinement by case law (2010–14)

At about the same time (that is, 2010), the court began to explain that Part 36 was a self-contained procedural code.[31] A body of case law also developed that addressed, amongst other things, the approach to be taken when a putative Part 36 offer was said to be defective in some way. **17.16**

Alignment with case law (2015)

In 2015, the Rules were changed—by way of the 78th update of the CPR—in such a way as to align them with the above body of case law.[32] The intention was also to simplify the Rules as far as possible to make them more accessible to court users—particularly litigants in person. The rules in Part 36 were renumbered. The associated Practice Direction was renamed, but on the whole was otherwise left unchanged. **17.17**

Transitional Provisions

The provisions in CPR, Part 36, changed on 5 April 2007 (the 44th update to the CPR)[33] and then again on 6 April 2015 (the 78th update).[34] The phrases 'original Part 36', 'pre-2015 Part 36' and 'present-day Part 36' are used accordingly. The following points may be made. **17.18**

- **Present-day Part 36 (6 April 2015 onwards)** Unless the contrary is stated or is obvious from the context, references to Part 36 are to provisions in Part 36 as it stood on the date of publication.
- **Pre-2015 Part 36 (5 April 2007–5 April 2015)** If the offer was made between 5 April 2007 and 6 April 2015, the regime that existed at that time will, on the whole, apply.[35]

---

27 *Carver v BAA plc* [2008] EWCA Civ 412.

28 See *Gibbon v Manchester City Council* [2010] EWCA Civ 726.

29 The amendment was made on 1 October 2011.

30 This was inserted by Civil Procedure (Amendment No 2) Rules 2011 (SI 2011/1979). The amended rule was the forerunner of the present-day CPR, r 36.17(2).

31 See *Gibbon v Manchester City Council* [2010] EWCA Civ 726. See also *F & C Alternative Investments (Holdings) Ltd & Ors Appellants v Barthelemy* [2012] EWCA Civ 843, at [57], *per* Davis LJ.

32 See the Explanatory Note of the Civil Procedure (Amendment No 8) Rules 2014 (SI 2014/3299).

33 See the Civil Procedure (Amendment No 3) Rules 2006 (SI 2006/3435).

34 It has been based on Sch 1 of the Civil Procedure (Amendment No 8) Rules 2014 (SI 2014/3299).

35 The Civil Procedure (Amendment No 8) Rules 2014 (SI 2014/3299), r 18.

Most of the relevant law can still be found in this book, but it has been relegated to the footnotes. More detail may be found in the second edition of this book in Chapters 14 and 15.

- **Original Part 36 (pre-6 April 2007)** In the very unlikely event that the offer in question was made before 5 April 2007, the original Part 36 may apply.[36] In any event, an offer made under the original Part 36 may be taken into account notwithstanding the fact that it was not accompanied by a payment in.[37] Further details of the old regimes can be found in the second edition of this book and in older editions of The White Book.

The Jurisdiction and Legal Framework of Part 36 Offers

17.19 This section deals with the rules that govern the making, disclosure and form of Part 36 offers. The following topics are addressed:

- the interpretation and nature of Part 36 (17.20);
- the time at which offers are made (17.26);
- types of claim and status of parties (17.30);
- the format and service of offers (17.39);
- the 'relevant period' (17.46);
- personal injury claims (17.48);
- clarity and adequacy of information (17.53); and
- disclosure of Part 36 offers to the court (17.57).

The interpretation and nature of Part 36

Self-contained code

17.20 CPR, Part 36, seeks to achieve certainty and to encourage early settlement of disputes by conferring costs benefits on parties who make realistic offers of settlement, the philosophy being that this will both benefit individual litigants and promote the administration of justice as a whole.[38] The need for certainty is regarded as being of particular importance, which is why Part 36 is regarded as a structured and highly prescriptive self-contained code.[39]

---

[36] Transitional provisions provide that offers made under the original Part 36 will have the consequences set out under the pre-2015 Part 36, but only if it would have had the consequences set out in the original Part 36: see the Civil Procedure (Amendment No 3) Rules 2006 (SI 2006/3435), r 7(2). It seems as though the court gives little weight to the procedural differences between the two regimes and, in particular, seems not to give weight to the fact that an offeror may have appropriately decided not to make a Part 36 payment: see *Cunningham v AST Express Ltd* [2009] EWCA Civ 767, at [33]; see also the second edition of this book, at para 14.53.

[37] Whilst technically *obiter*, see *French v Groupama Insurance Co Ltd* [2011] EWCA Civ 1119, at [35]–[39], *per* Rix LJ, who recited that the conditions that must be met are as follows: (a) the offer must be expressed in clear terms so that there is no doubt as to what is being offered; (b) the offer should be open for acceptance for at least 21 days and otherwise accord with the substance of a *Calderbank* offer; (c) the offer should be genuine and not a 'sham or non-serious in some way' (*Stokes Pension Fund v Western Power Distribution (South West) plc* [2005] EWCA Civ 854, at [41], per Waller LJ); and (d) the defendant should clearly have been good for the money when the offer was made.

[38] See *SG v Hewitt* [2012] EWCA Civ 1053, at [26], *per* Black LJ. See also *Abada v Gray and the Motor Insurers Bureau* (unreported), 25 June 1997, CA, in which Lord Woolf (then Master of the Rolls) made observations that remain relevant despite having been made in relation to the provisions of the Rules of the Supreme Court (RSC).

[39] See *Gibbon v Manchester City Council* [2010] EWCA Civ 726, at [4], *per* Moore-Bick LJ (who, at the time, was a member of the Civil Procedures Rule Committee that had recently drafted the Rules).

This is now made clear by CPR, r 36.1(1), which reads as follows: 'This Part contains a self-contained procedural code about offers to settle made pursuant to the procedure set out in this Part ("Part 36 offers").' One of the justifications for this is that Part 36 must be capable of being understood and followed by ordinary citizens who wish to conduct their own litigation;[40] indeed, Part 36 was drafted with these considerations in mind.[41]

Vos LJ had this to say about the way in which Part 36 should be interpreted (in the context of whether an offer that had been more generous to the offeree than was permitted by Part 36 should be regarded as being a valid Part 36 offer): **17.21**

> '[T]he words in Part 36 have been used precisely and carefully. If the Rules Committee had wanted Part 36 to be of more general in application to every type of case, it could easily have made it so. It seems to me that they did not.'[42]

Put otherwise, the provisions in CPR, Part 36, should not be moulded so as to fit circumstances that are different from those that are expressly set out.

Distinction between Part 36 and the law of contract Part 36 does not incorporate the law governing the formation of contracts.[43] That said, contract-like principles may come into play when interpreting the meaning of an offer[44] or where there is a need to determine the terms of the putative settlement, such as where there have been competing Part 36 offers passing back and forth.[45] **17.22**

Whilst a Part 36 offer will not be a contractual offer, it would seem that Part 36 is not so self-contained as to be incapable of giving rise to contractual consequences. For example, acceptance of a Part 36 offer is capable of amounting to a rejection of a contractual offer[46] and where the terms of the offer have to be contractual to be capable of enforcement, it seems that the court is able to regard them as being such.[47] The fact that, once accepted, a Part 36 offer is capable of giving rise to contractual consequences does not mean that Part 36 offers are, in themselves, contractual offers.[48] **17.23**

Distinction between Part 36 and Part 3 It is doubtful—if not unthinkable—that Part 36 is to be interpreted without reference to the overriding objective, but there are provisions in Part 3 that seem not to apply. For example, Elizabeth Laing J has found that the powers regarding the extension of time in Part 3 do not allow the court to vary the time limits **17.24**

---

40 *Ibid*, at [4].

41 See *ibid*, at [6].

42 *N J Rickard Ltd v Holloway* [2015] EWCA Civ 1631, at [27].

43 See *Gibbon v Manchester City Council* [2010] EWCA Civ 726, at [5], *per* Moore-Bick LJ.

44 See, eg, *C v D* [2011] EWCA Civ 646, at [55], *per* Rix LJ; cf *Shaw v Merthyr Tydfil County Borough* [2014] EWCA Civ 1678, at [19], *per* Maurice Kay LJ.

45 See, eg, *Rosario v Nadell Patisserie Ltd* [2010] EWHC 1886 (QB).

46 *DB UK Bank Ltd (t/a DB Mortgages) v Jacobs Solicitors* [2016] EWHC 1614 (Ch), at [23]–[27], *per* Andrew Hochhauser QC (sitting as a deputy High Court judge).

47 See, eg, *Orton v Collins* [2007] 1 WLR 2953, in which Peter Prescott QC (sitting as a deputy High Court judge) found that a right to land arising upon acceptance of a Part 36 offer was capable of being regarded as a contractual right for the purposes of s 2 of the Law of Property (Miscellaneous Provisions) Act 1989.

48 That said, whilst not binding and whilst it was, at the time of writing, subject to appeal, Judge Butler has found that a 'failed' Part 36 offer (ie an offer that was made under the post-6 April 2015 Rules, but which did not comply with the procedural requirements of CPR, r 36.5) was an offer that is capable of contractual acceptance, despite the fact that it was the offeror who argued that the offer was not a Part 36 offer: *Worrell v Nicholls* (unreported), 17 August 2017, Preston County Court, *per* Judge Butler.

in Part 36.[49] That said, other provisions may apply: whilst not binding, Master Yoxall has found (in the context of a putatively defective withdrawal of a Part 36 offer) that whilst Part 36 is a self-contained code, this does not exclude the court's general powers to remedy errors under CPR, r 3.10, as far as technically defective service is concerned.[50]

17.25 **Distinction between Part 36 and Part 44** Part 36 is not to be regarded as being an extension of Part 44 nor is it to be read as if it incorporates Part 44. Richard Davies J (sitting in the Court of Appeal) had this to say about the differences in the policies underlying Parts 36 and 44:

> 'Part 36 and Part 44 are separate regimes with separate purposes. Part 36 is a self-contained code dealing with offers of settlement made in accordance with and subject to the terms of Part 36, which specifies particular consequences in the event that such offers are not accepted. That those consequences include features which go far beyond that which might be ordered by way of costs under Part 44 ... While Part 36 is highly prescriptive in its terms, and highly restrictive of the exercise of any discretion by the court in any particular case, Part 44 confers on the court a discretion in almost the widest possible terms ... the broad terms in which the discretion conferred by Part 44 is expressed comes at the price of some uncertainty and some scope for argument as to costs.'[51]

Indeed, as of 6 April 2007, the separation of CPR, Parts 36 and 44, has been put beyond doubt by virtue of the fact that CPR, r 44.2(4)(c), now reads 'in deciding what order (if any) to make about costs, the court will have regard to all the circumstances, including ... any admissible offer ... which is not an offer to which costs consequences under Part 36 apply'. This is in contrast to what was said previously, which was 'any admissible offer ... (whether or not made in accordance with Part 36)'.[52]

The time at which offers are made

The time when offers may be made

17.26 Whilst the position under the original Part 36 was less clear,[53] it is now beyond doubt that an offer may be made at any time; indeed, there is an express provision that confirms that an offer may be made before the commencement of proceedings.[54] Similarly, an offer may be made before a counterclaim has been pleaded,[55] during an appeal[56] or—where the offer relates to costs—before commencement of a detailed assessment.[57]

---

[49] See *Titmus v General Motors UK Ltd* [2016] EWHC 2021 (QB), at [25].

[50] See *Thompson v Reeve* (unreported), 20 March 2017, QBD, *per* Master Yoxall.

[51] *Coward v Phaestos Ltd* [2014] EWCA Civ 1256, at [93], [94] and [101]. See also *Shovelar v Lane* [2011] EWCA Civ 802, at [52], *per* Ward LJ; *Webb (by her litigation friend) v Liverpool Women's NHS Foundation Trust* [2016] EWCA Civ 365, at [36]–[38], *per* Sir Stanley Burnton.

[52] See the Civil Procedure (Amendment No 3) Rules 2006 (SI 2006/3435); *Webb (by her litigation friend) v Liverpool Women's NHS Foundation Trust* [2016] EWCA Civ 365, at [33]–[38], *per* Sir Stanley Burnton.

[53] The original Part 36 provided that a Part 36 offer could be made at any time after proceedings had started (see CPR, r 36.2(4)(a)). Notwithstanding the fact that the court was specifically empowered to take such offers into account, it was argued that this rule meant that an offer made before the issue of proceedings was not to be regarded as being a Part 36 offer. The Court of Appeal rejected this argument: see *Huck v Robson* [2002] EWCA Civ 398, at [55].

[54] CPR, r 36.7(1).

[55] *AF v BG* [2009] EWCA Civ 757, at [17] and [18], *per* Lloyd LJ.

[56] CPR, r 36.7(1), as modified by CPR, r 36.4(2).

[57] See CPR, r 36.7(1), as modified by CPR, r 44.20(4).

An offer that is made before the issue of a claim form is capable of acceptance as a Part 36 offer. In that regard, the reference to 'proceedings' in CPR, r 36.13(1), is to be afforded a wide interpretation.[58] That said, if an offeree accepts an offer prior to the commencement of proceedings, whilst the claimant will have an entitlement to costs, they will not have the benefit of a deemed costs order.[59] **17.27**

The day on which time begins to run

A Part 36 offer is made when it is served on the offeree;[60] the original Part 36 merely provided that the offer must be 'received'.[61] In view of the change in the language and also in view of the signpost at the end of CPR, r 36.7,[62] it seems that the formalities relating to service now apply. That being so, CPR, Part 6, will be relevant (see 17.43; see also 43.133–43.137 for a discussion regarding the formalities of service, albeit in a different context). **17.28**

Where it is served within the UK,[63] a Part 36 offer will be deemed to be served on the day shown in Table 17.1.[64] **17.29**

Types of claim and status of parties

Types of claim to which offers may apply

A Part 36 offer may be made in respect of the whole or part[65] of any claim, counterclaim,[66] other additional claim, appeal or cross-appeal from a decision made at a trial[67] or by a tribunal,[68] or detailed assessment.[69] This includes any money claims, including claims for provisional damages[70] or periodic payments,[71] as well as non-monetary claims.[72] An offer may also relate to any issue that may arise in any of the above.[73] **17.30**

The following specific points can be made. **17.31**

- **Counterclaims** Where there is a counterclaim, a Part 36 offer may be made in respect of the claim, the counterclaim[74] or both.[75] Part 36 now expressly refers to CPR, rr 20.2

58 See *Thompson (a minor) & Ors v Bruce* [2011] EWHC 2228 (QB), at [38], *per* John Leighton Williams QC, disapproving the contrary finding of HHJ Platts in *Solomon v Cromwell Group Plc* (unreported) 2 August 2010, Manchester County Court; approved (in a different context) in *Solomon v Cromwell Group plc* [2011] EWCA Civ 1584.

59 See CPR, r 44.9(2). The effect of this is that it would mean that costs-only proceedings may be needed in default of agreement.

60 CPR, r 36.7(2).

61 See the original CPR, r 36.7; see also *Charles v NTL Group Ltd* [2002] EWCA Civ 2004.

62 That signpost says: '(Part 6 provides detailed rules about service of documents.)'

63 If the offer is to be served outside of the UK, then CPR, r 6.20, will apply.

64 See CPR, r 6.26.

65 See CPR, r 36.2(3).

66 See CPR, r 36.2(3)(a).

67 See CPR, r 36.2(3)(b).

68 It will also apply in appeals from certain tribunals; see, eg, *Blue Sphere Global Ltd v Revenue & Customs Commissioners* [2010] EWCA Civ 1448, which related to an appeal from a VAT and duties tribunal.

69 See CPR, r 47.20(4).

70 See CPR, r 36.19.

71 See CPR, r 36.18(2). This will only apply in a personal injuries claim.

72 This is implied by CPR, r 36.17(4)(d)(ii), and the fact that there is nothing within Part 36 to prevent an offer being made in non-monetary disputes or in respect of non-monetary issues.

73 CPR, rr 36.2(3) and 36.5(d).

74 CPR, r 36.2(3).

75 See CPR, r 36.5(1)(e).

Table 17.1 Service of Part 36 offers

Method of service	Deemed date of service
First-class post or equivalent	The second day after it was posted, left with, delivered to or collected by the relevant service provider, provided that day is a business day; if not, the next business day after that day
Document exchange	The second day after it was left with, delivered to or collected by the relevant service provider, provided that day is a business day; if not, the next business day after that day
Delivering the document to, or leaving it at, a permitted address	If it is delivered to or left at the permitted address on a business day before 4.30 pm, on that day; in any other case, on the next business day after that day
Fax	If the transmission of the fax is completed on a business day before 4.30 pm, on that day; in any other case, on the next business day after the day on which it was transmitted
Other electronic method	If the email or other electronic transmission is sent on a business day before 4.30 pm, on that day; in any other case, on the next business day after the day on which it was sent
Personal service	If the document is served personally before 4.30 pm on a business day, on that day; in any other case, on the next business day after that day

and 20.3,[76] which provide that counterclaims and other additional claims are treated as 'claims', and that references to a 'claimant or defendant include a party bringing or defending an additional claim'.[77] The effect of this is discussed at 17.33.

- **Contributory negligence** CPR, rr 36.2(3) and 36.5(d), expressly provide that offers may be made in respect of contributory negligence.[78]
- **Non-monetary offers** Offers may be made in disputes that are not about money.[79] Even where the dispute is about money, it is permissible for an offer to relate to non-monetary aspects of the claim. It is even possible to make offers in relation to factual issues (see, for example, 17.156).
- **More than one set of proceedings** It is a moot point whether a true Part 36 offer[80] may ever be made to pay or accept the net difference between a claim and another unrelated claim between the same parties. Leggatt J has explained that the court would not generally allow a party to combine the results of proceedings for the purposes of seeking the benefits of Part 36 because it may lead to injustice if proceedings were 'decoupled' and judgments were delivered at different times.[81]

---

76 See CPR, r 36.2.

77 See CPR, r 36.2 (in parentheses).

78 Goldring LJ has found that an offer in respect of contributory negligence may be construed as an offer in respect of liability, thereby bringing it within the category of a Part 36 offer: *Onay v Brown* [2009] EWCA Civ 775, at [28].

79 This is implied by CPR, r 36.17(4)(d)(ii), and the fact that there is nothing within Part 36 to prevent an offer being made in non-monetary disputes or in respect of non-monetary issues.

80 Even where the claims have become 'decoupled', it does not follow that the court will disregard a net offer. Leggatt J has explained that such an offer may be taken into account as being an 'admissible offer' under CPR, r 44.2: *Newland Shipping & Forwarding Ltd v Toba Trading FZC* [2014] EWHC 864 (Comm), at [17].

81 *Ibid*, at [13]–[16].

- **Future performance** Offers will usually relate to matters that are immediately in the control of the offeror, but this need not always be the case. Henderson J has confirmed that an offer may relate to an advantage or form of relief that the claimant would be able to obtain only at some later stage.[82] That said, where a defendant makes an offer to pay a sum of money in settlement of the claim, then unless it is an offer to pay provisional damages or periodical payments in a personal injuries case,[83] it must be an offer to pay a single sum of money.[84] Similarly, a defendant's offer that includes an offer to pay all or part of the sum at a date later than 14 days following the date of acceptance will not be treated as a Part 36 offer unless the offeree accepts the offer.[85]
- **Appeals and cross-appeals** A Part 36 offer may be made in respect of an appeal (or cross-appeal) from a decision made at a trial,[86] in which case the appellant and the respondent will be treated as being the 'claimant' and 'defendant', respectively.[87] To be effective, the offer must be made in the appeal proceedings themselves; where an offer has already been made in the proceedings that led to the appeal, it will need to be remade if it is to have a bearing on the costs of the appeal.[88]
- **Appeals in respect of interim decision and case/costs management decisions** Whilst there is no authority on the point, it seems that Part 36 offers may not be made in respect of appeals from interim decisions or case/costs management decisions (such as a costs management order). This is because such a decision would not be a decision 'made at a trial' within the meaning of CPR, r 36.2(3)(b)—presumably, to ensure that the provisions in Part 36 do not fan the flames of satellite litigation.
- **Detailed assessment proceedings** The provisions that enable Part 36 offers to be made in detailed assessment proceedings under CPR, Part 47, apply only where those proceedings commenced on or after 1 April 2013.[89] The receiving party and paying party are treated as if they were the claimant and defendant, respectively.[90] Whilst there is no authority on the point, it is probably not the case that a Part 36 offer may have the consequences of being a Part 36 offer in a solicitor-and-client assessment under s 70 of the Solicitors Act 1974 (see 36.77).

The only expressly exclusory rule in Part 36 is that CPR, Part 36, Section I, will not apply where CPR, Part 36, Section II applies[91]—that is, when a Part 36 offer is made in the context of the Pre-Action Protocol for Low Value Personal Injury Claims in Road Traffic Accidents **17.32**

82 *AB v CD & Ors* [2011] EWHC 602 (Ch), at [23].
83 See CPR, rr 36.18 and 36.19.
84 See CPR, r 36.6(1).
85 See CPR, r 36.6(2).
86 CPR, r 36.3(2)(b), specifically provides that a Part 36 offer may be made in appeal proceedings.
87 CPR, r 36.4(2).
88 See CPR, r 36.4(1). This is a codification of the judge-made law: see *P & O Nedlloyd BV v Utaniko Ltd* [2003] EWCA Civ 174, at [6], *per* Brooke LJ. See also *KR v Bryn Alyn Community (Holdings) Ltd (in liquidation)* [2003] EWCA Civ 383.
89 The Civil Procedure (Amendment) Rules 2013 (SI 2013/262), r 22(10).
90 See CPR, r 47.20(4).
91 See CPR, rr 36.1(3), 36.2(1) and 36.24. CPR, Part 36, Section II, applies to an offer to settle made in accordance with that Section where the parties have followed the Pre-action Protocol for Low Value Personal Injury Claims in Road Traffic Accidents or the Pre-action Protocol for Low Value Personal Injury (Employers' Liability and Public Liability) claims and have started proceedings under Part 8 in accordance with Practice Direction (PD) 8B.

(the RTA Protocol) or the Pre-Action Protocol for Low Value Personal Injury (Employers' Liability and Public Liability) Claims (the EL/PL Protocol). That said, once the claim leaves the protocol and is governed by CPR, Part 45, Section IIIA—that is, where post-Portal fixed costs become payable—Part I will apply (along with certain special provisions).[92]

The status of the parties

17.33 Part 36 refers mostly to claimants and defendants; other parties have an equivalent status, as is set out in Tables 17.2–17.5 below.

Table 17.2 Claim that is subject to set-off arising out of a counterclaim

Nominal status	Equivalent status for Part 36
Claimant in counterclaim	Claimant, where offer relates solely to counterclaim[93]
	Defendant, where offer relates to their liability after set-off[94] (but see 17.34–17.38)
Defendant in counterclaim	Defendant, where offer relates solely to counterclaim
	Claimant, where offer relates to their entitlement after set-off (but see 17.34–17.38)

Table 17.3 Claim in which there is any other type of additional claim (that is, a Part 20 claim that is not a counterclaim)[95]

Nominal status	Equivalent status for Part 36
Additional claimant	Claimant
Additional defendant	Defendant

Table 17.4 Appeal[96]

Nominal status	Equivalent status for Part 36
Appellant	Claimant
Respondent	Defendant

Table 17.5 Detailed assessment[97]

Nominal status	Equivalent status for Part 36
Receiving party	Claimant
Paying party	Defendant

92 See CPR, rr 36.20 and 36.21.
93 See CPR, r 20.3(1).
94 This is implied by CPR, r 36.5(1)(e).
95 See CPR, r 20.3(1).
96 See CPR, r 36.4(2).
97 See CPR, r 47.20(4).

Counterclaims It will usually be obvious whether an offeror is acting in the capacity of a claimant or a defendant, but occasionally there may be uncertainty. The present-day Part 36 expressly provides that where a party has a counterclaim or other additional claim, that party may be treated as though they were the claimant in respect of that claim.[98] Whilst the contrary is arguable,[99] this seems to be a codification of the pre-existing law.[100] The new provisions have, however, drawn attention to the fact that a defendant/counterclaimant is, in theory, able to make offers in one of three capacities: **17.34**

(1) a defendant's Part 36 offer in relation to the claim;
(2) a claimant's Part 36 offer in relation to the counterclaim; or
(3) an offer in respect of both the claim and the counterclaim.

The first two ought not to cause any conceptual difficulty, but the same is not true of the third (that is, an offer to pay or accept a sum of money that is intended to be the net difference between the claim and counterclaim) because it may not always be clear whether such an offer was being made as a claimant or as a defendant. This may be a point of pivotal importance if, for example, the offer were to be accepted, because it would determine who would be condemned to pay the costs of the proceedings.

Where the offer is made in respect of both the claim and the counterclaim: is there a need to determine the status of the offeror? It has been suggested that where, in a commercial claim, there is a claim and a counterclaim, and an offeror achieves a net result that beats an offer, it does not matter whether it was a claimant's offer or a defendant's offer. This argument is based on the notion that, in many commercial claims, the determinant of who is the claimant is often simply a matter of who got to the court first (see 6.63). Coulson J rejected that submission for the following reasons (amongst others): **17.35**

- the CPR expressly differentiate between the consequences of not accepting a claimant's Part 36 offer, on the one hand, and the consequences of not accepting a defendant's Part 36 offer, on the other, so it plainly matters which type of offer is under consideration; and
- it is important that the recipient of a Part 36 letter knows what sort of offer it is.[101]

---

[98] This is achieved by virtue of the cross-referencing to Part 20 in CPR, r 36.2.

[99] Prior to 6 April 2015, the pre-existing law had been anything but clear. Hildyard J had said that it was neither required nor permissible to go behind the formal status of the parties to determine which rules applied: *Procter & Gamble Co v Svenska Cellulosa Aktiebolaget SCA* [2012] EWHC 2839 (Ch), at [55]. He went on to say that the substance of the claim, and the issue of who was trying to prove the claim and who was trying to oppose it, were factors that could be taken into account for the purposes of deciding the issue of indemnity costs and interest. It appears not to have been drawn to Hildyard J's attention, however, that Lloyd LJ had found that a defendant could be treated as a claimant in respect of its counterclaim and be deemed to have made a 'claimant's Part 36 offer' in circumstances in which the offer was for the defendant to receive a net payment and therefore the defendant was, in substance, the claimant to the action: *AF v BG* [2009] EWCA Civ 757, at [16]–[21].

[100] See *AF v BG* [2009] EWCA Civ 757, at [16]–[21].

[101] See *Van Oord Ltd v Allseas UK Ltd* [2015] EWHC 3385 (TCC), at [16]–[19].

17.36 The second point above needs to be expanded upon. Coulson J had this to say about the importance of making the nature of the offer clear:

> '[B]ecause there is such a significant difference in the consequences of non-acceptance, depending on the proper construction of the letter, it is vital that a party making a Part 36 offer spells out, in terms which are unequivocal and free from ambiguity, the nature of the offer being made and the consequences which it says will flow from its non-acceptance by the recipient.'[102]

As such, the label given to the offer (or the label that would be necessarily implied by its terms) is a factor to which some importance may attach.

17.37 *Where the offer is made in respect of both the claim and the counterclaim: how is the status of the offeror to be determined?* Whilst there are conflicting authorities on the point[103] and whilst some of those authorities were decided under previous iterations of the CPR, it is probably the case that where a party makes an offer that encompasses both claim and counterclaim, that party's status as offeror is to be resolved by looking at the matter as a whole and not only by reference to a statement of intent recorded in the offer.[104] Thus, if a nominal defendant/counterclaimant were to make an offer, the fact that it purported to be a 'claimant's Part 36 offer' would not be determinative of that issue;[105] if, however, the counterclaim were to exceed the claim such that the balance was in the offeror's favour, then that party would be on firmer ground for arguing that they made the offer in the capacity of a claimant.[106] If the claim and the counterclaim had become so decoupled that they could no longer be said to be one set of proceedings, however, it would be arguable that an offer for the net difference should not be regarded as being a Part 36 offer at all[107] (see 17.31 under 'More than one set of proceedings').

17.38 Whilst it is no more than the editor's own creation,[108] the following list is intended to refer to factors that may be relevant to the issue of whether an offer is, in truth, a claimant's Part 36 offer or a defendant's:

- the relevant facts of the litigation and, in particular, the perceived status of the offeror given the way in which the competing claims were presented at the time the offer was made;
- the label attached to the offer (either expressly, or by necessary implication), and whether any clarification was made about its effect (such as 'for the avoidance of doubt ...');
- whether the offer is to pay a net amount of damages or debt or to receive a net amount;

---

[102] See *ibid*, at [17].

[103] See *Procter & Gamble Co v Svenska Cellulosa Aktiebolaget SCA* [2012] EWHC 2839 (Ch), at [55]; cf *AF v BG* [2009] EWCA Civ 757, at [16]–[21].

[104] See *AF v BG* [2009] EWCA Civ 757, at [16]–[18], *per* Lloyd LJ.

[105] Whilst there is no authority directly on the point, if a defendant were to phrase an offer in such way as to claim the status of claimant in circumstances in which that was plainly untrue, it is easily arguable that it should not be regarded as being a Part 36 offer at all. Similarly, if there were an insufficient nexus between the claim and the counterclaim to allow one to be set off against the other, a party who made an offer for the net liability may find that the court declines to regard it as being a relevant Part 36 offer at all.

[106] See *AF v BG* [2009] EWCA Civ 757, at [16]–[18], *per* Lloyd LJ.

[107] See, by way of analogy, *Newland Shipping & Forwarding Ltd v Toba Trading FZC* [2014] EWHC 864 (Comm), at [13]–[16], *per* Leggatt J.

[108] This list is based, to a large extent, on the factors that Coulson J regarded as being relevant in *Van Oord Ltd v Allseas UK Ltd* [2015] EWHC 3385 (TCC).

- whether the offer makes reference to paying or receiving costs in the event of it being accepted;
- whether the offer refers to the costs consequences of non-acceptance in terms that have the hallmarks of being a defendant's offer or a claimant's offer and, in particular, whether it makes mention of any of the claimant-only benefits of making a Part 36 offer (as set out at 17.81); and
- whether the offer, by its terms, is incompatible with it being either a claimant's offer or a defendant's offer.

The format and service of offers

Form N242A

The offer may be made in a completed Form N242A,[109] but in practice this is rarely done (despite judicial recommendation that it be used).[110] In practice, most Part 36 offers are made in the form of letters. **17.39**

Claimants and defendants

The following formalities apply to all Part 36 offers (made both by claimants and defendants). **17.40**

- **Writing** The offer must be in writing.[111]
- **Notice** The offer must 'make clear' that it is made pursuant to Part 36[112] or, if the offer was made before 6 April 2015, must state on its face that it is intended to have the consequences of CPR, Part 36, Section I.[113] There is no guidance as to what 'make clear' means, but one could easily argue that it is merely a more accessible way of saying 'state on its face or by clear reference'. It is worth noting that there is no requirement that the offer states that it is without prejudice save as to costs (although, in practice, this is commonly done).
- **'Relevant period'** Unless it is made less than 21 days before trial,[114] the offer must specify a period of not less than 21 days within which the defendant will be liable for the claimant's costs in accordance with CPR, rr 36.13 or 36.20, if the offer is accepted.[115]
- **Ambit** The offer must state whether it relates to the whole of the claim, to part of it or to an issue that arises in it and, if so, to which part or issue.[116]
- **Counterclaim** The offer must state whether it takes into account any counterclaim.[117] It is commonly the case that an offer is made in circumstances in which this would be entirely redundant, such as where the offer is made in detailed assessment proceedings. In such circumstances, offers tend not to comply with this requirement.

---

[109] See PD 36, para 1.1.
[110] See, eg, *Shah v Elliot* [2011] EW Misc 8, at [46], *per* Judge Platt.
[111] See CPR, r 36.5(1)(a) (or, if the offer was before 6 April 2015, CPR, r 36.2(2)(a), of the pre-2015 Part 36).
[112] See CPR, r 36.5(1)(b).
[113] See CPR, r 36.2(2)(b) of the pre-2015 Part 36.
[114] See CPR, r 36.5(2).
[115] See CPR, r 36.5(1)(c) (or, if the offer was before 6 April 2015, CPR, r 36.2(2)(c), of the pre-2015 Part 36).
[116] See CPR, r 36.5(1)(d) (or, if the offer was before 6 April 2015, CPR, r 36.2(2)(d), of the pre-2015 Part 36).
[117] See CPR, r 36.5(1)(e) (or, if the offer was before 6 April 2015, CPR, r 36.2(2)(e), of the pre-2015 Part 36).

If the claim is for damages for personal injuries, then further formalities may apply (see 17.48–17.52).

17.41 **Claimants** Hildyard J has said that there is no requirement that a claimant had to make the payment of costs a condition of their offer; instead—he found—Part 36 is to be read as requiring a claimant who sought their costs to specify a period of not less than 21 days within which the defendant would be liable to pay those costs if the offer were to be accepted.[118] This may be so, but Vos LJ has made it clear that this would not permit a claimant to make a 'drop hands' offer (that is, an offer under which, if accepted, no costs would be payable) that came within the ambit of CPR, Part 36 and, to that extent, Vos LJ disagreed with Hildyard J.[119]

17.42 **Defendants** Other than where it applies to provisional damages or to periodical payments (see 17.49–17.50), an offer by a defendant to pay a sum of money in settlement of a claim must be an offer to pay a single sum of money.[120] A defendant's offer that includes an offer to pay all or part of the sum at a date later than 14 days following the date of acceptance will not be treated as a Part 36 offer unless the offeree accepts the offer.[121] The requirement to make a Part 36 payment no longer exists (see 17.10–17.17).

Methods of service

17.43 It used to be the case that the rules for formal service of documents did not apply to Part 36 offers.[122] This is no longer the case (see 17.28). Other than as set out below, service may be effected in any of the following ways:

- personal service;[123]
- first-class post, document exchange or other service that provides for delivery on the next business day;[124]
- leaving the document at the opponent's address service;[125]
- fax,[126] email[127] or other electronic means; or
- any other method authorised by the court.[128]

---

[118] See *Procter & Gamble Co v Svenska Cellulosa Aktiebolaget SCA* [2012] EWHC 2839 (Ch), at [27]–[28], [44], [47], and [50].

[119] *N J Rickard Ltd v Holloway* [2015] EWCA Civ 1631, at [26].

[120] See CPR, r 36.6(1).

[121] See CPR, r 36.6(2).

[122] *Charles v NTL Group Ltd* [2002] EWCA Civ 2004.

[123] See CPR, r 6.20(1)(a). Service must be in accordance with CPR, r 6.22.

[124] See CPR, r 6.20(1)(b); PD 6A.

[125] See CPR, rr 6.20(1)(c) and 6.23.

[126] Service may be effected by fax (see CPR, r 6.20(1)(d)), in which case it need not also be effected in hard copy (PD 6A, para 4.3—which provision refers to 'electronic means' rather than 'fax or electronic means', but is generally regarded as applying to both). The party being served must have expressly indicated in writing that they are willing to accept service by fax and must have provided the requisite fax number (PD 6A, para 4.1). The unqualified inclusion of a fax number in the receiving party's headed paper or statement of parties would amount to such an express indication (PD 6A, para 4.1(2)(a)).

[127] Service may be effected by email (CPR, r 6.20(1)(d)); similar provisions relate to service by email as apply to service by fax (see PD 6A, para 4.1). Moreover, PD 6A, para 4.2, reads as follows: 'Where a party intends to serve a document by electronic means (other than by fax) that party must first ask the party who is to be served whether there are any limitations to the recipient's agreement to accept service by such means (for example, the format in which documents are to be sent and the maximum size of attachments that may be received).'

[128] See CPR, rr 6.20(1)(e) and 6.28.

Whilst not binding, Master Yoxall has found (in the context of a putatively defective withdrawal of a Part 36 offer) that whilst Part 36 is a self-contained code, this does not exclude the court's general powers to remedy errors under CPR, r 3.10, as far as technically defective service is concerned.[129] It is arguable that the same may apply to service of offers in certain circumstances.

Special provisions apply to companies,[130] limited liability partnerships[131] and persons outside the UK.[132] Where the party to be served is legally represented, the offer must be served on the legal representative.[133] 17.44

Extraneous and incompatible provisions

There are no exclusory provisions in Part 36, which means that offers may, where appropriate, contain provisions that are extraneous to Part 36. Thus a reference to the need to agree a Tomlin order as matter of recording the bargain would not be fatal to the offer being a Part 36 offer.[134] It is, however, almost certainly the case that a provision that was incompatible with Part 36 would invalidate the offer (see 17.62–17.66),[135] as would an offer to pay all or part of the sum at a date later than 14 days following the date of acceptance.[136] 17.45

The 'relevant period'

The offer must specify a period of not less than 21 days within which the defendant will, if the offer is accepted, be liable for the claimant's costs in accordance with CPR, rr 36.13 or 36.20.[137] The use of descriptive phrases such as the 'relevant acceptance period'[138] or 'this offer will be open for 21 days from the date of this letter, [that being] the relevant period'[139] are unobjectionable. Where there has been a failure to state any period at all, however, that would preclude the offer from being a Part 36 offer.[140] 17.46

The 'relevant period' is calculated as follows.[141] 17.47

- In the case of an offer made not less than 21 days before trial, the 'relevant period' is that period specified under the provisions referred to above or such longer period as the parties agree.
- Otherwise, the 'relevant period' is the period up to the end of such trial.

---

129 See *Thompson v Reeve* (unreported), 20 March 2017, QBD, *per* Master Yoxall.
130 See CPR, r 6.20(2).
131 See CPR, r 6.20(3).
132 If this is not the case, then other provisions apply: see PD 6B.
133 See PD 36, para 1.2.
134 *In the matter of Kilopress Ltd* (unreported), 22 April 2010, Ch D, *per* Norris J.
135 See, eg, *Howell v Lees-Millais* [2011] EWCA Civ 786, at [23], in which Neuberger MR said that an offer that excluded an entitlement to costs would, in general, not be a Part 36 offer; see also *London Tara Hotel Ltd v Kensington Close Hotel Ltd* [2011] EWHC 29 (Ch), at [27], in which Roth J found that an offer that imposed a restriction on the entitlement to costs was not a Part 36 offer. Similarly, see *Elliott v Shah* [2011] EW Misc 8.
136 See CPR, r 36.6(2).
137 CPR, r 36.5(1)(c).
138 *Onay v Brown* [2009] EWCA Civ 775.
139 *C v D* [2011] EWCA Civ 646, at [75].
140 See *PHI Group Ltd v Robert West Consulting Ltd* [2012] EWCA Civ 588, at [27]–[33], *per* Lloyd.
141 CPR, r 36.3(g).

In view of the fact that the 'relevant period' is always more than five days, Saturdays, Sundays, bank holidays, Christmas Day and Good Friday are included.[142]

Personal injury claims

17.48 Where the offer is a personal injury claim, additional requirements may apply where there is a claim for future pecuniary loss or for provisional damages, or where benefits may be deducted. Each is described in turn.

Future pecuniary loss

17.49 An offer that relates to a claim for future pecuniary loss must comply with the following.[143]

- It must state the amount of any offer to pay or to accept the whole or part of any damages in the form of a lump sum, and may state:
  - what part of the lump sum, if any, relates to damages for future pecuniary loss; and
  - what part relates to other damages to be paid or accepted in the form of a lump sum.
- It must state what part of the offer relates to damages for future pecuniary loss to be paid or accepted in the form of periodical payments and must specify:
  - the amount and duration of the periodical payments;
  - the amount of any payments for substantial capital purchases and when they are to be made; and
  - that each amount is to vary by reference to the retail prices index (or to some other named index), or that it is not to vary by reference to any index.
- It must state either that any damages that take the form of periodical payments will be funded in a way which ensures that the continuity of payment is reasonably secure in accordance with s 2(4) of the Damages Act 1996, or how such damages are to be paid and how the continuity of their payment is to be secured.

A failure to comply with these requirements will mean that the offer would not have the consequences specified in CPR, Part 36, Section I.[144]

Provisional damages

17.50 Where the offer is made in respect of a claim that includes a claim for provisional damages, it must specify whether or not the offeror is proposing that the settlement shall include an award of provisional damages.[145] Where the offeror is offering to make an award of provisional damages, the offer must also state:

- that the sum offered is in satisfaction of the claim for damages on the assumption that the injured person will not develop the disease or suffer the type of deterioration specified in the offer;
- that the offer is subject to the condition that the claimant must make any claim for further damages within a limited period; and
- what that period is.[146]

---

142 CPR, r 2.8(4).
143 CPR, r 36.18(4).
144 See CPR, r 36.18(2); see also the combined effect of CPR, rr 36.2(2) and 36.5(3).
145 CPR, r 36.19(1) and (2).
146 CPR, r 36.19(3).

A failure to comply with these requirements will mean that the offer would not have the consequences specified in CPR, Part 36, Section I.[147]

Deductible benefits

The Social Security (Recovery of Benefits) Act 1997 introduced a scheme for the recovery of certain benefits, including social security benefits paid or likely to be paid, if a compensation payment has been made to the injured person.[148] The scheme is administered by the Compensation Recovery Unit (CRU) within the Department for Work and Pensions. The underlying principle is that a person should not be compensated more than once for the injury the compensator has caused. No compensation payment may be made (other than certain exempt payments) unless the compensator has applied to the CRU for a certificate specifying the recoverable benefits that have been or are likely to be paid and the total amount to be repaid.[149] The scheme places responsibility for repaying the relevant benefits not on the injured person themselves, but on the compensator. The compensator will be liable to pay damages to the injured person and to pay the Secretary of State for Work and Pensions an amount equal to the total amount of the recoverable benefits.[150] Accordingly, section 8 of the 1997 Act provides for the reduction of compensation payments. **17.51**

Detailed provisions apply to Part 36 and deductible benefits (see CPR, r 36.22). They are not set out here in full, but, in brief, where a payment to a claimant following acceptance of an offer would be a compensation payment as defined in ss 1(4)(b) or 1A(5)(b) of the Social Security (Recovery of Benefits) Act 1997,[151] the offer should state whether it is made without regard to any liability for recoverable amounts or whether it is intended to include any deductible amounts;[152] a statement that the offer is 'net of CRU' will suffice to indicate that it is made without regard to any liability for recoverable amounts.[153] If the offer is inclusive of deductible benefits, it should state: **17.52**

- the amount of gross compensation;
- the name and amount of any deductible amount by which the gross amount is reduced; and
- the net amount of compensation.[154]

A failure to comply with these requirements (such as a failure to make it clear whether the offer was inclusive of deductible amounts or made without regard for any such amounts) will mean that the offer would not have the consequences specified in CPR, Part 36, Section I.[155]

Clarity and adequacy of information

No one would dispute that an offeree ought to be able to evaluate an offer by reference to a rational assessment of their own case, including the risk of incurring irrecoverable costs if **17.53**

[147] See CPR, r 36.18(2); see also the combined effect of CPR, rr 36.2(2) and 36.5(3).
[148] See Social Security (Recovery of Benefits) Act 1997, ss 1–3.
[149] See Social Security (Recovery of Benefits) Act 1997, ss 4 and 5.
[150] See Social Security (Recovery of Benefits) Act 1997, s 6.
[151] See CPR, r 36.22(2).
[152] CPR, r 36.22(3).
[153] See *Crooks v Hendricks Lovell Ltd* [2016] EWCA Civ 8, at [24], *per* Lindblom LJ.
[154] CPR, r 36.22(6).
[155] See the combined effect of CPR, rr 36.2(2) and 36.5(3).

they elect to continue the litigation.[156] To do this, the offeree must be able to understand the effect of the offer, in which regard two linked issues arise: first, the issue of whether the offeror has given the offeree adequate information relating to the offer; and secondly, whether the offer itself is lacking in clarity. A third issue of whether the offeree had sufficient information in general may be relevant, but that is an issue that would arise in the context of the injustice test (see 17.139) rather than in the context of whether the offer itself was a valid and clear offer.

Inadequate information

17.54 A lack of adequate information would (other than perhaps in an extreme case in which the information was actually misleading) not in itself be capable of nullifying an otherwise effective Part 36 offer. In this regard, Henderson J had this to say:

> '[It] would in my view be productive of much uncertainty if the validity, as opposed to the costs and interest consequences, of a Pt 36 offer were to depend on something as difficult to ascertain as the adequacy of the information supplied by the offeror to the offeree. In many cases it may well be reasonable for the offeror to supply no, or only limited, information when the offer is made, and to leave it to the offeree to come back with a request for further information. Any such request should then be dealt with in a spirit of co-operation, and (if it is not) the offeree is free to apply to the court for an order under [what is now CPR, r 36.8]. Alternatively, the offeree can decide whether or not to accept the offer as it stands, and if he decides to refuse it, but later fails to match or improve on it, he can argue that the usual adverse consequences should not follow, or should at least be mitigated, in reliance on [what is now CPR, r 36.17(5)(d)]. This is in my judgment a coherent and workable scheme, which respects the "demands of clarity and certainty in the operation of Pt 36" to which Moore-Bick LJ referred in *Gibbon v Manchester City Council* at 18.'[157]

Clarity of offers

17.55 In a pre-CPR case, Aldous J explained that, to be effective under the Rules of the Supreme Court (RSC), an offer had to be expressed in reasonably clear terms;[158] it was then open to the court to decline to give effect to an unclear offer as a matter of discretion.[159] More recently, Arden LJ has confirmed that where an offer is found to be difficult to evaluate and confusing, it is within the discretion of the court to find that a party cannot be penalised for not having accepted it.[160] It is possible, perhaps, for an offer to be so unclear as to fail to be a Part 36 offer at all, but under the present-day Rules the court would generally take such factors into account when deciding whether it would be unjust to allow the offeror to have the benefits of having made a Part 36 offer (see 17.136).[161] An offeree may have difficulty in relying on such an argument, however, because where an offeree is unsure about what is being offered, they may, within seven days of it being made, request that the offeror clarify it.[162] If the offeror

---

156 *AB v CD & Ors* [2011] EWHC 602 (Ch), at [23], *per* Henderson J, who was interpreting the application of the *obiter* comments of Moore-Bick LJ in *Gibbon v Manchester City Council* [2010] EWCA Civ 726, at [40].

157 *AB v CD & Ors* [2011] EWHC 602 (Ch), at [49].

158 *C&H Engineering v F Klucznic & Son Ltd* [1992] FSR 667.

159 *Ford v GKR Construction Ltd* [2000] 1 WLR 1397; although a pre-CPR case, see also *Burgess v British Steel plc* [2000] PIQR Q240, in which it was found that the knowledge of the offeree was sufficiently good to know whether to accept the offer. See also 17.177.

160 *Rio Properties Inc v Gibson Dunn & Crutcher* [2005] EWCA Civ 534.

161 See CPR, r 36.17(5)—in particular, subparagraphs (a) and (d).

162 See CPR, r 36.8(1).

fails to clarify the offer within seven days of having received any such request, the offeree may, unless the trial has started, make an application under Part 23[163] for an order that the offeror do so.[164] If the court allows such an application, it must specify the date on which the offer is to be treated as having been made.[165]

Where an offer is clarified, the whole of the relevant correspondence should be taken into account for the purposes of determining its scope and terms; thus, in a case in which an offer had originally been stated to 'not take into account any counterclaim', Simler J found that a clarification that stated that the offeror did not intend to bring a counterclaim meant that the offer, as originally formulated, had been modified so as to make it clear that it encompassed the whole of the dispute (including any putative counterclaim).[166] **17.56**

Disclosure of Part 36 offers to the court

A Part 36 offer will be treated as 'without prejudice except as to costs'.[167] Subject to certain exceptions, neither that fact nor the terms of any Part 36 offer may be communicated to the trial judge (or to the judge allocated in advance to conduct the trial) until 'the case has been decided'.[168] Sir Raymond Jack has explained that 'the case' means 'the proceedings' or 'the action'.[169] This restriction will not apply, however, where: **17.57**

- the defence of tender before claim has been raised;
- the proceedings have been stayed under CPR, r 36.14, following acceptance of a Part 36 offer;
- the offeror and the offeree agree in writing that the court should be permitted to see the offer; or
- the Part 36 offer in question relates solely to those parts of the litigation or those issues that have already been decided.[170]

Disclosure may be made to a judge who is hearing a dealing with interim matters and who will not be the trial judge.[171]

Split trials

A number of decisions in recent years have highlighted the difficulties arising out of the application of the pre-2015 Part 36 in the context of split trials or trials of preliminary issues—particularly concerns about the need to reserve the issue of costs until the conclusion of the whole claim.[172] It was mooted that a possible solution to that problem might, in an appropriate case, be to interpret the prohibition as referring to the conclusion of **17.58**

---

163 This is implied by the signpost after CPR, r 36.8(2).

164 See CPR, r 36.8(2).

165 See CPR, r 36.8(3).

166 See *Bailes v Bloom* (unreported), 23 November 2015, QBD.

167 CPR, r 36.16(1). This rule would apply only if the offer was made on or after 6 April 2015, or if the trial of any part of the claim or of any issue arising in it had started on or after 6 April 2015: see the Civil Procedure (Amendment No 8) Rules 2014 (SI 2014/3299), r 18(2). In all other circumstances, CPR, r 36.13, of the original Part 36 would apply instead.

168 CPR, r 36.16(2).

169 *Beasley v Alexander* [2012] EWHC 2715 (QB), at [12]–[14].

170 CPR, r 36.16(3).

171 Whilst now a very old authority, see *Williams v Boag* [1941] 1 KB 1, CA. It is worth noting that the editors of The White Book cite this authority as still carrying weight: see The White Book 2017, para 36.16.1.

172 See, eg, *Ted Baker plc v AXA Insurance UK Plc* [2012] EWHC 1779 (Comm).

each stage.[173] This is no longer necessary because the last of the exceptions listed above (see 17.57) allows the court to be told of the existence and terms of any Part 36 offer that deals solely with any issues that had already been decided.[174] This would be so in any claim (regardless of when the offer was made) in which a trial of any part of the claim or of any issue arising in it had started on or after 6 April 2015.[175] Similarly, the new provisions allow the trial judge to be told whether or not there are any other Part 36 offers[176]—although the terms of any such offer may not be disclosed,[177] which means that there will be cases in which it would be doubtful if the court would be able to make any rulings on costs at that stage.[178]

Where disclosure is given

17.59 The usual principle that there should be disclosure of the whole of the document will apply.[179] The fact that a Part 36 offer should not be disclosed to the court does not prevent other types of offer being disclosed.[180] The prohibition against disclosure is directory, not compulsory; thus the court would have the discretionary power to continue to hear the case notwithstanding the fact that it has inadvertently[181] or intentionally[182] been told about an offer.

Technical Shortcomings of Part 36 Offers

17.60 Where an offer substantially fails to comply with the procedural requirements set out above (see 17.39–17.52) the offeror will not be able to rely on it for the purposes of obtaining the benefits of Part 36.[183] Nonetheless, a non-compliant offer may still be taken into account as being an 'admissible offer' pursuant to CPR, r 44.2(4)(c). Where appropriate, the court will be able to make an order, known as an equivalent award, which closely mimics that which would have been made had the offer been a Part 36 (see 17.62).

17.61 As is set out below, there are several ways in which the court is able to overlook minor shortcomings in the format of an offer. There is, however, a limit to the extent that the court will overlook the flaws: as Davies LJ explained, 'it is not permissible wholly to

---

173 *AB v CD & Ors* [2011] EWHC 602 (Ch), at [18]–[20], *per* Hildyard J. See also *Ted Baker plc v AXA Insurance UK Plc* [2012] EWHC 1779 (Comm), at [12]–[19], *per* Eder J.

174 See CPR, r 36.16(3).

175 See the Civil Procedure (Amendment No 8) Rules 2014 (SI 2014/3299), r 18(2).

176 See CPR, r 36.16(4).

177 See CPR, r 36.16(4).

178 Whilst it related to the pre-2015 provisions, see *AB v CD & Ors* [2011] EWHC 602 (Ch), at [18]–[20], *per* Hildyard J. See also *Interactive Technology Corporation Ltd v Ferster* [2017] EWHC 1510 (Ch), at [9]–[11], in which Morgan J referred to the analysis in *HSS Hire Services Group plc v Builders Merchants Ltd* [2005] EWCA Civ 626 remaining apposite under the post-2015 Rules.

179 See *Virgin Atlantic Airways Ltd v Jet Airways (India) Ltd* [2012] EWHC 3318 (Pat), at [22]–[28], *per* Floyd J.

180 See *Ted Baker Plc v Axa Insurance UK Plc* [2012] EWHC 1779 (Comm), at [16], *per* Eder J.

181 *Garratt v Saxby* [2004] EWCA Civ 341, which case was decided under the original Part 36, but Henderson J has confirmed (albeit *obiter*) that it remains good law under the pre-2015 Part 36: see *AB v CD & Ors* [2011] EWHC 602 (Ch), at [16].

182 See *Virgin Atlantic Airways Ltd v Jet Airways (India) Ltd* [2012] EWHC 3318 (Pat), at [22]–[28], *per* Floyd J.

183 See CPR, r 36.2(2); see also *F & C Alternative Investments (Holdings) Ltd & Ors Appellants v Barthelemy* [2012] EWCA Civ 843, at [65], *per* Davis LJ.

discount a number of failures to comply with the requirements of Part 36 as the merest technicality'.[184] Moreover, it should not be forgotten that Part 36 expressly preserves the ability to make offers that are not Part 36 offers, which may be relevant to the issue of interpretation.[185]

Discretion, substantial compliance, waiver and estoppel

'Equivalent awards'

The requirements governing the form of Part 36 offers are mandatory.[186] This does not mean, however, that the court will disregard an offer merely because it failed to comply with those requirements. Whilst there are limits to such an approach (see 6.212) and whilst the interpretive approach set out at 17.67–17.76 is preferable, there is authority to support the notion that where an offer falls short of being a Part 36 offer by reason of '*de minimis* errors or obvious slips which mislead no one',[187] the court would be able to make a discretionary award—known as an equivalent award—that is similar to that which would have been made had the offer been free of technical defects.[188] In some cases in which the offer was made by a defendant, the practical effect can be similar to that of a Part 36 offer,[189] although the offeror would not be entitled to mechanistic benefits of Part 36.[190] This topic is addressed at 6.204–6.240. In contrast to defendants, the practical effect of 'admissible offers' made by claimants would never mimic the full effect of a Part 36, because many of the claimants' benefits under Part 36 are unique to that Part, such as enhanced interest and the additional amount (see 17.81). **17.62**

A similar approach was taken under both the original Part 36[191] and the pre-2015 Part 36.[192] Whilst the jurisdiction to make equivalent awards continues to exist, Rix LJ has **17.63**

---

[184] See *F & C Alternative Investments (Holdings) Ltd & Ors Appellants v Barthelemy* [2012] EWCA Civ 843, at [63].

[185] See CPR, r 36.2(2). This is a point that Maurice Kay LJ made in *Shaw v Merthyr Tydfil County Borough* [2014] EWCA Civ 1678, at [14].

[186] See *PHI Group Ltd v Robert West Consulting Ltd* [2012] EWCA Civ 588, at [25], *per* Lloyd LJ.

[187] See *F & C Alternative Investments (Holdings) Ltd & Ors Appellants v Barthelemy* [2012] EWCA Civ 843, at [63], *per* Davies LJ.

[188] See *ibid*, in which Davies LJ said (*obiter*) that 'perhaps there can be *de minimis* errors or obvious slips which mislead no one: but the general rule, in my opinion, is that for an offer to be a Part 36 offer it must strictly comply with the requirements', adding that (contrary to Underhill J's analysis in *Huntley v Simmonds* [2009] EWHC 406 (QB)) it was 'not permissible wholly to discount a number of failures to comply with the requirements of Part 36 as the merest technicality'. In a similar vein, Davies LJ said that, in *Fitzroy Robinson Ltd v Mentmore Towers Ltd* [2010] EWHC 98 (TCC), at [25], Coulson J went too far in awarding indemnity costs on the grounds that if '[those] offers [had] been made as Part 36 offers, then indemnity costs would have been payable as a matter of course'.

[189] See, eg, *PHI Group Ltd v Robert West Consulting Ltd* [2012] EWCA Civ 588, at [60] and [61], *per* Lloyd LJ.

[190] See *F & C Alternative Investments (Holdings) Ltd & Ors Appellants v Barthelemy* [2012] EWCA Civ 843, at [64], *per* Davies LJ. See also *Brit Inns Ltd (in liquidation) v BDW Trading Ltd* [2012] EWHC 2489 (TCC), at [34], *per* Coulson J; *French v Groupama Insurance Co Ltd* [2011] EWCA Civ 1119, at [41]; *Epsom College v Pierse Contracting Southern Ltd (formerly Biseley Construction Ltd) (in liquidation)* [2011] EWCA Civ 1449, at [54] *et seq*, *per* Rix LJ.

[191] *Hertsmere Primary Care Trust v Rabindra-Anandh* [2005] EWHC 320 (Ch), *per* Lightman J. This contrasts with *Brown v Mcasso Music Production* [2005] EWCA Civ 1546, in which Neuberger LJ found that an offer was defective in too many ways to be regarded as being equivalent to a Part 36 offer, albeit under the original Part 36 (the shortcomings included uncertainty as to whether it was without prejudice save as to costs and the fact that it was open for only seven days).

[192] See, eg, *Cunningham v AST Express Ltd* [2009] EWCA Civ 767, at [33], *per* Smith LJ.

explained that if the relevant formalities have not been observed, the mechanistic rules in Part 36 should not be applied;[193] hence an equivalent award should be made only where this is justified on the merits and not as a reflexive consequence of having made an offer.[194] Even where an offeror is not granted an equivalent award, they may still be awarded some valuable benefit (see 6.204–6.240).

17.64 Equivalent awards (or something very similar) may operate against an offeror if the offer were to be accepted; thus, in a case that an offer had been found to fall short of being a Part 36 offer because it related to an aspect of the claim that could not be the subject of a Part 36 offer, Morgan J awarded the offeree the costs of that aspect of the claim as a matter of discretion.[195]

Substantial compliance

17.65 Whilst the interpretative approach (17.67–17.76) is preferable and whilst there is no authority that uses the language of substantial compliance,[196] it is possible that this is another means by which minor technical shortcomings can be prevented from depriving an offeror of the benefits of having made an offer. Whilst he did not refer to substantial compliance by that name, Arnold J, for example, found that an offer that had been made jointly to two claimants who were married and who presented a united front throughout the litigation was not compliant notwithstanding the fact that, technically, the two had individual claims.[197] Such a forgiving approach would not be appropriate if the errors were not minor, however.[198]

Waiver and estoppel

17.66 Whilst it would be wrong to read too much into what may have been a passing remark, Jay J has said that where an offeree accepts a putatively defective offer without demur, this may amount to 'non-compliance [being] waived'.[199] (See 17.79 for more on this topic.) In a similar vein, Arnold J gave weight to the fact that a putatively defective offer contained the words 'If you think that this offer is defective or non-compliant with Part 36, you must let us know promptly', yet the offeree took no action upon receipt; indeed, Arnold J found (on the facts of the case in hand) that this estopped the offeree from impugning the validity of the offer.[200]

---

[193] *French v Groupama Insurance Co Ltd* [2011] EWCA Civ 1119, at [41]. See also *Epsom College v Pierse Contracting Southern Ltd (formerly Biseley Construction Ltd) (in liquidation)* [2011] EWCA Civ 1449, at [54] *et seq*, *per* Rix LJ. Even before this guidance was given, Underhill J had commented that an equivalent award would not be appropriate in every case in which there were technical defects, even if they could be characterised as causing no prejudice: *Huntley v Simmonds* [2009] EWHC 406 (QB).

[194] Ramsay J has commented that a factor that can be taken into account is whether the offeree raised the issue of any technical shortcoming at the time the offer was made: *Eiles v Southwark London Borough Council* [2006] EWHC 2014 (TCC), at [51].

[195] *Hertel & Anor v Saunders & Anor* [2015] EWHC 2848 (Ch), at [61].

[196] That said, in *Harper v Hussain* (unreported), 19 March 2008, Birmingham County Court, Judge McDuff QC analysed a case in a way that could have been phrased in terms of substantial compliance. The offer in that case failed to state whether it took into account any counterclaim, that being in a claim in which there was no counterclaim, and Judge McDuff QC found that it ought to be treated as being a Part 36 offer.

[197] See *Ali v Channel 5 Broadcast Ltd* [2018] EWHC 840 (Ch), at [41].

[198] See, eg, *Brown v Mcasso Music Production* [2005] EWCA Civ 1546, in which Neuberger LJ found that the defects (including ambiguity as to whether the offer was without prejudice save as to costs) were too great to allow it to be regarded as being a quasi-Part 36 offer.

[199] See *Haynes v Department for Business Innovation and Skills* [2014] EWHC 643 (QB), at [18].

[200] See *Ali v Channel 5 Broadcast Ltd* [2018] EWHC 840 (Ch), at [42]–[44].

Interpretation

Carnwarth LJ has said that where the Part 36 jurisdiction is expressly invoked, the court should generally take that statement at face value and, as far as possible, give effect to the consequences of CPR, Part 36, as envisaged by the Rules.[201] Rix LJ had this to say on the topic: 17.67

> 'Such a construction would save the Part 36 offer as a Part 36 offer and would also give to both parties the clarity and certainty which both Part 36 itself, and the offer letter ... aspire to ... Another principle or maxim of construction which is applicable in the present circumstances is that words should be understood in such a way that the matter is effective rather than ineffective (*verba ita sunt intelligenda ut res magis valeat quam pereat*).'[202]

In this way, Rix LJ interpreted the offer before him in such a way as to preserve the object of its stated intention—namely, that it be a Part 36 offer.[203] Thus, where an offer that states that it is intended to be a Part 36 offer has been unhappily worded, the notion that it should be interpreted in such a way as to retain that status appears to be the guiding principle, which principle Lewison LJ summarised as being 'validate if possible'.[204] 17.68

It should be noted, however, that (at least in so far as offers made before 6 April 2015 are concerned) there is a distinction to be made between offers that state that they are intended to have the consequences of Part 36 and offers that merely have a heading that says 'Part 36 offer'.[205] That said, since 6 April 2015, the test of whether an offer is a Part 36 offer is simple matter of whether it was made pursuant to CPR, Part 36 (see CPR, r 36.1), so it is possible that the approach now would be more forgiving than it has been. 17.69

The general approach to interpretation

The question is how a reasonable solicitor would have understood the offer in the context of the dispute as it stood at the time it was made;[206] the subjective intentions of the parties are irrelevant.[207] It is likely that the court would take into account the way in which the parties dealt with and reacted to the offer.[208] As to ambiguity, Rimer LJ had this to say: 17.70

> 'The relevance ... [of an] expressed intention to make [an] offer a Part 36 offer is that, if there are any ambiguities in it raising a question as to whether the offer does or does not comply with the requirements of Part 36, the reasonable man will interpret it in a way that is so compliant. That is because, objectively assessed, that is what the offeror can be taken to have intended.'[209]

---

[201] *Onay v Brown* [2009] EWCA Civ 775, [2010] 1 Costs LR 29, at [33].

[202] *C v D* [2011] EWCA Civ 646, at [54] and [55].

[203] *Ibid*, at [54] *et seq*. See also *Onay v Brown* [2009] EWCA Civ 775, at [27], *per* Goldring LJ; *Dutton v Minards* [2015] EWCA Civ 984, at [29], *per* Lewison LJ; *Procter & Gamble Co v Svenska Cellulosa Aktiebolaget SCA* [2012] EWHC 2839 (Ch), at [49], *per* Hildyard J.

[204] See *Dutton v Minards* [2015] EWCA Civ 984, at [31].

[205] *Shaw v Merthyr Tydfil County Borough* [2014] EWCA Civ 1678, at [16], *per* Maurice Kay LJ.

[206] *C v D* [2011] EWCA Civ 646, at [45], *per* Rix LJ, relying on *ICS v West Bromwich Building Society* [1998] 1 WLR 896, HL.

[207] *C v D* [2011] EWCA Civ 646, at [83], *per* Stanley Burnton LJ.

[208] In *Seeff v Ho* [2011] EWCA Civ 401, at [12], Thomas LJ (giving the judgment of the court) gave weight to the fact that the putative offer said on its face that if it was in any way defective or non-compliant, the offeree should inform the offeror straight away. Since the offeree raised no concerns in this regard, this was a factor that persuaded Thomas LJ to accept that a somewhat poorly drafted offer came within the ambit of Part 36. See also *Ali v Channel 5 Broadcast Ltd* [2018] EWHC 840 (Ch), at [41], *per* Arnold J.

[209] *C v D* [2011] EWCA Civ 646, at [75].

17.71 Stanley Burnton LJ put the matter more pithily: 'Any ambiguity in an offer purporting to be a Part 36 offer should be construed so far as reasonably possible as complying with Part 36.'[210] The words of an offer should be regarded as being effective rather than ineffective.[211] Rix LJ has cited, with approval, an extract from *Chitty on Contracts*[212] that propounds that if one interpretation makes the contract lawful and another makes it unlawful, the former is to be preferred.[213]

17.72 Offers under the original Part 36 and Part 36 payments are addressed in the footnotes.[214] An offer that was based on the original Part 36, but made after 5 April 2007, is likely to be found to be non-compliant.[215]

The interpretation of specific terms and issues

17.73 The following are examples of phrases that have fallen to be considered.

- **'open for 21 days'** These words should not be read as limiting the offer itself, but instead should be read as meaning that no attempt would be made to seek the court's permission to withdraw the offer within those 21 days.[216] If, however, an offer says that it may be accepted after the 'relevant period' only 'if the parties agree their liability [for] costs or the court provides its permission for late acceptance', it would not be capable of being a Part 36 offer.[217]
- **'we ... diarise expiry'** In the context of it being an offer made before 6 April 2015,[218] this was to be regarded as being a reference to the 'relevant period' rather than to the offer itself.[219]
- **'an acceptance period'** In so far as offers made before 6 April 2015 are concerned,[220] this phrase would almost certainly be interpreted as being a reference to the 'relevant period' rather than to the offer itself.[221]

---

210 *Ibid*, at [84]. This extract was cited with approval by Rix LJ in *Epsom College v Pierse Contracting Southern Ltd (formerly Biseley Construction Ltd) (in liquidation)* [2011] EWCA Civ 1449, at [66].

211 This being the maxim *verba ita sunt intelligenda ut res magis valeat quam pereat*.

212 *Chitty on Contracts* (30th edn, London: Sweet & Maxwell, 2008), vol 1, at para 12-081. 'If one construction makes the contract lawful and the other unlawful, the former is to be preferred ...'

213 *C v D* [2011] EWCA Civ 646, at [55].

214 Where an offer was made under the original Part 36, the matters set out at 17.11–17.14 would seem to be relevant. Smith LJ has said that where an offer made under the original Part 36 was made in good faith and held open for 21 days, it would put the claimant at risk on costs notwithstanding the fact that it was not backed up with a Part 36 payment: *Cunningham v AST Express Ltd* [2009] EWCA Civ 767, at [33]. Smith LJ also indicated that such an offer should be considered in the light of what is now CPR, r 44.2(3) (ie the 'general rule').

215 See *Shaw v Merthyr Tydfil County Borough* [2014] EWCA Civ 1678, at [16], *per* Maurice Kay LJ.

216 *C v D* [2011] EWCA Civ 646, at [54], *per* Rimer LJ. See also *Dutton v Minards* [2015] EWCA Civ 984, at [30], in which Lewison LJ noted that 'open for a period of 21 days' did not invalidate the offer as a Part 36 offer.

217 *Shaw v Merthyr Tydfil County Borough* [2014] EWCA Civ 1678, at [16], *per* Maurice Kay LJ.

218 This qualification is necessary because where an offer was made on or after 6 April 2015, it may be automatically withdrawn as a result of it containing terms to this effect: see CPR, r 36.9(4)(b).

219 *Epsom College v Pierse Contracting Southern Ltd (formerly Biseley Construction Ltd) (in liquidation)* [2011] EWCA Civ 1449, at [66], *per* Rix LJ. Similarly, see *Lilleyman v Lilleyman* [2012] EWHC 1056 (Ch), at [12], *per* Briggs J.

220 See the qualification in fn 210.

221 *C v D* [2011] EWCA Civ 646, at [24], *per* Rix LJ; see also *Onay v Brown* [2009] EWCA Civ 775, at [27], *per* Goldring LJ.

- **'if this offer is accepted ... more than 21 days from the date of this offer you will be liable for all our client's legal costs'** This phrase would not be interpreted in such a way as to prevent the court from deciding the issue of costs and, as such, would not result in the offer being invalid.[222]
- **'your client's reasonable costs'** Lewison LJ has held that an offer made by a defendant to pay 'your client's reasonable costs' should be read as being a reference to pay costs in the standard basis and, as such, was in accordance with the provisions of CPR, Part 36.[223]

There is nothing objectionable in specifying a period of 21 days as 'the relevant acceptance period'[224] or stating that 'this offer will be open for 21 days from the date of this letter, [that being] the relevant period'.[225] Lloyd LJ said this on the topic: **17.74**

> '[Counsel] submitted that [the] offer in the present case should be construed so as to find an implicit specification of a 21 day period for the purposes of rule 36.2(2)(c). I cannot accept that argument. The requirement in the rule that a period of not less than 21 days must be specified requires some explicit identification of a period of 21 or more days. Ambiguity may come in, and with it the principle of construction described, if a period is specified but there is some doubt as to the purpose for which it is specified. Here no period was specified at all, so there is no ambiguity which falls to be resolved.'[226]

Thus, if a suitable period is stated, but there is ambiguity as to what was meant, it may be possible to resolve that ambiguity in such a way as to preserve compliance.

Limits to interpretation

There are limits to the extent to which the court can overlook seemingly technical shortcomings. Maurice Kay LJ has pointed out that the exercise of construing a Part 36 offer is not an exercise in contractual interpretation.[227] He said that no process of construction, however liberal, would be able to bring about satisfaction of procedural requirements that were not fulfilled.[228] He declined to interpret an offer purposively. **17.75**

Some offers will, by their very substance, be incompatible with Part 36. **17.76**

- **Terms as to costs** An offer that excludes a liability to pay costs, for example, would, in general, not be a Part 36 offer[229] nor would an offer that imposed a restriction on the entitlement to costs[230] or which offered a global sum that was inclusive of costs.[231]

---

[222] *Wes Futures Ltd v Allen Wilson Construction Ltd* [2016] EWHC 2893 (TCC), at [12], *per* Coulson J.

[223] *Dutton v Minards* [2015] EWCA Civ 984, at [34], *per* Lewison LJ.

[224] *Onay v Brown* [2009] EWCA Civ 775.

[225] *C v D* [2011] EWCA Civ 646, at [75]. This case was decided before the requirement that Part 36 offers had to be served came into being, but it is easily arguable that references to 'the date of this letter' would be interpreted as meaning 'the date of service of this letter'.

[226] *PHI Group Ltd v Robert West Consulting Ltd* [2012] EWCA Civ 588, at [30].

[227] *Shaw v Merthyr Tydfil County Borough* [2014] EWCA Civ 1678, at [19].

[228] *Ibid*, at [16].

[229] *Howell v Lees-Millais* [2011] EWCA Civ 786, at [23], *per* Neuberger MR.

[230] *London Tara Hotel Ltd v Kensington Close Hotel Ltd* [2011] EWHC 29 (Ch), at [27], *per* Roth J. See also *Dutton v Minards* [2015] EWCA Civ 984, at [30], *per* Lewison LJ; *Elliott v Shah* [2011] EW Misc 8, *per* Judge Platt. See also *James v James* [2018] EWHC 242 (Ch), at [10]–[16], *per* Judge Paul Matthews (sitting as a judge of the High Court).

[231] See the comment of Rix LJ in *French v Groupama Insurance Company Ltd* [2011] EWCA Civ 1119, at [39].

- **No 'relevant period'** A complete failure to state the 'relevant period' (or any other period that could be taken as being the relevant period) would preclude the offer from being a Part 36 offer.[232]
- **Fetters on acceptance** If an offer says that it may be accepted after the 'relevant period' only if 'the parties agree their liability [for] costs or the court provides its permission for late acceptance', that would be incompatible with the offer being a Part 36 offer.[233]
- **Non-pleaded claims** Whilst it is a decision that, at the time of writing, was under appeal,[234] Morgan J has found that an offer that was in respect of a part of a claim that had been intimated, but not yet formally entered into the pleadings, was not capable of being a Part 36 offer.[235] (It should be noted that, in giving permission to appeal, Richards LJ said that there was 'force in the observation that it appears curious that a Part 36 offer can validly be made in respect of claims which are not yet the subject of any proceedings, but cannot be made in respect of claims which it is proposed to add in existing proceedings'.[236])

The status of offers that do not comply

17.77 Whilst it would be a rare occurrence, a party may seek to impugn the status of an offer whilst at the same time contending that it has been accepted. This would generally be an attempt to show that a compromise has been reached on a basis that is different from that which would have been reached if Part 36 had applied. This would be a dangerous tactic for either side to deploy because the court would, in general, tend towards interpreting the offer in such a way as to be complaint with the procedural requirements of Part 36 (see 17.67), but circumstances may arise in which the court is unable to do this. Where this is so, it invites the question of whether a non-compliant offer may be accepted in such a way as to bind the parties. This, of course, is not the same as whether it may be taken into account as an 'admissible offer' (see 17.62).

17.78 The nature of a putative Part 36 offer that is not compliant with the requirements of CPR, r 36.5, is anything but clear. There have been instances of the Court of Appeal referring to such an offer as being a contractual offer, but that was in circumstances in which the precise nature of the offer was not a matter that the court had to decide.[237] Whilst not binding, in a case in which the offeror chose to impugn its own offer, Judge Butler found that the offer was contractual and that it had been accepted to the offeree's detriment.[238] It is arguable that this was not the correct analysis, at least in so far as offers made on or after 6 April 2015 are concerned.[239]

---

[232] See *PHI Group Ltd v Robert West Consulting Ltd* [2012] EWCA Civ 588, at [27]–[33], *per* Lloyd LJ.

[233] *Shaw v Merthyr Tydfil County Borough* [2014] EWCA Civ 1678, at [16], *per* Maurice Kay LJ. Maurice Kay LJ commented that he agreed with Judge Behrens QC's analysis in *Thewlis v Groupama Insurance Company Ltd* [2012] EWHC 3 (TCC), at [28] and [29] (which was similarly worded), despite the fact that *Thewlis* had not only come in for a degree of academic criticism (see Regan, D, 'Is It or Isn't It?', *New Law Journal*, February 2012), but was also unpopular with many judges: see *Shaw v Merthyr Tydfil County Borough* [2014] EWCA Civ 1678, at [11].

[234] Confirmed in personal correspondence with the editor in June 2018.

[235] *Hertel & Anor v Saunders & Anor* [2015] EWHC 2848 (Ch), at [34]–[51]—in particular, at [41].

[236] *Ibid*, at [9].

[237] See, eg, *PHI Group Ltd v Robert West Consulting Ltd* [2012] EWCA Civ 588.

[238] *Worrell v Nicholls* (unreported), 17 August 2017, Preston County Court, *per* Judge Butler.

[239] This is because the definition of a Part 36 offer is now contained in CPR, r 36.1, and—unlike previous iterations of the CPR—that definition is separate from the provisions that deal with the effect of

For the avoidance of doubt, there is no reason to believe that an offeree is unable to accept a Part 36 offer merely because it is technically non-compliant with the procedural requirements of Part 36. In particular, in the vast majority of cases, the issue would never arise because both the offeree and the offeror will want the putative acceptance to bring the litigation to an end. If the parties were to give thought to the legal position, it would be likely that they would both say that they had waived any breaches (see 17.66). **17.79**

The Application and Effect of Part 36 Offers

Where offers are not accepted

The principles can be summarised as follows. **17.80**

- **Where the defendant beats their offer by adjudication** Where a claimant fails to obtain a judgment that is 'more advantageous' to them than the proposals contained in a Part 36 offer made by a defendant, then (unless the court considers it unjust to do so) it will award that defendant the costs from the date on which the 'relevant period' expired.
- **Where the claimant beats their offer by adjudication** Where a defendant fails to obtain a judgment that is 'at least as advantageous' as their opponent's Part 36 offer, unless the court considers it unjust, the defendant will pay costs on the indemnity basis *plus* enhanced interest and an uplift of the monies claimed.

Whilst, at first blush, it seems as if the test is not the same for a claimant as it is for a defendant, this is not so. This is because the references to 'more advantageous' and 'at least as advantageous' are both from the claimant's perspective; thus, in both instances, the offeror will receive the benefit of having made the offer if their opponent obtains a result that is either the same or not as advantageous (from the offeree's point of view) than the offer.

Where a claimant beats the offer

Where a claimant secures judgment that is 'at least as advantageous' to them as the proposals contained in a Part 36 offer that they had previously made, then, unless the court considers it unjust to do so, it will award the claimant costs on the indemnity basis, *plus* enhanced interest on both costs and damages, *plus* an additional amount based on a percentage of the damages (or, where there are no damages, a percentage of the claimant's costs).[240] The details of those benefits are as follows. **17.81**

- **Interest on damages** The interest will be at a rate not exceeding 10 per cent above base rate for some or all of the period starting with the date on which the 'relevant period' expired.[241] The topic of rates is addressed at 56.90–56.100 (where the offer was made

non-compliance with the procedural requirements of CPR, r 36.5. As such, any offer that is made pursuant to Part 36 will be a Part 36 offer, regardless of whether it is capable of having any of the consequences under that Part. Moreover, given the matters set out in 17.67–17.76 (that is, the court's approach to interpretation), it is arguable that where an offeror successfully impugns their own offer, that offer will not be capable of contractual acceptance because it was not clear what its effect would be. Further authority will be needed to decide these points.

[240] CPR, r 36.17(4).

[241] See CPR, r 36.17(4)(a).

in the substantive claim) and 56.115 (where the offer was made in detailed assessment proceedings).

- **Indemnity basis costs** The claimant will be entitled to costs (including any recoverable pre-action costs) on the indemnity basis from the date on which the 'relevant period' expired.[242]
- **Interest on the costs** The claimant will be entitled to interest on their costs at a rate not exceeding 10 per cent above base rate (again, see 56.90–56.100).[243]
- **An additional amount** Provided that the case has been decided and there has not been a previous similar order, the claimant will be entitled to an additional amount (limited to £75,000), calculated as 10 per cent of the first £500,000 and 5 per cent of any amount above that figure, but less than £1 million.[244] The additional amount is not compensatory, but is an additional amount awarded as an incentive.[245] Some judges have even described it as being penal in nature.[246] Whilst there are conflicting authorities on the point, it is probably the case that the starting figure will be the amount awarded inclusive of basic interest (or of any interest that may be due as a matter of contract), but exclusive of enhanced interest.[247]

17.82 The aforesaid benefits can be significant in financial terms, but Eady J has confirmed that a judge who is asked to depart from awarding them should not be tempted to make an exception merely because that judge thinks the regime itself harsh or unjust; rather, there must be something about the particular circumstances of the case that takes it out of the norm.[248]

17.83 It seems that the court is entitled to stand back and look at the totality of the benefits that the court is minded to award. For example, in a case in which he had allowed a relatively

242 See CPR, r 36.17(4)(b).

243 See CPR, r 36.17(4)(c).

244 See CPR, r 36.17(4)(d). Where there is no monetary award, the additional amount will apply to the claimant's costs rather than damages or debt. It may be that a money claim is advanced in the alternative to some other type of claim; where this is so, Warby J has said that the language of what is now CPR, r 36.14(4)(d), directs attention to the time at which the court is deciding whether to order payment of an additional amount and that 'the claim' means the claim in respect of which the court has given the judgment that is more advantageous than the offer: see *Elsevier Ltd v Munro* [2014] EWHC 2728 (QB), at [6]. This means that if the court did not need to rule on the issue of a money claim, the additional amount would be payable on the costs instead. It would generally not be appropriate to award an additional amount at an interim stage in the proceedings: see *JMX (a child by his mother and litigation friend, FMX) v Norfolk and Norwich Hospitals NHS Foundation Trust (No 2)* [2018] EWHC 675 (QB).

245 *OOO Abbott (A company incorporated in the Russian Federation) v Design Display Ltd* [2014] EWHC 3234 (IPEC), at [22], *per* Judge Birse. See also *Thai Airways International Public Co Ltd v KI Holdings Co Ltd (formerly known as Koito Industries Ltd)* [2015] EWHC 1476 (Comm), at [30], *per* Leggatt J.

246 *Cashman v Mid Essex Hospital Services NHS Trust* [2015] EWHC 1312 (QB), at [9], *per* Slade. See also *Sony/ATV Music Publishing LLC v WPMC Ltd (in liquidation)* [2017] EWHC 465 (Ch), at [10], *per* Arnold J.

247 See *Mohammed v The Home Office* [2017] EWHC 3051 (AB), at [23]–[29], in which Mr Edward Pepperall QC (sitting as a deputy judge of the High Court) disagreed with Judge Purle QC's analysis in *Watchorn v Jupiter Industries Ltd* [2014] EWHC 3003 (Ch), on the basis that not all alternative constructions of the relevant rule were drawn to his attention.

248 *Downing v Peterborough & Stamford Hospitals NHS Foundation Trust* [2014] EWHC Civ 4216 (QB), at [62] *et seq*, cited with approval in *Briggs v CEF Holdings Ltd* [2017] EWCA Civ 2363, at [20], *per* Gross LJ. Similar views were expressed by Judge Purle QC in *Watchorn v Jupiter Industries Ltd* [2014] EWHC 3003 (Ch). See also *Tiuta Plc v Rawlinson & Hunter (a firm)* [2016] EWHC 3480 (QB), at [21], *per* Andrew Baker J.

high rate of interest, Judge Waksman QC elected to allow a relatively modest additional amount.[249]

Other than where CPR, Part 45, Section IIIA, applies (see 50.290–50.296), the relevant provision are as follows (see CPR, r 36.17): **17.84**

'(1) Subject to rule 36.21, this rule applies where upon judgment being entered—

[...]

(b) judgment against the defendant is at least as advantageous to the claimant as the proposals contained in a claimant's Part 36 offer.

(2) For the purposes of paragraph (1), in relation to any money claim or money element of a claim, "more advantageous" means better in money terms by any amount, however small, and "at least as advantageous" shall be construed accordingly.

[...]

(4) Subject to paragraph (7), where paragraph (1)(b) applies, the court must, unless it considers it unjust to do so, order that the claimant is entitled to—

(a) interest on the whole or part of any sum of money (excluding interest) awarded, at a rate not exceeding 10% above base rate for some or all of the period starting with the date on which the "relevant period" expired;

(b) costs (including any recoverable pre-action costs) on the indemnity basis from the date on which the "relevant period" expired;

(c) interest on those costs at a rate not exceeding 10% above base rate; and

(d) provided that the case has been decided and there has not been a previous order under this sub-paragraph, an additional amount, which shall not exceed £75,000, calculated by applying the prescribed percentage set out below to an amount which is—

(i) the sum awarded to the claimant by the court; or

(ii) where there is no monetary award, the sum awarded to the claimant by the court in respect of costs—

Amount awarded by the court	**Prescribed percentage**
up to £500,000	10% of the amount awarded;
above £500,000 up to £1,000,000	10% of the first £500,000 and 5% of any amount above that figure

(5) In considering whether it would be unjust to make the orders referred to in paragraphs (3) and (4), the court must take into account all the circumstances of the case including—

(a) the terms of any Part 36 offer;

(b) the stage in the proceedings when any Part 36 offer was made, including in particular how long before the trial started the offer was made;

(c) the information available to the parties at the time when the Part 36 offer was made;

(d) the conduct of the parties with regard to the giving of or refusal to give information for the purposes of enabling the offer to be made or evaluated; and

(e) whether the offer was a genuine attempt to settle the proceedings.

(6) Where the court awards interest under this rule and also awards interest on the same sum and for the same period under any other power, the total rate of interest must not exceed 10% above base rate.

(7) Paragraphs (3) and (4) do not apply to a Part 36 offer—

(a) which has been withdrawn;

[249] See *Bataillion v Shone* [2015] EWHC 3177 (QB), at [27].

(b) which has been changed so that its terms are less advantageous to the offeree where the offeree has beaten the less advantageous offer;
(c) made less than 21 days before trial, unless the court has abridged the relevant period.'

17.85 Thus, where a claimant has beaten one of their own offers, they will generally be awarded the benefits of the offer from the date on which the 'relevant period' expired. Where an offer needs to be clarified,[250] the expiry of the 'relevant period' may be adjusted accordingly.[251] There is nothing in any of these provisions to oust the court's jurisdiction to make a discretionary award of costs on the indemnity basis.[252]

Miscellaneous points about whether an offer has been beaten

17.86 **'Near misses' in general** A 'near miss' is where an offeror come very close to 'beating' their own offer. There is now an express provision that says that a 'near miss' will not confer the benefit of the offer on the offeror, no matter how close it might be[253]—a rule that was introduced to reverse the decision in *Carver*[254] (see 17.99). In theory, *Carver* still applies to offers made before 1 October 2011 (albeit in an attenuated form),[255] but Tomlinson LJ has explained that it would rarely be the case that a *Carver* approach would be appropriate where the offeror was the claimant.[256] That said, the court would still have powers under CPR, r 44.2, so if the circumstances permitted (such as if the conduct of the offeree were poor), the court would be able to mark a 'near miss' with an award of indemnity costs even without invoking *Carver*. 'Near misses' in the context of defendants' offers are dealt with in more detail at 17.100–17.104.

17.87 **The relevance of payments on account** Where, in the absence of agreement to the contrary, a payment on account is made, it will be regarded as being a payment on account of the claim generally (and therefore also on account of the offer generally). This means that such a payment would not result in a concomitant increase in the amount offered.[257] Flaux LJ has explained that if a defendant offeror wishes to make a payment on account after an offer has been made and if this is intended to be in addition to the amount that has been offered, this must be made clear.[258]

Miscellaneous points about claimants' Part 36 offers

17.88 **The incidence of costs** The fact that a claimant would be entitled to costs on the indemnity basis if they beat their own offer does not mean that the court is entirely deprived of its discretion as to the incidence of costs. That said, the court is significantly more restricted in this regard than it was in years gone by.

---

[250] See CPR, r 36.8.

[251] *Colour Quest Ltd v Total Downstream UK plc* [2009] EWHC 823 (Comm), at [32], *per* David Steel J.

[252] Indeed, the offer itself can lead to an award of costs on the indemnity basis if the court is satisfied that it was unreasonable (as opposed to merely misjudged) not to accept it: see, eg, *D Morgan plc v Mace & Jones (a firm)* [2011] EWHC 26 (TCC), *per* Coulson J. That said, it should not be forgotten that CPR, r 44.2(4)(c), specifically provides that an 'admissible offer' will not include an offer to which costs consequences under Part 36 apply.

[253] See CPR, r 36.17(2).

[254] *Carver v BAA plc* [2008] EWCA Civ 412.

[255] See para 14.38 of the second edition of this book.

[256] *Acre 1127 Ltd (Formerly known as Castle Galleries Ltd) v De Montfort Fine Art Ltd* [2011] EWCA Civ 130.

[257] See *Littlestone v MacLeish* [2016] EWCA Civ 127.

[258] See *Gamal v Synergy Lifestyle Ltd* [2018] EWCA Civ 210, at [28]–[29].

As originally formulated, the CPR permitted the court to exercise its discretion under what is now CPR, r 44.2, in a way that was unfettered by the provisions in what is now CPR, r 36.17. In particular, Rix LJ found that the fact that Part 36 provided that a claimant was entitled to 'his costs' was not to be read as meaning 'all his costs'.[259] Thus, if the court were to wish to deprive an otherwise successful claimant of the costs of, say, an issue upon which they had failed, then the fact that that claimant had beaten a Part 36 offer would not have prevented the court from doing so. **17.89**

The present formulation of the CPR no longer permits such an approach. This is because both CPR, rr 44.2 and 36.17, have been amended so as to make it clear that they are separate jurisdictions.[260] This means that, when deciding what costs order to make under CPR, r 36.17, the court does not first exercise its discretion under CPR, r 44.2; its only discretion is that conferred by Part 36 itself.[261] This does not preclude the making of an issue-based or proportionate costs order, but—in the context of them having 'beaten' their offer—a claimant is to be deprived of costs after the expiry of the 'relevant period' only if the court considers that it would be unjust for the claimant to be awarded all or that part of those costs. Put otherwise, the 'injustice test' applies (see 17.118–17.163). When applying that test, Sir Stanley Burnton has explained that 'all the circumstances of the case' must be taken into account and that, in exercising its discretion, the court must take into account that the unsuccessful defendant could have avoided the costs of the trial if they had accepted the Part 36 offer.[262] **17.90**

Another factor that may be relevant is the fact that if a defendant is aware of the fact that an issues-based approach may ultimately be appropriate, there would be nothing to prevent them from making offers relating to the issues in question (as opposed to making an offer that relates to the whole claim). A failure to make issues-based offers may make it difficult for a defendant to argue that the court should take an issues-based approach when applying the injustice test.[263] **17.91**

'Equalling' an offer by judgment Where a claimant achieves a result upon judgment being entered that is the same as what they proposed in an offer they had previously made, the claimant will, colloquially, be said to have 'equalled' the offer.[264] Such a result would be regarded as being 'at least as advantageous' as the offer and therefore the claimant would be entitled to the benefits of having beaten the offer.[265] **17.92**

Summary judgment Under the original Part 36, a claimant would have been entitled to the benefit of having made a Part 36 offer only if they obtained the final result at **17.93**

---

[259] *Kastor Navigation Co Ltd v AXA Global Risks (UK) Ltd* [2004] EWCA Civ 277, at [135]–[139].

[260] See *Webb (by her litigation friend Perkins) v Liverpool Women's NHS Foundation Trust* [2016] EWCA Civ 365, at [33]–[36], *per* Sir Stanley Burnton.

[261] See *ibid*, at [37]; see also *ABC (A protected party proceeding by his wife and litigation friend DEF) v Barts Health NHS Trust* [2016] EWHC 500 (QB).

[262] See *Webb (by her litigation friend Perkins) v Liverpool Women's NHS Foundation Trust* [2016] EWCA Civ 365, at [38].

[263] See, eg, *ABC (A protected party proceeding by his wife and litigation friend DEF) v Barts Health NHS Trust* [2016] EWHC 500 (QB), at [17], *per* Judge McKenna (sitting as a judge of the High Court).

[264] The related point of how the court should deal with late acceptance of an offer is discussed at 17.177–17.187.

[265] Even under the original Part 36 (where the test was whether the claimant had been awarded more or whether they had secured a judgment that was more advantageous), the court often exercised its discretion pursuant to what is now CPR, r 44.2. Where the court did this, it would often find that an award on the indemnity basis was justified: *Read v Edmed* [2004] EWHC 3274 (QB).

trial.[266] Thus a claimant who had obtained summary judgment would not have received any such benefit[267] (although they would, of course, have been in a strong position to ask for a favourable costs award as a matter of discretion). The reference to 'trial' has long since been deleted from Part 36; instead, CPR, r 36.17(1)(b), now refers to 'judgment being entered'. As such, this would include a claim in which the claimant obtained a favourable summary judgment.

17.94 **More than one defendant** In a case in which there is more than one defendant, the claimant may wish to make an offer against more than one of them. This may be done severally (for example 'D1: £1,000 and D2: £2,000') or jointly (for example 'D1 and/or D2: £3,000'). If an offer is made jointly and if the court determines that one of the defendants has only a several liability, then if the amount payable by that defendant is less than the offer, the claimant may be denied the benefits of Part 36 as against that defendant. This may be so even where the claimant has beaten their own offer as against the defendants collectively. In view of this, it would often be wise for claimants to make offers that are joint alongside offers that are several (for example '£3,000 as against D1 and D2, £2,000 as against D2 and £1,000 as against D1').[268] That said, there seems to be a certain amount of flexibility in this regard.[269]

17.95 **Subrogated claims** The fact that a claim is a subrogated claim is irrelevant for the purposes of determining whether a claimant has beaten their own offer. In particular, it is wrong to say that a claimant could never be regarded as having beaten an offer if the burden of the claim was being borne by their insurers rather than by themselves personally.[270] Presumably, the same would apply in other situations in which a claimant had the benefit of a funder or some type.

17.96 **Offers to forgo costs or enhanced interest** When deciding whether a claimant has obtained a result that is at least as advantageous to them as their offer, offers to accept discounted costs are generally disregarded,[271] as are offers to forgo the 'uplift' element of any interest.[272] It is, however, arguable that a different approach should apply where the defendant has sought to restrict the claimant's entitlement to costs because that claim was dishonestly exaggerated,[273] but such an offer would probably be regarded as being an 'admissible offer' rather than a Part 36 offer. That said, whilst, in the editor's experience,

---

[266] See the original CPR, r 36.21.

[267] *Petrotrade Inc v Texaco Ltd (Note)* [2002] 1 WLR 947, at [58].

[268] See *Sycamore Bidco Ltd v Breslin* [2013] EWHC 583 (Ch), at [43]–[51], *per* Mann J.

[269] Whilst it related to an offer that had been made to rather than by the claimants, Arnold J found that an offer that had been made jointly to claimants who were married and who presented a united front throughout the litigation was effective notwithstanding the fact that, technically, they had individual claims: see *Ali v Channel 5 Broadcast Ltd* [2018] EWHC 840 (Ch), at [41].

[270] See *Greenwich Millennium Village Ltd v Essex Services Group Plc (Formerly Essex Electrical Group Ltd)* [2014] EWHC 1099 (TCC), at [37]–[39], *per* Coulson J.

[271] Whilst it related to the original Part 36, *Mitchell v James* [2002] EWCA Civ 997 is still regarded as being good law on this point. See also *Williams v Jervis* [2009] EWHC 1838 (QB) (in which Roderick Evans J declined to take such an offer into account); *Eiles v Southwark London Borough Council* [2006] EWHC 2014 (TCC).

[272] *Ali Reza-Delta Transport Co v United Arab Shipping Co* [2003] EWCA Civ 811.

[273] See *Walker Construction (UK) Ltd v Quayside Homes Ltd* [2014] EWCA Civ 93, at [92]–[95], *per* Gloster LJ.

they rarely carry much weight, such offers could be taken into account when considering whether an award of costs on the indemnity basis should be made under CPR, r 44.2.[274]

The relevance of costs in general Andrew Popplewell J has explained that costs should be disregarded for the purposes of determining whether a judgment against a defendant is at least as advantageous to the claimant as proposals contained in the latter's Part 36 offer.[275] **17.97**

Where a defendant beats the offer

If the discretion afforded by CPR, r 44.2(4)(c), is disregarded for a moment, the power to take a defendant's offer into account arises from the combined effects of CPR, r 36.14(1)(a) and (3). The relevant part of CPR, r 36.14, reads as follows: **17.98**

> '(1) Subject to rule 36.14A, this rule applies where upon judgment being entered—
> (a) a claimant fails to obtain a judgment more advantageous than a defendant's Part 36 offer;
> [...]
> (2) For the purposes of paragraph (1), in relation to any money claim or money element of a claim, "more advantageous" means better in money terms by any amount, however small, and "at least as advantageous" shall be construed accordingly.
> (3) Subject to paragraphs (7) and (8), where paragraph (1)(a) applies, the court must, unless it considers it unjust to do so, order that the defendant is entitled to—
> (a) costs (including any recoverable pre-action costs) from the date on which the "relevant period" expired; and
> (b) interest on those costs.
> [...]
> (5) In considering whether it would be unjust to make the orders referred to in paragraphs (3) and (4), the court must take into account all the circumstances of the case including—
> (a) the terms of any Part 36 offer;
> (b) the stage in the proceedings when any Part 36 offer was made, including in particular how long before the trial started the offer was made;
> (c) the information available to the parties at the time when the Part 36 offer was made;
> (d) the conduct of the parties with regard to the giving of or refusal to give information for the purposes of enabling the offer to be made or evaluated; and
> (e) whether the offer was a genuine attempt to settle the proceedings.'

CPR, r 36.17(7) and (8), goes on to add the following qualifications: **17.99**

> '(7) Paragraphs (3) and (4) of this rule do not apply to a Part 36 offer—
> (a) which has been withdrawn;
> (b) which has been changed so that its terms are less advantageous to the offeree, where offeree has beaten the less advantageous offer;

[274] See, eg, *Eiles v Southwark London Borough Council* [2006] EWHC 2014 (TCC), in which Ramsay J gave weight to an offer to discount costs that he had found not to be a Part 36 offer, but which was an 'admissible offer'.

[275] See *Transocean Drilling UK Ltd v Providence Resources plc* [2016] EWHC 2611 (Comm), at [16]–[17], [23]–[24] and [26]. The issue arose in a case in which judgment at first instance was for a certain amount of damages with no order as to costs, but on appeal the amount of damages was increased so as to overtop a Part 36 offer that had been made by the claimant. The defendant said that the offer had not been beaten because if the order that there be no order as to costs were taken into account, the defendant would have been worse off by having accepted the offer. Andrew Popplewell J rejected this argument as contrary to the purpose of Part 36, that purpose being to provide a clear rule that permitted easy determination of whether a party had or had not beaten an offer. He did, however, take the costs into account for the purposes of deciding whether it would be unjust to award the claimant the full benefit of the offer (see 17.159).

(c) made less than 21 days before trial, unless the court has abridged the relevant period.

(8) Paragraph (3) does not apply to a soft tissue injury claim to which rule 36.21 applies.'

Thus, where a defendant has beaten one of their own offers, they would generally be awarded costs[276] from the date on which the 'relevant period' expired. Where an offer needs to be clarified upon the request of the offeree,[277] the expiry of the 'relevant period' may be adjusted to take that need into account.[278] There is nothing in any of these provisions to oust the court's jurisdiction to make a discretionary award of costs.[279]

'More advantageous'

17.100 **'Near misses'** Where there has been a 'near miss' (that is, where the defendant has, on the face of it, failed to beat their own offer, but only by the narrowest of margins), two issues may arise:

(1) the court may have to determine whether, in truth, the result is or is not 'more advantageous' to the claimant than the offer; and
(2) the court may have to determine whether the offer should be taken into account when exercising its discretion as to costs.

Each is dealt with in turn.

17.101 *Whether offer has been beaten* Where the question is whether the claimant has failed to obtain a judgment that is more advantageous to them than a defendant's very similar Part 36 offer, as of 1 October 2011[280] the law has been as set out in what is now CPR, r 36.17(2):

> '(2) For the purposes of paragraph (1), in relation to any money claim or money element of a claim, "more advantageous" means better in money terms by any amount, however small, and "at least as advantageous" shall be construed accordingly.'

17.102 *Discretion* Where there has been a 'near miss', the court is at liberty to exercise its discretion pursuant to CPR, r 44.2.[281] One factor to be taken into account is whether any offers have been made.[282] The court has freedom in those circumstances to exercise its discretion to make an order that meets the justice of the situation. In an appropriate case, it is open to the court to make a percentage order.[283] Indeed, that approach was not wholly unknown, even under the original Part 36 regime.[284]

---

[276] Whilst the court has the power to order costs on the indemnity basis as a matter of discretion, the default position is that costs will be payable on the standard basis: see, eg, *Shalaby v London North West Healthcare NHS Trust* [2018] EWCA Civ 1323, at [51]–[55], *per* Singh LJ; *Excelsior Commercial & Industrial Holdings Ltd v Salisbury Hamer Aspden & Johnson (Costs)* [2002] EWCA Civ 879, at [19], *per* Woolf MR.

[277] See CPR, r 36.8.

[278] *Colour Quest Ltd v Total Downstream UK plc* [2009] EWHC 823 (Comm), at [32], *per* David Steel J, which case concerned claimants' offers, but the principles can only be the same.

[279] Indeed, the offer itself can lead to an award of costs on the indemnity basis if the court is satisfied that it was unreasonable (as opposed to merely misjudged) not to accept it: see, eg, *D Morgan plc v Mace & Jones (a firm)* [2011] EWHC 26 (TCC), *per* Coulson J.

[280] This was inserted by Civil Procedure (Amendment No 2) Rules 2011 (SI 2011/1979).

[281] *Straker v Tudor Rose (a firm)* [2007] EWCA Civ 368, at [3].

[282] CPR, r 44.2(4)(c); *Straker v Tudor Rose (a firm)* [2007] EWCA Civ 368, at [5]. See also *Hammersmatch Properties (Welwyn) Ltd v Saint-Gobain Ceramics & Plastics Ltd* [2013] EWHC 2227 (TCC), at [36].

[283] See, eg, *Owners, Demise Charters & Time Charterers of 'Western Neptune'* [2009] EWHC 1522 (Admlty).

[284] See, eg, *Firle v Datapoint* [2001] EWCA Civ 1106.

Where the court elects to exercise its discretion in this way, one or more of the parties may contend that the dispute would have settled if the other side had acted in a way more conducive to negotiation. Arguments such as this may be put with particular force when there has been a 'near miss'. Waller LJ said on this topic: 17.103

> 'If the judge is finding that the case would have settled as opposed to finding that there was a chance it would have settled, that could not have been other than a speculation. In my view it does not come well from a defendant who has [made an offer] to argue that if a claimant had been more reasonable he would have offered more. An investigation as to how negotiations would have gone is precisely the form of investigation which should be avoided. In a case about money a defendant has the remedy in his own hands where a claimant is being intransigent. He can [make a Part 36 offer to pay] the maximum sum he is prepared to pay.'[285]

Chadwick LJ expressed a similar view—in particular, expressing concern about the possibility of the court being drawn into 'a potentially lengthy, inquiry on incomplete material into "what would have happened if...?"'.[286] Ramsey J (a judge who had a particular interest in the law of costs) has confirmed that Chadwick LJ's comments continue to apply.[287] This is a topic that is dealt with in more detail at 6.73. 17.104

Barely 'beating' an offer A 'near miss' (see 17.100) should be distinguished from the situation in which there is a narrow failure on the part of the offeree to do better than the offer. In those circumstances, then unless it would be unjust to make such an order, the offeror will be entitled to the benefits of the offer[288]—an entirely different situation from a 'near miss'. 17.105

Measuring success: gauging the value of Part 36 offers

Interest and offers

Interest has to be taken into account when considering whether an offer has been beaten.[289] This is necessary to allow like to be compared with like. There is no express facility under Part 36 to make an offer that is exclusive of interest; instead, offers are presumed to include interest. In this regard, CPR, r 36.5(4), provides: 17.106

> '(4) A Part 36 offer which offers to pay or offers to accept a sum of money will be treated as inclusive of all interest until—(a) the date on which the period stated under rule 36.5(1) (c) expires; or (b) if rule 36.5(2) applies, a date 21 days after the date the offer was made ...'

CPR, r 36.5(2), applies if the offer is made less than 21 days before the start of the trial.

Where the offer and the judgment sum are sufficiently close to each other as to create doubt as to whether the offer has been beaten, it may be necessary to calculate the amount that would have been allowed had interest been calculated to the applicable date. In this regard, Brooke LJ endorsed the following extract from the 1999 edition of The White Book 17.107

---

285 *Straker v Tudor Rose (a firm)* [2007] EWCA 368, at [36].

286 *Johnsey Estates (1990) Ltd v Secretary of State for the Environment* [2001] EWCA Civ 535, at [32].

287 *Hammersmatch Properties (Welwyn) Ltd v Saint-Gobain Ceramics & Plastics Ltd* [2013] EWHC 2227 (TCC), at [36].

288 See, by way of analogy, *Fulham Leisure Holdings Ltd v Nicholson Graham & Jones* [2006] EWHC 2428 (Ch).

289 Although dealing with the original Part 36, see *Blackham v Entrepose UK* [2004] EWCA Civ 1109. More recently, see *Purrunsing v A'Court & Co* [2016] EWHC 1528 (Ch), *per* Judge Pelling QC (sitting as a deputy judge of the High Court).

(which extract is worded in pre-CPR language, but Brooke LJ confirmed that what is said remains good law under the CPR):

> '[If] the trial Judge awards £x by way of damages and the defendant has paid into Court £y, which exceeds £x, then a calculation may have to be made as to what the amount of interest would have been if judgment were given for £x at the date of the payment into Court. If such figure amounts to £a, and if £x + £a exceeds £y, the result would be that the amount recovered by the plaintiff will have exceeded the amount paid into Court by the defendant, so that the plaintiff will be entitled to be awarded the whole costs of the action. But it is thought that this calculation would not be very difficult and is likely to arise comparatively rarely.'[290]

17.108 Brooke LJ commented that this formulaic approach is to be preferred to a more general exercise of discretion, because the latter was not to be preferred because it would lead to inconsistencies between courts and between judges in the same court.

Non-monetary claims

17.109 Whilst it will not always be possible to carry out a straightforward comparison, it may be necessary to compare a non-monetary award with a non-monetary offer. Whilst the law is not wholly clear, the following comments can be made.

- **Quantifiable non-monetary claims** Where a fair quantitative evaluation is possible, then that may be an appropriate yardstick. This does not have to be an equivalent financial value, but often is expressed in such terms.[291] What is less clear, however, is whether and to what extent the court would be able to take other factors into account, if at all.[292]
- **Mixed monetary and non-monetary claims** Claims may embrace both monetary and non-monetary elements. Where this is so, then, when comparing the monetary elements, 'more advantageous' will mean better in monetary terms by any amount, however small, and 'at least as advantageous' shall be construed accordingly.[293] This much is clear, but what is less clear is how that finding would be influenced (if at all) by the court's findings about the non-monetary elements of the claim. The court will look at the whole of what was offered, and this may include apologies and offers of amends.[294]
- **Wholly non-monetary claims** Where a quantitative approach is not possible, the following comments of Sir Thomas Bingham MR are likely to apply:

> 'The judge must look closely at the facts of the particular case before him and ask: who, as a matter of substance and reality, has won? Has the plaintiff won anything of value which he could not have won without fighting the action through to a finish? Has the

[290] The White Book 1999, cited in *Blackham v Entrepose UK* [2004] EWCA Civ 1109, at [7].

[291] In a case involving the recovery of motor vehicles, for example, Chadwick LJ found that it was appropriate to analyse the 'advantage' in financial terms, because the claimant had offered to accept four collectable cars, but in the event had obtained six: *Neave v Neave* [2003] EWCA Civ 325. This case was decided under the original Part 36.

[292] The reason for this is because *Carver v BAA plc* [2008] EWCA Civ 412 has now been confined to its own facts. CPR, r 36.17(2), makes it clear that the *Carver* approach will not apply in 'any money claim or money element of a claim', but it leaves open the issue of what should happen in a claim that was not about money, but which was capable of being analysed in quantitative terms.

[293] CPR, r 36.17(2).

[294] See, eg, *KC v MGN Ltd (Costs)* [2013] EWCA Civ 3.

defendant substantially denied the plaintiff the prize which the plaintiff fought the action to win?'[295]

Similar considerations may arise in claims regarding non-monetary disputes about land,[296] chattels, etc. Whilst *obiter*, Ward LJ had the following to say about the range of factors that should be taken into account: 'It is quite clear that in non-money claims where there is no yardstick of pounds and pence by which to make the comparison, all the circumstances of the case have to be taken into account.'[297] Because there would be no other way of dealing with a wholly non-monetary claim that did not permit of a quantitative comparison, it is likely that these comments still apply to such claims.

- **Qualified offers and incomplete offers** The court is entitled to take into account any qualifications that may have attached to the offer.[298] Similarly, the court is entitled to take into account the fact that an offer did not apply to the whole of the claim. In a claim involving the rights to music, for example, Neuberger LJ found that it was open to the court to find that the offer had not been beaten where the defendant had secured a more advantageous result in respect of the monetary element, but not the non-monetary element.[299]

The point in time at which offer is to be compared with result

It may be that the question of whether an offer has been beaten depends on the point in time at which an offer is to be compared with the result (this being relevant where, for example, the comparison may be influenced by a fluctuating exchange rate). Both David Richards J[300] and Leggatt J[301] have found that the relevant point in time is when judgment is given (but see 17.106). **17.110**

Deductible benefits

The measure of whether an offer has been beaten is generally based on the applicable sums net of deductible benefits (usually known as net of CRU).[302] As has been explained in 17.51–17.52, offers may be expressed to be exclusive of deductible benefits,[303] but where this is not the case, an adjustment will need to be made for such benefits.[304] If appropriate, the court is permitted to wait until the outcome of an appeal in respect of the amount of detectible benefits for deciding the issue of whether the offer has been beaten.[305] **17.111**

295 *Roache v Newsgroup Newspapers Ltd* [1998] EMLR 161, at 168 (in the context of a defamation claim). Eady J has confirmed that these comments remain good law under the CPR: see *Jones v Associated Newspapers Ltd* [2007] EWHC 1489, at [14].

296 While it dealt with 'admissible offers' rather than Part 36 offers, see *MBI Inc v Riminex Investments Ltd* [2002] EWHC 2856 (QB).

297 *Carver v BAA plc* [2008] EWCA Civ 412, at [29] (which is probably still good law on that point, ie in respect of non-monetary claims).

298 See, eg, *Specsavers International Healthcare Ltd v Asda Stores Ltd (Costs)* [2012] EWCA Civ 494, at [36] and [37], *per* Kitchin LJ.

299 *Brown v Mcasso Music Production* [2005] EWCA Civ 1546.

300 See *Barnett v Creggy* [2015] EWHC 1316 (Ch), at [20]–[30].

301 See *Novus Aviation Ltd v Alubaf Arab International Bank BSC(c)* [2016] EWHC 1937 (Comm), at [22] and [23].

302 CPR, r 36.22(8); see also *Blackham v Entrepose UK* [2004] EWCA Civ 1109, in which Brooke LJ said that the like-for-like rule should be in relation to CRU.

303 CPR, r 36.22(3).

304 See *Crooks v Hendricks Lovell Ltd* [2016] EWCA Civ 8, at [39], *per* Lindblom LJ.

305 See *ibid*, at [32] and [33], *per* Lindblom LJ.

17.112 Determining the net sum of the offer ought to present no problems because it should have been stated in the offer.[306] The net sum of the judgment sum is derived by subtracting deductible amounts identified in the judgment.[307]

Special situations

17.113 **Appeals and Part 36 offers** CPR, r 36.3(4), provides that a Part 36 offer will have a bearing only on the costs of the proceedings in respect of which it is made and not on the costs of any appeal from the final decision in those proceedings.[308] This express provision reflects the way in which Brooke LJ interpreted the original Part 36.[309]

17.114 There is no authority on the topic of whether the costs consequences mentioned above would apply if a defendant's offer were to be beaten by judgment being entered by consent.[310] It would be possible to draw an analogy with the way in which the court deals with claimant's Part 36 offers,[311] but it could equally be argued that the policy considerations concerning defendants' Part 36 offers are different[312] and that this analogy is not appropriate.

17.115 **Costs budgets** If a party has failed to file a costs budget in time, under CPR, r 3.14, that party is treated as having filed a budget limited to court fees, which means that, in effect (and subject to obtaining relief from sanction), its recoverable costs are limited to court fees. Where that is the case, there may be little incentive for the opponent to settle in the face of a Part 36 offer from the party in default, because the costs risk if the offeree were to fail to beat the offer would be minimal.

17.116 The post-2015 CPR, r 36.23, addresses this difficulty by providing that, in certain circumstances (see 17.117), the defaulting party's recoverable costs for the purposes of Part 36 will be 50 per cent of the costs that would otherwise be recoverable, but will not be limited to court fees.

17.117 The circumstances in which the limitation will be lifted are particularised in CPR, r 36.23, as being when the following rules apply:

- CPR, r 36.13(5)(b) (where the offer is accepted after the expiry of the 'relevant period');
- CPR, r 36.17(3)(a) (where the claimant fails to beat a defendant's offer after the expiry of the 'relevant period'); and
- CPR, r 36.17(4)(b) (where a claimant is awarded costs on the indemnity basis from the date of expiry of the 'relevant period').[313]

---

306 CPR, r 36.22(6).

307 CPR, r 36.22(8).

308 See CPR, r 36.4(1).

309 *P & O Nedlloyd BV v Utaniko Ltd* [2003] EWCA Civ 174, at [6].

310 For the related issue of where an offer is accepted out of time or as a result of it being renewed, see 17.177–17.187.

311 *D Pride & Partners v Institute for Animal Health* [2009] EWHC 1617 (QB), at [33]. For a different, but related, point, see *Fitzpatrick Contractors Ltd v Tyco Fire & Integrated Solutions (UK) Ltd* [2009] EWHC 274 (TCC), at [28].

312 Not least because it would be in accordance with the overriding objective to discourage claimants from pursuing disproportionate claims that are capable of compromise: see *D Pride & Partners v Institute for Animal Health* [2009] EWHC 1817 (QB), at [33]. It could be argued that defendants should be encouraged to make realistic offers.

313 The meaning of CPR, r 36.23, in relation to CPR, r 36.17(4)(b), is anything but clear. This is because the limitation in CPR, r 3.14, does not apply at all where costs are awarded on the indemnity basis (see

It should be noted that CPR, r 36.23, applies only to the costs from expiry of the 'relevant period' onwards, which means that, where it is the claimant who is in default and the offer is accepted within the 'relevant period', the claimant will not avoid the limitation in CPR, r 3.14. Put otherwise, CPR, r 36.23, does not act retrospectively.

Discretion and Part 36: when the benefit of Part 36 would be 'unjust'

Unjust to make an award: the injustice test and discretion

With certain exceptions,[314] where an offeror has beaten their offer, then unless the court considers that it would be unjust to make such an award, the offeror will be entitled to the benefits of Part 36.[315] This test (which is referred to below as 'the injustice test') is in many ways the same as that which would apply where an offeree accepts an offer following the expiry of the 'relevant period' (see 17.177).[316] Because of this, it is convenient to deal with the tests—that is, that which applies where the offer has been beaten[317] and that which would apply where the offer has been accepted after the 'relevant period'[318]—together. It should be borne in mind, however, that, in practice, there are differences in the way in which the court applies the injustice test in these two situations (see 17.177–17.183, especially 17.181). **17.118**

Lewison LJ has explained that whether a particular outcome is unjust is essentially a value judgment, which is a matter for the judge at first instance.[319] He went on to explain that the making of a costs order that is not positively required by the Rules is a two-stage procedure: **17.119**

> '[T]he making of a costs order that is not positively required by the Rules is an exercise of judicial discretion. Thus, the judge must first decide whether or not applying the presumption of a default position in Part 36.10(5) would be unjust. If he decides that it would be, then he must go on to decide what other order to make.'[320]

The court is required to take into account all of the relevant circumstances, but the relevant factors will not always be the same for each of the benefits referred to in 17.81.[321] This may include the terms and circumstances of the relevant offer, even if those facts have already been taken into account for the purposes of determining whether the offer had been beaten.[322]

CPR, r 3.18); as such, it would appear that if the reference to CPR, r 36.17(4)(b), is to have any meaning, it is as a restriction on recoverable costs rather than a limited release of the restriction in CPR, r 3.14. This would be counter-intuitive, but it would not be wholly absurd, because it is possible that the restriction in CPR, r 36.17(4)(b), is to apply to a limited extent if the award on the indemnity basis has been made by reason of a Part 36 offer. That said, the wording of CPR, r 36.23, does not sit happily with that interpretation. The editor cannot help but wonder whether the reference to CPR, r 36.17(4)(b), is otiose and has no effect whatsoever.

314 They are set out in CPR, r 36.17(7), and relate to offers the offeror wishes to withdraw or change.
315 CPR, rr 36.17(3) (for defendants) and 36.17(4) (for claimants).
316 See CPR, r 36.13(5).
317 CPR, r 36.17.
318 CPR, r 36.13.
319 See *Dutton v Minards* [2015] EWCA Civ 984, at [26].
320 *Ibid.*
321 See *OMV Petrom SA v Glencore International AG* [2017] EWCA Civ 195, at [25], *per* Vos C.
322 See *Yentob v MGN Ltd* [2015] EWCA Civ 1292, at [20]–[22], *per* Arden LJ.

17.120 **'Just' and 'fair'** The burden is on the party who seeks to persuade the court that the normal orders would be unjust.[323] The injustice test is whether it would be unjust to make an order that affords the offeror the benefits of Part 36, not whether it would be unjust not to make such an order.[324] The court would fall into error if it were to fail to apply that test entirely[325] (although the test may be applied by implication rather than expressly[326]).

17.121 Whilst the injustice test is a threshold test, there is no requirement that the case be exceptional.[327] That said, Briggs J has said that 'the burden ... to show injustice is a formidable obstacle',[328] this being a description that Eder J also adopted.[329]

17.122 The words 'just' and 'fair' are often used interchangeably in the authorities. This is of no great importance. By way of example, whilst Longmore LJ has commented that 'it is open to the court to assess what the fairness of the situation demands',[330] Black LJ has explained that the question of what is unfair is the same as the question of what is unjust.[331] This is very different from the exercise of discretion under CPR, r 44.2,[332] that being a far more nuanced affair than a test of injustice. Ward LJ has explained that 'Part 36 trumps Part 44' in that regard.[333]

17.123 There are examples of the court exercising its discretion as to costs and *then* applying the injustice test,[334] but that would appear to be wrong in principle.[335] This should be distinguished from the court finding that the threshold has been met and then taking the factors in CPR, r 44.2(4), into account (see 17.126–17.128).

17.124 **Not all or nothing** There is no doubt that the injustice test is a threshold test, but this does not mean that it is an all-or-nothing affair; as Macur LJ put it, the court is 'not fettered by a bi-polar evaluation of [what is] "unjust"'.[336] Macur LJ went on to explain that the phrase 'unless it considers it unjust to do so' should be interpreted as meaning 'unless and to the extent of',[337] indicating that the court is able to adjust the award so as to avoid

323 See *Tiuta Plc v Rawlinson & Hunter (a firm)* [2016] EWHC 3480 (QB), at [14], *per* Andrew Baker J. See also *Optical Express v Associated Newspapers (Costs)* [2017] EWHC 2707 (QB), at [11], *per* Warby J.

324 *Huck v Robson* [2002] EWCA Civ 398, at [77], *per* Schiemann LJ. That said, it is not uncommon for judges to use the shorthand of whether it would be just to make the order sought: see, eg, *Jordan v MGN Ltd* [2017] EWHC 1937 (Ch), at [44], *per* Mann J.

325 See *Walker Construction (UK) Ltd v Quayside Homes Ltd* [2014] EWCA Civ 93, at [97], *per* Gloster LJ.

326 See, eg, *Yentob v MGN Ltd* [2015] EWCA Civ 1292, at [17], *per* Arden LJ.

327 See *SG v Hewitt* [2012] EWCA Civ 1053, at [25], *per* Black LJ.

328 *Smith v Trafford Housing Trust* [2012] EWHC 3320, at [13(d)], cited with approval in *Briggs v CEF Holdings Ltd* [2017] EWCA Civ 2363, at [20], *per* Gross LJ. See also *Optical Express v Associated Newspapers (Costs)* [2017] EWHC 2707 (QB), at [13]–[15], *per* Warby J.

329 *Ted Baker plc v AXA Insurance UK plc* [2014] EWHC 4178 (Comm), at [16], [17] and [23].

330 *Kunaka v Barclays Bank plc* [2010] EWCA Civ 1035, at [9] and [10].

331 *SG v Hewitt* [2012] EWCA Civ 1053, at [24].

332 *Matthews (a patient) v Metal Improvements Co Inc* [2007] EWCA Civ 215, *per* Chadwick LJ. This case was decided under the original Part 36, so it should be approached with some caution. It would probably not be helpful to draw any point of principle from it beyond the general statements made about the policy of Part 36.

333 See *Shovelar v Lane* [2011] EWCA Civ 802, at [52].

334 See, eg, the post-hearing discussion and Judge Hodge QC's *ex tempore* judgment on costs in *AW Group Ltd v Taylor Walton* [2013] EWHC 2610. (*Shovelar v Lane* [2011] EWCA Civ 802 had not been drawn to the judge's attention.)

335 *Ted Baker plc v AXA Insurance UK plc* [2014] EWHC 4178 (Comm), at [15], *per* Eder J.

336 *Thinc Group Ltd v Kingdom* [2013] EWCA Civ 1306, at [22].

337 *Ibid.*

injustice either by disallowing or curtailing the Part 36 benefits (see 17.81) or by adjusting the incidence of costs (or, presumably, both).[338] In a similar vein, Sir Colin MacKay has explained that the injustice test is to be (or, at least, may be) applied individually to each of those benefits rather than globally, which means that it is open to the court to allow the offeror the advantage of as many or as few of those benefits as would be appropriate on the facts of the case in hand.[339]

Eder J had this to say on the way in which the injustice test may operate so as to prevent a party's unreasonable behaviour being condoned: **17.125**

> 'It follows that the real question, in my view, is whether the [offeree] can show any relevant "injustice" so as to displace the general rule, bearing fully in mind that the burden of doing so is a "formidable obstacle" ... However, ... it seems to me that the fact that [an offeror] may make a Part 36 offer does not give such [a party] carte blanche to run any [case] whatsoever so as to entitle such [a party] necessarily to expect that the CPR Part 36 consequences will automatically to apply to those issues on which such [a party] lost.'[340]

Eder J went on to find that the offeror (a defendant) had acted unreasonably in the way it had 'left no stone unturned' in its defence and, as such, disallowed certain costs that otherwise would have been payable.[341]

Discretion once threshold has been met and double jeopardy Once the threshold of injustice has been met, the judge has a wide discretion as to the form of costs order. In this regard, Arden LJ had the following to say: **17.126**

> 'To my mind, the power of the court in this regard is a deliberate and important safety valve. For a case to be within the safety valve, however, the judge will in general need to find that the case has features which take it out of the ordinary principle and which demonstrate that it is unjust to impose the normal shifting of the costs risk. I would therefore, as Black LJ has done, interpret the existing CPR 36.10(4)(b) consistently with CPR 36.14(2) and thus as requiring the court to find that it is unjust not to order otherwise. Where those circumstances are present, however, the judge has a wide discretion as to the form of order that he substitutes.'[342]

It is not enough that a party demonstrates what would have happened under CPR, r 44.2,[343] although there is nothing to prevent the court from taking the factors in CPR, r 44.2(4), into account.[344] An example of the distinction between the exercise of discretion under CPR, r 44.2, and under the injustice test is a case in which Judge Keyser QC (sitting as a deputy judge of the High Court) found that a defendant had succeeded in general and had beaten its offer, but that it had also raised a number of bad points.[345] To take account of those points, he discounted the defendant's pre-offer costs by half, but he found that those points were not so bad as to justify a discount of the post-offer costs. **17.127**

---

338 *Davison v Leitch* [2013] EWHC 3092 (QB), at [73], *per* Andrews J.

339 See *RXDA v Northampton Borough Council* [2015] EWHC 2936 (QB), at [8] and [9].

340 *Ted Baker plc v AXA Insurance UK plc* [2014] EWHC 4178 (Comm), at [17].

341 *Ibid*, at [19].

342 *SG v Hewitt* [2012] EWCA Civ 1053, at [76].

343 See *Walsh v Singh (aka Buddha and Walsh)* [2011] EWCA Civ 80, at [7], *per* Arden LJ.

344 Arden LJ has explained that this is because they may serve as being a guide to the types of factor that are relevant to the exercise of the court's discretion under Part 36: see *ibid.*

345 *Altus Group (UK) Ltd v Baker Tilly Tax and Advisory Services LLP* [2015] EWHC 411 (Ch), at [22].

17.128 If, as a result of the threshold of injustice having been met, the court deprives an offeror of any of the Part 36 benefits as listed in 17.81, care must be taken not to visit double jeopardy on that party by unwittingly taking the same factors into account when exercising discretion as to costs in general.[346]

17.129 **Factors to be taken into account** Eady J has explained that while a judge may consider the effect of Part 36 to be harsh, that fact would not be a reason for denying the offeror the benefits of having made the offer.[347] CPR, r 36.17(5), gives specific guidance as to the factors that the court will take into account when considering whether or not it is just to make the award. Those factors are:

- the terms of any Part 36 offer;
- the stage in the proceedings at which any Part 36 offer was made, including, in particular, how long before the trial started the offer was made;
- the information available to the parties at the time when the Part 36 offer was made;
- the conduct of the parties with regard to the giving of or refusal to give information for the purposes of enabling the offer to be made or evaluated; and
- whether the offer was a genuine attempt to settle the proceedings.

Briggs J has noted that this list focuses on the circumstances of the making of the offer and the provision or otherwise of relevant information in relation to it, rather than upon the general conduct of the proceedings by the parties.[348] This may be so, but Black LJ has said that the 'factors specifically identified [in CPR, r 36.17(5)] as relevant cast quite a wide net on their own but they are not the only matters that fall for consideration and anything else which is relevant must be considered as well'.[349]

17.130 Both CPR, rr 36.17(5) and 13(6), say, in terms, that the court will take into account 'all the circumstances of the case'. The factors to be taken into account need not be limited to the financial aspect of the claim. In a claim in which the damages award by a court had not exceeded a defendant's Part 36 offer, for example, Briggs J found that it would have been unjust for the claimant to pay the defendant's costs because the claim was more about restoration of reputation and the conduct of the defendant's disciplinary proceedings than about money.[350] Whilst *obiter*, Eady J has given a hypothetical example that if—through no fault of their own—an offeree has rejected a Part 36 offer on the basis of inaccurate information, it may be unjust to allow the offeror the benefit of having made the offer.[351] This would be especially so where the offeree had been misled by the offeror or that party's advisers through (say) non-disclosure of a material fact or document.

17.131 One factor that is not on the list in CPR, r 36.17(5), is the amount of the costs claimed by the parties. Whilst he expressed considerable regret at having to make such a finding,

---

[346] See, eg, *Feltham v Bouskell* [2013] EWHC 3086 (Ch D), at [18], *per* Charles Hollander QC.

[347] *Downing v Peterborough & Stamford Hospitals NHS Foundation Trust* [2014] EWHC Civ 4216 (QB), at [61] *et seq*, *per* Eady J. Eady J made these comments in the context of an offer made by a claimant.

[348] *Lilleyman v Lilleyman & Anor* [2012] EWHC 1056 (Ch), at [16].

[349] *SG v Hewitt* [2012] EWCA Civ 1053, at [29]. See also *Lilleyman v Lilleyman & Anor* [2012] EWHC 1056 (Ch), at [16], *per* Briggs J; *Smith v Trafford Housing Trust* [2012] EWHC 3320, at [13(d)], *per* Briggs J.

[350] *Smith v Trafford Housing Trust* [2012] EWHC 3320 (Ch), at [14].

[351] *Downing v Peterborough & Stamford Hospitals NHS Foundation Trust* [2014] EWHC Civ 4216 (QB), at [62].

Ward LJ has confirmed that the court is not permitted to take that factor into account.[352] Similarly, Tomlinson LJ has explained that issues of quantum are matters for assessment rather than matters to be taken into account when making an order for costs.[353] Other factors that ought not to be taken into account (in the sense that they are irrelevant) are the incidence of costs as they would have been had the offer been accepted within the 'relevant period',[354] the fact that the offeree is funded under a conditional fee agreement or by way of after-the-event (ATE) insurance[355] and, where appropriate, the likely costs sanctions that may have been visited upon the parties if they had proceeded to trial.[356]

Conduct As mentioned above, the court would have to be persuaded that there was something unjust in applying the normal rule;[357] it is not enough that a party demonstrates what would have happened had the court been exercising its powers under CPR, r 44.2 (see 17.127).[358] The conduct of the parties may include the conduct throughout the whole of the proceedings; it is not limited to conduct after the offer was made.[359] There have been differing approaches as to the extent that the court takes into account any perceived difficulties that the offeree's legal advisers may have had in advising the offeree,[360] but, to the extent that this is a relevant fact, it seems rarely to be given much weight. **17.132**

There are instances of the court depriving the offeror of some or all of the benefits of their offer on the grounds of their poor conduct. An obvious example of where this would be appropriate would be where it transpired that the claimant's claim was fraudulent.[361] Judge Harris QC has said that the mere fact that a defendant chose to make a Part 36 offer rather than a costs-restricted *Calderbank* offer would not be a bar to that party arguing that it would be unjust to allow the claimant to have the whole of their costs.[362] That may be correct, but the fact that such a course of action would have been open to a defendant[363] may be a factor that the court can take into account.[364] **17.133**

[352] Whilst he was dealing with a matter to which Part 36 applied rather than Part 44, Ward LJ confirmed that the court must assume that the sums claimed will be assessed and that, as such, a seemingly excessive amount is not to be given weight, because the 'assessment will produce the right figure ... [and the paying party] will be properly condemned in that sum and no greater sum': *Shovelar v Lane* [2011] EWCA Civ 802, at [53].

[353] *United Marine Aggregates Ltd v G M Welding & Engineering Ltd* [2013] EWCA Civ 516, at [37].

[354] See *Walsh v Shanahan* [2013] EWCA Civ 675, at [12], *per* Rimer LJ.

[355] See *Briggs v CEF Holdings Ltd* [2017] EWCA Civ 2363, at [17], *per* Gross LJ.

[356] See *Jopling v Leavesley & Anor* [2013] EWCA Civ 1605, at [14], *per* Lewison LJ.

[357] *Fulham Leisure Holdings Ltd v Nicholson Graham & Jones* [2006] EWHC 2428 (Ch).

[358] See *Walsh v Singh (aka Buddha and Walsh)* [2011] EWCA Civ 80, at [7], *per* Arden LJ.

[359] *Thinc Group Ltd v Kingdom* [2013] EWCA Civ 1306, at [23], *per* Macur LJ. See also *Purser v Hibbs* [2015] EWHC 1792 (QB), in which Judge Moloney QC, after a tardy acceptance of a defendant's offer, refused to allow the claimant's poor conduct to prevent her from recovering her costs because it did not extend back to before the time when the offer was made.

[360] See *Briggs v CEF Holdings Ltd* [2017] EWCA Civ 2363, at [21]–[22], in which Gross LJ noted that, in *SG v Hewitt* [2012] EWCA Civ 1053, at [50 *et seq*, Black LJ seems to have had some regard to that factor, whereas in *Matthews v Metal Improvements Co Inc* [2007] EWCA Civ 215, at [34], Stanley Burnton J largely discounted it.

[361] See, eg, *Tuson v Murphy* (unreported), 6 April 2016, Oxford County Court, at [20], *per* Judge Harris QC; cf *Purser v Hibbs* [2015] EWHC 1792 (QB).

[362] See *Tuson v Murphy* (unreported), 6 April 2016, Oxford County Court, at [20].

[363] See *Summers v Fairclough Homes Ltd* [2012] UKSC 26, in which it was held that a defendant could protect his position by making an offer outside the framework of Part 36 to settle the genuine part of a claim on terms that the claimant pay his costs with regard to the fraudulent parts of the claim on an indemnity basis.

[364] See, eg, *Purser v Hibbs* [2015] EWHC 1792 (QB), at [17], *per* Judge Moloney QC.

17.134 There is no doubt that if a party 'orchestrat[es] a raft of evidence' against an opponent or performs sufficiently badly on cross-examination, they may be deprived of the benefits of having made an offer.[365] Similarly, where a claimant had raised a matter of fundamental importance to her case only in the course of opening trial, it was held to be open to the court to deprive her of part of the Part 36 benefits.[366]

17.135 The way the parties respond to offers may also be relevant. Macur LJ has made it clear that the need for objective reflection and assessment of any offer is particularly important in an action of relatively low monetary worth,[367] and this is a factor that the court can take into account as a reason not to deny the offeror the benefit of the offer. Offerees should be careful not to be seen as adopting a 'robust' approach to offers: in a less-than-flattering judgment, Macur LJ interpreted that word as meaning 'peremptory, dismissive and unco-operative, [conduct] that is deserving of opprobrium'.[368]

17.136 **Confusing offers** Although baffling offers may also be analysed in terms of whether they have been beaten (see 17.55), the court is able to find that it would be unjust to allow an offeror to take the benefit of such an offer. Arden LJ has confirmed that where an offer is found to be difficult to evaluate and confusing, it is within the discretion of the court to find that a party cannot be penalised for not having accepted it[369]—although it is also possible, perhaps, for the court to find that an offer is so unclear that it was not a Part 36 offer at all (see 17.55). Briggs J, however, has said that there are many areas of litigation in which there is complexity and legal uncertainty so as to give rise to a wide range of possible outcomes, and that the mere fact that a claim is complex would not, of itself, make it unjust for an offeror to have the benefits of Part 36.[370]

17.137 **Inadequate information** It may be that an offeree is unable to evaluate an offer because of a lack of information or time. Where this happens—assuming that the offeree's complaints were reasonable—it would be open to the court to deny the offeror the benefit of the offer,[371] either totally or over a stated period of time.[372] If the lack of information has resulted from an unreasonable failure on the part of the offeror to give disclosure, then that would be a factor that may satisfy the injustice test.[373]

---

365 See *Walsh v Singh (aka Buddha and Walsh)* [2011] EWCA Civ 80, at [17] and [31], *per* Arden LJ.

366 See, eg, *Feltham v Bouskell* [2013] EWHC 3086 (Ch D), at [9]–[10] and [13]–[16], *per* Charles Hollander QC.

367 *Thinc Group Ltd v Kingdom* [2013] EWCA Civ 1306, at [18].

368 *Ibid*, at [13].

369 *Rio Properties Inc v Gibson Dunn & Crutcher* [2005] EWCA Civ 534.

370 *Lilleyman v Lilleyman* [2012] EWHC 1056 (Ch), at [18].

371 *Ford v GKR Construction Ltd* [2000] 1 WLR 1397. Although a pre-CPR case, see *Burgess v British Steel plc* [2000] PIQR Q240, *per* Lord Woolf MR, in which it was found that the knowledge of the offeree was sufficiently good to know whether to accept the offer. See, eg, *Euro Asian Oil SA v Credit Suisse AG & Ors* [2016] EWHC 3340 (Comm), at [11] and [12], *per* Cranston J (no disclosure about the details of certain dealings between two other persons).

372 See, eg, *R v Secretary of State, ex p Factortame* (unreported) 18 October 2000, QBD, in which the offeree complained that it had not been able to evaluate an offer because it was not given adequate time to consider certain expert evidence. Toulson J afforded the offeree a degree of protection from the effect of the offer, but only up until a reasonable period of time for evaluating the evidence had elapsed.

373 See, eg, *Webb Resolutions Ltd v Waller Needham & Green (a firm)* [2012] EWHC 3529 (Ch), in which Mr John Baldwin QC (sitting as deputy judge of the Chancery Division) found the injustice test to be satisfied in a case in which the claimant had acted both unreasonably and against the letter and spirit of a pre-action protocol by refusing to comply with a request for certain disclosure.

Whilst other judges have taken a different view,[374] an example is a case in which Leggatt J found that it would be unjust to condemn a defendant to pay costs on the indemnity basis until after that party had received the claimant's expert evidence and had time to assimilate it.[375] **17.138**

The court is not generally impressed by the argument that the offeror gave inadequate costs information, because the offeree ought to assume that the costs will be reasonable once they have been assessed and, as such, a high claim for costs ought not to be a factor that would dissuade an offeree from accepting the offer.[376] **17.139**

The court also generally fails to be enthralled by the argument that an offeree was unable to accept an offer because evidence was uncertain or difficult to evaluate. Ward LJ, for example, had this to say on the topic: **17.140**

> 'It is almost inevitable in all litigation that the nature of the outcome cannot be certainly predicted until after the evidence has been given and even then there is no certainty as to the outcome until the judge has decided the case on that evidence. In this litigation the [evidence was such that] the litigation [was] all the more speculative. Far from there being a reason not to apply Part 36, it is in my judgment all the more reason for parties faced with that dilemma to make or to accept proper offers under Part 36. Not to beat the Part 36 offer has hazardous consequences as this case demonstrates. In these circumstances it is better to mediate than to litigate.'[377]

As such, an offeree who declines to accept an offer on the grounds that they are not able to assess the merits and value of the claim may be adopting a risky strategy. Similarly, declining to accept an offer in the hope that the expert evidence could be challenged would also be a risky strategy, because a mere shift of opinion by a party's experts would, in general, not be sufficient to justify the court denying the offeror the benefits of Part 36.[378] That said, as is set out below (see 17.142), circumstances may arise from time to time in which the court will afford a certain amount of leeway to an offeree where the evidence actually changed (as opposed to merely being uncertain). **17.141**

Evidential developments In a medically fascinating personal injury claim arising out of a collision between jet skis, Judge Denyer QC found that it would be unjust to require a claimant to pay a defendant's costs as a result of the former accepting the latter's Part 36 offer about two years after it was made, because of the fact that the medical evidence **17.142**

---

[374] In *Barclays Bank Plc v Christie Owen & Davies Ltd* (unreported), 24 November 2016, Ch D, at [26], Mr Spearman QC had this to say: 'To my mind, it would be very unfortunate if a CPR Part 36 offer did not have the typical effects indicated by the rule because the defendant could not make an informed assessment as to what to do, as that would tend towards the result that an offer would never be effective to produce the indemnity costs consequences and so forth unless made very late in the day or, if made earlier, would not be effective to trigger the indemnity costs regime until a much later date.'

[375] See *Thai Airways International Public Co Ltd v KI Holdings Co Ltd & Ors* [2015] EWHC 1476 Comm. This decision should, perhaps, be treated with caution, because many of the cases referred to in 17.139–17.141 were not drawn to the court's attention: see *Barclays Bank Plc v Christie Owen & Davies Ltd* (unreported), 24 November 2016, Ch D, at [23], *per* Richard Spearman QC.

[376] See *Mehjoo v Harben Barker (a firm)* [2013] EWHC 1669 (AB), at [29]–[35], *per* Silber J. See also *Thinc Group Ltd v Kingdom* [2013] EWCA Civ 1306, at [20] and [25], *per* Macur LJ.

[377] *Shovelar v Lane* [2011] EWCA Civ 802, at [53] and [54]. This was on the grounds that costs would be assessed at a reasonable sum on assessment.

[378] *Downing v Peterborough & Stamford Hospitals NHS Foundation Trust* [2014] EWHC Civ 4216 (QB), at [62], *per* Eady J. See also *Application in Private* [2017] EWHC 3606 (Comm), *per* Sir Jeremy Cooke.

radically changed after the offer was made.[379] Black LJ came to a similar conclusion in a case in which the prognosis in respect of a small child who had suffered brain damage had been difficult to determine.[380] Such cases are, however, at the very edge of what can be said to be the normal range of cases and it would not generally be appropriate to regard ordinary evidential developments as sufficient to satisfy the injustice test. In this regard, Gross LJ had this to say:

> '[It] is very important not to undermine the salutary purpose of Part 36 offers. It is important too that in considering often attractively advanced submissions as to uncertainty the court should not be drawn into microscopic examination of the litigation details. It is true that every case in this area is fact-specific but the important point is that there is a general rule which emerges from Part 36, namely, that if the offer is not accepted within time then the claimant bears the costs of the defendant until such time as the offer is accepted. If, of course, the offeree can show injustice, then a different situation will prevail—but it is up to the offeree to show injustice, not simply that it may have been difficult to form a view as to the outcome of the litigation. The whole point of the Part 36 offer is to shift the incidence of the risk as to costs onto the offeree. [It] is important not to undermine that salutary purpose.'[381]

Gross LJ went on to say that the conduct of the offeree may be relevant where reliance is placed on the fact that there were evidential developments, implying that if the offeree had requested a stay immediately after the offer had been made, this may have been a factor that would have been relevant.[382]

17.143 **Developments extraneous to the parties** It may be that an offeror finds themselves in the happy position of having beaten their offer as a result of serendipity rather than sound judgment. Where this is so, the injustice test may be satisfied. An example is a case in which a claimant beat its offer only because of a fall in the value of sterling as against the US dollar—and hence Leggatt J found that it would be unjust to allow the claimant the full benefit of the offer.[383] Another example is where Thirwall LJ (sitting as a judge of the High Court) found that it would be unjust to allow an offeror the benefit of an offer that had been beaten as a result of a change in the discount rate.[384]

17.144 **Relevance of experience of legal advisers** Whilst it would be rare for it to be regarded as being a significant factor of itself, the fact that a party was represented by experienced legal advisers may be relevant in the sense that it may add weight to the argument that that party was able to evaluate the offer properly. This would be particularly so where an experienced lawyer ought to have released the risks that the litigation posed.[385]

---

379 At the time the offer was made and for a considerable period thereafter, the medical evidence was that the claimant had suffered hypoxic brain damage as a result of a respiratory complication arising out of the collision, but, in due course, imaging taken at about the time of the collision confirmed that the claimant in fact had Pick's disease (a neurodegenerative disease that could mimic hypoxic damage): see *Hillier v Adams* (unreported), 17 March 2015, QBD, Bristol Civil Justice Centre, at [12].

380 See *SG v Hewitt* [2012] EWCA Civ 1053.

381 *Briggs v CEF Holdings Ltd* [2017] EWCA Civ 2363, at [36].

382 *Ibid*, at [39].

383 *Novus Aviation Ltd v Alubaf Arab International Bank BSC(c)* [2016] EWHC 1937 (Comm), at [18]–[26].

384 *Marsh v Ministry of Justice* [2017] EWHC 3185 (QB), at [50].

385 See, eg, *Bent v Highways and Utilities Construction & Anor* [2011] EWCA Civ 1539, at [2].

17.145 **Battle of offers** It may be that an offeree makes an offer that is less advantageous to them than the terms of an original offer made by their opponent. Where this is so, then (assuming all else to be equal) it would be open to the court to find that it would be unjust to award that party the benefit of the offer for the period after the expiry of the 'relevant period' following the original offer.[386] To give the court the ability to make such a finding, however, the other party (that is, the original offeror) would have to invoke the 'just-out-of-time jurisdiction' (see 17.173–17.175) unless the 'relevant period' following the subsequent offer had already expired. As can be seen from what is set out in respect of that jurisdiction, it would be a risk-laden strategy to make any assumptions about what the court would be likely to do where there has been a battle of offers.

17.146 **Partial success and failed issues** The mere fact that an offeror may have failed on a number of issues will not of itself make it unjust to displace the general rule that that party will be entitled to costs from the date of expiry of the 'relevant period'.[387]

17.147 **Not necessarily penal** In deciding whether it would be unjust to make such an award of costs on the indemnity basis, it should be remembered that an award under CPR, r 36.17, does not carry punitive overtones. Chadwick LJ had the following to say (albeit in the context of the original Part 36):

> 'To make the order carries no implied disapproval of the defendant's conduct; nor any stigma. Properly understood, the making of such an order in a case to which [the then equivalent of CPR, r 36.17(1)(b)] applies indicates only that the court, when addressing the task which it is set by that rule, has not considered it unjust to make the order for indemnity costs for which the rule provides.'[388]

In a similar vein (albeit in a case in which the parties' conduct comprised 'brinkmanship, professional discourtesy or a failure to appreciate the duty of each party to help the court to further the overriding objective of the procedural code'), Macur LJ said that costs on the indemnity basis gave 'credence to the significance of the effect of the Part 36 offer and [was] not a value judgment of the ... conduct in the lower court'.[389]

17.148 These comments undoubtedly remain true, but it should be borne in mind that Vos C has now explained that whilst use of the word 'penal' is 'probably unhelpful', the court has a discretion to include a non-compensatory element to the award.[390] This is discussed in more detail at 56.90–56.100.

17.149 **Offers to accept modest discounts** It has always been the case that an offer must be authentic in the sense that it involves a genuine element of concession on the part of the offeror (see 17.153).[391] The present-day Part 36 confirms this by specifically requiring the court to consider whether the offer was a genuine attempt to settle the

[386] See, eg, *Bailes v Bloom* (unreported), 23 November 2015, QBD, *per* Simler J.

[387] *Ted Baker plc v AXA Insurance UK plc* [2014] EWHC 4178 (Comm), at [17] and [22], *per* Eder J.

[388] *McPhilemy v Times Newspapers Ltd* [2001] EWCA Civ 993, at [9], echoing the comments of Lord Woolf MR in *Petrotrade Inc v Texaco Ltd* [2001] 4 All ER 853, at [62]–[64].

[389] *Thinc Group Ltd v Kingdom* [2013] EWCA Civ 1306, at [22].

[390] See *OMV Petrom SA v Glencore International AG* [2017] EWCA Civ 195, at [38].

[391] See, eg, *East West Corporation v DKBS* [2002] All ER(D) 361, at [14], in which Thomas J found that a claimant's offer to accept 100 per cent of the claim was a 'tactical ploy'. In a similar vein, see *R (on the application of MVN) v London Borough of Greenwich* [2015] EWHC 2663 (Admin), at [29], *per* Picken J.

proceedings,[392] which, presumably, is an attempt to draw the court's attention to the fact that it has the power to deny an offeror the full benefit of having made an offer if it was, in truth, a device to invoke Part 36 without any offer of genuine compromise. The term 'tactical offer' is sometimes used to describe such an offer, but—in the editor's view—this is not an appropriate terminology because all Part 36 offers are, in varying degrees, tactical.[393]

17.150 *The law prior to 6 April 2015* In a case (decided under the original Part 36) in which the offer was to accept 95 per cent of the full value of the claim, the Court of Appeal was divided as to what effect, if any, such an offer should have on the basis upon which costs were awarded—perhaps a reflection of the fact that the offer was close to being an offer to accept a *de minimis* reduction. Jonathan Parker LJ (dissenting) remarked:

> 'In order to qualify for the incentives provided by paragraphs (2) and (3) of the rule a claimant's Part 36 offer must represent at the very least a genuine and realistic attempt by the claimant to resolve the dispute by agreement. Such an offer is to be contrasted with one which creates no real opportunity for settlement but is merely a tactical step designed to secure the benefit of the incentives. That is not to say that the offer must be one which it would be unreasonable for the defendant to refuse; that would be too strict a test ... In some cases, an offer which allows only a small discount from 100 per cent success on the claim may be a genuine and realistic offer; in other cases, it may not. It is for the judge in every case to consider whether, in the circumstances of that particular case, and taking into account the factors listed in paragraph (5) of rule 36.21, it would be unjust to make the order sought.'[394]

17.151 Schiemann LJ and Tuckey LJ took a different view. In particular, Schiemann LJ went on to emphasise that where a claimant has made and beaten an offer to accept only a very small discount, the question is not whether it would be unjust to award costs on the indemnity basis, but whether it would be unjust *not* to award costs on the indemnity basis (see 17.120). He opined that it would have been unjust to deprive the offeror of the benefit of the offer mentioned above, but he went on to say:

> '[C]ircumstances can exist where, notwithstanding that a claimant has recovered in full after making a Part 36 offer for marginally less, he will not be awarded costs on the indemnity basis. I do not consider that Part 36 was intended to produce a situation in which a claimant was automatically entitled to costs on the indemnity basis provided only that he made an offer pursuant to Part 36.10 in an amount marginally less than the claim.'[395]

17.152 Tuckey LJ added these comments:

> 'I would however add that if it was self-evident that the offer made was merely a tactical step designed to secure the benefit of the incentives provided by the Rule (eg an offer to settle for 99.9% of the full value of the claim) I would agree with Jonathan Parker LJ that the judge would have a discretion to refuse indemnity costs.'[396]

---

392 CPR, r 36.17(5)(e).

393 Indeed, Norris J has made the point that all Part 36 offers are tactical in the sense that they are designed to take advantage of the incentives provided by Part 36: *Wharton v Bancroft* [2012] EWHC 91 (Ch), at [22].

394 *Huck v Robson* [2002] EWCA Civ 398, at [63].

395 *Ibid*, at [81].

396 *Ibid*, at [71].

Thus, in general, a pre-5-April-2007 offer to accept a modest discount would not result in an award of costs on the indemnity basis if it was merely a 'tactical step',[397] but otherwise it should not be disregarded. It seems that this continues to be the law under the pre-2015 Part 36, in which regard Henderson J had this to say: **17.153**

> 'The concept of an "offer to settle" is nowhere defined in Part 36. I think it clear, however, that a request to a defendant to submit to judgment for the entirety of the relief sought by the claimant cannot be an "offer to settle" within the meaning of Part 36. If it were otherwise, any claimant could obtain the favourable consequences of a successful Part 36 offer, including the award of indemnity costs, by the simple expedient of making an "offer" which required total capitulation by the defendant. In my judgment the offer must contain some genuine element of concession on the part of the claimant . . .'[398]

Thus Henderson J came to much the same conclusion as in the cases referred to above, but he did so by a different route—namely, that a putative offer that does not contain some genuine element of concession on the part of the offeror is not a Part 36 offer at all.

The law on and after 6 April 2015 As has already been explained, the present-day Part 36 now expressly requires the court to consider whether the offer was a genuine attempt to settle the proceedings.[399] It is not known whether this will change the way in which the court approaches such issues, but it is worth noting that the test of whether an offer is 'a genuine attempt to settle the proceedings' is not the same as a test of whether there was some 'genuine element of concession' or whether the offer was a 'tactical step'. It could be argued that the new test implies a need for a more earnest intent to bring the proceedings to an end than previously. That said, there have been instances of the court finding that an offer to accept a 5 per cent discount should not be dismissed as a derisory offer[400] and Foskett J has said that an argument that an offer to accept a 10 per cent discount in a clinical negligence case was not a genuine attempt to settle to proceedings could hardly ever succeed.[401] Moreover, it should not be forgotten that the purpose of the 78th update was to align Part 36 with case law (see 17.17); as such, it is easily arguable that the 'new' law is largely a continuation of that which has gone before. **17.154**

Offers for outcomes that are not available to the court It may be that the offer is for a result that would not, even theoretically, be an outcome that would be available to the court (such as where a claimant with an all-or-nothing claim offers to accept a modest discount). Edwards-Stuart J has found that this fact would not, of itself, result in the offeror being denied the benefits of having made the offer.[402] **17.155**

Offers in respect of factual issues There is no reason why an offer should not be made in respect of some aspect of the litigation that turns on a point of fact, but Picken J found, in the context of a disputed age assessment, that an 'offer' that a child's age should be as **17.156**

397 Indeed, such an offer was dismissed as being tactical in *Fotedar v St George's Healthcare NHS Trust (No 2)* [2005] All ER (D) 33 (QB).

398 *AB v CD & Ors* [2011] EWHC 602 (Ch), at [22].

399 CPR, r 36.17(5)(e).

400 See, eg, *Jockey Club Racecourse Ltd v Willmott Dixon Construction Ltd* [2016] EWHC 167 (TCC), *per* Edwards-Stuart J.

401 *JMX (a child by his mother and litigation friend, FMX) v Norfolk and Norwich Hospitals NHS Foundation Trust* [2018] EWHC 185 (QB), at [12].

402 *Jockey Club Racecourse Ltd v Willmott Dixon Construction Ltd* [2016] EWHC 167 (TCC), at [29]–[36].

asserted by the offeror was not an offer within the meaning of Part 36 because there was no element of compromise in such an offer.[403] Picken J was unpersuaded by the submission that the offer ought to be regarded as being a genuine offer because that would have resulted in costs savings,[404] but—whilst *obiter*—he did appear to accept that there was no reason in principle why a Part 36 offer should not apply to a disputed age assessment.[405]

17.157 **Apologies** In the context of a claim for misuse of private information, Arnold J has explained that the fact that a defendant offeror declined to make an apology or to agree to a statement in open court would not make it unjust for the offeree to bear the consequences of having failed to secure damages greater than had been offered.[406]

The relevance of costs

17.158 *The relevance of substantial costs being claimed* Warby J has commented that the mere fact that substantial costs are claimed is not a factor that should count against the court allowing a claimant the benefits of having made and beaten a Part 36 offer.[407] It should be noted, however, that, on the usual facts of the case before him (in which the 'additional amount' would have been payable on the costs rather than the damages because the claim was being treated as being a non-money claim), one of the reasons why Warby J decided that the injustice test was satisfied was because that 'additional amount' would be calculated by reference to the whole of the claimant's costs rather than those incurred since the date of the expiry of the relevant period.[408]

17.159 *Disputes solely about costs* It may be that the only dispute between the parties is the issue of costs and an offeree may wish to argue that it was reasonable not accept the offer if the parties were trying to resolve that dispute. This may be a reasonable argument in some circumstances, but it has its limits. In particular, it would rarely be appropriate for an offeree to proceed towards trial solely for the purposes of dealing with the issue of costs. Whilst it should be borne in mind that he did not expressly refer to the injustice test[409] and that, in any event, he ultimately decided the issue on other bases, Mann J had this to say about a case in which the claimant accepted a relatively low offer on the eve of trial:

> '... It would have been quite wrong and an abuse of the process to use court resources and have a 4–5 day trial involving all matters in issue on the pleadings when in fact the dispute was (on the facts) just about costs. ... The over-riding objective required that; the need to deal with matters proportionately meant that a trial was inappropriate. ... What would have been proportionate would have been for the defendant to accept that damages were agreed ... and agree that the court should determine the only outstanding issue of costs.'[410]

17.160 *The relevance of potential liability for costs* Whilst likely to be a rare occurrence, it may be that a defendant is able to point to the fact that if the offer had been accepted, it would

[403] See *R (on the application of MVN) v London Borough of Greenwich* [2015] EWHC 2663 (Admin), at [28].

[404] See *ibid*, at [43].

[405] See *ibid*, at [45].

[406] See *Ali v Channel 5 Broadcast Ltd* [2018] EWHC 840 (Ch) at [51].

[407] *Elsevier Ltd v Munro* [2014] EWHC 2728 (QB), at [8].

[408] See *ibid*, at [11] and [12].

[409] This is because Mann J was dealing with a pre-2015 Part 36 offer.

[410] *Jordan v MGN Ltd* [2017] EWHC 1937 (Ch), at [45], citing *Hanspaul v Ward* [2016] EWHC 1358 (Ch).

have resulted in liability for costs that could only have been avoided by not accepting the offer. For the reasons set out at 17.97, this would not be a good reason for finding that the claimant had failed to beat the offer, but it may be a factor that goes to whether it would be unjust to allow the claimant the benefit (or full benefit) of having made and beaten it. An example of this is a case in which Andrew Popplewell J found that it would be unjust to allow a claimant the benefit of an offer because it 'was, in commercial terms, and taking account of its costs consequences, too ambitious'.[411]

Specific persons A litigant's status may have a bearing on the way in which the injustice test is to be applied. **17.161**

- **Patients** Lang J has commented that the fact that the offeree lacks mental capacity would not of itself be sufficient to justify depriving an offeror the benefits of Part 36 (although it is a factor that may be taken into account).[412] It is likely that the points made about children (below) would also apply to patients.
- **Children** Both Black LJ[413] and Arden LJ[414] have concluded that the fact that the offeree is a child is not of itself sufficient to satisfy the test of injustice. Arden LJ went on to explain that this is because a child already has the protection of a litigation friend and of the need for the court's approval of any settlement, so they should not need any additional protection.[415]
- **Litigants in person** Whilst he was at pains to stress the fact that each case must be decided on its own facts, Longmore LJ found that the injustice test was met in a case in which the offeree was a litigant in person who accepted the offer after having been reminded of the existence of the offer by the offeror.[416] There is, however, no authority to suggest that litigants in person are entitled to expect such an approach.
- **Claimant or defendant?** If the reality is that it is the defendant who is trying to prove the claim and the claimant who is opposing it, this is a factor that can be taken into account.[417]
- **Part 20 defendants** The fact that an offeree was not able to accept an offer without a back-to-back agreement with its own Part 20 defendant is not a factor that would carry much weight.[418]
- **Adverse personal circumstances** Whilst she did not lay down any rule or guidance, Macur LJ rejected the notion that an offeree's personal circumstances mitigated the effect of failing to beat a Part 36 offer.[419]

---

[411] *Transocean Drilling UK Ltd v Providence Resources plc* [2016] EWHC 2611 (Comm), at [35].

[412] *Lumb v Hampsey* [2011] EWHC 2808 (QB), at [4]. It should be noted that Lang J was exercising a discretion that was less restrictive than it now is, because a test of injustice now applies; that said, this is the test that she applied notwithstanding the fact that, at the time, it was not an express requirement of the then Rules.

[413] *SG v Hewitt* [2012] EWCA Civ 1053, at [30]–[34].

[414] *Ibid*, at [78].

[415] See *ibid*, at [78], in which Arden LJ applied *Abada v Gray & MIB* (unreported), 9 May 1997, CA.

[416] *Kunaka v Barclays Bank plc* [2010] EWCA Civ 1035, at [9] and [10].

[417] *Procter & Gamble Co v Svenska Cellulosa Aktiebolaget SCA* [2012] EWHC 2839 (Ch), at [55]–[62], *per* Hilyard J.

[418] See *Greenwich Millennium Village Ltd v Essex Services Group Plc (Formerly Essex Electrical Group Ltd)* [2014] EWHC 1099 (TCC), at [36], *per* Coulson J.

[419] *Thinc Group Ltd v Kingdom* [2013] EWCA Civ 1306, at [20] (although this was in respect of a claimant's Part 36 offer).

- **Injured or unwell people** Whilst he was dealing with the matter under CPR, r 44.2, in the context of a withdrawn offer, Lewison LJ has commented that whilst a person may act reasonably in not accepting an offer at a time when there are uncertainties as to their prognosis, this may change if, with the passage of time, that person's prognosis becomes more certain.[420]

Interaction between Part 36 and Part 45

17.162 This topic is addressed in detail in Chapter 50. What follows is only a brief summary.

17.163 It may be the case that there is a putative conflict between the provisions of Part 36, which may pull in the direction of a party being awarded costs or being awarded costs on the indemnity basis, and Part 45, which may pull in the direction of costs being fixed. The following points may be made in this regard.

- **CPR, Part 45, Section IIIA** It may be that a claimant makes a Part 36 offer (either during the period when the claim is in the relevant Portal or otherwise); if so, then once the claim has exited the relevant Protocol, the claimant may obtain judgment that is more advantageous than that offer, in which case CPR, Part 45, Section IIIA, ostensibly applies. If this happens, then, as Dyson MR explained, the provisions in CPR, r 36.17(3) (as modified by CPR, r 36.21) will take precedence.[421] This is discussed in more detail at 50.287–50.296. Other situations regarding Part 36 offers are also addressed in those paragraphs.
- **CPR, Part 45, Section IV** Where a claimant is entitled to the benefit of having made and beaten a Part 36 offer, there is a tension between the provision of CPR, r 36.17(3), and the caps on costs in the Intellectual Property Enterprise Court Guide (IPEC). Judge Hacon considered *Broadhurst*, and whilst he did not find all of Dyson MR's observations to be relevant, on balance he found that CPR, r 36.17(3), takes precedence over the caps on costs in IPEC and that, as such, if a claimant is fortunate enough to beat their own Part 36 offer, neither the stage costs nor the overall cap will apply to any costs awarded on the indemnity basis as a result.[422] This is discussed in more detail at 50.336.

Acceptance, Rejection and Withdrawal of Part 36 Offers

Acceptance

17.164 Subject to certain restrictions relating to split trials (see 17.188),[423] then unless the court's permission is required (see 17.176), a Part 36 offer may be accepted at any time, including after the expiry of the 'relevant period'.[424] Rix LJ has confirmed that a Part 36 offer does

[420] *Rehill v Rider Holdings Ltd* [2014] EWCA Civ 42, at [14]–[22].

[421] *Broadhurst v Tan* [2016] EWCA Civ 94, at [22]–[28].

[422] *Phonographic Performance Ltd v Hagan* [2016] EWHC 3076 (IPEC), at [39].

[423] See CPR, r 36.12. This rule would apply in any case in which the trial of any part of the claim or of any issue arising in it started on or after 6 April 2015, regardless of when the offer was made: see the Civil Procedure (Amendment No 8) Rules 2014 (SI 2014/3299), r 18(2).

[424] CPR, r 36.11(2), or (in a case in which neither the offer was made nor any trial had started on or after 6 April 2015) CPR, r 36.9(2), of the pre-April 2015 Part 36: see the Civil Procedure (Amendment No 8) Rules 2014 (SI 2014/3299), r 18(2).

not cease to be capable of acceptance with the passage of time; it closes only with express withdrawal.[425]

Acceptance of an offer may take place in any of the following circumstances. **17.165**

- **Simple acceptance** This is where acceptance takes place within the 'relevant period' and without there being any need for permission (see 17.166). It is, by far, the most common mode of acceptance.
- **Acceptance were permission or adjudication is required** This is where, in the absence of agreement, the offeree must apply for permission before the offer can be accepted or the court is required to make a ruling as to costs (see 17.176).
- **Acceptance in particular circumstances** This is where there are particular circumstances that have a bearing on the offer, such as where there is a split trial or where the offer relates to only part of the claim (see 17.188).

The procedure of acceptance is addressed at 17.192.

Simple acceptance

This is the mode of acceptance that is by far the most common. Other than where the court's permission is required (see 17.176) and subject to certain restrictions concerning split trials (see 17.188), a Part 36 offer that has not been withdrawn may be accepted at any time during the 'relevant period'.[426] This is so regardless of whether or not the offeree has made a further offer[427] and regardless of the passage of time.[428] The claimant will be entitled to payment of the offered monies within the usual 14 days,[429] although the court now has power to vary that period.[430] The claimant is entitled to insist upon actual payment rather than having those monies set off against other monies.[431] **17.166**

Simple acceptance and costs Other than where permission to accept is required, then acceptance during the 'relevant period' will (where proceedings have been commenced[432]) result in the claimant acquiring a deemed entitlement to costs of the proceedings[433] up to the date of service of notice of acceptance,[434] payable on the standard basis.[435] This will include any costs incurred prior to the expiry of the 'relevant period' subject to any orders already made.[436] **17.167**

---

425 See *C v D* [2011] EWCA Civ 646, at [57].

426 See CPR, r 36.11(2), or (in a case in which neither the offer was made nor any trial had started on or after 6 April 2015), CPR, r 36.9(2), of the pre-April 2015 Part 36: see the Civil Procedure (Amendment No 8) Rules 2014 (SI 2014/3299), r 18(2).

427 See CPR, r 36.11(2).

428 See *C v D* [2011] EWCA Civ 646, at [57].

429 See CPR, r 36.14(6). If such sum is not paid within 14 days of acceptance of the offer, or such other period as has been agreed, the claimant may enter judgment for the unpaid sum: see CPR, r 36.14(6).

430 See *Titmus v General Motors UK Ltd* [2016] EWHC 2021 (QB), at [25]–[27], *per* Elizabeth Laing J. Whilst not binding see *Bingham v Abru Ltd* (unreported), 13 November 2015, Sheffield County Court, *per* Judge Robinson.

431 See *Cave v Bulley Davey (a firm)* [2013] EWHC 4246 (QB), *per* Judge Seymour QC.

432 See CPR, r 44.9(2).

433 The proceedings in question are the court proceedings to which the offer relates. Coulson J has explained that this would not include costs of other proceedings, such as prior adjudication proceedings: see *Wes Futures Ltd v Allen Wilson Construction Ltd* [2016] EWHC 2893 (TCC), at [8]–[18].

434 See CPR, rr 36.13(1) and 44.9(1)(b).

435 CPR, r 36.13(3).

436 *Ontulmus v Collett* [2014] EWHC 4117 (QB), at [91], *per* Warby J.

17.168 It seems to be the received view that—other than where the 'just-out-of-time jurisdiction' is invoked (see 17.173–17.175)—the court has no power to make any other costs order. In particular, where it was the claimant who made the offer, they would not be able to ask for costs on the indemnity basis,[437] and where the offer was made by a defendant, they would not be able to challenge the claimant's entitlement to costs.[438] Whilst it will rarely be necessary, the court will, however, be able to rule on the ambit of the offer, such as whether acceptance of the offer would cause one of a number of defendants to be liable for the costs of the other defendants.[439]

17.169 *Where there are multiple parties* Where there is more than one defendant and only one accepts an offer, the costs payable by that defendant will be limited to the cost of the proceedings against that defendant[440] (which will generally be costs attributable solely to that defendant's case *plus* their share of any generic costs).

17.170 It may be the case that, in a claim against two or more defendants, a Part 36 offer has been accepted so that the claim against only one of them has been compromised. Where this is so, the question may arise as to whether the defendant who has accepted the offer is liable for the costs of the whole of the proceedings or only those that relate specifically to that defendant. This is a question that will turn on the terms of the offer, but Jay J had the following to say about the meaning of the words 'the costs of the proceedings' in CPR, r 36.13(1):

> 'The ... issue turns on what is meant by the term, "the costs of the proceedings" ... I have no hesitation in concluding that the term means, in this context, "the costs of proceeding against the defendant against whom the deemed order has been made". Any broader definition would achieve obvious injustice and violate the language of the rule as seen in its proper contextual setting.'[441]

17.171 *Assignees, transferees and successors* Whilst the authorities on the point relate to pre-CPR payments into court rather than to Part 36 offers, it would seem that there is nothing so personal about a Part 36 offer that it would not be available to an assignee, transferee or successor of the offeree.[442] This is because the process of making offers is directed towards matching offers to claims, not to identifying an offer made to the claimant personally.[443]

17.172 **Simple acceptance of second or subsequent offer** For the reasons set out at 17.166,[444] if permission to accept is not required, then acceptance during the 'relevant period' will

---

437 See CPR, r 36.13(3). Whilst there is no authority specifically on the point, it seems that the generally received view (with which the editor concurs) is that unless the 'just-out-of-time jurisdiction' is invoked, the court does not have the power to deviate from costs being allowable on the standard basis.

438 The absence of any jurisdiction has been noted by Akenhead J in *Bellway Homes Ltd v Seymour (Civil Engineering Contractors) Ltd* [2013] EWHC 1890 (TCC), at [50] and [51].

439 See, eg, *Haynes v Department for Business Innovation and Skills* [2014] EWHC 643 (QB).

440 See *ibid*, *per* Jay J. Offers were made to ten defendants, but only one of them accepted; the claimant then discontinued against the others. Jay J found that the claimant was not entitled to recover all reasonable costs without those costs being disaggregated, apportioned or divided; on the contrary, the single paying party would pay its own individual costs, together with its share of the common costs.

441 *Ibid*, at [21].

442 See *Toprak Enerji Sanayi AS v Sale Tilney Technology Plc* [1994] 1 WLR 840.

443 See The White Book 2018, para 36.2.2.

444 Namely, the effect of CPR, r 36.13(3).

preclude the court from taking into account any other offers. In particular, where an offer has been renewed (or where an offer has been met with an identical counter-offer), the original offer will be disregarded if the most recent offer is accepted during its 'relevant period'.[445] In view of this, it would rarely be in the interests of an offeror to renew an offer (unless, of course, they were to want to do so for the purposes of achieving a compromise). If an offer were met with an identical counter-offer, then if the party who made the first offer wanted to rely on it, they should not accept the counter-offer during its 'relevant period'. One option would be to invoke the 'just-out-of-time jurisdiction' (see 17.173–17.175), but only if the risks of doing so are fully understood.

'Just-out-of-time jurisdiction' If an offeree wishes to accept an offer, but does not want the claimant to have the whole of their costs payable on the standard basis, the offeree has the option of invoking a device known as the just-out-of-time jurisdiction—that is, of waiting until immediately after the expiry of the 'relevant period' before accepting the offer.[446] This is intended to give the court the power to depart from the deeming provisions of CPR, r 36.13(1). The test that the court will apply will depend on whether the application is made by the claimant or the defendant. **17.173**

- **Defendant** If the jurisdiction is invoked by a defendant, the court will deprive the claimant of costs only if not to do so would be 'unjust'.[447] In theory, this will be so regardless of when the offer was made, but if the offer was made before 6 April 2015, it is arguable that a less restrictive test should apply in certain circumstances.[448] In general, the same test (that is, of injustice) will apply (see 17.180).
- **Claimant** If a claimant invokes the jurisdiction for the purposes of obtaining costs on the indemnity basis, then it is easily arguable that the court has a free hand to make whatever order it believes is appropriate.[449] It does not follow, however, that the court will automatically award costs on the indemnity basis in a case in which this would ordinarily happen under CPR, r 44.2, for the reasons set out at 17.182.

[445] In a case in which the most recent offer was on the same terms as the claimant had previously offered, Coulson J found that it would be wrong to import an indemnity costs presumption into what is now CPR, r 36.13: see *Fitzpatrick Contractors Ltd v Tyco Fire & Integrated Solutions (UK) Ltd* [2009] EWHC 274 (TCC), at [28].

[446] In *Dutton v Minards* [2015] EWCA Civ 984, at [11]–[13], it was noted that the offeree had waited until 1 minute after the expiry of the 'relevant period' to accept the offer. The existence of the jurisdiction has been acknowledged by Rix LJ in *Epsom College v Pierse Contracting Southern Ltd (formerly Biseley Construction Ltd) (in liquidation)* [2011] EWCA Civ 1449, at [64]. Moreover, the jurisdiction was intentionally invoked with successful results in *Bailes v Bloom* (unreported), 23 November 2015, QBD, *per* Simler J.

[447] See CPR, r 36.13(5) and (6).

[448] Whilst the original CPR, r 36.10(5), stated that the test was whether the court should 'order otherwise', this was often interpreted as being a test of whether the default order would be 'unjust': see *Lumb v Hampsey* [2011] EWHC 2808 (QB), at [6]. It is arguable, however, that where a party has invoked the 'just-out-of-time jurisdiction', the correct test is simply that which was stated—namely, whether the court should 'order otherwise'. Whilst there are no reported cases on the point, the editor's experience is that the court's approach was to decide the matter on the merits.

[449] This is because the presumptions in CPR, r 36.13(5), make no mention of the basis of costs. That said, the counter-argument is that Part 36 is a self-contained code and that, as such, the court is not able to exercise a discretion that is not expressly provided for within Part 36 itself.

17.174 It should be borne in mind that whilst the existence of the 'just-out-of-time jurisdiction' has been judicially acknowledged, it is very much on the fringes of received practice.[450] This is for the reasons given by Lewison LJ:

> 'The primary focus of [what is now CPR, r 36.13(5)] insofar as it enables a court to disapply the presumption is the costs incurred since the expiry of the relevant period. That is certainly how the point has arisen in previous cases. Here, by contrast, the Defendants seek to obtain advantage from the late acceptance of the Part 36 offer and, moreover, an advantage that relates to a period before the relevant period even began.'[451]

For the reasons set out below, it is a jurisdiction that—in the editor's view—ought to be invoked only rarely. Indeed, whilst it is no more than his opinion, this editor believes that it is best reserved for those cases in which it would be patently unfair to allow the offeror to benefit from a deemed order.[452]

17.175 *More than one offer and the 'just-out-of-time jurisdiction'* It may be that the reason why a party wishes to invoke the 'just-out-of-time jurisdiction' is because they are minded to accept a Part 36 offer (offer B) that an opponent has made in terms that are less favourable to that opponent than the terms of an offer (offer A) that the party in question had previously made; an example might be where the defendant had offered £10,000 (offer A), which, at a later stage, was met with a counter-offer to accept £9,000 (offer B). If the party who wishes to invoke the 'just-out-of-time jurisdiction' in respect of offer B is the defendant, then considerable caution ought to be exercised, for the following reasons.

(1) Even if one assumes that offer A was a Part 36 offer, acceptance of offer B would not mean that the costs consequences in CPR, r 36.17, would apply vis-à-vis offer A, because the failure on the part of the claimant to obtain an outcome more advantageous than offer A would not have come about as a result of judgment being entered.[453] In this regard, it should be noted that the purpose of making a Part 36 offer is to throw the risk of paying costs on the offeree if they fail to accept the offer within the 21-day period or to beat it at trial.[454]
(2) The primary focus of the rule that the 'just-out-of-time jurisdiction' invokes is on the costs incurred since the expiry of the relevant period, rather than on the period before that point in time (see 17.176).
(3) If the 'just-out-of-time jurisdiction' were to be invoked, the defendant would have to satisfy the injustice test to persuade the court to depart from the default

---

[450] Indeed, there are several authorities that say that if a defendant is justified in refusing to accept a Part 36 offer because it would be inappropriate for them to be condemned to pay the costs of the whole proceedings, this is a factor that the court can take into account: see, eg, *Fairclough Homes Ltd v Summers* [2012] UKSC 26, at [53]–[54], *per* Lord Clarke; *Medway Primary Care Trust v Marcus* [2011] EWCA Civ 750, at [51] and [52], *per* Tomlinson LJ; *Travelers Casualty and Surety Co of Canada v Sun Life Assurance Co of Canada (UK) Ltd* [2006] EWHC 2885 (Comm), at [86] *per* Christopher Clarke J. There was no mention of the just-out-of-time jurisdiction in any of those cases.

[451] *Dutton v Minards* [2015] EWCA Civ 984, at [42].

[452] Whilst in only a County Court case at first instance, the author has seen a defendant make successful use of the jurisdiction in a case in which the claimant made an offer to accept a tiny percentage of what he originally claimed, this being shortly after he had been served with evidence that proved beyond any doubt that he had fraudulently exaggerated his claim.

[453] *Dutton v Minards* [2015] EWCA Civ 984, at [38], *per* Lewison LJ.

[454] *Ibid*, at [39], referring to *SG v Hewitt* [2012] EWCA Civ 1053.

position—namely, that the claimant would be entitled to the whole of the costs (see 17.173–17.175).[455]

(4) It may be that, by accepting offer B, the defendant would achieve a reduction of the principal sum when compared with offer A, but this—as a starting point, at least—would be subject to the increase in costs since that offer had been made, that being a factor the court may take into account.[456]

(5) Finally, factual considerations may mean that the injustice test is not satisfied—in particular, that:
   - the court would be able to take into account any reasons the claimant may advance to justify the fact that offer A had not been accepted (such as insufficient information);[457] and
   - moreover, it may be relevant that acceptance of offer B meant that the defendant avoided the risk of a greater sum being entered against them if the action went to trial.[458]

Where adjudication is required

There are two ways in which the court may be asked to make a ruling: first, where the court's permission is required as a condition of acceptance (see CPR, r 36.11(3)); and secondly, where, in certain circumstances, there is a dispute about costs (see CPR, r 36.13(4)). The circumstances in which these provisions will apply are as follows. **17.176**

- **Where permission is required** The issue of whether permission is required may arise in the following circumstances.
  - **After start of trial** Permission is required to accept an offer after the trial[459] has started.[460] There is no implied term that an offer may not be accepted once the trial has begun,[461] but there will often (although not always[462]) be a degree of judicial reluctance to allow an offeree to accept an offer at such a stage.[463]

---

[455] *Dutton v Minards* [2015] EWCA Civ 984, at [41], *per* Lewison LJ.

[456] *Ibid*, at [22].

[457] See, eg, *ibid*, at [47].

[458] *Ibid*, at [22]; see also *ibid*, at [40].

[459] If the offer was made in respect of detailed assessment proceeding and if the assessment hearing had begun before 15 April 2015, the court lacked the power to give permission: see the 'old' CPR, rr 36.11(3)(d) and 47.20(4)(c). Where the assessment began after that date, then the court has the power to grant permission.

[460] Where the offer was made on or after 6 April 2015, or where a trial of any issue or part of the claim began on or after that date, the test for determining whether permission is required is whether the trial was 'in progress': see CPR, r 36.11(3)(d), and Civil Procedure (Amendment No 8) Rules 2014 (SI 2014/3299), r 18(2). This is defined as being from the time when the trial started until the time when judgment is given or handed down: see CPR, r 36.3(d). In the unlikely event that the offer had been made before 6 April 2015 and the trial in question had begun before that date—see the Civil Procedure (Amendment No 8) Rules 2014 (SI 2014/3299), r 18(2)—then the test of whether permission is needed is whether 'the trial has started': see CPR, r 36.9(3)(d), of the pre-April 2015 Part 36. In the even more unlikely event of the offer having been made before 5 April 2007, then it is doubtful whether an offer could be accepted after the hearing to which it related had begun: *Hawley v Luminar Leisure plc* [2006] EWCA Civ 30, at [29], *per* Brooke LJ. As such, the issue of permission would not arise.

[461] Coulson J doubted if there was ever a basis for coming to such a conclusion and went on to explain that such a conclusion would run counter to the provisions in what is now CPR, r 36.11(3)(d): see *Sampla v Rushmoor Borough Council* [2008] EWHC 2616 (TCC), at [39]–[41].

[462] See, eg, *Application in Private* [2017] EWHC 3606 (Comm), at [22], *per* Sir Jeremy Cooke.

[463] See, eg, *Houghton v PB Donoghue (Haulage & Plant Hire Ltd)* [2017] EWHC 1738 (Ch), at [7], in which Morgan J had this to say: '[If] an offeree, when he sees the way the wind is blowing in the trial, changes

- **After the end of trial** Unless the parties agree otherwise, an offer made before 6 April 2015 may not be accepted in the period between the end of the trial and the judgment being handed down.[464] Where the offer was made on or after that date, however, the court is able to grant permission.[465]
- **More than one defendant** Permission will be required where the offer has been made by one or more, but not all, of a number of defendants and where none of the conditions set out in the footnotes has been met.[466]
- **CRU** Permission is required where the offer includes deductible benefits, and where the 'relevant period' has expired and further deductible amounts have been paid to the claimant since the date of the offer.[467]
- **Fatal accidents** Permission is required where an apportionment is required for the purposes of the Fatal Accidents Act 1976 and the Law Reform (Miscellaneous Provisions) Act 1934.[468]
- **Change in circumstances** Rix LJ has confirmed that a significant change of circumstances would not give rise to a general ground on which the court's permission would be required to accept a Part 36 offer.[469]

• **Where a ruling on costs is required** In the absence of agreement on the point, the need for the court to rule on costs will arise where:
  - the 'relevant period' has expired—that is, where a Part 36 offer that relates to the whole of the claim is accepted after expiry of the 'relevant period' (see 17.177);[470]
  - less than 21 days before trial—that is, where a Part 36 offer that was made less than 21 days before the start of a trial is accepted (see 17.184);[471] and
  - offers regarding part of claim—that is, where a Part 36 offer that does not relate to the whole of the claim is accepted at any time,[472] but only if the offer

his attitude and wants to accept an offer that he previously did not want to accept, that is a change of circumstances which means that it may no longer be appropriate to allow the offeree to accept the offer which is still on the table.' In coming to this conclusion, Morgan J referred to similar comments made in *Capital Bank Plc v Stickland* [2004] EWCA Civ 1677, *Sampla v Rushmoor Borough Council* [2008] EWHC 2616 (TCC), at [45]–[55], and *Nulty v Milton Keynes Borough Council* [2012] EWHC 730 (QB), at [16]–[17].

464 This is because, under the pre-April 2015 Part 36, CPR, r 36.9(5), provided that 'unless the parties agree, a Part 36 offer may not be accepted after the end of the trial but before judgment is handed down'. In the unlikely event of an offeree wishing to accept an offer that was made before 5 April 2007, then Brooke LJ had 'no doubt at all that it carried an implied term that it would not be available for acceptance after the hearing ended and the court reserved judgment': *Hawley v Luminar Leisure plc* [2006] EWCA Civ 30, at [29].

465 See CPR, r 36.11(3)(d), which allows the court to grant permission if the trial is 'in progress'; CPR, r 36.3(d), defines 'in progress' as being 'from the time when it starts until the time when judgment is given or handed down'.

466 See CPR, rr 39n.11(3)(a) and 36.15(4). Permission will not be required if any of the situations in CPR, r 36.15(2) and (3) exist, which provisions read as follows: '(2) If the defendants are sued jointly or in the alternative, the claimant may accept the offer if—(a) the claimant discontinues the claim against those defendants who have not made the offer; and (b) those defendants give written consent to the acceptance of the offer. (3) If the claimant alleges that the defendants have a several liability to the claimant, the claimant may—(a) accept the offer; and (b) continue with the claims against the other defendants if entitled to do so.'

467 See CPR, rr 36.11(3)(b) and 36.22(3)(b). Any such application must contain the particulars set out in PD 36, para 3.3(1) and (2).

468 See CPR, rr 36.11(3)(c) and 41.3A.

469 See *C v D* [2011] EWCA Civ 646, at [20].

470 See CPR, r 36.13(4)(b).

471 See CPR, r 36.13(4)(a).

472 See CPR, r 36.13(4)(c). This will not apply, however, if the offer relates to only part of the claim, but within the 'relevant period' the claimant abandons the balance of the claim: see CPR, r 36.13(2).

was made by the claimant or the claimant abandons the balance of the claim (see 17.185).[473]

Adjudication and acceptance of Part 36 offers after the 'relevant period'

Late acceptance of Part 36 offers and the incidence of costs Where a Part 36 offer is accepted after the expiry of the 'relevant period', then, unless it would be unjust to do so, the offeree must pay the offeror's costs from the date of expiry of the 'relevant period' to the date of acceptance.[474] This test (the 'injustice test') is in many ways the same as would apply if the offer were to be beaten by way of a judgment,[475] but there are differences in the way in which the court will approach such a case. **17.177**

The fact that the injustice test on late acceptance is broadly the same as that which applies following judgment does not mean that acceptance of an offer should be equated with 'beating' that offer by obtaining judgment. This is because judgment and acceptance are wholly different. In particular, where an offer has been accepted, the claim will be stayed,[476] so (in the absence of consent[477]) it will not be open to the court to enter judgment.[478] This means that CPR, r 36.13(1) and (5), will apply and the court will be precluded from dealing with the matter in accordance with CPR, r 36.17(3) or (4).[479] This may have a significant bearing on the costs and interest that are payable, especially if the offer in question was made by the claimant. **17.178**

The injustice test is discussed in detail at 17.118–17.163. If the offer was made on or after 6 April 2015, the offeree would have to persuade the court not to apply the following presumption (CPR, r 36.13(5)): **17.179**

> '(5) Where [an offer has been accepted following the expiry of the "relevant period"] but the parties cannot agree the liability for costs, the court must, unless it considers it unjust to do so, order that—
> (a) the claimant be awarded costs up to the date on which the "relevant period" expired; and
> (b) the offeree do pay the offeror's costs for the period from the date of expiry of the "relevant period" to the date of acceptance.
> (6) In considering whether it would be unjust to make the orders specified in paragraph (5), the court must take into account all the circumstances of the case including the matters listed in rule 36.17(5).'

On the face of it, this injustice test appears to be a marked change from the test that applied before 6 April 2015 (which was that the court could make a different order as a matter of discretion[480]), but the reality was that the test the court used to apply was **17.180**

---

[473] See CPR, rr 36.13(4)(c) and 36.13(2).
[474] See CPR, rr 36.13(4)(b) and 36.13(5).
[475] See CPR, r 36.17(3) and (4).
[476] See CPR, r 36.13(1).
[477] See *Ontulmus v Collett* [2014] EWHC 4117 (QB), at [39] and [40], in which Warby J entered judgment without opposition.
[478] Whilst it related to the pre-April 2015 Part 36, see *Jolly v Harsco Infrastructure Services Ltd* [2012] EWHC 3086 (QB), at [13]–[15], *per* Cranston J.
[479] *Ibid.*
[480] See CPR, r 36.13(5) and (6), and compare those provisions with the original CPR, r 36.10(5).

broadly the same as the present-day test of injustice.[481] Lang J had this to say about the old test:

> 'The test which I apply is whether the usual costs order set out in [the equivalent of CPR, r 36.13(4)] should be departed from because it would be unjust for the [offeree] to pay the [offeror's] costs after the expiry of the relevant period, in the particular circumstances of this case. Such a departure would be the exception rather than the rule.'[482]

It therefore appears that the new wording is a codification of the established practice (in accordance with the points made at 17.17).

17.181 For the purposes of the injustice test, the main difference between late acceptance and 'beating' an offer at trial is that the offeror could have avoided being exposed to the consequences of CPR, r 36.13(5), by the expediency of withdrawing the Part 36 offer, or withdrawing it and replacing it with a *Calderbank* offer with restrictions on the costs that it was willing to pay.[483] In practice, this makes it particularly difficult for an offeror to avoid the ordinary costs consequences of Part 36.

17.182 *Late acceptance of Part 36 offers and the basis of costs* When an offer is accepted late, there is no reason to believe the court lacks the jurisdiction to make that order on the indemnity basis.[484] In a case in which, on the eve of trial, a claimant accepted an offer about 30 months after it had been made and in circumstances in which he had failed properly to respond to other offers made in the interim, Mann J condemned the claimant to pay costs on the indemnity basis.[485]

17.183 Where a defendant accepts an offer after the expiry of the 'relevant period', then, unless the court were to exercise its discretion in the claimant's favour, the entitlement to costs would ordinarily be on the standard basis—despite the fact that the claimant had secured a result that was 'at least as advantageous' as their offer.[486] Coulson J has made it clear that there is no presumption that costs should be payable on the indemnity basis where a Part 36 offer made by a claimant has been accepted after the expiry of the 'relevant period'.[487] Moreover, whilst his reasoning would hold good in only a minority of cases,

---

481 See, eg, *Lumb v Hampsey* [2011] EWHC 2808 (QB), in which Lang J applied a test of injustice for the purpose of then CPR, r 36.10(5). This approach was endorsed by the Court of Appeal in *SG v Hewitt* [2012] EWCA Civ 1053. The Court of Appeal took a similar view in *Matthews v Metal Improvements Co Inc* [2007] EWCA Civ 215, at [29], in relation to Part 36 as it was before it was revised in 2007. See also *Dutton v Minards* [2015] 984, at [15], *per* Lewison LJ.

482 *Lumb v Hampsey* [2011] EWHC 2808 (QB), at [6].

483 See *Tiuta Plc v Rawlinson & Hunter (a firm)* [2016] EWHC 3480 (QB), at [51], *per* Andrew Baker J. See also *Optical Express v Associated Newspapers (Costs)* [2017] EWHC 2707 (QB), at [22]–[23] and [27(3)], *per* Warby J.

484 This is because the default provisions (CPR, r 36.13(5)) make no mention of the basis of costs, so the test of 'unjustness' seems not to apply. See, eg, *Jordan v MGN Ltd* [2017] EWHC 1937 (Ch). Whilst *obiter* and not binding, see also *McKeown v Venton* (unreported), 12 June 2017, Liverpool County Court, at [6], [40] and [42], *per* Judge Graham Wood QC, citing *Petrotrade Inc v Texaco Ltd (Note)* [2002] 1 WLR 947.

485 See *Jordan v MGN Ltd* [2017] EWHC 1937 (Ch), at [62]–[67] and [72], *per* Mann J.

486 One reason why this is so is because the result would not amount to 'judgment being entered' and, as such, CPR, r 36.17(1), would not apply.

487 *Fitzpatrick Contractors Ltd v Tyco Fire & Integrated Solutions (UK) Ltd* [2009] EWHC 274 (TCC), at [28]. Whilst not binding, see also *Richardson v Wakefield Council* (unreported), 9 June 2017, Wakefield County Court, at [27]–[31], *per* Judge Gosnell; *McKeown v Venton* (unreported), 12 June 2017, Liverpool County Court, at [43], *per* Judge Graham Wood QC.

Tugendhat J has explained that where a claimant secures a commercial settlement that beats one of their own offers, it would not necessarily follow that the claimant should be afforded the benefit of their offer.[488] Tugendhat J's reasoning was that the provisions of Part 36 are there to promote a commercial approach to litigation in accordance with the overriding objective, not to reward claimants who pursue claims in which the costs outweigh the benefit. There is nothing in either of these judgments to suggest that it would not be open to the court to make an award on the indemnity basis if that is what the court thought was appropriate.

Less than 21 days before trial Where the offer was made less than 21 days before the start of trial, then, unless the parties are able to agree, the court will need to determine the issue of costs.[489] The presumptions referred to at 17.179 will not apply.[490] **17.184**

Offers in respect of part of the claim or the whole of the claim Where an offer is in respect of only part of the claim, that part will be stayed immediately upon the offer being accepted.[491] If the claimant abandons the balance of the claim, then, unless the court orders otherwise, the claimant will be entitled to the costs of the whole of that part of the claim up to the date of serving notice of acceptance.[492] If the claimant does not abandon the balance of the claim, then the court will have to determine the issue of costs.[493] There are similar provisions for claims to which CPR, Part 45, Section IIIA, applies[494] (see 50.288). **17.185**

It will not always be immediately apparent whether an offer can be said to relate to only a part of the claim. In a case in which the defendant had made an offer putatively in respect of only one aspect of the claimant's injuries (on the basis that the other injuries had allegedly been caused by someone else), Stadlen J found that the offer was capable of being accepted in respect of the whole claim and that the claimant was entitled to her costs accordingly.[495] **17.186**

The terms of the offer may be relevant. In a case in which the offer said, in terms, that the defendant would pay the whole of the costs, Lewison LJ found that this was a factor to be taken into account for the purposes of deciding whether the defendant was liable for the claimant's costs.[496] **17.187**

Miscellaneous circumstances

Split-trial cases Where there has been one trial or more, but not all issues in the case have been determined,[497] then a Part 36 offer that relates to only parts of the claim or issues that have already been decided can no longer be accepted.[498] Unless the parties agree, any other **17.188**

488 *D Pride & Partners v Institute for Animal Health* [2009] EWHC 1617 (QB), at [33]. On a different, but related point (ie late acceptance of an offer), see *Fitzpatrick Contractors Ltd v Tyco Fire & Integrated Solutions (UK) Ltd* [2009] EWHC 274 (TCC), at [28].
489 CPR, r 36.13(4)(a).
490 See CPR, r 36.13(5), which makes no mention of CPR, r 36.13(4)(a).
491 CPR r 36.14(3).
492 See CPR, r 36.13(2).
493 See CPR, r 36.13(4)(c).
494 See CPR, r 36.20(3).
495 *Sutherland v Turnbull* [2010] EWHC 2699 (QB), at [29]–[32].
496 See *Jopling v Leavesley & Anor* [2013] EWCA Civ 1605, at [10].
497 See CPR, rr 36.12(1) and 36m.3(e).
498 See CPR, r 36.12(2).

Part 36 offer (that is, any offer that relates to matters yet to be decided) cannot be accepted earlier than seven clear days after judgment is given or handed down in such a trial.[499] These provisions are subject to certain transitional provisions.[500]

17.189 **Where the claim has been stuck out** Kenneth Parker J has ruled that where a claim has been struck out (such as where there has been a failure to comply with an unless order), no Part 36 offer will remain open for acceptance.[501] He went on to say that the fact that the defaulting party might have made an application for relief from sanctions did not result in the offer being held 'on life support ... awaiting the ministering dispensation of relief by the Court so as to obviate final extinction'.[502]

17.190 **Claim and counterclaim** If an offer states that it takes into account the counterclaim, the claimant's entitlement to costs upon acceptance will include the costs incurred in dealing with that counterclaim.[503]

17.191 **Where CPR, Part 45, Section IIIA, applies** This topic is addressed at 50.287–50.289.

Procedure

17.192 Acceptance may be effected by serving written notice of acceptance on the offeror.[504] Form N242A may be used for this purpose because a draft notice of acceptance is incorporated within it.[505] The notice of acceptance must be served on the offeror and filed with the court in which the case is proceeding.[506] Where the party to be served is legally represented, the notice must be served on the legal representative.[507]

17.193 Where permission to accept is required, an application must be made in accordance with CPR, Part 23.[508] Unless the parties agree otherwise, any such application must be made to a judge other than a trial judge.[509] If the court grants permission to accept, it will, in default of agreement, also make an order dealing with costs.[510]

17.194 Where the application for permission is made after the 'relevant period' has expired and after further deductible amounts have been paid to the claimant since the date of the offer, the application for permission to accept the offer must: (a) state the net amount offered in the Part 36 offer, the deductible amounts that had accrued at the date the offer was made

---

[499] See CPR, r 36.12(3).

[500] These provisions will apply in any case in which the offer was made on or after 6 April 2015, or in which the trial of any part of the claim or of any issue arising in it started on or after 6 April 2015. This would be so regardless of when the offer was made: see the Civil Procedure (Amendment No 8) Rules 2014 (SI 2014/3299), r 18(2).

[501] *Joyce v West Bus Coach Services Ltd* [2012] EWHC 404 (QB), at [34] (although it was decided under the pre-2015 Part 36).

[502] *Ibid*, at [35]; see also *Super Group Plc v Just Enough* [2014] EWHC 3260 (Comm), *per* Flaux J.

[503] CPR, r 36.13(7). This is now a matter that is expressly set out in the CPR, but even before the present incarnation of Part 36, a defendant/counterclaimant was able to make an offer that could cover both claim and counterclaim.

[504] CPR, r 36.11(1).

[505] See PD 36, para 1.1.

[506] See PD 36, para 3.1.

[507] See PD 36, para 1.2.

[508] See PD 36, para 3.2.

[509] See PD 36, para 3.3.

[510] CPR, r 36.11(4).

and the deductible amounts that have subsequently accrued; and (b) be accompanied by a copy of the current certificate.[511]

Rejection of Part 36 offers

A Part 36 offer is not capable of being rejected in the sense that rejection will determine the offeree's right subsequently to accept it. It has been argued that the common law continues to apply to the extent that the notion of rejection of offers applies to Part 36 in just the same way as it applies to any other type of offer,[512] but first Coulson J[513] and then Moore-Bick LJ (with whom Sir Anthony May P and Carnwath LJ agreed)[514] rejected this analysis. Moore-Bick LJ had this to say on the point: **17.195**

> 'Basic concepts of offer and acceptance clearly underpin Pt 36, but that is inevitable given that it contains a voluntary procedure under which either party may take the initiative to bring about a consensual resolution of the dispute. Such concepts are part of the landscape in which everyone conducts their daily life. It does not follow, however, that Pt 36 should be understood as incorporating all the rules of law governing the formation of contracts, some of which are quite technical in nature. Indeed, it is not desirable that it should do so. Certainty is as much to be commended in procedural as in substantive law, especially, perhaps, in a procedural code which must be understood and followed by ordinary citizens who wish to conduct their own litigation.'[515]

Thus, in strictly legal terms, a rejection of a Part 36 offer is of no effect (other than, perhaps, as a background fact for the purposes of subsequently deciding the incidence of costs), although 'rejections' may continue to be made—and very frequently are made—for the purposes of advancing negotiations. **17.196**

Withdrawal or change of Part 36 offers

Provided that the offeree has not previously served notice of acceptance,[516] a Part 36 offer may be withdrawn, or its terms may be revised so as to make it more or less advantageous to the offeree (in which case it will be said to be 'improved' or 'downgraded', whichever is appropriate). **17.197**

The following provision will apply to any withdrawal or change, regardless of whether it is an improvement or a downgrade: **17.198**

> '36.9 (1) A Part 36 offer can only be withdrawn, or its terms changed, if the offeree has not previously served notice of acceptance.
>
> (2) The offeror withdraws the offer or changes its terms by serving written notice of the withdrawal or change of terms on the offeree.
>
> (Rule 36.17(7) deals with the costs consequences following judgment of an offer which is withdrawn.)

---

511 See PD 36, para 3.3.

512 That argument was based on an analogy with withdrawals under the original Part 36. Broadly speaking, Aldous LJ found that the common law did apply in the absence of an express provision that it should not: *Scammell v Dicker* [2001] 1 WLR 631. This is to be contrasted with payments into court, which were entirely procedural and not governed by the common law: see *Cumper v Pothecary* [1941] 2 KB 58, at 67, which was affirmed as being good law post-CPR in *Flynn v Scougall* [2004] EWCA Civ 873, at [26].

513 *Sampla v Rushmoor Borough Council* [2008] EWHC 2616 (TCC).

514 *Gibbon v Manchester City Council* [2010] EWCA Civ 726.

515 *Ibid*, at [6].

516 See CPR, r 36.9(1).

(3) Subject to rule 36.10, such notice of withdrawal or change of terms takes effect when it is served on the offeree.

(Rule 36.10 makes provision about when permission is required to withdraw or change the terms of an offer before the expiry of the relevant period.)

Thus a Part 36 offer can only be withdrawn, or its terms changed, if the offeree has not previously served notice of acceptance.[517] To withdraw or change an offer, the offeror must serve written notice of the withdrawal or change of terms on the offeree.[518] Where permission is not required, any such notice of withdrawal or change of terms takes effect when it is served on the offeree.[519]

17.199 The rules that govern improved offers (see 17.200) are different from those that govern withdrawn offers and downgraded offers (see 17.204).

Improved offers

17.200 As mentioned above, an offer may be improved—that is, the terms may be revised so as to make it more advantageous to the offeree.[520] The offeree is not the only one who stands to benefit from the improvement, because an improved offer will afford the offeror a higher level of costs protection than the original offer. Indeed, the lure of better costs protection is almost always the reason why offerors make improved offers.

17.201 **When the improvement may be made** Whilst there is no authority directly on the point, unless the offeree has served notice of acceptance,[521] an offer may be improved at any time, even before the expiry of the 'relevant period'.[522] No permission is required.[523] This is because an offeror would be at liberty to make a present-day Part 36 offer as and when they liked, so it would be pointless to try to limit the circumstances in which they may improve an offer. In this regard, it should be noted that an improved offer and a new offer are treated as being the same (see 17.202).

17.202 **The relationship of the new offer with the original offer** An improved offer will be treated as being a new offer on the improved terms.[524] Moreover, the original offer will not be treated as having been withdrawn[525] and, as such, it will continue to be capable of acceptance—a fact now expressly stated in Part 36, presumably to remind litigants that the

---

517 See CPR, r 36.9(1).

518 See CPR, r 36.9(2).

519 See CPR, r 36.9(3).

520 This is implied by CPR, r 36.9(5).

521 See CPR, r 36.9(1).

522 Where the original 'relevant period' has expired, then the ability to improve the offer without the permission of the court is conferred by CPR, r 36.9(4); where the 'relevant period' has yet to expire, then CPR, r 36.9(1), will apply, but (unlike changes that are not improvements) CPR, r 36.10, will not.

523 In particular, CPR, r 36.10, does not apply because that rule applies only to changes that would result in the changed offer being less advantageous to the offeree (see CPR, r 36.10(1)).

524 Where the offer was made on or after 6 April 2015, see CPR, r 36.9(5)(a). Some commentators have expressed doubt as to why this amendment was considered necessary. They point to the fact that the CPR have always distinguished between withdrawing an offer and changing its terms, so—they say—it is difficult to see why a variation of an existing offer might have been thought to result in its withdrawal. This is a valid point to make, but perhaps this amendment was simply to make the situation clearer. In particular, it reminds the parties that the consequences of the original offer will continue to apply despite the fact that the further offer has been made.

525 Where the offer was made on or after 6 April 2015, see CPR, r 36.9(5)(a); otherwise, see *Gibbon v Manchester City Council* [2010] EWCA Civ 726, at [17].

original offer may continue to have a bearing on the matter despite the fact that an improved offer has been made. The relevant provisions read as follows:

> '36.9 (5) Where the offeror changes the terms of a Part 36 offer to make it more advantageous to the offeree—
> (a) such improved offer shall be treated, not as the withdrawal of the original offer; but as the making of a present-day Part 36 offer on the improved terms; and
> (b) subject to rule 36.5(2), the period specified under rule 36.5(1)(c) shall be 21 days or such longer period (if any) identified in the written notice referred to in paragraph (2).'

Other than where the improvement is made less than 21 days before the start of trial, there will be a new 'relevant period' of 21 days (or such longer period as may be stated in the improved offer).[526]

Procedure As to procedure, an offeror improves their offer by serving written notice of the change of terms on the offeree.[527] Permission is not required, so that notice will take effect immediately upon it being served on the offeree.[528] Where the party to be served is legally represented, the notice must be served on the legal representative.[529] **17.203**

Withdrawal and downgrading

The adjectival law that governs the withdrawal of offers is, on the whole, the same as that which governs downgrades in the terms of offers. **17.204**

When the change may be made The topic of the withdrawal or downgrading of the terms of an offer may arise at the following times. **17.205**

- **Prior to expiry of the relevant period, but before trial** If the 'relevant period' has yet to expire, the offer may be withdrawn or downgraded, but only if either the court gives permission or the offeree does not serve notice of acceptance of the original offer during that period.[530] If, after service of a notice of withdrawal or change, the offeree serves a notice of acceptance of the original offer at any time prior to the expiry of the 'relevant period', then that acceptance has effect unless the offeror applies to the court for permission; such an application must be made promptly—that is, within seven days of the offeree's notice of acceptance, or before the start of trial if that is earlier.[531] If the offeree does not serve notice of acceptance to accept the original offer during that period, the notice of withdrawal or change will take effect immediately upon expiry of the 'relevant period'.[532]
- **Where the relevant period runs into trial** Sir Jeremy Cooke has noted that there is no express provision in Part 36 that deals with the situation in which the relevant period includes a period after the trial has begun—which is a period during which the offer could be accepted only with the permission of the court (see 17.176).[533] He concluded,

[526] See CPR, r 36.9(5)(b).
[527] See CPR, r 36.9(2).
[528] See CPR, r 36.9(3).
[529] See PD 36, para 1.2.
[530] See CPR, r 36.10(2).
[531] CPR, r 36.10(2)(a).
[532] See CPR, r 36.10(2). See also *Application in Private* [2017] EWHC 3606 (Comm), at [19], *per* Sir Jeremy Cooke.
[533] See *ibid*, at [22].

however, that the position is impliedly governed by CPR, r 36.10(3), which means that the court may allow the offer to be withdrawn or its terms changed if satisfied that there has been a change of circumstances since the making of the original offer and that it is in the interests of justice to give permission. Sir Jeremy Cooke went on to say that such a question was merely the obverse side of the coin to an application to accept the offer pursuant to CPR, r 36.11(3)(d) (see 17.176).[534]

- **After the expiry of the relevant period** Once the 'relevant period' has expired, then, provided that the offeree has not previously served notice of acceptance of the original offer, the offeror may withdraw or downgrade the offer without the permission of the court.[535] As is explained below (17.214–17.217), if an offer is withdrawn, the offer may still be taken into account as being an 'applicable offer' within the meaning of CPR, r 44.2(4)(c).[536]
- **After the end of the trial, but before judgment is handed down** In the period after the conclusion of the trial, but before judgment is handed down, an offer made before 6 April 2015 may be accepted only if the parties agree.[537] This means that, for all practical purposes, there would be no point in withdrawing or downgrading an offer. In a case in which a party did withdraw its offer immediately upon receiving the draft judgment, Silber J found that it should still be given the benefit of having made the offer.[538] If the offer was made on or after 6 April 2015, it is probable that the court would have discretion to decide the issue.[539]

17.206 **Notices of withdrawal or change** The offeror withdraws the offer or changes the terms of an offer by serving written notice of the withdrawal or change of terms on the offeree.[540] If the offer was made on or after 6 April 2015, then the notice of withdrawal may be given in the offer itself (see 17.219).[541] Other than where the court's permission is required to withdraw or change the offer, such notice of withdrawal or change of terms takes effect when it is served on the offeree.[542] Where the party to be served is legally represented, the notice must be served on the legal representative.[543]

17.207 **Procedure where permission is not required** After expiry of the 'relevant period', permission of the court is not required to change or withdraw a Part 36 offer. Provided that the offeree has

---

534 See *ibid*, at [24].

535 CPR, r 36.9(4)(a).

536 See the signpost at the end of CPR, r 36.17, which reflects the guidance given by Rix LJ in *Epsom College v Pierse Contracting Southern Ltd (formerly Biseley Construction Ltd) (in liquidation)* [2011] EWCA Civ 1449, at [54] *et seq*.

537 See CPR, r 36.9(5).

538 See *Mehjoo v Harben Barker (a firm)* [2013] EWHC 1669 (AB), at [23], in which Silber J seems to have worked on the basis that Part 36 continued to apply to the offer, but said that if he were wrong on that point, he would have considered giving effect to the offer under what is now CPR, r 44.2.

539 This is because CPR, r 36.11(3)(d), allows the court to grant permission to allow acceptance of an offer if the trial is 'in progress', whilst CPR, r 36.3(d), defines 'in progress' as being 'from the time when it starts until the time when judgment is given or handed down'. Given that Sir Jeremy Cooke has equated withdrawal and acceptance during trial as obverse sides of the same coin—see *Application in Private* [2017] EWHC 3606 (Comm), at [24]—it is arguable that the court has discretion to deal with an application to withdraw at any time prior to handing down judgment.

540 See CPR, r 36.9(2).

541 See CPR, r 36.9(4)(b).

542 See CPR, r 36.9(3).

543 See PD 36, para 1.2.

not previously served notice of acceptance, the offeror may withdraw the offer or downgrade its terms at any time[544] and without fetter.[545] This is achieved by serving notice of withdrawal or notice of change, as the case may be.[546]

Procedure where permission is required If the 'relevant period' has yet to expire, the offer may be withdrawn or downgraded, but only where the court gives permission or the offeree chooses not to serve notice of acceptance of the original offer.[547] The relevant provisions are set out in CPR, r 36.10: **17.208**

> '36.10 (1) Subject to rule 36.9(1), this rule applies where the offeror serves notice before expiry of the 'relevant period' of withdrawal of the offer or change of its terms to be less advantageous to the offeree.
>
> (2) Where this rule applies—
>
> (a) if the offeree has not served notice of acceptance of the original offer by the expiry of the relevant period, the offeror's notice has effect on the expiry of that period; and
>
> (b) if the offeree serves notice of acceptance of the original offer before the expiry of the relevant period, that acceptance has effect unless the offeror applies to the court for permission to withdraw the offer or to change its terms—
>
> (i) within 7 days of the offeree's notice of acceptance; or
>
> (ii) if earlier, before the first day of trial.
>
> (3) On an application under paragraph (2)(b), the court may give permission for the original offer to be withdrawn or its terms changed if satisfied that there has been a change of circumstances since the making of the original offer and that it is in the interests of justice to give permission.'

Where there is no dispute If notice of withdrawal or change is served during the 'relevant period' and if the offeree chooses not to serve notice of acceptance, the withdrawal or change will take effect upon the expiry of that period.[548] Similarly, if, upon receiving notice of acceptance, the offeror fails to make an application within certain time frames (see below), the notice of acceptance will take effect.[549] **17.209**

Notices and applications The issue of whether the offeror should be permitted to withdraw or downgrade an offer will arise only if the parties serve competing notices. Where the offeror serves notice of withdrawal or change during the 'relevant period', the outcome will depend on what the parties then do. If no notice of acceptance is served, then the withdrawal or change will take effect from the expiry of the 'relevant period'.[550] If, however, the offeree wishes to accept the offer, they will have the right to serve notice of acceptance at any time during the remainder of the 'relevant period'[551] and, if the offeree does this, the offeror must make an application either within seven days of the offeree's notice of acceptance or, if earlier, before the first day of trial.[552] The court will then decide whether to allow the offer to be accepted, or whether the offeror should be allowed to withdraw or **17.210**

544 See CPR, r 36.9(4)(a).
545 CPR, r 36.9(4).
546 CPR, r 36.9(2).
547 See CPR, r 36.10(2).
548 See CPR, r 36.10(2)(a).
549 See CPR, r 36.10(2)(b).
550 See CPR, r 36.10(2)(a).
551 See CPR, r 36.10(2).
552 See CPR, r 36.10(2)(b).

downgrade the offer.[553] If the offeror fails to make an application within those time limits, the notice of acceptance will take effect.[554]

17.211 *Discretion* Where the offeror has made an application in accordance with the provisions set out above, the court may give permission for the offer to be withdrawn or downgraded, but only if it is satisfied that (a) there has been a change of circumstances since the making of the original offer and (b) it is in the interests of justice to give permission.[555] The test that is set out in Part 36 applies only to offers made on or after 6 April 2015, but a very similar test will apply to offers made before that date.[556]

17.212 Whilst not in any way binding, there have been instances in which the court has declined to allow a party to withdraw an offer, despite the fact that the offeror's legal representative made a genuine mistake in formulating it.[557]

17.213 **Procedure on applying for permission** The permission of the court must, unless the parties agree otherwise, be sought by making an application under Part 23, which must be dealt with by a judge other than the trial judge.[558] Otherwise, the application may be made at trial or at any other hearing, but only if it is not to the trial judge.[559] As a general principle, applications should be made on notice.[560]

17.214 **The effect of a withdrawn or downgraded offer** CPR, Part 36, now expressly states that an offeror will not obtain the benefits of having made a Part 36 offer where (a) the offer has been withdrawn, (b) the offer has been changed so that its terms are less advantageous to the offeree, where the offeree has beaten the less advantageous offer, or (c) (unless the court has abridged the 'relevant period') the offer was made less than 21 days

[553] See CPR, r 36.10(2)(b) and (3). This rule reflects the guidance in *Flynn v Scougall* [2004] EWCA Civ 873, at [30], which was that where a notice of acceptance had been served, the court was permitted notionally to allow the stay to be lifted for the purpose of dealing with the application.

[554] See CPR, r 36.10(2)(b).

[555] See CPR, r 36.10(3).

[556] Leggatt J has held that the test to be applied when the court is considering whether to give a party permission to withdraw a Part 36 offer is whether there has been a sufficient change of circumstances to make it just to permit that party to do so: *Evans v Royal Wolverhampton Hospitals NHS Foundation Trust* [2014] EWHC 3185 (QB), at [52]. This is a test that was originally formulated by Goddard LJ: see *Cumper v Pothecary* [1941] 2 KB 58, at 70; *Flynn v Scougall* [2004] EWCA Civ 873. In *Application in Private* [2017] EWHC 3606 (Comm), at [38]–[39], Sir Jeremey Cooke said that 'what is envisaged is some radical alteration in circumstances which would justify an offeror departing from the valuation it had placed on the case when making the offer it did. A change in the subjective view of the offeror as to its prospects of success as a result of the way the case has panned out at trial would ... not suffice ... .' He went on to say that, '[w]here a party chooses to make a Part 36 ... offer, in the knowledge that evidence may emerge which is more favourable to it, the party must be taken to have assessed the potential upside and downside of further developments in the case when making the offer in the hope of securing an advantage in relation to costs should the offer not be accepted' (*ibid*, at [43]). See also *Manku v Seehra* (1985) 7 Con LR 90 (QBD), *per* Judge John Newey QC (subjective re-evaluation of the merits insufficient); *Marsh v Frenchay Healthcare NHS Trust* (2001) The Times, 13 March, QBD, *per* Curtis J (adverse surveillance evidence was sufficient); *MRW Technologies Ltd v Cecil Holdings Ltd & Anor* [2001] Lexis Citation 1882, *per* Garland J (multiple issues relating to disclosure and accountancy evidence was sufficient).

[557] See, eg, *Barret v Nutman* (unreported), 20 June 2014, Liverpool County Court, *per* DJ Clark.

[558] See PD 36, para 2.2(1).

[559] See PD 36, para 2.2(2).

[560] See *Evans v Royal Wolverhampton Hospitals NHS Foundation Trust* [2014] EWHC 3185 (QB), at [37], in which Leggatt J had this to say: 'As a general principle, applications should not be made without notice unless either giving notice would enable the offeree to take steps to defeat the purpose of the application or there has been literally no time to give notice before the urgent assistance of the court is required.'

before trial.[561] This reflects guidance previously given in the authorities.[562] This does not mean, however, that such an offer will be of no relevance at all when the court comes to exercise its discretion as to costs, because a withdrawn Part 36 offer is a species of 'admissible offer'.[563] Indeed, Part 36 makes express reference to the fact that the court will be able to take a withdrawn or downgraded offer into account when exercising its discretion as to costs.[564]

Ward LJ made the following comments about the effect of withdrawn offers: **17.215**

> 'The principal error in my judgment, was not to distinguish between the question whether the *Calderbank* letter was still on the negotiating table and the question whether its terms materially related to the result of the appeal. That it had lapsed, whether by rejection, non acceptance within a reasonable time, or its withdrawal, matters not. It remained material as a fact in the history of litigation. Had it been accepted within a reasonable time after it was made, and the learned Judge correctly found that it should have been because the Plaintiff eventually did less well than they had been offered, then there would have been no need for the appeal at all. An appeal became necessary because, without it, the wrong order would have stood uncorrected.'[565]

Thus a withdrawn offer remains relevant because it is part of the relevant history of the proceedings. In a similar vein, Mann J said that such an offer 'could play a part in a general assessment of the reasonableness or unreasonableness of the [offeree's] conduct, but it cannot be elevated to a position comparable to a living Part 36 offer merely because it has been beaten'.[566] On the facts of the case before him (in which the offer was being relied upon for the purposes of trying to obtain costs in the indemnity basis), Mann J said that it '[added] little'.[567]

Ward LJ was giving judgment in a pre-CPR decision, but there are several decisions made under the CPR that confirm the position.[568] Dyson LJ has confirmed that Ward LJ's analysis remains of strong persuasive force under the CPR;[569] similarly, whilst he was giving judgment in a case that was governed by the original CPR, Part 36, Longmore LJ has made it clear that the court should not disregard an offer merely because it may have **17.216**

561 See CPR, r 36.17(7).

562 See *French v Groupama Insurance Co Ltd* [2011] EWCA Civ 1119, at [41], *per* Rix LJ. See also *Epsom College v Pierse Contracting Southern Ltd (formerly Biseley Construction Ltd) (in liquidation)* [2011] EWCA Civ 1449, at [54] *et seq*, *per* Rix LJ. The position under the RSC was less clear: see *Bristol and West Building Society v Evans and Bullock* (unreported), 5 February 1996, CA; cf *The Toni* [1974] 1 Lloyd's Reports 489, at 496–7, in which Megaw LJ declined to give weight to an open offer that had been withdrawn. It is possible that the earlier cases would still apply in tribunals in which the CPR do not apply, but this seems not to be borne out in practice: see, eg, *Owners and/or Bareboat Charterers and/or Sub Bareboat Charterers of the Ship Samco Europe v Owners of the Ship MSC Prestige* [2011] EWHC 1656 (Admlty), at [27]. See also *Gulati v MGN Ltd* [2015] EWHC 1805 (Ch), at [20], *per* Mann J.

563 See the signpost at the end of CPR, r 36.17, which reflects the guidance given by Rix LJ in *Epsom College v Pierse Contracting Southern Ltd (formerly Biseley Construction Ltd) (in liquidation)* [2011] EWCA Civ 1449, at [54] *et seq*. See also *Ballard v Ballard* [2018] EWHC 370 (QB), at [20], *per* Foskett J.

564 See the signpost at the end of CPR, r 36.17.

565 *Bristol and West Building Society v Evans Bullock & Co (a firm)* (unreported), 5 February 1996, CA, at the third paragraph before the last.

566 See *Gulati v MGN Ltd* [2015] EWHC 1805 (Ch), at [22].

567 See *ibid*, at [23].

568 See the cases listed at nn 588–592; see also, eg, *Uwug Ltd (in liquidation) v Ball* [2015] EWHC 74 (IPEC).

569 *Stokes Pension Fund v Western Power Distribution (South West) plc* [2005] EWCA Civ 854.

been withdrawn.[570] In a personal injuries case, MacDuff J referred to a withdrawn offer as continuing to have 'costs potency'.[571] Teare J came to much the same conclusion in an admiralty case[572] and Rix LJ came to a similar conclusion in a dispute concerning negligent construction work.[573] Hence there can be little doubt that a withdrawn Part 36 offer is capable of influencing the incidence of costs.

17.217 When faced with a 'potent', but withdrawn, offer, an offeree may argue that there would be injustice in allowing that offer—which the offeree can no longer accept—to sit in the background operating against them. MacDuff J has acknowledged those concerns, but he rejected the argument by saying that if an offeree had failed to accept a reasonable offer that had subsequently been withdrawn, the offeree should appreciate their costs risk and take protective steps by making their own offer.[574] Teare J has explained that there is no reason why an offeree cannot protect themselves against future costs by making an offer in exactly the same terms as the one that puts them at risk.[575] More details about the effect of 'admissible offers' in general may be found at 6.207–6.243.

Implied and automatic withdrawal

17.218 **No implied withdrawal** The only ways in which a Part 36 offer can be withdrawn are by serving notice of withdrawal or by automatic withdrawal by the terms of the offer (and, where appropriate, obtaining the permission of the court). In particular, there is no such thing as an implied withdrawal—which was made clear by Moore-Bick LJ:

> 'In my view that leaves no room for the concept of implied withdrawal; it requires express notice in writing in terms which bring home to the offeree that the offer has been withdrawn. If justification for that requirement is sought, it can be found ... in the need for clarity and certainty in the operation of the Pt 36 procedure. [In] order to avoid uncertainty [the notice] should include an express reference to the date of the offer and its terms, together with some words making it clear that it is withdrawn.'[576]

The effect of this is that an offer can be accepted even though it has become obvious to all concerned that it was no longer an appropriate offer from the point of view of the offeror.[577] This means that where an offer ceases to be appropriate, the offeror must take the initiative and withdraw it.

17.219 **Time-limited offers** Where the offer contains a term that withdraws the offer after a stated period of time, then the offer will be (on the face of it) a time-limited

---

[570] *Farag v Commissioner of Police of the Metropolis* [2005] EWCA Civ 1814.

[571] *Pankhurst v White* [2010] EWHC 311 (QB), at [40]. This case was upheld on appeal, but this was on a different point: see *Pankhurst v (1) White and (2) Motor Insurers Bureau* [2010] EWCA Civ 1445.

[572] *Owners and/or Bareboat Charterers and/or Sub Bareboat Charterers of the Ship Samco Europe v Owners of the Ship MSC Prestige* [2011] EWHC 1656 (Admlty), at [26].

[573] *Epsom College v Pierse Contracting Southern Ltd (formerly Biseley Construction Ltd) (in liquidation)* [2011] EWCA Civ 1449, at [54] *et seq.*

[574] *Pankhurst v White* [2010] EWHC 311 (QB), at [36]. This reasoning was endorsed (albeit *obiter*) by Teare J in *Owners and/or Bareboat Charterers and/or Sub Bareboat Charterers of the Ship Samco Europe v Owners of the Ship MSC Prestige* [2011] EWHC 1656 (Admlty), at [23] and [26].

[575] *Owners and/or Bareboat Charterers and/or Sub Bareboat Charterers of the Ship Samco Europe v Owners of the Ship MSC Prestige* [2011] EWHC 1656 (Admlty), at [26].

[576] *Gibbon v Manchester City Council* [2010] EWCA Civ 726, at [17].

[577] See, eg, *Mahmood v Elmi* [2010] EWHC 1933 (QB), in which Cox J found that an offer had been accepted notwithstanding the fact that it had become clear that the value of the claim was more than eight times the amount of the offer.

offer. The approach to a putatively time-limited Part 36 offer will depend on when it was made.

- **Offer made before 6 April 2015** Before 6 April 2015, it was impossible to draft a Part 36 offer in such a way as to limit the period of time during which it may be accepted.[578] This had a bearing on the way in which the court interpreted offers that were capable of being read as including any such limit. Whilst it would not always be appropriate,[579] Rix LJ said that the court should reject competing interpretations that would result in the offer ceasing to be a Part 36 offer.[580] The following are examples.
  - **'Open for 21 days'** These words should not be read as limiting the offer itself, but instead should be read as meaning that no attempt would be made to seek the court's permission to withdraw the offer within those 21 days.[581]
  - **'We ... diarise expiry'** This reference is to be regarded as being a reference to the 'relevant period' rather than to the offer itself.[582]
  - **'An acceptance period'** This phrase would almost certainly be interpreted as being a reference to the 'relevant period' rather than to the offer itself.[583]
- **Offer made on or after 6 April 2015** Where the offer was made on or after 6 April 2015, it may now be automatically withdrawn as a result of it containing terms to this effect.[584] That said, since an offeree will not receive the benefits of a Part 36 offer where that offer has been withdrawn,[585] it is hard to see any advantage in making a Part 36 offer if it is to be automatically withdrawn in this way other than, for example, for the purposes of negotiation.

The provisions that govern offers made on or after 6 April 2015 read as follows: **17.220**

> '36.9 (4) Subject to paragraph (1), after expiry of the relevant period—
> (a) the offeror may withdraw the offer or change its terms without the permission of the court; or
> (b) the offer may be automatically withdrawn in accordance with its terms.'

578 *C v D* [2011] EWCA Civ 646, at [35]–[44], *per* Rix LJ.

579 See, eg, *Saigol v Thorney Ltd* [2014] EWCA Civ 556, at [22], in which Rimer LJ found that the judge making the costs order in the court below had misinterpreted an offer to settle expiring after 24 hours as being a Part 36 offer.

580 *C v D* [2011] EWCA Civ 646, at [54] *et seq*; see also *Onay v Brown* [2009] EWCA Civ 775, at [27], *per* Goldring LJ.

581 *C v D* [2011] EWCA Civ 646, at [54], *per* Rimer LJ.

582 *Epsom College v Pierse Contracting Southern Ltd (formerly Biseley Construction Ltd) (in liquidation)* [2011] EWCA Civ 1449, at [66], *per* Rix LJ. Similarly, see *Lilleyman v Lilleyman* [2012] EWHC 1056 (Ch), at [12], *per* Briggs J.

583 *C v D* [2011] EWCA Civ 646, at [24], *per* Rix LJ; see also *Onay v Brown* [2009] EWCA Civ 775, at [27], *per* Goldring LJ.

584 CPR, r 36.9(4)(b). Commentators have said that this change in the Rules was to deal with the anomalous fact that a Part 36 offer could be withdrawn after expiry of the 'relevant period' by sending a separate notice, but not by a notice contained in the offer itself (ie a Part 36 offer would be withdrawn by writing two letters, but not by writing only one).

585 See CPR, r 36.17(7).

Part VI

POINTS OF LAW REGARDING COSTS

18

THE INDEMNITY PRINCIPLE

This chapter deals with the following topics: **18.01**

- the indemnity principle in general (18.02):
  - the historical perspective (18.03);
  - policy matters (18.06);
  - the rule against profit (18.10);
  - the principle of individual application (18.11);
  - exceptions to the indemnity principle (18.15);
- evidencing the indemnity principle (18.24):
  - the two presumptions:
    - client liable for fees of the person whom the client engages (18.28); and
    - the *Bailey* presumption (18.30);
  - scrutiny by the court (18.40);
  - procedural issues (18.46);
  - the ethos of the CPR (18.51);
  - evidential issues relating to the indemnity principle (18.53);
- the indemnity principle in practice (18.58):
  - the principle of dual liability for costs (18.59);
  - subrogation (18.73);
  - miscellaneous issues:
    - the effect of undischarged funding certificates (18.79);
    - putative waiver of fees and the indemnity principle (18.82);
    - legal services provider acting on credit (18.85);
    - 'CFA Lites' (18.86); and
    - contractual problems (18.90);
  - *quantum meruit* (18.91);
  - estoppel (18.100);
- the costs of in-house staff (18.105):
  - the costs of in house legal staff (18.107);
  - the costs of in-house non-legal staff (18.115); and
- *pro bono* funding (18.121):
  - the jurisdiction relating to *pro bono* awards (18.123);
  - the discretion to make a *pro bono* awards (18.126);
  - costs protection and *pro bono* funding (18.130);
  - quantification of *pro bono* awards (18.131);
  - procedure and *pro bono* awards (18.132); and
  - Legal Services Act 2007, s 194 (18.136).

The Indemnity Principle in General

18.02 The indemnity principle may be described in the following way: an order for costs allows the receiving party to claim from the paying party no more than an indemnity in respect of the costs covered by the order; receiving parties therefore cannot recover a sum in excess of their liability to their own solicitors.[1] This principle applies both to the total amount claimed and to the individual sums that go to make up that total (see 18.11).

The historical perspective

18.03 Although the origins of the indemnity principle go back further,[2] its modern form was first expounded in 1860 (see 1.91) when Bramwell B said:

> 'Costs as between party and party are given by the law as an indemnity to the person entitled to them; they are not imposed as a punishment on the party who pays them, nor given as a bonus to the party who receives them. Therefore, if the extent of damnification can be found out, the extent to which costs ought to be allowed is also ascertained.'[3]

This established the principle that a litigant should not profit from litigation.

18.04 A decade later, this principle was given statutory force:

> 'The client who has entered into such [an] agreement shall not be entitled to recover from any other person under any order for the payment of any costs which are the subject of such agreement more than the amount payable by the client to his own attorney or solicitor under the same'.[4]

A provision not dissimilar to this remains on the statute books today (albeit only in relation to contentious business agreements).[5]

18.05 At the turn of the twentieth century, Fletcher Moulton LJ noted that the statutory provision referred to above (see 18.04) was an expression of an established common-law principle—although he went on to say that it was not purely declaratory.[6] By that stage, the indemnity principle had become established as the bedrock upon which other costs law was based.

Policy matters

18.06 It is often said that the indemnity principle is a doctrine undergoing a long process of attenuation.[7] As is discussed below, that is true in the sense that statute has intervened

[1] The definition is adapted from that given by Master Hurst in Practice Direction (Taxation: Indemnity Principle) [1998] 1 WLR 1674.

[2] See, eg, Limitation of Actions and Costs Act 1842, which provided that parties should be entitled to recover 'such full and reasonable indemnity as to all costs, charges, and expenses incurred in and about any action, suit or other legal proceedings as shall be taxed by the proper officer on that behalf'.

[3] *Harold v Smith* (1860) 5 H&N 381, at 385.

[4] Attorneys and Solicitors Act 1870, s 5.

[5] Solicitors Act 1974, s 60(3).

[6] *Gundry v Sainsbury* [1910] 1 KB 645, at 651.

[7] See, eg, the comments of Gray J in *Kitchen v Burwell Reed & Kinghorn Ltd* [2005] EWHC 1771 (QB), at [29]. Martin Rodger QC has questioned the need for the indemnity principle in determinations of costs applications under the Commonhold and Leasehold Reform Act 2002: see *Triplerose Ltd* [2016] EKUT 77 (LC), at [17]–[19].

to disapply the indemnity principle in certain specified circumstances. It is also true to say that there is no judicial appetite for some of the more ruthless challenges brought by paying parties.[8] This, perhaps, is why some liability insurers have, in the recent past, agreed to abide by an informal code by which challenges to the indemnity principle will be brought only within a very narrow window of opportunity.[9]

Nonetheless, there are those who make a powerful case for cherishing certain aspects of the indemnity principle. Speaking extrajudicially, Sir Anthony May, President of the Queen's Bench Division, remarked: **18.07**

> 'I rather think that a plea for reasonable costs, unrelated to a commercial rate or amount which is agreed to be payable by the client to the lawyer, risks steering the boat towards at least one whirlpool. In a world of "no win no fee" agreement, where is the measure of what are reasonable costs? Up to now, the main reference for what is reasonable is that which lawyers charge their clients in the market place ... If there were no such market, what is the measure of reasonableness?'[10]

Thus there are those in senior judicial posts who wish to preserve the indemnity principle for the purposes of maintaining some linkage between what is allowed between opposing parties and what the market in general will bear.[11] **18.08**

Notwithstanding this, in the late 2000s there were plans to abrogate the indemnity principle entirely. Speaking extrajudicially, Jackson LJ explained that this proposal was for a number of reasons—in particular, concerns about satellite litigation 'with no perceptible benefit either to court users or to society'.[12] He proposed that r 44.4(1) of the Civil Procedure Rules (CPR) be amended so as to make it clear that costs would be assessed by reference to reasonableness and, where appropriate, proportionality, rather than also by reference to the contractual relations between the receiving party and their legal advisers. That proposal was not implemented, but it is possible that this was due to lack of time rather than for policy reasons. **18.09**

The rule against profit

Despite the fact that the indemnity principle is rarely employed for the purposes of defeating a claim for unjust remuneration, the court has repeatedly emphasised its role of preventing parties from profiting from litigation.[13] That principle of restraint **18.10**

[8] See, eg, *Thornley v Lang* [2003] EWCA Civ 1484, at [5]–[9], *per* Lord Phillips of Worth Matravers MR. Whilst a criminal case, see also *R (McCormick) v Liverpool Justices* [2001] 2 All ER 705.

[9] The Personal Injury Multi-Track Code is a collaborative initiative between the Association of Personal Injury Lawyers, the Forum of Insurance Lawyers, various liability insurers and the Motor Insurers' Bureau. It applies to most personal injury claims (excluding asbestos claims and clinical negligence) where the accident occurred after 1 July 2008 and damages are expected to be over £250,000. Paragraphs 5.1 and 5.2 provide that challenges may be made only within 28 calendar days of the letter of claim.

[10] May, A, Untitled speech delivered at Cardiff Costs Conference, 19 June 2009.

[11] There are those who say that this view is misguided because it fails to take into account the fact that litigation is increasingly conducted on a conditional fee agreement (CFA) Lite basis (where there is no linkage at all between the amount the court allows and the amount the client would have been prepared to pay out of their own pocket). That criticism is misplaced because Sir Anthony May was not suggesting that it is desirable to have linkage in every case, but merely that there needs to be a sufficient prevalence of linkage to afford the court some measure of what is and is not reasonable.

[12] Jackson, R, *Review of Civil Litigation Costs: Final Report* (London: HMSO, 2010), ch 5, at para 3.4(i).

[13] See, eg, *Harold v Smith* (1860) 5 H&N 381, at 385.

seems to have developed hand in hand with other principles of restraint—namely, that not all losses incurred as a result of litigation will be afforded the status of costs and that the court will assess costs rather than charges (see 3.07).

The principle of individual application

18.11 By the end of the twentieth century, the indemnity principle had become well established as a general concept (see 18.03–18.05). What remained unclear was whether the indemnity principle operated only as a cap on the overall figure as assessed or whether it applied to each individual item in a bill of costs. The answer is the latter: in 1998, May LJ found that the proper application of the indemnity principle demands that the court looks at the detail of the work done rather than merely the total.[14] In particular, the hourly rate between the parties should never exceed that charged to the client.

18.12 The principle of individual application applies not only to formal written retainers, but also where other relationships exist between legal adviser and client, and this is so even where there is an unwritten agreement or an understanding arising from a long-standing relationship. Tucker J explained the rationale for this:

> 'It is desirable that there should be uniformity in approaches to taxation, and highly undesirable and confusing for different approaches to be adopted according to whether any agreement can be brought within the statutory definition of a [contentious business agreement].'[15]

18.13 The principle of individual application will usually present no conceptual difficulties. If, for example, the retainer limits the maximum hourly rate payable for the solicitor's work, that agreement will provide both the starting point and the ceiling for the hourly rate. Difficulties may arise where the retainer (or compromise between solicitor and client) provides for the payment of a single gross sum without specifying how that sum has been calculated; in those circumstances, it might be appropriate (depending on the facts) to make an apportionment of that sum.[16] An example might be where there has been a compromise between solicitor and client for a global sum that could properly be said to reflect a consistent reduction across the board.[17]

18.14 The principle of individual application ought not to be carried to extremes. If, for example, a solicitor has rounded down their costs in each interim statute bill, the court would generally assess the costs applicable to each item and then limit the amount allowed in each bill; there would usually be no attempt to apply the rounding down to each item individually (unless, of course, there was a particular reason to do so, such as a consistent rounding down that could properly be said to be a *de facto* reduction in the hourly rate). In a case in which a law firm was charging in euros, Mann J pragmatically rejected the argument that the indemnity principle required that the costs be paid in the same currency to avoid overpayments arising out of fluctuations in the exchange rate.[18] Moreover, whilst it is a judicial technique that has its limits, where the court wishes to allow a composite hourly rate in lieu

---

[14] *The General of Berne Insurance Co v Jardine Reinsurance Management Ltd* [1998] 2 All ER 301.

[15] *Nederlandse Reassurantie Groep Holding NV v Bacon & Woodrow (No 4)* [1998] 2 Costs LR 32, at 37.

[16] See *The General of Berne Insurance Co v Jardine Reinsurance Management Ltd* [1998] 2 All ER 301, at 310, overruling *Universal Thermosensors Ltd v Hibben* (unreported), 6 March 1992, Ch D, *per* Sir Donald Nicholls V-C.

[17] See, eg, *Botham v Khan* [2004] EWHC 2602 (QB), at [51] and [52].

[18] *Schlumberger Holdings Ltd v Electromagnetic Geoservices AS* [2009] EWHC 773 (Pat).

of a multitude of rates, some judges will occasionally afford themselves a certain amount of leeway (see 51.87–51.90).

Exceptions to the indemnity principle

Over the years, Parliament has created a number of exceptions to the indemnity principle. Until recently, these exceptions have been limited. **18.15**

Litigants in person

The first exception to the indemnity principle was made in April 1976 when the Litigants in Person (Costs and Expenses) Act 1975 came into force, s 1(1) of which permitted the recovery of costs by a litigant in person for work that they have carried out themselves in pursuance of their case. This was (and still is) an exception to the indemnity principle in the sense that the costs are payable as compensation rather than as an indemnity. **18.16**

Public funding

The next exception was originally made in February 1994, when provision was made for lawyers representing a publicly funded client to recover costs and to do so regardless of any rule of law that limited the costs recoverable to the amount that the client was liable to pay their legal services providers.[19] This was (and still is) an exception to the indemnity principle in the sense that the costs are limited only by the measure of reasonableness rather than also by the extent of the client's liability for their lawyer's fees. The wording of the current provision is as follows: **18.17**

> '21. (1) Subject to paragraphs (2) to (4), the amount of costs to be paid under a legally aided party's costs order or costs agreement must be determined as if that party were not legally aided.
>
> (2) Paragraph (3) applies only to the extent that the Lord Chancellor has authorised the provider under section 28(2)(b) of the Act to take payment for the civil legal services provided in the relevant proceedings other than payment made in accordance with the arrangements.
>
> (3) Where this paragraph applies, the amount of costs to be paid under a legally aided party's costs order or costs agreement is not limited, by any rule of law which limits the costs recoverable by a party to proceedings to the amount the party is liable to pay their representatives, to the amount payable to the provider in accordance with the arrangements.
>
> (4) The amount of costs to be paid under a legally aided party's costs order or costs agreement may include costs incurred in filing with the court, or serving on any other party to proceedings, a notice or any other document in accordance with regulations made under section 12 of the Act.'[20]

Paragraph 1.39 of the 2013 Standard Civil Contract Specification states: **18.18**

> '1.39 This Paragraph represents our authority pursuant to section 28(2)(b) of the Act, for you to receive payment from another party under a Client's costs order or Client's costs agreement (as defined in Legal Aid Legislation) and to recover those costs at rates in excess of those provided for in this Contract or any other contract with us. This applies in respect of both Licensed and Controlled Work and applies also to costs recovered in respect of Counsel's fees. It also applies notwithstanding any Costs Limit on a Certificate in Licensed Work cases.'

---

[19] See the Civil Legal Aid (General) Regulations 1989 (SI 1989/339), as amended, reg 107B(1) and (3)(b).
[20] Civil Legal Aid (Costs) Regulations 2013 (SI 2013/611), reg 21.

Exceptions under the CPR

18.19 A potentially greater, but as yet largely unrealised, intervention was made on 2 June 2003. This was as a result of the amendment made to s 51(2) of the Senior Courts Act 1981 (as amended[21]), which now reads:

> 'Without prejudice to any general power to make rules of court, such rules may make provision for regulating matters relating to the costs of those proceedings including, in particular, prescribing scales of costs to be paid to legal or other representatives or for securing that the amount awarded to a party in respect of the costs to be paid by him to such representatives is not limited to what would have been payable by him to them if he had not been awarded costs.'

Thus the Civil Procedure Rule Committee has been given the power to make rules that permit payment of costs that are unfettered by the indemnity principle.

18.20 In the early days following this amendment, there was concern about whether the Committee could lawfully be given the power to interfere with something as fundamental as the indemnity principle.[22] In particular, there were concerns that the Committee was set up to make rules 'governing ... practice and procedure',[23] and that the indemnity principle transcends those things. Those concerns may have influenced the Committee, because it has so far made only very limited use of this power. If CPR, Part 45, is put to one side for the moment, the only occasion on which the Committee has used its powers is to make a 'belt and braces' provision in respect of conditional fee agreement (CFA) Lites.[24]

18.21 That said, Simon J has relied upon s 51(2) of the Senior Courts Act 1981 (as amended) to dismiss an appeal in which he held that the indemnity principle does not apply where the Civil Procedure Rule Committee has made provision for fixed costs (see 50.81–50.106).[25]

18.22 Finally, it is worth clarifying that s 51(2) of the 1981 Act does not permit the Committee to abolish the indemnity principle (as opposed to setting it aside in accordance with the provisions of the CPR) and that it is generally accepted that primary legislation would be required to achieve that purpose.[26]

Agreements to disapply the indemnity principle

18.23 It is possible for the parties to agree to disapply the indemnity principle. Where this is done, it would require very clear words before expenditure that a client could not be required to meet under the terms on which that client engaged legal services providers could

---

21 This amendment was effected by s 31 of the Access to Justice Act 1999 and by the Access to Justice Act 1999 (Commencement No 10) Order 2003 (SI 2003/1241), art 2. Confusion can arise because it is often the case that a provision is cited by reference to the Act that made the amendment, rather than to the Act that was amended.

22 See, eg, Master O'Hare, 'In Defence of the Indemnity Principle', Paper presented to the Costs Forum, 30 November 2001.

23 See Civil Procedure Act 1997, s 1.

24 See the pre-2013 CPR, r 43.2(3), which provided: 'Where advocacy or litigation services are provided to a client under a conditional fee agreement, costs are recoverable under Parts 44–48 notwithstanding that the client is liable to pay his legal representative's fees and expenses only to the extent that sums are recovered in respect of the proceedings, whether by way of costs or otherwise.' It is described as being a 'belt and braces' provision because it is far from certain that CFA Lites breach the indemnity principle at all.

25 *Nizami v Butt* [2006] EWHC 159 (QB).

26 See, eg, Lord Chancellor's Department, *The Indemnity Principle: Programme of Change* (London: HMSO, 2002).

nonetheless be recovered from the paying party.[27] Thus an agreement to disapply the indemnity principle would, in general, not allow a receiving party to claim costs that fell outside the ambit of the agreement with their legal services provider.

Evidencing the Indemnity Principle

To prove compliance with the indemnity principle, it is necessary to demonstrate the existence of an enforceable retainer supporting all of the costs that are claimed. This can be done by relying on certain presumptions (see below) or by adducing evidence (usually, but not necessarily, in the form of a written retainer). **18.24**

Three issues need to be addressed: first, the extent to which a receiving party may rely solely on the presumptions to prove their retainer (18.26–18.29); secondly, the extent to which a receiving party is required to adduce evidence of the retainer (18.35–18.39); and thirdly, the way in which the court would take account of the evidence (18.40–18.45). It should be noted that CFAs may be treated differently from other retainers (see 18.38–18.39). **18.25**

The two presumptions relating to the indemnity principle

The law relating to non-conditional retainers differs from that relating to CFAs; each type of retainer is considered separately. It is assumed that the reader is familiar with the process of election—otherwise known as the *Pamplin* procedure[28] (see 46.40–46.59). **18.26**

Non-conditional retainers

Where the receiving party intended to enter into a private (that is, non-conditional) contract of retainer with their legal services provider, there are two presumptions upon which that party may rely. In practice, where the legal representative is a solicitor, the second is by far the more important of the two. **18.27**

First presumption: client liable for fees of the person whom they engage The first presumption is that a client is liable for the fees of a legal services provider whom they engage.[29] This presumption is rebuttable by evidence[30] and will not come into play if the work was carried out under a contract of retainer that is unenforceable.[31] Lloyd J explained the presumption in these terms: **18.28**

> 'Once it was shown ... that [the receiving party] was indeed the client, then a presumption arose that he was to be personally liable for the costs. That presumption could,

[27] *Motto & Ors v Trafigura Ltd & Anor (Rev 3)* [2011] EWCA Civ 1150, at [62], *per* Lord Neuberger MR.

[28] After *Pamplin v Express Newspapers Ltd* [1985] 1 WLR 689.

[29] See *Adams v London Improved Motor Builders Ltd* [1921] 1 KB 495, at 501. See also *R v Miller (Raymond)* [1983] 1 WLR 1056, at 1059–62, which was cited with approval in *Bailey v IBC Vehicles Ltd* [1998] 3 All ER 570, at 574. See also *Hazlett v Sefton Metropolitan Borough Council* [2000] 4 All ER 887; *Meretz Investments Ltd v ACP Ltd* [2007] EWHC 2635 (Ch).

[30] See *Blankley v Central Manchester and Manchester Children's University Hospitals NHS Trust* [2014] EWHC 168 (QB), at [47], *per* Phillips J, which was left undisturbed on appeal (see [2015] EWCA Civ 18).

[31] See, eg, *Radford & Anor v Frade & Ors* [2018] EWCA Civ 119. This was a case in which the solicitor and clients were working on the basis that there was a conditional fee agreement when, in truth, the written agreement did not cover the work in question. On the facts, there was an unwritten—and therefore unenforceable—conditional fee agreement in existence for much of the work. McCombe LJ found that this prevented the principle in *Adams v London Improved Motor Builders Ltd* [1921] 1 KB 495 from coming into play: see *ibid*, at [33]–[41] (esp [38]).

however, be rebutted if it were established that there was an express or implied agreement, binding on the solicitor, that [the receiving party] would not have to pay those costs in any circumstances.'[32]

18.29 This presumption has its limitations and in practice it is not as valuable to receiving parties as it might first appear. These issues are dealt with in more detail at 27.191–27.199. The presumption is usually taken as going to the indemnity principle itself—that is, it is usually accepted that proof of the primary fact (that the client has instructed the legal services provider) will imply the secondary fact (that there is an enforceable retainer).[33] It can be seen from the cases referred to at 27.191–27.199 that, in practice, the presumption can be afforded significant weight, but that tends to be only where the facts suggest the existence of a private retainer based on contract. Indeed, one could argue that the presumption is merely a presumption of fact rather than of law.[34]

18.30 **Second presumption: the *Bailey* presumption** The second presumption (which, as noted, is by far the more important of the two) is created by a solicitor lending their signature to the certificate to a bill of costs; hence a presumption is created that there has been no breach of the indemnity principle. An evidential analysis would be that, unless the contrary can be shown, there is a presumption that proof of the primary fact (that the bill of costs has been certified) will imply the secondary fact (that there has been no breach of the indemnity principle). The presumption—which is usually referred to as 'the *Bailey* presumption'[35]—is rebuttable by evidence and is probably best described as a rebuttable presumption of fact and law. *Bailey* was a pre-CPR decision, but there is no doubt that it remains good law.[36]

18.31 The effect of the presumption was explained by Henry LJ thus: 'The Court can (and should unless there is evidence to the contrary) assume that his signature to the bill of costs shows that the indemnity principle has not been offended.'[37]

18.32 Henry LJ went on to give his explanation of why a solicitors' signature should be given weight:

> 'In so signing he [the solicitor] certifies that the contents of the bill are correct. That signature is no empty formality ... The signature of the bill of costs under the Rules is effectively

[32] *R v Miller (Raymond)* [1983] 1 WLR 1056, at 1061. After having been elevated, Lloyd LJ affirmed this principle in *Ghadami v Lyon Cole Insurance Group Ltd* [2010] EWCA Civ 767, at [10]. The need to show 'an agreement ... not to have to pay those costs in any circumstances' is not a test of universal applicability; it applies only in cases in which the facts imply the existence of a retainer. See the discussion about *Byrne v Kunkel & Kunkel* [1999] 1 CL 349 in Chapter 27.

[33] See, eg, the way in which Banks LJ developed the notion of implied agency arising out of the fact of instruction by the member of a union (see 18.63). As an extreme example, see *Harrington v Wakeling* [2007] EWHC 1184 (Ch). It is arguable that this is an overly simplistic analysis and that the secondary fact is not that there is presumed to be an enforceable retainer, but that there is presumed just to be a retainer that would, in the absence of reason to believe otherwise, generally be enforceable. Indeed, one could argue that the presumption is merely a presumption of fact rather than of law.

[34] That is, the presumption may merely be an expression of the fact that where the client has given instructions and has not agreed that the legal representative will go unpaid, those are circumstances that would naturally lend themselves to the existence of an implied, but enforceable, private retainer. Similar presumptions may arise in the context of CFAs; hence the giving of instructions may be evidence of ratifying a collective CFA: *Kitchen v Burwell Reed & Kinghorn Ltd* [2005] EWHC 1771 (QB), at [16].

[35] After *Bailey v IBC Vehicles Ltd* [1998] 3 All ER 570.

[36] See, eg, *Burstein v Times Newspapers Ltd* [2002] EWCA Civ 1739.

[37] *Bailey v IBC Vehicles Ltd* [1998] 3 All ER 570, at 575.

the certificate by an officer of the Court that the receiving party's solicitors are not seeking to recover in relation to any item more than they have agreed to charge their client.'[38]

With the benefits bestowed by the *Bailey* presumption come onerous responsibilities, however. This was also explained by Henry LJ: '[The] other side of a presumption of trust afforded to the signature of an officer of the Court must be that breach of that trust should be treated as a most serious disciplinary offence.'[39] **18.33**

In a similar vein, Judge LJ emphasised that the responsibility extends to ensuring that the court is not misled: **18.34**

> 'As officers of the court, solicitors are trusted not to mislead or to allow the court to be misled. This elementary principle applies to the submission of a bill of costs. If a cap or similar arrangement had applied in this case, I should have expected [the receiving party's solicitors] to have disclosed that fact . . .'[40]

'Genuine issue' The *Bailey* presumption does not always apply (in the sense that it does not always arise). In particular, it does not apply where costs have been incurred under certain CFAs (see 18.38–18.39). In addition, it may be rebutted by evidence. The presumption will not be rebutted merely by putting the receiving party to proof of the secondary fact (that is, that there has been no breach of the indemnity principle),[41] instead, a 'genuine issue'—otherwise known as a 'genuine concern'—must be made out. This principle was stated by the Divisional Court (Lord Bingham CJ and Harrison J)[42] in a way which has since been approved by the Privy Council;[43] it has since been adopted by tribunals[44] and, to a limited extent, by courts in other common-law jurisdictions.[45] Harrison J, giving the judgment of the court, expounded the principle: **18.35**

> 'The need for a [receiving party] to give evidence to prove his entitlement to costs rather than relying on the presumption in his favour will not, however, arise if the defendant simply puts the [receiving party] to proof of his entitlement to costs. The [receiving party] would be justified in relying on the presumption in his favour. It would be necessary for the defendant to raise a genuine issue as to whether the [receiving party] is liable for his solicitors' costs before the [receiving party] would be called upon to adduce evidence to show that he is entitled to his costs.'[46]

The evidence must be sufficient to displace the secondary fact or at least to question it. There is a dearth of authority on what amounts to a 'genuine issue'. It may be that the absence of authority on the point is a reflection of the fact that the phrase speaks for itself (although there is another possible explanation[47]). It could be argued that the test is that the **18.36**

[38] *Ibid*, at 575.

[39] *Ibid*, at 576.

[40] *Ibid*, at 574. See also *GSD Law Ltd v Wardman & Ors* [2017] EWCA Civ 2144, at [39], *per* Newey LJ.

[41] *Burstein v Times Newspapers Ltd* [2002] EWCA Civ 1739, at [28]; *Hazlett v Sefton Metropolitan Borough Council* [2000] 4 All ER 887, at 893.

[42] *Hazlett v Sefton Metropolitan Borough Council* [2000] 4 All ER 887.

[43] The practice was approved by the Privy Council in *Kellar v Williams* [2004] UKPC 30, at [23].

[44] See, eg, *Triplerose Ltd Re Forth Banks Tower* [2016] UKUT 77 (LC).

[45] See, eg, *Heung Kong (Holdings) Ltd v Chan Wai Yip* [2002] HKCFI 631 (Hong Kong); *Curran v Finn* [2002] IEHC 124 (Republic of Ireland).

[46] *Hazlett v Sefton Metropolitan Borough Council* [2000] 4 All ER 887, at 893.

[47] The lack of authority could well reflect the fact that if the court were to find a genuine issue and if the receiving party were to be required to adduce evidence of the retainer, the cat would already be out of the bag by that stage, so an appeal would be pointless; as such, the only truly effective appeal would be one brought immediately after the decision to put the receiving party to their election. Such appeals are rare because they

paying party 'must show that there is a genuine reason for believing that it is not a proper [retainer]'[48]—that is, that the paying party must raise a *prima facie* case. One could raise an equally credible argument that the test is simply that there must be an issue that requires adjudication and that it must be genuine.

18.37 The fact that a receiving party is impecunious would not, of itself, give rise to a genuine issue[49] nor would the fact that a receiving party has received assistance from a third party, for example where an employer supports an employee by providing the assistance of its in-house legal staff.[50]

Conditional fee agreements

18.38 The first presumption (that the giving of instructions implies the existence of an enforceable retainer—see 18.28) is not capable of applying to CFAs because there can be no such thing as an enforceable implied CFA (see 29.17 and, by analogy, 27.214–27.215).

18.39 As to the *Bailey* presumption, the Court of Appeal has found that it should not extend to the written instrument of any agreement made under the Conditional Fee Agreements Regulations 2000.[51] It is possible that the same applies to other conditional fee agreements, as discussed at 29.44–29.52.

Scrutiny by the court

18.40 Although a receiving party may elect not to disclose their retainer documentation (if any) to their opponent, the receiving party has less freedom in so far as production to the court is concerned.

18.41 Where there is a dispute about the receiving party's liability to pay costs to their legal services providers, a request for a detailed assessment hearing must be accompanied by 'any agreement, letter or other written information provided by the legal representative to his client explaining how the legal representative's charges are to be calculated'.[52] Where a litigation is being funded by an insurer, the requisite documents ought to include those establishing a retainer between a legal services provider and an insurer.[53]

18.42 It has been argued that, for there to be a 'dispute' that is sufficient to engage to the requirement to provide the court with retainer documentation, the paying party must raise a *prima facie* case that there has been a breach of the indemnity principle.[54] There is no authority as to whether this argument is correct nor, in particular, as to whether a 'dispute' would be created by a paying party merely putting the receiving party to proof on the indemnity principle. If there is a need to prove that there is a 'dispute', the requisite threshold is, in practice, a low one.[55]

---

usually require the appellant to ask the court below to adjourn pending the appeal and that is a request that no party would relish making.

[48] *Hazlett v Sefton Metropolitan Borough Council* [2000] 4 All ER 887, at 894, *per* Harrison J.

[49] *Burstein v Times Newspapers Ltd* [2002] EWCA Civ 1739.

[50] See, eg, *Pepin v Watts* [2002] EWCA Civ 958, at [15]–[19].

[51] SI 2000/692.

[52] PD 47, para 13.2(i).

[53] See *Ilangaratne v British Medical Association* [2005] EWHC 2096 (Ch), at [38]–[39].

[54] See *ibid*, at [37].

[55] See *ibid*, at [37], where Warren J found that 'a surprisingly high rate' was sufficient to amount to a dispute.

18.43 It would be possible for a receiving party to refuse to comply with the requirement to provide retainer documents to the court, but (for obvious reasons) the more a receiving party protests, the more apprehensive both the court and the paying party would become. Depending on how they explain their actions, a receiving party's refusal to produce documentation to the court may result in that party being put to their election (which would mean that they would have to consider unveiling the retainer documentation to the paying party, as well as to the court).[56]

18.44 The act of providing retainer documentation to the court is different from the act of *relying* on that documentation: the first is merely the act of offering documents for inspection, whereas the latter is the act of using them for the purposes of establishing an affirmative case. The former would not entitle the paying party to see the documentation in the same way as the latter would. This issue is considered in detail at 46.49 and 46.60–46.66.

18.45 In summary, the receiving party would find it difficult to avoid offering up the retainer documentation for inspection by the court and any attempt to do so would expose them to the risk of losing credibility.

Procedural issues

18.46 Where the question of a genuine issue is raised by the paying party, the receiving party must be given adequate notice of the points that are going to be taken. Harrison J has explained that such notice should be sufficient to allow the receiving party to deal with the points properly and without the need for an adjournment.[57] It is implicit from the way in which Harrison J dealt with the matter that a paying party would be at risk on costs if the receiving party were taken by surprise.

18.47 While it will usually be the paying party who seeks to persuade the court that a genuine issue has been made out, the court is entitled to make such a finding of its own volition, as Lloyd J explained (albeit in the context of the first presumption rather than the *Bailey* presumption):

> 'In practice, of course, the taxing officer will have before him on the taxation the whole of the solicitor's file. If it appears to the taxing officer that there is doubt whether there was an express or implied agreement, binding on the solicitors, not to seek to recover the cost from the client, the taxing officer should ask for further evidence. It must then be for the taxing officer to come to a conclusion on the whole of the facts presented to him.'[58]

18.48 Indeed, the court is under a duty to consider the relevant material properly, as Judge LJ explained:

> 'The taxing officer is exercising a judicial function, with substantial financial consequences for the parties. To perform it, he is trusted properly to consider material which would normally be protected from disclosure under the rules of legal professional privilege. If, after reflecting on the material available to him, some feature of the case alerts him to the need to make further investigation or causes him to wonder if the information with which he is being provided is full and accurate, he may seek further information. No doubt he would begin by asking for a letter or some form of written confirmation or reassurance as appropriate. If this

[56] As an example of the way in which this can happen in practice, see *ibid.*
[57] *Hazlett v Sefton Metropolitan Borough Council* [2000] 4 All ER 887, at 893.
[58] *R v Miller* [1983] 1 WLR 1056, at 1061.

were to prove inadequate he might then make orders for discovery or require affidavit evidence. It is difficult to envisage circumstances in which the party benefiting from the order for costs will not have been anxious to provide the required information, but if all else fails, it would theoretically be open to him to order interrogatories.'[59]

18.49 Disclosure, where appropriate, may be in the form of redacted documents.[60] It is implicit from the way in which the Court of Appeal has commented upon redaction that the court ought to be put in a position to decide whether the redaction is fair;[61] common sense dictates that this would usually mean providing an unredacted copy of the retainer for the court.

18.50 As is discussed at 46.69–46.71, disclosure of the retainer would (with limited exceptions) be for the purposes of the detailed assessment only.

The ethos of the CPR

18.51 For the reasons set out above, both the paying party and the receiving party have certain legal rights that they can enforce if they wish, although the court has repeatedly encouraged parties to act cooperatively and reasonably in resolving any dispute about the indemnity principle. In so far as paying parties are concerned, Judge LJ gave the following guidance:

> 'An emphatic warning must be added against the over enthusiastic deployment of [the court's power to investigate the indemnity principle], particularly at the behest of the party against whom the order for costs has been made ... [The] danger of "satellite litigation" is acute. As far as possible consistent with the need to arrive at a decision which does broad justice between the parties, it must be prevented or avoided, and the additional effort required of the parties kept to the absolute minimum necessary for the taxing officer properly to perform his function.'[62]

It is implicit in this guidance that paying parties should not seek to bring disproportionate challenges. Any paying party who does so would be at risk on costs.

18.52 Likewise, Judge LJ encouraged receiving parties to act in a reasonable and cooperative way:

> '[In] view of the increasing interest taken in this issue by unsuccessful parties to litigation, coupled with the developing practice in relation to conditional fees, the extension of the "client care" letter and contentious business agreements ... in future, copies of the relevant documents (where they exist) or a short written explanation of the kind eventually provided in this case ... should normally be attached to the bill of costs. This will avoid skirmishes which add unnecessarily to the costs of litigation.'[63]

This means that whilst a receiving party is not legally obliged to disclose evidence of their retainer, they are encouraged to do so. Warren J has suggested that the onus to give voluntary disclosure of the relevant material is even greater under the CPR than it was when *Bailey* was decided.[64]

---

59 *Bailey v IBC Vehicles Ltd* [1998] 3 All ER 570, at 572.
60 See, eg, *Hollins v Russell* [2003] EWCA Civ 718, at [72].
61 *Ibid*, at [80].
62 *Bailey v IBC Vehicles Ltd* [1998] 3 All ER 570, at 573.
63 *Ibid*, at 575.
64 See *Ilangaratne v British Medical Association* [2005] EWHC 2096 (Ch), at [40].

Evidential issues relating to the indemnity principle

If a receiving party is put to their election, they will have to choose whether to rely upon the relevant retainer documentation or to prove compliance with the indemnity principle in some other way. There may be entirely valid reasons why a receiving party would choose not to rely upon the retainer documentation,[65] in which case evidence will usually be in the form of a witness statement given by the conducting legal services provider or the client (or both). That said, if a receiving party fails to explain why they have elected not to rely upon their written retainer, that party will (for obvious reasons) have difficulty in discharging the burden of proving that the retainer is enforceable. The fact that a client makes a witness statement evidencing the retainer will not always be sufficient; Scott Baker J has found that a costs judge is, in appropriate circumstances, entitled to view such evidence with some scepticism.[66] **18.53**

Cross-examination

Where a genuine issue has been made out, it will not necessarily follow that the court will allow a paying party to test the evidence with all of the rigour that might be appropriate in substantive litigation (although this may be appropriate in some cases).[67] The comments of Judge LJ have already been noted (see 18.52); other judges have said much the same. In a case in which the paying party sought permission to cross-examine the receiving party's solicitor, Latham LJ (giving the judgment of the court) said: **18.54**

> 'If there is no prospect that cross-examination could either undermine or further elucidate the respondent's case, to refuse to accede to the application will not be unfair and it would not breach the requirement of the overriding objective that the parties are on equal footing but would save expense and deal with the issues proportionately and expeditiously.'[68]

Notice of challenges

Where the receiving party gives disclosure of retainer documentation at a hearing, and where that disclosure prompts the paying party to raise factual queries that are contentious and which require determination, Mann J has commented that the receiving party ought to be given adequate time to adduce evidence to prove their case.[69] **18.55**

Evidence of payment not generally required

Where the receiving party has been put to their election, it is trite costs law that the issue is whether they have a liability to their legal services provider for costs, not whether the receiving party has actually paid those costs. In view of this, it would not usually be the case that a receiving party would be expected to produce evidence of payment. Robert Walker J has suggested (*obiter*) that there is no automatic right to see solicitor and client invoices.[70] Moreover, where work is done under a private retainer prior to entering into a CFA, the **18.56**

---

[65] The editor has seen one example in which the retainer documentation contained reference to the details of a sensitive family matter that were so embedded in the documentation that those details could not easily be redacted.

[66] *R (Ecclestone) v Legal Aid Board* [2001] EWHC 9008 (Costs).

[67] See, eg, *GSD Law Ltd v Wardman & Ors* [2017] EWCA Civ 2144.

[68] *Burstein v Times Newspapers Ltd* [2002] EWCA Civ 1739, at [28].

[69] *Fosberry & anor v HM Revenue and Customs* [2007] EWHC 2249 (Ch), at [46] (which case has also acquired a second neutral citation number, [2008] EWHC 3344 (Ch), and is also often reported as [2007] EWHC 3344 (Ch)); see also *Hazlett v Sefton Metropolitan Borough Council* [2000] 4 All ER 887, at 893.

[70] In *Mainwaring v Goldtech Investments Ltd* [1997] 1 All ER 467.

fact that invoices were not rendered to clients is not of itself sufficient for the court to infer that there was no enforceable retainer.[71] That said, where evidence of invoicing is adduced, it may be taken into account.[72]

Privilege

18.57 To date, the Court of Appeal has not found it necessary to rule on whether a retainer is a privileged document.[73] Rimer J has suggested that client care letters (or at least client care letters that do not give legal advice) are not privileged; that said, those comments were *obiter*.[74] Given that the process of election operates regardless of whether the retainer is privileged, this point will be academic in most instances.

The Indemnity Principle in Practice

18.58 This section addresses those disputes about the indemnity principle that are focused on issues other than the retainer itself. If the dispute is primarily about the effect or meaning of the contract of retainer, then the relevant issues are covered in Chapters 27–31.

The principle of dual liability for costs

18.59 It is often the case that organisations such as legal expense insurers, motoring organisations, unions and employers agree fund litigation on behalf of their clients, members or employees. Where there is one, the written retainer is often with the funder rather than the litigant, but it is not unusual for there to be no such document.[75]

18.60 Unless it can be proven that there was an agreement that the litigant would not, in any circumstances, be liable for the legal services providers' costs (or unless there is an express retainer that is in some way insufficient or unenforceable), there will have been no breach of the indemnity principle (see 18.63–18.66). As will be explained in the examples that follow, the matter can be analysed either in terms of agency, ratification or 'dual liability'. It is the last of these analyses that is usually preferred in practice, but in reality there is a great deal of overlap between them.

18.61 Similar analyses apply to collective CFAs (which are governed by written instruments that the client often does not see and does not sign). In those circumstances, the client's liability will be created as a result of the funder acting within its authority; an alternative view is that the client ratifies the agreement.[76] Provided that the client is aware of the fact that their legal services providers are instructed under such an agreement, the client's acceptance of the legal services providers' services will be sufficient to imply that the client has ratified or accepted their liability under that agreement.[77] The remainder of this discussion

---

[71] *Griffiths v Solutia (UK) Ltd* [2001] 1 Costs LR 99, at 106 (this case went to appeal, but not on this point).

[72] See, eg, *Radford & Anor v Frade & Ors* [2018] EWCA Civ 119, at [40].

[73] See *Hollins v Russell* [2003] EWCA Civ 718, at [79].

[74] *Dickinson v Rushmer* [2002] 1 Costs LR 128, at 132.

[75] See, eg, *Ilangaratne v British Medical Association* [2007] EWHC 920 (Ch), at [30] *et seq*. See also *Ghadami v Lyon Cole Insurance Group Ltd* [2010] EWCA Civ 767, in which the documentation was not compliant with the Solicitors' Code of Conduct 2007.

[76] *Thornley v Lang* [2004] 1 WLR 378, at [19].

[77] *Kitchen v Burwell Reed & Kinghorn Ltd* [2005] EWHC 1771 (QB), at [16].

is concerned primarily with non-conditional retainers, but many of the principles will also apply to conditional retainers.

The topic is dealt with from the viewpoint of a number of different types of funder: unions, insurers, motoring organisations, employers and the state, but what is said is of general application (that is, where any person pays costs on behalf of another person). This was made clear by Vos J in the following way: **18.62**

> '[It was] submitted that there was a difference between this case [in which a commercial entity had discharged the receiving party's costs] and the cases of unions and automobile associations, because there was some obligation in those cases as between the insurer and insured, or organisation and member, to discharge the fees on behalf of the client or insured. In my judgment, however, that is a distinction without a difference ... The question that the court has to answer in deciding in any particular case, where there is a party claiming to be indemnified with respect of costs is whether that person has paid or become liable to pay the costs. The question of who actually discharges the costs is not the relevant question ... In every case that I have cited the costs were actually discharged by some third party, by the insurer, by the Automobile Association, by the union or by someone else. It matters not that the third party has paid. What matters is whether ... the party claiming indemnity has "become liable to pay" those costs.'[78]

Unions

In the context of a claim funded by a union, Banks LJ offered the following analysis (which is based on agency, but could have been phrased in terms of dual liability): **18.63**

> 'It is said here that the plaintiff is not in a position to claim an indemnity, for two reasons, as I understand: one is that the firm who purported to act as his solicitors were not his solicitors at all; all they were were the solicitors for the union, and their only instructions were to act as solicitors for the union. The other is that, assuming the union instructed the solicitors to act as solicitors for the plaintiff, yet it was upon the terms that the solicitors should look solely to the union and not to the plaintiff for payment of their costs. Sankey J [the judge below] held that neither contention was well founded upon facts. He came to the conclusion that the solicitors were engaged to act as solicitors for the plaintiff by the union and that in so engaging the solicitors, the union were acting as agents of the plaintiff. In my opinion that view is correct. The learned Judge also found that there had been no arrangement either by the union or by the solicitors or by the plaintiff, that the solicitors should not under any circumstances, look to the plaintiff for payment of their costs. With that conclusion upon the facts I also agree.'[79]

He went on to mention a further step: **18.64**

> 'When once it is established that the solicitors were acting for the plaintiff with his knowledge and assent, it seems to me that he became liable to the solicitors for costs and that liability would not be excluded merely because the union undertook to pay the costs. It is necessary to go a step further and prove that there was a bargain, either between the union and the solicitors or between the plaintiff and the solicitors, that under no circumstances was the plaintiff to be liable for costs.'[80]

[78] See *Popat v Edwin Coe LLP* [2013] EWHC 4524 (Ch), at [33]–[35]. See also *Illumina Inc v Premaitha Health plc* [2018] EWHC 180 (Pat), at [38]–[47], *per* Henry Carr J.

[79] *Adams v London Improved Motor Coach Builders* [1919] 1 KB 495, at 500.

[80] *Ibid*, at 501. Younger LJ would have had more doubt as to the result but for *R v Archbishop of Canterbury* [1903] 1 KB 289, a case in which the Treasury Solicitor had intervened to act on the Archbishop's behalf in proceedings against him for *mandamus*, but without any express retainer by him. It was held that the Archbishop was potentially liable to the Treasury Solicitor for costs and could therefore recover the costs of

18.65 Although *obiter*, Atkin LJ analysed the same issue in terms of dual liability (that is, where both the funder and the litigant have a liability for the legal services providers' fees):

> 'In these circumstances I think that it is highly probable, though the matter has not been discussed, that the solicitors have a personal right against the trade union to receive a proper remuneration for their services. It has not been discussed, and we do not know the precise terms of the relationship between the trade union and the solicitors, but I assume there exists such an obligation. Nevertheless there is nothing inconsistent in that obligation co-existing with an obligation on the part of the plaintiff to remunerate the solicitors.'[81]

18.66 Regardless of how the situation is analysed, the paying party will not usually be able to make out a breach of the indemnity principle. This will not always be the case, however. Whilst there is some doubt as to whether it remains good law, the court has found that a union was acting as a maintainer in circumstances in which the support that was being provided was not mentioned in the members' handbook.[82] Even if this does remain good law, such cases will be rare.

Insurers

18.67 In a case involving an insurer as funder, it was argued that no costs had been incurred by the successful defendant because the insurer was bound to pay the costs. That argument was rejected. Viscount Dilhorne explained why:

> 'In this case the solicitors, no doubt first instructed by the insurance company, were the solicitors on record as solicitors for the respondent. They acted for him, and in the absence of proof of an agreement between him and them, or between them and the insurance company that he would not pay their costs, they could look to him for payment of the work done and his liability would not be excluded by the fact that the insurance company had itself agreed to pay their costs.'[83]

18.68 A similar conclusion is reached when the matter is analysed in terms of subrogation (see 18.73–18.77). It is not always necessary for the agreement between the insurer and the legal services provider to be in writing.[84] Where insurance is subject to an excess and where that excess is the only amount that the insured has been told must be paid, Lloyd LJ has confirmed that, in the absence of agreement to limit the fees to that amount, the indemnity principle will not act as a limit on the sums that must be paid.[85]

Motoring organisations

18.69 A similar conclusion is reached in circumstances in which the funder is a motoring organisation. Lord Denning explained why:

> '[It was suggested that the fees were not incurred by the receiving party] but were incurred by the Automobile Association because the Automobile Association undertook

his successful defence of the proceedings, even though he might never have been called upon by the Treasury Solicitor to make the liability good in reality. For Younger LJ, that case was decisive.

81 *Adams v London Improved Motor Coach Builders* [1919] 1 KB 495, at 505.

82 *Greig v National Amalgamated Union of Shop Assistants, Warehousemen and Clerks* (1906) 22 TLR 274; see also *Oram v Hutt* [1914] 1 Ch 98, CA; cf *Hill v Archbold* [1968] 1 QB 686, in which *Greig* and *Oram* were doubted.

83 *Davies v Taylor (No 2)* [1974] AC 225, at 230.

84 *Ilangaratne v British Medical Association* [2007] EWHC 920 (Ch), at [30] *et seq*, in which Briggs J found that negotiations may be admitted as being evidence of the fact of an agreement even if they would be inadmissible for the purposes of its interpretation. The agreement in that case was that there was a long-standing understanding that instructions sent to the legal representative by the insurer would give rise to a retainer between the insured and the legal representative on terms already agreed.

85 *Ghadami v Lyon Cole Insurance Group Ltd* [2010] EWCA Civ 767, at [25] and [26].

> the appeal and instructed their solicitors and paid them. I cannot accept this suggestion. It is clear that [the receiving party] was in law the party to the appeal. He was the person responsible for the costs. If the appeal had failed, he would be the person ordered to pay the costs. If the costs had not been paid, execution would be levied against him and not against the Automobile Association. The truth is that the costs were incurred by [the receiving party], but the Automobile Association indemnify him against the costs ... that is sufficient to satisfy the requirement that the costs were "incurred by him".'[86]

Employers

18.70 Lloyd J considered the situation in which the funder is an employer (in a case related to criminal, rather than civil, costs, but nothing turns on that):

> 'I would hold, following *Adams* [*v London Improved Motor Builders Ltd* [1921] 1 KB 495] and the other cases I have mentioned, that costs are incurred by a party if he is responsible or liable for those costs, even though they are in fact paid by a third party, whether an employer, insurance company, motoring organisation or trade union and even though the third party is also liable for those costs. It is only if he has agreed that the client shall in no circumstances be liable for the costs that they cease to be costs incurred by him, as happened in *Gundry v Sainsbury* [[1910] 1 KB 645]. In practice, of course, the taxing officer will have before him on the taxation the whole of the solicitors file. If it appears to the taxing officer that there is doubt whether there is an express or an implied agreement, binding on the solicitors, not to seek to recover the costs from the client the taxing officer should ask for further evidence. It must then be for the taxing officer to come to a conclusion on the whole of the facts presented to him. Unless those facts establish a clear agreement express or implied that in no circumstances will the solicitor seek to obtain payment from their client then the basic presumption stands ...'[87]

18.71 In a similar vein, Pill LJ declined to find that a genuine issue had been raised by virtue of the fact that a litigant (a police officer) had chosen to be represented by his employer's solicitors.[88]

The state

18.72 The fact that publicly funded clients do not have an agreement directly to pay their legal advisers does not undermine the indemnity principle.[89] In any event, the indemnity principle does not apply to costs properly claimed in respect of publicly funded work (see 18.17).

Subrogation

18.73 Subrogation is an equitable remedy that is based on restitution. It arises when an insurer admits a liability to the insured[90] and pays the insured the amount due under the contract of insurance.[91] Subrogation will then operate in such a way as to allow the insurer to be placed in the position of the insured. The insurer must sue or defend in the name of the

---

86 *Lewis v Avery (No 2)* [1973] 1 WLR 510, at 513, which case was doubted in *Davies v Taylor (No 2)* [1974] AC 225, but on a different point.

87 *R v Miller* [1983] 1 WLR 1056, at 1061.

88 See, eg, *Pepin v Watts* [2002] EWCA Civ 958, at [15]–[19].

89 *Daley v Diggers Ltd* [1951] 1 KB 661; *Starkey v Railway Executive* [1951] 2 All ER 902.

90 *Page v Scottish Insurance Corpn Ltd* (1929) 140 LT 571, CA.

91 *Castellain v Preston* (1883) 11 QBD 380, CA, at 389.

insured, not in its own name.[92] This distinguishes subrogation from assignment. The insurer must provide the insured with an indemnity against the costs of any proceedings the insurer commences or defends.[93]

18.74 It has been argued that, where a liability insurer brings a claim pursuant to its right of subrogation, that insurer cannot recover costs because any award would be in the name of the insured rather than the insurer. There are two ways in which this matter can be analysed. The first arises out of the way in which the Canadian judge, Middleton J, dealt with the issue: 'The costs awarded are in the same way the costs of the insurance company, though awarded in the name of the insured.'[94]

18.75 The effect of this (if it is good law, which it is usually accepted to be) is that if the insured is awarded costs of a subrogated claim, the insurer will be entitled to the benefit of that award of costs. This is in keeping with the way in which subrogation operates in litigation other than costs. In particular, subrogation will generally arise regardless of the nature of the legal right against the third party; it will, for example, arise when that right is tortious,[95] contractual[96] or statutory.[97] There is no reason to believe that it would not apply to a right to costs that may be regarded as being statutory[98] or contractual[99] (or both), as the case may be. In any event, for the reasons set out above (see 18.67–18.68), the fact that the insurer may be liable for the legal services providers' costs will not undermine the indemnity principle.[100]

18.76 The second way in which this issue may be analysed is as an instance of 'dual liability'. In this regard, Moore-Bick LJ had this to say:

> '[44] It is important to remember that although the proceedings are being conducted at the behest of the insurers, the parties to the litigation are in fact [the insured and his opponent]. Accordingly, any solicitors instructed in the matter were acting for him and he became liable for their costs: see *Davies v Taylor (No 2)* [1974] AC 225 ... and *Thornley v Lang* [2003] EWCA Civ 1484 ... to which Ward LJ has referred. However, since the insurers were entitled to direct the conduct of the litigation, they were entitled to decide whom he should instruct to act on his behalf...
>
> [45] As between [the insured and his opponent] the existence of a policy of insurance under which he had already been indemnified against his loss is in law irrelevant – it is *res inter alios acta*,[[101]] as it used to be said. The fact that the insurers are bound to indemnify him against the costs of the proceedings does not provide the council with a defence to a claim to recover the costs, any more than it provides it with a defence to a claim for the damage caused to his house.'[102]

---

[92] See *Clark v Blything Inhabitants* (1823) 2 B & C 254.

[93] *Dane v Mortgage Insurance Corpn* [1894] 1 QB 54, at 61.

[94] *Gough v Toronto & York Radial Railway Co* (1918) 42 OntLR 415, at 417. This is similar to the way in which rights in substantive litigation are transferred to the insurer: see, eg, *Finlay v Mexican Investment Corpn* [1897] 1 QB 517.

[95] See, eg, *Lister v Romford Ice and Cold Storage Co Ltd* [1957] AC 555.

[96] See, eg, *Castellain v Preston* (1883) 11 QBD 380.

[97] See, eg, *Ellerbeck Collieries Ltd v Cornhill Insurance Co Ltd* [1932] 1 KB 401.

[98] That is, a right to costs made pursuant to s 51 of the Senior Courts Act 1981.

[99] Where there is an agreement to pay costs.

[100] See, in particular, the discussion concerning *Davies v Taylor (No 2)* [1974] AC 225.

[101] Meaning 'a thing done between others'.

[102] *Sousa v London Borough of Waltham Forest Council* [2011] EWCA Civ 194, at [44].

Thus the arrangements between the insured and the insurer are of no concern to the paying party, and they do not give rise to a defence to a claim for costs. If this is correct, a right of subrogation is not necessary for the purposes of proving compliance with the indemnity principle and, whilst there is no authority on the point, it would seem that dual liability would exist even where that right was a contingent right (that is, if legal services providers were instructed before the right of subrogation arose). **18.77**

Miscellaneous issues relating to the indemnity principle

Generally speaking, the issue of the indemnity principle will turn on the enforceability of the contract of retainer—that is, if the retainer is found to be enforceable, it will usually follow that there has been compliance with the indemnity principle. This will not always be the case, as is explained below. **18.78**

The effect of undischarged funding certificates on other retainers

As is explained below, there is a prohibition against legal service providers seeking to 'top up' fees payable under a legal aid certificate.[103] In theory, this means that a paying party could rely on the fact that a receiving party has an undischarged certificate as giving rise to a breach of the indemnity principle in so far as recovery of costs under some other type of retainer (such as a CFA) is concerned. **18.79**

The law derives from Access to Justice Act 1999, s 10(1), which is in these terms: 'An individual for whom services are funded by the Commission as part of the Community Legal Service shall not be required to make any payment in respect of the services except where regulations otherwise provide.' Section 22(2) of the 1999 Act adds the following: **18.80**

> '(2) A person who provides services funded by the Commission as part of the Community Legal Service or Criminal Defence Service shall not take any payment in respect of the services apart from—
> (a) that made by way of that funding, and
> (b) any authorised by the Commission to be taken.'

Similar provisions have applied in years gone by.[104]

Davis LJ has explained that the prohibition created by the above is 'on the obligation to make, and entitlement to receive, payments for services on a concurrent basis'.[105] This means that there will be instances in which some other retainer is still enforceable even where the funding certificate has not been formally discharged.[106] Such cases may arise because the undischarged certificate has become 'spent'[107] or because there **18.81**

---

[103] See *Merrick v Law Society* [2007] EWHC 2997 (Admin).

[104] See Legal Aid Act 1974, s 8, and Legal Aid (General) Regulations 1980 (SI 1980/1894), reg 65. See also Legal Aid (General) Regulations 1989 (SI 1989/339), reg 64: 'Where a certificate has been issued in connection with any proceedings, the assisted person's solicitor or counsel shall not receive or be party to the making of any payment for work done in those proceedings during the currency of that certificate (whether within the scope of the certificate or otherwise) except such payments as may be made out of the fund.'

[105] See *Hyde v Milton Keynes NHS Foundation Trust* [2017] EWCA Civ 399, at [28].

[106] See *ibid*, at [31].

[107] In *Littaur v Steggles Palmer* [1986] 1 WLR 287, a client declined to pay their outstanding fees on the footing that, under Legal Aid Act 1974, s 8, and Legal Aid (General) Regulations 1980 (SI 1980/1894), reg 65, the solicitors were precluded from receiving any payment by reason of the fact that a certificate was still extant. Ackner LJ rejected that argument on the basis that the work under the certificate had been completed

has been a 'definite switch' to some other form of funding.[108] Davis LJ had this to say on the point:

> 'It is clear that the authorities [[109]] ultimately are focused on the justice and fairness of the individual outcome in each case, on substance rather than form. In all those cases it was said (as here) that none of the difficulties would have arisen had only a formal discharge been obtained. But that feature did not in any way prove determinative.'[110]

As such, a paying party would, in general, have difficulty in relying on the fact that a certificate was not formally discharged as giving rise to a breach of the indemnity principle.

Putative waiver of fees and the indemnity principle

18.82 If a legal services provider waives its fees, then that waiver may be passed along the line to the paying party in such a way as to diminish or extinguish the amount that the paying party has to pay. In practice, however, waiver (or, more accurately, acts akin to waiver) will not necessarily have this effect. This is not only because the waiver may fail for want of consideration (see 27.90), but also because acts akin to waiver generally do not totally extinguish the liability for costs. Two examples are given: agreements not to enforce and debts that have been written off as being bad.

18.83 **Agreement not to enforce** Mann J has found that if a legal services provider agrees to forgo enforcement of its entitlement by court proceedings, this will not amount to a total extinguishment of the client's liability in the sense that it will relieve the paying party of the burden of paying costs; that agreement was merely an agreement not to enforce liability in one particular way.[111]

18.84 **Bad debts** Patten J has found that if solicitors write off costs as being a bad debt (for accounting purposes), the contractual liability to pay costs will continue and, accordingly, the solicitors will be entitled to continue to rely on their lien.[112] There is no reason to believe that the same would not also apply to the indemnity principle.

Solicitor acting on credit and the indemnity principle

18.85 In a case in which it was suggested that a third party had been maintaining the claim, the receiving party's solicitor lodged an affidavit saying that he (personally) had been conducting the action on credit. Mustill LJ found that, in those circumstances, there was no maintenance; moreover, no adverse comment was made about the propriety of that situation.[113]

---

and that the certificate had therefore become spent: *ibid*, at [29B]. In a similar vein, see *Turner v Plasplugs Ltd* [1996] 2 All ER 939, at 943, *per* Sir Thomas Bingham MR. See also *Burridge v Stafford* [2000] WLR 927, at 943, in which (in a case in which a funded person became a litigant in person without the certificate being discharged) Woolf MR had this to say: '[A] legal aid certificate does not have to be discharged if it is spent so that a litigant is no longer receiving assistance under the certificate. By analogy it seems to me that the existence of a legal aid certificate which has not been discharged is merely for present purposes evidential.' See also *Mohamadi v Shellpoint Trustees Ltd* [2009] EWHC 1098 (Ch), at [24], *per* Briggs J.

[108] See *Hyde v Milton Keynes NHS Foundation Trust* [2017] EWCA Civ 399, at [45], *per* Davis LJ.

[109] See fn 107.

[110] *Hyde v Milton Keynes NHS Foundation Trust* [2017] EWCA Civ 399, at [41].

[111] *Harrington v Wakeling* [2007] EWHC 1184 (Ch).

[112] *Slatter v Ronaldsons* [2002] 2 Costs LR 267.

[113] *Singh v Observer Ltd* [1989] 3 All ER 777. This appeal was allowed by consent.

'CFA Lites' and the indemnity principle

What follows concerns 'CFA Lites'[114] (see 29.03 and 29.68). It has been argued that CFA Lites are inherently flawed and that they necessarily result in the indemnity principle being breached. This argument had some success in a case before a value added tax (VAT) tribunal in which a solicitor had agreed to charge only those costs received from the other side (if any), in which Macpherson J held that no order for costs could be made in those circumstances because there was nothing in respect of which an indemnity could apply.[115] His reasoning was based on the premise that, in the absence of an award of costs, the client had no liability and therefore no costs could be recovered. **18.86**

That case concerned the incidence of costs rather than the assessment of costs, but it is clear that Macpherson J very much had the indemnity principle in mind. His analysis has been criticised on the basis that it relies on circular reasoning. Commentators have also pointed out that the process of awarding and assessing costs does not create the liability, but merely discovers the amount due.[116] Regardless of whether Macpherson J's analysis was correct on the facts of the case before him, it is not binding on any court and is rarely followed.[117] **18.87**

In any event, where costs fall to be assessed under the CPR and where the agreement was made on or after 2 June 2003,[118] the concerns raised by Macpherson J will not arise. This is because the pre-2013 CPR, r 43.2(3), makes the following provision (also see 29.68): **18.88**

> '(3) Where advocacy or litigation services are provided to a client under a conditional fee agreement, costs are recoverable under Parts 44 to 48 notwithstanding that the client is liable to pay his legal representative's fees and expenses only to the extent that sums are recovered in respect of the proceedings, whether by way of costs or otherwise.'

It is a moot point whether this provision is necessary, because it is possible to draft a CFA Lite in such a way as to avoid the concerns raised by Macpherson J.[119] Nonetheless, it is also possible to make inadvertent errors in the drafting of a CFA Lite and, where this happens, CPR, r 43.2(3), may be relevant. That provision should not be regarded as setting aside the indemnity principle entirely; it merely prevents a CFA Lite from being unenforceable by reason of the fact that liability is linked to recovery. If a CFA Lite is unenforceable for other reasons, the indemnity principle will apply. **18.89**

Contractual problems

It is possible for an enforceable retainer to fail to satisfy the indemnity principle as a matter of contract. An example would be where the retainer is enforceable, but it does not apply to the claim in question. Another example would be where a CFA does not contain a definition of 'win'. These issues are dealt with at 31.29 and 29.63–29.64. **18.90**

---

[114] This discussion of 'CFA Lites' is intended not only to include those agreements that fall within the category of cases to which Conditional Fee Agreements Regulations 2000 (SI 2000/692), reg 3A, refers, but to any agreement under which the liability of the client is limited to those sums that are recovered in the litigation.

[115] *Commissioners of Customs & Excise v Vaz* [1995] STC 14.

[116] See, eg, *Kings Costs Team 'Costs Law Brief'* (2007) 157 NLJ 7278, at 890–1 (the editor was one of those commentators).

[117] See *Harrington v Wakeling* [2007] EWHC 1184 (Ch), at [14], in which it was distinguished on the facts.

[118] See the Civil Procedure (Amendment No 2) Rules 2003 (SI 2003/1242), r 6.

[119] This can be done, eg, by phrasing the 'Lite' provision in terms of waiver.

Quantum meruit

18.91 A claim for *quantum meruit* is a claim for payment for a reasonable sum for services provided. The term *quantum meruit* will usually refer to a right to payment arising from the unjust enrichment by one party at the expense of another, which right is an example of a restitutionary remedy. The term may also be used to refer to a contractual remedy, which in effect is an implied contractual term to pay a reasonable rate.

18.92 In so far as the law of costs is concerned, the issue of *quantum meruit* may arise in the following situations:

- where there is a written retainer that fails to specify the basis upon which the legal services provider will be paid;
- where there is no written retainer;
- where a contract of retainer has been found wanting for some reason; and
- where a contract of retainer has been repudiated.

Where there is no written retainer or where it fails to specify the basis of payment

18.93 The first two situations will, in general, present no conceptual difficulties. It will usually be self-evident that the agreement between the legal services provider and the client was not intended to be gratuitous; in those circumstances, the law will often imply an agreement that a reasonable fee be paid.[120] The issue of implied retainers is dealt with at 27.190–27.199 and the issue of Lloyd J's presumption is addressed at 18.28. Even where the court finds that there is an implied contract of retainer, not everything will be plain sailing for the receiving party: the court may, for example, decline to allow an uplift to take account of the complexity of the work.[121]

Where a written retainer is defective

18.94 It is trite law that a claim in *quantum meruit* cannot arise if there is an existing and enforceable contract to pay an agreed sum,[122] but what is less obvious is whether such a claim can arise in circumstances in which the retainer exists, but is not an enforceable contract.

18.95 It would seem that, in those circumstances, no claim in *quantum meruit* will arise. If the retainer is a contract that has been found to be unenforceable by reason of it being contrary to public policy, then no claim can be made in *quantum meruit*. This was made clear by Schiemann LJ:

> 'If the court, for reasons of public policy refuses to enforce an agreement that a solicitor should be paid it must follow that he cannot claim on a *quantum meruit* ... In the present case, what public policy seeks to prevent is a solicitor continuing to act for a client under a conditional normal fee arrangement. That is what [the solicitor] did. That is what she wishes to be paid for. Public policy decrees that she should not be paid.'[123]

---

[120] See *Kellar v Williams* [2004] UKPC 30, in which the Privy Council applied *Way v Latilla* [1937] 3 All ER 759, at 763.

[121] See *Adams v MacInnes* [2001] EWHC 9014 (Costs).

[122] *The Olanda* [1919] 2 KB 728.

[123] *Awwad v Geraghty & Co* [2001] QB 570, at 596; see also *Wild v Simpson* [1918–19] All ER Rep 682, at 693 (Duke LJ dissenting, albeit on other grounds).

Whilst his comments were *obiter* and based on hypothetical facts, Christopher Clarke J made similar comments in the context of an unenforceable CFA. In essence, he found that a client is not *unjustly* enriched in circumstances in which the enrichment has been as a result of the operation of statute.[124] **18.96**

It occasionally happens that a legal services provider accepts instructions on the assumption that a particular type of funding exists (such as public funding), but it later transpires that it had made a mistake. Burton J considered this issue in a case in which, through no fault of his own, the solicitor had carried out work outside of the scope of the legal aid certificate. Burton J had this to say: **18.97**

> 'Whatever inroads there now are into that indemnity principle as a result of express agreements between a solicitor and his client ... I do not consider that there is, at any rate yet, and certainly was not in this case between 1989 and 1997, any kind of implication in what was otherwise a legal aid arrangement that the client would be liable to his solicitor to make payment in respect of his costs in the event of there being no legal aid, but only in the event that he should be successful in recovering his costs against the opposite party. Or put another way, I do not consider that the plaintiff "freely accepted" the defendant's services on that basis.'[125]

A particular difficulty with the solicitor's argument was that the claim for *quantum meruit* was, in effect, a claim for payment of costs under an informal (and therefore unenforceable) CFA.[126] Whether a claim for *quantum meruit* can be made in other circumstances (such as where it is wrongly believed that a funder would pay the costs) is a moot point. **18.98**

Where a retainer has been repudiated

As to the last of the four situations referred to at 18.92, where a client repudiates a contract of retainer, the legal services provider may wish to rely on *quantum meruit* for the purposes of recovering fees for the work already done. Whilst this would be theoretically possible in so far as private contracts of retainer are concerned,[127] Judge Behrens (sitting as a judge of the High Court) has found that it is not possible in so far as CFAs are concerned.[128] **18.99**

Estoppel

Estoppel may arise in many guises, but in the present context there are three arguments that are most relevant: **18.100**

(1) that because the paying party has agreed to pay costs, they are estopped from contending that costs are not payable for want of compliance with the indemnity principle;

[124] *Forde v Birmingham City Council* [2009] EWHC 12 (QB), at [206]. He was unpersuaded that changes to the rules that govern solicitors had altered the lie of the land.

[125] *Bridgewater v Griffiths* [2000] 1 WLR 524, at 530.

[126] In *Radford & Anor v Frade & Ors* [2018] EWCA Civ 119, the issue of *quantum meruit* was raised in the context of an unenforceable conditional fee agreement that came into being by virtue of the fact that no one realised that the written CFA was limited only to certain procedural steps. McCombe LJ did not deal with *quantum meruit* expressly, but, by implication, he rejected the notion that it would apply in such circumstances.

[127] This argument could be based on cases such as *Planche v Colburn* (1831) 8 Bing 14 and *Chandler v Boswell* [1936] 3 ARE 179.

[128] See *Howes Percival LLP v Page* [2013] EWHC 4104 (Ch), at [311].

(2) that the notion of 'fair conduct'[129] would prevent the legal services provider's client from taking the point that an agreement was unenforceable and that, as a result, the paying party should also be estopped from taking the point;[130] and
(3) that a party is estopped from challenging the authority of the receiving party's legal services provider to act.

18.101 As to the first, whilst it is possible to envisage situations in which a paying party would be estopped from relying on the indemnity principle, those situations rarely arise in practice. In particular, it would rarely be the case that the receiving party would have volunteered the information that there was a problem with their retainer, so no estoppel would arise because the paying party would not have been put in a position in which they were able to acquiesce to that knowledge.[131]

18.102 As to the second of the two arguments, Schiemann LJ had this to say:

> '[Counsel] submits that the principle of fair conduct ... prevents [the client] from now taking the point that ... the agreement was champertous. I disagree for a number of reasons. One will suffice. The principle in that case does not prevent [the client] from asserting facts in his evidence. If those facts lead the court to the conclusion that the agreement was champertous then the court will refuse to enforce it whatever [the client's] attitude. Points on illegality are taken by the court of its own motion, not because of any consideration of fairness as between the two parties to the dispute but on wider considerations.'[132]

Thus the notion of 'fair conduct' has no real part to play. Schiemann LJ's comments were made in the context of a solicitor and client dispute, but they are likely to apply *a fortiori* to a dispute between the parties.

18.103 As to the third, Phillips J has explained that it is wrong in principle for an opponent to be estopped from challenging the authority of a receiving party's legal services provider.[133]

18.104 In summary, it would rarely be the case that a paying party would be estopped from relying on the indemnity principle and estoppel will certainly not arise out of the mere fact that the paying party has agreed to pay costs.

---

[129] See *Panchaud Frères Établissement Grains* [1970] 1 Lloyd's Rep 53.

[130] As articulated *ibid.*

[131] *Bridgewater v Griffiths* [2000] 1 WLR 524, at 530, relying on *Chitty on Contracts* (27th edn, London: Sweet & Maxwell, 1994), vol 1, para 3-081.

[132] *Awwad v Geraghty & Co* [2001] QB 570, at 595.

[133] See *Blankley v Central Manchester and Manchester Children's University Hospitals NHS Trust* [2014] EWHC 168 (QB), at [60], in which Phillips J had this to say: 'Solicitors acting in proceedings represent and warrant that they have the authority of the party they purport to represent. In the ordinary course, the opposing party does not in any sense agree that such authority in fact exists, nor share a common assumption as to its existence. The opposing party does not need to (and would be ill advised to) communicate any such agreement or assumption, precisely because it may later emerge that authority was absent or defective. The fact that the opposing party deals with solicitors without questioning their authority does not amount to such communication, and implies at most that the opposing party is relying upon the solicitors' warranty. Such reliance cannot give rise to any form of estoppel.' Phillips J's decision was upheld on appeal: [2015] EWCA Civ 18.

The Costs of In-house Staff

The next topic is whether a receiving party can recover costs for services rendered by persons who are also the receiving party's employees and, if so, how those costs are to be assessed. The term 'in-house' will be used to refer to such employees. **18.105**

The discussion distinguishes between legal and non-legal in-house staff. In so far as the former are concerned (that is, legal in-house staff), it should be noted that different considerations apply where the employer is in the business of providing legal services. That topic is dealt with at 59.38–59.53. **18.106**

The costs of in-house legal staff

Where costs are claimed for work done by in-house legal staff, those staff are—in a nutshell—given a notional status as independent practitioners. This achieves a rough approximation of the costs of employing them and therefore achieves justice without requiring the court to carry out the often disproportionate and difficult task of ascertaining the actual cost of employment.[134] The idea of notional fees being ascribed to legal services providers is nothing new.[135] **18.107**

Russell LJ laid down the following principles.[136] **18.108**

- The proper method of assessment is to assess the bill as though it were the bill of an independent solicitor.
- The hourly rate is assessed in the same way as it would be if it were the bill of an independent solicitor.
- It is a sensible and reasonable presumption that the figure arrived at on this basis will not infringe the indemnity principle.
- There may be special cases in which it appears reasonably plain that the indemnity principle will be infringed if the above method is used, but it would be impracticable and wrong to require a total exposition and breakdown of the activities and expenses of the in-house department with a view to ensuring that the principle is not infringed, and it is doubtful whether by any method certainty on the point could be reached.

There is no reason to believe that these points would not also apply to legal services providers who are not solicitors.

Russell LJ explained his reasoning in the following way: **18.109**

> 'Suppose a solicitor in independent practice with an assistant solicitor, two legal executives, clerks and typists and other overheads, who in year 1 works in fact exclusively for corporation X. For year 2 it is arranged that his whole office and staff is taken over as a department of corporation X, the solicitor also becoming an employee of the corporation at a salary commensurate with the profit made by him in year 1 doing the corporation's legal work. Suppose

[134] See the comments of Arden J in *Stubblefield v Kemp* [2001] 1 Costs LR 30, at [25].

[135] See *Crown & Stafford Stone v Eccleshall Magistrates' Court* [1988] 1 All ER 430 (in which a solicitor was allowed his notional fees for appearing in his own case in a magistrates' court); *R v Boswell; R v Halliwell* [1987] 2 All ER 513 (in which a barrister was allowed a notional fee for attending an appeal in respect of his own fees).

[136] *In re Eastwood, deceased; Lloyds Bank Ltd v Eastwood* [1975] Ch 112, at 132.

that in year 1 the corporation was successful in a piece of litigation in which in fact one of the legal executives did all the work: in taxing the corporation's costs the taxing master would apply the A and B conventional method and the figure for the discretionary item would be £75. Suppose in year 2 the corporation is successful in exactly comparable litigation, again with the legal executive doing the work: if the method of taxation adopted in this case were followed, only A (£45) would be allowed for the item, though the change would not have effected any saving to the corporation, who, instead of paying the profit to the solicitor in respect of that litigation, would have paid to him the equivalent in the form of a proportion of his salary. This example seems to us to demonstrate that there must be something wrong in an approach which uses only the A of the A B conventional method in the case of an employed solicitor.'[137]

18.110 Russell LJ's method came under attack in a case in which the paying party argued that whilst it may be correct to assign in-house staff a notional status, the quantum of costs should reflect the fact that the costs of running an in-house legal department may be lower than the costs of running an independent practice. In recognition of the fact that Russell LJ's judgment was binding, the paying party argued that these factors could be taken into account by adopting an 'A plus B' approach (see 51.24), but by assessing 'B' at nil. Elias J pithily rejected this argument: 'It is little short of fiction to say one is [to] apply the same method [as applied by Russell LJ] if in fact [one] is always allocating nothing under the B element.'[138] Elias J went on to acknowledge, however, that there might be 'special' cases in which it would not be appropriate to assess the in-house costs as if they were those of an independent practitioner.

18.111 It will occasionally be the case that the receiving party will, of its own volition, adduce accountancy evidence or produce a calculation similar to the 'Expense of Time' calculation. In a case in which this happened, the paying party argued that where such evidence was before the court, it should be taken into account. Buxton LJ rejected that argument and pointed to the considerable difficulty that would be caused by attempting to take such evidence into account.[139] That said—like Elias J—he too commented (*obiter*) that the usual method could be departed from in a special case. No guidance exists as to what might make a case 'special'.

18.112 Although not in a binding decision, Master Campbell has found that the fact that a party is also represented by independent solicitors does not preclude the recovery of costs in respect of in-house staff.[140]

18.113 In summary, the costs of in-house legal staff will generally be treated as if the work had been carried out by independent solicitors, but (in theory at least) the court can depart from that principle in special cases.

Government departments

18.114 It is often the case that government departments have accounting arrangements such that one department may pay a certain amount for legal services provided by another. Where this is so, the points made above about in-house solicitors will usually apply. Whilst not

---

[137] *Ibid*, at 131.
[138] *Maes Finance Ltd v WG Edwards & Partners* [2000] 2 Costs LR 198, at 200.
[139] *Cole v British Telecommunications plc* [2000] 2 Costs LR 310.
[140] *Ultraframe (UK) Ltd v Eurocell Building Plastics Ltd & Anor* [2006] EWHC 90069 (Costs).

binding, Mr CMG Ockelton, Vice President of the Upper Tribunal (Immigration and Asylum Chamber), has found that such payments are irrelevant for the purposes of the indemnity principle (see 51.82).[141]

The costs of in-house non-legal staff

To deal briefly with the recoverability of costs for services rendered by employees who are not (or who are not supervised by) in-house legal staff, it is necessary to stray slightly from the topic of the indemnity principle. **18.115**

It is trite law that costs are limited to legal costs.[142] Subject to certain exceptions, this means that a litigant is unable to recover the costs of work done by themselves that might otherwise have been carried out by a solicitor. It is convenient to call this principle the 'general prohibition'. The general prohibition is widely accepted as being correct as a matter of common law, having been accepted in many other common-law jurisdictions.[143] **18.116**

At this point, it is worth pausing to consider the mechanisms by which a party can avoid the operation of the general prohibition. This is helpful because it allows a distinction to be made between the indemnity principle and the other ways in which the costs of in-house staff (lawyers or otherwise) may be governed. In so far as they are relevant, the exceptions to the general prohibition are: **18.117**

- a litigant in person's costs, which are recoverable under the Litigants in Person (Costs and Expenses) Act 1975;
- a solicitor litigant's costs, which are now governed by CPR, r 46.8, and the associated practice direction;
- an employed (in-house) solicitor's costs, where they are acting in the course of their employment; and
- the costs of a limited number of categories of incidental work carried out by non-lawyers.

The relevance of these categories is that, where the work might otherwise have been carried out by a solicitor, the costs will be recoverable if they fall within any one of the first three categories (only the first of which relates to non-lawyers), but in all other circumstances they would be recoverable only if they were to fall within the last category. **18.118**

Whether the costs fall into the last category will depend on the facts of each case. In particular, it will depend on factors such as the nature of the work being undertaken, whether the receiving party is a litigant in person, etc. These matters go well beyond the topic of the indemnity principle and are considered elsewhere in this book (see, for example, 3.92–3.100 and 49.104–49.111), but their relevance to the indemnity principle is that it is clear from the way in which the court has dealt with such issues that there must actually be a *loss*; where there is no loss, there will be no costs. **18.119**

In summary, the costs of in-house non-legal staff may be recoverable in certain circumstances, but it will always be the case that a loss must be shown. **18.120**

---

[141] See *R (on the application of Bakhtiyar) v Secretary of State for the Home Department* [2015] UKUT 519 (IAC), at [31], *per* Mr CMG Ockelton. See also *Town Investments Limited and Ors v Department of the Environment* [1978] AC 359, at 399–401.

[142] *London Scottish Benefit Society v Chorley* (1884) 12 QBD 452.

[143] See, eg, the Irish case of *Henehan v Allied Irish Banks plc* (unreported), 19 October 1984, IEHC, *per* Findlay P; *Dawson & Anor (t/a AE Dawson & Sons) v Irish Brokers Association* [2002] IESC 36.

Pro Bono funding

18.121 '*Pro bono* funding' is an oxymoronic phrase that describes the practice of a legal services provider going without pay in the hope that a discretionary award to a 'prescribed charity' will be made in lieu of its fees.[144] It is a system that allows the court to lessen or negate the windfall from which a losing party would otherwise benefit as a result of the fact that the wining party's legal services provider was generous enough to act for free. The Access to Justice Foundation has this to say on the topic:

> 'Before October 2008 [when *pro bono* funding was introduced], the indemnity principle meant a party represented by *pro bono* lawyers could not obtain costs against the other side. The better resourced party therefore had an unfair advantage of litigating without normal costs risks. The introduction of *pro bono* costs aimed to help level the playing field for *pro bono* assisted parties, by preventing the losing party escaping an order for costs. In the process, a new form of funding would be created to support the provision of free legal help to those in need.'[145]

18.122 A pedant would say that *pro bono* awards are not for 'costs' at all, but are for monies payable in lieu of costs. Whilst this is correct and may occasionally be of practical relevance (see 18.127), for most purposes an award in lieu of costs can be thought of as being akin to a costs order. Indeed, there is express provision that, where appropriate, CPR, Parts 44–47, will, with appropriate modifications, apply (see 18.131).

The jurisdiction relating to *pro bono* awards

18.123 *Pro bono* funding is governed by Legal Services Act 2007, s 194, that section having been in force since 1 October 2008. The facility to make an award will apply only to legal services provided after that date;[146] in the Supreme Court, it applies only where the decision, order or judgment that is the subject of the appeal is made or given on or after 1 April 2013.[147] It does not apply in tribunals.[148] The 2007 Act refers to the legal representative[149] and the client by the letters 'R' (for representative) and 'P' (for party). The legal representative must provide representation free of charge, in whole or in part, but may continue to be a legal representative within the meaning of s 194 regardless of whether P has also been paid for legal services.[150] Put otherwise, a legal representative is able to act *pro bono* notwithstanding the fact that it was originally instructed on a private basis. 'Free of charge' means that R provides services not for or in expectation of fee, gain or reward.[151] That must be the basis on which the work was carried out at the time in question.[152]

---

[144] CPR, r 46.7(1) and (2).

[145] See Access to Justice Foundation, *Unlock Funds for Justice: Full Guidance and FAQs*, available online at http://www.atjf.org.uk/uploads/4/1/8/1/41811233/150819_full_guidance_landscape.pdf, at p 3.

[146] Legal Services Act 2007, s 194(11). *Pro bono* funding in the Supreme Court will be governed by Legal Aid, Sentencing and Punishment of Offenders Act 2012, s 61.

[147] See Legal Aid, Sentencing and Punishment of Offenders Act 2012, s 61(2).

[148] *Raftopoulou v Revenue & Customs Commissioners* [2015] UKUT 630 (TCC).

[149] Which is defined as a person exercising a right of audience or conducting litigation on the party's behalf: see Legal Services Act 2007, s 194(10).

[150] Legal Services Act 2007, s 194(1)(a) and (2).

[151] Legal Services Act 2007, s 194(10).

[152] See *Hurst v Denton-Cox* [2014] EWHC 3948 (Ch).

Where these conditions are met, the court may order an opponent to make a payment to a prescribed charity in respect of the legal representative's work (or, if only part of the representation was provided free of charge, in respect of that part).[153] A 'prescribed charity' is a charity prescribed by order.[154] At present, the only prescribed charity is the Access to Justice Foundation, which was established by the Law Society, Bar Council, CILEx and Advice Services Alliance to receive and distribute additional financial resources to support agencies and projects that provide free legal assistance to those in need.[155] That organisation distributes the monies received to 'regional legal support trusts' (although monies may also be distributed to other *pro bono* projects). The regional legal support trusts will, in turn, distribute to local advice agencies and law centres. **18.124**

An order under s 194 of the 2007 Act is not made for the benefit of P, but directly for the benefit of the prescribed charity.[156] The Access to Justice Foundation suggest the following wording: **18.125**

> 'The [party] must pay costs for *pro bono* representation on or before [date] to The Access to Justice Foundation (PO Box 64162, London WC1A 9AN), [summarily assessed at £____] [or] [to be assessed on the standard/indemnity basis if not agreed].'[157]

Where an order has been made, it is the represented party's responsibility to send a copy of the order to the prescribed charity within seven days of receipt.[158] This can be done by sending a scanned copy of the order to costs@ATJF.org.uk, or by posting a hard copy to: The Access to Justice Foundation, PO Box 64162, London WC1A 9AN. Payment may be by cheque payable to The Access to Justice Foundation or by bank transfer to account number 00018272, sort code 40-52-40, account name The Access to Justice Foundation.

The discretion to make a *pro bono* award

In considering whether to make an award, the court must have regard to whether an order would have been made if R had not been acting *pro bono*.[159] The CPR make it clear that the court may take into account the same factors as it would have taken into account when considering the incidence of costs generally.[160] It is notable that the Legal Services Act 2007 does not say that the court must disregard the fact that R is acting *pro bono*,[161] so it is arguable that the court is entitled to take that factor into account when deciding what order to make. That impression is entirely consistent with CPR, r 46.7(1), which reads: **18.126**

> '(1) Where the court makes an order under section 194(3) of the 2007 Act—
> (a) the court may order the payment to the prescribed charity of a sum no greater than the costs specified in Part 45 to which the party with *pro bono* representation would have been entitled in accordance with that Part and in respect of that representation had it not been provided free of charge; or

---

153 Legal Services Act 2007, s 194(3).
154 Legal Services Act 2007, s 194(8).
155 See Legal Services Act 2007 (Prescribed Charity) Order 2008 (SI 2008/2680), art 2.
156 CPR, r 46.7(1) and (2).
157 See Access to Justice Foundation, *Unlock Funds for Justice: Full Guidance and FAQs*, available online at http://www.atjf.org.uk/uploads/4/1/8/1/41811233/150819_full_guidance_landscape.pdf, at p 6.
158 CPR, r 46.7(3).
159 Legal Services Act 2007, s 194(4).
160 CPR, r 46.7(4)(a).
161 This is different from public funding, where such a provision does exist.

(b) where Part 45 does not apply, the court may determine the amount of the payment (other than a sum equivalent to fixed costs) to be made by the paying party to the prescribed charity by—
  (i) making a summary assessment; or
  (ii) making an order for detailed assessment, of a sum equivalent to all or part of the costs the paying party would have been ordered to pay to the party with pro bono representation in respect of that representation had it not been provided free of charge.'

18.127 Thus, whilst the court is limited in the sense that it cannot award more than would have been awarded had the services not been provided *pro bono*, it does not necessarily have to award the same amount. If a party had a mixture of *pro bono* and paid representation, the court will need to make two orders: a *pro bono* costs order for the *pro bono* work and a normal costs order for the fee-paid work.[162]

18.128 There is no guidance as to which factors the court can take into account when deciding whether to make an award. Although there is no authority on the point, it may be that the court is able to consider whether it is fair that the losing party is ordered to make a payment that is not intended to meet the interests of justice in the particular case in hand, but to achieve access to justice in the community as a whole. It could well be that one issue to be given particular emphasis is the financial strength of the losing party and whether they are insured.

18.129 As mentioned above, it is a moot point whether an award under s 194 of the 2007 Act is an order for 'costs' because it is a special type of order that is made for the benefit of a person who is not one of the parties. The relevance of this is that it is generally accepted that it is not possible to claim set-off.[163] If, therefore, the court wishes to take competing entitlements into account in such a way as to make an order for the net balance (which may be nil), this is best done at the stage of deciding the incidence of costs rather than at a later stage—that is, it is best for the court to make a single order that meets the justice of the situation generally. It is for this reason that the Access to Justice Foundation encourages *pro bono* representatives to ask the court to reserve orders for costs until the conclusion of the matter.[164]

Costs protection and *pro bono* funding

18.130 Persons who have the benefit of *pro bono* representation do not have any general costs protection. That said, there is limited protection in that a *pro bono* award may not be ordered against a party who 'was at all times' represented either *pro bono* or under Legal Services Commission (legal aid) funding.[165] It is not clear what the court will make of the phrase 'was at all times'. One could argue that it does not mean 'was at all material times' and that its true meaning is precisely what it says—namely, that a person must have had continuous and uninterrupted *pro bono* support throughout the whole of the claim.

162 The bill of costs, however, would be combined and split into parts: see PD 47, para 5.8(2).
163 Whilst not in any way a source of law, see Access to Justice Foundation, *Unlock Funds for Justice: Full Guidance and FAQs*, available online at http://www.atjf.org.uk/uploads/4/1/8/1/41811233/150819_full_guidance_landscape.pdf, at p 7.
164 See *ibid.*
165 See Legal Services Act 2007, s 194(5).

The quantification of *pro bono* awards

The award may be quantified by summary or detailed assessment.[166] The amount of any award under s 194(3) of the 2007 Act is limited to the amount that would have been awarded under a conventional costs order,[167] including where the order would have been for fixed costs.[168] **18.131**

Procedure and *pro bono* awards

In so far as proceedings commenced after 1 April 2013 are concerned,[169] the CPR expressly provide that where the court considers making or makes an order under s 194(3) of the 2007 Act, Parts 44–47 will apply with the following modifications:[170] **18.132**

- references to 'costs orders', 'orders about costs' or 'orders for the payment of costs' are to be read, unless otherwise stated, as if they refer to an order under s 194(3);
- references to 'costs' are to be read as if they referred to a sum equivalent to the costs that would have been claimed by, incurred by or awarded to the party with *pro bono* representation in respect of that representation had it not been provided free of charge; and
- references to 'receiving party' are to be read as meaning a party who has *pro bono* representation and who would have been entitled to be paid costs in respect of that representation had it not been provided free of charge.

As such, the adjectival law that relates to *pro bono* awards is, broadly speaking, the same as that which applies to costs proceedings in general.

As to the documentation that is required, Practice Direction (PD) 46, para 4.1, provides as follows: **18.133**

> 'Where an order is sought under section 194(3) of the Legal Services Act 2007 the party who has *pro bono* representation must prepare, file and serve a written statement of the sum equivalent to the costs that party would have claimed for that legal representation had it not been provided free of charge.'

Thus it would seem that a 'written statement of sum equivalent to costs' must be filed and served whenever a party seeks a *pro bono* costs award, which statement should be drafted as though the costs had been incurred by a legal representative who was not acting *pro bono*.[171] As such, it would seem that even where a party seeks a *detailed* assessment of the costs, a statement still has to be filed and served at the time that the order for a detailed assessment is sought. However, PD 47, para 5.8(2), implies that where a detailed assessment does take place, then a bill of costs is required—in particular, that where the award is submitted for detailed assessment, the bill must be **18.134**

---

[166] CPR, r 46.7(1)(b); CPD, art 10A.1.

[167] CPR, r 46.7(1).

[168] CPR, r 46.7(1)(a).

[169] Post-Jackson Civil Procedure Rules and practice directions relate to proceedings commenced after 1 April 2013. For earlier proceedings, CPR, r 44.3C, remains relevant, as well as the Costs Practice Direction (in particular, arts 4.2. 5.21, 6.2, 10A.1 and 10A.2). Those provisions are very similar to the present provisions, but if the reader wishes to read about them, they are covered in detail in the second edition of this book.

[170] CPR, r 46.7(4).

[171] PD 46, para 4.1.

divided into parts that distinguish between work that was provided *pro bono* and work that was not.[172]

18.135 Where the award has been assessed by way of detailed assessment, the presumption in CPR, r 47.20(1) (that the receiving party will be entitled to the costs of the assessment unless the court orders otherwise), does not apply. That said, the receiving party is able to apply for an order for the costs of the assessment under s 194(3) of the 2007 Act.[173]

Legal Services Act 2007, s 194

18.136 The wording of the *pro bono* section of the Legal Services Act 2007 is as follows:

> '194 **Payments in respect of pro bono representation**
>
> (1) This section applies to proceedings in a civil court in which—
> (a) a party to the proceedings ("P") is or was represented by a legal representative ("R"), and
> (b) R's representation of P is or was provided free of charge, in whole or in part.
>
> (2) This section applies to such proceedings even if P is or was also represented by a legal representative not acting free of charge.
>
> (3) The court may order any person to make a payment to the prescribed charity in respect of R's representation of P (or, if only part of R's representation of P was provided free of charge, in respect of that part).
>
> (4) In considering whether to make such an order and the terms of such an order, the court must have regard to—
> (a) whether, had R's representation of P not been provided free of charge, it would have ordered the person to make a payment to P in respect of the costs payable to R by P in respect of that representation, and
> (b) if it would, what the terms of the order would have been.
>
> (5) The court may not make an order under subsection (3) against a person represented in the proceedings if the person's representation was at all times within subsection (6).
>
> (6) Representation is within this subsection if it is—
> (a) provided by a legal representative acting free of charge, or
> (b) provided under arrangements made for the purposes of Part 1 of the Legal Aid, Sentencing and Punishment of Offenders Act 2012.[[174]]
>
> (7) Rules of court may make further provision as to the making of orders under subsection (3), and may in particular—
> (a) provide that such orders may not be made in civil proceedings of a description specified in the rules;
> (b) make provision about the procedure to be followed in relation to such orders;
> (c) specify matters (in addition to those mentioned in subsection (4)) to which the court must have regard in deciding whether to make such an order, and the terms of any order.
>
> (8) "The prescribed charity" means the charity prescribed by order made by the Lord Chancellor.
>
> (9) An order under subsection (8) may only prescribe a charity which—
> (a) is registered in accordance with section 30 of the Charities Act 2011,[[175]] and

---

172 PD 47, para 5.8(2).
173 See CPR, r 47.20(2).
174 As amended by Legal Aid, Sentencing and Punishment of Offenders Act 2012, Sch 5, para 68.
175 As amended by Charities Act 2011, s 127.

(b) provides financial support to persons who provide, or organise or facilitate the provision of, legal advice or assistance (by way of representation or otherwise) which is free of charge.

(10) In this section—

"legal representative", in relation to a party to proceedings, means a person exercising a right of audience or conducting litigation on the party's behalf;

"civil court" means—[176]

(a) the Supreme Court when it is dealing with a relevant civil appeal,
(b) the civil division of the Court of Appeal,
(c) the High Court, or
(d) the county court;[177]

"relevant civil appeal" means an appeal to the Supreme Court—

(a) from the High Court in England and Wales under Part 2 of the Administration of Justice Act 1969,
(b) from the Court of Appeal under section 40(2) of the Constitutional Reform Act 2005, or
(c) under section 13 of the Administration of Justice Act 1960 (appeal in cases of contempt of court) other than an appeal from an order or decision made in the exercise of jurisdiction to punish for criminal contempt of court;

"free of charge" means otherwise than for or in expectation of fee, gain or reward.

(11) The court may not make an order under subsection (3) in respect of representation if (or to the extent that) it is provided before this section comes into force.

[176] Amended, so as to embrace the Supreme Court, by Legal Aid, Sentencing and Punishment of Offenders Act 2012, s 61.

[177] Amended by Crime and Courts Act 2013, s 101.

19

PLURAL LIABILITY FOR AND PLURAL ENTITLEMENT TO COSTS

19.01 This chapter deals with the following topics:

- terminology and introduction (19.03);
- types of plural liability distinguished:
  - joint liability (19.05);
  - several liability (19.08);
  - joint and severable liability (19.09);
- the interpretation of contracts of retainer with more than one client (19.10);
- the interpretation of plural costs awards (19.11);
- joint liability of costs debtors (19.21):
  - full payment by one or more costs debtors (19.23);
  - partial payment by one or more costs debtors (19.24);
  - accord and satisfaction of costs (19.26);
  - reservation of the right to pursue other costs debtors (19.28);
  - promises not to sue (19.29);
- several liability of costs debtors (19.30);
- joint and several liability of costs debtors (19.31); and
- contributions between costs debtors (19.34).

19.02 Whilst the principles are explained with the focus on plural liability, they will tend to apply to plural entitlement too. The focus on plural liability is solely for illustrative purposes and to avoid repetition.

Terminology and Introduction

19.03 Where a liability or entitlement to costs attaches to more than one person, that liability or entitlement may be:

- joint;
- several; or
- joint and several.

The term 'plural liability' (or 'plural entitlement', as the case may be) is used to describe these circumstances. Where such a state of affairs exists, issues of distribution of costs may also arise, which topic is dealt with at 27.302–27.318 (in the context of retainers) and Chapter 20 (in the context of the assessment of costs).

Because most of the authorities that are referred to in this discussion derive from legal disciplines other than the law of costs, what is said in this chapter ought to be viewed as only a brief overview. Where a difficult point arises, research beyond what is set out herein will be required. **19.04**

Types of Plural Liability Distinguished

Joint liability

Joint liability is where two or more persons are ordered to pay the same costs, for example 'A and B will pay C's costs jointly'. Whilst the joint costs debtors may number two or more, they share a single obligation to pay costs. **19.05**

Special and often counter-intuitive rules apply to joint liability (see 19.24–19.28), but the essential characteristic is that payment in full by one joint costs debtor will discharge the indebtedness of the others (19.23). Thus, if A and B owe a joint liability for payment of costs of £1,000 to C, payment of £1,000 by A to C will discharge B's costs debt. **19.06**

The presence or absence of a joint liability depends not upon the manner in which the debtors are sued (or, in the context of costs debt, served with a notice of commencement), but upon the nature and quality of the liability alleged.[1] **19.07**

Several liability

Several liability is where two or more persons—possibly by the same order or by linked orders—are required to pay costs that are not the same, for example 'A will pay C's costs up to 1 January 2014 and B will pay C's costs thereafter'.[2] The effect is as though there were two or more costs orders. Full payment by one several costs debtor will not impact on the liability of the other costs debtors for their debts. Thus, if A and B each owe a several liability to C of £500, payment by A of A's £500 will have no bearing on B's costs debt. **19.08**

Joint and severable liability

Joint and severable liability is where two or more persons are ordered to pay the same costs not only jointly, but also individually. The effect of this is to disapply most of the special rules that apply to joint liabilities. The debt is, however, still owed jointly and, as such, may be enforced against either one of the debtors. Full payment by one will discharge the indebtedness of the other(s). If there are many costs debtors, it is not unusual for a series of awards to be made that distinguishes between them in the sense that the different costs debtors may bear differing total burdens (for example 'A, B and C will be jointly and severally liable for 50 per cent of D's costs, and A and B will be jointly and severally liable for the remainder').[3] **19.09**

1 See *Townsend v Stone Toms and Partners* [1981] 1 WLR 1153, CA.
2 See, eg, *Ilumina Inc v Premaitha Health plc* [2018] EWHC 180 (Pat).
3 See, eg, *Bal v Singh & Ors* [2018] EWHC 119 (Ch).

The Interpretation of Contracts of Retainer with More than One Client

19.10 The topic of contracts of retainer that involve more than one client is addressed in detail at 27.302–27.318. The topic of apportionment in general is addressed in Chapter 20.

The Interpretation of Plural Costs Awards

19.11 The issue of whether liability for costs is joint, several or joint and several is a matter of interpretation of the order or other document giving rise to an entitlement to costs.[4] The usual techniques of interpretation will apply.

19.12 The nature of an award involving more than one costs debtor or creditor will generally be apparent from the plain meaning of the words used, because an award will often state that a liability is to be borne jointly or jointly and severally. It will rarely be the case that awards will specifically state that a liability is to be borne severally, because that conclusion would usually be self-evident from the context. Thus, where the award is that A will pay the costs of the claim and B will pay the costs of a specified issue, that will create a severable liability in respect of the costs of that specified issue; it would be otiose to explicitly state the several nature of B's liability.

19.13 The interpretation of plural costs awards is not always such an undemanding task, however. A common situation is where a claim has successfully been brought against two defendants, both of whom have defended the claim separately. If, in such an instance, the claimant were to be awarded costs against both defendants where they were able to pursue only one of them (because, say, the other had become insolvent), the court would need to decide whether the claimant could recover the whole of the costs from that defendant. Whilst there is still room for argument on the point, the law probably is as explained by Lord Esher MR, who found that the liability of the defendants was not joint, but several, and said that to compel only one defendant to pay those costs would be 'absolutely contrary to natural justice'.[5] Fry LJ disagreed with Lord Esher's analysis, preferring instead to say that the issue was one of discretion for the trial judge rather than a matter that should be decided by the costs judge when interpreting the order:

> 'If natural justice requires that one defendant should not be liable for the costs occasioned solely by the act of the other defendant ... justice will be done if the Court or judge be asked to do it, but it cannot be done by the master. In my opinion the effect of the rule which has been laid down by the Master of the Rolls would be to vest in the master a discretion which by virtue of the rule belongs only to the judge.'[6]

19.14 That was more than a century ago. In more recent times, Davies J found that the judgment of Lord Esher should be preferred and that, over the years, it has become generally accepted that Fry LJ's judgment was the dissenting judgment.[7] Thus, where a single costs order is

---

4 See, by analogy, *Heaton & Ors v Axa Equity and Law Life Assurance Society plc & Anor* [2000] 4 All ER 673.

5 *Stumm v Dixon & Co and Knight* (1889) 22 QBD 529, at 531.

6 *Ibid*, at 536.

7 *CIBC Mellon Trust Co v Mora Hotel Corpn NV* [2003] EWHC 9037 (Costs).

made against two defendants who each defended the claim separately, the costs judge has the power to interpret an order that the claimant's costs should apply severally to each defendant in relation to the costs of the claimant's own defence.

Each entitling order ought to be interpreted individually. There are certain aids to interpretation that may be relevant, but they offer only limited assistance and are rarely determinative. General trends can be identified (some of which relate to agreements rather than costs orders, but the principles are broadly the same, especially where an order has been made by consent). They are set out below (19.16–19.20). **19.15**

Relevance of interests

It is open to the court to interpret an order in a way that accords with the interests of the parties[8]—that is, if their interests are joint, the order may be interpreted as joint, but if their interests are several, the order will generally be interpreted as being several. **19.16**

Silence as to severance

Under common law, a contract that provides for two or more persons to pay the same debt without that agreement making any provision for severance is a contract for a joint liability.[9] The fact that an order has been made by consent may be a relevant factor in the sense that it may be subject to the same analysis. **19.17**

Firms

Where the costs award has been made in respect of a partnership under the Partnership Act 1890, the liability of the partners of a firm is joint, not joint and several.[10] **19.18**

The irrelevance of impecuniosity

The ability of the parties to pay is usually an irrelevant factor. In particular, the ordinary meaning of the order must not be disregarded for reasons of convenience or hardship.[11] **19.19**

Fast-track trial costs

In a fast-track trial in which there is more than one claimant but only one defendant, the court may make only one award to the defendant of fast-track trial costs, for which the claimants are jointly and severally liable.[12] **19.20**

Joint Liability of Costs Debtors

In the context of costs, there are two types of joint liability: **19.21**

(a) where a costs creditor (that is, a receiving party) is owed a costs debt by more than one joint costs debtor (that is, the paying parties); and
(b) where a costs debtor owes a debt to more than one joint costs creditor.

---

[8] *Sorsbie v Park* (1843) 12 M & W 146.
[9] *White v Tyndall* (1888) 13 App Cas 263.
[10] Partnership Act 1890, s 9.
[11] *White v Tyndall* (1888) 13 App Cas 263.
[12] CPR, r 44.40(5).

As has been mentioned at 19.02, the focus is on joint liability—that is, (a) above—but this is only for illustrative purposes. With the necessary changes, the points made below would also generally apply to joint entitlement.

19.22 The special rules that are set out in 19.24–19.28 relate solely to joint liability (or entitlement, as the case may be); most do not relate to joint and several liability (or entitlement). Indeed, this is what distinguishes joint liability or entitlement from joint and several liability or entitlement.

Full payment by one or more costs debtors

19.23 Full payment of costs to only one of a number of joint costs creditors will discharge the costs debt to the others;[13] likewise, full payment of costs by one of a number of joint costs debtors will discharge the debt owed by the others.[14]

Partial payment by one or more costs debtors

19.24 The position is different where there has been a partial payment that has not been agreed between all of the relevant parties. Whether there has been an agreement that binds the other parties will depend on the construction of that agreement.

19.25 Where (without reservation) one of a number of joint costs creditors grants a release of the obligation to be paid costs, that release binds all.[15] Likewise, where a release is given by a costs creditor to one of a number of joint costs debtors, the release discharges the debt owed by all of the joint costs debtors.[16] This will not be the case if the release is given with a reservation of a right to claim against the other costs debtors.[17]

Accord and satisfaction of costs

19.26 A release may be purchased, in which case it is referred to as 'accord and satisfaction' (see, in a somewhat different context, 39.17). Where the liability is joint, the same principles apply to accord and satisfaction as will apply to release in general—in particular, that accord and satisfaction with one of a number of joint costs creditors will discharge the debt generally.[18] Accord and satisfaction with one of a number of joint costs debtors will also discharge the debt, unless there has been a reservation of right to pursue the other paying parties.[19] The making of a consent order may amount to accord and satisfaction.[20]

19.27 The payment of costs will count as consideration for the accord and satisfaction.[21] In practical terms, this means that if a costs creditor accepts payment of part of their costs from one joint costs debtor on the basis that the payment will discharge that party's liability for costs, the costs creditor must reserve the right to pursue the other costs debtors for the balance if that is the creditor's intended course of action.

---

13 *Powell v Brodhurst* [1901] 2 Ch 160 (albeit in the general, rather than costs, context).

14 *Mainwaring v Goldtech Investments Ltd (No 2)* [1999] 1 WLR 745. See also, in the general context, *Thorne v Smith* (1851) 10 CB 659; *Re EWA* [1901] 2 KB 642, CA.

15 *Ruddock's Case* (1599) 6 Co Rep 25a.

16 *Deanplan Ltd v Mahmoud* [1993] Ch 151.

17 *Tolstoy v Aldington* (1993) The Times, 16 December, CA.

18 *Wallace v Kelsall* (1840) 7 M & W 264.

19 *Watters v Smith* (1831) 2 B & Ad 889.

20 See *Morris v Wentworth-Stanley* [1999] 2 WLR 470.

21 *Thompson v Percival* (1834) 5 B & Ad 925.

Reservation of the right to pursue other costs debtors

Where judgment is obtained against one joint costs debtor, there is no reason why, if it is not satisfied, another joint costs debtor may not be pursued for the debt.[22] This principle will apply where a receiving party obtains a default costs certificate against a joint costs debtor whose ability to pay is in doubt (such as an insolvent paying party who has failed to file points of dispute); if those are the circumstances, then a different joint costs debtor may still be pursued. In general, the judgment (be it an order or a costs certificate) will be binding on all of the joint costs debtors. This may work to the debtor's advantage. An example would be where A and B are jointly liable to C for costs, but the court assesses the costs at nil as against A for want of compliance with the rules of court; in that case, that order will also apply to B. In this regard, Pill LJ commented: **19.28**

> 'This may be considered an undeserved windfall for [B] but appears to me the least unsatisfactory result following the serious default [C] by their solicitors. It would only be in an extreme case, such as the present, in which a taxing officer would wholly disallow costs against a party and there can be no legitimate complaint if the joint debtor is also released.'[23]

If, however, the reality is that an order against a joint costs debtor amounts to accord and satisfaction (such as where an assessment is brought to an end by way of a consent order that can properly be said to amount to accord and satisfaction), then the receiving party may well have compromised their right to pursue any other joint costs debtors (see 19.26–19.27).

Promises not to sue

A mere promise not to pursue a joint costs debtor will be treated as personal to that debtor and will not have the effect of releasing the other joint costs debtors from their debts.[24] **19.29**

Several Liability of Costs Debtors

There will usually be no difficulty in identifying several liability. No special rules apply. For all practical purposes, each several liability can be regarded as being its own separate costs order. **19.30**

Joint and Several Liability of Costs Debtors

The special rules that are set out at 19.24–19.28 relating to joint liability do not apply to joint and several liability. If there is doubt as to whether an order provides for joint liability or joint and several liability, then it would usually be prudent to assume that those rules apply for the purposes of approving the wording of any proposed compromise or consent order. **19.31**

---

[22] Civil Liability (Contribution) Act 1978, s 3, disapplying the common law to the contrary in *Kendall v Hamilton* (1879) 4 App Cas 504.

[23] *Mainwaring v Goldtech Investments Ltd (No 2)* [1999] 1 WLR 745, at 751.

[24] *Hutton v Eyre* (1815) 6 Taunt 289.

19.32 If costs are payable jointly and severally, and if there is accord and satisfaction in relation to the liability of one of the paying parties, that will not release the other paying parties from their liability to pay, but it will diminish their liability by the amount that has been paid. For example, if A and B are jointly and severally liable to C for costs of £1,000, and if C releases A from all further liability on the basis that A makes a contribution of £450, then C may pursue B for the remaining £550. In practice, this would mean that there would be an assessment of the full £1,000 and B would be ordered to pay C the assessed sum *less* £450.

19.33 If a contract is entered into that putatively provides for a joint and several liability in circumstances in which the debtor who made the contract did not have authority to bind the other debtor(s), then the several aspect of that agreement may still be enforceable against the debtor who entered into that contract.[25]

Contributions between Costs Debtors

19.34 Where a joint costs debtor (or a joint and several costs debtor) wishes partially or fully to discharge a joint costs debt, they may wish to seek a partial or full contribution from the other joint costs debtors. The starting point is the Civil Liability (Contribution) Act 1978, s 1 of which provides as follows:

> '(1) Subject to the following provisions of this section, any person liable in respect of any damage suffered by another person may recover contribution from any other person liable in respect of the same damage (whether jointly with him or otherwise).
>
> (2) A person shall be entitled to recover contribution by virtue of subsection (1) above notwithstanding that he has ceased to be liable in respect of the damage in question since the time when the damage occurred, provided that he was so liable immediately before he made or was ordered or agreed to make the payment in respect of which the contribution is sought.
>
> (3) A person shall be liable to make contribution by virtue of subsection (1) above notwithstanding that he has ceased to be liable in respect of the damage in question since the time when the damage occurred, unless he ceased to be liable by virtue of the expiry of a period of limitation or prescription which extinguished the right on which the claim against him in respect of the damage was based.
>
> (4) A person who has made or agreed to make any payment in *bona fide* settlement or compromise of any claim made against him in respect of any damage (including a payment into court which has been accepted) shall be entitled to recover contribution in accordance with this section without regard to whether or not he himself is or ever was liable in respect of the damage, provided, however, that he would have been liable assuming that the factual basis of the claim against him could be established.
>
> (5) References in this section to a person's liability in respect of any damage are references to any such liability which has been or could be established in an action brought against him in England and Wales by or on behalf of the person who suffered the damage.'

19.35 Section 2 of the 1978 Act goes on to provide that the assessment of the contribution shall be such as may be found by the court to be just and equitable, having regard to the extent of that person's responsibility for the damage in question.

---

[25] See *Rabiu v Marlbray Ltd* [2016] EWCA Civ 476.

As to the applicability of the Act, s 6 provides: **19.36**

> 'A person is liable in respect of any damage for the purposes of this Act if the person who suffered it . . . is entitled to recover compensation from him in respect of that damage (whatever the legal basis of his liability, whether tort, breach of contract, breach of trust or otherwise).'

The Civil Liability (Contribution) Act 1978 therefore refers to damages rather than costs. It also draws a distinction between 'damages' and 'damage' (see s 6(1)), so a point that may arise is whether a contribution in respect of costs may be sought under that Act. **19.37**

There are competing arguments on the point. In brief, the issue is whether costs can be said to have arisen from the original damage or whether they are merely a necessary incident of the subsequent claim. **19.38**

There is no easy answer to this question. It is necessary to examine a number of authorities (some of which apply only by analogy). The conclusion that is reached is that a contribution of costs may be made where a contribution in respect of damages is also awarded, but there is doubt as to whether a contribution may be awarded solely in respect of costs. **19.39**

It is best to deal with the authorities in the order in which they were decided; only the more recent case law is discussed. It is convenient to start with the following *obiter* comments of Judge Lloyd QC (sitting as a judge of the High Court): **19.40**

> 'Costs in a case such as this arise from the defendant's decision not to accept liability and not from the original cause of action . . . Even on a wide interpretation of either section 1 or section 2 of [the Civil Liability (Contribution) Act 1978] costs could not, therefore, form part of the loss or damage with respect to which a party is entitled to contribution.'[26]

Davies J came to a similar conclusion in a different case.[27]

Whilst adopting a different line of thinking and dealing with a slightly different point, Brooke LJ (with whom Beldham LJ agreed) found that Davies J's judgment should not be followed;[28] presumably, he would have said the same about Judge Lloyd's analysis. Brooke LJ's comments were *obiter* and related to the word 'payment' in s 1(4) of the Civil Liability (Contribution) Act 1978, but there is no reason to believe that a different interpretation should apply to the use of the word 'damages' elsewhere in the Act. **19.41**

In a different case, Henry LJ dealt with the issue of 'damages' generally and he came to much the same conclusion as Brooke LJ: **19.42**

> '[E]ven if part of the payment was expressed to be made in respect of [the claimant's] costs, we are not persuaded that the words of sections 2 or 6(1) of the Act preclude the making of a contribution order in respect of that part. Section 1(1) defines the person who is entitled "... to recover contribution ..." and the person from whom it may be recovered. Section 2(1) does not expressly limit the amount of contribution to the amount payable in respect of liability "... for the damage in question ..."—section 2(3) might, but would not necessarily have this effect; and section 6(1) again defines the person who can claim contribution, without expressly limiting his recovery to the "compensation" he is liable to pay to the injured person.'[29]

---

26 *Sainsbury plc v Broadway Malyan* [1998] 61 Con LR 31, at [8.3].

27 *Police Federation v Ryder* (1990) The Times, 30 July.

28 See *Adams v Associated Newspapers Ltd & Ors* (1999) EMLR 26.

29 *BICC Ltd v Parkman Consulting Engineers (a firm)* [2001] EWCA Civ 1621, (2002) BLR 64, at [121].

19.43 Brooke LJ's analysis was not drawn to Henry LJ's attention, but if it had been, it would probably have served only to bolster his view. Henry LJ went on to add the following comments:

> 'Our present view is that the 1978 Act enables the party claiming contribution to recover a contribution towards a payment made in respect of the injured party's costs: but it is sufficient for the purposes of the present case that the judge [in the court below] was entitled to have regard to the whole of the settlement figure paid in respect of "all claims".'[30]

Henry LJ therefore seems to have limited his conclusion to circumstances in which the compensation paid to the injured party was made up of both costs and damages, so it could be argued that his comments do not apply where the contribution is solely for costs. Ramsey J came to much the same conclusion as Henry LJ, in a case in which a lump sum was paid in respect of both costs and damages.[31]

19.44 Thus a contribution may be awarded where it is also awarded for damages, but it is not clear whether a contribution can be awarded solely for costs; it probably can, but there is some doubt about this. Where a contribution is payable, it will be for the party who seeks it to show that the amount claimed is reasonable.[32]

---

[30] *Ibid*, at [123].

[31] *Mouchel Ltd v Van Oord (UK) Ltd (No 2)* [2011] EWHC 1516 (TCC).

[32] See *German Property 50 Sarl v Summers-Inman Construction & Property Consultants LLP* [2009] EWHC 2968 (TCC), at [16], *per* Coulson J, citing the pre-CPR case of *Biggin & Co Ltd v Permanite Ltd* (1951) 2 KB 314, CA.

20

DISTRIBUTION: APPORTIONMENT AND DIVISION OF COSTS

This chapter examines 'distribution' of costs, that being the term that is used in this book to refer to the process of allotting costs by way of division or apportionment (or both), whichever is appropriate. It deals with the following topics: **20.01**

- terminology (20.03);
- types of distribution (20.05);
- an overview of distribution (20.06);
- the relevance of distribution at the time of making a costs order (20.11);
- the division of costs (20.13);
- the doctrine of equal apportionment (20.16):
  - the history of the doctrine of equal apportionment (20.20);
  - deviation from equal apportionment (20.26);
- apportionment as between legal services provider and two or more clients (20.34);
- the role of costs sharing agreements (20.40);
- distribution where there are reciprocal entitlements (20.50):
  - reciprocal entitlements arising out of claim and counterclaim (20.51);
  - reciprocal entitlements other than claim and counterclaim (20.63);
- distribution where an issues order has been made (20.64); and
- special orders (or directions) (20.66).

The following discussion deals with distribution of costs—that is, with the seemingly simple question of how much a party should pay (or receive, as the case may be) where two or more persons have an interest in the same order for costs. **20.02**

Terminology

It is necessary to use precise and unambiguous language. In particular, a clear distinction should be made between the following. **20.03**

- **Distribution** This is an umbrella term that—in this book at least—is used to mean the process of allotting costs by way of division or apportionment (or both), whichever is appropriate.
- **Apportionment** This is a question of law rather than fact. Whilst it is no more than the editor's formulation, the following definition may assist: apportionment is a question of law by which costs are distributed in a way that does not reflect the existence of any separately attributable components.

- **Equal apportionment** This is a doctrine that the starting point for any apportionment is that there will be equal apportionment (see 20.16–20.33).
- **Division** This is a question of fact, rather than law. Again, it is no more than the editor's formulation, but the following definition may be appropriate: division is a question of fact by which costs are distributed or disaggregated in a way that reflects any separately attributable components.
- **The *Medway Oil* principle** This is a rule of law that was articulated in *Medway Oil*.[1] It will apply only in certain circumstances, but where it does apply, it precludes apportionment (see 20.59–20.62).
- **Divisible** This is an adjective that is used to describe costs that are capable of division.
- **Indivisible** This is an adjective that is used to describe costs that are incapable of division. Such costs may be distributed by apportionment or not at all.

20.04 Unfortunately, not all authorities use any consistent terminology. By way of example, Warren J referred to division on a broad-brush basis as being 'apportionment',[2] whilst Jay J has used the term 'disaggregation'.[3]

Types of Distribution

20.05 Issues of distribution and apportionment may arise in the following circumstances.

- **As between legal services provider and client** This is question of examining the contract of retainer and the factual circumstances in which the costs were incurred. It may lead to division or apportionment, depending on the facts.
- **At the time of making a costs order** This is a matter for the exercise of discretion by the court awarding costs.
- **Where there are competing orders (cross-orders) as to costs** Unless there is a special order (which would be a considerable rarity), this will always lead to division and never to apportionment, this being because of the *Medway Oil* principle (see 20.59–20.62).
- **Where an issues order has been made** Whilst the contrary may (just about) be arguable, the *Medway Oil* principle will apply in the absence of a special order.
- **Distribution of costs where costs orders have been made against some, but not all, of the receiving party's opponents** This is question of examining the costs order and the nature of the costs that were incurred. It may lead to division or apportionment, depending on the facts and the terms of the order.

An Overview of Distribution

20.06 Often the most demanding aspect of this topic is identifying the precise question that needs to be answered. It may be necessary to break the question down into stages, because there is a hierarchy in the sense such that a limit on distribution at an anterior stage

---

[1] *Medway Oil and Storage Company Ltd v Continental Contractors Ltd* [1929] AC 88. Whilst *obiter*, Ward LJ has confirmed that this case remains good law under the CPR: *Burchell v Bullard* [2005] EWCA Civ 358, at [26]–[27].

[2] *Fourie v Roux & Ors* [2006] EWHC 1840 (Ch), at [14] and [15].

[3] *Haynes v Department for Business Innovation and Skills* [2014] EWHC 643 (QB), at [8].

may restrict the amount that may be allowed at a subsequent stage (see, for example, 20.33). Indeed, this is such an important point that the only safe way in which to deal with distribution is by methodically dealing with each relevant stage as if they were parts of a forensic sieve.

By way of example, the following stages may be relevant if the question of distribution arises at a detailed assessment. **20.07**

- **Stage One (the retainer)** This involves establishing whether there is anything in the contract of retainer that limits the amounts allowable as between legal services provider and client. If there is, then the indemnity principle will mean that no more than that amount may be allowed on assessment between opposing parties.
- **Stage Two (the order)** This requires establishing whether there is anything in the order for costs that has a bearing on the amounts allowable. If there is, then this will bind the judge who is carrying out the detailed assessment.
- **Stage Three (quantification)** Here, assessment involves whether any particular type of distribution—be that division, apportionment or both—is appropriate at the time of assessing the costs.

Figure 20.1 illustrates the way in which these stages would interact in a case in which the court had to deal with distribution (including apportionment) at a detailed assessment. **20.08**

That figure illustrates the fact that it is wrong to say that apportionment is not a matter that a cost judge will ever have to address. The reason why this statement is often made is because (other than where a special order exists) a costs judge carrying out an assessment has no power to exercise any *discretion* as to apportionment; hence it would not be open to a costs judge to exercise a discretion to award a receiving party only a proportion of their costs. A costs judge may, however, have to make rulings *about* apportionment, and that may mean that the court has to look at apportionment in detail. In particular, a costs judge may have to consider Stage One for the purposes of applying the indemnity principle (see 20.33); similarly, the court may have to consider whether the costs order imposes an apportionment (Stage Two). **20.09**

On the whole, however, when a costs judge is concerned with 'apportionment', that term will be used as an inaccurate colloquialism for what is more correctly called distribution. In particular, other than where a special order exists (which will be fleetingly rare), Stage Three is usually a matter of division (especially if the *Medway Oil* principle applies). **20.10**

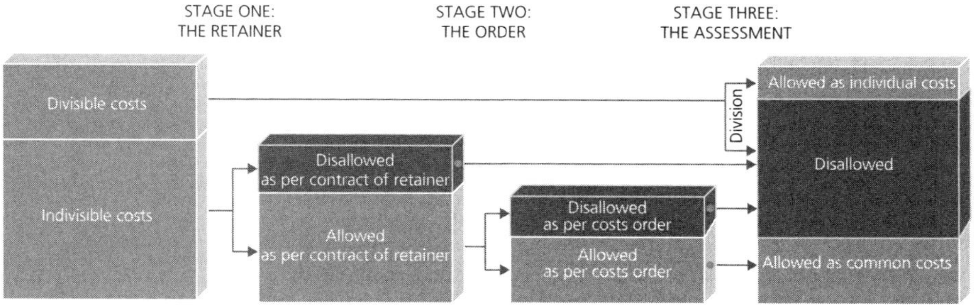

Figure 20.1 The three stages of the distribution of costs

Moreover, if the costs are divisible, the court will tend to look at division rather than apportionment and this will be so regardless of whether the issue arises during Stage One, Two or Three. For example, if a contract of retainer made between a solicitor, Client A and Client B were to say that Client A would bear 75 per cent of the common costs, that would be of no consequence if the costs in question could be divided equally between Client A and Client B.

The Relevance of Distribution at the Time of Making a Costs Order

20.11 The discussion in this chapter focuses on distribution in the context of detailed assessments, but what is described should also be borne in mind when a costs order is formulated. If this is not done, the eventual award of costs may be very different from what was intended. Unintended consequences may be avoided if the order makes it clear either that the paying party is to pay the costs attributable to a stated person's claims, or that a stated proportion of the costs incurred can properly be attributed to the issues in the paying claimant's claim.

20.12 Similar methodology to what is described in this chapter may be appropriate when exercising a discretion as to costs on a between-the-parties basis, especially in group litigation,[4] but also in other circumstances, such as where the *Medway Oil* principle applies.[5] This is discussed in more detail at 65.55–65.89 and Chapter 65 generally.

The Division of Costs

20.13 The division of costs is an entirely factual exercise by which the court will determine which costs (or divisible parts thereof) can be attributed solely to one category or the other. Thus, if counsel sees two clients in conference and spends 20 minutes dealing with the first client's affairs, 40 minutes dealing with the second client's affairs and 1 hour dealing with both jointly, a sixth of the conference would be attributable to the first client and a third to the second; the remainder would be indivisible.

20.14 If there is an absence of evidence before the court as to what the correct division should be, it would not be perverse for a costs judge to carry out a broad-brush division based on the number of categories into which costs were to be distributed.[6] This may have the appearance of being similar to apportionment, but is conceptually entirely different. This is particularly so in so far as the costs of issues are concerned (see 20.65).

20.15 There have been instances in which the court has applied something very similar to the doctrine of equal apportionment to the question of division in that it has dealt with

[4] See, eg, *Ward v Guinness Mahon plc* [1996] 1 WLR 894.

[5] See, eg, *Milanese v Leyton Orient Football Club Ltd (Costs)* [2016] EWHC 1263 (QB), at [21] and [22], in which Whipple J took *Medway Oil* into account when making an order for costs.

[6] *Haynes v Department for Business Innovation and Skills* [2014] EWHC 643 (QB), at [39], *per* Jay J.

the costs of issues on the rough-and-ready basis of the number of persons involved.[7] Jay J had this to say about such an approach:

> '[That] "rough and ready" approach ... was deprecated by Patten J in *Dyson*, precisely for the reason that it was unscientific and impressionistic. The general rule must be that evidence-based decisions are required, rather than an approach which simply identifies the number of [persons involved].'[8]

Jay J went on to say that, where appropriate, this general rule must 'yield in circumstances where it would be disproportionate to conduct a more punctilious exercise'.[9]

The Doctrine of Equal Apportionment

Unless there is reason to believe otherwise,[10] where costs are to be apportioned, the starting point is that there will be equal apportionment, this being the simple notion of equal shares. The doctrine of equal apportionment is a principle that Donaldson MR has said has age-old respectability, being based 'upon the Rhodian Law, the Rolls of Oleron and the maritime law of general average'.[11] **20.16**

The doctrine will, in general, apply to Stage One (that is, to apportionment as per the contract of retainer), but as Figure 20.1 shows, this may have a bearing on Stage Three—by virtue of the operation of the indemnity principle. **20.17**

For the avoidance of doubt, the doctrine of equal apportionment will apply only where the costs are to be apportioned. This means that it will not apply to Stage Two (because any distribution arising out of the order will be determined by the terms of the order rather than by the doctrine of equal apportionment). Unless it indirectly applies via the operation of the indemnity principle or by virtue of some 'special order' (see 20.66), neither apportionment nor the doctrine of equal apportionment will apply directly to Stage Three—and this will particularly be so in those cases in which the *Medway Oil* principle applies. **20.18**

In an extreme case, an order for costs may 'relate exclusively' to a certain party (or, for that matter, issue). Where that is the case, then there would be no apportionment at all and only those costs that could properly be attributed to that person (or issue) by division would be payable.[12] **20.19**

The history of the doctrine of equal apportionment

It is instructive to look at the development of the law of equal apportionment. This is necessary because older cases are still frequently cited, so it may be necessary to know something of their history to put those cases in context. **20.20**

---

[7] See, eg, *Fourie v Roux & Ors* [2006] EWHC 1840 (Ch), at [15] and [16], *per* Warren J.

[8] *Haynes v Department for Business Innovation and Skills* [2014] EWHC 643 (QB), at [38].

[9] *Ibid*, at [40].

[10] Where there is an agreement as to apportionment, that may be a factor that the court can take into account even when the paying party is not a counterparty to that agreement: see 20.29. See also *Coys of Kensington Ltd v Woollcombe Beer Watts (a firm)* (unreported), 18 February 1999, QBD, *per* Gardland J.

[11] *Davies v Eli Lilly & Co* [1987] 1 WLR 1136, at 1141.

[12] *Hay v Szterbin* [2010] EWHC 1967 (Ch), at [13], *per* Newey J.

Nineteenth-century cases on equal apportionment

20.21 In a mid-19th-century case, a masters' certificate[13] was obtained that explained the doctrine in this way:

> 'If one solicitor appears for three defendants, and the bill [ie the claim] is dismissed with costs as to one of them, the plaintiff can only be compelled to pay the costs of such proceedings as exclusively relate to that defendant, and one-third of the costs of the proceedings taken jointly for all three defendants.'[14]

The certificate went on to say: '[B]ut, nevertheless, the extent of the liability of the client may vary according to the circumstances of each case; in other words, according to the retainer of the solicitor.'[15]

20.22 The certificate was accepted (with some reservations) by the Court of Appeal in Chancery. Thus, whilst the principle of equal apportionment was something that could be expected to yield to what was recorded in the retainer, the practice in the courts of equity was that (where there was no contractual provision to the contrary) costs incurred jointly would be apportioned equally on a several basis.

20.23 This doctrine was both enduring and widespread.[16] According to Kelly CB, there was no difference between the practice in the courts of law and the practice in the courts of equity.[17] He confirmed that if there was a joint contract of retainer between the legal services provider and its clients, each client would be jointly liable for the whole costs, but that if there were separate contracts, each would be liable for their own costs and their own portion of the joint costs. As is mentioned at 20.35, Amphlett B has confirmed that the fact that the litigation may be conducted jointly does not necessarily make the liability joint.[18]

Early 20th-century cases on equal apportionment

20.24 An oft-quoted example of equal apportionment is *Beaumont v Senior and Bull*,[19] which is an early 20th-century case in which two defendants (D1 and D2) were represented by the same solicitor. It concerned costs between opposing parties, but it is useful in the present context because it shed light on the contract of retainer. D1's defence failed, but D2 was successful. There was no agreement as to how the costs should be shared. Costs followed the event in that both the claimant and D2 were awarded costs. D2's bill claimed all of the costs of the claim, but the costs judge allowed only those additional costs that had been occasioned by D2 as a result of being joined as a defendant. D2 appealed. The Divisional Court found that, in the absence of any agreement between the defendants as to how the costs of the defence should be shared, the defendants were each liable for an equal proportion of the costs of the defence.

20.25 Similar decisions followed and, in due course, the doctrine of equal apportionment became entrenched as established law. In 1919, for example, the principle was again approved by

13 This was a document similar to a short statement by a court assessor. It was a method whereby the then equivalent of a costs judge could give guidance to an appeal court.
14 *In re Colquhoun* (1854) 5 DM&G 35, at 37.
15 *Ibid.*
16 See, eg, *Keen v Towler* (1924) 41 TLR 86; *Davies v Chatwood* (1879) 40 LT 187.
17 *Burridge v Bellew* (1875) 32 LT 807, at 812.
18 *Ibid*, at 813 and 814.
19 *Beaumont v Senior and Bull* [1903] 1 KB 282.

the Court of Appeal in *Ellingsen*.[20] As in earlier cases,[21] the court expressed some reservations about the principle, but commented that, by that stage, it had become too well established to be disturbed. Subject to what is said at 20.26–20.33, that would appear to be the position today.

Deviation from equal apportionment

The doctrine of equal apportionment is capable of leading to injustice when applied rigidly. In view of this, cases other than those mentioned above heralded a more flexible approach. That said, there are significant limits to the extent to which the court can deviate from the principle. In particular, the exercise of adjustment will largely depend on the facts.[22] **20.26**

The case that is usually quoted as being an example of the flexible approach is *Korner v H Korner & Co Ltd*,[23] in which the Court of Appeal found that the doctrine was a rule of thumb that was convenient to apply in ordinary cases, but which should not be applied in every case if doing so would result in injustice. Singleton LJ found that the principle of equal apportionment was not appropriate in the case before him; this was largely because of the differences in the defences that had been raised by the defendants. Singleton LJ had this to say on the point: **20.27**

> 'I do not know of any authority which compels the court to follow the rule [of equal apportionment] which I have mentioned in every class of case, and even if to follow it would result in injustice. To do so would be to fly in the teeth of the generally accepted principle as stated in [*Ellingsen*] "that the successful party is to be recompensed the liability he has reasonably incurred in defending himself".'[24]

Thus the doctrine will yield so as to avoid injustice.[25]

No adjustment to take account of the justice of the situation

It should be noted that Singleton LJ did not go so far as to say that an adjustment should be made so as to *meet* the justice of the situation; rather, the adjustment that he made was to avoid injustice, and was based on the nature of the cases that each litigant had advanced and the different costs attributable thereto. Put otherwise, the adjustment was not based on some broader discretionary notion of what was fair and just. **20.28**

Where a party has incurred costs that cannot fairly be attributed to any co-litigants because of that party's behaviour, the court can take that fact into account, but in only a limited way.[26] It should also be noted that where inequality is an express term of the retainer, that may be a factor that the court can take into account even when the paying party is not a counterparty to that agreement.[27] **20.29**

---

[20] *Ellingsen v Det Skandinaviske Compani* [1919] 2 KB 567; see also *Keen v Towler* (1924) 41 TLR 86, in which Darling LJ did the same.

[21] In particular, *In re Colquhoun* (1854) 5 DM&G 35.

[22] See *Meretz Investments Ltd v ACP Ltd* [2007] EWHC 2635 (Ch).

[23] *Korner v H Korner & Co Ltd* [1951] Ch 11.

[24] *Ibid*, at 17

[25] See also *Meretz Investments Ltd v ACP Ltd* [2007] EWHC 2635 (Ch), in which, although he declined to exercise the power, Warren J found that the principle of equal apportionment was only a general rule that should not be allowed to produced injustice.

[26] See, eg, *Bank of Credit and Commerce International SA (in liquidation) v Ali* (No 5) [2000] 2 Costs LR 243 (group litigation in which the lead claimants were accused of dishonesty in the course of the litigation itself).

[27] See 20.49. See also *Coys of Kensington Ltd v Woollcombe Beer Watts (a firm)* (unreported), 18 February 1999, QBD, *per* Gardland J.

No adjustment to take account of the prominence of the persons involved

20.30 In a similar vein, Chadwick J had this to say about the relevance of the fact that some litigants may have played a more prominent part in the litigation than others:

> '[There is] no support in [the authorities] for the proposition that a pro-rata apportionment of the general costs of the action should be modified or "adjusted" on the ground that one client is more important, or more prominent in the litigation, than others. If costs cannot be attributed to particular clients on the basis of separate defences or separate issues, then they must be apportioned equally between all those clients for whose benefit they have been incurred.'[28]

Thus Chadwick J found that there was no support for the proposition that the adjustment should take into account the relative importance or prominence of the parties; rather, he found that it should be based solely on the issues raised and the costs that could be attributed to those issues.[29]

The influence of fraud

20.31 If a claimant were found to have been guilty of having advanced a fraudulent case, the court would be able to find that no part of those costs could be fairly attributed to the other litigant's claims and that therefore that litigant should personally bear the whole of those costs. Whilst he declined to exercise that power, Park J found that it existed.[30]

Umbrella ownership

20.32 It is often the case that legal and natural people are drawn into litigation because one party owns or is owned by another party. This would not mean that all of the costs would mechanistically vest in the ultimate owner. In particular, the fact that a corporate defendant was wholly owned by an individual defendant would not mean that the costs ought, without more, to be attributed to the individual defendant.[31]

The interaction between apportionment as per the contract of retainer and the indemnity principle

20.33 As has already been mentioned at 20.09, the position as between client and legal services provider may, through the operation of the indemnity principle, have a bearing on the positions as between opposing parties (also see Figure 20.1). Darling LJ had the following to say on the topic:

> '[A]lthough each of the four plaintiffs may be liable to the solicitor for the whole of the costs common to all of them, still as between themselves, each is liable to contribute one-fourth. From this it follows that ultimately each of the plaintiffs is only liable to pay one-fourth of the common costs, and that, therefore, as costs are given as an indemnity only, one-fourth is

28 *Bayliss v Kelly & Ors* [1997] 2 Costs LR 54, at 60.

29 In a similar vein, the fact that a corporate defendant was wholly owned by an individual defendant would not mean that the costs ought, without more, to be attributed to the individual defendant: see *Murphy v Rayner* [2013] EWHC 3878 (Ch), at [44], where Nicholas Strauss QC (sitting as a deputy High Court judge) explained that Sharp J's comments in *Legal Services Commission v F, A & V* [2011] EWHC 899 (QB) were *obiter* and did not establish a principle that the costs would be attributed to the individual.

30 *Bank of Credit and Commerce International SA (in liquidation) v Ali* (No 5) [2000] 2 Costs LR 243 (in the context of group litigation in which the lead claimants were accused of dishonesty in the litigation itself).

31 See *Murphy v Rayner* [2013] EWHC 3878 (Ch), at [44], where Nicholas Strauss QC (sitting as a deputy High Court judge) explained that Sharp J's comments in *Legal Services Commission v F, A & V* [2011] EWHC 899 (QB) were *obiter* and did not establish a principle that the costs would be attributed to the individual.

> all that the defendant should be called upon to pay to one plaintiff. To order the defendant to pay to the successful plaintiff more than one-fourth would be to order him to pay an amount in relief of the amount that the unsuccessful plaintiffs ought to pay.'[32]

This is an example of the fact that the stages referred to at 20.06 are capable of overlapping.

Apportionment as between Legal Services Provider and Two or More Clients

This section deals with the situation in which costs have been incurred for the benefit of two more clients, but where the instructions were given separately—that is, where the contract of retainer did not create a joint liability. Where this is so, then the doctrine of equal apportionment (and the principles that govern deviation therefrom) will be relevant (see 20.16). **20.34**

The topic of contracts of retainer that involve more than one client is addressed in detail at 27.302–27.318, but it is worth noting one or two points here. Kelly CB has said that if there was a joint contract of retainer between the legal services provider and its clients, each client would be jointly liable for the whole costs, yet if there were separate contracts, each would be liable for their own costs and their own portion of the joint costs.[33] Amphlett B has explained that the fact that the litigation may have been conducted jointly would not necessarily make the liability joint (see 27.310)[34]—that is, that the fact that co-litigants bring a claim jointly does not mean that each of them will bear a liability for the whole of the costs. **20.35**

What is set out below is likely to be particularly relevant in group litigation, in which case there may be a need to distinguish between common costs (those that need to be apportioned) and individual costs (those that do not need to be apportioned). This is addressed at 65.55–65.89. **20.36**

A flexible approach where a legal services provider represents a number of clients in the same claim

Chadwick J reviewed the authorities and listed a number of points that are similar to a forensic sieve.[35] His conclusions may be summarised in the following way. **20.37**

- Where a solicitor acts for a number of clients in the same claim on separate retainers, each client is entitled to have a separate bill, and to have that bill assessed as between only themselves and the solicitor.
- When assessing a client's bill, the court is to have regard to the overriding principle that the client is to be charged only for those costs properly attributable to the conduct of their own claim.
- Any costs relating solely to the claim of one client should be charged to that client, to the exclusion of the other clients.

---

32 *Keen & Ors v Towler* (1924) 41 TLR 86, PC.

33 *Burridge v Bellew* (1875) 32 LT 807, at 812.

34 *Ibid*, at 813 and 814.

35 *Bayliss v Kelly & Ors* [1997] 2 Costs LR 54. See also *Sayers v Merck SmithKline Beecham plc; X v Schering Healthcare Ltd; Afrika v Cape plc* [2001] EWCA Civ 2017, at [10]; *AB v Liverpool City Council* [2003] EWHC 1539 (QB).

- The court must have regard to the nature of the claims raised to determine whether there were distinct issues in relation to particular clients. If there were, the costs relating to those issues (so far as they can be indemnified) should be attributed accordingly.
- The general costs of the claim (that is, the costs that cannot be attributed to particular clients on the basis of separate claims or distinct issues) must be apportioned *pro rata*.
- It is irrelevant that the effect of an apportionment may be that the solicitor cannot recover some part of the apportioned costs (because, for example, one or more clients are insolvent).

20.38 Further principles may apply in group litigation. These are addressed at 65.58 (the default provision under CPR, r 46.6(4)) and 65.59 (the default position under the common law). Test claim costs are dealt with at 65.62.

Disclosure of the contract of retainer for the purposes of apportionment

20.39 Common sense dictates that the court would be hampered if the receiving party were to choose not to present their retainer to the court for scrutiny. The paying party would, no doubt, also wish to see it, not least because its interpretation is a matter of law upon which that party may wish to make submissions. Whilst there is no authority on the point, it could easily be argued that because the interpretation of the retainer is a matter of law rather than fact, the receiving party ought to be put to their election as a matter of course in much the same way as they would be if they were relying on a pre-November 2005 conditional fee agreement (see 29.44–29.48).[36]

The Role of Costs Sharing Agreements

20.40 For the reasons set out above (see 20.09 and Figure 20.1), apportionment will be subject to the indemnity principle, but it will not be dictated by it. To that extent, the contract of retainer will be relevant on the assessment of costs between opposing parties. The matter may be made more—or, hopefully, less—complex if there is a contract dealing with the issue of how co-litigants should share the burden of their costs. Such an agreement is known as a costs sharing agreement and may be express or implied.[37] There are two types of costs sharing agreement:

- a funding costs sharing agreement (FCSA)—an agreement that states co-litigants' relative or absolute contributions towards their own costs; and
- a liability costs sharing agreement (LCSA)—an agreement that states co-litigants' relative or absolute liability for an opponent's costs.

The two are often combined in the same written instrument (which itself is often included within a more general document, such as a litigation management agreement).

[36] When the editor drafts contracts of retainers for use by more than one client, he tends to bear this in mind and therefore (subject to instructions) attempts to draft them with an eye to voluntary disclosure. Where voluntary disclosure would be inappropriate, he usually tries to incorporate all of the relevant terms in a disclosable costs sharing agreement.

[37] See, eg, *Bank of Credit and Commerce International SA (in liquidation) v Ali* (No 5) [2000] 2 Costs LR 243, in which Park J found the existence of an implied costs sharing agreement.

Where it is express, a costs sharing agreement may be contained either within the relevant contract(s) of retainer or in a separate costs sharing agreement (which, as mentioned above, may itself be incorporated into a litigation management agreement). Separate costs sharing agreements are particularly common in the context of group litigation. A costs sharing agreement may be between the co-litigants alone or, if it is an FCSA, it may also embrace their legal services provider; where the latter is the case, then it will necessarily be linked to the relevant contract(s) of retainer. Costs sharing agreements often expressly state that they are subject to the court making a different costs sharing order; indeed, it is not uncommon for costs sharing agreements to be based on the assumption that the court is likely to make such an order and that, as such, what is said in the agreement is merely the default position. **20.41**

The effect of costs sharing agreements as between co-litigants

The existence of a costs sharing agreement will—obviously—have a bearing on the apportionment between co-litigants (unless, of course, the court makes a costs sharing order that provides otherwise). If it is an FCSA that is linked to the contract(s) of retainer, it may also have a bearing as between those persons and their legal services provider. For the reasons set out at 20.49, it may also have a bearing on apportionment between opposing parties. This means that the agreement may need to be taken into account by the costs judge during any assessment between opposing parties. In any event, it is not uncommon for the costs judge to be asked to assess costs not only between opposing parties, but also between co-litigants (especially where one co-litigant has settled the costs, but one or more of the others has not). Where this is the case, there will be considerable overlap between Stages One and Three. **20.42**

Where a costs sharing agreement exists, the court must ask itself how it should be regarded and whether it is bound by the agreement. The answer seems to be that the court would not be bound by such an agreement, but would only rarely make an order that would depart from it, even if such an agreement is merely implied. **20.43**

In *Bank of Credit and Commerce International SA v Ali & Ors*,[38] Park J had to decide how to apportion solicitor and client costs where there had been no written costs sharing agreement (although he did find that an implied FCSA existed). The costs related to a single issue in respect of which five lead claimants had been selected. All of these lead claims failed. The non-lead claimants alleged that this was as a result of dishonesty on the part of the lead claimants. Having ordered that the defendants should not pay costs, Park J went on to decide what should happen as between the claimants. He found that the costs should be borne by all of the claimants in equal measure. He found that there was an implied agreement—or 'clear understanding'—that the lead claimants' costs would be shared. **20.44**

Whilst *obiter*, Park J commented on whether he would have had the power to deal with the costs other than in accordance with that implied FCSA and concluded that he did: 'The answer [to the question of jurisdiction] would be yes, though it would be a very rare case where the judge would make an order which departed from what the group litigants had agreed.'[39] **20.45**

---

[38] *Ibid.*
[39] *Ibid*, at 250.

20.46 In making these comments, Park J said that the situation was similar to that in *Gomba Holdings (UK) Ltd v Minories Finacne Ltd*[40] (see 66.04), but that rather than the agreement being between opposing parties (as it was in *Gomba*), it was between parties on the same side. He summarised the position as follows:

> '[If] there is an agreement about the apportionment between group litigants of costs of proceedings, like a test case, the existence of the agreement does not exclude the statutory discretion of the court to make its own order, including an order which binds group litigants which are not strictly parties to the test case. However, where there are contractual rights and obligations the court's discretion should ordinarily be exercised so as to reflect those contractual rights and obligations.'[41]

20.47 Park J ultimately refused to depart from the terms of the 'clear understanding' that each claimant would bear a proportionate part of the lead claimant's costs. Amongst the many reasons he gave for coming to this decision was his desire not to set a precedent for lead claimants being stripped of the protection that costs sharing gave them; such a precedent, he explained, would be harmful to group litigation generally.[42] In commenting on the discreditable conduct of the lead claimants, he said that:

> '[T]o withdraw costs sharing on this ground would be the equivalent of fining the test case employees because of their discreditable conduct ... The process before me is not a penal process, and it would be wrong for me to exercise my discretion for penal purposes.'[43]

The relevance of the forms of funding of the co-litigants

20.48 The exact nature of the legal service provider's right to payment will not usually be relevant, even where the costs sharing agreement is between co-litigants with different types of retainer. In particular, Wright J has found that (in so far as group litigation is concerned) there is no distinction to be drawn between claimants who have legal aid and those who are funded by way of conditional fee agreements.[44] Similarly, Judge Cooke (sitting as a judge of the High Court) has found that where a number of persons who have instructed the same solicitors were awarded costs jointly, the fact that some of them left it to the others to enter into a representative contract of retainer would not justify any apportionment of the costs.[45]

The effect of costs sharing agreements as between opposing parties

20.49 Although the existence of a costs sharing agreement will not usually be relevant to entitlement to costs between opposing parties (as opposed to between co-litigants), this will not always be the case (especially where the agreement goes to costs incurred in jointly instructing the same legal services provider). For example, Garland J has found that where there is a costs sharing agreement between a defendant who was entitled to costs and a defendant who was not entitled to costs, that agreement might result in the paying party

40 *Gomba Holdings Ltd v Minories Finance Ltd* (No 2) [1993] Ch 171.
41 *Ibid*, at 252.
42 *Bank of Credit and Commerce International SA (in liquidation) v Ali* (No 5) [2000] 2 Costs LR 243, at 256.
43 *Ibid*, at 254.
44 *Hodgson v Imperial Tobacco Ltd (No 2)* [1998] 2 Costs LR 27.
45 See *Walker v Burton* [2013] EWHC 811 (Ch), at [44]–[48].

(the claimant) being liable for the entitled defendant's share of conducting the defendants' defence.[46] One way of analysing that decision is to regard the costs sharing agreement as having modified the retainer, thereby having a bearing on Stage One.

Distribution where there are Reciprocal Entitlements

Reciprocal entitlements may arise in one of two circumstances: where they arise out of claim and counterclaim (see 20.51); and where they arise in the absence of claim and counterclaim (see 20.63). **20.50**

Reciprocal entitlements arising out of claim and counterclaim

Cross-orders for costs will exist where parties reciprocally pay and receive costs (see 7.34–7.37). Where this is so, the court will determine which costs are allowable to each party. Divisible costs will be divided, that being a purely factual exercise. In the absence of a special order, indivisible costs will be dealt with according to the *Medway Oil* principle, that being a doctrine that is the antithesis of apportionment. In general, where reciprocal entitlements relate to claim and counterclaim, the costs are to be ascribed to the claim, other than where they can be said to relate solely to the counterclaim, in which case they will be ascribed to the counterclaim. **20.51**

Cross-orders (claim and counterclaim): the background to Medway Oil

The principal authority on this topic is *Medway Oil*,[47] which, in brief, established that where both a claim and a counterclaim succeed, the claim shall be treated as though it stood alone and the counterclaim should bear only the amount by which it has caused the costs of the proceedings to be increased. Unless the judge making the order for costs makes a special order (otherwise known as special directions), there will be no apportionment of costs that are putatively common to claim and counterclaim. **20.52**

***Medway Oil*: relevant history and background** *Medway Oil* is complex in terms of both the law it clarifies and its procedural history. To be able to understand the House of Lords' guidance, it is necessary to know something of that history. It is also worth bearing in mind that the issue that the court ultimately had to decide was whether costs should be apportioned between claim and counterclaim, or whether they should generally be ascribed to one or the other, without apportionment. **20.53**

Medway Oil: *the facts of* Medway Oil *Medway Oil* was a case in which a claim and counterclaim had each dismissed with costs. The sums involved were substantial. At the first appeal, the judge (who had also heard the trial itself) found that the defendant was entitled to the costs that it had incurred in defending the claim and the claimant was entitled only to such costs as it would not have incurred had it not been compelled to meet **20.54**

---

[46] *Coys of Kensington Ltd v Woollcombe Beer Watts (a firm)* (unreported), 18 February 1999, QBD. On the facts of that case, the costs sharing agreement was academic because it was an agreement for equal apportionment, so merely confirmed the position that would have existed if there had been no agreement.

[47] *Medway Oil and Storage Company Ltd v Continental Contractors Ltd* [1929] AC 88. Whilst *obiter*, Ward LJ has confirmed that this case remains good law under the CPR: *Burchell v Bullard* [2005] EWCA Civ 358, at [26]–[27].

the counterclaim (that is, that the costs should not be apportioned between the claim and the counterclaim).

20.55 The Court of Appeal disagreed (but ultimately was shown to have been wrong to do so): it found that the costs should be apportioned. The Court of Appeal found that there was no reason why the claimants should not be allowed costs incurred in resisting the counterclaim merely because the facts they put forward were common to both claim and counterclaim. It was held that the costs judge ought to have attributed to the counterclaim such portion of the common items as had arisen and been incurred by reason of the counterclaim.

20.56 Medway Oil: *development of the rule against apportionment* That ruling of the Court of Appeal was, however, at odds with existing authority (see 20.57). The matter consequently went to the House of Lords on a further appeal in which Viscount Haldane described the competing principles (that is, apportionment and non-apportionment) thus:

> 'One view is that as the costs of the issues were ... properly incurred in defeating the claim they should be given to the [defendant], the [claimant] getting only such extra costs as were incurred by reason of the counterclaim and but for it would not have been incurred. The other view is that the proper principle of [assessment] under a judgment such as the judgment in this case is that when one party has got the costs of a claim and another of a counterclaim, the [costs judge] ought to allow to each party all such costs as he has properly incurred in maintenance or resistance, as the case may be. When therefore the matters in controversy are common to both claim and counterclaim, the costs, so far as common to both claim and counterclaim, should be apportioned.'[48]

20.57 The House of Lords considered a line of authority[49] that established that where there has been success (or failure) on both the claim and the counterclaim, costs should not be apportioned between the claim and the counterclaim, but (in the absence of special directions) should instead be assessed as though the claim stood by itself.

20.58 The House of Lords noted that there were more recent authorities[50] that suggested a change of attitude: on the face of it, those authorities supported apportioning costs between the claim and the counterclaim. Viscount Haldane concluded that, properly analysed, those authorities did not support the practice of apportioning costs, but that they did support costs being *divided* between the claim and the counterclaim (assuming, of course, that the costs were capable of being so treated).[51] The distinction between division of costs and apportionment of costs depends on whether the item in question is divisible.[52] For example, a round road trip of 150 miles to take counsel's advice on both the claim and counterclaim would not be divisible, but a trip of 100 miles to see a witness in the claim, followed by a trip of 50 miles to see a witness in the counterclaim, would be divisible.

---

[48] *Medway Oil and Storage Company Ltd v Continental Contractors Ltd* [1929] AC 88, at 94.

[49] Beginning with *Saner v Bilton* (1879) 11 Ch D 416 and including: *Mason v Brentini* (1880) 15 Ch D 287; *Baines v Bromley* (1881) 6 QBD 691; *In re Brown* (1883) 23 Ch D 377; *Shrapnel v Laing* (1888) 20 QBD 334; *Atlas Metal Co v Miller* [1898] 2 QB 500, at 505.

[50] *Christie v Platt* [1921] 2 KB 1 (the dissenting view as expressed in the Irish case of *Crean v M'Millan* [1922] 2 IR 105).

[51] *Medway Oil and Storage Company Ltd v Continental Contractors Ltd* [1929] AC 88, at 100 and 101–2.

[52] For a discussion of the distinction between division and apportionment, see *Hay v Szterbin* [2010] EWHC 1967 (Ch), at [12] and [13], *per* Newey J.

The Medway Oil *principle*

The general principles of *Medway Oil* may be summarised in the following way. **20.59**

- Where there has been success on the claim and the counterclaim such that the claimant is awarded the costs of the claim and the defendant (that is, the counterclaimant) the costs of the counterclaim, the claimant will be entitled to the costs of the claim as if the claim stood by itself and the defendant will be entitled only to those costs attributable to the increase in costs that the counterclaim has caused.
- Where (as in *Medway Oil* itself) the positions are reversed such that both the claim and the counterclaim have failed (with costs), the defendant will be entitled to costs of the claim as if it stood by itself and the claimant will be entitled only to those costs attributable to the increase in costs that the counterclaim has brought about.
- Unless the trial judge gives 'special directions', there will be no apportionment of costs between the claim and the counterclaim.
- This will not, however, prevent costs that are capable of division being divided between the claim and the counterclaim.

The House of Lords recognised that whilst these principles had the merit of being conceptually easy to apply upon assessment, the result might be harsh on the unsuccessful party in the claim.[53] Viscount Haldane said: **20.60**

> 'My Lords, in the authorities which I have now cited successive Courts of Appeal have laid down a principle which is not only intelligible, but capable of being easily applied by the [costs judge]. It may work out apparently harshly in exceptional cases. But when these threaten to occur the remedy is to apply at the trial for special directions as to issues and details. The advantage of the principle is that it is a definite one, which lifts the subject out of the somewhat vague regions of apportionment.'[54]

The Medway Oil *principle where there is no formal counterclaim*

It is not always necessary for a defendant to bring a formal counterclaim to have the court take the existence of a counterclaim into account. Thus, in a case in which the parties had agreed that the issue of liability would dispose of both the claim and the counterclaim and that there was no need formally to issue a counterclaim, Smith LJ found that it was open to the court to take the notional counterclaim into account.[55] **20.61**

The Medway Oil *principle and Part 36*

Whilst not binding, Judge Gregory has found that references to the 'costs of proceedings' in r 36.13(1) of the Civil Procedure Rules (CPR), do not displace the *Medway Oil* principle where the counter-claimant's reciprocal entitlement to costs has come about as a result of the operation of that rule.[56] He went on to say that any other approach would 'seriously to deter a claimant who is also a Part 20 defendant, from seeking to compromise, in timely fashion and at proportionate cost, the Part 20 claim brought against them, and, as such, would hinder, rather than promote, the overriding objective'.[57] **20.62**

---

[53] See, eg, the facts of *Christie v Platt* [1921] 2 KB 17.
[54] *Medway Oil and Storage Company Ltd v Continental Contractors Ltd* [1929] AC 88, at 98.
[55] *Parkes v Martin* [2009] EWCA Civ 883.
[56] *Farnworth v Davies* (unreported), 4 March 2016, Liverpool County Court, *per* Judge Peter Gregory.
[57] *Ibid*, at [27].

Reciprocal entitlements other than claim and counterclaim

20.63 The rule in *Medway Oil* is capable of applying in other situations in which there are reciprocal entitlements to costs, such as where a successful claimant has to pay the costs of quantifying the damages from the date of an offer.[58]

Distribution where an Issues Order has been Made

20.64 The rule in *Medway Oil* is capable of applying where a party is successful overall, but is ordered to pay costs of certain issues. In these circumstances, the rule in *Medway Oil* would usually apply, in that apportionment would not be appropriate.[59]

Is apportionment ever appropriate as between issues?

20.65 It may be tempting to assume that where a party is entitled to the costs of certain issues, but not others, any indivisible costs ought to be apportioned between those issues. Ultimately, this is a question that will depend on the terms of the order for costs, but it should be borne in mind that—as a simple matter of logic—apportionment would rarely be appropriate in those circumstances. This is because (in the absence of a special order that gives the costs judge the power to apportion costs), any apportionment will be dictated solely by the contract of retainer. Contracts of retainer rarely deal with the costs of issues in a way that demands that costs be apportioned. This is in contrast to the way in which contracts of retainer with two or more clients deal with liability, in which case the doctrine of equal apportionment will apply by default. There is no logical basis for suggesting that the doctrine of equal apportionment would apply to issues.

Special Orders (or Directions)

20.66 Whilst they are rare, it would be possible for a special order to be made that either expressly affords a costs judge the power to apportion costs or expressly apportions those costs.[60]

---

58 *Cinema Press Ltd v Pictures & Pleasures Ltd* [1945] KB 356.

59 *Dyson Technology Ltd v Strutt* [2007] EWHC 1756 (Ch), esp at [55] and [56], *per* Patten J. Also see *Cinema Press Ltd v Pictures & Pleasures Ltd* [1945] KB 356, at 361, *per* Lord Goddard CJ.

60 See *Dyson Technology Ltd v Strutt* [2007] EWHC 1756 (Ch), esp at [46], *per* Patten J. As an example of a special costs order, see *Willcox v Kettell* [1937] 1 All ER 222, *per* Clauson J.

21

MUTUAL LIABILITIES AND SET-OFF

This short chapter deals with the following topics: **21.01**

- an overview (21.03);
- the jurisdictional basis of set-off (21.05);
- procedural issues of set-off (21.16); and
- set-off and discretion (21.21).

In the context of costs, the topic of set-off often arises when the court makes cross-orders as to costs. It is that situation which is considered in this chapter. Mention is also briefly made of the set-off of costs and damages. Set-off—or, more accurately, its common law cousin, 'abatement'[1]—may also apply in a solicitor-and-client setting, in which it can operate as a species of defence to a claim for unpaid solicitors' fees. This is addressed at 38.36–38.37. **21.02**

Overview

Where there are mutual liabilities for costs (that is, A is liable for B's costs and vice versa), set-off may operate to allow the smaller claim to be deducted from the larger claim, thereby leaving the party with the larger of the two to pay the balance. Mr Leggatt QC (sitting as a deputy judge of the High Court) summarised the principles in this way: **21.03**

> '(1) Where one party has a claim against another party who has a cross-claim, the two claims cannot be netted off so as to extinguish each liability to the extent of the other except by agreement or a judgment of the court and once both liabilities have been established by agreement or judgment.
>
> (2) Where, however, the two claims are for sums of money which are due and certain in amount, each party may raise a defence to the extent of its own claim in proceedings brought by the other (legal set-off).
>
> (3) In addition, where the two claims are (i) made reasonably and in good faith and (ii) so closely connected that it would be manifestly unjust to allow one party to enforce payment without taking into account the crossclaim, neither party may exercise any rights contingent on the validity of its claim except in so far as it exceeds the other party's claim (equitable set-off).
>
> (4) Under CPR r.40.13 and the court's inherent jurisdiction, the court has a discretion to order any judgment sum to be set off (in the sense of netted off) against any other such sum. The date at which such a set-off should be effected is the date on which the existence and amount of the two liabilities is or was established.

[1] *Mondel v Steel* (1841) 8 M & W 858.

(5) The approach which the court should adopt when ordering such a set-off between amounts payable in different currencies is: (i) to assess and add to each principal amount any interest accruing up to the date of the setoff; (ii) to convert the smaller amount into the currency of the larger amount at the exchange rate prevailing at that date; and (iii) to order payment of the balance.'[2]

21.04 Set-off is at the discretion of the court. If there is no order for set-off, then each claim may be enforced independently.

The Jurisdictional Basis of Set-off

Common law and equity

21.05 Whilst an oversimplification, set-off tends to arise in the following ways.

- **At law** The power to make an order for set-off at law is statutory.[3] It was a right to set off liabilities that are mutual (that is, between the same parties and in the same interest),[4] due and payable,[5] and capable of quantification.[6] The competing liabilities do not need to arise at the same time.[7]
- **In equity as preserved by statute** Historically, the power to make an order for equitable set-off operated to restrain a claimant proceeding in a claim where equity negated that claim; that power is now preserved by statute.[8] Equity has developed by analogy with set-off at law.[9] Where the right to set off arises at law, equity will recognise it, unless to do so would be inequitable.[10]

Denning MR has commented that these two strands have flowed together and combined so as to be indistinguishable.[11]

21.06 This traditional way of looking at set-off does not apply when the court is exercising its discretion as to the incidence of costs (other than, perhaps, as a guide). The court's power to make an award of set-off may analysed in two ways.

- **Section 51** Scott LJ has commented that, in so far as set-off involving only costs is concerned, the jurisdiction to make an order for set-off may be thought of as arising from s 51 of the Senior Courts Act 1981—but he went on to say that that analysis does not hold good where costs are set off against damages.[12]

---

[2] *Fearns v Anglo-Dutch Paint & Chemical Co Ltd* [2010] EWHC 2366 (Ch), at [50].

[3] See now Senior Courts Act 1981, s 49(2), which derived from the Supreme Court of Judicature (Consolidation) Act 1925 (repealed); in the County Court and its hearing centres, see County Courts Act 1984, s 72.

[4] *Inca Hall Rolling Mills Co Ltd v Douglas Forge Co* (1882) 8 QBD 179, at 183.

[5] *Stein v Blake* [1996] AC 243.

[6] *Hanak v Green* [1958] 2 QB 9.

[7] *Day & Dent Constructions Pty Ltd v North Australian Properties Pty Ltd* (1986) 150 CLR 85.

[8] See Senior Courts Act 1981, s 49(2), which refers to equitable defences.

[9] See *Halsbury's Laws of England* (LexisNexis, online), paras 659–660; see also *Rawson v Samuel* (1841) Cr & Ph 161.

[10] *Re Whitehouse & Co* (1878) Ch D 595.

[11] *Federal Commerce and Navigation Co Ltd v Molena Alpha Inc* [1978] QB 927, at 974.

[12] *Lockley v National Blood Transfusion Service* [1992] 1 WLR 492, at 496.

- **Inherent jurisdiction** Many judges have concluded that the court has an inherent jurisdiction to make an order that costs be set off against costs.[13] Neuberger J has found that this gives the court greater flexibility than it would have when applying the usual statutory and equitable principles (see 21.22) and Brooke LJ (giving judgment of the court) agreed with that analysis (see 21.23).[14]

Regardless of which analysis best suits the case in hand, the court has greater freedom over costs than it does when dealing with other types of set-off. In particular, the requirements of mutuality, etc—which will be referred to in this chapter as 'the requirements in *Hanak*'[15]) (see below)—do not need to be satisfied before the court can order that costs be set off against costs. Nonetheless, those requirements would normally be met because most (if not nearly all) cross-orders for costs will be made in circumstances in which they are met. **21.07**

The requirements in *Hanak* are that: **21.08**

- the monies relate to the same parties and the same interests;
- the amounts are quantifiable; and
- they become payable at the same time.

Thus the fine distinctions mentioned in 21.06 are usually little more than of academic interest.

The CPR and set-off

The Civil Procedure Rules (CPR) provide the mechanism by which orders for set-off may be made. CPR, r 16.6, makes provision for pleading set-off, but that provision is of only limited application to costs. In the present context, the more important provision is at CPR, r 44.12(1): **21.09**

> '(1) Where a party entitled to costs is also liable to pay costs, the court may assess the costs which that party is liable to pay and either—
> (a) set off the amount assessed against the amount the party is entitled to be paid and direct that party to pay any balance; or
> (b) delay the issue of a certificate for the costs to which the party is entitled until the party has paid the amount which that party is liable to pay.'

This provision permits set-off of costs in its traditional sense (that is, where a quantified sum is subtracted from another quantified sum). For the reasons set out above, the court will not be constrained by the requirements in *Hanak* when making an order under this provision.

The court has an even greater freedom, however, because—contrary to older practices[16]— CPR, r 44.2(6) and (7), permit the court to take set-off into account when making an order that a party be awarded only part of their costs. In those circumstances, the court is **21.10**

---

[13] *Izzo v Philip Ross* (2001) The Times, 9 August, Ch D, *per* Neuberger J. See also *Edwards v Hope* (1885) 14 QBD 922; *Reid v Cupper* [1915] 2 KB 147; *R (on the application of Burkett) v Hammersmith and Fulham London Borough Council* [2004] EWCA Civ 1342, at [44].

[14] *R (on the application of Burkett) v Hammersmith and Fulham London Borough Council* [2004] EWCA Civ 1342, at [38].

[15] After *Hanak v Green* [1958] 2 QB 9.

[16] See, eg, *Chell Engineering Ltd v Unit Tool and Engineering Co Ltd* [1950] 1 All ER 378.

unfettered in its discretion to do justice between the parties. The relevant principles are set out at 7.34–7.37.

Issues-based orders and set-off

21.11 There is no reason why set-off should not apply to an order that has been made on a general issues-based approach.[17]

Part 36 and set-off

21.12 Judge Seymour QC (sitting as a judge of the High Court) found that the wording of what is now CPR, r 36.14(6), was such that any damages payable as a result of the acceptance of a Part 36 offer must be paid and that the aforesaid rule did not permit of set-off of costs.[18]

Contract and set-off

21.13 It may be that the putative right to set-off arises under a contract such as an individual voluntary agreement (IVA) or a mortgage; where this is so, that right may be limited.[19]

Methods of funding and set-off

21.14 The way in which a party is funded is not something that would deprive the court of the jurisdiction to make an order of set-off. In particular, the fact that the Legal Services Commission (LSC) may have a proprietorial right arising out of the statutory charge will not prevent an order for set-off being made. In particular, in so far as the *Hanak* requirements apply, there will be no lack of mutuality arising out of the fact that the LSC has a right to a statutory charge.[20] The same seems not to be true, however, of awards made in respect of *pro bono* representation (see 18.129).

21.15 In summary, the court has wide powers to make an order for set-off. Whilst the requirements in *Hanak* may be a guide as to how the court should exercise its discretion, those requirements do not fetter the court.

Procedural Issues of Set-off

21.16 Where an application for set-off is made at the same time as the costs order itself, that application will merely form part of the parties' submissions as to costs, so there will be no formalities. Unless the subject matter of the claim is a putative entitlement to costs,[21] a party seeking set-off would not need to plead that contention. As to whether set-off should be mentioned in points of dispute, see 21.18.

---

[17] *Graham Calvert v William Hill Credit Ltd* [2008] EWCA Civ 888.

[18] See *Cave v Bulley Davey* [2013] EWHC 4246 (QB), at [5].

[19] An example being clause 7 of the Standard Conditions for IVAs, which allows for set-off where, before the commencement of the IVA, there had been mutual credits, mutual debts or other mutual dealings. This would not apply to costs liabilities that arose after the IVA had been made: see *Co-operative Bank plc v Phillips* [2014] EWHC 2862 (Ch), at [80] and [81], *per* Morgan J.

[20] *R (on the application of Burkett) v Hammersmith and Fulham London Borough Council* [2004] EWCA Civ 1342, following *Lockley v National Blood Transfusion Service* [1992] 1 WLR 492; overruling *Re A Debtor* (1981) The Times, 19 February, and *Anderson v Hills Automobiles (Woodford) Ltd* [1965] 1 WLR 745. See also *Hill v Bailey* [2003] EWHC 2835 (Ch); *Re Neckles* [2003] EWHC 685 (Ch).

[21] The CPR make provision for set-off to be pleaded as a defence (CPR, r 16.6), so where the claim is about costs, a claim to set-off ought to be pleaded.

Although there is no authority on the point, there is nothing within the CPR to suggest that the power to make an order for set-off vests only in the judge making the costs order. Indeed, the wording of CPR, r 44.12, seems specifically to envisage that the court may decide whether to make such an order at the end of the assessment. It would therefore seem that a costs judge has the power to make an order for set-off. **21.17**

There is nothing within the CPR that expressly requires a party seeking set-off to state its case in points of dispute. Such a party would be well advised to do so, however, because not only would this alert the court to the need to allocate the bills of costs to the same judge, but also it would alert the court to the need not to make an order of its own volition for a payment on account without first taking set-off into account. **21.18**

Where the issues concerning set-off place the matter beyond the jurisdiction of the County Court, the matter may be transferred to the High Court.[22] Where a party wishes to set off costs in different courts, written notice must be given to the courts concerned; the matter may then be transferred to a single court.[23] Where this happens and where, in the County Court, the orders have yet to be made, the counterpart court must send a copy of the order to the court that is dealing with the application.[24] **21.19**

In summary, in so far as costs are concerned, from a practical viewpoint there are almost no formalities relating to set-off. **21.20**

Set-off and Discretion

Whether to make an order for set-off is a matter that is within the court's discretion.[25] **21.21**

The breadth of the court's discretion

For the reasons set out at 21.07, the court is not constrained by the requirements in *Hanak*. Neuberger J has explained that this is because the power to order that costs be set off against costs arises from the court's inherent jurisdiction rather than solely from the doctrines of equitable or statutory set-off.[26] In the case before him, for example, Neuberger J observed (albeit *obiter*) that the court's inherent jurisdiction would have permitted him to make an order notwithstanding the fact that, on a *Hanak* analysis, there might have been a lack of mutuality in terms of the parties' identity. **21.22**

Brooke LJ agreed with Neuberger J's analysis: **21.23**

> 'In [*Lockley v National Blood Transfusion Service* [1992] 1 WLR 492] the court appears also to have been addressed on the basis of the rules as to set-off as a defence, and despite its perception ... that the "set-off" with which it was concerned was different and discretionary in nature, it reviewed those rules ... In truth, that step was not necessary, because the set-off ordered by Newman J, and by this court in *Lockley*, and by our predecessors in *Reid v Cupper*

[22] Senior Courts Act 1981, s 75.
[23] Senior Courts Act 1981, s 75.
[24] County Courts Act 1984, s 72.
[25] *Currie & Co v The Law Society* [1977] QB 990, at 1000, *per* May J.
[26] *Izzo v Philip Ross* (2001) The Times, 9 August, Ch D, *per* Neuberger J.

[[1915] 2 KB 147], is of a quite different nature from the type of set-off to which the rules of mutuality apply.'[27]

21.24 One of the passages in *Lockley* to which Brooke LJ referred was the following, in which Scott LJ analysed the matter by reference to the requirements in *Hanak*:

> 'The broad criterion for the application of set-off is that the plaintiff's claim and the defendant's claim are so closely connected that it would be inequitable to allow the plaintiff's claim without taking into account the defendant's claim. As it has sometimes been put, the defendant's claim must, in equity, impeach the plaintiff's claim.'[28]

21.25 Brooke LJ made it clear that whilst the matter could be analysed in that way, this was not a requirement:

> 'None of this has anything at all to do with a discretionary balance between two sums of costs. First, it is for the judge to decide, in his discretion, what costs order is appropriate. The exercise of striking a fair balance between such payments is quite different from the judge's task in a case of equitable set-off as just discussed, where he has to decide as a matter of law, not of discretion, what claims can be asserted, and then, but only then, decide whether the rules governing equitable set-off permit the one claim to be set-off against the other. Secondly, and illustrative of the point just made, no right to costs arises until the judge decides that the right exists. Since he has discretion in creating the right, so he has discretion in deciding the amount in which, and the form in which, that right should be enforced.'[29]

21.26 Brooke LJ went on to explain that technical objections to set-off founded on the notion of lack of mutuality 'simply beat the air'.[30]

21.27 Where the court is deciding the issue of set-off at the same time as deciding what costs order to make, the requirements in *Hanak* do not apply. There is no authority on the issue of whether the same applies when the topic of set-off is addressed at some later time. For the reasons set out at 21.07, however, that would rarely present any difficulties, because the requirements in *Hanak* would usually be met in circumstances in which cross-orders as to costs had already been made.

The form and effect of an order for set-off

21.28 There is nothing to prevent a court from making an order for set-off in respect of only a part of a party's costs. Where, for example, the litigation has lent itself to an issues-based order, the court may order set-off in respect of only those issues in respect of which there is a nexus.[31]

21.29 An order for set-off does not place the person against whom it is asserted under any obligation to pay; it merely reduces the amount that the person can recover.[32] Pre-CPR

---

[27] *R (on the application of Burkett) v Hammersmith and Fulham London Borough Council* [2004] EWCA Civ 1342, at [44].

[28] *Lockley v National Blood Transfusion Service* [1992] 1 WLR 492, at 496.

[29] *R (on the application of Burkett) v Hammersmith and Fulham London Borough Council* [2004] EWCA Civ 1342, at [46].

[30] *Ibid*, at [47].

[31] *Hashem v Shayif* [2009] EWHC 864 (Fam).

[32] *Hicks v Russell Jones & Walker* [2001] CP Rep 25, CA at [11]; *Hill v Bailey* [2003] EWHC 2835 (Ch); *R (on the application of Burkett) v Hammersmith and Fulham London Borough Council* [2004] EWCA Civ 1342, at [50].

authority suggests that a party cannot be compelled to claim set-off.[33] It may be that this principle has not survived the introduction of the CPR. In any event, the power to make percentage awards, etc, affords the court alternative means of dealing with the situation where there are competing rights to costs.

The exercise of discretion

As to the way in which the court should exercise its discretion, pre-CPR teaching was that, unless there were special circumstances, the court would lean towards making an order for set-off in appropriate cases.[34] Although *obiter*, Neuberger J seems to have found that guidance continued to have resonance under the CPR.[35] Nevertheless, there are other types of award that may achieve a similar or equally fair result (often in a more efficient manner) and those will usually be borne in mind as alternatives (see 7.34–7.37). **21.30**

In so far as claims and counterclaims are concerned, CPR, r 40.13, makes the following provisions relating to set-off: **21.31**

> '(1) This rule applies where the court gives judgment for specified amounts both for the claimant on his claim and against the claimant on a counterclaim.
>
> (2) If there is a balance in favour of one of the parties, it may order the party whose judgment is for the lesser amount to pay the balance.
>
> (3) In a case to which this rule applies, the court may make a separate order as to costs against each party.'

Potter LJ has confirmed that CPR, r 40.13(3), makes provision for the court to make a separate order for costs against each party according to its view of the justice of the case.[36]

Scott LJ has confirmed that the fact that a party is in receipt of public funding makes set-off no different from, and no more extensive than, the set-off available to or against parties who are not publicly funded.[37] **21.32**

Factors to be taken into account

The following circumstances may have a bearing on whether an order for set-off will be made. Some of the considerations will be encountered more commonly than others; indeed, it can be seen that, in the context of costs, some of the circumstances (such as a claim for costs being time-barred) are extremely unlikely to arise. They are mentioned only for the sake of completeness. **21.33**

[33] In the non-costs setting, see *Laing v Chatham* (1808) 1 Camp 252; *Jenner v Morris* (1861) 3 De GF & J 45; *Davis v Hedges* (1871) LR 6 QB 687; *Re Sturmey Motors Ltd, Rattray v Sturmey Motors Ltd* [1913] 1 Ch 16.

[34] *Puddephatt v Leith (No 2)* [1916] 2 Ch 168; *Currie & Co v The Law Society* [1977] QB 990.

[35] *Izzo v Philip Ross* (2001) The Times, 9 August, Ch D, *per* Neuberger J.

[36] *Boynton v Willers* [2003] EWCA Civ 904, at [39].

[37] *Lockley v National Blood Transfusion Service* [1992] 1 WLR 492, at 496.

Insolvency

21.34 Where a party is likely to be unable to pay costs, it would, in the absence of persuasive factors to make an order for set-off, be counter to common notions of good sense and justice to require the other party to pay, as opposed to set off, its costs.[38]

Assignment

21.35 Where one of the parties has assigned their right to costs to a third party, equity may, in certain circumstances, intervene to prevent set-off diminishing the third party's rights,[39] because it would be unconscionable to allow that entitlement to be negated.[40] Much will depend on timing and notice—issues that are dealt with in texts on equity.

Legal expenses insurance

21.36 A factor that may be relevant is whether set-off would have a bearing on whether a claim could be made under a policy of legal expenses insurance.

No mutuality and interest of justice

21.37 Where there is a lack of mutuality (such as where the cross-orders related to wholly separate issues[41] or where they arose in claims where parties were acting in different capacities), the court may decline to order set-off. For the reasons set out above, this would be a matter of discretion, rather than as a result of a failure to meet the requirements in *Hanak*. By way of example, both Neuberger J and Blofeld J have commented that, on the facts of the case before them, an order for set-off would not have been appropriate where the cross-orders related to entirely separate issues in the litigation.[42] In a case in which the claimant was a lead claimant in group litigation, Owen J refused to set off the claimant's proportionate share of the costs of trial of the generic issues against the claimant's damages, because this would not be fair and just: the claimant had sustained injury, and consequential loss and damage, and he would have succeeded in that action whether or not the generic issues had been litigated.[43]

Inchoate claims, unquantified claims and foreign currencies

21.38 Where a party has been awarded costs, but is not in a position to quantify those costs (such as where the court has declined to make a forthwith order or where the fees of an expert are required before the bill of costs can be finalised), it may not be appropriate—or, in some cases, even possible—to make an order for set-off at that time. Similarly, where costs are large and where the court has no bills of costs to assist it, it may be appropriate to defer any decision as to set off until more is known about the sums involved.[44] It may be that set-off

---

[38] In the costs setting, see *Revenue & Customs Commissioners v Xicom Systems Ltd* [2008] EWHC 1945 (Ch); *Fearns v Anglo-Dutch Paint & Chemical Co Ltd* [2010] EWHC 2366 (Ch). In a more general setting, see *Re Debtor (No 21 of 1950) (No 1)* [1951] Ch 313.

[39] See, as a costs example, *Izzo v Philip Ross* (2001) The Times, 9 August, Ch D, *per* Neuberger J, in which a *McKenzie* friend's entitlement to costs arising out of an order that had been assigned took precedence.

[40] See *Re Whitehouse & Co* (1878) 9 Ch D 595; *Re Paraguassu Steam Tramroad Co* (1872) 8 Ch App 254; *Mercer v Graves* (1872) LR 7 QB 499.

[41] See, eg, *Hashem v Shayif* [2009] EWHC 864 (Fam), in which the court made an order for set-off in respect of the costs of some of the issues, but not all.

[42] *Zappia Middle East Construction Co Ltd v Clifford Chance (a firm)* [2001] EWCA Civ 946, *per* Neuberger J, commenting on a previous decision by Blofeld J in the same case.

[43] *O v Ministry of Defence* [2006] EWHC 990 (QB).

[44] See *Amin v Amin* [2010] EWHC 827 (Ch), at [51].

needs to be made of one currency against another, in which case the approach is to assess and add to each principal amount any relevant interest up to the date of the set-off, then to convert the lesser sum into the currency of the greater sum at the exchange rate prevailing at that date, and then to order payment of the balance.[45]

Time-barred

Where one of the party's claims for costs is time-barred, the court may require that party to pursue their claim independently so as to afford the other party the opportunity to plead limitation.[46] **21.39**

Third parties

The positions of third parties other than assignees may be relevant (such as where a commercial funder may be denied monies if the funded party's costs were to be diminished by reason of set-off or where the rights of a *McKenzie* friend need to be taken into account).[47] That said, the fact that the financial burden on the LSC would be increased by an order for set-off is irrelevant, because it was its choice to fund the claim.[48] **21.40**

Unpaid solicitors

One particular type of third party merits particular mention—namely, solicitors. Where a receiving party has failed to pay their solicitor, the solicitor may take lien over the costs order in the hope that monies paid by the paying party will be recovered. If there are cross-orders as to costs and if the other party claims set-off, the court will have to decide whether to give precedence to the solicitor's lien or whether the rights of the paying party should prevail. Whilst there are older authorities to the contrary, the solicitor's lien would not normally disturb the paying party's right to set-off.[49] This will not always be so. In a case in which orders for costs were the fruits of the solicitor's labour and in which there were no good reasons to allow the solicitor's interest to be defeated, Pumfrey J declined to make an order for set-off.[50] **21.41**

In summary, the court has a very wide discretion as to whether to order set-off and that discretion is not constrained by the requirements in *Hanak*. An order for set-off may apply to all of a party's costs or to only a part of them. Many factors may be taken into account (even if they are to be afforded no or little weight), but the following are commonly found to be relevant: **21.42**

- the solvency of the parties;
- the rights of third parties, including the rights of assignees and (rarely) of a party's solicitor;
- the position concerning legal expenses insurance;
- mutuality; and
- whether a claim for costs is inchoate.

---

[45] *Fearns v Anglo-Dutch Paint & Chemical Co Ltd* [2010] EWHC 2366 (Ch), at [50] *et seq*, *per* Leggatt QC (sitting as a deputy judge of the High Court).

[46] A claim by way of set-off is deemed to be a separate action that commenced on the same date as the original action: see Limitation Act 1980, s 35(1)(b) and (2).

[47] *Izzo v Philip Ross* (2001) The Times, 9 August, Ch D, *per* Neuberger J.

[48] *Ahmad v Brent London Borough Council* [2011] EWHC 378 (QB), at [12], *per* Supperstone J.

[49] *Puddephatt v Leith (No 2)* [1916] 2 Ch 168.

[50] *Rohm Haas Co v Collag Ltd* [2002] IPD 25007.

22

AGENCY AND COSTS

22.01 This short chapter deals with the following topics:

- an overview of agency (22.02);
- solicitor agents (22.06);
- non-solicitor agents (22.08);
- specific relationships in which an issue of agency may arise (22.21):
  - costs draftspersons and costs lawyers (22.22);
  - counsel (22.25);
  - experts (22.26); and
  - medical agencies (22.27).

An Overview of Agency

22.02 The law of agency will apply where a person (the agent) is authorised to act as the representative of another person (the principal), such that the agent has the authority to create legal relations between the principal and third parties.[1] The agreement that is created is a principal–agent relationship. That relationship may be express or implied,[2] or may be created retrospectively by ratification.[3] In the present context (that is, costs incurred by persons said to be agents), an 'agent' is a person (often another solicitor) who, rather than being employed by the solicitor principal (or other authorised representative), is engaged to carry out work on their behalf. The third party to this principal–agent relationship is the client, who will ultimately be responsible for payment for the services rendered by the agent.

22.03 It is convenient to refer to 'the solicitor principal', 'the non-solicitor agent' and 'the solicitor agent' to describe the various persons who might be involved.

22.04 The main topic that is addressed in this section is whether an agent's fees are recoverable as profit costs or as a disbursement. The question is relevant for two reasons: first, it is relevant to the manner in which costs are to be presented in any statute bill or bill of costs; and secondly, it can have a bearing on the quantum of costs in that whilst no profit may be made on disbursements, it is permissible for a legal representative to make a profit when claiming profit costs (see 22.08–22.18).

---

1 *Re Nevill, ex p White* (1871) 6 Ch App 397, CA.
2 *Pole v Leask* (1863) 33 LJ Ch 155.
3 In a slightly different context, see 47.29.

This second of these two issues has become a noteworthy point in recent times, for two reasons: **22.05**

- a solicitor principal may, by charging the agent's services as if the solicitor principal had provided them itself, be able to make a considerable profit on services provided by an agent (because, in appropriate cases, a success fee may be charged); and
- the question of whether a fee can be regarded as having been incurred as a disbursement may have a bearing on its recoverability under the fixed costs regimes in Part 45 of the Civil Procedure Rules (CPR).

Solicitor Agents

A solicitor who is instructed by a client will, in general, have authority to instruct a solicitor agent.[4] There will, unless otherwise agreed, be no privity between the client and the solicitor agent,[5] and as such the agent will not be able to sue the client for its costs;[6] instead, the solicitor principal will be liable for the agent's costs.[7] If the client wishes to have the agent's fees assessed, this will be in the context of those being costs claimed by the principal.[8] If profit costs are incurred by a solicitor agent, the mere fact that the work has been delegated by the solicitor principal to the solicitor agent does not justify the agent's fee being regarded as a disbursement. This much is made clear by Stirling J: **22.06**

> 'It is well settled that between the client and the London agent of the country solicitor there is no privity. The relationship of solicitor and client does not exist between the client and the London agent. What is done by the London agent is part of the work done by the country solicitor for the client. The country solicitor does or may do part of the work personally. He does or may do part of his work through clerks whom he employs in the country. Or, if necessary ... he may do part of his work through a London agent. But as between the country solicitor and the client, the whole of the work is done by the country solicitor. It follows, therefore, that the items which make up the London agent's bill are not mere disbursements, but are items taxable in the strictest sense as between the client and the country solicitor, just as much as items in respect of work done by the country solicitor personally, or by the clerk whom he employs in the country.'[9]

These comments remain good law today.[10]

---

4 See *Re Bishop, ex p Langley, ex p Smith* (1879) 13 Ch D 110, CA. See also *Solley v Wood* (1852) 16 Beav 370. The solicitor would not impliedly have permission to instruct a different solicitor to act in his stead: *Re Becket, Purnell v Paine* [1918] 2 Ch 72, CA.

5 *Cobb v Becke* (1845) 6 QB 930; *Robbins v Fennell* (1847) 11 QB 248. See also *Gordon v Dalzell* (1852) 15 Beav 351.

6 See *Ward v Lawson* (1890) 43 Ch D 353, CA, at 360, *per* Cotton LJ; see also *Scrace v Whittington* (1823) 2 B & C 11.

7 *Scrace v Whittington* (1823) 2 B & C 11. This does not apply if the agent is an Irish solicitor: *Hyndman v Ward* (1899) 15 TLR 182. Because the principal solicitor is liable for the agent's fees and can be required to pay them regardless of whether the client has paid them, the solicitor principal is permitted to keep any interest recovered: *Ward v Lawson* (1890) 43 Ch D 353, CA.

8 *Wildbore v Bryan, ex p Wildbore* (1820) 8 Price 677.

9 *In re Pomeroy & Tanner* [1897] 1 Ch 284, at 287.

10 See *Agassi v Robinson* [2005] EWCA Civ 1507; *Crane v Canons Leisure Centre* [2007] EWCA Civ 1352, at [7]. See also *EMW Law LLP v Halborg* [2017] EWHC 1014 (Ch), at [20], *per* Newey J.

22.07 Where appropriate, the solicitor agent's fees will be charged as being the principal's profit costs. This is confirmed by Practice Direction (PD) 47, para 5.22(6), which provides:

> 'Agency charges as between a principal solicitors and their agents will be dealt with on the principle that such charges, where appropriate, form part of the principal solicitor's charges. Where these charges relate to head (1) in paragraph 5.12 (attendances at court and on counsel) they must be included in their chronological order in that head. In other cases they must be included in head (9) (attendances on London and other agents).'

It is implicit in this provision that whilst the agency fees should form part of the principal's own fees, the fact that an agent was engaged ought to be stated in the bill of costs. That said, the mere fact that there was an agreement that the supposed agent would be paid by the supposed principal would not give rise to a principal–agent relationship; if the agreement contemplated that the supposed agent would carry out work on their *own* behalf, then no agency would be created.[11] Thus an agent's fees should be charged as the principal's fees only where this is appropriate. An example in which this may not be appropriate would be where the putative agent was instructed directly by the lay client without the involvement of the principal; another example would be where the supposed agent was providing services (such as expert evidence) that could not be characterised as legal in nature.

Non-solicitor agents

22.08 For the reasons set out above, services provided by solicitor agents are, in appropriate cases, to be charged as though they had been provided by the solicitor principal. What is less clear is how the costs of a non-solicitor agent should be classified. The receiving party may, at different times, have reason to advance diametrically opposed arguments depending on the circumstances in which the costs are claimed.

22.09 The starting point is that a payment made by a solicitor may, in principle, be treated as a disbursement incurred through the agency of the solicitor.[12] There will be cases in which the payment will be a disbursement.

22.10 In certain circumstances, the work of a non-solicitor agent may be regarded as being equivalent to that of a fee earner employed by the solicitor. Indeed, May LJ has commented that the distinction between solicitor agents and non-solicitor agents is not as relevant to the issue of the nature of their fees as it might, at first blush, appear:

> 'I do not think that the classification of the cost of this work [ie the costs done by a non-solicitor agent] can sensibly depend on whether [the solicitor principals] did the work themselves, whether they delegated it to another solicitor or whether they delegated it to [agents] who were not solicitors.'[13]

It is implicit in this extract that one factor that is relevant is the nature of the services that are being provided.

---

[11] Although a non-costs case, see *Handley Page Ltd v Customs and Excise Commissioners and Rockwell Machine Tool Co Ltd* [1971] 2 Lloyd's Rep 298, CA.

[12] If authority were needed on the point, it can be implied from the way in which the Court of Appeal dealt with certain disbursements in *In Re Blair & Girling* [1906] 2 KB 131.

[13] *Crane v Canons Leisure Centre* [2007] EWCA Civ 1352, at [15].

22.11 The case that, until recently, was usually cited as the main authority in support of the proposition that non-solicitor agent's fees may be charged as if they were the fees of the solicitor principal fees is *Smith Graham*.[14] This was a case in which Hallett J allowed the fees of an enquiry agent (a retired police officer) as though the agent had been a fee earner. Hallett J's judgment was often cited, despite the fact that it involved a question of regulatory interpretation[15] rather than any issue of general applicability.

22.12 There was, until 2007 (see 22.13), a divergence of judicial opinion as to the effect of *Smith Graham*. Whilst some judges limited and distinguished *Smith Graham* by pointing to the fact that Hallett J had said that each case turns on its own facts,[16] others embraced the notion that agent's fees were capable of being charged as the principal's fees.[17] More recently, however, the court's approach has been to look at the facts, including (where appropriate):

- the nature of the work,
- the degree of supervision, and
- the terms of the retainer.

In addition, the extent to which the principal was authorised may also be a factor.

The nature of the work and the extent of supervision

22.13 As long ago as 2002, Senior Master Hurst had commented that a relevant factor was whether the putative principal had personal responsibility for the work that was being carried out.[18] Five years later, the Court of Appeal (including May and Hallett LJJ) caught up with the Senior Master, in a case that has become the main authority on the point: *Crane v Canons Leisure Centre*.[19] Unsurprisingly, Hallett LJ's approach was much the same as it had been when she was a puisne judge. May LJ had this to say:

> 'If [solicitor principals] properly choose to delegate their own work, they remain entitled to charge on their own account and the proper amount of the charge is not necessarily the same as the amount which they agree to pay to their subcontractor. It could be more or it could be less. In my view, the appellants are right to concentrate on whether the work is solicitors' work; and Master Hurst was right to say that a characteristic of such work is whether the solicitor remains responsible to the client for its proper conduct.'[20]

22.14 It is implicit in this passage that it will not always be the case that the work done by a person other than a solicitor will be regarded as being the costs of the solicitor who instructs that person. Clearly, the work has to be legal work for it to be characterised as profit costs (which is why the costs of an expert could never be regarded as profit costs). Likewise, counsel's fees are not regarded as profit costs.[21] Where other persons are instructed, however, the

---

14 *Smith Graham v Lord Chancellor's Department* [1999] 2 Costs LR 1.

15 Legal Aid in Criminal and Care Proceedings (Costs) Regulations 1989 (SI 1989/343), reg 2.

16 See, eg, Master Hurst's comments in *Claims Direct Test Cases Tranche 2* [2003] EWHC 9005 (Costs), at [115].

17 See, eg, *Stringer v Copley* (unreported), 17 May 2002, Kingston on Thames County Court, *per* HHJ Cook.

18 See *Claims Direct Test Cases Tranche 2* [2003] EWHC 9005 (Costs), at [80].

19 *Crane v Canons Leisure Centre* [2007] EWCA Civ 1352.

20 *Ibid*, at [14].

21 See the comments of Maurice Kay LJ *ibid*, at [28].

issue will turn on the facts of the case—on the nature of the work and the extent to which the solicitor principal remains responsible for the services that are provided.

22.15 The fact that there is an agreement between the putative principal and agent does not necessarily mean that a relationship of agency exists; where the agreement contemplates that the latter will carry out work on its own behalf, then no such relationship will be created.[22] In particular, where the solicitor merely 'rubber stamps' the work (to use Lord Jauncey's phrase), the work probably would be regarded as being a disbursement.[23]

The relevance of the retainer

22.16 The extent to which the solicitor principal remains responsible for the work done may depend on the wording of the retainer. There is no reason why a retainer should not expressly provide that work done by, say, a paginating bureau is a service for which the solicitor principal will (or will not) be responsible.[24] Whilst there is no authority on the point, it is likely that such a factor would be given significant weight in deciding the nature of the resultant fee (assuming, of course, that the provision in the retainer was not a sham).

22.17 Whilst his was a dissenting judgment, it is clear from the way in which Maurice Kay LJ dealt with the issue of whether a success fee is payable on work done by a costs draftsperson that another factor to be taken into account is the extent to which it is just and fair that the solicitor principal makes a profit.[25] On the facts of the case before them, Maurice Kay LJ's fellow judges did not agree with his analysis, but it may be that that is a factor that can be taken into account in other situations—most notably, the issue of reasonableness.

22.18 In particular, the fact that the costs of a non-solicitor agent are, in principle, the costs of the solicitor principal does not necessarily mean that the court will allow those costs in full. This is because the test of reasonableness will apply. If the court is satisfied that it was unreasonable of the solicitor principal to engage the services of a person whose costs would be charged as the principal's costs, then it is arguable that the costs may be restricted accordingly. Although there is no authority on the point, an example might be where a solicitor advocate was engaged in circumstances in which counsel would have been a cheaper and more appropriate option. Furthermore, a person cannot do through agency something that they cannot do themselves;[26] hence an enquiry agent cannot be instructed to carry out a task that the solicitor principal would not be able to do.

The relevance of authorisation

22.19 Finally, it is worth saying a word or two about principals who are not themselves entitled to conduct litigation. Where counsel has been instructed by a person who was not entitled to conduct litigation, counsel's fees cease to be recoverable in that litigation.[27] Whilst it

22 Although a non-costs case, see *Handley Page Ltd v Customs and Excise Commissioners and Rockwell Machine Tool Co Ltd* [1971] 2 Lloyd's Rep 298, CA.

23 *R v Legal Aid Board, ex p Bruce* [1992] 3 All ER 321, at 326.

24 In support of this, see the way in which Master Gordon-Saker addressed the issue of pagination agencies in *Ahmed v Aventis Pharma Ltd (Rev 1)* [2009] EWHC 90152 (Costs), at [12].

25 *Crane v Canons Leisure Centre* [2007] EWCA Civ 1352, at [14].

26 *Bateman v Mid-Wales Rly Co* (1866) LR 1 CP 499.

27 This is as a result of the operation of Solicitors Act 1974, s 25: see *Westland Helicopters Ltd v Al-Hejailan* [2004] EWHC 1625 (Comm).

should not be forgotten that, strictly speaking, counsel is not instructed as an agent (see 22.25), this seems to be in keeping with the doctrine that a person cannot do through someone else something that they cannot do themselves.[28] There is no reason to believe that the position would be any different for service providers other than counsel.

In summary, where a solicitor principal engages a non-solicitor to provide services, the services may or may not be part of the solicitor principal's fees, depending on the facts. Factors that will be relevant will include the nature of the work, the terms of engagement, the degree of supervision and the terms of the retainer. **22.20**

Specific Relationships in which an Issue of Agency May Arise

The following are examples only. Each case will turn on its own facts and there may be exceptions to the general points that are made. If, for example, a costs lawyer were to provide an expert opinion in a professional negligence case, a compelling case could be made out for that lawyer's fees not to be treated as being those of the solicitor principal. **22.21**

Costs draftspersons and costs lawyers

A costs draftsperson's fees are to be dealt with in exactly the same way as would the fees of any other non-solicitor agent. The same is true of costs lawyers. Given the nature of the services and responsibility that the solicitor principal must bear for the work, it is not surprising that the services will generally be treated as though they had been provided by a solicitor principal. This was confirmed by Hallett LJ: **22.22**

> '[To] determine whether or not these costs are properly described as base costs or disbursements, one must focus on the nature of the work done (whether it is solicitors' work) and where responsibility for the work lies. In my view, the work done by [the costs draftsperson] was undoubtedly solicitors' work. It was the type of work [the solicitors] were retained to do. [The solicitors] may have chosen to delegate their work, but they never relinquished control of it and responsibility for it. At every stage of the process [the costs draftsperson's] work was under [the solicitor's] supervision ... [Had] there been any failure on the part of [the costs draftsperson], [the solicitors] could have been held accountable. Given that background, for my part, I am satisfied that [the costs draftsperson's] work is properly described as work done "on behalf of the solicitors" and their fees are properly described as base costs ...'[29]

However, the decision of the court was not unanimous. Whilst May and Hallett LJJ opined that a costs draftsperson's fees are profit costs, Maurice Kay LJ believed otherwise. He recognised that his views might give rise to an anomalous and adventitious result in the way in which non-solicitor agents' fees are dealt with, but he justified this on the basis that he would 'prefer an anomalous conclusion to an unjust one'.[30] Other senior judges have expressed similar views, albeit extrajudicially.[31] **22.23**

In any event, where the services provided by a costs draftsperson or a costs lawyer are charged as profit costs, the bill of costs in which they are charged will usually make it clear **22.24**

---

[28] *Bateman v Mid-Wales Rly Co* (1866) LR 1 CP 499.
[29] *Crane v Canons Leisure Centre* [2007] EWCA Civ 1352, at [35]–[36].
[30] *Ibid*, at [29].
[31] See Jackson, R, *Review of Civil Litigation Costs: Final Report* (London: HMSO, 2010), para 10.5.25.

that the work has been done by a costs draftsperson. Indeed, on one reading of PD 47, this is mandatory.[32]

Counsel

22.25 For the reasons set out above, counsel's fees will not generally be regarded as services provided by the solicitor principal—that is, it is the received view that they are disbursements.[33] This includes any success fee charged by counsel.

Experts

22.26 Unless the expert is, in truth, merely carrying out administrative work for the solicitor, the services provided by an expert are not generally claimable as services provided by the solicitor principal. Whilst there is no authority on the point, one factor that is likely to be relevant is the fact that the services would not generally be capable of being said to be legal services.

Medical agencies

22.27 It is not clear whether the services provided by medical agencies are to be treated as the work done by the solicitor principal or as a disbursement. One of the reasons it is not clear is because the need for authority on the point has waned in the light of an agreement known as the *Woollard* agreement (see 52.69). Some medical agencies provide pagination services (that is, they sort and paginate medical records); those fees are often claimed as disbursements, but for the reasons set out above (see 22.16), this would not necessarily be the correct way in which they should be claimed. If the solicitor were to retain responsibility for the paginator's work (which would usually be the case), then those costs could reasonably be charged as profit costs.[34]

---

[32] See PD 47, para 5.22(6).

[33] See the comments of Maurice Kay LJ in *Crane v Canons Leisure Centre* [2007] EWCA Civ 1352, at [28].

[34] Whilst not binding, see *Ahmed v Aventis Pharma Ltd (Rev 1)* [2009] EWHC 90152 (Costs), at [19], *per* Master Gordon-Saker.

23

FINALITY, DELAY AND LIMITATION

23.01 This chapter examines when a decision becomes final in the sense that a party is precluded from controverting or reopening a decision that has been, or which ought to have been, made previously. It also covers the issue of delay in general. It deals with the following topics:

- finality and the law of costs (23.03);
- *res judicata* (23.07):
  - cause of action estoppel (or claim preclusion) (23.08);
  - issue estoppel (or issue preclusion) (23.19);
- abuse of process (23.28):
  - abuse of process in general (23.31);
  - the rule in *Henderson v Henderson* (23.34);
  - late arguments and proportionality (23.41);
  - conduct—the supposed rule in *Aaron v Shelton* (23.43);
  - special orders (23.49);
- delay and costs (23.50):
  - the disallowance of interest (23.57):
  - misconduct and delay (23.58);
- limitation (23.83):
  - limitation as between solicitor and client (23.85);
  - limitation and seeking orders for costs (23.103);
  - limitation and the assessment of costs (23.111);
  - bringing an action for an order for costs (23.116);
  - acknowledgement and part-payment (23.123); and
  - where limitation will not be permitted to stand as a defence (23.131).

23.02 The editor is grateful to Kenneth Handley AO C StJ QC (a former judge of the New South Wales Court of Appeal and one of the authors of *Res Judicata*[1]) for his guidance in writing this chapter.

Finality and the Law of Costs

23.03 The relevance of the concept of finality to the law of costs is twofold: first, it may have a bearing on the ability of a costs judge to enquire into that which has, or should have

[1] *Spencer Bower and Handley:* Res Judicata (4th edn, London: LexisNexis Butterworths, 2009).

been, previously determined in the substantive litigation; and secondly, it may have a bearing on the extent to which a costs judge may hear arguments that were, or which ought to have been, articulated at the time the costs order was made. Topics concerning finality of costs within costs proceedings (such as whether a further bill of costs may be presented after the first has already been assessed) are also briefly touched upon (see 23.39).

23.04 From ancient times, it has been a goal of the law that litigation must be capable of being brought to an end. Other than in appellate proceedings, the law seeks to discourage the same issues being litigated more than once.[2] To achieve this goal, costs orders are regarded as being final judgments (see 49.03) and restrictions are imposed on the extent to which parties are able to ask the court to examine issues that have been—or, on occasion, which should have been—examined before.

23.05 Unfortunately, there is a dearth of authority on the topic of finality in costs litigation and this means that it is usually necessary to seek guidance from the way in which similar issues are dealt with in substantive litigation. Analogous authorities may be helpful, but it should be borne in mind that costs litigation can differ markedly from substantive litigation. In particular, costs litigation has a much greater emphasis on adjectival law than is the case in substantive litigation, and this is especially true under the Civil Procedure Rules (CPR) now that the overriding objective focuses on the need to enforce compliance with rules, practice directions and orders.

23.06 Towards the end of this section, one or two topics are addressed for the purposes of explaining why the supposed rule in *Aaron v Shelton*[3] is no longer good law. If the reader is already able to put that authority out of mind, then 23.43–23.46 can be disregarded. Readers who are not familiar with that case may disregard paragraphs 23.43–23.46 entirely.

Res Judicata

23.07 *Res judicata* is a portmanteau term that is used to describe a number of different legal principles with different juridical origins.[4] It is used inconsistently, especially in older authorities.[5] In this book, it is used to refer to *res judicata* estoppel. That concept subdivides into 'cause of action estoppel' (or, to use a useful American phrase, 'claim preclusion') and 'issue estoppel' (or 'issue preclusion'). These concepts are wholly different from abuse of process, which is addressed later in this chapter (see 23.28). They are also different from the concept of preclusion by proportionality (see 23.47). Whilst the distinction between cause of action estoppel and issue estoppel is described, in the context of costs litigation there is so much overlap that that distinction is often of little practical relevance.

[2] *Arthur JS Hall v Simons* [2000] 3 All ER 673, at 701, *per* Lord Hoffmann.

[3] *Aaron v Shelton* [2004] EWHC 1162 (QB).

[4] *Virgin Atlantic Airways Ltd v Zodiac Seats UK Ltd (formerly Contour Aerospace Ltd)* [2013] UKSC 46, at [17], *per* Lord Sumption.

[5] In particular, it is often used to refer to 'merger of the cause of action' (*transit in rem judicatam*), which, whilst of importance in substantive litigation, is of little relevance to costs.

Cause of action estoppel (or claim preclusion)

Cause of action estoppel acts to ensure that a person is not vexed by the same claim twice. Lord Sumption had this to say on the point: **23.08**

> '[O]nce a cause of action has been held to exist or not to exist, that outcome may not be challenged by either party in subsequent proceedings. This is "cause of action estoppel". It is properly described as a form of estoppel precluding a party from challenging the same cause of action in subsequent proceedings.'[6]

In its most essential form, it will estop an entire cause of action. In the context of substantive litigation, it is usually described alongside 'merger of the cause of action in the judgment',[7] but in so far as costs litigation is concerned, this latter concept has little relevance; rather, its relevance is the fact that the estoppel will preclude a party from controverting points of law or fact that were necessarily decided by the earlier proceedings.[8] This would be as a result either of a determination that was expressly made or as a result of inferred judicial determination.

Whilst there is no costs authority on the point, an example might be where a claim is successfully brought for damages for personal injury and damage to the claimant's car arising out of a road traffic accident, and the paying party (the defendant) seeks to argue during the assessment that no costs should be allowed because the accident did not take place. The receiving party would respond by saying that the paying party is estopped from raising that point because the existence of the accident is a fact that was a necessary part of the claim. From the point of view of costs litigation, the effect would often be the same regardless of whether the estoppel were cause of action estoppel of issue estoppel, but this would not always be the case, especially if new material had come to light during the course of the assessment (see 23.27).[9] **23.09**

Cause of action estoppel where the facts are said to be incorrect

Cause of action estoppel will apply regardless of the correctness of the decision relied upon.[10] This is of particular relevance to costs litigation because it will sometimes be the case that the parties will come to question the correctness of a decision as a result of material that was not available to the trial judge (or to the parties when they agreed a consent order), but which becomes available during the detailed assessment. The earlier decision will be binding upon the parties unless overturned on appeal or otherwise set aside. Whilst giving judgment in a context other than costs litigation, Millett J had the following to say: '*Res judicata* ... gives effect to the policy of the law that the parties to a **23.10**

---

[6] *Virgin Atlantic Airways Ltd v Zodiac Seats UK Ltd (formerly Contour Aerospace Ltd)* [2013] UKSC 46, at [17].

[7] See Spencer Bower, G, Turner, AK, and Handley, KR, *The Doctrine of* Res Judicata (London: Butterworths, 1996), paras 176–183. See also *Virgin Atlantic Airways Ltd v Zodiac Seats UK Ltd (formerly Contour Aerospace Ltd)* [2013] UKSC 46, at [17], in which Lord Sumption said: '[T]here is the doctrine of merger, which treats a cause of action as extinguished once judgment has been given on it, and the claimant's sole right as being a right on the judgment.'

[8] See *Gregory v Molesworth* (1747) 3 Atk 626 for an early example of the application of this principle.

[9] See the discussion of this in Spencer Bower, G, Turner, AK, and Handley, KR, *The Doctrine of* Res Judicata (London: Butterworths, 1996), ch 7.

[10] In a setting other than costs, see *Myers v Casey* (1913) 17 CLR 90, at 114.

judicial decision should not afterwards be allowed to re-litigate the same question, even though the decision may be wrong.'[11]

23.11 Thus, if, in the example given at 23.09, documentation were to come to light during the detailed assessment that showed that the car did not belong to the claimant, the defendant would be estopped from taking that narrow point.

The effect and ambit of cause of action estoppel

23.12 The court's task in deciding whether a party is estopped is to identify the fact that is in question and then to decide whether that fact is included within the judgment on the claim. Such facts will generally be limited to those issues that have necessarily been decided by the claim.[12] This will include points that may not have been set out in the judgment in express terms, but which must have been decided for the court to make the finding that it made.[13] The ambit of the estoppel is narrow: the court will generally look only to those facts that—when examined with precision—can be said to have been necessarily included within the judgment on the claim.[14] Thus, in the example given at 23.09, cause of action estoppel would apply to a contention that the claimant was present at the scene of the accident, but it would not apply to a contention that the colour of the claimant's car was blue, and this would be so even if this were the most contentious point decided at trial.

23.13 The effect of a judgment for a claimant will usually be greater than that for a defendant. This is because a defendant is able to succeed if it is successful on only one point, but a claimant must prove an entire cause of action to succeed. The consequence of this is that where a defendant wishes to rely on their success in defending the claim, they must prove that the previous claim was decided on a basis that afforded them a defence in the subsequent claim.[15]

23.14 The ambit of cause of action estoppel will be decided primarily on the judgment, including, in an appropriate case, the reasons for the judgment.[16] Where there is ambiguity or uncertainty, it may be determined by examining the transcript of the hearing, the judge's notes, etc,[17] but where the judgment has clear meaning, no evidence (including the pleadings or the procedural history) is admissible to contradict that meaning.[18] Likewise, evidence may not be used for the purposes of denying a fact that has been pleaded and which must be taken to have been included within the judgment on the claim.[19] To continue to use the example given at 23.09, if alternative causes of action had been pleaded (such as negligence and a deliberate act), the transcript may help the costs judge to identify which cause of

---

11 *Crown Estate Commissioners v Dorset County Council* [1990] Ch 297, at 305.

12 *New Brunswick Rly Co v British and French Trust Corpn Ltd* [1938] 4 All ER 747.

13 *Patchett v Sterling Engineering Co Ltd* (1953) 71 RPC 61, which was reversed on other grounds on appeal ([1955] AC 534).

14 *New Brunswick Rly Co v British and French Trust Corpn Ltd* [1938] 4 All ER 747.

15 *Isaacs & Sons v Salbstein* [1916] 2 KB 139.

16 For a detailed discussion of this point, see *Spencer Bower and Handley:* Res Judicata (4th edn, London: LexisNexis Butterworths, 2009), paras 7.16 and 8.29.

17 See, eg, *Randolph v Tuck* [1961] 1 All ER 814.

18 *Gordon v Gonda* [1955] 2 All ER 762.

19 *Patchett v Sterling Engineering Co Ltd* (1953) 71 RPC 61, which was reversed on other grounds on appeal ([1955] AC 534).

action succeeded, but it may not be used to demonstrate that the judge accepted in oral argument that the accident did not take place. It is worth pausing here to add that where a claimant seeks more than one remedy and where they win but are not successful in all of them, the claimant will be presumed to have been denied the remedies not awarded and will not generally be able to claim them on a subsequent occasion.[20]

The earlier court (or tribunal[21] or arbitrator[22]) must have had jurisdiction to make its decision for estoppel to arise.[23] Judgment may have been obtained by consent,[24] by an admission[25] or by default,[26] but where the judgment has been obtained by default, it will be interpreted narrowly.[27] Where judgment is consensually entered with a reservation (such as a reservation that liability had not been admitted), it is arguable that the party who made the reservation would be able to rely on it even if it were inconsistent with the judgment.[28] Thus, in the example given at 23.09, if judgment were entered by consent without an admission of liability, it would, in theory, be open to the defendant to present their case on the assessment on the basis that they had not been responsible for the accident. **23.15**

Settled cases and cause of action estoppel

Whilst judgment entered by consent will give rise to cause of action estoppel, the situation is less clear where the claim has been brought to an end by compromise (including acceptance of a Part 36 offer). Under the Rules of the Supreme Court (RSC), it was established that where a claim had been concluded by the acceptance of the then equivalent of a Part 36 offer, whilst that would estop a similar claim being brought,[29] the defendant would not be estopped from subsequently asserting matters that contravened the material facts pleaded in the particulars of claim.[30] This is because a compromise is generally seen as being a device by means of which the proceedings are brought to an end.[31] The relevance of this from the costs point of view is that if the entitlement to costs arose by reason of a Part 36 offer being accepted, it would be consistent with these principles if the defendant were to be permitted to deny the facts of the claim (although, of course, the court would be able to take into account the fact that the defendant did not seek to prove that version of events by proceeding to trial). It is not known whether such an approach would be taken under the CPR. **23.16**

---

20 *Blake v O'Kelly* (1874) IR 9 Eq 54.

21 *Munir v Jang Publications Ltd* [1989] ICR 1.

22 *Associated Electric and Gas Insurance Services Ltd v European Reinsurance Co of Zurich* [2003] UKPC 11.

23 *Rogers v Wood* (1831) 2 B & Ad 245.

24 *Palmer v Durnford Ford (a firm)* [1992] 2 All ER 122. See also *Kinch v Walcott* [1929] AC 482, at 493, in which Lord Blandesburgh said 'in relation to this pleas of estoppel it is of no advantage to the appellant that the order [his opponent relied upon] ... was a consent order'.

25 *Boileau v Rutlin* (1848) 2 Exch 665.

26 *Huffer v Allen* (1866) LR 2 Exch 15.

27 See, eg, *New Brunswick Rly Co v British and French Trust Corpn Ltd* [1939] AC 1, [1938] 4 All ER 747, HL.

28 See, eg, in a context other than costs, the Australian case of *Isaacs v Ocean Accident* (1957) 58 SRNSW 69; cf *SCF Finance Co Ltd v Masri (No 3)* [1987] QB 1028, CA.

29 *Reardon Smith v Cayzer Irvine* (1929) Com Cas 270, at 280; *Hills v Co-operative Wholesale* [1940] 2 KB 435, CA.

30 See *Rigge v Burbidge* (1846) 15 M & W 598.

31 *Coote v Ford* [1895–99] All ER Rep 673.

New evidence and cause of action estoppel

23.17 It may be that fresh evidence comes to light during the assessment (or at some other time after the earlier judgment). In substantive litigation, the existence of fresh evidence would not ordinarily be an answer to cause of action estoppel.[32] There is no authority to confirm whether the same is true in costs litigation. If estoppel does apply, then if—in the example given at 23.09—a document were to come to light that showed that the car did not belong to the claimant and that they were not entitled to the damages for its repair, it would not be open to the defendant to argue that the claimant had failed to make out that part of the claim. In practice, however, this would not present too much of a problem for a paying party, because the ambit of the estoppel would be narrow, so it would not extend to whether it was reasonable to incur costs in proving that part of the claim. This may be why there is no costs authority on the point.

Procedure relating to cause of action estoppel

23.18 There are no special rules concerning procedure. The burden of proof lies with the party who seeks to rely on the estoppel.[33] In substantive litigation, where a party says that their opponent is estopped from raising a point, the estoppel may be decided either in advance of the trial by way of an application to strike out or that party may plead the estoppel and ask the court to deal with the matter in argument at the end of the trial.[34] If the same applies to costs litigation, then the estoppel should be set out in the points of dispute or the replies and thought ought to be given to deciding the question as a preliminary issue.

Issue estoppel (or issue preclusion)

23.19 If an issue has already been decided by a court of competent jurisdiction, it cannot subsequently be relitigated.[35] This is called issue estoppel. It means that even where the cause of action is not the same in the later action as it was in the earlier one, an issue that is necessarily common to both that was decided on the earlier occasion would be binding on the parties.[36]

23.20 In so far as costs litigation is concerned, issue estoppel is similar to cause of action estoppel, but it relates to *any* finding made in the earlier proceedings rather than only those that were part of the cause of action. This means that it is a wider doctrine than cause of action estoppel. However, the issue must have been a *necessary* part of the judgment (see 23.23) and not merely collateral to it.[37] In the example set out at 23.09, if the claimant were able to demonstrate that the court found that the claimant's car was blue, then the defendant would be issue estopped from saying otherwise, but only if that were a necessary part of the prior judgment.

---

[32] See the discussion of this in *Arnold v National Westminster Bank plc* [1988] 3 All ER 977. It may be possible to make out special circumstances to avoid the operation of the estoppel.

[33] *Isaacs & Sons v Salbstein* [1916] 2 KB 139, CA.

[34] *Carl Zeiss Stiftung v Rayner and Keeler Ltd (No 3)* [1969] 3 All ER 897.

[35] See, eg, *Thoday v Thoday* [1964] P 181, at 198, *per* Diplock LJ.

[36] *Virgin Atlantic Airways Ltd v Zodiac Seats UK Ltd (formerly Contour Aerospace Ltd)* [2013] UKSC 46, at [17], *per* Lord Sumption.

[37] See, eg, *Barrs v Jackson* (1842) 1 Y&C Ch Cas 585, at 596, *per* Knight Bruce V-C.

General principles of issues estoppel

The goal of issue estoppel is to prevent the same issue being litigated twice. Where an issue has arisen in litigation and where a party has had a finding made against them, that party is precluded from controverting that finding on a subsequent occasion.[38] The issue in question must have been the same one as that which was decided previously and it must arise between the same parties (or their privies).[39] The issue must have been decided finally,[40] with certainty[41] and by a court with jurisdiction.[42] Issue estoppel will exist regardless of whether the finding was made as a result of argument or not[43] and regardless of whether it is an issue of fact, law or both.[44] **23.21**

The ambit of issue estoppel

In determining the scope of estoppel, the court must determine the nature of the issue that was decided by the earlier proceedings. To demonstrate issue estoppel, the party seeking to resist the new claim needs to show that it raises an issue that (a) has already been litigated, (b) has already been decided and (c) was a necessary ingredient in the cause of action being advanced.[45] **23.22**

Lord Keith has explained that the issue in question must be one that forms: **23.23**

> '... a necessary ingredient in a cause of action [which] has been litigated and decided and in subsequent proceedings between the same parties involving a different cause of action to which the same issue is relevant [where] one of the parties seeks to re-open that issue.'[46]

This has caused some difficulty in ascertaining precisely what was involved in the earlier decision of the court. Lord Wilberforce suggested this formulation: **23.24**

> 'One way of answering this is to say that any determination is involved in a decision if it is a "necessary step" to the decision or a "matter which it was necessary to decide, and which was actually decided, as the groundwork of the decision" ... From this it follows that it is permissible to look not merely at the record of the judgment relied on, but at the reasons for it, the pleadings, the evidence ... and if necessary other material to show what was the issue decided ... The fact that the pleadings and the evidence may be referred to, suggest that the task of the court in subsequent proceedings must include that of satisfying itself that the party against whom the estoppel is set up did actually raise the critical issue, or possibly, though I do not think that this point has yet been decided, that he had a fair opportunity, or that he ought, to have raised it.'[47]

[38] *Mills v Cooper* [1967] 2 QB 459, [1967] 2 All ER 100. Similarly, where a separate issue is tried before the other issues in the case, the decision on the separate issue is binding on the parties and the court in the later stages of the case. In *Fidelitas Shipping* [1966] QB 630, CA, at 642, Diplock LJ said: 'Where the issue separately determined is not decisive of the suit the ... suit continues. Yet I take it to be too clear to need citation of authority that the parties to the suit are bound by the determination of the issue. They cannot subsequently in the same suit advance an argument or adduce further evidence directed to showing that the issue was wrongly determined.'

[39] *Blake v O'Kelly* (1874) IR 9 Eq 54.

[40] *Bobolas v Economist Newspaper Ltd* [1987] 3 All ER 121.

[41] See *Re Wright, Blizard v Lockhart* [1954] Ch 347, [1954] 2 All ER 98; *Re Koenigsberg, Public Trustee v Koenigsberg* [1949] Ch 348.

[42] *Rogers v Wood* (1831) 2 B & Ad 245.

[43] See *Re Koenigsberg, Public Trustee v Koenigsberg* [1949] Ch 348.

[44] *Jones v Lewis* [1919] 1 KB 328.

[45] See *Arnold v The National Westminster Bank plc* [1991] 2 AC 93.

[46] *Arnold v The National Westminster Bank plc* [1991] 2 AC 93, at 105.

[47] *Carl Zeiss Stiftung v Rayner and Keeler Ltd (No 2)* [1967] 1 AC 853, at 965.

23.25 The following are admissible for the purposes of deciding whether issue estoppel applies: the judgment;[48] the pleadings;[49] oral evidence;[50] and therefore (presumably) transcripts. The court must also determine whether the issue was fundamental or collateral to the prior judgment.[51] This can be of significant importance in substantive litigation, but it would be rare for a costs judge to controvert a finding of the trial judge unless there were a good reason to do so (such as new information coming to light).

23.26 Issue estoppel will apply to the determination of preliminary issues or interim matters decided earlier in the same action between the parties. The parties cannot subsequently, in those same proceedings, advance arguments or adduce further evidence directed to showing that the issue in question has been wrongly determined.[52]

New evidence and issue estoppel: 'special' circumstances

23.27 Unlike cause of action estoppel, the court is at liberty to find that the parties should not be fettered by issue estoppel where new evidence has come to light that would make it unfair for that fetter to exist.[53] The circumstances have to be 'special' and the evidence must be such that it could not, with due diligence on the part of the party who seeks to avoid the estoppel, have been put before the court during the earlier proceedings.[54] Ignorance of the matter previously omitted may be sufficiently special in substantive litigation[55] and whilst it is not known whether this concept applies to costs litigation, if it does, then it may be that if a costs judge discovers a document during the detailed assessment that controverts a finding of fact previously made, that judge may be at liberty to release the paying party from the fetter of estoppel.

Abuse of Process

23.28 The next doctrine is wider still—namely, abuse of process. This is discussed only briefly and chiefly for the purposes of highlighting that it will rarely be relevant in the context of costs litigation. In particular, it will not arise in the sense that the rule in *Henderson v Henderson*[56] will operate as between trial judge and costs judge (see 23.36–23.40).

23.29 Whether there is an abuse of process will turn on the facts of each case, but one important aspect of the doctrine that distinguishes it from *res judicata* estoppel is that it may preclude a party from raising an issue that was not raised during the earlier proceedings, but which ought to have been. Turning to the running example mentioned at 23.09, if the defendant were to say that they should not pay the costs of proving that the car had a red strip down

[48] *Shoe Machinery Co v Cutlan* [1896] 1 Ch 667.

[49] *Cribb v Freyberger* [1919] WN 22, CA.

[50] *Flitters v Allfrey* (1874) LR 10 CP 29.

[51] One test that has been suggested is that of whether the issue was capable of being appealed: see Spencer Bower, Turner and Handley, *The Doctrine of* Res Judicata (London: Butterworths, 1996), paras 202–205.

[52] See *Fidelitas Shipping Co Ltd v V/O Exportchleb* [1966] 1 QB 630, at 642, *per* Diplock LJ.

[53] See the principal speech given by Lord Keith in *Arnold v National Westminster Bank plc* [1991] 2 AC 93, at 106; see also *Chamberlain v DCT* (1988) 164 CLR 502.

[54] For an example of the court finding that due diligence could have resulted in the fresh material being put before the court in a context other than costs, see *McIlkenny v Chief Constable of West Midlands Police Force* [1980] QB 283, at 320.

[55] The older authorities on this point were Scottish, but Lord Keith has clarified that Scots law and English law are the same: *Arnold v National Westminster Bank plc* [1991] 2 AC 93, at 108.

[56] *Henderson v Henderson* (1843) 3 Hare 100.

the side and if they were to raise that issue for the very first time during the assessment itself, it may be open to the court to find that the defendant should have raised that argument before the trial judge when the court was considering the colour of the car generally, and that the defendant should be precluded from raising it on an assessment. For the reasons set out in this section and the next, it can be seen that whilst the costs judge will sometimes be precluded from hearing such tardy arguments, it will rarely be on the basis of abuse of process.

Nonetheless, abuse of process may apply in other circumstances, such as where it is said that an argument ought to have been raised at an earlier stage of the assessment. In view of this, the relevant law is set out in outline (see 23.31–23.32). The rule in *Henderson v Henderson* is addressed for similar reasons (see 23.34–23.40). **23.30**

Abuse of process in general

Some commentators have referred to abuse of process as an extended doctrine of *res judicata*.[57] There is undoubtedly a degree of overlap.[58] This probably arose out of the tendency for the narrower concept of *res judicata* to be assimilated by the wider concept of abuse of process,[59] but they are best treated as being related, but distinct. This is not least because there is authority that the principles of *res judicata* ought not to be extended beyond their present scope.[60] The onus of proving that an argument is an abuse of process rests with the person making that assertion.[61] **23.31**

Unlike *res judicata* estoppel, the doctrine of abuse of process does not depend on the earlier court having made a finding—that is, a party may be precluded from advancing an issue if the circumstances of the claim in general were such that that would be appropriate. In particular, inconsistency may amount to an abuse of process (that is, where one version of events is asserted at one stage and then a different version at a later stage).[62] In the running example mentioned at 23.09, if the claimant's entire case was based on the premise that they could not have seen and did not see the defendant's car, the court might preclude the claimant from arguing that they should be awarded the costs of obtaining expert evidence proving the efficacy of their brakes. Whilst it would be possible to analyse that situation in terms of abuse of process (that is, it is an abuse of the court to allow it to be used to recover costs that contradict the receiving party's own case), it is not difficult to see that it would usually be far simpler to analyse the matter in terms of reasonableness. **23.32**

The rule in *Henderson v Henderson* compared with estoppel

Coulson J had the following to say when comparing issue estoppel and the rule in *Henderson v Henderson*: **23.33**

> 'On a closer analysis, it can be seen that some of the elements of *Henderson* abuse are rather different to those arising under issue estoppel. For example, the principle is not, on any view,

[57] See Barnett, P, Res Judicata, *Estoppel, and Foreign Judgments* (Oxford: Oxford University Press, 2001), at para 6.02, where the author implies that this nomenclature is in use, but is not to be recommended.

[58] See, eg, *Lloyds TSB Bank Ltd v Cooke-Arkwright (a firm)* [2001] All ER (D) 127 (Oct), in which both were found to be available.

[59] See, eg, the comments of Toulson J in *Baker v Ian McCall International Ltd* [2000] CLC 189, at 196.

[60] *Howlett v Tarte* (1861) 10 CBNS 813; see also *Carl Zeiss Stiftung v Rayner & Keeler Ltd (No 2)* [1967] 1 AC 853.

[61] *Sweetman v Nathan* [2003] EWCA Civ 1115, at [34].

[62] In a context other than costs, see *Bradford and Bingley Building Society v Seddon* [1999] 4 All ER 217.

limited to the ingredients of a cause of action. In addition, the requirement that, in order for a finding of *Henderson* abuse, there needs to be a "broad merits-based judgment" means that the court must consider all the circumstances when analysing whether it is an abuse for a party now to raise an issue that it could have raised in either previous proceedings or in an earlier stage of the current proceedings. In addition, there will rarely be a finding of abuse without the court deeming the subsequent claim to amount to unjust harassment or oppression.'[63]

The rule in *Henderson v Henderson*

23.34 For the reasons set out above, in substantive litigation, abuse of process may be relevant where a party is precluded from advancing an issue on the grounds that they had opportunity to advance it on a previous occasion, but failed to avail themselves of that opportunity. In particular, where an issue could have been adjudicated upon during earlier proceedings, then the doctrine of abuse of process will, in appropriate circumstances, preclude that issue from being considered during the subsequent proceedings. This principle is usually referred to as being 'the rule in *Henderson v Henderson*'.[64] Wigram VC stated the rule in the following terms:

> '[W]here a given matter becomes the subject of litigation in, and of adjudication by, a court of competent jurisdiction, the court requires the parties to that litigation to bring forward their whole case, and will not (except under special circumstances) permit the same parties to open the same subject of litigation in respect of matter which might have been brought forward as part of the subject in contest, but which was not brought forward, only because they have, from negligence, inadvertence, or even accident, omitted part of their case. The plea of *res judicata* applies, except in special cases, not only to points on which the court was actually required by the parties to form an opinion and pronounce a judgment, but to every point which properly belonged to the subject of litigation, and which the parties, exercising reasonable diligence, might have brought forward at the time.'[65]

For many years, this rule was rarely invoked. The modern law on the subject began with the adoption of Wigram VC's statement of principle by the Privy Council in 1975, when Lord Kilbrandon referred to *Henderson v Henderson* as the authority for the 'wider sense' of *res judicata*, classifying it as part of the law relating to abuse of process.[66]

23.35 The modern approach to the rule in *Henderson v Henderson* is not to apply it mechanically. Lord Bingham had the following to say on the point:

> 'It is, however, wrong to hold that because a matter could have been raised in earlier proceedings it should have been, so as to render the raising of it in later proceedings necessarily abusive. That is to adopt too dogmatic an approach to what should in my opinion be a broad, merits-based judgment which takes account of the public and private interests involved and also takes account of all the facts of the case, focusing attention on the crucial question whether, in all the circumstances, a party is misusing or abusing the

---

63 *Seele Austria GmbH Co v Tokio Marine Europe Insurance Ltd* [2009] EWHC 255 (TCC), at [23].
64 *Henderson v Henderson* (1843) 3 Hare 100.
65 *Ibid*, at 114–16.
66 In *Yat Tung Investment Co Ltd v Dao Heng Bank Ltd* [1975] AC 581, at 589–90: see *Virgin Atlantic Airways Ltd v Zodiac Seats UK Ltd (formerly Contour Aerospace Ltd)* [2013] UKSC 46, at [19], *per* Lord Sumption.

process of the court by seeking to raise before it the issue which could have been raised before.'[67]

The mere fact that the issue could have been raised before, but was not raised, will not of itself amount to *Henderson* abuse.[68] A finding that an issue *could* have been raised is not the same as whether, in the round, that issue *should* have been raised.[69]

The rule in Henderson v Henderson *between costs proceedings and substantive proceedings*

Waller LJ has explained that the rule in *Henderson v Henderson* does not apply to costs litigation in the sense that if, at the time the costs order is made, a party remains silent about some fact or circumstance, that party will be precluded from relying on that fact or circumstance at the detailed assessment.[70] In so far as Jack J promulgated a different view in *Aaron v Shelton*,[71] he was mistaken. **23.36**

Waller LJ had this to say about the interaction between the then equivalent of CPR, rr 44.2 (the trial judge's role), and 44.4 (the costs judge's role): **23.37**

> 'In my view [r 44.2] and [r 44.4] are intended to work in harmony and it is intended that the parties' conduct (for example) may have to be considered under both. If what is sought is a special order as to costs which a costs judge should follow that obviously should be sought from the trial judge. If it is clear that a costs judge would be assisted in the assessment of costs by some indication from the trial judge about the way in which a trial has been conducted, a request for that indication should be sought. But none of this needs a rule as per *Henderson v Henderson* that a failure to raise a point before the trial judge will preclude the raising of a point before the costs judge.'[72]

As is explained below, there will still be circumstances in which a failure to raise a point before the trial judge will mean that it cannot be raised before the costs judge, but this will not be on the basis of abuse of process; rather, it is based on preclusion by proportionality. This is discussed at 23.41–23.49. **23.38**

The rule in Henderson v Henderson *and subsequent costs proceedings*

The rule in *Henderson v Henderson* still has relevance in the sense that it will be capable of applying to interactions *within* detailed assessment proceedings. This can be illustrated by referring to damages as an analogy: damages (other than provisional damages) must be assessed once and for all[73] and there is no reason to believe that costs are to be dealt with any differently. If the once-and-for-all principle does apply to costs, then that would explain why a receiving party would not be able to present a bill of costs for part of their costs and then, without the agreement of the paying party or an order of the court, present another bill of costs for the remainder.[74] The rule could also apply in other circumstances, such as **23.39**

---

[67] *Johnson v Gore Wood & Co* [2002] 2 AC 1, at 31.

[68] *Seele Austria GmbH Co v Tokio Marine Europe Insurance Ltd* [2009] EWHC 255 (TCC), at [24], *per* Coulson J.

[69] See *Dexter v Vlieland-Boddy* [2003] EWCA Civ 14; *Aldi Stores v WSP Group plc* [2007] EWCA Civ 1260.

[70] *Drew v Whitbread* [2010] EWCA Civ 53, at [30], which expanded on Waller LJ's comments made previously in *Northstar Systems Ltd v Fielding* [2006] EWCA Civ 1660.

[71] *Aaron v Shelton* [2004] EWHC 1162 (QB).

[72] *Drew v Whitbread* [2010] EWCA Civ 53, at [37].

[73] *Conquer v Boot* [1928] 2 KB 336, DC.

[74] Christopher Clarke J found that this was not permissible: *Harris v Moat Housing Group South Ltd* [2007] EWHC 3092 (QB), at [33].

where a party applies to a costs judge for relief from sanctions and subsequently seeks to apply for similar, but not identical, relief on a subsequent occasion.

23.40 The rule in *Henderson v Henderson* applies where judgment has been entered by consent and, in appropriate circumstances, to settlements generally.[75] Thus, presumably, if a bill of costs was presented and settled without reservation, this would prevent the receiving party from presenting a further bill of costs.

Late arguments and proportionality

23.41 For the reasons set out above, the rule in *Henderson v Henderson* does not apply between trial judge and costs judge. This does not mean, however, that arguments may be whimsically raised before a costs judge regardless of whether the trial judge was given opportunity to comment. This is not only because there will be the potential for estoppel in respect of anything that has already been decided (see 23.07–23.27), but also because the doctrine of preclusion by proportionality may apply (see 23.47).

23.42 It may be that a party wishes to raise an argument that was not raised before the trial judge. This invites the question of whether the costs judge would be able to hear it. In certain circumstances, a party would be precluded from raising a new argument: there is nothing new in this, because it has always been the case that there has been some regulation of the interaction between trial judge and costs judge.[76] For the reasons set out below, however, such preclusion would be rare and would not be based on abuse of process. The topic is best considered by looking at three issues: conduct; proportionality; and special orders.

Conduct: the supposed rule in *Aaron v Shelton*

23.43 In so far as conduct is concerned, it used to be believed that there was a rule—the rule in *Aaron v Shelton*[77]—which restricted the extent to which a costs judge could take conduct into account in circumstances in which it had not been raised before the trial judge. Jack J explained that supposed rule in this way:

> 'In my judgment, where a party wishes to raise in relation to costs a matter concerning the conduct of his opposing party (either before the litigation or during it), it is his duty to raise it before the judge making the costs order where it is appropriate to do so ... If he does not do so, it is not open to him when the costs come to be assessed to raise the same matter under CPR 44.5(3) as a ground for the reduction of the costs which he would otherwise have to pay ... Otherwise a party who thinks he has achieved an order which will get him his costs subject to the reasonableness of the amount, may on the assessment face an argument intended to deprive him of what he justifiably thought he had obtained.'[78]

23.44 This rule is no longer good law. The true law began to emerge two years after Jack J gave his guidance, when Waller LJ said that it was 'too broadly stated'.[79] Three years after that,

---

[75] See *Johnson v Gore Wood & Co (a firm)* [2001] 1 All ER 481.

[76] See, eg, *In re Frape, ex p Perrett (No 2)* [1894] 2 Ch 290, at 295, in which the court found that: 'The right of the client to dispute the solicitor's retainer as to this bill *in toto* was not reserved in the order as it ought to have been, if he was to have that right.' See also *Skuse v Granada Television Ltd* [1994] 1 WLR 1156, in which Drake J found that (on the facts of that particular case) the paying parties' failure to raise the issue of alleged maintenance at the time a costs order was made prevented them from raising the issue on the assessment.

[77] After *Aaron v Shelton* [2004] EWHC 1162 (QB).

[78] *Ibid*, at [20].

[79] *Northstar Systems v Fielding* [2006] EWCA Civ 1660, at [32] and [34].

in a different case, Waller LJ expanded on his previous comments and confirmed that the rule was not good law:

> 'In my view it would not be consistent with the express provisions of [CPR, rr] 44.3 and 44.5 and with the court's duty to see that costs are proportionate and reasonable to preclude a party raising a point highly material to that question because it had not been raised before the judge under [r] 44.3.'[80]

Thus a costs judge may take all aspects of the parties' conduct into account, regardless of whether it was raised before the costs judge. This is different from the position in analogous situations in substantive litigation,[81] but this is probably a reflection of the fact that the process of detailed assessment is an entirely different process. **23.45**

There is nothing in Waller LJ's guidance that should discourage a party from airing issues before the trial judge and from seeking the court's guidance. Waller LJ has advised that if it is clear that the costs judge would be assisted by some indication from the trial judge about the way in which a trial had been conducted, a request for that indication should be sought.[82] Whilst he was giving judgment at a time when the rule in *Aaron v Shelton* was still believed to be good law, Tomlinson J has confirmed that a trial judge is able to give guidance either in the order or in response to written questions; whilst it rarely happens, he also noted that a trial judge could, in an appropriate case, sit with the costs judge on the assessment.[83] **23.46**

Preclusion by proportionality

Whilst it has its legal foundations firmly in the overriding objective rather than in abuse of process, there is a mechanism by which a costs judge is able to decline to hear an argument where that argument ought to have been put before the trial judge. Waller LJ explained that mechanism in the following way: **23.47**

> 'There may not be circumstances in which a costs judge may be entitled to say, in the interests of keeping the costs of assessment proportionate, that a matter should have been brought up before the trial judge and a special order sought; for example, if it is to be argued that a witness in a long trial should never have been called because the evidence was irrelevant, a costs judge should not be required effectively to retry the case in order to adjudicate on the point; obviously a special order should be sought from the trial judge. But that is different from there being some form of rule founded on *Henderson v Henderson*, that a failure to raise a matter before the judge for [CPR, r] 44.3 purposes precludes the raising of the matter for [r] 44.5 purposes.'[84]

---

80 *Drew v Whitbread* [2010] EWCA Civ 53, at [41]. In the same case, at [31], Waller LJ explained that whilst Neuberger LJ had approved of Jack J's judgment in *Gray v Going Places Leisure Travel Ltd* [2005] EWCA Civ 189, that was in the context of considering the right time to deal with a wasted costs order.

81 In Chancery proceedings, for example, where an account is ordered, any special matter affecting the account should be brought forward at the trial, and if this is not done, it cannot be raised 'during the mechanical operation of taking an ordinary account': *Sanguineti v Stuckey's Banking Co (No 2)* [1896] 1 Ch 502, at 506.

82 *Drew v Whitbread* [2010] EWCA Civ 53, at [37].

83 *Three Rivers District Council v Bank of England* [2006] EWHC 816 (Comm): it should be noted that the comment about sitting with the costs judge was made in the context of an exceptionally complex matter.

84 *Drew v Whitbread* [2010] EWCA Civ 53, at [36].

23.48 Thus where the issue to be decided is so deeply buried in the substance of the trial that it would be inappropriate to require the costs judge to unearth it, it will stay where it lies.

Special orders

23.49 It is implicit in Waller LJ's analysis (see 23.37) that there will be occasions on which a 'special order' is required. Such an order will not be required merely for the purposes of reserving the right to argue some point about conduct (see 23.43–23.46), but it may be required if the court is to be asked to quantify the costs in a way that is distinguishable from an ordinary assessment of costs. Thus, if a paying party were to wish to argue that the claim had been exaggerated, for example, no special order would be required, but if the argument were that fixed costs should apply[85] or that a percentage reduction should be made,[86] then a special order would be required.

Delay and Costs

23.50 The main topic that is addressed in this section is delay occurring in the context of the detailed assessment process, but delay of other sorts, such as delay in obtaining or enforcing a costs order, is also touched upon.

23.51 It is assumed that the reader is familiar with the time limits for commencing detailed assessment proceedings and for requesting a detailed assessment hearing. These topics are dealt with in detail at 43.85 *et seq* and 43.117. Delay in the context of appeals is addressed at 45.35. Delay in the context of solicitor and client disputes is addressed at 36.32–36.36.

Delay generally

23.52 Most receiving parties are only too eager to have their costs quantified and paid, but, surprisingly, that is not always the case. Indeed, the problem of delay has blighted the processes for ascertaining costs since well before the introduction of the CPR.

23.53 There is a spectrum of consequences that may be visited upon a party who has delayed, some of which are more theoretical than real. In particular, whilst the issue of limitation is a topic that has the potential to arise, it does so exceptionally infrequently and it is included here only for the sake of completeness.

23.54 In so far as between-the-parties costs are concerned, the spectrum of consequences is as follows:

- disallowance of interest (dealt with at 56.50–56.53);
- the imposition of costs sanctions;
- disallowance of part or all of the costs claimed pursuant to CPR, r 44.11 (misconduct) (see 23.58–23.82); and
- disallowance of costs as a result of the claim for costs being statutorily time-barred.

[85] See *ibid.*

[86] Whilst on a slightly different point, see *Lahey v Pirelli* [2007] 1 WLR 998.

This list is not exhaustive. Those towards the top of the list are far more frequently encountered than those at the bottom.

There is very little authority on the issue of limitation in the context of costs, so it would be best to regard the analysis of that topic as being only a starting point for the purposes of further legal research. **23.55**

Whether a receiving party has been guilty of delay worthy of sanction will turn on the facts of each case, but not every instance of tardiness will result in sanction. It is not always practicable (or, occasionally, even possible) for a receiving party to comply with the time limits in the CPR. In particular, where the bill of costs is substantial, it may take longer to draft than the three-month time limit in CPR, r 47.7, allows. Thus the following pre-CPR comments of Walton J continue to have resonance: **23.56**

> 'Unless such time limit is to become an instrument of oppression – and there can be no conceivable logic or fairness in a deliberate act of oppression ... this time limit will be approached by the [costs judge] with due consciousness of its inappropriateness in many cases.'[87]

The disallowance of interest

Where there has been delay in commencing detailed assessment proceedings or where there has been delay in requesting a detailed assessment hearing, the court has the power to disallow the interest on costs.[88] That is an issue that must be addressed in the context of the court's discretion as to interest generally, which topic is discussed at 56.50–56.53. **23.57**

Misconduct and delay

CPR, rr 47.7 and 47.14(2), stipulate time limits during which the receiving party must commence detailed assessment proceedings and request a detailed assessment hearing (see 43.85 *et seq* and 43.117, respectively). Generally speaking, the receiving party has three months in which to do each, which typically means a total of six months between the date on which the costs order is made and the date by which a request for a detailed assessment should have been made. **23.58**

As mentioned above, delay in meeting these requirements may—and usually does—result in a disallowance of interest. Where the extent of the delay is such that a mere disallowance of interest would fail to meet the justice of the situation, the court is able to invoke its powers for dealing with misconduct (see CPR, r 44.11). Where the court invokes those powers, the costs themselves (rather than only interest) are at risk. **23.59**

The fact that interest may be disallowed is relevant to the issue of whether the court should invoke the power to disallow the costs itself, because the court may be able to impose a significant sanction by exercising its full powers concerning interest and this may be preferable to making a finding of misconduct (see 23.69). To fully understand the way in which the court exercises its discretion, it is necessary to know something of the history of the law, because otherwise the true significance of older authorities may be overlooked. **23.60**

---

[87] *Papathanassiou v Dutch Communication Co Ltd* (unreported), 9 May 1985, QBD, the transcript of which is no longer available.

[88] See CPR, rr 47.8(3) and 47.14(4), respectively.

The place of pre-CPR authority relating to delay

23.61 As will be explained below, the language used in authorities decided under the CPR is similar to those decided under the RSC. Both of those vocabularies refer to delay as being 'inordinate' and 'inexcusable'. This makes it tempting to rely on pre-CPR authorities. That temptation should be resisted,[89] however, because there are significant differences between the present regime and the corresponding prior regime, and those differences may escape the reader when presented with case reports that are taken out of historical context.

23.62 In particular, the CPR make provision for the paying party to obtain an 'unless order' requiring the receiving party to commence detailed assessment proceedings.[90] The corresponding provision under the RSC was different in that the paying party was able to apply to begin the proceedings directly.[91] This means that the opportunity to lay blame for delay solely at the feet of the receiving party is not the same under the CPR as it was under the RSC.

23.63 Moreover, the rules were in a state of flux even during the currency of the RSC. Very old cases, for example, were decided under a regime that would, to modern eyes, appear inflexible in the way in which it regards interest.

23.64 Rule changes are a matter of record and, accordingly, can be taken into account when considering older authorities, but there is one further factor that is less easy to recognise—namely, the court's attitude to prejudice. The court's stance subtly changed in the 15 or so years before the introduction of the CPR: prejudice used to be a condition precedent for the imposition of a sanction, but—following recommendations in a report chaired by the then equivalent of the senior cost judge[92]—not only were changes made to the RSC, but there was also a shift in the judicial approach towards the putative requirement of prejudice.[93] Indeed, shortly before the introduction of the CPR, it was often the case that, in so far as that requirement continued to exist, prejudice could be inferred from the delay itself.[94]

23.65 Pre-CPR authorities should therefore be avoided (unless, of course, those authorities have been affirmed in more recent cases). This chapter does not ignore pre-CPR cases entirely: where a pre-CPR authority gives guidance on a topic that is likely not to have changed as a result of the introduction of the CPR—such as the court's attitude to how long it ought to take to draft a bill of costs—then it has been cautiously included. In recognition of the fact that the reader is likely to encounter pre-CPR authorities

---

[89] Indeed, Longmore LJ has said that little guidance can be gleaned from older authorities decided under the CPR: *Haji-Ioannou v Frangos* [2006] EWCA Civ 1663, at [11].

[90] See CPR, r 47.8(2).

[91] See RSC, Ord 62, r 29(3).

[92] See the report dated 25 January 1983 of a working party on RSC, Ord 62, chaired by Master Horne.

[93] See, eg, *Pamplin v Fraser (No 2)* [1984] 2 All ER 694 and *Jones v Roberts* (1986) The Times, 2 August, which were two of the first cases in which it was held that it is not a prerequisite for the paying party to show prejudice.

[94] *London Borough of Enfield v P* [1996] 1 FLR 629.

when carrying out legal research, a brief summary of the pre-CPR law is given in the footnotes.[95]

The provisions under the CPR

In so far as it is relevant to the issue of delay, CPR, r 44.11, reads as follows: **23.66**

> '(1) The court may make an order under this rule where—
> (a) a party or his legal representative, in connection with a summary or detailed assessment, fails to comply with a rule, practice direction or court order; or
> (b) it appears to the court that the conduct of a party or his legal representative, before or during the proceedings which gave rise to the assessment proceedings, was unreasonable or improper.
>
> (2) Where paragraph (1) applies, the court may—
> (a) disallow all or part of the costs which are being assessed . . .'

The relationship between interest and misconduct

There is no halfway house between disallowing interest pursuant to CPR, r 47.8(3) (or r 47.14(4)), and disallowing costs pursuant to CPR, r 44.11. This means that, in the absence of a finding of misconduct, the court is not able to impose a sanction that is greater than a mere disallowance of interest.[96] In so far as commencement delay[97] **23.67**

---

[95] Order 62, r 28(4) provided as follows: 'Where a party entitled to costs—(a) fails without good reason to commence or conduct proceedings for the taxation of those costs in accordance with this Order or any direction, or (b) delays lodging a bill of costs for taxation, the taxing office may—(i) disallow all or part of the costs of taxation that he would otherwise have awarded that party; and (ii) after taking into account all the circumstances (including any prejudice suffered by any other party as a result of such failure or delay, as the case may be, and any additional interest payable under section 17 of the Judgments Act 1838 because of the failure or delay), allow the party so entitled less than the amount he would otherwise have allowed on taxation of the bill or wholly disallow the costs.'

In *London Borough of Enfield v P* [1996] 1 FLR 629, at 638, Holman J summarised the law as it was shortly before the introduction of the CPR in the following way: '(1) Subparagraphs (a) and (b) are conditions precedent or "triggers" to the exercise of the powers under (i) and (ii). (2) They are alternative triggers. (a) requires the absence of "good reason" but (b) does not. Delay alone suffices to trigger the power. Accordingly, (3) The delay does not have to be "inordinate and inexcusable" before the power is triggered. (4) If a trigger in either (a) or (b) applies, then the taxing officer has a discretion under (ii) to reduce the amount which would otherwise be allowed on taxation or to disallow the costs entirely. (5) The court is not limited to compensating prejudice to the paying party but can, in an appropriate case, make a further disallowance even if this confers a benefit on the paying party greater than pure compensation for his prejudice or loss. This is sometimes referred to as a "fine" or "punitive element". I think these terms are perhaps a little misleading. The essence of the court's task is to make an order which meets the overall justice of the case. But it is important to bear in mind that at least from the perspective of the receiving party and his solicitor any reduction beyond pure compensation will feel punitive. (6) Even a reduction in the costs calculated to compensate the paying party may have a "punitive" effect when viewed from the position of the receiving party. (7) In exercising the discretion the taxing office must take into account all the circumstances. (8) Relevant circumstances include the duration of the delay and the extent to which it is explained or excusable. (9) Relevant circumstances also include any, and if so what degree of, prejudice suffered by any other party and any additional interest payable under s 17 of the Judgments Act 1838 because of the delay. In an appropriate case prejudice can be inferred from the fact of delay even if no specific prejudice is established. However, prejudice is not a prerequisite to the exercise of the power.'

[96] Where the delay relates to commencing detailed assessment proceedings, it is arguable that the prohibition against 'imposing any other sanction' would apply only where: (a) no application has been made in accordance with CPR, r 47.8(1); and (b) it is the receiving party who has commenced detailed assessment proceedings. There is no authority for this proposition, however.

[97] That is, delay in commencing detailed assessment proceedings: see 43.85 *et seq*.

is concerned, the bar against other sanctions exists by reason of CPR, r 47.8(3), which reads as follows:

> '(3) If—
> (a) the paying party has not made an application [for an order requiring the paying party to commence detailed assessment proceedings]; and
> (b) the receiving party commences the proceedings later than the period specified in rule 47.7,
>
> the court may disallow ... [interest]
>
> [...]
>
> but will not impose any other sanction except in accordance with rule 44.11 (powers in relation to misconduct).'

Similar provisions, concerning delay in requesting a hearing, are made at CPR, r 47.14(4).

23.68 In a thorough review of the issue of misconduct and delay, Longmore LJ commented that there is a tension between CPR, r 47.8, and the then equivalent of r 44.11, and that the clue to resolving that tension is in the word 'misconduct' in the title of the latter.[98] Those words point to the nature of the court's discretion. He commented that some breaches of the rules can be more readily described as misconduct than others and that the rules contemplate costs judges being trusted to recognise misconduct when it occurs.[99]

23.69 In the same appeal, Arden LJ observed that the prescribed sanction of disallowance of interest is likely to be less controversial than disallowance of the costs themselves. This was for two reasons: first, it is more likely that opposing parties could agree a reduction in interest than a reduction in the costs themselves; and secondly, a finding of misconduct may cause disputes between solicitor and client as to who should bear the burden of the disallowed costs.[100] Longmore LJ explained that the court should hesitate before exercising any powers beyond the disallowance of interest (see 23.77), but it seems implicit in his analysis (and that of Arden LJ) that the court should, where appropriate, make full use of those powers concerning interest.

Jurisdictional threshold of what is 'misconduct' in the context of delay

23.70 In exploring the issue of what amounts to 'misconduct' in the context of delay, Longmore LJ used language that would not have been out of place under the RSC. In particular, he remarked:

> 'An inordinate and inexcusable delay which has prejudiced the paying party may well come within this category; excusable, although inordinate delay may not, especially if it has caused no prejudice. The important point is that, while a non-compliance with a rule, practice direction or court order is the only jurisdictional requirement for the exercise of the power contained in Rule 44.14, it will usually be appropriate as a matter of discretion to consider the extent of any misconduct which has occurred in the course of such non-compliance.'[101]

---

[98] *Haji-Ioannou v Frangos* [2006] EWCA Civ 1663, at [10].
[99] *Ibid*; see also the comments of Dyson LJ in *Lahey v Pirelli Tyres Ltd* [2007] EWCA Civ 91, at [29].
[100] *Haji-Ioannou v Frangos* [2006] EWCA Civ 1663, at [18].
[101] *Ibid*, at [10].

Thus the mere fact that delay is inordinate would not meet the jurisdictional threshold, but where the delay is also inexcusable, that threshold may well be met. Prejudice may be a factor, but it does not appear to be a necessary ingredient. Longmore LJ emphasised that the test is whether the delay amounts to misconduct: other findings may also be made (such as the delay being exceptional), but they do not define the requisite threshold. In particular, whilst Longmore LJ did not disagree with Warren J's analysis that there must be 'exceptional circumstances' before mere delay would justify the court invoking the then equivalent of CPR, r 44.11,[102] he emphasised that the delay must properly be categorised as being misconduct for any sanctions to be imposed. **23.71**

For the reasons set out at 23.61–23.65, care is required when seeking guidance from pre-CPR authorities. Nonetheless, the task of preparing a bill of costs under the RSC was not dissimilar to the same task under the CPR, so some guidance may be found from examining the way in which such a delay was classified as 'inordinate' under the RSC. It must be borne in mind, however, that the test is not whether the delay has been inordinate, but whether the delay amounts to misconduct; the issue of whether the delay is inordinate is merely a factor to be taken into account. Indeed, linguistically, a test of inordinacy is a fairly low threshold.[103] **23.72**

Elasticity of time limits in the context of misconduct Bearing these qualifications in mind, it is worth noting that Megarry V-C asserted that, for the delay to be inordinate, it must be shown that the period of time that has elapsed is materially longer than the period of time that is usually regarded by the courts and the profession as an acceptable period of time.[104] Some pre-CPR case examples are given in the footnotes, but they are, at best, no more than a guide as to the period of time during which a party can be expected to draft a bill of costs.[105] Whilst in a pre-CPR case, Walton J acknowledged that it would not always be possible to commence proceedings for assessment within three months and that this time limit was treated with a certain amount of 'elasticity'.[106] A similar approach tends to apply under the CPR, especially where larger bills fall to be considered. **23.73**

No preclusion arising out of unless orders There is one factor that may be dismissed as being irrelevant for the purposes of determining whether the court is able to exercise its jurisdiction under CPR, r 44.11, and that is whether an application for an unless order has been made. The jurisdiction under CPR, r 44.11, differs from that concerning **23.74**

---

[102] See *Less v Benedict* [2005] EWHC 1643 (Ch).

[103] The relevant entry in the *Oxford English Dictionary* (3rd edn, Oxford: Oxford University Press, 1989) is that 'inordinate' means 'not kept within orderly limits, immoderate, intemperate, excessive'.

[104] *Chapman v Chapman* [1985] 1 WLR 599, at 607.

[105] In *Papathanassiou v Dutch Communication Co Ltd* (unreported), 9 May 1985, QBD, a delay period of three months was not inordinate, but a delay of two years and seven months was held to be inordinately long. In *Drake & Fletcher Ltd v Clark* (1968) 112 SJ 95, a period of three-and-a-half years' delay was held to be inordinate. Similarly, in *Pamplin v Fraser (No 2)* (1984) 2 All ER 694, ten months' delay was held to be inordinate.

[106] *Papathanassiou v Dutch Communication Co Ltd* (unreported), 9 May 1985, QBD See also *Pauls Agriculture Ltd v Smith* (1993) 3 All ER 122, at 125, in which Walton J set out his views on this topic: 'I am fully aware that the 3-month period is not strictly adhered to by the profession and the courts in our jurisdiction. In fact, delay for about 3 months is quite normal and acceptable in the courts in which I preside. From the cases cited above, the period of 16 months delay, as has occurred in this case, is not within the limit of "elasticity" that may be acceptable in this jurisdiction and I therefore hold that such delay was inordinate.'

interest, in which case it is possible that the court may be fettered by such an application.[107] Notwithstanding this, whether an application for an unless order has been made may be relevant to the exercise of the court's discretion.

23.75 **Intention relating to delay** Intention may a relevant factor. Practice Direction (PD) 44, para 11.3, provides that 'conduct which is unreasonable or improper includes steps which are calculated to prevent or inhibit the court from furthering the overriding objective'. Thus, if the court was satisfied that delay was a deliberate tactical ploy (that is, an attempt to 'kick the matter off into the long grass'), then it would be open to the court to find that that amounted to misconduct.

Discretion

23.76 If the jurisdictional threshold is met, then the court must consider whether to impose a sanction and, if so, what sanction to impose.

23.77 **Loss of interest is the normal sanction** Longmore LJ deliberately refrained from giving detailed guidance as to when the court should exercise its powers under CPR, r 44.11. He did, however, explain that the court should make use of its powers to disallow interest—which is what he described as being the normal sanction for delay—but should hesitate before going any further:

> 'Of course delay is to be deprecated but where the relevant rule not only gives to the party at the receiving end of the delay the option of preventing further delay by himself taking the initiative but also spells out the normal sanction for penalising such delay (as Rule 47.8 does), it seems to me that the court should be hesitant to exercise further powers to impose further penalties by way of reducing otherwise allowable costs.'[108]

23.78 Longmore LJ's guidance has overshadowed older CPR decisions concerning delay and misconduct. Indeed, he commented that a detailed analysis of those cases would serve no useful purpose.[109] Nonetheless, one or two of those cases will be encountered from time to time in practice and, for this reason, they are briefly mentioned.

23.79 **Older cases decided under the CPR** (For the reasons set out at 23.77, the extent to which the cases referred to in this paragraph remain helpful is limited.) In a case in which there had been significant commencement delay that was not all the fault of the receiving party, Richards J found that no disallowance of costs ought to be made.[110] Factors that Richards J took into account were the facts that the paying party had not availed itself of the opportunity to apply for an unless order and that a fair assessment was still possible, notwithstanding the delay. In a different case, Park J considered how the court should exercise its discretion where costs were payable by the Legal Services Commission (LSC) in respect of services provided to an assisted person.[111] He found that delay in those circumstances was, if anything, positively beneficial to the LSC

[107] The argument concerning interest relies on a strict reading of CPR, r 47.8(3). It is possible to read that provision as saying that the court has the jurisdiction to disallow interest only where the paying party has not made an application for an unless order. This topic is discussed in more detail at 43.105–43.107. No such strict reading is possible in respect of CPR, r 44.11.

[108] *Haji-Ioannou v Frangos* [2006] EWCA Civ 1663, at [17].

[109] *Ibid*, at [11].

[110] *Botham v Khan* [2004] EWHC 2602 (QB).

[111] *Re Homes Assured plc* [2002] Costs LR 71.

and that whilst a delay of more than four years met the jurisdictional threshold, it was wrong to disallow the costs entirely.[112] Longmore LJ commented that Park J's analysis depended largely on provisions applicable to the assessment of publicly funded costs.[113] Finally, there is a case that has achieved some notoriety as a result of the commencement delay being about 20 years; had the assessment taken place, some of the costs that would have been assessed would have been incurred 40 years previously and the delay had caused the paying party to be hampered in terms of evidence: unsurprisingly, Chadwick LJ ruled that 'there must be finality in litigation' and ordered that assessment should not go ahead.[114]

Other cases Whilst it was in a family case, where a delay of just under three years was due to mismanagement rather than intention, Sumner J declined to disallow a substantial bill of costs in full because that would have been too drastic a penalty.[115] The court at first instance had ordered that unless the receiving party commenced assessment within seven days, the costs would be disallowed; on appeal, Sumner J held that whilst this was a serious delay and it was a matter of regret, complete disallowance of the costs would be disproportionate. He imposed a 20 per cent reduction to account for the delay. **23.80**

Procedure

There is no express requirement either in the CPR or in the accompanying practice directions that a request for disallowance of costs for delay should be made on application. Nonetheless, PD 47 provides that the court must give the party or legal representative in question a reasonable opportunity to answer a case of misconduct.[116] Unless the relevant persons are already at court, it would generally be that the party against whom the sanction is sought would be given notice of the hearing. In any event, it would always be sensible to inform the court of the fact that an application is likely to be made, because this would avoid the matter being allocated to an authorised court officer, who would lack the power to invoke CPR, r 44.11 (see 5.19).[117] **23.81**

Where the court has imposed a sanction under CPR, r 44.11(2), and where the receiving party is not present in person when the sanction is imposed, that party's solicitor must notify its client in writing no later than seven days after the solicitor receives notice of the order imposing the sanction.[118] The solicitor may be required to prove that it took reasonable steps to comply with that obligation.[119] **23.82**

Limitation

Whilst there are several Acts pertaining to limitation,[120] in so far as the law of costs is concerned, the only relevant one is the Limitation Act 1980. It is the effect of this Act that is **23.83**

112 *Ibid.*
113 *Haji-Ioannou v Frangos* [2006] EWCA Civ 1663, at [11].
114 *Weston v Weston* [2006] EWCA Civ 1554, at [30].
115 *Q v J* [2003] EWHC 251 (Fam).
116 See PD 47, para 11.2.
117 See CPR, r 47.3(1)(b)(i).
118 See CPR, r 44.11(3).
119 See PD 44, para 11.3.
120 See the Foreign Limitation Periods Act 1984 and the Limitation (Enemies and War Prisoners) Act 1945.

discussed in this section. The focus is on contentious business, but similar principles also apply to non-contentious business.

23.84 The following topics are discussed:

- whether a solicitor is able to enforce a claim for fees long after the work was done (23.85);
- whether a client is able to seek assessment of costs long after the work was done (23.100);
- whether a litigant is able to obtain an order for costs where the opportunity to ask for that order arose long ago (23.103);
- whether limitation would have any bearing on the court's ability to assess costs (23.111); and
- whether a receiving party is able to enforce an order long after it was made (23.116).

It is convenient, first, to explain the position as between solicitor and client, because that law, to an extent, governs the position between opposing parties.

Limitation as between solicitor and client

Jurisdiction under a contractual retainer

23.85 A solicitor's right to recover its fees will generally arise out of a simple contract.[121] The applicable section is s 5 of the Limitation Act 1980, which imposes a limitation period of six years beginning on the date on which the cause of action accrued: 'An action founded on simple contract shall not be brought after the expiration of six years from the date on which the cause of action accrued.'

Jurisdiction under a non-contractual retainer

23.86 Some contracts of retainer are expressly permitted by statute in the sense that, where certain conditions are met, statutory provision exists for the payment of fees.[122] Where this is the case, it is arguable that s 9(1) of the 1980 Act should apply (that section dealing with sums recoverable by statute),[123] but the counter-argument is that most statutory provisions relating to costs do not create a cause of action; rather, they merely stipulate the procedure. Regardless of which argument is correct, nothing will turn on the point because the limitation period is the same as that under Limitation Act 1980, s 5.

23.87 It will occasionally happen that a solicitor will seek to enforce a non-contractual right to payment by its client (such as where *quantum meruit* is claimed). In cases in which the court does not deal with argument by finding that there is an implied simple contract, it would be open to the court, in appropriate cases, to apply an express statutory limitation period other than that which relates to simple contract[124] or, alternatively, to apply the contractual limitation period by analogy.[125]

---

[121] This being a contract that has not been made by deed and which is not the very formal type of contract known as a contract of record.

[122] See, eg, Solicitors Act 1974, s 65(2).

[123] Which reads as follows: 'An action to recover any sum recoverable by virtue of any enactment shall not be brought after the expiration of six years from the date on which the cause of action accrued.'

[124] See, eg, Limitation Act 1980, s 21(3), which applies to non-fraudulent breach of trust. Caution must be exercised when the trust is said to be a constructive trust, because a limitation period will not always apply.

[125] In a context other than costs, see *De Seguros Imperio v Heath (REBX) Ltd* [2001] 1 WLR 112.

No discretion

Regardless of the way in which the solicitor's right to costs is studied, it will almost always be the case that a six-year limitation period will apply. In the context of a solicitor–client relationship, the court has no discretion to disapply the limitation period—the only exceptions to this being where the limitation period has been extended or postponed by reason of disability, fraud, etc (see 23.131–23.136). Thus unless a claim has been acknowledged (see 23.123–23.130), the issue of whether it is statute-barred will usually depend solely on whether the six-year limitation period has expired—and that is a mixed question of fact and law. **23.88**

When time begins to run

Time will begin to run from the date on which the cause of action accrued (or, more accurately, the day after, because the day on which the cause of action arose is excluded).[126] Ward LJ has confirmed that the following long-standing definition of 'cause of action' remains good law: 'Every fact which it would be necessary for the plaintiff to prove, if traversed, in order to support his right to the judgment of the court.'[127] **23.89**

The issue of when the cause of action accrued is a potentially difficult point in the context of solicitor and client costs because there are many stages in that relationship that may, at first blush, appear to be appropriate trigger points. In so far as contentious work is concerned, these might include: **23.90**

- the completion of an individual item of work;
- the completion of sufficient work to give rise to a natural break;
- the termination of the contract of retainer;
- the date of delivery of the bill of costs;
- the expiry of the month following the date of the delivery of the bill of costs; and
- the date on which costs are quantified by assessment or agreement.

In the context of conditional fee agreements, the points at which the claim is won or at which costs are assessed or paid may be added to this list.

The answer to the question of when time begins to run is that it begins at the moment the solicitor's right to be paid accrues: procedural factors—such as the need to allow a month to expire after serving a bill of costs—are of no relevance.[128] In particular: **23.91**

- whilst it is true to say that a solicitor cannot ordinarily sue a client for costs until the expiration of one month after delivery of a signed bill,[129] time runs against a solicitor from the time it has completed the work that allows it contractually to raise a bill and not from the delivery of the bill;[130] and

[126] *Marren v Dawson Bentley & Co Ltd* [1961] 2 QB 135.

[127] *Legal Services Commission v Rasool* [2008] EWCA Civ 154, at [16], citing (with approval) *Coburn v Colledge* [1897] 1 QB 702.

[128] As to the relevance of procedural provisions in general (ie not solely as they relate to costs), see *O'Connor v Isaacs* [1956] 2 All ER 417.

[129] Solicitors Act 1974, s 69(1).

[130] *Coburn v Colledge* [1897] 1 QB 702, CA.

- the fact that costs must be quantified (by assessment or by agreement) before they can be paid is a procedural issue only, so the fact that costs have not been quantified does not prevent time from starting to run.[131]

23.92 Lord Esher MR explained the relevance (or rather *ir*relevance) of the requirement to allow a month to expire before issuing proceedings:

> 'It does not provide that no solicitor shall have any cause of action in respect of his costs or any right to be paid till the expiration of a month from his delivering a signed bill of costs, but merely that he shall not commence or maintain any action for the recovery of fees, charges, or disbursements until then.'[132]

23.93 Procedural steps having been discounted as potential trigger points, the next question is how the court determines when the solicitor's right to be paid arose. Each case will be decided on its own merits, because each retainer will be different and the right to payment may arise in diverse ways. The retainer may or may not be an entire contract.[133] Where, for example, the retainer is a private retainer to provide services over a short period of time, the right to be paid is likely to arise immediately upon that work being complete.[134] Where an appeal is brought in the litigation that was the subject of the retainer, it may be the case that the right does not arise until the conclusion of that appeal,[135] but where the retainer is sufficiently lengthy to permit of natural breaks, then the right may arise piecemeal each time such a break occurs.[136] Termination of the retainer will start time running,[137] as will express or implied agreement that costs are due.[138] Whether time has begun to run under a conditional fee agreement will depend on the terms of the agreement: in some cases, the cause of action may accrue the moment the claim is won; in others, it may accrue at some later stage, such as when the costs against an opponent have been assessed or agreed.

Limitation and the effect of incidental work such as costs proceedings

23.94 It will often be the case that the retainer has concluded, but that work incidental to the retainer then needs to be carried out (such as dealing with the costs or dealing with receipt of damages). The nature of each retainer will turn on the facts, but generally such incidental work would be disregarded in the sense that it would not prevent time running in respect of the earlier work.[139]

---

[131] This is a necessary implication of *ibid.* It is also the analysis advanced by Aldous LJ in the analogous situation involving costs payable by the Legal Services Commission: see *Legal Services Commission v Rasool* [2008] EWCA Civ 154.

[132] *Coburn v Colledge* [1897] 1 QB 702, at 706.

[133] See 27.07–27.28. See *Underwood, Son & Piper v Lewis* [1894] 2 QB 306 for a discussion of this issue by Lord Esher MR.

[134] See, eg, *Baile v Baile* (1872) LR 13 Eq 497; *Bonser v Bradshaw* (1860) 25 JP 483.

[135] See, eg, *Harris v Quine* (1869) LR 4 QB 653. The issue will turn on the terms of the retainer.

[136] See 27.64–27.66 and 35.28–35.36. See, in particular, the analysis of Sir George Jessel MR in *In re Hall v Barker* (1893) 9 Ch D 538, at 545.

[137] See, eg, *Martindale v Falkner* (1846) 2 CB 706; see also *Underwood, Son and Piper v Lewis* [1894] 2 QB 306, CA.

[138] See 27.56–27.59 and 35.24. See, in particular, Lord Roskill's analysis in *Davidsons v Jones-Fenleigh* (1980) Costs LR (Core vol) 70, at 75.

[139] *Rothery v Munnings* (1830) 1 B & Ad 15; *Phillips v Broadley* (1846) 9 QB 744; *Re Nelson, Son and Hastings* (1885) 30 Ch D 1, CA.

Limitation where there is more than one type of costs debt

It will not always be the case that a retainer will cover only one type of work. Where a solicitor carries out work that touches upon differing matters, time will begin to run not in respect of the retainer as a whole, but in respect of each aspect of it.[140] If only some of the items included in the bill are statute-barred, the solicitor may claim for those items that are free of that barrier.[141] This, presumably, would apply where there have been natural breaks, interim invoices, etc. **23.95**

The effect of a successful limitation defence

The effect of a successful limitation defence is that the solicitor cannot enforce a claim for costs. The right itself continues to exist,[142] but the remedy of claim or legal set-off[143] is extinguished. The practical effect of this is that a bar will apply only where limitation is successfully raised as a defence to a claim; where it is not raised, the claim may be enforced in the usual way.[144] **23.96**

Trusts and limitation

Where a solicitor has acted for a trust and where its claim for costs has become statute-barred, the trustees are at liberty (subject to any contrary provision in the trust) to pay those costs notwithstanding the fact that they would be entitled to refuse to do so.[145] **23.97**

Lien and limitation

A creditor's lien is not something that is capable of becoming time-barred.[146] Thus a solicitor's lien for a statute-barred debt is not affected by the fact that the debt has become statute-barred.[147] **23.98**

Where its claim for costs is time-barred, a solicitor is not able to obtain a charging order pursuant to s 73 of the Solicitors Act 1974.[148] **23.99**

Late request for assessment of paid costs and accounts

Where a client has paid their solicitor, but wishes to have those costs assessed long after the work was done, the solicitor may wish to argue that the right to an assessment is statute-barred. There is no authority on the issue of whether an application for an assessment is capable of being statute-barred, which is probably a reflection of the fact that it would almost never be the case that a solicitor would need to rely on such an argument. This is because it would be able to rely on the fact that the court has no discretion to order that costs be assessed where more than 12 months have expired since payment[149] (see 36.04). (The issue would not arise where the costs had not been paid, because in those circumstances **23.100**

---

140 See *Phillips v Broadley* (1846) 9 QB 744.

141 See *Rothery v Munnings* (1830) 1 B & Ad 15; *Blake v Hummell* (1884) 51 LT 430; *Wilkinson v Smart* (1875) 24 WR 42.

142 See *Curwen v Milburn* (1889) 42 Ch D 424, CA, at 434, *per* Cotton LJ.

143 See *Smith v Betty* [1903] 2 KB 317, CA. The right to claim equitable set-off would not necessarily be extinguished: see *Filcross Securities Ltd v Midgeley* (unreported), 21 July 1998, CA.

144 See PD 16, para 13.1, which requires a defendant to particularise the basis of their defence.

145 *Budgett v Budgett* [1895] 1 Ch 202.

146 See *Spears v Hartly* (1800) 3 Esp 81.

147 *Higgins v Scott* (1831) 2 B & Ad 413; *Re Carter, Carter v Carter* (1885) 55 LJ Ch 230.

148 See Solicitors Act 1974, s 73(2).

149 *Harrison v Tew* [1990] 2 AC 523.

it would be the client, rather than the solicitor, who would be relying on the expiry of the limitation period.) If, in some preternatural circumstances, the issue were to arise, then, in view of the fact that Limitation Act 1980, s 38, provides that 'action' includes any proceeding in a court of law, there is no reason to believe that detailed assessment proceedings could not, in principle, be time-barred.[150]

23.101 The time within which a client must assert their right to an account is not limited to six years or to any other definite period.[151]

23.102 In summary, a solicitor's claim for its fees will generally be statute-barred within six years of the right to payment arising and the fact that certain tasks need to be carried out after the main work had been completed will not prevent time from running.

Limitation and seeking orders for costs

23.103 The issue here is whether a party who believes that they are entitled to costs may apply for an order long after the circumstances arose in which it was open to that party to make that application. For obvious reasons, this issue will arise where the putative right to costs arose before the claim was issued, so it would generally arise only as a result of an alleged compromise (which could either be a specific agreement to pay costs or an agreement to compromise the claim generally). It would not arise where a claim was discontinued, because in those circumstances an order for costs will be deemed to have been made.

23.104 As with costs between solicitor and client, more than one potential trigger point may be identified. In particular, it may be argued that time does not begin to run until after the costs have been quantified.

23.105 An analogous situation to a claim arising out of an alleged compromise would be where the LSC was attempting to recover costs from a formerly assisted person whose certificate had been revoked.[152] Dealing with just such a case, Ward LJ (with whom Smith and Wilson LJJ agreed) considered the issue of whether it was a requirement that costs should be assessed before a cause of action would accrue and, after having drawn upon non-costs cases in which quantification of a sum was not found to be necessary to start time running,[153] he concluded: 'In my judgment the fact that declaratory relief is available demonstrates to me that the process of ascertainment of the amount of costs is a mere procedural requirement, not an inherent element of the cause of action itself.'[154]

23.106 These comments suggest that time begins to run from the point not later than the moment at which the receiving party was put in a position to apply for a costs order. That point will depend on the facts of each case, but where (as will almost always be the case) it arose as a result of a compromise, time will run from the date on which that compromise was made.

---

150 It may be relevant that the 1980 Act does not apply to claims based on the court's inherent power over solicitors: *Bray v Stuart A West & Co* [1989] NLJR 753.

151 *Cheese v Keen* [1908] 1 Ch 245.

152 The analogy is not perfect: (a) most of the arguments addressed to Ward LJ were based on regulations that do not apply in other types of case; (b) the costs were recoverable by virtue of an enactment rather than by way of a contract of compromise; and (c) Ward LJ specifically mentioned the Legal Services Commission's ability to seek a declaration. The thrust of Ward LJ's analysis is likely to apply by analogy notwithstanding these imperfections.

153 In particular, *Hillingdon London Borough Council v ARC Ltd* [1999] Ch 139.

154 *Legal Services Commission v Rasool* [2008] EWCA Civ 154, at [29].

Contributions

Whilst there is no costs-specific authority on the point, the analysis set out above would not necessarily apply where a party sought a contribution towards its liability for costs under the Civil Liability (Contribution) Act 1978. In this regard, Limitation Act 1980, s 10(1), makes the following provisions: **23.107**

> 'Where under section 1 of the Civil Liability (Contribution) Act 1978 any person becomes entitled to a right to recover contribution in respect of any damage from any other person, no action to recover contribution by virtue of that right shall be brought after the expiration of two years from the date on which that right accrued.'

Thus a party has two years from the time when they become 'entitled to a right to recover a contribution' during which to bring their claim for a contribution.

There are three reasons for believing that time does not begin to run until the costs in respect of which the contribution is sought have been assessed. **23.108**

(1) An analogy may be drawn with the situation in which costs are payable between parties (where time does not begin to run until the costs have been quantified). In those circumstances Aldous LJ has found that there was 'nothing to enforce until the amount of costs had been certified' and that 'payment cannot be enforced without knowledge of what should be paid'.[155] Although the contrary is arguable (see below), a similar logic could apply to a party's right to seek a contribution.
(2) In respect of damages, time begins to run from the date of the assessment of quantum.[156] It could be argued that it would be curious if a different rule were to apply to costs.
(3) By the operation of CPR, r 47.1, the general rule will be that costs will not be assessed until the conclusion of proceedings. If time began to run from the date of the costs order rather than the date of quantification, a paying party could find themselves in the invidious position of having to seek a contribution before they had the right to apply for a hearing to have their own liability quantified.

However, the true law could be that costs are dealt with differently from damages, and that a paying party is required to obtain an order for a contribution first and then to deal with issues concerning quantum. There is no authority on the point. The problems outlined at 19.37–19.44 may also be relevant. **23.109**

In summary, the six-year limitation period will apply to a right to recover costs and time will begin to run as soon as the cause of action accrues. The position may be different in so far as contributions are concerned. **23.110**

Limitation and the assessment of costs

There is no authority on whether the expiry of a limitation period would have an impact on the way in which costs are assessed, so what is said here should be seen as nothing more than a framework for further legal research. **23.111**

For the reasons set out in the next section, a receiving party would not be at risk of being barred from enforcing their costs order until six years after the court has assessed the costs. **23.112**

[155] *Chohan v Times Newspapers Ltd* [2001] EWCA Civ 964, at [33].
[156] *Aer Lingus plc v Gildacroft Ltd* [2006] EWCA Civ 4.

Thus the only issue that will arise is whether the effect of the law as between solicitor and client has a bearing—as a result of the operation of the indemnity principle—on the position between the parties. Put another way, the question is whether a paying party is relieved of the burden of payment by virtue of the receiving party's solicitor's right to costs becoming statute-barred.

23.113 It will rarely be the case that a solicitor's bill of costs will have remained unpaid for a period of six years and it will be even more rarely be the case that the paying party would know about that state of affairs, even if it were to exist. The situation could arise, however, where the solicitors are acting for an impecunious client in the hope that the client would be able to discharge their fees out of the proceeds of the claim.

23.114 A paying party would have to overcome a number of problems before they could succeed in proving a breach of the indemnity principle, including that:

- the paying party would not find it easy to find out when invoices were rendered and whether they remained unpaid;
- the paying party would have to prove that there was a 'genuine issue' as to whether there had been a breach of the indemnity principle—that is, more than mere assertion would be required in that regard;[157]
- the paying party would have to prove that the debt had not been acknowledged by the client; and
- the court would have to be satisfied that it was open to a paying party to take such a point, given the fact that limitation will operate only when it is raised as a defence.[158]

In support of its argument on the last of these topics, the receiving party could point to the fact that, in the analogous situation of payment of statute-barred costs out of a trust, there is no principle that would prevent a trustee from declining to raise a limitation defence.[159]

23.115 In summary, a paying party would have difficulty in persuading the court to disallow costs by reason of those costs allegedly being statute-barred as between solicitor and client.

Bringing an action for an order for costs

23.116 The next question is whether a party who believes that they are entitled to costs can bring an action for an order for costs long after it was made. This is different from enforcement.[160] Various means by which an order may be enforced are briefly discussed at 43.407–43.414 and there are rules about enforcing judgments out of time,[161] which essentially provide that the permission of the court is required after the expiry of six years. Permission is not normally granted in contexts other than costs and there is no reason to believe that costs should be treated any differently.

---

157 See *Hazlett v Sefton Metropolitan Borough Council* [2000] 4 All ER 887 for a general discussion of this topic.

158 See, by way of analogy, *Garbutt v Edwards* [2005] EWCA Civ 1206, in which Arden LJ found that it was not ordinarily open to a paying party to take the point that an estimate of costs provided to a client should limit the costs payable between the parties. See also (in a non-costs context) *King v Victoria Insurance Co* [1896] AC 250, PC, at 254, concerning the ability of a stranger to intervene.

159 *Budgett v Budgett* [1895] 1 Ch 202.

160 See *Lowsley v Forbes* [1999] AC 329.

161 The provisions are an example of one of the few provisions of the RSC and CCR that are still in force: RSC, Ord 46, r 8; CCR, Ord 25 and Ord 26.

Section 24 of the Limitation Act 1980 provides: 23.117

'(1) An action shall not be brought upon any judgment after the expiration of six years from the date on which the judgment became enforceable.

(2) No arrears of interest in respect of any judgment debt shall be recovered after the expiration of six years from the date on which the interest became due.'

The limitation period applies regardless of the nature of the claim and, in particular, regardless of whether the original claim was advanced in law or in equity.[162]

There is therefore a limitation period of six years (in respect of both the costs and interest), after which no proceedings may be brought upon the order. As with the other circumstances discussed here, there is more than one potential trigger point. In particular, the trigger could be the date upon which the order was made or the date upon which the court issues a final costs certificate. 23.118

In contrast to the other circumstances mentioned, Aldous LJ (with whom Walker and Parker LJJ agreed) found that time does not begin to run until the costs have been quantified and certified.[163] In coming to this conclusion, Aldous LJ noted that, in a different case, Brandon J had found that the word 'enforceable' means enforceable by claim on the judgment, not by execution.[164] Aldous LJ found that that analysis was too restrictive and that time will run from the date on which judgment becomes enforceable by action or otherwise.[165] He concluded: 23.119

'The word "enforceable" must mean enforceable in a practical way according to law. There cannot be a right to bring an action which would amount to an abuse of process. Further, in the present case there was nothing to enforce until the amount of costs had been certified ... Payment cannot be enforced without knowledge of what should be paid.'[166]

Whilst he did not comment on the point, Aldous LJ's analysis is entirely in keeping with the restrictions imposed by CPR, rr 47.8(3)[167] and 47.15(4).[168]

Where the costs are to be assessed by detailed assessment, an order for costs will become statute-barred only six years after the issue of the final costs certificate. For obvious reasons, this will not apply where costs are assessed by summary assessment. Although there is no authority on the point, it is also probably the case that Aldous LJ's reasoning does not apply to foreign judgments.[169] 23.120

162 *Dunne v Doyle* (1860) 10 I Ch R 502.

163 *Chohan v Times Newspapers Ltd* [2001] EWCA Civ 964 (a case dealing with pre-CPR procedure, but which there is no reason to believe does not remain good law). Whilst only illustrative, Lord Neuberger MR came to a very similar conclusion in a case in which the Legal Services Commission sought to recoup fees overpaid to a barrister: see *Legal Services Commission v Henthorn* [2011] EWCA Civ 1415, at [56].

164 See *Berliner Industriebank Aktiengesellschaft v Jost* [1971] 1 QB 278, at 293.

165 *Chohan v Times Newspapers Ltd* [2001] EWCA Civ 964, at [18].

166 *Ibid*, at [33].

167 Which stipulates that the court may not impose any sanction for delay in commencing detailed assessment proceedings other than a disallowance of interest and any sanction made in accordance with CPR, r 44.11.

168 Which stipulates very similar restrictions relating to delay in requesting a detailed assessment hearing.

169 For a discussion of foreign judgment generally, see *Berliner Industriebank Aktiengesellschaft v Jost* [1971] 2 QB 463, at 470.

23.121 Where a costs order is statute-barred, the bar will apply to a statutory demand, as well as to other means of enforcement.[170]

23.122 In summary, whilst an order for costs cannot be enforced after the expiry of the six-year limitation period, that period does not run until the costs have been assessed.

Acknowledgement and part-payment

23.123 A fresh accrual of a claim may arise where a debt of costs is acknowledged or part-paid.[171] This may have the effect of extending a limitation period (and may do so repeatedly), but it will not have the effect of reviving a claim that has already become time-barred.[172]

23.124 In so far as it is relevant to the law of costs, Limitation Act 1980, s 29, provides as follows:

> '(5) Subject to subsection (6) below, where any right of action has accrued to recover—
> (a) any debt or other liquidated pecuniary claim; or
> (b) any claim to the personal estate of a deceased person or to any share or interest in any such estate;
>
> and the person liable or accountable for the claim acknowledges the claim or makes any payment in respect of it the right shall be treated as having accrued on and not before the date of the acknowledgement or payment.
>
> (6) A payment of a part of ... interest due at any time shall not extend the period for claiming the remainder then due, but any payment of interest shall be treated as a payment in respect of the principal debt.
>
> (7) Subject to subsection (6) above, a current period of limitation may be repeatedly extended under this section by further acknowledgements or payments, but a right of action, once barred by this Act, shall not be revived by any subsequent acknowledgement or payment.'

Is an unassessed claim for fees capable of falling within the ambit of Limitation Act 1980, s 29?

23.125 Lloyd LJ has confirmed that a solicitors' claim for costs, billed, but not yet fixed by assessment or agreement, is a claim that is capable of falling within the terms of s 29(5) of the Limitation Act 1980—that is, it is for a 'debt or other liquidated pecuniary claim'.[173] To the extent that authorities that deal with the question of whether a debt is liquidated for the purposes of insolvency suggest that a solicitor's claim for fees is unliquidated (see 40.123), they are distinguishable; this is because the legislation governing insolvency could be expected to impose stricter and more specific requirements than a provision about extending the running of time in the case of an acknowledged liability.[174] In a similar vein, the comments of Evans LJ in *Turner & Co v O Palomo*[175] (see 39.04) are distinguishable

---

[170] *Re a Debtor (No 647-SD-1999)* (2000) The Times, 10 April.

[171] See Limitation Act 1980, s 29(5).

[172] See Limitation Act 1980, s 29(7).

[173] See *Phillips & Co (a firm) v Bath Housing Co-operative Ltd* [2012] EWCA Civ 1591, at [5] *et seq*, in particular, at [46] and [47], *per* Lloyd LJ. In coming to this conclusion, Lloyd LJ relied on *Amantilla Ltd v Telefusion plc* (1987) 9 Con LR 139 and, by analogy, *Lagos v Grunwaldt* [1910] 1 KB 41. For a discussion of the development of the law, see *Creggy v Barnett* [2016] EWCA Civ 1004.

[174] See *Phillips & Co (a firm) v Bath Housing Co-operative Ltd* [2012] EWCA Civ 1591, at [40], *per* Lloyd LJ.

[175] *Turner & Co v O Palomo* [2000] 1 WLR 37, CA.

on the basis of their context—namely, the solicitor's entitlement to judgment, whether for a given amount or for an amount to be assessed.[176]

Putative acknowledgements in writing

Under Limitation Act 1980, s 30, the acknowledgement must be in writing and signed by the person making it, and it must be made to the person whose claim is being acknowledged. A letter that putatively acknowledges a debt may be interpreted in the light of extrinsic evidence.[177] **23.126**

Whilst it should be borne in mind that Lord Sumner has said that 'comparison with the words of other debtors is of little use' for the purposes of determining whether a letter amounts to an acknowledgement,[178] assistance can be obtained from looking at past cases in which an acknowledgement was found to have been made. **23.127**

- In a case in which the client complained that the amount claimed was '3–4 times higher than was anticipated and budgeted for', and went on to say that it would 'have no option but to put your invoice to one side until ... [there is] more time to deal with it in the detail which it warrants', Lloyd LJ found that this amounted to saying 'we owe you something', in that it referred to the claim, but did not take issue with the principle that something was payable.[179]
- Whilst not concerning costs, in a case in which the debtor had said, 'Sorry I cannot do you a cheque now', the Court of Appeal held that the letter amounted to saying 'I owe you money'.[180] In commenting on this case, Lloyd LJ noted that it made it clear that acknowledgement did not have to identify the amount of the debt.[181]

Putative acknowledgements by part-payment

The potential importance of a part-payment made by a client to a solicitor is that the client may lose the opportunity to assert a limitation defence. The same would rarely be true of interim payments between opposing parties, because those payments would usually be made only in the interval between the costs order being made and the costs being assessed, which is a period during which time does not begin to run in any event. **23.128**

When determining whether a payment amounts to an acknowledgement of a debt, the court will look not at the analysis that the court would place upon that payment after having had the benefit of legal argument, but at the position as it was understood by the parties at the time of the payment.[182] Thus a payment may be regarded as being a part-payment even if the monies were used for some other purpose (such as paying counsel). **23.129**

Putative acknowledgements by requesting further information

A request for particulars of costs is capable of being an acknowledgement. Cotton LJ, for example, found that a letter containing the following phrase was an acknowledgement: **23.130**

176 See *Phillips & Co (a firm) v Bath Housing Co-operative Ltd* [2012] EWCA Civ 1591, at [41].
177 See *ibid*, at [51].
178 *Spencer v Hemmerde* [1922] 2 AC 507, at 519.
179 See *Phillips & Co (a firm) v Bath Housing Co-operative Ltd* [2012] EWCA Civ 1591, at [53].
180 *Dungate v Dungate* [1965] 1 WLR 1477.
181 See *Phillips & Co (a firm) v Bath Housing Co-operative Ltd* [2012] EWCA Civ 1591, at [51].
182 *Kleinwort Benson Ltd v South Tyneside Metropolitan Borough Council* [1994] 4 All ER 972.

'Our client only requires you to deliver particulars of any unsettled bill of costs you may have against him.'[183]

Where limitation will not be permitted to stand as a defence

23.131 There are several circumstances in which the court may deny a party a limitation defence. Those circumstances are a mixed bag and no attempt is made to deal with the issues in any detail or in any particular order. What is set out below is no more than an aid to further legal research.

Lack of capacity

23.132 If, on the date on which a cause of action accrued, the party to whom it had accrued lacked capacity, time will not begin to run until that person ceases to be under a disability or dies.[184]

Children

23.133 If, on the date on which a cause of action accrued, the party to whom it had accrued was under the age of 18,[185] time will not begin to run until that person reaches majority or dies.[186]

Estoppel

23.134 The fact that the parties have been engaged in negotiation will not of itself prevent the paying party from relying on limitation as a defence,[187] but where the paying party has agreed a 'limitation holiday'[188] or where the paying party has given assurances that the receiving party will not be prejudiced by the delay caused by negotiation,[189] the paying party may be estopped from relying on limitation as a defence. The principles involved are those applicable to any estoppel and can be found in any textbook on equity. A promise not to rely on a limitation defence may result in the promisor being estopped from doing otherwise.[190] Such a promise may be given particular effect when it can also be interpreted as being an acknowledgement of the debt—in particular, a promise not to rely on a limitation defence combined with an acknowledgement of the costs may start time running afresh.[191]

Fraud

23.135 It may happen that a party finds that it has not asserted a right to costs by reason of a fraud being visited upon that party. Where this is the case, time will not begin to run until that party has discovered the fraud (or was in a position to discover the fraud by exercising reasonable diligence).[192]

23.136 In summary, whilst the court has no statutory discretion to disapply a limitation period, it is open to the court, in appropriate cases, to find that the debt has been acknowledged or that there are other circumstances that will prevent the defence of limitation from applying.

---

[183] *Curwen v Milburn* (1889) 42 Ch D 424, at 424.
[184] See Limitation Act 1980, s 28(1).
[185] See Family Law Reform Act 1969, s 1.
[186] See Limitation Act 1980, s 28(1).
[187] *Hewlett v LCC* (1908) 72 JP 136.
[188] See, eg, *Earl of Malmesbury, James Carleton Seventh v Strutt and Parker (a partnership)* [2008] EWHC 424 (QB).
[189] See, eg, *Seechurn v Ace Insurance Sa-Nv* [2002] EWCA Civ 67.
[190] *Paterson v Glasgow Corpn* (1908) 46 SLR 10.
[191] *Gardner v M'Mahon* (1842) 3 QB 561.
[192] Limitation Act 1980, s 32(1) (as amended).

24

HUMAN RIGHTS AND THE LAW OF COSTS

This chapter deals with the following topics concerning human rights: **24.01**

- Brexit (24.02);
- jurisdiction and governing bodies (24.03);
- effects, rights and remedies (24.13);
- determining incompatibility (24.23);
- specific topics relevant to the law of costs (24.32–24.33):
  - access to justice (24.34);
  - additional liabilities (24.43);
  - costs against the Courts Service (24.54);
  - privilege and election (24.55);
  - the right to privacy (24.56);
  - security for costs (24.58); and
  - wasted costs (24.59).

Brexit

This edition was written at a time when any attempt to deal with the impact of Brexit in detail would have been mere speculation. That said, it was possible to make the following points. **24.02**

- If and when it becomes law, the 'Great Repeal Bill 2016' will repeal the European Communities Act 1972—that is, the Act that took the UK into the European Union (EU) and which caused certain European laws to take precedence over laws passed in Parliament.[1] This should not, however, be conflated with the issue of what will happen to the Human Rights Act 1998 (HRA 1998), which is an entirely separate issue.
- The UK government's stated intention is that the *acquis communautaire*—the body of European legislation—will be copied across into domestic law.[2] This will not, however, mean that developments to EU legislation after Brexit will be treated in a similar fashion.
- The government plans to make use of 'Henry VIII powers' for the purposes of making adjustments to the law post-Brexit.[3]

---

[1] See Department for Exiting the European Union, *Legislating for the United Kingdom's Withdrawal from the European Union*, Cm 9446 (London: HMSO, 2017), at p 5.

[2] See *ibid*, at p 5.

[3] See *ibid*, at p 12; Great Repeat Bill 2016, cl 7.

- Withdrawal from the EU will have a significant impact on the legal framework that protects human rights in the UK. A complete withdrawal from the EU would mean that the UK would no longer have to comply with the human rights obligations contained within the EU treaties, the general principles of EU law (which include respect for fundamental rights), or EU directives and regulations protecting fundamental rights.[4]

In view of the above, what is written in this chapter is likely to be out of date within a year or so of publication; as such, the reader must conduct their own research to bring themselves up to date.

Jurisdiction and Governing Bodies

24.03 The starting point in any discussion about the law of human rights is the 1950 Convention for the Protection of Human Rights and Fundamental Freedoms, which is almost always referred to as the European Convention on Human Rights (ECHR). It is an international treaty by which all member states of the Council of Europe are bound. It was opened for signature in Rome on 4 November 1950 and was entered into force on 3 September 1953.

The European institutions

24.04 The European Court of Human Rights (ECtHR) was established under the ECHR for the purposes of hearing alleged violations of the human rights enshrined in the ECHR and its protocols. Applications can be made by individuals or by contracting states; the court may also issue advisory opinions. As of 1 June 2010, the European Commissioner for Human Rights has been allowed to intervene in applications as a third party[5] and the office of the Commissioner is an independent institution within the Council of Europe. The Commissioner's remit is to promote the awareness of and respect for human rights in member states; the Commissioner has no judicial role.

24.05 The ECtHR is not part of the EU[6] and should not be confused with the European Court of Justice (ECJ).[7] (The ECJ is the judicial institution of the EU, and is responsible for ensuring the uniform application and interpretation of EU law, *not* the ECHR.) That said, the ECJ often regards the ECHR as a guiding principle and, as such, its decisions are often woven with principles derived from the ECtHR. The two courts are geographically separate: the ECtHR is a supranational court based in Strasbourg, whilst the ECJ sits in Luxembourg.

24.06 Applications can be made to the ECtHR only after domestic remedies have been exhausted. This means that the applicant must have taken their case to the highest possible level of domestic jurisdiction. Applications must be lodged within six months following the last

---

[4] Joint Committee on Human Rights, *The Human Rights Implications of Brexit: Fifth Report of Session 2016-17*, HL 88, HC 695 (London: HMSO, 2016), p 3.

[5] See Protocol 14 to the ECHR.

[6] The EU now has a single legal identity and, by virtue of Protocol 14 ECHR, is now able to accede to the ECHR and be regulated as if it were a member state, but, at the time of writing, had yet to do so.

[7] Or, more formally, the Court of Justice of the European Union. By virtue of the Treaty of Lisbon 2009, the Court changed its name to the Court of Justice alongside its two subordinate chambers: the General Court (formerly the Court of First Instance) and the Civil Service Tribunal.

domestic judicial decision in the case. The applicant must be personally and directly a victim of a violation of the ECHR, and must have suffered a significant disadvantage as a result.

The ECtHR is divided into sections and chambers. A section is an administrative entity and a chamber is a judicial formation of the court within a given section. Court fees are not charged. At the time of writing, the ECtHR had a backlog of more than 120,000 cases and the listing time was several years. This is relevant in so far as costs law is concerned because supposedly 'recent' decisions may relate to costs regimes that are now either obsolete or nearly obsolete. **24.07**

The benefits conferred by the ECHR

The ECHR is split into parts and is supplemented by several protocols. The Articles in Part 1 of the ECHR create rights that are referred to as 'guaranteed rights'. The rights that are of most relevance in the context of the law of costs are Arts 6 (the right to a fair trial), 8 (the right to privacy) and, to lesser extent, 10 (the right to freedom of expression). Rights can be classified in the following ways. **24.08**

- **Express and implied rights** The Art 6, 8 and 10 rights referred to above are express rights. The ECHR is a 'living instrument' that is capable of growth and expansion,[8] and as a result there are, in addition to the express or core rights, a number of implied rights. An example of an implied right is the right to effective access to the court (see 24.34), which is a right implied by the right to a fair trial.
- **Absolute, limited and qualified rights** Whilst some rights are 'absolute' in the sense that they shelter the individual entirely from interference that is detrimental to them, but beneficial for the majority, most are 'qualified' in the sense that they may, in appropriate circumstances, be lawfully interfered with where the needs of the majority would justify such a step (see 24.16–24.29). In the context of the law of costs, an example (albeit a controversial one) might be a requirement to pay a success fee (see 24.43–24.53). Other rights are 'limited' in the sense that they are limited under express and defined circumstances.

With the exception of privilege, absolute and limited rights have no real part to play in the context of the law of costs. Qualified rights do occasionally play a part (albeit it only very rarely); the question will not usually be whether any given right exists or whether there has been interference with it, but whether the interference in question is lawful. This is addressed at 24.27–24.31.

The Human Rights Act 1998

The HRA 1998 came into force on 2 October 2000. Section 6 of the HRA 1998 provides that public bodies (including the courts[9]) must act in a way that is compatible with the ECHR. In so far as the law of costs is concerned, the most significant provision is that which relates to the interpretation of legislation: unless it is impossible to do otherwise, both primary and delegated legislation must be read so as to be compatible with the ECHR (see 24.03–24.17). This requirement is relevant in the context of the law of costs because, first, the power to award costs is nearly always statutory, and secondly, the procedure by **24.09**

---

[8] See *Brown v Stott* [2003] UKHL 21.
[9] See HRA 1998, s 6(3)(a).

which costs are assessed is typically governed by delegated legislation. In particular, the Civil Procedure Rules (CPR) are delegated legislation (see 4.37).

Persons who may rely on the Human Rights Act 1998

24.10 Section 7 of the HRA 1998 provides that a person who has a claim based on a breach of ECHR may bring proceedings against the public body in question or may rely on the relevant rights in legal proceedings. Only 'victims' are able to do this[10] and, in general, that category of persons will not include core public authorities (such as local authorities)[11] or representative bodies (such as trade unions).[12] Persons whose place of residence is outside the EU may still be 'victims'.[13]

24.11 The fact that claims may be brought only by victims rarely presents any problem in disputes concerning costs. This is because issues concerning both human rights and costs law usually arise in the context of interpretation of legislation in general rather than in the context of a specific claim brought under s 6 of the HRA 1998. Put otherwise, when issues arise, they tend to focus on the law rather than the litigants themselves. In any event, it is moot point as to whether a person needs to be a victim to require the court to interpret legislation in a way that is compatible with the ECHR.[14]

Authority of and conflicts with the ECtHR

24.12 Section 2 of the HRA 1998 requires (amongst other things) the domestic courts to take account of decisions of the ECtHR.[15] The House of Lords (now the Supreme Court) has repeatedly held that unless there are special circumstances, 'clear and constant reasoning' in ECtHR authorities should be followed even though they are not binding.[16] The doctrine of (domestic) precedent remains binding upon the lower courts, and where there is conflict between ECtHR authority and domestic authority, the latter will prevail.[17] The higher courts have greater freedom, however: in particular, where the Court of Appeal concludes that one of its previous decisions is inconsistent with a subsequent decision of the ECtHR, it may be able to depart from its previous decision.[18]

Effects, Rights and Remedies

24.13 In so far as the law of costs is concerned, a putative breach of the ECHR may have the following effects or consequences.

- It may result in the court interpreting a rule, regulation or provision in a way so as to avoid the putative breach.

---

10 For guidance as to who is a victim, see Art 34 ECHR. It is a category of persons that is interpreted more narrowly than the category of persons able to apply for judicial review.

11 See *Aston Cantlow and Wilmcote with Billesley Parochial Church Council v Wallbank* [2003] UKHL 37. Their Lordships commented, however, that hybrid public authorities that exercise both public and private functions may fall within the category of being a victim.

12 See *Director General of Fair Trading v Proprietary Association of Great Britain* [2001] EWCA Civ 1217.

13 See *Farrakhan v Secretary of State for the Home Department* [2001] EWHC 781 (Admin).

14 *R (on the application of Rusbridger) v Attorney General* [2003] UKHL 38, at [21], *per* Steyn.

15 See HRA 1998, s 2.

16 *R (Alconbury Developments Ltd) v Secretary of State for the Environment, Transport and the Regions* [2001] UKHL 23.

17 *Kay v Lambeth London Borough Council* [2006] UKHL 10.

18 *R (RJM (FC)) v Secretary of State for Work and Pensions* [2008] UKHL 63.

- It may result in the court making a declaration of incompatibility.
- It may result in the court awarding some other remedy, such as damages.

Interpretation

Section 3(1) of the HRA 1998 provides that, in so far as it is possible, both primary and secondary legislation must be interpreted in a way that is compatible with ECHR rights and freedoms. Lord Nicholls had this to say on the topic: '[Section 3] is a powerful tool whose use is obligatory. It is not an optional canon of construction. Nor is its use dependent on the existence of ambiguity. Further the section applies retrospectively.'[19] **24.14**

Whilst there is no authority on the point, it is likely that these principles apply to the practice directions and pre-action protocols. The relevant wording of s 3 of the HRA 1998 is as follows: **24.15**

> '(1) So far as it is possible to do so, primary legislation and subordinate legislation must be read and given effect in a way which is compatible with the Convention rights.
> (2) This section—
> (a) applies to primary legislation and subordinate legislation whenever enacted;
> (b) does not affect the validity, continuing operation or enforcement of any incompatible primary legislation; and
> (c) does not affect the validity, continuing operation or enforcement of any incompatible subordinate legislation if (disregarding any possibility of revocation) primary legislation prevents removal of the incompatibility.'

The ECtHR has explained that interpretation of ECHR should strike a fair balance between the demands of the general interest of the community and the requirements of the protection of the individual's fundamental rights.[20]

There are several mechanisms by which a legislative provision may be read in such a way as to be compatible with those rights. Respected commentators have noted that permissible techniques include 'reading down' words (that is, giving words a narrow meaning), 'reading broadly' and 'reading words in'.[21] Lord Nicholls has explained that s 3(1) of the HRA 1998 may require the court to depart from the *un*ambiguous meaning that the legislation in question would otherwise bear;[22] thus it is an exercise that may significantly differ from the traditional exercise of legislative interpretation, which is normally an exercise of interpreting words that are not unambiguous (see Chapter 31). **24.16**

There are, however, limits to the extent to which the court may depart from the words used. In particular, s 3 of the HRA 1998 is concerned with interpretation of legislation, not amendment. Lord Nichols had this to say on the topic: **24.17**

> 'Not all provisions in primary legislation can be rendered Convention compliant by the application of s 3(1). ... In applying s 3 courts must be ever mindful of this outer limit. The Human Rights Act reserves the amendment of primary legislation to Parliament ... Interpretation of statutes is a matter for the courts; the enactment of statutes, and the amendment of statutes, are matters for Parliament.'[23]

---

19 *Re S (Care Order: Implementation of Care Plan)* [2002] UKHL 10, at [37].
20 *Sporrong and Lönnroth v Sweden* (1982) 5 EHRR 35, at [69].
21 See, eg, Lester, Pannick and Herberg, *Human Rights Law and Practice* (3rd edn, London: LexisNexis).
22 *Ghaidan v Godin-Mendoza* [2004] UKHL 30, at [30].
23 In *Re S (Care Order: Implementation of Care Plan)* [2002] UKHL 10, at [37]–[40].

24.18 There is a distinction between 'vertical' and 'horizontal' application of human rights. The usual view of human rights law is that it applies 'vertically' (that is, from the state down to the individual) so as to protect individuals from the state.[24] Where an obligation begins to have an effect on the private duties and rights of citizens (that is, between individuals), then it is said to have 'horizontal effect'. Internationally, there is a certain amount of pressure in favour of expansion of horizontal effects, especially in so far as commercial entities are concerned.[25]

Declarations of incompatibility, etc

Primary legislation

24.19 The court has repeatedly reminded itself that judges will not act as legislators;[26] hence if primary legislation is incapable of being interpreted in a way that is consistent with ECHR rights and freedoms, the operation and enforcement of that legislation will continue to be valid.[27]

24.20 Where it is impossible to interpret primary legislation in a way that is compatible with the ECHR, the court may issue a 'declaration of incompatibility', thereby inviting Parliament to correct the legislation by way of a remedial order.[28]

Secondary legislation

24.21 If secondary legislation is inconsistent as a result of restrictions imposed by primary legislation, it too will continue to be valid; again, a declaration of incompatibility may be made. If, however, secondary legislation is inconsistent as a result of something other than restrictions imposed by primary legislation, the court is able directly to set aside the secondary legislation.[29] Not all judges have the power to do this.

Other remedies

24.22 Section 8 of the HRA 1998 provides that, where the court finds illegality of the sort contemplated above, the court may grant such relief or remedy, or may make such order as it considers just and appropriate. This may include an award of damages.

Determining Incompatibility

24.23 Whilst an oversimplification, an act of interference with a qualified right (which includes a failure to act[30]) will be lawful only if the following three conditions are met:

- it is prescribed by law (see 24.24–24.25);
- it is done for the purposes of securing a permissible aim (see 24.26); and

24 Whilst it relates to US law, rather than to this jurisdiction, see Knox, JH, 'Horizontal Human Rights Law' (2008) 102 Am J Int'l L 1.
25 See *ibid*, in which the author points out that many foreign governments, scholars and activists have urged the imposition of duties on corporations.
26 See, eg, *R v A* [2001] UKHL 25, at [103], *per* Lord Hope.
27 HRA 1998, s 3(2)(b).
28 See HRA 1998, s 4; CPR, r 40.20.
29 Under HRA 1998, s 6(1).
30 See HRA 1998, s 6(6).

- it is 'necessary in a democratic society' (see 24.27–24.29), which means that it must:
  - serve a pressing social need;
  - pursue a legitimate aim; and
  - be proportionate to the aims being pursued.

Each of these is considered in turn. In the context of the law of costs, the first two questions will rarely present any difficulty and the question will usually focus on whether the putative interference is an unlawful interference with a guaranteed right.[31]

Prescribed by law

There are three questions that must be answered when deciding whether an act of interference is prescribed by law. They were described by Lord Hope in this way: **24.24**

> 'The first is whether there is a legal basis in domestic law for the restriction. The second is whether the law or rule in question is sufficiently accessible to the individual who is affected by the interference, and sufficiently precise to enable him to understand its scope and foresee the consequences of his actions so that he can regulate his conduct without breaking the law. The third is whether, assuming that these two requirements are satisfied, it is nevertheless open to the criticism on the Convention ground that it was applied in a way that was arbitrary because, for example, it has been resorted to in bad faith or in a way that is not proportionate.'[32]

Where the act in question is prescribed by legislation (such as a requirement to allow fixed costs), then no difficulty will arise, but there are two species of rule that may cause problems in the context of costs litigation. **24.25**

- **Codes, protocols and guidelines** It may not be immediately obvious whether an act of interference that is prescribed by a code, a guideline or a protocol will be prescribed by law. In general, if the code, guideline or protocol is underpinned by legislation and if it is readily accessible, then it will be prescribed by law.[33] Of equal importance, however, is that a breach of a code, protocol or guideline may give rise to an inference that the act in question is not prescribed by law.[34]
- **Common law** It is possible for an act of interference to be prescribed by the common law,[35] but difficulties can arise if the law in question is in a state of development of flux (which is not unusual in the context of the law of costs). In particular, if the law is not wholly certain, argument can arise as to whether the law is sufficiently accessible and precise.[36]

---

[31] Examples include the right to privacy (the right) and the need to put a receiving party to their election (the putative interference), or the right to access to justice (the right) and the need to fund the administration of justice by charging court fees (the putative interference).

[32] *R (on the application of Rottman) v Metropolitan Police Commissioner* [2002] UKHL 20, at [35].

[33] See, eg, *R (on the application of Matthias Rath BV) v the Advertising Standards Authority Ltd* [2001] EMLR 22.

[34] See, eg, *R v Mason* [2002] EWCA Crim 385, in which a breach of Home Office guidelines was found to be relevant.

[35] See, eg, *R (on the application of Rottman) v Metropolitan Police Commissioner* [2002] UKHL 20, at [63].

[36] See, eg, *Douglas v Hello! Ltd* [2005] EWCA Civ 595, at [147].

Permissible aim

24.26 There must be a legitimate objective that justifies the means.[37] Whether the act is done for the question of securing that objective will depend on the circumstances.

Necessity and proportionality

24.27 An interference with a right must be proportionate to the legitimate aim pursued[38]—that is, there must be a reasonable relationship of proportionality between the means employed and the aim pursued.[39] Three criteria can be identified.[40]

- The legislative objective must be sufficiently important to justify limiting the guaranteed right.
- The measures designed to meet the legislative objective must be rationally connected to that objective and, in particular, they must not be arbitrary, unfair or based on irrational considerations.
- Those measures must be no more than is necessary to accomplish the legitimate objective. In particular, the more severe the detrimental effects of a measure,[41] the more important the objective must be if the measure is to be justified in a democratic society.

The word 'necessary' 'is not synonymous with indispensable, neither has it the flexibility of such expressions as admissible, ordinary, useful, reasonable or desirable ... it implies the existence of a "pressing social need"'.[42]

24.28 The court does not review the system of the domestic law *in abstracto*, but instead will form a view as to whether 'the manner in which this system was applied to or affected the applicants gave rise to any violations of rights'.[43] In the context of costs law, this would probably mean looking at the whole of the law, including practice directions, protocols, etc, rather than only at the isolated provision in question.

24.29 The court should strive to give effect to the general principle that there is a need to strike a fair balance between the demands of the general interest of the community and the requirements of the protection of the individual's guaranteed rights.[44] This will turn on whether the interference is 'proportionate to the legitimate aim pursued'.[45] Proportionality as used in this context is wholly different from the concept of proportionality as used in the CPR.

---

[37] *Fayed v United Kingdom* (1994) 18 EHRR 393, at [71].

[38] *Handyside v United Kingdom* (1976) 1 EHRR 737, at [49].

[39] *R v Dimsey* [2001] UKHL 46.

[40] *De Freitas v Permanent Secretary of Ministry of Agriculture, Fisheries, Lands and Housing* [1999] 1 AC 69, PC, at 80C–80H, *per* Lord Clyde.

[41] *R (Farrakhan) v Secretary of State for the Home Department* [2002] EWCA Civ 606, at [77].

[42] *Buckley v United Kingdom* (1996) 23 EHRR 101, at [76]; App No 27238/94 *Chapman v United Kingdom* (2001) 33 EHRR 399, at [92] and [110].

[43] *Hakansson and Sturesson v Sweden* (1990) 13 EHRR 1, at [46]. See similarly *Young, James and Webster v United Kingdom* (1981) 4 EHRR 38, at [53]; *Buckley v United Kingdom* (1996) 23 EHRR 101, at [59].

[44] App Nos 7151/75, 7152/75 *Sporrong and Lönnroth v Sweden* (1982) 5 EHRR 35, at [69].

[45] *Handyside v United Kingdom* (1976) 1 EHRR 737, at [49].

Margin of appreciation

A wide margin is afforded to those who make legislation and it will not be every interference with a victim's rights that will be unlawful. Where interference produces an excessive burden on an individual, the requisite balance will not be found.[46] Put another way, where there are exceptional circumstances and when a 'threshold of hardship' has been crossed, the court will find that there has been a violation of the victim's rights.[47] **24.30**

Whilst it is not for the UK courts to apply the margin of appreciation—that being a matter for the ECtHR—it is important that its existence is recognised domestically. This is for two prime reasons: first, it should be recognised that judges may lack the information or expertise to deal with the issue; and secondly, when the question requires the balancing of political factors, the executive will generally be better placed to deal with such things than the judiciary.[48] **24.31**

Specific Topics Relevant to the Law of Costs

In theory, any human rights issue may arise in the context of the law of costs (especially where the primary issue is right of access to the court), but in practice only Arts 6 (the right to a fair trial) and 8 (the right to privacy) have any general relevance. Article 10 (the right to freedom of expression) is also relevant to the issue of additional liabilities. Most of the topics are dealt with in other chapters; the relevant paragraphs may be found listed below (in alphabetical order). **24.32–24.33**

Access to justice

The right to a fair trial (Art 6 ECHR) is an absolute right that is given a broad and purposive interpretation,[49] but rights ancillary to it—which include the right of access to the court—will be subject to the balancing exercise referred to in 24.27–24.29.[50] This is not surprising because Art 6 'by its nature calls for regulation by the state, regulation which may vary in time and place according to the needs and resources of the community and of individuals'.[51] **24.34**

46 App No 8793/79 *James & Ors v United Kingdom* (1986) 8 EHRR 123, at [50]
47 *Velikovi & Ors v Bulgaria* (2009) 48 EHRR 27, at [50].
48 *Secretary of State for Home Department v Rehman* [2001] UKHL 47.
49 *Delcourt v Belgium* (1970) 1 EHRR 355, at [25].
50 See *Sunday Times v United Kingdom* [1979] ECHR 1, at [65].
51 *Golder v United Kingdom* (1975) 1 EHRR 524, at [38], quoted in *Ashingdane v United Kingdom* (1985) 7 EHRR 528, at [57]: 'Certainly, the right of access to the courts is not absolute but may be subject to limitations; these are permitted by implication since the right of access, "by its very nature calls for regulation by the state, regulation which may vary in time and place according to the needs and resources of the community and of individuals". In laying down such regulation, the contracting states enjoy a certain margin of appreciation. Whilst the final decision as to observance of the Convention's requirements rests with the court, it is no part of the court's function to substitute for the assessment of the national authorities any other assessment of what might be the best policy in this field.'

24.35 Notwithstanding the fact that it is not an absolute right,[52] the right of access to the court—or, more accurately, the right of *effective* access to a court[53]—is regarded as being of especial importance.[54] The ECtHR has said this on the topic:

> 'It would not be consistent with the rule of law in a democratic society or with the basic principle underlying art 6 para 1—namely that civil claims must be capable of being submitted to a judge for adjudication—if . . . a state could, without restraint or control by the Convention enforcement bodies, remove from the jurisdiction of the courts a whole range of civil claims or confer immunities from civil liability on large groups or categories of persons . . .'[55]

24.36 Access ought not be 'prohibitively expensive'.[56] Moreover, there must be an 'equality of arms' in that each party must be afforded a reasonable opportunity to present their case in conditions that do not put that party at a disadvantage vis-à-vis the other parties.[57]

24.37 Any limitation or restriction of the right of access must satisfy three requirements:

- it must not impair the essence of the right;
- it must be in pursuit of a legitimate aim; and
- it must comply with the principle of proportionality.[58]

24.38 Arguments concerning ECHR Art 6 are more common in cases before the ECtHR than their incidence in domestic law would suggest. This is somewhat curious given the fact that 'the ECHR is intended to guarantee not rights that are theoretical or illusory but rights that are practical and effective'.[59]

Case examples

24.39 Non-UK case examples include the following.

- **State funding** It has repeatedly been held that there will be cases in which an absence of legal representation (that is, an absence of state funding of some type) will deny effective access to the court.[60]
- **Fixed court fees** The imposition of a substantial and fixed court fee is capable of amounting to a disproportionate restriction on access to court.[61]

---

52 In *Golder v United Kingdom* (1975) 1 EHRR 524, at [38], the ECtHR said that the right of access '[b]y its very nature calls for regulation by the state, regulation which may vary in time and place according to the needs and resources of the community and of individuals'.

53 See, eg, *Airey v Ireland* (1979) 2 EHRR 305, at [26].

54 App No 6538/74 *Sunday Times v United Kingdom* (1979) 2 EHRR 245, at [65].

55 *Fayed v United Kingdom* (1994) 18 EHRR 393, at [65].

56 C-260/11 *Edwards v EA (No 2)* [2013] l WLR 2914, at [43] and [47]. This case confirms that the fact that proceedings have in fact been brought does not negate a complaint that the costs system is prohibitively expensive and incompatible with effective access to justice. It has been argued that one should look at the totality of the sums and consider whether it is so high as to not be in accordance with the ECHR: see *James v UK* (1986) 8 EHRR 123, at [50].

57 See *Dombo Beheer v The Netherlands* (1994) 18 EHRR 213, at [33]. See also *Steel & Morris v UK* [2005] EMLR 15, at [59].

58 *Ashingdane v United Kingdom* (1985) 7 EHRR 528, at [57].

59 App No 6289/73 *Airey v Ireland* (1979) 2 EHRR 305, at [24].

60 See App No 6289/73 *Airey v Ireland* (1979) 2 EHRR 305.

61 *Jedamski and Jedamska v Poland* (2007) 45 EHRR 47; see also, similarly, App No 28249/95 *Kreus v Poland* [2001] ECHR 394.

- **Stamp duty** A requirement to pay a substantial stamp duty as a prerequisite to access to the court has been held to amount to a disproportionate restriction on access to court.[62]
- **Sliding-scale court fees** A requirement to pay a court fee calculated as a high fixed percentage of the sums claimed has been found to be capable of being a disproportionate restriction on access to court.[63]
- **Blanket ban on waivers of court fees** A blanket ban on granting waivers from liability for court fees is capable of being unlawful.[64]

By contrast, the number of UK case examples is very limited. There are cases that concern the availability of legal aid,[65] but there are very few cases that deal with costs other than in the setting of public funding. Those that do exist include the following. **24.40**

- **Costs and expenses** The ECtHR has commented that the costs should not effectively bar access to court for impecunious litigants.[66]
- **Inequality of arms** The ECtHR has confirmed that an inequality of arms should not act as a bar to effective access to justice, whether as a result of an absence of representation[67] or as a result of inadequate representation.[68] That said, the mere fact that one side has leading counsel and the other lacks the funding to do likewise would not amount to an unlawful breach of Art 6.[69]

Where the putative breach has caused a party not to be represented, the tribunal in question will have to decide whether it can fairly dispose of the matter. Given the fact that it can constantly remind itself of the need to be fair and to make allowances, it is very much a matter for the tribunal in question.[70] The skill and experience of the litigant may be relevant in this regard.[71] **24.41**

It has been held that the court will exercise 'particularly rigorous scrutiny' in cases in which the issue is not access to justice over liability, but rather access to justice over some ancillary matter (in that instance, enforcement).[72] **24.42**

Additional liabilities

The question here is whether the system of shifting the burden of paying for unsuccessful litigation on to paying parties via the medium of additional liabilities is lawful. **24.43**

---

[62] App No 63945/00 *Weissman v Romania* [2011] ECHR 2204.

[63] *Stankov v Bulgaria* (2009) 49 EHRR 7, [2007] ECHR 582.

[64] App No 27888/04 *Tudor-Comert v Moldova*, 4 November 2008, ECtHR.

[65] These include *R (Jarrett) v Legal Services Commission* [2001] EWHC 389 (Admin); *McLean v Procurator Fiscal, Fort William* [2001] 1 WLR 2425; *Perotti v Collyer-Bristow (a firm)* [2003] EWCA Civ 1521. The threshold that the victim has to cross is very high—see *Perotti v Collyer-Bristow (a firm)* [2003] EWCA Civ 1521, at [31]—but examples do exist in which the court has found that funding was mandatory: see, eg, *Alliss v Legal Services Commission* [2002] EWHC 2079 (Admin).

[66] *Faulkner v United Kingdom* (2000) The Times, 11 January, ECtHR.

[67] App No 68416/01*Steel and Morris v United Kingdom* (2005) 41 EHRR 403.

[68] *R v Thakrar* [2001] EWCA Crim 1096.

[69] See *AG's Reference No 82A of 2000* [2002] EWCA Crim 215, at [14].

[70] *Re B and T (Care Proceedings: Legal Representation)* [2001] FCR 512.

[71] See *Pine v Solicitors' Disciplinary Tribunal* [2001] EWCA Crim 1574, in which the Court of Appeal found that a solicitor was not at a disadvantage representing himself before his professional body.

[72] App No 40765/02 *Apostol v Georgia*, 28 November 2006, ECtHR.

24.44 The first reported case in the House of Lords in which a party sought to argue that condemning a person to pay additional liabilities would be an unjustifiable violation of its guaranteed rights was the 2004 case of *Campbell v MGN Ltd*.[73] That said, similar issues had arisen in *Callery v Gray*,[74] a case decided in 2003 in which a five-judge House of Lords upheld a decision that a paying party was liable to pay certain additional liabilities. Whilst the arguments in *Callery* were not phrased in terms of human rights, their Lordships were asked to address the question of 'whether it is right in principle that a claimant's [additional] liability ... should be recoverable from the losing party'.[75] Indeed, the Court of Appeal (that is, the court below) had reached the view that 'the prejudice to defendants was not as clear as is suggested and that it was outweighed by the legislative policy and by a number of practical considerations' (the court then going on to list a number of factors that supported that finding).[76] Their Lordships commented adversely on much of what they saw. Lord Hoffmann, for example, said that he had 'considerable unease about the present state of the law,'[77] whilst Lord Scott (dissenting) said that 'if general policy considerations [were] to be brought into account, they tend strongly ... against allowing recovery [of the ATE premium in that case]'.[78] To that extent, at least, their Lordships looked at the overall justice of the situation.

24.45 Notwithstanding those concerns, their Lordships rejected the appeal and allowed the additional liabilities. Perhaps as a result of *Callery*, the mid-2000s saw costs practitioners focusing their attentions on the question of how much was payable on a case-by-case basis rather than on whether additional liabilities were recoverable per se. It is therefore no surprise that the first arguments based on right and freedoms enshrined in the ECHR came from a wholly different quarter: the privacy and publication claim of *Campbell*.[79] The defendant newspaper group had published an article about the claimant, who was a successful fashion model. The article said that the claimant, who had stated publicly that, unlike many others in the fashion business, she was not a drug addict, was in fact a drug user.

24.46 The arguments in *Campbell* arose in the context of the right of freedom of expression (that is, ECHR Art 10). The dispute arose not in the context of the assessment of costs, but in the context of a newspaper publisher seeking a prospective declaration that additional liabilities would not be recoverable. The publisher said that if additional liabilities were recoverable, they would be a 'sword of Damocles' that would have a 'chilling effect' on the ability of the press to speak freely. Their Lordships rejected that argument.[80]

24.47 The defendant was not happy with that result and sued the UK in the ECtHR. Their case reached the Fourth Chamber in 2011,[81] where the newspaper group argued that the UK government had breached its human rights by allowing the claimant to recover a success fee.

73 *Campbell v MGN Ltd* [2004] UKHL 22.
74 *Callery v Gray* [2002] UKHL 28.
75 See *ibid*, at [51], *per* Lord Hope.
76 *Callery v Gray (No 1)* [2001] EWCA Civ 1117, at [99].
77 *Callery v Gray* [2002] UKHL 28, at [18].
78 *Ibid*, at [121].
79 *Campbell v MGN Ltd* [2004] UKHL 22.
80 *Ibid*.
81 App No 39401/04 *MGN Ltd v United Kingdom* [2011] ECHR 66.

It is important to note that, by that stage, Sir Rupert Jackson had concluded the Civil Costs Review and that his Final Report contained a great deal of material that the newspaper group was able to deploy. In the event, the ECtHR gave great weight to Sir Rupert's criticisms of additional liabilities and, in doing so, it was highly critical of the whole philosophy of additional liabilities. The Court's decision may be summarised in the following way. **24.48**

- In the context of publication cases, the system of allowing very high success fees between opposing parties is an interference of the rights of expression guaranteed by ECHR Art 10.
- That interference did have a legitimate aim (namely, to facilitate access to justice), but the requirement that a paying party pays a success fee was disproportionate, having regard to that legitimate aim of achieving access to justice, because:
  - the CPR and the Costs Practice Direction (CPD) were not adequate for the purposes of limiting the success fee, because they fostered 'costs races';
  - the separate control of success fees (that is, control on the basis of risk rather than proportionality) was not effective at controlling costs; and
  - the Ministry of Justice had accepted (via the reasoning set out in Sir Rupert's report) that the overall burden of costs was disproportionate.

Conflict between Campbell v MGN Ltd *and* MGN Ltd v United Kingdom

There was (and still is) a head-on collision between the ECtHR's approach in *MGN Ltd v United Kingdom* and that of the House of Lords in *Campbell v MGN Ltd*. Where such a conflict exists, the domestic court will prevail.[82] If there was any doubt about that, such doubt was dispelled by Moore-Bick LJ, who, within only a couple of months of the ECtHR handing down its judgment, explained that *Campbell v MGN Ltd* was to be preferred.[83] Other judges have come to the same conclusion.[84] Indeed, as is set out below, the Supreme Court has said the same. **24.49**

Is it possible to distinguish the House of Lords' decision? At first blush, one would think that it would not be difficult to read *Campbell v MGN Ltd* narrowly (that is, in such a way as to focus on ECHR Art 8 rights only). One might also think that it would be far harder to do the same with *MGN Ltd v United Kingdom*, because the ECtHR's reliance on Sir Rupert's Jackson's Final Report meant that the decision went to the very heart of whether additional liabilities were rational and proportionate.[85] Moore-Bick LJ, however, took the opposite view: he found that *MGN Ltd v United Kingdom* should be read narrowly and that it was 'not remotely comparable' to the case before him, which concerned the assessment of costs.[86] Moore-Bick LJ also found that it was 'for Parliament to decide what arrangements viewed overall will best serve the general requirement for access to justice'.[87] **24.50**

---

[82] *Kay & Anor v London Borough of Lambeth & Anor* [2006] UKHL 10.

[83] *Sousa v London Borough of Waltham Forest Council* [2011] EWCA Civ 194, at [54].

[84] See, eg, *Miller v Associated Newspapers Ltd* [2016] EWHC 397 (QB), *per* Mitting J. See also *Eight Representative Claimants v MGN Ltd* [2016] EWHC 855 (Ch), *per* Mann J.

[85] See, in particular, *MGN Ltd v United Kingdom* [2011] ECHR 66, at [217].

[86] *Sousa v London Borough of Waltham Forest Council* [2011] EWCA Civ 194, at [54].

[87] *Ibid.*

24.51 The case in which Moore-Bick LJ was giving judgment was far from the ideal vehicle in which to develop the arguments. In particular, the paying party was itself a public authority and, as such, did not have any human rights to take into account.[88] There was, however, no appeal from his decision and liability insurers put their arguments on the back burner. One would have thought that this would have been whilst they awaited a better vehicle in which to air their arguments in the Supreme Court; whilst there may have been an element of this, it also has to be said that most insurers seemed to have very little appetite for the argument. Perhaps this was because they were focusing on the Civil Justice Review. Many people expected that to be an end of the matter.

24.52 In 2014, however, the argument reared its head again, at the end of an appeal in the Supreme Court, in the context of the paying party arguing that an order to pay additional liabilities infringed his Arts 6 and 1 rights (the latter being the right to peaceful enjoyment of one's possessions).[89] By a majority of 5:2,[90] the Supreme Court held that making an order that included additional liabilities would not amount to a breach. In particular, the Court found that considerable weight ought to be afforded to informed legislative choices, at least in so far as the legislature was seeking to reconcile the competing interests of different groups. It noted that Parliament had consulted widely before implementing the legislation that gave rise to additional liabilities, and that the drafters of the CPR and the CPD were best placed to determine how to strike an appropriate balance.

24.53 A similar matter came before the Supreme Court again in 2017, this time in the context of a publisher claiming that the imposition of additional liabilities infringed its Art 10 rights (which was the point that directly arose in *MGN Ltd*). All five of their Lordships[91] concluded that the challenge should be dismissed, although they declined to express a concluded view on the issue of whether the principle in *MGN Ltd* was part of domestic law.[92] They went on to say that even if that principle was part of domestic law, given the fact that receiving parties had embarked on the expectation that additional liabilities would be recoverable, it was difficult to see how their rights under Protocol 1, Art 1, could be defeated: it was a fundamental principle of any civilised system of government that citizens were entitled to act on the assumption that the law was as set out in legislation.[93]

Costs against the Courts Service

24.54 The topic of human rights and costs against the Courts Service is addressed at 64.04.

---

88 See, eg, *Aston Cantlow PCC v Wallbank* [2004] 1 AC 546, at [8], *per* Lord Nicholls. Whilst he did not refer to any authority, Moore-Bick LJ said that 'unless the liability to pay a success fee can be said to infringe the defendant's rights under the Convention (which is clearly not the case here), questions of proportionality and reasonableness do not arise': see *Sousa v London Borough of Waltham Forest Council* [2011] EWCA Civ 194, at [54].

89 *Coventry v Lawrence (No 3)* [2015] UKSC 50.

90 Lord Neuberger and Lord Dyson (with whom Lord Sumption and Lord Carnwath agreed) gave the joint leading judgment, and Lord Mance (with whom Lord Carnwath also agreed) gave a concurring judgment. Lord Clarke gave a dissenting judgment, with which Lady Hale agreed.

91 Lords Neuberger, Mance, Sumption, Hughes and Hodge.

92 See *Times Newspapers v Flood* [2017] UKSC 33, at [27]–[29] and [64].

93 *Ibid*, at [42]–[56]. That said, their Lordships did note that the position of one of the receiving parties was weaker than that of the others because they had entered into funding arrangements that provided for additional liabilities after *MGN Ltd v United Kingdom*: see *Times Newspapers v Flood* [2017] UKSC 33, at [57]–[63].

Privilege and election

The topic of human rights and the law of privilege and election during detailed assessments is addressed at 46.44. **24.55**

The right to privacy

The relevance of ECHR Art 8 is that the right to a private life includes the right to assert legal professional privilege.[94] It was for this reason that, shortly after the introduction of the CPR, CPR, r 48.7(3), was found to be *ultra vires*. This rule used to provide that the court may direct that privileged documents were to be disclosed for the purposes of dealing with applications for wasted costs, but it was revoked[95] after Toulson J found that it was incompatible with the right to a private life and declared it to be *ultra vires*.[96] **24.56**

The procedure of election pursuant to Practice Direction (PD) 47, para 13.13 (previously CPD, art 40.14), is compatible with the ECHR. This is addressed at 46.44. **24.57**

Security for costs

The topic of human rights and the law of security for costs is addressed at 15.73, 15.78 and 15.112. **24.58**

Wasted costs

The topic of human rights and the law of wasted costs is addressed at 9.97 and 9.203. **24.59**

---

[94] *R (on the application of Morgan Grenfell & Co Ltd) v Special Commissioners of Income Tax* [2002] UKHL 21.

[95] Civil Procedure (Amendment No 3) Rules 2000 (SI 2000/1317).

[96] *General Mediterranean Holdings SA v Patel* [2000] 1 WLR 272.

Part VII

THE OVERRIDING OBJECTIVE, PROPORTIONALITY AND RELIEF FROM SANCTIONS

25

PROPORTIONALITY AND COSTS

This chapter deals with the following topics: **25.01**

- the terminology of proportionality (25.02);
- the history of proportionality (25.04);
- individual proportionality (25.15):
  - transitional provisions (25.17);
  - individual proportionality and the management of claims (25.20);
  - the test of proportionality under the post-2013 method (25.29);
  - the test of proportionality under the pre-2013 method ('*Lownds* stage one') (25.37);
  - the measure of proportionate costs under the post-2013 method (25.47);
  - the measure of proportionate costs under the pre-2013 method ('*Lownds* stage two') (25.63); and
  - miscellaneous topics (25.69).

The Terminology of Proportionality

Proportionality is not a concept that is limited to the law of costs; it extends throughout the whole of the adjectival law in the civil courts. Whilst lawmakers in England and Wales seem to have resisted any attempt to make express reference to the point, other jurisdictions have recognised two distinct types of proportionality—that is, 'collective proportionality' and 'individual proportionality' (although they are rarely referred to by those names).[1] Whilst it is, to an extent, an artificial distinction, it is used in this book for the purposes of description. Collective proportionality is addressed at 26.26–26.47 and defined at 26.26; it may be relevant to costs management and to relief from sanctions, but is not—in general—relevant to the assessment of costs and therefore may largely be disregarded for present purposes. **25.02**

The following definitions apply in this chapter. **25.03**

- **Individual proportionality** This is proportionality as it applies to the costs of individual litigants. It is what costs practitioners understand 'proportionality' to mean.
- **Pre-2013 method** This is a reference to the test that used to apply prior to 1 April 2013 and, in some circumstances, will continue to apply (see 25.17). It is also known as the *Lownds* test.[2]

[1] See, eg, Sorabji, J, *English Civil Justice after the Woolf and Jackson Reforms: A Critical Analysis* (Cambridge: Cambridge University Press, 2014).

[2] After *Lownds v Home Office* [2002] EWCA Civ 365.

- **Post-2013 method** This is a reference to the test that, subject to the certain transitional provisions (see 25.17–25.19), now applies.

The History of Proportionality

25.04 As was said at the very start of this book (see 1.03–1.04), every decade or so policies relating to costs tend to be revised in what is a fluctuating process of evolution. This is certainly true of proportionality, both in this jurisdiction and abroad. In 2004, for example, one Australian commentator had this to say: 'There is a question whether proportionality is really something original, likely to have a beneficial impact on procedural law. Or whether it is simply old wine in new bottles, and likely to disappoint us.'[3] In England and Wales, there can be no doubt that the wine has repeatedly been decanted from bottle to bottle. By way of illustration, the measure of disproportionate costs under the post-2013 method (see 25.47–25.62) now seems to be much the same as that which was unsuccessfully advanced before the Court of Appeal in *Lownds* in 2002.[4] That proposed method was itself borrowed from a practice that had first been described in the authorities in 1997—namely, 'the *Singh* adjustment'[5]—which in turn bore a similarity to a method of assessment that was first described in 1989.[6] The approach that Woolf MR preferred in *Lownds* (that is, the pre-2013 method—see 25.37) was also borrowed: in essence, it was a restatement of an approach that was first formulated in 1875[7] (see 1.97), but which had been 'rebottled' twice—first in 1959 and then again in 1986 (see 1.129 and 1.144).

25.05 None of this is intended to be a criticism of the rulemakers or the senior judiciary; rather, it is a consequence of the fact that there is not—and never will be—a single 'right' answer to the question, 'how much is too much?' Given the fact that priorities will gently drift back and forth as the needs of society change, it is no surprise that the law is always perceived to be unsatisfactory.

25.06 The ancient history is addressed in Chapter 1, but, for present purposes, one does not need to go back any further than the beginning of the 17th century. In 1601, an Act was passed that limited the recovery of costs to a method of assessment that took into account the value of the claim (see 1.43).[8] That Act provided that where a claim had been issued in Westminster, if less than 40 shillings was recovered, no greater amount could be recovered

---

[3] Scott, I, 'Adjusting the Interests of Parties and Courts: Uniformity, Diversion and Proportionality', Paper presented at the 22nd Australian Institute of Judicial Administration Annual Conference, 17 September 2004, Sydney, at p 31.

[4] See *Lownds v Home Office* [2002] EWCA Civ 365, at [17] and [30]–[31], *per* Lord Woolf MR.

[5] That being 'the *Singh* adjustment', whereby the court, after having carried out an item-by-item assessment, would stand back and make a decision as to the monies claimed overall: after *R v SCTO, ex p Singh & Co* (1997) 1 Costs LR 49.

[6] See *Finley v Glaxo Laboratories Ltd* (1989) 106 Costs LR 106, at 111, *per* Hobhouse J: '[T]he district registrar is quite right that at the end of any assessment of this kind he should stand back for a moment and consider the implications and the overall picture presented by his decision on the detail.'

[7] RSC Ord 65, r 29.

[8] 43 Eliz I, c 6, which in modern terminology would be known as the Frivolous Suits Act 1601.

in costs. Successive Acts expanded the ambit of the rule (see 1.45),[9] but in practical terms the restriction had little practical effect.[10]

Things did not improve. Indeed, by the start of the 19th century one could have said that the civil law favoured procedure over all else (see 1.87). Those were the days when *Jarndyce v Jarndyce* would have borne an uncomfortable resemblance to reality.[11] According to 19th-century commentator William Blake Ogden: **25.07**

> '[Litigants] were sadly hampered in the year 1800 by cumbrous procedure and pedantic technicalities which caused suitors expense, delay, vexation and disgust. It took years for a merchant to recover a debt due to him. And half the actions were decided not on their real merits, but on questions of form and pleading'.[12]

This unattractive state of affairs changed in the 1870s with the coming into force of the Judicature Acts and the Rules of the Supreme Court (RSC) (see 1.92–1.94). Under those new Rules, the court had to show forbearance in the face of adjectival failure: **25.08**

> 'Non-compliance with any of these rules, or with any rule of practice for the time being in force, shall not render any proceedings void unless the court or judge shall so direct, but such proceedings may be set aside either wholly or in part as irregular, or amended, or otherwise dealt with in such manner and upon such terms as the court or judge shall think fit.'[13]

Thus procedural failings would be tolerated, at least to an extent. The then-new ethos came to be known as justice on the merits[14] and its sphere of influence reached far beyond issues of procedure. Indeed, the court's objective became the attainment of perfect individual justice (see 26.10–26.11).

Unsurprisingly, this was expensive. This was true not only in the sense that it led to the parties having to incur substantial costs, but also in the sense that it led to significant demands being placed on the resources of the court. This was due in part to the fact that the RSC made no mention of the court having to take into account its own resources. By the middle of the 20th century, it had become obvious that perfect justice was coming at too high a price. **25.09**

In 1953, the Committee on Supreme Court Practice and Procedure published the Evershed Report (see 1.129).[15] That report stated the principle that 'extravagant' costs should not be recoverable. It is now thought that this was an early forerunner of what would become modern proportionality.[16] That said, the changes that were made to the RSC did little to advance any such change in the law.[17] **25.10**

---

[9] The Limitation Act 1623 and then, in 1670, 22 & 23 Charles II, c 9, which in modern terminology would be known as the Duties on Law Proceedings Act 1670.

[10] The restriction would apply only if the court certified that it should, however, and the reality was that this almost never happened. Indeed, Baron Gilbert commented that the Act was 'pretty darkly penn'd and therefore I believe had very little or no effect': *Reeves v Butler* (1726) Gilb Rep 195, at 195. See also Sayer, J, *The Law of Costs* (London: Woodfall & Strahan, 1768), p 12; *Quick on Costs* (Thomson Reuters, online).

[11] This was the case in *Bleak House*, which 'became so complicated, that no man alive knew what it meant'; in the end, the whole estate was absorbed in costs: see Dickens, C, *Bleak House* (reprint, London: Wordsworth, 1993).

[12] Odgers, WB, 'Changes in Procedure and in the Law of Evidence', in Council of Legal Education (ed), *A Century of Law Reform: Twelve Lectures on the Changes in the Law of England during the Nineteenth Century* (London, Macmillan & Co, 1901), pp 203–40, at p 212.

[13] RSC 1883, Ord 70, r 1.

[14] See Zuckerman, A, 'The Revised CPR 3.9: A Coded Message Demanding Articulation' (2013) 32(2) CJQ 126.

[15] Evershed, R, *Final Report of the Committee on Supreme Court Practice and Procedure*, Cmnd 8878 (London: HMSO, 1953).

[16] See Jackson, R, *Review of Civil Litigation Costs: Final Report* (London: HMSO, 2010), ch 3, at para 3.1.

[17] See RSC Ord 62, r 28(2), in the 1959 revision of the RSC.

25.11 In the early 1990s, there was unease about the health of the civil litigation system in general and about costs in particular (see 1.142).[18] The Lord Chancellor asked Lord Woolf to carry out a review of civil justice. In his Interim Report, Lord Woolf highlighted the problem of 'excessive and unaffordable costs', and of 'disproportionate costs', commenting that 'the problem of costs is the most serious problem besetting our litigation system'.[19] In his Final Report, Lord Woolf identified a number of objectives, including making costs more 'proportionate' to the nature of the dispute and making the amount of costs more predictable.[20]

25.12 It was against that background that the Civil Procedure Rules (CPR) were formulated (see 1.156). From the earliest days of the CPR, proportionality was regarded as being a major precept upon which the effectiveness of those Rules would depend.[21] Indeed, their stated objective was (and still is) that litigation should be conducted in a proportionate manner and at a proportionate cost.[22] This was a fundamental difference that distinguished the CPR from the RSC.

25.13 In so far as the law of costs is concerned, however, almost all of the changes that were made in 1999 and 2000 (that is, when the CPR came into force and when the Woolf reforms were implemented) failed to contain costs within acceptable bounds. Even as early as 2003, it had become clear that there were problems. In this regard, Brooke LJ had this to say:

> 'Judges at every level must be astute to correct sloppy practice and to avoid at all costs slipping back to the bad old days when courts took a relaxed attitude to the need for compliance with rules and court orders, so that expensive and time-consuming satellite litigation was only too apt to flourish.'[23]

Professor Zuckerman has noted that 'notwithstanding such periodic exhortations, the court failed all too often to give effect to the overriding objective'.[24]

25.14 The failure of the Woolf reforms to contain costs led, in part, to the Jackson reforms (see 1.174). The policies that underlie the Jackson reforms are, in very broad terms, the same as those that underlay the Woolf reforms[25] (albeit with a greater emphasis on controlling costs) and, as such, the Jackson reforms could be regarded as a second attempt to implement the Woolf reforms. This is a topic that is dealt with in more detail in Chapters 1 and 26.

---

[18] See, eg, Heilbron, H, *Report of the General Council of the Bar and the Law Society of the United Kingdom Civil Justice on Trial: The Case for Change* (London: The Law Society, 1993).

[19] Lord Woolf, *Access to Justice: Interim Report to the Lord Chancellor on the Civil Justice System in England and Wales* (London: HMSO, 1995), ch 3, at paras 13–28.

[20] Lord Woolf, *Access to Justice: Final Report to the Lord Chancellor on the Civil Justice System in England and Wales* (London: HMSO, 1996), ch 7.

[21] See, eg, *Lownds v Home Office* [2002] EWCA Civ 365, at [1], *per* Lord Woolf CJ.

[22] See CPR, r 1.1.

[23] *Southern & District Finance Plc v Turner* [2003] EWCA Civ 1574, at [34]. See also *Mannion v Ginty* [2012] EWCA Civ 1667, at [18]; *Byrne v Poplar Housing and Regeneration Community Association Ltd* [2012] EWCA Civ 832.

[24] See Zuckerman, A, 'The Revised CPR 3.9: A Coded Message Demanding Articulation' (2013) 32(2) CJQ 123, at 126.

[25] Sorabji, J, *English Civil Justice after the Woolf and Jackson Reforms: A Critical Analysis* (Cambridge: Cambridge University Press, 2014).

Individual Proportionality

Individual proportionality seeks to contain costs so that no party is to bear a disproportionate burden of costs. This may be achieved either by managing costs (an *ex ante* mechanism) or by limiting costs on assessment (an *a posteriori* mechanism), or by both. The *a posteriori* mechanism will apply only where the costs are assessed on the standard basis (see 16.05). In so far as the *ex ante* mechanism is concerned (namely, case and costs management), there is often a degree of overlap between individual and collective proportionality (see 26.26), because those *ex ante* steps that are taken to preserve the court's resources will also tend to limit expenditure by the parties. The *a posteriori* mechanism, on the other hand, will always be individual rather than collective, because the court does not assess the usage of its own resources. **25.15**

The details of the applicable forensic method will depend on when the relevant work was done and whether it is the *ex ante* mechanism or the *a posteriori* mechanism that is being considered. As is explained below, the nature of the *a posteriori* mechanism is subject to transitional provisions in that there are two wholly distinct approaches: the pre-2013 and post-2013 methods. **25.16**

Transitional provisions

In so far as the *a posteriori* mechanism (namely, assessment) is concerned, the way in which the court approaches the issue of proportionality will depend on when the costs were incurred and when the claim was commenced. Where the claim was commenced before 1 April 2013 or where the costs incurred were for work done before that date, then the pre-2013 method will apply (see 25.37–25.46 and 25.63–25.68)—that is, the *Lownds* test, also known as the two-stage test.[26] The same is true of most additional liabilities (see 25.83–25.88), this being regardless of when the claim was commenced. In all other circumstances, however, the post-2013 method will apply (see 25.29–25.36 and 25.47–25.62). **25.17**

In cases that were commenced on or after 1 April 2013 but where work was carried out before that date, both methods will apply in the same assessment: the pre-2013 method will apply to the work done before that date and the post-2013 will apply thereafter.[27] **25.18**

In determining whether proceedings were commenced on or after 1 April 2013, proceedings are begun when the court issues a claim form at the request of the claimant (CPR, r 7.2(1)). A claim form is issued on the date entered on the form by the court (CPR, r 7.2(2)).[28] **25.19**

---

[26] See CPR, r 44.3(7).

[27] It should be noted that, on 6 April 2016, Practice Direction (PD) 47, para 5.8(7), was amended so as to ensure that, in such cases, the bill of costs to be assessed on the standard basis must be divided into parts to distinguish between costs shown as incurred for work done before 1 April 2013 and costs shown as incurred for work done on or after 1 April 2013.

[28] Davis LJ has explained that even though there may have been a delay between the court receiving the relevant documents and the court entering this date on the form, it is the latter that is determinative of the date of issue: see *Harrison v University Hospitals Coventry & Warwickshire NHS Trust* [2017] EWCA Civ 792, at [62].

Individual proportionality and the management of claims

25.20 CPR, rr 1.1(2)(a)–(d), permit the court to take account of individual proportionality for the purposes of managing claims—that is, the *ex ante* mechanism. The other subparagraphs in CPR, r 1.1(2), go to collective proportionality and are therefore addressed in Chapter 26 (see 26.29). They may, however, be just as relevant to the *ex ante* mechanism and therefore would need to be taken into account. For the purposes of the *ex ante* mechanism, the distinction between individual and collective proportionality is artificial, and is made only for the purposes of description. Both collective and individual proportionality will have a bearing on costs management, this being a topic that is addressed in Chapter 12. For obvious reasons, both forms of proportionality will also have a bearing on case management.

25.21 As of 1 April 2013,[29] the provisions that govern the *ex ante* mechanism of individual proportionality are as set out at CPR, r 1.1:

> '(1) These Rules are a new procedural code with the overriding objective of enabling the court to deal with cases justly and at proportionate cost.
>
> (2) Dealing with a case justly and at proportionate cost includes, so far as is practicable—
> (a) ensuring that the parties are on an equal footing;
> (b) saving expense;
> (c) dealing with the case in ways which are proportionate—
>   (i) to the amount of money involved;
>   (ii) to the importance of the case;
>   (iii) to the complexity of the issues; and
>   (iv) to the financial position of each party;
> (d) ensuring that it is dealt with expeditiously and fairly;
>
> [...]'

The importance of costs management and budgeting

25.22 These provisions will have a great role to play in the way in which the court manages the costs of the litigation—in particular, in budgeting. This topic is addressed at 12.99–12.103. The way in which a budget is taken into account at a detailed assessment is addressed at 12.137–12.165.

The importance of planning and legal project management

25.23 To give effect to the policy that litigation should be conducted in a proportionate manner and at proportionate cost (be that in a collective or an individual sense), it is necessary to identify those cases in which it is anticipated that costs might become disproportionate.[30] In comments that still have resonance even though the law has moved on, Lord Woolf MR emphasised the importance of planning and, in so doing, he adopted an approach that had originally been articulated by Judge Alton:

> 'In modern litigation, with the emphasis on proportionality, there is a requirement for parties to make an assessment at the outset of the likely value of the claim and its importance and complexity, and then to plan in advance the necessary work, the appropriate level of person to carry out the work, the overall time which would be necessary and appropriate spend on the various stages in bringing the action to trial and the likely overall cost. While

[29] See the Civil Procedure (Amendment) Rules 2013 (SI 2013/262).

[30] On this point, it is probable that *Lownds v Home Office* [2002] EWCA Civ 365, at [23], remains good law.

it was not unusual for costs to exceed the amount in issue, it was, in the context of modest litigation such as the present case, one reason for seeking to curb the amount of work done, and the cost by reference to the need for proportionality.'[31]

Formal planning of litigation (known as legal project management) has now become a specialism in its own right (see Chapter 41). Whilst an obvious point, a party who has taken the trouble to apply the principles set out in that chapter will find it far easier to persuade the court that its costs or proposed costs were proportionate. This may have a bearing on both the *ex ante* and the *a posteriori* mechanisms. Indeed, one could argue that *not* applying such methods would, in an appropriate case, count against a party. **25.24**

Individual proportionality and the assessment of costs

What follows is the *a posteriori* mechanism of applying proportionality (that is, what costs practitioners mean by 'proportionality' in the context of assessment of costs). It is trite costs law that, where the amount of costs is to be assessed on the standard basis, the court will allow only those costs that are proportionate to the matters in issue.[32] This invites the following questions. **25.25**

- Which factors does the court take into account for the purposes of deciding whether costs are proportionate or disproportionate (see 25.26)?
- What test does the court apply for deciding whether the costs are proportionate or disproportionate (see 25.37–25.46 for the pre-2013 method and 25.29–25.36 for the post-2013 method)?
- By which means does the court reduce disproportionate costs to a proportionate level—that is, what is the measure the court uses to determine the amount of proportionate costs (see 25.63–25.68 for the pre-2013 method and 25.47–25.62 for the post-2013 method)?

The factors that the court takes into account for the purposes of dealing with proportionality

The factors that the court has traditionally tended to take into account for the purposes of dealing with proportionality have been the 'seven pillars of wisdom' (of which there are now eight[33]), as set out in CPR, r 44.4(3): **25.26**

'The court must also have regard to—
(a) the conduct of all parties, including in particular—
    (i) conduct before, as well as during, the proceedings; and
    (ii) the efforts made, if any, before and during the proceedings in order to try to resolve the dispute;
(b) the amount or value of any money or property involved;
(c) the importance of the matter to all the parties;
(d) the particular complexity of the matter or the difficulty or novelty of the questions raised;
(e) the skill, effort, specialised knowledge and responsibility involved;
(f) the time spent on the case;
(g) the place where and the circumstances in which work or any part of it was done; *and*
(h) the receiving party's last approved or agreed budget.'

---

[31] *Jefferson v National Freight Carriers plc* [2001] EWCA Civ 2082, at [40].
[32] See CPR, r 44.3(2).
[33] Because the CPR have now added the need to take into account the receiving party's last approved or agreed budget: see CPR, r 44.4(3)(h).

25.27 That said, where—and only where—the post-2013 method applies, CPR, r 44.3(5), will apply (see 25.29), that being an entirely different rule. As is explained below, however, it is likely that, when applying that rule, the court must take into account all of the relevant circumstances and, in that regard, the 'seven pillars' may still have a bearing on the matter. It should be noted, however, that CPR, r 44.3(5), does not in any way expressly incorporate the 'seven pillars'.

The test of proportionality

25.28 The test of proportionality will depend on whether the pre-2013 or post-2013 methods apply (see 25.17).

25.29 **The test of proportionality under the post-2013 method** Where, and only where, the post-2013 method applies (see 25.17), then CPR, r 44.3(5), will identify the following indicators of proportionality:

> '(5) Costs incurred are proportionate if they bear a reasonable relationship to—
> (a) the sums in issue in the proceedings;
> (b) the value of any non-monetary relief in issue in the proceedings;
> (c) the complexity of the litigation;
> (d) any additional work generated by the conduct of the paying party; and
> (e) any wider factors involved in the proceedings, such as reputation or public importance.'

25.30 Thus the following factors are expressly identified:

- the sums in issue[34] (or non-monetary correspondent thereof);
- the complexity of the litigation;
- the conduct of the paying party; and
- any wider factors, such as reputation.

Costs will be proportionate if they bear a reasonable relationship to those factors.

25.31 Whilst it is no more than the editor's own thoughts on the matter, the appropriate method for deciding whether costs are proportionate or disproportionate pursuant to the post-2013 method may be as follows.

(1) The court should make itself aware of all of the relevant circumstances of the case. As in any assessment, these will include the 'seven pillars', but they may also include other factors, where appropriate.
(2) Having done this, the court should consider the factors in CPR, r 44.3(5) (including any relevant wider factors within the meaning of CPR, r 44.3(5)(e)), and—to the extent that they are relevant—should ask itself whether the costs bear a reasonable relationship to the cumulative effect of those factors. In doing so, the court should, where appropriate, weigh competing factors against each other.
(3) If the court is not satisfied that the costs are proportionate by reference to the factors in CPR, r 44.3(5), the court is at liberty to refer to any other relevant factor for the purposes of explaining why the costs are disproportionate. In this regard, the court is not fettered by the factors set out in CPR, r 44.3(5), but when evaluating what a

---

[34] Whilst not binding, Judge Dight has said that 'sums in issue in the proceedings' is the amount realistically in dispute: *May & Anor v Wavell Group Ltd & Anor* [2017] Lexis Citation 462, at [63]–[67].

proportionate amount should be, the court should base its judgment on the factors in CPR, r 44.3(5) (a topic that is addressed more fully at 25.47–25.62).

The editor's thinking in this regard is set out below. It should be noted that, in contrast to the pre-2013 method, under the post-2013 method the topic of proportionality is often addressed at the end of the item-by-item assessment rather than at the outset.

Are the factors in CPR, r 44.3(5), exhaustive or non-exhaustive? It should be noted that **25.32** CPR, r 44.3(5), does not expressly state that the list of factors is exhaustive, in contrast to the provisions as originally proposed by Sir Rupert Jackson.[35] That said, there is also nothing in the Rules to say that the list is *not* exhaustive. The editor's opinion (for what it is worth) is that—whilst all of the relevant circumstances should be taken into account (see 25.33)—the factors listed in CPR, r 44.3(5), are pivotal to the operation of the post-2103 method in that they provide a structure that will allow the court to make an evaluative judgment as to whether the costs are proportionate, but they should not be read as excluding other factors (such as extravagant conduct on the part of the receiving party) that may explain why costs are *dis*proportionate. Put otherwise, the court is at liberty to identify factors other than those in CPR, r 44.3(5) (including any of those factors listed in CPR, r 44.4(3)), as the cause of *dis*proportionate expenditure, but the court ought not to point to factors other than those in CPR, r 44.3(5), for the purposes of deciding that costs are affirmatively proportionate (or for the purposes of making an evaluative judgment as to what a proportionate amount of costs should be).

It is trite costs law that all of the circumstances must be taken into account[36] (provided, of **25.33** course, that they relate to the claim[37] and are relevant), but it is not clear how open-textured the reference to 'wider factors' in CPR, r 44.3(5)(e), is intended to be. Put otherwise, it is not clear how readily the court can add its own factors to the list in CPR, r 44.3(5), for the purposes of making an evaluative judgment as to what is proportionate. Again, whilst it is no more than the editor's own thoughts, it is likely that the provision should not be read as meaning *any* factor (without restraint), because this would deprive CPR, r 44.3(5), of its utility as a list. That said, the reference to 'wider factors' in CPR, r 44.3(5)(e), is likely to be wide enough to embrace issues of importance to only one of the parties, the prime example of which being that which is mentioned—namely, reputation. Issues such as examination of the actions of public bodies, clarification of the law, investigation of clinical errors and other such topics may also fall into this category.

---

[35] See Jackson, R, *Review of Civil Litigation Costs: Final Report* (London: HMSO, 2010), ch 3, at para 5.15. The original wording was: 'Costs incurred are proportionate if, and only if, they bear ...'

[36] In this regard, whilst not binding, in *May & Anor v Wavell Group Ltd & Anor* [2017] Lexis Citation 462, at [55], Judge Dight has said this: '[It] seems to me that the word proportionate is intended to have a consistent interpretation across rule 44.3(2), rule 44.3(5) and 44.4, which means that in considering proportionality the court is to have regard to all the circumstances (see CPR 44.4) which includes, but is not limited to, the further factors specified in CPR 44.4(3) even though they are not specifically referred to in CPR 44.3.' To that extent, the 'seven pillars' may be relevant: see, eg, *Savoye and Savoye Ltd v Spicers Ltd* [2015] EWHC 33 (TCC), at [16], in which Akenhead J took the seven pillars into account.

[37] Whilst not binding, Judge Smith has found that any issues to be taken into account must relate to the case itself—particularly that it is not permissible to take into account extraneous factors, such as the needs of the after-the-event (ATE) insurance industry in the context of block rating: see *Demouilpied v Stockport NHS Foundation Trust* (unreported), 4 November 2011, Manchester County Court, at [20]–[22].

25.34 *Are the factors in CPR, r 44.3(5), conjunctive or disjunctive?* A literal reading of CPR, r 44.3(5), would suggest that costs would be proportionate if they were to bear a reasonable relationship to each and every one of the factors set out in CPR, 44.3(5). This cannot possibly be correct, however, because very few claims would ever fall in that category. The only workable interpretation of this rule is that costs are proportionate if they bear a reasonable relationship to the *relevant* factors in CPR, 44.3(5), whichever they may be.[38]

25.35 The more difficult conundrum, however, is the question of what the court would make of a claim in which the costs, say, bore a reasonable relationship to complexity of the litigation (CPR, r 44.4(5)(c)), but not to the sums in issue (CPR, r 44.4(5)(a)). If those were the facts, then the competing interpretations would be as follows.

- **The disjunctive interpretation** Costs would be proportionate if they bore a reasonable relationship to *any* of the relevant factors in CPR, r 44.4(5).
- **The conjunctive interpretation** Costs would be proportionate if they bore a reasonable relationship to *all* of those relevant factors.

25.36 The disjunctive interpretation is difficult to reconcile with the fact that CPR, r 44.4(5), uses the conjunction 'and' rather than 'or'. Moreover, when Sir Vivien Ramsay (who, at the time, was responsible for the implementation of the Jackson reforms) spoke of this rule in the Implementation Lectures, he seemed to refer to the factors as being conjunctive.[39] That said, the conjunctive interpretation would mean that the costs of a modest claim with higher-than-expected costs could never be proportionate, even if it were fiendishly complex or if the costs had been inflated by the outlandish conduct of the paying party. This would be a curious way of dealing with costs. Again, whilst it is no more than the editor's own thoughts, perhaps the true law is that the court should have regard to the cumulative weight of the relevant factors and, in doing so, should weigh competing factors against each other.[40]

25.37 **The test of proportionality under the pre-2013 method (that is, '*Lownds* stage one')** What is said below relates only to those cases to which the pre-2013 method applies (see 25.06). The matters set out at 25.29–25.36 will not apply—particularly the factors in CPR, r 44.3(5), which will have no bearing on the matter.

25.38 The *Lownds* test—that is, the test that is to be applied under the pre-2013 method—is a two-stage test in which the first stage determines the test to be applied on the second stage. Lord Woolf MR had the following to say on the matter:

> '[What] is required is a two-stage approach. There has to be a global approach and an item by item approach. The global approach will indicate whether the total sum claimed is or

[38] In this regard, whilst not binding, it is relevant that, in *May & Anor v Wavell Group Ltd & Anor* [2017] Lexis Citation 462, at [55], Judge Dight said this (emphasis added): '[O]ne has to go back to the wording of sub-rule 44.3(5) and reach a judgment as to the amount of costs whose relationship with all the factors identified in that sub-rule is a reasonable one. Whether the relationship is reasonable is ... a matter of judgment, rather than discretion, and ... requires a costs judge to attribute weight, *and sometimes no weight*, to each of the factors (a) to (e).'

[39] Ramsey J, 'Implementation of Costs Reforms' (2013) 32(2) CJQ 112.

[40] In this regard, it is worth noting that District Judge Middleton has said (extrajudicially) that '[i]t is the combination of factors that determines the proportionate costs': see Middleton, S, 'Proportionality: CPR r 44.3(5) in Practice' (2018) 4 CPN 8, at 11. See also *May & Anor v Wavell Group Ltd & Anor* [2017] Lexis Citation 462, at [56] and [71], *per* Judge Dight.

appears to be disproportionate having particular regard to the [seven pillars of wisdom]. If the costs as a whole are not disproportionate according to that test then all that is normally required is that each item should have been reasonably incurred and the cost for that item should be reasonable. If on the other hand the costs as a whole appear disproportionate then the court will want to be satisfied that the work in relation to each item was necessary and, if necessary, that the cost of the item is reasonable.'[41]

Lord Woolf went on to give guidance as to procedure: **25.39**

'In a case where proportionality is likely to be an issue, a preliminary judgment as to the proportionality of the costs as a whole must be made at the outset. This will ensure that the costs judge applies the correct approach to the detailed assessment. In considering that question the costs judge will have regard to whether the appropriate level of fee earner or counsel has been deployed, whether offers to settle have been made, whether unnecessary experts had been instructed and the other matters set out in Part 44.5(3). Once a decision is reached as to proportionality of costs as a whole, the judge will be able to proceed to consider the costs, item by item, applying the appropriate test to each item.'[42]

Thus, if, at the outset of the assessment, the totality of the costs is, or appears to be, disproportionate, then, when the court assesses the individual items within the bill of costs, the court will apply a test of necessity rather than reasonableness, that being a more stringent test. **25.40**

Where the claim is a money claim, the value of the claim will be the amount of money involved, the measure of which will depend on whether the receiving party is a claimant or a defendant.[43] **25.41**

- **Claimant** The issue of whether the costs claimed by a claimant are proportionate is determined by having regard to the sum that it was reasonable for the claimant to believe that they might recover at the time they made the claim.
- **Defendant** The issue of whether the costs claimed by a defendant are proportionate is determined by having regard to the sum that it was reasonable for the defendant to believe that the claimant might recover, should the claimant have succeeded in their claim. A defendant would ordinarily be entitled to take the claimant's claim at face value, so the appropriate measure would normally be the amount that has been claimed.

It is the whole of the costs that needs to be considered: for the purposes of applying a measure of proportionality, the bill of costs may not be broken down into parts for consideration individually[44]—although, if the costs are not disproportionate in general, the court is allowed to disallow or reduce individual items on the grounds of proportionality.[45]

Arden LJ has commented that the exercise is more complex than comparing the costs with the value of the claim and scaling down the costs accordingly.[46] **25.42**

---

[41] *Lownds v Home Office* [2002] EWCA Civ 365, at [28]. To give effect to the CPR concept of proportionality, the Court of Appeal found it necessary to resurrect the pre-CPR concept that the court would allow only those costs that were 'necessary for the proper attainment of justice' (see RSC Ord 28(2)).

[42] *Lownds v Home Office* [2002] EWCA Civ 365, at [36].

[43] See *ibid*, at [39].

[44] *Motto & Ors v Trafigura Ltd & Anor* [2011] EWCA Civ 1150, at [50], *per* Lord Neuberger MR.

[45] See *Finglands Coachways Ltd v O'Hare* [2014] EWHC 1513 (QB), at [27] and [28], *per* Cranston J. See also *Giambrone v JMC Holidays Ltd* [2002] EWHC 2932, at [28] and [54], *per* Morland J.

[46] *Contractreal Ltd v Davies* [2001] EWCA Civ 928. Those comments preceded *Lownds*, however, and should be treated with some caution.

25.43 The test is whether the costs claimed are, *or appear to be*, disproportionate;[47] hence the presumption in CPR, r 44.3(2)(b), will apply[48] and any doubt as to whether the costs are disproportionate must be resolved in favour of the paying party. In particular, Moreland J has confirmed that, in the unlikely event that a costs judge is unable to say whether the bill viewed as a whole is proportionate or disproportionate, that judge will be obliged to carry out the detailed assessment on the basis that the costs are disproportionate.[49]

25.44 It is not necessary or reasonable to expect an experienced costs judge to go through the seven pillars of wisdom as a checklist.[50] However, where it applies, a failure to apply the two-stage test in *Lownds* is capable of being a procedural irregularity of a serious nature.[51]

25.45 *What is the approach if costs under both the pre-2013 and the post-2013 methods fall to be assessed?* Whilst not binding, Master O'Hare has found that where costs fall to be assessed under both the pre-2013 and the post-2013 methods, the former may be taken into account for the purposes of gauging the latter (although he was careful not to apply the post-2013 method to the costs that fell to be assessed under the pre-2013 method).[52] Master Rowley came to much the same conclusion.[53]

The measure of disproportionate costs in general

25.46 Once the court has determined that the costs claimed are disproportionate, then it will need to decide if it is going to reduce the costs, and if so, how. The forensic approach will depend on whether the pre-2013 or post-2103 method applies (see 25.17). That said, the matters set out at 25.69–25.103 are, where indicated, likely to apply regardless of which method applies.

25.47 **The measure of proportionate costs under the post-2013 method** What is set out below will apply only where the post-2013 method applies and the court has found that the costs are disproportionate.

25.48 Whilst there is likely to be a degree of overlap,[54] individual proportionality under the post-2103 method is conceptually distinct from both reasonableness and necessity. In particular, where costs have been found not to be proportionate in accordance with the provisions set out at 25.29–25.36, both reasonable expenditure[55] *and* necessary expenditure[56] may be disproportionate and therefore susceptible to reduction.

25.49 *Proportionality takes precedence over necessity* The reason why proportionality prevails over necessity is because CPR, r 44.3(2), acts in such a way as to disapply the *Lownds* test, an

47 *Lownds v Home Office* [2002] EWCA Civ 365, at [28], *per* Woolf MR.

48 That provision will always apply because the test of proportionality will apply only where the costs are assessed on the standard basis.

49 *Giambrone v JMC Holidays Ltd (formerly Sunworld Holidays Ltd)* [2002] EWHC 2932 (QB), at [33].

50 *Ortwein v Rugby Mansions Ltd* [2003] EWHC (Ch) 2077, at [23], *per* Lloyd J.

51 *Lloyds TSB Bank plc v Lampert* [2003] EWHC 249 (Ch).

52 See *Hobbs v Guy's & St Thomas' NHS Foundation Trust* (unreported), 2 November 2015, SCCO.

53 See *King v Basildon & Thurrock University Hospitals NHS Foundation Trust* (unreported), 20 November 2016, SCCO.

54 See, by analogy with the pre-2013 method, *Simms v The Law Society* [2005] EWCA Civ 849, at [24], *per* Carnworth LJ.

55 This is the necessary implication of CPR, r 44.2(a).

56 The authors of *Cook on Costs 2017* (LexisNexis, online), both of whom are costs judges, have said, at para 14.3, that it is 'glaringly apparent that proportionality [now] trumps necessity'.

essential component of which is the notion of necessity (see 25.64). CPR, r 44.3(2), reads as follows:

> 'Where the amount of costs is to be assessed on the standard basis, the court will—
> (a) only allow costs which are proportionate to the matters in issue. *Costs which are disproportionate in amount may be disallowed or reduced even if they were reasonably or necessarily incurred*; and
> (b) resolve any doubt which it may have as to whether costs were reasonably incurred or reasonable and proportionate in amount in favour of the paying party.
> (Factors which the court may take into account are set out in rule 44.4.)'[57]

Thus costs that are disproportionate may be disallowed or reduced even if they were reasonably *and* necessarily incurred.

There is no doubt that, once the court has determined that costs are disproportionate, the monies claimed may be reduced. What is less certain, however, is how this is to be done. **25.50**

It has been suggested that there should be a '*Lownds* +1'[58] or some other test that provides a formulaic method of assessment. The fact that there is no practice direction on this issue is, however, deliberate. This is because, when he was redesigning the principles of proportionality under the CPR, Sir Rupert Jackson sought to abide by the following words of advice given to Coleridge in 1796: 'Cultivate simplicity.'[59] This is why CPR, r 44.3(5), is as it is. **25.51**

There is no doubt that the relevant provisions are simple and short. In many ways, this is understandable: after all, a degree of flexibility is desirable and no one would dispute Blackstone's observation that *lex non exacte definit, sed arbitrio boni viri permittit* ('the law does not define exactly, but leaves something to the discretion of a just and wise judge').[60] One may, however, legitimately ask whether the rules are *too* simple and *too* short. It is certainly true to say that it is very difficult—for authors of textbooks, at least!—to describe any form of consistent forensic method that goes beyond generalities. **25.52**

In the editor's view, the starting point is a keynote speech given in 2014, in which Senior Master Gordon-Saker (speaking extrajudicially) said the following: **25.53**

> 'It is said that we will need guidance on how to apply the new test. I disagree. The guidance is already there. It is likely that somebody will in some case or another seek to appeal the approach that has been taken. But I would suggest that there is no reason to suppose that the court hearing the appeal will do other than restate the guidance that has already been given by Jackson LJ in his final report:
>
> > "... I propose that in an assessment of costs on the standard basis, proportionality should prevail over reasonableness and the proportionality test should be applied on a global basis. The court should first make an assessment of reasonable costs, having regard to the individual items in the bill, the time reasonably spent on those items and

---

[57] The added emphasis highlights amendments introduced in the 60th update of the CPR, which came into force on 1 April 2013: see the Civil Procedure (Amendment No 2) Rules 2013 (SI 2013/515).

[58] See Siabkin, N, and Farg, S, 'Will This New Matrix Control Litigation Costs?' (2013) 9 PIJL 10, at 12.

[59] See Jackson, R, 'Technical Aspects of Implementation: Third Lecture in the Implementation Programme', 31 October 2011, Foreword.

[60] Blackstone, W, *Commentaries on the Laws of England* (Oxford: Clarendon Press, 1765), vol 1, at p 42.

the other factors listed in CPR rule 44.5(3). The court should then stand back and consider whether the total figure is proportionate. If the total figure is not proportionate, the court should make an appropriate reduction. There is already a precedent for this approach in relation to the assessment of legal aid costs in criminal proceedings: see *R v Supreme Court Taxing Office ex p John Singh and Co* [1997] 1 Costs LR 49."

In the 15th implementation lecture on 29th May 2012—the lecture entitled "Proportionate Costs"—Lord Neuberger, then MR, quoted that passage and said that it seems likely that the courts will develop the approach to proportionality "as Sir Rupert described it" in that paragraph.'[61]

Thus, if Master Gordon-Saker is right, it would seem that proportionality will now revive 'the *Singh* adjustment'. This is noteworthy, because this was precisely the test that was urged upon the Court of Appeal by the paying party in *Lownds* more than 15 years ago.

25.54 Whilst he was speaking extrajudicially, Neuberger MR has said that 'it is ... true that proportionality can only be finally assessed at the end of a case'.[62] This would seem to be consistent with Master Gordon-Saker's comments and it certainly seems to have become standard practice.

25.55 What still remains a relative mystery, however, is how the adjustment ought to be made. Whilst no more than his own thoughts on the matter (which could well be wrong), the editor believes that it is no coincidence that those factors that are listed in CPR, r 44.3(5), are precisely those factors that would be of especial importance to clients of legal services providers. Clients do not care about reasonableness, necessity, time spent and other such niceties; indeed, they are often aghast at the so-called reasonable fees that their legal services providers charge. They care about more fundamental—usually commercial—matters, such as the amount at stake, how difficult the litigation is, how badly (or well) their opponents are behaving, etc. These are the factors that are listed in CPR, r 44.3(5), and are the factors that will tend to govern the extent to which clients are prepared to put their hands in their pockets.[63] If this is right, then—by analogy with other tests that govern the amounts of costs[64]—the test could well be the amount that a hypothetical reasonable litigant of adequate but not extravagant means would, in all of the relevant circumstances, regard as bearing a 'reasonable relationship' to the factors in CPR, r 44.3(5). Conceptually, this is not a difficult test to apply because—whilst an oversimplification—it boils down to a very simple question: 'Focusing on what really mattered to the litigants, what would a reasonable client have been prepared to pay in all of the relevant circumstances?' For obvious reasons, this will often be less than the 'reasonable' fees (or reasonable and necessary fees) that a line-by-line assessment may determine. In

61 Master Gordon-Saker, 'The Litigation Journey', Keynote speech for the Commercial Litigations Association, 1 October 2014.

62 See Lord Neuberger of Abbotsbury, Master of the Roll, 'Proportionate Costs: Fifteenth Lecture in Implementation Programme', 30 May 2012, at para 18.

63 Different analyses lead to much the same result. Whilst not binding, in *May & Anor v Wavell Group Ltd & Anor* [2017] Lexis Citation 462, at [56], Judge Dight said this: 'Whether the relationship between the costs and the relevant factors is reasonable requires an objective assessment and an objective balance to be undertaken in respect of them with a view to achieving the policy objectives of compensating the receiving party for his expenditure but not requiring the paying party to pay more than the litigation warranted.'

64 *Francis v Francis and Dickerson* [1956] P 87, at 91.

the editor's view, CPR, r 44.3(5), is merely a checklist that guides the court in answering this relatively simple question.

Again, whilst no more than his own views, the editor believes that the fact that no specific forensic method has been identified is intentional and that this is because the way in which the court will apply CPR, r 44.3(5), may vary from case to case.[65] In this regard, it is worth recalling Sir Rupert Jackson's quoting of Coleridge ('Cultivate simplicity') and Blackstone's comments (*lex non exacte definit, sed arbitrio boni viri permittit*), referred to at 25.51–25.52. If the costs that are claimed are grossly disproportionate (or if the costs have yet to be incurred), then a 'bottom-up' approach may be preferred (see 25.57–25.58), but if the costs can readily be brought within proportionate bounds by disallowing specific items or groups of items, then this may be the preferred approach.[66] In this regard, the court is likely to take into account its own resources and will be at liberty to deal with the matter in a way that does not lead it to become embroiled in lengthy, often pointless, arguments about the details of how the costs are to be brought within proportionate bounds. In this regard, the points made in Chapter 26 about collective proportionality may be relevant. **25.56**

Where a 'bottom-up' approach is appropriate, the editor can do little better than cite an article written by District Judge Middleton in *Civil Procedure News*, in which Middleton sought to provide practical guidance by reference to a number of worked examples.[67] That guidance focused on the *ex ante* mechanism (in particular, on budgeting), but the method that he described would, where appropriate, also apply to the *a posteriori* mechanism: **25.57**

> 'Start with a clean sheet of paper, on it list the issues that arise in the case and from these identify the relevant r.44.3(5) factors that are engaged. Only then can an informed view be taken as to the proportionate overall cost of conducting the claim/defence.'[68]

He went on to say that the approach should be 'factor-driven', with the focus firmly on the factors in CPR, r 44.3(5).[69] The purpose of the exercise would be to determine a range of costs that would establish what is and is not proportionate.

Whilst he stressed that the figures were only illustrative of the approach he was taking and should not be taken as setting any type of benchmark, District Judge Middleton went on to describe five hypothetical examples, which are summarised in Table 25.1.[70] **25.58**

Whilst District Judge Middleton did not approach the matter in the way suggested in 25.55, it is worth noting that the figures that he suggested are entirely in keeping with that method. He said that the 'assessment of proportionality is best undertaken ignoring the traditional costs components of hourly rate and time'.[71] This may be so in certain circumstances (such as where the costs have yet to be incurred), but—in the editor's view—when *assessing* costs, it is necessary at least to have regard to the component parts because they **25.58a**

[65] *May & Anor v Wavell Group Ltd & Anor* [2017] Lexis Citation 462, at [58].

[66] An example of this is *Hobbs v Guy's & St Thomas' NHS Foundation Trust* (unreported), 2 November 2015, SCCO, at [35], where Master O'Hare disallowed individual items of expenditure that appeared to be 'inconsistent with the true value of the claim'.

[67] Middleton, S, 'Proportionality: CPR r.44.3(5) in Practice' (2018) 4 CPN 8.

[68] *Ibid*, at 8.

[69] *Ibid*, at 11.

[70] *Ibid*, at pp 9–11.

[71] *Ibid*, at p 8.

Table 25.1 District Judge Middleton's five examples

Type of claim	Features of the claim	Proportionate range (excl VAT and court fees)
Simple contractual dispute over £200,000	Factual dispute as to whether payment of a sum of money was a gift or a loan Fact of the payment not in dispute; only its terms No relevant documentation Oral evidence required	CPR, r 44.3(5)(a), relevant £15,000–£20,000 for each party
Dispute over ownership of small piece of land that the claimant had been using for drainage purposes (septic tank and soakaways)	Issues of adverse possession may arise, as may issues concerning easement and responsibility for upkeep of septic tank May be a number of witnesses Ability to maintain drainage of importance to claimant Some complexity	CPR, r 44.3(5)(b), relevant £35,000–£40,000 for each party
Clinical negligence claim not exceeding £50,000, arising out of an allegedly negligent surgical perforation of the claimant's small bowel	Claimant suffered faecal peritonitis and claimed injury had caused her to have ongoing irritable bowel syndrome Breach, causation and quantum all disputed Relatively small special damages Defendant's solicitors involved only from issue of proceedings Significant complexity	CPR, rr 44.3(5)(a) and (c), relevant £52,500–£60,000 for claimant £47,500–£55,000 for defendant
Road traffic accident of around £100,000 relating to alleged damage to the claimant's spine and subsequent depression	Only quantum in dispute (no contributory negligence) Causation argument of some complexity because of pre-existing spinal symptoms, but psychiatric evidence agreed Orthopaedic experts on both sides Defendant's solicitors involved only from issue of proceedings	CPR, rr 44.3(5)(a) and (c), relevant £35,000–£40,000 for claimant £28,500–£33,500 for defendant
Solicitors' negligence claim for no more than £150,000 relating to the purchase of a property	Claimant said he was not advised of restriction on holiday lettings, and, as a result, paid more than property was worth and lost rental income Defendant said they were not told of claimant's intention to holiday-let property, that claimant was orally told of restriction and that, in any event, there was a failure to mitigate Two factual witnesses Both claimant and defendant had reputations to protect Defendant's solicitors involved only from issue of proceedings	CPR, rr 44.3(5)(a), (c) and (e), relevant £50,000–£57,500 for claimant £45,000–£52,500 for defendant

are relevant background facts.[72] In any event, the figures that District Judge Middleton allowed could easily have been reached by a traditional time-rate analysis, and some judges may prefer to take that approach, especially if they are less experienced. Put otherwise, District Judge Middleton's guidance should, perhaps, be regarded as being sage advice rather than a straightjacket.

Is more guidance required? There are those who cogently argue that more guidance is needed. Dr Sorabji (University College London) had this to say on the point: **25.59**

> 'Ideas such as what level of costs are proportionate in so far as individual litigation is concerned are not immediately obvious. What is needed is practical guidance from the Court of Appeal or via Practice Direction as to how the new theory, and particularly the application of both aspects of proportionality are to be implemented in practice so as to secure equitable access to justice for all court users.'[73]

He went on to add this:

> 'What cannot properly be done … is for [CPR, r 44.3(5)] to remain as it is on the face of the CPR, bereft of the ability to be applied simply, straightforwardly and, if it is ultimately to play a proper role to secure collective proportionality, consistently across all claims.'[74]

Professor Regan (an expert on the law of costs) put the matter in more colourful terms: 'I must say that in the current environment I would feel more comfortable as a crash test dummy than a costs judge.'[75]

It is not only academics that have been unimpressed by the new regime. Simon Gibbs (a well-respected costs lawyer and commentator) had this to say: **25.60**

> 'I have yet to meet a costs practitioner who believes that the new proportionality test is workable. More worryingly, I have yet to meet a costs judge who is able to explain by what margin, if any, a Bill of Costs in relation to routine litigation that has been assessed at £75,000.00 applying the reasonableness test should then be reduced down to if the amount in dispute was only £25,000.00.'[76]

The senior judiciary, however, have been less concerned. Lord Neuberger MR, speaking extrajudicially in 2012, had this to say about whether guidance should be given regarding proportionality: **25.61**

> 'Again the decision as to whether an item was proportionately incurred is case-sensitive, and there may be a period of slight uncertainty as the case law is developed. That is why I have not dealt with what precisely constitutes proportionality and how it is to be assessed. It would be positively dangerous for me to seek to give any sort of specific or detailed guidance in a lecture before the new rule has come into force and been applied. Any question relating to proportionality and any question relating to costs is each very case-sensitive, and when the two questions

---

72 In this regard, whilst not binding, in *May & Anor v Wavell Group Ltd & Anor* [2017] Lexis Citation 462, at [71], Judge Dight has said that he doubts 'that the proper interpretation of the rules requires or indeed entitles a costs judge at the end of an item by item assessment to impose a very substantial reduction on the overall figure without regard to the component parts'.

73 Sorabji, J, *English Civil Justice after the Woolf and Jackson Reforms: A Critical Analysis* (Cambridge: Cambridge University Press, 2014), p 245.

74 *Ibid*, at pp 245–6.

75 Regan, D, 'All Clear as *May v Wavell* Costs Overturned?' (2018) 168 NLJ 19.

76 GWS Law, 'New Proportionality Test', *Legal Costs Blog*, 24 October 2012, available online at http://www.gwslaw.co.uk/2012/10/new-proportionality-test-2/.

come together, that is all the more true. The law on proportionate costs will have to be developed on a case by case basis. This may mean a degree of satellite litigation while the courts work out the law, but we should be ready for that, and I hope it will involve relatively few cases.'[77]

25.62 One has to wonder whether Lord Neuberger MR would have taken the same view had he known that, more than half a decade later, there would still not be any overarching authority on the point. This, perhaps, was why Sir Rupert Jackson (speaking extrajudicially immediately before his retirement in 2018) said this:

> 'It was expected that there would be a cluster of test cases in which the Court of Appeal would apply the new rule to different scenarios. That has not happened. The profession is becoming impatient. The remedy lies in their own hands. The Court of Appeal can only decide the cases which come before it. As an interim measure I have discussed with DJ Middleton (who has huge experience of applying the proportionality rule, as well as writing about costs and teaching at the Judicial College) whether he could provide some practical assistance. He tells me that he will write an article for the April issue of *Civil Procedure News* in which he takes five different scenarios and explains how he would apply the proportionality rule if setting budgets in those cases ... Obviously that article will not have a higher status than any other article which appears in legal journals.'[78]

The article to which Sir Rupert referred is that which is described at 25.57–25.58. It is implicit in what Sir Rupert said that he believes that more guidance is required.

25.63 **The measure of proportionate costs under the pre-2013 method (that is, '*Lownds* stage two')** What is said below applies only under the pre-2013 method (see 25.17).[79]

25.64 If the court finds that the costs claimed are disproportionate in accordance with stage one of the *Lownds* test (see 25.37–25.46), a test of necessity will apply to each and every item in the bill of costs. It is not open to the court, on having made such a finding, to find that certain items only are proportionate and to apply a test of reasonableness to only those items.[80] (For the converse, where the court finds that the costs globally are proportionate, see 25.41.)

25.65 The requisite standard of necessity is not a fixed standard, but a variable standard—or a 'sensible' standard, as Lord Woolf MR put it.[81] Although the requisite standard is higher than that of reasonableness (or, in Moreland J's words, more 'stringent'[82]), it is still a standard that a competent practitioner should be able to achieve without undue difficulty.[83] In a similar vein, Lord Neuberger MR had this to say on the point:

> 'It does not seem to me to be a profitable or useful exercise for this court to describe in abstract the difference between assessing whether an item has been necessarily incurred and assessing whether an item has been reasonably incurred, save to confirm that the former hurdle is higher, but it does not carry with it the strictest sense of necessity.'[84]

---

[77] See Lord Neuberger of Abbotsbury, Master of the Roll, 'Proportionate Costs: Fifteenth Lecture in Implementation Programme', 30 May 2012, paras 14 and 15.

[78] See Jackson, R, 'Was It All Worth It?', Lecture to the Cambridge Law Faculty, 5 March 2018.

[79] See CPR, r 44.3(7).

[80] *Motto & Ors v Trafigura Ltd & Anor* [2011] EWCA Civ 1150, at [46].

[81] *Lownds v Home Office* [2002] EWCA Civ 365, at [37].

[82] *Giambrone v JMC Holidays Ltd (formerly Sunworld Holidays Ltd)* [2002] EWHC 2932 (QB), at [33].

[83] *Lownds v Home Office* [2002] EWCA Civ 365, at [37].

[84] *Motto & Ors v Trafigura Ltd & Anor* [2011] EWCA Civ 1150, at [52].

In deciding what is necessary, the conduct of the paying party (or any other opponent) is relevant. If they were uncooperative, then that may have rendered necessary costs that would otherwise have been unnecessary.[85] **25.66**

There is authority to suggest that if the court applies the two-stage test but finds that the costs continue to be disproportionate, then the correct approach is not to reduce the costs to a level that appears to be proportionate, but to revisit the item-by-item assessment in an effort to achieve further reductions.[86] **25.67**

As is set out below, three puisne judges have stressed the fact that a finding that a test of necessity will apply is not always a calamity for the receiving party. **25.68**

- Moreland J has commented that a finding that the costs are disproportionate does not penalise the receiving party nor does it determine the amount of the assessment; rather, it merely regulates the manner of the detailed assessment, and requires the receiving party to justify each item in the bill as being both necessary and reasonable.[87]
- Lewison J has commented that a finding of disproportionality does not shut out the receiving party from obtaining the costs of the exercise in question; rather, it requires that party to demonstrate that the costs were necessary.[88]
- Eady J has commented that the principle of proportionality does not always mean that corners need to be cut: in a case involving grave allegations, it may be that justice requires that significant time and money are spent in arriving at the right answer.[89]

Miscellaneous topics regarding whether costs claimed are disproportionate (both pre-2013 and post 2013 methods)

Much of what is set out below relates to cases decided under the pre-2013 method. That said, other than where the contrary is obvious from the context, a great deal of what is said is relevant (at least by analogy) to the post-2013 method. **25.69**

Judicial discretion and use of language Lewison J has commented that the issue of whether costs are disproportionate is one of judgement and 'feel', and that in this respect an experienced costs judge may take into account their experience of litigation generally.[90] There is no requirement that disproportionality has to 'jump off the page' or that the costs need to be obviously disproportionate.[91] Whilst not binding, Master Hurst has suggested that the following test of 'stepping into the client's shoes' may be of assistance in an appropriate case: **25.70**

> 'One way of testing the proportionality of the costs is to ask whether a litigant, paying the costs out of his own pocket, would have been prepared to pay that level of costs in order to achieve success. For the purpose of the test the Claimant must be deemed to be a person of adequate means. That is someone whose means are neither inadequate nor super abundant ...'[92]

---

[85] *Lownds v Home Office* [2002] EWCA Civ 365, at [38].
[86] *Hosking v Michaelides* [2003] EWHC 3029 (Ch).
[87] *Giambrone v JMC Holidays Ltd (formerly Sunworld Holidays Ltd)* [2002] EWHC 2932 (QB), at [32]–[33].
[88] *Ross v Stonewood Securities Ltd* [2004] EWHC 2235 (Ch), at [26].
[89] *Abu v MGN* [2002] EWHC 2345 (QB) (albeit that Eady J was not dealing with proportionality in the context of costs, but in a more general context).
[90] *Ross v Stonewood Securities Ltd* [2004] EWHC 2235 (Ch), at [27].
[91] *Giambrone v JMC Holidays Ltd (formerly Sunworld Holidays Ltd)* [2002] EWHC 2932 (QB), at [53], *per* Moreland J.
[92] *King v Telegraph Group Ltd* [2005] EWHC 90015 (Costs), at [54].

It is all but certain that these comments would apply under the post-2013 approach.

25.71 Under the pre-2013 method, the mere fact that a judge, having found that the costs are not disproportionate, refers to costs as being 'necessary' would not give rise to grounds for concern because that phrase may be meant in its ordinary sense to convey a notion of justification.[93]

25.72 **Appropriate use of court time** Moreland J has explained that a costs judge is not required to 'plough through [a] gargantuan mass of material' solely for the purposes of deciding whether the costs are or are not disproportionate; even in complex litigation, an experienced costs judge ought not to be required to spend more than an hour or two on the issue.[94] Of course, this would be less likely to be an issue under the post-2013 method because the issue will generally be addressed only after the court has carried out the item-by-item assessment.

25.73 **Proportionality and the financial positions of the parties** Akenhead J has explained that the financial positions of the parties may be relevant to the issue of proportionality: if, for example, an individual or a company is being sued for everything that they or it is worth, it may not be disproportionate for that individual or company to engage Queen's counsel (QC) even if the amount in issue is objectively not very large.[95] CPR, r 44.3(5), makes no mention of the financial position of the parties, but it is likely that this, in an appropriate case, would be a factor that the court could take into account under CPR, r 44.3(5)(e).

25.74 A paying party's impecuniosity could well be relevant to the case management of a claim, but it has no bearing on the application of the test of proportionality.[96]

25.75 **The relationship between proportionality and the value of the claim** As to the relevance of the value of claim, Lord Neuberger MR had this to say: '[T]he value of a claim in monetary terms, even where it is the only relief claimed, cannot be the sole guide to proportionality, although it will be a rare case where it is not a significant factor.'[97] These comments were made about the pre-2013 method, but they would undoubtedly still be true under CPR, r 44.3(5)(a).

25.76 When considering the amount of costs, the issue is whether it is fair to require the paying party to pay the sums that are claimed; the court should not be concerned with the position between solicitor and client.[98] There is no reason to believe that the position is any different under the post-2013 method.

25.77 It has long been recognised that the relationship between the costs incurred and the value of the claim may not be a reliable guide to whether the costs are disproportionate. Article

---

93 See *Finglands Coachways Ltd v O'Hare* [2014] EWHC 1513 (QB), at [26], *per* Cranston J.

94 *Giambrone v JMC Holidays Ltd (formerly Sunworld Holidays Ltd)* [2002] EWHC 2932 (QB), at [37]–[38]. It is not always easy to deal with issues so quickly: see, eg, Master Wright's comments in *Holland v PKF (a firm)* [2004] EWHC 9043 (Costs), at [58].

95 *Savoye and Savoye Ltd v Spicers Ltd* [2015] EWHC 33 (TCC), at [17(e)].

96 *Ilangaratne v British Medical Association* [2005] EWHC 2096 (Ch), at [10], On a related point, see also the pre-CPR case of *MB Building Contractors Ltd v Ahmed* (1998) The Independent, 23 November.

97 *Motto & Ors v Trafigura Ltd & Anor* [2011] EWCA Civ 1150, at [42].

98 *Habib Bank Ltd v Ahmed* [2004] EWCA Civ 805 (the Court of Appeal was carrying out a summary assessment, but notwithstanding this it is clear that they applied the two-stage *Lownds* test).

11.1 of the Costs Practice Direction (CPD) used to give the following guidance in that regard:

> 'In applying the test of proportionality the court will have regard to rule 1.1(2)(c). The relationship between the total of the costs incurred and the financial value of the claim may not be a reliable guide. A fixed percentage cannot be applied in all cases to the value of the claim in order to ascertain whether or not the costs are proportionate.'

It is likely that these comments would continue to have at least some resonance under the post-2013 method. That said, it should be borne in mind that a decision was taken not to publish a practice direction dealing with the operation of the CPR, r 44.3(5) (see 25.52). In any event, it should be noted that, even under the pre-2013 method, Black LJ had pointed out that this guidance says that the financial value of the claim *may* not be a reliable guide,[99] the implication being that, in some circumstances, it may be.

Low-value litigation and proportionality There will always be costs that are necessary for the conduct of the claim. In recognition of this, CPD, art 11.2, used to give the following guidance: **25.78**

> 'In any proceedings there will be costs which will inevitably be incurred and which are necessary for the successful conduct of the case. Solicitors are not required to conduct litigation at rates which are uneconomic. Thus in a modest claim the proportion of costs is likely to be higher than in a large claim, and may even equal or possibly exceed the amount in dispute.'

Whilst the points that are made remain factually correct, for the reasons set out in 25.48, it is not the case under the post-2013 method that costs that were necessarily, but disproportionately, incurred will be recoverable. That said, it is possible that such issues may still be taken into account in the context of CPR, r 44.3(5)(c) ('the complexity of the litigation').

Whilst no more than an aside, it is worth noting that other jurisdictions have, in a conscious effort to encourage settlement, attempted to make very small claims hard to afford.[100] **25.79**

High-value litigation and proportionality The new focus on proportionality in general seems to be having some effect in high-value commercial litigation. In a case in which the parties had spent £242,700 and £165,400, respectively, in the context of a claim worth US$119 million, Mr Justice Males described the costs of a one-day contested jurisdiction hearing as 'grossly disproportionate'.[101] He thought that it was extraordinary that the parties had spent over £400,000 to determine which court should decide the issue when both accepted that either court could decide it justly. He summarily assessed the costs at £75,000. **25.80**

Non-monetary factors and proportionality Not all claims are solely about money (as is now expressly recognised by CPR, r 44.3(5)(b)), so it may be necessary to take non-monetary factors into account.[102] Whilst there is no authority on the point, the principles at 17.109 may, by analogy, have a bearing. **25.81**

---

[99] See *Morgan v Spirit Group Ltd* [2011] EWCA Civ 58, at [38].

[100] Williams, P, *Report of the Review of Scales of Legal Professional Fees in General Jurisdictions* (Canberra: Attorney-General's Department, 1998), at n 64, c 4.

[101] *Vitol Bahrain EC v Nasdec General Trading LLC* (2013) 163 (7584) NLJ 20, at [11].

[102] Under the pre-2013 method, see *Cox v Carter v MGN Ltd* [2006] EWHC 1235 (QB), at [28], *per* Eady J.

25.82 **Value added tax (VAT) and proportionality** By established practice under the pre-2013 method,[103] the costs that are to be taken into account are the base costs (including disbursements), exclusive of VAT. The exclusion of VAT is because it could have had no bearing on the steps taken in the litigation. It is likely that the same approach will apply under the post-2013 method.

25.83 **Success fees and proportionality** Under the pre-2013 method (which is the appropriate method to use when assessing success fees[104]), a success fee would not be reduced simply on the grounds that, when it is added to reasonable and proportionate base costs, the total appears disproportionate.[105]

25.84 **After-the-event (ATE) premiums and proportionality** With the exception of certain clinical negligence premiums,[106] the pre-2013 method will continue to apply to the assessment of ATE premiums.[107]

25.85 Akenhead J, speaking of the pre-2013 method, has confirmed that the basic costs rules and practice about reasonableness and proportionality apply to ATE premiums, and that to the extent that a premium was unreasonable or disproportionate, it should be disallowed, at least on a standard basis assessment.[108] That said, the question of whether an additional liability is proportionate must be considered separately from the question of whether base costs are proportionate.[109] In practice, this means that unless there is a specific challenge to the proportionality of the premium, the court will tend to disregard it entirely for the purpose of proportionality. This does not mean that additional liabilities will escape the test of proportionality because it may be challenged individually.[110] Indeed, there are instances of the court reducing premiums *solely* on the grounds of proportionality (usually by finding that the particular choice of premium was disproportionate).[111]

25.86 Under the pre-2013 method, the test of proportionality applies in a way that takes into account the macroeconomic factors (see 54.136–54.137 and 54.144). In simplistic terms, the court recognises, as a matter of pragmatism, that if, for good macroeconomic reasons, the market dictates that it will not offer less expensive policies, then it would be 'necessary'

---

103 See *Giambrone v JMC Holidays Ltd (formerly Sunworld Holidays Ltd)* [2002] EWHC 2932 (QB), at [43], *per* Moreland J.

104 *BNM v MGN Ltd* [2017] EWCA Civ 1767, at [66]–[85], *per* Etherton MR.

105 See the now-revoked CPD, art 11.9.

106 Those premiums that are claimed pursuant to the Recovery of Costs Insurance Premiums in Clinical Negligence Proceedings Regulations 2013 (SI 2013/92) are subject to the post-2013 method. This is because those regulations are supplemented by PD 48, para 4.2, which states that 'the provisions in force in the CPR prior to 1 April 2013 relating to funding arrangements will not apply': see *BNM v MGN Ltd* [2017] EWCA Civ 1767, at [68], *per* Etherton MR. See also *Peterborough v Stamford Hospitals NHS Trust* [2017] EWCA 1941 (Civ), at [62], *per* Lewison LJ.

107 *BNM v MGN Ltd* [2017] EWCA Civ 1767, at [66]–[85], *per* Etherton MR.

108 *Redwing Construction Ltd v Wishart* [2011] EWHC 19 (TCC), at [15].

109 CPD, art 11.5.

110 Although not binding, Master Hurst's analysis in *King v Telegraph Group plc* [2005] EWHC 90015 (Costs), at [17]–[19], seems to support this view. Master Hurst concluded: 'Both the base costs and the success fee separately must be assessed at reasonable and proportionate figures but, if the two figures taken together appear, as they inevitably will, to be disproportionate, that is not a factor to be taken into account.'

111 See, eg, Baker in *Re RSA Pursuit Test Cases* [2005] EWHC 90003 (Costs); see also *Kelly v Black Horse Ltd* (unreported), 27 September 2013, SCCO, *per* Senior Costs Judge Hurst. Neither of these cases are binding.

(within the meaning of the *Lownds* test) for the receiving party to take out a policy that is less than ideally priced. Brooke LJ had the following to say on the topic:

> 'Necessity ... may be demonstrated by the application of strategic considerations which travel beyond the dictates of the particular case. Thus, it may include the unavoidable characteristics of the market in insurance of this kind. It does so because this very market is integral to the means of providing access to justice in civil disputes in what may be called the post-legal aid world.'[112]

In practical terms, this means that if a solicitor is reasonably tied to recommending a particular contract of insurance to all of its clients with relevant viable claims and if the receiving party can show that that was as a result of a legitimate need to avoid adverse selection, then the premium is likely to be allowed.

Not all judges agree with this, however. In a recent case that is not binding, Judge Smith found that the court is not permitted to take into account factors extraneous to the case itself, such as the interests of the ATE insurance industry.[113] It is not clear, however, whether Judge Smith had been made fully aware of the importance of macroeconomics and the constraints that it imposes on clients. That said, it is possible that his decision heralds a less tolerant approach towards the concerns of the insurance industry. **25.87**

One method of ensuring proportionality of premiums is to link them to the value of the claim. Whilst not binding, Master Hurst has found that such an approach is not, in principle, champertous.[114] A similar method is to link the premium to the level of costs generally. Again, Master Hurst has found that such a premium is untouched by the law of champerty.[115] **25.88**

The relationship between budgets and proportionality The authors of *Cook on Costs 2017* (both of whom are experienced costs judges) say that they: **25.89**

> '... remain firmly of the view that revisiting reasonableness and proportionality on assessment will be extremely rare and can only be done within an argument that there is "good reason" to depart from the budget—eg where decisions on reasonableness and proportionality have been made by the costs managing judge on the basis of a high value claim that transpires to have been exaggerated.'[116]

This is a topic that is addressed more fully at 12.159–12.160.

Capped costs and proportionality Where the costs claimed in a bill of costs have been limited or capped in some way, Lloyd J has commented (*obiter*) that the court should look at the proportionality or otherwise of the amount claimed, rather than at the original **25.90**

---

112 *Rogers v Merthyr Tydfil County Borough Council* [2006] EWCA Civ 1134, at [105].

113 See *Demouilpied v Stockport NHS Foundation Trust* (unreported), 4 November 2011, Manchester County Court, at [20]–[22].

114 *Pirie v Ayling* [2003] EWHC 9006 (Costs)—although this case is not binding (see the discussion at 30.48).

115 See *Re RSA Pursuit Test Cases* [2005] EWHC 90003 (Costs), at [283]–[297], esp [260]. On the facts of that case, in which the premium was in the same order of magnitude as the costs, he found that, for that approach to work, the costs upon which the premium is based must themselves be proportionate. This case is not binding, but is usually accepted as being highly persuasive.

116 *Cook on Costs 2017* (LexisNexis, online), para 14.3.

amount that might have been claimed had the cap or limit not been applied.[117] No doubt, this remains true under the post-2013 method.

25.91 **Proportionality and dishonesty** Whilst he was dealing with proportionality in a context other those discussed in this chapter, Waller LJ has made it clear that there is no general rule that a losing party who can establish dishonesty must receive all of their costs of establishing that dishonesty, however disproportionate they may be.[118] This will no doubt remain true under the post-2013 method, but an opponent's dishonesty would now undoubtedly fall within the ambit of CPR, r 44.3(5)(d).

25.92 **Proportionality and the costs of work relating to alternative dispute resolution (ADR)** Akenhead J has explained that where, in the course of ADR, work is carried out that duplicates the work done in proceedings, the court is able to take that work into account for the purpose of deciding whether the costs claimed are proportionate.[119] No doubt, the same remains the case under the post-2013 method.

25.93 **Settlements and hindsight** Where a claimant has settled a claim for an amount that is palpably less than they were seeking, the settlement sum may be good evidence of the true value of the claim. In a slightly different context (whether the small claims regime should apply[120]), Peter Smith J had the following to say—under the pre-2013 method—about a claim that had been exaggerated:

> 'It is appropriate that the costs which the claimant recovers on the expense claim should be measured by its recovery. They have recovered £5,000. Once again, they chose to take the £5,000. If they were not happy with that or they wanted to protect their costs position further, they could have proceeded to trial to seek an account and to seek to establish liability beyond that. They have chosen not to do so.'[121]

25.94 Similarly, Gloster LJ has said that, where a claim is said to be exaggerated, the trial judge may use hindsight for the purposes of testing that issue and making an order for costs.[122] This may be so, but this approach would not be permitted to make inroads into the principle that the court may not use hindsight for the assessment of costs. Lord Neuberger MR had this to say about the rule against hindsight:

> '[T]hat does not mean that one simply ignores the amount actually recovered, as it can provide some sort of reality check. For instance, where the sum eventually awarded or agreed is substantially less than the amount claimed, that may (and I emphasise "may") call into question the notion that the claim was genuinely or reasonably thought to be worth what it was claimed to be worth when it was first raised and while it was being prosecuted.'[123]

25.95 Whilst there is no authority on the point, it is likely that the same is true under the post-2013 method. This is because CPR, r 44.3(5)(c) and (b), expressly refers to what was in

---

[117] *Ortwein v Rugby Mansions Ltd* [2003] EWHC 2077 (Ch), at [31].

[118] *Ultraframe (UK) Ltd v Fielding* [2006] EWCA Civ 1660, at [36]. This lengthy judgment has, in this context, been summarised by Briggs J in *Bank of Tokyo-Mitsubishi UFJ Ltd v Baskan Gida Sanayi Ve Pazarlama AS* [2009] EWHC 1696 (Ch), at [15]–[19].

[119] *Savoye and Savoye Ltd v Spicers Ltd* [2015] EWHC 33 (TCC), at [17(c)].

[120] The incidence of costs.

[121] *E Ivor Hughes Educational Foundation v Leach* [2005] EWHC 1317 (Ch), at [25].

[122] *Walker Construction (UK) Ltd v Quayside Homes Ltd* [2014] EWCA Civ 93, at [91].

[123] *Motto & Ors v Trafigura Ltd & Anor* [2011] EWCA Civ 1150, at [42].

issue in the proceedings, and this is very different from the ultimate value of the amount or remedy awarded or agreed.

Case plans, time and proportionality One factor that often sways the court towards a finding that base costs are disproportionate is where the court is unable to find any coherent case plan in the receiving party's file of papers.[124] The points made at 25.23 are relevant in this regard. Akenhead J has made it clear that, when considering time, one can look at the total times claimed by the fees earners, saying—in a no doubt intentionally extreme hypothetical example—that if 3,000 hours of lawyers' time were to be incurred on a case that involved only a one-day hearing, that might well point to a disproportionate incurrence of time spent.[125] **25.96**

Compliance with pre-action protocols and proportionality Whilst non-compliance with a pre-action protocol may count against a party, compliance on the part of a receiving party will not necessarily mean that their costs are proportionate.[126] **25.97**

Discussions and correspondence between fee earners Each case will be determined on its own facts. The mere fact that there may have been a great deal of time spent in discussion or correspondence between fee earners—provided that it is recoverable in principle (see 49.66–49.67)[127]—does not necessarily mean that the resultant costs are disproportionate. **25.98**

Admissibility of notes from counsel A party may seek to rely on a note prepared by counsel—that is, counsel who was involved in the claim—for the purposes of persuading the court that the costs are proportionate or disproportionate, as the case may be. While dealing with such a note in the context of hourly rates rather than proportionality, Teare J has found that such notes are admissible notwithstanding the fact that they may be partly opinion.[128] **25.99**

Group litigation, test cases, etc, and proportionality Akenhead J has explained that the fact that a case is a test case or in the nature of a test case may be relevant to the issues of proportionality.[129] This is undoubtedly still true under the post-2013 method because it would be a 'wider factor' within the meaning of CPR, r 44.3(5)(e). **25.100**

Moreland J has explained that whilst it cannot be expected that group litigation involving very small claims should result in very small costs, there should be economies of scale even when each individual claimant has to be dealt with individually (see 65.91).[130] The test of proportionality applies to interim assessments in group litigation[131]—although, in practice, the court may have difficulty in applying the test if the totality of the costs is not **25.101**

---

124 See, eg, *O'Leary v Tunnelcraft Ltd* (2011) (unreported), 19 October 2011, SCCO, *per* Master O'Hare, in which the costs exceeded the claimant's solicitors' costs estimate and in which no case plan had been prepared.

125 *Savoye and Savoye Ltd v Spicers Ltd* [2015] EWHC 33 (TCC), at [17].

126 Whilst not binding, see *Prior v Silverline International Ltd* (unreported), 8 July 2015, Liverpool County Court, *per* Judge Wood QC.

127 See *TUI UK Ltd v Tickell* [2016] EWHC 2741 (QB), at [23]–[31], *per* Laing J.

128 *A v Chief Constable of South Yorkshire* [2008] EWHC 1658 (QB), at [22]–[23].

129 *Savoye and Savoye Ltd v Spicers Ltd* [2015] EWHC 33 (TCC), at [17(d)].

130 *Giambrone v JMC Holidays Ltd (formerly Sunworld Holidays Ltd)* [2002] EWHC 2932 (QB), at [52].

131 *Ibid*, at [48], *per* Morland J.

known to the judge who is carrying out the assessment, this being a common occurrence where the litigation settles piecemeal.

25.102 **Chains of Part 20 claims** Where there is a chain of Part 20 claims and where the costs liability passes down the chain to a single order at the end, the chain of bills of costs should generally be assessed at the same time and with reference to each other.[132]

25.103 **Appeals and appeals** Moreland J has expressed a firm view that appeals against decisions about the proportionality of costs are to be discouraged.[133]

132 *SCT Finance v Bolton* [2002] EWCA Civ 56, at [56], *per* Waller LJ.
133 *Giambrone v JMC Holidays Ltd (formerly Sunworld Holidays Ltd)* [2002] EWHC 2932 (QB), at [56]; Henriques J in *Young v JR Smart (Builders) Ltd* [2004] EWHC 103.

26

THE OVERRIDING OBJECTIVE, COLLECTIVE PROPORTIONALITY AND RELIEF FROM SANCTIONS

This chapter deals with the following topics: **26.01**

- the overriding objective (26.02);
- the historical approach under the Rules of the Supreme Court (RSC) and the County Court Rules (CCR) (26.09);
- the new approach to justice under the Civil Procedure Rules (CPR) (26.15);
- the overriding objective—early days and competing interpretations (26.17);
- collective proportionality (26.26); and
- relief from sanctions (26.48).

The Overriding Objective

The Civil Procedure Rules (CPR) were introduced in 1999 as a 'new procedural code'[1] (see 1.156) which was to usher in a new philosophy of litigation. As Lord Hobhouse said as long ago as 2003, the CPR marked an 'important shift in judicial philosophy [away] from the traditional philosophy that previously dominated the administration of justice'.[2] As will be explained below, it was a shift in philosophy that was intended to result in significant aspects of the approach to litigation under the Rules of the Supreme Court (RSC)[3] and County Court Rules (CCR)[4] being abandoned.[5] **26.02**

The new approach was encapsulated in two major innovations. First, the formal introduction of active case management[6]—that being a reform that has since expanded into active *costs* management—along with the imposition of a duty on parties to help the court to manage litigation effectively (see 26.06).[7] This was a radical inroad into the fundamental principle of party **26.03**

---

[1] CPR, r 1.1(1). For an extended discussion, see Sorabji, J, *English Civil Justice after the Woolf and Jackson Reforms: A Critical Analysis* (Cambridge: Cambridge University Press, 2014).

[2] *Three Rivers District Council & Ors v Governor and Company of the Bank of England (No 3)* [2003] 2 AC 1, at [153].

[3] SI 1776/1965.

[4] SI 1687/1981.

[5] *Hashtroodi v Hancock* [2004] EWCA Civ 652, at [16], *per* Dyson LJ.

[6] CPR, r 3.1.

[7] See further, on the scope of parties and their legal representatives' duty to assist the court, as well as the risk of adverse cost sanctions for a failure to carry out this duty appropriately: *Hertsmere Primary Care Trust v Rabindra-Anandh* [2005] EWHC 320 (Ch); *Hallam Estates Ltd v Baker* [2014] EWCA Civ 661; *Davies v Forrett* [2015] EWHC 1761 (QB); *Emmanuel v Revenue & Customs* [2017] EWHC 1253 (Ch).

autonomy, but it was not as radical as the second innovation, which was the introduction of an overarching purposive provision that guided the court and litigants in their approach to the proper conduct of litigation—namely, the overriding objective.

26.04 The overriding objective in its original iteration merely required the court to deal with cases justly, but, from 2013 onwards, it has required the court to deal with cases justly *and* at proportionate cost. The relevant provisions are set out in CPR, r 1.1, which now reads as follows:

> '(1) These Rules are a new procedural code with the overriding objective of enabling the court to deal with cases justly and at proportionate cost.
>
> (2) Dealing with a case justly and at proportionate cost includes, so far as is practicable—
> (a) ensuring that the parties are on an equal footing;
> (b) saving expense;
> (c) dealing with the case in ways which are proportionate—
> (i) to the amount of money involved;
> (ii) to the importance of the case;
> (iii) to the complexity of the issues; and
> (iv) to the financial position of each party;
> (d) ensuring that it is dealt with expeditiously and fairly;
> (e) allotting to it an appropriate share of the court's resources, while taking into account the need to allot resources to other cases; and
> (f) enforcing compliance with rules, practice directions and orders.'

There is no practice direction that supplements the overriding objective.

26.05 Thus the CPR are a procedural code with the objective of enabling the court to deal with cases justly and at proportionate cost—that is, so far as is practicable, enabling cases to be managed in a way that:

- ensures that the parties are on an equal footing;
- saves expense;
- is proportionate in terms of the amount of money involved, the importance of the case, the complexity of the issues and the financial position of each party;
- is expeditious and fair;
- uses an appropriate share of the court's resources, whilst taking into account the need to allot resources to other cases; and
- enforces compliance with rules, practice directions and orders.

The last two of these points give rise to issues that may be called 'collective proportionality', a fundamental concept that is addressed at 26.26–26.47.

26.06 CPR, r 1.3, adds the following: 'The parties are required to help the court to further the overriding objective.' Thus the parties are required to assist the court to achieve those objectives set out in 26.05.

26.07 Finally, CPR, r 1.4, gives the following guidance about how the court is to actively manage cases:

> '(1) The court must further the overriding objective by actively managing cases.
>
> (2) Active case management includes—
> (a) encouraging the parties to co-operate with each other in the conduct of the proceedings;
> (b) identifying the issues at an early stage;

(c) deciding promptly which issues need full investigation and trial and accordingly disposing summarily of the others;
(d) deciding the order in which issues are to be resolved;
(e) encouraging the parties to use an alternative dispute resolution procedure if the court considers that appropriate and facilitating the use of such procedure;
(f) helping the parties to settle the whole or part of the case;
(g) fixing timetables or otherwise controlling the progress of the case;
(h) considering whether the likely benefits of taking a particular step justify the cost of taking it;
(i) dealing with as many aspects of the case as it can on the same occasion;
(j) dealing with the case without the parties needing to attend at court;
(k) making use of technology; and
(l) giving directions to ensure that the trial of a case proceeds quickly and efficiently.'

As is explained below, early implementation of the overriding objective was flawed. The problem was that its meaning and application were not made clear. In particular, CPR, r 1.1, contained many open-textured terms,[8] each of which was capable of being interpreted and balanced against other terms with varying effect. Lack of clarity and certainty allowed litigants to take the path of least resistance, and hence to conduct litigation in much the same way as they did under the RSC and CCR (see 26.09–26.14). These things prevented the fundamental shift (see 26.02) that Lord Hobhouse had anticipated. As is explained below, since late 2013 onwards, there has been a change in judicial attitudes in the sense that the overriding objective is now being interpreted in a way that is more in keeping with what was originally intended. This, to a large extent, is because there is an appreciation of the need to take collective proportionality into account. **26.08**

The Approach under the Rules of the Supreme Court and County Court Rules

It is axiomatic—although sometimes forgotten—that the civil courts exist for the benefit of society as a whole; they are not, as the Supreme Court has made clear, simply the means to provide a private benefit to individual litigants engaged in the pursuit of judgment.[9] They exist—and their procedures exist—to enable persons to vindicate private and public law legal and equitable rights and obligations, thereby supporting democracy and the rule of law. This can be said to be their constitutional role. **26.09**

From the 1870s until the introduction of the CPR in 1999, the civil courts sought to fulfil that constitutional role in only one way: civil procedure was to be designed and operated so that individual civil disputes were decided on their substantive merits.[10] Their purpose—the then equivalent of the overriding objective—was to ensure that justice was done on the merits of each case.[11] This was achieved in a number of ways, as follows. **26.10**

[8] Waismann, F, 'Verifiability' (1945) 19 Proceedings of the Aristotelian Society 119; Hart, HLA, *The Concept of Law* (3rd edn, Oxford: Clarendon Press, 2012).
[9] *R (UNISON) v Lord Chancellor* [2017] UKSC 51, at [66] *et seq*.
[10] *Cropper v Smith* (1884) 26 Ch D 700, at 710 and 711.
[11] *Collins v The Vestry of Paddington* (1879–80) LR 5 QBD 368, at 380; *Kurtz v Spence* [1887] LR 36 Ch D 770, at 776.

- **Procedure was to be straightforward** Rules of pleading required parties to set out the facts underpinning their case, to provide a narrative and to define the scope of the dispute.[12] Parties were not to plead evidence nor were they to plead law; this was important because it ensured that procedural points could not be taken on the question of whether a statement of case articulated the 'right' law (a problem that had bedevilled the common-law courts prior to the introduction of the RSC).[13]
- **Wide latitude to plead and re-plead real issues** Parties were to be given wide latitude to ensure that their claims set out the real issues in dispute. If this meant that pleadings had to be amended to cure a pleading error or to clarify an issue, such an amendment was—even late in the day—generally to be allowed. The central issues in considering whether to grant permission to amend was whether amendment would facilitate the court's task in determining claims on their substantive merits and whether payment of costs could compensate the other party to the claim for any prejudice caused by the amendment.[14]
- **Tolerance of procedural error and non-compliance** In a similar vein, procedural mishaps and failings in compliance were not to stand in the way of determining claims on their substantive merits. Procedural non-compliance did not of itself invalidate claims. A remedy was to be permitted where, in the case of procedural error, the non-defaulting party could be compensated in costs for any prejudice caused by the default. Referring to *Cropper v Smith*,[15] Edmund Davies LJ described the following words of Bowen LJ as enunciating an 'all-embracing principle':

  > 'I know of no kind of error or mistake which, if not fraudulent or intended to overreach, the court ought not to correct, if it can be done without injustice to the other party. Courts do not exist for the sake of discipline, but for the sake of deciding matters in controversy, and I do not regard such amendment as a matter of favour or of grace ... It seems to me that as soon as it appears that the way in which a party has framed his case will not lead to a decision of the real matter in controversy, it is as much a matter of right on his part to have it corrected, if it can be done without injustice, as anything else in the case is a matter of right.'[16]

- **Specific promotion of justice on the merits** In addition to this general attitude towards procedural error and non-compliance, there were specific provisions.[17] The aim was to ensure that all of the relevant parties and issues were before the court in a single set of proceedings, so that all relevant matters, evidence, etc, could be decided at

[12] RSC Ord 18, r 7.

[13] Gordley, J, 'The Common Law in the Twentieth Century: Some Unfinished Business' (2000) 88 Cali L Rev 1815, at 1818.

[14] RSC Ord 20, r 8. See also *Tildesley v Harper* (1878) 10 Ch D 393, at 396 and 397; *Cropper v Smith* (1884) 26 Ch D 700, at 710 and 711; *Clarapede & Co v Commercial Union Association* (1883) 32 WR 262, at 263; *GL Baker Ltd v Medway Building & Supplies Ltd* [1958] 1 WLR 1216, at 1231; *Smith v Baron* (1991) The Times, 1 February, CA.

[15] *Cropper v Smith* (1884) 26 Ch D 700, at 710 and 711.

[16] *Associated Leisure v Associated Newspapers* [1970] 2 QB 450, at 457, *per* Edmund-Davies LJ, quoting *Cropper v Smith* (1884) 26 Ch D 700, at 710 and 711, *per* Bowen LJ.

[17] A liberal approach was, for instance, taken to joinder of parties and of issues, contrary to a far more restrictive approach that had prevailed in the common-law courts prior to the introduction of the RSC.

the same time.[18] Most significantly, a strongly liberal approach was taken to disclosure:[19] no stone was incapable of being turned in the pursuit of accurate findings of fact.

Thus procedure was—in the oft-repeated phrase—the 'handmaiden of justice'.[20] It was not to stand in the way of the court securing justice on the merits. Underpinning the justice-on-the-merits approach was a central assumption—namely, that the court's focus was always on 'the case in hand'[21] and on the imperative of ensuring that it concluded in a decision on the merits. **26.11**

The old approach to relief from the consequences of procedural error or non-compliance

The above philosophy was most obvious where there had been procedural error or non-compliance. Where such issues arose, the focus was on whether justice on the merits in the individual case was furthered by allowing whatever relief was sought. In particular, no consideration was given to the court's ability to secure justice on the merits in *other* cases. Put otherwise, the possibility that granting relief might or would have a negative impact on other court users did not form part of the test articulated in *Cropper v Smith* (see 26.10). **26.12**

The consequences of the old approach

This approach came at a price. It produced a number of adverse—and occasionally perverse—consequences. Disproportionate cost and delay were endemic, procedural obligations were complied with when convenient to the parties and applications for relief were transformed into hard-fought procedural battles.[22] **26.13**

This was only to be expected: if both the court and the parties were to concern themselves solely with securing justice on the merits, expenditure and time would inevitably be of secondary interest. Moreover, treating rules as if they were optional had two additional adverse consequences, as follows. **26.14**

- **Satellite litigation** It provided the impetus for a culture of satellite litigation, the focus of which was the question of whether the court should exercise its discretion to grant relief. This was not simply costly and time-consuming for the parties in the case in question, but also imposed an otherwise unnecessary burden on the court system.

---

[18] *The First Report of the Royal Commission to inquire into the Operation and Constitution of the High Court of Chancery, Courts of Common Law, Central Criminal Court, High Court of Admiralty, and other Courts in England, and into the Operation and Effect of the Present Separation and Division of Jurisdiction between the Courts*, No 4130 (London: HMSO, 1868–69) (the 1868 Report), para 6-12.

[19] This was under the test articulated by Brett MR in *Compagnie Financiere du Pacifique v Peruvian Guano Co* (1882) 11 QBD 55, under which, as Lord Woolf famously and critically described it, disclosure was 'virtually unlimited' in scope: Woolf, H, *Access to Justice: Interim Report to the Lord Chancellor on the Civil Justice System in England and Wales* (London: HMSO, 1995), pp 166–7.

[20] See, eg, *Smith v Barker* (1864) 2 H & M 498; *Re Coles & Ravenshear* [1907] 1 KB 1. See also Clark, C, 'The Handmaid of Justice' (1937–38) 23 Wash U LQ 297; *NML Ltd v Argentina* [2011] 2 AC 495, at [74].

[21] Piggot, D, 'Relief from Sanctions and the Overriding Objective' (2005) 24 CJQ 104, at 104.

[22] Woolf, H, *Access to Justice: Interim Report to the Lord Chancellor on the Civil Justice System in England and Wales* (London: HMSO, 1995), p 8.

- **Inappropriate focus** It diverted the focus away from justice on the merits.[23] Satellite litigation became a means to help a case to succeed other than on the merits. As Professor Zuckerman put it:

  '[T]he desire not to allow matters of procedure to stand in the way of doing justice on the merits created extensive scope for litigation that had nothing to do with the merits but which could well obstruct a merits based resolution to the dispute.'[24]

  This led to the overly adversarial approach to litigation that Lord Woolf identified as a barrier to access to justice.[25]

These things meant that the justice-on-the-merits approach tended to be self-defeating and, even where it was not, justice was achieved at unnecessary cost to the immediate parties and to the justice system as a whole.

The New Approach to Justice under the CPR

26.15 The CPR were intended to remedy these problems. The intention was to ensure that procedural rules, orders and directions were seen as being more than mere guidelines, and that an overly adversarial approach to litigation would no longer be taken. Unnecessary satellite litigation would become a thing of the past and cases would be dealt with at no more than proportionate cost, both to the parties and to the justice system as a whole.

26.16 The CPR were to achieve this through the overriding objective, which made explicit reference to how procedure was to operate.[26] Its introduction echoed the comparable introduction of an overriding objective into the US Federal Rules of Procedure in 1938.[27] Both objectives were intended to indicate a fundamental shift in approach by the courts—and by litigants—to the conduct of proceedings.[28] In the case of the Federal Rules, the shift was away from an approach that placed too great an emphasis on procedural compliance towards an approach that treated the achievement of justice on the merits as paramount.[29] In the case of the CPR, it indicated a shift away from justice on the merits towards a 'rationed and rational' approach to the conduct of proceedings.[30]

---

[23] See Zuckerman, A, 'Compliance with Process Obligations and Fair Trial', in Andenas, M (ed), *The Future of Transnational Civil Litigation* (London: British Institute of International and Comparative Law, 2004); Sorabji, J, *English Civil Justice after the Woolf and Jackson Reforms: A Critical Analysis* (Cambridge: Cambridge University Press, 2014), pp 69–74.

[24] Zuckerman, A, *Civil Procedure* (London: Butterworths, 2003), p 31.

[25] Woolf, H, *Access to Justice: Interim Report to the Lord Chancellor on the Civil Justice System in England and Wales* (London: HMSO, 1995), pp 7–8.

[26] *Ibid*, at p 215. See also Woolf, H, 'A New Approach to Civil Justice' [1996] Law Lectures for Practitioners (Hong Kong Law Journal Special Edition).

[27] See the Federal Rules of Civil Procedure, r 1.

[28] As Neuberger J put it, the overriding objective amounted to a public interest factor guiding procedure that was absent from the CPR's predecessors: see *Ropac Ltd v Inntrepreneur Pub Co (CPC) Ltd* [2001] L&TR 10, at [38].

[29] Bone, R, 'Improving Rule 1: A Master Rule for the Federal Rules' (2010) 87 Denver U L Rev 287, at 290.

[30] Issacharoff, S, *Civil Procedure* (3rd edn, New York: Foundation Press, 2012), p 196.

The Overriding Objective: Early Days and Competing Interpretations

As Dr Sorabji (an academic at University College London) points out, effecting a new approach to litigation—any new approach—requires three conditions to be satisfied: there must be clarity in the way in which it operates, it must be understood and it must be accepted.[31] This takes time: when, for example, justice on the merits came to prominence after the Judicature Act reforms in the 1870s (see 26.10), it took a generation of Court of Appeal authority before the then-new approach became embedded.[32] **26.17**

In so far as the CPR's overriding objective was concerned, all three conditions were unmet from the outset. The meaning of the overriding objective was neither clear nor well understood. It was not apparent whether it was simply an express restatement of the aim of securing justice on the merits or whether it was intended to be something other than that. In particular, there were two competing interpretations: the first—the conservative interpretation—is discussed at 26.19–26.21; the second—the progressive interpretation—at 26.22–26.23. As will be explained below, it is now known that the second ultimately prevailed. **26.18**

The conservative approach to the overriding objective

The conservative interpretation was that the overriding objective was no more than an express encapsulation of the aim of achieving justice on the merits—namely, that to deal with a case justly and at proportionate cost meant no more than to secure justice on the merits, albeit economically, efficiently and proportionately. Put otherwise, the overriding objective essentially did no more than articulate the *aim* of procedure and of procedural reformers since the 1870s. The express focus on cost, time and proportionality would simply make clear what reformers had always tried to achieve: that justice on the merits should come in reasonable time and at reasonable cost. Proportionality was merely an adjunct to this.[33] **26.19**

Such an interpretation had a good degree of judicial support. As May LJ put it (extra-judicially) in 2004, proportionality was no more than a reference to an inherent feature of justice and economy—that is, it went to the elimination of unnecessary expense and delay from the litigation process.[34] In a similar vein, Millett LJ (speaking shortly before the introduction of the CPR) said that 'the overriding principle is that justice must be done'.[35] **26.20**

---

[31] Sorabji, J, *English Civil Justice after the Woolf and Jackson Reforms: A Critical Analysis* (Cambridge: Cambridge University Press, 2014).

[32] From *Tildesley v Harper* (1876) 10 Ch D 393 to *Re Coles & Ravenshear* [1907] 1 KB 1; Sorabji, J, *English Civil Justice after the Woolf and Jackson Reforms: A Critical Analysis* (Cambridge: Cambridge University Press, 2014), pp 56–75.

[33] This, of course, left open the nature of proportionate cost, and its difference from necessary and reasonable costs. It was a difference that *Lownds v Home Office* [2002] EWCA Civ 365 rendered ineffective: see *Willis v Nicolson* [2007] EWCA Civ 199, at [19]. As May LJ also noted in 2009, the CPR approach to costs was one that gave 'only a nodding respect to proportionality': see May LJ, 'Speech at Cardiff Costs Conference', 19 June 2009, at p 13.

[34] See May, A, 'The ALI/UNIDROIT Rules of Transnational Civil Procedure', in Andenas, M, Andrews, N, and Nazazin, R (eds), *The Future of Transnational Civil Litigation: English Responses to the ALI/Unidroit Draft Principles and Rules of Transnational Civil Procedure* (London: British Institute of International and Comparative Law, 2004), p 44.

[35] *Mortgage Corpn v Sandoes* (unreported), 26 November 1996, Court of Appeal, at [30]; see also *Walsh v Missledine* [2000] CP Rep 74, at [82].

Time, expense and proportionality would, on this view, be secondary to that principle. If unnecessary expense and delay were avoided, then (the theory was) proportionality would fall into place because it was synonymous with economy and efficiency. At times, Brooke LJ (a major architect of the pre-Jackson landscape in the Court of Appeal) took a similar view: where use of resources and justice on the merits came into conflict, the former would take second place.[36] The editors of The White Book used to say much the same thing.[37]

26.21 This approach institutionalised and reinforced the approach that was extant under the RSC and CCR (see 26.09–26.14). It would reiterate and further embed the philosophy underpinning those old rules. As is now well known, the result was that the costs of litigation spiralled out of control.

The progressive approach to the overriding objective

26.22 The progressive interpretation of the overriding objective was markedly different. It echoed the views expressed in 2003 by Lord Hobhouse (see 26.02) and it interpreted the overriding objective not as being a reform that improved the ability of the court to achieve justice on the merits in individual claims,[38] but as heralding a 'rationed and rational'[39] approach to the delivery of justice—one that would ensure that no single claim would proceed at disproportionate cost either to the parties or to the justice system as a whole.[40] Equally, the progressive interpretation would enable the court to ensure that public resources were not wasted through inefficiency on the parts of litigants.[41] Dealing with cases justly and at proportionate cost would mean that the court was able, where appropriate, to temper the quality of justice—or even to deny justice on the merits entirely.[42]

26.23 According to the progressive interpretation, dealing with cases justly and at proportionate cost would not be a synonym for doing justice on the merits or merely for doing justice economically and efficiently; that would be only a part of what it meant.[43] To deal with a case 'justly' meant that each claim was to be allotted an equitable share of the court's resources. This would allow the claim to be pursued either to judgment on the merits or to a consensual resolution, but only within the limits of what was economic, efficient and proportionate.

---

[36] *Sayers v Clarke-Walker* [2002] EWCA Civ 645, at [25]. See also, eg, *Hannigan v Hannigan* [2000] EWCA Civ 159, at [36]–[38], in which Brooke LJ had this to say: '[T]he Civil Procedure Rules were drawn to ensure that civil litigation was brought up to a higher degree of efficiency. But one must not lose sight of the fact that the overriding objective … is to enable the court to deal with cases justly, and this means the achievement of justice as between litigants whose dispute it is the court's duty to resolve …'

[37] See, eg, The Right Hon Lord Justice Waller, *Civil Procedure* (London: Sweet & Maxwell, 2007), vol 1, at para 1.3.3; The Right Hon Lord Justice Waller, *Civil Procedure* (London: Sweet & Maxwell, 2009), vol 2, at para 11.8.

[38] See, eg, Dehn, C, 'The Woolf Report: Against the Public Interest?', in Zuckerman, A, and Cranston, R (eds), *Reform of Civil Procedure: Essays on 'Access to Justice'* (Oxford: Clarendon Press, 1995), at p 167.

[39] See Issacharoff, S, *Civil Procedure* (3rd edn, New York: Foundation Press, 2012), p 196.

[40] See *L (a child)* [2013] EWCA Civ 1778.

[41] See *Aon Risk Services Australia Ltd v Australian National University* [2009] HCA 27, at [23]–[25]; see also *Denton v White* [2014] EWCA Civ 906, at [45], *per* Dyson MR.

[42] See, eg, *Flaxman-Binns v Lincolnshire CC (Practice Note)* [2004] EWCA Civ 424, at [41]. See also the approach adopted by Dyson LJ in *Hashtroodi v Hancock* [2004] EWCA Civ 652.

[43] As explained by Lord Dyson MR (speaking extrajudicially) in 'The Application of the Amendments to the Civil Procedure Rules: 18th Lecture in the Implementation Programme', 22 March 2013, at [15]: 'Dealing with cases justly does not simply mean ensuring that a decision is reached on the merits. It is a mistake to assume it does.'

It is now unquestionably the case that the progressive interpretation is to be preferred. This was made clear by Lord Dyson MR in 2013: **26.24**

> '[T]he Woolf reforms and now the Jackson reforms were and are not intended to render the overriding objective ... subject to an overarching consideration of securing justice in the individual case. If that had been the intention, a tough application to compliance would have been difficult to justify and even more problematic to apply in practice. The fact that since 1999 the tough rules to which Lord Justice Brooke referred have not been applied with sufficient rigour is testament to a failure to understand that that was not the intention.
>
> The revisions [in 2013] to the overriding objective and to rule 3.9, and particularly the fact that rule 3.9 now expressly refers back to the revised overriding objective, are intended to make clear that the relationship between justice and procedure has changed. ... It has changed because doing justice is not something distinct from, and superior to, the overriding objective. Doing justice in each set of proceedings is to ensure that proceedings are dealt with justly and at proportionate cost. Justice in the individual case is now only achievable through the proper application of the CPR consistently with the overriding objective.'[44]

Thus justice on the merits was no longer the overriding objective.

One could argue that this ought to have been plain from the early days of the CPR. Indeed, Dyson MR and Vos LJ have said that 'what might be said to be the traditional approach of giving pre-eminence to the need to decide the claim on the merits ... should have disappeared following the Woolf reforms'.[45] **26.25**

Collective Proportionality

The progressive interpretation (as underpinned by the 2013 amendment to the overriding objective) ushers in the concept of collective proportionality. This may be said to be the 'the means by which substantive justice [may] be tempered in order to ensure that no single claim utilise[s] more than an equitable share of the justice system's resources'.[46] In view of this, it will apply to the management of claims—the *ex ante* mechanism referred to in 25.15—rather than as a factor specifically relevant to the assessment of costs. It has now become profoundly relevant both to case management and costs management. **26.26**

Because it goes to the question of the extent to which litigants are permitted to make use of the court's resources, collective proportionately is closely related to the question of whether the court should give relief from sanctions[47]—a topic that is addressed at 26.48–26.70. **26.27**

[44] See Lord Dyson MR, 'The Application of the Amendments to the Civil Procedure Rules: 18th Lecture in the Implementation Programme', 22 March 2013, at paras 25 and 26, as endorsed in *Mitchell v News Group Newspapers Ltd* [2013] EWCA Civ 1537, at [38] and [39].

[45] *Denton v White* [2014] EWCA Civ 906, at [81].

[46] Sorabji, J, *English Civil Justice after the Woolf and Jackson Reforms: A Critical Analysis* (Cambridge: Cambridge University Press, 2014), p 256.

[47] This is because of the belief that if the court is robust in the sense that it rarely affords relief from sanctions, litigants (in general) will try harder to comply with directions and this will promote collective proportionality. It is easy to see why a judge might believe that this link is significant, because, from a judge's perspective, non-compliance with directions is probably the most common cause of court time being wasted.

Early statements of the principles of collective proportionality

26.28 One of the first indications that the courts would consider not only the interests of individual parties, but also the wider interests of all litigants was given in 2012 in *Fred Perry (Holdings) Ltd v Brands Plaza Trading Ltd*,[48] in which there had been failure to comply with a number of directions. Jackson LJ had this to say:

> 'Non-compliance with the Civil Procedure Rules and orders of the court on the scale that has occurred in this case cannot possibly be tolerated. Any further grant of indulgence to the defendants in this case would be a denial of justice to the claimants and a denial of justice to other litigants whose cases await resolution by the court.'[49]

He went on to say that, post-2013, there would be 'significantly less indulgence' than had been the norm previously. Thus a clear indication was given that change was on the horizon.

26.29 Further early steps towards collective proportionality were taken by the making of comments in the Implementation Lecture series. In the 15th Implementation Lecture, Lord Neuberger MR—echoing previous comments[50]—explained that ensuring that individual claims were to be conducted at proportionate cost to the parties was only part of the approach required; the other part was ensuring that no single claim was afforded more than a proportionate share of the court's resources. As such, both the court and court users had to ensure that claims were managed consistently with that aspect of CPR, r 1.1(2)(e), which provides that claims must be allotted an appropriate share of the court's resources.[51] There was nothing new in what was being said,[52] but what was new was the fact that the then head of civil justice was signalling an intended and imminent shift in litigation culture.

26.30 When he became Master of the Rolls, Lord Dyson MR went further than his predecessor had gone. In the 18th Implementation Lecture, he set out a clear explanation of the underlying philosophy of the overriding objective under the progressive interpretation. Lord Dyson MR explained that dealing with cases justly did not only mean doing justice on the merits; he said that claims had to be managed in such a way that they would not utilise more than a proportionate share of the court's time and resources. He went on to say that the court would take a more robust approach to compliance, and that it would do so because the 'effective administration of justice' required it.[53] He also made it clear that such a robust approach was not unique to questions of compliance and relief; rather, it was

---

48 *Fred Perry (Holdings) Ltd v Brands Plaza Trading Ltd* [2012] EWCA Civ 224.

49 *Ibid*, at [1].

50 See fn 52.

51 Lord Neuberger of Abbotsbury, Master of the Roll, 'Proportionate Costs: Fifteenth Lecture in the Implementation Programme', 30 May 2012, at para 9.

52 This echoed what Lord Neuberger MR had previously said in 2010, in 'Costs, Management, Proportionality and Insurance', Personal Injuries Bar Association Lecture, 26 March 2010, at paras 19–21, and what he had said as Neuberger J in *Charlesworth v Relay Road Ltd & Ors* [2000] 1 WLR 230, at 235: '[E]ven where, in purely financial terms, the other party can be said to be compensated for a late amendment or late evidence by an appropriate award of costs, it can often be unfair in terms of the strain of litigation, legitimate expectation, the efficient conduct of the case in question, and the interests of other litigants whose cases are waiting to be heard, if such an application succeeds.'

53 Lord Dyson MR, 'The Application of the Amendments to the Civil Procedure Rules: 18th Lecture in the Implementation Programme', 22 March 2013, at para 31.

a universal approach required by the overriding objective, and hence would apply to case management and costs management.[54]

In 2014, the Supreme Court explicitly dealt with *Cropper v Smith* (see 26.10).[55] This was a case that focused on repeated and intentional non-compliance with court orders. The claimant relied on Bowen LJ's *dicta* from *Cropper* in arguing that relief should be granted. Lord Neuberger PSC summarised—and rejected—that argument in the following way: **26.31**

> '[Counsel for the claimant] relied on *Cropper v Smith* (1884) 26 Ch D 700, 710, where Bowen LJ said that he knew of "no kind of error or mistake which, if not fraudulent or intended to overreach, the Court ought not to correct, if it can be done without injustice to the other party". There are three problems for the [claimant] in this connection. The first is that these observations were made in connection with a proposed amendment to a pleading, ie an attempt by a litigant to do something which he would be entitled to do, but to do it late; whereas here we are concerned with a party who does not even now intend to obey a court order. Secondly, as the points made in the last few sentences of the immediately preceding paragraph of this judgment illustrate, there would be prejudice to the other parties if the [claimant's] current proposal was adopted. Thirdly and even more importantly, the approach laid down in *Cropper* has been overtaken by the CPR.'[56]

Thus *Cropper* has been overtaken by the CPR, this being something that has been confirmed at the very highest judicial level.

Collective proportionality under the CPR

Whilst in the early days of the CPR there were differing approaches (see 26.19–26.23), it is now known that the need to ensure fair and efficient usage of the court's resources was acknowledged in the first iteration of the overriding objective. The objective of the CPR was (according to the progressive interpretation, as set out in 26.22–26.23) no longer to assist the court in its quest for perfect justice on the merits, but to enable the court to deal with cases justly and at proportionate cost, whilst taking into account the need to allot resources to other cases.[57] This is collective proportionality in all but name. **26.32**

Collective proportionality is now unequivocally a part of the overriding objective (see CPR, r 1.1((2)(e) and (f)). The authors of *Cook on Costs 2017* comment on the fact that these provisions 'support the argument of those who believe justice has been compromised'.[58] This is correct, but this is for the reasons set out at 26.26–26.31. There are critics on both sides. For example, Professor Zuckerman has criticised the drafters of CPR, r 1.1(2), for having diluted the potency of collective proportionality by means of the use of 'such grotesquely anodyne language'.[59] **26.33**

Zuckerman may be right in saying that CPR, r 1.1, could be expressed in less open-textured language, but this did not stop Lord Neuberger MR (speaking extrajudicially) from supporting the notion of collective proportionality under the CPR: **26.34**

[54] *Ibid*, at para 31.
[55] See *Al Saud v Apex Global Management Ltd* [2014] UKSC 64.
[56] *Ibid*, at para 27.
[57] See CPR, r 1.1(2)(e).
[58] *Cook on Costs 2017* (LexisNexis, online), para 14.3.
[59] See Zuckerman, A, 'The Revised CPR 3.9: A Coded Message Demanding Articulation' (2013) 32(2) CJQ 123, at 125.

> '[P]arties, their advisers and the courts must always keep in mind the principle articulated at CPR 1.1(2)(e), as explained in Lord Woolf's Access to Justice Reports, and in the House of Lords decision, *Sutradhar v Natural Environment Research Council* [2006] 4 All ER 490 at [42]. In that case, Lord Hoffmann said that justice was not "priceless", and that, in the light of the "burden [which] a long and complicated trial would impose" upon the defendant, it would, "even if its resources were infinite ... be wrong to permit this case to proceed to trial".'[60]

Thus justice under the CPR is not solely about the parties; rather, it is about the parties *and* their usage of the resources of the civil justice system. Where it is necessary to ensure an equitable share of resources, justice under the CPR must be tempered.

The tempering of justice under the CPR and the need for consistency

26.35 Whilst the notion of tempering justice in the name of collective proportionality presents no conceptual difficulties, its practical implementation is a thornier issue. Consider, for example, the 'two-trial conundrum' in which there are two one-day trials, but the court's resources will permit a judge to sit for only one-and-a-half days and there is no possibility of the cases being adjourned to another day. It is conceptually easy to say that the time allotted to the two cases must be limited, but it is much harder to know how to achieve this in practice. Should the sitting time be apportioned? Should it be apportioned in accordance with the value of each claim? Should it be apportioned in accordance with their complexity? Or the number of witnesses? Or perhaps the issues that they raise? Even this simple illustration is fraught with difficulties.

26.36 The two-trial conundrum may also be used to illustrate (albeit, rather crudely) the link between collective proportionality and relief from sanctions (see 26.48). If the reason why the judge could sit for only one-and-a-half days was because of a failing on the part of one of the parties, what should happen? Should the burden be shared with the parties in the other claim? What about the opponent of the defaulting party? To what extent would it be fair to visit adversity upon them?

26.37 As will be seen from what is said below, there is no formula or test that would allow the court to adjudicate on an issue such as the two-trial conundrum in a way that would be consistent from court to court. In this regard, Sorabji has this to say:

> 'The problem in so far as collective proportionality is concerned is that no real consideration has yet been given regarding how to transform it into a concrete principle, or principles, that can properly be applied in case and costs management. It remains a nebulous concept. The Jackson Reforms do not assist to any great degree in this regard, as they did not focus on the issue, but were confined to the problem of costs between litigants.'[61]

26.38 Having noted the changes made by the Jackson reforms to the overriding objective, Zuckerman posed the following rhetorical question: 'How is the revised rule going to put an end to such flawed practices?'[62] In answer, Zuckerman pointed to the following comments

---

[60] See Lord Neuberger of Abbotsbury, Master of the Roll, 'Proportionate Costs: Fifteenth Lecture in the Implementation Programme', 30 May 2012, at paras 9 and 15.

[61] Sorabji, J, *English Civil Justice after the Woolf and Jackson Reforms: A Critical Analysis* (Cambridge: Cambridge University Press, 2014), pp 243–4.

[62] Zuckerman, A, 'The Revised CPR 3.9: A Coded Message Demanding Articulation' (2013) 32(2) CJQ 123, at 135.

made by Jackson LJ in 2012: '[L]itigants who substantially disregard court orders or the requirements of the CPR will receive significantly less indulgence than hitherto.'[63]

Zuckerman went on to say that whilst it was good to know that less indulgence would be shown to defaulting litigants in future, comments such those referred to above do not amount to a coherent policy.[64] Sorabji seems to agree with Zuckerman on that point, saying that what is needed is a concrete principle that can properly be applied in individual cases.[65] Zuckerman had this to say: **26.39**

> 'The ... revision [to the overriding objective] is in effect designed to revive the importance of the overriding objective as a case management tool capable of delivering efficient adjudication of civil claims; that is, adjudication on the merits within a reasonable time and by the use of proportionate court and litigant resources. But this cannot be achieved through bland words, however well intentioned.'[66]

The consequences of collective proportionality: general principles

The court system, like any other public service, operates with finite financial resources. As has been noted throughout the common-law world (see 26.46), the public interest requires those resources to be used 'fairly by State and citizen alike'.[67] This requires access to justice to be rationed so as to ensure that each party has a fair opportunity to put their case, but within the limited financial and temporal resources available. The proper administration of justice, as the Woolf reports had it, required the court to ensure that cases were managed so as to 'preserve access to justice for all users of the system [thereby ensuring] that individual users do not use more of the system's resources than their case requires'.[68] Lord Dyson MR—speaking extrajudicially in 2013 and echoing Lord Woolf MR[69]—had this to say on the topic: '[T]he proper administration of justice goes beyond the immediate parties to litigation. It requires the court to consider the needs of all litigants, all court-users. This idea finds expression in the overriding objective.'[70] **26.40**

This brings to light a significant contrast with the RSC and CCR (see 26.09–26.14). The focus under the old rules, as evidenced by the approach taken in *Cropper v Smith* (see 26.10), was straightforward: as long as any prejudice between parties could be cured by a payment of costs, the court should do what was necessary to facilitate a decision on the merits being achieved.[71] Whilst justice on the merits remains a factor, under the CPR **26.41**

[63] *Fred Perry (Holdings) Ltd v Brands Plaza Trading Ltd (t/a Brands Plaza)* [2012] EWCA Civ 224, at [50].

[64] See Zuckerman, A, 'The Revised CPR 3.9: A Coded Message Demanding Articulation' (2013) 32(2) CJQ 123, at 135.

[65] Sorabji, J, *English Civil Justice after the Woolf and Jackson Reforms: A Critical Analysis* (Cambridge: Cambridge University Press, 2014), pp 243–4.

[66] Zuckerman, A, 'The Revised CPR 3.9: A Coded Message Demanding Articulation' (2013) 32(2) CJQ 123, at 124.

[67] As explicitly recognised by the Court of Appeal in New Zealand in *Moevao v Department of Labour* [1980] 1 NZLR 464, at 481, and as endorsed by the High Court of Australia in *Aon Risk Services Australia Ltd v Australian National University* [2009] HCA 27.

[68] Lord Woolf, *Access to Justice: Final Report to the Lord Chancellor on the Civil Justice System in England and Wales* (London: HMSO, 1996), p 24. See also *Adoko v Jemal* (1999) The Times, 8 July, at [7]; *Charlesworth v Relay Road Ltd & Ors* [1999] CPLR 691.

[69] See, eg, Lord Woolf MR in *Beachley Property Ltd v Edgar* [1997] PNLR 197, at [6].

[70] Lord Dyson MR, 'The Application of The Amendments to The Civil Procedure Rules: 18th Lecture in the Implementation Programme', 22 March 2013, at para [17].

[71] See *Mitchell MP v News Group Newspapers Ltd* [2013] EWCA Civ 1537, at [1].

prejudice caused to other litigants now has to be considered.[72] This was necessary because—as the Court of Appeal stated on a number of occasions prior to 2013—prejudice arising in the conduct of particular claims did not simply affect the immediate parties; it also affected the administration of justice in general.[73]

The consequences of collective proportionality: individual cases

26.42 Where an individual claim proceeds in a way that is collectively disproportionate, then the court is able to bring that claim to an end prior to judgment. This means that justice on the merits could properly be denied.[74] Ralph Gibson LJ had this to say on the topic: 'Justice to the defendant and to the interests of other litigants may require that a claimant who ignores time limits prescribed by the rules forfeits the right to have his claim tried.'[75]

26.43 This new approach is thus one that treated justice on the merits as *part* of what it meant to provide a fair process for all litigants: justice on the merits was merely one aspect of procedural justice, just as economy, efficiency and proportionality were others. Laws LJ put it by stating the converse—namely, that those aspects of procedural justice were not part and parcel of what it meant to achieve substantive justice or a fair result.[76]

26.44 Unlike the conservative view discussed at 26.19–26.21, justice on the merits is not separate from or superior to procedural principles or commitments. Justice on the merits is not first amongst equals, nor is it a different species of procedural principle; it is merely one part of what was now meant by doing justice. It is on a par with efficiency, economy and proportionality.

The interplay between collective and individual proportionality

26.45 Sorabji points out that the difference between collective and individual proportionality is significant and essential.[77] Whilst it is an oversimplification of his observations, he expresses his concern that if collective and individual proportionality are not given their own identities, individual proportionality will tend to prevail, and that, in reality, the system of justice would then differ little from that which was provided under the RSC. He has

---

72 Examples of which were detailed in *Denton v White* [2014] EWCA Civ 906, at [89].

73 The point was reiterated in *UCB Corporate Services Ltd (formerly UCB Bank Plc) v Halifax (SW) Ltd* [1999] CPLR 691. See also *Charlesworth v Relay Road Ltd & Ors* [2000] 1 WLR 230 (in which Neuberger J specifically commented that compensating a party by way of costs in an individual case did not go to the issue of harm caused to other litigants by the manner in which that case had been conducted); *Arrow Nominees Inc v Blackledge* [2000] CP Rep 59; *Savings & Investment Bank Ltd v Fincken* [2003] EWCA Civ 1630; *Swain-Mason & Others v Mills & Reeve LLP* [2011] EWCA Civ 14.

74 *Flaxman-Binns v Lincolnshire County Council* [2004] EWCA Civ 424. See also Lord Neuberger MR, 'A New Approach to Justice: From Woolf to Jackson', in Meggit, G (ed), *Civil Justice Reform: What Has It Achieved?* (London: Sweet & Maxwell, 2010), para 20: 'Very many different types of cost can be said to be necessary to bring or defend a claim. They are costs which are incurred, as Woolf would have put it, to ensure the achievement of substantive justice. They are necessary to enable the court to decide cases on their merits. But such necessary costs are, as we all should well know by now, balanced now by an equal commitment to what Woolf described as procedural justice; that is to a fair, just and properly accessible justice system for all litigants. Procedural justice thus goes beyond the immediate concerns of individual litigants: it goes beyond what is necessary to achieve a decision on the merits in any individual case. In this way it is outward looking while necessity is inward looking.'

75 *Vinos v Marks & Spencer Plc* [2001] 3 All ER 784, at [26].

76 *Adoko v Jemal* (1999) The Times, 8 July, at [8].

77 Sorabji, J, *English Civil Justice after the Woolf and Jackson Reforms: A Critical Analysis* (Cambridge: Cambridge University Press, 2014), p 28.

observed that: 'individual justice, under the overriding objective, is limited by the need to secure distributive justice across all court users'.[78] In view of this, he suggests that the court should consider collective proportionality first and if the order sought is not collectively proportionate, it should be refused. Only if the order sought is collectively proportionate would the court go on to consider individual proportionality.

Collective proportionality in other jurisdictions

It is perhaps helpful to look at what has happened in one or two common-law jurisdictions that are said to have successfully implemented collective proportionality (or their versions of it).[79] **26.46**

- **Australia** In a case that has been called a 'triumph of case management', Gummow, Hayne, Crennan, Kiefel and Bell JJ delivered a joint judgment that dealt robustly with a defendant's request to amend its pleadings.[80] In brief, the court said that amendments that produce delay impact negatively on the entire court system and affect parties who wish to use the court system. The court went on to say that judicial officers must consider the wider public interest in the efficient use of limited court resources when deciding whether to grant applications to amend pleadings.
- **Canada** Similarly, Bell JJ has emphasised the need to regard collective proportionality as a practical and useful tool, not merely a rule to which lip service is given.[81] The Canadian equivalent of CPR, r 1.1, is by far the simpler of the two:[82] it merely provides that, applying the rules, the court shall make orders and give directions that are proportionate to the importance and complexity of the issues, and to the amount involved in the proceedings.

It is not possible to say that the evidence from other jurisdictions proves Sorabji's thesis—that is, that collective and individual proportionality need to be treated as being distinct from each other if the former is not to merge into the latter (see 26.45)—but equally there is nothing in that evidence to suggest that he is wrong. **26.47**

Relief from Sanctions

Where a party has failed to comply with a rule, practice direction or court order, any sanction for that failure to comply has effect unless the party in default applies for and obtains relief from the sanction (see CPR, r 3.8(1)). The power to give relief from sanctions is now closely bound up with collective proportionality (see 26.26–26.47). The power to afford relief derives from CPR, r 3.9, which reads as follows: **26.48**

> '(1) On an application for relief from any sanction imposed for a failure to comply with any rule, practice direction or court order, the court will consider all the circumstances of the case, so as to enable it to deal justly with the application, including the need—

[78] See *ibid*, at p 246.
[79] This is discussed at length *ibid*.
[80] *Aon Risk Services Australia Ltd v Australian National University* (2009) 258 ALR 14.
[81] *Marcotte v Longueil(ville)* [2009] 3 RCS 65, at [42].
[82] Canadian Rules of Civil Procedure, r 1.04. See also Osborne, QC, *Civil Justice Reform Project* (Ottawa, ON: Ministry of the Attorney General, 2007) (calling for increased attention to proportionality to the matter at stake and the step in the legal proceedings in awarding costs in litigation).

(a) for litigation to be conducted efficiently and at proportionate cost; and
(b) to enforce compliance with rules, practice directions and orders.'

Thus the factors that the court is expressly required to take into account bear a striking similarity to those that govern collective proportionality in the context of the overriding objective—namely, CPR, r 1.1(2)(e) and (f) (see 26.04). That said, as will be explained at 26.67, the court is not limited to taking *only* those factors into account; indeed, quite the opposite is true in that the court 'will consider all the circumstances of the case'.

26.49 In the context of costs law, the need to apply for relief from sanctions may arise in many circumstances, but the following are commonly encountered:

- where a party fails to comply with certain requirements concerning budgets (see 12.56–12.60);
- where a paying party fails to serve points of dispute, with the result that a default costs certificate is issued (see 43.158–43.160); and
- where a party is in default of an unless order (43.103–43.104).

Jurisdiction

26.50 It should be noted that, for CPR, r 3.9, to come into play, not only must there have been a default, but also a sanction must be imposed as a result of that default. Moreover, an application for relief from sanctions presupposes that the sanction has been properly imposed in principle; if a party wishes to contend that it was not appropriate to make the order, that should be by way of appeal or, exceptionally, by asking the court that imposed the order to vary or revoke it under CPR, r 3.1(7).[83]

26.51 CPR, r 3.9, does not apply where the 'sanction' is an order for the payment of costs. Where those are the circumstances, the party in default must appeal that order rather than make an application for relief from sanctions (see CPR, r 3.8(2)).

26.52 If an application is made prior to the breach occurring (such as where a party seeks an extension of time), that is referred to as an 'in-time application'.[84] If those are the circumstances, then what is said below will not apply.[85]

The approach prior to 1 April 2013

26.53 As originally drafted, CPR, r 3.9, made no mention of the factors relevant to collective proportionality. Instead, it was a checklist of nine factors to which the court was to have regard. It read as follows:

> '3.9 (1) On an application for relief from any sanction imposed for failure to comply with any rule, practice direction or court order the court will consider all the circumstances including—
> (a) the interests of the administration of justice;

---

[83] See *Mitchell v News Group Newspapers Ltd* [2013] EWCA Civ 1537, at [44], *per* Dyson MR. As to when it would be appropriate to make any application under CPR, r 3.1(7), see *Tibbles v SIG Plc (t/a Asphaltic Roofing Supplies)* [2012] EWCA Civ 518. In essence, this would normally be appropriate only where (a) there had been a material change of circumstances since the order was made, (b) the facts on which the original decision was made had been mis-stated or (c) there had been a manifest mistake on the part of the judge in formulating the order. Moreover, as the court emphasised, the application must be made promptly.

[84] *In re Guidezone Ltd* [2014] EWHC 1165 (Ch).

[85] As to the correct approach, see *Robert v Momentum Services Ltd* [2003] EWCA Civ 299; *Hallam Estates v Baker* [2014] EWCA Civ 661.

(b) whether the application for relief has been made promptly;
(c) whether the failure to comply was intentional;
(d) whether there is a good explanation for the failure;
(e) the extent to which the party in default has complied with other rules, practice directions, court orders and any relevant pre-action protocol;
(f) whether the failure to comply was caused by the party or his legal representatives;
(g) whether the trial date or the likely trial date can still be met if relief is granted;
(h) the effect which the failure to comply had on each party; and
(i) the effect which the granting of relief would have on each party.'

These factors were derived from pre-CPR authorities, the intention being that this would obviate the need to make extensive reference to judge-made law.[86] What actually happened, however, was that the checklist was treated as being a statutory code and this generated its own substantial body of judicial comment. In any event, for the reasons set out at 26.28–26.31, there was a concern that the relief from sanctions provisions were too generous.[87] **26.54**

The approach on and after 1 April 2013

The new provisions (as set out in 26.48) came into force on 1 April 2013.[88] The development of the law thereafter can best be described by examining two cases: *Mitchell v News Group Newspapers Ltd*[89] (see 26.56–26.59); and *Denton v TH White*[90] (see 26.60–26.70). It should be noted that the former was clarified—some would say qualified—by the latter. **26.55**

Mitchell v News Group Newspapers Ltd

Mitchell was a robust decision in late 2013 in which the court declined to give relief from sanctions to a party who had failed to comply with an (easily overlooked) prescriptive rule. The parties were required to submit costs budgets to the court in accordance with provisions similar to what is now CPR, Part 3, Section II. The claimant failed to do this in time, so the judge at first instance ordered that his costs should be restricted to court fees only.[91] Following the 18th Implementation Lecture (see 26.30) and Jackson LJ's indication in *Fred Perry* (see 26.28), one would have thought that the claimant would have realised that failure to comply with the rules would not be met with anything approaching indulgence. That said, it should be borne in mind that if the court had approached the question of relief applying the *Cropper* test (see 26.10) as reflected in the old CPR, r 3.9 (see 26.53–26.54), relief would almost certainly have been granted. In particular, there was no prejudice to the non-defaulting party that could not have been compensated for in costs, the non-compliance was inadvertent, it was not effected by malice or bad faith, and a fair trial was still possible. **26.56**

The first-instance judge who dealt with the application for relief applied the new approach. In particular, whilst she did not refer to collective proportionality by that name, her focus was on prejudice to other court users.[92] Relief was refused—a decision that was **26.57**

[86] *Bansal v Cheema* [2001] CP Rep 6.
[87] See also *Mitchell v News Group Newspapers Ltd* [2013] EWCA Civ 1537, at [24] and [35], *per* Dyson MR.
[88] See Civil Procedure (Amendment) Rules 2013 (SI 2013/262).
[89] *Mitchell v News Group Newspapers Ltd* [2013] EWCA Civ 1537.
[90] *Denton & Ors v TH White Ltd & Ors* [2014] EWCA Civ 906.
[91] This was not done by the operation of CPR, r 3.14, but by way of an order that drew upon that rule by way of analogy.
[92] *Mitchell MP v News Group Newspapers Ltd* [2013] EWHC 2355 (QB), at [28], [29] and [58].

subsequently upheld by the Court of Appeal. In so holding, the Court of Appeal expressly endorsed the views of Lord Dyson MR as given in the 18th Implementation Lecture (see 26.30).[93] The *Cropper* test—and, as such, its focus on justice on the merits—was thus consigned to history. The new approach—which has now been modified in *Denton* (see 26.60–26.70)—required the court to address two issues: first, whether the default or non-compliance was trivial; and secondly, if not, whether the applicant had discharged the heavy burden of proving that they should be granted relief from sanctions. In assessing these questions, issues of collective proportionality would feature heavily[94] (although the court did not refer to that principle by that name).

26.58 Looked at in terms of collective proportionality, the court's robustness made perfect sense: not only did the refusal act as a warning to others, but it also meant that the court's resources would not be squandered on litigants who had brought trouble upon themselves. Looked at from the point of view of individual justice, however, it was—in the eyes of many—little short of an abhorrence (because the penalty was wholly out of proportion to the culpability of the failure to comply).

26.59 Perhaps there were broad-minded court users who took a Benthamistic view that—on the whole—it would be beneficial to society to ensure that all court users studied the CPR and complied with the relevant provisions in full. Perhaps there were lawyers who eagerly looked forward to the benefits that collective proportionality would eventually bring. Perhaps so, but it was impossible to tell because of the deafening clatter of an entire profession preparing to weaponise *Mitchell*. Parties vied to use the tools of collective proportionality to inflict maximum damage on their opponents. As one commentator said: '[A]ll civility [had gone] out of civil litigation.'[95] A series of decisions in early 2014 bravely tried to follow the spirit of *Mitchell*, but, in long run, the Court of Appeal had to intervene and issue new guidance that placed more emphasis on individual justice. This was achieved in *Denton* (below).

Denton v TH White

26.60 In brief, the guidance given in *Denton* may be summarised as being that a judge should address an application for relief from sanctions in three stages.[96]

(1) The first stage is to identify and assess the seriousness and significance of the failure to comply with any rule, practice direction or court order that has engaged CPR, r 3.9(1) (see 26.61). If the breach is neither 'serious nor significant', the court is unlikely to need to spend much time on the second and third stages.
(2) Next is consideration of the reasons why the default occurred (see 26.66).
(3) Finally, the judge is to evaluate all of the circumstances of the case, so as to enable the court to deal justly with the application, including the needs:
    (a) for litigation to be conducted efficiently and at proportionate cost; and
    (b) to enforce compliance with rules, practice directions and orders (see 26.67).

---

93 *Ibid*, at [38] and [39].
94 *Ibid*, at [40] *et seq*.
95 Baksi, K, 'Featured Broadcast: *Mitchell* Sanctions Damaging to Litigation', *Law Society Gazette*, 17 June 2014.
96 See *Denton & Ors v TH White Ltd & Ors* [2014] EWCA Civ 906, at [24], *per* Dyson MR.

It should be noted that whilst the test explicated in *Denton* has placed more emphasis on individual justice than that adumbrated in *Mitchell*, there is still an emphasis on collective proportionality.

The first stage in *Denton* This stage involves the court looking at the 'seriousness and significance' of the breach. If a judge concludes that a breach is not serious or significant, then relief from sanctions will usually be granted and it will not usually be necessary to spend much time on the second or third stages. If, however, the court decides that the breach is serious or significant, then the second and third stages assume greater importance.[97] **26.61**

There is no reference to any test of triviality in CPR, r 3.9. Dyson MR has explained that it is nonetheless a useful concept in the context of the first stage because it requires the judge to focus on the question of whether a breach is serious or significant.[98] In this regard, it is worth bearing in mind that, in *Mitchell*, Dyson MR had said that if a breach is trivial, the court will usually grant relief provided that an application is made promptly: **26.62**

> 'If [the breach] can properly be regarded as trivial, the court will usually grant relief provided that an application is made promptly. The principle "*de minimis non curat lex*" (the law is not concerned with trivial things) applies here as it applies in most areas of the law. Thus, the court will usually grant relief if there has been no more than an insignificant failure to comply with an order: for example, where there has been a failure of form rather than substance; or where the party has narrowly missed the deadline imposed by the order, but has otherwise fully complied with its terms. We acknowledge that even the question of whether a default is insignificant may give rise to dispute and therefore to contested applications. But that possibility cannot be entirely excluded from any regime which does not impose rigid rules from which no departure, however minor, is permitted.'[99]

That said, the use of the word 'trivial' gave rise to sematic disputes. In *Denton*, Dyson MR explained that the focus of the enquiry at the first stage should not be on whether the breach has been 'trivial', but on whether the breach has been 'serious or significant'.[100]

Dyson MR expanded on this point in the following way: **26.63**

> 'It was submitted ... that the test of triviality should be replaced by the test of immateriality and that an immaterial breach should be defined as one which "neither imperils future hearing dates nor otherwise disrupts the conduct of the litigation". Provided that this is understood as including the effect on litigation generally (and not only on the litigation in which the application is made), there are many circumstances in which materiality in this sense will be the most useful measure of whether a breach has been serious or significant. But it leaves out of account those breaches which are incapable of affecting the efficient progress of the litigation, although they are serious ...We therefore prefer simply to say that, in evaluating a breach, judges should assess its seriousness and significance. We recognise that the concepts of seriousness and significance are not hard-edged and that there are degrees of seriousness and significance, but we hope that, assisted by the guidance given in this decision and its application in individual cases over time, courts will deal with these applications in a consistent manner.'[101]

[97] See *ibid*, at [28].
[98] See *ibid*, at [26].
[99] *Mitchell v News Group Newspapers Ltd* [2013] EWCA Civ 1537, at [40].
[100] See *Denton & Ors v TH White Ltd & Ors* [2014] EWCA Civ 906, at [26], *per* Dyson MR.
[101] See *ibid*, at [26].

26.64 Dyson MR went on to say that the assessment of the seriousness or significance of the breach should not—at least initially—involve a consideration of other unrelated failures that may have occurred in the past. At the first stage, the court should concentrate on an assessment of the seriousness and significance of the very breach in respect of which relief from sanctions is sought; prior breaches are a matter for the third stage.[102] That said, where the application for relief is in respect of a breach of an unless order, then it will be necessary to take into account the underlying breach.[103]

26.65 It may be that there is an application for relief in respect of more than one breach. Where this is so, the seriousness or significance of each should be considered separately for the purposes of the first stage, but they may be considered as a whole for the purposes of the third stage[104] (see 26.70).

26.66 **The second stage in *Denton*** In this stage, the court will consider why the default occurred. This stage cannot be derived from the express wording of CPR, r 3.9(1), but it is nonetheless important—particularly where the breach is serious or significant.[105] The court should consider why the failure or default occurred.

26.67 **The third stage in *Denton*** This is the formulation stage, during which the court will consider all of the circumstances of the case.[106] It is not the case that the first and second stages determines the third—that is, if there is a serious or significant breach and if there is no good reason for the breach, it does not follow that the application for relief from sanctions will necessarily fail.[107]

26.68 Dyson MR has made it clear that whilst the court may take into account all of the circumstances of the case, those factors expressly listed in CPR, r 3.9 (see 26.48), are to be given particular weight.[108]

- **Litigation to be conducted efficiently and at proportionate cost** Dyson MR has explained that this factor makes it clear that the court must consider the effect of the breach in every case.[109] If the breach has prevented the court or the parties from conducting the litigation (or other litigation) efficiently and at proportionate cost, that will be a factor weighing in favour of refusing relief.
- **The need to enforce compliance with rules, practice directions and orders** Dyson MR has said that this factor emphasises the importance of complying with rules, practice directions and orders.[110] He went on to say that the court must always bear in mind the need for compliance with rules, practice directions and orders, because the old lax culture of non-compliance is no longer tolerated.

---

[102] See *ibid*, at [27].
[103] See *British Gas Trading Ltd v Oak Cash and Carry Ltd* [2016] EWCA Civ 153.
[104] *McTear v Englehard* [2016] EWCA Civ 487, at [33], [34], [41] and [42].
[105] See *Denton & Ors v TH White Ltd & Ors* [2014] EWCA Civ 906, at [29], *per* Dyson MR.
[106] See *ibid*, at [31].
[107] See *ibid*, at [38].
[108] See *ibid*, at [32].
[109] See *ibid*, at [34].
[110] See *ibid*, at [34].

Dyson MR affirmed that the court must, in considering all of the circumstances of the case, give particular weight to these two important factors. Thus not only is collective proportionality relevant, but also it is a prominent feature of the test under *Denton*.

In addition to taking the above two factors into account, the court will take account of the seriousness and significance of the breach (which will have been assessed at the first stage) and any explanation (which will have been considered at the second stage). The more serious or significant the breach, the less likely it is that relief will be granted—unless there is a good reason for it. Where there is a good reason for a serious or significant breach, relief is likely to be granted. Where the breach is not serious or significant, relief is also likely to be granted.[111] **26.69**

Drawing on guidance given in *Mitchell*, the following miscellaneous points may be made about the operation of the third stage. **26.70**

- **The factors to be taken into account** Dyson MR said that, depending on the facts of the case, it may be appropriate to consider some, or even all, of the factors in the pre-April 2013 CPR, r 3.9 (see 26.48), as part of 'all of the circumstances of the case'.[112]
- **Burden** If the non-compliance cannot be characterised as trivial, then the burden is on the defaulting party to persuade the court to grant relief.[113]
- **Good reason** If there is a good reason for the breach, then relief will usually be granted.[114] For example, if the reason why a document was not filed with the court was that the party or their solicitor suffered from a debilitating illness or was involved in an accident, then, depending on the circumstances, that may constitute a good reason.[115]
- **Later developments** Later developments in the course of the litigation process are likely to be a good reason if they show that the period for compliance originally imposed was unreasonable, although the period seemed to be reasonable at the time, and could not realistically have been the subject of an appeal.[116]
- **Mere oversights and overworked lawyers** Merely overlooking a deadline, whether on account of overwork or otherwise, is unlikely to be a good reason. Dyson MR explained that he understood that solicitors may be under pressure and have too much work, but he went on to say that that would rarely be a good reason for delay: solicitors cannot take on too much work and expect to be able to persuade a court that this is a good reason for their failure to meet deadlines; they should either delegate the work to others in their firm or, if they are unable to do this, they should not take on the work at all.[117]

---

111 See *ibid*, at [35].
112 See *Mitchell v News Group Newspapers Ltd* [2013] EWCA Civ 1537, at [49].
113 See *ibid*, at [41].
114 See *ibid*, at [42] and [43], applying *Hashtroodi v Hancock* [2004] EWCA Civ 652 by analogy. See also *Denton & Ors v TH White Ltd & Ors* [2014] EWCA Civ 906, at [35], *per* Dyson MR.
115 See *Mitchell v News Group Newspapers Ltd* [2013] EWCA Civ 1537, at [41], *per* Dyson MR.
116 See *ibid*, at [41].
117 See *ibid*, at [41] and [48].

- **Promptness** Promptness of the application will be a relevant circumstance to be weighed in the balance along with all of the circumstances.[118] A lack of promptness may result in relief being denied.[119]
- **Prior or other breaches** Any past or other current breach of the rules, practice directions and court orders by the parties may also be taken into account as a relevant circumstance.[120]

118 See *Denton & Ors v TH White Ltd & Ors* [2014] EWCA Civ 906, at [36], *per* Dyson MR.
119 See, eg, *British Gas Trading Ltd v Oak Cash and Carry Ltd* [2016] EWCA Civ 153.
120 See *Denton & Ors v TH White Ltd & Ors* [2014] EWCA Civ 906, at [36], *per* Dyson MR.

Part VIII

AGREEMENTS BETWEEN LEGAL SERVICES PROVIDER AND CLIENT

27

CONTRACTS OF RETAINER (GENERAL PRINCIPLES)

This chapter deals with the following topics: **27.01**

- disambiguation:
  - the three meanings of the word 'retainer' (27.03);
  - the difference between the retainer and the retainer documentation (27.05);
- miscellaneous principles relating to contracts of retainer (27.06):
  - entire contracts in the context of contracts of retainer (27.07);
  - ambit and authority and contracts of retainer (27.29);
  - interim payments and contracts of retainer (27.38);
  - termination of contracts of retainer (27.67);
  - suspension of contracts of retainer (27.89);
  - waiver of rights under a contract of retainer (27.90);
  - withholding information about retainers and undue influence (27.91);
- factual disputes about retainers (27.92):
  - the evidential relevance of there being no written record (27.95);
  - codes of conduct regarding retainers (27.97);
- private retainers (27.102);
- business agreements (non-contentious and contentious) (27.107):
  - business agreements and agreements generally (27.109);
  - non-contentious business agreements (27.115);
  - contentious business agreements (27.135);
- implied retainers (27.190):
  - presumptions relating to retainers (27.191);
  - disputes about whether an implied retainer exists (27.200);
- oral retainers (27.207):
  - issues of fact relating to oral retainers (27.208);
  - issues of law relating to oral retainers (27.209);
- sham retainers (27.217);
- unlawful retainers and statutory prohibition (27.228):
  - statutory prohibition in the context of costs (27.229);
  - specific instances of express and implied statutory prohibition (27.259);
- retainers and similar contracts involving more than one client:
  - joint obligations (27.302);
  - the nature of obligations where there is a plurality of debtors (27.305);
  - costs sharing agreements (27.315);

- retainers with specific types of person:
  - retainers with companies, limited liability partnerships and members (27.319);
  - retainers with unincorporated associations (27.322);
  - retainers with trustees, executors, liquidators, etc (27.323);
  - 'retainers' with employees (27.324);
  - retainers with children or those who lack capacity (27.325); and
- terms commonly encountered in contracts of retainers (27.326).

27.02 The law relating to contracts of retainer is surprisingly complex and extensive. Since the second edition of this book, general consumer law has become increasingly relevant, both in terms of the formation of contracts of retainer and in terms of their effect. In view of this, those issues now have their own chapter—namely, Chapter 28. Conditional fee agreements (CFAs) and damages-based agreements (DBAs) are dealt with in Chapter 29. Champerty and maintenance are discussed in Chapter 30, and the interpretation of contracts of retainer is addressed in Chapter 31. Finally, the topic of the transfer of contracts of retainer between firms is addressed in Chapter 32, along with how to manage errors in contracts of retainer.

Disambiguation

The three meanings of the word 'retainer'

27.03 In the present context, there are three distinct, but overlapping, usages of the word 'retainer', as follows.[1]

- **Client care** This relates to the supply side of the retainer. In this regard, the word 'retainer' may be a reference to the terms on which legal services are supplied—or, as Bernard Livesey QC put it, 'the *fons et origo*[2] of a solicitor's duties ... [a] contract of engagement between himself and the client'.[3] Those terms are often referred to as 'client care' and are generally contained in a client care letter (which may or may not be supplemented with the legal service provider's standard terms and conditions).
- **Right to payment** This relates to the remuneration side of the retainer, whereby the word 'retainer' may also be a reference to the legal mechanism that gives rise to the legal services provider's right to be paid. Where the legal mechanism that gives rise to a right to payment is contractual, the supply side and the remuneration side of the retainer will, in general, be a single contract, but where the right is non-contractual (for example where the client has the benefit of legal aid), then a distinction ought to be made.
- **Professional relationship** Finally, the word 'retainer' may be used as a reference to the professional relationship that is created when a client instructs a legal services provider (thereby creating a duty of care) or to the fact that the giving of instructions is the representative's authorisation to act on behalf of the client.[4]

---

[1] Whilst rarely encountered in modern practice, when applied to counsel, the word 'retainer' may be a reference to a retaining fee, this being a sum of money paid to counsel for the purposes of securing their services. That type of retainer has nothing to do with the issues discussed in this chapter.

[2] Meaning 'source and origin'.

[3] *Phelps v Stewards (a firm)* [2007] EWHC 1561 (Ch), at [1], *per* Bernard Livesey QC (sitting as a judge of the Chancery Division), quoting from *Jackson and Powell on Professional Liability* (6th edn, London: Sweet & Maxwell, 2006), para 11-004.

[4] *Oxford English Dictionary* (3rd edn, Oxford: Oxford University Press, 2010): 'An authorisation given to an attorney to act in a case.'

Where the word 'retainer' or the phrase 'contract of retainer' is used in this book, then—unless the contrary is obvious from the context—it is a reference to the second of these concepts namely, the legal mechanism that gives rise to a right to payment. This is often true of the usage of that word in decided cases, but that is very far from always being the case.

Where the right to payment is contractual, the first and second of these concepts can be thought of as being the supply side and the remuneration side of the same contract. This does not mean that they will always be in the same document, however; indeed, it is often the case that they are not. In particular, the remuneration side of the contract is often set out in a separate document, such as a conditional fee agreement, a business agreement or a damages-based agreement. Where this is so, it is not uncommon for the court to look at the contract as a whole and to take into account all of the relevant documents, be they on the supply side or the remuneration side.[5] **27.04**

The difference between the retainer and the retainer documentation

A retainer and the written instrument that purports to create the retainer are not necessarily the same thing. In the context of a contractual retainer, for example, the contract—that is, the true bargain struck between client and legal services provider—may not be the same as the written instrument that purports to set out the relevant terms. In particular, the written instrument may contain errors, or it may have been qualified or amended by written or unwritten means. Interpretation of contracts of retainer is addressed in Chapter 31. **27.05**

Miscellaneous Principles Relating to Contracts of Retainer

Regardless of the finer points of how they are classified, the purpose of a retainer (be it contract of retainer or non-contractual retainer) is to govern the right to payment for the provision of legal services. This chapter focuses only on contracts of retainer. There are several miscellaneous points that need to be borne in mind when considering the nature and effect of a contract of retainer, as follows. **27.06**

- **Entire contract** A contract of retainer may or may not be an entire contract (see 27.07–27.28). This may be relevant because, where it is, then—unless there is reason to believe otherwise—the legal services provider will not be able to claim payment of fees until the conclusion of the matter to which it relates (see 27.08–27.09).
- **Ambit** The scope of a contract of retainer (or, for that matter, any retainer) may or may not cover the matter in hand (see 27.29–27.37). Where it fails to do this, this may have a bearing on the recoverability of fees for any work done beyond the ambit of the retainer (see 27.36).
- **Interim payments** A contract of retainer may or may not make provision for interim payments, be they payments on account or payments for discrete aspects of the services that have been provided (see 27.38–27.66).
- **Termination and suspension** A contract of retainer may or may not contain express provisions relating to termination (see 27.67–27.88). In general, whilst a client may

[5] See, eg, *Jones v Wrexham Borough Council* [2007] EWCA Civ 1356, at [17]. Other examples exist, such as *Utting v McBain* [2007] EWHC 3293 (QB), at [21]–[24].

terminate a contract at any time and for any reason, a solicitor may do so only in certain circumstances. It is possible for a contract of retainer to be suspended (see 27.89).

- **Waiver** Whilst rare, it is possible for a party to waive their rights under a contract of retainer (see 27.90).
- **Withholding information and undue influence** In certain circumstances, the fact that information was not given to a client may have a bearing on the contract of retainer (see 27.91).

The focus is on contracts of retainer made by solicitors, but, on the whole, the principles will also apply to contracts of retainer made by other legal services providers.

Entire contracts in the context of contracts of retainer

27.07 An entire contract (also known as a 'contract entire' or, in more modern parlance, an 'indivisible contract') is a contract that must be performed in its entirety—or at least substantially performed (see 27.24)—before payment of fees can be claimed. A memorable example is an undertaker who was not able to finish a funeral owing to the bursting of the coffin: he failed to perform the whole of his obligations under the contract and so was not able to raise a fee.[6]

27.08 Some, but by no means all, retainers are entire contracts under which a legal services provider is obliged to provide a complete basket of services (such as legal representation for the duration of a claim) before being entitled to claim payment of a fee. This is of potential significance for the following reasons.

- Except under the doctrine of substantial performance (see 27.24) and subject to certain other exceptions (see 27.25–27.28), a failure to perform the whole of the obligations would mean that the legal services provider would not generally be able to demand performance of the client's obligations (the most important of which would be the obligation to pay fees).[7]
- If those obligations were not performed in full, the legal services provider would not normally be able to claim payment *pro rata* nor would it ordinarily be able to bring a claim in restitution.[8]
- Similarly, the legal services provider would not be able to assert that there was an implied term that contradicted the express term that the contract was an entire contract (if such a term existed); therefore, the legal services provider would not be able to say that it was an implied term that there would be payment for part-performance.
- Finally, the legal services provider would not ordinarily be able to claim *quantum meruit* (see 18.91–18.99).

27.09 Thus, if a legal services provider failed to complete the task of providing the requisite legal services under an entire contract, then it will not ordinarily be entitled to payment, and this will be so even where the legal services provider were prevented from providing the requisite legal services by factors beyond its control.[9] There are ways in which the legal

[6] *Vigers v Cook* [1919] 2 KB 475, CA.
[7] See, eg, *Wild v Simpson* [1919] 2 KB 544.
[8] *Sumpter v Hedges* [1898] 1 QB 673, CA.
[9] See, eg, *Cutter v Powell* (1795) 6 Term Rep 320.

services provider may seek payment, but they would afford only sketchy and erratic relief (see 27.23–27.28).

In modern practice, however, it will rarely be the case that a legal services provider would feel the full force of these strictures because most modern retainers contain some sort of provision for payment in the event of incomplete performance. To that extent, they can be said not to be pure contracts entire. For example, in the case of a contract of retainer that provided that fees would be payable on a time basis and 'up to the date of termination', Sharp LJ found an attempt to avoid payment on the basis that the retainer was an entire contract to be 'unconvincing'.[10] **27.10**

The issue of whether a retainer is an entire contract may still be relevant in modern practice, however, for the following reasons, amongst others. **27.11**

- There continues to be modern-day contracts of retainer that are purely contracts entire and which contain no provisions regarding payment other than upon completion of the legal services obligations. Such contracts are most commonly seen in non-contentious work.
- Even where a provision for payment in the event of partial performance exists, the fact that the retainer is an entire contract may have a bearing on *when* a legal services provider is entitled to payment.
- If the legal services provider is a solicitor, the fact that the retainer is an entire contract may have a bearing on whether a client is entitled to an assessment. In particular, the client may wish to argue that a request for payment was a request only for interim payment on account and, in support of that argument, they may wish to contend that this must have been the case because the retainer was an entire contract.

Thus it is important to be able to distinguish between those retainers that are contracts entire and those that are not. That question can be fully addressed only if something is known of the history of the relevant law because, in ancient times, there was a stark difference between the way in which the common law and the courts of Chancery dealt with contracts of retainer. That difference narrowed over time, so the history of the development of the law is relevant for the purpose of putting older authorities in their correct context. The modern law is described at 27.21–27.22. **27.12**

Historical perspective: the common law and contracts entire

At the end of the 19th century, Lord Esher MR had the following to say about the way in which the common law looked at the issue: **27.13**

> 'When one considers the nature of a common law action, it seems obvious that the law must imply that the contract of the solicitor upon a retainer in the action is an entire contract to conduct the action to the end. When a man goes to a solicitor and instructs him for the purpose of bringing or defending such an action, he does not mean to employ the solicitor to take one step, and then give him fresh instructions to take another step, and so on; he instructs the solicitor as a skilled person to act for him in the action, to take all the necessary steps in it, and to carry it on to the end. If the meaning of the retainer is that the solicitor is to carry on the action to the end, it necessarily follows that the contract of the solicitor is an entire contract—that is, a contract to take all the steps which are necessary to bring the action to a conclusion.'[11]

[10] See *Harding Evans LLP v Spencer-White* [2017] EWCA Civ 434, at [26].
[11] *Underwood, Son & Piper v Lewis* [1894] 2 QB 306, at 309–10.

27.14 So the position at common law was that a retainer was capable of being an entire contract; indeed, it may well have been an entire contract if the instructions could be interpreted in that way. Lord Esher MR went on to say, however, that (at common law) there was a presumption that a retainer would be an entire contract:

> 'When it is shewn that there were no special terms, but only the ordinary retainer for the purposes of the action, the implication I have mentioned is that which every reasonable person would make, and therefore the implication which the law makes in such a case ... There may be circumstances which justify the solicitor in putting an end to the contract, but ... he cannot do so without giving reasonable notice. The result ... seems to me to be that, though there may be valid reasons for giving such a notice, if no such notice is given, the contract of the solicitor is an entire contract, and he cannot sue for his costs before the termination of the action.'[12]

27.15 Thus, unless there were terms to the contrary, at common law a retainer that had been entered into for the purposes of a claim would be presumed to be an entire contract. The legal services provider could end the contract by giving reasonable notice, but if it did so, no fees would be payable.[13]

27.16 Even in Victorian times, however, the application of the concept of the entire contract had its limitations—in particular, it had only very limited application in a case that could properly have been said to have comprised a succession of matters. In this regard, Sir George Jessel MR had this to say:

> 'If a man engages to carry a box of cigars from London to Birmingham, it is an entire contract, and he cannot throw the cigars out of the carriage half-way there, and ask for half the money; or if a shoemaker agrees to make a pair of shoes, he cannot offer you one shoe, and ask you to pay one half the price. That is intelligible. In my opinion, in the case of a solicitor there is not an implied contract of that kind. It bears no fair relation to the doctrine of entire contract. It is a series of services which, though nominally in relation to one matter, is in reality in relation to a succession of matters, and it is not within the doctrine of entire contract, because it is not within the mischief of it. It is not reasonable that a solicitor should engage to act on for an indefinite number of years, winding up estates, without receiving any payment on which he can maintain himself.'[14]

27.17 Therefore, if the legal services provider had been instructed for only a brief period of time, the court would be ready to infer the existence of an entire contract, but the same would not be true of a long-running matter that could properly be said to have been a series of services. In any event, it is trite law that a contract may contain both divisible and indivisible obligations,[15] so even in times gone by, it would have been open to the court to find that a contract of retainer was divisible to an extent that properly reflected the need of the legal services provider to get paid in a long-running matter.

Historical perspective: Chancery proceedings and entire contracts

27.18 The position in respect of Chancery proceedings was different from that at common law. The difference arose out of pragmatism rather than because equity offered a different legal

[12] *Ibid*, at 310.

[13] As an aside, it is worth mentioning that, in ancient times, the solicitor was not able to end the contract at all: so, if it failed to perform the requisite obligations, not only would it be unable to raise a fee, but also it would have been liable in damages for breach of contract.

[14] *In re Hall v Barker* (1893) 9 Ch D 538, at 543.

[15] See, eg, *Hoenig v Isaacs* [1952] 2 All ER 176.

exposition. This was because, in time gone by, Chancery proceedings were prone to lasting much longer than common-law claims—a situation that Lord Esher MR described in the following way:

> 'If a solicitor undertakes to carry through a legal transaction, the law is that he cannot send in a final bill of costs until that transaction is completed; the law on the point is the same in equity as at common law. But in equity the nature of many of the suits is such that they can be divided into stages, and the Court may treat the legal transaction as finished although the suit has not been carried to its final conclusion; this is a most important feature of Chancery proceedings. The ordinary procedure in equity is for the matter to go on to the stage of decree. In many suits there may be successive decrees; but the decision or decree has to be worked out—a process which may take years ... In an ordinary common law action, the duties of the solicitor are completed when judgment is pronounced: the client gets nothing by the action until that time; though the circumstances of each action may differ, the law applicable to them is the same.'[16]

The positions in Chancery proceedings and in common-law claims were therefore at opposite ends of a spectrum. In particular, there was no presumption in the former because each case was decided on its own facts. Sir George Jessel MR had the following to say on the topic: **27.19**

> 'Of course a suit in equity which might relate to a number of different matters might be continued to such a period of time that, if the doctrine extended to suits in equity, one might be compelled, if the case called for discussion and decision, to limit its application to some period or periods during the suit short of the final disposal of it.'[17]

This analysis was approved by Lindley LJ, who commented that it 'is for those who maintain the contrary view to shew some good grounds'.[18]

Thus the position at the end of the 19th century was that different types of case were dealt with in different ways: where it was an unremarkable common-law case, the legal services would generally have been regarded as having been provided under an entire contract; where it was a long-running case, the court would look at each stage individually. In addition, there was a gradual evolution in the law that moderated the rigid common-law analysis. Roskill LJ had this to say on the topic: 'After the fusion of law and equity it is plain that gradually, as common law cases became more complicated, the former rigid common law rule was mitigated on pragmatic grounds.'[19] **27.20**

The modern approach to entire contracts

The modern approach is to decide the issue on the circumstances of each case (the most prominent of which would, of course, be the terms of the contract of retainer). It is not clear whether any of the old presumptions continue to apply, but, even if they do, their practical effect would be greatly diminished by the following factors. **27.21**

- The prevalence of conditional fee agreements means that, in many cases, the legal services provider will necessarily be paid only upon the conclusion of the matter. For obvious

[16] *In re Romer & Haslam* [1893] 2 QB 286, at 293.
[17] *In re Hall v Barker* (1893) 9 Ch D 538, at 543.
[18] *Re Nelson, Son and Hastings* (1885) 30 Ch D 1, at 14.
[19] *Davidsons v Jones-Fenleigh* (1980) Costs LR (Core vol) 70, at 72.

reasons, that type of retainer would generally be an entire contract and this would be so regardless of the type of claim to which it applied (see 27.22).

- In non-conditional contentious cases conducted by a solicitor, the solicitor's statutory right[20] to charge payments on account in contentious business (see 27.40–27.41) often makes the issue of the nature of the retainer somewhat academic.
- The prevalence of standard terms and conditions means that the issue of partial performance is usually dealt with expressly in the retainer. This means that the nature of the retainer can usually be determined by examining it terms, rather than by looking at the nature of the case to which it relates.

In any event, as has been mentioned at 27.10, any attempt by a client to rely on an overly technical analysis will often fail to find favour.

27.22 The following miscellaneous points may be added.

- **Conditional fee agreements** Whilst there is no authority on the point, it is difficult to envisage an ordinary conditional fee agreement that is not an entire contract (or, more accurately, which does not have obligations that are non-divisible). An exception to this is discounted conditional fee agreements (where a discounted fee is payable regardless of whether the case is won), but even in those circumstances the agreement may be drafted in such a way as to make it an entire contract. Another possible exception would be where an agreement is so heavily qualified with contingent provisions that the reality is that payment would be made regardless of the stage at which the agreement terminated. A more common exception would be where the agreement provides for payment of disbursements regardless of the outcome of the claim: if that were the case, then it would be open to the court to find that the agreement is an entire contract, but only in part (that is, that it contains both divisible and non-divisible obligations).
- **Retainers relating to appeals** The position in respect of appeals is much the same as it is in respect of proceedings at first instance. Indeed, if a legal services provider is instructed on an appeal and if that legal services provider had been instructed in the court below, the contract will (in the absence of reason to believe otherwise) generally cover both proceedings.[21] This is often not the case with conditional fee agreements, however, because many such agreements expressly state that they will not cover an appeal brought by the client against a final order.
- **Options and stages** A retainer may have options to cover only certain aspects of the matter (such as an option that it may or may not apply beyond a particular stage in the proceedings); that does not necessarily mean that the retainer is not an entire contract in respect of those parts to which it applies.[22] Where, however, a contract is for the provision of piecemeal services (that is, services in many stages), then it would be open to the court to find that it was not an entire contract.[23]

[20] See Solicitors Act 1974, s 65(2).

[21] *Harris v Quite* (1969) LR 4 QB 653.

[22] See, by analogy, *J Rosenthal & Sons Ltd v Esmail* [1965] 1 WLR 1117, HL at 1131, *per* Lord Pearson.

[23] Whilst it related to a surveyor's retainer rather than a solicitor's, see *Smales v Lea* [2011] EWCA Civ 1325.

- **'General retainers'** Where a legal services provider agrees 'to act generally' for a person, Slesser LJ has stated that it would not be correct to imply a term that it is to continue to act without payment throughout the life of the client.[24]

The effect of a retainer being an entire contract

Where a retainer is an entire contract, the starting position is that the legal services provider is entitled to payment only if it discharges the entirety of its obligations under that retainer.[25] That said, most modern-day retainers will contain provision for payment of a reasonable sum in the event of unforeseen circumstances preventing the legal services provider from performing those obligations. Even where no such provision exists, there are mechanisms that permit a charge to be raised in certain limited circumstances, including those set out below. The points made about 'natural breaks' also ought to be noted (see 27.64–27.66 and 35.28–35.36). **27.23**

Substantial performance Where the obligations have been substantially performed such that there are only minor or inconsequential matters outstanding, the doctrine of substantial performance may allow the legal services provider to claim payment,[26] such payment being subject to an adjustment in respect of those tasks that the provider has not completed.[27] An example might be where a legal services provider has agreed to carry out a transaction for a fixed sum, but, whilst they have been able to effect the transaction, certain formalities remain outstanding for reasons beyond its control. **27.24**

Acceptance of partial performance Where the original retainer is an entire contract and where it can be inferred that the client has agreed that a new retainer (or an amended retainer) should be made for performance of lesser obligations, payment may be demanded upon performance of those lesser obligations.[28] The client must have had the opportunity to accept or reject the part-performance (that is, the performance of the lesser obligations) and they must have chosen to accept.[29] It would not generally be relevant that the part-performance was as a result of the legal services provider's own decision[30] (such as where a legal services provider wishes to withdraw from a case for personal reasons). **27.25**

Partial performance under a contentious business agreement Where a solicitor is prevented from performing its obligations under a contentious business agreement, s 63 of the Solicitors Act 1974 will, in some circumstances (that is, death, incapacity or disinstruction of the solicitor), permit an allowance of an appropriate amount, which **27.26**

---

24 *Warmingtons v McMurray* [1937] 1 All ER 562. In a different case, Tuckey LJ has stated that a general retainer is an entire contract: see *Donsland Ltd (a firm) v Van Hoogstraten* [2002] EWCA Civ 253. That, however, was in the context of considering whether the solicitor had authority to act, rather than considering a solicitor's right to payment, and it probably should not be taken as authority for the proposition that the retainer cannot be broken down into its constituent parts for the purpose of considering remuneration.

25 See *Wild v Simpson* [1919] 2 KB 544. As a modern example of this principle in operation, see *Richard Buxton (a firm) v Mills-Owens* [2008] EWHC 1831 (QB), which decision was reversed on appeal on the grounds that the solicitor had been entitled to terminate ([2010] EWCA Civ 122).

26 In a non-costs context, see *H Dakin & Co Ltd v Lee* [1916] 1 KB 566, CA.

27 *Hoenig v Isaacs* [1952] 2 All ER 176, CA.

28 See *Astilleros Canarios SA v Cape Hatteras Shipping Co SA, The Cape Hatteras* [1982] 1 Lloyd's Rep 518; *Appleby v Myers* (1867) LR 2 CP 651.

29 *Sumpter v Hedges* [1898] 1 QB 673, CA.

30 In a non-costs context, see *Appleby v Myers* (1867) LR 2 CP 651, at 65, *per* Blackburn J.

amount will usually be assessed on a basis that takes the terms of the agreement into account (see 27.182–27.184).

27.27 **Frustration and repudiation** Where a client frustrates the performance of the legal services provider's obligations and where the legal services provider has performed services that are of valuable benefit to the client, the legal services provider may recover such sums as the court deems fit.[31] There are three stages to the process: first, the court must identify the benefit bestowed on the client (which will be provision of legal services); then, it must value that benefit (that is, assess the value of those services); and finally, it must award a sum that is just.[32]

27.28 Even where a retainer is an entire contract, the legal services provider is entitled to terminate that arrangement without being in breach of contract (assuming, of course, that they have the right to terminate in general, which right is dealt with in more detail at 27.70–27.75). If a client repudiates the contract of retainer (such as by stating a clear intention not to pay the legal services provider), then the legal services provider may be entitled to accept that repudiation, in which case it will be entitled to payment of damages assessed on a loss-of-chance basis.[33]

Ambit and authority and contracts of retainer

27.29 This section discusses whether work can be said to fall within the ambit of a retainer and, if not, what effect this would have on the legal services provider's ability to recover fees. This topic would usually be relevant to whether a client—and, by extension, a paying party—is liable for fees putatively payable in accordance with the retainer in question, but it may also be relevant to other issues, such as whether a legal services provider bore such-and-such a risk of loss under a conditional fee agreement.[34]

Ambit

27.30 Whether work is within the ambit of the retainer is a matter of contractual interpretation. Whilst no special principles apply, common sense dictates that the purpose of a retainer is to facilitate the provision of legal services and that therefore where the court is faced with two competing interpretations, one of which would embrace those services and one of which would not, a purposive construction would favour the former over the latter. An example of this is a 'general retainer' (which is a retainer to look after a person's affairs generally): Tuckey LJ said that the lack of specific instructions in those circumstances ought not to be construed as limiting the ambit of the retainer.[35]

---

[31] See the Law Reform (Frustrated Contracts) Act 1943. An example of this happening in practice is *Howes Percival LLP v Page* [2013] EWHC 4104 (Ch), *per* Judge Behrens (sitting as a judge of the High Court).

[32] In an analogous context other than costs, see *BP Exploration Co (Libya) Ltd v Hunt (No 2)* [1979] 1 WLR 783, at 801, *per* Goff J.

[33] See *Howes Percival LLP v Page* [2013] EWHC 4104 (Ch), at [259]–[264] and [316] (on the assessment of damages), *per* Judge Behrens (sitting as a judge of the High Court).

[34] An example of this is *O'Brien v Shorrock and MIB* [2015] EWHC 1630 (QB), at [15]–[21], in which Edis J found that a success fee should be assessed on the basis that recovery of compensation under the Untraced Drivers Agreement did not fall within the ambit of a conditional fee agreement and that, as such, the prospect that compensation may be obtained in that way rather than through civil litigation was a risk that could be reflected in the allowable success fee.

[35] *Donsland Ltd (a firm) v Van Hoogstraten* [2002] EWCA Civ 253, at [27]. This was in a context other than costs, but that part of Tuckey LJ's reasoning probably does apply to the ambit of the retainer for the purposes of costs.

The background facts will often be of relevance to the issue of ambit. An example of this is a case in which a claimant who had been injured in a road traffic accident brought a claim in the knowledge that there was a possibility that he would fail but still be awarded compensation through the Untraced Drivers Agreement. In view of the fact that the latter could not be said to be 'damages' and in view of the fact that costs are, in general, not payable under the Untraced Drivers Agreement, Edis J found that recovery of compensation under that Agreement did not fall within the ambit of the claimant's conditional fee agreement and therefore would not have counted as a 'win' for the purposes of assessing the success fee.[36] **27.31**

It is not uncommon for the court to find that the work carried out by a legal services provider fell within the ambit of the retainer despite the fact that, on a literal interpretation, the retainer did not correctly describe that work.[37] Whilst only a decision refusing permission to appeal (and therefore not a decision that should be cited in court), Maurice Kay LJ found that it was not incumbent upon a solicitor to draft the contract of retainer in such a way as to embrace all areas into which the claim may develop.[38] If this is correct, then retainers may have a certain amount of malleability. **27.32**

Whilst the court will often determine the ambit of contract of retainer in a purposive way, the court has other tools that may be used to avoid an unjust outcome. It may, for example, be able to find an implied term that covers the work in question or, in an appropriate case, it may even find that an entire implied retainer has been created (see 27.190–27.206).[39] It may also find that there has been an implied variation of the retainer.[40] To avoid difficulties arising out of the rule that there can be no liability for the costs incurred without authority before the retainer was made,[41] it would be open to the court to rely on the presumption that authority to incur fees may be implied by virtue of the fact that instructions were given.[42] There have also been instances of the court finding that the client is estopped from denying the applicability of the retainer.[43] **27.33**

Retainers are not always so pliable, however. In a case in which a conditional fee agreement referred to the actual defendant, but not to a potential defendant, Floyd LJ said that the claimant had been right to accept that the agreement could cover only the cost of the named (that is, the actual) defendant.[44] Although not binding, Judge Stewart QC **27.34**

---

36 *O'Brien v Shorrock and MIB* [2015] EWHC 1630 (QB), at [15]–[21].

37 Whilst not binding, in a case in which the name of the person against whom the claim had been brought differed from the opponent named in the retainer, Master Gordon-Saker found that the work carried out fell within the ambit of the retainer because the person named as the opponent conducted business on behalf of the true opponent: see *Brierley v Prescott* [2006] EWHC 90062 (Costs). See also *Scott v Transport for London* (unreported), 23 December 2009, Hastings County Court, *per* Judge Hollis; *Brooks v DC Leisure Management Ltd* [2013] EW Misc 17 (CC), *per* Judge Cotter QC.

38 *Blair v Danesh* [2009] EWCA Civ 516.

39 As an example, see *Meretz Investments Ltd v ACP Ltd* [2007] EWHC 2635 (Ch).

40 Whilst not binding, see *Scott v Transport for London* (unreported), 23 December 2009, Hastings County Court, *per* Judge Hollis; *Brooks v DC Leisure Management Ltd* [2013] EW Misc 17 (CC), *per* Judge Cotter QC.

41 *Re Watson, ex p Phillips* (1887) 19 QBD 234, CA.

42 See, eg, *Bolden v Nicholay* (1857) 3 Jur NS 884.

43 Whilst not binding, see *Scott v Transport for London* (unreported), 23 December 2009, Hastings County Court, *per* Judge Hollis.

44 See *Engeham v London & Quadrant Housing Trust* [2015] EWCA Civ 1530, at [10].

found that where a conditional fee agreement stated that the opponent was person A, but the claim was pursued against a person B, the work done in respect of person B did not fall within the ambit of the contract of retainer.[45] He rejected the notion that a purposive construction would permit the court to find otherwise. Judge Stewart QC also rejected the argument that the claimant had elected to treat the contract as covering the claim against person B and that it is not for a stranger to the contract (that is, the paying party) to intervene with an argument to the contrary.[46] There are examples (none of which are binding) of the court taking a similar approach to that taken by Judge Stewart QC in circumstances in which the claim was brought under the Fatal Accidents Act 1976, but the retainer was in respect of the Law Reform (Miscellaneous Provisions) Act 1934.[47] That said, there are also examples of Judge Stewart's analysis not finding favour with other judges.[48]

27.35 There are other reasons why the court may not be overly liberal in so far as interpretation is concerned, not least being that the contract of retainer is an important factor in deciding the duty that a legal services provider owes to its client. In general, the court will not extend that duty far beyond the express bounds of the retainer, although an extension might be appropriate in narrow circumstances in which there was a close factual and legal connection between the retainer and the issue in question.[49]

Work carried out beyond the ambit of the retainer

27.36 Where work has been carried out beyond the ambit of the written contract of retainer, it does not necessarily follow that the legal services provider will be unable to require payment for services rendered. As set out above (see 27.30–27.37), the court may interpret the agreement in such a way as to embrace the work that has been done, but, even where this is not the case, there are mechanisms by which a right to fees may be enforced. The following points may be made in this regard.

- **Presumption in favour of payment and implied retainers** There have been examples of the court simply relying on the rebuttable presumption that a person who instructs a legal services provider will be liable for the legal services provider's reasonable costs (see 27.190–27.194).[50] In a similar vein, the court may find that the facts of the matter give rise to an implied retainer (see 27.190–27.206). Where the work has been carried out on a conditional fee basis, it would not usually be possible for the receiving party to rely on these principles, because it is a statutory requirement that conditional fee agreements are in writing.[51]
- **Estoppel** There have been instances of the court finding that the client in question is estopped from denying the fact that the retainer covers the work for which they gave instructions,[52] but this is a rare finding and each case must be decided on its own facts.

[45] *Law v Liverpool City Council* (unreported), 10 May 2005, Liverpool County Court.
[46] This was an argument based on *King v Victoria Insurance Co* [1896] AC 250.
[47] See, eg, *Pacey v The Ministry of Defence* [2009] EWHC 90138 (Costs).
[48] Whilst *obiter* (and whilst not binding in any event), Judge Hollis QC has said that he does not accept Judge Stewart's reasoning: *Brooks v DC Leisure Management Ltd* [2013] EW Misc 17 (CC), at [41].
[49] Whilst it related to financial advisers rather than to legal services providers, see *Denning v Greenhalgh Financial Services* [2017] EWHC 143 (QB), at [43], [46], [51]–[58] and [64]–[65], *per* Green J.
[50] As an example, see *Meretz Investments Ltd v ACP Ltd* [2007] EWHC 2635 (Ch).
[51] See Courts and Legal Services Act 1990 (as amended), s 58(3)(a).
[52] See, eg, *Scott v Transport for London* (unreported), 23 December 2009, Hastings County Court, at [10], *per* Judge Hollis.

Phillips J has explained that any such estoppel would not prevent an opponent from raising a challenge.[53]

- ***Quantum meruit*** For the reasons set out at 18.91–18.99, it would be difficult for a legal services provider to rely on *quantum meruit.*
- **Litigation friends** It may be argued that the retainer was with a litigation friend, but the work had been done for the benefit of a child or person who lacks capacity. For the reasons set out in the footnotes, that argument would usually fail by reason of the litigation friend's non-contractual ability to recover their fees from the property of the person whom they represent.[54]

Authority

Another issue that may arise is whether work was carried out with the authority of a client. Authority may be express[55] or implied[56] and it may be given in advance or retrospectively by way of ratification.[57] An agent who has been given authority to act generally will have authority to instruct a legal services provider.[58] This applies to insurers who appoint legal services providers to act on behalf of an insured.[59] It also applies to legal services providers who themselves instruct agents,[60] but it would not permit a legal services provider to instruct a different legal services provider to act in its stead.[61] **27.37**

Interim payments and contracts of retainer

What follows addresses the contractual aspects of interim payments (that is, payments made prior to the conclusion of the matter). Other aspects of interim payments (such as procedure, amount, etc) are addressed at 35.06–35.36. Much of what follows applies only to contracts of retainer with solicitors. **27.38**

The circumstances in which a solicitor may render a bill are: **27.39**

- in accordance with s 65(2) of the Solicitors Act 1974 (see 27.40–27.41);
- by express agreement (see 27.42–27.55);

[53] See *Blankley v Central Manchester and Manchester Children's University Hospitals NHS Trust* [2014] EWHC 168 (QB), at [60] (aff'd [2015] EWCA Civ 18), in which Phillips J had this to say: 'Solicitors acting in proceedings represent and warrant that they have the authority of the party they purport to represent. In the ordinary course, the opposing party does not in any sense agree that such authority in fact exists, nor share a common assumption as to its existence. The opposing party does not need to (and would be ill advised to) communicate any such agreement or assumption, precisely because it may later emerge that authority was absent or defective. The fact that the opposing party deals with solicitors without questioning their authority does not amount to such communication, and implies at most that the opposing party is relying upon the solicitors' warranty. Such reliance cannot give rise to any form of estoppel.'

[54] In particular, CPR, r 21.12, makes express provision for the recovery of expenses, including costs. Thus the person whom the litigation friend represents would be liable for the costs not by reason of having a direct contractual liability, but by reason of the CPR making express provision that the litigation friend's fees can be recovered. Whilst there is no authority on the point, the mechanism by which that liability is created probably has more in common with a costs order than with an obligation arising out of a contract.

[55] See, eg, *Pickford v Ewington* (1835) 4 Dowl 453; *May v Sherwin* (1883) 27 Sol Jo 278, CA.

[56] See, eg, *Tomlinson v Broadsmith* [1896] 1 QB 386, CA. See also *Court v Berlin* [1897] 2 QB 396, CA.

[57] *Terrell v Hutton* (1854) 4 HL Cas 1091, at 1099, *per* Lord Cranworth.

[58] *Re Frampton, ex p Frampton* (1859) 1 De GF & J 263, CA.

[59] See *Walsh v Julius* (1927) The Times, 13 July; *Luck v Meyler* (1928) 72 Sol Jo 337.

[60] See *Re Bishop, ex p Langley, ex p Smith* (1879) 13 Ch D 110, CA. See also *Solley v Wood* (1852) 16 Beav 370.

[61] *Re Becket, Purnell v Paine* [1918] 2 Ch 72, CA.

- by implied agreement (see 27.56–27.63);
- where there is a 'natural break' in the matter (see 27.64, 27.66 and 35.28–35.36); and
- upon termination of the retainer (see 27.67), although this would not technically be an interim payment.

Payments on account in contentious business

27.40 In cases in which the retainer relates to contentious business conducted by a solicitor, the solicitor has a statutory right to ask for a payment on account.[62] This means that it is not necessary for the contract of retainer to contain any express provision in this regard (although it often will).

27.41 Payments on account are dealt with in more detail at 35.10–35.14, but for present purposes—namely, the contractual aspects of the matter—it is sufficient to say that, in a contentious matter, if a client refuses or fails to make a payment that the solicitor has reasonably requested, the solicitor's remedy is to withdraw from the retainer. The position of a non-solicitor legal services provider is less certain and it is for this reason that retainers with non-solicitor legal services providers ought to contain express provisions dealing with non-payment.

Terms for payment of interim payments

27.42 Where a retainer makes provision for interim payments, a distinction needs to be made between whether that provision is (a) for payments on account or (b) for interim statute bills. That issue will turn on two things: first, what is said in the retainer; and secondly, the nature of, and circumstances in which, the invoice in question was rendered. The former is discussed here and the latter, at 35.15–35.27.

27.43 Most standard-form retainers make provision for interim payments, often on a set date of each calendar month or at intervals no more frequent than monthly. This will, however, often leave open the issue of whether those provisions permit a solicitor to render interim statute bills.

27.44 **The desirability of certainty** It is desirable, from a consumer protection point of view, to make the situation clear in an express and transparent way. Judge LJ had the following to say on that topic:

> 'The desirability of such arrangements is likely to be reinforced by the increasing impact of the Civil Justice Reforms on a client's entitlement to be kept properly informed of his escalating financial obligations at each stage of the proceedings. As clients should know exactly where they stand throughout the process, it is reasonable to anticipate that questions of their own costs, and payment, should be arranged at an early stage in the process.'[63]

Many well-drafted contracts of retainer put the matter beyond all doubt—in particular, often containing a clarificatory provision along the lines of the following:

> 'Any invoice that is delivered prior to the termination of the agreement will be an interim statute bill unless the contrary is expressly stated on its face; this means that unless the

[62] See Solicitors Act 1974, s 65(2). The statutory right is different from the other types of right to ask for payment, for the following reasons: the right is to ask for a payment on account, not to enforce it; the right relates to payments on account of fees incurred or yet to be incurred, rather than payments in final discharge of fees already incurred; and there are no fetters as to the time(s) when requests may be made.

[63] *Abedi v Penningtons* [2000] 2 Costs LR 205, at 221.

invoice says otherwise, it will be a self-contained statute bill for all work done and expenses incurred the period covered by that invoice and time will immediately begin to run for the purposes of the matters set out in [the provisions relating to solicitor and client assessments]. We reserve the right to claim payments on account, but if we do this, this will be stated on the face of the invoice.'

Retainers that make provision for both interim statute bills and payments on account Many retainers contain provision for both interim statute bills and payments on account. In particular, retainers will commonly contain a clarificatory provision that says that, unless the contrary is stated on the face of the invoice, invoices rendered prior to the conclusion of the retainer are (or are not) to be treated as being interim statute bills (see the example above). **27.45**

Retainers that make provision for both payments on account and interim statute bills, and which do not contain such a clarificatory provision are prone to giving rise to problems. This is because disputes may arise about the true status of invoices rendered prior to the conclusion of the matter. If, for example, there is a series of detailed invoices, there may be a dispute about whether time began to run for the purposes of s 70 of the Solicitors Act 1974 on the dates on which each was delivered or only on the date on which the final invoice was delivered (or at all).[64] Such issues may need to be decided on the basis of factors other than the terms of the contract of retainer, which topic is addressed in detail at 35.86 and 36.15–36.16. **27.46**

Retainers that make no express provision for interim payments Where a contract of retainer does not make express provision for interim payments (be those on account or otherwise), then the court may have to consider whether there are any implied provisions. This is addressed at 27.56–27.59. **27.47**

A contract of retainer that does not make express provision for interim payments may be varied by subsequent agreement. In particular, cases may arise in which it is said that there was an express agreement that interim statute bills may be rendered, but that the agreement was not reduced into writing. Where there is a dispute about such facts, Denning LJ made it clear that the solicitor may have to suffer the effects of having failed to make a written record of what was said.[65] If the agreement was with a consumer client, the points made in 27.55 may also be relevant. **27.48**

If the contract of retainer does not make provision for the delivery of interim statute bills, the mere fact that a solicitor states in correspondence that there was no proposal to invoice any further amount would not convert a request for payment on account into an interim bill. This is so regardless of whether the solicitor also indicated that, in the absence of an application for assessment, proceedings for the amounts already invoiced would be brought.[66] **27.49**

Retainers that are ambiguous as to whether they allow for interim statute bills If a contract of retainer makes an ambiguous provision for interim payments, the court may have **27.50**

[64] As an example, see *Bari v Rosen (t/a RA Rosen & Co Solicitors)* [2012] EWHC 1782 (QB), [2012] 5 Costs LR 851. See also *Vlamaki v Sookias & Sookias* [2015] EWHC 3334 (QB).
[65] *Griffiths v Evans* [1953] 2 All ER 1364, at 1369.
[66] See *Vlamaki v Sookias & Sookias* [2015] EWHC 3334 (QB), at [38], *per* Walker J.

to decide whether it allows a solicitor to render interim statute bills. The points made in Chapter 31 about contractual interpretation may be relevant in that regard. In addition, the points made below may be made.

27.51 *The role of* contra proferentem *and asymmetry of information* Where appropriate, it would be open to the court to have regard to the following two points: (a) the fact that, where a contract of retainer has been drafted by the solicitor, the principle of *contra proferentem* may apply (see 31.40); and (b) the fact that the solicitors were lawyers, whereas the client was not[67] (meaning that there would be asymmetry of information, in the sense that the client could not be expected to know the relevant legal principles). For the reasons set out below, it seems that these two principles may have a significant bearing on the way in which the court will construe a contract of retainer, at least in a case in which the client was not a lawyer.

27.52 *Seemingly conflicting authorities* Having made the above two points, Walker J went on to say the following about the way in which the court is likely to approach a dispute about the effect of a contract of retainer:

> 'Those observations underscore the impracticality and unfairness to a client if a retainer has the effect that interim bills are final in relation to the period that they cover, with resultant drastic limitations on the ability of the client to make use of statutory provisions for assessment. Thus, for example, a client who followed [a certain] complaints procedure ... would, without knowing it, be giving up the statutory right to taxation within 1 month of delivery of the bill. These drastic limitations, and the inevitable recognition of the factual matrix found in [point (b)] above, in my view constitute sound reasons for strictly applying [point (a)] above. Application of such a concession carries with it a corollary: unless the retainer makes it unambiguous, the client will not be able to say that under the retainer bills are final in relation to the period that they cover. However that corollary, to my mind, is unlikely to cause injustice to either side.'[68]

27.53 Thus, according to this analysis, if there is ambiguity as to whether a contract of retainer allows a solicitor to deliver interim statute bills, that ambiguity ought generally to be resolved against that construction. Walker J found that the words 'a bill for our charges and expenses at the end of each month while the work is in progress' and 'a final bill after completion of the work' were ambiguous, and hence did not give rise to a right to render interim statute bills.[69] Indeed, he went so far as to suggest that, to avoid any ambiguity, there would have to be a specific statement telling the client that the bill 'at the end of each month' would be final as to work and expenses during the period covered by the bill.[70]

27.54 This, however, was markedly different from the way in which Keith J had dealt with a very similar issue five years earlier. In particular, Keith J had found that, in a contract of retainer that distinguished between 'interim bills' and 'requests for payment on account', the former was a reference to interim statute bills.[71] Walker J distinguished

---

67 *Ibid*, at [15].
68 *Ibid*, at [15]. See also *Bari v Rosen (t/a Rosen & Co Solicitors)* [2012] EWHC 1782 (QB).
69 *Vlamaki v Sookias & Sookias* [2015] EWHC 3334 (QB), at [19]–[27], *per* Walker J.
70 *Ibid*, at [24].
71 See *R (on the application of Scott Halborg, trading under the style of Halborg & Co, Solicitors) v Law Society* [2010] EWHC 38 (Admin), at [23].

Keith J's analysis on the basis that, in the case before him, the solicitors had conceded that the two points referred to in 27.51 applied, whereas those points had not been raised in the case before Keith J.[72] That may be so, but the reality is that those two points would almost always apply (other than, perhaps, if the client was unusually experienced in legal matters or was themselves a lawyer); as such, it does seem that there is a conflict between the approaches of Keith J and Walker J. Whilst it is no more than the editor's opinion, Walker J's approach is probably to be preferred. This is not only because it builds upon an approach taken by Spencer J in another case,[73] but also because it reflects the general trend towards increased consumer protection that has arisen since Keith J's judgment. Indeed, as is explained immediately below, present-day consumer protection legislation strongly supports Walker J's approach, at least in so far as consumers are concerned.

Consumer protection legislation Whilst there is no authority on the point, if the client were a consumer, then the points made by Walker J (see 27.52) are likely to be all the more true, given the effect of regs 9(1), 10(1) and 13(1) of the Consumer Contracts (Information, Cancellation and Additional Charges) Regulations 2013.[74] This is because Schs 1 and 2 of those Regulations require a legal services provider to explain 'the arrangements for payment' before the contract of retainer is made (see 28.71–28.76).[75] Moreover, if the contract was made on or after 1 October 2015, any such information would be treated as being included as a term of the contract of retainer (see 28.30–28.33 and 28.81).[76] Whilst it is no more than the editor's opinion, it seems likely that, where the client is a consumer, the combination of Walker J's analysis and the aforesaid provisions is that a solicitor may deliver such to a consumer client only if it was expressly stated that an interim bill would be final as to work and expenses during the period it covered. **27.55**

Implied provisions regarding interim payments

The question here is whether a retainer contains an implied term that permits the legal services provider to render interim statute bills. Much of what is said applies only to solicitors. The topic of contractual implication in general is discussed in Chapter 31. There is a great deal of overlap between this topic and the topic of 'natural breaks' (see 27.64–27.66). The points made at 27.54 and 27.55 are also likely to be relevant. **27.56**

Where the circumstances permit, it is possible for a contract of retainer to contain an implied provision that the solicitor is entitled to deliver interim statute bills. Each case will turn on its own facts, but the circumstances in which such a provision may arise include: **27.57**

- where the client has received invoices that purport to be interim statute bills and where they have paid them without demur;

[72] *Vlamaki v Sookias & Sookias* [2015] EWHC 3334 (QB), at [26], *per* Walker J.
[73] See *Bari v Rosen (t/a Rosen & Co Solicitors)* [2012] EWHC 1782 (QB).
[74] SI 2013/3134.
[75] See also, in particular, the advice given by the Competition and Markets Authority (CMA), reproduced at 28.72.
[76] Consumer Contracts (Information, Cancellation and Additional Charges) Regulations 2013 (SI 2013/3134), reg 9(3). Consumer Rights Act 2015, s 50, also has this effect.

- where the solicitor and client had previously conducted business on the basis that interim statute bills would be delivered; and
- where there was a custom that interim statute bills would be delivered.

For the reasons set out in 27.54 and 27.55, it is unlikely that the court would be now willing to find that there was such an implied provision where the client is a consumer or where there was asymmetry of information (or both).

27.58 Although the points made immediately above ought to be borne in mind, Simon Brown LJ has confirmed that interim statute bills may become payable by virtue of what can be inferred from the circumstances, as well as by virtue of what is set out in the retainer.[77] In particular, where a client has received what purported to be interim statute bills and where they have paid them without demur, that would be a factor to be taken into account. Roskill LJ had this to say on the topic:

> 'If the client's reaction is to pay the bill in its entirety without demur it is not difficult to infer an agreement that that bill is to be treated as a complete self-contained bill of costs to date ... Looking at each of [the bills], it seems to me, applying the principles laid down in [*In re Romer & Haslam* [1893] 2 QB 286], that there was a clear intention on the part of the [solicitors], and indeed a plain agreement to be inferred from the conduct of the parties that those bills should be treated as completely self-contained bills covering the period down to the relevant date given.'[78]

27.59 Cogent evidence of implication is required (see 27.60) and Simon Brown LJ has said that the mere fact of payment would not of itself usually be sufficient.[79] This is particularly true in cases in which the issue is whether the invoices were requests for payments on account rather than interim statutes bills. It should also be borne in mind that, in appropriate circumstances, a series of invoices delivered over a period of time may constitute a single bill, known as a *Chamberlain* bill (see 36.15).[80] If those were the circumstances, then the fact that the interim invoices were received and paid would say very little about whether the solicitor was entitled to render interim statute bills.

27.60 **Evidence of implied provisions for the delivery of interim statute bills** Cogent evidence is required before the court will conclude that there is an implied provision that interim statute bills may be rendered. This is because the delivery of an interim statute bill starts time running for the purposes of s 70 of the Solicitors Act 1974 and, as such, is potentially prejudicial to the client. Fulford J explained that the onus is on the solicitor to explain matters clearly to the client:

> 'In particular the party must know what rights are being negotiated and dispensed with in the sense that the solicitor must make it plain to the client that the purpose of sending the bill at that time is that it is to be treated as a complete self-contained bill of costs to date'.[81]

---

77 *Abedi v Penningtons* [2000] 2 Costs LR 205.

78 *Davidsons v Jones-Fenleigh* (1980) Costs LR (Core vol) 70, at 75.

79 *Abedi v Penningtons* [2000] 2 Costs LR 205, at 219, citing *In re Romer & Haslam* [1893] 2 QB 286, at 298, *per* Bowen LJ. See also *R (on the application of Scott Halborg, trading under the style of Halborg & Co, Solicitors) v Law Society* [2010] EWHC 38 (Admin), at [25], *per* Keith J.

80 After *Chamberlain v Boodle & King* [1982] 1 WLR 1443. See also *Re Cartwright* (1873) LR 16 Eq 469; *Bari v Rosen (t/a RA Rosen & Co Solicitors)* [2012] EWHC 1782.

81 *Adams v Al Malik* [2003] EWHC 3232 (QB), at [48].

The points made by Walker J, as set out at 27.52–27.54, seem to support this view.

Where there is a factual dispute, a legal services provider may find that the court prefers the client's evidence if the former has not made a written record of what was said and done (see 27.92–27.101). However, where the disputed fact is something that would not normally be recorded in writing, then this principle has less relevance. **27.61**

The effect of the Solicitors Code of Conduct 2007 (now revoked) Although there is no authority on the point, where the retainer was made before 6 October 2011, the Solicitors' Code of Conduct 2007 may have had a bearing on the issue. This is because it contained a requirement to give advice about the retainer and to confirm that information in writing[82] (see 27.98). A failure to comply with those requirements would be a factor to be taken into account, but it would not necessarily mean that the court would reject the solicitor's contentions.[83] **27.62**

The effect of the SRA Code of Conduct 2011 The Solicitors Regulation Authority (SRA) Code of Conduct 2011 contains no express requirement that the terms of the retainer be in writing;[84] rather, it states an 'indicative behaviour' (IB)—which is not a binding requirement—that information must be given in 'a clear and accessible form which is appropriate to the needs and circumstances of the client'[85] (see 27.99–27.101 for more detail). It is possible that this implies a need for the terms of the retainer to be in written form, but there is no authority on this point. **27.63**

Natural breaks and contracts of retainer

The next question is whether the retainer is such that interim statute bills may be rendered when there is a 'natural break' in the proceedings or matter to which the retainer relates. This topic is closely allied to the topic of implied provisions (see 27.56–27.59), but it is a topic of some significance because if a client pays an invoice and only subsequently learns that it was an interim statute bill, they may unwittingly have set off down a path towards losing the right to have that bill assessed. **27.64**

A natural break will arise where one part of the proceedings or matter draws to a close and another begins. Unless there is provision to the contrary (such as an express or implied term in the retainer), then such a natural break will allow the solicitor to deliver a statute bill for the work that has already been done during that part which has drawn to a close. Lord Esher MR described a natural break in the following way: '[The] conclusion of a definite and distinct part of the legal transaction as would entitle the solicitors to send in a final bill of costs.'[86] Because of the lack of certainty as to what constitutes a natural break, however, Cranston J has said that solicitors should rely on that concept in only the clearest of cases.[87] **27.65**

---

82 See rr 2.03(1) and 2.03(5), and, in respect of conditional fee agreements, r 2.03(2).

83 Whilst dealing with the indemnity principle and, in particular, hourly rates, see *Ghadami v Lyon Cole Insurance Group Ltd* [2010] EWCA Civ 767, at [27], *per* Lloyd LJ.

84 There are provisions relating to complaints and service provision, but not to fees: see SRA Code of Conduct 2011, O(1.9) and O(1.10).

85 See SRA Code of Conduct 2011, IB(1.19).

86 *In re Romer & Haslam* [1893] 2 QB 286, at 293.

87 *Minkin v Cawdery Kaye Fireman & Taylor* [2011] EWHC 177 (QB), at [28], citing with approval from *Cordery on Solicitors* (now *Cordery on Legal Services*, LexisNexis, online). Cranston J's decision was reversed on appeal ([2012] EWCA Civ 546), but on a different point.

27.66 Not all retainers will allow the solicitor to render a statute bill in the event of there being a natural break. Whether a retainer prohibits or permits such a thing will be a matter of contractual interpretation. The following points may be made.

- **Express confirmation regarding 'natural breaks'** It is often the case that a contract of retainer will expressly confirm that interim statute bills may be delivered after a natural break. In the editor's experience, this is usually done by referring to bills being rendered 'at other times' (that is, other than regular bills) or 'at an appropriate stage', rather than by using the phrase 'natural breaks'. For the reasons set out at 27.52–27.54, it is doubtful whether such a provision would be effective against a consumer client unless that client was specifically told that any such bill would be a statute bill.
- **Implied confirmation regarding 'natural breaks'** A facility to render interim statute bills may be implied. This is discussed at 27.56–27.59. Indeed, on one analysis, a natural break is little more than a species of implied contractual term.
- **Provisions that are contrary to 'natural breaks'** Retainers may contain provisions that mean that the solicitor is not entitled to rely on the concept of 'natural breaks'. It is rare for a retainer to contain an express provision to that effect, but such a provision may exist by implication (such as where the retainer lists the situations in which interim statute bills may be delivered, but makes no mention of natural breaks).[88] The matters set out at 27.52–27.54 may also be relevant.
- **Provisions that supersede 'natural breaks'** It is often the case that a retainer will make express provision for the delivery of interim statute bills at regular intervals. Whilst such provisions would usually make the issue academic, it may be that the express provisions are so thorough as to leave little room for the notion of natural breaks.
- **The nature of the retainer** Whilst the nature of the retainer will be relevant, it will rarely be determinative of the issue of whether there has been a natural break. In particular, a finding that the retainer is an entire contract will be of only limited relevance. This is because the whole point of the doctrine of natural breaks is to allow interim payment of costs in circumstances in which the retainer is an entire contract.

Termination of contracts of retainer

27.67 The termination of a retainer may have many consequences in so far as costs are concerned. It may also have other consequences, especially where the act of termination was at the behest of the legal services provider. This book focuses solely on the law of costs; in particular, issues of negligence are not discussed and professional conduct is discussed only to the very limited extent that it is relevant to the law of costs. Legal services providers contemplating terminating a retainer should ensure that it is professionally proper for them to do so, but this book makes no attempt to address that issue in any depth.

The circumstances in which termination may arise

27.68 A retainer may (or may not) be terminated in many ways, but the following merit specific mention:

- termination by the client (see 27.69);
- termination by the legal services provider (see 27.70–27.75);

[88] This would be an example of the principle *expressio unius est exclusio alterius* ('to express one thing is to exclude another').

- termination by reason of death (see 27.76–27.78);
- termination by reason of incapacity (see 27.79–27.81 and 60.64);
- putative termination by reason of insolvency on the part of the client (see 27.82); and
- putative termination by insolvency or inability to practise on the part of the legal services provider (see 27.83).

Termination of a contract of retainer should be distinguished from suspension, which is addressed at 27.89.

Termination by the client A client may end the retainer at any time and for any reason.[89] Many retainers contain an express provision to this effect.[90] In any event, unless the retainer is an entire contract, the common law will give rise to the existence of an implied right to terminate.[91] Where the client is a consumer, they may also be given a statutory right to cancel the retainer, as is discussed at 28.89–28.94, but technically this would not be termination of the retainer (that is, it would be cancellation *ab initio* instead). A client may, where appropriate, treat a retainer as having been terminated if the legal services provider is guilty of misconduct of a type that is incompatible with it carrying out the work.[92] Moreover, a disclaimer of liability under the retainer may be accepted as repudiation thereof.[93] **27.69**

Termination by the legal services provider Subject to giving reasonable notice, a solicitor may terminate only for good reason (or 'good cause', as it is referred to in the Solicitors Act 1974). Examples of when it would be reasonable to give notice of an intention to terminate include a breakdown in confidence between solicitor and the client, where the solicitor believes the case to be not properly arguable,[94] where the client misleads the solicitor[95] or where the solicitor is unable to obtain proper instructions.[96] One could argue that at least some of these circumstances would not be termination by the solicitor per se, but would be acceptance of a repudiatory breach on the part of the client. Be that as it may, a solicitor is professionally obliged to give reasonable notice of termination: the SRA Code of Conduct 2011 (which has applied since 6 October 2011) provides that 'ceasing to act for a client without good reason and without providing reasonable notice' may be an indicative behaviour demonstrating a failure to comply with the Principles.[97] If the termination took place before that date, then the Solicitors' Code of Conduct 2007 would have applied, the relevant part of which read as follows: **27.70**

> 'If there is good reason to cease acting, you must give reasonable notice to the client. What amounts to reasonable notice will depend on the circumstances. For example, it would normally be unreasonable to stop acting for a client immediately before a court hearing

[89] See, eg, *Re Galland* (1885) 31 Ch D 296, CA, at 300, *per* Chitty J. See also para 8 of the Guidance to r 2.01 of the Solicitors' Code of Conduct 2007.

[90] See, eg, para 7 of the various incarnations of the Law Society model conditional fee agreement.

[91] *JH Milner & Son v Percy Bilton Ltd* [1966] 1 WLR 1582.

[92] *Re Smith* (1841) 4 Beav 309.

[93] *Hawkes v Cottrell* (1858) 3 H & N 243, at 245; see also *Howes Percival LLP v Page* [2013] EWHC 4104 (Ch), *per* Judge Behrens (sitting as a judge of the High Court).

[94] *Richard Buxton (a firm) v Mills-Owen* [2010] EWCA Civ 122.

[95] See, eg, *Kris Motor Spares Ltd v Fox Williams LLP* [2009] EWHC 2813 (QB).

[96] See, eg, Solicitors' Code of Conduct 2007, para 8 of the Guidance to r 2.01.

[97] See SRA Code of Conduct 2011, IB(1.26).

where it is impossible for the client to find alternative representation ... There may be circumstances where it is reasonable to give no notice.'[98]

27.71 In addition to being a professional requirement, the duty to give reasonable notice also exists in law[99] and there is no reason to believe that this would not apply to legal services providers who are not solicitors.

27.72 A failure to give reasonable notice (or to putatively terminate a contract for a reason other than 'good cause') may amount to repudiatory breach of contract on the part of the solicitor. It is trite law that a repudiatory breach by one party cannot unilaterally terminate the contract; instead, the innocent party may elect between termination and affirmation of the contract. Unless and until the innocent party terminates the contract, it subsists.[100] Where a solicitor wrongly treats a contract of retainer as having been terminated, this may mean that no fees at all may be charged.[101]

27.73 From the costs point of view, the most important 'good cause' arises out of Solicitors Act 1974, s 65(2), which reads:

> 'If a solicitor who has been retained by a client to conduct contentious business requests the client to make a payment of a sum of money, being a reasonable sum on account of the costs incurred or to be incurred in the conduct of that business and the client refuses or fails within a reasonable time to make that payment, the refusal or failure shall be deemed to be a good cause whereby the solicitor may, upon giving reasonable notice to the client, withdraw from the retainer.'

Crane J has found the reference to a 'reasonable sum' to be a reference to an amount that it was reasonable to request at that particular time.[102] Toulson J has found that a request by a solicitor for 90 per cent of outstanding costs was unreasonable in the context of those costs being disputed.[103]

27.74 The Guidance to the Solicitors' Practice Rules 1990 used to stipulate that if a contract of retainer is for the solicitor to be remunerated by way of an agreed fee, the solicitor may not terminate the retainer by reason of that work becoming unremunerative.[104] This provision was not repeated in the Solicitors' Code of Conduct 2007 nor is it repeated in the SRA Code of Conduct 2011. Those codes contain only general provisions relating to termination (see 27.70).

27.75 Where appropriate, a solicitor's right to terminate will exist regardless of whether the retainer is a private retainer or a conditional fee agreement. This was made clear by Lord Woolf MR:

---

[98] Solicitors' Code of Conduct 2007, para 9 of the Guidance to r 2.01.

[99] See *Underwood, Son & Piper v Lewis* [1894] 2 QB 306, at 313, *per* Lord Esher MR, and at 315, *per* A L Smith LJ, More recently, see *Cawdery Kaye Fireman & Taylor v Minkin* [2012] EWCA Civ 546, at [29] and [30], but it should be noted that a distinction may be drawn between termination and suspension (see [30]), and that, in any event, the contract may provide for immediate termination for unreasonable refusal to pay monies already billed (see [30]).

[100] See *Société Générale, London Branch v Geys* [2012] UKSC 63; see also *Budana v The Leeds Teaching Hospitals NHS Trust & Anor* [2017] EWCA Civ 1980, at [38], *per* Gloster LJ.

[101] *Minkin v Cawdery Kaye Fireman & Taylor* [2011] EWHC 177 (QB), at [38]. Cranston J's decision was reversed on appeal ([2012] EWCA Civ 546), but not on this point.

[102] *Collyer Bristow v Robichaux* (unreported), 20 July 2001, QBD.

[103] In *Wong v Vizards* [1997] 2 Costs LR 46, at 52.

[104] Law Society, *The Guide to the Professional Conduct of Solicitors* (8th edn, London: Law Society, 1999), §13.03, para 5.

'The lawyer has however the right, if the need should arise, to cease to act for a client under a CFA in the same way as a lawyer can cease to act in the event of there being a conventional retainer.'[105]

Putative termination by superseding retainer It is possible for two contracts of retainer to coexist (such as where a client instructs a legal services provider to provide litigation services under a conditional fee agreement whilst at the same time instructing the same legal services provider to provide non-contentious work on a privately paying basis), but, in general, if one contract of retainer is, on the facts, replaced by another, the first will be terminated. By way of example, in a case in which a client had instructed a solicitor privately and then entered into a conditional fee agreement, McCombe LJ said that he could 'find no room, on the facts . . . , for the two types of express retainer to have subsisted side by side or for the original retainer to spring back into life, when, contrary to all expectations, the CFA did not cover all the steps taken'.[106] **27.76**

Putative termination by death Although the death of a counterparty will not generally discharge a contract,[107] many retainers contain a provision that death is a stipulated event that will result in termination. Termination by death will not be a breach of contract.[108] Retainers often provide that a personal representative of a deceased client may continue the retainer by subsequent agreement. A personal representative may continue the retainer by adopting it, in which case, they will incur a personal liability.[109] **27.77**

Where a contract is a general retainer (that is, a contract arising out of instructions to do generally what is necessary in a person's affairs), the death of the client will not necessarily result in the contract of retainer being terminated; rather, the solicitor will remain instructed to the extent that it must continue to do what is necessary to protect and preserve the client's interests.[110] In any event, the solicitor will be entitled to sue for work already done if the client dies[111]—although there is less certainty about whether the personal representative of a deceased solicitor is entitled to sue for the fees incurred before the solicitor's death.[112] **27.78**

Putative termination by loss of capacity The issue of whether loss of capacity terminates a contract of retainer is one of the few circumstances in which it is necessary to make a clear distinction between the various meanings of the word 'retainer' (see 27.03). **27.79**

Loss of mental capacity has, in the past, been regarded as being an event that terminates a solicitor's authority (that is, the third meaning of the word 'retainer' as set out at **27.80**

---

[105] *Hodgson v Imperial Tobacco Ltd* [1998] 1 WLR 1056, at 1065. See also *Kris Motor Spares Ltd v Fox Williams LLP* [2009] EWHC 2813 (QB).

[106] *Radford & Anor v Frade & Ors* [2018] EWCA Civ 119, at [32].

[107] See, in a context other than costs, *Werner v Humphreys* (1841) 2 Man & G 853.

[108] *Pool v Pool* (1889) 61 LT 401.

[109] *Re Bentinck, Bentinck v Bentinck* (1893) 37 Sol Jo 233.

[110] *Donsland Ltd (a firm) v Van Hoogstraten* [2002] EWCA Civ 253.

[111] *Whitehead v Lord* (1852) 7 Exch 691.

[112] See *Underwood, Son and Piper v Lewis* [1894] 2 QB 306, CA, at 313, *per* Lord Esher MR. That said, see also the Law Reform (Frustrated Contracts) Act 1943, s 1.

27.03),[113] but it cannot be said with certainty that this remains good law. In a case in which it was not necessary to decide the issue, Richards LJ had this to say on the point:

> 'There is much to be said in favour of a fresh examination or reconsideration of [this principle]. It is potentially unfair and unsatisfactory for a client's supervening incapacity to have the effect of terminating automatically the solicitor's authority to act on the client's behalf in the litigation, exposing the solicitor to the risk of liability to other parties for breach of warranty of authority in respect of steps taken in the litigation even when the solicitor is not aware of the incapacity, and depriving him of authority to take any steps to protect the client's position when he does become aware of it—to the extent that it is said that he acts without authority, albeit apparently in accordance with good practice, in applying to the court for the appointment of a deputy and/or litigation friend. One might at least expect the principle to be qualified so that (i) the solicitor retains authority to act so long as he is unaware of the incapacity and (ii) he retains authority to take necessary steps in consequence of the incapacity,[[114]] including an application to the court for the appointment of a deputy and/or litigation friend, when he does become aware of it. It might also be preferable to talk in terms of "suspension" rather than "termination" of authority, on the basis that the solicitor's authority is restored if the client regains capacity or a litigation friend is appointed to continue the litigation on the client's behalf.'[115]

27.81 Be that as it may, the mere fact that loss of capacity may determine the authority of the solicitor to act does not mean that it terminates the remuneration aspects of the contract of retainer (that is, the second meaning of the word 'retainer' as set out at 27.03). Indeed, in the case before Richards LJ, counsel for the paying party accepted that loss of capacity would not, as a matter of law, bring an end to the contract of retainer.[116] It was argued that, notwithstanding this, the contract of retainer was frustrated (because an incapable client was said to be unable to give instructions), but Richards LJ rejected that argument.[117]

27.82 **Putative termination by insolvency on the part of the client** Where a client becomes bankrupt and where a legal services provider carries out no work for the trustee or assignee, that will usually give rise to termination,[118] but, in other circumstances, the retainer will pass to the trustee or assignee.[119] Any claim for costs against the client will become a bankruptcy debt,[120] which will be payable out of the property held by the trustee. Few legal services providers would be prepared to continue acting on the basis that they are unsecured creditors, so the practical effect of a client's bankruptcy would generally be to terminate the retainer. However, there would be nothing to prevent a legal services provider entering into a new retainer with the trustee (or agreeing to continue to act on the basis that it was given some form of security), if that is what they wished to do. In so far as corporate insolvency is concerned, the legal services provider's retainer is not terminated by the removal of the liquidator who retained it and this is so even if, at the relevant time, no replacement had been appointed.[121]

---

[113] *Yonge v Toynbee* [1910] 1 KB 215, CA, overruling *Smout v Ilbery* (1842) 10 M & W 1 and approving *Collen v Wright* (1857) 8 E & B 647, Ex Ch.

[114] There is authority for this proposition: see *The Fore Street Warehouse Co Ltd v Durrant & Co* (1883) 10 QBD 471.

[115] *Blankley v Central Manchester and Manchester Children's University Hospitals NHS Trust* [2015] EWCA Civ 18, at [36].

[116] *Ibid*, at [28].

[117] *Ibid*, at [38].

[118] In a context other than costs, see *Jennings' Trustee v King* [1952] Ch 899. See also *Re Moss* (1866) LR 2 Eq 345 at 348, *per* Lord Romily.

[119] See Insolvency Act 1986, s 283(1).

[120] See Insolvency Act 1986, s 322.

[121] See *R v Lord Mayor of London, ex p Boaler* [1893] 2 QB 146, DC.

Putative termination by insolvency or inability to practise on the part of the legal services provider Where the solicitor is practising on their own account and where they become bankrupt, the bankruptcy will usually result in the retainer being terminated, not as a result of a contractual provision, but as a result of the fact that the solicitor would lose the ability to practise.[122] The same is true of injury sufficient to prevent the solicitor from practising,[123] disqualification from practice[124] and imprisonment.[125] The client may, however, subsequently enter into a new retainer with an intervener. Likewise, whilst there is ancient authority for the proposition that, where a legal services provider (including a solicitor) transfers its business to someone else, that will terminate the retainer,[126] there is ample scope for the court to avoid injustice by finding that the retainer was novated or otherwise adopted by the new legal services provider.[127] Indeed, this is often done by express means, as is discussed at 32.02–32.41. Where a firm is dissolved, that will, in general, terminate the firm's retainer,[128] but again there is usually scope for the court to avoid injustice in that regard. **27.83**

The effect of termination

The effect of termination will depend on the terms of the contract of retainer and on the facts, and so may differ from case to case. The following general points can, however, be made. **27.84**

- Lawful termination will not generally result in the client being discharged from the accrued rights under the retainer[129]—that is, the legal services provider's right to be paid for work already done.
- Termination of the retainer will not always bring the relationship between legal services provider and client to an end. In particular, where a conditional fee agreement has been terminated, the client will often be placed under an ongoing contractual obligation to inform the legal services provider if the case is subsequently 'won'.
- Likewise, termination will not necessarily result in a final crystallisation of the client's liability for costs. The example given above illustrates this: it may be, for example, that whilst the client became liable to pay base costs immediately upon termination, they would become liable to pay a success fee if they were subsequently to win the claim.

Another example of a terminated retainer continuing to have effect is where a legal services provider is required to carry out 'run-off' work, such as preparing a detailed bill of costs, either for a solicitor-and-client assessment or for use in recovering costs from an opposing party. Many retainers will expressly provide that such work is to be payable under the terms of the retainer. Likewise, if a client instructs a legal services provider in circumstances in which that provider has a continuing duty to the court, then it is likely **27.85**

---

122 See the Solicitors Act 1974, s 15(1).

123 *Forney v Bushe* (1954) 104 L Jo 604.

124 See *Re Smith* (1861) 9 WR 396, *per* Kindersley V-C.

125 Whilst it may no longer be good law, see *Scott v Fenning* (1845) 15 LJ Ch 88.

126 *Colegrave v Manley* (1823) Turn & R 400.

127 This can certainly be done by consent: see *Budana v The Leeds Teaching Hospitals NHS Trust & Anor* [2017] EWCA Civ 1980.

128 *Griffiths v Griffiths* (1843) 2 Hare 587; see also *Rawlinson v Moss* (1861) 30 LJ Ch 797.

129 *Richard Buxton (a firm) v Mills-Owen* [2010] EWCA Civ 122; see also *Minkin v Cawdery Kaye Fireman & Taylor* [2011] EWHC 177 (QB), at [32]. Cranston J's decision was reversed on appeal ([2012] EWCA Civ 546), but on a different point.

that the legal services provider would be able to charge for any work done in discharging that duty.[130]

27.86 One class of retainer merits specific mention—namely, conditional fee agreements. Most conditional fee agreements used by solicitors prior to 1 April 2013 were based on the Law Society's Model Agreement. Whilst the exact wording may vary, that agreement usually contained the following provision:

> 'You can end the agreement at any time. We then have the right to decide whether you must:
> - pay our basic charges and our disbursements including barristers' fees when we ask for them; or
> - pay our basic charges, and our disbursements including barristers' fees and success fees if you go on to win your claim for damages.'

This is known as the election provision and, where it applies, the solicitor had a right to decide whether to be paid basic charges straight away or to be paid basic charges and a success fee only in the event of success. It was (and still is) desirable for an election to be made not only expressly, but also at an early stage.[131] Conditional fee agreements made on or after 1 April 2013 may also contain elections provisions.

Wrongful termination

27.87 Whilst the effect of wrongfully terminating a retainer may sound in damages, disciplinary action or both, from the point of view of the law of costs, the effect is usually limited—unless the retainer is an entire contract (see 27.88). In particular, the wrongfulness of a termination will rarely result in the loss of the right to be paid for legal services that have already been provided.[132]

27.88 The situation is different if the retainer is an entire contract because the termination will go hand in hand with the failure to discharge the requisite obligations. This means that wrongful termination is capable of resulting in the legal services provider being disentitled to raise a fee (see 27.23). Atkin LJ has explained that, in those circumstances, *quantum meruit* would also be prohibited on policy grounds[133] (albeit on grounds that are now nearly a century old).

Suspension of contracts of retainer

27.89 It is possible for a contract of retainer to contain a provision that it be suspended—that is, a provision that the supply of legal services be put on hold pending some event (usually payment of fees). Whilst he acknowledged that there is a degree of overlap between suspension and termination, Ward LJ found that they should be regarded as distinct and distinguishable concepts.[134] On the facts of the case before him (which were unremarkable other

---

[130] See *Lady De la Pole v Dick* (1885) 29 Ch D 351, CA, at 356–7.

[131] This is because disputes could arise. If the client lost the claim before an election was made and if the solicitor then claimed base charges in accordance with the first limb of the election provision, that solicitor may be accused of having delayed its decision for the purposes having its cake and eating it.

[132] Nelson J, for example, has commented, *obiter*, that if a solicitor charges more than it is entitled to charge and then terminates the retainer as a result of a refusal to pay, this would usually amount merely to a breach of contract and would not automatically disentitle the solicitor to fees for the work already done: *Wilson v William Sturges & Co* [2006] EWHC 792 (QB).

[133] *Wild v Simpson* [1918–19] All ER Rep 682, at 693 (Duke LJ dissenting, albeit on other grounds).

[134] *Cawdery Kaye Fireman & Taylor v Minkin* [2012] EWCA Civ 546, at [30].

than the fact that the retainer made express provision for suspension), Ward LJ found that it was not necessary to imply a provision that the solicitor would suspend the retainer only after having given reasonable notice.[135] Ward LJ went on to find that (assuming it to be in accordance with the terms of the retainer) suspension did not amount to termination of the contract and that it would be wrong to regard suspension as absolving the client from performing their obligations under the contract.[136]

Waiver of rights under a contract of retainer

Whilst a putative waiver of the right to be paid fees would clearly be a factor that the court could take into account for assessing the amount payable as a matter of reasonableness, if a client is to rely on waiver as negating the legal services provider's contractual right to payment, the waiver must be supported by consideration. In this regard, Tugendhat J held that a promise did not become contractually binding simply because the making of the promise was potentially advantageous to the promisor.[137] Likewise, the act of writing costs off for taxation purposes would not extinguish the contractual right to payment.[138] **27.90**

Withholding information about retainers and undue influence

This topic is only touched upon here. If a legal services provider invites a client to enter into a contract of retainer without giving the client the information that was needed to allow them to decide whether to accept that invitation, this is capable of invalidating the contract of retainer. An example would be where a firm of solicitors allowed a client to enter into a contingency fee agreement without giving that client certain information that would make it clear to the client that the risk of an ongoing dispute was very low.[139] The topic of undue influence may also arise, this being addressed (albeit in the context of managing 'broken retainers') at 32.44–32.53. **27.91**

Factual Disputes About Retainers

This section deals with how the court would address a factual dispute about a contract of retainer where that dispute has arisen between legal services provider and client. Where it is a paying party who wishes to challenge the retainer, they will usually (but not always) need to establish a 'genuine issue' or 'genuine concern' that there has been a breach of the indemnity principle. A paying party would also have to overcome the rebuttable presumption that (broadly speaking and subject to certain exceptions) a person who instructs a legal services provider will be liable for its fees. These issues are dealt with at 18.24–18.57. **27.92**

Factual disputes about retainers are dealt with in much the same way as any other factual dispute. The legal burden (otherwise known as the burden of persuasion) will usually **27.93**

135 *Ibid*, at [30].
136 *Ibid*, at [44].
137 *Ashia Centur Ltd v Barker Gillette LLP* [2011] EWHC 148 (QB), at [20].
138 *Slatter v Ronaldsons* [2002] 2 Costs LR 267.
139 Whilst it related to a decision of the Legal Ombudsman rather than a decision taken upon assessment, see *Ejiofoer (t/a Mitchell and Co Solicitors) v Legal Ombudsman* [2016] EWHC 1933 (Admin), at [45], *per* Wyn Williams J.

remain with the legal services provider, who must prove the existence of an enforceable retainer as a condition for the recovery of its fees.[140]

27.94 The evidential burden (otherwise known as the burden of adducing evidence) will shift between the parties, depending on the point that is being asserted and who is asserting it. There is, however, a presumption in favour of the legal services provider that a client is liable for the fees of a legal services provider whom the client has engaged.[141] This presumption is rebuttable and, in effect, is a presumption that (subject to certain exceptions) there will be an implied retainer unless the contrary can be shown. This topic is addressed at 27.191–27.194 and 18.28–18.29.

The evidential relevance of there being no written record

27.95 Where there is a dispute between a legal services provider and a client concerning the terms or existence of a contract of retainer, one factor that will be given weight is the presence or absence of a written instrument of retainer (that is, a document, or documents, that record the terms of the retainer). If there is a written instrument, it will—obviously—be taken into account, but if it is absent, that will create a rebuttable evidential presumption in the client's favour (but only in so far as disputed terms are concerned). The principle was described by Denning LJ in this way:

> 'On this question of retainer, I would observe that where there is a difference between a solicitor and his client on it, the courts have said for the last 100 years or more that the word of the client is to be preferred to the word of the solicitor, or, at any rate more weight is to be given to it: ... The reason is plain. It is because the client is ignorant and the solicitor is, or should be, learned. If the solicitor does not take the precaution of getting a written retainer, he has only himself to thank for being at variance with his client over it and must take the consequences.'[142]

27.96 On a similar point, Rougier J said this:

> 'It seems to me that the underlying basis for this principle must be that it is the client who actually knows what he wants the solicitor to do, and so it is the solicitor's business to ascertain the client's wishes accurately, bearing in mind the possibility that the client, through ignorance of the correct terminology, may not have correctly expressed it.'[143]

Peter Smith J has confirmed that this principle is not limited to situations in which the legal services provider ought to have recognised the possibility of misapprehension and sought clarification accordingly.[144] This principle is ancient,[145] but Butterfield J has confirmed it as being good law.[146] Indeed, Denning LJ's words may have particular resonance

---

[140] This being a reflection of the generally applicable principle, as explained by Davies LJ in *Chapman v Oakleigh Animal Products Ltd* (1970) 8 KIR 1063, CA, at 1072, that the onus of proof is on the claimant.

[141] See *Adams v London Improved Motor Builders Ltd* [1921] 1 KB 495, at 501. See also *R v Miller (Raymond)* [1983] 1 WLR 1056, at 1059–62, which was cited with approval in *Bailey v IBC Vehicles Ltd* [1998] 3 All ER 570, at 574; *Hazlett v Sefton Metropolitan Borough Council* [2000] 4 All ER 887.

[142] *Griffiths v Evans* [1953] 2 All ER 1364, at 1369.

[143] *Gray & Anor v Buss & Merton (a firm)* [1999] PNLR 882, at 892.

[144] *Sibley & Co v Reachbyte Ltd* [2008] EWHC 2665 (Ch), at [44]–[50].

[145] See *Re Paine* (1912) 28 TLR 201, *per* Warrington J. Older authorities exist—see, eg, *Allen v Bone* (1841) 4 Beav 493 and *Crossley v Crowther* (1851) 9 Hare 384—but they appear to suggest that there is a rule of law that operates against the solicitor. To the extent that they do so, those authorities are probably no longer good law.

[146] *Fereidooni v Pettman Smith* [2001] EWHC 9007 (Costs).

in modern practice, because of the way in which the various codes of conduct have addressed the issue of written confirmation about costs (see below). In the context of a contract of retainer with a consumer client, the matters set out in 28.30, 28.47–28.49, 28.67–28.88 and 28.100 may also have a bearing.

Codes of conduct regarding retainers

The codes of conduct that guide solicitors have, to varying extents over the years, always made provision for certain information to be given to clients. The exact provisions depend on when the work was done. Where the contract was made after 1 July 2007, but before 6 October 2011, the following provisions in the Solicitors' Code of Conduct 2007 applied: 'Any information about the cost must be clear and confirmed in writing.'[147] **27.97**

The reference to 'the cost' was a reference to the cost to the client of instructing the solicitor and it included information about the retainer. The Solicitors' Code of Conduct 2007 also imposed the following obligations: **27.98**

'**2.03 Information about the cost**

(1) You must give your client the best information possible about the likely overall cost of a matter both at the outset and, when appropriate, as the matter progresses. In particular you must:
(a) advise the client of the basis and terms of your charges;
(b) advise the client if charging rates are to be increased;
(c) advise the client of likely payments which you or your client may need to make to others;
(d) discuss with the client how the client will pay, in particular:
  (i) whether the client may be eligible and should apply for public funding; and
  (ii) whether the client's own costs are covered by insurance or may be paid by someone else such as an employer or trade union;
(e) advise the client that there are circumstances where you may be entitled to exercise a lien for unpaid costs;
(f) advise the client of their potential liability for any other party's costs; and
(g) discuss with the client whether their liability for another party's costs may be covered by existing insurance or whether specially purchased insurance may be obtained.'[148]

In so far as retainers made before 1 July 2007 were concerned, similar provisions existed under the Solicitors Practice Rules 1990.[149]

Contracts of retainer made on or after 6 October 2011 will be subject to the SRA Code of Conduct 2011, which does not contain the same words as appeared in the previous codes. This does not, however, mean that the principle described by Denning LJ at 27.95 is any less important. Indeed, the corresponding provisions in the SRA Code of Conduct 2011 include the following: **27.99**

'**Outcomes**

You must achieve these outcomes:

O(1.1) you treat your clients fairly;

[...]

[147] Solicitors' Code of Conduct 2007, para 2.03(5).
[148] Solicitors' Code of Conduct 2007, para 2.03(1).
[149] See Solicitors' Costs Information and Client Care Code 1999, para 3(3).

O(1.6) you only enter into fee agreements with your clients that are legal, and which you consider are suitable for the client's needs and take account of the client's best interests;

[...]

O(1.12) clients are in a position to make informed decisions about the services they need, how their matter will be handled and the options available to them;

O(1.13) clients receive the best possible information, both at the time of engagement and when appropriate as their matter progresses, about the likely overall cost of their matter;

O(1.14) clients are informed of their right to challenge or complain about your bill and the circumstances in which they may be liable to pay interest on an unpaid bill;

O(1.15) you properly account to clients for any financial benefit you receive as a result of your instructions;

[...]

Fee arrangements with your client

[...]

IB(1.13) discussing whether the potential outcomes of the client's matter are likely to justify the expense or risk involved, including any risk of having to pay someone else's legal fees;

IB(1.14) clearly explaining your fees and if and when they are likely to change;

IB(1.15) warning about any other payments for which the client may be responsible;

IB(1.16) discussing how the client will pay, including whether public funding may be available, whether the client has insurance that might cover the fees, and whether the fees may be paid by someone else such as a trade union;

IB(1.17) where you are acting for a client under a fee arrangement governed by statute, such as a conditional fee agreement, giving the client all relevant information relating to that arrangement;

IB(1.18) where you are acting for a publicly funded client, explaining how their publicly funded status affects the costs;

IB(1.19) providing the information in a clear and accessible form which is appropriate to the needs and circumstances of the client;

IB(1.20) where you receive a financial benefit as a result of acting for a client, either:

- paying it to the client;
- offsetting it against your fees; or
- keeping it only where you can justify keeping it, you have told the client the amount of the benefit (or an approximation if you do not know the exact amount) and the client has agreed that you can keep it;

IB(1.21) ensuring that disbursements included in your bill reflect the actual amount spent or to be spent on behalf of the client.

[...]

IB(1.26) ceasing to act for a client without good reason and without providing reasonable notice;

IB(1.27) entering into unlawful fee arrangements such as an unlawful contingency fee.'

27.100 Where the retainer is a conditional fee agreement made before 6 October 2011, there were additional topics that ought to have been discussed (and, for the reasons set out above, recorded in writing). They were as follows:

'(2) Where you are acting for the client under a conditional fee agreement, (including a collective conditional fee agreement) in addition to complying with 2.03(1) above and 2.03(5) and (6) below, you must explain the following, both at the outset and, when appropriate, as the matter progresses:

(a) the circumstances in which your client may be liable for your costs and whether you will seek payment of these from the client, if entitled to do so;
(b) if you intend to seek payment of any or all of your costs from your client, you must advise your client of their right to an assessment of those costs; and
(c) where applicable, the fact that you are obliged under a fee sharing agreement to pay to a charity any fees which you receive by way of costs from the client's opponent or other third party.'[150]

Breach of these obligations would be most unlikely to have the effect of making a retainer unenforceable (especially when the challenge is made by a paying party[151]), but, from an evidential point of view, a legal services provider may find it difficult to explain the absence of a written record in the event that it is at odds with the client over a matter that ought to have been recorded in writing. **27.101**

Private Retainers

A private retainer is an ordinary, archetypal contract of retainer by means of which the client agrees to pay the legal services provider for work on an unconditional basis (usually on the basis of an hourly rate). Contentious and non-contentious business agreements are sometimes classified as being varieties of private retainer, but, to avoid confusion, that classification is not used in this book. The distinction between a private retainer and a business agreement can be a fine one, however (as is explained at 27.109–27.165). **27.102**

Private retainers are usually created by one or both of two documents, as follows. **27.103**

- **Client care letters** A client care letter is a letter that, as the name implies, sets out the basis upon which the legal services provider will provide services to the client. It will usually deal with many issues other than costs (such as the details of the person with conduct of the matter, the complaints procedure, etc). It may also give initial advice about the claim.
- **Terms and conditions** This is usually a standard document that contains the terms and conditions upon the basis of which the legal services providers will provide legal services. Standard-form terms and conditions exist.

At the time of writing, retainers were still being encountered that were made before 6 October 2011 but after 1 July 2007. As such, the Solicitors' Code of Conduct 2007 may still apply. That Code required that certain information be given both orally and in writing (see 27.97 and 27.98), and the requisite information was usually given in one or both of the documents referred to above. The Guidance to the Solicitors' Code of Conduct 2007 made it clear that the solicitor was not required to be inflexible about the information that they gave in any given case. Moreover, the Code advised that overly complex or lengthy documents may not be helpful.[152] **27.104**

[150] Solicitors' Code of Conduct 2007, para 2.03(2).
[151] See *Garbutt v Edwards* [2005] EWCA Civ 1206.
[152] Paragraphs 13 and 22 of the Guidance to r 2.01 of the Solicitors' Code of Conduct 2007.

27.105 The requirements under the SRA Code of Conduct 2011 (which will apply to contracts of retainer made on or after 6 October 2011) are less easy to pin down (see 27.99). If, and in so far as, a need to confirm the terms of the retainer can be implied into that Code, it is most unlikely that any such requirement would be any more demanding than that which existed previously, because the SRA Code of Conduct 2011 specifically refers to itself as a flexible code that focuses on outcomes rather than on laying down prescriptive guidance. That said, solicitors would be storing up trouble for themselves if they were to fail to set themselves high standards in this regard; disregarding aspects of the SRA Code of Conduct 2011 would be a very risky strategy.[153]

27.106 When drafting a private retainer, the drafter would do well to consider whether any of the provisions mentioned at 27.326–27.339 need to be included. Thought also ought to be given to the matters set out in Chapter 28.

Business Agreements (Non-contentious and Contentious)

27.107 Business agreements fall into two categories, non-contentious and contentious, each of which has its own statutory regime. The following topics are addressed:

- business agreements and agreements generally (27.109–27.110):
- purported compromises and agreements to restrict assessments under the common law (27.111–27.114);
- non-contentious business agreements (27.115–27.134); and
- contentious business agreements (27.135–27.189).

27.108 Broadly speaking, business agreements differ from other contracts of retainers in that, unless they are set aside, they are enforceable without the client having a right to a full assessment.[154] However, the court has many powers to regulate business agreements, one of which is to set the agreement aside on the basis that it is unfair or unreasonable. Clients should not assume that the court will readily intervene in this regard, however. Mustill J had the following to say on the point: '[From] a practical point of view the agreement of the client is strongest evidence that the fee is reasonable.'[155]

Business agreements and agreements generally

27.109 The distinction between business agreements and other forms of retainer can sometimes be a fine one. A client care letter that has been signed by both the solicitor and the client could easily (and inadvertently) be a business agreement.

27.110 Both contentious and non-contentious business agreements are governed by primary legislation—namely, the Solicitors Act 1974. Certain requirements are stipulated in that Act (as are addressed below), but there is nothing that expressly stipulates what will happen in

[153] Whilst he was dealing with the Solicitors Practice Rules 1990 rather than the SRA Code of Conduct 2011, Auld LJ (sitting in the Divisional Court) said that there was a heavy onus on a solicitor to establish that its client is so sophisticated in matters of litigation and so attentive to the cost implications of the litigation in question that the then requirements to give information about costs could be disregarded: *Darby v Law Society* [2003] EWHC 2270 (Admin), at [27].

[154] In the case of a non-contentious business agreement, the agreement will be enforceable without the client having the right to a remuneration certificate and this will be the case even for bills rendered before 11 August 2009.

[155] *Walton v Egan* [1982] QB 1232, at 1238.

the event of non-compliance. That topic is most easily addressed by looking at the history of business agreements. A summary of the modern law may be found at 27.111–27.114 and, as can be seen, there are—or at least may be—differences between what may happen depending on whether the work that was being carried out was contentious or non-contentious, but, regardless of those differences, it will generally be the case that the solicitor will not go unremunerated for any work done.

Purported compromises and agreements to restrict assessments under the common law

At common law, an agreement by a solicitor to be paid a predictable sum (as opposed to a fee to be assessed) was not necessarily regarded as being void, but it was looked upon with suspicion.[156] It was not uncommon for such agreements to be found to be unenforceable[157] (in the sense that the agreement to pay a predictable sum was unenforceable, not in the sense that there was no right to enforce payment at all[158]). The common law was described by Fletcher-Moulton LJ in these terms: **27.111**

> 'At that date [ie before the introduction of statutory regulation] agreements between a solicitor and his client as to the terms on which the solicitor's business was to be done were not necessarily unenforceable. They were, however, viewed with great jealousy by the Courts, because they were agreements between a man and his legal adviser as to the terms of the latter's remuneration, and there was so great an opportunity for the exercise of undue influence, that the Courts were very slow to enforce such agreements where they were favourable to the solicitor unless they were satisfied that they were made under circumstances that precluded any suspicion of an improper attempt on the solicitor's part to benefit himself at his client's expense.'[159]

Thus the position at common law was that agreements restricting the client's right to challenge their solicitor's fees were often not enforced and that this was often on grounds that were not dissimilar to presumed undue influence. A similar line of thought applied to agreements to settle accounts for costs already incurred by taking a gross sum before delivery of a bill (see 39.12). In so far as costs yet to be incurred were concerned, a solicitor could not, in general, enter into a bare agreement that fees would not be assessed[160] and any agreement to preclude the right to an assessment had to be shown to be favourable to the client to be enforceable.[161] In particular, there is no reason why a solicitor could not agree to limit its fees.[162] Further examples are given in the footnotes.[163] **27.112**

---

[156] *In re Whitcombe* (1844) 8 Beav 140, Many of the applicable cases dealt primarily with verbal agreements.

[157] For example, a textbook pre-dating the introduction of statutory control records that such agreements were held to be binding only 'not infrequently', which implies that they were also held *not* to be binding: *Cordery on Solicitors* (3rd edn, London: LexisNexis, 1996), p 261.

[158] Where the court found the agreement to be unenforceable, the solicitor would still be able to recover fees, but those fees would be subject to an assessment: see *Saunderson v Glass* (1742) 2 Atk 296; *Philby v Hazle* (1860) 8 CBNS 647, at 652; *O'Brien v Lewis* (1863) 32 LT (Ch) 569.

[159] *Clare v Joseph* [1907] 2 KB 369, at 376.

[160] See, eg, *Balme v Paver* (1821) Jac Rep 305; *Scougall v Campbell* (1826) 3 Russ 545.

[161] See *Re Newman* (1861) 30 Beav 196; *Re Cawley & Whatley* (1870) 18 WR 1125.

[162] *Scarth v Rutland* (1866) LR 1 CP 642, at 643, *per* Earl CJ. This case is often cited as authority for the proposition that if the client has failed to plead a defence of non-delivery of a detailed bill, the solicitor could recover in an action on the agreement—but it is unlikely that this remains good law.

[163] The following is a list of agreements that have been found to be enforceable, but it is important to note that many of the categories—ie (a), (b) and (c)—would be likely now to be subject to statutory provisions concerning conditional fee agreements: (a) agreeing not to charge in the event of non-recovery of costs (*Jennings v Johnson* (1873) LR 8 CP 425); (b) agreeing not to charge in the event of failure

27.113 When the statutory regime was first introduced, the position was much the same: agreements that did not comply with the legislative requirements were impeached.[164] Where this happened, the then statutory regime expressly provided that the solicitor's costs would be assessed as if the agreement had never been made.[165]

27.114 The same is broadly true today, although there is—or, at least, may be—a difference in the way in which the court will deal with contentious and non-contentious business (see 27.211–27.213). If an agreement falls short of being a business agreement (be it contentious or non-contentious), the solicitor will lose the benefit of Solicitors Act 1974, s 60(1), and, as a result, the costs will generally be subject to an assessment. The failed agreement may form the basis of that assessment—and, to this extent, the costs will be assessed in accordance with that agreement even though it has failed—but (equally) those costs will be recovered only to the extent that they were reasonably incurred and reasonable in amount. That said, it may be that, in certain circumstances, the client could rely on the underlying common law (in which case the client may still be able to rely on the agreement), but, as is explained in 27.211, it is possible that this would be the case only if the agreement were a contentious business agreement.

Non-contentious business agreements

27.115 The following topics are addressed:

- the requirements of a non-contentious business agreement (27.119–27.125);
- unintended non-contentious business agreements (27.126);
- agreements concerning security for solicitors' fees (27.127);
- the effect of a non-contentious business agreement (27.128–27.131);
- termination of a non-contentious business agreement (27.132); and
- objections on the grounds that the agreement is unfair or unreasonable (27.133–27.134).

27.116 Non-contentious business agreements (like contentious business agreements) are a creation of statute.[166] The principal characteristic of a non-contentious business agreement is that it is a contract of retainer that, subject to certain safeguards, will allow the solicitor to recover fees as if they were an ordinary debt. This means that the client would not ordinarily be entitled to an assessment of those fees. A lesser form of non-contentious business agreement exists that permits only the hourly rate to be treated in this way, thereby leaving the client free to ask the court to ascertain the reasonableness of the time claimed.

(*Tabram v Horne* (1827) 1 Man & Ry 228; *Galloway v Corpn of London* (1867) LR 4 Eq 90, at 97; *Turner v Tennant* (1846) 10 Jur 429; *Gundry v Sainsbury* [1910] 1 KB 645); (c) agreeing to charge disbursements only (*Jones v Reade* (1836) 5 A & E 529); and (d) agreements to restrict costs (*Moon v* Hall (1864) 17 CB(NS) 760; *Re Owen; ex p Payton* (1885) 52 LT 628). See also *Re a Solicitor (No 2)* [1956] 1 QB 155, which (albeit *obiter*) affirmed *Clare* and *Jennings* as being good law. See also *Electrical Trades Union v Tarlo* [1964] Ch 720 (oral retainer related to both contentious and non-contentious work: contentious part found to be enforceable).

[164] *In re Russell Son & Scott* [1885] 30 Ch D 114, at 116.

[165] Attorneys and Solicitors Act 1870, s 9.

[166] Whilst not given their modern title, they were first created by Attorneys and Solicitors Act 1870, s 2, and given something similar to their modern form in Solicitors' Remuneration Act 1881, s 8.

The modern legislation is at Solicitors Act 1974, s 57,[167] which provides: **27.117**

> '(1) Whether or not any order is in force under section 56,[[168]] a solicitor and his client may, before or after or in the course of the transaction of any non-contentious business by the solicitor, make an agreement as to his remuneration in respect of that business.
>
> (2) The agreement may provide for the remuneration of the solicitor by a gross sum or by reference to an hourly rate, or by a commission or percentage, or by a salary, or otherwise, and it may be made on the terms that the amount of the remuneration stipulated for shall or shall not include all or any disbursements made by the solicitor in respect of searches, plans, travelling, taxes, fees or other matters.
>
> (3) The agreement shall be in writing and signed by the person to be bound by it or his agent in that behalf.
>
> (4) Subject to subsections (5) and (7), the agreement may be sued and recovered on or set aside in the like manner and on the like grounds as an agreement not relating to the remuneration of a solicitor.
>
> (5) If on any assessment of costs the agreement is relied on by the solicitor and objected to by the client as unfair or unreasonable, the costs officer may enquire into the facts and certify them to the court, and if from that certificate it appears just to the court that the agreement should be set aside, or the amount payable under it reduced, the court may so order and may give such consequential directions as it thinks fit.
>
> (6) Subsection (7) applies where the agreement provides for the remuneration of the solicitor to be by reference to an hourly rate.
>
> (7) If, on the assessment of any costs, the agreement is relied on by the solicitor and the client objects to the amount of the costs (but is not alleging that the agreement is unfair or unreasonable), the costs officer may enquire into—
> (a) the number of hours worked by the solicitor; and
> (b) whether the number of hours worked by him was excessive.'

It should be noted that the reference to payment by percentage expressly authorises agreements under which the amount of the fee paid to the solicitor is based on results. This is a type of agreement that is often referred to as a contingency fee agreement (although this would include what would now be called conditional fee agreements). Spencer J has confirmed that an agreement under which the fee is based on a percentage of the monies recovered is 'perfectly lawful'.[169] The enforceability of such an agreement is expressly preserved by the legislation relating to conditional fee agreements and certain damages-based agreements.[170] This is addressed in detail at 29.03, 29.145–29.148 and 29.185–29.191. **27.118**

The requirements of a non-contentious business agreement

The requirements of a non-contentious business agreement are that: **27.119**

- it must be in writing (see 27.120–27.121);[171]

---

167 By Courts and Legal Services Act 1990, s 98.

168 That order is the Solicitors' (Non-Contentious Business) Remuneration Order 2009 (SI 2009/1931).

169 *Bolt Burdon Solicitors v Tariq & Ors* [2016] EWHC 811 (QB), at [144(i)]. Spencer J went on to confirm that because a non-contentious business agreement relates to non-contentious work, the Damages-Based Agreements Regulations 2013 (SI 2013/609) do not apply: *ibid*, at [150].

170 See Courts and Legal Services Act 1990 (as amended), ss 58(5) and 58AA(9).

171 Solicitors Act 1974, s 57(7).

- it must be signed by the person to be bound by it (or their agent on the person's behalf) (see 27.122);[172] and
- it must state the terms of the remuneration (a provision implied by Solicitors Act 1974, s 57(3)) (see 27.123–27.125).[173]

27.120 **Written form** Section 57(3) of the Solicitors Act 1974 provides that the agreement must be in writing. A non-contentious business agreement does not necessarily need to be a single document; a series of documents may suffice.[174] Stanley Burnton LJ has confirmed that there is no requirement that a non-contentious business agreement must not be in the same written instrument as a contentious business agreement.[175]

27.121 The absence of a written agreement as to the sums payable will usually mean that the agreement is unenforceable as a non-contentious business agreement (see 27.114). This would usually be to the client's advantage and the solicitor's disadvantage, but this will not always be the case. Pearson J, for example, made a finding that a client could not rely on an oral agreement that the solicitor would charge *less* than the ordinary rate of remuneration.[176] Where it is said that there is an oral agreement as to the sums payable, there is an apparent anomaly between the way in which the law treats non-contentious and contentious costs, which anomaly is dealt with at 27.211. The authorities on that point are somewhat old, however, and the points made at 27.213 should also be noted; it is possible that the modern law is that non-contentious business agreements are to be treated the same as contentious business agreements, in which case the points made at 27.162 will apply.

27.122 **Signature** Section 57(3) of the 1974 Act provides that the agreement must be signed by the 'person bound by it or his agent in that behalf'. This does not necessarily mean that the agreement must be signed by both the solicitor and client for it to be of effect. Lindley LJ had the following to say on the point:

> 'What is meant by an agreement signed by the person to be bound? The subsection does not mean signed by both parties, because only one is required to sign. It means that the person to sign is the person who seeks to get rid of the agreement, and who is sought to be bound by it. Here the client seeks to get rid of the agreement, and he is the person who signs it. In such a case it is sufficient for him to sign it whatever the solicitor may do.'[177]

(The reference to getting 'rid of the agreement' was made in the context of an application by a client for assessment notwithstanding the existence of an agreement.) Thus the agreement must be signed by the person against whom it is sought to be enforced or their agent.

27.123 **Statement of terms** Solicitors Act 1974, s 57(2) (as amended), specifies the methods by which payment may be calculated. It provides that:

- the agreement may or may not encompass disbursements;

---

[172] Solicitors Act 1974, s 57(3).

[173] *Bake v French (No 2)* [1907] 2 Ch 215.

[174] *Ibid.*

[175] *Bilkus v Stockler Brunton (a firm)* [2010] EWCA Civ 101, at [50]–[53].

[176] In *In re a Solicitor* [1956] 1 QB 157. Whilst *obiter*, that case affirmed the view that oral agreements in relation to contentious work were enforceable.

[177] *In re Frape, ex p Perrett* [1893] 2 Ch 284, at 294.

- payment may be independent of outcome, such as by gross sum, reference to an hourly rate[178] or a salary;
- payment may be dependent on outcome, such as payment of a percentage or of a commission; and
- other methods of payment may be used.

As such, any lawful method of calculation of fees may be incorporated into a non-contentious business agreement.

The terms of remuneration should be expressed in the agreement[179] and the points made at 27.148–27.150 about specificity (in respect of contentious business agreements) may be relevant by analogy. Where work has already been carried out, the words 'agreed costs' are not, of themselves, sufficient to satisfy that requirement,[180] but where the detail of the agreement could be implied, that phrase is capable of being sufficient.[181] **27.124**

The Solicitors Act 1974, s 57(1), provides that an agreement may be made 'before or after or in the course of the transaction of any non-contentious business by the solicitor', which means that the agreement may be retrospective in effect. It is therefore no bar to the creation of an agreement that the work to which it relates has already been completed or is in the process of being completed. **27.125**

Unintended non-contentious business agreements

It is possible for a non-contentious business agreement to be formed without that being the subjective intention of the counterparties. Whilst this may happen regardless of whether the agreement was made before, during or after the transaction to which it relates, the effect can be particularly unexpected when the agreement is retrospective.[182] An extreme example is a receipted account, which—if sufficiently clear and detailed, and if signed—may be capable of giving rise to a binding agreement.[183] The mere taking of a bill of exchange will not be sufficient, however.[184] Another example is where a client waives their right to a bill in writing after having been given details about the costs: this can give rise to a binding agreement and this may be so even where no bill has been delivered.[185] It should be borne in mind, however, that most of the authorities concerning unintended agreements are at least a century old, and it is possible that modern-day courts—with their greater emphasis on consumer protection—would be reluctant to find that a client has unintentionally agreed to forgo the right to a detailed assessment. The points made at 27.154 (about contentious business agreements) may be relevant in that regard. **27.126**

[178] This provision came about as a result of the amendments effected by Courts and Legal Services Act 1990, s 98.
[179] *Bake v French (No 2)* [1907] 2 Ch 215.
[180] *In re Baylis* [1896] 2 Ch 107, at 119.
[181] *In re Frape, ex p Perrett* [1893] 2 Ch 284.
[182] See Solicitors Act 1974, s 57(1).
[183] See *In Re Thompson ex p Baylis* [1894] 1 QB 462. It should be noted, however, that, despite the impression given in the Law Reports, the client in that case had already received a statute bill: see the report in the *Law Journal* (63 LJ (QB) 187), referred to by Chitty J in *In re Baylis* [1896] 2 Ch 107, at 114.
[184] *Ray v Newton* [1913] 1 KB 249; see also *Martin Boston & Co (a firm) v Levy* [1982] 1 WLR 1434.
[185] *Bake v French (No 2)* [1907] 2 Ch 215.

Agreements concerning security for solicitors' fees

27.127 Agreements concerning security for a solicitor's fees do not fall within the ambit of Solicitors Act 1974, s 57.[186] Whilst *obiter*, Mustill J had the following to say:

> '[Solicitors Act 1974, s 57] seems to be concerned with the ascertainment of the amount of the remuneration, rather than the way in which it is to be paid—so that an agreement as to the source of the funds which are to be used for paying the bill lies outside the scope of the section.'[187]

The effect of a non-contentious business agreement

27.128 The principal effect of a non-contentious business agreement is that it may be treated 'as an agreement not relating to the remuneration of a solicitor', which means that the client may lose the right to challenge the level of fees by way of a detailed assessment.[188] In particular, a solicitor may sue upon a non-contentious business agreement as if it were any other debt.[189] This is differs from contentious business agreements, under which the court's approval is required to enforce the agreement.[190] If, upon enquiry, the court finds that the agreement is unfair or unreasonable, however, it may be set aside or the amount payable under it may be reduced (see 27.133).[191]

27.129 A non-contentious business agreement may provide for remuneration to be by reference to an hourly rate. Where that is the case, the court may assess the number of hours worked by the solicitor.[192] That would be an exercise virtually indistinguishable from an ordinary assessment other than that the hourly rate would not fall to be assessed—but that would usually be the case anyway because, in modern practice, the rate would almost always be approved by the client in any event. The court may carry out that assessment without making a finding that the agreement was unfair or unreasonable; if, however, either of those thresholds were to be met, the court may set aside the agreed rate and reduce it.[193]

27.130 **Interpretation of non-contentious business agreements** The terms of an agreement must be precise and unambiguous.[194] If the agreement contains a one-sided ambiguous provision that has been inserted by the solicitor, the *contra proferentum* rule may apply in the client's favour.[195] Similarly, where the contract was made prior to 1 October 2015,[196] reg 7 of the Unfair Terms in Consumer Contracts Regulations 1999[197] provides that a consumer contract is to be 'expressed in plain, intelligible language' and that, if there is doubt about the meaning of a written term, the interpretation that is most favourable to the consumer shall prevail. After that date, the provisions of Part 2 of the Consumer Rights Act 2015 may have a bearing (see 28.40–28.44).

---

186 *In re an undertaking by Wingfields, Halse and Trustram, Jonesco v Evening Standard Co* [1932] 2 KB 340 (which related to law that did not distinguish between contentious and non-contentious law, however).
187 *Walton v Egan* [1982] 3 WLR 352, at 357.
188 Solicitors Act 1974, s 57(4).
189 Solicitors Act 1974, s 57(4).
190 Solicitors Act 1974, s 61(1).
191 Solicitors Act 1974, s 57(5).
192 Solicitors Act 1974, s 57(5) and (6).
193 Solicitors Act 1974, s 57(5).
194 *Chamberlain v Boodle & King* [1982] 3 All ER 188.
195 *R a Debtor (No 1594 of 1992)* (1992) The Times, 8 December.
196 See Consumer Rights Act 2015 (Commencement No 3, Transitional Provisions, Savings and Consequential Amendments) Order 2015 (SI 2015/1630) art 6(4).
197 SI 1999/2083.

In a case in which a non-contentious business agreement contained a provision that a solicitor would be entitled to 50 per cent of monies recovered under a compensation scheme, Spencer J found that there was no basis for implying a term that that fee would be based only on the compensation that was obtained through the solicitor's efforts and noted that the implication of such a term would pose insurmountable difficulties of interpretation.[198] Spencer J also found that there was no basis for restricting the payment so that it was calculated on the basis of the compensation net of tax.[199] **27.131**

Termination of a non-contentious business agreement

Beyond what is said about termination of retainers generally at 27.67–27.88, a non-contentious business agreement may be terminated at will. There are no formalities in this regard. **27.132**

Objections on the grounds that the agreement is unfair or unreasonable

It will be recalled that Solicitors Act 1974, s 57(5), reads as follows: **27.133**

> '(5) If on any assessment of costs the agreement is relied on by the solicitor and objected to by the client as unfair or unreasonable, the costs officer may enquire into the facts and certify them to the court, and if from that certificate it appears just to the court that the agreement should be set aside, or the amount payable under it reduced, the court may so order and may give such consequential directions as it thinks fit.'

If one goes back to mid-Victorian times, it can be seen that this is based on a similar provision that was made prior to the distinction being drawn between contentious and non-contentious business.[200] This caused Spencer J to look for guidance in the authorities from around that time.[201] As a result, he concluded that issues of fairness and reasonableness must be considered separately: fairness, he said, relates principally to the manner in which the agreement came to be made, whilst reasonableness relates principally to the terms of the agreement.[202] This is addressed in more detail (in the context of contentious business agreements) at 27.175–27.177. If the agreement is found to be unfair, then it will be set aside and the points made at 27.114 will apply. **27.134**

Contentious business agreements

The following topics are addressed: **27.135**

- the form and content of contentious business agreements (27.142–27.155);
- the effect of contentious business agreements (27.156–27.159);
- a comparison between contentious business agreements and other types of retainer (27.160–27.165);
- the enforcement and examination of contentious business agreements (substantive issues) (27.166–27.177);
- contentious business agreements where the client is acting in a representative capacity (27.178–27.181 and 60.37);
- contentious business agreements where there is only partial performance (27.182–27.184);
- reopening a contentious business agreement (27.185); and

---

198 *Bolt Burdon Solicitors v Tariq & Ors* [2016] EWHC 811 (QB), at [77], [78], [81], [82], [84] and [85].

199 *Ibid*, at [102]–[110].

200 See Attorneys' and Solicitors' Act 1870, ss 8 and 9.

201 In particular, he found the judgment of Lord Esher MR in *In Re Stuart, ex p Cathcart* [1893] 2 QB 201 to be helpful: see *Bolt Burdon Solicitors v Tariq & Ors* [2016] EWHC 811 (QB), at [148].

202 *Bolt Burdon Solicitors v Tariq & Ors* [2016] EWHC 811 (QB), at [149].

- procedural issues relating to contentious business agreements (27.186–27.189).

27.136 Contentious business agreements (like their non-contentious counterparts) are governed by primary legislation—in particular, by Solicitors Act 1974, ss 59–63. They are often referred to as CBAs, but that abbreviation is not used in this book because it is prone to being confused with the abbreviation commonly used for conditional fee agreements (CFAs).

27.137 A contentious business agreement is a retainer that, subject to certain safeguards, will allow the solicitor to recover fees for contentious work as if they were an ordinary debt—although a special procedure must be used in order to do this (see 27.170–27.172 and 27.186–27.188). The principal effect of this is that the costs will not ordinarily be subject to assessment (or, if the agreement provides for payment by an hourly rate, the rate will not ordinarily be subject to assessment). However, judicial control continues to exist in an attenuated form, in that the court is able to set aside a contentious business agreement if it is found to be unfair or unreasonable (see 27.166 *et seq*).

27.138 The modern provisions are set out in Solicitors Act 1974, ss 59–63. They were amended by the Courts and Legal Services Act 1990 to introduce an express facility to charge by reference to hourly rates. The wording of the modern provision derives from the Solicitors Act 1957, but similar provisions existed well before this. To understand the effect of contentious business agreements, it is necessary to know something of the common law and of the history of the jurisdiction.

The relationship of the Solicitors Act 1974 with the common law

27.139 The original statutory provisions were introduced by the Attorneys and Solicitors Act 1870 (see 1.82–1.84). Notwithstanding the fact that, in Victorian times, no distinction was made between contentious and non-contentious work, s 4 of the 1870 Act was similar in many ways to the provisions that govern the form, content and effect of modern contentious business agreements.[203] It should be noted, however, that what is said below arguably applies only to contentious business agreements (see 27.211).

27.140 Those early statutory provisions were purely enabling provisions; they were not intended to be restrictive in any way. Fletcher Moulton LJ had this to say on the point:

> 'It is to be remarked in the first place that this is a purely enabling, and not a disabling, section, and the Court would not, unless forced to do so, construe such a section so as to take away or alter powers already in existence, except indeed by extending them.'[204]

He went on to say that 'the specific provisions of s 4 did no more than provide and regulate a procedure for the control of such agreements; they did not in substance alter the law affecting them'.[205]

27.141 Thus those early statutory provisions did not restrict the ability of clients and solicitors to negotiate terms of engagement. The relevance of this is that, where a putative contentious business agreement did not comply with the requisite statutory requirements, it would be judged according to the underlying common law (see 27.111) and, as such, may or may not have been found to be enforceable. In particular, to the extent that it was favourable to the client, it could be enforced by the client.

---

[203] Solicitors Act 1974, s 59.
[204] *Clare v Joseph* [1907] 2 KB 369, at 376.
[205] *Ibid.*

The form and content of contentious business agreements

The form and content of a modern contentious business agreement is governed by Solicitors Act 1974, s 59, and by the authorities that clarify that section. The requirements are that: **27.142**

- the agreement is in writing (see 27.144);[206]
- it must contain terms going to the amount of costs, or to the method by which those costs are to be calculated (see 27.145–27.147);[207] and
- it must be sufficiently specific to allow the client to know what is being proposed (see 27.148–27.150).[208]

It is a moot point whether a contentious business agreement needs to be signed, which point is addressed at 27.151–27.153. Whilst it is not a requirement under the Solicitors Act 1974, it is arguable that a solicitor is now under a duty to give notice of the fact that an agreement is a contentious business agreement (see 27.154–27.155).

Solicitors Act 1974, s 59, provides as follows: **27.143**

> '(1) Subject to subsection (2), a solicitor may make an agreement in writing with his client as to his remuneration in respect of any contentious business done, or to be done, by him (in this Act referred to as a "contentious business agreement") providing that he shall be remunerated by a gross sum or by reference to an hourly rate, or by a salary, or otherwise, and whether at a higher or lower rate than that at which he would otherwise have been entitled to be remunerated.
>
> (2) Nothing in this section or in sections 60 to 63 shall give validity to—
> (a) any purchase by a solicitor of the interest, or any part of the interest, of his client in any action, suit or other contentious proceeding; or
> (b) any agreement by which a solicitor retained or employed to prosecute any action, suit or other contentious proceeding, stipulates for payment only in the event of success in that action, suit or proceeding; or
> (c) any disposition, contract, settlement, conveyance, delivery, dealing or transfer which under the law relating to bankruptcy is invalid against a trustee or creditor in any bankruptcy or composition.'

Writing Section 59(1) of the Solicitors Act 1974 provides that a contentious business agreement must be in writing. With appropriate adjustments, the points made at 27.120–27.121 (about non-contentious business agreements) will apply. **27.144**

Terms as to costs Section 59(1) provides that a contentious business agreement may require that a solicitor be remunerated 'by a gross sum or by reference to an hourly rate, or by a salary, or otherwise, and whether at a higher or lower rate than that at which he would otherwise have been entitled to be remunerated'. This requirement will overlap with the requirement that the agreement is sufficiently specific (see 27.148–27.150). Denning MR has explained that the agreement must relate to the solicitor's remuneration itself, rather than only to some variable aspect of the way in which the solicitor's bill will be drawn up (see 27.146).[209] Mann J had this to say about this requirement: 'The purpose of **27.145**

[206] Solicitors Act 1974, s 59(1).
[207] Solicitors Act 1974, s 59(1). See also *Chamberlain v Boodle & King* [1982] 1 WLR 1443, at 1445.
[208] *Chamberlain v Boodle & King* [1982] 1 WLR 1443, at 1445.
[209] *Chamberlain v Boodle & King* [1982] 1 WLR 1443.

a [contentious business agreement] is to fix the fees, or provide a fixing mechanism, so that the parties (and in particular the client) knows where they stand.'[210]

27.146 The retainer that was before Denning MR did little more than make provision for a number of different rates to be paid in respect of different fee earners and, even then, those rates were not fixed. He had this to say about that:

> '[It] seems to me that this is not an agreement as to remuneration at all. It is simply an indication of the rate of charging on which the solicitors propose to make up their bill. It is by no means an agreement in writing as to remuneration ... It is impossible to say that this was a contentious business agreement in writing such as to deprive the client of his right to have it taxed.'[211]

It should be noted that this was before the statutory provisions were changed so as to expressly include retainers dealing with hourly rates.

27.147 It therefore seems that a contentious business agreement must be an agreement that can properly be said to be an agreement as to what will be charged, rather than only a general indication as to the way in which the costs will be calculated. Even where there has been a mere general indication, however, the agreed figures will still be relevant in the sense that they will be taken into account when considering the reasonableness of the costs.[212]

27.148 **Sufficiently specific** For an agreement to comply with the requirements of Solicitors Act 1974, s 59, Denning MR held that it 'must be sufficiently specific—so as to tell the client what he is letting himself in for by way of costs'.[213] Mann J put much the same point in the following way: 'The essence of a [contentious business agreement] is certainty ... Since the client is disadvantaged [by entering into a contentious business agreement], the agreement has to be in writing, and it has to be sufficiently certain.'[214]

27.149 The requirement that the agreement be sufficiently specific is similar to (and may overlap with) the requirement that the amount or method be stated (see 27.147), but there are differences between the two. In particular, an agreement may lack specificity in a way that relates to something other than the quantum of the solicitor's fees. Each case will turn on its own facts, but the following are examples:

- where the retainer is a general retainer rather than a retainer relating to a specific case and where it had not been adapted for use in the case in hand;[215]
- where the agreement contemplated the execution of a more formal document;[216]
- where the retainer afforded a facility for the solicitor's fees to be adjusted to take account of the nature of the case;[217] and
- where the agreement was contained in a series of letters, which had not been signed by the client.[218]

---

210 *Wilson v The Spectre Partnership* [2007] EWHC 133 (Ch), at [16(b)].
211 *Chamberlain v Boodle & King* [1982] 1 WLR 1443, at 1445.
212 See CPR, r 46.9(2)(a) and (b).
213 *Chamberlain v Boodle & King* [1982] 1 WLR 1443, at 1445.
214 *Wilson v The Spectre Partnership* [2007] EWHC 133 (Ch), at [15].
215 *Ibid.*
216 See, in a context other than costs, *Tiverton Estates Ltd v Wearwell Ltd* [1975] Ch 146, which was considered in *Martin Boston & Co (a firm) v Levy* [1982] 1 WLR 1434.
217 *Wilson v The Spectre Partnership* [2007] EWHC 133 (Ch), at [16(b)].
218 *Chamberlain v Boodle & King* [1982] 1 WLR 1443, at 1445.

Whilst they are not express requirements, there are two other issues that merit attention, not least because they may be important factors in deciding whether the requirements have been satisfied and whether the agreement should be set aside. The first is the need for a signature (see 27.151–27.153); the second is the extent to which the client must be put on notice that the agreement is intended to be a contentious business agreement (see 27.154–27.155). **27.150**

Signature In contrast to non-contentious business agreements (see 27.122), there is no express statutory requirement that a contentious business agreement be signed. There are (ancient) *obiter* comments to the effect that a signature is necessary,[219] but it is doubtful whether those authorities represent the modern law.[220] Denning MR has held that if a client is to be deprived of their right to an assessment, they should at least sign the agreement,[221] but that was in the context of the putative agreement being contained in letters, rather than a specific document, and in the context of the agreement being found to be insufficiently specific to be a contentious business agreement. **27.151**

Even if there is a requirement that a contentious business agreement is to be signed, a failure by the solicitor to sign will not necessarily prevent that solicitor from enforcing that agreement.[222] This would be on the basis that the client had signed it, so that there can be no doubt that the client was prepared to be bound by its terms. The points made at 27.122 about non-contentious business agreements may be relevant in that regard. **27.152**

Although there is no specific authority on the point, it would be open to a client to argue that, if the circumstances were such that they could reasonably have expected to have been given the opportunity to sign the retainer, it would be unfair to afford the solicitor the benefits of it being a contentious business agreement.[223] **27.153**

Notice Neither the Solicitors Act 1974 nor the authorities stipulate that the client must be put on notice that if they make the agreement, they will lose the right to claim an assessment as of right. That said, in so far as contracts made before 6 October 2011 are concerned, it is difficult to see how a solicitor could have complied with para 2.30 of the Solicitors' Code of Conduct 2007[224] without having told the client that their right to an assessment would be negated if they were to agree to enter into a contentious business agreement. The SRA Code of Conduct 2011 is less specific (see 27.63), and it is likely that the court would not find that code helpful in deciding what was and was not required for the purposes of creating a fully enforceable contract of retainer. That said, where the client is a consumer and where the agreement was made on or after 13 June 2014, reg 9(1) of the Consumer Contracts (Information, Cancellation and Additional Charges) Regulations 2013[225] would impose a duty to give certain information (see 28.67–28.88, and in particular, 28.71–28.72) and it **27.154**

---

[219] *In re Lewis, ex p Munro* (1876) 1 QBD 724.

[220] See *In re Thompson, ex p Bayliss* [1894] 1 QB 462.

[221] *Chamberlain v Boodle & King* [1982] 1 WLR 1443, at 1445.

[222] *Bake v French (No 2)* [1907] 2 Ch 215; *In re Thompson, ex p Bayliss* [1894] 1 QB 462, at 464; *In re Jones* [1895] 2 Ch 719. A contrary decision—*Pontifex v Farnham* (1892) 41 WR 238—was confined to its own facts in *Bake v French (No 2)* [1907] 2 Ch 215.

[223] See, by way of analogy, *Martin Boston & Co (a firm) v Levy* [1982] 1 WLR 1434, in which there is a discussion about the effect of a client having a reasonable expectation of the agreement being executed in a more formal form.

[224] This provides that 'if you intend to seek payment of any or all of your costs from your client, you must advise your client of their right to an assessment of those costs'.

[225] SI 2013/3134.

is difficult to see how a solicitor could comply with those requirements without telling the client something as fundamental as the possible loss of the right to an assessment.

27.155 Whilst the court would no doubt take into account the way in which a contentious business agreement described itself, the presence or absence of a label is not determinative of the issue of whether a contract of retainer is a contentious business agreement. In particular, the fact that a retainer is not referred to as being a contentious business agreement does not preclude it from being one. Mann J has explained that the test is whether the retainer meets the criteria for a contentious business agreement, not whether the counterparties referred to it in that way.[226] Although there is no authority on the point, the court would probably place weight on an express provision that the agreement was not a contentious business agreement and, even if the court did not do so, it would be open to the client to argue that, in light of that provision, the agreement was unfair within the meaning of Solicitors Act 1974, s 61(2)(b), in that it gave misleading information.

The effect of contentious business agreements

27.156 Broadly speaking, the effect of a contentious business agreement is that (unless it is set aside) the client will lose the right to a detailed assessment of whichever fees have been agreed.[227] Moreover, the solicitor may commence proceedings for its fees without having to wait for the expiry of one month after the delivery of the bill.[228]

27.157 Not all contentious business agreements are intended to preclude assessment entirely; this is because some agreements fix only certain aspects of the costs. Thus, whilst some contentious business agreements may contain provisions fixing all of the solicitor's fees (such as a fixed fee), others may fix only part of those fees (such as where the agreement provides for payment by reference to an agreed hourly rate). Where an hourly rate has been set, the court may ascertain the number of hours worked by the solicitor[229] and, to that extent, there may be an assessment. The court may carry out that exercise without making a finding that the agreement was unfair or unreasonable; if, however, the agreement were to be found to be unfair or unreasonable, then the court could set the rate aside or reduce it.[230]

27.158 A number of the relevant provisions are set out in Solicitors Act 1974, s 60 (as amended), which reads as follows:

> '(1) Subject to the provisions of this section and to sections 61 to 63, the costs of a solicitor in any case where a contentious business agreement has been made shall not be subject to assessment or (except in the case of an agreement which provides for the solicitor to be remunerated by reference to an hourly rate) to the provisions of section 69.
>
> (2) Subject to subsection (3), a contentious business agreement shall not affect the amount of, or any rights or remedies for the recovery of, any costs payable by the client to, or to the client by, any person other than the solicitor, and that person may, unless he has otherwise agreed, require any such costs to be assessed according to the rules for their assessment for the time being in force.

226 *Wilson v The Spectre Partnership* [2007] EWHC 133 (Ch).
227 Solicitors Act 1974, s 60(1).
228 See Solicitors Act 1974, s 60(1), which sets aside s 69(1).
229 See Solicitors Act 1974, s 61(4A) and (4B).
230 See Solicitors Act 1974, s 61(2) and (4).

(3) A client shall not be entitled to recover from any other person under an order for the payment of any costs to which a contentious business agreement relates more than the amount payable by him to his solicitor in respect of those costs under the agreement.

(4) A contentious business agreement shall be deemed to exclude any claim by the solicitor in respect of the business to which it relates other than—
(a) a claim for the agreed costs; or
(b) a claim for such costs as are expressly excepted from the agreement.

(5) A provision in a contentious business agreement that the solicitor shall not be liable for his negligence, or that of any employee of his, shall be void if the client is a natural person who, in entering that agreement, is acting for purposes which are outside his trade, business or profession.

(6) A provision in a contentious business agreement that the solicitor shall be relieved from any responsibility to which he would otherwise be subject as a solicitor shall be void.'

The effect of these provisions may be summarised in the following way. **27.159**

- **No assessment** Section 60(1) of the 1974 Act precludes an assessment of fees that are the subject of a contentious business agreement—although this will not be the case if the court finds that the agreement should be set aside as being unfair or unreasonable (see 27.166–27.177). Where the contentious business agreement provides for remuneration by reference to an hourly rate, the time claimed (but not the rate) may be assessed (see 27.157).
- **Third parties** Section 60(2) provides that a contentious business agreement does not affect the costs payable by or to a third party and that the third party may require the costs to be assessed. Where a third party is paying the solicitor's fees, the indemnity principle would usually apply and, in view of this, the solicitor would not be able to seek more from the third party than it could from its own client, the effect of which is that, for all practical purposes, the third party can elect whether to have the costs assessed or to pay the amount stipulated in the agreement.
- **Indemnity principle preserved** Section 60(3) creates a statutory version of the indemnity principle. Hansard records that it was included in anticipation of the possibility of the indemnity principle being abolished.[231] This, of course, has not happened, so, to that extent, it is otiose.
- **Ambit** Section 60(4) limits the effect of a contentious business agreement to that which has been agreed.
- **Limitation on liability** Section 60(5) restricts the extent to which a solicitor can limit its liability for negligence. Section 60(6) and the last 12 or so words of s 60(5) have been inserted by the Legal Services Act 2007 to regulate the growing trend to insert clauses that limit a liability in negligence.[232] These issues go beyond the remit of this book and are not discussed further.

Comparison between contentious business agreements and other types of retainer

Oral retainers and other types of contract of retainer in general To understand the effect of the statutory provisions mentioned above, it is necessary to know how the law treats agreements that fix (or which are intended to fix) the quantum of a solicitor's fees, but **27.160**

[231] Hansard, HL Deb, col GC64 (2 July 1972).
[232] See Ashford, P, 'Negligence Claims: The Ins and Outs of Limiting Your Liability' (2007) 58 PILJ 21.

which are not regarded as contentious business agreements. Oral agreements fall within this category (see 27.210–27.213) and are a good indicator of how many other types of contract would be treated. By comparing the effect of the statutory provisions with that of the common law, it is possible to determine what difference the statutory provisions make.

27.161 As was set out at 27.140, Fletcher Moulton LJ has explained that the statutory provisions relating to contentious business agreements were intended to be enabling, rather than disabling.[233] In the case before him, Fletcher Moulton LJ went on to find that the oral agreement in question was enforceable by the client notwithstanding its unwritten form.[234] Similar conclusions have been reached in other cases in which the agreement in question has been found to fall short of being a contentious business agreement (see the footnotes to 27.112). This is a reflection of the principle that the common law generally, but not always, allows enforcement against the solicitor (see 27.111 and 27.210).

27.162 Where the solicitor intends to rely on an oral agreement as against its client, however, the common law will apply in that it will, in general, be enforceable only if favourable from the client's perspective.[235] In line with the principles set out at 27.211, oral agreements cannot be relied upon against the client so as to act unfavourably from the client's point of view.[236] Thus, when compared with the position under the common law, the effect of compliance with the statutory provisions concerning contentious business agreements is to put the status of the agreement beyond doubt (subject, of course, to it not being set aside), whereas, without compliance, there is considerable potential for doubt because the uncertainties of the common law will prevail.

27.163 **Conditional fee agreements and their relationship to contentious business agreements** Most conditional fee agreements expressly state that they are not contentious business agreements. It is not clear what effect, if any, such a statement would have. There is no reason why a conditional fee agreement should not also be a contentious business agreement; indeed, there are *obiter* comments to suggest that, in appropriate circumstances, this would be the case.[237]

27.164 Whilst on the topic of conditional fee agreements, it is worth saying that, unlike the legislation governing non-contentious business agreements (see 27.118), there is nothing within the legislation governing contentious business agreements that deals with contingency fee agreements.[238] As such, what is set out in this section should not be regarded as being an alternative mechanism by which conditional free agreements may be found to be enforceable.

27.165 **Agreements that provide for security of payment** An agreement that provides for security of payment (rather than for the method or the amount of payment) would not

---

[233] *Clare v Joseph* [1907] 2 KB 369, at 376.

[234] The agreement that was found to be enforceable was a conditional fee agreement.

[235] *In re Fernandes* (1878) WN 57; *In re Russell, Son v Scott* (1885) 30 Ch D 114.

[236] *Chamberlain v Boodle & King* (1980) 124 SJ 186, subsequently upheld on appeal ([1982] 1 WLR 1443); *Martin Boston & Co (a firm) v Levy* [1982] 1 WLR 1434 (arguable defence to a claim by solicitors for fees for contentious work under oral agreement).

[237] *Hollins v Russell* [2003] EWCA Civ 718, at [93].

[238] See Solicitors Act 1974, s 59(2). Whilst not binding, for a discussion on this topic, see Master Hurst's judgment in *Tel-Ka Talk Ltd v Revenue & Customs Commissioners* [2010] EWHC 90175 (Costs), at [134] *et seq*.

be a contentious business agreement simply by reason of it being in writing, etc.[239] The points made at 27.127 (about non-contentious business) are likely to apply by analogy. The provisions relating to contentious business agreements do not impose a requirement that agreements for security of payment be made in writing[240] (although, of course, other legislation may impose such an obligation, depending on the nature of the security that is involved).

The enforcement and examination of contentious business agreements (substantive issues)

'Enforcement' in this context is used to mean the court adjudicating upon and enforcing the specific terms of an agreement. If the court declines to enforce the terms of a contentious business agreement, that does not mean that the court will find the entire contract of retainer to be unenforceable; it merely means that the court will determine the amount payable on the basis of what is reasonable and/or in accordance with the common law. **27.166**

Solicitors Act 1974, s 61, provides as follows: **27.167**

> '(1) No action shall be brought on any contentious business agreement, but on the application of any person who—
> (a) is a party to the agreement or the representative of such a party; or
> (b) is or is alleged to be liable to pay, or is or claims to be entitled to be paid, the costs due or alleged to be due in respect of the business to which the agreement relates,
>
> the court may enforce or set aside the agreement and determine every question as to its validity or effect.
>
> (2) On any application under subsection (1), the court—
> (a) if it is of the opinion that the agreement is in all respects fair and reasonable, may enforce it;
> (b) if it is of the opinion that the agreement is in any respect unfair or unreasonable, may set it aside and order the costs covered by it to be assessed as if it had never been made;
> (c) in any case, may make such order as to the costs of the application as it thinks fit.
>
> (3) If the business covered by a contentious business agreement (not being an agreement to which section 62 applies) is business done, or to be done, in any action, a client who is a party to the agreement may make application to a costs officer of the court for the agreement to be examined.
>
> (4) A costs officer before whom an agreement is laid under subsection (3) shall examine it and may either allow it, or, if he is of the opinion that the agreement is unfair or unreasonable, require the opinion of the court to be taken on it, and the court may allow the agreement or reduce the amount payable under it, or set it aside and order the costs covered by it to be assessed as if it had never been made.
>
> (4A) Subsection (4B) applies where a contentious business agreement provides for the remuneration of the solicitor to be by reference to an hourly rate.
>
> (4B) If on the assessment of any costs the agreement is relied on by the solicitor and the client objects to the amount of the costs (but is not alleging that the agreement is unfair or unreasonable), the costs officer may enquire into—
> (a) the number of hours worked by the solicitor; and
> (b) whether the number of hours worked by him was excessive.

---

[239] *In re Jackson* [1915] 1 KB 371 (which, for present purposes, did not distinguish between contentious and non-contentious work).

[240] *In re an undertaking by Wingfields, Halse and Trustram, Jonesco v Evening Standard Co* [1932] 2 KB 340.

(5) Where the amount agreed under any contentious business agreement is paid by or on behalf of the client or by any person entitled to do so, the person making the payment may at any time within twelve months from the date of payment, or within such further time as appears to the court to be reasonable, apply to the court, and, if it appears to the court that the special circumstances of the case require it to be re-opened, the court may, on such terms as may be just, re-open it and order the costs covered by the agreement to be assessed and the whole or any part of the amount received by the solicitor to be repaid by him.

(6) In this section and in sections 62 and 63 "the court" means—

(a) in relation to an agreement under which any business has been done in any court having jurisdiction to enforce and set aside agreements, any such court in which any of that business has been done;

(b) in relation to an agreement under which no business has been done in any such court, and under which more than £50 is payable, the High Court;

(c) in relation to an agreement under which no business has been done in any such court and under which not more than £50 is payable, any county court which would, but for the provisions of subsection (1) prohibiting the bringing of an action on the agreement, have had jurisdiction in any action on it;

and for the avoidance of doubt it is hereby declared that in paragraph (a) "court having jurisdiction to enforce and set aside agreements" includes [the[241]] county court.'

27.168 Thus there are three separate functions contained within the section, as follows.

- **The power to enforce** There is the jurisdiction to enforce the contentious businesses agreement, which power is contained in Solicitors Act 1974, s 61(1) and (2).
- **The power to examine** There is the jurisdiction to examine the contentious business agreement, which power is contained in Solicitors Act 1974, s 61(3), (4), (4A) and (4B).
- **The power to reopen** There is the power to reopen a contentious business agreement, which power is contained in Solicitors Act 1974, s 61(5).

The first two of these topics are addressed immediately below. The last of these topics—along with some other topics arising out of s 61—is considered at 27.185.

27.169 **The jurisdiction to enforce and the jurisdiction to examine** Historically, the jurisdictions to enforce and to examine were entirely separate:[242] an application under one jurisdiction would not have precluded an application under the other.[243] This is still theoretically true, but—in view of the fact that, in most circumstances, the issues would be almost identical under both jurisdictions—it is doubtful whether a court applying the overriding objective would suffer the same arguments to be put more than once.

27.170 Solicitors Act 1974, s 61(1), precludes an action being brought on a contentious business agreement,[244] but provides an alternative mechanism by which an agreement may be enforced upon application. It is within the court's discretion whether to enforce it, that discretion turning on whether the agreement is fair and reasonable. If it is found to be unfair

[241] At the time of writing, this amendment had yet to come into force generally: see the Crime and Courts Act 2013, s 17(5), Sch 9, Pt 3, para 52(1)(b) and (2), and (as to date of commencement) s 61(3).

[242] In the Attorneys and Solicitors Act 1870, these powers were contained in separate sections.

[243] *Stuart, ex p Cathcart, In Re* [1893] 2 QB 201, at 204. See also *In re Simmons & Politzer* [1954] 2 QB 296, in which it was held that a failure to comply with certain statutory requirements concerning examination by the court could be a reason to set aside upon reopening the matter (although those statutory requirements no longer exist and, to that extent, *Simmons & Politzer* is no longer good law).

[244] A solicitor is, however, able to bring an action for failure on the part of the client to instruct the solicitor under the terms of the agreement: *Rees v Williams* (1875) LR 10 Exch 200.

or unreasonable, the court may set the agreement aside and order the fees to be assessed as if it had never been made.[245] There is a similar jurisdiction that may be exercised upon examination of the agreement: if the court finds that the agreement is unfair or unreasonable, the court is given the power not only to set aside the agreement, but also to reduce the amount payable under it.[246]

There is some ambiguity as to how the jurisdiction to enforce operates, which ambiguity is discussed at 27.186–27.188. In particular, it is not wholly clear when the court's permission is required. **27.171**

From the client's point of view, the effect of these two jurisdictions is that if a client is not content with the solicitor's costs, they are able to ask the court to determine whether the agreement is fair and reasonable.[247] If it is, then the court will allow the agreement (which, in effect, means that the court will permit it to be enforced without further enquiry); if it is not, then the court will set aside the agreement, in which case the costs will be subject to assessment or, in the alternative, the court may reduce the amount payable under it.[248] **27.172**

The effect of setting aside a contentious business agreement The setting aside of an agreement will not have the effect of automatically negating the solicitor's ability to recover fees. This is because there will usually be an underlying enforceable retainer that will allow the solicitor to recover those fees (subject, of course, to the court regarding those costs as being reasonable, and to the underlying common law and to any other relevant law). Where there is doubt about this (such as where the contentious business agreement is also a conditional fee agreement, in which case it might be said that, by setting that agreement aside, there could be no implied agreement to step into its place), it would be open to the court to make an order under Solicitors Act 1974, s 61(4), to reduce the amount payable under the agreement. As such, it would rarely be the case that the court would be forced to send the solicitor away without any payment at all. **27.173**

Scrutiny of an agreement that provides for an hourly rate Where the agreement provides for payment by way of an hourly rate, the court may assess the number of hours worked and it may do so without having to make a finding that the agreement is unfair or unreasonable.[249] This, of course, would be the case only if there were also no binding agreement as to the number of hours worked. **27.174**

'Fair' and 'reasonable' What is fair and reasonable will depend on the facts of each case. The test is whether the agreement is fair and reasonable; the court looks at each of these matters as being discrete topics. Esher MR had the following to say on the point: **27.175**

> 'With regard to the fairness of such an agreement, it appears to me that this refers to the mode of obtaining the agreement, and that if a solicitor makes an agreement with a client who fully understands and appreciates that agreement that satisfies the requirement as to fairness. But the agreement must also be reasonable, and in determining whether it is so the matters covered by the expression "fair" cannot be re-introduced.'[250]

245 Solicitors Act 1974, s 61(2)(b).
246 Solicitors Act 1974, s 61(4).
247 Solicitors Act 1974, s 61(3); cf s 61(1), which implies a similar jurisdiction.
248 Solicitors Act 1974, s 61(4); cf s 61(2), which implies a similar jurisdiction.
249 Solicitors Act 1974, s 61(4A) and (4B).
250 *In re Stuart, ex p Cathcart, In Re* [1893] 2 QB 201, at 205.

Spencer J has confirmed (albeit in the context of non-contentious business agreements) that this approach remains good law[251] (see 27.134).

27.176 Whilst there is no authority on the point, it is likely that, in deciding whether the agreement is fair, the court would take into account the prevailing standards that the client was entitled to expect the solicitor to meet, so the quality and content of the advice given pursuant to the prevailing codes of conduct may be relevant. It is also possible that the court would take into account any relevant consumer protection legislation.

27.177 In considering what is reasonable, the court should not carry out a *de facto* detailed assessment.[252] Even so, it is difficult to see how the court could decide whether the agreement is reasonable without coming to *some* approximate view of what would have been allowed had the agreement not existed.

Contentious business agreements where the client is acting in a representative capacity

27.178 It used to be the case that all contentious business agreements needed to be examined by the court before payment could be received.[253] That rule no longer applies, but the court does still have a role to play in that regard in certain circumstances in which the client is acting in a representative capacity.

27.179 Solicitors Act 1974, s 62, provides as follows:

> '**62 Contentious business agreements by certain representatives**
>
> (1) Where the client who makes a contentious business agreement makes it as a representative of a person whose property will be chargeable with the whole or part of the amount payable under the agreement, the agreement shall be laid before a costs officer of the court before payment.
>
> (2) A costs officer before whom an agreement is laid under subsection (1) shall examine it and may either allow it, or, if he is of the opinion that it is unfair or unreasonable, require the opinion of the court to be taken on it, and the court may allow the agreement or reduce the amount payable under it, or set it aside and order the costs covered by it to be assessed as if it had never been made.
>
> (3) A client who makes a contentious business agreement as mentioned in subsection (1) and pays the whole or any part of the amount payable under the agreement without it being allowed by the officer or by the court shall be liable at any time to account to the person whose property is charged with the whole or any part of the amount so paid for the sum so charged, and the solicitor who accepts the payment may be ordered by the court to refund the amount received by him.
>
> (4) A client makes a contentious business agreement as the representative of another person if he makes it—
>
> (a) as his guardian,
> (b) as a trustee for him under a deed or will,
> (c) as a deputy for him appointed by the Court of Protection with powers in relation to his property and affairs, or
> (d) as another person authorised under that Act to act on his behalf.'

[251] *Bolt Burdon Solicitors v Tariq & Ors* [2016] EWHC 811 (QB), at [149].

[252] *Re Templeton and Cox* (1909) 101 LT 144, CA.

[253] See Solicitors Act, 1932, s 60 (which was the old requirement); *In re Simmons & Politzer* [1954] 2 QB 296.

Thus, where a contentious business agreement is made by a client who is acting as a representative of another person, the court's approval must be sought before any payment is made under that agreement. If the court's approval is not sought, then the solicitor may be required to account for any monies paid, as may the representative person. These provisions protect children or persons who lack capacity from abuse; they are comparable to the provisions requiring the compromise of a solicitor and client bill to be approved by the court. **27.180**

Solicitors Act 1974, s 62(4)(c) and (d), refers to persons who lack capacity. The reference to 'that Act' in s 62(4)(d) is not wholly clear: the subsection was inserted by the Mental Capacity Act 2005[254] and may be a reference to that Act. If this is right, then a client will be acting in a representative capacity if they make the agreement for another person authorised under the Mental Capacity Act 2005 to act on that person's behalf. **27.181**

Contentious business agreements where there is only partial performance

Where, by reason of death, loss of capacity or (in some circumstances) disinstruction, a solicitor is prevented from performing its obligations under a contentious business agreement, the court may make an allowance for the work done. This is as a consequence of Solicitors Act 1974, s 63, which reads as follows: **27.182**

> '**63 Effect on contentious business agreement of death, incapability or change of solicitor**
>
> (1) If, after some business has been done under a contentious business agreement but before the solicitor has wholly performed it—
> (a) the solicitor dies, or becomes incapable of acting; or
> (b) the client changes his solicitor (as, notwithstanding the agreement, he shall be entitled to do),
>
> any party to, or the representative of any party to, the agreement may apply to the court, and the court shall have the same jurisdiction as to enforcing the agreement so far as it has been performed, or setting it aside, as the court would have had if the solicitor had not died or become incapable of acting, or the client had not changed his solicitor.
>
> (2) The court, notwithstanding that it is of the opinion that the agreement is in all respects fair and reasonable, may order the amount due in respect of business under the agreement to be ascertained by assessment, and in that case—
> (a) the costs officer, in ascertaining that amount, shall have regard so far as may be to the terms of the agreement; and
> (b) payment of the amount found by him to be due may be enforced in the same manner as if the agreement had been completely performed.
>
> (3) If in such a case as is mentioned in subsection (1)(b) an order is made for the assessment of the amount due to the solicitor in respect of the business done under the agreement, the court shall direct the costs officer to have regard to the circumstances under which the change of solicitor has taken place, and the costs officer, unless he is of the opinion that there has been no default, negligence, improper delay or other conduct on the part of the solicitor, or any of his employees, affording the client reasonable ground for changing his solicitor, shall not allow to the solicitor the full amount of the remuneration agreed to be paid to him.'

[254] Mental Capacity Act 2005, s 67(1), and Sch 6, para 22(1) and (3).

27.183 One effect of these provisions is to limit the potentially harsh effect of a contentious business agreement being an entire contract (see 27.23 for a description of those potential consequences). In particular, if a solicitor is unable to complete its obligations under the agreement because the solicitor dies, loses capacity or because the client withdraws instructions without reasonable grounds, then the court will award a sum to be assessed (or, if circumstances permit, payment in full). If, however, the client had reasonable grounds for terminating the retainer, the court will be able to assess the costs and, in doing so, will be able to take the solicitor's default, negligence, improper delay or other conduct, if any, into account.

27.184 Solicitors Act 1974, s 63(3), permits the court to take account of default or negligence, improper delay or other conduct on the part of the solicitor (or any of its employees) that may have given the client reasonable grounds for instructing another solicitor. It is clear that the default or negligence can be taken into account in such a way as to reduce the solicitor's fees to a level that is lower than they would have been had the agreement been fully performed, but what is less clear is whether the court is able to allow an amount that is less than a reasonable amount. It is arguable that the court does have this power, but there is no authority on that point.

Reopening a contentious business agreement

27.185 If the liability under a contentious business agreement has been discharged, the person who made the payment may apply to the court for the matter to be reopened and the costs assessed. The court may make such an order only if there are 'special circumstances' within the meaning of Solicitors Act 1974, s 61(5). Unlike statute bills in general, there is no absolute bar to an assessment after the expiry of 12 months following payment. In particular, the section provides that the court may reopen the matter 'within such further time as appears to the court to be reasonable'. This gives rise to the somewhat anomalous situation that a client who has paid their solicitor costs for a period exceeding one year may be in a better position if they paid them under a formal contentious business agreement than they would have been in had there been no such agreement.

Procedural issues relating to contentious business agreements

27.186 **Enforcement of a contentious business agreement (procedural issues)** There is some ambiguity as to how the jurisdiction to enforce under Solicitors Act 1974, s 61(1), operates. There are two schools of thought: the first is that the court's permission must be sought before any application to enforce is made; the second is that the court's permission to enforce the agreement is required only if and when the agreement becomes contentious. In quoting a passage from *Cook on Costs 2006*, Mann J had this to say:

> '[One of the parties] drew my attention to a passage in *Cook on Costs* [2006] at para 6.9 in which the editor suggests that an action could be commenced without what he calls the "permission" of the court to enforce the agreement, and that the statutory bar would only be called into play if the point was taken. He says "... it is only if the solicitor wishes to rely on the contentious business agreement that he needs permission to proceed". If the point were not taken then the solicitor would be able to benefit from a default or summary judgment (assuming, of course, that the conditions necessary for those forms of judgment existed) ... I confess I have difficulty understanding the passage in *Cook*. If there is a [contentious business agreement], and the solicitor sues for fees due under it, it seems to me that he would be enforcing the [contentious business

agreement]. I do not understand how he can claim the fees due under it without enforcing it.'[255]

On the facts of the case before him, it was not necessary for Mann J to clarify the correct procedure, but it seems that he subscribed to the first school of thought. In any event, the phrase 'no action shall be brought' in s 61(1) of the 1974 Act does not prevent a claim being brought for breach of a contentious business agreement.[256] **27.187**

Any claim should be made by the procedure under Part 8 of the Civil Procedure Rules (CPR) or, in existing proceedings, by application.[257] Where the claim is issued in the High Court in London, it must be issued in the Senior Courts Costs Office (SCCO),[258] unless it is a claim under Solicitors Act 1974, s 63, in which case it may (but does not have to) be issued in the SCCO.[259] This topic is addressed in more detail at 36.43–36.45. **27.188**

Seeking approval of a contentious business agreement by a person acting in a representative capacity Where the client has been acting in a representative capacity and where they are required seek the court's approval of the agreement, the procedure for laying the agreement before the court is the CPR, Part 8, procedure (or, in existing proceedings, by application).[260] Where the claim is issued in the High Court in London, it must be issued in the SCCO.[261] **27.189**

Implied Retainers

This section addresses the issue of implied retainers. For obvious reasons, this is a topic that will be relevant only if there is no express contract of retainer that covers the fees in question. There are, in the present context, three modes of implication: **27.190**

- implication arising out of the relationship between the counterparties (that is, the legal services provider and client) (see 27.191–27.194);
- implication by law (see 27.195–27.197); and
- implication by custom or usage (see 27.198–27.199).

The topics addressed in Chapter 31 (at 35.57–35.73) may also be relevant.

Presumptions relating to retainers

The presumption in favour of payment

The first of these modes of implication is often of pivotal relevance in the context of there being no express contract of retainer covering the fees in question. Where it is a necessary inference from the words or conduct used that a contract has come into being, then an implied contract, including a contract for services such as a retainer, will exist.[262] Stirling J had this to say on the point: **27.191**

255 *Wilson v The Spectre Partnership* [2007] EWHC 133 (Ch), at [13].
256 *Rees v Williams* (1875) LR 10 Ex 200.
257 CPR, r 67.3(2).
258 See PD 67, paras 2.1 and 1(2)–(5).
259 See PD 67, paras 2.1 and 1(6).
260 CPR, r 67.3(2); PD 67, para 1(5).
261 PD 67, para 2.1(1).
262 See, eg, *Harrods Ltd v Harrods (Buenos Aires) Ltd* (1998) The Times, 1 June, CA; *Re Chappell, ex p Ford* (1885) 16 QBD 305, CA.

'It is quite plain that no formal or express retainer was ever given ... but that was not necessary, for although no such express retainer has been given, the relation may subsist, and its existence may be inferred from the acts of the parties. If any authority for that proposition be required, it will be sufficient to refer to the decision of the Court of Appeal in the case of *Bean v Wade* 2 Times LR 157.'[263]

27.192 Whilst it was a case in which the issue related to duty of care rather than liability for fees, the leading case on when a retainer will come into existence by implication is *Dean v Allin & Watts*,[264] in which Lightman J (with whom Robert Walker and Sedley LJJ agreed) had this to say:

'As a matter of law, it is necessary to establish that [the solicitors] by implication agreed to act for [the client]: an implied retainer could only arise where on an objective consideration of all the circumstances an intention to enter into such a contractual relationship ought fairly and properly to be imputed to the parties. In *Searles v Cann and Hallett* [1993] PNLR 494 the question arose whether the solicitors for the borrowers impliedly agreed to act as solicitors for the lenders. Mr Philip Mott QC (sitting as a deputy judge of the Queen's Bench Division) held that there was nothing in the evidence which clearly pointed to that conclusion. He went on:

"No such retainer should be implied for convenience, but only where an objective consideration of all the circumstances make it so clear an implication that [the solicitor himself] ought to have appreciated it." '[265]

A test of necessity will apply.[266] In so far as solicitors are concerned, Arnold J has stated the test is as follows: was there conduct by the parties that was consistent only with the firm being retained as solicitors for the client?[267]

27.193 Once it has been established that the client did engage the legal services provider in that capacity, then there will be a rebuttable presumption that a client will be liable for the provider's fees.[268] Whilst that presumption can be analysed in other ways, for practical purposes it is a presumption that that will be an implied term of the retainer unless the contrary can be shown.

27.194 Lloyd J explained the presumption in this way:

'Once it was shown ... that [the receiving party] was indeed the client, then a presumption arose that he was to be personally liable for the costs. That presumption could, however, be rebutted if it were established that there was an express or implied agreement, binding on the solicitor, that [the client] would not have to pay those costs in any circumstances.'[269]

---

263 *Morgan v Blyth* [1891] 1 Ch 337, at 355.

264 *Dean v Allin & Watts* [2001] EWCA Civ 758.

265 *Ibid*, at [33].

266 For a discussion of necessity in the context of implied terms generally, see *Marks and Spencer plc v BNP Paribas Securities Services Trust Company (Jersey) Ltd & Anor* [2015] UKSC 72, at [15]–[22], *per* Neuberger PSC. For a recent example of this test being applied in the context of a contract of retainer, see *Harding Evans LLP v Spencer-White* [2017] EWCA Civ 434, at [31], *per* Sharp LJ. For older examples, see *Harrods Ltd v Harrods (Buenos Aires) Ltd* (1998) The Times, 1 June, CA; *Re Chappell, ex p Ford* (1885) 16 QBD 305, CA.

267 See *Caliendo v Mischon De Reya* [2016] EWHC 150 (Ch), at [682].

268 See *Adams v London Improved Motor Builders Ltd* [1921] 1 KB 495, at 501. See also *R v Miller (Raymond)* [1983] 1 WLR 1056, at 1059–62, which was cited with approval in *Bailey v IBC Vehicles Ltd* [1998] 3 All ER 570, at 574; *Hazlett v Sefton Metropolitan Borough Council* [2000] 4 All ER 887.

269 *R v Miller (Raymond)* [1983] 1 WLR 1056, at 1061. See also *Ghadami v Lyon Cole Insurance Group Ltd* [2010] EWCA Civ 767, at [10], in which Lloyd LJ reaffirmed this principle. The need to show 'an agreement ... not to have to pay those costs in any circumstances' is not, however, a test of universal applicability;

That presumption may be rebutted either upon evidence or by operation of the law (or both).

The presumption that a reasonable amount will be paid

The second mode of implication—namely, by law—may also have a role to play in the context of the law of costs. In particular, it is an implied term of a consumer contract for services that the person providing services will be paid reasonable remuneration for those services. As of 1 October 2015, statute has provided as follows: **27.195**

> '51 **Reasonable price to be paid for a service**
> (1) This section applies to a contract to supply a service if—
> (a) the consumer has not paid a price or other consideration for the service,
> (b) the contract does not expressly fix a price or other consideration, and does not say how it is to be fixed, and
> (c) anything that is to be treated under section 50 [of the Consumer Rights Act 2015] as included in the contract does not fix a price or other consideration either.
>
> (2) In that case the contract is to be treated as including a term that the consumer must pay a reasonable price for the service, and no more.
> (3) What is a reasonable price is a question of fact.'[270]

The reference to s 50 of the Consumer Rights Act 2015 is a reference to certain terms that may be included in a contract by reason of things said or written by the lawyer (28.29–28.39).

Where the client is not a consumer (or if the client was a consumer, but the contract was made prior to 1 October 2015), then s 15(1) of the Supply of Goods and Services Act 1982 may imply a similar term (see 28.156). **27.196**

The statutory provisions imply only terms rather than entire contracts. It would, however, rarely be the case that the very existence of a retainer was in dispute, especially in the context of the presumption mentioned at 27.194. **27.197**

Custom or usage

The third mode of implication—namely, by custom or usage—will most often be encountered in cases involving commercial clients, but it may also arise in other circumstances, such as where a private client habitually instructs their family's solicitor. Another example may be where an insolvency practitioner instructs a firm on a 'recoveries only' basis of remuneration.[271] In certain circumstances, evidence of custom and usage is admissible for the purposes of implying a term into a contract.[272] **27.198**

---

it applies only in those cases in which the facts imply the existence of a retainer. See the discussion about *Byrne v Kunkel & Kunkel* [1999] 1 CL 349 elsewhere in this work.

[270] See the Consumer Rights Act 2015, s 51. If the contract was made prior to 1 October 2015, then Supply of Goods and Services Act 1982, s 15, would have implied similar terms. The 1982 Act still applies in business-to-business transactions.

[271] See, eg, *Stevensdrake Ltd v Hunt* [2016] EWHC 342 (Ch), at [107], *per* Judge Simon Barker QC (sitting as a judge of the High Court).

[272] In a context other than costs, see *Cunliffe-Owen v Teather and Greenwood* [1967] 1 WLR 1421, which deals with the custom in the stock exchange.

27.199 A legal services provider's claim for costs could not usually be founded upon estoppel by convention;[273] something more would usually be required than merely asserting that the client is estopped from denying the existence of a retainer by reason of their long-standing relationship with the legal services providers. However, for the reasons set out above, it would rarely be necessary for the legal services provider to have to seek to rely on such a principle.

Disputes about whether an implied retainer exists

27.200 The analysis that follows focuses on the contractual relationship between legal services provider and client, but much of what is said would also apply to a dispute between opposing parties. An opposing party would, however, have the additional hurdle of proving a 'genuine issue' (see 18.35–18.39).

27.201 A dispute between legal services provider and client about the existence or terms of an enforceable retainer may turn on disputed facts. The topic of how the court deals with such disputed facts is discussed at 27.95: in essence, the client will be given the benefit of the fact that the legal services provider failed to keep a written record of the retainer. In general, however, this will go only to the terms of the retainer; the presumption referred to at 27.191 would generally make it difficult for a client to argue that there was no contract of retainer at all.

27.202 For the reasons set out in the extract from Lloyd J's judgment at 27.194, the client would have to clear a high hurdle to rebut the presumption that fees were payable in principle. This is because (subject to what is said below about the operation of the law) they must prove that there was an express or an implied term, binding on the legal services provider, that the client would not have to pay the legal services provider's fees in any circumstances. The advantages that the presumption affords the legal services provider are not, however, necessarily as great as they may at first appear, for the following reasons.

- The need to show 'an agreement ... not to have to pay those costs in any circumstances' is not a test of universal applicability; rather, it applies only in cases in which the facts imply the existence of an enforceable contractual retainer. This would not be the case if, for example, the solicitor were engaged under what was intended to be a conditional fee agreement (see 27.204).
- In view of the fact that solicitors (and many other legal services providers) are professionally obliged to confirm certain costs information in writing (see 27.97–27.99), the fact that there is no written retainer is something that may be afforded some weight. That said, there are instances of the court affording such a matter very little weight.[274] For example, Slade J has said that the absence of a client care letter does not affect the liability of the client if they had acquiesced in the instruction of the solicitors on their behalf by a third party.[275] Moreover, Lang J seems to have given weight to the fact that

[273] In a setting other than costs, see *Baird Textiles Holdings Ltd v Marks & Spencer plc* [2001] EWCA Civ 274; as to the requirement of necessity, see *The Aramis* [1989] 1 Lloyd's Rep 213.

[274] *Ghadami v Lyon Cole Insurance Group Ltd* [2010] EWCA Civ 767, both at [27], *per* Lloyd, and also in general (the client had not received the client care documentation to which he was entitled, but the court found that that did not preclude liability and that the lack of a stated hourly rate did not prevent the court from allowing a reasonable rate).

[275] *Culkin v Wirral Independent Appeals Panel* [2011] EWHC 1526 (QB), at [18].

the Guidance to the Code of Conduct 2007 explains that 'it is not envisaged or intended that a breach ... should invariably render a retainer unenforceable'.[276] These cases seem to illustrate the fact that each case will turn on its own facts.

- In older cases, it may also be relevant that, prior to 1 April 2013, the CPR and the Costs Practice Direction (CPD) required a legal services provider to give certain information about the level of costs.[277]

The first of these points is illustrated by a decision of Judge Cowell[278]—or, more accurately, by the way in which that case was commented upon by Burton J in a similar case,[279] as is explained below. In Judge Cowell's case, the action was pursued to trial, with all parties acting on the erroneous assumption that the receiving party was legally aided. In fact, there was no legal aid certificate and, as a result, the paying party argued that there was no retainer. Judge Cowell came to the following conclusion: **27.203**

> '[A] party is presumed to be liable for his costs until proved otherwise and [none of the parties] had discharged the burden upon them to prove the existence of an express or implied agreement between [the receiving party] and his former solicitors that he would never have to pay their costs in any circumstances ... In the absence of such an agreement, the mere lack of legal aid did not mean there was a breach of the indemnity principle ...'[280]

Burton J, *obiter*, strongly disagreed with that analysis, essentially on the basis that the facts did not support the notion that the counterparties had intended to enter into a private retainer: **27.204**

> 'I cannot accept the judge's conclusion ... There surely cannot be a question, in a legal aid, or presumed legal aid, situation, that there has to be proved the existence of an express or implied agreement that the legally aided plaintiff would never have himself to pay his solicitor's costs (save any shortfall as referred to above): the burden must surely be exactly the reverse, namely, that there would have to be established an express or implied agreement, or at any rate a quasi-contractual obligation upon such a client, that he would be personally liable to pay his solicitor in some unforeseen situation ...'[281]

Thus the approach of the court is take into account all of the facts, including the nature of the retainer that was intended (if any), but not created. If that retainer was something other than a private retainer, then it may not be open to the court to find that an implied private retainer takes its place. This is perhaps akin to the principle that terms which were expressly agreed may not be contradicted by implied terms.[282] **27.205**

An unwelcome feature of implied retainers is that they rarely contain any specific terms as to the legal services provider's remuneration. Even if it can be shown that a contractual liability to pay exists, it will not usually be possible to say that the counterparties had decided upon a specific hourly rate (although this may be possible if the client, without **27.206**

---

276 *Fladgate LLP v Harrison* [2012] EWHC 67 (AB), at [39].

277 See CPD, art 6.4(2).

278 *Byrne v Kunkel & Kunkel* [1999] 1 CL 349.

279 *Bridgewater v Griffiths* [2000] 1 WLR 524.

280 *Byrne v Kunkel & Kunkel* [1999] 1 CL 349, as recited in *Bridgewater v Griffiths* [2000] 1 WLR 524, at 533.

281 *Bridgewater v Griffiths* [2000] 1 WLR 524, at 533.

282 *Expressum facit cessare tacitum*, meaning 'what is expressed makes what is implied silent'. In a context other than costs, see *Lynch v Thorne* [1956] 1 WLR 303, CA.

demur, discharged invoices that stated the rate). Where it is not possible to find that a specific rate was agreed, it is open to the court to find an implied term that the rate would be reasonable.[283] Applying an implied term as to the hourly rate will not always be a straightforward task; there may, for example, be a dispute about whether there is provision that the rates may be uplifted to take account of the complexity of the work.[284] On the whole, the court will be reluctant to allow a legal services provider something such as an uplift that has not been expressly agreed.[285] This topic is also addressed at 31.70.

Oral Retainers

27.207 It is trite costs law that retainers do not need to be in writing[286] and that the word 'retainer' can legitimately be used to refer to an unwritten agreement to supply legal services.[287] Whilst oral retainers are, by definition, express contracts, specific terms will often need to be implied and, to that extent, the discussion above on implied retainers will be relevant, as will the matters discussed in Chapter 31 (see 31.57–31.73).

Issues of fact relating to oral retainers

27.208 Where the client disputes the terms of an oral retainer, the court will usually give weight to the fact that there is no written retainer (see 27.92). In general terms, where the legal services provider has failed to keep a written record of the retainer, there will be an evidential presumption in the client's favour. Older cases that suggest that this presumption was a rule of law, rather than an evidential presumption,[288] are probably no longer good law.

Issues of law relating to oral retainers

27.209 There are three types of oral retainer that merit particular attention:

- agreements that were intended to be business agreements (see 27.210–27.213);
- oral conditional fee agreements (see 27.214–27.215); and
- oral agreements made away from the legal services provider's place of business (see 27.216).

Oral 'business agreements'

27.210 The solicitor and client may have entered into an oral agreement that certain aspects of the remuneration are to be fixed or to be determined in a particular way (such as an agreement to apply a discount or an agreement that there will be a fixed fee). Such an agreement will be analogous to a contentious business agreement or non-contentious business agreement,

283 See *Ghadami v Lyon Cole Insurance Group Ltd* [2010] EWCA Civ 767, at [27].

284 See, eg, *Adams v MacInnes* [2001] EWHC 9014 (Costs).

285 Whilst dealing with implied terms rather than implied retainers, see *Bilkus v Stockler Brunton (a firm)* [2010] EWCA Civ 101, at [54], *per* Stanley Burnton LJ.

286 See, eg, *Owen v Ord* (1828) 3 C & P 349; *Wiggins v Peppin* (1839) 2 Beav 403; *Bird v Harris* [1881] WN 5, CA.

287 Historically, see *Bouvier's Law Dictionary* (6th edn, 1856), vol 2, p 472/1: 'Although it is not indispensable that the retainer should be in writing ... it is very expedient.' See also *Oxford English Dictionary* (3rd edn, Oxford: Oxford University Press, 2010), which cites Abbott US Digest (Ser i) II. 340/1 (1874): 'A mere parol retainer is sufficient to authorise an attorney to commence a suit.'

288 See *Allen v Bone* (1841) 4 Beav 493, *per* Lord Langdale MR; *Crossley v Crowther* (1851) 9 Hare 384; *Atkinson v Abbot* (1855) 3 Drew 251.

as the case may be. Whether such an agreement would be regarded as being a 'failed' business agreement or as being merely akin to a business agreement is a moot point,[289] but, regardless of this, even where such an agreement is found to be unenforceable, it will be only the agreement as to the amount (or method of determining the amount) that will be of no effect; the underlying retainer will remain extant and enforceable.

The precise effect of such agreements will depend on whether the work to which an agreement relates is contentious or non-contentious. There are some inconsistencies and ambiguities in the authorities, but the following is fair description of law (although the points made at 27.213 should be noted). **27.211**

- **Contentious business** Where the agreement relates to contentious business, it cannot be relied upon against the client (in the sense that it causes an adverse result from the client's point of view),[290] but, in appropriate circumstances, it can be relied upon against the solicitor.[291] Put otherwise, where the agreement is favourable to the client, it may be enforced, but where it is not favourable to the client, then it will not be enforced. The reason for this is that the legislation governing contentious business agreements is regarded as being enabling legislation that does not supplant the common law (see 27.240 and 27.261) and, as such, if the agreement 'fails', then it will be judged according to the common law—specifically, according to that body of law which developed before legislation was made (in 1870) making provision for business agreements.[292] It is said that this applies to agreements for costs already incurred,[293] but it is possible that that principle is no longer good law and, certainly, other common-law jurisdictions have moved away from that position.[294] The points made at 27.52 may also be relevant in that regard.
- **Non-contentious business** Where the agreement relates to non-contentious business, it would usually be held to be unenforceable as against *both* parties, even where it would otherwise be to the client's advantage.[295] This is because, in contrast to the legislation governing contentious business agreements, the legislation governing non-contentious business agreements[296] is generally regarded as being *dis*abling in the sense that agreements that do not comply cannot be enforced.[297]

---

[289] It is probably the former: see *Barclays plc v Villers* [2000] 1 All ER (Comm) 357, at 367.

[290] *Chamberlain v Boodle & King* (1980) 124 SJ 186, subsequently upheld on appeal ([1982] 1 WLR 1443); *Martin Boston & Co (a firm) v Levy* [1982] 1 WLR 1434 (arguable defence to a claim by solicitors for fees for contentious work under oral agreement).

[291] See, eg, *Gundry v Sainsbury* [1910] 1 KB 99 (verbal agreement that client would pay no costs). As an early example, see *Jennings v Johnson* (1873) LR 8 CP 425 (agreement similar to a modern-day CFA Lite). See also *Re a Solicitor (No 2)* [1956] 1 QB 155, which, *obiter*, affirmed *Clare* and *Jennings* as being good law; *Electrical Trades Union v Tarlo* [1964] Ch 720 (oral retainer related to both contentious and non-contentious work; contentious part found to be enforceable); *In re a Solicitor* [1956] 1 QB 157 (which, whilst *obiter*, affirmed the view that oral agreements in relation to contentious work were enforceable as against the solicitor).

[292] That being the Attorneys and Solicitors Act 1870.

[293] *Re Russell, Son & Scott* (1885) 30 Ch D 114.

[294] See, eg, *Bear v Waxman* [1912] VLR 292; Anderson and Rowland JJ in *D'Alessandro & D'Angelo v Cooper* (unreported), 21 June 1996, WASC, Full Ct, *per* Kennedy, Rowland and Anderson JJ. Both cases found no bar to cost agreements in Western Australia covering past services.

[295] In *In re a Solicitor* [1956] 1 QB 157, for example, Pearson J found that a client could not rely on an oral agreement that his solicitor would charge less than the ordinary rate of remuneration.

[296] This originally being the Solicitors' Remuneration Act 1881, s 8(1).

[297] *In re a Solicitor* [1956] 1 QB 157.

27.212 The distinction between these two types of agreement was illustrated by a case in which the agreement related in part to contentious business and in part to non-contentious business, in which Wilberforce J found that the part of the agreement that related to contentious work was enforceable by the client, but that the remainder was unenforceable.[298]

27.213 It is not wholly clear whether the distinction between these two types of agreement is still good law; this is because it appears to have been founded on—or at least justified by—statutory provisions that are no longer in force. In particular, Pearson J[299] explained the difference on the basis that the then provisions relating to contentious business[300] were more liberal than those relating to non-contentious business.[301] The presently available authorities relating to oral agreements should therefore be viewed with some caution because it is arguable that the proper interpretation of the modern provisions—namely, s 57 of the Solicitors Act 1974—is not the same as that set out above. Moreover, where the client is consumer, the matters referred to at 28.30–28.36 (regarding the effect of s 50 of the Consumer Rights Act 2015) may have a bearing.

Oral conditional fee agreements

27.214 Any oral conditional fee agreement would be unenforceable by reason of it not being in writing.[302] This will apparently be so even if it is in respect of non-contentious business. Indeed, whilst its function was merely to describe the law rather than to create it, the Guidance to the (now-revoked) Solicitors' Code of Conduct 2007 offered the following narrative: 'It is acceptable to enter into a contingency fee arrangement for non-contentious matters ... but you should note that to be enforceable the arrangement must be contained in a non-contentious business agreement.'[303]

27.215 This state of affairs has come about as a result of a combination of the common law and the express statutory prohibition created by s 58(1) of the Courts and Legal Services Act 1990 (as amended). That provision renders unenforceable any conditional fee agreement that does not comply with the requirements of that section, one of which is that the agreement must be in writing. There is an exception to this prohibition in that s 58(5) of the 1990 Act reads: 'If a conditional fee agreement is an agreement to which section 57 of the Solicitors Act 1974 (non-contentious business agreements between solicitor and client) applies, subsection (1) shall not make it unenforceable.' In view of the fact that one of the requirements of Solicitors Act 1974, s 57, is that the agreement should be in writing, the exception does not operate in such a way as to permit such a thing as an enforceable oral conditional fee agreement.

Oral agreements made away from the legal services provider's place of business

27.216 An oral retainer made at a place other than the solicitor's place of business may be unenforceable if there has been a failure to give a written notice of right to cancel in accordance with the relevant consumer protection legislation. That topic is discussed in Chapter 28 (see 28.97–28.99 and 28.195–28.200).

---

298 *Electrical Trades Union v Tarlo* [1964] Ch 731.
299 *In re a Solicitor* [1956] 1 QB 157.
300 Then Attorneys and Solicitors Act 1870, s 4; now Solicitors Act 1974, s 59.
301 Then Solicitors Act 1932, s 57; now Solicitors Act 1974, s 57.
302 See Courts and Legal Services Act 1990 (as amended), s 58(1) and (3)(a).
303 Paragraph 45 of the Guidance to r 2.04 of the Solicitors' Code of Conduct 2007.

Sham Retainers

A sham retainer will exist where the parties have created a written instrument that is intended to give either the court or the paying party the appearance of having created legal rights and obligations different from the real legal rights and obligations that they actually intended to create.[304] **27.217**

In the past, sham retainers were usually used in the context of the client being unable or unwilling to pay their legal services provider's fees in the event of the claim being lost. A legal services provider would often agree to charge only if the case was successful, but would not make that agreement openly because such agreements were unlawful: the term 'speccing agreement' was applied to such agreements.[305] Given the fact that conditional fee agreements are now lawful, speccing agreements are largely of historical interest only. **27.218**

Sham agreements are not wholly extinct, however. Sham agreements may arise in relatively innocent circumstances. If, for example, it forms the basis of the retainer, an assurance 'not to worry' about fees may suffice.[306] More commonly, however, sham agreements will arise out of a more conscious attempt to deceive. Current-day examples may include where the written instrument records an hourly rate that the client is not prepared to pay and will not pay, and has secretly agreed that they will not pay this rate with their legal services provider. **27.219**

Whether an agreement is a sham will depend on the facts. Arden LJ gave the following guidance (here paraphrased and adapted to apply to the law of costs).[307] **27.220**

- In the case of a written retainer, the court is not restricted to examining the four corners of the written instrument; rather, it may examine external evidence, which may include the counterparties' explanations and the way in which the retainer was used.
- The test of intention is a subjective test: the counterparties must have intended to create different rights and obligations from those set out in the written instrument, and they must also have intended to give a false impression of those rights and obligations to third parties.
- The fact that the terms of the retainer are uncommercial or artificial does not mean that the retainer is a sham.
- The fact that parties subsequently depart from the terms of the retainer does not necessarily mean that they never intended the retainer to be effective and binding.
- The intention must be a common intention shared by both legal services provider and client.

A distinction should be made between an intention that forms the basis of the retainer and an intention that is merely the exercise of discretion within the parameters of the **27.221**

---

[304] This definition is adapted from *Snook v London & West Riding Investments Ltd* [1967] 2 QB 786, at 802.

[305] That term also applied to some types of informal conditional fee agreement that are not sham agreements.

[306] *British Waterways Board v Norman* (1993) 26 HLR 232: whilst the Court of Appeal did not use the term 'sham agreement', that was clearly its conclusion.

[307] *Stone v Hitch* [2001] EWCA Civ 63.

retainer. Tuckey J had the following to say (*obiter*), in the context of a putative speccing agreement:

> 'If . . . it is made clear that the client is liable for costs irrespective of the outcome of proceedings, there can be no objection to the solicitors agreeing that such liability need not be discharged until the end of those proceedings, if any, is known. At that stage, provided that it has not formed the basis of the agreement with the client, it would be open to the solicitors, if the circumstances warranted it, to decide not to enforce their right to be paid, in the event that some or all of their costs were unrecovered from the other party to the proceedings.'[308]

27.222 Both Kennedy LJ and Jowitt J have approved of those comments, but in doing so they remarked that if a legal services provider always (or nearly always) waived its fees in the event of the claim being lost, the court could draw the inference that that formed the basis of the agreement.[309]

The relevance of the fact that client cannot afford to pay to whether a retainer is a sham

27.223 The mere fact that the legal services provider knows that the client will not be able to afford to pay does not prove that the retainer is a sham. Latham LJ (giving the judgment of the court) had this to say on the topic:

> 'Whilst the client's impecuniosity may be relevant to determining what the true nature of the agreement was, the mere fact that the solicitor may have been conducting the action on credit or continuing an action in the knowledge of his client's lack of means does not justify a conclusion that he was unlawfully maintaining the action.'[310]

27.224 Mustill LJ has commented that there is nothing improper in a solicitor acting in a case for a meritorious client who, to their knowledge, cannot afford to pay if the case is lost.[311] In a similar vein, Sir Christopher Bellamy found that the fact that a client was paying a monthly contribution that was far lower than the value of services being provided did not give rise to the inference that the retainer was a sham.[312]

Evidential matters concerning sham retainers

27.225 For obvious reasons, the issue of whether a retainer was a sham will generally arise at the behest of a paying party. The court will not usually allow such a party to test the retainer by cross-examination unless there is substance to the allegations; this will not only be on the basis of the presumption afforded by the certificate to the bill of costs, but also on the wider basis of proportionality. Indeed, it was in the context of a paying party wishing to prove the existence of a sham retainer that Latham LJ made the following famous comment: 'Satellite litigation about costs has become a growth industry, and one that is a blot on the civil justice system. Costs Judges should be astute to prevent such proceedings from being protracted by allegations that are without substance.'[313]

---

308 *British Waterways Board v Norman* (1993) 26 HLR 232, at 243.
309 *Wells v Barnsley Metropolitan Borough Council* (1999) The Times, 12 November, QBD.
310 *Burstein v Times Newspapers Ltd* [2002] EWCA Civ 1739, at [21].
311 *Singh v Observer Ltd* [1989] 3 All ER 777. See also *A Ltd v B Ltd* [1996] 1 WLR 665; *Thai Trading Co (a firm) v Taylor* [1998] 3 All ER 65, at 72.
312 Whilst not binding, see *Albion Water v Water Services Regulation Authority* [2007] CAT 1.
313 *Burstein v Times Newspapers Ltd* [2002] EWCA Civ 1739, at [29].

Where fraud or impropriety are alleged, the accused party may be able to rely on the rebuttable presumption that their acts have been in accordance with the law and what is ethically right.[314] Cogent evidence is required to prove fraud. Whilst some have said that, where fraud is alleged, the standard of proof approaches the criminal standard,[315] the better analysis is that the standard remains the same, but the more serious the allegation, the more unlikely it is and the more cogent the evidence needs to be to be capable of proving it.[316] In this regard, Lord Carswell has explained that the standard or proof (albeit in the context of a criminal matter) is 'finite and unvarying': **27.226**

> '[I]n some contexts a court or tribunal has to look at the facts more critically or more anxiously than in others before it can be satisfied to the requisite standard. The standard itself is, however, finite and unvarying. Situations which make such heightened examination necessary may be the inherent unlikelihood of the occurrence taking place, ... the seriousness of the allegation to be proved or, in some cases, the consequences which could follow from acceptance of proof of the relevant fact. The seriousness of the allegation requires no elaboration: a tribunal of fact will look closely into the facts grounding an allegation of fraud before accepting that it has been established. The seriousness of consequences is another facet of the same proposition: if it is alleged that a bank manager has committed a minor peculation, that could entail very serious consequences for his career, so making it the less likely that he would risk doing such a thing. These are all matters of ordinary experience, requiring the application of good sense on the part of those who have to decide such issues. They do not require a different standard of proof or a specially cogent standard of evidence, merely appropriately careful consideration by the tribunal before it is satisfied of the matter which has to be established.'[317]

In summary, whilst sham agreements may still be encountered from time to time, they are much less common than they were before conditional fee agreements became lawful. The issue of whether a retainer is a sham is determined in exactly the same way as the issue of whether any other contract is a sham. Each case will turn on its own facts. **27.227**

Unlawful Retainers and Statutory Prohibition

The topic of unlawful retainers is dominated by the concepts of express and implied statutory prohibition. It is worth pausing to note that there is a distinction between statutory prohibition (which will be determined by a process of statutory interpretation) and common-law prohibition (which is less well defined and which will turn on issues of public policy). There is an overlap between these two things—in particular, the mechanism by which statute may prohibit a retainer may be mediated by public policy (of which examples follow). The distinction between statutory interpretation and public policy may not always be clear, especially in the context of costs law, which is heavily regulated by legislation. Some commentators have said that the distinction 'no longer serves any useful purpose, and ought to be abandoned'.[318] This may or may not be so, but it is certainly the **27.228**

[314] See, in a non-costs context, *Constantine Steamship Line Ltd v Imperial Smelting Corpn Ltd* [1942] AC 154; *Low v Guthrie* [1909] AC 278, HL.

[315] See the discussion in *Hornal v Neuberger Products Ltd* [1957] 1 QB 247; see also *Miles v Cain* (1989) The Times, 15 December, CA.

[316] *Dellow's Will Trusts, Lloyds Bank Ltd v Institute of Cancer Research* [1964] 1 All ER 771.

[317] *R (on the application of D) v Life Sentence Review Commissioners* [2008] UKHL 33, at [28].

[318] See Greig, DW, and Davis, LJR, *The Law of Contract* (Sydney: Law Book Co, 1987), p 1116.

case that, in appropriate circumstances, Parliament's intention—as expressed in legislation—may be regarded as reflecting public policy and as being a measure of it.[319] This will be of obvious relevance when interpreting a provision in statute, but it may also be relevant when considering other supposed prohibitions; the fact that something is not prohibited by statute may be relevant in those circumstances.

Statutory prohibition in the context of costs

27.229 This area of the law has developed not in the context of costs, but in that of claims being brought against defendants who have sought to defend the claim on the basis that the contract is illegal. There are many conflicting decisions. In general, there are two mechanisms by which a contract of retainer may be prohibited by statute: by express statutory prohibition and by implied statutory prohibition.

Express statutory prohibition

27.230 Express statutory prohibition will exist where a statute expressly states that a contract is unlawful or unenforceable.[320] An example is a conditional fee agreement: if such an agreement does not comply with the requirements of s 58 of the Courts and Legal Services Act 1990 (as amended), it will be unenforceable as a direct result of the operation of statute. This is discussed in more detail in Chapter 29 (see 29.14 *et seq*).

Implied statutory prohibition

27.231 Implied statutory prohibition differs from express statutory prohibition in that the effect of the statute will not be set out in express terms, which means that the court must ascertain its meaning by a process of statutory interpretation. When considering whether a retainer is unenforceable by reason of implied statutory prohibition, the procedure is identical to that used in any other branch of the law. Devlin J clarified that procedure, as that:

- it must be determined whether the statutory intention was to prohibit contracts at all; and
- it must be determined whether the contract under consideration belongs to the class of contract that the statute intended to prohibit.[321]

27.232 There are three ways in which a contract may be unlawful in the absence of express statutory prohibition:

(1) the contract may be an agreement to inflict a legal wrong (see 27.235–27.237);
(2) the agreement itself may be objectionable on the basis that it is unlawful or on the basis that the counterparties have inflicted a legal wrong while in the process of forming it (see 27.238–27.245); or
(3) the counterparties may inflict a legal wrong while in the process of performing the agreement (see 27.246–27.251).

---

[319] See, eg, Steyn LJ's comments in *Giles v Thompson* [1993] 3 All ER 321, at 331, where, in the context of champerty, he said: 'There is, of course, no more cogent evidence of a change of public policy than the expression of the will of Parliament.' See also *Awwad v Geraghty* [2001] QB 570, at 600; *Bevan Ashford v Geoff Yeandle (Contractors) Ltd (in liquidation)* [1999] Ch 239.

[320] Where a statute expressly provides that a retainer is unenforceable, there is no need to inquire as to the meaning of that provision, because its meaning and effect will be evident from the express language used: see Williams, GL, 'The Legal Effect of Illegal Contracts' (1942–44) 8 CLJ 51, at 58–69, for a discussion of this topic in general.

[321] *St John Shipping Corpn v Joseph Rank Ltd* [1957] 1 QB 267.

The term 'legal wrong' is used in the sense that it includes both acts and omissions. In the context of costs, examples of these things would include: 27.233

- in category (1), an agreement with a claims referral company to provide unregulated and unlawful insurance;
- in category (2), failure to abide by the provisions in the code of conduct that prohibit certain forms of contingency fee agreement; and
- in category (3), accepting an unlawful commission paid by an after the event (ATE) insurer.

The effect of a retainer being in the first category will generally be greater than the effect of a retainer being in the third category.

In discussing each of these categories, the focus is on statutes (and delegated legislation), but it is worth noting that the principles may also, with the appropriate modifications, apply to non-statutory forms of prohibition, such as a failure to comply with non-statutory professional guidance. 27.234

The first category of implied statutory prohibition: contracts to commit a legal wrong 27.235
Contracts in this category are agreements to do something that is, by the operation of statute, illegal. Such an agreement will—unsurprisingly—not generally be enforced by the courts;[322] this is because the court will not be used as a vehicle to carry out illegal acts or otherwise to inflict legal wrongs.[323] Lord Bingham CJ explained the principle thus: 'If the court were to allow its process to be used to enforce agreements of this kind, the risk would inevitably arise that such agreements would abound ... to the detriment of the public.'[324]

It would rarely be the case that a retainer would also be a contract to commit a legal wrong. This is because the supply of legal services is not an inherently unlawful activity. However, a contract that relates to legal funding, but which is not a retainer, may be an agreement to commit a legal wrong, for example an illegal agreement to share fees.[325] Where the facts are such that the objectionable contract is so entwined with the retainer that the two should stand or fall together, it may be said that the objectionable contract (or the objectionable part of the contract) is 'tainted with illegality'. 27.236

A contract to commit a legal wrong would usually be unenforceable (in the sense that no fees at all may be enforced). As is implied above, it is important to identify the correct contract when considering the issue of enforceability. If, for example, a legal services provider has agreed with a claims management agency to provide unlawful insurance, the starting point would be that the agreement with the claims management company would be unenforceable rather than the contracts of insurance themselves.[326] There may be statutory provisions that make the situation clearer: in the example just given, statute would expressly 27.237

[322] This does not mean that the entirety of the contractual obligations will become unenforceable nor does it mean that the court would have no discretion; in the example given (unlawful insurance), the court has the power to exercise its discretion to allow the agreement to be enforced.

[323] The principle may be summed up in the Latin phrase *ex dolo malo non oritur action*, meaning 'no court will lend its aid to a man who founds his cause of action upon an immoral or illegal action'.

[324] *Mohammed v Alaga & Co* [2000] 1 WLR 1815, at 1824. Strictly speaking, Bingham CJ was dealing with a case that was in the second category rather than the first.

[325] *Ibid.*

[326] For an example that dealt with similar issues, see *Dix v Townend & Anor* [2008] EWHC 90117 (Costs).

provide the court with discretion to order that the obligations arising under the contract of insurance would be enforceable.[327]

27.238 **The second category of implied statutory prohibition: prohibited contracts and formation** A contract in the second category would be an agreement that is prohibited by statute or which has been constructed in a way that is prohibited by statute (or both). Such a contract may or may not be unenforceable.

27.239 *The mechanism by which prohibited contracts may be unenforceable* The mechanism by which statute may cause a contract in the second category to be unenforceable was explained by Megarry J:

> 'Where a contract is made in contravention of some statutory provision then, in addition to any criminal sanctions, the Courts may in some cases find that the contract itself is stricken with illegality ... If the statute ... provides that one of the parties must satisfy certain requirements ... before making any contract of the type in question, then the statutory prohibitional requirement may well be sufficiently linked to the contract for questions to arise of the illegality of any contract made in breach of the statutory requirement.'[328]

27.240 The fact that such a mechanism exists does not mean that the court will be quick to find that a contract will be 'stricken with illegality', as Megarry J put it. Devlin J had this to say on the topic:

> 'If a contract has as its whole object the doing of the very act which the statute prohibits, it can be argued that you can hardly make sense of a statute which forbids an act and yet permits to be made a contract to do it; that is a clear implication. But unless you get a clear implication of that sort, I think that a court ought to be very slow to hold that a statute intends to interfere with the rights and remedies given by the ordinary law of contract. Caution in this respect is, I think, especially necessary in these times when so much of commercial life is governed by regulations of some sort or another; which may easily be broken without wicked intent.'[329]

27.241 The court is therefore sympathetic to the plight of persons who are heavily regulated. In a similar vein, Sachs LJ referred to persons 'flounder[ing] in a mass of statutes, orders and regulations governing their daily affairs'.[330] Some would say that those words have even more resonance in the context of costs than they had in the context in which they were originally spoken. The relevance of this sympathetic attitude is that it does not follow that merely because a retainer has been created in a way that breaches some statutory provision, it will be unenforceable.

27.242 Contracts that are prohibited by legislation commonly arise in the context of costs; they may be found to be unenforceable, but this will not always be the case. The mechanism by which a contract or retainer may be found to be unenforceable is not dissimilar to the mechanism by which contracts in the first of the three categories in 27.232 are found to be unenforceable. May LJ, for example, explained that there was no distinction of substance or quality between an unlawful retainer and an unlawful agreement to share professional fees.[331]

---

[327] See Financial Services and Markets Act 2000, s 28.
[328] *Curragh Investments Ltd v Cook* [1974] 1 WLR 1559, at 1563.
[329] *St John Shipping Corpn v Joseph Rank Ltd* [1957] 1 QB 267, at 288.
[330] *Shaw v Groom* [1970] 2 QB 504, at 522.
[331] *Awwad v Geraghty* [2001] QB 570, at 598–599.

Public policy and prohibited contracts As to the interplay between public policy and statutory prohibition, Phillips MR had this to say: **27.243**

> 'Where the law expressly restricts the circumstances in which agreements in support of litigation are lawful, this provides a powerful indication of the limits of public policy in analogous situations. Where this is not the case, then we believe one must today look at the facts of the particular case and consider whether those facts suggest that the agreement in question [is contrary to public policy].'[332]

As was explained by Schiemann LJ,[333] the court defers to Parliament on issues as significant as what is and is not permissible in terms of conditional funding. The practical effect of this is that whilst the court recognises that there is a distinction between Parliament's role in making legislation and the court's role in adjudicating upon issues of public policy, the court may conclude that the latter is reflected in the former. In the context of a putative breach of the Solicitors Practice Rules 1990, Lord Bingham CJ had this to say: **27.244**

> 'Section 31 [of the Solicitors Act 1974] confers power on the Law Society to make, with the concurrence of the Master of the Rolls, subordinate legislation governing the professional practice and conduct of solicitors ... When making such subordinate legislation, the Law Society is acting in the public interest and not (should there be any conflict) in the narrower interests of the solicitors' profession (see *Swain v Law Society*).'[334]

Lord Bingham CJ went on to say that where the concurrence of the Master of Rolls is required, this is for the purpose of guaranteeing that the interests of the public are fully safeguarded.

Sufficiency of penalties for prohibited contracts Where, instead of an express provision that a contract is unenforceable, statute imposes a penalty for a prohibited act or omission, one issue that will arise is whether that penalty will, of itself, be sufficient to defeat the mischief that the provision was intended to address. In the context of costs, this will often mean examining the power that the Solicitors Regulation Authority (SRA) has to punish solicitors and to award compensation to clients. These were factors that Arden LJ took into account when considering whether a failure to provide an estimate of costs should have the effect of making the retainer unenforceable and she concluded that the SRA's powers were sufficient for upholding the purpose of the statute.[335] Presumably, the converse could be argued in an appropriate case. **27.245**

The third category of implied statutory prohibition: performance An agreement in the third category would be a contract that was performed in a way that was contrary to statute; such an agreement would rarely be unenforceable. In all areas of the law, the court draws a distinction between the creation of a contract and its performance. This was explained by Browne-Wilkinson J in the following way: **27.246**

> 'The fact that a party has in the course of performing a contract committed an unlawful or immoral act will not by itself prevent him from further enforcing that contract unless the contract was entered into with the purpose of doing that unlawful or immoral act or the contract itself (as opposed to the mode of his performance) is prohibited by law.'[336]

---

332 *R v Secretary of State for Transport, ex p Factortame* [2002] EWCA Civ 932, at [36].
333 *Awwad v Geraghty* [2001] QB 570, at 593.
334 *Mohammed v Alaga & Co (a firm)* [2000] 1 WLR 1815, at 1823.
335 *Garbutt v Edwards* [2005] EWCA Civ 1206, at [39]–[41].
336 *Coral Leisure Group Ltd v Barnett* [1981] ICR 503, at 509.

27.247 It is often not an easy task to recognise that the retainer is within the third, rather than the second, category. This is because the unlawful performance of a retainer often takes place at about the same time as the retainer was made.[337] This can be an important issue because, as mentioned above, a retainer falling within the third category will usually not be unenforceable.

27.248 *Harmless collaterality* The phrase 'harmless collaterality'[338] has been used to describe the relationship between a legal wrong and an agreement that has been performed in an unlawful way. Although she did not refer to it by that name, Arden LJ had this to say:

> 'The fact that statute imposes a requirement to take some step … is not of itself sufficient to render the performance of a contract in disregard of that step unlawful and unenforceable … What the court has to do is to determine the effect of the requirement as a matter of the true construction of the statutory provision.'[339]

27.249 Arden LJ was addressing harmless collaterality in the context of a contract of retainer, but there are many instances of the court coming to very similar conclusions in other contexts.[340]

The position of the paying party who seeks to rely on statutory prohibition

27.250 Another factor that can have a bearing on the matter is whether the person who seeks to prove the alleged unenforceability of the retainer is the client or the paying party.

27.251 It is often said that the court is less willing to make a finding of unenforceability when the person who advances that argument is the paying party—a stranger to the contract who is seeking to catch a windfall—rather than the client. This is some truth in that,[341] but, in so far as the isolated issue of whether there is implied statutory prohibition is concerned, it does not seem to be borne out by the authorities. It may, however, be highly relevant to the exercise of the court's discretion (where such discretion exists) or to the issue of whether the court will allow argument on the point. This is a topic that is addressed in detail in Chapter 18.

27.252 **Morality and the issue of who seeks to benefit** Most of the authorities on implied statutory prohibition have arisen not in the context of costs, but in the more general context of defendants seeking to impugn their own agreements. This is relevant because such persons are, if anything, morally in a more objectionable position than a paying party who seeks to rely on a breach of the indemnity principle. In view of this, it is worth examining the way in which the court dealt with moral objections.

27.253 The answer is that the law is largely unperturbed by the duplicity of the arguments and prefers to grant a windfall rather than to give either of the counterparties the benefit of an unlawful contract. Lord Mansfield explained thus:

---

[337] An example would be where a solicitor fails to account to a client for a commission.

[338] *Imageview Management Ltd v Jack* [2009] EWCA Civ 63, at [30], *per* Jacob LJ.

[339] *Garbutt v Edwards* [2005] EWCA Civ 1206, at [35].

[340] The general approach is illustrated by a case in which auctioneers had sought to take a secret profit. The issue was whether that legal wrong disentitled them to their fee. The court found that it did not: *Hippisley v Knee Bros* [1905] 1 KB 1. See also *Kelly v Cooper* [1993] AC 205; *Boardman v Phipps* [1967] 2 AC 46; *The Peppy* [1997] 2 Lloyd's Rep 722.

[341] See, eg, the comments of Gilligan J in the Irish case of *Boyne v Dublin Bus* [2006] IEHC 209.

'The objection, that a contract is immoral or illegal as between plaintiff and defendant, sounds at all times very ill in the mouth of the defendant. It is not for his sake, however, that the objection is ever allowed; but it is founded in general principles of policy, which the defendant has the advantage of, contrary to the real justice, as between him and the plaintiff, by accident, if I may say so. The principle of public policy is this: *ex dolo malo non oritur actio*. No Court will lend its aid to a man who founds his cause of action upon an immoral or illegal act. If, from the plaintiff's own stating or otherwise, the cause of action appears to arise *ex turpi causa*, or the transgression of a positive law of this country, there the Court says he has no right to be assisted. It is upon that ground the Court goes; not for the sake of the defendant, but because they will not lend their aid to such a plaintiff. So if the plaintiff and defendant were to change sides, and the defendant was to bring his action against the plaintiff, the latter would then have the advantage of it; for where both are equally in fault, *potior est conditio defendentis*.'[342]

Thus, in contexts other than the law of costs, an illegal contract will be found to be unenforceable not because such a decision would bring justice to a wrongly pursued defendant, but because public policy requires that the contract itself should be struck down and that neither party should have the benefit of it. **27.254**

The same appears to be true in the context of costs. In the well-known case of *Garbutt v Edwards*,[343] Arden LJ did not make any distinction between the status of a client and the status of the paying party. In so far as implied statutory prohibition was concerned, the only distinction she drew between the two was as follows: **27.255**

'In making these rules [ie the Solicitors' Practice Rules 1990], the Council of the Law Society is acting in the public interest, and the rules have the force of subordinate legislation (see *Swain v Law Society* [1982] 2 All ER 827, [1983] AC 598). The inference I would draw is that the code is there to protect the legitimate interests of the client, and the administration of justice, rather than to relieve paying parties of their obligations to pay costs which have been reasonably incurred.'[344]

In so far as the implied statutory prohibition itself was concerned, Arden LJ took that distinction no further (although she did rely on that distinction in other contexts). The way in which she dealt with the issue suggests that the position of the paying party is to be taken into account only for the purposes of interpreting the statute (such as in identifying the mischief) and this reflects the approach in other areas of the law. **27.256**

Contractual provisions are the same, whoever takes the point Whilst he was dealing with a point other than implied statutory prohibition,[345] Hughes LJ confirmed that the source of the contention (that is, whether the challenge came from the client or the paying party) cannot alter the construction of the agreement; the contractual position as between the legal services provider and the client must be the same, whoever takes the point.[346] **27.257**

Practice and discretion Whilst, in theory, it makes no difference whether the person who seeks to rely on implied statutory prohibition is the client or the paying party, in practice **27.258**

---

342 *Holman v Johnson* (1775) 1 Cowp 341, at 343.

343 *Garbutt v Edwards* [2005] EWCA Civ 1206 (she did make this decision in relation to an alternative ground of appeal relating to the effect of an estimate of the issue of quantum, but that is a different matter).

344 *Ibid*, at [31].

345 Namely, the issue of whether a retainer could constructively be said to be a CFA Lite.

346 *Jones v Wrexham Borough Council* [2007] EWCA Civ 1356, at [83].

it can make a difference, not least because a paying party will not find it as easy to marshal the relevant evidence as would the client. Moreover, where the court has the power to exercise its discretion as to whether a retainer is or is not enforceable, the fact that the challenge was brought by the paying party rather than the client could well be a relevant factor (see, for example, 27.285—albeit in the context of express rather than implied statutory prohibition).

Specific instances of express and implied statutory prohibition

Conditional fee agreements

27.259 This topic is discussed in detail in Chapter 29. It is mentioned here only as an example of express statutory prohibition. That example is created by s 58(1) of the Courts and Legal Services Act 1990 (as amended):

> 'A conditional fee agreement which satisfies all of the conditions applicable to it by virtue of this section shall not be unenforceable by reason only of its being a conditional fee agreement; but ... any other conditional fee agreement shall be unenforceable.'

Thus this provision expressly states that non-compliance with the provision in that Act will lead to the disobedient retainer being unenforceable.

Contingency fee agreements and damages-based agreements

27.260 Again, this topic is discussed in detail in Chapter 29, but is mentioned here for the purposes of dealing with statutory prohibition. It has repeatedly been said that the Solicitors' Practice Rules 1990 had a force equivalent to that of a schedule to a statute.[347] The same is true of the Rules' successor—namely, the Solicitors' Code of Conduct 2007 (see 4.15). Those provisions have now been replaced by the SRA Code of Conduct 2011, but it is likely that the same general principle applies (at least to an extent). That said, what is set out below applies only to contracts of retainer made before 6 October 2011, because the relevant provisions have not been replicated in the SRA Code of Conduct 2011 (see 27.266).

27.261 **Contingency fee agreements made before 6 October 2011** The Solicitors' Code of Conduct 2007 defined the phrase 'contingency fee' in the following way: 'A "contingency fee" is defined in rule 24 (Interpretation) as any sum (whether fixed, or calculated either as a percentage of the proceeds or otherwise) payable only in the event of success.'[348] The Guidance to r 2.04 of that Code stated that this definition was sufficiently broad to include conditional fee agreements.[349]

27.262 Rule 2.04 of the 2007 Code imposed the following prohibition:

> '(1) You must not enter into an arrangement to receive a contingency fee for work done in prosecuting or defending any contentious proceedings before a court of England and Wales, a British court martial or an arbitrator where the seat of the arbitration is in England and Wales, except as permitted by statute or the common law.

---

347 See, in particular, *Swain v The Law Society* [1983] 1 AC 598.

348 Solicitors' Code of Conduct 2007, r 24, and para 41 of the Guidance to r 2.04.

349 See para 44 of the Guidance to r 2.04 of the Solicitors' Code of Conduct 2007. The definition in r 24 certainly is wide enough to include most conditional fee agreements, but it could be argued that it does not include agreements under which the fees are payable in the event of something happening other than success.

> (2) You must not enter into an arrangement to receive a contingency fee for work done in prosecuting or defending any contentious proceedings before a court of an overseas jurisdiction or an arbitrator where the seat of the arbitration is overseas except to the extent that a lawyer of that jurisdiction would be permitted to do so.'[350]

Thus, in so far as retainers made between 1 July 2007 and 6 October 2011 were concerned, contingency fees were prohibited other than to the extent that they were permitted by statute or common law. The Solicitors' Practice Rules 1990 imposed a very similar prohibition for work done after 8 January 1999;[351] before that date, similar (but more restrictive) provisions applied.[352] **27.263**

Thus 'contingency fee' agreements (including conditional fee agreements) were prohibited. May LJ made the following comments about the provisions contained in the 1990 Rules (which, presumably, also apply to the provisions in the Solicitors' Code of Conduct 2007): **27.264**

> 'They are secondary legislation having the force of statute ... The Rules regulate professional practice, but breach of the Rules is unlawful in addition to being a breach of professional practice ... Although no doubt not every trifling breach of the Solicitors' Practice Rules would render a transaction with which it was concerned unenforceable, in my view an arrangement to receive a contingency fee contrary to rule 8(1) would make the fee agreement which it comprised unenforceable.'[353]

There is therefore an implied statutory prohibition against a 'contingency fee' agreement relating to contentious business. The only exceptions to that prohibition are where the agreement is permitted by statute or the common law (see Chapter 29). **27.265**

Contingency fee agreements made on or after 6 October 2011 There is, in the editor's opinion, no implied statutory prohibition against 'contingency fee' agreements (including conditional fee agreements) arising out of the SRA Code of Conduct 2011. This is because the 2011 Code says no more than that entering into unlawful fee arrangements such as an unlawful contingency fee is indicative of the solicitor not having complied with its Principles.[354] As such, the SRA Code of Conduct 2011 appears to follow the law rather than to shape it. In any event, the SRA Code of Conduct 2011 is less prescriptive than its predecessors (see 4.16). This is, however, only the editor's opinion and, as such, it may be incorrect. In any event, it is a point that would rarely be of practical relevance because the position is now expressly governed by legislation. **27.266**

---

350 Similar provisions relating to overseas clients could be found at Solicitors' Code of Conduct 2007, r 15.02.

351 '(1) A solicitor who is retained or employed to prosecute or defend any action, suit or other contentious proceeding shall not enter into any arrangement to receive a contingency fee in respect of that proceeding, save one permitted under statute or by the common law. (2) Paragraph (1) of this rule shall not apply to an arrangement in respect of an action, suit or other contentious proceeding in any country other than England and Wales to the extent that the local lawyer would be permitted to receive a contingency fee in respect of that proceeding.'

352 A different, more restrictive, form of wording was used up until 8 January 1999: 'A solicitor who is retained or employed to prosecute any action, suit or other contentious proceeding shall not enter into any arrangement to receive a contingency fee in respect of that proceeding.'

353 *Awwad v Geraghty* [2001] QB 570, at 598.

354 See IB(1.27) and OP(1.3).

Other breaches of the codes of conduct

27.267 The applicable principles are those explained at 27.231. In particular, where a retainer is said to be unenforceable by reason of implied statutory prohibition, the correct way of addressing that issue is to apply Devlin J's two-stage test (see 27.231).

27.268 Whilst the true meaning of each provision must be determined by a process of statutory interpretation and whilst that meaning would be the same regardless of whether the argument was raised by the client or by the paying party, the general thrust of Arden LJ's judgment in *Garbutt v Edwards*[355] was that a failure to adhere strictly to the then code of conduct (in that instance, the Solicitors' Practice Rules 1990) would not render a contract of retainer unenforceable. The fact that other common-law jurisdictions have come to similar conclusions strongly implies that this is a principle of general application and that, as such, it applies to both the Solicitors' Code of Conduct 2007 and the SRA Code of Conduct 2011.[356]

27.269 One factor that appeared to have a bearing on Arden LJ's analysis was that although the Solicitors' Practice Rules 1990 made no provision for non-compliant retainers to be rendered unenforceable, it made express provision for compensation to be payable to the client for inadequate professional services (those provisions qualifying the power conferred by Solicitors Act 1974, s 37A). It is perhaps relevant that the Solicitors' Code of Conduct 2007 did nothing to diminish those powers—and whilst those powers do not seem to be part of the SRA Code of Conduct Rules 2011 themselves (or the associated SRA Disciplinary Rules 2011), the Legal Ombudsman now has very similar powers.

27.270 In summary, whilst each case must be considered individually, a failure to comply with the requirements of the prevailing code of conduct would not generally result in the retainer being found to be unenforceable.

Consumer protection regulations

27.271 These are addressed in Chapter 28.

Provisions relating to insurance

27.272 The provisions relating to insurance are potentially relevant to a contract of insurance in two ways.

- **Quasi-insurance** It has been argued that an agreement to provide an indemnity for adverse costs is an agreement to provide insurance and that where a legal services provider provides such an indemnity in an unregulated fashion, this has the effect of making the contract of retainer unenforceable (see 27.273–27.286).
- **Ineptly provided after-the-event (ATE) insurance** It may be that a solicitor carries out the task of arranging ATE insurance and it does so in such an inept way that the contract of retainer is put at risk (see 27.287–27.301).

27.273 **Quasi-insurance: whether a retainer is an insurance policy** Two issues arise in relation to quasi-insurance: the first is whether such an agreement is contrary to the rules

355 *Garbutt v Edwards* [2005] EWCA Civ 1206.

356 See, eg, *Boyne v Dublin Bus* [2006] IEHC 209; *A & L Goodbody Solicitors v Colthurst* (unreported) 5 November 2003, High Court of Ireland.

of champerty; the second, whether the agreement is contrary to the legislative provisions regulating insurance. For the reasons set out below, it is now known that there is almost no scope for the court to find that a contract of retainer is unenforceable for either of these reasons. The topic of champerty is addressed first. As is explained in Chapter 30, the law of champerty still very much applies to legal services providers acting in that capacity; it is, however, a necessary ingredient that the putative champerter be acting contrary to public policy. Lord Neuberger MR had this to say on this topic:

> 'Access to justice is an essential ingredient of a modern civilised society, but it is difficult to achieve for the great majority of citizens, especially with the ever reducing availability of legal aid. This has been accompanied by a shift in legislative policy towards favouring the relaxation of previously tight professional ethical constraints, in order to enable a variety of more flexible funding arrangements (which some applaud and others believe give too much weight to consumerism and involve expensive regulation). In these circumstances, I find it hard to accept that, by shouldering the risk of an adverse order for costs against his client, a solicitor is acting contrary to public policy, which is, of course, the basis for the law of champerty.'[357]

Lord Neuberger MR went on to say that he rejected the idea that such cases are to be dealt on a case-by-case basis.[358] There has been a degree of academic criticism of this decision, but Lord Neuberger MR readily pointed out that 'the rule against champerty is not entirely logical in its extent or limits'[359] and, as such, it is an analysis that is unashamedly based on current-day policy. **27.274**

Lord Neuberger MR also considered whether an arrangement that a legal services provider bears the risk of adverse costs orders could be said to be unlawful maintenance. He concluded that it could not, because maintenance involves an element of assisting one of the parties 'without justification or excuse' and, as Lord Phillips had found before him,[360] Lord Neuberger MR could not envisage a legal services provider acting in that capacity doing so without justification or excuse.[361] **27.275**

The next topic is the relevance of the legislation that governs insurance (a detailed discussion of which can be found in Chapter 34). That legislation provides for an express statutory prohibition that, subject to the court ordering otherwise, will prevent an unregulated contract of insurance from being enforced against the client. For the reasons set out below, the question of whether the express statutory prohibition applies will turn on whether, taking the contract as whole, it can be said to have as its principal object the provision of insurance. If the answer to that question is in the negative, then the contract will not be unenforceable by reason of the express statutory prohibition. As will be explained below, Lord Neuberger MR has said that that question will almost always be answered in the negative. **27.276**

The Financial Services and Markets Act 2000 creates an express statutory prohibition that it labels 'the general prohibition'. The general prohibition is part of the machinery that circumscribes 'regulated activities' and it is described at 34.43–34.59. What is and is not a 'regulated activity' is defined by the Financial Services and Markets Act 2000 (Regulated **27.277**

357 *Morris v London Borough of Southwark* [2011] EWCA Civ 25, at [49].
358 *Ibid*, at [57].
359 *Ibid*, at [51].
360 *R v Secretary of State for Transport, ex p Factortame* [2002] EWCA Civ 932, at [76].
361 *Morris v London Borough of Southwark* [2011] EWCA Civ 25, at [53].

Activities) Order 2001.[362] Providing ATE insurance as a principal is a regulated activity. On 14 January 2005, the 2001 Order was amended[363] and, from that date, the act of giving advice about ATE insurance also became a regulated activity.

27.278 One aspect of the express prohibition is created by Financial Services and Markets Act 2000, s 26, which (to the extent that it is relevant) reads:

> '(1) An agreement made by a person in the course of carrying on a regulated activity in contravention of the general prohibition is unenforceable against the other party.
>
> [...]
>
> (3) "Agreement" means an agreement—
> (a) made after this section comes into force; and
> (b) the making or performance of which constitutes, or is part of, the regulated activity in question.'

Thus, where a solicitor makes a contract in the course of carrying on a regulated activity in contravention of the general prohibition, that agreement will be rendered unenforceable against the client, but only if the making or performance of the contract constitutes, or is part of, the regulated activity in question.

27.279 Section 26 relates to agreements made by a person in contravention of the general prohibition. Section 27 of the 2000 Act introduces a similar provision that relates to agreement made through such a person. In so far as it is relevant, it reads:

> '(1) An agreement made by an authorised person ("the provider")—
> (a) in the course of carrying on a regulated activity (not in contravention of the general prohibition), but
> (b) in consequence of something said or done by another person ("the third party") in the course of a regulated activity carried on by the third party in contravention of the general prohibition, is unenforceable against the other party.
>
> [...]
>
> (3) "Agreement" means an agreement—
> (a) made after this section comes into force; and
> (b) the making or performance of which constitutes, or is part of, the regulated activity in question carried on by the provider.'

This creates an express statutory prohibition that is similar to that described above, but which is one step removed in that the contract will be unenforceable not as an effect of the involvement of the person who made the contract, but as a result of the involvement of a person who said or did something that led to its creation.

27.280 These provisions invite the question as to whether a contract of retainer that also provides for an indemnity for adverse costs falls within the ambit of these provisions. This would be the case only if the contract in question could be said to be a contract of insurance. A detailed discussion of what is and is not insurance is beyond the scope of this book, but, subject to what is said below at 27.283, the following is generally accepted as describing the requisite constituents:

---

[362] SI 2001/544.

[363] Financial Services and Markets Act 2000 (Regulated Activities) (Amendment) Order 2004 (SI 2004/1610).

'The payment of one or more sums of money, commonly called premiums, by one party ("the policyholder"). In return for these payments the other party ("the insurer") undertakes to pay a sum of money on the happening of a specified event ... The event must be one which is adverse to the interests of the policyholder.'[364]

In so far as contracts of retainers are concerned, Lord Neuberger MR approved of the following findings in the court below: **27.281**

'45. I have been referred to the following extract from *McGillivray on Insurance Law*. I do not apologise for quoting it, word-for-word, reflecting as it does my own view,

"It is sometimes necessary to decide, in the context of fiscal or regulatory legislation, whether a contract containing insurance and non-insurance elements should be classified wholly or partly as a contract of insurance. The inclusion of indemnity provisions within a contract, or the supply of services, neither makes the indemnifier an insurer, nor justifies describing the contract as wholly or partly one of insurance. Where a contract for sale, or for services, contains elements of insurance, it will be regarded as a contract of insurance only if, taking the contract as whole, it can be said to have as its principal object the provision of insurance."

46. In my judgment, this, on any view, was a contract for the provision of legal services. The indemnity clause, whether looked at individually or as part of the contract, was a subsidiary part of the contract. ... [T]his was a contract for the provision of legal services, with an indemnity clause whereby the solicitor undertook to pay the opponent's costs, in the event that that became necessary. To characterise it as a contract of insurance, albeit that the indemnity created some principles similar to an insurance contract, is to go too far ...'[365]

Thus a contract of retainer could almost never be said to be a contract of the type that would engage the regulatory framework governing insurance. It is, perhaps, possible that a legal services provider could cross the line and conduct its business in such a way as to make the provision of legal services a subsidiary element, but there are no instances of any such findings ever having been made. **27.282**

Lord Neuberger MR's analysis has received a certain amount of academic criticism, but two points are worth making. The first is that the law has always avoided being overly rigid in its view of what is and is not insurance. In this regard, Templeman J had the following to say: **27.283**

'It does not follow that the definition given by Channell J [at 27.280] in a case based on the facts with which he was concerned and applied by me to the case in which I am now concerned is an exhaustive definition of insurance. There may well be some contracts of guarantee, some contracts of maintenance which might at first sight appear to have some resemblance to the definition laid down by Channell J and which, on analysis, are not found to be true contracts of insurance at all.'[366]

The second point is that this is not the first time that the court has found that a contract for something that may, at first blush, appear to be insurance should not be regarded as such. An example of this arose in the context of a scheme to give discretionary legal assistance to members of a mutual professional organisation: Megarry V-C drew a distinction between **27.284**

[364] *Prudential Insurance Co v IRC* [1904] 2 KB 658, at 336, *per* Channell J.

[365] *Morris v London Borough of Southwark* [2011] EWCA Civ 25, at [59], quoting Birds, J, *MacGillivray on Insurance Law* (London: Sweet & Maxwell, 2008).

[366] *Department of Trade and Industry v St Christopher Motorists Association Ltd* [1974] 1 All ER 395, at 401.

contracts *of* insurance and contracts *for* insurance.[367] This was an analysis very similar to Lord Neuberger MR's analysis, as set out at 27.281.

27.285 Nonetheless, it is still theoretically possible that a legal services provider could cross the line and enter into an agreement that was not a contract of retainer, but was a contract of insurance. Even if this were to happen, it would not necessarily follow that the contract would be unenforceable against the client. This is because Financial Services and Markets Act 2000, s 28, gives the court discretion to allow the contract to be enforced against the client:

> '(1) This section applies to an agreement which is unenforceable because of section 26 or 27.
>
> [...]
>
> (3) If the court is satisfied that it is just and equitable in the circumstances of the case, it may allow—
> (a) the agreement to be enforced; or
> (b) money and property paid or transferred under the agreement to be retained.
>
> (4) In considering whether to allow the agreement to be enforced or (as the case may be) the money or property paid or transferred under the agreement to be retained the court must—
> (a) if the case arises as a result of section 26, have regard to the issue mentioned in subsection (5); or
> (b) if the case arises as a result of section 27, have regard to the issue mentioned in subsection (6).
>
> (5) The issue is whether the person carrying on the regulated activity concerned reasonably believed that he was not contravening the general prohibition by making the agreement.
>
> (6) The issue is whether the provider knew that the third party was (in carrying on the regulated activity) contravening the general prohibition.
>
> (7) If the person against whom the agreement is unenforceable—
> (a) elects not to perform the agreement, or
> (b) as a result of this section, recovers money paid or other property transferred by him under the agreement, he must repay any money and return any other property received by him under the agreement.
>
> (8) If property transferred under the agreement has passed to a third party, a reference in section 26 or 27 or this section to that property is to be read as a reference to its value at the time of its transfer under the agreement.
>
> (9) The commission of an authorisation offence does not make the agreement concerned illegal or invalid to any greater extent than is provided by section 26 or 27.'

Section 28(4) is worded in mandatory terms. In view of the guidance given by Lord Neuberger MR, as set out at 27.273, it is difficult to think of circumstances in which it could be argued that this provision would give rise to a breach of the indemnity principle. Examples might include where the contract was a tripartite agreement with an unregulated third party that was, in some way, objectionable on public policy grounds.

27.286 In summary, whilst it remains a theoretical possibility, for all practical purposes a contract of retainer would not be made unenforceable solely by reason of it containing a provision for an indemnity in respect of an opponent's costs.

---

[367] *Medical Defence Union Ltd v Department of Trade* [1979] 2 All ER 421, at 431.

Ineptly provided ATE insurance and the enforceability of retainers This section addresses the steps that need to be taken to avoid a breach of the 'general prohibition' (see 27.277 and 34.43). For the reasons set out above, it is likely that the only circumstances in which a legal services provider would need to concern itself with such issues would be where it is dealing with insurance provided by an insurer, which instance would usually arise in the context of the legal services provider arranging ATE insurance. As is set out above (see 27.278), a breach of the general prohibition is capable of rendering unenforceable a contract made 'in the course of carrying on a regulated activity', although it is not known whether this would be interpreted sufficiently widely to mean that a contract of retainer made at the same time as an ATE policy would be regarded as having been made 'in the course of carrying on a regulated activity'. Given the sentiments expressed by Lord Neuberger MR relating to quasi-insurance (see 27.281), this would seem unlikely, but it cannot be ruled out entirely and, as such, compliance remains an issue that deserves to be addressed. In any event, it is desirable not to breach the general prohibition for reasons unrelated to retainers. **27.287**

The relevant law follows a tortuous path through statute, delegated legislation and rules of professional conduct, but an overview is as follows. **27.288**

- Effecting or carrying out a contract of ATE insurance as a principal is a regulated activity, as is giving advice about ATE insurance.
- Carrying out either of these activities without also complying with the relevant regulatory regime would amount to a breach of the general provision.
- Certain professionals are exempt from many of the requirements imposed by the Financial Services and Markets Act 2000, but only if and to the extent that they comply with certain rules.
- In so far as solicitors are concerned, the task of formulating those rules is delegated to the SRA in its role as a designated professional body.
- Those rules (which are discussed at 34.47–34.59) have been formulated in such a way as to lie alongside the prevailing rules of professional conduct and compliance with those rules will mean that the solicitor avoids breaching the general prohibition.

The starting point is Financial Services and Markets Act 2000, s 327, which section exempts certain persons from the general prohibition, but only if: **27.289**

- that person is a member of a profession (or controlled or managed by one or more such members);
- that person accounts to their client for any commission received;
- the activity in question is 'incidental to the provision of professional services';
- the activity is of a certain permitted type and is not of a prohibited type; and
- the activity is the only regulated activity carried on by that person (other than regulated activities in relation to which they are an exempt person).

These provisions permit certain firms to be treated as 'exempt professional firms' and to carry on 'exempt regulated activities'. These firms will not need to be regulated by the Financial Conduct Authority (FCA), but will be able to carry on exempt regulated activities under the supervision of a designated professional body. A designated professional body must formulate rules to regulate the way in which regulated activities are performed. **27.290**

27.291 The SRA is a designated professional body. There are two sets of relevant rules, both of which were made by the procedure described above and both of which have the force of statute (see 34.47–34.59):

- the SRA Financial Services (Scope) Rules 2001 (the Scope Rules); and
- the SRA Financial Services (Conduct of Business) Rules 2001 (the Conduct of Business Rules).[368]

Both were amended on 14 January 2005 to include ATE insurance, again on 1 July 2007 to take account of the introduction of the Solicitors Code of Conduct 2007 and then again on 6 October 2011 to take account of the SRA Code of Conduct 2011. They are referred to as rules governing 'specialist services' under the SRA Code of Conduct 2011.

27.292 The Scope Rules include the following:

- a list of prohibited activities;
- basic conditions that must be satisfied; and
- restrictions relating to particular types of activity.

27.293 Like the Financial Services and Markets Act 2000 (Regulated Activities) Order 2001,[369] the Scope Rules were amended on 14 January 2005 to encompass ATE insurance. In the present context, the most important provisions are that:

- a solicitor may provide 'insurance mediation activities' (a definition that includes giving advice about ATE insurance) only if registered with the FCA;
- the advice must arise out of, or be complementary to, the provision of a professional service to the client; and
- the solicitor must account to the client for any pecuniary reward or other advantage received from a third party.

27.294 Registration with the FCA is not the same as being regulated by the FCA: registration is a straightforward administrative process, whereas regulation is much more involved. The issue of whether advice is complementary to the provision of legal services would depend on the facts of the case in hand and whilst it is implicit that there will be a limit to what could be regarded as being complementary, there is no authority as to where the line should be drawn.

27.295 As to the third of these requirements (accounting for any pecuniary reward), it was once not unusual for solicitors to be paid a commission for recommending a contract of insurance. The requirement to account to the client does not mean that the commission necessarily has to be paid to the client. In this regard, the SRA Code of Conduct 2011 reads as follows:

> 'O(1.15) You must achieve these outcomes: you properly account to clients for any financial benefit you receive as a result of your instructions.
>
> [...]
>
> IB(1.20) where you receive a financial benefit as a result of acting for a client, either:
> (a) paying it to the client;

[368] These used to be known as the Solicitors' Financial Services (Scope) Rules 2001 and the Solicitors' Financial Services (Conduct of Business) Rules 2001, respectively.

[369] SI 2001/544.

(b) offsetting it against your fees; or
(c) keeping it only where you can justify keeping it, you have told the client the amount of the benefit (or an approximation if you do not know the exact amount) and the client has agreed that you can keep it.'[370]

Up until 6 October 2011, the Solicitors' Code of Conduct 2007 made the following provisions: **27.296**

> 'If you are a principal in a firm you must ensure that your firm pays to your client commission received over £20 unless the client, having been told the amount, or if the precise amount is not known, an approximate amount or how the amount is to be calculated, has agreed that your firm may keep it.'[371]

Even under those rules, however, the £20 limit did not apply to commissions paid on ATE insurance. This is because Financial Services and Markets Act 2000, s 327(3), overrode that limit:

> 'P [ie the solicitor] must not receive from a person other than his client any pecuniary reward or other advantage, for which he does not account to his client, arising out of his carrying on of any of the activities.'

Solicitors therefore need to—and have always needed to—account for all ATE commissions, regardless of size.

The Conduct of Business Rules require that solicitors give 'status disclosure' (see 34.52–34.57), which in essence means that the solicitor should explain that they are not authorised by the FCA, but are regulated by the SRA. In particular, the solicitor is required to give the client the following information in writing: **27.297**

- a statement that the firm is not authorised by the FCA;
- the name and address of the firm;
- the nature of the regulated activities carried on by the firm and the fact that they are limited in scope;
- a statement that the firm is regulated by the SRA; and
- a statement explaining that complaints and redress mechanisms are provided though SRA regulation.

Moreover, the following statement must be made in writing: **27.298**

> '[This firm is]/[We are] not authorised by the Financial Conduct Authority. However, we are included on the register maintained by the Financial Conduct Authority so that we can carry on insurance mediation activity, which is broadly the advising on, selling and administration of insurance contracts. This part of our business, including arrangements for complaints or redress if something goes wrong, is regulated by the Solicitors Regulation Authority. The register can be accessed via the Financial Conduct Authority website at [https://www.fca.org.uk/register]'[372]

The Guidance Notes to the Conduct of Business Rules suggest that this information may be given in the client care letter.

[370] Provisions concerning overseas practice can be found at OP(1.1).
[371] Solicitors' Code of Conduct 2007, r 2.06.
[372] See SRA Financial Services (Conduct of Business) Rules 2001, r 3.3.

27.299 The Conduct of Business Rules provide that certain records must be kept.[373] In essence, the client's instructions need to be recorded, as must any relevant instructions given to any other person. A record most also be kept of the commissions received and of how that commission has been accounted. These records must be kept for at least six years.[374]

27.300 In so far as ATE insurance is concerned, the solicitor must comply with the provisions of Appendix 1 of the Conduct of Business Rules,[375] which imposes three obligations: to disclose certain information; to advise the client whether the ATE insurance is suitable; and to give the client a 'demands and needs statement'. These topics are addressed in Chapter 34 (at 34.47–34.59).

27.301 In summary, whilst it is extremely unlikely that it would ever operate in such a way as to render a contract of retainer unenforceable, there is a statutory mechanism that provides a means by which a contract of retainer could be found to be unenforceable by reason of it having been associated in some way with a breach of the 'general prohibition'.

Retainers and Similar Contracts Involving More than One Client

Joint obligations

27.302 A retainer may relate to more than one client in one of two ways: expressly and impliedly.

- **Expressly** The retainer may expressly refer to more than one client, either in a single document that refers to all of the client counterparties or by way of a number of documents referring to only one client each, but which are expressly linked so as to form a collective whole. An example of the latter would be where a number of seemingly separate retainers in group litigation are expressly linked by an overarching fee-sharing agreement.
- **Impliedly** In contrast, clients may be jointed in the same contract of retainer by implication. The context in which this usually arises is where several seemingly separate documents are linked in such a way that each must be read in the context of the others. An example would be where co-litigants each have their own retainer, but where their instructions are to incur costs that are to be shared amongst them.

Plurality of debtors

27.303 Regardless of the mechanism by which they are created, retainers will exist where there is a plurality of costs debtors. Where this is the case, the costs debtors will have joint obligations. The law of joint obligations is not beyond criticism. In 1949, Glanville Williams remarked on the subject: 'This [work] discusses a difficult and seriously defective part of the common law ... I do not suppose any lawyer can read the pages that follow without astonishment that the law can be so involved, inconvenient and unjust.'[376]

---

[373] See Solicitors' Financial Services (Conduct of Business) Rules 2001, r 5, which must be read in conjunction with r 4.

[374] See Solicitors' Financial Services (Conduct of Business) Rules 2001, r 9.

[375] See Solicitors' Financial Services (Conduct of Business) Rules 2001, r 8A.

[376] Williams, GL, *Joint Obligations: A Treatise on Joint and Joint and Several Liability in Contract, Quasi-Contract and Trusts in England* (London: Butterworth & Co, 1949), p 3.

Modern commentators have confirmed that this comment is still applicable today,[377] so what is said below should be regarded only as a general overview of the topic; further legal research may be required in more demanding cases. 27.304

The nature of obligations where there is a plurality of debtors

Where there is a plurality of debtors (in this context, paying clients), the obligation to discharge a costs debt may be several, joint or joint and several. 27.305

- **Several costs liability** This means that each costs debtor has a separate obligation to pay a share of the costs. The costs creditor is able to pursue each individual debtor for no more than their own share of the total and, as such, the issue of contributions between the costs debtors does not arise.
- **Joint costs liability** This means that there is only one obligation to pay costs and that obligation would be owed by all the costs debtors. The costs creditor is able to recover the whole of the debt from any solvent debtor or from any number of them. The liability does not give rise to any rights as between the costs debtors that would enable any of them to seek a contribution from the others.
- **Joint and several costs liability** This means that there is one obligation to pay costs and that obligation is owed by all of the costs debtors, but, as between themselves, the obligation gives rise to rights to seek contributions so as to divide the obligation into shares.

These topics are covered in detail in Chapter 21, which focuses on orders for costs between opposing parties, but the general principles are the same. For present purposes, it is necessary only to know that these three categories exist. 27.306

Whether the obligation is joint, several or joint and several will depend on the wording of the contract of retainer. There are two other factors that may be of relevance: first, the nature of instructions (that is, whether the instructions were given jointly or separately); and secondly, the interest that the clients have in the subject matter of the instructions (that is, whether the interest that the clients have in the matter is joint or several). If one focuses on these two factors, the following categories of plural liability can be described: 27.307

- separate instructions in separate matters (see 27.308);
- separate instructions in joint matters (see 27.309);
- joint instructions in separate matters (see 27.310–27.312); and
- joint instructions in joint matters (see 27.313–27.314).

Separate instructions in separate matters

This situation would occur when the clients' interests in the subject matter of the retainer are separate and where the instructions are also separate. For obvious reasons, it will usually follow that any given client will bear the full liability for the costs incurred as a result of their instructions and that the obligation to pay will be several[378] (unless, of course, the retainer provides otherwise). Chadwick LJ has said that the obligation to pay will be several where separate clients give separate instructions on discrete issues that can be said to be separate.[379] 27.308

[377] Brownsword, R, *The Law of Contract* (London: LexisNexis Butterworths, 2007), para 6.336.
[378] This will not always be the case. Where a client is a test-claimant in group litigation, for example, those costs may be categorised as being common costs: see CPR, r 46.6(b)(ii).
[379] *Bayliss v Kelly & Ors* [1997] 2 Costs LR 54, at 59.

Separate instructions in joint matters

27.309 This situation will arise where persons who are otherwise unconnected instruct a legal services provider who then carries out work that is of benefit to all of them. An example is where several claimants pursue a claim based on similar facts against a single defendant and where the retainers are, on the face of it, separate; in those circumstances, each claimant will generally be liable only for the costs attributable to their own claim, together with their share of the costs that were common to the claim generally. The principle of equal apportionment will apply to the common costs, as is discussed at 20.16–20.25.

Joint instructions in separate matters

27.310 This situation would occur when the client's interests in the subject matter are separate, but instructions are given jointly. The mere fact that the instructions are given to the same solicitor (even if those instructions overlap) is not enough to allow a conclusion to be drawn that there is a joint retainer. Amphlett B had this to say on the topic:

> '[T]he mere fact that the several defendants appear by the same solicitor, that they join in putting in the same answer, join in the same affidavits, and attend joint consultations, would not, to my mind, amount to evidence that there was any joint retainer.'[380]

27.311 In the modern context, these comments would still apply as a consequence of the need to give clients a degree of consumer protection. There is, in particular, a need to ensure that a client does not become liable for the costs of others without realising that that is the case. An example is where a solicitor was instructed by cohabitees to prepare wills conferring mutual benefits, in which case the court found that the obligations were several.[381] Another example is where a number of directors were sued in their personal capacities and where they gave joint instructions to a solicitor to 'take such steps as you may consider necessary in the matter', in which case the obligation was found to be several.[382]

27.312 It will, however, not always be the case that where the client's interests are separate, their obligations will also be separate. An example is a retainer that covered two tenants in common (that is, each had a separate and distinct interest in the property); in view of the nature of the instructions, the court found that the liability was joint and several.[383]

Joint instructions in joint matters

27.313 Where the solicitor is acting for litigants pursuing a joint cause of action upon the receipt of joint instructions, the starting point will be that the retainer imposes a joint liability unless the contrary can be shown.[384] For the reasons set out above (see 27.310), a distinction must be drawn between clients giving instructions jointly and clients merely giving overlapping instructions to the same solicitor. Whilst there is no authority on the point, it would be in keeping with the modern emphasis on client care that a joint liability would be created only where the clients were made aware of the fact that they were each assuming a liability for all of the costs, including those for legal services that might be of benefit to the others. There is, however, no authority to confirm that analysis.

---

380 *Burridge v Bellew* (1875) 32 LT 807, at 812. See also the New Zealand case of *Longreach Oil Ltd v Southern Cross Exploration* NL 1988 NSW Lexis 9762.

381 *Hall v Meyrick* [1957] 2 QB 455.

382 *Davies v Chatwood* (1879) 11 Ch D 244.

383 *Furlong v Scallan* (1875) IR 9 Eq 202.

384 *Starving v Cousins* (1835) 1 Gale 159. See also, eg, *Burridge v Bellew* (1875) 32 LT 807.

It will be clear from the examples given above that each case will turn on its own facts. There is, however, one legal principle that dominates the topic of joint obligations: the principle of equal apportionment. This is addressed in detail in Chapter 20 (see, in particular, 20.34–20.37). **27.314**

Costs sharing agreements

Where litigation involves more than one client and where costs will be incurred in respect of issues that are common to the clients (or some of them), it may be appropriate to enter into a costs sharing agreement. This can be done by way of a simple agreement to share a part of the costs or, in a more demanding case, it can be made more robust by way of a system of interlocking indemnities. The way in which such a system works is that all of the contributors are jointly and severally liable for all of the costs, but each contributor is able to rely on a full indemnity from the other contributors for all but their own share of the costs.[385] **27.315**

A costs sharing agreement would almost always deal with the clients' liability for their own legal services provider's fees—known as a funding costs sharing agreement (FCSA) (see 65.07)—but many agreements also make provision for sharing the burden of an adverse costs order—known as a liability costs sharing agreement (LCSA). Where the agreement contains an LCSA, care ought to be taken to ensure that it does not conflict with any provisions that may have been made for ATE insurance—in particular, that the additional exposure that an LCSA may impose upon a litigant does not cause them to exceed the extent of cover. **27.316**

Where the retainer is such that the legal services provider's fees, or part of them, are dependent on recovery of costs from the opponent—such as in the case of a simple conditional fee agreement, or CFA Lite—then any FCSA should make it clear whether the liability for an adverse costs order is to be set off against costs recovered. It should leave no doubt as to whether it is the client or the legal services provider who bears the brunt of that risk. **27.317**

In group litigation, the costs sharing agreement—be it an FCSA, an LCSA, or both—may need to be approved by the court and, in any event, will be subject to the court's supervision. These issues are discussed in more detail in Chapter 65. **27.318**

Retainers with Specific Types of Person

Retainers with companies, limited liability partnerships and members

Companies are generally presumed to have the capacity to enter into simple contracts such as contracts of retainer or costs sharing agreements. The fact that a company's constitution prohibits it from entering into a particular type of contract will not be a reason for calling into question its capacity to do so[386]—although its constitution may stipulate the **27.319**

[385] This scheme has not been approved by any court, but neither has it ever been challenged.

[386] See Companies Act 2006, s 39; in relation to unregistered companies, see the Unregistered Companies Regulations 2009 (SI 2009/2436). Special provisions apply to charities: see Companies Act 2006, s 42; Charities Act 1993 ss 50, 60 (s 50 as amended by the Charities Act 2006 s 75(1), and Sch 8, paras 96 and 143); if the agreement was made after 14 March 2012, see Charities Act 2011 ss 251, 260 and 261.

method by which it is permitted to make a contract (see below). Moreover, where a person is dealing with a company in good faith, the power of the directors to bind the company or to authorise others to do so is deemed to be free of any limitation under the company's constitution.[387]

27.320 Ancient provisions[388] that required a retainer to be in writing and made under seal no longer apply.[389] It is still possible for a contract (including a contract of retainer[390]) to be made under a company's seal,[391] but it is far more common for a contract to be made on behalf of a company by a person signing it acting with the company's authority, be that authority express or implied.[392] Certain formalities apply. Those that have applied since 6 April 2008 are as follows:

> '(1) Under the law of England and Wales ... a document is executed by a company—
> (a) by the affixing of its common seal, or
> (b) by signature in accordance with the following provisions.
>
> (2) A document is validly executed by a company if it is signed on behalf of the company—
> (a) by two authorised signatories, or
> (b) by a director of the company in the presence of a witness who attests the signature.
>
> (3) The following are "authorised signatories" for the purposes of subsection (2)—
> (a) every director of the company, and
> (b) in the case of a private company with a secretary or a public company, the secretary (or any joint secretary) of the company.
>
> (4) A document signed in accordance with subsection (2) and expressed, in whatever words, to be executed by the company has the same effect as if executed under the common seal of the company.'[393]

Even where the contract must be written (such as where it is a conditional fee agreement or a damages-based agreement), there is no absolute requirement that the contract is signed

[387] See Companies Act 2006, s 40; in relation to unregistered companies, see the Unregistered Companies Regulations 2009 (SI 2009/2436). These presumptions are there to ensure that a company cannot seek to evade its contractual obligations by pointing to restrictions in its constitution, so it is a moot point whether the company itself would be able to rely on these principles for the purposes of complying with the indemnity principle.

[388] See *Arnold v Poole Corpn* (1842) 4 Man & G 860.

[389] See Corporate Bodies' Contracts Act 1960, s 1, not least because companies are no longer required to have a seal: see Companies Act 2006, s 45.

[390] If authority were needed on the point, see *A-G v Brecon Corpn* (1878) 10 Ch D 204.

[391] See Companies Act 2006, s 43. Different rules apply to deeds (see s 46 of the 2006 Act). Different rules also apply to companies formed and registered under the Companies Act 1985 (unless it is an existing company, as defined in that Act). Section 1 of the 1985 Act says, in essence, that if the contract is required to be in writing, it may be made by the company if it is signed by any person acting under its authority, express or implied, but if the contract is not required to be in writing, it can be made by parol by any person acting with the company's authority, express or implied.

[392] See Companies Act 2006, ss 43 and 44(1). Different rules apply to deeds (see s 46 of the 2006 Act). Different rules also apply to companies formed and registered under the Companies Act 1985 (unless it is an existing company, as defined in that Act). Section 1 of the 1985 Act says, in essence, that if the contract is required to be in writing, it may be made by the company if it is signed by any person acting under its authority, express or implied, but if the contract is not required to be in writing, it can be made by parol by any person acting with the company's authority, express or implied.

[393] Companies Act 2006, s 44. Special rules apply to composite execution clauses (ie where one natural person signs on behalf of several companies in a single written instrument): see the Regulatory Reform (Execution of Deeds and Documents) Order 2005 (SI 2005/1906).

'by and on behalf of' the company.[394] Whilst there is a presumption that an agreement is presumed to be duly executed, that presumption does not apply to contracts of retainer.[395] That said, a company is able to enter into an unwritten or an implied contract of retainer,[396] so unless the contract was of a type that needed to be in writing, it would be open to the court to rely on the presumption described at 27.191–27.199 for the purposes of making a finding that there was a unwritten or implied contract of retainer. It is arguable that company may use its trading name for the purposes of entering into a contract.[397] Whilst each case will be highly dependent on its own facts, authority exists—albeit rather old authority—for the proposition that where a company is not bound by a retainer, its individual members may be.[398]

A limited liability partnership (LLP) has unlimited capacity.[399] Every member of an LLP is the agent of the LLP, but an LLP is not bound by anything done by a member in dealing with a person if (a) the member in fact has no authority to act for the LLP by doing that thing, and (b) the person knows that the member has no authority, or does not know or believe them to be a member of the LLP.[400] In so far as formalities are concerned, for an agreement made on or after 1 October 2009, the same provisions that apply to limited companies apply to LLPs (with the references to directors being read as if they were references to members[401]), but this is without prejudice to the status of each member of the LLP as its agent. **27.321**

Retainers with unincorporated associations

An unincorporated association may not make a contract of retainer as an entity in its own right; the retainer will be with the committee or the other persons who acted with authority in giving instructions to the legal services provider.[402] **27.322**

Retainers with trustees, executors, liquidators, etc

Unless it is expressly agreed otherwise,[403] a trustee or executor is personally liable for the monies payable under a retainer.[404] A trustee has a right to an indemnity from the fund (see 66.36). Where there is more than one trustee, a retainer with one will bind the others only if there is express authority to that effect.[405] A liquidator (unlike a trustee in **27.323**

[394] Whilst dealing with agreements other than contracts of retainer, see *Williams v Redcard Ltd* [2011] EWCA Civ 466.

[395] It applies only to purchasers of property: see Companies Act 2006, s 44(5).

[396] See Companies Act 2006, ss 43 and 44.

[397] See, eg, *OTV Birwelco Ltd v Technical & Guarantee Co Ltd* [2002] 4 All ER 668.

[398] *Robinson v Price* (1886) 2 TLR 242.

[399] See Limited Liability Partnerships Act 2000, s 1(3).

[400] See Limited Liability Partnerships Act 2000, s 6.

[401] See Limited Liability Partnerships (Application of Companies Act 2006) Regulations 2009 (SI 2009/1804), reg 4. For agreements made before 1 October 2009, the situation is not so clear due to an oversight by the government when implementing the Regulatory Reform (Execution of Deeds and Documents) Order 2005 (SI 2005/1906), which failed to include reference to LLPs.

[402] See *Flemyng v Hector* (1836) 2 M & W 172; *Jones v Hope* [1880] WN 69, CA.

[403] *Blyth v Fladgate* [1891] 1 Ch 337, at 359, *per* Stirling J.

[404] *Staniar v Evans, Evans v Staniar* (1886) 34 Ch D 470, at 477, *per* North J.

[405] See *Luke v South Kensington Hotel Co* (1879) 11 Ch D 121, CA; *Brazier v Camp* (1894) 9 R 852, CA.

bankruptcy[406]) is not personally liable for costs;[407] as such, it is desirable that it is expressly recorded that the legal services provider will look only to the assets for its fees.[408]

'Retainers' with employees

27.324 Provided that there is no infringement of the relevant rules of professional conduct, a solicitor may enter into an agreement to be paid a salary as an employee. That would usually be in the form of a contract for employment. It is a moot point whether such a contract can properly be regarded as being a contract of retainer in the ordinary sense, but such arrangements are lawful even where costs that are recovered beyond the salary are to be paid to the employer.[409] By analogy with the authorities decided under the common law, it is likely that this principle has survived Solicitors Act 1974, s 60(3), on the basis that the costs are assessed as if an independent solicitor had carried out the work.[410]

Retainers with children or those who lack capacity

27.325 This is addressed in Chapter 60.

Terms Commonly Encountered in Contracts of Retainers

27.326 There are many provisions that may be incorporated into a retainer for the purposes of clarification, and to pre-empt unusual and difficult situations. Many such provisions, which may be incorporated into any contractual retainer regardless of its type, are discussed below. It should be noted that a skilled drafter would generally consider including many more provisions than those set out below.[411]

Specific terms often found in contracts of retainer

'Unusual' costs

27.327 Where a client wishes to incur fees or disbursements that would be regarded as being 'unusual' in the sense that they are unlikely to be recovered from an opposing party, it is good practice to obtain the client's express consent to those costs being incurred. It is often the case that contracts of retainer expressly deal with this point. The provisions of CPR, r 46.9(3)(c), are relevant in that regard, because such monies are likely to be disallowed on a solicitor-and-client assessment if the client was not informed that they might not be recovered from an opposing party (see 37.06). Likewise, where the client wishes to incur costs in the County Court that are not likely to be recovered in that court (see 37.18), disputes can be avoided if it is expressly recorded that the client agrees to pay those costs notwithstanding that fact. Where notice has been given, the matter may need to be kept under review. In particular, it would generally not be appropriate to give a generic notice

---

406 The difference between a liquidator and a trustee in bankruptcy is that the assets are vested in the latter, but not in the former.

407 *Re Anglo-Moravian Hungarian Junction Rly Co, ex p Watkin* (1875) 1 Ch D 130, CA.

408 *Re Hermann Loog Ltd* (1887) 36 Ch D 502.

409 *Galloway v Corpn of London* (1867) LR 4 EQ 90.

410 For a discussion of this point in the context of the indemnity principle, see *In re Eastwood, deceased; Lloyds Bank Ltd v Eastwood* [1975] Ch 112.

411 For pragmatic guidance as to drafting contracts generally, the reader would do well to see Adams, K, *A Manual of Style for Contract Drafting* (2nd edn, Chicago, IL: American Bar Association, 2008).

about 'unusual' expenditure, and then to rely solely on that notice as and when specific unusual fees are incurred or disbursements are paid.

Destination of interest

Where interest is recovered from an opposing party, it belongs to the client. If the client had already paid fees and disbursements during the course of the litigation, then no problem would arise, because any interest would properly be payable only to the client. If, however, it is the legal services provider who has borne the brunt of funding the litigation, then it may have a legitimate claim to the interest. Disputes may be avoided by including an express provision that deals with the destination of any such interest. Lord Ackner had this to say on the topic: **27.328**

> '[For the legal services provider to recover the interest the retainer must contain] an express agreement between the solicitor and his client that any interest recovered on costs and disbursements after judgment is pronounced but before the [costs judge's] certificate is obtained, which costs and disbursements have not in fact been paid prior to taxation, shall as to the interest on the costs belong to the solicitor and as to the interest on disbursements be held by him for and on behalf of the person or persons to whom the disbursements are ultimately paid.'[412]

Costs recovered

Sir Stephen Sedley has explained that it would be sensible for contracts of retainer to contain a provision that deals with disputes regarding monies payable by opponents.[413] He has implied that contracts of retainer may include provisions that forestall any attempt by a client to compromise the amount of costs payable.[414] The following is an example (written by the editor) of such a provision: **27.329**

> 'Without prejudice to the Solicitors' lien, where there is a dispute as to who is entitled to any monies (or part thereof) paid or payable by the Opponent, in the absence of agreement to do otherwise, those monies (or, if appropriate, the disputed part thereof) must be paid into an escrow account (or into court) pending resolution of that dispute. Where the dispute is about how much is payable as Basic Charges, Disbursements, etc, then the Client agrees that, in the absence of the Solicitors' written consent, the Client will not in any circumstances or at any time (even after this Agreement has been terminated) seek to agree those monies (or any part thereof) with the Opponent.'

Forum

It may be sensible to include a contractual provision expressly stating the jurisdiction in which any dispute concerning costs will be litigated. This would be particularly true where the client is out of the jurisdiction or where the litigation is conducted in a different jurisdiction (including Scotland). **27.330**

Severability clause

Some retainers contain a provision that permits an objectionable provision to be severed from the rest of the agreement in the event of the contract of retainer being found to be unenforceable because of that objectionable provision. The prime reason why this is included is not because of the possibility of a dispute arising between the legal services provider and **27.331**

412 *Hunt v RM Douglas (Roofing) Ltd* [1990] 1 AC 398, HL, at 407.
413 *Khans Solicitor (A Firm) v Chifuntwe & Anor* [2013] EWCA Civ 481, at [30].
414 *Ibid*, at [37].

the client, but because of the possibility of an opposing party raising an argument based on the indemnity principle. An example would be where the legal services provider was anxious about the possibility of a particular provision being seen as an unlawful contingency fee agreement. Whilst the inclusion of a severability clause will rarely cause any harm, it is doubtful whether it is a provision that is capable of having its intended effect.[415]

Force majeure *clause*

27.332 Retainers often include a *force majeure* clause that makes it clear that if the legal services provider is prevented from discharging its obligations by reason of some factor that is outside of its control, then the provider will not be prejudiced by reason of any delay in performing the contract.

Variation-in-writing clause

27.333 Retainers often contain a restriction that, to be effective, any variation should be in writing. The intention is to avoid factual disputes about the terms of the retainer. Where the counterparties are sure that the written retainer is exactly as they would like, the inclusion of such a restriction is unobjectionable. Harm can be caused, however, in circumstances in which the client's needs change during the course of the litigation. An example would be where a retainer expressly states that it would not cover an appeal, but this provision was supposedly overridden by a subsequent oral agreement that it would do so. If, as is often the case, no one turns their mind to the issue of whether a variation should be effected in writing, disputes can arise as to the ambit of the retainer (especially if the retainer was a conditional fee agreement, which must be in writing).

Deemed signature clause

27.334 It can often be the case that one or more of the counterparties has failed to sign the contract of retainer. Equally, the original signed document may go missing. To deal with these contingencies, it is possible to incorporate a term whereby the retainer will be deemed to have been signed in the event of the client continuing to give instructions after receipt of their copy of the retainer. It would be sensible to regard any such term as being only a back-up provision.

Deemed increase clause

27.335 Almost all written contracts of retainer that provide for time-based charging make provision for the hourly rates to be reviewed. It is possible to make provision for a deemed increase to be made. Examples include linking the rates to the local 'guideline' rates or merely increasing the rate by a fixed percentage each year. It is possible to draft a retainer in such a way as to provide for a deemed increase to apply only if and to the extent that no agreed increase has been made.

ADR clauses

27.336 Whilst they are far from common, some retainers include an express provision concerning alternative dispute resolution (ADR). Examples include a provision for the matter to be decided by a barrister of more than ten years' call, or by mediation or arbitration. Where the sums involved are likely to be small, it is also possible to provide that any claim (including

[415] Whilst not binding, see *Oyston v The Royal Bank of Scotland plc* [2006] EWHC 90053 (Costs), at [36]. See also *Aratra Potato Co Ltd v Taylor Joynson-Garrett* [1995] 4 All ER 695, at 710, *per* Garland J.

an assessment) will be treated as a small claim and that the small-claims costs regime will apply. Whilst there is no authority on the topic, a solicitor would be well advised to take care not to impinge too much on the client's right to a detailed assessment; where it is proposed to restrict that right, thought ought to be given to making a formal business agreement.

Where the contract of retainer is with a consumer, the Alternative Dispute Resolution for Consumer Disputes (Competent Authorities and Information) Regulations 2015[416] may need to be taken into account (see 28.53), as may reg 10 of the Provision of Services Regulations 2009[417] (see 28.51 and 27.338). Similarly, where the contract was made prior to 1 October 2015[418] and the client was a consumer, care would have been required not to create a provision that was in breach of Sch 2, para 1(q), to the Unfair Terms in Consumer Contracts Regulations 1999[419] (which was a provision that confirmed that mandatory arbitration clauses were unfair). It was for this reason that ADR clauses in consumer contracts of retainer generally tend to afford the client a choice as to whether ADR should be used. **27.337**

FCA declaration and declaration pursuant to the Provision of Services Regulations 2009

Retainers often contain provisions concerning the solicitor's status with the FCA (that is, whether they are registered or not). The FCA publishes a standard paragraph that ought to be included (see 27.298). There is no need for those issues to be dealt with in the contract of retainer itself. The Provision of Services Regulations 2009[420] impose certain obligations to provide clients with information about the compulsory professional indemnity insurance, value added tax (VAT) number, non-judicial dispute resolution procedures and information regarding the Solicitors' Code of Conduct (see 28.47).[421] These issues are often addressed in the client care letter, but there is no reason why they cannot be addressed in the contract of retainer itself (if this is separate). **27.338**

Notices concerning the retainer

It may often be the case that where a retainer is made at a place that is not the legal services provider's place of business, certain notices must be made. This is addressed at 28.76 *et seq.* **27.339**

[416] SI 2015/542.

[417] SI 2009/2999. These implemented Directive 2006/123/EC of the European Parliament and of the Council of 12 December 2006 on services in the internal market, OJ L 376/36.

[418] See Consumer Rights Act 2015 (Commencement No 3, Transitional Provisions, Savings and Consequential Amendments) Order 2015 (SI 2015 No 1630), art 6(4).

[419] SI 1999/2083.

[420] SI 2009/2999.

[421] The following information should be provided: the legal representative's VAT number (r 8(1)(g)); details concerning the legal representative's compulsory professional indemnity insurance, including the contact details of the insurer(s) and the territorial coverage of the insurance (r 8(1)(n)); details of how to access the detailed professional rules applicable to the legal representative (r 9(1)(d)); and details of complaint resolution procedures (r 10(1)). The legal representative must also inform clients of the role of the Legal Ombudsman in resolving disputes and where further information can be obtained in this respect.

28

CONTRACTS OF RETAINER, ETC (CONSUMER ISSUES)

28.01 This chapter deals with the following topics:

- the legal services market and consumers:
  - overview of consumers in the legal services sector (28.02);
  - overview of general protection for individual consumers and small businesses (28.04);
- general consumer protection legislation (present day) (28.16):
  - the EU legislative background (28.17);
  - the Consumer Rights Act 2015 (in general) (28.22);
  - the Consumer Rights Act 2015, Part 1 (deemed terms) (28.29);
  - the Consumer Rights Act 2015, Part 2 (unfair terms) (28.40);
  - the Provision of Services Regulations 2009 (28.45);
  - the Alternative Dispute Resolution for Consumer Disputes (Competent Authorities and Information) Regulations 2015 (28.53);
  - the Consumer Contracts (Information, Cancellation and Additional Charges) Regulations 2013 (28.58);
  - the Consumer Protection from Unfair Trading Regulations 2008 (28.101);
  - remedies afforded to consumer clients (28.134);
- general consumer protection legislation (recently revoked in part):
  - the Unfair Terms in Consumer Contracts Regulations 1999 (now partially superseded) (28.149);
  - the Supply of Goods and Services Act 1982 (now partially superseded) (28.156);
  - the Unfair Contract Terms Act 1977 (now partially superseded) (25.159);
- general consumer protection legislation (older revoked provisions):
  - the Cancellation of Contracts Made in a Consumer's Home or Place of Work etc Regulations 2008 (now superseded) (28.163);
  - the Consumer Protection (Distance Selling) Regulations 2000 (now revoked) (28.201);
  - the Electronic Commerce (EC Directive) Regulations 2002 (now revoked) (28.213);
  - the Consumer Protection (Cancellation of Contracts Concluded Away from Business Premises) Regulations 1987 (now revoked) (28.214);
- general protection legislation for businesses (present day):
  - provisions relating to business that have already been addressed (28.215);
  - the Business Protection from Misleading Marketing Regulations 2008 (28.216); and
  - remedies for businesses (28.217).

The Legal Services Market and Consumers

Overview of consumers in the legal services sector

The provision of legal services to consumers in England and Wales is estimated to generate annual turnover of around £11–12 billion[1] (over a third of the £26–27 billion turnover generated by the legal services industry in general). This includes both contentious and non-contentious work. Figure 28.1 illustrates the legal needs of individual consumers in 2014, based on information provided by the Competition and Markets Authority (CMA). **28.02**

The legal needs of small business in 2015, based on the same source, were as illustrated in Figure 28.2. **28.03**

Overview of general protection for individual consumers and small businesses

Legislation exists that affords consumers and businesses certain baseline protections when purchasing services, including legal services. The CMA takes the view that those protections apply regardless of whether the legal services provider is or is not authorised.[2] The nature of the protection afforded depends on whether the purchaser of those services is an individual consumer (see 28.05–28.10) or a business (see 28.11–28.14). **28.04**

Baseline consumer protection regulation for individual consumers

In so far as present-day legislation is concerned, a 'consumer' is an individual who is acting for purposes that are wholly or mainly outside their trade, business, craft or profession (see 28.26). A 'trader' is a person who is acting for purposes relating to their trade, business or profession, whether acting personally or through another person acting in **28.05**

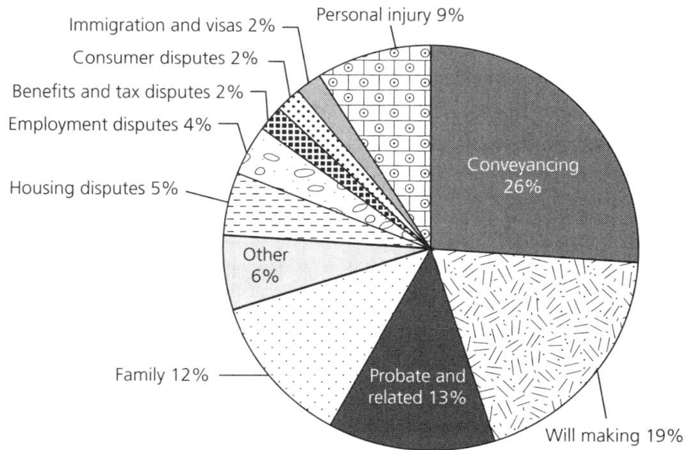

Figure 28.1 Legal needs of individual consumers, 2014

Source: CMA, *Legal Services Market Study: Final Report* (London: HMSO, 2016), p 36

[1] This is the CMA's estimate, based on data from the Law Society: see CMA, *Legal Services Market Study: Final Report* (London: HMSO, 2016), p 35.

[2] See *ibid*, at Appx E, para 2 *et seq*.

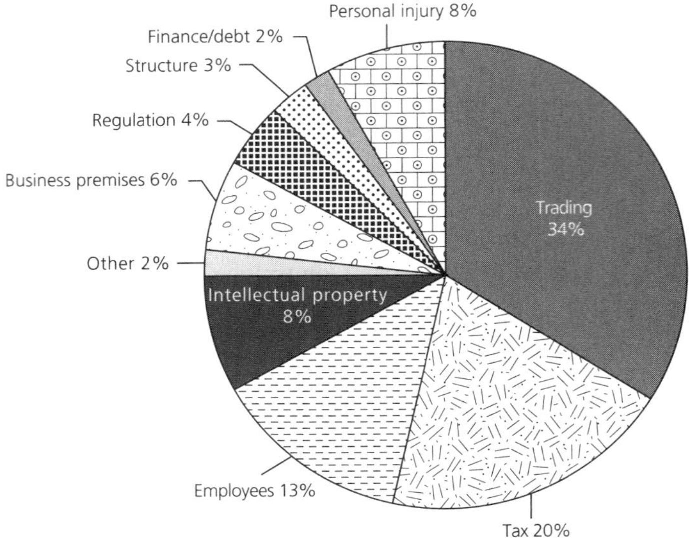

Figure 28.2 Legal needs of small businesses, 2015
Source: CMA, *Legal Services Market Study: Final Report* (London: HMSO, 2016), p 36

their name or on their behalf (see 28.27). For obvious reasons, persons who provide fee-based legal services will be traders. Such persons are referred to in this chapter as 'legal services providers'.

28.06 **Current legislation relating to consumers** The following legislation may be relevant where an individual consumer purchases legal services:

- the Consumer Rights Act 2015 (see 28.22)—both Part 1 (deemed terms) see (28.29) and Part 2 (unfair terms) (see 28.40);
- the Provision of Services Regulations 2009[3] (see 28.45);
- the Alternative Dispute Resolution for Consumer Disputes (Competent Authorities and Information) Regulations 2015[4] (see 28.53);
- the Consumer Contracts (Information, Cancellation and Additional Charges) Regulations 2013[5] (see 28.58); and
- the Consumer Protection from Unfair Trading Regulations 2008,[6] as amended by the Consumer Protection (Amendment) Regulations 2014[7] (see 28.101).

[3] SI 2009/2999.
[4] SI 2015/542.
[5] SI 2013/3134. These Regulations give domestic effect to Directive 2011/83/EU of the European Parliament and of the Council of 25 October 2011 on consumer rights, OJ L 304/64, 22 November 2011 (the Consumer Rights Directive).
[6] SI 2008/1277. These Regulations implement Directive 2005/29/EC of the European Parliament and of the Council of 11 May 2005 concerning unfair business-to-consumer commercial practices in the internal market, OJ L 149/22, 11 June 2005 (the Unfair Commercial Practices Directive).
[7] SI 2014/870.

In addition, contracts of retainer may, in some circumstances, give rise to consumer credit agreements—but this would give rise to issues that are beyond the scope of this book.

Present-day legislation listed according to the protections afforded to consumers The legislation referred to above gives rise to an interlocking series of rights and protections. These are described in detail below, but, in essence, legislation gives consumers the following protections. **28.07**

- Legal services providers (including, for the avoidance of doubt, unauthorised legal services providers[8]) are required to supply services with reasonable care and skill.[9]
- Certain representations made by the legal services provider (likely to include the giving of estimates) will become terms of the contract of retainer (see 28.30–28.33) and may be revised only with the client's consent.[10]
- Where the price has not been agreed, legal services providers must provide a service for a reasonable price (see 28.37).[11]
- Where a specific time of delivery has not been agreed, legal services providers must carry out the service within a reasonable time (see 28.38–28.39).[12]
- Legal services providers must deal fairly with consumers when entering into agreements or when seeking to impose terms through the giving of notices (see 28.40–28.44).[13]
- Legal services providers must give certain information about their businesses (see 28.45–28.52).[14]
- In certain circumstances, legal services providers must provide information regarding alternative dispute resolution (ADR) (see 28.53–28.57).[15]
- Legal services providers must give certain stipulated pre-contract information (see 28.67–28.88).[16]
- In some circumstances, consumers ought to be given a right to cancel (see 28.89–28.96).[17]
- Legal services providers must not make use of commercial practices that are misleading, or which are aggressive or banned (see 28.101–28.133).[18]

---

[8] The CMA takes the view that an unauthorised legal services provider is likely to be held to the same standard of reasonable care and skill as an authorised legal services provider, particularly if they hold themselves out as providing a service of comparable quality to an authorised provider or where they employ, or claim to employ, qualified legal advisers: see CMA, *Legal Services Market Study: Final Report* (London: HMSO, 2016), at Appx E, para 50.

[9] See Consumer Rights Act 2015, s 49. The test of assessing reasonable care and skill is 'what the reasonably competent [provider] would do having regard to the standard normally adopted in his profession': see *Midland Bank Trust Co Ltd v Hett, Stubb & Kemp* [1979] Ch 384, at 403.

[10] See Consumer Rights Act 2015, s 50.

[11] See Consumer Rights Act 2015, s 51.

[12] See Consumer Rights Act 2015, s 52.

[13] Consumer Rights Act 2015, Pt 2. In addition, traders cannot unilaterally change the service as they have described it in the information they have given under the Contracts (Information, Cancellation and Additional Charges) Regulations 2013 (SI 2013/3134) or otherwise where the consumer has relied on that information: see Consumer Rights Act 2015, Pt 1, s 50.

[14] The Provision of Services Regulations 2009 (SI 2009/2999).

[15] The ADR for Consumer Disputes (Competent Authorities and Information) Regulations 2015 (SI 2015/542).

[16] The Contracts (Information, Cancellation and Additional Charges) Regulations 2013 (SI 2013/3134).

[17] *Ibid.*

[18] Consumer Protection from Unfair Commercial Practices Regulations 2008 (SI 2008/1277).

28.08 **Remedies afforded to consumers by present-day legislation** Where a legal services provider fails to comply with consumer protection legislation, the consumer may, in some instances, be entitled to a statutory remedy. The type of remedy will depend on the type of breach. The remedies include: the right to unwind the contract of retainer (see 28.137–28.139); the right to a discount (see 28.140–28.142); the right to a price reduction (see 28.146–28.148); and—whilst unlikely to have any bearing on the law of costs—the right to damages or repeat performance (see 28.145). Many of these provisions operate by implying terms into the consumer client's contract of retainer.

28.09 **Recently revoked (or partially revoked) legislation** In so far as consumers are concerned, the following legislation used to apply, but has now been revoked and therefore will apply only to older contracts of retainer:

- the Unfair Terms in Consumer Contracts Regulations 1999[19] (see 28.149–28.155);
- the Supply of Goods and Services Act 1982 (see 28.156–28.158); and
- the Unfair Contract Terms Act 1977 (see 28.159–28.162).

Table 28.1 may help in determining whether any of these older regulations apply. It should be noted that the last two items on this list will, in general, continue to apply where the client is not a consumer (see 28.11 and 28.215).

28.10 **Older legislation** Regulations that are even older may be relevant if the retainer in question was made some years ago:

- the Cancellation of Contracts Made in a Consumer's Home or Place of Work etc Regulations 2008[20] (see 28.163–28.200);
- the Consumer Protection (Distance Selling) Regulations 2000[21] (as amended) (see 28.201–28.212);
- the Electronic Commerce (EC Directive) Regulations 2002[22] (see 28.213); and
- the Consumer Protection (Cancellation of Contracts Concluded Away from Business Premises) Regulations 1987[23] (as amended) (see 28.214).

Again, Table 28.1 may assist in determining which regulations apply.

[19] SI 1999/2083. These Regulations gave domestic effect to Council Directive 93/13/EEC of 5 April 1993 on unfair terms in consumer contracts, OJ L 95/29, 21 April 1993 (the Unfair Terms in Consumer Contracts Directive).

[20] SI 2008/1816. These Regulations gave domestic effect to the now-revoked Council Directive 85/577/EEC of 20 December 1985 to protect the consumer in respect of contracts negotiated away from business premises, OJ L 372/31, 31 December 1985 (the Doorstep Selling Directive).

[21] SI 2000/2334. These Regulations gave domestic effect to the now-revoked Directive 97/7/EC of the European Parliament and of the Council of 20 May 1997 on the protection of consumers in respect of distance contracts, OJ L 144/19, 4 June 1997.

[22] SI 2002/2013. As their name suggests, these Regulations incorporate Directive 2000/31/EC of the European Parliament and of the Council of 8 June 2000 on certain legal aspects of information society services, in particular electronic commerce, in the Internal Market, OJ L 178/1, 17 July 2000 (the E-Commerce Directive) into UK law.

[23] SI 1987/2117. These Regulations gave domestic effect to the now-revoked Doorstep Selling Directive (Directive 85/577/EEC).

Table 28.1 An overview of consumer legislation

Issue in question	Consumer: present day	Business: present day	Consumer: pre-1 October 2015	Consumer: pre-13 June 2014	Consumer: older
Which informational regulations need to be considered for the purposes of making a new contract of retainer?	Consumer Contracts (Information, Cancellation and Additional Charges) Regulations 2013, SI 2013/3134 Provision of Services Regulations 2009, SI 2009/2999 Alternative Dispute Resolution for Consumer Disputes (Competent Authorities and Information) Regulations 2015, SI 2015/542	Provision of Services Regulations 2009, SI 2009/2999	Consumer Contracts (Information, Cancellation and Additional Charges) Regulations 2013, SI 2013/3134 Provision of Services Regulations 2009, SI 2009/2999	Consumer Protection (Distance Selling) Regulations 2000, SI 2000/2334 Cancellation of Contracts Made in a Consumer's Home or Place of Work etc Regulations 2008, SI 2008/1816	Electronic Commerce (EC Directive) Regulations 2002, SI 2002/2013 Consumer Protection (Cancellation of Contracts Concluded Away from Business Premises) Regulations 1987, SI 1987/2117
Does the issue concern notices of the right to cancel (or a similar such right)?	Consumer Contracts (Information, Cancellation and Additional Charges) Regulations 2013, SI 2013/3134	n/a	Consumer Contracts (Information, Cancellation and Additional Charges) Regulations 2013, SI 2013/3134	Consumer Protection (Distance Selling) Regulations 2000, SI 2000/2334 Cancellation of Contracts Made in a Consumer's Home or Place of Work etc Regulations 2008, SI 2008/1816	Consumer Protection (Cancellation of Contracts Concluded Away from Business Premises) Regulations 1987, SI 1987/2117
Does the issue concern misleading or aggressive practices?	Consumer Protection from Unfair Commercial Practices Regulations 2008, SI 2008/1277	Business Protection from Misleading Marketing Regulations 2008, SI 2008/1276	Consumer Protection from Unfair Commercial Practices Regulations 2008, SI 2008/1277		

(continued)

Table 28.1 Continued

Issue in question	Consumer: present day	Business: present day	Consumer: pre-1 October 2015	Consumer: pre-13 June 2014	Consumer: older
Does the issue concern pre-contract counselling?	Consumer Contracts (Information, Cancellation and Additional Charges) Regulations 2013, SI 2013/3134	n/a	Consumer Contracts (Information, Cancellation and Additional Charges) Regulations 2013, SI 2013/3134	Consumer Protection (Distance Selling) Regulations 2000, SI 2000/2334 Cancellation of Contracts Made in a Consumer's Home or Place of Work etc Regulations 2008, SI 2008/1816	
Does the issue concern the duty to deal fairly with clients?	Consumer Rights Act 2015, Pt 2	Unfair Contract Terms Act 1977	Unfair Terms in Consumer Contracts Regulations 1999, SI 1999/2083 Unfair Contract Terms Act 1977		
Does the issue concern the giving of information about the legal services provider's business?	Provision of Services Regulations 2009, SI 2009/2999				
Does the issue concern the price that will be paid where no price has been agreed in advance?	Consumer Rights Act 2015, s 51	Supply of Goods and Services Act 1982, s 15			
Does the issue concern the time that the lawyer may take to perform the services?	Consumer Rights Act 2015, s 52	Supply of Goods and Services Act 1982, s 14			

Baseline consumer protection regulation for businesses

Persons who are seeking advice or assistance for their trade, business or profession are not consumers for the purposes of consumer protection legislation and therefore do not have the statutory protections afforded by that legislation. There is, however, a similar (albeit less extensive) body of legislation that applies to business-to-business transactions. **28.11**

Relevant current legislation relating to businesses The following legislation may be relevant where a business purchases legal services: **28.12**

- the Supply of Goods and Services Act 1982 (see 28.156–28.158);
- the Unfair Contract Terms Act 1977 (see 28.159–28.162);
- the Provision of Services Regulations 2009[24] (see 28.45–28.52); and
- the Business Protection from Misleading Marketing Regulations 2008[25] (see 28.216).

Present-day legislation listed according to the protections afforded to businesses The effect of this legislation may be summarised in the following way (only some of which points are relevant to the law of costs). **28.13**

- Legal services providers must provide certain information about their business (see 28.45–28.52).[26]
- Legal services providers must not advertise through the use of false statements of fact, concealment of important facts or by creating a false impression (see 28.216).[27]
- Legal services providers must carry out their services with reasonable care and skill, and within a reasonable time. If no price has been fixed in advance, their fees must be reasonable (see 28.156).[28]
- Certain restrictions are imposed on the types of terms that may be used in business-to-business contracts (see 28.159–28.162).[29]

Remedies afforded to businesses These are briefly addressed at 28.217–28.218. **28.14**

Identifying the applicable provisions (both consumers and businesses)

Table 28.1 may assist in deciding which provisions apply. The date on which the contract was concluded is usually the relevant starting point. **28.15**

General Consumer Protection Legislation (Present Day)

Where a legal services provider makes a contract of retainer with a consumer, that contract will be subject to consumer protection legislation. The applicable provisions will depend on the time, place and method by which the contract of retainer was made (see Table 28.1). **28.16**

The EU legislative background

Nearly all of the provisions referred to in this chapter owe their existence to the European Union (EU). This is not surprising, because the treaty that founded the EU specifically **28.17**

[24] SI 2009/2999.
[25] SI 2008/1276.
[26] See the Provision of Services Regulations 2009 (SI 2009/2999).
[27] The Business Protection from Misleading Marketing Regulations 2008 (SI 2008/1276).
[28] See the Supply of Goods and Services 1982.
[29] See the Unfair Contract Terms Act 1977.

stipulated that one of the EU's purposes was to contribute to protecting the economic interests of consumers.[30] Put otherwise, the need to protect the interests of consumers is a cardinal purpose of the *acquis* of the EU.

EU directives and regulations

28.18 The principal means by which the EU discharges its duties to protect consumers is by adopting directives and, less commonly, regulations.[31] Directives require member states to set and enforce certain standards, leaving it to the states to implement the directives in domestic law,[32] meaning that individual consumers do not have any directly enforceable rights arising out of directives; regulations, meanwhile, are directly binding in their entirety and give rise to directly enforceable rights.[33] The way in which the UK gives effect to directives is through primary and secondary legislation: primary legislation usually creates the legislative framework[34] and secondary legislation puts flesh on the bones.[35]

Brexit

28.19 It is not likely that, in the absence of specific legislation to the contrary, the UK's withdrawal from the EU (commonly known as Brexit) will have any real bearing on the matters set out in this chapter. This is because the UK government has said that when the European Communities Act 1972 is repealed, the *acquis communautaire*—that is, the body of existing EU law—will be converted into domestic law.[36]

Harmonisation and 'gold-plating'

28.20 Consumer protection directives are generally 'minimum harmonisation directives', which means that they tend to set minimum standards that must be met.[37] 'Maximum harmonisation directives' exist too,[38] but are not relevant for present purposes.

28.21 Other than where a maximum harmonisation directive applies, the measures adopted by the EU do not prevent member states from introducing more stringent protective measures (provided that such measures are compatible with the EU treaties and also provided that the European Commission has been notified).[39] This is often referred to as 'gold-plating'.

---

[30] See Treaty on the Functioning of the European Union (TFEU), Art 169.1.

[31] TFEU, Art 288.

[32] See TFEU, Art 288.

[33] TFEU, Art 288.

[34] The Cancellation of Contracts Made in a Consumer's Home or Place of Work etc Regulations 2008 (SI 2008/1816) go further than that, in that they deal with certain issues highlighted by a 2002 campaign initiated by Citizens Advice. The Doorstep Selling Regulations are therefore specific to the UK.

[35] This is not always the case, however: see, eg, the Consumer Protection Act 1987, Pt I, ss 1–9.

[36] See Prime Minister's Office, 'The Government's Negotiating Objectives for Exiting the EU: PM Speech', 17 January 2017, available online at https://www.gov.uk/government/speeches/the-governments-negotiating-objectives-for-exiting-the-eu-pm-speech

[37] The Consumer Protection (Cancellation of Contracts Concluded Away from Business Premises) Regulations 1987 (SI 1987/2117) (as amended), for example, came into being to give domestic effect to the Doorstep Selling Directive (Directive 85/577/EEC). This was achieved under the *vires* of European Communities Act 1972, s 2(2), which makes general provision for regulations to be made to implement any EC obligation of the UK.

[38] One of which is the Unfair Commercial Practices Directive (Directive 2005/29/EC), which gave rise to the Unfair Trading Regulations 2008 (SI 2008/1277).

[39] See TFEU, Art 169.4. The Cancellation of Contracts Made in a Consumer's Home or Place of Work etc Regulations 2008 (SI 2008/1816), for example, deal with certain issues highlighted by a 2002 campaign initiated by Citizens Advice. They are therefore specific to the UK and they go further than is provided for in the relevant directive.

Both primary[40] and secondary[41] legislation have been used to gold-plate EU legislation. It is arguable that the Cancellation of Contracts Made in a Consumer's Home or Place of Work etc Regulations 2008[42] are an example of this.[43]

The Consumer Rights Act 2015 (in general)

Brief overview

In so far as it is relevant, the Consumer Rights Act 2015 creates a framework that consolidates and enhances consumer rights, covering contracts for services and the law relating to unfair terms in consumer contracts. It is in three Parts, but only the first two are relevant to the law of costs: **28.22**

- Part 1 covers legislation regarding deemed terms (see 28.29–28.39); and
- Part 2 covers legislation regarding unfair terms (see 28.40–28.44).

Legislative history and background

Legislative history and consequential amendments The Consumer Rights Act 2015, which received royal assent on 26 March 2015 and came into force on 1 October 2015, was a consolidating Act that was made with the intention of simplifying the law.[44] As part of the consolidation, many statutory provisions familiar to practitioners either disappeared or ceased to apply to consumers. In particular, the Act replaced the Unfair Terms in Consumer Contracts Regulations 1999,[45] the Unfair Contract Terms Act 1977 (but only in relation to individual consumers) and the Supply of Goods and Services Act 1982 (but, again, only in relation to consumers). **28.23**

Legislative background The Consumer Rights Act 2015 implemented part of the Consumer Rights Directive.[46] The Directive was passed in October 2011 and came into force in all EU member states in 2014, replacing Directive 85/577/EEC.[47] **28.24**

---

40 See, eg, Consumers, Estate Agents and Redress Act 2007, ss 59 and 62(3)(f), which allowed the 'gold-plate' aspects of the Cancellation of Contracts Made in a Consumer's Home or Place of Work etc Regulations 2008 (SI 2008/1816) to be made.

41 See, eg, the Cancellation of Contracts Made in a Consumer's Home or Place of Work etc Regulations 2008 (SI 2008/1816).

42 SI 2008/1816.

43 When the Doorstep Selling Directive (Directive 85/577/EEC) was initially given domestic effect in the form of the Consumer Protection (Cancellation of Contracts Concluded Away from Business Premises) Regulations 1987 (SI 1987/2117) (as amended), it related only to unsolicited visits. As a result of Citizens Advice's campaign, the protection afforded to consumers was extended in 2008 to include solicited visits, under the *vires* of Consumers, Estate Agents and Redress Act 2007, ss 59 and 62(3)(f). The policy underpinning that extension was explained thus by Baroness Vadera, Under-Secretary of State of the sponsoring department (Hansard, HL Deb, col GC80, 2 July 2008): 'The purpose of the proposed new regulations is to extend to solicited visits the cooling-off period and cancellation rights that currently apply to contracts made during unsolicited visits by traders; and to require that a notice of the right to cancel the contract be prominently and clearly displayed in the same document where the contract is completed wholly or partly in writing.' Hence this had nothing to do with EU directives.

44 Consumer-protection law began as judge-made law, which was then supplemented with domestic legislation, both primary and secondary. Those laws were then overlaid and changed by EU legislation. This led to complexity; indeed, there was general agreement across consumer groups that the law was fragmented, unclear and couched in legalistic language. See the Explanatory Memorandum to the Consumer Rights Act 2015, para 5.

45 SI 1999/2083.

46 Directive 2011/83/EU of the European Parliament and of the Council of 25 October 2011 on consumer rights, OJ L 304/64, 22 November 2011.

47 Council Directive 85/577/EEC of 20 December 1985 to protect the consumer in respect of contracts negotiated away from business premises, OJ L 372/31, 31 December 1985. This is why the Consumer

28.25 In August 2012, a consultation by the Department for Business Innovation and Skills (BIS) sought views on implementing the Consumer Rights Directive—in particular, highlighting those areas in which the UK had flexibility in the way the Directive might be applied.[48] A government response was published in August 2013, following which partial implementation was achieved by way of delegated legislation—largely, the Consumer Contracts (Information, Cancellation and Additional Charges) Regulations 2013[49] (see 28.58 and 28.61). The remainder of the Directive was given domestic implementation by the Consumer Rights Act 2015: as far as appropriate, that Act was made consistent with the Directive, 'with the intention of achieving overall a simple, coherent framework of consumer legislation'.[50]

Definitions of 'consumer' and 'trader'

28.26 'Consumer' includes any individual 'acting for purposes that are wholly or mainly outside that individual's trade, business, craft or profession'.[51] This is a slightly wider definition than the corresponding definition in previous legislation because it may encompass individuals who enter into contracts for a mixture of business and personal reasons. It should be noted that this definition is consistent with that used in other harmonisation legislation (see, for example, 28.66 and 28.107). It should also be noted that this definition is somewhat wider than that which existed under older legalisation (see 28.171).

28.27 A 'trader' is defined as a person acting for purposes relating to that person's trade, business, craft or profession, whether acting personally or through another person acting in the trader's name or on the trader's behalf.[52] Again, this definition is now consistent with that used in other harmonisation legislation. By analogy with older legislation (see 28.169 and 28.170), it is all but certain that this definition includes legal services providers.

No diminution of existing rights

28.28 Nothing in the Consumer Rights Act 2015 detracts from any enactment or rule of law that imposes a stricter duty on the legal services provider.[53] Furthermore, the provisions of that Act are subject to any other enactment that defines or restricts the rights, duties or liabilities arising in connection with any service.[54] Whilst there is no authority on the point, the effect of this is that it is likely that the Consumer Rights Act 2015 and the Solicitors Act 1974 operate in tandem in the context of contracts of retainer; in consequence, a consumer will enjoy the benefits of the protective elements of both.

Protection (Distance Selling) Regulations 2000 (SI 2000/2334) and the Cancellation of Contracts Made in a Consumer's Home or Place of Work etc Regulations 2008 (SI 2008/1816) were superseded by new regulations: see Consumer Contracts (Information, Cancellation and Additional Charges) Regulations 2013 (SI 2013/3134), reg 2.

[48] BIS, *UK Implementation of the Consumer Rights Directive 2011/83/EU* (London: HMSO, 2012).

[49] SI 2013/3134. These Regulations give domestic effect to the Directive 2011/83/EU of the European Parliament and of the Council of 25 October 2011 on consumer rights, OJ L 304/64, 22 November 2011 (the Consumer Rights Directive).

[50] See the Explanatory Memorandum to the Consumer Rights Act 2015, para 13.

[51] See Consumer Rights Act 2015, s 2(3).

[52] See Consumer Rights Act 2015, s 2(2).

[53] See Consumer Rights Act 2015, s 53(1).

[54] See Consumer Rights Act 2015, s 53(2).

The Consumer Rights Act 2015, Part 1 (deemed terms)

Part 1 of the Consumer Rights Act 2015 applies to all terms in contracts between a legal services provider and a consumer entered into on or after 1 October 2015, but does not apply to any notice provided or communicated before that date.[55] **28.29**

Information given by a legal services provider is to be binding

The relevant provisions are in s 50 of the Consumer Rights Act 2015, which reads as follows: **28.30**

> '**50 Information about the trader or service to be binding**
>
> (1) Every contract to supply a service is to be treated as including as a term of the contract anything that is said or written to the consumer, by or on behalf of the trader, about the trader or the service, if—
> (a) it is taken into account by the consumer when deciding to enter into the contract, or
> (b) it is taken into account by the consumer when making any decision about the service after entering into the contract.
>
> (2) Anything taken into account by the consumer as mentioned in subsection (1)(a) or (b) is subject to—
> (a) anything that qualified it and was said or written to the consumer by the trader on the same occasion, and
> (b) any change to it that has been expressly agreed between the consumer and the trader (before entering into the contract or later).
>
> (3) Without prejudice to subsection (1), any information provided by the trader in accordance with regulation 9, 10 or 13 of the Consumer Contracts (Information, Cancellation and Additional Charges) Regulations 2013 (SI 2013/3134) is to be treated as included as a term of the contract.
>
> (4) A change to any of the information mentioned in subsection (3), made before entering into the contract or later, is not effective unless expressly agreed between the consumer and the trader.
>
> (5) See section 54 for a consumer's rights if the trader is in breach of a term that this section requires to be treated as included in a contract.'

Thus anything that is communicated (orally or in writing) to a consumer client that they then take into account for the purposes of deciding whether to give instructions (or what those instructions should be) will be included as a term of the contract of retainer. In particular, the following will be included as terms: **28.31**

- anything that is said or written to the consumer, by or on behalf of the legal services provider, about the provider or the service it intends to supply, but only if it is taken into account by the consumer when either deciding to enter into the contract or making any decision about the service after entering into the contract;[56] and

[55] See Consumer Rights Act 2015 (Commencement No 3, Transitional Provisions, Savings and Consequential Amendments) Order 2015 (SI 2015/1630), art 6(1).

[56] See Consumer Rights Act 2015, s 50(1). This is subject to anything that qualified it and was said or written to the consumer by the legal service provider on the same occasion, and to any change to it that has been expressly agreed between the consumer and the legal service provider before entering into the contract or later: see Consumer Rights Act 2015, s 50(2).

- any information provided by the legal services provider in accordance with regs 9, 10 or 13 of the Consumer Contracts (Information, Cancellation and Additional Charges) Regulations 2013[57] (see 28.58–28.84).

28.32 These are new provisions (that is, there were no similar provisions in the Supply of Goods and Services Act 1982). Their purpose is to allay the likelihood of dispute about whether information given by a legal services provider (or any trader) has become an express term of the contract. They also provide for incorporation into the contract of the mandatory pre-contractual information that is required under the 2013 Regulations.

28.33 These provisions are potentially of considerable importance in so far as the law of costs is concerned. In particular:

- supposedly informal agreements as to the amount that a client will pay are, if relied upon, likely to be contractually binding and, whilst there is no authority on the point, one could easily envisage circumstances in which this could lead to a breach of the indemnity principle;
- quotations are, when relied upon by a consumer client, almost certain to be contractually binding; and
- it is easily arguable that unrevised and unqualified estimates, when relied upon by a consumer client, will also be contractually binding (see 38.58–38.59 for more detail).

28.34 **Revisions to information given** A change to any of the information mentioned pursuant to regs 9, 10 or 13 of the 2013 Regulations made before entering into the contract or later is not effective unless expressly agreed between the consumer and the legal services provider.[58] This may be relevant if, for example, that change is to the estimated fees that the legal services provider intends to charge.

28.35 **Remedies** If the trader does not conform to the requirements of this provision, the consumer is entitled to the new remedies under the right to repeat performance under Consumer Rights Act 2015, s 55, or the right to a price reduction under s 56 (see 28.145–28.148).[59]

28.36 **No contracting out** It should be noted that the rights that are conferred on consumers are not implied terms of the contract, but are to be treated as terms.[60] The legal services provider cannot contract out of those statutory rights and cannot limit its liability for breach of these clauses to less than the contract price.[61]

Reasonable price to be paid for a service

28.37 Section 51 of the Consumer Rights Act 2015 reads as follows:

> '**51 Reasonable price to be paid for a service**
>
> (1) This section applies to a contract to supply a service if—
>
> (a) the consumer has not paid a price or other consideration for the service,

---

57 SI 2013/3134. See Consumer Rights Act 2015, s 50(3).

58 See Consumer Rights Act 2015, s 50(4).

59 See Consumer Rights Act 2015, s 49(2).

60 It was hoped by legislators that setting out the obligations in this way would assist users of this legislation (who might not all be legal service providers, but may include consumers and those advising consumers within consumer-oriented organisations) and would explain the true nature of the thinking that the Act required: see Andrews, C, *Enforcement of Consumer Rights and Protections* (London: Butterworths Law, 2012), para 5.7.

61 See Consumer Rights Act 2015, s 57.

(b) the contract does not expressly fix a price or other consideration, and does not say how it is to be fixed, and
(c) anything that is to be treated under section 50 as included in the contract does not fix a price or other consideration either.

(2) In that case the contract is to be treated as including a term that the consumer must pay a reasonable price for the service, and no more.

(3) What is a reasonable price is a question of fact.'

Services to be performed within a reasonable time

Section 52 of the Consumer Rights Act 2015 reads as follows: **28.38**

'**52 Service to be performed within a reasonable time**

(1) This section applies to a contract to supply a service, if—
(a) the contract does not expressly fix the time for the service to be performed, and does not say how it is to be fixed, and
(b) information that is to be treated under section 50 as included in the contract does not fix the time either.

(2) In that case the contract is to be treated as including a term that the trader must perform the service within a reasonable time.

(3) What is a reasonable time is a question of fact.

(4) See section 54 for a consumer's rights if the trader is in breach of a term that this section requires to be treated as included in a contract.'

The CMA give the following as an example: **28.39**

'[W]here, for instance, a consumer consults a legal services provider to obtain an emergency injunction. If the terms of the contract do not express when the injunction will be applied for or obtained then it is implied by section 52, that it will be applied for or obtained within a reasonable time (for instance, same day or the next day).'[62]

Consumer Rights Act 2015, Part 2 (unfair terms)

Part 2 of the Consumer Rights Act 2015 applies to all terms (including negotiated terms) in contracts between legal services providers and consumers entered into on or after 1 October 2015.[63] It also applies to consumer notices provided or communicated on or after that date.[64] **28.40**

Test of unfairness

The Consumer Rights Act 2015 applies a test of fairness to terms in consumer contracts. A standard term is unfair 'if contrary to the requirements of good faith, it causes a significant imbalance in the parties' rights and obligations arising under the contract, to the **28.41**

[62] See CMA, *Legal Services Market Study: Final Report* (London: HMSO, 2016), Appx E, para 53.

[63] See Consumer Rights Act 2015 (Commencement No 3, Transitional Provisions, Savings and Consequential Amendments) Order 2015 (SI 2015/1630), art 6(4).

[64] *Ibid.* A consumer notice is defined by Consumer Rights Act 2015, s 61, as wording that relates to rights or obligations as between a trader and a consumer. It includes all announcements, whether or not in writing, and any other communication or purported communication. It does not matter whether the notice is expressed to apply to a consumer, as long as it is reasonable to assume it is intended to be seen or heard by a consumer. A consumer notice can, for instance, include online representations or material advertised in the trader's office.

detriment of the consumer'.[65] The test is applied by looking at the words and how they could be used. It takes into consideration the services that are being supplied, how a term relates to other terms in the contract and all of the circumstances at the time the term was agreed.[66] The Consumer Rights Act 2015 also applies substantially the same test of fairness to consumer notices.[67]

The effect of an unfair term or notice

28.42 An unfair term of a consumer contract[68] or unfair consumer notice[69] is not legally binding on the consumer, but the consumer is permitted to rely on the term or notice if they choose to do so.[70]

'Greylisted' items

28.43 The Consumer Rights Act 2015 provides an indicative and non-exhaustive list of consumer contract terms that may be regarded as unfair.[71] These are known as greylisted terms. All of these terms are subject to the fairness test, but are not necessarily unfair.[72]

28.44 In the context of the provision of legal services, examples of greylisted terms include:

- any term that has the object and effect of requiring the consumer who fails to fulfil their obligation under a contract of retainer (or, for that matter, any contract) to pay a disproportionately high sum in compensation,[73] which instance may (according to the CMA) occur where the terms of a legal services provider's contract specify a disproportionately high rate of interest that will be charged against all outstanding invoices;[74] or
- a term that has the object or effect of enabling the trader to terminate a contract for an indeterminate duration without reasonable notice except where there are good grounds for doing so,[75] which (again, according to the CMA) means that a term that allows a legal services provider to terminate a contract without notice is unfair because it has the potential of allowing the legal services provider to withdraw from the contract during an important stage of a case—just before trial, for instance.[76]

The Provision of Services Regulations 2009

28.45 As of 28 December 2009, the Provision of Services Regulations 2009[77] have been giving domestic effect to the Services in the Internal Market Directive.[78]

---

[65] See Consumer Rights Act 2015, s 62(4).
[66] See Consumer Rights Act 2015, s 62(5).
[67] See Consumer Rights Act 2015, s 62(6).
[68] See Consumer Rights Act 2015, s 62(1).
[69] See Consumer Rights Act 2015, s 62(2).
[70] See Consumer Rights Act 2015, s 62(3).
[71] See Consumer Rights Act 2015, s 63(1), which refers to Sch 2, Pt 1.
[72] See Consumer Rights Act 2015, s 63(2).
[73] See Consumer Rights Act 2015, Sch 2, Pt 1, para 6.
[74] See CMA, *Legal Services Market Study: Final Report* (London: HMSO, 2016), Appx E, para 59.
[75] See Consumer Rights Act 2015, Sch 2, Pt 1, para 8.
[76] See CMA, *Legal Services Market Study: Final Report* (London: HMSO, 2016), Appx E, para 59.
[77] SI 2009/2999.
[78] Directive 2006/123/EC of the European Parliament and of the Council of 12 December 2006 on services in the internal market, OJ/L 376/36, 27 December 2006.

Ambit (both consumer and business-to-business)

The 2009 Regulations apply to 'providers'[79] and 'recipients'[80] of a service,[81] rather than to 'traders' and 'consumers'. As such, they apply in business-to-business transactions as well as to business-to-consumer transactions. **28.46**

General information that must be given

In so far as legal services providers are concerned, the CMA say that the following information ought to be given.[82] **28.47**

- **The provider's name, and the provider's legal status and form** The provider's legal status and form includes whether it is a sole trader, partnership, limited liability partnership (LLP) or limited company. This information informs the recipient of the type of entity the legal services provider is and the extent of its liability.
- **The geographic address at which the provider is established** This will be, for instance, the registered office of a company.
- **Details by which the provider may be contacted rapidly and communicated with directly** This is particularly relevant for, for instance, criminal law practitioners, which may need to be accessible out of office hours to provide advice and assistance. Methods of communication includes email and by mobile telephone number.
- **If the provider is registered in a trade or other similar public register, the name of that register and the provider's registration number, or equivalent means of identification in that register** For instance, where the legal services provider is registered with the Solicitors Regulatory Authority (SRA), the SRA identity (ID) number must be provided.
- **Where the activity is subject to an authorisation scheme in the UK, the particulars of the relevant competent authority** For instance, details of the SRA must be provided if the legal services provider is authorised by the regulator to provide the service.
- **Where the activity is subject in another European Economic Area (EEA) state to a scheme equivalent to an authorisation scheme, the particulars to the authority involved or the single point of contact in that state** This is likely to apply where legal services providers have a presence in EEA states. In this scenario, legal services providers must provide details of an equivalent SRA scheme that is recognised in the EEA state and a single point of contact.
- **Where the provider exercises an activity that is subject to value added tax (VAT), the VAT identification number** This is self-explanatory.
- **Where the provider is carrying out a regulated profession, any professional body or similar institution with which the provider is registered, the professional title and**

---

[79] A provider is a person who provides or offers to provide a service and who is an EEA national or is established in an EEA state: see Provision of Services Regulations 2009 (SI 2009/2999), paras 4 and 5(4).

[80] 'Recipient' is defined as a person who is an EEA national or who is established in an EEA state, who, for professional or un-professional purposes, uses or wishes to use the service. This is a broad definition and includes consumers who are seeking legal advice in their personal capacity, as well as individuals seeking legal advice in their professional/business capacity: see Provision of Services Regulations 2009 (SI 2009/2999), paras 4 and 5(3).

[81] A services is an economic activity normally provided for remuneration and which is not a contract for employment. 'Remuneration' should be interpreted broadly, eg money or payment in kind (but excluding wages or salaries): see Provision of Services Regulations 2009 (SI 2009/2999), paras 4 and 2. A service can be business-to-business or business-to-individual activity. Legal services providers generally provide a service for remuneration and therefore fall within the scope of this definition.

[82] See CMA, *Legal Services Market Study: Final Report* (London: HMSO, 2016), Appx E, para 62.

the EEA state in which that time has been granted For instance, a solicitor might state: 'I am authorised to act as a solicitor in the UK by the Solicitors Regulatory Authority.'

- **The general terms and conditions, if any, used by the provider** This is self-explanatory.
- **The existence of contractual terms, if any, that are used concerning the competent courts or the law applicable to the contract** These terms must be provided if they exist. They may, for instance, include a statement that the English courts have jurisdiction or that the contract is governed by English law.
- **The price of a service where price is predetermined by the provider for a given type of service** The price of a service may, in certain circumstances, be predetermined by the legal services provider, such as where the legal services provider charges a fixed fee for a conveyance transaction or for a will-drafting service.
- **The main features of the service, if not already apparent from the context** This is likely to include a description of the key features of the service offered by the provider, such as commercial disputes, family matters (divorce, child arrangement orders, family mediation), personal injury matters, etc.
- **The contact details of the insurer or guarantor and the territorial coverage of the insurance or guarantee** If the legal services provider is subject to a requirement to hold professional liability insurance, information about that cover—in particular, the contact details of the insurer and the territorial coverage—must be provided.

Means by which information may be made available

28.48 Information can be made available in any or all of the following ways:

- at the legal services provider's own initiative;
- by being made easily accessible to the recipient at the place where the service is provided or the contract concluded (such as the legal services provider's offices);
- by being made easily accessible by the recipient electronically by means of an address they supply, for example by providing the exact address of where the information can be found on a publicly available website; and
- by being made easily accessible in any information documents that are supplied to the recipient in which a detailed description of the service is given.[83]

28.49 All of the above information must be given in a clear and unambiguous manner so that it can be easily understood to enable the recipient to make an informed decision; the information must also be given in good time before the contract is concluded or before the service is provided, when there is no written contract.[84] This is so that the recipient has enough time to consider the information and alter their decision about entering into a contract.

Contact details that must be given

28.50 The provider of a service must provide contact details to which complaints and requests for information may be sent. Those contact details must include: (a) a postal address, fax number or email address; (b) a telephone number; and (c) where the service provider has an official address, that address (which means the address that a person is

[83] See Provision of Services Regulations 2009 (SI 2009/2999), reg 8(2).
[84] See Provision of Services Regulations 2009 (SI 2009/2999), reg 11.

required by law to register, notify or maintain for the purpose of receiving notices or other communications).[85]

Requirement to declare non-judicial dispute resolution procedures

Where the legal services provider is subject to a code of conduct (or is a member of a professional body) that provides for recourse to a non-judicial dispute resolution procedure, the recipient must be told of this fact. This must be done in any information document in which the legal services provider gives a detailed description of the service, specifying how to access detailed information about that procedure.[86] **28.51**

Information that must be given upon request

Additionally, legal services providers must supply certain further information if the recipient asks for it[87]—although they may choose to make the information available in all cases if they prefer. In so far as legal services are concerned, the CMA says that such further information may include: **28.52**

- were the price is not predetermined by the legal services provider or an exact price cannot be given, the method for calculating the price so that it can be checked by the recipient, or a sufficiently detailed estimate, which will include the hourly chargeable rate and the likely number of hours the legal services provider will engage;
- where the legal services provider is authorised, a reference to the professional rules applicable in the UK (that is, the SRA Code of Conduct) and how these can be accessed, so that recipients can easily find the rules, for example on a website;
- information on any other activities carried out by the legal services provider that are directly linked to the service in question and on the measures taken to avoid conflicts of interest, which information should be included in any document in which the legal services provider gives a detailed description of its services; and
- any codes of conduct to which the legal services provider is subject and the websites from which these codes are available, specifying the language version available (for example, a legal services provider may be subject to the Paralegal Practitioners' Code of Conduct).[88]

The Alternative Dispute Resolution for Consumer Disputes (Competent Authorities and Information) Regulations 2015

The Alternative Dispute Resolution for Consumer Disputes (Competent Authorities and Information) Regulations 2015[89] implement many of the provisions of the Directive on Consumer Alternative Dispute Resolution (ADR).[90] In so far as is relevant, the Regulations came into force on 9 July 2015.[91] They are unlikely to have a direct bearing on issues relating to the law of costs, but they may be relevant to the formation of contracts of retainer **28.53**

[85] See Provision of Services Regulations 2009 (SI 2009/2999), reg 7.
[86] See Provision of Services Regulations 2009 (SI 2009/2999), reg 10.
[87] See Provision of Services Regulations 2009 (SI 2009/2999), reg 9.
[88] See CMA, *Legal Services Market Study: Final Report* (London: HMSO, 2016), Appx E, para 64.
[89] SI 2015/542.
[90] Directive 2013/11/EU of the European Parliament and of the Council of 21 May 2013 on alternative dispute resolution for consumer disputes, OJ L 165/63, 18 June 2013.
[91] See the Alternative Dispute Resolution for Consumer Disputes (Competent Authorities and Information) Regulations 2015 (SI 2015/542), reg 1.

and to dispute resolution between client and legal services provider; as such, they merit a brief mention. The Regulations do not apply to business-to-business transactions.

Definitions of 'consumer' and 'trader'

28.54 The definitions of 'consumer' and 'trader' under the 2015 Regulations are the same as those under the Consumer Rights Act 2015 (see 28.26–28.27).[92]

Consumer information by traders

28.55 The potentially relevant provisions are found in reg 19 of the 2015 Regulations:

> '**Consumer information by traders**
>
> 19 (1) Where a trader is obliged to use alternative dispute resolution services provided by an ADR entity under—
> (a) an enactment; or
> (b) the rules of a trade association to which the trader belongs, the trader must provide the name and website address of the ADR entity—
> (c) on the trader's website, if the trader has a website; and
> (d) in the general terms and conditions of sales or service contracts between the trader and a consumer.
>
> (2) Where a trader has exhausted its internal complaint handling procedure when considering a complaint from a consumer relating to a sales contract or a service contract, the trader must inform the consumer, on a durable medium—
> (a) that the trader cannot settle the complaint with the consumer;
> (b) of the name and website address of an ADR entity which would be competent to deal with the complaint, should the consumer wish to use alternative dispute resolution; and
> (c) whether the trader is obliged, or prepared, to submit to an alternative dispute resolution procedure operated by that ADR entity.
>
> (3) The trader information requirements set out in paragraphs (1) and (2) apply in addition to any information requirements applicable to traders regarding out-of-court redress procedures contained in any other enactment.'

28.56 Thus neither consumers nor legal services providers are required to use ADR unless the latter is required to do so under a statutory instrument, or if it is committed to using an ADR as a condition of membership of a trader or profession, or if ADR is a term of the contract between the provider and consumer. At the time of writing, only the last of these conditions is likely to be met in the context of the provision of legal services. That said, where a legal services provider has exhausted its internal complaints-handling process relating to a service provided, the legal services provider must inform the consumer, on a durable medium:

- that the legal services provider cannot settle the complaint with the consumer;
- of the name and address of a certified ADR entity that would be competent to deal with the complaint; and
- whether the legal services provider is prepared to submit to an ADR procedure operated by an ADR entity.

28.57 There is no reason to believe that a failure to comply with these provisions would lead to any difficulty in so far as the indemnity principle is concerned. Indeed, it is difficult to see

[92] See the Alternative Dispute Resolution for Consumer Disputes (Competent Authorities and Information) Regulations 2015 (SI 2015/542), reg 3.

how any such failure could give rise to any issues of recoverability of costs even between the legal services provider and the client. That said, whilst there is no authority on the point, if the client were able to show that they would have been attracted by ADR, any such failure could well be a relevant factor relating to the costs of a solicitor and client assessment.

The Consumer Contracts (Information, Cancellation and Additional Charges) Regulations 2013

Brief overview

On 13 June 2014, the Consumer Contracts (Information, Cancellation and Additional Charges) Regulations 2013[93] replaced the Consumer Protection (Distance Selling) Regulations 2000[94] (see 28.201) and the Cancellation of Contracts Made in a Consumer's Home or Place of Work etc Regulations 2008[95] (see 28.163). They impose requirements to provide information and to make available a prescribed means of cancelling the contract of retainer. The exact requirements depend on whether the contract or retainer is an 'on-premises contract' (see 28.69–28.73), an 'off-premises contract' (see 28.74–28.80) or a 'distance contract' (see 28.81–28.82). In addition, there are separate provisions that apply to distance contracts that are made solely by electrical communications methods (see 28.83–28.86). **28.58**

Background

The 2013 Regulations give partial domestic implementation to the Consumer Rights Directive[96] (see 28.25 for a description of the remainder of its implementation). **28.59**

To the extent that it is relevant to the 2013 Regulations, the Directive: **28.60**

- imposes an obligation that a trader must provide certain information (for example on the main characteristics of the services) before the consumer will be bound by a contract;
- creates certain cancellation rights (during so-called cooling-off periods) for contracts concluded at a distance or off-premises; and
- introduces various measures aimed at protecting consumers from hidden charges once they have entered into a contract.

Part of the Consumer Rights Directive was implemented as the Consumer Rights (Payment Surcharges) Regulations 2012;[97] much of the remainder was implemented with effect from 13 June 2014 as the Consumer Contracts (Information, Cancellation and Additional Charges) Regulations 2013.[98] The last part was implemented by the Consumer Rights Act 2015 (see 28.25). **28.61**

Vires

The 2013 Regulations were made in exercise of the powers conferred on the Secretary of State by s 2(2) of the European Communities Act 1972.[99] **28.62**

---

93 SI 2013/3134.

94 SI 2000/2334.

95 SI 2008/1816.

96 Directive 2011/83/EU of the European Parliament and of the Council of 25 October 2011 on consumer rights, OJ L 304/64, 22 November 2011.

97 SI 2012/3110.

98 SI 2013/3134.

99 See the introductory paragraph to the Consumer Contracts (Information, Cancellation and Additional Charges) Regulations 2013 (SI 2013/3134).

Ambit

28.63 The 2013 Regulations apply to contracts between a 'consumer' and a 'trader' (see 28.26–28.27).[100]

28.64 The 2013 Regulations provide that they will apply to contracts entered into on or after 13 June 2014;[101] for contracts made from that date onwards, neither the Consumer Protection (Distance Selling) Regulations 2000[102] nor the Cancellation of Contracts Made in a Consumer's Home or Place of Work etc Regulations 2008[103] will apply.[104] Whilst there are several classes of contract to which the 2013 Regulations do not apply,[105] none of those excluded classes encompass contracts of retainer.

28.65 **Terms used** The 2013 Regulations refer to three types of consumer contract: distance contracts;[106] on-premises contracts; and off-premises contracts.[107] The requirements relating to distance contracts are likely to apply where legal services providers send contractual documents to consumers by post and consumers return signed copies by the same means, which is common practice with conveyancing, wills and probate,[108] as well as in many personal injury claims.

28.66 In addition, the following terms are used in the 2013 Regulations in such a way as to define their ambit or operation.

- **'Durable medium'** This means paper or email, or any other medium that: (a) allows information to be addressed personally to the recipient; (b) enables the recipient to store the information in a way that is accessible for future reference for a period that is long enough for the purposes of the information; and (c) allows the unchanged reproduction of the information stored.[109]

---

[100] See Consumer Contracts (Information, Cancellation and Additional Charges) Regulations 2013 (SI 2013/3134), reg 4.

[101] See Consumer Contracts (Information, Cancellation and Additional Charges) Regulations 2013 (SI 2013/3134), reg 1(2).

[102] SI 2000/2334.

[103] SI 2008/1816.

[104] See Consumer Contracts (Information, Cancellation and Additional Charges) Regulations 2013 (SI 2013/3134), reg 2.

[105] See Consumer Contracts (Information, Cancellation and Additional Charges) Regulations 2013 (SI 2013/3134), reg 6.

[106] 'Distance contract' means a contract concluded between a trader and a consumer under an organised distance sales or service-provision scheme without the simultaneous physical presence of the trader and the consumer, with the exclusive use of one or more means of distance communication up to and including the time at which the contract is concluded: see Consumer Contracts (Information, Cancellation and Additional Charges) Regulations 2013 (SI 2013/3134), reg 5.

[107] The difference between an 'off-premises contract' and an 'on-premises contract' is addressed by Consumer Contracts (Information, Cancellation and Additional Charges) Regulations 2013 (SI 2013/3134), reg 5, which reads as follows: ' "[O]ff-premises contract" means a contract between a trader and a consumer which is any of these—(a) a contract concluded in the simultaneous physical presence of the trader and the consumer, in a place which is not the business premises of the trader; (b) a contract for which an offer was made by the consumer in the simultaneous physical presence of the trader and the consumer, in a place which is not the business premises of the trader; (c) a contract concluded on the business premises of the trader or through any means of distance communication immediately after the consumer was personally and individually addressed in a place which is not the business premises of the trader in the simultaneous physical presence of the trader and the consumer; (d) a contract concluded during an excursion organised by the trader with the aim or effect of promoting and selling goods or services to the consumer; "on-premises contract" means a contract between a trader and a consumer which is neither a distance contract nor an off-premises contract.'

[108] See CMA, *Legal Services Market Study: Final Report* (London: HMSO, 2016), Appx E, para 36.

[109] *Ibid.*

- **'Service contract'** This means a contract, other than a sales contract, under which a trader supplies, or agrees to supply, a service to a consumer and the consumer pays, or agrees to pay, the price.[110]

Pre-contract information requirements under the Consumer Contracts (Information, Cancellation and Additional Charges) Regulations 2013

The information requirements of the 2013 Regulations apply to all types of contract (specifically, to distance contracts, on-premises contracts and off-premises contracts).[111] They provide that information is made available to the client. For the avoidance of doubt, this information is in addition to the information that must be given pursuant to the Provision of Services Regulations 2009[112] (see 28.45–28.47), although there may be a certain amount of overlap. Information is made available only to the extent that the consumer can reasonably be expected to know how to access it.[113] **28.67**

The information that needs to be given will depend on the nature of the contract or retainer, the types being: **28.68**

- on-premises contracts, such as contracts of retainer made at a solicitors' offices (see 28.69–28.73);
- off-premises contracts, such as contracts of retainer made during a visit to a client's home (see 28.74–28.80);
- distance contracts not made by electronic means, such as contracts of retainer made by phone or post (see 28.81–28.82 and 28.86); and
- contracts made by electronic means, such as contracts of retainer made via a website (see 28.83–28.85).

On-premises contracts of retainer On-premises contracts of retainer are contracts that are neither off-premises contracts nor distance contracts;[114] rather, they are contracts that are entered into between a legal services provider and consumer at the legal services provider's place of business. This embraces a broad range of contracts: according to the CMA, it is a category that includes the majority of contracts of retainer concluded between legal services providers and consumers.[115] **28.69**

Regulatory provisions relating to on-premises contracts of retainer In so far as they are relevant, the following provisions apply to on-premises contracts: **28.70**

> '9 (1) Before the consumer is bound by an on-premises contract, the trader must give or make available to the consumer the information described in Schedule 1 in a clear and comprehensible manner, if that information is not already apparent from the context.
>
> [...]

[110] *Ibid.*

[111] See Consumer Contracts (Information, Cancellation and Additional Charges) Regulations 2013 (SI 2013/3134), reg 7. Part 2 does not apply to off-premises contracts under which the payment to be made by the consumer is not more than £42: see reg 7(4).

[112] SI 2009/2999.

[113] See Consumer Contracts (Information, Cancellation and Additional Charges) Regulations 2013 (SI 2013/3134), reg 8.

[114] See Consumer Contracts (Information, Cancellation and Additional Charges) Regulations 2013 (SI 2013/3134), reg 5.

[115] See CMA, *Legal Services Market Study: Final Report* (London: HMSO, 2016), Appx E, para 43.

(3) Any information that the trader gives the consumer as required by this regulation is to be treated as included as a term of the contract.

(4) A change to any of that information, made before entering into the contract or later, is not effective unless expressly agreed between the consumer and the trader.'[116]

28.71 Thus, before making on-premises contracts of retainer, unless it is already apparent legal services providers must provide consumers with the information set out in Sch 1 to the 2013 Regulations—that is, a reference to the following provisions (which are reproduced only in so far as they are relevant to contracts of retainer):

'The information referred to in regulation 9(1) is—
(a) the main characteristics of the ... services, to the extent appropriate to the medium of communication and to the ... services;
(b) the identity of the trader (such as the trader's trading name), the geographical address at which the trader is established and the trader's telephone number;
(c) the total price of the ... services inclusive of taxes, or where the nature of the goods or services is such that the price cannot reasonably be calculated in advance, the manner in which the price is to be calculated;
[...]
(e) where applicable, the arrangements for payment, ... performance, and the time by which the trader undertakes to ... perform the service;
(f) where applicable, the trader's complaint handling policy;
[...]
(i) the duration of the contract, where applicable, or, if the contract is of indeterminate duration or is to be extended automatically, the conditions for terminating the contract; ...'

28.72 *The CMA's guidance regarding on-premises contracts of retainer* Having regard to the information specified in Sch 1 (see 28.71), the CMA advises that legal services providers should provide the following pre-contract information to consumers and that they should do so before they are bound by any on-premises contract of retainer.[117]

- **The main characteristics of the service** Consumers should be given sufficient information about the service to enable them to make informed decisions. This is likely to include a description of the legal service, for instance 'advice and assistance in relation to the purchase of 123 Avenue Road'.
- **The identity of the trader, including geographic address and telephone number** In some instances, the geographic address may not be obvious—particularly where the legal services provider has multiple premises. Consumers should be provided with this information, including a contact telephone number.
- **The total price of the service, including taxes** This is likely to be straightforward where a solicitor is charging a fixed fee (such as in conveyancing transaction). However, where a fixed fee cannot be calculated, the consumer should be provided with the best possible information about the overall cost of their matter (such as an hourly rate plus the number of hours that are likely to be engaged). If there are likely to be any disbursements (such as court fees, land registry fees), then, where possible, these should be factored into the price. It could be material information, under the 2013 Regulations, for the provider

[116] Consumer Contracts (Information, Cancellation and Additional Charges) Regulations 2013 (SI 2013/3134), reg 9.

[117] See CMA, *Legal Services Market Study: Final Report* (London: HMSO, 2016), Appx E, paras 45 and 46.

to set out some typical estimates of how much the work is likely to cost, based on the different sorts of likely scenarios.

- **Arrangements for payment, delivery and performance, and the time that the trader will take to perform the service** This may include setting out what steps the legal services provider will take, estimated timescales and how frequently it will get in contact, as well as how payment can be received.
- **The length of the contract if fixed or, if the contract is of indeterminate duration or will be automatically extended, the conditions for terminating that contract** Most contracts for legal services providers are for an indeterminate period. Consumers should therefore be provided with information on how they can cancel their contract.
- **Where applicable, the legal services provider's complaints-handling policy** Where applicable, information on the legal services provider's complaints-handling policy should also be provided. For instance, in the case of authorised legal services providers, details of the role of the Legal Ombudsman in resolving disputes and where further information can be obtained in this respect should be provided to consumers.

Deemed terms relating to on-premises contracts of retainer Any of the above information **28.73** that a legal services provider gives the consumer is treated as included as a term of the contract of retainer[118] (see 28.30–28.33).[119]

Off-premises contracts of retainer There are several types of off-premises contract, the **28.74** following two of which are (according to the CMA[120]) most likely to be relevant to the provision of legal services:

- a contract concluded in the simultaneous physical presence of the legal services provider and the consumer, in a place that is not the business premises of the legal services provider;[121] and
- a contract concluded on the business premises of the legal services provider or through any means of distance communication immediately after the consumer was personally and individually addressed in a place that is not the business premises of the legal services provider in the simultaneous physical presence of the legal services provider and the consumer.[122]

There are two other types of contract that fall within the definition of off-premises **28.75** contracts:

- a contract for which an offer was made by the consumer in the simultaneous physical presence of the trader and the consumer, in a place that is not the business premises of the trader; and

[118] Consumer Contracts (Information, Cancellation and Additional Charges) Regulations 2013 (SI 2013/3134), reg 9(3).

[119] Consumer Rights Act 2015, s 50, also has this effect.

[120] See CMA, *Legal Services Market Study: Final Report* (London: HMSO, 2016), Appx E, para 37.

[121] These situations may occur where, for instance, a legal services provider engages in door-to-door sales during which its representative enters into a contract of retainer at a consumer's home. It could also include a situation in which the representative of a legal services provider is invited to a consumer's home to take instructions and, as part of that process, a contract of retainer is concluded.

[122] These situations may occur where, for instance, a legal services provider supplies information to a consumer at their home, but the consumer does not immediately enter into a contract of retainer and only later signs it at the legal services provider's offices (or, alternatively, signs and returns the contract by post).

- a contract concluded during an excursion organised by the trader with the aim or effect of promoting and selling goods or services to the consumer.

According to the CMA, these types of off-premises contract are unlikely to be encountered in a legal context.[123] This is no doubt right, but it remains the case that they will be encountered from time to time and, as such, they are briefly addressed.

28.76 *Regulatory provisions that apply to off-premises contracts of retainer* In so far as they are relevant to contracts of retainer, the following provisions apply to off-premises contracts:

> '10 (1) Before the consumer is bound by an off-premises contract, the trader—
> (a) must give the consumer the information listed in Schedule 2[[124]] in a clear and comprehensible manner, and
> (b) if a right to cancel exists, must give the consumer a cancellation form as set out in Part B of Schedule 3.
>
> (2) The information and any cancellation form must be given on paper or, if the consumer agrees, on another durable medium and must be legible.
>
> (3) The information referred to in paragraphs (l), (m) and (n) of Schedule 2 may be provided by means of the model instructions on cancellation set out in part A of Schedule 3; and a trader who has supplied those instructions to the consumer, correctly filled in, is to be treated as having complied with paragraph (1) in respect of those paragraphs.
>
> (4) If the trader has not complied with paragraph (1) in respect of paragraph (g), (h) or (m) of Schedule 2, the consumer is not to bear the charges or costs referred to in those paragraphs.

[123] See CMA, *Legal Services Market Study: Final Report* (London: HMSO, 2016), Appx E, fn 19.

[124] Consumer Contracts (Information, Cancellation and Additional Charges) Regulations 2013 (SI 2013/3134), Sch 2, provides as follows: 'The information referred to in regulations 10(1) and 13(1) is (subject to the note at the end of this Schedule)—(a) the main characteristics of the ... services, to the extent appropriate to the medium of communication and to the ... services; (b) the identity of the trader (such as the trader's trading name); (c) the geographical address at which the trader is established and, where available, the trader's telephone number, fax number and e-mail address, to enable the consumer to contact the trader quickly and communicate efficiently; (d) where the trader is acting on behalf of another trader, the geographical address and identity of that other trader; (e) if different from the address provided in accordance with paragraph (c), the geographical address of the place of business of the trader, and, where the trader acts on behalf of another trader, the geographical address of the place of business of that other trader, where the consumer can address any complaints; (f) the total price of the ... services inclusive of taxes, or where the nature of the ... services is such that the price cannot reasonably be calculated in advance, the manner in which the price is to be calculated, ... (h) in the case of a contract of indeterminate duration ... the total costs per billing period or (where such contracts are charged at a fixed rate) the total monthly costs; ... (j) the arrangements for payment ... performance, and the time by which the trader undertakes to ... to perform the services; (k) where applicable, the trader's complaint handling policy; (l) where a right to cancel exists, the conditions, time limit and procedures for exercising that right in accordance with regulations 27 to 38; ... (n) that, if the consumer exercises the right to cancel after having made a request in accordance with regulation 36(1), the consumer is to be liable to pay the trader reasonable costs in accordance with regulation 36(4); (o) where under regulation ... 36 ... the right to cancel may be lost ... the circumstances under which the consumer loses the right to cancel; ... (r) the existence of relevant codes of conduct, as defined in regulation 5(3)(b) of the Consumer Protection from Unfair Trading Regulations 2008, and how copies of them can be obtained, where applicable; (s) the duration of the contract, where applicable, or, if the contract is of indeterminate duration or is to be extended automatically, the conditions for terminating the contract; (t) where applicable, the minimum duration of the consumer's obligations under the contract; ... (x) where applicable, the possibility of having recourse to an out-of-court complaint and redress mechanism, to which the trader is subject, and the methods for having access to it.'

(5) Any information that the trader gives the consumer as required by this regulation is to be treated as included as a term of the contract.

(6) A change to any of that information, made before entering into the contract or later, is not effective unless expressly agreed between the consumer and the trader . . .'[125]

The CMA's guidance regarding off-premises contracts of retainer Having regard to the information specified in Sch 2,[126] the CMA recommends that legal services providers provide the following types of pre-contract information to consumers (in addition to the information outlined for on-premises contracts at 28.71–28.72).[127] **28.77**

- **Legal services provider's number, fax number and email address** This is self-explanatory.
- **The identity and geographic address of any third-party trader if the legal services provider is acting on their behalf** This generally applies to conveyancing transactions in which legal services providers act for both the purchaser and the mortgage lender.
- **Address to which complaints should be sent** If the address for complaints is different from the business address, then this should be stipulated. This is likely to be relevant where the legal services provider has multiple offices.
- **In the case of a contract of indeterminate duration or a contract containing a subscription, the total costs per billing period or (where such contracts are charged at a fixed rate) the total monthly costs** If the consumer has an ongoing retainer for an indeterminate period, the legal services provider should give an estimate of costs for each stage.
- **Costs associated with using distance communication to conclude the contract** This is unlikely to be relevant to legal services contracts, which are likely to be concluded in writing in the majority of cases. However, if a consumer has the option of concluding a contract by telephone using a premium number, then this should be highlighted to the consumer.
- **Information on the conditions, time limits and procedures for exercising a right to cancel** The right to cancel applies only to distance and off-premises contracts. Information requirements include the time limit for cancellation (14 days from the date on which the contract was entered into) and the procedure for cancellation.
- **Notification that if the consumer asks the legal services provider to start the work within the cancellation period, the consumer will be responsible for paying the reasonable costs of the service if the contract is cancelled** The consumer loses the right to cancel the service contract if the service has been fully performed at their request and they acknowledge that they would lose their right to cancel once the contract was completed. This is likely to apply in urgent cases, such as in relation to an emergency injunction or a will, or to any work that the consumer wishes to commence immediately.
- **Notification if there are no cancellation rights for specific services or circumstances in which the consumer will lose those rights** This is likely to apply where the consumer asks the legal services provider to start the work within the cancellation period.
- **The existence of relevant codes of conduct and how copies of these can be obtained** In respect of authorised legal services providers, this is likely to be the SRA Handbook or the Bar Standards Board (BSB) Handbook for barristers, or any other codes to which

[125] Consumer Contracts (Information, Cancellation and Additional Charges) Regulations 2013 (SI 2013/3134), reg 10.

[126] See fn 124.

[127] See CMA, *Legal Services Market Study: Final Report* (London: HMSO, 2016), Appx E, para 41.

authorised legal services providers are subject. Legal services providers should inform consumers how they can access these codes (for example by supplying links to the appropriate website).

- **Where applicable, the existence and the conditions of deposits or other financial guarantees to be paid or provided by the consumer at the request of the trader** This includes money that a consumer is required to pay up front ('on account') to the legal services provider. This may apply in conveyance transactions in which money on account is needed to enable the conveyancer to undertake searches.
- **The possibility of recourse to an out-of-court complaint and redress mechanism to which the trader is subject and the methods for accessing it** In the case of authorised legal services providers, details of the Legal Ombudsman, which handles complaints against solicitors and barristers, should be provided to consumers.

28.78 The CMA say that this information ought to be given in a 'retainer letter' before the consumer is bound by the contract. The information must be given on paper or, *if the client agrees*, on another durable medium.[128] This would rarely present a problem because it would normally be sufficient to ask the client for permission during the off-premises attendance.

28.79 *Documentation relating to off-premises contracts* The legal services provider must provide a signed copy of the contract of retainer or other confirmation of the contract[129] and this must either be on paper or, if the client agrees, on another durable medium.[130] The copy or confirmation must include all of the information set out above (unless that information has already been provided),[131] and it must be provided within a reasonable time after the conclusion of the contract and before performance begins of any service supplied under the contract (see also 28.87–28.88).[132]

28.80 *Deemed terms relating to off-premises contracts* Any information that a legal services provider supplies pursuant to the requirements of an off-premises contract or the requirements of a distance contract is treated as being incorporated as a term of the contract (see also 28.30–28.33).[133]

28.81 **Distance contracts of retainer (in general)** In so far as they are relevant to contracts of retainer, the following provisions apply to distance contracts:

> '13 (1) Before the consumer is bound by a distance contract, the trader—
> (a) must give or make available to the consumer the information listed in Schedule 2 in a clear and comprehensible manner, and in a way appropriate to the means of distance communication used, and

---

[128] See Consumer Contracts (Information, Cancellation and Additional Charges) Regulations 2013 (SI 2013/3134), reg 10(2).

[129] See Consumer Contracts (Information, Cancellation and Additional Charges) Regulations 2013 (SI 2013/3134), reg 12(1).

[130] See Consumer Contracts (Information, Cancellation and Additional Charges) Regulations 2013 (SI 2013/3134), reg 12(3).

[131] See Consumer Contracts (Information, Cancellation and Additional Charges) Regulations 2013 (SI 2013/3134), reg 12(2).

[132] See Consumer Contracts (Information, Cancellation and Additional Charges) Regulations 2013 (SI 2013/3134), reg 12(4).

[133] Consumer Contracts (Information, Cancellation and Additional Charges) Regulations 2013 (SI 2013/3134), regs 10(5) and 13(6). Consumer Rights Act 2015, s 50, also has this effect.

(b) if a right to cancel exists, must give or make available to the consumer a cancellation form as set out in part B of Schedule 3.

(2) In so far as the information is provided on a durable medium, it must be legible.

(3) The information referred to in paragraphs (l), (m) and (n) of Schedule 2 may be provided by means of the model instructions on cancellation set out in part A of Schedule 3; and a trader who has supplied those instructions to the consumer, correctly filled in, is to be treated as having complied with paragraph (1) in respect of those paragraphs.

(4) Where a distance contract is concluded through a means of distance communication which allows limited space or time to display the information—

(a) the information listed in paragraphs (a), (b), (f), (g), (h), (l) and (s) of Schedule 2 must be provided on that means of communication in accordance with paragraphs (1) and (2), but

(b) the other information required by paragraph (1) may be provided in another appropriate way.

(5) If the trader has not complied with paragraph (1) in respect of paragraph (g), (h) or (m) of Schedule 2, the consumer is not to bear the charges or costs referred to in those paragraphs.

(6) Any information that the trader gives the consumer as required by this regulation is to be treated as included as a term of the contract.

(7) A change to any of that information, made before entering into the contract or later, is not effective unless expressly agreed between the consumer and the trader.'[134]

The requirements relating to distance contracts are similar to those relating to off-premises contracts, but, for the reasons set out below, they are marginally less exacting. The main differences are that: **28.82**

- the requirement to give information is such that it needs to be given in a way appropriate to the means of distance communication used;[135]
- the need to obtain the client's consent to provide the contract on a durable medium (as opposed to on paper) is not required;[136] and
- where there is limited space or time to give information, certain information[137] needs to be given by the primary means of distance communication, whereas other information may be given in a different way.[138]

[134] Consumer Contracts (Information, Cancellation and Additional Charges) Regulations 2013 (SI 2013/3134), reg 13.

[135] See Consumer Contracts (Information, Cancellation and Additional Charges) Regulations 2013 (SI 2013/3134), reg 13(1)(a).

[136] See Consumer Contracts (Information, Cancellation and Additional Charges) Regulations 2013 (SI 2013/3134), reg 13(2); cf reg 10(2).

[137] The information is listed in Sch 2, paras (a) (type of services), (b) (identity of trader), (f) (total price), (g) (price, but not applicable to retainers), (h) (price per billing period), (l) (details of right to cancel) and (s) (details of duration of contract and right to terminate).

[138] See Consumer Contracts (Information, Cancellation and Additional Charges) Regulations 2013 (SI 2013/3134), reg 13(4). That other information is listed in Sch 2, paras (c) (geographic location), (d) (identity of any other trader), (e) (address for complaints), (j) (arrangements for payment), (k) (complaint handling policy), (o) (circumstances in which right to cancel may be lost) and (r) (existence of Codes of Conduct). Paragraphs (l), (m) and (n) are dealt with by the 'model instructions' referred to at Consumer Contracts (Information, Cancellation and Additional Charges) Regulations 2013 (SI 2013/3134), reg 13(3).

28.83 **Distance contracts of retainer concluded by electronic means** If the contract is a distance contract made by electronic means, then (in so far as they are relevant to contracts of retainer) the following provisions will apply:

> '14 (1) This regulation applies where a distance contract is concluded by electronic means.
>
> (2) If the contract places the consumer under an obligation to pay, the trader must make the consumer aware in a clear and prominent manner, and directly before the consumer places the order, of the information listed in paragraphs (a), (f), (g), (h), (s) and (t) of Schedule 2.
>
> (3) The trader must ensure that the consumer, when placing the order, explicitly acknowledges that the order implies an obligation to pay.
>
> (4) If placing an order entails activating a button or a similar function, the trader must ensure that the button or similar function is labelled in an easily legible manner only with the words 'order with obligation to pay' or a corresponding unambiguous formulation indicating that placing the order entails an obligation to pay the trader.
>
> (5) If the trader has not complied with paragraphs (3) and (4), the consumer is not bound by the contract or order.
>
> (6) The trader must ensure that any trading website through which the contract is concluded indicates clearly and legibly, at the latest at the beginning of the ordering process ... which means of payment are accepted.'[139]

28.84 Thus, where the contract of retainer is a distance contract made by electronic means, then the relevant provisions are different from the provisions that govern other types of contract. In particular:

- whilst the trader needs to give much the same information as with other distance contracts,[140] the trader must ensure that the customer has explicitly acknowledged that, by placing the order (that is, giving instructions), an obligation to pay will be created; and
- if placing an order entails activating a button or similar function (such as through an e-signing service), the button must be clearly marked as giving rise to an obligation to pay.[141]

28.85 *The effect of non-compliance with provisions relating to contracts concluded by electronic means* A failure to comply with these provisions will result in the agreement being unenforceable against the client[142]—something that could cause difficulties in complying with the indemnity principle. This must be borne in mind if the contract of retainer is to be signed by certain proprietary electronic means because they may be interpreted as falling within the ambit of a mechanism that is a 'button or similar function'.

---

[139] Consumer Contracts (Information, Cancellation and Additional Charges) Regulations 2013 (SI 2013/3134), reg 14.

[140] See Consumer Contracts (Information, Cancellation and Additional Charges) Regulations 2013 (SI 2013/3134), reg 14(2). The differences are that precedence is given to the information listed in Sch 2, paras (a) (type of services), (f) (total price), (g) (price, but not applicable to retainers), (h) (price per billing period), (s) (details of duration of contract and right to terminate) and (t) (minimum duration of the contract).

[141] See Consumer Contracts (Information, Cancellation and Additional Charges) Regulations 2013 (SI 2013/3134), reg 14(3) and (4).

[142] See Consumer Contracts (Information, Cancellation and Additional Charges) Regulations 2013 (SI 2013/3134), reg 14(5).

Additional requirements relating to distance contracts made by telephone There are further requirements that apply where a distance contract is concluded by telephone: **28.86**

> '15 If the trader makes a telephone call to the consumer with a view to concluding a distance contract, the trader must, at the beginning of the conversation with the consumer, disclose—
> (a) the trader's identity,
> (b) where applicable, the identity of the person on whose behalf the trader makes the call, and
> (c) the commercial purpose of the call.'[143]

It is difficult to imagine circumstances in which a competent legal services provider would fail to comply with these (very basic) requirements.[144]

Confirmation of distance contracts Once a distance contract of retainer has been concluded (by whatever means), it will need to be confirmed. The relevant provisions are as follows: **28.87**

> '16 (1) In the case of a distance contract the trader must give the consumer confirmation of the contract on a durable medium.
>
> (2) The confirmation must include all the information referred to in Schedule 2 unless the trader has already provided that information to the consumer on a durable medium prior to the conclusion of the distance contract.
>
> [...]
>
> (4) The confirmation must be provided within a reasonable time after the conclusion of the contract, but in any event
>
> [...]
>
> (b) before performance begins of any service supplied under the contract.
>
> (5) For the purposes of paragraph (4), the confirmation is treated as provided as soon as the trader has sent it or done what is necessary to make it available to the consumer.'[145]

Thus, within a reasonable period after making it:[146] **28.88**

- a copy of the contract must be provided in a durable form[147] (such as by email or sent via the post on paper);
- that confirmation must contain all of the information in Sch 2[148] (other than to the extent that the information has already been provided on a durable medium);[149] and
- work must not begin until that confirmation has been provided.[150]

---

143 Consumer Contracts (Information, Cancellation and Additional Charges) Regulations 2013 (SI 2013/3134), reg 15.
144 The only obvious exception would be where the contract was made by a referral agency that did not properly explain what it was doing.
145 Consumer Contracts (Information, Cancellation and Additional Charges) Regulations 2013 (SI 2013/3134), reg 16.
146 See Consumer Contracts (Information, Cancellation and Additional Charges) Regulations 2013 (SI 2013/3134), reg 16(4).
147 See Consumer Contracts (Information, Cancellation and Additional Charges) Regulations 2013 (SI 2013/3134), reg 16(1).
148 See fn 124.
149 See Consumer Contracts (Information, Cancellation and Additional Charges) Regulations 2013 (SI 2013/3134), reg 16(2).
150 See Consumer Contracts (Information, Cancellation and Additional Charges) Regulations 2013 (SI 2013/3134), reg 16(4).

The confirmation will be regarded as having been provided as soon as it is sent to the client.[151]

Right to cancel under the Consumer Contracts (Information, Cancellation and Additional Charges) Regulations 2013

28.89 Clients have a right to cancel distance and off-premises contracts of retainer. The right to cancel exists for a prescribed time, known as the cancellation period. That period begins when the contract is concluded; the point at which it ends will depend on whether there has been compliance with the information requirements of the Consumer Contracts (Information, Cancellation and Additional Charges) Regulations 2013.[152]

- **Normal cancellation period** For present purposes (that is, in relation to contracts of retainer), where the requisite information has been given in accordance with the aforesaid provisions, the cancellation period finishes 14 days after the day on which the contract was concluded.[153]
- **Cancellation period extended for breach of information requirement** If the legal services provider provides the client with the requisite information late, but within 12 months after the contract of retainer was made,[154] then the cancellation period will end once 14 days have expired after the consumer received that information.[155] If there has been a failure to provide information about the right to cancel, the cancellation period ends 12 months after the day on which it would have ended had there been full compliance with the requirements to provide information[156] (that is, a year and a fortnight after the contract was first made).

28.90 The relevance of this to contracts of retainer is that where there has been a failure to provide the requisite information about the client's right to cancel, the cancellation period is extended for up to a year and a fortnight. In view of the fact that the client is, during that time, theoretically permitted to cancel the agreement without having to pay for the work done,[157] this could cause problems with the indemnity principle. There is, however, no authority on that point.

28.91 **The right of a client to cancel** The client may cancel a distance contract or off-premises contract of retainer at any time during the cancellation period without giving any reason and without incurring any liability.[158] The only relevant exception to this is that if a client

[151] See Consumer Contracts (Information, Cancellation and Additional Charges) Regulations 2013 (SI 2013/3134), reg 16(5).

[152] SI 2013/3134.

[153] See Consumer Contracts (Information, Cancellation and Additional Charges) Regulations 2013 (SI 2013/3134), reg 30(1) and (2).

[154] The relevant provision is Consumer Contracts (Information, Cancellation and Additional Charges) Regulations 2013 (SI 2013/3134), reg 31(2). The wording is slightly curious in that, rather than referring to the day after the contract was made, it refers to 'the period of 12 months beginning with the first day of the 14 days mentioned in regulation 30(2) to (6)'.

[155] See Consumer Contracts (Information, Cancellation and Additional Charges) Regulations 2013 (SI 2013/3134), reg 31(2).

[156] See Consumer Contracts (Information, Cancellation and Additional Charges) Regulations 2013 (SI 2013/3134), reg 31(3).

[157] See Consumer Contracts (Information, Cancellation and Additional Charges) Regulations 2013 (SI 2013/3134), reg 36(6)(b) and (1).

[158] See Consumer Contracts (Information, Cancellation and Additional Charges) Regulations 2013 (SI 2013/3134), reg 29(1).

has asked for work to begin before the end of the cancellation period, the client will be liable to pay for the work done.[159]

The following provisions apply to cancellations. 28.92

- **Communication of request to cancel** If a client wishes to cancel a contract, they must inform the legal services provider of that fact.[160] Whilst the client is at liberty to use the form provided for that purpose, cancellation may be effected by the client giving any clear statement setting out the decision to cancel the contract.[161]
- **Timing of request to cancel** It is the time when the cancellation was sent that is important: the client is to be treated as having cancelled the contract within the cancellation period if the communication was sent before the end of that period.[162]

The effect of cancellation by the client Where a distance contract or off-premises contract is cancelled in accordance with the above provisions, the cancellation brings the obligations of the parties to perform the contract to an end. Where this happens, the following terms will apply[163] as if they were included within the contract.[164] 28.93

- The legal services provider must reimburse all payments received from the client by no later than 14 days after the day on which the legal services provider was informed of the client's decision to cancel the contract.[165]
- That reimbursement must be by the same means of payment as the client used for the initial transaction, unless the client has expressly agreed otherwise.[166]
- No fee shall be payable in respect of the reimbursement.[167]

Moreover, where a contract of retainer is cancelled in compliance with these provisions, then any 'ancillary contracts' are also cancelled.[168] Whilst there is no authority on the point, it is likely that this would include after-the-event (ATE) insurance policies and disbursement funding loans, because they would be services 'related to' the main contract of retainer being provided either by the trader or a third party on the basis of an arrangement between the third party and the trader within the meaning of reg 38(3) of the 28.94

[159] See Consumer Contracts (Information, Cancellation and Additional Charges) Regulations 2013 (SI 2013/3134), regs 29(1)(d) and 36(4).

[160] See Consumer Contracts (Information, Cancellation and Additional Charges) Regulations 2013 (SI 2013/3134), regs 32(1) and (2).

[161] See Consumer Contracts (Information, Cancellation and Additional Charges) Regulations 2013 (SI 2013/3134), reg 32(3).

[162] See Consumer Contracts (Information, Cancellation and Additional Charges) Regulations 2013 (SI 2013/3134), reg 32(5).

[163] See Consumer Contracts (Information, Cancellation and Additional Charges) Regulations 2013 (SI 2013/3134), reg 33.

[164] See Consumer Contracts (Information, Cancellation and Additional Charges) Regulations 2013 (SI 2013/3134), reg 34(13).

[165] See Consumer Contracts (Information, Cancellation and Additional Charges) Regulations 2013 (SI 2013/3134), reg 34(6).

[166] See Consumer Contracts (Information, Cancellation and Additional Charges) Regulations 2013 (SI 2013/3134), reg 34(7).

[167] See Consumer Contracts (Information, Cancellation and Additional Charges) Regulations 2013 (SI 2013/3134), reg 34(8).

[168] See Consumer Contracts (Information, Cancellation and Additional Charges) Regulations 2013 (SI 2013/3134), reg 38.

Consumer Contracts (Information, Cancellation and Additional Charges) Regulations 2013.[169]

28.95 *Work carried out within the cancellation period* The legal services provider must not supply legal services before the end of the cancellation period unless (a) the client has made an express request to this effect and (b), in the case of an off-premises contract, that request has been made on a durable medium.[170]

28.96 Whether there is a right to payment for work carried out during the cancellation period depends on whether there has been compliance with the requirements to provide information and on whether the work was carried out early as a result of the request made by the client.

- **Where there has been a request and there has been full compliance** In these circumstances, the legal services provider will be entitled to payment. The following provisions will apply:

  '(4) Where the service is supplied in response to a request in accordance with paragraph (1) [ie a request that the work is carried out early], the consumer must (subject to paragraph (6) [see the bullet points below]) pay to the trader an amount—
  (a) for the supply of the service for the period for which it is supplied, ending with the time when the trader is informed of the consumer's decision to cancel the contract, in accordance with regulation 32(2), and
  (b) which is in proportion to what has been supplied, in comparison with the full coverage of the contract.

  (5) The amount is to be calculated—
  (a) on the basis of the total price agreed in the contract, or
  (b) if the total price is excessive, on the basis of the market value of the service that has been supplied, calculated by comparing prices for equivalent services supplied by other traders.'[171]

- **Where there has been no request** Whilst harsh, the 2013 Regulations provide that if the service provided before the end of the cancellation period was not supplied in response to an express request that work should begin, then the client bears no responsibility for paying for that work, either in full or in part.[172] Moreover, if the contract is an off-premises contract, the client's request must have been made on a durable medium.[173]
- **Where there has been a failure to provide information** Where the legal services provider has failed to provide the client with (a) information concerning the conditions, time limit and procedures for exercising the right to cancel, or (b) the information that, if the consumer exercises the right to cancel after having made a request that work begins before the cancellation period, the client would be liable to pay for that work, then the

---

[169] SI 2013/3134.

[170] See Consumer Contracts (Information, Cancellation and Additional Charges) Regulations 2013 (SI 2013/3134), reg 36(1).

[171] Consumer Contracts (Information, Cancellation and Additional Charges) Regulations 2013 (SI 2013/3134), reg 36(4) and (5).

[172] See Consumer Contracts (Information, Cancellation and Additional Charges) Regulations 2013 (SI 2013/3134), reg 36(6)(b) and (1).

[173] See Consumer Contracts (Information, Cancellation and Additional Charges) Regulations 2013 (SI 2013/3134), reg 36(6)(b) and (1).

client will bear no responsibility for paying for the work carried out during the cancellation period, either in full or in part.[174]

The consequences of not complying with the Consumer Contracts (Information, Cancellation and Additional Charges) Regulations 2013 Whilst often overlooked in the context of costs law, the most important consequence of not complying with the 2013 Regulations is that non-compliance may amount to a criminal offence.[175] There are several arguments that could be used for the purposes of showing that a failure to comply is, for one reason or another, capable of leading to a breach of the indemnity principle. Some of the arguments are as follows—although none are supported by authority.[176] **28.97**

- **Contracts other than distance contracts made by electronic means** It is arguable that the words 'before the consumer is bound by a [contract]' (which appear at the start of regs 9, 10 and 13 of the 2013 Regulations) are to be interpreted as creating a condition precedent—namely, that the contract will not be binding unless and until there has been compliance. There are, however, competing interpretations and it could well be the case that those words are there merely to identify the point in time at which the requisite information should be given.[177]
- **Distance contracts concluded by electronic means** The provisions relating to distance contracts concluded by electronic means make explicit reference to the contract being unenforceable in the event of non-compliance, but only where the non-compliance is a failure to ensure that (a) the client explicitly acknowledges that the order implies an obligation to pay and (b) any button (or similar) that is used to make the contract is labelled, in an easily legible manner only, with the words 'order with obligation to pay' (or a corresponding unambiguous formulation indicating that placing the order entails an obligation to pay).[178] This may be a problem if the contract is made using certain proprietary methods of effecting an electronic signature.

---

[174] See Consumer Contracts (Information, Cancellation and Additional Charges) Regulations 2013 (SI 2013/3134), reg 36(6)(a).

[175] In particular, a criminal offence would be committed if the legal services provider were to fail to give notice of the right to cancel: see Consumer Contracts (Information, Cancellation and Additional Charges) Regulations 2013 (SI 2013/3134), reg 19. A person convicted of that crime is liable, on summary conviction, to a fine not exceeding level 5 on the standard scale. There is a defence of due diligence: see Consumer Contracts (Information, Cancellation and Additional Charges) Regulations 2013 (SI 2013/3134), reg 20.

[176] It is possible that the fact that an offence has been committed could have a bearing on the recoverability of costs by reason of the concept of 'implied statutory prohibition', but that argument would probably not be necessary because there are several express statutory provisions (as set out below).

[177] In support of that interpretation is the fact that each of the aforesaid paragraphs contains a provision that says that if certain requirements are not satisfied, the client is not to bear the charges or costs referred to in those paragraphs; if the true interpretation of the words 'before the consumer is bound' is that it creates a condition precedent, then the provision relating to individual requirements would be otiose. This suggests that the true interpretation is not that it creates a condition precedent. Similarly, whilst its general wording is very different from the paragraphs that say 'before the consumer is bound ...', the provisions relating to distance contracts concluded by electronic means make explicit reference to the contract being unenforceable in the event of non-compliance: see Consumer Contracts (Information, Cancellation and Additional Charges) Regulations 2013 (SI 2013/3134), reg 14(5). This rather suggests that if the true meaning of the 2013 Regulations were that non-compliance generally would result in the index contract being unenforceable, this would be explicitly stated.

[178] See Consumer Contracts (Information, Cancellation and Additional Charges) Regulations 2013 (SI 2013/3134), reg 14(5).

- **All cancellable contracts** Where there has been a failure to provide information about the right to cancel, then the cancellation period will continue to run until it reaches 12 months (that is, a year) after the end of the 14-day period that would have applied if the information had been given when it ought to have been given.[179] In practice, this means that there will be a period of a year and a fortnight during which the client could, if they so wished, cancel the contract of retainer at no cost.[180] It could be argued that, where the right not to pay existed (such as where the requisite information had not been given and the case had settled only a few months after the contract had been made), it would be unreasonable of the client not to exercise that right.

28.98 Many other such arguments exist. That said, if a paying party were to try to rely on some of the above arguments, it is entirely possible that they would be defeated, for the reasons given by Arden LJ in *Garbutt v Edwards*.[181] This topic is (in very general terms) discussed at 27.268–27.269.

28.99 In any event, under the heading 'Effect on contract of failure to provide information', reg 18 of the 2013 Regulations has the following to say:

> '18 Every contract to which this Part applies is to be treated as including a term that the trader has complied with the provisions of—
> (a) regulations 9 to 14 [these being the requirements to give information], and
> (b) regulation 16 [this being the requirement to confirm a distance contract].'

As such, the client is able to rely on the relevant terms notwithstanding the fact that they were not informed of them. Again, this may have a bearing on the extent to which a paying party would be able to rely on a putative breach of the provisions.

28.100 **Evidential matters regarding compliance with the Consumer Contracts (Information, Cancellation and Additional Charges) Regulations 2013** In general, the ordinary civil burden of proof will apply, but this is subject to the following provisions.

- Where there is a dispute about the trader's compliance with any provision of regs 10–16 of the 2013 Regulations (the provisions about giving the client information), it is for the legal services provider to prove its compliance.[182]
- Where there is a dispute about when a contract was cancelled, it is for the consumer to show that the contract was cancelled within the cancellation period.[183]

A failure to give notice of the client's right to cancel is a criminal offence and, as such, the right to freedom from self-incrimination applies.[184] Whilst there is no authority on

---

[179] See Consumer Contracts (Information, Cancellation and Additional Charges) Regulations 2013 (SI 2013/3134), reg 31(3).

[180] See Consumer Contracts (Information, Cancellation and Additional Charges) Regulations 2013 (SI 2013/3134), reg 36(6)(b) and (1).

[181] *Garbutt v Edwards* [2005] EWCA Civ 1206, at [35] *et seq*.

[182] See of the Consumer Contracts (Information, Cancellation and Additional Charges) Regulations 2013 (SI 2013/3134), reg 17(1). That burden does not apply to proceedings for an offence under reg 19 (ie criminal proceedings), or relating to compliance with an injunction, interdict or order under reg 45: see Consumer Contracts (Information, Cancellation and Additional Charges) Regulations 2013 (SI 2013/3134), reg 17(2).

[183] See Consumer Contracts (Information, Cancellation and Additional Charges) Regulations 2013 (SI 2013/3134), reg 32(6).

[184] See Consumer Contracts (Information, Cancellation and Additional Charges) Regulations 2013 (SI 2013/3134), reg 26. The precise extent to which this may have a bearing on (civil) costs proceedings is not

the point, if a receiving party's legal services provider were to try to rely on this, it would probably prompt the court to put the receiving party to their election on the point and, as such, it is unlikely to be of much practical relevance on an assessment between opposing parties.

The Consumer Protection from Unfair Trading Regulations 2008

Overview

The Consumer Protection from Unfair Trading Regulations 2008[185] are in place to guard against sharp practices and rogue traders. The Explanatory Note to the Regulations reads as follows: **28.101**

> 'The [2008 Regulations] introduce a general prohibition on traders in all sectors engaging in unfair commercial (mainly marketing and selling) practices against consumers. It will put in place a comprehensive framework for dealing with sharp practices and rogue traders who deliberately set out to exploit loopholes in existing legislation.'[186]

Whilst they have almost no bearing on the recoverability of costs under a contract of retainer,[187] the 2008 Regulations are relevant to the law of costs in that they have a bearing on the way in which contracts of retainer are formed. This means that mistakes and wrongdoings in that regard are capable of giving rise to regulatory breaches. This is to be avoided because many such breaches are criminal offences. **28.102**

Unfair commercial practices are prohibited,[188] as are any unfair practices contained within any code of conduct.[189] The following constitute unfair practices: **28.103**

- practices that contravene the requirements of professional diligence and materially distort, or are likely to materially distort, the economic behaviour of the average consumer (see 28.111–28.113);
- misleading actions (see 28.114–28.118);
- misleading omissions (see 28.119–28.123);
- aggressive practices (see 28.124–28.128); and
- certain proscribed banned practices (see 28.129–28.130).

Vires

The 2008 Regulations came into force on 26 May 2008. They gave domestic effect to the Unfair Commercial Practices Directive.[190] It was thought that, to comply with the Directive, it would be easier to repeal much of the existing consumer law and to make new **28.104**

known, but if a legal services provider were to attempt to rely on the right against self-incrimination as being an explanation for its silence on the issue of compliance, then presumably it would fail to discharge the burden of proof referred to above.

185 SI 2008/1277.

186 Consumer Protection from Unfair Trading Regulations 2008 (SI 2008/1277), Explanatory Note on p 48 of the print version.

187 See Consumer Protection from Unfair Trading Regulations 2008 (SI 2008/1277), reg 29.

188 Consumer Protection from Unfair Trading Regulations 2008 (SI 2008/1277), reg 3(1).

189 See Consumer Protection from Unfair Trading Regulations 2008 (SI 2008/1277), reg 4.

190 Directive 2005/29/EC of the European Parliament and of the Council of 11 May 2005 concerning unfair business-to-consumer commercial practices in the internal market, OJ L 149/22, 11 June 2005.

law.[191] That said, parts of the 2008 Regulations are modelled on the Trade Descriptions Act 1968.[192]

28.105 On 1 October 2014, the 2008 Regulations were amended in such a way as to allow them to continue to apply to consumers under the Consumer Rights Act 2015.[193] The government also implemented most of the recommendations made by the Law Commission following its findings that the law regarding consumer rights to redress for misleading or aggressive practices was fragmented, complex and unclear.[194] The new provisions gave consumers the right to unwind a contract (or payment) or to receive a discount on the price paid (see 28.135–28.142).

Terminology

28.106 Rather confusingly, the 2008 Regulations refer only to 'products', but this is defined as meaning any goods or services[195] and, as such, would include the provision of legal services.

28.107 **The meanings of 'consumer' and 'trader'** The definitions of 'consumer'[196] and 'trader'[197] are the same as those given in the Consumer Rights Act 2015 (see 28.26–28.27).

28.108 **The meaning of 'average customer'** The 2008 Regulations refer to the 'average customer'. This certainly does not mean 'a moron in a hurry';[198] rather, the average customer is expected to be 'reasonably circumspect'[199] or 'reasonably well-informed and reasonably observant and circumspect'.[200] Kitchin J summarised his understanding of the issue in this way:

> 'The concept of a typical or average consumer is a familiar one in European consumer law extending also into the law of registered trade marks. Such a person is generally assumed to be reasonably well informed and reasonably observant and circumspect, and to read the relevant documents and to seek to understand what is being read. The standard is a variable one and must, I believe, take colour from the context. For example, consumers who are financially sophisticated may be expected to bring to bear a greater understanding of the meaning and implications of the terms of a contract than consumers who are vulnerable as a result of their naivety or credulity.'[201]

---

191 See the Explanatory Note to the Consumer Protection from Unfair Trading Regulations 2008 (SI 2008/1277), para 3. In particular, Consumer Protection Act 1987, Pt 3, concerning misleading price indications was repealed.

192 See the Explanatory Note to the Consumer Protection from Unfair Trading Regulations 2008 (SI 2008/1277), para 3.18.

193 See Consumer Rights Act 2015, Sch 1, para 3. The enforcement provision of the Consumer Protection from Unfair Trading Regulations 2008 (SI 2008/1277) was, however, revoked on 1 October 2015: see Consumer Rights Act 2015, Sch 2, paras 114 and 115.

194 Law Commission and Scottish Law Commission, *Consumer Redress for Misleading and Aggressive Practices*, Cm 8323, Law Com 332 (London: HMSO, 2012).

195 See Consumer Protection from Unfair Trading Regulations 2008 (SI 2008/1277), reg 2(1), as amended by Consumer Protection (Amendment) Regulations 2014 (SI 2014/870), para 2(6).

196 Consumer Protection from Unfair Trading Regulations 2008 (SI 2008/1277), reg 2(1) as amended by Consumer Protection (Amendment) Regulations 2014 (SI 2014/870), para 2(3).

197 See Consumer Protection from Unfair Trading Regulations 2008 (SI 2008/1277), reg 2(1) as amended by Consumer Protection (Amendment) Regulations 2014 (SI 2014/870), para 2(7).

198 See Foster J in *Morning Star Co-Operative Society Ltd v Express Newspapers Ltd* [1979] FSR 113, at 117.

199 Case C740/93 *Verein gegen Unwesen in Handel und Gewerbe Köln v Mars GmbH* [1995] ECR I-1923, at [24].

200 Case C-210/96 *Gut Springenheide GmbH and Rudolf Tusky v Oberkreisdirektor des Kreises Steinfurt—Amt für Lebensmittelüberwachung* [1998] ECR I-46571, at [31].

201 *Office of Fair Trading v Ashbourne Management Services Ltd* [2011] EWHC 1237 (Ch), at [128].

As will be explained below, the 'average customer' may be required to know something about the legal services market. There is no authority on the extent to which a legal services provider has to explain its services, but (whilst they do not relate specifically to the legal services industry) the following comments about 'alternative products' by Briggs LJ may be instructive: **28.109**

> '[T]he critical question ... is whether the average consumer can be said to need to obtain that information from the trader in question, rather than obtain it (for example) by shopping around, and finding out for himself whether something better, or cheaper, is on offer. Generally, inward-facing information [ie information about the company's own practices/prices, etc.] is likely to be available only from the trader in question, because it is information about that trader, or its goods or services. By contrast, information about alternative or competing products may generally be supposed to be available in the marketplace, to the extent that a particular consumer wishes to obtain it before deciding whether to make a purchase from the trader in question. In short, shopping around for information about alternative products (whether goods or services) is characteristic of the reasonably well informed, observant and circumspect consumer.'[202]

Briggs LJ went on to say that the expectation that the average consumer will make enquiries about alternative competing products was no more than a general assumption or starting point and therefore one that may yield to particular aspects of the context in which the alleged omission arose.[203] Whilst it is no more than the editor's opinion, many of the situations in which a consumer may seek the advice of a solicitor are such that even the most robust and inquisitive 'average customer' would find it difficult to make their own inquiries. **28.110**

Professional diligence and material distortion

A commercial practice is unfair if (a) it contravenes the requirements of professional diligence and (b) it materially distorts, or is likely to materially distort, the economic behaviour of the average consumer with regard to the product.[204] **28.111**

The meaning of terms The following points can be made. **28.112**

- **'Professional diligence'** This is defined as follows:

  > '... the standard of special skill and care which a trader may reasonably be expected to exercise towards consumers which is commensurate with either—
  > (a) honest market practice in the trader's field of activity, or
  > (b) the general principles of good faith in the trader's field of activity.'[205]

  The word 'special' is not intended to require more than would reasonably be expected of a trader in that field of activity.
- **'Honest market practice' or 'good faith'** There is no definition of the terms 'honest market practice' or 'good faith' in the legislation, but (whilst not admissible as an aid to

---

[202] *Secretary of State for Business, Innovation and Skills v PLT Anti-Marketing Ltd* [2015] EWCA Civ 76, at [31].

[203] *Ibid*, at [32].

[204] See Consumer Protection from Unfair Trading Regulations 2008 (SI 2008/1277), reg 3(3)(a) and (b).

[205] Consumer Protection from Unfair Trading Regulations 2008 (SI 2008/1277), reg 2(1).

interpretation), the CMA says that the principles require traders to deal with transactions professionally and fairly, as judged by a reasonable person.[206]

- **'Material distortion'** This is defined as 'appreciably to impair the average consumer's ability to make an informed decision thereby causing him to take a transactional decision that he would not have taken otherwise'.[207] For a commercial practice to fall within this prohibition, it must impair the average consumer's ability to make an informed decision and that impairment must be significant enough to alter the average consumer's decision. This means that practices that do not affect, or which are unlikely to affect, the economic behaviour of the average consumer are unlikely to fall within this prohibition.[208]

28.113 **Examples of infringing actions** In so far as the provision of legal services is concerned, the CMA give the following examples that could infringe on this provision:

- offering incorrect advice on the consumer's options, leading to the consumer commissioning work that is unnecessary;
- falsely claiming that the legal services provider employs qualified solicitors and barrister when it does not;
- failing to provide adequate information to a consumer about the time that will be engaged in progressing the consumer's case and the likely costs;
- failing to comply with recognised standards in the legal services industry, such as the SRA Code of Conduct; and
- failing to deal with complaints either at all or in an honest, fair, reasonable and professional manner.[209]

Misleading actions

28.114 **General** A commercial practice will be a misleading action if:

- it contains false information and is therefore untruthful in relation to any of certain prescribed factors (see below) or if it, or its overall presentation, in any way deceives, or is likely to deceive, the average consumer in relation to any of those factors, even if the information is factually correct; and
- it causes, or is likely to cause, the average consumer to take a transactional decision they would not have otherwise taken.[210]

28.115 In so far as they are relevant to contracts of retainer, the prescribed list of factors[211] includes:

- the nature, attributes and rights of the trader (that is, identity, qualifications, status, awards and distinctions[212]);
- the consumer's rights or the risks the consumer may face;
- the price or the manner in which the price is calculated;

---

206 See CMA, *Legal Services Market Study: Final Report* (London: HMSO, 2016), Appx E, para 16.

207 Consumer Protection from Unfair Trading Regulations 2008 (SI 2008/1277), reg 2(1).

208 Whilst not admissible as an aid to interpretation, see CMA, *Legal Services Market Study: Final Report* (London: HMSO, 2016), Appx E, para 17.

209 See *ibid*, Appx E, para 18.

210 Consumer Protection from Unfair Trading Regulations 2008 (SI 2008/1277), reg 5(2).

211 See Consumer Protection from Unfair Trading Regulations 2008 (SI 2008/1277), reg 5(4).

212 See Consumer Protection from Unfair Trading Regulations 2008 (SI 2008/1277), reg 5(6). This list has been reordered so as to make it more relevant to contracts of retainer.

- the existence of a specific price advantage;
- the extent of the trader's commitments;
- the motives for the commercial practice; and
- the nature of the sales process.

Thus, if the legal services provider misleads a client about its qualifications, for example, that may amount to a breach, but only if it would pass the objective test of whether an 'average consumer' would have been misled.[213] The 2008 Regulations pay particular regard to vulnerable groups of consumer, such as the elderly.[214]

Trade marks and competitors A commercial practice is a misleading action if it concerns any marketing of a product (including comparative advertising) that creates confusion with any products, trade marks, trade names or other distinguishing marks of a competitor.[215] **28.116**

Codes of conduct A commercial practice is a misleading action if it concerns any failure by a trader to comply with a commitment contained in a code of conduct with which the trader has undertaken to comply, if (a) the trader indicates in a commercial practice that they are bound by that code of conduct, and (b) the commitment is firm and capable of being verified and is not aspirational, and it causes, or is likely to cause, the average consumer to take a transactional decision that they would not have taken otherwise, taking account of its factual context and of all its features and circumstances.[216] **28.117**

Examples of misleading actions The CMA give the following examples of what, in a legal setting, may amount to a misleading action: **28.118**

- where a legal services provider states that a legal service will cost a certain sum of money (for example a fixed price) if, in fact, it is likely to cost more than this; or
- where an unregulated legal services provider falsely claims that it is subject to the SRA Code of Conduct and this representation causes the average consumer to make a transactional decision they would not have otherwise made (for example retaining the services of an unauthorised legal services provider, as opposed to an authorised legal services provider).[217]

Misleading omissions

A commercial practice is a misleading omission if, in its factual context and taking account of certain prescribed matters,[218] it omits material information, hides material information, **28.119**

[213] 'Average consumer', in this context, means an average client who is reasonably well informed, reasonably observant and circumspect: see Consumer Protection from Unfair Trading Regulations 2008 (SI 2008/1277), reg 2(2) and (4).

[214] See Consumer Protection from Unfair Trading Regulations 2008 (SI 2008/1277), reg 2(5), which reads: 'In determining the effect of a commercial practice on the average consumer ... where a clearly identifiable group of consumers is particularly vulnerable to the practice or the underlying product because of their mental or physical infirmity, age or credulity in a way which the trader could reasonably be expected to foresee ... reference to the average consumer shall be read as referring to the average member of that group.'

[215] See Consumer Protection from Unfair Trading Regulations 2008 (SI 2008/1277), reg 5(3)(a).

[216] See Consumer Protection from Unfair Trading Regulations 2008 (SI 2008/1277), reg 5(3)(b).

[217] See CMA, *Legal Services Market Study: Final Report* (London: HMSO, 2016), Appx E, para 21.

[218] Consumer Protection from Unfair Trading Regulations 2008 (SI 2008/1277), reg 6(2), provides that those factors are: (a) all of the features and circumstances of the commercial practice; (b) the limitations of the medium used to communicate the commercial practice (including limitations of space or time); and (c) where the medium used to communicate the commercial practice imposes limitations of space or time, any measures taken by the trader to make the information available to consumers by other means.

provides material information in a manner that is unclear, unintelligible, ambiguous or untimely, or fails to identify its commercial intent, unless this is already apparent from the context, and, as a result, it causes, or is likely to cause, the average consumer to take a transactional decision they would not have otherwise taken.[219]

28.120 **Factors to be taken into account** The court will take into account certain factors that are not unlike those that relate to misleading actions other than that the need to provide more complex advice is governed by a test of 'professional diligence'[220]—an objective test that is based on the professional practices of the market.[221] In so far as they are relevant, the following provisions set out factors that will automatically be regarded as material information:

> '(4) Where a commercial practice is an invitation to purchase, the following information will be material if not already apparent from the context in addition to any other information which is material information under paragraph (3)—
> (a) the main characteristics of the product, to the extent appropriate to the medium by which the invitation to purchase is communicated and the product;
> (b) the identity of the trader, such as his trading name, and the identity of any other trader on whose behalf the trader is acting;
> (c) the geographical address of the trader and the geographical address of any other trader on whose behalf the trader is acting;
> (d) either—
> (i) the price, including any taxes; or
> (ii) where the nature of the product is such that the price cannot reasonably be calculated in advance, the manner in which the price is calculated;
> [...]
> (f) the following matters where they depart from the requirements of professional diligence—
> (i) arrangements for payment,
> [...]
> (iii) arrangements for performance,
> (iv) complaint handling policy;
> (g) for products and transactions involving a right of withdrawal or cancellation, the existence of such a right.'[222]

28.121 **Meaning of invitation to purchase** An invitation to purchase takes place where a trader provides sufficient details of the product and price to enable the consumer to decide whether to purchase that service. According to the case law of the Court of Justice of the European Union (CJEU), this is not a high threshold; in particular, it is not necessary for the putative invitation to include an actual opportunity to purchase or for it to appear in proximity to, and at the same time as, such an opportunity.[223] The thinking behind this

[219] See Consumer Protection from Unfair Trading Regulations 2008 (SI 2008/1277), reg 6(1).

[220] See Consumer Protection from Unfair Trading Regulations 2008 (SI 2008/1277), reg 6(4)(f), which (in so far as they are relevant) focuses on arrangements for payment, arrangements for performance and the legal services provider's complaint handling policy.

[221] Consumer Protection from Unfair Trading Regulations 2008 (SI 2008/1277), reg 1(1), provides that 'professional diligence' means the standard of special skill and care that a trader may reasonably be expected to exercise towards consumers that is commensurate with either (a) honest market practice in the trader's field of activity, or (b) the general principle of good faith in the trader's field of activity.

[222] Consumer Protection from Unfair Trading Regulations 2008 (SI 2008/1277), reg 6(4).

[223] Case C-122/10 *Konsumentombudsmannen v Ving Sverige AB* [2011] WLR (D) 181, at [29]–[35].

is to ensure that consumers are given the key information they need to make an informed purchasing decision, such as fully inclusive pricing.

Examples of misleading omissions The CMA gives the following as examples of invitations to purchase in the context of legal services: **28.122**

- retainer letters that enable consumers to purchase the service by signing and returning it; and
- information provided on a legal services provider's website about its services, including likely prices.[224]

Similarly, the CMA give the following as examples of possible misleading omissions: **28.123**

- failing to provide a consumer with full information on fees and charges, such as how they are calculated and when they will be payable, before that consumer becomes contractually bound;
- failing to adequately highlight or draw to a consumer's attention unusual or surprising terms in the provider's terms and condition, such as, in a claim for compensation, any deductions that the legal services provider will make from the consumer's damages award; and
- failing to set out, in a clear and unambiguous manner, any codes of practice by which the legal services provider is bound.[225]

The editor will add a specific example of something that—whilst there is not authority on the point—is likely to qualify as a misleading omission: a failure to provide information about the need to pay a success fee out of damages.

Aggressive commercial practices

A commercial practice is 'aggressive' if, through the use of harassment, coercion or undue influence, it significantly impairs, or is likely significantly to impair, the average consumer's freedom of choice or conduct in relation to the provision of legal services[226] and it thereby causes, or is likely to cause, the consumer to take a transactional decision they would not have taken otherwise.[227] **28.124**

'Undue influence' is defined as 'exploiting a position of power in relation to the consumer so as to apply pressure, even without using or threatening to use physical force, in a way which significantly limits the consumer's ability to make an informed decision'.[228] **28.125**

---

[224] See CMA, *Legal Services Market Study: Final Report* (London: HMSO, 2016), Appx E, para 26.

[225] See *ibid*, Appx E, para 27.

[226] Consumer Protection from Unfair Trading Regulations 2008 (SI 2008/1277), reg 7(2), provides that: 'In determining whether a commercial practice uses harassment, coercion or undue influence account shall be taken of (a) its timing, location, nature or persistence; (b) the use of threatening or abusive language or behaviour; (c) the exploitation by the trader of any specific misfortune or circumstance of such gravity as to impair the consumer's judgment, of which the trader is aware, to influence the consumer's decision with regard to the product; (d) any onerous or disproportionate non-contractual barrier imposed by the trader where a consumer wishes to exercise rights under the contract, including rights to terminate a contract or to switch to another product or another trader; and (e) any threat to take any action which cannot legally be taken.' Regulation 7(3)(b) goes on to explain that ' "undue influence" means exploiting a position of power in relation to the consumer so as to apply pressure, even without using or threatening to use physical force, in a way which significantly limits the consumer's ability to make an informed decision'.

[227] See Consumer Protection from Unfair Trading Regulations 2008 (SI 2008/1277), reg 7(1).

[228] Consumer Protection from Unfair Trading Regulations 2008 (SI 2008/1277), reg 7(3)(b).

28.126 Factors to be taken into account The 2008 Regulations list factors that will be taken into account when determining whether a commercial practice is aggressive:

> '(2) In determining whether a commercial practice uses harassment, coercion or undue influence account shall be taken of—
> (a) its timing, location, nature or persistence;
> (b) the use of threatening or abusive language or behaviour;
> (c) the exploitation by the trader of any specific misfortune or circumstance of such gravity as to impair the consumer's judgment, of which the trader is aware, to influence the consumer's decision with regard to the product;
> (d) any onerous or disproportionate non-contractual barrier imposed by the trader where a consumer wishes to exercise rights under the contract, including rights to terminate a contract or to switch to another product or another trader; and
> (e) any threat to take any action which cannot legally be taken.'[229]

28.127 Examples of aggressive practices The CMA say that a commercial practice may significantly impair a consumer if, for example, the legal services provider stays in a consumer's home for so long that the consumer feels compelled to sign a contract. The CMA says that a breach would be established if it could be shown that a consumer would have been likely to have taken a different decision had it not been for the unfair commercial practice adopted by the legal services provider.[230]

28.128 In addition, the CMA give the following examples of aggressive practices:

- pressurising a consumer to enter into a contract for the supply of a legal service, for example pressurising a client who has asked for a will to be drawn up to appoint the legal services provider as executor or to accept provision of a will-holding service;
- refusing to allow a consumer to cancel their contract in circumstances in which a cancellation period applies and has not expired; and
- intimidating, pressurising or coercing consumers into dropping complaints against the legal services provider, for example by using threatening or abusive language or behaviour.[231]

Whilst there is no authority on this point, it is possible that being involved in some pressure-selling techniques (such as automated cold-calling) could fall within this category.[232]

Proscribed unfair practices

28.129 Schedule 1 of the 2008 Regulations sets out certain activities that are, by definition, unfair in all circumstances and are prohibited (banned practices), irrespective of the effect that these practices will have on consumers. The main activities that are potentially relevant to contracts of retainer are all related to professional claims that are false.

28.130 Examples of proscribed unfair practices The CMA provides the following examples (with reference to the banned practice) that may amount to a prohibited commercial practice in the context of legal services providers.[233]

---

229 Consumer Protection from Unfair Trading Regulations 2008 (SI 2008/1277), reg 7(2).

230 See CMA, *Legal Services Market Study: Final Report* (London: HMSO, 2016), Appx E, para 31.

231 See *ibid*, Appx E, para 33.

232 Indeed, Consumer Protection from Unfair Trading Regulations 2008 (SI 2008/1277), Sch 1, para 26, provides that the following is unfair: 'Making persistent and unwanted solicitations by telephone, fax, e-mail or other remote media except in circumstances and to the extent justified to enforce a contractual obligation.'

233 See CMA, *Legal Services Market Study: Final Report* (London: HMSO, 2016), Appx E, para 34.

- **Claiming to be a signatory to a code of conduct when the trader is not** For example, an unauthorised legal services provider may claim that it is bound by the SRA Code of Conduct when it is not.
- **Displaying a trust mark, quality mark or equivalent without having obtained the necessary authorisation** For example, a legal services provider may display a Law Society Accreditation Quality Assurance mark on its website when it does not have authorisation from the Law Society to do so.
- **Claiming that a trader (including their commercial practice) or a product has been approved, endorsed or authorised by a public or private body when the trader, the commercial practices or the product has not, or making such a claim without complying with the terms of the approval, endorsement or authorisation** For example, a legal services provider may claim that its wills service is accredited by the Law Society's Wills and Inheritance Quality Scheme when it is not.
- **Conducting personal visits to a consumer's home, ignoring the consumer's request to leave or not to return, except in circumstances and to the extent justified to enforce a contractual obligation** For example, the representative of a legal services provider may enter a consumer's home during a doorstep selling process and later fail to leave when the consumer asks them to do so.
- **Making persistent and unwanted solicitations by telephone, fax, email or other remote media except in circumstances and to the extent justified to enforce a contractual obligation** For example, a legal services provider may repeatedly contact a consumer by telephone and by email to persuade that consumer to enter into a contract for the provision of legal services when the consumer has specifically asked the provider to cease doing so.

The effect of non-compliance

A failure to comply with the 2008 Regulations will often amount to a criminal offence[234]— although there is a defence of due diligence.[235] **28.131**

Remedies for non-compliance

Non-compliance and costs incurred before 1 October 2014 In so far as costs incurred before 1 October 2014 are concerned, provided that the contract of retainer was also made before that date, a breach would have been of no real effect in so far as the contract of retainer was concerned, because reg 29 of the 2008 Regulations provided (and still does provide) that an agreement shall not be void or unenforceable by reason only of a breach of the Regulations. As such, there would have been, for example, no breach of the indemnity principle.[236] **28.132**

---

234 See Consumer Protection from Unfair Trading Regulations 2008 (SI 2008/1277), regs 8–16. A person convicted on indictment is liable to a fine or imprisonment for a term not exceeding two years, or both.

235 See Consumer Protection from Unfair Trading Regulations 2008 (SI 2008/1277), reg 17.

236 One could possibly seek to adapt the *ex turpi causa* principle (or to apply the *in bonam partem* rule of statutory construction). Consumer Protection from Unfair Trading Regulations 2008 (SI 2008/1277), reg 29, however, specifically protects the agreement from invalidity and/or unenforceability by reason only of a breach of the Regulations. It therefore seems to be strongly arguable that the provision of this express exemption from the normal consequences of illegality leaves little room for reliance on general principles of law or canons of statutory interpretation.

28.133 If the contract of retainer was made on or after 1 October 2014, then a breach may, if certain conditions were satisfied (see below), give rise to a 'right to redress' (see below).[237]

The remedies afforded to consumer clients

28.134 There are several common-law remedies available to a client who has been subject to a breach of the protection legislation outlined above, with the main remedy being an award for damages (which is also available as a legislative remedy).[238] These remedies are also all available to consumers and, where appropriate, businesses. They are, however, unlikely to be relevant to the law of costs. There are four legislative remedies that are worth mentioning because they may be of some importance to the law of costs:

- the 'right to redress' (see 28.135–28.136)[239] under the 2008 Regulations, as amended by Consumer Protection (Amendment) Regulations 2014,[240] including:
  - the right to unwind (see 28.137–28.139);[241] and
  - the right to a discount (see 28.140–28.142);[242]
- the 'right to enforce terms about services' (see 28.143–28.144)[243] under the Consumer Rights Act 2015, including:
  - the right to require repeat performance (see 28.145);[244] and
  - the right to a price reduction (see 28.146–28.148).[245]

Right to redress under the Consumer Protection from Unfair Trading Regulations 2008 (as amended)

28.135 If the contract of retainer was made on or after 1 October 2014, then a breach may, if certain conditions are satisfied (see 28.136), give rise to a 'right to redress'.[246] The relevant provisions read as follows:

> '**When does a consumer have a right to redress?**
>
> 27A (1) A consumer has a right to redress under this Part if—
> (a) the conditions in this regulation are met, and
> (b) the conditions (if any) in the following provisions of this Part for the availability of that right are met.

---

[237] See Consumer Protection (Amendment) Regulations 2014 (SI 2014/870), reg 1(3), which reads as follows: '[The new provisions] come into force on 1st October 2014 and apply in relation to contracts entered into, or payments made, on or after that date.'

[238] See Consumer Protection from Unfair Trading Regulations 2008 (SI 2008/1277), reg 27J, as amended by the Consumer Protection (Amendment) Regulations 2014 (SI 2014/870).

[239] See Consumer Protection from Unfair Trading Regulations 2008 (SI 2008/1277), regs 27A and 27B, as amended by the Consumer Protection (Amendment) Regulations 2014 (SI 2014/870).

[240] SI 2014/870.

[241] See Consumer Protection from Unfair Trading Regulations 2008 (SI 2008/1277), regs 27E and 27F, as amended by the Consumer Protection (Amendment) Regulations 2014 (SI 2014/870).

[242] See Consumer Protection from Unfair Trading Regulations 2008 (SI 2008/1277), reg 27I, as amended by the Consumer Protection (Amendment) Regulations 2014 (SI 2014/870).

[243] See Consumer Rights Act 2015, s 54.

[244] See Consumer Rights Act 2015, s 55.

[245] See Consumer Rights Act 2015, s 56.

[246] See Consumer Protection (Amendment) Regulations 2014 (SI 2014/870), reg 1(3), which reads: '[The new provisions] come into force on 1st October 2014 and apply in relation to contracts entered into, or payments made, on or after that date.'

(2) The first condition is that—
(a) the consumer enters into a contract with a trader for the sale or supply of a product by the trader (a "business to consumer contract"), [or]
[...]

(4) The second condition is that—
(a) the trader engages in a prohibited practice in relation to the product,
[...]

(6) The third condition is that the prohibited practice is a significant factor in the consumer's decision to enter into the contract ...

What does "prohibited practice" mean in this Part?

27B (1) In this Part "prohibited practice" means a commercial practice that—
(a) is a misleading action under regulation 5, or
(b) is aggressive under regulation 7.
[...]'[247]

Thus, if a legal services provider were to engage in commercial practices that were either misleading (see 28.119) or aggressive (see 28.124)—as defined by regs 5 and 7 of the 2008 Regulations, respectively—and if those practices were to be a significant factor in the client decision to enter into a contract of retainer with that legal services provider, then the client would have a right to redress. This means that a consumer who enters into a contract for legal services with a legal services provider or who pays a provider for a supply of legal services has a 'right to redress' if the legal services provider engages in a practice that comprises misleading action or in an aggressive commercial practice in relation to the services. It should be noted that the 2008 Regulations (as amended by the 2014 Regulations) do not provide a mechanism for redress for misleading omissions and banned practices. What is meant by 'redress' will depend on whether the client elects to unwind the contract or to seek a discount. **28.136**

The right to unwind The provisions relating to unwinding read as follows: **28.137**

'**When does the right to unwind apply to a business to consumer contract?**

27E (1) A consumer has the right to unwind in respect of a business to consumer contract if the consumer indicates to the trader that the consumer rejects the product, and does so—
(a) within the relevant period, and
(b) at a time when the product is capable of being rejected.

(2) An indication under paragraph (1) may be something that the consumer says or does, but it must be clear.

(3) In paragraph (1)(a) "the relevant period" means the period of 90 days beginning with the later of—
(a) the day on which the consumer enters into the contract, and
(b) the relevant day.

(4) In this Part "the relevant day" means the day on which—
[...]
(b) the performance of the service begins,
[...]

[247] Consumer Protection from Unfair Trading Regulations 2008 (SI 2008/1277), regs 27A and 27B, as amended by the Consumer Protection (Amendment) Regulations 2014 (SI 2014/870).

(8) For the purposes of paragraph (1)(b), a product remains capable of being rejected only if—

[...]

(b) the service has not been fully performed,

[...]

How does the right to unwind work in the case of a business to consumer contract?

27F (1) Where a consumer has the right to unwind in respect of a business to consumer contract—

(a) the contract comes to an end so that the consumer and the trader are released from their obligations under it,

(b) the trader has a duty to give the consumer a refund (subject as follows)

[...]

(2) The consumer's entitlement to a refund works as follows.

(3) To the extent that the consumer paid money under the contract, the consumer is entitled to receive back the same amount of money (but see paragraphs (7) to (10)).

[...]'[248]

28.138 Thus the right to unwind must be exercised while the services remain capable of being rejected and within a period of 90 days. If the consumer exercises this right, the contract comes to an end and the consumer is entitled to a refund (subject to certain conditions set out in the Regulations).

28.139 It is not clear exactly how these provisions would apply in the context of costs, but it is easily arguable that a client could unwind an entire contract of retainer provided that this was done within the relevant time limits. It is, however, highly unlikely that a paying party could rely on the right to unwind for proving a breach of the indemnity principle, because it is clear that the right to unwind would apply only upon the client electing to exercise that right. As such, any such attempt would almost certainly be defeated, for the reasons given by Arden LJ in *Garbutt v Edwards*.[249]

28.140 **The right to a discount** The provision relating to the right to a discount reads as follows:

'**How does the right to a discount work?**

27I (1) A consumer has the right to a discount in respect of a business to consumer contract if—

(a) the consumer has made one or more payments for the product to the trader or one or more payments under the contract have not been made, and

(b) the consumer has not exercised the right to unwind in respect of the contract.

(2) If the consumer has made one or more payments, the consumer has the right to receive back from the trader the relevant percentage of the payment or payments.

(3) If one or more payments have not been made, the consumer has the right—

(a) to reduce by the relevant percentage as many of those payments as is appropriate having regard to the seriousness of the prohibited practice,

[...]

[248] Consumer Protection from Unfair Trading Regulations 2008 (SI 2008/1277), regs 27E and 27F, as amended by the Consumer Protection (Amendment) Regulations 2014 (SI 2014/870).

[249] *Garbutt v Edwards* [2005] EWCA Civ 1206, at [35] *et seq*.

(4) Subject to paragraph (6), the relevant percentage is as follows—
(a) if the prohibited practice is more than minor, it is 25%,
(b) if the prohibited practice is significant, it is 50%,
(c) if the prohibited practice is serious, it is 75%, and
(d) if the prohibited practice is very serious, it is 100%.

(5) The seriousness of the prohibited practice is to be assessed by reference to—
(a) the behaviour of the person who engaged in the practice,
(b) the impact of the practice on the consumer, and
(c) the time that has elapsed since the prohibited practice took place.

[...]

(8) The application of this regulation does not affect any of the other rights and liabilities under the contract.'[250]

Thus, if a consumer has the right to a discount, it will be for 25 per cent, 50 per cent, 75 per cent or 100 per cent of past or future payments under the contract of retainer, depending on the seriousness of the breach, the impact of the practice on the consumer and the time that has elapsed. Exercising this right of redress has no effect on any other rights and liabilities that may arise under the contract, but a consumer cannot recover twice for the same loss. **28.141**

Again, it is not clear exactly how these provisions would apply in the context of costs, but it would seem that if a legal services provider were to engage in even minor aggressive or misleading commercial practices, the client would be entitled to a discount. This is potentially of significant importance as between clients and legal services providers. The points made above about *Garbutt v Edwards* would almost certainly apply if the point were to be raised by a paying party.[251] This topic is discussed at 27.268–27.269. **28.142**

The right to enforce terms about services under the Consumer Rights Act 2015

In so far as it is relevant, s 54 of the Consumer Rights Act 2015 reads as follows: **28.143**

'**54 Consumer's rights to enforce terms about services**

(1) The consumer's rights under this section and sections 55 and 56 do not affect any rights that the contract provides for, if those are not inconsistent.

[...]

(3) If the service does not conform to the contract, the consumer's rights (and the provisions about them and when they are available) are—
(a) the right to require repeat performance (see section 55);
(b) the right to a price reduction (see section 56).

[...]

(5) If the trader is in breach of what the contract requires under section 52 (performance within a reasonable time), the consumer has the right to a price reduction (see section 56 for provisions about that right and when it is available).

[...]'

[250] Consumer Protection from Unfair Trading Regulations 2008 (SI 2008/1277), reg 27I, as amended by the Consumer Protection (Amendment) Regulations 2014 (SI 2014/870).
[251] *Ibid.*

28.144 Thus, if a legal services provider's service does not conform to the contract of retainer, the client may be entitled to repeat performance or to a price reduction. In particular, where the contract of retainer is not performed with reasonable care and skill or within a reasonable time, then the consumer may have such a right.

28.145 **The right to require repeat performance** This is a right to require the legal services provider to take the steps necessary to perform the service again so that it conforms with the contract. If the consumer requires such repeat performance, the legal services provider must provide it within a reasonable time, but without causing significant inconvenience to the consumer.[252] The legal services provider must also bear any necessary costs incurred in repeating performance of the contract. The availability of repeat performance as redress in the legal services sector depends entirely on the facts of the case and, in particular, the point at which the consumer raises a complaint or seeks a remedy.

28.146 **The right to a price reduction** The right to a price reduction is governed by s 56 of the Consumer Rights Act 2015, which reads as follows:

> '56 **Right to price reduction**
>
> (1) The right to a price reduction is the right to require the trader to reduce the price to the consumer by an appropriate amount (including the right to receive a refund for anything already paid above the reduced amount).
>
> (2) The amount of the reduction may, where appropriate, be the full amount of the price.
>
> [...]
>
> (4) A refund under this section must be given without undue delay, and in any event within 14 days beginning with the day on which the trader agrees that the consumer is entitled to a refund.
>
> (5) The trader must give the refund using the same means of payment as the consumer used to pay for the service, unless the consumer expressly agrees otherwise.
>
> (6) The trader must not impose any fee on the consumer in respect of the refund.'

28.147 Thus this is a right to require the legal services provider to reduce the price payable by the consumer to an appropriate amount. It includes the right to receive a refund for anything already paid above a reduced amount and may include the full amount of the price.

28.148 This is potentially of significant importance in so far as the relationship between a solicitor and client is concerned. This is not only because it provides a statutory mechanism by which a client may seek to avoid paying for 'shoddy work' (see 37.36), but also because it appears to provide a mechanism that allows a client to seek a reduction in their liability for fees that is not dependent on them being exposed to the risk of a solicitor-and-client assessment. Indeed, one could argue that the *generalia specialibus non derogant* canon of statutory interpretation[253] does not preclude the operation of the two separate statutory regimes (that is, that they are complementary) and that the client is at liberty to elect which regime to rely upon. If this is correct, then this is a significant strengthening of the position of clients. There is, however, no authority on this topic.

---

252 See Consumer Rights Act 2015, s 55.

253 That is, that the provisions of a general statute must yield to those of a special one.

General Consumer Protection Legislation (Recently Revoked in Part)

The Unfair Terms in Consumer Contracts Regulations 1999 (now partially superseded)

Where the contract was made prior to 1 October 2015,[254] the Unfair Terms in Consumer Contracts Regulations 1999[255] continue to govern unfair terms in contracts concluded between a 'seller or supplier' and a consumer.[256] Where the contract was made after that date, the provisions of Pt 2 of the Consumer Rights Act 2015 will apply instead (see 28.40–28.44). **28.149**

'Consumer', in this context, means any natural person who is acting for purposes that are outside their trade, business or profession,[257] whilst 'seller or supplier' means any natural or legal person who is acting for purposes relating to their trade, business or profession.[258] A consumer client and a legal services provider would ordinarily fall within those categories. **28.150**

In so far as contracts of retainer are concerned, the important aspects of the 1999 Regulations are contained in reg 5, which reads as follows: **28.151**

> '5 (1) A contractual term which has not been individually negotiated shall be regarded as unfair if, contrary to the requirement of good faith, it causes a significant imbalance in the parties' rights and obligations arising under the contract, to the detriment of the consumer.
>
> (2) A term shall always be regarded as not having been individually negotiated where it has been drafted in advance and the consumer has therefore not been able to influence the substance of the term.
>
> (3) Notwithstanding that a specific term or certain aspects of it in a contract has been individually negotiated, these Regulations shall apply to the rest of a contract if an overall assessment of it indicates that it is a pre-formulated standard contract.
>
> (4) It shall be for any seller or supplier who claims that a term was individually negotiated to show that it was.'

Contracts of retainer with consumers would normally fall squarely within the category of contracts regarded as not having been individually negotiated. This means that if there is a provision in such a contract, it would be regarded as being 'unfair' if, contrary to the requirement of good faith, it were to cause a significant imbalance in the rights and obligations of the legal services provider to the detriment of the client.[259] The 1999 Regulations provide a number of examples of what would be regarded as being unfair.[260] By analogy to some of those examples, it is arguable that some provisions commonly found in contracts of retainer are 'unfair' and the following is a (non-exhaustive) list. **28.152**

- **Unfair accounting** Whilst there is no authority on the point, a provision that says that the legal services provider may keep monies that otherwise would be accounted for to the

[254] See Consumer Rights Act 2015 (Commencement No 3, Transitional Provisions, Savings and Consequential Amendments) Order 2015 (SI 2015/1630), art 6(4).

[255] SI 1999/2083.

[256] See Unfair Terms in Consumer Contracts Regulations 1999 (SI 1999/2083), reg 4(1).

[257] See Unfair Terms in Consumer Contracts Regulations 1999 (SI 1999/2083), reg 3(1).

[258] See Unfair Terms in Consumer Contracts Regulations 1999 (SI 1999/2083), reg 3(1).

[259] See Unfair Terms in Consumer Contracts Regulations 1999 (SI 1999/2083), reg 5(1).

[260] See Unfair Terms in Consumer Contracts Regulations 1999 (SI 1999/2083), Sch 2.

client (such as commission, or the interest received between the parties, or the benefit of a Part 36 enhancement of costs), could be at risk if there is no objective reason why those monies should be paid to the legal services provider rather than the client.

- **Transfer of control** Now rarely seen, a requirement that the client relinquishes control of the case to the legal services provider would almost certainly be regarded as being unfair (as well as unlawful for other reasons).
- **Mandatory arbitration** Provisions requiring the client to engage in arbitration, rather than litigation, may be regarded as being unfair.[261]
- **Small print** Irrevocably binding a client to terms with which they had no real opportunity of becoming acquainted before the conclusion of the contract would be regarded as being unfair.[262]
- **Termination at will** Whilst most legal services providers are prevented by professional rules from terminating a retainer at will, termination provisions are occasionally encountered, especially in conditional fee agreements. They are of doubtful legality because enabling the legal services provider to terminate a contract of indeterminate duration without reasonable notice except where there are serious grounds for doing so would be regarded as being 'unfair'.[263]

28.153 The assessment of whether a term is unfair is subject to the following provisions:

> '6 (1) ... [T]he unfairness of a contractual term shall be assessed, taking into account the nature of the ... services for which the contract was concluded and by referring, at the time of conclusion of the contract, to all the circumstances attending the conclusion of the contract and to all the other terms of the contract or of another contract on which it is dependent.
>
> (2) In so far as it is in plain intelligible language, the assessment of fairness of a term shall not relate–
> (a) to the definition of the main subject matter of the contract, or
> (b) to the adequacy of the price or remuneration, as against ... services supplied in exchange.'[264]

Thus the issue of fairness will be gauged by reference to the circumstances as they were at the time the contract of retainer was concluded.

The effect of a term being 'unfair'

28.154 The effect of an unfair term in a contract of retainer is that that term is not binding on the client.[265] The contract itself will continue to bind the parties if it is capable of continuing in existence without the unfair term[266] and this will almost always be the case in respect of contracts of retainer. Whilst there is no authority on the point, the power to find that a term is unfair adds to the means by which the court may avoid injustice that may otherwise be caused by the irrebuttable presumptions in r 46.9(3) of the Civil Procedure Rules (CPR). This is addressed in more detail at 37.34.

261 See Unfair Terms in Consumer Contracts Regulations 1999 (SI 1999/2083), Sch 2, para 1(q).
262 See Unfair Terms in Consumer Contracts Regulations 1999 (SI 1999/2083), Sch 2, para 1(i).
263 See Unfair Terms in Consumer Contracts Regulations 1999 (SI 1999/2083), Sch 2, para 1(g); see also Sch 2, para 1(f), which deals with rights to unilaterally dissolve the contract.
264 Unfair Terms in Consumer Contracts Regulations 1999 (SI 1999/2083), reg 6.
265 See Unfair Terms in Consumer Contracts Regulations 1999 (SI 1999/2083), reg 8(1).
266 See Unfair Terms in Consumer Contracts Regulations 1999 (SI 1999/2083), reg 8(2).

OFT guidance

The Office of Fair Trading (OFT)—the CMA's predecessor—produced the following checklist aimed at allowing businesses to ensure that their terms of business were fair: **28.155**

> 'The following list provides some areas to consider when reviewing your terms. If you are unsure whether the terms you are using are fair, you should seek guidance from a legal professional.
> - Use ordinary words and avoid legal or technical language as much as possible.
> - Consider whether the meaning of your terms are clear and not open to a number of interpretations.
> - Make written terms legible (for example, consider whether font size and print quality is easily readable).
> - Consider whether your written contract is reader-friendly (for example, are short sentences and subheadings used?).
> - Check terms don't have the potential to be misleading.
> - Consider whether the price and main subject matter terms are highlighted as well as intelligible.
> - Ensure your terms don't give your business an unfair advantage.'

The Supply of Goods and Services Act 1982 (now partially superseded)

Where there is a contract for the supply of a service,[267] then if (a) Ch 2 of Pt 1 of the Consumer Rights Act 2015 does not apply (that is, if the client is not a consumer)[268] or (b) the client is a consumer who entered into the contract before 1 October 2015,[269] the following terms will be implied. **28.156**

- **Reasonable care and skill** Where the supplier is acting in the course of a business, there will be an implied term that the supplier will carry out the service with reasonable care and skill.[270]
- **Reasonable period of time** Where a supplier is acting in the course of a business and the time for the service to be carried out is not stipulated or otherwise agreed in the course of dealing between the parties, there is an implied term that the supplier will carry out the service within a reasonable period of time.[271]
- **Reasonable charge** Where the payment for the service is not determined by the contract or otherwise agreed between the parties, there will be an implied term that the party contracting with the supplier will pay a reasonable charge.[272]

Where the client is a consumer who made the contract on or after 1 October 2015, then the three terms referred to above will be implied by ss 49(1), 52 and 51 of the 2015 Act, respectively. **28.157**

The provisions in the Supply of Goods and Services Act 1982 were capable of applying to contracts of retainer, but there was a specific exclusion relating to advocacy services. **28.158**

---

[267] A contract for the supply of services is a contract under which a person (namely, 'the supplier') agrees to carry out a service: see Supply of Goods and Services Act 1982, s 12(1).

[268] See Consumer Rights Act 2015, Sch 1, paras 37–52.

[269] Consumer Rights Act 2015 (Commencement No 3, Transitional Provisions, Savings and Consequential Amendments) Order 2015 (SI 2015/1630), art 3.

[270] Supply of Goods and Services Act 1982, ss 12 and 13.

[271] See Supply of Goods and Services Act 1982, s 14(1).

[272] See Supply of Goods and Services Act 1982, s 15(1).

In particular, the implied term to carry out the service with reasonable care and skill did not apply to services of an advocate in court or before any tribunal, inquiry or arbitrator, which included the carrying out of preliminary work directly affecting the conduct of the hearing.[273] This exclusion was made to preserve the immunity from suit that counsel enjoyed at the time (that is, in 1982); despite the fact that that immunity ceased to exist decades ago, that exclusion has not been expressly revoked. Fortunately, there is no such exclusion in the corresponding provisions in the Consumer Rights Act 2015. It will continue to apply, however, where the client is not a consumer.

The Unfair Contract Terms Act 1977 (now partially superseded)

28.159 Where (a) the client is not a consumer[274] or (b) the client is a consumer who entered into the contract before 1 October 2015,[275] then the Unfair Contract Terms Act 1977 may apply. If the client is a consumer and the contract was made on or after 1 October 2015, then Pt 2 of the Consumer Rights Act 2015 will apply instead (see 28.40–28.44).

28.160 The 1977 Act contains a number of provisions that may be relevant to contracts of retainer. Most of those provisions turn on a test of 'reasonableness' and, as such, it is best to start with an explanation as to what is meant by that test.

The test of reasonableness

28.161 The issue of whether a term is reasonable is a question of whether it was a fair and reasonable term to be included in the contract having regard to the circumstances that were, or ought reasonably to have been, known to or in the contemplation of the parties when the contract was made.[276] In so far as it is relevant, Sch 2 of the Unfair Contract Terms Act 1977 gives the following guidance about the question of whether a term is reasonable:

> '[Regard will be had to any of] ... the following which appear to be relevant—
> (a) the strength of the bargaining positions of the parties relative to each other, taking into account (among other things) alternative means by which the customer's requirements could have been met;
> (b) whether the customer received an inducement to agree to the term, or in accepting it had an opportunity of entering into a similar contract with other persons, but without having to accept a similar term;
> (c) whether the customer knew or ought reasonably to have known of the existence and extent of the term (having regard, among other things, to any custom of the trade and any previous course of dealing between the parties); and
> (d) where the term excludes or restricts any relevant liability if some condition is not complied with, whether it was reasonable at the time of the contract to expect that compliance with that condition would be practicable.'

Specific provisions

28.162 The Unfair Contract Terms Act 1977 makes the following specific provisions that may be relevant to a contract of retainer.

273 See Supply of Services (Exclusion of Implied Terms) Order 1982 (SI 1982/1771), reg 2.
274 See Consumer Rights Act 2015, Sch 4, paras 2–27.
275 Consumer Rights Act 2015 (Commencement No 3, Transitional Provisions, Savings and Consequential Amendments) Order 2015 (SI 2015/1630), art 3.
276 See Unfair Contract Terms Act 1977, s 11(1).

- **Variation of a contract** Unreasonable variation of a contract is not permitted where the contract of retainer[277] is with a consumer and is based on the legal services provider's standard terms and conditions.[278] This could be relevant, for example, where the contract of retainer provided for a partner fee earner to carry out the work, but the solicitors unreasonably reallocated the conduct of the matter to an associate. The client's reaction to the putative variation may be relevant: in particular, if the client decides not to terminate the contract and treat it as repudiated, then this is a factor that the court can take into account, but it would not be determinative of whether the variation was reasonable.[279] Similarly, if the client terminated the agreement and elected to treat it as repudiated, then that would not be determinative of the fact that the variation was *un*reasonable.[280]
- **Notices given to clients** Notices are often given to clients. Where the notice is given to a client who is a consumer, then—unless the notice is one that has contractual effect (such as a notice that is referred to in the contract of retainer itself)—the requirement of reasonableness is that it should be fair and reasonable to allow reliance on the notice, having regard to all of the circumstances obtaining when the notice took effect.[281]
- **Choice-of-law clauses** Whilst they usually point to England and Wales, some contracts of retainer seek to invoke other jurisdictions. Where the client is a consumer, then such a provision will usually be void. This is because, with certain irrelevant exceptions,[282] contracts of retainer made with a consumer in the UK[283] cannot contain a clause that ousts that jurisdiction.[284]
- **Indemnity and exclusion clauses** It is frequently the case that contracts of retainer contain exclusions or limitations that seek to limit the extent to which a client is entitled to compensation in the event of some wrongdoing on the legal services provider's part. The approach of the court will depend on whether the contract of retainer is with a consumer or with a business.

---

277 It can safely be assumed that the legal services provider will always be acting in the course of a business, because Unfair Contract Terms Act 1977, s 14, provides that ' "business" includes a profession'.

278 See Unfair Contract Terms Act 1977, s 3, which provides as follows: '**3 Liability arising in contract** (1) This section applies as between contracting parties where one of them deals as consumer or on the other's written standard terms of business. (2) As against that party, the other cannot by reference to any contract term—(a) when himself in breach of contract, exclude or restrict any liability of his in respect of the breach; or (b) claim to be entitled—(i) to render a contractual performance substantially different from that which was reasonably expected of him, or (ii) in respect of the whole or any part of his contractual obligation, to render no performance at all, except in so far as (in any of the cases mentioned above in this subsection) the contract term satisfies the requirement of reasonableness.'

279 See Unfair Contract Terms Act 1977, s 9(2).

280 See Unfair Contract Terms Act 1977, s 9(1).

281 See Unfair Contract Terms Act 1977, s 11(3). The actual wording of this provision is slightly more complex than is set out in the text: 'In relation to a notice (not being a notice having contractual effect), the requirement of reasonableness under this Act is that it should be fair and reasonable to allow reliance on it, having regard to all the circumstances obtaining when the liability arose or (but for the notice) would have arisen.'

282 See the Unfair Contract Terms Act 1977, s 26.

283 Unfair Contract Terms Act 1977, s 27(2), makes the following provisions: 'This Act has effect notwithstanding any contract term which applies or purports to apply the law of some country outside the United Kingdom, where ... [in] the making of the contract one of the parties dealt as consumer, and he was then habitually resident in the United Kingdom, and the essential steps necessary for the making of the contract were taken there, whether by him or by others on his behalf.'

284 Unfair Contract Terms Act 1977, s 27(2).

- **Business** In commercial matters, the apportionment of risks by the parties will generally be upheld, especially where the parties are not of unequal bargaining power and where risks are ordinarily borne by insurance.[285] That said, exclusion clauses are often interpreted narrowly and a widely drafted clause may be interpreted as being of very little effect as a result.[286] The issue of whether the exclusion is clear or is 'buried' in the small print may be a relevant factor to the way in which the court interprets the clause,[287] as may the issue of whether the exclusions are clearly set out in terms of layout of the contract.[288] A further consideration is what remedy the innocent party would have in the event of a breach of contract.[289]
- **Consumer** Unreasonable indemnity clauses are not easily enforceable in the context of contracts of retainer with a person who deals as a consumer,[290] because such clauses are subject to a test of reasonableness.[291] The issue of whether the indemnity clause is reasonable is an issue that the court will take into account, assessing: (a) the resources that the legal services provider could expect to be available to them for the purpose of meeting the liability should it arise; and (b) how far it was open to the legal services provider to cover itself by insurance.[292]

General Consumer Protection Legislation (Older Revoked Provisions)

The Cancellation of Contracts Made in a Consumer's Home or Place of Work etc Regulations 2008 (now superseded)

28.163 Where a contract of retainer was made between 1 October 2008 and 13 June 2014, and where it was made at the client's home or place of work, or during an excursion, then the Cancellation of Contracts Made in a Consumer's Home or Place of Work etc Regulations 2008[293] (known as the Doorstep Selling Regulations) are likely to apply.[294] As of 13 June 2014, however, those Regulations were superseded by the Consumer

---

[285] See, eg, *Photo Production Ltd v Securicor Transport Ltd* [1980] AC 827, at 843 and 851.

[286] This is particularly so where the clause attempts to deal with 'indirect loss': see, eg, *GB Gas Holdings Ltd v Accenture (UK) Ltd & Ors* [2010] EWCA Civ 912.

[287] See, eg, *Kudos Catering (UK) Ltd v Manchester Central Convention Complex Ltd* [2013] EWCA Civ 38.

[288] See, eg, *Markerstudy Insurance Co Ltd & Ors v Endsleigh Insurance Services Ltd* [2010] EWCH 281 (Comm), in which the court held that the lack of subparagraphs meant that a poorly drafted provision 'contaminated' the whole of the clause.

[289] Again, see *Kudos Catering (UK) Ltd v Manchester Central Convention Complex Ltd* [2013] EWCA Civ 38.

[290] A party deals as consumer if (a) they neither make the contract in the course of a business nor hold themselves out as doing so and (b) the other party *does* make the contract in the course of a business: see Unfair Contract Terms Act 1977, s 12(1).

[291] See Unfair Contract Terms Act 1977, s 3, which provides: '4 **Unreasonable indemnity clauses** (1) A person dealing as consumer cannot by reference to any contract term be made to indemnify another person (whether a party to the contract or not) in respect of liability that may be incurred by the other for negligence or breach of contract, except in so far as the contract term satisfies the requirement of reasonableness. (2) This section applies whether the liability in question—(a) is directly that of the person to be indemnified or is incurred by him vicariously; (b) is to the person dealing as consumer or to someone else.'

[292] See Unfair Contract Terms Act 1977, s 11(4).

[293] SI 2008/1816.

[294] They revoked and replaced the Consumer Protection (Cancellation of Contracts Concluded Away from Business Premises) Regulations 1987 (SI 1987/2117).

Contracts (Information, Cancellation and Additional Charges) Regulations 2013[295] (see 28.58–28.100). If the contract was made after that date, then the new provisions will apply; if the contract was made before 1 October 2008, then the Consumer Protection (Cancellation of Contracts Concluded Away from Business Premises) Regulations 1987 may apply[296] (see the second edition of this book, at para 8.364).

Vires

The Doorstep Selling Regulations owed their origins to an EU directive.[297] Whilst their predecessors merely gave domestic effect to that directive, the Doorstep Selling Regulations went further in that they addressed a number of purely domestic concerns. They were made under two discrete powers: the first (concerning unsolicited visits) was the *vires* created by s 2(2) of the European Communities Act 1972; and the second (concerning solicited visits) was the *vires* created by ss 59 and 62(3)(f) of the Consumers, Estate Agents and Redress Act 2007.[298] **28.164**

Human rights issues

Jackson LJ has explained that the Doorstep Selling Regulations were not incompatible with Art 1 of the European Convention on Human Rights (ECHR), which prohibits a public authority from depriving a person of their possessions except in the public interest and subject to conditions provided by law. This is because, where there was a want of documentary compliance with the Doorstep Selling Regulations, the result was that any putative entitlement to payment under the contract never existed in the first place.[299] **28.165**

Application

Regulation 5 of the Doorstep Selling Regulations defines their ambit of application: **28.166**

> '**Scope of application**
>
> 5. These Regulations apply to a contract, including a consumer credit agreement, between a consumer and a trader which is for the supply of goods or services to the consumer by a trader and which is made—
> (a) during a visit by the trader to the consumer's home or place of work, or to the home of another individual;
> (b) during an excursion organised by the trader away from his business premises; or
> (c) after an offer made by the consumer during such a visit or excursion.
>
> 6. (1) These Regulations do not apply to—
> (a) any contracts listed in Schedule 3 (Excepted Contracts);
> (b) a cancellable agreement;
> (c) a consumer credit agreement which may be cancelled by the consumer in accordance with the terms of the agreement conferring upon him similar rights as if the agreement were a cancellable agreement; or

---

295 See Consumer Contracts (Information, Cancellation and Additional Charges) Regulations 2013 (SI 2013/3134), reg 2.

296 SI 1987/2117.

297 The Doorstep Selling Directive (Directive 85/577/EEC).

298 Consumers, Estate Agents and Redress Act 2007, s 59, defines the ambit of the power to make purely domestic provisions. It refers to 'consumers' and 'traders'; the definitions of these words are discussed below. Section 62(3)(f) is merely a procedural provision requiring that regulations modifying any Act must be laid before Parliament.

299 *Salat v Barutis* [2013] EWCA Civ 1499, at [26] and [27].

(d) a contract made during a solicited visit or a contract made after an offer made by a consumer during a solicited visit where the contract is—

[. . .]

(2) Where any agreement referred to in paragraph (1)(b), (c) or (d)(iii) is a related credit agreement the provisions of regulations 11 and 12 shall apply to the cancellation of that agreement.

(3) A solicited visit means a visit by a trader, whether or not he is the trader who supplies the goods or services, to a consumer's home or place of work or to the home of another individual, which is made at the express request of the consumer but does not include—

(a) a visit by a trader which is made after he, or a person acting in his name or on his behalf—
   (i) telephones the consumer (otherwise than at the consumer's express request) and indicates during the course of the telephone call (either expressly or by implication) that he, or the trader in whose name or on whose behalf he is acting, is willing to visit the consumer; or
   (ii) visits the consumer (otherwise than at the consumer's express request) and indicates during the course of that visit (either expressly or by implication) that he, or the trader in whose name or on whose behalf he is acting, is willing to make a subsequent visit to the consumer; or

(b) a visit during which the contract which is made relates to goods and services other than those concerning which the consumer requested the visit of the trader, provided that when the visit was requested the consumer did not know, or could not reasonably have known, that the supply of such goods or services formed part of the trader's commercial or professional activities.'

28.167 Thus the Doorstep Selling Regulations used to apply when a 'trader' made a contract with a 'consumer' during certain types of 'visit' and 'excursion'. This invites discussion of the following topics:

- whether legal services providers are 'traders' (see 28.168–28.170) and clients, 'consumers' (see 28.171–28.173);
- the types of contract to which the Regulations apply (see 28.174–28.177);
- the types of visit and excursion to which the Regulations apply (see 28.178–28.184); and
- the effect of contracting out (see 28.185).

28.168 **Legal services providers as 'traders'** The Doorstep Selling Regulations defined 'trader' as 'a natural or legal person who, for the transaction in question, acts in his commercial or professional capacity, and anyone acting in the name or on behalf of a trader'.[300]

28.169 Notwithstanding the reference to a trader acting in a 'professional capacity', one could argue that Parliament did not intend the word 'trader' to include legal services providers. If, for example, one looks at the relevant consultation papers, parliamentary debates, etc,[301] there is a lack of any express reference to legal services providers. Indeed, the Recital to the Doorstep Selling Directive made it clear that the main target was tradespeople such

[300] In additions, Consumers, Estate Agents and Redress Act 2007, s 59, defines 'trader' by reference to the Doorstep Selling Directive (Directive 85/577/EEC), in which the definition is given at Art 2 and is very similar to that given in the Regulations.

[301] The editor is unable to find any mention in Hansard that contracts of retainer were intended to fall within the ambit of the Regulations. The same is true of the minutes of the House of Commons General Committee on Delegated Legislation (see Second Delegated Legislation Committee, 30 June 2008).

as double-glazing sales representatives. In view of what Jackson LJ had to say in a case in which he was forced to find against a trader (a removals provider), it is almost certain that any such argument would fail:

> 'I reach this decision with regret. For consumer protection regulations to apply in the circumstances of this case is, in my view, inappropriate. Many removal firms are small businesses. They necessarily visit customers at home in order to assess the proposed work. It must often happen that the remover and the customer enter into an agreement at the customer's home. Once the deal is done, the remover must incur costs in preparing for the move. He may also turn away other work during the relevant period. If the customer has seven days grace in which to cancel the contract, the remover is put in an impossible position. I express hope that the Department for Business, Innovation, and Skills will review the Doorstep Selling Regulations in the light of this case and consider whether any amendments are appropriate. It may, for example, be thought appropriate to include removal contracts in the list of "excepted contracts" in Schedule 3 to the Regulations.'[302]

In view of all of this, the court is not likely to be swayed by an argument that it would be overly harsh to visit the full force of the Doorstep Selling Regulations on a particular type of trader (including legal services providers).

There are, in any event, other reasons why the court is likely to interpret the Doorstep Selling Regulations as including legal services providers. First and foremost, there are cases in which the court has considered the Regulations without making any mention of the issue of whether a legal services provider is a 'trader'.[303] Secondly, the Doorstep Selling Regulations were silent as to contracts made with legal services providers, yet they expressly excluded certain other types of contract (see 28.176–28.177).[304] Thirdly, derogations from an individual right conferred by a directive will rarely be implied and will usually be interpreted narrowly[305]—especially where the right is for the benefit of a consumer.[306] And finally, it could be argued that the nature of the services is barely relevant and that the Regulations are there to protect 'the consumer not because he purchases certain goods but because of the way in which the goods are purchased or the contract concluded'.[307] **28.170**

The meaning of 'consumer' Section 59 of the Consumers, Estate Agents and Redress Act 2007 defines 'consumer' by reference to the Doorstep Selling Directive, which definition is given at Art 2: ' "[C]onsumer" means a natural person who, in transactions covered by this Directive, is acting for purposes which can be regarded as outside his trade or profession ...' The Doorstep Selling Regulations themselves include similar definitions at reg 2(1): ' "[C]onsumer" means a natural person who in making a contract to which these Regulations apply is acting for purposes which can be regarded as outside his trade or profession ...' **28.171**

---

302 See *Robertson v Swift* [2012] EWCA Civ 1794, at [58]—a decision that was reversed in part on appeal, but on a different point ([2014] UKSC 50).

303 See *Cox v Woodlands Manor Care Home* [2015] EWCA Civ 415, esp at [14]; *Howes Percival LLP v Page* [2013] EWHC 4104 (Ch), *per* Judge Behrens (sitting as a judge of High Court).

304 This was a point that the ECJ took into account when considering any analogous argument that credit hire agreements should be excluded from the scope of the Doorstep Selling Directive (Directive 85/577/EEC): see *Heininger & Anor v Bayerische Hypo und Vereinsbank AG* [2004] All ER (EC) 1, at [30]–[32].

305 See, eg, Case C-222/84 *Johnston v Chief Constable of the Royal Ulster Constabulary* [1986] 3 All ER 135, at 158.

306 Case C-203/99 *Veedfald v Århus Amtskommune* [2001] ECR I-3569, at [15].

307 *Per* Advocate General Alber in *Travel-Vac SL v Antelm Sanchís* [1999] All ER (EC) 656, at 662.

28.172 Thus a consumer is natural person who is not acting in the course of their trade or profession.[308] There is, however, scope for arguing that these conditions will not be met if the supply of legal services is for a purpose that is connected with a person's trade or profession[309]—in contrast with the present-day legislation, which requires only that the person be acting 'wholly or mainly outside that individual's trade, business, craft or profession' (see 28.26). Whilst there is no authority on the point, it is possible that the ambit of the older definition would not include the situation in which legal services are provided both to a client and a funder, such as an insurer or a union.[310]

28.173 Whilst he was addressing legislation that was only analogous to the Doorstep Selling Regulations,[311] Field J has found that, where there are two linked contracts (a principal contract and contract that is ancillary to the principal contract), both must have been executed as a consumer for the Regulations to apply.[312] Again, this may be of relevance where, for example, the retainer is formed as a result of the client already having a contract of legal expenses insurance or a contract of union membership.

28.174 **When the contract was made** The Doorstep Selling Regulations did not apply to contracts that were made before 1 October 2008[313] or which were made on or after 13 June 2014.[314] Contracts that pre-dated that period were governed, if at all, by the Consumer Protection (Cancellation of Contracts Concluded Away from Business Premises) Regulations 1987.[315]

28.175 **The type of contract and how it was made** Certain types of contract were excluded from control (see 28.176–28.177). Where the agreement is not an excepted contract, then the following issues may arise:

- the question of what is meant by 'visit' and 'excursion' (see 28.178–28.184);
- the relevance of the contract being signed after a visit or excursion, or of it being made conditional upon some future event (see 28.181–28.182);
- the relevance of there having been more than one visit or excursion (see 28.183);
- the relevance of whether the visit or excursion was solicited (see 28.184); and
- the extent to which a trader can 'contract out' of the Doorstep Selling Regulations (see 28.185).

28.176 *Excepted contracts* Certain contracts were expressly excepted from the Doorstep Selling Regulations. Whilst many of those contracts are, like certain types of contract of retainer,

---

[308] This would seem not to include a person in a partnership, association or co-operative: see Case C-215/08 *E Friz GmbH v Carsten von der Heyden*, Opinion of AG Trstenjak, 8 September 2009 (unreported).

[309] Case C-45/96 *Bayerische Hypothetken v Dietzinger* [1998] 1 WLR 1035, at [18]–[23], in which the ECJ found that guaranteed repayment of a debt contracted by another person who, for his part, was active within the course of his trade or profession was sufficient to disapply the Doorstep Selling Directive (Directive 85/577/EEC). See also *Barclays Bank plc v Kufner* [2008] EWHC Comm 2319, at [28], *per* Field J.

[310] That said, the ECJ has held that a contract which benefits a stranger standing outside the contract is not excluded from the scope of the Directive on the sole ground that the benefit of the contract is intended for the use of that third party: see Case C-45/96 *Bayerische Hypothetken v Dietzinger* [1998] 1 WLR 1035.

[311] Unfair Terms in Consumer Contracts Regulations 1999 (SI 1999/2083).

[312] *Barclays Bank plc v Kufner* [2008] EWHC Comm 2319, at [28], *per* Field J.

[313] See Cancellation of Contracts Made in a Consumer's Home or Place of Work etc Regulations 2008 (SI 2008/1816), reg 4(3).

[314] See Consumer Contracts (Information, Cancellation and Additional Charges) Regulations 2013 (SI 2013/3134), reg 2.

[315] SI 1987/2117.

subject to other forms of regulatory control, contracts of retainer are not amongst those that are excepted.[316] However, Sch 3, para 6, to the Regulations does except '[a]ny contract not falling within paragraph 5 under which the total payments to be made by the consumer do not exceed £35'.

It may be the case that some conditional fee agreements fall within this category—in particular, agreements that do not permit the legal services provider, in any circumstances, to recover monies from its client beyond those that are recovered from the opponent. There is, however, no binding authority on this point[317] and the counter-arguments are easy to muster. **28.177**

Visits and excursions The Doorstep Selling Regulations will apply to a contract that is made in the following circumstances: **28.178**

- during a visit by the trader to the consumer's home or place of work, or to the home of another individual;
- during an excursion organised by the trader away from their business premises; and
- after an offer made by the consumer during such a visit or excursion.[318]

If one draws an analogy with cases concerning sales representatives, the mere fact that a legal services provider habitually visits a place (such as a union's offices) will not make that place its place of business.[319] **28.179**

There is no definition of 'excursion' within the Doorstep Selling Regulations. In a case in which a trader had invited a consumer to go to a specified place that was different from the premises where the trader usually carried on his business, the European Court of Justice (ECJ) found that any resulting contract had to be considered to have been concluded 'during an excursion organised by the trader'.[320] That said, Slade J (in a decision that was upheld on appeal) found that the ECJ had not been asked to rule on the meaning of the word 'excursion' and went on to say the following: **28.180**

> 'Regulation 5(a) contains the word "visit" and Regulation 5(c) both "excursion" and "visit". A different meaning must be given to each otherwise the inclusion of both would be otiose. In my judgment, the ordinary meaning of the word excursion carries with it a degree of organisation. If a person goes on a cruise they would have to travel to join a ship. Whilst on the ship they may dock at a port and go site-seeing. The latter would be an excursion and the former would not. In my judgment, the mere fact of having to travel to a destination where services are offered does not constitute the travel and events on arrival an "excursion".'[321]

As such, it seems that an 'excursion' implies an element of organisation that goes beyond merely travelling to a destination.

[316] Cancellation of Contracts Made in a Consumer's Home or Place of Work etc Regulations 2008 (SI 2008/1816), reg 6.

[317] Whilst not binding, in *Hurley v Makuni* (unreported), 28 September 2012, Manchester County Court, Regional Costs Judge Moss rejected the argument that a CFA Lite fell within this category.

[318] Cancellation of Contracts Made in a Consumer's Home or Place of Work etc Regulations 2008 (SI 2008/1816), reg 5.

[319] See *In the matter of Tag World Services Ltd* [2008] EWHC Ch 1866, at [24].

[320] *Travel-Vac SL v Antelm Sanchís* [1999] All ER (EC) 656.

[321] See *Kupeli v Cyprus Turkish Airlines* [2016] EWHC 1125 (QB), at [23], affirmed on appeal ([2017] EWCA Civ 1037).

28.181 *Signed after a visit or excursion or made conditional upon some future event* If a retainer is signed by both parties during the visit or excursion, then it will usually be clear that the retainer was made during that visit or excursion. Judge Mackie QC (sitting as a judge of the High Court) has confirmed that if, following a visit, revisions are made to the resulting agreement without a further visit or exclusion, that revised agreement will not be caught by the Doorstep Selling Regulations.[322]

28.182 If a contract is signed during a visit or excursion on the basis that it will become binding only upon the happening of some future event, then it will still have been made during that visit or excursion; hence, in a case in which a retainer was said to be conditional upon an ATE insurer agreeing to provide cover, Underhill LJ found that it had been made at the time it was signed rather than at the time that cover was provided.[323]

28.183 *One visit or more than one visit or excursion* Jackson LJ has explained that the use of the phrase 'during a visit' does not limit the Doorstep Selling Regulations so that they apply only if there was one visit;[324] rather, the Doorstep Selling Regulations apply if the consumer's home was the place where the contract was concluded. This is so irrespective of whether there were earlier negotiations between the parties at the consumer's home.[325] In a case in which there were ongoing discussions about the contract of retainer, Judge Behrens (sitting as a deputy judge of the High Court) found that a visit that took place part-way through those discussions was mere 'happenstance' and that, for the Regulations to engage, the offer needed to be an offer in the ordinary legal sense of that word, rather than an offer that was subject to ongoing negotiations.[326]

28.184 *Solicited and unsolicited visits* Whilst the Doorstep Selling Regulations draw a distinction between solicited and unsolicited visits, that distinction is not likely to be relevant to legal services providers or their retainers (because the distinction matters only in respect of certain specified types of contract and that group does not include contracts of retainer).[327]

28.185 **Contracting out** There is only limited scope to contract out of the provisions of the Doorstep Selling Regulations. In particular, any contractual term will be void if it is inconsistent with a regulatory provision for the protection of the consumer. This will be so where the contractual term purports to impose a duty or liability on the consumer that is additional to or different from those specified in the Doorstep Selling Regulations.[328]

The effect of cancellation under the Doorstep Selling Regulations

28.186 Where the relevant requirements have been satisfied, a contract of retainer will not be unenforceable for want of compliance with the Doorstep Selling Regulations, but

---

322 See *W v Veolia Environmental Services (UK) plc* [2011] EWHC 2020 (QB), at [54].

323 *Cox v Woodlands Manor Care Home* [2015] EWCA Civ 415, at [11]–[13], *per* Underhill LJ.

324 *Robertson v Swift* [2012] EWCA Civ 1794, at [41]—a decision that was reversed in part on appeal, but on a different point ([2014] UKSC 50).

325 *Ibid.*

326 See *Howes Percival LLP v Page* [2013] EWHC Ch 4104, at [241].

327 See Cancellation of Contracts Made in a Consumer's Home or Place of Work etc Regulations 2008 (SI 2008/1816), reg 6(d).

328 Cancellation of Contracts Made in a Consumer's Home or Place of Work etc Regulations 2008 (SI 2008/1816), reg 15.

the client will have the right to cancel it during 'the cancellation period' (which is seven days).[329]

General points A cancelled retainer will be treated as if it had never been made. A cancellation notice sent by post is taken to have been served at the time of posting, whether or not it is actually received. Where a cancellation notice is sent by email, it is taken to have been served on the day on which it was sent.[330] **28.187**

Where a written request was made Where a client had entered into a 'specified contract' (the definition of which includes contracts of retainer) and where they intended the legal services provider to start work before the end of the cancellation period, that request had to be made in writing.[331] If the client were to subsequently cancel the retainer, they would be obliged to 'pay in accordance with the reasonable requirements of the cancelled contract for ... services that were supplied before the cancellation'.[332] **28.188**

Where no written request was made If the client made no written request to begin work immediately and if they cancelled the contract within the cancellation period, the legal services provider would have gone unremunerated. It was not permissible for the legal services provider to charge a penalty or lump sum upon renunciation of the contract.[333] **28.189**

Monies held on account Where a contract was cancelled, any monies paid on account were refundable and any securities taken in respect of fees would have been treated as never having been taken.[334] The provisions concerning payments on account permitted the solicitor to deduct payment for services already rendered (if any such monies were properly payable), but the same was not true of securities, which had to be returned in whole. This, presumably, applied to lien, charging orders and security for costs taken pursuant to Solicitors Act 1974, s 65(1). **28.190**

Related agreements Cancellation of the retainer would have had the effect of cancelling any related credit agreement (such as a disbursements funding loan).[335] Where this happened, the legal services provider had to tell the creditor and any monies paid by the client had to be reimbursed. There were also provisions concerning interest that were dependent on the nature of the credit agreement[336]—but that topic is beyond the scope of this book. **28.191**

---

[329] Cancellation of Contracts Made in a Consumer's Home or Place of Work etc Regulations 2008 (SI 2008/1816), reg 7(1) and 2.

[330] Cancellation of Contracts Made in a Consumer's Home or Place of Work etc Regulations 2008 (SI 2008/1816), reg 8.

[331] Cancellation of Contracts Made in a Consumer's Home or Place of Work etc Regulations 2008 (SI 2008/1816), reg 9.

[332] Cancellation of Contracts Made in a Consumer's Home or Place of Work etc Regulations 2008 (SI 2008/1816), reg 9(2).

[333] *Travel-Vac SL v Antelm Sanchis* [1999] All ER (EC) 656.

[334] Cancellation of Contracts Made in a Consumer's Home or Place of Work etc Regulations 2008 (SI 2008/1816), reg 10.

[335] Cancellation of Contracts Made in a Consumer's Home or Place of Work etc Regulations 2008 (SI 2008/1816), reg 11(1).

[336] Cancellation of Contracts Made in a Consumer's Home or Place of Work etc Regulations 2008 (SI 2008/1816), reg 12.

The requirements of the Doorstep Selling Regulations

28.192 Where the Doorstep Selling Regulations applied, the following requirements had to be satisfied.

- The legal services provider had to give the client a written notice of their right to cancel the retainer, which notice had to be given at the time the contract of retainer was made or, if the contract was made after the visit or excursion, at the time the offer was made.[337]
- That notice ought to have:
  - been dated;
  - indicated the right of the client to cancel the contract within the cancellation period;
  - been easily legible;
  - contained the following information:
    - the identity of the legal services provider (including trading name, if any); and
    - the legal service provider's reference, code or other details to enable the contract or offer to be identified;
  - contained a cancellation form in the manner set out in Pt II of Sch 4 to the Doorstep Selling Regulations, that being provided as a detachable slip and completed by or on behalf of the legal service provider in accordance with the notes;
  - contained the name and address (including any email address, as well as the postal address) of the person to whom a cancellation notice ought to have been given;
  - contained a statement that the consumer had a right to cancel the contract and that that right could have been exercised by delivering, or sending (including by email) a cancellation notice to the person mentioned above at any time within the period of seven days, starting with the day of receipt of the notice of the right to cancel the contract;
  - contained a statement that notice of cancellation would have been deemed to have been given as soon as it was posted or sent to the legal services provider or, in the case of email, on the day on which it was sent;
  - contained a statement that the consumer was able to use the cancellation form provided;
  - indicated, if applicable, that the consumer would be required to pay for the services supplied if services were provided with their written agreement before the end of the cancellation period; and
  - indicated, if applicable, that a related credit agreement (such as a disbursement funding loan) would have been automatically cancelled if the retainer had been cancelled.[338]

28.193 This notice ought to have been incorporated into the written instrument of retainer.[339] Whilst not binding on any court in this jurisdiction, McCloskey J found that it was not necessary that the notice of the right to cancel should be on the same piece of paper as the rest of the contract and that separate pieces of paper suffice to comprise one document:

> 'It is unclear whether [the relevant documents] were physically attached to each other by means of a staple or paper clip or otherwise. However, I am of the opinion that the

[337] Cancellation of Contracts Made in a Consumer's Home or Place of Work etc Regulations 2008 (SI 2008/1816), reg 7(2).

[338] Cancellation of Contracts Made in a Consumer's Home or Place of Work etc Regulations 2008 (SI 2008/1816), reg 7(3) and Sch 4.

[339] Cancellation of Contracts Made in a Consumer's Home or Place of Work etc Regulations 2008 (SI 2008/1816), reg 7(4).

requirements of the Regulations are designed to ensure that the agreement and cancellation notice are packaged together in a manner which ensures that the hirer appreciates their inextricable linkage and has brought to his attention his right to cancel the agreement. "Incorporation" in my view, is to be understood in this sense.'[340]

McCloskey J found that the documents were part of a package and that, when viewed as a whole, the component parts of that package were inseparable. The notice must be set out in a separate box with the heading 'Notice of the Right to Cancel'. It also ought to have had as much prominence as any other information in the retainer (apart from the heading, the parties and any information inserted in handwriting).[341]

For the reasons set out at 28.188, a legal services provider who sought to be paid for services provided prior to cancellation had to ensure that the client had confirmed that fact in writing. **28.194**

Non-compliance with the Doorstep Selling Regulations

Regulation 7(6) of the Doorstep Selling Regulations reads as follows: 'A contract to which these Regulations apply shall not be enforceable against the consumer unless the trader has given the consumer a notice of the right to cancel and the information required in accordance with this regulation.' This provision (which is the only provision in the Doorstep Selling Regulations concerning enforceability) appears to be subtler and more specific than a bare statement that non-compliance will result in the contract being unenforceable. It would not be open to the court to find that the effluxion of time negated the client's right to claim the benefit of the Doorstep Selling Directive.[342] **28.195**

Non-compliance is a criminal offence, but such issues are beyond the scope of this book. A defence of due diligence may apply. **28.196**

The Doorstep Selling Regulations between the parties

Whilst not binding on any court in this jurisdiction, McCloskey J has found that, where a third party is liable to pay (albeit in a context other than costs), that amount will be nil if there has been a breach of the Doorstep Selling Regulations.[343] As such, the indemnity principle would seem to apply.[344] **28.197**

It is also not clear whether a receiving party is obliged to lodge documents proving compliance with the Doorstep Selling Regulations at court pursuant to Practice Direction (PD) 47, para 13.2(i). This is because that provision requires the lodging of documents **28.198**

---

[340] *Clarke v McCullough* [2012] NIQB 104, at [27]. See also *Guerrero v Nykoo* (unreported), 25 October 2010, Cardiff County Court, *per* HHJ Vosper QC. HHJ Vosper QC came to that view by drawing an analogy with consumer credit cases—in particular, *Carey v HSBC Bank Plc* [2009] EWHC 3417 (QB), [2010] Bus LR 1142. HHJ Armstrong came to much the same conclusion in *Orley v Viewpoint Housing Association Ltd* (unreported), 7 December 2010, Gateshead County Court.

[341] Cancellation of Contracts Made in a Consumer's Home or Place of Work etc Regulations 2008 (SI 2008/1816), reg 7(5).

[342] See, by analogy, the comments of Advocate General Léger in *Heininger & Anor v Bayerische Hypo und Vereinsbank AG* [2004] All ER (EC) 1, at [60]–[65]; cf Case C-412/06 *Annelore Hamilton v Volksbank Filder eG* [2008] ECR I-2383, at [46], in which the ECJ distinguished *Heininger*.

[343] *Clarke v McCullough* [2012] NIQB 104, at [25]. In coming to that conclusion, McCloskey cited, with approval, *Wei v Cambridge Power and Light* (unreported), 10 September 2010, Cambridge County Court, *per* HHJ Maloney QC.

[344] See also *Cox v Woodlands Manor Care Home* [2015] EWCA Civ 415.

'explaining how the legal services provider's charges are to be calculated' and it is a moot point whether cancellation notices, etc, fall within this category.

28.199 There is no reason in principle why a paying party should not put CPR, Part 18, requests to a receiving party, but whether a receiving party would be required to answer those requests would be in the discretion of the court, to be decided on the facts of the case.

28.200 If a receiving party's legal services provider knows that there has been a breach of the requirements of the Doorstep Selling Regulations and if they know that, as a result of that breach, the retainer is unenforceable (that is, there is no credible contrary argument), then (in the editor's view) it would be improper for that provider to certify a bill of costs if that bill gives the impression that there has been no breach of the indemnity principle. Care should be taken in this regard, because improperly certifying a bill of costs is a serious disciplinary offence.[345]

The Consumer Protection (Distance Selling) Regulations 2000 (now revoked)

28.201 The Consumer Protection (Distance Selling) Regulations 2000[346] (known as the Distance Selling Regulations) implemented Directive 97/7/EC.[347] They came into force on 31 October 2000 and were significantly amended on 6 April 2005. In brief, they provided for a cooling-off period during which the client was able to cancel the retainer; where this happened, the contract of retainer was treated as if it had not been made. As of 13 June 2014, those Regulations were superseded by the Consumer Contracts (Information, Cancellation and Additional Charges) Regulations 2013[348] (see 28.58); if the contract was made after that date, then the new provisions will apply.

28.202 For most purposes, the relevance of the Distance Selling Regulations is that where a legal services provider failed to inform the client that the retainer could have lasted more than 30 days, the retainer could, arguably, be rendered void *ab initio*. This, however, is on a strict reading of the Distance Selling Regulations and there is no authority to confirm that this would happen in practice.

Application

28.203 The Distance Selling Regulations applied to retainers that were made exclusively by means of distance communication. Such arrangements were (and still are) commonplace in low-value personal injury work. Distance communication is likely to have included letters, telephone attendances, video attendances, email and fax.[349] The use of distance communication had to be exclusive—that is, up to and including the moment at which the retainer was made, distance communication had to have been the *only* means by which the legal services provider communicated with the client.[350]

[345] *Bailey v IBC Vehicles Ltd* [1998] 3 All ER 570.

[346] SI 2000/2334.

[347] Directive 97/7/EC of the European Parliament and of the Council of 20 May 1997 on the protection of consumers in respect of distance contracts, OJ L 144/19, 4 June 1997.

[348] See Consumer Contracts (Information, Cancellation and Additional Charges) Regulations 2013 (SI 2013/3134), reg 2.

[349] Consumer Protection (Distance Selling) Regulations 2000 (SI 2000/2334), Sch 1.

[350] Consumer Protection (Distance Selling) Regulations 2000 (SI 2000/2334), regs 3(1) and 4.

Requirements

The Distance Selling Regulations required the legal services provider to provide the client with certain information. In so far as they related to the provision of legal services, the requirements were as follows. **28.204**

- In the case of telephone communication, the identity of the legal services provider and the commercial purpose of the call had to be made clear at the beginning of the conversation.[351]
- The legal services provider had to provide:
  - the identity of its firm and—where the retainer required payment in advance—their address (including the address to which complaints should be made);[352]
  - a description of the main characteristics of the services to be provided;
  - the price of the services, including all taxes;
  - the arrangements for payment, delivery or performance;
  - the existence of a right of cancellation and the conditions under which that right could be exercised;[353]
  - the period for which the offer of services remained valid.[354]
- The legal services provider had to ensure that the above information was provided in a clear and comprehensible manner appropriate to the means of distance communication used. This ought to have been done with due regard to the principles of good faith in commercial transactions and the principles governing the protection of those who are unable to give their consent, such as children.[355]
- The legal services provider had to ensure that its commercial purpose was made clear when providing the information required.[356]

The information mentioned above had to be supplied in writing or in some other durable medium, and it ought to have been given either prior to the conclusion of the contract of retainer (that is, before it was made) or in good time thereafter. In any event, it ought to have been given prior to the termination of the retainer.[357] **28.205**

The need to provide information regarding cancellation The provisions relating to pre-cancellation work changed on 6 April 2005. **28.206**

- **Pre-2005** Where the legal services provider intended to be paid for pre-cancellation work, then the client had to be told in writing or another durable medium that they would not be able to cancel the retainer once work had begun.[358] The client's agreement to this provision would be implied by giving instructions to begin work.[359]
- **Post-2005**[360] After that date, the legal services provider had to inform the client in writing or another durable medium that if the client agreed to services starting within what otherwise would have been the cancellation period, the right to cancel would be

[351] Consumer Protection (Distance Selling) Regulations 2000 (SI 2000/2334), reg 7(4).
[352] Consumer Protection (Distance Selling) Regulations 2000 (SI 2000/2334), reg 8(2)(c).
[353] Consumer Protection (Distance Selling) Regulations 2000 (SI 2000/2334), reg 8(2)(e).
[354] Consumer Protection (Distance Selling) Regulations 2000 (SI 2000/2334), reg 7(1)(a).
[355] Consumer Protection (Distance Selling) Regulations 2000 (SI 2000/2334), reg 7(2).
[356] Consumer Protection (Distance Selling) Regulations 2000 (SI 2000/2334), reg 7(3).
[357] Consumer Protection (Distance Selling) Regulations 2000 (SI 2000/2334), reg 8.
[358] Consumer Protection (Distance Selling) Regulations 2000 (SI 2000/2334), reg 8(3).
[359] Consumer Protection (Distance Selling) Regulations 2000 (SI 2000/2334), reg 13(1)(a).
[360] Consumer Protection (Distance Selling) (Amendment) Regulations 2005 (SI 2005/689).

lost. Where a legal services provider provided that information before beginning work and where the client agreed to work beginning before the expiry of the cancellation period, there was no right to cancel.[361]

Other than as set out above, there could have been no contracting out of the provisions of the Distance Selling Regulations.[362]

28.207 **The need to avoid the 30-day trap** Unless there was agreement to the contrary, the legal services provider had to perform the retainer (that is, finish its work) within 30 days of the retainer being made. For obvious reasons, this would rarely have been possible in the context of contracts of retainer. The Distance Selling Regulations provided that if there was no agreement that the work would take longer than 30 days and if the contract was not performed within 30 days, then, from the legal services provider's point of view, the retainer would be treated as if it had not been made. With most retainers to which the Distance Selling Regulations applied, a failure to agree that the legal services provider's work would take longer than 30 days was capable of giving rise to difficulties in proving compliance with the indemnity principle. There is, however, no authority to confirm that the court would apply the Distance Selling Regulations in such a harsh way.[363]

Cancellation

28.208 The cancellation period varied depending on the circumstances. For the reasons set out at 28.206, however, after 6 April 2005, where there had been full compliance with the Distance Selling Regulations and where work had begun with the client's agreement during what otherwise would have been the cancellation period, the right to cancel would have been lost.

- **Full compliance** Where the requirements set out at 28.204 had been complied with prior to the retainer being made, the cancellation period would have ended on the expiry of the period of seven working days, beginning with the day after the day on which the contract was concluded.[364]
- **Late compliance** In general,[365] if the requirements were met late, then the cancellation period ended on the expiry of the period of seven working days beginning with the day after the day on which the client received the requisite information. After 6 April 2005, however, if the work had been completed within seven working days of the retainer having been made, then the cancellation period would have ended on the date that work was completed.[366]
- **No compliance** In all other circumstances (that is, where the requisite information had not been given), the cancellation period ended on the expiry of the period of three months and seven working days, beginning with the day after the day on which the contract was concluded.[367]

---

[361] Consumer Protection (Distance Selling) Regulations 2000 (SI 2000/2334), regs 8, 12 and 13 (as amended).

[362] Consumer Protection (Distance Selling) Regulations 2000 (SI 2000/2334), reg 25.

[363] Consumer Protection (Distance Selling) Regulations 2000 (SI 2000/2334), reg 19.

[364] Consumer Protection (Distance Selling) Regulations 2000 (SI 2000/2334), regs 12(2) and 2(1). A 'working day' is defined as all days other than Saturdays, Sundays and public holidays.

[365] Where work has begun within the initial seven-day period, see Consumer Protection (Distance Selling) Regulations 2000 (SI 2000/2334), reg 12(3)(a).

[366] After 2005, see Consumer Protection (Distance Selling) Regulations 2000 (SI 2000/2334), reg 13(1)(a).

[367] Consumer Protection (Distance Selling) Regulations 2000 (SI 2000/2334), reg 12.

Notice of cancellation If the client gave notice of cancellation during the cancellation period, that notice would have cancelled the retainer. The retainer would be treated as if it had never been made.[368] The client would not be able to cancel the retainer if the legal services provider had given notice prohibiting cancellation. Notice of cancellation may have been given by post, fax or email. Where the evidence is that it was sent by post, it was regarded as having been given regardless of whether or not it had been received.[369] 28.209

If the retainer was cancelled, any sums paid on account had to be returned, as did any securities that had been taken.[370] Any related credit agreement (such as a disbursement funding loan) would have been automatically cancelled.[371] 28.210

Failure to give the requisite information

Where the legal services provider failed to provide the requisite information in accordance with the Distance Selling Regulations, the cancellation period was extended by three months. The retainer would not have been unenforceable for want of compliance. 28.211

If a retainer had been cancelled in circumstances in which the legal services provider had failed to give notice of the effect of beginning work during the first seven days of the retainer (see above), then it is arguable that the legal services provider would be entitled to *quantum meruit* on the basis that the effect of cancellation was not to make the retainer unenforceable (in which case, an action in *quantum meruit* would not lie), but to cancel the retainer *ab initio*. In those circumstances (that is, valuable services being provided in the absence of a contract), it may be open to the court to find that the legal services provider is entitled to *quantum meruit*. That said, the comments of Schiemann LJ in *Awwad v Geragthy & Co*[372] would present the legal services provider with some difficulties. These issues are discussed in more detail at 27.267–27.268. 28.212

The Electronic Commerce (EC Directive) Regulations 2002 (now revoked)

This topic is addressed in the second edition of this book, at para 8.395. 28.213

Consumer Protection (Cancellation of Contracts Concluded away from Business Premises) Regulations 1987 (now revoked)

This topic is addressed in the second edition of this book, at para 8.364. 28.214

General Protection Legislation for Businesses (Present Day)

Provisions relating to business that have already been addressed

The following provisions have already been described in the context of provisions that, until recently, applied to consumers: 28.215

- the Supply of Goods and Services Act 1982 (see 28.156–28.158);

[368] Consumer Protection (Distance Selling) Regulations 2000 (SI 2000/2334), reg 10.
[369] Consumer Protection (Distance Selling) Regulations 2000 (SI 2000/2334), reg 10(4).
[370] Consumer Protection (Distance Selling) Regulations 2000 (SI 2000/2334), reg 14.
[371] Consumer Protection (Distance Selling) Regulations 2000 (SI 2000/2334), reg 15.
[372] *Awwad v Geragthy & Co* [2001] QB 570, at 596.

- the Unfair Contract Terms Act 1977 (see 28.159–28.162); and
- the Provision of Services Regulations 2009[373] (see 28.45–28.52);

Whilst these provisions no longer apply to consumers, they continue to apply where the purchaser of legal services is a business.

The Business Protection from Misleading Marketing Regulations 2008

28.216 In addition to the aforesaid provisions, the Business Protection from Misleading Marketing Regulations 2008[374] are the business-to-business equivalent of the Consumer Protection from Unfair Trading Regulations 2008.[375] They are, however, unlikely to be relevant to the law of costs and, as such, are beyond the scope of this book.

Remedies for businesses

28.217 Businesses do not have a 'right to redress' (see 28.135) under the Consumer Protection from Unfair Trading Regulations 2008[376] (as amended) or the 'right to enforce terms about services' (see 28.143) under the Consumer Rights Act 2015 because the relevant provisions do not apply to business-to-business transactions. Therefore, if a legal services provider has either acted negligently in providing advice or assistance to a business, then—provided that this is not fairly excluded from the contract or contrary to an agreed contract—the business can seek a remedy by bringing an action for breach of contract or in tort for, for example, negligence.

28.218 There are several remedies for breach of contract, such as award of damages, specific performance, rescission and restitution. The main remedy is an award of damages and this is the same for tortious loss, the main remedy for which is also financial compensation for damages. This will rarely be relevant in the context of the law of costs.

[373] SI 2009/2999.
[374] SI 2008/1276.
[375] SI 2008/1277.
[376] SI 2008/1277.

29

CONTRACTS OF RETAINER (CONDITIONAL FEE AGREEMENTS AND DAMAGES-BASED AGREEMENTS)

This chapter deals with conditional fee agreements and damages-based agreements. In particular, it deals with the following topics: **29.01**

- the language of conditional fee agreements (29.02);
- types of conditional fee agreement (29.03);
- conditional fee agreements and the statutory law (29.04);
- the basic requirements of all modern enforceable conditional fee agreements (29.14);
- older conditional fee agreements (29.24):
  - identifying the correct provisions (29.33);
  - genuine issues in the context of conditional fee agreements (29.44);
  - materiality (29.53);
  - individual regulations—breach and materiality (29.55);
  - the effect of a breach of the CFA Regulations 2000 (29.106);
- collective conditional fee agreements (29.111);
- retrospectivity and conditional fee agreements (29.132);
- damages-based agreements (29.141);
- conditional fee agreements, damages-based agreements and the common law (29.179):
  - non-contentious matters (29.185);
  - contentious matters (29.192);
  - persons other than lawyers (29.198);
- the history of conditional fee agreements (29.203); and
- the relevant regulations (29.217).

The Language of Conditional Fee Agreements

The law of conditional fee agreements and damages-based agreements has its own vocabulary. Some of the following words and phrases (which are listed in alphabetical order) are time-expired, informal or not universally accepted, but they are all commonly encountered nonetheless. **29.02**

- **Additional liability** 'Additional liability', in this context, refers to success fees and percentage increases. Whilst the present iteration of the Civil Procedure Rules (CPR) no longer defines this term, CPR, r 43.2(o), used to read: ' "[A]dditional liability" means the percentage increase, the insurance premium, or the additional amount in respect of provision made by a membership organisation, as the case may be.'

- **Base costs** Again, the CPR no longer define base costs, but Costs Practice Direction (CPD), art 2.2, used to read as follows: ' "[B]ase costs" means costs other than the amount of any additional liability.' The term 'basic costs' is also often used to mean the same thing.
- **Collective element** This is a term that refers to that part of a collective conditional fee agreement which contains the standard terms of the agreement.[1]
- **Damages-based payment** This is the payment payable to a legal representative who has successfully represented a client under a damages-based agreement. It is determined by reference to the amount of the financial benefit obtained.
- **Funder** Regulation 1(2) of the now-revoked Collective Conditional Fee Arrangement Regulations 2000[2] (the CCFA Regulations 2000) offered the following definition, which is still encountered from time to time: ' "[F]under" means the party to a collective conditional fee agreement who, under that agreement, is liable to pay the legal representative's fees.' This usage of the word has nothing to do with the use of the same word in the context of maintenance and non-party costs orders nor does it having anything to do with litigation funders.
- **Percentage increase** Regulation 3(3) of the Conditional Fee Agreements Regulations 2000[3] (the CFA Regulations 2000) used to afford the following definition,[4] which is very similar to that which used to be given by CPR, r 43.2(l): ' "[P]ercentage increase" means the percentage by which the amount of the fees which would be payable if the agreement were not a conditional fee agreement is to be increased under the agreement.' The difference between a success fee and a percentage increase is that the former is a sum of money, whereas the latter is expressed in terms of a percentage. In practice, however, the term 'success fee' is often used to mean percentage increase.
- **Postponement charge** This is also known as the postponement element[5] and a charge for postponement.[6] It is that part of the success fee which (where it is claimed) compensates the legal representative for the fact that it will not be able to issue interim invoices. Regulation 3(1)(b) of the now-revoked CFA Regulations 2000 gave the following definition: '[That part] of the percentage increase, if any, [which] relates to the cost to the legal representative of the postponement of the payment of his fees and expenses.' In this book, the phrase is used to refer both to the charge itself and to the percentage that is used to calculate it.
- **Quantum risk** This is a risk that arises out of a conditional fee agreement providing for no payment of base costs for work carried out after the client has failed to secure a result that is more advantageous to them than an opponent's Part 36 offer.[7]

---

[1] Under the Collective Conditional Fee Arrangement Regulations 2000 (SI 2000/2988) (CCFA Regulations 2000), it was that part of the agreement which was referred to by regs 4 and (where the agreement provides for a success fee) 5.

[2] SI 2000/2988 (CCFA Regulations 2000).

[3] SI 2000/692 (as amended).

[4] This definition is almost identical to that which appears at Collective Conditional Fee Arrangement Regulations 2000 (SI 2000/2988), reg 5(3).

[5] For an example of this phrase being used, see *Sidhu v Sandhu* [2008] EWHC 90108 (Costs), at [19].

[6] See, eg, *Utting v McBain* [2007] EWHC 90085 (Costs), at [23].

[7] For an example of it being used, see *Haines v Sarner* [2005] EWHC 90009 (Costs), at [15].

- **Success fee** Section 58A(2)(b) of the Courts and Legal Services Act 1990 (as amended) provides:

  'A conditional fee agreement provides for a success fee if it provides for the amount of any fees to which it applies to be increased, in specified circumstances, above the amount which would be payable if it were not payable only in specified circumstances.'

  So a success fee will be a fee that is payable only in specified circumstances (which almost always means that the case has been won) and which exceeds the amount that would have been payable if it were not payable only in specified circumstances. The percentage increase is used to calculate the success fee (see above).

Types of Conditional Fee Agreement

Conditional fee agreements and damages-based agreements come in many different forms. The following are often encountered in practice. **29.03**

- **Ordinary conditional fee agreements** This is what is usually meant by the initialism 'CFA'. If the claim is successful, the legal representative will be paid its full base costs, together with a success fee (where there is one); if it is unsuccessful, the legal representative will receive no such fees. Disbursements may or may not be payable in the event of a win, depending on the terms of the agreement. If the client 'wins', but fails to beat a Part 36 offer, fees incurred after the 'relevant period' relating to the offer may or may not be forfeited, depending on the type of agreement; if such fees are not payable, the agreement is said to 'provide for a quantum risk'. For agreements made on or after 1 April 2013, the success fee (if there is one) is generally payable by the client and is not recoverable from an opponent; where the agreement was made before that date, then the success fee is generally recoverable from an opponent, but is often restricted such that the percentage increase is no higher than that payable by the opponent.
- **CFA Lites** The phrase 'CFA Lite'[8] was originally a light-hearted term, but it has gained currency and is now an accepted label.[9] The main characteristic of this type of agreement is that, in ordinary circumstances, the client will be liable only for those fees that are recovered from the opponent. Disbursements may or may not be treated in this way, depending on the terms of the agreement. If the agreement was made before 1 April 2013, then a success fee may have been (and usually was) payable, but was limited to the monies recovered from the other side; if it was made on or after that date, then—by

[8] The phrase 'CFA Lite' originally referred only to the type of agreement made under Collective Conditional Fee Arrangement Regulations 2000 (SI 2000/2988), reg 3A (as amended), under which the client was 'liable to pay his legal representative's fees and expenses only to the extent that sums [were] recovered in respect of the relevant proceedings, whether by way of costs or otherwise'. The 2000 Regulations were revoked on 1 November 2005, but the use of the term has continued; the term has therefore come to mean any CFA under which the legal representative's fees are limited to those costs recovered in the litigation. Many modern-day CFA Lites would not satisfy the original requirements—in particular, it is not uncommon for disbursements to be payable regardless of the outcome of the claim.

[9] See, eg, *Jones v Wrexham Borough Council* [2007] EWCA Civ 1356, in which Waller LJ repeatedly used the term. See also *Munkenbeck & Marshall v Harold* [2005] EWHC 356 (TCC); Phillips MR, Speech made to the Law Society Litigation Conference, 2003.

definition—no CFA Lite could provide for a success fee.[10] That said, there is a type of conditional fee agreement (which is occasionally referred to as a 'CFA Max') that allows for an *ir*recoverable success fee (which is usually deducted from damages) to be paid on whatever base fees are recovered from an opponent.

- **Discounted conditional fee agreements** This is often shortened to 'dCFA'.[11] The legal representative's fees are payable in full if the case is won, but a discounted fee (usually expressed in terms of a discounted hourly rate) will apply if the case is not won. A success fee may or may not be payable. This type of agreement is particularly popular with solicitors who have a predominately defendant practice, because it allows liability insurers to fund the litigation at a discount, but in such a way as to ensure that the solicitor has an incentive to succeed. Discounted conditional fee agreements are also often used in combination with litigation (third-party) funding. Where the agreement was made before 1 April 2013, the fact that a success fee may be payable by an opponent was thought to encourage settlement and some legal representatives saw that as a significant advantage.
- **Discounted CFA Lites** This is often shortened to 'dCFA Lite'[12] and, as its name implies, is a cross between a discounted conditional fee agreement and a CFA Lite in that a discounted fee is payable if the case is lost, but if the case is won, the legal representative is entitled to be paid those fees recovered from whichever opponent is ordered to pay costs. Such agreements are popular with commercial litigators and with solicitors who have a predominately insurance-based practice, including those who do work funded by before-the-event (BTE) insurance.
- **Collective conditional fee agreements** A conditional fee agreement will be a collective conditional fee agreement[13]—or 'CCFA'—if it is based on a standard set of terms that the client (or funder) has agreed in advance and which are intended to apply in general to a defined class of cases. All of the types of agreement mentioned above have their collective equivalents. Thus, in addition to ordinary CCFAs, there are also CCFA Lites, dCCFAs, dCCFA Lites, etc. The advantage of collective conditional fee agreements is that they are robust and are administratively easy to implement on a case-by-case basis.
- **Damages-based agreements** The initialism 'DBA' is gaining currency.[14] The term 'contingency fee agreement' is also used, but this is a term that is apt to cause confusion because it can mean different things in different circumstances (see below). Under such an agreement, the amount of the legal representative's fee is quantitatively linked to the amount of damages or debt recovered (or, in non-contentious matters, to the price

[10] Except in certain types of claim in which success fees are still recoverable between opposing parties.

[11] Another term is a 'guaranteed fee agreement'. The term 'partial fee agreement' is occasionally used, especially when the agreement applies to a barrister. There is supposed to be a distinction between a partial fee agreement and a discounted CFA, but it is not a distinction that is important: a partial fee agreement is supposed to create two retainers, one of which is payable privately and the other of which is payable conditionally.

[12] The term 'insurers' CFA' is also gaining currency.

[13] The ambit of the term has widened since it was first used. The term was originally used to refer to an agreement that purported to comply with the Collective Conditional Fee Arrangement Regulations 2000 (SI 2000/2988) (as amended), but now that those Regulations have been revoked, the term is used to refer to any form of conditional retainer the terms of which are contained in an umbrella agreement (often referred to as the 'collective element') that applies to clients in general (or to a class of clients).

[14] See, eg, the comments in Ministry of Justice, *Regulating Damages-based Agreements*, CP 10/09 (London: HMSO, 2009), p 3.

received, the premium levied, etc). Section 58AA of the Courts and Legal Services Act 1990 (as amended) provides the following statutory definition:

> '(a) a damages-based agreement is an agreement between a person providing advocacy services, litigation services or claims management services and the recipient of those services which provides that—
> (i) the recipient is to make a payment to the person providing the services if the recipient obtains a specified financial benefit in connection with the matter in relation to which the services are provided, and
> (ii) the amount of that payment is to be determined by reference to the amount of the financial benefit obtained.'[15]

The fact that this definition applies to agreements in both contentious and non-contentious business is confirmed by s 58AA(9) of that Act,[16] which makes certain provision relating to damages-based agreements that are also non-contentious business agreements.

- **Contingency fee agreements** The term 'contingency fee agreement' can be used to mean different things in different contexts. This can cause difficulties because the two most common usages mean radically different things. As is explained above, the term is often used to mean a subset of conditional fee agreements (as broadly interpreted) under which the legal representative's fee is calculated by reference to the amount of money that is recovered for the client.[17] An example in a non-contentious setting would be where the legal representative sought to recover a percentage of the price of sale of a business; an example in a contentious setting would be where the fee was a percentage of the damages or debt recovered (this being a 'damages-based agreement', as defined above). The other way in which the phrase is used is to mean *any* conditional fee agreement of *any* sort.[18] There is nothing wrong with either of these usages, but, to avoid confusion, neither is adopted in this book.

Conditional Fee Agreements and the Statutory Law

Statutory definition

As of 1 April 2000 (with savings as to existing cases), the relevant statutory provisions have been—and still are—ss 58 and 58A of the Courts and Legal Services Act 1990 (as amended). Section 58(2)(a) provides: '[A conditional fee agreement is an] agreement with a person providing advocacy or litigation services which provides for his fees and expenses, or any part of them, to be payable only in specified circumstances.' **29.04**

Thus the statutory definition of a conditional fee agreement is that it: **29.05**

- is with a person providing litigation services or advocacy services; and
- provides that their fees, or any part of them, are payable only in specified circumstances.

[15] Courts and Legal Services Act 1990, s 58AA(3)(a), as amended by Coroners and Justice Act 2009, s 154.

[16] Which was inserted by Legal Aid, Sentencing and Punishment of Offenders Act 2012, s 45(10).

[17] See Anon, 'Criminal Solicitors Gear up for Mile-high Club' (2002) 99 LSG 11, at 41, for an example of the emergence of this usage.

[18] See, eg, the Solicitors' Code of Conduct 2007, which defined a contingency fee as 'any sum (whether fixed, or calculated either as a percentage of the proceeds or otherwise) payable only in the event of success'. The SRA Code of Conduct 2011 seems to use the phrase in that way too, but it is not possible to be sure of this because it contains no express definition.

29.06 The definition depends on the meaning of 'litigation services' and 'advocacy services'. These are defined by s 119 of the 1990 Act in this way:

- 'litigation services' means any services that it would be reasonable to expect a person who is exercising, or contemplating exercising, a right to conduct litigation in relation to any proceedings, or contemplated proceedings, to provide; and
- 'advocacy services' means any services that it would be reasonable to expect a person who is exercising, or contemplating exercising, a right of audience in relation to any proceedings, or contemplated proceedings, to provide.[19]

As can be seen, both of these definitions depend on the meaning of 'proceedings'.

29.07 If, for a moment, one looks at matters other than conditional fee agreements, the 1990 Act defines 'proceedings' as 'proceedings in any court'.[20] If that default definition were to apply, the meaning of 'proceedings' would be narrow (which would mean that the class of retainers that would fall within the category of conditional fee agreements would also be narrow). There is, however, a definition that applies only to conditional fee agreements and damages-based agreements, and that definition is much wider than the default definition. It reads as follows:

> 'In section 58 and this section (and in the definitions of "advocacy services" and "litigation services" as they apply for their purposes) "proceedings" includes any sort of proceedings for resolving disputes (and not just proceedings in a court), whether commenced or contemplated.'[21]

Thus ss 58 and 58A of the 1990 Act will apply to *any* class of proceedings[22] for resolving disputes and not only to those in a court.[23] The converse is that this definition will not cover retainers that do not relate to disputes or which relate to disputes but do not relate to proceedings.

29.08 The CPR no longer refer to conditional fee agreements, but, when they did, they adopted the statutory definition. They did this by making specific provision for costs to be recovered pursuant to conditional fee agreements and then by linking that provision to the statutory definition mentioned above.[24]

Contractual interpretation and unintended conditional fee agreements

29.09 The next question is how the statutory definition of a conditional fee agreement is to be applied in practice. An issue that commonly arises is whether a retainer has inadvertently become a conditional fee agreement by reason of a conditional waiver (that is, a putative

---

19 These definitions have been unaffected by the amendments made by the Legal Services Act 2007.

20 Courts and Legal Services Act 1990, s 119 (as amended).

21 Courts and Legal Services Act 1990, s 58A(4) (as amended).

22 The definition is somewhat circular because it defines 'proceedings' by reference to a definition that includes that very same word. There is no authority on how that word is to be interpreted—in particular, there is no authority on the issue of whether it would include work that is traditionally regarded as being non-contentious, such as work in tribunals.

23 Until Courts and Legal Services Act 1990, s 58, was amended by the Access to Justice Act 1999, CFAs that related to arbitral proceedings did not fall within the statutory regime: *Bevan Ashford (a firm) v Geoff Yeandle (Contractors) Ltd (in liquidation)* [1999] Ch 239.

24 CPR, r 43.2(4).

agreement to waive fees if the case is unsuccessful). That waiver may, for example, have been made by the legal representative in a client care letter.

The issue of waiver will often (but not always) be academic if the retainer was made on or after 1 November 2005, because the document that effected the waiver would usually itself meet the minimal statutory requirements that remained after the revocation of the CFA Regulations 2000 (see 29.14–29.18). Unintended conditional fee agreements made before that date, however, would rarely meet the then requirements (see 29.55–29.105), so, in those circumstances, a finding that a retainer had accidentally become a conditional fee agreement would often render it unenforceable. **29.10**

That said, this would not always be the case. When just such a case presented itself to Dyson LJ, he dealt with the matter by interpreting the phrase 'contemplated' proceedings in Courts and Legal Services Act 1990, s 58A(4) (see 29.07), in a pragmatically narrow way.[25] The client care letter contained the following putative waiver: 'If your claim is disputed by your opponent and you decide not to pursue your claim then we will not make a charge for the work we have done to date.' Dyson LJ explained that, as a matter of construction, work carried out before the decision to proceed with a contested claim could not be characterised as being 'litigation services' and he found that the waiver was intended to apply to fees for modest pre-litigation services. He reminded himself that s 119(1) of the 1990 Act defined 'litigation services' by reference to whether there were 'contemplated proceedings'; he went on to say this: **29.11**

> ' "[C]ontemplated proceedings" are proceedings of which it can be said that there is at least a real likelihood that they will be issued. Until the potential defendant disputes the claim, it is not possible to say that proceedings are contemplated. Advising a client as to whether he or she has a good *prima facie* case and writing a letter of claim are not enough to amount to litigation services.'[26]

There is, however, a limit to the extent to which a legal services provider is able to avoid its services being 'litigation services'. In a case in which the solicitors were not on the record but were simply assisting other solicitors who were, Lewison LJ found that there had been a supply of 'litigation services'.[27] **29.12**

As with the interpretation of any contract, the court is not restricted to looking solely at the four corners of the written instrument. Where appropriate, it may take into account other matters, such as other documents, correspondence, and standard terms and conditions.[28] Whilst dealing with a slightly different point—that is, the effect of a retainer, rather than whether a retainer was a conditional fee agreement—Waller LJ found that a client care letter and a conditional fee agreement could be taken into account in deciding how the retainer would operate in practice: **29.13**

> 'I can see no reason why the court should not look at the whole package produced by the solicitor, the CFA agreement, the [client care] letter explaining to the client

---

[25] In *Gaynor v Central West London Buses Ltd* [2006] EWCA Civ 1120.

[26] *Ibid*, at [17].

[27] See *Rees v Gateley Wareing (a firm) & Ors* [2014] EWCA Civ 1351, at [57]–[62].

[28] See, eg, *Munkenbeck & Marshall v Harold* [2005] EWHC 356 (TCC), in which industry standard terms and conditions were incorporated into an agreement.

the effect of the agreement, and indeed the insurance policy recommended by the solicitor.'[29]

Other examples of a similar approach exist.[30] There is no reason to believe that, in an appropriate case, the court would adopt a different approach when considering whether a retainer was a conditional fee agreement within the meaning of Courts and Legal Services Act 1990, s 58(2)(a).

The Basic Requirements of all Modern Enforceable Conditional Fee Agreements

29.14 The starting point for all conditional fee agreements (regardless of when they were made) is Courts and Legal Services Act 1990, s 58(1):

> 'A conditional fee agreement which satisfies all of the conditions applicable to it by virtue of this section shall not be unenforceable by reason only of its being a conditional fee agreement; but (subject to subsection (5))[31] any other conditional fee agreement shall be unenforceable.'

29.15 The 'conditions' that must be satisfied are set out at s 58(3):

> 'The following conditions are applicable to every conditional fee agreement—
> (a) it must be in writing;
> (b) it must not relate to proceedings which cannot be the subject of an enforceable conditional fee agreement; and
> (c) it must comply with such requirements (if any) as may be prescribed by the Lord Chancellor.'

29.16 Thus, to be enforceable, any conditional fee agreement to which s 58(3) of the 1990 Act relates must:

- be in writing (see 29.17);
- not relate to proceedings that cannot be the subject of an enforceable conditional fee agreement (see 29.18); and
- comply with the applicable delegated legislation.

As will be explained below, this last point will be relevant to older agreements (see 29.24–29.110) and to any agreement that provides for a success fee (see 29.19–29.23).

The requirement to be in writing

29.17 Whether a conditional fee agreement is in writing will be a matter of fact. Whilst there is no authority directly on the point, it is almost certain that any conditional fee agreement that is not in writing would be unenforceable and this would be so regardless of whether

[29] *Jones v Wrexham Borough Council* [2007] EWCA Civ 1356, at [17]. Although he ultimately came to the conclusion that the agreement was unenforceable, in *Utting v McBain* [2007] EWHC 3293 (QB), at [21]–[24], Blake J took into account a letter that had been sent to the client at about the same time that the CFA was made.

[30] See, eg, *Forde v Birmingham City Council* [2009] EWHC 12 (QB), at [73]–[78].

[31] The issues meant by the reference to 'subsection 5' relate to non-contentious work.

it is in respect of contentious or non-contentious work, this being for the reasons given at 29.190.

Prohibited conditional fee agreements

The types of proceeding that cannot be the subject of an enforceable conditional fee agreement are set out in Courts and Legal Services Act 1990, s 58A(1). They are: **29.18**

- criminal proceedings (apart from proceedings under s 82 of the Environmental Protection Act 1990); and
- family proceedings.[32]

Proceedings under s 82 of the Environmental Protection Act 1990 are proceedings brought in the magistrates' court for an order abating a statutory nuisance. For the reasons set out at 29.20, whilst a conditional fee agreement in that type of claim is permissible, it may not provide for a success fee.

Further requirements where there is a success fee

Conditional fee agreements may—and, until recently, almost always did—provide for success fees. That type of agreement is defined by s 58(2)(b) of the 1990 Act: **29.19**

> '[A] conditional fee agreement provides for a success fee if it provides for the amount of any fees to which it applies to be increased, in specified circumstances, above the amount which would be payable if it were not payable only in specified circumstances.'

If the agreement was made before 1 April 2013, the success was, in principle, recoverable between opposing parties; for agreements made on or after that date, the success fee must be paid by the client (or, if the client is funded by someone else, by that other person).[33] Transitional provisions apply (see 54.04–54.09 and 54.15–54.37).

In addition to those conditions stipulated in s 58(3) of the 1990 Act, the following further conditions (in s 58(4)) apply to conditional fee agreements that provide for success fees: **29.20**

> 'The following further conditions are applicable to a conditional fee agreement which provides for a success fee—
> (a) it must relate to proceedings of a description specified by order made by the Lord Chancellor;
> (b) it must state the percentage by which the amount of the fees which would be payable if it were not a conditional fee agreement is to be increased; and
> (c) that percentage must not exceed the percentage specified in relation to the description of proceedings to which the agreement relates by order made by the Lord Chancellor.'

[32] 'Family proceedings' are defined by Courts and Legal Services Act 1990, s 58A(2), as being proceedings under the following: the Matrimonial Causes Act 1973; the Adoption and Children Act 2002; the Domestic Proceedings and Magistrates' Courts Act 1978; Matrimonial and Family Proceedings Act 1984, Pt III; Children Act 1989, Pts I, II and IV; Family Law Act 1996, Pt IV; Female Genital Mutilation Act 2003, Sch 2, Pt 1; Civil Partnership Act 2004, Pt 2, Ch 2 (proceedings for dissolution etc of civil partnership), Sch 5 (financial relief in the High Court or a county court etc), Sch 6 (financial relief in magistrates' courts etc), Sch 7 (financial relief in England and Wales after overseas dissolution etc of a civil partnership); and the inherent jurisdiction of the High Court in relation to children.

[33] See Courts and Legal Services Act 1990, s 58A(6), as amended by Legal Aid, Sentencing and Punishment of Offenders Act 2012, s 45(4).

Any properly constituted conditional fee agreement may provide for a success fee unless it relates to proceedings under s 82 of the Environmental Protection Act 1990.[34]

29.21 The percentage increase must not exceed 100 per cent (that is, the success fee must not exceed the base costs).[35] If this percentage is exceeded, the retainer is unenforceable;[36] likewise if no single or discernible figure is stated.[37] It would not be permissible simply to sidestep the legislation by finding that the failure to state the percentage invites the conclusion that the agreement did not provide for a success fee at all.[38] The statement of the success fee would generally be included in the agreement or in a linked risk assessment made at about the same time as the agreement, but, where circumstances allow, it may be possible for a statement to be made by reference to a document that was made prior to the agreement itself.[39]

29.22 For the purpose of gauging compliance, the measure of the percentage increase is not the costs at risk, but the fees that would have been sought had the agreement not been a conditional fee agreement.[40] This may be relevant in the event that the agreement is a discounted conditional fee agreement. An example illustrates this: if the amount that would have been charged had the agreement not been a conditional fee agreement is £100 per hour and if the amount that is charged in the event of a loss is £25 per hour, the maximum permissible success fee would be 100 per cent of £100 per hour, rather than 100 per cent of the costs at risk (that is, £75 per hour).

29.23 Where the agreement was made on or after 1 April 2013 and where the claim is for personal injuries, the following further provisions apply:

> '(4A) The additional conditions are applicable to a conditional fee agreement which—
> (a) provides for a success fee, and
> (b) relates to proceedings of a description specified by order made by the Lord Chancellor for the purposes of this subsection.
>
> (4B) The additional conditions are that—
> (a) the agreement must provide that the success fee is subject to a maximum limit,
> (b) the maximum limit must be expressed as a percentage of the descriptions of damages awarded in the proceedings that are specified in the agreement,
> (c) that percentage must not exceed the percentage specified by order made by the Lord Chancellor in relation to the proceedings or calculated in a manner so specified,[[41]] and
> (d) those descriptions of damages may only include descriptions of damages specified by order made by the Lord Chancellor in relation to the proceedings.'[42]

---

[34] Conditional Fee Agreements Order 2013 (SI 2013/689), art 2.

[35] Conditional Fee Agreements Order 2013 (SI 2013/689), art 3.

[36] See *Jones v Caradon Catnic Ltd* [2005] EWCA 1821.

[37] See, eg, *Pirta v Shahi* (unreported), 2 July 2015, Birmingham County Court, at [31]–[36], *per* District Judge Griffiths, in which the success fee was said to be '12.5–100% of our basic charges'.

[38] Whilst *obiter*, see *Pentecost v John* [2015] EWHC 1970 (QB), at [30], *per* Turner J.

[39] As an example of this, see *ibid*, in which a collective CFA was novated, but no new statement of the success fee was made following the novation; Turner J found that the original statement was sufficient.

[40] *Evans v Gloucestershire County Council* [2008] EWCA Civ 21, at [27].

[41] This is specified by Conditional Fee Agreements Order 2013 (SI 2013/689), art 5.

[42] The new provisions in Courts and Legal Services Act 1990, s 58, were added by Legal Aid, Sentencing and Punishment of Offenders Act 2012, s 44(6).

Older Conditional Fee Agreements

The law set out below applies only to conditional fee agreements (as opposed to collective conditional fee agreements) entered into on or after 1 April 2000 but before 1 November 2005. Such agreements are still encountered from time to time, but they are now rare. As such, this edition of this book contains less detail than in previous editions. If the agreement was made before 1 April 2000, then the second edition of this book ought to be consulted. **29.24**

Where the conditions referred to above are met, the 'requirements' stipulated in Courts and Legal Services Act 1990, s 58(3)(c) (see 29.15) are the Conditional Fee Agreements Regulations 2000[43] (the CFA Regulations 2000). If the requirements of those Regulations are not met, the conditional fee agreement will be unenforceable.[44] Whether a putative breach of the Regulations will have that result will depend on whether the breach is a 'material' breach (see 29.53–29.54). Materiality is a doctrine that arises from case law; it is not mentioned in the CFA Regulations 2000 themselves. **29.25**

It is convenient to deal with materiality in some detail, but to allow the reader to see the wood for the trees, it is worth considering the overall method by which a putative breach is considered. The following forensic sieve is a useful framework—although it may not be appropriate in every case. **29.26**

(1) The court will consider whether a retainer is a conditional fee agreement to which the CFA Regulations 2000 apply and, if it is, which specific regulations apply to the case in question (see 29.33–29.40).
(2) If the CFA Regulations 2000 do apply, the court will (in the context of costs between opposing parties) consider whether there is a 'genuine issue' that there has been non-compliance with those Regulations (see 29.44–29.52).
(3) If appropriate, the court will ask itself whether the agreement, when properly construed, is in breach of one or more of the requirements of the Regulations (see 29.55–29.110) and, if so, whether that breach—either on its own or in conjunction with any other such breach—has had a materially adverse effect either upon the protection afforded to the client or upon the proper administration of justice (see 29.53–29.54).

The need to avoid an overzealous approach

Cautionary comments have been made about the risk of an overzealous approach to the CFA Regulations 2000. Whilst only two are mentioned, many others exist. The following comments of Latham LJ are often cited (despite the fact that the court was concerned with something other than the CFA Regulations 2000): **29.27**

> 'The Deputy Costs Judge is to be commended for ensuring that the detailed assessment did not become an excuse for further expensive litigation at the behest of a disappointed but persistent litigant. Satellite litigation about costs has become a growth industry, and one that is a blot on the civil justice system. Costs Judges should be astute to prevent such proceedings from being protracted by allegations that are without substance.'[45]

---

[43] SI 2000/692 (as amended).

[44] See Courts and Legal Services Act 1990, s 58(1).

[45] *Times Newspapers Ltd v Burstein* [2002] EWCA Civ 1739, at [29].

29.28 Citing those comments with approval in another case, Brooke LJ added the following remarks of his own:

> 'The court should be watchful when it considers allegations that there have been breaches of the Regulations. The parliamentary purpose is to enhance access to justice, not to impede it, and to create better ways of delivering litigation services, not worse ones. These purposes will be thwarted if those who render good service to their clients under CFAs are at risk of going unremunerated at the culmination of the bitter trench warfare which has been such an unhappy feature of the recent litigation scene.'[46]

The relevance of consumer protection

29.29 The other side of the coin is that the intention of Parliament ought not to be thwarted. The court has often reminded itself that it cannot be said to be irrational that Parliament chose to impose a harsh regime upon those who are charged with ensuring that their clients' rights are properly protected. Dyson LJ had this to say on the point (in the context of a discussion on materiality):

> 'Parliament was painting with a broad brush … Parliament considered that the need to safeguard the interests of clients was so important that it should be secured by providing that, if any of the conditions were not satisfied, the CFA would not be enforceable and the solicitor would not be paid. To use the words of Lord Nicholls again [in *Wilson v First County Trust Ltd (No 2)* [2003] UKHL 40, [2004] 1 AC 816], this is an approach of punishing solicitors *pour encourager les autres*. Such a policy is tough, but it is not irrational.'[47]

Similar comments have been made by Laws LJ, also in the context of materiality.[48]

29.30 Where legislation is capable of inflicting punitive or harsh consequences upon individuals, it is commonly interpreted in such a way that the obligations it imposes are read narrowly. It is also commonly the case that, where the purpose of legislation is to protect consumers, those obligations will be read widely. In so far as the CFA Regulations 2000 are concerned, these factors pull in opposite directions, or, at least, may do so. Dyson LJ (giving judgment of the court) found that the need for a narrow interpretation did not outweigh the need for a wide interpretation:

> 'The purpose of the Regulations is to protect clients, not the financial interests of solicitors. In our judgment, the Regulations should be construed by giving the plain language in which they are expressed its normal and natural meaning.'[49]

Clarke MR has stated much the same thing—namely, that the CFA Regulations 2000 should be interpreted in such a way as to promote, rather than detract from, consumer protection.[50]

---

[46] *Hollins v Russell* [2003] EWCA Civ 718, at [224], cited with approval by Clarke LJ in *Tankard v John Fredricks Plastics Ltd* [2008] EWCA Civ 1375, at [51].

[47] *Garrett v Halton Borough Council; Myatt v National Coal Board* [2006] EWCA Civ 1017, at [30].

[48] See *Jones v Caradon Catnic Ltd* [2005] EWCA 1821, at [33]–[36], referred to with approval by Dyson LJ in *Myatt v National Coal Board* [2006] EWCA Civ 1017, at [40]–[41].

[49] Dyson LJ in *Garrett v Halton Borough Council; Myatt v National Coal Board* [2006] EWCA Civ 1017, at [40]–[41].

[50] *Tankard v John Fredricks Plastics Ltd* [2008] EWCA Civ 1375, at [43].

Clarity

Although the Court of Appeal has yet to find that an agreement is unenforceable solely for want of clarity, it has repeatedly said that a lack of clarity would place an agreement at risk of being found to be unenforceable.[51] **29.31**

Similarity of approach regardless of the identity of challenger

Hughes LJ has confirmed that the construction of the agreement is not influenced by the source of the challenge; the contractual position as between the solicitor and the client must be the same, whoever takes the point.[52] This does not mean, however, that the paying party will necessarily be permitted to take the same points that a client would be able to take (see Chapter 18). The fact that many clients show no real interest in the advice being given to them is not a good reason for failing to give effect to the intention of Parliament.[53] **29.32**

Identifying the correct provisions

This is the first question in the forensic sieve at 29.26. The first step is to identify whether the retainer is a conditional fee agreement within the meaning of Courts and Legal Services Act 1990, s 58(2)(a). This is an issue that is dealt with at 29.04–29.07. It is not an issue that will present any difficulty in the majority of cases; difficulties may arise where transitional provisions need to be considered and in determining which delegated legislation applies. This is addressed below. **29.33**

Where an agreement was made before 1 November 2005

If the retainer was entered into on or after 1 November 2005, then the CFA Regulations 2000 will not apply, because they were revoked on that date.[54] Difficulties may arise where a conditional fee agreement was entered into before 1 November 2005, but where a further conditional fee agreement was made after that date. The relevant transitional provisions read as follows: 'The [CFA Regulations 2000] shall continue to have effect for the purposes of a conditional fee agreement entered into before 1 November 2005.'[55] **29.34**

Thus, whilst there is no authority directly on the point, the test seems not to be whether *any* conditional fee agreement was entered into before 1 November 2005, but whether the particular conditional fee agreement in question was entered into before that date.[56] Disputes may arise where the 'old' and 'new' retainers are very similar or identical (or, in extreme cases, merely the old retainer re-signed). Although there is no guidance on the point from the higher courts, that issue is likely to be a mixed question of fact and law as to whether the new agreement is, in fact, genuinely a new agreement. **29.35**

---

[51] As an example, see *ibid*, at [45] (discussion about whether inconsistent advice about panel membership would amount to a breach); *Hollins v Russell* [2003] EWCA Civ 718, at [152]–[154] (discussion about the importance of the clarity of the Law Society Conditions).

[52] *Jones v Wrexham Borough Council* [2007] EWCA Civ 1356, at [83].

[53] *Garrett v Halton Borough Council; Myatt v National Coal Board* [2006] EWCA Civ 1017, at [102].

[54] Conditional Fee Agreements (Revocation) Regulations 2005 (SI 2005/2305), regs 1 and 2.

[55] Conditional Fee Agreements (Revocation) Regulations 2005 (SI 2005/2305), reg 3(1).

[56] This position has to be contrasted with the Access to Justice Act 1999 (Transitional Provisions) Order 2000 (SI 2000/900), for example, which is worded in a much broader way.

29.36 Disputes may also arise where the 'new' retainer purports retroactively to replace the 'old' retainer in such a way as to make compliance with the CFA Regulations 2000 irrelevant. These issues are discussed in detail at 29.132–29.139.

Where the 'CFA Lite' provisions may apply

29.37 Where the agreement is one to which the CFA Regulations 2000 apply, the next issue will be to determine whether the agreement in question was governed by the provisions introduced on 2 June 2003 regulating CFA Lites (the Lite provisions).[57] Those provisions were significantly less burdensome than those that applied to other types of conditional fee agreement.

29.38 Unsurprisingly, a major factor in deciding whether the Lite provisions applied was whether the agreement had been made on or after 2 June 2003. Whilst there is no authority on the point and whilst there are no transitional provisions, the received view is that the Lite provisions applied only to agreements that had been made on or after 2 June 2003 (for the reasons set out in the footnotes).[58]

29.39 To qualify as being regulated by the Lite provisions, not only must the agreement have been made on or after 2 June 2003 and before 1 November 2005 (see 29.34), but also it would have had to satisfy the following conditions (see 29.67).

- The client's liability to pay their legal representative's fees and expenses, including disbursements other than the after-the-event (ATE) premium,[59] must have been limited to the sums that were recovered, whether by way of costs or otherwise.[60]
- The exceptions to this must have been limited to instances in which the client:
  - fails to cooperate with the legal representative;
  - fails to attend any medical or expert examination or court hearing that the legal representative reasonably requests them to attend;
  - fails to give necessary instructions to the legal representative;
  - withdraws instructions from the legal representative;
  - is an individual who is adjudged bankrupt, or who enters into an arrangement or a composition with their creditors, or against whom an administration order is made;
  - is a company for which a receiver, administrative receiver or liquidator is appointed; or
  - dies and their estate becomes liable for the fees.[61]

29.40 Examples of circumstances in which the 'failure to cooperate' exception would apply would include where the client asks the solicitor to work in an improper way or where the client deliberately misleads the solicitor.[62] Rejecting the legal representative's

[57] Conditional Fee Agreements (Miscellaneous Amendments) Regulations 2003 (SI 2003/1240), reg 2.

[58] There are no transitional provisions relating directly to reg 3A, so the court is required to draw such inferences it can as to what it considers Parliament to have intended: see (in a context other than costs) *Cardshops Ltd v John Lewis Properties Ltd* [1983] QB 161. The CPR contain provisions that are related to reg 3A, but which will apply only where the agreement was entered into on or after 2 June 2003: see CPR, r 43.2(7); Civil Procedure (Amendment No 2) Rules 2003 (SI 2003/1242), r 6. In view of this, it is a reasonable inference that the same applies to the regulations themselves.

[59] See *Jones v Wrexham Borough Council* [2007] EWCA Civ 1356, at [51].

[60] See Conditional Fee Agreements Regulations 2000 (SI 2000/692) (as amended), reg 3A(1).

[61] See Conditional Fee Agreements Regulations 2000 (SI 2000/692) (as amended), regs 5 and 5A(1).

[62] *Jones v Wrexham Borough Council* [2007] EWCA Civ 1356, at [49].

advice concerning settlement would not necessarily amount to a 'failure to cooperate'.[63]

Whether a CFA Lite can be found by looking beyond the agreement itself The court may take into account all of the relevant circumstances in deciding whether these conditions have been met rather than only the written instrument itself (see Chapter 31 for a general discussion of this topic). This may include documents other than the agreement, such as the client care letter. Waller LJ (with whom Hughes and Longmore LJJ agreed) had this to say on the topic: **29.41**

> 'The important point is that if and insofar as [the paying party] would seek to look at the CFA on its own, and construe that CFA strictly, I would reject that approach ... The correct approach in my view is to ask the question, has the solicitor produced an arrangement for a CFA under which the client would not be liable for any own-side costs or expenses (apart from the circumstances defined by [reg 3(5) of the Conditional Fee Agreement Regulations 2000 (as amended)]other than those that are actually recovered from the other side or from insurers.'[64]

On the facts of the case before him, Waller LJ found that, when the agreement was read in conjunction with the client care letter, the client had been insulated from paying his solicitor's profit costs.

Whether insurance can give rise to a CFA Lite One particular circumstance that may arise is where the liability for costs may be covered by legal expenses insurance that sits alongside the agreement. This may be relevant because it is not unusual for such policies to cover a party's own disbursements in such a way that the client is protected from the risk of having to pay those monies. If a policy of that type is combined with a conditional fee agreement that insulates the client from the risk of paying profit costs, then the overall effect may be the same as a CFA Lite. This, however, would be the case only if the indemnity provided by the policy could be taken into account. **29.42**

Waller LJ found that any such indemnity could be taken into account. The issue turned on whether the words 'or otherwise' in reg 3A(1) of the CFA Regulations 2000 included the proceeds of an ATE policy. Waller LJ summarised his views in this way: **29.43**

> 'I can see no reason why the court should not look at the whole package produced by the solicitor, the CFA agreement, the [client care] letter explaining to the client the effect of the agreement, and indeed the insurance policy recommended by the solicitor.'[65]

The possibility of the insurer avoiding its liabilities is not to the point.[66]

Genuine issues in the context of conditional fee agreements

The second question in the forensic sieve at 29.26 will arise only where the challenge to the conditional fee agreement is made by a paying party. The paragraphs that follow focus on the way in which the *Bailey* presumption[67] applies to conditional fee agreements. If the **29.44**

---

[63] *Ibid*, at [54]; *ibid*, at [96]–[97], Hughes LJ came to the conclusion that, on the facts of the case before him (in which the solicitor had a very high degree of control over the claim), a failure to accept a recommendation concerning an offer could amount to a failure to cooperate.

[64] *Ibid*.

[65] *Ibid*, at [27].

[66] *Ibid*, at [13]–[22] and [42].

[67] After *Bailey v IBC Vehicles Ltd* [1998] 3 All ER 570.

reader is not familiar with the general principles, what follows ought to be read in conjunction with 18.35–18.50 and Chapter 18 generally.

29.45 In brief, the Court of Appeal has explained that the *Bailey* presumption should not extend to the written instrument of a conditional fee agreement made under the CFA Regulations 2000—although it is a moot point whether it applies to other types of conditional fee agreement[68] (see 29.49–29.50). Thus, in so far as the CFA Regulations 2000 are concerned, there is a need to distinguish between those regulations that depend on the written instrument for compliance (that is, regs 2, 3, 3A and 5) and those that turn on other factors (that is, reg 4(1)–(6)). The receiving party will be able to rely on the *Bailey* presumption in respect of the latter, but not in respect of the former.

'Genuine issues' and the written instrument

29.46 In *Hollins v Russell*,[69] Brooke LJ identified five reasons why (in the context of an agreement to which the CFA Regulations 2000 applied) the *Bailey* presumption should not apply to the written instrument of a conditional fee agreement. He explained that the receiving party should normally be put to their election in relation to the conditional fee agreement itself. Brooke LJ's reasons can be summarised as follows.

- **Significance of the nature of the argument** The challenge in *Bailey* went only to a part of the profit costs (the hourly rate), but challenges in respect of conditional fee agreements usually go to the entirety of the profit costs. Challenges in respect of conditional fee agreements are therefore more significant. Brooke LJ had this to say on that point: 'The challenge to a bill of costs must surely move several ratchets up the scale once the challenge changes from a challenge to the figures produced to a challenge to the principle of paying anything at all.'[70]
- **Complexity of the issues** With non-conditional retainers, the matters that are normally the subject of a certificate are conventional matters; this is not so with compliance with the CFA Regulations 2000, because they introduced a level of complexity that was unknown when *Bailey* was decided.
- **Legitimate interest in the terms** The CPR and the CPD (as they then were) required that only basic information be given about a conditional fee agreement,[71] yet the paying party may reasonably have required more. For example, the paying party might have needed to know how a 'win' had been defined in the agreement.
- **Not solely matters of fact** The question of whether a conditional fee agreement is enforceable is principally a matter of law. This is distinct from whether costs are properly claimed in cases not involving conditional fee agreements, because such issues are generally questions of fact and are likely to be within a solicitor's peculiar expertise. In view of this difference, the certificate may not be sufficient in the context of conditional fee agreements.
- **Policy and efficient use of court time** There are policy reasons for not extending the *Bailey* presumption to conditional fee agreements. Given the complexity of

[68] A decision in the County Court has confirmed that collective CFAs ought to be dealt with in a similar way: *Woollam v Cleanaway Ltd* (unreported), 26 July 2004, Chester County Court, *per* HHJ Halbert.

[69] *Hollins v Russell* [2003] EWCA Civ 718.

[70] *Ibid*, at [64].

[71] The Civil Procedure Rule Committee responded to Brooke LJ's remarks by proposing amendments to the CPD (see below).

the issues, Brooke LJ thought that it was not appropriate to impose on costs judges the responsibility of acting as a filter to see that the relevant regulations had been complied with in every respect, because this would inevitably be a time-consuming task.

In view of these factors, Brooke LJ came to the conclusion that the *Bailey* decision should not be extended beyond the facts with which it was dealing—namely, that of a conventional bill. He went on to say: **29.47**

> '[Where] there is a [conditional fee agreement], a costs judge should normally exercise his discretion under the Costs Practice Direction and the *Pamplin* procedure [ie the process of election[72]] so as to require the receiving parties (subject to their right of election preserved by paragraph 40.14 of the Costs Practice Direction and the *Goldman* case[[73]]) to produce a copy of their [conditional fee agreements] to the paying parties.'[74]

Whilst not binding, a decision in the County Court has confirmed that collective conditional fee agreements ought to be dealt with in a similar way.[75] **29.48**

'Genuine issues' where the agreement was made on or after 1 November 2005

What is not clear is whether the decision not to extend the *Bailey* presumption (see 29.46) holds good when the conditional fee agreement was entered into after the revocation of the CFA Regulations 2000. Clearly, many of the reasons given by Brooke LJ for disapplying the principle in *Bailey* (see 29.46) will not apply to such agreements. The matter can be argued either way and there have been conflicting first-instance decisions on the point.[76] Changes to the CPD were mooted, but they did not materialise.[77] The position in law is not wholly clear, but there remains wisdom in the words quoted with reverence by Brooke LJ[78] and initially spoken by Louis Brandeis J shortly before he was nominated to the Supreme Court of the United States: 'Sunlight is said to be the best of disinfectants; electric light the most efficient policeman.'[79] **29.49**

Clearly, Brooke LJ intended to encourage parties to go about dealing with the indemnity principle in a transparent way. But, where disclosure is not given voluntarily, the court is still required to exercise its discretion. As a result, a receiving party cannot be put to their election until such time as the court has considered the matter judicially. Although not binding, there have been decisions in which it has been found that a receiving party may not be put to their election until after points of dispute have been served.[80] If this is the true state of the law, then the practical effect is that a receiving party will be able to defer deciding whether to give disclosure until after they know the paying party's case. **29.50**

---

72 After *Pamplin v Express Newspapers* [1985] 1 WLR 689.
73 *Goldman v Hesper* [1988] 1 WLR 1238.
74 *Hollins v Russell* [2003] EWCA Civ 718, at [71].
75 *Woollam v Cleanaway Ltd* (unreported), 26 July 2004, Chester County Court, *per* Judge Halbert.
76 See *Vinayak & Anor (t/a Doctors Chambers) v Lovegrove & Eliot (a firm)* [2007] EWHC 90096.
77 It was proposed to introduce a new CPD, art 32.5(1)(d).
78 *Hollins v Russell* [2003] EWCA Civ 718, at [71].
79 Brandeis, L, *Other People's Money—and How the Bankers Use It* (Louisville, KY: Brandeis School of Law, 1914); only the first half was quoted by Brooke LJ.
80 See *Cole v News Group Newspapers* (unreported), 18 October 2006, SCCO, *per* Master Howarth.

Redaction

29.51 The agreement may be disclosed in redacted form.[81] It is, however, implicit from the way in which the Court of Appeal has commented upon redaction that the court ought to be put in a position to decide whether it is fair.[82] This would generally mean providing an unredacted copy of the retainer to the court.

Genuine issues and factors other than the written instrument

29.52 A paying party will often wish to see not only the written instrument of the agreement, but also evidence of compliance with reg 4 of the CFA Regulations 2000 (see 29.77–29.101). Where those are the circumstances, the costs judge should not require attendance notes to be disclosed unless there is a 'genuine issue' as to whether there has been compliance with reg 4.[83] Put otherwise, *Bailey* will apply. Brooke LJ commented that the adequacy of the explanation given to the client is largely a matter of fact, so that it is appropriate that the paying party should have to rebut the presumption arising from the fact that the receiving party's solicitor, an officer of the court, has signed the certificate of accuracy.[84] Whilst common sense dictates that there is a limit to the extent to which such evidence can be taken into account before a finding of a 'genuine issue' becomes inescapable, it would seem that evidence may be adduced for the purposes of rebutting an allegation that a 'genuine issue' exists.[85]

Materiality

29.53 For a breach of the CFA Regulations 2000 to be found to be unenforceable, it must be a 'material' breach—namely, it must have had a materially adverse effect either upon the protection afforded to the client or upon the proper administration of justice.[86] The Court of Appeal has given the following guidance:

> 'Costs judges should ask themselves the following question: "Has the particular departure from a regulation or requirement in section 58 [of the Courts and Legal Services Act 1990], either on its own or in conjunction with any other such departure in this case, had a materially adverse effect either upon the protection afforded to the client or upon the proper administration of justice?".'[87]

29.54 The following points may be made about materiality.

- **Materiality is to be determined by reference to the circumstances at the time the agreement was made** The enforceability of the agreement is determined on the date it was made. Drawing an analogy with consumer credit cases,[88] Dyson LJ said: 'We see no reason for departing from the general rule that the legal character of a contract must be determined (or determinable) at its commencement.'[89]

---

81 See, eg, *Hollins v Russell* [2003] EWCA Civ 718, at [72].

82 *Ibid*, at [80].

83 *Ibid*, at [81].

84 *Ibid*, at [81].

85 See, eg, *Thornley (a child) v MoD* [2010] EWHC 2584 (QB), at [27], *per* HHJ Behrens (sitting as a judge of the High Court).

86 *Hollins v Russell* [2003] EWCA Civ 718, at [107] and [221].

87 *Ibid*, at [221]. It seems as if Lord Woolf MR foresaw the test of materiality long before *Hollins*: in *Hodgson & Ors v Imperial Tobacco* [1998] 1 WLR 1056, at 1065, he said (of a CFA) '[i]f it materially departs from the legislative requirements it will not be enforceable'.

88 Specifically, he referred to *MacMillan Williams v Range* [2004] EWCA Civ 294.

89 *Garrett v Halton Borough Council; Myatt v National Coal Board* [2006] EWCA Civ 1017, at [36].

- **Potential, rather than actual, consequences** In considering whether a breach is material, it is the potential, rather than the actual, consequences[90] of the breach that are relevant. Causation and harm are irrelevant (other than to the extent that actual harm may shed light on the potential for loss), so the court does not need to find that there has been actual detriment to find that there has been a material breach. Dyson LJ explained the rationale behind this in the following way:

  '[It] is fallacious to say that a breach is trivial or not material because it does not in fact cause loss to the client in the particular case. The scheme has the wider purpose of providing for client protection (as well as the proper administration of justice).'[91]

  Thus, if, for example, there has been a failure to make adequate enquiries about the possible existence of alternative means of funding, the fact that no alternative means of funding actually existed would be irrelevant for the purposes of considering materiality. However, it might be helpful to have regard to what actually happened, because that may shed light on the potential consequences of a breach.[92]
- **Limits of the concept of materiality** The concept of materiality has its limitations. In particular, Laws LJ has commented that it must not be allowed to undermine the force of Courts and Legal Services Act 1990, s 58(1).[93] This seems to be particularly relevant in cases in which the breach is binary—in the sense that it either has been committed or it has not—with no room for gradations of severity between those two extremes.[94]
- **Trivial and small breaches** Brooke LJ has confirmed that the maxim *de minimis non curat lex* (meaning 'the law does not care about very small matters') must be applied when a court considers whether there has been compliance with the CFA Regulations 2000.[95] Breaches that are 'literal but trivial and immaterial' or 'marginal' will be regarded as being immaterial.[96] That said, the Court of Appeal has stopped short of saying that the concept of materiality is merely an expression of that principle.[97] Breaches that are not immaterial for other reasons would rarely be immaterial solely because they are very small. In the context of declarable interests under reg 4(2)(e), for example, Clarke MR has commented that it would be difficult to envisage such a situation.[98]
- **Multiple breaches** When considering whether the effect of multiple breaches is material, it is permissible to consider them in aggregate, rather than only individually.[99]

---

90 *Ibid*, at [27]–[39]. The first instance of this was *Jones v Caradon Catnic Ltd* [2005] EWCA Civ 1821, in which a breach was found to be material on the basis that it had the potential for causing harm to the administration of justice.

91 *Garrett v Halton Borough Council; Myatt v National Coal Board* [2006] EWCA Civ 1017, at [32].

92 *Ibid*, at [39].

93 *Jones v Caradon Catnic Ltd* [2005] EWCA Civ 1821, at [34].

94 Whilst not binding, an example is *Preece v Caerphilly County Borough Council* (unreported), 15 August 2007, Cardiff County Court, at [18], *per* HHJ Hickinbottom (now Hickinbottom J) (a decision concerning a total failure to sign an agreement).

95 *Hollins v Russell* [2003] EWCA Civ 718, at [50].

96 See *Garrett v Halton Borough Council; Myatt v National Coal Board* [2006] EWCA Civ 1017, at [31]; *Jones v Caradon Catnic Ltd* [2005] EWCA Civ 1821, at [34].

97 *Garrett v Halton Borough Council; Myatt v National Coal Board* [2006] EWCA Civ 1017, at [31].

98 *Tankard v John Fredricks Plastics Ltd* [2008] EWCA Civ 1375, at [47].

99 *Fosberry & anor v HM Revenue and Customs* [2007] EWHC 2249 (Ch), at [46], which has also acquired a second neutral citation number—[2008] EWHC 3344 (Ch)—and is also often cited as [2007] EWHC 3344 (Ch).

- **Materiality and substantial compliance** The test of materiality can be analysed in terms of substantial compliance.[100] It has been argued that the test of materiality is often applied in a way that is impermissible under that doctrine and that, as such, it should be viewed in 'a wider habitat'. Whilst some judges have found that approach to be of assistance,[101] many have not. In particular, Mann J has concluded that the approach did not shed any significant illumination on how the test of materiality should be applied.[102]

Individual regulations: breach and materiality

29.55 This section deals with breaches of the CFA Regulations 2000—that is, it concerns the third question in the forensic sieve at 29.26. It applies only to those agreements to which the CFA Regulations 2000 apply (which will rarely be the case in modern-day practice). Each of the regulations—which Phillips MR has described as 'extremely detailed'[103]—is addressed in turn.

Regulation 2(1) of the CFA Regulations 2000

29.56 Regulation 2(1) required that the agreement defined its own ambit and that it incorporated a number of provisions clarifying its effect. It therefore went to the written instrument of the agreement.

29.57 The regulation provides as follows:

> '2 (1) A conditional fee agreement must specify—
> (a) the particular proceedings or parts of them to which it relates (including whether it relates to any appeal, counterclaim or proceedings to enforce a judgment or order),
> (b) the circumstances in which the legal representative's fees and expenses, or part of them, are payable,
> (c) what payment, if any, is due—
> (i) if those circumstances only partly occur,
> (ii) irrespective of whether those circumstances occur, and
> (iii) on the termination of the agreement for any reason, and
> (d) the amounts which are payable in all the circumstances and cases specified or the method to be used to calculate them and, in particular, whether the amounts are limited by reference to the damages which may be recovered on behalf of the client.'

Other than CFA Lites (see 29.37–29.40), this regulation applies to all conditional fee agreements to which the CFA Regulations 2000 apply, including those that were made with an additional legal representative, those that provided for a success fee and those in which the legal representative was a membership organisation.

29.58 The following issues regarding reg 2(1) of the CFA Regulations 2000 may arise.

- **Clarity** The court may be influenced by the clarity with which the agreement has been expressed. In a case in which he was able to interpret the agreement in a way that was

---

[100] See, eg, *Hollins v Russell* [2003] EWCA 718, at [106], in which Brooke LJ said that 'conditions are sufficiently met when there has been substantial compliance with, or in other words no material departure from, what is required'.

[101] See, eg, *Preece v Caerphilly County Borough Council* (unreported), 15 August 2007, Cardiff County Court, *per* HHJ Hickinbotton.

[102] *Fenton v Holmes* [2007] EWHC 2476 (Ch), at [40].

[103] *Thornley v Lang* [2003] EWCA Civ 1484, at [11].

favourable to the legal representative, Brooke LJ commented that his findings might have been different had the agreement been less clear.[104]

- **The meaning of the word 'specify' and implied terms** The requirement to 'specify' should be read as meaning that the thing must be stated explicitly.[105] For the reasons set out below, this can be achieved either by the agreement dealing expressly with the matter in terms that reflect the above requirements or by the way in which the agreement operates as a whole.[106]
- **Provisions relating to hourly rates** Retainers often make provision for hourly rates to be increased, but may fail to state the mechanism by which that increase will be calculated. Eady J noted (*obiter*, but without disapproval) that a costs judge had found that the requirement was satisfied by an implied term that any increase would be fair and reasonable.[107] In view of Brooke LJ's comments about the meaning of the word 'specify' (see above), that decision (as described to Eady J) ought to be treated with some caution (although the same conclusion can be reached in other ways).
- **Provisions relating to termination** In a case in which the agreement failed to specify what would happen in the event of termination prior to the conclusion of the claim, Mann J found that there had been a breach of reg 2(1) of the CFA Regulations 2000. In coming to this conclusion, he reminded himself that the requirement was to 'specify' and he found that the process he was being asked to accept was 'close to a process of implication rather than mere construction'.[108] He did not express a view as to whether that breach was material.
- **Method by which amounts are calculated** Crane J has emphasised that the Regulations choose the word 'method' rather than, for example, the word 'formula' or some other such word. He said that no formula is required and that, in his view, a method that relied on the old 'A plus B' analysis was compliant.[109]
- **Unexpected developments and provisions relating to appeals** Whilst it was a decision refusing permission to appeal and therefore not a decision that should be cited to any court, Maurice Kay LJ refused permission for a paying party to argue that the conditional fee agreement in question ought to have been drafted in such a way as to embrace all areas into which the claim may develop.[110] Although *obiter*, Mann J explained that there was nothing objectionable about an agreement that did not expressly refer to whether it covered an appeal brought by an opponent, which view he came to because it was clear from the provisions that the legal representative was contractually bound to act in the client's best interests and that this extended to representing the client on an appeal brought by an opponent.[111]
- **Need to state whether there is a cap when there is no cap** Brooke LJ rejected the argument that the requirement was to state the existence of a damaged-based cap only if

[104] *Hollins v Russell* [2003] EWCA Civ 718, at [128].

[105] See the comments of Brooke LJ in *Hollins v Russell* [2003] EWCA Civ 718, at [125], in which he drew upon *BWE International Ltd v Jones* [2003] EWCA Civ 298, at [29], as an example of that approach.

[106] See also *Myler v Williams* [2003] EWHC 1587 (QB), at [23], *per* Crane J.

[107] *Cox v MGN Ltd* [2006] EWHC 1235 (QB), at [75].

[108] *Fosberry & anor v HM Revenue and Customs* [2007] EWHC 2249 (Ch), at [43], which case has also acquired a second neutral citation number—[2008] EWHC 3344 (Ch)—and is also often cited as [2007] EWHC 3344 (Ch).

[109] *Myler v Williams* [2003] EWHC 1587 (QB), at [32].

[110] *Blair v Danesh* [2009] EWCA Civ 516.

[111] *Fenton v Holmes* [2007] EWHC 2476 (Ch), at [58]–[63].

there was a cap.[112] (The effect of this finding was significantly ameliorated by his other findings in relation to the cap, as follows below.)

- **Failure to state a cap** Where there has been literal non-compliance with the requirement to state whether there is a damages-based cap, it would often be open to the court to find that such a breach lacks materiality. Whilst *obiter*, Brooke LJ explained that, where an agreement was otherwise clear as to its effect (that is, it was clear that there was no cap), any failure to refer expressly to the absence of a cap was immaterial.[113]
- **Very early Law Society model agreements** Brooke LJ has specifically commented that no problem will arise where the post-July 2000 version of the Law Society model agreement is used.[114] The version that existed between April and July 2000 was less felicitously drafted, however, reading: 'If you win your claim, you pay our basic charges, our disbursements and a success fee. The amount of the success fee is not based on or limited by reference to the damages.' When read in isolation, this provision failed to comply with the requirement to state whether there was a damages-based cap, because it specified only whether the success fee was limited by reference to the damages, rather than whether the costs generally were limited. Brooke LJ went on to explain that the agreement must be read as whole and that other provisions made it clear that there was no cap.[115] There was therefore no breach.

Regulation 2(2) of the CFA Regulations 2000

29.59 Regulation 2(2) imposed a requirement that the agreement contain a statement of compliance with the relevant requirements of reg 4 (see 29.77–29.101): 'A conditional fee agreement to which regulation 4 applies must contain a statement that the requirements of that regulation which apply in the case of that agreement have been complied with.' This was usually done by way of a brief statement in the body of the agreement.

29.60 This regulation applied to all conditional fee agreements to which reg 4 applied, which means that it applied to all agreements to which the CFA Regulations 2000 applied, except CFA Lites (see 29.37), and except those between legal representatives and an additional legal representative. As far as the editor is aware, there have been no authoritative decisions in which a breach of this regulation has, of itself, led to an agreement being found to be unenforceable.

Regulation 3(1)(a) of the CFA Regulations 2000

29.61 Regulation 3(1)(a) stipulated that the agreement must specify the reasons for setting the percentage increase at the level stated: 'A conditional fee agreement which provides for a success fee—(a) must briefly specify the reasons for setting the percentage increase at the level stated in the agreement ...' It applied to all types of agreement that provided for a success fee other than CFA Lites (see 29.37). This included those with an additional legal representative and those in which the legal representative was a membership organisation.

---

[112] In particular, Brooke LJ rejected the notion that there was significance in the fact that the Conditional Fee Agreements Regulations 1995 (SI 1995/1675) required solicitors to state 'whether or not' there was a cap, but the Conditional Fee Agreements Regulations 2000 (SI 2000/692) referred only to 'whether' there was a cap: see *Hollins v Russell* [2003] EWCA Civ 718, at [123]–[124].

[113] *Ibid*, at [120] *et seq*.

[114] *Ibid*, at [118].

[115] In particular, para 4 of the standard terms and conditions made it clear that the client was liable for all of the legal representative's basic charges and success fee: see *ibid*, at [126]–[127].

The requirements of this regulation were usually met by including a brief narrative risk assessment. Wilson LJ has confirmed that compliance with reg 3(1)(a) is an issue that could be decided with regard to the background (which, in the case before him, included the fact that the client was assisted by a shrewd and intelligent lawyer).[116] In those circumstances, references to 'the fact that if you lose, we will not earn anything' and 'our assessment of the risks of your case' were regarded as being sufficient.

Regulation 3(1)(b) of the CFA Regulations 2000

In so far as drafting errors were concerned, breach of reg 3(1)(b) was probably the most common cause of older conditional fee agreements being found to be unenforceable. This regulation related to the 'postponement charge' (defined at 29.02). It required the agreement to specify the percentage increase that had been used to calculate the postponement charge: **29.62**

> '3 (1) A conditional fee agreement which provides for a success fee—
> [...]
> (b) must specify how much of the percentage increase, if any, relates to the cost to the legal representative of the postponement of the payment of his fees and expenses.'

It applied to all types of agreement—other than CFA Lites (see 29.37)—that provided for a success fee, including those with an additional legal representative and those in which the legal representative was a membership organisation.

In general, the court approached the issue of compliance by reference to the agreement as properly interpreted rather than by reference to what was literally set out in the agreement. That process has been referred to as 'prior interpretation' or 'anterior interpretation' (see 31.29). Although there is no authority on the point, it is probably true to say that the process of interpretation should not be permitted to develop into a process of implication.[117] **29.63**

Two topics arise, as follows. **29.64**

- **The effect of failing to entirely state the postponement charge** Blake J has confirmed that the duty to state the postponement charge existed even if there was no intention to levy it. That, however, was in the context of the agreement having made reference to the postponement charge; he commented that his conclusion might have been different had the agreement been entirely silent on that matter.[118] The court is not limited to looking at the body of the agreement when deciding whether the postponement charge has been specified. An example of the court going beyond the corpus of the agreement was a case in which Burton J held that the details given in the schedule were, when properly interpreted, sufficiently clear to satisfy the requirement.[119] Where the court finds that there has been a complete failure to state the postponement charge and where the court finds that this does amount to a breach, it may be relevant to

---

[116] *Bray Walker Solicitors (A Firm) v Silvera* [2010] EWCA Civ 332, at [25].

[117] Mann J dealt with similar issues in *Fosberry & anor v HM Revenue and Customs* [2007] EWHC 2249 (Ch), at [43], which case has also acquired a second neutral citation number—[2008] EWHC 3344 (Ch)—and is also often cited as [2007] EWHC 3344 (Ch).

[118] *Utting v McBain* [2007] EWHC 3293 (QB), at [9]–[11].

[119] *Sidhu v Sandhu* (unreported), 5 May 2009, QBD.

the issue of materiality that, in general, a party is not entitled to benefit from their own breach.[120]

- **The effect of a postponement charge that is unclear or unintelligible** It was not uncommon for an agreement to contain terms concerning the postponement charge that were in conflict, unclear or, in an extreme case, unintelligible. Whilst the last of these circumstances would usually be beyond rescue, the process of 'anterior interpretation' may offer a route by which the court may find compliance in appropriate cases (see 31.29). The process of anterior interpretation may go to breach or materiality.[121] The following points may be made about inconsistencies and ambiguities.
  - **Inconsistency** An early example of anterior interpretation was a case in which there was an inconsistency between what was said in the body of the agreement and what was recorded in the risk assessment.[122] The paying party said that the ambiguity could not be resolved; the Court of Appeal expressed its disagreement in fairly forceful terms.[123] Brooke LJ (giving judgment of the court) had this to say: 'Taken together, [the terms in the body] prevail over the risk assessment schedule, and thus on its true construction the CFA in this case complies with the Regulations.'[124]
  - **Ambiguity** Ambiguous terms will usually present more of a problem than inconsistent terms, because the task may not be as easy as choosing which interpretation is correct; rather, the agreement may be so disorganised that it is impossible to tell what it means. In a case in which the body of the agreement had made it clear that a postponement charge existed and was chargeable notwithstanding the fact that it was impossible to discern what that charge was, Brooke LJ found that the court below had been entitled to find that there had been a breach.[125] Other examples of ambiguity giving rise to non-compliance with reg 3(1)(b) exist.[126] In a case in which the risk assessment recorded that postponement had been taken into account for the purpose of setting the level of the success fee, Mann J found that the fact that it had been mentioned was capable of implying that the postponement charge existed and he went on to say that if it was unquantified, that may amount to a material breach.[127]

Regulation 3(2) of the CFA Regulations 2000

29.65 Regulation 3(2) was made up of three parts, the first of which ensured that the court would be able to see why the success fee had been set at the level stated in the agreement, and

[120] In a setting other than costs, see *Micklefield v SAC Technology Ltd* [1990] 1 WLR 1002; *Richco International Ltd v Alfred C Toepfer GmbH* [1991] 1 Lloyd's Rep 136; *Little v Courage* [1995] CLC 164, at 168, *per* Millett LJ.

[121] An example of the court finding that a breach of reg 3(1)(b) was immaterial was *Brennan v Association Asphalt Ltd* [2006] EWHC 90052 (Costs), but it is important to note that an appeal from that decision was allowed by consent, thereby diminishing the persuasive value of that case.

[122] *Tichband v Hurdman* [2003] EWCA Civ 718, which was one of the cases heard at the same time as *Hollins v Russell.* The corpus of the agreement said that the postponement charge was nil, but the risk assessment indicated that it had been taken into account in calculating the success fee.

[123] Brooke LJ called the paying party's arguments 'as unattractive as they are unmeritorious': see *Tichband v Hurdman* [2003] EWCA Civ 718, at [132].

[124] *Ibid*, at [134].

[125] *Spencer v Wood* [2004] EWCA Civ 352, at [17].

[126] See, eg, *Utting v McBain* [2007] EWHC 3293 (QB), at [21]–[25].

[127] *Fosberry & anor v HM Revenue and Customs* [2007] EWHC 2249 (Ch), at [46], which case has acquired a second neutral citation number—[2008] EWHC 3344 (Ch)—and is also often cited as [2007] EWHC 3344 (Ch).

the second and third of which ensured that (subject to the court ordering otherwise) the percentage increase paid by the client would be no higher than that recovered from an opponent. Blake J has likened this to the 'reverse of the indemnity principle'.[128] Regulations 3(2) read as follows:

> '3 (2) If the agreement relates to court proceedings, it must provide that where the percentage increase becomes payable as a result of those proceedings, then—
> (a) if—
> (i) any fees subject to the increase are assessed, and
> (ii) the legal representative or the client is required by the court to disclose to the court or any other person the reasons for setting the percentage increase at the level stated in the agreement, he may do so,
> (b) if—
> (i) any such fees are assessed, and
> (ii) any amount in respect of the percentage increase is disallowed on the assessment on the ground that the level at which the increase was set was unreasonable in view of facts which were or should have been known to the legal representative at the time it was set, that amount ceases to be payable under the agreement, unless the court is satisfied that it should continue to be so payable, and
> (c) if—
> (i) sub-paragraph (b) does not apply, and
> (ii) the legal representative agrees with any person liable as a result of the proceedings to pay fees subject to the percentage increase that a lower amount than the amount payable in accordance with the conditional fee agreement is to be paid instead, the amount payable under the conditional fee agreement in respect of those fees shall be reduced accordingly, unless the court is satisfied that the full amount should continue to be payable under it.'

The regulation applied only to agreements that both provided for a success fee and related to court proceedings. It applied regardless of whether the agreement was with an additional legal representative or whether it was with a membership organisation. It did not apply to CFA Lites.

The following miscellaneous points may be made about reg 3(2) of the CFA Regulations 2000. **29.66**

- **Total failure to include disclosure provision** A total failure to include the disclosure provisions will give rise to a material breach. Mann J rejected the argument that the provisions were immaterial because they were solely for the benefit of the legal representative (in the sense that non-compliance would do no more than impair the legal representative's ability to recover a high success fee); instead, he found that the disclosure provisions had a role to play in the administration of justice:

> 'Assuming that any written assessment is a privileged document, absent reg 3(2)(a), the receiving party would have the option of disclosing it in order to assist its case, or not disclosing it and proving the case otherwise. It might be that, by refusing to disclose the document, the case of that party would be damaged ... [Regulation 3(2)(a)] probably has the effect of overruling such privilege as might otherwise have existed in any risk assessment documents germane to the CFA. It effectively requires the client to consent in advance to the disclosure of the material. That being the practical purpose of the reg 3(2)(a) provision

128 *Bray Walker Solicitors (A Firm) v Silvera* [2008] EWHC 3147 (QB), at [71].

and, therefore, of reg 3(2)(a) itself, it seems to me that the legal purpose ... is that it furthers the administration of justice.'[129]

- **Partial failure to include limiting provisions** In a different case, Mann J found that an agreement that included the first limiting provision, but not the second, was in breach of reg 3(2). He was not persuaded by the fact that the agreement stated that the success fee might be limited by agreement.[130]
- **The extent of the limiting provisions** It has been argued that the limiting provisions do not—as implied above—relate only to the success fee, but also to base costs. That argument has had a degree of success at first instance (although not to the extent that any breach has ever been found to be material), but it has not been developed or pursued for many years.[131]

Regulation 3A of the CFA Regulations 2000

29.67 What follows should be read in conjunction with 29.37–29.40, because they relate only to CFA Lites. The provisions of reg 3A are as follows:

> '3A (1) This regulation applies to a conditional fee agreement under which, except in the circumstances set out in paragraph (5) and (5A), the client is liable to pay his legal representative's fees and expenses only to the extent that sums are recovered in respect of the relevant proceedings, whether by way of costs or otherwise.
>
> (2) In determining for the purposes of paragraph (1) the circumstances in which a client is liable to pay his legal representative's fees and expenses, no account is to be taken of any obligation to pay costs in respect of the premium of a policy taken out to insure against the risk of incurring a liability in the relevant proceedings.
>
> (3) Regulations 2, 3 and 4 do not apply to a conditional fee agreement to which this regulation applies.
>
> (4) A conditional fee agreement to which this regulation applies must—
>
> (a) specify—
>
> (i) the particular proceedings or parts of them to which it relates (including whether it relates to any appeal, counterclaim or proceedings to enforce a judgment or order); and
>
> (ii) the circumstances in which the legal representative's fees and expenses, or part of them, are payable; and
>
> (b) if it provides for a success fee—
>
> (i) briefly specify the reasons for setting the percentage increase at the level stated in the agreement; and
>
> (ii) provide that if, in court proceedings, the percentage increase becomes payable as a result of those proceedings and the legal representative or the client is ordered to disclose to the court or any other person the reasons for setting the percentage increase at the level stated in the agreement, he may do so.

[129] *Fenton v Holmes* [2007] EWHC 2476 (Ch), at [46]–[49].

[130] *Fosberry & anor v HM Revenue and Customs* [2007] EWHC 2249 (Ch), at [43], which case has also acquired a second neutral citation number—[2008] EWHC 3344 (Ch)—and is also often cited as [2007] EWHC 3344 (Ch).

[131] See *Ghannouchi v Houni Ltd & Ors* [2004] EWHC 9002 (Costs). It seems that the last time this point was mentioned in the SCCO was 2006—see *Oyston v The Royal Bank of Scotland plc* [2006] EWHC 90053—which was also the last time it was mentioned in legal journals: see Gore, A, 'Access to Justice in Personal Injury Cases' (2006) 2 JPI Law 189.

(5) A conditional fee agreement to which this regulation applies may specify that the client will be liable to pay the legal representative's fees and expenses whether or not sums are recovered in respect of the relevant proceedings, if the client—
(a) fails to co-operate with the legal representative;
(b) fails to attend any medical or expert examination or court hearing which the legal representative reasonably requests him to attend;
(c) fails to give necessary instructions to the legal representative;
(d) withdraws instructions from the legal representative;
(e) is an individual who is adjudged bankrupt or enters into an arrangement or a composition with his creditors, or against whom an administration order is made; or
(f) is a company for which a receiver, administrative receiver or liquidator is appointed.

(5A) A conditional fee agreement to which this regulation applies may specify that, in the event of the client dying in the course of the relevant proceedings, his estate will be liable for the legal representative's fees and expenses, whether or not sums are recovered in respect of those proceedings.

(6) Before a conditional fee agreement to which this regulation applies is made, the legal representative must inform the client as to the circumstances in which the client or his estate may be liable to pay the legal representative's fees and expenses, and provide such further explanation, advice or other information as to those circumstances as the client may reasonably require.'

Thus reg 3A created a mechanism whereby a simplified agreement (namely, a CFA Lite) could be created without it having to comply with regs 2, 3 and 4 of the CFA Regulations 2000. It applied to all CFA Lites made on or after 2 June 2003, but before 1 November 2005, including those with additional legal representatives and those in which the legal representative was a membership organisation. There used to be a provision in the CPR that disapplied the indemnity principle for CFA Lites;[132] that provision has now been omitted from the CPR, but transitional provisions mean that it will still apply where the agreement was made before 1 April 2013.[133] **29.68**

Broadly speaking, reg 3A had two functions: **29.69**

- it regulated the circumstances in which a legal representative was able to look to the client for payment under a CFA Lite; and
- it imposed a number of requirements that—when viewed in the context of the client's liability being otherwise limited to what was recovered—afforded a degree of protection not dissimilar to that afforded by the CFA Regulations 2000 in general.

Regulation 3A contained a number of conditions—'the Lite conditions' (see 29.72–29.73)—that needed to be satisfied before the agreement could be said to be a CFA Lite (thereby disapplying regs 2, 3 and 4). Once those conditions had been met, then a number of requirements—'the Lite requirements' (see 29.74–29.76)—applied, which were similar to, but less onerous than, the requirements that applied to other types of conditional fee agreement. **29.70**

Disputes about reg 3A are often about whether the Lite conditions have been satisfied—an issue that is discussed elsewhere in this chapter (see 29.37–29.40). A failure to satisfy the **29.71**

[132] CPR, r 43.2(3), which brings into force the provisions in Senior Courts Act 1981, s 51(2), as amended by Access to Justice Act 1999, s 31.
[133] See CPR, r 48n.1.

Lite conditions will mean that the agreement is not a CFA Lite; it may, however, still be an enforceable agreement if it happens to comply with regs 2, 3 and 4 of the CFA Regulations 2000. It is possible for an agreement to satisfy the Lite conditions, but not the Lite requirements. If this happens, the agreement will be an unenforceable CFA Lite (unless, of course, it also happens to comply with regs 2, 3 and 4 of the CFA Regulations 2000).

29.72 **The Lite conditions** Regulation 3A(1) (see 29.67) created the most important aspect of the Lite conditions, which, essentially, was that the client would not be liable for the legal representative's fees or disbursements (other than an ATE premium) beyond those that were recovered in the litigation.

29.73 Regulations 3A(5) and (5A) provided that the client may be required to personally pay the legal representative's fees and expenses, but only in certain stipulated circumstances, such as a failure on the part of the client to cooperate with the legal representative or where the client fails to give necessary instructions (see 29.39–29.40).

29.74 **The Lite requirements** The Lite requirements are set out in regs 3(4) and (6) (see 29.67). In common with regs 2, 3 and 4, a legal representative entering into a CFA Lite was required to ensure that certain information had been given to the client and that certain provisions had been incorporated into the agreement itself.[134] In particular, a CFA Lite was required to include:

- a provision that specified the particular proceedings, or parts of them, to which the agreement related, including whether it related to:
  - any appeal;
  - any counterclaim; or
  - any proceedings to enforce a judgment or order; and
- a provision that specified the circumstances in which the legal representative's fees and expenses, or part of them, were payable.

29.75 Before a CFA Lite was signed, the legal representative was required to inform the client as to the circumstances in which the client or their estate may be liable to pay the legal representative's fees and expenses. The legal representative was required to provide such further explanation, advice or other information about those circumstances as the client may reasonably request.

29.76 Where it provided for a success fee, a CFA Lite had to include:

- a brief statement of the reasons for setting the percentage increase at the level stated in the agreement; and
- a provision that if the percentage increase were to become payable as a result of court proceedings, then:
  - if any fees subject to the increase were assessed and
  - if the legal representative or the client was required by the court to disclose to the court or any other person the reasons for setting the percentage increase at the level stated in the agreement,

  they may do so.

[134] See Conditional Fee Agreements Regulations 2000 (SI 2000/692) (as amended), reg 3A(6) and (4), respectively.

There is no binding authority dealing with these requirements in the specific context of reg 3A, but there is no reason to believe that the principles relating to regs 2, 3, and 4 would not apply.

Regulation 4(2) of the CFA Regulations 2000 (in general)

Regulation 4 imposed a number of obligations. It is convenient first to take an overview and then to consider each obligation in turn. There was a certain amount of overlap between the obligations. **29.77**

Regulation 4(2) must be read in conjunction with reg 4(1) (see 29.79): the latter created a requirement that the client be given pre-contract counselling and the former stated what that information should be. There was also a requirement that if the client reasonably required any further explanation, advice or other information, it should be provided. A number of general points can be made about reg 4(2). **29.78**

- **Situations in which reg 4(2) did not apply** There are three situations in which reg 4(2) either did not apply or, if it applied, was entirely redundant, as follows.
  - **CFA Lites** As is explained in at 29.66, reg 4 did not apply to agreements that were CFA Lites.
  - **Additional legal representatives** Regulation 4 (in general) did not apply to agreements made between a legal representative and additional legal representatives.
  - **Membership organisations** Where the legal representative was a body to which s 30 of the Access to Justice Act 1999 applied (that is, a membership organisation[135]) and where there were no circumstances in which the client may have been personally liable to pay any costs in respect of the proceedings, then reg 4(1) did not apply.[136] This had the effect of making reg 4(2) redundant.[137]
- **Delegation** Subject to certain safeguards, a legal representative was permitted to delegate responsibilities under reg 4 to unqualified persons. More than 100 years ago, Lord Blackburn had the following to say about delegation in general: 'There are some matters as to which though he may delegate them and need not do them in person but may employ a clerk, yet he would be required to see that that clerk had competent knowledge.'[138] After having reminded himself of what Lord Blackburn had said, Brooke LJ came to the conclusion that delegation under reg 4 was permissible, provided that the person to whom the task was delegated was competent and appropriately supervised:

  > 'Each situation must be considered on its own facts. Parliament wishes to foster new ways of rendering litigation services, and provided that the performance of the regulation 4 duties is appropriately delegated, and the duties are properly performed under appropriate

---

[135] Thirteen organisations have been approved since the powers were introduced: AA Legal Service; British Cycling Federation; Defence Police Federation; Durham Colliery Overmen Deputies and Shotfirers Retired Members Group; Engineering Employers' Federation; Police Federation of England and Wales; RAC Motoring Services; the Cyclist Touring Club; the London Cycling Campaign; British Triathlon Federation; the Co-operative Group; the National Union of Students; and the British Association of Social Workers.

[136] See Conditional Fee Agreements Regulations 2000 (SI 2000/692), reg 4(4).

[137] This catered for organisations that wished to support their members via their own in-house legal staff rather than by engaging external lawyers through a collective CFA.

[138] *Law Society v Waterlow* (1883) 8 App Cas 407, at 415, quoted in *Hollins v Russell* [2003] EWCA Civ 718, at [178].

supervision, we cannot see that Parliament's intentions are being thwarted if the solicitor delegates more widely than is allowed for in [the paying parties'] primary argument before us. We would not wish to be prescriptive about the form which that supervision should take, provided that an appropriate system has been set up.'[139]

Sub-delegation was also permissible. Brooke LJ emphasised that it was essential that the legal representative had a degree of supervisory control over the sub-delegates:

'Quality control, however, is all important, and if a solicitor abjures his duty to maintain supervisory responsibility, through an established framework for reporting and accountability, over the ... representatives when they visit his client's home on his behalf, it is likely that it would be found that it was not he who gave the information he was required by regulation 4 to give, and that the regulation has therefore been broken.'[140]

- **Advice based on a mistake of law** Irwin J has concluded that giving advice that was based on an error of law was not compliant with reg 4 and that this would be so even where that error was understandable in human terms.[141]
- **Relevance to enforceability** Regulation 4(2) related to requirements that had to be satisfied before the conditional fee agreement was made. It has been argued that those requirements ought to be regarded as being something distinguishable from the agreement itself and that therefore a failure to satisfy those requirements would not put the agreement at risk. Brooke LJ rejected that argument, essentially on policy grounds (namely, that pre-contract warnings are an important part of a regime that goes to consumer protection); he also rejected it on textual grounds.[142] Thus, if there has been a material breach of reg 4(2), the agreement will be unenforceable.

Regulation 4(2)(a) of the CFA Regulations 2000

29.79 Regulation 4(2)(a), when read in conjunction with reg 4(1), stipulated that the client must be told of the circumstances in which they may be liable to pay the costs of the legal representative in accordance with the agreement:

'4 (1) Before a conditional fee agreement is made the legal representative must—
(a) inform the client about the following matters, and
(b) if the client requires any further explanation, advice or other information about any of those matters, provide such further explanation, advice or other information about them as the client may reasonably require.

(2) Those matters are—
(a) the circumstances in which the client may be liable to pay the costs of the legal representative in accordance with the agreement ...'

---

139 *Hollins v Russell* [2003] EWCA Civ 718, at [195].
140 *Ibid*, at [217].
141 *Crook v Birmingham City Council* [2007] EWHC 1415 (QB), at [28]. In the case, Irwin J was dealing with the breach related to reg 4(2)(c), but there is no reason to believe that the principle does not also apply to the other regulations.
142 He cited three reasons in *Hollins v Russell* [2003] EWCA Civ 718, at [111]: (a) Courts and Legal Services Act 1990, s 58A(3)(a) (as amended), clearly characterises the requirements in the Conditional Fee Agreements Regulations 2000 (SI 2000/692) as among those with which the agreement must comply; (b) the words 'applicable to it' (as used in Courts and Legal Services Act 1990, s 58(1)) are able to encompass steps taken by one of the parties before the agreement is made; and (3) reg 2(2) requires a CFA to state that reg 4 has been complied with, thus making compliance part of the obligation under the CFA.

The requisite information had to be given orally (whether or not it was also given in writing).[143] Regulation 4(2)(a) applied to all conditional fee agreements made after 1 April 2000 and before 1 November 2005, except those referred to in the first bullet point of 29.78. The duty was to explain the circumstances in which costs may have been payable under the agreement, rather than to explore hypothetical situations that might arise.[144]

Regulation 4(2)(b) of the CFA Regulations 2000

Regulation 4(2)(b), when read in conjunction with reg 4(1), stipulated that the client should be told the circumstances in which they would be able to seek an assessment of the fees and expenses of the legal representative: **29.80**

> '4 (2) Those matters are—
>
> [...]
>
> (b) the circumstances in which the client may seek assessment of the fees and expenses of the legal representative and the procedure for doing so ...'

The requisite information had to be given orally (whether or not it was also given in writing).[145] Regulation 4(2)(b) applied to all conditional fee agreements made after 1 April 2000 and before 1 November 2005, except those referred to in the first bullet point of 29.78.

Regulation 4(2)(c) of the CFA Regulations 2000

Regulation 4(2)(c), when read in conjunction with reg 4(1), required the legal representative to say whether it considered that the client's risk of incurring liability for costs in respect of the proceedings to which the agreement related was insured against under an existing contract of insurance: **29.81**

> '4 (2) Those matters are—
>
> [...]
>
> (c) whether the legal representative considers that the client's risk of incurring liability for costs in respect of the proceedings to which agreement relates is insured against under an existing contract of insurance ...'

The information had to be given orally (whether or not it was also given in writing).[146] Regulation 4(2)(c) applied to all conditional fee agreements made after 1 April 2000 and before 1 November 2005, except those referred to in the first bullet point of 29.78.

The burden of considering the availability of BTE insurance lay with the legal representative, rather than the client. Unless circumstances permitted otherwise (see 29.83), the client ought not to have been asked the 'ultimate question'—as Dyson LJ put it—of whether the client had BTE insurance that would have covered the legal expenses of bringing the claim.[147] Indeed, in many cases, the client should simply have been asked to produce any home and motor insurance policies that they may have had, thereby leaving **29.82**

---

[143] Conditional Fee Agreements Regulations 2000 (SI 2000/692), reg 4(5).

[144] *Bray Walker Solicitors (A Firm) v Silvera* [2008] EWHC 3147 (QB), at [75], affirmed on appeal ([2010] EWCA Civ 332).

[145] Conditional Fee Agreements Regulations 2000 (SI 2000/692), reg 4(5).

[146] Conditional Fee Agreements Regulations 2000 (SI 2000/692), reg 4(5).

[147] *Garrett v Halton Borough Council; Myatt v National Coal Board* [2006] EWCA Civ 1017, at [55], [62], and [72].

it to the legal representative to read them and form a view as whether legal expenses insurance already existed.[148]

29.83 A 'calibrated' approach was required when considering the issue of what was reasonably required under reg 4(2)(b) of the CFA Regulations 2000. Dyson LJ identified five categories of relevant factors, as follows.[149]

- **Category one: nature of the client** Some clients may have been sufficiently knowledgeable and intelligent to be able to answer the 'ultimate question' (see 29.82), but few would fall into this category. The legal representative bore the burden of being responsible for forming a view as to whether the client's answers could reasonably be relied upon.
- **Category two: the circumstances of the instructions** The legal representative was not required to carry out investigations that would have been unreasonable in the circumstances of the case in question. By way of example, Brooke LJ described as 'ridiculous' the notion that full BTE enquiries be required for an 80-year-old woman who was still in hospital after recently having been discharged from an intensive therapy unit.[150]
- **Category three: the nature of the claim** If it was unlikely that standard BTE policies would have applied to the claim in question, the legal representative may have been justified in taking fewer investigative steps than might otherwise have been the case.
- **Category four: the cost of ATE cover** The cost of ATE cover was a relevant factor.[151]
- **Category five: previous enquiries** Where the claim had been referred by a referral agency, it was often the case that the agent had already investigated the question of the availability of BTE cover. Whether it was reasonable to rely on that information was a matter for the legal representative to decide, using its own judgement.

29.84 The standard of enquiries was not the same as that required for the purposes of considering whether ATE insurance was required—those enquiries often being referred to as '*Sarwar* enquiries' (see 54.198).[152] Dyson LJ made it clear that the two were not a single standard:

> '[It] follows that the regulation 4(2)(c) duty does not require solicitors slavishly to follow the detailed guidance given by this court in [*Sarwar v Alam* [2001] EWCA Civ 1401, which dealt with the standard applicable to ATE]. In particular, the statement at para 45 that a solicitor should normally invite a client to bring to the first interview any relevant policy should be treated with considerable caution. It has no application in high volume low value litigation conducted by solicitors on referral by claims management companies.'[153]

29.85 The following miscellaneous points may be made about reg 4(2)(c) of the CFA Regulations 2000.

- **Timing** Although not binding, Master Wright found that the requirement that advice had to be given before the agreement was made did not mean that it needed to be given

---

148 *Ibid*, at [78].

149 *Ibid*, at [71]–[76].

150 *Hollins v Russell* [2003] EWCA Civ 718, at [138], cited by Dyson LJ in *Garrett v Halton Borough Council; Myatt v National Coal Board* [2006] EWCA Civ 1017, at [73].

151 Dyson LJ noted that this was also a factor relevant to the standard of enquiries required for the purposes of ATE insurance.

152 After *Sarwar v Alam* [2001] EWCA Civ 1401.

153 *Garrett v Halton Borough Council; Myatt v National Coal Board* [2006] EWCA Civ 1017, at [70]. On this issue generally, see *ibid*, at [66]–[70]; *Hollins v Russell* [2003] EWCA Civ 718, at [139].

at precisely the same time as the agreement was made.[154] Where, however, the requisite enquiries were carried out after the agreement had already been made, Judge Stewart QC found that that deprived the client of proper advice and that did amount to a material breach.[155]

- **Expired BTE and insurance other than BTE** In a case in which the costs incurred had already exceeded the level of cover under a pre-existing BTE policy, Judge Behrens (sitting as a judge of the High Court) found that there was no obligation to advise that BTE cover existed.[156] Whilst not binding, Judge MacDuff found that the duty to make enquiries under reg 4(2)(c) was not limited to making enquiries about BTE insurance, but would, in appropriate circumstances, have included a duty to make enquiries about the existence of ATE insurance that may already have been incepted.[157]
- **ATE insurance already incepted** In a similar vein, Waller LJ said (*obiter*) that the onus to give advice would exist even where it was known that ATE insurance had already been incepted.[158]

Regulation 4(2)(d) of the CFA Regulations 2000

Regulation 4(2)(d), when read in conjunction with reg 4(1), required the legal representative to state whether other methods of financing the costs of the claim were available, and if so, how they would apply to the client and the proceedings in question: **29.86**

> '4 (2) Those matters are—
> [...]
> (d) whether other methods of financing those costs are available, and, if so, how they apply to the client and the proceedings in question ...'

The requisite information had to be given orally (whether or not it was also given in writing).[159] Regulation 4(2)(d) applied to all conditional fee agreements made on or after 1 April 2000, but before 1 November 2005, except those referred to in the first bullet point of 29.78.

The following points may be made about reg 4(2)(d) of the CFA Regulations 2000. **29.87**

- **Insurance already in existence** The duty to give advice continued to exist even where the client had pre-existing insurance. Where this was so, the client ought to have been given advice about whether that insurance was appropriate to use for funding the matter.[160]
- **ATE insurance already incepted** See the points made at 29.85.
- **Impracticable funding options** Irwin J has commented that reg 4(2)(d) did not impose a duty to give advice about methods of funding that, for all practical purposes, would not have been available.[161]

---

154 *White v Revell* [2006] EWHC 90054 (Costs).
155 *Cooper v Morgan* (unreported), 29 September 2006, Liverpool County Court.
156 *Thornley (a child) v MoD* [2010] EWHC 2584 (QB), at [20]–[28].
157 *Berry v Spousals* (unreported), 24 April 2007, Birmingham County Court.
158 *Jones v Wrexham Borough Council* [2007] EWCA Civ 1356, at [62].
159 Conditional Fee Agreements Regulations 2000 (SI 2000/692), reg 4(5).
160 *Jones v Wrexham Borough Council* [2007] EWCA Civ 1356, at [62].
161 *Crook v Birmingham City Council* [2007] EWHC 1415 (QB), at [34].

- **Complex funding options** In circumstances in which complex funding options existed, Christopher Clarke J explained (*obiter*) that it would have been reasonable to look at the matter in the round and at whether the advice was reasonable in all of the circumstances.[162]
- **Timing** See the points made at 29.85.
- **English not the client's first language** Blake J declined to find that there had been a breach of reg 4(2) by reason of the fact that the client (whose first language was Italian) had been given a written explanation in English, especially where he had the benefit of a translator easily to hand.[163]
- **Failure to give advice about protection from adverse costs** Irwin J has commented (*obiter*) that if the breach was such that the client had been given inadequate advice about how to manage the possibility of an adverse costs order, then that would amount to a material breach unless the advice had been only minimally deficient.[164]
- **Failure to give advice about the availability of public funding** This issue tended to arise only in housing disrepair claims and clinical negligence claims, because these were the two types of claim in relation to which, at the time, legal aid was most readily available. There are examples of the court having found that a failure to give advice about the minutiae of public funding would not have amounted to a material breach;[165] equally, an affirmative and reasonable decision not to burden the client with detailed advice would not have amounted to a breach.[166] Many examples of material breach, however, exist.[167]

Regulation 4(2)(e) of the CFA Regulations 2000

29.88 The purpose of reg 4(2)(e), when read in conjunction with reg 4(1), was to ensure that the legal representative acted and gave advice independently of its own interest.[168] Regulation 4(2)(e) read as follows:

> '4 (1) Before a conditional fee agreement is made the legal representative must—
> (a) inform the client about the following matters, and
> (b) if the client requires any further explanation, advice or other information about any of those matters, provide such further explanation, advice or other information about them as the client may reasonably require.
>
> (2) Those matters are—
> [...]
> (e) whether the legal representative considers that any particular method or methods of financing any or all of those costs is appropriate and, if he considers that a contract of insurance is appropriate or recommends a particular such contract—
> (i) his reasons for doing so, and
> (ii) whether he has an interest in doing so.'

---

162 *Forde v Birmingham City Council* [2009] EWHC 12 (QB), at [200].

163 *Bray Walker Solicitors (A Firm) v Silvera* [2008] EWHC 3147 (QB), at [73], affirmed on other grounds on appeal ([2010] EWCA Civ 332, at [25]). It was probably relevant that the client was a relatively sophisticated businessman.

164 *Crook v Birmingham City Council* [2007] EWHC 1415 (QB), at [35].

165 *Ibid.*

166 *Forde v Birmingham City Council* [2009] EWHC 12 (QB).

167 These include *Bowen v Bridgend County Borough Council* [2004] EWHC 9010 (Costs) and *Hughes & Ors v London Borough of Newham* [2005] EWHC 90019 (Costs), neither of which is binding.

168 *Tankard v John Fredricks Plastics Ltd* [2008] EWCA Civ 1375, at [13]–[15].

The regulation applied to all conditional fee agreements made after 1 April 2000, but before 1 November 2005, except those referred to in the first bullet point of 29.78.

Unlike the other provisions in reg 4(2), under reg 4(2)(e) the requisite information had to be given orally *and* in writing.[169] Provided that it was sufficiently clear, the latter requirement could have been met by a written explanation that was contained within the agreement itself.[170] **29.89**

The following miscellaneous points may be made about reg 4(2)(e) of the CFA Regulations 2000. **29.90**

- **Nature of the interest** There was no reason to interpret the requirement to declare any interest as narrowly as meaning only a *direct* financial interest.[171] The applicable test was an objective one: Clarke MR explained that a declarable interest would have arisen if a reasonable person with knowledge of the relevant facts would have thought that the existence of the interest might have affected the advice given.[172]
- **Panel membership** This topic is discussed in detail at 29.91.
- **No interest** The requirement to declare an interest under reg 4(2)(e)(ii) did not extend to declaring the absence of an interest: the word 'whether' in the regulation was read as meaning 'if'. Brooke LJ explained the rationale behind that interpretation:

  'The mischief which this regulation was introduced to remedy was the risk that the client's legal representative might induce the client to enter into insurance arrangements in which he had an interest. If he had no interest, then there was no identified mischief.'[173]

- **ATE insurance already incepted** See the points made at 29.85.
- **BTE insurance already in existence** The duty to give advice pursuant to reg 4(2)(e) existed even where the client had pre-existing insurance (that is, even where the client had BTE insurance). In those circumstances, the client ought to have been given advice about whether the insurance would be appropriate to use.[174]
- **Timing** There is no reason to believe that the points made at 29.85 concerning the other provisions under reg 4(2) do not also apply to reg 4(2)(e).
- **Incorrect statement of interest** The obligation to state whether a legal representative had an interest was an obligation to state those details correctly; it would not have been sufficient merely to state whether there was an interest if that statement was incorrect, even if the legal representative believed that what it had said was correct.[175]
- **Clarity** As is the case with reg 4 in general, any advice that was given ought to have been clear; inconsistent advice (such as the client being told about the existence of an interest, but the agreement saying something else) would not be sufficient to discharge the legal representative's duty.[176]

---

[169] Conditional Fee Agreements Regulations 2000 (SI 2000/692), reg 4(5).
[170] Although dealing with a different aspect of reg 4(2), there is no reason to believe that the analysis in *Hollins v Russell* [2003] EWCA Civ 718, at [152]–[154], would not also apply.
[171] *Garrett v Halton Borough Council; Myatt v National Coal Board* [2006] EWCA Civ 1017, at [91].
[172] *Ibid.*
[173] *Hollins v Russell* [2003] EWCA Civ 718, at [144].
[174] *Jones v Wrexham Borough Council* [2007] EWCA Civ 1356, at [62].
[175] *Garrett v Halton Borough Council; Myatt v National Coal Board* [2006] EWCA Civ 1017, at [94].
[176] *Tankard v John Fredricks Plastics Ltd* [2008] EWCA Civ 1375, at [45].

- **Complexity and materiality** On the facts of a palpably complicated matter, Irwin J found that a failure to give advice about the detail of funding lacked materiality because the correct advice would have been so complex, with risks and opportunities 'all hedged about with uncertainty', that it would not have made any difference to the client's decision as to how to fund the claim.[177]
- **The Conduct of Business Rules** Whilst Dyson LJ did not say that the two standards were the same, he made *obiter* comments to the effect that compliance with the requirements imposed by the Solicitors' Financial Services (Conduct of Business) Rules 2001 (which coincided with the CFA Regulations 2000 for about ten months in 2005) would have been sufficient to comply with the obligations under reg 4(2)(e)(ii).[178]

Panel membership in the context of the CFA Regulations 2000

29.91 The points made below concern panel membership. It should be read in conjunction with 29.88–29.90. The focus of this section is reg 4(2)(e) of the CFA Regulations 2000, but what is set out below would probably apply in any situation in which a legal representative is required to declare an interest. In so far as reg 4(2)(e) was concerned, the argument that paying parties most often advanced was that if a firm made a profit from cases referred to it as a result of being on a panel, that panel membership had value and ought to have been declared.

29.92 A number of different types of panel existed (and still do exist), the two most common being an 'insurance panel' (where the legal representative is, by virtue of its membership, able to obtain a particular contract of insurance for its clients) and a 'referral panel' (where the legal representative receives referrals from a referral agency and is usually required to recommend a particular contract of insurance in return). Panel membership may also bring with it 'delegated authority', which is the power to bind the insurer by incepting a contract of insurance without direct reference to the insurer.

29.93 Clarke MR has confirmed that the fact that a legal representative was a member of a panel did not necessarily mean that there was a declarable interest for the purposes of reg 4(2)(e).[179] Every type of panel membership was capable of generating a declarable interest, so each case had to be considered on its own facts. At one end of the spectrum, where a legal representative was dependent on referrals as the 'lifeblood' of its practice (to use a word adopted by Dyson LJ), that would have created an indirect, but declarable, interest;[180] at the other end of the spectrum, where the panel membership was principally for the purposes of obtaining high-quality insurance for the benefit of clients, that would usually not have amounted to a declarable interest.[181]

29.94 **Panel membership: list of relevant factors** It is possible to identify the following factors as being relevant to the issue of whether panel membership gave rise to a declarable interest:

- the motive for a legal representative's membership of the panel, including whether the legal representative was attracted to the panel by the high quality of the insurance;

[177] *Crook v Birmingham City Council* [2007] EWHC 1415 (QB), at [28].
[178] *Garrett v Halton Borough Council; Myatt v National Coal Board* [2006] EWCA Civ 1017, at [103].
[179] *Tankard v John Fredricks Plastics Ltd* [2008] EWCA Civ 1375, at [17]–[18].
[180] *Garrett v Halton Borough Council; Myatt v National Coal Board* [2006] EWCA Civ 1017, at [97].
[181] See *Tankard v John Fredricks Plastics Ltd* [2008] EWCA Civ 1375, at [17]–[20].

- the motive of the panel organisation for requiring panel membership, including whether the concern of the underwriter was merely to avoid adverse selection of cases;
- the extent to which the legal representative was dependent on the referrals;
- whether failure to comply with recommending a policy would have led to a cessation of referral of cases;
- whether there had been reviews to ensure that continued membership of the panel was in clients' bests interests; and
- the closeness of the business relationship between the legal representative and the referrer.[182]

Clarke MR has clarified (*obiter*) that it would not be sufficient to declare the existence of a declarable interest without giving any indication as to its nature. The requisite standard entailed explaining to the client the nature of the benefits to the legal representative in remaining on the panel—and doing so with sufficient clarity for the client to understand what those benefits were.[183] It would not have been sufficient for a legal representative merely to inform the client that it was recommending a policy because that was the only policy that it was free to recommend, because this would have told the client nothing of the benefit that accrued to the legal representative through continuing membership of the panel.[184] **29.95**

The following miscellaneous points may be made about panel membership. **29.96**

- **Exclusivity agreements** The fact that a legal representative was required to use a particular insurer exclusively was not, of itself, something that created a declarable interest. Clarke MR explained that this was because such an arrangement might be necessary to avoid adverse selection of cases and that, in any event, it did not affect the advice that is given to the client.[185]
- **Rebates** Some panels operated (and still do operate) a rebate scheme, whereby a membership fee was payable upon subscription to the panel, but a rebate or partial rebate was given in the event of a certain number of policies being incepted. Clarke MR confirmed (by implication) that, in principle, such a scheme could amount to a declarable interest, but qualified this by saying that the court must look at the size of the rebate in the context of the legal representative's turnover; on the facts of the case before him, he found that the rebate was a 'minute fraction of turnover'.[186]
- **Bare declaration of panel membership** The mere fact that the client had been made aware of a legal representative's panel membership would not have been a sufficient declaration. This was because a client could not have been expected to infer from that information that the recommendation may have been dictated by the legal representative's

[182] This list is nothing more than the editor's interpretation of the authorities; it is not intended to be exhaustive. That said, it is heavily based on *ibid.*

[183] *Ibid*, at [37], [38] and [43].

[184] *Ibid*, at [44]. Any dicta to the contrary in *Garrett v Halton Borough Council; Myatt v National Coal Board* [2006] EWCA Civ 1017 should not be followed.

[185] *Tankard v John Fredricks Plastics Ltd* [2008] EWCA Civ 1375, at [25]–[26], referring to *Rogers v Merthyr Tydfil CBC* [2006] EWCA Civ 1134, at [113]–[114].

[186] *Tankard v John Fredricks Plastics Ltd* [2008] EWCA Civ 1375, at [32]–[33]. The rebate was in the order of £250.

financial interests. Indeed, a lay person might have believed that panel membership was a mark of quality control.[187]

- **Evidence of causal link** Waller LJ has clarified (*obiter*) that, where a firm was obliged to recommend a particular form of insurance, it was an 'obvious inference not requiring any evidence' that ignoring that provision would cause damage to the legal representative's business relationship with the person to whom that promise was made.[188]

Regulation 4(3) of the CFA Regulations 2000

29.97 Regulation 4(3) stipulated that, before an agreement was made, the legal representative had to explain its effect to the client: 'Before a conditional fee agreement is made the legal representative must explain its effect to the client.' The explanation had to be given both orally and in writing.[189] The regulation applied to all conditional fee agreements, except those made between a legal representative and an additional legal representative,[190] and except CFA Lites.[191] It applied regardless of whether the legal representative was a membership organisation.

29.98 There is no reason to believe that the general points made in the discussion on reg 4(2) about reasonableness, timing, etc, do not also apply to reg 4(3) (see 29.85, 29.87 and 29.90). These points are not repeated here, but they are—depending on the facts of the case—likely to have been relevant to a putative breach of reg 4(3). In essence, each case must be decided on its own facts and the requisite standard was one of reasonableness.

29.99 Compliance is generally a matter of fact and degree. An example of a case in which the requisite standard had not been met was where a new agreement had been made without the client having been told that it did not cap the fees in a similar way to a prior agreement.[192] Not all such cases have turned on questions of fact, however, and the process of anterior interpretation may be relevant (see 31.29). Whilst he did not refer to it by that name, Stanley Burnton J carried out that process in a case in which the client had been told that the agreement would be effective from a certain date, but the agreement itself had been backdated and bore a different date.[193] He found that there had been a literal breach, but that it was not material, coming to this conclusion because, on a true interpretation of the agreement, the date from which it was effective and the date that the client had been told about were one and the same.[194]

29.100 It has been argued that where an agreement contains inconsistent terms, this gives rise to an inadequate written explanation for the purposes of complying with reg 4(3). In the context of an agreement that had failed to set out all of the material terms and which had to be read in conjunction with another document, Mann J said that the suggestion that this could amount to a breach was a 'bad point'.[195]

---

187 *Garrett v Halton Borough Council; Myatt v National Coal Board* [2006] EWCA Civ 1017, at [99]–[100].

188 *Jones v Wrexham Borough Council* [2007] EWCA Civ 1356, at [66].

189 Collective Conditional Fee Agreements Regulations 2000 (SI 2000/2988), reg 4(5).

190 Collective Conditional Fee Agreements Regulations 2000 (SI 2000/2988), reg 4(6).

191 Collective Conditional Fee Agreements Regulations 2000 (SI 2000/2988), reg 3A(3).

192 *Langsam v Beachcroft LLP & Ors* [2011] EWHC 1451 (Ch), *per* Roth J.

193 *Holmes v Alfred McAlpine Homes (Yorkshire) Ltd* [2006] EWHC 110 (QB).

194 *Ibid*, at [21]. The judgment does not record the reasons why Stanley Burnton J did not conclude that there had been no breach at all, which (on the face of it) was a finding that was open to him.

195 *Fenton v Holmes* [2007] EWHC 2476 (Ch), at [65].

Stanley Burnton J commented (*obiter*) that if the circumstances were that a client had been given incorrect advice about the scope of the agreement, it would be open to the court to find that there was no material breach, because (on the facts of the case before him) if the client had been given the correct advice, any sensible client would have agreed to what was being proposed.[196] **29.101**

Regulation 5 of the CFA Regulations 2000

Regulation 5 required that the agreement was signed by both the client and the legal representative: **29.102**

> '5 (1) A conditional fee agreement must be signed by the client and the legal representative.
>
> (2) This regulation does not apply in the case of an agreement between a legal representative and an additional legal representative.'

This regulation applied to all conditional fee agreements, except those between the legal representative and an additional legal representative.[197] As with any document, the signature had to be in a place that governed the document.[198]

Although not binding, Judge Hickinbottom has found that a total failure to sign a conditional fee agreement would amount to a material breach; as to materiality, he found that if an agreement had not been signed, then a less scrupulous legal representative might, for example, have been tempted to enforce its right to be paid in the event of the claim failing.[199] Mann J came to a very similar conclusion: **29.103**

> 'I am afraid that I have difficulty in seeing how a failure to sign important contractual documentation can ever be capable of falling within [the definition of being immaterial]. Parliament not only prescribed that a CFA be in writing ... it also required that it be in writing and signed by both parties. There are clear policy considerations underlying both of these requirements. They achieve that the terms of the agreement (which are capable of impacting not only on the parties to it, but upon a paying party in litigation) are clear and clearly subscribed to. These considerations clearly have implications, both in terms of consumer protection for the client and in terms of the administration of justice.'[200]

Regulation 6 of the CFA Regulations 2000

Regulation 6 imposed an obligation that arose only where the agreement had been amended to cover further proceedings or parts thereof. An example would be where an agreement had been amended to cover an appeal brought by the client against a final order. The regulation provided as follows: **29.104**

> '6 Where an agreement is amended to cover further proceedings or parts of them—
>
> (a) regulations 2, 3, 3A and 5 apply to the amended agreement as if it were a fresh agreement made at the time of the amendment, and

---

196 *Holmes v Alfred McAlpine Homes (Yorkshire) Ltd* [2006] EWHC 110 (QB), at [21]. It is not clear whether this point was extensively argued before Stanley Burnton J, so those comments should be treated with some caution.

197 Conditional Fee Agreements Regulations 2000 (SI 2000/692), reg 5(2) (as amended).

198 *Caton v Caton* (1867) LR 2 HL 127.

199 *Preece v Caerphilly County Borough Council* (unreported), 15 August 2007, Cardiff County Court, at [18].

200 *Fenton v Holmes* [2007] EWHC 2476 (Ch), at [55]. The case with which Mann J was dealing did not concern the agreement itself, but a letter upon which the receiving party was forced to rely to prove compliance with one of the other requirements of the Conditional Fee Agreements Regulations 2000 (SI 2000/692) (as amended).

(b) the obligations under regulation 4 apply in relation to the amendments in so far as they affect the matters mentioned in that regulation.'

This regulation continues to have effect for the purposes of agreements made between 1 April 2000 and 1 November 2005.[201]

29.105 Where the agreement had been varied, the following would apply:

- regs 2, 3, 3A and 5 applied to the amended agreement as if it were a fresh agreement made at the time of the amendment; and
- in so far as they were relevant, the obligations under reg 4 would apply to the variation.

The effect of a breach of the CFA Regulations 2000

As between legal representative and client

29.106 Where they apply, the effect of a material breach of the CFA Regulations 2000 is to render the agreement unenforceable.[202] The only exception to this is if the agreement is a non-contentious business agreement that is complaint with s 57 of the Solicitors Act 1974 (see 27.115–27.134, 29.145–29.148 and 29.185–29.191).[203]

29.107 For all practical purposes, there is a further exception in that, where fixed recoverable costs applied, an opposing party would be liable for those costs regardless of the enforceability of the agreement. Whilst Simon J has explained the policy behind this principle,[204] it is not wholly clear how the legal representative would be able to claim those costs from the client. It is possible that the client may hold those costs on constructive trust for the legal representative, but that analysis is far from perfect when looked at in any detail,[205] as are most other analyses.[206] Nonetheless, no client has had sufficient strength of feeling to generate any authority on the point.

29.108 Brooke LJ has confirmed that there is no basis for the proposition that the extent to which the agreement is to be rendered unenforceable ought to be tailored so that it is proportionate to the culpability of the breach.[207]

As between opposing parties

29.109 Other than as set out above (that is, in relation to fixed recoverable costs[208]) and properly constructed CFA Lites (see 18.186–18.189), the indemnity principle applies to

---

[201] See Conditional Fee Agreements (Revocation) Regulations 2005 (SI 2005/2305), reg 3(1). It could be argued, however, that the words 'fresh agreement' in Conditional Fee Agreements Regulations 2000 (SI 2000/692) (as amended), reg 6(1), release the legal representative from some of the obligations imposed by that regulation.

[202] Courts and Legal Services Act 1990 (as amended), s 58(1).

[203] Courts and Legal Services Act 1990 (as amended), s 58(5).

[204] *Nizami v Butt* [2006] EWHC 159 (QB), at [23]–[25].

[205] Not least because it would be an equitable remedy that would go against the grain of Courts and Legal Services Act 1990, s 58(1).

[206] Another possibility is that the order of the court in some way affords the legal representative a proprietorial right to the costs, in the sense that the costs are to be paid to the legal representative rather than to the client, but there is nothing in CPR, Part 45, Section II, which suggests that that is the correct analysis. A further analysis is that whilst the agreement may be unenforceable, the legal representative is able to claim a right to any monies that come into its hands by other means.

[207] *Spencer v Wood* [2004] EWCA Civ 352.

[208] There is also an exception created by CPR, r 43.2(3), but, for present purposes, that can be disregarded, because it has no bearing on unenforceable retainers.

conditional fee agreements. It is not correct to say that the statutory provisions concerning enforceability are operative only between solicitor and client rather than between opposing parties.[209]

Some types of disbursement (most noticeably, paid disbursements) may have been recovered notwithstanding a breach of the indemnity principle. Recoverable and irrecoverable costs are each addressed in turn. **29.110**

- **Recoverable costs** Where disbursements are recoverable by a mechanism other than via an unenforceable agreement—such as where ATE premium is recoverable under a contract of insurance[210] or where the client was directly responsible for payment to a third party[211]—the enforceability of the agreement would be irrelevant.
- **Irrecoverable costs** Unless, and to the extent that, fixed recoverable costs are recoverable, all profit costs incurred under an unenforceable agreement would be irrecoverable. Disbursements other than those mentioned above would also be irrecoverable.[212]

Collective Conditional Fee Agreements

This section deals, first and foremost, with those collective conditional fee agreements that were made on or after 30 November 2000 and before 1 November 2005, which agreements had to comply with the Collective Conditional Fee Agreements Regulations 2000[213] (as amended) (the CCFA Regulations 2000).[214] Surprisingly, this is a situation that is still encountered in practice because some insurers are still using documentation that is very old. There has, since 1 November 2005, been an absence of any regulatory control of collective conditional fee agreements per se, but, in view of the fact that collective agreements are now mostly used as an administratively efficient means of creating individual contracts of retainer based on a standardised template, it is likely that those individual contracts are subject to the same regulatory control as conditional fee agreements[215] (see 29.114). **29.111**

The structure of a collective conditional fee agreement

Any collective conditional fee agreement will contain a 'collective element', which is the framework document setting out the terms agreed between the funder and the legal representative. The collective element does not refer to specific proceedings; instead, it provides **29.112**

[209] *Hollins v Russell* [2003] EWCA 718, at [92]–[95].

[210] *Ibid*, at [114].

[211] *Ibid*, at [115]. This was so even if the monies had been paid out of a client account.

[212] Whilst some CFAs with additional legal representatives did attempt to provide for a direct liability between the client and the additional legal representative, the vast majority did not, so the fees of the additional legal representative would stand or fall with the fees of the legal representative.

[213] SI 2000/2988 (CCFA Regulations 2000).

[214] There was no requirement that they comply with the CFA Regulations 2000: see Conditional Fee Agreements Regulations 2000 (SI 2000/692) (as amended), reg 8. See also *Thornley v Lang* [2003] EWCA Civ 1484, at [13], [17], [18] and [20].

[215] This is in marked distinction to the position under the Collective Conditional Fee Arrangement Regulations 2000 (SI 2000/2988), which displaced the Conditional Fee Agreements Regulations 2000 (SI 2000/692) entirely: see *Thornley v Lang* [2003] EWCA Civ 1484, at [13], [17], [18] and [20].

for fees to be payable on a standard basis in relation to a class (or several classes) of proceedings.[216] A true collective conditional fee agreement involves persons acting in three capacities: the funder, the client and the legal representative. The funder and the client may be the same person. There never has been any requirement that the collective element refers to specific clients;[217] indeed, specific clients are mentioned only very rarely in the collective element.

29.113 As with individual conditional fee agreements, collective conditional fee agreements have always been able to provide for success fees.[218] Similarly, a collective conditional fee agreement may be a 'CCFA Lite';[219] under the CCFA Regulations 2000, the qualifying criteria for an agreement to be a CCFA Lite were very similar to those that applied to CFA Lites.[220]

29.114 In isolation, the collective element cannot form a contract of retainer because the client is not a counterparty to it. To form a contract of retainer relating to a claim, it must in some way be 'applied' so as to bring the client, the funder and the legal representative into contractual relations. The exact mechanism by which this is achieved is a moot point, but one aspect of the matter is beyond question: no retainer regulated by the CCFA Regulations 2000 would have been a conditional fee agreement in the sense that it had to comply with the CFA Regulations 2000. Put otherwise, the two regulatory regimes that ran between 2000 and 2005 were mutually exclusive.[221] The present-day position is less clear, but it is likely that (in the absence of any legislation specific to collective conditional fee agreements) the contract that is ultimately formed with the client is an agreement that must comply with the prevailing legislation relating to conditional fee agreements (see 29.14).

29.115 Phillips MR has said that a retainer comes into being as a result of the funder, acting with the authority of the client, agreeing to use it in an individual case—although he also mentioned an alternative analysis, that the agreement is ratified by the client.[222] Gray J seems to have accepted that analysis.[223] Regardless of the exact mechanism by which the agreement is applied, the end result is that the client and the funder have a dual liability for the legal representative's fees.[224] The contract of retainer can probably be best thought of as being a tripartite agreement whereby, for the time being, the client has agreed to be bound by the terms of the collective element, usually in return for assistance with funding the litigation.

---

216 Collective Conditional Fee Arrangement Regulations 2000 (SI 2000/2988) (as amended), reg 3(1).

217 Collective Conditional Fee Agreements Regulations 2000 (SI 2000/2988) (as amended), reg 3(2).

218 Collective Conditional Fee Arrangement Regulations 2000 (SI 2000/2988) (as amended), reg 5.

219 See the amendments made by Conditional Fee Agreements (Miscellaneous Amendments) Regulations 2003 (SI 2003/1240) and Conditional Fee Agreements (Miscellaneous Amendments) (No 2) Regulations 2003 (SI 2003/3344).

220 Collective Conditional Fee Arrangement Regulations 2000 (SI 2000/2988) (as amended), reg 5(5), (6) and (7).

221 Conditional Fee Agreements Regulations 2000 (SI 2000/692) (as amended), reg 8; see also the comments of Phillips MR in *Thornley v Lang* [2003] EWCA Civ 1484, at [13], [17], [18] and [20].

222 *Thornley v Lang* [2003] EWCA Civ 1484, at [20], drawing on the line of authority that is described at 18.59 *et seq*.

223 *Kitchen v Burwell Reed & Kinghorn Ltd* [2005] EWHC 1771 (QB), at [16].

224 *Thornley v Lang* [2003] EWCA Civ 1484.

Regulatory control of older collective conditional fee agreements

For agreements created in the present day, there are no regulations or orders that relate specifically to collective conditional fee agreements. Between 30 November 2000 and 1 November 2005, however, the CCFA Regulations 2000 applied, which were much less exacting than the CFA Regulations 2000.[225] The requirements could be split into four groups: **29.116**

- those provisions that applied to all collective conditional fee agreements (see 29.117);
- those provisions that applied to all collective conditional fee agreements other than where the agreement was with an additional legal representative (see 29.118);
- those provisions that applied to any collective conditional fee agreement that provided for a success fee (see 29.119); and
- those provisions that applied to any collective conditional fee agreement that provided for a success other than for where the agreement was a CCFA Lite (see 29.120).

Application of the CCFA Regulations 2000

Any collective conditional fee agreement Under the CCFA Regulations 2000, a collective conditional fee agreement had to satisfy the following requirements.[226] **29.117**

- It needed to specify the circumstances in which the legal representative's fees and expenses, or part of them, would become payable.[227]
- It needed to provide that, after accepting instructions in relation to any specific proceedings, the legal representative was obliged to confirm its acceptance of instructions in writing to the client.

Any agreement that was not an agreement with an additional legal representative Under the CCFA Regulations 2000, other than agreements with additional legal representatives, a collective conditional fee agreement was required to satisfy the following further requirements.[228] **29.118**

- It needed to say that, when accepting instructions in relation to any specific proceedings, the legal representative had an obligation to inform the client as to the circumstances in which they or their estate would be liable to pay the costs of the legal representative.
- It needed to say that if the client reasonably required any further explanation, advice or other information about the agreement, it would be given.

Any agreement that provided for a success fee (including a CCFA Lite) If the collective conditional fee agreement was made between 30 November 2000 and 1 November 2005, and if it provided for a success fee, it needed to abide by the following requirements: **29.119**

> '(1) Where a collective conditional fee agreement provides for a success fee the agreement must provide that, when accepting instructions in relation to any specific proceedings the legal representative must prepare and retain a written statement containing—
> (a) his assessment of the probability of the circumstances arising in which the percentage increase will become payable in relation to those proceedings ("the risk assessment");

[225] *Ibid*, at [11], *per* Phillips MR.

[226] Collective Conditional Fee Agreements Regulations 2000 (SI 2000/2988) (as amended), reg 4.

[227] Those circumstances may include the fact that the legal representative's fees and expenses are payable only to the extent that sums are recovered in respect of the proceedings, whether by way of costs or otherwise: see Collective Conditional Fee Agreements Regulations 2000 (SI 2000/2988) (as amended), reg 4(1A).

[228] Collective Conditional Fee Agreements Regulations 2000 (SI 2000/2988) (as amended), reg 4.

(b) his assessment of the amount of the percentage increase in relation to those proceedings, having regard to the risk assessment; and
(c) the reasons, by reference to the risk assessment, for setting the percentage increase at that level.

(2) If the agreement relates to court proceedings it must provide that where the success fee becomes payable as a result of those proceedings, then—
(a) if—
(i) any fees subject to the increase are assessed, and
(ii) the legal representative or the client is required by the court to disclose to the court or any other person the reasons for setting the percentage increase at the level assessed by the legal representative,
he may do so ...'[229]

29.120 **Any agreement that provided for a success fee, but which was not CCFA Lite** Any collective conditional fee agreement made between 30 November 2000 and 1 November 2005 that was not a CCFA Lite, but which provided for a success fee, needed to comply with the following requirements.[230]

- It needed to match the success fee paid by the client with the success fee allowed by the court.[231]
- It needed to match the success fee paid by the client with the success fee recovered by consent from an opponent.[232]

The effect of a breach of the CCFA Regulations 2000

29.121 What follows relates only to collective conditional fee agreements to which the CCFA Regulations 2000 continue to apply.

29.122 Properly drafted collective conditional fee agreements were, and still are, robust. For the reasons set out below, where the collective element is compliant with the CCFA Regulations 2000, it would (even now) be rare that its use would give rise to an unenforceable contract of retainer. One could envisage dull-witted misuse of such an agreement that may give rise to problems, but such circumstances hardly ever arise.

Transitional cases: where the collective element was made before 1 November 2005, but was 'applied' to an individual case after that date

29.123 It would be possible for an older collective element to have been incompetently drafted in the sense that it failed to comply with the CCFA Regulations 2000 or failed to effect the

[229] Collective Conditional Fee Agreements Regulations 2000 (SI 2000/2988) (as amended), reg 5.

[230] Collective Conditional Fee Agreements Regulations 2000 (SI 2000/2988) (as amended) reg 5(2)(b) and (c), and (4).

[231] If the agreement related to court proceedings, it ought to have provided that, where the success fee became payable, then, if any such fees are assessed by the court and if any amount in respect of the percentage increase is disallowed on the assessment on the ground that the level at which the increase was set was unreasonable in view of facts that were or should have been known to the legal representative at the time it was set, that amount would cease to be payable unless the court is satisfied that it should continue to be so payable.

[232] The agreement ought to have provided that if the situation mentioned above does not apply and if the legal representative agrees with any person liable as a result of the proceedings to pay fees subject to the percentage increase that a lower amount than the amount payable in accordance with the CFA is to be paid instead, the amount payable shall be reduced accordingly, unless the court is satisfied that the full amount should continue to be payable under it.

creation of any contracts of retainer at all, but, given the passage of time since such a document would have first been used, such circumstances will rarely be encountered in modern practice because any serious problems would have come to light years ago. If they were to occur, the agreement would be unenforceable.[233] That would not, however, necessarily mean that the legal representative would be burdened by an unenforceable contract of retainer, because it is possible that the court would find that, where the collective element is unenforceable, any instructions received after 1 November 2005 should be regarded as being outside the scope of the agreement and that the enforceability of the retainer should be judged on that basis (see also 29.125–27.127).

To be compliant with the CCFA Regulations 2000, the collective element was required to contain the contractual provisions mentioned at 29.117. In effect, the contract had to say that the client had been told that their legal representatives had accepted instructions under a collective conditional fee agreement. Whilst he was sitting in the County Court rather than the High Court, Field J found that non-performance of those obligations did not result in unenforceability by reason of the operation of the CCFA Regulations 2000.[234] **29.124**

Breach of the CCFA Regulations 2000: enforceability, damages and remedies for non-performance

If a failure to comply with the provisions of the CCFA Regulations 2000 is to have any effect at all, one must look at the contract of retainer itself rather than only the collective element. Gray J has found that the obligations that need to be set out in the collective element were not conditions precedent for the formation of a contract of retainer.[235] Whilst not binding, Master Wright has found that non-performance of those contractual obligations would not preclude the legal representative from enforcing the obligation that it be paid its fees.[236] Gray J has said (*obiter*) that non-performance of those contractual obligations might sound in damages or might give rise to an entitlement on the part of the client to repudiate the retainer.[237] **29.125**

Where the collective element has been competently drafted, it is difficult to think of circumstances in which the retainer would be rendered unenforceable by reason of a lack of compliance with the CCFA Regulations 2000. Indeed, the function of the Regulations appears to be to afford the client contractual remedies rather than to render retainers unenforceable. **29.126**

Whether the contractual obligations mentioned above have been performed will be a matter of the construction of the correspondence sent by the legal representative to the client.[238] There is no need for the detail of the proposal to be set out; the client's agreement **29.127**

233 Courts and Legal Services Act 1990, s 58(1) (as amended).

234 *Various Claimants v Gower Chemicals Ltd* (unreported), 28 February 2007, Swansea County Court.

235 *Kitchen v Burwell Reed & Kinghorn Ltd* [2005] EWHC 1771 (QB), at [17].

236 *Various Claimants v Gower Chemicals Ltd* (unreported), 12 March 2008, SCCO.

237 *Kitchen v Burwell Reed & Kinghorn Ltd* [2005] EWHC 1771 (QB), at [17]. This was an analysis also adopted by Field J in *Various Claimants v Gower Chemicals Ltd* (unreported), 28 February 2007, Swansea County Court.

238 *Kitchen v Burwell Reed & Kinghorn Ltd* [2005] EWHC 1771 (QB), at [13], *per* Gray J. It is clear from that judgment that the correspondence needs only to refer to the collective CFA, rather than to the details of the retainer.

may be inferred from their tacit acceptance of the proposal and the fact that they had continued to give instructions.[239]

Application of the CCFA Regulations 2000: the indemnity principle

29.128 The indemnity principle applies to collective conditional fee agreements in just the same way as it applies to other conditional fee agreements. The CCFA Regulations 2000 do not create a right that allows the paying party to be paid independently of the indemnity principle.[240] For the reasons set out above, however, it would rarely be the case that non-compliance would result in a breach of the indemnity principle, because the CCFA Regulations 2000 seem to go more to ensuring that the client had certain contractual rights than to the indemnity principle.

Collective conditional fee agreement in use in the present day

29.129 The use of collective conditional fee agreements (albeit those not governed by the CCFA Regulations 2000) is becoming increasingly widespread.[241] Some solicitors continue to use agreements drafted before the revocation of the CCFA Regulations 2000, whilst most are choosing to draft new agreements.

29.130 It is not only claimant solicitors who are benefiting from the administrative efficiency of collective conditional fee agreements; liability insurers and local government organisations also commonly require legal services to be provided under such agreements. This is particularly so where they wish to formalise previously unlawful arrangements by which a discounted hourly rate was paid in the event of costs not being recovered from an opposing party. Once that informal arrangement has been formalised by way of a discounted collective conditional fee agreement, it is easy to make it lawful.[242]

29.131 Collective conditional fee agreements are now becoming a part of counsel's practice, especially where a solicitor habitually instructs the same chambers.[243] The first and second editions of this book stated that such arrangements were not commonplace, but that is no longer true.

Retrospectivity and Conditional Fee Agreements

Solicitor and client

29.132 There is nothing within the Courts and Legal Services Act 1990 (as amended) nor in the secondary legislation made under it that precludes conditional fee agreements being retrospective.[244] From the solicitor and client point of view, there is nothing inherently objectionable or unlawful about a conditional fee agreement having retrospective

---

[239] *Ibid*, at [15].
[240] *Thornley v Lang* [2003] EWCA Civ 1484, at [19].
[241] Indeed, some solicitors are extending the concept in that they are using framework documents in the absence of a funder; a document such as that would probably be best thought of as a set of standard terms and conditions rather than as a true collective CFA.
[242] *Gloucestershire County Council v Evans* [2008] EWCA Civ 21.
[243] See Goodridge, M, 'On Target?', *Counsel*, January 2006, pp 24–5.
[244] See *Pentecost v John* [2015] EWHC 1970 (QB), at [30], *per* Turner J.

effect.[245] Megaw J had this to say on the point (albeit in a context other than the law of costs):

> '[T]here is no principle of English Law which provides that a contract cannot in any circumstances have retrospective effect, or that, if it purports to have, in fact, retrospective effect, it is in law a nullity .... Often, as I say, the ultimate contract expressly so provides. I can see no reason why, if the parties so intend and agree, such a stipulation should be denied legal effect.'[246]

Indeed, it will often be in the client's interests to retrospectively replace a retainer with a conditional retainer: by designating pre-agreement work as being conditional, the client's liability for costs will be contingent upon the outcome of the litigation and many clients would see this as an advantage.[247] **29.133**

Thus the issue will not usually be whether the counterparties are at liberty to enter into a retrospective agreement in principle,[248] but whether the agreement makes provision for retrospective application. That will be a matter of contractual interpretation. In this regard, Lord Neuberger MR had this to say: **29.134**

> '[A]ny CFA which limits the client's liability to work done after the CFA is entered into, cannot extend to work done before that date. Equally, although of course solicitors and their clients can agree terms otherwise the natural presumption in a contract by which a person engages a solicitor to act for him must be, in the absence of such a term, that he is agreeing to pay for work done in the future, not for work already done.'[249]

Most conditional fee agreements (including, in particular, those based on the Law Society models) apply to those legal services that have been supplied from 'now'.[250] The question, therefore, is what is meant by 'now'. Stanley Burnton J has confirmed that it is a reference to the date on which the agreement is made (which may or may not be the date that appears on the face of the agreement).[251] Where an agreement does apply from 'now', pre-agreement work will usually be claimed under an express or implied private retainer, and will therefore be payable regardless of the outcome of the claim and will not attract a success fee. Where these are the circumstances, the agreement will not be retrospective in effect. **29.135**

Not all conditional fee agreements are worded in this way, however. A conditional fee agreement may expressly cover work carried out before the agreement was made. An **29.136**

---

245 *Motto & Ors v Trafigura Ltd & Anor (Rev 3)* [2011] EWCA Civ 1150, at [61]. Edis J has confirmed that '[t]he practice of "back-dating" CFAs is not improper as a matter of contract between solicitor and client' (the reference to 'backdating' being a reference to making the agreement retrospective): see *O'Brien v Shorrock and MIB* [2015] EWHC 1630 (QB), at [44]. See also *Forde v Birmingham City Council* [2009] EWHC 12 (QB), at [123]–[127]. As an early example of the court tolerating a retrospective agreement, see *Arkin v Borchard Lines* (unreported), 19 June 2001, QBD, *per* Coleman J. See also *King v Telegraph Group Ltd* [2005] EWHC 90015 (Costs); *Northern and Shell Plc v John Laing Construction Ltd* [2002] EWHC 2258 (TCC), at [40], *per* Judge Thornton QC (sitting as a High Court judge), upheld on appeal ([2003] EWCA Civ 1035).

246 *Trollope and Colls Ltd v Atomic Power Constructions Ltd* [1963] 1 WLR 333, at 339.

247 *Forde v Birmingham City Council* [2009] EWHC 12 (QB), at [123]–[127].

248 An exception to this is where it is suggested that the solicitor has acted improperly, in which case issues of undue influence and informed approval may arise.

249 *Motto & Ors v Trafigura Ltd & Anor (Rev 3)* [2011] EWCA Civ 1150, at [61].

250 This being a consequence of the way in which base costs are defined.

251 *Holmes v Alfred McAlpine Homes (Yorkshire) Ltd* [2006] EWHC 110 (QB), at [20]. See also *Motto & Ors v Trafigura Ltd & Anor (Rev 3)* [2011] EWCA Civ 1150, at [61].

agreement that covers 'all work from the date of instruction, including work carried out before this agreement was made' will have made express provision for a retrospective application. Moreover, retrospective effect may arise by implication.[252] Whilst there is no authority on the point, the court may be able to imply such a term in circumstances in which the client has been assured that they would not pay any costs beyond those that were recoverable from the other side. That said, whilst retrospective effect may be implied into a contract (including a conditional fee agreement), the circumstances must demonstrate that this was clearly the intention of the parties.[253]

Between the parties

29.137 Although disputes about base costs may arise from time to time (see below), disputes between opposing parties about retrospective conditional fee agreements tend to focus on the recoverability of the success fee (where such a fee is recoverable). This is a topic that is addressed at 54.54–54.56.

29.138 It is most unlikely that the court would allow costs that came into existence as the result of the receiving party voluntarily accepting a liability after they became entitled to costs. While he was discussing contentious business agreements, rather than conditional fee agreements, Irwin J made the following (*obiter*) comments:

> 'I would be hesitant to conclude that any CBA entered into by a Claimant, after an adverse Costs Order had been made ... could be held to alter retrospectively the rights and obligations as between claimant and solicitor. The reason is obvious. To uphold a retrospective re-arrangement in circumstances like that, would be to uphold the retrospective revision of—or even creation of—the defendant's costs liability.'[254]

So, if the supposedly retrospective agreement had been made after the entitlement to costs had already been decided, it is highly doubtful that that would have any bearing at all on the paying party's liability. This would certainly apply to a success fee, but it may well also apply to base costs. Whilst not binding, there are persuasive decisions that point in that direction.[255]

29.139 Beyond this, there is no particular reason to believe that base costs that are sought under a retrospective conditional fee agreement should be treated any differently from base costs that were sought under any other type of retainer. From the paying party's point of view, the nature of the retainer is usually irrelevant, so the only issues that will need to be decided are those that would apply between solicitor and client.

Backdating

29.140 Stanley Burnton J had the following to say about backdating (that is, placing a date upon the agreement that pre-dates the date on which it was actually made):

> 'I would emphasise ... that the back-dating of documents as was done in this case is generally wrong. It is wrong to seek to give an agreement retrospective effect by back-dating it.

---

[252] Whilst *obiter*, see *Northern and Shell Plc v John Laing Construction Ltd* [2002] EWHC 2258 (TCC), at [40(2)], *per* Judge Thornton QC (sitting as a High Court judge), upheld on appeal ([2003] EWCA Civ 1035).

[253] *Trollope & Colls v Atomic Power Construction Ltd* [1963] 1 WLR 333, at 339.

[254] *Crook v Birmingham City Council* [2007] EWHC 1415 (QB), at [36].

[255] See, eg, *Kellar v Williams* [2004] UKPC 30; *Oyston v Royal Bank of Scotland* [2006] EWHC 90053 (Costs). More recently, see *Engeham v London & Quadrant Housing Trust* [2015] EWCA Civ 1530.

> If it is agreed that a written agreement should apply to work done before it is entered into, it should be correctly dated with the date on which it is signed and expressed to have retrospective effect, ie to apply to work done before its date. Back-dating is liable to mislead third parties, and is liable to lead to the suspicion that it was done in order to mislead third parties, including a court before which the agreement is to be placed.'[256]

Intentional backdating would therefore be improper.

Damages-based Agreements

The law as set out below relates to agreements made on or after 1 April 2013[257] (or 12 November 2009, if it related to an employment matter).[258] The law governing an agreement that was made between 12 November 2009 and 1 April 2013, and which relates to an employment matter, is not separately set out, but—other than the fact that regulations that were then in force had different paragraph numbers—the law was much the same as it is now. **29.141**

Notwithstanding the fact that damages-based agreements have now become lawful, they remain a singularly unpopular choice. This is, at least in part, because of perceived defects in the way in which the regulations work. **29.142**

The starting point is s 58AA of the Courts and Legal Services Act 1990 (as amended), which reads as follows: **29.143**

> '**58AA Damages-based agreements**
>
> (1) A damages-based agreement which satisfies the conditions in subsection (4) is not unenforceable by reason only of its being a damages-based agreement.
>
> (2) But (subject to subsection (9)) a damages-based agreement which does not satisfy those conditions is unenforceable.
>
> (3) For the purposes of this section—
>
> (a) a damages-based agreement is an agreement between a person providing advocacy services, litigation services or claims management services and the recipient of those services which provides that—
>
> (i) the recipient is to make a payment to the person providing the services if the recipient obtains a specified financial benefit in connection with the matter in relation to which the services are provided, and
>
> (ii) the amount of that payment is to be determined by reference to the amount of the financial benefit obtained;
>
> [...]
>
> (4) The agreement—
>
> (a) must be in writing;
>
> (aa) must not relate to proceedings which by virtue of section 58A(1) and (2) cannot be the subject of an enforceable conditional fee agreement or to proceedings of a description prescribed by the Lord Chancellor;
>
> (b) if regulations so provide, must not provide for a payment above a prescribed amount or for a payment above an amount calculated in a prescribed manner;

[256] *Holmes v Alfred McAlpine Homes (Yorkshire) Ltd* [2006] EWHC 110 (QB), at [23].

[257] See Legal Aid, Sentencing and Punishment of Offenders Act 2012, s 45(13).

[258] See Coroners and Justice Act 2009, s 154.

(c) must comply with such other requirements as to its terms and conditions as are prescribed; and
(d) must be made only after the person providing services under the agreement has complied with such requirements (if any) as may be prescribed as to the provision of information.

(5) Regulations under subsection (4) are to be made by the Lord Chancellor and may make different provision in relation to different descriptions of agreements.

(6) Before making regulations under subsection (4) the Lord Chancellor must consult—
(a) the designated judges,
(b) the General Council of the Bar,
(c) the Law Society, and
(d) such other bodies as the Lord Chancellor considers appropriate.

(6A) Rules of court may make provision with respect to the assessment of costs in proceedings where a party in whose favour a costs order is made has entered into a damages-based agreement in connection with the proceedings.

(7) In this section—
"payment" includes a transfer of assets and any other transfer of money's worth (and the reference in subsection (4)(b) to a payment above a prescribed amount, or above an amount calculated in a prescribed manner, is to be construed accordingly);
"claims management services" has the same meaning as in Part 2 of the Compensation Act 2006 (see section 4(2) of that Act).

(7A) In this section (and in the definitions of "advocacy services" and "litigation services" as they apply for the purposes of this section) "proceedings" includes any sort of proceedings for resolving disputes (and not just proceedings in a court), whether commenced or contemplated.

(8) Nothing in this section applies to an agreement entered into before the coming into force of the first regulations made under subsection (4).

(9) Where section 57 of the Solicitors Act 1974 (non-contentious business agreements between solicitor and client) applies to a damages-based agreement other than one relating to an employment matter, subsections (1) and (2) of this section do not make it unenforceable.

(10) For the purposes of subsection (9) a damages-based agreement relates to an employment matter if the matter in relation to which the services are provided is a matter that is, or could become, the subject of proceedings before an employment tribunal.'

(11) Subsection (1) is subject to section 47C(8) of the Competition Act 1998.[[259]]'

29.144 Thus a damages-based agreement is an agreement between a client and a person providing advocacy services, litigation services or claims management services,[260] which provides (a) that the client is to make a payment (known as a damages-based payment) if they obtain a specified financial benefit and (b) that the amount of that payment is to be determined by reference to the amount of the financial benefit obtained. It is arguable that the ambit of that section is not limited only to those agreements under which a percentage of

[259] This subparagraph was created by an amendment made on 1 October 2015 by Consumer Rights Act 2015, Sch 8, para 37. Competition Act 1998, s 47C(8) reads: 'A damages-based agreement is unenforceable if it relates to opt-out collective proceedings.'

[260] This phrase has the same meaning as in Part 2 of the Compensation Act 2006 (see s 2 of that Act): see Courts and Legal Services Act 1990, s 58AA(7) (as amended).

the damages is payable,[261] but that is the type of arrangement that is generally regarded as typifying a damages-based agreement.

A damages-based agreement that either (a) satisfies the conditions referred to below or (b) (if it does not relate to an employment matter) is a non-contentious business agreement to which s 57 of the Solicitors Act 1974 applies will not be unenforceable by reason only of its being a damages-based agreement, but—by virtue of s 58AA(2) of the Courts and Legal Services Act 1990—a damages-based agreement that does not fall within one of these categories will be unenforceable.[262] The conditions set out in the 1990 Act are that the agreement: **29.145**

- must be in writing;
- must not relate to proceedings that, by virtue of s 58A(1) and (2), cannot be the subject of an enforceable conditional fee agreement or to proceedings of a description prescribed by the Lord Chancellor;
- must not provide for a payment above a prescribed amount or for a payment above an amount calculated in a prescribed manner;
- must comply with such other requirements as to its terms and conditions as are prescribed; and
- must be made only after the person providing services under the agreement has provided prescribed information (if any).[263]

The prescribed matters are set out in delegated legislation—specifically, the Damages-Based Agreements Regulations 2013[264] (the DBA Regulations 2013), the wording of which can be found at 29.219. First, the topic of non-contentious business agreements will be addressed, then each of the relevant regulations will be addressed in turn.

In addition, as of 1 October 2015, the Competition Act 1998 has provided that a damages-based agreement will be unenforceable if it relates to opt-out collective proceedings.[265] **29.146**

Non-contentious business agreements and damages-based agreements

Section 58AA(9) of the Courts and Legal Services Act 1990 provides that, where s 57 of the Solicitors Act 1974 (non-contentious business agreements between solicitor and client) applies to a damages-based agreement other than one relating to an employment matter, s 58AA(1) and (2) of the 1990 Act do not make it unenforceable. The effect of this is that if a damages-based agreement relates to non-contentious business other than in an **29.147**

[261] Indeed, it is arguable that an ordinary CFA that takes offers into account may, in some circumstances, fall within the ambit of s 58AA. In any event, the Law Society offers the following guidance in its *Practice Note: Damages-based Agreements Regulations* (27 May 2010): 'You should be aware, however, that a conditional fee agreement may amount to a DBA for the purposes of the Act where the amount of the costs and/or of any success fee payable under the agreement is to be determined by reference to the amount of any financial award obtained. This would be the case if a conditional fee agreement provided for different levels of success fee dependent on the size of the financial award or capped the costs and/or success fee by reference to the level of that award.'

[262] See Courts and Legal Services Act 1990, s 58AA(1), (2) and (9), as amended by Coroners and Justice Act 2009, s 154, and Legal Aid, Sentencing and Punishment of Offenders Act 2012, s 45.

[263] Courts and Legal Services Act 1990, 58AA(4) (as amended).

[264] SI 2013/609.

[265] See Competition Act 1998, s 47C(8), and Courts and Legal Services Act 1990, s 58AA(11), as added by Consumer Rights Act 2015, Sch 8, para 37.

employment matter and if it is compliant with s 57 of the Solicitors Act 1974, the issue of whether it is enforceable is governed by the common law. This is the reason why 'contingency fee agreements' (as they are often called) are not unenforceable in tribunals that are not 'courts' (see 29.186–29.191, but also see 3.34–3.36). This is also the reason why agreements to pay a 'value charge' are enforceable. The requirements of s 57 of the Solicitors Act 1974 are discussed at 27.115–27.125.

29.148 Oral contracts of retainer relating to non-contentious business will not satisfy those requirements—and such agreements would generally be unenforceable even where they are not damages-based agreements (see 27.210–27.213). Written agreements may satisfy those requirements, however, and the fact that such an agreement is a damages-based agreement will not make it unenforceable under the common law, because the common-law principle that damages-based agreements are unenforceable arises out of the law of champerty and champerty does not apply to non-contentious work (See 29.185–29.191 and 30.04). This issue is addressed in detail in the context of conditional fee agreements at 29.185–29.191; the same principles apply to damages-based agreements.

Damages-based agreements and the DBA Regulations 2013

Ambit and reg 3

29.149 Regulation 3 of the DBA Regulations 2013 (which applies to all damages-based agreements) requires that the agreement defines its own ambit and that it incorporates a number of provisions clarifying its effect. It therefore goes to the written instrument of the agreement. The agreement must specify:

- the claim or proceedings, or parts of them, to which the agreement relates;
- the circumstances in which the representative's payment, expenses and costs, or part of them, are payable; and
- the reason for setting the amount of the payment at the level agreed, including having regard to, where appropriate, whether the claim or proceedings is one of several similar claims or proceedings.[266]

Payment and reg 4

29.150 Regulation 4 of the DBA Regulations 2013 applies only to agreements concerning matters other than employment matters.[267] Its purpose is to restrict the monies payable by the client, which it does in two ways: first, by restricting the types of payment that may be made; and secondly, by imposing a limit on the amount that may be paid.

- **Types of payment** The types of payment that may be paid by the client are restricted to:
  – the damages-based payment,[268] net of any costs[269] and (where relevant) any sum in

[266] See Damages-Based Agreements Regulations 2013 (SI 2013/609), reg 3(a), (b) and (c), respectively. Employment matters are matters that are—or could become—the subject of proceedings before an employment tribunal.

[267] See Damages-Based Agreements Regulations 2013 (SI 2013/609), reg 4.

[268] This is referred to in the Regulations as being a 'payment', which reg 1(2) defines as that part of the sum recovered in respect of the claim or damages awarded that the client agrees to pay the representative, and excludes expenses, but includes, in respect of any claim or proceedings to which these Regulations apply other than an employment matter, any disbursements incurred by the representative in respect of counsel's fees.

[269] This includes fixed costs under CPR, Part 45: see Damages-Based Agreements Regulations 2013 (SI 2013/609), reg 4(1)(a).

respect of counsel's fees that have been paid or are payable by another party to the proceedings; and
- any expenses incurred by the representative, net of any amount that has been paid or is payable by another party to the proceedings.

- **Limits on damages-based payment** The limits will depend on whether the claim is a personal injuries claim[270] or a claim at first instance.
  - **Personal injuries claims** Where the claim is a personal injuries claim, the only sums from which the damages-based payment shall be met are (a) general damages recovered for pain, suffering and loss of amenity, and (b) damages recovered for pecuniary loss other than future pecuniary loss, net of any sums recoverable by the government's Compensation Recovery Unit (CRU). Where the claim is at first instance, the agreement must not provide for a payment above an amount that, including value added tax (VAT), is equal to 25 per cent of those monies. Whilst not expressly stated in the Regulations, it is implied that if a claim reaches the stage of an appeal, the damages-based fee may be anything up to 100 per cent of those monies. This may still prove attractive to many claimants, however, because damages for future pecuniary loss would be ring-fenced.
  - **Claims other than personal injuries claims** Where the claim is a first-instance claim that is not a personal injuries matter, the agreement must not provide for a payment above an amount that, including VAT, is equal to 50 per cent of the sums ultimately recovered by the client. Whilst not expressly stated, it is implied that if a non-personal injuries matter reaches an appeal, the damages-based fee is potentially 100 per cent of the damages. Presumably, clients would agree to pay such a proportion of their damages only if there were something other than the recovery of damages that made success on appeal attractive (such as establishing a point of principle or avoiding an adverse costs order made at first instance).

It is an express requirement of reg 4 that no damages-based agreement that relates to a matter other than an employment matter shall provide for any payment beyond those that are stipulated (which, in essence, is the damages-based fee plus disbursements not relating to counsel). Many commentators have said that this restriction makes damages-based agreements so unattractive to legal representatives that the intention to enhance access to justice has been thwarted. In particular, they point to the fact that if the agreement is terminated for whatever reason, no payment may be made for work already carried out. They also point to the fact that a legal representative would be limited to the damages-based payment even if costs on an hourly rate basis would be recoverable from the opponent—in contrast to regimes in other jurisdictions (such as Montreal) that allow for payment of costs recovered between opposing parties irrespective of the amount of the damages-based payment. **29.151**

There is a further reason why legal representatives are less than impressed with the commercial realities of the DBA Regulations 2013, albeit that it is a reason that applies only to claims for personal injuries. If one compares the monies that are recoverable under a damages-based agreement and the monies that are recoverable under a conditional fee agreement, it would almost always be the case that the former is less **29.152**

[270] Damages-Based Agreements Regulations 2013 (SI 2013/609), reg 4.

attractive, from the legal representative's point of view, than the latter. This is because the limit that restricts the damages-based payment is almost the same as the limit that restricts the amount of a success fee. This is curious because, under a damages-based agreement, the damages-based payment is the *only* payment that can be made to the legal representatives, whereas, under a conditional fee agreement, the success fee is payable in addition to base costs. In a claim for personal injuries, the only circumstances in which a damages-based agreement would be significantly more attractive to a legal representative would be where it was anticipated that the amount of general damages and past losses are likely to be significantly higher than the amount of base costs likely to be incurred. In the vast majority of personal injuries claims, this will not be the case (or even close to being the case).

Pre-contract counselling and reg 5

29.153 Regulation 5 of the DBA Regulations 2013 applies only to employment matters[271]—that is, matters that are, or could become, the subject of proceedings before an employment tribunal.[272] It imposes an obligation to provide pre-contract information. There is no corresponding provision in matters other than employment matters—that is, there is no express need for pre-contract counselling—although it is possible that a failure to give appropriate advice could lead to findings of duress.[273] Regulation 5 imposes a number of obligations, nearly all of which are reminiscent of reg 4 of the CFA Regulations 2000. There are two parts to reg 5 of the DBA Regulations 2013: the first creates a requirement that the client receives information in writing; the second stipulates what that information should be. There is also a requirement that the client must be given any further explanation, advice or other information that they may request.[274]

29.154 It is likely that, subject to certain safeguards, a legal representative is permitted to delegate functions under reg 5 to an unqualified, but properly supervised, person (see, by analogy, the second bullet point at 29.78).

29.155 **Regulation 5(2)(a)** This regulation applies only to employment matters. When read in conjunction with reg 5(1), it stipulates that the client must receive a written explanation of the circumstances in which they may seek a review of the costs and expenses. The reference to 'expenses' is a reference to disbursements,[275] but the reference to 'costs' is less straightforward, because that word is defined in the following way: ' "costs" means the total of the representative's time reasonably spent, in respect of the claim or proceedings, multiplied by the reasonable hourly rate of remuneration of the representative.'[276]

---

[271] Damages-Based Agreements Regulations 2013 (SI 2013/609).

[272] Damages-Based Agreements Regulations 2013 (SI 2013/609), reg 1(2), defines 'claim for personal injury' as having the same meaning as in CPR, r 2.3.

[273] Whilst, technically, it related to a non-contentious business agreement, see *See Ejiofoer (t/a Mitchell and Co Solicitors) v Legal Ombudsman* [2016] EWHC 1933 (Admin), at [45].

[274] Damages-Based Agreements Regulations 2013 (SI 2013/609), reg 5(1).

[275] See Damages-Based Agreements Regulations 2013 (SI 2013/609), reg 1(2), which provides that 'expenses' means disbursements incurred by the representative, including counsel's fees and the expense of obtaining an expert's report.

[276] See Damages-Based Agreements Regulations 2013 (SI 2013/609), reg 1(2).

Costs are different from the 'payment' (that is, the damages-based payment), which is defined in this way: ' "payment" means a part of the sum recovered in respect of the claim or damages awarded that the client agrees to pay the representative and excludes expenses.'[277] **29.156**

Thus it would seem that the legal representative is required to explain only the procedure relating to those fees that are paid on a time basis, rather than the procedures (such as they are) that also relate to the damages-based payment. This may be an oversight, but equally it may be a reflection of the fact that if a client has agreed a damages-based payment and if that payment is enforceable, it would be difficult for the amount of that payment subsequently to be challenged. Put another way, it is possible that Parliament intended that clients are not to be given false hope by being told that they are able to challenge damages-based payments at a later stage when, in fact, this is likely to be very difficult. **29.157**

By analogy with the CFA Regulations 2000, it is likely that the duty under reg 5(2)(a) of the DBA Regulations 2013 is to explain the circumstances in which costs may be payable under the agreement, rather than to explore hypothetical situations that might arise in the litigation[278] (see, by analogy, 29.79). **29.158**

Regulation 5(2)(**b**) This regulation applies only to employment matters. When read in conjunction with reg 5(1), it stipulates that the client must be told in writing about the dispute resolution service provided by the Advisory, Conciliation and Arbitration Service (ACAS) in regard to actual and potential claims. **29.159**

There is no guidance as to what the client must be told, but common sense dictates that, at the very least, the client must be told of the existence of these services. It is not clear, however, whether the client must also be told whether they are available as a means of resolving the specific claim to which the proposed damages-based agreement relates. **29.160**

Regulation 5(2)(**c**) This regulation, when read in conjunction with reg 5(1), requires the legal representative to state in writing whether other methods of pursuing the claim or financing the proceedings exist and, if so, how they relate to the claim or proceedings in question. It applies only to employment matters. **29.161**

It is likely that, by analogy with the CFA Regulations 2000, the burden of considering the availability of BTE insurance, etc, lies with the legal representative. These issues are addressed detail at 29.86 and 29.87. **29.162**

The Law Society offers the following advice: **29.163**

> '[A solicitor should] discuss with [its] client other methods of funding which may be available to the client including any public funding and/or *pro bono* help. This would also include funding by a conditional fee agreement or on an hourly rate, depending on what would be in the client's best interest and on [the solicitor's] willingness to undertake the case on that basis.'[279]

---

[277] See Damages-Based Agreements Regulations 2013 (SI 2013/609), reg 1(2).

[278] See *Bray Walker Solicitors (A Firm) v Silvera* [2008] EWHC 3147 (QB), affirmed on appeal ([2010] EWCA Civ 332).

[279] Law Society, *Practice Note: Damages-based Agreements Regulations* (27 May 2010).

It is not clear whether the need to advise about the availability of *pro bono* funding extends to making enquiries of the providers of such services, but it is arguable that such enquiries ought to be carried out in cases in which this would be a reasonable funding option (which is commonly the case in employment matters).

29.164 **Regulation 5(2)(d)** This regulation applies only to employment matters. When read in conjunction with reg 5(1), it requires the legal representative to state in writing the point at which expenses (that is, disbursements) become payable.

29.165 Regulation 1(2) defines 'expenses' as meaning disbursements incurred by the representative, including counsel's fees and the expense of obtaining an expert's report.

29.166 **Regulation 5(2)(e)** This regulation applies only to employment matters. The purpose of reg 5(2)(e), when read in conjunction with reg 5(1), is to ensure that the legal representative provides a fully inclusive estimate of expenses.[280] It is worth noting that there is no requirement to provide an estimate of either the damages-based payment or, if there are any, the time-based costs.

Amendments and reg 6

29.167 Regulation 6 of the DBA Regulations 2013 relates to certain types of amendment. It reads as follows: 'In an employment matter, any amendment to a damages-based agreement to cover additional causes of action must be in writing and signed by the client and the representative.' There would appear to be no express requirement to revisit any of the matters in reg 5 in the event of an amendment being made.

Amount of the damages-based fee in employment matters and reg 7

29.168 Regulation 7 of the 2013 Regulations provides that, in an employment matter, the amount prescribed for the purposes of s 58AA(4)(b) of the Courts and Legal Services Act 1990 (that is, the maximum amount of the damages-based payment) is the amount that, including VAT, is equal to 35 per cent of the sum ultimately recovered by the client in the claim or proceedings. The amount of the damages-based payment must include any transfer of assets and any other transfer of money's worth.[281]

29.169 The Law Society has this to say about the effect of this cap:

> 'The cap of 35 per cent applies to the amount recovered by the client and not the award. Consequently, you will not be able to recover any costs from the client without first recovering all or part of the award from the unsuccessful opponent.'[282]

There is a respectable argument that this guidance is not correct as a matter of strict legal interpretation, but it is no doubt correct as a matter of practice.

29.170 The Law Society's guidance continues: 'This figure [ie the cap] need not include counsel's fees or other disbursements but if these are to be charged separately you must state this in the agreement.'[283] To the extent that it is admissible as an extrinsic aid to interpretation,

[280] *Tankard v John Fredricks Plastics Ltd* [2008] EWCA Civ 1375, at [13]–[15].
[281] See Courts and Legal Services Act 1990, s 58AA(7), as amended by Coroners and Justice Act 2009, s 154.
[282] Law Society, *Practice Note: Damages-based Agreements Regulations* (27 May 2010).
[283] *Ibid.*

when speaking to the draft Regulations in the House of Lords, Lord Bach explained that the cap excluded counsel's fees,[284] and this is now confirmed in reg 1(2).

Termination and reg 8

There are no specific provisions allowing for termination of a damages-based agreement where it relates to a matter other than an employment matter. This is a surprising omission that has led some commentators to say that a damages-based agreement that does not relate to an employment matter is not capable of being terminated. Perhaps the better analysis is that the agreement can be terminated only if provision is made for termination in its terms; there is, however, no authority on this point. What is not in doubt, however, is the fact that, if it were to be terminated, such an agreement could not provide for payment for the work carried out. This is because reg 4 of the DBA Regulations 2013 prohibits payments other than the payment stipulated therein. Thus, for all practical purposes, to the extent that termination is permitted, this would be at the expense to the solicitor of all remuneration and, for obvious reasons, it would be a rare event for a legal representative to invoke such a right. Indeed, many legal representatives would probably wish to avoid the possibility of the agreement being terminated by writing a *non*-termination provision into the agreement. Whilst it is questionable whether such a provision would always bind a client, it would afford at least some protection to a legal representative as the case draws closer to a conclusion. **29.171**

Regulation 8 of the 2013 Regulations imposes a number of restrictions on what can and cannot be done if one of the parties is considering terminating an agreement that relates to an employment matter: **29.172**

> '**8 Terms and conditions of termination in an employment matter**
>
> (1) The additional requirements prescribed for the purposes of section 58AA(4)(c) of the Act are that the terms and conditions of a damages-based agreement must be in accordance with paragraphs (2), (3) and (4).
>
> (2) If the agreement is terminated, the representative may not charge the client more than the representative's costs and expenses for the work undertaken in respect of the client's claim or proceedings.
>
> (3) The client may not terminate the agreement—
> (a) after settlement has been agreed; or
> (b) within seven days before the start of the tribunal hearing.
>
> (4) The representative may not terminate the agreement and charge costs unless the client has behaved or is behaving unreasonably.
>
> (5) Paragraphs (3) and (4) are without prejudice to any right of either party under the general law of contract to terminate the agreement.'

These provisions are self-explanatory. The reference to 'costs' is a reference to time-based costs.[285] The need to prevent termination by the client after settlement or within seven days of the tribunal hearing is to prevent clients from taking the benefit of the legal representatives' efforts and then converting the method of payment to a time-based method by the simple expedient of terminating the agreement. **29.173**

[284] Hansard, Lords, 25 Mar 2010, col 1153.
[285] See Damages-Based Agreements Regulations 2013 (SI 2013/609), reg 1(2).

29.174 The Law Society offers the following guidance as to what might constitute unreasonable conduct sufficient to justify termination:

> 'The definition of "unreasonable" is likely to include circumstances in which a client refuses to accept an appropriate settlement, and requires you to act in a way which is contrary to the Code of Conduct. There are many other examples of "unreasonable" behaviour and it may be appropriate for you to explain these to the client at the start of the case.'[286]

If a client were to refuse to accept an appropriate settlement, it would not necessarily be in the solicitor's interest to terminate the agreement, because time-based costs may be less than it would like. As such, the power to terminate is by no means as powerful a sanction as it is in the context of conditional fee agreements.

Breaches of the Damages-Based Agreements Regulations 2013

29.175 Whilst there is no authority on the point, it is arguable that putative breaches of the DBA Regulations 2013 would be subject to a test of materiality similar to that which is described at 29.53 *et seq*.

Damages-based agreements and the indemnity principle

29.176 For the reasons set out above, a failure to comply with the requirements of the DBA Regulations 2013 may result in the agreement being unenforceable. In this regard, it is relevant that CPR, r 44.18, provides as follows:

> '44.18 (1) The fact that a party has entered into a damages-based agreement will not affect the making of any order for costs which otherwise would be made in favour of that party.
>
> (2) Where costs are to be assessed in favour of a party who has entered into a damages-based agreement—
> (a) the party's recoverable costs will be assessed in accordance with rule 44.3; and
> (b) the party may not recover by way of costs more than the total amount payable by that party under the damages-based agreement for legal services provided under that agreement.'

29.177 Some commentators have said that this provision creates an unnecessary difficulty. They point to the fact that—on the face of it, at least—given the way in which reg 4 of the DBA Regulations 2013 is drafted, the client is liable only for that part of the damages-based payment which is not recovered between opposing parties. They say that a provision such as that would work only if the CPR were to set aside the indemnity principle for the purposes of recovering costs incurred under damages-based agreements. CPR, r 44.18, does not do this; if anything, it reaffirms the indemnity principle. There is no authority to say whether this assertion has merit, but it is certainly arguable.

29.178 Likewise, some commentators have noted that, pursuant to *General of Berne Insurance Co v Jardine Reinsurance Management Ltd*,[287] items of costs are recoverable only if the client is liable for those items individually. They say that if time-based costs are going to be

[286] Law Society, *Practice Note: Damages-based Agreements Regulations* (27 May 2010).
[287] *General of Berne Insurance Company v Jardine Reinsurance Management Ltd* [1998] 1 WLR 1231.

recovered (which seems to be the implication of CPR, r 44.18(2)(a)), this means that the indemnity principle would need to be set aside. Again, there is no authority to confirm whether this argument has merit.

Conditional Fee Agreements, Damages-based Agreements and the Common Law

If legislation is disregarded so as to examine the underlying common law, conditional fee agreements (including damages-based agreements) relating to contentious business are, according to conventional teaching, unlawful. Denning MR described the thinking behind this in the following way (although note that he used the word 'contingency' where the word 'conditional' is usually used today): **29.179**

> 'English law has never sanctioned an agreement by which a lawyer is remunerated on the basis of a "contingency fee", that is that he gets paid the fee if he wins, but not if he loses. Such an agreement was illegal on the ground that it was the offence of champerty.'[288]

The objection was to the conditionality of the agreement, not the fact that it might afford the legal representative a success fee. Indeed, in years gone by, the common law has held conditional normal fee agreements to be unenforceable[289]—even that an agreement to give a one-fifth discount in the event of failure was contrary to public policy and therefore unenforceable.[290] **29.180**

It is easily arguable that the common law has moved on since the policy described by Denning MR was first formulated and it may well be that the common law now would tolerate some forms of conditional fee agreement.[291] Indeed, other common-law jurisdictions have found that certain types of conditional fee agreement are lawful.[292] This is largely irrelevant, however, because the common law has been rendered obsolete by statute, so the matters below are relevant only in jurisdictions where ss 58, 58A and 58AA of the Courts and Legal Services Act 1990 (as amended) do not apply. **29.181**

---

[288] *Wallersteiner v Moir (No 2)* [1975] 1 All ER 849, at 860. It is worth noting that Denning MR went on to find that the retainer was lawful; it was the other two members of the court (Buckley and Scarman LJJ) who found that CFAs should remain unlawful at common law.

[289] *British Waterways Board v Norman* (1993) 26 HLR 232. The correctness of this decision was doubted in *Thai Trading Co (a firm) v Taylor* [1998] 3 All ER 65, at 71, but *Thai Trading* itself was found to be wrongly decided on the basis that the court had not taken into account professional rules that banned such agreements: *Awwad v Geraghty* [2001] QB 570. Those rules no longer exist and, as such, it is probable that such agreements are lawful. Moreover, cases in other common-law jurisdictions have indicated that the general principle in *Thai Trading* was correctly decided: see, eg, *Law Society of Singapore v Kurubalan s/o Manickam Rengaraju* [2013] SGHC 135.

[290] *Aratra Potato Co Ltd v Taylor Joynson Garrett (a firm)* [1995] 4 All ER 695. This case was also said to be 'wrongly decided' in *Thai Trading Co (a firm) v Taylor* [1998] 3 All ER 65, at 73; indeed, at 72, Millett LJ said '[i]f this is the law then something has gone badly wrong'.

[291] See, in particular, *Thai Trading Co (a firm) v Taylor* [1998] 3 All ER 65, at 69; *Kellar v Williams* [2004] UKPC 30, at [21].

[292] See, eg, *Law Society of Singapore v Kurubalan s/o Manickam Rengaraju* [2013] SGHC 135, in which it was held that an attorney is able to act for an impecunious client in the expectation of payment only if the case were won.

29.182 In 2003, the Privy Council considered an appeal from one of those jurisdictions (the Turks and Caicos Islands).[293] Lord Carswell commented on an agreement that was arguably a normal-fee conditional fee agreement:

> 'It then has to be considered whether the fee agreement ... constituted a conditional fee agreement. In approaching this issue, their Lordships wish to make it plain that they are not to be taken as accepting without question the traditional doctrine of the common law that all such agreements are unenforceable on grounds of public policy. The content of public policy can change over the years, and it may now be time to reconsider the accepted prohibition in the light of modern practising conditions.'[294]

Lord Carswell went on to refer to the well-known (but wrongly decided) case of *Thai Trading Co v Taylor*,[295] in which the Court of Appeal had found that a normal-fee conditional fee agreement was lawful under the common law.

29.183 Thus, when freed from the constraints of statute (or, in the case of Court of Appeal, when it wrongly believed that it had been so freed), two of the most senior courts in the land have expressed the view that there is nothing inherently objectionable about normal-fee conditional fee agreements. One would imagine that very few consumers would take issue with them.

29.184 For the reasons set out at 29.181, in England and Wales, such considerations are of academic interest only—although it is worth noting that Courts and Legal Services Act 1990, s 58(1), provides that a conditional fee agreement that satisfies all of the relevant conditions shall not be unenforceable 'by reason *only* of its being a conditional fee agreement' (emphasis added). Thus, if a conditional fee agreement is unenforceable for some other reason, compliance with s 58 will not restore its enforceability. In view of this, it is worth examining the following three topics.

- **Where costs relate to work that is non-contentious** This is worth examining (see 29.185) because the Courts and Legal Services Act 1990 disapplies itself where the agreement is a non-contentious business agreement[296] and, in those circumstances, the common law may be of importance.
- **Where costs relate to work that is contentious** This is worth examining (see 29.192) because it may be relevant to damages-based agreements made before 1 April 2013 (or 12 November 2009, if it relates to an employment matter) or conditional fee agreements made before 7 July 1995.
- **Where the costs relate to work carried out by persons other than authorised persons** This is worth looking at because it is a topic that commonly arises in practice (see 29.198).

Conditional fee and damages-based agreements in the context of the common law (non-contentious business)

29.185 This section discusses the enforceability of agreements relating to non-contentious business. Provided that they govern only non-contentious business, what is said below is true of all damages-based agreements (other than those made on or after 12 November 2009 in employment matters) and all conditional fee agreements.

---

293 *Kellar v Williams* [2004] UKPC 30.

294 *Ibid*, at [21]. Gray J has approved of those comments (*obiter*) in the context of a collective CFA: *Kitchen v Burwell Reed & Kinghorn Ltd* [2005] EWHC 1771 (QB).

295 *Thai Trading Co v Taylor* [1998] QB 781.

296 See Courts and Legal Services Act 1990, s 58(5).

To put the common law in context, it is necessary to explain the statutory backdrop. On 1 April 2000, Courts and Legal Services Act 1990, s 58(5), was amended to read: 'If a conditional fee agreement is an agreement to which section 57 of the Solicitors Act 1974 (non-contentious business agreements between solicitor and client) applies, subsection (1) shall not make it unenforceable.'[297] **29.186**

Thus, if the agreement was made on or after 1 April 2000[298] and if it is a non-contentious business agreement to which s 57 of the Solicitors Act 1974 applies, s 58(1) of the Courts and Legal Services Act 1990 (as amended) will not make it unenforceable.[299] This means that, where an agreement falls short of complying with the requirements of s 58 of the 1990 Act, it gets a second chance:[300] it will survive as an enforceable agreement if (a) it complies with the requirements under s 57 of the 1974 Act and (b) is not rendered unenforceable under the common law. Similar provisions apply to damages-based agreements under s 58AA(9) of the 1990 Act (see 29.143). **29.187**

The requirements of non-contentious business agreements are described at 27.115–27.125. It can be seen that most written agreements would qualify. The remainder of this section deals with the common law. That said, it is worth noting that Lewison LJ has explained that s 57 of the Solicitors Act 1974 will not apply if the work was carried out by a solicitor for the purposes of proceedings.[301] If those conditions are met, then the business is contentious business, and s 57 will not validate an agreement for a contingent fee for that business.[302] **29.188**

The common law tends to look favourably on conditional fee agreements and damages-based agreements in non-contentious business. In particular, the common law tends not render such agreements unenforceable, because the common-law principles that would otherwise render a conditional fee agreement unenforceable for policy reasons have their origins in champerty—a concept that tends to apply only to contentious business (see 30.04, although see also 30.14 and 3.34–3.36). Thus, if an agreement made on or after 1 April 1990 is one that is compliant with s 57 of the Solicitors Act 1974, then the fact that it is a conditional fee agreement or a damages-based agreement will, in general, not make it unenforceable. **29.189**

As has already been discussed in the context of 'oral retainers' (see 27.207–27.216), unwritten agreements in non-contentious work are generally unenforceable.[303] This applies regardless of whether the agreement is a conditional fee agreement, a damages-based agreement or some other type of agreement. In any event, where it was made on or after 1 April 2000, an unwritten agreement will fall outside the ambit of ss 58(5) or 58AA(9) of the Courts and Legal Services Act 1990 (as amended) (that is, it would not be a non-contentious **29.190**

---

[297] The amendment was made by Access to Justice Act 1999, s 27(1).

[298] Agreements relating to non-contentious work made before 1 April 2000 were the subject of differently worded legislation and were governed exclusively by the common law. There was no express savings provision of the type that exists now: see Courts and Legal Services Act 1990, s 58, as amended by Access to Justice Act 1999, s 27(1). If this analysis is correct, then pre-2000 agreements relating to non-contentious work were (and still are) governed by the common law.

[299] To this extent, the common law relating to such agreements survives, because a non-contentious business agreement that does not comply with Courts and Legal Services Act 1990, s 58(1), will be enforceable only to the extent that the common law permits it to be.

[300] See *Kel-Ta Talk Ltd v Revenue & Customs Commissioners* [2011] STC 497.

[301] See *Rees v Gateley Wareing (a firm) & Ors* [2014] EWCA Civ 1351, at [28].

[302] *Ibid*, at [29].

[303] In *In re a Solicitor* [1956] 1 QB 157, for example, Pearson J found that a client could not rely on an oral agreement that his solicitor would charge less than the ordinary rate of remuneration.

business agreement compliant with s 57 of the Solicitors Act 1974) and, as such, it would be unenforceable by reason of ss 58(1) or 58AA(2) of the 1990 Act (because an agreement that is governed by those sections must be in writing if it is to be enforceable).

29.191 Finally, to be enforceable at common law, the agreement must have certainty and, in particular, it must contain intelligible success criteria.[304]

Conditional fee and damages-based agreements in the context of the common law (contentious business)

29.192 What follows has largely been eclipsed by statute and is mostly of historical interest only.

The influence of legislation

29.193 Whilst it applies only to damages-based agreements made before 1 April 2013,[305] there is authority to suggest that a damages-based agreement relating to contentious work would be enforceable if it were to comply with the requirements relating to *conditional* fee agreements. It has to be stressed, however, that the received view seems to be that what is set out immediately below is not good law.

29.194 Judge Rich QC (sitting in the High Court) had this to say on the topic (in the context of the agreement in question being, in effect, a damages-based agreement):

> '[The] mere fact that an arrangement was a conditional fee agreement, as defined in the Act, was accepted by Parliament when the 1990 Act was passed, as enough to make it unenforceable for champerty, whatever the basis of remuneration for which it provided. [Section] 58(1) [of the Courts and Legal Services Act 1990] relieves the party from such unenforceability in respect of such an agreement, which satisfies all the relevant conditions ... There is, in my judgment, no room for treating it, nonetheless, as unenforceable for champerty. The requisite conditions remain satisfied, even if the percentage uplift is calculated by reference to the amount recovered, provided only that it does not exceed 100 per cent.'[306]

If this is correct, an agreement made before 1 April 2013 that is compliant with s 58 of the 1990 Act will not be unenforceable solely by reason of it being some form of conditional fee agreement. If and to the extent that a damages-based agreement can be said to be a conditional fee agreement, then if it was made before 1 April 2013, it would (on Judge Rich's analysis) be enforceable if it were to comply with provisions relating to conditional fee agreements.

29.195 Whilst there is no authority on the point, the received view is that this analysis is not correct. There are several arguments in support of the received view, the most cogent of which is that a damages-based agreement should not be regarded as being a type of conditional fee agreement. The effect of this would be that the enforceability of such an agreement would be governed by the common law and the received view is that this would mean that an agreement relating to contentious business would be unenforceable. To the extent that it would be admissible, there is material to suggest that Parliament made a distinction between damages-based agreements and conditional fee agreements. For example, the Ministry of Justice has said this:

---

[304] Whilst dealing with contingency fee agreements in a context other than costs, see *Derek Hodd Ltd v Climate Change Capital Ltd* [2013] EWHC 1665 (Ch).

[305] After that date, there was express statutory provision relating to damages-based agreements and it would be difficult to argue that the common law still applies.

[306] *Benaim (UK) Ltd v Davies Middleton & Davies Ltd* [2004] EWHC 737 (TCC), at [35].

'[Damages-based agreements] ... are not permitted in litigation ... Extending DBAs to litigation would be a major step which raises a number of issues, not least costs shifting and the apportionment of costs between parties. We have no current plans to extend the use of DBAs more widely, but it makes sense to include a provision to allow for this should that be considered to be in the public interest.'[307]

This was, however, in 2009 and, as such, is very unlikely to be regarded as admissible for the purposes of interpreting an Act that was made in 1990. Moreover, some of the Ministry's legal reasoning is not as clear as it could be.[308] Perhaps the only thing that can be said with certainty is that the law relating to the enforceability of damages-based agreements made before 1 April 2013 is not entirely clear.

The underlying common law

The matters under this heading are relevant only to damages-based agreements made before 1 April 2013 and to conditional fee agreements made before 7 July 1995; even then, the relevance is only potential. For the reasons set out below, it is (just about) arguable that agreements made before those dates are enforceable—but this would be contrary to received teaching on the issue. **29.196**

The common-law prohibition against conditional fee agreements and damages-based agreements arose out of the law of champerty (which is discussed in more detail in Chapter 30). Whilst champerty itself is an ancient concept, it was not until the 1860s that the court focused on the issue of contracts of retainer. This was one of the issues that arose out of a profound crisis between 1859 and 1863 concerning the conduct of the Bar—in particular, five notorious cases of counsel's misconduct. The resultant litigation not only clarified the common law in respect of damages-based agreements,[309] but also clarified other points of law, such as the common-law principle that counsel's retainer is non-contractual.[310] The relevance of this is that the principle that conditional fee and damages-based agreements are unlawful arose out of a 19th-century crisis, and it may well be that the policy considerations that applied then have no resonance now (see, for example, 29.210). In this regard, it is perhaps worth mentioning that, in many other common-law jurisdictions, the law has developed in such a way as to permit damages-based agreements under the common law, in circumstances in which they were previously believed to be prohibited by statute.[311] Contingency fees in personal injury litigation in the United States, for example, are the norm, rather than the exception.[312] As long ago as 1994, Lord Mustill commented (*obiter*) that the rule against damages-based agreements was in the course of attenuation and that it survived, 'so far as it survive[d] at all', largely as a rule of professional conduct.[313] Perhaps **29.197**

[307] Ministry of Justice, *Regulating Damages-based Agreements*, CP 10/09 (London: HMSO, 2009), p 3.

[308] In particular, it would seem that the Ministry of Justice believes that Solicitors Act 1974, s 59, prohibits damages-based agreements: see Ministry of Justice, *Regulating Damages-based Agreements*, CP 10/09 (London: HMSO, 2009), para 18, to form a view as to whether that is correct.

[309] Pue, WW, 'Moral Panic at the English Bar: Paternal vs Commercial Ideologies of Legal Practice in the 1860s' (1990) 15(1) Law and Social Inquiry 49.

[310] *Kennedy v Broun* (1863) 32 LJ (CP) 137.

[311] See, eg, the Canadian cases of *Bergel & Edson v Wolf* (2000) 50 OR (3d) 777 (SCJ), *per* Justice Spiegel, and *McIntyre Estate v Ontario (Attorney-General)* [2001] OJ 713 (SCJ), *per* Justice Wilson.

[312] See the American Bar Association Model Rules of Professional Conduct (2004), r 1:5 (fees).

[313] *Giles v Thompson* [1994] 1 AC 142, at [15]. Phillips MR has criticised Lord Mustill's analysis, but largely on the basis that Lord Mustill was focusing on the common law rather than the statutory law: *R v Secretary of State for Transport, ex p Factortame* [2002] EWCA Civ 932, at [44].

the only conclusion that can be reached is that the common law is not something that is set in stone and that what may have been unlawful many years ago may now be seen as being acceptable—even desirable.[314]

Conditional fee agreements and persons other than lawyers

29.198 Persons who do not have rights to conduct litigation or rights of audience are not authorised litigators. Section 58(1) of the Courts and Legal Services Act 1990 (as amended) applies only to authorised litigators, for the following reasons.[315]

- This is the natural reading of s 58(1) of the 1990 Act.
- This conclusion is supported by the delegated legislation that was made under that Act, which reads as though the term 'legal representative' applies to a person conducting litigation or exercising rights of audience on behalf of a litigant.
- Reference to Hansard[316] shows that the provisions of s 58 of the 1990 Act were not intended to apply to those who were not conducting the litigation or appearing as advocates.
- There is good reason why principles of maintenance and champerty should apply with particular rigour to those conducting litigation or appearing as advocates.

29.199 Thus the common law (and, in particular, the law of champerty) will apply to those who are not authorised litigators. Each case must be decided on its own facts. The law of champerty is discussed in Chapter 30.

29.200 Whilst not binding, an example of a champertous arrangement is a case in which Master Hurst found that an unqualified cost negotiator was acting as a champerter: his retainer provided that his fees were based on the reduction in costs that he was able to secure.[317] Examples of the court declining to make a finding of champerty are commonplace, however, and include contingency fees claimed by a surveyor for carrying negotiations[318] and surveyors' fees that were conditional on successfully obtaining planning permission.[319]

29.201 A word of caution should be made here: it cannot be assumed that, because they are not an authorised litigator, a person will be completely unregulated. An example would be where fees are charged by persons providing claims management services, which are regulated by the Compensation Act 2006, Pt 2, and associated delegated legislation.[320] So it should not be assumed that, just because a person is not an authorised litigator, the only question that needs to be asked is whether their retainer is champertous.

29.202 In summary, persons who are not authorised litigators are not bound by Courts and Legal Services Act 1990, s 58(1), so the enforceability of such a person's retainer is to be gauged principally by the common law—most notably, the law of champerty. Other legislation may supervene, however, depending on the status of the person and the nature of the work they are carrying out.

---

[314] See, eg, the comments of Steyn LJ in *Giles v Thompson* [1993] 3 All ER 321, at 331–2.
[315] *R (Factortame Ltd) v Transport Secretary (No 8)* [2002] EWCA Civ 932, at [54].
[316] Hansard, HC Deb, 26 January 1999, pp 962 and 964.
[317] *Ahmed v Powell* [2003] EWHC 9011 (Costs).
[318] *Pickering v Sogex Services (UK) Ltd* [1982] 1 EGLR 42.
[319] *Picton Jones & Co v Arcadia Developments Ltd* [1989] 1 EGLR 43.
[320] Compensation (Claims Management Services) Regulations 2006 (SI 2006/3322).

The History of Conditional Fee Agreements

Very little of what follows here remains good law. It is included in this book only for interest and to allow older authorities to be put in their correct context. The focus is on the modern history, so ancient law is mentioned only briefly. **29.203**

Early 20th century (and before)

Pre-eminent judges have commented that English common law has never sanctioned conditional fee agreements.[321] It is, however, far from certain that this is correct. Whilst there are cases of some antiquity that give credence to that view,[322] there are examples of even the higher courts tolerating what appears to be overt conditional funding.[323] As recently as the early 20th century, the Court of Appeal expressed no disapproval of an informal conditional fee agreement in a case that was subsequently specifically approved of in *Gundry v Sainsbury*.[324] In the late 19th century, the Court of Common Pleas found that an agreement by an attorney with a client 'to charge him nothing if he lost the action, and to take nothing for costs out of any money that might be awarded to him in such action' was entirely unobjectionable.[325] Indeed, Bovill CJ went so far as to say that 'a promise not to charge anything for costs is not champerty'.[326] **29.204**

Mid-20th century

By the mid-20th century, the modern notion that conditional fee agreements had always been abhorrent had become ingrained.[327] From 1936 onwards, the Law Society issued rules governing solicitors that forbade conditional fee agreements, which created an implied statutory prohibition of such agreements. That said, even Lord Denning MR (whom many would regard as having been a proponent of that view) suggested that public policy should favour conditional fee agreements in certain circumstances.[328] The perception was that statutory intervention would be required to allow lawful conditional fee agreements to be made. **29.205**

In 1966, the Law Commission proposed that maintenance and champerty should be decriminalised, but it refused to recommend making conditional fee agreements lawful; rather, it suggested that this was a question 'upon which the professional bodies as well as **29.206**

---

321 See, eg, the comments of Lord Denning MR in *Wallersteiner v Moir (No 2)* [1975] QB 373, at 393.

322 Indeed, by as early as 1870, there was statutory recognition that CFAs were unenforceable. In particular, in 1870, the equivalent of the Solicitors Act 1974 provided that 'nothing [herein] ... shall give validity to ... any agreement by which a solicitor retained or employed to prosecute any action, suit or other contentious proceeding, stipulates for payment only in the event of success in that action, suit or proceeding ...'.

323 See *Clare v Joseph* [1907] 2 KB 369 at 376; *Ladd v London Road Car Co* [1900] LT 80; *Jennings v Johnson* (1873) LR 8 CP 425.

324 *Gundry v Sainsbury* [1910] 1 KB 645, approving *Clare v Joseph* [1907] 2 KB 376.

325 *Jennings v Johnson* (1873) LR 8 CP 425.

326 *Ibid*, at 426. See also *Ladd v London Road Car Co* [1900] LT 80; cf the comments of Kennedy LJ in *Wells v Barnsley Metropolitan Borough Council* (1999) The Times, 12 November, QBD, in which he says of *Ladd* that the only thing that was approved of was the willingness of the solicitor to act for an impecunious client who would probably not be able to pay if he were to lose.

327 As an early example, see *In re A Solicitor, ex p Law Society* [1912] 1 KB 302. See also Lord Esher MR's comment in *Pittman v Prudential Deposit Bank Ltd* (1896) 13 TLR 110, at 111.

328 Those circumstances being derivative actions: see *Wallersteiner v Moir (No 2)* [1975] QB 373, at 395G.

the public must have further time for reflection before any solutions can or should be formulated'.[329] Parliament accepted the recommendation not to alter the law of conditional fee agreements.[330] After due reflection and consultation, it was decided to take the matter no further.[331]

1970s

29.207 Giving judgment in the mid-1970s, Lord Denning MR rejected the proposal that the fact that champerty had been decriminalised in some way gave legitimacy to conditional fee agreements.[332] He took the opportunity to explain that, in his view, the common law viewed such agreements with abhorrence and he also explained that the Law Society's rule against conditional fee agreements was a reflection of public policy (as opposed to a self-standing reason to imply a prohibition). In 1979, the Royal Commission on Legal Services examined the topic, and concluded that there would be a conflict of interest between litigants and their lawyers if conditional fee agreements were to be permitted.[333]

1980s

29.208 A very similar view was taken in 1987 by a Law Society working party, which concluded that it would be impossible to overcome the ethical and consumer protection problems posed by such funding arrangements. Shortly thereafter, however, the position began to change. In 1988, the Report of the Review Body on Civil Justice[334] suggested a re-examination of the topic. In 1989, the view of the executive began to change,[335] as did that of the Law Society. Indeed, the latter asked to seek an opportunity to remove the statutory bars on contingency fees.

1990s

29.209 Within a short time, the legislature concluded that changes were required. The statutory mechanism by which enforceable conditional fee agreements could be made was put in place in 1990.[336] The necessary delegated legislation did not come into force until 1995,[337] however, and then it permitted conditional fee agreements to be made in only a limited range of proceedings.[338] The common law continued to apply to agreements that did

[329] Law Commission, *Proposals for Reform of the Law Relating to Champerty and Maintenance*, Law Com 7 (London: HMSO, 1966), para 19.

[330] Criminal Law Act 1967, s 14(2), read: 'The abolition of criminal and civil liability under the law of England and Wales for maintenance and champerty shall not affect any rule of that law as to the cases in which a contract is to be treated as contrary to public policy or otherwise illegal.'

[331] Law Commission, *Sixth Annual Report 1970–71*, Law Com 47 (London: HMSO, 1971), pp 7–8, paras 33–35.

[332] *Wallersteiner v Moir (No 2)* [1975] QB 373, at 393.

[333] Benson, H, *Lord Chancellor's Department: Royal Commission on Legal Services*, LCO 19 (London: HMSO, 1976–79).

[334] Hodgson, M, *Civil Justice Review: Report of the Review Body on Civil Justice*, Cm 394 (London: HMSO, 1988), paras 384–389.

[335] See Lord Chancellor's Department, *Contingency Fees*, Cm 571 (London: HMSO, 1989); Lord Chancellor's Department, *Legal Services: A Framework for the Future*, Cm 740 (London: HMSO, 1990).

[336] Courts and Legal Services Act 1990, s 58 (as original).

[337] See the Conditional Fee Agreements Regulations 1995 (SI 1995/1675) and the Conditional Fee Agreements Order 1995 (SI 1995/1674).

[338] The first Order was brought into force on 5 July 1995; this limited CFAs to personal injury cases, insolvency cases and cases before the European Court of Human Rights. In July 1998, the range of proceedings was extended as far as possible under the Courts and Legal Services Act 1990 to all civil proceedings, other than family cases.

not fall within that range, which resulted in a number of agreements being found to be unenforceable.[339]

In 1998, the Court of Appeal decided a case that gave rise to the term '*Thai Trading* agreement'[340] (an informal agreement that the client will not be charged if the claim is not successful). The court found that the agreement was enforceable, but this was because the parties had failed to direct the court's attention to the implied statutory prohibition arising out of the Law Society's rules (see 29.205). However, *Thai Trading* did give an insight into what the court would have said had it not been encumbered by the implied statutory prohibition. In particular, Millett LJ (with whom Hutchinson and Kennedy LJJ agreed) had the following to say: **29.210**

> 'The fear that lawyers may be tempted by having a financial incentive in the outcome of litigation to act improperly is exaggerated, and that there is a countervailing public policy in making justice readily accessible to persons of modest means. Legislation was needed to authorise the increase in the lawyer's reward over and above his ordinary profit costs. It by no means follows that it was needed to legitimise the long-standing practice of solicitors to act for meritorious clients without means, and it is in the public interest that they should continue to do so.'[341]

That analysis was followed for a brief period of time,[342] but, before long, it soon came to light that it was wrong.[343] In any event, in more recent times, Lord Neuberger MR has commented that *Thai Trading* is an anomalous case that is inconsistent with subsequent decisions of the Court of Appeal—particularly where the question is whether a legal representative acting in that capacity is a champerter.[344] **29.211**

When the Court of Appeal came to consider the issue again (this time in the light of the implied statutory prohibition), Schiemann LJ had this to say: **29.212**

> 'I share Lord Scarman's reluctance[[345]] to develop the common law at a time when Parliament was in the process of addressing those very problems. It is clear from the careful formulation of the statutes and regulations that Parliament did not wish to abandon regulation altogether and wished to move forward gradually. I see no reason to suppose that Parliament foresaw significant parallel judicial developments of the law ... I would therefore hold that acting for a client in pursuance of a conditional normal fee agreement, in circumstances not sanctioned by statute, is against public policy.'[346]

Thus the court deferred to Parliament. It is worth noting, however, that Schiemann LJ was careful to point out that his findings were limited to findings on the law as it stood in 1993; there are those who say that conditional fee agreements (or, at least, conditional fee **29.213**

---

[339] See, eg, *British Waterways Board v Norman* (1993) 26 HLR 232; *Aratra Potato Co Ltd v Taylor Joynson Garrett* [1995] 4 All ER 695.

[340] After *Thai Trading Co v Taylor* [1998] QB 781.

[341] *Ibid*, at 790.

[342] See, eg, *Bevan Ashford (a firm) v Geoff Yeandle (Contractors) Ltd (in liquidation)* [1999] Ch 239.

[343] See *Hughes v Kingston upon Hull City Council* [1999] QB 1193. See also *Leeds City Council v Carr* (1999) The Times, 12 November, in which a differently constituted Divisional Court doubted *Thai Trading Co v Taylor* [1998] QB 781.

[344] *Morris v London Borough of Southwark* [2011] EWCA Civ 25, at [39].

[345] In *Wallersteiner v Moir (No 2)* [1975] QB 373.

[346] *Awwad v Geraghty & Co (a firm)* [2001] QB 570, at 593.

agreements that do not provide for a success fee) are no longer unlawful at common law. This issue is discussed in more detail at 29.197.

29.214 At about the same time (that is, in 1999), the Nuffield Foundation published a study that showed that clients did not generally fully understand conditional fee agreements.[347] Also in 1999, the Law Society issued more detailed and demanding guidance for solicitors, which required them to give more information, and to give some of that information both orally and in writing.[348] In September 1999, the Lord Chancellor issued a new consultation paper that focused more on the mechanics of conditional fee agreement than their desirability.[349] This was in the context of government planning to phase out public funding for most types of claim.[350]

2000s

29.215 The way had been paved for a more widespread implementation of conditional fee agreements. In February 2000, the Lord Chancellor published the government's conclusions following his 1999 consultation. Although the Law Society and the senior costs judge had said that the rules recently introduced by the Law Society ensured that clients would be given adequate information, the government decided to make it a regulatory requirement that a certain level of information be given (those requirements mirroring the Law Society's requirements). This gave rise to the CFA Regulations 2000.

29.216 A timetable for reforming public funding had already been set. It left little—some would say insufficient—time for consideration of the proposed Regulations, which came into force in April 2000. There had been no opportunity for consultation. The 'costs war' began a few months later, when paying parties began to rely on a doctrine that had previously been a relative rarity in costs litigation—namely, the indemnity principle. An attempt was made in 2003 to amend the Regulations in such a way as to make compliance with them easier,[351] but those amendments had little impact. The Regulations were revoked entirely in November 2005.[352] For practical purposes, the only restriction on conditional fee agreements is that the success fee should not exceed 100 per cent nor should they be used in criminal and family matters.

The Relevant Regulations

The Conditional Fee Agreements Regulations 2000 (revoked)

29.217 The CFA Regulations 2000, operative between 1 April 2000 and 1 November 2005, read as follows:

> **'1 Citation, commencement and interpretation**
>
> (1) These Regulations may be cited as the Conditional Fee Agreements Regulations 2000.
>
> (2) These Regulations come into force on 1 April 2000.

[347] Yarrow, S, and Abrams, P, *Nothing to Lose? Clients' Experiences of Using Conditional Fees: Summary Report* (London: University of Westminster, 1999).

[348] Law Society, *Solicitors' Costs Information and Client Care Code* (September 1999).

[349] Lord Chancellor's Department, *Conditional Fees: Sharing the Risks of Litigation* (London: HMSO, 1999).

[350] See the Access to Justice Act 1999, the relevant parts of which did not come into force until 2000.

[351] The Conditional Fee Agreements (Miscellaneous Amendments) Regulations 2003 (SI 2003/1240).

[352] The Conditional Fee Agreements (Revocation) Regulations 2005 (SI 2005/2305).

(3) In these Regulations—
"client" includes, except where the context otherwise requires, a person who—
 (a) has instructed the legal representative to provide the advocacy or litigation services to which the conditional fee agreement relates, or
 (b) is liable to pay the legal representative's fees in respect of those services; and
"legal representative" means the person providing the advocacy or litigation services to which the conditional fee agreement relates.

2 Requirements for contents of conditional fee agreements: general

(1) A conditional fee agreement must specify—
(a) the particular proceedings or parts of them to which it relates (including whether it relates to any appeal, counterclaim or proceedings to enforce a judgment or order),
(b) the circumstances in which the legal representative's fees and expenses, or part of them, are payable,
(c) what payment, if any, is due—
 (i) if those circumstances only partly occur,
 (ii) irrespective of whether those circumstances occur, and
 (iii) on the termination of the agreement for any reason, and
(d) the amounts which are payable in all the circumstances and cases specified or the method to be used to calculate them and, in particular, whether the amounts are limited by reference to the damages which may be recovered on behalf of the client.

(2) A conditional fee agreement to which regulation 4 applies must contain a statement that the requirements of that regulation which apply in the case of that agreement have been complied with.

3 Requirements for contents of conditional fee agreements providing for success fees

(1) A conditional fee agreement which provides for a success fee—
(a) must briefly specify the reasons for setting the percentage increase at the level stated in the agreement, and
(b) must specify how much of the percentage increase, if any, relates to the cost to the legal representative of the postponement of the payment of his fees and expenses.

(2) If the agreement relates to court proceedings, it must provide that where the percentage increase becomes payable as a result of those proceedings, then—
(a) if—
 (i) any fees subject to the increase are assessed, and
 (ii) the legal representative or the client is required by the court to disclose to the court or any other person the reasons for setting the percentage increase at the level stated in the agreement,
 he may do so,
(b) if—
 (i) any such fees are assessed, and
 (ii) any amount in respect of the percentage increase is disallowed on the assessment on the ground that the level at which the increase was set was unreasonable in view of facts which were or should have been known to the legal representative at the time it was set,
 that amount ceases to be payable under the agreement, unless the court is satisfied that it should continue to be so payable, and
(c) if—
 (i) sub-paragraph (b) does not apply, and
 (ii) the legal representative agrees with any person liable as a result of the proceedings to pay fees subject to the percentage increase that a lower amount than the amount payable in accordance with the conditional fee agreement is to be paid instead,

the amount payable under the conditional fee agreement in respect of those fees shall be reduced accordingly, unless the court is satisfied that the full amount should continue to be payable under it.

(3) In this regulation 'percentage increase' means the percentage by which the amount of the fees which would be payable if the agreement were not a conditional fee agreement is to be increased under the agreement.

3A Requirements where the client's liability is limited to sums recovered

(1) This regulation applies to a conditional fee agreement under which, except in the circumstances set out in paragraph (5) and (5A), the client is liable to pay his legal representative's fees and expenses only to the extent that sums are recovered in respect of the relevant proceedings, whether by way of costs or otherwise.

(2) In determining for the purposes of paragraph (1) the circumstances in which a client is liable to pay his legal representative's fees and expenses, no account is to be taken of any obligation to pay costs in respect of the premium of a policy taken out to insure against the risk of incurring a liability in the relevant proceedings.

(3) Regulations 2, 3 and 4 do not apply to a conditional fee agreement to which this regulation applies.

(4) A conditional fee agreement to which this regulation applies must—

(a) specify—

 (i) the particular proceedings or parts of them to which it relates (including whether it relates to any appeal, counterclaim or proceedings to enforce a judgment or order); and

 (ii) the circumstances in which the legal representative's fees and expenses, or part of them, are payable; and

(b) if it provides for a success fee—

 (i) briefly specify the reasons for setting the percentage increase at the level stated in the agreement; and

 (ii) provide that if, in court proceedings, the percentage increase becomes payable as a result of those proceedings and the legal representative or the client is ordered to disclose to the court or any other person the reasons for setting the percentage increase at the level stated in the agreement, he may do so.

(5) A conditional fee agreement to which this regulation applies may specify that the client will be liable to pay the legal representative's fees and expenses whether or not sums are recovered in respect of the relevant proceedings, if the client—

(a) fails to co-operate with the legal representative;

(b) fails to attend any medical or expert examination or court hearing which the legal representative reasonably requests him to attend;

(c) fails to give necessary instructions to the legal representative;

(d) withdraws instructions from the legal representative;

(e) is an individual who is adjudged bankrupt or enters into an arrangement or a composition with his creditors, or against whom an administration order is made; or

(f) is a company for which a receiver, administrative receiver or liquidator is appointed.

(5A) A conditional fee agreement to which this regulation applies may specify that, in the event of the client dying in the course of the relevant proceedings, his estate will be liable for the legal representative's fees and expenses, whether or not sums are recovered in respect of those proceedings.

(6) Before a conditional fee agreement to which this regulation applies is made, the legal representative must inform the client as to the circumstances in which the client or his estate may be liable to pay the legal representative's fees and expenses, and provide such further explanation, advice or other information as to those circumstances as the client may reasonably require.

4 Information to be given before conditional fee agreements made

(1) Before a conditional fee agreement is made the legal representative must—

(a) inform the client about the following matters, and

(b) if the client requires any further explanation, advice or other information about any of those matters, provide such further explanation, advice or other information about them as the client may reasonably require.

(2) Those matters are—

(a) the circumstances in which the client may be liable to pay the costs of the legal representative in accordance with the agreement,

(b) the circumstances in which the client may seek assessment of the fees and expenses of the legal representative and the procedure for doing so,

(c) whether the legal representative considers that the client's risk of incurring liability for costs in respect of the proceedings to which agreement relates is insured against under an existing contract of insurance,

(d) whether other methods of financing those costs are available, and, if so, how they apply to the client and the proceedings in question,

(e) whether the legal representative considers that any particular method or methods of financing any or all of those costs is appropriate and, if he considers that a contract of insurance is appropriate or recommends a particular such contract—

  (i) his reasons for doing so, and

  (ii) whether he has an interest in doing so.

(3) Before a conditional fee agreement is made the legal representative must explain its effect to the client.

(4) In the case of an agreement where—

(a) the legal representative is a body to which section 30 of the Access to Justice Act 1999 (recovery where body undertakes to meet costs liabilities) applies, and

(b) there are no circumstances in which the client may be liable to pay any costs in respect of the proceedings,

paragraph (1) does not apply.

(5) Information required to be given under paragraph (1) about the matters in paragraph (2)(a) to (d) must be given orally (whether or not it is also given in writing), but information required to be so given about the matters in paragraph (2)(e) and the explanation required by paragraph (3) must be given both orally and in writing.

(6) This regulation does not apply in the case of an agreement between a legal representative and an additional legal representative.

5 Form of agreement

(1) A conditional fee agreement must be signed by the client and the legal representative.

(2) This regulation does not apply in the case of an agreement between a legal representative and an additional legal representative.

6 Amendment of agreement

Where an agreement is amended to cover further proceedings or parts of them—

(a) regulations 2, 3, 3A and 5 apply to the amended agreement as if it were a fresh agreement made at the time of the amendment, and

(b) the obligations under regulation 4 apply in relation to the amendments in so far as they affect the matters mentioned in that regulation.

7 Revocation of 1995 Regulations

The Conditional Fee Agreements Regulations 1995 are revoked.

8 Exclusion of collective conditional fee agreements

These Regulations shall not apply to collective conditional fee agreements within the meaning of regulation 3 of the Collective Conditional Fee Agreements Regulation 2000.'

The Collective Conditional Fee Agreements Regulations 2000 (revoked)

29.218 The CCFA Regulations 2000,[353] operative between 1 April 2000 and 1 November 2005, read as follows:

'**1 Citation, commencement and interpretation**

(1) These regulations may be cited as the Collective Conditional Fee Agreements Regulations 2000, and shall come into force on 30 November 2000.

(2) In these Regulations, except where the context requires otherwise—

"client" means a person who will receive advocacy or litigation services to which the agreement relates;

"collective conditional fee agreement" has the meaning given in regulation 3;

"conditional fee agreement" has the same meaning as in section 58 of the Courts and Legal Services Act 1990;

"funder" means the party to a collective conditional fee agreement who, under that agreement, is liable to pay the legal representative's fees;

"legal representative" means the person providing the advocacy or litigation services to which the agreement relates.

2 Transitional provisions

These Regulations shall apply to agreements entered into on or after 30 November 2000, and agreements entered into before that date shall be treated as if these Regulations had not come into force.

3 Definition of "collective conditional fee agreement"

(1) Subject to paragraph (2) of this regulation, a collective conditional fee agreement is an agreement which—

(a) disregarding section 58(3)(c) of the Courts and Legal Services Act 1990, would be a conditional fee agreement; and

(b) does not refer to specific proceedings, but provides for fees to be payable on a common basis in relation to a class of proceedings, or, if it refers to more than one class of proceedings, on a common basis in relation to each class.

(2) An agreement may be a collective conditional fee agreement whether or not—

(a) the funder is a client; or

(b) any clients are named in the agreement.

4 Requirements for contents of collective conditional fee agreements: general

(1) A collective conditional fee agreement must specify the circumstances in which the legal representative's fees and expenses, or part of them, are payable.

(1A) The circumstances referred to in paragraph (1) may include the fact that the legal representative's fees and expenses are payable only to the extent that sums are recovered in respect of the proceedings, whether by way of costs or otherwise.

(2) A collective conditional fee agreement must provide that, when accepting instructions in relation to any specific proceedings the legal representative must—

[353] The Collective Conditional Fee Arrangement Regulations 2000 (SI 2000/2988) have been amended twice, by the Conditional Fee Agreements (Miscellaneous Amendments) Regulations 2003 (SI 2003/1240) and by the Conditional Fee Agreements (Miscellaneous Amendments) (No 2) Regulations 2003 (SI 2003/3344). This was the most up-to-date version (prior to their revocation).

(a) inform the client as to the circumstances in which the client or his estate may be liable to pay the costs of the legal representative; and
(b) if the client requires any further explanation, advice or other information about the matter referred to in sub-paragraph (a), provide such further explanation, advice or other information about it as the client may reasonably require.

(3) Paragraph (2) does not apply in the case of an agreement between a legal representative and an additional legal representative.

(4) A collective conditional fee agreement must provide that, after accepting instructions in relation to any specific proceedings, the legal representative must confirm his acceptance of instructions in writing to the client.

5 Requirements for contents of collective conditional fee agreements providing for success fees

(1) Where a collective conditional fee agreement provides for a success fee the agreement must provide that, when accepting instructions in relation to any specific proceedings the legal representative must prepare and retain a written statement containing—
(a) his assessment of the probability of the circumstances arising in which the percentage increase will become payable in relation to those proceedings ("the risk assessment");
(b) his assessment of the amount of the percentage increase in relation to those proceedings, having regard to the risk assessment; and
(c) the reasons, by reference to the risk assessment, for setting the percentage increase at that level.

(2) If the agreement relates to court proceedings it must provide that where the success fee becomes payable as a result of those proceedings, then—
(a) if—
    (i) any fees subject to the increase are assessed, and
    (ii) the legal representative or the client is required by the court to disclose to the court or any other person the reasons for setting the percentage increase at the level assessed by the legal representative,
  he may do so,
(b) if—
    (i) any such fees are assessed by the court, and
    (ii) any amount in respect of the percentage increase is disallowed on the assessment on the ground that the level at which the increase was set was unreasonable in view of facts which were or should have been known to the legal representative at the time it was set
  that amount ceases to be payable under the agreement, unless the court is satisfied that it should continue to be so payable, and
(c) if—
    (i) sub-paragraph (b) does not apply, and
    (ii) the legal representative agrees with any person liable as a result of the proceedings to pay fees subject to the percentage increase that a lower amount than the amount payable in accordance with the conditional fee agreement is to be paid instead,
  the amount payable under the collective conditional fee agreement in respect of those fees shall be reduced accordingly, unless the court is satisfied that the full amount should continue to be payable under it.

(3) In this regulation "percentage increase" means the percentage by which the amount of the fees which would have been payable if the agreement were not a conditional fee agreement is to be increased under the agreement.

(4) Sub-paragraphs (b) and (c) of paragraph (2) do not apply to a collective conditional fee agreement under which, except in the circumstances set out in paragraph (6) and (7), the client is liable to pay his legal representative's fees and expenses only to the extent that sums are recovered in respect of the proceedings, whether by way of costs or otherwise.

(5) In determining for the purposes of paragraph (4) the circumstances in which a client is liable to pay his legal representative's fees and expenses, no account is to be taken of any obligation to pay costs in respect of the premium of a policy taken out to insure against the risk of incurring a liability in the relevant proceedings.

(6) A collective conditional fee agreement to which paragraph (4) applies may specify that the client will be liable to pay his legal representative's fees and expenses whether or not sums are recovered in respect of the relevant proceedings, if the client—

(a) fails to co-operate with the legal representative;
(b) fails to attend any medical or expert examination or court hearing which the legal representative reasonably requests him to attend;
(c) fails to give necessary instructions to the legal representative;
(d) withdraws instructions from the legal representative.
(e) is an individual who is adjudged bankrupt or enters into an arrangement or a composition with his creditors, or against whom an administration order is made; or
(f) is a company for which a receiver, administrative receiver or liquidator is appointed.

(7) A collective conditional fee agreement to which paragraph (4) applies may specify that, in the event of the client dying in the course of the relevant proceedings, his estate will be liable for the legal representative's fees and expenses, whether or not sums are recovered in respect of those proceedings.

6 Form and amendment of collective conditional fee agreement

(1) Subject to paragraph (2), a collective conditional fee agreement must be signed by the funder, and by the legal representative.

(2) Paragraph (1) does not apply in the case of an agreement between a legal representative and an additional legal representative.

(3) Where a collective conditional fee agreement is amended, regulations 4 and 5 apply to the amended agreement as if it were a fresh agreement made at the time of the amendment.'

The Damages-Based Agreements Regulations 2013

29.219 The DBA Regulations 2013 came into force on 1 April 2013[354] (in so far as employment matters were concerned) and they read as follows:

'1 Citation, commencement, interpretation and application

(1) These Regulations may be cited as the Damages-Based Agreements Regulations 2013 and come into force on 1st April 2013.

(2) In these Regulations—

"the Act" means the Courts and Legal Services Act 1990;

"claim for personal injuries" has the same meaning as in Rule 2.3 of the Civil Procedure Rules 1998;

"client" means the person who has instructed the representative to provide advocacy services, litigation services (within section 119 of the Act) or claims management services (within the meaning of section 4(2)(b) of the Compensation Act 2006) and is liable to make a payment for those services;

"costs" means the total of the representative's time reasonably spent, in respect of the claim or proceedings, multiplied by the reasonable hourly rate of remuneration of the representative;

"employment matter" means a matter that is, or could become, the subject of proceedings before an employment tribunal;

354 Almost identical regulations, the Damages-Based Agreements Regulations 2010 (SI 2010/1206), had been in operation since 7 April 2010.

"expenses" means disbursements incurred by the representative, including the expense of obtaining an expert's report and, in an employment matter only, counsel's fees;

"payment" means that part of the sum recovered in respect of the claim or damages awarded that the client agrees to pay the representative, and excludes expenses but includes, in respect of any claim or proceedings to which these regulations apply other than an employment matter, any disbursements incurred by the representative in respect of counsel's fees;

"representative" means the person providing the advocacy services, litigation services or claims management services to which the damages-based agreement relates.

(3) Subject to paragraphs (4), (5) and (6), these Regulations shall apply to all damages-based agreements entered into on or after the date on which these Regulations come into force.

(4) Subject to paragraph (6), these Regulations shall not apply to any damages-based agreement to which section 57 of the Solicitors Act 1974(5) (non-contentious business agreements between solicitor and client) applies.

(5) In these Regulations—

(a) regulation 4 does not apply; and

(b) regulations 5, 6, 7 and 8 only apply,

to any damages-based agreement in respect of an employment matter.

(6) Where these Regulations relate to an employment matter, they apply to all damages-based agreements signed on or after the date on which these Regulations come into force.

2 Revocation of 2010 Regulations and transitional provision

(1) Subject to paragraph (2), the Damages-Based Agreements Regulations 2010(6) ("the 2010 Regulations") are revoked.

(2) The 2010 Regulations shall continue to have effect in respect of any damages-based agreement to which those Regulations applied and which was signed before the date on which these Regulations come into force.

3 Requirements of an agreement in respect of all damages-based agreements

The requirements prescribed for the purposes of section 58AA(4)(c) of the Act are that the terms and conditions of a damages-based agreement must specify—

(a) the claim or proceedings or parts of them to which the agreement relates;

(b) the circumstances in which the representative's payment, expenses and costs, or part of them, are payable; and

(c) the reason for setting the amount of the payment at the level agreed, which, in an employment matter, shall include having regard to, where appropriate, whether the claim or proceedings is one of several similar claims or proceedings.

4 Payment in respect of claims or proceedings other than an employment matter

(1) In respect of any claim or proceedings, other than an employment matter, to which these Regulations apply, a damages-based agreement must not require an amount to be paid by the client other than—

(a) the payment, net of—

(i) any costs (including fixed costs under Part 45 of the Civil Procedure Rules 1998); and

(ii) where relevant, any sum in respect of disbursements incurred by the representative in respect of counsel's fees,

that have been paid or are payable by another party to the proceedings by agreement or order; and

(b) any expenses incurred by the representative, net of any amount which has been paid or is payable by another party to the proceedings by agreement or order.

(2) In a claim for personal injuries—

(a) the only sums recovered by the client from which the payment shall be met are—

(i) general damages for pain, suffering and loss of amenity; and

(ii) damages for pecuniary loss other than future pecuniary loss,

net of any sums recoverable by the Compensation Recovery Unit of the Department for Work and Pensions; and

(b) subject to paragraph (4), a damages-based agreement must not provide for a payment above an amount which, including VAT, is equal to 25% of the combined sums in paragraph (2)(a)(i) and (ii) which are ultimately recovered by the client.

(3) Subject to paragraph (4), in any other claim or proceedings to which this regulation applies, a damages-based agreement must not provide for a payment above an amount which, including VAT, is equal to 50% of the sums ultimately recovered by the client.

(4) The amounts prescribed in paragraphs (2)(b) and (3) shall only apply to claims or proceedings at first instance.

5 Information required to be given before an agreement is made in an employment matter

(1) In an employment matter, the requirements prescribed for the purposes of section 58AA(4)(d) of the Act are to provide—

(a) information to the client in writing about the matters in paragraph (2); and

(b) such further explanation, advice or other information about any of those matters as the client may request.

(2) Those matters are—

(a) he circumstances in which the client may seek a review of costs and expenses of the representative and the procedure for doing so;

(b) the dispute resolution service provided by the Advisory, Conciliation and Arbitration Service (ACAS) in regard to actual and potential claims;

(c) whether other methods of pursuing the claim or financing the proceedings, including—

(i) advice under the Community Legal Service,

(ii) legal expenses insurance,

(iii) pro bono representation, or

(iv) trade union representation,

are available, and, if so, how they apply to the client and the claim or proceedings in question; and

(d) the point at which expenses become payable; and

(e) a reasonable estimate of the amount that is likely to be spent upon expenses, inclusive of VAT.

6 Additional causes of action in an employment matter

In an employment matter, any amendment to a damages-based agreement to cover additional causes of action must be in writing and signed by the client and the representative.

7 Payment in an employment matter

In an employment matter, a damages-based agreement must not provide for a payment above an amount which, including VAT, is equal to 35% of the sums ultimately recovered by the client in the claim or proceedings.

8 Terms and conditions of termination in an employment matter

(1) In an employment matter, the additional requirements prescribed for the purposes of section 58AA(4)(c) of the Act are that the terms and conditions of a damages-based agreement must be in accordance with paragraphs (2), (3) and (4).

(2) If the agreement is terminated, the representatives may not charge the client more than the representative's costs and expenses for the work undertaken in respect of the client's claim or proceedings.

(3) The client may not terminate the agreement—
(a) after settlement has been agreed; or
(b) within seven days before the start of the tribunal hearing.

(4) The representative may not terminate the agreement and charge costs unless the client has behaved or is behaving unreasonably.

(5) Paragraphs (3) and (4) are without prejudice to any right of either party under general law of contract to terminate the agreement.'

30

CONTRACTS OF RETAINER (CHAMPERTY AND MAINTENANCE)

30.01 This chapter deals with the following topics:

- introduction (30.02);
- maintenance:
  - the ancient law of maintenance—historic aspects (30.04);
  - the elements of maintenance (modern law) (30.06);
  - assignment of causes of action and debts (30.10);
  - collateral interests (30.11);
  - public policy (30.13);
  - largely a question of fact (30.16);
  - the relevance of analogous statutes (30.17);
- champerty:
  - the relationship of champerty to maintenance (30.18);
  - the ancient law of champerty—development and history (30.19);
  - the administration of and access to justice (30.20);
  - wanton and officious intermeddling (30.22);
  - public policy (30.25);
  - the modern approach (30.26); and
- case examples relating to maintenance and champerty (30.32).

Introduction

30.02 Many years ago, the topics of champerty and maintenance were highly relevant to the law of costs, but this is no longer the case. The range of circumstances in which they continue to have any practical relevance has dwindled. The following is a non-exhaustive list of those circumstances that now may arise in the context of costs litigation:

- where a non-party has meddled in the litigation and where a non-party costs order is sought against that person 9.21–9.31;
- where a contract of retainer is said to be champertous by reason of the retainer providing for an objectionable method of remuneration;[1]
- where a contract of retainer is said to be tinged with illegality by reason of the legal representative having an objectionable interest in the litigation;[2]

[1] See, eg, *Benaim (UK) Ltd v Davies Middleton & Davies Ltd* [2004] EWHC 737 (TCC).
[2] See, eg, *Dix v Townend & Anor* [2008] EWHC 90117 (Costs).

- where a person other than a legal representative seeks payment for services rendered and where that payment is sought as costs, but is said not to be recoverable by reason of it being based on an objectionable method of remuneration;[3] and
- where a person other than a legal representative seeks payment for services rendered and where that payment is sought as costs, but is said not to be recoverable by reason of that person's champertous involvement in the litigation.

Even this short list may be undergoing a process of attenuation. In particular, the ascendancy of litigation funding (see Chapter 33) may further reshape public policy, ultimately diminishing the relevance of maintenance and champerty almost to vanishing point. At present, however, costs practitioners need to know the law of maintenance and champerty—or at least need to know where to find that law. **30.03**

Maintenance

The ancient law of maintenance: historic aspects

Chitty on Contracts describes maintenance in the following way: 'A person is guilty of maintenance if he supports litigation in which he has no legitimate concern without just cause or excuse'.[4] As such, it tends to apply only to contentious business (although see 30.14 and 3.34–3.36). The doctrines of maintenance and champerty developed to combat abuses in late medieval England. The perception was that barratry[5] was common, and that unscrupulous nobles and royal officials were lending their names to bolster the credibility of doubtful and fraudulent claims.[6] Speaking extrajudicially in the early 17th century, Lord Chief Justice Coke described the origins of maintenance in this way: 'Maintenance, *manutenentia*, is derived from the verb *manutenere*, and signifieth in law a taking in hand, bearing up, or *upholding* of quarrels and sides, to the disturbance or hindrance of common right.'[7] These comments were made in the context of the court previously having been anxious to prevent a wide range of maintenance; indeed, in times past, the phrase 'maintenance' had been used to apply not only to those who gave support in civil claims, but also to those who sought to maintain robbers, heretics and even 'a new sect coming from beyond the sea, clad in white garments'.[8] Clearly, the ancient law of maintenance had very different aims from the modern law, so whilst scrutiny of the ancient law is of interest, it rarely helps in any practical way.[9] **30.04**

Maintenance used to be a misdemeanour[10] and was also a tort for which damages were recoverable. In the mid-20th century, legislation was enacted that abolished both the tort **30.05**

[3] See, as a counter-example, *Pirie v Ayling* [2003] EWHC 9006 (Costs).

[4] *Chitty on Contracts* (28th edn, London: Sweet & Maxwell, 1999), vol 1, para 17-050.

[5] This being the frequent incitement of lawsuits and quarrels. *The Case of Barratry* (30 Eliz 8 Rep 36) defined 'barratry' in the following way: 'A common barrator is a common mover or stirrer up on maintainer or suits, quarrels, or parties, either in Courts, or in the county . . .'

[6] Winfield, PH, 'The History of Maintenance and Champerty' [1919] Law QR 35, at 50.

[7] 1 Coke Litt 368b.

[8] Parliamentary Rolls III, 125b, and III, 428a (1399), cited in Winfield, PH, *The History of Conspiracy and Abuse of Legal Procedure* (Cambridge: Cambridge University Press, 1921), p 134.

[9] Indeed, LCJ Coke himself made a distinction between 'special' and 'general' maintenance, which is not susceptible to modern analysis: see Winfield, PH, *The History of Conspiracy and Abuse of Legal Procedure* (Cambridge: Cambridge University Press, 1921), pp 136–8.

[10] Champerty Act 1275 (3 Ed I (St West I) c 25).

and the crime,[11] but law relating to the enforceability of contracts for maintenance was expressly preserved.[12] To that extent, the common law remains relevant.

The elements of maintenance (modern law)

30.06 In brief, maintenance is the intermeddling by a disinterested party for the purposes of encouraging a lawsuit.[13] For the reasons set out below, the elements of maintenance can be summarised as being that:

- the putative maintainer has wantonly and officiously intermeddled with the dispute of another person;
- in particular, the putative maintainer does so whilst having no collateral or other interest in the dispute (see 30.11); and
- the maintainer does this without having just cause or excuse.

30.07 Thus the modern law of maintenance focuses upon those who meddle in the disputes of others. That policy was described by Fletcher Moulton LJ in the following terms: 'It is directed against wanton and officious intermeddling with the disputes of others in which the [maintainer] has no interest whatever, and where the assistance he renders to one or the other party is without justification or excuse.'[14]

30.08 Similarly, Lord Denning MR described maintenance as '[i]mproperly stirring up litigation and strife by giving aid to one party to bring or defend a claim without just cause or excuse'.[15] The phrase 'wanton and officious intermeddling' does not mean that the person concerned is acting in an arbitrary and capricious manner, but merely that they do not have a sufficient interest in the subject matter of the claim to justify their involvement.[16]

30.09 What amounts to maintenance will depend on the facts of the case. In ancient times, maintenance might have been by word, writing, countenance or deed.[17] In the late 18th century, the law even went so far as to provide that volunteering information would suffice.[18] Whilst exceptions exist,[19] anything of this nature would not ordinarily be regarded as being maintenance today. Maintenance now tends to focus on financial aid, such as direct funding, or the provision of legal or other services. In so far as the law of costs is concerned, it is the provision of legal services that is usually of importance, because it is that which may be the link between maintenance (or, more usually, champertous maintenance) and the retainer, this being a relationship that may taint the retainer with illegality.

---

[11] Criminal Law Act 1967, ss 13(1) and 14(1).

[12] Specifically, Criminal Law Act 1967, s 14(2), provided that s 14(1) 'shall not affect any such rule of law as to the cases in which a contract is to be treated as contrary to public policy or otherwise illegal'.

[13] Curzon, LB, *Dictionary of Law* (6th edn, Harlow: Longman, 2002), p 260.

[14] *British Cash and Parcel Conveyors Ltd v Lamson Store Service Co Ltd* [1908] 1 KB 1006, at 1014. More recently cited with approval by Lord Mustill in *Giles v Thompson* [1994] 1 AC 142, at 161. See also *Alabaster v Harness* [1895] 1 QB 339, CA, at 342, *per* Lord Esher MR; *Wallis v Duke of Portland* (1797) 3 Ves 494.

[15] *Re Trepca Mines Ltd (No 2)* [1963] Ch 199, at 219.

[16] See *Simpson (as assignee of Catchpole) v Norfolk & Norwich University Hospital NHS Trust* [2011] EWCA Civ 1149, at [22], *per* Moore-Bick LJ.

[17] 2 Co Inst 212, *per* LCJ Coke.

[18] *Master v Miller* (1791) 4 Term Rep 320, at 340.

[19] See, eg, *Fraser v Buckle* [1996] 2 IRLM 34 and other cases given as examples below.

Assignment of causes of action and debts

There is one further way in which a person may be found to be guilty of maintenance in a way that is relevant to costs—that is, where a claim is supposedly assigned from one person to another. Whilst debts can be assigned for a purchase price,[20] the common law abhorred the assignment of a bare cause of action in tort.[21] This was because, in ancient times, this would have allowed a doubtful or fraudulent claim to be transferred to a person of influence or power, who (in a legal system that was still influenced by patronage) could then expect a sympathetic hearing in court proceedings.[22] Where the agreement to assign is struck down as being champertous, there are many ways in which the receiving party could be denied costs. Whilst there is no authority on the point, the range of mechanisms extends from the court finding that the maintainer has been meddling in a claim that had not been validly assigned all the way through to the court merely finding that the retainer is tainted with illegality. **30.10**

Collateral interests

Not every act of meddling will amount to maintenance: even in ancient times, assistance with litigation was permissible when the assistor had a legitimate interest in the outcome of the claim (or if they had a reasonable belief in such an interest).[23] This was not confined to cases in which the person in question had a financial or commercial interest in the outcome; it extended to other circumstances in which social, family or other ties justified the person's support of the litigation.[24] Viscount Haldane had this to say about who could be regarded as having a legitimate interest: **30.11**

> 'Such an interest is held to be possessed when in litigation a master assists his servant, or a servant his master, or help is given to an heir, or a near relative, or to a poor man out of charity, to maintain a right which he might otherwise lose.'[25]

Examples and counter-examples of legitimate interests are given at 30.32–30.54. The interest must not arise out of the agreement to provide assistance[26]—that is, it must be a pre-existing interest. Where the likely benefit is far greater than the interest, the court may find that no legitimate interest exists.[27]

In addition to 'community of interest'—as a shared financial interest is often called—assistance may be justified on the basis that it is provided as an act of charity,[28] or on **30.12**

[20] See, eg, *Camdex International Ltd v Bank of Zambia (No 1)* [1998] QB 22.

[21] As a modern example, see *Simpson (as assignee of Catchpole) v Norfolk & Norwich University Hospital NHS Trust* [2011] EWCA Civ 1149, at [15] *et seq.*

[22] See *Giles v Thompson* [1993] 3 All ER 321, at 328, cited by Baroness Hale in *Massai Aviation Services v Attorney-General* [2007] UKPC 12, at [15].

[23] See *Alabaster v Harness* [1895] 1 QB 339, CA.

[24] *Thai Trading Co (a firm) v Taylor* [1998] 3 All ER 65, at 69, *per* Millett LJ.

[25] *Neville v London Express Newspaper Ltd* [1919] AC 368, at 389. See also *Bradlaugh v Newdegate* (1883) 11 QBD 1, at 11, in which Lord Coleridge CJ spoke of 'the interest which consanguinity or affinity to the suitor give to the man who aids him, or the interest arising from the connection of the parties, eg as master and servant ...'. See also *Condliffe v Hislop* [1996] 1 WLR 753, in which it was held that it was not unlawful for a mother to provide limited funds to finance her bankrupt son's action for defamation, and *Thai Trading Co (a firm) v Taylor* [1998] 3 All ER 65, at 70.

[26] *Giles v Thompson* [1993] 3 All ER 321, at 333 (which was appealed, but on other grounds).

[27] *Advanced Technology Structures Ltd v Cray Valley Products Ltd* [1993] BCLC 723, CA.

[28] See *Jennings v Johnson* (1873) LR 8 CP 425; *Holden v Thompson* [1907] 2 KB 489.

the basis that it is provided out of kinship[29] or religious ties.[30] Financial institutions are permitted to fund litigation where this is part of the service that they provide: this is the mechanism that permits a bank to offer a disbursement funding loan and is the mechanism by which a legal expenses insurer is able to fund the provision of legal services.[31] It probably by means of this mechanism that litigation funding avoids the label of maintenance.[32]

Public policy

30.13 From the beginning of the 20th century (and probably much earlier), it was recognised that public policy must change with the times.[33] Danckwerts LJ had this to say on the point:

> 'The law of maintenance depends upon the question of public policy, and public policy is not a fixed and immutable matter. It is a conception which, if it has any sense at all, must be alterable by the passage of time.'[34]

30.14 In modern times, the law became much more tolerant of the intervention by one person in the claim of another.[35] By the late 20th century, the stage had been reached at which, for example, a car hirer was able to conduct a road traffic accident claim for the purposes of recovering its fees.[36] As is explained in Chapter 33, litigation funding has also become something to be tolerated, if not actively promoted. The change in the law of champerty (which is discussed at 30.18–30.31) has been equally as noticeable.

30.15 The law of maintenance and champerty is not confined to proceedings in court,[37] but it does not apply to all forms of dispute resolution procedures. It has, for example, been found not to apply to licensing magistrates.[38]

Largely a question of fact

30.16 The issue of whether there has been maintenance will largely be a matter for the tribunal of fact. When considering a contract (including a contract of retainer), the matter will not simply be one of contractual interpretation; in particular, the court may go behind a written agreement and draw its own conclusions as to the parties' intentions.[39]

The relevance of analogous statutes

30.17 Notwithstanding the fact that the issue of whether there has been maintenance will largely be a matter of fact (see 30.16), legal issues may arise. In particular, the common law can

[29] As to the limits of this doctrine, see *Burke v Greene* (1814) 2 Ball & B 517; *Bradlaugh v Newdegate* (1883) 11 QBD 1, at 11.

[30] *Rothewel v Pewer* (1431) YB 9 Hen 6, p 64, pl 713.

[31] See, eg, *Martell v Consett Iron Co Ltd* [1955] Ch 363, at 416.

[32] See *Arkin v Borchard* [2005] EWCA Civ 655.

[33] See, eg, *British Cash and Parcel Conveyors Ltd v Lamson Store Service Co Ltd* [1908] 1 KB 1006, at 1013.

[34] *Hill v Archbold* [1968] 1 QB 686, at 697.

[35] See, eg, *Thai Trading Co (a firm) v Taylor* [1998] 3 All ER 65, at 69, *per* Millett LJ, which is no longer good law, but was found to be wrong on bases other than the discussion of what amounts to champertous maintenance. That said, Lord Neuberger MR has urged caution in respect of this case generally: see *Morris v London Borough of Southwark* [2011] EWCA Civ 25, at [24].

[36] *Giles v Thompson* [1994] 1 AC 142, at 161.

[37] See, eg, *In re Trepca Mines Ltd (No 2)* [1963] Ch 199, at 220, 225 and 226.

[38] *Saville Bros Ltd v Langman* (1898) 79 LT 44, CA.

[39] *Rees v De Bernardy* [1896] 2 Ch 437.

take its lead from statute.[40] An example is a case in which the court was asked to declare whether a conditional fee agreement in arbitral proceedings was lawful (at a time when statute did not apply to arbitral proceedings). Sir Richard Scott V-C drew an analogy with the statutory provisions relating to court proceedings and, effectively, found that any agreement that would have met those statutory requirements would be free from any public policy objection.[41]

Champerty

The relationship of champerty to maintenance

Chitty on Contracts describes champerty in the following way: '[Champerty] occurs when the person maintaining another stipulates for a share of the proceeds of the action or suit.'[42] Champerty is generally regarded as being a subspecies of maintenance;[43] it is typically said to be maintenance in which there is a notion of division of the spoils. The phrase 'champertous maintenance' is used in this book to describe that state of affairs.[44] That said, Lord Neuberger MR has pointed out that it is possible to have champerty without maintenance, because the latter involves an element of assisting one of the parties 'without justification or excuse', yet this is not a necessary ingredient of the former.[45] This distinction is more relevant than it might first appear, because one of the most important modern-day applications of champerty is in the context of legal representatives acting in that capacity, and both Lord Phillips[46] and Lord Neuberger MR[47] have explained that such a person can hardly be said to be providing assistance without justification or excuse. **30.18**

The ancient law of champerty: development and history

Lord Mustill has commented that champerty is so ancient that its 'origins can no longer be traced'.[48] What can be said, however, is that the focus of concern has shifted over the centuries. In the 14th century, the concern was to combat unprincipled nobles and royal officials lending their names to strengthen the credibility of doubtful and fraudulent claims in return for a share of the property recovered.[49] By the 19th century, the focus had shifted **30.19**

---

[40] 'There is, of course, no more cogent evidence of a change of public policy than the expression of the will of Parliament': *Giles v Thompson* [1993] 3 All ER 321, at 331, *per* Steyn LJ.

[41] *Bevan Ashford (a firm) v Geoff Yeandle (Contractors) Ltd (in liquidation)* [1999] Ch 239. This case applied authority (*Thai Trading Co (a firm) v Taylor* [1998] 3 All ER 65), which was subsequently found to be wrongly decided and so was probably itself wrongly decided, but it remains illustrative of the principle that public policy can be influenced by statute.

[42] *Chitty on Contracts* (28th edn, London: Sweet & Maxwell, 1999), vol 1, para 17-054.

[43] See *Morris v London Borough of Southwark* [2011] EWCA Civ 25, at [52], *per* Lord Neuberger MR.

[44] See Pearson LJ's comments in *Re Trepca Mines Ltd (No 2)* [1963] Ch 199, at 226. See also *Hickman v Kent or Romney Marsh Sheepbreeders' Association* (1920) 151 LT Jo 5, CA ('every champerty is maintenance'); *Ellis v Torrington* [1920] 1 KB 399, at 412.

[45] *Morris v London Borough of Southwark* [2011] EWCA Civ 25, at [53].

[46] *R v Secretary of State for Transport, ex p Factortame* [2002] EWCA Civ 932, at [76].

[47] *Morris v London Borough of Southwark* [2011] EWCA Civ 25, at [53].

[48] *Giles v Thompson* [1994] 1 AC 142, at 153. The earliest solid reference the editor can find is the Champerty Act 1275 (3 Ed I (St West I) c 25), but it is generally thought that the statute merely increased the punishment for champerty and that it had existed for many centuries before it was mentioned in statutes or ordinances: see Winfield, PH, *The History of Conspiracy and Abuse of Legal Procedure* (Cambridge: Cambridge University Press, 1921), p 138.

[49] Winfield, PH, 'The History of Maintenance and Champerty' [1919] Law QR 35, at 50.

from the person who was being sued to the person whose claim it was. In particular, there was concern that, where such people were unable to litigate for want of finance, they might be tempted to enter into an 'improvident bargain' that would unfairly diminish their rights.[50]

The administration of and access to justice

30.20 Modern-day concerns focus principally on the administration of justice. As Steyn LJ commented: 'The doctrine of champerty serves to protect only the integrity of English public justice. It is based not on grounds of morality but on a concern to protect the administration of civil justice in this country.'[51]

30.21 In addition to this change in its aims, public policy has, in recent years, also focused on access to justice. Both Lord Hoffmann[52] and Baroness Hale[53] have commented on the fact that the illegality of champertous funding agreements may act to deter poor persons from obtaining legal redress. The fact that litigation funding is now tolerated (see Chapter 33) is a natural extension of such a line of thought.

Wanton and officious intermeddling

30.22 There are features of maintenance that are particularly relevant where champerty is alleged. One such feature is the fact that the champerter will not have a legitimate interest in the claim. Lord Mustill has noted that that aspect of champerty can still be well described as 'a wanton and officious intermeddling without justification or excuse'.[54] The phrase 'wanton and officious intermeddling' can be traced at least as far back as the end of the 18th century[55] and has become shorthand for one of the two main ingredients of champerty (the other being division of the spoils). It does not mean that the person concerned is acting in an arbitrary and capricious manner, but merely that they do not have a sufficient interest in the subject matter of the claim to justify taking an assignment.[56] Another phrase that is often heard is that the champerter might be tempted, for their own personal gain, 'to inflame the damages, to suppress evidence, or even to suborn witnesses'—these being famous words originally spoken by Denning MR in the mid-1960s[57] and which have been instrumental in shaping the law of champerty ever since.[58]

30.23 Whilst there can be no champerty where there is no notion of giving assistance, it is not necessary that the giving of assistance must of itself be unlawful maintenance. This is because the public policies that inform the two doctrines are different and allow for different

[50] *Hutley v Hutley* (1873) LR 8 QB 112; see also *Rees v De Bernady* [1896] 2 Ch 437.

[51] *Giles v Thompson* [1993] 3 All ER 321, at 332. See also *Papera Traders Co Ltd v Hyundai (Merchant) Marine Co Ltd (No 2)* [2002] 2 Lloyd's LR 692.

[52] *Norgeln Ltd v Reeds Rains Prudential Ltd* [1999] 2 AC 1, at 11.

[53] *Massai Aviation Services v Attorney-General* [2007] UKPC 12, at [13].

[54] *Giles v Thompson* [1994] 1 AC 142, at 153 and 161. The phrase was used by Fletcher Moulton LJ in *British Cash and Parcel Conveyors Ltd v Lamson Store Service Co Ltd* [1908] 1 KB 1006, at 1014.

[55] *Wallis v Duke of Portland* (1797) 3 Ves 494.

[56] See *Simpson (as assignee of Catchpole) v Norfolk & Norwich University Hospital NHS Trust* [2011] EWCA Civ 1149, at [22], *per* Moore-Bick LJ.

[57] *Trepca Mines Ltd (No 2)* [1963] 1 Ch 199, at 219.

[58] See, eg, *R v Secretary of State for Transport, ex p Factortame* [2002] EWCA Civ 932, at [36].

exceptions.[59] So an act of maintenance may be acceptable when carried out in isolation, but may become objectionable when it is combined with the notion of division of the spoils.[60] An example is providing assistance as an act of charity: such assistance may take on an altogether less innocent air if the maintainer puts altruism to one side and demands their share of the proceeds.

The mere fact that litigation services have been provided in return for a promise in the share of the proceeds is not by itself sufficient to justify a finding of champerty.[61] **30.24**

Public policy

As has been noted in the discussion of maintenance (see 30.04–30.17—especially 30.13–30.14), public policy is not static, but is something that evolves.[62] Lord Phillips said that, 'because the question of whether maintenance and champerty can be justified is one of public policy, the law must be kept under review as public policy changes'.[63] Champerty used to be a crime and a tort for which damages were recoverable. Sections 13(1) and 14(1) of the Criminal Law Act 1967 abolished both the tort and the crime, but the law relating to the enforceability of contracts was preserved. In modern times, the pendulum has swung in the direction of restricting the scope of what is champertous,[64] but it should not be assumed that the pendulum will not swing back again. Indeed, developments in other common-law jurisdictions demonstrate that champerty continues to be relevant. **30.25**

- **Republic of Ireland** Champerty and maintenance continue to be crimes in Ireland. Litigation funding remains unlawful on the grounds of champterty.[65] That said, the Irish courts have recently begun to tolerate after-the-event (ATE) insurance policies.[66]
- **Hong Kong** In Hong Kong, champerty and maintenance were long thought to have been obsolete concepts relegated to textbooks on legal history, but they have been revived in recent years, in response to the prevalence of 'recovery agents' (a particularly aggressive species of claims farmer).

[59] *Thai Trading Co (a firm) v Taylor* [1998] 3 All ER 65, at 69, *per* Millett LJ. This case is no longer good law, but it was found to be wrong on bases other than the discussion of what amounts to champertous maintenance.

[60] An example is where assistance is provided by a person whose only interest in the matter is that they are acting out of kinship or to assist the poor; where that person seeks to take a share of the profits, any defence arising out of that interest will no longer be available: see *Cole v Booker* (1913) 29 TLR 295; *Hutley v Hutley* (1873) LR 8 QB 112.

[61] *R (Factortame) Ltd v Secretary of State for Transport (No 8)* [2003] QB 381. See also Underhill J's analysis in *Mansell v Robinson* [2007] EWHC 101 (QB).

[62] In the context of champerty rather than only maintenance, see *R v Secretary of State for Transport, ex p Factortame* [2002] EWCA Civ 932, at [31]–[33].

[63] *Ibid*, at [32].

[64] See, eg, *Thai Trading Co (a firm) v Taylor* [1998] 3 All ER 65, at 69, *per* Millett LJ. This case is no longer good law, but it was found to be wrong on bases other than the discussion of what amounts to champertous maintenance.

[65] See *Thema International Fund PLC v HSBC Institutional Trust Services (Ireland) Ltd* [2011] IEHC 357; more recently, *Persona Digital Telephony Ltd & Sigma Wireless Networks Ltd v The Minister for Public Enterprise* [2017] IESC 27.

[66] See *Greenclean Waste Management Ltd v Leahy (No 2)* [2014] IEHC 314, reversed on other grounds on appeal ([2015] IECA 97).

- **Australia** Whilst the arguments have so far failed to find favour, defendants to class actions have been seeking to rely on arguments closely related to champerty for the purpose of arguing against litigation funding (see 33.13).

The modern approach

30.26 The modern approach to champerty has been explained by Phillips MR as follows:

> 'Where the law expressly restricts the circumstances in which agreements in support of litigation are lawful, this provides a powerful indication of the limits of public policy in analogous situations. Where this is not the case, then we believe one must today look at the facts of the particular case and consider whether those facts suggest that the agreement in question might tempt the allegedly champertous maintainer for his personal gain, to inflame the damages, to suppress evidence, to suborn witnesses or otherwise to undermine the ends of justice.'[67]

30.27 Thus the elements of champerty are:

- whether the putatively champertous maintainer has an interest in the litigation, such as an agreement to share the spoils of the claim; and
- whether the agreement might tempt the putatively champertous maintainer, for their own personal gain, to inflame the damages, to suppress evidence or to suborn witnesses; or
- whether the agreement offends against public policy in that it might undermine the ends of justice.

30.28 The correct approach is not to ask whether the agreement has in fact caused the corruption of public justice; instead, the court must consider the tendency of the agreement to tempt the putatively champertous maintainer, for their own personal gain, to inflame the damages, to suppress evidence, to suborn witnesses or otherwise to undermine the ends of justice.[68] This implies an element of moral culpability and some judges have noted that the court is often reluctant to make a finding of champerty.[69]

Contracts of retainer

30.29 In so far as the indemnity principle is concerned, the focus is mostly on the retainer in question rather than the claim as a whole; hence issues such as whether the retainer is 'tinged with illegality' might arise. The following points may be made in that regard.

- It is not permissible to disregard the champertous contract of retainer and look at what would have happened had it not existed. In particular, Atkin LJ has confirmed that, where a person is engaged to carry out work under a champertous contract, they are not able to seek payment on the basis of *quantum meruit* or on the basis of an earlier, non-champertous, agreement.[70]
- The client's motives and methods need not necessarily be taken into account when considering the issue of whether the contract of retainer is champertous. In particular, a retainer will not be tinged with illegality merely because the solicitor knows that its client

---

67 *R v Secretary of State for Transport, ex p Factortame* [2002] EWCA Civ 932, at [36].
68 Whilst the decision was appealed on other grounds, see *Giles v Thompson* [1993] 3 All ER 321, at 333; *Trendtex Trading Corpn v Crédit Suisse* [1982] AC 629.
69 See *London and Regional (St George's Court) Ltd v Ministry of Defence* [2008] EWHC 526 (TCC), at [103], in which Coulson J cited, with approval, *Papera Traders Co Ltd v Hyundai (Merchant) Marine Co Ltd (No 2)* [2002] 2 Lloyds LR 692.
70 *Wild v Simpson* [1919] 2 KB 544.

has made a champertous agreement to share the proceeds with a third party; rather, the solicitor would have to participate in the champertous arrangement for the retainer to be champertous. Denning LJ has indicted that the participation must be active participation in the sense that the solicitor must voluntarily carry out a positive act of assistance,[71] but his comments were made in the context of champerty being a criminal offence and it is entirely possible that the court would view the matter differently today.

The second of these points does not mean that the court is unable to look beyond the retainer. Although there is no authority on the point, it is easy to envisage circumstances in which a retainer could be found to be unenforceable by reason of the conduct of the solicitor, for example where it has knowingly referred clients to a person who would fund the claim in a way that was champertous. **30.30**

The court's own volition

Christopher Nugee QC (sitting as a deputy judge of the High Court) has commented (*obiter*) that whilst the court is able to make a finding of champerty of its own volition, it should do so only where it can clearly see that the contract is illegal.[72] **30.31**

Case Examples Relating to Maintenance and Champerty

The following are examples and counter-examples of maintenance and champertous maintenance. Very old cases have been disregarded. Only the briefest of descriptions of the facts is given—as an aid to, rather than a substitute for, further legal research. It should be borne in mind that many of the following examples would now be regarded as being lawful (and possibly even in line with public policy) by reason of the intervention of statute. **30.32**

The provision of legal services by a lawyer for a share of the proceeds (early 20th century onwards)

Where a solicitor agreed to represent a client for a share of the proceeds, the solicitor was found to have entered into a champertous agreement.[73] Whilst an extreme example, Waller LJ found that there was 'no clearer case of wanton and officious intermeddling' than a case in which a solicitor had initiated, funded and personally directed the proceedings.[74] **30.33**

Financial support in a commercial context (late 19th century)

A 'genuine pre-existing financial interest in maintaining the solvency of the person whose action he maintains' may be sufficient to avoid a finding of champerty.[75] Where, for example, litigation was funded by brokers who had a 4–5 per cent interest in the placement of the **30.34**

---

[71] *In re Trepca Mines Ltd (No 2)* [1963] Ch 199.

[72] *Ladiaev v Vallen* [2008] EWHC 1271 (Ch), at [105].

[73] *Wild v Simpson* [1919] 2 KB 544. See also *Haseldine v Hosken* [1933] All ER Rep 1 and the cases cited in that case, which include *Earle v Hopwood* (1861) 30 LJCP 217 and *Ford v Radford* (1920) 36 TLR 658. For a discussion of this topic in the context of the Courts and Legal Services Act 1990 (as amended) see 29.141–29.178 and 30.20–30.21. Whilst it was only a finding of *prima facie* case, see *Media Cat Ltd v Adams & Ors* [2011] EWPCC 010.

[74] *Nordstern Allgemeine Versicherungs AG v Internav Ltd* [1999] 2 Lloyd's Rep 139, at 142.

[75] *Trendtex Trading Corpn v Crédit Suisse* [1980] AC 629, at 668, *per* Oliver LJ, affirmed on appeal at [1982] AC 679.

contracts that were being litigated, no champerty existed, because their involvement came 'nowhere near' being wanton and officious intermeddling.[76] At the other end of the spectrum was a director who gave financial support to a specialist to bring a libel action arising out of adverse comments made about the specialist's own comments about the director's company's products, which was found to amount to maintenance.[77] Perhaps in the middle of the spectrum is where a consultancy undertook the effort, cost and risk of applying for *Norwich Pharmacal* orders and making claims against alleged copyright infringers in return for 'a handsome share of the proceeds', which Arnold J found not to be champertous, largely because it did not prevent the court from properly managing the case.[78]

Litigation support in a trade union setting (early 20th century)

30.35 Where a union funded a libel claim against a member's employer, that not being a stated benefit of membership, that was found to be maintenance.[79]

Litigation support in the context of a charity or other beneficial organisation (early 20th century)

30.36 Where a charity funded an action and provided litigation services to an examiner who wished to bring a defamation claim, that was found to be maintenance.[80]

Litigation support in the context of a commercial interest (early 21st century)

30.37 In response to the recognition that an overzealous application of the law of maintenance is capable of denying persons access to justice, the concept of a 'genuine commercial interest' has developed.[81] A contract between persons who had entered into a joint venture that one would provide the other with assistance in unrelated litigation was held not to be champertous, because the joint venture would have been adversely affected by a poor outcome in that litigation, so the supposed champerter had a genuine commercial interest in the matter.[82]

Assignment of a bare cause of action (early and mid-20th century to present day)

30.38 The common law abhorred the assignment of a bare cause of action.[83] The assignment of a bare right to bring a claim can be struck down as a transaction savouring of maintenance.[84] Where the facts permit, this can be the case even where the rights are debts that must be sued upon to be able to benefit from them.[85]

---

76 *Stocznia Gdanska SA v Latvian Shipping Co* [2001] BCC 174.

77 *Alabaster v Harness* [1895] 1 QB 339, CA.

78 *Golden Eye (International) Ltd v Telefonica UK Ltd* [2012] EWHC 723 (Ch), at [99].

79 *Greig v National Amalgamated Union of Shop Assistants, Warehousemen and Clerks* (1906) 22 TLR 274. See also *Oram v Hutt* [1914] 1 Ch 98, CA; cf *Hill v Archbold* [1968] 1 QB 686, in which *Greig* and *Oram* were doubted.

80 *Scott v National Society for Prevention of Cruelty to Children and Parr* (1909) 25 TLR 789.

81 See the discussion by Baroness Hale in *Massai Aviation Services v Attorney-General* [2007] UKPC 12, at [17].

82 *Crittenden v Bayliss* [2002] All ER (D) 92.

83 As modern examples, see *Simpson (as assignee of Catchpole) v Norfolk & Norwich University Hospital NHS Trust* [2011] EWCA Civ 1149, at [15]; *Skywell (UK) Ltd v Revenue & Customs Commissioners* [2012] UKFTT 611 (TC), at [19]. See also *Trendtex Trading Corpn v Crédit Suisse* [1982] AC 629.

84 *Glegg v Bromley* [1912] 3 KB 474, CA.

85 *Laurent v Sale & Co (a firm)* [1963] 2 All ER 63; cf *Camdex International Ltd v Bank of Zambia* [1996] 1 WLR 721, in which it was made clear that there is a distinction between assignment of a debt to a purchaser and an agreement that had maintenance or champerty as its object.

Assignment of a cause of action where the assignee has a commercial interest (late 20th and early 21st centuries)

An example of a genuine commercial interest was where a co-defendant settled as against the claimant, but took the claimant's claim against the other co-defendants.[86] Another example would be a 'borrowing' arrangement under which a subcontractor borrows the name of the main contractor for the purposes of pursuing a claim in which it has an interest.[87] **30.39**

Assignment of an associated cause of action (early 20th century)

Assignment of an associated right to bring a claim (such as where it is associated with a property transaction or a legitimate business interest) is not maintenance.[88] **30.40**

Trafficking in litigation (late 20th century)

Where an assignment of a cause of action would have been permissible by reason of the assignee having a legitimate business interest in the matter, it would amount to maintenance if the assignee were to take it for the purposes of reassigning it to a third party with no interest in the matter.[89] **30.41**

Assignment of a bare cause of action by a trustee or liquidator (late 20th century)

A trustee in bankruptcy or liquidator is in a privileged position in that it will not be contrary to public policy for such a person to assign a cause of action or to realise its value for the purposes of satisfying the demands of creditors.[90] A transaction such as that would not be maintenance. Where such a transaction is carried out, it would not be open to the court to make a pre-emptive order that a trustee in bankruptcy who assigns the claim will not be liable for costs of a successful defendant if the assigned claim fails.[91] **30.42**

Funding insolvent persons (late 20th century)

Whilst liquidators and trustees in bankruptcy may be able to assign a cause of action for payment of a sum of money in return, it does not follow that a person may fund an insolvent person to bring a claim. That would, in appropriate circumstances, amount to maintenance.[92] **30.43**

Funding a liquidator (late 20th century)

The funding of a liquidator to bring a claim against the directors of the liquidated company was found to be capable of amounting to maintenance (especially where the funders had a degree of control over the litigation).[93] **30.44**

---

86 See, eg, *Brownton v Edward Moore Inbucon Ltd* [1985] 3 All ER 499.

87 For a discussion of this, see Patterson, L, 'Identity Crisis' (2008) 23 Building 69; see also *London and Regional (St George's Court) Ltd v Ministry of Defence* [2008] EWHC 526 (TCC).

88 See the discussion in *Trendtex Trading Corpn v Crédit Suisse* [1982] AC 629; *Martell v Consett Iron Co Ltd* [1954] 3 All ER 339.

89 *Trendtex Trading Corpn v Crédit Suisse* [1982] AC 629.

90 *Circuit Systems Ltd (in liquidation) v Zuken-Redac (UK) Ltd* [1999] 2 AC 1, at 2.

91 *Hunt (trustee in bankruptcy of Harb) v Harb & Ors* [2011] EWCA Civ 1239, at [19], [26] and [28].

92 *Grovewood Holdings plc v James Capel & Co Ltd* [1995] Ch 80.

93 *Re Oasis Merchandising Services Ltd* [1998] Ch 170.

Supply of information for the purposes of litigation (late 19th century)

30.45 It will not necessarily be maintenance (or, at least, not champertous maintenance) to supply information in return for a share of the proceeds,[94] but it may become maintenance if the agreement itself involves court proceedings.[95]

Assisting with a dispute resolution procedure other than litigation (late 20th century)

30.46 Providing services for the purpose of representing a person in a valuation court in return for a conditional fee was not maintenance (or, at least, not champertous maintenance), because the dispute resolution procedure was found to be administration, rather than litigation.[96] The provision of services by a surveyor in a planning inquiry for a conditional fee was held not to be maintenance for similar reasons.[97]

The deduction of legal costs (late 20th century)

30.47 In the context of family law, in a claim against a husband who was better able to fund the litigation than was the wife, Wilson J held that an agreement to deduct legal costs of proceedings from a divorce award was not champertous or unlawful.[98]

ATE policies and litigant funding (early 21st century)

30.48 Whilst it is an issue that almost never arises in this jurisdiction, Hogan J (an Irish judge) has found that ATE policies are not necessarily champertous,[99] despite the fact that, in so far as maintenance and champerty are concerned, the Irish courts tend to be less flexible than English courts. Although not in a binding decision, Master Hurst has found that calculating an ATE premium as being 20 per cent of the damages awarded in a road traffic accident claim was not champertous on the basis that the insurer was seeking to profit from the insurance rather than from the litigation.[100] Litigation (third-party) funding is lawful in England and Wales,[101] but this is not the case in many other common-law jurisdictions.[102]

The provision of support services to an expert (early 21st century)

30.49 Where a firm of accountants had agreed to provide services on a contingency fee basis, but where it was not acting as experts and where it had limited its role to providing support services for other accountants who were acting as experts, its involvement was not champertous.[103]

---

[94] *Hutley v Hutley* (1873) LR 8 QB 112. Even in ancient times, there was nothing objectionable about an agreement merely to give information in return for a share of the proceeds where the informant took no further part in the litigation: see *Stanley v Jones* (1831) 7 Bing 369; *Spyre v Porter* (1856) 7 E & B 58.

[95] See the Irish case of *Fraser v Buckle* [1996] 2 IRLM 34.

[96] *Pickering (t/a City Agents) v Sogex Services (UK) Ltd* [1982] 1 EGLR 42.

[97] *Picton Jones & Co v Arcadia Developments Ltd* [1989] 1 EGLR 43.

[98] *Sears Tooth (a firm) v Payne Hick Beach (a firm) & Ors* [1997] 2 FLR 116.

[99] *Greenclean Waste Management Ltd v Leahy (No 2)* [2014] IEHC 314, reversed on other grounds on appeal ([2015] IECA 97).

[100] *Pirie v Ayling* [2003] EWHC 9006 (Costs).

[101] See the discussion of 'commercial funders' at 9.32 and at 33.08–33.26. See also *Arkin v Borchard* [2005] EWCA Civ 655.

[102] See, eg, the Irish case of *Thema International Fund PLC v HSBC Institutional Trust Services (Ireland) Ltd & Ors* [2011] IEHC 357.

[103] *R v Secretary of State for Transport, ex p Factortame* [2002] EWCA Civ 932.

The provision of investigative services (early 21st century)

Underhill J declined to find that an agreement made by a journalist to use his investigative skills to assist a person to bring a claim in return for a percentage of the damages was champertous.[104] **30.50**

Expert witnesses and professional assistance (early 21st century to present day)

Phillips MR has commented (*obiter*) that the dangers of allowing an expert to be funded on a conditional basis were great, so it would be 'very rare indeed' that the court would be prepared to consent to an expert being funded in such a way.[105] In contrast, Cresswell J found that the involvement of a marine recovery specialist on a contingent basis was not champertous for several reasons, one of which was the fact that the activities of the specialist were subject to the control of the claimant's solicitors and therefore the specialists had only a limited opportunity to influence the outcome.[106] Similarly, Judge Seymour QC (sitting in the Technology and Construction Court) found that an agreement to provide consultancy services in return for a share of the damages was not champertous.[107] **30.51**

Beneficial associations (late 20th century)

Where an organisation exists to provide benefits for its members, it may have an interest in funding its members' claims. An example would be where a trade union brought actions on behalf of its members for damages arising out of industrial accidents[108] or where a union funded liable actions.[109] **30.52**

Shared interest in a pastime (mid-20th century)

Where the members of an angling club gave assistance to a claim that dealt with the pollution in a river, they were held to have a genuine interest in the matter.[110] **30.53**

Interest in land (early 21st century)

Where a person has an interest in property and where that interest may be affected by the litigation, they may have a sufficient interest to justify providing assistance in that litigation.[111] **30.54**

---

[104] *Mansell v Robinson* [2007] EWHC 101 (QB).

[105] *R v Secretary of State for Transport, ex p Factortame* [2002] EWCA Civ 932, at [72]–[73]; cf Chadwick LJ's comments in *Hamilton v Al Fayed & Ors* [2002] EWCA Civ 665, at [69].

[106] *Papera Traders Co Ltd v Hyundai (Merchant) Marine Co Ltd (No 2)* [2002] 2 Lloyds LR 692.

[107] *Dal-Sterling Group plc v WSP South & West Ltd* (unreported), 18 July 2001, TCC, *per* HHJ Seymour QC.

[108] See *Bourne v Colodense Ltd* (1998) The Times, 4 February; *Allen v Francis* [1914] 3 KB 1065, CA, at 1067.

[109] *Hill v Archbold* [1968] 1 QB 686; cf *Greig v National Amalgamated Union of Shop Assistants, Warehousemen and Clerks* (1906) 22 TLR 274 and *Oram v Hutt* [1914] 1 Ch 98, CA.

[110] *Martell v Consett Iron Co Ltd* [1955] Ch 363, at 387.

[111] *London and Regional (St George's Court) Ltd v Ministry of Defence* [2008] EWHC 526 (TCC); *Alabaster v Harness* [1894] 2 QB 897. In the context of liability to pay rent, see *Findon v Parker* (1843) 11 M & W 675.

31

CONTRACTS OF RETAINER (INTERPRETATION AND IMPLIED TERMS)

31.01 The discussion in this book is only the briefest of introductions to contractual interpretation; specialist texts ought to be consulted for a more detailed discussion. This chapter deals with the following topics:

- overview of contractual interpretation (31.02);
- background facts and contractual interpretation (31.05);
- the role of commercial common sense (31.14);
- the interpretation of inconsistent terms (31.34);
- the interpretation of ambiguous terms (31.38);
- the interpretation of mistakenly drafted contracts (31.41);
- the interpretation of contracts of retainer in which terms are seemingly missing (31.48);
- the roles of joinder (31.52) and severance (31.56);
- the implication of contractual terms in general (31.57); and
- specific implied terms in the context of contracts of retainers (31.69).

Overview of the Interpretation of Contracts of Retainer

31.02 The construction of a contract of retainer (or any contract) is a question of law.[1] The starting point—which has been reaffirmed many times—is the following speech of Lord Hoffmann:

> '(1) Interpretation is the ascertainment of the meaning which the document would convey to a reasonable person having all the background knowledge which would reasonably have been available to the parties in the situation in which they were at the time of the contract.
>
> (2) The background was famously referred to by Lord Wilberforce as the "matrix of fact", but this phrase is if anything an understated description of what the background may include. Subject to the requirement that it should be reasonably available to the parties and to the exception mentioned next, it includes absolutely anything which would have affected the way in which the language of the document would have been understood by a reasonable man.
>
> (3) The law excludes from the admissible background the previous negotiations of the parties and their declarations of subjective intent. They are admissible only in an action for rectification. The law makes this distinction for reasons of practical policy and, in

[1] *Woodhouse AC Israel Cocoa Ltd SA v Nigerian Produce Marketing Co* [1972] AC 741, at 770, *per* Lord Salmon.

this respect only legal interpretation differs from the way we interpret utterances in ordinary life . . .

(4) The meaning which a document (or any other utterance) would convey to a reasonable man is not the same thing as the meaning of its words. The meaning of words is a matter of dictionaries and grammars; the meaning of a document is what the parties using those words against the relevant background would reasonably have been understood to mean . . .

(5) The rule that words should be given their "natural and ordinary meaning" reflects the common-sense proposition that we do not easily accept that people have made linguistic mistakes, particularly in formal documents. On the other hand, if one would nevertheless conclude from the background that something must have gone wrong with the language, the law does not require judges to attribute to the parties an intention which they plainly could not have had . . .'[2]

Thus interpretation is the ascertainment of the meaning that the document would convey to a reasonable person having all of the background knowledge that was reasonably available to the parties at the time the contract was made. That process: **31.03**

- will take into account the 'matrix of fact'—or, in more modern parlance, the background facts (see 31.05–31.08);
- will not take into account the previous negotiations of the parties—although they may be admissible for the purposes of rectification (see 32.67–32.74);
- is not the same as merely determining the meaning of the words used; and
- may, in an appropriate case, permit the court to work on the basis that the parties made a mistake in their use of language (see 31.41–31.47).

In 2015, Lord Neuberger gave the following summary of what the process of interpretation involves: **31.04**

> 'When interpreting a written contract, the court is concerned to identify the intention of the parties by reference to "what a reasonable person having all the background knowledge which would have been available to the parties would have understood them to be using the language in the contract to mean", to quote Lord Hoffmann in *Chartbrook Ltd v Persimmon Homes Ltd* . . . And it does so by focussing on the meaning of the relevant words . . . in their documentary, factual and commercial context. That meaning has to be assessed in the light of (i) the natural and ordinary meaning of the clause, (ii) any other relevant provisions of the [contract], (iii) the overall purpose of the clause and the [contract], (iv) the facts and circumstances known or assumed by the parties at the time that the document was executed, and (v) commercial common sense, but (vi) disregarding subjective evidence of any party's intentions.'[3]

Background Facts and Contractual Interpretation

As has been mentioned above, the 'matrix of fact' (that is, the background facts) may be relevant. What follows (see 31.06–31.13) focuses on issues that are likely to be relevant to the interpretation of contracts of retainer. **31.05**

[2] *Investors Compensation Scheme v West Bromwich Building Society* [1998] 1 WLR 896, HL, at 912.

[3] *Arnold v Britton* [2015] UKSC 36, at [15], citing Lord Hoffmann in *Chartbrook Ltd v Persimmon Homes Ltd* [2009] UKHL 38, at [14].

31.06 In 2015, Lord Neuberger restated the law[4] in such a way as to cause some commentators to say that he had recalibrated the extent to which the court gives weight to the background facts,[5] but it has now been made clear that this was not so.[6] Lord Hodge has explained that 'textualism and contextualism are not conflicting paradigms in a battle for exclusive occupation of the field of contractual interpretation'.[7]

31.07 If—as will often be the case with contracts of retainer—the contract in question has been tightly drafted, then it may not be necessary to have much regard to the background facts; the opposite may be true of the interpretation of an informal, brief or complex contract (especially if the contract was drafted in a commercial context). Lord Hodge noted that, in circumstances in which professionals were involved in the creation of the contract (which, again, is common in so far as contracts of retainer are concerned), the contract may not achieve 'a logical and coherent text because of, for example, the conflicting aims of the parties, failures of communication, differing drafting practices, or deadlines which require the parties to compromise in order to reach agreement'.[8] In these circumstances, it may be necessary to examine the background facts.

31.08 In this regard, Lord Clarke had the following to say:

> '[T]he ultimate aim of interpreting a provision in a contract, especially a commercial contract, is to determine what the parties meant by the language used, which involves ascertaining what a reasonable person would have understood the parties to have meant. As Lord Hoffmann made clear in the first of the principles he summarised in the *Investors Compensation Scheme* case [see 31.02], the relevant reasonable person is one who has all the background knowledge which would reasonably have been available to the parties in the situation in which they were at the time of the contract.'[9]

Hindsight is not permissible

31.09 Lord Neuberger made the following points about what may and may not be taken into account as being background facts:

> 'When interpreting a contractual provision, one can only take into account facts or circumstances which existed at the time that the contract was made, and which were known or reasonably available to both parties. Given that a contract is a bilateral, or synallagmatic, arrangement involving both parties, it cannot be right, when interpreting a contractual provision, to take into account a fact or circumstance known only to one of the parties.'[10]

Thus the court may take into account only that knowledge which would reasonably have been available to the parties in the situation in which they were at the time of the contract.[11] Hindsight is not permitted.

---

4 *Arnold v Britton* [2015] UKSC 36.

5 See, eg, Havelock, R, 'Return to Tradition in Contractual Interpretation' (2016) 27(2) KJL 188.

6 See *Wood v Capita Insurance Services Ltd* [2017] UKSC 24, at [9], *per* Lord Hodge (with whom Lord Neuberger, Lord Mance, Lord Clarke and Lord Sumption agreed). Lord Hodge made it clear that *Arnold v Britton* [2015] UKSC 36 was not a recalibration of the approach summarised in *Rainy Sky v Kookmin Bank* [2011] UKSC 50.

7 *Wood v Capita Insurance Services Ltd* [2017] UKSC 24, at [13].

8 *Ibid.*

9 See *Rainy Sky SA v Kookmin Bank* [2011] UKSC 50, at [14].

10 *Arnold v Britton* [2015] UKSC 36, at [21].

11 See also *Zoan v Rouamba* [2000] 2 All ER 620, at [36]; that said, see *White v White* [2001] UKHL 9, [2001] 2 All ER 43.

If unanticipated circumstances arise, one or both parties may be tempted to use hindsight for the purposes of showing that a particular interpretation lacks business common sense. Lord Neuberger had this to say on the topic: **31.10**

> '[C]ommercial common sense is not to be invoked retrospectively. The mere fact that a contractual arrangement, if interpreted according to its natural language, has worked out badly, or even disastrously, for one of the parties is not a reason for departing from the natural language. Commercial common sense is only relevant to the extent of how matters would or could have been perceived by the parties, or by reasonable people in the position of the parties, as at the date that the contract was made.'[12]

Matters of law as background facts

The background facts may include the state of the law.[13] Lord Hoffmann has commented (*obiter*) that the parties are unlikely to have intended to agree to something that was inherently unlawful or legally ineffective.[14] Those comments that often have particular resonance where the dispute concerns the enforceability of a retainer (see 31.29)—especially where the challenge is brought by a stranger to the contract (that is, a paying party who seeks to avoid paying costs in reliance upon the indemnity principle). There is, however, a limit to the extent that clients can be expected to know the law. By way of example, Walker J declined to interpret a contract of retainer on the basis that the client, who was not a lawyer, ought to have known that interest would be payable only if statute bills (as opposed to mere requests for payments on account) had been delivered; instead, he approached the matter on the basis of 'an objective reader without special knowledge of [the Solicitors] Act 1974'.[15] **31.11**

Evidential matters and background facts

Expert evidence may be admissible as to what the parties to the contract would reasonably have known or as to any market practice that might inform how the reasonable person would understand the document.[16] That said, the court often will dismiss evidence of the commercial purpose of the contract as too argumentative and trespassing on the legal sphere.[17] **31.12**

Evidence of prior negotiations

As has already been mentioned (see 31.02), Lord Hoffmann explained that the law excludes from the admissible background the previous negotiations of the parties and their declarations of subjective intent.[18] This is known as the rule against parol evidence. Not everyone agrees that the rule is as absolute as was stated by Lord Hoffmann,[19] but, in practical terms, disputes concerning supposedly prior negotiations regarding contracts of retainer rarely arise. This is because discussions regarding the terms of the retainer tend to be **31.13**

---

12 *Arnold v Britton* [2015] UKSC 36, at [19].
13 *Zoan v Rouamba* [2000] 2 All ER 620, at [36].
14 *Bank of Credit and Commerce International SA (in liquidation) v Ali* [2001] UKHL 8, at [39].
15 *Vlamaki v Sookias & Sookias* [2015] EWHC 3334 (QB), at [23].
16 See *Crema v Cenkos Securities plc* [2010] EWCA Civ 1444.
17 See, eg, *US Bank Trustees Ltd v Titan Europe 2007-1 (NHP) Ltd* [2014] EWHC 1189 (Ch), at [24].
18 *Investors Compensation Scheme v West Bromwich Building Society* [1998] 1 WLR 896, HL, at 912.
19 See, eg, Lord Nicholls, 'My Kingdom for a Horse: The Meaning of Words' (2005) 121 LQR 577.

admissible for other reasons (usually arising out of the fact that the legal services provider had a duty to give advice about funding).[20]

The Role of Commercial Common Sense

31.14 Where the words and the commercial intent are clear and plain, interpreting a contract will pose no problems. The exercise is, however, often a more nuanced process of balancing the clarity of the words against the commerciality of the outcome: the clearer the words, the more extreme the outcome must be to displace them. What follows is a discussion of how the court deals with such matters.

31.15 If the outcome is so uncommercial as to lead to the conclusion that something has gone wrong with the language, the court may be able to depart entirely from words used (see 31.30).

The relationship between the meaning of the words used and business common sense

31.16 In *Investors Compensation Scheme Ltd*,[21] Lord Hoffmann confirmed that the changes in approach over the previous 30 years or so meant that any concept of a 'legal' interpretation—a strict adherence to the words used—was dead. In particular, it was no longer the case that parties would be tripped up by linguistic accidents; instead, the courts would seek to find 'the meaning which the document would convey to a reasonable person having all the knowledge which would have been available to the parties in the situation in which they were in at the time of the contract'.[22]

31.17 During the 2000s, there was a gradual acceptance of business common sense being an increasingly significant factor in this regard.[23] Indeed, in 2011, Lord Clarke explained that if there are two possible constructions, the court is entitled to prefer that construction which is consistent with business common sense and to reject the other.[24]

31.18 By 2015, however, Lord Neuberger gave the following guidance:

> '[T]he reliance placed in some cases on commercial common sense and surrounding circumstances ... should not be invoked to undervalue the importance of the language of the provision which is to be construed. The exercise of interpreting a provision involves identifying what the parties meant through the eyes of a reasonable reader, and, save perhaps in a very unusual case, that meaning is most obviously to be gleaned from the language of the provision. Unlike commercial common sense and the surrounding circumstances, the parties have control over the language they use in a contract. And, again save perhaps in a very unusual case, the parties must have been specifically focussing on the issue covered by the provision when agreeing the wording of that provision.'[25]

---

[20] See, eg, *Stevensdrake Ltd v Hunt* [2016] EWHC 342 (Ch), at [100], *per* Judge Simon Barker QC (sitting as a judge of the High Court).

[21] *Investors Compensation Scheme v West Bromwich Building Society* [1998] 1 WLR 896, HL.

[22] *Ibid*, at 912.

[23] For an historical overview, see Gibbons, K, 'The Strange Death of Literal England', Clifford Chance Client Briefing, November 2009.

[24] See *Rainy Sky SA v Kookmin Bank* [2011] UKSC 50, at [31].

[25] *Arnold v Britton* [2015] UKSC 36, at [17].

Thus care must be taken not to undervalue the importance of the language of the provision that is to be construed. This is not, however, a rejection of Lord Hoffmann's test in favour of some traditional 'plain meaning' approach—a point that Lord Hodge made clear in 2017.[26] He explained that Lord Neuberger's comments were not 'a recalibration' of the approach summarised by Lord Clarke, as set out at 31.08.[27]

As to the extent to which the court may depart from the natural meaning of the words used in cases in which they have not been clearly drafted, Lord Neuberger made the following comments: **31.19**

> '[W]hen it comes to considering the centrally relevant words to be interpreted, I accept that the less clear they are, or, to put it another way, the worse their drafting, the more ready the court can properly be to depart from their natural meaning. That is simply the obverse of the sensible proposition that the clearer the natural meaning the more difficult it is to justify departing from it. However, that does not justify the court embarking on an exercise of searching for, let alone constructing, drafting infelicities in order to facilitate a departure from the natural meaning. If there is a specific error in the drafting, it may often have no relevance to the issue of interpretation which the court has to resolve.'[28]

Thus the clearer the words, the more extreme the outcome must be to displace them. This echoed the comments that Aikens LJ had said two years previously (in 2013): **31.20**

> ' "[C]ommercial common sense" is not to be elevated to an overriding criterion of construction and, secondly ... the parties should not be subjected to "... the individual judge's own notions of what might have been the sensible solution to the parties' conundrum" ... still less should the issue of construction be determined by what seems like "commercial common sense" from the point of view of one of the parties to the contract.'[29]

The place of business common sense in general

For the reasons set out above, the modern approach to contractual interpretation does not place undue emphasis on business common sense, but instead ensures that the importance of the language of the provision in question is respected. This does not mean, however, that the court will disregard business common sense. Indeed, in modern times, it has always been the case that the court will strive to interpret contracts (including contracts of retainer) in such a way as to be commercially coherent while seeking to avoid a plainly unreasonable result. For the reasons set out at 31.26–31.29, this has been a particularly important aspect of interpreting contracts of retainer that are said be ineffective or unenforceable. **31.21**

The following speeches of the House of Lords are worth noting. **31.22**

- Speaking as long ago as 1974, Lord Reid had this to say on the point:

> 'The fact that a particular construction leads to a very unreasonable result must be a relevant consideration. The more unreasonable the result the more unlikely it is that the parties can

---

26 *Wood v Capita Insurance Services Ltd* [2017] UKSC 24, at [8]–[14].
27 *Ibid*, at [9].
28 *Arnold v Britton* [2015] UKSC 36, at [18].
29 *BMA Special Opportunity Hub Fund Ltd v African Minerals Finance Ltd* [2013] EWCA Civ 416, at [24].

have intended it, and if they do intend it the more necessary it is that they shall make that intention abundantly clear.'[30]

- In a similar vein, speaking in 1985 in the context of a commercial matter other than the law of costs, Lord Diplock said this: 'If a detailed semantic and syntactical analysis of words in a commercial contract is going to lead to a conclusion that flouts business common sense, it must be made to yield to business common sense.'[31]
- And, in 2005, Lord Bingham said this:

> 'The task of the court is to ascertain and give effect to the intentions of the contracting parties, so that a business sense will be given to business documents ... [The court] must seek to give effect to the contract as intended, so as not to frustrate the reasonable expectations of businessmen.'[32]

31.23 For the reasons set out at 31.19 and 31.20, all of these comments still have resonance today. In the context of the interpretation of retainers, in particular, the avoidance of unreasonable results and the notion that the contract should make commercial sense may be of particular relevance.[33]

No rewriting of the contract

31.24 Notwithstanding the court's desire to avoid unreasonable results, Peter Gibson LJ has explained that there are limits to the extent to which the court is able to depart from what is written in the instrument of the contract:

> 'The court is entitled to look at those consequences because the more extreme they are, the less likely it is that commercial men will have intended an agreement with that result. But the court is not entitled to rewrite the bargain which they have made merely to accord with what the court thinks to be a more reasonable result.'[34]

Thus the court is not entitled to rewrite the contract.

31.25 In a similar vein, Lord Neuberger made the following observation regarding the interplay between commercial common sense and seemingly imprudent bargains:

> 'While commercial common sense is a very important factor to take into account when interpreting a contract, a court should be very slow to reject the natural meaning of a provision as correct simply because it appears to be a very imprudent term for one of the parties to have agreed, even ignoring the benefit of wisdom of hindsight. The purpose of interpretation is to identify what the parties have agreed, not what the court thinks that they should have agreed.'[35]

---

[30] *L Schuler AG v Wickman Machine Tools Sales Ltd* [1974] AC 235, at 236; followed in *SimplySure Ltd & Anor v Personal Touch Financial Services Ltd* [2016] EWCA Civ 461.

[31] *Antaios Compania Naviera v Salen Rederierna* [1985] AC 191, at 221.

[32] *The Starsin* [2004] 1 AC 715, HL, at [9]–[12].

[33] As an example of this, see *Manning v Kings College Hospital NHS Trust* [2011] EWHC 2954 (QB) (see 31.25).

[34] *Kazakstan Wool Processors (Europe) Ltd v Nederlandsche Credietverzekering Maatschappij* [2000] 1 All ER (Comm) 708, at 719.

[35] *Arnold v Britton* [2015] UKSC 36, at [20]. See also *US Bank Trustees Ltd v Titan Europe 2007-1 (NHP) Ltd* [2014] EWHC 1189 (Ch), at [25], *per* Mr Richard Snowden QC (sitting as a deputy judge of the High Court).

That said, where appropriate, the court may be inclined to generosity in this regard.[36]

Avoidance of interpretations that render the contract ineffective or unenforceable

Contractual ineffectiveness Where there are competing interpretations and where one of the interpretations may lead to a commercially sound result (such as a retainer being enforceable), the court may prefer the commercially coherent result over an incoherent result. In particular, the court will seek to avoid an interpretation that destroys the contract.[37] In this regard, Lord Hoffmann commented that 'the parties are unlikely to have intended to agree to something unlawful or legally ineffective'.[38] **31.26**

Speaking in the context of offers rather than contracts of retainer, Rix LJ had this to say: **31.27**

> 'Another principle or maxim of construction ... is that words should be understood in such a way that the matter is effective rather than ineffective (*verba ita sunt intelligenda ut res magis valeat quam pereat*) ... There are numerous instances of the application of this maxim. This is how *Chitty on Contracts*, 30th ed, 2008, Vol 1, at para 12-081 refers to this rule:
>
> > "If the words used in an agreement are susceptible of two meanings, one of which would validate the instrument or the particular clause in the instrument, and the other render it void, ineffective or meaningless, the former sense is to be adopted. This rule is often expressed in the phrase *ut res magis valeat cum* [*sc. quam*] *pereat*. Thus, if by a particular construction the agreement would be rendered ineffectual and the apparent object of the contract would be frustrated, but another construction, though by itself less appropriate looking to the words only, would produce a different effect, the latter interpretation is to be applied, if that is how the agreement would be understood by a reasonable man with a knowledge of the commercial purpose and background of the transaction. So, where the words of a guarantee were capable of expressing either a past or a concurrent consideration, the court adopted the latter construction, because the former would render the instrument void. If one construction makes the contract lawful and the other unlawful, the former is to be preferred ...".'[39]

Where the challenge is brought by a paying party, there will be a certain amount of overlap between these principles and *contra proferentem* (see 31.40). The extent to which the court will seek to preserve the effect of a contract of retainer in such a way is limited, however; in particular, Warby J has pointed out that it would have no application at all in cases in which the words were clear.[40] **31.28**

Contractual unenforceability In so far as costs litigation is concerned, the points made at 31.21–31.27 are relevant because the court has repeatedly confirmed that it is legitimate to interpret a contract of retainer as part of the process of deciding whether it is enforceable. This topic has already been touched upon at 29.63–29.64, where—in the context of regulatory compliance—it was referred to as 'prior interpretation' (otherwise known as anterior **31.29**

---

[36] As an example of this, see *Manning v Kings College Hospital NHS Trust* [2011] EWHC 2954 (QB). See also *Solly v Forbes* (1820) 2 Brod & Bing 38, at 48; *Haigh v Brooks* (1839) 10 Ad & El 309.

[37] See, eg, *Kredietbank Antwerp v Midland Bank plc* [1998] Lloyd's Rep Bank 173.

[38] *Bank of Credit and Commerce International SA (in liquidation) v Ali* [2001] UKHL 8, at [39].

[39] *C v D* [2011] EWCA Civ 646, at [55].

[40] *Radford v Frade* [2016] EWHC 1600 (QB), at [28], *per* Warby J. This decision was affirmed on appeal ([2018] EWCA Civ 119), but on a different point.

interpretation.[41] It is an example of the court taking into account the state of the law as being part of the background against which the retainer is to be interpreted (see 31.11), this being a well-established method by which (in the words of Lord Hoffmann) the court 'takes into account that the parties are unlikely to have intended to agree to something unlawful or legally ineffective'.[42]

31.30 **Mistakes** It may be that the parties' use of language has gone so badly wrong that the court is able to conclude that the parties made a mistake and used the wrong words or syntax.[43] The approach that the court may take in such circumstances is discussed at 31.42–31.47.

31.31 That said, Lord Hoffmann emphasised that the court 'does not readily accept that people have made mistakes' in formal documents.[44] Lord Neuberger MR (citing Lord Hoffman) explained that, before the court can be satisfied that something has gone wrong, the court has to be satisfied both that there has been 'a clear mistake' and that it is clear 'what correction ought to be made'.[45]

The relevance of the use of standard wording and model contracts

31.32 Where the parties choose to use standard wording, the context of an individual transaction becomes of significance. Whilst he was dealing with a matter other than contract of retainer, Andrew Smith J had this to say on the point:

> '[W]hen parties choose to use for a contract a standard wording ... generally their own circumstances at the time of the contract will not affect the interpretation of the wording. By choosing standard wording, parties usually evince an intention that the wording as incorporated into their contract should be given its usual meaning.'[46]

31.33 In the context of costs law, this may be relevant if, for example, a solicitor chooses to use a standard contract of retainer, such as the template conditional fee agreements published by the Law Society. That said, whilst it is generally true to say that some standard forms are 'intended to be normative, and to apply in many different situations and with as much straightforward application as possible',[47] model contracts of retainer tend to drafted in such a way as to permit their adaptation to the matter in hand. As such, it would be a mistake to regard model contracts of retainer as necessarily being normative.

---

[41] An example of prior interpretation is *Tichband v Hurdman* [2003] 1 WLR 2487, in which the Court of Appeal resolved a conflict between what was said in the body of a conditional fee agreement and what was said in the risk assessment. The court applied the Conditional Fee Agreements Regulations 2000 (SI 2000/692) to the agreement as interpreted, thereby saving the agreement. The court considered the enforceability of the retainer not on the basis of what it said upon its face in literal terms, but on the basis of what—properly interpreted—it was understood to mean. Other examples exist: see, eg, *Jones v Wrexham Borough Council* [2007] EWCA Civ 1356; for an example of the limits of the approach of prior interpretation, see *Jones v Caradon Catnic Ltd* [2005] EWCA Civ 1821.

[42] *Bank of Credit and Commerce International SA (in liquidation) v Ali* [2001] UKHL 8, at [39].

[43] See *Pink Floyd Music Ltd & Anor v EMI Records Ltd* [2010] EWCA Civ 1429, at [20], *per* Lord Neuberger MR.

[44] *Chartbrook Ltd v Persimmon Homes Ltd* [2009] UKHL 38, at [20].

[45] See *Pink Floyd Music Ltd & Anor v EMI Records Ltd* [2010] EWCA Civ 1429, at [20], *per* Lord Neuberger MR, citing Lord Hoffman in *Chartbrook Ltd v Persimmon Homes Ltd* [2009] UKHL 38, at [22]–[24].

[46] *SwissMarine Corpn Ltd v O W Supply & Trading A/S* [2015] EWHC 1571 (Comm), at [27].

[47] *Lehman Brothers Finance SA v SAL Oppenheim jr & Cie KGAA* [2014] EWHC 2627 (Comm), at [25].

The Interpretation of Inconsistent Terms

A problem that often arises in the context of costs litigation is where a contract of retainer contains inconsistent terms. This usually happens because a firm's standard terms and conditions have been unthinkingly incorporated without the drafter standing back to look at the effect of the totality of their efforts. Steyn J had this to say about the issue of inconsistent terms (albeit in a context other than costs litigation): 'This question must be approached on the basis that the court's duty is to reconcile seemingly inconsistent provisions if that result can conscientiously and fairly be achieved.'[48] Likewise, Rix LJ endorsed the following extract from a well-known textbook: 'The court is reluctant to hold that parts of a contract are inconsistent with each other, and will give effect to any reasonable construction which harmonises such clauses.'[49] **31.34**

Where there are inconsistent terms, the first port of call will be the retainer itself: many retainers will make express provision for the resolution of conflicts caused by drafting errors. Indeed, standard terms often contain a provision that expressly defers to the instrument into which they have been incorporated. **31.35**

In any event, the court will strive to give effect to that term which records the true intentions of the counterparties.[50] Whilst they should not be afforded the status of rules and should always be viewed in the context of Lord Hoffmann's guidance, as set out at 31.02, a number of older judicial methods can be described which (depending on the facts) may still be of some help in the interpretation of contracts of retainer. **31.36**

- **Bespoke terms** Generally speaking, where a standard term conflicts with a bespoke term, the latter will prevail.[51] Thus, if the body of a client care letter provides for one hourly rate, but standard terms and conditions provide for a different hourly rate, the former will usually prevail over the latter.
- **Incorporation of documents** In a similar vein, where a contract incorporates the terms of another document and the terms of that other document conflict with the terms of the contract, the terms of the contract will (depending on facts) tend to prevail.[52]
- **Terms repugnant to the contract as a whole** Where a term is repugnant to the contract as a whole, it may, in appropriate circumstances, be rejected.[53] In the context of costs, an example might be where a typographical error has led to a supposed hourly rate of nil (see 31.45).

---

[48] *The Brabant* [1967] 1 QB 588, at 589.

[49] *C v D* [2011] EWCA Civ 646, at [51], endorsing Lewison, K, *The Interpretation of Contracts* (4th edn, London: Sweet & Maxwell, 2004), para 9.13.

[50] *Love v Rowtor Steamship Co Ltd* [1916] 2 AC 527, at 535.

[51] *Glynn v Margetson & Co* [1893] AC 351; see also *Robertson v French* (1803) 4 East 130; cf *Smith v Royce Properties Ltd* [2001] EWCA 949, in which Tuckey LJ was careful to point out that there is no presumption of law.

[52] See the comments of Buckley LJ in *Modern Building Wales Ltd v Limmer and Trinidad Co Ltd* [1975] 1 WLR 1281, CA. See also *Sabah Flour and Feed Mills Sdn Bhd v Comfez Ltd* [1988] 2 Lloyd's Rep 18, CA; *Adamastos Shipping Co Ltd v Anglo-Saxon Petroleum* [1959] AC 133, at 178.

[53] *Adamastos Shipping Co Ltd v Anglo-Saxon Petroleum* [1959] AC 133; see also *Glynn v Margetson & Co* [1893] AC 351, *per* Lord Halsbury, LC.

- **Later repugnant clause** Where a clause in a contract is followed by a later clause that destroys the effect of the first clause, the later clause is generally rejected as repugnant. If, however, the later clause can be read as qualifying, rather than destroying, the effect of the first clause, then the two are to be read together and effect given to both.[54] An example might be where a non-contentious retainer makes provision for payment by way of an hourly rate and a value charge, but where that provision is supposedly destroyed by a later clause, which provides for payment on the basis of only an hourly rate. If the latter seemingly destroyed the entitlement to the value charge, then the former would probably prevail, but if they were capable of being read together, the former would probably be read as if it had been qualified by the latter.
- **Terms as to quantum** A contract that provides for two mutually inconsistent measures of quantum is not unusual (in the context of costs, for example where it provides for two inconsistent hourly rates). It is usually possible to decide that one is to be preferred over the other without the contract itself being at risk.[55] This may be relevant if it is argued that the retainer is void for uncertainty.

Some of these examples may properly be regarded as falling into the category of mistakes (see 31.41–31.47).

Case examples

31.37 Most authorities relate to contracts other than retainers, but there are one or two examples that relate specifically to contracts of retainer. For example, Hodge J had to decide what to make of a conditional fee agreement that had been adapted to provide for a bespoke definition of 'win' with such ineptitude that the term was afforded two mutually inconsistent definitions. Hodge J resolved the conflict by preferring that interpretation which best suited the unusual purpose to which the retainer had been put; as a result, the costs were recoverable in accordance with the true intentions of the counterparties.[56]

The Interpretation of Ambiguous Terms

31.38 Ambiguous terms are more troublesome. This is because the court's task is often more complex and nuanced than merely choosing between two competing terms. There are many examples that may be found in textbooks on the law of contracts, but it should not be forgotten that each case will be decided on its own facts.

31.39 It will often be the case that ambiguity arises only by reason of a detailed forensic examination of the retainer by a paying party. Where this is the case, it may be appropriate to ensure that the examination of the retainer does not descend into an inappropriate level of detail. Speaking in a context other than costs, Neill LJ indicated: 'Construction is a composite exercise neither uncompromisingly literal nor unswervingly purposive. The instrument must speak for itself but must do so *in situ* and not be transported to the laboratory

[54] *Forbes v Git* [1922] 1 AC 256, *per* Lord Wrenbury.
[55] *Love and Stewart Ltd v Rowtor Steamship Co Ltd* [1916] 2 AC 527, HL.
[56] *Wood v Worthing & Southlands Hospitals NHS Trust* (unreported), 18 October 2004, QBD. Another similar example has already been mentioned at 10.39.

for microscopic analysis.'[57] Those comments may well have resonance in cases in which the facts cry out for a common-sense approach rather than an overly legalistic one.

Contra proferentem

Another principle that may occasionally be of assistance is *contra proferentem*.[58] This principle (which is not a rule of law, but merely an aid to interpretation) is that where a contract is ambiguous, the ambiguity should be resolved against the proferens (that is, the person who drafted it).[59] In the context of retainers, that will almost always be the legal representative. It is very much a principle of last resort.[60] In any event, Warby J has pointed out that it would have no application at all in cases in which the words were clear.[61] **31.40**

The Interpretation of Mistakenly Drafted Contracts

The principles discussed in this section have been described as 'common-law rectification'.[62] They are to be distinguished from the principles discussed at 32.67–32.74 on equitable rectification, which are entirely different. **31.41**

As was mentioned in 31.30, it is open to the court, in appropriate cases, to conclude that the parties must, for whatever reason, have used the wrong words or syntax.[63] Whilst the court does not readily accept that such mistakes have been made (especially in formal documents),[64] where the court does reach that conclusion, a clear mistake may be corrected as a matter of interpretation. In particular, if (a) it is clear that something has gone wrong with the language and (b) it is clear what a reasonable person would have understood the parties to have meant, there is no 'limit to the amount of red ink or verbal rearrangement or correction which the court is allowed'.[65] **31.42**

Brightman LJ had this to say on the topic: **31.43**

> 'It is clear on the authorities that a mistake in a written instrument can, in limited circumstances, be corrected as a matter of construction without obtaining a decree in an action for rectification. Two conditions must be satisfied: first, there must be a clear mistake on the face of the instrument: secondly, it must be clear what correction ought to be made in order to cure the mistake. If those conditions are satisfied, then the correction is made as a matter of construction. If they are not satisfied, then either the Claimant must pursue an action for

---

[57] *International Fina Services AG v Katrina Shipping Ltd, The Fina Samco* [1995] 2 Lloyd's Rep 344, at 350; see also *Sinochem v Mobil* [2000] 1 All ER (Comm) 474.

[58] 'Against (*contra*) the one bringing forth (the *proferens*)'.

[59] See *Tam Wing Chuen v Bank of Credit and Commerce Hong Kong Ltd* [1996] 2 BCLC 69; see also Unfair Terms in Consumer Contracts Regulations 1999 (SI 1999/2083), reg 7(2). For an example of this principle being applied in the context of a contract of retainer, see *Vlamaki v Sookias & Sookias* [2015] EWHC 3334 (QB), at [15] *per* Walker J.

[60] *Sinochem v Mobil* [2000] 1 All ER (Comm) 474, at 483.

[61] *Radford v Frade* [2016] EWHC 1600 (QB), at [28]. Warby J's decision was affirmed on appeal ([2018] EWCA Civ 119), but on a different point.

[62] McMeel, G, *The Construction of Contracts* (Oxford: Oxford University Press, 2007), paras 17.02–17.20.

[63] *Mannai Investment Co Ltd v Eagle Star Life Assurance Co Ltd* [1997] 3 All ER 352, *per* Lord Steyn, cited with approval by Lord Hoffmann in *ICS v West Bromwich Building Society* [1998] 1 WLR 896, HL, at 912.

[64] See *Chartbrook Ltd v Persimmon Homes Ltd* [2009] UKHL 38, at [15]; *Enviroco Ltd v Farstad Supply A/S, The Far Service* [2009] EWCA Civ 1399, at [21].

[65] *Chartbrook Ltd v Persimmon Homes Ltd* [2009] UKHL 38, at [25].

rectification or he must leave it to a court of construction to reach what answer it can on the basis that the uncorrected wording represents the manner in which the parties decided to express their intention.'[66]

31.44 Examples (albeit not relating to contracts of retainer) include where the contract named the wrong party,[67] where it misnamed one of the parties[68] or even where a name had been omitted entirely from the final draft.[69] That said, there are limits to the circumstances in which the court will engage in verbal rearrangement or correction: if, for example, the putative error relates to a term that has been defined by the contract itself, then in general the court will correct that meaning only if not to do so would lead to an absurd result.[70]

Inconsistent terms included by mistake

31.45 Where a term has been mistakenly incorporated and where that term is inconsistent with the specific purpose of the contract, the court may decline to give that term effect. Lord Halsbury said:

> 'Looking at the whole of the instrument, and seeing what one must regard ... as its main purpose, one must reject words, indeed whole provisions, if they are inconsistent with what one assumes to be the main purpose of the contract.'[71]

31.46 Thus, if a retainer mistakenly contained a provision that suggested that legal services would be provided for no charge, the court may, in appropriate circumstances, decline to give effect to that provision.

Contracts drafted under pressure of time

31.47 The court recognises that mistakes may easily arise in complex documents drafted at short notice.[72] Some retainers are certainly complex and, in the context of commercial litigation, they may also be entered into with considerable urgency. This may be a factor that the court takes into account.

The Interpretation of Contracts of Retainer in which Terms are Seemingly Missing

31.48 A retainer may be found wanting on the basis that an essential term (such as a term that identifies the parties) is absent. By analogy with cases relating to formalities of other types of written instrument, it is not always the case that detail is required if the requisite elements can be implied. It may be possible, for example, for the court to find that, because the parties are identified, other details are implied.[73] This can be of use where the retainer

---

[66] *East v Pantiles Plant Hire Ltd* [1982] 2 EGLR 111, at 116.
[67] *Wilson v Wilson* (1854) 5 HL Cas 40.
[68] *Nittan (UK) Ltd v Solent Steel Fabrications Ltd* [1981] 1 Lloyd's Rep 633.
[69] Although now a very old case, see *Lord Say and Seals Case* (1711) 10 Mod Rep 40; see also *Protank Shipping Inc v Total Transport Corpn, The Protank Orinoco* [1997] 2 Lloyd's Rep 42, at 46.
[70] *City Inn (Jersey) Ltd v Ten Trinity Square Ltd* [2008] EWCA Civ 156, at [8].
[71] *Glynn v Margetson & Co* [1893] AC 351, at 357. See also *Alexander (as representative of the Property118 Action Group) v West Bromwich Mortgage Company Ltd* [2016] EWCA Civ 496.
[72] *Static Control Components (Europe) Ltd v Egan* [2004] EWCA Civ 392.
[73] Whilst now very old cases, see *Potter v Duffield* (1874) LR 18 Eq 4 and *Rossiter v Miller* (1878) 3 App Cas 1124.

documentation is little more than an introductory letter. In other circumstances, it may be sufficient to identify the subject matter of the contract to allow other details to be implied.[74]

Such an approach has its limitation, however. Where the contract of retainer is subject to legislative control, it may be that the missing term is one that is required to be there. Where this is so, Brooke LJ has explained that the word 'specify' is to be read as meaning that the thing must be stated explicitly.[75] **31.49**

Waiver and submission

In contexts far removed from the law of costs, the court has permitted counterparties to demonstrate compliance with formalities by the related mechanisms of 'waiver' and 'submission'. These concepts are mentioned here more for the sake of completeness than because they are likely to be of practical relevance. **31.50**

- **Waiver** Where a requisite term has been omitted and where that term would have been entirely in favour of one of the counterparties, that person may 'waive' the benefit of the omitted term and enforce the contract notwithstanding the omission.[76] This concept is likely to be of limited use in the context of contracts of retainers because there is authority (albeit now rather old) that material terms may not be waived.[77]
- **Submission** The converse of waiver is submission: where, if it had been included, an omitted term would have been wholly for another person's benefit, a person may submit to that term as if it had been included.[78]

It is possible that such an analysis may be of use if a receiving party seeks to waive or submit for the purposes of demonstrating compliance with the indemnity principle, but this would be entirely unsupported by any modern authority. **31.51**

Joinder and Severance in the Context of Interpretation

Joinder

A useful judicial tool is the ability of the court to take other written instruments into account when construing the retainer. This is based on the premise that where documents form part of the same transaction, they should be interpreted together.[79] **31.52**

Although this facility has been affirmed in the context of contracts of retainer only in the last decade or so,[80] it is by no means a new concept. Indeed, it is a well-established principle **31.53**

---

[74] *Caddick v Skidmore* (1857) 2 De G&J 52; *Plant v Bourne* [1897] 2 Ch 281.

[75] See the comments of Brooke LJ in *Hollins v Russell* [2003] EWCA Civ 718, at [125], in which he drew upon *BWE International Ltd v Jones* [2003] EWCA Civ 298, at [29] as an example of that approach.

[76] *North v Loomes* [1919] 1 Ch 378.

[77] *Hawkins v Price* [1947] Ch 645.

[78] For obvious reasons, such an approach would not find universal favour, as is evidenced by the fact that, even in contexts other than costs, it is a principle that is often rejected by the court: see *Martin v Pycroft* (1852) 2 De GM&G 785; *Burgess v Cox* [1951] Ch 383; *Scott v Bradley* [1971] Ch 850.

[79] *Burchell v Clark* (1876) 2 CPD 88.

[80] *Jones v Wrexham Borough Council* [2007] EWCA Civ 1356. Some commentators would disagree with the suggestion that this was an example of joinder.

and has even come to the aid of counterparties in the face of legislation that expressly contemplated the inclusion of all of the relevant terms in one document.[81]

31.54 Ideally, where documents are to be joined, one document should refer to the other,[82] but if this is not the case, it may be possible to introduce oral or other evidence to establish the nexus.[83]

31.55 Costs examples exist.[84] Whilst it was based on a concession, Mann J accepted that a letter could be joined to a conditional fee agreement for the purposes of complying with a requirement of the (now revoked) Conditional Fee Agreements Regulations 2000.[85]

Severance

31.56 It is, in principle, open to the court to find that a retainer can be salvaged by the court severing the objectionable part from the unobjectionable remainder. In support of this notion, Christopher Clarke J has made *obiter* comments to the effect that he could see no reason why, in an appropriate case, the court could not strike its blue pencil through the objectionable provision.[86] Most cases will not be appropriate, however. This is because where the retainer is objectionable by reason of it being contrary to public policy, it would—in general—itself be contrary to public policy to permit severance.[87]

Implied Terms

The general law of implied terms

31.57 Implying terms into a contract has traditionally been treated as distinct from construing a contract, but there is a certain amount of overlap. In 2009, there was a blurring of the distinction between the implication of terms and construction of the contract,[88] but there

[81] See, eg, *Pearce v Gardener* [1897] 1 QB 688, in which a letter was coupled with the envelope in which it was delivered.

[82] See, eg, the discussion in *Boydell v Durmmond* (1809) 11 East 142, at 158.

[83] See, eg, the *obiter* analysis of Jenkins LJ in *Timmins v Moreland Street Property Ltd* [1958] Ch 110, at 120.

[84] *Jones v Wrexham Borough Council* [2007] EWCA Civ 1356, at [17]. Other examples exist. Whilst, ultimately, he came to the conclusion that the agreement was unenforceable, Blake J took into account a letter that had been sent to the client at about the same time as the conditional fee agreement was made: *Utting v McBain* [2007] EWHC 3293 (QB), at [21]–[24]. See also *Radford v Frade* [2016] EWHC 1600 (QB), at [20]–[22], in which Warby J found that it would have been wrong to have ignored a risk assessment as part of contract when seeking to construe a conditional fee agreement; at [24], he went on to find that whilst a covering letter may have been extraneous to the agreement itself, it was part of the 'package' and was therefore something to be taken into account. Warby J's decision was affirmed on appeal ([2018] EWCA Civ 119), but on a different point.

[85] SI 2000/692; *Fenton v Holmes* [2007] EWHC 2476 (Ch), at [24]–[27].

[86] *Forde v Birmingham City Council* [2009] EWHC 12 (QB), at [151], relying on *The Great Peace* [2002] EWCA Civ 14 and *Brennan v Bolt Burdon* [2004] EWCA Civ 1017.

[87] See *Aratra Potato Co Ltd v Taylor Joynson-Garrett* [1995] 4 All ER 695, at 701, *per* Garland J. See also *Awwad v Geraghty* [2001] QB 570, at 600, in which Shiemann LJ noted that it would be contrary to public policy to go beyond that which Parliament has provided. Whilst not binding, see *Oyston v The Royal Bank of Scotland plc* [2006] EWHC 90053 (Costs), at [54].

[88] In *Attorney General of Belize v Belize Telecom Ltd* [2009] UKPC 10, at [21], implied terms were brought within the interpretative fold. The single question was put: does the supposed implied term 'spell out in express words what the instrument, read against the relevant background, would reasonably be understood to mean'? In other words, interpretation and implication became part of the same process.

was a retreat from this position in 2015.[89] The effect of this is that the notions of 'business efficacy' and 'officious bystanders' (see 31.59)—known to every first-year law student—remain of use.

The two types of implication

There are two types of contractual implied term, as follows.[90] **31.58**

- **Factual implication** Factual implication refers to a term being implied into a contract, in the light of the express terms, commercial common sense and the facts known to both parties at the time the contract was made.
- **Legal implication** Legal implication arises because, unless such a term is expressly excluded, the law—sometimes by statute; sometimes through the common law—effectively imposes certain terms into certain classes of relationship.

Factual implication may include implication by custom or usage (see 31.63–31.68).

Factual implication

The development of the law There have been many judicial observations about the nature of the requirements that have to be satisfied before a term can be implied into a contract. They include the following. **31.59**

- **Business efficacy** Bowen LJ observed that, in all of the cases in which a term had been implied, 'it will be found that ... the law is raising an implication from the presumed intention of the parties with the object of giving the transaction such efficacy as both parties must have intended that at all events it should have'.[91] Scrutton LJ said that '[a] term can only be implied if it is necessary in the business sense to give efficacy to the contract' and added that a term would be implied only if:

  '... it is such a term that it can confidently be said that if at the time the contract was being negotiated the parties had been asked what would happen in a certain event, they would both have replied "Of course, so and so will happen; we did not trouble to say that; it is too clear".'[92]

- **'Officious bystander'** MacKinnon LJ observed that, '[*p*]*rima facie* that which in any contract is left to be implied and need not be expressed is something so obvious that it goes without saying', and then—reflecting what Scrutton LJ had said 20 years earlier—famously added that a term would be implied only 'if, while the parties were making their bargain, an officious bystander were to suggest some express provision for it in their agreement, they would testily suppress him with a common "Oh, of course!" '.[93]

In 1977, Lord Simon summarised the law in the following way: **31.60**

> '[F]or a term to be implied, the following conditions (which may overlap) must be satisfied: (1) it must be reasonable and equitable; (2) it must be necessary to give business efficacy

[89] See *Marks and Spencer plc v BNP Paribas Securities Services Trust Co (Jersey) Ltd & Anor* [2015] UKSC 72, at [26]–[31], *per* Neuberger PSC.

[90] See *ibid*, at [15] *per* Neuberger PSC, referring to *Société Générale, London Branch v Geys* [2012] UKSC 63, at [55], *per* Lady Hale.

[91] *The Moorcock* (1889) 14 PD 64, at 68.

[92] *Reigate v Union Manufacturing Co (Ramsbottom) Ltd* [1918] 1 KB 592, at 605.

[93] *Shirlaw v Southern Foundries (1926) Ltd* [1939] 2 KB 206, at 227.

to the contract, so that no term will be implied if the contract is effective without it; (3) it must be so obvious that "it goes without saying"; (4) it must be capable of clear expression; (5) it must not contradict an express term of the contract.'[94]

31.61 In 1995, Sir Thomas Bingham MR cited Lord Simon's summary and extended it:

'The question of whether a term should be implied, and if so what, almost inevitably arises after a crisis has been reached in the performance of the contract. So the court comes to the task of implication with the benefit of hindsight, and it is tempting for the court then to fashion a term which will reflect the merits of the situation as they then appear. Tempting, but wrong. ... [I]t is not enough to show that had the parties foreseen the eventuality which in fact occurred they would have wished to make provision for it, unless it can also be shown either that there was only one contractual solution or that one of several possible solutions would without doubt have been preferred ...'[95]

31.62 **The modern approach** More recently, Lord Neuberger, having cited both Lord Simon and Sir Thomas Bingham MR, added a number of comments of his own.[96]

- **No requirement of proof of actual intention**

'Lord Steyn rightly observed[97] that the implication of a term was "not critically dependent on proof of an actual intention of the parties" when negotiating the contract. If one approaches the question by reference to what the parties would have agreed, one is not strictly concerned with the hypothetical answer of the actual parties, but with that of notional reasonable people in the position of the parties at the time at which they were contracting.'[98]

- **No implication on the grounds of fairness alone**

'A term should not be implied into a detailed commercial contract merely because it appears fair or merely because one considers that the parties would have agreed it if it had been suggested to them. Those are necessary but not sufficient grounds for including a term.'[99]

- **Reasonableness and equitableness add little**

'[It] is questionable whether Lord Simon's first requirement, reasonableness and equitableness [see 31.58], will usually, if ever, add anything: if a term satisfies the other requirements, it is hard to think that it would not be reasonable and equitable.'[100]

- **Business necessity and obviousness may be alternatives**

'[A]lthough Lord Simon's requirements are otherwise cumulative, I would accept that business necessity and obviousness ... can be alternatives in the sense that only one of them

---

94 See Privy Council case of *BP Refinery (Westernport) Pty Ltd v President, Councillors and Ratepayers of the Shire of Hastings* (1977) 52 ALJR 20, at 26, *per* Lord Simon (speaking for the majority, which included Viscount Dilhorne and Lord Keith).

95 See *Philips Electronique Grand Public SA v British Sky Broadcasting Ltd* [1995] EMLR 472, at 482.

96 See *Marks and Spencer plc v BNP Paribas Securities Services Trust Co (Jersey) Ltd & Anor* [2015] UKSC 72, at [21].

97 In *Equitable Life Assurance Society v Hyman* [2002] 1 AC 408, at 459.

98 See *Marks and Spencer plc v BNP Paribas Securities Services Trust Co (Jersey) Ltd & Anor* [2015] UKSC 72, at [21].

99 *Ibid.*

100 *Ibid.*

needs to be satisfied, although I suspect that in practice it would be a rare case where only one of those two requirements would be satisfied.'[101]

- **Importance of formulating the correct question**

  '[I]f one approaches the issue by reference to the officious bystander, it is "vital to formulate the question to be posed by [him] with the utmost care", to quote from Lewison, *The Interpretation of Contracts* 5th ed (2011), para 6.09.'[102]

- **Necessity[103] is not a test of absolute necessity**

  '[N]ecessity for business efficacy involves a value judgment. It is rightly common ground on this appeal that the test is not one of "absolute necessity", not least because the necessity is judged by reference to business efficacy. It may well be that a more helpful way of putting Lord Simon's second requirement is, as suggested by Lord Sumption in argument, that a term can only be implied if, without the term, the contract would lack commercial or practical coherence.'[104]

Factual implication by custom or usage Factual implication by custom or usage will most often be encountered in cases involving commercial clients, but it may also arise in other circumstances, such as where a private client habitually instructs the family solicitor.[105] Another example may be where an insolvency practitioner instructs a firm on a 'recoveries only' basis of remuneration.[106] **31.63**

Where the counterparties are acting in the course of their businesses (that is, where both the legal representative and the client are businesses, and are acting in that capacity), evidence of custom and usage is admissible for the purposes of implying a term into a contract.[107] **31.64**

---

101 *Ibid.*

102 *Ibid.*

103 For a discussion of necessity in the context of implied terms generally, see *Marks and Spencer plc v BNP Paribas Securities Services Trust Co (Jersey) Ltd & Anor* [2015] UKSC 72, at [15]–[22], *per* Neuberger PSC. For a recent example of this test being applied in the context of a contract of retainer, see *Harding Evans LLP v Spencer-White* [2017] EWCA Civ 434, at [31], *per* Sharp LJ. For older examples, see *Harrods Ltd v Harrods (Buenos Aires) Ltd* (1998) The Times, 1 June, CA; *Re Chappell, ex p Ford* (1885) 16 QBD 305, CA. Support for the notion that a term will be implied only if it satisfies the test of business necessity is to be found in a number of observations made in the House of Lords. Notable examples included Lord Pearson (with whom Lord Guest and Lord Diplock agreed) in *Trollope & Colls Ltd v North West Metropolitan Regional Hospital Board* [1973] 1 WLR 601, at 609, and Lord Wilberforce, Lord Cross, Lord Salmon and Lord Edmund-Davies in *Liverpool City Council v Irwin* [1977] AC 239, at 254, 258, 262 and 266, respectively. More recently, the test of 'necessary to give business efficacy' to the contract in issue was mentioned by Lady Hale in *Société Générale, London Branch v Geys* [2012] UKSC 63, at [55], and by Lord Carnwath in *Arnold v Britton* [2015] UKSC 36, at [112].

104 See *Marks and Spencer plc v BNP Paribas Securities Services Trust Co (Jersey) Ltd & Anor* [2015] UKSC 72, at [21], *per* Lord Neuberger.

105 By way of example, there is one term that would be implied by custom in almost every implied retainer, regardless of whether the client was a business or a private individual, ie the basis of charging by 6-minute units. That term would be implied on the basis that the court does not commonly use any other method for quantifying time.

106 See, eg, *Stevensdrake Ltd v Hunt* [2016] EWHC 342 (Ch), at [107], *per* Judge Simon Barker QC (sitting as a judge of the High Court).

107 In a context other than costs, see *Cunliffe-Owen v Teather and Greenwood* [1967] 1 WLR 1421, which deals with the custom in the stock exchange.

31.65 *Custom, usage and estoppel by convention* A legal representative's claim for costs could not usually be founded upon estoppel by convention;[108] something more would usually be required than merely asserting that the client is estopped from denying the existence of a retainer by reason of their long-standing relationship with the legal representative. However, for the reasons set out above, the legal representative would often be able to point to something more.

31.66 Estoppel by convention may, however, work in a client's favour. In a case in which an insolvency practitioner had instructed a firm on the basis that it would be paid only out of monies recovered, Judge Simon Barker QC (sitting as a judge of the High Court) found that the firm was estopped from claiming fees in the absence of any such recovery.[109] Indeed, Judge Barker even went so far as to find (technically *obiter*) that the firm would have been guilty of presumed undue influence had it tried to impose any other arrangements upon the insolvency practitioner without specifically alerting him to those new arrangements.[110]

Legal implication

31.67 Terms may be implied by the operation of legislation or common law. This is a topic that is best addressed in the context of specific terms (see 31.69 *et seq*).

31.68 It should be noted that the rights that are conferred on consumers by the Consumer Rights Act 2015 and associated legislation are not *implied* terms of the contract, but are to be treated *as* terms (see 28.30–28.31).[111] For present purposes, however, the distinction is not that important.

Specific Implied Terms, Deemed Terms and Presumptions in the Context of Contracts of Retainers

Rebuttable presumption that the client is liable for fees

31.69 Once it has been established that the client did engage the legal services provider in that capacity, then (should the facts support such a conclusion) there will be a rebuttable presumption that a client will be liable for the provider's fees.[112] Whilst that presumption can be analysed in other ways, for practical purposes it is a presumption that that will be an implied term of the retainer unless the contrary can be shown. This is a topic that is addressed in more detail in 18.28–18.29 and 27.191–27.197.

---

[108] In a setting other than costs, see *Baird Textiles Holdings Ltd v Marks & Spencer plc* [2001] EWCA Civ 274. As to the requirement of necessity, see *The Aramis* [1989] 1 Lloyd's Rep 213.

[109] *Stevensdrake Ltd v Hunt* [2016] EWHC 342 (Ch), at [107].

[110] *Ibid*, at [114].

[111] Legislators hoped that setting out the obligations in this way would assist users of this legislation (who might not all be legal service providers, but consumers and those advising consumers within consumer-oriented organisations) and would explain the true nature of the thinking that the Act required: see Andrews, C, *Enforcement of Consumer Rights and Protections* (London: Butterworths Law, 2012), para 5.7.

[112] See *Adams v London Improved Motor Builders Ltd* [1921] 1 KB 495, at 501. See also *R v Miller (Raymond)* [1983] 1 WLR 1056, at 1059–62, which was cited with approval in *Bailey v IBC Vehicles Ltd* [1998] 3 All ER 570, at 574. See also *Hazlett v Sefton Metropolitan Borough Council* [2000] 4 All ER 887.

Implied terms regarding hourly rates

31.70 Where it is not possible to find that a specific rate was agreed, it is open to the court to find an implied term that the rate would be a reasonable rate.[113] Applying an implied term as to the hourly rate will not always be a straightforward task; there may, for example, be a dispute about whether there is provision that the rates may be uplifted to take account of the complexity of the work.[114] On the whole, the court will be reluctant to allow a legal representative something such as an uplift that has not been expressly agreed.[115]

Implied terms regarding interim payments

31.71 This is addressed at 27.56–27.63.

Deemed terms in contracts of retainer with consumers

31.72 Where the contract of retainer is with a consumer and where it was made on or after 1 October 2015, then the following will apply.

- Information given by a legal services provider will be binding as terms (see 28.29–28.33).[116]
- Where no price has been agreed, the legal services provider's fees will be reasonable (see 28.37).[117]
- Where no specific terms have been agreed, the services are to be performed within a reasonable time (see 28.38).[118]

Where the agreement was made before 1 October 2015, then Table 28.1 may assist in finding the relevant legislation.

Implied terms in contracts of retainer with business clients

31.73 Where there is a contract for the supply of a service,[119] then, if (a) Ch 2 of Pt 1 of the Consumer Rights Act 2015 does not apply (that is, if the client is not a consumer)[120] or (b) the client is a consumer who entered into the contract before 1 October 2015,[121] the following terms will be implied:

- **Reasonable care and skill** Where the supplier is acting in the course of a business, there will be an implied term that the supplier will carry out the service with reasonable care and skill.[122]

---

113 See *Ghadami v Lyon Cole Insurance Group Ltd* [2010] EWCA Civ 767, at [27].

114 See, eg, *Adams v MacInnes* [2001] EWHC 9014 (Costs).

115 Whilst dealing with implied terms rather than implied retainers, see *Bilkus v Stockler Brunton (a firm)* [2010] EWCA Civ 101, at [54], *per* Stanley Burnton LJ.

116 See Consumer Rights Act 2015, s 50.

117 Consumer Rights Act 2015, s 52.

118 Consumer Rights Act 2015, s 52.

119 A contract for the supply of services is a contract under which a person (namely, 'the supplier') agrees to carry out a service: Supply of Goods and Services Act 1982, s 12(1).

120 See Consumer Rights Act 2015, Sch 1, paras 37–52.

121 Consumer Rights Act 2015 (Commencement No 3, Transitional Provisions, Savings and Consequential Amendments) Order 2015 (SI 2015/1630), art 3.

122 Supply of Goods and Services Act 1982, ss 12 and 13.

- **Reasonable period of time** Where a supplier is acting in the course of a business and the time for the service to be carried out is not stipulated or otherwise agreed in the course of dealing between the parties, there is an implied term that the supplier will carry out the service within a reasonable period of time.[123]
- **Reasonable charge** Where the payment for the service is not determined by the contract or otherwise agreed between the parties, there will be an implied term that the party contracting with the supplier will pay a reasonable charge.[124]

[123] See Supply of Goods and Services Act 1982, s 14(1).
[124] See Supply of Goods and Services Act 1982, s 15(1).

32

CONTRACTS OF RETAINER (TRANSFER OF CONTRACTS OF RETAINER AND THE MANAGEMENT OF ERRORS)

This chapter deals with the following topics: **32.01**

- the transfer of contracts of retainer (32.02);
  - methods of transferring contracts of retainer (32.05);
  - assignment (32.08);
  - novation (32.34);
- the management of defective contracts of retainer (32.42):
  - the position between legal services provider and client (32.43);
  - remedial steps that may be taken before the entitlement to costs has arisen (32.56); and
  - remedial steps that may be taken after the entitlement to costs has arisen (32.65).

The Transfer of Contracts of Retainer (Assignment, etc)

It may be that a legal services provider wishes to hand over the rights and obligations under a contract of retainer to another legal services provider, known as transfer of the contract of retainer. The circumstances in which such a need tends to arise were described by Gloster LJ: **32.02**

> '[T]he instructed firm might have ceased to practise in a particular area . . .; a client may have wished for their case to continue to be dealt with by an individual solicitor who had moved firms . . .; conversely, a client might have lost confidence in one firm and wished to instruct a new firm; or the instructed firm might have become a new entity through merger . . . or by the incorporation of a firm which had previously existed as a partnership.'[1]

The need to effect a transfer often arises in the context of personal injury litigation,[2] but it may arise in any area of practice.

In the past, the need to effect a transfer tended to arise out of a desire to preserve the right to recover success fees between opposing parties. In recent times, however, the focus has been more on convenience, because transfer will obviate the need to make entirely new contracts of retainer—something that could be administratively burdensome if a large number of clients were involved. **32.03**

[1] *Budana v The Leeds Teaching Hospitals NHS Trust & Anor* [2017] EWCA Civ 1980, at [35].
[2] For a discussion as to why this is so, see *ibid*, at [30]–[36].

32.04 This chapter deals with consensual transfers. It should be borne in mind that certain assignments may occur by the operation of law. Examples of this include the transfer of rights of a deceased person to their personal representatives and the transfer of choses in action to a trustee in bankruptcy.[3] These topics are, however, beyond the scope of this book. What follows focuses on transfer as between legal services providers.

Methods of transferring contracts of retainer

32.05 There are two aspects to the issue of transfer:

- the transfer of accrued rights and benefits (such as the right to payment for fees already billed or the right to render invoices for work in progress); and
- the transfer of the contractual relations that allow a legal services provider to charge fees for work yet to be done.

32.06 Over recent years, transfers in respect of both of the above have generally been attempted by way of a type of assignment known as a *Jenkins* assignment.[4] As is explained at 32.12, there can be no doubt that this was (and still is) an appropriate way of dealing with the accrued rights and benefits. In so far as the right to claim fees for work yet to be done is concerned, however, it is now known that assignment is not a means by which a transfer may be effected (see 32.19). As such, *Jenkins* assignments do work in the way that they were intended to work. That said, nearly all competent attempts to carry out a *Jenkins* assignment would result in the contract of retainer being novated and—for the reasons set out below (see 32.39–32.41)—the practical effect of this would be almost the same as was intended. In particular, it is now known that the mere fact that a pre-April 2013 conditional fee agreement was transferred by way of (unintended) novation would not negate the right on the part of the client to recover a success fee from their opponent for work yet to be done at the point of transfer.

32.07 To explain the relevant law, it is necessary to deal first with both the law of assignment and the doctrine of privity. This is despite the fact that it is now known that assignment will be effective only in so far as accrued rights and benefits are concerned. Once those topics have been dealt with, then the law of novation is addressed (see 32.34–32.37). As will be seen, novation is the means by which the right to charge fees for work yet to be done may be transferred from firm to firm and, as such, is of greater practical relevance than assignment.

Assignment

32.08 An assignment is the immediate transfer of an existing proprietary right—vested or contingent—from the assignor to the assignee.[5] Put otherwise, it is the rights and benefits under a contract that are assigned, not the contract itself.[6] In broad terms, the properties that are

[3] See Insolvency Act 1986, ss 283(1), 306 and 436.

[4] After *Jenkins v Young Brothers Transport Ltd* [2006] EWHC 151 (QB). See the evidence of the Law Society referred to by Gloster LJ at *Budana v The Leeds Teaching Hospitals NHS Trust & Anor* [2017] EWCA Civ 1980, at [36].

[5] *Norman v Federal Comr of Taxation* (1963) 109 CLR 9, at 26, *per* Windeyer J.

[6] *Linden Gardens Trust Ltd v Lenesta Sludge Disposals Ltd* [1994] 1 AC 85, at 103, *per* Lord Browne-Wilkinson.

transferred are the choses in action[7] that are governed by, or which have been created by, the contract in question.[8]

Privity

The doctrine of privity is that a contract is unable to confer rights or to impose obligations arising under it on any persons except the parties to the contract. The assignment of a right or benefit under a contract does *not* create privity of contract between the assignee and person who is obliged to confer that right (that person being known as the obligor).[9] The effect of the assignment is merely procedural in that it allows the assignee to issue proceedings in their own name and to give a good discharge under the contract.[10] **32.09**

In the context of contracts of retainer, the relevance of the parties not being brought into privity means that it would be wrong to talk of assignment *of* the contract of retainer; instead, one needs to focus on (and distinguish between) benefits and burdens *under* the contract of retainer (see 32.20–32.23). As will be explained below, only benefits may be assigned in the present context. This is why *Jenkins* assignments do not work in the way that the putative assignor and assignee may have intended. **32.10**

The converse of this is that if the parties were brought into privity, the transfer would not have been an assignment, but instead would have been a novation. This is relevant to attempted assignments of benefits and burdens (that is, of the right to be paid fees in return for work yet to be done), because it will almost always be the case that the new legal services provider and the client will be brought into privity by the fact that the latter gives instructions to the former. This is addressed in more detail at 32.25–32.27. **32.11**

Benefits and rights already accrued at the point of assignment

For obvious reasons, if fees have already become payable at the point of transfer, they would merely be a costs debt and, as such, could be assigned without difficulty. Furthermore, Gloster LJ has confirmed that there is no reason, in principle, why more general rights and benefits under a contract of retainer should not be capable of assignment.[11] This would include the right to recover a costs debt, but would also include the right to render fees for work in progress.[12] As to work already carried out under a conditional fee agreement where the case has yet to be 'won', one needs to look at the topic of future property (see below). As can be seen, it seems that the right to payment for such work is capable of being assigned. **32.12**

[7] For present purposes, a chose in action may be defined as 'all personal rights of property which can only be claimed or enforced by action, and not by taking physical possession': see *Torkington v Magee* [1902] 2 KB 427, at 430, *per* Channell J. That said, it should be noted that Channell J went on to explain that there is no requirement that the right be capable of being enjoyed only by way of action: see *ibid*, at 431. This is relevant to contracts of retainer because it would otherwise mean that assignment be limited to actions for breach of contract, which would not include claims for fees. This case was reversed on appeal ([1903] 1 KB 644), but on a different point.

[8] *Investors Compensation Scheme Ltd v West Bromwich Building Society* [1998] 1 WLR 896, at 915, *per* Lord Hoffmann.

[9] *Tolhurst v Associated Portland Cement Manufacturers (1900) Ltd* [1902] 2 KB 660, at 668, *per* Collins MR.

[10] *Tolhurst v Associated Portland Cement Manufacturers (1900) Ltd* [1903] AC 414, at 424, *per* Lord Lindley.

[11] *Budana v The Leeds Teaching Hospitals NHS Trust & Anor* [2017] EWCA Civ 1980, at [46].

[12] *Ibid.*

32.13 **Future property and conditional fee agreements** 'Future property' is a phrase that is used to refer to property (in this context, a right to fees) that may come into existence at some point in the future. It is something other than a chose in action and is therefore not capable of *immediate* assignment (see 32.28–32.30).[13] An example closely analogous to fees payable under a contract of retainer is income, such as royalties that have not yet become payable.[14] The right to payment at some point in the future may be assignable without difficulty, but—of course—payment itself would be made only at some point in the future.

32.14 For the avoidance of doubt, the notion of 'future property' is not an impediment to assignment of the right to be paid for work already done under a conditional fee agreement. One reason why this is so is because equity will intervene to regard the transaction as an agreement to assign.[15] For example, where the consideration under such an agreement is executed by the assignee—namely, the new legal services provider—then the original legal services provider may hold the relevant property on trust for the new provider as and when it acquires the right to be paid.[16] That said, the need to rely any principle of equity will rarely arise in the context of conditional fee agreements because the issue of assignment tends to become contentious only *after* fees have become payable and, in those circumstances, the assignment is likely to be regarded as being a valid assignment under s 136 of the Law of Property Act 1925 (see 32.29–32.30).

32.15 In any event, there are strong practical reasons for not applying the notion of future property—or, for that matter, any of the putative technical bars to assignment of rights and benefits—too rigidly. Whilst not binding, Judge Graham Wood QC had this to say on the topic:

> 'In my judgment, the proposition that an assignment of the benefit of a [conditional fee] agreement could only be effective in equity at the time the contingency arose would have a chilling effect on the efficacy of business arrangements which for a whole host of reasons legal service providers may wish to enter into. If [counsel for the party trying to impugn the assignment] is correct with his proposition, a solicitor who had a number of [conditional fee] agreements in progress but who wished to cease to practise, could not transfer or assign those agreements unless he or they continued to exist as a legal entity. They would have no value for assignment if the solicitor taking over the conduct of the case could not recover the benefit of the work undertaken.'[17]

Having rehearsed the principles set out in 32.14, Judge Graham Wood QC went on to find, on the facts of the case before him, that the assignment was valid. In so far as his judgment related to benefits and rights (as opposed to burdens and obligations), what he said remains good law.

32.16 Thus it seems that a right to fees already incurred under a contract of retainer may be assigned, regardless of whether those fees have actually become payable at the point of transfer. In this regard, it is worth noting that, whilst he did not deal with the topic in any detail, Lord Sumption has expressed the view that the right to payment for work already carried out under a conditional fee agreement may be assigned in principle.[18]

---

[13] See *Norman v Federal Comr of Taxation* (1963) 109 CLR 9, at 24, *per* Windeyer J.
[14] See, eg, *Re Trytel* [1952] 2 TLR 32.
[15] Whilst not a costs case, see *Norman v Federal Comr of Taxation* (1963) 109 CLR 9, at 24, *per* Windeyer J.
[16] See *Palette Shoes Pty Ltd v Krohn* (1937) 58 CLR 1, at 27, *per* Dixon J; *Tailby v Official Receiver* (1888) 13 App Cas 523.
[17] *Jones v Spire Healthcare Ltd* [2016] 3 Costs LO 487, at [119].
[18] *Plevin v Paragon Personal Finance Ltd* [2017] UKSC 23, at [6].

The relevance of personal contracts Generally speaking, where a contractual benefit is personal, it may not be assigned.[19] Similarly, a personal contractual obligation may not be performed by someone else.[20] The question of whether a contract is a personal contract will depend on the circumstances (including the terms of the contract): whilst contracts of retainer are capable of being personal contracts,[21] this will not generally be the case, especially in so far as personal injury litigation is concerned. Gloster LJ had this to say on the point: **32.17**

> 'Whereas generally a contract between a solicitor and his client might well be regarded as a personal contract from the point of view of both the solicitor and the client, the question is fact specific and depends on the individual retainer. Given the circumstances in which most claimant personal injury litigation is now conducted ... the CFA between a client and his solicitor in such a case lacks the features of a personal contract. What the client wants is representation by a competent practitioner and not necessarily representation by a specific individual (whom he or she may probably never meet).'[22]

In any event, even where a contract of retainer can be said to contain a personal element, this would not prevent assignment to an assignee of a legal services provider's right to payment for work done.[23] Put otherwise, the fact that a contract of retainer may be said to be a personal contract does not appear to prevent the legal services provider from assigning the right to be paid for work already carried out (or, for that matter, any other benefit) to another person. **32.18**

Transfer of the right to be paid for work yet to be done

The issue of the right to be paid for work yet to be done at the point of transfer is a more difficult point, because any putative assignment would not merely be of the benefits and rights under the contract of retainer, but of the burdens and obligations, and, in particular, of the legal services provider's obligation to carry out the work for which it seeks payment. As is explained below, there are two reasons why such a putative assignment (namely, a *Jenkins* assignment) would fail as an assignment—that is, because: **32.19**

- it is not possible (for present purposes) to assign burdens and obligations; and
- the fact that the client consents to the new legal services provider being instructed will, in general, give rise to a new contract of retainer and this will result in an unintended novation.

As such, whilst any such putative assignment would (if competently executed) be a valid *transfer* of the right to charge for work yet to be done, this would be by way of novation, rather than assignment. For the reasons set out at 32.38, however, this seems to be of little

[19] See *Chitty on Contracts* (32nd edn, London: Sweet & Maxwell, 2015), paras 19-055–19-056; *Tolhurst v Portland Cement* [1902] 2 KB 660, at 668, *per* Collins MR.

[20] See, eg, *Griffith v Tower Publishing Co* [1897] 1 Ch 21; *Nokes v Doncaster Amalgamated Collieries Ltd* [1940] AC 1014.

[21] Where the excellence the service provided depends on the input of the service provider, it is more likely that the obligation will be regarded as being personal: see *Johnson v Raylton, Dixon & Co* (1881) 7 QBD 438, at 444, *per* Cotton LJ.

[22] *Budana v The Leeds Teaching Hospitals NHS Trust & Anor* [2017] EWCA Civ 1980, at [47]. See also, by way of analogy, *Johnson v Raylton, Dixon & Co* (1881) 7 QBD 438, at 454, *per* Brett LJ; *Phillips v Alhambra Palace Co* [1901] 1 KB 59.

[23] *Budana v The Leeds Teaching Hospitals NHS Trust & Anor* [2017] EWCA Civ 1980, at [49] and [51(i)], *per* Gloster LJ, citing *Plevin v Paragon Personal Finance Ltd* [2017] UKSC 23.

practical relevance, especially in so far as pre-April 2013 conditional fee agreements are concerned.

32.20 **The putative assignment of obligations and burdens** It is trite law that whilst an unqualified benefit of a contract may usually be freely assigned, the burden of a contract generally may not.[24] For the reasons set out at 32.19, this principle—if it is applied—would prevent a legal services provider from assigning the right to charge for work yet to be done to another legal services provider.

32.21 It used to be thought that the 'conditional benefit principle' (see 32.22) could, in certain circumstances, act in such a way as to circumvent this problem.[25] This was the basis on which *Jenkins* assignments were thought to operate and has been the basis on which most putative assignments have been structured over the last decade. For the reasons set out at 32.24–32.27, it is now known that it is not possible to rely on that principle for the purposes of transferring the right to charge fees for work yet to be done from one legal services provider to another by way of assignment—although it is worth noting that Davis LJ, in a dissenting judgment, came to the opposite conclusion.[26] Indeed, on the basis of the law as it is presently understood to be, one could even go so far as to say that it is not possible to assign *any* obligations and burdens arising under a contract of retainer.[27]

32.22 The conditional benefit principle may be stated in this way: where a right under a contract is conditional upon, or qualified by, performance of some obligation in return for which the right has been granted, an assignee of the benefit of such right will be entitled to exercise the right only upon satisfying that obligation.[28] Speaking in a context other than contracts of retainer, Megarry V-C had the following to say on the topic:

> 'An instrument may be framed so that it confers only a conditional or qualified right, the condition or qualification being that certain restrictions shall be observed or certain burdens assumed, such as an obligation to make certain payments. Such restrictions or qualifications are an intrinsic part of the right: you take the right as it stands, and you cannot pick out the good and reject the bad. In such cases it is not only the original grantee who is bound by the burden: his successors in title are unable to take the right without also assuming the burden. The benefit and the burden have been annexed to each other *ab initio*, and so the benefit is only a conditional benefit.'[29]

---

[24] See, eg, *Scarf v Jardine* (1882) 7 App Cas 345, at 351, *per* Lord Selborne; *Tolhurst v Associated Portland Cement* [1902] 2 KB 660, at 668, *per* Collins MR; *Southway Ltd v Wolff* [1991] 57 BLR 33, at 52–3, *per* Bingham LJ; *Linden Gardens Trust Ltd v Lenesta Sludge Disposals Ltd* [1994] 1 AC 85, at 103, *per* Lord Browne-Wilkinson.

[25] See, eg, *Jenkins v Young Brothers Transport Ltd* [2006] EWHC 151 (QB). See also *Jones v Spire Healthcare Ltd* [2016] 3 Costs LO 487, at [78], *per* Judge Graham Wood QC; *Azim v Tradewise Insurance Services Ltd* [2016] EWHC B20 (Costs). These cases are no longer good law. It is worth noting that, even before this was known, some judges took a different view: see, eg, *Webb v Bromley London Borough Council* (unreported), 18 February 2016, SCCO, at [45] and [46], *per* Master Rowley.

[26] *Budana v The Leeds Teaching Hospitals NHS Trust & Anor* [2017] EWCA Civ 1980, at [89]–[105].

[27] *Budana v The Leeds Teaching Hospitals NHS Trust & Anor* [2017] EWCA Civ 1980, at [62(iv)], *per* Gloster LJ.

[28] See *Tito v Waddell (No 2)* [1977] 1 Ch 106, at 290, *per* Megarry V-C; *Rhone v Stephens* [1994] 2 AC 310, at 322, *per* Lord Templeman; *Davies v Jones* [2010] 1 P&CR 22, at [27], *per* Morritt Ch.

[29] *Tito v Waddell (No 2)* [1977] Ch 106, at 290. See also *Wilkinson v Kerdene* [2013] EWCA Civ 44; *Elwood v Goodman* [2014] Ch 442.

Whether or not the conditional benefit principle applies will—in general, rather than only in respect of contracts of retainer—turn on the terms of the contract in question.[30] More important for present purposes is the fact that it will apply only where the benefits and obligations are linked to each other in a dependent fashion.[31] Put otherwise, there needs to be more than a mere incidental combination of assignment and performance by persons other than the original contracting parties. An example unrelated to the law of costs would be where a person is granted the 'benefit' of the right of admission by way of ticket to an event: they may be under the 'burden' of producing the ticket to the event organisers.[32] The fact that that 'burden' exists would not prevent assignment of the benefit, because in reality it would merely be a condition. **32.23**

The non-availability of the conditional benefit principle in cases regarding contracts of **32.24**
retainer Until recently, it was thought that the conditional benefit principle was capable of applying to contracts of retainer in the sense that the benefit (namely, the right to be paid for work yet to be done) was conditional on the burden (namely, the obligation to carry out that work). Whilst Davis LJ dissented on the point,[33] it is now known that this is not the case. Gloster LJ (with whom Beatson LJ agreed) had this to say on the topic:

> 'In my view Rafferty J [in *Jenkins v Young Brothers Transport Ltd* [2006] EWHC 151 (QB)] wrongly sought to enlarge the scope, or the application, of the conditional benefit principle. The authorities show that it is a rule of limited scope; see e.g. *Rhone v Stephens* [1994] 2 AC 310. The imposition of the burden does not occur merely as a result of the taking of an incidental benefit, but only where a conscious decision is taken to exercise the benefit in circumstances where the burden that follows is directly related and correlates with the benefit taken; see e.g. *Thamesmead Town Ltd v Allotey* (1998) 20 HLR 1052 at 1060. Her view appears to have been that, simply because the solicitors' benefit—the right to payment—was conditional on the burden (undertaking the work), the principle applied. If that was the correct analysis, it is difficult to see why the burdens or obligations in any contract would not be capable of assignment. As [counsel for the paying party] submitted, her analysis does

[30] *Tito v Waddell (No 2)* [1977] Ch 106, at 297.

[31] See *Pan Ocean Shipping Co Ltd v Creditcorp, The Trident Beauty* [1994] 1 All ER 470, [1994] 1 WLR 161; *Radstock Co-operative and Industrial Society v Norton-Radstock UDC* [1967] Ch 1094.

[32] This is an example given by Furmston, M, *The Law of Contract* (London: Butterworths, 2010), para 6.293.

[33] In *Budana v The Leeds Teaching Hospitals NHS Trust & Anor* [2017] EWCA Civ 1980, at [97] and [98], Davis LJ said the following: 'I can see that it can be said that, in substance, there is not being assigned here the right simply to receive payment of costs, including success fee, in the event of the claimant's claim being successful, to which the professional services required to achieve that success are but an ancillary link. It can be said that, if anything, it is more the other way round: [the new firm] took on the obligation of providing professional services to the claimant (in fact, took on the entire contract) in the hope that they would reap the benefit, in the form of costs and success fee, if the claim succeeded ... [The] conclusion which I reach in this case does not, I think, depart unacceptably from the principles underlying the application of the doctrine of conditional benefit, to the extent that such principles are applicable. My decision is ultimately based on what I consider to be the effect of the tripartite contractual arrangements, based on the proper interpretation of those contractual arrangements: an effect which all parties clearly intended to achieve. If it is, in legal theory, necessary to style this as an extension of the principle of conditional benefit as applied in the context of CFAs (and I am not altogether sure that it is necessary) then that is an incremental extension which, in the present context of CFAs, I am prepared to make ... I agree with Judge Graham Wood QC when he said, in the course of his judgment in the County Court in the case of *Jones v Spire Healthcare Ltd* (11 May 2016) and in which he followed and applied the decision in Jenkins, that it would be "unduly restrictive" to deny the parties the effect of what they intended.'

> no more than identify the essential nature of a contract for services, namely that the right to payment arises from performance of the relevant service. If that is sufficient conditionality, then the effect of Rafferty J's judgment goes far wider even than the 'pure' benefit and burden principle which was rightly identified as being flawed and was rejected by the House of Lords in *Rhone v Stephens*.'[34]

Thus, as a matter of law, the conditional benefit principle will not apply to contracts of retainer in so far as work yet to be carried out is concerned.

32.25 *The effect of giving instructions* There is another reason why the conditional benefit principle will not apply, this being because the new legal services provider (that is, the assignee) would almost always need to obtain the client's consent before providing legal services. Indeed, in the editor's experience, express written permission is usually obtained in this regard, often by way of a deed or explicitly in correspondence. The effect of this is that the putative *Jenkins* assignment would, in truth, be a novation because the client and the new legal services provider would be brought into privity. Gloster LJ has confirmed that this would leave no room for the application of the conditional benefit principle.[35] Beatson LJ agreed with Gloster LJ, but Davis LJ dissented.

32.26 Bingham LJ had this to say on the point (albeit not in a case not concerning contracts of retainer):

> 'It is in general permissible for A, who has entered into a contract with B, to assign the benefit of that contract to C. This does not require the consent of B, since in the ordinary way it does not matter to B whether the benefit of the contract is enjoyed by A or by a third party of A's choice such as C. But it is elementary law that A cannot without the consent of B assign the burden of the contract to C, because B has contracted for performance by A and he cannot be required against his will to accept performance by C or anyone other than A. If A wishes to assign the burden of the contract to C he must obtain the consent of B, upon which the contract is novated by the substitution of C for A as a contracting party.'[36]

In practical terms, the effect of this is that it would not be possible to rely on the conditional benefit principle, even if (contrary to what is said at 32.24) that principle were capable of applying as a matter of law. As to what happens when a putative assignment leads to an unintended novation, see 32.34.

32.27 For the avoidance of doubt, the conditional benefit principle is not capable of acting in such a way as to prevent novation in the circumstances referred to above.[37]

The mechanisms of assignment

32.28 For the reasons set out above, the benefits and rights under a contract of assignment may be assigned and, indeed, this is often done. What follows deals with the mechanisms by which any such assignment may be effected—namely, assignment in law (see 32.29–32.30) and equitable assignment (see 32.31–32.32).

---

34 *Ibid*, at [62(vi)].

35 See *ibid*, at [55] and [62(i)], *per* Gloster LJ, citing *Tolhurst v Portland Cement* [1902] 2 KB 660, *per* Sir Richard Collins MR, and *Southway Ltd v Wolff* [1991] 57 BLR 33, at 52–3, *per* Bingham LJ.

36 *Southway Ltd v Wolff* [1991] 57 BLR 33, at 52–3.

37 *Budana v The Leeds Teaching Hospitals NHS Trust & Anor* [2017] EWCA Civ 1980, at [45], *per* Gloster LJ.

Assignment in law Legal assignment (otherwise known as statutory assignment) is governed by s 136 of the Law of Property Act 1925.[38] Compliance with the provisions set out therein will generally mean that an assignment has taken place. The following points may be made. **32.29**

- **Intention** Section 136(1) of the Law of Property Act 1925 requires an intention to assign—that is, an intention to make a transfer that is both immediate and irrevocable.
- **Consideration** Consideration is not required for an assignment under s 136 of the Law of Property Act 1925.[39]
- **In writing** Whilst there are no requirements as to form,[40] an assignment under s 136 of the Law of Property Act 1925 must be in writing and 'under the hand of' (which means signed by) the person making the assignment.[41]
- **Notice** In so far as assignments in general are concerned, express notice in writing of the assignment must be given to the obligor[42] (who, in this context, would be the client), although no notice need be given to the assignee.[43] Constructive notice would never be sufficient,[44] although there are no requirements in s 136 as to who is to give notice.[45] There are no formalities as to the notice, but it must be sufficiently clear to allow the client to know where they stand.[46] Notice may be included in the deed of assignment[47] (and often is in the context of contracts of retainer[48]).
- **Absolute assignment** Section 136 of the Law of Property Act 1925 applies only to absolute assignments.[49] An assignment will not be absolute if it is conditional,[50] but, for the reasons set out in 32.13–32.16, this is not a principle that causes problems in practice in so far as the right to be paid for work done under a conditional fee agreement is concerned.

---

[38] See *Jenkins v Young Brothers Transport Ltd* [2006] EWHC 151 (QB), at [14] (which remains good law on this point). Broadly speaking, the requirements are: (a) that the assignment is absolute; (b) that it must be in writing under the hand of the assignor; and (c) that express notice in writing thereof must be given to the debtor (ie the client).

[39] *Re Westerton* [1919] 2 Ch 104; *Harding v Harding* (1886) 17 QBD 442; *Holt v Heatherfield Trust Ltd* [1942] 2 KB 1, at 5.

[40] *Re Westerton* [1919] 2 Ch 104.

[41] It is a moot point whether an agent can sign: see *Wilson v Wallani* (1880) 5 Ex D 155; cf *Re Diptford Parish Lands* [1934] Ch 151.

[42] Notice may not, in general, be given to someone else—see *Consolidated Trust Co Ltd v Naylor* (1936) 55 CLR 423, at 439, *per* Dixon J—even if the obligor is illiterate: see *Amalgamated General Finance Co Ltd v C E Golding & Co Ltd* [1964] 2 Lloyd's Rep 163.

[43] See *Grey v Australian Motorists & General Insurance Co Pty Ltd* [1976] 1 NSWLR 669.

[44] *Consolidated Trust Co Ltd v Naylor* (1936) 55 CLR 423, at 439, *per* Dixon J.

[45] See *Anning v Anning* (1907) 4 CLR 1049, at 1059, *per* Griffith CJ.

[46] See *Court Line Ltd v Aktiebologet Gotaverken, The Halcyon the Great* [1984] 1 Lloyd's Rep 283.

[47] *Van Lynn Developments Ltd v Pelias Construction Co Ltd* [1969] 1 QB 607, at 615, *per* Widgery LJ; see also *Curran v Newpark Cinemas Ltd* [1951] 1 All ER 295.

[48] Although where this is so, the deed would need to be received by the client rather than merely shown to them: whilst not binding, see *Brown v Bank of Australasia* [1915] VLR 453. See also *Holt v Heatherfield Trust Ltd* [1942] 2 KB 1.

[49] See *Durham Bros v Robertson* [1898] 1 QB 765, at 773.

[50] An assignment will be conditional if it does not take effect immediately, but will take place only upon the performance of a condition or the happening of some uncertain event—see, eg, *Durham Bros v Robertson* [1898] 1 QB 765, at 773, *per* Chitty LJ—or if it reserves a power to deal with that which is purportedly being assigned—see, eg, *Court Line Ltd v Aktiebologet Gotaverken, The Halcyon the Great* [1984] 1 Lloyd's Rep 283—or if it ceases upon the happening of some event: see, eg, *Grey v Australian Motorists & General Insurance Co Pty Ltd* [1976] 1 NSWLR 669.

32.30 A statutory assignment is effective from the date of the notice rather than the date of making the instrument that sets out the terms of the assignment.[51] As soon as notice has been given, the original legal services provider ceases to be able to claim fees under the contract of retainer.[52]

32.31 **Equitable assignment** A transaction that fails to satisfy the requirements of s 136 of the Law of Property Act 1925 may still be upheld as a valid equitable assignment.[53] There is no prescribed form of such an assignment.[54] The principal requirement for such an assignment is that the intended assignor must have an intention to immediately dispose of the whole or part of their interest.[55] Valuable consideration is generally not required.[56] The subject matter of an equitable assignment (which, in the present context, would be the benefits under the contract of retainer) must be sufficiently identified.[57] There have been instances of the court finding that there has been equitable assignment of rights under conditional fee agreements.[58]

32.32 Whilst the contrary is arguable,[59] equitable assignment merely creates rights in the assignee with no corresponding disposal of rights by the assignor.[60] To the extent that this is correct, they are not true assignments. In practical terms, however, this is of limited relevance to the issue of contracts of retainer.

32.33 **Contractual bars to assignment** It may be that a contract of retainer contains a contractual bar to assignment; such provisions are lawful and tend to be effective.[61]

Novation

32.34 In the present context, novation will generally occur where there is an agreement with the client that the new legal services provider will continue to operate on the terms of the original contract of retainer with the old legal services provider.[62] More generally, it may be defined and distinguished from assignment in the following way:

> 'A novation consists of an agreement between what would be all the parties to an assignment (the assignor, the assignee and the obligor) under which, for valuable consideration, the contract between the "assignor" and "obligor" is discharged and a new contract, again made for valuable consideration, is entered into between the "obligor" and "assignee". A novation may also occur between the parties to a contract agreeing for valuable consideration to discharge one contract and to enter into a replacement contract.'[63]

---

[51] See *Holt v Heatherfield Trust Ltd* [1942] 2 KB 1.

[52] See *Gustavson v Haviland* [1919] 1 Ch 38.

[53] See *William Brandt's & Sons v Dunlop Rubber Co Ltd* [1905] AC 454, at 461, *per* Lord Macnaghten.

[54] See *Brandt's Sons & Co v Dunlop Rubber Co* [1905] AC 454, at 462; *Re Wale* [1956] 1 WLR 1346, at 1350; *Allied Carpets Group Plc v MacFarlane* [2002] EWHC 1155, at [32]–[33].

[55] See *Norman v Federal Comr of Taxation* (1963) 109 CLR 9.

[56] See *Holt v Heatherfield* [1942] 2 KB 1.

[57] See *Percival v Dunn* (1885) 29 Ch D 128.

[58] See, eg, *French v Hartman* [2014] EWHC 1682 (QB).

[59] See *Chitty on Contracts* (32nd edn, London: Sweet & Maxwell, 2015), at para 19.006.

[60] See Edelman, J, and Elliott, S, 'Two Conceptions of Equitable Assignment' (2015) 131 LQR 228. See also Furmston, M, *The Law of Contract* (London: Butterworths, 2010), para 6.281; Furmston, M, 'Assignment' (1998) 13 JCL 42.

[61] See, eg, *Linden Gardens Trust Ltd v Lenesta Sludge Disposals Ltd* [1994] 1 AC 85, at 106.

[62] *Budana v The Leeds Teaching Hospitals NHS Trust & Anor* [2017] EWCA Civ 1980, at [62(iii)], *per* Gloster LJ.

[63] See Furmston, M, *The Law of Contract* (London: Butterworths, 2010), para 6.264.

Thus there are two species of novation: where the original contract of retainer is (with the consent of the client) transferred to a new legal services provider; and where it is replaced by an entirely new contract of retainer. The focus of this discussion is on the former, but it is worth bearing in mind that the latter may be relevant from time to time (such as where a firm wishes to revise its contracts of retainer in bulk, in which case novation by way of a master deed may be an administratively convenient way of effecting such a change). **32.35**

Novation must be consensual.[64] Indeed, for the reasons set out at 32.25, the fact that consent is given will generally mean that a transfer of a contract of retainer will be by way of novation even where it was originally intended that it be by way of a *Jenkins* assignment. In contrast to assignment, valuable consideration is required,[65] but this requirement would almost always be met in the context of a transfer of a contract of retainer from one firm to another, because the agreement to supply legal services in return for a fee would suffice. **32.36**

The fact that novation creates a new contract of retainer means—a pedant may say—that there is no *transfer* of rights.[66] For the reasons set out below, however, this is of little practical relevance because novation is so close to being a transfer as to be almost indistinguishable. This is why, in this book, novation is described as being a means of transfer. **32.37**

Novation of pre-April 2013 conditional fee agreements

It used to be the generally received view that recent novation of a pre-April 2013 conditional fee agreement would create a new, post-April 2013, conditional fee agreement that was distinguishable from the antecedent agreement, thereby extinguishing any ongoing right on the part of the client to recover a success fee from an opponent. This is why the predominant intended method by which conditional fee agreements have been transferred from one firm to another has been by way of *Jenkins* assignment (see 32.06). **32.38**

It is now known, however, that the fact that a pre-April 2013 conditional fee agreement has been novated is not a bar to the recovery of success fees for work done after the novation. Gloster LJ has said that the question is not a bald one of whether a transfer was an assignment or novation, but whether the true effect of the contractual arrangements between the parties means that the receiving party had to pay a success fee under a conditional fee agreement that was entered into before 1 April 2013.[67] Gloster LJ went on to find that, for the purposes of the legislation governing success fees, an antecedent conditional fee agreement is capable of remaining in existence—as a contract valid as its date of creation—notwithstanding its transfer as between successive firms of legal services providers and that this would be so notwithstanding the fact that the client assented to such a transfer, thereby giving rise to a novation.[68] As to the effect that this had on the recoverability of any success fee, she had this to say: **32.39**

> '[T]he fact that there was a new contract does not mean that, for the purposes of section 44(6) of [the Legal Aid, Sentencing and Punishment of Offenders Act 2012], the success fee

[64] Consent is required: see *Rasbora Ltd v JCL Marine Ltd* [1977] 1 Lloyd's Rep 645; *The Blankenstein* [1985] 1 WLR 435.

[65] As to the requirement of consideration, see *Scarf v Jardine* (1882) 7 App Cas 345, at 351.

[66] See *Rasbora Ltd v JCL Marine Ltd* [1977] 1 Lloyd's Rep 645.

[67] *Budana v The Leeds Teaching Hospitals NHS Trust & Anor* [2017] EWCA Civ 1980, at [43].

[68] *Ibid*, at [51(ii)] and [51(iii)], *per* Gloster LJ, relying on *Plevin v Paragon Personal Finance Ltd* [2017] UKSC 23.

payable by the claimant to [the new legal services providers], as a result of the contractual arrangements, did not qualify as "a success fee payable by ... [the receiving party] *under a conditional fee agreement entered into before*" 1 April 2013.'[69]

32.40 Gloster LJ had this to say on the point:

> 'I accept the [receiving party's] submissions in relation to the construction of section 44 of [the Legal Aid, Sentencing and Punishment of Offenders Act 2012]. It is clear that the modern approach to statutory interpretation takes account of the apparent policy of that legislation ... Moreover, the policy of LASPO is also clear. In *Plevin* Lord Sumption, giving judgment for the majority, stated at [21] that:
>
> > "The purpose of the transitional provisions of LASPO, in relation to both success fees and ATE premiums, is to preserve vested rights and expectations arising from the previous law. That purpose would be defeated by a rigid distinction between different stages of the same litigation."
>
> Similarly, in my judgment, that purpose would be defeated by an overtechnical application of the doctrine of novation so as to prevent any litigant, who had begun a claim under a CFA prior to 1 April 2013, from recovering costs in respect of a success fee, simply because a novation had occurred as a result of a change in the constitution of the firm of solicitors acting for her, or as a result of conduct of her claim case being transferred, for whatever reason, to a new firm of solicitors. ... [W]here, as here, the parties expressly provide by their contractual arrangements that their vested rights and expectations, under the previous CFA entered into under the previous law, should be continued, I see no difficulty in construing section 44 to give effect to that intention.'[70]

32.41 Thus, whilst each case will turn on wording of the relevant documentation, there is no reason, in principle, why novation—intended or otherwise—will of itself extinguish the right to recover a success fee. In practical terms, this means that the fact that an intended *Jenkins* assignment of the benefit and burdens of a pre-April 2013 conditional fee agreement has unintentionally resulted in novation will be of little consequence.

The Management of Defective Contracts of Retainer

32.42 This section deals with the question of how contracts of retainer that contain errors should be managed. Its focus is necessarily on the remedial steps that a receiving party (or their legal services provider) may take. The topic is dealt with in three parts:

- the position between legal services provider and client (see 32.43);
- the remedial steps that may be taken before the entitlement to costs has arisen (see 32.56); and
- the remedial steps that may be taken after the entitlement to costs has arisen (see 32.65).

For the avoidance of doubt, the words 'remedy' and 'remedial' refer to solutions and palliations, rather than to any formal notion of legal remedy.

[69] *Ibid*, at [70].
[70] *Ibid*, at [72]–[75].

The position between legal services provider and client

Subject to any contrary law or regulatory provision, a legal services provider and its client may agree to be bound by any obligations that they care to negotiate, which means that (in principle) there is no reason why a contract of retainer cannot be amended or replaced with retrospective effect. Some of these issues have already been discussed in Chapters 27 and 29. There are, however, two aspects of the matter that merit further scrutiny: the first is the issue of undue influence—that is, the issue of whether asking a client to 'mend' a defective retainer amounts to undue influence (see 32.44); and the second, that of consideration (see 32.54). **32.43**

Remedial steps and undue influence

Where a legal services provider believes that the contract retainer is at risk of being unenforceable or otherwise ineffective, it may ask the client to take steps to deal with the situation—in particular, to make a new contract of retainer or to amend or rectify the existing one. If such a step were to be taken, this may lead to the client being asked to accept a liability that otherwise they might not have had; all other things being equal, this could be seen as asking the client to act against their rational self-interest. **32.44**

In the absence of justification, these circumstances may be capable of giving rise to issues of undue influence. This is a ground of relief developed by the courts of equity for the purposes of ensuring that the influence of one person over another is not abused. If a person makes an agreement in the context of a relationship of trust and confidence, the law may scrutinise the manner in which that agreement came into being—in particular, whether there was an abuse of that relationship. If the descendent agreement was procured by unacceptable means, it will not be permitted to stand.[71] This may have a bearing on the legal service provider's ability to recover fees. **32.45**

Actual and presumed undue influence Undue influence may be actual or presumed. The latter arises in certain classes of relationship between two persons in which one has acquired a measure of influence over the other.[72] A solicitor–client relationship automatically falls within that category;[73] indeed, there is an irrebuttable presumption of influence as between solicitor and client.[74] There is no particular reason to believe that the same would not be true of other types of legal services provider. **32.46**

Unlike actual undue influence (where something must be done to twist the mind of a complainant), presumed undue influence may arise as a result of inactivity. Put otherwise, once the relationship of trust has been demonstrated to exist, the issue may turn on what has *not* been done, such as the giving of impartial advice.[75] **32.47**

An example of a case in which the court found (*obiter*) that a client would have been able to rely on presumed undue influence was where an insolvency practitioner had instructed a firm on the basis that it would be paid only out of monies recovered: Judge Simon Barker **32.48**

---

71 *Huguenin v Baseley* (1807) 14 Ves 273, at 300.

72 *Royal Bank of Scotland v Etridge (No 2)* [2002] 2 AC 773, at [8]–[18].

73 This was accepted before Christopher Clarke J in *Forde v Birmingham City Council* [2009] EWHC 12 (QB).

74 *Royal Bank of Scotland v Etridge (No 2)* [2002] 2 AC 773, at [18]; *Willis v Barron* [1902] AC 271, HL.

75 *Daniel v Drew* [2005] EWCA 507.

QC (sitting as a judge of the High Court) found that the firm was estopped from claiming fees in the absence of any such recovery[76] and he went on to say that the firm would have been guilty of presumed undue influence had it tried to impose any other arrangements upon the insolvency practitioner without specifically alerting him to those new arrangements.[77] It has to be stressed, however, that it is rare for the court to make such findings, for the reasons given below.

32.49 **The relevance of 'ordinary motives'** In general, there will be no undue influence if the descendant contract of retainer came about as a result of 'ordinary motives'.[78] Christopher Clarke J found that a willingness on the part of a client to assist in the recovery of costs from a paying party could be said to arise from such motives: 'The ordinary motives of ordinary persons do not exclude doing the decent thing, even if some persons would not be minded to do so.'[79] Notwithstanding the fact that there had been no undue influence on the facts before him, Christopher Clarke J found that there was no reason in principle why a paying party should not be able to assert that there has been undue influence.[80] It is, however, very rare for such arguments to succeed.

32.50 **The effect of undue influence** A contract of retainer obtained as a result of undue influence is voidable, not void. It remains effective until set aside; such relief may be given on terms such as payment of a reasonable sum for services actually rendered.[81] Whilst his comments were technically *obiter*, Christopher Clarke J declined to hold that a failure by a solicitor to put its client's interests first would have the effect of turning any retainer resulting from that failure into a prohibited contract, but he went on to say that such a finding would have an effect of which Draco would have approved.[82] This is illustrative of the fact that a paying party who seeks to rely on undue influence is likely to face an uphill struggle.

32.51 It has been said that Christopher Clarke J's attention was not drawn to the long line of authorities (pre-dating statutory intervention concerning business agreements) that dealt with the way in which the common law viewed agreements restricting a client's right to an assessment. Those authorities supposedly demonstrate that the common law often found such agreements to be unenforceable, on bases that were almost indistinguishable from presumed undue influence (see 27.111–27.114). There may be some merit in that argument, but it should be borne in mind that it was generally not the contracts of retainer themselves that were found to be unenforceable, but the putative agreements that precluded the assessment of the fees payable under those contracts. It is therefore debatable whether Christopher Clarke J would have derived much assistance from those authorities.

---

76 *Stevensdrake Ltd v Hunt* [2016] EWHC 342 (Ch), at [107].

77 *Ibid*, at [114].

78 See *National Westminster Bank plc v Morgan* [1985] AC 686, at 704, approved in *Royal Bank of Scotland v Etridge (No 2)* [2002] 2 AC 773 and applied in *Forde v Birmingham City Council* [2009] EWHC 12 (QB).

79 *Forde v Birmingham City Council* [2009] EWHC 12 (QB), at [106].

80 *Ibid*, at [110]. Whilst it is not wholly clear from the judgment, it seems that Christopher Clarke J made these comments after having had his attention drawn (*ibid*, at [114]) to *Garbutt v Edwards* [2006] 1 WLR 2907.

81 See *Forde v Birmingham City Council* [2009] EWHC 12 (QB), at [111], citing *Johnson v EBS Pensioner Trustees Ltd* [2002] EWCA Civ 164 and *O'Sullivan v Management Agency & Music Ltd* [1985] 1 QB 429.

82 *Forde v Birmingham City Council* [2009] EWHC 12 (QB), at [114].

Nothing unfair about asking for payment of fees Christopher Clarke J found that there is nothing unfair about a legal services provider asking for payment of its fees, this having the effect of rendering the Unfair Terms in Consumer Contracts Regulations 1999[83] irrelevant.[84] There is no reason to believe that the position would be any different under the present-day consumer protection legislation discussed in Chapter 24 (assuming, of course, that there was compliance with that legislation in general). **32.52**

Success fees and undue influence It may be that the antecedent contract of retainer is a pre-April 2013 conditional fee agreement under which the client had an expectation that the success fee, if any, would be recovered from the opponent. If that type of agreement were to be entirely replaced retrospectively with a post-April 2013 conditional fee agreement that provided for a success fee, then the client would not be able to recover that fee and would have to bear the brunt of it personally. It would be arguable that the new agreement was obtained through undue influence, especially if the legal services provider claimed to be entitled to the new agreement as a matter of right. It is for this reason that it is not common to see defective pre-April 2013 conditional fee agreements replaced with agreements that provide for success fees. **32.53**

Remedial steps and consideration

There is nothing objectionable in principle about a legal services provider and a client agreeing that a contract of retainer should be replaced, amended or, where appropriate, rectified.[85] Where consideration is needed, the fact that the legal services provider would continue to act for the client would, in general, suffice.[86] Likewise, if the descendant retainer is on terms more favourable to the client than the first, then that too would amount to effective consideration.[87] **32.54**

If they were particularly concerned about consideration, the counterparties would be at liberty to create the descendant contract of retainer by way of deed. If properly executed, that would remove the need for consideration entirely. This is briefly discussed at 32.58. **32.55**

Remedial steps that may be taken before the entitlement to costs has arisen

The following paragraphs examine the way in which a retainer may be amended, replaced or rectified in the event of it being found merely to be at risk (that is, where the putative defect comes to light prior to any order for costs being made). The focus is on contentious business, but most of the points that are made will also apply to non-contentious business. **32.56**

The principles are broadly the same regardless of the type of retainer in question. Where the putatively defective retainer is a conditional fee agreement that provides for a success **32.57**

---

83 SI 1999/2083.

84 *Forde v Birmingham City Council* [2009] EWHC 12 (QB), at [158]–[162].

85 See, eg, *Plevin v Paragon Personal Finance Ltd* [2017] UKSC 23, at [9]–[14], esp [13] and [14], *per* Lord Sumption.

86 The notion of the continued provision of legal services amounting to good consideration is nothing new: see Duke LJ's dissenting judgment in *Wild v Simpson* [1919] 2 KB 544. In a more modern context, see *Forde v Birmingham City Council* [2009] EWHC 12 (QB), at [81]–[92].

87 *Forde v Birmingham City Council* [2009] EWHC 12 (QB), at [81]–[92], in which Clarke J distinguished *Foakes v Beer* (1884) 9 App Cas 605 and relied on the reasoning in *Williams v Roffey Bros & Nicholls (Contractors) Ltd* [1991] 1 QB 1, at 18: 'Consideration there must still be but, in my judgment, the courts nowadays should be more ready to find its existence so as to reflect the intention of the parties to the contract.'

fee, thought ought to be given to the recoverability of the success fee and the extent to which the client could fairly be asked to make a contribution thereto. In some circumstances, thought may also need to be given to the effect of *Simmons v Castle*[88] (see 54.195–54.196). Legal services providers need to take care not to allow their clients to enter into unfair bargains, not least because this would mean that the descendent agreement would be potentially unenforceable by reason of undue influence (see 32.55). The issues discussed in Chapter 24 may also be relevant.

Rectification and amendment

32.58 If the error in the contract of retainer is simply a typographical or printing error, then it may be possible to correct the putatively defective contract of retainer by way of a deed of rectification. Rectification in general is addressed at 32.67. It would be appropriate when both the legal services provider and client were in agreement that the contract of retainer does not properly record the intended terms. This is to be distinguished from amendment, which would change the contract of retainer, rather than merely remedy the incorrect way in which it was recorded.

32.59 **Deeds and formalities** There is no rule that a deed must be used if a contract of retainer is to be rectified or amended, but a deed is generally preferred to a simple contract, because it would be enforceable even in the absence of consideration.[89]

32.60 In the present context, a deed may be defined as a written instrument that is executed with the necessary formality and by means of which a client's obligation to pay for legal services is created or confirmed.[90] In respect of deeds made by individuals, the ancient common-law requirements have been abolished[91] and replaced by the following statutory requirements (which are set out only in so far as they are relevant to contracts of retainer).[92]

- The deed must make it clear on its face that the parties to it intended it to be a deed. It can do this by describing itself as a deed or by expressing itself to be executed or signed as a deed, or by some other means.
- The deed must be validly executed as a deed:
  - by that person, or a person authorised to execute it in the name or on behalf of that person; or
  - by one or more of those parties, or a person authorised to execute it in the name or on behalf of one or more of those parties.
- The deed must have been signed by the individual in the presence of a witness who attests the signature (or at their direction and in their presence and the presence of two witnesses who each attest the signature).
- The deed must be delivered as a deed.

---

88 *Simmons v Castle* [2012] EWCA Civ 1039.

89 As to consideration, see *Morley v Boothby* (1825) 3 Bing 107, at 111–12, *per* Best CJ.

90 Adapted from the definition in Law Commission, *Execution of Deeds and Documents by or on Behalf of Bodies Corporate*, CP143 (London: HMSO, 1998).

91 Law of Property (Miscellaneous Provisions) Act 1989, s 1(1) (as amended). The common-law requirements related to the types of materials on which a deed must be written and how it must be sealed.

92 See Law of Property (Miscellaneous Provisions) Act 1989, s 1 (as amended).

32.61 The position concerning registered companies and limited liability partnerships is more complex because the common law continues to apply. Moreover, the memoranda and articles of association may prescribe additional formalities.[93] Under the common law, a deed made by a company must be made under seal, but the effect of this requirement is significantly diminished by the fact that a company registered under the Companies Act 1985 is no longer required to have a common seal.[94] Generally speaking, where a deed has been signed by a director and the secretary of a company, or by two directors, and where it has been expressed to be executed by the company, that document has the same effect as if it had been executed under the common seal of the company.

32.62 Other formalities exist.[95] In view of the fact that the exact formality requirements may depend on the type of corporation, and on what is written in the memoranda and articles of association (or other document setting out the constitution of the corporation), advice must be taken before a deed is executed on behalf of a corporation.

32.63 Finally, care also ought to be taken to ensure that any formalities are complied with in respect of a rectified contract of retainer. In theory, rectification will operate *ab initio*, but a cautious legal services provider would wish to work on the basis that the effect of the deed may be to unintentionally create an amendment or even a novated retainer. Whilst now unlikely to be encountered, if the putatively defective contract of retainer is a pre-1 April 2013 conditional fee agreement, it may be necessary to consider whether notice of funding ought to be re-served.

Miscellaneous practice points

32.64 The following general points may be made.

- **Whether to create one retainer or two** Where there is a possibility that the retrospective element of the descendant contract of retainer may be unlawful or unenforceable (perhaps because of an unusual aspect of the case that makes a finding of undue influence a real possibility), then thought ought to be given to making two contracts of retainer rather than one. The first (which is often a contentious business agreement) would apply to costs that have already been incurred; the second (which is often a CFA Lite, but may be any type of contractual retainer) would apply to costs yet to be incurred. Other combinations may be appropriate, depending on the circumstances.
- **The use of contentious business agreements** Each case will turn on its own facts, but where the descendant retainer is not intended to be a conditional fee agreement, then it would be sensible to enter into a contentious business agreement, rather than a non-statutory (that is, ordinary) private retainer. This is because there is express statutory provision that a contentious business agreement may be retrospective.[96]
- **Conditional or non-conditional replacement** Where the original contract of retainer was a conditional fee agreement, thought should be given to whether the descendent contract ought to be a conditional or non-conditional retainer. If the reality is that the

93 See *Clarke v Imperial Gas Light and Coke Co* (1832) 4 B & Ad 315, at 324.
94 See Law of Property (Miscellaneous Provisions) Act 1989, s 36A (as amended).
95 See, eg, Law of Property Act 1925, s 74A (as amended).
96 See Solicitors Act 1974, s 59(1).

success fee is not likely to be recovered and that the condition of a 'win' is almost certainly going to be met, then it may be best to enter into a new retrospective contentious business agreement (see above) rather than to run the risk, however slight, that the court might find some difficulty arising out of the use of a conditional fee agreement.

- **Redundancy** Thought ought to be given to incorporating redundant (that is, back-up) provisions in the descendant retainer. This can be done in one of two ways: the first is to stipulate that if the descendant is found to be unenforceable, inapplicable or void, then the counterparties agree to rely on the antecedent retainer as if the changes had never been made;[97] the second is to make the descendant contract of retainer itself redundant, in the sense that it comes into play only if a finding is made that the antecedent contract is unenforceable, inapplicable or void. This is not recommended, however, because it may lead to the descendent being formed only after the entitlement to costs has arisen (see 32.65).
- **Severability clauses, assignment clauses, etc** Thought ought to be given to including a severability clause. The descendant retainer is likely to be the subject of intense scrutiny and, as such, it must be as robust as possible. Thus it is normally advisable to include provisions concerning all eventualities, such as assignment, insolvency, etc (see 27.327–27.339).
- **Interest** The antecedent contract of retainer may have made provision for the payment of interest in the event of non-payment. If this is the case, then it may be necessary to make provision within the descendant contract for ensuring that that interest is not charged in an inappropriate or unfair way.
- **Consumer legislation** Descendant retainers are often made by distance communication methods or in clients' homes, so there is the possibility that consumer protection regulations may apply. This topic is addressed at 28.81 *et seq*. Indeed, the matters referred to in Chapter 28 ought to be borne in mind generally.
- **The cost of taking advice about defective retainers** The costs of remedying problems with contracts of retainer are not likely to be recoverable from an opposing party. A receiving party would be well advised not to claim the costs of taking remedial steps in the bill of costs because this may give the paying party an unwelcome insight into the receiving party's affairs.
- **Proper disclosure to the court and the paying party** It would be improper to submit a bill of costs that gives a misleading impression. Practice Direction (PD) 47, para 5.11(3), requires that the bill of costs should set out 'a brief explanation of any agreement or arrangement between the receiving party and his legal services providers which affects the costs claimed in the bill'. Although there is no authority on the point, common sense dictates that that requirement should not be interpreted so narrowly as to mislead by omission.

Remedial steps that may be taken after the entitlement to costs has arisen

32.65 If an entitlement to costs has already crystallised, there is not a great deal that can usefully be done to remedy any problems with the contract of retainer—although rectification of a genuine error may still be available (see 32.67). This is because any steps taken (with the possible exception of rectification where there was evidence of genuine mistake in the way

[97] See, eg, *Forde v Birmingham City Council* [2009] EWHC 12 (QB), at [79]–[80].

in which the retainer was recorded) would generally be ineffective as against the paying party. Lord Carswell had this to say on the point:

> 'It was quite open to the [receiving party] and his attorneys to vary the fee agreement ... if they so wished ... If, however, [the variations] were likely to produce a larger costs bill than the original framework ... the [paying party] would be entitled simply to refuse to accept the amended basis and require the respondent to revert to the original framework ... [The paying party] could do so on the ground ... that that amendment had come into existence subsequent to the making of the costs basis and so could be disregarded by the paying party if he wished.'[98]

Lord Carswell was giving an opinion on the Privy Council, so his comments are not binding, but McCombe LJ has confirmed that they ought to be followed.[99] McCombe LJ went on to clarify that the bar against retrospective amendments after the costs order has been made is not a mere point of reasonableness, but a point of principle, and in doing so he affirmed the following comments of Warby J in the court below: 'The liability to pay costs crystallises at that point and, although its quantum will remain to be worked out, that process must be governed by the liabilities of the receiving party as they stand at that time.'[100]

Where a party finds themselves with a putatively defective contract of retainer in circumstances in which they have already become entitled to costs, they would, for all practical purposes, have only very limited options. Rare situations aside,[101] those options would be as follows. **32.66**

- **Interpretation (or 'common-law rectification')** The first port of call would usually be to try to persuade the court to interpret the contract of retainer as being enforceable and effective (see 31.41–31.47).
- **Rectification** Where the error is a mere error in the way in which the true contract of retainer has been recorded, then rectification may be available (see 32.67–32.74).
- ***Quantum meruit*** This is addressed at 18.91–18.99. As can be seen, *quantum meruit* is rarely available in the context of a defective contract of retainer.

Rectification

Rectification is an equitable remedy that may be available in cases in which the written instrument does not accurately record what the counterparties intended it to say. In effect, the court rectifies the document so that it reflects the true intentions of the counterparties. The following paragraphs deal largely with rectification on evidence; rectification by deed is addressed at 32.58–32.63. **32.67**

Cozens-Hardy MR described rectification in this way: 'The essence of rectification is to bring the document which was expressed and intended to be in pursuance of a prior agreement into harmony with that prior agreement.'[102] It is important to distinguish between **32.68**

---

98 *Kellar v Williams (Appeal No 13 of 2003)* [2004] UKPC 30, at [20].

99 *Radford & Anor v Frade & Ors* [2018] EWCA Civ 119, at [44]–[47].

100 *Ibid*, at [49], affirming *Radford & Anor v Frade & Ors* [2016] EWHC 1600 (QB), at [67], *per* Warby J.

101 Such as set-off of costs against monies owed by the solicitor to the client. The arguments are complex: *Cosslett (Contractors) Ltd) v Bridgend County Borough Council* [2001] UKHL 58 would be a good place to start.

102 *Lovell and Christmas Ltd v Wall* [1911–13] All ER Rep Ext 1630, at 1634.

rectification and interpretation—or 'common-law rectification', as it is sometimes called (see 31.41). Where the argument is that the factual circumstances of the case are such that the only reasonable conclusion is that a particular term meant something other than what it at first appears to say, the argument is then one of interpretation, rather than rectification. Where the argument is that the written instrument incorrectly records the true agreement between the counterparties, then that would imply a need for (true) rectification. Lord Neuberger had the following to say on the topic:

> 'If it is a question of interpretation, then the document in question has, and has always had, the meaning and effect as determined by the court, and that is the end of the matter. On the other hand, if it is a question of rectification, then the document, as rectified, has a different meaning from that which it appears to have on its face . . .'[103]

The issue of interpretation ought to be addressed before any attempt is made to rectify the document.[104] However, there is no reason, in principle, why the arguments cannot be advanced in the alternative.

32.69 The fact that the antecedent contract of retainer is unenforceable by reason of its failure to comply with a statutory provision will not prevent it from being capable of rectification.[105] It is not known whether the same applies when the issue is whether there has been compliance with regulations concerning retainers.

32.70 The court will grant relief only where relief is required and will not grant it where it is not required. That said, the fact that there may be no dispute between the counterparties is not a bar to the granting of relief.[106] (This will often be relevant in the context of contracts of retainer because the dispute is frequently brought on by a stranger to the contract—namely, the paying party—rather than by the counterparties themselves.)

32.71 The remedy of rectification will not extend to subject matter that the parties did not consider at the time the contract was made. This is so even if it can be shown that they *would* have come to the requisite agreement *if* they had turned their minds to the matter.[107] In practical terms, this often presents a considerable obstacle in so far as contracts of retainer are concerned, because the 'mistaken' provision in the antecedent document is often, in truth, a consequence of a lack of intention, rather than an inaccurately expressed intention.

32.72 The antecedent instrument will not be ignored and 'convincing proof' would normally be required to contradict it.[108] Again, this may cause difficulties in the context of contracts of retainer: if, for example, the correspondence was vague and inconclusive—as it often is—a claim for rectification may fail for want of evidence as to what the parties really meant by their agreement.

32.73 Rectification may not be available where it impinges upon the rights of a third party. There is a respectable argument for saying that this would include the paying party.[109]

---

103 *Marley v Rawlings* [2014] UKSC 14, at [36]–[40].

104 *Sloggett and Perry v Stroud* [2000] Lexis Citation 2052, CA, at [19], *per* Chadwick LJ.

105 See *United States v Motor Trucks Ltd* [1924] AC 196.

106 See *Seymour v Seymour* (1989) The Times, 16 February.

107 See *Harlow Development Corpn v Kingsgate (Clothing Productions) Ltd* (1973) 226 EG 1960.

108 *Thomas Bates v Wyndham's (Lingerie) Ltd* [1981] 1 WLR 505, at 521.

109 In particular (and in addition to the principles already mentioned arising from *Kellar*, etc), the court will not rectify a document where a third party has purchased an interest for value without notice: *Garrard*

However, where the interest has not been acquired for value, a claim for rectification would not necessarily be defeated by the existence of a third party.[110] The issue of whether rectification is available for the purposes of restoring a paying party's liability arising out of a mistaken retainer is very much a moot point.[111]

In summary, rectification is fraught with legal difficulties and it is often challenging from the factual point of view. It tends to be an option of last resort. **32.74**

---

v Frankel (1862) 30 Beav 445. In addition, the provision of an indemnity by a third party may qualify as an interest: see *Nurdin & Peacock plc v DB Ramsden & Co* [1999] 1 All ER 941.

[110] See *Load v Green* (1846) 15 M & W 216.

[111] Irwin J was asked to express an *obiter* view on this issue, but he declined, presumably because he felt that the issue merited more than only an *obiter* comment: *Crook v Birmingham City Council* [2007] EWHC 1415 (QB).

Part IX

AGREEMENTS WITH FUNDERS AND INSURERS

33

LITIGATION FUNDING

This chapter deals with the following topics: **33.01**

- introduction (33.03);
- public policy and relevant history (33.04):
  - history and comparative law (33.08);
- future developments:
  - regulation (33.27);
  - blurring the boundaries (33.30);
  - alternative business structures (33.31);
- present legislative control (33.32);
- the provision of litigation funders to consumers (33.34);
- availability and practice (33.59):
  - types of claim (33.64);
  - minimum values (33.65);
  - acceptance of cases (33.67);
  - remuneration (33.69);
  - after-the-event insurance (33.71);
  - independent legal advice (33.72);
  - control of litigation (33.73);
  - contractual provisions (33.74); and
- disclosure of funding (33.85).

The editor is grateful to Kevin de Haan QC and Nick Rowles-Davies (Chief Executive Officer, Chancery Capital) for their expert assistance in writing this chapter. For more detail than is set out below, see Rowles-Davies, N, *Third-party Litigation Funding* (Oxford: Oxford University Press, 2014). **33.02**

Introduction

An agreement for litigation funding—the preferred name for what used to be called third-party funding—is an agreement whereby a stranger to a dispute provides funding (other than insurance) in return for a share of the proceeds. It also goes by the names of litigation financing, professional funding and—occasionally, in older authorities—sponsoring. Speaking extrajudicially, Jackson LJ defined 'litigation funding' in the following way: **33.03**

> '[Litigation funding is the] funding of litigation by a party who has no pre-existing interest in the litigation, usually on the basis that (i) the funder will be paid out of the proceeds of

any amounts recovered as a consequence of the litigation, often as a percentage of the recovery sum; and (ii) the funder is not entitled to payment should the claim fail.'[1]

Public Policy and Relevant History

33.04 If such an arrangement were to be adjudged by the law as it stood in or before the early 1980s, then—with one or two exceptions relating to insolvency—litigation funding would have been condemned as being champertous. Indeed, prior to 1967, the creation of such an agreement may even have been a criminal offence. Champerty, however, is a doctrine based on public policy, and that means that it is far from immutable (see 30.13–30.14 and 30.25). The chronology set out below explains how public policy has changed so that, far from regarding it as being repugnant, public policy has now come to embrace certain types of litigation funding as desirable. It should be noted that the same is true in many (but not all[2]) other common-law jurisdictions (see 30.25).

33.05 It is not possible to point to 'the' authority that confirmed the legality of litigation funding nor is it possible to point to any such legislation; rather, litigation funding has become lawful by a piecemeal process that, in part, has been the result of tacit acceptance and extrajudicial commentary. The prime example of tacit acceptance is *Arkin v Borchard Lines Ltd*,[3] in which the Court of Appeal ruled on an ancillary matter without passing any adverse comment on the fact that the litigation had been funded by way of a litigation funding agreement (see 33.14). As has been explained in the discussion of champerty in Chapter 30, up until the mid-1960s a litigation funding agreement would have been not only unenforceable, but also illegal in the criminal sense. 'Sponsoring' was permitted in the context of insolvency,[4] but that was restricted in scope[5] and, in any event, bore no more than a passing resemblance to modern-day litigation funding.

33.06 The law has changed beyond recognition since those days. Speaking extrajudicially in 2009,[6] Jackson LJ identified the following benefits of litigation funding that now seem to be generally accepted as justifying its existence on policy grounds.

---

[1] Jackson, R, *Review of Civil Litigation Costs: Preliminary Report* (London: HMSO, 2009), vol 1, p viii.

[2] See, eg, *Thema International Fund PLC v HSBC Institutional Trust Services (Ireland) Ltd* [2011] IEHC 357; more recently, *Persona Digital Telephony Ltd & Sigma Wireless Networks Ltd v The Minister for Public Enterprise* [2017] IESC 27. Both explain that litigation funding continues to be champertous in Ireland.

[3] *Arkin v Borchard Lines Ltd* [2005] EWCA Civ 655.

[4] In *Guy v Churchill* (1888) 40 Ch D 481, there was an assignment on terms that the assignee would continue the action in his name and pay to the trustee in bankruptcy 25 per cent of any net recovery. Chitty J upheld the assignment. The decision was followed by the Court of Appeal in *Ramsey v Hartley* [1977] 2 All ER 673, [1977] 1 WLR 686, in which the trustee assigned a cause of action to the bankrupt in consideration of receiving 35 per cent of any net recovery. See also *Seear v Lawson* [1880] 15 Ch D 426.

[5] In *Grovewood Holdings plc v James Capel & Co Ltd* [1994] 2 BCLC 782, [1995] Ch 80, there was no outright assignment of the cause of action, but a sponsorship arrangement under which the action was pursued in the name of the company, but at the expense of the sponsors and with the assistance of, but not subject to the control of, the liquidator. In the result, the action was stayed as champertous. See *Rawnsley v Weatherall Green & Smith North Ltd* [2009] EWHC 2482 (Ch), *per* HHJ Behrens, for a discussion of this area of the law.

[6] Jackson, R, *Review of Civil Litigation Costs: Final Report* (London: HMSO, 2010), ch 11, para 1.2. He also commented that third-party funding would become more important if success fees were to become irrecoverable between opposing parties.

- Litigation funding promotes access to justice by providing an additional—or for some, their only—means of funding litigation.
- Notwithstanding the fact that a successful claimant with litigation funding will be liable to the funder for a percentage of their winnings, that is a better position to be in than to recover no winnings at all.
- The use of litigation funding does not impose additional financial burdens upon paying parties.[7]
- The screening process used by litigation funders tends to filter out unmeritorious cases, which is of benefit to opposing parties.

Given the fact that other senior judges, such as Lord Neuberger NR,[8] have commented favourably on litigation funding (again, extrajudicially) and also given the fact that Jackson LJ's comments were made following extensive public consultation, it can safely be said that the policies that underlay the rules of champerty no longer hold sway over the law. **33.07**

History and comparative law

To fully understand the relevant public policy, it is necessary to look at the history of litigation funding both in this country and in other common-law countries.[9] It is also necessary to consider the development of conditional funding generally. To that extent, there is a degree of overlap with the history of conditional fee agreements (see 29.203). The law in other common-law jurisdictions is also relevant, for two reasons: first, policy-makers now, more than ever, look at what is happening in other common-law jurisdictions; and secondly, funders tend to be global investors, rather than domestic entities, and are therefore well equipped to argue that more conservative jurisdictions are behind the times. **33.08**

Up to and including 1995

Whilst, in the UK, the crime of champerty was abolished in the 1960s, it was not until the 1980s that Parliament felt able to enact legislation making conditional fee agreements lawful (see 29.208–29.209). At that stage, there was no mention of litigation funding, but the acceptance of conditional funding in any form was a significant step that laid the groundwork for further developments. Despite it being enacted in 1990, that legislation did not come into force until 1995 (see 29.209); when it did, it was a significant event. With hindsight, it can be seen that the Rubicon had been crossed. Similar developments were taking place in other jurisdictions: in the 1990s, for example, Australian legislation was passed that also permitted conditional funding.[10] **33.09**

---

[7] As set out fn 46, Courts and Legal Services Act 1990 (as amended), s 58B(8), does, in fact, contain provision requiring the payment of any amount payable under a litigation funding agreement, but this is not in force and it might be argued that it is unlikely ever to come into force other than, perhaps, in the context of a small, barrister-driven contingency legal aid fund.

[8] See his comments, made in a press release dated November 2011, in which he welcomed the Code of Conduct of Litigation Funders.

[9] For a full analysis of this topic, see Mulheron, R, 'Third-party Funding: A Changing Landscape' (2008) 27(3) CJQ 312.

[10] It would be excessive to give the historic details, but in 1995 administrators and liquidators were given powers that allowed them to dispose of company assets in such a way as to make a profit from something similar to litigation funding.

33.10 There were also developments in the common law. In 1994, the House of Lords—dealing with issues that bore a degree of similarity to litigation funding[11]—explained that the approach to public policy was more nuanced than had previously been believed. Their Lordships established that the question of whether an agreement claiming a stake in litigation was objectionable is to be answered by asking whether the agreement under scrutiny has a 'tendency to corrupt public justice', and they determined that this issue turns on the nature and surrounding circumstances of the agreement in question.[12] The relevance of this is that a funding agreement would not be struck down automatically as a matter of law merely because it belonged to a certain class of agreement. It must be stressed, however, that, at this stage, litigation funding of the type that is seen today was not regarded as lawful.

Early 2000s

33.11 In the late 1990s and early 2000s, the court repeatedly demonstrated a flexible and pragmatic approach to cases that previously would have been characterised as champertous.[13] By way of example, in a case in which litigation had been funded by shipping brokers who had a 4–5 per cent interest in the placement of certain contracts that they gave up in return for a 55 per cent interest in the proceeds of the litigation, the Court of Appeal found that no champerty existed because the funders 'had no opportunity to influence the conduct of any proceedings abusively', and because their involvement came 'nowhere near' being wanton and officious intermeddling.[14]

33.12 Moreover, the use of conditional funding had become a quotidian means of providing legal services. Many commentators said that the long-standing objections that had been relied upon to justify the law of champerty relating to funders began to sound hoary and hollow.

33.13 In 2002, the Court of Appeal (in the UK) clarified the law of champerty in such a way as to permit persons other than solicitors to enter into agreements in which payment of their fees was dependent on success: it was established that the mere fact that litigation services had been provided in return for a share of the proceeds was not, by itself, sufficient to justify a finding of unenforceability.[15] It was at about this time that modern-day litigation funding agreements started to emerge. That said, it was a slow start, not least because litigation funders in other common-law jurisdictions suffered a series of setbacks, largely as a result of funders trying to sequester to themselves an excessive degree of control over the litigation.[16]

---

[11] A putatively champertous car hire agreement.

[12] *Giles v Thompson* [1994] 1 AC 142.

[13] See, eg, *Papera Traders Co Ltd v Hyundai (Merchant) Marine Co Ltd (No 2)* [2002] 2 Lloyd's Rep 692, in which marine claims assessors carried out work on a 'no cure, no pay' basis under which they would be entitled to a fee of 5 per cent of the recovered amount. Cresswell J found that this was not objectionable, largely because the defendant was protected from any claim for excessive fees by the process of assessment under CPR, Part 47.

[14] *Stocznia Gdanska SA v Latvian Shipping Co* [2001] BCC 174, at 205.

[15] *R (Factortame Ltd & Ors) v Secretary of State for Transport, Local Government and Regions (No 8)* [2002] EWCA Civ 932.

[16] See, eg, the Australian case of *Clairs Keeley (a firm) v Treacy & Ors* (2003) 28 WAR 139, which was stayed because the court found that the fact that the case had been assigned to the funder meant that the litigation was proceeding without reference to the plaintiff in any way. Likewise, in *Marston v Statewide Independent Wholesalers Ltd* [2003] NSWSC 816, the funder had contractually prevented communication between the solicitors and the plaintiffs, which—unsurprisingly—was held to be an abuse of process.

Mid-2000s

The legality of litigation funding agreements in the UK was confirmed by the Court of Appeal in 2005,[17] but this was by way of what was *not* said rather than by way of an express ruling. The matter was an application for a non-party costs order in a claim that had plainly and openly been funded by a litigation funder. The court *could* have disposed of that application by finding that litigation funding was an anathema that should inevitably lead to the funder being condemned in costs to the maximum extent, but instead the court pragmatically weighed the interests of all of the persons involved (including the interests of the funder) and determined, in the round, how much, if any, the funder should contribute to its opponent's costs. In particular, the court found that the funder should be potentially liable for costs up to the limit of its investment (this being the '*Arkin* cap', which is discussed at 9.38–9.44). The way in which the court approached that issue implied that litigation funding was in some ways desirable, but, more importantly, it strongly implied that it was lawful. Phillips MR explained the benefits of litigation funding as being that: **33.14**

- professional funders would be likely to cap the funds that they provide to limit their exposure to a reasonable amount;
- this would have a salutary effect in keeping costs proportionate; and
- professional funders would also have to consider, with even greater care, whether the prospects of the litigation are sufficiently good to justify the support that they are asked to give.[18]

Thus litigation funding had become accepted as lawful and in accordance with public policy. Rowles-Davies has the following to say about *Arkin*: **33.15**

> 'By its decision in *Arkin*, the Court of Appeal established a framework within which professional funders could operate and understand the extent of the commercial risks they ran by being involved, with a view to profit, in funding the other party's litigation. Generally, unless they had entered into champertous agreements ... where their degree of control of the litigation, or their anticipated reward from it, was outside acceptable limits, funding would not be exposed to unlimited costs liabilities of third parties. The case struck a balance between competing considerations that, on the one hand, a successful party should recover costs which another party has caused him to incur, and on the other hand, that it was public policy to help to ensure access to justice. The consequence of capping funders' exposure to another party's costs is, of course, that such other party is left to bear a proportion of its own costs which otherwise it might never have been incurred. It is such parties who, in this context, to that extent, pay the price of giving effect to the public policy of enabling access to justice.'[19]

The topic of the funder's potential liability for adverse costs is discussed in detail at 9.37–9.44.

It is also worth noting that—at about the same time—the Australian courts were recording the benefits of litigation funding in almost exactly the same terms as those used by Phillips MR.[20] Indeed, the rise of conditional funding in Australia then gathered pace. In 2006, the High Court of Australia[21] handed down decisions that, for all practical **33.16**

[17] *Arkin v Borchard Lines Ltd* [2005] EWCA Civ 655.

[18] *Ibid*, at [42].

[19] Rowles-Davies, N, *Third-party Litigation Funding* (Oxford: Oxford University Press, 2014), para 2.67.

[20] See, eg, *Fostif Pty Ltd v Campbells Cash & Carry Pty Ltd* (2005) 63 NSWLR 203, at [100]; *QPSX Ltd v Ericsson Australia Pty Ltd (No 3)* (2005) 219 ALR 1, at [54].

[21] This being a court the decisions of which are binding on all courts in Australia.

purposes, abolished the common-law rules against champerty and maintenance.[22] It said this about the age-old concerns that underlay those rules: '[T]o meet these fears by adopting a rule in either form would take too broad an axe to the problems that may be seen to lie behind the fears.'[23]

33.17 Thus, in Australia, questions of illegality and public policy would be answered according to the prevailing circumstances (that is, on the facts of each case). This echoed the position in the UK (see 33.13–33.14). The High Court of Australia noted that existing substantive and procedural rules were, in general, sufficient to protect court processes.[24]

Late 2000s

33.18 In early 2007, in the UK, the Civil Justice Council spoke positively about litigation funding.[25] This reinforced the view that public policy now tolerated such agreements. In that same year, the Office of Fair Trading (OFT) recommended that litigation funding ought to be encouraged in private competition claims (a type of litigation that is notoriously difficult to fund),[26] because the OFT hoped that this would discourage anti-competitive practices—something that was obviously in the public interest.

33.19 In Australia—where funding was being used primarily for class actions—defendants were complaining that the involvement of funders was not facilitating the resolution of disputes, but allowing lawyers to stir up disputes, and defendants also brought a number of technical challenges. On the whole, however, most of the challenges based on policy were rejected.[27]

33.20 Speaking extrajudicially in 2008, retired English judge Sir Gavin Lightman said that 'throwing aside the shackles of the past law' on champerty and maintenance 'would release litigants and funders from rules which are positively damaging to the public'.[28] The Master of the Rolls made similar comments. Some commentators began to discuss why litigation funding was not being more widely adopted;[29] other commentators noted that recent developments in the law of conditional fee agreements would be a boon to the future development of litigation funding.[30] Thus the debate in the UK had got to the stage at which policymakers were looking at how litigation funding could be given a more prominent role in the litigation landscape.

---

[22] See *Campbells Cash and Carry Pty Ltd v Fostif Pty Ltd* (2006) 229 CLR 386; *Mobil Oil Australia Pty Ltd v Trendlen Pty Ltd* [2006] HCA 42.

[23] *Campbells Cash and Carry Pty Ltd v Fostif Pty Ltd* (2006) 229 CLR 386, at [91].

[24] *Ibid*, at [92].

[25] Civil Justice Council, *Improved Access to Justice: Funding Options and Proportionate Costs* (London: HMSO, 2007).

[26] Office of Fair Trading, *Private Actions in Competition Law: Effective Redress for Consumers and Businesses*, OFT916 (London: HMSO, 2007).

[27] For example, in *Jeffery and Katauskas Pty Ltd v Rickard Constructions Pty Ltd* (2009) 239 CLR 75, the High Court rejected the argument that a failure by the litigation funder to provide security for costs amounted to an abuse of process. Similarly, in *Deloitte Touche Tohmatsu v JP Morgan Portfolio Services Ltd* (2007) 158 FCR 417, the full Federal Court summarily rejected arguments by the appellant that there was an abuse of process, essentially relying on *Campbells Cash and Carry Pty Ltd v Fostif Pty Ltd* (2006) 229 CLR 386 and *Mobil Oil Australia Pty Ltd v Trendlen Pty Ltd* [2006] HCA 42.

[28] Rose, N, 'Radical Shake-up Needed in Funding of Litigation', *Law Society Gazette*, 20 March 2008.

[29] Ciumei, C, 'A More Open Competition' (2008) 158(7321) NLJ 691.

[30] Friel, S, 'Funding Manoeuvres' (2009) 159(7369) NLJ 707.

Also in 2008, Coulson J made certain comments regarding representations and warranties that are generally regarded as being of relevance to funders[31] (albeit in a case that did not concern litigation funding).[32] The claimant was contractually obliged to refurbish a property in which it had acquired a leasehold interest. There was an agreement with the defendant under which the claimant sublet the property to the defendant and agreed to carry out refurbishment works. Those works were carried out by a builder. A dispute arose between the claimant and the builder, but they settled on the basis that the builder was entitled to pursue and, if necessary, enforce the claims against the defendant; indeed, the builder was given 'full and unfettered' control of such claims. This gave rise to the question of whether the settlement agreement between the claimant and the builder was champertous, and hence unlawful. Moreover, the claimant had given a warranty that it had not done, and would not do, anything to prejudice the claim—a fact that the defendant thought pointed towards champerty. Coulson J disagreed: he found that the builder had an entirely legitimate financial interest in the outcome of the present proceedings; indeed, he found that the case was 'as far from ... champerty as it is possible to get'.[33] In particular, the warranty did not assist the defendant. **33.21**

Rowles-Davies has this to say about the importance of Coulson J's judgment: **33.22**

> 'Coulson J's reasoning is significant for the operation of third party funding. In practice funders will require warranties and representations, as to the truth of instructions and alignment of conduct in a fashion supportive of their case, from those who seek their assistance. This is not unreasonable given the very substantial investment that funders must frequently make ... The judgment recognizes that such commitments are not sought so as to interfere with the integrity of the proceedings, and should not be construed in that fashion.'[34]

Thus Coulson J's decision was regarded as being confirmation that funders were able to seek certain warranties and declarations from their clients. To that extent at least, the funder was permitted a degree of control over the litigation.

In 2009, the Jackson Review called for comments about whether the common law of champerty and maintenance ought to be replaced by a regulatory framework. Following consultation, Jackson LJ (speaking extrajudicially) concluded that whilst it was not necessary to abolish champerty and maintenance, litigation funding was to be encouraged (see 33.05); although he believed that it was too early to impose a legislative regulation, he did recommend a voluntary code (see 33.27).[35] The issue of regulation arose in Australia too, albeit in the context of contested cases, rather than consultation.[36] **33.23**

---

[31] For a more detailed discussion of this topic, see Rowles-Davies, N, *Third-party Litigation Funding* (Oxford: Oxford University Press, 2014), paras 2.68–2.72.

[32] *London & Regional (St George's Court) Ltd v Ministry of Defence* [2008] EWHC 526 (TCC).

[33] *Ibid*, at [108].

[34] Rowles-Davies, N, *Third-party Litigation Funding* (Oxford: Oxford University Press, 2014), para 2.72.

[35] Jackson, R, *Review of Civil Litigation Costs: Final Report* (London: HMSO, 2010), ch 11, paras 2.1–2.12.

[36] In *Brookfield Multiplex Ltd v International Litigation Funding Partners Pte Ltd* (2009) 256 ALR 427, the defendant in funded proceedings challenged the propriety of the litigation funding arrangements, citing the lack of regulation as a relevant factor.

Early 2010s

33.24 The effect of these developments has been to shift the focus away from legality and towards regulation, both in the UK and elsewhere.[37] The Australian courts have concluded that litigation funding arrangements are, where appropriate, to be treated as investment products and that they are to be regulated in that way,[38] but the practical effect of such findings is limited.[39] No specific regulations had, at the time of writing, been made (other than to require that funders have in place a process for managing conflicts of interest), but debate on the topic is ongoing.[40] The Law Council of Australia has noted that, despite clear rulings by the Australian High Court as to the legality of litigation funding (see 33.14), there continued to be satellite litigation on the topic.[41] The Australian courts are, in some ways, a few years ahead of the UK in terms of the arguments that are likely to arise, so it is possible that the UK will follow suit. That said, there is less willingness in the UK to deal with the issue of champerty on a case-by-case basis[42] and this may be enough to save the UK from excessive satellite litigation.

33.25 In the UK, the Civil Justice Council has recommended that a voluntary association ought to be established.[43] As is explained at 33.27–33.29, this was achieved in November 2011, when the Association of Litigation Funders of England & Wales (ALF) was formed and published its rules of membership. The Code of Conduct for Litigation Funders was also first published at this time—a development that the Master of the Rolls has welcomed.[44]

33.26 Litigation funding became far more prevalent in the 2010s. It has been suggested that one of the drivers of this growth was the fact that the global financial crisis of 2007–08 and subsequent economic recession caused cash flow problems for solicitors and clients alike, and that this forced some firms to be more innovative in the way in which they funded cases.[45]

---

[37] See, eg, Law Council of Australia, 'Regulation of Third-party Litigation Funding in Australia', Position paper, June 2011; see also *International Litigation Partners Pte Ltd v Chameleon Mining NL* [2011] NSWCA 50, in which the New South Wales Court of Appeal dealt with a litigation funding agreement as if it were any other financial product.

[38] In *International Litigation Partners Pte Ltd v Chameleon Mining NL* [2011] NSWCA 50, at [45] (see also the headnote), the New South Wales Court of Appeal found that the funder must hold a financial services licence because the funding agreement was a 'financial product' which involved 'managed risk'.

[39] The practical effect of decisions to treat litigation funders as financial service providers is limited because of ASIC Class Order 10/333, which exempts litigation funders from holding a financial services licence.

[40] In 2011, the Law Council of Australia concluded that only guidelines were necessary for the purpose of regulating lawyers and that either guidelines or regulations would be sufficient for regulating funders: see Law Council of Australia, 'Regulation of Third-party Litigation Funding in Australia', Position paper, June 2011, at para 70. In 2014, the Australian Productivity Commission published a report entitled *Access to Justice Arrangements*, in which it recommended regulation and licensing of litigation funders. The government response to the Commission report, released in April 2016, was silent on the subject of regulation of litigation funding.

[41] See Law Council of Australia, 'Regulation of Third-party Litigation Funding in Australia', Position paper, June 2011, para 54.

[42] See, eg, *Morris v London Borough of Southwark* [2011] EWCA Civ 25, at [57], *per* Lord Neuberger MR.

[43] Annex D to the CJC's 2009 submission to the Jackson Review, which submission is no longer available online.

[44] See his comments made in a press release dated November 2011, in which he welcomed the Code of Conduct of Litigation Funders.

[45] See Rowles-Davies, N, *Third-party Litigation Funding* (Oxford: Oxford University Press, 2014), para 3.08.

Future Developments

Regulation

Whilst a statutory framework for regulation exists, it is not yet in force and is largely ignored.[46] There are those who say that it will never come into force (or, at least, that there are parts of it that will never come into force).[47] Some commentators have noted that there is an absence of regulation of litigation funding.[48] That may be so, but this is probably because the focus has been on self-regulation, rather than legislation. Of particular concern, it has been said, is the absence of any solvency requirements.[49] This is in marked contrast to insurers, who, for many years, have had to satisfy the financial regulators as to their solvency. Speaking extrajudicially in 2009, Jackson LJ recommended a voluntary code,[50] echoing the thoughts of a number of academics.[51] Shortly thereafter, the Civil Justice Council published a draft voluntary code of conduct, but Jackson felt that that code did not go far enough in terms of consumer protection.[52] A new (voluntary) Code of Conduct for Litigation Funders was first published in November 2011, revised in November 2016 and then revised again in January 2018. That Code does not apply to funders who are already the subject of statutory regulation; thus, if funding is provided by a bank—and, **33.27**

[46] That framework is Courts and Legal Services Act 1990, s 58A, as amended by Access to Justice Act 1999, s 28: '**58B Litigation funding agreements.** (1) A litigation funding agreement which satisfies all of the conditions applicable to it by virtue of this section shall not be unenforceable by reason only of its being a litigation funding agreement. (2) For the purposes of this section a litigation funding agreement is an agreement under which—(a) a person ("the funder") agrees to fund (in whole or in part) the provision of advocacy or litigation services (by someone other than the funder) to another person ("the litigant"); and (b) the litigant agrees to pay a sum to the funder in specified circumstances. (3) The following conditions are applicable to a litigation funding agreement—(a) the funder must be a person, or person of a description, prescribed by the Secretary of State; (b) the agreement must be in writing; (c) the agreement must not relate to proceedings which by virtue of section 58A(1) and (2) cannot be the subject of an enforceable conditional fee agreement or to proceedings of any such description as may be prescribed by the Secretary of State; (d) the agreement must comply with such requirements (if any) as may be so prescribed; (e) the sum to be paid by the litigant must consist of any costs payable to him in respect of the proceedings to which the agreement relates together with an amount calculated by reference to the funder's anticipated expenditure in funding the provision of the services; and (f) that amount must not exceed such percentage of that anticipated expenditure as may be prescribed by the Secretary of State in relation to proceedings of the description to which the agreement relates. (4) Regulations under subsection (3)(a) may require a person to be approved by the Secretary of State or by a prescribed person. (5) The requirements which the Secretary of State may prescribe under subsection (3)(d)—(a)include requirements for the funder to have provided prescribed information to the litigant before the agreement is made; and (b) may be different for different descriptions of litigation funding agreements. (6) In this section (and in the definitions of "advocacy services" and "litigation services" as they apply for its purposes) "proceedings" includes any sort of proceedings for resolving disputes (and not just proceedings in a court), whether commenced or contemplated. [. . .] (8) A costs order made in any proceedings may, subject in the case of court proceedings to rules of court, include provision requiring the payment of any amount payable under a litigation funding agreement. (9) Rules of court may make provision with respect to the assessment of any costs which include fees payable under a litigation funding agreement.'

[47] In particular, it is close to inconceivable that the provision permitting recovery of funding monies between opposing parties (see s 58B(8)) will ever come into force.

[48] See, eg, Pirozzolo, R, 'Opinion: Funder the Cosh', *The Lawyer*, 11 August 2009.

[49] *Ibid.* See also Jackson, R, *Review of Civil Litigation Costs: Final Report* (London: HMSO, 2010), ch 11.

[50] Jackson, R, *Review of Civil Litigation Costs: Final Report* (London: HMSO, 2010), ch 11, para 6.1. This is an issue that has been considered by the Civil Justice Council.

[51] See, eg, Mulheron, R, 'Third-party Funding: A Changing Landscape' (2008) 27(3) CJQ 312.

[52] Jackson, R, *Review of Civil Litigation Costs: Final Report* (London: HMSO, 2010), ch 11, para 6.1.

accordingly, is regulated—then the Code would not apply. Equally, the Code applies only to those litigation funders who are members of the ALF.

33.28 In addition to provisions concerning confidentiality, promotional literature, etc, the Code of Conduct for Litigation Funders 2018 contains provisions relating to solvency,[53] client counselling[54] and conduct of cases.[55] It also contains the following provisions concerning the contents of any litigation funding agreement:

> '10. The LFA [litigation funding agreement] shall state whether (and if so to what extent) the Funder or Funder's Subsidiary or Associated Entity is liable to the Funded Party to:
> 10.1 meet any liability for adverse costs that results from a settlement accepted by the Funded Party or from an order of the Court;
> 10.2 pay any premium (including insurance premium tax) to obtain costs insurance;
> 10.3 provide security for costs; and
> 10.4 meet any other financial liability.'[56]

33.29 The Code of Conduct for Litigation Funders 2018 also provides that:

> '11. The LFA shall state whether (and if so how) the Funder or Funder's Subsidiary or Associated Entity may:
> 11.1 provide input to the Funded Party's decisions in relation to settlements;
> 11.2 terminate the LFA in the event that the Funder or Funder's Subsidiary or Associated Entity:
> 11.2.1 reasonably ceases to be satisfied about the merits of the dispute;
> 11.2.2 reasonably believes that the dispute is no longer commercially viable; or
> 11.2.3 reasonably believes that there has been a material breach of the LFA by the Funded Party.
>
> 12. The LFA shall not establish a discretionary right for a Funder or Funder's Subsidiary or Associated Entity to terminate a LFA in the absence of the circumstances described in clause 11.2.
>
> 13. If the LFA does give the Funder or Funder's Subsidiary or Associated Entity any of the rights described in clause 11, the LFA shall provide that:
> 13.1 if the Funder or Funder's Subsidiary or Associated Entity terminates the LFA, the Funder or Funder's Subsidiary or Associated Entity shall remain liable for all funding obligations accrued to the date of termination unless the termination is due to a material breach under clause 11.2.3;

[53] Both Code of Conduct of Litigation Funders 2018, paras 9.4 and 9.5, and Rules of the Association of Litigation Funders, r 3.15, deal with the capital adequacy provisions for funders, including maintaining access to adequate financial resources to cover funding obligations for a 36-month period, access to a minimum of £5 million of capital, and ongoing obligations of disclosure and audit in that regard.

[54] Code of Conduct of Litigation Funders 2018, para 9.1, provides that a funder will 'take reasonable steps to ensure that a Funded Party shall have received independent advice on the terms of the LFA prior to its execution, which obligation shall be satisfied if the Funded Party confirms in writing to the Funder that the Funded Party has taken advice from the solicitor instructed in the dispute'.

[55] Code of Conduct of Litigation Funders 2018, para 9.2, prevents the funder from taking 'any steps that cause or are likely to cause the Funded Party's solicitor or barrister to act in breach of their professional duties', whilst para 9.3 provides that the funder will 'not seek to influence the Funded Party's solicitor or barrister to cede control or conduct of the dispute to the Funder'.

[56] Code of Conduct of Litigation Funders 2018, para 10.

13.2 if there is a dispute between the Funder or Funder's Subsidiary or Associated Entity and the Funded Party about settlement or about termination of the LFA, a binding opinion shall be obtained from a Queen's Counsel who shall be instructed jointly or nominated by the Chairman of the Bar Council.'

Blurring the boundaries

Some commentators have noticed that the boundary between litigation funding and after-the-event (ATE) insurance has become blurred in the sense that many funders now limit their funding to adverse costs and that some insurers are prepared to agree to provide an indemnity for the costs of security for costs applications.[57] Indeed, it is now commonplace for insurers to provide a deed of indemnity or bond for the purposes of security for costs.[58] Most litigation funders say that it is condition of funding that adequate ATE insurance is obtained. This has led certain funders to forge close relationships with ATE providers, with a view to ensuring that there is adequate cover for adverse costs across their 'portfolio', or book, of investments. Indeed, many of those who work in litigation funding have a background in ATE insurance and vice versa. **33.30**

Alternative business structures

With the introduction of alternative business structures (ABSs) under the Legal Services Act 2007, it is possible that risk may be more widely spread in the future (at least amongst lawyers), but that this will do nothing to stifle innovation.[59] It is certainly true to say that funders are already seeking to forge links with lawyers who previously would not have considered such links, such as barristers in independent practice. **33.31**

Present Legislative Control

There is, at present, nothing to suggest that the UK is likely to follow the Australian lead and actively seek to regulate litigation funders by means of the state's general powers to regulate financial services providers (see 33.24). That said, where funding is offered to consumers, then they will, where appropriate, become entitled to the protection of the Consumer Credit Act 1974 and the Consumer Credit Act 2006 and the Financial Services and Markets Act 2000. For the reasons set out at 33.34–33.58, however, there is doubt as to whether it is possible to provide litigation funding (as it is presently understood) to consumer clients. **33.32**

At present, most funding agreements are with commercial clients and it seems that voluntary regulation is not only lawful (see 33.42), but also the preferred method of control. The same also seems to be true of the role of solicitors: prior to 6 October 2011, there was a provision that prevented solicitors from entering into certain agreements with funders **33.33**

[57] Amey, M, 'Litigation Funding' (2009) 61 Litigation Funding 24.

[58] See Pirozzolo, R, 'Opinion: Insurers and Third-party Funders Should Work Together', *The Lawyer*, 1 December 2008.

[59] It is noteworthy that Burford Capital, a funder listed on the Alternative Investment Market (AIM), has an alternative business structure (ABS) licence and formed Burford Law in 2015, an ABS law firm that supports and complements Burford Capital's judgment enforcement business.

of personal injury claims,[60] but it is noticeable that those provisions have no counterpart in the Solicitors' Regulation Authority (SRA) Code of Conduct 2011[61]—presumably, because claims management services are regulated by other means (namely, the Compensation Act 2006).

The Provision of Litigation Funders to Consumers

33.34 Over the last few years, litigation funders have extended the range of their business activities to provide funding to consumer clients, in contrast to more traditional funding, which has historically been provided only to commercial clients. For the reasons set out in 33.36–33.58, such practices are of questionable legality. There are two aspects to the matter: first, whether a litigation funder who provides funding to consumer clients needs to be an authorised person for the purposes of the Financial Services and Markets Act 2000 (see 33.36–33.50); and secondly, whether a litigation funding agreement with a consumer client is capable of being compliant with the Consumer Credit Act 1974 and its associated delegated legislation (see 33.51–33.58).

33.35 As will be explained, whilst there is no authority on the point, it seems likely that it is extremely difficult, if not impossible, to provide traditional litigation funding to consumers. It is worth noting that academic lawyers have recently raised similar concerns about litigation funding in other jurisdictions.[62]

The Financial Services and Markets Act 2000

33.36 Whilst some litigation funders are authorised persons for the purposes of the Financial Services and Markets Act 2000, many are not. What follows is a discussion of the relevance of the fact that a funder may not be authorised. As will be explained, this tends not to cause problems if the funded client is a business (see 33.42), but it creates considerable problems if the funded client is a consumer.

33.37 The starting point is the 'general prohibition', which is defined in s 19 of the Financial Services and Markets Act 2000 in the following way:

> '19 **The general prohibition**
> (1) No person may carry on a regulated activity in the United Kingdom, or purport to do so, unless he is—

[60] Solicitors' Code of Conduct 2007, para 9.01(4)–(6), used to provide as follows: '(4) You must not, in respect of any claim arising as a result of death or personal injury, either: (a) enter into an arrangement for the referral of clients with; or (b) act in association with, any person whose business, or any part of whose business, is to make, support or prosecute (whether by action or otherwise, and whether by a solicitor or agent or otherwise) claims arising as a result of death or personal injury, and who, in the course of such business, solicits or receives contingency fees in respect of such claims. (5) The prohibition in para 9.01(4) shall not apply to an arrangement or association with a person who solicits or receives contingency fees only in respect of proceedings in a country outside England and Wales, to the extent that a local lawyer would be permitted to receive a contingency fee in respect of such proceedings. (6) In para 9.01(4) and (5) "contingency fee" means any sum (whether fixed, or calculated either as a percentage of the proceeds or otherwise howsoever) payable only in the event of success in the prosecution or defence of any action, suit or other contentious proceedings.'

[61] Indeed, serious thought was given to the relevant provisions being excluded from the Solicitors Code of Conduct 2007: see *Cook on Costs 2011* (LexisNexis, online), para 41.18.

[62] See, eg, Skiba, PM, and Xiao, J, 'Consumer Litigation Funding: Just Another Form of Payday Lending?', available online at https://scholarship.law.duke.edu/cgi/viewcontent.cgi?article=4840&context=lcp

(a) an authorised person; or
(b) an exempt person.
(2) The prohibition is referred to in this Act as the general prohibition.'

In so far as it is relevant, s 22 of the Financial Services and Markets Act 2000 defines 'regulated activities' as follows: **33.38**

'22 **Regulated activities**
(1) An activity is a regulated activity for the purposes of this Act if it is an activity of a specified kind which is carried on by way of business and—
(a) relates to an investment of a specified kind . . . ;
[. . .]
(4) "Investment" includes any asset, right or interest.
(5) "Specified" means specified in an order made by the Treasury . . .'

Regulated activities are, in broad terms, defined in Sch 2 to the Financial Services and Markets Act 2000. In so far as it is relevant, the making of investments is not a regulated activity, but dealing in investments and arranging deals in investments are, as is managing investments.[63] **33.39**

Activities of a 'specified kind' are, however, defined by the Financial Services and Markets Act 2000 (Regulated Activities) Order 2001.[64] In so far as it is relevant, art 60B of that Order provides as follows: **33.40**

'60B **Regulated credit agreements**
(1) Entering into a regulated credit agreement as lender is a specified kind of activity.
(2) It is a specified kind of activity for the lender or another person to exercise, or to have the right to exercise, the lender's rights and duties under a regulated credit agreement.
"credit agreement"—
(3) In this article—
(a) . . . means an agreement between an individual or relevant recipient of credit ("A") and any other person ("B") under which B provides A with credit of any amount;
[. . .]
"exempt agreement" means a credit agreement which is an exempt agreement under articles 60C to 60H, but where only part of a credit agreement falls within a provision of articles 60C to 60H, only that part is an exempt agreement under those articles;
"regulated credit agreement" means—
(a) in the case of an agreement entered into on or after 1st April 2014, any credit agreement which is not an exempt agreement . . .
[. . .]'

Thus, whilst litigation funding would not generally fall within the ambit of the general definition of 'regulated activities' (see 33.39), it would fall within the ambit of being a 'specified' activity if it were to be a regulated credit agreement. This would not be so, however, if the agreement were to be an 'exempt agreement'.

63 See the Financial Services and Markets Act 2000, Sch 2, Pt 1, esp paras 2, 3 and 6.
64 SI 2001/544.

33.41 An exempt agreement is a credit agreement that is defined as such under arts 60C–60H of the Financial Services and Markets Act 2000 (Regulated Activities) Order 2001.[65] In particular, art 60C provides as follows:

> '**60C Exempt agreements: exemptions relating to the nature of the agreement**
> (1) A credit agreement is an exempt agreement for the purposes of this Chapter in the following cases.
> [...]
> (3) A credit agreement is an exempt agreement if—
> (a) the lender provides the borrower with credit exceeding £25,000, and
> (b) the agreement is entered into by the borrower wholly or predominantly for the purposes of a business carried on, or intended to be carried on, by the borrower.'

33.42 This is likely to be the reason why most litigation funding has not fallen within the ambit of the definition of regulated credit agreements, because, historically, most litigation funding has been provided to businesses for the purposes of commercial disputes and the amounts that have been involved have almost always been substantially in excess of £25,000.

33.43 There is nothing in the Financial Services and Markets Act 2000 (Regulated Activities) Order 2001 that provides that an agreement to provide credit to consumers would be exempt.[66] This is not surprising, as the whole point of the legislation delegated under the Financial Services and Markets Act 2000 is to protect consumers.

33.44 The foregoing discussion invites the question of whether a litigation funding agreement would be regarded as a credit agreement. 'Credit' is defined as including 'a cash loan and any other form of financial accommodation'.[67] This definition is broad, because it was intended to comprehend all existing forms of consumer credit facility and any new forms that may be devised. According to the editors of *Goode: Consumer Credit Law and Practice*, the purpose of this definition is to ensure that nothing that may fairly be regarded as credit shall fall outside the Act, whether by accident or through a deliberate evasion.[68] At the heart of the statutory definition of 'credit' are two ideas: (a) lending—that is, an advance in cash or its equivalent; and (b) financial accommodation, such as a deferral of what would otherwise be an immediate obligation to pay for goods, services or some other value received.

33.45 Whilst there is no authority on the point and whilst each case would have to be decided on its own facts, it is likely that most litigation funding would fall within the definition of a credit agreement, because litigation funding usually involves the advancement of cash (namely, the deployed funding) and a financial accommodation in the sense that there is a deferral of what would otherwise have been an immediate obligation to repay those monies. Indeed, many, if not most, litigation funding agreements directly provide for repayment of the deployed funding out of damages (usually as an item that takes priority over other potential deductions). Moreover, where litigation funding is provided to consumers, it tends

---

[65] SI 2001/544.

[66] See Financial Services and Markets Act 2000 (Regulated Activities) Order 2001 (SI 2001/544), Ch 14A.

[67] See Financial Services and Markets Act 2000 (Regulated Activities) Order 2001 (SI 2001/544), art 60L(1).

[68] See *Goode: Consumer Credit Law and Practice* (London: LexisNexis, 1999), para 5.8.

to be provided to 'individuals' (either in the sense that each funded client has a funding agreement directly with the funder or in the sense that, in group litigation, funding is made available to them via a working committee under a costs sharing agreement).

In view of these things, where litigation funding is extended to consumers, this may create a regulated credit agreement for the purposes of the Financial Services and Markets Act 2000 (Regulated Activities) Order 2001.[69] If this is so, then the funder must be either an authorised or exempt person if they are to avoid contravening the general prohibition (see 33.37). Many litigation funders are not authorised, so this invites the question of whether they would be exempt. **33.46**

Certain persons are exempted from the general prohibition, but, in the present context, this would be so only if the following conditions were met: **33.47**

- they were a member of a profession (or controlled or managed by one or more such members);
- they accounted to their clients for commission received;
- the relevant activities were 'incidental to the provision by him of professional services';
- the relevant activities were of a certain permitted type and were not of a prohibited type; and
- the relevant activities were the only regulated activities carried out (other than regulated activities in relation to which the person in question may be an exempt person).[70]

These provisions permit solicitors to be treated as 'exempt' in certain circumstances. Such persons are permitted to carry on activities known as exempt regulated activities without being regulated by the Financial Conduct Authority (FCA); instead, they are under the supervision of the SRA, which is known as a designated professional body. The provisions that allow solicitors to be treated as exempt are contained in Part XX of the Financial Services and Markets Act 2000, which is why the exemption is often known as the Part XX exemption. **33.48**

It is difficult to see how Part XX exemption could apply to a litigation funder, even if a solicitor were involved in the provision of funding. It is true that the SRA Financial Services (Scope) Rules 2001 (as amended)[71] permit solicitors to enter into regulated credit agreements as lenders where the agreement in question relates exclusively to the payment of disbursements or professional fees due to the firm,[72] and it is also true that those Rules permit solicitors to exercise a lender's rights and duties under a regulated credit agreement in similar circumstances.[73] In general, however, the involvement of a solicitor will not be in either of these capacities for the purposes of litigation funding. **33.49**

In view of these matters, where a litigation funder who is not an authorised person provides funding to consumer clients, this—depending on the facts—would be in breach of **33.50**

69 SI 2001/544.
70 See Financial Services and Markets Act 2000, s 327.
71 The Scope Rules were made under ss 31, 79 and 80 of the Solicitors Act 1974, ss 9 and 9A of the Administration of Justice Act 1985, and s 83 of the Legal Services Act 2007, with the approval of the Legal Services Board under Legal Services Act 2007, Sch 4, para 19.
72 See SRA Financial Services (Scope) Rules 2001 (as amended), para 2.1(p).
73 See SRA Financial Services (Scope) Rules 2001 (as amended), para 2.1(q).

the general prohibition. Where this is so, not only would the funder have committed a criminal offence,[74] but also the agreement would be unenforceable (subject to the court ordering otherwise).[75]

The Consumer Credit Act 1974

33.51 The Consumer Credit Act 1974 imposes regulation on certain contracts relating to credit and on certain aspects of ancillary credit business. Much of the detailed machinery of the legislation is implemented by way of regulations made under the Act.

33.52 Although the Consumer Credit Act 1974 is described as an Act for the protection of consumers, 'consumer' is not defined within it and, in any event, the Act was amended some years ago to refer instead to 'individuals'. There is no doubt, however, that it covers not only individuals in the sense of single natural people, but also small partnerships and other unincorporated associations.[76]

33.53 Central to the functioning of much of the Consumer Credit Act 1974 is the term 'credit', which has already been addressed at 33.44–33.45. One could argue that many, if not most, traditional litigation funding agreements would be for 'credit'.

33.54 For the purposes of the Consumer Credit Act 1974 and in so far as it is relevant, a consumer credit agreement is defined in the following way:

> '8 **Consumer credit agreements**
> (1) A consumer credit agreement is an agreement between an individual ("the debtor") and any other person ("the creditor") by which the creditor provides the debtor with credit of any amount.
> [...]
> (3) A consumer credit agreement is a regulated credit agreement within the meaning of this Act if it—
> (a) is a regulated credit agreement for the purposes of Chapter 14A of Part 2 of the Regulated Activities Order ... ;
> [...]'

33.55 The reference to 'Chapter 14A of Part 2 of the Regulated Activities Order' is, rather confusingly, a reference to arts 60B–60M of the Financial Services and Markets Act 2000 (Regulated Activities) Order 2001.[77] This topic has already been addressed (see 33.41–33.43). It seems that traditional litigation funding would generally qualify as the provision of a consumer credit agreement.

33.56 Consumer credit agreements are highly regulated. It would be extremely difficult—if not impossible—to provide traditional litigation funding in a way that would comply with those

---

[74] See Financial Services and Markets Act 2000, s 23.

[75] See Financial Services and Markets Act 2000, ss 20 and 26.

[76] 'Individual' is defined as including partnerships consisting of two or three persons, not all of whom are bodies corporate, and unincorporated bodies not consisting entirely of bodies corporate: see Consumer Credit Act 1974 s 189(1). This is similar to the definition found in the Financial Services and Markets Act 2000 (Regulated Activities) Order 2001 (SI 2001/544), art 60L(1). Loans to companies are outside the scope of the Consumer Credit Act 1974.

[77] SI 2001/544.

requirements.[78] As such, s 65(1) of the Consumer Credit Act 1974[79] would make any such agreement enforceable against the client only on the order of the court. Put otherwise, it would be *prima facie* unenforceable—and this would be so even if the funder were an authorised person or an exempt person for the purposes of the Financial Services and Markets Act 2000.

The court's discretion under s 65(1) of the Consumer Credit Act 1974 is a structured discretion. It is governed by s 127 of that Act, which (in so far as it is relevant) reads as follows: **33.57**

> '127 **Enforcement orders in cases of infringement**
>
> (1) In the case of an application for an enforcement order under—
> (a) section 65(1) (improperly executed agreements), or
> [...]
> the court shall dismiss the application if, but ... only if, it considers it just to do so having regard to—
> (i) prejudice caused to any person by the contravention in question, and the degree of culpability for it; and
> (ii) the powers conferred on the court by subsection (2) and sections 135 and 136.
>
> (2) If it appears to the court just to do so, it may in an enforcement order reduce or discharge any sum payable by the debtor or hirer, or any surety, so as to compensate him for prejudice suffered as a result of the contravention in question.'

(The reference to ss 135 and 136 is to the powers of the court to impose conditions or to vary the infringing agreement.)

It is not known how the court would exercise its discretion under these provisions. Presumably, each case would be decided on its own facts. **33.58**

Availability and Practice

Litigation funding has grown from an obscurity into a mainstream industry. As of January 2009, fewer than 100 claims in England and Wales were funded by litigation funders.[80] The number of funded cases has increased significantly since then and whilst the numbers are still relatively small due to the requirements of single case litigation funding, the market is now mature, rather than nascent. **33.59**

Whilst an oversimplification, litigation funding tends to be available in the following circumstances: **33.60**

- where the party seeking funding is a claimant or counterclaimant (although this is not an absolute requirement);[81]

[78] It may be possible to provide a form of funding to consumers by way of a contract for differences, but even this would be fraught with difficulties.

[79] Which reads: 'An improperly-executed regulated agreement is enforceable against the debtor or hirer on an order of the court only ...'

[80] Pirozzolo, R, Personal communication with the author, 25 November 2009.

[81] See Rowles-Davies, N, *Third-party Litigation Funding* (Oxford: Oxford University Press, 2014), paras 3.20–3.32. Defendant litigation funding is the smallest of small print, but is possible if the client and funder can agree on what will amount to a 'win' and what the terms of remuneration should be. In practice, this tends to be possible only where the litigation is about how a sum of money is to be divided rather than a simple claim for debt or damages.

- where the claim is large—that is, six or seven figures (see 33.65)—and where the defendant is adjudged to be able to satisfy any judgment made against them;
- where the prospects of success are very good—usually at least 70 per cent likely to succeed (see 33.67); and
- where the risks can be shared with both an ATE insurer and the client's lawyers (see 33.67), and where the lawyers are experienced and competent at the type of claim in question.[82]

33.61 In the same way that ATE insurers work on the basis of the actuarial principles of adequacy and equity (see 54.158), litigation funders look to achieve an appropriate return on their investment, the quantification of which return is known as gearing. Put otherwise, litigation funders seek to invest in claims that, if successful, will repay their investment, together with a reward. The business model that has traditionally been used has sought a reward of about three times the investment value,[83] usually being calculated as a percentage of the damages or debt that is the subject of the claim (see 33.69). This is on the basis that if the claim fails, the investment will not be repayable—known as the non-recourse basis of funding. With new entrants into the market, funders are being more flexible in terms of gearing, but, on the whole, funders tend to focus on monetary claims of high value (see 33.65). To date, the claims that have been funded have been predominantly insolvency claims, professional negligence claims, securities litigation and tax disputes.

33.62 Litigation funding has evolved over the last few years and funders are beginning to adapt their financing models in other ways. The single-case funding model of paying legal fees on behalf of a specific claimant is still the main focus, but there are now funders who provide funding of a much broader type. In particular, funding may be available for portfolios of claims within firms, such as where a funder assists with cash flow and disbursement funding in return for payments that are calculated in a way that is analogous to the way in which conditional fee agreements or a damages-based agreements operate.

33.63 The following paragraphs (see 33.65–33.73) set out the factors that may be relevant to whether any given individual case is suitable for litigation funding. Each funder will, however, have its own selection criteria.

Types of claim

33.64 In theory, subject to it being lawful, litigation funding ought to be available in any type of claim; in practice, it is far more prevalent in commercial claims. That said, it is not unknown in other types of claim, such as matrimonial,[84] personal injuries[85] and insolvency.

---

[82] Highly respected legal commentator Michael Cook refers to an additional requirement—namely, that the costs of pursuing the matter are proportionate to the size of the claim: see *Cook on Costs 2012* (LexisNexis, online), para 41.4.

[83] Pirozzolo, R, 'Opinion: Insurers and Third-party Funders Should Work Together', *The Lawyer*, 1 December 2008.

[84] As early as 2008, Key Business Finance Corporation Plc and Barclays Plc offered legal funding for matrimonial cases; that said, those facilities were more akin a consumer credit agreement than a true funding agreement. 'Proper' litigation funding is now available, an example of which is the products offered by Woodsford Litigation Funding.

[85] For example, Online Finance and Funding Ltd (t/a Claims Funding) offers a non-recourse product whereby the profit element is obtained in the form of interest on the sum advanced.

Minimum values

Most litigation funders have a threshold for the value of the claim below which they will not offer funding. Funders tend to operate on the basis that their funding is 10–20 per cent of the value of the likely proceeds. They like to have this ratio to allow for the potential for budget increases and reductions in the likely damages as the case progresses. **33.65**

Trade publications exist that give up-to-date information about the state of the market.[86] The market has grown significantly since early 2010, because new litigation funders continue to enter the market. **33.66**

Acceptance of cases

The purpose of litigation funding is to cover costs and make a profit, so it is a necessary requirement of funding that the case in question has good prospects of success. Funders take care in choosing their cases, often electing to carry out their own risk assessments, but the potential for loss can be enormous.[87] As such, some will accept only about 10 per cent of referrals. Most will invest only if there is at least a 70 per cent chance of success[88] (although see 33.70). Most will also require the client's solicitor to demonstrate faith in the strength of the case by agreeing to expose themselves to at least a degree of risk; hence a solicitor would normally be expected to enter into a discounted conditional fee agreement under which at least 30 per cent of their fees were at risk .[89] **33.67**

Whilst a seemingly obvious point, Stanley Burnton LJ has explained that a person with a claim would be ill advised to allow the primary limitation period to expire whilst they were trying to arrange funding.[90] The correct thing to do would be to issue and serve proceedings, and then to seek a stay whilst funding arrangements were made. **33.68**

Remuneration

Remuneration is typically between 10 per cent and 40 per cent of the value of the claim, but it may be higher and is usually calculated as the greater of a percentage of damages or a multiple of the capital actually invested (for example three times investment *plus* the return of the invested sum itself). This may start low and rise over the duration of the case as the perceived risk increases; such arrangements are broadly in line with arrangements in other jurisdictions.[91] **33.69**

The market is made up of two types of funder: established professional funders (whose core business is funding) and hedge-fund funders (who usually commit a smaller percentage of their capital assets to funding than established funders). Because a higher proportion **33.70**

---

[86] A table of third-party funders and their products can often be found in a table in *Litigation Funding* magazine.

[87] If proof were needed on that point, it can be found in the (infamous) case of *Excalibur Ventures LLC v Texas Keystone Inc* [2013] EWHC 2767 (Comm); [2013] EWHC 4278 (Comm), a case in which the claimant lost on every single point in a five-month trial. The funder's losses were tens of millions of pounds.

[88] *Arkin v Borchard Lines Ltd* [2005] EWCA Civ 655, at [161].

[89] See Rowles-Davies, N, *Third-party Litigation Funding* (Oxford: Oxford University Press, 2014), para 3.12.

[90] See *Cecil v Bayat* [2011] EWCA Civ 135.

[91] The percentages in Australia are usually between 25 and 40 per cent: see Standing Committee of Attorneys-General, *Litigation Funding in Australia* (Sydney: Standing Committee of Attorneys-General, 2006), pp 4 and 7.

of their capital is committed to funding (and therefore at risk), established professional funders are typically less willing to take risks than hedge-fund funders. It is for this reason that established funders will generally abide by fixed actuarial methods; hedge-fund funders will often be more willing to negotiate a bespoke package and may therefore be willing to accept a greater degree of risk.[92] For obvious reasons, if a funder accepts a high degree of risk, its remuneration is likely to be correspondingly higher.

After-the-event insurance

33.71 A funder is potentially liable for costs, at least to the extent that it has funded the claim[93] (see 9.38–9.44). In view of this, it is often a necessary requirement for funding that appropriate ATE insurance is put in place.[94] This may be on the basis that it provides cover for both sides' costs (in which case the funder will expect to be repaid its investment regardless of the outcome of the litigation), but this type of funding has now become relatively rare because a 'both sides' insurance policy is now almost impossible to obtain.[95] The premium may or may not be recoverable, depending on when the policy was incepted.[96] It is worth pausing here to note that insurers and funders are usually able to coexist in harmonious accord, and may even form close working relationships (see 33.30). This is partly due to their having mutual clients, but also because they have complementary roles (that is, the funder classically funds own costs and disbursements, whilst the insurer classically indemnifies adverse costs). Whilst there is a degree of overlap (see 33.30), on the whole funders and insurers tend to trade in sufficiently dissimilar markets to avoid direct competition. By way of example, whilst litigation funders seek clients with claims that have at least a 70 per cent chance of success (see 33.67), insurers tend, as a rule, to consider claims that have at least a 60 per cent chance of success.[97]

Independent legal advice

33.72 The Code of Conduct for Litigation Funders 2018 states that a funder will take reasonable steps to ensure that the litigant has received independent advice on the terms of the litigation funding agreement.[98] This is in line with experience from the United States, which

[92] Delaney, J, 'Litigation Insurance and Funding' (2008) 19(6) Cons Law 20.

[93] *Arkin v Borchard Lines Ltd* [2005] EWCA Civ 655, at [41]. The court explained that the restriction on the funder's liability will not apply if the agreement falls foul of the policy considerations that render an agreement champertous. In these circumstances, the funder may have an unlimited liability.

[94] See Rowles-Davies, N, *Third-party Litigation Funding* (Oxford: Oxford University Press, 2014), para 3.12. See also Jackson, R, *Review of Civil Litigation Costs: Preliminary Report* (London: HMSO, 2009), vol 1, p 161. Exceptions do exist, however: see, eg, *Stone & Rolls Ltd (in liquidation) v Moore Stephens (a firm)* [2009] UKHL 39, which was funded without ATE insurance.

[95] See Rowles-Davies, N, *Third-party Litigation Funding* (Oxford: Oxford University Press, 2014), para 3.12.

[96] This will depend on whether the ATE policy was a pre-commencement funding arrangement. In any event, it is worth noting that where both ATE insurance and litigation funding are required, and where the former is purchased at the behest of funder, it is a moot point whether the premium would be recoverable from a paying party. It has been suggested that the premium ought not to be recoverable because the expenditure could be categorised as part of the funder's business overheads: see Langdon-Down, G, 'Litigation Funding: Place Your Bets', *Law Society Gazette*, 21 May 2009.

[97] Pirozzolo, R, 'Opinion: Insurers and Third-party Funders Should Work Together', *The Lawyer*, 1 December 2008.

[98] Code of Conduct for Litigation Funders 2018, para 9.1.

suggests that, in appropriate cases, clients should be advised to take independent legal advice about the proposed method of funding.[99]

Control of litigation

The Code of Conduct for Litigation Funders 2018 provides that a funder will 'not seek to influence the Funded Party's solicitor or barrister to cede control or conduct of the dispute to the Funder'.[100] This provision is probably otiose, however, because fears that their involvement may otherwise be seen as champertous have generally stopped funders from exercising any significant control over funded litigation.[101] **33.73**

Contractual provisions

Litigation funding agreements ought to be drafted only by funding specialists, but the following general points can be made. **33.74**

Precedence condition

It is sensible to ensure that the agreement is drafted by a drafter who has had prior sight of the draft contracts of retainer and the ATE policies, and who ought to be asked to ensure that there are no conflicts. It is good practice to include a provision that stipulates which document will take precedence in the event of a conflict. **33.75**

Reporting provision and representations as to truth

Funders will frequently require representations, or even warranties, as to the truth of instructions and 'alignment of conduct in a fashion supportive of the case'.[102] This is generally regarded as not posing a risk to the enforceability of the funding agreement (see 33.21).[103] **33.76**

Whilst not something that is required by the Code of Conduct for Litigation Funders 2018, it is good practice to include a reporting provision that states in specific terms what the legal representative is expected to report to the funder. That provision must not require such a level of reporting that it might lead to allegations of 'wanton intermeddling' and champerty. **33.77**

Management provision

The Code of Conduct for Litigation Funders 2018 states that agreements should state whether (and, if so, how) the funder may provide input to the litigant's decisions in relation to settlements.[104] It is good practice to set out, in terms, what the funder is not permitted to do (that is, to limit the funder's influence, so that it will not be accused of controlling the litigation). **33.78**

Termination provision

The Code of Conduct for Litigation Funders 2018 sets out the following provisions concerning termination: **33.79**

> '11. The LFA shall state whether (and if so how) the Funder or Funder's Subsidiary or Associated Entity may:
>
> [...]

[99] Wheeler, J, 'Welcome to the Party' (2008) 158(7342) NLJ 1491.
[100] See Code of Conduct for Litigation Funders 2018, para 9.3.
[101] Jackson, R, *Review of Civil Litigation Costs: Preliminary Report* (London: HMSO, 2009), vol 1, p 163.
[102] Rowles-Davies, N, *Third-party Litigation Funding* (Oxford: Oxford University Press, 2014), para 2.72.
[103] *Ibid.* See also *London & Regional (St George's Court) Ltd v Ministry of Defence* [2008] EWHC 526 (TCC).
[104] See Code of Conduct for Litigation Funders 2018, para 11.1.

11.2 terminate the LFA in the event that the Funder or Funder's Subsidiary or Associated Entity:
(i) reasonably ceases to be satisfied about the merits of the dispute;
(ii) reasonably believes that the dispute is no longer commercially viable; or
(iii) reasonably believes that there has been a material breach of the LFA by the Funded Party.'

33.80 Importantly, the Code also provides that the agreement shall not establish a discretionary right for a funder to terminate an agreement in the absence of the circumstances described in clause 11.2.[105] The Code then goes on to make the following provision:

'13. If the LFA does give the Funder or Funder's Subsidiary or Associated Entity any of the rights described in clause 11 the LFA shall provide that:
13.1 if the Funder or Funder's Subsidiary or Associated Entity terminates the LFA, the Funder or Funder's Subsidiary or Associated Entity shall remain liable for all funding obligations accrued to the date of termination unless the termination is due to a material breach under clause 11.2.3;
[...]'

33.81 David Donaldson QC (sitting as a deputy judge of the High Court) has explained that where a funding agreement imposes on a client an obligation to provide information to their funder and where that funder has taken reasonable steps to obtain information, it will be entitled to decide whether to terminate the agreement on the basis of the information given.[106]

Priorities provision

33.82 Whilst not something that is dealt with in the Code of Conduct for Litigation Funders 2018, it is often helpful to include within an agreement (or as a schedule to an agreement) a record of priorities (that is, an agreement dealing with who is to be paid what if the sums recovered in the litigation are insufficient to satisfy all of the parties' contractual entitlements). This is often referred to as 'the waterfall of priorities'. Where other stakeholders are involved—such as ATE insurers—a separate agreement, known as a priorities agreement, could be appropriate. It is particularly important to record the order of priority of payments from the proceeds of a case in the situation in which the funder (expecting a return of invested funds and an uplift), the ATE insurer (expecting a deferred and contingent premium) and the lawyers (expecting the uplift on a contingent retainer) have taken some contingent risk. Paying attention to these issues at the beginning of the litigation will lessen the chances of disputes at its conclusion.

Disputes resolution procedure

33.83 The Code of Conduct for Litigation Funders 2018 provides that if there is a dispute between the funder and the litigant about settlement or about termination of the agreement, a binding opinion shall be obtained from a Queen's Counsel, who shall

[105] See Code of Conduct for Litigation Funders 2018, para 12.
[106] See *Harcus Sinclair (a firm) v Buttonwood Legal Capital Ltd* [2013] EWHC 1193 (Ch).

be instructed jointly or nominated by the chair of the Bar Council.[107] This requirement does not provide the parties any route of appeal; it is good practice to ensure that both the funder and the litigant are fully aware of this fact before the agreement is made.

Adverse event provision, security for costs, etc

The Code of Conduct for Litigation Funders 2018 provides as follows: **33.84**

> '10. The LFA shall state whether (and if so to what extent) the Funder or Funder's Subsidiary or Associated Entity is liable to the Funded Party to:
> 10.1 meet any liability for adverse costs that results from a settlement accepted by the Funded Party or from an order of the Court;
> 10.2 pay any premium (including insurance premium tax) to obtain adverse costs insurance;
> 10.3 provide security for costs; and
> 10.4 meet any other financial liability.'

It is usually convenient to set these details out in a schedule to the agreement. Unless the entire risk is borne by the ATE insurer, there also ought to be a record of who pays what and in which circumstances (that is, who would be responsible for adverse costs orders, who would pay for top-up insurance, etc).

Disclosure of Funding

It is often the case that an opponent will want to know whether a party has the benefit of litigation funding and, if so, what the terms of that funding are. Whilst there is no obligation on a funded party to disclose the fact of its funding arrangement, that party will usually want to tell the other side because it might encourage settlement. Moreover, that party will want to leverage the psychological advantage over their opponent that an independent third party has faith in the merits of the claim. **33.85**

That said, there will be occasions on which the funded party would want to keep the fact of funding confidential. Whilst there have been occasions on which the court has ordered that the identity of the funders should be disclosed,[108] there is no authority in this jurisdiction as to what information (if any) a funded party should *ordinarily* disclose. Funders often refer to the fact that Lord Neuberger has said that there is no obligation on either party to disclose how a case is being funded,[109] but those comments were extra-judicial (as well as being in the abstract). Those who point to Lord Neuberger's comments may well ultimately be right in what they say, but the reality is that the court has **33.86**

[107] See Code of Conduct for Litigation Funders 2018, para 13.2.

[108] See, eg, *R v SSHD, ex p Osman* [1993] COD 204, in which the Divisional Court (Kenney LJ and Waterhouse J) thought that it was *prima facie* right that the third parties who had supported the litigation should be ordered to meet the costs orders made against the applicant, and hence ordered the applicant and his solicitors to disclose their identities.

[109] Lord Neuberger, 'From Barratry, Maintenance and Champerty to Litigation Funding', Harbour Litigation Funding First Annual Lecture, 8 May 2013, available online at https://www.harbourlitigationfunding.com/wp-content/uploads/2015/09/lord_neuberger_harbour_annual_lecture_8_may_2013.pdf

yet to address the issue and it is entirely possible that future decisions will make it clear that funded parties are under a duty to disclose.

33.87 There are many decisions in other common-law jurisdictions that seem to set a precedent that certain limited disclosure should, in general, be given. The Supreme Court of New Zealand has explained that funded parties should disclose the fact that they have a funding agreement, the identity and location of the funder, and whether the funder is subject to the jurisdiction of the New Zealand courts.[110] That said, the court also said that there is no obligation to disclose the financial means of the funder or the terms upon which funding can be withdrawn. Similarly, the High Court in the Isle of Man has ordered that disclosure be given[111] and even US federal courts have insisted on a certain amount of disclosure[112] (albeit limited in extent).

33.88 One area in which the issue of disclosure of a funder has been considered recently is in relation to an application for security for costs. The Commercial Court ordered a claimant to disclose the identity of a litigation funder and whether that funder would benefit from a share of any proceeds of the action. The order for disclosure was made on the basis that there was good reason to believe that the claimant was in receipt of litigation funding and that an application for security for costs would have reasonable prospects of success.[113]

33.89 Despite this general trend, there can be no doubt that there is a limit to the extent to which a funded party can be forced to give disclosure, because an application for extensive disclosure would almost certainly run into problems regarding privilege.[114] That said, it is worth noting that the Supreme Court of New Zealand went on to say that the *terms* of the funding agreement itself may need to be disclosed where the agreement is relevant to any application for security for costs or third-party costs order against the funder.[115]

33.90 Even if an opponent were to be told of a funding agreement and even if they were to manage to persuade the court that it was in some way unlawful, it is doubtful whether this would have much of a bearing on the conduct of the claim. This is because an opponent of a funded party would probably not be entitled to stay proceedings even if a funding agreement were deemed champertous.[116]

---

110 *Waterhouse v Contractors Bonding Ltd* [2013] NZSC 89.

111 See, eg, *Tomlinson v Thane Investments Ltd* (unreported), 2 March 2006, Chancery Division of the High Court in the Isle of Man, in which it was directed that the name of the third party funding the action be disclosed.

112 See, eg, *Del Webb Communities, Inc v Partington*, 652 F3d 1145, 1156 (9th Cir 2011), which is often cited in US federal courts as authority for the proposition that disclosure is usually limited to equity shareholdings in the party above a certain level. That said, see also *Trust for the Certificate Holders of the Merrill Lynch Mortgage Investors, Inc v Love Funding Corpn*, 591 F3d 116 (2d Cir 2010); *Trust for the Certificate Holders of the Merrill Lynch Mortgage Investors, Inc v Love Funding Corpn*, 13 NY3d 190 (NY 2009).

113 See *Wall v RBS plc* [2016] EWHC 2460 (Comm). The defendant bank wished to make an application for security for costs against the funder under CPR, r 25.14. The claimant refused to confirm whether he was in receipt of funding. The bank applied for disclosure of the identity of the funder and whether it was funding in return for a share of the proceeds (to satisfy the conditions of CPR, r 25.14(2)(b)). See also *In the Matter of Hellas Telecommunications (Luxembourg)* [2017] EWHC 3465 (Ch), *per* Snowdon J. This case dealt with a similar application as that in *Wall* and confirmed the ability to require disclosure of third-party funding arrangements in these circumstances, but went on to say that where disclosure may present material prejudice, then protection to the funder could be dealt with by way of a confidentiality club.

114 See, eg, *Guinness Peat Properties Ltd v The Fitzroy Partnership* [1987] 1 WLR 1027.

115 *Waterhouse v Contractors Bonding Ltd* [2013] NZSC 89.

116 Whilst now rather an old case, see *Martell v Consett Iron Co* [1955] 1 Ch 363.

34

LEGAL EXPENSES INSURANCE

This chapter deals with the following topics: **34.01**

- the nature of legal expenses insurance in general (34.02);
- before-the-event (BTE) insurance (34.04);
- after-the-event (ATE) insurance (34.21):
  - the market in ATE insurance (34.22);
  - availability of ATE insurance (34.28);
  - accessing the market for ATE insurance (34.34);
- top-up insurance (34.38);
- challenges to the ATE premiums (34.41);
- formalities relating to ATE insurance (34.42); and
- rights against legal expenses insurers (34.60).

Only the funding and contractual aspects of legal expenses insurance are dealt with in this chapter; the recoverability of ATE premiums between opposing parties is addressed in Chapter 54.

The editor is grateful to Mr Rocco Pirozzolo for his help in writing this chapter.

The Nature of Legal Expenses Insurance in General

Legal expenses insurance—otherwise known as legal protection insurance—is a type of **34.02** general insurance that is in a separate class for authorisation purposes[1] (see 34.42). It protects the insured against either or both of the risks of: (a) having to incur costs (that is, own-side costs) or (b) having to satisfy an adverse costs award. It may, depending on the terms of the policy, apply both to those who bring claims and to those who defend them. As a general rule,[2] legal expense insurance does not cover the damages in the litigation itself; that would be the function of other types of general insurance, such as liability insurance. Other types of insurance are often bundled with legal expenses insurance, usually by insurers other than the legal expenses insurer (to avoid conflicts of interest).

There are, in broad terms, three types of legal expenses insurance, as follows. **34.03**

[1] Financial Services and Markets Act 2000 (Regulated Activities) Order 2001 (SI 2001/544), art 3(1) and Sch 1, Pt 1, para 17.

[2] Awards of compensation that the insured is ordered to pay may be covered by before-the-event (BTE) policies relating to employment disputes purchased by businesses. This will always be subject to the terms of the policy and the limit of indemnity.

- **Before-the-event (BTE) insurance** With BTE insurance, the policy is generally incepted before the litigation occurs or is in sight (see 34.04).
- **After-the-event (ATE) insurance** With ATE insurance, the policy is incepted after the litigation has come into sight (often after the dispute has arisen or the proceedings have been commenced) (see 34.21).
- **Top-up insurance** With top-up insurance, the policy is incepted (or an existing policy is extended) so as to cover costs that might exhaust the cover provided by a pre-existing policy (see 34.38).

Before-the-event Insurance

34.04 Before-the-event insurance is taken out by those wishing to protect themselves against potential litigation costs that could be incurred in the future. Like most types of general insurance, it is purchased before the need for its use has arisen and, as a result, is generally modestly priced on the principle that 'the many pay for the few'.

The origins of BTE insurance

34.05 In 1911, a fatal accident took place during the Le Mans motor race in France. The persons who were injured were uninsured, so they contributed to a common fund for the purposes of financing their claims. This prompted a German motoring club, Deutsche Automobil Schutz (DAS), to increase its membership contributions to form a common fund for the benefit of its members. The popularity of the scheme was such that members of the general public applied to join. The concept of BTE insurance in continental Europe then spread. In the 1970s, it began to be sold in the UK.

34.06 In the early 1980s, BTE insurance began to be offered by insurers other than specialist legal expenses insurers.[3] Associations between insurers became closer and it became common—as it still is—for it to be offered as an adjunct to other financial products, such as household insurance or motor insurance (see 34.04).

The prevalence of BTE insurance

34.07 Before-the-event insurance is now commonplace in the UK. However, it is difficult to know how many individuals or businesses have this cover. Certainly, the 'adding on' of legal expenses insurance as a section of cover to other types of insurance—such as motor or household policies—has helped to distribute this cover amongst individuals and households.

34.08 Another common way of distributing BTE insurance has been by bundling the cover as part of a package of benefits known as affinity group packages, these being packages that are put together for particular types of business or trade.[4] These may include non-insurance benefits, such as help with lobbying, networking, etc. In addition, stand-alone policies for

[3] For a full historical perspective, see Jenkins, D, *The History of Insurance* (London: Pickering & Chatto, 2000).

[4] Affinity group insurance is available for a variety of businesses such as travel agents, hairdressers, the police, prison officers, etc. It is far more common for businesses to obtain this insurance through affinity group packages than by any other means. In addition, the Federation of Small Businesses, which includes many small-to-medium-sized enterprises (SMEs) and micro-businesses amongst its members, includes BTE insurance for its members on this affinity basis.

both businesses and consumers exist, but such insurance is less common in the UK than it is in certain other European countries.[5]

It used to be the case that BTE insurance for individuals was often bundled for free with other types of insurance, but this practice has now waned.[6] Premiums for cover purchased as an add-on to home or motor cover tends now to be in the region of £15–25 for a limit of indemnity of £50,000–100,000. Many such policies provide access to a legal helpline. **34.09**

In 2014, the Financial Conduct Authority (FCA) published its findings following a market study of general insurance add-ons, in which it expressed concern about the fact that consumers were acquiring BTE insurance not because of an affirmative choice, but because they did not opt out of incepting such cover.[7] As a result, on 1 April 2016, the FCA banned opt-out selling and consumers will now either have to affirmatively opt in or purchase cover as part of a bundled package to which they subscribe.[8] Given that motor and household insurance is now often purchased on comparison websites and that consumers may be motivated to maximise savings on their premiums, there are concerns that this may reduce the take-up of BTE insurance. Given the fact that additional liabilities are no longer recoverable between opposing parties, this may have an adverse effect on access to justice. There is, however, a lack of data on this point.[9] **34.10**

The contents of BTE policies

Whilst each policy will turn on its own terms, general consumer BTE insurance will typically afford cover for the following types of dispute: **34.11**

- personal injury claims, fatal accident claims and claims for clinical negligence;
- contractual disputes (although some types of consumer transaction may be excluded);
- property disputes (including boundary disputes, nuisance, landlord and tenant, etc); and
- employment disputes, including proceedings in an employment tribunal.[10]

A BTE policy will typically contain the following contractual provisions. **34.12**

- **Limits of cover** Policies define the limit of cover, usually by reference to a period of insurance (which is often defined by reference to the date of the occurrence that gave rise

[5] Of the 25 million households in the UK in 2008, between 10 million and 15 million have BTE insurance as an add-on to household insurance: see Jackson, R, *Review of Civil Litigation Costs: Final Report* (London: HMSO, 2010), para 8.5.1. However, surveys conducted since 2009 indicate that the figure may be much lower: see Civil Justice Council, *The Law and Practicalities of Before-the-Event Insurance* (London: HMSO, 2017), pp 97–101.

[6] See *Cook on Costs 2017* (LexisNexis, online), para 9.3: 'There are a number of motor and household insurance policies which have included BTE cover for free. That practice has reduced for two reasons. The first is that its inclusion was, for some insurers, simply a tactic at the height of the "costs wars", to cause claimants some difficulty in recovering the cost of ATE premiums (and success fees). That imperative appears to have waned. More recently, the comparison websites have obliged insurers to place a nominal cost against add-ons such as BTE insurance so that the policies can be compared against other providers. Anecdotally, this has caused the take up of BTE insurance to drop considerably where potential policyholders look to minimise the cost of their insurance.'

[7] Financial Conduct Authority, *General Insurance Add-ons: Provisional Findings of Market Study and Proposed Remedies*, MS14/1 (London: FCA, 2014).

[8] See Civil Justice Council, *The Law and Practicalities of Before-the-Event Insurance* (London: HMSO, 2017), pp 92–6, for a useful summary.

[9] See *ibid.*

[10] Jackson, R, *Review of Civil Litigation Costs: Final Report* (London: HMSO, 2010), para 8.5.2.

to the claim), to a specific geographical territory, to a specified limit of indemnity or cap and to other such matters.

- **Persons covered** Policies often provide cover for persons other than the policyholder (such as cover for passengers travelling in the policyholder's car). Members of the same household may be covered, even where they are not members of the same family.
- **Exclusions** All policies contain exclusions. These may be significant if the policy has been created for a specific purpose. In a policy designed for commercial use, for example, personal injury claims or claims for loss or damage to property may be excluded.
- **Notification requirement** Policies generally contain a notification requirement. Whilst the precise terms of the requirement will be a matter of construction, there is usually a requirement that the insured must notify the insurer as soon as they become aware of any cause, event or circumstance that has given, or is likely to give, rise to a claim. This does not mean that the insurer must be told the moment that the dispute arises, but will (depending on the terms of the policy) generally be regarded as being a reference to a likely need for adjudication, arbitration or litigation.[11]
- **Merits requirement** Policies will typically provide that, for a cover to apply, the insured must have a reasonable prospect of success in the notified proceedings. Whilst the wording of any such merits requirement may differ from policy to policy, a reference to 'more likely to succeed than not' is generally taken to refer to prospects of success being at least 51 per cent.[12] Policies often provide that counsel's opinion is sought on the merits.
- **Ongoing notification requirement** All policies contain ongoing notification requirements, often that the insured is required to immediately inform the insurer of any alteration that may materially affect its assessment of the risk.
- **Appointed representative provision** Whilst insureds have a degree of choice (see 34.16), most policies provide that the insurer is at liberty to nominate an appointed legal representative. Once this is done, then the appointed legal representative will be under certain obligations to the insurer.
- **Cooperation requirement** All policies stipulate that the insured must cooperate in the prosecution or defence of their case.[13]
- **Basis of payment** Cover is almost always limited to reasonable costs. Many policies stipulate that these will be limited to costs on the standard basis (see also 34.13).
- **Mitigation requirement** In a similar vein, policies tend to contain a provision that the insured will take reasonable steps to keep the amounts payable under the policy as low as reasonably possible.
- **Disclosure requirement** Policies tend to provide that certain documentary disclosure be given to the insurer upon request.
- **Discretion** Whilst policies are rarely entirely discretionary,[14] many policies provide that the insurer must agree that the merits requirement is met. Cover may be withdrawn

[11] See, eg, *Laker Vent Engineering Ltd v Templeton Insurance Ltd* [2009] EWCA Civ 62.

[12] The Financial Ombudsman Service (FOS) notes that, in complaints made to it by BTE policyholders who were concerned about the rejection of their claim because of inadequate merits, it also applies a 'balance of probabilities' assessment: FOS, 'Online Technical Resource', available online at http://www.financial-ombudsman.org.uk/publications/technical_notes/legal-expenses.html

[13] That such requirements are lawful was confirmed in *Denso Manufacturing UK Ltd v Great Lakes Reinsurance (UK) plc* [2017] EWHC 391 (Comm), *per* Sara Cockerill QC.

[14] Whilst technically not insurance, cover provided by medical defence organisations tends to be discretionary.

by the insurer at a later stage in circumstances identified in the policy. A common example would be where the insurer believes that the prospects of success have deteriorated such that the merits requirement is no longer satisfied. The policyholder usually has a contractual right to contest that assessment.

In addition, there are certain regulatory requirements that govern issues such as the structure of the policy and issues relating to conflicts of interest (see 34.15).

It used to be the case that BTE policies often did not provide cover for the client's own legal services provider's fees (that is, 'own-side costs'). This was logical because when success fees were recoverable between opposing parties, legal services providers often preferred to act under conditional fee agreements as this would maximise their income. Indeed, it was not unknown that the extent of cover would be adjusted on an ad hoc basis so as to allow legal services providers to enter into such agreements.[15] Now that success fees are irrecoverable between opposing parties, things have changed: it now tends to be the case that BTE policies afford cover for the fees of both sides' legal services providers. **34.13**

Restrictions on the use of BTE insurance

By the operation of an EU directive,[16] a person who has the benefit of BTE insurance has the right to choose the lawyer who will act for them.[17] That directive is given domestic implementation by secondary legislation[18]—namely, the Insurance Companies (Legal Expenses Insurance) Regulations 1990.[19] Those Regulations apply to the most commonly encountered types of BTE insurance.[20] For present purposes, the relevant provisions are at reg 6: **34.14**

> '(1) Where under a legal expenses insurance contract recourse is had to a lawyer (or other person having such qualifications as may be necessary) to defend, represent or serve the interests of the insured in any inquiry or proceedings, the insured shall be free to choose that lawyer (or other person).

---

[15] See *Cook on Costs 2017* (LexisNexis, online), para 9.4.

[16] Directive 2009/138/EC of the European Parliament and of the Council of 25 November 2009 on the taking-up and pursuit of the business of Insurance and Reinsurance, OJ L 335/1, 17 December 2009 (the Solvency II Directive).

[17] The wording of Art 6 of the relevant Directive is as follows: '6(1) Where under a legal expenses insurance contract recourse is had to a lawyer (or other person having such qualifications as may be necessary) to defend, represent or serve the interests of the insured in any inquiry or proceedings, the insured shall be free to choose that lawyer (or other person). (2) The insured shall also be free to choose a lawyer (or other person having such qualifications as may be necessary) to serve his interests whenever a conflict of interests arises. (3) The above rights shall be expressly recognised in the policy.'

[18] That legislation is made under European Communities Act 1972, s 2(2).

[19] SI 1990/1159.

[20] The exceptions, under Insurance Companies (Legal Expenses Insurance) Regulations 1990 (SI 1990/1159), reg 3, are: (a) legal expenses insurance contracts concerning disputes or risks arising out of, or in connection with, the use of seagoing vessels; (b) where the cover is for the purpose of defending or representing the insured in an inquiry or proceedings that is at the same time in the insurer's own interest under such cover; or (c) cover provided by an assistance insurer where that cover is provided under a contract of which the principal object is the provision of assistance for persons who fall into difficulties while travelling, while away from home or while away from their permanent residence, and where the costs are incurred outside the state in which the insured normally resides.

(2) The insured shall also be free to choose a lawyer (or other person having such qualifications as may be necessary) to serve his interests whenever a conflict of interests arises.

(3) The above rights shall be expressly recognised in the policy.'[21]

34.15 The Regulations go on to provide that policies must mention the right of the insured to have recourse to arbitration in the event of a dispute arising between the insured and the insurer.[22] They also stipulate the structure of the policy[23] and they make provision for managing potential conflict of interest.[24]

34.16 Similarly, the Court of Justice of the European Union (CJEU) has confirmed that insureds have the right to engage lawyers[25] of their own choice.[26] This precludes insurers from stipulating that their own employees must act on behalf of insureds.[27] Burton J has explained that the right of election exists even if the insured seeks to change their lawyers.[28] It is often said (wrongly) that an insured is permitted to exercise a right to choose at all times, regardless of whether proceedings had been issued.[29] That is not so,

---

[21] This regulation does not apply to insurance in relation to seagoing vessels or to insurance provided as a benefit of membership of motoring organisations such as the AA or the RAC: see Insurance Companies (Legal Expenses Insurance) Regulations 1990 (SI 1990/1159), reg 7.

[22] See Insurance Companies (Legal Expenses Insurance) Regulations 1990 (SI 1990/1159), reg 8.

[23] Under Insurance Companies (Legal Expenses Insurance) Regulations 1990 (SI 1990/1159), reg 4, legal expenses cover must be contained in a separate policy (reg 4(a)) or, where that cover is provided under a policy relating to one or more other classes of general insurance business, a separate section of the policy relating to that cover only (reg 4(b)) and specifying the nature of that cover.

[24] Insurance Companies (Legal Expenses Insurance) Regulations 1990 (SI 1990/1159), reg 5, reads as follows: '(1) An insurance company carrying on legal expenses insurance business shall adopt at least one of the following arrangements. (2) The company shall ensure that no member of staff who is concerned with the management of claims under legal expenses insurance contracts, or with legal advice in respect of such claims, carries on at the same time any similar activity—(a) in relation to another class of general insurance business carried on by the company, or (b) in any other insurance company, having financial, commercial or administrative links with the first company, which carries on one or more other classes of general insurance business. (3) The company shall entrust the management of claims under legal expenses insurance contracts to an undertaking having separate legal personality, which shall be mentioned in the separate policy or section referred to in regulation 4. If that undertaking has financial, commercial or administrative links with another insurance company which carries on one or more other classes of general insurance business, members of the staff of the undertaking who are concerned with the processing of claims, or with providing legal advice connected with such processing, shall not pursue the same or a similar activity in that other insurance company at the same time. (4) The company shall, in the policy, afford the insured the right to entrust the defence of his interests, from the moment that he has the right to claim from the insurer under the policy, to a lawyer of his choice or, to the extent that the law of the relevant forum so permits, to any other appropriately qualified person.'

[25] HHJ Seymour (sitting as a judge of the High Court) has confirmed that this would include counsel in the context of direct public access: *Pine v DAS Legal Expenses Insurance Co Ltd* [2011] EWHC 658 (QB).

[26] Case C-199/08 *Eschig v UNIQA Sachversicherung AG* [2009] ECR 1-08295.

[27] Case C-442/12 *Sneller v DAS Nederlandse Rechtsbijstand Verzekeringsmaatschappij NV* [2014] Lloyd's Rep IR 238, at [29].

[28] Burton J has found that an insured has the right to change lawyers: see *Brown-Quinn & Anor v Equity Syndicate Management Ltd & Anor* [2011] EWHC 2661 (Comm), at [29] *et seq*. Whilst there was a successful appeal to the Court of Appeal, this point survived.

[29] This is not surprising given the fact that when Case C-199/08 *Eschig v UNIQA Sachversicherung AG* [2009] ECR 1-08295 was handed down, the FSA gave guidance that needed to be retracted and corrected. The FSA's reaction to *Eschig* was to overstate its effect (see the letter from Mr K Hogg to insurers dated July 2010) and, in particular, it wrongly stated that *Eschig* was authority for the proposition that the right to choose arose before proceedings had been begun. This needed to be corrected following criticism by the insurance industry: see, eg, Lee, M, 'Freedom Fighters', *Solicitors Journal*, 4 October 2010. That correction was effected by way of the FSA issuing a revised letter (dated 12 August 2010), which included explanatory footnotes. Those footnotes are not entirely clear and this has led some commentators to say that, even now, the FSA's guidance is confused and ambiguous.

however; rather, it is a right that is usually regarded as applying only once proceedings have been issued.[30]

Any contractual term that seeks to limit the right of election would be in breach of the Solvency II Directive,[31] but this does not mean that the right to choose may never be curtailed.[32] Longmore LJ has explained that BTE insurers are permitted to limit the costs for which they are liable (such as to a particular hourly rate), but not if it means that the remuneration offered was so insufficient as to render the insured's freedom of choice meaningless.[33] **34.17**

The suitability of BTE insurance generally

For obvious reasons, it would not be unreasonable to reject insurance that was unsuitable for its proposed purpose. In particular, the fact that certain restrictions may legitimately exist (see 34.16) means that BTE insurance will not always be suitable for the case in hand. **34.18**

Phillips MR has explained that if a claimant possesses BTE cover that appears to be suitable, then, in the ordinary course of events, the claimant should be referred to the insurer—although he made it clear that that guidance was specifically limited to small, personal injury claims in which the value of the claim would be likely to be no more than about £5,000 (in 2001).[34] That guidance, however, was made in the context of the alternative being the use of conditional fee agreements, which provided for a recoverable success fee. It is likely that a legal services provider would now be expected to advise a client about using BTE cover wherever it is available. Indeed, Indicative Behaviour (IB)(1.16) of the Solicitors' Regulation Authority (SRA) Code of Conduct 2011 provides that solicitors ought to discuss 'how the client will pay, including ... whether the client has insurance that might cover the fees'. **34.19**

This does not mean, however, that a client would be obliged to use BTE insurance; indeed, a client would have an absolute right to decline to use a policy if they so wished. Moreover, it will not always be the case that a party's decision to eschew a seemingly suitable policy would be regarded as being unreasonable—a topic that may arise if the insured **34.20**

---

[30] Other than for the mistake they made regarding Case C-199/08 *Eschig v UNIQA Sachversicherung AG* [2009] ECR 1-08295, the FOS interpreted the 1990 Regulations as meaning that the right to choose is triggered only when negotiations have been completed and proceedings have to be begun: see the decisions of the Insurance Ombudsman against Cornhill Insurance plc, 3 May 2002, and against DAS, 17 June 2002.

[31] This was the true *ratio* in Case C-199/08 *Eschig v UNIQA Sachversicherung AG* [2009] ECR 1-08295.

[32] Case C-293/10 *Stark v DAS Oesterreiche Algemeine Rechtsschutzversicherung AG* [2011] ECR I-04711, at [33], in which the court said: 'Consequently, freedom of choice ... does not mean that Member States are obliged to require insurers, in all circumstances, to cover in full the costs incurred in connection with the defence of an insured person, irrespective of the place where the person professionally entitled to represent that person is established in relation to the court of administrative authority with jurisdiction to deal with a dispute, on condition that that freedom is not rendered meaningless. That would be the case if the restriction imposed on the payment of those costs were to render de facto impossible a reasonable choice of representative by the insured person. In any event, it is for the national courts, if an action is brought before them in this regard, to determine whether or not there is any such restriction.'

[33] *Brown-Quinn & Anor v Equity Syndicate Management Ltd & Anor* [2012] EWCA Civ 1633, at [28] and [29]. In Case C-442/12 *Sneller v DAS Nederlandse Rechtsbijstand Verzekeringsmaatschappij NV* [2014] Lloyd's Rep IR 238, at [27], the Eighth Chamber of the CJEU found that it is not a requirement that member states impose such a requirement, but the court went on to say that it was permissible for them to do so.

[34] *Sarwar v Alam* [2001] EWCA Civ 1401, at [41].

were potentially able to claim additional liabilities from an opponent (see 54.191 *et seq*). The following points may be made in this regard.

- **Legitimate restrictions** An example might be where there are no panel solicitors who were reasonably local to the receiving party and where the client did not want to (or was unable to) instruct an off-panel solicitor under the terms of the policy,[35] perhaps because the hourly rate under the policy was not sufficient to allow the insurer to instruct a solicitor of their own choice (see 34.17).
- **Adverse conditions** In a similar vein, policies may include conditions that make it difficult or impossible to make a claim for the purposes of the matter in hand. That said, it is not uncommon for the court to read such conditions restrictively.[36]
- **Limit of cover** It may be that the limit of cover is too low to fund the whole of the claim. Where this is so, it may be reasonable to set up a different form of funding entirely, but it may be equally reasonable to exhaust the policy first and then to apply for top-up cover (see 34.38). Another option would be to combine the policy with other methods of funding.[37]
- **Cover provided by an opponent's policy** An issue that may arise is whether a claimant may reasonably reject funding afforded by the defendant's BTE policy. In the context of low-value, modest personal injury claims, Phillips MR has said that the claimant would be expected not to reject that form of funding, but that if the defendant were to fail to cooperate, that would be sufficient reason to justify eschewing it.[38]
- **Size of the claim** The size of the claim may be a relevant factor.[39]

After-the-event Insurance

34.21 After-the-event insurance protects against liability for costs (which may include the insured's own costs) in specific proceedings. Policies are incepted after the dispute or cause of action has arisen and hence the name. In view of the fact that ATE insurance is not based on the 'many pay for the few' principle, premiums tend to be considerably higher than those for BTE policies.

---

[35] *Chappell v De Bora's of Exeter (a firm)* [2004] EWHC 90020 (Costs), *per* HHJ Overend. Despite the 'EWHC' reference, this was a county court case and is not binding.

[36] An example is *Laker Vent Engineering Ltd v Templeton Insurance Ltd* [2009] EWCA Civ 62, in which the policy stipulated that the insurer be notified as soon as the insured became aware of any event that had given, or was likely to give, rise to a construction claim. Aikens LJ found that that stage would be reached only where adjudication, arbitration or litigation was likely to be required to resolve the dispute.

[37] See, eg, *Smith v Interlink Express Parcels Ltd* [2007] EWHC 90095 (Costs), in which counsel's success fee was justified on the basis that it was reasonable to use the limited BTE cover on counsel, but instead to fund counsel by way of a conditional fee agreement. This case is not binding.

[38] *Sarwar v Alam* [2001] EWCA Civ 1401, at [48].

[39] In this regard, Philips MR had this to say *ibid*, at [56]: 'We are not ... persuaded by the ... contention that there is such a strong public interest in maintaining a client's freedom of choice of legal adviser that this should override the appropriateness of a claim as small as that with which we are concerned on this appeal being handled by a BTE insurer with or without the assistance of a panel solicitor. The philosophy contained in CPR, r 1.1(2)(c), and the express provisions of CPR, r 44.5, require the court to ensure that no costs are incurred which are not reasonable and proportionate.' See also *R v Legal Aid Board, ex p Duncan* [2000] COD 159, which dealt with a similar issue in the context of public funding.

The market in ATE insurance

The origins of ATE insurance

In July 1995, conditional fee agreements were introduced in England and Wales (see 1.155), at a time when the legal aid regime still funded many civil claims. An ATE insurance product was developed to insure a claimant for adverse costs and their own disbursements; that insurance was provided by Lexington and administered by its agent, Abbey Legal Protection. Within the space of only a few years, Lexington exited the market with significant losses—perhaps the result of the premiums being too low for the cover provided (that is, £85 for £100,000 of cover). **34.22**

In due course, legal aid was all but withdrawn for the majority of civil claims, especially personal injury claims (see 1.163–1.167). This led, in early 2000, to the true birth of an ATE insurance market. The spur for this was the ability to recover ATE insurance premiums from opposing parties (see 1.157). Various syndicates in Lloyd's of London formed a significant part of the early market in these early years. **34.23**

Types of claim covered by ATE insurance post-2013

The claims in which ATE premiums remain recoverable from an unsuccessful opponent are as follows: **34.24**

- clinical negligence proceedings[40] (see 54.38–54.41);
- publication and privacy proceedings (see 54.35–54.37); and
- mesothelioma proceedings (see 54.22–54.30).

For all other claims, the ATE premiums are not recoverable from an unsuccessful opponent and are to be paid by the policyholder. Although insolvency proceedings had been 'carved out' of the reform ending recoverability of premiums on 1 April 2013, the premiums for these claims ceased to be recoverable from 6 April 2016 (see 54.31–54.34).

Types of ATE insurance by type of premium The following types of premium may be encountered: **34.25**

- **Single premium** A policy that provides for a single premium will stipulate that a single premium will be payable in full regardless of the outcome of the claim. This may or may not be deferred (see below).
- **Deferred premium** A deferred premium is a premium (which may be single or staged) that is not payable upon inception of the policy, but instead is payable either upon conclusion of the insured claim (whatever the outcome of that claim) or upon termination of the policy, whichever occurs first. In this instance, a deferred premium is often combined with own-premium cover if the claim is unsuccessful (see 34.26). The phrase 'deferred premium' is often loosely used to refer to a premium that is payable only if the claim is successful; whilst it is true to say that such a premium is a deferred premium, this term is also used to describe many other types of premium and it is therefore not a usage to be encouraged. The more accurate description would be to refer to this type of

[40] If an ATE policy insures more than the cost of the expert reports on liability and causation, then it needs to distinguish the recoverable premium for such reports from the irrecoverable premium that relates to other risks, such as other disbursements and adverse costs, because these need to be paid by the policyholder.

premium as a 'contingent premium' because the obligation to pay the premium depends on a successful outcome being achieved, as defined in the policy wording.

- **Staged premium** A staged premium (also often called a stepped premium or a rebated premium) is a premium that is quantified by reference to the stage at which the claim concludes. The premium may be calculated as a diminishing rebate or as an escalating premium: the amount payable increases (or the potential rebate deceases) if the litigation fails to conclude before the certain predefined stage. Such policies may provide for the premiums to be paid either in instalments, by way of deferred premiums or by way deposit premiums (see below). The term 'rebated' is usually reserved for premiums that have been paid at inception on the basis that it will be partially refunded if the claim settles early (that is, it is a policy that provides for a diminishing discount).
- **Deposit premium** A deposit premium is paid before the policy is incepted, with the balance of the premium being deferred (see above). The deposit premium is non-refundable. The deferred premium may be for a single amount or it may be staged.

34.26 **Types of ATE insurance by type of cover** The precise nature of the cover provided by an ATE policy will be a matter of construction, but the following types may be encountered.

- **Adverse-only cover** This is cover solely for the purposes of covering an opponent's costs.
- **Own-disbursements cover** This is cover for the insured's own disbursements (either including or excluding counsel). What is and is not a disbursement will be a matter of contractual interpretation. The word 'disbursement' may be defined in the policy as including the premium itself; this is one mechanism by which own-premium cover (below) might be provided where the policy is a pre-commencement funding arrangement (see 54.23).
- **Both sides' costs cover** This is a form of cover that extends beyond adverse costs and the insured's own disbursements to include the insured's own solicitor's fees. Such cover enables a claimant or defendant to hedge against the fees that they are paying their solicitors if they are unsuccessful in the litigation; such policies are often used in combination with discounted conditional fee agreements.
- **Own-premium cover** Whilst it will only be available if the policy is a pre-commencement funding arrangement, own-premium cover exists where either the claim is unsuccessful and the premium (which is usually deferred) is insured under the policy, or the claim is successful, but the full premium is not awarded on a summary or detailed assessment from an opponent.[41] The premium may be deferred, but it may also be payable upon inception. Where it is payable on inception, it would usually be covered by a disbursement funding loan, which will be paid off by the insurer in the event of an adverse outcome. Own-premium cover is also called premium shortfall waiver and premium indemnity guarantee.[42]

34.27 **Types of ATE insurance by type of claim** The following types of claim merit a mention.

- **Personal injuries** After-the-event cover continues to be available for personal injuries claims, as well as clinical negligence claims (see below). One of the aims of introducing

[41] Hughes LJ was obviously impressed by this type of policy because he has commented that it was 'remarkable': *Jones v Wrexham Borough Council* [2007] EWCA Civ 1356, at [75].

[42] Amey, M, 'PIG of a Problem' (2010) 68 Litigation Funding 20.

qualified one-way costs shifting (QOCS) (see Chapter 8) was that claimants would not require ATE insurance for adverse costs, given the costs protection afforded by the new regime. If the cover were to be restricted to own disbursements, then the limit of indemnity and the premium would be significantly lower; that said, the operation of QOCS still exposes a claimant to an adverse costs risk, such as for failing to beat a Part 36 offer. As a result, ATE policies for personal injury claims (and clinical negligence claims) tend to continue to insure adverse costs. This has meant that the limits of indemnity are higher than would otherwise have been the case; as a result, premiums tend to be commensurately higher. Anecdotally, the uptake for ATE cover in personal injuries litigation has fallen dramatically since the introduction of QOCS.

- **Clinical negligence** The points made above have resonance in clinical negligence cases because QOCS applies, but, in view of the fact that own-side disbursements tend to be much higher and that premiums are still recoverable in that regard (see 54.38–54.41), uptake tends to be much higher.
- **Insolvency-related claims** There is invariably little or no money available in the insolvent estate to fund insolvency-related claims. Solicitors and barristers are typically expected to enter into conditional fee agreements. Equally, ATE insurers are often asked to offer a fully deferred premium whereby the premium is paid from the recoveries in the litigation. With premiums no longer recoverable after 6 April 2016, the focus is on whether the realistic value of any recoveries (whether achieved by way of a settlement or at trial) is sufficient to pay the legal advisers and other expenses, such as the ATE premium, and also to provide a return to the creditors. Unsurprisingly, certain claims that were previously brought before 6 April 2016 are now no longer economically viable.

The availability of ATE insurance

The ATE insurance market has been through a period of transition since the Jackson reforms. The focus has shifted away from personal injuries claims to insuring commercial disputes, as a natural consequence of the reforms. Whilst the market continues to cater for claimants with personal injuries and clinical negligence claims (see 34.27), the ability of the market to insure a broad range of commercial disputes has developed over the last few years. **34.28**

Personal injuries and clinical negligence claims tend to continue to be insured by solicitors operating delegated authority schemes (see 34.36). Insurers operate these schemes by imposing a predefined matrix of premiums that will apply; those premiums are block-rated, in that actuaries will have modelled a basket of similar claims, allowing for the consequences of successes and losses in the life cycle of the litigation to be taken into account. This contrasts with the approach that is taken when a one-off claim is submitted for insurance, and the risk is individually assessed by the insurer and priced accordingly; an individual assessment of claims is common for commercial disputes, particularly where significant limits of indemnity are requested. **34.29**

There are now more insurers willing to insure commercial disputes than before April 2013. Some insurers have a ceiling on the limit of indemnity for which they are able to provide cover.[43] That said, there are insurers who are able to provide limits of indemnity of up to **34.30**

[43] An example of this is *Premier Motorauctions v PWC LLP* [2016] EWHC 2610, in which four insurers were required to build a limit of indemnity of £5 million.

(and beyond) £5 million. Higher limits are of particular interest to litigation funders who are keen to offset the *Arkin* risk[44] (see 33.71 and 9.38–9.44). Indeed, the growth of the litigation funding market in England and Wales, as well as globally, has driven the growth of the ATE insurance market.

34.31 The ATE insurance market has developed solutions to bespoke requests as it repositions itself following the Jackson reforms. The following deserve a mention.

- **Insurance for defendants** After-the-event insurance has traditionally been regarded as a product for claimants. Cover is now available for defendants who would otherwise be uninsured or underinsured. There has, however, been only limited interest in this type of cover.
- **Anti-avoidance clauses** Apart from being a way of transferring cost risk, ATE insurance has also become a way of providing security for costs (or of avoiding an order for security for costs being made). Whilst an appropriately framed ATE policy may provide adequate security, concerns may be raised about the possibility of the insurer avoiding the policy for non-disclosure or misrepresentation by the insured. Some insurers are willing to endorse their policies in such a way as to afford a degree of comfort that this will not happen; such an endorsement is known as an anti-avoidance clause and may have a significant bearing on the way in which the court deals with an application for security for costs (see 15.39).
- **Insurance for solicitors' fees** Insurance for solicitors' fees may be provided in two ways. If the solicitor is being paid all or part of their hourly rate under a discounted fee agreement, then those fees can be insured under a both sides' costs policy (see above). An alternative product is available for firms who act under a damages-based agreement whereby a percentage of their work in progress may be insured (the cover would, typically, not exceed 50 per cent of their hourly rate). This would need to be coupled with additional cover for adverse costs and own disbursements to provide the comprehensive cover of a both sides' costs policy.

34.32 In general, the availability of ATE insurance will be subject to a merits test.[45] As a general rule, ATE providers seek prospects of success of at least 60 per cent, although there are exceptions to this. By comparison, BTE insurance typically adopts a merits threshold that the claim or defence is more likely than not to succeed (namely, at least 51 per cent). It would be usual for counsel's opinion to be sought upon the merits.

34.33 Historically, the ATE insurance market tended not to quote unless the solicitors were acting under a full or discounted conditional fee agreement. The reason for this approach was that insurers expected solicitors to show confidence in the merits of their clients' claims by exposing themselves to risk. For discounted conditional fee agreements, a discount of at least 30 per cent would typically be expected to demonstrate that there was sufficient 'skin in the game'. However, there has been a shift away from this approach: there are now

[44] After *Arkin v Borchard Lines Ltd & Ors* [2005] EWCA Civ 655.

[45] See, eg, *Persimmon Homes Ltd v Great Lakes Reinsurance (UK) plc* [2010] EWHC 1705 (Comm), in which the policy in question stipulated that the prospects of success had to be 51 per cent or better. See also *Winterthur Swiss Insurance Co v AG (Manchester) Ltd (in liquidation)* [2006] EWHC 839 (Comm), in which a similar term applied.

several insurers who are willing to quote even if the legal team is being paid in full under a private retainer.

Accessing the market for ATE insurance

The market can be approached in a variety of ways. Many legal services providers and litigation funders have their own preferred ATE providers; where this is not the case, insurance brokers may be used. A list of ATE providers and brokers may be found in a table at the back of The Law Society's magazine *Litigation Funding*. This table, which is not meant to be exhaustive, also gives a snapshot of the type of insurance that may be available. **34.34**

The stage at which to apply for ATE insurance

To improve the chances of obtaining ATE insurance, it is sensible to approach the market as soon as a reasonable risk assessment has been made. This is typically shortly before the issue of proceedings. By this stage, the parties would have set out their respective positions in any pre-action correspondence and counsel may have advised on the merits. Whilst ATE insurance can be applied for at any time, as a general rule, insurers are not willing to quote for cover where the action is close to the trial date. Invariably, by this stage, all efforts to settle have failed and the parties to the dispute may have both been advised that they will succeed at trial. Such an application would normally be regarded as selecting a risky case to be insured (known as adverse selection or cherry-picking) and so invariably insurers would decline to quote. **34.35**

Delegated authority and ATE insurance

Delegated authority modifies the administrative process by which a policy comes into existence. A solicitor with delegated authority is able to incept a policy without first having to obtain case-specific authority from the insurer or from an intermediary (as the agent for an insurer). It is often combined with block rating (see 54.164). Delegated authority will arise out of an agreement between the insurer and the solicitor whereby the solicitor is authorised, as the insurer's agent, to hold the 'underwriting pen'; that agreement will almost always include provisions that are intended to avoid adverse selection (see 54.136–54.137). **34.36**

Components of the premium A premium may be made up of the following four elements: burning costs, risk/profit costs, administrative costs and distribution commission.[46] **34.37**

- **Burning costs** These are the costs of meeting claims. Such costs may also be called the basic pure underwriting cost. Broadly speaking, there are two ways in which burning costs may be calculated: 'individual rating' (whereby the risk is assessed in each case or each category of risk and the premium is set accordingly); and 'block rating' (whereby a uniform premium, or series of premiums, is charged for any case that is deemed to have adequate prospects of success).[47] The term 'individual assessment' is also often used.

---

46 *Callery v Gray (No 2)* [2001] EWCA Civ 1246, at [21]–[26]. See also CPD, art 11.10.

47 'Block rating' is a phrase that is used to describe a portfolio or book of claims, of the same or a similar type, where it is expected that the claims will be insured on or before a particular point in time (such as before sending a letter of claim). This approach is based on the insurance principle of 'the many paying for the few', so that there is a spread of risk across cases that are expected to be insured. This approach is adopted where there is a large number of claims and is therefore particularly suitable for cases dealt with by delegated authority.

- **Risk/profit costs** This will include the insurer's profit, but will not necessarily be limited to that; rather, it may include the costs of reinsurance.
- **Administrative costs** These include items such as personnel, premises, issuing costs, processing costs and claims administration.
- **Distribution commission** This covers advertising, marketing and commissions paid to brokers, underwriting agents or other intermediaries.

In addition, there may be monies that are claimed as being part of a premium, but which are not. These monies are discussed at 54.172–54.174.

Top-up Insurance

34.38 Top-up insurance is additional cover that is taken out with a view to allowing litigation to continue in the event that the limit of indemnity under a BTE policy or an ATE policy is—or is anticipated to be—close to being reached.[48] The need may arise in the context of an appeal where the original policy was for the first-instance trial or it may arise during the first-instance claim.

34.39 As a rule of thumb, the limit of indemnity under a BTE policy may be thought of as being equally attributable to (a) the insured's own solicitor's costs and disbursements, and (b) adverse costs. Where the limit of cover is close to being reached, then the insured's legal representative would generally be able to deal with the former by offering to enter into a conditional fee agreement or by obtaining litigation funding. As such, the focus for the purposes of top-up tends to be on the latter—namely, adverse costs.

34.40 The following points may be made.

- **Top-up from BTE insurance** Because BTE policies are written on the basis of 'the many paying for the few', it is not common for BTE insurers to grant additional cover; where the limit of cover under a BTE policy is close to being reached, it will generally be necessary to go to the ATE market for a separate top-up policy.
- **Top-up from ATE insurance** Where it is an ATE policy that requires the limit of indemnity to be increased, it would be usual for the policyholder to re-approach the ATE insurer who has already insured its case to quote for the additional cover. Any quote would require an additional premium to be paid.

Challenges to the After-the-event Premiums

34.41 On one level, once an insured has agreed to enter into an ATE policy, it will be unable to challenge its terms. In particular, the agreement will generally be directly enforceable between the insured and the insurer, so the issue of a solicitor-and-client assessment may not arise. That said, some of the consumer protections referred to in Chapter 28 may apply. Moreover, whilst at the time of writing his decisions was subject to appeal, Soole J has

[48] For an example of a policy being topped up, see *Plevin v Paragon Personal Finance Ltd* [2017] UKSC 23, at [16], *per* Lord Sumption.

found that (in consumer setting, at least) an ATE premium may be an 'actual disbursement' (and therefore amenable to assessment). This is discussed in detail at 52.04.

Formalities Relating to After-the-event Insurance

Whilst legal expense insurance is classified as being a form of general insurance, it is in a separate class for the purposes of regulation.[49] The discussion below looks at the potential relevance of non-compliance with the regulatory provisions. In particular, this chapter examines the topic of whether a policy that is not compliant with the formalities is enforceable against the insured. For the avoidance of doubt, this book does not deal with compliance generally (as opposed to compliance in so far as it relates to costs). **34.42**

The general prohibition and ATE insurance

The Financial Services and Markets Act 2000 creates a general prohibition that forbids persons who are neither authorised nor exempt from engaging in certain regulated activities. Contravening the general prohibition is a criminal offence.[50] The general prohibition is phrased in the following terms: **34.43**

> '(1) No person may carry on a regulated activity in the United Kingdom, or purport to do so, unless he is—
> (a) an authorised person; or
> (b) an exempt person.
> (2) The prohibition is referred to in this Act as the general prohibition.'[51]

What is and is not a regulated activity is defined by the Financial Services and Markets Act 2000 (Regulated Activities) Order 2001,[52] which is often referred to as 'the RAO'. On 14 January 2005, the RAO was amended in such a way as to provide that giving advice about ATE insurance is a regulated activity. **34.44**

Certain persons are exempted from the general prohibition, but only if: **34.45**

- they are a member of a profession (or controlled or managed by one or more such members);
- they account to their clients for commission received;
- the relevant activities are 'incidental to the provision by him of professional services';
- the relevant activities are of a certain permitted type and are not of a prohibited type; and
- the relevant activities are the only regulated activities carried out (other than regulated activities in relation to which the person in question may be an exempt person).[53]

These provisions permit solicitors to be treated as 'exempt'. Such persons are permitted to carry on activities known as exempt regulated activities without being regulated by the FCA; instead, they are under the supervision of the SRA, which is known as a designated professional body. The provisions that allow solicitors to be treated as exempt are contained **34.46**

[49] Financial Services and Markets Act 2000 (Regulated Activities) Order 2001 (SI 2001/544), art 3(1) and Sch 1, Pt 1, para 17.
[50] See Financial Services and Markets Act 2000, s 23.
[51] See Financial Services and Markets Act 2000, s 19.
[52] SI 2001/544.
[53] See Financial Services and Markets Act 2000, s 327.

in Pt XX of the Financial Services and Markets Act 2000, which is why the exemption is often known as the Part XX exemption.

The SRA Financial Services (Scope) Rules 2001

34.47 For a Part XX exemption to exist, the designated professional body must have created certain rules. For that purpose, the SRA (acting with statutory authority[54]) has made the SRA Financial Services (Scope) Rules 2001 (the Scope Rules). Those Rules define the scope of the exempt regulated activities that may be undertaken and they list certain basic conditions that must be met. They also list certain prohibitions and restrictions. If the Scope Rules are breached, then the solicitor or firm may have contravened the general prohibition (which is a criminal offence).[55]

34.48 Like the RAO (see 34.44), the Scope Rules were amended on 14 January 2005 to encompass ATE insurance. In so far as the law of costs is concerned, the most important provisions are that:

- a solicitor may provide 'insurance mediation activities' only if registered with the FCA;
- the relevant activity must arise out of, or be complementary to, the provision of a particular professional service to a particular client; and
- the solicitor must account to a client for any pecuniary reward or other relevant advantage received from a third party.

The first of these provisions needs no explanation: whilst a solicitor does not need to be regulated by the FCA, they do need to be registered. The second of these provisions would rarely be relevant in the context of the law of costs.[56] The third may be relevant in that it is not unusual for solicitors to be paid a commission for recommending a particular contract of insurance; if that commission is not accounted for correctly, then the entire premium may be put at risk.

34.49 The issue of commissions has is addressed at 54.154. In essence, a solicitor needs to account for all commissions, regardless of size. The solicitor may be permitted to keep a commission, but only if the client consents to this.

34.50 Where a contract is made in contravention of the general prohibition by an unauthorised person, it will be unenforceable.[57] That said, the court would have discretion in the matter, that discretion being exercised in the following way:

> '(3) If the court is satisfied that it is just and equitable in the circumstances of the case, it may allow—
> (a) the agreement to be enforced; or
> (b) money ... paid ... under the agreement to be retained.

---

[54] The Scope Rules are made under Solicitors Act 1974, ss 31, 79 and 80, Administration of Justice Act 1985, ss 9 and 9A, and Legal Services Act 2007, s 83, with the approval of the Legal Services Board under Legal Services Act 2007, Sch 4, para 19.

[55] Financial Services and Markets Act 2000, s 23.

[56] It could become relevant if a solicitor were to become overly involved in distributing and marketing a particular form of insurance; it might also become relevant if a solicitor were to be in the habit of conspiring to write 'ghost insurance'.

[57] Financial Services and Markets Act 2000, ss 26 and 27, make similar provisions concerning contracts made through an unauthorised person.

(4) In considering whether to allow the agreement to be enforced or (as the case may be) the money ... paid ... under the agreement to be retained the court must—

(a) if the case arises as a result of section 26 [ie where the contract has been made by an authorised person], have regard to the issue mentioned in subsection (5); or

(b) if the case arises as a result of section 27 [ie where the contract has been made through an authorised person], have regard to the issue mentioned in subsection (6).

(5) The issue is whether the person carrying on the regulated activity concerned reasonably believed that he was not contravening the general prohibition by making the agreement.

(6) The issue is whether the provider knew that the third party was (in carrying on the regulated activity) contravening the general prohibition.

(7) If the person against whom the agreement is unenforceable—

(a) elects not to perform the agreement, or

(b) as a result of this section, recovers money paid or other property transferred by him under the agreement,

he must repay any money and return any other property received by him under the agreement.'[58]

Thus the test is what is just and equitable, and, in this regard, the court will take into account whether the solicitor knew that it was acting in breach of the general prohibition.

The SRA Financial Services (Conduct of Business) Rules 2001

In addition to the Scope Rules, the SRA has made the SRA Financial Services (Conduct of Business) Rules 2001 (the Conduct Rules). **34.51**

The solicitor is required to give the client a degree of pre-contract counselling. One of the topics that must be addressed is 'status disclosure', which means that the solicitor must give the client certain information in writing.[59] The solicitor must give some of that information in a prescribed way.[60] **34.52**

The Conduct Rules require that certain records be kept.[61] In essence, records need to be kept of the instructions received from the client, the instructions given by the solicitor to another person to effect a transaction, of the commissions received and of how the solicitor has accounted to the client for those commissions. These records must be kept for at least six years.[62] **34.53**

---

58 See Financial Services and Markets Act 2000, s 38.

59 See SRA Financial Services (Conduct of Business) Rules 2001, para 3. That information is: a statement that the firm is not authorised by the FCA; the name and address of the firm; the nature of the regulated activities carried on by the firm and the fact that they are limited in scope; a statement that the firm is regulated by the Law Society; and a statement explaining that complaints and redress mechanisms are provided through Law Society regulation.

60 See SRA Financial Services (Conduct of Business) Rules 2001, para 3(3). The following statement must be made in writing: '[This firm is]/[We are] not authorised by the Financial Conduct Authority. However, we are included on the register maintained by the Financial Conduct Authority so that we can carry on insurance mediation activity, which is broadly the advising on, selling and administration of insurance contracts. This part of our business, including arrangements for complaints or redress if something goes wrong, is regulated by Solicitors Regulation Authority. The register can be accessed via the Financial Conduct Authority website at www.fca.org.uk/register.'

61 See SRA Financial Services (Conduct of Business) Rules 2001, paras 5 and 6.

62 See SRA Financial Services (Conduct of Business) Rules 2001, para 9.

34.54 In so far as ATE insurance is concerned, a solicitor must comply with the provisions of 'Appendix 1'.[63] Broadly speaking, that appendix requires solicitors to do three things:

- they must disclose certain information (see 34.55);
- they must consider whether the ATE insurance is suitable (see 34.58); and
- they must prepare a 'demands and needs statement' (see 34.59).

Disclosure under the Conduct of Business Rules

34.55 The solicitor must take reasonable steps to communicate information to the client in a way that is 'clear, fair and not misleading'.[64] The solicitor must declare the basis upon which its recommendation is made,[65] including the following in particular.

- Where a solicitor recommends an ATE policy, they must inform the client whether they have given advice on the basis of a 'fair analysis' of a sufficiently large number of insurance contracts available on the market to enable them to make a recommendation regarding which contract of insurance would be adequate to meet the client's needs.[66]
- If the answer to the question above is in the negative, the solicitor must:
  - advise whether they are contractually obliged to conduct insurance mediation activities with only one or more insurance undertakings;
  - advise the client that they can request details of the insurance undertakings with which the solicitor conducts business; and
  - provide the client with such details on request.[67]

34.56 Thus the Conduct Rules recognise that a solicitor's recommendation might be influenced by commercial realities. Indeed, the Law Society used to offer the following guidance on the Conduct Rules:

> 'The Law Society is aware that some firms have entered into contracts with introducers whereby they are obliged to effect for their client a particular type of insurance contract eg if there is a conditional fee agreement. These arrangements are acceptable provided, of course, that the particular insurance policy is suitable for the client's needs and the solicitor has informed the client of the constraint.'[68]

The SRA's current guidance does not go this far, but it does say that certain indicative behaviours relating to introductions to third parties do not apply to general insurance (which includes ATE insurance).

34.57 The information outlined at 34.55 must be provided to the client on paper or on any other durable medium available and accessible to the client.[69]

---

63 See SRA Financial Services (Conduct of Business) Rules 2001, para 8A.
64 See SRA Financial Services (Conduct of Business) Rules 2001, Appx, para 1.
65 See SRA Financial Services (Conduct of Business) Rules 2001, Appx, para 1(2) and (3).
66 See SRA Financial Services (Conduct of Business) Rules 2001, Appx, para 1(2).
67 See SRA Financial Services (Conduct of Business) Rules 2001, Appx, para 1(3).
68 See at para 9.7 of the 2010 Guidance on SRA Financial Services (Conduct of Business) Rules 2001, Appx, para 1(3).
69 See SRA Financial Services (Conduct of Business) Rules 2001, Appx, para 1(4).

Suitability under the Conduct of Business Rules

Before a solicitor can recommend an ATE policy, it must take reasonable steps to ensure that the recommendation is suitable to the client's needs and meets their demands. In this regard, a solicitor must: **34.58**

- consider relevant information already held;
- obtain details of any relevant existing insurance;
- identify the client's requirements and explain to the client what they need to disclose;
- assess whether the level of cover is sufficient for the risks that the client wishes to insure; and
- consider the relevance of any exclusions, excesses, limitations or conditions.[70]

Where a solicitor recommends a contract of insurance that does not meet the needs of the client and where this is because no such contract is available in the market, the client must be told those facts.[71]

Demands and needs statements

The solicitor must give the client a demands and needs statement.[72] This must be provided to the client before the policy is finalised. That statement must: **34.59**

- set out the client's demands and needs on the basis of the information provided by the client;
- explain the reason why the solicitor is recommending that contract of insurance;
- reflect the complexity of the insurance contract being proposed; and
- be on paper or on any other durable medium available and accessible to the client.[73]

Rights Against Legal Expenses Insurers

It may be that a costs creditor (such as a receiving party or a legal services provider) is unable to enforce against a costs debtor (such as a paying party or a client) because of the latter's insolvency. Where this is the case and where the debtor had the benefit of legal expenses insurance, there are several mechanisms by which the creditor may try to recover its monies directly from the insurer; as is explained below, any such attempt would be an uphill struggle. **34.60**

The Third Parties (Rights against Insurers) Acts

If an insured becomes liable to a third party for monies covered by a legal expenses policy, the third party would ordinarily be able to claim against the insured; that liability would, in turn, be covered by the insurer. If the insured were to become insolvent, however, the third party would not, at common law, be able to proceed against the insured in the usual way, because they would simply become a general creditor. **34.61**

[70] See SRA Financial Services (Conduct of Business) Rules 2001, Appx, para 2.
[71] See SRA Financial Services (Conduct of Business) Rules 2001, Appx, para 2.
[72] See SRA Financial Services (Conduct of Business) Rules 2001, Appx, para 3.
[73] See SRA Financial Services (Conduct of Business) Rules 2001, Appx, para 3.

34.62 On 1 August 2016, the Third Parties (Rights against Insurers) Act 2010 came into force. Where, under any contract of insurance (including a legal expenses policy), a person is insured against liabilities to third parties that they may incur, then, in the event of the insured becoming bankrupt or insolvent (or, if it is a body corporate, in the event of it being wound up, entering administration or being dissolved), the rights against the insurer under the policy are, with certain limitations,[74] transferred to the third party. In practical terms, this means that a receiving party or a legal services provider may be able to claim directly from a legal expenses insurer.

34.63 The 2010 Act defines a 'relevant person' as—in essence—the person who has become bankrupt or otherwise insolvent. There are provisions relating both to natural persons[75] and to corporate bodies.[76] The Act also defines a 'third party' as the person to whom the rights of the relevant person under the contract against the insurer in respect of the liability[77] are transferred.[78] In essence, if a 'relevant person' incurs a liability against which they are insured or if a person who is subject to such a liability becomes a 'relevant person', then the rights of the relevant person are transferred to and vest in the third party. The insurer is able to assert any defence that it would have been able to assert against the insured.[79]

---

[74] Such as a territorial limitation: see, eg, *Catalyst Managerial Services v Libya Africa Investment Portfolio* [2017] EWHC 1236 (Comm), at [5].

[75] Third Parties (Rights against Insurers) Act 2010, s 4(1) (as amended), makes the following provisions: '(1) An individual is a relevant person if any of the following is in force in respect of that individual in England and Wales—(a) a deed of arrangement registered in accordance with the Deeds of Arrangement Act 1914, (b) an administration order made under Part 6 of the County Courts Act 1984, (c) an enforcement restriction order made under Part 6A of that Act, (d) subject to subsection (4), a debt relief order made under Part 7A of the Insolvency Act 1986, ie a voluntary arrangement approved in accordance with Part 8 of that Act, or (f) a bankruptcy order made under Part 9 of that Act. (4A) A body corporate or unincorporated body is a relevant person if it is in insolvency under Part 2 of the Banking Act 2009.'

[76] Third Parties (Rights against Insurers) Act 2010, s 6(1) and (2), makes the following provisions: '(1) A body corporate or an unincorporated body is a relevant person if—(a) a compromise or arrangement between the body and its creditors (or a class of them) is in force, having been sanctioned in accordance with s 899 of the Companies Act 2006, or (b) the body has been dissolved under section 1000, 1001 or 1003 of that Act, and the body has not been—(i) restored to the register by virtue of section 1025 of that Act, or (ii) ordered to be restored to the register by virtue of section 1031 of that Act. (2) A body corporate or an unincorporated body is a relevant person if, in England and Wales—(a) a voluntary arrangement approved in accordance with Part 1 of the Insolvency Act 1986 is in force in respect of it, (b) an administration order made under Part 2 of that Act is in force in respect of it, (c) there is a person appointed in accordance with Part 3 of that Act who is acting as receiver or manager of the body's property (or there would be such a person so acting but for a temporary vacancy), (d) the body is, or is being, wound up voluntarily in accordance with Chapter 2 of Part 4 of that Act, (e) there is a person appointed under section 135 of that Act who is acting as provisional liquidator in respect of the body (or there would be such a person so acting but for a temporary vacancy), or (f) the body is, or is being, wound up by the court following the making of a winding-up order under Chapter 6 of Part 4 of that Act or Part 5 of that Act.'

[77] Third Parties (Rights against Insurers) Act 2010, s 1(4), provides that 'liability is established only if its existence and amount are established; and, for that purpose, "establish" means establish—(a) by virtue of a declaration under section 2 or a declarator under section 3, (b) by a judgment or decree, (c) by an award in arbitral proceedings or by an arbitration, or (d) by an enforceable agreement.' The third party may bring proceedings to enforce the rights against the insurer without having established the relevant person's liability; but the third party may not enforce those rights without having established that liability: see Third Parties (Rights against Insurers) Act 2010, s 1(3).

[78] See Third Parties (Rights against Insurers) Act 2010, s 1(2).

[79] In this regard, Third Parties (Rights against Insurers) Act 2010, s 2(4), reads: 'Where proceedings are brought under subs (2)(a) the insurer may rely on any defence on which the insured could rely if those proceedings were proceedings brought against the insured in respect of the insured's liability to P.' There are also provisions concerning set-off: see Third Parties (Rights against Insurers) Act 2010, s 10.

Moreover, where the liability of the insured to the third party is less than the liability of the insurer to the insured, no rights are transferred in respect of the difference.[80] The third party may bring proceedings against the insurer for either or both of (a) a declaration as to the insured's liability and (b) a declaration as to the insurer's potential liability.[81]

Transitional provisions apply.[82] In essence, the 2010 Act will apply other than where the insured became insolvent and the liability was incurred before 1 August 2016. Where both of those conditions are met, then the Third Parties (Rights against Insurers) Act 1930 will continue to apply. For the reasons set out in the second edition of this book, at paras 21.323–21.326, it would be difficult, if not impossible, for a third party to make use of the 1930 Act where the insurance was BTE insurance (although it is arguable that the use of that Act could be made if the policy in question were an ATE policy).[83] In essence, the difficulty arises because the 1930 Act applies only where a person or company takes out *liability* insurance.[84] **34.64**

The Contracts (Rights of Third Parties) Act 1999

The Contracts (Rights of Third Parties) Act 1999[85] will, in certain circumstances, apply to contracts of insurance. That Act makes provision for persons who are not a party to a contract to enforce the contract; it will apply only (a) where the contract expressly provides that the third party may enforce it or (b) where there is a term that purports to confer a benefit on them.[86] The third party must be expressly identified in the contract by name, or as a member of a class, or as answering a particular description.[87] It is doubtful whether the 1999 Act would assist a third party seeking to enforce against a legal expenses insurer: Toulson J found it to be of little assistance in a case in which a solicitor sought to enforce his fees against the BTE insurer of an insolvent insured.[88] That said, Judge Behrens refused to allow an application to strike out a claim brought against an ATE insurer partly on the basis that it may have been possible to rely on the 1999 Act.[89] **34.65**

[80] See Third Parties (Rights against Insurers) Act 2010, s 8.

[81] See Third Parties (Rights against Insurers) Act 2010, s 2(2).

[82] In so far as it is relevant, Third Parties (Rights against Insurers) Act 2010, Sch 3, para 3, provides that the Third Parties (Rights against Insurers) Act 1930 will continue to apply in relation to cases in which the bankruptcy or insolvency and the liability under the policy both arose before commencement day.

[83] Whilst there was no analysis of the point in the judgment and whilst it is not clear if *Tarbuck v Avon Insurance plc* [2001] 2 All ER 503 was drawn to the court's attention, in *Persimmon Homes Ltd & Anor v Great Lakes Reinsurance (UK) plc* [2010] EWHC 1705 (Comm), David Steel J heard an application under the 1930 Act in which the insurer had underwritten an after the event policy. He ultimately dismissed that application on the facts, but he seemed impliedly to accept that the claim was arguable as a matter of law: see *Persimmon*, at [2].

[84] See Third Parties (Rights against Insurers) Act 1930 s 1(1). See also *Tarbuck v Avon Insurance plc* [2001] 2 All ER 503 at 509.

[85] It applies to contracts entered into or renewed after 11 May 2000.

[86] Unless, on a proper construction of the contract, it appears that the parties did not intend the term to be enforceable by the third party: see Contracts (Rights of Third Parties) Act 1999, s 1(1) and (2).

[87] See Contracts (Rights of Third Parties) Act 1999, s 1(3).

[88] *Tarbuck v Avon Insurance plc* [2001] 2 All ER 503, at 509.

[89] See *Beecham Peacock Solicitors LLP v Enterprise Insurance Co plc* [2014] EWHC 2194 (QB), at [48], *per* Judge Behrens.

Other mechanisms

34.66 There are several other mechanisms by which a third party (such as a solicitor) may try to enforce an insurer's obligations under a legal expenses policy. They include the following.

- **Implied contract** Whilst relating primarily to insurance in respect of adverse costs, it has been argued that, where a solicitor agrees to refer a client to an insurer and write the policy on behalf of the insurer and where, in doing so, the solicitor agrees to enter into a conditional fee agreement to provide legal services to the client, a contractual obligation is created pursuant to which the solicitor can enforce the insurer's duty to honour its obligations under the policy. Cooke J rejected that argument, likening the solicitors to 'cover holders' and asserting that there was nothing unusual in an arrangement that a person is given authority to arrange insurance; hence he found that no such term could be implied by reference to either the business efficacy or officious bystander test.[90]
- **Implied term within policy, restitution and the Civil Liability (Contribution) Act 1978** In the case referred to above, the solicitors (who had already made significant payments in respect of adverse costs that they said ought to have been paid by the insurers) submitted that there was an implied agreement between them and the insurer as surety and debtor, and/or that they were entitled to payment by reason of the Civil Liability (Contribution) Act 1978 and/or the law of restitution. Cooke J agreed: he made no finding as to which of those mechanisms was the correct mechanism (that being 'a matter of indifference'), but he explained that the insurers did have a duty that the law would enforce.[91]
- **Declaration** A solicitor who seeks to ensure that it is appointed under a contract of insurance held by one of its would-be clients is entitled to seek a declaration to that effect.[92]
- **Trust** It is possible for a third party to gain rights as a result of the operation of a trust.[93] There is, however, no authority for the proposition that such a mechanism would assist a costs creditor in obtaining payment from a legal expenses insurer.
- **Road traffic accident cases** Likewise, provisions exist concerning the rights of third parties involved in road traffic accident cases,[94] but there is no authority to suggest that they are relevant in the present context.

---

[90] *Greene Wood McLean LLP (in administration) v Templeton Insurance Ltd* [2010] EWHC 2679 (Comm), at [33], [42], [44], [45] and [48]–[50].

[91] *Ibid*, at [65]–[72].

[92] This is implied by *Brown-Quinn & Anor v Equity Syndicate Management Ltd & Anor* [2011] EWHC 2661 (Comm), at [28], following a decision that was made after argument, but which is not recorded in the written judgment.

[93] See, eg, *Bowskill v Dawson* [1955] 1 QB 13, [1954] 2 All ER 649, CA (which was an express trust); *Hepburn v A Tomlinson (Hauliers) Ltd* [1966] AC 451, [1966] 1 All ER 418, HL (in which the party was a bailee).

[94] See Road Traffic Act 1988, s 151.

Part X

COSTS AS BETWEEN SOLICITOR AND CLIENT

35

INVOICES AND BILLS

This chapter deals with the following topics: 35.01

- the distinction between invoices and statute bills (35.02);
- interim invoices:
  - interim statute bills (35.06);
  - requests for payment on account (35.10);
  - distinguishing interim statute bills from bills for a payment on account (35.15);
  - natural breaks and interim invoices (35.28);
- internal invoices (35.37);
- statute bills generally (35.40):
  - the requirements of a statute bill:
    - reasonably complete (35.47);
    - sufficient narrative (35.52);
    - signed (35.72);
    - delivered (35.85);
  - erroneous bills—amendment, withdrawal, and substitution (35.87);
  - gross sum bills and requests for bills containing detailed items (35.99);
- the consequences of failing to comply with Solicitors Act 1974, s 69 (35.109):
  - payment (35.112);
  - statutory demands (35.113);
  - set-off (35.114);
  - loss of protection (35.115);
- how disbursements are treated in a statute bill (35.116); and
- the power to order delivery of a bill (35.120).

The Distinction between Invoices and Statute Bills

An invoice is a commercial document by which a solicitor claims monies for services rendered (or to be rendered) or disbursements disbursed (or to be disbursed). Beyond this, whilst non-payment of an invoice may give rise to certain legal consequences, an invoice per se has no special legal status. 35.02

An invoice may or may not be a bill within the meaning of s 69(2) of the Solicitors Act 1974 (as amended); the term 'statute bill' is used in this book to describe a bill *bona fide* compliant with that section. In contrast to other types of invoice, an invoice that is a statute bill will have significant legal status, not least because it will be the document upon which a solicitor will be able to found a claim for payment of fees. 35.03

35.04 All statute bills will be invoices, but not all invoices will be statute bills. Indeed, some invoices will—by intention—not be statute bills; this may often be true of invoices rendered part-way through a retainer (so-called interim invoices). Such invoices that are not, in themselves, *bona fide* compliant with the 1974 Act are merely requests for payments on account (see 35.06 and 35.10–35.14). Moreover, some invoices (known as internal invoices) are created only for tax and accounting purposes without there being an intention that they be sent to the client, this being where the client has been informed of the monies they have to pay by some other means, known as a 'written notification' of costs (see 35.12).

35.05 Disputes often arise as to the status of invoices. Such disputes tend to arise because the status of the invoice will determine whether the solicitor is able to bring a claim for payment of fees, whether time has begun to run for the purposes of the client's right to a detailed assessment, or both.

Interim Invoices

Interim statute bills

35.06 Interim statute bills must be distinguished from requests for payment on account: interim statute bills are bills *bona fide* compliant with the requirements of Solicitors Act 1974, s 69(2), and—whilst interim—they are discrete and entire statute bills in their own right. In particular, subject to certain procedural requirements, a solicitor can sue upon an interim statute bill and a client can apply to have it assessed; neither of these steps can be taken if the invoice is a mere request for payment on account.

35.07 For reasons set out at 35.87–35.98, an interim statute bill is a final bill in the sense that it is complete and, once rendered, cannot readily be withdrawn, replaced or amended. It is interim only in the sense that it is rendered during the currency of the retainer; the description of it being interim does not meant that it is provisional or transient.

35.08 The requirements that apply to statute bills generally will apply to interim statute bills. Those requirements are discussed in detail at 35.42–35.86.

35.09 Interim statute bills may be issued only if and to the extent that the retainer permits this, be that as expressly provided by the contract of retainer, as impliedly permitted as a matter of construction, or as a result of a type of factual implication known as a 'natural break' (see 27.64–27.66 and 35.28–35.35).

Requests for payment on account

35.10 Requests for payment on account—or, as they are often called, interim invoices on account—are not bills upon which a solicitor can found a claim for payment; rather, they are mere requests for payment on account of monies that may (or may not) be billed at some point in the future. They may be for fees or disbursements that have already been incurred but not yet billed, or they may be for (or include) a reasonable allowance for such monies yet to be incurred.[1]

[1] In so far as contentious business is concerned, see Solicitors Act 1974, s 65(1). Whilst not a source of law, also see IB(1.21) of the SRA Code of Conduct 2011 (as amended in 2017).

Although a solicitor cannot bring a claim on a request for payment on account, such invoices may, in certain circumstances, be of significance in other ways. If, on the one hand, such a request were to be for more than the client was content to pay, it might precipitate an application for delivery of a statute bill under s 68(1) of the Solicitors Act 1974 (see 35.120–35.129). If, on the other, a client refuses to make a reasonable interim payment on account, then—where the work is contentious—this may amount to 'good cause' to terminate the retainer pursuant to Solicitors Act 1974, s 65(2). That provision reads as follows: 35.11

> 'If a solicitor who has been retained by a client to conduct contentious business requests the client to make a payment of a sum of money, being a reasonable sum on account of the costs incurred or to be incurred in the conduct of that business and the client refuses or fails within a reasonable time to make that payment, the refusal or failure shall be deemed to be a good cause whereby the solicitor may, upon giving reasonable notice to the client, withdraw from the retainer.'

There does not need to be an agreement to this effect in respect of contentious work.[2]

In any event, even though it will not be a statute bill, a request for a payment on account may have a significant bearing on the way in which a solicitor deals with any monies they hold for the client in question (including any monies received from the client's opponent). This is because monies that have been properly 'earmarked for costs' become office monies and, as such, not only *may* they be treated as office monies, but—as a matter of professional conduct—they *must* be transferred into an office account within 14 days.[3] This is in contrast to monies held on account generally, which will remain client monies unless and until they are 'earmarked for costs'.[4] According to the Solicitors Regulation Authority (SRA) Accounts Rules 2011 (as amended), monies will be 'earmarked for costs' if they are specific sums relating to a statute bill or 'other written notification of costs',[5] the latter being a request for payment (which, in the editor's view, may be in the form of correspondence rather than a commercial invoice as such). That said, the earmarking ought not to go beyond the amount of costs and disbursements incurred[6] or paid[7] to date. Payments on account of costs generally, and of unpaid professional disbursements specifically,[8] will remain client monies and must remain in a client account.[9] 35.12

Because a request for payment on account (or a 'written notification') is not a document that is subject to formalities, the requirements that are described at 35.42–35.86 do not apply.[10] This means that there is no requirement that such a request should contain a 35.13

---

[2] See Solicitors Act 1974, s 65(2).

[3] See SRA Accounts Rules 2011 (as amended), rr 17.2 and 17.3.

[4] See SRA Accounts Rules 2011 (as amended), r 17.4.

[5] See SRA Accounts Rules 2011 (as amended), r 17.7.

[6] *Vlamaki v Sookias & Sookias* [2015] EWHC 3334 (QB), at [10], *per* Walker J. This may include unpaid disbursements for which the solicitor has incurred a liability to the payee, but not yet paid (eg travel agents' charges, taxi fares, courier charges or Land Registry search fees, payable on credit): see Guidance Note (i)(c) to r 17 of the SRA Accounts Rules 2011 (as amended).

[7] See Guidance Note (i)(a) to r 17 of the SRA Accounts Rules 2011 (as amended).

[8] See Guidance Note (i)(b) to r 17 of the SRA Accounts Rules 2011 (as amended).

[9] See SRA Accounts Rules 2011 (as amended), rr 12.2(c), 12.2(e), 14.1, 17 and 18—but note the provision made for receipts from the Legal Aid Agency.

[10] Other formalities may apply if the document is a commercial invoice that is intended to be a VAT invoice: see, eg, Council Directive 2006/112/EC of 28 November 2006 on the common system of value added tax, OJ L 347/1, 11 December 2006, Art 226.

narrative, that it be signed, etc.[11] It must, however, be for no more than a 'reasonable sum'.[12] Crane J has found this to mean that it must be for an amount that it is reasonable to request at the time the request is made.[13]

35.14 If a solicitor claims more than a reasonable amount, that solicitor may not be able to rely upon the request for the purposes of withdrawing their services pursuant to Solicitors Act 1974, s 65(2) (see 35.11). This may result in the solicitor being in breach of contract if they subsequently withdraw those services (see 27.72).[14] Toulson J has found (albeit *obiter*) that a request by a firm of solicitors for 90 per cent of its costs was unreasonable in the context of those costs being disputed and that, as a consequence, the subsequent termination of the retainer was unlawful.[15] The topic of unlawful termination is addressed in more detail at 27.70–27.75.

Distinguishing interim statute bills from requests for a payment on account

35.15 Whether an interim invoice is an interim statute bill or a request for payment on account is an issue that will turn on the facts of each case.[16]

35.16 Whilst far from being an exhaustive list, the following factors may be relevant in distinguishing an interim statute bill from a request for payment on account:

- the terms of the contract of retainer (see 35.17–35.18);
- the information given to the client (see 35.19–35.21);
- the absence or presence of a natural break at the time the invoice was requested (see 35.22 and 35.28–35.35);
- the form of the invoice (or 'written notification') (see 35.23);
- the conduct of the parties (see 35.24–35.25);
- the subject matter of the invoice (see 35.26); and
- whether a balance has been carried forward (see 35.27).

The contract of retainer

35.17 The starting point will generally be examining the terms of the contract of retainer, as retainers will often expressly stipulate whether an interim invoice is to be regarded as a request for a payment on account or an interim statute bill. For example, it is often the case that a retainer will say that an interim invoice is not to be treated as an interim statute bill

---

[11] The editor has been unable to find any rule or authority that says that an invoice that is not intended to be a statute bill has to be sent to the client. In this regard, IB(1.20)(c) of the SRA Code of Conduct (as amended in 2017) merely provides that 'the solicitor must have told the client the amount of the benefit (or an approximation . . .) and the client has agreed that you can keep it'. If the editor's researches are correct, then it would seem permissible for a solicitor to issue interim invoices internally and to simply request payment in correspondence. Indeed, this seems to be confirmed by r 17.2 of the SRA Accounts Rules 2011 (as amended), which reads as follows: 'If you properly require payment of your fees from money held for a client or trust in a client account, you must first give or send a bill of costs, or other written notification of the costs incurred, to the client or the paying party.'

[12] *Collyer Bristow v Robichaux* (unreported), 20 July 2001, QBD.

[13] *Ibid.*

[14] This is because if a retainer is terminated without good reason, then the solicitor may not be able to require the client to pay for work done up to this point: *Underwood Son & Piper v Lewis* [1894] 2 QB 306. As a counter-example, see *Minkin v Cawdery Kaye Fireman & Taylor (a firm)* [2012] EWCA Civ 546, in which Ward LJ found that care should be taken to distinguish termination from suspension of services.

[15] See *Wong v Vizards* [1997] 2 Costs LR 46, at 52.

[16] *In re Romer & Haslam* [1893] 2 QB 286, at 293.

unless it says, upon its face, that it is a 'final bill' (or some other such term). Such contractual safeguards are often included for the purpose of allowing revisions to be made to the sums earmarked for costs upon the determination of the retainer. The retainers of some firms (especially larger firms with sophisticated accounting facilities) will often say precisely the opposite, this being because such firms are generally more confident in their ability to charge the right amount at any given time and they are more concerned about being able to promptly bring a claim for their fees in the event of non-payment.

As with any contract, issues of interpretation may arise. The general principles of the interpretation of contracts of retainer are addressed in Chapter 31. The more specific issue of whether a contract of retainer permits the delivery of interim statute bills is addressed in detail at 27.42–27.63. **35.18**

The information given to the client and consumer issues

Where a client has not been told that they will be sent an interim statute bill—which may be relevant because delivery of such a bill would start time running for the purposes of Solicitors Act 1974, s 70(2)—then that will be a factor that will militate against the invoice being an interim statute bill. In this regard, Fulford J made the following points about consumer protection: **35.19**

> 'In particular the party must know what rights are being negotiated and dispensed with in the sense that the solicitor must make it plain to the client that the purpose of sending the bill at that time is that it is to be treated as a complete self-contained bill of costs to date'.[17]

The more recent observations made by Walker J, as set out at 27.52–27.54, seem to support this view.

Similarly, in a case in which the contract of retainer was ambiguous in the sense that it said that the client could have an assessment 'at any time', Spencer J found that this assurance was incompatible with the notion that time started to run for the purposes of s 70 of the 1974 Act prior to the termination of the retainer and that, as such, the retainer did not provide for delivery of interim statute bills.[18] **35.20**

The *contra proferentum* rule may apply (see 31.40). Similarly, whilst there is no authority directly on the point, the Consumer Contracts (Information, Cancellation and Additional Charges) Regulations 2013[19] and—where the contract of retainer was made on or after 1 October 2015—the provisions of the Consumer Rights Act 2015 may also be relevant (see 28.31 and 28.71–28.76). **35.21**

The absence or presence of natural breaks

If a retainer makes no express provision for interim statute bills and if invoices are rendered at times that cannot be said to coincide with natural breaks, then that will be a factor that **35.22**

[17] *Adams v Al Malik* [2003] EWHC 3232 (QB), at [48], in which Fulford J made reference to the judgment of Roskill LJ in *Davidsons v Jones-Fenleigh* [1980] 124 SJ 204. See also *Vlamaki v Sookias & Sookias* [2015] EWHC 3334, at [11], *per* Walker J.

[18] *Bari v Rosen (t/a Rosen & Co Solicitors)* [2012] EWHC 1782 (QB), at [35].

[19] SI 2013/3134.

militates against those invoices being interim statute bills.[20] This issue is considered more fully at 35.28–35.35 and 27.64–27.66.

The form of the invoice or 'written notification'

35.23 Where an invoice bears, upon its face, a description of its intended effect, then this will be a factor to be taken into account. An invoice may say that it is a statute bill (or that it is not). This will be particularly relevant if the contract of retainer provides that an interim invoice should or should not be regarded as an interim statute bill (see 35.17). The form of the putative invoice may also be relevant. If it is a notification in correspondence as to the fees that will be deducted from client monies, for example, then it is likely to be a mere 'written notification' of the type envisaged by r 17.2 of the SRA Accounts Rules 2011 (as amended) (see 35.12). Such a notification would be a request for a payment on account and this would be so even if the solicitor created (but did not deliver) an internal invoice for accounting purposes.[21]

The parties' conduct

35.24 Roskill LJ has explained that the reaction of the parties is a factor relevant to whether an invoice should be treated as an interim statute bill: 'If the client's reaction is to pay the bill in its entirety without demur it is not difficult to infer an agreement that that bill is to be treated as a complete self-contained bill of costs to date.'[22] In the editor's view, it would be wrong to read too much into Roskill LJ's comments, especially given the fact that, in the present-day legal services industry, contracts of retainer are usually so lengthy and complex that clients (especially consumer clients) could easily misunderstand the nature of the request being made of them. The reaction of a client is, perhaps, of most relevance where the issue is whether there has been a natural break (see 35.28–35.41, especially 35.34).

35.25 If there was no right to deliver interim statute bills, the mere fact that a solicitor states in correspondence that there was no proposal to seek any further amount would not convert a request for payment on account into an interim statute bill—and this would be so even if the solicitor were also to say that proceedings would be commenced for the amounts already invoiced.[23]

The subject matter of the invoice

35.26 Where an invoice is for work yet to be done or (with one or two exceptions[24]) for professional disbursements yet to be paid or disbursements yet to be incurred, it can (to that extent at least) be only a request for payment on account because those monies would be client monies (see 35.12). Similarly, if an invoice were to exclude mark-up on the hourly rate in circumstances in which such a charge would be expected (such as where a mark-up is provided for in the contract of retainer), then that too would suggest that the invoice was a mere request for a payment on account.

---

20 See, eg, *In re Hall v Barker* (1893) 9 Ch D 538, in which a series of bills was found to have been rendered at natural breaks.

21 See, eg, *Parvez v Mooney Everett Solicitors Ltd* [2018] EWHC 62 (QB), *per* Soole J.

22 *Davidsons v Jones-Fenleigh* (1980) Costs LR (Core vol) 70, at 75.

23 See *Vlamaki v Sookias & Sookias* [2015] EWHC 3334 (QB), at [38], *per* Walker J.

24 A disbursement may have been incurred notwithstanding the fact that it may not have been paid. For example, if a solicitor declines to afford its client any credit, a request for payment may be made on the basis that the solicitor is merely acting as agent for the client.

Carrying forward a balance

Where there is a series of invoices, the fact that a balance had been carried forward from one invoice to the next would suggest that it is a series of requests for payment on account[25]—although where the series comprises a running account, it may, when properly analysed, constitute a single statute bill that is finally delivered only upon completion of the series, that being known as a *Chamberlain* bill[26] (see 36.15–36.16). It is the carrying forward that is relevant, not the fact that credit may have been recorded for sums already paid. **35.27**

Natural breaks and interim invoices

One of the factors mentioned thus far has been whether there has been a natural break in the claim or matter to which the retainer relates. The following is only a brief summary, with its focus firmly on the nature of the invoice. For a discussion of contractual issues relating to natural breaks, see 27.64–27.66. **35.28**

The time-honoured position at common law used to be that a contract of retainer was a contract entire (see 27.13–27.15), which meant that a solicitor could not charge for their services unless and until they had performed the entirety of their obligations under that contract. In long-running cases, this was capable of causing injustice, not only because the solicitor was kept out of their fees until the conclusion of the claim, but also because the solicitor may have been unable to secure payment at all if, for some reason, they were prevented from discharging their obligations (see 27.16–27.17). **35.29**

That potential for injustice is ameliorated by the doctrine of the 'natural break'. Sir George Jessel MR explained the need for that doctrine by posing the following rhetorical question: **35.30**

> '[E]ven if it were right [that a retainer is an entire contract], there must be a break somewhere. In the case of a Chancery suit I have shewn what sort of break you may have. In the case of winding up there are all sorts of breaks. Is it to be supposed that, because a few matters are undisposed of, the solicitor is not to be paid until the final termination?'[27]

Sir George Jessel MR went on to answer that question in the negative.

Giving judgment at about the same time, but in a different case, Lord Esher MR explained the mechanism of the doctrine: **35.31**

> '[When] the award was given there was a break—that is, such a conclusion of a definite and distinct part of the legal transaction as would entitle the solicitors to send in a final bill of costs, such as might in Chancery be sent in at the stage of decree.'[28]

As to whether a bill is a statute bill or merely a request for a payment on account, Lord Esher MR said: **35.32**

> 'Whether in the case of a series of bills each bill has been sent in as a final bill, or whether they are mere statements of account shewing how far the expenses have gone up to the time of sending them in, is a question of fact to be determined on the evidence in each case, and it is a question which cannot be determined in any case upon the finding of the Court in any other case.'[29]

[25] See, eg, *In re Romer & Haslam* [1893] 2 QB 286.
[26] After *Chamberlain v Boodle & King* [1982] 1 WLR 1443.
[27] *Hall v Barker* (1893) 9 Ch D 538, at 545.
[28] *In re Romer & Haslam* [1893] 2 QB 286, at 294.
[29] *Ibid.*

35.33 The issue of whether an interim invoice was an interim statute bill or a request for a payment on account is therefore a question of fact and law. The law will be relevant in that the terms of the retainer may shed light on the nature of the interim invoice,[30] but that will usually be only one factor amongst many. Another way of looking at the doctrine is to regard a natural break as implied by the combination of an invoice that does not exclude the delivery of interim statute bills and circumstances that make it appropriate that such a bill be delivered.

35.34 Whether there has been a natural break will, to some extent, depend on the way in which the solicitor and client comported themselves at the time when the invoice was rendered (see 35.24). That is a factor to be taken into account, but Simon Brown LJ has explained that it should not be given so much weight that the solicitor is, in effect, allowed to create a natural break at will.[31]

35.35 Although there is no authority specifically on the point, the court will often bear in mind the fact that clients are reliant on their legal advisers as to the status of any invoice that is delivered. Judge LJ had this to say (*obiter*) about the need for there to be express agreement about the terms upon which payments would be made:

> 'The desirability of such arrangements is likely to be reinforced by the increasing impact of the Civil Justice Reforms on a client's entitlement to be kept properly informed of his escalating financial obligations at each stage of the proceedings. As clients should know exactly where they stand throughout the process, it is reasonable to anticipate that questions of their own costs, and payment, should be arranged at an early stage in the process.'[32]

35.36 If a solicitor has failed to heed this guidance, they must bear the risk that the court finds that the bill they intended to sue upon is, in truth, a mere request for a payment on account.

Internal Invoices

35.37 The foregoing discussion has largely focused on documents that have been created for the purposes of being sent to the client. Over the last 15 years or so, it has become widespread practice in some sectors of the legal services industry (particularly personal injury) for clients merely to be told in correspondence about the fees that they must pay—known as a 'written notification' (see 35.12). Indeed—whilst it is probably a breach of the SRA Accounts Rules 2011—it is not unheard of for clients not to be told anything of the fact that specific costs recovered from an opponent have been taken as fees and transferred from the solicitor's client account into their office account. Such practices may happen, but there are myriad reasons why a solicitor would be unable to escape the need to raise an invoice of some kind, not least amongst which is the need to create an actual tax point for value added tax (VAT) purposes (see 55.06). Regardless of whether it is professionally

---

[30] An example would be where an invoice was rendered under a provision in a conditional fee agreement that allowed for immediate payment of costs of a successful hearing. In those circumstances, the nature of the retainer itself would strongly—possibly conclusively—indicate that such an invoice was an interim statute bill.

[31] *Abedi v Penningtons* [2000] 2 Costs LR 205.

[32] *Ibid*, at 221.

proper to do so,[33] invoices created for accounting and taxation purposes are commonly intended to lie within the solicitor's file and never be sent to the client. Such invoices may usefully be referred to as 'internal invoices'.

Internal invoices are not capable of being statute bills (unless, of course, the solicitor subsequently elects to deliver such a document to the client as a statute bill) and this would be so even if such an invoice were to come into the possession of the client at some later stage. Moreover, the court lacks the power under s 68 of the Solicitors Act 1974 (see 35.120) to order a solicitor to deliver an internal invoice as a statute bill. In this regard, Soole J had the following to say: **35.38**

> '[A] document is not a bill of costs [ie a statutory bill] unless it is sent by the solicitor to the client as a demand or claim of the sum therein stated to be due ... [It] is only the solicitor who can determine the content and terms of what is *his* demand or claim for payment. Neither the client nor the Court can make that determination on his behalf. ... [The] Court's power under s.68 to order a solicitor to deliver a bill of costs does not entitle the Court to order (nor therefore the client to seek) delivery of a specific identified document and thereby to determine the terms and content of the solicitor's demand or claim for payment. It is for the solicitor to provide "a bill" of his costs; and for the process of assessment to deal with any challenge thereto.'[34]

Soole J went on to say this: **35.39**

> 'The client can be in no better position if the relevant document has come into his possession otherwise than in the character of a delivered bill of costs [ie a statute bill]. There is no principled basis to treat it differently from a document which remains in the possession of the solicitors. It is unnecessary to determine whether or not there was a breach of the Solicitors Accounts Rules. Even if there was, this does not entitle the client to treat an undelivered bill of costs as if it had been delivered. To do so would again allow the client to determine the terms and content of the solicitor's demand or claim for payment.'[35]

Statute Bills Generally

A solicitor may render a statute bill for services rendered in contentious or non-contentious business. A bill may be either a gross sum bill—that is, a bill that summarises the costs as a whole (see 35.99–35.108)—or a detailed bill. The right to render a gross sum bill in non-contentious business may be open to challenge (see 35.58). **35.40**

To a large extent, the law is the same for all statute bills—contentious or non-contentious, gross sum or detailed—but there are certain requirements that are specific to certain types of bill. It is convenient to deal with the general principles first (see 35.42–35.86), followed by the specific topics (see 35.99–35.108). **35.41**

The requirements of a statute bill

The relevant law derives from Solicitors Act 1974, s 69. Those provisions relate to statute bills for services rendered in both contentious and non-contentious business. **35.42**

---

33 Soole J did not make a finding on this point in *Parvez v Mooney Everett Solicitors Ltd* [2018] EWHC 62 (QB), at [60]. The editor's views may be found at fn 12.
34 *Ibid*, at [56]–[58] (emphasis original).
35 *Ibid*, at [59]–[60].

35.43 The 1974 Act sets out the circumstances in which a solicitor may bring a claim for fees and prescribes certain requirements for statute bills. Since 7 March 2008,[36] the relevant provisions have read as follows:

> '**69 Action to recover solicitor's costs**
>
> (1) Subject to the provisions of this Act, no action shall be brought to recover any costs due to a solicitor before the expiration of one month from the date on which a bill of those costs is delivered in accordance with the requirements mentioned in subsection (2); . . .
>
> (2) The requirements referred to in subsection (1) are that the bill must be—
> (a) signed in accordance with subsection (2A), and
> (b) delivered in accordance with subsection (2C).
>
> (2A) A bill is signed in accordance with this subsection if it is—
> (a) signed by the solicitor or on his behalf by an employee of the solicitor authorised by him to sign, or
> (b) enclosed in, or accompanied by, a letter which is signed as mentioned in paragraph (a) and refers to the bill.
>
> (2B) For the purposes of subsection (2A) the signature may be an electronic signature.
>
> (2C) A bill is delivered in accordance with this subsection if—
> (a) it is delivered to the party to be charged with the bill personally,
> (b) it is delivered to that party by being sent to him by post to, or left for him at, his place of business, dwelling-house or last known place of abode, or
> (c) it is delivered to that party—
> (i) by means of an electronic communications network, or
> (ii) by other means but in a form that nevertheless requires the use of apparatus by the recipient to render it intelligible,
>
> and that party has indicated to the person making the delivery his willingness to accept delivery of a bill sent in the form and manner used.
>
> (2D) An indication to any person for the purposes of subsection (2C)(c)—
> (a) must state the address to be used and must be accompanied by such other information as that person requires for the making of the delivery;
> (b) may be modified or withdrawn at any time by a notice given to that person.
>
> (2E) Where a bill is proved to have been delivered in compliance with the requirements of subsections (2A) and (2C), it is not necessary in the first instance for the solicitor to prove the contents of the bill and it is to be presumed, until the contrary is shown, to be a bill *bona fide* complying with this Act.
>
> (2F) A bill which is delivered as mentioned in subsection (2C)(c) is to be treated as having been delivered on the first working day after the day on which it was sent (unless the contrary is proved).
>
> [. . .]
>
> (5) In this section references to an electronic signature are to be read in accordance with section 7(2) of the Electronic Communications Act 2000 (c 7).
>
> (6) In this section—
> "electronic communications network" has the same meaning as in the Communications Act 2003 (c 21);

[36] If the older law is required, then the unamended statute ought to be consulted: see the Legal Services Act 2007, s 177 and Sch 16, Pt 1, paras 1, 64(1) and (3). Transitional provisions apply: see Legal Services Act 2007, Sch 22, para 14.

"working day" means a day other than a Saturday, a Sunday, Christmas Day, Good Friday or a bank holiday in England and Wales under the Banking and Financial Dealings Act 1971 (c 80).'

Thus there are express statutory requirements that a bill must be signed (electronically or otherwise) and that it must be delivered (electronically or otherwise).

Compliance with those express requirements will not necessarily result in the bill being a statute bill *bona fide* compliant with the Solicitors Act 1974. This is because of the operation of s 69(2E), which states that a bill that complies with those requirements will be a bill *bona fide* complying with the 1974 Act 'unless the contrary is shown'. Put another way, compliance with the express requirements will create a presumption of compliance with s 69 in general, but that presumption may be rebutted. This is because, in addition to the express requirements, there are implied requirements—in particular, that a statute bill must be reasonably complete (see 35.47–35.51) and that there must be a sufficient narrative that tells the client what is being claimed (see 35.52–35.71). **35.44**

Where a solicitor seeks to bring a claim upon an invoice, there can be no bill other than a statute bill *bona fide* compliant with s 69(2) of the Solicitors Act 1974. Chitty J made it clear that it is wrong to say that a bill that is not *bona fide* compliant with the 1974 Act has the status of a bill in a different legal sense[37]—although, of course, it may be an invoice, such as a request for a payment on account (see 35.10–35.14), or an internal invoice for accounting purposes (see 35.37–35.39). Specifically, an account stated[38] will not suffice to allow a solicitor to sue unless it is a valid bill[39] (or, of course, a valid agreement to pay a certain amount[40]). A mere 'written notification of the costs incurred' made in correspondence pursuant to r 17.2 of the SRA Accounts Rules 2011 (as amended) would not generally amount to a statute bill.[41] **35.45**

It is convenient to deal first with the implied requirements—that is, the completeness of the statute bill and the sufficiency of the narrative (see 35.47–35.70)—and then to consider the express requirements—that is, the signature and delivery (see 35.72–35.86). **35.46**

The first (implied) requirement of a statute bill: it must be reasonably complete

A statute bill must be reasonably complete. If, for example, an invoice is rendered to a client that is for the shortfall in the recovery of costs that have otherwise been paid by a third party, that document would not be a reasonably complete bill.[42] A statute bill must be adequate to serve its purpose of informing the client of the basis upon which it was prepared and to enable the court to investigate its propriety.[43] An invoice that particularised a **35.47**

---

[37] In *Re Baylis* [1896] 2 Ch 107, at 110.

[38] An account stated is a statement between a costs creditor and a costs debtor that a certain sum is owing.

[39] *Eicke v Nokes* (1834) 1 M & Rob 359; *In Re Baylis* [1896] 2 Ch 107, at 111.

[40] If an oral retainer is made and then the agreed sum is acknowledged in the form of an account stated after payment has been made by deduction, that acknowledgement will not be sufficient to give rise to a retrospective business agreement: *Re Fernandes* [1878] WN 57.

[41] Whilst there is no authority on the point, the editor's view is that this would be so even if the solicitor had produced an internal invoice for accounting purposes that, had it been delivered, would have been a statute bill.

[42] *Cobbett v Wood* [1908] 2 KB 420. It is commonly the case that where a solicitor is paid in part by way of costs recovered from an opponent and in part by deductions from a client's damages, an invoice is sent to the client only for the latter. Such invoices would not generally be statute bills (although the contrary is arguable).

[43] *Ibid.* See also *Philby v Hazle* (1860) 8 CBNS 647 (bill containing only some of the items that were agreed to form part of the services rendered).

number of items but which specified a putatively agreed charge in respect of only some of them, was found not to be sufficient in that regard.[44]

35.48 Whilst there is no authority to confirm the point, it seems that the legal burden of proving that the bill is not complete lies with the client (assuming, of course, that it is the client who is challenging the veracity of the putative bill). This is because of the effect of s 69(2E) of the Solicitors Act 1974 (see 35.43).

35.49 Slade J has found that, for an invoice to be a statute bill in the context of it being a bill that covers a period of time, it must include all of the costs incurred during the period to which it relates, including disbursements.[45] Slade J went on to say that this would be so even notwithstanding the practical difficulties that a solicitor may have in including disbursements (such as ensuring that experts and counsel have rendered fee notes for all work done during the period in question).[46] In this regard, Slade J had this to say:

> 'The Master was bound by statute as explained in authority to hold that an interim statute bill must contain a bill of all costs including profit costs and disbursements in respect of agreed periods of time. Any practical difficulties which this requirement may cause to the solicitor are outweighed by the certainty given to the client, safeguarded by statute and authority, of knowing the total amount of costs they are being asked to pay. The client needs to know the total costs incurred over a certain period to enable them to form an evidenced based view of whether to exercise their right under Section 70 to challenge the bill.'[47]

At the time of writing, Slade J's decision was under appeal, but if it is found to be correct, it will necessitate a significant change in the way in which legal services are provided to clients in cases in which it is the solicitor's intention to render regular statute bills (which is a very common commercial arrangement). This is because counsel and experts frequently provide fee notes only at *ir*regular intervals (often for good reason, such as the need to focus their minds on the client's case). Indeed, one could say that Slade J has discovered a new implied requirement of a statute bill—that is, that if it relates to a period of time, there is an implied requirement of currency (that is, it must be up to date).

35.50 It should be noted that Slade J made no mention in her judgment of having been referred to *Aaron v Okoye*[48]—a case that arguably may have caused her to come to a different conclusion (although it is distinguishable on the facts). In *Aaron*, two bills were rendered, the first of which did not include counsel's fees,[49] but the second of which did. The first bill expressly referred to the fact that counsel's fees had not been included. Hobhouse LJ had this to say on the point:

> 'The first bill made it clear that counsel's fees were not being included and a covering letter adequately reminded [the client] of the reason why that was so. [The client] was not deceived. She was not led astray in any way and there is no general principle which precludes the solicitor from then including the relevant item in a later bill when it is proper for him to do so.'[50]

---

[44] *Wilkinson v Smart* (1875) 24 WR 42; see also *Blake v Hummel* (1884) 1 TLR 22.
[45] See *Slade & Company Solicitors v Boodia* [2017] EWHC 2699 (QB), at [20]–[33].
[46] See *ibid*, at [53]–[58].
[47] *Ibid*, at [53].
[48] *Aaron v Okoye* [1998] 2 Costs LR 6.
[49] This being necessary because of the operation of para 2 of App 2 to Ord 62.
[50] *Aaron v Okoye* [1998] 2 Costs LR 6, at 12.

Hobhouse LJ was at pains to point out that the client had the right to assess both the first and the second bills (the implication being that both were statutory bills).

The fact that a statute bill contains items it ought not to contain will not necessarily negative that bill; the solicitor's claim may be maintained for the residue.[51] **35.51**

The second (implied) requirement of a statute bill: the narrative must be sufficient

A narrative is a description of the work to which the bill relates. It should not be confused with the detail in a detailed bill, although the two may overlap or even be the same. A gross sum bill (see 35.99) may have an informative narrative running to many pages, but, in the absence of a breakdown of the fees, it will still be a gross sum bill. It is good practice to ensure that a statute bill explains, upon its face or reverse, the client's rights to challenge or complain about the monies claimed.[52] This is often done by preprinting that information on the reverse of the bill. Such information would not, however, generally go to the sufficiency of the narrative. **35.52**

Whilst not an express statutory requirement, the need to provide a sufficient narrative is not merely a matter of good practice, but also a matter of principle: for a bill to be *bona fide* compliant with the Solicitors Act 1974, it must have a sufficient narrative for that purpose.[53] Not only must the work to which the bill relates be adequately described, but also the nature of the bill must be tolerably clear (see 35.69). **35.53**

Because it is an implied rather than express requirement, the Solicitors Act 1974 is silent as to what constitutes a sufficient narrative. Indeed, there is neither help nor hint in the Act in this regard;[54] instead, the details of the requirement are judge-made. Ward LJ has summarised the appropriate test in the following way: **35.54**

> '[T]he burden on the client under section [69(2E) of the 1974 Act] to establish that a bill for a gross sum in contentious business will not be a bill "*bona fide* complying with the 1974 Act" is satisfied if the client shows:
> (a) that there is no sufficient narrative in the bill to identify what it is he is being charged for, and
> (b) that he does not have sufficient knowledge from other documents in his possession or from what he has been told reasonably to take advice whether or not to apply for that bill to be taxed.'[55]

Thus (subject to the discussion about non-contentious business at 35.57–35.59), when considering the adequacy of a narrative of a putative statute bill, the court is not constrained to examine only what is found on the face of that document, but may also take into account the client's own knowledge of the work for which fees are sought. This is an approach that has been articulated by the courts since at least the mid-19th century[56] and it continues to be the case today.[57] **35.55**

51 *Pilgrim v Hirschfeld* (1863) 3 New Rep 36.

52 In this regard, see O(1.15) of the SRA Code of Conduct 2011 (as amended in 2017).

53 *Garry v Gwillim* [2002] EWCA Civ 1500, at [59]–[60]. See also *Haigh v Ousey* (1857) 7 El & Bl 578; *Cook v Gillard* (1852) 1 E & B 26. More recently, see *Bloomsbury Law v MacPhearson* [2016] EWHC 3395 (QB), at [3], *per* Lewis J.

54 *Garry v Gwillim* [2002] EWCA Civ 1500, at [15].

55 *Ibid*, at [70]. See also *Rahimian v Allan Janes LLP* [2016] EWHC B18 (Costs), at [30], *per* Master Gordon-Saker ('A bill must contain sufficient information to enable the client to obtain advice as to its detailed assessment'); *Eversheds (a firm) v Osman* [2000] 1 Costs LR 54, at 61–63, *per* Nourse LJ.

56 See, eg, *Cook v Gillard* (1852) 1 E & B 26.

57 See, eg, *Barclays plc v Villers* [2000] 1 All ER (Comm) 357, at 367.

35.56 This is certainly the case where the putative bill is for services rendered in contentious business, but it is not wholly clear whether Ward LJ's test (see 35.54) applies to bills relating to non-contentious business. This is because, on the face of it, Ward LJ specifically limited his test to the former.

35.57 It should also be noted that Denning LJ previously articulated a different test (albeit *obiter*) for bills relating to non-contentious business:

> '[T]he question is: what must a solicitor's bill for non-contentious business now contain? It need not contain detailed charges as it used to do before 1920 ... But I think that it must contain a summarised statement of the work done, sufficient to tell the client what it is for which he is asked to pay.'[58]

35.58 Thus Denning LJ's test appears to be a significantly more demanding test, from the solicitor's point of view, than that articulated by Ward LJ. In particular, Denning LJ's test does not seem to take into account the client's own knowledge. On a related point, it is worth noting that it used to be the case that a solicitor had a recognised implied right to render a gross sum bill (see 35.99) in non-contentious work, in which case that bill would stand as the final bill without there being a right to a more detailed bill, but (whilst the contrary is arguable based on Australian authority[59]), there is a good case for saying that the right to render a gross sum bill in non-contentious work no longer exists.[60] In the absence of English authority on the point, a cautious solicitor would do well to ensure that they render only reasonably detailed bills for non-contentious work.

35.59 In any event, whilst the contrary is arguable, it seems that Ward LJ's test is the correct test in a modern setting even for bills for non-contentious work. Ward LJ made the following comments, which suggest that Denning LJ's test (see 35.57) should be regarded as *obiter* and made without the benefit of full legal argument:

> 'For my part, I do not feel bound to treat Denning LJ's dictum as binding upon me though it is obviously hugely persuasive. I have already explained why it was *obiter*. Given the way the question was addressed, I cannot believe Lord Denning was laying down an exhaustive statement of the principle or intending to say that the client's knowledge was immaterial. He

---

[58] *Re a Solicitor: In Re a taxation of costs* [1955] 2 QB 252, at 272.

[59] The contrary analysis is that s 64 of the Solicitors Act 1974 relates solely to contentious business because the common law has always permitted gross sum bills in non-contentious work: see the Australian case of *Patel v Sica* [1982] VR 273, at 276–7.

[60] The implied right came about in the following way, as outlined by Denning MR in *Re A Solicitor* [1955] 2 All ER 283, at 287: 'By the Order of 1920 ... a solicitor was authorised to charge a gross sum for non-contentious business, in lieu of detailed charges, but it was provided that the client could insist within six months on a detailed bill of charges, just as if no gross sum were permissible. In 1953 a new order, the Solicitors' Remuneration Order, 1953, was made, which made great alterations in the method of charging for non-contentious business. The solicitor is now entitled ... to "Such sum as may be fair and reasonable, having regard to all the circumstances of the case ..." This, I think, means a lump sum as before, but, whereas previously the client could afterwards insist on a detailed bill of charges, he now has no right to have the lump sum split up into items. He is, however, given a valuable new right. He can require the solicitor to put the bill before the Law Society, so that the Law Society can see whether the sum charged is fair and reasonable.' The implied ability to render a gross sum bill was dependent on the words 'such sum as may be fair and reasonable', but the present incarnation of the relevant legislation—the Solicitors' (Non-Contentious Business) Remuneration Order 2009 (SI 2009/1931)—no longer contains those words, commensurate with the fact that the right to a remuneration certificate no longer exists. As such, it is at the very least arguable that the ability to render gross sum bills for non-contentious work has ceased to exist.

did not have the benefit of argument addressed to him on the rulings in *Haigh v Ousey*[61] and the other cases to which I have referred.'[62]

It is also worth noting that Ward LJ mentioned two cases in which Denning LJ's test had been applied to invoices for services rendered in contentious business.[63] In doing so, he made no effort to suggest that one test should apply to contentious business, but another test should apply to non-contentious business. This seems to suggest that there is only a single test. **35.60**

In any event, Mance LJ has made it clear that Ward LJ's test (which was based on an analysis of older authorities) may not always be appropriate in every case: 'In some future case [it may] be relevant to consider how far interpretation of the concept and purpose of "a gross sum bill" ... can be determined by reference to Victorian authority.'[64] **35.61**

Although it should be borne in mind that older authorities may have had their day and may no longer be good law, it is worth reciting some case examples (not least because the older authorities do crop up from time to time in practice). **35.62**

Is the client able to judge the bill's fairness? There is old authority to the effect that a bill should enable the client to judge its fairness, and should enable a legal representative to give advice upon it and to judge the propriety of the items claimed.[65] In view of the matters set out at 35.52–35.62 and in view of the fact that that authority pre-dated the ability to render a gross sum bill, it would seem that it is now largely of only historical interest. That said, in very general terms, it is a point that remains good law.[66] **35.63**

Numerous errors An invoice containing a large number of obviously erroneous details was found to be a document that could not properly be assessed.[67] **35.64**

Computer printouts A computer printout may, in appropriate circumstances, either be a narrative or supplement a narrative. In a case in which the narrative merely referred to 'general matters', Nourse LJ found that the printout provided all of the necessary detail.[68] In contrast, in a case in which a solicitor had agreed to provide printouts from time to time, the court found that the failure to do so cast doubt on the sufficiency of the narrative.[69] **35.65**

Narrative omitted by implied agreement Where a sophisticated client forgoes their right to a narrative, the fact that there is no narrative will not necessarily preclude the court from finding that the invoice is a statute bill.[70] **35.66**

---

61 *Haigh v Ousey* (1857) 7 El & Bl 578.
62 *Garry v Gwillim* [2002] EWCA Civ 1500, at [62].
63 *Re A Solicitor* (unreported), 10 October 1994, QBD, *per* Mr Christopher Clarke QC (sitting as a deputy judge); *Ring Sights Holding Co Ltd & Anor v Lawrence Graham* (unreported), 8 October 2001, Ch D, *per* Nigel Davis J.
64 *Garry v Gwillim* [2002] EWCA Civ 1500, at [76]–[78].
65 *Haigh v Ousey* (1857) 7 E & B 578.
66 See, eg, *Bloomsbury Law v MacPhearson* [2016] EWHC 3395 (QB), at [9], *per* Lewis J; *Garry v Gwillim* [2002] EWCA Civ 1500, at [60]–[62].
67 *Slingsby v Attorney-General* [1918] P 236.
68 *Eversheds (a firm) v Osman* [2000] 1 Costs LR 54.
69 *Bari v Rosen (t/a Rosen & Co Solicitors)* [2012] EWHC 1782 (QB).
70 *Barclays plc v Villers* [2000] 1 All ER (Comm) 357, at 367.

35.67 **'For professional services'** In the absence of other compensating material (see, for example, 35.63), a putative bill that merely states that it was 'for professional services' would usually be inadequately narrated.[71]

35.68 **Where there are several courts** A bill containing a number of items of work relating to different courts was found to be sufficient: the individual items were clearly described[72] (see also 35.70).

35.69 **Intended purpose** In a case in which a solicitor relied on a schedule-like document, Tomlinson LJ declined to find that the document was a statute bill because the circumstances in which it was sent and its general appearance gave the impression that its purpose was to be used for recovering costs from an opponent.[73] The discussion at 35.37–35.39 may be relevant in this regard.

35.70 **The client's own knowledge** Where a bill had been split into parts relating to work in different courts, Lord Campbell CJ found that it did have a sufficient narrative in light of the client's own knowledge of the work carried out.[74]

35.71 **Superfluous information** A bill that failed to mention the name of the court in which the business was transacted was held to be valid because it was clear that the client neither wanted nor needed that information to be set out in the bill.[75]

The third (express) requirement of a statute bill: the bill must be signed

35.72 The law concerning signatures is now set out in Solicitors Act 1974, s 69(2A):

> '(2A) A bill is signed in accordance with this subsection if it is—
> (a) signed by the solicitor or on his behalf by an employee of the solicitor authorised by him to sign, or
> (b) enclosed in, or accompanied by, a letter which is signed as mentioned in paragraph (a) and refers to the bill.'

From 7 March 2008,[76] this provision has replaced the previous iteration of Solicitors Act 1974, s 69(2)(a), which, in effect, provided that only a solicitor or a partner could sign the bill. Transitional provisions apply,[77] but will now rarely be relevant.

35.73 It should be noted that, even under the old provisions, Irwin J found that the requirement that a bill be signed is directory rather than mandatory.[78] He explained that his conclusion

---

[71] The authority that has been cited in support of this proposition for many years is *Re Kingsley* (1978) 122 Sol Jo 457, but the case report makes no real mention of the issue in hand. Nonetheless, whilst *obiter*, Swift J has confirmed that if the only material available to the client was such sparse detail as 'for professional services', that would plainly be insufficient as a narrative: *Carter-Ruck (a firm) v Mireskandari* [2011] EWHC 24 (QB), at [80]–[86].

[72] *Keene v Ward* (1849) 13 QB 513. In so far as they suggest the contrary, neither *Martindale v Falkner* (1846) 2 CB 706 nor *Ivimey v Marks* (1847) 16 M & W 843 remain good law.

[73] *Kingston Solicitors v Reiss Solicitors* [2014] EWCA Civ 172. See also *Parvez v Mooney Everett Solicitors Ltd* [2018] EWHC 62 (QB).

[74] *Cook v Gillard* (1852) 1 E & B 26. See also *Cobbett v Wood* [1908] 1 KB 590, at 594, *per* Pickford J.

[75] *Cozens v Graham* (1852) 12 CB 398, at 406, *per* Maule J.

[76] See Legal Services Act 2007, s 177, and Sch 16, Pt 1, paras 1, 64(1) and (3).

[77] Legal Services Act 2007, Sch 22, para 14.

[78] *Megantic Services Ltd v Dorsey & Whitney* [2008] EWHC 2662 (QB). Some commentators have questioned the correctness of this decision in the light of *R v Soneji* [2006] 1 AC 340, which seems to discourage the distinction between mandatory and directory requirements.

was based on a purposive interpretation of the Solicitors Act 1974.[79] Even before Irwin J clarified the law in this way, a liberal approach was not unknown. Where fees were sought by a 'recognised body' within the meaning of the Administration of Justice Act 1985, for example, an employee of that body was permitted to sign.[80] Victorian authority suggests that a signature by an employee in the firm's name was not a sufficient signature to satisfy the requirements of legislation.[81] The legislation now expressly provides that employees are able to sign, but, even under the pre-7 March 2008 provisions, it is questionable whether the Victorian approach remained good law.

In a context other than the law of costs, Popplewell J has explained that, generally speaking, a signature is the writing or otherwise affixing of a person's name, or a mark to represent their name, with the intention of authenticating the document as being that of, or binding on, the person whose name is so written or affixed.[82] **35.74**

The general law relating to requirements to sign written instruments ought not to be forgotten (although not all of it will apply to signatures on bills). In particular, the court often adopts a purposive approach when considering whether there has been compliance with legislation that requires a signature.[83] As with any written instrument, the signature must be in a place that governs the document[84]—although that would rarely be contentious, because bills tend to be fairly compact and formulaic documents. **35.75**

Electronic signatures Electronic signatures are now permitted, because the Solicitors Act 1974 Act now makes specific provision for a bill to be signed electronically, at s 69(2B) and (5) (see 35.43). An electronic signature is: **35.76**

> '... so much of anything in electronic form as—
> (a) is incorporated into or otherwise logically associated with any electronic communication or electronic data; and
> (b) purports to be so incorporated or associated for the purpose of being used in establishing the authenticity of the communication or data, the integrity of the communication or data, or both.'[85]

Regulation 2 of the Electronic Signature Regulations 2002[86] defines electronic signature as 'data in electronic form which are attached to or logically associated with other electronic data and which serve as a method of authentication'. **35.77**

It is a moot point whether the printed name of a solicitor (or their firm) in an electronic invoice that was not digitally certified would suffice. This is because such a document would lack the necessary safeguards—such as an asymmetric encryption system based on a public key infrastructure (PKI)—that would allow its authenticity and integrity **35.78**

---

79 See *Zuliani v Veira* [1994] 1 WLR 1149 PC (UK).
80 Administration of Justice Act 1985, Sch 2, para 29.
81 *In re Frape, ex p Perrett* [1893] 2 Ch 284, at 291, citing (with approval) *Evans v Hoare* [1892] 1 QB 593. See also *Angell v Tratt* (1883) 1 Cab & El 118.
82 *Bassano v Toft* [2014] EWHC 377 (QB), at [42].
83 See, eg, *Wood v Smith* [1992] 3 WLR 583; cf *Firstpost Homes Ltd v Johnson* [1996] 1 WLR 67.
84 *Caton v Caton* (1867) LR 2 HL 127.
85 Electronic Communications Act 2000, s 7(2). The Act was the (partial) domestic implementation of (now-repealed) Directive 1999/93/EC of the European Parliament and of the Council of 13 December 1999 on a Community framework for electronic signatures, OJ L 13/12, 19 January 2000.
86 SI 2002/318.

to be easily verified. This is why, in so far as financial contracts such as mortgages are concerned, the authenticity and integrity of electronic signatures are normally based on a PKI, which is backed by a digital certificate issued by a regulated certification service provider.

35.79 A prudent solicitor would probably ensure both authenticity and integrity by putting a PKI in place, but, at the time of writing, this was very much the exception. It is easily arguable that a putative electronic signature that is not backed by such a PKI (or something similar) should not be regarded as sufficient, because whilst the solicitor would be able to prove authenticity by other means (such as producing records from email servers), the client would be at a considerable disadvantage in this regard. Put otherwise, it is easily arguable that if no PKI were in place, the solicitor could repudiate the putative signature all too easily (which would defeat its very purpose). That said, the legislation referred to above does not prescribe any particular method by which a solicitor must ensure authenticity or integrity of data, and (in the editor's view) it would be open to the court to give whatever weight it thought appropriate to the evidence of authenticity and integrity in any given case. In this regard, it is probably worth noting that, in 2001, the Law Commission expressed the common-sense view that the typing of the name or its automatic addition to the email was capable of indicating to the recipient that the signatory had the necessary authenticating intention.[87]

35.80 **Stamps, printed signatures, marks, descriptions etc** A signature placed by means of a rubber stamp containing a facsimile representation of a suitable signature was found to be sufficient to satisfy the purposes of s 65 of the Solicitors Act 1932.[88] There is no reason to believe that the law has become any more restrictive in this regard. Although contrary examples do exist, it may be relevant that a printed signature is capable of being regarded as sufficient in contexts other than the law of costs.[89] In the editor's experience, a printed signature, or the name of the solicitor or firm, on a paper document is generally regarded as sufficient. Similarly, a signature need not consist of a name, but may be a letter by way of mark, even where the party executing the mark is able to write.[90] The signature may consist of a description of the signatory, if sufficiently unambiguous.[91]

35.81 A signature in the solicitor's business name was a good signature by the solicitor for the purposes of the Solicitors Act 1932.[92] Likewise, a recognisable abbreviation of the solicitor's firm's name would be sufficient—although the Court of Appeal has said that it is sensible to use a firm's full name.[93] Again, there is no reason to believe that the law has become

---

[87] See Law Commission, *Electronic Commerce: Formal Requirements in Commercial Transactions—Advice from the Law Commission* (London: HMSO, 2001); Law Commission, *Financial Law Panel Report: E-commerce—Review of Legal Implications: Proof and Evidence* (London: HMSO, 2000). See also, by way of analogy, *Bassano v Toft* [2014] EWHC 377 (QB), at [44], *per* Popplewell J; *Golden Ocean Group Ltd v Salgaocar Mining Industries PVT Ltd* [2012] 2 All ER (Comm) 978, at [32].

[88] *Goodman v J Eban Ltd* [1954] 1 QB 550.

[89] See, eg, *Schneider v Norris* (1814) 2 M&S 286.

[90] *Baker v Dening* (1838) 8 Ad & E 93.

[91] Whilst not related to statutory bills, examples include 'Your loving mother' (*In re Cook* [1960] 1 All ER 689) or 'Servant to Mr Sperling' (*In re Sperling* (1863) 3 Sw & Tr 272).

[92] *Goodman v J Eban Ltd* [1954] 1 QB 550.

[93] *Bartletts de Reya v Byrne* (1983) 127 Sol Jo 69, CA.

any more restrictive in this regard, especially in light of Irwin J's clarification of the pre-7 March 2008 law (see 35.73).

Accompanying emails and letters An unsigned bill accompanied by a signed letter is capable of being sufficient if there is a nexus between the letter and the bill.[94] Whilst there is no direct authority on the point, it is likely, by analogy to consumer credit agreements, that the same would be true of a signature contained separately in an email.[95] **35.82**

Where a solicitor has died, become bankrupt or has assigned rights to another, the executor, administrator and assignee of the solicitor may sign the bill.[96] This is so even if the assignee is a lay person.[97] **35.83**

Signature through conduct Where an unsigned bill is delivered, it is open to the court to find that the client should be taken, through their conduct, to have accepted that the bill was signed.[98] Similarly, if a solicitor seeks to gain advantage over their client through the ruse of not signing a bill, it may be open the court to find that it should be treated as having been signed.[99] Whilst dealing with a case in a context other than costs, Roxburgh J found that the court can investigate the circumstances to see whether a document came into being as a perfect instrument and that if, on the evidence, it finds that it did, the court is not prevented from so holding by any impediment in law.[100] **35.84**

The fourth (express) requirement of a statute bill: the bill must have been delivered

Solicitors Act 1974, s 69(2C) and (2D) (as amended), provides as follows: **35.85**

> '(2C) A bill is delivered in accordance with this subsection if—
> (a) it is delivered to the party to be charged with the bill personally,
> (b) it is delivered to that party by being sent to him by post to, or left for him at, his place of business, dwelling-house or last known place of abode, or
> (c) it is delivered to that party—
> (i) by means of an electronic communications network, or
> (ii) by other means but in a form that nevertheless requires the use of apparatus by the recipient to render it intelligible,
>
> and that party has indicated to the person making the delivery his willingness to accept delivery of a bill sent in the form and manner used.
>
> (2D) An indication to any person for the purposes of subsection (2C)(c)—
> (a) must state the address to be used and must be accompanied by such other information as that person requires for the making of the delivery;
> (b) may be modified or withdrawn at any time by a notice given to that person.'

94 *Penley v Anstruther* (1883) (1) 52 L J (Ch) 367.

95 *Bassano v Toft* [2014] EWHC 377 (QB), at [44], *per* Popplewell J. See also *Golden Ocean Group Ltd v Salgaocar Mining Industries PVT Ltd* [2012] 2 All ER (Comm) 978, at [32].

96 Solicitors Act 1974, s 68(3).

97 *Ingle v M'Cutchan* (1884) 12 QBD 518; *Penley v Anstruther* (1883) (1) 52 L J (Ch) 367. *Medlicott v Emery* (1933) All ER Rep 655 is often quoted as being authority on this point, but this seems to be an error.

98 *Re Gedye* (1851) 14 Beav 56; *Young v Walker* (1847) 16 M&W 446; *In re Sutton & Elliot* (1883) 11 QBD 337, at 379.

99 See *Re Firm of Solicitors, ex p D'Aragon* (1887) 3 TLR 815, referred to by Soole J in *Parvez v Mooney Everett Solicitors Ltd* [2018] EWHC 62 (QB), at [61].

100 *Leeman v Stocks* [1951] Ch 941; cf *Firstpost Homes Ltd v Johnson* [1996] 1 WLR 67, which suggests that the principle in that case is not to be applied more widely than it currently is.

This amended section replaces old Solicitors Act 1974, s 69(2)(b),[101] which contained provisions that were almost identical to those now contained in s 69(2C)(b). To this extent, the law relating to the old s 69(2)(b) is preserved.

35.86 The following miscellaneous points may be made about delivery of bills.

- **Bar against unintended delivery** A document is not a statute bill unless it is sent by the solicitor to the client as a demand or claim for payment.[102] It is only the solicitor who can determine the content and terms of what is their demand or claim for payment. If the client comes into possession of a draft bill that was not delivered as a demand or claim for payment, neither the client nor the court can make that determination on the solicitor's behalf (see 35.37–35.39).[103]
- ***Chamberlain* bills (that is, bills delivered in parts)** Where a series of invoices is properly regarded as being one statute bill delivered in parts, delivery will not take place until the whole bill (that is, the entirety of its parts) has been delivered.[104] Time will not start to run for the purposes of Solicitors Act 1974, s 70, until the last part of the bill has been delivered.[105]
- **Agents, employees, etc** Delivery may be to an agent of the client or to the party chargeable.[106] An employee or servant of the client may take delivery at a person's business or home.[107] Delivery to a liability insurer is capable, in appropriate circumstances, of being delivery to the insured.[108]
- **Qualified bills** A bill containing a qualification or a condition may be delivered even if that qualification is that the bill may be replaced at a later stage by another bill.[109]
- **New solicitors** Where a former client has instructed new solicitors, delivery to those new solicitors will suffice only if the client has given authority that this may be done[110] or if the court has so ordered.[111]
- **More than one client** Where a number of clients are jointly liable to pay the bill, delivery to one is capable of being delivery to each.[112]

Erroneous statute bills: amendment, withdrawal, and substitution

35.87 A solicitor is bound by the bill that they have delivered and—except by operation of Solicitors Act 1974, s 64(2), or by consent or order of the court—the solicitor cannot withdraw it, strike it out or vary or add items.[113] This may be true even where a bill has been

---

101 The changes took place on 7 March 2008. If the older law is required, then the unamended statute ought to be consulted: see Legal Services Act 2007, s 177 and Sch 16, Pt 1, paras 1, 64(1) and (3). Transitional provisions apply: see Legal Services Act 2007, Sch 22, para 14.

102 See *Parvez v Mooney Everett Solicitors Ltd* [2018] EWHC 62 (QB), at [56], *per* Soole J, relying on *Kingstons Solicitors v Reiss Solicitors* [2014] EWCA Civ 172.

103 See *Parvez v Mooney Everett Solicitors Ltd* [2018] EWHC 62 (QB), at [57], *per* Soole J.

104 *Chamberlain v Boodle & King* [1982] 1 WLR 1443, at 1446.

105 See *Re Cartwright* (1873) LR 16 Eq 469.

106 *Daubney v Phipps* (1849) 18 LJQB 337; *Re Bush* (1844) 8 Bear 66.

107 *Macgregor v Keily* (1849) 3 Ex 794.

108 *Solicitors Indemnity Fund Ltd v Hewitson & Harker* [2010] EWCA Civ 147, at [12].

109 In *Re Thompson* (1885) 30 Ch D 441.

110 *Spier v Barnard* (1863) 8 LT 396.

111 *Vincent v Slaymaker* (1810) 12 East 372.

112 *Mant v Smith* (1859) 4 H&N 324; *Crowder v Shee* (1808) 1 Camp 437.

113 *Rezvi v Brown Cooper (a firm)* [1997] Costs LR 109, at 120, approving a passage from *Cordery on Solicitors* (9th edn, London: Butterworths, 1994). See also *Saad v Griffin* [1908] 2 KB 510, CA; *Davis v*

delivered, but not signed.[114] One of the principal justifications for this is that the court wishes to prevent solicitors from abusing the rights of clients by, for example, lodging a bill that they believe to be unjustifiable, but then—only when the client takes legal advice and complains—withdrawing it and submitting a bill that is easier to defend.[115] Lord Romilly MR put it this way:

> 'The reason and justice of this is obvious, and it appears to me to rest not less on principle than on practice. If one species of alteration be made, any other might. Who is to determine what alteration might or might not be made and if any alteration may be made? and if any alteration may be made, it is clear that a bill could be altered to meet the turn which the taxation was taking.'[116]

These general rules are subject to the provisions of Solicitors Act 1974, s 64(2). In particular, where a solicitor renders a gross sum bill for contentious work and where a client requests a detailed bill in lieu of a gross sum bill, the detailed bill will stand in place of the gross sum bill, which will then be of no effect. This is considered in more detail at 35.99–35.108. The detailed bill may be for a greater amount than the original gross sum bill.[117] **35.88**

Where a solicitor has delivered a gross sum bill, there is nothing to prevent the solicitor from delivering a detailed breakdown of that bill.[118] In those circumstances, the detailed breakdown would not replace the gross sum bill, but would merely be an aid for the purposes of assessing the costs claimed therein. This illustrates the fact that a detailed breakdown is not necessarily the same as a detailed bill. **35.89**

Reservation of the right to withdraw or alter a bill

A solicitor may reserve the right to withdraw the bill or to alter it on conditions.[119] This can be done only if those conditions are both fair and clearly and fully stated to the client. An example might be where the bill is provisional by reason of a need to estimate counsel's fees (although see 35.48). Where the condition is, in reality, an unjustified reservation of a right to redeliver a *different* bill—or, as Cotton LJ drily put it, to render 'a bill which contains charges which I [the solicitor] cannot sustain on taxation'[120]—that condition will usually be rejected, leaving the solicitor bound by the original bill. **35.90**

Consensual withdrawal of a bill

A client may give their consent to a bill being withdrawn and such consent may be impliedly given where the client agrees to an assessment of a new bill delivered in substitution of a previous bill.[121] Where this happens, the court may take the withdrawn bill into account when carrying out the assessment. **35.91**

Dysart [1855] 25 LJ Ch 122; *Re Heather* (1870) LR 5 Ch App 694; *Re Thompson* (1885) 30 Ch D 441, at 448. Of historical interest, see also *In re Carven* (1845) 8 Beav 436, at 438.

[114] *Re Jones* (1886) 54 LT 648.

[115] *Rezvi v Brown Cooper (a firm)* [1997] Costs LR 109, at 119.

[116] *Re Catlin* (1854) 18 Beav 508, at 519–20.

[117] *In re Taxation of Costs; In re Solicitors* [1943] KB 69.

[118] See Solicitors Act 1974, s 64(4) (as amended); CPR, r 46.10(2).

[119] See, as a modern example, *Aaron v Okoye* [1998] 2 Costs LR 6.

[120] In *Re Thompson* (1885) 30 Ch D 441, at 450. See also *Lumsden v The Shipcote Land Co* [1906] 2 KB 433, at 436, *per* Vaughan Williams LJ (albeit *obiter*). Historically, see *In re Walters* (1845) 9 Beav 299.

[121] *Rezvi v Brown Cooper (a firm)* [1997] Costs LR 109, esp 118 and 119 for discussion regarding *Loveridge v Botham* (1797) 1 Bos & P 49 772.

Withdrawal or amendment with the permission of the court

35.92 Whilst it was originally the case that the court had no jurisdiction to allow a solicitor to withdraw their bill,[122] that rule ceased to be absolute at the turn of the 20th century and the court now does have a discretion in that regard. There is authority to the effect that typographical or arithmetical errors in a bill may be corrected by the court, but omissions may not,[123] but it is not clear whether this latter constraint remains good law, not least because it seems a rather anachronistic rule that has not been applied for over a century.[124]

35.93 Notwithstanding these general principles, which—at the very least—discourage amendments and corrections, the court has a wide discretion to make an order that avoids injustice. Where, for example, a bill contains an accidental omission, the court may, in exceptional circumstances, allow that bill to be withdrawn and substituted.[125] In this regard, Lord Nolan (sitting in the Privy Council) had this to say:

> '[It] by no means follows that an action brought on a bill which fails to satisfy one or more of the statutory requirements or which contains erroneous items must necessarily be dismissed without consideration of the merits. It has long been established that a court, confronted with a defective bill, is entitled to look into all the circumstances of the case and in appropriate cases to allow the solicitor to withdraw the bill and to deliver a fresh one.'[126]

35.94 Stanley Burnton LJ has, however, made it clear that it is a jurisdiction that should be exercised only where there has been a genuine mistake or error on the part of the solicitor when preparing their original bill.[127]

35.95 There is a distinction between the withdrawal of a bill with the court's consent (which would, for example, mean that any current proceedings might have to be abandoned) and amendment of the bill with the court's consent (which may avoid that necessity). Wright J, sitting on a review of detailed assessment, held that he had power to permit the solicitors to amend their original bill of costs to insert the necessary words 'not paid' against unpaid disbursements. He said (*obiter*) that it would have been in the power of a costs officer to do the same.[128] More recently, a costs judge's power to allow amendment of a solicitor's bill was not questioned at first instance or before the Court of Appeal.[129]

35.96 If a claim is brought on a defective bill, the court has a discretionary power to allow the solicitor to withdraw the bill and to bring a new claim. There is also authority that the court may allow a solicitor to replace a bill without bringing new proceedings,[130] but that

---

122 See, eg, *Re Catlin* (1854) 18 Beav 508, at 520, *per* Romilly MR; *Re Thompson* (1885) 30 Ch D 441, at 448, *per* Cotton LJ.

123 *In re Grant, Bulcraig & Co* [1906] 1 Ch 124.

124 See, in particular, *Polak v Machioness of Winchester* [1956] 2 All ER 660; *Zuliani v Veira* [1994] 1 WLR 1149, PC; CPR, r 3.1(m).

125 *Polak v Marchioness of Winchester* [1956] 2 All ER 660, at 668, *per* Jenkins LJ. See also *Chappell v Mehta* [1981] 1 All ER 349.

126 *Zuliani v Veira* [1994] 1 WLR 1149. The WLR is only a short report; this extract is taken from (1994) 45 WIR 188, at 194.

127 *Bilkus v Stockler Brunton (a firm)* [2010] EWCA Civ 101, at [57]–[59].

128 *Tearle & Co (a firm) v Sherring* (unreported), 29 October 1993, QBD, *per* Wright J.

129 *Bilkus v Stockler Brunton (a firm)* [2010] EWCA Civ 101, at [57]–[59].

130 *Zuliani v Veira* [1994] 1 WLR 1149, PC. See also *Tearle & Co (a firm) v Sherring* (unreported), 29 October 1993, QBD, *per* Wright J, which concerned an accidental failure to comply with Solicitors Act 1974, s 67.

authority is a decision of the Privy Council that relies on a foreign statutory provision with no obvious counterpart in English law, so it may not be as persuasive as it may appear at first sight. Nonetheless, it is possible that r 3.1(2)(m) of the Civil Procedure Rules (CPR) may permit the court to allow a bill to be replaced without the need for new proceedings (although this is by no means a certainty).

If the court does order substitution of a bill (other than as a result of Solicitors Act 1974, s 64(2)), the court will be able to take that into account when the costs of the assessment fall to be determined. Whether or not the court can take a gross sum bill into account when it has been replaced by a detailed bill pursuant to s 64(2) is a moot point because the 1974 Act says that the gross sum bill will be of 'no effect'. **35.97**

For the avoidance of doubt, it is worth stating that these general rules apply only to assessments made under Solicitors Act 1974 or if a claim is brought on a statute bill by a solicitor; they do not apply to assessments between opposing parties[131] or where the court has merely referred a solicitor's charges to a costs judge for an assessment of a reasonable charge for the work done.[132] Indeed, Practice Direction (PD) 47, para 13.10, specifically states that (unless the court orders otherwise), on a between-the-parties assessment, a party may vary its bill of costs without requiring the permission of the court. **35.98**

Gross sum bills and requests for bills containing detailed items

The modern position is now governed by Solicitors Act 1974, s 64, which makes the following provisions: **35.99**

> '(1) Where the remuneration of a solicitor in respect of contentious business done by him is not the subject of a contentious business agreement, then, subject to subsections (2) to (4), the solicitor's bill of costs may at the option of the solicitor be either a bill containing detailed items or a gross sum bill.
>
> (2) The party chargeable with a gross sum bill may at any time—
>
> (a) before he is served with a writ or other originating process for the recovery of costs included in the bill, and
>
> (b) before the expiration of three months from the date on which the bill was delivered to him,
>
> require the solicitor to deliver, in lieu of that bill, a bill containing detailed items; and on such a requirement being made the gross sum bill shall be of no effect.
>
> (3) Where an action is commenced on a gross sum bill, the court shall, if so requested by the party chargeable with the bill before the expiration of one month from the service on that party of the writ or other originating process, order that the bill be assessed.
>
> (4) If a gross sum bill is assessed, whether under this section or otherwise, nothing in this section shall prejudice any rules of court with respect to assessment, and the solicitor shall furnish the costs officer with such details of any of the costs covered by the bill as the costs officer may require.'[133]

[131] See PD 47, para 13.10(1). See also (historically) CPD, para 40.10; *Davis v Dysart (No 2)* (1855) 21 Beav 124, at 132.

[132] *Lumsden v Shipcote Land Co* [1906] 2 KB 433; *Rollinsone v Eversheds* (unreported), 11 May 1993, CA.

[133] Minor terminological changes were, at the time of writing, due to be made by the Legal Services Act 2007, s 177 and Sch 16, Pt 1, paras 1 and 60. It is likely that they will have been made by the time the book is published; none of the changes alter the meaning of the extract.

Thus, where work is contentious and where there is no contentious business agreement in place,[134] a solicitor may elect either to deliver a gross sum bill or to deliver a bill containing detailed items (which is usually referred to simply as a 'detailed bill'). As to non-contentious work, it is likely that there is a right to render gross sum bills (see 35.58), but this is not certain.

35.100 If the solicitor chooses to deliver a gross sum bill relating to contentious work, the client may, within certain time limits (see Solicitors Act 1974, s 64(2), cited at 35.99), request a detailed bill. If the client makes such a request, the detailed bill will replace the gross sum bill, which will then be of no effect.[135] This may mean that the solicitor can recover an amount that exceeds the amount originally charged.[136] It follows that a client who requests a detailed bill may ultimately pay more than they would have paid had they dealt with the matter on the basis of a gross sum bill.

35.101 In so far as contentious work is concerned, a detailed bill delivered pursuant to Solicitors Act 1974, s 64(2)—that is, at the client's request—should not be confused with a detailed breakdown served pursuant to s 64(4) of the 1974 Act or CPR, r 46.10(2). If a gross sum bill falls to be assessed, the court will often order the solicitor to prepare a detailed breakdown pursuant to r 46.10(2). That would not entitle the solicitor to submit a new bill; it would be the same bill (that is, the original gross sum bill) rather than the breakdown that will be the subject of assessment. It will often be the case that the detailed breakdown is capable of justifying costs that are higher than those claimed in the bill. If this is the case, then the costs will be limited to those sums claimed in the bill.[137]

35.102 A request for greater detail may be characterised, on the one hand, as a request for a detailed bill pursuant to Solicitors Act 1974, s 64(2), or, on the other, merely as a request for clarification of the gross sum bill. For the foregoing reasons, the distinction can be important. This question is determined by looking at the substance of the demand, because it would not be right to allow an overly technical interpretation of the language to defeat the purpose of the request[138]—and this is particularly so where the person making the request is a layperson.[139]

35.103 Megarry J offered guidance about how to categorise demands for detail that are said to be requests for a detailed bill pursuant to Solicitors Act 1974, s 64(2):

> 'It seems to me that before proviso (a) of section 64 is brought into play there must be something which can fairly be described as a request or requirement that the solicitors should deliver to the client a detailed bill to replace the gross sum bill already delivered: and although I do not think that any particular form of words need be employed, the substance of what is relied upon must amount to a request or requirement of this kind.'[140]

---

[134] Contentious business agreements often provide for fixed or partially fixed costs, so the provisions concerning detail are less relevant.

[135] *Madurasinghe v Penguin Electronics (a firm)* [1993] 1 WLR 989.

[136] *In re Taxation of Costs; In re Solicitors* [1943] KB 69. See also *Polak v Marchioness of Winchester* [1956] 2 All ER 660.

[137] It is good practice to make this clear on the face of the detailed breakdown. An example would be: 'This breakdown supports costs of £*x*, but the amount claimed is limited to £*y* in accordance with the bill delivered on . . .'

[138] *Penningtons (a firm) v Brown* (unreported), 30 April 1998, CA.

[139] *Ibid.*

[140] *Carlton v Theodore Goddard & Co* [1973] 1 WLR 623, at 626.

For the foregoing reasons, a finding that a request is a request for a detailed bill would usually be to the client's disadvantage. This is a factor that the court can take into account when resolving doubt as to whether a request is a request for a detailed bill pursuant to Solicitors Act 1974, s 64(2), or merely a request for clarification. Sir John Vinelott gave the following guidance about the resolution of doubt: 'If there is doubt as to the way in which the letter should be interpreted, the doubt should be resolved in favour of the client for whose protection these provisions were enacted.'[141] **35.104**

Where the solicitor is in doubt as to what their client is requesting, Megarry J explained that the solicitor should seek clarification from their client: 'If in doubt . . . the solicitors, before embarking on the work, can always inquire whether some equivocal communication that they have received is or is not intended to be a requirement under the proviso.'[142] The absence of such an inquiry would be a factor that might be taken into account.[143] **35.105**

There are nonetheless limits to the extent to which the court will shield the client as a consumer or layperson. In particular, the client's knowledge or understanding of the law (or lack thereof) will not prevent the court from categorising a request for detail (as opposed to clarification) as being a request for a detailed bill.[144] Pill LJ has found that the court should not be influenced in its construction of a request for detail by the fact that a client may be condemned to pay a greater sum than they would have paid had they not made the request.[145] **35.106**

One or two case examples illustrate the court's approach. **35.107**

- The following statement (which had been drafted by the client's new solicitors) was found not to amount to a request for a detailed bill pursuant to Solicitors Act 1974, s 64(2), because it could not be said to be a request or a requirement: 'Accordingly, it would seem that there is no alternative but for your bill to be prepared and lodged for taxation.'[146]
- A request for 'a full breakdown of your firm's bill' did amount to a request for a detailed bill, even in circumstances in which that request also indicated an intention to have 'the bill' (that is, the gross sum bill) assessed.[147]

Where a detailed bill is delivered in circumstances in which the client has made no request, the assessment will proceed on the basis of the original gross sum bill.[148] The solicitor will not be able to withdraw and substitute the gross sum bill unless either the client consents or the court so orders. That said, the superfluous detailed bill may still be of use, in that it may be able to stand as the breakdown of costs pursuant to CPR, r 48.10(2). **35.108**

---

[141] *Penningtons (a firm) v Brown* (unreported), 30 April 1998, CA, at the antepenultimate paragraph of the transcript, *per* Sir John Vinelott.

[142] *Carlton v Theodore Goddard & Co* [1973] 1 WLR 623, at 626.

[143] See, eg, *Penningtons (a firm) v Brown* (unreported), 30 April 1998, CA, in which Pill LJ implicitly adopted this line of thinking.

[144] *Ibid.*

[145] *Ibid.*

[146] *Carlton v Theodore Goddard & Co* [1973] 1 WLR 623, at 625.

[147] *Penningtons (a firm) v Brown* (unreported), 30 April 1998, CA.

[148] *Carlton v Theodore Goddard & Co* [1973] 1 WLR 623.

The Consequences of Failing to Comply with Solicitors Act 1974, s 69

35.109 Should an invoice fail to meet the requirements of Solicitors Act 1974, s 69, then s 69(1) provides that no claim shall be brought for the recovery of any costs due; as such, any such invoice would be unenforceable.

35.110 If a claim is brought on a defective bill, see the discussion at 35.92–35.98.

35.111 Whilst no claim may be brought on a defective bill, the solicitor's fees and disbursements may be capable of being recovered in other ways (see 35.115–35.114). In practice, however, it is rare that the court would find that a bill was a defective statute bill (as opposed to something else, such as an interim invoice on account) and it is even rarer for the court to refuse a request to withdraw a bill.

Payment

35.112 The fact that a bill is not compliant with Solicitors Act 1974, s 69, will not render it incapable of being paid as a demand for payment nor does it prevent a solicitor from deducting payment from client monies, this being because it would be a 'written notification of costs' (see 35.12).[149] As to whether it may be paid for the purposes of the Solicitors Act 1974, however, see 36.18–36.28.

Statutory demand

35.113 It may or may not be the case that a solicitor is permitted to serve a statutory demand in respect of a defective bill. This issue frequently arises in practice because solicitors commonly seek to take active steps against former clients before the expiry of the one-month time limit under Solicitors Act 1974, s 69(1). There is authority that service of a statutory demand for payment of a solicitor's costs does not constitute the bringing of an action.[150] That may be true, but it has been successfully argued that a solicitor's bill is not, prior to an assessment, a 'liquidated debt' for the purposes of bankruptcy proceedings.[151] This is dealt with in more detail at 40.123–40.128.

Set-off

35.114 Where a solicitor is a debtor to a client who has outstanding fees, the solicitor may set off the sum due to them even though they have not complied with the requirements of Solicitors Act 1974, s 69.[152] This is a discretionary remedy that may be refused, however.[153]

Where there has been a loss of protection

35.115 Circumstances may arise in which the client may lose the benefit of the protection afforded by Solicitors Act 1974, s 69(1), such that an invoice may be enforceable notwithstanding

---

149 See SRA Accounts Rules 2011 (as amended), r 17.7.

150 *In re A Debtor (No 88 of 1991)* [1993] Ch 286, in which Sir Donald Nicholls V-C went on to say (*obiter*) that a bankruptcy petition probably should be regarded as being an action for the purposes of s 69(1).

151 See *Truex v Toll* [2009] EWHC 369 (Ch); *Klamer v Kyriakides & Braier (a firm)* [2005] BPIR, Ch D (which is not binding, because it was a master's decision); Insolvency Act 1986, s 267(2)(b).

152 *Ex p Cooper* (1854) 14 CB 663; *Harrison v Turner* (1847) 10 QB 482; *Brown v Tibbits* (1862) 11 CBNS 855.

153 See, eg, *Currie & Co v Law Society* [1977] QB 990.

the fact that it is not a statute bill. Where, for example, a solicitor and client compromise a claim for the solicitor's costs and state an account showing a balance in the solicitor's favour, a claim may be brought by the solicitor for that balance. This is because the compromised sum would be for more than the mere remuneration in issue and, as such, the compromise would fall outside the ambit of s 69(1).[154] Likewise, a solicitor may sue upon a promissory note given in respect of costs[155] and, in an appropriate case, they may even foreclose a mortgage taken as security on the costs.[156] Similarly a solicitor is able to sue on a dishonoured cheque[157] or letter of credit,[158] but Warner J has made it clear that this jurisdiction ought not to be allowed to afford the solicitor a means of avoiding the consumer protection provisions in the Solicitors Act 1974[159] (see 40.11).

How Disbursements are Treated in a Statute Bill

Solicitors Act 1974, s 67, provides as follows: **35.116**

> 'A solicitor's bill of costs may include costs payable in discharge of a liability properly incurred by him on behalf of the party to be charged with the bill (including counsel's fees) notwithstanding that those costs have not been paid before the delivery of the bill to that party; but those costs—
> (a) shall be described in the bill as not then paid; and
> (b) if the bill is assessed, shall not be allowed by the costs officer unless they are paid before the assessment is completed.'

The words 'properly incurred by him on behalf of the party to be charged with the bill' have the effect of defining disbursements for the purposes of this section. Other definitions of disbursements exist; they are only peripherally relevant for present purposes and are dealt with in Chapter 31. Payments that neither law nor custom require a solicitor to make (such as purchase monies for land) ought not to be categorised as disbursements and should appear in the cash account, rather than the bill.[160] Agents' fees should appear in the bill, but this will be generally as profit costs, rather than disbursements,[161] and this includes the fees of any costs lawyer or costs draftsperson who may have been instructed as the solicitor's agent.[162]

Slade J has recently found that, for an invoice to be a statute bill that relates to a period of time, it must include all of the costs incurred during the period to which it relates and that this should include all disbursements, including those that relate to services provided by counsel and experts during that period[163] (see 35.48). In any event, disbursements that **35.117**

[154] *Turner v Willis* [1905] 1 KB 468. If the agreement merely relates to the costs, then the client will usually not lose protection: *Re Fernandes* [1878] WN 57.
[155] *Jeffreys v Evans* (1845) 14 M&W 210.
[156] *Thomas v Cross* (1864) 29 JP 4.
[157] See *Nova (Jersey) Knit Ltd v Kammgarn Spinnerei GmbH* [1977] 1 WLR 713, HL.
[158] See *Safa Ltd v Banque du Caire* [2000] All ER (D) 1010.
[159] *Martin Boston & Co (a firm) v Levy* [1982] 1 WLR 1434.
[160] See *Re Remnant* (1849) 11 Beav 603 (purchase money); *Re Buckwell* [1902] 2 Ch 596 (security for costs); *Prothero v Thomas* (1815) 6 Tuant 196 (monies payable to an opponent); PD 47, para 6.6(b).
[161] *Pomeroy v Tanner* [1897] 1 Ch 285.
[162] *Crane v Cannons Leisure* [2007] EWCA Civ 1352.
[163] See *Slade & Company Solicitors v Boodia* [2017] EWHC 2699 (QB), at [20]–[33]. At the time of writing, this decision was subject to appeal.

have been paid ought to be entered into the bill where appropriate,[164] even where they have been paid directly by the client,[165] such as where the client has offered a cheque made payable to counsel.[166]

35.118 Unpaid disbursements merit particular attention. If they are not described in the bill of costs as unpaid, then the protection offered by Solicitors Act 1974, s 67, will be lost and they will be irrecoverable against the client.[167] If disbursements are correctly described as unpaid in the bill of costs but remain unpaid at the time of assessment, they will, by virtue of s 67, be disallowed. This includes counsel's fees. Indeed, because of the non-contractual nature of some counsel's fees (generally where counsel was instructed before 2013—see 53.04–53.05), there may be no enforceable debt at all until the fees have been paid.[168] Although there is no authority on the point, there is no particular reason to believe that this rule does not apply to counsel's fees where counsel has been instructed under a conditional fee agreement.[169] It is commonly the case that unpaid disbursements are, accidentally or otherwise, not always described within the bill as being unpaid. The court has the power to order that such a bill be withdrawn and substituted with a revised bill, but there is pre-CPR authority to suggest that the court also has the power to allow such a bill to be amended to include the necessary words (see 35.95).

35.119 Acton J has confirmed that a client cannot evade liability by instructing the solicitor not to pay disbursements that have been properly incurred. Put otherwise, disbursements are recoverable from the client even though the payment is made by the solicitor after the client has stated that they do not propose to pay the disbursement.[170]

The Power to Order Delivery of a Bill

35.120 Solicitors Act 1974, s 68 (as amended), gives the court the power to order a solicitor to deliver a bill:

> '(1) The jurisdiction of the High Court to make orders for the delivery by a solicitor of a bill of costs, and for the delivery up of, or otherwise in relation to, any documents in his possession, custody or power, is hereby declared to extend to cases in which no business has been done by him in the High Court.
>
> (2) The County Court shall have the same jurisdiction as the High Court to make orders making such provision as is mentioned in subsection (1) in cases where the bill of costs or

---

[164] *Re Seal, ex p Crickett* (1893) 37 Sol Jo 842, CA.

[165] *Re Metcalfe* (1862) 30 Beav 406.

[166] *Devereux v White & Co* (1896) 13 TLR 52.

[167] See *Smith v Howes* [1922] 1 KB 592, which dealt with the then rules of court, which were very similar to Solicitors Act 1974, s 67. It can be seen that the provision was introduced to avoid the stringency of the decision in *Sadd v Griffin* [1908] 2 KB 510, which effectively prevented the recovery of any disbursements that were unpaid at the time the bill was delivered. See also *Re A Taxation of Costs* [1936] 1 KB 523. Other common-law jurisdictions have followed *Sadd*: see, eg, *Vilensky v Banning* (unreported), 20 June 1996, WA Sup Ct, *per* Kennedy, Ipp and Rowland JJ, a decision of the Full Court of Western Australia.

[168] *Re Taxation of Costs; Re A Solicitor* [1936] 1 KB 523.

[169] For the avoidance of doubt, the provisions concerning unpaid counsel's fee apply only on a solicitor-and-client assessment; they have no role to play between opposing parties.

[170] *Medlicott v Emery* [1933] All ER 655.

the documents relate wholly or partly to contentious business done by the solicitor in [the County Court].[171]

(3) In this section and in sections 69 to 71 "solicitor" includes the executors, administrators and assignees of a solicitor.'

The court may be asked to exercise this power in circumstances such as where a solicitor has paid themselves by deduction or where the solicitor proposes to take sums paid on account as being final payment without delivering a statute bill—something that commonly happens (see 35.37–35.39). The application is often combined with an application to deliver a cash account. A solicitor principal may require a solicitor agent to deliver a bill.[172]

The orders that the court is able to make are set out in CPR, r 67.2(1): **35.121**

'Where the relationship of solicitor and client exists or has existed, the orders which the court may make against the solicitor, on the application of the client or his personal representatives, include any of the following—

(a) to deliver a bill or cash account;
(b) to pay or deliver up any money or securities;
(c) to deliver a list of the moneys or securities which the solicitor has in his possession or control on behalf of the applicant;
(d) to pay into or lodge in court any such money or securities.'

The power to order a solicitor to deliver a bill does not extend to allowing the court to order a solicitor to deliver a specific internal invoice (see 35.38–35.39).

Where the solicitor alleges that it has a claim for costs against the client, the court may make an order securing the payment of the costs or protecting the solicitor's lien.[173] **35.122**

Whether the court makes an order under Solicitors Act 1974, s 68, is matter of discretion.[174] **35.123**
The power to order delivery of a bill is wider than the power to refer a bill for assessment. The court may order delivery of a bill notwithstanding the fact that the court may not have jurisdiction to order that the bill be assessed.[175] The power to order delivery has always been exercised irrespective of the question of whether the bill may be submitted for assessment:[176] the two jurisdictions are quite distinct.[177] The court should bear in mind that it will be for the client to consider, after they have received the bill, whether they will or will not apply for an assessment.[178]

The court may refuse to exercise its discretion to order delivery, such as where a client had left it very late (six years) to make their application.[179] The court will not make orders that are pointless, which means that if there has been an agreement as to the costs[180] or if costs **35.124**

171 As amended.
172 *Re A Solicitor* (1909) 54 Sol Jo 67.
173 CPR, r 67.2(3).
174 *In re Solicitor; In re a Taxation of Costs* [1953] Ch 480.
175 *Duffet v McEvoy* (1885) 10 App Cas 300.
176 *In re West, King & Adam, ex p Clough* [1892] 2 QB 102, at 108.
177 *Duffet v McEvoy* (1885) 10 App Cas 300.
178 *In Re Blackmore* (1851) 13 Beav 154.
179 *In re a Solicitor; In re Taxation of Costs* [1947] Ch 274.
180 *In re Van Laun, ex p Chatterton* [1907] 1 KB 155; on appeal ([1907] 2 KB 23), the Court of Appeal confirmed that, in respect of different bills rendered between the same parties, a trustee could require delivery to know the sums to be paid from the estate.

have been settled by a third party, the need for a bill will no longer exist.[181] In this regard, Lord Evershed MR had the following to say:

> 'It seems, therefore, quite plain to me that as a matter of general principle it is not right to say that a client, who has made an agreement for paying a lump sum for non-contentious business, has an unqualified right to come and ask for a bill. His right to require a bill is limited to cases where he can show, on the facts of the particular case, to the satisfaction of the court that there is something which as a matter of general principle or private right, or both, the court ought to look into.'[182]

35.125 That said, where the solicitor resists an order on the basis that bills have already been delivered, it would not be pointless to make an order if putative bills were to contain an insufficient narrative to qualify as bills. Lewis J had this to say on the issue:

> 'I do not consider that [the order that a bill be delivered] will lead to any unfairness. Indeed, it seems it will result in a sensible procedure for the resolution of the dispute about whether or not the costs are reasonable and are payable.'[183]

35.126 Costs must exist before the court can order delivery of a statute bill. Thus, in a case in which a solicitor had procrastinated to such an extent that he was unable to draw up a bill and had relinquished his right to be paid, North J declined to make an order.[184] Likewise, no order would be made where a solicitor declines to raise a charge.[185] Even in those circumstances, the solicitor may be ordered to provide a cash account.[186] That said, pre-CPR authority indicates that if the solicitor claims no costs, and swears that they have retained no client monies, the solicitor will generally not be required to furnish a cash account.[187]

35.127 The costs must be legal costs. If the work that has been done is work that cannot properly be regarded as professional work, the party chargeable will not have the right to apply for delivery of a bill.[188]

35.128 If the application for an order is made within existing proceedings, it must be made by application notice in accordance with CPR, Part 23. Where it is not made in existing proceedings, it is made under the Part 8 procedure.[189] The application will usually be made to the Senior Courts Costs Office (SCCO), but this need not necessarily be the case.[190]

35.129 If the court allows the application, it will make an order in the form of Precedent K of the Schedule of Costs Precedents annexed to the Costs Practice Direction (CPD).

---

181 *Re Chapman* (1903) 20 TLR 3, CA.
182 *Rutter v Sheridan-Young* [1958] 1 WLR 444, at 453. See also *Re Palmer* (1890) 45 Ch D 291.
183 *Bloomsbury Law v MacPhearson* [2016] EWHC 3395 (QB), at [20].
184 In *Re Landor (a solicitor)* [1899] 1 Ch 818.
185 *Re Griffith* (1891) 7 TLR 268; *Sparrow v Johns* (1838) 3 M & W 600, 150 ER 1284.
186 CPR, r 67.2(1)(a).
187 *Re Landor* (1899) 1 Ch 818.
188 *Re Fanshaw* [1905] WN 64.
189 CPR, r 67.2(2).
190 PD 67, para 2.1(2).

36

SOLICITOR-AND-CLIENT ASSESSMENTS

This chapter addresses the procedural aspects of solicitor-and-client assessments. In particular, it deals with the following topics: **36.01**

- assessments on the application of either the party chargeable or the solicitor (36.03):
  - the meaning of 'party chargeable' (36.07);
  - the time of delivery (36.14);
  - the meaning of 'payment' (36.18);
  - the meaning of 'one month' and '12 months' (36.29);
  - assessment as of right (36.30);
  - assessment as a matter of discretion (36.31);
  - 'special circumstances' (36.32);
  - procedural issues (36.39);
  - the scope of the assessment (36.54);
  - the costs of the assessment (36.57);
- assessments and accounts on the application of third parties (36.79):
  - assessments under s 71 of the Solicitors Act 1974 (36.81);
  - claims for account and declarations (36.84);
  - who pays whom (36.85);
  - the difference between applications under s 71(1) and those under s 71(3) (36.86);
  - meaning of 'a person other than the party chargeable with the bill' (36.91);
- the assessment hearing and the procedure leading up to the assessment hearing (36.96); and
- costs certificates and interim payments (36.113).

This chapter deals with applications for the assessment of costs. This is not the same as claims brought by solicitors for the payment of costs, which topic is addressed in Chapter 40. **36.02**

Assessments on the Application of the Party Chargeable or the Solicitor

The law governing the right to solicitor-and-client assessments derives from s 70 of the Solicitors Act 1974: **36.03**

> '(1) Where before the expiration of one month from the delivery of a solicitor's bill an application is made by the party chargeable with the bill, the High Court shall, without requiring any sum to be paid into court, order that the bill be assessed and that no action be commenced on the bill until the assessment is completed.
>
> (2) Where no such application is made before the expiration of the period mentioned in subsection (1), then, on an application being made by the solicitor or, subject to subsections

(3) and (4), by the party chargeable with the bill, the court may on such terms, if any, as it thinks fit (not being terms as to the costs of the assessment), order—
(a) that the bill be assessed; and
(b) that no action be commenced on the bill, and that any action already commenced be stayed, until the assessment is completed.

(3) Where an application under subsection (2) is made by the party chargeable with the bill—
(a) after the expiration of 12 months from the delivery of the bill, or
(b) after a judgment has been obtained for the recovery of the costs covered by the bill, or
(c) after the bill has been paid, but before the expiration of 12 months from the payment of the bill,

no order shall be made except in special circumstances and, if an order is made, it may contain such terms as regards the costs of the assessment as the court may think fit.

(4) The power to order assessment conferred by subsection (2) shall not be exercisable on an application made by the party chargeable with the bill after the expiration of 12 months from the payment of the bill.'

36.04 Thus the ease with which a 'party chargeable' (see 36.07) may obtain an order for assessment under s 70 of the Solicitors Act 1974 diminishes with the effluxion of time; this can be summarised as follows.

- If an application for an assessment is made within one month of the delivery of a bill, the court will order that the bill be assessed as a matter of right (see 36.30).
- If the application is made after the expiry of one month, but before 12 months have passed, the court has an unfettered discretion to order an assessment (see 36.31), but only if the bill has not been paid and only if judgment has not been obtained for the recovery of the costs covered by the bill.
- If the application is made after the expiry of 12 months, after the bill has been paid or after judgment has been obtained, the court may order an assessment, but only if 'special circumstances' can be made out; the same applies if the bill has been paid for a period of less than 12 months (or judgment has been obtained) (see 36.32–36.38).
- If the application is made after the expiry of 12 months from the payment of a bill, the court has no power under the Solicitors Act 1974 to order an assessment of that bill—although the court may still have the power to order a non-statutory quantification of costs (see 39.03–39.07).

36.05 The received view is that if the last of these circumstances applies (that is, more than 12 months have elapsed since payment of the bill), then that is an absolute bar to an assessment under the 1974 Act.[1] This is arguably wrong, however, because an absolute bar may be contrary to a person's rights under Art 6(1) of the European Convention on Human Rights (ECHR). Lord Mance had this to say on the topic:

'I consider that ... [certain statutory provisions] ... can and should all be read subject to the qualification that the court must have a discretion in exceptional circumstances to extend time for both filing and service, where such statutory provisions would otherwise

[1] See Solicitors Act 1974, s 70(4); *Harrison v Tew* [1990] 2 AC 523. This applies where the application is made by a liquidator following payment made by the now-insolvent company: *Forsinard Estate Ltd v Dykes* [1971] 1 WLR 232. For the rights of a *cestui que* trust in respect of a bill delivered to a trustee, see *Re Downes* (1844) 5 Beav 425; *Re Brown* (1867) LR 4 Eq 464.

> operate to prevent an appeal in a manner conflicting with the right of access to an appeal process held to exist under [A]rt 6(1) in *Tolstoy Miloslavsky*.[2] The High Court must have power in any individual case to determine whether the operation of the time limits would have this effect. If and to the extent that it would do so, it must have power to permit and hear an out of time appeal which a litigant personally has done all he can to bring and notify timeously.'[3]

This was in the context of an extradition claim, which—of course—is a very different matter from a mere assessment of costs. It is, however, possible that there may be circumstances in which an absolute bar to assessment could be said to engage with a person's rights under Art 6(1) ECHR. Exceptional circumstances would have to exist and the client would have to show that they had done all they could to make an application in time.[4] Perhaps the greatest difficulty that a person who sought to rely on Art 6(1) would encounter, however, would be the facts that even if they were to be absolutely denied an assessment under the Solicitors Act 1974, the court would still be able to carry out a non-statutory quantification of costs (see 39.03–39.07), and that, as such, that person would still have access to the court, albeit not quite the access that they would ideally have liked.[5] **36.06**

The meaning of 'party chargeable with the bill'

The party chargeable is usually the client (that is, the person who receives the legal services), but this will not always be the case. If, for example, a mother has entered into a contract of retainer to pay the costs incurred by her daughter, then the mother would be a party chargeable. Identification of the party chargeable will usually be a question of fact, but points of law may arise from time to time (see, for example, 36.10). **36.07**

The following circumstances concerning parties chargeable merit specific discussion: **36.08**

- where the client is a professional client (see 36.09);
- where there is group litigation in which common costs are shared (see 36.10);
- where there are joint contracts of retainer involving joint costs debtors (see 36.11);
- where the party chargeable is acting in a representative capacity or as a trustee (see 36.12); and
- where the assessment is a quantification of the solicitor's claim against assets (see 36.13).

The 'party chargeable' where the client is a professional client

The fact that a solicitor's client is themselves a solicitor is no bar to the instructing solicitor being a party chargeable. Where a solicitor instructs another solicitor as their agent, the instructing solicitor may be a party chargeable notwithstanding the principal–agent relationship.[6] Likewise, where a solicitor is a trustee entitled under the trust to charge for their professional services and where they deliver a bill to a co-trustee, the co-trustee is a party chargeable.[7] **36.09**

---

[2] *Tolstoy Miloslavsky v United Kingdom*, App No 18139/91 (1995) 20 EHRR 442.

[3] *Pomiechowski v District Court of Legnica, Poland* [2012] UKSC 20, at [39].

[4] *R (Adesina & Ors) v The Nursing & Midwifery Council* [2013] EWCA Civ 818, at [15], *per* Maurice Kay LJ.

[5] The costs consequences of a non-statutory assessment might also be significantly different: see *Ahmud & Co v MacPherson* [2015] EWHC 2240 (QB); cf *Smith v Edwardes* (1888) 22 QBD 103.

[6] *In re Wilde (a solicitor)* [1910] 1 Ch 100. See also *Jones v Roberts* (1838) 8 Sim 397; *Toghill v Grant, Re Boord* (1840) 2 Beav 261.

[7] *In re HP Davies & Son* [1917] 1 Ch 216.

Group litigation and the 'party chargeable'

36.10 Where, in group litigation, each party has their own contract of retainer, it will usually be that each party would be a party chargeable in the sense that they would be liable for their individual costs and a share of the common costs. This means that there would ordinarily be more than one party chargeable for the common costs (either as joint costs debtors or as individual costs debtors, depending on the terms of the retainer and any attendant costs sharing agreement). To prevent a multiplicity of assessments, the court will, so far as possible, direct a single assessment in the presence of all of the relevant parties.[8] See Chapter 65 for further comments on the management of such matters.

The 'party chargeable' where there are joint retainers

36.11 Where a retainer is joint—that is, where there is single costs debt for which more than one client is liable (see 19.05–19.07)—any client may be the party chargeable, regardless of whether the co-clients refuse to join or object to the assessment.[9]

The 'party chargeable' where there are joint representatives and trustees

36.12 A party chargeable may include a personal representative,[10] a trustee in bankruptcy[11] or a liquidator[12] of the client. In a similar vein to the point made above, any one of a number of trustees can obtain an order for assessment of work done for the trust, regardless of whether the co-trustee refuses to join or raises an objection.[13]

Quantification of a claim against assets

36.13 Where the purpose of the exercise is solely to find out how much the solicitor is able to claim against the assets of an estate or trust, it is arguable[14] that the court can carry out an assessment under the general jurisdiction of the court rather than under the Solicitors Act 1974. If this is correct, then the issue of whether the party seeking the assessment is a party chargeable would not arise.[15] In an appropriate case, thought ought to be given to whether a claim for an account ought to be made (see 36.84) or—whilst not likely to be helpful—an application for an assessment under s 71(3) of the Solicitors Act 1974 (see 36.79–36.83).

The time of delivery

36.14 The time of delivery will usually be a matter of fact to be determined on the evidence. Points of law may arise, however, such as where the bill is one of a series of requests for payment and where the client is a company in the process of being wound up. Other points of law may arise from time to time (see 27.38–27.66).

---

8 Whilst a very old case, see, by analogy, *In re Salaman* [1894] 2 Ch 201.

9 *Lockhard v Hardy* (1841) 4 Beav 224. See also *Re Hair* (1847) 10 Beav 187; *Re Lewin* (1853) 16 Beav 608.

10 *Jefferson v Warrington* (1840) 7 M&W 137.

11 *Re Allingham* (1886) 32 Ch D 36, CA.

12 *In re Foss, Bilbrough, Plaskitt & Foss* [1912] 2 Ch 161.

13 *Hazard v Lane* (1817) 3 Mer 285, at 290.

14 It is not wholly clear whether this remains good law; it is arguable either way. See *Harrison v Tew* [1990] 2 AC 523; cf *Turner & Co v Palomo SA* [2000] 1 WLR 37. The situation is arguably comparable to the latter, in which case the jurisdiction will exist.

15 *In re Foss, Bilbrough, Plaskitt & Foss* [1912] 2 Ch 161; *In re Palace Restaurants* [1914] 1 Ch 492.

Time of delivery where there is a series of bills

It may be necessary to examine the nature of the retainer to determine the time of delivery in law (see 27.38–27.66). If the bill related to an entire contract[16] and if there was a series of invoices that could properly be regarded as forming a single bill, time will not begin to run until delivery of the final bill.[17] This is because the bill is not delivered until the whole of it has been delivered. A bill that has been sent to the client in instalments is sometimes referred to as a *Chamberlain* bill.[18] Up until the stage at which the whole of the bill has been delivered, the instalments are usually regarded as being requests for payment on account.[19] Circumstances that would favour a series of invoices being a *Chamberlain* bill include: **36.15**

- where there is no contractual right to render interim statute bills[20] and where the invoices were delivered in the absence of natural breaks;
- where the invoices have not, in themselves, been complete statute bills because they have omitted items, such as disbursements;[21]
- where the invoices were delivered over a short period of time;[22] and
- where the invoices have a nexus between them (such as where a running total is carried over from one invoice to the next or where there is overlap between the periods the invoices cover).[23]

In the editor's experience, it is becoming increasingly common for courts to regard series of invoices as comprising *Chamberlain* bills, largely because such an approach is generally perceived as being in the interests of protecting clients. One of the reasons why the court tends to be inclined to do this is that it may be difficult for a client to challenge an interim statute bill. Whilst he was dealing with a different point, Jacobs J had the following to say on that topic: **36.16**

> '[There is a] modern practice of solicitors of sending bills on a regular basis which are complete bills, not interim bills. That causes difficulty when you have litigation which is ongoing. The client is called upon by these provisions to challenge an interim bill within one month, if he wants to do it as of right; and if he does not challenge it within twelve months then he has to show "special circumstances" to challenge his solicitors' bill. That puts him in an impossible position. Either he challenges his solicitors' bill—the very solicitor who is

---

[16] This will, in general, not be a finding open to the court where the retainer is a general retainer (ie a retainer that does not relate to a single case): see *Warmingtons v McMurray* [1936] 2 All ER 745. The fact that the contract of retainer is a general retainer is not, however, a bar to a series of invoices being a *Chamberlain* bill: *Bari v Rosen (t/a Rosen & Co Solicitors)* [2012] EWHC 1782 (QB).

[17] *Chamberlain v Boodle & King* [1982] 1 WLR 1443. As to timing, see *Re Street* (1870) LR 10 Eq 165. See also *Warmingtons v McMurray* [1936] 2 All ER 745; for a more recent example, *Bari v Rosen (t/a Rosen & Co Solicitors)* [2012] EWHC 1782 (QB).

[18] After *Chamberlain v Boodle & King* [1982] 1 WLR 1443. See *Bari v Rosen (t/a Rosen & Co Solicitors)* [2012] EWHC 1782 (QB), at [47].

[19] *Bari v Rosen (t/a Rosen & Co Solicitors)* [2012] EWHC 1782 (QB), at [37].

[20] This was an important feature of the *Chamberlain* bill in *Bari v Rosen (t/a Rosen & Co Solicitors)* [2012] EWHC 1782 (QB).

[21] See, eg, *Slade & Co Solicitors v Boodia* [2017] EWHC 2699 (QB), at [20]–[33], *per* Slade J.

[22] See *Bari v Rosen (t/a Rosen & Co Solicitors)* [2012] EWHC 1782 (QB), at [58], in which Spencer J found that a period of nine months was a sufficiently short period of time to permit of a finding that the invoices were parts of a *Chamberlain* bill.

[23] See, eg, *Bari v Rosen (t/a Rosen & Co Solicitors)* [2012] EWHC 1782 (QB), at [58]. See also the facts of *Chamberlain v Boodle & King* [1982] 1 WLR 1443 itself.

now acting for him—and continues using that solicitor at the same time; or he has to change solicitor, all in the middle of litigation when he is facing another enemy.'[24]

Winding up

36.17 Where a bill is delivered to a company that is subsequently wound up, the practice has been to treat the case as if the rights of the parties had remained just as they were at the time of the winding-up. It would follow that if a bill were to be delivered more than 12 months before the winding-up, there would be a need to show special circumstances, but if the bill were to be delivered less than 12 months before the winding-up, there would be no need to show special circumstances—and this would be so even if more than 12 months had elapsed between delivery and application. The authorities are unclear as to whether such an order may be said to be made under the Solicitors Act 1974. Given the clear terms in which time limits are set in s 70 of that Act and the practice in such cases of adding the costs of the assessment to the solicitor's claim in the winding-up, it is suggested that it may not.[25]

The meaning of 'payment'

36.18 The following conditions must be satisfied before a transfer of money can properly be said to be a 'payment' within the meaning of Solicitors Act 1974, s 70:

- there must have been delivery of a statute bill;[26] and
- the client must have been aware of the fact that the putative payment had been made.[27]

Both of these are largely issues of fact. The following case examples illustrate the way in which the court addresses those issues.

Putative payments where there is no bill or the putative bill is not bona fide *complaint with the 1974 Act*

36.19 There can be no payment in the complete absence of a statute bill.[28] This is true even if there has been an agreement as to the amount payable (such as would happen if a solicitor were to rely on a settled account).[29] Lord Romilly wearily explained this point: 'I have held over and over again that there can be no payment . . . before the bill has been delivered and the client has had the opportunity of seeing the items.'[30]

36.20 What is less clear is whether there can be payment of a demand for payment that is properly made under the contract of retainer and which gives the client sufficient information to know what is being charged, but which is, in some way, not a statute bill *bona fide* compliant with s 69(2) of the Solicitors Act 1974. There is, for example, Victorian authority to suggest that payment of a bill that was defective in the sense that it had not been signed

---

[24] *Harrods Ltd v Harrods (Buenos Aires) Ltd* [2014] 6 Costs LR 975, at [20], *per* Jacobs J.

[25] *Re James, ex p Quilter* (1850) 4 De G & Sm 183; *Re Park, Cole v Park* (1888) 41 Ch D 326; *Re Brabant* (1879) 23 Sol Jo 779; *Re Marseilles Extension Rly and Land Co, ex p Evans* (1870) LR 11 Eq 151; *In re Foss, Bilbrough, Plaskitt & Foss* [1912] 2 Ch 161.

[26] *Re Foster* [1920] 3 KB 306. See also *In re West, King & Adam, ex p Clough* [1892] 2 QB 102.

[27] See *In re Bignold* (1845) 9 Beav 269, at 270. See also the other footnotes in the case examples.

[28] *Re Callis* (1901) 49 WR 316; *Re Foster* [1920] 3 KB 306.

[29] *In re Frape, ex p Perrett* [1893] 2 Ch 284. See also *In re Baylis* [1896] 2 Ch 107.

[30] *In re Street* (1870) Law Rep 10 Eq 165, CA, at 167. See also *In re Blackmore* (1851) 13 Beav 154; *In re Stogdon* (1887) 56 LJ (Ch) 420, in which Chitty J approved and followed *In re Street*. See also *In re Baylis* [1896] 2 Ch 107, in which the Court of Appeal upheld Chitty J's analysis.

would start time running for the purposes of the then equivalent of s 70 of the 1974 Act.[31] In particular, Brett MR had this to say:

> '[The reference to a bill in that Act] includes an unsigned bill, and consequently, if it has been paid, and more than a year has afterwards elapsed, it cannot be ordered for taxation. Otherwise, after a bill of costs has been delivered and paid and settled, a client may, at any time afterwards have the whole matter re-opened, because the bill was not a signed one. This ought not to be done ...'[32]

It would be easy to dismiss Brett MR's decision as relating to legislation long since repealed were it not for the fact that Lord Lowry appears to have referred to it with apparent approval under the 1974 Act.[33] In any event, whilst the wording of the Victorian Act was (markedly) different from the wording of the present-day Act, the character of the legislative scheme was much the same. As such, it is arguable that Brett MR's analysis remains good law and that whilst there can be no payment in the complete absence of a document that could be said to have been a statute bill, there can be payment if that document was only technically not a statute bill. If this is right, this may be of relevance in a modern setting because—since about 2014—it has become increasingly common for former clients to attempt to reopen seemingly settled business with their former solicitors. Whether Brett MR's comments remain good law is, in many ways, a matter of policy and, as such, may need to be revisited to take account of modern concerns and practices, but—in view of the fact that former clients now tend to have the ability to make use of the Legal Ombudsman scheme (see 39.22–39.34)—it could well be that Brett MR's comments continue to have resonance. The contrary, however, is easily arguable. **36.21**

Payment by deduction and the client's knowledge

There can be no payment if the client is ignorant of it. If a solicitor pays their bills by deduction without the knowledge of their client, that will not amount to payment within the meaning of Solicitors Act 1974, s 70,[34] and it would also be a breach of the Solicitors Regulation Authority (SRA) Accounts Rules 2011 (as amended) (see 35.12). Mere acquiescence on the part of the client would not suffice.[35] Payment by deduction with the client's agreement may, however, be regarded as payment.[36] **36.22**

Partial payment

In the absence of accord and satisfaction (see 39.17–39.18), where a payment is only partial (that is, where a costs debt is not extinguished by the payment), it is not a payment within the meaning of Solicitors Act 1974, s 70, but is merely a payment on account.[37] **36.23**

---

[31] That is, the Solicitors Act 1843 (6 & 7 Vict c 73), s 41.

[32] *In re Sutton & Elliot* (1883) 11 QBD 337, at 379. See also *Re Firm of Solicitors, ex p D'Aragon* (1887) 3 TLR 815.

[33] *Harrison v Tew* [1990] 2 AC 523, at 535. See also Dillon LJ's comments in the Court of Appeal: *Harrison v Tew* [1989] QB 307, at 331.

[34] *In re Jackson* [1915] 1 KB 371, at 381 and 383; *In re Stogdon* (1887) 56 LJ (Ch) 420.

[35] See *Re Ingle* (1855) 25 LJ Ch 169; *In re West, King & Adam, ex p Clough* [1892] 2 QB 102; *Re Foss, Bilborough & Co* [1912] 2 Ch 161.

[36] *Forsinard Estates v Dykes* [1971] 1 WLR 232. See also *Re David* (1861) 30 Beav 278; *Hitchcock v Stretton* [1892] 2 Ch 343; *Re Thompson* [1894] 1 QB 462.

[37] *Re Woodard* (1869) 18 WR 37.

Payment by negotiable instruments

36.24 Presenting a negotiable instrument (such as a promissory note, a bill of exchange or a cheque) will amount to payment only if and when it is honoured.[38] The date of payment is the date on which it is honoured rather than the date on which it is presented.[39] A client is entitled to a bill regardless of whether they have offered a negotiable instrument as payment.[40] A solicitor cannot evade their obligation to deliver a statute bill by taking a bill of exchange from their client for an agreed amount (see 40.11)[41] nor (arguably) can the solicitor do so by suing on a dishonoured cheque.[42]

Where delivery comes after monies are paid

36.25 Provided that the monies were, at all times, referable to the bill in question, the court is able to find that there has been payment notwithstanding the fact that delivery came after the transfer of monies.[43] This was explained by Stirling J in the following terms:

> '[If] no bill of costs is delivered at all, then there is no payment . . . , yet if a bill is delivered after a payment previously made, then the Court may look at the whole circumstances, and come to the conclusion that the payment which has been made is referable to the bill which is subsequently delivered, and, in that case, unless the Court finds special circumstances such as would justify the [assessment] of a bill . . . , it is not a matter of course that the bill should be [assessed].'[44]

36.26 Payment is made at the time of delivery and, as such, the client will be able to ask for an assessment as of right only during the first calendar month following delivery; after this, to have an assessment, the client will have to show special circumstances as a result of the fact that payment would have been made (see 36.32–36.38). There are limits to the extent to which a solicitor can rely on a bill delivered after payment, however; whilst persuasive rather than binding, Australian case law confirms that delivery of a bill after payment will not cure the original failure to deliver a proper bill.[45]

Charges and mortgages

36.27 The giving of a mortgage with a covenant to pay is not equivalent to payment of the bill.[46]

Putative compromise

36.28 Disputes about whether there has been a payment often arise in a context in which it is said that the payment compromised the dispute between the solicitor and client. These issues are dealt with at 39.15–39.16.

---

[38] *Sayer v Wagstaff* (1844) 14 LJ Ch 116.

[39] *Re Romer & Haslam* [1893] 2 QB 286; *Ray v Newton* [1913] 1 KB 249, at 256.

[40] *Ray v Newton* [1913] 1 KB 249, CA.

[41] *Ibid.*

[42] *Martin Boston & Co (a firm) v Levy* [1982] 1 WLR 1434.

[43] *In re Thompson ex p Baylis* [1894] 1 QB 462, at 463. See also *Hitchcock v Stretton* [1892] 2 Ch 343; cf *In re Street* (1870) Law Rep 10 Eq 165, CA (in which not only was no bill delivered, but also the solicitor was himself the trustee).

[44] *Hitchcock v Stretton* [1892] 2 Ch 343, at 351, setting out his interpretation of *Ex p Hemming* (1879) 28 LT 144.

[45] *Woolf v Trebilco* [1933] VLR 180, at 190. In a similar vein, if an oral retainer is made and then the agreed sum is acknowledged in the form of an account stated after payment has been made by deduction, that acknowledgement will not be sufficient to give rise to a retrospective business agreement: *Re Fernandes* [1878] WN 57.

[46] *In re Van Laun, ex p Chatterton* [1907] 1 KB 155.

The meaning of 'one month' and of '12 months'

The reference to 'one month' is a reference to one calendar month.[47] This is discussed in more detail at 40.05. Similarly, the reference to '12 months' is a reference to 12 calendar months. The day of delivery is excluded, as is the day on which proceedings are commenced.[48] The period ends when an application for an assessment is made: Carnwath LJ has made it clear that what is required is an actual application for an assessment, rather than a mere request for an assessment.[49] **36.29**

Assessment as of right

Where the application is made before the expiry of a month since the delivery of the bill, the client's right to an assessment is absolute.[50] There can be no defence on the merits.[51] It would be wrong to impose conditions (such as a requirement to make an interim payment).[52] **36.30**

The court's discretion

Where the application is made after the first month following delivery, but where the need to show special circumstances has not yet arisen, the matter will be in the court's discretion. Many of the factors listed at 36.36 will be relevant, but there will be no need to show 'special circumstances'.[53] The court is free to order the client to make a payment on account or to pay money into court.[54] Cozens-Hardy MR has commented that the court is able to take this into account when exercising its discretion.[55] **36.31**

Special circumstances

Where the application for an assessment is made more than 12 months after delivery of the statute bill, then, to have the costs assessed, the client will have to show that 'special circumstances' exist.[56] Once the client has lost the right to an assessment as of right, the same is true if the application is made after the bill has been paid (within 12 months of payment) or if the application is made after judgment has already been obtained for recovery of the sums claimed.[57] **36.32**

Special circumstances are not confined to pressure, overcharge or fraud; the existence of such circumstances is a matter of degree and of discretion to be exercised in the circumstances of the particular case.[58] Circumstances need to be considered in **36.33**

---

47 Interpretation Act 1978, Sch 1.

48 *Blunt v Heslop* (1838) 4 A&E 577.

49 *Solicitors Indemnity Fund Ltd v Hewitson & Harker* [2010] EWCA Civ 147, at [12].

50 See Solicitors Act 1974, s 70(1).

51 *Szekeres v Alan Smeath & Co* [2005] EWHC 1733 (Ch), *per* Pumfrey J.

52 *Re Brockman* [1908–10] All ER Rep 364.

53 In the editor's experience, the bar is set low—at least if the application is made reasonably promptly. Whilst not binding (and *obiter*), Master Rowley has said that, in 'most cases', a client 'can be confident that the assessment will be allowed ... albeit on the likelihood of some payment on account of the costs are ... to be assessed': see *Eurasian Natural Resources Corpn Ltd v Dechert LLP* [2017] EWHC B4 (Costs), at [12].

54 Although the court may not impose terms as to the costs of the assessment: Solicitors Act 1974, s 70(2).

55 *Re Brockman* [1908–10] All ER Rep 364.

56 See Solicitors Act 1974, s 70(3)(a).

57 See Solicitors Act 1974, s 70(3)(b) and (c).

58 See *In re Hirst & Capes* [1908] 1 KB 982, affirmed by the House of Lords ([1908] 1 AC 416).

context[59] and 'special' means 'special', not 'exceptional'.[60] Lewison J had this to say on the topic:

> 'Whether special circumstances exist is essentially a value judgment. It depends on comparing the particular case with the run of the mill case in order to decide whether a detailed assessment in the particular case is justified, despite the restrictions contained in Section 70(3).'[61]

36.34 When the court is asked to consider more than one factor, it should consider those factors in aggregate, rather than individually.[62]

Special circumstances relating to third parties

36.35 Where the application is brought by a third party under s 71 of the Solicitors Act 1974, s 71(2) states that the court may take into account circumstances that affect the applicant, but do not affect the party chargeable with the bill. Langley J has confirmed that the mere fact that the third party did not have control over the litigation would not of itself be sufficient to amount to special circumstances.[63] This would be largely of academic interest, however, because, in most circumstances, it would be better for the third party to bring a claim for an account rather than to apply an assessment under s 71 (see 36.84) and, as such, the issue of special circumstances would not ordinarily arise.

Case examples relating to special circumstances

36.36 The following case examples are not intended to be a statement of the law—indeed, some of them are decisions of costs judges and are therefore not binding; rather, they are meant only to be illustrative.

- **Agreement to assess (or not to assess)** An agreement between the parties that there would be a detailed assessment is as powerful a special circumstance as it is possible to have.[64] A mutual understanding (as opposed to an express agreement) that the bill would be assessed is also capable of amounting to a special circumstance.[65] On a related note, it is no defence to an application for an assessment made by a client to say that there has been a verbal agreement as to the quantum of costs.[66]
- **Excessive costs** Special circumstances may exist where a client shows that costs are unreasonably high,[67] that there has been overcharging[68] or that costs are such that they call

59 See *Kris Motor Spares Ltd v Fox Williams LLP* [2009] EWHC 2813 (QB), in which Holroyde J declined to find special circumstances arising out of a reservation of a right to assessment because the client had sought an assessment only after the solicitor had refused to provide legal services on favourable terms.

60 *Riley v Dibb Lupton Alsop*, sub nom *A v BCD (a firm)* (1997) 147 NLJ 1422, at 1422, *per* Sedley J. See also *Stone Rowe Brewer LLP v Just Costs Ltd* [2015] EWCA Civ 1168, at [69], *per* Sales LJ (albeit in the context of Solicitors Act 1974, s 70(10)).

61 *Falmouth House Freehold Co Ltd v Morgan Walker LLP* [2010] EWHC 3092 (Ch), at [13], cited with approval by Sales LJ in *Stone Rowe Brewer LLP v Just Costs Ltd* [2015] EWCA Civ 1168, at [66], and by Spencer J in *Bari v Rosen (t/a Rosen & Co Solicitors)* [2012] EWHC 1782 (QB), at [67].

62 *Sanders v Isaacs* [1971] 1 WLR 240; *Kundrath v Henry Kwatia & Gooding* [2005] 2 Costs LR 279.

63 *Barclays plc v Villers* [2000] 1 All ER (Comm) 357, at 369.

64 *Arrowfield Services Ltd v BP Collins (a firm)* [2003] EWHC 830 (Ch); [2005] 2 Costs LR 171.

65 *Barnes v Stones (a firm)* [2007] EWHC 90069 (Costs), *per* Master Simons; see also *BFS Investments plc v Manches plc* [2007] EWHC 90082 (Costs), *per* Master Gordon-Saker. Neither of these is binding.

66 In relation to contentious costs, see *In re Russell Son & Scott* (1885) 30 Ch D 114; in relation to non-contentious costs, *In re West, King & Adam, ex p Clough* [1892] 2 QB 102 at 106.

67 *Re Norman* (1886) 16 QBD 673.

68 *Re a Solicitor* [1961] Ch 491.

for an explanation[69]—although it would be wrong to allow such concerns to override the requirement to show special circumstances. An explicably high level of fees will not, however, of itself amount to special circumstances (see below).[70]

- **Substantial costs** The fact that a significant amount of costs has been claimed will, in general, simply be a factor that may be taken into account,[71] but there have been instances of the court finding that the fact that very substantial costs were incurred over a short period of time was a factor that magnified the effect of any other factors.[72]
- **Pressure brought to bear** Where a client is discouraged from seeking an assessment in a case in which the recovery of costs was questionable, the court may find that special circumstances are made out.[73] In general, the client should be able to identify the areas in which there has been alleged overcharging.[74]
- **Interim billing** The mere fact that it would be difficult for a client to issue proceedings in respect of interim bills would not, in general, give rise to special circumstances, but there have been instances of the court finding that a client's need to maintain a special relationship with a particular solicitor is a factor that can be taken into account in this regard.[75]
- **Poor client care and poor information** A refusal on the part of a solicitor to give further details about their costs has been held not to amount to special circumstances,[76] but incorrect advice about the assessment process might amount to special circumstances.[77] If the solicitor is unable to provide information that would allow the costs to be recovered from an opponent, that may be a factor that would count towards there being special circumstances.[78]
- **Inaccurate estimates** Providing inaccurate estimates may suffice. In this regard, it should be noted that the court now tends to expect a higher quality of estimates than would have been acceptable in the past.[79] One could argue that estimates ought to be at

69 *Re Robinson* (1867) LR 3 Ex 4. Whilst not binding, in the context of estimates having been given to a client that were exceeded by a substantial margin, Master Rowley drew guidance from the discussion of the phrase 'calling for an explanation' in cases concerning estimates of costs between opposing parties: *Eurasian Natural Resources Corpn Ltd v Dechert LLP* [2017] EWHC B4 (Costs), at [16]–[17]. See, eg, *Leigh v Michelin Tyre Plc* [2003] EWCA Civ 1766, at [26], *per* Dyson; *Mastercigars Direct Ltd v Withers LLP* [2007] EWHC 2733 (Ch), at [99], *per* Morgan J.

70 See *Winchester Commodities Group Ltd v RD Black & Cl* [2000] BCC 310, in which the high level of fees was explicable on the basis of the specialist nature of the work. See also *Re Cartwright* (1873) LR 16 Eq 469.

71 See, eg, *Falmouth House Freehold Co Ltd v Morgan Walker LLP* [2010] EWHC 3092 (Ch), at [11], *per* Lewison J, referring to *Winchester Commodities Group Ltd v RD Black & Co* [2000] BCC 310.

72 Whilst not binding, see *Eurasian Natural Resources Corpn Ltd v Dechert LLP* [2017] EWHC B4 (Costs), at [66], *per* Master Rowley.

73 *Kralj v Birkbeck Motague* (unreported), 18 February 1988, CA.

74 *Re Boycott* (1885) LR 29 Ch D 571.

75 Whilst not binding, see *Eurasian Natural Resources Corpn Ltd v Dechert LLP* [2017] EWHC B4 (Costs), at [88]–[90], *per* Master Rowley.

76 *Re Metal Distributors (UK) Ltd* [2004] EWHC (Ch).

77 *Kundrath v Henry Kwatia & Gooding* [2005] 2 Costs LR 279.

78 *Bari v Rosen (t/a Rosen & Co Solicitors)* [2012] EWHC 1782 (QB), at [63].

79 Whilst not binding, in *Eurasian Natural Resources Corpn Ltd v Dechert LLP* [2017] EWHC B4 (Costs), at [51]–[56], Master Rowley had this to say on the point: '[The solicitor said] that work was difficult to predict ... in every estimate he has given. But any such difficulty is in my view wholly insufficient to cover the gap between the estimates and the reality. [The solicitor's] phrasing is redolent of costs estimates from ten or more years ago where a solicitor would routinely say that the costs to be incurred were impossible to predict.' Master Rowley went on to find that there were special circumstances.

least passably accurate in cases that are subject to costs management or which were suitable for legal project management.

- **Incorrect advice about the process of assessment** Where solicitors wrongly advised a client that, to have her costs assessed, she would have had to have made an upfront payment of 40 per cent of the costs as claimed, the court found that special circumstances had been made out by reason of the misleading advice that the client had received.[80]
- **Errors in the bill and with billing in general** The presence of gross errors or blunders in the bill may give rise to special circumstances.[81] The presence of costs charged as a result of a mistake as to the law may do the same.[82] Irregularities with interim bills may give rise to special circumstances.[83]
- **Delivery of bill with reservations** Where a bill is delivered with a reservation that a further bill may follow, that is capable of amounting to special circumstances.[84]
- **Delay caused by other dispute resolution processes** It used to be the case that a client was able to apply to the Legal Complaints Service for a 'remuneration certificate' stating the correct amount of costs payable.[85] If that procedure took more than 12 months to complete, then that would be a factor that was capable of giving rise to special circumstances.[86] The remuneration certificate procedure no longer exists, but the same principle also applies to other unavoidable delays, such as those caused by an appellate process.[87] Whilst it is no more than his own view, the editor believes that the same principle would also apply where it was appropriate to make a complaint to the Legal Ombudsman.
- **Prejudice caused by delay** Where a client has delayed in making an application for an assessment, the presence or absence of prejudice caused by that delay may be a relevant factor. Where the solicitors have themselves caused or contributed to the delay (by, for example, the tardy preparation of a detailed breakdown of costs), then that would be a factor that could be taken into account.[88]
- **Payment of a bill with reservations** Special circumstances may arise where a client pays a bill with an express reservation of the right to assess.[89] Of itself, a reservation may not be sufficient to amount to special circumstances, but, taken in conjunction with other factors (such as the solicitor asserting lien), special circumstances may be made out.[90]
- **Payment without demur** The fact that the client paid the bills without demur is a factor that may be taken into account.[91] That said, where the payment is made in

[80] *Kundrath v Henry Kwatia & Gooding* [2005] 2 Costs LR 279.

[81] *Re Norman* (1886) 16 QBD 673.

[82] *Re G* (1909) 53 SJ 469.

[83] Whilst not binding, see *Eurasian Natural Resources Corpn Ltd v Dechert LLP* [2017] EWHC B4 (Costs), at [94]–[95], *per* Master Rowley.

[84] *Harris v Yarm* [1960] Ch 256.

[85] See the Solicitors' (Non-Contentious Business) Remuneration Order 2009 (SI 2009/1931); see also ch 19 of the second edition of this book.

[86] *Riley v Dibb Lupton Alsop*, sub nom *A v BCD (a firm)* (1997) 147 NLJ 1422, *per* Sedley J.

[87] *Pine v Law Society* (unreported), 26 October 2004, QBD, *per* HHJ Maddocks (sitting as a High Court judge). See also *Bari v Rosen (t/a Rosen & Co Solicitors)* [2012] EWHC 1782 (QB), at [64].

[88] *Barnes v Stones (a firm)* [2007] EWHC 90069 (Costs), *per* Master Simons (not binding).

[89] *Re Tweedie* [1909] WN 110; *Re Solicitors* (1934) 50 TLR 327.

[90] *Sanders v Isaacs* [1971] 1 WLR 240. See also *Kris Motor Spares Ltd v Fox Williams LLP* [2009] EWHC 2813 (QB), *per* Holroyde J.

[91] *Barclays plc v Villers* [2000] 1 All ER (Comm) 357, at 369.

circumstances in which the client was actively seeking an assessment, the fact of payment would rarely count against them;[92] indeed, payment under protest may be a factor in a client's favour.[93] Likewise, where the client is contractually obliged to make interim payments, the fact that payments were made without demur will not generally count against them for the purposes of considering special circumstances.[94]

- **Unpaid disbursements** The fact that disbursements may not have been paid at the time the bill was delivered has been held not to amount to a special circumstance.[95] Non-payment of counsel's fees by a solicitor agent has been held not to constitute special circumstances.[96]
- **Personal stress and associated health problems** In a case in which a client complained that the dispute with her solicitors had caused her considerable personal stress and (unspecified) health problems, Master Rogers found that no special circumstances had been made out (although he took into account the fact that the client was herself a solicitor, and that she had been given clear advice as to how and when to apply for an assessment).[97]
- **Sophisticated clients** The fact that the client is an experienced litigant acting on the advice of experienced solicitors may be relevant.[98]
- **Other bills subject to assessment** The fact that a client may be entitled to an assessment of a number of bills will not, in general, be a factor that will justify a finding of special circumstances in respect of other bills that the solicitor may have delivered.

It is worth noting that Master Rogers has commented that the court is often prepared to find special circumstances where, in the past, special circumstances would not have been found.[99] If this is correct, older cases, such as some of those set out above, should be approached with some caution. That said, it should not be forgotten that the circumstances must be *special*: the bar may be lower than it was in the past, but not so low as to allow the court free rein, because this would defeat the will of Parliament.[100] **36.37**

Appeals

An appellate court will not readily interfere with a decision as to special circumstances[101] (especially where the court at first instance was a specialist cost judge[102]), but successful appeals are not entirely unknown under the Civil Procedure Rules (CPR).[103] **36.38**

---

92 On a slightly different point, see *Re Simmons and Politzer* [1954] 2 All ER 811.

93 See *Bari v Rosen (t/a Rosen & Co Solicitors)* [2012] EWHC 1782 (QB), at [61].

94 See *ibid*, at [44], where the fact of payment was discussed, and at [60], where it was not referred to as being relevant to special circumstances.

95 *Re Massey* (1909) 101 LT 517.

96 *Re Nelson, Son and Hastings* (1885) 30 Ch D 1, CA.

97 *Sharif v The Law Society* [2005] EWHC 90018 (Costs).

98 *Ingrams v Sykes* (1987) 137 NLJ 1135.

99 Although not binding, see Master Rogers' comments in *Sharif v The Law Society* [2005] EWHC 90018 (Costs), at [23].

100 See, by way of analogy, *Stone Rowe Brewer LLP v Just Costs Ltd* [2015] EWCA Civ 1168, at [69], *per* Sales LJ.

101 See *Re Cheeseman* [1891] 2 Ch 289, CA.

102 *Falmouth House Freehold Co Ltd v Morgan Walker LLP* [2010] EWHC 3092 (Ch), at [13].

103 See, eg, *Kundrath v Henry Kwatia & Gooding* [2005] 2 Costs LR 279.

Procedural issues concerning assessments and related matters

Bringing the claim (or application)

36.39 The procedural details relating to claims for solicitor-and-client assessments are somewhat fragmented in that they are found in Practice Direction (PD) 46, para 6, CPR, r 67.3, and PD 67, paras 1–4. Further administrative requirements are set out in the Senior Court Costs Office (SCCO) Guide 2018.[104] The application for an assessment is made by the procedure under CPR, Part 8 (or, in existing proceedings, on application),[105] and must be made in the matter of the solicitor.[106]

36.40 Precedent J of the Schedule of Costs Precedents at the end of PD 47 is a model claim form.[107] The claim (or application) must[108] be accompanied by the bill and, where there is one, the conditional fee agreement under which the costs were incurred. If the original bill is not available, a copy will suffice,[109] but it ought to be certified by or on behalf of the applicants as being a true and complete copy.[110] Three copies of the claim form and order sought should be sent to the court.[111] Once the payment of the fee has been processed, then, in the SCCO, the application will be passed to the application clerk in Room 7.12 Thomas More Building, Royal Courts of Justice, who will put the file before a costs judge; the costs judge will then allocate a date for a directions hearing.[112] The court will send out the application to the parties unless, for example, the applicant requests permission to serve it.[113]

36.41 If the claim is uncontested (that is, if the parties agree that there should be an assessment), then there is no need to file evidence with the Part 8 claim.[114] Evidence will not always be needed even if the claim is contested, but if the client needs to show special circumstances, then evidence may be required.[115] Where the retainer is disputed[116] (see 36.42–36.45) or where it is said that there has been a compromise, then these aspects of the claim should ordinarily be pleaded (that is, pleaded in the claim itself as opposed to

---

104 See HMCTS, *Senior Court Costs Office Guide 2018* (London: HMSO, 2018), para 26.4. The applicant must send or bring the following items to the SCCO: (a) three copies of the claim form, with the draft order sought; (b) a cheque for the fee, made payable to HM Courts and Tribunals Service (HMCTS); and (c) the original bill(s) or copies of the original(s), certified by or on behalf of the applicants as being true and complete copies.

105 CPR, r 67.3(2); PD 46, para 6.4.

106 Solicitors Act 1974, s 72(1).

107 PD 46, para 6.4.

108 By analogy with other types of litigation, it is likely that a procedural error will not necessarily lead to the claim being struck out: see, eg, *Szekeres v Alan Smeath & Co* [2005] EWHC 1733 (Ch), in which Pumfrey J refused, in the absence of prejudice to the defendant, to dismiss a claim where the claim form contained a number of minor deficiencies.

109 PD 46, para 6.4.

110 Whilst not a source of law, see HMCTS, *Senior Court Costs Office Guide 2018* (London: HMSO, 2018), para 26.4(a)(iii).

111 See *ibid*, at para 26.4(a)(i).

112 *Ibid*, para 26.4(b).

113 *Ibid*, para 26.4(b), which goes on to say that: 'The application will usually be listed for a short appointment (15 minutes). If a second hearing is needed the matter will be adjourned to a new date with a longer time estimate.'

114 PD 67, para 4. See also HMCTS, *Senior Court Costs Office Guide 2018* (London: HMSO, 2018), para 26.4(c).

115 PD 67, para 2.2A.

116 See, eg, *Re Inderwick* (1884) LR 25 Ch D 279.

being held over for the points of dispute). The same is true where the client seeks more than only an assessment of costs.

Disputed retainers, business agreements and the interpretation of retainers Where the client disputes the existence of the retainer (as opposed to merely its terms), then they may wish to dispute the entirety of the bill. Where the application for an assessment has been made by the solicitor, then the client is at liberty to argue this point on the assessment itself (that is, the client is at liberty to plead this point for the first time in the points of dispute).[117] Where, however, the application has been made by the client, then there is authority—albeit pre-CPR authority—that, without a special order, the client is precluded from raising such an argument in that way.[118] It is entirely possible that, under the CPR, this is no longer good law, but, notwithstanding this, a client who disputes the retainer would be well advised to plead their case fully in the claim form, because this will allow the court either to address that issue at trial or to make a special order that the costs judge is entitled to address this issue on the detailed assessment. Where the issue is merely the interpretation of the contract of retainer, the costs judge has jurisdiction to determine that issue for the purposes of the detailed assessment,[119] but that jurisdiction is not an exclusive jurisdiction.[120] **36.42**

Whilst technically not a claim for an assessment, any claim challenging a contentious business agreement should be made by the Part 8 procedure (or, in existing proceedings, by application).[121] Where the claim is issued in the High Court in London, it *must* be issued in the SCCO,[122] unless it is a claim under Solicitors Act 1974, s 63, in which case it *may* be issued in the SCCO.[123] Where the agreement relates to business done in the County Court and its hearing centres—or where no business has been done in any court with jurisdiction to enforce and set aside agreements, and the amount payable under the agreement is less than £50—the appropriate court in which to bring the claim is the County Court; in all other circumstances, the appropriate court is the High Court.[124] Where a claim is made in the High Court in London, it must be issued in the SCCO;[125] if made outside of London, it may be transferred to the SCCO.[126] **36.43**

---

[117] Whilst now rather old, see *Re Jones* (1887) 36 Ch D 105; *Re Graham & Wigley* (1908) 52 SJ 684; *Re Wingfield & Blew* (1904) 2 Ch 665, at 675.
[118] *Re Herbert* (1887) 34 Ch D 504; *Re Frape* [1894] 2 Ch 290.
[119] See, eg, *Re Hirst & Capes* [1908] AC 416.
[120] *Mosley v Kitson* (1912) 57 SJ 12.
[121] CPR, r 67.3(2).
[122] See PD 67, para 2.1, which refers to PD 67, paras 1(1)–(5). The circumstances in which the claim must be issued in the SCCO are where any of the following claims are brought: (a) an application under Solicitors Act 1974, s 57(5), for a costs officer to enquire into the facts and certify whether a non-contentious business agreement should be set aside or the amount payable under it reduced; (b) a claim under Solicitors Act 1974, s 61(1), for the court to enforce or set aside a contentious business agreement and determine questions as to its validity and effect; (c) a claim by a client under Solicitors Act 1974, s 61(3), for a costs officer to examine a contentious business agreement as to its fairness and reasonableness; (d) where the amount agreed under a contentious business agreement has been paid, a claim under Solicitors Act 1974, s 61(5), for the agreement to be reopened and the costs assessed; and (e) proceedings under Solicitors Act 1974, s 62, for the examination of a contentious business agreement, where the client makes the agreement as a representative of a person whose property will be chargeable with the amount payable.
[123] See PD 67, para 2.1, which refers to PD 67, para 1(6).
[124] See Solicitors Act 1974, s 61(6).
[125] See PD 67, para 2.1(1), which refers to PD 67, para 1(2) and (3).
[126] See PD 67, para 2.2.

36.44 If a claim is issued in the County Court where Solicitors Act 1974, s 61(6) provides that it ought to have been brought in the High Court, the County Court will lack the power to deal with the issue (although it would have the power to transfer the matter to the SCCO).[127]

36.45 Where the client has been acting in a representative capacity and where they must seek the court's approval of the agreement, the procedure for laying the agreement before the court is the Part 8 procedure (or, in existing proceedings, by application).[128] Where the claim is issued in the High Court in London, it must be issued in the SCCO.[129]

36.46 **Formalities and applications by informal means** Although an application for an assessment should normally be made formally, there is authority to suggest that it is possible for it to be made informally (for example by letter).[130] It must amount to an actual application, however;[131] the mere reference to the fact that an application will be made would not be sufficient.[132] There used to be a requirement that where a claim for an assessment was made by a solicitor, that solicitor had to provide a certificate of compliance with the Solicitors Act 1974.[133] This requirement no longer exists under the CPR, but it would be sensible to confirm compliance in the pleadings.

36.47 **Venue** The claim (or application) for an assessment must be made in the High Court unless the costs relate to contentious business done in the County Court *and* the amount to be assessed is within the financial limit specified in Solicitors Act 1974, s 69(3) (£5,000 at time of writing).[134] If those are the circumstances, then the assessment may (but not must[135]) proceed in the County Court.[136] Up to 22 April 2014, the claim had to be made in the same county court in which the business had been carried out,[137] but following the creation of the single County Court,[138] this rule no longer applies (although see 36.50).

---

127 County Courts Act 1984, s 42. See also *R (on the application of Srinivasans Solicitors) v Croydon County Court* [2011] EWHC 3615 (Admin). This case was subject to appeal ([2013] EWCA Civ 249), but on a different point.

128 CPR, r 67.3(2); PD 67, para 2.1, which refers to PD 67, para 1(5).

129 PD 67, para 2.1(1).

130 *Connollys (a firm) v Harrington* [2002] All ER (D) 268 (May), *per* Judge Chapman (sitting as a judge of the High Court). That said, see *Solicitors Indemnity Fund Ltd v Hewitson & Harker* [2010] EWCA Civ 147, at [12].

131 *Solicitors Indemnity Fund Ltd v Hewitson & Harker* [2010] EWCA Civ 147, at [12].

132 *Truex v Toll* [2009] EWHC 369 (Ch), at [42].

133 RSC, Ord 106, r 5A.

134 See Solicitors Act 1974, s 69(3), as amended by the High Court and County Courts Jurisdiction Order 1991 (SI 1991/724), art 2(7) and (8) and Sch, Pt 1.

135 CPR, r 67.3(3)(c)(ii).

136 See CPR, r 67.3(1)(a).

137 See the old CPR, r 67.3(1)(a)(ii). To the extent that it continues to apply, the fact that a solicitor may have made an application in a particular County Court hearing centre for a charging order under County Courts Act 1984, s 73, does not mean that the claim for the assessment must subsequently be issued in that centre: *Jones v Twinsectra Ltd* [2002] EWCA Civ 668.

138 See by the Crime and Courts Act 2013, s 17; Crime and Courts Act 2013 (Commencement No 10 and Transitional Provisions) Order 2014 (SI 2014/954).

There is a requirement that claims for assessments based in the High Court in London[139] are to be issued in the SCCO.[140] Claims based outside London may be issued there if the claimant believes that doing so would be appropriate[141] (which would often be the case, given the specialist nature of solicitor-and-client assessments). Similarly, an application made in existing High Court proceedings may be referred to the SCCO.[142] In any event, an application made in the 'wrong' court can, in theory, be struck out; in practice, it is likely to be transferred.[143] **36.48**

Where the client wishes to challenge a contentious business agreement, the points regarding venue that are set out at 36.43–36.45 will apply. **36.49**

It may be that the proceedings begin when a solicitor brings an action for their costs. Where the claim relates to contentious business done in the County Court and its hearing centres, and where it is within the financial limit of that court's jurisdiction as specified in Solicitors Act 1974, s 69(3) (£5,000 at time of writing),[144] the claim may be made in the County Court. Where the claim cannot be made in the County Court, it *must* be made in the High Court.[145] It used to be the case that the claim had to be brought in the same county court in which the business was done,[146] but it is arguable that this is no longer the case now that there is a single County Court served by County Court hearing centres. That said, in view of the fact that the power of any district judge who hears the matter would be limited to proceedings in the district registry of which they are the district judge or proceedings in the County Court hearing centre within the district of that district registry,[147] it would usually be best to bring proceedings in the same centre. **36.50**

The order for an assessment

Model forms of order that the court may make are set out in the Schedule of Costs Precedents.[148] They comprise Precedent K (an order for delivery of a bill), Precedent L (an order for an assessment at the client's request) and Precedent M (an order for an assessment at the solicitor's request). It is common practice for a timetable to be incorporated into the order, dealing with service of a breakdown of the bill, service of points of dispute, any reply and the request for a hearing date.[149] Where the claim is brought by the solicitor in a case in which the only dispute between the parties is the amount payable, the court may order that judgment be entered for the amount assessed. Whilst, **36.51**

139 This will be the case where the appropriate office is any of the following County Court hearing centres: Barnet; Bow; Brentford; Bromley; Central London; Clerkenwell and Shoreditch; Croydon; Edmonton; Ilford; Kingston; Lambeth; Mayors and City of London; Romford; Uxbridge; Wandsworth; West London; Willesden; Woolwich. See PD 47, para 4.2.

140 See PD 67, paras 2.1 and 4.2.

141 PD 67, para 2.1.

142 PD 67, para 2.2.

143 See County Courts Act 1984, s 42.

144 That limit was last amended in 1991: see the High Court and County Courts Jurisdiction Order 1991 (SI 1991/724), art 2(7) and (8), and Sch, Pt I.

145 CPR, r 67.3(1)(b).

146 CPR, r 67.3(1)(a); Solicitors Act 1974 (as amended), s 68(2).

147 See CPR, r 67.3(3)(c).

148 See PD 46, para 6.5. The Schedule can be found at the end of PD 47.

149 See HMCTS, *Senior Court Costs Office Guide 2018* (London: HMSO, 2018), para 26.5(c). A specimen order is included in the Appendix to the Guide.

historically, this has been referred to as a '*Smith v Edwardes* order',[150] it is now something that is expressly provided for by statute:

> 'The certificate of the costs officer by whom any bill has been assessed shall, unless it is set aside or altered by the court, be final as to the amount of the costs covered by it, and the court may make such order in relation to the certificate as it thinks fit, including, in a case where the retainer is not disputed, an order that judgment be entered for the sum certified to be due with costs.'[151]

Such orders are still encountered, but they are not strictly necessary, because, from 1986 onwards, costs officers (that is, any judge carrying out the assessment) have had the power to enter judgment.[152]

The hearing of an application for an assessment

36.52 Where an application is made by a litigant in person, an order for detailed assessment will not ordinarily be made in the absence of the parties, because the litigant in person is usually required to attend so that the costs judge can explain the 'one-fifth rule'.[153] If no one attends on behalf of the respondent, the costs judge may make the order sought conditional upon adequate proof of service of the application.[154] Where the application is allowed, the costs of the application will usually be treated as being part of the costs of the detailed assessment.[155] Procedural points relating to detailed assessment hearings are addressed at 36.96–36.112.

Orders that the detailed assessment be stayed

36.53 In a case in which a client had repeatedly failed to articulate its case properly such that it had already left the 'last-chance saloon', Teare J found that it was open to the court to stay the detailed assessment proceedings indefinitely, even if this effectively brought an end to the assessment.[156] This was a case in which the solicitor had already been paid, but it is unlikely that anything turns on that. Teare J went on to find that such a stay did not amount to a breach of Art 6 ECHR.[157]

The scope of the assessment

36.54 Usually, an assessment will be in respect of the whole of the bill, but Solicitors Act 1974, s 70(5) and (6), empower the court to restrict the ambit of the assessment:

> '(5) An order for the assessment of a bill made on an application under this section by the party chargeable with the bill shall, if he so requests, be an order for the assessment of the profit costs covered by the bill.

[150] In *Smith v Edwardes* (1888) 22 QBD 103, the Court of Appeal stated that such an order should, as a matter of good practice, preserve the right of the parties to take the benefit of the one-fifth rule. This is not the modern approach: judgments for solicitors' costs to be assessed do not generally incorporate such a provision and, in *Ahmud & Co v MacPherson* [2015] EWHC 2240 (QB), Males J took the view that the solicitor, having obtained judgment for costs to be assessed, was in a similar position to a party with judgment for damages to be assessed and awarded the costs of assessment accordingly.

[151] See Solicitors Act 1974, s 72(4).

[152] This was not always the case. Prior to 1986, taxing masters were not part of the court, as defined in RSC, Ord 1, r 4(1) and (2). In practice, the court will normally issue a final costs certificate in accordance with PD 46, para 6.19.

[153] Whilst not a source of law, see HMCTS, *Senior Court Costs Office Guide 2018* (London: HMSO, 2018), para 26.5(a).

[154] See *ibid*, para 26.5(b).

[155] See *ibid*, para 26.5(d).

[156] *Mount Eden Land Ltd v Speechly Bircham LLP* [2014] EWHC 169 (QB), at [17] and [18].

[157] *Ibid*, at [19].

(6) Subject to subsection (5), the court may under this section order the assessment of all the costs, or of the profit costs, or of the costs other than profit costs and, where part of the costs is not to be assessed, may allow an action to be commenced or to be continued for that part of the costs.'

Thus the party chargeable is at liberty to elect to limit the assessment to profit costs only and, subject to this right, the court has a discretionary power to order that all of the costs, or the profit costs, or the costs other than profit costs be assessed. Where only part of the costs are to be assessed, the court can order that any claim in respect of the undisputed part may be commenced or continue.

The significance of the facility to limit the assessment to only a part of the bill is that only that part will be subject to the one-fifth rule (see 36.58).[158] The effect of this can have a dramatic bearing on the risks of an adverse costs order being made at the conclusion of the assessment and can make the difference between an assessment being economically viable or not. The following example illustrates this: if the costs to be assessed are £10,000, and if this comprises undisputed counsel's fees of £8,001 and disputed profit costs of £1,999, it will be impossible for the party chargeable to satisfy the one-fifth rule. By obtaining an order that only the profit costs are assessed, a chance of satisfying the one-fifth rule is restored. **36.55**

'Bills' rendered by persons other than solicitors or authorised persons

Only bills that have been rendered by a person who is either a solicitor recognised under the Solicitors Act 1974 or a recognised body under the Administration of Justice Act 1985 are capable of assessment under the 1974 Act. If a person who does not fall into one of these categories has rendered the putative 'bill', the assessment or application will be struck out for want of jurisdiction.[159] **36.56**

The costs of the assessment

In so far as it is relevant to the costs of the assessment, Solicitors Act 1974, s 70, provides: **36.57**

'(7) Every order for the assessment of a bill shall require the costs officer to assess not only the bill but also the costs of the assessment and to certify what is due to or by the solicitor in respect of the bill and in respect of the costs of the assessment.

[...]

(9) Unless—

(a) the order for assessment was made on the application of the solicitor and the party chargeable does not attend the assessment, or

(b) the order for assessment or an order under subsection (10) otherwise provides,

the costs of an assessment shall be paid according to the event of the assessment, that is to say, if the amount of the bill is reduced by one fifth, the solicitor shall pay the costs, but otherwise the party chargeable shall pay the costs.

(10) The costs officer may certify to the court any special circumstances relating to a bill or to the assessment of a bill, and the court may make such order as respects the costs of the assessment as it may think fit.

[...]

158 See Solicitors Act 1974, s 70(12), which expressly states that the one-fifth rule will relate only to the costs being assessed.

159 See *Assaubayev v Michael Wilson & Partners Ltd* [2014] EWHC 821 (QB), at [169]–[183], *per* Walker J.

(12) In this section "profit costs" means costs other than counsel's fees or costs paid or payable in the discharge of a liability incurred by the solicitor on behalf of the party chargeable, and the reference in subsection (9) to the fraction of the amount of the reduction in the bill shall be taken, where the assessment concerns only part of the costs covered by the bill, as a reference to that fraction of the amount of those costs which is being assessed.'

36.58 At the heart of these provisions is the 'one-fifth rule', which, in effect, provides that where the amount of the bill is reduced by a fifth, the solicitor pays the costs of the assessment; otherwise, the party chargeable pays the costs. Sales LJ had this to say on the topic:

> 'Section 70(9) provides for a basic and simple default rule that the costs of the assessment should follow the event (i.e. be paid by the losing to the winning party), where the "event" (i.e. the criterion of who has won and who has lost) is defined by reference to whether a reduction in the amount of the bill of one fifth has been achieved by the client in the assessment.'[160]

This is subject to the court finding special circumstances, in which case the court may make some different order (see 36.68–36.76).

One-fifth rule

36.59 A number of points can be made about the measure of the one-fifth rule, relating to:

- the rationale for the one-fifth rule (see 36.60–36.61);
- disbursements and the one-fifth rule (see 36.62);
- discounted bills and the one-fifth rule (see 36.63);
- gross sum bills and the one-fifth rule (see 36.64);
- more than one bill and the one-fifth rule (see 36.65);
- excluded items and the one-fifth rule (see 36.66–36.67);
- more than one solicitor's costs and the one-fifth rule (see 36.68);
- costs already assessed and paid and the one-fifth rule (see 36.69); and
- value added tax (VAT) and the one-fifth rule (see 36.70).

36.60 **The rationale for the one-fifth rule** Sales LJ has explained the rationale for the one-fifth rule as follows:

> 'Disputes between solicitors and clients regarding the amount of solicitors' bills can be substantial, and the costs of resolving them can likewise be substantial. ... Both client and solicitor benefit from knowing in advance what the basic default rule is governing the costs of an assessment, and what ordinarily counts as winning and losing, so that they can make a rational calculation of the risks involved in proceeding with a disputed assessment before a costs judge. The costs of conducting underlying legal proceedings may already be considerable, and it is in the interests of the parties and the court that the parties have a reasonable idea of where they stand before they incur yet more costs in arguing about those costs and that arguments about the incidence of the costs of arguing about costs should be kept within reasonable parameters in an effort to prevent them becoming disproportionate. In this context, reasonable protection for the expectations of the parties formed on the basis of the default rule is important.'[161]

36.61 There are those who would dispute whether this theory translates into practical benefits. In particular, many costs practitioners would point out that the one-fifth rule makes it difficult

[160] *Wilsons Solicitors LLP v Bentine* [2015] EWCA Civ 1168, at [5].
[161] *Ibid*, at [7].

for parties to gauge the likely influence of any offers that may have been made and that, as such, it actually leads to increased uncertainty. Others would point to the fact that the costs of solicitor-and-client assessments are, in general, not only high, but notoriously high—often because each side is desperately trying to get over the line. Indeed, expert commentators have questioned the need for a statutory one-fifth rule where rules of court are easily capable of creating a more flexible and fair system of dealing with the costs of assessment.[162] Be that as it may, there is no likelihood of the one-fifth rule being replaced in the foreseeable future.

Disbursements and the one-fifth rule Other than where the scope of the assessment has been restricted to exclude such monies, the one-fifth rule will be applied to the costs inclusive of disbursements.[163] **36.62**

Discounted bills and the one-fifth rule If a bill has been discounted after delivery, it is the undiscounted figure that is used for the purposes of applying the one-fifth rule.[164] The rationale behind this rule was explained by Baggallay LJ: **36.63**

> 'I think it would be exceedingly pernicious to lay down a rule which would enable a solicitor whose bill exceeded what could be allowed on taxation, to oblige his client, by a device of this kind [ie a discount], to have his bill taxed at a greater risk as to costs than if a bill had been delivered for the amount which the solicitor had stated his willingness to accept.'[165]

However, the fact that the solicitor was prepared to give a discount may be relevant as giving rise to special circumstances.[166]

Gross sum bills and the one-fifth rule In the same vein, where a gross sum bill is being assessed with the benefit of a detailed breakdown, it is the gross sum bill (and the reductions thereto) that is relevant for the purposes of applying the one-fifth rule, not the detailed breakdown.[167] **36.64**

Multiple bills and the one-fifth rule Where a number of bills have been delivered under the same contract of retainer, but only some of which are the subject of assessment, only the costs in those that are being assessed will be taken into account for the purposes of applying the one-fifth rule. If there are, for example, two orders for the assessment of two separate bills, the one-fifth rule will be applied separately to each bill as assessed.[168] Whilst her decision was reversed on appeal on a different point, Andrews J has explained that where there is one order for assessment of a number of bills, the approach is different: **36.65**

> 'Thus if there is only one action and one order for assessment, then even though that order may provide for the assessment of more than one bill, for the purposes of the one-fifth rule, the costs judge will add up the total of the amounts of the fees that he has awarded, and the total of how much was claimed under all of the bills, and will then compare those two figures to see if the client has reduced the overall amount by more than one-fifth. That is the normal practice, and that is how it should be done.'[169]

---

162 See, eg, Heining, M, 'Out of Date?' (2014) 164(7593) NLJ 9.

163 *Re Haigh* (1849) 12 Beav 307.

164 *In re Carthew, In re Paull* (1884) 27 Ch D 485; see also *Re Mackenzie* (1894) 69 LT 751.

165 *In re Carthew, In re Paull* (1884) 27 Ch D 485, at 494.

166 *In re Paull* (1884) 27 Ch D 485, although, in that case, the court did not depart from the rule that costs should follow the assessment.

167 See *obiter* comments in *Re Mackenzie* (1894) 69 LT 751.

168 *Devereux v White & Co* (1896) 13 TLR 52.

169 *Stone Rowe Brewer LLP v Just Costs Ltd* [2014] EWHC 219 (QB), at [23] and [24].

Thus it is the aggregate that is measured, not the amounts claimed in each individual bill. For the reasons set out at 36.72–36.76, however, the court is able to descend more into the detail for the purposes of dealing with special circumstances.

36.66 **Items excluded for want of retainer and the one-fifth rule** Where items are disallowed because the business to which they related fell beyond the ambit of any retainer, those items are not to be disregarded for the purpose of applying the one-fifth rule.[170] In particular, Sales LJ has made it clear that 'there is no good reason to divide up different elements within the bill for the purposes of application of the one fifth rule'.[171] As is explained in 36.76, it used to be the case that costs that were disallowed for want of an applicable retainer were disregarded for the purposes of the one-fifth rule. Sir Bernard Rix has explained that one of the reasons why this is no longer the correct approach is because the wording of the relevant legislation has changed from referring to that which was 'taxed off' to referring to that which was 'reduced'.[172]

36.67 **Cash accounts** For the avoidance of doubt, items in the cash account are excluded.[173]

36.68 **More than one solicitor's costs and the one-fifth rule** Where a solicitor includes another solicitor's costs in their own bill, it will be the combined total that will be relevant for the purposes of applying the one-fifth rule. This will be so even if the principal solicitor's own costs are reduced by less than one-fifth.[174]

36.69 **Costs already assessed and paid and the one-fifth rule** Costs are not excluded from the one-fifth rule merely by virtue of them having been already assessed[175] and paid.[176] Where the monies in question are actual disbursements (see 52.04), then even where the client has themselves paid those monies (such as where the client has sent a cheque directly to counsel), those monies must appear in the bill. Put otherwise, the payment must, where appropriate, be entered as credit in the cash account rather than regarded as being expunged from the bill.[177]

36.70 **VAT and the one-fifth rule** Whilst there is no binding authority on the point, VAT is generally excluded as being something beyond the solicitor's control.[178]

Special circumstances and the costs of the assessment

36.71 Where special circumstances are made out, the court has:

> '... a general power to vary the ordinary statutory rule [ie the one-fifth rule], and where it is inequitable in the special circumstances certified that the statutory rule should be

---

170 See *Wilsons Solicitors LLP v Bentine* [2015] EWCA Civ 1168, at [21], *per* Sales LJ, overruling *Re Taxation of Costs; Re a Solicitor* [1936] 1 KB 523 and *White v Milner* (1794) 2 H Bl 357—and, by extension, *Mills v Revett* (1834) 1 A&E 856: see *Wilsons Solicitors LLP v Bentine* [2015] EWCA Civ 1168, [22]–[36]. Sales LJ pointed out that *In re Clark* (1851) 13 Beavan 173, aff'd on appeal ((1851) 1 De Gex M & G 43) had overruled *White v Milner* (1794) 2 H Bl 357, yet had not been drawn to the attention of the court in *Re Taxation of Costs; Re a Solicitor* [1936] 1 KB 523: see *Wilsons Solicitors LLP v Bentine* [2015] EWCA Civ 1168, at [37]–[41].

171 *Wilsons Solicitors LLP v Bentine* [2015] EWCA Civ 1168, at [21].

172 *Ibid*, at [75] and [76].

173 *Re Haigh* (1849) 12 Beav 307.

174 *In re Fletcher and Dyson* [1903] 2 Ch 688.

175 This may happen where, for example, an assessment has been carried out on behalf of the client, but then a further assessment is carried out for a person making an application under Solicitors Act 1974, s 71.

176 *Re Osborn and Osborn* [1913] 3 KB 862.

177 *Ibid*, at 869; *Re Richards* [1912] 1 Ch 49, at 53.

178 This is the view expressed by the editors of The White Book.

applied, the Court should exercise its discretion in favour of the solicitor or the client as the case may be.'[179]

The reference to special circumstances being 'certified' is an anachronism[180] that has nothing to do with costs certificates of the type mentioned in 36.113.

The Solicitors Act 1974 gives no guidance as to what may constitute 'special circumstances'. After having explained that 'special' does not mean 'exceptional',[181] Sales LJ had this to say: **36.72**

'It is better not to gloss the language used in section 70(10), albeit one should bear in mind when applying that provision that one is looking for something significant and out of the ordinary course which justifies departing from the prima facie one fifth rule set by Parliament.'[182]

Sales LJ went on to say that the process of determining whether there were special circumstances was 'the sort of value judgment ... which a costs judge ... is well-placed to make', and that, when deciding whether special circumstances existed, there was no reason in principle why the court should not have regard to the way in which particular issues arose in the proceedings and the outcome achieved in relation to them.[183] **36.73**

Arden LJ had this to say on the way in which the court should approach s 70(10) of the Solicitors Act 1974: **36.74**

'My approach to section 70(10) is as follows. I accept that the statutory policy expressed in section 70(9) is not necessarily made irrelevant by a finding that there are special circumstances under section 70(10). It may be that, in deciding what order to make under section 70(10), the court will consider it appropriate to take into account the fact that Parliament intended that claimants under section 70 should have some protection. But, I do not consider that it has to be given weight in every case where there are special circumstances. The wide words used by Parliament in section 70(10) make it clear that the court may, dependent on the circumstances, decide to give the section 70(9) outcome no substantial weight. It is, as I see it, a factor to which the costs judge may give weight according to the circumstances of the case. This is so even though bills of costs would normally be aggregated for the purpose of ascertaining who was the winner under section 70(9). The simple fact is that that provision is not a requirement under section 70(10). The weight to be given under section 70(10) to who is the statutory winner under section 70(9) is a matter for the discretion of the Master or costs judge, and this Court should not interfere unless the result is perverse or the Master or costs judge has misdirected himself on a matter of law.'[184]

---

179 *In re Davies* [1912] 1 Ch 49, at 54, *per* Parker J.

180 Prior to 1986, taxing masters used to certify matters to be sent back to the High Court for further consideration. This now almost never happens. As Sales LJ explained, in *Wilsons Solicitors LLP v Bentine* [2015] EWCA Civ 1168, at [6]: '[T]he costs judge conducting an assessment simply identifies any relevant special circumstances in the course of his ruling on the assessment and makes the appropriate order. This is a sensible way of proceeding, but care needs to be taken to ensure that the relevant "special circumstances" are properly identified in the ruling, if no formal certificate is to be drawn up.'

181 And, in doing so, citing *Riley v Dibb Lupton Alsop* (1997) 147 LJ 1422.

182 *Stone Rowe Brewer LLP v Just Costs Ltd* [2015] EWCA Civ 1168, at [69]. It should be noted that this formulation appears to be in conflict with previous cases, such as a case in which Sedley J found that 'special' does not mean 'exceptional': see *Riley v Dibb Lupton Alsop*, sub nom *A v BCD (a firm)* (1997) 147 NLJ 1422.

183 *Stone Rowe Brewer LLP v Just Costs Ltd* [2015] EWCA Civ 1168, at [70].

184 *Ibid*, at [114].

36.75 It is worth bearing in mind that Sir Bernard Rix cautioned against an overly mathematical approach to dealing with issues.[185] On the facts of the case before them, neither Arden LJ nor Sales LJ agreed with him, but it would be possible to envisage circumstances in which such an approach would be inappropriate.

36.76 **Miscellaneous points** The following miscellaneous points may be made about special circumstances relating to the costs of assessment.

- **Properly made offers** If an offer has been made at what Parker J called the 'proper time' (which, in the modern day, would be likely to mean reasonably early) and if the offeror secures an award that is more advantageous to them than was their own offer, that offer would be capable of amounting to special circumstances.[186] As to offers made under CPR, Part 36, see 36.77.
- **Inopportune offers** Where an offer is made that is not made at the proper time or where it is unclear, that may negate the effect of that offer. By way of example, an offer that does not state the costs consequences of its acceptance may be given less weight as a result.[187]
- **Items claimed in error** Where disbursements have been claimed in the bill in error, but in such a way as to mislead no one, the fact that the one-fifth rule would have been satisfied had the error not been made may amount to special circumstances.[188]
- **Poor conduct** A failure to engage in mediation or to attempt to negotiate is capable of giving rise to special circumstances.[189] Taking 'tortuous' points of law that went nowhere may also amount to special circumstances.[190]
- **Reductions made for want of retainer** It used to be the case that if a dispute between the parties was about whether the costs fell within the ambit of the retainer, any costs that were disallowed as a result were not be taken into account for the purposes of the one-fifth rule.[191] The rationale for this was (as Lord Eldon put it) that 'you [the client] shall not come here and say, the Master has taken off more than a one-[fifth], when you yourself state not that he has taken it off, but that you have taken it off'.[192] The effect of this was that a client could win hands down, but still fail to satisfy the one-fifth rule. For the reasons set out at 36.66, it is now known that this approach was wrong in law. That said, Sales LJ has explained that, when deciding whether special circumstances existed, there was no reason in principle why the court should not have had regard to the way in which particular issues arose in the proceedings and the outcome achieved in relation to them.[193] Indeed, this is precisely what happened at first instance (a decision that Sales LJ restored).

---

185 *Ibid*, at [85].

186 *Angel Airlines (a Romanian company in liquidation) v Dean & Dean* [2008] EWHC 1513 (QB).

187 Whilst not dealing with the one-fifth rule, see *Tramountana Armadora SA v Atlantic Shipping Co SA, The Vorros* [1978] 2 All ER 870 (Comm).

188 *In re Richards* [1912] 1 Ch 49.

189 *Allen v Colman Coyle LLP* [2007] EWHC 90075 (Costs), *per* Master Simons.

190 See *Bentine v The Official Solicitor and Wilsons Solicitors LLP* [2013] EWHC 3098 (Ch), at [60], revd on appeal ([2015] EWCA Civ 1168), but on a different point.

191 See *Re Taxation of Costs* [1936] 1 KB 523, at 531, *per* Lord Eldon; *Bentine v The Official Solicitor and Wilsons Solicitors LLP* [2013] EWHC 3098 (Ch), at [38], *per* Proudman J.

192 See *Re Taxation of Costs* [1936] 1 KB 523, at 531.

193 *Stone Rowe Brewer LLP v Just Costs Ltd* [2015] EWCA Civ 1168, at [70].

- **Putative lack of information** In a case in which a litigant in person had been sent a gross sum bill, Morris J found, on the facts of the case before him, that the lack of information was a factor that the costs judge should have taken into account—and all the more so given the fact that no detailed breakdown was provided for a period of more than six months after one was requested.[194]
- **Small cases in which the client is a litigant in person** Morris J had this to say about the suggestion that a litigant in person should be treated identically to other litigants for the purposes of s 70(10) of the Solicitors Act 1974: 'I take account of the fact that requiring the taking of legal advice is not necessarily realistic in cases where small amounts of costs are in issue, such as in this case.'[195] It was said that, instead of applying for a detailed assessment, the litigant in person ought to have made an application under s 64(2) of the Solicitors Act 1974. Morris J disagreed. He said that a litigant in person could not have known this, that the court did not mention this during the mandatory hearing referred to at 36.52, and that the SCCO Guide made no mention of it. These were all factors that were capable of contributing towards the existence of special circumstances.

Part 36 and solicitor-and-client assessments

It is not clear whether a party to a solicitor-and-client assessment is able to make a Part 36 offer in such a way as to obtain the benefit of CPR, Part 36, Section I, as opposed to it being an offer that may amount to 'special circumstances' (see 36.76). Whilst no more than his own view, the editor doubts that a Part 36 offer would have the consequences of that Section (unless, perhaps, it were to be accepted). This is because s 70 of the Solicitors Act 1974 provides its own checks and balances, and it is, in many ways, a self-contained code; one could easily argue that it would subvert the intention of Parliament, as expressed in s 70, to add an adjectival gloss that either diluted or bolstered the one-fifth rule. In any event, there would be practical problems with applying CPR, Part 36: who, for example, would be regarded as the claimant? Would it be the solicitor (who claims the costs) or the client (who claims a reduction in those costs)? If the client were the claimant, then how would the court calculate the 'additional amount'? Moreover, one could argue that if CPR, Part 36, were to have a role to play in solicitor-and-client assessment under s 70 of the Solicitors Act 1974, this would be expressly set out in CPR, r 46.9, in much the same way as it is set out in CPR, r 47.20(4). **36.77**

Non-attendance of one or more parties at the detailed assessment hearing

Solicitors Act 1974, s 70(8), specifically provides that if, after due notice of any assessment, either party fails to attend, the costs officer may proceed with the assessment notwithstanding the absence of the party or parties in question. Whilst the context was wholly different (namely, non-attendance following a debarring order in an assessment between opposing parties), Langley J has commented that it would never be appropriate merely to 'rubber-stamp' costs; rather, he found that an assessment must take place regardless of who attended to make submissions.[196] Where the assessment was made on the **36.78**

[194] *Parissis v Matthias Gentle Page Hassan Holdings LLP* [2017] EWHC 761 (QB), at [22] and [23].

[195] *Ibid*, at [24].

[196] *Days Healthcare UK Ltd v Pihsiang Machinery Manufacturing Co Ltd* [2006] EWHC 1444 (QB), at [30].

application of the solicitor and where the party chargeable fails to attend, the one-fifth rule would not apply.[197]

Assessments and Claims for Account on the Application of Third Parties

36.79 This section deals with the options available to a person who is liable to pay another person's costs.[198] Archetypally, this situation will arise where a mortgage stipulates that one party will pay the other party's costs, but there are many other circumstances in which a third-party liability may arise (see 36.92). The formal terminology—which is used in this part of this book—is that a person who has primary liability is the 'party chargeable' and a person who has secondary liability is the 'third party'.[199] The party chargeable is usually the client. The third party is able to step into the shoes of the party chargeable for the purposes of obtaining an assessment, but, for the reasons set out below, this would rarely be an appropriate step to take. This is because the court is severely restricted in what it can and cannot do in such an assessment (see 36.82). In view of this, the appropriate jurisdiction will depend on the nature of the dispute.

- **Where the dispute is about the reasonableness of the costs that the third party is to pay** Where the dispute is about how much the third party is to pay to the party chargeable in respect of the solicitors' fees, then, whilst it is theoretically open to the third party to do so, applying for an assessment under s 71(1) of the Solicitors Act 1974 would rarely be appropriate. This is because the court would, in general, be unable to reduce items on the grounds of reasonableness unless the points that were raised were precisely the same as could have been raised between the party chargeable and the solicitor. Where, as will almost always be the case, the third party wishes to object to the costs on grounds that go beyond the objections that could be raised by the party chargeable, the third party should bring a claim (usually a Part 8 claim in the Chancery Division or the County Court), either for an account or for a declaration as to what is payable as between the party chargeable and the third party.
- **Where the dispute is solely about whether the third party is liable in principle for the monies claimed** Whilst such circumstances will be rare, it may be that the dispute is limited to whether the third party is liable in principle for the monies claimed. Where this is so, then it may be appropriate to seek an assessment under s 71 of the Solicitors Act 1974, but only if the points that arise all fall within the very limited range of issues that the court is able to decide under that jurisdiction (see 36.82); in all other circumstances, it would be better to apply for an account or declaration (see above). Where it is appropriate to make an application under s 71, then the precise jurisdiction will depend on the following.

[197] See Solicitors Act 1974, s 70(9)(a).

[198] For the avoidance of doubt, this does not include persons who are ordered to pay costs as between opposing parties.

[199] The term 'third party' in this sense should not be confused with an 'entitled third party', as defined in Solicitors' (Non-contentious Business) Remuneration Order 2009 (SI 2009/1931), art 2. The two are entirely different.

- **Where the party chargeable is a trustee, executor or administrator** Where (a) the solicitor was instructed by a trustee, executor or administrator and (b) the third party has an interest in the monies out of which the solicitor is going to be paid or has been paid, then it is open to the third party to apply for an assessment under s 71(3) of the 1974 Act.
- **All other cases** Where those two conditions have not been met, then the application should be made under s 71(1).

It should be noted that, where the party chargeable has already paid the solicitor, the scope for arguing that costs were unreasonably incurred is so limited as to barely exist. As such, where the solicitors have already been paid, it would almost never be appropriate to apply for an assessment as opposed to an account (or declaration, as the case may be). **36.80**

Assessments under s 71 of the Solicitors Act 1974

The relevant law is set out in Solicitors Act 1974, s 71 (as amended): **36.81**

> '(1) Where a person other than the party chargeable with the bill for the purposes of section 70 has paid, or is or was liable to pay, a bill either to the solicitor or to the party chargeable with the bill, that person, or his executors, administrators or assignees may apply to the High Court for an order for the taxation of the bill as if he were the party chargeable with it, and the court may make the same order (if any) as it might have made if the application had been made by the party chargeable with the bill.
>
> (2) Where the court has no power to make an order by virtue of subsection (1) except in special circumstances it may, in considering whether there are special circumstances sufficient to justify the making of an order, take into account circumstances which affect the applicant but do not affect the party chargeable with the bill.
>
> (3) Where a trustee, executor or administrator has become liable to pay a bill of a solicitor, then, on the application of any person interested in any property out of which the trustee, executor or administrator has paid, or is entitled to pay, the bill, the court may order—
> (a) that the bill be taxed on such terms, if any, as it thinks fit; and
> (b) that such payments, in respect of the amount found to be due to or by the solicitor and in respect of the costs of the taxation, be made to or by the applicant, to or by the solicitor, or to or by the executor, administrator or trustee, as it thinks fit.
>
> (4) In considering any application under subsection (3) the court shall have regard—
> (a) to the provisions of section 70 as to applications by the party chargeable for the taxation of a solicitor's bill so far as they are capable of being applied to an application made under that subsection;
> (b) to the extent and nature of the interest of the applicant.
>
> (5) If an applicant under subsection (3) pays any money to the solicitor, he shall have the same right to be paid that money by the trustee, executor or administrator chargeable with the bill as the solicitor had.
>
> (6) Except in special circumstances, no order shall be made on an application under this section for the taxation of a bill which has already been taxed.
>
> (7) If the court on an application under this section orders a bill to be taxed, it may order the solicitor to deliver to the applicant a copy of the bill on payment of the costs of that copy.'[200]

[200] The points made previously about the amendments made by the Legal Services Act 2007 are repeated.

36.82 Despite the fact that the court has long since acknowledged that the intended purpose of s 71 of the Solicitors Act 1974 is to make it easier for third parties to obtain an assessment of the sums for which they are liable,[201] it has not been interpreted in a way that would give effect to that intended purpose. Indeed, s 71 is applied in such a way as to make it almost *in*operable for that purpose. This is because of the principle—which appears to be strictly applied—that a third party may bring in the objections that the party chargeable could bring in, but no more.[202] That principle expurgates s 71 of almost all utility, for the following reasons.

- The dispute is usually between the third party and the party chargeable. By the time the third party applies for an assessment, the party chargeable will almost always have approved the disputed monies (usually by paying them to the solicitor or by agreeing to pay them). Put otherwise, the disputed monies will usually be monies that the party chargeable believes are properly payable.
- CPR, r 46.9, will apply and, because the disputed monies will usually have been 'approved' by the party chargeable, the third party will be unable to argue that those costs were unreasonably incurred or are unreasonable in amount (see 37.06–37.07).
- The practical effect of this is that s 71 assessments are almost of no use to anyone, because where the costs have been approved (such as by being paid without reservation), the only bases upon which items may be disallowed[203] are:
  - where the disputed item relates to business for which the third party is not liable (such as where the item relates to a different claim or matter); and
  - where the disputed item would be allowable as against the party chargeable only on the basis of advice that it would not be recoverable against the third party, and therefore is to be treated as subject to a special arrangement between client and solicitor.[204]

36.83 Cozens-Hardy J has explained that, where the client has sanctioned the costs (either by paying them or by other means), it is not open to the third party to object to the amount claimed on the grounds that the payments sanctioned by the client are excessive.[205] Similarly, Lloyd LJ has found that, unless the same point could be made in an assessment brought under Solicitors Act 1974, s 70, it is not open to the court, on an assessment under s 71, to substitute a lower amount for a higher one on the basis that something is allowable, but that the amount claimed is unreasonably high.[206] He went on to say that, where the

---

201 See, eg, *Re Abbott* (1861) 4 LT 576, in which Romilly MR said that the predecessor to s 71 was introduced to shorten the remedy available to a third party.

202 See *Re Massey* (1865) 34 Beav 463, at 470, *per* Romilly MR; see also *Re Brown* (1867) LR 4 Eq 464. For a discussion of the history of this provision, see *Tim Martin Interiors Ltd v Akin Gump LLP* [2011] EWCA Civ 1574, at [32] *et seq* and [82] *et seq*, *per* Lloyd LJ.

203 *Tim Martin Interiors Ltd v Akin Gump LLP* [2011] EWCA Civ 1574, at [83], relying on *Re Gray* [1901] 1 Ch 239, at 246.

204 It has long been the case that a third party cannot be at risk of being liable to the party chargeable for a sum that is recoverable by the solicitor from the party chargeable only if the solicitor has advised the client that it would not be recoverable from the third party: see *Tim Martin Interiors Ltd v Akin Gump LLP* [2011] EWCA Civ 1574, at [74], *per* Lloyd LJ. See also *Re Cohen & Cohen* [1905] 2 Ch 137, CA.

205 *Re Gray* [1901] 1 Ch 239, at 246, cited with approval by Lloyd LJ in *Tim Martin Interiors Ltd v Akin Gump LLP* [2011] EWCA Civ 1574, at [77].

206 *Tim Martin Interiors Ltd v Akin Gump LLP* [2011] EWCA Civ 1574, at [82]. To the extent that *Re Longbotham & Sons* [1904] 2 Ch 152 can be read as saying otherwise, it is not a correct statement of the law: see Lloyd LJ's comments in *Tim Martin Interiors Ltd v Akin Gump LLP* [2011] EWCA Civ 1574, at [48] *et seq*.

party chargeable has agreed the bill and paid it, such an argument would not be open to the third party. After having reviewed an impressively wide range of authorities, Lloyd LJ had the following to say:

> 'I do not accept that either [the authorities] or the statute allow the court to alter the amount of an item in the bill in respect of which something is properly chargeable, but where the court considers that the amount claimed is excessive and unreasonable, so that a lower amount should be allowed, unless that could be done on an assessment under section 70, as between the solicitor and the client directly. I therefore agree with Lewison J [in the court below] who said:
>
> > "On an assessment under section 71 the court is entitled to interfere with the hourly rate agreed between the solicitor and the client; but only to the extent that it could have interfered with it at the behest of the client."
>
> 'He went on to point out that in a case where the client had agreed the rate there was very little scope for such interference, because of the presumption under CPR rule 48.8(2)(b) [now CPR, r 46.9(2)(b)].'[207]

Claims for account and declarations

Lloyd LJ has acknowledged that the above interpretation imposes a 'serious limitation' on the extent to which an assessment under s 71 of the Solicitors Act 1974 is able to resolve a dispute about how much a third party is required to pay.[208] He went on to explain that, rather than applying for an assessment, the better option would be to make a claim for an account. Lloyd LJ said that, in cases in which a claim for an account is not the right approach, it may be necessary to claim a declaration as to the amount properly due[209]—although this may not always be something that the third party can do because the issue of whether the court will deal with such a request will be fact-specific.[210] If the third party disputed the reasonableness of costs claimed, the court could order that the issue be determined by a costs judge.[211] As to procedure, Lloyd LJ had this to say: **36.84**

> 'Instead of seeking an assessment under section 71, therefore, in almost all cases a ... [third party] should bring a claim for an account of the sums due ... I doubt that such proceedings for an account nowadays would be much more complex than assessment proceedings. In practice the [third party] would issue a claim form, perhaps under Part 8, in the Chancery Division or, where appropriate, in the county court, and on the first hearing before the Master or District Judge he would apply for an order that the costs in dispute be referred for assessment, normally to the SCCO. From then on, the procedure would be as for an assessment under section 70, but with the right parties contesting it, namely the [third party and the party chargeable]. The costs judge will have the necessary expertise, and will be able to decide the dispute, on ordinary principles and processes of assessment,

---

207 See *Tim Martin Interiors Ltd v Akin Gump LLP* [2011] EWCA Civ 1574, at [84].

208 See *ibid*, at [84].

209 *Ibid*, at [101].

210 Lloyd LJ suggests, *ibid*, at [101], that an account in the case of a trust or the administration of an estate may be sought. That may be so, but in *Chopping v Cowan & Dewey* (unreported), 17 April 2013, Ch D, Master Marsh found that the beneficiary of an estate had no absolute right to an account; there must be a basis for such an order. Where full accounts have been provided, an order for an account must be based upon established breaches of trust, or at least a case made out for further factual inquiry, before expenditure incurred will be investigated in detail. For further consideration by the master of the circumstances in which it might be appropriate to order an account, see *Henchley & Ord v Thompson* [2017] EWHC 225 (Ch).

211 *Tim Martin Interiors Ltd v Akin Gump LLP* [2011] EWCA Civ 1574, at [25]–[27].

> in an economical and efficient manner. Once the assessment is complete, the result would be reported to the Master or District Judge, and the account would proceed on that basis. Somewhat more by way of steps in the proceedings would be necessary than for an ordinary assessment, but not a great deal. If there are other issues in dispute as well they can be dealt with in whatever is the appropriate way, by the Master or District Judge or, if necessary, by a judge.'[212]

Thus it is possible, in an appropriate case, to treat a claim for an account as if it were a claim for an assessment.

Who pays whom?

36.85 Where the third party claims an account (or a declaration), there will usually be no doubt as to who is to pay whom, because the dispute would be between the 'correct parties' (as Lloyd LJ described them[213]) and, as such, determining the amount payable by or to the third party is usually a straightforward affair. The same is not necessarily true if the third party seeks an assessment under s 71 of the Solicitors Act 1974. In this regard, the following points can be made.

- **Disallowed items** Where the court finds that the third party has no liability for an item of costs, such items are left out of the assessment altogether. This means that the solicitor remains entitled to pursue the party chargeable for those monies[214] and, as such, the solicitor will not be required to repay those monies to either the party chargeable or the third party.
- **The effect of obtaining an order for an assessment** Older authorities relating to the amount that the third party is to pay ought to be treated with some caution because, prior to 1986, third parties had to undertake to pay the amount assessed, that undertaking being a condition for getting an order for an assessment.[215] This meant that, in theory, a third party could be ordered to pay the solicitor more than they were liable to pay the party chargeable. That said, the court deployed a number of methods to ensure that this did not happen.[216] Nowadays, the court has more flexibility, because it is able to determine who pays whom at the end of the assessment, and Lloyd LJ has said that there is no reason to suppose that an s 71 assessment can increase the third party's liability for costs to the party chargeable.[217] In particular, the fact that they have obtained an order determining what is payable as between party chargeable and solicitor will not in itself mean that the third party is required to pay those monies.[218]
- **Overpayments and refunds** Where the third party has already paid the party chargeable, who, in turn, has paid the solicitor, and where the court finds that the party chargeable is liable for the whole of those monies, but the third party is not, then the

---

[212] *Ibid*, at [100].

[213] See *ibid*, at [98].

[214] *Ibid*, at [95] *et seq*, *per* Lloyd LJ.

[215] See *Re Fyson* (1846) 9 Beav 117, at 119, *per* Lord Langdale MR, discussed in detail in *Tim Martin Interiors Ltd v Akin Gump LLP* [2011] EWCA Civ 1574, at [35]–[37].

[216] See, eg, *Re Negus* [1895] 1 Ch 73; *Re Gray* [1901] 1 Ch 239, at 245–6 and 248. See also *Re Denne & Secretary of State for War* (1884) 51 LT 657.

[217] *Tim Martin Interiors Ltd v Akin Gump LLP* [2011] EWCA Civ 1574, at [85], *per* Lloyd LJ.

[218] See *Re Fyson* (1846) 9 Beav 117, at 119, *per* Lord Langdale MR, discussed in detail in *Tim Martin Interiors Ltd v Akin Gump LLP* [2011] EWCA Civ 1574, at [32]–[45].

court should not order the solicitor to refund monies to the third party; instead, the court should leave the third party to pursue an account as against the party chargeable.[219] Put otherwise, the liability to repay lies with the party chargeable, not with the solicitor.

The difference between applications made under Solicitors Act 1974, s 71(1) and (3)

There is a distinction to be drawn between an application made pursuant to Solicitors Act 1974, s 71(1), and an application made pursuant to s 71(3). Applications made under s 71(1) are made by persons who are 'as if he were the party chargeable' (that is, the applicant steps into the shoes of the party chargeable). Section 71(2) provides that, in so far as there is a need to consider special circumstances, the court can take into account factors that affect the applicant, but do not affect the party chargeable. Section 71(1) gives the court the same powers in the case of an applicant as the court would have had if the application had been made by the person chargeable under s 70. These powers would be limited, where appropriate, by the absolute bar on ordering an assessment of any bills that had been paid for more than 12 months.[220] **36.86**

The same is not true, however, of an application made under Solicitors Act 1974, s 71(3). Such an application is made by 'a person interested' in the property out of which the bill is to be paid, rather than by a person 'as if he were the party chargeable', so different considerations apply. In particular, it has been held that the absolute limit on ordering an assessment of any bills that had been paid for more than 12 months does not apply to applications made under s 71(3).[221] Section 71(4)(a) specifically requires the court to have regard to the provisions of s 70 in so far as they are capable of being applied to an application by a person interested in chargeable property. Judge Rich QC (sitting as a deputy High Court judge) offered his guidance: **36.87**

> 'I have decided that there is a discretion [to order assessment of a bill on application under s 71(3) notwithstanding the fact that that bill has been paid for more than 12 months]. It is, however, a discretion to be exercised in circumstances where the Court is required to have regard to the fact that there would be no power to order a taxation on the application of the chargeable party. It will, therefore, in my judgment, be for the Applicant, who is interested in the chargeable property, to persuade the Court that it should nonetheless order a taxation at his request, and that the considerations of finality which justify the rule in respect of the chargeable party should not prevail upon the present application. In my judgment, some special circumstances precluding a more timely application would have to be shown to invoke the court's discretion.'[222]

Where the application is made under Solicitors Act 1974, s 71(3), it is specifically provided by s 71(4)(b) that the court is to have regard to the extent and nature of the interest of the applicant. Thus, for example, if an applicant under s 71(3) were liable to pay only a small part of the costs sought, that would be a factor to take into account. **36.88**

---

219 See *Tim Martin Interiors Ltd v Akin Gump LLP* [2011] EWCA Civ 1574, at [91]–[94], *per* Lloyd LJ.

220 Solicitors Act 1974, s 70(4).

221 *McIlwraith v McIlwraith* [2002] EWHC 1757 (Ch), *per* HHJ Rich QC (sitting as a deputy High Court judge).

222 *Ibid*, at [32].

36.89 Regardless of whether the application is made 'as if he were the party chargeable' (s 71(1)) or by 'a person interested' (s 71(3)), the court will need to find special circumstances before ordering an assessment (or, rather, reassessment) of a bill that has already been assessed.[223]

36.90 Finally, where the court orders an assessment by a third party, whether under its powers conferred by s 71(1) or by s 71(3), the assessment itself will proceed as if it were at the request of the party chargeable.[224] Whilst only persuasive, rather than binding, the Supreme Court of Victoria has found that the legislation is aimed at the relationship between solicitor and party chargeable, not at that between solicitor and the third party.[225]

The meaning of 'a person other than the party chargeable with the bill'

36.91 Robert Walker LJ has emphasised the general applicability of Solicitors Act 1974, s 71(1):

> 'Section 71 is of general application. It recognises that the person chargeable with the bill may not be ultimately liable to pay the costs thereby claimed. Its evident purpose is to confer on one with a secondary liability for those costs a right comparable to that possessed by the person primarily liable. Given that, for the reasons I have already explained, the Law Society is entitled to have the bills taxed under section 70. Parliament is unlikely to have intended that there should be degrees of secondary liability, some of which are excluded from the ambit of section 71.'[226]

36.92 Examples of those who might successfully make an application under this section include:

- a person who has provided a guarantee for another person's costs;[227]
- a tenant who is contractually liable to pay their landlord's costs;
- a purchaser who has agreed to pay costs incurred by a vendor;
- an insurer who has to pay costs incurred by its insured;[228]
- a mortgagor who is liable to pay the mortgagee's costs;
- solicitors who are liable to meet the costs intervention in their practices;[229]
- a person who agrees to pay costs as between solicitor and client as part of a compromise[230] or other agreement; and
- liquidators of companies.

Indeed, Rolt LJ has said that 'if a person who is not chargeable thinks fit to pay the bill it is open to him to do so, and if he does so, he should be entitled to have that bill assessed as the party chargeable therewith might himself have done'.[231]

36.93 The fact that the contract under which the person who applies for the assessment is itself the subject of a dispute will not necessarily prevent that person from applying for an

---

223 Solicitors Act 1974, s 71(6).
224 *Re Massey* (1865) 34 LJ Ch 492.
225 *Re Lawler* (1878) 4 VLR 8.
226 *Pine v Law Society* [2002] EWCA Civ 175, at [27].
227 See the *obiter* examples given by Cockburn CJ in *In re Heritage, ex p Docker* (1878) 3 QBD 726.
228 See, eg, *Brown-Quinn & Anor v Equity Syndicate Management Ltd & Anor* [2011] EWHC 2661 (Comm).
229 See, eg, *Pine v Law Society* [2002] EWCA Civ 175.
230 Not to be confused with a party who has been ordered to pay the costs of an opponent in litigation: see *Re Cohen & Cohen* [1905] 2 Ch 137.
231 *Re Newman* (1867) 2 Ch App 707, at 717.

assessment. In particular, questions as to the construction of the agreement to pay costs would not ordinarily be a bar to an assessment.[232]

Despite the wide applicability of Solicitors Act 1974, s 71(1), not everyone who believes that they are liable to pay costs would be able to make an application; the question will turn upon whether they fall within the wording of the section. Examples of unsuccessful applications under earlier legislation include: **36.94**

- a party who voluntarily accepted a liability for another person's costs;[233]
- a person who was liable to pay costs solely as a result of being a taxpayer;[234]
- a person who agreed to pay a fixed sum to an opponent's solicitor for that solicitor's trouble in promoting a composition between himself and his creditors;[235] and
- a person who agreed to pay a sum to his opponent's solicitors on discontinuing proceedings.[236]

If a person is unable to bring themselves within the category of a person other than the party chargeable with the bill, they cannot bring themselves within the category of a party chargeable by pointing to the fact that the solicitors had made them into a 'quasi-client' by virtue of the fact that the solicitors kept that person up to date with what services the solicitors were providing.[237]

The meaning of 'any person interested in the property'

This relates to s 71(3) of the Solicitors Act 1974, which relates to any person interested in any property out of which a trustee, executor or administrator has paid, or is entitled to pay, a solicitor's bill. This would include a creditor who, seeking assessment of a bill paid by the deceased, has obtained a judgment in an administration.[238] It does not extend so far as to permit a bankrupt to obtain an assessment of a bill paid by the trustee in bankruptcy.[239] **36.95**

The Assessment Hearing and Procedure Leading up to the Assessment Hearing

Where the court orders a solicitor-and-client assessment, it will adhere to the guidance given in CPR, r 46.10: **36.96**

> '46.10 (1) This rule sets out the procedure to be followed where the court has made an order under Part III of the Solicitors Act 1974 for the assessment of costs payable to a solicitor by the solicitor's client.
>
> (2) The solicitor must serve a breakdown of costs within 28 days of the order for costs to be assessed.

[232] *In re Hirst & Capes* [1908] 1 KB 982.
[233] *Re Becke* (1843) 5 Beav 506. See also *Langford v Nott* (1820) 1 Jac & W 291; *Re Cookson* (1886) 30 SJ 305.
[234] *Re Barber* (1845) 14 M&W 720.
[235] *In re Heritage, ex p Docker* (1878) 3 QBD 726.
[236] *Re Morris* (1872) 27 LT 554.
[237] *Barrett v Rutt-Field* [2006] TLR 1505.
[238] *Re Jones & Everett* [1904] 2 Ch 363.
[239] *In re Leadbitter* (1878) 10 Ch D 388.

(3) The client must serve points of dispute within 14 days after service on the client of the breakdown of costs.

(4) The solicitor must serve any reply within 14 days of service on the solicitor of the points of dispute.

(5) Either party may file a request for a hearing date—
(a) after points of dispute have been served; but
(b) no later than 3 months after the date of the order for the costs to be assessed.

(6) This procedure applies subject to any contrary order made by the court.'

36.97 On the face of it, these directions appear to be mandatory: both the CPR and PD 46—and, when it applied, the now-revoked Costs Practice Direction (CPD)—refer to these steps as ones that must be taken.[240] The contrary is arguable, however. In any event, there is nothing within either the CPR or PD 46 to prevent the court from amending the directions.

36.98 The court will usually also make an order in the form of Precedent L (or, if the application has been made by the solicitor, Precedent M). The form of Precedent L has been the subject of judicial criticism, Morgan J finding that it ought—but fails—to reflect the wording of Solicitors Act 1974, s 70(2)(b) (that is, 'no action be commenced on the bill, and ... any action already commenced on the bill be stayed, until the assessment is completed').[241] Practitioners may wish to ask the court to depart from Precedent L accordingly.

The breakdown of costs

36.99 The breakdown of costs referred to in CPR, r 46.10(2), is a document that contains the following.[242]

- **Detailed breakdown** Unless the bill itself is a detailed bill, the breakdown must contain details of the work done under each of the bills sent for assessment.[243]
- **Cash account** In applications under Solicitors Act 1974, s 70, the breakdown must include a cash account.[244]

A model breakdown is provided at Precedent P of the Schedule of Costs Precedents annexed to PD 47.

Fee notes

36.100 Copies of counsel's fee notes and the fee notes of any experts should also be served. Written evidence as to any other disbursement exceeding £250 should be provided, which will usually mean the appropriate vouchers or receipted invoices.[245]

---

[240] See CPR, r 46.10; PD 46, para 6.3.
[241] *Mastercigars Direct Ltd v Withers LLP* [2007] EWHC 2733 (Ch), at [145].
[242] PD 46, para 6.6.
[243] Where the bill relates to contentious business, the requirement to serve a detailed breakdown in respect of a gross sum bill is not only set out at CPR, r 46.10(2), but also set out at Solicitors Act 1974, s 64(4).
[244] A cash account is an account that includes money received by the solicitor to the credit of the client and sums paid out of that money on behalf of the client, but excludes outgoing payments that were made in satisfaction of the bill (or any items contained therein): PD 46, para 6.6(b).
[245] See PD 46, para 6.7.

Points of dispute

It used to be the case that, as far as practicable, points of dispute had to comply with the requirements for assessments between opposing parties.[246] That requirement does not appear in PD 46. That said, in the absence of any other guidance on the point, costs lawyers and costs draftspersons are likely to continue to draft their points of dispute in a similar format to that used for between-the-parties assessments. **36.101**

Request for a hearing

The time for requesting a detailed assessment hearing is within three months of the date of the order for costs to be assessed.[247] No specific penalty is mentioned in the event of default. The request must be in a prescribed form (Form N258C), which must contain an estimate of the length of the hearing[248] and must be accompanied by: **36.102**

- the order sending the bill for assessment;
- the bill;
- the solicitor's breakdown of costs and any invoices or accounts served with that breakdown;
- a copy of the points of dispute;
- a copy of the replies, if any; and
- a statement signed by the party filing the request or their legal representative, giving the names and addresses for service of all parties to the proceedings.[249]

Upon receipt of the request, the court may give directions, set the matter down for directions or set the matter down for the assessment.[250] There used to be a requirement to serve a copy of the points of dispute, annotated as necessary to show which items have been agreed and their value, and to show which items remain in dispute.[251] There also used to be a requirement to include as many copies of the points of dispute so annotated as there are other parties entitled to attend the assessment.[252] Neither of these provisions now apply. **36.103**

The right to be heard and attendance

Unless the court gives permission, it will hear only the solicitor whose bill it is and those parties who have served points of dispute, and it will rule only upon items specified in the points of dispute.[253] The assessment can proceed even if the parties do not attend (see 36.78). If a party ignores notices of hearing and does not attend, that party may have difficulty in appealing any decision that the court then makes.[254] **36.104**

---

246 CPD, art 56.9.
247 CPR, r 46.10(5)(b); PD 46, para 6.9.
248 PD 46, paras 6.10 and 6.11.
249 PD 46, paras 6.10.
250 PD 46, para 6.12.
251 See CPD, art 56.10(d).
252 See CPD, art 56.10(e).
253 PD 46, para 6.14.
254 See, eg, *Snowden v Ministry of Defence* [2001] EWCA Civ 1524.

Variation of documents

36.105 Permission is not required to vary a breakdown of costs, points of dispute or a reply, but the court may disallow the variation or permit it only upon conditions, including conditions as to the payment of any costs caused or wasted by the variation.[255] The power to vary a statute bill is highly restricted, as is explained at 35.87–35.98.

Filing of papers

36.106 Unless the court directs otherwise, the solicitor must file the papers in support of the bill not less than seven days and not more than 14 days before the date for the assessment hearing.[256] Unless the court orders otherwise, any order in proceedings in the SCCO to which PD 67 applies shall be drawn up and served by the party who made the relevant claim or application.[257]

Privilege and client papers

36.107 Where a client brings professional negligence proceedings against their solicitor, it would generally be the case that this would amount to an implied waiver of privilege in respect of all relevant materials.[258] To an extent, the same applies where there is a solicitor-and-client assessment, but any waiver is limited[259] and is certainly not to the whole world.[260] To this extent, the points made about assessments between opposing parties also apply to assessments between solicitor and client (see 46.69–46.71). Gloster LJ had this to say on the point:

> '[T]here is no reason why implied waiver should not be limited in scope: an implied waiver is for a specific and limited purpose (such as to enable a solicitor to defend the proceedings brought by a former client), and LPP [legal professional privilege] is so important a principle of the legal system that an implied exclusion of it should be confined in scope. Nor is there any justification for there to be a more expansive approach to the loss of LPP in the context of a detailed assessment concerning own solicitor costs than in the context of the detailed assessment concerning *inter partes* costs. The client is entitled to at least as much protection of LPP if it is the client's own solicitor with whom there is a dispute. And indeed, as the judge recognised at paragraph 15 of his judgment, solicitor-own client assessment disputes are in one sense more supervisory than the adversarial context of *inter partes* assessment.'[261]

36.108 Indeed, Gloster LJ went on to point out that Lord Millett had previously explained that the concept of limited waiver is of general application, designed to ensure that the loss of legal professional privilege (given its fundamental importance) is limited to that which is necessary to protect other interests.[262]

---

[255] PD 46, para 6.15.
[256] PD 46, para 6.16.
[257] See PD 67, para 5.
[258] See, eg, *Paragon Finance plc v Freshfields* [1999] 1 WLR 1183, at 1188E–G, *per* Lord Bingham CJ; *Lillicrap v Nalder & Son* [1993] 1 WLR 94, at 99, *per* Dillon LJ.
[259] See *Dechert LLP v Eurasian Natural Resources Corpn Ltd* [2016] EWCA Civ 375, at [46], *per* Gloster LJ, who referred to *B v Auckland District Law Society* [2003] 2 AC 736. See also *Goddard v Nationwide Building Society* [1987] 1 QB 670, at 685, *per* Nourse LJ; *National Westminster Bank plc and another v Brice Droogleever (a firm)* [2003] EWHC 1821 (Ch), at [130], *per* Lindsay J.
[260] *Dechert LLP v Eurasian Natural Resources Corpn Ltd* [2016] EWCA Civ 375, at [51], *per* Gloster LJ.
[261] *Ibid*, at [50].
[262] See *ibid*, at [52], referring to *B v Auckland District Law Society* [2003] 2 AC 736, at [66]–[71].

Hearings may be heard in private

The general rule is that hearings are in public (see CPR, r 39.2(1)),[263] but a hearing, or any part of it, may be in private if: 36.109

- publicity would defeat the object of the hearing;
- it involves matters relating to national security;
- it involves confidential information (including information relating to personal financial matters) and publicity would damage that confidentiality;
- a private hearing is necessary to protect the interests of any child or protected party;
- it is a hearing of an application made without notice and it would be unjust to any respondent for there to be a public hearing;
- it involves uncontentious matters arising in the administration of trusts or in the administration of a deceased person's estate; or
- the court considers this to be necessary, in the interests of justice (see CPR, r 39.2(3)).

These exceptions seek to encapsulate both the general rule of open justice and the particular cases in which it may be appropriate to depart from it.[264]

The subject matter of a solicitor-and-client assessment may be confidential. Whilst *obiter*, Gloster LJ has explained that the right not to incriminate oneself and the presumption of innocence under Art 6 ECHR means that if a public hearing would expose a client to a risk of incrimination, the court is able to sit in private, either for the whole of the hearing or for the relevant part of it.[265] This would be so regardless of whether there had been any actual or possible waiver of legal professional privilege.[266] A decision to sit in private would not, however, predicate that any judgment should not be published.[267] 36.110

After the hearing

After the detailed assessment hearing is concluded, the court will generally: 36.111

- complete the court copy of the bill, so as to show the amount allowed;
- determine the result of the cash account;
- award the costs of the detailed assessment hearing in accordance with Solicitors Act 1974, s 70(8); and
- issue a final costs certificate showing the amount due.[268]

There used to be a rule that said that, unless the court ordered otherwise, the final costs certificate would include an order to pay the sum it certified.[269] That provision no longer exists as an express rule, but common sense dictates that this is what would happen if no request for a different figure were made. Circumstances in which the court may order otherwise would include where the assessment was brought by a third party and the amount payable by that third party is less than the amount payable by the party chargeable.[270] 36.112

---

[263] See also *Dechert LLP v Eurasian Natural Resources Corpn Ltd* [2016] EWCA Civ 375, at [38], *per* Gloster LJ; HMCTS, *Senior Court Costs Office Guide 2018* (London: HMSO, 2018), para 13.1.

[264] *X v Dartford and Gravesham NHS Trust* [2015] EWCA Civ 96, at [10].

[265] *Dechert LLP v Eurasian Natural Resources Corpn Ltd* [2016] EWCA Civ 375, at [43].

[266] *Ibid*, at [44].

[267] *Ibid*, at [45].

[268] PD 46, para 6.19.

[269] CPD, art 56.19 (now revoked).

[270] See *Tim Martin Interiors Ltd v Akin Gump LLP* [2011] EWCA Civ 1574, at [34].

Costs Certificates in Solicitor-and-client Assessments and Interim Payments

36.113 There used to be an express provision that referred to the power to issue interim costs certificates in solicitor-and-client assessments.[271] That power seems no longer to be expressly stated. It is possible that this is because it was regarded as being otiose in view of the power to make an interim award pursuant to the combined effect of Solicitors Act 1974, s 70(6),[272] and CPR, r 25.1(1)(k).[273] That said, that power is limited to making an award of those monies that the court holds the client to be liable to pay, so it seems not to be as broad as the power to issue an interim costs certificate. In view of this, perhaps the true law is that the power conferred by CPR, r 47.18, applies to solicitor-and-client assessments, as well as to assessment between opposing parties.

36.114 In contrast to the way in which the power to issue an interim costs certificate in general has been treated (see 36.101), the power to issue an interim costs certificate in favour of the client has been preserved as express rule.[274] Such a certificate may be issued, for example, where the cash account shows that the client has overpaid.

36.115 There is no provision within the CPR for a default costs certificate to be issued in solicitor-and-client assessments.[275] However, if a party simply refuses to cooperate, the Solicitors Act 1974 specifically provides that the costs officer may hear the assessment *ex parte*.[276]

36.116 Unless it is set aside or amended, the costs certificate will be final; unless the retainer is disputed,[277] the costs officer is able to enter judgment for the amount certified.[278]

---

[271] CPD, art 56.17, which used to refer to CPR, r 47.15, as being applicable to solicitor-and-client assessments.

[272] Which allows a claim to be commenced or continued for parts of the bill that are not to be the subject of an assessment.

[273] CPR, r 25.1(1)(k), permits payment by a defendant on account of 'any damages, debt or other sum (except costs) which the court may hold the defendant liable to pay'. Rightly or wrongly, the reference to 'except costs' is generally interpreted as being a reference to costs of the claim, rather than costs that are the subject of the claim.

[274] PD 46, para 6.18.

[275] See PD 46, para 6.8.

[276] Solicitors Act 1974, s 70(8).

[277] This qualification arises from Solicitors Act 1974, s 72(4). It is not wholly clear what it means; one interpretation is that it refers to the situation in which the issue of enforceability of the retainer is to be decided at trial and the assessment is only a quantification exercise.

[278] Solicitors Act 1974, s 72(4).

37

THE BASIS OF ASSESSMENT BETWEEN SOLICITOR AND CLIENT

This chapter deals with the following topics: **37.01**

- the basis of the assessment of costs as between solicitor and client (37.02);
- the details of assessment between solicitor and client:
  - the solicitor and client presumptions (37.06);
  - the County Court restriction (37.18);
  - the Solicitors' (Non-Contentious Business) Remuneration Order 2009 (37.24);
  - the assessment of percentage increases as between solicitor and client (37.30); and
- consumer issues (37.32).

The Basis of the Assessment of Costs as between Solicitor and Client

Solicitor-and-client costs are assessed on the indemnity basis.[1] This means that, subject to what is said below, r 44.3(3) of the Civil Procedure Rules (CPR) applies (at least by analogy): **37.02**

> 'Where the amount of costs is to be assessed on the indemnity basis, the court will resolve any doubt which it may have as to whether costs were reasonably incurred or were reasonable in amount in favour of the receiving party.'

Thus, when assessing costs as between solicitor and client, the court will not allow costs that have been unreasonably incurred or which are unreasonable in amount. Any doubt as to reasonableness is to be resolved in favour of the solicitor. The concept of proportionality will not apply (other than perhaps, in the sense that it may be a manifestation of the tests of reasonableness). It is worth pausing here to note that—strictly speaking—CPR, r 44.3(3), does not directly apply to non-contentious costs (see 37.24), but, for practical purposes, little turns on this. In particular, whilst CPR, r 44.3(3), may not apply as a matter of law, for all practical purposes it accurately describes the way in which non-contentious costs are assessed. **37.03**

A general discussion of the indemnity basis may be found in Chapter 16 (see 16.09–16.12). With appropriate modifications, the points made therein apply to the assessment of costs as between solicitor and client. The modifications are as follows. **37.04**

- Both contentious and non-contentious costs are subject to certain presumptions that apply only as between solicitor and client (see 37.06–37.07).

[1] See CPR, r 46.9(3); PD 46, para 6.2.

- Where contentious costs incurred in the County Court and its hearing centres are to be assessed as between solicitor and client, a provision known as 'the County Court restriction' applies (see 37.08–37.23). (It should be noted that this is entirely different from the jurisdictional restriction referred to in 36.43 and 36.50.)
- Different (but not dissimilar) rules apply to the assessment of non-contentious costs—namely, the Solicitors' (Non-Contentious Business) Remuneration Order 2009[2] (see 37.24–37.29).
- Specific rules apply to the assessment of percentage increases as between solicitor and client (see 37.30–37.31).

37.05 In addition, whilst there is no authority on the point, it is possible that consumer protection legislation now has a significant bearing on the way in which costs may be assessed in certain circumstances (see 37.32–37.36 and Chapter 28 in general).

The Details of Assessment as between Solicitor and Client

The solicitor-and-client presumptions

37.06 There are certain presumptions—known as the solicitor-and-client presumptions—that pre-date the CPR,[3] but which are now expressed within them. In particular, CPR, r 46.9, reads as follows:

> '(1) This rule applies to every assessment of a solicitor's bill to his client except a bill which is to be paid out of the Community Legal Service Fund under the Legal Aid Act 1988 or the Access to Justice Act 1999 . . .
>
> [. . .]
>
> (3) Subject to paragraph (2), costs are to be assessed on the indemnity basis but are to be presumed—
> (a) to have been reasonably incurred if they were incurred with the express or implied approval of the client;
> (b) to be reasonable in amount if their amount was expressly or impliedly approved by the client;
> (c) to have been unreasonably incurred if—
> (i) they are of an unusual nature or amount; and
> (ii) the solicitor did not tell his client that as a result he might not recover all of them from the other party.'

37.07 Thus costs are:

- assumed to have been reasonably incurred if they were incurred with the express or implied approval of the client;
- assumed to be reasonable in amount if their amount was expressly or impliedly approved by the client; and
- assumed to have been unreasonably incurred if:
  - they are of an unusual nature or amount; and
  - the solicitor did not tell their client that, as a result, they might not recover all of their costs from the other party.

---

[2] SI 2009/1931.
[3] RSC, Ord 62, r 15.

Are the presumptions rebuttable?

It is not clear whether the solicitor-and-client presumptions are rebuttable, although—for the reasons set out in 37.10–37.13—this is a largely abstract point, because judge-made law has created a different mechanism through which the court is able to avoid injustice. It is true to say that Practice Direction (PD) 46, para 6.2, provides that 'the presumptions in r 46.9(3) are rebuttable', but this direction is not in accordance with prior judge-made law (see 37.09) and it is far from clear whether a Practice Direction is able to forge the CPR in this way (see 4.50). There is a strong case for saying that PD 46, para 6.2, is *ultra vires* and that the solicitor-and-client presumptions are not rebuttable (that is, that they are 'conclusive presumptions'). **37.08**

The topic of rebuttability vexed Holland J when he was considering the pre-CPR equivalent of the presumptions.[4] He found that the first two presumptions (concerning approval) were theoretically rebuttable, but went to say that he could conceive no basis upon which such a rebuttal could take place.[5] Holland J expressed concern that, if left unmitigated, a presumption that could not be rebutted could lead to injustice.[6] Holland J was unable to find anything in the notion of rebuttal that afforded clients refuge, but he did go on to discover the concept of 'informed approval' (see 37.10). It seems that subsequent cases have focused on that test rather than on the putative rebuttability afforded by PD 46, para 6.2.[7] Whilst no more than his own view, the editor believes that Holland J's test is to be preferred to the putative rebuttability afforded by PD 46, para 6.2, and that the latter should be regarded as either *ultra vires* or an imperfectly worded expression of Holland J's test. **37.09**

'Approval' and informed approval Having found (albeit on the basis of rules that were not precisely the same as the present-day rules) that, for all practical purposes, the presumption of approval is not rebuttable (see 37.08), Holland J went on to explicate the notion of informed approval: **37.10**

> 'I talked of "informed" approval and even with reflection I adhere to that concept. To rely on the [clients'] approval the solicitor must satisfy me that it was secured following a full and fair exposition of the factors relevant to it so that the [clients], lay persons as they are, can reasonably be bound by it.'[8]

Thus a client must have given informed approval if they were to be bound by the presumption of approval; if a client's putative approval was not informed, then the court would be able to assess the costs unhindered by those presumptions. In a more recent case (decided under the CPR), Soole J had this to say: **37.11**

> 'I do not accept that the "approval" of the client is satisfied by the mere fact of the client's consent to the relevant type or amount of cost to be incurred. The language of "approval" evidently requires something more. I respectfully agree with Holland J in *Macdougall* that approval requires an informed consent. It follows that the simple refrain of freedom of contract establishes neither the presumptions nor the reasonableness of the success fee in the particular case.'[9]

---

4 *MacDougall v Boote Edgar Estekin* [2001] 1 Costs LR 118.

5 *Ibid*, at 122.

6 An unscrupulous solicitor, for example, could cajole their client into approving rates that were not only unreasonable, but also outlandish.

7 See, eg, *Herbert v HH Law Ltd* [2018] EWHC 580 (QB), *per* Soole J.

8 *MacDougall v Boote Edgar Estekin* [2001] 1 Costs LR 118, at 122.

9 *Herbert v HH Law Ltd* [2018] EWHC 580 (QB), at [41].

Thus there can be no doubt that Holland J's analysis has survived the coming into force of the CPR.

37.12 On the facts of the case before him (in which an hourly charging rate of £300 per hour was claimed at a time when such rates were palpably high), Holland J found that the information that had been given to the clients was insufficiently frank and detailed as to make their approval informed. The following factors featured in his reasoning:

- the fact that the clients had not been given a fair and full explanation of the likely recovery of costs on a between-the-parties assessment;
- his finding that there was no logical basis for charging the hourly rate that was claimed (the solicitors had increased their hourly rate in a seemingly arbitrary way); and
- the fact that the clients had not been told how the higher rate would impact upon the sums that they would have to pay generally.[10]

37.13 Soole J has confirmed that 'the requirement of approval is [not] directed only at cases where the client has been misled by the solicitor'.[11] On the facts of the case before him (which concerned the amount of a success fee), Soole J was able to find an absence of informed approval arising out of the fact that the solicitor had failed to explain a business model that resulted in a high percentage increase being charged as a matter of routine[12] (see 37.31). In any event, it is worth noting that if a client found themselves having to argue against a seemingly unfair or excessive fee or other item of costs, their argument could now be bolstered by reference to consumer protection legislation (see 37.32–37.37).

37.14 **'Unusual nature or amount'** Whilst there is a surprising dearth of authority on the point, it is likely that what amounts to costs that are unusual in nature or amount will be a question of fact (or, where appropriate, fact and law). The contractual issues relating to 'unusual costs' are addressed at 27.327.

37.15 PD 46, para 6.1, has this to say on the topic:

> '6.1 A client and solicitor may agree whatever terms they consider appropriate about the payment of the solicitor's charges. If however, the costs are of an unusual nature, either in amount or the type of costs incurred, those costs will be presumed to have been unreasonably incurred unless the solicitor satisfies the court that the client was informed that they were unusual and that they might not be allowed on an assessment of costs between the parties. That information must have been given to the client before the costs were incurred.'

Thus the CPR places emphasis on what the client was told (or not told). To this extent, there is overlap with the approval presumptions.

37.16 Examples of costs that have been disallowed as being 'unusual in nature or amount' are rare, but they include the costs of using leading counsel to draft pleadings[13] (at a time when the use of leading counsel for such work would have given rise to 'special fees').[14]

---

[10] *MacDougall v Boote Edgar Estekin* [2001] 1 Costs LR 118, at 122–125.

[11] *Herbert v HH Law Ltd* [2018] EWHC 580 (QB), at [42].

[12] *Ibid*, at [47] and [49]. At the time of writing, this decision was subject to appeal. This decision, if it survives appeal, is likely to be of some importance, because this is a common arrangement in certain sectors of the legal services industry—especially personal injury and clinical negligence.

[13] *Re Cohen & Cohen* [1905] 1 Ch 345, *per* Swinfen Eady J, appealed on a different point at [1905] 2 Ch 137.

[14] See Rules of the Supreme Court 1883, Order LXV, r 27(29).

Conflicting presumptions

Whilst the editor is not aware of such a state of affairs ever having occurred, it is possible that competing presumptions could come into conflict (such as if a client were to give their approval to costs of an unusual nature without being told that those costs might not be recoverable in full from their opponent). If such a situation were to arise, then—whilst there is no authority on the point—it would be open to the court to find that they had cancelled each other out.[15] Alternatively, the concept of 'informed approval' (see 37.10–37.13) could be invoked, in which case the presumption in favour of the solicitor would yield to that in favour of the client. Furthermore, if the client were a consumer, then the matters referred to at 37.33 and 37.34 regarding consumer protection may apply. **37.17**

The County Court restriction

CPR, r 46.9(2), reads as follows: **37.18**

> '(2) Section 74(3) of the Solicitors Act 1974(a) applies unless the solicitor and client have entered into a written agreement which expressly permits payment to the solicitor of an amount of costs greater than that which the client could have recovered from another party to the proceedings.'

The effect of this is that, unless it is disapplied by agreement (see 37.23), s 74(3) of the Solicitors Act 1974 will apply to the assessment of costs as between solicitor and client. That section imposes a restriction on the amount of costs recoverable in the County Court and its hearing centres. It reads as follows: **37.19**

> '(3) The amount which may be allowed on the assessment of any costs or bill of costs in respect of any item relating to proceedings in the county court shall not, except in so far as rules of court may otherwise provide, exceed the amount which could have been allowed in respect of that item as between party and party in those proceedings, having regard to the nature of the proceedings and the amount of the claim and of any counterclaim.'

Thus, in so far as it applies, s 74(3) will limit the amount that the client has to pay to that amount which could have been allowed had the costs been payable between opposing parties.

Application of the County Court restriction

This seemingly wide-ranging restriction has been held to apply only where the CPR imposes limits as to the level of costs recovery, as was explained by Hughes J: **37.20**

> 'I am satisfied that section 74(3) exists to apply a cap where there are limits under the rules to the level of costs recoverable as between the parties. The subsection remains in the same form as it has in 1974. At that time, costs in the County Court were in most cases recovered on one or other of five scales, according to the amount of money in dispute ... The section was designed to limit the costs between solicitor and client to those scales, in the same way as the scales limited costs recoverable as between the parties ... Under the [CPR] the express reference to section 74(3) which appears in rule [46n.9(2)], shows that the section does not simply survive but is intended still to bite. And bite it does whenever there are fixed costs ...'[16]

[15] In a setting other than the law of costs, see *Monkton v Tarr* (1930) 23 BWCC 504, CA.

[16] *Lynch v Paul Davidson Taylor (a firm)* [2004] EWHC 89 (QB), at [15]–[19].

37.21 Thus the restriction applies where there is a principled limit to the sums that may be recovered between the parties. It will not apply where the putative limit would merely be an incidental part of the ordinary assessment of costs.

37.22 This means that Solicitors Act 1974, s 74(3), can be disregarded for the purposes of most assessments. It is of potential relevance where a solicitor seeks to recover more than fixed costs in a case in which fixed costs would apply—although many fixed costs relate to pre-issue work (which is non-contentious), so even this limited sphere of influence is not as great as it first appears.

Disapplication of the County Court restriction by consent

37.23 CPR, r 46.9(2), provides a mechanism by which the County Court restriction can be disapplied by consent. It reads as follows:

> 'Section 74(3) of the Solicitors Act 1974(a) applies unless the solicitor and client have entered into a written agreement which expressly permits payment to the solicitor of an amount of costs greater than that which the client could have recovered from another party to the proceedings.'

In practice, many (if not most) well-written retainers contain a provision that addresses this point, so—for all practical purposes and taking into account the matters set out in 37.20–37.23—it would be a rare case in which Solicitors Act 1974, s 74(3), would have any practical bearing.

Non-contentious costs

37.24 Non-contentious costs are assessed on what can be termed the 'fair and reasonable basis'.[17] In substance, that basis is merely a subcategory of the indemnity basis (and is usually referred to as such—to the extent that the phrase 'fair and reasonable basis' is almost never heard in practice). Nonetheless, whilst part of the same family, it is distinguishable from other bases of assessment. Specifically, CPR, rr 44.3(3) and 44.4(3), are disapplied by r 44.3(6), which reads:

> 'Where the amount of a solicitor's remuneration in respect of non-contentious business is regulated by any general orders made under the Solicitors Act 1974, the amount of the costs to be allowed in respect of any such business which falls to be assessed by the court will be decided in accordance with those general orders rather than this rule and rule 44.4.'

37.25 Thus the assessment of non-contentious costs does not have its foundations in the 'pillars of wisdom' in CPR, r 44.4(3); rather, the strikingly similar nine factors in art 3 of the Solicitors' (Non-Contentious Business) Remuneration Order 2009[18] will apply. That provision reads as follows:

> 'A solicitor's costs must be fair and reasonable having regard to all the circumstances of the case and in particular to—
> (a) the complexity of the matter or the difficulty or novelty of the questions raised;

---

[17] The term 'fair and reasonable basis' derives from Solicitors' (Non-Contentious Business) Remuneration Order 2009 (SI 2009/1931), art 3, and its predecessors. A pedant may object to the term on the grounds that it does not describe the basis upon which costs are to be assessed, but merely one measure that comprises the appropriate basis. The term has, in the past, been used to describe other bases of assessment, so some caution must be exercised when it is encountered in older authorities.

[18] SI 2009/1931. Similar provisions appeared in the Solicitors' Remuneration Order 1972 (SI 1972/1139) and the Solicitors' (Non-Contentious Business) Remuneration Order 1994 (SI 1994/2616).

(b) the skill, labour, specialised knowledge and responsibility involved;
(c) the time spent on the business;
(d) the number and importance of the documents prepared or considered, without regard to length;
(e) the place where and the circumstances in which the business or any part of the business is transacted;
(f) the amount or value of any money or property involved;
(g) whether any land involved is registered land within the meaning of the Land Registration Act 2002;
(h) the importance of the matter to the client; and
(i) the approval (express or implied) of the entitled person or the express approval of the testator to –
    (i) the solicitor undertaking all or any part of the work giving rise to the costs; or
    (ii) the amount of the costs.'

It is worth noting that other jurisdictions have very similar lists, one of the most complete being a 12-point list used in the United States.[19]

It can be seen that with one exception (namely, conduct), each of the original seven pillars also appears in the nine factors. (Conduct does not apply because, in most instances, there would be no opposing parties and therefore there would be no occasion on which issues of conduct may arise.) The three further factors that the court is to take into account are: the number and importance of the documents prepared or perused (without regard to length);[20] whether any land involved is registered land; and any approval given by the client (or person paying). This last factor is amplified in CPR, r 46.9, which is addressed at 37.06–37.17. **37.26**

CPR, r 46.9, refers to the indemnity basis, yet the only definition of the indemnity basis in the CPR is in r 44.3, which—as mentioned in 37.25—is a rule that expressly disapplies itself for the purposes of assessing non-contentious costs. This is not a conundrum that is capable of causing any real interpretative difficulty, however, because there can be no doubt about what is meant by the indemnity basis. **37.27**

For most practical purposes, the basis of assessment of non-contentious costs is the same as that of contentious costs. The only significant difference is that the court may need to take into account nine factors rather than the fewer factors that are the 'pillars of wisdom' (see 37.25). It is, perhaps, because of this similarity that the term 'fair and reasonable basis' is so infrequently heard. **37.28**

Although the *basis* of assessment of non-contentious costs is (almost) the same as the basis on which contentious costs are assessed, the *method* of assessment is often markedly **37.29**

---

[19] That list was laid out in *Johnson v Georgia Highway Express* 488 F 2d 714, 717–19 (5th Cir, 1974): '(a) The time and labour required; (b) The novelty and difficulty of the questions involved; (c) The skill requisite to perform the legal service properly; (d) The fact that acceptance of the case made it impossible to take on other cases; (e) Any customary fee for similar work; (f) Whether the fee was fixed or contingent; (g) Any degree of urgency imposed by the client or the circumstances; (h) The amount of money involved or awarded and the results obtained; (i) The experience, reputation and ability of the attorney; (j) The undesirability of being associated with the case; (k) The nature and length of the professional relationship of the attorney with the client; (l) Awards in similar cases.'

[20] The prohibition against taking the length of documents into account has its origins in the need to deal with the problem that vexed ancient courts of lawyers writing overly long documents to enhance their fees, as discussed in Chapter 1.

different. In particular, much greater emphasis is often placed on the value of money or property involved. This factor is often reflected in an element of charge known as the value element, which, if significant, will overshadow other aspects of the assessment. Thus, whilst the law may be much the same regardless of whether the costs are contentious or non-contentious, the way in which the law is applied often markedly differs. As Longmore LJ noted: 'There are significant differences in the circumstances in which charges are made for contentious and non-contentious business and the approach to such charges can properly differ even though the same factors fall to be taken into account.'[21]

Percentage increases

37.30 CPR, r 46.9(4), (which relates to success fees) reads as follows:

> '(4) Where the court is considering a percentage increase, whether on the application of the legal representative under rule 44.16 or on the application of the client, the court will have regard to all the relevant factors as they reasonably appeared to the solicitor or counsel when the conditional fee agreement was entered into or varied.'

This is self-explanatory and needs no elaboration.

37.31 Soole J has confirmed that CPR, r 46.9, should be read as a whole and that, as such, the solicitor-and-client presumptions (referred to at 37.06–37.07) apply,[22] but that the risk borne by the solicitor is likely to be the prime factor in the determination of appropriate amount where those presumptions do not apply.[23] On the facts of the case before him (in which the firm of solicitors took no account of the risk in the individual case and provided for a 100 per cent percentage increase in all cases by reason of its particular business model), Soole J took the view that the solicitor-and-client presumptions did not apply, because informed approval would have required the firm's reasoning to be clearly explained to clients before they entered the conditional fee agreement in question.[24]

Consumer Protection Issues

37.32 Whilst, technically, they would operate by having a bearing on the contractual relationship between solicitor and client rather than by modifying the basis of assessment, there are four consumer protection provisions that may have a particular bearing on the way in which costs are assessed as between solicitor and client. It has to be stressed, however, that circumstances in which it would be appropriate to invoke any of the following would arise only rarely and that, even then, there is a complete absence of authority on the point. Indeed, what follows should properly be regarded as being little more than the editor's thoughts as to how the law could be applied in certain circumstances.[25]

---

[21] *Jemma Trust Co Ltd v Liptrott* [2003] EWCA Civ 1476, at [26], *per* Longmore LJ.
[22] *Herbert v HH Law Ltd* [2018] EWHC 580 (QB), at [46].
[23] *Ibid*, at [44] and [50].
[24] *Ibid*, at [47] and [49].
[25] Whilst he could easily be wrong, it is the editor's view that some of the provisions referred to below are capable of having a significant bearing on the way in which solicitor and client costs are assessed. There are two competing factors at play: the first is that consumer protection legislation is, in general, interpreted as being of broad application; the second is that where sector-specific legislation exists, it will, in general, prevail.

Representations are incorporated

As is explained at 28.30–28.33, s 50 of the Consumer Rights Act 2015 means that supposedly informal agreements as to the amount that a consumer client will pay are, if relied upon by the client, contractually binding as terms of the contract of retainer; the rights that are conferred are not *implied* terms of the contract of retainer, but are to be treated *as* terms.[26] This would generally be relevant where, for example, the client seeks to rely upon an assertion that an estimate was given (see 38.58–38.59), but—subject to the qualification that there is no authority on the topic—it is easy to envisage circumstances in which incorporated representations could lead to a modification of the basis of assessment. An example would be a seemingly informal assurance to limit costs to those that would be recoverable between opposing parties (as opposed to actually recovered), which could well modify the basis of assessment such that, for all practical purposes, the standard basis applied. **37.33**

Unfair terms

The Consumer Rights Act 2015 applies a test of fairness to terms in consumer contracts (see 28.41). An unfair term of a consumer contract[27] is not legally binding on a consumer.[28] A term is unfair, 'if contrary to the requirements of good faith, it causes a significant imbalance in the parties' rights and obligations arising under the contract, to the detriment of the consumer'.[29] Whilst there is no authority on the point, one could envisage circumstances in which this may have a bearing on the basis upon which costs are assessed as between solicitor and client, such as where a solicitor sought to invoke the approval presumption (see 37.06–37.07) without having afforded the client a proper explanation as to whether this would be appropriate. There would, obviously, be overlap with Holland J's concept of 'informed approval', as expanded upon by Soole J (see 37.10–37.13), or even undue influence, but—whilst no more than the editor's opinion—the consumer protection provisions may go much further than that in certain circumstances. **37.34**

The Consumer Rights Act 2015 also applies substantially the same test of fairness to consumer notices.[30] An unfair consumer notice[31] is not legally binding on the consumer.[32] **37.35**

The right to a discount

The right to a discount is potentially of significant importance in so far as the relationship between a solicitor and client is concerned not only because it provides a statutory **37.36**

One could argue that the other provisions referred to in this chapter fall into the latter category and should therefore take precedence. The editor does not take that view, because those other provisions can, in no way, be regarded as being primarily consumer protection provisions. In any event, the former act upon the retainer, whereas the latter do not; the relevance of this is that there is no logical reason why the law should preclude the parties from entering into a contract that (either *de facto* or *de jure*) modifies the basis of assessment.

[26] It was hoped by legislators that setting out the obligations in this way would assist users of this legislation (who might not all be legal service providers, but may be consumers and those advising consumers within consumer-oriented organisations) and would explain the true nature of the thinking that the Act required: see Andrews, C, *Enforcement of Consumer Rights and Protections* (London: Butterworths, 2012), para 5.7.

[27] See Consumer Rights Act 2015, s 62(1).

[28] See Consumer Rights Act 2015, s 62(3).

[29] See Consumer Rights Act 2015, s 62(4).

[30] See Consumer Rights Act 2015, s 62(6).

[31] See Consumer Rights Act 2015, s 62(2).

[32] See Consumer Rights Act 2015, s 62(3).

mechanism through which a client may seek to avoid paying for 'shoddy work' (see 28.146–28.148), but also because it appears to provide a mechanism that allows a client to seek a reduction in their liability for fees that is not dependent on their being exposed to the full rigours of a solicitor-and-client assessment. If this is correct, then this is a significant strengthening of the position of clients. There is, however, no authority on this topic. In particular, there is no authority on whether a consumer client would be able to contend for a discount in the context of a solicitor-and-client assessment.

The right to a price reduction

37.37 The right to require the legal services provider to reduce the price payable by the consumer to an appropriate amount includes the right to receive a refund for anything already paid above a reduced amount and may include the full amount of the price (see 28.146–28.147).

38

QUANTUM BETWEEN SOLICITOR AND CLIENT

38.01 This chapter examines the finer points relating to the assessment of fees and disbursements between solicitor and client. The broader points—namely, the basis of assessment, the solicitor-and-client presumptions, etc—are dealt with in Chapter 37. This chapter deals with the following topics:

- non-contentious costs—hourly rates and value charges (38.04);
- non-contentious costs—the limited role of authority and comparators (38.08);
- hourly rates (38.09);
- the value charge (38.15):
  - the purpose of the value charge (38.16);
  - the weight to be given to factors other than value (38.22);
  - the weight to be given to value (38.28);
- shoddy work (38.35);
- inadequate advice regarding funding options (38.41);
- estimates and assurances on a solicitor-and-client basis (38.43):
  - the duty to give estimates (38.44);
- putative waiver of fees (38.80);
- assurances about how services will be provided (38.81);
- interest between solicitor and client (38.86):
  - interest on non-contentious costs (38.89);
  - interest on contentious costs (38.92);
  - judgment debt interest (38.93);
  - discretion generally (38.95); and
  - the Late Payment of Commercial Debts (Interest) Act 1998 (38.97).

38.02 This chapter assumes that the reader has a working knowledge of the quantification of costs in general. If this is not the case, then the reader is referred to other chapters in this book.

38.03 The precise method of assessment may differ depending on whether the work in question was contentious or non-contentious. Much of the focus of this chapter is on the assessment of non-contentious costs as between solicitor and client. This is because the method of assessment of contentious costs (as opposed to the basis of assessment) is so similar to the assessment of costs between opposing parties that what is said in Part XIII of this book can stand as a description of that method. There are, however, certain qualifications that apply to the assessment of contentious costs as between solicitor and client, and these are set out in this chapter. The reader should consult the relevant part of Part XIII first and then the relevant part of this chapter.

Non-contentious Costs: Hourly Rates and Value Charges

38.04 Although there are many means by which solicitors may calculate their fees for non-contentious work, two stand out as deserving of scrutiny: hourly rates (38.09–38.14) and the value charge (38.15–38.34).

Terminology: 'value charge' and 'value element'

38.05 As used in this book, the term 'value charge' is not the same as 'value element'.

- **Value element** This is 'the value of the money or property involved'[1] and, as such, is one of the factors that is taken into account for the purposes of ascertaining the amount payable. Where a great deal of money or valuable property is involved, then that fact is referred to as the value element and may be reflected either in an enhanced hourly rate or in a separate value charge.
- **Value charge** This is a separate charge that is assessed in such a way as to reflect the value element.

This nomenclature is not standard and is used in this book only for the purposes of description.[2] It should be noted that the two terms are often used inconsistently and interchangeably elsewhere. It should also be noted that what is set out in this chapter has little to do with the notion of 'value' in so far as it relates to value-based pricing (see Chapter 42).

How the value element is reflected in hourly rates

38.06 Where the value element (or, for that matter, any relevant factor) is reflected in the hourly rate, solicitors are encouraged to set a single all-inclusive rate rather than a rate that is intended to be enhanced for 'care and conduct'.[3]

38.07 Paragraphs 38.09–38.14 and 38.15–38.34 deal, respectively, with hourly rates and value charges as separate topics, but it should be remembered that they are both fees for legal services rendered and that, as such, both should be ascertained collectively, as well as individually. While there will inevitably be a degree of overlap, duplication must be avoided. Duplication may perniciously disguise itself: where, for example, an allowance has already been made for complexity, value, time and responsibility, care needs to be taken not to give excessive weight to the number of documents, because to do so would be to count those factors twice over.[4] Likewise, it is important to stand back and look at the overall charge so as to ensure that the total is not excessive;[5] to that extent, the hourly rates and the value

---

1 See Solicitors' (Non-contentious Business) Remuneration Order 2009 (SI 2009/1931), art 3(f).

2 Indeed, the two terms are used interchangeably in other texts and in the authorities.

3 See, eg, Law Society, 'Practice Advice Service: Non-contentious Costs', July 2012, p 10. This advice is not specifically repeated in the Law Society's Price and Service Transparency Toolkit, but is entirely consistent with what is said in that publication, albeit in a more detailed way. In the editor's view, the old guidance better describes the law than the present guidance, although technically it is now a historical document. The old guidance may be found only on WayBack Machine, under http://www.lawsociety.org.uk/new/documents/20120/noncontentiouscosts.pdf

4 *Property and Reversionary Investment Corpn Ltd v Secretary of State for the Environment* [1975] 2 All ER 436, at 442.

5 See *Treasury Solicitor v Regester* [1978] 1 WLR 446, at 450. See also, by analogy with the 'A plus B approach', *Leopold Lazarus Ltd v Secretary of State for Trade and Industry* (1976) Costs LR, core vol 62.

charge are assessed collectively. Longmore LJ had this to say (in the context of non-contentious probate):

> 'In an estate of small or medium value, it may be appropriate for a solicitor to limit his charges to a percentage of the estate's value or to charge a percentage together with an appropriately modest hourly rate. For a high-value estate it may also be appropriate to charge a percentage together with an hourly rate because, if one is to take value into account ... that will mean that the charges will have one element of comparative certainty. An hourly rate, although certain of itself, is subject to the variable that the number of hours worked cannot be ascertained until the business is completed. It must always be remembered that, once the business is completed, it is the solicitor's duty to have charged no more than is fair and reasonable in all the circumstances and the costs judge will be able to look at the matter in the round.'[6]

Non-contentious Costs: The Limited Role of Authority and Comparators

The ascertainment of non-contentious costs is a matter that must be decided on the facts of the case or matter in question. Donaldson J has explained that comparable cases are to be used only as a cross-check of the fairness and reasonableness of sums allowed, and that it would be wrong in principle to seek to find a comparable case and then to 'adjust' or 'correct' it, so that it can be used as a primary indicator of value.[7] To an extent, this is true of all issues concerning the quantum of costs, but it is especially true of non-contentious costs, because non-contentious costs turn more on what was agreed between solicitor and client than do other species of costs, which tend more to turn on what is inherently reasonable. This is particularly true where the solicitor has used value-based pricing for setting their fees (see Chapter 42). **38.08**

Hourly Rates

There is a chapter in this book that deals solely with hourly rates (see Chapter 51), but it focuses on rates between the opposing parties rather than rates between solicitor and client. That said, subject to what follows, many of the principles set out in that chapter also apply to the assessment of rates between solicitor and client (but only where those rates are not subject to the solicitor-and-client presumptions referred to in 37.06–37.07). **38.09**

The three most important factors that distinguish the two types of assessment are that: **38.10**

- the basis of assessment between solicitor and client is on the indemnity basis, whereas, between opposing parties, it is more commonly on the standard basis (see 37.02–37.04);
- certain presumptions apply as between solicitor and client (see 37.06–37.07); and
- hourly rates are, in general, governed by the contract of retainer, rather than solely by reference to what is reasonable (or reasonable and proportionate).

[6] *Jemma Trust Co Ltd v Liptrott* [2003] EWCA Civ 1476, at [24].

[7] *Treasury Solicitor v Regester* [1978] 2 All ER 920, at 924.

38.11 The second and third of these factors are, in combination, usually enough to determine the hourly rate that the solicitor is able to charge the client. In this regard, it will be recalled that r 46.9(3)(b) of the Civil Procedure Rules (CPR) provides that costs are assumed to be reasonable in amount if their amount was expressly or impliedly approved by the client (see 37.06). Whilst it is (just about) arguable that this presumption is rebuttable (see 37.08–37.09) and whilst any approval must have been 'informed' before the presumptions apply (see 37.10–37.13) the reality is that CPR, r 46.9(3)(b), will apply in the vast majority of cases and the rates that will be allowed will be those that were agreed. It will only be where the 'approval' presumption does not apply that the first of the three factors (that is, assessment on the indemnity basis) will be relevant. In the rare instance in which that point is reached, however, then the process becomes a simple matter of deciding what was reasonable and that will be much the same as an assessment between opposing parties (as set out in Chapter 51).

A forensic sieve for the assessment of hourly rates between solicitor and client

38.12 In view of the above, the following forensic sieve—which is only the editor's formulation and has not been approved by any court—is intended to be a time-efficient way of assessing the hourly rate between solicitor and client.

(1) Does the contract of retainer provide for an identifiable hourly rate?
  (a) If no, then go to question 4.
  (b) If yes, then go to the next question.
(2) Did the client give 'informed approval' of that rate (see 37.10–37.13)?
  (a) If no, then go to question 4.
  (b) If yes, then go to the next question.
(3) (i) Is the rate for an 'unusual' amount and (ii) did the solicitors fail to tell the client that, as a result, they might not recover the whole of the rate from the other party (see 37.14–37.16)?
  (a) If the answer to both (i) and (ii) is yes, then go to question 4.
  (b) If the answer to either of these questions is no or if there is no other party, then go to the next question.
(4) Is the work contentious or non-contentious?
  (a) If contentious, then assess the rates in much the same way as one would between opposing parties, but on the indemnity basis and in accordance with the presumptions in CPR, r 46.9(3).
  (b) If non-contentious, then go to question 5.
(5) Does the case or matter have a significant 'value element' (that is, is the value a significant factor)?
  (a) If no, then assess the rate on the indemnity basis and in accordance with the nine factors listed at 37.25. Unless there is reason to believe otherwise, the rate that is set will be the allowable rate.
  (b) If yes, then go to question 6.
(6) Is the intention to reflect the value of the case or matter in a separate value charge, or is the intention to reflect it in the hourly rate?
  (a) If the intention is to reflect the value of the case or matter in the hourly rate, then assess the rate on the indemnity basis and in accordance with the nine factors

listed at 37.25, including value. Unless there is reason to believe otherwise, the rate that is set will be the allowable rate.

  (b) If the intention is to reflect value in a separate value charge, then set that charge (see 38.15–38.34) and assess the rate on the indemnity basis in accordance with the nine factors listed at 37.25, but not including value, then go to the next question.

(7) Does the combination of the value charge and the hourly rate give rise to excessive remuneration overall?
  (a) If no, then the rate that has been set will be the allowable rate.
  (b) If yes, then go back and adjust the figures accordingly.

As the sieve implies, where the costs relate to non-contentious business, the value of the case or matter (that is, the value element) may have a significant influence on the amount allowed. If a great deal of money is involved, for example, the value element may allow the solicitor to command a high hourly rate as an alternative to a value charge. This is in contrast with both contentious costs and costs between opposing parties, in which value would have only a limited influence on the rates allowable. To a limited extent, the matters discussed in Chapter 42 (on value-based pricing) may have a bearing in this regard—although it should be noted that the notion of 'value' in value-based pricing is very different from the notion of value in the present context (see 42.24–42.25). **38.13**

Where the costs are non-contentious, then the factors that are relevant to their assessment are the nine factors in the Solicitors' (Non-Contentious Business) Remuneration Order 2009[8] (see 37.25). Two additional points merit special attention, as follows. **38.14**

- **The adrenaline factor** This is a factor arising out of a need to work under time pressure (see 38.23–38.24).
- **The bath-time factor** This is a factor that takes into account the contribution that a professional person's musings outside business hours make to the quality of the service they provide (see 38.25–38.26).[9]

These are described in the context of the value charge, but what is said in that context would also apply to an assessment of hourly rates (see 38.24 and 38.26).

The Value Charge

This topic is addressed in three parts: first, the purpose of the value charge; secondly, the role of factors other than value; and thirdly, the role of the value element—that is, the factor described in art 3(f) of the Solicitors' (Non-Contentious Business) Remuneration **38.15**

[8] SI 2009/1931.

[9] Such as 'in the train or car home, or in the bath, or even whilst watching television': *Maltby v DJ Freeman & Co* [1978] 1 WLR 431, at 435, *per* Walton J.

Order 2009[10] (see 37.25). It is important to bear in mind the distinction made between the value charge and the value element (see 38.05).

The purpose of the value charge

38.16 The ascertainment of costs is simply a matter of measurement. Like all systems of measurement, the starting point is to identify the dimensions that are going to be measured. Contentious costs tend to be either one-dimensional (for example fixed costs) or two-dimensional (that is, hourly rate and time spent), but whilst non-contentious costs may also be one- or two-dimensional, they are also commonly three-dimensional (that is, hourly rate, time spent and value charge). The existence of this third dimension makes it easier to take all of the relevant factors into account in such a way as to give rise to a fee that, overall, is fair and reasonable. Put otherwise, it makes for a very flexible system of charging. In a labour-intensive matter concerning a small amount of money, the fee would usually be predominantly—or even wholly—made up of a time charge (that is, the product of the hourly rate and the time spent), but if large sums were involved and time were a scarce luxury, the value charge would probably assume much greater prominence. This flexibility must not give rise to a lack of transparency, however, and this is addressed in more detail at 38.18.

The value charge reaffirmed . . .

38.17 The value charge is a well-established way of charging for the supply of non-contentious legal services, but in recent times it has been challenged as being so long-abiding as to be anachronistic. It would be far better—it has been argued—to do away with the idea of a value charge entirely and to ensure that the value element is reflected in the hourly rate—and *only* in the hourly rate (where that is the proposed means of charging). In 2003, the Court of Appeal rejected that argument.[11] In essence, Longmore LJ noted that there are significant differences between contentious and non-contentious business, and that those differences explain the need for and justify the value charge.[12] That said, whilst recognising that value charges continue to have a role to play, Longmore LJ cautioned that solicitors must address themselves to whether their overall remuneration is fair and reasonable, taking into account all of the relevant factors set out in (the then equivalent of) the Solicitors' (Non-Contentious Business) Remuneration Order 2009.[13]

. . . and then side-lined

38.18 There is no doubt that the law is as set out above, but the notion of levying a discrete value charge does appear to be becoming less commonly encountered. In particular, it is noticeable that the Law Society's Price and Service Transparency Toolkit[14]—which was

[10] SI 2009/1931.

[11] See *Jemma Trust Co Ltd v Liptrott* [2003] EWCA Civ 1476.

[12] *Ibid*, at [22]–[28]. In summary, Longmore LJ noted that, with contentious business, it is usually difficult to ascribe a 'value' to the money or property involved. He also commented that, in contentious business, it is ordinarily necessary to know the charges at the outset (because that information will be required for providing costs estimates, recovering the costs of interim hearings, etc), whereas the same is not true of non-contentious work, where the charges can be assessed at conclusion on a basis that is fair and reasonable in all of the circumstances.

[13] SI 2009/1931. The then equivalent was the Solicitors' (Non-Contentious Business) Remuneration Order 1994 (SI 1994/2616).

[14] See online at http://www.lawsociety.org.uk/support-services/advice/articles/price-and-service-transparency-toolkit/

published in response to calls from the Competition and Markets Authority (CMA) for greater transparency in the way in which legal services providers charge for their services—makes no mention of value charges. Indeed, the tenor of that document turns the notion of 'value' on its head in the sense that it now refers to the *added* value that the solicitor brings to the matter rather than the value of the subject matter of the instructions. The matters set out in Chapter 42 (on value-based pricing) seem to support the notion that the perception of what is meant by 'value' is undergoing a process of change.

The need to focus on all aspects of the matter as opposed to focusing on time spent and hourly rate

There is a need to avoid being overly preoccupied with time spent and rate charged. Donaldson J had this to say on the point: **38.19**

> 'The magnetic attraction of [the time spent] as a foundation for assessment of fair and reasonable remuneration is that, in the absence of an approved scale applied to value, it is the only figure which is readily calculable. It is an attraction which must be sternly resisted in cases of this sort where one or more of the other factors is such as to dwarf it into insignificance.'[15]

Thus there is a need to give appropriate weight to all of the factors in the then equivalent of the Solicitors' (Non-Contentious Business) Remuneration Order 2009[16] and it would be a mistake to focus solely on time. Donaldson J went on to say this: **38.20**

> 'This is not to say that the calculation [of time] has no value. It has a real value in all cases. Thus, if calculated accurately, it informs a solicitor of the minimum figure which he must charge if he is not to make an actual loss on the transaction. Second, it gives him an idea of the relationship between the overheads attributable to the transaction and the profit accruing to him. This latter point is plainly relevant in the broad sense that the nature of some transactions will justify much larger profits than others of a more routine type. But we must stress that it is only one of a number of crosschecks on the fairness and reasonableness of the final figure. The final figure will result from an exercise in judgment, not arithmetic, whatever arithmetical cross-checks may be employed.'[17]

The correct approach is a matter of judgement, rather than logic: all of the relevant circumstances should be taken into account, but this must be done without giving excessive weight to any of them. **38.21**

The weight to be given to factors other than value

Any one of the factors listed in the Solicitors' (Non-Contentious Business) Remuneration Order 2009[18] might be germane to the assessment of non-contentious costs (see 37.24–37.26). As noted at 38.14, two factors merit a specific mention: 'the adrenaline factor' and 'the bath-time factor' (although neither of these are specifically referred to in the 2009 Order). **38.22**

---

[15] *Treasury Solicitor v Regester* [1978] 1 WLR 446, at 450.

[16] See fn 13. This sentiment was recently affirmed by the Court of Appeal: *Jemma Trust Co Ltd v Liptrott* [2003] EWCA Civ 1476, at 656.

[17] *Treasury Solicitor v Regester* [1978] 1 WLR 446, at 451.

[18] SI 2009/1931.

The adrenaline factor

38.23 The adrenaline factor can be described as being that element of exigency which arises when a solicitor is required to work under a time pressure, with little or no margin for error. It can be placed within either art 3(e) of the 2009 Order ('place and circumstance') or art 3(h) ('importance'), or both. Donaldson J described it in this way:

> '[W]hat was the factor or factors, if any, which distinguished this transaction from the general run of such transactions. The answer was clearly the "adrenalin" [*sic*] factor. By this we mean that the solicitor had not only to work fast but had absolutely no margin for error. The transaction had to be completed by 31 July, come what might ... This caused us to look towards the top rather than the bottom of the bracket. In a different case, we might have found that there was plenty of time and that the transaction was very similar to one with which the solicitors had previously been concerned for the same client. This would have caused us to look in a reverse direction.'[19]

38.24 The adrenaline factor may be reflected in the hourly rate or the value charge. The latter would be particularly appropriate when, as would often be the case, the time pressure was such that the solicitor did not have the benefit of being able to devote as much time to the matter as they would have liked.

Bath-time factor

38.25 The bath-time factor is a recognition of the fact that no matter how accurate a solicitor's time-recording system might be, it will not record time spent thinking about the client's affairs whilst going about other business. It was described by Walton J in these terms:

> 'In a good many cases—although by no means all—[the actual time recorded] the logical starting point, in that it gives in itself a good indication of the weight of the matter as a whole. I would, however, make one gloss; however meticulously time records are kept, this will always, save in the plainest of all possible cases, represent an undercharge. No professional man, or senior employee of a professional man, stops thinking about the day's problems the minute he lifts his coat and umbrella from the stand and sets on the journey home. Ideas—often very valuable ideas—occur in the train or car home, or in the bath, or even whilst watching television. Yet nothing is ever put down on a time sheet—or can be put down on a time sheet—adequately to reflect this out of hours devotion of time. Thus, it will be a rare bill which can be simply compounded of time and value; there must always be a third element—usually under the second head.'[20]

38.26 Donaldson J held a similar view, but he expressed it by cautioning against giving excessive weight to the time that has been recorded, rather than by recommending that an affirmative adjustment be made for time not recorded:

> 'It also follows that it is wrong always to start by assessing the direct and indirect expense to the solicitor, represented by the time spent on the business. This must always be taken into account, but it is not necessarily, or even usually, a basic factor to which all others are related. Thus, although the labour involved will usually be directly related to, and reflected by, the time spent, the skill and specialised knowledge involved may vary greatly for different parts of that time. Again not all time spent on a transaction necessarily lends itself to being recorded, although the fullest possible records should be kept.'[21]

---

19 *Treasury Solicitor v Regester* [1978] 2 All ER 920, at 933.

20 *Maltby v DJ Freeman & Co* [1978] 1 WLR 431, at 435.

21 *Property and Reversionary Investment Corpn Ltd v Secretary of State for the Environment* [1975] 1 WLR 1504, at 1509, recited by Donaldson J in *Treasury Solicitor v Regester* [1978] 1 WLR 446, at 450.

As with the adrenaline factor, the bath-time factor may be reflected in either the hourly rate or the value charge. For the reasons set out at 38.07, it would usually not be appropriate to reflect it in both.

Disputes between opposing parties and non-contentious work

38.27 The costs incurred in a dispute that settled before proceedings were issued are non-contentious costs (see 3.23–3.30) and so, in theory, they ought to be assessed by reference to the factors in the Solicitors' (Non-Contentious Business) Remuneration Order 2009.[22] In practice, however, this rarely—if ever—happens. The costs of disputes between opposing parties are usually assessed without the court giving much thought to whether the work was contentious or not. Not only do judges not make the distinction, but also they prefer to treat the costs of all potential litigation as if they were incurred in actual litigation. Only a pendant could object to that approach. The distinction between contentious and non-contentious costs can become relevant, however, especially if the recoverability of the costs claimed depends on the costs being non-contentious.[23]

The weight to be given to value

38.28 Whilst it is not wholly clear what its current guidance is,[24] the Law Society used to recommend that, in certain spheres of work, such as probate, mortgages, commercial leases and domestic conveyancing, it may be appropriate to include a value element in the method of charging.[25] Even if the Law Society has now ceased to give guidance in this area, there is no reason to believe that the guidance it used to give was wrong in any way. The value element may be included within the hourly rate or as a separate charge (that is, as a value charge), but not duplicatively in both (see 38.07).

38.29 Similarly, the Law Society used to recommend that, where there is no specific guidance in the individual subject area, the charges set out in Table 38.1—known as the 'general regressive scale'—may assist in formulating an overall charging structure.

Table 38.1 The general regressive scale

Value band	Percentage (%)
Up to £400,000	0.5%
On next £600,000 (maximum value £1 million)	0.375%
On next £1,500,000 (maximum value £2.5 million)	0.25%
On next £2,500,000 (maximum value £5 million)	0.125%
On next £5,000,000 (maximum value £10 million)	0.1%

Note: This scale is based on work done in 2003. It could be argued that it should be updated.

[22] SI 2009/1931.

[23] See, eg, *Bilkus v Stockler Brunton (a firm)* [2010] EWCA Civ 101, in which a finding that certain work was contentious deprived a solicitor of a £50,000 value charge. Another example would be where the contract of retainer was a contingency fee agreement in a case in which only the common law applied.

[24] The Law Society website says that its Practice Advice Service guidance on non-contentious costs has been withdrawn because of the sea change in costs that occurred on 1 April 2013: personal communication with the editor, August 2017. The guidance has not been replaced.

[25] Law Society, 'Practice Advice Service: Non-contentious Costs', July 2012, p 16 *et seq*.

38.30 The following practice areas merit particular mention: probate and estates; domestic conveyancing; leasehold work; and acting on a mortgage (or remortgage).

Probate and estates

38.31 The Law Society used to recommend[26] that the estate be divided into two parts: the value of the deceased's residence; and the value of the rest of the estate. There is no reason to believe that its advice was incorrect or that it has now become wrong (although one could argue that other methods of pricing services are becoming more relevant, such as value-based pricing of the type described in Chapter 42). Where the solicitor is not acting as an executor, a value charge of 1 per cent of the value of the gross estate *less* residence *plus* 0.5 per cent of the value of the residence would be reasonable. Where the solicitor is acting as an executor, these figures could reasonably rise to 1.5 per cent and 0.75 per cent, respectively. Where the estate has a high value, then the regressive scale set out in Table 38.2 may be appropriate.[27]

Table 38.2 The probate and estates regressive scale

Value	Percentage (%)
Up to £1 million	1.5%
£1 million to £4 million	0.5%
£4 million to £8 million	0.1666%
£8 million to £12 million	0.0833%
Over £12 million	0.0416%

Note: This scale is based on work done in 2003. It could be argued that it should be updated.

Domestic conveyancing

38.32 Whilst its current guidance is silent on the point, the Law Society used to recommend[28] either taking a broad view of the circumstances or applying the general regressive scale (see Table 38.1). There is no reason to believe that this recommendation is wrong in any way.

Leasehold work

38.33 It would be reasonable to charge an hourly rate and a value charge for leasehold work. The value charge can be calculated as half the yearly rent multiplied by the unexpired term of the lease (limited to 20 years), *plus* any premium payable by the lessee and *less* any payable by the lessor, and then applying the general regressive scale (see Table 38.1). The resultant figure should then be reviewed to ensure that it is fair and reasonable, having regard to all of the circumstances.[29]

[26] See Law Society, 'Practice Advice Service: Non-contentious Costs', July 2012, pp 10 and 11; Law Society, 'Practice Advice Service: Non-contentious Costs', July 2012, pp 16 and 17.

[27] *Jemma Trust Co Ltd v Liptrott* [2003] EWCA Civ 1476, at 656, affirming the approach originally articulated by Walton J in *Maltby v D J Freeman & Co* [1978] 1 WLR 431.

[28] Law Society, 'Practice Advice Service: Non-contentious Costs', July 2012, pp 11 and 12.

[29] This was the advice that the Law Society used to give: *ibid*, p 12. Its current guidance is silent on the point, however.

Table 38.3 The mortgage regressive scale

Status	Percentage (%)
When acting for purchaser/mortgagor	0.25%
When acting for the mortgagee alone	0.5%
When acting for purchaser/mortgagor	0.25%
When acting for the mortgagee alone	0.5%

Acting on a mortgage or remortgage

Many lenders have their own scales, but where this is not the case, the Law Society used to suggest the scale laid out in Table 38.3 in mortgage or remortgage cases other than very high-value cases.[30] The current guidance issued by the Law Society is silent on the point, but there is no reason to believe that the old guidance was, or has become, wrong. **38.34**

Shoddy Work

It has long been established that a legal representative cannot recover costs from a client where deficient professional performance has negated the benefit of that work.[31] In the past, this may have been analysed as a result of non-performance of an entire contract[32] or an example of the doctrine of abatement. There is now an additional remedy available to consumer clients arising out of the consumer protection provisions referred to in Chapter 28 (especially at 28.146–28.148). In addition, s 63(3) of the Solicitors Act 1974 may apply (see 38.38–38.39). **38.35**

Abatement

The right of abatement will arise where a solicitor (or any trader) claims fees, but the client has an unliquidated counterclaim arising out of a breach of the contract for the supply of those services. Where those are the circumstances, the client may be entitled to deduct the counterclaim. It is a right that is a true defence at common law[33] and is distinct from set-off.[34] That said, there would be no reason why set-off could not be pleaded in the alternative. Where a client wishes to rely on a right of abatement, they must show that the breach of contract directly reduced the value of the services rendered;[35] hence not all **38.36**

30 *Ibid*, p 13.

31 *In re Massey and Carey* (1884) 26 Ch D 459. As a modern example of this (albeit it one concerning a barrister instructed directly rather than a solicitor), see *Dunn v Glass Systems (UK) Ltd* [2007] EWHC 1901 (QB), in which fees were disallowed on the basis that they were for drafting prolix pleadings that would have led to the litigation being unmanageable.

32 For an example of this (albeit only by analogy), see *PC Harrington Contractors Ltd v Systech International Ltd* [2012] EWCA Civ 1371, in which an arbitrator was denied costs for carrying out work that led to an unenforceable judgment (because he had breached rules of natural justice).

33 Although there is no modern authority relating to solicitors, it is probable that the true defence mentioned above is unaffected by the laws relating to limitation: see Limitation Act 1980, s 35(3).

34 See *Mondel v Steel* (1841) 8 M & W; *Aries Tanker Corpn v Total Transport Ltd* [1977] 1 WLR 185, HL. As to the principles by which legal set-off may operate as a defence, see *Hanak v Green* [1958] 2 QB 9, at 16.

35 *Mellowes Archital Ltd v Bell Properties Ltd* (1997) 87 BLR 26, CA.

counterclaims arising out of a solicitor–client relationship would suffice, but a counterclaim for shoddy work would ordinarily be capable of passing that test.

38.37 Abatement is an ancient doctrine, but, in a modern context, the solicitor's fees would either be diminished by a counterclaim or they would be assessed as being nil—or close to nil—as a result of the value of the work being negated by the solicitor's shortcomings. The abatement would not diminish the costs incurred prior to the provision of deficient services.[36] Some retainers seek to preclude the client from claiming abatement or set-off for shoddy work (or at all), but such provisions are probably not enforceable.[37]

Solicitors Act 1974, s 63(3)

38.38 There is another mechanism through which the court is able to take shoddy work into account, but it is available only where the work has been carried out under a contentious business agreement—and even then only when the client changes solicitors before the solicitor has fully performed their obligations. In those (somewhat unlikely) circumstances, Solicitors Act 1974, s 63(3), may apply, which reads:

> 'If [where the client changes solicitors] an order is made for the assessment of the amount due to the solicitor in respect of the business done under the agreement, the court shall direct the costs officer to have regard to the circumstances under which the change of solicitor has taken place, and the costs officer, unless he is of the opinion that there has been no default, negligence, improper delay or other conduct on the part of the solicitor, or any of his employees, affording the client reasonable ground for changing his solicitor, shall not allow to the solicitor the full amount of the remuneration agreed to be paid to him.'

38.39 This provision permits the court to take account of default or negligence, so presumably it allows the court to take account of substandard work. It is clear that negligence can be taken into account in such a way as to reduce the solicitor's fees to a level that is lower than they would have been had the agreement been fully performed. What is less clear is whether the court is able to take that conduct into account in such a way as to allow a figure that is lower than the amount that is a reasonable amount: it is arguable that the court does have this power, but there is no authority to confirm this.

The Ombudsman

38.40 It is open to a client to complain to the Legal Ombudsman (previously known as the Legal Services Ombudsman) for the purposes of obtaining a reduction in the fees payable. The relevant provisions are discussed at 39.22–39.34. This option was created at broadly the same time as the long-standing provisions concerning inadequate professional services were revoked,[38] which is probably no coincidence (because the Ombudsman has the powers to deal with shoddy work).

---

[36] *Lewis v Samuel* (1846) 8 QB 685.

[37] Although not a costs case, see *Hong Kong & Shanghai Banking Corpn v Kloeckner & Co AG* [1990] 2 QB 514. Also see Part 2 of the Consumer Rights Act 2015.

[38] Those provisions were contained in Solicitors Act 1974, s 37A, and were repealed by Legal Services Act 2007, ss 177 and 210, Sch 16, Pt 1, paras 1 and 39, and Sch 23, on 1 January 2009.

Inadequate Advice Regarding Funding Options

If a solicitor fails to give appropriate advice regarding the funding options available to a client or potential client, this may result in some or all of that solicitor's fees and disbursements being irrecoverable. In a case in which a firm of solicitors allowed a client to enter into a conditional fee agreement rather than take advantage of union-funded legal aid, Hickenbottom J found that it was open to the costs judge to assess the fees and disbursements at nil, on the basis that it was not reasonable to incur costs in those circumstances.[39] It would not be appropriate to approach such a situation as if it were a case in which the reduction in costs should be assessed on a 'loss of chance' basis.[40] **38.41**

It is becoming increasingly common for consumer clients to pursue their former solicitors for after-the-event (ATE) insurance premiums and success fees deducted from damages in cases in which the client had other suitable means of funding that could have been used to avoid those costs being incurred.[40a] **38.42**

Estimates and Assurances on a Solicitor-and-client Basis

The following discussion deals with two topics: **38.43**

- the extent to which a client is able to rely on the fact that an estimate has been exceeded (or not been given when it ought to have been, as the case may be); and
- the extent to which a client is able to rely on an assurance that legal services would be provided in a particular manner (such as by a particular grade of fee earner or by a particular person).

The duty to give an estimate

There are many ways in which a duty to provide an estimate may arise: **38.44**

- as a professional duty;
- as a result of the giving of specific instructions or under the rules of court;
- under the common law;
- under an agreed term in the retainer; and
- as a result of an obligation imposed by consumer legislation.

Any one of these may be relevant to the assessment of costs, but the first (namely, professional duty) is particularly relevant. This is because it will exist in all cases. That said, the matters referred to in 38.58–38.59 relating to consumer clients may be of greater importance in the future; indeed, the law described in those paragraphs could be a game-changer in certain circumstances.

As is explained below, the extent and nature of the professional duty will turn on when the estimate was, or should have been, given. **38.45**

---

[39] See *McDaniel & Co (a firm) v Clarke* [2014] EWHC 3826 (QB), at [27].
[40] See *ibid*, at [26] and [27].
[40a] See Friston, M, Key tips on solicitor/client costs (2 September 2018), Practical Law Dispute Resolution Blog, http://disputeresolutionblog.practicallaw.com/key-tips-on-solicitorclient-costs/

The professional duty to provide estimates

38.46 **Before 1 July 2007** Prior to 1 July 2007, a solicitor's obligations arose out of the Solicitors' Costs Information and Client Care Code 1999.[41] The solicitor in question was under an obligation to give the client the 'best information possible' about the likely overall costs, including a breakdown between fees, value added tax (VAT) and disbursements.[42] There was a requirement that all information given orally be confirmed in writing.[43]

38.47 **Between 1 July 2007 and 5 October 2011** Between these dates, the matter was governed by the Solicitors' Code of Conduct 2007. During that period, the solicitor continued to have a duty to give the best information possible about the likely overall cost of a matter at the outset. Any information about costs had to be clear and confirmed in writing,[44] and ought to have been given as soon as possible after the solicitor had agreed to act.[45] In so far as estimates were concerned, the solicitor was required to:

- advise the client of the basis and terms of the solicitor's charges;
- advise the client if charging rates were to be increased;
- advise the client of likely payments that may need to be made; and
- discuss with the client how the client would pay—in particular:
  - whether the client may be eligible and should apply for public funding; and
  - whether the client's own costs were covered by insurance or may be paid by someone else, such as an employer or trade union.[46]

38.48 There was a requirement to carry out a cost–benefit analysis. In particular, the solicitor was required to discuss with their client whether the potential outcomes of the case

[41] Where the fee was based on time spent, the solicitor was under an obligation to clearly explain the time that was likely to be spent in dealing with a matter: see Solicitors' Costs Information and Client Care Code 1999, para 4(b). Under para 4(c), giving 'the best information possible' would have included: agreeing a fixed fee; giving a realistic estimate; giving a forecast within a possible range of costs; or explaining to the client the reasons why it is not possible to fix, or give a realistic estimate or forecast of, the overall costs, and giving instead the best information possible about the cost of the next stage of the matter. Where the client was a privately paying client, the solicitor was at liberty to tell them that they could set an upper limit on the solicitor's costs for which they might be liable without further authority—although this would appear not to have been a mandatory requirement. Where such a limit was set, it should not have been (and still should not be) exceeded without first obtaining the client's consent: see para 4(d). The solicitor ought to have made it clear at the outset if an estimate, quotation or other indication of cost was not intended to be fixed: see para 4(e). A cost–benefit analysis ought to have been carried out and the solicitor in question was required to discuss whether the likely outcome in a matter justified the expense or risk involved: see para 4(f). The solicitor ought to have kept the client properly informed about costs as the matter progressed—in particular, under para 6(b)–(d): unless agreed otherwise, the solicitor ought to have said how much the costs were and this ought to have been done at regular intervals (at least every six months); the solicitor ought to have explained any changed circumstances that were likely to have had a bearing on the amount of costs, the degree of risk involved or the cost–benefit to the client of continuing with the matter; and the solicitor ought to have informed the client in writing as soon as it appeared that a costs estimate or agreed upper limit might or would be exceeded.

[42] Solicitors' Costs Information and Client Care Code 1999, para 4(1).

[43] Solicitors' Costs Information and Client Care Code 1999, para 3(a)–(c).

[44] Solicitors' Code of Conduct 2007, para 2.03(5), and para 27 of the Notes thereto.

[45] Paragraph 18 of the Guidance to para 2.03 of the Solicitors' Code of Conduct 2007.

[46] Solicitors' Code of Conduct 2007, para 2.03(1).

justified the expense or risk involved, including, if relevant, the risk of having to pay an opponent's costs.[47] The solicitor was not required to give information where it was inappropriate to do so.[48]

On and after 6 October 2011 The present-day provisions are contained in the Solicitors Regulation Authority (SRA) Code of Conduct 2011 (as amended in 2017), which are not as prescriptive as the provisions that preceded them. The relevant provisions read as follows: **38.49**

> 'You must achieve these outcomes:
>
> O(1.12) clients are in a position to make informed decisions about the services they need, how their matter will be handled and the options available to them;
>
> O(1.13) clients receive the best possible information, both at the time of engagement and when appropriate as their matter progresses, about the likely overall cost of their matter;
>
> [...]
>
> Acting in the following way(s) may tend to show that you have achieved these outcomes and therefore complied with the Principles:
>
> IB(1.13) discussing whether the potential outcomes of the client's matter are likely to justify the expense or risk involved, including any risk of having to pay someone else's legal fees;
>
> IB(1.14) clearly explaining your fees and if and when they are likely to change;
>
> IB(1.15) warning about any other payments for which the client may be responsible;
>
> IB(1.16) discussing how the client will pay, including whether public funding may be available, whether the client has insurance that might cover the fees, and whether the fees may be paid by someone else such as a trade union;
>
> IB(1.17) where you are acting for a client under a fee arrangement governed by statute, such as a conditional fee agreement, giving the client all relevant information relating to that arrangement;
>
> IB(1.18) where you are acting for a publicly funded client, explaining how their publicly funded status affects the costs;
>
> IB(1.19) providing the information in a clear and accessible form which is appropriate to the needs and circumstances of the client.'

It is not known how the court will interpret these provisions. Notwithstanding the shift from a prescriptive approach to an outcomes-based approach, similarities with the previous incarnations of the Code of Conduct are far greater than the differences. Solicitors would be storing up trouble for themselves if they were not to set themselves high standards in this regard.[49] **38.50**

[47] Solicitors' Code of Conduct 2007, para 2.03(6).

[48] Paragraph 18 of the Guidance to para 2.03 of the Solicitors' Code of Conduct 2007.

[49] By way of example, in *Darby v Law Society* [2003] EWHC 2270 (Admin), at [27], Auld LJ (sitting in the Divisional Court) said that there was a heavy onus on a solicitor to establish that their client is so sophisticated in matters of litigation and so attentive to the cost implications of the litigation in question that the then requirements (under the Solicitors' Practice Rules 1990) to give information about costs could be disregarded.

38.51 It should be noted that the duty to provide information is an ongoing duty under O(1.13) (in which O means 'outcome'). Where a revised estimate is given, that may be taken into account as the applicable estimate.[50]

38.52 The Law Society's Price and Service Transparency Toolkit refers to the need to give estimates (especially of time likely to be spent if the solicitor's fees are to be charged on an hourly rate basis).[51] Unlike the SRA Code of Conduct 2011, the Toolkit is not made pursuant to any statutory powers, and—in the editor's view—is not likely to be given much weight other than as a document that sets out best practices.

Duties to provide estimates other than the professional duty

38.53 In addition to the professional duty to provide estimates, there are other ways in which the duty may (or may not) arise.

38.54 **Contractual duties to provide estimates** A duty to provide an estimate may arise out of express or implied terms within the retainer.[52] That said, in the ordinary run of things, the fact that the professional duty to provide an estimate exists would not give rise to a corresponding implied contractual duty (see 38.74).[53] This may no longer be so in certain circumstances if the client is a consumer, however (see 38.58–38.59 and 38.68–38.71).

38.55 **Instructions and the duty to provide estimates** Where the client gives instructions that expressly or impliedly require that an estimate be given, that will create a duty that may be relevant, especially if the client can show reliance.[54]

38.56 **Practice directions and the duty to provide estimates** Where an estimate is served and filed in court proceedings, the Costs Practice Direction (CPD) used to provide that the legal representative also had to serve the estimate on the client.[55] This included the circumstances in which the estimate was served by reason of a change in the funding arrangement.[56] It would seem that, post 1 April 2013, the CPR no longer contain such a requirement. That said, in a case that is subject to costs management, it is difficult to see how a solicitor could properly not take instructions on the draft budget, so it is easily arguable that—for all practical purposes—they would remain under a duty to keep their client informed in this regard.

---

[50] *Harrison v Eversheds LLP* [2017] EWHC 2594 (QB), at [41]–[44], *per* Slade J.

[51] See Law Society, 'Price and Service Transparency Toolkit', p 5, online at http://www.lawsociety.org.uk/support-services/advice/articles/price-and-service-transparency-toolkit/

[52] For an example of a case in which an express duty to provide estimates was regarded as creating a duty, see *Eversheds LLP v Cuddy* (unreported), 17 December 2009, SCCO, *per* Master Campbell.

[53] *Mastercigars Direct Ltd v Withers LLP* [2007] EWHC 2733 (Ch), at [107]–[111].

[54] For an example of a case in which an express duty to provide estimates was regarded as creating a duty, see *Eversheds LLP v Cuddy* (unreported), 17 December 2009, SCCO, *per* Master Campbell.

[55] CPD, art 6.4(1). The relevant provision read as follows:'(1) When—(a) a party to a claim which is outside the financial scope of either the small claims track or the fast track files an allocation questionnaire; or (b) a party to a claim which is being dealt with on the fast track or the multi track files a pre-trial check list (listing questionnaire), that party must also file an estimate of costs and serve a copy of it on every other party, unless the court otherwise directs. Where a party is represented, that party's legal representative must in addition serve a copy of the estimate on that party. (2) Where a party who is required to file and serve a new estimate of costs in accordance with Rule 44.15(3), is represented; and the legal representative must in addition serve the new estimate on that party. (3) This paragraph does not apply to litigants in person.'

[56] See CPD, art 6.4(2); CPR, r 44.15(3).

General consumer law and the duty not to provide unrealistic estimates A solicitor is under an obligation not to give an unrealistic estimate to secure the work. If they were to fail in this regard, then the solicitor would be guilty of a criminal offence,[57] as well as in breach of the SRA Code of Conduct 2011.[58] **38.57**

Consumer legislation and the duty to provide estimates As is explained in more detail in Chapter 28, on 13 June 2014 the Consumer Contracts (Information, Cancellation and Additional Charges) Regulations 2013[59] came into force. The new Regulations imposed requirements to provide certain information. In so far as an 'on-premises' contract is concerned, Sch 1 to the 2013 Regulations imposes a requirement to provide 'the total price of the ... services inclusive of taxes, or where the nature of the goods or services is such that the price cannot reasonably be calculated in advance, the manner in which the price is to be calculated'. A very similar provision applies to 'off-premises' and distance contracts.[60] **38.58**

It is arguable that these provisions are a game-changer, because they appear to impose a requirement that the solicitor—or any legal services provider—must give a 'total price' unless this 'cannot reasonably be calculated in advance'. One could easily argue that, when dealing with a consumer client, this imposes a duty to provide an all-inclusive price unless this cannot reasonably be done (which, in the editor's view, would be the case in only a minority of cases). If this is right, then when they are dealing with a consumer, it may be that it is no longer open to a solicitor—or any legal services provider—simply to elect to provide legal services on the traditional, open-ended basis of an hourly rate. Such an arrangement would need to be justified, which, in the majority of cases, would be hard to do (and almost impossible to do if the solicitor were under a professional duty to provide such an estimate). There is, however, no authority on this point. **38.59**

The relevance of estimates in general

It will rarely be the case that a figure *bona fide* intended to be an estimate would be regarded as being a binding quote.[61] The relevance of any such figure would be a matter of contractual interpretation, to be decided on the facts of the matter in hand. Slade J had this to say on the matter: **38.60**

> 'An estimate is to be distinguished from a quotation of fees: an offer which is accepted. An estimate is what it says. It gives an idea, which from a professional firm can be taken as reasonably and carefully made taking into account all relevant considerations, of what the future costs of work on a case is likely to be. A solicitor cannot be held to be restricted to recovering the exact sum set out in an estimate. However, a client is entitled to place reliance on the estimate. The nature, degree and reasonableness of that reliance will no doubt be but one factor in the view taken on an assessment under Section 70 of the Solicitors Act 1974 of how much more than the estimate it is reasonable for the client to pay.'[62]

[57] See Consumer Protection Act 1987, Pt III, ss 20 and 21, which deal with misleading price indications.

[58] See SRA Code of Conduct 2011, O(8.1), IB(8.7) and IB(8.9).

[59] SI 2013/3134.

[60] See Consumer Contracts (Information, Cancellation and Additional Charges) Regulations 2013 (SI 2013/3134), Sch 2, para (f).

[61] *Wong v Vizards* [1997] 2 Costs LR 46, at 48. See also *Harrison v Eversheds LLP* [2017] EWHC 2594 (QB), at [38], *per* Slade J.

[62] *Harrison v Eversheds LLP* [2017] EWHC 2594 (QB), at [63].

38.61 While a pedant would say that the law was merely clarified rather than changed, in 2007 there was a shift in the juridical approach towards cases in which estimates had been exceeded.[63] To understand that shift, it is necessary to know something of the history of the law.

38.62 The starting point is the approach adopted by Toulson J in *Wong v Vizards*,[64] the facts of which were remarkable only in that an estimate had been exceeded. Toulson J found that it was permissible to reduce the allowable costs to the level of the estimate and then to add back an allowance that 'effectively allowed to the solicitor a margin of approximately 15% over the worst case estimate'.[65] This gave rise to a method of assessing costs on a solicitor-and-client assessment where the court would allow the figure stated in the estimate *plus* a margin—typically between 10 per cent and 20 per cent.[66]

38.63 In 2007, Morgan J clarified the law in such a way as to discourage the use of that method.[67] He explained that Toulson J was not expounding a point of principle. Morgan J held that, where an estimate has been exceeded, the approach is not to allow the figure in the estimate to be adjusted by a margin, but to use the estimate as a yardstick against which the reasonableness of the costs finally claimed may be measured:

> 'This is not to say that I would reject altogether the idea that a margin might offer something useful. As I indicated earlier, when saying that an excess of the final bill over the estimate calls for an explanation, this reaction is heavily dependent upon the extent of the excess. A modest excess does not call for much explanation and a substantial excess calls for a great deal of explanation.'[68]

Morgan J was at pains to point out that his comments were not in any way at odds with what Toulson J had said previously.[69]

38.64 Morgan J's approach appears at first to be different from the approach between opposing parties (in which regard PD 44, para 3, specifically mentions a margin of 20 per cent where a budget is exceeded), but in truth they are the same. This is because the 20 per cent is simply a threshold beyond which an explanation is required. If that explanation is unsatisfactory, then the amount by which the estimate has been exceeded will be a factor that the court will take into account. It will not operate as a cap, either on a solicitor-and-client basis[70] or between opposing parties.

38.65 Morgan J's approach invites the obvious question of whether the court is at liberty to allow an amount that is lower than the amount that would be justified on a line-by-line assessment. Whilst *obiter*, he confirmed that it was:

---

[63] Some commentators have said that the law has not been clarified, but that there is simply a divergence of judicial option: see, eg, Morgan, J, 'Estimating the Damage', *Litigation Funding*, April 2009, pp 14–15.

[64] *Wong v Vizards* [1997] 2 Costs LR 46.

[65] *Ibid*, at 50.

[66] See, eg, *Reynolds v Stone Rowe Brewer (a firm)* [2008] EWHC 497; *Anthony v Ellis & Fairburn (a firm)* [2000] 2 Costs LR 277.

[67] *Mastercigars Direct Ltd v Withers LLP* [2007] EWHC 2733 (Ch), at [118].

[68] *Ibid*, at [104].

[69] See *Wong v Vizards* [1997] 2 Costs LR 46, at 49.

[70] Whilst it dealt with the law as it used to be under the CPD, see *Mastercigars Direct Ltd v Withers LLP* [2007] EWHC 2733 (Ch), at [106].

> '[E]ven if the solicitor has spent a reasonable time on reasonable items of work and the charging rate is reasonable, the resulting figure may exceed what it is reasonable in all the circumstances to expect the client to pay and, to the extent that the figure does exceed what is reasonable to expect the client to pay, the excess is not recoverable.'[71]

The test is what it is reasonable to expect the client to pay. To that extent, the client does not need to show that they relied upon the estimate for the court to take the estimate into account (and, in particular, does not need to establish an estoppel).[72] Where the client is able to show reliance, then the court would give greater weight to that estimate.[73] In any event, deviation from an estimate is something that requires explanation and justification: in a case in which the estimate in respect of profit costs had been exceeded by a factor of just under three, Slade J found that it was not sufficient merely to point to the fact that certain additional and unforeseen work had been required, and that an opponent's estimate of costs (as set out in Precedent H) had also increased.[74] **38.66**

Up until 13 June 2013, this was the state of the law. Whilst there is no authority on the point, the approach to estimates may have changed for contracts made with consumer clients on or after that date. This is not only because of the requirement to give the information referred to at 38.58–38.59, but also because any information that the solicitor—or any legal services provider—gives pursuant to the Consumer Contracts (Information, Cancellation and Additional Charges) Regulations 2013[75] is to be treated as included as a term of the contract.[76] Moreover, a failure to provide an estimate would also be relevant by virtue of reg 18 of the 2013 Regulations (see 28.99). One could easily argue that there is no reason why solicitors should be excused from the effect of these provisions merely because, historically, their estimates have been treated as non-binding. **38.67**

A further potentially relevant change in the law took place on 1 October 2015, when s 50 of the Consumer Rights Act 2015 came into force. It reads as follows: **38.68**

> '**50 Information about the trader or service to be binding**
>
> (1) Every contract to supply a service is to be treated as including as a term of the contract anything that is said or written to the consumer, by or on behalf of the trader, about the trader or the service, if—
> (a) it is taken into account by the consumer when deciding to enter into the contract, or
> (b) it is taken into account by the consumer when making any decision about the service after entering into the contract.
>
> (2) Anything taken into account by the consumer as mentioned in subsection (1)(a) or (b) is subject to—
> (a) anything that qualified it and was said or written to the consumer by the trader on the same occasion, and

[71] *Ibid*, at [102].

[72] Whilst the point went by consent, see *Harrison v Eversheds LLP* [2017] EWHC 2594 (QB), at [38], *per* Slade J.

[73] See, eg, *ibid*, at [63].

[74] See *ibid*, at [45]–[70].

[75] SI 2013/3134.

[76] See Consumer Contracts (Information, Cancellation and Additional Charges) Regulations 2013 (SI 2013/3134), reg 9(3), in relation to on-premises contracts, and regs 10(5) and 13(6), in relation to off-premises contracts and distance contracts, respectively.

(b) any change to it that has been expressly agreed between the consumer and the trader (before entering into the contract or later).

(3) Without prejudice to subsection (1), any information provided by the trader in accordance with regulation 9, 10 or 13 of the Consumer Contracts (Information, Cancellation and Additional Charges) Regulations 2013 (SI 2013/3134) is to be treated as included as a term of the contract.

(4) A change to any of the information mentioned in subsection (3), made before entering into the contract or later, is not effective unless expressly agreed between the consumer and the trader.

(5) See section 54 for a consumer's rights if the trader is in breach of a term that this section requires to be treated as included in a contract.'

38.69 Thus anything that is said or written that a consumer client then takes into account for the purposes of deciding whether to give instructions (or what those instructions should be) will be included as a term of the contract of retainer. The relevance of this is that any spoken or written estimate is capable of becoming part of the contract, not only those that are given pursuant to the 2013 Regulations.

38.70 In addition, traders (including solicitors) cannot unilaterally change the service as they have described it in the information they have given under the Consumer Contracts (Information, Cancellation and Additional Charges) Regulations 2013[77] or otherwise where the consumer has relied on that information.[78] The CMA has specifically referred to the fact that these restrictions apply to lawyers.[79]

38.71 There is no doubt that these new provisions are intended to strengthen the protection afforded to consumers. It would be difficult to argue that solicitors—or any legal services provider—are exempt. As such, one would not expect the Consumer Rights Act 2015 merely to maintain the *status quo* in so far as solicitors are concerned. In particular, it would be surprising if an estimate that was a contractual term were to be afforded exactly the same status as an estimate that was not. One could easily argue that the better analysis is that where a consumer is able to prove that an estimate is a contractual term, that estimate should be binding unless the lawyer is able to prove otherwise by reference to the estimate being qualified or changed in accordance with s 50(2) of the 2015 Act. There is, however, no authority on that point.

38.72 It is also worth noting that the CMA has specifically cited 'failing to provide adequate information to a consumer about the time that will be engaged in progressing the consumer's case and the likely costs' as a breach of the Consumer Protection from Unfair Trading Regulations 2008,[80] reg 3(1),[81] this being a criminal office (see 28.102).[82]

38.73 The following miscellaneous points can be made about estimates.

77 SI 2013/3134. See Consumer Protection Act 2015, s 50(4).

78 See Consumer Protection Act 2015, s 50(2)(b).

79 See CMA, *Legal Services Market Study: Final Report* (London: HMSO, 2016), p 28.

80 SI 2008/1277.

81 See CMA, *Legal Services Market Study: Final Report* (London: HMSO, 2016), Appx E, para 18.

82 See Consumer Protection from Unfair Trading Regulations 2008 (SI 2008/1277), regs 8–16.

Revised estimates In a case in which there was nothing to suggest otherwise, Morgan J found that the professional requirements to provide updated costs information were not to be implied as terms of the contract of retainer.[83] Morgan J rejected the argument that the ambit of the retainer was limited to the work set out in the estimate.[84] Thus, unless there is reason to believe otherwise, a failure to give a revised estimate would seem to be merely a factor to be taken into account. Some retainers, however, contain express terms that impose obligations to provide revised estimates at certain times; where this is so, it would easily be arguable that a failure to discharge those obligations should, at the very least, be a factor that is given significant weight. Furthermore, where the client is a consumer, the points made at 38.67–38.72 may have a bearing. **38.74**

Where a revised estimate is given in an attempt to correct an underestimate (as opposed to as a result of a change in the facts), then it is open to the court to find that weight should be given to the original, rather than to the revised estimate.[85] For the reasons given at 38.70, this is likely also to be the case in certain circumstances if a consumer client is able to prove that the original estimate was a contractual term. In any event, where a revised estimate is given, the court is able to take it into account as being the starting point.[86] **38.75**

Qualified estimates In a case in which the client sought to justify his failure to pay an interim invoice on the grounds that an estimate had been exceeded, Ward LJ had to consider the effect of the following qualification given by the solicitor: **38.76**

> 'We only give estimates as a guide. Thus we will make every attempt to ensure their accuracy, we cannot guarantee that the final charge will not exceed the estimate. This is because there are many factors outside our control which may affect the level of costs.'[87]

Ward LJ had the following to say about the effect of this qualification: **38.77**

> 'The complaint that the bill exceeded the estimate cannot stand in the face of the fact that [the above provision] made [it] plain ... that estimates were not intended to be fixed or binding and that other factors might mean that the estimate would be varied from time to time.'[88]

It would, however, be wrong to read too much into this *ratio*, because Ward LJ was dealing with a refusal to pay interim invoices in a case in which there were sound reasons for the estimate having been exceeded—and that is very different from the more common situation in which the estimate was not adequately revised or was palpably unrealistic from the outset. In the context of a conditional estimate (an estimate such as 'if the matter settles after exchange of pleadings ...'), Sir Oliver Popplewell found that the conditionality of the estimate did not give rise to implied authority that it may be exceeded with impunity.[89] Furthermore, where the client is a consumer, the points made at 38.67–38.72 may have a bearing. **38.78**

---

[83] *Mastercigars Direct Ltd v Withers LLP* [2007] EWHC 2733 (Ch), at [107]–[111].
[84] *Ibid*, at [112].
[85] *Reynolds v Stone Rowe Brewer (a firm)* [2008] EWHC 497, at [67] *et seq*.
[86] *Harrison v Eversheds LLP* [2017] EWHC 2594 (QB), at [41]–[44], *per* Slade J.
[87] *Cawdery Kaye Fireman & Taylor v Minkin* [2012] EWCA Civ 546, at [7].
[88] *Ibid*, at [336].
[89] *Anthony v Ellis & Fairburn (a firm)* [2000] 2 Costs LR 277, at 283.

38.79 **Incomplete estimates and poor estimates** It may be that a solicitor says that the estimate was so wide of the mark that it ought to have been obvious that it was wrong; whilst it is possible to envisage cases in which it would succeed, that argument would ordinarily not find favour.[90] Whilst dealing with the interpretation of a contract, rather than the effect of an estimate, Hughes LJ has indicated that if a client is not told about a potential liability for costs, they will not be required to pay them.[91] The implication is that if an estimate is given in relation to one aspect of the matter and then costs are incurred in another, the costs of the latter may not be recoverable. The extent to which this applies to estimates is not known.

Putative Waiver of Fees

38.80 Whilst a putative waiver of fees would be a factor that the court could take into account for the purposes of assessment, if a client is to rely on waiver as negating or limiting the solicitor's contractual right to payment, it must be supported by consideration that must come from the client. Tugendhat J has held that there was no consideration in the fact that the solicitor might benefit from having waived their fees (see 27.90).[92] In a similar vein, the act of writing off costs for accounting purposes would not of itself extinguish the contractual right to payment.[93]

Assurances About How Services Will be Provided

38.81 In the same way that clients can expect to be given reasonably accurate information about costs, they are also entitled to receive reasonably accurate information about the way in which legal services are to be provided. In particular, they should be told the status of the persons who are carrying out the work.[94] Although only of descriptive value, the notes to the now-superseded Solicitors' Code of Conduct 2007 gave the following guidance:

> 'The status of the person dealing with your client must be made absolutely clear, for legal and ethical reasons. For example, a person who is not a solicitor must not be described as one, either expressly or by implication. All staff having contact with clients, including reception, switchboard and secretarial staff, should be advised accordingly.'[95]

38.82 There are two circumstances in which this requirement may become relevant to the issue of costs: the first is where the client has made a specific request concerning the provision of legal services and that request is not met; the second is where the solicitor's conduct has led to a reasonable expectation about the way in which legal services will be provided. Each is dealt with in turn.

---

[90] Whilst not in any way binding, see *Billington v Downs Solicitors LLP* (unreported), 16 January 2012, SCCO, *per* Master Leonard.

[91] In *Jones v Wrexham Borough Council* [2007] EWCA Civ 1356, at [94].

[92] *Ashia Centur Ltd v Barker Gillette LLP* [2011] EWHC 148 (QB), at [20].

[93] *Slatter v Ronaldsons* [2002] 2 Costs LR 267.

[94] Whilst it has now been superseded, see Solicitors' Code of Conduct 2007, para 2.02(2).

[95] See para 19 of the Guidance to para 2.02 of the Solicitors' Code of Conduct 2007. A similar provision existed prior to 1 July 2007: see Solicitors Practice Rules 1990, r 15(2)(a).

Specific request regarding the supply of legal services

A failure to comply with a specific request may lead to a complete failure to perform the solicitor's obligations and this would be capable of wholly negating the solicitor's right to payment under the contract of retainer. In a case in which the client had asked for a solicitor, but was allocated an unqualified fee earner, Schiemann LJ found that the fact that the client had asked to see 'a solicitor' resulted in the retainer being a contract for the provision of legal services by *a solicitor* and he found that the purported performance of the contract by someone other than a solicitor was no performance at all; therefore no costs were payable.[96] Underhill J has found that, in an appropriate case, the question will turn on the client's knowledge, both at the time they gave instructions and throughout the retainer generally, the implication of which is that if a client becomes aware of the true status of the person providing the legal services and if they continue to accept those services without demur, then the client will find it difficult to persuade the court that the services were not the same as those they required.[97] As to the types of evidence that might be relevant, see 38.84. Underhill J also raised the question of whether adequate supervision by a solicitor may, in certain circumstances, amount to the provision of legal services by a solicitor: whilst he made no findings in that regard, he implied that this was possible.[98] The points made at 38.67–38.72 about consumer contracts may, with appropriate modifications, have a bearing in a case involving a client who is a consumer. **38.83**

Solicitor's conduct

The expectation that the work be done in a certain way or by a certain person may arise from the conduct of the solicitor. In a case in which a fee earner had said he was a practising solicitor when, in fact, he was not, Brooke LJ found that the fee earner had misrepresented his status and that this had created a situation similar to that mentioned at 38.83.[99] Whilst he was dealing with a case in which there had been a specific request, Underhill J explained that the court's findings will be based on all of the circumstances and not only the contents of the client care letter.[100] The factors that Underhill J took into account included: the fee earner's standard professional practice as to whether he would explain his status to his clients; the client's reaction on learning of the true status of the fee earner; and any note about the fee earner's status on the firm's letterhead.[101] **38.84**

It would seem that similar principles apply when the solicitor makes representations about instructing counsel. Whilst not in a case involving the assessment of fees, Sir Brian Leveson severely criticised a solicitor who had indicated that he would instruct an experienced barrister, but then delegated to a far less experienced advocate.[102] Presumably, the same would apply to experts and other service providers. **38.85**

---

96 *Pilbrow v Pearless de Rougement & Co* [1999] 3 All ER 355.

97 *Manches LLP v Green (t/a Green Denman & Co)* [2008] EWHC 917 (QB), at [71].

98 *Ibid*, at [70].

99 *Adrian Alan Ltd v Fuglers* [2002] EWCA Civ 1655.

100 *Manches LLP v Green (t/a Green Denman & Co)* [2008] EWHC 917 (QB), at [83].

101 *Ibid*, at [84].

102 See *R (on the application of Akram) v Secretary of State for the Home Department* [2015] EWHC 1359 (Admin).

Interest between Solicitor and Client

38.86 The following paragraphs should be read in conjunction with Chapter 56. These comments are a coda to that chapter in that they add one or two specific points about interest payable by a client to their solicitor.

38.87 Unless interest is allowed under the court's statutory powers to make a discretionary award, interest will be payable on a contractual basis in accordance with the terms of the retainer. In so far as non-contentious costs are concerned, there is, in addition, delegated legislation that allows interest to be awarded on unpaid fees (see 38.89).[103]

38.88 Unless the client had been told that the law would not generally allow a solicitor to claim such a rate, a solicitor is not able to enforce a putatively agreed rate of interest where it markedly exceeds the rates that would be allowed under s 35A of the Senior Courts Act 1981.[104] Moreover, a solicitor is not able to divert monies paid on account in such a way as to leave disbursements unpaid (and therefore attracting interest).[105]

Interest on non-contentious costs

38.89 In so far as bills delivered on or after 11 August 2009 are concerned, art 5 of the Solicitors' (Non-Contentious Business) Remuneration Order 2009[106] (as amended) makes the following default provisions:

> '**Interest**
>
> 5 (1) A solicitor may charge interest on the unpaid amount of his costs plus any paid disbursements and value added tax, subject to the remainder of this article.
>
> (2) Where an entitlement to interest arises under paragraph (1), and subject to any agreement made between a solicitor and client, the period for which interest may be charged runs from one month after the date of delivery of a bill.
>
> (3) Subject to any agreement made between a solicitor and client, the rate of interest must not exceed the rate for the time being payable on judgment debts.
>
> (4) Interest charged under this article must be calculated, where applicable, by reference to—
> (a) the amount specified in a determination of costs by the Law Society under Schedule 1A to the Solicitors Act 1974;
> (aa) the fees specified in a direction made by the ombudsman under section 137(2)(b)(i) of the Legal Services Act 2007;[[107]] or
> (b) the amount ascertained on assessment if an application has been made for the bill to be assessed.'

As such, a client is afforded a period of grace of one month.

---

[103] It is a moot point whether that right is enforceable as a direct right conferred by legislation or indirectly by way of an implied contractual right. It is probably the former: see *Walton v Egan* [1982] 3 WLR 352.

[104] *Clifford Harris & Co v Solland International Ltd* [2005] EWHC 141 (Ch), at [50], *per* Mr Nugee QC (sitting as a deputy judge of the High Court).

[105] *Hartland v Murrell* (1873) LR 16 Eq 285.

[106] SI 2009/1931.

[107] This subparagraph was inserted by the Solicitors' (Non-Contentious Business) Remuneration (Amendment) Order 2010 (SI 2010/2262) and it applied from 6 October 2010. It provides for interest that may be charged on solicitors' unpaid costs to be calculated by reference to the fees contained in a direction made by an ombudsman of the Office for Legal Complaints under Legal Services Act 2007, s 137(2)(b)(i).

It is possible for a client to agree interest in such a way as to create a non-contentious business agreement relating to interest. Such an agreement may be enforced in just the same way as any other non-contentious business agreement.[108] The relevance of this is that the one-month period of grace referred to above may not apply.[109] **38.90**

In so far as bills rendered before 11 August 2009 are concerned, art 14 of the Solicitors' (Non-Contentious Business) Remuneration Order 1994[110] provided as follows: **38.91**

> 'Interest
>
> 14. (1) After the information specified in article 8 has been given to an entitled person in compliance with articles 6 or 7, a solicitor may charge interest on the unpaid amount of his costs plus any paid disbursements and value added tax, subject to paragraphs (2) and (3) below.
>
> (2) Where an entitlement to interest arises under paragraph (1), and subject to any agreement made between a solicitor and client, the period for which interest may be charged may run from one month after the date of delivery of a bill, unless the solicitor fails to lodge an application within one month of receipt of a request for a remuneration certificate under article 4, in which case no interest is payable in respect of the period between one month after receiving the request and the actual date on which the application is lodged.
>
> (3) Subject to any agreement made between a solicitor and client, the rate of interest must not exceed the rate for the time being payable on judgment debts.
>
> (4) Interest charged under this article must be calculated, where applicable, by reference to the following—
>
> (a) if a solicitor is required to obtain a remuneration certificate, the total amount of the costs certified by the Council to be fair and reasonable plus paid disbursements and value added tax;
>
> (b) if an application is made for the bill to be taxed, the amount ascertained on taxation;
>
> (c) if an application is made for the bill to be taxed or a solicitor is required to obtain a remuneration certificate and for any reason the taxation or application for a remuneration certificate does not proceed, the unpaid amount of the costs shown in the bill or such lesser sum as may be agreed between the solicitor and the client, plus paid disbursements and value added tax.'

Wyn Williams J has found that where interest is claimed in compliance with the provisions of art 14, those provisions do not confer upon the court a discretionary power to disallow that interest or to reduce its amount.[111]

Interest on contentious costs

It is a moot point whether interest is necessarily payable on unpaid contentious costs. If the retainer makes provision for interest, then it will be payable in accordance with those provisions, but it is often the case that no provision is made. Where this is so, then interest cannot be claimed as of right, but it can be awarded pursuant to Senior Courts Act 1981, s 35A, or County Courts Act 1984, s 69(1). **38.92**

---

[108] See *Walton v Egan* [1982] 3 WLR 352, which related to the 1972 equivalent of the Solicitors' (Non-Contentious Business) Remuneration Order 2009 (SI 2009/1931).

[109] See subpara (2) in the regulation cited at 38.89.

[110] SI 1994/2616.

[111] *Lake v Hunt Kid Law Firm LLP (in administration)* [2011] EWHC 766 (QB), at [26], in which Wyn Williams J found it very difficult to read s 35A of the Senior Courts Act 1981 as conferring a power to reduce or extinguish interest that is payable as a consequence of a provision wholly independent of that section.

Judgment debt interest

38.93 Judgment debt interest may accrue on debts for which there is already a judgment, but, in the County Court and its hearing centres, this will be subject to the £5,000 limit mentioned at 56.18. As to the time from which interest runs, art 2(2) of the County Courts (Interest on Judgment Debts) Order 1991[112] reads as follows: 'In the case of a judgment or order for the payment of a judgment debt, other than costs, the amount of which has to be determined at a later date, the judgment debt shall carry interest from that later date.'

38.94 At first blush, this appears to mean that interest is payable on costs from the moment at which there is an order for costs to be assessed—which would be the position between opposing parties (see 56.10)—rather than from the date of the certificate quantifying those costs. This is probably not the correct interpretation; it is more likely that the reference to 'costs' is a reference to 'costs awarded pursuant to s 51 of the Senior Courts Act 1981'. This would not only accord with the common-sense view that a solicitor's unpaid fees should be treated in exactly the same way as any other professional's unpaid fees, but it also accords with the notion that art 2(2) is written in this way merely to reflect the fact that the *incipitur* rule applies to costs awarded by the court, whereas the *allocatur* rule applies to all other monies (see 56.23).

Discretion generally

38.95 For the reasons set out at 38.91, it will commonly be the case that the court will lack the power to reduce or extinguish interest where that interest is payable as a consequence of compliance with art 14 of the Solicitors' (Non-Contentious Business) Remuneration Order 1994.[113] Where interest is payable under contract, or where interest is payable as a result of the operation of legislation similar to art 14, it is difficult to see why any other reasoning would apply. As such, the exercise of ascertaining the amount of interest payable between solicitor and client will typically be limited to finding the start date and the end date (both being questions of mixed fact and law), and to determining the applicable rate or rates (this being question of interpretation).

38.96 Where a general discretion does arise, the relevant factors will be much the same as those described in Chapter 56. Whilst *obiter*, Wyn Williams J has confirmed that the court's primary purpose when making an award of interest is to compensate the recipient for the fact that they have been precluded from obtaining a return on the money rightfully kept from them.[114] Wyn Williams J explained that the fact that the party liable for that interest may have been out of pocket for whatever reason (in that case, because a payment into court had been made) would not generally count as a sufficient reason to justify a reduction in the interest properly payable.

The Late Payment of Commercial Debts (Interest) Act 1998

38.97 The Late Payment of Commercial Debts (Interest) Act 1998 (as amended) addresses the issue of late payment of monies by businesses to businesses. In essence, it implies a term

[112] SI 1991/1184.
[113] SI 1994/2616.
[114] *Ibid*, at [34] and [35]; Wyn Williams J cited, with approval, the decision of Christopher Clarke J in *Fattal v Walbrook Trustees (Jersey) Ltd & Anor* [2009] EWHC 1674 (Ch), at [26].

into an applicable contract that it will carry a high level of simple interest. The Act was originally the domestic implementation of Directive 2000/35/EC.[115] On 16 March 2013, that directive was replaced by Directive 2011/7/EU,[116] domestic implementation of which was achieved by the amendments made to the Act by the Late Payment of Commercial Debts Regulations 2013.[117] The new provisions are not retrospective: they will not apply to contracts made prior to 16 March 2013.[118]

Broadly speaking, the Late Payment of Commercial Debts (Interest) Act 1998 (as amended) will apply when payment is 30 days late.[119] Where both parties are businesses and where there is no other enactment that provides for the payment of interest, then the 1998 Act may apply. 'Business' includes the liberal professions and the activities of any government department or local or public authority,[120] and therefore unequivocally embraces solicitors. Consumer credit agreements, mortgages, pledges, charges and other securities are excluded.[121] The debt must be a 'qualifying debt' and a debt will not be a qualifying debt if, or to the extent that, it consists of a sum to which a right to interest or to charge interest applies by virtue of any enactment.[122] Similarly, a debt will not be a qualifying debt if, or to the extent that, a right to demand interest on it pursuant to some other right to interest is exercised.[123] **38.98**

From 16 March 2013 onwards, statutory interest would generally start to run from the day after the agreed date for payment of the debt. Where no date was agreed, statutory interest would generally start to run from the date 30 days after the creditor performed its obligations, or the debtor received the invoice, whichever is later. The provisions depend on the nature of the debtor, as follows. **38.99**

- **Public authorities** Where a public authority purchases goods or services, statutory interest will start to run on outstanding payments from 30 days after the supplier's invoice is received or services are received, or the services are verified and accepted (where provided for by statute or contract), whichever is the later.[124]
- **Other organisations and businesses** Where a payment period has not been agreed, statutory interest will start to run on outstanding payments from 30 days after the supplier's invoice is received or services are received, or the services are verified and accepted (where provided for by statute or contract), whichever is the later.[125]

Where a payment period is specified in the contract, statutory interest will start to run from that date. However, if that agreed payment period is more than 60 days after the events listed above, then statutory interest will begin to run from the date 60 days after **38.100**

[115] Directive 2000/35/EC of the European Parliament and of the Council of 29 June 2000 on combating late payment in commercial transactions, OJ L 200/35, 8 August 2000.

[116] Directive 2011/7/EU of the European Parliament and of the Council of 16 February 2011 on combating late payment in commercial transactions (recast), OJ L 48/1, 23 February 2011.

[117] SI 2013/395.

[118] Late Payment of Commercial Debts Regulations 2013 (SI 2013/395), reg 1.

[119] Late Payment of Commercial Debts (Interest) Act 1998, s 4.

[120] See Late Payments of Commercial Debts (Interest) Act 1998 (as amended), s 2(7).

[121] Late Payments of Commercial Debts (Interest) Act 1998 (as amended), s 2(5).

[122] See Late Payments of Commercial Debts (Interest) Act 1998 (as amended), s 3(2).

[123] See Late Payments of Commercial Debts (Interest) Act 1998 (as amended), s 3(3).

[124] Late Payments of Commercial Debts (Interest) Act 1998 (as amended), s 3A.

[125] Late Payments of Commercial Debts (Interest) Act 1998 (as amended), s 3B.

the events, despite the express contractual term, unless the longer payment period agreed between the parties is not 'grossly unfair' to the supplier.[126] However, if statutory interest has been ousted by the provision of a 'substantial contractual remedy', statutory interest will not apply and these provisions will have no effect. Any attempt to exclude or limit this right is subject to the test of reasonableness set out in the Unfair Contract Terms Act 1977.[127]

38.101 From the point of view of costs between opposing parties, it will almost never be the case that the 1998 Act will apply, because it will apply only to a contract for the supply of goods or services where the purchaser and the supplier are each acting in the course of a business.[128] In practical terms, the Late Payment of Commercial Debts (Interest) Act 1998 will apply only to solicitor-and-client costs or under an indemnity for costs—and even then only rarely. It is thought, however, that it does apply to the Unified Contract under which lawyers are paid legal aid.[129]

38.102 Where the Late Payment of Commercial Debts (Interest) Act 1998 does apply, the applicable rate of interest is at least 8 percentage points over 'the reference rate'[130] (the rate announced from time to time by the Monetary Policy Committee of the Bank of England). Compensation for late payment of a fixed charge of £40, £70 or £100 is payable depending on the size of the debt (under £1,000, under £10,000 and higher, respectively).[131] Where the contract was made on or after 16 March 2013, then if the reasonable costs of the creditor in recovering the debt are not met by the fixed sum, the creditor shall also be entitled to a sum equivalent to the difference between the fixed sum and those costs.[132]

[126] See Late Payments of Commercial Debts (Interest) Act 1998 (as amended), s 3C.

[127] See Late Payments of Commercial Debts (Interest) Act 1998 (as amended), s 5A(4).

[128] Late Payment of Commercial Debts (Interest) Act 1998 (as amended), s 2(1). Furthermore, a debt does not carry (and shall be treated as never having carried) statutory interest if or to the extent that a right to demand interest on it, which exists by virtue of any rule of law, is exercised: see Late Payments of Commercial Debts (Interest) Act 1998 (as amended), s 3(2) and (3).

[129] See Law Society, *Practice Note: Late Payments from the LSC*, 21 March 2012.

[130] Late Payment of Commercial Debts (Rate of Interest) (No 3) Order 2002 (SI 2002/1675), art 4.

[131] See Late Payments of Commercial Debts (Interest) Act 1998, s 5A, as amended by the Late Payment of Commercial Debts Regulations 2002 (SI 2002/1674).

[132] See Late Payment of Commercial Debts (Interest) Act 1998 (as amended), s 5A(2A).

39

CLIENTS' RIGHTS AND REMEDIES (ALTERNATIVE MEANS OF RESOLVING DISPUTES AND COMPROMISE)

This short chapter examines a miscellaneous rights and remedies by means of which a client can challenge the fees payable without asking for a statutory assessment. This includes the most attractive remedy of all: compromise. In particular, this chapter deals with the following topics: 39.01

- remuneration certificates (now obsolete) (39.02);
- non-statutory assessments (*Turner & Co v Palomo*[1] quantifications) (39.03);
- disputed compromise, including accord and satisfaction, and promissory estoppel (39.08); and
- the Legal Ombudsman and the Solicitors Regulation Authority (39.22).

Remuneration Certificates (Now Obsolete)

A remuneration certificate was a certificate issued by the Legal Complaints Service on behalf of the Law Society. It gave an opinion as to the amount properly chargeable. It is now an obsolete procedure; the current-day equivalent (which has applied since 11 August 2009[2]) is described at 39.22–39.34. In the unlikely event that more information is sought on the procedure, see the second edition of this book, which contains a full description at para 19.01. 39.02

Non-statutory Assessments (*Turner & Co v Palomo* Quantifications)

A non-statutory assessment—also known as a *Turner & Co v Palomo* assessment[3]—is a rough-and-ready assessment that the court may carry out when it is unable to carry out an assessment under the Solicitors Act 1974. Males J has said that it is analogous to an assessment of damages.[4] Whether the court is able to carry out an assessment pursuant to s 70 (or s 71) of the Solicitors Act 1974 (a 'statutory assessment') will depend on a number of factors, including whether the bill has been paid, as well as the period of time that has 39.03

[1] After *Turner & Co v O Palomo SA* [2000] 1 WLR 37.
[2] See Solicitors' (Non-contentious Business) Remuneration Order 2009 (SI 2009/1931), art 1(3).
[3] After *Turner & Co v O Palomo SA* [2000] 1 WLR 37.
[4] See *Ahmud & Co Solicitors v MacPherson* [2015] EWHC 2240 (QB), at [11] and [26].

expired between the delivery of the bill and the application for an assessment (see 36.04 *et seq*). Circumstances will exist in which the court is precluded from making an order for a statutory assessment.[5] Where this is the case, it may be open to the court to order that there be a non-statutory ascertainment of the quantum of costs, which is referred to in this book as a 'non-statutory assessment'.

39.04 The jurisdiction to make such an order stems from the fact that a claim brought by a solicitor for their fees is a claim for a reasonable (unliquidated) sum.[6] The court is therefore able to rule on the reasonableness of the sums claimed in much the same way as it would on any other claim for payment for services rendered. The jurisdiction was first exercised under the Rules of the Supreme Court (RSC)[7] and, unsurprisingly, continues to exist under the Civil Procedure Rules (CPR).[8] Whilst there is no authority directly on the point,[9] it is probable that the jurisdiction also exists by reason of the fact that, unless there is statutory provision to the contrary, the court's inherent jurisdiction permits it to ensure that the solicitor, as an officer of the court, is remunerated properly and no more for the work they have done.[10] It is possible that there is a separate jurisdiction that permits a solicitor principal to have the costs of a solicitor agent assessed, under the court's jurisdiction to regulate officers of the court,[11] but there is no modern authority on that point.

39.05 Where practicable, the assessment should be heard by a costs judge, whose task will be to assess the costs and to enter judgment for the assessed amount.[12] Where it would be inappropriate to transfer the matter to a costs judge (such as where the application to transfer the matter to a costs judge has been made very late in the day), the assessment may be carried out by a trial judge.[13]

39.06 Although there is no authority on the point, common sense dictates that the client ought not to be able to escape an assessment on the indemnity basis simply by placing themselves in a position in which they were unable to ask for a statutory assessment. This probably explains why, anecdotally, non-statutory assessments are a less rigorous process than statutory assessments, in that the court tends to paint with a broader brush and is less inclined to hear detailed argument (especially from the client). If this is correct, the client would be ill-advised to allow their right to a statutory assessment to lapse on a carefree assumption that a non-statutory assessment will be similar to a statutory assessment.

---

[5] See, eg, *Harrison v Tew* [1990] 2 AC 523 although also see 36.05–36.06.

[6] The fact that a solicitor's claim for fees in the circumstances of the case before him was for an unliquidated sum was confirmed by Evans LJ in *Turner & Co v O Palomo SA* [2000] 1 WLR 37, at 52. See also *Thomas Watts & Co (a firm) v Smith* [1998] 2 Costs LR 59, at 73, *per* Sir Richard Scott VC. The fact that a claim for solicitor's fees may be regarded as being liquidated for the purposes of s 29 of the Limitation Act 1980 does not detract from Evans LJ's analysis: see *Phillips & Co (a firm) v Bath Housing Co-operative Ltd* [2012] EWCA Civ 1591, at [41], *per* Lloyd LJ. See also *Allen v Jarvis* (1869) LR 4 Ch 616.

[7] *Thomas Watts & Co (a firm) v Smith* [1998] 2 Costs LR 59; *Turner & Co (a firm) v O Palomo SA* [2000] 1 WLR 37.

[8] See, eg, *Truex v Toll* [2009] EWHC 396 (Ch); *King v Rothschild Trust* [2002] EWHC 1346 (Ch).

[9] The authority referred to below, ie *Sutton v Sears* [1959] 3 All ER 545, related to sums payable under a legal aid certificate rather than to sums payable under a private contract of retainer.

[10] See *Sutton v Sears* [1959] 3 All ER 545, at 550. In a similar vein, Judge Chapman (sitting as a judge of the High Court) has found that Solicitors Act 1974, s 70, does not oust the court's inherent jurisdiction to order assessment of a solicitor's invoices: see *Connollys (a firm) v Harrington* [2002] All ER (D) 268 (May).

[11] See *Storer & Co v Johnson* (1890) 15 App Cas 203, HL.

[12] *Thomas Watts & Co (a firm) v Smith* [1998] 2 Costs LR 59, at 74.

[13] *King v Rothschild Trust* [2002] EWHC 1346 (Ch).

The parties to a non-statutory assessment will not be afforded the protection of the one-fifth rule. This is because the assessment is akin to an assessment of damages and therefore governed by CPR, r 44.2[14] (and presumably Part 36, where appropriate). It is not entirely clear how the court would determine 'success' for the purposes of dealing with costs, so the parties—particularly the client—would each be well advised to make either a Part 36 offer or, at least, an admissible offer. Factors that the court may take into account include the client's delay, the amount of the reduction, the efforts that have been taken to settle the dispute and the fact that the parties were at liberty to make offers without being impeded by the need to show special circumstances before the court could take those offers into account.[15] **39.07**

Disputed Compromise

A disputed compromise will exist where one of the parties claims that the amount of fees or disbursements due has been agreed, but the other contends that this is not so. **39.08**

Most of the authorities cited in the next few paragraphs were decided long ago, so it could be the case that they are no longer good law. In particular, the concept of consumer protection plays a much greater role today than it did in times past. This is relevant because (unlike in disputed compromise in other spheres of the law) the effect of the putative agreement does not turn solely on the law, as it is often also a matter of discretion (see 39.12, 39.14, 39.15 and 39.19). In view of these qualifications, what follows ought to be regarded as setting the boundaries of what the law will permit as opposed to a guide to what a present-day court would actually decide. **39.09**

The counterparties to a contract of retainer may reach agreement—or, from a consumer protection point of view, may negotiate away their rights—in a number of ways,[16] including: **39.10**

- a written agreement forming a contentious or non-contentious business agreement;
- an oral agreement as to the amount to be charged;
- a compromise of the bill (not being accord and satisfaction);
- accord and satisfaction;
- a promise giving rise to promissory estoppel; and
- a subsequent promise or waiver.

Each is discussed in turn. There is considerable overlap between these categories; indeed, it could be said that the distinction between some of them is so fine as to be artificial.

Disputed business agreements, etc

Whether there has been a written agreement that forms a contentious or non-contentious business agreement will be a matter of fact and law, to be determined on the evidence and in accordance with the principles set out at 27.107–27.189. The following case examples may be relevant in the present context (that is, where there is a dispute as to whether there was intended to be agreement as to the amount payable). **39.11**

[14] *Ahmud & Co Solicitors v MacPherson* [2015] EWHC 2240 (QB), at [21]–[26], *per* Males J.
[15] *Ibid.*
[16] Other mechanisms would include composition with creditors and account stated or release by deed.

- A memorandum signed by the client and the solicitor may be sufficient to amount to a contentious business agreement.[17]
- A memorandum signed retrospectively is capable of amounting to a contentious business agreement, even though a lower amount had initially been agreed.[18]
- Where there is no consideration, an admission that the costs debt exists or a promise to pay it would not be sufficient to preclude a subsequent assessment.[19]
- A receipt given for monies paid in 'full and final settlement of all outstanding costs' would, in general, not preclude an assessment in circumstances in which the monies were paid for the purposes of securing a release of papers held under lien.[20]
- A signed memorandum is capable of binding a party chargeable, even though it was the client (rather than the party chargeable) who had affixed their signature.[21]

39.12 Many of these cases were decided on the basis not of whether there was an agreement in principle, but of whether it was fair to allow that agreement to bind the parties and the statutory provisions that allow the court to exercise its discretion in this way continue to exist.[22] The court therefore has considerable freedom to arrive at a conclusion that avoids injustice. Where no bill had been delivered, agreements to compromise a costs debt for a fixed sum were enforceable if the solicitor could show that the agreement had been made fairly and with proper knowledge on both sides.[23] That said, the relationship between solicitor and client is a fiduciary relationship and, as such, the burden of proving these things is not easy to shift.[24]

Disputed oral agreements

39.13 Whether there has been a binding oral agreement is a matter of fact and law, to be determined on the evidence and in accordance with the principles set out at 27.207–27.213. As can be seen from what is said in those paragraphs, there is a distinction to be drawn between contentious and non-contentious business.

39.14 In the days before the court drew that distinction, it was established that an oral agreement by a solicitor to take a gross sum from their client in lieu of costs was not void, although it was regarded by the court 'with jealousy'[25] (which, in more modern language, means that it would have been viewed with some circumspection). Thus, even in ancient times, the court was not overly ready to allow an oral agreement to be enforced in such a way as to cause detriment to the client. Whilst there remains room for argument on the point, a reasonably accurate generalisation is that an oral agreement as to non-contentious work is

---

17 *Bake v French (No 2)* [1907] 2 Ch 215, following *Re Jones* [1895] 2 Ch 719, applied in *In re Thompson ex p Baylis* [1894] 1 QB 462, at 463. *Bake* doubted the earlier case of *Pontifex v Farnham* (1892) 62 LJQB 344.

18 *In re Thompson, ex p Baylis* [1894] 1 QB 462. This case was criticised in *Re Simmons and Politzer* [1954] 2 All ER 811, but that criticism was based on a provision that no longer exists (ie the need for an agreement to be approved before it can be enforced).

19 *Truex v Toll* [2009] EWHC 369 (Ch), at [36].

20 *Re Simmons and Politzer* [1954] 2 All ER 811.

21 *Turner v Hand* (1859) 27 Beav 561. In a similar vein, see *Re Stogdon, ex p Baker* (1887) 51 JP 565; cf *Re Blackmore* (1851) 13 Beav 154.

22 See Solicitors Act 1974, ss 57(5) and 61(4).

23 *Stedman v Collett* (1854) 17 Beav 608; *Clare v Joseph* [1907] 2 KB 369, at 376.

24 *Tyrrell v Bank of London* (1862) 10 HLC 26, at 44; *Re Van Laun, ex p Chatterton* [1907] 2 KB 23, at 29.

25 *In re Whitcombe* (1844) 8 Beav 140.

not enforceable against either of the parties[26] and an oral agreement as to contentious work is not enforceable against the client[27] (see 27.211). It has to be said, however, that there is uncertainty as to whether these principles remain good law: other common-law jurisdictions have moved towards examining such agreements on an ordinarily contractual basis (see 27.211, fn 294). In any event, where no bill has been delivered, that would be a factor that the court could take into account.[28]

Disputed agreements relating to a bill

This category is broader than the two categories mentioned above in that it is the alleged compromise of the bill itself that falls to be considered, rather than any putative agreement about what that bill should contain. The question of whether a bill has been compromised will be an issue of fact and law. The fact that a purported compromise could, in certain circumstances,[29] be said to be a retrospective contentious or non-contentious business agreement (see 39.11–39.12) is relevant because if the court finds that the agreement is a business agreement, it has the power to set it aside.[30] The modern approach seems to be to decide these issues on a discretionary basis.[31] **39.15**

An early example (circa 1860) of the principle of consumer protection is a case in which the court found that a compromise was not binding because the bill that had been delivered did not comply with the then statutory requirements for a statute bill.[32] **39.16**

Accord and satisfaction

In the present context, 'accord and satisfaction' means that a client has purchased their release from the obligation to discharge their costs debt and that they have done so by means of valuable consideration that is not payment of the debt in full. It is akin to an agreed part-payment. Subject to what is said below, part-payment of a debt (in general, as opposed to a costs debt) will not normally suffice as satisfaction because there would have been no consideration for the remainder of the debt.[33] This would normally be true even where part-payment would be commercially useful to the creditor for reasons of cash flow.[34] **39.17**

---

[26] In *In re a Solicitor* [1956] 1 QB 157, for example, Pearson J found that a client could not rely on an oral agreement that his solicitor would charge less than the ordinary rate of remuneration.

[27] *Chamberlain v Boodle & King* (1980) 124 SJ 186, subsequently upheld on appeal ([1982] 1 WLR 1443). See also *Martin Boston & Co (a firm) v Levy* [1982] 1 WLR 1434 (arguable defence to a claim by solicitors for fees for contentious work under an oral agreement).

[28] *In re West, King & Adam, ex p Clough* [1892] 2 QB 102. See also *Re Ingle* (1855) 25 LJ Ch 169, in which the court gave particular weight to the fact that the client was poorly educated.

[29] There is authority that a compromise can operate independently of the Solicitors Act 1974 (*Re Morris* (1872) 27 LT 554), but it is doubtful if this remains good law and, in any event, it does not accord with the modern approach, which is generally determined on the basis of discretion: see *Re Heritage, ex p Docker* (1878) 3 QBD 726; *Ingrams v Sykes* (1987) 137 NLJ 1135; *Barclays plc v Villers* [2000] 1 All ER (Comm) 357, at 367.

[30] See Solicitors Act 1974, ss 57(5) and 61(4). As an early example, see the comments of Sir George Jessel MR in *Re Attorneys & Solicitors Act* (1870) 1 Ch D 575.

[31] See *Barclays plc v Villers* [2000] 1 All ER (Comm) 357, at 367. As older examples, see *Re Heritage, ex p Docker* (1878) 3 QBD 726; *Ingrams v Sykes* (1987) 137 NLJ 1135.

[32] *Philby v Hazle* (1860) 8 CBNS 647; see also *Wilkinson v Smart* (1875) 24 WR 42.

[33] *Pinnel's Case* (1602) 5 Co Rep 117a.

[34] *Foakes v Beer* (1884) 9 App Cas 605; cf *Williams v Roffey Bros & Nicholls (Contractors) Ltd* [1991] 1 QB 1, at 18, *per* Glidewell LJ: 'Consideration there must still be but, in my judgment, the courts nowadays should be more ready to find its existence so as to reflect the intention of the parties to the contract'.

Costs debts are treated differently, however, because most costs debts are for unliquidated sums;[35] where this is so, payment of a sum agreed between the parties is capable of amounting to good consideration.[36]

39.18 This means that it is relatively easy for the parties to negotiate a compromise that amounts to accord and satisfaction. That said, there are no modern authorities on this point, which is probably a reflection of the fact that, where evidence exists that would support a finding of accord and satisfaction, that evidence would also support a finding that there is a business agreement for the agreed sum (see 39.11–39.12). This would be a much more attractive finding from the court's point of view because it would mean that the court would have the discretionary power to set the agreement aside. Where, however, the purchase of the release is made with something that is entirely extraneous to the costs, a finding of accord and satisfaction may be the only finding open to the court.

Promissory estoppel

39.19 Estoppel is a discretionary equitable remedy whereby a promisor may be prevented (that is, estopped) from disputing the quantum of the costs debt. This may happen where they have made a promise (such as a promise to pay that debt in a particular sum) and where that promise has caused the promisee to adversely alter their position. A detailed discussion of this topic is beyond the scope of this book. There are no authorities directly on costs debts,[37] but there are many authorities dealing with promissory estoppel in general.[38] The absence of specific authority could be a reflection of the fact that a solicitor asserting estoppel would probably face difficulties arising out of the fact that it would be seen as an attempt to circumvent the consumer protection afforded by the Solicitors Act 1974. In any event, Proudman J has confirmed that seeking to enforce a costs debt is not of itself a sufficient alteration of position to found an estoppel; otherwise, there would be an estoppel in almost every case.[39]

Subsequent promise or waiver

39.20 Whilst unrelated to promissory estoppel in terms of its legal foundations, the effect of a subsequent promise (that is, a promise or ratification after the original bargain has been struck) will often lead to a result that is very similar to the operation of promissory estoppel. Whilst not binding, Australian judge Anderson J has explained the principles in this way:

> 'In [*Kennedy v Brown*[40]] it was held that the request to perform the services, followed by performance, created an implied contract to pay a reasonable amount; and that the subsequent promise to pay a stipulated amount (or to pay at a stipulated rate) is in the nature of

---

[35] See *Thomas Watts & Co (a firm) v Smith* [1998] 2 Costs LR 59; *Turner & Co (a firm) v O Palomo SA* [2000] 1 WLR 37.

[36] *Wilkinson v Byers* (1834) 1 Ad & El 106.

[37] There is a negative authority in which it was found that there was no estoppel: see *Truex v Toll* [2009] EWHC 396 (Ch).

[38] See the *High Trees* principles, as explained in *Central London Property Trust Ltd v High Trees House Ltd* [1947] KB 130.

[39] *Truex v Toll* [2009] EWHC 369 (Ch), at [41].

[40] *Kennedy v Broun* (1863) 13 CBNS 677, 143 ER 268.

> an admission by the promisor of what is a reasonable amount, ie the subsequent promise is evidence against the promisor of what is a reasonable amount. In [*Re Casey's Patents; Stewart v Casey*[41]], it was held that the subsequent promise was "a positive bargain which fixes the amount of that reasonable remuneration on the faith of which the service was originally rendered". In both these explanations the later express promise to pay a specified sum was treated as nothing more than a refinement of the earlier implied promise to pay a reasonable sum, the consideration for both promises being the actual performance of the work.'[42]

Similarly, whilst relating to a topic other than costs, the Privy Council has confirmed that an act done or service performed before the giving of a promise to make a payment can be consideration for the promise.[43] That said, a subsequent acknowledgment of an agreed fee will not necessarily result in a favourable outcome from the solicitor's point of view because it will not necessarily result in an oral retainer being converted into a business agreement.[44] In a similar vein, an assurance or putative waiver given by the solicitor will not necessarily produce a favourable outcome from the client's point of view because it may fail for want of consideration (see 27.90). **39.21**

The Legal Ombudsman and the Solicitors Regulation Authority

There are, in essence, two mechanisms by which a dissatisfied client may pursue a complaint about their solicitor's fees: **39.22**

- the Solicitors Regulation Authority (SRA); and
- the Legal Ombudsman (formerly known as the Legal Services Ombudsman).[45]

The SRA is able to investigate breaches of the SRA Code of Conduct 2011 (as amended), but will not investigate issues concerning poor services (such as excessive fees) unless the services are supplied in such a way as to give rise to a breach of the Code. In particular, only the Legal Ombudsman has the power of redress (that is, the power to award compensation or reduce fees).[46] The focus of the next few paragraphs is mainly on the Legal Ombudsman.

Governance

The SRA is governed by the Legal Services Board (LSB) and is thereby accountable to Parliament. The Legal Ombudsman is established by the Office for Legal Complaints (OLC), which, in turn, is also accountable to the LSB and thereby to Parliament. **39.23**

---

41 *Re Casey's Patents; Stewart v Casey* [1892] 1 Ch 104, at 115–16.

42 *D'Alessandro & D'Angelo v Cooper* (unreported), 2 June 1996, WASC, Full Ct, *per* Kennedy, Rowland and Anderson JJ, at p 9 of the reasons.

43 *Pao On v Lau Iu Long* [1980] AC 614, at 629–30, *per* Lord Scarman.

44 If an oral retainer is made and then the agreed sum is acknowledged in the form of an account stated after payment has been made by deduction, that acknowledgement will not be sufficient to give rise to a retrospective business agreement: *Re Fernandes* [1878] WN 57.

45 This book focuses solely on the use of those mechanisms for the purpose of dealing with a dispute about costs; it makes no attempt to deal with the wider regulatory aspects of the matter.

46 See Legal Services Act 2007, s 157.

Jurisdiction

39.24 The following points can be made about the Legal Ombudsman's jurisdiction.

- **The nature of the complaint** A complaint is ordinarily excluded from the jurisdiction if the client has not first used the solicitor's complaints procedures.[47] The complaint must be about *services* provided to the solicitor, either directly or at the request of an intermediary.[48] This does not mean, however, that the Legal Ombudsman is unable to deal with complaints relating to the amounts of costs. In this regard, in 2013, Phillips J said that it would be an artificial and unworkable distinction if the Ombudsman could consider the quality and levels of services, but not issues of wrongful charging or overcharging.[49] Similarly, Wyn Williams J has explained that the Legal Ombudsman may examine the quality of advice given about funding (in that case, the lack of advice about the terms and consequences of the contingency fee agreement).[50] Presumably as a result of these decisions, the Scheme Rules 2018 have been amended so as to make express provision to the amount of fees (see, for example, 39.30).
- **Complainants** Individuals and most businesses (including charities) are able to make complaints,[51] but public bodies and their agents may not.[52]
- **Respondents** Whilst the focus of this chapter is on solicitors' fees, the Legal Ombudsman is able to consider complaints against any 'authorised person' (see 3.48 and 3.77). The client, but not the solicitor, may complain about a barrister instructed by the solicitor.[53] It is a moot point as to whether the Ombudsman has jurisdiction to deal with a complaint about unregulated legal practitioners (such as a costs draftsperson) who have not been instructed via the agency of a solicitor (or other authorised person). The editor's personal communications with the Ombudsman indicates that the following approach would be taken (although it has to be stressed that this personal communication must not be taken as authoritative):

  > 'If the consumer had engaged the unqualified costs adviser directly the situation would be more complicated. Assuming that the work was on a paid basis and related to costs litigation then the draftsman has probably been conducting litigation. The Act says this is "reserved legal activity" and that to do it without proper qualification or authorisation is a criminal offence. In practice the Ombudsman would look at whether the costs draftsman had led the client to believe they were authorised to do the work. If they suggested they were [*sic*] would be likely to accept their claim that they were authorised, and so within [the Ombudsman's] jurisdiction. It might be unappealing for a costs draftsman to argue they were not within the Ombudsman's jurisdiction because what they were doing was in fact an offence. At least one consequence is that they would lose any entitlement to their fees.'[54]

- **Employees** Any act or omission by a person in the course of the person's employment is to be treated as also an act or omission by the person's employer, whether or not it was done with the employer's knowledge or approval.[55]

---

[47] See Legal Services Act 2007, s 126; Scheme Rules 2018, para 4.1. As to the discretion, see Scheme Rules 2018, paras 4.2 and 4.3.

[48] See Legal Services Act 2007, s 128(4). There are additional provisions allowing beneficiaries of an estate or trust to complain about administration, etc.

[49] *Layard Horsfall Ltd v Legal Ombudsman* [2013] EWHC 4137 (QB), at [21] and [22]. See also *Ejiofoer (t/a Mitchell and Co Solicitors) v Legal Ombudsman* [2016] EWHC 1933 (Admin), at [37], *per* Wyn Williams J.

[50] See *Ejiofoer (t/a Mitchell and Co Solicitors) v Legal Ombudsman* [2016] EWHC 1933 (Admin), at [31].

[51] See Scheme Rules 2018, para 2.1, for details.

[52] See Legal Services Act 2007, s 128(5)(b).

[53] See the Scheme Rules 2018, para 2.4.

[54] Note by Anthony Rich, General Counsel, Legal Ombudsman, prepared on 2 February 2012.

[55] See Legal Services Act 2007, s 131.

- **Legal proceedings** The Legal Ombudsman may (but does not have to) summarily dismiss a complaint if it would be better dealt with by legal proceedings or if it has previously been dealt with by legal proceedings.[56] It should be noted that the fact that legal proceedings have been begun is *not* a bar to making a complaint; indeed, if the court proceedings have been stayed for the purposes of allowing the Legal Ombudsman to deal with a complaint, there is no power to dismiss a complaint on this ground.[57] As such, whilst it may be necessary for a client to *issue* a Part 8 claim form for an assessment to preserve the right to an assessment, it would never be necessary for them to *continue* proceedings if the solicitor were willing to stay for the purposes of allowing the matter to be dealt with by the Legal Ombudsman. Neither the solicitor nor the client may institute or continue legal proceedings in respect of a matter that was the subject of a complaint after the time when a determination by the Ombudsman becomes binding and final,[58] but the client has the power to reject the determination, in which case it will have no effect on the legal rights of any party.[59]
- **Delay and time limits** Ordinarily, a complainant must refer a complaint to the Legal Ombudsman within (a) six years from the act or omission, or (b) three years from when the complainant should reasonably have known there was cause for complaint, whichever is later.[60] If there are exceptional circumstances—such as serious illness—these time limits may be extended.[61] Phillips J has held that it would be unrealistic and absurd to require a client to bring complaints regarding poor service or poor advice about fees prior to those fees being invoiced.[62]

Every month, the Legal Ombudsman publishes an article in the *Law Society Gazette* in which he gives an indication of the type of cases he refers and how he decides those cases. **39.25**

Charges and fees

Unless a costs order is made against the complainant (see 39.33), the Legal Ombudsman's service is free to the complainant. The respondent, however, will generally be charged what is known as a case fee,[63] which—at the time of writing—was £400.[64] **39.26**

Powers and determination

The Legal Ombudsman may dismiss a complaint without consideration of the merits if: **39.27**

- They consider the complaint, or part of it, to be frivolous, or vexatious, or totally without merit:

---

56 See Legal Services Act 2007, s 133(4). See also Scheme Rules 2018, para 5.7.
57 See Scheme Rules 2018, para 5.7(f).
58 See Legal Services Act 2007, s 140(11). See also Scheme Rules 2018, paras 5.46–5.56.
59 See, in particular, Scheme Rules 2018, para 5.54.
60 See Scheme Rules, para 4.5; Legal Services Act 2007, s 133.
61 See Scheme Rules, para 4.7.
62 *Layard Horsfall Ltd v Legal Ombudsman* [2013] EWHC 4137 (QB), at [29] and [30].
63 This is governed by Legal Services Act 2007, s 136: '**136 Charges payable by respondents** (1) Scheme rules must require respondents, in relation to complaints under the ombudsman scheme, to pay to the OLC such charges as may be specified in the rules. (2) The rules must provide for charges payable in relation to a complaint to be waived (or wholly refunded) where—(a) the complaint is determined or otherwise resolved in favour of the respondent, and (b) the ombudsman is satisfied that the respondent took all reasonable steps to try to resolve the complaint under the respondent's complaints procedures.'
64 See Scheme Rules 2018, para 6.3.

- the complaint, or part of it, would be better dealt with under another ombudsman scheme, by arbitration or by other legal proceedings;
- there has been undue delay;
- the subject of the complaint, or part of it, has previously been dealt with under another ombudsman scheme, by arbitration or by other legal proceedings; or
- there are other compelling reasons why it is inappropriate for the complaint to be dealt with under the ombudsman scheme.[65]

The Legal Ombudsman has wide procedural powers,[66] including the power to compel parties to attend to give evidence and to produce documents.[67]

39.28 The powers of the Legal Ombudsman, upon determination, are as follows:

> '137 **Determination of complaints**
>
> (1) A complaint is to be determined under the ombudsman scheme by reference to what is, in the opinion of the ombudsman making the determination, fair and reasonable in all the circumstances of the case.
>
> (2) The determination may contain one or more of the following—
> (a) a direction that the respondent make an apology to the complainant;
> (b) a direction that—
> (i) the fees to which the respondent is entitled in respect of the services to which the complaint relates ("the fees") are limited to such amount as may be specified in the direction, and
> (ii) the respondent comply, or secure compliance, with such one or more of the permitted requirements as appear to the ombudsman to be necessary in order for effect to be given to the direction under sub-paragraph (i);
> (c) a direction that the respondent pay compensation to the complainant of such an amount as is specified in the direction in respect of any loss which has been suffered by, or any inconvenience or distress which has been caused to, the complainant as a result of any matter connected with the complaint;
> (d) a direction that the respondent secure the rectification, at the expense of the respondent, of any such error, omission or other deficiency arising in connection with the matter in question as the direction may specify;
> (e) a direction that the respondent take, at the expense of the respondent, such other action in the interests of the complainant as the direction may specify.
>
> (3) For the purposes of subsection (2)(b) "the permitted requirements" are—
> (a) that the whole or part of any amount already paid by or on behalf of the complainant in respect of the fees be refunded;
> (b) that the whole or part of the fees be remitted;
> (c) that the right to recover the fees be waived, whether wholly or to any specified extent.
>
> (4) Where—
> (a) a direction is made under subsection (2)(b) which requires that the whole or part of any amount already paid by or on behalf of the complainant in respect of the fees be refunded, or

---

65 See Legal Services Act 2007, s 133(4). The details are given in Scheme Rules 2018, para 5.7.

66 See Legal Services Act 2007, s 133.

67 See Legal Services Act 2007, s 133(3)(e), but see the limit, at s 133(5), that the Ombudsman may not compel the giving of evidence of the production of a document which that person could not be compelled to produce in court proceedings.

(b) a direction is made under subsection (2)(c),

the direction may also provide for the amount payable under the direction to carry interest from a time specified in or determined in accordance with the direction, at the rate specified in or determined in accordance with scheme rules

(5) The power of the ombudsman to make a direction under subsection (2) is not confined to cases where the complainant may have a cause of action against the respondent for negligence.'[68]

Wyn Williams J has explained that if the Legal Ombudsman determines that a contract of retainer has been entered into as a result of inadequate advice, s 137 of the Legal Services Act 2007 would require the Ombudsman to determine the complaint by reference to what they thought was fair and reasonable in all of the circumstances. In particular, it would become permissible for them to reach a view about the fairness and reasonableness of the effect of the contract of retainer in question.[69] **39.29**

In so far as fees are concerned, the Scheme Rules 2018 provide as follows: **39.30**

'If the determination contains a direction to limit fees to a specified amount, it may also require the authorised person to ensure that:
a) all or part of any amount paid is refunded;
b) interest is paid on that refund from a specified time;
c) all or part of the fees are remitted;
d) the right to recover the fees is waived, wholly or to a specified extent; or
e) any combination of these.'[70]

If the Legal Ombudsman makes a direction that restricts or limits a solicitor's fees under s 137(2), then any applicable interest that is to be charged on the solicitor's unpaid fees is to be calculated by reference to the limited fee that has been directed by the Ombudsman.[71] **39.31**

These powers are limited, however, in accordance with s 138 of the Legal Services Act 2007:[72] **39.32**

'**138 Limitation on value of directions under the ombudsman scheme**

(1) Where a determination is made under the ombudsman scheme in respect of a complaint, the total value of directions under section 137(2)(c) to (e) contained in the determination must not exceed £50,000.

(2) For this purpose the total value of such directions is the aggregate of—
(a) the amount of any compensation specified in a direction under subsection (2)(c) of section 137, and
(b) the amount of any expenses reasonably incurred by the respondent when complying with a direction under subsection (2)(d) or (e) of that section.

(3) For the purposes of determining that total value, any interest payable on an amount within subsection (2)(a) of this section, by virtue of section 137(4), is to be ignored.'

---

[68] See Legal Services Act 2007, s 137.

[69] See *Ejiofoer (t/a Mitchell and Co Solicitors) v Legal Ombudsman* [2016] EWHC 1933 (Admin), at [40].

[70] See Scheme Rules 2018, para 5.40.

[71] The Solicitors (Non-Contentious Business) Remuneration (Amendment) Order 2010 (SI 2010/2262).

[72] As amended by the Legal Services Act 2007 (Alteration of Limit) Order 2012 (SI 2012/3091).

Costs orders

39.33 The Legal Ombudsman has the power to award costs against the respondent in favour of the complainant.[73] He also has power to award costs against the complainant, but only if, in his opinion, that person acted so unreasonably that it is appropriate in all of the circumstances of the case to make such an award.[74] Awards of costs are rare.[75] Interest may be added to the costs.[76]

Acceptance or rejection of the determination

39.34 The Legal Ombudsman must notify the parties of his determination.[77] If the complainant notifies the Ombudsman that the determination is accepted by the complainant, it is binding on the respondent and the complainant, and is final.[78] It may be enforced via the court.[79]

73 See Legal Services Act 2007, s 133(3)(h).
74 See Legal Services Act 2007, s 133(3)(i).
75 Scheme Rules 2018, para 5.39, expressly states this.
76 See Legal Services Act 2007, s 133(6).
77 See Legal Services Act 2007, s 139.
78 See Legal Services Act 2007, s 140(4).
79 See Legal Services Act 2007, s 141.

40

SOLICITORS' RIGHTS AND REMEDIES (PROCEEDINGS, LIEN, CHARGING ORDERS AND EQUITABLE INTERFERENCE)

This chapter describes the rights that a solicitor may assert when faced with a client who either will not pay or is at risk of defaulting on payment. It deals with the following topics: **40.01**

- suing for recovery of fees (40.02);
- obtaining payments on account (40.31);
- withdrawal of services under a contract of retainer (40.33);
- lien (40.36);
- solicitors' charging orders under the Solicitors Act 1974 (40.89);
- solicitors' charging orders under the Charging Orders Act 1979 (40.99);
- solicitors' security for costs (40.100);
- equitable interference (40.106); and
- statutory demands and bankruptcy (40.121).

Rights against legal expenses insurers are addressed at 34.60–34.66.

Suing for Recovery of Fees

This section deals with the topics of whether, how and when a solicitor is able to bring a claim for payment of their fees. It relates to fees for which a statute bill was rendered on or after 11 August 2009.[1] **40.02**

Whilst this book deals only briefly with the commercial aspects of engaging in solicitor-and-client litigation, a decision to litigate would be a significant step, fraught with risks. The authors of *Cook on Costs* have the following to say on the point: **40.03**

> 'Litigation is meant to be the last resort and never a truer statement was made in the context of solicitors and their clients. Things have normally gone badly wrong if you are contemplating the issuing of proceedings or taking other forceful steps to recover your fees from your client. The irrecoverable cost of pursuing the client—in terms of lost fee earning and management time—should make you stop and consider whether a deal, any deal, with this client might be better in the long run. Learning lessons on what to do (or not do) next time

---

[1] Prior to 11 August 2009, there were minor differences between the procedure for contentious and non-contentious business; since that date, those differences have ceased to exist. If the claim relates to non-contentious work and if the bill in question was delivered on or after that date, then the reader is referred to the second edition of this book for the relevant provisions.

will be more palatable if a large amount of the costs of pursuing the client are not thrown away in addition.'[2]

General principles

40.04 Solicitors, like most professionals, are able to sue for their unpaid fees by bringing a claim. This, however, is subject to certain safeguards. In general terms, those safeguards are as follows.

- **The right to deliver a bill** The solicitor must have a right to issue and enforce a statute bill (see 27.39). In general, this will mean that chargeable work has been carried out and that:
  - the contract of retainer has come to an end, giving rise to a right to render a final statute bill (see 27.67–27.88);
  - there has been a 'natural break' in the matter, giving rise to a right to render an interim statute bill (see 27.64–27.66 and 35.28–35.36); or
  - the client has expressly agreed to allow the solicitor to render an interim statute bill (see 27.42–27.55), or there has been an implied agreement to that effect (see 27.56–27.63).
- **A *bona fide* bill must exist** A statute bill must have been drawn up in a way that is *bona fide* compliant with the express and implied requirements applicable to statute bills (see 35.42–35.84).
- **The bill must have been delivered** The statute bill must have been delivered in a way that complies with s 69(2C) and (2D) of the Solicitors Act 1974 (see 35.85–35.86).
- **No order barring a claim** There must have been no order preventing a claim being brought pending assessment (see 36.03 and 40.07–40.08).
- **One month must have elapsed since delivery** In general, no less than one month must have expired from the date on which the applicable statute bill was delivered (see 35.43 and 40.05–40.06).

Only the last two of these points are addressed in this chapter; the other points are addressed elsewhere, as indicated.

The one-month period after delivery

40.05 The day of delivery is excluded, as is the day on which proceedings are commenced.[3] The reference to one month is a reference to one calendar month.[4] *Halsbury's Laws of England* has the following to say about what that means in practice:

> 'When the period prescribed is a calendar month running from any arbitrary date the period expires upon the day in the succeeding month corresponding to the date upon which the period starts, save that, if the period starts at the end of a calendar month which contains more days than the next succeeding month, the period expires at the end of that succeeding month. If a period of one calendar month includes the last day of February there must be 29 or 28 days, according as the year is or is not a leap year.'[5]

---

[2] *Cook on Costs 2017* (LexisNexis, online), para 3.1.

[3] *Blunt v Heslop* (1838) 4 Ad & El 577.

[4] Interpretation Act 1978, Sch 1.

[5] See *Halsbury's Laws of England* (5th edn, London: LexisNexis, 2015), vol 97, para 311. See also Case 152/85 *Misset v EC Council* [1987] ECR 223.

This is known as the corresponding date rule. It can give rise to anomalies, but where the period expires on the last day of a month containing fewer days than that in which it began, it would be wrong to take into account anomalies arising by comparison with periods commencing on adjacent days.[6] If the bill is sent by post, delivery is on the day on which, in the ordinary course of events, it would be delivered.[7]

There are exceptions to the general rule that the client is afforded a month's grace. They are set out in the Solicitors Act 1974, s 69(1): **40.06**

> 'If there is probable cause for believing that the party chargeable with the costs—
> (a) is about to quit England and Wales, to become bankrupt or to compound with his creditors, or
> (b) is about to do any other act which would tend to prevent or delay the solicitor obtaining payment,
>
> the High Court may, notwithstanding that one month has not expired from the delivery of the bill, order that the solicitor be at liberty to commence an action to recover his costs and may order that those costs be assessed.'[8]

Where the client has applied for an assessment

A claim for payment of fees is not the same as a claim for an assessment (a topic that is addressed in detail in Chapter 36). Where an application for an assessment has been made, this can have a bearing on how the court deals with the claim for fees. Where that application was made within one month of the bill being delivered, the court will—as of the client's right, rather than as a matter of discretion—order both that the bill be assessed and that no claim may be commenced until the assessment has been completed.[9] If, contrary to the Solicitors Act, s 69(1) (see 35.43), the solicitor had already issued a claim during the one-month grace period, then whilst the Solicitors Act 1974 contains no express provision on the point, it is likely that the court would either stay the claim or strike it out as an abuse of process. **40.07**

Where an application is made after the expiry of the one-month period, the court has the discretionary power to order that there be an assessment. Jurisdictional and discretionary issues (including special circumstances) are discussed at 36.31–36.38. Where the court makes an order that the costs be assessed, it may also order that no claim may be commenced on the bill (or, if it has already been commenced, that it be stayed).[10] A claim may be stayed pending resolution of a complaint to the Legal Ombudsman;[11] if this happens, then—whilst the client will have the power to reject the determination of the Ombudsman—the solicitor will (subject to certain safeguards) be bound by any such determination.[12] Given the notoriously high cost of solicitor-and-client assessments, it would often be in both parties' interests to try to resolve the dispute in this way. **40.08**

---

[6] Whilst not binding, see *University of Cambridge v Murray* [1993] ICR 460, EAT.

[7] *Browne v Black* [1912] 1 KB 316, CA.

[8] As amended by Legal Services Act 2007, s 177 and Sch 16, Pt 1, paras 1 and 60.

[9] Solicitors Act 1974, s 70(1) see 36.03.

[10] Solicitors Act 1974, s 70(2) and (3) see 30.04.

[11] If this happens, the Legal Ombudsman would lack the power to dismiss the complaint on the ground that proceedings were ongoing: see Scheme Rules 2018, para 5.7(f).

[12] See Legal Services Act 2007, s 140(11). See also Scheme Rules 2018, paras 5.46–5.56, esp para 5.54.

Claims based on dishonoured cheques, promissory notes, etc

40.09 Where a person tenders a cheque (or other such instrument) in payment of a costs debt and where that offer is accepted for consideration, a new contract will be formed between the payor and the payee, that contract being distinct from the contract of retainer.[13] If the cheque is subsequently not honoured, then the payee (that is, the solicitor) will be entitled to sue upon the cheque,[14] in accordance with the so-called cheque rule.

40.10 Similar points can be made about letters of credit,[15] promissory notes[16] and agreed statements of account.[17] Other than where the cheque has been countermanded, the client will need to be given 'notice of dishonour'.[18] The payee will usually make an application for summary judgment, which means that the test that is generally applied is whether the defendant (that is, the client) has a real prospect of successfully defending the claim,[19] which defences may include:

- a total defence (for example a total failure of consideration,[20] fraud[21] or illegality of the underlying contract[22]);
- a partial defence (for example misrepresentation[23] or an objection to the amount of costs claimed[24]); or
- a counterclaim for set-off (for example based on professional negligence).

Most importantly in the present context, it is possible for a payor to raise a partial defence that they have been overcharged.[25] Given the matters set out in Chapter 28, this is now more likely to arise than it was in the past.

40.11 Where the court finds that a full or partial defence has a real prospect of success, it will generally stay the claim pending an assessment (because the issues that are raised in full and partial defences tend to be ones that are best dealt with by a costs judge). In any event, the client is entitled to a statute bill regardless of whether they have offered a cheque as payment.[26]

---

[13] Whilst not dealing specifically with costs, see *Nova (Jersey) Knit Ltd v Kammgarn Spinnerei GmbH* [1977] 1 WLR 713, HL.

[14] *Ibid.* As to the importance of the rule and the need to preserve it, see *Cebora v SIP* [1976] 1 Ll R 271.

[15] See *Safa Ltd v Banque du Caire* [2000] All ER (D) 1010.

[16] *Jeffreys v Evans* (1845) 14 M&W 210.

[17] *Turner v Willis* [1905] 1 KB 468. If the agreement merely relates to the costs, then the client will usually not lose protection: *Re Fernandes* [1878] WN 57.

[18] See Bills of Exchange Act 1882, s 50(2)(c).

[19] See CPR, r 24.2(a)(ii).

[20] As to the importance of the lack of consideration being total rather than partial, see *Lamont v Hyland* [1950] 1 KB 585. *Diamond v Graham* [1968] 1 WLR 1061 emphasised that the consideration need not be given by the payee directly to the payor.

[21] See, eg, *Solo Industries v Canara Bank* [2001] All ER (D) 34 (Jul). The mere assertion or allegation of fraud would not be sufficient: see *Bolivinter Oil SA v Chase Manhattan Bank* [1984] 1 Ll R 251, at 257.

[22] See, eg, *Crockfords Club Ltd v Mehta* [1992] 1 WLR 355, CA. This has obvious ramifications if the dispute between the solicitor and the client relates to whether the retainer is enforceable.

[23] *Ibid* is usually quoted as authority on the point, but a better case in the context of costs litigation is *Safa Ltd v Banque du Caire* [2000] 2 All ER (Comm) 567, at 579, in which Waller LJ said: 'If there was a misrepresentation by a beneficiary ... and there was a real prospect of such being established at the trial, it would seem to me that a court would be entitled not to give summary judgment.'

[24] See, eg, *AEG v Lewis* (1992) The Times, 29 December, CA.

[25] See *Nova (Jersey) Knit Ltd v Kammgarn Spinnerei GmbH* [1977] 1 WLR 713, at 720c–d; *Thoni GmbH v RTP* [1979] 2 Ll R 282, CA. See also *AEG v Lewis* (1992) The Times, 29 December, CA.

[26] *Ray v Newton* [1913] 1 KB 249, CA.

Whilst not binding,[27] Warner J has made it clear that the cheque rule should not be used so as to allow solicitors to side-step the provisions of the Solicitors Act 1974, saying: '[A] solicitor cannot escape from the provisions of the legislation relating to solicitors' remuneration by taking a cheque from his client and suing on the cheque.'[28] Warner J went on to suggest that it is arguable that the consumer protection afforded by the requirement to wait a month following delivery of a statute bill would be defeated if a solicitor were to be permitted to sue upon the cheque within that period.[29]

For the foregoing reasons, a solicitor would normally be in no better a position having sued on a cheque than they would have been had they sued for their fees in the usual way. If the solicitor believes that the client is about to become insolvent, however, their ability to sue on a cheque may become of practical use, because (where it is available) a summary judgment can typically be obtained more promptly than a claim for fees brought in reliance on the contract of retainer. **40.12**

Venue

A claim brought by a solicitor for fees is wholly different from a claim for an assessment. This means that the procedural requirements under r 67.3(1) of the Civil Procedure Rules (CPR) do not apply and that the solicitor is free to choose the venue in accordance with Practice Direction (PD) 7, paras 2.1–2.4. Where appropriate, however, it would be sensible to have regard to the issue of where any assessment would be heard if the client were to counterclaim for an assessment (see 40.17 and 40.19). **40.13**

Evidential issues and disclosure

In general, admissibility of evidence will not be an issue, but the following points are worth making. **40.14**

- **Confidential material** Where material is confidential (such as where the subject matter of the instructions was something that, if made public, could incriminate the client), it would be open to the court to deal with matters in private (see 36.109–36.110).
- **Privilege and client papers** It may be that there has been an implied waiver of privilege over client papers; this is addressed at 36.107–36.108 (also see 46.60–46.66).
- **Without-prejudice correspondence (as between the parties)** This is addressed at 6.213–6.218.
- **Without-prejudice correspondence (as between persons other than the parties)** It may be that one of the parties wishes to rely putatively on without-prejudice communications that did not pass between the parties, but between one of them and a third party (such as where a solicitor agent sues a solicitor principal for their fees and the former wants to see without-prejudice correspondence with the client). The without-prejudice rule is capable of extending beyond the parties to the relevant negotiations.[30]

---

27 This is because Warner J was dealing with an application for summary judgment and, as such, he was not deciding the merits of the issues, but merely determining whether the client's arguments had a real chance of success.

28 *Martin Boston & Co (a firm) v Levy* [1982] 1 WLR 1434, at 1440.

29 *Ibid*, at 1441.

30 See *Rush & Tompkins Ltd v GLC* [1989] 1 AC 1280, at 1301, *per* Lord Griffiths; more recently, *Ofulue v Bossert* [2009] UKHL 16, at [37], *per* Lord Rodger.

This may or may not prevent compulsory disclosure of that correspondence,[31] but it would not be a bar to one or more of the correspondents from voluntarily showing that correspondence to a third party.[32] Newey J has explained that the notion of common interest privilege (see 46.11) would not apply by analogy in those circumstances.[33]

Procedure

40.15 As to procedure, it is not wholly clear whether a claim for unpaid fees may be brought by a claim under CPR, Part 7. CPR, r 67.3(2), provides that a claim for 'an order under Part III of the Act' must be made by Part 8 claim form (unless it is made in existing proceedings), but it is arguable that a claim for unpaid fees is not an order under Pt III of the Solicitors Act 1974, because that Act does not create the cause of action; it merely provides a means of regulating it. Regardless of the theoretical considerations, the Part 8 procedure would usually be the appropriate procedure simply as a matter of convenience and also to avoid the problems that may be caused if the client were not to file an acknowledgement of service or defence (see 40.24).

Declarations

40.16 Whilst a slight digression, it is worth noting that if there is a dispute as to the effect of a contract of retainer, it would be open to a solicitor (or client) to seek declaratory relief.[34]

Non-contentious work

40.17 A claim brought by a solicitor for their costs is not a claim for an assessment, so the procedural requirements under CPR, r 67.3(1), do not apply. If, however, the court were to order that there be an assessment, that assessment would have to proceed in the High Court.[35] This means that it is often sensible to bring the claim in the High Court in the first place, in anticipation of an application being made for an assessment.

Contentious work

40.18 Where a contentious business agreement does more than provide for remuneration by reference to an agreed hourly rate, the costs incurred under that agreement will not be subject to assessment[36] (unless, of course, the court sets the agreement aside). This is discussed in detail at 27.156–27.159.

40.19 The points made at 40.17 about the appropriate court are repeated here: where the claim relates to contentious business done in the County Court and its hearing centres and where the claim is within the financial limit of that court's jurisdiction (that is, less than £5,000),[37] then the County Court will be able to hear the assessment.[38] This may be a factor to take

[31] See *Rabin v Mendoza & Co* [1954] 1 WLR 271. See also *Muller v Linsley & Mortimer* [1996] 1 PNLR 74; *EMW Law LLP v Halborg* [2017] EWHC 1014 (Ch), at [64], *per* Newey J.

[32] See *EMW Law LLP v Halborg* [2017] EWHC 1014 (Ch), at [44] and [45], *per* Newey J.

[33] See *ibid*, at [46]–[50].

[34] See, eg, *Colemans-CTTS LLP v O'Keefe* [2014] EWHC 4099 (QB), *per* Judge Seymour QC (sitting as a deputy High Court judge). See also *Ultimate Products Ltd v Woolley* [2014] EWHC 1919 (Ch).

[35] See CPR, r 67.3(1)(b).

[36] Solicitors Act 1974, s 60(1).

[37] See Solicitors Act 1974, s 69(3), as amended by High Court and County Courts Jurisdiction Order 1991 (SI 1991/724), art 2(7) and (8) and Sch, Pt 1 of the Schedule.

[38] CPR, r 67.3(1)(a).

into account when deciding where proceedings should be issued. Errors in this regard may mean that the court lacks *vires* to make the order sought[39] (see 36.43–36.44).

Summary judgment

Where the claim is resisted on a point of principle—as opposed to merely on quantum—and where the client has no real prospect of success, the court is entitled to give summary judgment in favour of the solicitor. The test is whether the client has no real prospect of successfully defending the claim or issue.[40] **40.20**

An application for summary judgment may be based on: **40.21**

- a point of law (including a question of construction of a document); or
- the evidence that can reasonably be expected to be available at trial or the lack thereof; or
- a combination of these things.[41]

Unless the court acts of its own initiative, it would be for the solicitor to make an application on notice.[42] Other than where the court gives permission, the application must not be made until the client has filed an acknowledgement of service or a defence. Written evidence must be served in advance of the hearing.[43]

Examples of reported cases are surprisingly scarce. Turner J gave summary judgment in a case in which the client repeatedly changed her case, proceeding with each new argument only when the previous argument had been shown to be untenable.[44] **40.22**

It is not only solicitors who may apply for summary judgment; in an appropriate case, it would also be open to a client to seek summary judgment on the claim under CPR, r 24.2(a)(i)—and this would avoid the need to seek a strike-out for abuse of process.[45] **40.23**

Default judgment

A default judgment is a judgment that is entered as a result of the client having failed to file an acknowledgement of service or a defence within the requisite period of time.[46] Although there is no authority on the point, there are two reasons why a solicitor would, in general, be well advised not to make an application for default judgment. In particular, there are two reasons why a solicitor would do well to avoid the risk of having to make an application by the simple expedient of using the Part 8 procedure rather than the Part 7 procedure. **40.24**

- **Abuse of process** Default judgments may not be made in claims brought by way of the CPR, Part 8 procedure.[47] For the reasons set out at 40.15, it not wholly clear whether CPR, r 67.3(2), precludes a claim for a solicitor's cost being brought under the Part 7

---

39 See *R (on the application of Srinivasans Solicitors) v Croydon County Court* [2011] EWHC 3615 (Admin), which decision was the subject of an appeal ([2013] EWCA Civ 249), but on a different point.
40 CPR, r 24.2(a)(ii).
41 PD 24, para 1.3.
42 See PD 24, para 2, for the relevant procedure.
43 CPR, r 24.5(1)–(4).
44 *Penningtons (a firm) v Abedi* (unreported), 30 July 1999, QBD.
45 *Alpha Rocks Solicitors v Alade* [2015] EWCA Civ 685, at [21], *per* Vos LJ.
46 CPR, rr 12.1 and 12.3(1); PD 12, para 1.1.
47 CPR, r 12.2(b).

procedure. If it does, then it could be argued that it would be an abuse of process to allow default judgment to be entered in a claim that has been brought in defiance of a mandatory rule.

- **No specified amount of money** It used to be the case that, where a default judgment was sought, it was entered for the amount claimed; there is now doubt as to whether this is the correct procedure. This is because of the growing body of case law relating to the statutory demands (see 40.121–40.129) that makes it clear that claims for solicitors' fees are not liquidated sums.[48] Although there are arguments to the contrary,[49] one could easily argue that it would be inconsistent if one rule were to apply to statutory demands, but another to civil claims. If this argument were to succeed, then default judgment may be obtained only for an 'amount of money to be decided by the court'[50]—and this may lead to disputes as to what this means.

40.25 These problems can be avoided by using the Part 8 procedure. If the client fails to serve an acknowledgement of service in time, then they will be able to attend the hearing of the claim, but may not take part in the hearing unless the court gives permission.[51] The solicitor would be entitled to ask the court to deal with the matter on this basis, but on the merits.

40.26 In any event, if the solicitor uses the Part 7 Procedure, they would be unable to apply for default judgment in any of the following circumstances:

- where the client has applied to strike out the claim;
- where the client has applied for summary judgment;
- where the client has satisfied the whole claim (including the costs); or
- where the client has filed an admission, together with a request for time to pay.[52]

If the court were to make an order for an amount of money to be decided by the court, then it would either allocate the matter to a track or give directions (or both).[53]

Strike-out

40.27 It may be that a client wishes to apply for the claim to be struck out in accordance with CPR, r 3.4, which reads as follows:

> '3.4 (1) In this rule and rule 3.5, reference to a statement of case includes reference to part of a statement of case.
>
> (2) The court may strike out a statement of case if it appears to the court—
>
> (a) that the statement of case discloses no reasonable grounds for bringing or defending the claim;

---

[48] See *Klamer v Kyriakides & Braier (a firm)* [2005] BPIR Ch D, a decision of Master Simmonds; *Truex v Toll* [2009] EWHC 369 (Ch), in which Proudman J accepted, without demur, the agreement between the parties that such a bill is not for a liquidated sum. See also *In Re Laceward Ltd* [1981] 1 WLR 133, at 137.

[49] It could be argued that, unless the fees were obviously excessive, it would be an abuse of process to afford the defendant the opportunity to have the fees assessed, because this would undermine the provisions in Solicitors Act 1974, s 70. It could also be argued that the cases concerning statutory demands can be distinguished on the basis that they relate to an enforcement procedure, as opposed to a civil claim, which (at the stage of default judgment) is a procedure of ascertainment rather than enforcement.

[50] CPR, r 12.4(1).

[51] See CPR, r 8.4(2).

[52] CPR, r 12.3(3).

[53] CPR, r 12.7(2).

(b) that the statement of case is an abuse of the court's process or is otherwise likely to obstruct the just disposal of the proceedings; or
(c) that there has been a failure to comply with a rule, practice direction or court order.
[...]'

The first of these grounds (namely, no reasonable grounds for bringing the claim) is unlikely to apply in the context of claims brought by a solicitor for their fees, although it is possible that an unmeritorious defence could be struck out. **40.28**

The second (namely, abuse of the court's process or if otherwise likely to obstruct the just disposal of the proceedings) may apply if, for example, a client says that the claim that is being brought against them is fraudulent. In a context other than a claim for fees, Mummery LJ held that a strike-out may be appropriate 'where a claimant [was] guilty of misconduct in relation to proceedings which is so serious that it would be an affront to the court to permit him to continue to prosecute the claim, then the claim may be struck out for that reason'.[54] It would be very rare that the court would allow such an application in the context of a claim brought by a solicitor for their fees. Vos LJ had this to say on the topic: **40.29**

> 'In my judgment, the court should exercise caution in the early stages of a case in striking out the entirety of a claim on the grounds that a part has been improperly or even fraudulently exaggerated. That is because of the draconian effect of so doing and the risk that, at a trial, events may appear less clear cut than they do at an interlocutory stage. The court is not easily affronted, and in my judgment the emphasis should be on the availability of fair trial of the issues between the parties. As CPR Part 3.4(2)(b) itself says, "[t]he court may strike out a statement of case if... the statement of case is an abuse of the court's process or *is otherwise likely to obstruct the just disposal of the proceedings*".'[55]

On the facts of the case before him (in which it was said that a bill had been backdated and work had been charged for when it had not been done), Vos LJ went on to find that it had been inappropriate to strike out the claim without testing the evidence at trial.[56]

As to the third of the grounds (namely, failure to comply with a rule, practice direction or court order), *Denton*[57] will apply (see 26.48–26.70). **40.30**

Payments on Account and Interim Payments

The most secure two forms of security that a solicitor can have are possession of cash or of cleared funds. There is no reason why a client should not be asked to pay part or **40.31**

[54] *Masood v Zahoor (Practice Note)* [2009] EWCA Civ 650, at [71], *per* Mummery LJ, relying on *Arrow Nominees Inc v Blackledge* [2000] BCLC 167.

[55] *Alpha Rocks Solicitors v Alade* [2015] EWCA Civ 685, at [22], emphasis added by Vos LJ. See also (albeit in a context other than claims for fees) *Summers v Fairclough Homes* [2012] 1 WLR 2004, at [49], in which Lord Clarke said: 'The draconian step of striking a claim out is always a last resort, *a fortiori* where to do so would deprive the claimant of a substantive right to which the court had held that he was entitled after a fair trial. It is very difficult indeed to think of circumstances in which such a conclusion would be proportionate. Such circumstances might, however, include a case where there had been a massive attempt to deceive the court but the award of damages would be very small.'

[56] *Alpha Rocks Solicitors v Alade* [2015] EWCA Civ 685, at [26]–[28].

[57] *Denton v TH White Ltd* [2014] EWCA Civ 906.

all of the costs debt pending an assessment (or, for that matter, pending any other dispute resolution procedure). Indeed, if the client applies for an assessment that is not as of right, it is commonly the case that the court will make an order that a substantial part of the debt be paid on account, that order being a condition for allowing any such application.[58] These issues are addressed at 36.31. If relations between the solicitor and client have reached such a nadir that the client will not tolerate the solicitor having use of the money, an escrow account[59] or a separate designated client account (previously known as a special client account) may prove to be an acceptable compromise, with the monies being released only with the consent of both parties or upon order of the court.

40.32 The following miscellaneous topics might be relevant to the issue of whether a voluntary payment on account should be made (some of which would be appropriate if only the client were to wish to continue to instruct the solicitor).

- **Subsequent effect of voluntary payment** Although payment without demur may be a factor that may count against a client who subsequently seeks an assessment,[60] it will rarely be the case that a voluntary payment will count against the client if it is made without prejudice to the right to seek an assessment.[61] This will be especially true if the payment is only a part-payment.[62]
- **Overpayment** The court has the power to order the solicitor to return any monies that have been overpaid.[63]
- **Deposit-against-services retainer** Whilst it is rarely seen in this jurisdiction, the deposit-against-future-services retainer is a well-regarded method of ensuring payment that is often seen in the United States and is not uncommon in Australia.[64]
- **Agreements to pay interim invoices in return for continued representation** Where a solicitor agrees to carry out further work on condition that the client pays outstanding invoices, Roger Wand QC (sitting as a deputy judge of the High Court) found that the supply of those further services was consideration for that agreement and the client could not resile from it.[65]

---

[58] See, eg, *Re Brockman* [1908–10] All ER Rep 364. See also *Eurasian Natural Resources Corpn Ltd v Dechert LLP* [2017] EWHC B4 (Costs), at [12], *per* Master Rowley.

[59] In this context, an escrow account is an account in which money is held until specific conditions are met.

[60] *Barclays plc v Villers* [2000] 1 All ER (Comm) 357, at 369.

[61] See, eg, *Re Simmons and Politzer* [1954] 2 All ER 811, in which payment to secure release of papers did not preclude an assessment.

[62] *Re Callis* (1901) 49 WR 316; *Re Woodard* (1869) 18 WR 37.

[63] *Barclays plc v Villers* [2000] 1 All ER (Comm) 357, at 367.

[64] See Robinson, MA, *Winning Alternatives to the Billable Hour: Strategies That Work* (3rd edn, Chicago, IL: American Bar Association, 2008), pp 102–3. As to Australia, this issue will be addressed in the new edition of *Quick on Costs* (LexisNexis, online), ch 5. A deposit-against-future-services retainer is a variant of an annual or monthly retainer whereby a fixed amount is paid every year or every month, but rather than those monies being in full and final payment for the services rendered, they are payments on account (ie they are either used to pay bills that have been issued or they are held on account, usually in trust, for future costs). At the end of the retainer, the final bill will be delivered and, if necessary, corrected, and either the legal representative will refund the balance or the client will make good the shortfall, whichever is appropriate. This may be appropriate if the client wishes to continue to instruct the solicitor.

[65] See *Francis v Solomon Taylor & Shaw (a firm)* [2013] EWHC 9 (Ch), at [21]–[25].

Withdrawal of Services under a Contract of Retainer

When a solicitor is faced with a client who will not pay, but who has an ongoing matter, one option would be to terminate the contract of retainer (perhaps under s 62(5) of the Solicitors Act 1974) and to sue on the unpaid statute bills. This would certainly be an option, but there is also a 'very different remedy'—to use Ward LJ's phrase—namely, to withdraw the provision of legal services and to suspend the contract of retainer.[66] **40.33**

Suspension of a retainer may be a more effective remedy than termination, because clients tend not to like changing solicitors and, if they are forced to do so, it tends to cause them to become entrenched; suspension lessens that risk. Moreover, suspension puts the ball squarely in the client's court in the sense that, if the client chooses not to pay, it would generally be open to the court to find that whilst the solicitor merely suspended the retainer, the client terminated it.[67] This may be relevant in cases in which it is said that the retainer was a contract entire. **40.34**

Ward LJ said that whilst notice was required for termination of a retainer, there was no requirement for a client to be given notice in advance of the retainer being suspended.[68] Ward LJ rejected the argument that such a requirement was implied by the provision that permitted suspension. If the client were to want to continue to instruct the solicitor, the options referred to in 40.32 may be worth considering. **40.35**

Lien

This book is about costs, and therefore the following is merely an overview that is intended to assist costs practitioners and generalists. Where a complex issue of lien arises, it would be advisable to consult more in-depth texts, such as *Halsbury's Laws of England*.[69] **40.36**

Retaining lien

In certain circumstances, a solicitor will have a right to claim lien. Where this happens, the client is known as the lienor and the solicitor as the lien holder. Where lien is claimed as a result of property being in the solicitor's possession, it is known as a retaining lien. This is by far the most common type of lien encountered in costs practice and it may be claimed as a self-help remedy without the benefit of an order of the court.[70] A retaining lien is a type of general lien,[71] which can be defined as a rule that entitles a person lawfully in possession of property to retain that property until all of their lawful claims against the owner are satisfied.[72] Notwithstanding the fact that they are discouraged on policy grounds,[73] **40.37**

[66] *Minkin v Cawdery Kaye Fireman & Taylor (a firm)* [2012] EWCA Civ 546, at [30].

[67] This is precisely what happened in *ibid.*

[68] *Ibid.*

[69] *Halsbury's Laws of England* (5th edn, London: LexisNexis, 2015), vol 68.

[70] Compare this with particular lien: *see Bozon v Bolland* (1839) 4 My & Cr 354; *Re Fuld (No 4)* [1968] P 727; *James Bibby Ltd v Woods and Howard* [1949] 2 KB 449.

[71] A general lien allows a person in possession of property to retain that property until all of the owner's debts owed to the person (in general) have been satisfied.

[72] See *Selwyn's Abridgment of the Law of Nisi Prius* (13th edn, London: Stevens & Sons, 1869), p 1312.

[73] 'General liens are a great inconvenience to the generality of traders, because they give a particular advantage to certain individuals who claim to themselves a special privilege against the body (at large) of creditors

retaining liens apply not only to solicitors, but also to bankers, factors, stockbrokers, warehouse keepers and insurance brokers. In general, there are two ways in which a retaining lien may arise: the first is through contract; the second is by a common-law right arising from custom.[74] In so far as solicitors are concerned, retaining liens usually arise out of express terms in the contract of retainer. The right to claim a retaining lien will exist only if possession of the property has been rightfully obtained[75] with the client's consent.[76] In general, this will not be the case where monies were paid by mistake[77] nor will it generally be the case where monies or goods are obtained by the wrongful act of a third party.[78] Other circumstances in which a retaining lien may or may not arise are addressed at 40.48 *et seq.*

Particular lien

40.38 A particular lien may arise at common law where monies (whether costs or damages) have been recovered in litigation by the efforts of the solicitor, or where a solicitor's work (or that of some other type of legal services provider) has added value in some other way, such as where a conveyancer has prepared papers for conveyancing,[79] or where an arbitrator has written an award, but claims lien over it pending remuneration.[80] A particular lien will not attach if the property was recovered by negotiation[81] nor will it attach to real estate.[82] A particular lien is similar to, but distinct from, the statutory rights described at 40.89 *et seq* (that is, charges, etc).[83] Given the fact that equitable lien is now becoming so established (see 40.39–40.42), it will rarely be the case that a solicitor would need to rely on only a particular lien.

Equitable lien

40.39 Where the circumstances permit (see 40.41), a solicitor may be able to claim an equitable lien over property in respect of which they have carried out work. It is a right that has existed since the late 18th century,[84] but which, in the early 19th century, was developed as

instead of coming in with them for an equal share of the insolvent's estate': *Rushforth v Hadfield* (1805) 6 East 519, at 528. Whilst only persuasive, see also the decision of the Irish Supreme Court in *In the Matter of Galdan Properties Ltd (in liquidation)* [1988] IR 213, at 215.

[74] See, eg, *Re Southern Livestock Producers Ltd* [1963] 3 All ER 801, at 802.

[75] *Griffiths v Hyde* (1809) Dorset Summer Assizes, 2 Selw NP 1320; see also *Wickens v Townshend* (1830) 1 Russ & M 361. Indeed, a person who has obtained possession by misrepresentation may not set up a lien to which he might otherwise have been entitled: *Madden v Kempster* (1807) 1 Camp 12, NP.

[76] *Gibson v May* (1853) 4 De GM & G 512.

[77] See *Scottish Metropolitan Assurance Co v P Samuel & Co* [1923] 1 KB 348. As to payment under mistake of fact generally, see *Chase Manhattan Bank NA v Israel-British Bank (London) Ltd* [1981] Ch 105. See also *Woolwich Equitable Building Society v IRC (No 2)* [1993] AC 70, HL; *Kleinwort Benson Ltd v Lincoln City Council* [1999] 2 AC 349.

[78] This is discussed in *Halsbury's Laws of England* (5th edn, London: LexisNexis, 2015), vol 68, para 824. See also *Buxton v Baughan* (1834) 6 C & P 674. Where a negotiable instrument has been obtained by a wrongful act of another, the solicitor may assert lien if it obtained the instrument in good faith and without notice of the wrongdoing: see *Brandao v Barnett* (1846) 12 Cl & Fin 787, HL, at 805. See also Bills of Exchange Act 1882, s 27(3).

[79] See *Hollis v Claridge* (1813) 4 Taunt 807; see also *Steadman v Hockley* (1846) 15 M & W 553.

[80] See, eg, *DTC (CNC) Ltd v Gary Sergeant & Co (a firm)* [1996] 2 All ER 369, [1996] 1 WLR 797.

[81] *Megeurditchian v Lightbound* [1917] 2 KB 298, CA, at 302, *per* Swinfen Eady LJ.

[82] See *Shaw v Neale* (1858) 6 HL Cas 581 (the case that resulted in Parliament passing legislation that led to solicitors' charging orders).

[83] *Re Clarke's Settlement Fund* [1911] WN 39, at 40.

[84] The first case in which it was recognised was *Welsh v Hole* (1779) 1 Dougl KB 238. See also *Read v Dupper* (1795) 6 Term Rep 361; *Ormerod v Tate* (1801) 1 East 464.

a means of achieving access to justice.[85] Such a lien is a right over the fruits of a solicitor's labour (whether those fruits are in the hands of the solicitor or not), rather than a mere right to retain property in the solicitor's possession. In view of this, Lord Briggs has explained that whilst it is called a lien, it is better analysed as a form of equitable charge.[86] He explained the rationale for the charge in this way:

> 'In its traditional form it is the means whereby equity provides a form of security for the recovery by solicitors of their agreed charges for the successful conduct of litigation, out of the fruits of that litigation. It is a judge-made remedy, motivated not by any fondness for solicitors as fellow lawyers or even as officers of the court, but rather because it promotes access to justice. Specifically it enables solicitors to offer litigation services on credit to clients who, although they have a meritorious case, lack the financial resources to pay up front for its pursuit.'[87]

An equitable lien differs from a retaining lien in that it is not merely defensive,[88] but also must be actively enforced[89] (that is, it requires a court order,[90] without which it may not be asserted[91]). Sir Stephen Sedley provided this summary (which was cited with approval by Lord Briggs): **40.40**

> '[T]he law is today (and, in our view, has been for fully two centuries) that the court will intervene to protect a solicitor's claim on funds recovered or due to be recovered by a client or former client if (a) the paying party is colluding with the client to cheat the solicitor of his fees, or (b) the paying party is on notice that the other party's solicitor has a claim on the funds for outstanding fees. The form of protection ought to be preventative but may in a proper case take the form of dual payment.'[92]

Having cited this summary, Lord Briggs went on say that: equity depends upon the solicitor having a claim for their charges against the client; there must be something in the nature of a fund against which equity can recognise that the claim extends (usually a debt owed by an opponent to the solicitor's client, which debt owes its existence—at least in part—to the solicitor's services to the client); and, for equity to intervene, there must be something sufficiently affecting the conscience of the payer, either in the form of collusion to cheat the solicitor or notice of the solicitor's claim against, or interest in, the fund.[93] Lord Briggs went on to say that the solicitor's claim is limited to the unpaid amount of their charges.[94] Where the circumstances, permit, a solicitor may be able to claim an equitable lien in respect of monies that would have been due under a CFA Lite.[95] **40.41**

---

85 See *Ex p Bryant* (1815) 1 Madd 49; *Gould v Davis* (1831) 1 Cr & J 415.

86 *Gavin Edmondson Solicitors Ltd v Haven Insurance Co Ltd* [2018] UKSC 21, at [3] and [37], *per* Lord Briggs. In this regard, Lord Briggs referred to the following cases, *ibid* at [34]–[35]: *Barker v St Quintin* (1844) 12 M & W 441, at 443, *per* Baron Parke; *Mason v Mason and Cottrell* [1933] P 199, at 214, *per* Lord Hanworth MR; *In re Fuld dec'd (No 4)* [1968] P 727, at 736, *per* Scarman J.

87 *Gavin Edmondson Solicitors Ltd v Haven Insurance Co Ltd* [2018] UKSC 21, at [1].

88 See *ibid*, at [2].

89 *Bozon v Bolland* (1839) 4 My & Cr 354.

90 *Re Fuld (No 4)* [1968] P 727.

91 *James Bibby Ltd v Woods and Howard* [1949] 2 KB 449.

92 *Khans Solicitor (a firm) v Chifuntwe & Anor* [2013] EWCA Civ 481, at [33], cited in *Gavin Edmondson Solicitors Ltd v Haven Insurance Co Ltd* [2018] UKSC 21, at [36]–[37].

93 *Ibid*, at [7].

94 *Ibid*, at [7].

95 *Ibid*, at [37]–[44].

40.42 It has long been the case that if an attempt has been made to frustrate the solicitor's right to the lien, then (in certain circumstances) the court may take additional steps that go beyond that lien.[96] Those additional steps are known as equitable interference and are dealt with at 40.106 *et seq*. As can be seen, whilst equitable interference is a long-established remedy, it is capable of having effect in very modern settings, such as allowing a solicitor to recover fixed fees under the Pre-Action Protocol for Low Value Personal Injury Claims in Road Traffic Accidents in circumstances under which the liability insurer for the opponents of their clients sought to frustrate their entitlement to be paid those fees by settling claims directly with those clients.[97]

Lien holders' duty to take care of retained property

40.43 A solicitor who holds property belonging to another is a bailee of those items, which means that, unless there has been an agreement to the contrary or there are special circumstances, they will owe a duty of care to take care of the retained property.[98] This includes a duty to exercise reasonable care in the safekeeping and management of the property.[99] Whilst the contrary is arguable, the solicitor would generally not be able to charge the lienor for the costs of keeping the property (such as storage fees).[100]

The effect of a retaining lien

40.44 The starting point is that a solicitor with a retaining lien is entitled to refuse access to the retained property, be that by the client or their successors,[101] or by any new solicitor instructed by the client. Where that property is the client's file (or any other documents belonging to the client), the solicitor may refuse to allow any copies to be taken[102] or to allow the documents to be inspected.[103] This can apply even in family cases.[104] The solicitor may retain property against the client, against third parties[105] and against all persons claiming through the client, and it may do this until the costs debt is discharged *in full*.[106] A retaining lien will attach to the whole of the costs debt, not only a part of it that has a nexus

---

96 See, eg, *Re Sullivan v Pearson, ex p Morrison* (1868) LR 4 QB 153, at 156, *per* Blackburn J. See also *Guy v Churchill* (1887) 35 Ch D 489, at 497, *per* Cotton LJ.

97 *Gavin Edmondson Solicitors Ltd v Haven Insurance Co Ltd* [2018] UKSC 21.

98 See *Scarfe v Morgan* (1838) 4 M & W 270, at 279, 284 and 289; see also *Great Western Rly Co v Crouch* (1858) 3 H & N 183, Ex Ch.

99 See *Great Western Rly Co v Crouch* (1858) 3 H & N 183, Ex Ch; *Nightingale v Tildsley* [1980] CLY 134, Wolverhampton County Court.

100 *Somes v British Empire Shipping Co* (1860) 8 HL Cas 338; cf *China Pacific SA v Food Corpn of India, The Winson* [1982] AC 939, HL, at 962–3, *per* Lord Diplock, and at 964, *per* Lord Simon of Glaisdale.

101 Such as personal representatives (*Re Watson* (1884) 53 LJ Ch 305), a trustee in bankruptcy (*Re Watters* (1881) 7 LR Ir 531) or, in the case of a company, a liquidator (*Re Aveling Barford Ltd* [1988] 3 All ER 1019).

102 See *Leo Abse & Cohen v Evan G Jones (Builders) Ltd* (1984) 128 Sol Jo 317; see also *Hemsworth, ex p Underwood* (1845) de G 190.

103 See *Leo Abse & Cohen v Evan G Jones (Builders) Ltd* (1984) 128 Sol Jo 317; *Re Biggs and Roche* (1897) 41 Sol Jo 277.

104 *Hughes v Hughes* [1958] P 224. See also *Halsbury's Laws of England* (5th edn, London: LexisNexis, 2015), vol 66, para 1003, quoted with approval by Morgan J (sitting in the Court of Appeal) in *French v Carter Lemon Camerons LLP* [2012] EWCA Civ 1180, at [27].

105 See *Loescher v Dean* [1950] 1 Ch 491; see also *Irwin Mitchell v HMRC* [2008] EWCA Crim 1741, at [37], *per* Toulson LJ.

106 *Hawkes, Re; Ackerman v Lockhart* [1898] 2 Ch 1, CA.

with the retained property.[107] The client must be personally liable for the costs debt; where this is not the case, no lien will attach.[108]

A retaining lien is not a right of action in itself,[109] but instead a defence to a claim in respect of the retained property. This has both advantages and disadvantages for the solicitor. On the one hand, the solicitor will be able to claim lien even where the costs debt is statute-barred;[110] on the other hand, a lien will confer no power to sell the property or to dispose of it for profit. Whilst the contrary is arguable[111] and whilst there are exceptions,[112] a retaining lien confers a mere personal right, which means that (unless the owner consents) it cannot be transferred to a third party simply by transferring the retained property.[113] **40.45**

The effect of a particular lien

Particular lien usually relates to the proceeds of litigation. As with a retaining lien, the lien holder may refuse to allow inspection or copying of the owner's papers. Unlike a retaining lien, however, a particular lien does not extend to the costs debt generally, but only to that part of the debt which pertains to the recovery of the retained property.[114] **40.46**

The principal benefit of a particular lien is that where notice is given to the party liable to discharge the order for costs, damages, etc, that person would be at risk of being held accountable to the solicitor if they were to comply with that order in disregard of the lien.[115] Indeed, a claim may be brought against a person (such as a former partner of a solicitor) who acted contrary to the lien.[116] **40.47**

The extent and acquisition of a retaining lien

As a general rule, a retaining lien may extend to any money[117] that has come into the solicitor's possession,[118] but only to the extent that it does not exceed the costs debt.[119] A retaining lien may apply to deeds,[120] documents[121] or personal chattels,[122] but not—as **40.48**

---

[107] This is in contrast to a particular lien: see *Donald v Suckling* (1866) LR 1 QB 585, at 612–13, *per* Blackburn J, and at 618–19, *per* Cockburn CJ.

[108] *Lightfoot v Keane* (1836) 1 M & W 745.

[109] *Tappenden (t/a English and American Autos) v Artus* [1964] 2 QB 185, at 194–195, CA, *per* Diplock LJ, who said that lien is a self-help remedy, triggered by the performance of work that improves a chattel of which the performer has lawful possession, and does not depend on any implied contractual term.

[110] *Higgins v Scott* (1831) 2 B & Ad 413.

[111] The editors of *Halsbury's Laws of England* (5th edn, London: LexisNexis, 2015), vol 68, para 820, have noted that it is arguable that the decisions in the next footnote afford one of several indications that common-law possessory liens are beginning to be recognised as a limited form of property interest.

[112] There are cases in which a retaining lien was assignable in which a secured debt was also assigned: see *Bull v Faulkner* (1848) 2 De G & Sm 772. See also the Australian case concerning accountants: *Vered v Inscorp Holdings Ltd* (1993) 31 NSWLR 290, NSW SC. See also *Gordon v Gordon* [2002] EWCA Civ 1884, [2002] All ER (D) 308 (Dec).

[113] *Donald v Suckling* (1866) LR 1 QB 585, at 612–13, *per* Blackburn J, and at 618–19, *per* Cockburn CJ.

[114] *Re Bayly's Estate, ex p Humphrey* (1860) 12 I Ch R 315.

[115] *Ross v Buxton* (1889) 42 Ch D 190.

[116] See, eg, *FPH Law v Brown* [2016] EWHC 1681 (QB).

[117] *Re Phoenix Life Assurance Co, Howard and Dolman's Case* (1863) 1 Hem & M 433, at 444.

[118] It is the legal entity that took possession that is relevant: *Re Forshaw* (1847) 16 Sim 121. A solicitor's successors may also take possession: *Pelly v Wathen* (1849) 7 Hare 351.

[119] *Re Dee Estates Ltd, Wright v Dee Estates Ltd* [1911] 2 Ch 85, CA.

[120] *Ibid.*

[121] *Re Markby, ex p Markby Assignees* (1864) 11 LT 250.

[122] *Friswell v King* (1846) 15 Sim 191, in which lien extended to evidence that was to be relied upon at trial.

a general rule—to costs debtors' wills,[123] public records or orders made by the court.[124] In contrast to the situation in which lien is claimed over money, the solicitor may assert lien over goods regardless of whether the value of the retained items exceeds the costs debt.[125] Indeed, in the absence of fraud, the court is normally unwilling to interfere to assess the value of the lien[126]—a reflection of the fact that retaining liens are generally thought of as self-help remedies.

40.49 Lien may attach regardless of whether the property has intrinsic value.[127] There are limits, however. In particular, retaining lien will not extend to allowing a creditor to assert lien over an electronic database. This is because the information contained on a database is not a physical object capable of possession independently of the medium in which it was held.[128]

40.50 Lien may be claimed only where there is debt that is due, not where it is merely accruing.[129] Moreover, a solicitor may not set up a lien that is inconsistent with their retainer.[130] This means that if there was an agreement to defer payment of fees until the conclusion of the matter, lien would not attach until that point had been reached.[131] Similarly, where the retainer is a contract entire that makes no provision for interim billing, it is arguable that lien would attach only upon completion of the matter to which the retainer relates.[132] Where, however, the retainer permits interim billing, then there is authority to suggest that lien will attach to work in progress (that is, to fees that have been earned, but not billed), in which regard Toulson LJ had this to say (in the context of whether a client had an interest over the retained monies):

> 'Once [the solicitors] had earned that amount in fees [ie the amount of the monies over which lien is claimed], the value of [the client's] interest in the fund was reduced to nil. ... The bill, if properly served, reflects the solicitors' entitlement to payment by virtue of the work done. Once they were entitled to payment of that sum, [the client's] "interest" in the relevant account became literally nominal ...'[133]

Toulson LJ went on to explain that the solicitors' lien was not annulled by the fact that, at the time they claimed lien, they had yet to comply with certain billing requirements under the Solicitors Accounts Rules 1998.[134]

---

[123] *Balch v Symes* (1823) 1 Turn & R 87.

[124] *Bird v Heath* (1848) 6 Hare 236.

[125] *Gebruder Naf v Ploton* (1890) 25 QBD 13, CA.

[126] *Ibid; Segbedzi v Glah* (1989) New LJ 1303, CA.

[127] *Hughes v Hughes* [1958] P 224.

[128] *Your Response Ltd v Datateam Business Media Ltd* [2014] EWCA Civ 281, [2014] All ER (D) 156 (Mar).

[129] See *Freeport Electronics Ltd v Habib Bank Ltd* [2007] EWHC 1149 (QB), at [136].

[130] Whilst not relating specifically to solicitors, see *Re Southern Livestock Producers Ltd* [1963] 3 All ER 801, at 807, *per* Pennycuick J.

[131] See, by analogy, *Chase v Westmore* (1816) 5 M & S 180.

[132] Again, see, by analogy, *ibid.* Moreover, it may be of relevance that lien does not ordinarily arise under a contract for services until after the work has been carried out: see, eg, *Pinnock v Harrison* (1838) 3 M & W 532, at 535, *per* Parke B.

[133] *Irwin Mitchell v HMRC* [2008] EWCA Crim 1741, [2009] 1 WLR 753, at [32]. See also, by analogy, *Re K* [1990] 2 QB 298, which concerned a lien claimed by a bank.

[134] Whilst it is doubtful that it made any difference to the outcome, it should be noted that not all of the relevant law relating to statute bills was drawn to Toulson LJ's attention.

Not acting as a solicitor

To be entitled to a retaining lien, the solicitor must, at the time the retained property came into their possession, have been acting in the course of their engagement as a solicitor on behalf of the costs debtor or their successors.[135] Thus, where the retained property has come into a solicitor's possession whilst they were acting in a personal, rather than a professional capacity, the solicitor will, in general, not be able to claim lien. Examples include where a solicitor was acting as a mortgagee for a client,[136] where a solicitor was acting as a land agent[137] and where the debt had arisen as a result of a mere loan.[138] **40.51**

Monies and property held for a purpose (including trusts)

Where the property comes into the solicitor's possession as trustee, then a retaining lien will generally not apply;[139] likewise, a retaining lien would not extend to property held by a solicitor who, subsequent to receipt, has constituted themselves as a trustee.[140] If property is held on trust, but is subsequently (lawfully) retained by the solicitor for other purposes, then a retaining lien may attach.[141] **40.52**

Where, under a contract, monies are placed in the solicitor's hands for only a particular purpose, then lien will generally not attach.[142] Where the solicitor's words or conduct merit such a finding, it is open to the court to find that a purpose trust exists.[143] The court does not need to go so far as this to find that lien is excluded, however.[144] Sir Robin Jacob has explained that the absence of a purpose trust does not automatically mean that a lien will arise, because there is room for an 'undistributed middle' (as he called it).[145] In so far as monies in a client account are concerned, he explained that the key question was whether it was there 'for general purposes' or for a particular purpose, the existence of which may be evidenced by receipts,[146] covering letters,[147] what was said orally[148] and correspondence generally.[149] If the particular purpose has become time-expired, then the solicitor may be **40.53**

---

[135] *Re Long, ex p Fuller* (1881) 16 Ch D 617.

[136] *Vaughan v Vanderstegen* (1854) 2 Drew 408; cf *Re Riddell, Public Trustee v Riddell* [1936] 2 All ER 1600.

[137] See, eg, *Re Walker, Meredith v Walker* (1893) 68 LT 517, in which the solicitor acted as a land agent and lien was found not to attach.

[138] *Re Taylor, Stileman and Underwood* [1891] 1 Ch 590.

[139] See *Halvanon Insurance Co Ltd v Central Reinsurance Corpn* [1988] 3 All ER 857; *Hicks v Wrench* (1821) 6 Madd 93. Whilst only persuasive, the decision of the Irish Supreme Court *In the Matter of Galdan Properties Ltd (in liquidation)* [1988] IR 213 makes it clear that if a third party supplies property to a solicitor for a specific purpose and held to the third party's order, no lien will attach.

[140] *Lloyd v Gough* (1894) 70 LT 725; *Re Clark, ex p Newland* (1876) 4 Ch D 515.

[141] *Re Mid-Kent Fruit Factory* [1896] 1 Ch 567.

[142] See *Walker v Birch* (1795) 6 Term Rep 258. See also *Brandao v Barnett* (1846) 12 Cl & Fin 787, HL. Where a particular purpose is shown, then the solicitors will, in theory, still have a general retaining lien, but that general lien is subject to the purpose.

[143] See, eg, *Barclays Bank v Quistclose Investments Ltd* [1968] 3 All ER 651, HL; *Twinsectra Ltd v Yardley* [2002] UKHL 12; *Templeton Insurance Ltd v Penningtons Solicitors LLP* [2006] EWHC 685 (Ch).

[144] See *Withers LLP v Langbar International Ltd* [2011] EWCA Civ 1419, at [22], in which Sir Robin Jacob explained that if the reason why monies were placed in a client account was inconsistent with the putative lien, then there would be no lien. In deciding whether there was inconsistency, a key question was whether money in a client account was there 'for general purposes' or for a particular purpose.

[145] *Ibid*, at [33].

[146] See, eg, *Walker v Birch* (1795) 6 Term Rep 258.

[147] See, eg, *Buchanan v Findlay* (1829) 9 B & C 738.

[148] See, eg, *Burn v Brown* (1817) 2 Stark 272.

[149] See, eg, *Bock v Gorrissen* (1860) 2 De G F & J 434, CA in Ch.

able to rely on the lien without those monies being subject to that purpose.[150] If a client wishes to avoid any lien arising, then this must be done by way of a special agreement to that effect.[151]

Escrow accounts

40.54 Where monies are paid into an escrow account controlled by a solicitor, such monies are akin to monies paid into court. This means that the solicitor is acting as a bare trustee and will therefore not be entitled to assert a retaining lien.[152] Where monies come to be paid out of the account, a particular lien may attach at that point.[153] If it is said that the monies were paid into the escrow account for a particular purpose, then the matters described in 40.52 will become relevant.

Client accounts

40.55 Lord Hoffmann had the following to say about monies held in client accounts: 'Money in a solicitor's client account is held on trust. The only question is the terms of that trust.'[154] The terms of the trust will be governed by any undertaking given by the solicitor as to the purposes for which the money will be applied.[155] Notwithstanding the fiduciary nature of the nexus between them,[156] the relationship between solicitor and client is not inherently that of trustee and beneficiary.[157] That said, given the facts that a solicitor has an obligation to keep separate accounts of clients' monies[158] and that a client's monies are, for the purposes of the Insolvency Act 1986, regarded as being held by the solicitor for another person,[159] clients' monies are, to those limited extents, held on trust. These trusts are not, however, of a type that would prevent money in the client account from being subject to a lien. If, by express agreement or otherwise, a solicitor's actions or words justify such a finding, it may become a trustee in a more general sense[160] and this could have a bearing on lien. In particular, if the solicitor were to say that the monies were paid to them for a particular purpose, then a purpose trust may be created (see 40.52). Finally, on a slightly different topic, it should be noted that the fact that the professional rules may require a bill to be submitted to the client before money can be transferred from a client account to an office account will not prevent money in the client account from being subject to a lien.[161]

---

150 See *Ex p Sterling* (1809) 16 Ves 258.

151 See *ibid.*

152 *Halvanon Insurance Co Ltd v Central Reinsurance Corpn* [1988] 1 WLR 1122.

153 *Ibid*; see also *Knight v Knight* [1925] Ch 835.

154 *Twinsectra Ltd v Yardley* [2002] UKHL 12, at [12].

155 See *ibid; Re Bell's Indenture, Bell v Hickley* [1980] 3 All ER 425.

156 See, eg, *Oswald Hickson Collier & Co v Carter-Ruck* [1984] AC 720.

157 See *Fyler v Fyler* (1841) 3 Beav 550. See also *Midland Bank Trust Co Ltd v Hett, Stubbs and Kemp (a firm)* [1979] Ch 384; *John Mowlem Construction plc v Neil F Jones & Co* [2004] EWCA Civ 768.

158 *Plunkett v Barclays Bank Ltd* [1936] 2 KB 107, at 117. See also SRA Accounts Rules 2011, para 13.

159 *Re A Solicitor* [1952] Ch 328.

160 Examples include: *Re Bell's Indenture, Bell v Hickley* [1980] 3 All ER 425, [1980] 1 WLR 1217; *Bulkley v Wilford* (1834) 2 Cl & Fin 102, HL, at 177; *Harpham v Shacklock* (1881) 19 Ch D 207, CA. As a counter-example, see *Islamic Republic of Iran Shipping Lines v Denby* [1987] 1 Lloyd's Rep 367 (monies paid as a bribe to a solicitor not held in trust), although the correctness of this decision must be in doubt following *FHR European Ventures LLP v Cedar Capital Partners LLC* [2014] UKSC 45.

161 *Irwin Mitchell v HMRC* [2008] EWCA Crim 1741, [2009] 1 WLR 753. Indeed, SRA Accounts Rules 2011, r 11, expressly provides that those Rules will not deprive a solicitor of any recourse or right—whether by way of lien, set-off, counterclaim, charge or otherwise—against monies standing to the credit of a client account.

Registration and matters concerning companies

Where a solicitor who is an incorporated body has retaining lien, it would seem that the lien is not something that needs to be registered as a company charge.[162] As to insolvency, winding up and administration, see 40.79. **40.56**

Privilege and papers belonging to the solicitor

The mere fact that papers may be privileged would not give the solicitor a right to claim lien over them.[163] If, however, the papers belong to the solicitor (such as papers created on a file following the termination of a retainer[164]), then the solicitors will be entitled to refuse access (although this would not be as a result of lien). **40.57**

The extent and acquisition of a particular lien

The principles applying to particular lien are different from those that apply to retaining liens. Where lien is claimed over monies paid by an opponent, those monies must have been recovered in the litigation in respect of which the solicitor was, at the material time, retained.[165] Recovery by way of negotiation would not generally give rise to a particular lien.[166] A particular lien may attach to almost any form of property except maintenance payments[167] and real property.[168] In particular, it may extend to an award of costs[169] and to money paid into court as security for costs.[170] **40.58**

Relief from lien

Difficulties may arise where, in the midst of litigation, the solicitor asserts lien over the client's file of papers. In those circumstances, the court may afford the client relief from lien by ordering delivery up of the papers[171] or by ordering the solicitor to allow the lienor (or their legal advisers) to inspect the papers.[172] Whether the court would do this will depend on the circumstances. For descriptive purposes, the following scenarios may be identified: **40.59**

- where the solicitor discharges themselves from the retainer (see 40.61);
- where the retainer is still extant and where the solicitor continues to act (see 40.66); and
- where the client has determined the retainer by withdrawing instructions (see 40.67).

The distinction between these three scenarios will usually be a question of fact, but occasionally points of law may arise. The following miscellaneous points may be made. **40.60**

- **Want of payment** If termination of the retainer has arisen as a result of the solicitor determining the retainer for want of payment, this would typically be characterised as

---

162 This is the view of the editors of *Halsbury's Laws of England* (5th edn, London: LexisNexis, 2015), vol 68, para 821. See also *Re Hamlet International plc (in administration), Trident International Ltd v Barlow* [1999] 2 BCLC 506.

163 See, eg, *Cherrilow Ltd v Osmond Solicitors and Richard Butler-Creagh* [2011] EWHC 3443 (QB), *per* Eady J.

164 See, eg, *DR Sheridan v Higgins* [2012] EWHC 547 (Ch).

165 *Re Sullivan v Pearson, ex p Morrison* (1868) LR 4 QB 153.

166 *Megeurditchian v Lightbound* [1917] 2 KB 298, CA.

167 *Cross v Cross* (1880) 43 LT 533.

168 *Shaw v Neale* (1858) 6 HL Cas 581.

169 *Campbell v Campbell and Lewis* [1941] 1 All ER 274, CA; *Pounset v Humphreys* (1837) Coop Pr Cas 142.

170 *Hall v Hall* [1891] P 302, CA.

171 See CPR, r 25.1(c)(ii).

172 See CPR, r 25.1(c)(ii).

discharge by the solicitor, rather than by the client,[173] and this would be so regardless of whether the solicitor's right to interim payments was express or implied.[174]

- **Dissolution of the solicitor's firm** Dissolution of a firm would generally amount to determination of the retainer by the solicitor.[175]
- **Constructive determination** Discharge by the client as a result of misconduct on the part of the solicitor would ordinarily be capable of amounting to constructive discharge by the solicitor.[176] Although there is no authority on the point, the converse is also probably true (that is, that poor conduct on the part of the client may amount to constructive determination by them).

Lien where the solicitor discharges themselves

40.61 Lord Eldon pithily summed up the fact that a solicitor's rights are subordinate to the need for justice: 'A solicitor cannot, by virtue of his lien, prevent the king's subject from obtaining justice.'[177] Other than in exceptional cases (see 40.62), where a solicitor terminates the retainer during ongoing litigation, the court will make a mandatory order for delivery of the client's papers—normally against an undertaking by the new solicitor to preserve the lien of the original solicitor. This practice was described by Templeman LJ:

> '[The] practice of the court ... in order to save the client's litigation from catastrophe, [is to order] the solicitor to hand over the client's papers to the client's new solicitors, provided the new solicitors undertake to preserve the original solicitor's lien and to return the papers to the original solicitor, for what they are worth, after the end of the litigation.'[178]

Templeman LJ did not suggest a particular form of the mandatory order, but the order made in that case has become the *de facto* standard form (albeit in a more up-to-date form). It provides that the new solicitor will:

- hold the documents delivered to it subject to the first solicitor's lien;
- allow the original solicitor and the costs draftsperson or costs lawyer reasonable access to the documents for the purpose of preparing their bill of costs;
- progress the litigation in an active manner; and
- restore said documents to the original solicitor upon conclusion of the litigation.

40.62 A mandatory order will not be made in every case nor will it always be made in the standard form.[179] Roch LJ has commented (*obiter*) that the court's task is to weigh the principle that a client should not be deprived of material relevant to the conduct of their case and so be 'driven from the judgment seat' against the principle that litigation should be conducted with due regard to the interest of the solicitor, and he implied that it was relevant that

[173] *Robins v Goldingham* (1872) LR 13 Eq 440, which was approved in *Gamlen Chemical Co (UK) Ltd v Rochem Ltd* [1980] 1 WLR 614 and *Ismail v Richards Butler (a firm)* [1996] 2 All ER 506. As an earlier example, see *Webster v Le Hunt* (1861) 9 WR 804.

[174] *Bluck v Lovering & Co* (1886) 35 WR 232.

[175] *Griffiths v Griffiths* (1843) 2 Hare 587.

[176] *Hannaford v Hannaford* (1871) 24 LT 86; see also *French v Carter Lemon Camerons LLP* [2012] EWCA Civ 1180, at [31].

[177] *Commerell v Poynton* (1818) 1 Swan 1, at 2.

[178] *Gamlen Chemical Ltd v Rochem Ltd* [1980] 1 WLR 614, at 624.

[179] *Ibid*, at 625; see also *A v B* [1984] 1 All ER 265.

solicitors are the court's own officers and that they should not be left without payment of that which is due to them.[180]

Each case will turn on its own facts. Goff LJ has confirmed that much would depend on the nature of the case, the stage that the litigation has reached, the conduct of the solicitor and of the client, and the 'balance of hardship' that might result from the order the court is asked to make.[181] **40.63**

Where the new solicitor accepts the standard obligations, that would ordinarily be the only security to which the old solicitor would be entitled, but, in exceptional cases, the court may order that further security be given.[182] **40.64**

Where the standard obligations (or any obligations) are accepted by way of an undertaking, the court will lack the *vires* to relieve the new solicitor of the burden of compliance.[183] **40.65**

Lien where the solicitor is still acting

Where the solicitor continues to act, the issue of lien over the client's papers will be more academic than practical, because the client will not feel the effect of the lien: their claim will proceed with the benefit of the papers. Although there is no authority on the point, if the client were to make an application for delivery up, the court would probably treat that as if the client had terminated (or was about to terminate) the retainer. **40.66**

Lien where the client terminates the retainer

Where the retainer has been determined by the client, the solicitor would not ordinarily be ordered to deliver up the client's file. Hodson LJ explained the relevant principles: 'There is no doubt that a solicitor who is discharged by his client during an action, otherwise than for misconduct, can retain any papers in the cause in his possession until his costs have been paid.'[184] **40.67**

Similarly, Morgan J (sitting in the Court of Appeal) approved of the following description of the law, as set out in *Halsbury's Laws of England*: **40.68**

> 'In the event of a change of solicitors in the course of an action, the former solicitor's retaining lien is not taken away but his rights in respect of it may be modified according to whether he discharges himself or is discharged by the client. If he is discharged by the client otherwise than for misconduct he cannot, so long as his costs are unpaid, be compelled to produce or hand over the papers ...'[185]

It is possible that there are exceptions to this position. In particular, there are two mechanisms by which the court may order delivery up (or something very similar to delivery up).

---

[180] *Bentley v Gaisford* [1997] QB 627.

[181] *Gamlen Chemical Ltd v Rochem Ltd* [1980] 1 WLR 614, at 625, in which the Court of Appeal approved the speech of Lord Cottenham LC in *Heslop v Metcalfe* (1837) 3 M & C 183, at 190: 'I think the principle should be, that the solicitor claiming the lien, should have every security not inconsistent with the progress of the cause.'

[182] *Ismail v Richards Butler (a firm)* [1996] 2 All ER 506.

[183] *Hughes v Hughes* [1958] P 224.

[184] *Ibid*, at 227.

[185] *French v Carter Lemon Camerons LLP* [2012] EWCA Civ 1180, at [28], citing *Halsbury's Laws of England* (5th edn, London: LexisNexis, 2015), vol 66, para 1003.

Mechanisms whereby delivery up may be ordered

40.69 **Equitable jurisdiction** The court has an equitable jurisdiction to order delivery up if, as a matter of conscience, it would be inappropriate for the lien to be enforced.[186] This would be so even if the court had previously ordered that the lienor is entitled to delivery up if certain monies are paid into court under CPR, r 25.1(1)(m).[187]

40.70 **Rules of court** CPR, r 25.1(1)(m), provides that the court may make 'an order permitting a party seeking to recover personal property to pay money into court pending the outcome of the proceedings and directing that, if he does so, the property shall be given up to him'. There is a surprising lack of authority on the point, but Hart J has accepted that the jurisdiction to make an order overriding lien does exist.[188]

Case examples concerning delivery up

40.71 Regardless of which jurisdiction applies, the exceptions tend to apply where the rights of third parties would be affected by the lien. Each case will turn on its own facts, but the following are examples.

- **Documents required for trust managed by the court** The Court of Appeal in Chancery found that solicitors for the trustees of an estate under the administration of the court should be ordered to produce documents required for the management of the estate.[189]
- **Rights owed by client to third parties** A solicitor's lien is only available as against its client and persons claiming through them; it does not enable the solicitor to refuse production to anyone to whom its client was bound to produce the documents.[190] This is an example of the principle that, between the solicitor and third parties, the solicitor has no greater right to refuse production of documents on which they have a lien than the client would have if the documents were in their own possession.[191]
- **Representative claims** The solicitor may be ordered to deliver up where the property is required for the purposes of a representative claim.[192]

Law Society guidance concerning delivery up

40.72 Regardless of the position *de jure*, the Law Society has given the following guidance, which, whilst no longer part of the prevailing code of conduct, is still sage advice:

> 'When you cease acting for a client, you will need to consider what should be done with the paperwork. You must hand over the client's files promptly on request subject to your right to exercise a lien in respect of outstanding costs. You should try to ensure the client's position is not prejudiced, and should also bear in mind his or her rights under the Data Protection Act 1998. Undertakings to secure the costs should be used as an alternative to the exercise of a lien if possible. There may be circumstances where it is unreasonable to exercise a lien, for example, where the amount of the outstanding costs is small and the value or importance of the matter is very great.'[193]

---

[186] *Slatter v Ronaldsons* [2002] 2 Costs LR 267, at 274. See also (albeit in a criminal setting) *R v Onuigbo (aka Okoronkwo)* [2014] EWCA Crim 65, at [50].

[187] See *Ismail v Richards Butler (a firm)* [1996] QB 711, [1996] 2 All ER 506, followed in *Slatter v Ronaldsons (a firm)* [2001] All ER (D) 251 (Dec).

[188] *Paragon Finance plc v Rosling King* (unreported), 26 May 2000, Ch D.

[189] *Belaney v Ffrench* (1872) 8 Ch 918.

[190] *Furlong v Howard* (1804) 2 Sch & Lef 115.

[191] *Hawkes, Re; Ackerman v Lockhart* [1898] 2 Ch 1, CA.

[192] *Simmonds v Great Eastern Rly Co* (1868) 3 Ch App 797; *Ross v Laughton* (1813) 1 Ves & B 349.

[193] See para 11 of the Guidance to Solicitors' Code of Conduct 2007, r 2.01.

A failure on the part of a solicitor to comply with its professional obligations would not, of itself, ordinarily be grounds for the court exercising its equitable discretion to order delivery up.[194]

Loss of lien

Case examples of loss of lien

A solicitor's lien may be extinguished in a number of ways. The following are examples (each of which is dealt with in turn): **40.73**

- tender or discharge (see 40.74);
- waiver and abandonment (see 40.76);
- taking alternative securities (see 40.77);
- liquidation, receivership or bankruptcy (see 40.79);
- parting possession (including, in some circumstances, where this is done for the purposes of preserving property) (see 40.80); and
- (in some circumstances) silence (see 40.83).

It is a matter of some practical importance that the act of taking alternative security may give rise to waiver (see 40.77).

Tender or discharge First and foremost, lien will be lost upon full payment of the costs debt.[195] In practice, this is often the only way in which a client can secure release of papers where they are the one who has terminated the retainer. The payment must be a full payment; this is because (in the absence of accord and satisfaction) a debt cannot be discharged by payment of a lesser sum.[196] **40.74**

Payment must be made, not merely ordered.[197] Where the solicitor demands a larger sum than was originally claimed, that demand will not be regarded as being a waiver of lien.[198] While it is doubtful that it remains good law, there is ancient authority to the effect that, upon discharge, the solicitor must deliver up not only the file, but also the working papers (such as drafts and copies).[199] It is likely that the modern interpretation would be that the working papers belong to the solicitor as their property and that they could be retained.[200] **40.75**

Waiver or abandonment A solicitor may lose lien by way of waiver (or, as it is sometimes called, 'abandonment'). This can be done expressly or impliedly. The editors of *Halsbury's Laws of England* say that waiver may arise where: **40.76**

- a claim has been abandoned for a number of years;[201]
- there is general conduct from which a waiver can be inferred;[202]

---

194 *Slatter v Ronaldsons* [2002] 2 Costs LR 267, at 277.

195 *Re Emma Silver Mining Co, Re Turner* (1875) 24 WR 54.

196 *Foakes v Beer* (1884) 9 App Cas 605. See also *Hardingham v Allen* (1848) 5 CB 793; *Jenkyns v Brown* (1849) 14 QB 496.

197 *Re Aikin's Estate* [1894] 1 IR 225.

198 See, eg, *Albemarle Supply Co Ltd v Hind & Co* [1928] 1 KB 307.

199 *Re Horsfall* (1827) 7 B&C 528.

200 See, by analogy, *Leicestershire County Council v Michael Faraday & Partners Ltd* [1941] 2 KB 205. See also *Chantrey Martin (a firm) v Martin* [1953] 2 QB 286; *Wentworth v de Montfort* (1988) 15 NSWLR 348.

201 See, eg, *Re Noble, ex p Douglas* (1833) 3 Deac & Ch 310.

202 See, eg, *Jarl Trä AB v Convoys Ltd* [2003] EWHC 1488 (Comm).

- the party claims to retain goods on grounds different from those on which it rests its claim for lien and makes no mention of lien;[203] or
- having a lien on goods for a general balance, the party claims a lien on them merely for a particular debt.[204]

40.77 **Taking alternative securities** One way in which implied waiver can come into existence is by a solicitor taking alternative security for their costs (such as a charge over a client's house) without explaining to the client that the solicitor intends to reserve their lien.[205] Richards J explained matters in this way:

> 'It is well established that, at least in certain circumstances, the taking of security by a solicitor will be treated as a waiver of his right to a common law lien. This principle is shortly stated in *Cordery on Solicitors* at para L [954]:
>
> > "... if a solicitor takes security for costs generally and that security is inconsistent with his lien and the solicitor does not in doing so reserve the lien then *prima facie* he will be taken to have abandoned it." '[206]

40.78 This is not a rule of law, but an inference to be drawn from the facts. As Kay LJ explained:

> 'I take it that the true rule is ... that in every case where you have to consider whether a lien has been waived you must weigh all the circumstances of that particular case ... A solicitor has a duty to perform towards his client to represent to his client all the facts of the case in a clear and intelligible manner and to inform him of his rights and liabilities, and where you find a solicitor dealing with his client and taking from him such a security as was given in this case, not expressly reserving his right of lien ... the inference ought to be against the continuance of the lien.'[207]

As is explained at 40.84, it will not always be the case that taking alternative security will amount to waiver.

40.79 **Winding up, liquidation, receivership, bankruptcy, etc** The court will, in general, recognise a retaining lien where it arose after the commencement of the winding up of a company, but only if the court has not yet made a winding-up order; once the winding-up order has been made, then the right to claim lien is lost.[208] Where an administration order is made against a lienor, then the usual restrictions and formalities that affect the enforcement of security over the property of a company in administration will apply.[209] Lien that arises before a bankruptcy order was made will continue to be effective against creditors.[210]

---

[203] See, eg, *Cannee v Spanton* (1844) 8 Scott NR 714.

[204] See, eg, *Morley v Hay* (1828) 7 LJOSKB 104. See *Halsbury's Laws of England* (5th edn, London: LexisNexis, 2015), vol 68, para 852.

[205] See, eg, *In re Taylor, Stileman & Underwood* [1891] 1 Ch 591. See also *In re Galland* (1885) 31 Ch D 296; *Cowell v Simpson* (1809) 16 Ves 275; *In re Douglas Norman & Co* [1898] 1 Ch 199.

[206] *Clifford Harris & Co v Solland International Ltd* [2004] EWHC 2488, (Ch), at [13].

[207] *Taylor, Stileman & Underwood* [1891] 1 Ch 591, at 600.

[208] See *Re Wiltshire Iron Co, ex p Pearson* (1868) 3 Ch App 443.

[209] See *Halsbury's Laws of England* (5th edn, London: LexisNexis, 2015), vol 68, para 836, for details.

[210] See *Re Bushell, ex p Great Western Rly Co* (1882) 22 Ch D 470, CA. See also *Hammonds v Thomas Muckle & Sons* [2006] BPIR 704; *Re Born* [1900] 2 Ch 433.

Parting possession To keep a retaining lien, a solicitor must either preserve their lien (see 40.82) or have continuous possession of the retained property.[211] A solicitor may lose lien if they part with possession of that property,[212] even if this was by mistake.[213] There is no such thing as a notional retaining lien and, as such, the court does not have the power merely to find that lien existed when there was no possession.[214] Loss of lien will not occur in every circumstance in which possession passes to someone else, however, because lien may be preserved. In particular, lien may be preserved where possession passes to another person for a specific reason on the expressly stated or implied basis[215] that lien is maintained.[216] Examples of lien being preserved in this way include: **40.80**

- where an undertaking is given and the undertaker holds the property to the solicitor's account (see 40.85);
- where the property is given for the purposes of allowing an arbitrator to make an award;[217] and
- where the court has made an order requiring the solicitor to part with the property on the basis that lien is preserved.[218]

In general, recovery of the previously retained property will not result in restoration of the lien where that lien was a retaining lien, but if the lien is a particular lien, then it would not necessarily be lost by a temporary loss of possession.[219] In any event, where the property has been recovered after the owner had obtained it by fraud, then the lien will be rejuvenated—and this would be so even if the property was recovered by subterfuge.[220] **40.81**

Preservation of property Where, to preserve the property, it is necessary to order that it be delivered up, the court may make such an order, but the solicitor's security would ordinarily be preserved by the client being required to make a suitable payment into court[221] (or into an escrow account). **40.82**

Silence when proving the costs debt Lien may be lost if the solicitor is silent about it when proving the costs debt in insolvency proceedings.[222] **40.83**

[211] See *Pennington v Reliance Motor Works Ltd* [1923] 1 KB 127, in which it was held that the loss of possession is the loss of the lien and the lien cannot be subsequently regained because possession is regained. See also *Rust v McNaught* (1917) 144 LT Jo 76 (on appeal (1918) 144 LT Jo 440, CA).

[212] *Re Phoenix Life Assurance Co, Howard and Dollman's Case* (1863) 1 Hem & M 433.

[213] See *Dicas v Stockley* (1836) 7 C & P 587; *Bligh v Davies* (1860) 28 Beav 211.

[214] See, eg, *The Gaupen* [1925] WN 138; cf *Albemarle Supply Co Ltd v Hind & Co* [1928] 1 KB 307, CA, in which there was an element of agreement between the parties that went further than the court was able to impose.

[215] *Watson v Lyon* (1855) 7 de GM & C288 discusses implied reservations.

[216] See *Caldwell v Sumpters* [1972] Ch 478, [1971] 3 All ER 892, rev'd on a different point on appeal ([1972] Ch 478, CA), in which a solicitor was found not to have lost lien where he had delivered client's papers to third party under an express undertaking that the third party would hold to the solicitor's order. See also *Bentley v Gaisford* [1997] QB 627, [1997] 1 All ER 842, CA.

[217] *Whalley v Halley* (1829) 8 LJOSKB 6.

[218] *Re Till, ex p Parsons* (1871) 19 WR 325.

[219] *Rose v CMS Operations Ltd* [2002] EWHC 59 (Ch), [2002] All ER (D) 20 (Jan).

[220] See *Earl of Bristol v Wilsmore* (1823) 1 B & C 514; *Hawse v Crowe* (1826) Ry & M 414.

[221] *Richards v Platel* (1841) 10 LJ Ch 375.

[222] *Re Safety Explosives Ltd* [1904] 1 Ch 226.

Counter-examples concerning loss of lien

40.84 As counter-examples, the following are circumstances in which lien would not ordinarily be lost.

- **Writing off bad debts** Writing off the cost debt as bad debt would not ordinarily result in a loss of lien and this would be so even if the solicitor's liability for tax had been adjusted accordingly.[223]
- **Taking consistent securities** Where a charge is taken on an asset that is unrelated to the retained property, and where there is no inconsistency between those securities and the lien, then there would be no waiver.[224]
- **Taking security for specific costs** In a similar vein, where a client gives securities for the purpose of securing payment of particular costs (such as counsel's fees), the lien in general is unaffected.[225]
- **The effluxion of time** The fact that the costs debt is statute-barred will not result in the loss of retaining lien[226] or particular lien.[227]

Undertakings to hold to order

40.85 Where solicitor A has a retaining lien over documents handed over to solicitor B, solicitor A may specify that the documents be 'held to order' (or 'held to account', which means much the same thing). Where this is so, the legal possession of the documents remains with solicitor A, thus preserving their lien.[228] An undertaking may arise in either of two ways, as follows.

- **Express undertaking** An express undertaking may be made orally or in writing. Obligations ought to be well thought out, because the court lacks the *vires* to relieve solicitor B of the burden of compliance.[229]
- **Implied undertaking** An implied acceptance of an undertaking may arise if solicitor B retains documents that have been offered conditionally on an undertaking.[230]

40.86 Where an undertaking is given over the client's papers, it may be that there is no express agreement as to the extent to which solicitor B may use and distribute those papers. The value of solicitor A's lien might be substantially negated if solicitor B were to use the papers in a way that advanced the client's claim. If this were to happen, the lien would continue to exist, but its value would be diminished. There is therefore a distinction to be drawn between the fact of solicitor A's lien and its value.

40.87 Although Sir Richard Scott V-C dissented, Roch and Henry LJJ have held that the use that solicitor B could make of the documents was impliedly limited so as to preserve to solicitor

---

223 *Slatter v Ronaldsons* [2002] 2 Costs LR 267.

224 See the discussion in *Clifford Harris & Co v Solland International Ltd* [2005] EWHC 141 (Ch), *per* Christopher Nugee QC. See also *Balch v Symes* (1823) 1 Turn & R 87.

225 *In re John Morris* [1908] 1 KB 473.

226 *Re Broomhead* (1847) 5 Dow & L 52.

227 *Higgins v Scott* (1831) 2 B & Ad 413.

228 Whilst only persuasive, see the decision of the Irish Supreme Court in *In the Matter of Galdan Properties Ltd (in liquidation)* [1988] IR 213.

229 *Hughes v Hughes* [1958] P 224.

230 *Caldwell v Sumpters* [1972] Ch 478, [1971] 3 All ER 892, rev'd on a different point on appeal ([1972] Ch 478, CA).

A every security not inconsistent with the progress of the client's litigation. They held that, unless it was necessary for the purposes of the litigation, it would be a breach of the undertaking to copy the documents to the client wholesale.[231]

A breach of an undertaking will not necessarily sound in damages (or other relief). This is because the jurisdiction to order compensation will normally be exercised only where the conduct of the solicitor is inexcusable and such as to merit reproof.[232] That said, the court normally affords significant weight to undertakings given by a solicitor. **40.88**

Solicitors' Charging Orders

Under the Solicitors Act 1974, s 73

A solicitors' charging order will be available where, in the course of court proceedings, a solicitor is instrumental in recovering money on behalf of their client. The usual order is that the solicitor will be given a charge over a between-the-parties costs order. It is a statutory provision that was originally introduced to extend particular lien to cover real property;[233] as such, there is a certain degree of overlap between solicitors' charging orders and particular lien (see 40.39). **40.89**

The relevant statutory provisions are contained in Solicitors Act 1974, s 73: **40.90**

> '(1) Subject to subsection (2), any court in which a solicitor has been employed to prosecute or defend any suit, matter or proceedings may at any time—
> (a) declare the solicitor entitled to a charge on any property recovered or preserved through his instrumentality for his assessed costs in relation to that suit, matter or proceeding; and
> (b) make such orders for the assessment of those costs and for raising money to pay or for paying them out of the property recovered or preserved as the court thinks fit;
>
> and all conveyances and acts done to defeat, or operating to defeat, that charge shall, except in the case of a conveyance to a *bona fide* purchaser for value without notice, be void as against the solicitor.
>
> (2) No order shall be made under subsection (1) if the right to recover the costs is barred by any statute of limitations.'

The following points may be made about these provisions. **40.91**

- **'Any court'** 'Any court' means any civil court.[234] Thus money recovered by other means (such as by the police as a result of a criminal investigation) would not be chargeable.[235] The phrase 'any court' is not intended to distinguish between levels of judge; a judge is not limited to dealing only with proceedings and costs in their own court.[236]

---

[231] *Bentley v Gaisford* [1997] QB 627, at 643. Roch LJ effectively adopted the test for when an application is made to the court for release of documents following termination of the retainer by the solicitor: *Heslop v Metcalfe* (1837) 3 M & C 183.

[232] *Udall v Capri Lighting Ltd* [1988] 1 QB 907, at 917, *per* Balcombe LJ.

[233] See *Guy v Churchill* (1887) 35 Ch D 489, at 490—esp the submissions, which refer to the Common Law Procedure Act 1860, (23 & 24 Vict, c. 126), s 28.

[234] *Re Humphreys, ex p Lloyd-George and George* [1898] 1 QB 520, CA, at 525.

[235] *Ibid.*

[236] *Re Deakin* [1900] 2 QB 489; *Mastercigars Direct Ltd v Withers LLP* [2007] EWHC 2733 (Ch), at [137].

- **'Been employed'** The phrase 'been employed' does not mean that the solicitor's retainer has to have been with the person against whom the charge is sought (although this will usually be the case).[237] The words 'shall be employed' are not used in the future tense; rather, the use is conditional and they do not tie the employment down to any particular time.[238]
- **'Property'** 'Property' includes both real and personal property.[239] That word is to be construed widely and to encompass choses in action, which may include an order for costs where no assessment has yet taken place.[240]
- **'Recovered or preserved'** It is a statutory prerequisite to making a charging order that property be 'recovered or preserved'.[241] The following are examples of cases in which this was found to be so:
  - where a sum of money was recovered for costs (but not by compromise);[242]
  - where a sum of money was recovered for costs with no other monies being recovered;[243]
  - where a sum of money was recovered for damages;[244] and
  - where a beneficial interest was obtained in real property held under a trust for sale.[245]

40.92 In contrast, the following are case examples in which it was found that monies were not recovered or preserved:

- where money had been paid into court as security for costs of proceedings that were later abandoned;[246]
- where an administration order had been made, but not executed;[247]
- where a costs order was made by compromise;[248] and
- where money was paid into court with a denial of liability, but the client proceeded with the claim and recovered a smaller sum.[249]

40.93 Property may be preserved even though the value of it diminishes while under the solicitor's control—and this would be so even if the property yielded little or nothing for the client.[250] The fact that a fund had been lodged prior to a solicitor being retained would not preclude the solicitor preserving the fund.[251] The fact that a fund has been diminished by way of a collusive compromise will not preclude the solicitor taking a charge[252] (see also 40.112).

---

237 *Bonser v Bradshaw* (1860) 30 LJ Ch 159, in which the retainer was with a litigation friend, but the order was sought against a person who, when the retainer was made, was a child.

238 *Colver v Adams* (1881) 6 QBD 622, *per* Grove J.

239 *Redfern & Son v Rosenthall Bros* (1902) 86 LT 855, CA.

240 *Fairfold Properties Ltd v Exmouth Docks Co Ltd (No 2)* [1993] Ch 196.

241 *Re Blake, Clutterbuck v Bradford* [1945] Ch 61.

242 *Campbell v Lewis* [1941] 1 All ER 274; see also *Al-Abbas v As-Dabbagh* [2002] EWCA Civ 1962.

243 *Re Blake, Clutterbuck v Bradford* [1945] 1 Ch 61.

244 *Marie Gartz (No 2)* [1920] 1 P 460.

245 *National Westminster Bank Ltd v Stockman* [1981] 1 WLR 67.

246 *The Dirigo* [1920] P 425.

247 *Pinkerton v Easton* (1873) LR 16 Eq 490.

248 *Al-Abbas v As-Dabbagh* [2002] EWCA Civ 1962, at [25].

249 *Westacott v Bevan* [1891] 1 QB 774, DC. For a full treatment of the issue of monies not recovered or preserved, see *Halsbury's Laws of England* (5th edn, London: LexisNexis, 2015), vol 44(1), para 264, from which these examples are taken.

250 *Re Turner* [1907] 2 Ch 126; see also *White v Hyde* [1933] P 105.

251 *Wimbourne v Fine* [1952] 2 All ER 681.

252 *Twynam v Porter* (1870) LR 11 Eq 181; see also *Moxon v Sheppard* (1890) 24 QBD 627.

Money paid into court as security for costs would not be property that had been recovered or preserved.[253]

As to the exercise of the court's discretion, a solicitor must make out a *prima facie* case that, without the charging order, they will not obtain their costs.[254] Where the solicitor makes out this *prima facie* case, the court will generally make the order unless there is reason for not doing so.[255] The court will take the interests of the client into account. This may be reflected in the form that the order takes.[256] **40.94**

The solicitor's conduct is relevant to the exercise of the court's discretion: it may decline to make the order if the solicitor's conduct or inactivity would make it unjust that the interest of other parties should come second to the solicitor's interests.[257] **40.95**

Miscellaneous points concerning solicitors' charging orders

The following miscellaneous points can be made. **40.96**

- **No need to wait until the expiry of one month** Morgan J has clarified that the bar against commencing proceedings within one month of delivery of a bill does not apply to applications for charging orders.[258]
- **No mandatory need for an assessment** Notwithstanding the use of the phrase 'assessed costs' in Solicitors Act 1974, s 73(1)(a), there is no need for the court to order that there be a solicitor-and-client assessment of costs.[259]
- **Waiver (inconsistent securities)** The right to a charging order may be lost if the solicitor seeks a remedy that is inconsistent with the continuance of the charging order. This may happen, for example, if a solicitor seeks and accepts security for costs.[260]
- **Competing securities, set-off, etc** Where solicitors have competing charging orders, then, in general, the order of the solicitor who had conduct of the claim upon conclusion will take priority. This was explained by Kay J in the following way:

  > '[If the first solicitor] is discharged ... he could not compel the client to go on with the suit for the purpose of enforcing the lien. He is entirely at the client's mercy. If the client employs another solicitor why should not that solicitor have the first charge on the fund? It seems quite right; because the charge really only becomes effective when the fund has been recovered, and it is always subject to the chance whether the fund will be recovered or not. Of course, if the fund is sufficient to pay both, no question need arise; but if it is not, it seems quite fair that the solicitor who has conducted the action to a conclusion and has been the means of actually bringing the fund into the hands of his client by conducting the cause up to the point when the fund is recovered should have the first claim on the fund.'[261]

  Where a party seeks set-off that would diminish or negative the value of a solicitor's charging order, the court should bear the solicitor's position in mind. The protectable

[253] *Rhodes v Sugden* (1885) 29 Ch D 517.
[254] *Harrison v Harrison* (1888) 13 PD 180, CA, at 184.
[255] *Dallow v Garrold, ex p Adams* (1884) 13 QBD 543.
[256] *Jackson v Smith, ex p Digby* (1884) 53 LJ Ch 972, at 975.
[257] *Higgs v Higgs* [1934] 1 P 95.
[258] *Mastercigars Direct Ltd v Withers LLP* [2007] EWHC 2733 (Ch), at [144]–[146].
[259] *Fairfold Properties Ltd v Exmouth Docks Co Ltd (No 2)* [1993] Ch 196.
[260] *Groom v Cheesewright* (1885) 1 Ch 730.
[261] *In re Wadsworth, Rhodes v Sugden* (1886) 34 Ch D 155, at 159.

interest conferred by statute should be upheld unless there are good reasons to the contrary. This would be the case notwithstanding the fact that an order for set-off would not prejudice the party for whom the solicitors were acting: that factor is irrelevant.[262]

- **Insolvency and competing interests** It may be that, after monies being recovered or preserved and by reason of a solicitor's efforts, the client becomes insolvent. If this is so, then, in general, the solicitor's right will take precedence over other creditors who seek to take the benefit of those efforts.[263] In this regard, it should be borne in mind that the original statutory provisions that have now become s 73 of the Solicitors Act 1974[264] were enacted to extend a solicitor's particular lien to cover real property; as such, precedence is often analysed in terms of lien.[265]
- **Child clients** A charging order may be obtained even where the work was done on behalf of a child.[266]
- **Assignment** An assignee of a solicitor's right to costs may apply for a charging order.[267]
- **Notice by way of injunction** Whilst, technically, it has more to do with particular lien than charging orders, the court seems to retain an ancient jurisdiction to make an injunction restraining the client from receiving payment in the litigation without giving notice to the solicitor.[268]

Procedure relating to solicitors' charging orders

40.97 Unless there are already existing proceedings, the application is made by way of a claim under CPR, Part 8.[269] A costs judge has the jurisdiction to hear an application for a charging order.[270] In particular, a costs judge sitting in the Senior Courts Costs Office (SCCO) will have jurisdiction to hear an application notwithstanding the fact that they have not heard the proceedings in respect of which the solicitors were instructed.[271]

40.98 As has been explained at 5.15, the County Court does not have jurisdiction to hear bills relating to contentious business that exceed £5,000 and this includes applications for solicitor's charging orders.[272] The High Court may make an order in respect of arbitral proceedings.[273] The power to make an order is capable of being delegated to a registrar in bankruptcy.[274]

---

262 *Rhom & Haas Co v Collag Ltd* (2002) IPD 25007.

263 See, eg, *Scholey v Peck* [1893] 1 Ch 709, at 711, *per* Romer J. See also *Clutterbuck v Bradford* [1945] Ch 61, at 67, *per* Greene MR; *Re Born* [1900] 2 Ch 433, at 435, *per* Farwell J. As to particular lien in those circumstances, see *Hammonds v Thomas Muckle & Sons* [2006] BPIR 704; *Re Born* [1900] 2 Ch 433.

264 Namely, the Common Law Procedure Act 1860, (23 & 24 Vict, c. 126), s 28.

265 See, eg, *Guy v Churchill* (1887) 35 Ch D 489, at 490–491, *per* Cotton LJ (and the preceding submissions) and *Haymes v Cooper* (1864) 33 Beav 431, both of which were referred to by Master Campbell in *Addleshaw Goddard LLP v Wood & Anor* [2015] EWHC B12 (Costs), at [36]–[38].

266 *Baile v Baile* (1872) LR 13 Eq 497. See also *Greer v Young* (1881–85) All ER Rep 513; *Bonser v Bradshaw* (1860) 25 JP 483.

267 *Briscoe v Briscoe* [1892] 3 Ch 543.

268 *Hobson v Shearwood* (1845) 8 Beav 486.

269 CPR, r 67.3(2).

270 *Mastercigars Direct Ltd v Withers LLP* [2007] EWHC 2733 (Ch), at [139].

271 *Ibid*, at [137]–[139], drawing on CPR, rr 67.1(1)(b) and 67.3(3); PD 67, paras 2.1(2) and 3.2.

272 *Jones v Twinsectra Ltd* [2002] EWCA Civ 668.

273 Arbitration Act 1996, s 44.

274 *Re Wood, ex p Fanshawe* [1897] 1 QB 314.

Under the Charging Orders Act 1979

Where a solicitor obtains judgment against a former client for their costs, they may ask the court to make a charging order in respect of those monies.[275] The details of this subject are beyond the scope of this book. What may be relevant, however, is the fact that the court lacks the power to make a charging order absolute where the sums claimed are unassessed costs (that is, where there has been no assessment).[276] **40.99**

Solicitors' Security for Costs

Whilst it will be of value only where its use is contemplated before the work is done, Solicitors Act 1974, s 65(1), makes provision for security to be taken for the solicitor's fees for contentious work: 'A solicitor may take security from his client for his costs, to be ascertained by assessment or otherwise, in respect of any contentious business to be done by him.' **40.100**

Article 3 of the Solicitors' (Non-Contentious Business) Remuneration Order 2009[277] makes a similar provision for security in non-contentious business: 'A solicitor may take from his client security for the payment of any costs, including the amount of any interest to which the solicitor may become entitled under article 14 [of that Order].' **40.101**

Solicitors considering taking security for costs should consider the following guidance given by the Solicitors Regulation Authority (SRA), which, whilst not carried over into the SRA Code of Conduct 2011 (as amended), still has resonance: **40.102**

> 'Whilst you are entitled to take security for costs you should be aware of the risk of the court finding undue influence. Before you do take a charge over a client's property it is advisable, therefore, to suggest the client consider seeking independent legal advice. Such advice would not normally be essential unless the terms of the proposed charge are particularly onerous or would give you some unusual benefit or profit. It is, however, important always to ensure that the client understands that a charge is being taken and the effect of such a charge.'[278]

If a first legal charge is to be obtained over a client's property, care should be taken to ensure that the solicitor does not inadvertently enter into a regulated mortgage contract as a lender. Standard textbooks on financial regulation should be consulted on this matter. **40.103**

An agreement for security that is not an agreement as to the amount or method of payment does not need to comply with the formalities relating to contentious and non-contentious business agreements.[279] **40.104**

Obtaining security for costs can, in certain circumstances, result in loss of lien (see 40.77). This will be particularly likely if there is no express reservation of lien. **40.105**

---

275 Charging Orders Act 1979, s 1(1).

276 *Monte Developments Ltd (in administration) of Court Management Consultants Ltd* [2010] EWHC 3071 (Ch).

277 SI 2009/1931.

278 Paragraph 43 of the Guidance to r 3 of the Solicitors Code of Conduct 2007.

279 *In re an undertaking by Wingfields, Halse and Trustram, Jonesco v Evening Standard Co* [1932] 2 KB 340.

Equitable Interference by the Court

40.106 It may be that, as a result of their solicitor's[280] efforts, a client (or ex-client) has become entitled to receive money from an opponent. Those monies may be costs or they may be damages out of which the solicitor is entitled to take fees by way of deduction. It occasionally happens that a client seeks to negotiate directly with the paying party (often after terminating the retainer), in an attempt to avoid the solicitor ever coming into possession of the monies. This may be in a deliberate—possibly fraudulent—attempt on the part of the client to frustrate the solicitor's right to payment,[281] but it may also be at the behest of an opponent.[282] This section addresses the way in which the court would deal with such a situation. In particular, it describes a pragmatic extension of the notion of equitable lien (see 40.39), known as equitable interference.

40.107 The court has long since recognised that, in reality, the only monies available for payment of a solicitor's fees are often those recovered from an opponent.[283] The fact that solicitors are prepared to act on that basis is in the interests of access to justice and, in view of this, the court will often seek to protect solicitors from clients who would keep them out of their money.[284] Thus, where an opponent has paid (or is contemplating paying) monies directly to a client, the court will, where appropriate, order that party—or, occasionally, that party's legal representatives or insurer (see 40.110)—to make the payment directly to the solicitor, on the grounds that the client lacked (or lacks) the ability to give good receipt for the monies. This may result in that party (or legal representative or insurer, as the case may be) being forced to make a second payment.[285]

Jurisdiction under which a remedy may be sought

40.108 Orders for equitable interference are often referred to as being based on lien,[286] but they are probably better thought of as being a form of equitable intervention or charge ordered by the court. In this regard, Lord Hanworth MR had this to say:

> 'The nature of a solicitor's lien ... is merely a *right to claim the equitable interference* of the court, who may order that the judgment obtained by the solicitor's client do stand as security for her costs and that payment of such an amount as will cover them be made to the solicitor in the first instance.'[287]

---

[280] It is possible that particular lien may apply to other types of legal representative too: see *Gavin Edmondson Solicitors Ltd v Haven Insurance Co Ltd* [2018] UKSC 21, at [1], *per* Lord Briggs. That said, many of the authorities refer to the court's need to ensure that its own officers are paid (or words to that effect) and, as such, it is arguable that other legal representatives are in a different position: see, eg, *Re Fuld (No 4)* [1968] P 727, at 739.

[281] See, eg, *Khans Solicitor (a firm) v Chifuntwe & Anor* [2013] EWCA Civ 481.

[282] See, eg, *Gavin Edmondson Solicitors Ltd v Haven Insurance Co Ltd* [2018] UKSC 21.

[283] For example, in *Ex p Bryant* (1815) 1 Madd 49, at 52, Sir Thomas Plumer V-C said that 'business is often transacted by solicitors for needy clients, merely on the prospect of having their costs under the doctrine as to lien'.

[284] *Re Fuld (No 4)* [1968] P 727, at 739.

[285] See *Gavin Edmondson Solicitors Ltd v Haven Insurance Co Ltd* [2018] UKSC 21, at [30], *per* Lord Briggs. See also *Khans Solicitor (a firm) v Chifuntwe & Anor* [2013] EWCA Civ 481, at [33], *per* Sir Stephen Sedley.

[286] Thus, in *Ross v Buxton* (1889) 42 Ch D 190, at 202, the court referred to the need for the paying party to 'satisfy ... the lien'.

[287] *Mason v Mason and Cottrell* [1933] P 199, CA, at 214, emphasis added. This analysis was cited with approval by Lord Briggs in *Gavin Edmondson Solicitors Ltd v Haven Insurance Co Ltd* [2018] UKSC 21, at [35].

Lord Goddard CJ has gone so far as to say that the term 'lien' is a misnomer.[288] He went on to speak approvingly of the following explanation given by Cockburn CJ: **40.109**

> 'There is no such thing as a lien except upon something of which you have possession . . . although we talk of an attorney having a lien upon a judgment, it is in fact only a claim or right to ask for *the intervention of the court for his protection*, when, having obtained judgment for his client, he finds there is a probability of the client depriving him of his costs.'[289]

More recently, Lord Briggs has said that the term 'equitable charge' may be more appropriate.[290]

The court's powers are not limited to the making of orders against the opponent itself; in an appropriate case, an order may, for example, be made against the opponent's legal representatives[291] or liability insurer.[292] The fact that the amount of costs has not yet been determined by way of an assessment is no bar, in principle, to the court intervening.[293] Similarly, the fact that the solicitor is acting under a CFA Lite would not, of itself, be a bar.[294] **40.110**

Discretion

As with any equitable remedy, equitable interference is discretionary. Scarman J has explained that the court will take into account the same considerations as those that would have been taken into account had the solicitor applied for a charging order.[295] It is therefore arguable that a solicitor must make out a *prima facie* case that, without the interference of the court, it will not obtain their costs.[296] This may be putting it too highly, but it would be broadly in keeping with the guidance given by Sir Thomas Plumer VC that the duty of the court is to intervene only if it is necessary for the solicitor's protection—, and then only to the extent that it is necessary to safeguard the lien.[297] Sir Thomas Plumer VC went on to say that the court must not prejudice the rights of the client,[298] this also being similar to the approach taken when an application for a solicitor's charging order is made (see 40.94). **40.111**

The modern approach to equitable interference was summarised by Sir Stephen Sedley.[299] That summary is set out at 40.40 (in the context of equitable lien) and is not repeated here, but it can be seen that the court will intervene to protect a solicitor's claim on funds recovered, or due to be recovered, by a client or former client if (a) the paying party is colluding with the client to cheat the solicitor of their fees (see 40.114), or (b) the paying party is on notice that the other party's solicitor has a claim on the funds for outstanding fees (see 40.115). **40.112**

---

288 *Bibby v Woods* [1949] 2 KB 449, at 453.
289 *Mercer v Graves* (1872) LR 7 QB 499, at 503, emphasis added.
290 *Gavin Edmondson Solicitors Ltd v Haven Insurance Co Ltd* [2018] UKSC 21, at [3].
291 *Ross v Buxton* (1889) 42 Ch D 190, at 202.
292 See, eg, *Gavin Edmondson Solicitors Ltd v Haven Insurance Co Ltd* [2018] UKSC 21.
293 This is because it would be absurd if the lien were to be defeated by the client's failure to have the costs assessed and, in this regard, equity looks on as done that which ought to be done: see *Re Fuld (No 4)* [1968] P 727, at 737.
294 *Gavin Edmondson Solicitors Ltd v Haven Insurance Co Ltd* [2018] UKSC 21, at [37]–[44], *per* Lord Briggs.
295 *Re Fuld (No 4)* [1968] P 727, at 739.
296 See, by analogy, *Harrison v Harrison* (1888) 13 PD 180, CA, at 184.
297 *Re Fuld (No 4)* [1968] P 727, at 737.
298 *Ibid.*
299 *Khans Solicitor (a firm) v Chifuntwe & Anor* [2013] EWCA Civ 481, at [33].

40.113 The conduct of the client and the paying party are both relevant,[300] as are the reasons the client gives for having sought payment directly from the paying party. The fact that the client may achieve reductions on an assessment is a factor that may be taken into account.[301]

Fraud on the part of the client

40.114 There is no doubt that where a client and a paying party collude for the purposes of keeping a solicitor out of their monies, the court has the power to interfere.[302] For example, in a case in which the transaction between client and paying party was 'a distinct case of a cheat ... done with the intention of cheating [the solicitors] of [their] costs', Kekewich J made an order that the paying party should pay costs directly to the solicitors.[303] Similarly, in a case in which the transaction between the client and the paying party had been 'a mere shuffle between the plaintiff and defendant ... to cheat the attorney of his lien', Lord Kenyon gave judgment for the solicitor, because this corresponded with 'convenience, good sense and justice'.[304]

Notice given to the paying party

40.115 Notwithstanding older authorities to the contrary,[305] it is now clear that if—despite being put on notice of the need to pay monies to the solicitor rather than the client—an opponent (or someone acting on their behalf) makes a payment directly to the client, then the court has the power to interfere. As is explained at 40.116–40.120, the court has that power even if there has been no fraud or no collusion between the client and the paying party.

40.116 That power has its origins in an 18th-century case in which Lord Mansfield CJ said this:

> 'He may stop it *in transitu* if he can lay hold of it. If he apply to the Court, they will prevent its being paid over till his demand is satisfied. I am inclined to go still farther, and to hold that, if the attorney give notice to the defendant not to pay till his bill should be discharged, a payment by the defendant after such notice would be in his own wrong, and like paying a debt which has been assigned, after notice. But I think we cannot go beyond those limits.'[306]

---

300 See, eg, *ibid.*

301 See, eg, *Re Fuld (No 4)* [1968] P 727, at 740.

302 *Khans Solicitor (a firm) v Chifuntwe & Anor* [2013] EWCA Civ 481, at [33], cited with approval by Lord Briggs in *Gavin Edmondson Solicitors Ltd v Haven Insurance Co Ltd* [2018] UKSC 21, at [36]–[37].

303 *Re Margetson and Jones* [1897] 2 Ch 314, at 321. In *Re Fuld (No 4)* [1968] P 727, at 739, Scarman J commented that Kekewich J's decision shows 'how extensive are the powers of the court to protect and enforce solicitors' lien for [their] costs on the fruits of litigation won by [their] exertions'. Whilst on a slightly different point, see *Manley v The Law Society* [1981] 1 WLR 335, CA, in which it was held that where a solicitor colludes with its client to deprive the Legal Aid Agency of its statutory charge, equity would intervene to prevent the solicitors from making any claims on the fund for those costs.

304 See *Welsh v Hole* (1779) 1 Doug 238, at 239, referred to by Sir Stephen Sedley in *Khans Solicitor (a firm) v Chifuntwe & Anor* [2013] EWCA Civ 481, at [13]. See also *Ormerod v Tate* (1801) 1 East 463.

305 See, eg, *The Hope* (1883) 8 PD 144, CA, in which it was held that an order would not be made upon a defendant to pay to the plaintiff's solicitor the costs of an action for a seaman's wages that has been settled by the parties without the intervention of the plaintiff's solicitor, unless he could clearly establish collusion between the parties to deprive him of his costs.

306 *Welsh v Hole* (1779) 1 Doug 238, at 239, cited with approval by Lord Briggs in *Gavin Edmondson Solicitors Ltd v Haven Insurance Co Ltd* [2018] UKSC 21, at [30].

Thus, where a paying party acts in contravention of a notice to pay only the solicitor, it would not obtain good receipt for monies paid directly to the client.[307]

Lord Mansfield CJ's comments were *obiter*, however, and for a long time there was uncertainty as to what the true law was. Matters are now clearer because Sir Stephen Sedley has found that notice alone (that is, without fraud or collusion) may suffice.[308] He went on to speak approvingly of the following decision of Stirling J: **40.117**

> '[W]here a valid compromise has been entered into under which a sum of money, the fruit of the action, is coming to the plaintiff, the defendant or his solicitor is not at liberty, after express notice by the plaintiff's solicitor of his claim to a lien, to pay that sum over to the plaintiff in disregard of the notice.'[309]

Notice may be implied (such as by the operation of a pre-application protocol). Lloyd Jones LJ had this to say on the topic: **40.118**

> 'I can see no reason in principle why implied notice should not be sufficient for the operation of the principle stated in *Khans* ... Express notice acts as in parallel with collusion. Both involve a similar degree of moral culpability on the part of the paying party so as to justify the court in ordering a double payment. A party must either collude in defeating the lien or must know that payment is being made against the background of a dispute and that the payment will have the effect that the lien may be defeated. However, to my mind, equitable intervention will be just as appropriate where implied notice of such matters is given. In any event, I am satisfied that the present case is one of express notice. [The paying party's] knowledge of and participation in the scheme established by the Protocol and the Portal meant that it was well aware of the interest of [the receiving party's solicitors] in receiving its fixed costs and other sums due under the Protocol scheme. Furthermore, it has not been disputed that [the paying party's] objective in entering into the compromise agreements was to defeat that interest.'[310]

Bona fide negotiations and the effect of compromise on the solicitor

Notwithstanding what is set out at 40.106–40.118, there is no reason why a client cannot take control of their affairs and enter into proper negotiations with their opponent. In this regard, Stirling J has explained that: **40.119**

> '[A] *bona fide* compromise entered into before verdict or judgment, and even after notice of the solicitor's claim for costs, is good, and will not be set aside or affected at the instance of the solicitors unless collusion or fraudulent conspiracy exists between the parties.'[311]

Similarly, Sir Stephen Sedley has explained that where the client has come to an agreement with the paying party about the amount of costs payable, unless there is something in the contract of retainer to forestall that agreement, it will be binding on the solicitor in terms of its amount.[312]

---

307 See also *Read v Dupper* (1795) 6 TR 361, at 362, *per* Kenyon CJ.
308 *Khans Solicitor (a firm) v Chifuntwe & Anor* [2013] EWCA Civ 481, at [22].
309 *Ibid*, quoting Stirling J in *Ross v Buxton* (1889) LR 42 Ch D 190, at 202.
310 *Gavin Edmonson Solicitors Ltd v Haven Insurance Co Ltd* [2015] EWCA 1230, at [29], affirmed on appeal ([2018] UKSC 21).
311 *Ross v Buxton* (1889) 42 Ch D 190, at 201.
312 *Khans Solicitor (a firm) v Chifuntwe & Anor* [2013] EWCA Civ 481, at [37].

Procedure

40.120 Sir Stephen Sedley has explained that where the solicitor is concerned about the possibility of payment being made directly to a client, the solicitor should apply for an order that the monies be paid into court pending resolution of any dispute as between the solicitor and the client.[313] Where such an application is not made and where payment is made to an ex-client, who then makes off with the money, then an application can be made for a 'dual payment' order[314]—that is, an order that the paying party must make a payment to the solicitor regardless of whether it has already made a payment to the client.

Statutory Demands and Bankruptcy Proceedings

40.121 When a solicitor is faced with a client who will not pay, one option that might cross their mind would be to serve a statutory demand. Whether a solicitor is able to do this will turn on the facts of each case, but (for the reasons set out below) it is an option that would exist only very infrequently. In any event, the Law Society advises that solicitors should be wary of issuing statutory demands,[315] because there is a power to set them aside on the grounds of injustice.[316]

Statutory demands

40.122 A statutory demand is a precursor to a petition for bankruptcy.[317] There are a number of conditions that must be satisfied at the date of presentation. For the purposes of most solicitor-and-client disputes, those conditions are that:

- the costs debt (that is, the amount outstanding) is at least equal to £750;
- the costs debt that is relied upon is a liquidated sum;
- the costs debt is one that the costs debtor (that is, the client or the party chargeable) has no reasonable prospect of being able to pay; and
- there is no outstanding application to set aside the statutory demand.

Usually, the matter will turn on whether the costs debt that is relied upon is a liquidated sum. For the reasons set out next, this is a condition that is rarely met.

Liquidated vs unliquidated

40.123 An unassessed bill that is entirely free of agreement is not a bill for a liquidated sum for the purposes of insolvency.[318] Where this is so, it is not possible to serve a statutory demand for the full amount of the bill.[319] The fact that a client may have acknowledged the solicitor's

---

313 *Ibid*, at [34].

314 *Ibid*, at [33].

315 See Law Society, 'Practice Advice Service: Non-contentious Costs', July 2012, p 26.

316 See *Re a Debtor (No 88 of 1991)* [1992] 4 All ER 301; *Marshalls (a firm) v A Debtor* [1993] Ch 286; *Shalson v DF Keane Ltd* [2003] EWHC 599 (Ch).

317 It is issued pursuant to Insolvency Act 1986, s 268. See also s 267 of the 1986 Act.

318 Compare this with the position under Limitation Act 1980, s 29: see *Phillips & Co (a firm) v Bath Housing Co-operative Ltd* [2012] EWCA Civ 1591, at [40], *per* Lloyd LJ.

319 See *Klamer v Kyriakides & Braier (a firm)* [2005] BPIR 1142, Ch D, a decision of Master Simmonds; *Blavo v The Law Society* [2017] EWHC 561 (Ch), a decision of Judge Klein (sitting as a judge of the High Court). See also *Truex v Toll* [2009] EWHC 369 (Ch), in which Proudman J accepted, without demur, the agreement between the parties that such a bill is not for a liquidated sum; *In Re Laceward Ltd* [1981] 1 WLR 133, at 137. This approach is in line with the analogous law in relation to accountants' bills, where Vinelott J

invoices does not turn an unliquidated costs debt into a liquidated costs debt nor does it give rise to estoppel.[320]

Some bills will have been agreed. In particular, where a business agreement exists, there may be agreement as to part of the costs (such as hourly rates, etc). There are conflicting authorities on whether a statutory demand can be issued in those circumstances. In the past, the court took a view as to whether the undisputed amount exceeded the threshold; indeed, in ancient times, there was a practice of sending costs for a provisional assessment to determine that point.[321] Proudman J has found that a solicitor may not issue a statutory demand even where the supposed agreement relates to costs that exceed the £750 threshold. That said, she commented that her conclusion was at odds both with standard Chancery practice and previous decisions,[322] and that she was 'hesitant' about it.[323] At least one Chancery master has come to a similar conclusion, however.[324] **40.124**

It may well be that the modern approach differs from that which used to exist in times past,[325] but there are contrary arguments that have yet to be decided.[326] **40.125**

Conversion to a liquidated sum

An unliquidated costs debt can be converted into a liquidated costs debt by agreement or conduct. Proudman J said that this may happen by means of: **40.126**

- an agreement for consideration—that is:
  - an agreement as to a fixed amount;
  - an agreement as to hourly rates and time spent in consideration of future services;
  - a compromise agreement; or
- conduct giving rise to an estoppel according to established principles.[327]

The agreement would not have to be for an expressly stated sum; a costs debt will not be unliquidated merely by virtue of the fact that an arithmetical calculation needs to be performed to ascertain the sums due.[328] **40.127**

---

held that it would be an abuse of process for a firm of accountants to serve a statutory demand for the amount of their bill: see *Re a Debtor No 32 of 1991 (No 2)* [1994] BCC 524, at 527. See also *Wallace LLP v Yates* [2010] EWHC 1098 (Ch), in which Morgan J found that the meaning of 'immediately payable' in Insolvency Act 1986, s 268, referred to sums that had to be both liquidated and payable immediately.

[320] *Truex v Toll* [2009] EWHC 396 (Ch).

[321] See, eg, *Re Ford* (1838) 3 Deac 494, Mont & Ch 97.

[322] See, eg, *Re a Debtor No 833 of 1993 and No 834 of 1993* [1994] NPC 82, in which Vinelott J found that the mere fact that the costs might be reduced was not a reason to set aside a statutory demand if the reduced amount would still be above £750.

[323] *Truex v Toll* [2009] EWHC 369 (Ch), at [38].

[324] *Klamer v Kyriakides & Braier (a firm)* [2005] BPIR 1142, Ch D.

[325] One of Proudman J's reasons for departing from previous decisions was because those decisions were made before it was established that the quantum of a solicitor's bill could be investigated even if an assessment under the Solicitors Act 1974 had been precluded: see *Truex v Toll* [2009] EWHC 369 (Ch), at [24] *et seq*, relying on cases such as *In Turner & C v O Palomo SA* [2000] 1 WLR 37.

[326] In particular, if Proudman J's analysis is correct, it would seem to be at odds with the position relating to limitation, in respect of which a claim for a solicitor's fees is capable of being a liquidated claim within the meaning of Limitation Act 1980, s 29(5): see *Byatt v Nash* [2002] All ER (D) 353.

[327] *Truex v Toll* [2009] EWHC 369 (Ch), at [26]–[40], esp [30].

[328] *Re a Debtor No 32 of 1991 (No 2)* [1994] BCC 524, at 527.

40.128 It seems implicit in Proudman J's reasoning that an agreed costs debt will be liquidated notwithstanding the fact that the court has the power to set the agreement aside (see 27.128–27.129 and 27.173). Where there is a dispute about whether there has been a compromise, the court may have to determine that dispute. That topic is addressed at 39.08–39.21, but one aspect of that topic needs particular emphasis because it is commonly encountered in practice: a mere admission of the fees, unsupported by consideration or estoppel, would ordinarily be insufficient to convert a costs debt into a liquidated sum.[329]

One-month period

40.129 It is, for the sake of completeness, worth recording that service of a statutory demand does not constitute the bringing of a claim and that the solicitor is therefore not precluded from issuing a statutory demand under the provisions concerning the one-month period stipulated in Solicitors Act 1974, s 69(1).[330] That narrow point remains good law, but it is rarely of practical relevance.

Bankruptcy proceedings

40.130 The following points are made subject to the foregoing points. Indeed, much of what is set out below would be academic in most cases because no statutory demand could be issued.

40.131 There is nothing innate about a solicitor's costs that would prevent the solicitor from issuing a bankruptcy petition in an effort to recover unpaid costs; it need not be the case that the solicitor is in a position to bring a *claim* for its costs.[331] That said, the solicitor would have to prove the costs debt, and, in appropriate cases, the court may order that a statute bill be drawn up and that the costs be assessed. There is, however, no immutable requirement that a statute bill be delivered.[332] If the circumstances permit (such as where there is a fixed sum retainer), the court may accept that the solicitor has proved the costs debt without delivering a statute bill.[333] Where this is done, the court may enlist the assistance of a costs judge in deciding the correctness of the solicitor's assertions.[334]

40.132 It may be that, for whatever reason, the amount claimed is difficult to ascertain. Where this is so, it is open to the court to order that a nominal amount be payable, thereby permitting the solicitor to vote at a creditor's meeting.[335]

---

329 *Truex v Toll* [2009] EWHC 369 (Ch), at [36].

330 *In re A Debtor (No 88 of 1991)* [1993] Ch 286, in which Sir Donald Nicholls V-C went on to say (*obiter*) that a bankruptcy petition probably should be regarded as being an action for the purposes of s 69(1).

331 See *Ex p Sutton* (1805) 11 Ves 163 and, in more modern times, *Re a Debtor No 833 of 1993 and No 834 of 1993* [1994] NPC 82.

332 *Re Potts, ex p Établissements Callot and De Schrijver v Leonard Tubbs & Co and Official Receiver* [1934] Ch 356, at 362 and 364, *per* Farwell J.

333 *Eicke v Nokes* (1829) Mood & M 303.

334 Whilst ancient authority, see *Re Hallett's Estate* (1880) 13 Ch D 318.

335 See, eg, *Rowbury v Official Receiver* sub nom *Re Mark Forstater (Keystone Law LLP)* [2015] EWHC 2951 (Ch).

Part XI

PRACTICE ISSUES

41

LEGAL PROJECT MANAGEMENT

This chapter deals with the following topics:[1] **41.01**

- terminology (41.03);
- history (41.05);
- the aims of legal project management (41.07);
- the relevance of legal project management to costs as between solicitor and client (41.08);
- the relevance of legal project management to costs as between parties (41.10);
- legal project management distinguished from other concepts (41.11);
- the phases of legal project management (41.13):
  - initiation (41.15);
  - planning (41.22);
  - execution and control (41.48);
  - completion (41.60); and
- non-traditional legal project management (41.61).

Whilst the editor is a Fellow of the International Institute of Legal Project Management (IILPM), this is only an honorary award, so the real expertise in writing this chapter derives not from him, but from Mr Antony Smith (solicitor and director of Legal Project Management Ltd) and Mr Roger Quick (an eminent commentator on Australian costs), to whom the editor is most grateful. **41.02**

Terminology

Project management has a vocabulary of its own, nearly all of which is irrelevant for the purposes of the law and practice of costs. The following terms, however, do need to be understood.[2] **41.03**

- **'Project'** This may be defined as a 'unique, transient endeavour undertaken to achieve planned objectives'. In the context of the provision of disputatious legal services (namely,

---

[1] This chapter does not attempt to address the topic of legal project management in any detailed way; rather, it is limited to that which is relevant to the law and practice of costs. For a more detailed explication of the topic, see publications such as Bowes, E, *The Lawyer's Guide to Legal Project Management* (London: Ark Group, 2017) or Hassett, J, *Legal Project Management, Pricing and Alternative Fee Arrangements: What Firms Are Doing* (Boston, MAL: LegalBizDev, 2013).

[2] Unless otherwise stated, the quoted definitions are those used by the Association for Project Management (APM), available online at https://www.apm.org.uk/

those that relate to contentious business or to disputes that may become contentious), this may be the pursuance of a claim, the defence of a claim, or some other such matter. In the context of non-disputatious legal services (such as conveyancing), a project may be any discrete matter to which instructions relate.

- **'Scope'** This may be defined as 'the totality of the outputs, outcomes and benefits and the work required to produce them'. In a contentious matter, the scope of a project may not be the same as the ambit of the client's instructions because the court or tribunal may or may not allow a client free rein. That said, the ambit of instructions would, in general, limit the scope of the project. As is set out at 41.16, the act of defining the scope of the project is a pivotal initial step in the process of legal project management. Moreover, there is an ongoing need to revise the scope (see 41.55).
- **'Stakeholders'** These are the persons who have an interest in the project. This will always include the client, but may also include others, such as litigation funders, insurers and legal services providers. In some instances, even opponents may be classed as stakeholders.
- **'Objectives'** These may be defined as 'predetermined results towards which effort is directed'. The objectives will almost always be client-led (see 41.18).
- **'Deliverables'** These may be defined as a 'package of work that will be delivered to, and formally accepted by, a stakeholder'. In the context of litigation that is subject to costs management orders, this will include completion of phases as set out in the approved or agreed budget. In other contexts, it may include any measurable result that is sought by a client. There are two types of deliverable: 'interim deliverables', which are to be used in subsequent tasks on the project, and 'final deliverables', which are of intrinsic benefit to the client upon conclusion of the project.
- **'Products'** These are similar to deliverables and, in many instances, will be the same. In the present context, products will generally be discrete legal services, which may be 'external outputs' (such as particulars of claim) or 'internal outputs' (such as internal reviews or work done on disclosed documents).
- **'Activities'** An activity may be defined as 'a task, job, operation or process consuming time and possibly other resources; the smallest self-contained unit of work in a project'. Both activities *and* tasks, as defined for the purposes of the Civil Procedure Rules (CPR) (see 49.21), will fall within the definition of activities for the purposes of legal project management. Indeed, the words 'task' and 'activity' are often used interchangeably.
- **'Phase'** This may be defined as a 'major subdivision of a life cycle'. It should be noted that—whilst there may be some overlap—the use of this word for the purposes of traditional legal project management is not coterminous with the use of this word in the CPR (see 41.13).
- **'Constraints'** Constraints are limitations to the successful completion of the project. They are factors that may prevent work from being accomplished. As is mentioned at 41.24, the most important constraints are the ambit of instructions, the availability of funding and the need to adhere to a timetable. In the context of litigation that is the subject of a costs management order, the approved or agreed budget may be a relative constraint. Other constraints may arise out of legal, ethical, geographic or technical issues, or out of matters specific to the legal services provider, such as the availability of personnel or access to information technology.

- **'Value'** This may be defined as 'a standard, principle or quality considered worthwhile or desirable'. This is a concept that is relevant to value-based pricing, which is addressed in detail in 42.16–42.38. It is also relevant to project control (see 41.51).
- **'Funding'** This may be defined as 'the means by which the capital required to undertake a project, programme or portfolio is secured and then made available as required'. In the context of litigation, it is likely that funding would be far more complex than merely the amount that the client (personally) would be willing to pay—in particular, the legal services provider may have to work within (or at least have regard to) the limits imposed by a costs management order.
- **'Quality'** This may be defined as 'the fitness for purpose or the degree of conformance of the outputs of a process or the process itself'.
- **'Baseline'** This may be defined as 'the reference levels against which a project, programme or portfolio is monitored and controlled'.
- **'Forecast expenditure'** This may be defined as 'the estimated and predicted use of money'. In the context of litigation, it is likely to be based on time spent (plus disbursements).
- **'Actual expenditure'** This may be defined as those 'costs that have been charged to the budget and for which payment has been made, or accrued'. In the context of litigation, there are two factors that need to be taken into account (although they will generally be linked); they are the amount that the client is willing to pay, and the amount that is likely to be recovered from an opponent. As is shown by Figure 41.2—which may be found after 41.27—the latter can be particularly important in the context of cases that are subject to a costs management order.
- **'Actual progress'** This may be defined as a 'measure of the work that has been completed for comparison with the baseline'.

Many of these words have meanings that are different from those used in general costs practice or as defined in the CPR. For the avoidance of doubt, unless the context suggests otherwise, in this chapter the words are used with the defined, rather than general, meanings. **41.04**

History

The term 'legal project management' first appeared in the United States around 2008 when it was associated with the need to manage matters involving extensive disclosure. The concept then expanded to refer to the need for management not only of more general aspects of litigated claims, but also of non-disputatious matters—especially those concerned with regulatory compliance, banking and finance. **41.05**

In the UK, there is now a nascent, but ever-growing, profession of specialist legal project managers (see 41.36). **41.06**

The Aims of Legal Project Management

The primary aim of legal project management is to achieve the objectives, whilst complying with relevant constraints (see 41.24). The secondary—more ambitious—goal is to optimise the use of resources to meet those objectives. **41.07**

The Relevance of Legal Project Management to Costs as between Solicitor and Client

41.08 It is said that legal services providers who use legal practice management techniques have greater confidence in their pricing strategies than those who do not.[3] Smith says that this increased confidence has been a 'big driver behind the increased adoption of [legal practice management]'.[4] This is hardly surprising given the ever-forward march of contracts of retainer that eschew time-based charging, such as fixed pricing agreements, damages-based agreements (29.141–29.178) and retainers based on value-based pricing (42.16–42.38). The fact that consumer protection law is becoming more relevant (see Chapter 28) is also a factor.

41.09 Legal project management and contracts of retainer that eschew time-based charging go hand in glove. In this regard, Smith has this to say:

> '[C]onsider a basic fixed price [agreement] ... After agreeing a fixed price with a client, "all" a lawyer has to do is make sure matters are completed satisfactorily within cost so as to leave the lawyer with a reasonable profit. The essence of applied [legal project management] is that it should ensure lawyers:
> - scope the extent of the work to be done, and clearly agree that scope with the client
> - plan the delivery of the work, including assigning appropriate resources
> - execute the work as planned
> - monitor how the work is progressing
> - keep all stakeholders (especially the client) fully informed.'[5]

Thus, if the amount that a client is willing to pay is constrained or fixed, legal project management is a necessity to ensure that the metaphoric hand does not grow too large for the glove. It is also necessary to ensure that effort is not wasted by virtue of a client authorising work that will either prove purposeless or lead to an unacceptable level of irrecoverable costs (see Figure 41.2).

The Relevance of Legal Project Management to Costs as between Parties

41.10 Whilst an obvious point, if the claim is such that a costs management order is likely to be made, then the techniques of legal project management—and of preparing costs breakdown structures, in particular (see 41.41–41.45)—will be relevant.

Legal Project Management Distinguished from Other Concepts

Legal project management distinguished from legal practice management

41.11 Whilst some writers do not make the distinction,[6] legal *project* management may be distinguished from legal *practice* management on the basis that the former is not

---

[3] See Jessen, N, and Baccus, B, 'Legal Project Management', *Association of Corporate Counsel*, 1 January 2012, available online at http://www.acc.com/legalresources/quickcounsel/lpm.cfm

[4] See Smith, A, 'An Introduction to Legal Project Management' (2013) 24(1) Computer & Law Magazine of SCL 2.

[5] See *ibid*, at 3.

[6] See, eg, the definition adopted by Hassett, J, *Legal Project Management, Pricing and Alternative Fee Arrangements: What Firms Are Doing* (Boston, MA: LegalBizDev, 2013), pp 107–8.

Table 41.1 Differences between legal practice management and legal project managements

	Legal practice management	Legal project management
Processes and projects	Legal practice management deals with processes, which tend to be permanent or semi-permanent fixtures within a legal practice. The phrase 'business-as-usual processes' may be used to describe such matters.	Legal project management deals with projects, which are temporary, with well-defined start, middle and end points.
Permanence	Legal practice management tends to deal with activities that are repetitive, permanent or semi-permanent.	Legal project management tends to deal with activities that are limited in ambit, which do not need to be repeated or which need to be repeated to only a limited extent.
Focus	Legal practice management tends to be focused on the business—namely, looking at legal services provider's processes. In theory, this covers everything from the recruitment of new staff through to rendering invoices to clients.	Legal project management is focused on matters external to the business, namely, the efficient delivery of legal services to specific clients, in accordance with their needs and expectations.
Ambit	Legal practice management tends to be run as 'programmes', which are collections of related activities, with the emphasis being on making sure that the legal services provider obtains benefits for future use.	Most of the time (but not always), legal project management is concerned with individual, stand-alone projects in which the focus is on delivering defined outputs within time, cost and quality constraints.

about improving the business processes of legal services providers, but is instead about managing individual projects, be those cases, matters or other instructions.[7] For obvious reasons, there is a degree of overlap between the two, but Table 41.1 illustrates the most significant differences.

Legal project management distinguished from pricing

Legal project management is linked to the pricing of legal services (see 41.41). Baker (a US expert on the topic) has this to say on the point: **41.12**

> 'Even if your firm only "bills by the hour" project management is vital, as you must plan how work that comes in is allocated, what resources are allocated to it, what are the deadlines, and the myriad other issues that proper project management deals with. This is simply a table stake of operating an effective organisation; it is not tied to pricing.'[8]

Thus legal project management may be required even where none of the fee structures referred to at 41.08 are present.

[7] Baker, R, *Implementing Value Pricing: A Radical Business Model for Professional Firms* (Chichester: John Wiley & Sons, 2011), pp 303–4.

[8] *Ibid*, p 300.

The Phases of Legal Project Management

41.13 Whilst other models exist—such as agile project management (see 41.61) and lean project management—the project management methodology that is most immediately relevant to the law and practice of costs is traditional legal project management. This is what is described in the greater part of this chapter (see 41.14–41.60).

41.14 For the purposes of description, traditional legal project management may be thought of as having the following sequential phases, although, in practice, there will be considerable overlap between the putative stages:

- initiation (see 41.15);
- planning (see 41.22);
- execution and control (see 41.48); and
- completion (see 41.60).

Project initiation

41.15 Traditional project management starts with the initiating processes, which, in a legal setting, would generally comprise the receipt of instructions and gathering an understanding of the client's objectives. This information would then determine the scope of the project. If the initiation stage is performed badly, the project is not likely to be managed well.

Defining the scope

41.16 The scope of the project will need to be defined, usually in the form of a short scope statement followed by a more detailed, narrative description. This may take place either towards the end of initiation process or during the initial planning stage, depending on the nature of the matter. The Association of Corporate Counsel (ACC) has this to say on the topic:

> 'Defining the project's scope is the starting point for effective project management. The scope identifies what the project is to encompass and what it is to accomplish, and is the foundation for subsequent planning and project management. A clearly defined scope will make it easier to determine the project's phases and timeline, staffing, and budget.'[9]

As is discussed at 41.55, it will be necessary to keep the scope under review from time to time.

41.17 **Project initiation document** A document—perhaps the most important document—that legal project managers will produce during the project initiation stage is the project initiation document (PID). The purpose of a PID is to record the essential facts of the project in light of initial planning and scoping work.

[9] See Jessen, N, and Baccus, B, 'Legal Project Management', *Association of Corporate Counsel*, 1 January 2012, available online at http://www.acc.com/legalresources/quickcounsel/lpm.cfm

There is no set format, but a well-crafted PID would generally contain the following elements, many of which have obvious parallels with draft budgets prepared for costs management purposes (see 12.21–12.42).[10] **41.18**

- **Scope statement** The scope statement defines—often in a single sentence—what it is intended that the project will accomplish.
- **Scope details** This will contain the detail of what the project is intended to accomplish.
- **Stakeholders** Project stakeholders ought to be identified, as a precursor to a more complete stakeholder analysis that may take place at a later stage (see 41.46).
- **Objectives** These will be the stakeholder's objectives and, as such, will answer the specific question: what does success look like? Smith has the following to say on the topic:

  '[Legal project management] provides a method or protocol for scoping new matter engagements, which refers to client objectives and what success looks like from the client's point of view. These should be recorded quickly and simply, using a template, and then referred to throughout the matter.'[11]

- **Assumptions** Assumptions are expressions of the beliefs that underpin the project. They may or may not be the same as those used for costs management purposes and are usually stated more comprehensively. One assumption that is so obvious that it may safely be left unsaid is that the relationship between ambit, funding and timetable—that is, scope, costs and time (see 41.26)–must be maintained.
- **Deliverables** Both interim and final deliverables (see 41.03) ought to be identified.
- **Constraints** Constraints should be identified and described. Risks (see below) should not be categorised as constraints, because constraints are *known* facts rather than uncertain events.
- **Risks** There would usually be a summary of foreseeable risks, including, where appropriate, any plans that may mitigate those risks.
- **Project organisation structure** Ideally, each project ought to have a structure—in the sense of something that ultimately may be expressed in an organisation breakdown structure (see 41.35). In practice, unless an unusually large number of persons are involved, the structure will be implied by the organisation of the relevant department or team carrying out the work.
- **Resource requirements statement** This is a statement of the skills required and number of personnel with the relevant skills who are likely to be needed to complete the project. Where appropriate, there should also be a summary of any requisite non-human resources.
- **Roles definition (or team definition)** This tends to follow on from the organisation structure and resource requirements statement. Each person—whether a fee earner or not—ought to have a defined role.
- **Outline communications plan** A plan needs to be formulated as to how and when there should be communication with the stakeholders (see 41.46).

[10] This list is based on Baker, R, *Implementing Value Pricing: A Radical Business Model for Professional Firms* (Chichester: John Wiley & Sons, 2011), p 300. For further comments on this, see *Quick on Costs* (Thompsons Reuters, online), paras 1170–1200.

[11] Smith, A, 'Future Projections', *Managing for Success*, August 2012, p 23.

- **Outline schedule** A concise list of project milestones should be created, with target dates for each. These will then be used for project control and earned value analysis (see 41.51).
- **Initial project budget** An estimate of cost to completion ought to be made. This will eventually lead to an estimate of the budget at completion (see 41.44).
- **Project change control** This will state whether the scope statement or scope details may be changed and, if so, what the process for dealing with change requests is (see 41.55).
- **Approval** This will record whether the project manager (or other appropriate person) has approved the scope.

41.19 As can be seen, a PID serves several purposes. It is a high-level document that is used to communicate key features of the project to the relevant stakeholders: stakeholders should understand what the project will—and will not—deliver. In mature project environments, PIDs are also used to obtain approval of the project from key stakeholders; indeed, this is often done by them signing the PID. Legal services providers should be aware that, in a consumer setting, this may give rise to obligations under the Consumer Rights Act 2015 (see 28.30–28.33).

41.20 *The relationship between project initiation document and contract of retainer* There may or may not be a close relationship between the contents of the PID and the contract of retainer. Where the latter is a fixed-price agreement, a damages-based agreement or other such agreement that eschews charging by the hour, the relationship is likely to be a close one. Where this is so, it would usually be sensible to draft the PID and the contract of retainer in such a way as to identify and deal with:

- the purpose of the contract of retainer;
- specific measurable objectives;
- details of deliverables;
- expected timetabling;
- exclusions or 'carve-outs', as well as assumptions;
- foreseeable risks; and
- the anticipated breakdown of costs (or reference thereto).[12]

41.21 In many cases (especially matters involving consumers), the PID will become part of the contract of retainer. In view of this, it is essential that care is taken not to be overly rigid in the way in which matters are defined, because errors in this regard may lead to a breach of the indemnity principle.

Project planning

41.22 Once the PID has been drafted and work on the project has begun, a more detailed plan ought to be produced. This is an ongoing task. The main purpose is to make plans for the use of time and resources, and to set a budget; in a legal setting, this means looking at those activities that may be required to achieve the objectives and to deliver deliverables. Risks

[12] Adapted from Hassett, J, *The LegalBizDev Survey of Alternative Fees* (Boston, MA: LegalBizDev, 2009), p 15.

need to be identified and, if they are in any way significant, a plan needs to be put in place for their management.

Project planning can be time-consuming and there is often a temptation to spend as little time as possible on this task in favour of simply getting on with the work. No matter how great that temptation may be, it is worth bearing in mind that research shows that high-performing project managers spend twice as much time on planning as their peers.[13] There is a reason for this: time spent planning in advance pays dividends later on in the project. In any event, it would be a risky strategy indeed to scrimp on planning in a matter that is likely to be the subject of a costs management order. **41.23**

Constraints and the project management triangle

Planning will be dependent on constraints. In a legal setting, those constraints will generally be as follows. **41.24**

- **Scope** The scope of project (as per the client's instructions or as per directions of the court, whichever is appropriate or to be given precedence) is a fundamental constraint.
- **Funding** This is a reference to the monies that are available to pay for the project. Depending on the nature of the contract of retainer, funding may or may not be constrained by the amounts set out in a costs management order (where there is one), but even where the client wishes to pay more than is provided for in the approved or agreed budget, the amounts therein will still be a relevant factor (see 41.27).
- **Timetable** The timetable (either in the sense of what the client requires or in the sense of what the court has ordered, whichever is most pressing) will be a significant constraint.

These factors act as a constraint on quality. The way in which this works is often depicted in the form of the 'project management triangle',[14] which—when adapted so as to suit legal projects—is shown at Figure 41.1. Many other variations on this theme exist—in particular, the triangle is often depicted with 'personnel' or 'persons' in the place of 'scope'—but the general meaning of such variants is broadly the same. **41.25**

The triangle illustrates the fact that expanding the amount of funding, for example, will grant the legal services provider the opportunity to provide higher-quality services or to allow the ambit of the instructions to expand (or both). It is important to bear in mind, however, that—once the baseline has been set—the triangle is depicted so as to be equilateral; hence, if quality is to be maintained, each side must be balanced against the other two. Put otherwise, the relationship between ambit, funding and timetable (that is, scope, costs and time) must be maintained if effort is not to be wasted. **41.26**

This means that an increase in time available, for example, will not result in an improvement in quality if the client's instructions (that is, ambit) continue to be a limiting factor. Whilst an obvious point, it also means that the mere fact that a client is more demanding (thereby increasing ambit) will not result in increased quality. This would particularly be so (even if the client were willing to pay more) in the context of litigated matters, because the limiting factor may well be the 'triangle' as directed by the court. This is illustrated in **41.27**

---

13 See Crowe, A, *Alpha Project Managers: What the Top 2% Know That Everyone Else Does Not* (Kennesaw, GA: Velociteach, 2010).

14 This is also often referred to as the 'iron triangle'.

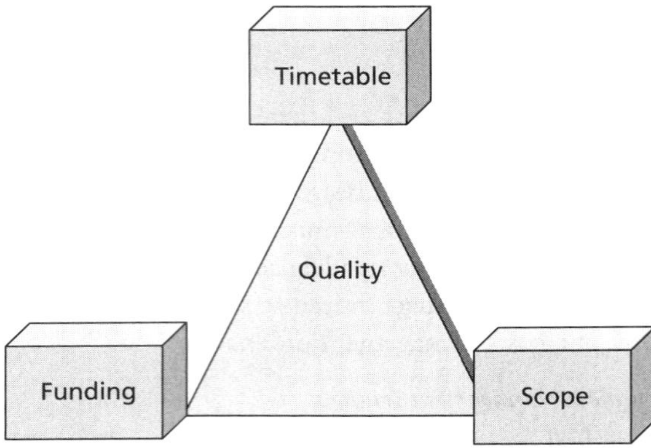

Figure 41.1 Project management triangle

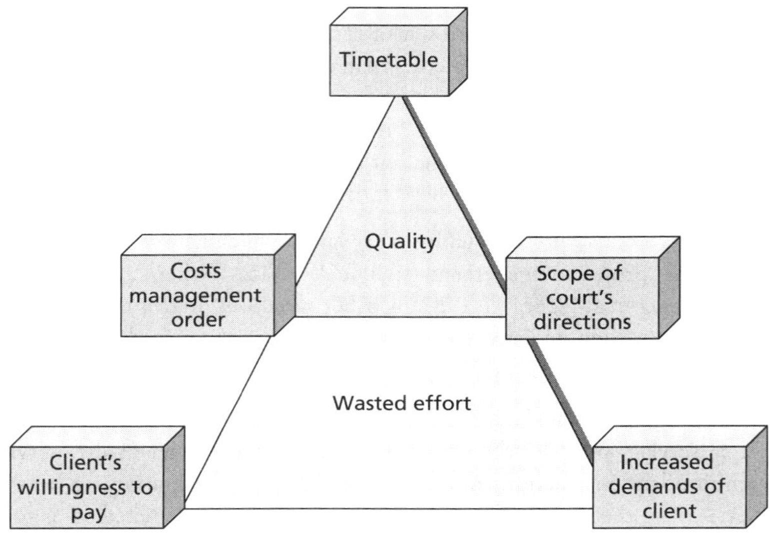

Figure 41.2 Project management triangle in which effort is wasted

Figure 41.2. As can be seen, a significant mismatch between what the client wants or demands and what the court has ordered will generally lead to wasted effort.

Project plans and breakdown structures

41.28 A project plan comprises several detailed plans (see 41.29). In general, legal project managers will take certain aspects of the matter and break them down—or 'decompose' them—into smaller and more manageable components in the form of breakdown structures. A breakdown structure may be represented in a number of ways. In this book, the examples are graphical (see Figures 41.3 and 41.4), tabular (see Table 41.2) and by way of an indented list (see 41.31).

41.29 In so far as legal project management is concerned, the following breakdown structures are often encountered:

- product breakdown structures (see 41.30);
- work breakdown structures (see 41.33);
- organisational breakdown structures (see 41.35);
- risk breakdown structures (see 41.40);
- cost breakdown structures and budgets at completion (see 41.41);
- contract breakdown structures—but only in large or complex matters (see 41.39); and
- communications plans (see 41.46).

Other types of breakdown structure and other plans exist, but they are not likely to be of relevance to traditional legal project management.

41.30 **Product breakdown structures** Product-based planning is a well-known concept in project management. In essence, it is designed to encourage project managers to consider all items needed to deliver a project as 'products'. In the context of legal services providers, this will mean discrete legal services, which may be external outputs (such as particulars of claim) or internal outputs (such as advices or work done on disclosure). In many regards, the products are the deliverables referred to in 41.03.

41.31 The following is an example of a product breakdown structure (relating to the instruction of counsel):

'1. Instruct counsel
  1.1. Establish need for counsel
  1.2. Identify any specialist area sought
  1.3. Identify level of expertise sought
2. Consult in-house database
  2.1. Select potential counsel
3. Telephone chambers clerk
  3.1. Confirm expertise
  3.2. Confirm availability
  3.3. Any potential conflict?
  3.4. Confirm cost
4. Prepare brief to counsel
  4.1. Summary of facts and issues—chronological order
  4.2. Highlight particular facts and issues of relevance
  4.3. Enclose copies of all relevant documents
    4.3.1. Relevant documents disclosed to date
    4.3.2. Draft witness statements
    4.3.3. Draft experts report(s)
  4.4. Statement about what is required of counsel
    4.4.1. List of specific questions for counsel to answer'

One could say that this is no more than a basic checklist and, in some respects, this is true. The point, however, is that the concept of product-based planning should help a legal services provider to focus on the product required (in this case, the brief to counsel), and so generate ideas as to what is required to produce the product.

41.32 As can be seen, a product breakdown structure breaks the services down into their constituent parts. Ideally, once a product breakdown structure has been formulated, a product flow diagram should be created, the purpose of which is to show *when* the constituent components are required, bearing in mind the sequential flow of the project.

41.33 **Work breakdown structures** The work breakdown structure has been formally defined by the Project Management Institute (PMI) as 'a hierarchical decomposition of the total scope of work to be carried out by the project team to accomplish the project objectives and create the required deliverables'.[15] Less formally, it may be described as a 'to do' list, with the focus being on the *work* that needs to be done, rather than the *outputs* of the project. It is this that distinguishes a work breakdown structure from a product breakdown structure.

41.34 A work breakdown structure is a low-level document. The PMI says that such a document ought to refer to 'the planned work [that] is contained within the lowest level of [work breakdown structure] components, which are called workpackages'.[16] A work breakdown structure may—and usually should—provide the framework for budgeting and timetabling.[17] That said, it is not itself a schedule nor is it a chronological listing; rather, it specifies what will be done, not how or when it will be carried out. Table 41.2 is an example.

41.35 **Organisational breakdown structures (and the role of legal project managers)** Organisational breakdown structures define organisational relationships. They are used as the framework for assigning work responsibilities. They may be in the form of indented lists, tables or charts.

41.36 At the centre of any organisational breakdown structure is a legal project manager. On one level, every legal project will have a project manager in the sense that there will be a fee earner who will oversee the work being carried out. This may be all that is required on less-demanding matters. There is, however, now a specialism of legal project management and specialist legal project managers; it is difficult to say how many legal project managers there are in England and Wales, but it is a growing profession.

41.37 Many legal project managers will be members of either the PMI[18] or the Association for Project Management (APM).[19] Some are also now members of the International Institute of Legal Project Management (IILPM), which provides 'education internationally recognised qualifications, global certifications and ongoing support to build [members'] legal project management competence and expertise'.[20] Some are legally qualified.

41.38 Within law firms and in-house legal departments, the most common structure is where legal project managers become members of workgroups made up of fee earners and non-fee earners who are focused on particular areas of practice. To that extent, legal project managers will have niche specialisms. They will often be operational team leaders and, as such, will be responsible for what might be called the 'mechanics' of the delivery of legal services to clients. In essence, they will strive to ensure that fee earners are relieved of the

---

[15] See Project Management Institute, *A Guide to the Project Management Body of Knowledge* (5th edn, Newtown Square, PA: PMI, 2013), p 12.

[16] See *ibid*, p 126.

[17] Booz, Allen & Hamilton, 'Earned Value Management Tutorial: Module 2—Work Breakdown Structure', available online at https://www.energy.gov/sites/prod/files/maprod/documents/EVMModule2.pdf

[18] See https://www.pmi.org/

[19] See https://www.apm.org.uk/

[20] See http://www.iilpm.com/

Table 41.2 Example of a work breakdown structure (in tabular form)

WBS No	Activity/Task	Elapsed effort (days)	Dependencies	Earliest start date	Latest finish date	HR budget internal (£)	HR budget external (£)	Equipment, materials & consumables (£)	Person responsible
1	Expert document review								
1.1	Collect all relevant documentation	0.5		01/11/18	02/11/18	500.00			FL
1.2	Send all relevant documentation to expert (courier)	0.10	1.1	01/11/18	02/11/18			25.00	FL
1.3	Expert reads documentation	1	1.2	03/11/18	06/11/18		2,000.00		CD
1.4	Expert tests software								
1.4.1	Write test cases	2	1.1; 1.2	07/11/18	10/11/18		4,000.00		CD
1.4.2	Set up technical test environment	1		13/11/18	14/11/18		2,000.00	750.00	CD
1.4.3	Software testing	2	1.2.1; 1.2.2	14/11/18	17/11/18		4,000.00		CD
1.5	First draft expert report								
1.5.1	Expert writes up report	2	1.2.3	20/11/18	23/11/18		4,000.00		CD
1.5.2	Expert report sent to legal team (courier)	0.10		24/11/18	24/11/18			25.00	CD
1.5.3	Internal review by legal team	0.25	1.3.1; 1.3.2	27/11/18	27/11/18	3,225.00			FL, CS, RM
				Column totals		£3,725.00	£16,000.00	£800.00	
				HR budget internal		£3,725.00			
				HR budget external		£16,000.00			
				Equipment, materials & consumables		£800.00			
				Total budget		**£20,525.00**			

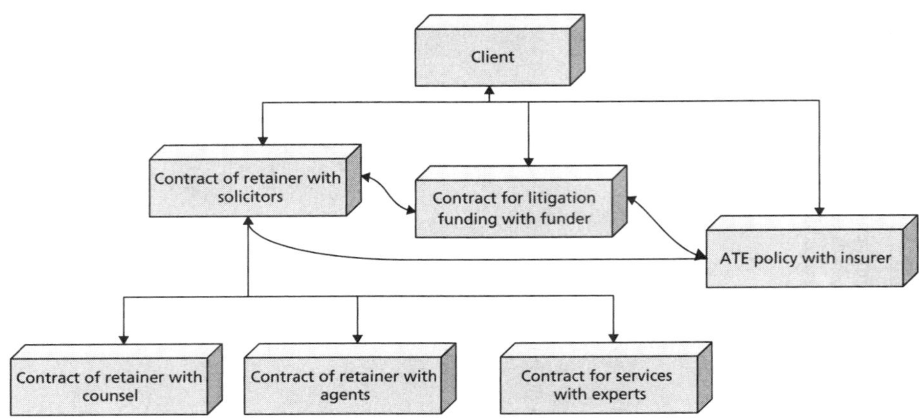

Figure 41.3 Example of a contract breakdown structure

burden of project administration so that they are able to devote more time to their core activity—namely, providing legal services.

41.39 **Contract breakdown structures** In project management in settings other than the provision of legal services, a contract breakdown structure is a hierarchal arrangement of head contractors, subcontractors, suppliers, etc, which is arranged to show the overall supply chain feeding goods and services into the project. Such structures are often unnecessary in legal project management, but, in a complex matter, a contract breakdown structure may look like Figure 41.3.

41.40 **Risk breakdown structures** A risk breakdown structure is a hierarchically organised depiction of the identified risks arranged in categories. The structure is organised by source, so that the total risk exposure of the project can be more easily understood and planning for the risk more easily accomplished. It would be rare that a costs practitioner would become involved with such matters, but they are nonetheless relevant to legal project management.

41.41 **Cost breakdown structures and budgets at completion** The cost breakdown structure sets out the costs of a project by reference to some form of categorisation. In the context of legal services, that may be based on the categories used for cost management, those used in a traditional bill of costs or those used for electronic coding, such as the Legal Electronic Data Exchange Standard (LEDES™).

41.42 A cost breakdown structure is at the lowest level of breakdown structures in general, but it is often combined with the work breakdown structure—or parts thereof (see 41.33). A (very) basic graphical example of this is set out in Figure 41.4.

41.43 A cost breakdown structure will generally be used for the purposes of cost estimation. They are often drafted with the assistance of costs lawyers or costs draftspersons. The following steps will generally be necessary for passably accurate costs estimation.[21]

- **Understand the size of the project** Until all project tasks have been understood, it is difficult to appreciate the size of the project—which means that estimators should

[21] Adapted from Smith, A, 'An Educated Guess', *Litigation Funding*, December 2012, p 18.

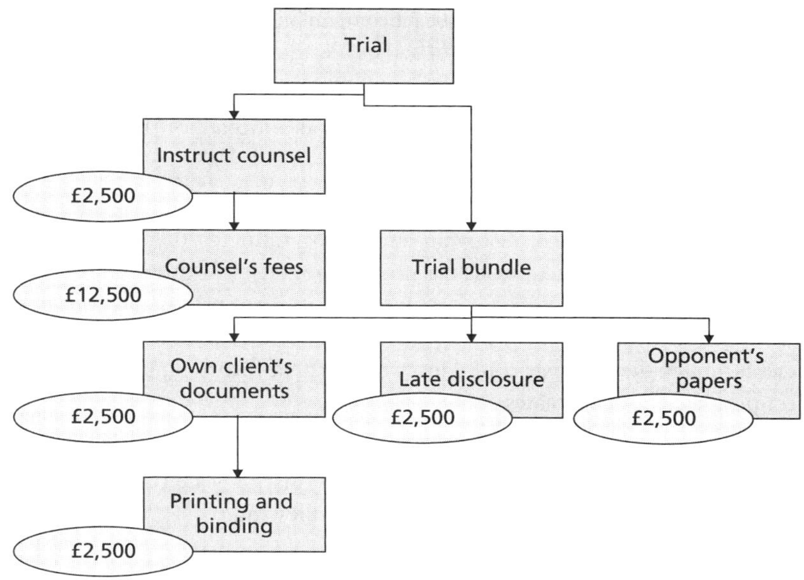

Figure 41.4 Example of a cost breakdown structure

concentrate on understanding all of the activities and phases before they begin the task of preparing an estimate. This will generally be achieved by preparing a product breakdown structure (see 41.30) and a work breakdown structure (see 41.33).

- **Create a costs breakdown structure** For each phase (whether phases in a draft budget or otherwise), activities should be identified and listed (which, for the avoidance of doubt, would include 'tasks'). Where appropriate, activities should be broken down into sub-tasks (because it is easier to appreciate the effort required to complete a series of smaller tasks than it is that of a much larger task)—although activities ought not be broken down to such an extent that the sub-tasks are no longer meaningful.
- **Ensure that estimates are done by those who will perform the work** The fee earners who will carry out the work ought to be involved in preparing the costs breakdown structure. Where appropriate, the work of non-fee earners—often unseen by those not directly involved in task execution—must be factored in.
- **Consider a team-based approach** With larger projects, it may be appropriate to have estimates prepared by the team that will carry out the work. That said, it is worth bearing in mind that those people may not necessarily be best placed to assign figures to the activities listed in the costs breakdown structure. An 'obvious approach' (according to Smith) is for the fee earner who is going to carry out the work to produce a draft costs breakdown structure and a costs lawyer or costs draftsperson to then provide the figures.
- **Use comparative estimates, where possible** In general, estimating is best carried out with the benefit of historical data of previous projects, which is known as comparative estimating. Most legal services providers will have such data easily available. Smith offers the following advice on the topic:

> 'While it is true that there are often plenty of similarities between cases, it is equally true that, when looked at in detail, many cases have some unique attributes. So use the historic data as a means of developing and sanity checking your current estimates. Historic data is

an absolutely vital tool, but it should not be relied upon blindly—past performance is not a cast-iron guarantee of future performance.'[22]

41.44 A cost breakdown structure may conclude with, or lead to, an estimate of the budget at completion (BAC), which is—as its name implies—an estimate of the total expenditure upon conclusion of the matter.

41.45 It is permissible—if not necessary—to plan to revise estimates as the project progresses. In particular, it is permissible to deploy an 'estimating funnel'—that is, an estimate that is intended to become more accurate as the project progresses. If this method is deployed, then provision will have to be made for any appropriate assumptions and contingencies in any draft budget. This may be illustrated by Figure 41.5, the 'cone of uncertainty', which is a representation of the fact that confidence in estimated future expenditure will grow as the project progresses and estimates are revised.

41.46 **Stakeholder engagement and communications plans** Stakeholder engagement is the process of communicating with stakeholders to ensure that they are content with what has been achieved and what is proposed. It involves the following.

- **Identifying stakeholders** All stakeholders ought to be identified.
- **Assessing needs** The needs of stakeholders ought to be identified and assessed.
- **Assessing roles** The roles of stakeholders ought to be identified, including both those that may contribute to the success of the project and those that may threaten it.

Once such an assessment has been carried out, a communications plan will need to be formulated. This will deal with issues such as the mode, content and frequency of

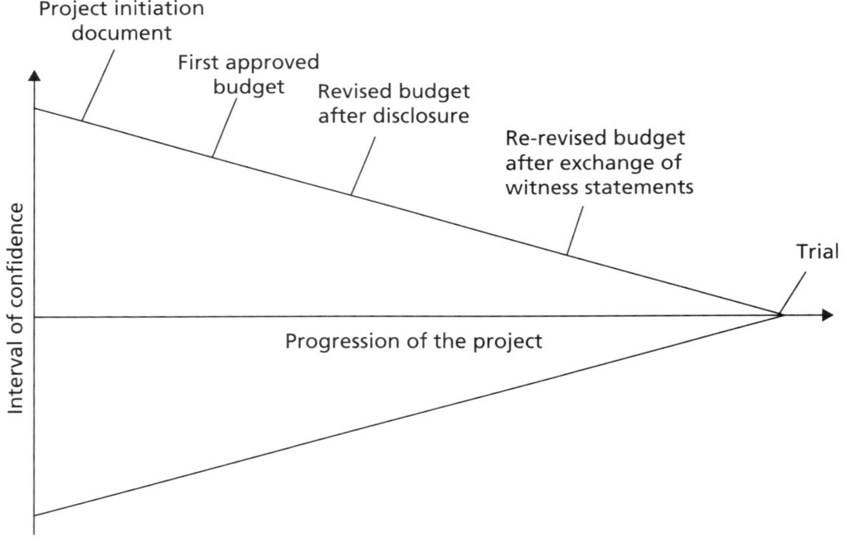

Figure 41.5 The cone of uncertainty

[22] *Ibid.*

communications. Any such plan may need to be revised in light of the progress of the project or the changing needs of the stakeholders.

In a modest matter, a communications plan is likely to be implied by the client care documentation, but it should not be forgotten that one of the main benefits of legal project management is better communication between legal services provider and client.[23] As such, even if there is no pressing need for a specific communication plan, there will be a need to ensure that the benefit of better communication is not denied to the client. In any event, in a more complex matter (especially one involving many stakeholders), a formal plan may be of assistance. **41.47**

Project execution and control

This stage, as its name implies, encompasses the performance of those tasks and activities identified during the planning stage, as set out in the work breakdown structure. This will, in the context of the project being carried out by a team, require a project manager to co-ordinate people and resources. **41.48**

Project control may be thought of as a form of ongoing audit. Its purpose is to keep the project on track, on time and on budget (that is, within the available funding). This means that a view needs to be taken as to whether there are problems and what actions need to be taken to deal with them. **41.49**

Project control tools

Whilst some will have only limited application in the context of legal projects, the following project control tools may be deployed (amongst others): **41.50**

- earned value analysis (see 41.51–41.54);
- cost–benefit analysis;
- value–benefit analysis;
- simulation calculations;
- risk-profile analyses;
- milestone trend analysis; and
- cost trend analysis.

Project control and earned value analysis The purpose of project control is to identify variances from the baseline by means of regular observation and measurement.[24] In this way, the cone of uncertainty (see 41.45 and Figure 41.5) will be narrowed. For obvious reasons, it will be necessary to compare actual progress with the baseline. In so far as the practice of costs is concerned, the most important aspect of project control will be the comparison of actual expenditure and work done against (baseline) forecast expenditure and planned work. **41.51**

The reason why both expenditure and work done need to be examined is that whilst project expenditure (cost) may be progressing as planned, this may not be true of work done. This is where earned value analysis becomes relevant. In brief, the steps of earned value analysis are as follows. **41.52**

[23] See, eg, Smith, A, 'Future Projections', *Managing for Success*, August 2012, p 23.

[24] Baker, R, *Implementing Value Pricing: A Radical Business Model for Professional Firms* (Chichester: John Wiley & Sons, 2011), pp 303–4.

(1) The project plan (including a costs breakdown structure and an estimate of budget at completion) will need to be created upon initiation of the project (see 41.22–41.47).
(2) At a point in time (often a predetermined point known as a milestone), the following are either taken into account or estimated:
   - the 'actual cost of the work performed';
   - the 'budgeted cost of the work performed'—that is, the amount that the work actually performed ought to have cost, according to the original (or revised) project plan; and
   - the 'budgeted cost of the work scheduled'—that is, the amount that the work that ought to have been done ought to have cost, according to the original (or revised) project plan.
(3) Once this has been done, the variances between actual and projected progress (in terms of both cost and work done) may be determined.
(4) This will then allow a revised budget at completion—known as the estimate at completion (EAC)—to be formulated.

41.53 The purpose behind earned value analysis is to allow the legal project manager to take stock of progress to date and to manage the remainder of the project in such a way as to best achieve the project objectives within the project constraints. For the reasons set out at 41.09, this will be necessary even if the client is insulated from having to pay the difference because they benefit from a contract of retainer that eschews time-based charging.

41.54 If the proceedings are subject to a costs management order, then some form of earned value analysis will be necessary for the purposes of knowing whether an application needs to be made to revise the approved or agreed budget. In this regard, it should be noted that it will be necessary to calculate costs on a time basis regardless of the nature of the contract of retainer. This is an aspect of the matter that would generally best be handled by a costs lawyer or costs draftsperson.

Change requests

41.55 It may be (and, in practice, almost always will be) that the scope of the project will need to be amended in some way. Where this is necessary, the request is known as a change request; such a request may or may not be granted. In the context of litigation, a change request would depend on the nature of the constraint to which it relates. Thus, if the constraint is the timetable set by the court, the request would comprise a request to the client for instructions to make an application, and—should such instructions be given—then the application itself. In the context of a litigated matter, a change request may be no more than a request for revised instructions or a request to amend a costs management order.

41.56 A change request may have a significant bearing on issues relating to costs. The precise nature of the influence it will have will depend on whether one is looking at the matter as between legal services provider and client (see 41.57), or as between opposing parties (see 41.59).

Change requests as between legal services provider and client

41.57 Depending on what is written into the contract of retainer, a change request may result in a need for a change in the fees ultimately charged to the client. If the contract of retainer provides for fees to be calculated by reference to the time spent, then it may be that nothing needs to be done other than to inform the client of the new estimate; if the client is a consumer, however, this may give rise to the issues discussed at 28.34. If the contract of retainer is not based on time spent (that is, if it is a so-called alternative fee agreement), then—depending on what the agreement says—a change request may result in a renegotiated fee. Smith had this to say on the point (his comments being in the context of there being some form of alternative fee agreement in place):

> 'The concept of change control to manage scope change has assumed particular importance in light of [contracts of retainer that eschew time-based charging]. If there is a process whereby scope change is flagged up, discussed and the means of dealing with the change agreed with the client then this should help everyone feel more relaxed about the [fee arrangement] in question. Of central importance here is the acknowledgement that prices may need to be re-quoted in light of any agreed change in scope. It follows that [fee arrangements] should be clearly recorded and documented. However, there is an obvious potential issue with change control procedures in the context of supplying legal services. Lawyers by nature and training have a tendency to go for detailed definitions and robust interpretation of wording. I would suggest that arguing with clients over minutiae of an [fee arrangement] is not a good strategy for a lawyers' long-term success. Hence common sense and sensitivity should be applied as counterweight to an overly legalistic interpretation of the agreement and what amounts to "change of scope" in any given set of circumstances.'[25]

It should be noted that, for the reasons set out at 29.151 and 29.171, it is extremely dif- **41.58**
ficult to vary the terms of a damages-based agreement in such a way as to accommodate a change request. On the basis of the law as it was understood to be at the time of writing, it would not be possible to incorporate a contractual right to do this.

Change requests and their relevance as between opposing parties

In a case that is not subject to a costs management order, a change request is likely to be **41.59**
reflected only in the work done, but if the case is subject to such an order, then the request may give rise to a need to amend the budget.

Project completion

Completion includes the formal acceptance of the project, which ends the project and is **41.60**
marked by administrative activities (such as archiving files, final billing, etc). A post-project review may take place, for the purposes of learning from the way in which the project was managed. This is particularly important in projects that were subject to costs management orders because the data that may be gleaned may be directly relevant to future cases.

Non-traditional Legal Project Management

As was noted at 41.13, this chapter deals mostly with the traditional approach to legal **41.61**
project management. There are, however, other approaches—most notably, 'agile' project management. That species of project management was born of a reaction to the perceived bureaucratic nature of traditional project management.

Agile project management is a lighter methodology, with greater emphasis on the persons **41.62**
who are carrying out the work being given more responsibility for defining and revising the

---

[25] See Smith, A, 'An Introduction to Legal Project Management' (2013) 24(1) Computer & Law Magazine of SCL 2, at 3.

scope of the project and the schedule of deliverables. In essence, those who carry out the work will manage the work in 'sprints', which are periods of time—usually of between two and six weeks. At the end of each sprint, the persons responsible for carrying out the work will liaise closely with the client to discuss what has been achieved and how outstanding work is to be done.

41.63 Whilst agile project management is distinguishable from traditional project management, the two are not mutually exclusive. As such, it is possible to combine the two methodologies such that agile project management takes place within the framework of traditional project management. For example, the issue of taking witness statements may be part of a traditional project management plan, but may be dealt with as being a 'sprint'.

42

VALUE-BASED PRICING AND PRACTISING WITHOUT RECORDING TIME

This chapter deals with the following topics: **42.01**

- introduction (42.02);
- theories of value (42.04);
- the state of the market (42.05);
- costs-plus pricing (42.09);
- value-based pricing (42.16):
  - the advantages and disadvantages of value-based pricing (42.19);
  - the method of value-based pricing (42.24);
  - value from the client's perspective (42.25);
  - pricing options based on level of service (42.26);
  - contracts of retainer and pricing options (42.28);
  - legal project management and value-based charging (42.31);
  - post-project reviews (42.35);
- the chief value officers (42.37);
- pricing strategies, analytics and reporting (42.39);
- practising without recording time (42.43):
  - why recording time may not be necessary (42.48); and
  - alternatives to recording time (42.56).

Introduction

This chapter is a departure from the usual style of this book, in the sense that it is less heavily referenced than other chapters and also necessarily contains statements of opinion. This is because the subject matter is relatively new in this jurisdiction. To compensate for this, the editor has co-authored this chapter with two renowned experts on value-based pricing—namely, Ron Baker and John Chisholm, both of the VeraSage Institute in California. Where quotes are attributed to Baker and Chisholm without a reference, this is to the original, unedited text written by them for the purposes of this book. **42.02**

Managing partners may wish to note that what is set out in this chapter is, of necessity, only a small part of what Baker and Chisholm have to say as this is a book on costs, rather than a book on practice management.[1] They would also do well to note that there is **42.03**

[1] For more detail on practice management, see Baker, R, *Implementing Value Pricing: A Radical Business*

evidence from the United States that firms that *proactively* engage in value-based charging are more than twice as likely to report higher profitability in respect of that type of business when compared to firms that are reactive in that regard.[2] In an increasingly global market, they should also note the inexorable rise in value-based pricing in other jurisdictions.

Theories of Value

42.04 Theories of value are about how, why and to what degree persons value things, including the provision of services. For present purposes—namely, the provision of legal services—there are two competing theories of value, as follows.

- **The labour theory of value** This is a theory that posits that a service's value is intrinsic to the service provided[3] and is determined by the amount of labour or effort expended in providing that service. In so far as legal services are concerned, its most commonly encountered manifestation is costs-plus pricing (see 42.09).
- **The subjective theory of value** This theory eschews the notion that services have only an intrinsic value, positing instead that value depends on the subjective needs and wants of the client.[4] Put otherwise, it places a value on services by determining what those services mean to the particular client (or category of clients) in question.[5] Its most commonly encountered manifestation is value-based pricing (see 42.16), which is the main topic addressed in this chapter.

The State of the Market

42.05 In professions other than the law—accountancy in particular—and in the law in many other jurisdictions, the subjective theory of value has already gained considerable traction: many service providers routinely price their services according to the external value created (as perceived and determined by the client), rather than the basis of internal costs incurred in generating those services. In particular, the use of value-based pricing (see 42.16) is becoming commonplace.

42.06 This chapter examines the issue of whether the same should be so in certain circumstances in this jurisdiction. It should be borne in mind, however, that (in disputatious matters—namely, contentious matters and matters that may become contentious) the perception of value in England and Wales has historically been distorted by the fact that reasonable and proportionate costs have been—and, in many cases, still are—routinely recoverable between opposing parties. This has had the following effects that have discouraged subjective measures of value:

Model for Professional Firms (Hoboken, NJ: John Wiley & Sons, 2011).

[2] See, eg, Clay, TS, and Seeger, EA, *Law Firms in Transition 2011: An Altman Weil Flash Survey*, available online at http://www.altmanweil.com/LFiT2011/

[3] Zimmerman, M, 'Intrinsic vs Extrinsic Value', *Stanford Encyclopedia of Philosophy*, 24 December 2014, available online at https://plato.stanford.edu/entries/value-intrinsic-extrinsic/

[4] Investopedia, 'Subjective Theory of Value', available online at https://www.investopedia.com/terms/s/subjective-theory-of-value.asp

[5] BusinessDictionary.com, 'Utility Theory', available online at http://www.businessdictionary.com/definition/utility-theory.html

- there is, in many cases, a need to record time for the purposes of recovering costs from an opponent and, as a result, it is only natural that this has become the predominant method of determining value; and
- the fact that fees may be recoverable from an opponent has created a situation in which recovery of those costs will, of itself, often be perceived as justifying further expenditure, especially if those costs become significant.

These two factors have historically made it difficult for legal services providers to supply **42.07** legal services in disputatious matters on any basis other than the traditional (that is, hourly rate) basis of charging. As will be explained at 42.09, this method is a manifestation of the labour theory of value known as costs-plus pricing. Conditional fee agreements and, to a much lesser extent, damages-based agreements have effected a modest degree of change, but there has yet to develop any predominant culture of pricing legal services on that basis. That said, value-based charging is gaining traction, especially in so far as non-disputatious legal services (such as commercial transactions, conveyancing, non-contentious probate, etc) are concerned.

That may be the situation now and it undoubtedly will continue to be so for certain cases **42.08** for the foreseeable future, but, for the reasons set out at 42.11, there are many circumstances in which costs-plus pricing may no longer be desirable (and certainly is not necessary). Where this is so, there may be business advantages to a legal services provider (and to clients) in adopting other methods of pricing, such as value-based pricing. In particular, in certain cases, it may be possible to avoid the need to record time entirely. Baker and Chisholm have the following to say on that topic:

> 'Clients buy outcomes, not hours. No one cares about the labor pains, they want to see the baby. Yet law firms not only measure the labor pains, they bill for them in six-minute contractions. Being a professional means taking responsibility for providing a result, not delivering a series of tasks. It's one of the reasons hourly billing is unprofessional—it atomizes everything into a task, distracting attention away from creating an outcome.'

As will be explained below, Baker and Chisholm suggest that there are other and better methods by which business performance may be measured than by recording time (see 42.56).

Costs-plus Pricing

Costs-plus pricing is a form of pricing that is largely based on the labour theory of value. **42.09** It is a pricing strategy in which the fees for services rendered are determined by adding a mark-up to the costs of providing those services.[6] It may be described in the following way:

Service → Cost → Price (including profit element) → Value → Client

This, in essence, is what happens when a legal services provider sets an hourly rate that includes a profit element, which is generally what happens when a client instructs a legal services provider in this jurisdiction.

[6] Lewis, WC, Jain, SK, and Petersen, CH, *Managerial Economics* (4th edn, London: Pearson Education, 2006).

42.10 Costs-plus pricing used to happen expressly under the 'A plus B' method of determining hourly rates that preceded the Civil Procedure Rules (CPR) (see 51.24–51.37); it now happens in a way that is arguably less transparent, in the sense that the profit element is now rarely considered in isolation (see 51.38–51.39). In non-disputatious matters (such as non-contentious probate and conveyancing), there may be a degree of overlap with the subjective theory of value, in the sense that the profit element—the 'plus' in 'costs-plus'—may still expressly be based on subjective factors (see 38.19–38.21), but there is very little overlap in disputatious matters because the profit element tends to be governed by the rate (or those rates) that the legal services provider aspires to recover between opposing parties on behalf of its client. These tend to be set according to objective measures, such as guideline hourly rates, historical pricing strategies and other such matters.

42.11 Costs-plus pricing may still be appropriate in those cases in which it is expected that assessed costs (as opposed to fixed costs) may be recovered from an opponent, because this would be commensurate with the method by which such costs would be ascertained by the court. For the reasons set out below, however, such an approach may no longer be necessary in an increasingly large range of circumstances.

- **Non-disputatious matters and disputatious matters in which there is no jurisdiction to allow costs** Whilst an obvious point, if there is no opponent to pay costs, there is no pressing need to adopt cost-plus pricing, and the same point may be made about cases before tribunals in which there is no power to award costs.
- **Fixed costs** Where costs are fixed, costs-plus pricing may not be necessary because the court will (subject to certain escape provisions) allow costs between opposing parties according a method that would be wholly different.
- **Proportionality** Under the post-2013 method of assessing proportionate costs (see 25.47–25.58), the court will disallow costs that are disproportionate even if they were incurred in providing legal services that were necessarily required. As such, in lower-value matters, a dogged adherence to costs-plus pricing may ultimately be self-defeating because such fees are unlikely to be recovered as costs.
- **Budgeted cases** Where costs are subject to a costs management order, then (in general) budgeted costs will be assessed only where there is 'good reason' to depart from the budget (see 12.137–12.165). This being so, the need to charge on a costs-plus basis is lessened—especially where the matter is subject to efficient legal project management (see Chapter 41).
- **Cases in which costs are unlikely to be assessed as between opposing parties** There are many circumstances (such as claims that proceed on the small claims track) in which it is very unlikely that costs will be recovered between opposing parties. Where this is so, an adherence to costs-plus pricing may not always be appropriate.

42.12 For all of these reasons (and others), there is now a significant and ever-expanding category of cases and matters in which costs-plus pricing is not mandatory. It is also worth bearing in mind that many judges have a strong dislike of costs-plus pricing (in the form of hourly rates). For example, Neuberger MR (speaking extrajudicially) said that it 'at best leads to inefficient practices, [and] at worst it rewards and incentivises inefficiency'.[7] Many academics

[7] See Lord Neuberger, 'Keynote Address: Fourteenth Lecture in the Implementation Programme', 11 May 2012, para 17.

have said much the same thing, for example Susskind saying that it 'penalises ... well run legal business whose systems and processes enable it to conclude matters rapidly'.[8]

In any event, there is no reason why costs-plus pricing should dictate the amount that the client is asked actually to *pay*. In particular, it is easy to draft contracts of retainer that allow for the recovery of costs from an opponent on a traditional costs-plus (hourly rate) basis, but which restrict the amount that the client actually pays to a different amount. This can be done, for example, by inserting a clause that says that the only way in which a legal services provider may enforce the difference between those two amounts is by causing the client to recover those monies from an opponent. As such, there would rarely be a need to adhere rigidly to costs-plus pricing as between legal services provider and client—and this would be so even in cases that do not fall within the categories outlined in 42.11. **42.13**

It should also be noted that costs-plus pricing is rarely a successful business strategy in markets that are perfectly competitive. This may be highly relevant in the future, because the Competition and Markets Authority (CMA) is in the process of making changes to the legal services market that are intended to increase competition significantly.[9] In particular, if—as is planned—legal services providers are required to be transparent in terms of hourly rates, there will be little competitive advantage in offering legal services that are based solely on that method of charging. This is one of the reasons why the Law Society has published its Price and Service Transparency Toolkit.[10] **42.14**

In view of the above, it is worth examining other methods by which the fees that the client actually pays are valued. In particular, it is worth examining value-based pricing. **42.15**

Value-based Pricing

Value-based pricing is a pricing strategy that sets fees primarily by reference to the perceived or estimated value of the service to the client, rather than according to the cost of those services or their historical prices.[11] It inverts the chain illustrated at 42.09 by recognizing the fact that the client is the ultimate and sole arbiter of value as between client and legal services provider, and hence it may be depicted as: **42.16**

Client → Value → Price (including profit element) → Cost → Service

Thus value-based pricing turns the order of cost-plus pricing on its head. The costs of carrying out the work do not determine the price, less still the value; instead, the price justifies the costs that can be profitably invested for the purposes of making the service desirable for the client. Baker and Chisholm have this to say on the point: **42.17**

[8] Susskind, R, *The End of Lawyers? Rethinking the Nature of Legal Services* (Oxford: Oxford University Press, 2010), p 151.

[9] See CMA, *Legal Services Market Study: Final Report* (London: HMSO, 2016).

[10] Law Society, *Price and Service Transparency Toolkit* (London: Law Society, 2016), available online at http://www.lawsociety.org.uk/support-services/advice/articles/price-and-service-transparency-toolkit/

[11] Adapted from Hinterhuber, A, 'Value Delivery and Value-based Pricing in Industrial Markets', in Woodside, AG, Golfetto, F, and Gibbert, M (eds) *Creating and Managing Superior Customer Value* (Bingley: Emerald Group, 2008), pp 381–448.

> 'A coat is not worth eight times as much as a hat because it takes eight times as long to make it. Rather, manufacturers are willing to devote eight times as long to the making of a coat because customers value it eight times more than a hat. The cause and effect is the exact opposite of the conventional wisdom of hourly billing.'

42.18 It should be noted that, in this context, value does not mean the objective value of the claim or matter; it is therefore entirely different from the notions of 'value' that may apply to the seven (now eight) 'pillars of wisdom' (see 25.26). It is the subjective value of the services from the client's perspective, which has a similar meaning to 'value' in the context of legal project management (see 41.03), but is not the same as earned value analysis (see 41.51–41.54), because that is a project control tool, rather than a mechanism for setting price.

The advantages and disadvantages of value-based pricing

42.19 Whilst each case or matter (or each category of case or matter) will turn on its own facts, there are potential advantages to value-based pricing, for both clients and legal services providers. From a client's perspective, the benefits may include certainty of price and increased choice of pricing options. From the legal services provider's point of view, the benefits may include:

- increased competitive advantage;
- an increased ability to select profitable instructions; and
- the possibility of avoiding the administrative overhead of recording time (see 42.43–42.57).

42.20 As to the first of these factors—namely, competitive advantage—it should be noted that value-based charging does not mean that legal services providers will offer their services for a lower overall fee than would be the case under costs-plus pricing. Indeed, in general, quite the opposite would be true. This is because value-based pricing allows legal services providers to target certain sectors of the market (or to tailor their pricing to suit individual clients) in such a way as to encourage the client to pay a premium for the services that the sector or category of client to which they belong values. For example, if a client particularly values the ability to speak to a senior fee earner at very short notice, then this is something for which they may be willing to pay. Moreover, where value-based pricing is combined with legal project management (or where the services being provided are likely to be much the same from case to case), value-based pricing allows a legal services provider to reject instructions at the very outset in those matters in which the client is unable or unwilling to pay a price that will allow a reasonable profit to be made.

42.21 Whilst an obvious point, it should always be borne in mind that a legal services provider is under a duty to act in its client's best interests. In particular, the Solicitors Regulation Authority (SRA) Code of Conduct 2011 provides that legal services providers who are subject to that Code must enter into only those fee agreements that it considers suitable for the client's needs and which take account of the client's best interests.[12] It would therefore be professionally improper to implement value-based pricing in an overly aggressive way. That said, provided that a client is offered a choice (see 42.26 and 42.28) and is given appropriate advice about other methods of funding, there is no reason why value-based pricing

[12] See SRA Code of Conduct, O(1.6).

cannot be used to charge a premium for services that the client in question particularly values. The guidance given generally in the Law Society's Price and Service Transparency Toolkit[13] may be relevant in this regard.

Value-based pricing does have disadvantages, however. In this jurisdiction, the most obvious disadvantage is that it is not the method by which costs between opposing parties are assessed; as such, it may not be appropriate (and certainly not easy) to implement value-based pricing in those cases in which costs are likely to be awarded on the basis that they are to be assessed. That said, for the reasons set out at 42.13, this does not rule out value-based charging entirely, because it is possible to draft contracts of retainer in such a way as to allow for both value-based charging *and* the recovery of costs on a time basis from an opponent. Another disadvantage is that it will usually be necessary to know in advance how much it is likely to cost to provide the requisite legal services and this will not always be knowledge that is easy to obtain. In particular, whilst large cases will lend themselves to legal project management and smaller cases may be easy to gauge by reference to historical data, mid-sized cases may be more problematic (although less so if they are subject to costs management). That said, there is the potential for considerable profit from such cases and, as such, value-based pricing should not be ruled out. **42.22**

The reality is that, in this jurisdiction at the present time, value-based charging is likely to be easiest to implement in cases in which costs are not likely to be assessed as between opposing parties (such as high-volume personal injury work, to which CPR, Part 45, applies, will writing, non-contentious probate, conveyancing, etc) and larger cases in which legal project management will be used. Internationally, value-based pricing is already well established in 'commoditised' cases—although, anecdotally, in this jurisdiction, clients with such cases tend to focus on cost, rather than value. Perhaps this will change as legal services providers take notice of the potential benefits of value-based pricing. In any event, as legal project management become more prevalent and the ambit of CPR, Part 45, grows, the use of value-based pricing is likely to expand considerably. **42.23**

The method of value-based pricing

Baker suggests that certain steps ought to be taken to implement value-based pricing.[14] The following list is based on Baker's list, but has been adapted to suit this jurisdiction. **42.24**

- **Initial discussion with client** Baker suggests that, at the outset, there ought to be a conversation with the client that is along the following lines: 'We will undertake this engagement only if we can agree, to our mutual satisfaction, that the value we are creating is greater than the price we are charging you. Is that acceptable?' (As to what is meant by 'value' in this context, see 42.25.)
- **Price-led costing** Baker says that the correct approach is to 'price the customer, not the service'. This means that the legal services provider must listen to the client and offer its services on a basis that reflects what the client perceives to be of value.

[13] Law Society, *Price and Service Transparency Toolkit* (London: Law Society, 2016), available online at http://www.lawsociety.org.uk/support-services/advice/articles/price-and-service-transparency-toolkit/

[14] Adapted from Baker, R, *Implementing Value Pricing: A Radical Business Model for Professional Firms* (Hoboken, NJ: John Wiley & Sons, 2011), pp 118–24.

- **Pricing options** Baker suggests that, in general, clients ought to be offered three options—what he calls 'Goldilocks pricing'. For the reasons set out at 42.21, this would be a wise course of action notwithstanding Baker's advice. Baker suggests that thought ought to be given to how best to present those options to the client and, in particular, to whether to offer the cheapest or the most expensive option first. This is sage advice, but the duties referred to at 42.21 should always be borne in mind. Pricing analytics may assist in knowing what pricing options to offer (see 42.39).
- **Contract of retainer** Baker suggests that the most appropriate type of retainer in a case to which value-based charging applies is a fixed-priced agreement. That is no doubt correct in many US states, but other types of contract of retainer may be appropriate in this jurisdiction (see 42.28). Indeed, it is possible to create value solely by offering an imaginative contract of retainer (see 42.28–42.30).
- **Implement legal project management** In matters that require it, legal project management ought to be implemented. In particular, Baker advises focusing on ensuring that the scope of the project is properly defined (see 41.16) and that appropriate use is made of 'change requests' (see 41.55–41.59). He also recommends that capacity and cash-flow modelling is carried out.
- **Post-project review** Finally, Baker advises that any project or matter should conclude with a post-project review (see 41.60), otherwise known as an after-action review.

In addition, Baker suggests that firms should appoint a chief value officer (see 42.37).

Value from the client's perspective

42.25 From a client's perspective in this jurisdiction, 'value' is likely to include matters such as:

- expertise, experience and specialism (especially where this is likely to lessen exposure to risk or increase the ability to manage that risk);
- innovative solutions to problems (especially where those solutions are based on intellectual property or information systems that are not easily available elsewhere);
- predictability as to the fees payable;
- deferment of payment of fees[15] or discounts;
- turnaround time for providing legal services and the ability to carry out work urgently;
- excellent client care, communication and accessibility;
- access to financial services, such as access to after-the-event (ATE) insurance or litigation funding;[16]
- innovative fee structures, such as weekly, monthly or yearly retainers;
- conditional funding (whether on the basis of conditional fee agreements, damages-based agreements or other such fee arrangements); and
- ring-fencing of damages or certainty as to how much the client will actually pay in addition to monies recovered from an opponent.

[15] Care should be taken not to create a contract of retainer that is governed by the Consumer Credit Acts.

[16] This may be a factor to be taken into account, but it would probably be professionally improper to charge a client a premium for providing such services.

Pricing options based on level of service

It can be seen from the above list that it would usually be easy—even in an unremarkable matter—to offer a client a range of options based on different levels of service or other such matters that the client regards as having value. This is where Baker's 'Goldilocks' pricing'—offering three options—becomes relevant. **42.26**

It should be noted that it is not the case that value-based charging necessarily means that the legal services provider tries to 'upsell' its services by offering superior services at a premium. Indeed, quite the opposite may be true: if, for example, a client were particularly concerned about cost, it may appropriate to offer a lower level of service at a discount because the client would see value in the discount. That would still be value-based pricing, but such an approach may be very much in the interests of the legal services provider because it may result in high volumes of work or a better quality of work. **42.27**

Contracts of retainer and pricing options

In addition to the client being offered differing levels of service, the client may be offered a range of fee structures. Indeed, those fee structures may, of themselves, add value (as can be seen from the list in 42.25). The phrase 'alternative fee agreements' is often used to refer to such structures—although this phrase tends to be restricted to fee agreements that are 'alternative' in the sense that they are not based solely on hourly billing, rather than 'alternative' in the sense that they comprise a range of options.[17] **42.28**

Whilst Baker is a strong advocate of fixed-price agreements, in this jurisdiction the following may be offered (all of which lend themselves to value-based pricing): **42.29**

- fixed-fee agreements (including on a case-by-case basis,[18] a per task basis, a flat monthly retainer basis[19] or a yearly retainer basis[20]);
- volume purchase discounts;[21]
- damages-based agreements (in which case, the 'value' to the client could be reflected in the level of the damages-based payment);
- contingency fee agreements (in non-contentious matters only); and
- fixed-fee conditional fee agreements (in which a fixed fee is payable only in the event of success).

[17] The American Bar Association has the following to say on the point: 'AFAs are not about charging more than what an hourly rate might be — they are about charging an appropriate fee based on what value the client receives and how that client perceives value. Alternative billing should be based on what is fair and reasonable both to the client and the lawyer. Keeping track of time should be the lawyer's measure of cost, not necessarily a measure of the value he or she is providing the clients in their legal needs.' See Robertson, MA, 'Marketing Alternative Fee Arrangements' (2011) 37(5) Law Practice, online at https://www.americanbar.org/publications/law_practice_magazine/2011/september_october/alternative_fee_arrangements.html

[18] It is not only consumers who are attracted by such fee arrangements; Pfizer Inc, for example, often instructs lawyers on this basis: see *ibid.* In any event, 48 per cent of consumer clients who purchase legal services now pay for them via a fixed fee, with the number being higher in more commoditised areas such as conveyancing (in which it is 68 per cent): see Legal Services Board, *Prices of Individual Consumer Legal Services Research Report* (West Malling: OMB Research, 2016), available online at https://research.legalservicesboard.org.uk/wp-content/media/Prices-of-Individual-Consumer-Legal-Services.pdf

[19] Cisco Systems often engages legal services providers on this basis: see ibid.

[20] Tyco International often engages lawyers on this basis: see *ibid.*

[21] See Law Society, *Price and Service Transparency Toolkit* (London: Law Society, 2016), p 5, available online at http://www.lawsociety.org.uk/support-services/advice/articles/price-and-service-transparency-toolkit/

Where any of the above are used, it may be possible to avoid having to record time (see 42.43).

42.30 In addition to the above, it may be possible to offer fee structures that are a hybrid of value-based pricing and costs-plus pricing. Again, those fee structures may, of themselves, add value. The following may fall into that category:

- conditional fee agreements (in which case, the 'value' to the client could be reflected in the success fee, but only within the limits of that which is reasonable);
- contracts of retainer that ring-fence damages;
- contracts of retainer that limit the amount that the client will pay in addition to those monies that are recovered in costs from an opponent (see 42.13); and
- other hybrid agreements (such as those that provide for both a blended hourly rate and some other means of charging).

Where any of the above are used, it would generally be necessary to record time and this would mean that the benefits of not recording time (see 42.43) would be lost. This is one of the main reasons why Baker recommends the use of non-hybrid fee agreements.

Legal project management and value-based pricing

42.31 Where value-based pricing leads to any of the contracts of retainer referred to at 42.29, then it would be necessary for the legal services provider to know in advance what the cost of the legal services is likely to be (that is, the cost to the legal services provider, not the client); if it were otherwise, the legal services provider could easily make a loss. It would also be desirable to know the anticipated cost in advance of entering into any of the contracts of retainer listed at 42.30. In smaller or 'commoditised' cases, the anticipated cost may be obvious from historical data,[22] but where this is not the case, then legal project management may be required.

42.32 Legal project management is addressed in Chapter 41. As can be seen, it is a process that often focuses on the time and cost of providing legal services (see, for example, the discussion of work breakdown structures at 41.33–41.34). That may be so, but it would be a mistake to believe that this implies that legal project management must go hand in hand with costs-plus pricing. Legal project management may work well with costs-plus pricing,[23] but it also works well with value-based pricing. This is because legal project management tends to be a prospective exercise in which project control tools are used to ensure that costs are controlled, thereby allowing the legal services to be priced on a basis that is limited, but not dictated, by the cost of providing the services. As to the prospective nature of legal project management, Baker and Chisholm have the following to say:

> 'Project management is about forecasting the future looking forward. Timesheets look backwards. By definition, by the time you see something on a timesheet, it is no longer manageable. This is the equivalent of timing your cookies with your smoke alarm.'

[22] In this regard, the American Bar Association gives the following advice: 'Data mine your files. Your closed files may well be your greatest resource in determining what might work for AFAs.' See *ibid*; see also Heineman Jr, BW, 'Getting Your Fix', *Corporate Counsel*, September 2009, p 74.

[23] Indeed, Baker, R, *Implementing Value Pricing: A Radical Business Model for Professional Firms* (Hoboken, NJ: John Wiley & Sons, 2011), p 119, has the following to say on that point: 'Even if your firm only "bills by the hour" project management is vital, as you must plan how work that comes in is allocated, what resources are devoted to it, what are the deadlines, and the myriad other issues that proper project management deals with. This is simply a table stake of operating an effective organization; it is not at all tied to pricing.'

In any event, the focus on time in legal project management tends to be on timetabling and duration, rather than on time, as a determinant of fees. This is relevant to value-based pricing because adherence to a timetable and the efficient provision of legal services is likely to be a factor that a client will regard as being valuable.[24] Baker and Chisholm have this to say on the topic: 'Like FedEx [a logistics firm], firms should measure turnaround time, both at the firm-wide level and team-member level. This is what the clients care about. Shouldn't we use the same measurements the clients do to assess our success?' **42.33**

That said, the cost of having fee earners spending time on a matter—or 'effort', in the parlance of legal project management—will have a direct bearing on the cost of providing the legal services in question. This is a 'constraint' for the purposes of legal project management, in the sense that fees (however calculated) must not fall below that level. As Baker and Chisholm point out, the need to know about such matters is something that needs to be addressed prospectively, rather than retrospectively. **42.34**

Post-project reviews

Post-project reviews (also known as after-action reviews) are, as their name implies, reviews that look back at what happened during the provision of legal services. In management circles, much is made of the fact that they were an invention of the US Army, but, notwithstanding this, they have utility in the context of the provision of legal services. Baker and Chisholm have this to say on the point: **42.35**

> 'Perhaps we ignore innovations in the military because its mission—to break things and kill people—is so divergent from that of a business organization. But this is far too parochial an attitude; and once again we discover a useful practice from another sector. Here are the questions you need to ask in each AAR:
>
> - What was supposed to happen?
> - Why actually happened (the "ground truth")?
> - What were the positive and negative factors here?
> - What have we learned and how can we do better next time?'

A full exposition of what happens during a post-project review is beyond the scope of this book, but Baker and Chisholm provide more guidance in an excellent podcast.[25] **42.36**

Chief Value Officers

Baker advocates that each firm should appoint a chief value officer (CVO), otherwise known as a pricing director. He has this to say on the point: **42.37**

> 'Pricing is far too important to the viability of the company to be left to mediocre pricers. No other area—not cost cutting, efficiency increases or growth—can have as large an

[24] This is what Eliyahu M Goldratt pointed out in his book, *The Goal*, which explains his 'theory of constraints': Goldratt, EM, *The Goal* (Barrington, MA: North River Press, 1984).

[25] See Baker, R, and Kless, E, 'The Best Learning Method Ever Devised: After Action Reviews', *The Soul of Enterprise*, Episode #15, 13 October 2014, available online at https://www.thesoulofenterprise.com/tsoe/aar

impact on profitability as does pricing. It is time for organizations to recognize that, if they are serious about pricing their offerings commensurate with the value they create, they need to establish a core group of enthusiastic pricers to make pricing a core competency within the firm.'[26]

There are examples of legal services providers in the UK that have already appointed chief value officers, although these presently tend to be only very large firms.[27]

42.38 A chief value officer would be responsible for ensuring the creation and maximisation of value, and for attending to pricing strategy and analytics. This may involve ensuring a consistent approach to pricing within a firm and that pricing policies are well understood by all concerned. This can be particularly important for larger firms—especially those with many offices.

Pricing Strategies, Analytics and Reporting

42.39 The (complex) issues of pricing strategies, analytics and reporting are largely beyond the scope of this book, but the following brief comments can be made.

42.40 The first, and perhaps most important, point to make is that whilst it is always appropriate to offer clients value for money, it would rarely be sensible simply to try to undercut competitors' prices; rather, a balance has to be struck. Mark Striving, a US pricing consultant, has the following comments to make on the topic:

> 'First, pricing can be very destructive. When you lower your prices, that certainly hurts your competitors. When they retaliate, and they almost certainly will, that will hurt you as well. In the end, the most likely result is lower industry profits, including yours.
>
> Second, you can't un-explode a nuclear bomb. Similarly, it is extremely difficult to raise prices again once a price war begins. Companies rarely want to unilaterally raise prices and risk giving up market share to their competitors. Coordinating price increases in an industry is challenging and it's illegal if done through direct communication.
>
> Third, pricing can be considered a deterrent. Your competitors are much less likely to lower prices if they believe you are going to follow suit and not let them easily take your market share. The real trick to this is to monitor and control your costs. You never want to be in the position where a competitor can price below your cost of doing business.'[28]

42.41 In the context of value-based pricing, whilst it may be appropriate to offer a discount (see 42.27), in general the better business practice would be to strive to keep prices high to reflect the provision of value. Whilst an obvious point, it is far easier to do this if a legal services provider is able to distinguish themselves by offering innovative services or by offering commonplace services in an innovative way. Indeed, Baker and Chisholm place great emphasis on innovation.

[26] Baker, R, 'What's a Chief Value Officer and How Can It Give You a Competitive Advantage?', available online at https://quickbooks.intuit.com/r/pricing-strategy/whats-a-chief-value-officer-and-how-can-it-give-you-a-competitive-advantage/

[27] Baker & McKenzie, for example, has had one since 2011.

[28] Stiving, M, 'Pricing is … the Nuclear Bomb of Business', *pragmaticpricing.com*, 12 September 2013, available online at https://pragmaticpricing.com/2013/09/12/pricing-is-the-nuclear-bomb-of-business/

Pricing analytics and reporting is a process by which data is collected to allow pricing strategies to be set. Richard Burcher (a UK consultant on legal pricing) gives the following advice: 42.42

- 'Focus attention not on how much data you can extract from practice management and other software but on producing actionable insights to the right people at the right time.
- Collate and make available as much historical analysis of pricing and profitability as possible, and ensure the firm applies this learning, especially when setting fixed fee arrangements. Toby Brown, one of the founders of the P3 legal pricing group, regularly presents to groups of law firm pricing and analytics managers and recommends that firms also mine the date from their experience base of lost tenders and pitches to learn what pricing positions have not worked.
- Invest in proper analytics capability, and not simply something cobbled together in an Excel spreadsheet.'[29]

Practising without Recording Time

The only circumstances in which it would, for the purposes of providing a service to clients, be mandatory to record time spent would be where there was a need to do so for the purposes of recovering costs from an opponent or for regulatory purposes. This would cover many civil disputes between opposing parties, but not those in which (a) costs were not recoverable in principle or (b) costs were necessarily fixed. Moreover, there will be circumstances—such as where a claim proceeds on the small claims track—in which the chances of costs being awarded and then assessed (either by way of summary or detailed assessment) are so remote that it would be reasonable not to record time prospectively, but instead to rely on retrospective estimates of time spent, should the need arise. As such, there will be many circumstances in which there would be no obvious need to record time for the purposes of protecting the client's position as regards the recovery of costs. As the ambit of CPR, Part 45, grows, that state of affairs will become increasingly common. 42.43

This invites the question of whether it is necessary to record time for business purposes. There are two aspects to this topic: first, whether it is necessary to record time for the purpose of billing clients; and secondly, whether it is necessary to record time for the purposes of providing information about the business. 42.44

The first question is easy to answer: there will be a need to record time for the purposes of billing only if this is required by the contract of retainer. Thus, if any of the contracts of retainer described at 42.29 are used, that need will not exist. 42.45

The second question is less easy to answer: opinions are divided on the issue. There are those who say that it is a business imperative. In its Legal Project Management Best Practices Series, for example, LexMundi has this to say: 42.46

> 'It seems that for firms using steadily more [alternative fee arrangement] pricing, timekeeping is even more important now than it was in the days when hourly rate pricing ruled supreme. In this new market, firms with the greatest insight are most likely to succeed, and they need ever more accurate, comprehensive and timely information about productivity and utilization in order to manage profitability and engineer continuous improvement in

[29] Burcher, R, 'So, You're Going to Nail This Pricing Business in 2015?', *Validatum.com*, 29 January 2015, no longer available online.

efficiency. Without that data, the firm is forced back to the kind of broadbrush financial reporting that passed for "business intelligence" a decade ago.'[30]

42.47 This is certainly one point of view, but Baker and Chisholm strongly argue against such an approach. They say that, in appropriate circumstances, time recording is neither necessary nor desirable. This book does not attempt to resolve the dispute, but it does aim to explain why Baker and Chisholm take that view. They cite the fact that legal services providers wrongly point to four reasons why time recording is necessary:

- for the purposes of pricing;
- for the purposes of legal project management;
- to evaluate the efficiency of fee earners; and
- for cost accounting and business intelligence purposes.

Each is addressed in turn. It should be noted that the editor has adapted Baker and Chisholm's arguments to better suit this jurisdiction.

Why time recording may not be necessary

Is time recording needed for the purposes of pricing?

42.48 For the reasons set out elsewhere in this chapter, where it is appropriate to offer value-based pricing, time recording will not be necessary for the purposes of pricing. This would certainly be true in so far as any individual case was concerned, but, for the reasons set out at 42.52 *et seq*, Baker and Chisholm also make a powerful case for it not being true in so far as the firm (or relevant part thereof) is concerned.

Is time recording needed for the purposes of legal project management?

42.49 For the reasons set out at 42.31–42.34, the focus on 'time' for the purpose of legal project management is not the same as time recording in the sense of keeping timesheets in the traditional sense. In particular, legal project management tends to focus on timetabling and duration. Moreover, the whole point of legal project management is to manage effort prospectively (that is, during planning) and, provided that project management tools are appropriately used, there is no need to slavishly keep timesheets. That said, the single biggest outlay that legal services providers have is the cost of employing staff, so if traditional time recording is not used, it must be replaced with some other form of information management system. Those may or may not have regard to time spent, but, for the reasons set out below, there is no need for them to be based on traditional time recording.

Is time recording needed for to evaluate the efficiency of fee earners?

42.50 The argument here (in support of time recording) is that the only way of knowing whether fee earners are performing efficiently is to measure the hours that they spend engaging in profitable work. Indeed, many fee earners will be familiar with targets laid out in terms of billable hours. Whilst no one would advocate turning a blind eye to a fee earner who never engages with their keyboard (see 42.56), Baker and Chisholm point out that monitoring time spent is not a good indicator of effectiveness in the context of value-based pricing. They would no doubt agree with the comments made by Michael Cook as long ago as the

[30] LexMundi, *Best Practices Guide to Implementing Alternative Fee Arrangements and Next Generation Pricing Strategies*, Legal Project Management Best Practices Series, 2016, available online at https://static1.squarespace.com/static/58a0a009a5790a7c3fc0fdb8/t/5965838ef7e0abde9da27e4b/1499825039119/LEX_BestPracticesAlternateFee.pdf

1990s, when—in his own inimitable way—he described billing by the hour as the 'painful plodders' charter'.[31] In the context of costs-plus pricing, that charter would benefit the firm; in the context of value-based pricing, it benefits no one.

Baker and Chisholm go further, pointing out that efficiency (which is mathematical ratio) is not the same as effectiveness. They go on to say this: 'Efficiency cannot be meaningfully defined without regards to your purpose, desires, and preferences. It cannot simply be reduced to output per man-hour. It is inextricably linked to what people want—and at what cost people are willing to pay.' **42.51**

Is time recording needed for cost accounting purposes?

Cost accounting is an accounting method that aims to capture the costs of providing services by assessing the input costs of each step, as well as fixed costs (such as depreciation of capital equipment). It will first measure and record these costs individually, then compare input results to output or actual results, to aid company management in measuring financial performance.[32] It is possible to use cost accounting to describe a business's external condition, but it offers little insight into the particular inner relationships that determine results.[33] **42.52**

One may think that a legal services provider would need to engage in time recording for the purposes of cost accounting. That may be true in certain circumstances, but Baker and Chisholm say that this would not be a reason to engage in that activity if value-based pricing (or, for that matter, any system of pricing not based on cost-plus pricing) is to be used, because cost accounting may not be required at all in such circumstances. They point out that Toyota Motor Manufacturing has never employed any standard form of cost accounting,[34] because it has deployed project management in its place—and the effect of this is that Toyota sets a budget, then works to that budget. Toyota has *information* systems in place (for the purposes of ensuring that it is working to plan), but no standard cost accounting systems. Costing takes place in advance, rather than retrospectively. **42.53**

In any event, Baker and Chisholm assert that time recording is not a good way of cost accounting. They have this to say on the point: **42.54**

> 'Your hourly rate is not even an accurate cost allocation method. This is for the following reasons:
> 1. It is inclusive of profit: There is no such thing as allocating profit in cost accounting. That is profit forecasting, not cost accounting. Opportunity cost has no place in cost accounting either, as it is an economic concept, not a cost accounting concept.
> 2. Even if you remove the profit component from your hourly rate, it still bears no relationship to your firm's actual costs. Since most firms establish their hourly rates based upon reverse competition—that is, what your competitors charge—the cost component

[31] See Cook, MJ, *Cook on Costs* (London: Butterworths, 2000), p 191. That said, see the Irish case of *Sheehan v Corr* [2016] IECA 168, at [118], in which Cregan J said that that argument was 'unsustainable'.

[32] Investopedia, 'Cost Accounting', available online at https://www.investopedia.com/terms/c/cost-accounting.asp

[33] Johnson, HT, and Bröms, A, *Profit beyond Measure: Extraordinary Results through Attention to Work and People* (Boca Raton, FL: Productivity Press, 2000). H. Thomas Johnson is an American accounting historian, professor of business administration at Portland State University and one of the pioneers of the activity-based costing movement. The book *Profit beyond Measure* is a seminal work in which Johnson and Bröms profile Toyota and Scania as two manufacturers that do not have a standard cost accounting system.

[34] *Ibid.*

is completely arbitrary. I have yet to encounter more than a handful of firms that actually tie out their cost per hour to the general ledger.
3. With the timesheet, you are attempting to run a Profit & Loss statement on every hour of work logged. This is absurd, since your firm is an interdependent system and cannot be atomized into a series of recorded hours. What matters is profitability across the entire firm, the same logic we use with our investment portfolios, which contain different levels of risk and reward assets.
4. The hourly cost allocation gives no weight to the lifetime value of the client—and the lifetime value of the firm to the client.

These are egregious errors for the accounting profession to commit, given its supposed fastidiousness when it comes to dealing with numbers.'

42.55 The second of the points that Baker and Chisholm make above is particularly relevant in this jurisdiction, because, over the last few years, there has developed an almost complete disconnect between the 'Expense of Time' calculation and hourly rates (see 51.27–51.43).

What are the alternatives to time recording in matters that are subject to value-based pricing?

42.56 Baker and Chisholm certainly do not advocate that time recording should be abandoned with nothing put in its place; instead, they suggest several key performance indicators (KPIs) that may take its place in matters in which value-based pricing is used. They say that it may be appropriate to select different KPIs for different clients (or categories of clients) and that, in some instances, it may be appropriate to discuss with clients which KPIs should be used.

42.57 The KPIs that Baker and Chisholm point to as being particularly well suited to use in matters subject to value-based pricing include the following.

- **Turnaround time** Baker and Chisholm say that law firms should be diligent about tracking when each matter comes in, establishing a desired completion date and measuring the proportion of matters that are completed on time. They say that turnaround time can be tracked at the firm-wide level, as well as the fee-earner level, and that turnaround time (unlike time recording) is a leading indicator of performance, in the sense that poor turnaround times in respect of any given fee earner may alert a firm to problems before they became entrenched.
- **Innovation revenue** This metric maps revenue from services introduced in recent years against the legal service provider's innovation in offering additional services to its clients. Again, it has the advantage over time recording of being a leading indicator of performance.
- **Actual client referrals** This, for obvious reasons, is a useful metric for a firm. Again, it has the advantage of being a leading indicator.
- **Number and quality of client contacts** Baker and Chisholm say that many clients who disinstruct legal services providers do so because of perceived indifference on the part of the latter, and they suggest that monitoring the number and quality of client contacts is a useful way of preventing this. Such an approach would go hand in hand with the points made about stakeholder engagement and communications plans at 41.46.
- **Value gap** This measurement attempts to gauge the gap between how much the firm could be yielding from its clients compared to how much it is actually yielding.

Part XII

ASSESSMENTS, APPEALS AND ALTERNATIVE DISPUTE RESOLUTION BETWEEN OPPOSING PARTIES

43

DETAILED ASSESSMENTS BETWEEN OPPOSING PARTIES

This chapter deals with the procedural aspects of detailed assessments between opposing parties. In particular, it deals with the following topics: **43.01**

- the venue for detailed assessment proceedings:
  - venue—the 'appropriate office' (43.02);
  - allocation within the judiciary (43.10);
- case management in detailed assessment proceedings (43.25);
- the form and content of the bill of costs (43.29):
  - old-style bills of costs (43.33);
  - bills of costs—contents (43.38);
  - new-style bills of costs (43.43);
- commencement of detailed assessment proceedings (43.51):
  - commencement—miscellaneous points (43.55);
  - when proceedings may be commenced (43.60);
  - late commencement and delay (43.85);
- points of dispute (43.108):
  - format (43.109);
  - content (43.111);
  - variation (43.125);
  - time limits (43.126);
  - service (43.135);
  - failure to serve (43.139);
- default costs certificates (43.140):
  - issue (43.142);
  - setting aside (43.149);
  - *pro bono* work (43.165);
- replies to points of dispute (43.166):
  - format (43.167);
  - procedure (43.168);
  - content (43.171);
- requesting an assessment (43.176):
  - time limits (43.177);
  - form of request (43.178);

- accompanying documents (43.181);
- fees (43.186);
- delay (43.190);

• provisional assessments (43.196):
- history and pilots (43.198);
- jurisdiction (43.200);
- procedure (43.207);
- costs (43.229);

• agreed costs and putative agreements (43.239):
- uncontested agreements as to costs (43.240);
- disputes regarding putatively settled costs ('contested agreements') (43.250);

• offers to settle detailed assessment proceedings (43.252);

• detailed assessment hearings (43.302):
- preparation (43.305);
- statements of costs for detailed assessment hearings (43.309);
- submissions (43.312);
- disclosure of offers (43.315);
- judgments (43.317);
- determination of issues of fact (43.320);
- issues as between legal services provider and client (43.326);

• liability for costs of detailed assessment proceedings (43.327):
- incidence (43.329);
- interest (43.370);
- procedure (43.373);
- rules and directions (43.374);

• interim costs certificates (43.376);
- jurisdiction (43.377);
- discretion (43.378);
- procedure (43.379);

• final costs certificates and the conclusion of the assessment (43.383):
- final filing (43.384);
- final costs certificates (43.388);
- the wording of relevant provisions (43.392);

• discontinuing costs proceedings and withdrawal (43.394):
- the wording of the relevant provisions (43.395);
- discontinuance without consent (43.403);
- discontinuance with consent (43.406); and

• enforcement (43.407).

The Venue for Detailed Assessment Proceedings

The 'appropriate office'

Rule 47.4 of the Civil Procedure Rules (CPR) refers to assessments being dealt with by the 'appropriate office'—that is, the court office that will deal with the assessment.[1] The CPR makes provision for cases to be referred to or between courts.[2] **43.02**

The following points may be made about 'appropriate offices'.[3] **43.03**

- **County Court hearing centres and district registries in London** Where a detailed assessment is initially dealt with by a County Court hearing centre or High Court district registry in London, the appropriate office will, in general, be the Senior Courts Costs Office (SCCO).[4]
- **County Court hearing centres and district registries outside of London** Where the costs order was made whilst the matter was being dealt with by a district registry or a County Court hearing centre outside London, the appropriate office will, in general, be that district registry or hearing centre.

---

[1] There is a difference between an assessment being transferred to a court and a case being referred to a court as the appropriate office (see CPR, r 47.4(4)). The former will mean that the assessment and any subsequent appeal will be heard at the destination court, but the latter means that whilst the assessment would usually be heard at the destination court, any subsequent appeal would revert back to the originating court. For a discussion of this, see *The Public Service Ombudsman for Wales v Heesom* [2015] EWHC 3306 (QB).

[2] See CPR, r 47.4, which provides: '(1) All applications and requests in detailed assessment proceedings must be made to or filed at the appropriate office. (Practice Direction 47 sets out the meaning of "appropriate office" in any particular case) (2) The court may direct that the appropriate office is to be the Costs Office. (3) In the County Court, a court may direct that another County Court hearing centre is to be the appropriate office. (4) A direction under paragraph (3) may be made without proceedings being transferred to that court. (Rule 30.2 makes provision for the transfer within the County Court of proceedings for detailed assessment of costs.)'

[3] See PD 47, para 4.1, which provides: 'For the purposes of rule 47.4(1) the "appropriate office" means—(a) the district registry or County Court hearing centre in which the case was being dealt with when the judgment or order was made or the event occurred which gave rise to the right to assessment, or to which it has subsequently been transferred; (b) where a tribunal, person or other body makes an order for the detailed assessment of costs, a County Court hearing centre (subject to paragraph 4.2); or (c) in all other cases, including Court of Appeal cases, the Costs Office.' See also HM Courts & Tribunals Services, *Senior Courts Costs Office Guide* (London: HMSO, 2018), para 10.7.

[4] PD 47, para 4.2, makes the following provisions: '(1) This paragraph applies where the appropriate office is any of the following County Court hearing centres: Barnet, Bow, Brentford, Bromley, Central London, Clerkenwell and Shoreditch, Croydon, Edmonton, Ilford, Kingston, Lambeth, Mayors and City of London, Romford, Uxbridge, Wandsworth, West London, Willesden and Woolwich. (2) Where this paragraph applies—(a) the receiving party must file any request for a detailed assessment hearing in the Costs Office and, for all purposes relating to that detailed assessment (other than the issue of default costs certificates and applications to set aside default costs certificates), the Costs Office will be treated as the appropriate office in that case; (b) default costs certificates should be issued and applications to set aside default costs certificates should be issued and heard in the relevant County Court hearing centre; and (c) unless an order is made under rule 47.4(2) directing that the Costs Office as part of the High Court shall be the appropriate office, an appeal from any decision made by a Costs Judge shall lie to the Designated Civil Judge for the London Group of County Court hearing centres or such judge as the Designated Civil Judge shall nominate. The appeal notice and any other relevant papers should be lodged at the Central London Civil Justice Centre.'

- **Specialist lists** Where the claim was in the Administrative Court, the Technology and Construction Court or the Planning Court, the appropriate office will not necessarily be the SCCO, because these courts are specialist lists within the Queen's Bench Division[5] and, as such, the appropriate office will be the relevant district registry.
- **Other courts** In all other cases,[6] including Court of Appeal cases, the appropriate office will be the SCCO.
- **Tribunals, etc** Where the order was made by a tribunal, person or other body, the appropriate office will be a County Court hearing centre.

Referral to the SCCO

43.04 Regardless of where it originated, any court has the power to refer an assessment to the SCCO.[7] The following will be relevant to the exercise of the court's discretion:

- the size of the bill of costs;
- the difficulty of the issues involved;
- the likely length of the hearing;
- the cost to the parties; and
- any other relevant matter.[8]

43.05 Whether a court is able to refer an assessment to a regional costs judge is another factor that can, perhaps, be added to this list. The points made at 43.09 would probably also apply, if only by analogy. In general, if a case is only part heard, it will not be suitable for transfer to the SCCO unless the parties consent to the assessment starting afresh.[9]

Transfer between courts and hearing centres

43.06 Any County Court hearing centre has the power to refer a matter to any other County Court hearing centre.[10] The relevant procedure for specifying the appropriate office is set out in Practice Direction (PD) 47, para 4.3(1), which provides: 'A direction under rule 47.4(2) or (3) specifying a particular court, registry or office as the appropriate office may be given on application or on the court's own initiative.'

Transfer and its effect

43.07 An assessment may be transferred to a new court, rather than merely referred to that court as the appropriate office. If a case is transferred, then the effect is to transfer not only the assessment itself, but also the administrative responsibility and any subsequent appeal.

---

[5] See *The Public Service Ombudsman for Wales v Heesom* [2015] EWHC 3306 (QB), at [30], [42] and [47]–[54], *per* Hickenbottom J.

[6] Other than, of course, for matters in the Supreme Court.

[7] See CPR, r 47.4(2).

[8] See PD 47, para 4.3(2), which provides as follows: 'Unless the Costs Office is the appropriate office for the purposes of Rule 47.4(1) an order directing that an assessment is to take place at the Costs Office will be made only if it is appropriate to do so having regard to the size of the bill of costs, the difficulty of the issues involved, the likely length of the hearing, the cost to the parties and any other relevant matter.'

[9] Whilst not a source of authority, this is the advice given in SCCO, *Notes for New Deputy Masters* (London: HMSO, 2013), p 4.

[10] See CPR, r 47.4(3).

CPR, r 30.2, deals with transfers generally. In so far as it is relevant to detailed assessments, it makes the following provisions: **43.08**

'(1) A county court may order proceedings before that court, or any part of them ... to be transferred to another county court if it is satisfied that—
(a) an order should be made having regard to the criteria in rule 30.3; or
(b) proceedings for—
  (i) the detailed assessment of costs;
  [...]
could be more conveniently or fairly taken in that other county court.

[...]

(3) An application for an order under paragraph (1) or (2) must be made to the county court where the claim is proceeding.

(4) The High Court may, having regard to the criteria in rule 30.3, order proceedings in the Royal Courts of Justice or a district registry, or any part of such proceedings (such as a counterclaim or an application made in the proceedings), to be transferred—
(a) from the Royal Courts of Justice to a district registry; or
(b) from a district registry to the Royal Courts of Justice or to another district registry.

(5) A district registry may order proceedings before it for the detailed assessment of costs to be transferred to another district registry if it is satisfied that the proceedings could be more conveniently or fairly taken in that other district registry.

(6) An application for an order under paragraph (4) or (5) must, if the claim is proceeding in a district registry, be made to that registry.'

CPR, r 30.3, gives guidance on the factors to be taken into account when considering whether a matter should be transferred: **43.09**

'(1) Paragraph (2) sets out the matters to which the court must have regard when considering whether to make an order under—
(a) section 40(2), 41(1) or 42(2) of the County Courts Act 1984 (transfer between the High Court and a county court [*sic*]);
(b) rule 30.2(1) (transfer within the County Courts); or
(c) rule 30.2(4) (transfer between the Royal Courts of Justice and the district registries).

(2) The matters to which the court must have regard include—
(a) the financial value of the claim and the amount in dispute, if different;
(b) whether it would be more convenient or fair for hearings ... to be held in some other court;
(c) the availability of a judge specialising in the type of claim in question;
(d) whether the facts, legal issues, remedies or procedures involved are simple or complex;
(e) the importance of the outcome of the claim to the public in general;
(f) the facilities available at the court where the claim is being dealt with and whether they may be inadequate because of any disabilities of a party or potential witness;
(g) whether the making of a declaration of incompatibility under section 4 of the Human Rights Act 1998 has arisen or may arise;
(h) in the case of civil proceedings by or against the Crown, as defined in rule 66.1(2), the location of the relevant government department or officers of the Crown and, where appropriate, any relevant public interest that the matter should be tried in London.'

Allocation within the judiciary

Only issues concerning allocation are addressed in this chapter; jurisdictional issues are addressed in Chapter 5 (see 5.05–5.10 and 5.17–5.19). **43.10**

43.11 Judges and court officers who assess costs are formally referred to as 'costs officers'.[11] There are three types of costs officer who have recognised specialist skills in the ascertainment of civil costs:

- costs judges and deputy costs judges (see 5.03 and 43.12);
- regional costs judges (see 43.16); and
- authorised court officers (see 5.07 and 43.19).

In addition, generalist district judges will hear a significant number of detailed assessments and, when they act in that role, they too are costs officers.

Costs judges

43.12 The office of taxing master was created when the Court of Chancery Act 1842[12] abolished the Chancery Office of the Six Clerks (see 1.73). Specialist Chancery taxing masters used to exist up until the early 1900s, but that post has now been abolished as a separate appointment (see 1.106).

43.13 The term 'costs judge' is defined by CPR, r 44.1(1), as a 'taxing master of the Senior Courts'; all such judges (whether full-time or part-time) are based in the SCCO. In recognition of their specialist status, costs judges (regardless of gender) are usually addressed as 'Master'. Where the occasion demands, a costs judge will sit as a deputy district judge of the principal registry of the Family Division, or as deputy district judge of the County Court. Where a costs judge sits in one of those capacities, they will be vested with all of the powers of the relevant court.[13]

43.14 Other than to the extent that individual judges may not be available, cases are assigned on a fixed rotational basis (to ensure that there is no bias). Each incoming file is referred to a Master, who will determine whether the case is suitable for provisional assessment. If it is not, they will then assess the time estimate by reference to the points of dispute and the replies.

43.15 The file may be referred to a deputy costs judge for hearing. Deputies generally undertake civil or family cases listed for no more than two days. They do not hear solicitor-and-client assessments (see 5.08). They often hear routine applications, such as setting aside default costs certificates.[14]

Regional costs judges

43.16 Regional costs judges are district judges who have nurtured an interest in costs. The SCCO Guide 2018 defines them in the following way:

> 'A District Judge who has been appointed to sit in both the County Court and the District Registry of the High Court to carry out detailed assessments in most of the larger and more difficult cases in each region of England and Wales.'[15]

A regional costs judge may sit either in a County Court hearing centre or in the appropriate district registry of the High Court.

[11] See CPR, r 44.1(1). In practice, authorised court officers are almost always referred to as 'costs officers'; the formal usage of that phrase is almost never encountered in practice.

[12] An Act for abolishing certain offices of the High Court of Chancery in England, 5 & 6 Vict c 103.

[13] CPR, r 2.4.

[14] SCCO, *Notes for New Deputy Masters* (London: HMSO, 2013), p 4.

[15] HM Courts & Tribunals Services, *Senior Courts Costs Office Guide* (London: HMSO, 2018), Glossary.

The criteria for referral to a regional costs judge are as follows: **43.17**

'... the time estimate for the detailed assessment exceeds on day; and/or the sum claimed exceeds £100,000; and/or complex arguments on points of law, or an issue affecting a group of similar cases, are identified in the points of dispute or the reply or are referred to in argument at a detailed assessment hearing.'[16]

The following guidance is given on procedure: **43.18**

'Once a request for detailed assessment in Form N258 has been filed at court the bill will be referred to a District Judge who will consider whether it falls within the criteria for reference to a Regional Costs Judge. If it does, the bill will be referred to the appropriate Regional Costs Judge who will then decide whether to accept it and will give any directions required, including directions as to listing.

If a party wishes to make submissions as to whether any particular detailed assessment fulfils the criteria for reference to a Regional Costs Judge, or as to the most convenient court for any hearing before a Regional Costs Judge, they should first consult the other parties or their legal representatives before making submissions to the court. It is helpful if such submissions are filed with the court when the request for detailed assessment is lodged. If possible the parties should attempt to agree the reference to the Regional Costs Judge, any directions and the most convenient venue.'[17]

At the time of writing, there were 33 regional costs judges (see Table 68.2); no circuit was without a regional costs judge.

Authorised court officers

An authorised court officer is a civil servant (see 5.17) who hears those detailed assessments that are deemed appropriate for an unqualified tribunal. The correct title is 'court officer', but common usage has corrupted the term to 'costs officer'. Senior court officers are referred to as 'principal officers'; less senior court officers are referred to as 'senior executive officers' (SEOs). **43.19**

There are no authorised court officers outside the SCCO (although some costs officers are willing to travel to hear assessments in the provinces). Assessments are allocated to authorised court officers only if the sums claimed are less than £110,000, inclusive of additional liability, but exclusive of value added tax (VAT). In the SCCO, bills not exceeding £50,000 (exclusive of VAT) will generally be allocated to a costs officer as a matter of course.[18] The parties may agree that the assessment should not be heard by an authorised court officer.[19] If there is disagreement on this point, an application may be made for directions.[20] **43.20**

PD 47, para 3, gives the following guidance (also see 5.18): **43.21**

'3.1 The court officers authorised by the Lord Chancellor to assess costs in the Costs Office and the Principal Registry of the Family Division are authorised to deal with claims where the base costs excluding VAT do not exceed £35,000 in the case of senior executive officers, or their equivalent, and £110,000 in the case of principal officers.

[16] *Ibid*, para 1.1(c).
[17] *Ibid*, para 1.1(c).
[18] *Ibid*, para 12.4.
[19] See PD 47, para 3.2.
[20] See PD 47, para 3.3.

3.2 Where the receiving party, paying party and any other party to the detailed assessment proceedings who has served points of dispute are agreed that the assessment should not be made by an authorised court officer, the receiving party should so inform the court when requesting a hearing date. The court will then list the hearing before a costs judge.

3.3 In any other case a party who objects to the assessment being made by an authorised court officer must make an application to the costs judge under Part 23 setting out the reasons for the objection.'

43.22 In deciding whether or not a case is suitable for an authorised court officer, it may be relevant to consider the powers that they have. Those powers are set out in CPR, r 47.3:

'(1) An authorised court officer has all the powers of the court when making a detailed assessment, except—

(a) power to make a wasted costs order as defined in rule 46.8;
(b) power to make an order under—
    (i) rule 44.11 (powers in relation to misconduct);
    (ii) rule 47.8 (sanction for delay in commencing detailed assessment proceedings);
    (iii) paragraph (2) (objection to detailed assessment by authorised court officer); and
(c) power to make a detailed assessment of costs payable to a solicitor by that solicitor's client, unless the costs are being assessed under rule 46.4 (costs where money is payable to a child or protected party).

(2) Where a party objects to the detailed assessment of costs being made by an authorised court officer, the court may order it to be made by a costs judge.

(Practice Direction 47 sets out the relevant procedure.)'

43.23 Thus an authorised court officer neither has penal powers nor (for all practical purposes) is able to hear solicitor-and-client assessments. The restrictions relating to delay are not limited to misconduct; they also prevent an authorised court officer from adjudicating on the disallowance of interest.

43.24 CPR, r 3.2, empowers an authorised court officer to refer a juridical step to a costs judge.[21] It permits a referral of only part of an assessment. For example, if there is a dispute about the indemnity principle, a court officer may refer that part of the assessment only to a judge, but reserve the rest of the assessment to themselves.

Case Management in Detailed Assessment Proceedings

43.25 In most detailed or provisional assessments (with the possible exception of assessments of the costs of group litigation and very large bills), no case management will ordinarily be required. That said, where appropriate, any party can apply for case management directions, such as the exchange of witness statements and attendance for cross-examination, or directions concerning the detailed assessment of 'linked bills'.[22] Moreover, the SCCO Guide 2018 provides that, in the case of bills of costs exceeding £500,000, timetable directions may be given fixing a series of dates for the detailed assessment hearing.[23]

[21] It provides as follows: 'Where a step is to be taken by a court officer—(a) the court officer may consult a judge before taking that step; (b) the step may be taken by a judge instead of the court officer.'

[22] HM Courts & Tribunals Services, *Senior Courts Costs Office Guide* (London: HMSO, 2018), para 20.3, under 'Case management directions'.

[23] *Ibid.*

Costs management

In the case of larger bills in the SCCO in which a significant amount of court time and costs will be involved, the court will consider whether to order budgets to be prepared by the parties in relation to the costs of detailed assessment with a view to making a costs management order.[24] **43.26**

Orders that the detailed assessment be stayed

In a case in which a party had repeatedly failed to articulate its case properly such that they had already left the 'last-chance saloon', Teare J found that it was open to the court to stay the detailed assessment proceedings indefinitely, even if this effectively brought an end to the assessment.[25] This was a case concerning a solicitor-and-client assessment in which the solicitor had already been paid, but it is unlikely that anything turns on that. Teare J went on to find that such a stay did not amount to a breach of Art 6 of the European Convention on Human Rights (ECHR).[26] **43.27**

Debarring orders

Langley J has confirmed that if a party fails to meet its obligations under an order, the court is able to exercise its inherent jurisdiction, as preserved by CPR, r 3.1(1), to debar that party from taking any further part in the detailed assessment pending compliance with the order (see 43.382).[27] Langley J went on to say that such an order could also be justified as the exercise of the general power of the court to debar a party in contempt.[28] **43.28**

The Form and Content of Bills of Costs

This section deals with the form and content of bills of costs. There are two styles of bills of costs: the old-style bill of costs (which is a paper document), and the new-style bill of costs (which is an electronic document that is capable of being presented in paper form). The old-style bill of costs is likely to still be in use for many years, so both the old and the new styles are described in this section (see 43.33 and 43.43 respectively). **43.29**

The issue of whether the old- or new-style bill of costs is to be used is governed by PD 47, para 5.1, which reads as follows: **43.30**

> '5.1 In the circumstances provided for in this paragraph, bills of costs for detailed assessment must be in electronic spreadsheet format and compliant with paragraphs 5.A1 to 5.A4 ("electronic bills") while in all other circumstances bills of costs may be electronic bills or may be on paper ("paper bills") and compliant with paragraphs 5.7 to 5.21. Precedents A, B, C and D in the Schedule of Costs Precedents annexed to this Practice Direction are model forms of paper bills of costs for detailed assessment. The circumstances in which bills of costs must be electronic bills are that—
>
> (a) the case is a Part 7 multi-track claim, except—

24 *Ibid.*

25 *Mount Eden Land Ltd v Speechly Bircham LLP* [2014] EWHC 169 (QB), at [17] and [18].

26 *Ibid*, at [19].

27 *Days Healthcare UK Ltd v Pihsiang Machinery Manufacturing Co Ltd* [2006] EWHC 1444 (QB), at [18]–[20], [23] and [25]–[27]. See also *Hammond Suddard Solicitors v Agrichem International Holdings Ltd* [2001] EWCA Civ 2065, at [48], *per* Clarke LJ.

28 *Days Healthcare UK Ltd v Pihsiang Machinery Manufacturing Co Ltd* [2006] EWHC 1444 (QB), at [23].

(i) for cases in which the proceedings are subject to fixed costs or scale costs;
(ii) cases in which the receiving party is unrepresented; or
(iii) where the court has otherwise ordered; and
(b) the bills of costs relate to costs recoverable between the parties for work undertaken after 6 April 2018 ("the Transition Date").

43.31 Thus the new-style bill of costs *must* be used in the following circumstances:

- where the case is a Part 7 multitrack claim, except:
  - for cases in which the proceedings are subject to fixed costs or scale costs;
  - for cases in which the receiving party is unrepresented; or
  - where the court has otherwise ordered; and
- the bill of costs relates to costs recoverable between the parties for work undertaken after 6 April 2018 (that date being referred to as 'the transition date').

In all other circumstances, the old-style bill of costs *may* be used.

43.32 Further transitional provisions apply. They are found in PD 47, para 5.A4, which reads as follows:

> '5.A4 Where a bill of costs otherwise falls within paragraph 5.1(a) but work was done both before and after the Transition Date, a party may serve and file either a paper bill or an electronic bill in respect of work done before that date and must serve and file an electronic bill in respect of work done after that date.'

Thus, where the receiving party is required to use a new-style bill of costs (see 43.31), but work was carried out before 6 April 2018, they may, at their option, use an old-style bill of costs for that work. It is not likely, however, that many receiving parties would wish to do that, because presenting the costs in that way would be time-consuming and cumbersome.

The format of old-style bills of costs

43.33 The form and content of old-style bills of costs continues to be governed by PD 47, para 5.7. To an extent, this guidance also relates to new-style bills of costs (see 43.46). It reads as follows:

> '5.7 A bill of costs may consist of such of the following sections as may be appropriate—
> (1) title page;
> (2) background information;
> (3) items of costs claimed under the headings specified in paragraph 5.12;
> (4) summary showing the total costs claimed on each page of the bill;
> (5) schedules of time spent on non-routine attendances; and
> (6) the certificates referred to in paragraph 5.21.
>
> If the only dispute between the parties concerns disbursements, the bill of costs shall be limited to items (1) and (2) above, a list of the disbursements in issue and brief written submissions in respect of those disbursements.'

43.34 Old-style bills of costs are paper documents. That said, where they are capable of being copied electronically, the receiving party is required, on request, to supply the paying party with a copy in its native format (for example in MS Excel, MS Word or an equivalent), and they must do so free of charge and within seven days after receipt of the request.[29]

---

[29] PD 47, para 5.6.

The overall layout of bills of costs

The Precedent A old-style bill of costs may be found at Figure 43.1. The following points can be made about the overall structure. **43.35**

- **Title page** The title page is intended to set out:
  - the full title of the proceedings;
  - the name of the party whose bill of costs it is and a description of the document granting the right to an assessment;[30]
  - the VAT number of the legal representative or other person in respect of whom VAT is claimed; and
  - details of all relevant legal aid certificates, Legal Services Commission (LSC) certificates and relevant amendment certificates.[31]
- **Background information** Background information is often referred to as 'the narrative' (which must be distinguished from 'the narrative column': see below). In general, it contains the following:
  - a brief description of the proceedings up to the date of the notice of commencement;
  - a statement of the status of the legal representatives in respect of whom costs were claimed[32] and (if those costs are calculated on the basis of hourly rates) the hourly rates claimed for each such person (see 51.46); and
  - a brief explanation of any agreement or arrangement between the receiving party and their legal representatives that affected the costs claimed.[33]
    - Where the receiving party has the benefit of a pre-commencement funding arrangement, the background information often also contained the statement of reasons for setting the success fee at the level claimed (see 54.124).
- **Columns** The numbered items of cost are set out on pages divided into columns.[34] The column on the extreme left is the 'narrative column' (a column in which the items are described).[35] The columns to the right of the narrative column are the 'arithmetic columns' (that is, those columns that contain the amounts claimed).[36] There are three formats in ordinary usage,[37] as follows, the first of which is by far the most common.

---

30 These are defined at PD 47, para 13.3, in the following way: ' "The document giving the right to detailed assessment" means such one or more of the following documents as are appropriate to the detailed assessment proceedings: (a) a copy of the judgment or order of the court giving the right to detailed assessment; (b) a copy of the notice served under rule 3.7 (sanctions for non-payment of certain fees) where a claim is struck out under that rule; (c) a copy of the notice of acceptance where an offer to settle is accepted under Part 36 (Offers to settle); (d) a copy of the notice of discontinuance in a case which is discontinued under Part 38 (Discontinuance); (e) a copy of the award made on an arbitration under any Act or pursuant to an agreement, where no court has made an order for the enforcement of the award; (f) a copy of the order, award or determination of a statutorily constituted tribunal or body.'

31 See PD 47, para 5.10.

32 Other than guidance that used to be given as to the use of the term 'legal executive' (see CPD, art 4.5), the CPR do not prescribe the way in which the status of the fee earners should be described. That said, it is almost universally the case that this is done by reference to Grades A– D.

33 See PD 47, para 5.11.

34 See PD 47, para 5.17.

35 See now-revoked CPD, art 4.17, for a usage of this phrase.

36 CPD, art 4.17.

37 Precedents A, B and C in the Schedule of Costs Precedents annexed to **PD 47**, illustrate various model forms of bills of costs. All three types are illustrated there.

SCHEDULE OF COSTS PRECEDENTS

PRECEDENT A: MODEL FORM OF BILL OF COSTS

IN THE HIGH COURT OF JUSTICE 2011 – B – 9999

QUEEN'S BENCH DIVISION

BRIGHTON DISTRICT REGISTRY

BETWEEN

AB Claimant

- and –

CD Defendant

CLAIMANT'S BILL OF COSTS TO BE ASSESSED PURSUANT TO THE ORDER DATED 2ND APRIL 2013

VAT NO. 33 4404 90

In these proceedings the claimant sought compensation for personal injuries and other losses suffered in a road accident which occurred on 1st January 2011 near the junction between Bolingbroke Lane and Regency Road, Brighton, East Sussex. The claimant had been travelling as a front seat passenger in a car driven by the defendant. The claimant suffered severe injuries when, because of the defendant's negligence, the car left the road and collided with a brick wall.

The defendant was later convicted of various offences arising out of the accident including careless driving and driving under the influence of drink or drugs.

In the civil action the defendant alleged that immediately before the car journey began the claimant had known that the defendant was under the influence of alcohol and therefore consented to the risk of injury or was contributory negligent as to it. It was also alleged that, immediately before the accident occurred, the claimant wrongfully took control of the steering wheel so causing the accident to occur.

The claimant first instructed solicitors, E F & Co, in this matter in July 2011. The claim form was issued in October 2011 and in February 2012 the proceedings were listed for a two day trial commencing 25th July 2012. At the trial the defendant was found liable but the compensation was reduced by 25% to take account of contributory negligence by the claimant. The claimant was awarded a total of £78,256.83 plus £1,207.16 interest plus costs.

The claimant instructed E F & Co under a retainer which specifies the following hourly rates.

Partner - £217 per hour plus VAT
Assistant Solicitor - £192 per hour plus VAT
Other fee earners - £118 per hour plus VAT

Except where the contrary is stated the proceedings were conducted on behalf of the claimant by an assistant solicitor, admitted November 2008.

Item No.	*Description of work done*	*VAT £*	*Disburse-ments £*	*Profit Costs £*
	8th July 2011 - EF & Co instructed			
1.	7th October 2011 – Claim issued			
2.	Issue fee		685.00	
	21st October 2011 – Particulars of claim served 25th November 2011 – time for service of defence extended by agreement to 14th January 2012			
3.	Fee on allocation		220.00	
	20th January 2012 – case allocated to multi-track 9th February 2012 – Case management conference at which costs were awarded to the claimant and the costs were summarily assessed at £400 (paid on 24th February 2012)			
	23rd February 2012 – Claimant's list of documents			
	12th April 2012 – Part 36 Offer £25,000			
	13th April 2012 – Filing pre-trial checklist			
4.	Paid listing fee		110.00	
5.	Paid hearing fee		1090.00	
	25th July 2012 – Attending first day of trial: adjourned part heard Engaged in court 5.0 hours £960.00 Engaged in conference 0.75 hours £144.00 Travel and waiting 1.5 hours £288.00			
6.	Total solicitors fee for attending			1392.00
7.	Counsel's fee for trial (Miss GH)	400.00	2000.00	
8.	Fee of expert witness (Dr IJ)		850.00	
9.	Expenses of witnesses of fact		84.00	
	26th July 2012 – Attending second day of trial when judgment was given for the claimant in the sum of £78,256.53 plus £1207.16 interest plus costs			
	To summary:	**400.00**	**5039.00**	**1392.00**

Item No.	Description of work done	VAT £	Disburse-ments £	Profit Costs £
	Engaged in Court 3.00 hours £576.00			
	Engaged in conference 1.5 hours £288.00			
	Travel and waiting 1.5 hours £288.00			
10.	Total solicitor's fee for attending			1,152.00
11.	Counsel's fee for second day (Miss GH)	190.00	950.00	
	Claimant			
12.	8th July 2011 – First instructions: 0.75 hours by Partner:			162.75
	Other timed attendances in person and by telephone – See Schedule 1			
13.	Total fee for Schedule 1 – 7.5 hours			1,440.00
14.	Routine letters out and telephone calls – 29 (17+12) total fee			556.80
	Witnesses of Fact Timed attendances in person, by letter out and by telephone – See Schedule 2			
15.	Total fee for Schedule 2 – 5.2 hours			998.40
16.	Routine letters out, e-mails and telephone calls – 8 (4+2+2) total fee			153.60
17.	Paid travelling on 10th October 2011	4.59	22.96	
	Medical Expert (Dr IJ)			
18.	11 September 2011 – long letter out 0.33 hours fee			63.36
19.	31st January 2012 – long letter out 0.25 hours fee			48.00
20.	23rd May 2012 – telephone call 0.2 hours fee			38.40
21.	Routine letters out and telephone calls – 10 (6+4) total fee			192.00
22.	Dr IJ's fee for report	-	500.00	
	Defendant and his solicitor			
23.	8th July 2011 – timed letter sent 0.5 hours fee			96.00
24.	19th February 2012 – telephone call 0.25 hours fee			48.00
25.	Routine letters out and telephone calls – 24 (18+6) total fee			460.80
	Communications with the court			
26.	Routine letters out and telephone calls – 9 (8+1) total fee			172.80
	To summary:	**194.59**	**1,472.96**	**5,582.91**

3

Item No.	Description of work done	VAT £	Disburse-ments £	Profit costs £
	Communications with counsel			
27.	Routine letters out, e-mails and telephone calls – 19 (4+7+8) total fee			364.80
	Work done on documents			
28.	Timed attendance – see Schedule 3 Total fees for Schedule 3 – 0.75 hours at £217, 44.5 hours at £192, 12 hours at £118			10,122.75
	Work done on negotiations 23rd March 2012 – meeting at offices of solicitors for the Defendant Engaged - 1.5 hours £288 Travel and waiting – 1.25 hours £240			
29.	Total fee for meeting			528.00
	Other work done Preparing and checking bill Engaged solicitor – 1 hour £192 Engaged: Costs draftsman – 4 hours (at £110) £480			
30.	Total fee on other work done			672.00
31.	VAT on solicitor's fees (20% of £18,662.46)	3,731.49		
32.	VAT on Counsel's fees (20% of £3,950.00)	790.00		
	To summary:	**4,521.49**		**11,687.55**
	Summary			
	Page 2	**400.00**	**5,039.00**	**1,392.00**
	Page 3	**194.59**	**1,472.96**	**5,582.91**
	Page 4	**4,521.49**		**11,687.55**
	Totals:	**5,116.08**	**6,511.96**	**18,662.46**
	Grand Total			**30,290.50**

4

Figure 43.1 Precedent A: the old-style bill of costs (non-legal aid)

- **A three-column format**[38] Profit costs are claimed in the left-hand arithmetic column, disbursements in the middle arithmetic column and VAT in the right-hand arithmetic column.
- **A four-column format** In this format, the two left-most arithmetic columns contain profit costs and disbursements and VAT, respectively, and the two right-most arithmetic columns are left blank to record the amounts allowed.
- **A six-column format** This is either an expanded version of the four-column format (that is, with profit costs and disbursements each occupying one column) or it is a version in which one set of arithmetic columns relates to claims against the paying party and the other to claims against the LSC—although schedules are the prescribed option in LSC cases[39] (see 43.183).

• **Chronological entries** The next component of the bill of costs is often referred to as the 'chronology'. It comprises items such as the court fees, conferences, court hearings, etc. The intention is that, in addition to costs that relate to the entry in question, it includes items that would assist the court even though they bore no charge (so-called non-chargeable items). This would include, for example, orders and other major chronological landmarks.[40]

• **Attendances and routine items** Immediately after the chronological entries come the attendances and routine items. The order in which they are set out is not prescribed by any rule, but convention dictates that they be as follows:
  - attendances on the receiving party;
  - attendances on the paying party and/or any other party;
  - attendances on witnesses, including expert witnesses;
  - attendances on and by agents;
  - attendances on others;
  - non-chronological attendances on the court; and
  - non-chronological attendances on counsel.

• **Documents** The next item is often referred to as the 'documents item'. It is a record of time spent on documents, usually set out in a schedule to the bill of costs.

• **Additional liabilities** Where the receiving party has the benefit of a pre-commencement funding arrangement that provides for a success fee, such fees are usually claimed after each chronological item and then after the documents item for each part of the bill of costs. Alternatively, success fees are claimed at the end of each part of the bill of costs. After-the-event (ATE) premiums are often found towards the end of the bill of costs, but it is also common for them to be claimed as disbursements elsewhere in the bill of costs.

• **Costs of preparing and checking the bill of costs** The costs of drafting and checking the bill of costs (together with a success fee thereupon, if appropriate) are usually the final items to be claimed.

• **Summary** At the end of the bill of costs is a summary of the total costs claimed. It has to show the total profit costs and disbursements claimed separately from the total VAT.[41] Where the bill of costs is divided into parts (see 43.36), there must be a summary that gives

---

38 The narrative column is disregarded when describing a bill by reference to the number of columns it contains.

39 See PD 47, para 13.2(i)(iv).

40 In this regard, PD 47, para 5.16 provides as follows: '5.16 In each part of the bill of costs which claims items under head (1) in paragraph 5.12 (attendances at court and upon counsel) a note should be made of—(1) all relevant events, including events which do not constitute chargeable items; (2) any orders for costs which the court made (whether or not a claim is made in respect of those costs in this bill of costs).'

41 See PD 47, para 5.20.

the totals for each part. If each page of the bill of costs gives a page total (which is common, but not mandatory, practice), the summary also has to set out the totals for each page.[42]

- **Certificates** The bill of costs has to be signed and has to bear the 'appropriate certificates'.[43] This would always include:
  - a certificate as to accuracy and as to the indemnity principle;[44] and
  - a certificate as to interest and payments.[45]
  - Where appropriate, it also includes:
  - a certificate in respect of disbursements not exceeding £500;[46] and
  - a certificate as to recovery of VAT.[47]
  - In addition, if the receiving party has the benefit of a pre-commencement funding arrangement and where a legal representative wishes to claim a higher success fee from its client than that which is to be recovered from the paying party, there needs to be a certificate in accordance with pre-April 2013 Costs Practice Direction (CPD), art 20.6.[48] Other provisions apply where the receiving party was publicly funded.[49]
- **Schedules** If the number of attendances and communications (other than routine communications) in any one head of costs is 20 or more, those items have to be relegated to a schedule.[50]

Division of the bill of costs into parts

PD 47, para 5.8, gives guidance as to when a bill of costs ought to be divided into parts. To an extent, this guidance relates to new-style bills of costs (see 43.46) as well as to old-style bills of costs. It reads as follows: **43.36**

> '5.8 Where it is necessary or convenient to do so, a bill of costs may be divided into two or more parts, each part containing sections (2), (3) and (4) above. Circumstances in which it will be necessary or convenient to divide a bill into parts include the following—
>
> (1) Where the receiving party acted in person during the course of the proceedings (whether or not that party also had a legal representative at that time) the bill must be divided into different parts so as to distinguish between;
> (a) the costs claimed for work done by the legal representative; and
> (b) the costs claimed for work done by the receiving party in person.

42 Ibid.

43 See PD 47, para 5.21.

44 See precedent (1) in Schedule F to the Schedule of Costs Precedents annexed to PD 47.

45 See precedent (2) in Schedule F to the Schedule of Costs Precedents annexed to PD 47.

46 See precedent (5) in Schedule F to the Schedule of Costs Precedents annexed to PD 47.

47 See precedent (6) in Schedule F to the Schedule of Costs Precedents annexed to PD 47.

48 That rule provides that the certificate must state the following: that the amount of the percentage increase is disputed, either in respect of counsel's fees or the solicitor's fees; whether the solicitor will make an application for an order that the aforesaid shortfall remains payable by its client; that the solicitor has given its client an explanation in accordance with CPD, art 20.5; and whether the client wishes to attend court when the amount of any relevant percentage increase is to be decided. A precedent can be found in ch 44 of the second edition of this book.

49 In all cases in which the client is publicly funded, the certificate must include a certificate as to interest of assisted person/LSC-funded client, pursuant to Civil Legal Aid (General) Regulations 1989 (SI 1989/339), reg 119; where appropriate, it will also contain consent to the signing of the certificate within 21 days of detailed assessment, pursuant to regs 112 and 121. See precedents (3) and (4) in Schedule F to the Schedule of Costs Precedents annexed to PD 47.

50 See PD 47, para 5.18.

(2) Where the receiving party had *pro bono* representation for part of the proceedings and an order under section 194(3) of the Legal Services Act 2007 has been made, the bill must be divided into different parts so as to distinguish between—
    (a) the sum equivalent to the costs claimed for work done by the legal representative acting free of charge; and
    (b) the costs claimed for work not done by the legal representative acting free of charge.

(3) Where the receiving party was represented by different legal representatives during the course of the proceedings, the bill must be divided into different parts so as to distinguish between the costs payable in respect of each legal representative.

(4) Where the receiving party obtained legal aid or LSC funding or is a person for whom civil legal services (within the meaning of Part 1 of the Legal Aid, Sentencing and Punishment of Offenders Act 2012) were provided under arrangements made for the purposes of that Part of that Act in respect of all or part of the proceedings, the bill must be divided into separate parts so as to distinguish between—
    (a) costs claimed before legal aid or LSC funding was granted or before civil legal services were provided;
    (b) costs claimed after legal aid or LSC funding was granted or after civil legal services were provided; and
    (c) any costs claimed after legal aid or LSC funding ceased or after civil legal services ceased to be provided.

(5) Where the bill covers costs payable under an order or orders under which there are different paying parties the bill must be divided into parts so as to deal separately with the costs payable by each paying party.

(6) Where the bill covers costs payable under an order or orders, in respect of which the receiving party wishes to claim interest from different dates, the bill must be divided to enable such interest to be calculated.

(7) Where the case commenced on or after 1 April 2013, the bill covers costs for work done both before and after that date and the costs are to be assessed on the standard basis, the bill must be divided into parts so as to distinguish between costs shown as incurred for work done before 1 April 2013 and costs shown as incurred for work done on or after 1 April 2013.

(8) Where a costs management order has been made, the costs are to be assessed on the standard basis and the receiving party's budget has been agreed by the paying party or approved by the court, the bill must be divided into separate parts so as to distinguish between the costs claimed for each phase of the last approved or agreed budget, and within each such part the bill must distinguish between the costs shown as incurred in the last agreed or approved budget and the costs shown as estimated.

(9) Where a costs management order has been made and the receiving party's budget has been agreed by the paying party or approved by the court, (a) the costs of initially completing Precedent H and (b) the other costs of the budgeting and costs management process must be set out in separate parts.'

43.37 Each part of a bill of costs usually ends by way of a summary of the costs claimed; each such summary is then itself summarised in the grand summary at the end of the bill of costs.[51]

Contents

43.38 The next few paragraphs discuss heads of costs and items of costs. Other aspects of the contents of bills of costs are discussed in Chapter 49.

[51] PD 47, para 5.20.

Heads of costs

The following heads of costs are defined at PD 47, para 5.12, which reads as follows: **43.39**

> '5.12 The bill of costs may consist of items under such of the following heads as may be appropriate:
> (1) attendances on the court and counsel up to the date of the notice of commencement;
> (2) attendances on and communications with the receiving party;
> (3) attendances on and communications with witnesses including any expert witness;
> (4) attendances to inspect any property or place for the purposes of the proceedings;
> (5) attendances on and communications with other persons, including offices of public records;
> (6) communications with the court and with counsel;
> (7) work done on documents;
> (8) work done in connection with negotiations with a view to settlement if not already covered in the heads listed above;
> (9) attendances on and communications with London and other agents and work done by them;
> (10) other work done which was of or incidental to the proceedings and which is not already covered in the heads listed above.'

Where appropriate, agency charges form part of the principal solicitor's charges (see 22.08–22.20 and Chapter 22 in general). Where those charges relate to attendances at court and on counsel, they have to be included in chronological order under the relevant head; otherwise, they must be included as a separate head under 'attendances on London and other agents'.[52] The reason for this requirement is to ensure that the court is not wrongly led to believe that work carried out by agents was carried out by the principal solicitors. **43.40**

Items of costs

PD 47, para 5.13, provides for the following details: **43.41**

> 'In respect of each of the heads of costs:
> (1) "communications" means letters out e-mails out and telephone calls;
> (2) communications, which are not routine communications, must be set out in chronological order;
> (3) routine communications must be set out as a single item at the end of each head.'

Each item has to be consecutively numbered.[53] Directions are given in respect of the following types of item. **43.42**

- **Routine communications** Routine outgoing letters, routine outgoing emails and routine telephone calls (either outgoing or incoming) would, in general, be allowed on a unit basis of 6 minutes (see 49.97). Other electronic communications are allowed on a time basis (see 49.98–49.99). As set out above, PD 47, para 5.13, provides that routine communications must be set out as a single item at the end of each head, and this is generally interpreted as meaning that the numbers of letters, emails and telephone calls have to be shown separately, as well as cumulatively.

52 See PD 47, para 5.22(6).
53 PD 47, para 5.15.

- **Success fee** Where a party claims a success fee under a pre-commencement funding arrangement, the amount of the success fee must be shown separately from the base fee, either in the appropriate arithmetic column or in the narrative column.[54]
- **Costs of preparing the bill of costs** Other than the costs of preparing and checking it, the bill of costs must not contain any costs relating solely to the detailed assessment proceedings.[55]

The format of new-style bills of costs

43.43 By the time this book is published, the new-style bill of costs will—subject to transitional provisions (see 43.30–43.32)—be mandatory. The new-style bill of costs is primarily an electronic document that may exist in two forms: a spreadsheet version and a PDF version (the latter of which may be printed in hard copy). It is a document that relies on costs being claimed according to phase, task and activity, which topic is addressed at 49.42–49.401. A summary may be found on the inside of the cover at the end of this book.

43.44 The new-style bill of costs is introduced by PD 47, paras 5.A1 and 5.A2, which reads as follows:

> '5.A1 A model electronic bill in pdf format is annexed to this Practice Direction as Precedent S and a link to an electronic spreadsheet version of the same model bill is provided in paragraph 5.A2 of this Practice Direction.
>
> 5.A2 Electronic bills may be in either the spreadsheet format which can be found online at http://www.justice.gov.uk/courts/procedure-rules/civil or any other spreadsheet format which—
> (a) reports and aggregates costs based on the phases, tasks, activities and expenses defined in Schedule 2 to this Practice Direction;
> (b) reports summary totals in a form comparable to Precedent S;
> (c) allows the user to identify, in chronological order, the detail of all the work undertaken in each phase;
> (d) automatically recalculates intermediate and overall summary totals if input data is changed;
> (e) contains all calculations and reference formulae in a transparent manner so as to make its full functionality available to the court and all other parties.'

43.45 Thus there is a model new-style bill of costs (known as Precedent S) that is available in both PDF and spreadsheet format. Use of Precedent S is not mandatory, because any spreadsheet format may be used that:

- reports and aggregates costs based on the phases, tasks, activities and expenses (a topic addressed at 49.42–49.401);
- reports summary totals in a form comparable to Precedent S;
- allows the user to identify, in chronological order, the detail of all of the work undertaken in each phase (which, in practice, means that each entry will need to be dated);
- automatically recalculates intermediate and overall summary totals if input data is changed; and
- contains all calculations and reference formulae in a transparent manner, so as to make its full functionality available to the court and all other parties.[56]

---

[54] See now-revoked CPD, art 4.17(1). For an example, see Precedent A or Precedent B in the Schedule of Costs Precedents annexed to the CPD.

[55] PD 47, para 5.19.

[56] See PD 47, para 5.A2.

PD 47, para 5.A3, reads as follows: **43.46**

> '5.A3 The provisions of paragraphs 5.7 to 5.21 of this Practice Direction shall apply to electronic bills insofar as they are not inconsistent with the form and content of Precedent S. Where those paragraphs require or recommend division of the bill into parts, electronic bills (unless the format of the bill already provides the requisite information, for example in identifying the costs within each phase) should incorporate a summary in a form comparable to the "Funding and Parts Table" in Precedent S to provide the information that would otherwise be provided by its division into parts.'

So the provisions relating to old-style bills of costs will continue to apply to new-style **43.47** bills of costs, other than where the former is incompatible with the latter. In particular (to the extent that it is necessary, given the layout of the new-style bill of costs), the requirements to divide the bill of costs into parts (see 43.36) will continue to apply in the sense that there should be a 'funding and parts table' that allows the costs in each virtual part to be summarised (see 43.49). Many, if not most, of the formatting requirements set out at 43.35 will, on the face of it, be incompatible with the new-style bill of costs. Whilst no more than the editor's own thoughts on the matter, it is likely that the requirements relating to the contents of the title page and the background information will continue to apply, as will the stipulations regarding the costs of preparing and checking the bill of costs relating to certificates. The requirements relating to columns will, obviously, not apply nor will the requirements relating to schedules. Chronological entries, additional liabilities and summaries are likely to fall into place automatically given the way in which costs are recorded in the new-style bill of costs.

Serving and filing new-style bills of costs

PD 47, para 5.1, reads as follows: **43.48**

> '5.1A Whenever electronic bills are served or filed at the court, they must also be served or filed in hard copy, in a manageable paper format as shown in the pdf version of Precedent S. A copy of the full electronic spreadsheet version must at the same time be provided to the paying party and filed at the court by e-mail or other electronic means.'

The wording of the paragraph is intended to take into account that the paying party may not accept service by electronic means; this is why the electronic spreadsheet must be 'provided' rather than 'served'.

The layout of the new-style bill of costs (Precedent S)

In its electronic form, Precedent S (the model form of the new-style bill of costs) comprises **43.49** the following components (known as worksheets).

- **Worksheet 1: front sheet** This cites the administrative details of the case.
- **Worksheet 2: certificates** This refers to certificates as to accuracy, the indemnity principle, VAT, etc.
- **Worksheet 3: synopsis** This is the equivalent of the 'background information'; as such, will contain a brief explanation as to what the claim was about, what work was done and who carried out the work. It also clarifies the structure of the bill of costs.
- **Worksheet 4: master chronology** This records the chronological steps taken during the litigation.
- **Worksheet 5: legal team** This records the names of the relevant fee earners, their status and grade, the hourly rates claimed and any success fee claimed in respect of counsel.

- **Worksheet 6: funding and parts table** This describes the parts of the bill of costs. Where appropriate, it also records details such as the applicable rate of VAT, any limit imposed by the indemnity principle and the success fees claimed by the receiving party's solicitors.
- **Worksheet 7: table of costs as summarily assessed** This worksheet records any relevant costs that have been summarily assessed.
- **Worksheet 8: main summary by phase** This is a summary of the costs that are claimed and, as such, is the main reference point in Precedent S. The summary is set out phase by phase. Worksheet 8 also summarises the total amount of the bill, but—in breach of PD 47, para 5.A2(d)—it does not automatically recalculate if input data is changed; rather, this recalculation has to be done manually (see 43.50).
- **Worksheet 9: summary by task, activity and expenses** This is a summary of the amounts claimed under any chosen task, activity or expense.
- **Worksheet 10: summary of costs as claimed vs amount in last budget** This summarises the amounts in the most recent approved or agreed budget and will compare those amounts with the sums claimed.
- **Worksheet 11: main summary by parts** This summarises the costs claimed in each part of the bill of costs (see 43.36).
- **Worksheet 12: summary of communications** This summarises the communications.
- **Worksheet 13: print version** This is a printable presentation of the data contained in the bill of costs.
- **Worksheet 14: detailed bill** This will be a table that contains the detail of the costs claimed, presented in a printable form.
- **Worksheet 15–17: reference and look-up tables** These will contain tables for use in drafting and interpreting the bill of costs.

Precedent S in practice

43.50 The following comments are made about the practicalities of using Precedent S, based on the assumption that the user is working in Microsoft Excel 2016 for Windows.

- **Enable editing** If Precedent S has been provided by email or has been downloaded from the Internet, it will usually be locked to editing. It must be unlocked by selecting 'Enable editing'.
- **Preservation of data** Precedent S does not record changes (unless tracking is turned on, which is cumbersome to use). As such, it is advisable to keep a copy of the bill as originally drawn. Moreover, it is advisable to adjust the 'AutoRecover' feature to make a backup copy every minute or so (the default being every 10 minutes, which could lead to loss of data). In MS Excel 2016, this can be done by selecting File > Options > Save.
- **The need to refresh the data** A useful reference point is worksheet 8 (main summary by phase); the total amount of the bill of costs is at the top right-hand corner, opposite 'Total Bill'. It should be noted that Precedent S does *not* calculate totals automatically; this has to be done manually by selecting Data > Refresh All. This will cause the entire bill to recalculate automatically.
- **Making edits** Changes to the amounts allowed in any cell may be made by first left-clicking on that cell, then either typing directly into that cell or typing into the Formula bar at the top of the screen. If the intention is to insert a formula rather than a figure, this must be done by writing the formula into the Formula bar rather than into the cell itself. Care must be taken not to unwittingly overwrite formulas—and this is especially

important where the formulas are 'pivot table' entries, because overwriting such may radically alter the way in which the total is calculated.

- **Navigation** Precedent S worksheets are selected by clicking on the numbered tabs at the bottom of the screen. They can also be selected by using [CTRL]+[PgUp] or [CTRL]+[PgDn]. The worksheets can be dragged to different locations. Once the required worksheet has been selected, it is possible to move to the top or bottom of a column quickly by using [CTRL]+[↑] or [CTRL]+[↓], respectively.
- **Hiding and unhiding columns** Columns may be hidden to make navigation of the bill easier (which may be necessary if the bill is being read on a small screen). This can be done by selecting the column in question at the top of the screen, then right-clicking and selecting 'Hide'. Columns may be unhidden either by selecting the adjacent columns, right-clicking and selecting 'Unhide', or by selecting all columns (by pressing [CTRL]+[A] or by clicking on the triangle at the top left), right-clicking, and selecting 'Unhide'.
- **Sorting and reordering** Entries in worksheet 14 (which contains the detail of the costs claimed) can be sorted or reordered by clicking on the filter arrow (a small inverted triangle at the top of every column). It should be noted that the available functions are not limited to reordering the data; in particular, it will usually be possible to sort the data (such as by selecting only that work which was done in a particular year or month).
- **Isolating entries and subtotalling** It may be necessary to isolate entries in any given column (such as to isolate only counsel's fees). This can be done by left-clicking on the filter arrow on the relevant column and then unticking 'Blanks'. It is then possible to create a subtotal of those entries by using the AutoSum feature. It should be noted that this may not always work as expected in Precedent S; it may be necessary to enter the relevant formula manually, in the form of '=Subtotal(9,x1:x2)', where x1 and x2 defines the range of cells to be summated. It should be noted that, where this is done, only hours are shown (that is, the minutes are not shown).
- **Clearing filters** If filters have been applied, they can be cleared by selecting the 'Data' tab on the ribbon and then left-clicking on 'Clear' (or, if it is highlighted, by left-clicking on 'Filter').
- **Hourly rates** Hourly rates may be changed by making the appropriate changes to the figures in worksheet 5 (legal team, hourly rates and counsel's success fees); those changes will then propagate themselves throughout the bill when Data > Refresh All is activated. Care needs to be taken to avoid inadvertently changing the rates that apply to budgeted costs; the editor understands that Precedent S will soon be revised to make this easier. If the bill has not been drafted in such a way as to allow this to be done easily, a certain amount of manual recalculation may be required.
- **Restricting the costs according to a budget** At present, Precedent S does not allow the user to choose whether the costs are to be restricted to the amounts allowed in the budget (those amounts being recorded in worksheet 10). A manual adjustment may have to be made in this regard; the figures in the right-hand column on worksheet 10 (namely, 'Departure from the Last Approved/Agreed Budget') may be used for this purpose.
- **Comments** Whilst it should be regarded as no more than an aid to the person using Precedent S, it is possible to add comments to any given cell by right-clicking within it and selecting 'Insert Comment'. Comments can be deleted by right-clicking the cell (rather than the Comment itself) and selecting 'Delete Comment'.

Commencement of Detailed Assessment Proceedings

43.51 The procedure for commencing detailed assessment proceedings is unusual, in the sense that the court is not involved in the process. Commencement happens when the following are served on the paying party[57] (and, where applicable, on any 'other relevant person' as specified in PD 47):[58]

- a notice of commencement,[59] which is in a prescribed form (Form N252);[60]
- a copy of the bill of costs (or, where work spans 6 April 2018 such that both new- and old-style bills are drawn up, copies);[61]
- copies of the fee notes of counsel and of any expert in respect of fees claimed in the bill;[62]
- written evidence as to any other disbursement that is claimed and which exceeds £500;[63] and
- a statement giving the name and address[64] for service of any person upon whom the receiving party intends to serve the notice of commencement.[65]

43.52 As of 1 October 2015,[66] there is an additional requirement, in that if a costs management order has been made, a breakdown of the costs claimed for each phase of the proceedings must also be served.[67] The present provision, PD 47, para 5.2(f) (which has since been amended), now reads as follows:

> '(f) if a costs management order has been made (and if the same information is not already fully provided in an electronic bill), a breakdown of the costs claimed for each phase of the proceedings. Precedent Q in the Schedule of Costs Precedents annexed to this Practice Direction is a model form of breakdown of the costs claimed for each phase of the proceedings.'

---

57 See CPR, r 47.6(1).

58 See CPR, r 47.6(2). PD 47, para 5.5, provides as follows: '(1) For the purposes of rule 47.6(2) a "relevant person" means: (a) any person who has taken part in the proceedings which gave rise to the assessment and who is directly liable under an order for costs made against him; (b) any person who has given to the receiving party notice in writing that he has a financial interest in the outcome of the assessment and wishes to be a party accordingly; (c) any other person whom the court orders to be treated as such. (2) Where a party is unsure whether a person is or is not a relevant person, that party may apply to the appropriate office for directions. (3) The court will generally not make an order that the person in respect of whom the application is made will be treated as a relevant person, unless within a specified time he applies to the court to be joined as a party to the assessment proceedings in accordance with Part 19 (Parties and Group Litigation).'

59 See CPR, r 47.6(1)(a); PD 47, para 5.2(a).

60 See PD 47, para 5.2(a).

61 See CPR, r 47.6(1)(b); PD 47, para 5.2(b).

62 See PD 47, para 5.2(c).

63 See PD 47, para 5.2(d).

64 The SCCO informally requests that email addresses are included in the statement of parties: SCCO, 'Request Made to Members of the Association of Law Costs Draftsmen', 26 January 2010. See also HM Courts & Tribunals Services, *Senior Courts Costs Office Guide* (London: HMSO, 2018), para 13.2, which implies the same.

65 See PD 47, para 5.2(e).

66 See the Civil Procedure (Amendment No 4) Rules 2015 (SI 2015/1569), r 8.

67 See CPR, r 47.6(1)(c); PD 47, para 5.2(f). Precedent Q in the Schedule of Costs Precedents annexed to PD 47 is a model form of breakdown of the costs claimed for each phase of the proceedings (see PD 47, para 5.1A).

The standard form (that is, Form N252) can be found at Figure 43.2. **43.53**

As can be seen, the notice of commencement must be completed to show the following as separate items: **43.54**

- the total amount of the costs claimed in the bill; and
- the extra sum that will be payable by way of fixed costs and court fees if a default costs certificate is obtained.[68]

Miscellaneous points

Where there are additional liabilities

If the receiving party had a pre-commencement funding arrangement (see 54.18), then the pre-April 2013 CPD will continue to apply for the purposes of assessing the relevant additional liabilities. The requirements under the old regime and the new are not entirely the same.[69] Whilst the contrary is arguable, a receiving party would do well to assume that, where there are differences, documents should be served, rather than not served.[70] In the unlikely event that a receiving party seeks an assessment in respect of additional liabilities only, then (assuming that the case was not budgeted) the only documents that are likely to be relevant are those listed in the pre-April 2013 CPD.[71] **43.55**

The status of persons who have been served with notices of commencement

Persons who (in addition to the paying party and the receiving party) have been served as 'other relevant persons' are parties to the detailed assessment proceedings.[72] **43.56**

Service of notices of commencement

The provisions that govern service of notices of commencement are largely the same as those that govern service of points of dispute (see 43.138). In addition, PD 47, para 5.4, provides as follows: **43.57**

> '5.4 Where the notice of commencement is to be served outside England and Wales the date to be inserted in the notice of commencement for the paying party to send points of dispute is a date (not less than 21 days from the date of service of the notice) which must be calculated by reference to Section IV of Part 6 as if the notice were a claim form and as if the date to be inserted was the date for the filing of a defence.'

It should be noted that estoppel by convention may prevent a paying party from complaining about defective service of a notice of commencement if both parties mistakenly assumed that service had been effective and proceeded on that basis.[73] Similarly, if service is effected against a party who is a joint costs debtor, any other joint costs debtor will be bound by decisions of the court notwithstanding the fact that they may not have been served (see 19.23 and 19.28).[74] **43.58**

---

[68] See PD 47, para 5.3.

[69] The provisions in the pre-April 2013 CPD may be found at CPD, arts 32.5–32.7.

[70] This is because CPR, r 48.1, provides that the provisions of the CPD will apply as they were in force immediately before 1 April 2013, with such modifications (if any) as may be made by a practice direction on or after that date. As such, it is arguable that the differences (which are all additions) are modifications.

[71] The relevant provision is the pre-April 2013 CPD, art 32.4, which reads as follows: 'If the detailed assessment is in respect of an additional liability only, the receiving party must serve on the paying party and all other relevant persons the following documents: (a) a notice of commencement; (b) a copy of the bill of costs; (c) the relevant details of the additional liability; and (d) a statement giving the name and address of any person upon whom the receiving party intends to serve the notice of commencement.'

[72] See CPR, r 47.6(3).

[73] See *Edray v Canning* [2015] EWHC 2744 (Ch).

[74] See, eg, *Mainwaring v Goldtech Investments Ltd (No 2)* [1999] 1 WLR 745, CA.

Notice of commencement of assessment of bill of costs

In the	
Claim No.	
Claimant (include Ref.)	
Defendant (include Ref.)	

To the claimant(defendant)

Following an (*insert name of document eg. order, judgment*) dated (copy attached) I have prepared my Bill of Costs for assessment. The Bill totals *£ If you choose to dispute this bill and your objections are not upheld at the assessment hearing, the full amount payable (including the assessment fee) will be £ (together with interest (*see note below*)). I shall also seek the costs of the assessment hearing

Your points of dispute must include

- details of the items in the bill of costs which are disputed
- concise details of the nature and grounds of the dispute for each item and, if you seek a reduction in those items, suggest, where practicable, a reduced figure

You must serve your points of dispute by (*insert date 21 days from the date of service of this notice*) on me at:- (*give full name and address for service including any DX number or reference)*

You must also serve copies of your points of dispute on all other parties to the assessment identified below *(you do not need to serve your points of dispute on the court).*

I certify that I have also served the following person(s) with a copy of this notice and my Bill of Costs:- *(give details of persons served)*

If I have not received your points of dispute by the above date, I will ask the court to issue a default costs certificate for the full amount of my bill *(see above*)* plus fixed costs and court fee in the total amount of £

Signed (Claimant)(Defendant)('s solicitor) **Date**

Note: Interest may be added to all High Court judgments and certain county court judgments of £5,000 or more under the Judgments Act 1838 and the County Courts Act 1984.

The court office at

is open between 10 am and 4 pm Monday to Friday. When corresponding with the court, please address forms or letters to the Court Manager and quote the claim number.

N252 Notice of commencement of assessment of bill of costs (12.99) *The Court Service Publications Unit*

Figure 43.2 Form N252: the notice of commencement

Finality and multiple bills of costs

A receiving party is not able to present a bill of costs for part of their costs and then, without the agreement of the paying party or an order of the court, present another bill of costs for the remainder.[75] **43.59**

When proceedings may be commenced

Where costs are to be ascertained by detailed assessment, the general rule is that the assessment will take place only upon the conclusion of the proceedings to which they relate. In this regard, CPR, r 47.1, makes the following provisions: 'The general rule is that the costs of any proceedings or any part of the proceedings are not to be assessed by the detailed procedure until the conclusion of the proceedings but the court may order them to be assessed immediately.' **43.60**

'Forthwith orders'

An order that provides for an immediate assessment is known as a forthwith order (see 7.80–7.81). Such an order would usually be made at the same time as the award of costs, but it may be made at a subsequent stage.[76] What follows is a discussion of the powers that a costs judge may exercise in the absence of a pre-existing forthwith order; for a discussion of the powers of the trial judge to make a forthwith order, see 7.82–7.99. **43.61**

Applications to a costs judge for permission to commence or continue proceedings **43.62**
Upon application, a costs judge may make an order permitting detailed assessment proceedings to be commenced or to continue.[77] There can be little doubt that a costs judge is permitted to make an award if they find that the proceedings have, in fact, concluded or if the parties give their consent in writing. What is less clear is whether a costs judge has the power to order (in a contested application) that, notwithstanding the fact that they are continuing, the proceedings will be treated as if they had concluded.

The wording of the relevant provisions—PD 47, paras 1.2–1.4, is as follows: **43.63**

> '1.2 The court may order or the parties may agree in writing that, although the proceedings are continuing, they will nevertheless be treated as concluded.
>
> 1.3 A party who is served with a notice of commencement ... may apply to a costs judge or a District Judge to determine whether the party who served it is entitled to commence detailed assessment proceedings. On hearing such an application the orders which the court may make include: an order allowing the detailed assessment proceedings to continue, or an order setting aside the notice of commencement.
>
> 1.4 A costs judge or a District Judge may make an order allowing detailed assessment proceedings to be commenced where there is no realistic prospect of the claim continuing.'

[75] Christopher Clarke J found that this was not permissible: *Harris v Moat Housing Group South Ltd* [2007] EWHC 3092 (QB), at [33].

[76] An example of this is *GB Gas Holdings Ltd v Accenture (UK) Ltd* [2010] EWHC 2928 (Comm), at [32] and [33], in which Hamblin J acknowledged the existence of the jurisdiction in cases in which the proceedings were in the Commercial Court, but the costs in question had been incurred on an interim appeal.

[77] This is implied by PD 47, paras 1.3 and 1.4.

43.64 As can be seen, these provisions seem to envisage a costs judge having the power to make any one of three orders:

- an order that proceedings be treated as if they had concluded;[78]
- an order that proceedings be allowed to continue; and[79]
- an order allowing detailed assessment proceedings to be commenced because there is no realistic prospect of the claim continuing.[80]

43.65 Until recently, it was not clear whether a costs judge would, in the absence of a pre-existing forthwith order or the parties' consent, have the power to allow detailed assessment proceedings to be commenced (or to continue) in proceedings that were still ongoing in any way. David Richards LJ has now put the matter beyond doubt, saying this: 'The primary function of costs judges is to assess costs when an assessment is due, not to decide whether there should be an assessment.'[81] Thus a costs judge does *not* have the power to make a forthwith order as a matter of discretion.

43.66 David Richards LJ added the following comments:

> 'The [receiving parties] rely on paragraph 1.3 of [PD 47], ... They submit that it confers jurisdiction on a costs judge to make an order for assessment. The terms of paragraph 1.3 make clear that it is not a general jurisdiction, but arises (if at all) only where a paying party served with a notice of commencement applies to the costs judge to determine whether the other party is entitled to commence detailed assessment proceedings. The wording of paragraph 1.3 makes clear that the entitlement should pre-date the commencement of the assessment proceedings and that the costs judge's function is to determine whether the entitlement exists. The second sentence does not, in my judgment, envisage that the costs judge has a discretion to order an assessment where none exists but is, as Patten J said of the predecessor provision in [*Crystal Decisions (UK) Ltd v Vedatech Corpn* [2007] EWHC 1062 (Ch),] at [78] "consequential and contingent upon the power for the costs judge to decide whether the party serving a notice of commencement is entitled to do so". If the costs judge holds that the receiving party was entitled to commence an assessment, he or she may make an order allowing it to continue. Alternatively, the costs judge could stay the proceedings until a more appropriate time in the future.'[82]

43.67 The reference to Patten J's comments were to the following paragraph from a judgment (albeit *obiter*) about similar provisions[83] in the now-revoked CPD:

> 'I am far from persuaded that [the then equivalent of the provision set out above] in fact gives to the costs judge power to order the continuation of a detailed assessment in circumstances where the Court making the original order for costs has not done so. The power contained in [the then equivalent of the second sentence in PD 47, para 1.3,] to allow the assessment to continue seems to me to be consequential and contingent upon the power contained in [the then equivalent of the first sentence in PD 47, para 1.3,] for the costs judge to decide whether the party serving a notice of commencement is entitled to do so. The reference to being entitled to do so must be a reference to the terms of CPR 47.1 and calls for

---

[78] See PD 47, para 1.2.
[79] See the second sentence of PD 47, para 1.3.
[80] See PD 47, para 1.4.
[81] See *Khaira v Shergill* [2017] EWCA Civ 1687, at [62].
[82] See *ibid*, at [63].
[83] CPD, art 28.1(4)(a) and (b), was very similarly worded to the first and second sentences of PD 47, para 1.3, respectively.

a judicial determination of whether under that rule the party in question is entitled to proceed. It would be odd for the costs judge to be entitled to allow the assessment to continue notwithstanding a ruling that CPR 47.1 did not justify an immediate assessment and I do not consider that [the then equivalent of the second sentence in PD 47, para 1.3,] conferred on the costs judge any such dispensing power. The only Court entitled to permit a deviation from the general rule is the Court making the costs order. If that power is not exercised, the costs judge must apply the general rule.'[84]

Thus, when presented with a contested application in a case in which no pre-existing forthwith order has been made, the role of a costs judge would be limited, at most, to (a) determining whether a forthwith order was required on the facts of the particular case and/or (b) determining whether the proceedings had, as a matter of fact, concluded. Put otherwise, a costs judge would have no general discretion to, in effect, make a forthwith order. **43.68**

The meaning of 'concluded' The guidance about when proceedings are concluded in PD 47, para 1.1, may be relevant: 'For the purposes of rule 47.1, proceedings are concluded when the court has finally determined the matters in issue in the claim, whether or not there is an appeal, or made an award of provisional damages under Part 41.' **43.69**

Thus proceedings will be regarded as being concluded if the court has 'finally determined the matters in issue in the claim', and this will be so regardless of whether there is an appeal and regardless of whether an award of provisional damages has been made. The making of an award of provisional damages will be treated as a final determination of the matters in issue. 'Concluded' does not mean that there is no possibility of the parties ever again coming before the court.[85] **43.70**

What is less clear is whether *part* of the proceedings may be regarded as being concluded. There is, perhaps, a tension between what is set out in CPR, r 47.1, which expressly refers to 'any part of the proceedings', and what is set out in PD 47, para 1.1. Respected commentators have suggested that CPR, r 47.1, should be read as permitting an immediate assessment of any part of the proceedings that has concluded.[86] Whilst it is no more than his opinion, the editor takes a different view: he reads CPR, r 47.1, as *prohibiting* the immediate assessment of costs of a part of the proceedings rather than as *permitting* it. There is, however, no authority on the point. **43.71**

Treated as being concluded by consent There can be little doubt that the parties may agree that the proceedings may be treated as being concluded even where they are continuing. In this regard, PD 47, para 1.2, reads as follows: 'The court may order or the parties may agree in writing that, although the proceedings are continuing, they will nevertheless be treated as concluded.' **43.72**

[84] See *Crystal Decisions (UK) Ltd v Vedatech Corpn* [2007] EWHC 1062 (Ch), at [78].

[85] Whilst it is a pre-CPR authority, in a case in which a claim had been tried and the court had given final judgment that included the reservation of certain enquiries to future hearings, Morritt J found that since the original cause of action had merged in the judgment, the claim was concluded. This was despite the fact that those enquiries may require judicial consideration at some later point: *Mölnlycke AB v Proctor & Gamble Ltd (No 6)* [1993] FSR 154, Patents Ct, at 156.

[86] See, eg, *Cook on Costs 2017* (LexisNexis, online), para 28.6.

43.73 *Treated as being concluded by order* As can be seen above, in addition to stating that the parties may agree to the case being treated as being concluded, PD 47, para 1.2, states that the court may order that the proceedings be treated as concluded even where they are continuing. For the reasons set out at 43.65, it seems that is not a power that could properly be exercised by a costs judge.

43.74 **Appeals and 'forthwith' orders** Appeals may present problems of their own, including in the following situations:

- pending appeals and stays in general (see 43.75);
- pending appeals where the outcome of the appeal has the potential to change the incidence of costs (see 43.78); and
- concluded appeals where the appeal court has made an order for costs (see 43.79).

43.75 *Pending appeals from final determinations and stays in general* It will be recalled from 43.69 that PD 47, para 1.1, provides that proceedings are concluded when the court has finally determined the matters in issue in the claim 'whether or not there is an appeal'. This implies that an appeal from a final determination of the claim and the proceedings in the court below are, to that extent and in some regards, separate proceedings. This is confirmed by CPR, r 47.2, which reads: 'Detailed assessment is not stayed pending an appeal unless the court so orders.'

43.76 As such, the party who has been awarded costs in the court below will not only *be able* to commence detailed assessment proceedings immediately, but will *be under a duty* to do so within the time limits referred to at 43.85. These rules arguably reflect pre-CPR authorities in which proceedings progressing towards trial and appeals therefrom were, in many regards, separate proceedings for the purposes of costs.[87] In this regard, David Richards LJ had this to say:

> 'The matters in issue in the claim are not finally determined until the court at first instance has finally ruled on them, but once it has done so the proceedings are for these purposes concluded even if there is an appeal.'[88]

Thus, where the claim has been finally decided, the proceedings are regarded as being concluded and this is so regardless of whether there is an appeal from that decision.

43.77 This may cause a quandary because the parties may have legitimate reasons for wanting to postpone the assessment until after the appeal from the final determination of the claim. If it is the paying party who wants to postpone matters, then, in the absence of forbearance on the part of the receiving party, the paying party has no option but to apply for a stay. As to procedure, PD 47, para 2, provides that such an application 'may be made to the court whose order is being appealed or to the court which will hear the appeal', which (strongly) implies that no such application may be made to a costs judge. If it is the receiving party who seeks to postpone the assessment pending an appeal, then they may

[87] See *Hawksford Trustees Jersey Ltd (Trustee of The Bald Eagle Trust) v Stella Global UK Ltd* [2012] EWCA Civ 987, at [42], [44], [45] and [58], *per* Rix LJ, at [22], [23], [24] and [34], *per* Patten LJ (dissenting), and at [62], *per* Etherton LJ. As an example of the pre-CPR authorities, see *Masson Templier & Co v De Fries (Costs)* [1910] 1 KB 535; *Wright v Bennett* [1948] 1 KB 601. See also Morritt LJ's discussion of this topic in *Morris v Bank of America National Trust (appeal against striking out)* [2001] 1 All ER 954.

[88] See *Khaira v Shergill* [2017] EWCA Civ 1687, at [39].

similarly apply for a stay, but another option would be simply to delay serving the notice of commencement. This latter option is fraught with danger, however, because it would expose the receiving party to the sanctions referred to at 43.94.

Pending appeals where the outcome of the appeal may change the incidence of costs Where the outcome of an appeal from a final determination is not capable of impacting on the incidence of costs, the only issue that the receiving party has to address is whether they should incur the costs of applying for a stay or whether it would be better to run the risk of having to bear the sanctions referred to at 43.94. If, however, there is a real risk that the appeal may alter the incidence of costs, the receiving party is in a much more difficult position because it may not be worth incurring the costs of detailed assessment proceedings if the order may not survive the forthcoming appeal. **43.78**

Concluded interlocutory appeals where the appeal court has made an order for costs It will be recalled that, prior to the coming into force of the CPR, proceedings progressing towards trial and appeals therefrom were regarded as separate proceedings for the purposes of costs (see 43.76). It will also be recalled that this seems to have been carried over into the CPR, in the sense that detailed assessment proceedings are not automatically stayed pending appeal (see 43.75). As such, one may have thought that no forthwith order would be required in respect of the costs of an interlocutory appeal because the same would be regarded as being the costs of separate proceedings. This, however, would be wrong: whilst there used to be conflicting authorities on the point, David Richards LJ has now explained that such appeal proceedings are not separate proceedings for the purposes of CPR, r 47.1.[89] He had the following to say on the topic: **43.79**

> 'The issue of whether there is an automatic immediate assessment of costs depends on its meaning and effect. Unless CPR 47.1 has no application at all to appeals, the effect of paragraph 1.1 of [PD 47] is, in my judgment, that there is no automatic detailed assessment of the costs of an interlocutory appeal and that an order of the court is required, consistently with the views of the judges in this court and in the High Court who have previously considered this point.'[90]

In arriving at this conclusion, David Richards LJ made reference to the following *obiter* comments of Patten J: **43.80**

> 'The purpose of CPR 47.1 is to lay down a general rule that the costs of part of the proceedings are not to be assessed until the conclusion of the proceedings as a whole unless the Court orders them to be assessed immediately, which the Court of Appeal did not. The order made by the Court of Appeal is therefore governed by this general rule and although it would have been open to the Court of Appeal to order an immediate assessment (see e.g. *Morris v Bank of America* [2000] 1 AER 954) it did not do so. [The decision in the court below] effectively re-writes CPR 47.1 and cannot stand.'[91]

Thus Patten J took the view that a forthwith order was a necessity before the costs of an interlocutory appeal could be assessed prior to the conclusion of the first-instance proceedings as a whole. By implication, Hamblen J came to the same conclusion in a case in which

[89] See *Khaira v Shergill* [2017] EWCA Civ 1687, at [41]–[53].
[90] See *ibid*, at [52].
[91] See *Crystal Decisions (UK) Ltd v Vedatech Corpn* [2007] EWHC 1062 (Ch), at [77].

he was asked to make an order that costs previously incurred in an interlocutory appeal should be assessed forthwith.[92]

43.81 This is as one would expect it to be, because the appeal court would know whether proceedings were going to continue in another court and, as such, it would be in an ideal position to decide whether or not to make a forthwith order. Master Campbell—giving judgment more a decade ago—pointed out that, as a matter of practice, a party could be expected to seek a forthwith order from the appeal court.[93] Furthermore, even in the days before the CPR, the guidance given by the Court of Appeal was that 'when there [was] doubt as to whether or not an order results in the "conclusion of the cause or matter" the wise course [was] to ask the court . . . for consent to proceed to taxation forthwith'.[94]

43.82 It may be that an appeal court has made an order for costs that does not contain a 'forthwith' order and that the matter then proceeds in the court below (or some other court). Where this is so, Hamblen J has explained that the court in which the matter proceeds would have jurisdiction to order that the costs in the appeal court be assessed forthwith.[95] This may—arguably—continue to be so if the appeal proceeded in the same court (such as where both were in the County Court and its hearing centres), but it is now known that the High Court does not have the power to make such an order where the appeal was in the Court of Appeal.[96]

43.83 **Additional liabilities** Success fees may present problems, because a receiving party would usually be reluctant to disclose any risk assessment until the conclusion of the case. The comments made at 7.91 apply.

43.84 *Group litigation* Group litigation can create difficulties, as discussed at 7.92–7.93.

Late commencement and delay

Period of time allowed

43.85 As a general rule, the period for beginning detailed assessment proceedings is three months from the date on which the receiving party became entitled to costs, as outlined in Table 43.1.[97]

43.86 The CPR do not stipulate what should happen where there is no forthwith order in proceedings that are ongoing litigation. This topic is discussed in more detail (in the context of appeals) at 7.87–7.90.

Counting days

43.87 The three-month period is measured in calendar months.[98] It is implicit from PD 47, para 6.2, that time will stop running upon compliance with CPR, r 47.6(1) (that is,

---

92 See *GB Gas Holdings Ltd v Accenture (UK) Ltd & Ors* [2010] EWHC 2928 (Comm), at [28].
93 *Bottin (International) Investments Ltd v Venson Group plc* [2005] EWHC 90005 (Costs), at [44].
94 *In re Harrods (Buenos Aires) Ltd* (unreported), 10 March 1993, CA, *per* Sir Mervyn Davies. This case is not reported, but it is cited in *Bottin (International) Investments Ltd v Venson Group plc* [2005] EWHC 90005 (Costs), at [45].
95 See *GB Gas Holdings Ltd v Accenture (UK) Ltd & Ors* [2010] EWHC 2928 (Comm), at [28].
96 See *Khaira v Shergill* [2017] EWCA Civ 1687, at [60] and [61], *per* David Richards LJ.
97 See CPR, r 47.7.
98 See CPR, r 2.10.

Table 43.1 Time to commencement

Source of right to detailed assessment	Time by which detailed assessment proceedings must be commenced
Judgment, direction, order, award or other determination	Three months after the date of the judgment etc
	Where detailed assessment is stayed pending an appeal, three months after the date of the order lifting the stay
Discontinuance under CPR, Part 38	Three months after the date of service of notice of discontinuance under CPR, r 38.3
	Three months after the date of the dismissal of application to set the notice of discontinuance aside under CPR, r 38.4
Acceptance of an offer to settle under CPR, Part 36	Three months after the date on which the right to costs arose

service of a notice of commencement and a copy of the bill of costs). PD 47, para 6.2, reads: 'The detailed assessment proceedings are commenced by service of the documents referred to. Permission to commence assessment proceedings out of time is not required.'

Variation of time limits

Both the court and the parties have the power to vary the three-month period. This may happen upon application, retrospectively or by consent. It is worth noting that the issue is of only limited importance, because (other than in egregious cases in which the delay amounts to misconduct) the court lacks the powers to prevent a receiving party from commencing detailed assessment proceedings.[99] **43.88**

Extending period by application Where a party wishes to vary the time for commencing detailed assessment proceedings in default of agreement to that effect, the court has power pursuant to CPR, Part 3, to make the appropriate order. PD 47, para 6.1, confirms this: 'The time for commencing the detailed assessment proceedings may be extended or shortened either by agreement (rule 2.11) or by the court (rule 3.1(2)(a)). Any application is to the appropriate office.' It is rare for permission to be refused. That said, the court will take the overriding objective into account, and it may be that—under the post-April 2013 version of that rule—permission will be less frequently granted. It used to be said that, in cases of complexity, the court would take into account the matters that used to be listed in CPR, r 3.9 (relief from sanctions),[100] but it is not known whether this continues to be the case under the post-April 2013 version of that rule.[101] In any event, it is easily arguable that that approach ought never to have applied to detailed assessment proceedings.[102] Indeed, it is a general principle that, unless it is made retrospectively, an **43.89**

[99] See CPR, r 47.8(3).

[100] Whilst it related to a different type of application, the case that was generally cited in support of this analysis of the law was *Sayers v Clarke Walker* [2002] EWCA Civ 645.

[101] Because, *ibid*, at [20], Brooke LJ referred to 'the checklist' in CPR, r 3.9; he did not say that where a party seeks an extension of time, they should be treated as though they were applying for relief from sanctions.

[102] This is because there is no automatic or mandatory penalty arising out of the receiving party's tardiness. As such, it is not necessary for the court to consider giving relief from sanctions, because it is open to the court to decline to impose sanctions in the first place.

application for an extension of the time is not to be equated with an application for relief from sanctions.[103]

43.90 **Extending time retrospectively** CPR, r 3.1(2)(a), stipulates that the application for an extension may be made after the time for compliance has expired. This would often be otiose, however, because permission to commence assessment proceedings out of time is not required.[104] If the issue were to arise, then, for the reasons given immediately above, it is easily arguable that the court would treat the application as if it were a request for relief from sanctions.

43.91 **Extending time by consent** It is generally accepted that parties may agree to vary the period of time for serving notice of commencement. This will often happen, for example, where either the bill of costs is large and will take more than three months to draft or the parties are in active negotiations. This power is exercisable under CPR, r 2.11, as is made clear by PD 47, para 6.1 (see 43.89). The court has the power to make a different order from that which the parties have agreed,[105] but, in practice, this would almost never happen because the extension would usually be agreed prior to the court's involvement.

43.92 This generally received view may be wrong, however. This is because the combined effect of CPR, r 3.8(3) and (4), is that where a rule requires a party to do something within a specified time and where that rule 'specifies the consequence of failure to comply', the time for doing the act in question may not be extended by agreement between the parties for more than a period of 28 days.[106] CPR, r 47.8(3), does 'specify a consequence'—namely, that late commencement will result in the court having the power to disallow interest. One could argue that CPR, r 47.8(3), does not specify a consequence because it will have effect only if the court exercises its discretion to disallow interest, but this would be a difficult argument to run in the light of the authorities (albeit ones relating to law other than costs).[107]

43.93 It has been said that the law is unclear in this regard.[108] That may be so, but it is not easy to envisage circumstances in which a party would want to rely on the supposed illegality of an agreed extension (unless, of course, as a reason to decline a request for an extension). No paying party would want to argue that an extension was unlawful, and if a receiving party were to try to impugn the legality of an extension from which it had benefited, one would imagine that the court would afford that party short shrift.

Sanctions for delay

43.94 Tardiness on the part of the receiving party may be as a result of delay in commencing detailed assessment proceedings or delay in requesting a detailed assessment

[103] See *Hallam Estates Ltd v Baker* [2014] EWCA Civ 661, at [26], *per* Jackson LJ; *Robert v Momentum Services Ltd* [2003] EWCA Civ 299, at [33].

[104] PD 47, para 6.1.

[105] In a context other than costs, see *Ropac Ltd v Inntrepreneir Pub Co* [2001] CP Rep 31.

[106] Whilst *obiter* and on a slightly different point, it is worth noting that in *Hallam Estates Ltd v Baker* [2014] EWCA Civ 661, at [12], Jackson LJ referred to the 28-day limit as applying in the context of costs litigation.

[107] See *Primus Telecommunications Netherlands BV v Pan European Ltd* [2005] EWCA Civ 273, at [58] and [59], which concerned CPR, r 32.10, but the relevant wording is similar to CPR, r 47.8(3). See also *Papa Johns (GB) Ltd v Doyley* [2011] EWHC 2621(QB).

[108] See Underwood, K, 'Provisional Assessment', 6 March 2015, available online at https://kerryunderwood.wordpress.com/2015/03/06/provisional-assessment-2/

hearing, or both. Where there has been any such delay, a paying party has two potential remedies: it may apply for an unless order, or it may seek sanctions against the receiving party.

The topic of sanctions is addressed in Chapter 23, starting at 23.50. What follows is a discussion of the paying party's ability to apply for an unless order. It should be noted that, for the reasons set out at 43.105 and 43.106, it is possible that the two remedies are mutually exclusive. **43.95**

Jurisdiction and unless orders CPR, r 47.8(1), provides as follows: **43.96**

> 'Where the receiving party fails to commence detailed assessment proceedings within the period specified—
> (a) in rule 47.7; or
> (b) by any direction of the court,
>
> the paying party may apply for an order requiring the receiving party to commence detailed assessment proceedings within such time as the court may specify.'

CPR, r 47.8(1), allows the court to make one component of an unless order—namely, the part that imposes the deadline by which proceedings must be commenced. The other component—namely, the penalty in default—is governed by CPR, r 47.8(2), which provides as follows: **43.97**

> 'On an application under paragraph (1), the court may direct that, unless the receiving party commences detailed assessment proceedings within the time specified by the court, all or part of the costs to which the receiving party would otherwise be entitled will be disallowed.'

Almost identical provisions to those set out above govern delay in requesting a detailed assessment hearing.[109]

Paying parties' applications for unless orders: without-notice applications Where appropriate, applications may be made without notice. Where this is so, the paying party will bear a duty of candour.[110] **43.98**

Paying parties' applications for unless orders: payments out of the CLS Fund or by the Lord Chancellor Special provisions apply where the costs are payable out of the Community Legal Service (CLS) Fund or by the Lord Chancellor, under Part 1 of the Legal Aid, Sentencing and Punishment of Offenders Act 2012.[111] **43.99**

---

[109] See CPR, r 47.14(2) and (3), which provides as follows: '(2) Where the receiving party fails to file a request in accordance with paragraph (1), the paying party may apply for an order requiring the receiving party to file the request within such time as the court may specify. (3) On an application under paragraph (2), the court may direct that, unless the receiving party requests a detailed assessment hearing within the time specified by the court, all or part of the costs to which the receiving party would otherwise be entitled will be disallowed.'

[110] See, eg, *FN v Secretary of State for the Home Department* [2015] EWHC 3057 (QB).

[111] CPR, r 47.8(4) and (5), reads as follows: '(4) Where the costs to be assessed in a detailed assessment are payable out of the Community Legal Service Fund, this rule applies as if the receiving party were the solicitor to whom the costs are payable and the paying party were the Legal Services Commission. (5) Where the costs to be assessed in a detailed assessment are payable by the Lord Chancellor under Part 1 of the Legal Aid, Sentencing and Punishment of Offenders Act 2012, this rule applies as if the receiving party were the solicitor to whom the costs are payable and the paying party were the Lord Chancellor.'

43.100 **Discretion and unless orders** The fact that the court has the power to make an unless order does not mean that it will necessarily exercise that power. An unless order would, in the absence of further judicial scrutiny, ordinarily visit significant consequences on the defaulting party; as such, it is not a trivial order to make. Moore-Bick LJ had this to say on the topic (albeit in a context other than the law of costs):

> '[A further] consequence is that before making conditional orders, particularly orders for the striking out of statements of case or the dismissal of claims or counterclaims, the judge should consider carefully whether the sanction being imposed is appropriate in all the circumstances of the case. Of course, it is impossible to foresee the nature and effect of every possible breach and the party in default can always apply for relief, but a conditional order striking out a statement of case or dismissing the claim or counterclaim is one of the most powerful weapons in the court's case management armoury and should not be deployed unless its consequences can be justified. I find it difficult to imagine circumstances in which such an order could properly be made for what were described in *Keen Phillips v Field* [2006] EWCA Civ 1524, [2007] 1 WLR 686 as "good housekeeping purposes".'[112]

43.101 There is no reason to believe that the power to make an unless order in detailed assessment proceedings should be exercised with any lesser degree of care; hence an unless order will not be made other than where 'its consequences can be justified'. In a similar vein, Dame Janet Smith had this to say: 'The CPR are intended to make solicitors comply with orders or to face the consequences with their eyes open. They are not intended to create traps for the unwary or slightly incompetent.'[113]

43.102 There have been instances in which the court has made an unless order under CPR, r 47.8(2), without a hearing and without giving the receiving party opportunity to be heard. Whilst she was dealing with the topic in the context of litigation other than costs, Dame Janet Smith has said that she 'deprecates [that] practice'.[114]

43.103 **Unless orders and relief** If a party knowingly fails to comply with an unless order, that party will often be denied relief.[115] That said, it is not unknown for parties to consent to an unless order as a convenient procedural accommodation for the purposes of case management and, where this has happened, non-compliance would ordinarily be correspondingly less serious.[116] Indeed, the court has the power to afford relief in relation to any unless order that the parties have agreed; the fact that the order was made by consent is a fact that would be a relevant, but not decisive, factor.[117]

43.104 If the court is to be asked to grant relief from the effect of an unless order, this should normally be considered at a hearing.[118] A refusal to grant relief may be vitiated if the court fails to give reasons.[119]

---

112 *Marcan Shipping (London) Ltd v Kefalas* [2007] EWCA Civ 463, at [36].
113 *Ryder plc v Beever* [2012] EWCA Civ 1737, at [62].
114 *Ibid.*
115 See, eg, *Eden v Rubin* [2011] EWHC 3090 (QB), at [51], *per* Coulson J; see also *Rybak & Ors v Langbar International Ltd* [2010] EWHC 2015 (Ch), *per* Morgan J (deliberately destroying computer files).
116 *Pannone LLP v Aardvark Digital Ltd* [2011] EWCA Civ 803, at [33], *per* Tomlinson LJ.
117 *Ibid*, at [31].
118 See *Vernon v Spoudeas* [2010] EWCA Civ 666, at [25], *per* Ward LJ, citing *Collier v Williams* [2006] EWCA Civ 20, at [38], *per* Dyson LJ. In a similar vein, see also *Ryder plc v Beever* (2012) [2012] EWCA Civ 1737, at [62], *per* Dame Janet Smith.
119 *Vernon v Spoudeas* [2010] EWCA Civ 666, at [31] *et seq*, per Ward LJ.

Orders vs interest CPR, r 47.8(3), makes the following further provisions: **43.105**

'If—

(a) the paying party has not made an application in accordance with paragraph (1); and
(b) the receiving party commences the proceedings later than the period specified in rule 47.7, the court may disallow all or part of the interest otherwise payable to the receiving party under—
  (i) section 17 of the Judgments Act 1838; or
  (ii) section 74 of the County Courts Act 1984,

but will not impose any other sanction except in accordance with rule 44.11 (powers in relation to misconduct).'

The effect of these provisions is ambiguous. In particular, the effect of the words 'if the paying party has not made an application' is not clear. These words could be read as meaning that the act of making an application for an unless order would preclude the court from subsequently disallowing interest. Equally, the rule as a whole could be read as giving the court the power to impose whatever sanction it adjudges to be appropriate. There is no authority on which interpretation is correct, but the first of these two interpretations has prevailed in a number of cases decided at first instance. **43.106**

If the correct interpretation is that the court has no power to disallow interest once an application for an unless order has been made, then that would not give rise to any particular unfairness.[120] It should be noted, however, that there is no authority to confirm that that analysis is correct. **43.107**

Points of Dispute

Points of dispute contain the paying party's objections to the receiving party's costs. In practice, they tend to be akin to a hybrid between a counter-schedule and an abbreviated skeleton argument. **43.108**

Format

In so far as it is practicable, points of dispute must follow Precedent G of the precedents annexed to PD 47,[121] which can be found at Figure 43.3. As can be seen, points of dispute are made up of a repeating series of three rows, the first of which contains the paying party's objections, and the second and third of which are left empty for the receiving party's replies and the court's findings, respectively. **43.109**

There used to be a direction that stated that where points of dispute had been prepared on a computer, a copy of the computer file had to be provided free of charge upon request.[122] That provision no longer exists (possibly because it was thought to be so obvious a duty as to be implied). **43.110**

---

[120] That interpretation could be justified on the basis that a paying party who is faced with an apparently tardy opponent has a choice: either it can make an application to the court (in which case it would give up its rights concerning interest, but may benefit by way of an immediate order) or it can let the matter rest (in which case, it would not benefit by way of an immediate order, but may benefit by interest being disallowed).

[121] See PD 47, para 8.2.

[122] See now-revoked CPD, art 35.6.

SCHEDULE OF COSTS PRECEDENTS
PRECEDENT G: POINTS OF DISPUTE

IN THE HIGH COURT OF JUSTICE

QUEEN'S BENCH DIVISION **Claim number: 2000 B 9999**

OXBRIDGE DISTRICT REGISTRY

B E T W E E N

WX **Claimant**

- and -

YZ **Defendant**

POINTS OF DISPUTE SERVED BY THE DEFENDANT

Point 1 General point	Rates claimed for the assistant solicitor and other fee earners are excessive. Reduce to £158 and £116 respectively plus VAT.
	Receiving Party's Reply:
	Costs Officer's Decision:
Point 2 Point of principle	The claimant was at the time a child/protected person/insolvent and did not have the capacity to authorise the solicitors to bring these proceedings.
	Receiving Party's Reply:
	Costs Officer's Decision:
Point 3 (6), (12), (17), (23), (29), (32)	(i) The number of conferences with counsel is excessive and should be reduced to 3 in total (9 hours). (ii) There is no need for two fee earners to attend each conference. Limit to one assistant solicitor in each case.
	Receiving Party's Reply:
	Costs Officer's Decision:
Point 4 (42)	The claim for timed attendances on claimant (schedule 1) is excessive. Reduce to 4 hours.
	Receiving Party's Reply:
	Costs Officer's Decision:
Point 5 (47)	The total claim for work done on documents by the assistant solicitor is excessive. A reasonable allowance in respect of documents concerning court and counsel is 8 hours, for documents concerning witnesses and the expert witness 6.5 hours, for work done on arithmetic 2.25 hours and for other documents 5.5 hours. Reduce to 22.25 hours.
	Receiving Party's Reply:
	Costs Officer's Decision:
Point 6 (50)	The time claimed for preparing and checking the bill is excessive. Reduce solicitor's time to 0.5 hours and reduce the costs draftsman's time to three hours.
	Receiving Party's Reply:
	Costs Officer's Decision:

Served on .... [date] by ....[name] [legal representative of] the Defendant.

Figure 43.3 Precedent G: points of dispute and replies

Content

PD 47, para 8.2, gives guidance as to the contents of points of dispute: **43.111**

> '8.2 Points of dispute must be short and to the point. They must follow Precedent G in the Schedule of Costs Precedents annexed to this Practice Direction, so far as practicable. They must:
> (a) identify any general points or matters of principle which require decision before the individual items in the bill are addressed; and
> (b) identify specific points, stating concisely the nature and grounds of dispute. Once a point has been made it should not be repeated but the item numbers where the point arises should be inserted in the left hand box as shown in Precedent G.'

Much of this differs from what was in the CPD. The post-2013 provisions require paying parties to be brief and to group similar items together, so that each argument is stated only once. This is in contrast to the old provisions, which stipulated that each disputed item be identified, together with reasons.

Although there is no prescribed structure, the following sequence of objections is commonly encountered (but only in so far as the topics arise): **43.112**

(1) any issue arising out of the certificates;
(2) any issue concerning misconduct and delay in the assessment proceedings;
(3) the indemnity principle;
(4) proportionality (although this is often found at the end);
(5) estimates;
(6) hourly rates; and
(7) the individual items.

Brevity and prolixity

It should be noted that Precedent G is almost terse in its language. This reflects the fact that points of dispute ought to be short and to the point.[123] There is, however, a limit to the extent to which points of dispute can be shortened. Whilst he was dealing with a case governed by the pre-April 2013 CPD, Teare J had this to say about a schedule that a paying party had been ordered to produce because its points of dispute had been overly pithy: **43.113**

> 'All that was required, [counsel for the paying party] submitted, was a schedule which identified which items were disputed as briefly as possible. However, such a literal interpretation does not take sufficient account of the problem which had arisen at the detailed assessment. The Master would, I think, have been surprised at the suggestion that all that was required was a list of the items of dispute with no explanation as to why the items were in dispute. I have no doubt that when he ordered that [the paying party sets] out as "briefly as possible in a schedule those items that remain in dispute" he was reflecting and emphasising the requirement in the Costs Practice Direction that the nature and grounds of dispute be stated "concisely".'[124]

Thus overly short objections do not assist the court, but there are at least two other reasons why a paying party would be unwise to strive for supreme succinctness, as follows. **43.114**

- CPR, r 47.14(6), provides that, unless the court gives permission, only items specified in the points of dispute may be raised at a detailed assessment hearing. As such, it would a risky strategy not to counter every item to which objection is taken.

---

[123] See PD 47, para 8.2.
[124] *Mount Eden Land Ltd v Speechly Bircham LLP* [2014] EWHC 169 (QB), at [11].

- If the bill of costs is to be subject to provisional assessment, then—unless the paying party wants to risk incurring the costs of a post-provisional hearing—it may be the case that the only information that the court will have about its case is that which is in the bill of costs and points of dispute.

43.115 That said, prolixity would also be unwise. Prior to 1 April 2013, it was commonplace for points of dispute to be highly repetitive and formulaic. Sir Rupert Jackson (writing extra-judicially) had this to say on the topic:

> 'Points of dispute are said to be overlong, therefore expensive to read and expensive to reply to. . . . [T]hese pleadings are in large measure formulaic and are built up from standard paragraphs held by solicitors on their databases. In addition, there are lengthy passages in the points of dispute . . . dealing with time spent on documents. It would be better if the points of dispute . . . concentrated on the reasoning of the bill, not the detailed items . . . they should, where practical, deal with items compendiously, rather than repeat the same objection time and time again.'[125]

This is why PD 47, para 8.2, says that 'once a point has been made it should not be repeated but the item numbers where the point arises should be inserted in the left hand box as shown in Precedent G' (see 43.111).

Offers

43.116 **Individual offers** There used to be a requirement that each objection be accompanied by a corresponding offer (for example 'Item 42 is excessive . . . Offer 12 minutes').[126] That requirement no longer exists, but it remains the case that it is good practice to make an offer where this is practicable. Indeed, Precedent G illustrates this (see Figure 43.3).

43.117 Where appropriate, it is good practice to summate the individual objections made and to state the total time offered. If, for example, there are half a dozen objections to the documentary work, it would be appropriate to say: 'In summary, the paying party offers 6 hours.' This is particularly true in cases in which the bill of costs is likely to be provisionally assessed, because it is unlikely that the court would have the time to carry out the necessary arithmetic.

43.118 **Open global offers** There is now an express requirement to make an open global offer. It reads as follows:

> '8.3 The paying party must state in an open letter accompanying the points of dispute what sum, if any, that party offers to pay in settlement of the total costs claimed. The paying party may also make an offer under Part 36.'[127]

43.119 The reference to 'if any' makes it clear that a paying party may, if it so wishes, make a 'nil' open global offer. This invites the question of whether it is open to a paying party to make no offer at all. On a strict reading of PD 47, para 8.2, this would not be permissible, but it is difficult to see what sanction could reasonably and proportionately be imposed on a paying party who made no offer instead of a 'nil' offer. That said, there is no authority on the point.

43.120 It is not wholly clear what the purpose is of the open global offer. In particular, it is noticeable that there is no requirement that it be based on the maximum reductions possible in the light of the points of dispute (which, at least, would have been an identifiable purpose). The editor must confess to being perplexed as to what the purpose of the open global offer

---

[125] Jackson, R, *Review of Civil Litigation Costs: Final Report* (London: HMSO, 2010), ch 45, para 2.7.
[126] See CPD, art 35.3(3).
[127] PD 47, para 8.3.

is—but at least he is in good company, because other commentators have come to much the same view.[128]

In view of the fact that no one knows what the open global offer is for, it is not surprising that many paying parties make 'nil' offers. Indeed, this is so commonplace that the notion of the open global offer is becoming somewhat hard to justify. **43.121**

Reliance on budgets and estimates

If a paying party claims to have reasonably relied on a budget filed by a receiving party, or if the paying party wishes to rely upon the costs shown in the budget to dispute the reasonableness or proportionality of the costs claimed, that party must serve a statement setting out its case in the points of dispute.[129] Whilst there is no authority on the point, it is likely that this would also apply if the paying party were to wish to rely on a pre-1 April 2013 estimate of costs. **43.122**

Additional liabilities

Where the receiving party has a pre-commencement funding arrangement and their bill includes a claim for additional liabilities, a paying party may wish to ask about alternative means of funding, which request may be made in the points of dispute. In this regard, CPD, art 35.7 (which still applies to such matters), used to read as follows: **43.123**

> '(1) Where the receiving party claims an additional liability, a party who serves points of dispute on the receiving party may include a request for information about other methods of financing costs which were available to the receiving party.
>
> (2) Part 18 (further information) and the Practice Direction Supplementing that part apply to such a request.'

Part 18 will apply to any such request. This means that the request must be concise and strictly confined to matters that are reasonably necessary and proportionate to enable the paying party to prepare its own case or to understand the case it has to meet.[130] In so far as it is relevant, PD 18, para 1.6, gives the further following guidance: **43.124**

> '(1) A Request ... must—
> [...]
> (b) ... state that it is a Request made under Part 18, identify the [party making the request and the party receiving the request] and state the date on which it is made,
> (c) set out in a separate numbered paragraph each request for information or clarification,
> [...]
> (e) state the date by which the first party expects a response to the Request.
>
> (2) ...
> (a) A Request ... may, if convenient, be prepared in such a way that the response may be given on the same document.
> (b) To do this the numbered paragraphs of the Request should appear on the left hand half of each sheet so that the paragraphs of the response may then appear on the right.
> (c) Where a Request is prepared in this form an extra copy should be served for the use of the second party.'

---

[128] It is also worth noting that Simon Gibbs (a well-regarded commentator on costs) is also perplexed as to the purpose of open global offers: see Gibbs, S, 'It's a Mystery' (2013) 157(25) Solicitors Journal 19.

[129] PD 44, para 3.3.

[130] See PD 18, para 1.2.

Variation

43.125 If the paying party wishes to raise an argument that has not been articulated in the points of dispute, those points of dispute may be varied. The same is true of bills of costs and replies to points of dispute. Permission is not generally required, as is made clear by PD 47, para 13.10:

> '(1) If a party wishes to vary that party's ... points of dispute ... an amended or supplementary document must be filed with the court and copies of it must be served on all other relevant parties.
>
> (2) Permission is not required to vary ... points of dispute ... but the court may disallow the variation or permit it only upon conditions, including conditions as to the payment of any costs caused or wasted by the variation.'

The first of these paragraphs is often overlooked. It states that if a party wishes to vary its bill of costs, points of dispute or replies, a copy of the amended document must be filed at court. This requirement is rarely complied with where the variation takes place before a request has been made for a hearing.

Time limits

43.126 CPR, r 47.9, lays down the relevant procedure:

> '(1) The paying party and any other party to the detailed assessment proceedings may dispute any item in the bill of costs by serving points of dispute on—
> (a) the receiving party; and
> (b) every other party to the detailed assessment proceedings.
>
> (2) The period for serving points of dispute is 21 days after the date of service of the notice of commencement.
>
> (3) If a party serves points of dispute after the period set out in paragraph (2), that party may not be heard further in the detailed assessment proceedings unless the court gives permission.
>
> (Practice Direction 47 sets out requirements about the form of points of dispute).'

43.127 The time limit for serving points of dispute is 21 days after the date of service of the notice of commencement.[131] There used to be a provision that expressly stated that where a notice of commencement was served on a party outside England and Wales, the period within which that party should serve points of dispute was to be calculated by reference to CPR, Part 6, Section IV as if the notice of commencement had been a claim form and as if the period for serving points of dispute had been the period for filing a defence.[132] That provision seems no longer to exist, but the same is implied by PD 47, para 5.4, which reads as follows:

> '5.4 Where the notice of commencement is to be served outside England and Wales the date to be inserted in the notice of commencement for the paying party to send points of dispute is a date (not less than 21 days from the date of service of the notice) which must be calculated by reference to Section IV of Part 6 as if the notice were a claim form and as if the date to be inserted was the date for the filing of a defence.'

43.128 Where it is expressed as being a number of days, the time for serving points of dispute is computed in 'clear days'. CPR, r 2.8, provides:

> '[...]
>
> (2) A period of time expressed as a number of days shall be computed as clear days.

---

[131] See CPR, r 47.9(2).

[132] See now-revoked CPD, art 35.4(2).

(3) In this rule "clear days" means that in computing the number of days—
(a) the day on which the period begins; and
(b) if the end of the period is defined by reference to an event, the day on which that event occurs are not included.'

In view of the fact that the relevant period is always more than five days, Saturdays, Sundays, bank holidays, Christmas Day and Good Friday are included within the calculation,[133] but where the last day is a day on which the court office is closed, service may be effected in time if made on the next day on which the court office is open.[134] **43.129**

Consensual extensions of time

The time for serving points of dispute may be varied. PD 47, para 8.1, provides: 'Time for service of points of dispute may be extended or shortened either by agreement (rule 2.11) or by the court (rule 3.1(2)(a)). Any application is to the appropriate office.' **43.130**

It is generally accepted that parties have a free hand to consensually vary the period of time for serving points of dispute. The power to vary by consent is exercisable under CPR, r 2.11, as is made clear by PD 47, para 8.1. This received view may be wrong, however, in that it is easily arguable that the parties do not have the power to extend time for more than 28 days. This is because the combined effect of CPR, r 3.8(3) and (4), is that where a rule requires a party to do something within a specified time and where that rule specifies the consequence of failure to comply, the time for doing the act in question may not be extended by agreement between the parties for more than a period of 28 days.[135] This undoubtedly applies to an application for an extension of time to serve points of dispute because the rules stipulate the sanction (namely, the fact that the paying party may not be heard further unless the court gives permission).[136] In practice, however, this issue does not arise. **43.131**

In any event, Jackson LJ has made *obiter* comments to the effect that receiving parties should act reasonably when asked to grant an extension of time: **43.132**

> 'A variety of circumstances may arise in which one or other party (however diligent) may require a modest extension of time. Under rule 1.3 the parties have a duty to help the court in furthering the overriding objective. The overriding objective includes allotting an appropriate share of the court's resources to an individual case. Therefore legal representatives are not in breach of any duty to their client, when they agree to a reasonable extension of time which neither imperils future hearing dates nor otherwise disrupts the conduct of the litigation. On the contrary, by avoiding the need for a contested application they are furthering the overriding objective and also saving costs for the benefit of their own client.'[137]

Debarring orders for late service As to the provision that a defaulting paying party may not be heard further unless the court gives permission (see 43.127), the authors of *Cook on Costs* (who are both experienced judges) make the following point: **43.133**

> 'This is very much a backstop provision aimed at enabling a court to deal with one of several paying parties who serves his points of dispute late and takes little or no part until much later in proceedings. It would be a very rare case indeed that a court would decline

---

[133] CPR, r 2.8(4).
[134] CPR, r 2.8(5).
[135] It is worth noting that in *Hallam Estates Ltd v Baker* [2014] EWCA Civ 661, at [12], Jackson LJ referred to the 28-day limit as applying in the context of costs litigation.
[136] *Ibid.*
[137] See *ibid.*

to give permission for a party liable to pay the costs assessed by the court to be heard on that assessment.'[138]

As such, it seems unlikely that a paying party would find itself debarred from being heard further simply as a result of tardiness[139]—but this does not mean that it could never happen.

Applications to extend time

43.134 Provided that the applicant filed their application notice before expiry of the permitted time period, an application for an extension of the time to serve points of dispute is not an application for relief from sanctions, and that would be the case even if the court were to deal with the application after the expiry of the relevant period.[140]

Service

43.135 What follows relates to service of points of dispute, but it also relates to service of bills of costs and replies.

43.136 Service of documents generally is governed by CPR, Part 6, Section III. Other than as set out below, service may be effected by:

- personal service;[141]
- first-class post, document exchange or other service that provides for delivery on the next business day;[142]
- leaving the document at the opponent's address service;[143]
- fax, email or other electronic means (see below); or
- any other method authorised by the court.[144]

Special provisions apply to companies[145] and limited liability partnerships.[146]

Service of documents by email

43.137 Service may be effected by email.[147] Restrictions apply, but in relation to costs litigation, it is fair to say that many judges do not give them much weight.[148] Broadly speaking, the recipient must have expressly indicated in writing that they are willing to accept service by electronic means.[149] The unqualified inclusion of an email address in the receiving party's headed paper or statement of parties would amount to such an indication.[150] Where a party

---

138 See *Cook on Costs 2017* (LexisNexis, online), para 28.24.

139 That said, a paying party's failure to articulate its case properly may result in sanctions. Whilst it was a solicitor-and-client matter, see *Mount Eden Land Ltd v Speechly Bircham LLP* [2014] EWHC 169 (QB), referred to at 36.53.

140 See *Hallam Estates Ltd v Baker* [2014] EWCA Civ 661, at [26], *per* Jackson LJ, approving *Re Guidezone Ltd* [2014] EWHC 1165 (Ch) and *Robert v Momentum Services Ltd* [2003] EWCA Civ 299, at [33].

141 See CPR, r 6.20(1)(a). Service must be in accordance with CPR, r 6.22.

142 See CPR, r 6.20(1)(b); PD 6A.

143 See CPR, rr 6.20(1)(c) and 6.23.

144 See CPR, rr 6.20(1)(e) and 6.28.

145 See CPR, r 6.20(2).

146 See CPR, r 6.20(3).

147 See CPR, r 6.20(1)(d).

148 Whilst not binding, see, eg, *Brett v Colchester Hospital University NHS Foundation Trust* (unreported), 7 April 2014, SCCO, in which Master O'Hare commented that the requirements regarding email were largely historical.

149 PD 6A, para 4.1(1).

150 PD 6A, para 4.1(2)(b).

seeks to serve a document by electronic means, it should first seek to clarify with the party who is to be served whether there are any limitations to the recipient's agreement to accept service by such means, including the format in which documents are to be sent and the maximum size of attachments that may be received.[151] Where a document is served by electronic means, the party serving the document is not obliged also to effect service in hard copy.[152]

Service of documents by fax

Service may be effected by fax,[153] in which case it need not also be effected in hard copy.[154] The receiving party must have expressly indicated in writing that it is willing to accept service by fax and must have provided the requisite fax number.[155] Again, the unqualified inclusion of a fax number in the receiving party's headed paper or statement of parties would amount to such an express indication.[156] Whilst a slight digression, it should be noted that documents may not be filed by fax in the SCCO, because that court no longer has a fax machine. **43.138**

Failure to serve

If a party serves points of dispute after the requisite period, they may not—in theory—be heard further in the detailed assessment proceedings unless the court gives permission (see 43.127).[157] In practice, however, this almost never happens (see 43.133). If the period of time for serving points of dispute has expired and if points of dispute have not been served, then the receiving party may file a request for a default costs certificate (see 43.142).[158] **43.139**

Default Costs Certificates

A default costs certificate certifies the amount that the paying party must pay consequent upon that party having failed to file points of dispute. It is issued in an amount that is based on the sum claimed in the bill of costs, rather than a sum that the court has judged to be reasonable. **43.140**

A default costs certificate will be effective only against the paying party; it will not be effective against the CLS Fund or the Lord Chancellor.[159] The default costs procedure does not apply to solicitor-and-client assessments.[160] **43.141**

Issue

A default costs certificate is issued only upon application.[161] Where the relevant court is a County Court hearing centre or a High Court district registry in London, default costs certificates should be issued in the relevant hearing centre or registry, not in the SCCO.[162] **43.142**

---

[151] PD 6A, para 4.2.
[152] PD 6A, para 4.3.
[153] See CPR, r 6.20(1)(d).
[154] PD 6A, para 4.3. Whilst this provision refers to 'electronic means' rather than to 'fax or electronic means', it is generally regarded as applying to both.
[155] PD 6A, para 4.1.
[156] PD 6A, para 4.1(2)(a).
[157] CPR, r 47.9(3).
[158] CPR, r 47.9(4).
[159] PD 47, para 10.4.
[160] PD 46, para 6.8.
[161] The procedure is governed by PD 47, para 10.1.
[162] See PD 47, para 4.2(2)(b).

43.143 The jurisdiction is defined by CPR, r 47.9:

> '(4) The receiving party may file a request for a default costs certificate if—
> (a) the period set out in paragraph (2) for serving points of dispute has expired; and
> (b) the receiving party has not been served with any points of dispute.
>
> (5) If any party (including the paying party) serves points of dispute before the issue of a default costs certificate the court may not issue the default costs certificate.'

Timing of applications

43.144 Whilst *obiter*, Jackson LJ has commented that if the receiving party wishes to obtain a default costs certificate, they must file the request (a) after expiry of the time permitted for serving the points of dispute and (b) before the points of dispute are served.[163] Whilst not binding, Judge Wood QC has found that the words 'may not issue' in CPR, r 47.9(5), do not confer a discretion, but are 'strictly prohibitive'.[164] The effect of this is that the court is not able to issue a default costs certificate if the paying party serves points of dispute in the interval between an application being made and a certificate being issued.

43.145 It is implicit from these provisions that the receiving party must inform the court if points of dispute are received after a request for a default costs certificate has been made, but before a certificate has been issued.

The form of application and certificates

43.146 The model form of request[165] for a default costs certificate contains two certificates:

- a certificate confirming that the paying party has been served with the notice of commencement, the bill of costs and a copy of the document giving rise to the detailed assessment; and
- a certificate confirming that points of dispute have not been served.

43.147 It is mandatory that the model form is used and it must be signed by the receiving party or their legal representative.[166] The request must be accompanied by the document giving rise to the detailed assessment[167] (which will usually be a costs order). No further evidence is required. That said, the request must provide sufficient information to enable the court to process the request and, in this regard, it should be borne in mind that, where the request is made to the SCCO, there will be no court file, so the only paperwork that the court will have will be the form of request and its attachments.

Costs of issue of a default costs certificate

43.148 Unless the court orders otherwise, fixed costs are payable upon the issue of a default costs certificate.[168] Where the certificate has been made in the context of costs-only proceedings, the court is able to award the receiving party the costs of those proceedings.[169]

---

163 *Hallam Estates Ltd v Baker* [2014] EWCA Civ 661, at [36].
164 See *Cadwallader v Akzo Nobel UK* (unreported), 16 June 2014, Liverpool County Court, at [15], *per* Judge Wood QC.
165 Forms N254 and N255—Form N255 (HC) for the High Court—which are a request for a default costs certificate and the certificate itself, respectively.
166 PD 47, para 10.1(1).
167 PD 47, para 10.1(2).
168 PD 47, paras 10.7 and 10.8
169 See *Tasleem v Beverly* [2013] EWCA Civ 1805.

Setting aside

CPR, Part 47, used to provide that where a receiving party discovers that its notice of commencement failed to reach the paying party at least 21 days before the default costs certificate had been issued, the onus was on the receiving party to take active steps to have it set aside[170]—but that provision seems no longer to exist. That said, it remains the case that a receiving party is able to make an application to have a default costs certificate set aside, should that party feel that this is appropriate.[171] Where this is done, the application may be dealt with by a court officer, rather than a judge.[172] **43.149**

In view of the above, the onus now appears to be on the paying party to make an application for the certificate to be set aside. Such an application will be dealt with by a costs judge or a district judge.[173] **43.150**

CPR, r 47.12, gives the following guidance: **43.151**

> '(1) The court will set aside a default costs certificate if the receiving party was not entitled to it.
>
> (2) In any other case, the court may set aside or vary a default costs certificate if it appears to the court that there is some good reason why the detailed assessment proceedings should continue.
>
> (Practice Direction 47 contains further details about the procedure for setting aside a default costs certificate and the matters which the court must take into account.)
>
> (3) Where the court sets aside or varies a default costs certificate in detailed assessment proceedings pursuant to an order under section 194(3) of the Legal Services Act 2007, the receiving party must send a copy of the order setting aside or varying the default costs certificate to the prescribed charity.'

There are two bases upon which a paying party may bring an application to set aside a default costs certificate: **43.152**

- where the receiving party was not entitled to it; and
- where there is 'some good reason' why the detailed assessment proceedings should continue.[174]

Each is considered in turn.

Procedure for setting aside

An application to set aside on the basis of 'good reason' must be supported by evidence.[175] It is implicit within the provisions of PD 47 that the application ought to be accompanied by: **43.153**

- a copy of the bill of costs;
- a draft of the points of dispute that the paying party proposes to serve if the application is successful; and
- a copy of the default costs certificate.[176]

Where the relevant court is a County Court hearing centre or High Court district registry in London, the application should be made to the court that issued the certificate rather than to the SCCO.[177] **43.154**

---

170 See the pre-April 2013 version of CPR, r 47.12(3).
171 This is implied by PD 47, para 11.1.
172 PD 47, para 11.1.
173 PD 47, para 11.1.
174 CPR, r 47.12
175 PD 47, para 11.2(1); see also CPR, r 3.9(2).
176 PD 47, para 11.2(3).
177 See PD 47, para 4.2(2)(b).

Setting aside as of right

43.155 If the receiving party was not entitled to the default costs certificate, then the court has no option but to set it aside.[178] If one bears in mind the circumstances in which a receiving party is able to apply for a default costs certificate[179] (see 43.143), the following are the circumstances in which the court would have to take that course of action:

- where there had been a failure to serve a notice of commencement;
- where the certificate had been issued before the requisite period[180] had expired; or
- where points of dispute had been served before the certificate was issued.[181]

This list is not exhaustive; other similar circumstances might include where the bill of costs was grossly defective or where there had been an agreement between the parties that a default costs certificate would not be issued.

43.156 **Estoppel by convention and setting aside default costs certificates** It should be noted that estoppel by convention may prevent a paying party from complaining about defective service of a notice of commencement if both parties had mistakenly assumed that service had been effective and proceeded on that basis.[182]

43.157 **Errors in default costs certificates and setting aside** The certificate may contain an error that, if uncorrected, would award the receiving party costs to which it was not entitled. That would not necessarily be reason to set it aside;[183] it would, of course, be reason to vary it.

Setting aside for 'good reason'

43.158 An application to set aside for good reason is generally regarded as an application for relief from sanctions. It has been argued, however, that such issues are decided under a different set of rules from CPR, r 3.9, and that therefore the test in *Denton*[184] does not apply—an argument that has been accepted in a number of first-instance cases.[185] That said, it is noticeable that Jackson LJ made no mention of such an analysis in a case in which the issue of relief from sanctions and *Mitchell*[186] arose in the context of a party seeking to extend time for serving points of dispute.[187]

43.159 **Relevant factors** In practice, certain factors are regarded as being particularly relevant. Whilst many of the authorities referred to below were decided under the pre-April 2013 provisions, they are still indicative of the factors on which the court tends to focus—namely:

---

178 CPR, r 47.12(1).

179 CPR, r 47.9(4).

180 CPR, r 47.9(2). This period is 21 days after service of the notice of commencement.

181 In addition to CPR, r 47.9(5), see *Hallam Estates Ltd v Baker* [2014] EWCA Civ 661, at [36], *per* Jackson LJ.

182 See *Edray v Canning* [2015] EWHC 2744 (Ch).

183 See the comments in *Meghani v Nessfield Ltd* [2008] EWHC 2827 (Ch), at [7], which indicate that, on an earlier occasion, Collins J rejected the argument that a miscalculation was reason to set aside the certificate.

184 *Denton v TH White Ltd* [2014] EWCA Civ 906.

185 Whilst not binding, see, eg, *Brett v Colchester Hospital University NHS Foundation Trust* (unreported), 7 April 2014, SCCO, in which Master O'Hare commented that the requirements regarding email were largely historical.

186 *Mitchell v News Group Newspapers Ltd* [2013] EWCA Civ 1537.

187 See *Hallam Estates Ltd v Baker* [2014] EWCA Civ 661.

- the punctuality with which the application to set aside was made;[188]
- the reasons why points of dispute were not served in time and whether this failure was intentional or accidental;[189]
- whether there was a good explanation for the failure to serve points of dispute on time,[190] such as serious illness;[191]
- the extent to which the points of dispute were out of time and the efforts (or lack thereof) that were made by the receiving party to prompt the paying party to serve them;
- the merits of the bill and, in particular, whether the objections in the draft points of dispute are likely to result in a significant reduction in the allowable costs;[192]
- whether the application was accompanied by the bill of costs, draft points of dispute and a default costs certificate;[193]
- the amount of costs claimed and whether it would be proportionate to allow a detailed assessment to proceed;[194]
- the effect that granting relief would have on the parties;[195] and
- the overall justice of the situation and whether any prejudice can be compensated for by an award of costs.[196]

Brooke LJ had the following to say (*obiter*) about the last of these factors: **43.160**

> 'The overriding objective necessarily implied that dealing with a case justly included actually dealing with the case. If the deputy judge had made any other order, he would have shut out the council entirely from pursuing the disputed points in relation to costs, and both sides agreed that the amount of costs were very substantial indeed.'[197]

It may be that the court would take a different view under the *Denton* test.

Power to make an order that amount of costs on account is paid as a condition to setting aside a certificate PD 47, para 11.3, seeks to draw attention to CPR, rr 3.1(3) (which enables the court, when making an order, to make it subject to conditions) and 44.2(8) (which enables the court to order a party whom it has ordered to pay costs to pay an amount on account before the costs are assessed). That direction goes on to state that a costs judge may exercise the power of the court to make an order under CPR, r 44.2(8), notwithstanding the fact that they did not make the order about costs that led to the issue of the default costs certificate. **43.161**

188 PD 47, para 11.2(2); CPR, r 3.9(1)(b). See also the unnamed case mentioned in *Seray-Wurie v London Borough of Hackney* [2002] EWCA Civ 909, at [10]; *Bagley v Branch* [2007] EWHC 2344 (Ch), *per* Kitchen J.

189 *Smolen v Solon Co-operative Housing Services Ltd* [2005] EWCA Civ 1567.

190 See *ibid.*

191 In general, any illness has to be serious in the sense that it incapacitates the paying party. An example of this is a case in which a paying party had a series of illnesses and operations, including a short stay in intensive care, but failed to persuade the court that this was sufficient because he failed to prove that he was unable to give instructions: *Omatov v Macaria Investment Ltd* [2015] EWHC 2799 (Ch).

192 *Ford v Labrador* [2003] UKPC 41; *Seray-Wurie v London Borough of Hackney* [2002] EWCA Civ 909.

193 PD 47, 11.2(3).

194 *Ford v Labrador* [2003] UKPC 41.

195 *Ibid.*

196 *Ibid.*

197 *Seray-Wurie v London Borough of Hackney* [2002] EWCA Civ 909, at [11].

Punctuality

43.162 On the facts of the case before him (in which the paying party was hampered by practical problems), Gibbs J commented that it was difficult to imagine a more prompt application to set aside than three days.[198] This indicates that the court will take into account the paying party's circumstances, including any difficulties that they may encounter (but see 43.163). It also—perhaps—gives a broad indication of the time scales that would be regarded as being sufficiently prompt.

Procrastination

43.163 Where a paying party (who acted in person throughout) failed entirely to serve points of dispute, Jack J declined to allow an appeal against a decision not to set the certificate aside. He found (*obiter*) that procrastination by the paying party may be factor to be taken into account, even if the paying party is disadvantaged as a result of illness.[199] Thus there appears to be a limit to the extent to which the court will take the paying party's circumstances into account.

Procedural irregularities

43.164 Whilst rare, it will occasionally be the case that the process by which a default costs certificate came into being was flawed by reason of procedural irregularity, an example being a case in which a judge effectively allowed a default costs certificate against one party to turn into a costs order against a third party, without the judge giving thought to the issue of how much, if anything, that person should pay.[200] Where this happens, the correct way of dealing with the issue would be by way of appeal. Where the certificate itself contains an error, see 43.157.

***Pro bono* work**

43.165 Where a lawyer acts *pro bono* under Legal Services Act 2007, s 194, the following two provisions will apply.

- Where a receiving party obtains a default costs certificate in detailed assessment proceedings pursuant to an order under s 194(3) of the 2007 Act, that party must send a copy of the default costs certificate to the prescribed charity.[201]
- Where the court sets aside or varies a default costs certificate in detailed assessment proceedings pursuant to an order under s 194(3), the receiving party must send a copy of the order setting aside or varying the default costs certificate to the prescribed charity.[202]

Replies to Points of Dispute

43.166 Replies are the receiving party's comments on the objections raised in the points of dispute. They are optional,[203] but as, the editors of the White Book say:

---

198 Unreported case mentioned in *Seray-Wurie v London Borough of Hackney* [2002] EWCA Civ 909, at [10].
199 *Smolen v Solon Co-Operative Housing Services Ltd* [2005] EWCA Civ 1567.
200 *Salekipour v Parmar* [2013] EWCA Civ 1376. This case was only an application for permission to appeal and, as such, ought not to be cited in court.
201 CPR, r 47.11(3).
202 CPR, r 47.12(3).
203 CPR, r 47.13(1).

'[Whilst] there is no obligation upon the receiving party to serve a reply . . ., if the receiving party fails to do so, this may be a factor taken into account . . . when the court is considering what order to make in respect of the costs of the detailed assessment proceedings.'[204]

Format

It used to be the case that replies could either be presented as a separate document prepared by the receiving party *de novo* or included within the same document as the points of dispute.[205] That provision has not been carried over into PD 47 from the CPD. Where practicable, replies need to be set out in the style of Precedent G[206] (that is, the same precedent as is used for points of dispute) (see Figure 43.3). Whilst the contrary is arguable,[207] it would seem, as a matter of common sense, that, where practicable, the receiving party should use the same document as the paying party. Moreover, where the bill of costs is to be subject to provisional assessment, it is a requirement that combined points of dispute and replies be filed.[208] In any event, to the extent that the receiving party has a choice, there can be no doubt that a failure to file a combined document will make the court's task much harder than it would otherwise be—and this would do the receiving party no favours. **43.167**

Procedure

Where a party to the detailed assessment proceedings serves points of dispute, the receiving party may serve a reply on the other parties to the assessment proceedings.[209] The time for doing so is within 21 days after service of the points of dispute,[210] but, in practice, late service will not usually result in any adverse consequences other than those that sound in costs (see 43.169). There used to be a requirement that replies be signed by the party serving them or by their solicitor, but this is no longer the case. **43.168**

Unless the receiving party has disobeyed a specific order, no default sanction will be imposed for the late service of replies.[211] This does not mean that a receiving party may ignore the option to serve replies with impunity; if they fail to serve replies in circumstances in which such sensible intervention would have saved costs, a receiving party may be ordered to bear the costs thrown away. **43.169**

Anecdotally, some courts have upheld points of dispute to which there have been no replies. In this regard, the editor wholly agrees with the authors of *Cook on Costs 2017* (both of whom are experienced judges) who say that such a practice is 'simply wrong' and that it 'runs counter to the aim of limiting replies to aspects which are helpful'.[212] **43.170**

---

[204] See White Book 2018, para 47.13.1.
[205] See pre-April 2013 CPD, art 39.1(2).
[206] See PD 47, para 12.2.
[207] PD 47, para 13.2 (which deals with the documents that need to be filed at court along with the bill of costs), refers to points of dispute and replies as if they were (or as if they were capable of being) separate documents.
[208] See PD 47, para 14.3(e).
[209] See CPR, r 47.13(1).
[210] CPR, r 47.13(2).
[211] Whilst not binding, as an example of a case in which the court refused to impose a sanction for putative non-compliance with CPR, r 47.13(2), see *Sullivan v Rollingsons Solicitors* (unreported), 21 March 2014, Liverpool County Court, *per* DDJ Mulrooney.
[212] See *Cook on Costs 2017* (LexisNexis, online), para 28.26.

Content

43.171 PD 47, para 12.1, provides that replies must be limited to points of principle and concessions only; they must not contain general denials, specific denials or standard-form responses. The intention underpinning these directions is to avoid the highly repetitious, uninformative documents that used to be served before April 2013. Whilst there is no authority on the point, a degree of common sense is needed in applying this rule. For example, if the whole assessment turns on the indemnity principle, it would not be appropriate for the receiving party to remain silent on that issue in the mistaken belief that its case is a general denial.

43.172 Where the bill of costs is likely to be the subject of provisional assessment, it should not be forgotten that it is possible that the replies will be the only opportunity that the receiving party gets to state its case. Where appropriate, it is good practice to assist the court by stating facts that otherwise could be gleaned only by a detailed reading of the receiving party's file of papers. In this regard, it is unlikely that a judge would complain if the replies were to contain entries such as 'the letter was six pages long' or 'the trial was only a fortnight away': these, strictly speaking, are neither concessions nor points of principle, but they are points that are likely to make the court's task easier.

43.173 In a similar vein, where a number of concessions are made in respect of timed work, it is good practice to summate the individual concessions and to state the total time that is counter-offered. If, for example, there were to be half a dozen concessions made in relation to the documentary work, it would be good practice to say 'once the above concessions have been taken into account, the time claimed is 5 hours 12 minutes'.

Additional liabilities and replies

43.174 There are other more specific instances in which a failure to serve replies may result in adverse consequences. Both relate to additional liabilities and, as such, will be of interest only if the receiving party has the benefit of a pre-commencement funding arrangement. The first is where the receiving party has failed to reply to an objection to counsel's success fee. This may result in a finding against the receiving party, because CPD, art 20.4, makes the following provisions, which suggest that an absence of a response may be taken as tacit acceptance of the challenge raised:

> '(1) Where detailed assessment proceedings have been commenced, and the paying party serves points of dispute ... which show that he is seeking a reduction in any percentage increase charged by counsel on his fees, the solicitor acting for the receiving party must within 3 days of service deliver to counsel a copy of the relevant points of dispute and the bill of costs or the relevant parts of the bill.
>
> (2) Counsel must within 10 days thereafter inform the solicitor in writing whether or not he will accept the reduction sought or some other reduction. Counsel may state any points he wishes to have made in a reply to the points of dispute, and the solicitor must serve them on the paying party as or as part of a reply.
>
> (3) Counsel who fails to inform the solicitor within the time limits set out above will be taken to accept the reduction unless the court otherwise orders.'

43.175 The second instance is where a receiving party has the benefit of a staged ATE policy. Where this is so, CPD, art 39.2, provides that where there is a dispute about the insurance premium in a staged policy, it will normally be sufficient for the receiving party to set out in any replies the reasons for choosing the particular insurance policy and the basis on which the insurance premium is rated, whether block rated or individually rated.[213] For obvious reasons, if a receiving party fails to take advantage of this provision and remains silent, they may have given up the chance to prove their case at minimal cost.

Requesting an Assessment

If the parties, after having exchanged points of dispute and replies, are still unable to agree the amount of costs claimed, their next step would be to ask the court for an assessment. The onus lies with the receiving party. **43.176**

Time limits

Where points of dispute have been served, the receiving party must file a request for an assessment, and it must do so within three months of the expiry of the period for commencing detailed assessment proceedings as specified in CPR, r 47.7, or as specified by the court.[214] This means that, in general, the receiving party must request an assessment no later than six months after the right to costs arose. **43.177**

The form of request

CPR, r 47.14, refers to such a request as being 'a request for a detailed assessment hearing'; perhaps the better term is that it is a request for an assessment. This is because, in smaller cases (see 43.196), the court will direct that there should be a provisional assessment;[215] the court would offer a detailed assessment hearing only if the parties were not satisfied with the court's provisional assessment of the costs. It will only be in larger cases that the request will be treated as being a request for a detailed assessment hearing.[216] **43.178**

A request for an assessment is made by way of standard form (Form N258), use of which is mandatory.[217] If the assessment proceedings have been a very long-running affair, then it may be appropriate to use a pre-April 2013 version of that form.[218] Figure 43.4 is the present-day version of the form. **43.179**

The same form is used regardless of whether the costs qualify for a provisional assessment or not and should state the estimated length of hearing[219] (assuming, of course, that the matter goes to a hearing). The court will decide whether to offer provisional assessment on the basis of the information given by the receiving party on the face of the form. As can be seen from Figure 43.4, the receiving party is required to select which of the following two confirmations is correct: **43.180**

> 'I confirm the costs claimed are £75,000 or less and I ask the court to undertake a provisional assessment.'
>
> 'I confirm the costs claimed are over £75,000 and I ask the court to arrange a detailed assessment hearing.'

---

213 It should be noted that CPD, art 39.2, contains a typographical error: the reference to 'CPD, art 19.4(3A)' was clearly intended to be a reference to CPD, art 19.4(3)(c).
214 See CPR, r 47.14(1;) PD 47, para 13.1.
215 See CPR, r 47.15(7).
216 See CPR, r 47.14(1).
217 See PD 47, para 13.2. A different style of standard form (Form N258A) must be used for publicly funded work.
218 This is because the new form asks questions that are inappropriate to cases in which the detailed assessment proceedings began before 1 April 2013 (see 43.178). The editor is grateful to Simon Gibbs (costs lawyer) for pointing this out.
219 See PD 47, para 13.2(i).

Request for provisional/ detailed assessment
(general form)

Name of court	
Claim no.	
Claimant (include Ref.)	
Defendant (include Ref.)	

I certify that the Notice of Commencement was served on the paying party ______________________
(and give details of any other party served with the notice)

on ______________ *(insert date)*

I enclose *(tick as appropriate)*

☐ the document giving the right to detailed assessment;

☐ the Notice of Commencement;

☐ the bill of costs;

☐ the paying party's points of dispute, annotated as necessary in order to show (1) which items have been agreed and their value and (2) which items remain in dispute and their value (Precedent G);

☐ points in reply (if any);

☐ a statement giving the names, addresses for service and references of all persons to whom the court should give notice of the hearing;

☐ the relevant details of any additional liability claimed;

☐ copies of all the orders made by the court relating to the costs of the proceedings which are to be assessed;

☐ any fee notes of counsel and receipts or accounts for other disbursements relating to items in dispute;

☐ [where there is a dispute as to the receiving parties ability to pay] the client care letter delivered to the receiving party or the legal representative's retainer;

☐ I confirm the costs claimed are **£75,000 or less** and I ask the court to undertake a **provisional assessment.**

I also enclose *(tick as appropriate)*

☐ an additional copy of the bill, including a statement of the costs claimed in respect of the detailed assessment based on the assumption that there will not be an oral hearing; and

☐ the offers made (those marked 'without prejudice save as to costs' or made under Part 36 must be contained in a sealed envelope, marked 'Part 36 or similar offers', but not indicating which party or parties have made them).

☐ I confirm the costs claimed are **over £75,000** and I ask the court to arrange a detailed **assessment hearing.**

☐ I believe the hearing will take ☐ *(give estimate of time court should allow).*

I enclose the fee of £__________ Fee Account no. ☐

Signed ______________________ **Date** ______________
(Claimant)(Defendant)('s legal representative)

Please address forms or letters to the Operational Delivery Manager and quote the claim number.

N258 Request for detailed assessment hearing (general form) (05.14)

Figure 43.4 Form N258 (post April 2013)

Accompanying documents

Certain documents must be filed at court at the time the request is made. Whilst the form is the same regardless of whether the costs qualify for provisional assessment (that is, Form N258), the documents that must be filed depend on whether or not the costs qualify for a provisional assessment. This means that the receiving party must take a view as to whether the costs qualify in that regard. **43.181**

Documents for requesting a hearing

The following is a composite list[220] of documents that must be filed at court when asking for a detailed assessment hearing (that is, where the costs do not qualify for a provisional assessment). If the request relates to costs that qualify for a provisional assessment, then the documents listed at 43.185 will also need to be filed. **43.182**

The editor has tried to group documents by type. The order and names of the groups are merely his invention. **43.183**

- **Court forms**
  - Form N258 (that is, the request for an assessment)[221]
  - A copy of the notice of commencement of detailed assessment proceedings[222]
- **Administrative details**
  - A statement signed by the receiving party or the legal representative, giving the name, email address, address for service, reference and telephone number of[223]
    - the receiving party,
    - the paying party and
    - any other person who has served points of dispute or who has informed the receiving party of a financial interest in the assessment,

    and, where appropriate, giving an estimate of the length of time an assessment hearing will take[224]
- **Court orders**
  - A copy of the document giving the right to detailed assessment[225]
  - Copies of all orders made by the court relating to the costs that are to be assessed[226]
- **Retainer documentation**
  - Any agreement, letter or other written information provided by the legal representative to the client explaining how the legal representative's charges are to be calculated (but only where there is a dispute concerning the indemnity principle)[227]

---

220 The list takes into account the provisions in PD 47, para 8.3, and PD 47, para 13.2, as well as the guidance given on Form N258.
221 See CPD, art 13.2.
222 See PD 47, para 13.2(a).
223 See PD 47, para 5.2, which is invoked by PD 47, para 13.2(j).
224 See PD 47, para 13.2(g).
225 See PD 47, paras 13.2(c) and 13.3.
226 See PD 47, para 13.2(g).
227 See PD 47, para 13.2(i).

- **Costs 'pleadings'**
  - The bill of costs[228]
  - A copy of the points of dispute[229] and replies,[230] annotated as necessary to show which items have been agreed and their value, as well as which items remain in dispute and their value[231]
  - As many copies of the annotated points of dispute as there are persons who have served points of dispute[232]
- **Proof of expenditure**
  - Copies of any fee notes of counsel or fee notes of expert witnesses that were served with the notice of commencement[233]
  - Copies of any written evidence as to any other disbursement that is claimed and which exceeds £500[234]
- **Legal aid documentation**
  - If the receiving party is an assisted person, or LSC-funded client, or other person to whom civil legal services have been provided, then also:[235]
    - The legal aid certificate, LSC certificate, the certificate recording the determination of the Director of Legal Aid Casework and relevant amendment certificates, any authorities and any certificates of discharge or revocation or withdrawal
    - A certificate in the form of Precedent F(3) of the Schedule of Costs Precedents
    - If that other person has a financial interest in the detailed assessment hearing and wishes to attend, their postal address, to which the court will send notice of any hearing
    - If the rates payable out of the LSC fund or by the Lord Chancellor under Part 1 of the Legal Aid, Sentencing and Punishment of Offenders Act 2012 are prescribed rates, a schedule to the bill of costs setting out all of the items in the bill that are claimed against other parties, calculated at the legal aid prescribed rates, with or without any claim for enhancement[236]
  - A copy of any default costs certificate in respect of costs claimed in the bill of costs[237]

In addition to the above, if the receiving party seeks an interim costs certificate, it is good practice to include the relevant application.

43.184 In addition, the SCCO Guide 2018 says that the receiving party should also file a note of any dates upon which, to the knowledge of that party, a detailed assessment hearing would be inconvenient for any party likely to attend.[238]

---

228 PD 47, para 13.2(b).
229 See PD 47, para 13.2(e).
230 PD 47, para 13.2(f).
231 See PD 47, para 13.2(d).
232 See PD 47, para 13.2(e).
233 See PD 47, para 5.2, which is invoked by PD 47, para 13.2(h).
234 PD 47, para 5.2.
235 See PD 47, para 13.2(l), which is invoked by PD 47, para 14.3(b).
236 Further information as to this schedule is set out in PD 47, para 17.
237 PD 47, para 13.2(v).
238 HM Courts & Tribunals Services, *Senior Courts Costs Office Guide* (London: HMSO, 2018), para 12.5.

Documents for provisional assessment

Where the costs qualify for provisional assessment, then all of the documents referred to at 43.183 must be filed,[239] as well as the following. **43.185**

- **Costs 'pleadings'**
  - An additional copy of any old-style bill of costs, including a statement of the costs claimed in respect of the detailed assessment, drawn on the assumption that there will not be a post-provisional hearing following the provisional assessment[240]
  - Completed Precedent G (that is, points of dispute and any replies)[241]
- **Offers**
  - The paying party's open letter accompanying the points of dispute, stating what sum, if any, that party offers to pay in settlement of the total costs claimed (see 43.119)[242]
  - Any other offers that have been made[243]
- **Additional liabilities (if relevant)**[244]
  - Where there is a pre-commencement conditional fee agreement:
    - a statement showing the amount of costs that have been summarily assessed or agreed and the percentage increase that has been claimed in respect of those costs
    - a statement of the reasons for the percentage increase given, in accordance with the Conditional Fee Agreements Regulations 2000,[245] reg 3(1)(a) or 5(1)(c)
  - Where there is a pre-commencement ATE policy, a copy of the insurance certificate, showing:
    - whether the policy covers the receiving party's own costs, or their opponent's costs, or their own costs and their opponent's costs
    - the maximum extent of that cover
    - the amount of the premium paid or payable
  - Where there is a pre-commencement agreement under s 30 of the Access of Justice Act 1999, a statement setting out the basis upon which the receiving party's liability for the additional amount is calculated

Where any of the offers were made on a 'without-prejudice save as to costs' basis or under CPR, Part 36, those offers must be contained in a sealed envelope, marked 'Part 36 or similar offers'. The envelope must not indicate which party or parties made those offers (if any).[246]

Fees

The Ministry of Justice is empowered to levy a fee for the court's services.[247] It is the Ministry's stated aim that court fees should be set, so far as possible, at levels that reflect the full cost of the process involved.[248] **43.186**

---

[239] See PD 47, para 14.3(b).
[240] See PD 47, para 14.3(c).
[241] See PD 47, para 14.3(e).
[242] See PD 47, paras 14.3(b) and 8.3.
[243] See PD 47, para 14.3(d).
[244] CPD, art 32.5.
[245] SI 2000/692.
[246] See PD 47, para 14.3(d).
[247] Courts Act 2003, s 92.
[248] See Ministry of Justice, *Civil Court Fees 2008*, CP31/08 (London: HMSO, 2008), para 2.

Table 43.2 Court fees for detailed assessment

Sums claimed	Fee payable
Does not exceed £15,000	£369
Exceeds £15,000 but does not exceed £50,000	£734
Exceeds £50,000 but does not exceed £100,000	£1,106
Exceeds £100,000 but does not exceed £150,000	£1,480
Exceeds £150,000 but does not exceed £200,000	£1,848
Exceeds £200,000 but does not exceed £300,000	£2,772
Exceeds £300,000 but does not exceed £500,000	£4,620
Exceeds £500,000	£6,160

43.187 A little over a decade ago, fees for detailed assessment were modest; in 2008, following consultation, they were significantly increased.[249] Whilst the fees were listed in Sch 1 to the Civil Proceedings Fees (Amendment) Order 2014,[250] that Order merely reproduced the 2008 fees. Initially, despite the fact that other court fees were significantly increased in 2015,[251] the fees for detailed assessment escaped change; on 25 July 2016, they too were increased.[252]

43.188 Where the only costs to be assessed are publicly funded costs, a fee of £220 is payable.[253] In all other cases, a sliding scale will apply, as set out in Table 43.2, that scale being based on the sums claimed.[254]

43.189 Where the bill contains both publicly funded costs and costs payable between the parties, the fees will be attributed proportionately on the basis of the amounts allowed.[255]

Delay

43.190 The paying party may not apply for a hearing; instead, where the receiving party has failed to apply for a hearing within the period mentioned above, the paying party may file a request for an order requiring the receiving party to file a request.[256]

Unless orders

43.191 The court may direct that, unless the receiving party requests a detailed assessment hearing within a certain time, all or part of the costs to which the receiving party would otherwise be entitled will be disallowed.[257] Such an order is usually referred to as an 'unless order'.

[249] Civil Proceedings Fees Order 2008 (SI 2008/1053), art 1(1).
[250] SI 2014/874.
[251] Civil Proceedings and Family Proceedings Fees (Amendment) Order 2015 (SI 2015/576).
[252] See the Civil Proceedings, First-tier Tribunal, Upper Tribunal and Employment Tribunals Fees (Amendment) Order 2016 (SI 2016/807).
[253] Civil Proceedings Fees Order 2008 (SI 2008/1053) (as amended), Sch 1, Fee 5, para 5.1.
[254] Civil Proceedings Fees Order 2008 (SI 2008/1053) (as amended), Sch 1, Fee 5, para 5.2.
[255] Civil Proceedings Fees Order 2008 (SI 2008/1053) (as amended), Sch 1, Fee 5, para 5.2.
[256] CPR, r 47.14(2).
[257] CPR, r 47.14(3).

There is no reason why the guidance given by Moore-Bick LJ about unless orders in general would not apply (see 43.100).[258] He reminded himself that an unless order is one of the most powerful weapons in the court's case management armoury and that it should be deployed only if 'its consequences can be justified'. He also reminded himself that it would be difficult to imagine circumstances in which such an order could properly be made for 'good housekeeping purposes'. Notwithstanding that guidance, it is commonplace for unless orders to be made against receiving parties who repeatedly fail to progress matters. Further points about unless orders can be found at 43.100. **43.192**

Power to disallow interest

Subject to what is said below, where the receiving party has made a request for an assessment that is out of time, the court will, at the time the costs are assessed, be able to disallow interest, but (in the absence of misconduct) the court must not impose any other sanction.[259] **43.193**

Orders vs interest

The provisions that govern the court's power to disallow interest read as follows: **43.194**

> '(4) If—
> (a) the paying party has not made an application in accordance with paragraph (2); and
> (b) the receiving party files a request for a detailed assessment hearing later than the period specified in paragraph (1),
>
> the court may disallow all or part of the interest otherwise payable to the receiving party under—
> (i) section 17 of the Judgments Act 1838; or
> (ii) section 74 of the County Courts Act 1984,
>
> but will not impose any other sanction except in accordance with rule 44.11 (powers in relation to misconduct).'[260]

These provisions are capable of being read restrictively, in the sense that the court is not able to disallow interest if the paying party has filed a request for an order pursuant to CPR, r 47.14(2). There is no authority on that point, but if that interpretation is correct, then, where the detailed assessment has ground to a halt after service of the point of dispute, the paying party must elect either to make an application for an unless order and to forgo disallowance of interest, or to bide their time and ask the court to disallow interest if and when the assessment is revived. If this analysis is correct, the least attractive option would be to allow many months to pass and then to make an application. **43.195**

Provisional Assessments

If the parties, after having exchanged points of dispute and replies, are still unable to settle the costs, they are likely to need the assistance of the court. This means that the court needs to be asked to carry out an assessment. The form that is used to do this (Form N258) is titled a 'Request for Provisional/General Detailed Assessment' (see Figure 43.4); the same form is used regardless of whether the claim for costs qualifies for a provisional assessment. **43.196**

[258] *Marcan Shipping (London) Ltd v Kefalas* [2007] EWCA Civ 463, at [36].
[259] CPR, r 47.14(4).
[260] CPR, r 47.14(4).

The receiving party must certify whether the claim for costs is for £75,000 or less; if that condition is met, then certain documents need to be filed at court at the time the request is made (see 43.183 and 43.185). Where the claim for costs is for more than that figure, Form N258 will be regarded as a request for a detailed assessment and a more limited set of documents must be filed (see 43.183). It is a moot point whether the limit of £75,000 is inclusive or exclusive of VAT: in the SCCO, the limit is applied inclusive of VAT, but practices in some other courts are to apply it exclusive of VAT.

43.197 A provisional assessment is a dispute resolution procedure in which the court provisionally assesses costs on paper in the absence of the parties. It is similar to a mandatory form of early neutral evaluation (see 48.58), but differs in the sense that it is potentially binding. It is provisional in the sense that either the receiving party or the paying party is permitted to be heard at a hearing (a post-provisional hearing) if they are dissatisfied with the provisional assessment.

History and pilots

43.198 The provisional assessment procedure was created on the back of extrajudicial recommendation by Sir Rupert Jackson.[261] He relied heavily on the results of a pilot scheme (see 43.199), but he also drew attention to the fact that the procedure had been used successfully in Hong Kong since 2009.[262] This was undoubtedly correct, but Sir Rupert did not need to look so far afield for inspiration: a short trip over the Irish Sea to the Isle of Man would have taken him to a jurisdiction with decades of experience of provisional assessments.[263] Indeed, whilst they often go by other names, procedures for provisionally assessing costs can be found in many jurisdictions, both in England and Wales,[264] and in other common-law jurisdictions.[265]

The pilot schemes

43.199 Under Sir Rupert's supervision, a pilot scheme was set up in the Leeds, York and Scarborough county courts. It was due to run from 1 October 2010 to 30 September 2012, but, in the event, it published a preliminary report nine months early.[266] It was clear that the pilot was a success, both with the judiciary[267] and with court users.[268] Sir Rupert recommended that the pilot be extended nationally for 'all bills up to

---

[261] That recommendation was, for all practical purposes, made in Jackson, R, *Report on the Provisional Assessment Pilot* (London: HMSO, 2012), para 4.1.

[262] See *ibid*, para 1.1.

[263] See Rules of the High Court of Justice 2009, O48A, r 28(1). It is hard not to chuckle, however, when one learns that, in 2009, the Tynwald abolished this procedure, in an attempt to better harmonise with the UK mainland: see Administration of Justice Act 2008 (Statutes of the Isle of Man 2008 c14).

[264] See, eg, RSC Ord 62, r 31. Moreover, provisional assessment was used for quantifying the amounts payable by the Legal Aid Agency (or its predecessors), for assessing costs payable in the Privy Council (see Judicial Committee of the Privy Council PD 8 (Costs), para 14) and for assessing costs in the Supreme Court (UKSC PD 13, para 14).

[265] See, eg, the Supreme Court of Western Australia Consolidated Practice Direction (2009), para 4.7.2. See also the 'provisional taxation' procedure in Hong Kong, Rules of the High Court 2008, O62, r 21B.

[266] See Jackson, R, *Report on the Provisional Assessment Pilot* (London: HMSO, 2012).

[267] See *ibid.*

[268] Whilst the evidence is only anecdotal, it is said that the pilot was so popular that litigants from outside Leeds, York and Scarborough used to commence litigation there. The pilot's success was largely attributable to the hard work of recently retired regional costs judge District Judge Hill.

£25,000',[269] but this was not necessary because, in the event, provisional assessments were incorporated into the CPR.

Jurisdiction

Ambit

Any claim for costs of £75,000 or less will qualify for provisional assessment[270] (see 43.202). There is no guidance as to whether this sum is inclusive of VAT, success fees and ATE premiums, but in the SCCO it is usually regarded as inclusive of all three. A claim for interest is not made at the time the request is made and, as such, it is almost certain that it is to be excluded for determining the amount claimed. **43.200**

The rule has applied since 1 April 2013[271] and applies only to detailed assessment proceedings commenced on or after that date.[272] **43.201**

Jurisdiction

The jurisdiction[273] to carry out a provisional assessment now derives from CPR, r 47.15(1)—a provision that came into force on 1 April 2013 (see 43.201). It reads as follows: **43.202**

> '(1) This rule applies to any detailed assessment proceedings commenced in the High Court or the County Court on or after 1 April 2013 in which the costs claimed are the amount set out in paragraph 14.1 of the practice direction supplementing this Part, or less.'

The amount referred to is £75,000;[274] hence the provisional assessment procedure applies only to those cases in which the costs claimed are £75,000 or less.

CPR, r 47.15(2), goes on to say this: 'In proceedings to which this rule applies, the parties must comply with the procedure set out in Part 47 as modified by paragraph 14 Practice Direction 47.' **43.203**

The effect of this is to elevate PD 47, so that it becomes a source of law (see 4.49). The relevant part of PD 47, para 14.2, reads as follows: **43.204**

> '14.2 The following provisions of Part 47 and this Practice Direction will apply to cases falling within rule 47.15—
> (1) rules 47.1, 47.2, 47.4 to 47.13, 47.14 (except paragraphs (6) and (7)), 47.16, 47.17, 47.20 and 47.21; and
> (2) paragraphs 1, 2, 4 to 12, 13 (with the exception of paragraphs 13.4 to 13.7, 13.9,[[275]] 13.11 and 13.14), 15, and 16, of this Practice Direction.'

[269] See Jackson, R, *Report on the Provisional Assessment Pilot* (London: HMSO, 2012), para 4.1.

[270] See CPR, r 47.15(1); PD 47, para 14.1.

[271] CPR, r 47.15, was created by Civil Procedure (Amendment) Rules 2013 (SI 2013/262), r 16, applying to any detailed assessment proceedings commenced on or after 1 April 2013 (see r 2). A pedant would point out that CPR, r 47.15(5), was amended in 2013 and the amended provisions have effect from 1 October 2013: see Civil Procedure (Amendment No 7) Rules 2013 (SI 2013/1974), r 2.

[272] Rather confusingly, the transitional provisions are not contained in Civil Procedure (Amendment) Rules 2013 (SI 2013/262), r 22, but are set out in CPR themselves, at r 47.15(1).

[273] The pilot scheme enjoyed its own jurisdiction (the details of which are no longer relevant, but which can be found in the second edition of this book). The jurisdiction derived from PD 51E, which in turn derived its power from CPR, r 51.2. It is of no continuing relevance.

[274] PD 47, para 14.1, reads as follows: 'The amount of costs referred to in rule 47.15(1) is £75,000.'

[275] PD 47, para 14.2, states that PD 47, para 13.9, does not apply to provisional assessments. This is somewhat curious, because—in what is presumably a typographical error—there is no PD 47, para 13.9.

This is an unusual provision because PD 47 governs the rules of court. Presumably, the aim was to afford the Master of the Rolls a degree of flexibility without having to go to the trouble of laying the new provisions before Parliament.

43.205 This list of provisions is so long that it is easier to focus on those parts of CPR, Part 47, that do *not* apply, which are as follows.

- **CPR, r 47.3** Powers of an authorised court officer
- **CPR, r 47.14(6)** Provisions relating to what can and cannot be raised at the hearing
- **CPR, r 47.14(7)** Provisions that deal with the procedure on appeal and when time starts to run
- **CPR, r 47.18** Provisions relating to the detailed assessment procedure where costs are payable out of the CLS Fund
- **CPR, r 47.19** Provisions relating to the detailed assessment procedure where costs are payable out of a fund other than the CLS Fund
- **CPR, r 47.22–47.24** Provisions relating to appeals from authorised court officers

The rules and directions that have been excluded are, in general, those that relate to detailed assessment hearings—as one would expect.

43.206 It is, however, less easy to understand why the provisions relating to authorised court officers should be excluded (a putative exclusion that arises out of the fact that CPR, r 47.3, has been excluded). If it is true to say that authorised court officers are not permitted to conduct provisional assessments, it would be a strange state of affairs, not least because PD 47, para 14, expressly preserves the applicability of CPR, r 47.21 (which is a provision that relates solely to the power to appeal a decision of an authorised court officer). Whilst there is no authority on the point, it is likely that the putative exclusion of CPR, r 47.3, is simply an error. This would be in keeping with the fact that, in the SCCO, authorised court officers carry out the majority of the provisional assessments.[276]

Procedure

43.207 As to procedure, CPR, r 47.15(3) and (4), reads as follows:

> '(3) The court will undertake a provisional assessment of the receiving party's costs on receipt of Form N258 and the relevant supporting documents specified in Practice Direction 47.
>
> (4) The provisional assessment will be based on the information contained in the bill and supporting papers and the contentions set out in Precedent G (the points of dispute and any reply).'

Thus the rules imply that the procedural details are addressed in PD 47.

Requests

43.208 PD 47, para 14.3, reads as follows:

> '14.3 In cases falling within rule 47.15, when the receiving party files a request for a detailed assessment hearing, that party must file—
> (a) the request in Form N258;
> (b) the documents set out at paragraphs 8.3 and 13.2 of this Practice Direction;

[276] Ms Hazel Ford, Private communication with the author, 12 January 2015.

(c) an additional copy of the bill, including a statement of the costs claimed in respect of the detailed assessment drawn on the assumption that there will not be an oral hearing following the provisional assessment;
(d) the offers made (those marked "without prejudice save as to costs" or made under Part 36 must be contained in a sealed envelope, marked "Part 36 or similar offers", but not indicating which party or parties have made them);
(e) completed Precedent G (points of dispute and any reply).'

It should be noted that Form N258 is titled 'Request for Provisional/General Detailed Assessment' (that is, it is the same form as is used for requesting a detailed assessment). The receiving party is asked to choose one of the following confirmations: **43.209**

> 'I confirm the costs claimed are £75,000 or less and I ask the court to undertake a provisional assessment.'
>
> 'I confirm the costs claimed are over £75,000 and I ask the court to arrange a detailed assessment hearing.'

There is no option to ask for a detailed assessment in cases in which more than £75,000 is claimed. If the parties were to agree that they wanted a provisional assessment but were not entitled to one, it would be open to them to apply under CPR, r 3.1(2)(m), for an early judicial neutral evaluation (see 48.62–48.64), but, given the fact that such evaluations tend to take up a great deal of court time, it is a moot point whether the court would accede to such a request. **43.210**

Where the parties are entitled to a provisional assessment, there is no right to demand a detailed assessment without a foregoing provisional assessment. That said, if either or both parties have good reasons why there should be no provisional assessment, the court has the power to proceed directly to a detailed assessment[277] (see 43.212). **43.211**

Unsuitable cases

Not all cases are suitable for provisional assessment. In view of this, CPR, r 47.15(6), makes the following provisions: 'The court may at any time decide that the matter is unsuitable for a provisional assessment and may give directions for the matter to be listed for hearing. The matter will then proceed under rule 47.14 without modification.' **43.212**

Thus, if the court takes the view that the matter is unsuitable for a provisional assessment, the court will direct that the matter must be listed for hearing; where this happens, the rules relating to provisional assessments cease to apply. The court will often make such an order where the issues that are raised are too numerous, complex or contentious to be addressed without the benefit of oral submissions. **43.213**

Prior to the assessment

Once the relevant documents have been received, where appropriate, the court will allocate the matter to a judge or authorised court officer. In the SCCO, the parties are usually told in advance who will be carrying out the provisional assessment. PD 47, para 14.4(1), sets the following timetable: 'On receipt of the request for detailed assessment and the supporting papers, the court will use its best endeavours to undertake a provisional assessment within 6 weeks. No party will be permitted to attend the provisional assessment.' **43.214**

[277] See CPR, r 47.15(6).

43.215 In some courts and hearing centres (most notably, the SCCO), there is a policy of asking receiving parties to lodge their papers (that is, attendance notes, correspondence, etc) for the purposes of the provisional assessment. Many other courts and hearing centres actively discourage this practice. The court will usually write to the parties to tell them what to do in this regard.

The assessment itself

43.216 No party will be permitted to attend the provisional assessment.[278] That said, it is open to the judge to adjourn the provisional assessment whilst making enquiries of the parties.

43.217 The CPR contain no guidance as to how the judge is to carry out the assessment. The editor's forensic method (which may or may not be correct) is to read the bill of costs, points of dispute and replies, and then to scan through the beginning and the end of the receiving party's file. Where appropriate, he will also read the contract of retainer. Few judges will read everything. In view of this, if a receiving party wants the court to take note of something that only a close reading of the files would reveal, this ought to be stated (preferably in the narrative or the replies).

The post-provisional hearing

43.218 There is no guidance in the CPR as to how the court should conduct a post-provisional hearing. It is implicit from the provisions cited above that the hearing will deal only with those items that the parties (or either one of the parties) has identified.

43.219 In certain jurisdictions that have had experience of provisional assessments, the post-provisional hearing is referred to as the 'review'[279] and the figure that has been provisionally assessed as the 'order *nisi*'.[280] These are useful shorthand terms, but they are not standard terms in this jurisdiction.

43.220 It has been suggested that the word 'review', in CPR, r 47.15(8)(a), means that the hearing will be a review in the sense that it will be for the party who challenges the provisional assessment to show that it was wrong. The arguments against this interpretation are cogent, however, as follows.

- In contrast to the word 'review' as used in the context of appeals,[281] there is nothing to define the test to be applied, less still anything to say that the appropriate test is whether the initial decision was wrong.
- The word 'review' has been used in other jurisdictions to mean re-examination of the costs.[282]
- The *Oxford English Dictionary* defines 'review' as meaning '[t]o re-examine; to reconsider'; hence the use of the word is entirely in keeping with the notion that the post-provisional hearing is merely a matter of the court looking again at the costs that are claimed.

---

278 PD 47, para 14.4(1).

279 See, eg, Isle of Man Rules of the High Court of Justice 2009, O48A, r 28(1). In any event, CPR, r 47.15(8)(a), refers to the costs 'which are sought to be reviewed at the hearing', so one could say that a post-provisional hearing should be referred to as a review.

280 See Hong Kong, Rules of the High Court 2008, O62, r 21B.

281 See CPR, r 52.11(1)–(3).

282 See, eg, Isle of Man Rules of the High Court of Justice 2009, O48A, r 28 (1).

Thus, whilst the contrary is arguable, it seems that the test to be applied on a post-provisional hearing is the same as that which would be applied at a detailed assessment hearing. That said, it is inevitable that when a judge is asked to reconsider an earlier finding, they are likely to ask themselves whether the original finding was right. This being so, there is a danger that a post-provisional hearing may *de facto* become a review similar to an appeal. That said, whilst it has famously been said that it would be inappropriate for a judge hearing an appeal to be 'drawn into an exercise calculated to add a little here or knock off a little there',[283] there is no reason at all why a judge conducting a post-provisional hearing should not do just that. There is, however, no authority on this point. **43.221**

Whilst not binding, in a case in which a bill of costs was assessed at nil on provisional assessment after the receiving party had failed to file a disputed conditional fee agreement, Judge Wood QC found that there was no need for relief from sanctions before a post-provisional hearing could take place.[284] **43.222**

Record of findings

Once the provisional assessment has concluded, the judge will record their findings and return the papers to the receiving party. PD 47, para 14.4(2), provides as follows: **43.223**

> '(2) Once the provisional assessment has been carried out the court will return Precedent G (the points of dispute and any reply) with the court's decisions noted upon it. Within 14 days of receipt of Precedent G the parties must agree the total sum due to the receiving party on the basis of the court's decisions. If the parties are unable to agree the arithmetic, they must refer the dispute back to the court for a decision on the basis of written submissions.'

Thus the court's provisional findings are to be recorded in the document based on Precedent G (that is, the points of dispute and replies). This direction is, however, at odds with PD 47, para 47.15(7), which implies that the court will record its findings in the bill of costs. Few (if any) judges will record their reasons in both the bill of costs *and* in the points of dispute and replies. Indeed, there is often insufficient room in the bill of costs for the court to state its reasons. **43.224**

In any event, it is often not convenient for the court to record its findings on the combined points of dispute and replies. This is because the relevant MS Word file is rarely available. This is the reason why some judges set out their findings in a separate document. Other judges simply write in hand on the bill of costs (or, sometimes, the points of dispute and replies); where this is so, they will often use a pen that writes in a colour other than black, so that the alterations can clearly be seen.[285] **43.225**

After the assessment

CPR, r 47.15(7)–(9), reads as follows, all of which is self-explanatory: **43.226**

> '(7) When a provisional assessment has been carried out, the court will send a copy of the bill, as provisionally assessed, to each party with a notice stating that any party who wishes to challenge any aspect of the provisional assessment must, within 21 days of the receipt of

[283] *Mealing-McLeod v Common Professional Examination Board* [2000] 2 Costs LR 223, at 224, *per* Buckley J.
[284] *Mehmi v Pincher* (unreported), 10 September 2015, Liverpool County Court.
[285] See *Cook on Costs 2017* (LexisNexis, online), para 30.9.

the notice, file and serve on all other parties a written request for an oral hearing. If no such request is filed and served within that period, the provisional assessment shall be binding upon the parties, save in exceptional circumstances.

(8) The written request referred to in paragraph (7) must—

(a) identify the item or items in the court's provisional assessment which are sought to be reviewed at the hearing; and

(b) provide a time estimate for the hearing.

(9) The court then will fix a date for the hearing and give at least 14 days' notice of the time and place of the hearing to all parties.'

43.227 Thus, if the parties (or either of them) are dissatisfied with the provisional assessment, they are able to ask for a post-provisional hearing. That request must (other than in exceptional circumstances) be filed and served within 21 days of receipt of the record of provisionally assessed costs. The parties must provide a time estimate for the hearing and they must identify the item(s) that they wish to be reviewed.

43.228 If the parties are content with the provisional assessment, the receiving party is able to file the completed bill of costs and request a final costs certificate. The appropriate procedure is explained at 43.383.

Costs

Where there has been no post-provisional hearing

43.229 **The incidence and basis of costs** Where there has been no post-provisional hearing, there are no specific rules governing the incidence of costs of provisional assessments. In view of this, the generally received view is that the provisions of CPR, r 47.20, apply[286] and that, as such, the costs of provisional assessments that do not proceed to a post-provisional hearing are subject to the same provisions that govern the incidence of costs of detailed assessment in general.

43.230 **The amount of costs** There are, in contrast, specific restrictive provisions that govern the amount of costs of provisional assessments that do not proceed to a post-provisional hearing. Those provisions read as follows:

'(5) In proceedings which do not go beyond provisional assessment, the maximum amount the court will award to any party as costs of the assessment (other than the costs of drafting the bill of costs) is £1,500 together with any VAT thereon and any court fees paid by that party.'[287]

43.231 Thus, unless the matter goes beyond a provisional assessment, the maximum that can be awarded to a party for the costs of the provisional assessment is £1,500 *plus* VAT (where appropriate) and court fees. This limit will apply even if the receiving party has 'beaten' their own Part 36 offer.[288]

---

[286] This is because that rule applies in 'detailed assessment proceedings' and provisional assessment is a subtype thereof. Put otherwise, it is likely that all proceedings commenced by notice of commencement are detailed assessment proceedings, regardless of whether they are destined for a detailed assessment hearing.

[287] See CPR, r 47.15(5).

[288] See *Lowin v W Portsmouth & Co* [2017] EWCA Civ 2172, at [38]–[44], in which Asplin LJ distinguished the reasoning in *Broadhurst v Tan* [2016] EWCA Civ 94 to the conflict between the provisions of CPR, Part 36, and CPR, r 47.15(5).

Whilst not binding on any judge, there have been first-instance decisions that point to the fact that the £1,500 cap encompasses the costs of costs-only proceedings.[289] **43.232**

The stage at which the court will consider any offers Whilst the receiving party is required to lodge a sealed envelope containing Part 36 (or similar) offers (see 43.208), many (if not most) judges will not open that envelope until it has been confirmed that neither party will seek a post-provisional hearing. This is because they do not want to have to recuse themselves for having seen the parties' offers. Indeed, many judges will leave the issue of costs to the parties, with liberty to apply should they not be able to reach agreement. Obviously, if a Part 36 offer (or other offer) has been 'beaten', that is likely to have a bearing on the incidence and/or basis of costs (although the cap referred to at 43.231 will still apply).[290] **43.233**

Disputes solely about costs It may be that the only dispute between the parties is who should pay the costs of the provisional assessment. PD 47, para 14.6, makes the following provisions in that regard: **43.234**

> '14.6 If a party wishes to be heard only as to the order made in respect of the costs of the initial provisional assessment, the court will invite each side to make written submissions and the matter will be finally determined without a hearing. The court will decide what if any order for costs to make in respect of this procedure.'

Where there has been a post-provisional hearing

Where a post-provisional hearing has been requested, specific provisions apply to the incidence of costs. In particular, CPR, r 47.15(10), reads as follows: **43.235**

> '(10) Any party which has requested an oral hearing, will pay the costs of and incidental to that hearing unless—
> (a) it achieves an adjustment in its own favour by 20% or more of the sum provisionally assessed; or
> (b) the court otherwise orders.'

Thus, if a post-provisional hearing has been requested, then a test similar to the one-fifth rule comes (see 36.58) into play. There is, however, one crucial difference: where it is carrying out a provisional assessment, the court has what appears to be an unfettered discretion to make whatever order it believes is appropriate; there is no need for the court to find 'special circumstances'. **43.236**

Whilst the discretion may be unfettered, it is structured. In this regard, PD 47, para 14.5, makes the following provisions: 'When considering whether to depart from the order indicated by rule 47.15(10) the court will take into account the conduct of the parties and any offers made.' **43.237**

Bearing all of these matters in mind, if one or both parties have requested a post-provisional hearing, the costs of the assessment are, in general, dealt with in the following way. **43.238**

- **Costs awarded to the paying party** If the costs as finally assessed are 80 per cent or less of the amount provisionally assessed, or if the receiving party was the one who asked for

---

[289] See, eg, *Harding v Warrington Borough Council* (unreported), 4 November 2014, Burnley County Court, *per* District Judge Clarke.

[290] See *Lowin v W Portsmouth & Co* [2017] EWCA Civ 2172, at [38]–[44].

the hearing and the amount allowed is not more than 120 per cent of the amount provisionally assessed, the costs of the assessment will be awarded to the paying party.[291]

- **Costs awarded to the receiving party** If the costs as finally assessed are 120 per cent or more than the amount provisionally assessed, or if the paying party was the one who asked for the hearing and the amount allowed is more than 80 per cent of the amount provisionally assessed, the costs of the assessment will be awarded to the receiving party.[292]
- **No order for costs** Where both parties asked for the hearing and where the amount allowed is greater than 80 per cent, but less than 120 per cent, of the sum that had been provisionally assessed, then neither party will be awarded their costs.[293]
- **Poor conduct** Where a party is guilty of poor conduct, they will be at risk of forfeiting their own costs and may even be at risk of having to pay their opponent's costs.

Whilst there is no authority on the point, it is likely that the costs of the provisional assessment are excluded for the purposes of applying the rules set out above.[294]

Agreed Costs and Putative Agreements

43.239 The following discussion explains the procedure where both parties have agreed the amount of the costs claimed. The topic of disputes in which one party denies the putative agreement is dealt with at 39.08 and, in so far as procedure is concerned, at 43.250.

Uncontested agreements as to costs

43.240 If detailed assessment proceedings are settled, the receiving party must immediately give notice of that fact to the court. The rules suggest that this ought to be done by fax,[295] but this rule is somewhat out of date because the SCCO no longer has a fax machine. PD 47, para 9.1, gives the following guidance about what may be done next:

> '9.1 Where the parties have agreed terms as to the issue of a costs certificate (either interim or final) they should apply under rule 40.6 (Consent judgments and orders) for an order that a certificate be issued in the terms set out in the application. Such an application may be dealt with by a court officer, who may issue the certificate.'

43.241 PD 47, para 9.4, goes on to say this:

> '9.4 (1) The receiving party may discontinue the detailed assessment proceedings in accordance with Part 38 (Discontinuance).
>
> (2) Where the receiving party discontinues the detailed assessment proceedings before a detailed assessment hearing has been requested, the paying party may apply to the appropriate office for an order about the costs of the detailed assessment proceedings.

---

291 See CPR, r 47.15(10).

292 See CPR, r 47.15(10).

293 See, by analogy, PD 51E, para 8(2). The court has the power to adopt that approach under CPR, r 47.15(10).

294 The pilot schemes expressly stated this: see PD 51E, para 8(1), (2) and (3). It is, however, unlikely that the costs of the provisional assessment are both determinative of and influenced by the costs of the provisional assessment.

295 PD 47, para 13.8(2).

(3) Where a detailed assessment hearing has been requested the receiving party may not discontinue unless the court gives permission.

(4) A bill of costs may be withdrawn by consent whether or not a detailed assessment hearing has been requested.'

Thus PD 47 refers to three mechanisms by which the detailed assessment proceedings can be brought to an end: **43.242**

- by applying for a final costs certificate (see 43.338);
- by discontinuing the detailed assessment proceedings; and
- by withdrawing the bill of costs on terms (see 43.342).

There is one further mechanism that ought to be borne in mind (not least because it is so frequently encountered): the Tomlin order (see 43.246).

Final costs certificates

CPR, r 47.10, provides guidance as to how to apply for a final costs certificate in an agreed amount: **43.243**

'(1) If the paying party and the receiving party agree the amount of costs, either party may apply for a costs certificate (either interim or final) in the amount agreed.

(Rule 47.16 and rule 47.17 contain further provisions about interim and final costs certificates respectively.)

(2) An application for a certificate under paragraph (1) must be made to the court which would be the venue for detailed assessment proceedings under rule 47.4.'

PD 47, para 9.1 (see 43.343), adds further detail in that it makes it clear that the application should be made in accordance with CPR, r 40.6. PD 47, para 9.3, confirms that the parties are at liberty to ask the court to make an order for a specified sum: 'Nothing in rule 47.10 prevents parties who seek a judgment or order by consent from including in the draft a term that a party shall pay to another party a specified sum in respect of costs.' **43.244**

Thus, where the parties wish to conclude matters in the most formal way, an application may be made for a final costs certificate. **43.245**

Tomlin orders

If the compromise embraces matters of which the court is not seized (which is not uncommon in commercial disputes) or which deals with matters that the parties wish to keep confidential, a Tomlin order can be a convenient way of encapsulating the compromise.[296] A potential disadvantage of this is that the parties may have to return to court for the purposes of enforcing the compromise (because the schedule of a Tomlin order gives rise to contractual rights, rather than rights that have been ordered by the court). Many judges lack enthusiasm for Tomlin orders and, in view of this, where there is no particular reason to use a Tomlin order, a final costs certificate or other such order is generally to be preferred.[297] The form and requirements of Tomlin orders are discussed at 7.70–7.79. **43.246**

---

[296] A form of wording can be found at 7.71.

[297] See the discussion on this point in Godwin, H, 'Disposing of Claims: Final Orders, Please' (2014) 158(10) Solicitors Journal 27.

Withdrawal and discontinuance

43.247 The other two ways in which a detailed assessment can come to an end are withdrawal or discontinuance on agreed terms. Where a detailed assessment hearing has been requested, the receiving party may not discontinue unless the court gives permission.[298] Where the receiving party discontinues before a detailed assessment hearing has been requested, the paying party may apply to the appropriate office for an order about the costs of the detailed assessment proceedings.[299]

43.248 Neither of these can be recommended, for two reasons: first, because both discontinuance and withdrawal would lead to difficulties if there were a need to take a matter back before the court; and secondly, because neither of them necessarily precludes further detailed assessment proceedings. Even a Tomlin order is generally to be preferred to withdrawal or discontinuance.

43.249 It is worth noting that, once a detailed assessment hearing has been requested, there is no means by which the receiving party can unilaterally extricate itself from those proceedings without the permission of the court. This is because (a) permission is required to discontinue and (b) withdrawal can be effected only by consent.[300]

Disputes regarding putatively settled costs ('contested agreements')

43.250 A 'contested agreement' will arise where one party believes that there has been a binding agreement as to the amount of costs payable, but the other party (or parties) says otherwise.

43.251 PD 47, para 9.2, provides the following procedural guidance:

> '9.2 Where in the course of proceedings the receiving party claims that the paying party has agreed to pay costs but that the paying party will neither pay those costs nor join in a consent application under paragraph 9.1, the receiving party may apply under Part 23 for a certificate either interim or final to be issued.'

Whether there has been a compromise will be a matter of fact and law, which topic is addressed at 39.08 *et seq* (albeit in the context of disputes between solicitor and client).[301]

Offers to Settle Detailed Assessment Proceedings

43.252 What follows deals with the form, content and acceptance of offers. The topic of offers and the incidence of the costs of the detailed assessment is addressed in the discussion beginning at 43.329. Where appropriate, the two sections should be read in conjunction.

Types of offer in detailed assessment proceedings

43.253 Whilst any party is entitled to make any type of offer, at any time, the styles of offer that generally tend to be encountered are:

- offers made pursuant to CPR, r 36.5, as modified by CPR, r 47.20 ('Part 36 offers') (see 43.254);

---

298 See PD 47, para 9.4(3).
299 See PD 47, para 9.4(2).
300 See PD 47, para 9.4(2) and (4).
301 None of the special rules set out therein that apply to solicitor-and-client disputes will apply to purported compromises between opposing parties; hence the effect of the consumer protection provisions in the Solicitors Act 1974 should be disregarded.

- offers made in accordance with pre-April 2013 CPR, r 47.19 ('Part 47 offers') (see 43.280);[302]
- other offers made 'without prejudice save as to costs' ('admissible offers' and *Calderbank* offers[303]) (see 43.298);
- commercial offers (see 43.299); and
- global open offers (see 43.119).

Where detailed assessment proceedings were commenced before 1 April 2013, the provisions relating to Part 47 offers will continue to apply (see 43.280), even if the offer itself was made after that date.[304] Where proceedings were commenced on or after that date, offers are generally governed instead by Part 36 (see below).[305]

Part 36 offers in detailed assessment proceedings

The provisions that enable Part 36 offers to be made in detailed assessment proceedings do not apply where those proceedings commenced before 1 April 2013.[306] If proceedings were commenced before that date, then the provisions that govern Part 47 offers—namely, CPR, rr 47.18 and 47.19, as they were immediately before 1 April 2013—will continue to apply (see 43.280). The topic of what effect a Part 36 offer may have if the offeror 'beats' its own offer is addressed at 43.342 *et seq.* **43.254**

The form of offers If detailed assessment proceedings were commenced on or after 1 April 2013, both paying and receiving parties are at liberty to make Part 36 offers regarding the costs claimed. The form and content of such offers is governed by CPR, r 36.5. In essence, CPR, r 47.20(4), adapts Part 36, so that it applies to detailed assessment proceedings.[307] When these adaptations are made, CPR, r 36.5, reads as follows: **43.255**

> '36.5 (1) A Part 36 offer must—
> (a) be in writing;
> (b) make clear that it is made pursuant to Part 36;
> (c) specify a period of not less than 21 days within which the [paying party] will be liable for the [receiving party's] costs in accordance with rule 36.13 or 36.20 if the offer is accepted;
> (d) state whether it relates to the whole of the claim or to part of it or to an issue that arises in it and if so to which part or issue; and
> (e) state whether it takes into account any counterclaim.
>
> (Rule 36.7 makes provision for when a Part 36 offer is made.)

[302] Pre-April 2013 CPR, r 47.19, used to implicitly provide that the parties may each make offers to settle the detailed assessment proceedings and that those offers may be made without prejudice other than as to the costs of the detailed assessment proceedings.

[303] After *Calderbank v Calderbank* [1975] 3 All ER 333, CA.

[304] Civil Procedure (Amendment) Rules 2013 (SI 2013/262), r 22(10).

[305] Civil Procedure (Amendment) Rules 2013 (SI 2013/262), r 22(10).

[306] Civil Procedure (Amendment) Rules 2013 (SI 2013/262), r 22(10).

[307] In particular, references in CPR, Part 36, to a 'claimant' should be regarded as referring to a 'receiving party', and references to a 'defendant', to a 'paying party'; references in CPR, Part 36, to a 'trial' should be regarded as referring to a 'detailed assessment hearing'; references in CPR, Part 36, to a detailed assessment hearing being 'in progress' are references to the period from the time when the hearing starts until the bill of costs has been assessed or agreed; references in CPR, Part 36, to 'judgment being entered' should be regarded as referring to the completion of the detailed assessment; and references in CPR, Part 36, to a 'judgment' being advantageous or otherwise are to be regarded as being references to the outcome of the detailed assessment.

(2) Paragraph (1)(c) does not apply if the offer is made less than 21 days before the start of a [detailed assessment hearing].

[...]

(4) A Part 36 offer which offers to pay or offers to accept a sum of money will be treated as inclusive of all interest until—

(a) the date on which the period specified under rule 36.5(1)(c) expires; or

(b) if rule 36.5(2) applies, a date 21 days after the date the offer was made.'

43.256 Thus, if an offer is to comply with the provisions of Part 36, it must:

- be in writing;
- make clear that it is made pursuant to Part 36;
- specify a period of not less than 21 days[308] within which the paying party will be liable for the costs of the assessment if the offer is accepted;
- state whether it relates to the whole of the assessment, or to only part of it, or to an issue that arises in it and, if so, to which part or issue; and
- state whether it takes into account any counterclaim (which, presumably, would mean any countervailing entitlement to costs).

Some of these requirements (the last in particular) seem out of place in the context of detailed assessment proceedings, but there is no reason to believe that they can be disregarded for that reason. If, however, there is countervailing entitlements to costs, it would be unwise to make an offer for the net amount payable, because the court may decline to give effect to such an offer (because the court is likely to regard opposing entitlements as separate proceedings).

43.257 Where the offer is made by a paying party, the following provisions apply: '[A] Part 36 offer by a [paying party] to pay a sum of money in settlement of a claim must be an offer to pay a single sum of money.'[309]

43.258 **When to make an offer** A Part 36 offer is made when it is served on the offeree (see 17.28).[310] Part 36 offers may be made at any time during detailed assessment proceedings.[311] PD 47 confirms that such an offer may be made at the same time as making a mandatory open offer pursuant to PD 47, para 8.3[312]—that is, the offer that is made when points of dispute are served (see 43.119).

43.259 *Early Part 36 offers in detailed assessment proceedings* There is no prohibition against Part 36 offers being made prior to the commencement of detailed assessment proceedings;[313] indeed, they commonly are.

43.260 *Late Part 36 offers in detailed assessment proceedings* In theory, a Part 36 offer may be made at any stage up to the eve of the assessment, but, subject to what is said below, if such an

---

[308] This requirement does not apply if the offer is made less than 21 days before the hearing: see CPR, r 36.5(2), as modified by CPR, r 47.20(4).

[309] See CPR, r 36.6, as modified by CPR, r 47.20(4).

[310] See CPR, r 36.7(2).

[311] CPR, r 36.7(1), reads as follows: 'A Part 36 offer may be made at any time, including before the commencement of proceedings.'

[312] See PD 47, para 8.3.

[313] See CPR, r 36.7(1). Whilst a pre-CPR case, see also *Platt v GKN Kwikform Ltd* [1992] 1 WLR 465.

offer were to be made on or after the 21st day before the hearing, the offeror would not be entitled to the full range of the benefits afforded by Part 36. This is because those benefits will, in general, begin to accrue only from the expiry of the 'relevant period'—normally a 21-day period after the offer was made.[314] A (somewhat anomalous) exception to this is where a receiving party makes an offer on or after the 21st day before the hearing: if that party were subsequently to 'beat' such an offer, they would *prima facie* be entitled to an uplift on the costs claimed in the bill of costs.[315] That said, if the offer was made very late in the day, it is entirely possible that the court would consider it unjust to allow that uplift (see CPR, r 36.17(5)(b)).

The content of Part 36 offers

Interest Offers in general—that is, offers that are not Part 36 offers—may be net or gross of interest. For the reasons set out below, it seems possible that, if an offer is to be an effective Part 36 offer, it must be inclusive of interest. If this is correct, then if a party wishes to obtain the benefits of making a Part 36 offer to pay £*(x)* in respect of costs, they must recalculate their offer as £*(x* + interest). For the reasons set out below, it is arguable that a party is able, in principle, to expressly exclude interest, but it is a moot point whether this would be a wise course of action. **43.261**

The starting point is, perhaps, PD 47, para 19, which gives the following guidance: **43.262**

> '19 Where an offer to settle is made, whether under Part 36 or otherwise, it should specify whether or not it is intended to be inclusive of the cost of preparation of the bill, interest and VAT. Unless the offer states otherwise it will be treated as being inclusive of these.'

Thus, on the face of it, an offer that is silent as to interest will be deemed to include those monies. This is not a new provision; indeed, it reflects the position under both the CPD[316] and under the Rules of the Supreme Court (RSC).[317] **43.263**

PD 47, para 19, implies that is it permissible to make an offer that is stated to be exclusive of interest. When Part 47 offers were the predominant type of offer, this caused no difficulties. Indeed, such offers were the norm, because offers that were exclusive of interest were far more convenient, both for practitioners and for judges (especially in cases in which payments on account had been made). Now that Part 36 offers have taken their place, however, the situation is not so clear. This is because CPR, r 36.5(4), reads as follows: **43.264**

> '(4) A Part 36 offer which offers to pay or offers to accept a sum of money will be treated as inclusive of all interest until—
> (a) the date on which the period specified under rule 36.5(1)(c) [that being the 'relevant period'] expires; or
> (b) if rule 36.5(2) applies [ie if made less than 21 days before trial], a date 21 days after the date the offer was made.'

Thus, on the face of it, a Part 36 offer will be regarded as being inclusive of interest calculated to the last day of the 'relevant period', that period usually being 21 days after it was made.

---

[314] See CPR, r 36.17(3) and (4).
[315] See CPR, r 36.17(4)(d). This is because that subparagraph makes no mention of the 'relevant period'.
[316] CPD, art 46.2.
[317] *Bell v Mahoney* (unreported), 17 May 1991, Ch D, in which an offer that was 'in full settlement of your claim for costs' was deemed to be inclusive of interest.

43.265 This invites the question of whether it is possible to make a Part 36 offer that is exclusive of interest. If a paying party were to make a Part 36 offer to pay '£*(x)*, exclusive of interest', there are three ways in which this could be interpreted:

(1) that the offer relates only to that part of the claim which did not comprise interest;
(2) that the words 'exclusive of interest' are to be regarded as being of no effect; and
(3) that the court could find that the offer fell short of being a Part 36 offer entirely.

As to the first, it should be noted that CPR, r 36.5(1)(d), provides that an offer may 'state whether it relates to the whole of the claim or to part of it'; as such, it is arguable that it is open to a party to make an offer that relates only to the costs (and not to interest).

43.266 It is difficult to know which of these interpretations is correct. Judge Robert Owen QC has found that the third interpretation is correct—namely, that an offer that is stated to be exclusive of interest is not a Part 36 offer.[318] However, this decision is not binding on any court and, in the editor's view, it should be treated with some caution because it seems that the provisions of CPR, r 36.5(1)(d), were not drawn to the judge's attention. Moreover, it seems that the judge regarded CPR, r 36.5(4), as imposing a condition that must be satisfied, whereas only CPR, r 36.5(1) and (3), use the word 'must'.

43.267 In the editor's opinion—which could well be wrong—the first interpretation is to be preferred. This is because interest on costs is different from interest on damages, in that interest on costs does not form part of the claim itself: interest on damages is pleaded as an integral part of the claim and will merge with the judgment, whereas interest on costs is judgment debt interest payable *on* the claim and will not merge with any judgment. Moreover, PD 47, para 19, states that Part 36 offers regarding costs can be net of interest, which was not only the norm prior to 1 April 2013, but also by far the most sensible and least confusing way of making offers in detailed assessment proceedings. This being so, it would be surprising if CPR, r 36.5(4), were to take precedence over CPR, r 36.5(1)(d), in such a way as to prevent a party from making an effective Part 36 offer that is exclusive of interest. That said, it should not be forgotten that whilst it is permissible to use practice directions as an extrinsic aid to interpretation of the CPR,[319] they are, at best, only a weak aid.[320]

43.268 Notwithstanding the above, it would be unwise to assume that it is open to a party to freely make a Part 36 offer that is exclusive of interest. By far the safest thing to do (in the absence of binding authority on the point) would be to make Part 36 offers that are inclusive of interest. At first blush, this appears to be no more than a minor inconvenience, but in truth it can be problematic if interim payments or payments on account have been made. Perhaps 'best practice' is to make the offer inclusive of interest, but to explain the way in which that offer was calculated. This would then allow the court and the parties to more easily gauge whether that offer has been 'beaten' at the conclusion of the assessment.

[318] See *Potter v Sally Montague Hair and Spa* (unreported), 7 October 2016, Nottingham County Court, at [22]–[26].

[319] As to the principle that a practice direction may be used as an aid to interpretation of the CPR, see *Van Aken v London Borough of Camden* [2002] EWCA Civ 1724, at [36].

[320] See *Godwin v Swindon Borough Council* [2001] EWCA Civ 1478, at [11].

VAT, etc A Part 36 offer that is silent on the issue of VAT will be regarded as including such.[321] The same applies to the costs of preparing the bill of costs.[322] **43.269**

Restrictions on payment In general, if an offer is made that qualifies the offeree's rights, it will carry less weight than it otherwise would have carried. In particular, if a paying party's Part 36 offer is to pay all or part of the monies at a date later than 14 days following the date of acceptance, it will not be treated as a Part 36 offer unless the offeree accepts it.[323] **43.270**

Partial and conditional offers Where a significant point of principle exists (such as a point concerning the indemnity principle), an offer may be expressed in conditional terms, such as 'subject to you proving that there has been no breach of the indemnity principle, the defendant offers the sum of £--------'. A pedant may argue that such an offer is not a true Part 36 offer and this may be so (depending on the wording of the offer), but even if such an argument were to succeed, there is no reason to believe that it would not be taken into account as an admissible offer or a *Calderbank* offer. **43.271**

Offers in budgeted cases Following *Merrix v Heart of England NHS Foundation Trust*,[324] there is a peculiarity in the way in which the ability to make Part 36 offers in provisional assessments works in cases that have been budgeted. Deputy Master Campbell (writing extrajudicially) had this to say on the point: **43.272**

> 'Where does *Merrix* fit in? It gives the receiving party yet another string to its bow. Suppose that the case has been budgeted, and a case management order has been made. Under *Merrix*, the court is bound to allow the costs approved or agreed in the budget unless good reason can be shown not to do so. In these circumstances, an alert receiving party can pitch its Part 36 offer safe in the knowledge that in all likelihood, the budgeted costs will be allowed and that if, for the purposes of settlement, a modest reduction is offered for the unbudgeted costs which the paying party rejects, there will be a real expectation that the receiving party will beat its own offer.'[325]

There is no doubt that what Deputy Master Campbell says is correct, but it should be borne in mind that the court would have the power under CPR, r 36.17(3), to deny a receiving party the benefit of that provision where it would be unjust to allow it. **43.273**

It would, of course, also be open to the paying party to make an offer. Indeed, a paying party who does not make a valid and effective Part 36 offer is highly likely to be condemned in costs. Moreover, to a certain extent, the fact that costs may have been budgeted may also allow the paying party to make an effective offer. **43.274**

Any party making a Part 36 offer will need to consider carefully the incurred costs in its formulation. Moreover, two further points must be borne in mind, as follows.[326] **43.275**

- If there are any additional liabilities, they are not budgeted.[327]

---

321 See PD 47, para 19.
322 PD 47, para 19.
323 See CPR, r 36.6(2).
324 *Merrix v Heart of England NHS Foundation Trust* [2017] EWHC 346 (QB).
325 Campbell, C, 'Provisional Benefits' (2017) 108 Litigation Funding 8, at 10.
326 *Ibid*, p 11.
327 See *Various Claimants v MGN* [2016] EWHC 1894 (Ch), *per* Mann J.

- Unless the offer states otherwise, the offer will be treated as being inclusive of the costs of preparing the bill of costs, interest and VAT.[328]

43.276 **Acceptance** See 17.166–17.175 for acceptance during the 'relevant period' and 17.177–17.183 for acceptance after the 'relevant period'.

43.277 Whilst not binding, Judge Seys Llewellyn QC has found that provisional assessments are part of the detailed assessment procedure and that (pursuant to what is now CPR, r 36.11(3)(d)) an offeree therefore needs permission to accept an offer after the provisional assessment has begun.[329]

43.278 **Procedural points** For the purposes of CPR, r 36.17, detailed assessment proceedings are regarded as an independent claim.[330] The rules for formal service of documents as contained in CPR, Part 6, now apply to Part 36 offers (see 17.43–17.44).

43.279 If, after acceptance of a Part 36 offer, the accepted sum is not paid within 14 days or such other period as has been agreed, the offeree may apply for a final costs certificate for the unpaid sum.[331]

Part 47 offers in detailed assessment proceedings

43.280 Where detailed assessment proceedings commenced before 1 April 2013, CPR, rr 47.18 and 47.19, as they were in force immediately before 1 April 2013 (and the relevant parts of the CPD), will continue to apply.[332] This is so even in relation to offers made after that date or which are yet to be made.

43.281 **Form of offers** It is implicit from pre-April 2013 CPR, r 47.19(1), that a Part 47 offer is required to be in writing and to be expressed to be 'without prejudice save as to costs' of the detailed assessment proceedings.

43.282 **When to make an offer** Subject to the conditions referred to in 43.280, Part 47 offers can be made at any time,[333] including prior to the commencement of detailed assessment proceedings.[334]

43.283 Where it continues to apply, the CPD provides that where a Part 47 offer is made by the paying party, it should be made within 14 days of service of the notice of commencement.[335] Similarly, where it is made by the receiving party, it ought to be made within 14 days of service of the points of dispute.[336] These directions are rarely heeded, however, because it is difficult to make an offer without the benefit of having drafted points of dispute or the replies, whichever is appropriate. Indeed, the reality is that Part 47 offers were commonly made right up until the eve of the assessment hearing. That said, an offer that is

---

328 See PD 47, para 19.

329 See *Shepard v Hughes* (unreported), 28 January 2015, Mold County Court, at [17]–[20], *per* Judge Seys Llewellyn QC.

330 See CPR, r 47.20(7).

331 CPR, r 47.20(4)(d).

332 Civil Procedure (Amendment) Rules 2013 (SI 2013/262), r 22(10).

333 Whilst a pre-CPR case, see *Platt v GKN Kwikform Ltd* [1992] 1 WLR 465.

334 Whilst a pre-CPR case, see *ibid.* In so far as Part 36 offers are concerned, see CPR, r 36.7(1).

335 See now-revoked CPD, art 46.1. In this context, 'days' are clear days, but include weekends and bank holidays: CPR, r 2.8(3) and (4).

336 See now-revoked CPD, art 46.1. In this context, 'days' are clear days, but include weekends and bank holidays: CPR, r 2.8(3) and (4).

made late (that is, outside of the time limits set out above) is generally afforded less weight than offers made at an earlier stage,[337] which topic is discussed at 43.361.

The content of Part 47 offers

Interest Part 47 offers may be net or gross of interest. Where it still applies (see 43.280), CPD, art 46.2, gives the following guidance: **43.284**

> 'Where an offer to settle is made it should specify whether or not it is intended to be inclusive of the cost of preparation of the bill, interest and value added tax (VAT). The offer may include or exclude some or all of these items but the position must be made clear on the face of the offer so that the offeree is clear about the terms of the offer when it is being considered. Unless the offer states otherwise, the offer will be treated as being inclusive of all these.'

Thus an offer that is silent as to interest will be deemed to include it. This reflects the position under the RSC[338] and continues to be the case under CPR, Part 36 (see 43.261).[339]

VAT, etc A Part 47 offer that is silent on the issue of VAT will be regarded as including it.[340] The same applies to the costs of preparing the bill of costs.[341] **43.285**

Withdrawal and expiry Provided that it has not been accepted, a Part 47 offer may be withdrawn at any time.[342] What is less clear is whether an offeror may subsequently rely upon a withdrawn offer for the purposes of influencing the court's decision as to the incidence of costs. There is no authority on the point, but it may be that a withdrawn offer can to be taken into account in such a way as to afford it less weight than would have been the case had it not been withdrawn. **43.286**

Expiry of offers by the effluxion of time In general (that is, in contexts other than costs), an offer will expire after a reasonable period of time.[343] What amounts to a 'reasonable' period of time will be a matter for the tribunal of fact. It is an issue that will turn on factors such as the nature of the offer[344] (and, in particular, on whether it was inclusive of costs[345]), the subsequent conduct of the parties and whether there was any implied renewal of the offer.[346] It is quite possible that true Part 47 offers (namely, offers that do not include any costs) never expire, solely by reason of the effluxion of time—a point that is arguable either way. **43.287**

Offers limited by time A Part 47 offer may terminate at a time specified in the offer.[347] It is not uncommon to see offers stated to be open for acceptance for a period of 21 days. **43.288**

---

337 CPD, art 46.1; *Wills v Crown Estate Commissioners* [2003] EWHC 1718 (Ch), at [31].

338 *Bell v Mahoney* (unreported), 17 May 1991, Ch D, in which an offer that was 'in full settlement of your claim for costs' was deemed to be inclusive of interest.

339 See PD 47, para 19.

340 CPD, art 46.1.

341 CPD, art 46.1.

342 In a context other than costs, see *Payne v Cave* (1789) 3 Term Rep 148.

343 See, eg, *Meynell v Surtees* (1855) 25 LJ Ch 257.

344 In a context other than costs, see *Ramsgate Victoria Hotel Co Ltd v Montefiore* (1866) LR 1 Exch 109.

345 In a context other than costs, see *Wakefield (t/a Wills Probate and Trusts of Weybridge) v Ford* [2009] EWHC 122 (QB).

346 In a context other than costs, see *Dunlop v Higgins* (1848) 1 HL Cas 381.

347 The authority that is often cited in this regard is persuasive only (because it is not English): *Barrick v Clark* [1951] SCR 177, [1950] 4 DLR 529, Supreme Court of Canada.

43.289 **Variation** Any offer may be varied, but a variation that is disadvantageous to the offeree will be seen as an implied withdrawal of the original offer.[348] If, however, the variation is on such terms as to costs that it affords the offeree a further chance to accept the original offer, it may be seen as being a form of a renewal.[349] In appropriate circumstances, that may add to the weight subsequently to be given to that offer.

43.290 **Rejection** As with any offer based on contract, a clear and unambiguous rejection of an offer will determine the offeree's ability to accept it.[350] Whilst a trite point, it is worth reciting that a counter-offer is usually interpreted as being an implied rejection.[351]

43.291 **Acceptance** There are no formalities governing the acceptance of Part 47 offers, which means that an offer may be accepted by any method, such as by written acceptance, by oral acceptance or by the offeree's conduct. An offer may be accepted by the offeree's agent[352] (such as their costs draftsperson).

43.292 *Very late acceptance* An offer may contain an implied term that it may not be accepted after a particular stage in the proceedings has been reached. By analogy, it is unlikely that an offer can be accepted after commencement of the detailed assessment hearing.[353] Moreover, there is little doubt that an offer may not be accepted after the conclusion of the hearing.[354]

43.293 *The effect of acceptance* Acceptance of a Part 47 offer will result in a compromise of the costs to which the offer relates. Unless there is reason to believe otherwise, acceptance of a Part 47 offer made in the context of costs-only proceedings will not compromise the costs of the Part 8 proceedings.[355]

43.294 In some circumstances, such as where one of the parties is a child or a person who lacks capacity, the court's approval may be required before the compromise is enforceable—issues that are touched upon (albeit only briefly) elsewhere in this book (see 60.38–60.39).

43.295 **Procedural points** Where a Part 47 offer is for the costs of a claim that settled without the need for the issue of proceedings, it will not, by default, be taken to include the costs of any subsequent cost-only proceedings.[356]

Admissible offers in detailed assessment proceedings

43.296 The term 'admissible offer' derives from CPR, r 44.2(4)(c). Strictly speaking, CPR, r 44.2, does not apply to detailed assessments, but the terminology may be used by analogy. An offer that has failed to comply with the relevant formalities (that is, the formalities relating to Part 36 offers or, for offers made before 1 April 2013, those relating to Part 47 offers) may fall into the category of admissible offer. An offer that includes something other than

348 In a context other than costs, see *Gilkes v Leonino* (1858) 4 CBNS 485.
349 In a context other than costs, see *Dunlop v Higgins* (1848) 1 HL Cas 381.
350 In a context other than costs, see *Thornbury v Bevill* (1842) 1 Y & C Ch Cas 554.
351 See *Hyde v Wrench* (1840) 3 Beav 334, at 337; *Norfolk County Council v Dencare Properties Ltd* (unreported), 9 November 2005, CAT.
352 *Earl v Mawson* (1973) 228 Estates Gazette 529; aff'd (1974) 232 Estates Gazette 1315, CA.
353 While dealing with CPR, Part 36, rather than CPR, Part 47, see *Hawley v Luminar Leisure plc* [2006] EWCA Civ 30, at [26].
354 In a non-costs context, see *Bright v Low* 1940 SC 280.
355 This being because a Part 47 offer is 'a written offer to settle the costs of the proceedings which gave rise to the assessment proceedings'.
356 *Crosbie v Munroe* [2003] EWCA Civ 350.

the costs of the proceedings that gave rise to the detailed assessment may be treated in a similar manner.[357]

It is a moot point whether an 'all-inclusive' offer (that is, an offer inclusive of the costs of the assessment) is an admissible offer. Regardless of how it is categorised, it would often be difficult to take an all-inclusive offer into account in determining incidence of costs.[358] The practical effect of this is that an all-inclusive offer will afford the offeree a lesser degree of costs protection—if any at all—than an offer that excludes those costs. This disadvantage has to be balanced against the benefit that, if accepted without qualification, an all-inclusive offer would bring a complete end to the detailed assessment (that is, there would be no need to deal with the costs of the assessment). **43.297**

Calderbank *offers in detailed assessment proceedings*

In the present context, there is, for all practical purposes and in principle, no difference between a *Calderbank* offer and an admissible offer.[359] **43.298**

Commercial offers (or without-prejudice offers) in detailed assessment proceedings

It may be that an offeror wishes to make an offer that is not intended to afford that party any costs protection, but is made solely in an attempt to dispose of the matter on a commercial basis. Such an offer would ordinarily be expressly stated to be 'without prejudice' (as opposed to 'without prejudice save as to costs'). **43.299**

Whilst not binding, Judge Hughes QC has found that, unless there is reason to believe otherwise (such as the offeree stating that it reserves the right to raise a further claim), acceptance of a commercial offer will compromise the costs of negotiation.[360] **43.300**

Hybrid offers in detailed assessment proceedings

More than one type of offer may be made at any one time (or at different times). In particular, PD 47, para 8.3, confirms that a Part 36 offer may be made at the time that points of dispute are served—that is, the time when mandatory open offers are also made. **43.301**

Detailed Assessment Hearings

Once it has received a request for a detailed assessment hearing, the court will fix a date. Alternatively, the court will give directions or fix a date for a preliminary appointment.[361] Unless the court orders otherwise, if the only dispute between the parties concerns disbursements, the hearing will take place in the absence of the parties, on the basis of the documents, and the court will issue its decision in writing.[362] **43.302**

---

[357] See, eg, *Morris v Wiltshire and Woodspring District Council* [2002] 1 Costs LR 167, at [24].

[358] This is because the court would have to estimate the value of the costs at the detailed assessment at the time the offer was made.

[359] A pedant would say that an admissible offer is a term of art that refers to CPR, r 44.3(4)(c), and that, because that provision does not apply to the costs of detailed assessments, the term '*Calderbank* offer'—after *Calderbank v Calderbank* [1975] 3 All ER 333, CA—is to be preferred.

[360] See *Longman v Feather & Black (a firm)* (unreported), 18 February 2008, Southampton County Court.

[361] PD 47, para 13.4.

[362] PD 47, para 13.5.

43.303 In the SCCO, listing times vary according to the numbers of cases received and the resources available to the court. Historically, cases assigned to costs officers were usually given a date for hearing not more than three months later than the date on which the request for a hearing was filed, whereas cases assigned to masters have usually been given a date for hearing not more than eight months later than the date on which the request for a hearing was filed.[363]

43.304 From about April 2016 onwards, the SCCO has operated a group listing scheme under which cases that are likely to be heard within a single day are allocated to a group list, which will usually be heard on the Monday or Tuesday of the second week of the month. Cases with a gross value of £75,000–£200,000 are eligible. The benefits of group listing are that the case will usually be heard relatively quickly (usually within two or three months); the only significant disadvantage is that the case will not be allocated to any given costs judge until shortly before the hearing.

Preparation for hearings

Notices

43.305 The court will, in due course, give at least 14 days' notice of the hearing.[364] Special notice provisions may apply from time to time—the following, in particular.

- **Misconduct** If the court intends to rule on whether there has been misconduct within the meaning of CPR, r 44.11, it must give the party or legal representative in question a reasonable opportunity to attend a hearing to give reasons why it should not make such an order.[365]
- **Additional liabilities** Special rules apply where a legal representative seeks an order that the amount payable under a pre-commencement funding agreement shall continue to be payable by its client even if not recovered from the paying party.[366] Similarly, special rules apply where counsel may have an interest in the assessment of additional liabilities.[367]

---

363 HM Courts & Tribunals Services, *Senior Courts Costs Office Guide* (London: HMSO, 2018), para 12.5.

364 PD 47, para 13.6.

365 PD 44, para 11.1.

366 Where the receiving party has the benefit of a pre-commencement funding agreement and where the paying party serves points of dispute seeking a reduction in any percentage increase, then if that legal representative intends to apply for an order that any amount of the percentage disallowed as against the paying party shall continue to be payable by its client, that legal representative must, within 14 days of service of the points of dispute, give to its client a clear written explanation of (a) the nature of the relevant point of dispute and the effect it would have if it were to be upheld in whole or in part by the court, and (b) the client's right to attend any subsequent hearings at court when the matter is raised: see pre-April 2013 CPD, art 20.5. The solicitor acting for the receiving party must, within seven days of receiving, from the court, notice of the date of the assessment hearing, notify its client and, if appropriate, counsel, in writing, of the date, time and place of the hearing: see pre-April 2013 CPD, art 20.7(1). One reason for this is that a very large number of seemingly contested detailed assessments settle shortly before the detailed assessment hearing.

367 Where the receiving party has the benefit of a pre-commencement funding arrangement with counsel and where the amount of any percentage increase recoverable by counsel may be affected by the outcome of the application, the solicitor issuing the application must serve on counsel a copy of the application notice and notice of the hearing as soon as practicable, and in any event at least two days before the hearing. Counsel may make written submissions or may attend and make oral submissions at the hearing: see pre-April 2013 CPD, art 10.2.

Venue and time

Any request to vary the date of the hearing must be made in accordance with CPR, Part 23.[368] Likewise, a request to vary directions must be made upon application[369] (even if the variation is sought by consent[370]). In practice, this latter requirement is not always rigidly enforced. The hearing will be in public unless the court orders otherwise.[371] **43.306**

Filing papers

PD 47 provides that, unless the court directs otherwise, the receiving party must file the papers in support of the bill of costs not less than 7 and not more than 14 days before the hearing date.[372] A number of County Court hearing centres have their own practices, which local costs practitioners will be expected to know; in particular, some courts will discourage early filing, preferring instead that the papers be made available on the day of the assessment itself. **43.307**

The following provisions apply in respect of the papers to be filed in support of the bill of costs: **43.308**

> '13.12 The papers to be filed in support of the bill and the order in which they are to be arranged are as follows—
> (i) instructions and briefs to counsel arranged in chronological order together with all advices, opinions and drafts received and response to such instructions;
> (ii) reports and opinions of medical and other experts;
> (iii) any other relevant papers;
> (iv) a full set of any relevant statements of case;
> (v) correspondence, file notes and attendance notes;
> [...]'[373]

Statements of costs for detailed assessment hearings It used to be the case that, unless the court ordered otherwise, there was no need to file or serve a statement of costs of the detailed assessment.[374] This is no longer the case. In this regard, PD 44, para 9.5, will apply by default. It reads as follows: **43.309**

> '(1) It is the duty of the parties and their legal representatives to assist the judge in making a summary assessment of costs in any case to which paragraph 9.2 above applies, in accordance with the following subparagraphs.
>
> (2) Each party who intends to claim costs must prepare a written statement of those costs showing separately in the form of a schedule—
> (a) the number of hours to be claimed;

[368] PD 47, para 13.8(1)(b) and (3).
[369] PD 47, para 13.8(4).
[370] PD 47, para 13.8(1)(c) and (4).
[371] See CPR, r 39.2; PD 39A, para 1.2. The circumstances in which the court may order otherwise are limited in the following way (CPR, r 39.2(3)): 'A hearing, or any part of it, may be in private if—(a) publicity would defeat the object of the hearing; (b) it involves matters relating to national security; (c) it involves confidential information (including information relating to personal financial matters) and publicity would damage that confidentiality; (d) a private hearing is necessary to protect the interests of any child or protected party; (e) it is a hearing of an application made without notice and it would be unjust to any respondent for there to be a public hearing; (f) it involves uncontentious matters arising in the administration of trusts or in the administration of a deceased person's estate; or (g) the court considers this to be necessary, in the interests of justice.'
[372] PD 47, para 13.11.
[373] PD 47, para 13.12.
[374] See now-revoked CPD, art 45.3.

(b) the hourly rate to be claimed;
(c) the grade of fee earner;
(d) the amount and nature of any disbursement to be claimed, other than counsel's fee for appearing at the hearing;
(e) the amount of legal representative's costs to be claimed for attending or appearing at the hearing;
(f) counsel's fees; and
(g) any VAT to be claimed on these amounts.

(3) The statement of costs should follow as closely as possible Form N260 and must be signed by the party or the party's legal representative. Where a party is—
(a) an assisted person;
(b) a LSC funded client;
(c) a person for whom civil legal services (within the meaning of Part 1 of the Legal Aid, Sentencing and Punishment of Offenders Act 2012) are provided under arrangements made for the purposes of that Part of that Act; or
(d) represented by a person in the party's employment,

the statement of costs need not include the certificate appended at the end of Form N260.

(4) The statement of costs must be filed at court and copies of it must be served on any party against whom an order for payment of those costs is intended to be sought as soon as possible and in any event—
(a) for a fast track trial, not less than 2 days before the trial; and
(b) for all other hearings, not less than 24 hours before the time fixed for the hearing.'

Filing papers in electronic format

43.310 The Electronic Working Pilot Scheme (PD 51O) does not apply to the SCCO and the SCCO does not have access to documents that have been filed at other courts in accordance with that Scheme. Moreover, given the nature of the papers that need to be lodged, the creation of a single PDF document with bookmarks would not be cost-effective other than for very modest cases. The SCCO Guide 2018 points out that there is no other provision within the CPR that bears on the use of electronic documents. It goes on to say the following (which is, in many ways, a reflection of the fact that there is limited access to the Internet in the SCCO):

> '[T]he use of electronic documents in support of the receiving party's bill of costs is entirely a matter of discretion for each of the Costs Judges. Practices will vary and, in some respects, will depend entirely upon the individual circumstances of the case. The following comments can therefore be regarded as no more than a broad indication of what may be acceptable in any given case:
>
> Laptops loaded with documents separated into folders or similar so that navigating the documents is relatively easy is the preferred option. Memory sticks or flash drives are considered to be problematic regarding security and are unlikely to be accepted. Similarly, Internet based file hosting services which allow access to documents centrally are not considered to be secure and also suffer from the fragile Wi-Fi reception.
>
> If the Judge is prepared to use a laptop to view documents at a hearing, the receiving party needs to consider the possibility of providing (a) passwords and (b) training on the particular system as necessary before the hearing takes place. Experience has shown that ease of access to email traffic in particular is likely to determine whether viewing documents electronically is likely to be helpful.'[375]

[375] HM Courts & Tribunals Services, *Senior Courts Costs Office Guide* (London: HMSO, 2018), para 12.5.

Where a laptop has been provided to the court, the court may require the receiving party to remove it from the court premises each evening during the assessment.[376] **43.311**

Submissions

Unless the court gives permission, only the following persons may be heard on the detailed assessment: **43.312**

- the receiving party;
- the paying party;
- any other relevant person who has served points of dispute under CPR, r 47.9 (see 43.51); and
- in certain circumstances,[377] any barrister who has an interest in the outcome of the assessment of certain success fees.[378]

Although there is no prescriptive rule on the point, the court will generally work through the objections in the points of dispute sequentially. Items may be taken out of turn where the court so directs, such as where the court leaves the issue of hourly rates until the later stages of the hearing.[379] Moreover, some judges will ask the parties if there are issues that are preventing the parties from settling and, if there are, many judges will deal with those issues first. **43.313**

Unless the court says otherwise, only those items specified in the points of dispute may be challenged at the hearing.[380] That said, the court must allow justice to be done. In this regard, Peter Smith J found that it was wrong not to hear a paying party on a 'totally new' point even though an adjournment had been granted previously to allow the same party to put a different 'totally new' point.[381] **43.314**

Disclosure of offers

Neither the existence nor the terms of any Part 47 offers[382] or a Part 36 offer[383] may be communicated to the court until the stage is reached at which the court will hear submissions as to the costs of the detailed assessment. **43.315**

If, without proper cause, the existence of an offer is communicated to the court, that may or may not be grounds for recusal. Whilst dealing with the issue of recusal in a context other than costs, Lord Hope has described the appropriate test as being whether a fair-minded and informed observer, having considered the facts, would conclude that there was a real possibility that the tribunal would be biased.[384] Whether inadvertent disclosure of an offer would lead to the possibility of bias would depend on the facts of the case. **43.316**

[376] *Ibid*, para 14.6.
[377] Where counsel has a pre-commencement funding arrangement and they seek to recover a shortfall in the success fee, counsel will be entitled to be heard or to make written submissions (presumably limited to the issues in which they have an interest): CPD, art 20.7(2).
[378] See CPR, r 47.14(5).
[379] See, eg, Duerden, J, 'Detailed Assessment: A Judge's Advice on Preparation' (2008) 66 PILJ 2.
[380] CPR, r 47.14(6).
[381] *Rye v The Liquidator of Ashfield Nominees Ltd* [2005] EWHC 1189 (Ch).
[382] See pre-April 2013 CPR, r 47.19(2).
[383] See CPR, r 36.16(2).
[384] *Magill v Weeks* [2001] UKHL 67.

Judgments and reasons

43.317 A reasoned judgment must be given. Although dealing with criminal, rather than civil costs, Richards LJ has confirmed that when the court disallows costs, it is incumbent on the court to provide some explanation, however brief.[385] Where a party is concerned that inadequate reasons have been given, it should generally invite the judge to consider whether to expand upon those reasons before complaining about their inadequacy to an appeal court.[386]

43.318 The court will usually give judgment on each item individually. In keeping with the general principle that a judgment takes effect from the time at which the judge pronounces it and the subsequent entry of it is in obedience to the rules of court,[387] time for lodging an appellant's notice used to run from the moment at which judgment was given, rather than from the conclusion of the assessment.[388] The practical effect of this was that judges were often asked—in fact, were very frequently asked—to order that time did not begin to run until the conclusion of the assessment. Perhaps because of this, the position now is that if an assessment is carried out at more than one hearing, then, for the purposes of CPR, r 52.12(2), time for appealing shall not start to run until the conclusion of the final hearing, unless the court orders otherwise.[389]

43.319 The court will make a note in the bill of costs of any disallowances or reductions that it has made.[390] With a paper bill of costs, this is usually done by adding a manuscript note, generally in red ink, but with an electronic bill of costs, this may be done digitally. PD 47 requires the court to record the disallowance or reduction of the sums claimed,[391] but, more often than not, with paper bills of costs, the court will record the time that has been allowed, rather than the actual sums. The court will then leave the task of carrying out the arithmetic to the parties.

Determination of issues of fact

43.320 Occasionally, an issue of fact will need to be decided on the basis of formal evidence (or, more accurately, on the basis of formal evidence beyond that which is contained within the receiving party's file of papers). The 'general rule' is that evidence will be by witness statement, unless the court directs otherwise.[392]

Cross-examination

43.321 Where cross-examination is not merited, the general rule will apply and the court will refuse permission. Indeed, it is uncommon for a costs judge to allow witnesses to be cross-examined unless there is substance in the allegations of fact. Latham LJ had the following to say on the topic:

> 'The mere fact that [an] issue has been raised is not of itself sufficient. If there is no prospect that cross-examination could either undermine or further elucidate the respondent's case, to

[385] *Budgens Stores Ltd v Hastings Magistrates Court* [2009] EWHC 1646 (Admin). In a more general context, see *English v Emery Reimbold & Strick Ltd* [2002] EWCA Civ 605.

[386] *Paulin v Paulin* [2009] EWCA Civ 221, at [30].

[387] *Holtby v Hodgson* (1889) 24 QBD 103.

[388] *Kasir v Darlington & Simpson Rolling Mills Ltd* [2001] 2 Costs LR 228, *per* Popplewell J.

[389] CPR, r 47.14(7). This provision does not apply where the final hearing was concluded before 1 April 2013: Civil Procedure (Amendment) Rules 2013 (SI 2013/262), r 22(9).

[390] PD 47, para 16.1.

[391] PD 47, para 16.2.

[392] CPR, r 32.6(1).

refuse to accede to the application will not be unfair and it would not breach the requirement of the overriding objective that the parties are on equal footing but would save expense and deal with the issues proportionately and expeditiously.'[393]

The court will take into account the cogency of the points to which the disputed facts relate. In a case in which the costs judge had found the paying party's allegations of an unlawful retainer to be ill-founded, Underhill J found that the costs judge had been entitled to refuse permission to cross-examine the receiving party's solicitor.[394] **43.322**

Where cross-examination is merited, it will not always be appropriate for it to be heard in the context of a detailed assessment rather than a trial. Neuberger J commented thus on the range of issues that may be encountered: '[There were issues] more appropriate for a High Court judge than a Costs Judge, in some respects equally appropriate for a High Court judge and a Costs Judge, and in some respects more appropriate for a Costs Judge.'[395] **43.323**

Referral to trial judge

Where an assessment involves weighty issues (such as where a professional person's integrity is impugned), it is possible for the adjudication of that matter to be referred to a trial judge for a trial of those issues.[396] In practice, this very rarely happens. **43.324**

Hearsay

In costs litigation, it will often be the case that evidence will be hearsay. It is trite evidential law that hearsay evidence is generally admissible in civil proceedings, but a party proposing to adduce it is obliged to give notice of its intention to do so in accordance with the rules of court.[397] CPR, r 33.3, provides, however, that this requirement does not apply to evidence at hearings other that trials and, as such, the requirement to serve a hearsay notice will almost never arise in the context of costs litigation. That said, PD 32, para 18.2(2), provides that a witness statement must indicate 'the source for any matters of information or belief', so, to that extent, notice of hearsay evidence does need to be given. **43.325**

Issues as between legal services provider and client

It may be that, in respect of a pre-commencement funding arrangement, the receiving party's legal representative wishes to retain part or all of the success fee not recovered from the paying party. Where that is the case, the court will deal with the assessment between the opposing parties first, and then with the position as between solicitor (or counsel) and client.[398] The court may proceed without an adjournment, but only if the client is present in court, the persons affected agree to there being no adjournment and the court is satisfied that the issue can be fairly decided in that way.[399] In any other case, the court will give directions and fix a date for the hearing of the issues between solicitor and client.[400] **43.326**

393 *Burstein v Times Newspapers Ltd* [2002] EWCA Civ 1739, at [28].
394 *Chaffe v Kingsley* [2006] EWHC 3412 (QB).
395 *Rosling King v Rothschild Trust* [2002] EWHC 1346 (Ch), at [20].
396 This could be done under CPR, rr 30.5 or 3.1(2)(m).
397 See Civil Evidence Act 1995, s 2(1).
398 CPD, art 20.8(1).
399 CPD, art 20.8(2).
400 CPD, art 20.8(3).

Liability for Costs of Detailed Assessment Proceedings

43.327 The incidence of the costs of assessment is usually a topic of fundamental practical importance. An order to pay those costs will usually obliterate any financial benefit that the party in question would otherwise have obtained from the proceedings.

43.328 There are three regimes that govern the costs of assessments. The first is that which applies when the matter goes no further than a provisional assessment (see 43.229). That said, the special provisions relating to provisional assessment apply only to the amounts of costs (see 43.230) and, in all other regards, the general provisions set out below will apply. The second regime will apply where there has been a post-provisional hearing (see 43.235). In all other circumstances, the third regime (as set out below) will apply.

Incidence

43.329 This discussion addresses the factors relevant to the incidence of costs of detailed assessments in general. It assumes that there has been no misconduct. If there has been misconduct, then the matters set out at 9.100–9.102 may apply.

Presumption

43.330 The CPR provide that the receiving party is entitled to the costs of the detailed assessment except where any Act, rule or practice direction provides otherwise, or where the court orders otherwise.[401] Thus there is a presumption in favour of the receiving party. This presumption is not unique to the CPR; indeed, it is arguable that a similar presumption also exists at common law.[402] The presumption will not apply where that party has *pro bono* representation in the detailed assessment proceedings.[403]

Factors to be taken into account

43.331 In deciding whether to make some other order, the court must have regard to all of the circumstances, including:

- the conduct of all of the parties (see 43.334);
- the amount, if any, by which the bill of costs has been reduced (see 43.336); and
- whether it was reasonable for a party to claim the costs of a particular item or to dispute that item (see 43.339).[404]

43.332 Although there is no authority on the point, the wording of the CPR is such that the requirement to take these factors into account appears to be mandatory, rather than directory. That said, it is not commonly the case that the court will expressly refer to each in turn, because they are so well understood by most experienced costs judges.

[401] CPR, r 47.20(1).

[402] See, eg, *Horsford v Bird* [2006] UKPC 55, in which the Privy Council approved of *Chrulew v Borm-Reid & Co* [1992] 1 WLR 176.

[403] That said, that party may apply for an order in respect of that representation under Legal Services Act 2007, s 194(3): see CPR r 47.20(2). See also CPR r 44.9(3).

[404] CPR r 47.20(3).

Where appropriate, the court will take any relevant offers into account. The way in which the court will do that will depend on whether the offer was a Part 36 offer (see 43.342) or a Part 47 offer (see 43.356).[405] The form and nature of such offers are discussed at 43.252. **43.333**

Conduct The conduct of the parties is a factor that should be taken into account.[406] An example of the type of conduct that might be relevant is failing to make an application at the time that it ought to have been made.[407] Common sense dictates that, on grounds of relevance alone, the court should be slow to take into account conduct during the proceedings that gave rise to the bill of costs. If, however, belligerent conduct has been carried forward into the assessment, then that might be relevant (see, by analogy, 6.78 *et seq*). Moreover, if that conduct was so poor as to amount to the misconduct, then the matters discussed at 9.100–9.102 may be relevant. **43.334**

A factor that will often be given weight is an offeree's willingness to enter into negotiations once an offer has been made.[408] Each case will turn on its own facts, but, in general, a mere failure to make an offer will not be sufficient to deprive a party of its costs.[409] A failure to respond reasonably to an offer of ADR, however, may easily have that effect (see 6.118 *et seq*). **43.335**

Amount of reduction The amount by which the costs have been reduced is a factor that ought to be taken into account.[410] Each case must be decided on its own facts: it is not possible to say that a reduction beyond a fixed percentage will displace the presumption that the receiving party will be awarded costs. In particular, there is no basis in principle for drawing an analogy with the regime governing solicitor-and-client assessments (where the incidence of costs is largely governed by the one-fifth rule). The two regimes are based on wholly different underlying policies and, in any event, are procedurally dissimilar. **43.336**

With the comments made immediately above firmly in mind, it is worth noting that Judge Griggs declined to interfere with a decision to deprive the receiving party of costs in a case in which the amount recovered was about 65 per cent of that claimed.[411] On the facts of the case before him—which were unremarkable—Judge Griggs believed that it was within the ambit of the court's discretion to give weight to a reduction of 35 per cent. Similarly, Mitting J found that a reduction of 25 per cent (largely attributable to a reduction in hourly rates) was a factor that should count against the receiving party in so far as the costs of the assessment were concerned.[412] Likewise, Christopher Clarke J declined to interfere with a decision to deprive the receiving parties of their costs in a case in which their costs **43.337**

---

[405] See pre-April 2013 CPR, r 47.19.

[406] See CPR, r 47.20(3)(a).

[407] See, eg, *Manning (Personal Representatives) v King's College Hospital NHS Trust* [2011] EWHC 3054 (QB), at [38]–[42], in which the claimant lost 25 per cent of its costs as a result of failing to apply for relief from sanctions at the appropriate time.

[408] See, eg, *Bufton v Hill* [2002] EWHC 9024 (Costs), in which Silber J addressed this issue in the context of publicly funded persons and found that whilst he could not take the offers themselves into account, he could take into account the parties' conduct in responding to those offers.

[409] *Horsford v Bird* [2006] UKPC 55, at [15].

[410] See CPR, r 47.20(3)(b).

[411] *Palmer v Milbrook Beds Ltd* (unreported), 23 February 2007, Torquay County Court.

[412] *Lewis v The Royal Shrewsbury Hospital* (unreported) 20 May 2005, QBD (reported in brief as SCCO Summary No 15 of 2005). The order he made was no order for costs, but this took into account other factors, such as the fact that the claimant had lost a significant point (namely, the hourly rates).

had been reduced by 60 per cent (where the reductions were made primarily because of the absence of attendance notes) and he afforded the following explanation:

> 'Here the reduction was very large and the reason for the reduction was in large measure because the solicitors had failed to keep attendance notes. Such a failure materially contributes to the length and cost of assessment proceedings ... [It] leads to a scrambling around among the papers when the costs are queried to seek to work out what was done at different stages often without any clear answer, followed by a guessing game on the part of the Costs Judge.'[413]

As can be seen from Christopher Clarke J's comments, there seems—as one would expect—to be the potential for a degree of overlap between the reduction and the receiving parties' conduct.

43.338 Notwithstanding the above, it is open to the court to make allowances for the fact that a ruling on a point of principle has had a significant bearing on the amount of costs ultimately allowed.[414] Similarly, it is open to the court to take into account the fact that the receiving party has made concessions in the replies to the points of dispute. This will not necessarily be the receiving party's saving grace, however: in a case in which significant concessions had been made that diminished the costs claimed from 82 per cent to 63 per cent, District Judge Ian Besford (a highly experienced regional costs judge) found that the reduction was still 'exceptional and must be a significant factor when assessing liability for the costs of [the] assessment'.[415]

43.339 **'Reasonable to claim' or 'reasonable to dispute'** The question of whether it was reasonable for a party to claim the costs of a particular item or to dispute that item is a factor that should be taken into account.[416] Whether it was reasonable for a party to claim the costs of a particular item or to dispute that item is an issue that will turn on the facts of each case. It is implicit in the CPR that the court may make an order that takes into account the costs of issues or groups of issues; this may be done in a variety of different ways (such as by making a percentage order or by allowing costs from a specified date).

43.340 Receiving parties who claim everything but the kitchen sink are likely to find themselves in difficulty. This is for the reasons given by District Judge Ian Besford:

> 'This was an assessment on a standard basis where the costs are assessed on the basis that the paying party should pay what is reasonable and proportionate. It is incumbent on [the receiving party] when presenting a bill to "stand back" and prune any aspect that is likely to be irrecoverable on a standard assessment. To do anything other can be seen as failing to further the overriding objective and being opportunist.'[417]

These comments are not binding, but they are unquestionably correct.

43.341 There will often be overlap between questions of whether it was reasonable to claim or dispute specific items and questions of conduct generally. An example of this is a case in which

---

413 *Fattal v Walbrook Trustees (Jersey) Ltd* [2009] EWHC 1674, at [61].

414 Whilst not binding, see *Horsford v Bird* [2006] UKPC 55, at [15].

415 See *Morris v Sandahtay* (unreported), 2 February 2015, Kingston-upon-Hull County Court, at [20] and [29].

416 See CPR, r 47.20(3)(c).

417 See *Morris v Sandahtay* (unreported), 2 February 2015, Kingston-upon-Hull County Court, at [30].

a paying party took every imaginable point in opposition to the fact that the receiving party had changed solicitors part-way through the claim: Globe J found that the court was entitled to condemn him to pay the costs of both firms attending the assessment to deal with those points.[418] Another example is where a receiving party claimed an outrageously high hourly rate: £400 for a Grade C fee earner in Kingston-upon-Hull.[419]

Part 36 offers As has been explained at 43.254, where detailed assessments were commenced on or after 1 April 2013, it is open to the parties to make Part 36 offers. In this regard, the detailed assessment proceedings are to be regarded as an independent claim.[420] The following is only a brief overview; more detail on Part 36 offers can be found in Chapter 15. **43.342**

Paying parties 'beating' their own offers Subject to certain exceptions,[421] where a receiving party fails to obtain a judgment[422] more advantageous than a paying party's Part 36 offer, then, unless it considers it unjust to do so (see 43.344), the court must order that the paying party is entitled to (a) costs (including any recoverable pre-assessment costs) from the date on which the 'relevant period' expired and (b) interest on those costs.[423] **43.343**

In considering whether it would be unjust to award those benefits, the court must take into account all of the circumstances of the case, including: **43.344**

- the terms of the offer;
- the stage at which it was made, including, in particular, how long before the assessment it was made;
- the information available to the parties at the time it was made;
- the conduct of the parties with regard to the giving of or refusal to give information for the purposes of enabling the offer to be made or evaluated; and
- whether the offer was a genuine attempt to settle the proceedings.[424]

Receiving parties 'beating' their own offers Subject to certain exceptions,[425] where a receiving party 'beats' its own Part 36 offer—that is, where the receiving party obtains judgment[426] against the paying party that is at least as advantageous to the receiving party as the proposals contained in its Part 36 offer[427]—then, unless the court believes that it would be unjust to make such an award, that party will be entitled to the following. **43.345**

[418] *Shah v Breed* [2013] EWHC 232 (QB), at [36].

[419] See *Morris v Sandahtay* (unreported), 2 February 2015, Kingston-upon-Hull County Court, at [28], *per* Regional Costs Judge Besford.

[420] See CPR, r 47.20(7).

[421] This will not be so, however, where the offer in question has (a) been withdrawn, (b) changed so that its terms are less advantageous to the receiving party where it has 'beaten' the less advantageous offer, (c) been made less than 21 days before the assessment hearing, unless the court has abridged the relevant period: see CPR, r 36.17(7).

[422] A reference to a 'judgment' being advantageous or otherwise is to the outcome of the detailed assessment: see CPR, r 47.20(4)(e).

[423] See CPR, r 36.17(3).

[424] CPR, r 36.17(5).

[425] Where the offer in question has (a) been withdrawn, (b) changed so that its terms are less advantageous to the receiving party where it has 'beaten' the less advantageous offer, (c) been made less than 21 days before the assessment hearing, unless the court has abridged the relevant period: see CPR, r 36.17(7).

[426] A reference to a 'judgment' being advantageous or otherwise is to the outcome of the detailed assessment: see CPR, r 47.20(4)(e).

[427] See CPR, r 36.17(2).

- **Interest on costs in the bill of costs** The receiving party will be entitled to interest on the whole or part of the costs awarded (excluding interest), at a rate not exceeding 10 per cent above base rate,[428] for some or all of the period starting with the date on which the 'relevant period' expired[429] (the topic of rates being addressed at 56.90–56.96).
- **Indemnity basis costs of the assessment** The receiving party will be entitled to costs of the assessment (including any recoverable pre-assessment costs) on the indemnity basis from the date on which the 'relevant period' expired.[430]
- **Interest on the costs of the assessment** The receiving party will be entitled to interest on its costs of the assessment at a rate not exceeding 10 per cent above base rate (again, see 56.90–56.96).[431]
- **An additional amount** Provided that the bill of costs has been assessed and provided that the receiving party has not been a previous similar order, it will be entitled to an additional amount (limited to £75,000), calculated as 10 per cent of the first £500,000 of costs in the bill of costs and 5 per cent of any amount that is above that figure, but less than £1 million.[432]

43.346 Slade J has noted that the 'additional amount' awarded under CPR, r 36.14(3)(d), is penal.[433] She also noted that policy reasons for this are set out in Lord Justice Jackson's report:

> 'Lord Justice Jackson in his "Review of Civil Litigation Costs: Final Report" of December 2009 considered at paragraph 3.9 that "the claimant was insufficiently rewarded and the defendant insufficiently penalised when the claimant has made an adequate offer." To remedy this defect Lord Justice Jackson proposed an addition to CPR 36.14(3) of a new sub-paragraph (d). The proposed rule was enacted with some refinements but with the same purpose as that in the draft. When outlining in paragraph 3.15 the benefits of the proposed reform, Lord Justice Jackson considered that the third benefit of the proposed new rules would be that "in those cases which do go to trial, despite the claimant having made an adequate offer, the claimant will recover a significantly larger sum".'[434]

43.347 It is often the case that enhanced interest and any 'additional amount' is ultimately paid to the receiving party's lawyers rather than to the receiving party personally. It should be noted, however, that it is trite law that these monies will, by default, belong to the client rather than to their lawyers;[435] as such, a receiving party's lawyers would properly be able to take those monies only if this is something for which their contract of retainer made specific provision.

---

[428] Where the court awards any such interest, and where it also awards interest on the same costs and for the same period under any other power, the total rate of interest must not exceed 10 per cent above base rate: see CPR, r 36.17(6).

[429] CPR, r 36.17(4)(a).

[430] See CPR, r 36.17(4)(b).

[431] See CPR, r 36.17(4)(c).

[432] See CPR, r 36.17(4)(d). Where there is no monetary award, the additional amount will apply to the claimant's costs rather than to damages or debt.

[433] *Cashman v Mid Essex Hospital Services NHS Trust* [2015] EWHC 1312 (QB), at [9]. See also *Sony/ATV Music Publishing LLC v WPMC Limited (in liquidation)* [2017] EWHC 465 (Ch), at [10], *per* Arnold J.

[434] *Cashman v Mid Essex Hospital Services NHS Trust* [2015] EWHC 1312 (QB), at [8].

[435] Indeed, in *ibid*, Slade J was told that an additional sum of some £17,000 would be passed on to the client without deduction.

Whether 'unjust' In considering whether it would be unjust to award the benefits referred to above, the court must take into account all of the circumstances of the case, including: **43.348**

- the terms of the receiving party's offer;
- the stage at which it was made, including, in particular, how long before the assessment it was made;
- the information available to the parties at the time it was made;
- the conduct of the parties with regard to the giving of or refusal to give information for the purposes of enabling the offer to be made or evaluated; and
- whether the offer was a genuine attempt to settle the proceedings.[436]

The following general points may be made (in addition to those made in the context of Part 36 offers in general at 17.118–17.161). **43.349**

- **Perceived unfairness of the rules** Whilst he was dealing with a case concerning damages rather than costs, Sir David Eady (sitting as a High Court judge) had the following comments to make about the relevance of any perception that the Part 36 regime itself is harsh or unjust:

  > 'It is elementary that a judge who is asked to depart from the norm, on the ground that it would be "unjust" not to do so, should not be tempted to make an exception merely because he or she thinks the regime itself harsh or unjust. There must be something about the particular circumstances of the case which takes it out of the norm.'[437]

  Slade J appears to have endorsed these comments in a case concerning detailed assessment.[438]
- **The amount of the reduction** In a case in which the bill of costs had been reduced by a considerable amount (33.7 per cent), Slade J found that the costs judge had fallen into error by finding that it would be unjust to make an award, partly because: 'It is the terms of the Part 36 offer not the level of the sums claimed in the bill of costs which are to be considered under CPR 36.14(4).'[439]
- **Misleading information** Whilst he was dealing with a case concerning damages rather than costs, Sir David Eady (sitting as a High Court judge) had the following comments to make about misleading information:

  > 'One could imagine that a court might well think it "unjust" to order indemnity costs if the individual defendant had rejected a Part 36 offer on the basis of inaccurate information through no fault of his own and, especially, where he has been misled by the claimant or his advisors through (say) non-disclosure of a material fact of document.'[440]

- **Lack of information or lack of clarification** Whilst it was not a matter upon which she commented, in a case before Slade J, it was suggested that a lack of information (in particular, a lack of clarification) may be a relevant factor.[441]

---

436 CPR, r 36.17(5).

437 *Downing v Peterborough & Stamford Hospitals NHS Foundation Trust* [2014] EWHC 4216 (QB), at [62].

438 See, in general, *Cashman v Mid Essex Hospital Services NHS Trust* [2015] EWHC 1312 (QB), esp at [19].

439 See *ibid*, esp at [23].

440 *Downing v Peterborough & Stamford Hospitals NHS Foundation Trust* [2014] EWHC 4216 (QB), at [62].

441 See, in general, *Cashman v Mid Essex Hospital Services NHS Trust* [2015] EWHC 1312 (QB), esp at [15].

43.350 *The measure of offers* 'More advantageous' means better in money terms by any amount, however small, and 'at least as advantageous' shall be construed accordingly.[442] Unless the offer in question states otherwise, it will be treated as being inclusive of VAT, interest and the costs of preparing the bill of costs.[443]

43.351 *Early offers* There is no prohibition against Part 36 offers being made prior to the commencement of detailed assessment proceedings.[444] When considering whether it would be unjust to allow an offeror to have the benefits of Part 36, the court must take into account the stage at which the offer was made and the information available to the parties at the time it was made.[445]

43.352 *Late offers* When considering whether it would be unjust to allow an offeror to have the benefits of Part 36, the court must take into account the stage at which the offer was made.[446] Offers made less than 21 days before the assessment hearing will, in general, be of little relevance, because the benefits of Part 36 will generally[447] begin to accrue only from the expiry of the 'relevant period'—normally 21 days.[448]

43.353 *Withdrawn offers* This topic is addressed at 17.214–17.217. In essence, the court is able to take the offer into account, but the offeror will not be entitled to the benefits of Part 36.[449]

43.354 *Technically deficient offers* It may be that an offer fails, in some minor way, to comply with the requirements of Part 36. While dealing with the analogous provisions under the RSC, Roderick Evans J found that a minor technical shortcoming would not necessarily deprive the offer of effect.[450]

43.355 *Procedural points* If the offer is unclear, the offeree has the right to ask, within seven days of the Part 36 offer being made, the offeror to clarify the offer.[451]

43.356 **Part 47 offers** Where the assessment proceedings commenced before 1 April 2013, a Part 47 offer made either before or after that date may have a considerable effect on the incidence of the costs of those proceedings, especially where the offer has been made by the paying party. In essence, if a paying party makes an offer at a reasonably early stage of the assessment and if it achieves a result that is more advantageous from its point of view (that is, if they 'beat' the offer), that party may be awarded the costs of the assessment.[452] Offers made by the receiving party may have a similar effect, but, given the fact that a receiving

---

442 See CPR, r 36.17(2).
443 See PD 47, para 19.
444 See CPR, r 36.7(1). Whilst a pre-CPR case, see also *Platt v GKN Kwikform Ltd* [1992] 1 WLR 465.
445 CPR, r 36.17(5)(b) and (c).
446 CPR, r 36.17(5)(b).
447 A (somewhat anomalous) exception to this is where a receiving party makes an offer on or after the 21st day before the hearing. If that party subsequently 'beats' that offer, it would *prima facie* be entitled to an uplift on the costs claimed in the bill of costs: see CPR, r 36.17(4)(d). If the offer were to be made very late in the day, it is entirely possible that the court would consider it unjust to allow that uplift: see CPR, r 36.17(5)(b).
448 See CPR, r 36.17(3) and (4).
449 CPR, r 36.17(7).
450 *Morris v Wiltshire* [2002] 1 Costs LR 167.
451 CPR, r 36.8(1).
452 The importance of this factor was highlighted by Master O'Hare who, speaking extrajudicially, labelled it as one of his 'top ten mistakes' for a paying party not to have made a sensible offer: O'Hare, 'Detailed Assessments: The Top Ten Mistakes' (2000) 149(6919) NLJ 51.

party would already have the benefit of the presumption that it will be awarded its costs, that effect is usually masked.

The measure of offers A Part 47 offer that is silent as to the cost of preparation of the bill, interest and VAT will be treated as being inclusive of those monies.[453] Adjustments may have to be made to ensure that like is compared with like. When making adjustments for interest, it is the amount of interest payable at the time of the offer that is relevant, not the interest that (absent the offer) would have been payable at the time of the assessment. Unless there is reason to believe otherwise, the appropriate date on which the offeree could reasonably have accepted the offer is often taken as being seven days after the date of the offer.[454] **43.357**

Fully inclusive offers Offers may be stated to be 'fully inclusive' or 'all-inclusive', in which case they may (in appropriate circumstances) be regarded as being inclusive of the costs of assessment.[455] This may cause the offeror some difficulties. If the analogous situation under CPR, Part 36, sheds any light on the topic, it can be seen that the court is generally slow to agree to make complex and speculative findings solely for the purpose of deciding whether the offer has been beaten.[456] For the reasons set out at 43.297, it is doubtful whether such an offer can be categorised as being a Part 47 offer; it may, however, be classified as an admissible offer, in which case it would often be afforded at least some weight. Offers that are inclusive of costs tend to expire with the effluxion of time.[457] **43.358**

Costs-only proceedings Unless there is reason to believe otherwise, a Part 47 offer should not be taken as being inclusive of the costs of bringing costs-only proceedings.[458] The offer may have a bearing on both the costs of the assessment and the costs of the Part 8 claim.[459] **43.359**

Early Part 47 offers Pre-CPR authority confirms that offers may be taken into account if they were made before the bill of costs was served.[460] There is no reason to believe that the same is not true under the CPR. Where appropriate, a paying party may wish to argue that the offer was made at such an early stage that it had not been given the information necessary to be able to evaluate it; that argument would stand little chance of succeeding unless the offeror had refused to allow a subsequent acceptance of the offer. **43.360**

Late Part 47 offers The CPD expressly provided that where, without 'good reason', a Part 47 offer is made after the expiry of the 14-day period following receipt of the bill of costs (see 43.367), the offer is likely to be given less weight than otherwise would have been the case.[461] Peter Smith J had the following to say about the policy behind that principle: **43.361**

> 'This appeal emphasises the need for paying parties who wish to protect themselves against the costs consequences of CPR 47.19 to make realistic settlement offers at the beginning of

453 See CPD, art 46.2. To the extent that it applies, see also PD 47, para 19.
454 See, eg, *Morris v Wiltshire* [2002] 1 Costs LR 167.
455 See *ibid* for a discussion of how such an offer ought to be interpreted.
456 See, by way of analogy, *Mitchell v James* [2002] EWCA Civ 997.
457 *Wakefield (t/a Wills Probate and Trusts of Weybridge) v Ford* [2009] EWHC 122 (QB).
458 *Crosbie v Munroe* [2003] EWCA Civ 250.
459 *Ibid.*
460 *Platt v GKN Kwikform Ltd* [1992] 1 WLR 465.
461 CPD, art 46.1.

the detailed assessment proceedings and not at the end. The Court is bedevilled with late settlements. The procedures in CPR 47.19 are designed to promote early reasonable offers and parties should bear this in mind in the future.'[462]

In practice, however, the court is usually sympathetic to practical considerations.

43.362 *Withdrawn Part 47 offers* This topic is addressed at 43.286. In essence, the court is able to take the offer into account, but, in doing so, it may give it less weight than would have been the case had it not been withdrawn.

43.363 *Technically deficient Part 47 offers* It may be that an offer fails, in some minor way, to comply with the requirements of CPR, r 47.19 (as it was before 1 April 2013). While dealing with the analogous provisions under the RSC, Roderick Evans J found that a minor technical shortcoming would not necessarily deprive the offer of effect.[463]

43.364 *Part 47 offers relating to funded persons* The pre-1 April 2013 CPR used to provide that, in so far as a funded person is concerned, a Part 47 offer will not have the consequences specified under CPR, r 47.19, unless the court so orders.[464] Silber J appears to have accepted (*obiter*) the consensual view of the parties that Part 47 offers are of no relevance as against a funded person.[465] Whether the parties were correct to come to that view is a moot point, but Silber J did explain that, while the offers themselves may not be of relevance, the court was able to look at the conduct of the receiving party in choosing to accept or reject the offer.[466] A funded person is therefore not able to dismiss offers with impunity.

43.365 *Set-off* Although each case will turn on its own facts, the effect of an offer will not be diminished merely because it contains a provision for set-off of other sums that are not in dispute.[467]

43.366 *Part 47 offers made by receiving parties* A receiving party that beats its own Part 47 offer will not ordinarily benefit, in the sense that it will be awarded costs that might otherwise not have been awarded. This is because, in the ordinary run of things, that party would be entitled to costs even if the offer were to be disregarded. The benefit to a receiving party of making an offer is subtle: the fact that an offer has been made may be used to defeat an argument that there was a reluctance to negotiate, or it may be a factor to be taken into account when one or more factors in CPR, r 47.18 (as it was before 1 April 2013), conspire to deprive that party of costs. In some circumstances, it may be a factor that would justify an award of costs on the indemnity basis (although there is no authority to suggest that this should be the ordinary consequence of a receiving party beating its offer).

---

[462] *Wills v Crown Estate Commissioners* [2003] EWHC 1718 (Ch), at [31].

[463] *Morris v Wiltshire* [2002] 1 Costs LR 167.

[464] Pre-April 2013 CPR, r 47.19, reads as follows: 'The Costs Practice Direction provides that rule 47.19 does not apply where the receiving party is a LSC funded client or an assisted person, unless the court orders otherwise.' CPD, art 46.4, reads as follows: 'Where the receiving party is an assisted person or an LSC funded client, an offer to settle without prejudice save as to the costs of the detailed assessment proceedings will not have the consequences specified under rule 47.19 unless the court so orders.'

[465] *Bufton v Hill* [2002] EWHC 9024 (Costs).

[466] This approach, if correct, is similar to the effect of CPR, r 27.14(2A), which states (in relation to costs on the small claims track): 'A party's rejection of an offer in settlement will not of itself constitute unreasonable behaviour under paragraph (2)(d) but the court may take it into consideration when it is applying the unreasonableness test.'

[467] *Morris v Wiltshire and Woodspring District Council* [2002] 1 Costs LR 167, at 173.

Costs incurred before the offer was made It is a curious feature of detailed assessments that where a paying party has beaten its offer, that party is often awarded the entire costs of the assessment rather than only those costs that post-date the offer. If this practice is correct, the following points (which are not supported by authority) could be said in its justification. **43.367**

- The practice could merely be a reflection of the fact that, where a paying party makes a Part 47 offer within the 14-day period stipulated in the CPD,[468] the costs of the assessment would usually be nil, or close to nil.
- The requirement to pay the whole of the paying party's costs could be seen as being a fair levy to pay for the presumption in the receiving party's favour.

However, whilst not binding, the Privy Council seems to have treated an offer as having a bearing on the incidence of costs only from the date on which the offer should reasonably have been accepted.[469] It is certainly within the court's discretion to treat an offer in that way. **43.368**

Roderick Evans J has commented that where the court is minded to make an order that differentiates between costs incurred before and after the offer, the relevant date is not the date of the offer, but a date that is based on the offeree having had a reasonable period of time—seven days, on the facts of the case before him—in which to consider the offer.[470] **43.369**

Interest

CPR, r 47.20(6), makes the following provision: 'Unless the court otherwise orders, interest on the costs of detailed assessment proceedings will run from the date of default, interim or final costs certificate, as the case may be.' **43.370**

Thus, unless the court orders otherwise, interest on the costs of the assessment will run from the date of the default, interim or final costs certificate to which the costs relate. Presumably, interest on the costs of interim applications will run from the date of the order for costs, as would be the case with any other order for costs. **43.371**

There are transitional provisions that CPR, r 47.20(6), does not apply where the date of the default, interim or final costs certificate (as the case may be) was before 1 April 2013.[471] This invites the obvious question as to what the law is if this provision does not apply. There used to be a provision in the CPD that was almost identical to CPR, r 47.20(6),[472] but that seems not to have been preserved by the relevant transitional provisions.[473] The pre-CPR position, which was judge-made, was that interest on the costs of the assessment was payable from the date on which the receiving party was awarded the costs that appear in the bill of costs.[474] Whilst it is certainly arguable that the effect of the transitional provisions is to restore the pre-CPR position, it is difficult to believe that this is what was intended. **43.372**

468 CPD, art 46.1.

469 *Horsford v Bird* [2006] UKPC 55.

470 *Morris v Wiltshire and Woodspring District Council* [2002] 1 Costs LR 167, at [25].

471 See Civil Procedure (Amendment) Rules 2013 (SI 2013/262), r 22(11).

472 See pre-April 2013 CPD, art 45.5(1).

473 See Civil Procedure (Amendment) Rules 2013 (SI 2013/262), r 22(11).

474 *Ross v Bowbelle (Owners)* [1997] 1 WLR 1159.

Procedure

43.373 Statements of costs should be served and filed in advance of the hearing (see 43.309). As a general rule, the court will assess the receiving party's costs of the detailed assessment proceedings and add them to the bill of costs.[475] If the costs of the detailed assessment proceedings are awarded to the paying party, the court will either assess those costs summarily or make an order for them to be decided by detailed assessment.[476]

Rules and directions

43.374 The wording of CPR, r 47.20(1), is as follows:

> '(1) The receiving party is entitled to the costs of the detailed assessment proceedings except where—
> (a) the provisions of any Act, any of these Rules or any relevant practice direction provide otherwise; or
> (b) the court makes some other order in relation to all or part of the costs of the detailed assessment proceedings.
>
> (2) Paragraph (1) does not apply where the receiving party has *pro bono* representation in the detailed assessment proceedings but that party may apply for an order in respect of that representation under section 194(3) of the 2007 Act.
>
> (3) In deciding whether to make some other order, the court must have regard to all the circumstances, including—
> (a) the conduct of all the parties;
> (b) the amount, if any, by which the bill of costs has been reduced; and
> (c) whether it was reasonable for a party to claim the costs of a particular item or to dispute that item.
>
> (4) The provisions of Part 36 apply to the costs of detailed assessment proceedings with the following modifications—
> (a) "claimant" refers to "receiving party" and "defendant" refers to "paying party";
> (b) "trial" refers to "detailed assessment hearing";
> (c) in rule 36.9(5), at the end insert "or, where the Part 36 offer is made in respect of the detailed assessment proceedings, after the commencement of the detailed assessment hearing.";
> (d) for rule 36.11(7) substitute "If the accepted sum is not paid within 14 days or such other period as has been agreed the offeree may apply for a final costs certificate for the unpaid sum.";
> (e) a reference to "judgment being entered" is to the completion of the detailed assessment, and references to a "judgment" being advantageous or otherwise are to the outcome of the detailed assessment.
>
> (5) The court will usually summarily assess the costs of detailed assessment proceedings at the conclusion of those proceedings.
>
> (6) Unless the court otherwise orders, interest on the costs of detailed assessment proceedings will run from the date of default, interim or final costs certificate, as the case may be.
>
> (7) For the purposes of rule 36.14, detailed assessment proceedings are to be regarded as an independent claim.'

[475] This used to be expressly stated in CPD art 45.1, but PD 47 is silent on the point. It is nonetheless the case that the receiving party's costs of the assessment will be added to the bill of costs.
[476] CPR r 47.20(5).

PD 47, para 19, gives the following further guidance: **43.375**

> '19 Where an offer to settle is made, whether under Part 36 or otherwise, it should specify whether or not it is intended to be inclusive of the cost of preparation of the bill, interest and VAT. Unless the offer states otherwise it will be treated as being inclusive of these.'

Interim Costs Certificates

An interim costs certificate is an order for an interim payment of costs, which is made after the receiving party has filed a request for a detailed assessment hearing. A payment made pursuant to an interim costs certificate should be distinguished from a payment on account (see 14.02 *et seq*). **43.376**

Jurisdiction

The court has no power[477] to issue an interim costs certificate until the receiving party has filed a request for a detailed assessment hearing.[478] Once this has been done, CPR, r 47.16, will become relevant: **43.377**

> '(1) The court may at any time after the receiving party has filed a request for a detailed assessment hearing—
> (a) issue an interim costs certificate for such sum as it considers appropriate;
> (b) amend or cancel an interim certificate.
>
> (2) An interim certificate will include an order to pay the costs to which it relates, unless the court orders otherwise.
>
> (3) The court may order the costs certified in an interim certificate to be paid into court.
>
> (4) Where the court—
> (a) issues an interim costs certificate; or
> (b) amends or cancels an interim certificate,
>
> in detailed assessment proceedings pursuant to an order under section 194(3) of the Legal Services Act 2007, the receiving party must send a copy of the interim costs certificate or the order amending or cancelling the interim costs certificate to the prescribed charity.'

Discretion

The fact that a party is entitled to costs is simply a factor to be taken into account; it does not give rise to a presumption that the receiving party is entitled to an interim award.[479] The factors discussed at 14.10–14.14 would be relevant to interim costs certificates. Put otherwise, the court often takes into account the same factors regardless of whether the application is for an interim costs order or an order for a payment on account of costs. **43.378**

---

[477] Senior Courts Act 1981, s 32(5) (which prevents the court making an interim payment in respect of costs), is disapplied for the purposes of costs proceedings by s 32(4) of that Act.

[478] See CPR, r 47.16(1).

[479] *Blakemore v Cummings* [2009] EWCA Civ 1276. In *German Property 50 Sarl v Summers-Inman Construction & Property Consultants LLP* [2009] EWHC 2968 (TCC), at [11], Coulson J appears to have said the opposite, but his attention seems not to have been drawn to *Blakemore v Cummings*.

Procedure

43.379 The relevant procedure is to make an application under CPR, Part 23.[480] Further procedural guidance is given by CPR, r 47.16 (see 43.377). At any time after the receiving party has filed a request for a detailed assessment hearing, the court may issue an interim costs certificate for such sum as it considers appropriate.[481] If a certificate has already been issued, it may amend or cancel it.[482] Unless the court orders otherwise, an interim certificate will include an order to pay the costs to which it relates.[483] The court may order the costs certified in an interim certificate to be paid into court.[484]

Stays and enforcement

43.380 If a paying party wishes to apply for a stay of enforcement of an interim costs certificate, that party may apply to a judge of the court office that issued the certificate or (if it is a different court) to the court that has general jurisdiction to enforce the certificate.[485] Enforcement proceedings may not be issued in the SCCO.[486]

Interim costs certificates: pro bono *work*

43.381 Where the court makes such an order in detailed assessment proceedings pursuant to an order under s 194(3) of the Legal Services Act 2007, the receiving party must send a copy of the interim costs certificate, or the order amending or cancelling the interim costs certificate, to the prescribed charity.[487]

Non-compliance

43.382 Langley J has explained that if a paying party fails to meet its obligations pursuant to an order to make a payment on account, that party may be debarred from taking any further part in the detailed assessment pending discharge of those obligations (see 43.28).[488] There is no reason to believe that the position would be any different if the obligation were to arise under an interim costs certificate; indeed, in the editor's experience, such orders are commonly made.

Final Costs Certificates and the Conclusion of the Assessment

43.383 Once the detailed assessment hearing has ended, it is the responsibility of the legal representative appearing for the receiving party, or the receiving party in person, to remove the papers filed in support of the bill of costs.[489] If it is not possible to remove the papers immediately after a hearing in the SCCO, the receiving party may, with the permission of the

---

480 PD 47, para 15.
481 See CPR, r 47.16(1).
482 See CPR, r 47.16(1).
483 See CPR, r 47.16(2).
484 See CPR, r 47.16(3).
485 PD 47, para 16.11.
486 PD 47, para 16.12.
487 See CPR, r 47.16(4).
488 *Days Healthcare UK Ltd v Pihsiang Machinery Manufacturing Co Ltd* [2006] EWHC 1444 (QB), at [18]–[20], [23] and [25]–[27]; see also *Hammond Suddard Solicitors v Agrichem International Holdings Ltd* [2001] EWCA Civ 2065, at [48], *per* Clarke LJ.
489 PD 47, para 13.14.

court, leave the papers with a court clerk for collection within the next seven days.[490] If the papers have been supplied in electronic format on a laptop, the laptop must be removed at the end of the hearing.[491]

Final filing

Whilst, in practice, it is a requirement that is generally disregarded, the rules provide that a completed bill must be filed with the court within 14 days of the end of a detailed assessment hearing.[492] At the same time as filing the completed bill, the receiving party must also file receipted fee notes and accounts in respect of disbursements.[493] There are exceptions to this, however, in that counsel's fees that do not exceed £500 and which have been duly discharged do not need to be dealt with in this way.[494] **43.384**

Calculations

PD 47, para 16.1, provides that the court must make a note in the bill of costs of any disallowances or reductions it has made. The receiving party must make clear the correct figures agreed or allowed in respect of each item and must recalculate the summary of the bill of costs appropriately.[495] Once those details have been noted to it, that bill of costs is referred to as the 'completed bill'.[496] **43.385**

Delay in filing the completed bill

It will occasionally happen that the receiving party will fail to file a completed bill. In practice, this will usually be where the bill of costs has been assessed in an amount that is lower than monies that have already been paid on account. Where the receiving party is delaying things in this way, the paying party may make an application seeking an appropriate order under CPR, r 3.1 (that is, the court's general powers of management).[497] **43.386**

Pro bono *work and completion*

Where a person has been represented *pro bono* and the court has made an order on a detailed assessment for the benefit of a prescribed charity (that is, under s 194(3) of the Legal Services Act 2007), the receiving party must send a copy of the final costs certificate to the prescribed charity.[498] **43.387**

Final costs certificates

Once final filing has been attended to, the court will consider issuing a final costs certificate. This is a document that will state the amount of costs that have been assessed and, unless the court orders otherwise, include an order to pay the costs to which it relates.[499] A separate certificate will be issued for each person entitled to costs.[500] **43.388**

---

490 HM Courts & Tribunals Services, *Senior Courts Costs Office Guide* (London: HMSO, 2018), para 14.3.
491 *Ibid*, para 14.6.
492 PD 47, para 16.3; CPR, r 47.17(2).
493 PD 47, para 16.4.
494 See Precedent F(5) in the Schedule to the CPD, which is referred to by CPD, art 42.4.
495 PD 47, para 16.2.
496 CPR, r 47.17(1).
497 PD 47, para 16.6.
498 CPR, r 47.17(6).
499 CPR, r 47.17(5).
500 PD 47, para 16.9.

Deferral

43.389 There are two circumstances in which the court may defer issuing a final costs certificate, as follows.

- **Unpaid fees** The court will not issue a final costs certificate until all relevant court fees payable on the assessment have been paid.[501]
- **Unpaid costs** Where a party is both entitled to costs and is required to pay costs, CPR, r 47.17(4), permits a costs judge to delay the issue of a party's final costs certificate until that party has paid the amount that it is liable to pay. CPR, r 47.17(4), echoes that provision.

Contents

43.390 Form N256 is the model form of final costs certificate.[502] The certificate must show the amount of costs that have been agreed or which have been allowed on detailed assessment and, where applicable, the amount agreed or allowed in respect of VAT.[503] There is no need to record the amounts of profit costs and disbursements separately (although those figures would ordinarily be recorded in the completed bill). The model form gives the court the option of separately recording the amount allowed for the costs of the detailed assessment; this may be necessary where interest on those costs runs from a different date from that which relates to interest on the remainder of the costs. There is also provision for the court to state the relevant dates separately.

Miscellaneous points

43.391 The following miscellaneous topics may, from time to time, present themselves.

- **Payments already made** If the court makes an order that costs be paid, there is also provision for the court to set out amounts that have already been paid on account and to state the balance that remains due.
- **Outstanding payments** If the court is aware that previous orders or interim costs certificates have gone unpaid, the certificate may contain an endorsement such as '... and, no sums having been paid under the order of Mr Justice X dated ... or under the interim certificate dated ...'.[504]
- **Changes to the rate of VAT** Where there has been a change in the rate of VAT, and where that change has been made between the end of the detailed assessment and the court issuing the final costs certificate, an application may be made for the detailed assessment to be varied so as to take account of that change of rate. Once the final costs certificate has been issued, no such variation will be permitted.[505]
- **Enforcement and stays** If the final costs certificate includes an order that costs be paid, that order may be enforced in the usual way.[506] The receiving party will have become a judgment creditor and the paying party, a judgment debtor.[507] If a paying party wishes

[501] PD 47, para 16.5.
[502] PD 47, para 16.10.
[503] PD 47, para 16.7.
[504] HM Courts & Tribunals Services, *Senior Courts Costs Office Guide* (London: HMSO, 2018), para 19.3(c).
[505] CPR, r 44; PD 44, para 2.10.
[506] CPR, r 70.1(2)(d).
[507] CPR, r 70.1(2)(a) and (b).

to apply for a stay of enforcement of a final costs certificate, it may apply to a costs judge of the court office that issued the certificate or to the court (if it is a different court) that has general jurisdiction to enforce the certificate.[508]

- **Instalments** A final costs certificate may make provision for payment in instalments. That said, where a certificate containing an order to pay has already been issued, the court lacks the power to vary that order so that the certified amount is to be paid in instalments.[509]
- **Interest** The SCCO Guide 2018 provides that 'only in an exceptional case (e.g. where enforcement proceedings on a final costs certificate are to be taken abroad) will a final costs certificate record the amount of interest accrued up to the date of the certificate and/or the daily rate of interest accruing thereafter'.[510] It goes on to say that 'to obtain such a certificate the receiving party should apply, on notice to the paying party, justifying the rate of interest claimed and, where payments on account have been made, explaining the effect which such payments have had on the calculation of interest'.[511]

Wording of relevant provisions

CPR, r 47.17, provides: **43.392**

> '47.17 (1) In this rule a "completed bill'" means a bill calculated to show the amount due following the detailed assessment of the costs.
>
> (2) The period for filing the completed bill is 14 days after the end of the detailed assessment hearing.
>
> (3) When a completed bill is filed the court will issue a final costs certificate and serve it on the parties to the detailed assessment proceedings.
>
> (4) Paragraph (3) is subject to any order made by the court that a certificate is not to be issued until other costs have been paid.
>
> (5) A final costs certificate will include an order to pay the costs to which it relates, unless the court orders otherwise.
>
> (Practice Direction 47 deals with the form of a final costs certificate.)
>
> (6) Where the court issues a final costs certificate in detailed assessment proceedings pursuant to an order under section 194(3) of the 2007 Act, the receiving party must send a copy of the final costs certificate to the prescribed charity.'

The wording of PD 47, para 16, is as follows: **43.393**

> '16.1 At the detailed assessment hearing the court will indicate any disallowance or reduction in the sums claimed in the bill of costs by making an appropriate note on the bill.
>
> 16.2 The receiving party must, in order to complete the bill after the detailed assessment hearing make clear the correct figures agreed or allowed in respect of each item and must recalculate the summary of the bill appropriately.
>
> 16.3 The completed bill of costs must be filed with the court no later than 14 days after the detailed assessment hearing.
>
> 16.4 At the same time as filing the completed bill of costs, the party whose bill it is must also produce receipted fee notes and receipted accounts in respect of all disbursements except

[508] PD 47, para 16.11.

[509] *Gittins v Serco Home Affairs* [2012] EWHC 651 (Ch), at [43]–[53], *per* Judge Behrens.

[510] HM Courts & Tribunals Services, *Senior Courts Costs Office Guide* (London: HMSO, 2018), para 17.2.

[511] *Ibid*, para 17.2.

those covered by a certificate in Precedent F(5) in the Schedule of Costs Precedents annexed to this Practice Direction.

16.5 No final costs certificate will be issued until all relevant court fees payable on the assessment of costs have been paid.

16.6 If the receiving party fails to file a completed bill in accordance with rule 47.16 the paying party may make an application under Part 23 (General Rules about Applications for Court Orders) seeking an appropriate order under rule 3.1 (The court's general powers of management).

16.7 A final costs certificate will show:

(a) the amount of any costs which have been agreed between the parties or which have been allowed on detailed assessment;

(b) where applicable the amount agreed or allowed in respect of VAT on the costs agreed or allowed.

This provision is subject to any contrary provision made by the statutory provisions relating to costs payable out of the Community Legal Service Fund or by the Lord Chancellor under Part 1 of the Legal Aid, Sentencing and Punishment of Offenders Act 2012.

16.8 A final costs certificate will include disbursements in respect of the fees of counsel only if receipted fee notes or accounts in respect of those disbursements have been produced to the court and only to the extent indicated by those receipts.

16.9 Where the certificate relates to costs payable between parties a separate certificate will be issued for each party entitled to costs.

16.10 Form N257 is a model form of interim costs certificate and Form N256 is a model form of final costs certificate.

16.11 An application for an order staying enforcement of an interim costs certificate or final costs certificate may be made either:

(a) to a costs judge of the court office which issued the certificate; or

(b) to the court (if different) which has general jurisdiction to enforce the certificate.

16.12 An interim or final costs certificate may be enforced as if it were a judgment for the payment of an amount of money. However, proceedings for the enforcement of interim costs certificates or final costs certificates may not be issued in the Costs Office.'

Discontinuing Costs Proceedings and Withdrawal

43.394 The topic of discontinuance has already been addressed in the context of compromise at 43.240. The present discussion addresses the topic in a wider, more general, context.

The wording of the relevant provisions

43.395 The starting point is PD 47, para 9.4, which provides:

'(1) The receiving party may discontinue the detailed assessment proceedings in accordance with Part 38 (Discontinuance).

(2) Where the receiving party discontinues the detailed assessment proceedings before a detailed assessment hearing has been requested, the paying party may apply to the appropriate office for an order about the costs of the detailed assessment proceedings.

(3) Where a detailed assessment hearing has been requested the receiving party may not discontinue unless the court gives permission.

(4) A bill of costs may be withdrawn by consent whether or not a detailed assessment hearing has been requested.'

Thus CPR, Part 38, will apply unless the parties agree that the bill of costs is to be withdrawn (see 43.247).

If a detailed assessment hearing has been requested, the receiving party may not discontinue unless the court gives permission—although it is not known if this would also apply if a party had merely requested a provisional assessment. If no detailed assessment hearing has been requested, then the paying party is at liberty to apply for an order concerning the costs of the assessment. **43.396**

CPR, r 38.2(1), reads as follows: **43.397**

> '38.2 (1) A claimant may discontinue all or part of a claim at any time.
> (2) However—
> (a) a claimant must obtain the permission of the court if he wishes to discontinue all or part of a claim in relation to which—
> (i) the court has granted an interim injunction; or
> (ii) any party has given an undertaking to the court;
> (b) where the claimant has received an interim payment in relation to a claim (whether voluntarily or pursuant to an order under Part 25), he may discontinue that claim only if—
> (i) the defendant who made the interim payment consents in writing; or
> (ii) the court gives permission;
> (c) where there is more than one claimant, a claimant may not discontinue unless—
> (i) every other claimant consents in writing; or
> (ii) the court gives permission.
>
> (3) Where there is more than one defendant, the claimant may discontinue all or part of a claim against all or any of the defendants.'

Surprisingly, there is nothing in the CPR to say that references to 'claimants' and 'defendants' in CPR, Part 38, should, for the purposes of detailed assessments, be regarded as being references to 'receiving parties' and 'paying parties', respectively, but perhaps it was felt that this was not necessary because any other interpretation would lead to absurdity. **43.398**

CPR, r 38.3, provides as follows: **43.399**

> '(1) To discontinue a claim or part of a claim, a claimant must—
> (a) file a notice of discontinuance; and
> (b) serve a copy of it on every other party to the proceedings.
>
> (2) The claimant must state in the notice of discontinuance which he files that he has served notice of discontinuance on every other party to the proceedings.
>
> (3) Where the claimant needs the consent of some other party, a copy of the necessary consent must be attached to the notice of discontinuance.
>
> (4) Where there is more than one defendant, the notice of discontinuance must specify against which defendants the claim is discontinued.'

Whether the proceedings should be determined by discontinuance or withdrawal will, as a matter of practice, depend on whether the paying party consents to the receiving party's proposal. **43.400**

CPR, r 38.7, reads as follows: **43.401**

> 'A claimant who discontinues a claim needs the permission of the court to make another claim against the same defendant if—
> (a) he discontinued the claim after the defendant filed a defence; and

(b) the other claim arises out of facts which are the same or substantially the same as those relating to the discontinued claim.'

43.402 One could easily argue that, in the context of detailed assessment proceedings, the reference to a defence should be regarded as being a reference to points of dispute. There is, however, no authority on that point.

Discontinuance without consent

43.403 Detailed assessment proceedings may be discontinued by the procedure in CPR, Part 38,[512] which may be brought to bear at any time and at any stage in the proceedings.[513] The paying party will ordinarily be entitled to the costs of the assessment,[514] but an application may be made for a different order.[515] Permission will be required in the following circumstances:

- where an application has already been made for a hearing date;[516]
- where a payment on account has been made or ordered and where an interim costs certificate has been issued;[517] and
- where there is more than one receiving party and it is not the case that all of the other receiving parties agree.[518]

43.404 The fact that there is more than one paying party and the receiving party wishes to discontinue against some, but not all, of them will not, of itself, mean that permission must be obtained.[519]

Challenging discontinuance

43.405 CPR, r 38.2(4), reads as follows:

> '(1) Where the claimant discontinues under rule 38.2(1) the defendant may apply to have the notice of discontinuance set aside.
>
> (2) The defendant may not make an application under this rule more than 28 days after the date when the notice of discontinuance was served on him.'

As such, a paying party has the right to challenge discontinuance by applying to have the notice of discontinuance set aside. This may be done, however, only if no more than 28 days have passed since the notice of discontinuance was served. Such applications tend to be made in circumstances in which the discontinuer is seeking to obtain a collateral advantage by discontinuing.[520]

---

512 PD 47, para 9.4(1).
513 CPR, r 38.2(1).
514 CPR, r 38.6.
515 PD 47, para 9.4(2).
516 PD 47, para 9.4(3)
517 CPR, r 38.2(b).
518 CPR, r 38.2(c).
519 CPR, r 38.2(3).
520 Whilst not a case concerning costs, see *High Commissioner for Pakistan in the UK v National Westminster Bank* [2015] EWHC 55 (Ch), at [78]–[83], in which Henderson J set aside a notice of discontinuance on the grounds that the claimant was attempting to obtain a collateral advantage by trying to avoid the effect of a waiver of sovereign immunity.

Discontinuance with consent

Where the parties consent, the bill of costs may be withdrawn (see 43.247). The advantage of this is that the court's permission is not required.[521] In view of the fact that withdrawal is procedurally less cumbersome than discontinuance, withdrawal would often be the preferred option. It should be borne in mind that, while the CPR make express provision for subsequent proceedings to be brought in the case of discontinuance,[522] there is no such provision in the case of withdrawal. This does not mean that new proceedings cannot be brought following withdrawal, but parties who are contemplating compromise should be aware that there might be dispute about this if it is the receiving party's intention to bring new proceedings. **43.406**

Enforcement

This book does not attempt to deal with the issue of enforcement in any detail; hence only a brief introduction to the subject is offered here. **43.407**

The means of enforcing costs debts

A costs order for a stated amount is an enforceable judgment debt,[523] as is an interim or final costs certificate.[524] Where such an order or certificate exists, the receiving party will have become a judgment creditor and the paying party, a judgment debtor.[525] The judgment creditor is generally able to recover the costs of enforcement. This is because s 15(3) and (4) of the Courts and Legal Services Act 1990 (as amended) provides as follows: **43.408**

> '(3) Where a person takes steps to enforce a judgment or order of the High Court or a county court for the payment of any sum due, the costs of any previous attempt to enforce that judgment shall be recoverable to the same extent as if they had been incurred in the taking of those steps.
>
> (4) Subsection (3) shall not apply in respect of any costs which the court considers were unreasonably incurred (whether because the earlier attempt was unreasonable in all the circumstances of the case or for any other reason).'

As can be seen, the effect of these provisions is to allow recovery of all of the costs of enforcement, rather than only the costs of those steps that ultimately led to a successful recovery of the judgment debt.

Broadly speaking, the decision as to how to enforce a costs order will depend on the nature of the judgment debtor's assets. The following is a summary. **43.409**

- Where goods and chattels are owned by the judgment debtor, a warrant of execution would be appropriate.
- Where fixed assets are owned by the judgment debtor, a charging order would be appropriate.

---

[521] PD 47, para 9.4(4).
[522] CPR, r 38.7.
[523] CPR, r 70.1(2)(d).
[524] See PD 47, para 16.12. There is no express provision dealing with default costs certificates, but the fact that they may be enforced is implied by PD 47, para 10.6.
[525] CPR, r 70.1(2)(a) and (b).

- Where the judgment debtor is employed, an attachment of earnings order may be appropriate.
- Where the judgment debtor has savings or other monies in the bank, a third-party debt order may be appropriate.

43.410 Where the nature of the debtor's assets is not known, an application may be made for an oral examination of the debtor's assets and liabilities.

43.411 Enforcement proceedings may not be issued in the SCCO.[526]

Stays

43.412 If a paying party wishes to apply for a stay of enforcement of a final costs certificate, it may apply to a costs judge of the court office that issued the certificate or to the court (if it is a different court) that has general jurisdiction to enforce the certificate.[527]

Methods

43.413 The enforcement of costs certificates is broadly the same as the enforcement of any other form of order, so a costs order may be enforced by means of:

- a writ of control (previously known as *fieri facias*) or warrant of execution;[528]
- a third-party debt order;[529]
- a charging order, stop order or stop notice;[530]
- in the County Court and its hearing centres, an attachment of earnings order;[531]
- the appointment of a receiver;[532] and
- by way of insolvency proceedings (although, technically, this would not be a form of enforcement).

43.414 The following is a (very) brief description of the various methods of enforcement.

- **Warrant of execution** A warrant of execution is an order that gives a bailiff the authority to take goods from the judgment debtor's home or business. If the sum outstanding is more than £5,000, the County Court is not able to issue a warrant.
- **Attachment of earnings order** An attachment of earnings order is an order that is sent to the judgment debtor's employer, ordering it to take money from the debtor's earnings and to pay that money to the creditor (via the court). Obviously, this method may not be used in respect of a debtor who is unemployed or self-employed.
- **Third-party debt order** A third-party debt order (also known as a garnishee order) usually applies to a building society or bank that holds an account in the debtor's name, but it is not restricted to those circumstances. Andrew Smith J has explained that a third-party debt order may apply even where the costs have yet to be assessed or agreed.[533]

---

[526] PD 47, paras 16.12 (in respect of a final or interim costs certificate) and 10.6 (in respect of a default costs certificate).
[527] PD 47, paras 16.11 (in respect of a final or interim costs certificate) and 10.5 (in respect of a default costs certificate).
[528] CPR, Parts 83 and 84.
[529] CPR, Part 72.
[530] CPR, Part 73.
[531] CCR, Ord 27.
[532] CPR, Part 69.
[533] See *Travellers Insurance Co Ltd v Advani* (unreported), 10 May 2013, QBD, in which the court applied *O'Driscoll v Manchester Insurance Committee* [1915] 3 KB 499 and considered *Dawson v Preston (Law Society, Garnishees)* [1955] 1 WLR 1219.

- **Charging order** A charging order prevents the judgment debtor from disposing of their assets (usually land) without discharging their judgment debt. In some circumstances, this may lead to an order for sale of the assets. The court lacks power to make a charging order absolute where the sums claimed are unassessed costs.[534]
- **Statutory demand** In view of the fact that an order for a stated amount is for a liquidated sum, another option would be to issue a statutory demand.[535] This would be as a precursor to a bankruptcy petition (in the case of an individual) or to a winding-up petition (in the case of a company). This would be an option only if the outstanding monies were in excess of £750.

[534] *Monte Developments Ltd (in administration) of Court Management Consultants Ltd* [2010] EWHC 3071 (Ch).

[535] Insolvency Act 1986, ss 123(1)(a) or 222(1)(a).

44

SUMMARY ASSESSMENTS

44.01 This chapter deals with the following topics:

- entitlement to a summary assessment (44.03);
- discretionary power to order that there be no summary assessment (44.14):
  - delay and lack of time (44.15);
  - substantial costs (44.18);
  - substantial objections (44.19);
  - complex objections (44.20);
  - challenges to the indemnity principle (44.21);
  - conditional fee agreements (44.22);
  - litigants in person (44.23);
  - no fetter (44.24);
- procedure:
  - general procedure (44.25);
  - failure by a party to serve statement (44.28);
  - assessment of additional liabilities (44.37).

44.02 Rule 44.1 of the Civil Procedure Rules (CPR) defines summary assessment in this way: ' "[S]ummary assessment" means the procedure whereby costs are assessed by the judge who has heard the case or application.' Summary assessment has also been described as a procedure whereby the court makes an award for a stated amount of costs, rather than for costs to be assessed or for fixed costs.[1]

Entitlement to a Summary Assessment

44.03 The court's power to carry out a summary assessment is contained in CPR, r 44.6(1), and in Practice Direction (PD) 44, para 8.1, which paraphrases CPR, r 44.6(1). CPR, r 44.6(1) provides as follows:

> '(1) Where the court orders a party to pay costs to another party (other than fixed costs) it may either—
> (a) make a summary assessment of the costs; or
> (b) order detailed assessment of the costs by a costs officer,
> unless any rule, practice direction or other enactment provides otherwise.

[1] This was the definition that used to be given at CPR, r 43.3; the new and the old definitions are entirely compatible with each other.

(Practice Direction 44—General rules about costs sets out the factors which will affect the court's decision under paragraph (1).)'

The detail is contained in PD 44, para 9, rather than in the CPR themselves. Moreover, some of the provisions in the now-revoked Costs Practice Direction (CPD) continue to be relevant (see 44.38).

The 'general rule' and specific provisions for summary assessment

There is a 'general rule' that costs will be summarily assessed at the end of certain hearings. PD 44, para 9.2, expresses that rule in the following way: **44.04**

'9.2 The general rule is that the court should make a summary assessment of the costs—
(a) at the conclusion of the trial of a case which has been dealt with on the fast track, in which case the order will deal with the costs of the whole claim; and
(b) at the conclusion of any other hearing, which has lasted not more than one day, in which case the order will deal with the costs of the application or matter to which the hearing related. If this hearing disposes of the claim, the order may deal with the costs of the whole claim,
unless there is good reason not to do so, for example where the paying party shows substantial grounds for disputing the sum claimed for costs that cannot be dealt with summarily.'

As can be seen, there must be a 'good reason' not to assess costs to which the general rule in PD 44, para 9.2, would otherwise apply[2]—a topic that is addressed at 44.14–44.24.

In addition to this general rule, there are specific provisions concerning certain types of litigation. CPR, Part 45, Section IV, for example, provides that, with certain exceptions, all costs in the Intellectual Property Enterprise Court (IPEC) will be assessed by way of summary assessment.[3] More detail on this topic can be found at 50.337–50.338. Similarly, in the Court of Appeal, the costs of the following types of hearing tend to be dealt with by summary assessment: **44.05**

- contested directions hearings;
- applications for permission to appeal at which the respondent is present;
- dismissal list hearings in the Court of Appeal at which the respondent is present;
- appeals from case management decisions; and
- appeals listed for one day or less.[4]

The present incarnation of PD 52 omits this list, but it is unlikely that this indicates a change of policy against carrying out summary assessments in such circumstances.

Summary of specific provisions for summary assessment

For the reasons set out at 44.04 and 44.05, a summary assessment is likely to take place at the conclusion of the following types of hearing: **44.06**

- any fast-track trial (when the whole of the costs of the claim will be assessed summarily);[5]

[2] PD 44, para 9.9.
[3] See CPR, rr 45.30(3) and 63.26.
[4] This is taken from the pre-1 April 2013 iteration of PD 52, para 14. See also *Clearwell International Ltd v (1) MSL Group Holdings Ltd* (unreported), 16 November 2012, CA.
[5] PD 44, para 9.2(a).

- any hearing lasting less than one day[6] (or any appeal hearing in the Court of Appeal that was listed for or lasted one day or less[7]);
- any contested directions hearing in the Court of Appeal;[8]
- any application for permission to appeal in the Court of Appeal at which the respondent is present;[9]
- any dismissal list hearings in the Court of Appeal at which the respondent is present;[10]
- any appeals from case management decisions in the Court of Appeal;[11] and
- any hearing in the IPEC, subject to certain exceptions (see 50.337–50.338).[12]

44.07 In general, the costs to be assessed would be the costs of the application or matter to which the hearing related,[13] but PD 44 expressly provides that where a claim has been disposed of by a hearing lasting one day or less, the general rule will apply to the assessment of the costs of the whole of the claim.[14]

Discretion to carry out a summary assessment

44.08 The court's powers to carry out a summary assessment are not limited to the situations set out at 44.06, however, PD 44, para 9.1, confirms this in the following way: 'Whenever a court makes an order about costs which does not provide only for fixed costs to be paid the court should consider whether to make a summary assessment of costs.'

44.09 Thus the court has general discretion summarily to assess the costs of *any* case other than those that provide only for fixed costs. Whilst there is no presumption in favour of summary assessment, the court is required to address its mind to the matter. The Commercial Court Guide has this to say on the topic:

> 'Active consideration will generally be given by the Court to adopting the summary assessment procedure in all cases where the schedule of costs of the successful party is no more than £100,000, but the parties should always be prepared for the Court to assess costs summarily even where the costs exceed this amount.'[15]

44.10 It would seem that there is also no presumption in favour of detailed assessment. In particular, Wilson J has explained that there is no presumption in favour of detailed assessment in cases in which the hearing lasts more than one day.[16] This was in the context of a family matter, but there is no reason to believe that the position is any different in civil matters.

44.11 The editors of *Cook on Costs 2017* go so far as to say 'that summary assessments should be carried out in preference to detailed assessment as often as possible'.[17] One could

---

[6] PD 44, para 9.2(b).
[7] PD 52, para 14, as it used to be before 1 April 2013.
[8] *Ibid.*
[9] *Ibid.*
[10] *Ibid.*
[11] *Ibid.*
[12] *Ibid.*
[13] See PD 44, para 9.2(b).
[14] PD 44, para 9.2(b).
[15] HM Courts & Tribunals Service, *Commercial Court Guide* (10th edn, London: HMSO, 2017), para F14.2.
[16] *Q v Q (Family Division: Costs; Summary Assessment)* [2002] 2 FLR 668.
[17] See *Cook on Costs 2017* (LexisNexis, online), para 27.4.

argue that this is putting the point a shade too strongly in view of the matters referred to immediately above, but it is certainly true to say that it is not uncommon for substantial costs to be summarily assessed.[18] It is also certainly true to say that both paying and receiving parties would derive significant benefits from seeking a summary assessment where this would be practicable and where there is nothing to contraindicate such a step.

Exceptions to the 'general rule' regarding summary assessments

There are exceptions to the general rule in PD 44, para 9.2 (see 44.04), as follows. **44.12**

- **Legal aided party** There will be no summary assessment where the receiving party is an assisted person, a client funded by the Legal Services Commission (LSC)[19] or a person who is receiving civil legal services under Part 1 of the Legal Aid, Sentencing and Punishment of Offenders Act 2012.[20]
- **Children and protected persons** Unless their legal representative has waived the right to further costs, there will be no summary assessment where the receiving party is a child or a protected party.[21] This bar applies only where costs are payable *to* a child or protected party; PD 44 expressly provides that the court has the power to make a summary assessment of costs payable *by* a child or protected party.[22] Special provisions apply to children (but not protected persons) where the claim is a personal injury claim in which the damages are £25,000 or less and it is proposed to make a deduction of a success fee or sum payable under a damages-based agreement[23] (see 60.40–60.42).
- **Mortgagees and mortgagors** Unless they ask the court to make an order for their costs to be paid by another party, there will be no summary assessment of a mortgagee's costs incurred in mortgage possession proceedings or other proceedings relating to a mortgage.[24] Respected commentators have said that this is to reflect the fact that the mortgagee is in an advantageous position[25] and that, in any event, a mortgagee tends not seek an award of costs because they are entitled to recover the costs under the terms of the mortgage.[26] The wording of PD 44, para 9.3, is as follows:

  > 'The general rule in paragraph 9.2 [that the court should make a summary assessment of the costs] does not apply to a mortgagee's costs incurred in mortgage possession proceedings or other proceedings relating to a mortgage unless the mortgagee asks the court to make an order for the mortgagee's costs to be paid by another party.'

---

[18] See, eg, *Sony Communications AB v SSH Communications Security Corpn* [2016] EWHC 2985 (Pat).

[19] PD 44, para 9.8, which reads: 'The court will not make a summary assessment of the costs of a receiving party who is an assisted person or [Legal Services Commission] funded client or who is a person for whom civil legal services (within the meaning of Part 1 of the Legal Aid, Sentencing and Punishment of Offenders Act 2012) are provided under arrangements made for the purposes of that Part of that Act.'

[20] This is the modern equivalent of a funded client. The categories to which it applies are set out in Sch 1, Pt 1, to the Legal Aid, Sentencing and Punishment of Offenders Act 2012. That Part is subject to the exclusions in Sch 1, Pt 2. The types of case it includes are family cases involving vulnerable people or children, judicial review, environmental claims, etc.

[21] PD 44, para 9.9(1).

[22] PD 44, para 9.9(2).

[23] See CPR, r 21.12(1A)(b) (in combination with CPR, r 46.4(5)(b), and PD 21, para 11).

[24] PD 44, para 9.3.

[25] See, eg, *Cook on Costs 2014* (LexisNexis, online), para 36.2.

[26] See, eg, *ibid*, para 27.11.

Compromise and summary assessments

44.13 Where an application is made with the consent of both parties, they ought not simply to attend court in the expectation that they will be entitled to a summary assessment as of right; instead, they should seek to agree those costs. PD 44, para 9.4, gives the following guidance:

> 'Where an application has been made and the parties to the application agree an order by consent without any party attending, the parties should seek to agree a figure for costs to be inserted in the consent order or agree that there should be no order for costs.'[27]

Discretionary Power to Order that there be No Summary Assessment

44.14 The court has the discretionary power not to assess costs summarily.[28] Whilst, in theory, it is not binding (see 4.50), PD 44, para 9.9, states that there must be 'good reason' not to assess costs to which the general rule in PD 44, para 9.2, would otherwise apply. The following miscellaneous points can be made about the exercise of the court's discretion not to carry out a summary assessment.

Delay and lack of time

44.15 Lack of time would generally be considered to be a good reason for not carrying out a summary assessment,[29] but mere weariness on the part of the court or the parties would not. This was made clear by the former Judicial Studies Board (JSB) in its advice to judges:

> 'You may be tired at the end of a case and lack enthusiasm for dealing with the costs, but this does not entitle you to order detailed assessment, which may be to the detriment of the lay clients on both sides. The receiving party will have to involve himself in the additional expenditure of preparing a bill, and will be kept out of his money for longer than he need be. If enforcement is necessary it is preferable to be able to pursue the total of the judgment debt and costs, instead of first recovering the debt, and several months later having to start once more on the enforcement process, this time for the costs. By then the paying party may have successfully divested himself of assets, paid other creditors, or disappeared. As regards the paying party, he also may incur further expense in instructing his lawyers to deal with the bill, whilst interest on the costs will continue to accrue.'[30]

44.16 This guidance was not in any way binding, but it did articulate the problems that may be consequent to a decision not to carry out a summary assessment (those being further cost, delay and the potential for a multiplicity of enforcement proceedings).

---

[27] This provision was amended on 1 April 2013; the old wording used to provide that if the parties could not agree the costs position, attendance on the appointment would be necessary. The removal of that provision is not likely to deny a party the right to be heard, however, because if their opponent stubbornly refuses to agree to pay costs, they would have the sanction of not agreeing the application, in which case everything (including the issue of costs) would come before the court. Whether the court would look favourably on a party who did that, however, would depend on the facts.

[28] See PD 44, para 9.2. It is arguable that the court lacks the *vires* to make such an order in the Intellectual Property Enterprise Court (IPEC) (see 50.337–50.338).

[29] Whilst it does not appear in PD 44, now-revoked CPD, art 13.2, used to give this as an example.

[30] Judicial Studies Board, *Civil Bench Book* (c. 2010), para 8.42.

Where the court does not carry out an immediate summary assessment, the outstanding issues must be resolved within a reasonable period of time. The European Court of Human Rights (ECtHR) has found that a delay—of four years!—was a breach of Art 6(1) of the European Convention on Human Rights (ECHR).[31] **44.17**

Substantial costs

Costs of a complex and weighty claim may not be suitable for summary assessment.[32] The Guide to the Summary Assessment of Costs gives the following advice: **44.18**

> 'It may not be appropriate to carry out a summary assessment if a case lasts more than half a day or involves leading Counsel since in those circumstances the case is likely to be complex and weighty. It will often be unwise for the court summarily to assess costs in a matter which is not simple and straightforward, unless the difference between the parties is comparatively small, or unless the correct allowance appears clear.'[33]

This guidance concerns hearings in the Court of Appeal, but there is no reason to believe that it would not also have resonance in other circumstances. That said, it should be borne in mind that there have been instances of the court summarily assessing the costs of very weighty litigation (especially in cases that have been costs managed).[34] It also ought to be borne in mind that the guidance is now over a decade old.

Substantial objections

PD 44, para 9.2, states that where the paying party shows substantial grounds for disputing the sum claimed, that may amount to good reason for not assessing the costs summarily. **44.19**

Complex objections

Complex legal arguments about the costs might justify a detailed assessment. In a case in which there were arguments over the hourly charging rates of employed solicitors, for example, a detailed assessment was thought appropriate.[35] **44.20**

Challenges to the indemnity principle

By the same token, a credible challenge to the indemnity principle would not normally be suitable for summary assessment.[36] **44.21**

Conditional fee agreements

The JSB advised that the existence of a conditional fee agreement or other such funding arrangement would not, of itself, be a good reason to order a detailed assessment.[37] **44.22**

---

[31] See *Robins v United Kingdom*, App no 22410/93 (1997) 26 EHRR 527. This did not relate to the summary assessment under the CPR, but it did deal with a directly analogous type of procedure.

[32] As an example of this, see *Euroil Ltd v Cameroon Offshore Petroleum Sarl* [2014] EWHC 215 (Comm).

[33] See HM Courts & Tribunals Services, *Guide to the Summary Assessment of Costs* (London: HMSO, 2005), para 65(1).

[34] See, eg, *Sony Communications AB v SSH Communications Security Corpn* [2016] EWHC 2985 (Pat).

[35] *R v Cardiff City Council, ex p Brown* (unreported), 11 August 1999, QBD.

[36] *Ibid.*

[37] Judicial Studies Board, *Civil Bench Book* (c. 2010), para 8.42.

Litigants in person

44.23 Where a litigant in person wishes to demonstrate pecuniary loss,[38] it may be necessary to afford them more time to obtain evidence and prepare their case. That would be capable of amounting to a good reason not to carry out a summary assessment.

No fetter

44.24 Where PD 44 (or any other practice direction) provides that a summary assessment is the ordinary method by which costs will be assessed, a decision to summarily assess the costs will rarely be corrected on appeal. In a case in which £22,000 was claimed on a Form N260 that provided very little information about those costs, the Court of Appeal declined to find that the judge had been wrong to carry out a summary assessment.[39]

Procedure in General

44.25 The parties are expected to assist the court by preparing for a summary assessment.[40] This begins with the completion of the model form that records the sums claimed—namely, Form N260.[41] It should be noted that the model form has changed twice in recent years (first in April 2013 and then again in June 2015) and, as such, it would be wise to ensure that the most recent version is being used. The present version contains a schedule for the details of the work done on documents.[42] The form does not allow costs to be set out in a way that accords with the phases of a budget, which will not present any problems when the costs in question have not been the subject of a costs management order, but if the costs have been the subject of such an order, then it may be appropriate to provide a phasic breakdown in some other document, such as by adapting Precedent Q for this purpose.

44.26 It will usually assist the court if the paying party's statement of costs is placed before the court in addition to that of the receiving party.[43] Indeed, in the editor's experience, refusal to do this will often be met with judicial disapproval.

44.27 PD 44, para 9.5, gives the following guidance:

> '9.5 (1) It is the duty of the parties and their legal representatives to assist the judge in making a summary assessment of costs in any case to which paragraph 9.2 above applies, in accordance with the following subparagraphs.
>
> (2) Each party who intends to claim costs must prepare a written statement of those costs showing separately in the form of a schedule—
> (a) the number of hours to be claimed;
> (b) the hourly rate to be claimed;
> (c) the grade of fee earner;
> (d) the amount and nature of any disbursement to be claimed, other than counsel's fee for appearing at the hearing;

[38] *Neil v Stephenson* [2001] EWCA Civ 627.

[39] *Bryen & Langley Ltd v Boston* [2005] EWCA Civ 973.

[40] See PD 44 para 9.5(1); see also *Clearwell v MSN* [2012] EWCA 1440, at [5], *per* Smith J.

[41] See PD4 4, para 1.2.

[42] Akenhead J has explained that Form N260 provides for a schedule to be filled in for work done on documents, with there being envisaged a one-line description of work for each item of work. He went on to find, however, that it would be disproportionate to disallow the documentary time as a result of having failed to do this: see *Group M UK Ltd v Cabinet Office* [2014] EWHC 3863 (TCC), at [15] and [16].

[43] *Clearwell v MSN* [2012] EWCA 1440, at [5], *per* Smith J.

(e) the amount of legal representative's costs to be claimed for attending or appearing at the hearing;
(f) counsel's fees; and
(g) any VAT to be claimed on these amounts.

(3) The statement of costs should follow as closely as possible Form N260 and must be signed by the party or the party's legal representative. Where a party is—
(a) an assisted person;
(b) a LSC funded client;
(c) a person for whom civil legal services (within the meaning of Part 1 of the Legal Aid, Sentencing and Punishment of Offenders Act 2012) are provided under arrangements made for the purposes of that Part of that Act; or
(d) represented by a person in the party's employment,
the statement of costs need not include the certificate appended at the end of Form N260.

(4) The statement of costs must be filed at court and copies of it must be served on any party against whom an order for payment of those costs is intended to be sought as soon as possible and in any event—
(a) for a fast track trial, not less than 2 days before the trial; and
(b) for all other hearings, not less than 24 hours before the time fixed for the hearing.'

Where the costs in question relate to an appeal, PD 52A, para 5.3, provides that any statement of costs must show the amount claimed for the skeleton argument separately.

Failure by a party to serve statement of costs

It may happen that the receiving party failed to file and serve a statement of costs in accordance with the relevant provisions. In 2001, Neuberger J gave detailed guidance about how the court should deal with that situation.[44] That guidance is, in many ways, no longer good law post-*Denton*,[45] but Neuberger J's description of the following options that would be available to the court continues to apply. **44.28**

- **Immediate summary assessment** The paying party may be afforded a short adjournment to consider the statement of costs, following which a summary assessment would be carried out. The fact that the paying party may not have had much time to consider the statement of costs is a factor that can be taken into account.
- **Delayed summary assessment** The matter may be stood over for a summary assessment at a later date (either on the basis of paper submissions or otherwise).
- **Detailed assessment** The matter may be sent for a detailed assessment on the basis that there are appropriate sanctions as to costs.[46]

Neuberger J explained that if there were aggravating factors,[47] it might be correct to deprive a defaulting party of its costs entirely.

It is relevant that PD 44, para 9.6, now reads as follows: **44.29**

'9.6 The failure by a party, without reasonable excuse, to comply with paragraph 9.5 will be taken into account by the court in deciding what order to make about the costs of the claim,

[44] *MacDonald v Taree Holdings Ltd* [2001] 1 Costs LR 147.
[45] *Denton v TH White Ltd* [2014] EWCA Civ 906.
[46] This is what happened, for example, following *Wheeler v The Chief Constable of Gloucestershire Constabulary* [2013] EWCA Civ 1791.
[47] This approach was also taken by Nugee J in *Kingsley v Orban* [2014] EWHC 2991 (Ch).

hearing or application, and about the costs of any further hearing or detailed assessment hearing that may be necessary as a result of that failure.'

44.30 This invites the question of how the court is to deal with a failure, without reasonable excuse, to serve a statement of costs in accordance with PD4 4, para 9.5(4). Akenhead J has explained that *Denton*[48] applies and that a failure to comply is capable of being a 'serious and significant' breach.[49] On the facts of the case before him (in which the receiving party had served the statement of costs only three hours before a hearing, albeit for understandable reasons), Akenhead J had the following to say about the third stage in *Denton*:

'(a) The failure to comply with the Practice Direction was at the lower end of serious.
(b) Unlike the provisions relating to costs and management budgets which expressly impose a sanction (unless other factors suggest that the sanction should not be imposed), no sanction is expressly identified in the Practice Direction. Paragraph 9.6 of the Practice Direction simply requires the Court to take the failure into account.
(c) Exactly the same arguments of principle and of quantification of costs would have been argued and have had to be addressed in any event. ...
(d) Having decided that in principle that [the receiving party] should have its reasonable costs ... it would be unjust to refuse it any quantified sum simply because for understandable reasons it did not file its Statement of Costs more than 24 hours before the handing down judgment. The prejudice or detriment suffered by [the paying party] is minimal, other than possibly its incurring a small amount of costs (say £2,000) over and above what it would have incurred in any event if the Statement of Costs had been served more than 24 hours before the handing down. To punish [the receiving party] for its failure in effect to the tune of some £40,000 plus would to most right thinking people be wholly disproportionate. The additional cost can be taken off any summary assessment to which [the receiving party] is found to be entitled.'[50]

Thus, even post-*Denton*, it does not follow that a failure to comply with PD 44, para 9.5(4), will result in significant adverse consequences being visited upon the receiving party.

44.31 It should be noted that it would arguably be open to the court to disallow costs entirely,[51] but the editor is not aware of any cases in which this has happened. Indeed, such an outcome would be very far removed from what tends to happen in practice. The approach of Akenhead J has already been mentioned (see 44.30). In a similar vein, Nugee J said (in the context of an appeal) that 'it would have been preferable for the [court below] to have granted [the paying party] a short adjournment of 15 minutes or so had he asked for it to consider any points arising on the schedule', but he declined to interfere with the assessment made in the court below (in which no additional time had been given to the paying party).[52] Similarly, in a matter in which a statement had been filed, but not served, Warby J made only a modest reduction in the amount that was allowed, the amount of that reduction being based on the additional costs occasioned by the failure to serve the statement.[53]

---

48 *Denton v TH White Ltd* [2014] EWCA Civ 906.

49 See *Group M UK Ltd v Cabinet Office* [2014] EWHC 3863 (TCC), at [10] and [11].

50 See *ibid*, at [14].

51 This is because PD 44, para 9.5(2), refers to the fact that a party intending to seek costs must prepare a statement of costs, and PD 44, para 9.5(4), states that this must be filed and served by the prescribed time before the hearing. As such, it is arguable that this creates a condition precedent to the recovery of costs.

52 *Kingsley v Orban* [2014] EWHC 2991 (Ch), at [22].

53 *Simpson v MGN Ltd* [2015] EWHC 126 (QB).

The court may order (usually with the parties' consent) that costs be assessed on paper following written representations from both parties. In the editor's experience, this is not an uncommon way of dealing with a failure to comply with PD 44, para 9.5(4). Where this has happened and where the court has made an order as to the amount allowed, it would not generally be open to the parties to subsequently ask for a detailed assessment; if the parties were dissatisfied with the result, the proper route would be to appeal.[54] **44.32**

Remittal of assessments

It is not possible for the judge who made the costs order to remit the matter to a costs judge for a *summary* assessment. This is because of a provision in PD 44, para 9.7: **44.33**

> 'The court awarding costs cannot make an order for a summary assessment of costs by a costs officer. If a summary assessment of costs is appropriate but the court awarding costs is unable to do so on the day, the court may give directions as to a further hearing before the same judge.'

Thus, if the court is minded to remit the matter to a costs judge, this must be for a detailed assessment, rather than a summary assessment.

It used to be thought that the only judge who was in a position to carry out a summary assessment was the judge who had made the order. This was explained by Sir Swinton Thomas in the following way: **44.34**

> 'The important words in 13.8 are the words "a further hearing before the same judge". The reasoning behind that rule is clear. It is that only the person who has actually heard the case and knows about it is in a position to make a summary assessment of costs.'[55]

This is no longer good law, for two reasons: first, PD 44, para 9.7, now refers to the fact that the court *may* give directions as to a further hearing before the same judge (whereas the 2001 equivalent used the word 'must'); and secondly, the overriding objective is now worded differently.[56] Coulson J had this to say on the point: **44.35**

> 'It is often the case that a summary assessment is the only just and proportionate way to deal with costs. It would be absurd if such an exercise could not be undertaken because of, say, the death or indisposition of the judge who conducted the original hearing or made the original order, or because he or she is on circuit and is unable to deal with the matter when it arises. Some degree of flexibility must be permissible.'[57]

This means that if there is going to be an adjournment for a summary assessment at a later date, it may or may not be reserved to the judge who made (or who intends to make) the costs order. Coulson J also said this, however, which makes it clear that it would, in general, be appropriate for the same judge to deal with the matter: **44.36**

> 'Obviously, in the majority of cases, it will be appropriate, even necessary, for the same judge to conduct the summary assessment. If, for example, there was a contested hearing,

---

[54] See *Emmott v Michael Wilson & Partners* [2013] EWHC 3690 (Comm), *per* Judge Mackie QC.

[55] *Mahmood v Penrose* [2002] EWCA Civ 457, at [12]. However, the rule that only the judge who made the order can summarily assess the costs has, from time to time, been broken by the Court of Appeal itself. In *Bryen & Langley Ltd v Boston* [2005] EWCA Civ 973, for example, the court indicated that if the quantum of costs in the court below had not been agreed, it would have been minded to assess those costs.

[56] See *Transformers and Rectifiers Ltd v Needs Ltd* [2015] EWHC 1687 (TCC), at [13]–[18], *per* Coulson J.

[57] *Ibid*, at [10].

and the detail of any summary assessment exercise carried out thereafter depended on the views formed by the judge about the parties' submissions, or the witnesses, or their conduct generally, then it would be inappropriate for any other judge to attempt the exercise. But an inflexible rule that the same judge must, in every case, conduct the summary assessment, cannot be derived from the CPR.'[58]

Assessment of additional liabilities

Summary assessment upon the conclusion of the proceedings

44.37 Subject to any necessary modifications,[59] the provisions of the now-revoked CPD that concern funding arrangements will continue to apply where the receiving party has the benefit of a pre-commencement funding arrangement—which will generally mean a conditional fee agreement or after-the-event (ATE) policy made before 1 April 2013.[60] The same is also true of those parts of the CPR that used to relate to additional liabilities. Where, at the conclusion of proceedings, a party with a pre-commencement funding arrangement seeks to have its additional liabilities summarily assessed, that party should ensure that all relevant documentation is to hand and is available for the court. The relevant guidance continues to be that which used to be contained in CPD, art 14.9:

> '14.9 In order to facilitate the court in making a summary assessment of any additional liability at the conclusion of the proceedings the party seeking such costs must prepare and have available for the court a bundle of documents which must include—
> (1) a copy of every notice of funding arrangement (Form N251) which has been filed by him;
> (2) a copy of every estimate and statement of costs filed by him;
> (3) a copy of the risk assessment prepared at the time any relevant funding arrangement was entered into and on the basis of which the amount of the additional liability was fixed.'

Assessment of costs incurred while the claim is ongoing

44.38 Additional liabilities pose a potential problem when costs are summarily assessed prior to the conclusion of proceedings, because:

- the court will not know whether the proceedings will be determined in favour of the receiving party and therefore it may not be known whether a success fee will be payable; and
- the receiving party may have a legitimate interest in keeping the quantum of the success fee confidential.

These are the reasons why the assessment of additional liabilities is usually postponed until the conclusion of the proceedings.

44.39 CPR, r 44.3A, used to provide as follows:

> '(1) The court will not assess any additional liability until the conclusion of the proceedings, or the part of the proceedings, to which the funding arrangement relates.
>
> ("Funding arrangement" and "additional liability" are defined in rule 43.2.)
>
> (2) At the conclusion of the proceedings, or the part of the proceedings, to which the funding arrangement relates the court may—
> (a) make a summary assessment of all the costs, including any additional liability;

[58] *Ibid*, at [8].
[59] See CPR, r 48.1(1).
[60] See CPR, r 48.2, for more details.

(b) make an order for detailed assessment of the additional liability but make a summary assessment of the other costs; or
(c) make an order for detailed assessment of all the costs.

(Part 47 sets out the procedure for the detailed assessment of costs.)'

For the reasons set out, these provisions above continue to apply where the receiving party has the benefit of a pre-commencement funding arrangement.

Similarly, CPD, art 13.12, gave the following guidance: **44.40**

> '13.12 (1) Attention is drawn to rule 44.3A which prevents the court from making a summary assessment of an additional liability before the conclusion of the proceedings or the part of the proceedings to which the funding arrangement relates. Where this applies, the court should nonetheless make a summary assessment of the base costs of the hearing or application unless there is a good reason not to do so.'

Thus the court was (and still is) encouraged to summarily assess the base costs even if the additional liabilities are to be held over to another time.

In much the same vein, the CPD, arts 14.1 and 14.2, gave the following further guidance: **44.41**

> '14.1 The existence of a conditional fee agreement or other funding arrangement within the meaning of rule 43.2 is not by itself a sufficient reason for not carrying out a summary assessment.
>
> 14.2 Where a legal representative acting for the receiving party has entered into a conditional fee agreement the court may summarily assess all the costs (other than any additional liability).'

No summary assessment of only the additional liabilities

It would not be correct to make a summary assessment of the success fee and then to remit **44.42** the base costs to a costs judge for a detailed assessment. This used to be confirmed by CPD, art 3.1: 'Rule 43.3 defines summary assessment. When carrying out a summary assessment of costs where there is an additional liability the court may assess the base costs alone, or the base costs and the additional liability.'

45

COSTS APPEALS AND REVIEWS

45.01 This chapter deals with the following topics:

- introduction (45.02);
- terminology (45.04);
- appeals under CPR, Part 47, Section VIII:
  - general points concerning appeals from authorised court officers (45.05);
  - the timing of appeals from authorised court officers (45.08);
  - records of what was said in hearing below (45.10);
- appeals under CPR, Part 52 (45.14):
  - the tests to be applied on appeal and how those tests are applied in practice (45.16);
  - the appeals procedure under CPR, Part 52 (45.32);
  - costs in the appeal court and below (including interest on overpaid costs) (45.57);
  - topics likely to arise during an appeal hearing (45.60);
  - assessors (45.66);
  - second appeals (45.70); and
- judicial review (45.73).

Introduction

45.02 There are four means by which a party may challenge the outcome of an assessment of costs. The first is the regime created by Part 47, Section VIII, of the Civil Procedure Rules (CPR) and Practice Direction (PD) 47, para 47.20, which applies where the assessment was carried out by an authorised court officer (ACO). The second is the general appeals procedure under CPR, Part 52 and PDs 52A–52E, which is by far the most important regime and is likely to be the only one that most readers will encounter. The third is the regime in the Supreme Court, which is not addressed in this book. Last, and most certainly least, are judicial reviews, which are relevant only in those rare cases in which there are no means of appealing the judge who made the order that the applicant wishes to challenge (see 45.73).

45.03 On 3 October 2016, CPR, Part 52, was amended[1] (along with the provisions regarding the destinations of appeals[2]) to streamline the appeals process in the Court of Appeal and to

---

[1] See the Civil Procedure (Amendment No 3) Rules 2016 (SI 2016/788); Ministry of Justice, *86th Update: Practice Direction Amendments*, available online at https://www.justice.gov.uk/courts/procedure-rules/civil/pdf/update/86th-update-pd-making-document.pdf

[2] See Access to Justice Act 1999 (Destination of Appeals) Order 2016 (SI 2016/917), art 7, which revoked the Access to Justice Act 1999 (Destination of Appeals) Order 2000 (SI 2000/1071).

consolidate and reorder provisions relating to appeals in general.[3] Transitional provisions apply.[4]

Terminology

The following points may be made about the terminology of costs appeals. **45.04**

- **'Appeal'** The word 'appeal' is not defined in the CPR, but it is generally taken to mean the transference of a case from an inferior court to a higher court or tribunal for the purpose of asking the higher court to revise or reverse the decision of the inferior court. The word 'appeal' may be used in such a way as to include an appeal by way of case stated.[5]
- **Appellant** An appellant is the person who is appealing.[6] It used to be difficult to know how to refer to a would-be appellant who had yet to be granted permission to appeal. This problem now no longer exists because the CPR expressly states that appellant 'means a person who brings or seeks to bring an appeal'.[7] As such, the days of long-winded phrases such as 'the applicant for permission to appeal' have gone.
- **Respondent** This means 'a person other than the appellant who was a party to the proceedings in the lower court and who is affected by the appeal'; where appropriate, it will also mean a 'person who is permitted by the appeal court to be a party to the appeal'.[8]
- **'Appeal court'** This means the court to which the appeal in question is being made, which may or may not be the Court of Appeal,[9] but the words 'appeal court' should not be regarded as being shorthand for 'Court of Appeal'. Whilst it is not a phrase that is used in the CPR, the phrase 'appeals court' is also often used in practice.
- **'Lower court'** The CPR stipulate that this means 'the court, tribunal or other person or body from whose decision the appeal in question is brought'.[10] Whilst it is not defined in the CPR, the term 'court below' is often used to mean the same thing.
- **'Appeal notice'** This is not the same as 'appellant's notice' (see below); rather, an 'appeal notice' is a more general phrase that may include an appellant's notice or a respondent's notice.[11] In this regard, it is worth noting the following.
  - **'Appellant's notice'** This is the document that begins the appeal. It must be submitted using Form N161 (or Form N164 on the small claims track).[12] Time limits

---

[3] See Explanatory Memorandum to Civil Procedure (Amendment No 3) Rules 2016 (SI 2016/788), para 2.2.

[4] In so far as destinations are concerned, see Civil Procedure (Amendment No 3) Rules 2016 (SI 2016/ 788), art 8, which provided as follows: 'Where a person has filed a notice of appeal or applied for permission to appeal before the date on which this Order comes into force—(a) this Order shall not apply to the appeal to which that notice or application relates; and (b) that appeal shall lie to the court to which it would have lain before that date.' See also Civil Procedure (Amendment No 3) Rules 2016 (SI 2016/788), r 16.

[5] CPR, r 52.1(3)(a).

[6] This may, albeit rarely, include a person who was not a party to the proceedings, but who was adversely affected by them: see *George Wimpey UK Ltd v Tewkesbury Borough Council* [2008] EWCA Civ 12.

[7] CPR, r 52.1(3)(d).

[8] CPR, r 52.1(3)(e).

[9] CPR, r 52.1(3)(b).

[10] CPR, r 52.1(3)(c).

[11] CPR, r 52.1(3)(f).

[12] PD 52, para 4.2.

apply (in general, 21 days in which to file the notice,[13] followed by seven days in which to serve it).[14] Where the appellant seeks permission from the appeal court, that application must be made in the appellant's notice.[15]

- **Respondent's notice** This is usually submitted using Form N162. Any respondent may file and serve such a document,[16] but this is mandated only where the respondent is themselves seeking permission to appeal, or where they wish to ask the appeal court to uphold the decision of the lower court for reasons different from or additional to those given by that court.[17]

Appeals Under CPR, Part 47, Section VIII

General points concerning appeals from authorised court officers

45.05 Appeals from decisions of ACOs are governed by CPR, Part 47, Section VIII. CPR, Part 52 does not apply,[18] so the appeal will not count as a 'first' appeal for the purposes of the destination of any subsequent appeal.[19]

45.06 CPR, Part 47, Section VIII, is a discrete procedure that is dissimilar to and unconnected with any other appeals procedure in the CPR.[20] In particular:

- the appellant is not required to obtain permission to appeal;[21]
- the appeal will always proceed by way of a rehearing, rather than a review;[22] and
- the appeal will be heard by a court that would itself have been capable of hearing the matter at first instance.[23]

For all practical purposes, an appeal under CPR, Part 47, Section VIII, will proceed as if it were an assessment. It is only natural that the parties and the court will, from time to time, refer to the court officer's reasoning, but the appeal court is not in any way bound by it. In practice, appellants often choose to structure their submissions around what the

---

[13] See CPR, r 52.13(2), which reads: 'The appellant must file the appellant's notice at the appeal court within—(a) such period as may be directed by the lower court (which may be longer or shorter than the period referred to in sub-paragraph (b)); or (b) where the court makes no such direction, and subject to the specific provision about time limits in rules 52.8 to 52.11 and Practice Direction 52D, 21 days after the date of the decision of the lower court which the appellant wishes to appeal.'

[14] See CPR, r 52.13(3), which reads: '[U]nless the appeal court orders otherwise, an appellant's notice must be served on each respondent—(a) as soon as practicable; and (b) in any event not later than 7 days, after it is filed.'

[15] See CPR, r 52.13(2).

[16] See CPR, r 52.13(1).

[17] See CPR, r 52.13(2).

[18] See CPR, r 52.1(2), which states: 'This Part does not apply to an appeal in detailed assessment proceedings against a decision of an authorised court officer.' See also PD 52A, para 2.2(b).

[19] This used to be expressly stated in Access to Justice Act 1999 (Destination of Appeals) Order 2000 (SI 2000/1071), art 5(a); Civil Procedure (Amendment No 3) Rules 2016 (SI 2016/788) makes mention of ACOs, but PD 52A, para 3.5 (as amended by the 86th Update) makes the position clear.

[20] Although there is no authority on the point, these differences are probably a reflection of the fact that an ACO is not a judge in the sense that they are required to have both legal qualifications and experience of legal practice.

[21] This is implied by CPR, r 47.21, and made explicit by PD 47, para 20.2.

[22] See CPR, r 47.24(a); PD 47, para 20.4.

[23] CPR, r 47.22; PD 47, para 20.4.

ACO said, but that is very different from there being a requirement to show that the court officer's conclusions were 'wrong'.

The procedure is governed by CPR, r 47.23, which reads as follows: **45.07**

> '(1) The appellant must file an appeal notice within 21 days after the date of the decision against which it is sought to appeal.
> (2) On receipt of the appeal notice, the court will—
> (a) serve a copy of the notice on the parties to the detailed assessment proceedings; and
> (b) give notice of the appeal hearing to those parties.'

As is set out below, this rule is supplemented by PD 47, para 20.

The timing of appeals from authorised court officers

An appellant's notice must be filed within 21 days of the court officer's decision[24] and this is so even if the appellant has not yet been able to obtain a suitable record of that decision.[25] The form that the appellant should use is Form N161.[26] This is a somewhat inconvenient requirement because that form is ill-suited to appeals under CPR, Part 47, Section VIII.[27] **45.08**

The appellant does not need to serve the appellant's notice on the other parties, because this is something that the court will do.[28] In contrast to the position under CPR, Part 52 (see 45.33), it seems that time starts running on the date of the individual decision that is the subject of the appeal, not the date on which the assessment finished.[29] **45.09**

A record of what was said in the hearing below

Where possible, the appellant must obtain a suitable record of what was said in the court below.[30] This requirement may seem rather odd, given the fact that an appeal from a decision of an authorised officer is a rehearing rather than a review, but in practice it is often convenient to know what the ACO had to say. If there is an official recording of the **45.10**

---

[24] CPR, r 47.23.

[25] PD 47, para 20.6.

[26] PD 47, para 20.3.

[27] In particular, §2 requires the appellant to state the status of the judge whose decision they wish to appeal, yet 'ACO' is not one of the options. Moreover, §6 requires the appellant to state grounds of appeal, but this may not be appropriate if the appellant merely wants the court to have another look at their points of dispute or points in reply. The editor's suggestions are as follows. Sections 1, 3, 4, 5, 9 and 10 usually present no difficulties. In §2, in response to the question, 'What is the status of the Judge whose decision you want to appeal?', a note needs to be added that explains what an ACO is. Where appropriate, the box next to 'final decision' should be ticked. It may also be necessary to explain that the issue of allocation is not relevant because detailed assessments are not allocated in the way that other claims are. As to §§6 and 7, a list of grounds should be prepared on a separate sheet, but there is no reason why this could not refer to the detailed points in the points of dispute or replies. As to §8, it may be best to tick the second box and to say, 'The appeal court is asked to review the assessment and to issue a new final costs certificate for the newly assessed amount.'

[28] CPR, r 47.23(2).

[29] This is because CPR, r 47.14(7), does not apply to appeals under CPR, Part 47, Section VIII, and, as such, *Kasir v Darlington & Simpson Rolling Mills Ltd* [2001] 2 Costs LR 228 continues to be good law in this regard. In any event, see CPR, r 47.23(1).

[30] PD 47, paras 20.5 and 20.6. It may not always be possible to obtain that record within the time in which the appellant's notice must be filed. Where this is the case, the appellant's notice should be completed to the best of the appellant's ability; it may then be amended with the permission of the costs judge or district judge hearing the appeal.

hearing, then an approved transcript ought to be obtained.[31] If not, the following would be acceptable:

- the court officer's comments written on the bill;[32] or
- a note prepared by one of the advocates (which, if possible, ought to be agreed) and approved by the ACO.[33]

45.11 The rule that banned the use of photocopies of the original transcript[34] no longer to applies. Similarly, there is no requirement to obtain 'written reasons' from the court officer.[35]

Litigants in person and appeals from decisions of ACOs

45.12 Where an unrepresented party wishes to appeal, but there is no official record of the ACO's reasons, it is the duty of the representative of any would-be respondent to make their note of the ACO's reasons available to the would-be appellant, promptly and free of charge.[36]

45.13 Similarly, where the appellant was represented before the ACO, but is now acting in person, it is the duty of the appellant's former advocate to make a note available.[37] The appellant in person should submit the note of the reasons to the court hearing the appeal.[38]

Appeals Under CPR, Part 52

45.14 With the exception of what has been said above about ACOs (see 45.05), the procedure governing appeals will be found not in Parts 44–47, but instead in a place that has no special regard for the differences between costs and other types of money—namely, CPR, Part 52. That Part is easily navigable because certain changes were made in 2012 that simplified matters considerably.[39] In particular, the related practice directions have now also been split into parts and sections, as follows.

- **PD 52A, Appeals in general**
  - Section I, Practice directions supplementing Part 52
  - Section II, Introduction
  - Section III, Destinations of appeal

[31] PD 47, para 20.5.
[32] PD 47, para 20.5(a).
[33] PD 47, para 20.5(b).
[34] This being CPD, art 48.3 (which, for the avoidance of doubt, is no longer good law).
[35] PD 47, para 20.2.
[36] PD 47, para 20.5.
[37] PD 47, para 20.5.
[38] PD 47, para 20.5.
[39] In 2011, a subcommittee chaired by Moore-Bick LJ recommended that changes be made to the procedures governing civil appeals. The opportunity was taken to reduce the text and to simplify the operation of CPR, Part 52: see The White Book, para 52.0.10. This led to the creation of five new practice directions (PDs 52A–52E). Those new provisions came into force on 1 October 2012: see the Civil Procedure (Amendment No 2) Rules 2012 (SI 2012/2208). Further changes were made in October 2016, for the purposes of streamlining the appeals process in the Court of Appeal and consolidating the provisions relating to appeals in general: see Explanatory Memorandum to Civil Procedure (Amendment No 3) Rules 2016 (SI 2016/788), para 2.2.

  - Section IV, Obtaining permission to appeal
  - Section V, Skeleton arguments
  - Section VI, Disposing of applications and appeals by consent
  - Section VII, Reopening appeals
  - Section VIII, Transitional provisions
- **PD 52B, Appeals in the County Court and High Court**
  - Section I, Application
  - Section II, Venue for appeals and filing of notices and applications
  - Section III, Extending time in which to appeal
  - Section IV, Initiating an appeal
  - Section V, Case managing the appeal; orders of the court
  - Section VI, Conduct of the appeal
  - Section VII, Determination of applications
  - Section VIII, Hearings
- **PD 52C, Appeals to the Court of Appeal**
- **PD 52D, Statutory appeals and appeals subject to special provision**
- **PD 52E, Appeals by way of case stated**

As can be seen, it is easy to identify the relevant provisions. The practice directions give a fair amount of guidance, but it should not be forgotten that practice directions are not sources of law. The editors of The White Book had this to say on the point: **45.15**

> 'The information contained in those Practice Directions summarises and presents in an intelligible form a large amount of quite complicated legislation dealing with rights of appeal and "routes" of appeal. This is a great benefit for practitioners. However, it must be remembered that the material in the Practice Directions is not the source of the law relating to the exercise of rights of appeal but merely an explanation of its effects.'[40]

Before dealing with the niceties of procedure, it is best to examine the nature of the tests that the appeal court will apply.

The tests to be applied on appeal and how those tests are applied in practice

Appeals under CPR, Part 52, nearly always proceed by way of review, rather than a rehearing.[41] In particular, the court will allow an appeal only if the decision of the lower court was 'wrong' or it was 'unjust because of a serious procedural or other irregularity in the proceedings'.[42] The second of these tests is rarely relevant in the practice of costs, so it is not discussed any further.[43] **45.16**

---

40 See The White Book, para 52.0.4.

41 Whilst the test is a simple question of whether it is in the interests of justice that there should be a rehearing (CPR, r 52.21(1)(b)), in practice it is rare for the court to go down that route. This topic was considered by the Court of Appeal in *Audergon v La Baguette Ltd* [2002] EWCA Civ 10. It is clear that, for the matter to proceed as a rehearing, there must be some element of injustice of a serious procedural or other irregularity. The fact that the court at first instance did not give reasons for its decision is not, of itself, a reason to have a rehearing: see *Secretary of State for Trade and Industry v Lewis* [2001] 2 BCLC 597. That said, there have been examples of the Court of Appeal proceeding by way of a rehearing (especially if the effect of this would be to settle a large number of related cases), including *U v Liverpool County Council* [2005] EWCA Civ 475 and *Rogers v Merthyr Tydfil County Borough Council* [2006] EWCA Civ 1134.

42 CPR, r 52.21(3).

43 For a discussion of this topic, see *Storer v British Gas plc* [2000] 2 All ER 440; see also *Tanfern Ltd v Cameron-MacDonald* [2000] 2 All ER 801, at 809.

45.17 The general approach to an appeal that proceeds by way of a 'review' of the decision in the court below was described by Woolf LJ thus:

> 'Before the court can interfere it must be shown that the judge has either erred in principle in his approach or has left out of account or has taken into account some feature that he should or should not have considered or that his decision was wholly wrong because the court is forced to the conclusion that he has not balanced the various factors fairly in the scales.'[44]

This passage continues to be regularly cited, both in this jurisdiction[45] and in other common-law jurisdictions.[46]

45.18 As a rule, the appeal court will be loath to interfere with a discretionary decision on costs. Wilson LJ had the following to say about the ethos underlying that approach:

> 'This is an appeal ... in relation to costs. As such, it is overcast, from start to finish, by the heavy burden faced by any appellant in establishing that the judge's decision falls outside the discretion in relation to costs ... For reasons of general policy, namely that it is undesirable for further costs to be incurred in arguing about costs, this court discourages such appeals by interpreting such discretion very widely.'[47]

45.19 Baron J (with whom both Arden and Davis LJJ agreed) had this to say about appeals concerning the exercise of discretion in the court below:

> 'The conclusions which I derive from the authorities are that:
>
> a. the overriding objective requires cases to be dealt with justly. CPR 1.1(2)(d) demands that the Court deals with cases "expeditiously and fairly". Fairness requires the position of both sides to be considered and this is in accordance with Article 6 [of the European Convention on Human Rights].
> b. fairness can only be determined by taking all relevant matters into account (and excluding irrelevant matters).
> c. it may be, in any one scenario, that a number of fair outcomes are possible. Therefore a balancing exercise has to be conducted in each case. It is only when the decision of the first instance judge is plainly wrong that the Court of Appeal will interfere with that decision.
> d. unless the Appeal Court can identify that the judge has taken into account immaterial factors, omitted to take into account material factors, erred in principle or come to a decision that was impermissible ... the decision at first Instance must prevail.'[48]

Baron J was dealing with a topic unrelated to costs, but her comments seem to have been an attempt to deal with the exercise of discretion as it is generally, rather than as it was in the narrow confines of the particular appeal before the court.

45.20 Having stated the general approach, the following specific types of appeal are now considered:

- appeals concerning the incidence of costs (see 45.21);
- appeals concerning the amount of costs (see 45.23);

[44] *AEI Rediffusion Music Ltd v Phonographic Performance Ltd* [1999] 1 WLR 1507, at 1523; see also *Tanfern Ltd v Cameron-Macdonald* [2000] 1 WLR 1311, at 1317, *per* Brooke LJ.

[45] As a recent example, see *Grant & Anor v Baker* [2016] EWHC 1782 (Ch), at [43].

[46] See, eg, *Harlequin Property (SVG) Ltd v Cellate Caribbean Ltd* (2013) 85 WIR 68, at [33], in which Burgess JA referred to *AEI Rediffusion Music Ltd v Phonographic Performance Ltd* [1999] 1 WLR 1507 as applying in a Barbadian case.

[47] *SCT Finance v Bolton* [2002] EWCA Civ 56, at [1].

[48] See *Asiedu v Dhillon* [2012] EWCA Civ 1020, at [33].

- appeals in which the court below failed to give reasons or failed to cite the law properly (see 45.25);
- appeals concerning summary assessments (see 45.27);
- appeals concerning case management decisions (see 45.28);
- appeals against interim decisions (see 45.29); and
- appeals in which the court below did not hear the substantive claim to which the costs relate (see 45.30).

Appeals concerning the incidence of costs

An appellant who seeks to challenge a decision as to the incidence of costs will find that they have a heavy burden to shift. Waller LJ, for example, has said that an appellant must show that the court below had gone 'seriously wrong' before they could expect to succeed: **45.21**

> 'It is well known that this court will be loath to interfere with the discretion exercised by a judge in any area but so far as costs are concerned that principle has a special significance. The judge has the feel of a case after a trial which the Court of Appeal cannot hope to replicate and the judge must have gone seriously wrong if this court is to interfere.'[49]

Sir Murray Stuart-Smith explained the circumstances in which the appeal court might be persuaded to interfere: **45.22**

> 'Costs are in the discretion of the trial judge, and this court will only interfere with the exercise of that discretion on well-defined principles. As I said in *Roache v News Group Newspapers Ltd* [1998] EMLR 161, [at] 172:
>
>> "Before the court can interfere it must be shown that the judge has either erred in principle in his approach, or has left out of account, or taken into account, some feature that he should, or should not, have considered, or that his decision is wholly wrong because the court is forced to the conclusion that he had not balanced the various factors in the scale".'[50]

Thus the appeal court will interfere in an appropriate case, but that would usually be on the basis that the court below made an error in its method, such as taking into account an irrelevant factor, failing to take into account a relevant factor, or making a decision that lay beyond the ambit of conclusions open to the court. Whilst there are instances of the court accepting appellants' arguments,[51] the third of these arguments—that is, ambit—is especially difficult to prove.

Appeals concerning the amount of costs

Appeals concerning the quantum of costs are notoriously challenging from the appellant's point of view.[52] One of the reasons for this is that the court will draw a distinction between a decision that was wrong and a decision that is merely an alternative imperfect solution **45.23**

[49] *Straker v Turner Rose (a firm)* [2007] EWCA Civ 368, at [2].

[50] *Adamson v Halifax plc* [2002] EWCA Civ 1134, at [16]; see also Viscount Cave LC in *Donald Campbell & Co Ltd v Pollak* [1927] AC 732.

[51] An example of this is *Lowe v W Machell Joinery Ltd* [2011] EWCA Civ 798, at [12], in which the Court of Appeal allowed an appeal despite commenting that 'the legitimate ambit of the discretion afforded by the rules to the court determining the question of costs is unusually wide'.

[52] See Laing J in *TUI UK Ltd v Tickell & Ors* [2016] EWHC 2741 (QB), at [16].

to that which would have been adopted by the appeal court. Lord Fraser had this to say on the point:

> 'Certainly it would not be useful to inquire whether different shades of meaning are intended to be conveyed by words such as "blatant error" used by the President in the present case, and words such as "clearly wrong", "plainly wrong" or "simply wrong" used by other judges in other cases. All these various expressions were used in order to emphasise the point that the appellate court should only interfere when they consider that the judge of first instance has not merely preferred an imperfect solution, which is different from an alternative imperfect solution which the Court of Appeal might or would have adopted, but has exceeded the generous ambit within which a reasonable disagreement is possible.'[53]

Lord Fraser's comments were made prior to the introduction of the CPR, but there are many authorities that confirm their continuing relevance.[54]

45.24 Buckley J had these oft-quoted observations to make about the approach generally taken in appeals concerning the quantum of costs:

> 'A Judge will allow an appeal ... if satisfied that the decision of the Costs Judge was wrong ... That is easy to apply to matter of principle or construction. However, where the appeal includes challenges to the details of the assessment, such as hours allowed in respect of a particular item, the task in hand is one of assessment or judgment rather than principle. There is no absolute answer ... I would regard it as inappropriate for the Judge on appeal to be drawn into an exercise calculated to add a little here or knock off a little there. If the Judge's attention is drawn to items which with the advice of Assessors he feels should, in fairness, be altered, doubtless he will act. That is a matter for his good judgment.'[55]

It would be wrong to regard these cautionary words as if they were rigid rules, however—as is shown by the fact that Buckley J went on to make about a dozen modest adjustments, some of which were as small as allowing an extra 15 minutes.

Appeals in which the court below failed to give reasons or failed to cite the law properly

45.25 In the context of an appeal in which it was said that the court at first instance had not fully understood the law, Ward LJ quoted the following passage from a speech of Lord Hoffmann, adding his own emphasis:

> 'The exigencies of daily court room life are such that reasons for judgment will always be capable of having been better expressed. This is particularly true of an unreserved judgment such as the judge gave in this case but also of a reserved judgment based upon notes, such as was given by the District Judge. *These reasons should be read on the assumption that, unless he has demonstrated the contrary, the judge knew how he should perform his functions and which matters he should take into account. This is particularly true when the matters in question are* [well known]. An appellate court should resist the temptation to subvert the principle that they should not substitute their own discretion for that of the judge by a narrow textual analysis which enables them to claim that he misdirected himself.'[56]

---

53 *G v G (Minors: Custody Appeal)* [1985] 1 WLR 647, at 652.

54 See, eg, *Griffiths v Solutia UK Ltd* [2001] EWCA Civ 736; *Higgs v Camden & Islington Health Authority* [2003] EWHC 15 (QB).

55 *Mealing-McLeod v Common Professional Examination Board* [2000] 2 Costs LR 223, at 224.

56 *Cambertown Timber Merchants Ltd v Sidhu* [2011] EWCA Civ 1041, at [35], citing Lord Hoffmann in *Piglowska v Piglowski* [1999] 1 WLR 1360, at 1372 (emphasis added by Ward LJ).

It ought to be apparent from a judgment why one side has lost and the other has won, and a failure to give reasons is itself capable of standing as a ground of appeal.[57] As to the duty to give reasons in respect of a cost order, Woolf CJ said: **45.26**

> 'As is to be expected, the decision of the judge in relation to costs was expressed succinctly. A judge is not expected to give a detailed decision as to why he is making an order. However, if he is going to make an order for costs which is not the normal order expected under the particular provisions of the CPR, then the parties are entitled to know the basis of that order and the judge is required to explain that so far as is necessary to do.'[58]

Those comments were made in the context of litigation in general, but they also apply to costs. Burton J, for example, has made similar comments in the context of the duty to give reasons for disallowance made during a summary assessment.[59] Where a judge makes an issues-based order, the reasons will normally be readily apparent from the judgment in the substantive matter.[60] In so far as the assessment of costs is concerned, Hart J has commented that it will sometimes be impossible—and sometimes undesirable—for the costs judge to spell out the exact process of reasoning that has led to the final figure. He noted that a decision as to quantum will frequently be the result of 'a triangulation' between a variety of relatively unfixed possible positions and that that process is based very much on expert 'feel'.[61] For obvious reasons, an appeal court would be reluctant to find that a judge had erred simply by reason of not having described every step taken in that process. Similarly, Peter Smith J has said that the appellate court should not be tempted into a detailed analysis of each and every reason or argument put forward and allegedly not dealt with by the judge at first instance.[62]

Appeals concerning summary assessments

Until only recently, a summary assessment was not regarded as a 'final decision' for the purposes of CPR, Part 52. The effect of this was to make it even easier for the court to dismiss any attempt to challenge an assessment on an appeal. Indeed, the editors of The White Book had this to say about the prospects of such an appeal: **45.27**

> 'A summary assessment of costs is not a "final decision" for the purposes of the Destination Order (Practice Direction 52A para. 3.8(2)). The rules in Part 52 apply. No appeal may be made without permission. As a practical matter, and for obvious reasons, it is unlikely that permission will be granted.'[63]

Whilst the recent changes to the Destination Order[64] and the practice direction have negated the need to decide whether the assessment was a 'final decision' (see 45.39), only the most Panglossian of appellants would expect this to make much of a difference.

---

57 *English v Emery Reimbold & Strick Ltd* [2002] EWCA Civ 605.
58 *Excelsior Commercial & Industrial Holdings Ltd v Salisbury Hamer Aspden & Johnson (Costs)* [2002] EWCA Civ 879, at [20].
59 *Sterling Publications Ltd v Burroughs* [2000] 2 Costs LR 155.
60 *Early Red Corpn NV v Glidepath Holdings BV* [2005] EWCA Civ 525.
61 *Jemma Trust Co Ltd v Liptrott & Ors (No 2)* [2004] EWHC 1404 (Ch), at [26].
62 *Sibley & Co v Reachbyte Ltd* [2008] EWHC 2665 (Ch), at [39].
63 See The White Book 2016, para 52.1.3.3.
64 That is, the Access to Justice Act 1999 (Destination of Appeals) Order 2016 (SI 2016/917).

Appeals concerning case management decisions

45.28 A party who wishes to appeal a case management decision will usually have an uphill struggle. PD 52A, para 4.6, has this to say on the point:

> '4.6 Where the application is for permission to appeal from a case management decision, the court dealing with the application may take into account whether—
> (a) the issue is of sufficient significance to justify the costs of an appeal;
> (b) the procedural consequences of an appeal (e.g. loss of trial date) outweigh the significance of the case management decision;
> (c) it would be more convenient to determine the issue at or after trial.
> Case management decisions include decisions made under rule 3.1(2) and decisions about disclosure, filing of witness statements or experts' reports, directions about the timetable of the claim, adding a party to a claim and security for costs.'

Appeals in respect of interim decisions

45.29 Enduring decisions about the incidence of costs are often taken during the litigation, rather than at the end (such as where a party is awarded the costs of an application). This may cause litigants to ask the court to reconsider its earlier decisions in the light of the outcome of the case. A request to reconsider earlier orders ought to be made by way of an appeal, rather than application (see 10.09 *et seq*), but even if the correct procedure is followed to the letter, the court is not likely to be receptive to such an appeal. Indeed, it will often dismiss such as an attempt to re-litigate an interim costs order with the benefit of hindsight.[65] A claimant is not able to extinguish the jurisdiction to appeal an interim costs order by the expedient of discontinuing the claim.[66]

Appeals against decisions in which the lower court did not hear the substantive claim

45.30 Where the parties have settled everything other than the costs and where the parties ask the lower court to rule on the incidence of costs without that court having heard the substantive issues, the appeal court will—in the absence of an error of principle—be reluctant to interfere. Wilson LJ has said that the parties can reasonably be expected to accept the court's decision unless it could be shown that the decision was 'manifestly unjust'.[67] Gross LJ has queried why such a test should be applied, but he was prepared to apply it nonetheless.[68] In any event, David Richards LJ has noted that not all of the relevant authorities were drawn to Gross LJ's attention.[69] As such, it seems that the test of whether the decision was 'manifestly unjust' applies. David Richards LJ had this to say on the point:

> 'However the approach is expressed, I consider that these authorities show that an appellate court will be even more reluctant than in the case of a costs order after a contested hearing to interfere with a costs order made at the request of the parties after they have settled the substantive issues between them.'[70]

45.31 Where, however, there has been an error of principle, the appeal court may interfere.[71] In particular, in the case referred to above, Gross LJ found that the fact that the court below

65 *Koshy v Deg-Deutsche Investitions und Entwicklungs Gesellschaft Gmbh* [2003] EWCA Civ 1718.

66 See *Safeway v Twigger* [2010] EWCA Civ 1472, at [58], *per* Pill LJ.

67 *BCT Software Solutions Ltd v C Brewer & Sons Ltd* [2003] EWCA Civ 939, at [8]. See also *Venture Finance Plc v Mead & Anor* [2005] EWCA Civ 325; *Bray (t/a the Building Company) v Bishop & Anor* [2009] EWCA Civ 768.

68 See *Patience v Tanner* [2016] EWCA Civ 158, at [33].

69 *Powles & Anor v Reeves & Anor* [2016] EWCA Civ 1375, at [25], those authorities being *Venture Finance Plc v Mead & Anor* [2005] EWCA Civ 325 and *Bray (t/a the Building Company) v Bishop & Anor* [2009] EWCA Civ 768.

70 *Powles & Aonr v Reeves & Anor* [2016] EWCA Civ 1375, at [26].

71 See, eg, *Lay v Drexler* [2007] EWCA Civ 464, plus *Venture Finance Plc v Mead & Anor* [2005] EWCA Civ 325 and *Bray (t/a the Building Company) v Bishop & Anor* [2009] EWCA Civ 768.

had failed to take into account a factor that ought to have been taken into account resulted in an outcome that was 'manifestly unjust'.[72]

The appeals procedure under CPR, Part 52

The following miscellaneous procedural points may be made (which are broadly in the order that they would arise in the appeal process). **45.32**

The timing of appeals under CPR, Part 52

Filing Unless the court[73] or rule[74] directs otherwise, the appellant's notice must be filed within 21 days after the date of the decision of the lower court to which the appeal relates.[75] The lower court is, at any time,[76] able to direct that a different date for filing is to apply,[77] but an extension should be granted only if there is 'good reason' to do so[78] and should not be granted retrospectively (that is, after the appeal court has become seized of the matter by virtue of an appellant's notice having been filed).[79] In any event, the lower court should bear in mind that it is able to leave the question of whether time should be extended to the appeal court.[80] **45.33**

The time for lodging an appellant's notice used to run from the date on which the specific decision in question was made.[81] This provision was singularly ill-suited to costs litigation because it was often impossible to know part-way through an assessment whether a decision would be worth appealing. Notwithstanding the points made above, costs judges fell into the habit of almost always allowing applications for orders that time should not start until the assessment had finished; indeed, the court would often make such an order of its own volition. Provided that the final hearing was not concluded before 1 April 2013,[82] there is now no difficulty in this regard, because CPR, r 47.14(7) provides that: 'If an assessment is carried out at more than one hearing, then for the purposes of rule 52.12 time for appealing shall not start to run until the conclusion of the final hearing, unless the court orders otherwise.' **45.34**

An application to vary the time limit should be made to the appeal court, rather than the lower court.[83] In addition, PD 52B, Section III, gives the following guidance: **45.35**

> '3.1 A party may apply to the lower court for an extension of time in which to file an appellant's notice. The application must be made at the same time as the appellant applies to the lower court for permission to appeal.

---

72 See *Patience v Tanner* [2016] EWCA Civ 158, at [40].

73 Specific provision for this is made in CPR, r 52.12(2)(a).

74 Whilst they are not likely to be relevant to matters relating to costs, there are specific provisions about time limits in CPR, rr 52.8–52.11 and PD 52D.

75 CPR, r 52.12(2)(b).

76 Whilst she was discussing a version of the CPR that was worded very differently from the present iteration, this was the conclusion that Arden LJ reached in *Aujla v Sanghera* [2004] EWCA Civ 121, at [17]. There is no reason to believe that the position has changed.

77 That being CPR, r 52.12(2); see also *Aujla v Sanghera* [2004] EWCA Civ 121, at [14], *per* Arden LJ.

78 Whilst it is now relatively old authority that related to a much earlier update of the CPR, see *Aujla v Sanghera* [2004] EWCA Civ 121, at [17], in which Arden LJ explained that the power of the appeal court to grant an extension is not negated by the rule that stated that an application to vary the time limit for filing an appellant's notice had to be made to the appeal court. CPR, r 52.12(1), is almost identically worded to CPR, r 52.6(1), so Arden LJ's comments seem to continue to be good law.

79 See *ibid*, at [18].

80 *Ibid*, at [17]–[19].

81 This was the conclusion that Popplewell J reached in *Kasir v Darlington & Simpson Rolling Mills Ltd* [2001] 2 Costs LR 228.

82 See (Civil Procedure (Amendment) Rules 2013 (SI 2013/262), r 22(9).

83 See CPR, r 52.15(1).

3.2 Where the time for filing an appellant's notice has expired, the appellant must include an application for an extension of time within the appellant's notice (form N161 or, in respect of a small claim, form N164) stating the reason for the delay and the steps taken prior to making the application.

3.3 The court may make an order granting or refusing an extension of time and may do so with or without a hearing. If an order is made without a hearing, any party seeking to set aside or vary the order may apply, within 14 days of service of the order, for a hearing.'

Other than in 'wholly exceptional circumstances'—to use Law LJ's phrase[84]—extreme delay will defeat an application for permission to appeal.[85]

45.36 **Service** Unless the appeal court orders otherwise, an appellant's notice must be served on each respondent as soon as practicable and, in any event, no later than seven days after it is filed.[86]

No automatic stay when an appeal is brought

45.37 If a party commences appeal proceedings, the mere existence of that appeal will not automatically stay matters in so far as costs are concerned. This is so regardless of whether the appeal relates to the parties' entitlement to costs[87] (such as where the appellant says it should have won in the substantive litigation) or whether it relates to the assessment of costs[88] (such as where the appellant says that it should not be required to pay any costs because there was a breach of the indemnity principle).

45.38 Both the lower court and the appeal court are able to grant a stay.[89] In practice, stays are often granted in cases in which a credible challenge has been raised in respect of the receiving party's entitlement to costs, this being for the pragmatic reason that it is best to wait until it is known what is and is not payable before proceeding with an assessment.

Destination court under CPR, Part 52, and the 'leapfrog' procedure

45.39 The rules that dealt with destination courts were radically changed on 3 October 2016.[90] Transitional provisions exist.[91] The new regime is refreshingly simple: out go lawyerly distractions—such as the fine distinctions between 'interim' and 'final decisions'[92]—and in comes a simple principle that, for first appeals, the appeal is heard by a judge who is one step up the ladder. If one focuses solely on costs litigation and if one disregards rarities, the entire regime can be summarised simply as in Table 45.1.[93]

---

[84] *Compagnie Noga D'Importation et D'Exportation SA v Abacha* [2003] EWCA Civ 1101, at [7].

[85] In *ibid*, for example, there had been a delay of more than four years in asking for permission to appeal an interim costs order; permission was (robustly) refused.

[86] See CPR, r 52.12(3).

[87] See CPR, r 47.2; PD 47, para 2.

[88] CPR, r 52.16.

[89] PD 47, para 2; CPR, r 52.16.

[90] See the Access to Justice Act 1999 (Destination of Appeals) Order 2016 (SI 2016/917); Ministry of Justice, *86th Update: Practice Direction Amendments*, available online at https://www.justice.gov.uk/courts/procedure-rules/civil/pdf/update/86th-update-pd-making-document.pdf. Article 7 of the 2016 Order has revoked the Access to Justice Act 1999 (Destination of Appeals) Order 2000 (SI 2000/1071).

[91] Access to Justice Act 1999 (Destination of Appeals) Order 2016 (SI 2016/917), art 8, provides as follows: 'Where a person has filed a notice of appeal or applied for permission to appeal before the date on which this Order comes into force—(a) this Order shall not apply to the appeal to which that notice or application relates; and (b) that appeal shall lie to the court to which it would have lain before that date.' In the interests of saving space, the old provisions are not repeated in this edition, but they can be found in the second edition of this book.

[92] In this regard, PD 52A, paras 3.6–3.8, have been omitted and PD 52A, para 3.5, now says that '[t]he destinations ... apply in relation to first appeals, whether the decision is interim or final'.

[93] This is based on PD 52A, Table 1, which itself paraphrases the provisions in the Access to Justice Act 1999 (Destination of Appeals) Order 2016 (SI 2016/917).

Table 45.1 Destination courts

Court	Deciding judge	Destination
County Court	District judge (including masters who are sitting as deputy district judges and other deputies)	Circuit judge[94]
	Recorder	High Court judge or certain designated civil judges[95]
	Circuit judge	High Court judge or a 'section 9 judge'[96]
High Court	Master (including a costs judge) or district judge	High Court judge or a 'section 9 judge'[97]
	High court judge	Court of Appeal
Intellectual Property Enterprise Court (IPEC)	District judge	Enterprise judge
	Enterprise judge	Court of Appeal
Any court	Authorised court officer (ACO)	Master (specifically, a costs judge)
	Any judge in a case that 'leapfrogs'	Court of Appeal
	Any judge hearing an appeal (other than where a master is hearing an appeal from an ACO)	Court of Appeal

As can be seen, there are no changes regarding second appeals: the destination court for second appeals continues to be the Court of Appeal.[98] For the avoidance of doubt, however, this would not be the case if the first appeal were by an appeal from a decision of an ACO.[99] **45.40**

Leapfrogs Where the court believes that an appeal would raise an important point of principle or practice, or where it considers that there is some other compelling reason for the Court of Appeal to hear it, that court may order the appeal to be transferred directly to the Court of Appeal,[100] this procedure being known as leapfrogging. Whilst Lord Phillips MR has pointed out that it is only the appeal itself that may be transferred, rather than the application for permission to appeal,[101] in cases of doubt, there is a statutory provision[102] that **45.41**

[94] The designated civil judge in any given area, in consultation with the presiding judge, has responsibility for allocating appeals to circuit judges: see PD 52A, para 4.5.

[95] The designated civil judge in question must be authorised, under para (5) of the table in s 9(1) of the Senior Courts Act 1981, to act as a judge of the High Court: see PD 52A, para 4.4(b).

[96] This is a judge who has been authorised, under paras (1), (2) or (4) of the table in s 9(1) of the Senior Courts Act 1981, to act as a judge of the High Court: see PD 52A, para 4.4(a).

[97] See PD 52A, para 4.3.

[98] PD 52A, para 4.7. See also the Access to Justice Act 1999 (Destination of Appeals) Order 2016 (SI 2016/917), art 6, which reads: 'Where—(a) an appeal is made to the county court or the High Court (other than from the decision of an officer authorised to assess costs by the Lord Chancellor); and (b) on hearing the appeal the court makes a decision, an appeal shall lie from that decision to the Court of Appeal and not to any other court.'

[99] Where a costs judge hears an appeal against the detailed assessment of costs made by an ACO, any appeal against the costs judge's ruling is treated as a 'first appeal', not a 'second appeal': see Access to Justice Act 1999 (Destination of Appeals) Order 2016 (SI 2016/917), art 6(a).

[100] See CPR, r 52.23(1). It is a power conferred by Access to Justice Act 1999, s 57.

[101] See *In the Matter of Claims Direct Test Cases* [2002] EWCA Civ 428, at [23].

[102] Access to Justice Act 1999, s 57(1)(a).

permits the matter to be referred to the Master of the Rolls for his or her consideration.[103] The practical effect of this is that the lower court must either decide the issue of permission for itself or must refer the matter to the Master of Rolls. If the lower court refuses permission to appeal, it lacks the power to direct that any subsequent appeal should be heard in the Court of Appeal.[104]

45.42 It is fair to say that the Court of Appeal would generally prefer not to spend its time dealing with mundane disputes about costs. This may be why Buxton LJ had this to say in a case that had been 'leapfrogged' to the Court of Appeal by the then senior costs judge:

> 'I would therefore uphold the decision of the senior costs judge in its entirety. While I understand why the senior costs judge gave permission to appeal, and did so without limitation, this court has had to reconsider a series of matters that are questions neither of law nor of principle, but rather issues of fact or judgment on which the court is likely to be slow to differ from the assessment of the very expert tribunal below. If in future similar cases should come before the costs judges, they, and this court, are likely, when considering applications for permission to appeal, to need to see detailed grounds of appeal, and to require specific demonstration that those grounds do indeed raise matters of principle suitable for the consideration of this court.'[105]

Thus, before making an order to leapfrog a case to the Court of Appeal, a costs judge ought to see detailed grounds of appeal and must be satisfied that those grounds raise matters of principle suitable for consideration by the Court of Appeal.

Venue for appeals

45.43 If an appeal is brought in the County Court in respect of an assessment that was transferred to the Senior Courts Costs Office (SCCO) from a hearing centre in London, then PD 47, para 4.2(c), is likely to apply. It reads as follows:

> '[U]nless an order is made under rule 47.4(2) directing that the Costs Office as part of the High Court shall be the appropriate office, an appeal from any decision made by a costs judge shall lie to the Designated Civil Judge for the London Group of County Court hearing centres or such judge as the Designated Civil Judge shall nominate. The appeal notice and any other relevant papers should be lodged at the Central London Civil Justice Centre.'

Thus papers are to be lodged at the Central London Civil Justice Centre—which is no great hardship for costs practitioners because that Centre is housed in the same building as the SCCO.

Appellant's notice and grounds

45.44 The appellant's notice must be filed at the appeal court,[106] along with the supporting documentation. The requisite documentation depends on whether the appeal is to the County Court or High Court,[107] or to the Court of Appeal.[108] In the High Court and County

[103] See *Clark (Inspector of Taxes) v Perks* [2001] 1 WLR 17, at [9].

[104] *7E Communications Ltd v Vertex Antennentechnik GmbH* [2007] EWCA Civ 140.

[105] *Sharratt v London Central Bus Co (No 2)* [2004] EWCA Civ 575, at [47].

[106] CPR, r 52.12(2).

[107] PD 52B, para 4.2, reads as follows: 'Documents to be filed with the appellant's notice: The appellant must file with the appellant's notice—(a) three copies of the appellant's notice and one additional copy for each respondent; (b) a copy of the sealed order under appeal; (c) where an application was made to the lower court for permission to appeal, a copy of any order granting or refusing permission to appeal together with a copy of the reasons, if any, for allowing or refusing permission to appeal; and (d) grounds of appeal, ...'

[108] The relevant parts of PD 52C, para 3, read as follows: '(3) At the same time as filing an appellant's notice, the appellant must provide for the use of the court three copies of the appellant's notice and one copy of

Court, the grounds of appeal must be set out on a separate sheet attached to the appellant's notice, outlining 'in simple language, clearly and concisely, why the order of the lower court was wrong or unjust because of a serious procedural or other irregularity'.[109] Similar, but more exacting, provisions apply in the Court of Appeal.[110] It is now no longer necessary to state for each ground whether the appeal is on a point of law or against a finding of fact.[111]

Respondent's notice to an appeal

A respondent may file a respondent's notice. If they are seeking permission to appeal from the appeal court, or if they wish to ask the appeal court to uphold the order of the lower court for reasons different from or additional to those given by the lower court, then a respondent's notice must be filed.[112] **45.45**

Documents to be filed with appellant's notice

PD 52B, Section IV, gives the following guidance about what needs to be filed at the time that the appellant's notice is filed: **45.46**

> 'The appellant must file with the appellant's notice—
> (a) three copies of the appellant's notice and one additional copy for each respondent;
> (b) a copy of the sealed order under appeal;
> (c) where an application was made to the lower court for permission to appeal, a copy of any order granting or refusing permission to appeal together with a copy of the reasons, if any, for allowing or refusing permission to appeal; and
> (d) grounds of appeal, which must be set out on a separate sheet attached to the appellant's notice and must set out, in simple language, clearly and concisely, why the order of the lower court was wrong or unjust because of a serious procedural or other irregularity (Rule 52.21(3)).'

Skeleton arguments

Whilst, in theory, they are optional,[113] in practice appellants will always file and serve a skeleton argument. The purpose of a skeleton argument is to assist the court by setting out, **45.47**

---

each of the following—(a) the sealed order or tribunal determination being appealed; (b) any order granting or refusing permission to appeal, together with a copy of the judge's or tribunal's reasons for granting or refusing permission to appeal; (c) any witness statements or affidavits relied on in support of any application included in the appellant's notice; (d) in cases where the decision of the lower court was itself made on appeal, the first order, the reasons given by the judge who made it, and the appellant's notice of appeal against that order;(e) in a claim for judicial review or a statutory appeal, the original decision which was the subject of the application to the lower court; (f) the order allocating the case to a track (if any); (g) the appellant's skeleton argument in support of the appeal; (h) the approved transcript of the judgment. (4) The appellant must also provide to the court one copy of the appellant's notice for each respondent for sealing by the court and return to the appellant for service. (5) Where the appellant applies for permission to appeal, additional documents are required: see Section 4 of this Practice Direction. (6) Provisions in relation to the skeleton argument are set out in paragraph 31.'

[109] PD 52B, para 4.2(d).

[110] PD 52C, para 5, reads as follows: '5 (1) The grounds of appeal must identify as concisely as possible the respects in which the judgment of the court below is—(a) wrong; or (b) unjust because of a serious procedural or other irregularity, as required by rule 52.11(3). (2) The reasons why the decision under appeal is wrong or unjust must not be included in the grounds of appeal and must be confined to the skeleton argument.'

[111] This used to be a requirement imposed by PD 52, para 3.2.

[112] CPR, r 52.13(2).

[113] Guidance is given in PD 52B, Section VIII, that suggests that the parties should file and serve skeleton arguments only where the complexity of the issues justify them. It has to be said that this in no way reflects what happens in reality, given that appellants almost always draft detailed skeleton arguments.

as concisely as practicable, the arguments upon which a party intends to rely.[114] PD 52A, para 5.1, gives the following guidance:

'[...]

(2) A skeleton argument must—

- be concise;
- both define and confine the areas of controversy;
- be set out in numbered paragraphs;
- be cross-referenced to any relevant document in the bundle;
- be self-contained and not incorporate by reference material from previous skeleton arguments;
- not include extensive quotations from documents or authorities.

(3) Documents to be relied on must be identified.

(4) Where it is necessary to refer to an authority, a skeleton argument must—
(a) state the proposition of law the authority demonstrates; and
(b) identify the parts of the authority that support the proposition.
If more than one authority is cited in support of a given proposition, the skeleton argument must briefly state why.

(5) The cost of preparing a skeleton argument which—
(a) does not comply with the requirements set out in this paragraph; or
(b) was not filed within the time limits provided by this Practice Direction (or any further time granted by the court),
will not be allowed on assessment except as directed by the court.'

The parties should consider what other information the appeal court will need. This may include a list of persons who feature in the case or glossaries of technical terms.[115] A chronology of relevant events will be necessary in most appeals.[116]

45.48 In the Court of Appeal, the following additional provisions will apply:

'(1) Any skeleton argument must comply with the provisions of Section 5 of Practice Direction 52A (and in particular must be concise) and must in any event—
(a) not normally exceed 25 pages (excluding front sheets and back sheets);
(b) be printed on A4 paper in not less than 12 point font and 1.5 line spacing (including footnotes);
(c) be labelled as applicable (e.g. appellant's PTA skeleton, appellant's replacement skeleton, respondent's supplementary skeleton), and be dated on its front sheet.
(2) (a) Any skeleton argument that does not comply with the requirements of paragraph 31.1(a), (b) and (c)—
(i) will be returned to its author by the Civil Appeals Office; and
(ii) may not be re-filed unless and until it complies with those requirements; and
(b) if the skeleton argument is re-filed out of time—
(i) it must be served on all other parties to the appeal; but
(ii) the party re-filing it must make an application under Part 23 to obtain the permission of the court in advance of the hearing in order to rely on it.

(3) Where an appellant has filed a skeleton argument in support of an application for permission to appeal, the same skeleton argument may be relied upon in the appeal or the appellant may file an appeal skeleton argument (Timetable Section 5, Part 1).

[114] This is expressly stated at PD 52A, para 5.1.
[115] PD 52A, para 5.2.
[116] PD 52A, para 5.2.

(4) At the hearing the court may refuse to hear argument on a point not included in a skeleton argument filed within the prescribed time.

(5) The court may disallow the cost of preparing an appeal skeleton argument which does not comply with these requirements or was not filed within the prescribed time.'[117]

Permission to appeal under CPR, Part 52, in general

As a rule, permission to appeal will be required in all costs appeals—other than those from an ACO (see 45.05). This will generally be so even if permission is not required to appeal the matter to which the costs relate.[118] An application may be made to the lower court at the time the decision appealed against is made, or it may be made to the appeal court in the appellant's notice.[119] The editors of The White Book say that an appellant would generally be well advised to apply for permission to the lower court at the time of judgment, for the following reasons.[120] **45.49**

- The judge below would be fully seized of the matter and so the application will take minimal time. Indeed, the judge may have already decided that the case raises questions fit for appeal.
- An application at that stage would involve neither party in additional costs.
- No harm would be done if the application were to fail: the appellant would still enjoy two bites at the cherry.
- If the application were to succeed, the parties would avoid the expensive and time-consuming permission stage in the appeal court.
- No harm would be done if the application were to succeed, even if the appellant subsequently decides not to appeal.

If the lower court refuses permission, the application may be renewed in the appeal court.[121] If the appeal court refuses permission on paper (as it very often does in costs cases[122]), the appellant has the right to request an oral hearing, which is done by sending a request to the court (usually in the form of a letter). This must be done within seven days after service of the notice that permission has been refused,[123] but the court does have the power pursuant to CPR, r 3.1(2)(a), to extend that period.[124] Permission to appeal will be granted only where the court considers that the appeal would have a real prospect of success or where there is some other compelling reason why the appeal should be heard.[125] Lord Woolf MR has explained that 'real' means that the prospect of success must be realistic, rather than fanciful.[126] Buckley J has emphasised that permission to appeal should not be granted 'simply to allow another trawl through the bill, in the absence **45.50**

[117] PD 52C, para 31.

[118] See, eg, *Hosking v Michaelides* [2003] EWHC 3029 (Ch), in which it was held that permission was required to appeal a summary assessment of costs in insolvency proceedings, even though permission would not have been required to appeal the proceedings themselves.

[119] CPR, r 52.3(2).

[120] See The White Book, para 52.3.6.

[121] CPR, r 52.3(3).

[122] A notable example of this is *Lownds v Home Office* [2003] EWCA 365, which was initially rejected on the papers on the grounds that it raised no point of principle.

[123] CPR, r 52.3(4) and (5).

[124] See *Slot v Isaac* [2002] EWCA Civ 481, at [15].

[125] CPR, r 52.3(6).

[126] See *Swain v Hillman* [2001] All ER 91, at [10].

of some sensible and significant complaint'.[127] Moreland J made a similar point, but in terms that were more forceful:

> '[There is] a trend in litigation, which in my judgment I condemn as deplorable, satellite litigation about costs which is hugely wasteful of both professional time and expensive resources. If the trend were allowed to continue, it would tend to render nugatory the "overriding objective" of the CPR.'[128]

45.51 Where the judge who granted permission was misled, permission to appeal may be revoked.[129]

Conditional permission to appeal under CPR, Part 52

45.52 The court may impose conditions on the granting of permission to appeal.[130] The court may, for example, make an order for security for costs (see 15.12–15.18 and 15.50–15.51). The court may also make conditions as to the incidence of costs. This is relatively common in costs litigation—especially in the Court of Appeal. If, for example, the appellant's insurer wishes to clarify the law, permission may be granted on terms that the appellant must bear the costs of the appeal.[131] It is not possible to appeal a decision relating to permission to appeal (see 45.54). This means that if the lower court has granted permission on terms that are not acceptable to the appellant, the appellant's only courses of action would be (a) to abandon the prospective appeal, (b) to accept the terms or (c) to treat the conditional permission as a refusal of permission to appeal and to make a fresh application for permission to the appellate court.[132]

Submissions and hearings relating to permission to appeal under CPR, Part 52

45.53 Respondent's submissions should be filed at the permission stage only if they are addressed solely to the question of whether the appeal satisfied the relevant threshold test or if there was some material inaccuracy in the papers placed before the court; submissions on the merits should be left to the appeal itself.[133] In the County Court or High Court, a respondent who has been served with an appeal bundle and who considers that relevant documents have been omitted may, within seven days of receipt of the bundle, file and serve on all parties a respondent's supplemental appeal bundle, containing copies of other relevant documents.[134] Respondents are not expected to attend unless the court so directs.[135] In the High Court and the County Court, the following provisions will apply to the costs of the application for permission to appeal:

> '8.1 Attendance at permission hearings: Where a respondent to an appeal or cross-appeal attends the hearing of an application for permission to appeal, costs will not be awarded to the respondent unless—

---

[127] *Mealing-McLeod v Common Professional Examination Board* [2000] 2 Costs LR 223, at 224.

[128] *Giambrone v JMC Holidays Ltd (formerly Sunworld Holidays Ltd)* [2002] EWHC 2932 (QB), at [3].

[129] *Angel Airlines SA v Dean & Dean Solicitors* [2006] EWCA Civ 1505.

[130] See CPR, r 52.9.

[131] As happened, for example, in *Jones v Caradon Catnic Ltd* [2005] EWCA Civ 1821.

[132] *R (ex p Medical Justice) v Secretary of State for the Home Department* [2011] EWCA Civ 269, at [8], *per* Lord Neuberger MR.

[133] *Jolly v Jay* [2002] EWCA Civ 277.

[134] See PD 52B, para 8.2.

[135] See PD 52C, para 16(2), in the Court of Appeal. There is no express provision that deals with this issue in the High Court or County Court, but PD 52B, para 8, implies that the respondent is not required to attend unless the court so orders.

(a) the court has ordered or requested attendance by the respondent;
(b) the court has ordered that the application for permission to appeal be listed at the same time as the determination of other applications;
(c) the court has ordered that the hearing of the appeal will follow the hearing of the application if permission is granted; or
(d) the court considers it just, in all the circumstances, to award costs to the respondent.'[136]

In the Court of Appeal, the following very similar provisions will apply:

'20. (1) In most cases an application for permission to appeal will be determined without the need for the respondent to file submissions or attend a hearing. In such circumstances an order for costs will not normally be made in favour of a respondent who voluntarily makes submissions or attends a hearing.

(2) If the court directs the respondent to file submissions or attend a hearing, it will normally award costs to the respondent if permission is refused.'[137]

Refusal of permission to appeal (refusal)

No appeal may be brought from a decision to refuse permission to appeal.[138] The inherent jurisdiction of the court to review decisions of officials of the court does not permit the Court of Appeal to review a puisne judge's refusal to grant permission.[139] **45.54**

Appeal hearings, appeal bundles, etc

In so far as procedure is concerned, an appeal in respect of costs is exactly the same as any other appeal. The provisions can be found in CPR, Part 52, and PDs 52A–52C. The only papers that the appeal court will need will be those that are itemised in PD 52;[140] there is no need to file the receiving party's file of papers (as would happen in a detailed assessment). A suitable record of the judgment in the court below will be required.[141] **45.55**

---

136 PD 52B, para 8.1.

137 PD 52C, para 20.

138 See Access to Justice Act 1999, s 54(4); CPR, r 52.3(3). See also *R (on the application of Sivasubramaniam) v Wandsworth County Court* [2002] EWCA Civ 1738.

139 *Riniker v University College London* [2001] 1 Costs LR 20, in which Robert Walker LJ (with whom Brooke LJ agreed) commented that by no stretch of language or thought could a High Court judge's refusal to grant permission to appeal be regarded as a decision taken as a delegate of the Court of Appeal. In this regard, the Court of Appeal reminded itself that its jurisdiction is wholly statutory and that it has no original jurisdiction.

140 In this regard, PD 52B, para 6.4, provides as follows: '6.4 Documents relevant to the appeal: (1) Subject to any order made by the court, the following documents must be included in the appeal bundle—(a) a copy of the appellant's notice; (b) a copy of any respondent's notice; (c) a copy of any appellant's or respondent's skeleton argument; (d) a copy of the order under appeal; (e) a copy of the order of the lower court granting or refusing permission to appeal together with a copy of the judge's reasons, if any, for granting or refusing permission; (f) a copy of any order allocating the case to a track; (g) a transcript of the judgment of the lower court or other record of reasons (except in appeals in cases which were allocated to the small claims track and subject to any order of the court). (2) The following documents should also be considered for inclusion in the appeal bundle but should be included only where relevant to the appeal—(a) statements of case; (b) application notices; (c) other orders made in the case; (d) a chronology of relevant events; (e) witness statements made in support of any application made in the appellant's notice; (f) other witness statements; (g) any other documents which any party considers would assist the appeal court.'

141 PD 52B, para 6.2, provides as follows: '6.2 Transcript of the judgment of the lower court or other record of reasons: Except where the claim has been allocated to the small claims track, the appellant must obtain a transcript or other record of reasons of the lower court as follows—(a) where the judgment has been officially recorded, the appellant must apply for an approved transcript as soon as possible and, in any event, within 7 days of the filing of the appellant's notice; (b) where the judgment under appeal has been handed down in writing, the appellant must obtain and retain a copy of the written judgment; (c) in any other case,

Appeals against legal aid assessments

45.56 Appeals against legal aid assessment must be notified to the Ministry of Justice. This rule will not be applied in such a way as to cause injustice.[142]

Costs in the appeal court and below (including interest on overpaid costs)

45.57 The court hearing an appeal may, unless it dismisses the appeal, make orders about the costs of the proceedings giving rise to the appeal, as well as the costs of the appeal itself.[143] Where an appeal results in a reversal of a costs order and where costs have already been paid under that order, the court may order the party who has to repay costs to also pay interest on those costs.[144] This topic is addressed in more detail at 56.103–56.107. Where the court makes an order granting permission to appeal, the order will be deemed to include an order for the applicant's costs in the case.[145]

45.58 The small claims provisions apply to the costs of an appeal brought against a decision in a small claim.[146] This is also true of second appeals.[147] Sir Stanley Burnton has added that whilst CPR, r 52.9A, confers power to limit costs of an appeal, it does not confer power to award costs where there is a provision of the CPR precluding a costs order.[148]

45.59 Whilst it would rarely be of relevance in an appeal regarding costs, it is worth noting that, in a case in which costs recovery is normally limited or excluded at first instance, an appeal court may make an order that the recoverable costs of an appeal will be limited to the extent that the court specifies (see 13.102 and 50.378).[149]

Topics likely to arise during an appeal hearing

New evidence and Ladd v Marshall

45.60 Unless it gives permission, the appeal court will not receive evidence that was not before the lower court.[150] To justify the reception of fresh evidence, three conditions must be fulfilled:

- it must be shown that the evidence could not have been obtained with reasonable diligence for use in the court below;
- the evidence must be such that, if given, it would probably have an important influence on the result of the case, although it need not be decisive; and

---

the appellant must cause a note of the judgment under appeal to be made and typed. The parties to the appeal should agree the note, which should then be sent to the judge of the lower court for approval. The parties and their advocates have a duty to make, and to co-operate in agreeing, a note of the judgment.'

[142] In *Edwards & Ors v Roche Products Ltd* [2003] EWHC 9022 (Costs), Fulford J permitted a funded party (in reality, his counsel) to recover the costs of an appeal pursuant to Civil Legal Aid (General) Regulations 1989 (SI 1989/339) (as amended), reg 113(2), notwithstanding the fact that the Lord Chancellor's Department had not been kept informed of the appeal to the extent that it should have been. Fulford J did not impose any sanction because the Lord Chancellor's Department (the forerunner of the Ministry of Justice) had indicated that it did not wish to intervene and, as a result, there was no prejudice.

[143] See CPR, r 44.10(4).

[144] *Bim Kemi AB v Blackburn Chemicals Ltd* [2003] EWCA Civ 889.

[145] CPR, r 44.10(2); see also *A Practice Statement (Judicial Review: Costs)* (2004) The Times, 20 May, QBD.

[146] See CPR, r 27.14(2), which reads: 'The court may not order a party to pay a sum to another party in respect of that other party's costs, fees and expenses, including those relating to an appeal, except [those allowed under the small claims regime].'

[147] See *Akhtar v Boland (Costs)* [2014] EWCA Civ 943, at [7], *per* Sir Stanley Burnton; *Conlon v Royal Sun Alliance Insurance plc* [2015] EWCA Civ 92, at [15], *per* Kitchin LJ.

[148] *Akhtar v Boland (Costs)* [2014] EWCA Civ 94, at [7].

[149] See CPR, r 52.9A.

[150] CPR, r 52.11(2)(b).

- the evidence must be such as is presumably to be believed—that is, it must be apparently credible, although it need not be incontrovertible.[151]

Bringing in new points on appeal

In a similar vein, if a point was not taken during the detailed assessment, the appeal court may refuse to hear the point.[152] An appellant will bear a heavy burden when trying to persuade the appeal court to hear a point that was not taken or which was abandoned in the court below. In this regard, Peter Gibson LJ had this to say: **45.61**

> 'In general the court expects each party to advance his whole case at the trial. In the interests of fairness to the other party this court should be slow to allow new points, which were available to be taken at the trial but were not taken, to be advanced for the first time in this court. That consideration is the weightier if further evidence might have been adduced at the trial, had the point been taken then, or if the decision on the point requires an evaluation of all the evidence and could be affected by the impression which the trial judge receives from seeing and hearing the witnesses. Indeed it is hard to see how, if those circumstances obtained, this court, having regard to the overriding objective of dealing with cases justly, could allow that new point to be taken.'[153]

Thus the appellant must seek to discharge the burden of showing that the case would not have been conducted differently had the points that are raised on appeal been raised in the court below.[154] Where those points are factual and where the court below heard live evidence, that burden will be difficult to shift. At the other end of spectrum will be where the appellant seeks to raise a new point of law.[155] Where, for example, the new point goes to jurisdiction, then the court is more likely to be persuaded to hear it.[156] It has long been the case that an appeal court ought not to entertain a question of law raised for the first time before it unless it is satisfied beyond doubt that the facts, if fully investigated, would have supported the new plea.[157] The burden lies with the appellant, rather than the respondent: Arden LJ explained that the court cannot reasonably expect the respondent to be specific about the evidence they would have adduced had the point been raised earlier.[158] She explained that if there is any area of doubt, the benefit of that doubt must be given to the respondent; it is that party which should have raised the point at trial who should bear any risk of prejudice. **45.62**

Much will also turn on the way in which the case was put in the court below. If, for example, the point had been raised and then abandoned, the stage that had been reached at the time of abandonment will be relevant. In respect of a case in which the putatively new point had been raised in pleadings, but expressly disavowed at an early stage of trial (that **45.63**

---

[151] *Ladd v Marshall* [1954] 1 WLR 1489, which was confirmed to be good law under the CPR in *Hertfordshire Investments Ltd v Bubb* [2000] All ER (D) 1052 and, more recently, in *Muscat v Health Professions Council* [2009] EWCA Civ 1090.

[152] In the context of costs litigation, see *Ross v Stonewood Securities Ltd* [2004] EWHC 2235 (Ch), at [29], *per* Lewison J.

[153] *Jones v MBNA International Bank* [2000] EWCA Civ 514, at [38]. See also *Australia and New Zealand Banking Group Ltd v Société Générale* [2000] 1 All ER (Comm) 682, which confirmed the approach taken in *Jones*.

[154] For a discussion of this, see *Lowe v W Machell Joinery Ltd* [2011] EWCA Civ 794, at 59 *et seq*; see also *Mullarkey v Broad (in the matter of Southill Finance Ltd, in liquidation)* [2009] EWCA Civ 2, at [49].

[155] Whilst a pre-CPR case, see *Pittalis v Grant* [1989] QB 605, which is often cited as authority for the proposition that the court should generally permit new points of law.

[156] See, eg, *Hardy v Sefton Metropolitan Borough Council* [2006] EWHC 1928 (Admin), *per* Walker J; see also *Pittalis v Grant* [1989] QB 605.

[157] See *Connecticut Fire Insurance Co v Kavanagh* [1892] AC 473.

[158] *Crane v Sky In-home Ltd* [2008] EWCA Civ 978, at [21].

is, before the evidence had been heard), Lloyd LJ said this: 'A party who seeks to advance a different case, in circumstances such as this, bears a heavy burden as regards showing that the case could not have been conducted differently, in any material respect, as regards the evidence.'[159] If, however, the point is abandoned after evidence had been heard (such as during closing submissions), that burden will be easier to discharge.[160]

Findings of fact and appeals

45.64 The appeal court will ordinarily decline to interfere with the lower court's findings of fact unless it reached a decision that no reasonable court would have reached on the material available or pivotal factors that ought to have been taken into account were not taken into account.[161] This principle will be of only limited application in many costs disputes, however, because the putatively disputed facts will, in general, be the inferences to be drawn from undisputed documentary evidence. Ward LJ had this to say on that topic:

> '[Counsel] submits that this is a finding of fact which cannot be said to be wrong and that we should, therefore, not interfere with it. That is not strictly correct. The primary facts were not in dispute and were for the trial judge to find but the inferences to be drawn from those facts are matters for us as much as for the judges below. Whether the facts give rise to a reasonable justification for [a certain course of action] is a value judgment, a conclusion of mixed fact and law, which is either right or wrong: it is not an exercise of discretion which admits of a range of choices in which there is a generous ambit for decision-making. The costs judge is expert in his field and his views command respect but we have had the invaluable assistance of our assessor and so are not in any weaker position. Whilst I do, therefore, pay deference to the conclusions of the courts below, I am not bound by them and I am free to decide whether they were right or wrong.'[162]

Material not referred to in the judgment and appeals

45.65 The appeal court will be reluctant to find that the lower court took into account factors that were not referred to in the judgment.[163]

Assessors

45.66 The appeal court may sit with assessors[164] and often will do so when the appeal is from a costs judge.[165] Where the court does sit with assessors, the responsibility for its decision will lie with the judge, but it is not uncommon for the judge to refer to the fact that the assessors were in agreement.[166]

45.67 One of the assessors will usually be a costs judge; the other will often be a practising barrister or solicitor, depending on the nature of the case. Circuit judges hearing appeals from district judges may or may not sit with an assessor[167]—practices vary from court to court.

---

[159] *Mullarkey v Broad (in the matter of Southill Finance Ltd, in liquidation)* [2009] EWCA Civ 2, at [49].

[160] See, eg, *Slack & Partners Ltd v Slack* [2010] EWCA Civ 204.

[161] *Designers Guild Ltd v Russell Williams (Textiles) Ltd* [2000] 1 WLR 2416. Whilst a Scottish case, this principle was reaffirmed in *McGraddie v McGraddie & Anor (Scotland)* [2013] UKSC 58.

[162] *Cawdery Kaye Fireman & Taylor v Minkin* [2012] EWCA Civ 546, at [35].

[163] *MacDonald v Taree Holdings* [2001] 1 Costs LR 147, at 150.

[164] CPR, r 35.15.

[165] See HM Courts & Tribunals Service, *Senior Courts Costs Office Guide* (London: HMSO, 2006), para 13.5.

[166] See, eg, *G (by her mother and litigation friend M) v Kingston upon Hull City Council* (unreported), 18 September 2013, Kingston-upon-Hull County Court, at [5], *per* Judge Jeremy Richardson QC.

[167] See County Courts Act 1984 (as amended), s 63.

Not less than 21 days before making any such appointment, the court will notify each party in writing of the name of the proposed assessor, of the matter in respect of which the assistance of the assessor will be sought and of the qualifications of the assessor to give that assistance. If so advised, any party may object to the assessor.[168] **45.68**

It would ordinarily be the court's responsibility to make arrangements for the attendance of assessors, rather than that of the parties. In view of this, Leggatt LJ described as 'surprising' a circuit judge's decision not to grant an adjournment to enable assessors to sit with him except on terms that the paying party (whose appeal it was) paid the costs thrown away.[169] **45.69**

Second appeals

Second appeals are to the Court of Appeal,[170] but this would not be so if the 'first' was by an appeal from a decision of an ACO.[171] For all but the most exceptional costs case, the Court of Appeal will be the final court of appeal, because the responsibility for overseeing costs litigation rests primarily with that court, rather than with the Supreme Court. This was explained by Lord Bingham thus: **45.70**

> 'The responsibility for monitoring and controlling the developing practice in a field such as this lies with the Court of Appeal and not the House, which should ordinarily be slow to intervene. The House cannot respond to changes in practice with the speed and sensitivity of the Court of Appeal.'[172]

The Court of Appeal will not give permission to bring a second appeal unless it considers that the appeal would have a real prospect of success. In addition, the appeal must raise an important point of principle or practice, or there must be some other compelling reason for hearing it.[173] In view of this, an application to make a second appeal must identify, in the grounds of appeal, the important point of principle or practice, or the compelling reason that is said to justify the grant of permission to appeal.[174] **45.71**

The Court of Appeal has no jurisdiction to hear an application for permission to appeal in a case in which the court at first instance and a judge hearing a subsequent application have both refused permission—and this is so even where it is said that the Court of Appeal should hear the matter by reason of an inherent jurisdiction.[175] However, where the subject of the second application is a decision ancillary to it (such as a decision on the costs of the application), those may be regarded as being separate decisions in respect of which a further application may be made.[176] **45.72**

---

[168] PD 35, paras 7.1 and 7.2.

[169] *Laurence v Singh* [1997] 1 Costs LR 58, at 61.

[170] PD 52A, para 4.7. The Court of Appeal used to be barred from hearing appeals in discretionary costs matters unless the court below had been given permission (see, originally, Judicature Act 1873, s 49), but the scope of that restriction was cut back by the court taking a narrow view as to what was 'discretionary': see *Jones v Curling* (1884) 13 QBD 262, at 267 and 271. In any event, the restriction was abolished entirely by Courts and Legal Services Act 1990, ss 7(2), 125(7) and Sch 20, repealing Senior Courts Act 1981, s 18(1)(f).

[171] Where a costs judge hears an appeal against the detailed assessment of costs made by an ACO, any appeal against the costs judge's ruling is treated as a 'first appeal', not a 'second appeal': see Access to Justice Act 1999 (Destination of Appeals) Order 2000 (SI 2000/1071), art 5(a).

[172] *Callery v Gray* [2002] UKHL 28, at [8]; see also *Girvan v Inverness Farmers Dairy* 1998 SC (HL) 1, at 21D–21G.

[173] CPR, r 52.7.

[174] See PD 52C, para 5A.

[175] *Riniker v University College London* [2001] 1 WLR 13, applying Access to Justice Act 1999, s 54(4). See also, in a more general setting than the law of costs, *Clark (Inspector of Taxes) v Perks* [2001] 1 WLR 17, at 20.

[176] *Riniker v University College London* [2001] 1 WLR 13; see also *Jolly v Jay* [2002] EWCA Civ, at [51]–[52].

Judicial Review

45.73 Occasionally, a judge at first instance will exercise a jurisdiction that is not amenable to appeal within the regime outlined in this chapter. This will usually be in the context of criminal costs, but it could also include examples of the court acting in an arbitral role, such as where the court is assessing the costs of a non-statutory inquiry. Another example would be where the court has refused permission to appeal and there is no further route of appeal. Where the usual route of appeal is unavailable, the question may arise as to whether the judge's decision is amenable to judicial review.

45.74 Generally speaking, the decisions of costs judges in the High Court are not susceptible to challenge by way of judicial review, because the court does not judicially review its own decisions.[177] That said, where there is 'a gap in the rules', the High Court has an inherent jurisdiction to control the exercise of the authority of the court where that authority has been delegated to a costs judge.[178] Decisions of judges in the county courts used to be amenable to judicial review,[179] but this is probably no longer the case in relation to the County Court (now a single court of record) and its hearing centres.[180] It is not yet known whether the High Court will regard decisions made by County Court judges as analogous to decisions of costs judges.

45.75 Where the power to review is available, Maurice Kay LJ has emphasised that it is a jurisdiction that will be exercised sparingly.[181] There has to be a 'real injustice' before it could properly be invoked.[182] Nonetheless, case examples do exist in which it is difficult to identify any 'real injustice'.[183] The jurisdiction to review cannot be invoked in such a way as to do something that is inconsistent with the CPR.[184]

45.76 The Supreme Court has held that judicial review by the High Court of a refusal by the Upper Tribunal of permission to appeal to itself was available, but that it was limited to the application of the criteria for second-tier appeals—namely, where either the proposed appeal raises some important point of principle or practice, or there was some other compelling reason.[185]

---

177 *R v SCTO, ex p John Singh & Co* [1997] 1 Costs LR 49.

178 *R v Taxing Officer, ex p Bee-Line Roadways International Ltd* (1982) The Times, 11 February. The Times report is very brief; lengthier extracts from Woolf J's judgment can be found quoted in *In re Macro (Ipswich) Ltd* [1997] 1 Costs LR 128, at 136.

179 *R (on the application of Strickson) v Preston County Court & Ors* [2007] EWCA Civ 1132; *R v His Honour Judge Sir Donald Hurst, ex p Smith* [1960] 2 All ER 385. See also *R (on the application of Srinivasans Solicitors) v Croydon County Court* [2011] EWHC 3615 (Admin). This used to include the power to review decisions not to grant permission to appeal: see *R (on the application of Sivasubramaniam) v Wandsworth County Court* [2002] EWCA Civ 1738.

180 See Crime and Courts Act 2013, s 17.

181 See also *Brewer v SCCO* [2009] EWHC 986 (QB), which involved the same parties in which the lower court's decision was quashed by reason of its failure to conduct a hearing.

182 *R v SCTO, ex p John Singh & Co* [1997] 1 Costs LR 49, at 51; see also, eg, *R (on the application of Brewer) v Supreme Court Costs Office* [2006] EWHC 1955 (Admin).

183 *In re Macro (Ipswich) Ltd* [1997] 1 Costs LR 128, at 139, *per* Ferris J. It is not clear whether this authority remains good law: see *R (on the application of Strickson) v Preston County Court & Ors* [2007] EWCA Civ 1132, which suggests that the test is different from that applied by Ferris J.

184 *Tombstone Ltd v Raja* [2008] EWCA Civ 1444.

185 *R (on the application of Cart) v Upper Tribunal; R (on the application of MR (Pakistan)) v Upper Tribunal (Immigration and Asylum Chamber) & Anor* [2011] UKSC 28.

46

EVIDENTIAL ISSUES AND PRIVILEGE

This chapter describes the adjectival law that governs the fact-finding process in detailed assessments. It deals with the following topics: **46.01**

- overview (46.03);
- legal professional privilege (46.04):
  - types of privilege (46.06)
  - what is and is not privileged (46.13);
- the filing of documents at court (46.28):
  - the duty to file adverse material (46.32);
  - the 'escalator of enquiry' relating to adverse material (46.36);
  - documents filed in error (46.38);
- the process of election:
  - the principles of election (otherwise known as the *Pamplin* principles[1]) (46.40);
  - the procedure of election and the court's discretion (46.45);
  - the relevance of proportionality to election (46.57);
  - implied waiver of privilege (46.60);
  - limited waiver of privilege (46.67);
  - withdrawal of waiver of privilege (46.68);
  - the consequences of electing to disclose documents (46.69);
  - the consequences of electing not to disclose documents (46.72);
- disclosure in cases of fraud (46.75);
- disclosure of non-privileged material (46.76); and
- the procedure relating to evidential issues (46.77).

In addition, the following topics are addressed elsewhere in this book: **46.02**

- evidential issues relating to without prejudice correspondence are addressed at 6.213–6.218;
- the role of testimony and hearsay evidence is briefly addressed at 43.325; and
- evidential issues relating to appeals are dealt with at 45.60–45.65.

[1] After *Pamplin v Express Newspapers Ltd* [1985] 1 WLR 689.

Overview

46.03 Costs litigation treads a path that cautiously obviates the need for mandatory disclosure of the type seen in substantive litigation. This is necessary because the particulars of the work that has resulted in the costs in question being incurred may be—and often are—subject to legal professional privilege. There are two concepts that are central to the issue of how the court deals with evidence in the context of disputes about costs, as follows.

- **Filing** This is the process of lodging documents for inspection by the court (see 46.28) and is usually done by lodging the receiving party's file at court a few days before the assessment hearing (see 47.307–47.308 and 47.310). The fact that a document has been filed in this way does not mean that the receiving party has expressed an intention to rely on it. It is a moot point whether a receiving party is under a duty to file material that undermines its case (see 46.32–46.41).
- **Election** This is the process by which the receiving party chooses—that is, 'elects'—whether to rely on a document or whether to maintain a claim of privilege over it. These options are mutually exclusive: if a receiving party chooses not to rely on a document they may continue to assert privilege over it, but if they wish to rely on it they must waive privilege *pro tem* for the purposes of the assessment. These topics are addressed in detail at 46.40–46.74.

Legal Professional Privilege

46.04 Legal professional privilege is an essential right at common law.[2] Gloster LJ has said that it is 'fundamental to the administration of justice and ... a fundamental human right'.[3]

46.05 Where it exists and is not waived or negated, legal professional privilege is absolute and not subject to any form of balancing exercise of weighing competing public interests against each other. In this regard, Lord Taylor CJ had this to say:

> 'The principle ... is that a man must be able to consult his lawyer in confidence, since otherwise he might hold back half the truth. The client must be sure that what he tells his lawyers in confidence will never be revealed without his consent. Legal professional privilege is thus much more than an ordinary rule of evidence, limited in its application to the facts of a particular case. It is a fundamental condition on which the administration of justice as a whole rests. ... Nobody doubts that legal professional privilege could be modified, or even abrogated, by statute ... [but] whatever inroads may have been made by Parliament in other areas, legal professional privilege is a field which Parliament has so far left untouched.'[4]

---

[2] See *R (Morgan Grenfell & Co Ltd) v Special Commissioner of Income Tax* [2003] 1 AC 563, at [7]. See also *Three Rivers District Council v Governor and Company of the Bank of England* [2004] UKHL 48, at [25]; reaff'd in *McE v Prison Service of Northern Ireland* [2009] UKHL 15.

[3] See *Dechert LLP v Eurasian Natural Resources Corpn Ltd* [2016] EWCA Civ 375, at [39]. Gloster LJ went on to cite *R v Derby Magistrates' Court, ex p B* [1996] AC 487, at 507D, *per* Lord Taylor; *R (Morgan Grenfell & Co Ltd) v Special Commissioners* [2003] 1 AC 563, at [7], *per* Lord Hoffmann; *Three Rivers District Council v Governor and Company of the Bank of England* [2004] UKHL 48, at [25], *per* Lord Scott.

[4] *R v Derby Magistrates' Court, ex p B* [1996] AC 487, at 507.

To the extent that it putatively derogates from the right to assert legal professional privilege, any rule of court (or other secondary legislation) would be *ultra vires*.[5]

Types of privilege

For present purposes, the following types of privilege can be identified (only the first three of which are forms of legal professional privilege): **46.06**

- advice privilege (otherwise known as legal advice privilege) (see 46.08–46.09);
- litigation privilege (see 46.10);
- common interest privilege (see 46.11);
- without-prejudice privilege (which is addressed at 6.213–6.218); and
- other types of privilege (see 46.12).

Only the first two types are dealt with in any detail in this chapter. There is considerable overlap between them, but, in essence, advice privilege will apply to confidential communications with lawyers where those communications were made for the purposes of obtaining legal advice, whereas litigation privilege will apply where communications are made for the purposes of preparing for litigation. There are differences between the two, especially in so far as communications with persons other than lawyers are concerned (see 46.22).

References to 'lawyers' or 'lawyer' in this chapter should not be read as being confined to solicitors; in general, the points made extend to confidential communications with any lawyer, including lawyers from other jurisdictions.[6] **46.07**

Advice privilege

Correspondence passing between a party (or their predecessors in title) and their lawyers are privileged from production, but only if they are confidential and written to, or by, the lawyers acting in their professional capacity for the purpose of legal advice or assistance.[7] This principle has long been extended to non-litigious business. Where these conditions are not met, however, the correspondence is unlikely to be covered by legal advice privilege.[8] **46.08**

The following points may be made about advice privilege. **46.09**

- **Prerequisites** The communications must have been confidential. They must also have been made in the context of a professional lawyer–client relationship.[9]
- **Nature of advice** The nature of the advice does not need to be limited to advice about legal rights and obligations.[10]

---

[5] In its first incarnation, the CPR contained a provision (then CPR, r 48.7(3)) that putatively gave the court the *vires* to order a party to disclose privileged documents. It soon became apparent that the provision was *ultra vires*: see *General Mediterranean Holdings SA v Patel* [2000] 1 WLR 272.

[6] See, eg, *Wheeler v Le Marchant* (1881) 17 Ch D 675, at 679; *Macfarlan v Rolt* (1872) LR 14 Eq 580.

[7] See *O'Shea v Wood* [1891] P 286, CA; *Gardner v Irvin* (1878–79) LR 4 Ex D 49, at 53, CA; *Kennedy v Lyell* (1883) LR 23 Ch D 387, at 404.

[8] See *Original Hartlepool Collieries v Moon* (1874) 30 LT 193, at 585; *Moseley v Victoria Co* (1886) 55 LT 482.

[9] *Minter v Priest* [1930] AC 558; see also *Wilden Pump Engineering Co v Fusfeld* (1985) FSR 159, CA (Civ Div).

[10] *Three Rivers District Council v Governor and Company of the Bank of England* [2004] UKHL 48.

- **Information received from third parties** Advice privilege extends to information that any lawyer receives in a professional capacity from a third party and which they convey to their client for the purposes of giving legal advice.[11]
- **Communications made through third parties** The fact that a communication was made through a third party employed as a clerk or agent of the lawyer will not detract from the fact that advice privilege may attach.[12] The same will apply if the third party is engaged by the client for the purposes of conveying information to or from the lawyer.[13]
- **Information in the public domain** The mere fact that a document contains information that is in the public domain will not result in loss of advice privilege.[14]
- **Information already disclosed to an opponent** Advice privilege will not extend to a communication that took place with an opponent or in the presence of an opponent.[15]
- **Other jurisdictions** Advice privilege may apply even if the lawyer in question is based in another jurisdiction.[16]

Litigation privilege

46.10 Communications made for the purposes of preparing for litigation[17] and items referred to or enclosed with such communications will generally be covered by 'litigation privilege'.[18] The important point about litigant privilege is that it will apply regardless of whether those communications were between the receiving party and their lawyers, or between their lawyers and a third party (such as an expert or a non-professional agent). This will be so regardless of whether the communication was conveyed via an agent.[19]

Common interest privilege

46.11 Common interest privilege arises where a party voluntarily discloses a document that is privileged in its hands to another party who has a common interest in the subject matter of the communication or in litigation in connection with which the document was brought into being. In such circumstances, provided that disclosure is given in recognition of the fact that the parties share a common interest, the document will also be privileged in the hands of the second party.[20]

Other types of privilege

46.12 Other types of privilege exist, but may be discounted for present purposes.[21]

---

[11] *Re Sarah C Getty Trust, Getty v Getty* [1985] 3 WLR 302.

[12] See *Wheeler v Le Marchant* (1881) LR 17 Ch D 675, CA, at 682.

[13] See *Reid v Langlois* (1849) 1 Mac & G 627; *Hooper v Gumm* (1862) 2 John & H 602.

[14] *Ainsworth v Wilding* [1900] 2 Ch 315.

[15] *Ibid*; cf *Feuerheerd v LGO Co* [1918] 2 KB 565. See also *Gore v Harris* (1851) 21 LJ Ch 10.

[16] *Garfield v Fay* [1968] P 306.

[17] This means that the communications must have come into existence after litigation had become contemplated or had commenced and they must have been made with a view to such litigation, either for the purpose of obtaining or giving advice in regard to it or for the purpose of obtaining or collecting evidence: see *Anderson v Bank of British Columbia* (1875–76) LR 2 Ch D 644, at 649. See also *Wheeler v Le Marchant* (1881) LR 17 Ch D 675, at 681.

[18] See *Three Rivers District Council v Governor and Company of the Bank of England* [2004] UKHL 48, at [10].

[19] *Anderson v Bank of British Columbia* (1875–76) LR 2 Ch D 644, at 650.

[20] See Thanki, B, et al, *The Law of Privilege* (2nd edn, Oxford: Oxford University Press, 2011), para 6.16, cited with approval in *EMW Law LLP v Halborg* [2017] EWHC 1014 (Ch), at [46], *per* Newey J.

[21] Privilege against self-incrimination may arise in theory; in practice, it would rarely arise in the context of a detailed assessment.

What is and is not privileged

Where the topic arises in the context of costs, the court may have to determine whether a document is or is not subject to legal professional privilege. The following points may be made in that regard. **46.13**

Specific types of document

Bills and invoices In general, bills and invoices for a lawyer's fees are subject to legal professional privilege (which may be either advice privilege or litigation privilege, depending on the circumstances). Turner V-C came to this conclusion on the basis that 'an attorney's bill of costs is, in truth, his history of the transaction in which he has been concerned'.[22] Whilst there is no authority directly on the point, there is no reason to believe that the same would not apply to invoices that were not statute bills, provided, of course, that they were sufficiently detailed to amount to a history of the transactions between lawyer and client. **46.14**

Turner V-C's comments seem still to be good law. Aldous J, for example, appears to have accepted a concession made by leading counsel that bills were privileged, commenting that 'the reasonable solicitor would have been in no doubt that the legal bills were privileged documents'.[23] Rimer J also seems to have accepted this as the correct position, but he went on to say that calculations made in relation to bills are not privileged[24] (although, they probably would be if they were to contain sufficient detail so as to record the history of the transactions between lawyer and client). **46.15**

Client care letters A client care letter may be privileged, depending on the nature of its contents and the context in which it was written.[25] Rimer J commented (albeit *obiter*) that a letter merely setting out the terms on which the lawyer will act was not privileged.[26] If only parts of the letter relate to legal advice, it would not be appropriate to try to hive off the rest of the letter as not being privileged[27]—although it may be appropriate, in some circumstances, for it to be redacted.[28] **46.16**

Administrative records Brooke LJ has confirmed that not every document generated in the course of a retainer will be privileged.[29] Whilst not a binding decision, Judge Grenfell found that certain automated records of time spent were not privileged.[30] In the context of a criminal matter, Bingham CJ found that records of the times of attendances were not privileged.[31] **46.17**

Insurance policies This topic is addressed at 54.174. **46.18**

---

[22] *Chant v Brown* (1851) 9 Hare 790, at 794. Whilst in a wholly different context, Tindall CJ has found that 'the attorney's bill may be called the history of the cause': *Waller v Lacey* (1840) 133 ER 245, at 251.

[23] *International Business Machines Corpn v Phoenix International (Computers) Ltd* [1995] 1 All ER 413, at 424.

[24] *Dickinson v Rushmer* [2002] 1 Costs LR 128, at [12]–[13].

[25] For general guidance, see *Balabel v Air India* [1988] Ch 317, esp at 330.

[26] *Dickinson v Rushmer* [2002] 1 Costs LR 128, at [13].

[27] See *Balabel v Air India* [1988] Ch 317. See also *The Sagheera* [1997] 1 Lloyd's Rep 160, at 168.

[28] Whilst on a slightly different point, see *Stein v Blake* (2000) 97(43) LSG 38, *per* Neuberger J.

[29] *Hollins v Russell* [2003] EWCA Civ 718, at [77].

[30] *Stables v York City Council* (unreported), 13 October 2008, Leeds County Court.

[31] *R v Manchester Crown Court, ex p Rogers* [1999] 1 WLR 832.

46.19 **Litigation funding (third-party agreements)** In the context of an application for security of costs, Sir Donald Rattee addressed the issue of whether a litigation funding agreement should be disclosed, deciding that it should not—but it was notable that at no stage did he contemplate that the agreement might be privileged.[32] Also see 33.85–33.90.

46.20 **Counsel's papers** Instructions and briefs to counsel are privileged, as are counsel's advices and opinions.[33] Similarly, documents that come into existence merely as materials to be sent to counsel are privileged.[34] Drafts prepared by counsel may also be privileged,[35] but a mere note on a brief as to the outcome of a trial would not.[36]

46.21 **Expert reports** A report obtained by a lawyer from an expert for the purposes of litigation will be covered by litigation privilege, but if it was obtained for other purposes, it will be covered neither by litigation nor advice privilege.[37]

46.22 **Documents written by advisers who are not lawyers** Documents that are communications with non-lawyers are subject to litigation privilege if, and only if, they came into existence for the purpose of obtaining legal advice in existing or anticipated proceedings.[38] Surprisingly, advice privilege will not attach to communications between a professional non-lawyer (such as an accountant) and their client, even if the purpose of those communications was to obtain legal advice.[39] The same applies to other non-lawyer advisers, such as human resources consultants.[40]

46.23 **Communications made prior to litigation** Privilege may be claimed in respect of communications made with a lawyer acting in a professional capacity, even if those communications were not made in anticipation of litigation.[41] Whilst an obvious point, instructions given by the client to their lawyer are privileged.[42]

46.24 **Communications with employees of clients of corporate clients** Privilege does not automatically attach to all communications with corporate clients. In particular, the 'client', for the purposes of the advice privilege, will be limited to those employees who are authorised to seek and receive legal advice, which means that the advice privilege will not extend to information provided by other employees—and this will be so even if they are providing information for the purpose of it being communicated to a lawyer.[43]

---

[32] *Reeves v Sprecher* [2007] EWHC 3226 (Ch).

[33] See *Bristol Corpn v Cox* (1884) LR 26 Ch D 678; *Curtis v Beaney* [1911] P 181; *Lowden v Blakey* (1889) LR 23 QBD 332.

[34] See *Southwark Water Co v Quick* (1878) 3 QBD 315, at 320; see also *The Palermo* (1883) LR 9 PD 6.

[35] *Pearse v Pearse* (1846) 1 De G & S 12; *Bolton v Liverpool Corpn* (1833) 1 My & K 88, at 93; *Vigneron-Dahl Ltd v Pettit* [1925] WN 177.

[36] *Walsham v Stainton* (1863) 2 H & M 1; *Nicholl v Jones* (1865) 2 H & M 588.

[37] *Wheeler v Le Marchant* (1881) 17 Ch D 675, at 683, CA, *per* Brett LJ. See also *Smith v Daniel* (1874) 18 LR Eq 649.

[38] *Seabrook v British Transport Commission* [1959] 1 WLR 509, *per* Havers J.

[39] *R (on the application of (1) Prudential Plc) v Special Commissioner of Income Tax* [2010] EWCA Civ 1094, aff'd at [2013] UKSC 1.

[40] *New Victoria Hospital v Ryan* [1993] ICR 201, EAT.

[41] *Lawrence v Campbell* (1859) 4 Drew 485.

[42] *Bristol Corpn v Cox* (1884) 26 Ch D 678.

[43] See, eg, *Three Rivers District Council & Ors v The Governor and Company of the Bank of England (No 5)* [2003] EWCA Civ 474; *The RBS Rights Issue Litigation* [2016] EWHC 3161 (Ch).

Internal documents Where privilege applies to lawyer–client communications, internally circulated documents or extracts from documents are also privileged.[44] In particular, communications between lawyers in the same firm will tend to be privileged,[45] as may communications with agents.[46] The mere fact that privileged documents were made available to solicitor agents would not amount to an implied waiver as against that agent.[47] Similarly, communications with in-house lawyers will tend to be privileged (but only if it otherwise qualifies as being privileged).[48] **46.25**

Communications with third parties for purposes other than litigation In general, communications with persons other than the client for purposes other than obtaining legal advice will not be covered by privilege.[49] That said, there might be other reasons why they cannot be disclosed (such as the privilege that attaches to without-prejudice material). **46.26**

Marshalled documents Documents that have been marshalled by a lawyer with a view to existing or contemplated litigation are, in principle, subject to litigation privilege,[50] but this will not cloak otherwise unprivileged documents.[51] In particular, documentation that comes into being for some purpose other than to instruct a lawyer or to form part of its brief are not privileged and do not become privileged merely because they are sent to a lawyer as part of its instructions.[52] **46.27**

Filing Documents at Court

PD 47, para 13.11, obliges a receiving party to file material in support of its bill. It reads as follows: **46.28**

> 'Unless the court directs otherwise the receiving party must file with the court the papers in support of the bill not less than 7 days before the date for the detailed assessment hearing and not more than 14 days before that date.'

Papers ought to be filed in the following order: **46.29**

- instructions and briefs to counsel arranged in chronological order, together with all advices, opinions and drafts received, and response to such instructions;
- reports and opinions of medical and other experts;
- any other relevant papers;
- a full set of any relevant pleadings, to the extent that they have not already been filed in court; and
- correspondence, files and attendance notes.[53]

---

44 *Bank of Nova Scotia v Hellenic Mutual War Risk Association (Bermuda) Ltd, The Good Luck* [1992] 1 AC 233.
45 *Mostyn v West Mostyn Coal Co* (1876–77) LR 2 CPD 547.
46 *Hughes v Biddulph* (1827) 4 Russ 190; *Bolton v Liverpool Corpn* (1833) 1 My & K 88, at 96.
47 See *EMW Law LLP v Halborg* [2017] EWHC 1014 (Ch), at [69], *per* Newey J.
48 *Alfred Crompton Amusement Machines Ltd v Commissioners of Customs and Excise (No 2)* [1974] AC 405.
49 *Ibid.* In a costs context, see *Hollins v Russell* [2003] EWCA Civ 718, at [77].
50 *Learoyd v Halifax Banking Co* [1893] 1 Ch.686, at 690.
51 *Chadwick v Bowman* (1885–86) LR 16 QBD 561.
52 *Dubai Bank Ltd v Galadari* [1989] 3 All ER 769, CA.
53 PD 47, para 13.12. Some courts ask that a bundle is prepared, but most do not.

Where the claim is in respect of additional liabilities on their own, then only those papers that are relevant to those liabilities need to be filed.[54]

46.30 These are the documents that must be filed prior to the hearing; they are in addition to those that ought already to have been filed at the time the hearing was requested (see 43.182–43.185).

46.31 The requirement to file documents in accordance with PD 47, para 13.11, invites the question of whether the receiving party is under a compulsion to file material that is adverse to its case. That is not an easy question to answer.

The duty to file adverse material

46.32 Prior to the coming into force of the Civil Procedure Rules (CPR), the Rules of the Supreme Court (RSC) were interpreted as giving rise to a duty to file adverse material. In particular, Aldous LJ held that the duty to lodge material at the court was 'a duty . . . to disclose to the taxing master all relevant papers . . . [including] those which support the claim and those which undermine the claim'.[55] As is explained below, it is not known whether any such duty continues to exist.

The duty to file written documents other than the retainer

46.33 Neither the CPR nor PD 47 make any mention of a duty to file adverse material. Indeed, PD 47, paras 13.11 and 13.12, speak of papers '*in support* of' a bill of costs, so it could easily be argued that this excludes (or at least does not include) documents that are adverse to the bill.

46.34 That said, it is possible that a duty to file adverse documentation exists, for the following reasons.

- **'In support of'** It may be that the words 'in support of the bill' in PD 47, para 13.11, should be read as a reference to papers that are relevant to the bill, rather than only to those that bolster it.
- **Judge-made duty** Similarly, it is possible that Aldous LJ's broad interpretation of the RSC (see 46.32) should continue to be applied to the CPR, which approach would be entirely consistent with the court's duty to take adverse material into account (see 46.36–46.39).
- **Professional duty** It is easily arguable that filleting the file so as to create a false impression would be a breach of a solicitor's duty not to mislead the court.

There is no authority on any of these points, but a solicitor would be very unwise to take a chance with the third (not least because an experienced costs judge will spot a filleted file within moments of seeing the papers).

The duty to file written instruments of retainer

46.35 PD 47 expressly provides that where compliance with the indemnity principle is disputed, a request for a hearing should be accompanied by 'any agreement, letter or other written information provided by the legal representative to the client explaining how the legal representative's charges are to be calculated'.[56] Whilst it is arguable that this does not include documentation that has become irrelevant (such as retainer documentation that had

[54] In this regard, CPD, art 40.12, remains of relevance.
[55] *Bourns Inc v Raychem Corpn* [1999] 3 All ER 154, at 162.
[56] PD 47, para 13.2(i).

been replaced by more recent documentation), it is difficult to see how a receiving party could comply with this provision without disclosing all of the relevant documents. Any attempt to be selective in this regard might be viewed as an attempt to mislead the court.

The 'escalator of enquiry' relating to adverse material

Where the court discovers something untoward in the receiving party's file, it will begin a process that can usefully be thought of as being an 'escalator of enquiry'. Judge LJ had the following to say on the topic: **46.36**

> 'The taxing officer is exercising a judicial function ... he is trusted properly to consider material which would normally be protected from disclosure under the rules of legal professional privilege. If ... some feature of the case alerts him to the need to make further investigation or causes him to wonder if the information with which he is being provided is full and accurate, he may seek further information. No doubt he would begin by asking for a letter or some form of written confirmation or reassurance as appropriate. If this were to prove inadequate he might then make orders for discovery or require affidavit evidence. It is difficult to envisage circumstances in which the party benefiting from the order for costs will not have been anxious to provide the required information, but if all else fails, it would theoretically be open to him to order interrogatories. However, if the stage has been reached where interrogatories might reasonably be ordered, the conclusion that the receiving party had not been able to satisfy the taxing officer about the bill, or some particular aspect of it, would seem inevitable.'[57]

Judge LJ's comments were made under the RSC, but they are generally regarded as having continuing relevance under the CPR.

An example of an escalator would be as follows. **46.37**

(1) The receiving party may be put to their election in respect of the documentation that has caused the court to become concerned.
(2) If the receiving party's response does not satisfy the court, then the receiving party may be asked to provide an informal explanation via their representative.
(3) If that does not satisfy the court, then the court may require the receiving party to provide an explanation in a witness statement or (in more serious cases) by affidavit.
(4) If that does not satisfy the court, then the receiving party may be required to answer questions under CPR, Part 18, or to offer their witnesses for cross-examination.
(5) If the court still remains dissatisfied, it may draw inferences against the receiving party (but see 46.72–46.74).

Documents filed in error

It occasionally happens that the court has sight of a document that it was not supposed to see (such as a Part 36 offer relating to costs). Where this happens, the court's primary concern will be to ensure that the parties are not prejudiced as a result. The court will do its best to discharge its duties without recusing itself, but this may not be possible. Hobhouse J had this to say on the topic: **46.38**

> 'The trained legal mind normally has no difficulty in preventing irrelevant or improper material from influencing its decision. Occasionally a master may feel embarrassed by what he

[57] In the context of privilege in relation to retainers, in *Bailey v IBC Vehicles Ltd* [1998] 3 All ER 570, at 572.

has seen, and knows that the respondent has not seen, and cannot be told about. In such a case, the master can [order] that the taxation of one or more items be dealt with by another taxing master'.[58]

46.39 Whilst dealing with the issue of recusal in a context other than costs, Lord Hope has described the appropriate test as being whether a fair-minded and informed observer, having considered the facts, would conclude that there was a real possibility that the court would be biased.[59]

The Process of Election

The principles of election

46.40 Election is to costs litigation what disclosure is to substantive litigation. This is true only to a limited extent, however, because election and disclosure differ in terms of procedure and philosophy.

46.41 Election prevents a receiving party from having their evidential cake and eating it. In particular, it prevents the receiving party from asserting privilege over a document upon which they intend to rely. The receiving party must decide—or elect—whether to rely on the document (in which case, their opponent will see it) or whether to assert privilege over it (in which case, they will not be able to rely on it).

46.42 The process of election—which came to be known as the *Pamplin* procedure[60]—was first described by Hobhouse J in the mid-1980s. PD 47, para 13.13, is its present-day incarnation:

> 'The court may direct the receiving party to produce any document which in the opinion of the court is necessary to enable it to reach its decision. These documents will in the first instance be produced to the court, but the court may ask the receiving party to elect whether to disclose the particular document to the paying party in order to rely on the contents of the document, or whether to decline disclosure and instead rely on other evidence.'

46.43 As has already been explained at 46.05, where privilege exists and has not been waived or abrogated, it is absolute; it is not subject to any type of balancing exercise by which competing public interests are weighed against each other.[61] Where necessary, the right of the paying party to see the relevant documents will prevail over the right of the receiving party to claim privilege; the latter will be preserved, however, in the sense that (in the absence of fraud) a receiving party would never be ordered to disclose privileged documents.[62]

46.44 Pumfrey J has confirmed that the method of election presents no incompatibility with the principles articulated by the European Court of Human Rights.[63]

---

[58] *Pamplin v Express Newspapers Ltd* [1985] 1 WLR 689, at 697.

[59] *Magill v Weeks* [2001] UKHL 67.

[60] After *Pamplin v Express Newspapers Ltd* [1985] 1 WLR 689, at 695.

[61] See *R v Derby Magistrates' Court, ex p B* [1996] AC 487, at 491; see also *South Coast Shipping Co Ltd v Havant Borough Council* [2002] 3 All ER 779, at 793.

[62] See *South Coast Shipping Co Ltd v Havant Borough Council* [2002] 3 All ER 779, at 794.

[63] *Ibid*, at 793, referring to the European Convention on Human Rights (ECHR), as set out in Sch 1 to the Human Rights Act 1998.

The procedure of election and the court's discretion

The informal approach

One of the most striking features of election is that, in practice, it is rarely necessary to invoke it. This is because nearly all detailed assessments are dealt with on an informal basis, at least in part. In practical terms, this means that the paying party will not insist on seeing each and every document that is placed before the judge, but instead will trust the judge to carry out a proper examination of those documents and to ensure fair play. This courteous and efficient fact-finding procedure suffices for all but the most contentious of assessments. **46.45**

Davies J has described this informal procedure as 'sensible, pragmatic and time and cost saving'.[64] He also highlighted the fact that where a party unnecessarily departs from it, that party can be penalised in costs.[65] **46.46**

Hobhouse J had this to say about the benefits of an informal approach: **46.47**

> '[It will be] very rare for the full formality of these steps [relating to election] to be gone through. Most [paying parties] appreciate that once they have drawn to the master's attention the possibility that an item of charge may be unnecessary or may be being overvalued, their interests are best served by allowing the master to look at the relevant documents and form his own judgment. The [paying party] will normally achieve little or nothing by asking to see the documents as well. The master is well aware of the criteria he has to apply and is highly experienced in the exercise of assessment he has to undertake.'[66]

The court will actively encourage the informal approach. In particular, the Court of Appeal has said that a costs judge should use 'all his expertise and tact' to avoid a party being put to its election.[67]

The formal approach

The informal approach will not always be appropriate. Where there is doubt about this, the court's task is to identify the stage at which the receiving party will need to put to their election; that stage may never be reached, but if it is, the matter must then proceed on a formal footing. **46.48**

The fact that the judge has read the documents filed at court (see 46.29–46.30) does not mean that the receiving party has waived their right to claim privilege nor does it give rise to any problems of natural justice. This is because the costs judge is able to disregard what they have seen if the receiving party subsequently chooses not to rely on the documents in question.[68] **46.49**

It may be, however, that a decision needs to be made as to what the judge should and should not take into account. Once that stage has been reached, the costs judge has a *duty* to put the receiving party to their election. This was explained by Hobhouse J thus: **46.50**

---

64 *Gower Chemicals Group Litigation* [2008] EWHC 735 (QB), at [15]; see also *Pamplin v Express Newspapers Ltd* [1985] 1 WLR 689.

65 *Gower Chemicals Group Litigation* [2008] EWHC 735 (QB), at [34].

66 *Pamplin v Express Newspapers Ltd* [1985] 1 WLR 689, at 697.

67 *Goldman v Hesper* [1988] 1 WLR 1238, at 1245. This was a pre-CPR case, but it is doubtful whether this aspect of the law is any different under the CPR.

68 See *Pamplin v Express Newspapers Ltd* [1985] 1 WLR 689, at 695, which, although a pre-CPR authority, remains authoritative on this point.

'An issue of fact may emerge which necessitates ... making formally or informally a finding of fact. In such a situation, the master may have to ask the [receiving party] what evidence he wishes to rely upon in support of the contested allegation of fact. The [paying party] may then take the stand that if the claimant wishes to adduce evidence, he [the paying party] wishes to see it and comment on or contradict it. This will mean that the [receiving party] will then have to elect whether he wants to use the evidence and waive his privilege or seek to prove what he needs in some other way.

... [I]t is the duty of the master, if the respondent raises a factual issue, which is real and relevant and not a sham or fanciful dispute, to require the claimant to prove the facts upon which he relies.'[69]

46.51 In a post-CPR case, Rimer J came to much the same conclusion:

'[The situation] was one which involved an issue of fact which the costs judge had to decide. It appears to me to be obvious that as soon as it became clear that the [receiving party] was proposing to support his own case on the point by reference to documents which he was not willing to disclose to the [paying party], the costs judge should have considered whether that course was consistent with one of the most basic principles of natural justice, namely the right of each side to know what the other party's case is and to see the documentary material that he is relying on so that he can make his own comments on it.'[70]

46.52 Pumfrey J has explained that the need to put a receiving party to their election may arise where the document is of sufficient importance for the judge to take it into account:

'Once the document is of sufficient importance to be taken into account in arriving at a conclusion as to recoverability, then, unless otherwise agreed, it must be shown to the paying party or the receiving party must content itself with other evidence.'[71]

The other side of the coin—whether the court may decline to put a party to their election on the basis that the document is of insufficient importance to be taken into account—is discussed at 46.57 and 46.59.

46.53 The issue of election will not arise unless there is a need to adjudicate upon a contentious issue. No such issue will arise if the receiving party is able to rely on a presumption in their favour. It is for this reason that the receiving party could expect not to be put to their election over a private retainer (unless, of course, the presumption is rebutted).

46.54 A receiving party will not be put to their election solely for the purposes of testing their evidence. This was noted by Pumfrey J in the following way:

'It does not seem to me that the principles set out above require privileged material available to the receiving party to be disclosed for the purpose of testing the evidence given ... The solution is imperfect, but is dictated by the existence of the privilege: ... either both or neither can deploy the privileged material. The familiar rule that the other party is entitled to see the disclosable material even if the party which possesses it does not deploy it can have no application when the material is privileged.'[72]

Thus the process of election is not to be used to force disclosure of documents upon which the receiving party does not intend to rely.

---

69 *Ibid*, at 696.
70 *Dickinson v Rushmer* [2002] 1 Costs LR 128, at [32].
71 *South Coast Shipping Co Ltd v Havant Borough Council* [2002] 3 All ER 779, at 793.
72 *Ibid*, at 794.

Miscellaneous points concerning election

Blanket election The court will generally not tolerate blanket applications for a party to be put to their election (such as an unfocused application in respect of the receiving party's entire file).[73] **46.55**

Waiver limited to assessment The fact that a receiving party is able to reassert privilege in subsequent contexts is a factor the court is permitted to take into account.[74] **46.56**

Proportionality and election

In a case concerning a disputed retainer, Pumfrey J made the following observations, which, at first blush, seem to suggest that a costs judge is at liberty to decline to put a party to their election on the grounds of proportionality: **46.57**

> 'I would expect that in the great majority of cases the paying party would be content to agree that the costs judge alone should see privileged documents. Only where it is necessary and proportionate should the receiving party be put to his election.'[75]

However, Rimer J came to a conclusion that seems to be at odds with Pumfrey J's analysis: **46.58**

> 'I do not attach much weight to [the] submissions as to the need for proportionality in relation to the procedure applicable on a detailed assessment of costs. I interpret the substance of this submission to be that a detailed assessment of costs is essentially ancillary to the main litigation and so justifies the court in adopting something of a broad-brush approach to the performance of the exercise. I do not subscribe to that view. A claim by one party to recover costs from another may well in practice prove to be just as important, perhaps even more so, to one or other or both sides as the resolution of the substantive issues in the action.'[76]

These seemingly antagonistic observations are reconcilable: proportionality will play a role where the costs judge is using 'all his expertise and tact' to avoid the need to put a party to their election (see 46.47), but, once that need is made out, the process of election will not be cut back on grounds of proportionality—although it should be borne in mind that Rimer J's comments were made before the overriding objective was amended in 2013 and it is possible that the amendment has lessened the force of his comments. Even if Rimer J's comments still carry weight, however, this does not mean that a paying party is able to insist on the court putting the receiving party to their election in respect of every letter, attendance note and file note; at the very least, a paying party who took that approach would be at risk of being condemned in costs. **46.59**

Implied waiver of privilege

The fact that a receiving party accepts that they should be put to their election does not preclude that party from subsequently asserting privilege. If the receiving party impliedly elects to rely on a document, however, then they will lose that opportunity. This would give rise to implied, unintended waiver of privilege. **46.60**

The court tends to be slow to find that a receiving party has unwittingly waived privilege. Hobhouse J had the following to say on the topic: **46.61**

> '[It] will normally be a matter of express waiver only. It should always be possible to avoid having to get involved with implied waiver ... A [receiving party] should not have imposed

73 See, eg, *Pamplin v Express Newspapers Ltd* [1985] 1 WLR 689, which is an example of this.
74 *South Coast Shipping Co Ltd v Havant Borough Council* [2002] 3 All ER 779, at 785j.
75 *Ibid*, at 793j.
76 *Dickinson v Rushmer* [2002] 1 Costs LR 128, at [29].

on him an unintended waiver unless fairness to both parties really does necessitate that result.'[77]

46.62 The way in which the court allows a receiving party to retain their right to privilege is by ensuring that they have the opportunity to withdraw the document in question. This was explained by Gray J thus:

> 'When a party lodges a privileged document for detailed assessment in order to claim the costs of it, if the other party wishes to see it to dispute that claim for costs the [receiving party] must be given the right to elect to withdraw it and not claim costs or he must disclose it.'[78]

46.63 There is no doubt that a receiving party who has merely filed a document at court should be given the opportunity to withdraw it, but what is less clear is whether such a party should be allowed to do so if the document has been handed up to the court during the assessment.

46.64 Rimer J held that a decision to hand a document to the judge would pre-empt the decision that the receiving party be put to their election. He had this to say on the point:

> 'The costs judge did not *direct* the production to him of the relevant documents, and so the procedure contemplated by that rule [ie the then equivalent of PD 47, para 13.14] was strictly not engaged at all. The judge saw the documents because the [receiving party] voluntarily chose to hand them to him in support of his case ... [This] was a simple situation in which the [receiving party] chose to prove his version of a disputed issue of fact by reference to certain documents. In my view, the basic principle is that, if he wanted to do so, fairness required him also to disclose the documents to the [paying party].'[79]

46.65 It is commonly the case that retainer documentation is handed up to the costs judge in the expectation that those documents will not be shown to the paying party unless and until the court finds that a 'genuine issue' has been made out. Such a practice is unwise, because it may give rise to unintended waiver. Rimer J had this to say on the point:

> 'A paying party raises an issue about [the indemnity principle] by advancing factual assertions which serve to put it in question ... Faced with those assertions, the [receiving party] had a choice as to what course to follow. He could have asked the costs judge to direct whether he regarded the [paying party] as having raised an issue on which he, the [receiving party] needed to provide further evidence ... Alternatively, he could, as he did, pre-empt any decision by the judge on that point ... The fact that the [receiving party] thought it appropriate to adopt the latter course is perhaps the best indication that the issue the [paying party] had raised was a genuine one—or at least the [receiving party] so regarded it.'[80]

46.66 Likewise, Gray J has indicated (albeit *obiter*) that where a client care letter is affirmatively relied upon, it ought to be 'standard practice' that it be made available to the paying party.[81] Where, however, the documents are in the hands of the judge solely as a result of the procedure envisaged by PD 47, para 13.2(i) (see 46.35), there will have been no waiver.[82]

---

77 *Pamplin v Express Newspapers Ltd* [1985] 1 WLR 689, at 698.
78 *Adams v MacInnes* [2001] EWHC 9014 (Costs).
79 *Dickinson v Rushmer* [2002] 1 Costs LR 128, at [30].
80 *Ibid*, at [31].
81 *Adams v MacInnes* [2001] EWHC 9014 (Costs).
82 *Giambrone v JMC Holidays Ltd* [2002] EWHC 495 (QB) at [34 ii)], *per* Nelson J.

Limited waiver of privilege

Disclosure of documents does not necessarily mean that privilege is lost—in particular, disclosure may be given for limited and specific purposes.[83] Whilst speaking in a context other than the law of costs, Neuberger MR has explained that the question of whether waiver is limited is to be determined by reference to all of the circumstances of the alleged waiver and, in particular, what was expressly or impliedly communicated between the person sending and the person receiving, the documents in question and what they must or ought reasonably to have understood.[84] **46.67**

Withdrawal of waiver of privilege

It is possible to withdraw a waiver of privilege. To be effective, however, the waiver must be withdrawn before it has resulted in documents being inspected by the paying party.[85] **46.68**

The consequences of electing to disclose documents

As has been explained at 46.67, disclosure of documents does not necessarily mean that privilege is lost—in particular, disclosure may be given for limited and specific purposes.[86] This is particularly true in the context of costs litigation. In particular, any disclosure of privileged documentation for the purposes of the assessment is, with very limited exceptions, for that purpose only, which means that voluntary waiver or disclosure during an assessment would not prevent the owner of the document from reasserting its privilege in any subsequent context.[87] This principle was memorably illustrated by Aldous LJ by reference to 'Mr Bloch's cat': **46.69**

> 'As to Mr Bloch's "cat" [Mr Bloch being one of the advocates], in all cases where there is disclosure upon terms the "cat is out of the bag". There is no need to put it back. Documents disclosed for a limited purpose can only be used for that purpose. Of course difficulties arise, but that is not the fault of the person making the disclosure nor the law which protects the confidences of the person disclosing the documents.'[88]

In a similar vein, Taylor LJ had this to say: **46.70**

> '[O]nce a party puts forward privileged documents as part of his case for costs some measure of their privilege is temporarily and *pro hac vice* relaxed ... Any disclosure of privileged documents which does have to be made in the exercise of the taxing officer's discretion would in my judgment be only for the purposes of the taxation.'[89]

---

[83] See *B v Auckland District Law Society* [2003] 2 AC 736, at [68], *per* Lord Millett.

[84] *Berezovsky v Hine* [2011] EWCA Civ 1089, at [27]–[29]. See also *Brown v Guardian Royal Exchange plc* [1994] 2 Lloyd's Rep 325, at 328, as discussed by Aikens J in *Winterthur Swiss Insurance Co v AG (Manchester) Ltd (in liquidation)* [2006] EWHC 839 Comm, at [74].

[85] *Goldman v Hesper* [1988] 1 WLR 1238, at 1240.

[86] See *B v Auckland District Law Society* [2003] 2 AC 736, at [68], *per* Lord Millett.

[87] *Bourns Inc v Raychem Corpn* [1999] 3 All ER 154, at 159, *per* Aldous LJ; *Goldman v Hesper* [1988] 1 WLR 1238, at 1244C–H, *per* Taylor LJ. See also *Dechert LLP v Eurasian Natural Resources Corpn Ltd* [2016] EWCA Civ 375, at [38], *per* Gloster LJ (albeit in the context of solicitor-and-client assessments); *B v Auckland District Law Society* [2003] 2 AC 736 (disclosure given with express reservations as to the right to assert privilege); *British Coal Corpn v Dennis Rye Ltd (No 2)* [1988] 1 WLR 1113.

[88] *Bourns Inc v Raychem Corpn* [1999] 3 All ER 154, at 159.

[89] *Goldman v Hesper* [1988] 1 WLR 1238, at 1244C–H. See also *Bourns Inc v Raychem Corpn* [1999] 3 All ER 154, at 162c, *per* Aldous LJ.

Gloster LJ has confirmed that these principles have survived the CPR.[90]

46.71 Thus there will be no need to 'put the cat back in the bag' for the purposes of a subsequent (non-costs) dispute or hearing—because the cat would not have been let out of that particular bag in the first place.

The consequences of electing not to disclose documents

The burden of proof

46.72 A refusal to disclose a document will place the receiving party at the disadvantage of having to rely on what inevitably will be imperfect evidence. Where the burden of proof lies with the receiving party (which will almost always be the case where they have been put to their election), this may cause the receiving party to fail to shift that burden.

No adverse inferences

46.73 If a party declines to waive privilege, it would be wrong to regard such a refusal per se as giving rise to an adverse inference,[91] although in the context of the detailed assessments, other circumstances may weigh heavily in the balance.

No assumptions

46.74 Where a receiving party chooses not to disclose a document, it would be wrong to make assumptions about their motives. In particular, the court will usually bear in mind that the receiving party may have a legitimate interest in not adducing the most obvious or complete evidence.[92]

Disclosure in Cases of Fraud

46.75 Where it is necessary for the purposes of defeating fraud, the receiving party may be ordered to disclose privileged material—but the party seeking disclosure must provide 'strong evidence' before the court will make such an order.[93]

Disclosure of Non-privileged Material

46.76 A paying party may contend that a certain document is not privileged and that it ought to be disclosed without the receiving party being given the option of withdrawing it. Whilst there is no binding authority on the point, that argument has occasionally found favour in the County Court.[94]

---

[90] *Dechert LLP v Eurasian Natural Resources Corpn Ltd* [2016] EWCA Civ 375, at [49]. See also *Hollins v Russell* [2003] EWCA 718, at [56].

[91] See, eg, *Reed Executive plc v Reed Business Information Ltd* [2004] EWCA Civ 887, at [36].

[92] *Pamplin v Express Newspapers Ltd* [1985] 1 WLR 689, at 697.

[93] *Skuse v Granada Television* [1994] 1 WLR 1156, at 1166, relying on the principle set out in *Derby & Co Ltd v Weldon (No 7)* [1990] 1 WLR 1156. By analogy, see 6.218.

[94] See, eg, *Stables v York City Council* (unreported), 13 October 2008, Leeds County Court, *per* HHJ Grenfell.

Procedure Relating to Evidential Issues

The topics of timing and of whether the document in question should be shown to the court before a ruling is made are both dealt with at 46.48–46.54. **46.77**

In general, there are no procedural formalities pertaining to election, because the issue of whether the receiving party should be put to their election will arise as an integral part of the detailed assessment. Receiving parties are, however, encouraged to consider giving advance disclosure in appropriate cases. The Senior Courts Costs Office (SCCO) Guide 2018 offers the following advice: **46.78**

> 'The production of documents at a detailed assessment hearing may well cause substantial delay to that hearing and may prejudice or embarrass any appeal made in the proceedings in which the costs were awarded or in any similar proceedings between the same parties. Receiving parties should therefore consider in advance what voluntary disclosure to their opponents they are willing to make and how such disclosure can be achieved before the detailed assessment hearing without substantially damaging any privilege they wish to retain.'[95]

That guidance goes on to say that, in appropriate cases, the court may order that the issue of election be tried as a preliminary issue. Where this is so, the issues to be tried should be clearly defined and, where appropriate, reduced into writing.[96] **46.79**

[95] HM Courts & Tribunals Services, *Senior Courts Costs Office Guide* (London: HMSO, 2018), para 18.3.

[96] *Lahey v Pirelli Tyres* [2007] EWCA Civ 91, at [5]. See also O'Hare, J, 'Applications about CFAs in Detailed Assessments', Presentation at Sweet & Maxwell Professional Conference, February 2007, p 6.

47

REPRESENTATION AND RIGHTS OF AUDIENCE

47.01 This chapter deals with representation. It deals with the following topics:

- notification (47.04);
- persons who are not authorised persons (47.05):
  - independent costs draftspersons (47.07);
  - employed costs draftspersons (47.09);
  - *McKenzie* friends and expert assistants (47.10);
- authorised persons:
  - solicitors, barristers, etc (47.12); and
  - costs lawyers (47.13).

It then goes on to deal with the following topics concerning representation:

- restriction of a right of audience (47.17);
- advocates who wish to be heard on the topic of their own fees (47.18);
- the actual and ostensible authority of costs practitioners (47.23);
- bankrupt persons who wish to be heard (47.30); and
- companies (47.32).

The linked topic of whether the costs of an independent costs draftsperson (as opposed to a costs lawyer) are recoverable is addressed at 22.22–22.25.

47.02 As has been explained in Chapter 3, the acts of conducting litigation and of exercising of a right to be heard are both 'reserved legal activities' within the meaning of the Legal Services Act 2007 (see 3.49).[1] The question of whether a person is entitled to carry out such an activity is to be determined solely in accordance with the provisions of the 2007 Act (see 3.80).[2]

47.03 It is an offence for a person to carry on a reserved legal activity without being entitled to do so.[3] A person would have such an entitlement only if they were an 'authorised person' or an 'exempt person' in relation to the activity in question (see 3.48–3.91).[4] Authorised persons are subject to approved regulators.[5] They include costs

[1] Legal Services Act 2007, s 12(1).
[2] See Legal Services Act 2007, s 13(1).
[3] See Legal Services Act 2007, s 14(1).
[4] See Legal Services Act 2007, s 13(2).
[5] See Legal Services Act 2007, s 18(1)(a).

lawyers,[6] solicitors, barristers, etc. The rights of the various classes of person are set out at 47.07–47.13.

Notification

Practice Direction (PD) 39A, para 5.1, provides that, at any hearing, the court ought to be given the following written notification about the persons who appear before it: **47.04**

> '5.1 At any hearing, a written statement containing the following information should be provided for the court:
> (1) the name and address of each advocate,
> (2) his qualification or entitlement to act as an advocate, and
> (3) the party for whom he so acts.

Persons who are not Authorised Persons

Persons who cannot be said to be authorised persons are often encountered in costs litigation. They include *McKenzie* friends and costs draftspersons (as distinct from costs lawyers). A person who is not an authorised person may be heard only if the court gives permission, in which case they will become an exempt person for the purposes of the matter for which permission was granted.[7] **47.05**

The general approach to the issue of representation by unauthorised persons was addressed by Woolf CJ: **47.06**

> 'It is very important that courts, without going into the matter in a disproportionate way, do satisfy themselves that it is right to extend rights of audience to those who are not properly qualified. The courts are at a disadvantage and the public can be at a disadvantage if rights of audience are too readily given to those who do not have the necessary qualifications.'[8]

This confirms that the court is careful to ensure that, where they seek to represent others, only qualified or otherwise suitable persons appear before it. These concerns continue to apply today (see 3.88).

Independent costs draftspersons

It is often said that independent costs draftspersons have a concessionary right of audience arising out of the legal fiction that they are temporary employees of their instructing solicitors (see 3.88).[9] This may or may not be so, but it is not necessary to invoke such strained analyses, because the court is able to hear from any person to whom it grants permission **47.07**

[6] See the Association of Law Costs Draftsmen Order 2006 (SI 2006/3333). As of 31 October 2011, that body has delegated its regulatory role to the Costs Lawyer Standards Board (CLSB).

[7] Legal Services Act 2007, Sch 3, para 1(2).

[8] *Clarkson v Gilbert & Ors* [2000] EWCA Civ 3018, at [24] of the transcript.

[9] See, eg, HM Courts & Tribunals Services, *Senior Courts Costs Office Guide* (London: HMSO, 2018), para 1.2(d). The authority that is usually given in this regard is *Waterson Hicks v Eliopoulos* (1995) Costs LR core vol 363, at 373, *per* Evans LJ, but that case actually deals with authority as an agent, rather than rights of audience. Other cases that deal with the point include: *Claims Direct Test Cases Tranche 2* [2003] EWHC 9005 (Costs), at [115]; *Crane v Canons Leisure Centre* [2007] EWCA Civ 1352, at [12], *per* May LJ.

to be heard.[10] In practice, the court's concerns tend to focus not on legal fictions, but on whether there is a proper chain of command from the client (or insurer, as the case may be) to the advocate. This is relevant because it is only by reason of such a chain of command that an authorised body is able to exert an influence over the authorised person (or those who instruct him). The legal fiction may, however, occasionally become relevant, such as where an independent costs draftsperson appears on behalf of a litigant in person. If those are the circumstances, the costs draftsperson may be treated as a *McKenzie* friend[11] (see 47.10–47.11).

47.08 Although not binding on any court, the following comments of Senior Master Hurst illustrate the way in which the issue of representation by independent costs draftspersons is often addressed:

> 'There is nothing in my view inherently wrong in a requirement by an insurance company that, when costs come to be determined, a particular firm of costs draftsmen should be instructed. Those instructions must come from the instructing solicitors who have themselves been properly instructed and who are required to consider the claim for costs and advise the client. It is abundantly clear in this case that [the unauthorised persons] were attempting to run the detailed assessment proceedings without reference to the Defendant's solicitors under the umbrella of the correspondence to which I have referred, which does not, for the reasons I have given, achieve its objective.'[12]

Other judges have expressed similar sentiments (see 3.88).[13]

Employed costs draftspersons

47.09 A distinction needs to be drawn between independent costs draftspersons and costs draftspersons who are employed by firms that are themselves 'authorised persons' (3.86–3.87). This is because the latter will have rights of audience arising out of the fact of their employment (see 3.86): the fact that they are employed by an authorised person will cause an employed costs draftsperson to become an exempt person.[14] Whilst the court has a discretionary power to grant wider rights in respect of other types of hearing,[15] an employed costs draftsperson's right to be heard will generally be limited to chambers.[16]

McKenzie friends and expert assistants

47.10 Where an unauthorised person seeks to assist a litigant in person, the court has the power to allow that person to be heard.[17] That person is referred to as a *McKenzie* friend.[18] In general, a *McKenzie* friend should be granted rights of audience only if there is 'good reason'

---

[10] See Legal Services Act 2007, Sch 3, para 1(2).

[11] See HM Courts & Tribunals Services, *Senior Courts Costs Office Guide* (London: HMSO, 2018), para 1.2(d).

[12] *Ahmed v Powell* [2003] EWHC 9011 (Costs), at [36].

[13] See, eg, Hill, R, 'Right of Audience', *Law Society Gazette*, 20 September 2010.

[14] *Kynaston v Carroll* [2011] EWHC 2179 (QB), at [6]–[8], *per* Bennett J (albeit only in the capacity of a judge hearing an application for permission to appeal).

[15] See Legal Services Act 2007, Sch 3, para 1(2).

[16] See Legal Services Act 2007, Sch 3, para 1(7) (see 3.87).

[17] See Legal Services Act 2007, s 19, and Sch 3, para 1(2) (or, before 1 January 2010, Courts and Legal Services Act 1990, ss 27(2)(b) and 28(2)(c), respectively). See also *Clarkson v Gilbert* (2001) The Times, 4 July, CA.

[18] After *McKenzie v McKenzie* [1971] P 33.

or there are 'special circumstances'.[19] In so far as costs litigation is concerned, the Senior Courts Costs Office Guide 2018 describes the court's approach as follows:

> 'With regard to *McKenzie* Friends, the only right is that of the litigant to have reasonable assistance. A *McKenzie* Friend has no right to act as such. A *McKenzie* Friend is not entitled to address the court. A *McKenzie* Friend who does so becomes an advocate and that requires the grant of a right of audience from the court. As a general rule, a litigant in person who wishes to have a *McKenzie* Friend will be allowed to do so unless the judge is satisfied that fairness and the interests of justice do not so require. The court can prevent a *McKenzie* Friend from continuing to act in that capacity where the assistance given impedes the efficient administration of justice.'[20]

The person who seeks to provide assistance may be qualified, in the sense that they are a member of a body other than an approved regulator; in some circumstances, this would allow the litigant to recover their costs under affirmative powers conferred by the Civil Procedure Rules (CPR), but only where the work comprised the provision of expert assistance in assessing costs (see 3.95–3.96). Unauthorised persons who fall within that category are: **47.11**

- any law costs draftsperson who is a member of the Academy of Experts; or
- any law costs draftsperson who is a member of the Expert Witness Institute.[21]

Whilst this would no doubt be a factor that the court would take into account when deciding whether to allow an unauthorised expert assistant to be heard, these provisions do not go so far as to bestow an automatic right of audience on a person who falls within one of the categories. In the editor's experience, however, it is rare for the court to decline the assistance of an experienced costs draftsperson (regardless of whether they fall into either of the categories above), because of the technical nature of the issues that tend to arise in costs litigation.

---

[19] Lord Neuberger and Wall LJ have jointly issued *Practice Guidance (*McKenzie *Friends: Civil and Family Courts)* [2010] 1 WLR 1881 (revising the previous 2008 Direction). *McKenzie* friends are able to do the following (subject to the court ordering otherwise): (a) provide moral support for litigants; (b) take notes; (c) help with case papers; and (d) quietly give advice on any aspect of the conduct of the case. They are *not* able to do the following (subject to the court ordering otherwise): (a) act as the litigants' agent in relation to the proceedings; (b) manage litigants' cases outside court, for example by signing court documents; or (c) address the court, make oral submissions or examine witnesses. Courts should be slow to grant any application from a litigant for a right of audience or a right to conduct litigation to a *McKenzie* friend. This is because a person exercising such rights must ordinarily be properly trained, be under professional discipline (including an obligation to insure against liability for negligence) and be subject to an overriding duty to the court. The court should be prepared to grant such rights only where there is good reason to do so, taking into account all of the circumstances of the case. Such grants should not be extended to lay persons automatically or without due consideration. They should not be granted for mere convenience. Examples of the type of special circumstances that have been held to justify the grant of a right of audience are: (a) that person is a close relative of the litigant; (b) health problems preclude the litigant from addressing the court, or conducting litigation, and the litigant cannot afford to pay for a qualified legal representative; and (c) the litigant is relatively inarticulate and prompting by that person may unnecessarily prolong the proceedings. At the other end of the spectrum, the court may make an order that prevents a person being assisted by a *McKenzie* friend. Examples of circumstances in which this might arise are: (a) the assistance is being provided for an improper purpose; (b) the assistance is unreasonable in nature or degree; (c) the *McKenzie* friend is subject to a civil proceedings order or a civil restraint order; (d) the *McKenzie* friend is using the litigant as a puppet; (e) the *McKenzie* friend is directly or indirectly conducting the litigation; and (f) the court is not satisfied that the *McKenzie* friend fully understands the duty of confidentiality.

[20] See HM Courts & Tribunals Services, *Senior Courts Costs Office Guide* (London: HMSO, 2018), para 1.2(h).

[21] CPR, r 48.6(3)(c); historically, see also CPD, art 52.1.

Authorised Persons

Solicitors, barristers, etc

47.12 Solicitors, barristers and chartered legal executives are able to carry on most reserved legal activities, including nearly all of those that relate to the law of costs—at least at first instance (see 3.80). The fact that a person is authorised does not mean that the court is obliged to hear them,[22] but where it refuses to do so, the court must give its reasons (see 47.17).[23]

Costs lawyers

47.13 A costs lawyer is a specialist costs practitioner who is regulated by the Costs Lawyers Standards Board (CLSB). It is a status that first came into existence on 31 December 2011. As of 26 March 2014, costs lawyers have enjoyed the following rights:

> 'As a Costs Lawyer you are a regulated person under the [Legal Services Act 2007] and are authorised to carry on the following reserved legal activities:
> - The exercise of a right of audience
> - The conduct of litigation
> - The administration of oaths
>
> Provided that you are instructed to deal only with matters that relate to costs, you may conduct proceedings and represent clients in any court or tribunal, including any criminal court or courts martial, the Supreme Court or the Privy Council where:
> - the proceedings are at first instance; or
> - the proceedings include an appeal below the level of the Court of Appeal or Upper Tribunal, are on a first appeal (other than in the Court of Appeal) and the appeal itself relates to costs; or
> - the proceedings do not fall within either of the categories above, but your instructions are limited to dealing with the costs of the proceedings; or
> - the court or tribunal grants permission for you to conduct proceedings or to represent a client (or both).
>
> Where proceedings relate to other matters, in addition to costs, the rights referred to above apply only to those parts of the proceedings (if any) that:
> - relate solely to costs; or
> - when they relate to other issues, solely those issues that are not in dispute.'[24]

47.14 Thus, other than certain appeals, a costs lawyer is able to appear in any matter in which their instructions relate only to costs. This invites the obvious question of what is meant by 'relates to costs'. The CLSB's Code of Conduct: Cost Lawyers 2014 has this to say on the point:

> 'A matter "relates to costs" if it relates to payments for legal representation, including payments in respect of *pro bono* representation under s 194 of the LSA and/or to payments made for bringing or defending any proceedings, but only if and to the extent that those monies are not damages. For the avoidance of doubt, this includes:
> - Costs between opposing parties including costs management and budgeting.

[22] The court has discretion in this regard: see 47.17.
[23] Legal Services Act 2007, s 192(2).
[24] See CLSB Code of Conduct: Costs Lawyers 2014, pp 1–2.

- Solicitor and client costs but not if and to the extent that issues of negligence arise when a Lawyer competent to deal with allegations of negligence ought to be instructed instead.
- Legal aid, criminal costs, wasted costs or costs against third parties.'[25]

The Code of Conduct also makes it clear that a costs lawyer will be an authorised person notwithstanding the fact that their instructions cover issues that do not relate to costs, but only where those issues have been agreed. **47.15**

Where a costs lawyer lacks a right to be heard (such as in an appeal in the Court of Appeal), the court has the power to grant the appropriate right, in which case the costs lawyer will become an excepted person for that purpose.[26] Whilst only a decision on application for permission to appeal, Burnett J has found that a costs lawyer is able to delegate the task of appearing in court to an employee under their direct supervision.[27] **47.16**

Discretion Not to Hear an Authorised Person

The court has the power to refuse to hear from a person who would otherwise have enjoyed a right of audience. The relevant provisions are as follows: **47.17**

> '**192 Powers of court in respect of rights of audience and conduct of litigation**
>
> (1) Nothing in this Act affects the power of any court in any proceedings to refuse to hear a person (for reasons which apply to that person as an individual) who would otherwise have a right of audience before the court in relation to those proceedings.
>
> (2) Where a court refuses to hear a person as mentioned in subsection (1), it must give its reasons for refusing.
>
> (3) Where—
>
> (a) immediately before the commencement of section 13 (entitlement to carry on reserved legal activities), or
>
> (b) by virtue of any provision made by or under an enactment passed subsequently,
>
> a court does not permit the appearance of advocates, or permits the appearance of advocates only with leave, no person may exercise a right of audience before the court, in relation to any proceedings, solely by virtue of being entitled to do so under this Act.
>
> (4) But a court may not limit the right to appear before the court in any proceedings to only some of those who are entitled to exercise that right by virtue of this Act.
>
> (5) A court may not limit the right to conduct litigation in relation to proceedings before the court to only some of those who are entitled to exercise that right by virtue of this Act.
>
> (6) In this section "advocate", in relation to any proceedings, means a person exercising a right of audience as a representative of, or on behalf of, any party to the proceedings.'[28]

[25] See *ibid*, pp 1–2.
[26] See Legal Services Act 2007, Sch 3, para 1(2).
[27] *Kynaston v Carroll* [2011] EWHC 2179 (QB), at [6]–[8].
[28] Legal Services Act 2007, s 192.

Advocates who Wish to be Heard on their Own Fees

47.18 There is a lack of judicial consensus as to whether the court should hear an advocate who seeks to be heard on the topic of their own fees. The court usually tolerates (and occasionally encourages) the attendance of solicitors at detailed assessments, but, as is set out below, it is often less accommodating where it is counsel who seeks to be heard.

47.19 There are competing factors that may affect counsel's ability to assist the court: counsel will usually know a great deal about the claim and would be able to assist the court in that regard, but might lack objectivity—especially if they have a financial interest in the matter. It was this latter factor that troubled Cazalet J:

> 'Mr B, who was junior counsel in the main case, also appeared before us in this review of taxation. As was to be expected of him, he made his submissions in a balanced and measured way. However, I do not consider that, as a general rule, counsel who has appeared in the substantive case should be instructed to appear at taxation of costs review concerning the same case and involving his own fees. Although we do not suggest that there is any professional impropriety in this, such a course could lead to submissions being confused with evidence and possible loss of objective assessment.'[29]

47.20 Leveson J, however, came to a different conclusion. Giving judgment in a case concerning criminal costs, he believed that counsel could assist:

> 'Whatever might have been the position in 1995 [when Cazalet J made the comments above], and with very great respect to [him], I do not accept that his concerns have the same validity today. After all, summary assessment of costs (albeit at a much reduced level) not infrequently requires counsel to justify their own brief fee or challenge that of an opponent ... Furthermore, solicitors regularly appear on assessments to justify their own costs (with or without the assistance of costs draftsmen) and there is no reason to believe that barristers are less able sensibly to justify their own fees. Obviously, if any member of the bar (or indeed a solicitor for the rules are the same) feels so emotionally involved in a case that he wishes to instruct and advocate to appear on his behalf, he is perfectly entitled to do so. However, it does not seem to me that this should justify his being indemnified against the costs of so doing (over and above that which he would himself have been entitled to recover) ...'[30]

47.21 The comments of Leveson J are not binding, not least because they relate to a criminal case. The difference between criminal and civil costs is significant, and ought not to be overlooked.[31] Perhaps the law is that each case must be decided on its own facts and that the court should take into account all of the relevant factors (which would include those mentioned by both Cazalet J and Leveson J). Regardless of whether counsel is able to be heard, there can usually be no objection to counsel preparing a written note to be handed to the costs judge; whether such a note is to be regarded as evidence or a submission is a

[29] *F v F* [1995] 2 FLR 702, at 713D.

[30] *Jackson v Lord Chancellor* [2003] EWHC 626 (QB), at [12].

[31] In particular, in a criminal case, counsel will usually be engaged in a well-defined exercise, the purpose of which will be apparent to all concerned (ie they will be fighting their corner for the purposes of getting paid). The same would not necessarily be true in a civil matter, because counsel may or may not have an interest in the matter (or, at the very least, may fear that they are at risk of not getting paid even if the legal niceties suggest otherwise).

moot point, but there is little doubt that, in principle, the court is entitled to take such a note into account.[32]

The Senior Courts Costs Office Guide 2018 says that if counsel appears on their own behalf, they are not entitled to a fee. It goes on to say that 'counsel's clerks ... do not have any right of audience', but that, 'in an exceptional case, counsel's clerk may be allowed a hearing on behalf of counsel if counsel so requests in writing and if the Costs Judge or Costs Officer so allows'.[33] **47.22**

The Authority of Costs Practitioners

The following discussion examines the topic of when representatives have the authority to bind their clients. It does not attempt a detailed analysis of the issue; rather, it deals with this issue only from the standpoint of costs litigation. A brief discussion of the language and principles of agency can be found at 22.02–22.05. **47.23**

Where a person is represented by counsel or by a solicitor, then, unless there is reason to believe otherwise, both the court and their opponent are entitled to assume that the representative has actual authority both to represent and to bind the person who instructs them. A solicitor retained under a 'general retainer' will have actual authority for the purposes of preserving and protecting its client's interests; this would be so even where there was an absence of specific instructions.[34] The ambit of authority in other cases must be determined on the facts. That said, an agent will have implied authority to carry out all acts that are necessary or ordinarily incidental to the exercise of their express authority; hence the agent's authority will not be limited solely to the principal's precise commands.[35] **47.24**

Where there is an absence of actual authority, the court may find that the representative has 'ostensible' or 'apparent' authority.[36] This would allow the court to interpret the actions of the representative as if they had actual authority in relation to those actions. In the context of company law rather than costs, Lord Hatherly explained the concept of ostensible authority: **47.25**

> 'When there are persons conducting the affairs of the company in a manner which appears to be perfectly consonant with the articles of association, those so dealing with them externally are not to be affected by irregularities which may take place in the internal management of the company.'[37]

Where a solicitor or counsel negotiates a compromise, they will, in the ordinary run of things, have ostensible authority to do so. This will be so unless the compromise takes in **47.26**

[32] See *Armitage v Nurse* [2000] 2 Costs LR 231.

[33] See HM Courts & Tribunals Services, *Senior Courts Costs Office Guide* (London: HMSO, 2018), para 1.2(g).

[34] *Donsland Ltd (a firm) v Van Hoogstraten* [2002] EWCA Civ 253.

[35] See, eg, *Gavaghan v Edwards* [1961] 2 QB 220, [1961] 2 All ER 477, CA, in which the legal representatives were found to have authority to make a memorandum recording an agreement.

[36] See *Royal British Bank v Turquand* (1856) 6 E&B 327; *Criterion Properties plc v Stratford UK Properties LLC* [2004] UKHL 28. Circumstances may also exist in which agency by estoppel may be created, which, in the present context, is similar to a finding of ostensible authority: see the discussion of this concept in *Rama Corpn Ltd v Proved Tin and General Investments Ltd* [1952] 2 QB 147.

[37] *Mahoney v East Holyford Mining Co* (1875) LR 7 HL 869, at 894.

matters collateral to the claim. A matter would not be collateral to the claim unless it were to take in extraneous subject matter, such as a compromise of a claim for damages that took into account a debt entirely unrelated to the claim. A compromise would not take in matters collateral to the claim merely because it resulted in the parties coming to an agreement that the court could not itself have ordered.[38]

47.27 The position in respect of costs draftspersons is not so clear, because neither the court nor an opponent can be sure that a person who describes themselves as such is under any form of professional duty, still less that they owe a duty to ensure that they have authority. Neill LJ made the following *obiter* comments about the issue of ostensible authority of costs draftspersons:

> 'On the facts of the present case, however, I do not find it necessary to reach a final decision as to the ostensible authority of an independent costs draftsman, but I am inclined to the view that where a solicitor sends a costs draftsman to a taxation the other parties to the litigation are entitled to assume in the absence of any information to the contrary or unless the sums involved are very large, that the costs draftsman has the same authority as the solicitor would have had to consent to orders which are not plainly collateral to the matters before the taxation officer.'[39]

47.28 Evans LJ agreed and added the following comments of his own:

> 'As regards the authority, actual or apparent, of an independent costs draftsman who attends before the taxing officer, it should be remembered that he can appear on behalf of the party only as a duly authorised representative of the solicitor who has instructed him to be there. The scope of his apparent authority would be the same, in my judgment, as that of any costs draftsman employed by the firm.'[40]

These comments seem to have narrowed the gap between the authority of employed costs draftspersons and that of independent costs draftspersons. In so far as costs lawyers are concerned, it might be relevant that they are subject to a professional duty to keep clients properly informed as to the progress of their instructions.[41]

47.29 Thus, unless there is reason to believe otherwise or unless the sums involved are very large, a costs draftsperson will be regarded as having authority to speak for and to bind the person who instructs them, as will a costs lawyer. Another way of analysing the matter would be to say that costs draftspersons have implied authority to act in accordance with the customs of their profession, which would include having authority to bind their clients.[42] Even where a representative does not have actual or ostensible authority, the subsequent conduct of the person who instructed that representative may ratify their actions.[43] Ratification must be by adoption of the agent's acts or by acquiescence thereto;[44] ratification may be express or it may be implied, usually by conduct.[45] This means that it is not always the case that the

38 *Waugh v HB Clifford & Sons Ltd* [1982] Ch 374.
39 *Waterston Hicks v Eliopoulos* (1995) Costs LR core vol 363, at 372.
40 *Ibid*, at 373.
41 See ACL Code of Conduct 2011, art 6.8.
42 Whilst a non-costs case, see *Lienard v Dresslar* (1862) 3 F & F 212.
43 See *OPM Property Services Ltd v Venner* [2004] EWHC 427 (Ch); see also *Re Vimbos Ltd* [1900] 1 Ch 470.
44 *Lythgoe v Vernon* (1860) 5 H & N 180.
45 *Soames v Spencer* (1822) 1 Dow & Ry KB 32.

costs draftsperson would need to have had actual authority at the time that the agreement, offer or concession was made.

Bankrupt Persons

47.30 Between the date of the bankruptcy order and the appointment of the trustee, a bankrupt retains the right of audience in relation to their estate. The Official Receiver is the receiver and manager of the debtor's estate during this time.[46]

47.31 Following the appointment of a trustee, the bankrupt has no right to be heard unless the court makes an order under s 303 of the Insolvency Act 1986 (or, of course, unless the litigation relates to matters that have arisen after the bankruptcy). Indeed, a bankrupt person relinquishes all control over their estate to the trustee and, as such, is not able to take any steps in relation to their estate.[47]

Companies

47.32 CPR, r 39.6, provides that a company or other corporation may be represented at trial by an employee if: (a) the employee has been authorised by the company or corporation to appear at trial on its behalf; and (b) the court gives permission. An assessment, however, is not a trial. The Senior Courts Costs Office Guide 2018 points out that PD 39A, para 5, applies to all hearings, the implication being that it is the procedure to be followed at an assessment hearing.[48] The relevant part of PD 39A, para 5, reads as follows:

> '5.2 Where a party is a company or other corporation and is to be represented at a hearing by an employee the written statement should contain the following additional information:
> (1) The full name of the company or corporation as stated in its certificate of registration.
> (2) The registered number of the company or corporation.
> (3) The position or office in the company or corporation held by the representative.
> (4) The date on which and manner in which the representative was authorised to act for the company or corporation, e.g. _________ 19____: written authority from managing director; or _________ 19____: Board resolution dated _________ 19____ .
>
> 5.3 Rule 39.6 is intended to enable a company or other corporation to represent itself as a litigant in person. Permission under rule 39.6(b) should therefore be given by the court unless there is some particular and sufficient reason why it should be withheld. In considering whether to grant permission the matters to be taken into account include the complexity of the issues and the experience and position in the company or corporation of the proposed representative.
>
> 5.4 Permission under rule 39.6(b) should be obtained in advance of the hearing from, preferably, the judge who is to hear the case, but may, if it is for any reason impracticable or inconvenient to do so, be obtained from any judge by whom the case could be heard.
>
> 5.5 The permission may be obtained informally and without notice to the other parties. The judge who gives the permission should record in writing that he has done so and supply a copy to the company or corporation in question and to any other party who asks for one.'

[46] See Insolvency Act 1986, s 287.
[47] See Insolvency Act 1986, ss 311 and 312.
[48] See HM Courts & Tribunals Services, *Senior Courts Costs Office Guide* (London: HMSO, 2018), para 1.2(c).

48

ALTERNATIVE DISPUTE RESOLUTION OF COSTS DISPUTES

48.01 This chapter deals with alternative dispute resolution (ADR) in the context of disputes about the amounts of costs. It deals with the following topics:

- costs ADR in general:
  - a definition of ADR and types of costs ADR (48.04);
  - the benefits of costs ADR (48.06);
  - policy, the CPR and ADR (48.08);
  - proposing ADR and responding to such proposals (48.11);
- costs mediation:
  - the nature of costs mediation (48.13);
  - the benefits and drawbacks of mediation (48.15);
  - mediators and mediation providers (48.17);
  - facilitative and evaluative mediation (48.29);
  - the funding of mediations and costs (48.50);
- early neutral evaluation (48.58):
  - the procedure of early neutral evaluation (48.62);
  - the funding of early neutral evaluation (48.64);
- costs arbitration (48.65):
  - the nature of costs arbitration (48.66);
  - jurisdictional issues (48.69);
  - the principles of arbitration (48.73);
  - arbitration agreements (48.76);
  - procedural issues (48.78);
  - pendulum arbitration (48.87);
  - arbitration awards (48.93);
  - the funding of arbitration proceedings (48.95); and
  - the costs of arbitration (48.97).

48.02 In common with many practitioners, the editor knows that ADR works,[1] but confesses to being less than expert on its key points. He has therefore sought the assistance of people who are experts on the topic—namely, Deputy Master Campbell (now a consultant at

[1] A poll of costs mediators carried out in 2017 has revealed that around 85 per cent of costs cases settle on the day. Some mediators report that they see 100 per cent of their cases settling on the day or within five days, once instructions have been taken.

Kain Knight and a mediator with Costs Alternative Dispute Resolution), Jonathan Dingle (costs mediator, arbitrator and course leader for the Society of Mediators) and Matthew Smith of Kings Chambers.

Much of what follows draws on *The Jackson ADR Handbook*,[2] which should be consulted for a more in-depth analysis of ADR in general.[3] **48.03**

Costs ADR in General

A definition of ADR and types of costs ADR

The term 'alternative dispute resolution' has no universally agreed definition, but the Civil Procedure Rules (CPR) define it as a 'collective description of methods of resolving disputes otherwise than through the normal trial process'.[4] The authors of *The Jackson ADR Handbook* use the term to mean 'the full range of alternatives to litigation potentially available to resolve a civil dispute'.[5] They go on to draw a distinction between adjudicative and non-adjudicative forms of ADR: **48.04**

> 'An ADR process may result in a binding decision being made by a third party (adjudicative) or by the parties themselves by agreement (non-adjudicative). There may be a relatively formal procedure (as in arbitration) or substantial flexibility (as in negotiation). The process may be paper-based, internet-based, or involve meetings. The process may be evaluative (with proposals for a fair outcome being made) or facilitative.'[6]

The forms of ADR that are most commonly encountered in the context of costs disputes are: **48.05**

- mediation (both facilitative and evaluative) (see 48.13);
- early neutral evaluation (ENE) (see 48.58); and
- arbitration (including pendulum arbitration) (see 48.65).

By far the most common is facilitative mediation.

The benefits of costs ADR

Once a costs order has been made, the parties are not bound to resolve the issue of the amount of costs payable by way of detailed assessment. Costs may be agreed and frequently are, but where that does not happen and where negotiations have seemingly broken down, the parties may agree to engage in ADR. The authors of *The Jackson ADR Handbook* have this to say on the importance of such methods of dispute resolution: **48.06**

> 'In the resolution of a civil dispute, anyone is entitled to a fair opportunity to put their case, within a reasonable time, at a reasonable cost, and with appropriate independent input to

[2] Blake, S, Browne, J, and Sime, S, *The Jackson ADR Handbook* (Oxford: Oxford University Press, 2016). The book was not written by Sir Rupert Jackson, but in response to his recommendation that an authoritative handbook should be written that deals in detail with the topic of ADR: see *ibid*, para 1.14, referring to Jackson, R, *Review of Civil Litigation Costs: Final Report* (London: HMSO, 2010), recommendation 75.

[3] Reference may also be made to Dingle, J, and Sephton, J, *Practical Mediation* (Minehead: LawBrief, 2017).

[4] See the Glossary to the CPR.

[5] Blake, S, Browne, J, and Sime, S, *The Jackson ADR Handbook* (Oxford: Oxford University Press, 2016), para 1.02.

[6] *Ibid*, para 1.03.

ensure fairness. The quality of justice in the courts of England and Wales is very well respected. However, there are circumstances in which options other than litigation may be more cost effective, quicker, or flexible, while still resulting in a fair outcome. The potential litigant should be sufficiently aware of, and appropriately advised about, other options. Alternative dispute resolution (ADR) has a long and respected history in this jurisdiction. It has received increasing support from the Civil Procedure Rules 1998 and associated Practice Directions, the judiciary, and developments in government policy. We have reached the stage, not least following the introduction of the Jackson Reforms from 1 April 2013, when resolution through ADR processes needs to be given serious consideration as part of resolving almost any civil dispute, forming part of case and costs management. Rises in court fees and limits in the availability of legal aid funding are also making the potential use of ADR more attractive.'[7]

48.07 Parties may wish to consider ADR as an alternative to detailed assessment for wide-ranging reasons. Some are obvious; others, less so. They include the following.[8]

- **Saving of expense** If ADR is successful, it can avoid both the payment of court fees (see 43.186) and the expense of attending detailed assessment. If mediation or early neutral evaluation—in particular—are carried out at a sufficiently early stage, the savings may be considerable. Costs savings are less likely with arbitration, but they may still be made (especially with pendulum arbitration and paper-based arbitration).
- **Speed of settlement** Mediation and early neutral evaluation (but, in general, not arbitration) may take place quickly and at an early stage, which may be particularly important where the parties have other business concerns to be getting on with—especially where the parties wish to have an ongoing business relationship. For receiving parties, ADR may result in accelerated receipt of the money; for insured paying parties, it may mean a more prompt closure of the book of business for the insurer.
- **Choice of form and forum** Persons who engage in ADR will be able to choose both the form of ADR and the ADR provider. This may be of particular importance where the dispute calls for expertise of a certain type (which tends to be common in disputes about costs).
- **Choice of venue and timing** ADR will afford the parties the benefit of being able to choose the location for ADR and the dates on which it will take place.
- **Control of process** Whilst many ADR providers will have their own method of working and will use their own standard contractual documentation, the parties will, in general, have a degree of freedom as to the procedure to be adopted. This is particularly true of mediation and early neutral evaluation.
- **Flexibility of process** In mediation and early neutral evaluation, the process of ADR will, in general, be considerably more flexible than that of detailed assessment. This is less true of arbitration, but there is still a degree of flexibility in this regard (especially with pendulum arbitration).
- **Confidentiality** Court hearings are generally held in public; confidentiality may be more easily preserved through ADR.
- **Use of a problem-solving approach** Commercial considerations often apply. In particular, it may be that the parties wish to have a continuing business relationship and,

[7] *Ibid*, para 1.01.
[8] Adapted from *ibid*, paras 2.30–2.40.

where this is so, dealing with costs in a cooperative and problem-solving way may yield benefits.

- **Risk management** Any or all of the parties may have difficulties with their cases; risk may be more easily controlled through ADR than through litigation. For example, a receiving party may have a potentially defective conditional fee agreement: by proceeding to a detailed assessment, they may end up with nothing, but by making sensible use of ADR, they may benefit from a less harsh outcome. Similarly, a paying party who has turned down an offer under CPR, Part 36, may be at risk of having to pay an 'additional sum' *plus* enhanced interest if they were to proceed to an assessment (see 17.81 and 43.345). Such a risk may be best managed through ADR.

Policy, the CPR and ADR

Whilst there are no provisions dealing specifically with the ADR of costs disputes, the CPR and its associated practice directions and protocols are redolent of support for ADR in general, as are court guides and court-based mediation schemes. The following are of particular note.[9] **48.08**

- **The overriding objective** Those aspects of the overriding objective that go to saving expense and ensuring that cases are dealt with expeditiously (see CPR, r 1.1(2)) are entirely consistent with the use of ADR.[10] Indeed, parties may be expected to draw perceived obstacles to ADR to the court's attention at a sufficiently early stage of the proceedings to allow those obstacles to be overcome.[11]
- **Case management** CPR, r 1.4(2)(a), expressly provides that the court must encourage the parties to cooperate with each other in the conduct of the proceedings. Moreover, CPR, r 1.4(2)(e), specifically requires the court to encourage the parties to use ADR if the court considers that appropriate. The court has the power to stay proceedings[12]—a power that is often used for the purposes of facilitating ADR. Indeed, the court may even give guidance—which may be robust—relating to the use of ADR.[13]
- **Court guides and schemes** Whilst the Senior Court Costs Office (SCCO) Guide 2018 makes no mention of ADR of costs disputes, other court guides do.[14] There have been, and still are, many court-based mediation schemes[15]—albeit not ones that encompass costs disputes.
- **Costs management** Whilst they would rarely apply to detailed assessment proceedings, costs management orders tend to make specific provision for ADR.

In addition to these specific provisions, there is considerable judicial enthusiasm for ADR in general, and for mediation in particular. Dyson LJ had the following to say on the topic: **48.09**

---

9 Adapted from *ibid*, para 1.05.

10 See, eg, *Dyson v Leeds City Council* [2000] CP Rep 42, *per* Lord Woolf.

11 See, eg, *PGF II SA v OMFS Co* [2012] EWHC 83 (TCC).

12 See CPR, r 3.1(f).

13 See, eg, *Brookfield Construction (UK) Ltd v Mott Macdonald Ltd* [2010] EWHC 659 (TCC), *per* Coulson J.

14 See, eg, Chancery Guide, Appx 1 and 15; Queen's Bench Division Guide, para 6.6; Technology and Construction Court Guide, para 7 and Appx E.

15 Examples include a pilot scheme in the Central London County Court in 1996 and a mediation scheme in the Court of Appeal, which was established in 1997. Indeed, on 30 March 2012, it was announced that there would be a pilot under which all cases in the Court of Appeal would be referred to mediation unless the court ordered otherwise.

'Parties sometimes need to be encouraged by the court to embark on an ADR. The need for such encouragement should diminish in time if the virtue of ADR in suitable cases is demonstrated even more convincingly than it has been thus far. The value and importance of ADR have been established within a remarkably short time. All members of the legal profession who conduct litigation should now routinely consider with their clients whether their disputes are suitable for ADR. But we reiterate that the court's role is to encourage, not to compel. The form of encouragement may be robust.'[16]

In a similar vein, Lord Neuberger (speaking extrajudicially) described ADR as 'litigation's invaluable twin'.[17]

48.10 It is not only the court that encourages ADR as a matter of policy; parties may do so too. Most notably, government departments tend to engage in ADR as a matter of policy.[18] Again, this is an approach that is encouraged by the courts.[19]

Proposing ADR and responding to such proposals

48.11 The authors of *The Jackson ADR Handbook* give the following advice about how and when ADR should be proposed:

'Reasonable consideration of the use of ADR ... might include the following:

- advice from the lawyer to the client on the potential benefits of ADR, the types of ADR that might best suit the case, and the timing of the use of ADR;
- evidence of consideration of ADR options by the client, and the decision taken;
- if no form of ADR is thought appropriate, specific reasons why;
- a proposal to the other side as regards the reasonable use of ADR;
- a request to the other side in relation to any particular steps identified to facilitate the use of ADR;
- if the decision taken by a client might not be considered objectively reasonable, advice for the lawyer as regards the potential risks;
- the provision of sufficient information about the matters in dispute for the other party to make informed decisions about settlement, or reasons why it was inappropriate to provide such information;
- that proceedings were only started as a matter of last resort, because settlement could not be further explored at that time.'[20]

48.12 They go on to give the following advice about how to respond to any such proposal:

'Responding to a proposal in relation to ADR made ... might include the following:

- if the proposal is accepted, any terms in relation to the acceptance;
- if a proposal is refused, sufficient reasons to show that the refusal was reasonable. A failure to reply might be seen as a refusal to engage in ADR. A rejection of the use of ADR before

---

16 *Halsey v Milton Keynes General NHS Trust* [2004] EWCA Civ 576, at [11].

17 See Lord Neuberger, 'Equity, ADR, Arbitration and the Law: The Fourth Keating Lecture', Lincoln's Inn, 19 May 2010. See also Jackson, R, 'The Role of Alternative Dispute Resolution in Furthering the Aims of the Civil Litigation Costs Review: Eleventh Implementation Lecture', RICS Expert Witness Conference, 8 March 2012.

18 See, eg, Lord Chancellor's Department, 'Government Pledges to Settle Legal Disputes out of Court', Press Notice 117/01, 23 March 2001.

19 See, eg, *R (Cowl) v Plymouth City Council* [2001] EWCA Civ 1935, at [25], in which Lord Woolf said that a 'failure to adopt [ADR], in particular where public money is involved, [is] indefensible'.

20 Blake, S, Browne, J, and Sime, S, *The Jackson ADR Handbook* (Oxford: Oxford University Press, 2016), para 8.21.

the issue of proceedings may be penalised, though the failure will be balanced against other factors ...

- if there is concern about the use of ADR that might be addressed, that the concern is raised with the other party at that time;
- if there may be q request for further relevant information before a decision on ADR is taken;
- if one form is ADR is not thought suitable, a more appropriate form may be proposed, and this is best done at the time and not in a latter unrelated offer;
- letter may usefully address the '*Halsey* factors'[21] relevant to the use of ADR ... but should do so in ways which engage sufficiently with the details of the case in question.'[22]

The *Halsey* factors are addressed in detail at 6.123–6.139.

Costs Mediation

The nature of costs mediation

Mediation is a non-adjudicative method of ADR. The authors of *The Jackson ADR Handbook* define it as '[a] non-adjudicative dispute resolution process under which the parties agree to try to reach a settlement of their dispute with the assistance of an independent third party using a process agreed by the parties'.[23] As is explained below, there are two styles of costs mediation: the facilitative style (see 48.29); and the evaluative style (see 48.48). **48.13**

Costs mediation is markedly different from detailed assessment proceedings. In particular, the parties—often referred to as 'participants'—may: **48.14**

- appoint the mediator (in contrast with detailed assessment, in which the court allocates the matter to a judge);
- fix a mutually convenient date on which the mediation will take place (in contrast with detailed assessment, in which the court will set the hearing date, usually without consulting the parties);
- choose the venue for the mediation (in contrast with detailed assessment, in which the court will, in general, determine the venue);
- decide how long the mediation is to last (in contrast with detailed assessment, in which the court will adjourn part-heard if business cannot be completed in the time available);
- agree how much the mediator will be paid (in contrast with detailed assessment, in which a prescribed court fee is payable);
- agree and sign a mediation agreement under which provision may—and usually is—made for all matters discussed at the mediation to remain confidential (in contrast which court proceedings, in which what is said is generally recorded and may enter the public domain);
- make offers and proposals of any kind, whilst at the same time retaining control over the effect of any such offers (in contrast with court proceedings, in which the judge may take the matter out of the parties' hands and offers may have ongoing effects);

[21] After *Halsey v Milton Keynes General NHS Trust* [2004] EWCA Civ 576.

[22] Blake, S, Browne, J, and Sime, S, *The Jackson ADR Handbook* (Oxford: Oxford University Press, 2016), para 8.20.

[23] *Ibid*, Glossary and Abbreviations.

- inform the mediator of any offers of settlement (in contrast with court proceedings, in which the judge hearing the assessment is generally kept in ignorance of such offers);
- decide which documents, materials and position statements, if any, are to be made available to the mediator (in contrast with court proceedings, in which certain documents must be lodged at court and the receiving party may be put to their election—see 46.40–46.74);
- retain a degree of control over how the mediation will progress (in contrast with court proceedings, in which the judge will have control over such matters);
- agree on the extent to which the proceedings should be adversarial (in contrast with court proceedings, which are always adversarial);
- agree not to be bound by any opinions or views that the mediator may express (in contrast with court proceedings, in which the parties will, subject to appeal, be bound by decisions of the judge);
- choose whether and when to terminate the mediation for any or no reason (in contrast with detailed assessment proceedings, in which the parties will generally be able to terminate the court proceedings only by settlement or by one side capitulating);
- choose to continue discussions after the mediation has concluded (in contrast with court proceedings, in which a decision of the court will generally be enforced in accordance with its terms); and
- choose to bring absolute finality to the dispute by settling the dispute (in contrast with court proceedings, in which a decision of a judge may be amenable to appeal).

The benefits and drawbacks of mediation

48.15 The authors of *The Jackson ADR Handbook* point to the following potential benefits of mediation:

> 'The main potential benefits of mediation are:
> - a neutral third party can help a party to see the strengths and weaknesses of a case more clearly;
> - a mediator can help parties step outside an adversarial framework and entrenched positions, so mediation may work where negotiation has failed;
> - a mediator can make possible offers and concessions look more acceptable;
> - a robust and experienced mediator can help to find a way forward even in a relatively intractable dispute;
> - the structure of mediation allows a lawyer and client time to review offers and options in a way that may not be possible in negotiation;
> - the flexibility of mediation can be used to advantage, for example letting an party make a statement of particular personal importance; mediation generally achieves good success rates and party satisfaction.'[24]

48.16 They go on to draw attention to the following drawbacks:

> 'The main potential drawbacks of mediation are:
> - success depends on the abilities of the mediator;
> - mediation can increase costs if a case might have been resolved by negotiation, or if the mediation fails;
> - mediation may need to be approached with skill by a mediator and by lawyers if a party tries to misuse the process, etc to get an unjustified result in a weak case;

[24] *Ibid*, para 2.22.

- mediation may not work if the parties are deeply antagonistic;
- mediation can be more difficult where one or both parties are not represented, and/or not fully advised in advance.'[25]

Procedural matters in mediation

Mediators and mediation providers

There is no specific formal regulation of costs mediators. That said, the Civil Mediation Council was set up in 2003 for the purposes of developing standards for training and practice,[26] and some mediators are accredited with that body, whilst all organisations registered with that body will comply with its standards. That body complies with the EU Code of Conduct for Mediators. **48.17**

In a technical field such as costs ADR, experience has shown that the more skilled and experienced the mediator, the better the chances of success will be. An understanding of costs law will generally be a prerequisite for any costs mediator, as would be a knowledge of mediation (preferably gained as a result of formal costs mediation training).[27] At the time of writing, there were about 20 regularly practising costs mediators in England and Wales; the small size of the pool means that practitioners tend to be commensurately experienced. **48.18**

Mediators may or may not provide their services under the auspices of a provider organisation. One such organisation is Costs Alternative Dispute Resolution (CADR)—the only dedicated costs mediation service currently active. Other panels of mediators—including CEDR, MediateLegal and Clerksroom—offer mediators who have a costs practice. Trust Mediation offers costs mediation in the context of personal injury and contributory negligence. As far as the editor is aware, CADR is the only panel to require its members to have undertaken a costs mediation course involving facilitative and evaluative costs mediation training. It may be that others will follow suit in the future. **48.19**

In a costs mediation, it is usual for the mediator to have knowledge of relevant costs law. Indeed, many mediators are former costs judges or are barristers who specialise in costs. The mediator's role is not to decide issues or points of law, but it is generally advantageous for a mediator to have an understanding of how a costs judge might adjudicate upon the matters preventing settlement. **48.20**

In contrast to proceedings in court, it is for the parties to decide who should speak and in what order. The more that the mediator can foster and encourage discussions between the parties, and the less that they participate themselves in cross-table talk, the better—because the mediator's skill is in the restarting of a conversation and the reopening of a line of communication between the parties that has broken down. **48.21**

The mediator must be neutral and must not pressurise or otherwise coerce parties into a settlement; use of skills such as listening, tact, diplomacy and patience are much more likely to yield results. **48.22**

[25] *Ibid*, para 2.23.

[26] See http://www.civilmediation.org

[27] There is only one course that includes costs mediation and evaluation skills: that offered by mediation charity The Society of Mediators.

48.23 In a specialised field such as costs, it is probable that the mediator will be known to the parties, but that does not of itself place the mediator in a position of conflict. Since the mediator will not, in general, be making decisions or deciding issues, being known to the parties is unlikely to present any difficulty in practice. That said, it is for the parties to choose the mediator: if one prospective mediator has a close professional or personal connection with one or other of the parties, their appointment will not be agreed and the parties will need to look elsewhere. In the rare case that a conflict of interest emerges after the mediator has accepted the appointment or when the mediation has begun, it is within the power of all three to terminate the mediation with immediate effect.

The timing of costs mediation

48.24 In general, costs mediation may take place at any time after the costs order is made, but it is likely that the parties will wish to mediate with the benefit of a bill of costs, points of dispute and replies (if any). As such, mediation tends to take place only after those documents have been served.

48.25 Early mediation tends to result in greater savings than later mediation. In particular, if mediation takes place before detailed assessment proceedings have been commenced, the court fee will be saved, which may result in substantial savings.

Mediation agreements

48.26 In general, the participants will be required to enter into a mediation agreement, which is a contract that both defines the contractual relationship between the participants and the mediator, and establishes certain rules in relation to the conduct of the mediation. A typical mediation agreement will deal with the following matters.

- **Administrative details** This will include matters such as the identity of the participants, the identity of the mediator, the venue for the mediation, and the date and time on which it will take place.
- **The ambit of the mediation** This will define (or at least identify) the dispute that will be the subject of the mediation. This need not be the entirety of the dispute that exists between the participants.
- **The role of the mediator** Most agreements will make it clear that the mediator is independent and impartial, and will—unless the participants agree otherwise or the law so requires—be bound by a duty of confidentiality. Where appropriate, many agreements expressly record the fact that the mediator is obliged to adhere to whichever code of conduct they are governed by. Agreements may also provide that the mediator does not provide legal or professional advice and will not deliver a judgment or award.
- **Payment and indemnification of the mediator** Most agreements will set out the terms of payment of the mediator's fees. Many will also provide that:
  - the mediator may not be required to disclose their notes of the mediation and that they may not be required to give evidence; and
  - should the mediator incur costs in resisting any attempt to force disclosure or the giving of evidence, the participant who seeks to do so will be required to provide an indemnity in respect of those costs.
- **Authority** Most mediation agreements require the signatories to confirm that they have authority to settle the dispute.

- **Confidentiality** Nearly all mediation agreements contain a provision that enshrines the confidential nature of the mediation (see 48.43). In addition, it is common for agreement to confirm the fact that communications passing between the participants for the purposes of trying to settle the dispute are subject to the 'without prejudice' doctrine (see 48.43 and 48.44).
- **Settlement** Many agreements stipulate that any settlement reached will become binding only upon it being reduced into writing and signed by the participants.
- **Termination** Most agreements will provide for ways in which the mediation can be terminated. Usually, this will be by agreement or by settlement, but provision will be made under which the mediator is at liberty to end the mediation at their discretion, without giving reasons.
- **Costs** Many agreements also make provision as to the costs of the mediation (such as each participant will bear its own costs unless the court orders otherwise, where the mediation has not resulted in a settlement and has proceeded to a detailed assessment, or the participants otherwise agree).
- **Cancellation** Most agreements stipulate how fees will be paid in the event that the mediation is cancelled, either because the dispute has been settled or for other reasons. Usually, a reduced fee is payable depending upon how close to the date fixed for the mediation the cancellation occurs.

The terms of a mediation agreement may be enforced by the courts,[28] including by way of injunction.[29] **48.27**

The conclusion of mediations

Upon conclusion of a mediation, it will generally be for the parties to draw up and execute a settlement agreement. **48.28**

Facilitative mediation and evaluative mediation

Facilitative mediation

Most costs mediations will be in—or at least will contain elements of—the facultative style, which is where the mediator helps the participants to resolve the dispute by facilitating negotiations. Indeed, this is the primary form of mediation. The authors of *The Jackson ADR Handbook* have this to say about that style of mediation: **48.29**

> 'Although the mediator is there as a facilitator, the mediator's role is not a passive one. The facilitative mediator will:
> - ask questions that test the strengths and weaknesses of each side's case;
> - explore each party's situation and help them identify what they really need or want to achieve from the dispute;
> - encourage the parties to think about the likely outcome of the litigation and the costs of obtaining that outcome;
> - focus each party's attention on their underlying objectives and needs, rather than on a strict analysis and evaluation of the merits of their case;
> - help the parties work out a creative solution that is in their best interests;

---

28 See, eg, *Brown v Rice* [2007] EWHC 625 (Ch).

29 *Venture Investment Placement Ltd v Hall* [2005] EWHC 1227 (Ch).

- assist the parties to negotiate more effectively by formulating offers in a way that may be more attractive to the other side, and considering the timing and staging of offers and concessions.'[30]

48.30 As can be seen, a mediator who adopts the facilitative style does not express an opinion on the merits of each party's case or the likely outcome of the dispute. This distinguishes facilitative mediation from evaluative mediation (see 48.48).

48.31 **Preparation for facilitative mediation (and mediation in general)** There will often be a degree of contact between the participants and the mediator in advance of the mediation, as an opportunity for a decision to be taken as to what papers the mediator should see. The authors of *The Jackson ADR Handbook* suggest the following list of matters that the mediator may wish to consider:

- '[C]heck that the parties understand the process;
- obtain information on any particular needs and objectives that each party may have;
- discuss practical matters such as the venue, the date and time of the mediation, the duration of the mediation, and any special arrangements that need to be made for any of the parties;
- identify the individuals who should attend the mediation, advise on the document to be provided and the preparation that each of the parties should do for the mediation;
- set the timetable for the mediation and the dates by which steps should be taken by each party in order to prepare for the mediation. This is usually also set out in an letter to the parties;
- explore who is intending to take lead in the negotiations and the opening plenary session, and the role that the lay client will have;
- explore with the lawyers, particularly where the lay client is a public body, a company, partnership or backed by an insurer, that the representative attending the mediation has full authority to settle the dispute, whatever emerges during the negotiation process, or at the very least robust arrangements are in place to seek additional authority where necessary. If he or she has not, the mediator will try to persuade the lawyer to ensure that someone more senior, who has the appropriate authority, attends the mediation;
- form a view of the personalities of the parties involved and the way they interact with the other parties and the strength of feeling they have in respect of the issues;
- discuss how to approach and structure the mediation.'[31]

48.32 In the context of costs mediation, the participants will wish to consider which documents the mediator will see in advance. Whilst there is no requirement for bundles to be agreed, it is helpful if key documents common to the participants can be placed into a joint (core) bundle. These will include the bill of costs, points of dispute and replies (if any), any offers made by the parties, any relevant court orders and a transcript of the court judgment at trial (if there is one). Excessive documentation will do nothing other than cause the costs of the mediation to rise; as such, the joint bundle should be kept as short as reasonably possible. Indeed, some mediators will stipulate that it should not exceed a certain length. Materials that might have been relevant to the case itself—such as experts' reports, witness statements and legal authorities—should be avoided; here, the focus is on simplicity, rather than legal points-scoring or elaborate forensic analysis.

---

[30] Blake, S, Browne, J, and Sime, S, *The Jackson ADR Handbook* (Oxford: Oxford University Press, 2016), para 14.06.

[31] *Ibid*, para 14.48.

In addition, confidential bundles—namely, bundles prepared for disclosure only to the mediator—may be prepared. In a costs mediation, these may contain documents that the receiving party has possession of, but has not yet elected to disclose. These are likely to be the receiving party's solicitor's files of working papers, including the privileged correspondence passing between them, but the use of such materials at the mediation is likely to be of limited use to the mediator and none to the other participant. **48.33**

Position statements may be prepared. It is a matter for the participants to decide if they should be exchanged or merely made available to the mediator. Position statements should not be akin to skeleton arguments setting out submissions of law, but should be limited to the key issues that have hitherto prevented settlement. Often, these will be arguments about hourly rates, compliance with the indemnity principle, proportionality and the level of any success fee. Provided that they are succinct and identify the principal issues upon which the participants cannot agree, and set out the offers and counter-offers made, position statements can be an invaluable aid to the mediator. **48.34**

The authors of *The Jackson ADR Handbook* suggest that a position statement should contain the following (this being in the context of mediation in general).[32] **48.35**

- **Heading** A position statement should be marked 'without prejudice and for use in mediation only'.
- **Status** If a position statement is to be shown only to the mediator, this should be stated on its face.
- **Formalities** A position statement should record the date and time of the mediation, the name of the mediator, the persons who will attend on behalf of the relevant participant and their connection with the dispute.
- **Facts** A position statement should briefly record the facts of the dispute.
- **Issues** A position statement should identify the issues in dispute—both legal and factual—and should highlight those that are of particular importance.
- **Outline of case** A position statement should state the relevant participant's stance in relation to those issues—and this ought to be done in a non-confrontational way.
- **Interests and objectives** A position statement should identify the relevant participant's key objectives.
- **Further information that is required** A position statement should identify any further information, if any, that the relevant participant needs to be able to negotiate effectively.
- **Negotiations** A position statement should list the offers that have been made to try to settle the dispute or any part of it.

Procedure during a facilitative mediation Whilst procedure may vary, facilitative mediations typically take place in both joint session, when all participants and the mediator are in attendance, and in private session (otherwise known as closed sessions or caucuses), when the mediator speaks with each participant in private. **48.36**

There are no rules about who can attend the mediation. It is not always necessary for participants to be legally represented. It is, however, essential that there is someone there on behalf of each participant who has authority to settle: there is no purpose to be served in **48.37**

[32] *Ibid*, para 14.67.

attending a costs mediation unless there is access to a decision maker who has the power to authorise a settlement. Ideally, such a person ought to physically attend the mediation, but it is permissible for instructions to be taken by telephone.

48.38 Typically, a facilitative mediation will, if successful, go through the following stages.[33]

(1) **The opening stage** The process will commonly start with an initial joint session (often referred to as a plenary session), chaired by the mediator. The participants will often make an opening statement in which they will state their positions in relation to the disputed issues and their desire to resolve those issues.
(2) **The exploration (or information) stage** During this stage, the mediator will garner information, both about the dispute and the participants' proposals. The stage may take place either in joint session or in private session (or a mixture of the two). In addition, the mediator may probe the underlying issues and carry out a 'reality test' (which means that the mediator will try to help the participants to better understand the strengths and weaknesses of their respective cases).
(3) **The negotiation (or bargaining) stage** During this stage, the mediator will facilitate negotiation. This tends to take place in a series of private sessions. The mediator both will act as a 'shuttle diplomat' and will attempt to devise strategies to help the participants to overcome any issues that are preventing settlement.[34]
(4) **The settlement (or closing) stage** During this stage—which tends to take place in joint session—the participants will (if the mediation has been successful) draft and sign written terms of settlement. If the mediation has not been successful, the mediator will record this and will summarise the closing positions of the participants, in an effort to facilitate post-mediation discussions.

48.39 It is acceptable for there to be discussion between lawyers (such as counsel-to-counsel discussions), but the participants must be kept informed of what is discussed.[35] Similarly, it is often the case that if the participants are legally represented, they will be encouraged to speak directly to each other, with or without their legal representatives in attendance.

48.40 **Disclosure of documents in the context of mediation** There is no general duty of disclosure in mediation proceedings other than that which may exist as a result of ongoing proceedings in court. In non-costs mediations, a duty of disclosure may arise as a result of the operation of pre-action protocols, but this is not the case with mediations about the amount of costs. Documents may be released voluntarily, either to the mediator alone (see 48.33) or to the mediator and other participants (see 48.32). The formal procedure of election (see 46.40–46.74) does apply in costs mediations.

48.41 Where documents are revealed only to the mediator, the mediator will generally be under a duty not to reveal those documents to the other participants; instead, the mediator will bear them in mind for the purposes of facilitating negotiations. If, however, a mediator is asked to put an offer that is directly contradicted by a document, the mediator may decline to do so if the offeree has not seen that document.[36]

[33] See *ibid*, para 15.04.
[34] Details of these techniques may be found *ibid*, para 15.19.
[35] See *ibid*, para 5.19.
[36] See *ibid*, para 14.80.

Whilst there is no duty of disclosure, care ought to be taken not to withhold documents that might be relevant. In the context of a mediation of costs between opposing parties, withholding material documents may lead to any settlement being overturned for misrepresentation. If the parties are in a fiduciary relationship—which may be the case if the mediation is between legal services provider and client—allegations of material non-disclosure may also arise.[37] **48.42**

Privacy and confidentiality in the context of mediation Whilst there is no general absolute right of privacy,[38] there are many protections that afford the participants to a mediation a degree of confidence that the proceedings will remain both private and confidential (unless otherwise agreed). **48.43**

- **Contractual confidentiality clauses** Under the terms of nearly all mediation agreements, everything said and done during the course of a mediation is confidential. This means that the parties are free to make without-prejudice admissions that might assist in reaching a settlement, but which will not thereafter be binding. Settlement agreements may contain additional confidentiality clauses. A potential risk that a confidentiality clause may be breached may be restrained by way of an injunction.[39]
- **Standards of ADR providers** Mediators will, independently of any contractual provisions, normally follow a mediation code of conduct that is likely to include a duty of confidentiality.[40]
- **Regulatory standards** Where they apply, regulatory standards may impose a duty of confidentiality.[41]
- **The doctrine protecting 'without prejudice' communications** This is addressed at 6.213–6.218. Exceptions to the rule may apply, such as where there is a dispute about what was agreed during mediation, and those exceptions are addressed at 6.218.
- **Legal professional privilege** This is addressed at 46.04–46.27. For the avoidance of doubt, revealing documents that otherwise would be privileged would not amount to a waiver of privilege, albeit that parties would wish to consider carefully before disclosing such material, since the existence of those will remain within the knowledge of both parties, albeit that copies cannot be taken or shown to the court.
- **Professional duties of confidentiality** All professional codes of conduct that bind mediators and legal services providers include duties in relation to client confidentiality.[42]

Briggs J (writing extrajudicially) has suggested that there is an additional and separate 'mediation privilege',[43] but there is no binding authority on that point.

There are, however, limits to the extent to which the above principles will apply. In particular, whilst the court will tend not to dissect the mediation for the purposes of deciding **48.44**

[37] See *ibid*, para 14.79.

[38] See *Farm Assist Ltd (in liquidation) v The Secretary of State for the Environment, Food and Rural Affairs (No 2)* [2009] EWHC 1102 (TCC).

[39] *Venture Investment Placement Ltd v Hall* [2005] EWHC 1227 (Ch).

[40] See Blake, S, Browne, J, and Sime, S, *The Jackson ADR Handbook* (Oxford: Oxford University Press, 2016), paras 13.29–13.43.

[41] See, eg, EU Code of Conduct for Mediators, para 4.

[42] See Blake, S, Browne, J, and Sime, S, *The Jackson ADR Handbook* (Oxford: Oxford University Press, 2016), paras 5.05 and 6.11–6.13.

[43] See Briggs, J, 'Mediation Privilege?' (2009) 159 NLJ 506, at 550.

what is and is not covered by the 'without prejudice' doctrine,[44] it is open to the court to find that the doctrine does not apply to certain types of information. The authors of *The Jackson ADR Handbook* give the following examples (amongst others).[45]

- The doctrine will not protect information that is disclosable for some other reason.
- The doctrine will not apply to peripheral matters, such as terms of payment in relation to which settlement in principle is not in dispute.[46]
- The doctrine does not apply to matters of detail in respect of an open admission[47] nor does it apply to open admissions in general.
- The doctrine does not apply to open offers.
- The words 'without prejudice' may not be used to conceal something that should be conveyed in open correspondence.[48]

The topic of exceptions to the 'without prejudice' doctrine in general is addressed at 6.218.

48.45 Whilst not binding, Master Haworth has held that information provided about costs in the run-up to a mediation was covered by the confidentiality clause of the mediation agreement, but matters of pure fact were different.[49] He found that costs information in the form of a statement of facts could be distinguished from other documents and could be referred to in the detailed assessment—in that instance, the defendant's costs estimates when preparing for the mediation for the purpose of calculating an after-the-event (ATE) insurance premium.

48.46 In a similar vein, when deciding who should pay the costs of hard-fought proceedings in tort, Jack J had this to say on the topic of confidentiality:

> 'The claimants' position at the mediation was plainly unrealistic and unreasonable. Had they made an offer which better reflected their true position, the mediation might have succeeded. It would be wrong to say more. As far as I am aware, the courts have had not to consider the situation where a party has agreed to mediate, but has then taken unreasonable position in the mediation. It is not dissimilar in effect to an unreasonable refusal to engage in mediation. For a party who agrees to mediation then causes the mediation to fail by his reason of unreasonable position in the mediation is in reality in the same position as a party who unreasonably refuses to mediate.'[50]

48.47 Where an observer to the mediation is to attend (for example if a participant wishes to bring a friend or supporter), an observer's agreement must be signed under which the observer agrees to preserve the confidentiality of the process. If the attendance is opposed, the observer cannot attend the mediation.

---

[44] See *Unilever plc v Proctor & Gamble Co* [2000] 1 WLR 2436; *Williams v Hull* [2009] EWHC 2844 (Ch). See also (specifically in the context of mediation) *Mason v Walton on Thames Charity* [2010] EWHC 1688 (Ch).

[45] Blake, S, Browne, J, and Sime, S, *The Jackson ADR Handbook* (Oxford: Oxford University Press, 2016), para 5.23.

[46] *Bradford & Bingley plc v Rashid* [2006] UKHL 37.

[47] *Ibid.*

[48] *Buckinghamshire County Council v Moran* [1990] Ch 623.

[49] *Savings Advice Ltd v EDF Energy Customers Ltd* [2017] EWHC B1 (Costs).

[50] *James Carleton Seventh of Malmesbury & Ors v Strutt & Parker* [2008] EWHC 424 (QB), at [72].

Evaluative mediation

48.48 Most evaluative mediations (which are also known as directive mediations) will begin in the facilitative style (see 48.29), but—should the participants agree—will then progress to a stage at which the mediator will evaluate the available material and express an opinion on the merits. In a costs setting in particular, an evaluative mediator may be asked to recommend a range of options for settlement. Any such evaluation would not be binding on the participants (namely, it would not be adjudicative), but would merely be intended to assist them in their negotiations and, once delivered, the participants will be asked to deliberate upon it. The mediator cannot impose an evaluative mediation on the participants, but if an impasse is reached using facilitative mediation, the mediator is able to suggest that the evaluative process be adopted, in which case both participants must jointly sign a certificate providing their consent. Evaluative mediation includes the following.

- **Mediator comment** This is a means by which the mediator is authorised to make such informal comment on the merits or substance of the case, including potential options for resolution, as they believe appropriate.
- **Suggested settlements** The mediator may make a suggestion as to the basis for settlement that, in all of the circumstances, appears to them to be capable of meeting the interests of the participants.
- **Non-binding evaluation** This is a means by which the mediator may give a non-binding evaluation either orally at the mediation or in writing at a later date (for which an additional fee is generally payable).

The points made about pendulum arbitration (see 48.87) may also be worth bearing in mind. As far as the editor is aware, pendulum arbitration has not yet been used as an adjunct to mediation, but there is no reason why this should not be done.

48.49 Evaluative mediation is not without its disadvantages. The authors of *The Jackson ADR Handbook* have this to say on the topic:

> 'Evaluative mediation does have some perceived disadvantages:
> - An evaluation is likely to favour one side's case over another. This can lead to a perception that the mediator is not neutral and unbiased and this may destroy the effectiveness of the mediation process;
> - There is also a perception that evaluative mediators can coerce the parties into settlement;
> - In some cases, an evaluation can result in a hardening of position on the part of the party whole case is more likely to succeed, with the consequence that the parties are likely to become more entrenched in their positions;
> - The mediator will also seldom be provided with all of the documentation in a case. Any evaluation that is provided may not be based on complete information and may therefore be misleading. Providing an evaluation may also expose the mediator to a potential claim in negligence.'[51]

They go on to say, however, that evaluative mediation has its advantages—in particular, the fact that it may lead negotiations to progress more rapidly and 'provide a reality check that is needed to enable the parties to move towards settlement'.[52]

[51] Blake, S, Browne, J, and Sime, S, *The Jackson ADR Handbook* (Oxford: Oxford University Press, 2016), para 14.11.

[52] *Ibid*, para 14.13.

The funding of mediations and costs

Funding mediation and mediators' fees

48.50 Liability for the fees of the mediator will be covered by the mediation agreement. In general, the fee will be shared equally by the participants, although it may be agreed that the fee become part of the costs in the claim in general.[53] A mediator's fee is fixed by the contract and may not (unless there are provisions to the contrary) be assessed in so far as the mediator's right to payment is concerned.[54]

The costs of the mediation

48.51 Subject to there being no contractual agreement to the contrary (see 48.52), the costs of mediation may, in principle, be recovered as costs of court proceedings (see 49.133–49.137).

48.52 The mediation agreement will, in general, make provision for the costs of the mediation. In the context of costs mediations, the usual term is that the participants will initially bear their own costs, but that the costs will then become part of the costs of the detailed assessment proceedings in the event that the mediation is not successful. The reason for this is not only to take account of the presumption in CPR, r 47.20(1) (see 43.330), but also to ensure that the parties are not deprived of the benefit of having made Part 36 offers. That said, the participants are at liberty to come to some other arrangement, such as that the participants will each bear their own costs regardless of any order that the court may subsequently make. Costs of the mediation may also be shifted by agreement reached during the mediation itself.

The costs consequences of an unreasonable refusal to mediate in costs disputes

48.53 Judicial encouragement to engage in ADR has gathered strength over the past two decades. It is now trite costs law that an unreasonable refusal to participate in mediation is likely to sound adversely in the incidence (or possibly basis) of costs. This is addressed in detail at 6.118–6.139; the following discussion builds upon the principles set out in Chapter 6, with emphasis on costs disputes.

48.54 When one party makes an offer to mediate and the other party rejects it without reasonable excuse, the latter will be at risk on costs, both in terms of the incidence of costs and the basis of costs. Although no binding judgment has yet been given that deals with this topic in the context of costs disputes, decisions at first instance have reflected this principle. Master O'Hare, for example, had this to say (in the context of a paying party—and NHS trust—having unreasonably refused an offer of mediation):

> 'I want to end with a brief note of caution about sanctions imposed on parties who unreasonably refuse to mediate. Case law on this topic is largely about penalties imposed on parties who are in other respects the successful party. In *Halsey* and in other cases, penalties were imposed upon winners. ... If the party unwilling to mediate is the losing party, the normal sanction is an order to pay the winner's costs on the indemnity basis, and that means they will have to pay their opponent's costs even if those costs are not proportionate to what was at stake. This penalty is imposed because a court wants to show its disapproval of their conduct. I do disapprove of this defendant's conduct but only as from the date they are likely to have received the July offer to mediate.'[55]

---

[53] *Ibid*, para 7.16.
[54] Whilst not binding, see *National Westminster Bank v Feeny* [2006] EWHC 90066 (Costs).
[55] *Reid v Buckinghamshire Healthcare NHS Trust* [2015] EWHC B21 (Costs), at [10]–[12].

Master O'Hare went on to make an order for costs on the indemnity basis from the date on which the NHS trust refused to mediate.

In a similar vein, Master Simons had this to say (also in relation to an NHS trust): **48.55**

> '[The paying parties] say they did not enter into the mediation because the parties were so far apart. The claimants were unreasonable in their offer and the offers that were put forward by the defendants were much closer to the actual settlement than, in fact, were the offers made by the claimant and these are factors that should be taken into account ... [P]arties should be encouraged to enter into mediation and if one party fails to enter into mediation and that failure is unreasonable ... [The] defendants have not given any reasonable reason why they refuse to engage in mediation and I am satisfied that there should be an appropriate sanction ... It took three months for them to reject and they gave no good reason other than the fact that the case had already been set down for a detailed assessment ... I think that the correct sanction is that the claimant should receive their costs on the indemnity basis on their 80% costs, as a sanction for the defendant's failing to engage in mediation.'[56]

As can be seen, Master Simons made an award of costs on the indemnity basis from the start of the costs proceedings.

The conduct of the NHS trusts in these two cases drew heavy criticism from Sir Henry Brooke, a strong advocate of mediation, who had the following to say (extrajudicially): **48.56**

> 'In each case the defendants were ordered to pay the claimant on an indemnity basis, not the usual standard basis ... They also had to pay interest at the rate of 8% [per annum] on the unpaid costs until the date of judgment. They also had to pay their own costs of the detailed assessment: in the first case, where they failed to "beat" a part 36 offer, they had to pay the claimant a 10% uplift of £13,000 on the award of costs as well. ... If, by way of illustration, the taxpayer had to pay £50,000 in each case more than he would have had to pay if those representing the [NHS Litigation Authority] had behaved prudently and reasonably, that would mean £100,000 of public money went down the drain for no real purpose. Oh dear.'[57]

A similar conclusion was reached by the Master Judge Gordon-Saker (in a matter that did not involve an NHS trust): **48.57**

> 'It seems to me that there has been a blanket refusal by the defendant to engage in any sort of alternative dispute resolution ... Accordingly, I have no hesitation in concluding that the defendant has behaved unreasonably in failing to engage in the process of discussing at least the possibility of alternative dispute resolution and mediation in particular ... The defendant's conduct is unreasonable to a high degree and such to justify an award of costs on the indemnity basis.'[58]

Early Neutral Evaluation

Early neutral evaluation (ENE) is a form of non-adjudicative ADR in which a neutral third party provides an assessment (usually in written form) of some or all of the issues in a dispute. It is particularly valuable in cases in which the outcome of the dispute turns on **48.58**

---

56 *Bristow v Princess Alexander Hospital NHS Trust* [2015] EWHC B22 (Costs), at [2]–[11].

57 Brooke, H, 'The Cost of the NHSLA's Refusals to Mediate', 9 January 2016, available online at https://sirhenrybrooke.me/2016/01/09/the-cost-of-the-nhslas-refusals-to-mediate/

58 *Various Claimants v Mirror Group Newspapers Ltd* (unreported), 4 October 2016, SCCO, at p 3 of the transcript.

limited issues—especially where those issues require a degree of expertise in their resolution. As such, it is particularly well suited to costs disputes that involve points of principle.

48.59 The evaluation is not binding, but is instead intended to help the parties to evaluate the merits of their respective cases, thereby facilitating settlement. To that extent, it bears some similarity to evaluative mediation (see 48.48), but the two are not the same. The authors of *The Jackson ADR Handbook* have this to say on the topic:

> 'ENE differs from mediation in that mediation is essentially a facultative process. ENE is an advisor and evaluative process. However, there is a close similarity between ENE and evaluative mediation ... [T]he term ENE is used when a neutral third party is asked to evaluate a dispute, without themselves becoming involved in any way in the negotiations between the parties. It is this disengagement from the negotiation process that distinguishes ENE from evaluative mediation.'[59]

48.60 In certain spheres of practice, early neutral evaluation may take place within the court system (that is, by a judge), but there is no such facility for costs disputes. As such, evaluators tend to be counsel in independent practice or retired costs judges.

48.61 As is implied by its name, early neutral evaluation tends to be employed in the early stages of a dispute, but it may be deployed at any stage. It may be combined with other forms of ADR, such as mediation. As to those cases in which it may be most beneficial, the authors of *The Jackson ADR Handbook* have this to say:

> 'The rationale for ENE is that an unbiased evaluation of one or more issues in the case and/or the likely outcome by a neutral party, such as a judge or an expert, will help the parties subsequently to settle the dispute by negotiation or even mediation. It can be particularly useful where one or more of the parties has taken an unrealistic and entrenched view of one or more of the issues, or the case as a whole, and would benefit from an assessment of the particular issue or the case by an independent person.'[60]

The procedure of early neutral evaluation

48.62 Unlike most other forms of ADR, early neutral evaluation does not necessarily have to be a consensual process, because it is possible for a party to unilaterally seek an evaluation of some or all of the issues that are preventing settlement. That said, it is most often a process that is carried out on the basis of instructions being given jointly by the parties; where this is so, the parties will jointly agree the ambit and content of the instructions. The evaluator may wish to hear oral submissions, but this is unusual in the context of costs disputes.

48.63 The evaluator will generally give their evaluation in writing and this may or may not contain detailed reasons. The evaluation is non-binding and confidential to the parties.

The funding of early neutral evaluation

48.64 The cost of early neutral evaluation will depend on whether the evaluation will take place on the basis of written submissions alone. The evaluator's fee is likely to turn on the complexity of the case, and the degree of expertise and time required.

---

[59] Blake, S, Browne, J, and Sime, S, *The Jackson ADR Handbook* (Oxford: Oxford University Press, 2016), para 22.02.

[60] *Ibid*, para 22.06.

Costs Arbitration

Arbitration is an example of adjudicative ADR. In particular, it is a form of ADR that will be conducted by an arbitrator (or a panel of arbitrators), who will make a binding decision—known as an award—on the merits of the matter. The process is consensual, in the sense that the parties will be able to agree in advance what the process should be, but often the parties agree to delegate the task of deciding procedural issues to the arbitrator. **48.65**

The nature of costs arbitration

Arbitration may involve a hearing (which, in a costs context, may be very similar to a detailed assessment), or it may take place on the basis of written submissions only. **48.66**

The authors of *The Jackson ADR Handbook* have this to say on the benefits of arbitration: **48.67**

> 'The main attractions of arbitration are that:
> - the parties can select an arbitrator with appropriate expertise and experience;
> - the process is private, unlike a trial in open court;
> - many aspects of the process can be tailored to the needs of a specific dispute;
> - the process can be relatively structured, if that is attractive to the parties;
> - the process can be relatively simple and cost effective if the dispute is decided the basis of written submissions rather than a hearing.'[61]

They go on to make the following points about the potential drawbacks of arbitration: **48.68**

> 'The potential drawbacks of arbitration are that:
> - arbitration is not necessarily a cost-saving option if a process similar to trial is used;
> - the parties leave the final decision to a third party, and will be bound by it;
> - an arbitration process cannot deal easily with a party who fails to cooperate, as an arbitrator will not have the wide powers or a judge;
> - the arbitrator needs to be selected with care as regards expertise, experience, etc, to ensure the parties will have confidence in the award made.'[62]

Jurisdictional issues

Sources of arbitral law

The sources of arbitral law are statute, the common law and international conventions, but only the first is relevant in the present context. In particular, non-international costs arbitration is governed by the Arbitration Act 1996 (as amended). **48.69**

An arbitration will touch upon three areas of law: **48.70**

- the law that governs the substance of the dispute between the parties (which, in the present context, will be the entitlement to costs);
- the law of the arbitration agreement (often referred to as the 'proper law of the arbitration agreement' (see 48.71); and
- the procedural law of the arbitration (which may be referred to as the 'curial law of the arbitration') (see 48.72).

---

61 *Ibid*, para 2.05.
62 *Ibid*, para 2.07.

The proper law of the arbitration agreement

48.71 The proper law of the arbitration agreement governs the validity, interpretation and effect of the agreement in question.[63] It may be that parties are obliged to engage in arbitration as a result of a pre-existing contract between them; where this is so, any arbitration agreement that is then created will be subject to its own proper law.[64] The proper law of the arbitration does not necessarily have to be the law of England and Wales, but in the context of costs dispute, it generally will be.

The procedural law of the arbitration

48.72 The procedural law of the arbitration will govern the arbitration proceedings, and will include the conduct of the arbitration and the powers of the court to oversee matters.[65] Unless there is agreement to the contrary, in the context of non-international costs arbitrations, the procedural law will be that which applies in England and Wales.[66]

The principles of arbitration

48.73 Arbitrations in England and Wales are governed by the general principles that are set out in s 1 of the Arbitration Act 1996 (as amended):

> 'The provisions of this Part are founded on the following principles, and shall be construed accordingly—
> (a) the object of arbitration is to obtain the fair resolution of disputes by an impartial tribunal without unnecessary delay or expense;
> (b) the parties should be free to agree how their disputes are resolved, subject only to such safeguards as are necessary in the public interest;
> (c) in matters governed by this Part the court should not intervene except as provided by this Part.'

48.74 Where parties agree to arbitration, Lord Hoffmann has said that their agreement implies the following:

> 'They want [the matter] decided by a tribunal which they have chosen, commonly on the grounds of such matters as its neutrality, expertise and privacy, the availability of legal services at the seat of the arbitration and the unobtrusive efficiency of its supervisory law. Particularly in the case of international contracts, they want a quick and efficient adjudication and do not want to take the risks of delay and, in too many cases, partiality, in proceedings before a national jurisdiction.'[67]

48.75 The Arbitration Act 1996 (as amended) regulates arbitrations in two ways.

- it contains mandatory provisions that apply regardless of any agreement between the parties to the contrary;[68] which provisions are set out in Sch 1 to the Act;[69] and

---

63 See *James Miller & Partners Ltd v Whitworth Street Estates (Manchester) Ltd* [1970] AC 583.

64 *Black-Clawson International Ltd v Papierwerke Waldhof-Aschaffenburg AG* [1981] 2 Lloyd's Rep 44.

65 See *James Miller & Partners Ltd v Whitworth Street Estates (Manchester) Ltd* [1970] AC 583.

66 See *ibid.*

67 *Premium Nafta Products Ltd (20th Defendant) & Ors v Fili Shipping Co Ltd & Ors* [2007] UKHL 40, at [6].

68 See Arbitration Act 1996 (as amended), s 4(1).

69 Schedule 1 refers to the following sections in the Arbitration Act 1996 (as amended): ss 9–11 (stay of legal proceedings); s 12 (power of court to extend agreed time limits); s 13 (application of Limitation Acts); s 24 (power of court to remove arbitrator); s 26(1) (effect of death of arbitrator); s 28 (liability of parties for fees and expenses of arbitrators); s 29 (immunity of arbitrator); s 31 (objection to substantive jurisdiction of

- it contains non-mandatory provisions that apply by default, but which may be departed from should the parties agree.[70]

Arbitration agreements

An arbitration agreement is an agreement to submit present or future disputes to arbitration, whether they are contractual or not.[71] In the context of costs disputes, this tends either to be an agreement entered into specifically for the purposes of dealing with the issue of costs or to arise out of a prior agreement between the parties to submit to arbitration. It should be borne in mind, however, that a general agreement to submit to arbitration would not necessarily imply that an award of costs is to be assessed by that means; this is because s 63(4) of the Arbitration Act 1996 (as amended) provides that the court may assess costs incurred in arbitral proceedings. **48.76**

If the provisions of the Arbitration Act 1996 (as amended) are to apply, then the agreement must be in writing.[72] This condition may be met if the agreement is made in writing, whether or not it is signed by the parties, if the agreement is made by exchange of communications in writing or if the agreement is evidenced in writing.[73] **48.77**

Procedural issues

The procedure in arbitrations

Subject to the mandatory provisions referred to at 48.75, the procedure to be adopted will depend on what the parties have agreed. In the context of costs disputes, the procedure is often similar to a detailed assessment. In general, there will be four stages to a costs arbitration: **48.78**

(1) commencement (see 48.79);
(2) a preliminary hearing (see 48.80–48.82);
(3) a pre-hearing conference (see 48.83); and
(4) the hearing itself (see 48.84).

That said, arbitrations may be carried out on the basis of written submissions alone,[74] in which case any or all of the stages may either be avoided or dealt with without the need for personal attendance.

Commencement of arbitration The parties are free to agree when arbitral proceedings are to be regarded as commenced.[75] If there is no agreement, then (provided that there is **48.79**

tribunal); s 32 (determination of preliminary point of jurisdiction); s 33 (general duty of tribunal); s 37(2) (items to be treated as expenses of arbitrators); s 40 (general duty of parties); s 43 (securing the attendance of witnesses); s 56 (power to withhold award in case of non-payment); s 60 (effectiveness of agreement for payment of costs in any event); s 66 (enforcement of award); ss 67 and 68 (challenging the award: substantive jurisdiction and serious irregularity), and ss 70 and 71 (supplementary provisions; effect of order of court) in relation to those sections; s 72 (saving for rights of person who takes no part in proceedings); s 73 (loss of right to object); s 74 (immunity of arbitral institutions, etc.); and s 75 (charge to secure payment of solicitors' costs).

[70] See Arbitration Act 1996 (as amended), s 4(2).
[71] See Arbitration Act 1996 (as amended), s 6(1).
[72] See Arbitration Act 1996 (as amended), s 5(1).
[73] See Arbitration Act 1996 (as amended), s 5(2).
[74] See Arbitration Act 1996 (as amended), s 34.
[75] See Arbitration Act 1996 (as amended), s 14(1).

an extant arbitration agreement), a party may commence proceedings by serving a notice of arbitration (or a notice to appoint an arbitrator) on the other party or parties.[76]

48.80 **Preliminary meeting** As to the preliminary meeting, the authors of *The Jackson ADR Handbook* have this to say:

> 'A preliminary meeting will often be convened shortly after the tribunal is appointed. It is an opportunity for the parties to meet, but its main purpose is as a forum for the tribunal to discuss jurisdictional matters and to make procedural directions for the preparation of evidence needed for deciding the reference. There is no set agenda for preliminary meetings. It may well be possible for directions to be agreed between the parties, which will make a preliminary meeting less necessary. It is becoming increasing common to hold preliminary meetings by conference telephone calls or through video-conferencing.'[77]

48.81 Unless the parties agree otherwise, it will be for the arbitrator to decide procedural issues.[78] Section 35 of the Arbitration Act 1996 (as amended) provides as follows:

> '(1) It shall be for the tribunal to decide all procedural and evidential matters, subject to the right of the parties to agree any matter.
>
> (2) Procedural and evidential matters include—
> (a) when and where any part of the proceedings is to be held;
> (b) the language or languages to be used in the proceedings and whether translations of any relevant documents are to be supplied;
> (c) whether any and if so what form of written statements of claim and defence are to be used, when these should be supplied and the extent to which such statements can be later amended;
> (d) whether any and if so which documents or classes of documents should be disclosed between and produced by the parties and at what stage;
> (e) whether any and if so what questions should be put to and answered by the respective parties and when and in what form this should be done;
> (f) whether to apply strict rules of evidence (or any other rules) as to the admissibility, relevance or weight of any material (oral, written or other) sought to be tendered on any matters of fact or opinion, and the time, manner and form in which such material should be exchanged and presented;
> (g) whether and to what extent the tribunal should itself take the initiative in ascertaining the facts and the law;
> (h) whether and to what extent there should be oral or written evidence or submissions.
>
> (3) The tribunal may fix the time within which any directions given by it are to be complied with, and may if it thinks fit extend the time so fixed (whether or not it has expired).'

48.82 In the context of a costs arbitration, further issues that may need to be addressed would include:

- what papers are to be provided to the arbitrator (including whether the arbitrator should have access to the receiving party's file); and
- the basis on which the arbitrator should deal with the costs of the arbitration (see 48.101–48.104).

[76] See Arbitration Act 1996 (as amended), s 14(4).

[77] Blake, S, Browne, J, and Sime, S, *The Jackson ADR Handbook* (Oxford: Oxford University Press, 2016), para 25.13.

[78] See Arbitration Act 1996 (as amended), s 59(1).

Pre-hearing conference The authors of *The Jackson ADR Handbook* have this to say about pre-hearing conferences: **48.83**

> 'If the arbitration is of some complexity it may be sensible to hold a pre-trial hearing or conference. This will usually take place a number of weeks before the expected start of the hearing. The main purpose is to review what has been done in preparation for the hearing, to assess whether the parties are going to be ready for the hearing, and to make directions.'[79]

The hearing In most costs disputes, the hearing will bear a similarity to a detailed assessment. That said, it is within the power of the arbitrator to proceed in a different way—in particular, if they so choose, to frame the hearing as inquisitorial rather than adversarial.[80] Moreover, special types of arbitration may take place, such as pendulum arbitrations (see 48.87). **48.84**

The implicit duty of confidentiality and privacy in arbitrations

It is ingrained in arbitral law that proceedings are private[81] and confidential.[82] The process itself will be confidential,[83] but this will not extend to documents that would not otherwise be confidential.[84] In general terms, the comments made at 48.43–48.47 will apply. **48.85**

As to disclosure, the parties will normally agree on the extent of mutual disclosure. If there is no agreement, the arbitrator may determine the issue. In arbitration in general, it tends not to be acceptable for documents to be disclosed only to the arbitrator, but costs mediations tend to follow the process of election, much as in a detailed assessment. **48.86**

Pendulum arbitration

Pendulum arbitration[85] is a method of ADR that has yet to be used for costs disputes in this jurisdiction, but there is reason to believe that it may be a highly effective means of resolving disputes solely relating to quantum. **48.87**

At heart, the method involves the parties to a dispute agreeing to be bound by the decision of arbitration. This, however, is not on the basis that the arbitrator is free to select a figure of their own choosing; rather, the arbitrator must make a binary choice between offers that have been made by the parties. The reason why such a method is so well suited to costs disputes is that it forces the parties to compete to make the most reasonable offer; if the arbitrator believes that the opponent's offer is the more reasonable, then the outcome will be based on the opponent's offer. **48.88**

As long ago as 1995, Zuckerman (an Oxford academic) had the following to say of something very similar to pendulum arbitration: **48.89**

> 'One possible measure for discouraging litigation is the pendulum system of adjudication under which the judge can only decide to accept the plaintiff's claim in full or, alternatively,

---

[79] Blake, S, Browne, J, and Sime, S, *The Jackson ADR Handbook* (Oxford: Oxford University Press, 2016), para 25.16.

[80] See Arbitration Act 1996 (as amended), s 34(2).

[81] *Oxford Shipping Co Ltd v Nippon Yusen Kaisha* [1984] 2 All ER 835.

[82] *Ali Shipping Corpn v Shipyard Trogir* [1999] 1 WLR 314.

[83] *Dolling-Baker v Mettet* [1990] 1 WLR 1205.

[84] *Milsom v Ablyazov* [2011] EWHC 955 (Ch).

[85] Otherwise known as final offer arbitration, last best offer arbitration, straight choice arbitration, flip-flop arbitration and, perhaps most famously, baseball arbitration.

wholly accept the defendant's defence and reject the plaintiff's claim altogether. Under this system a judge has no jurisdiction to award part only of the claim or accept part only of a defence. It stands to reason that a judge faced with such a choice will tend to decide in favour of the party whose position is closest to what the judge believes to be the correct solution. Hence, a party who advances an excessive claim or defence runs a serious risk of losing everything. Accordingly, this feature of the system provides a powerful mechanism for narrowing the divergence between the competing positions of plaintiffs and defendants, with the result that mutually agreed settlements become much more likely.'[86]

48.90 The implications for resolving costs disputes are obvious. Moreover, pendulum arbitration would be a useful adjunct to mediation in the sense that the parties' final offers at mediation could form the basis of the offers of arbitration. Indeed, there is no reason why a suitably qualified mediator could not act as the pendulum arbitrator.

48.91 There are four recognised variations of pendulum arbitration (in addition to the base method referred to above).

- **'Night baseball' arbitration**[87] This entails the arbitrator making a decision before receiving details of the final offers of the parties. Whichever final offer is closer to the decision of the arbitrator is the one that then binds the parties.
- **Double-offer arbitration** This entails each party making a primary offer (which constitutes the maker's preferred solution) and a secondary offer (which is intended to be an offer the arbitrator is more likely to prefer). Game theory suggests that the parties' secondary offers are likely to be similar, but empirical evidence does not support this.[88] In such a method, the arbitration agreement would generally provide that convergence of offers resulted in a binding compromise.
- **Pendulum arbitration with third-party assistance** This may take various forms. The third-party assistance can be an independent person or panel that makes findings of fact or which proposes solutions in addition to the final offers of the parties. The arbitrator is then permitted to rely on such findings of fact or, indeed, to prefer the solution offered by the independent third party over those offered by the parties.
- **Issue-by-issue final-offer arbitration** This entails the making of offers with regard to individual specified issues within the overall dispute. It affords the arbitrator the opportunity to craft an arbitrated compromise by selecting the offers relating to particular issues. Whilst that can lead to fears that an arbitrator will merely split the difference between the parties in so far as is possible by charting a course through the issue-based offers, it can also generate the uncertainty necessary to lead the parties to compromise.

48.92 For those interested in attempting pendulum arbitration, the American Arbitration Association's International Centre for Dispute Resolution (ICDR) publishes supplementary rules.[89] It will be seen that those rules provide for the final offers to be in a

---

[86] Zuckerman, A, 'A Reform of Civil Procedure: Rationing Procedure Rather than Access to Justice' (1995) 22 JLS 155, at 178.

[87] The name derives from the fact that pendulum arbitration had its origins in resolving disputes regarding the pay of US baseball players.

[88] Zeng, D, Nakamura, S, and Ibaraki, T, 'Double-offer Arbitration' (1996) 31 Mathematical Social Sciences 147; Dickinson, DL, 'Bargaining Outcomes with Double-offer Arbitration' (2005) 8(2) Experimental Economics 145.

[89] See https://www.adr.org/sites/default/files/Final%20Offer%20Supplementary%20Arbitration%20Procedures.pdf

single monetary amount, exclusive of interest and the costs of arbitration. Although the arbitrator is limited to choosing only one of the final offers submitted by the parties, the award must be reasoned, stating the rationale for the selection of one offer over the other.

Arbitration awards

Types of arbitral award

In so far as costs arbitrations are concerned, there are three types of award that may be made, as follows. **48.93**

- **Interim awards** These are awards on issues that do not dispose of the arbitration in general.[90]
- **Main awards** These are awards that dispose of the arbitration in general.[91]
- **Costs awards** These are awards in respect of costs (see 48.98).

The effect of award and enforcement

Enforcement of awards is either by bringing a claim on the award on the High Court or by the summary procedure in s 66(1) of the Arbitration Act 1996 (as amended). **48.94**

The funding of arbitration proceedings

Arbitration will generally be significantly more expensive than other forms of ADR, although arbitration based on only paper submissions will often be less so.[92] The Chartered Institute of Arbitrators (CIArb) provides costs-controlled arbitration rules for dispute where no more than £50,000 is at stake.[93] **48.95**

The fees of an arbitrator are not amenable to assessment because they are a matter of contract. For the avoidance of doubt, any assessment of the costs of arbitration will have no bearing on the arbitrator's right to be paid their fees.[94] **48.96**

The costs of arbitration

Definition

The costs of the arbitration include: **48.97**

- the arbitrator's fees and expenses;
- the fees and expenses of any arbitral institution that may have provided access to the arbitrator; and
- the legal or other costs of the parties.[95]

Costs will include the costs of, or incidental to, any proceedings to determine the amount of the recoverable costs of the arbitration.[96]

---

90 See Arbitration Act 1996 (as amended), s 47.
91 See Arbitration Act 1996 (as amended), ss 46–58.
92 Blake, S, Browne, J, and Sime, S, *The Jackson ADR Handbook* (Oxford: Oxford University Press, 2013), para 7.18.
93 *Ibid*, para 7.19, referring to http://www.ciarb.org
94 See Arbitration Act 1996 (as amended), s 63(7).
95 See Arbitration Act 1996 (as amended), s 59(1).
96 See Arbitration Act 1996 (as amended), s 59(2).

48.98 An agreement that a party is to pay the whole or part of the costs of the arbitration in any event would be valid only if made after the dispute in question has arisen.[97]

Awards of costs in arbitrations

48.99 Whilst an arbitrator does not have an inherent power to make an award of the costs of the arbitration, the parties may agree to give the arbitrator that power.[98] Once an award has been made, the costs may be assessed by a court.[99]

48.100 Unless the parties agree otherwise, the arbitrator must award costs on the basis that costs should follow the event other than to the extent that it would be appropriate to do otherwise.[100] This may cause problems in the context of arbitrations about the amount of costs, because it may not be immediately apparent who is the successful party. As such, it is common for the parties to agree that the rules that govern costs in detailed assessment proceedings will apply.

48.101 **Recoverable costs in arbitral proceedings** As with many other aspects of arbitrations, it is open to the parties to agree what costs of the arbitration are to be recoverable.[101] If there is no such agreement, then the arbitrator may decide the issue.[102] In particular, it is open to the arbitrator to assess the costs to be allowed; where this is done, the arbitrator must specify the basis on which the costs have been ascertained, along with the amount allowed for each item.[103] Unless the arbitrator (or the court) directs otherwise, the costs will be assessed on the standard basis.[104]

48.102 If the arbitrator elects not to assess the costs, then any party may make an application to the court for an assessment.[105]

48.103 In so far as the arbitrator's fees and expenses are concerned, then, unless agreed otherwise, only reasonable fees will be allowed as between the parties.[106] An application may be made to the court for a determination on the point.[107] For the avoidance of doubt, any such determination will not have a bearing on the amount that the arbitrator is paid.[108]

48.104 Subject to the parties agreeing otherwise, the arbitrator may direct that the recoverable costs of the arbitration, or of any part of the proceedings, are to be limited to a specified amount.[109] That amount may be varied at any stage, but if this is done, it must be sufficiently in advance of the incurring of costs to which it relates or the taking of any steps in the proceedings that may be affected by it for the limit to be taken into account.[110]

---

97 See Arbitration Act 1996 (as amended), s 60.
98 See Arbitration Act 1996 (as amended), s 61(1).
99 See CPR, r 44.1(2)(a)(i).
100 See Arbitration Act 1996 (as amended), s 61(2).
101 See Arbitration Act 1996 (as amended), s 63(1).
102 See Arbitration Act 1996 (as amended), s 63(1).
103 See Arbitration Act 1996 (as amended), s 63(3).
104 See Arbitration Act 1996 (as amended), s 63(5).
105 See Arbitration Act 1996 (as amended), s 63(4); CPR, r 44.1(2)(a)(i).
106 See Arbitration Act 1996 (as amended), s 64(1).
107 See Arbitration Act 1996 (as amended), s 64(2).
108 See Arbitration Act 1996 (as amended), s 64(4).
109 See Arbitration Act 1996 (as amended), s 65(1).
110 See Arbitration Act 1996 (as amended), s 65(2).

Part XIII

QUANTIFICATION OF COSTS BETWEEN OPPOSING PARTIES

49

THE ASSESSMENT OF COSTS IN GENERAL (INCLUDING THE ASSESSMENT OF TIME)

This chapter deals with the following topics: **49.01**

- the absence of any power to controvert an order for costs (49.03);
- the principles of assessment of time:
  - the *Gibson* principles (49.07);
  - Sachs J 'sensible solicitor' (49.08);
  - the duty to consider the relevant material (49.09);
- time recording (49.12) and estimated time (49.15);
- classification into 'phases', 'tasks' and 'activities' (overview) (49.21);
- 'phases' and 'tasks' under the CPR (49.23);
- defined 'activities' under the CPR (including a discussion of certain types of work that fall therein):
  - 'Appear For/Attend' (A1) (49.51);
  - 'Communicate (with Counsel)' (A2) (49.56);
  - 'Communicate (with Client)' (A3) (49.58);
  - 'Communicate (Witnesses)' (A4) (49.60);
  - 'Communicate (Experts)'(A5) (49.61);
  - 'Communicate (Other Party(s)/Other Outside Lawyers)' (A6) (49.62);
  - 'Communicate (Other External)' (A7) (49.63);
  - 'Communicate (Internally within Legal Team)' (A8) (49.65);
  - 'Billable Travel Time' (A9) (49.76);
  - 'Plan, Prepare, Draft, Review' (A10) (49.81);
- other activities:
  - the costs of marshalling the facts (49.104);
  - the costs of funding (49.112);
  - the costs of legal research (49.117);
  - 'solicitor and client' work (49.121);
  - the costs of an isolated counterclaim (49.124);
  - the costs of preparing material that was not used (49.125);
  - subsequent conduct and amendments (49.126);
  - the costs of dealing with the media (49.127);
  - the costs of administrative work and work of an administrative nature (49.130);
  - the costs of negotiation and mediation (49.132);
  - the costs of preparing and checking the bill of costs (49.140);

- costs incurred in particular circumstances:
  - costs incurred prior to issue of proceedings (49.147);
  - costs incurred after the order for costs was made (49.151);
  - costs incurred during a stay (49.152);
  - costs of inquests and other proceedings in the context of a civil claim (49.154);
  - costs incurred at first instance and on appeal (49.157);
  - the costs of statutory and non-statutory inquiries (49.158);
  - the costs of claims other than the claim in hand (49.159);
  - the costs of the administration of an estate (49.161);
  - the costs as damages and contractual right to costs (49.163); and
- the EW-UTBMS code-set (otherwise known as J-Codes) and LEDES™ (49.165).

49.02 This chapter deals with the ascertainment of costs as between opposing parties. It is assumed that the reader is familiar with the bases on which costs are assessed and the method that applies to each of those two bases (see Chapter 16). It is also assumed that the reader is familiar with the test of proportionality (see Chapter 25) and how the court deals with costs that are the subject of a costs management order (see Chapter 12). The focus in this chapter is on the general principles that govern the assessment of costs, with particular emphasis on the assessment of time. Specific topics (such as hourly rates, disbursements, counsel's fees, etc) are dealt with in other chapters.

The Assessment Must Not Controvert the Order for Costs

49.03 It is trite costs law that, as long as it stands and has not been revised or successfully appealed, an order for costs to be assessed will bind a costs judge such that they will be obliged to give effect to it. In particular, a costs judge is not able to assess costs in a way that is inconsistent with the entitling order. These principles were established in *Cope v United Dairies (London) Ltd*[1] and are entirely consistent with the way in which orders for assessment in other branches of the law are regarded.[2]

49.04 In reality, *Cope* is nowhere near as clear on the point as it is reputed to be, but the notion that a costs judge lacks the power to controvert an order for costs has now become so ingrained in the fabric of costs law that it could not be sensibly challenged.

[1] *Cope v United Dairies (London) Ltd* (1968) Costs LR Core vol 23, in which the defendant was awarded costs against a legally aided claimant who had failed to progress his claim following discharge of his certificate. The costs order did not distinguish between the claimant's liability for costs incurred before the discharge of his legal aid certificate and his liability for costs after discharge. The costs judge refused to assess those costs that had been incurred prior to the discharge of the legal aid certificate, because he believed that part of the order to be *ultra vires*. The defendant successfully appealed that refusal and, in allowing the appeal, Megaw J impliedly held that a costs judge would not be permitted to refuse to carry out an order for assessment on the ostensible basis that he considered it to be wrong or *ultra vires*: see *ibid*, at 24.

[2] A common-law judgment for damages to be assessed is binding on the court conducting the assessment: *Thomas v Bunn* [1991] AC 362. An enquiry as to title under a decree for specific performance is limited to the title that the vendor must show under the contract proved at the trial and the officer of the court conducting the enquiry cannot consider whether a different contract exists that imposed a lesser obligation on the vendor: *McGrory v Alderdale Estate Ltd* [1918] AC 503, at 511, where Viscount Haldane said, '[t]he terms of the decree have ... superseded and excluded all other evidence, and it is too late, if the decree remains unaltered, to try to import new terms in the course of inquiries which follow merely consequently'.

The following points may be made. **49.05**

- **Interpretation of orders** Whilst an obvious point, the bar against controversion would not prevent a costs judge from interpreting an order for costs.
- **Special orders** Whilst rare, it is possible for the court to make special orders that afford costs judges wider powers than they would ordinarily have (such as where a costs judge is given the power to apportion costs).
- **The absence of a special order and reservations** The power to make special orders is generally most relevant in terms of the absence of any such order. In particular, if a party wishes to raise a point on an assessment that ought to have been the subject of a special order, then the fact that a special order was not made will usually prevent that argument being put.[3]
- **Deemed orders** The points made at 49.03 apply to deemed orders, as well as to orders made by adjudication.[4]
- **Orders made in respect of interim matters** Mann J has explained that a costs judge lacks the power to assess at nil an order for costs made in respect of an interim matter if to do so would controvert the order.[5]

The Principles of Accounting for Costs

There are three classic principles that apply to the assessment of costs in general, as follows: **49.06**

- that the issue of whether costs are to be admitted in principle will be decided according to the *Gibson* principles[6] (see 49.07);
- that the reasonableness of costs will be gauged from the viewpoint of Sachs J's 'sensible solicitor' (see 49.08); and
- that the court will consider all the relevant material (see 49.09).

These principles pre-date proportionality and costs management, but they continue to apply nonetheless.

[3] Whilst *obiter*, Waller LJ gave the following as an illustrative example, in *Drew v Whitbread* [2010] EWCA 53, at [36]: if it is to be argued that a witness in a long trial should never have been called because the evidence was irrelevant, a costs judge should not be required to effectively retry the case to adjudicate on the point because that is something that ought to have been reflected in a special order. See also *In re Frape, ex p Perrett (No 2)* [1894] 2 Ch 290, at 295, in which the court found: 'The right of the client to dispute the solicitor's retainer as to this bill *in toto* was not reserved in the order as it ought to have been, if he was to have that right.' See also *Skuse v Granada Television Ltd* [1994] 1 WLR 1156, in which Drake J found that (on the facts of that particular case) the paying parties' failure to raise the issue of alleged maintenance at the time a costs order was made prevented them from raising the issue on the assessment.

[4] See *Lahey v Pirelli Tyres Ltd* [2007] EWCA Civ 91, at [22].

[5] *Business Environment Bow Lane Ltd v Deanwater Estates Ltd* [2009] EWHC 2014 (Ch), at [1]. The question that Mann J had to answer was: 'Where a claimant has picked up one or more costs orders in its favour on the way to a trial, but fails very badly at the trial (for example due to exaggeration), can the costs judge assess those costs at nil on the footing that they were not, as it turned out, reasonably incurred because they had been incurred in an action that sought an exaggerated sum which should never have been claimed?' Mann J answer the question in the negative. It should be noted that Mann J did not have the benefit of Waller LJ's guidance in *Drew v Whitbread* [2010] EWCA 53 and in *O'Beirne v Hudson* [2010] EWCA 52. It is possible that his conclusion would have been different had he had this guidance.

[6] After *Re Gibson's Settlement Trusts* [1981] Ch 179.

The *Gibson* principles

49.07 Although rarely encountered in express terms in modern-day practice, Megarry V-C identified the three strands of reasoning that the court will take into account when gauging whether costs are to be allowed in principle.[7] They are known as 'the *Gibson* principles' (after the case in which they were first articulated). Originally, they related equally to profit costs and disbursements, but they have come to have particular resonance where the issue is whether profit costs can be recovered for certain types of work.[8] The three strands are:

- whether the work was of use and service in the claim;
- whether the work was of relevance to an issue in the claim; and
- whether the need for the work can be attributed to the paying party's actions or omissions.[9]

Each of these strands must be decided in the receiving party's favour if the costs in question are to be recoverable in principle.

Sachs J's 'sensible solicitor' and the rule against wrongful retrospection

49.08 It is trite costs law that costs should not be assessed with hindsight, but the 'sensible solicitor' test, as explicated by Sachs J, deals with more than only wrongful retrospection:

> 'The correct viewpoint to be adopted by a taxing officer is that of a sensible solicitor sitting in his chair and considering what in the light of his then knowledge is reasonable in the interests of his lay client ... [It] is wrong for a taxing officer to adopt an attitude akin to a revenue official called upon to apply rigorously one of those Income Tax Act Rules as to expenses which have been judicially described as "jealously restricted" and "notoriously rigid and narrow in their operation." I should add that, as previously indicated, the lay client in question should be deemed a man of means adequate to bear the expense of the litigation out of his own pocket – and by "adequate" I mean neither "barely adequate" nor "superabundant".'[10]

Whilst these comments can apply to any item of costs, they are particularly relevant to profit costs, not least because profit costs are the costs over which a solicitor has most control.

The duty to examine material

49.09 Where profit costs are challenged, the receiving party will usually place file notes, letters, etc, before the court in support of the costs claimed. This may be formally (as a result of the court exercising its discretion to put the receiving party to their election) or informally

---

[7] See *Re Gibson's Settlement Trusts* [1981] Ch 179, at 185, in which Megarry V-C drew on *Frankenburg v Famous Lasky Film Service Ltd* [1931] 1 Ch 428 and *Société Anonyme Pêcheries Ostendaises v Merchants Marine Insurance Co* [1928] 1 KB 750.

[8] See, eg, *Ross v Owners of the Bowbelle (Review of Taxation under Ord 62 r 35)* (1997) 2 Lloyd's Rep 196 (Note) QBD (Admlty); *Roach v Home Office* [2009] EWHC 312 (QB).

[9] Some authorities—including *Re Gibson's Settlement Trusts* [1981] Ch 179 itself—refer to the third strand as pertaining to the 'conduct' of the paying party. The way in which Megarry V-C applied that test makes it clear that the issue is not whether the receiving party has been vexed by poor conduct, but whether the need for the work can be attributed to the paying party's endeavours.

[10] *Francis v Francis and Dickerson* [1956] P 87, at 91.

without the issue of election ever arising (see 46.45–46.47). The following points may be made about the court's duty to examine the relevant material. That said, nothing that follows is intended to promote a laborious approach to the quantification of costs; the fact that the law permits time to be scrutinised in minute detail[11] does not mean that every assessment should proceed in that way.

The need for an adequate examination

Whilst the case before him related to the assessment of criminal, rather than civil, costs, Maurice Kay LJ (sitting in the Divisional Court) explained that where a costs judge finds that costs are to be admitted in principle, the documentation must be adequately examined before an assessment of quantum can be made.[12] Whilst that may be so as a matter of law, a more informal approach pertains in practice, in that run-of-the-mill items are often assessed without sight of the documents. This is especially true in so far as provisional assessments are concerned. **49.10**

Extrapolating from a sample and broad-brush assessments

Where the court is daunted by the prospect of carrying out a line-by-line assessment (such as where there is a lengthy schedule), it may adopt a broad-brush method based on an extrapolation of the assessment of a sample of the items. Park J has commented that, where this is so, the court should be mindful of the fact that if the sample is unrepresentative, errors may be made that may serve to substantially distort the accuracy of that method.[13] In a similar vein (but in the context of the court seeking to disallow the costs of pursuing an exaggerated claim), Kennedy LJ found that it would be wrong in principle to apply a percentage discount in lieu of an item-by-item assessment. He explained that the correct approach was to go through the bill on an item-by-item basis and only then (if appropriate) to apply a percentage reduction.[14] **49.11**

Time Recording and Estimated Time

Time recording, computer printouts, attendance notes, etc

In a well-run practice, time will always be recorded (either manually by keeping file or attendance notes, or electronically by making an entry in a computerised practice management system). Despite its obsolescence, the following guidance from a 1986 practice direction still has resonance: **49.12**

> 'Properly kept and detailed time records are helpful in support of a bill provided they explain the nature of the work as well as recording the time involved. The absence of such

---

[11] Some judges have been in favour of a very detailed approach. In *Chamberlain v Boodle & King* [1982] 1 WLR 1443, at 1445, Denning MR, for example, had this to say (in his own inimitable way): 'These rates are over a pound a minute. It would seem that there must be a very good system of timing—almost by stopwatch—if that is to be the rate of payment.'

[12] *R (on the application of Brewer) v Supreme Court Costs Office* [2006] EWHC 1955 (Admin), at [24]–[26].

[13] See, eg, *Arab Monetary Fund v Hashim* (unreported), 30 June 2000, Ch D, *per* Park J, in which the costs judge allowed 80 per cent of a senior grade fee earner's time, but, on closer scrutiny, an allowance of 90 per cent was the appropriate extrapolation.

[14] *Booth v Britannia Hotels Ltd* [2002] EWCA Civ 579.

records may result in the disallowance or diminution of the charges claimed. They cannot be accepted as conclusive evidence that the time recorded either has been spent or if spent, is "reasonably" chargeable.'[15]

Thus keeping an accurate record of what was done will assist in the recovery of costs, but the mere fact that a contemporaneous record was kept would not be conclusive on the issue of whether the costs claimed were recoverable.

(Over)reliance on computerised records and coding

49.13 Practice management systems exist that automatically record work as it is carried out. Many will allow this to be done in the form of Uniform Task-Based Management System for England and Wales (EW-UTBMS) codes (otherwise known as J-Codes) or some other UTBMS-based system. Automated time recording is a useful adjunct for the purposes of assessment, but overreliance on automated records is a risky strategy. Payne J had the following to say on the matter:

> 'I ought to add that this case illustrates the dangers which are present if reliance is placed on a modern system of recording, without at the same time retaining the old and well tried practice of keeping attendance notes showing briefly the time taken and the purport of the work done day by day. It may be that this case will invite attention to the importance of appreciating the limits to which the computer system can be used in cases where taxation of costs must follow litigation and to the necessity of preserving as well the use of the traditional systems.'[16]

Payne J made these comments in the very early days of computerised time recording (the 1970s) and before the advent of coding, but there is nothing to suggest that they have ceased to apply.[17] Indeed, it is easier to create a false impression using numbers and codes than it is to do so using words, so modern coding systems provide the perfect *tabula rasa* onto which works of great fiction may—inadvertently or otherwise—appear. As such, it could easily be argued that Payne J's words of caution continue to be relevant. That said, a distinction should be made between mere codes and detailed entries, which—in effect—are file or attendance notes that are merely kept in digital form.

Absence of attendance or file notes

49.14 The best evidence of time spent continues to be the file or attendance note (be it in digital or paper form). This does not mean, however, that a solicitor is under a duty to keep such a record. Hart J had this to say on the point:

> '[It] seems to me wrong to speak of an "obligation" to keep attendance notes. That language suggests that failure to keep attendance notes is a duty [*sic*], breach of which will be visited by the sanction of total or partial disallowance. The true position is that in both kinds of work the burden is on the solicitor not only to show that the time claimed has been spent but that it has been reasonable to spend that time. The keeping of an attendance note is one way, but not the only way, in which this can be demonstrated.'[18]

---

[15] *Practice Direction (Supreme Court Taxing Office) No 1 of 1986* (unreported), February 1986, SCTO, at n 13.

[16] *Re Kingsley* (1978) 122 Sol Jo 457. The passage quoted is not in the report, but may be found on the last page of the transcript.

[17] Indeed, the authors of *Cook on Costs 2014* (LexisNexis, online), para 31.26, cite *Re Kingsley* (1978) 122 Sol Jo 457.

[18] *Jemma Trust Co Ltd v Liptrott & Ors (No 2)* [2004] EWHC 1404 (Ch), at [43].

Hart J went on to say that a failure to keep file or attendance notes would expose the receiving party to the risk of being unable to prove the reasonableness of the time spent. Where there is a complete absence of any record of time spent, then costs may still be claimed, but this would have to be on the basis of estimated time. This is dealt with at 49.15–49.19.

Estimated time

Estimated time is time that is claimed notwithstanding the absence of a contemporaneous record of the time spent. It is time that has been estimated retrospectively, usually either by the legal representative who did the work, or by the costs lawyer or costs draftsperson who prepared the bill. Two topics arise: firstly, the question of whether costs based on estimated time are recoverable in principle (see 49.17–49.18); and secondly, the question of how much ought to be allowed (see 49.19). **49.15**

There is—surprisingly, one may think—no requirement within either the Civil Procedure Rules (CPR) or the associated practice directions that estimated time should be stated to be such in the bill. It is nonetheless good practice to state the fact that time has been estimated—usually by marking the entry with an 'e' or some other suitable symbol. Best practice would be also to state the basis upon which the time has been estimated (for example '12 mins (e); estimate based on two-page attendance note', or 'the time has been estimated at 6 minutes per page'). **49.16**

The recoverability of estimated time in principle

There will be occasions on which it is not possible to record time. Parker J gave as an example an exceptionally complex case in which short, but important, discussions arose in an environment of exigency.[19] He found that it would be 'wholly impractical in some instances to keep [attendance] notes'.[20] Parker J found that there is no reason in principle why the court should not accept that actual time was spent notwithstanding the absence of a contemporaneous time recording. Brooke J came to a similar conclusion, finding that the general rule is that costs are not made irrecoverable solely by reason of being based on estimated time.[21] **49.17**

Where time is estimated, the court is entitled to require the receiving party to explain the basis upon which the estimate was made. This may involve the receiving party being put to their election in respect of the material upon which the estimate was based. Whether or not the court allows the time will be a matter of fact to be decided on the evidence, but the material the court may take into account is not limited to the presence or absence of attendance notes, as Parker J explained: **49.18**

> 'The right to charge cannot depend upon the question whether discussions are recorded or unrecorded. It must depend, initially, upon whether they in fact took place and occupied the time claimed. If they are recorded in attendance notes, this will no doubt ordinarily be accepted as sufficient evidence of those facts. If they are not so recorded it may well be that

[19] *In re Frascati* (unreported), 2 December 1981, QBD.

[20] *Ibid*, quoted in *Brush v Bower Cotton & Bower* [1993] 4 All ER 741, at 753.

[21] Although a pre-CPR case, the authority that is usually cited on this point is *Brush v Bower Cotton & Bower* [1993] 4 All ER 741, at 753, in which Brooke J reviewed the authorities on the point.

the claimant is unable to satisfy the taxing officer or master as to the facts. But neither the presence nor the absence of an attendance note is conclusive.'[22]

Assessment of the amount of estimated time

49.19 The time that will be allowed will depend on the nature of the claim that is made. In particular, it will depend on the cogency of the available evidence and the type of work carried out. The following comments may be made.

- **Long attendances** Brooke J has warned that claims for unrecorded long attendances are likely to be 'viewed with very considerable care' and that it would be in only an unusual case that any substantial allowance would be made for unrecorded time.[23]
- **Short attendances** It is implicit in what is said about long attendances that the court will not necessarily be perturbed by the fact that there is no record of the time spent in short attendances (although, of course, the award may be less generous than it otherwise might have been). A complete absence of a record of the fact of the attendance will rarely be overlooked entirely (see 49.18).
- **Repeated failure to record time** Where there is a habitual failure to record the time spent, very significant reductions are the norm. For example, in a case in which 350 hours of unrecorded time had been claimed, Park J described an allowance of 100 hours as 'generous'.[24]
- **'Padding' of the bill** Whilst a colloquial expression, a bill may be said to be 'padded' if it contains multiple claims for short attendances or other work that are not recorded but which are said to be implied by the nature of the work being carried out. An example would be where short file reviews are habitually claimed before writing routine letters. Whilst he did not refer to it by that name, Evans J found that the court is entitled to disallow costs that are the result of padding, this being on the basis that there is no presumption that the time that is recorded in a file is an under-recording of the time spent.[25]

Most of the cases referred to above are pre-CPR; given the fact that neither the Rules of the Supreme Court (RSC) nor the CPR have anything significant to say about estimated time, they probably remain good law. That said, as with all pre-CPR cases, they ought to be viewed with appropriate caution.

Phases, Tasks and Activities under the CPR

49.20 By the time this book is published, it is likely that certain costs will have to be entered into an electronic bill of costs that reports and aggregates costs according to certain defined phases, tasks and activities. Whilst it is not an official term, the phrase 'CPR code-set' may be used to refer to the system of coding that appears in Precedent S (which was the most recent version of the electronic bill of costs that was available at the time of writing). It

[22] *In re Frascati* (unreported), 2 December 1981, QBD. The transcript of this case is no longer available, but the quoted text is referred to in *Brush v Bower Cotton & Bower* [1993] 4 All ER 741, at 753, and in Cook, M, *Cook on Costs* (London: Butterworths, 1991), p 23.

[23] *Brush v Bower Cotton & Bower* [1993] 4 All ER 741, at 742.

[24] *Arab Monetary Fund v Hashim* (unreported), 30 June 2000, Ch D.

[25] *Johnson v Reed Corrugated Cases Ltd* [1992] 1 All ER 169, at 187. This was in response to the suggestion that *Maltby v D J Freeman & Co* [1978] 2 All ER 913, at 916, was authority for the proposition that an allowance ought to be routinely made for unrecorded time.

should be borne in mind, however, that that 'code-set' is not a proper code-set of the type described at 49.176; rather, it is merely the remnants that were left after the EW-UTBMS code-set was stripped out of the pilot electronic bill of costs (see 49.167). Indeed, it is probably not right to afford it the status of a code-set.

Code-sets, phases, tasks, activities and expenses

Case-specific data is recorded in the form of one or more of a series of code-sets. The CPR code-set (or any code-set that is described in this chapter) works at three different levels of generality, as follows.[26] **49.21**

- **Phase** The highest level is the 'phase', such as 'Initial and Pre-Action Protocol Work'.
- **Task** The intermediate level is the 'task'. Each phase comprises a number of tasks; hence the phase 'Issue/Statements of Case' may include tasks such as 'Review of Other Party/Opponents' Statement of Case'.
- **Activity** The lowest level of generality is the 'activity', for example 'Communicate (with Client)'.

Thus there are phase codes and task codes (see 49.23–49.49), and there are activity codes (see 49.50–49.102). In addition, there are expense codes, which deal with disbursements. Codes in the CPR code-set are denoted either by their descriptive title (such as the examples given above) or by two- or three-digit alphanumeric codes. There are 15 defined phases (P1–P15), 41 defined tasks (T1–T41), 10 activities (A1–A10), and 10 expenses (X1–X10). A summary of the CRP code-set may be found on the inside back cover of this book.

The background to the CPR code-set

As is explained in detail at 49.175, the CPR code-set had its origins in a coding system known as EW-UTBMS codes (otherwise known as J-Codes), a code-set belonging to the Uniform Task-Based Management System (UTBMS)[27] that was created for use in England and Wales. Should the receiving party so wish, J-Codes may still be used; in view of this, they are described at the end of this chapter (see 49.165–49.189). **49.22**

Phases and tasks under the CPR

Under the CPR, there are 15 coded phases and 41 coded tasks, as set out below (with phase codes and task codes in parentheses). Unless otherwise stated, the phases and tasks correspond with those that are used for the purposes of budgeting—that is, for Precedent H (see 12.26). Some of the latter phases and tasks deal with costs that would never fall within the ambit of a budget (such as the costs of a detailed assessment); as such, many of those latter codes have no budgeting counterpart. Each phase is dealt with in turn. **49.23**

Phase Code 1 (P1), 'Initial and Pre-Action Protocol Work' Phase One is defined as: 'Work relating to the obtaining of instructions, identification of witnesses, dealing with locus and evidential issues, dealing with and identifying legal issues arising from the case **49.24**

[26] See Nelson, D, *Jackson Review of Civil Litigation Costs: UTBMS Drafting Group—Civil Litigation J-Code Set Overview and Guidelines*, 27 July 2014, available online at http://utbms.com/jackson-ew-utbms/, p 7.

[27] See http://utbms.com/. The UTBMS was originally produced through collaborative effort between the American Bar Association, the American Corporate Counsel Association, and a group of major corporate clients and law firms, coordinated and supported by Price Waterhouse LLP (now PricewaterhouseCoopers).

and strategy, and dealing with any protocol related matters, if not covered elsewhere.' It corresponds with the 'Pre-Action Costs' phase in Precedent H.

49.25 Phase 1 encompasses the following three tasks.

- **'Factual investigation' (T1)** 'Work required to understand the facts of the case including instructions from the client and the identification of potential witnesses[.]'
- **'Legal investigation' (T2)** 'Includes identification of the legal issues raised by the case facts and developing the strategy for the case.'
- **'Pre-action protocol (or similar) work' (T3)** 'Communications at an initial stage in compliance with pre-action protocol including letters before action and responses.'

49.26 There is clearly the potential for overlap between T1 and T3, not least in terms of communications with the client for the purposes of establishing the facts. Whilst there is no authority on the point, perhaps the best way of dealing with overlap is to enter the time in the most specific category (which, in this instance, would be T1). Indeed, whilst no more than the editor's own observation, it seems that—in general—specific tasks precede more general tasks; as such, if in doubt, a rule of thumb would be to include work in the first potentially applicable task.

49.27 **Phase Code 2 (P2), 'Issue/Statements of Case'** Phase 2 is defined in the following way: 'Covers issue and acknowledgment of proceedings, Statements of Case and Further Information requests/responses. Includes taking instructions, making inquiries and searches, researching, drafting, editing, filing and all meetings and communications for the purpose of such documents.'

49.28 Phase 2 encompasses the following four tasks.

- **'Issue and Serve Proceedings and Preparation of Statement(s) of Case' (T4)** 'Work related to effecting service, including dealing with process servers or the foreign process office; work in preparation of claims, petitions and any other originating process, Statements of Case, Part 20 proceedings, including reviewing those of other parties whether or not a responsive document is served. Includes all work with counsel thereon and all dealings with client and others in connection therewith. In appeals includes Appellants' and Respondents' Notices and supporting skeleton arguments.'
- **'Review of Other Party(s)' Statements of Case' (T5)** 'Considering Other Party(s)' Claim Form and Statements of Case.'
- **'Requests for Further Information' (T6)** 'Preparing and considering requests for Further Information and responses thereto.'
- **'Amendment of Statements of Case' (T7)** 'Preparing and considering amendments to originating process, Statements of Case, Part 20 proceedings. In appeals refers to amendments to Appellants' and Respondents' Notices and supporting skeleton arguments.'

49.29 **Phase Code 3 (P3) and Task Code 8 (T8), 'Case Management Conference'** Phase 3 is defined as: 'Work relating to such hearings and the preparation for them, including [pre-trial review] PTR and CMC's [*sic*]. This does not include interim applications heard at the same time (excludes costs management).' It comprises only one task (T8) and corresponds with the case management conference (CMC) phase in Precedent H.

Phase Code 4 (P4), 'Disclosure' Phase 4 is defined as: 'Work relating to gathering and reviewing documents for potential disclosure, preparing disclosure lists and practical steps of disclosure.' **49.30**

Phase 4 encompasses the following four tasks. **49.31**

- **'Preparation of the disclosure report and the disclosure proposal'** (T9) 'Preparation of the disclosure report and the disclosure proposal to comply with obligations that came in on 1-April-2013 (applicable to both manual and e-disclosure). All Disclosure related work required for the CMC. Additionally, this task encompasses work such as determining the location of documents, letters to client re disclosure obligations and setting up client based disclosure teams.'
- **'Obtaining and reviewing documents'** (T10) 'Obtaining and reviewing documents to determine relevance (applicable to both manual and e-disclosure).'
- **'Preparing and serving disclosure lists'** (T11) 'Preparing and serving disclosure lists (applicable to both manual and e-disclosure).'
- **'Inspection and review of the other side's disclosure for work undertaken after exchange of disclosure lists'** (T12) 'Inspection and review of the other side's disclosure for work undertaken after exchange of disclosure lists (applicable to both manual and e-disclosure).'

Phase Code 5 (P5), 'Witness Statements' Phase 5 is defined as: 'Work that relates to the identification of potential witnesses and preparing their evidence for trial (excludes witness evidence in relation to interim applications).' **49.32**

Phase 5 encompasses the following two tasks. **49.33**

- **'Taking, preparing and finalising witness statement(s)'** (T13) 'Work involved in identifying appropriate witnesses, tracing and communicating with same, taking instructions for, preparing and serving witness statements or affidavits, preparing and serving witness summaries, preparing and serving any notices under Civil Evidence or similar Acts, preparing and serving witness summonses, including reviewing other materials for these purposes and all dealings with client, witnesses, inquiry agents, counsel, Other Party(s) and others in relation to own side witness statements.'
- **'Reviewing Other Party(s)' witness statement(s)'** (T14) 'Considering Other Party(s)' witness statements, affidavits, witness summaries, Civil Evidence Act or similar notices, reviewing same in context of other evidence and material, considering strategy to deal with issues raised.'

Phase 6 (P6), 'Expert reports' Phase 6 is defined as: 'Work that relates to the identification of potential experts and preparing their evidence for trial (excludes expert evidence in relation to interim applications).' **49.34**

Phase 6 encompasses the following three tasks. **49.35**

- **'Own expert evidence'** (T15) 'Identifying and interviewing experts and consultants (testifying or non-testifying), working with them, and developing expert reports. Reviewing case in the light of such evidence. Considering questions asked by Other Party(s) of own experts and experts' responses. Arranging experts' discussions; considering reports of experts' discussions; includes all communications or other work with counsel, and all communications with Other Party.'

- **'Other Party(s)' expert evidence' (T16)** 'Considering Other Party(s)' expert evidence, preparing and asking questions of their experts, considering replies, reviewing case in light of such evidence.'
- **'Joint expert evidence' (T17)** 'As [T15] (own expert evidence) with appropriate modifications.'

49.36 **Phase Code 7 (P7) and Task Code 18 (T18), 'Pre-Trial Review'** Phase 7 is defined as: 'Work in preparing for and attending any Pre Trial Review (excluding Costs Management).' It comprises a single task (T18) and corresponds to the 'PTR' task in Precedent H.

49.37 **Phase Code 8 (P8), 'Trial preparation'** Phase 8 is defined as: 'Work for the preparation of the trial not included in the other phases.' It encompasses the following tasks.

- **'Preparation of trial bundles' (T19)** 'Time spent identifying documents for inclusion in the trial bundles, working with the other parties to agree the trial bundles, preparing and updating the trial bundles.'
- **'General work regarding preparation for trial' (T20)** 'All other time spent in preparing for and supporting a trial, including developing overall trial strategy, preparing own witnesses for trial, working on cross-examination, preparing opening and closing arguments, identifying documents for use at trial, preparing demonstrative materials, making any physical arrangements for trial etc[.]'

49.38 **Phase Code 9 (P9), 'Trial'** Phase 9 is defined as: 'Covers preparation for advocacy including written trial submissions and all other work from the first day on which a trial or appeal begins or, if settled, was due to begin.'

49.39 Phase 9 encompasses the following three tasks.

- **'Advocacy' (T21)** 'Preparation by advocates of written and oral openings, closings or skeleton arguments; preparation for examination of witnesses; preparation of and for all applications made during trial; considering all submissions of other parties; attendance of advocates during trial. Includes all dealings by advocates with others (e.g. solicitors, clients, witnesses) for these purposes.'
- **'Support of advocates' (T22)** 'Work by lawyers other than advocates relating to the above matters and all attendances at court on trial days including conferences or meetings before or after court and travel and waiting. Where there is a substantial gap between trial days, work should be allocated to whichever is the more appropriate of the Trial Preparation and Trial phases.'
- **'Judgment and post-trial activity' (T23)** 'Considering draft judgments, preparing and considering any written responses to the court, submissions or skeleton arguments in relation to judgment or consequential orders, preparation for and attendance at hearings when reserved judgments handed down or consequential orders considered, all dealings relating to form of judgment or order. Includes all meetings and communications relating thereto.'

49.40 **Phase Code 10 (P10), 'ADR/Settlement'** Phase 10 is defined as: 'Work that is directed to settlement including [alternative dispute resolution] ADR.' It corresponds with the 'ADR/settlement discussions' in Precedent H and comprises the following two tasks.

- **'Mediation'** (T24) 'Work related to proposals for mediation, preparation and attendance at the mediation and any follow-up work.'
- **'Other Settlement Matters'** (T25) 'Work that is directed to settlement including Part 36 and other offers and consequent negotiations (includes all forms of ADR other than mediation).'

This is a topic that is addressed in detail at 49.132–49.139.

Phase Code 11 (P11), 'Interim Applications and Hearings (Interlocutory Applications)' Phase 11 is defined as: 'Work covering all proposed and actual interim applications and hearings. Includes taking instructions, making inquiries, research, preparing and filing applications, supporting evidence and skeleton arguments including reviewing those of other parties whether or not a responsive document is served, preparing for and attending hearings and all meetings and communications for the purpose of such applications or hearings.' Rather confusingly, P11 corresponds with the 'contingencies' in Precedent H; it will also include work that would fall within the ambit of Practice Direction (PD) 3E, para 7.9 (see 12.06). **49.41**

Phase 11 encompasses the following array of tasks. **49.42**

- **'Applications relating to originating process or Statement of Case or for default or summary judgment'** (T26) 'Includes applications as to service or jurisdiction, to strike out or amend all or part of a claim or Statement of Case, or for the variation of parties.'
- **'Applications for an injunction or committal'** (T27) 'Work performed related to applications for an injunction or committal.'
- **'Applications for disclosure or Further Information'** (T28) 'Work performed related to applications for disclosure or Further Information[.]'
- **'Applications concerning evidence'** (T29) 'Work performed related to applications concerning evidence[.]'
- **'Applications relating to Costs alone'** (T30) 'Includes applications for security for costs, costs capping and protective costs orders. Does not include budgeting or costs management orders which are dealt with [under 'costs management']. Does not include applications proceeding as to costs alone where a substantive application for some other relief has settled.'
- **'Permission applications'** (T31) 'All permission applications where permission to proceed is required, such as in judicial review proceedings or on appeal.'
- **'Other applications'** (T32) 'All other types of application not covered by the categories above.'

Phase Code 12 (P12) and Task Code 33 (T33), 'Funding' Phase 12 is defined as: 'All work relating to reviewing funding options, securing funding and reports to funders during the life of the case.' It comprises only one task (T33). This Phase has no counterpart in Precedent H. **49.43**

Given that the costs of funding are not recoverable between opposing parties (see 49.112), it is not entirely clear why this phase/task has been included in a code-set that is intended for use between opposing parties. Perhaps its purpose is to allow the court to explicitly identify the costs of funding so that they can be excluded—support for which view may be gleaned from the fact that Sir Rupert Jackson said, in the context of Legal Electronic Data Exchange Standard (LEDES™) coding, that provision must be made for work that is not **49.44** chargeable to be allocated to a separate file[28] (see 49.170). The points made at 49.181 may also be relevant. Given the fact that the CPR code-set was modelled on the EW-UTBMS code-set, it may be that P12/T33 has been carried over; if this is so, then it is not the case that the inclusion of P12/T33 necessarily implies that the costs of funding are recoverable between opposing parties.

49.45 **Phase Code 13 (P13), 'Budgeting incl. costs estimates'** Phase 13 is defined as: 'All work throughout the life of the case relating to budgeting and costs management, excluding the "costs assessment" and "funding" related work and preparation for and attendance at any costs management hearing, all of which have discrete phases.'

49.46 Phase 13 encompasses the following three tasks.

- **'Budgeting—own side's costs' (T34)** 'Preparing budgets solely for the client and monitoring costs incurred for the purposes of any required variations. Performing budgetary work related to obtaining third party funding/[after-the-event] ATE insurance.'
- **'Budgeting—Precedent H' (T35)** 'Initially completing Precedent H—This task is confined to preparing and compiling the first budget required by the court in the form of Precedent H.'
- **'Budgeting—between the parties' (T36)** 'Work on budgeting between the parties following initial completion of the first budget, including the monitoring of costs incurred against the budget and any applications for variation of a budget.'

This phase has no counterpart in Precedent H (other than that the limits imposed by PD 3E, para 7.2, will appear on the first page of the relevant budget). The costs of budgeting are addressed at 12.130–12.136.

49.47 **Phase Code 14 (P14) and Task Code 37 (T37), 'Costs Management Conference'** Phase 14 is defined as: 'Work in preparing for and attending any Costs Management Conference/Hearing including the hearing of any applications to vary a budget.' It comprises just one task (T37). It has no counterpart in Precedent H.

49.48 **Phase Code 15 (P15), 'Costs Assessment'** Phase 15 is defined as: 'Work related to the assessment or agreement of costs following trial or settlement of the underlying action.' For obvious reasons, it has no counterpart in Precedent H.

49.49 Phase 15 encompasses the last four of the tasks.

- **'Preparing costs claim' (T38)** 'Includes the reconciliation of the costs claimed to any approved budget in and the preparation of the bill of costs for detailed assessment' (see 49.140).
- **'Points of dispute, Replies and Negotiations' (T39)** 'Work on the formal procedural steps under CPR 47 following service of a bill of costs together with Part 36 and other offers to settle costs and consequent negotiations[.]'
- **'Hearings' (T40)** 'Includes preparation for and attendance at hearings for directions and interim certificate applications as well as the detailed assessment itself[.]'

[28] Jackson, R, *Review of Civil Litigation Costs: Final Report* (London: HMSO, 2010), ch 45, para 5.5.

- **'Post Assessment Work (Excluding Hearings)' (T41)** 'Includes post-hearing calculations and all other work required to finalise the amounts due for principal, interest and the costs of the assessment[.]'

Activities as Defined in the CPR

There are ten activities that are listed, as follows (with the activity code in parentheses). **49.50**

- **'Appear For/Attend' (A1)** 'Any appearance for or attendance at a scheduled event related to the matter (see 49.51–49.55);
- **'Communicate (with Counsel)' (A2)** 'Any communication by letter, fax, email, telephone, meetings and conferences with own-side Counsel' (see 49.56–49.57).
- **'Communicate (with client)' (A3)** 'Any communication by letter, fax, email, telephone, meetings and conferences with client' (see 49.58–49.59).
- **'Communicate (witnesses)' (A4)** 'Any communication by letter, fax, email, telephone, meetings and conferences with witnesses' (see 49.60).
- **'Communicate (experts)' (A5)** 'Any communication by letter, fax, email, telephone, meetings and conferences with experts' (see 49.61).
- **'Communicate (Other Party(s)/other outside lawyers)' (A6)** 'Any communication by letter, fax, email, telephone, meetings and conferences with opposing lawyers or other outside lawyers not representing the client' (see 49.62).
- **'Communicate (other external)' (A7)** 'Any communication by letter, fax, email, telephone, meetings and conferences with other external parties not already categorised within these activity codes' (see 49.63–49.64).
- **'Communicate (internally within legal team)' (A8)** 'Any internal communications within firm' (see 49.65–49.75).
- **'Billable Travel Time' (A9)** 'Includes time spent waiting associated with the matter when other billable services are not performed for the client' (see 49.76–49.80).
- **'Plan, Prepare, Draft, Review' (A10)** 'Any planning or preparation associated with a matter; Any drafting or revision or other preparation of documents or other material; Any review or analysis of documents or other material; Any handling of documents, files or data' (see 49.81–49.95).

Each activity code is now dealt with in turn. Communications in general are addressed at 49.96–49.102.

'Appear For/Attend' (A1)

This activity is defined in the following way: 'Any appearance for or attendance at a scheduled event related to the matter.' In general, this will include attendances in court at trial or at any other scheduled event, either with or without counsel. **49.51**

Sitting behind counsel at trial

The rule that a solicitor had to attend counsel at trial[29] was amended as long ago as 3 April 2001 and was abolished entirely on 5 October 2011; there is now no professional rule that requires counsel to be attended by their instructing solicitors in court (either at trial or at all). That said, whilst it now no longer applies, the following (selective) extract from the **49.52**

[29] Solicitors' Practice Rules 1990, r 20.04.

Solicitors' Code of Conduct 2007 is a useful guide as to the circumstances in which attendance would generally be required:

> '8. Whenever you instruct an advocate—whether counsel or a solicitor advocate—you will need to decide whether it is in the interests of your client and the interests of justice for you, or a responsible representative of your firm, to attend the proceedings. In reaching this decision you will need to consider what is necessary for the proper conduct of the case, taking into account the nature and complexity of the case and the capacity of the client to understand the proceedings. For example, you, or your representative, should normally attend:
> [...]
> (c) where the client may have difficulty in giving or receiving instructions or in understanding the proceedings, for example if the client is a child, has inadequate knowledge of English, or suffers from a mental illness or some other disability;
> (d) where the client is likely to disrupt proceedings if the advocate appears alone;
> (e) where the advocate is representing more than one party to the hearing;
> [...]
> (g) where there are a large number of witnesses in the case;
> (h) ...; or
> (i) where issues are likely to arise which question the client's character or your conduct of the case.'[30]

For obvious reasons, the clear majority of hearings will be far removed from these situations; more commonplace reasons for permitting the attendance of solicitors at trial would be where there is a need to care for witnesses or where there is a need to keep a handwritten note, etc. Special provisions apply to fast-track trials (see 50.350–50.361).

More than one fee earner attending or appearing at a scheduled event

49.53 The attendance of more than one fee earner at a trial or at another scheduled event will need to be justified. The court may take into account the fact that if only one fee earner were to attend, they would be able to liaise with other fee earners by telephone.[31] Where there is more than one claimant or more than one defendant and where there is no conflict between them, then the costs of separate representation may not be justified.[32]

More than one fee earner sitting behind counsel in the Court of Appeal

49.54 While dealing with the issues of costs in the context of summary assessment, rather than the detailed assessment of costs, the Guide to the Summary Assessment of Costs gives the following advice:

> 'Although it is usually reasonable to have a senior fee earner sitting with Counsel in the Court of Appeal, it is not usually reasonable to have two fee earners. The second fee earner may be there for training purposes only.'[33]

[30] Solicitors' Code of Conduct 2007, r 11 (Litigation and advocacy), Guidance note. That said, see *Motto & Ors v Trafigura Ltd & Anor* [2011] EWCA Civ 1150, at [112]: Lord Neuberger MR has explained that the mere fact that a solicitor is obliged to do something does not mean that the costs of that task are recoverable between opposing parties; as such, it does not necessarily follow that attendance will be deemed reasonable even if the case falls within one of the categories set out above.

[31] See *Intergraph (UK) Ltd v Wolfson Microelectronics plc* [2012] EWHC 1862 (Ch), at [8], *per* Mr Snowdon QC.

[32] *Birmingham City Council v H (a minor)* [1994] 2 WLR 31, at 33, *per* Lord Keith.

[33] See HM Courts & Tribunals Service, *Guide to the Summary Assessment of Costs* (London: HMSO, 2005), para 65.

Where there is more than one appellant or respondent and where there is no conflict between them, then the costs of separate representation may not be justified[34]—particularly in the context of appeals, because the issues will be well defined. Lord Keith has commented that, where appropriate, it is the duty of counsel and solicitors to consider this issue carefully.[35]

Appointments in the Court of Appeal in general

In respect of appointments in the Court of Appeal, the following further guidance is given: **49.55**

> 'Although many appointments in the Court of Appeal merit the attendance of a senior fee earner familiar with the case, the most minor appointments may not. For example, on an application in the dismissal list in a case tried in Newcastle, if Counsel who was briefed for the trial attends it may be unreasonable for a solicitor familiar with the case to travel from Newcastle to attend also. In order to arrive at a notional figure to represent the instruction of and costs of an agent, it may be appropriate to disallow most of the travel time and travelling expenses claimed by the solicitor.'[36]

'Communicate (with counsel)' (A2)

This activity is defined in the following way: 'Any communication by letter, fax, email, telephone, meetings and conferences with own-side Counsel.' Thus conferences with counsel now fall within the same activity code as communications with counsel (and, no doubt, with their clerk). This dispenses with the time-honoured practice that attendances on court and counsel are dealt with as closely related items. **49.56**

Attendances upon counsel in chambers (including conferences)

Attendances on counsel are treated in the same way as any other attendance. Brooke J has made it clear that it is irrelevant whether counsel raises a fee and it is irrelevant whether counsel has specific instructions on the point being discussed[37]—although the second of these factors may be highly relevant to counsel's fee (see 53.42–53.44). **49.57**

'Communicate (with client)' (A3)

This activity is defined in the following way: 'Any communication by letter, fax, email, telephone, meetings and conferences with client.' The topic of communications in general is addressed at 49.96–49.102. The topic of the costs of travelling to see a client is addressed at 49.77. The costs of a party relying on inappropriately long statements are addressed at 49.84–49.85. Beyond this, no special principles apply. **49.58**

That said, there are certain anecdotal measures that—despite that some would say they are entirely spurious—are often encountered in practice. One of them has found its way into the Guide to the Summary Assessment of Costs (albeit in the context of appeals): **49.59**

> 'Although the solicitor may have spent many hours with the client, the client should have been warned that little of this time is recoverable against a losing party. Reasonable time

---

[34] *Birmingham City Council v H (a minor)* [1994] 2 WLR 31, at 33, *per* Lord Keith.

[35] *Ibid.*

[36] See HM Courts & Tribunals Service, *Guide to the Summary Assessment of Costs* (London: HMSO, 2005), para 66. That document suggests actual figures for the following types of hearing in the Court of Appeal: contested directions hearings; applications for permission to appeal at which the respondent is present; appeals from case management decisions; and dismissal list hearing at which the respondent is present. See the current edition of the Guide for the up-to-date figures.

[37] *Brush v Bower Cotton & Bower* [1993] 1 WLR 1328, at 1352.

spent receiving instructions and reporting events should not greatly exceed the time spent on attending the opponents.'[38]

This is one of many ratios and measures that are said to be of use in assessing the costs of attendance upon the client. Whilst some of them are surprisingly reliable, none of them are supported by any authority.[39]

'Communicate (witnesses)' (A4)

49.60 This activity is defined in this way: 'Any communication by letter, fax, email, telephone, meetings and conferences with witnesses.' The topic of communications in general is addressed at 49.96–49.102. The costs of a party relying on inappropriately long statements are addressed at 49.84. Beyond this, no special principles apply.

'Communicate (experts)' (A5)

49.61 This activity is defined in the following way: 'Any communication by letter, fax, email, telephone, meetings and conferences with experts.' The topic of communications in general is addressed at 49.96–49.102. Beyond this, no special principles apply.

'Communicate (Other Party(s)/other outside lawyers)' (A6)

49.62 This activity is defined as: 'Any communication by letter, fax, email, telephone, meetings and conferences with opposing lawyers or other outside lawyers not representing the client.' The topic of communications in general is addressed at 49.96–49.102. Beyond this, no special principles apply.

'Communicate (other external)' (A7)

49.63 This activity is defined in the following way: 'Any communication by letter, fax, email, telephone, meetings and conferences with other external parties not already categorised within these activity codes.' The topic of communications in general is addressed at 49.96–49.102. It seems that non-scheduled attendances upon the court will fall within this activity code; such costs are recoverable under the CPR in just the same way as are the costs of any other attendance. The notion that the costs of communicating with the court should be subsumed within costs generally is an obsolete doctrine that applied to the intricate scale of fees that existed before 1986 (see 1.137–1.139).[40]

Attendances at court for the purposes of issuing

49.64 In general, the costs of personal attendance at court to issue documents would be largely disallowed on the basis that the same chore could be carried out by post. Where the receiving party can show a degree of urgency, however, an allowance may be made. Thus, in a case in which urgency was compounded by the fact that 'local experience [was that

---

[38] See HM Courts & Tribunals Service, *Guide to the Summary Assessment of Costs* (London: HMSO, 2005), para 65(6).

[39] One anecdotal measure (which the editor has found to be surprisingly reliable) is that if the number of telephone calls to a client exceeds half of the number of letters, then this suggests a degree of duplication or a degree of solicitor-and-client work. Another is that the total time spent on attending upon the client is usually less than half of the documentary time. None of these rules are supported by authority and are nothing more than a method by which a paying party or the court can be alerted to the possibility of unreasonable or irrecoverable costs.

[40] See *Brush v Bower Cotton & Bower* [1993] 1 WLR 1328, at 1352, for a discussion of this point.

applications] can take several days to be processed', Edwards-Stuart J made an allowance for personal attendance.[41]

'Communicate (internally within legal team)' (A8)

This activity is defined as such: 'Any internal communications within firm.' There are several ways in which such communication may take place and—as is explained below—not all of them will result in costs being incurred that are recoverable between opposing parties. **49.65**

Office memoranda and discussions between fee earners

Whilst not binding, Master O'Hare offered this view on the costs of communications between colleagues in the same firm: **49.66**

> 'In my judgment it is always, or almost always, inappropriate for a claim to be made for letters sent by one fee earner to another fee earner in the same firm. The allocation of tasks between them is part of the irrecoverable overhead of the firm. If the senior fee earner needs to be informed of some aspect of a matter he should simply read the relevant attendance notes when the file is sent to him.'[42]

These comments were made in the context of work having been delegated, but they would generally also apply where there has been no delegation. There is no reason to believe that the mere fact that work of this nature now falls within an activity code means that the costs of such work necessarily become recoverable.

Much the same points could be made about the costs of discussions between colleagues in the same firm (as opposed to where there has been an exchange of memoranda). It would, however, be open to the court to make an allowance for the time that would have been spent reading into the file. Moreover, in a matter in which there were 205 claimants and most of the work had been carried out by paralegals under supervision, Laing J found that it would be unrealistic to suggest that no discussions between fee earners should be allowed.[43] This goes to illustrate that each case will be decided on its own facts. **49.67**

Delegation and supervision

Delegation occurs where a duty is entrusted to another; *supervision* occurs where the execution or performance of a task is superintended. The former will usually arise in the context of the person who has conduct of the matter enlisting the help of a more junior colleague; the latter may arise in that context or in the context of someone who has conduct of the matter asking for help from a more senior colleague. **49.68**

Delegation and supervision give rise to the same potential problem, in that both require a degree of interaction between colleagues. The time spent interacting may be objected to on the basis that it was not required or on a more intrinsic basis that such work is not chargeable in principle. **49.69**

[41] *Price v Carter* [2010] EWHC 1737 (TCC), at [9].

[42] *In re Radcliffe* [2004] EWHC 90039 (Costs), at [20]; see also *Senior Courts Taxing Office (SCTO) Practice Direction No 2 of 1992* (unreported), c. September 1992, para 1.8.

[43] *TUI UK Ltd v Tickell & Ors* [2016] EWHC 2741 (QB), at [23]–[31], *per* Laing J.

49.70 That intrinsic objection arises out of the fact that some types of supervision are properly characterised as being the costs of running a practice, rather than the costs of litigation. Whilst he was dealing with a criminal case, Mustill J had this to say on the topic:

> 'Every senior solicitor will wish to keep an eye on what is going on in his office, to make sure that it is operating efficiently, and that the standards set by the senior solicitor, who bears the ultimate responsibility for the proper conduct of all work carried out by the practice, are being scrupulously maintained. Again, a senior solicitor who has proper regard for his broader responsibilities will find it necessary to discuss matters with his more junior staff, as a method of practical instruction, with a view to making them better fitted to perform their allotted work. Very often in both of these spheres the solicitor may occupy some time on a particular case. It would not, however, by any means necessarily follow that this time would be attributed to the preparation of that case, so as to entitle the solicitor to remuneration under [the relevant Regulation]. It would simply be part of the overhead expense incurred by the solicitor in the proper conduct of his practice.'[44]

49.71 As can be seen, Mustill J made no mention of reasonableness. Thus the court may disallow costs, not because they were unreasonably incurred (such as where there has been duplication of effort), but because they are irrecoverable in principle. There is no generally accepted way of referring to that principle, but the phrases 'costs that are absorbed within the overhead' and 'costs of running a practice' are as good as any.

49.72 There is a limit to the amount of work that will be disallowed in this way, however, and once that limit has been reached, then a receiving party will have to demonstrate that the delegation or supervision was reasonably required. Mustill J has explained that the burden will lie with the receiving party to provide an explanation as to why this was so.[45]

49.73 **Delegation** There is nothing wrong in principle with delegation; indeed, there have been instances of the court finding that a receiving party unreasonably *failed* to delegate.[46] Although there is no authority on the point, common sense dictates that, where they are allowed in principle, the costs of delegation will be recoverable only to the extent that the overall costs do not exceed those that would have been incurred had the delegation not taken place (see, by way of analogy, 49.75). That will be a question of fact. An allowance will generally be made for the delegatee to familiarise themselves with the necessary material.[47] Indeed, Edwards-Stuart J impliedly made an allowance for the fact that a very junior fee earner might not have been fully familiar with the relevant procedure (in the context of the procedure being an unusual one—namely, commercial arbitration).[48]

49.74 **Supervision by the person with conduct of the file** Supervision may be provided by the person who has conduct of the litigation; where this is so, the points made immediately

[44] *R v Sandhu* (1984) 29 November, SCTO, reported in Senior Courts Taxing Office (SCTO), *Taxing Masters Compendium* (London: SCTO, 1984), Appx 7. That the principles referred to in that case have survived the introduction of the CPR is suggested by the fact that it was extensively relied upon by Master O'Hare in *In re Radcliffe* [2004] EWHC 90039 (Costs).

[45] *R v Sandhu* (1984) 29 November, SCTO, reported in Senior Courts Taxing Office (SCTO), *Taxing Masters Compendium* (London: SCTO, 1984), Appx 7.

[46] See, eg, *Dawe v Idg Communications Ltd* [2013] EWPCC 33.

[47] Whilst a criminal case, see, eg, *R v Sandhu* (1984) 29 November, SCTO, reported in Senior Courts Taxing Office (SCTO), *Taxing Masters Compendium* (London: SCTO, 1984), Appx 7.

[48] *Price v Carter* [2010] EWHC 1737 (TCC), at [11].

above would apply. It would be open to the court to allow the supervisee a lower rate than would have been allowed if they had been entrusted to carry out the task in hand without supervision—that is, if they had been a delegatee rather than a supervisee[49] (see 51.79).

Supervision of the person with conduct of the file Where the person with conduct of the file is supervised by a more senior colleague, the court will usually consider the effect of that supervision on the overall amount of costs. If, for example, the fact that the supervision has taken place has resulted in the matter being allocated to a junior fee earner, the costs of supervision may well be justifiable. Mustill J had these comments to make on the issue: **49.75**

> 'There must be many cases where, once the case has been allocated to a fee earner of the appropriate grade he or she can be allowed to carry on the work unaided, without any need for intervention by someone more senior. On the other hand, there may equally be cases where, if and when the matter is in the hands of someone who could ordinarily be considered competent to deal with it, there might be an unexpected turn of events where the senior solicitor's extra experience and weight would be an essential reinforcement.'[50]

Mustill J went on to say that costs may be allowable if there has been an unexpected turn of events such that the senior fee earner's extra experience and weight could be said to be 'an essential reinforcement'.

'Billable Travel Time' (A9)

This activity is defined in the following way: 'Includes time spent waiting associated with the matter when other billable services are not performed for the client.' Under the CPR, travelling time is claimed at the same rate as other work (unless, of course, the retainer provides for a lower rate).[51] This is made clear by PD 47, para 5.22(3), which provides: 'Where travelling and waiting time is claimed, this should be allowed at the rate agreed with the client unless this is more than the hourly rate on the assessment.' **49.76**

Travelling to attend upon client

Hallett J (sitting with Master Hurst as an assessor) has confirmed that unless the client is housebound or in hospital, it is normal for a client to visit the solicitor at their offices rather than the other way around.[52] Whilst each case will turn on its own facts, it would be reasonable to infer that the costs of travelling to see a client who is *not* housebound or in hospital would, absent justification, be irrecoverable as a matter of reasonableness. **49.77**

Travelling that saves other costs

In considering the reasonableness of the time claimed for travelling, the court is entitled to examine the entirety of the costs and, in particular, is entitled to look at the savings that **49.78**

[49] *Giambrone v JMC Holidays Ltd* [2002] EWHC 495 (QB), at [7]–[13], *per* Nelson J.

[50] *R v Sandhu* (1984) 29 November, SCTO, reported in Senior Courts Taxing Office (SCTO), *Taxing Masters Compendium* (London: SCTO, 1984), Appx 7, quoted by Master O'Hare in *In re Radcliffe* [2004] EWHC 90039 (Costs).

[51] Although a criminal case, see, by analogy, *R (on the application of Schwartz) v Highbury Corner Magistrates Court* [2009] EWHC 1397 Admin.

[52] *Ledward v Kent & Medway Health Authority* [2003] EWHC 2551 (QB), at [24].

may have been made as a result. Thus, where travelling has reduced the need to engage agents, this is a factor that can be taken into account. Likewise, if travelling has meant that the use of a distant solicitor has reduced the hourly rate, then this too is a factor that may be taken into account.[53]

Travelling rendered unnecessary by technology

49.79 If the travelling could have been avoided by the use of technology, the time may be disallowed. Whilst not dealing specifically with costs, Carnwath LJ had this to say on the topic:

> 'It is incumbent on those advising parties appearing before this, or any, court to take all the steps they can in accordance with CPR Rules 1.1 and 1.3 to reduce the cost of the proceedings. This includes taking advantage of such cost-saving facilities as video-conferencing whenever they are available and it is appropriate to use them.'[54]

Public transport v private car

49.80 Where public transport is reasonably easily available and where it would be more efficient in terms of time, it would be open to the court to find that the costs of travelling by private car were allowable only if and to the extent that this resulted in a saving in costs.[55]

'Plan, Prepare, Draft, Review' (A10)

49.81 This activity is defined in the following way: 'Any planning or preparation associated with a matter; Any drafting or revision or other preparation of documents or other material; Any review or analysis of documents or other material; Any handling of documents, files or data.' This very broad activity includes what previously would have been referred to as 'the documents item'.

49.82 Article 4.16(2) of the now-revoked Costs Practice Direction (CPD) used to provide that, in principle, a bill of costs may contain the following documentary work:

> 'Work done on documents: preparing and considering documentation, including documentation necessary to comply with Practice Direction (Pre-action Conduct) or any relevant pre-action protocols where appropriate, work done in connection with arithmetical calculations of compensation and/or interest and time spent collating documents.'

The provisions in PD 47 are not so descriptive, now simply saying that a bill of costs may contain 'work done on documents'.[56] It is not yet known whether anything turns on this. Generally speaking, documentary time will be assessed without regard to any special rules or principles.

Short documents

49.83 Buxton LJ has confirmed that short documents do not draft themselves,[57] the implication being that pithiness comes at a price.

---

53 *Ledward v Kent & Medway Health Authority* [2003] EWHC 2551 (QB), at [17].
54 *Black v Pastouna & Anor* [2005] EWCA Civ 1389, at [14].
55 Whilst a criminal case, see *R v Slessor* [1997] Costs LR (Core Vol) 438 (a case decided on 1 October 1984).
56 See PD 47, para 5.12(7).
57 *R (on the application of Roudham & Larling Parish Council) v Breckland Council* [2008] EWCA Civ 714, at [28].

Prolixity and long witness statements

49.84 Unjustifiable prolixity may result in costs being disallowed.[58] Where, for example, a party uses its witness statements as a platform on which to rehearse its case (rather than merely as a platform for presenting its evidence), then costs consequences may follow. Whilst speaking about the incidence of costs rather than their amount, Peter Smith J had this to say:

> 'The purpose of my criticism is to put down a marker for all of the legal profession to take on board, that witness statements are supposed to be live evidence of witnesses. Drafting long witness statements with craggy submissions and masses of documents and then, in effect, throwing those witnesses to the wolves without preparing them is one of the many failings of the use of witness statements.'[59]

49.85 Similarly, whilst not a source of law, the Chancery Guide gives the following guidance:

> 'It is incumbent on solicitors and counsel not to allow the costs of preparation of witness statements to be unnecessarily increased by over-elaboration of the statements. Any unnecessary elaboration may be the subject of a special order as to costs.'[60]

Disorganised documentation and opponents' prolixity

49.86 Edwards-Stuart J has implied that where one party causes another to carry out work because of the disorganised nature of the documentation the first party has served, this is a factor that may be taken into account.[61] He went on to say the same about prolix documentation.[62]

Checking documents

49.87 It will often be the case that documents need to be checked before some step can be taken (such as checking whether a client has given authority for an offer to be made) and this will often take far less than 6 minutes. Where this is so, it is permissible for the court to allow some, but not all, such items (that is, to discount the time by not allowing all of the items as claimed).[63]

Reading in, duplication and new legal representation

49.88 While each case will turn on its own facts, time spent by one fee earner reading into a file after having received it from another fee earner is generally irrecoverable.[64] The same may apply where solicitors duplicate counsel's work.[65] Where costs have been duplicated by reason of a new firm being instructed, the 'reading in' costs of the new firm will generally be disallowed, but each case must be decided on its own facts and if the work of the first

---

[58] Whilst it concerned a barrister instructed directly, rather than a solicitor, see *Dunn v Glass Systems (UK) Ltd* [2007] EWHC 1901 (QB), in which fees were disallowed on the basis that they were for drafting prolix pleadings that would have led to the litigation being unmanageable.

[59] *A&E Television Networks LLC v Discovery Communications Europe Ltd* [2013] EWHC 276 (Pat), at [18].

[60] HM Courts & Tribunals Service, *Chancery Guide* (London: HMSO, 2016), para 19.7.

[61] *Price v Carter* [2010] EWHC 1737 (TCC), at [15].

[62] *Ibid*, at [16]–[18].

[63] See *TUI UK Ltd v Tickell & Ors* [2016] EWHC 2741 (QB), at [46]–[48], *per* Laing J.

[64] Although of only persuasive value, this is confirmed by HM Courts & Tribunals Service, *Guide to the Summary Assessment of Costs* (London: HMSO, 2005), para 65(7).

[65] *Ibid*.

was of questionable quality, then it may be appropriate to disallow that firm's fees instead. In any event, care must be taken to ensure that costs are not disallowed twice.[66]

Collating documents

49.89 Article 4.6(7) of the CPD used to state, in terms, that the costs of time spent collating documents were, in principle, recoverable under the CPR. As was mentioned at 49.82, PD 47 has rid itself of the specific reference to collating documents; whether this is intended to have any bearing on the recoverability of costs of collating documents is not known. Moreover, it is not wholly clear what is meant by 'collate': it is often taken to be a reference to sorting and marshalling documents, but the *Oxford English Dictionary* suggests that, when used in its legal sense, 'collate' means bringing documents together for comparison to ascertain points of agreement and difference.

49.90 Given the fact that the reference to collation of documents has not been carried over into PD 47, and given the fact that there are grounds for saying that 'collate' means more than only sorting and bundling documents, it would now be arguable that the costs of sorting and bundling documents should no longer be regarded as documentary work. There is, however, no authority on the point. Moreover, even if the court were to find that the collation of documents is not documentary work, it would be within the court's powers simply to allow the costs of collation under PD 47, para 5.12(10).[67]

The relevance of heavy documentation

49.91 It has been argued that differences in the wording between the RSC and the CPR mean that the court is unable to give weight to the fact that a case was heavy in terms of documentary work. Lloyd J rejected that submission: in an appropriate case, the court can give weight to the amount of documentary work involved[68]—and this may be so in terms of both the documentary time itself and the seven (now eight) pillars of wisdom.

Work done over a long period of time

49.92 Where a claim is long-running, work may, of necessity, have been carried out piecemeal. Donaldson J had the following to say about multiple small items of work carried out over a long period of time:

> 'The bill of costs showed that the solicitors were engaged for 30 hours in the relevant period. Most of this time was made up of short items spread over a period. This did not mean that what was done was of little importance or required little skill. Far from it ... It is in some ways more difficult to pick up the thread continually over a period than to do the same work more or less continuously.'[69]

It should be noted that this was a pre-CPR case concerning non-contentious costs. Its relevance in the present context is merely to illustrate the fact that it is not necessarily unreasonable to incur costs in multiple, short bursts.

---

[66] See, eg, *Shah v Breed* [2013] EWHC 232 (QB), at [29]–[34], in which Globe J found that a global discount (of 20 per cent) imposed by the trial judge took account of any duplication and that it was within the powers of the costs judge not to make a further reduction.

[67] This reads: '[O]ther work done which was of or incidental to the proceedings and which is not already covered in the heads listed above.'

[68] *Ortwein v Rugby Mansions* [2003] EWHC 2077 (Ch), at [24], *per* Lloyd J.

[69] *Property and Reversionary Investment Corpn Ltd v Secretary of State for the Environment* [1975] 1 WLR 1504, at 1507E.

Decision not to use counsel

It is open to the court to take into account the amount that would have been charged by counsel if they had been instructed to carry out the work—as also confirmed by the Guide to the Summary Assessment of Costs.[70] **49.93**

Costs of drafting attendances notes

If the time claimed is reasonable, there is no reason why time cannot be claimed for drafting attendance notes. Brooke J said: **49.94**

> 'Work properly and reasonably done in furthering the client's interests may reasonably include the preparation of attendance and file notes recording what work has been done. The time spent in preparation of these notes should be recorded. The emphasis must always be on the question whether this work is reasonable.'[71]

This does not mean that time will always be allowed in addition to the time allowed for the attendance itself. Whilst speaking in the context of costs capping, rather than the assessment of costs, Hallett J has indicated that additional note-drafting time should *not* ordinarily be allowed: **49.95**

- where the note could have been drafted during the attendance itself;
- where the note could have been drafted whilst travelling; and
- where there is more than one fee earner in attendance.[72]

Communications (in general)

Communications are defined as 'letters out, e-mails out, and telephone calls'.[73] Incoming correspondence and emails are in a different category because they are either discretionary ('electronic communications'[74]) or generally not recoverable at all (routine incoming correspondence) (see 49.100). **49.96**

Routine communications

Routine communications are 'letters out, e-mails out and telephone calls which because of their simplicity should not be regarded as letters or e-mails of substance or telephone calls which properly amount to an attendance'.[75] Such communications will, in general, be allowed on a unitary basis of 6 minutes each, the charge being calculated by reference to the appropriate hourly rate.[76] For obvious reasons (that is, that the correspondence will speak for itself), a solicitor is not required to record the time spent preparing routine correspondence such as letters or emails. **49.97**

Timed communications

The term 'real communications' is occasionally used to mean communications that are not routine communications.[77] Such communications are assessed on a time basis. PD **49.98**

---

[70] See HM Courts & Tribunals Service, *Guide to the Summary Assessment of Costs* (London: HMSO, 2005), para 65(5).
[71] *Brush v Bower Cotton & Bower* [1993] 1 WLR 1328, at 1349.
[72] *Ledward v Kent & Medway Health Authority* [2003] EWHC 2551 (QB), at [50].
[73] See PD 47, para 5.13(1).
[74] See PD 47, para 5.22(2).
[75] See PD 47, para 5.14.
[76] See PD 47, para 5.22(1).
[77] See, eg, Harrison, J, 'Costs a Bomb' (2007) 137 NLJ 56.

47, para 5.22(2), provides that the court may, in its discretion, allow a time charge for preparation of 'electronic communications', but only if the time taken has been recorded. If the number of communications other than routine communications is 20 or more, the claim for the costs of those items in that section of the bill of costs should be for the total only, and should refer to a schedule in which the full record of dates and details is set out.[78]

SMS texts, etc

49.99 Perhaps as a result of long-standing criticism that it did not reflect modern practice,[79] now-revoked CPD, art 4.16(2), was updated so that it dealt with 'electronic communications other than e-mail'. The present rules refer only to 'electronic communications'[80]—a phrase that is not defined, but which is likely to include short messaging service (SMS) communications (that is, text messages), multimedia messaging service (MMS) communications and instant messaging (IM), including Skype. PD 47, para 5.22(2), provides as follows: 'The court may, in its discretion, allow an actual time charge for preparation of electronic communications sent by legal representatives, which properly amount to attendances provided that the time taken has been recorded.'

Incoming correspondence

49.100 In general, no costs are allowed for incoming correspondence (including emails). This is because the allowance for outgoing letters and emails will include an allowance for perusing and considering incoming correspondence. PD 47 implicitly provides that no separate charge should be made for incoming correspondence,[81] but it is a moot point whether this applies to all or only routine correspondence. Most judges interpret the rule to mean the latter.

Perfunctory letters

49.101 Whilst not binding, Master O'Hare has found that, in certain circumstances, letters of an administrative nature (such as a covering letter) may justify an allowance of 3 minutes rather than a full allowance of a full 6 minutes.[82]

Circular letters

49.102 In group litigation involving anything more than a handful of litigants, there will often be a need to dispatch volleys of letters that differ very little from litigant to litigant. Such letters are often referred to as 'circular letters'. Each case will turn on its own facts, but in a case in which the letters were substantially the same, Nelson J found that a full allowance of 6 minutes for each would be inappropriate. Nonetheless, he found that some allowance ought to be made for 'thinking time' and (on the facts of the case before him) he allowed 2 minutes per letter.[83] A part of this allowance will be for printing and postage costs; where a significant number of letters is involved, this becomes the predominant cost. Where this is

[78] See PD 47, para 5.18.

[79] See, eg, Harrison, J, 'Costs a Bomb' (2007) 137 NLJ 56.

[80] See PD 47, para 5.22(2).

[81] This is implied by PD 47, para 5.22(1), which reads: 'The unit charge for letters out and e-mails out will include perusing and considering the routine letters in or e-mails in.'

[82] *In re Walker* (unreported), c. November 2002, SCCO, *per* Master O'Hare—a decision he confirmed as being correct in *In re Radcliffe* [2004] EWHC 90039 (Costs).

[83] *Giambrone v JMC Holidays Ltd* [2002] EWHC 495 (QB), at [7]–[13], *per* Nelson J.

so, one option is for the court to allow a stated amount of costs (often in the order of £5) rather than an amount of time.

Activities that are not Specifically Defined in the CPR

This section deals with the costs of certain specified activities to which 'the *Gibson* principles'[84] (see 49.07) will apply. It should be emphasised that whilst costs will usually be assessed in accordance with those principles, it is rare for them to be referred to expressly. **49.103**

The costs of marshalling the facts

The phrase 'marshalling the facts' is used to refer to the task of gathering and organising evidence. It does not refer to the costs of actually formulating the evidence and exercising professional judgement in selecting which parts of it will be relied upon, but only to the task of gathering together the material that will allow those tasks to be completed. **49.104**

The topic commonly arises in one of two guises: it may arise in the context of the work having been carried out by the solicitor, in which case the issues will be simply whether it is, by its nature, irrecoverable; or it may arise where the work has been carried out by the receiving party personally, or by their employees or agents, in which case there will be the additional consideration of whether that person is able to recover costs at all (see 3.100). **49.105**

Although it is arguable that it has been overtaken by the CPR,[85] the general rule is that the costs of marshalling the facts are not recoverable because they are not 'legal costs' (see 3.13–3.14). This is because they are the costs of being a litigant, rather than the costs of litigation.[86] As Bingham J put it, they are the costs 'a litigant must bear ... to prove his own case'.[87] **49.106**

This does not mean that such work would always be irrecoverable. Each case will turn on its own facts. **49.107**

Technical or expert marshalling of facts

If the work was of a technical nature or if it had an expert flavour to it, then an allowance may be made.[88] **49.108**

Academic work and marshalling the facts

The principle mentioned immediately above would not extend to work that merely had an academic flavour to it; in a case in which the receiving party had to prepare a schedule of academic books lost as a result of the paying party's negligence, Douglas Brown J declined to find that the costs of carrying out that work were recoverable.[89] **49.109**

---

[84] After *Re Gibson's Settlement Trusts* [1981] Ch 179.

[85] See, eg, *Papera Traders Co Ltd & Ors v Hyundai Merchant Marine Co Ltd & Anor* [2003] EWHC 9018 (Costs), at [73] *et seq*, in which it was said that *Amec Process & Energy Ltd v Stork Engineers & Contracts (No 3)* [2002] All ER (D) suggested that *Re Nossen's Patent* [1969] 1 All ER 775 and *Richards & Wallington (Plant Hire) Ltd v Monk & Co* (1984) Costs LR Core vol 79 had been overtaken. For the converse view, see *Sisu Capital Fund Ltd & Ors v Tucker* [2005] EWHC 2321 (Ch), in which Warren J declined to follow *Amec*.

[86] See the extensive discussion in *London Scottish Benefit Society v Chorley* [1884] 13 QBD 872, at 877; see also Chapter 5.

[87] *Richards & Wallington (Plant Hire) Ltd v Monk & Co* (1984) Costs LR Core vol 79, at 83.

[88] See *Re Nossen's Patent* [1969] 1 All ER 775, in which Lloyd-Jacob J contemplated making an allowance for work of a technical nature.

[89] *Stockinger v Highdorn Co Ltd* [2001] All ER (D) 62 (Apr) (QBD).

Non-legal professional work and marshalling the facts

49.110 The mere fact that the work was carried out by persons who were professionals or office holders would not displace the general rule that costs of marshalling the facts are not recoverable.[90]

Extensive work relating to factual material

49.111 In a family case in which the wife had asked complex questions about the husband's accounts, Bennett J determined that the test to be applied was 'whether the instruction of [a lawyer] to draft the answers and all such necessary work to enable him to do that, was reasonable' (most of the work related to factual material rather than drafting).[91] Bennett J asked himself whether the receiving party could be expected to collate, marshal and present the information without expert assistance. He found that it was reasonable to engage a lawyer to carry out the work in question.

The costs of funding

49.112 For present purposes, it is useful to distinguish between:

- financing costs (such as interest on a disbursement funding loan);
- administrative costs (such as the costs of preparing invoices, paying cheques, etc); and
- the profit costs arising from professional advice concerning the methods of funding the claim (that is, the costs of funding advice).

It is the costs of funding advice (the third category above) that is the focus of the immediate discussion. It is well established that financing costs (the first category) cannot be recovered from an opposing party[92] and that administrative costs (the second) could not properly be characterised as legal costs at all.[93]

49.113 After a long period of no binding authority on the issue of the recoverability of the costs of funding advice, Lord Neuberger MR has now confirmed that such costs are *not* recoverable.[94]

49.114 In a pre-CPR case that has been affirmed as still being good law,[95] Purchas LJ said: '[B]y established practice and custom funding costs have never been included in the category of expenses, costs or disbursements envisaged by ... statute or [the then rules of court].'[96] Part of Purchas LJ's reasoning was that costs of funding are not costs. This analysis is still

[90] *Sisu Capital Fund Ltd & Ors v Tucker* [2005] EWHC 2321 (Ch) (office holders not entitled to recover fees). Although not binding, see *Cuthbert v Gair* (unreported), 26 September 2009, SCCO, *per* Master Haworth (loss adjusters not entitled to recover fees).

[91] *D v D* [2002] 2 Costs LR 312, at 318.

[92] See *Hunt v RM Douglas (Roofing) Ltd* (1987) The Times, 23 November, CAT, cited by the Court of Appeal in *Claims Direct Test Cases* [2003] EWCA Civ 136, at [35]. See also *Bushwell Properties v Vortex Properties* [1975] 2 All ER 214, *per* Evans J.

[93] See the extensive discussion in *London Scottish Benefit Society v Chorley* (1884) 13 QBD 872, at 877; see also Chapter 5.

[94] *Motto & Ors v Trafigura Ltd & Anor* [2011] EWCA Civ 1150, at [104]–[114].

[95] The confirmation was given by Brooke LJ in *Claims Direct Test Cases* [2003] EWCA Civ 136, at [35], and then again in *Motto & Ors v Trafigura Ltd & Anor* [2011] EWCA Civ 1150, at [105].

[96] *Hunt v RM Douglas (Roofing) Ltd* (1987) The Times, 23 November, CAT, at the antepenultimate page of the official transcript.

good law,[97] but Lord Neuberger MR's analysis is more easily understood in the context of modern legal practice:

> 'The time, expertise and effort devoted by solicitors to identifying a potential claimant, and negotiating the terms on which they are to be engaged by the claimant, in connection with litigation, cannot, in my view, be properly described as an item incurred by the client for the purposes of the litigation. Until the [conditional fee agreement] CFA is signed, the potential claimant is not merely not a claimant: he is not a client. When advising a potential claimant on the terms and effect of the CFA, the solicitors are acting for themselves, not for the potential claimant: the solicitors are negotiating with him as a prospective client, not for him as an actual client.'[98]

The fact that funding advice must be given as a matter of professional conduct is not sufficient to render the costs associated with that work recoverable. In this regard, Lord Neuberger MR has explained that the mere fact that a solicitor is obliged to do something under the Solicitors Regulation Authority (SRA) Code of Conduct 2011 does not mean that the solicitor can charge for it.[99] **49.115**

The costs of giving advice about legal expenses insurance is similarly irrecoverable between opposing parties. Lord Neuberger MR has explained that such costs are not so much a cost of the litigation as they are a cost that was collateral to litigation—namely, a cost incurred to ensure that the client was not at risk on costs.[100] **49.116**

The costs of legal research

Legal research is work that is carried out for the purposes of discovering the law and should be distinguished from work carried out for the purposes of applying the law.[101] **49.117**

Each case will be decided on its own facts, but, in general, the costs of legal research will not be allowed if the solicitor could have been expected to have known the law in question. Lord Donaldson MR explained this by referring to legal knowledge as the solicitor's 'stock in trade': **49.118**

> 'Solicitors, like barristers and Judges, are not to be expected to carry a knowledge of all the law in their heads. They have to consider rules, regulations, text books and authorities or get others to undertake the research for them. If the problem is difficult or outside the scope of their experience, they will wish to discuss it with others who are more qualified (whether professionally or otherwise) and in some circumstances may have to remunerate those who they consult. But knowledge of the law, however acquired or recalled,

---

[97] The receiving party argued that the particular monies in question (interest) were capable of quantification and that this therefore undermined the conclusion that they were not costs; this, the receiving party argued, was because part of Bowen LJ's seminal analysis of what are and are not costs was of the question of whether the monies in question could readily be quantified (see 3.06). Purchas LJ rejected this analysis, finding that to categorise measurable costs of funding as costs 'would be an extension of the existing category of "legal costs" which is not under the prevailing circumstances warranted': *Hunt v RM Douglas (Roofing) Ltd* (1987) The Times, 23 November, CAT, at the antepenultimate page of the official transcript.

[98] *Motto & Ors v Trafigura Ltd & Anor* [2011] EWCA Civ 1150, at [108].

[99] See *ibid*, at [112]. It is worth noting that it does not always follow that because work is mandatory, it will be remunerated: see, eg, *In re Radcliffe* [2004] EWHC 90039 (Costs), at [16], in which Master O'Hare described the costs of certain mandatory requirements in the Court of Protection as being work that had to be carried out 'to obtain the right to undertake the work which is remunerated'.

[100] *Motto & Ors v Trafigura Ltd & Anor* [2011] EWCA Civ 1150, at [114].

[101] Time claimed for applying the law is recoverable: *Loveday v Renton (No 2)* [1992] 3 All ER 184, at 190.

is their stock in trade … In so far as expenses involved in added to or replenishing this stock in trade, it is an overhead expense and not something which can be charged to the client …'[102]

49.119 Although his decision relates to counsel's fees rather than profit costs, Garland J observed that there may be cases that give rise to legal issues that are so unusual or infrequent that time ought to be allowed for discovering the law—although he stressed that each case should be decided on its own facts and according to the lawyer's professed expertise.[103] A factor that may be relevant is the judicial level at which the matter is to be heard. It is, for example, not unknown for a modest allowance to be made for researching the law in the Court of Appeal.[104] In a similar vein, Swinton Thomas LJ has noted that counsel cannot be expected to be 'a walking law library'.[105] Presumably, the same applies to solicitors, if not more so.

49.120 The costs of legal research will not be transformed into something else merely by reason of the solicitor instructing a specialist to carry out the work. Where this is done and where the law is such that the solicitor could reasonably have been expected to know it without seeking specialist advice, then the cost will usually be disallowed. Arden J has commented that such costs are incurred by the solicitor using the specialist for their own purposes—namely, to replenish their own stock in trade.[106]

'Solicitor and client' work

49.121 A person has the right to retain the solicitor of their choice[107] and (subject to rules of professional conduct), that person has the right to give whatever instructions they like. Where this results in costs being disallowed as being 'solicitor and client' in nature, this arises not by the operation of an exclusory principle, but because there is a fissure between that which it is reasonable for a receiving party to pay their solicitor and that which it is reasonable for a paying party to pay that receiving party.

49.122 The fissure is there by design rather than happenstance. This was explained by Malins V-C:

> 'It is of great importance to litigants who are unsuccessful that they should not be oppressed into having to pay an excessive amount of costs … I adhere to the rule which has already been laid down that the costs chargeable under a taxation as between party and party are all that are necessary to enable the adverse party to conduct the litigation and no more. Any charges merely for conducting litigation more conveniently may be called luxuries and must be paid by the party incurring them.'[108]

---

[102] *R v Legal Aid Board, ex p Bruce* [1991] 1 WLR 1231, at 1237–8. This case went to the House of Lords, where Lord Jauncey approved of selected parts of this extract: [1992] 3 All ER 321, at 326.

[103] *Perry v Lord Chancellor* (1994) The Times, 26 May, QBD.

[104] See, eg, *Hornsby v Clarke Kenneth Leventhal (a firm)* [2000] 2 Costs LR 295.

[105] *Johnson v Valks* (2000) WL 362603, 15 March 2000, CA, at [18] of the official transcript.

[106] *In the Matter of Tina Jayne Cloughton* (unreported), c 1999, Ch D, *per* Arden J.

[107] See *Watts v Official Solicitor* [1936] 1 All ER 249, CA. See also *Oswald Hickson Collier & Co v Carter-Ruck* [1984] AC 720, CA, in which it was held that a restraint-of-trade clause in a contract was contrary to public policy, because it sought to prevent a client from instructing the solicitor of his choice. See also *Edwards v Worboys* [1984] AC 724.

[108] *Smith v Buller* (1875) LR 19 Eq 473, at 474.

Speaking extrajudicially in a peer-reviewed journal, Master Hurst has confirmed that what Malins V-C had to say remains relevant under the CPR.[109]

Convenience is not the only motivation that may lead a receiving party to incur costs that are ultimately deemed to be solicitor-and-client costs. The costs of keeping the client informed for accounting purposes or for purposes of complying with reporting obligations would fall into that category.[110] Hallett J has indicated that the costs of acting as counsellor in an emotionally charged matter might not be recoverable against the paying party.[111] That type of work is often referred to as 'hand-holding', but the fact that it has this label does not mean that it is rendered irrecoverable as a result; as with all work that is said to be 'solicitor and client' in nature, the issue is one of reasonableness and degree, rather than principle, and there is no authority for the proposition that an exclusory principle can be made out. **49.123**

The costs of an isolated counterclaim

Where a counterclaimant is awarded costs, the appropriate measure of costs will depend on whether that counterclaimant is also ordered to pay costs. If so, then the principles set out at 20.50–20.63 will apply. If they have not been ordered to pay costs, then the costs of a counterclaim could legitimately include costs relating to the perusal and consideration of issues in the claim, because the party in question will need to keep abreast of the claim for the purposes of managing the counterclaim.[112] **49.124**

The costs of preparing material that was not used

Prematurity

Speaking of a costs regime long since passed, Lord Hanworth referred to the following extract from a master's certificate[113] dealing with material thrown away: **49.125**

> 'We have always acted upon the principle that the costs of all work in preparing, briefing, or otherwise relating to affidavits or pleadings, reasonably and properly and not prematurely done, down to the time of any notice which stops the work, are allowable; and ... the Taxing Master, having regard to the circumstances of each case, must decide whether the work was reasonable and proper and the time for doing it had arrived.'[114]

This extract illustrates the fact that it is possible to carry out work prematurely. If the benefit of that work is ultimately thrown away, the costs may be disallowed on the basis that the work ought not to have been carried out until it was known whether

[109] Master Hurst, 'Going Round in Circles' (2006) 25 CJQ 546. Master Hurst commented that this was despite the fact that the test of necessity to which Malins V-C referred has been replaced by a test of reasonableness.

[110] *Intergraph (UK) Ltd v Wolfson Microelectronics plc* [2012] EWHC 1862 (Ch), at [9], *per* Mr Snowdon QC.

[111] *Ledward v Kent & Medway Health Authority* [2003] EWHC 2551 (QB), at [54].

[112] *Re a Company (No 004081 of 1989)* [1995] 2 All ER 155, at 162, *per* Lindsay J.

[113] This was a formal document used to state some aspect of the law or practice.

[114] See the certificate referred to in *Harrison v Leutner* (1881) 16 Ch D 559, at 559–60, as 'a working rule which properly exhibits the discretion which is entrusted to the Masters' by Lord Hanworth MR in *Société Anonyme Pêcheries Ostendaises v Merchants Marine Insurance Co* [1928] 1 KB 750, at 758.

there was a need for it. There is no reason to believe that this line of thinking does not still apply.

Subsequent conduct and amendments

49.126 It is trite law that costs must not be assessed with hindsight (see 49.08). That said, it is possible to negate an entitlement to costs by subsequent conduct. A decision not to use a witness statement for no good reason could, for example, be interpreted as being a waiver of the right to claim the associated costs. Likewise, the costs of amendments will often be disallowed, either by disallowing the costs thrown away or by disallowing the costs of carrying out the amendment (or a combination of the two).

The costs of dealing with the media

49.127 Proceedings in court may attract a degree of media attention. It may be that costs are claimed for liaison with the media or for advice about media relations.

49.128 In a judgment that preceded the CPR, Clarke J confirmed that there are three strands of reasoning—which rely heavily on the *Gibson* principles set out at 49.07—that are relevant to the issue of whether the costs of dealing with the media are recoverable:

- whether the work was of use and service in the claim;
- whether the work was of relevance to an issue in the claim; and
- whether the need for the work can be attributed to the paying party's conduct.[115]

In practice, these three strands of reasoning amount to a three-part test. Clarke J explained that the work of protecting the receiving party from what may be unwelcome pressure from different parts of the media may well satisfy that test, depending on the facts.

49.129 In some cases (especially high-profile cases), such costs may be said to be not a necessary incident of the claim, but an integral part of it, in the sense that the media were being used as a method of putting pressure on an opponent. Clarke J has made it clear that costs incurred in that way are not likely to be recoverable: 'Civil claims should be pursued in the civil Courts and not through the media.'[116]

Administrative work and work of an administrative nature

49.130 For the reasons set out at 3.85–3.87, an employed fee earner's unqualified status will not preclude a charge being made for their work. That said, work carried out by the most junior members of a team may be administrative in nature, in which case it may be objectionable on the basis that it was not 'fee earners' work'.

49.131 Subject to the terms of the retainer, it is the nature of the work that is relevant, not the fact that it may have been carried out by an unqualified person. Brooke J has confirmed that where the work can properly be described as clerical or administrative work, it must go unremunerated; where, however, there were features of the work that would have been properly charged had it been carried out by the solicitor, then, to that extent, it

[115] *Ross v Owners of the Bowbelle (Review of Taxation under Ord 62 r 35)* (1997) 2 Lloyd's Rep 196 (Note) QBD (Admlty), at 210. The three strands were drawn from Megarry V-C's analysis in *Re Gibson's Settlement Trusts* [1981] Ch 179.

[116] *Ross v Owners of the Bowbelle (Review of Taxation under Ord 62 r 35)* (1997) 2 Lloyd's Rep 196 (Note) QBD (Admlty), at 210.

ought to be allowed.[117] Each case will turn on its own facts, to be decided on the available evidence.[118]

The costs of negotiation and mediation

Negotiation

In principle, the costs of negotiation may be included within both a budget[119] and a bill of costs.[120] This is true even if the negotiation went to interim remedies such as security for costs, interim custody of the property that is the subject of the claim, etc.[121] Whilst there is no authority on the point, for the reasons set out below in respect of mediation, it is arguable that costs negotiation conducted well before the issue of proceedings are not recoverable. **49.132**

Mediation

Whilst it has been noted that there is room for argument on the point,[122] the costs of mediation are generally regarded as being recoverable in principle.[123] This would certainly be the case where the mediation agreement provided for the recovery of such costs or does not preclude such costs[124] (see 48.52). **49.133**

The following factors, however, may prevent or restrict such costs from being recovered: **49.134**

- where the mediation agreement precludes or restricts recovery;
- where the mediation took place well before the issue of proceedings; and
- (possibly) where the receiving party did not properly engage in the mediation.

Where the mediation agreement putatively precludes recovery It is commonly the case that mediation agreements contain a provision that each party will bear its own costs and expenses of its participation in the mediation; other agreements may provide that the expenses of mediation (including the mediator's fee) will be borne equally by the parties. Where such a restriction exists, then it will generally be open to the court to disallow those costs between opposing parties.[125] **49.135**

---

117 *Brush v Bower Cotton & Bower* [1993] 1 WLR 1328, at 1353.

118 On a related point, the need to produce evidence of allegedly high overheads was recognised by Eady J in *Cox and Carter v MGN Ltd* [2006] EWHC 1235 (QB), at [59]–[60], in which the judge commented favourably on *Various Claimants v TUI UK Ltd* (unreported), 11 August 2005, SCCO, *per* Master Hurst. Presumably, the same would apply by analogy.

119 This is implied by the use of the phrase 'ADR/Settlement' in both Precedent H and Precedent Q.

120 See PD 47, para 5.12(8), which provides that the bill may contain 'work done in connection with negotiations with a view to settlement if not already covered in the heads listed above'.

121 *National Westminster Bank v Kotonou* [2009] EWHC 3309 (Ch), *per* Briggs J.

122 *North Oxford Golf Club v A2 Dominion Homes Ltd* [2013] EWHC 852 (QB), at [20], *per* Royce J.

123 As an early example, see *Eagleson v Liddell* [2001] EWCA Civ 155, in which the costs order following the appeal included the costs of a mediation. See also the use of the phrase 'ADR/Settlement' in both Precedent H and Precedent Q.

124 See, eg, *Roundstone Nurseries Ltd v Stephenson Holdings Ltd* [2009] EWHC 1431 (TCC), at [52], in which Coulson J concluded that mediation costs were recoverable because there had been no agreement that they would be borne by each party regardless of the outcome and no agreement that one or other party could not subsequently seek them. See also *Chantrey Vellacott v The Convergence Group Plc* [2007] EWHC 1774 (Ch), at [226]–[229], *per* Rimer J.

125 The example that is usually quoted in this regard is *National Westminster Bank v Feeney* [2006] EWHC 90066 (Costs). This case was appealed to Eady J, who dismissed the appeal, but there is no transcript of his judgment: see *North Oxford Golf Club v A2 Dominion Homes Ltd* [2013] EWHC 852 (QB), at [18], *per*

49.136 The whole of the mediation agreement (including any attached schedules) must be taken into account. Many agreements contain a standard provision that, at first blush, appears to impose an obligation on each party to bear their own costs of the mediation; on closer inspection of the agreement, it can often be seen that the provision is qualified in such a way as to make that nothing more than the starting position. It will often be necessary to interpret the costs order alongside the mediation agreement to determine the true meaning of the order (assuming, of course, that the mediation agreement is admissible). Side letters may also play a role.[126]

49.137 **Where the mediation that failed took place well before the issue of proceedings** Although it related to an application for security for costs, rather than a detailed assessment, Coulson J has found that the costs of a stand-alone mediation that failed to prevent the commencement of proceedings were not likely to be recoverable:

> 'Unlike the costs incurred in a pre-action protocol, I do not believe that the costs of a separate pre-action mediation can ordinarily be described as "costs of and incidental to the proceedings." On the contrary, it seems to me to be clear that they are not. They are the costs incurred in pursuing a valid method of alternative dispute resolution ... As a matter of general principle, therefore, I do not believe that the costs incurred in respect of such a procedure are recoverable under s 51 [of the Senior] Courts Act 1981.'[127]

He went on to explain that the costs of mediation may be recoverable if they were incurred in an attempt to comply with pre-action protocols.[128]

49.138 **Where the receiving party did not properly engage in the mediation** There have been instances of the court (at the stage of making an order for costs) having regard to events during the mediation itself.[129] This is certainly permissible if the parties consent to this, but would otherwise be a questionable practice.[130] That said, some mediation agreements provide that the mediator will be entitled to prepare a brief report for the court dealing with the conduct of the parties during the mediation.

49.139 Where costs are being assessed, the issue would simply be one of reasonableness. Whilst there is no authority on the point, if the court was unable to find evidence that the receiving party had properly engaged in the mediation, then it is conceivable that costs may be disallowed as a result.

The costs of preparing and checking the bill of costs

49.140 The costs of preparing and checking the bill are recoverable between the parties.[131] The following miscellaneous points can be made (see 49.141–49.146).

Royce J. Another example is *North Oxford Golf Club* itself, at [16] and [17], but Royce J was dealing only with an application for permission to appeal.

126 See, eg, *North Oxford Golf Club v A2 Dominion Homes Ltd* [2013] EWHC 852 (QB), at [15], *per* Royce J.

127 *Lobster Group Ltd v Heidelberg Graphic Equipment Ltd* [2008] EWHC 413 (TCC), at [16].

128 See *ibid*, this being a separate judgment in that case.

129 See, eg, *Chantrey Vellacott v The Convergence Group Plc* [2007] EWHC 1774 (Ch), at [228]–[229], in which Rimer J took the parties' negotiating positions into account.

130 See, eg, Star, J, 'Time for a New Privilege?' (2016) 343 PLJ 26.

131 See PD 47, para 5.19: 'The bill of costs must not contain any claims in respect of costs or court fees which relate solely to the detailed assessment proceedings other than costs claimed for preparing and checking the bill.'

The status of the signatory

Where a receiving party has been represented by a firm of solicitors, the issue may arise as to whether the bill of costs needs to be signed by a partner (or a director, or member, as the case may be). The requirement that a partner certifies the bill of costs was a pre-CPR requirement that no longer applies.[132] PD 47, para 5.21, reads as follows: 'The bill of costs must contain such of the certificates, the texts of which are set out in Precedent F of the Schedule of Costs Precedents annexed to this Practice Direction, as are appropriate.' Precedent F straightforwardly stipulates that 'all certificates must be signed by the receiving party or by his solicitor'. Therefore, where a junior solicitor has had conduct of the claim, that person is able to certify the bill of costs, regardless of their status within the firm. **49.141**

More than one firm

Where a receiving party has been represented by more than one solicitor or firm, the question may arise as to whether the paying party is liable for the costs of preparation of only one certificate, or for the costs of the preparation of a certificate for each solicitor or firm. It is implicit from the guidance given in Precedent F that the latter position is correct.[133] **49.142**

Time claimed for checking the bill

It is not uncommon for only peppercorn times to be allowed for checking the bill of costs, but this will not always be the case. Hooper J found that 30 minutes was insufficient for checking two bills of costs where there was a need to carry out a degree of cross-checking between the two; rather, he allowed several hours for the task.[134] **49.143**

The costs of preparing the bill

Hourly rate Whilst only persuasive, rather than binding, the Privy Council refused to disturb an hourly rate for drafting work of £160 (relating to costs incurred in about 2005).[135] The judgment in that case does not make it clear whether their Lordships had the benefit of a costs assessor. Many judges are less generous than this and will allow a different (lower) rate for drafting bills of costs than they will allow for costs advocacy. A rate equivalent to a Grade D (or occasionally Grade C) is not unusual for routine bills of costs, with higher rates being reserved for weightier bills. Hourly rates of £126–£135 are not uncommon for drafting work. **49.144**

Appeals from assessments of time The allowance of costs for preparing the bill of costs is a matter that lies peculiarly within the expertise of costs judges; hence it would be difficult to disturb such a decision on appeal.[136] **49.145**

Success fee Where the solicitor is engaged under a conditional fee agreement that provides for a success fee and where the costs draftsperson is engaged by the solicitor, rather **49.146**

---

[132] See RSC Ord 62, r 29(7)(c)(iii); Matrimonial Causes (Costs) Rules 1988 (SI 1988/1328), r 13(iii) (Form and contents of bills of costs lodged in Principal Registry as from 3 October 1988).

[133] That guidance reads: 'Where the bill claims costs in respect of work done by more than one firm of solicitors, certificate (1), appropriate completed, should be signed on behalf of each firm.'

[134] *Pritchard and Riccio v Ford Motor Co Ltd* [1997] 1 Costs LR 39. This was a pre-CPR case, so ought to be treated with some caution because there was no allowance for preparing the bill of costs under the RSC, when the regime was not the same as it is at present.

[135] *Horsford v Bird* [2006] UKPC 55.

[136] *Ibid.*

than by the client directly, the success fee will be recoverable on the costs draftsperson's fees for preparing the bill of costs.[137] This topic is addressed in detail at 22.22–22.24.

Costs Incurred in Particular Circumstances

Costs incurred prior to issue

49.147 Whilst there can be no liability for costs incurred before the retainer was made[138] (unless, of course, the contract of retainer is expressly retrospective), the court has long had the power to determine whether costs incurred prior to issue were reasonably required for the attainment of justice and, if so, to allow those costs.[139] This may be so even where the matter settled prior to the issue of proceedings.[140] It has been argued that the words 'of and incidental to proceedings' in s 51(a) of the Senior Courts Act 1981 (as amended) qualify costs orders in such a way as to make pre-issue costs irrecoverable. This is not so, because the words 'of and incidental' are words of extension, rather than words of restriction.[141] Lord Hanworth MR said this on the topic:

> 'It appears to me ... that there is power in the Master to allow costs incurred before action brought, and that if the costs are in respect of materials ultimately proving of use and service in the action, the Master has a discretion to allow these costs, which he probably will exercise in favour of the party incurring them, because they have been made use of during the course of the action.'[142]

49.148 Lord Hanworth's words continue to have resonance today. In particular, it remains the case that costs need not necessarily have been incurred in contemplation of the actual proceedings that were ultimately brought; the court is permitted to focus on the use to which they were put, rather than on the use for which they were originally incurred.[143] This does not offend against the rule precluding the use of hindsight because the question is whether it was reasonable to make use of the work that had already been carried out (the alternative being to redo the work). Care should be taken to read the order, however, because different words used therein may have wholly different meanings.[144]

---

[137] *Crane v Canons Leisure Centre* [2007] EWCA Civ 1352.

[138] *Re Watson, ex p Phillips* (1887) 19 QBD 234, CA. The practical effect of this rule is limited, because authority will usually be implied by virtue of instructions being given: see *Bolden v Nicholay* (1857) 3 Jur NS 884. See also 27.33.

[139] *Société Anonyme Pêcheries Ostendaises v Merchants Marine Insurance Co* [1928] 1 KB 750. See also *Gibson's Settlement Trusts* [1981] Ch 179; *Roach v Home Office* [2009] EWHC 312 (QB).

[140] An example of this is *Lee v Birmingham City Council* [2008] EWCA Civ 891, at [34], in which Hughes LJ (giving judgment of the court) took into account repairs that had been effected before the claim was issued, saying: '[T]he effect of the claim is to get the work done, then providing that the landlord was liable for the disrepair the tenant ought to recover the reasonable costs of achieving that result.'

[141] *Gibson's Settlement Trusts* [1981] Ch 179, at 184, *per* Megarry V-C, thereby limiting *Re Fahy's Will Trusts* [1962] 1 All ER 73 to its own facts.

[142] *Société Anonyme Pêcheries Ostendaises v Merchants Marine Insurance Co* [1928] 1 KB 750, at 757; see also *Frankenburg v Famous Lasky Film Service Ltd* [1931] 1 Ch 428.

[143] See *Admiral Management Services Ltd v Para-Protect Europe Ltd* [2002] EWHC 233 (Ch), in which Stanley Burton J found that costs incurred before solicitors had been instructed were, in principle, recoverable if they resulted in material that was ultimately used.

[144] See, eg, *Newall v Lewis* [2008] EWHC 910 (Ch), in which Briggs J found that the order in question referred to 'costs of' rather than 'costs of and incidental'.

Where costs were properly incurred under a pre-action protocol, Lord Woolf CJ has explained that this is a factor that goes to those costs being recoverable in principle: 'Where an action is commenced and a costs order is then obtained, the costs awarded will include costs reasonably incurred before the action started, such as costs incurred in complying with the pre-action protocol.'[145] This used to be reflected in the CPD[146] and it is something that has been confirmed in several authorities.[147] PD 47, however, does not specifically mention pre-action protocols.[148] The relevance of this is not known—although it would be very surprising, in this context, if anything significant were to turn on it. **49.149**

The fact that the receiving party is a defendant in no way negates their ability to recover pre-issue costs.[149] That said, Judge Coulson QC has confirmed that costs incurred in responding to issues subsequently not included from the claim would not ordinarily be recoverable, explaining that they would become recoverable only in exceptional circumstances.[150] Whilst he was dealing with the incidence of costs rather than the assessment of costs, Tugdenhat J ruled that, in a case in which the claimant brought an abusive claim, the defendant should not have its costs pre-issue because it would not have been able to seek an order for those costs if the abusive claim had not been brought[151]—but perhaps this is best regarded as an illustration that each case must be determined on its own facts. **49.150**

Costs incurred after the order for costs was made

Where proceedings have been brought to an end by way of a final costs order, the receiving party may have to carry out further work for the purposes of concluding the claim. After having reviewed competing authorities on the point, Sir Christopher Staughton came to the following conclusion: 'In my judgment, the fees of [the receiving party's] solicitors reasonably incurred in procuring that the settlement be carried out can fairly be described as being party of the costs of the action.'[152] That case was pre-CPR, but the fact that such costs continue to be recoverable is confirmed by PD 47, para 5.12(1), which states that a bill of costs may include: 'Attendances on the court and counsel up to the date of the notice of commencement.' The reference to 'attendances on the court and counsel' is a somewhat old-fashioned way of referring to the chronology in a bill of costs; it is not intended to limit the recoverable costs in any way. **49.151**

[145] *Callery v Gray* [2001] EWCA Civ 1117, at [54(ii)]. See also *Lee v Birmingham City Council* [2008] EWCA Civ 891, at [11]–[16], *per* Hughes LJ (giving judgment of the court).

[146] See CPD, art 4.6(7), which used to provide that a bill of costs may include documentation necessary to comply with the Practice Direction (Pre-Action Conduct) or any relevant pre-action protocols, where appropriate.

[147] See *McGlinn v Waltham Contractors Ltd* [2005] EWHC 1419 (TCC), at [6], *per* HHJ Coulson QC (now Coulson J); *Roundstone Nurseries Ltd v Stephenson Holdings Ltd* [2009] EWHC 1431 (TCC), at [48], *per* Coulson J; *Citation Plc v Ellis Whittam Ltd* [2012] EWHC 764 (QB), at [16], *per* Tugendhat J (who emphasised that pre-action costs may be recoverable, not that they will always be recoverable).

[148] CPD, art 4.6(7), used to refer to 'work done on documents: preparing and considering documentation, including documentation necessary to comply with Practice Direction (Pre-Action Conduct) or any relevant pre-action protocols where appropriate, work done in connection with arithmetical calculations of compensation and/or interest and time spent collating documents', whilst PD 47, para 5.12(7), simply refers to 'work done on documents'. It is not yet known if anything turns on this.

[149] *Bright's Trustee v Sellar* [1904] 1 Ch 370.

[150] *McGlinn v Waltham Contractors Ltd* [2005] EWHC 1419 (TCC), at [11].

[151] *Citation Plc v Ellis Whittam Ltd* [2012] EWHC 764 (QB), at [28].

[152] *Wallace v Brian Gale & Associates (a firm)* [1998] 2 Costs LR 53, at 56. See also *Krehl v Park* (1875) 10 Ch App 334; cf *Thomas v Cunard Whitestar Line* [1950] 2 All ER 1157.

Costs incurred during a stay

49.152 The court has the power to stay the whole or part of any proceedings or judgment, either generally or until a specified date or event.[153] The Glossary to the CPR defines a stay in the following terms: 'A stay imposes a halt on proceedings, apart from taking any steps allowed by the Rules or the terms of the stay. Proceedings can be continued if a stay is lifted.'

49.153 That definition is similar to pre-CPR definitions, so the following comments of Lord Harnworth MR probably remain good law:

> 'Then comes the more important point upon which the appeal has been presented to us. MacKinnon J has held, apparently, that the stay of proceedings included in the order for ship's papers prevents any costs incurred while that stay was operative from being recovered. I take note that the stay is of "All further proceedings." It is not a stay of activities, the steps which prudence dictates are not forbidden. The question whether the steps that are taken are or are not premature is a matter for the Taxing Master. I agree with the answer made by Sir George King in these terms: "I do not understand that the order entirely paralyses the plaintiff so that he cannot do anything by way of preparation for his real proceedings. If this is so, the question whether any act by the plaintiff during that period is or is not premature must be like every other question about premature acts, a question of reasonableness to be decided by me." I think that Sir George King has rightly answered the objection carried in.'[154]

The stay therefore temporarily brings the proceedings to a halt, but it does not bring a halt to the gamut of activities that a solicitor may need to engage in for the purposes of managing the claim. Costs reasonably incurred in managing the claim will, in principle, continue to be recoverable notwithstanding the stay. This will be particularly true if the purpose of the stay is to enable the parties to attempt to reach a compromise or to engage in ADR.

The costs of inquests and other proceedings in the context of civil claims

49.154 It may be necessary for a party to attend proceedings other than the civil claim (such as an inquest, criminal proceedings, etc), whether specifically in contemplation of a civil claim or for other purposes. The question may then arise of whether the costs of the non-costs-bearing proceedings were 'of and incidental'—the wording of s 51 of the Senior Courts Act 1981 (as amended)—to the costs-bearing proceedings.

49.155 It has been argued that the court lacks the power to make an award of costs incurred in proceedings other than the civil claim. It has also been argued that the fact that the tribunal in the non-costs-bearing proceedings lacks the power to make an award of costs is relevant in the sense that the civil court should not make an order that the other tribunal would be unable to make. Davis J rejected these submissions, finding that the costs of attending non-costs-bearing proceedings may be of and incidental to the costs-bearing proceedings[155] and that attending other proceedings may very often be the most efficient way of investigating the claim. He also found that while the receiving party's purpose of attending the non-costs-bearing proceedings may be a factor to be taken into account, it cannot be determinative of the matter.[156]

---

[153] CPR, r 3.1(2)(f).

[154] *Société Anonyme Pêcheries Ostendaises v Merchants Marine Insurance Co* [1928] 1 KB 750, at 757; see also *Whiteley Exerciser Ltd v Gamage* [1898] 2 Ch 405.

[155] This being the wording of the general power to award costs in Senior Courts Act 1981, s 51.

[156] *Roach v Home Office* [2009] EWHC 213 (QB), esp [57].

There are nevertheless limits to the extent to which costs of non-costs-bearing proceedings can be regarded as being 'of and incidental' to the costs-bearing proceedings. In particular, the costs of the other proceedings must be 'subordinate costs', as explained by Arden LJ: **49.156**

> 'The expression "of and incidental to" is a time-hallowed phrase in the context of costs [which] has received a limited meaning, [in particular] the words "incidental to" have been treated as denoting some subordinate costs to the costs of the action. If [counsel for the receiving party] was right in this action it would mean that the costs of some very substantial proceedings would be treated as costs of and incidental to other proceedings.'[157]

Examples abound of the court declining to find that costs of other proceedings are subordinate to the civil claim; a small number of examples are given at 49.157–49.164.

Costs at first instance and on appeal

As a general (but highly variable) rule, a trial and an appeal are treated as separate proceedings for the purposes of costs.[158] The costs of providing documents to counsel in proceedings at first instance could not be regarded as costs 'incidental to' the proceedings in the Court of Appeal and therefore did not form part of the costs of the appeal: the costs had been incurred in the lower court and the bundle of documents was simply passed on to counsel for use in the appeal.[159] **49.157**

Statutory and non-statutory inquiries

Jupp J has held that, on the facts of the case before him, the costs of an inquiry held pursuant to a reference to the secretary of state were not costs 'incidental' to the claim in which the reference was made.[160] **49.158**

Other civil proceedings

There is no reason in principle why costs incurred in proceedings should not be recovered in other proceedings where the work carried out was common to both. Thus, in a claim that had been dismissed on wholly procedural (that is, technical) grounds, Rimer LJ ordered that if the claimant were to bring a new claim, all steps that had been taken in the first claim subsequent to its issue would be deemed to be steps taken in the new claim and the costs of such steps were to be deemed as incurred in the new claim.[161] In practice, however, it is rare for a court to deal with costs in this way.[162] Donaldson MR has held that the costs of an action ordered to be paid by a charterer to a subcharterer were not costs 'incidental to' the charterer's defence of an action by the owner, even though the unsuccessful proceedings against the subcharterer were the inevitable consequence of the owner's unsuccessful action against the charterer.[163] **49.159**

---

[157] *Contractreal Ltd v Davies* [2001] EWCA Civ 928, at [41]; see also *In re Llewellin* (1887) 37 Ch D 317.

[158] Whilst it related to additional liabilities, see *Hawksford Trustees Jersey Ltd (Trustee of The Bald Eagle Trust) v Stella Global UK Ltd* [2012] EWCA Civ 987, at [43] *et seq*, *per* Rix LJ. See also *Masson Templier & Co v De Fries (Costs)* [1910] 1 KB 535. That said, see *Plevin v Paragon Personal Finance Ltd* [2017] UKSC 23.

[159] *Wright v Bennett* [1948] 1 QB 601, at 606, CA, *per* Somervell LJ.

[160] *Department of Health v Envoy Farmers Ltd* [1976] 1 WLR 1018.

[161] See *Millburn-Snell & Ors v Evans* [2011] EWCA Civ 577, at [15], *per* Rimer LJ (with whom Lord Neuberger MR and Hooper LJ agreed).

[162] For example, the editor asked for such an order following the judgment in *Kingstons Solicitors v Reiss Solicitors* [2014] 6 Costs LR 998, but his request was rejected out of hand.

[163] *Aiden Shipping v Interbulk Ltd* [1985] 1 WLR 1222, at 1226.

Multiple statutory demands

49.160 It may be that a party has served multiple statutory demands, but has brought proceedings on only one of them. Where this is so, the serving party will generally not be entitled to the costs of those statutory demands that proceeded that which was the basis for the proceedings in which the costs order was made.[164]

Administration of an estate and setting up trusts

49.161 Whilst not binding, Judge Jeremy Richardson QC has found that the costs of setting up a trust fund for a successful claimant (a minor with autism) were special damages and ought not to be recoverable as costs between opposing parties.[165]

49.162 In a case in which success in a claim resulted in a need to carry out administrative estate work that otherwise would not have been required, Willmer J found that the fact that the administrative work had been carried out after the conclusion of the proceedings demonstrated that those costs were in no way necessary to enable him to conduct the claim.[166] This decision was pre-CPR and ought to be approached with appropriate caution, but whether the work was carried out before or after the conclusion of the claim is likely still to be a factor that the court is able to take into account.

Costs as damages and contractual rights to costs

49.163 Where a person's attendance at proceedings other than the civil claim is as a result of an opponent's default and where costs have been incurred which are not likely to be recoverable as costs, then it may be possible to claim those costs as damages, which topic is addressed in general terms at 3.38.

49.164 In a case in which the Leasehold Valuation Tribunal had declined to add costs to a service charge, Arden LJ found that the fact that the landlord had a contractual right to costs permitted the court to allow those costs.[167] This topic is addressed in general terms at 66.02–66.29.

The EW-UTBMS Code-set (Otherwise Known as J-Codes)

49.165 As is explained at 49.167, there is now an approved UTBMS code-set for use in civil litigation in England and Wales—namely, the EW-UTBMS code-set (otherwise known as J-Codes).

49.166 The CPR code-set referred to earlier in this chapter (see 49.20 *et seq*) is based on the EW-UTBMS code-set, which is part of the Uniform Task-Based Management System (UTBMS): a system originally developed under the auspices of the Legal Electronic Data Exchange Standard (LEDES™) Oversight Committee (see 49.168). Those codes were originally developed for the purposes of 'classifying legal services performed by a legal vendor in an electronic invoice submission' in the United States.[168] The original UTBMS code-sets

[164] See *Stratford-on-Avon District Borough Council v Clarke* [2015] EWHC 1539 (Ch), *per* Mr John Jarvis QC (sitting as a deputy judge of the High Court).

[165] See *G (by her mother and litigation friend M) v Kingston upon Hull City Council* (Unreported), 18 September 2013, Kingston upon Hull County Court, at [66] and [67].

[166] *Thomas v Cunard Whitestar Line* [1950] 2 All ER 1157.

[167] See *Chaplair Ltd v Kumari* [2015] EWCA Civ 798, at [19]–[26]. Those costs were allowable despite the fact that the case had been allocated to the small claims track.

[168] See http://utbms.com/

were highly geared towards use in that jurisdiction, but the EW-UTBMS code-set has been adapted for use in England and Wales (and hence the 'EW' prefix).

The EW-UTBMS code-set was approved by the LEDES™ Oversight Committee in 2014. The original intention was that its use would be coupled with the new electronic bill of costs, but in April 2016 Sir Rupert Jackson recommended that this should no longer be so (see 49.175).[169] This meant that the EW-UTBMS codes were removed from the model electronic bill of costs. Nonetheless, they left their imprint and it is this that gave rise to what is referred to earlier in this chapter as the 'CPR code-set'. The EW-UTBMS code-set still has relevance, however, in that it may be used at the option of the receiving party. **49.167**

LEDES™

No description of the EW-UTBMS code-set would be complete without referring to LEDES™, which is the body that oversees UTBMS code-sets. LEDES™ (pron. /liːdz/) is the trade name of the Legal Electronic Data Exchange Standard Oversight Committee, a US body that was first created in 1995 and became incorporated in 2000 as a Californian non-profit mutual benefit corporation. It is responsible for overseeing the formats and syntaxes described below. **49.168**

The LEDES™ Oversight Committee is charged with the task of creating and maintaining open standard formats for the electronic exchange of billing information between corporations and law firms.[170] It sets itself high standards—in particular, aiming for its coding systems to be simple, unambiguous and able to meet the needs of law firms, their corporate clients and their suppliers of legal software.[171] The LEDES™ billing standards are the Committee's most recognised 'brand' (for want of a better word). Indeed, those e-billing standards are accepted as the industry-specific electronic data interchange (EDI)[172] standards for the system-to-system exchange of legal e-billing information.[173] **49.169**

The history of the EW-UTBMS code-set

In his Final Report, Sir Rupert Jackson said that there should be codes for different tasks.[174] He suggested that bills of costs should be based on the 'phase, task, activity' format, as used by the UTBMS.[175] Sir Rupert added that any new format must provide for work that is not chargeable or work that is written off to be allocated to a separate file.[176] He said that if bills were to be prepared along the lines suggested, there would potentially be large savings in time and costs.[177] **49.170**

[169] See Jackson, R, 'The New Form Bill of Costs: Keynote Address to the Law Society's Civil Litigation Conference', 21 April 2016, para 5.2.

[170] See https://ledes.org/

[171] LEDES' work is based on five basic principles: keep it simple; make it unambiguous; diverge from existing formats as little as absolutely necessary; ask only for information the law firm is typically able to provide from its financial system; and meet the needs of corporations, law firms and legal industry software vendors to the maximum extent possible consistent with the first four criteria.

[172] That is, the transfer of structured data, by agreed message standards, from one computer system to another without human intervention.

[173] See http://utbms.com/

[174] Jackson, R, *Review of Civil Litigation Costs: Final Report* (London: HMSO, 2010), ch 45, para 2.3.

[175] *Ibid*, para 5.7.

[176] *Ibid*, para 5.5.

[177] *Ibid*, para 5.5.

The Association of Costs Lawyers Working Group

49.171 In September 2010, the Association of Costs Lawyers (ACL) established a working group to consider Sir Rupert's proposals for a new format. Its first report was published in October 2011.[178] In essence, it said that the use of UTBMS code-sets would be one way of dealing with the majority of Sir Rupert's concerns.

The Jackson Review Project Steering Committee

49.172 On 24 April 2012, there was a meeting of interested parties to discuss the feasibility of adapting a UTBMS code-set to meet the requirements of civil litigation in this jurisdiction. That group became the Jackson Review Project Steering Committee. It was initially chaired by Jeremy Morgan QC, but, on his retirement in 2013, Alexander Hutton QC took the lead. Two subcommittees were created, as follows.

- **The Jackson Review Bill Group** This group was responsible for the development of a new model bill of costs.
- **The Jackson Review Drafting Group** This group was responsible for the development of a new set of UTBMS time-recording codes for use in England and Wales.

49.173 By September 2013, a draft EW-UTBMS code-set had been drawn up by the Jackson Review Drafting Group and it was sent to Sir Vivien Ramsey (the judge who, at the time was overseeing the Jackson reforms) for approval. On 30 July 2014, Lord Dyson, Sir Rupert Jackson and Master Hurst jointly wrote to the LEDES™ Oversight Committee to ask it for ratification of the draft codes. On 11 September 2014, the Committee announced that it had endorsed the new UTBMS litigation code-set for use in England and Wales; hence the code-set came into being.

Implementation

49.174 It was originally envisaged that the EW-UTBMS code-set would be adopted by the legal profession on an industry-wide basis. The intention was that task codes initially recorded by fee earners would be fed directly into the bills of costs, which would then be presented to the court for assessment. The LEDES™ Oversight Committee also said that it was 'envisaged the J-Codes [would] be used extensively to analyse the Bill-of-Costs by the losing litigant, in order to minimize their costs'.[179]

49.175 In reality, however, it was very unlikely that these aspirations could ever have been realised in any brief time frame. By January 2016, the Civil Procedure Rule Committee had come to the conclusion that it was 'too soon' to make the new bill of costs—which, at that stage, was based on the EW-UTBMS code-set—compulsory. In a speech delivered to the Law Society in April 2016, Sir Rupert Jackson acknowledged that there was 'a state of deadlock' in this regard.[180] He said that the industry needed 'practical proposals to break the deadlock and advance the discussion', and he proposed that references to the EW-UTBMS code-set should be removed from the electronic bill of costs. He went on to say that doing so would allow 'greater flexibility', in that the CPR should allow practitioners to prepare that bill in

[178] Association of Costs Lawyers, *Modernising Bills of Costs: First Report of the Jackson Working Group* (Diss: ACL, 2011).

[179] See http://utbms.com/

[180] See Jackson, R, 'The New Form Bill of Costs: Keynote Address to the Law Society's Civil Litigation Conference', 21 April 2016, para 3.8.

any manner of their choosing, whether with the assistance of J-Codes, automatically generated by an Excel spreadsheet or by hand.[181] Thus usage of the EW-UTBMS code-set is entirely optional.

Coding and the EW-UTBMS code-set ('J-Codes')

The UTBMS stable is home to many different code-sets for many types of work, including code-sets for US litigation ('L-Codes'), for bankruptcy ('B-Codes') and for the work of patent attorneys ('P-Codes'). The EW-UTBMS code-set is similar to the code-set that contains L-Codes, but it has been adapted both to correspond with the phases of English litigation and to map to the codes used for budgeting.[182] **49.176**

The following benefits have been attributed to the EW-UTBMS code-set.[183] **49.177**

- It enables courts and other parties to easily perform analysis of costs and legal fees at different levels using the same set of data, including the comparison of actual costs to budgeted costs.
- It facilitates conformity in costs breakdowns across the court system by providing a common set of budgeting and time-recording codes.
- It enables data, in the form of time entries (including task and activity codes), to be entered only once into a solicitor's system, from which data it should be possible to produce cost reports and bills at different levels of detail for different purposes.
- It is intuitive enough for all organisations to adopt easily.
- It is compatible with existing time-recording systems in terms of length and format.
- It enables and assists in the analysis of costs during the process of cost recovery between opposing parties.

Code protocol

The EW-UTBMS codes are four characters long—namely, two letters followed by two digits—and are structured as follows.[184] **49.178**

- **Character 1, the code-set identifier** This defines the code-set and, as such, is always a 'J' for phase codes and task codes; activity codes and expense codes use the prefixes 'A' and 'X', respectively.
- **Character 2, the phase identifier** This is a letter[185] that identifies the phase group.
- **Characters 3 and 4, the phase/task identifiers** These define the relevant phase or task (or both).

A code ending in two zeros (that is, 00) identifies only the phase (for example JA00, JB00).[186] Those that end in other numbers define tasks; hence JA01, JA02/JB01, JB02 are

---

[181] See *ibid*, para 5.2.

[182] See Nelson, D, *Jackson Review of Civil Litigation Costs: UTBMS Drafting Group—Civil Litigation J-Code Set Overview and Guidelines*, 27 July 2014, available online at http://utbms.com/jackson-ew-utbms/, p 5.

[183] See *ibid*, p 5.

[184] See *ibid*, p 10.

[185] Note that this differs from the US-centric litigation code-set, because it uses a numeric digit to identify the phase group.

[186] Note that the US-centric code-set identifies the phase in a similar way, using numerics in the hundreds (ie L100, L200).

all task codes. Other UTBMS codes (such as expense codes and activity codes) are composed of a letter followed by three digits.

The codification of profit costs

49.179 Both time and rate may be codified. Time spent may be coded with phase and task codes in combination with activity codes. Thus there is a hierarchy, with phases at the top, tasks in the middle and activities at the bottom. The hourly rate may be coded with grade codes (see 49.184).

49.180 **EW-UTBMS phase codes** Phase codes are the highest-level category in the coding hierarchy. The purpose of the phase is to contain a series of predefined tasks or steps, which means that the phase is often inferred by the task code. Phase codes may be entered or amended at any time; in particular, they do not have to be entered at the time entry is made.

49.181 It will be recalled that the EW-UTBMS code-set was developed so that the phases correspond with those in Precedent H. There are, however, several phases (and corresponding tasks) that do not appear in Precedent H. Those phases and tasks (such as funding) may relate to costs that are not recoverable between opposing parties, and the Jackson Review Drafting Group has said that the inclusion of such codes enables such costs to be identified and captured at the stage when time is recorded. As such, it does not follow that the mere fact that a code exists for any given type of work means that costs for that work are recoverable between opposing parties.

49.182 **EW-UTBMS task codes** Task codes are entered at the point of recording the time entry. They provide information about the type of work that was done.

49.183 **EW-UTBMS activity codes** These are codes intended to describe how work is accomplished (for example 'communicating', 'drafting'). The activity code-set is common to all tasks codes and is entered at the point of recording.

49.184 **EW-UTBMS grade codes** The grade of fee earner can also be coded, as laid out in Table 49.1.[187]

49.185 **The codification of disbursements** Likewise, there is a separate set of expense codes, which are independent of phase, task and activity codes.

LEDES™ files

49.186 LEDES™ is a set of file format specifications intended to standardise EDI in the legal services industry. Formats commonly used for EDI in other industries (such as e-purchasing) include spreadsheets, fixed-width files, comma separated variable (.csv) files, and SAP intermediate document (IDOC) files; this is a significant barrier to EDI because the costs of setting up file-conversion systems are usually very high.[188] The actual file format began as a

[187] See Nelson, D, *Jackson Review of Civil Litigation Costs: UTBMS Drafting Group—Civil Litigation J-Code Set Overview and Guidelines*, 27 July 2014, available online at http://utbms.com/jackson-ew-utbms/, p 27.

[188] Where there has been a mismatch of this type, cloud-based software as a service (SAAS) has been used to carry out the necessary conversion. There is no reason why the same could not happen with LEDES.

Table 49.1 EW-UTBMS grade codes

Experience	Grade code	Grade description
PQE 8 years+	A	A Solicitors with more than eight years' post-qualification experience (PQE), including at least eight years' litigation experience
PQE 7–8 years	B	B Solicitors and legal executives with more than four years' PQE, including at least four years' litigation experience
PQE 5–6 years	B	
PQE 4–5 years	B	
PQE 3–4 years	C	C Other solicitors and legal executives,* and fee earners of equivalent experience
PQE 2–3 years	C	
PQE 1–2 years	C	
PQE 0–1 years–newly qualified	C	
Trainee (year 2)	D	D Trainee solicitors, paralegals and other fee earners
Trainee (year 1)	D	
Paralegal	D	

* 'Legal executive' means a Fellow of the Chartered Institute of Legal Executives (CILEX).

pipe-delimited plain text file (.txt). In about 2000, the file format changed to an extensible markup language (XML) file.[189] The chronology is as follows.

- **LEDES 1998** was the first LEDES™ format, created in 1998, but no longer in use.
- **LEDES 1998B** is a .txt file. There is also an international version.[190] The standard was adopted in 1998 and it is by far the most commonly used LEDES™ format. Pipe-delimited plain text has an inherently rigid structure, which means that if a user wishes to add their own fields or notes, they can do so only by departing from the 'standard'. The LEDES™ Oversight Committee has noted that many users have attempted to do this only to discover that they have defeated the purpose of the standard. LEDES 1998B is inefficient in that invoice-level data is repeated on every line item even though it is needed only once (because it does not vary per line). Notwithstanding these drawbacks, law firms prefer it for its simplicity and familiarity.
- **LEDES 2000** is an XML format adopted in 2000. One advantage of LEDES 2000 is that although the structure is very well defined, the specification defines 'extend' segments, allowing the insertion of client-specific fields without breaking the format or violating the standard. Despite this, adoption of this newer standard has been slow.
- **XML E-Billing versions 2 and 2.1** are improved versions of LEDES 2000. The first was ratified in 2006, but has yet to see adoption.
- **LEDES Budget Standard** was ratified in 2006. This XML format is intended to facilitate the exchange of budget data between law firms and clients.

[189] See http://utbms.com/

[190] LEDES 1998B-INTL (international) is a pipe-delimited plain text file, based on the LEDES 1998B standard. This format was designed to accommodate legal bills generated outside of the United States. It includes all of the fields in the LEDES 1998B format, plus additional ones. The format was proposed in 2004 by the Legal IT Innovators Group (LITIG). The LEDES Oversight Committee (LOC) ratified the format in 2006.

49.187 As such, whilst .txt files are by far the most common, the most modern formats have an XML file extension. That format focuses mainly on documents, but it is also widely used for arbitrary data structures,[191] such as web pages. The relevance of this is that it provides a means for recording versioning, which may be an important point given that the data will be used for many purposes (such as making offers, assessing the costs, billing clients, etc).

49.188 LEDES™ files have been designed in such a way as to allow individual files to be sent electronically—via EDI value added network (VAN), applicability statement 2 (AS2), File Transfer Protocol (FTP), FTPS (that is, secure FTP), HTTPS (secure Hypertext Transfer Protocol), or by email—along with an invoice.[192] This combination of electronic invoicing and LEDES™ files is known as 'e-billing'. Existing software (such as practice management systems) may not use the same format as is used for LEDES™ coding. Where there has been a mismatch of this type in other EDI contexts (such as e-purchasing), cloud-based software as a service (SaaS) has been used to carry out the necessary conversion. There is no reason why the same could not happen with LEDES™.

49.189 As far as the editor is aware, there is no published standard for ensuring authenticity, integrity and non-repudiation (all of which would be required if a LEDES™ file were to be digitally signed). As such, it would be up to individuals to make their own such arrangements in this regard. This could cause problems when a receiving party wishes to certify a file.

[191] Fennell, P, 'Extremes of XML: Keynote Address', XML London 2013, available online at http://xmllondon.com/2013/presentations/fennell/, p 80.

[192] See http://utbms.com/

50

FIXED COSTS, COSTS ON THE SMALL CLAIMS TRACK AND FAST-TRACK COSTS

This chapter deals with the following topics: **50.01**

- the language of fixed costs, predictable costs, etc (50.04);
- the history of fixed costs (50.07);
- CPR, Part 45, Section I—fixed commencement costs, fixed enforcement costs, etc (50.48):
  - the circumstances in which fixed costs will apply (50.49);
  - fixed commencement costs (50.55);
  - miscellaneous fixed costs (the costs of service) (50.61);
  - fixed judgment costs (50.62);
  - fixed enforcement costs (50.66);
- CPR, Part 45, Section II—fixed recoverable costs (50.67):
  - ambit (50.68);
  - definitions (50.72);
  - amount (50.79);
  - procedure (50.95);
  - putative premature issue of claims (50.97);
- pre-April 2013 CPR, Part 45, Sections III, IV and V—fixed success fees (50.102);
- CPR, Part 45, Section III and the related Portal—Portal costs (50.150):
  - jurisdiction and associated rules (50.153);
  - exit from the relevant protocol (50.170);
  - fixed costs (50.173);
  - Portal costs stage by stage (50.191);
  - the consequences of non-compliance (50.254);
- CPR, Part 45, Section IIIA—post-Portal fixed costs (50.267);
- CPR, Part 45, Section IV—scale costs for claims in the Intellectual Property Enterprise Court (50.312);
- CPR, Part 45, Section V—fixed costs: HM Revenue & Customs (50.342);
- CPR, Part 45, Section VI—fast-track trial costs (50.345):
  - the amount of fast-track trial costs (50.350);
  - the power to award more or less than fast-track trial costs (50.356);
  - fast-track trial costs where there is more than one claimant or defendant (50.362);
- CPR, Part 45, Section VII—costs limits in Aarhus Convention claims (50.368);
- costs on the small claims track:
  - general provisions (50.369);
  - the applicability of the small claims restriction (50.371); and
  - unreasonable behaviour (50.400).

50.02 Fixed costs are governed by Part 45, Sections I–III, IIIA and IV–VII of the Civil Procedure Rules (CPR). All of these sections are addressed in this chapter (including the pre-1 April 2013 provisions) other than Section VII (Aarhus Conventions claims), which is described at 13.78–13.99. This chapter also deals with the rules that govern costs on the small claims track.

50.03 The editor is grateful to Professor Fenn (emeritus professor of economics at the University of Nottingham), Judge Hacon (presiding judge of the Intellectual Property Enterprise Court) and Kevin Latham of counsel (Kings Chambers) for their assistance with parts of this chapter.

The Language of Fixed Costs, Predictable Costs, etc

50.04 The CPR define fixed costs as those costs 'the amounts of which are fixed by rules of court, whether or not the court has a discretion to allow some other or no amount'.[1] The term 'scale costs' is also used,[2] but scale costs tend to act as limits rather than fix the sums payable.

50.05 Table 50.1 (overleaf) sets out the nomenclature that is used in this book. As can be seen, other terms exist, but they often have ambiguous meanings; for this reason, those other terms are best avoided.

50.06 Whilst not a term that is encountered in the CPR themselves, 'predictable costs' is often used to refer to costs that are fixed in the sense that they are quantified by the application of a set formula; indeed, it was a phrase that was used by both Lord Woolf[3] and Sir Rupert Jackson.[4] The term 'predictive costs' is also often heard, but is best avoided, not least because it is grammatically incorrect. In any event, neither of those phrases are used in this book because they are ambiguous in the sense that they have been used to refer both to costs payable under CPR, Part 45, Section II, and to costs payable under Section III.

The History of Fixed Costs

50.07 The following historical topics are addressed in this section:

- the modern fascination with hourly rates (see 50.08);
- the pre-Woolf history (broadly from Elizabethan times to the mid-1990s) (see 50.10);
- the Woolf reforms (see 50.15);
- between Woolf and Jackson—fixed success fees and fixed recoverable costs (see 50.19);
- early fixed costs under Jackson (see 50.21);
- the original RTA Portal (see 50.26);
- general developments following the original RTA Portal (see 50.27);
- publication of the revisions to the RTA Portal (see 50.44); and
- a retrospective reflection (see 50.45).

---

1 See CPR, r 44.1.

2 See, eg, CPR, r 45.31.

3 See, eg, Lord Woolf, *Access to Justice: Final Report to the Lord Chancellor on the Civil Justice System in England and Wales* (London: HMSO, 1996), ch 7, paras 2 and 4.

4 See, eg, Jackson, R, *Review of Civil Litigation Costs: Final Report* (London: HMSO, 2010), ch 15, para 3.1.

Table 50.1 The nomenclature of fixed costs

Section	Terms preferred in this book	Other terms
Section I	Fixed commencement costs Fixed judgment costs Fixed enforcement costs Miscellaneous fixed costs	Fixed costs
Section II	Fixed recoverable costs	Predictable (or predictive) costs
Sections III, IV and V (pre-April 2013)	Fixed success fees	Fixed recoverable costs
Section III	Portal costs	Predictable (or predictive) costs
Section IIIA	Post-Portal fixed costs	Fixed recoverable costs Expanded fixed recoverable costs Predictable costs Expanded predictable costs
Section IV	Scale costs	
Section V	HMRC charges	
Section VI	Fast-track trial costs	
Section VII	n/a	

This summary does not extend beyond 2014 because developments since that date are ongoing and any attempt to address such issues would quickly become out of date.

The modern fascination with hourly rates

Fixed costs are nothing new. Indeed, quite the opposite is true: it is time-based charging that is the newcomer (see 1.135–1.136 and 51.03–51.11). In the 18th century and early-to-mid-19th century, costs tended to be fixed by court directions (see 1.94).[5] As is explained at 50.12, towards the end of the 19th century the system of directions was replaced by a more formal system of fixed costs based on rules of court—namely, 'scale charges'. The rules originally stipulated the amounts that would be payable between solicitor and client, but over time they came to govern costs between opposing parties (see 50.13). **50.08**

Scale charges continued to exist in one form or another until as recently as 1998. By that stage, the hourly rate had taken hold (see 51.12). The fact that the pendulum is now swinging back towards fixed fees should not come in any way as a surprise; the only surprise is the fact that the newcomer—time-based charging—has been allowed to hold sway for so long. **50.09**

[5] Q Le Riche's *Handy Book on the Taxation of Common Law Costs* (London: IR Taylor, 1859), for example, is largely a collection of 'Directions to Masters of the Courts', setting out, in tabular form, the various amounts that would be allowed for certain categories of case in certain courts. The allowance for taking instructions in a case worth £20 in the Court of Common Pleas, for example, was 3s 4d—and this was so regardless of the complexity of the matter.

The pre-Woolf history of fixed costs

The 40-shilling rule

50.10 The first tariff-based costs regime of which reliable records exist was the 40-shilling rule introduced during the reign of Elizabeth I (see 1.43–1.44). That rule did not fare well: as is explained at 1.46–1.47, a hostile judiciary thwarted it with such unrelenting consistency that it became a near-irrelevance. This was despite the legislature's repeated efforts to breathe life into it during Stuart and early Georgian times (see 1.59 and 1.66). That said, the 40-shilling rule limped on for an astonishingly long time: whilst, by then, it had withered to little more than an obscure footnote, a version of it continued to exist until as recently as 2014 (see 58.03).

Scale costs from 1883 to 1998

50.11 Notwithstanding the failure of the 40-shilling rule, the need for effective restraint of costs was ever-present. In 1828, Lord Brougham strenuously argued for fixed costs between solicitor and client (see 1.75). His arguments failed before Parliament, but, as has been mentioned above (see 50.08), many courts had already created direction-based tariffs. In practice, those tariffs often applied in such a way as to moderate costs as between solicitor and client.

50.12 Later in the 19th century, those tariffs were replaced with scale charges in the form of Appendix N of the Rules of the Supreme Court 1883 (see 1.94–1.96). As a matter of law, the new scale charges operated as between solicitor and client (that is, the relevant rule read 'solicitors should be entitled to charge and be allowed the fees set forth'[6]). The effect of this, however, was mitigated by the fact that the Attorneys' and Solicitors' Act 1870 had come into force only a few years earlier, s 4 of which permitted solicitors to enter into agreements by which they could be paid 'at a greater ... rate [to that] which [they] would otherwise be entitled to be remunerated'[7]—the forerunner of modern-day business agreements (see 1.84). This meant that a solicitor was able to charge more than scale costs, but only if this had been expressly agreed in writing.

50.13 In time, scale charges began to refer to costs as between opposing parties rather than between solicitor and client—although they continued to have an influence on the amounts charged between solicitor and client by virtue of the then equivalents of the County Court restriction (see 37.18–37.23). Scale charges grew to cover a large range of cases, especially in the county courts.

50.14 Scale costs were remarkably resilient. They existed in one guise or another right up to the eve of the introduction of the CPR.[8] Indeed, some were carried over into the CPR in the form of Part 45, Section 1 (namely, fixed commencement costs, fixed judgment costs, etc).

---

6 See RSC 1883, Ord LXV, r 8.

7 The court had the power to disallow any fees 'improperly incurred', however: see Attorneys' and Solicitors' Act 1870, s 4; RSC 1883, Ord LXV, r 11.

8 Albeit only in the county courts: see 1.139.

The Woolf reforms

Notwithstanding the fact that scale costs were already widely in use, there was a perception that the costs of litigation were too uncertain. This was largely because, during the 20th century, the linkage between scale costs and charges as between solicitor and client had become weakened (put otherwise, scale costs increasingly governed the position only between opposing parties). In any event, charging by way of hourly rates gradually took hold in the High Court (see 1.136 and 51.10). It was said that the way in which costs were ascertained had become incomprehensible to many litigants and that this induced the fear of the unknown.[9] This proved to be the catalyst for change. **50.15**

In 1994, the Lord Chancellor asked Lord Woolf MR to carry out a review of the civil justice system (see 1.145). In his Interim Report, Lord Woolf highlighted the problem of 'excessive and unaffordable costs' and of 'disproportionate costs', commenting that 'the problem of costs [was] the most serious problem besetting our litigation system'.[10] In his Final Report, Lord Woolf identified several objectives, including making costs more proportionate to the nature of the dispute and making the amount of costs more predictable.[11] **50.16**

Lord Woolf's academic advice

Lord Woolf MR commissioned Professor Zuckerman of Oxford University to consider ways in which costs could be controlled. Zuckerman said that a system of fixed recoverable costs (or something similar) was the only way of achieving access to justice at predictable and proportionate cost.[12] One of the many proposals that Zuckerman made was that costs could be fixed by means of 'prospective budget-setting'. It is fair to say that the legal profession did not embrace this suggestion with enthusiasm: **50.17**

> 'The paper occasioned a general outcry from the legal profession. Prospective budget-setting was seen as unworkable, unfair and likely to be abused by the creation of inflated budgets. The ability of judges to be involved in the hard detail of matters such as cost was generally doubted. The imposition of fixed fees, even relating only to *inter partes* costs, was seen as unrealistic and as interference with parties' rights to decide how to instruct their own lawyers. There was widespread concern that these suggestions heralded an attempt to control solicitor and own client costs. The restrictions were generally seen as "artificial and unworkable".'[13]

This put paid to the notion of costs being managed by what is now known as costs management. Some other method of controlling costs was required.

Lord Woolf's recommendations

In so far as multitrack claims were concerned, Lord Woolf proposed that the problem of costs would be solved by case management, rather than by orders limiting the expenditure **50.18**

[9] See Lord Woolf, *Access to Justice: Final Report to the Lord Chancellor on the Civil Justice System in England and Wales* (London: HMSO, 1996), overview, para 2.

[10] Lord Woolf, *Access to Justice: Interim Report to the Lord Chancellor on the Civil Justice System in England and Wales* (London: HMSO, 1995), ch 3, paras 13–28.

[11] Lord Woolf, *Access to Justice: Final Report to the Lord Chancellor on the Civil Justice System in England and Wales* (London: HMSO, 1996), ch 7.

[12] See *ibid.*

[13] *Ibid*, ch 7, paras 16–17.

of recoverable costs. Moreover, contrary to what is often believed, Lord Woolf had no plans to introduce fixed fees on the multitrack.[14] His intentions for the fast track, however, were not only that there should be fixed fees for trial (which were introduced as early as 2000), but also that there should be staged fixed costs for the litigation itself.[15] The latter were not introduced until 2013, however, and even then only for personal injury claims (see 50.21–50.25).

Between Woolf and Jackson: fixed success fees and fixed recoverable costs

50.19 In the aftermath of the Access to Justice Act 2000, there was considerable satellite litigation that had its genesis in the fact that defendants believed that the recoverability of additional liabilities had weakened cost-control incentives. This prompted the Civil Justice Council to initiate a process of quasi-mediation in an attempt to negotiate an industry-wide solution to the twin problems of the drain on the resources of the court and the rising cost burden imposed by additional liabilities. Professors Paul Fenn (then an academic economist at the University of Nottingham) and Neil Rickman (an economist from the University of Surrey) were asked to produce an evidenced-based report[16] that would assist with this process. This, in 2003, led to the introduction of fixed recoverable costs (which related to non-litigated lower-value road traffic accident claims) and fixed success fees (which related to certain personal injury claims).[17]

50.20 Professors Fenn and Rickman were subsequently asked by the Civil Justice Council to evaluate the effect of these new provisions. In 2007, they submitted a further evidence-based report.[18] While they found that the impact of the new provisions was broadly in line with expectations, they noted that defendants continued to have concerns about their ability to control costs. Pressure was put on the Ministry of Justice to introduce a new scheme by which low-value road traffic accident claims could be subject to lower fixed costs (see 50.26).

The Jackson reforms: early fixed costs under Jackson

50.21 In 2009, Sir Rupert Jackson carried out his review (see 1.171). In his Preliminary Report, Sir Rupert stated that it was the unanimous view of his panel of assessors that his reforms should seek to achieve a fixed costs system for all fast-track cases.[19]

50.22 In September and October 2009, the Civil Justice Council held a series of 'facilitative meetings' with stakeholders, at Jackson's request.[20] In essence, the aim was to set fixed costs for fast-track personal injury cases that related to claims other than lower-value

[14] *Ibid*, chs 5 and 7.

[15] *Ibid*, ch 4.

[16] See Fenn, P, and Rickman, N, *Costs of Low Value RTA Claims 1997–2002* (London: Civil Justice Council, 2003).

[17] For more details (including a more detailed chronology), see Fenn, P, and Rickman, N, 'Fixing Lawyers' Fees *ex Ante*: A Case Study in Policy and Empirical Legal Studies' (2011) 8(3) Journal of Empirical Legal Studies 533.

[18] See Fenn, P, and Rickman, N, *Monitoring the Fixed Recoverable Costs Scheme, Part I (The Effects of the Scheme on the Outcome of Claims) and Part II (The Effects of the Scheme on Case Handling)* (London: Civil Justice Council, 2007).

[19] Jackson, R, *Review of Civil Litigation Costs: Preliminary Report* (London: HMSO, 2009), ch 22.

[20] See Jackson, R, *Review of Civil Litigation Costs: Final Report* (London: HMSO, 2010), ch 1, para 4.6. These meetings are described *ibid*, at ch 15. This related to employer's liability and public liability claims.

road traffic accidents. It is clear from the reports of those meetings that they were co-operative and constructive. Where stakeholders were unable to agree, Sir Rupert acted in a quasi-judicial capacity to resolve any stubborn issues. The way in which he and those who assisted him dealt with the matter was refreshingly transparent; there is insufficient space in this book to do justice to that topic, but a brief summary may be found in the footnotes.[21] One of the results of those discussions was the proposed matrix of fixed costs that may be found at Annex 5 of Sir Rupert's Final Report, which matrix relates to personal injury claims.

In that Final Report, Sir Rupert noted that opinions were divided along 'party lines'.[22] He rejected the notion that the introduction of fixed costs would be a reform weighted towards savings for defendants and insurers; instead, he concluded that there was a high public interest in making litigation costs in the fast track both proportionate and certain.[23] **50.23**

Sir Rupert concluded that it would be premature to embark upon any scheme of fixed costs or scale costs in respect of lower-value multitrack cases. The priority, he said, was to be (a) to achieve a comprehensive scheme of fixed or predictable costs in the fast track and (b) to introduce a scheme of capped scale costs for lower-value multitrack cases in what is now the Intellectual Property Enterprise Court.[24] He went on to say that, once those reforms had been implemented, there would need to be a period of evaluation.[25] Sir Rupert suggested that a costs council be set up to keep fixed costs under review,[26] and that reviews should be conducted every year by 'a well informed and independent body, which commands the respect of all parties'.[27] **50.24**

Sir Rupert's recommendations were, by and large, adopted, with many of the relevant changes made on 1 April 2013. The most significant recommendation that was not adopted at that time was that the costs of non-personal injury claims in the fast track be fixed. **50.25**

The Ministry of Justice reforms: the original RTA Portal

Independently of the matters referred to in 50.21–50.25, in October 2009 the Ministry of Justice—having consulted widely—published a policy report that confirmed plans to **50.26**

[21] Those present used, as their starting point, data compiled by Professor Fenn, whose figures were an estimate of the actual profit costs incurred in fast-track personal injury cases settled between 2006 and 2009: *ibid*, ch 15, para 5.4. Those data were then adjusted for inflation using the Consumer Price Index (CPI) for miscellaneous services (DKB9): *ibid*, ch 15, para 5.4. They were then discounted to take account of the costs savings associated with costs being fixed. This adjustment was in the order of £100 per claim. This discount was intended to leave an allowance for the overhead required to provide information on inputs/costs so that the fixed cost regime can be properly reviewed and regulated: *ibid*, ch 15, para 5.9. An allowance was then made for the average costs of instructing counsel: *ibid*, ch 15, para 5.10. No reduction was made to take account of the likely costs savings that were anticipated as a result of the (then) forthcoming ban on referral fees: *ibid*, ch 15, fn 14. Whilst he stressed that the matter should be kept under review, Sir Rupert said that other competing arguments cancelled each other out: *ibid*, ch 15, para 5.9. He then adjusted the figures to provide an incentive to defendants to settle at an early stage: *ibid*, ch 15, para 5.14.

[22] *Ibid*, ch 7, para 4.7.

[23] *Ibid*, ch 15, para 5.8.

[24] *Ibid*, ch 16, para 2.9.

[25] *Ibid*, ch 16, para 2.10.

[26] *Ibid*, executive summary, para 2.11.i.

[27] *Ibid*, ch 6, paras 2.8 and 2.9.

implement new methods of resolving low-value (that is, up to £10,000) personal injury claims arising out of road traffic accidents (RTAs).[28] On 30 April 2010 and following further consultation, this led to the creation of the RTA Protocol and its associated Portal.[29]

General developments following the original RTA Protocol

50.27 In due course, that initial protocol (that is, the RTA Protocol) underwent a number of revisions that increased its ambit vertically, horizontally and collaterally. In addition, the amounts payable in cases that were disposed of via the RTA Portal were revised. In summary, the changes—which all came into being on 31 July 2013—were as follows.

- **Vertical expansion** There was a vertical expansion of the RTA Protocol in that the ceiling was raised to £25,000.
- **Horizontal expansion** There was a horizontal expansion in the form of the EL/PL Protocol.[30]
- **Collateral expansion** There was a collateral extension in the sense that new provisions in CPR, Part 45, Section IIIA, came into force, which created a framework for dealing with costs in cases that had ceased to follow one of the Protocols, ultimately giving rise to 'post-Portal fixed costs'.
- **Revision of amounts payable** In addition, there was a downward revision of the amounts payable in road traffic accident cases.

50.28 The way in which these revisions were carried out was in marked contrast to the transparent way in which Sir Rupert had dealt with the (then) entirely separate matters in 2009 that led to his Final Report (see 50.21–50.25). Indeed, the tale can fairly be said to be the paradigm case of how to ignore expert advice and how to please one group of stakeholders whilst antagonising the other. It should be borne in mind that the two strands of the reforms were separate: on the one hand, there were the Portal-related matters that were being reviewed by the Ministry of Justice; on the other, Sir Rupert Jackson's review. Sir Rupert was not significantly involved in the former. It was only at a later stage that the Ministry of Justice adopted some of Sir Rupert's recommendations (ultimately giving rise to post-Portal fixed costs).

Solving Disputes in the County Court

50.29 The story begins with *Solving Disputes in the County Court*, a consultation started by the Ministry of Justice in 2011 in the form of a questionnaire that required a reply by June 2011.[31] The consultation focused on the County Court and mooted a range of options.

50.30 On 9 February 2012, the Ministry of Justice published its response,[32] in which it made the following claim:

> 'There was general support for extending the scheme for low value road traffic accident claims (RTA PI scheme), and for introducing a similar simplified claims procedure on a fixed

---

[28] See Ministry of Justice, *Low Value Personal Injury Claims in Road Traffic Accidents* (London: HMSO, 2009).

[29] See Civil Procedure (Amendment) Rules 2010 (SI 2010/621), r 1(2).

[30] See Civil Procedure (Amendment No 6) Rules 2013 (SI 2013/1695).

[31] This can be found online at https://consult.justice.gov.uk/digital-communications/county_court_disputes

[32] Ministry of Justice, *Creating a Simpler, Quicker and More Proportionate System: A Consultation on Reforming Civil Justice in England and Wales—The Government Response*, Cm 8274 (London: HMSO, 2012).

costs basis for other personal injury claims. However, since the scheme only began operating in April 2010, and there was a lack of evidence as to its effectiveness, ... respondents advised caution in extending the scheme, or introducing similar schemes, too quickly.'[33]

The Ministry concluded that there was a need for 'caution', because the RTA Protocol and its associated Portal had been in place for only a short time. It went on to say (in terms) that it did not have sufficient management information to carry out an adequate impact assessment.[34] **50.31**

It is worth pausing here to note that the Ministry of Justice had instructed Professor Fenn to write a report dealing with the issue of extension of the RTA Protocol and its associated Portal.[35] The main thrust of Fenn's report was that it was too early to make any decisions on the data that was then available and that the matter ought to be reviewed once more data was available. As is explained next, it would seem that the Ministry of Justice ultimately disregarded most of Fenn's advice, in the context of it having had a draft of his report from a relatively early stage.[36] **50.32**

Notwithstanding the fact that it recognised a need for caution, the Ministry committed to extending the RTA Protocol vertically, to include claims up to £25,000, and horizontally, to incorporate employer's liability and public liability claims.[37] It also committed to reducing the monies payable under the RTA Portal so that they (supposedly) 'more accurately reflect[ed] the time taken to carry out the necessary work, bearing in mind the efficiencies gained from electronic document exchange ... and in the light of the recent ban on referral fees'.[38] **50.33**

Whilst the absence of an adequate impact assessment may have been a concern, it would seem that at this point the Ministry at least acknowledged the need for caution and, to that extent, was following the advice it had received. What Prime Minister David Cameron did next (see below) was consequently somewhat surprising. **50.34**

David Cameron's 'insurance summit'

On about 14 February 2012, Cameron hosted an 'insurance summit'—that is, a private meeting with only one group of stakeholders (insurers) present.[39] The fact that it was a unilateral meeting gave rise to complaints about the lack of transparency and barbed references to the fact that some of the insurers were donors to the prime minister's political party.[40] A judicial review was brought, but it failed, on the basis that discussions with one interest **50.35**

---

33 *Ibid*, p 8.

34 See *ibid*, p 10.

35 That report was Fenn, P, *Evaluating the Low Value Road Traffic Accident Process*, MoJ Research Series 13/12 (July 2012).

36 Personal communication with Professor Fenn, dated 6 March 2018.

37 Ministry of Justice, *Creating a Simpler, Quicker and More Proportionate System: A Consultation on Reforming Civil Justice in England and Wales—The Government Response*, Cm 8274 (London: HMSO, 2012).

38 This description being taken from the Explanatory Notes to the Civil Procedure (Amendment No 6) Rules 2013 (SI 2013/1695).

39 See *R (on the application of Association of Personal Injury Lawyers v Secretary of State for Justice)* [2013] EWHC 1358 (Admin), at [21].

40 See Thompsons Solicitors, 'Ministry of Justice: Call for Evidence—Extending the Road Traffic Accident Scheme: Response from Thompsons Solicitors', May 2012, available online at http://www.thompsonstradeunionlaw.co.uk/information-and-resources/pdf/thompsons-response-extending-rta-scheme.pdf, pp 1 and 2.

group (that is, insurers) did not amount to consultation.[41] That may be so, but it was a step that caused palpable resentment.[42]

Jonathan Djanogly's call for evidence

50.36 On 28 February 2012, Parliamentary Under-Secretary of State for Justice Jonathan Djanogly MP issued a call for evidence regarding the extension of the RTA Protocol and the amounts payable under it. His letter recorded the fact that, on 5 January, the Prime Minister had announced that the RTA Protocol and its associated Portal would be extended.[43] In addition, his letter went on to raise the following points:

> 'As you are aware, Lord Justice Jackson also recommended a ban of referral fees in personal injury cases alongside the reform of Contingency Fee Agreements, both of which are being taken forward in the Legal Aid, Sentencing and Punishment of Offenders (LASPO) Bill currently before Parliament. As a result of these changes, and as I indicated in November when the Bill was at report stage, we are reviewing the fixed recoverable costs in the RTA scheme. You will also be aware that at the recent Number 10 insurance summit, the Prime Minister committed to reducing these costs.'

50.37 That call for evidence was not received well by the claimant lobby, because it seemed to be based on some 'extremely premature assumptions'.[44] Moreover, the claimant lobby felt that the Ministry was acting with a sense of haste that was hard to reconcile with its own conclusions that the RTA Protocol was relatively new and needed time to 'bed in' (see 50.31). The fact that the Ministry delayed publication of Fenn's report (see 50.32) until after the call for evidence had closed did not help (although this was probably as a result of the need for the Ministry to complete its own peer review process[45]). In short, many people in the claimant lobby felt that the consultations were merely going through the motions—that the Ministry had already decided what it wanted to do.

50.38 On 22 October 2012, the Civil Procedure Rule Committee asked for comments on its draft protocols for the extended schemes,[46] which consultation was targeted at those who had responded to the Ministry of Justice's earlier call for evidence (see 50.36). That consultation closed on 23 November 2012—a mere month after it had begun. On 19 November 2012, the Ministry of Justice published an analysis of responses to its call for evidence.[47]

---

[41] See *R (on the application of Association of Personal Injury Lawyers v Secretary of State for Justice)* [2013] EWHC 1358 (Admin), at [36]–[46], *per* Elias LJ.

[42] The author is bound by 'Chatham House rules', but he personally attended meetings at which such views were not only expressed, but also expressed in very strong terms.

[43] This, if it was correct, was before the matters referred to above, although the author has not been able to find confirmation of this.

[44] See Thompsons Solicitors, 'Ministry of Justice: Call for Evidence—Extending the Road Traffic Accident Scheme: Response from Thompsons Solicitors', May 2012, available online at http://www.thompsonstradeunionlaw.co.uk/information-and-resources/pdf/thompsons-response-extending-rta-scheme.pdf, p 2.

[45] Personal communication with Professor Fenn, dated 6 March 2018.

[46] The facts are set out in Thompsons Solicitors, 'Civil Procedure Rule Committee Consultation on the Draft Protocols in an Expanded RTA Scheme: Response by Thompsons Solicitors', November 2012, available online at https://www.thompsonstradeunion.law/media/1990/civil-procedure-rule-committee-consultation-on-the-draft-protocols-in-an-expanded-rta-scheme-november-2012-thompsons-solicitors.pdf, p 1.

[47] See Ministry of Justice, 'Analysis of Responses to the Call for Evidence in Relation to Extension of the Road Traffic Accident Personal Injury Scheme', 19 October 2012, available online at https://consult.justice.gov.uk/digital-communications/extension-rta-scheme/results/detailed-analysis.pdf

At the same time, Parliamentary Under-Secretary of State Helen Grant MP began another consultation.[48] In its response issued in January 2013, the Civil Justice Council stated that fixed-fee proposals for personal injury work were unrealistic and should wait until at least 2014. The Ministry ultimately rejected this advice (see 50.42). **50.39**

The Ministry's findings

On 27 February 2013, the Ministry of Justice published its findings.[49] In a letter dated the same day, Secretary of State for Justice Chris Grayling MP wrote to stakeholders to say that: **50.40**

- a full evaluation of the existing scheme was not required to inform a decision about extending the RTP Protocol vertically to £25,000;
- revision of the fees payable under the RTA Protocol would commence at the end of April 2013; and
- the new Protocols carrying out these horizontal and collateral extensions would be implemented from the end of July 2013.

He added: 'Since sufficiently representative and comprehensive data in this area is not readily obtainable for all of the reforms, I do not wish to commit at this stage to a formal review fixed in 12 months' time.'

The Ministry said that whilst a high number of responses had been received in the most recent consultation, many of these, particularly from claimant lawyers, took the form of 'campaign' letters that did not provide detailed evidence as to the appropriate level of costs.[50] One could easily argue that many of those responses were, in fact, cogent and reasoned. **50.41**

As to the suggestion that it ought to have allowed the rules to 'bed in' before making any significant changes, the Ministry had this to say: **50.42**

> '[The] Government is not convinced by the argument set out by some respondents, including the Civil Justice Council (CJC), that the Government should wait to see how the range of civil justice reforms currently underway have bedded in, or until further analysis has been completed before proceeding with any reduction in fixed recoverable costs or extension of the RTA scheme. The Government is not clear what further data or evidence would be available in the near future which would make a sufficiently material difference to the current proposals to justify delaying their implementation.'[51]

On the face of it, this would seem to have been a significant and seemingly capricious departure from the Ministry's stance, as expressed in its response to the *Solving Disputes* consultation (see 50.31). Moreover, some of the conclusions that the Ministry reached did not seem to have been based on published evidence.[52] That said, the Ministry of Justice **50.43**

[48] See Grant, H, 'Extension of the RTA PI Scheme: Proposals on Fixed Recoverable Costs', 19 November 2012, available online at http://www.justice.gov.uk/downloads/publications/policy/moj/rta-pi-scheme.pdf

[49] Ministry of Justice, 'Extension of the Road Traffic Accident Personal Injury Scheme: Proposals on Fixed Recoverable Costs—Consultation Response', 27 February 2013, available online at https://consult.justice.gov.uk/digital-communications/extension-rta-scheme/results/rta-costs-response.pdf

[50] *Ibid*, para 1.

[51] *Ibid*, para 5.

[52] In particular, there was no evidence in the public domain to support the £700 across-the-board reduction in costs resulting from the referral fee ban.

went on to say that it was prepared to review and assess the effectiveness of the scheme should evidence be provided to demonstrate that this was necessary—but it did not wish to commit to a formal review fixed every 12 months.[53]

Publication of the 2013 revisions to the Portal

50.44 The rules for the extended Portal were published on 12 July 2013—a mere 12 working days before they were due to come into force. The then President of the Law Society had the following to say about this:

> 'Solicitors have an impossible task of advising their clients about procedures and costs liabilities. Many of those clients have an existing retainer with their solicitor which may cause them to incur additional liabilities which they will not be aware of. Clients will have agreed an hourly-rate basis for work done but fixed costs may result in a shortfall on recovery if they are successful.'[54]

She added:

> 'These far-reaching changes to civil litigation costs are to be implemented in less than four weeks' time. The government appears to be hell-bent on disruption, by failing to give the profession the notice they reasonably need. This could have a severe effect on access to justice for many thousands of accident victims.'[55]

Notwithstanding the force in these comments, the 65th update to the Civil Procedure Rules[56] came into force as planned on 31 July 2013.

A retrospective reflection

50.45 In a personal communication with the editor in early 2018,[57] Prof Fenn made the following comments:

> '[T]he provisions have not caused the degree of disruption to the personal injury market that might have been expected. [My] view is that this is due to the relaxation of the prior requirement that success fees reflect the risk of losing (and indeed the removal of the previous recommended success fee levels from the CPR). Success fees are now almost universally set at 100% with a 25% cap, and this has gone a long way to masking the effect of the reduced recoverable costs. Whether this is a sensible approach to fixing costs is a moot point.'

50.46 Put otherwise, the personal injury industry has responded to fixed costs by placing part of the burden for funding claims on clients (usually in the form of a success fee). Given the fact that there is now a nascent industry that is encouraging former clients to seek repayment of costs deducted from damages (see 36.21), one could argue that Fenn is right to question whether the present arrangements are sensible—not only because of the problems that this may cause in terms of access to justice, but also because of the drain that claims brought by former clients could place upon the courts' resources. It may be that fixed costs have not solved the problem, but have merely shifted it to a different arena. It is possible

[53] Ministry of Justice, 'Extension of the Road Traffic Accident Personal Injury Scheme: Proposals on Fixed Recoverable Costs—Consultation Response', 27 February 2013, available online at https://consult.justice.gov.uk/digital-communications/extension-rta-scheme/results/rta-costs-response.pdf, para 4.

[54] Law Society, 'New Civil Procedure Rules Will Lead to Major Disruption', 11 July 2013, available online at http://www.lawsociety.org.uk/news/stories/new-civil-procedure-rules-will-lead-to-major-disruption/

[55] *Ibid.*

[56] Civil Procedure (Amendment No 6) Rules 2013 (SI 2013/1695).

[57] Dated 7 March 2018.

that thought will have to be given to revising the amounts that are payable under the regimes described in this chapter so that they better reflect the cost of carrying out the work, thereby allowing legal services providers to make deductions from damages that are more acceptable to former clients (such as success fees that are based on risk and risk alone, rather than on the business needs of the person providing legal services). This, however, is very much a matter for policymakers.

A great deal of work has been carried out since about 2014 for the purposes of attempting to extend fixed costs to areas other than those described in this chapter (such as clinical negligence). That work is ongoing and, as such, it would not be appropriate to deal with that topic in this book (not least because any discussion would be out of date by the time this book was printed). It is worth noting, however, that, on 7 May 2018, CPR, Part 45, Section IIIA, was extended so as to include package travel claims, in response to concern about the costs of such claims. **50.47**

CPR, Part 45, Section I: Fixed Commencement Costs, Fixed Enforcement Costs, etc

This section deals with CPR, Part 45, Section I, which contains provisions for: **50.48**

- fixed commencement costs (see 50.55);
- miscellaneous fixed costs (which might be better termed fixed costs of service) (see 50.61);
- fixed costs on entry of judgment (see 50.62); and
- fixed enforcement costs (see 50.66).

Other than where is otherwise obvious from the context, these costs are referred to collectively as 'fixed costs'.

Circumstances in which fixed costs will apply

Broadly speaking, unless the court orders otherwise (see 50.52–50.54), fixed costs will apply where a claim was for a specified amount of money and where it was short-lived by reason of it having settled, having gone by default or having been disposed of by way of summary judgment. In these circumstances, fixed commencement costs will be payable (see 50.55), with or without fixed costs on entry of judgment (see 50.62) and/or miscellaneous fixed costs, depending on the circumstances.[58] In addition, fixed enforcement costs may be payable (see 50.66). **50.49**

CPR, r 45.1(2), sets out the circumstances in which fixed costs will apply: **50.50**

> 'This Section applies where—
> (a) the only claim is a claim for a specified sum of money where the value of the claim exceeds £25 and—
> (i) judgment in default is obtained under rule 12.4(1);
> (ii) judgment on admission is obtained under rule 14.4(3);
> (iii) judgment on admission on part of the claim is obtained under rule 14.5(6);
> (iv) summary judgment is given under Part 24;

[58] These provisions had, in essence, been carried over from Ord 38 of the County Court Rules 1981.

(v) the court has made an order to strike out a defence under rule 3.4(2)(a) as disclosing no reasonable grounds for defending the claim; or
(vi) rule 45.4 applies;

(b) the only claim is a claim where the court gave a fixed date for the hearing when it issued the claim and judgment is given for the delivery of goods, and the value of the claim exceeds £25;
(c) the claim is for the recovery of land, including a possession claim under Part 55, whether or not the claim includes a claim for a sum of money and the defendant gives up possession, pays the amount claimed, if any, and the fixed commencement costs stated in the claim form;
(d) the claim is for the recovery of land, including a possession claim under Part 55, where one of the grounds for possession is arrears of rent, for which the court gave a fixed date for the hearing when it issued the claim and judgment is given for the possession of land (whether or not the order for possession is suspended on terms) and the defendant—
(i) has neither delivered a defence, or counterclaim, nor otherwise denied liability; or
(ii) has delivered a defence which is limited to specifying his proposals for the payment of arrears of rent;

(e) the claim is a possession claim under Section II of Part 55 (accelerated possession claims of land let on an assured shorthold tenancy) and a possession order is made where the defendant has neither delivered a defence, or counterclaim, nor otherwise denied liability;
(f) the claim is a demotion claim under Section III of Part 65 or a demotion claim is made in the same claim form in which a claim for possession is made under Part 55 and that demotion claim is successful; or
(g) a judgment creditor has taken steps under Parts 70 to 73 to enforce a judgment or order.'

50.51 It is worth noting that where the claim is for possession under Part 55 and no arrears of rent is claimed (CPR, r 45.1(2)(c)), or where the claim is a demotion claim (CPR, r 45.1(2)(f)), the requisite circumstances will exist only where 'fixed commencement costs ... [are] stated on the claim form'. It therefore seems that, to this limited extent, a claimant may elect whether or not to seek those costs.[59] The wording of CPR, r 45.1(5), is in keeping with this, in that it reads 'the claim form *may* include a claim for fixed commencement costs' (emphasis added). If this is right and if a claimant were unreasonably to elect not to claim fixed costs, it is likely that the court would have the power to award costs as if fixed commencement costs had been claimed.[60] Each case would have to be decided on its own facts, but it would be difficult to object to the court taking fixed costs into account as a measure (amongst others) of what reasonable costs should be.

The court's discretion regarding fixed costs

50.52 Generally speaking, where the conditions set out in CPR, r 45.1(2), are met, the claimant's costs of the claim will be limited to fixed costs (plus court fees).[61] CPR, r 45.1(1), states that the court has discretion to allow costs other than (or in place of) fixed costs: 'This Section sets out the amounts which, unless the court orders otherwise, are to be allowed in respect of legal representatives' charges.'

59 Indeed, CPR, r 45.1(5), states that 'the claim form may include a claim for fixed commencement costs', which impliedly confirms the claimant's right to choose.

60 There is no authority directly on this point, but *Drew v Whitbread plc* [2010] EWCA Civ 53 and *O'Beirne v Hudson* [2010] EWCA Civ 52 seem to make this point by analogy.

61 See CPR, r 45.1(4).

Likewise, CPR, r 45.3(1), confers a discretion in cases in which the defendant has paid the sums claimed within a short period of time after commencement: **50.53**

> '(1) Where—
> (a) the only claim is for a specified sum of money; and
> (b) the defendant pays the money claimed within 14 days after service of particulars of claim on him, together with the fixed commencement costs stated in the claim form,
>
> the defendant is not liable for any further costs unless the court orders otherwise.'

The paradigm example of where the court may 'order otherwise' is where the defendant articulates a seemingly cogent defence—thereby putting the claimant to the trouble of 'front-loading' the claim—only to then change their stance capriciously and without explanation immediately upon being served with proceedings.[62] Another example (relating to costs payable under CPR, r 45.8) is a case in which Ramsay J 'ordered otherwise' because of the amount of work that was required on behalf of a party seeking a charging order.[63] **50.54**

Fixed commencement costs

Fixed commencement costs will apply only to claims for a specified sum of money where the value of the claim is more than £25.[64] No sum in respect of legal representatives' charges will be allowed where the only claim is for a sum of money or goods not exceeding £25.[65] **50.55**

The monies claimed must be a specified sum.[66] Damages or debt may be claimed as a sum to be assessed, but this will expose the claimant to a risk that the court could find that a specified sum should have been claimed instead, in which case the costs would have been limited to fixed commencement costs. The archetypal case in which that type of dispute may arise is a 'bent metal' road traffic accident case in which the repairs had already been carried out prior to issue. There is no authority on the point, but the distinction between liquidated and unliquidated damages may be of relevance. *Halsbury's* has this to say about that difference: **50.56**

> 'The parties may agree by contract that a particular sum is payable on the default of one of them. If the agreement is not obnoxious as a "penalty", such a sum constitutes "liquidated damages" and is payable by the party in default. The term is also applied to sums expressly made payable as liquidated damages under a statute. In every other case, where the court has to quantify or assess the damages or loss, whether pecuniary or non-pecuniary, the damages are "unliquidated".'[67]

Thus the issue may turn on whether the court would, in default of payment, have had to quantify or assess the monies claimed.

---

[62] See, eg, *Amber Construction Services Ltd v London Interspace HG Ltd* [2007] EWHC 3042 (TCC), referred to with apparent approval in *Whaleys (Bradford) Led v Bennett & Anor* [2017] EWCA Civ 2143, at [16]–[18], *per* Newey LJ.

[63] *Marche v Newham London Borough Council* [2014] EWHC 1521 (TCC), at [20]. It is worth noting, however, that the receiving party was not able to produce a statement of costs and hence Ramsay J ascertained the costs as being the same as the monies set out in CPR, r 45.8.

[64] See CPR, r 45.1(3).

[65] CPR, r 45.1(3).

[66] CPR, r 45.1(2)(a).

[67] *Halsbury's Laws of England* (5th edn, London: LexisNexis, 2015), vol 12(1) (reissue), para 808.

The amount of fixed commencement costs

50.57 The amount of fixed commencement costs depends on whether the claim is for money or property, or for land or demotion. Where the claim is for money or property, Table 1 applies (see CPR, r 45.2, and Table 50.2 below); where the claim is for land or demotion, Table 3 applies (see Table 50.3 below). In both cases, an additional amount under Table 4 (see Table 50.4 below) may be payable if the circumstances are appropriate. The relevant court fee is payable in addition (see CPR, r 45.1(3)).

50.58 There is nothing in either CPR, Part 45, Section I, or Practice Direction (PD) 45 to confirm whether or not value added tax (VAT) is payable in addition to the amounts of fixed commencement costs that are stated. Whilst it is no more than the editor's view, it is likely that they are exclusive of VAT, because this would otherwise unfairly penalise a party who was not registered for VAT. The contrary is arguable, however, not least because other sections in CPR, Part 45, expressly refer to VAT being payable in certain circumstances. That said, this is probably explained by the fact that, unlike the other sections in CPR, Part 45, most of Section I was largely carried over word-for-word from the County Court Rules 1981.[68]

50.59 CPR, Part 45, Section I, Table 1, is reproduced here as Table 50.2.

Table 50.2 Fixed costs on commencement of a claim for the recovery of money or goods

Relevant band	Where the claim form is served by the court or by any method other than personal service by the claimant	Where— • the claim form is served personally by the claimant; and • there is only one defendant	Where there is more than one defendant, for each additional defendant personally served at separate addresses by the claimant
Where— • the value of the claim exceeds £25 but does not exceed £500	£50	£60	£15
Where— • the value of the claim exceeds £500 but does not exceed £1,000	£70	£80	£15
Where— • the value of the claim exceeds £1,000 but does not exceed £5,000; or • the only claim is for delivery of goods and no value is specified or stated on the claim form	£80	£90	£15
Where— • the value of the claim exceeds £5,000	£100	£110	£15

[68] See Ord 38 of the County Court Rules 1981.

CPR, Part 45, Section I, Table 3, is reproduced here as Table 50.3. **50.60**

Table 50.3 Fixed costs on commencement of a claim for the recovery of land or a demotion claim

Where the claim form is served by the court or by any method other than personal service by the claimant	Where— • the claim form is served personally by the claimant; and • there is only one defendant	Where there is more than one defendant, for each additional defendant personally served at separate addresses by the claimant
£69.50	£77.00	£15.00

Miscellaneous fixed costs (costs of service)

CPR, Part 45, Section I, Table 4 (see CPR, r 45.7)—reproduced here as Table 50.4— **50.61** permits further allowances in cases in which the costs of service are higher than the norm. For some reason, they go under the heading 'miscellaneous fixed costs' rather than 'fixed costs of service' (which is what they are).

Table 50.4 Miscellaneous fixed costs

[Service]	[Cost]
For service by a party of any document required to be served personally including preparing and copying a certificate of service for each individual served	£15.00
Where service by an alternative method is permitted by an order under rule 6.8 for each individual served	£53.25
Where a document is served out of the jurisdiction—	
(a) in Scotland, Northern Ireland, the Isle of Man or the Channel Islands;	£68.25
(b) in any other place	£77.00

Fixed judgment costs

Fixed judgment costs will apply to a claim where fixed commencement costs are recoverable and where the court was required to enter judgment. **50.62**

Where the claim is for money or property, the applicable rule will be CPR, r 45.4, which reads as follows: **50.63**

> 'Where—
> (a) the claimant has claimed fixed commencement costs under rule 45.2; and
> (b) judgment is entered in a claim to which rule 45.1(2)(a) or (b) applies in the circumstances specified in Table 2, the amount to be included in the judgment for the claimant's legal representative's charges is the total of—
>   (i) the fixed commencement costs; and
>   (ii) the relevant amount shown in Table 2.'

CPR, Part 45, Section I, Table 2, is reproduced here as Table 50.5. **50.64**

Table 50.5 Fixed costs on entry of judgment in a claim for the recovery of money or goods

	Where the amount of the judgment exceeds £25 but does not exceed £5,000	Where the amount of the judgment exceeds £5,000
Where judgment in default of an acknowledgement of service is entered under rule 12.4(1) (entry of judgment by request on claim for money only)	£22.00	£30.00
Where judgment in default of a defence is entered under rule 12.4(1) (entry of judgment by request on claim for money only)	£25.00	£35.00
Where judgment is entered under rule 14.4 (judgment on admission), or rule 14.5 (judgment on admission of part of claim) and claimant accepts the defendant's proposal as to the manner of payment	£40.00	£55.00
Where judgment is entered under rule 14.4 (judgment on admission), or rule 14.5 (judgment on admission of part of claim) and court decides the date or time of payment	£55.00	£70.00
Where summary judgment is given under Part 24 or the court strikes out a defence under rule 3.4(2)(a), in either case, on application by a party	£175.00	£210.00
Where judgment is given on a claim for delivery of goods under a regulated agreement within the meaning of the Consumer Credit Act 1974 and no other entry in this table applies	£60.00	£85.00

50.65 Where the claim is for land or demotion, the applicable rule will be CPR, r 45.6, which reads as follows:

> '(1) Where—
> (a) the claimant has claimed fixed commencement costs under rule 45.5; and
> (b) judgment is entered in a claim to which rule 45.1(2)(d) or (f) applies, the amount to be included in the judgment for the claimant's legal representatives' charges is the total of—
> (i) the fixed commencement costs; and
> (ii) the sum of £57.25.
>
> (2) Where an order for possession is made in a claim to which rule 45.1(2)(e) applies, the amount allowed for the claimant's solicitor's charges for preparing and filing—
> (a) the claim form;
> (b) the documents that accompany the claim form; and
> (c) the request for possession,
> is £79.50.'

There is nothing in either CPR, Part 45, Section I, or PD 45 to confirm whether or not VAT is payable in addition to the amounts of fixed judgment costs that are stated in Part 45, but (for the reasons given in 50.58), it likely that VAT is payable in addition.

Fixed enforcement costs

50.66 Certain fixed costs are allowed upon enforcement (see CPR, r 45.8). The relevant sums are set out in CPR, Part 45, Section I, Table 5, reproduced here as Table 50.6.

Table 50.6 Fixed enforcement costs

For an application under rule 70.5(4) that an award may be enforced as if payable under a court order, where the amount outstanding under the award:	
exceeds £25 but does not exceed £250	£30.75
exceeds £250 but does not exceed £600	£41.00
exceeds £600 but does not exceed £2,000	£69.50
exceeds £2,000	£75.50
On attendance to question a judgment debtor (or officer of a company or other corporation) who has been ordered to attend court under rule 71.2 where the questioning takes place before a court officer, including attendance by a responsible representative of the legal representative.	for each half hour or part, £15.00
On the making of a final third party debt order under rule 72.8(6)(a) or an order for the payment to the judgment creditor of money in court under rule 72.10(1)(b):	
if the amount recovered is less than £150	one-half of the amount recovered
otherwise	£98.50
On the making of a final charging order under rule 73.8(2)(a):	£110.00 The court may also allow reasonable disbursements in respect of search fees and the registration of the order.
Where a certificate is issued and registered under Schedule 6 to the Civil Jurisdiction and Judgments Act 1982, the costs of registration	£39.00
Where permission is given under RSC Order 45, rule 3 to enforce a judgment or order giving possession of land and costs are allowed on the judgment or order, the amount to be added to the judgment or order for costs—	
(a) basic costs	£42.50
(b) where notice of the proceedings is to be to more than one person, for each additional person	£2.75
Where a writ of control as defined in rule 83.1(2)(k) is issued against any party	£51.75
Where a writ of execution as defined in rule 83.1(2)(l) is issued against any party	£51.75
Where a request is filed for the issue of a warrant of control under rule 83.15 for a sum exceeding £25	£2.25
Where a request is filed for the issue of a warrant of delivery under rule 83.15 for a sum exceeding £25	£2.25
Where an application for an attachment of earnings order is made and costs are allowed under CCR Order 27, rule 9 or CCR Order 28, rule 10, for each attendance on the hearing of the application	£8.50

There is nothing in either CPR, Part 45, Section I, or PD 45 to suggest that VAT is payable in addition to the amounts of fixed enforcement costs that are stated above.

CPR, Part 45, Section II: Fixed Recoverable Costs

50.67 CPR, Part 45, Section II, includes a self-contained code for calculating fixed recoverable costs and disbursements payable to claimants in certain non-litigated road traffic accident claims in which liability has been admitted and the value of the claim is no more than £10,000. It also contains a mechanism for the claimant to apply for a higher sum. As is explained below, these provisions have now been made far less important than they once were. They are of historical importance, however, because they were the first significant fixed costs to be created under the CPR (see 50.19–50.20).

Ambit

50.68 Fixed recoverable costs (that is, CPR, Part 45, Section II) apply only where the following conditions[69] are met:

- the claim has been compromised[70] such that the damages in respect of personal injury, property or both[71] do not exceed £10,000,[72] as calculated in accordance with CPR, r 26.8(2);[73]
- the claim has been commenced under the costs-only procedure (CPR, r 46.14(1))—which means that it is a non-litigated claim in respect of damages—or is a claim for approval of a settlement under CPR, r 21.10(2);
- the dispute arises from a road traffic accident that occurred on or after 6 October 2003;[74]
- the claimant is not a litigant in person;[75]
- the case does not fall within the scope of the Untraced Drivers Agreement[76]—although cases that fall within the scope of the Uninsured Drivers Agreement (dated 13 August 1999) will be included;[77]
- if a claim had been issued for the amount of the agreed damages, the small claims track would not have been the normal track;[78] and
- neither CPR, Part 45, Section IIIA[79] nor Section III apply.[80]

[69] CPR, r 45.9(1)–(3); PD 45, paras 2.2 and 2.3.
[70] Although not binding, see *Lloyds TSB Group plc v Allen* (unreported), 20 October 2005, Medway County Court, *per* Judge Cryan, in which fixed recoverable costs were denied for want of agreement as to damages.
[71] CPR, r 45.9(2)(b).
[72] CPR, r 45.9(2)(c).
[73] See PD 45, para 2.2.
[74] CPR, r 45.9(2)(a); PD 45, paras 2.1 and 2.2.
[75] CPR, r 45.9(3)(a).
[76] See PD 45, para 2.4. That said, it is questionable whether a practice direction can qualify the operation of the CPR in this way.
[77] See PD 45, para 2.4.
[78] See PD 45, para 2.2.
[79] This will apply only to claims started under the RTA Protocol in which the claim notification form was sent on or after 31 July 2013: see Civil Procedure (Amendment No 6) Rules 2013 (SI 2013/1695), r 10.
[80] CPR, r 45.9(3)(b).

It is the final two restrictions that are, in practice, now the most important, for the following reasons. **50.69**

- The limit governing the small claims track (£10,000[81]) is now the same as the upper limit beyond which CPR, Part 45, Section II, ceases to apply.[82] This means that the latter will almost never apply to 'bent metal' claims or to claims for personal injuries for less than £1,000.
- The fact that the influence of the Pre-Action Protocol for Low Value Personal Injury Claims in Road Traffic Accidents (the RTA Protocol) has been expanded vertically so as to cover claims that have exited the Protocol (see 50.27) means that there is very little scope left for CPR, Part 45, Section II.[83] Indeed, in practice, Section II now encompasses only those claims that are *excluded* from the RTA Protocol (see 50.158).

Cases settled by acceptance of a Part 36 offer

Whilst it is arguable that it is no longer good law,[84] Moore-Bick LJ has explained that the fact that the claim may have been compromised by way of the procedure in Part 36 does not avoid the operation of CPR, Part 45, Section II.[85] **50.70**

Older cases that exit the RTA Portal

Whilst it is not now a situation that is likely to arise, if the RTA Portal was engaged by way of a claim notification form being sent before 31 July 2013, then CPR, Part 45, Section II, would continue to be capable of applying if the case were subsequently to exit the RTA Portal.[86] If this were to happen, credit would need to be given for any Stage 1 and Stage 2 fixed costs that had been paid by the defendant.[87] **50.71**

Definitions

The CPR define certain words and phrases as follows: **50.72**

- 'personal injuries' includes any disease and any impairment of a person's physical or mental condition;[88]
- 'road traffic accident' means an accident resulting in bodily injury to any person or damage to property caused by, or arising out of, the use of a motor vehicle on a road or other public place in England and Wales;[89]
- 'motor vehicle' means a mechanically propelled vehicle intended for use on roads;[90] and

[81] See CPR, r 26.6.
[82] See CPR, r 45.9(2)(c).
[83] This will apply only to claims started under the RTA Protocol in which the claim notification form was sent on or after 31 July 2013: see Civil Procedure (Amendment No 6) Rules 2013 (SI 2013/1695), r 10.
[84] Because of the way in which the Court of Appeal dealt with an analogous situation in *Broadhurst & Anor v Tan & Anor* [2016] EWCA Civ 94. That said, in *Williams v The Secretary of State for Business, Energy & Industrial Strategy* [2018] EWCA Civ 852, at [46], Coulson LJ made reference to *Solomon v Cromwell Group plc* [2011] EWCA Civ 1584 and, in doing so, he did not suggest that it was wrongly decided or old law.
[85] See *Solomon v Cromwell Group plc* [2011] EWCA Civ 1584, at [22]–[26].
[86] This is the effect of the transitional provisions in Civil Procedure (Amendment No 6) Rules 2013 (SI 2013/1695), r 10.
[87] See CPR, r 45.28.
[88] CPR, r 2.3.
[89] CPR, r 45.9(4)(a).
[90] CPR, r 45.9(4)(b).

- 'road' means any highway and any other road to which the public has access, and includes bridges over which a road passes.[91]

50.73 The language used in CPR, Part 45, Section II, bears a striking similarity to that used in the Road Traffic Acts—in particular, to Road Traffic Act 1988, s 145. If the analogy is apt, then the questions of what CPR, r 45.9, means by a 'road', 'motor vehicle', etc, are to be determined by the tribunal of fact, that tribunal having properly directed itself as to the law.[92]

What is the 'use' of motor vehicle?

50.74 Although the CPR define the words and phrases set out above, there is no definition of the word 'use' (that is, in 'use of motor vehicle')—and there is considerable room for disagreement on this point. If, for example, a lorry carrying explosive material were to explode and cause injury to bystanders, the issue could be argued either way. Some guidance may be obtained by looking at the way in which similar phrases have been interpreted when they have been used in the Road Traffic Acts—in particular, the Road Traffic Act 1988.

50.75 The Court of Appeal considered a case in which a driver had run out of petrol, got out of her car to cross the road to reach a colleague and been killed by a passing car. The issue was whether the death arose out of the use of the deceased's car. Rose LJ held that it did[93] and, in giving judgment, impliedly approved of an Australian decision in which Windeyer J had said:

> 'The words "injury caused by or arising out of the use of the vehicle" postulate a causal relationship between the use of the vehicle and the injury. "Caused by" connotes a direct or proximate relationship of cause and effect. "Arising out of" extends this to a result that is less immediate; but it still carries a sense of consequence. It excludes cases of bodily injury in which the use of a vehicle is a merely [casual[94]] concomitant not considered to be, in a relevant causal sense, a contributing factor.'[95]

50.76 Rose LJ also commented that one factor that may be relevant to the issue would be the injured person's reasons or motive for carrying out the activity that led to the injury. The definition of 'use of a vehicle on a road' should not be stretched too far, however: whilst it was not a case concerning CPR, Part 45, Silber J found that the victims of a London taxi driver who lured women into his taxi, then sedated and sexually assaulted them, did not sustain injuries that 'ar[o]se out of the use of a vehicle on a road'.[96] Whilst not binding, Judge Cotter QC has found that the phrase 'caused by, or arising out of the use of, a motor vehicle on the road' in CPR, r 45.9, included a case in which a driver was hit by a falling tree because, at the time, the driver was subject to road traffic regulations

[91] CPR, r 45.9(4)(c).

[92] *Cutter v Eagle Star Insurance Co Ltd* [1998] 1 WLR 1647.

[93] *Dunthorne v Bentley* (1996) RTR 428, CA, in respect of Road Traffic Act 1988, s 145(3)(a). In a similar vein, whilst not binding, see *Scheider v Door2Door PTS Ltd* [2011] EWHC 90210 (Costs), in which Master Campbell found that it was not necessary for there to be vehicular movement for there to be a road traffic accident for the purposes of CPR, Part 45, Section II.

[94] This word is mistranscribed in most UK reports. The word that was used is indeed 'casual', but many UK reports use the word 'causal': see the original transcript of the Australian Legal Information Institute.

[95] *Government Insurance Office of New South Wales v R J Green & Lloyd Pty Ltd* (1966) 114 CLR 437, at 447.

[96] *Axn & Ors v (1) Worboys* [2012] EWHC 1730 (QB), at [58]–[65].

and duties.[97] Similarly, in a case in which the claimant was injured as she was being lifted in a wheelchair on a platform attached to a vehicle, Judge Darroch found that this amounted to the use of a motor vehicle within the meaning of CPR, Part 45,[98] as did Master Campbell in a case in which a claimant had been injured getting into a stationary minibus.[99] As a counter-example, in a case in which the claimant stepped and fell upon a defect in the road whilst unloading luggage from his car, Judge Gore QC found that CPR, Part 45, did not engage because 'arising out of' excludes cases of bodily injury in which the use of the vehicle is merely a casual concomitant to, as opposed to causally contributing factor in, the causation of the accident and bodily injury.[100]

The meaning of other words relating to the use of a motor vehicle

The Road Traffic Acts may also assist in the interpretation of other words and phrases in CPR, Part 45. The House of Lords said that the word 'road' should be given its ordinary meaning.[101] The issue of whether the putative road was a place 'to which the public had access' is, to a large extent, a question of fact;[102] the law may be relevant, but a finding that the putative road is privately owned will not be determinative of issue.[103] It should be borne in mind that whilst there are similarities between CPR, Part 45, Section II, and certain sections in the Road Traffic Acts, the latter were enacted for a purpose far removed from the issue of whether fixed costs should apply. In view of this, it should not always be assumed that what is said of one automatically applies to the other. **50.77**

Judge Main QC has found that where a tram uses a road that has been adapted for use by trams, the tram is a 'motor vehicle' and CPR, Part 45, engages.[104] **50.78**

Amount

Where fixed recoverable costs apply, the only costs that may be recovered are: **50.79**

- fixed recoverable costs in accordance with CPR, r 45.11 (see 50.80–50.82),
- disbursements allowed in accordance with CPR, r 45.12 (see 50.83–50.85), including counsel's fees in certain circumstances (see 50.86); and
- where appropriate, a success fee allowed in accordance with the pre-April 2013 CPR, r 45.11 (see 50.88),[105]

plus VAT, where appropriate.[106]

---

[97] *Orange v Taylor* (unreported), 21 January 2014, Exeter County Court, at [11] and [25]–[30].

[98] *Griffin v Wishbech Phab Club* (unreported), 11 July 2011, Norwich County Court.

[99] See *Scheider v Door2Door PTS Ltd* [2011] EWHC 90210.

[100] *O'Brien v Sandown Court Management Co* (unreported), 21 July 2011, Liverpool County Court, at [11].

[101] *Cutter v Eagle Star Insurance Co Ltd* [1998] 1 WLR 1647. This too was in respect of Road Traffic Act 1988, s 145(3)(a), but also took into account the effects of Road Traffic Act 1991, ss 1 and 2.

[102] See *Cox v White* [1976] RTR 248, at 248, *per* Kilner Brown J.

[103] See *Harrison v Hill* (1931) SLT 598, *per* Lord Blackburn. On the similar and linked topic of what is a 'public place', see *Paterson v Ogilvy* [1957] JC 42 (field used in connection with an agricultural show was a public place). See also *Rodger v Normad* [1995] SLT 411 (on a similar point concerning a school playground); *Bowman v DPP* [1991] RTR 263 (multistorey car park was a public place); *DPP v Coulman* [1993] RTR 230 (immigration lane at dockyard was a public place); *R (on application of Lewis) v DPP* [2004] EWHC 3081 Admin (a public house car park was a public place); *May v DPP* [2005] EWHC 1280 (a customer car park was a public place).

[104] See *Stagecoach Group plc v Wilson* (unreported), 21 December 2016, Manchester County Court.

[105] See CPR, r 48.2, for the savings provisions.

[106] CPR, r 45.10.

The amount of profit costs

50.80 Subject to the matters set out below, fixed recoverable costs are calculated on the basis of a fixed sum *plus* a variable percentage of the value of the claim. The amount is the total of:

- £800; *plus*
- 20 per cent of the damages agreed up to £5,000; *plus*
- 15 per cent of the damages agreed between £5,000 and £10,000.[107]

50.81 The amount allowable may be increased by 12.5 per cent in cases in which the claimant lives or works in and around London.[108] Where appropriate, VAT is payable in addition to the figures above.[109] The amount payable is fixed: the indemnity principle does not apply.[110]

50.82 The following provisions apply when calculating the amount of damages.[111]

- Account must be taken of both general and special damages and interest.
- Any interim payments made must be included.
- Where the parties have agreed an element of contributory negligence, the amount of damages attributed to that negligence must be deducted.
- Any amount required by statute to be paid by the compensating party directly to a third party, such as sums paid by way of compensation recovery payments and National Health Service (NHS) expenses, must not be included.

Disbursements

50.83 There are restrictions on the disbursements that may be allowed,[112] but the court may allow disbursements that have arisen as a result of a particular feature of the dispute,[113] such as a need for an interpreter.[114] Other than this—unless the claim involves a child or a protected party, as defined in CPR, Part 21—the only allowable disbursements are the costs associated with:

- medical records;
- a medical report;
- a police report;
- an engineer's report;
- a search of the records of the Driver and Vehicle Licensing Agency (DVLA); and

---

107 CPR, r 45.11; PD 45, para 2.5.

108 PD 45, para 2.6. The areas are those served by the County Court hearing centres at Barnet, Bow, Brentford, Central London, Clerkenwell and Shoreditch, Edmonton, Ilford, Lambeth, Mayors and City of London, Romford, Wandsworth, West London, Willesden and Woolwich, and (outside London) the County Court hearing centres at Bromley, Croydon, Dartford, Gravesend and Uxbridge.

109 See CPR, r 45.11(3).

110 *Nizami v Butt* [2006] EWHC 159 (QB).

111 PD 45, para 2.3.

112 CPR, r 45.12.

113 CPR, r 45.12.

114 Whilst not binding, see, eg, *Madej v Maciszyn* [2013] Lexis Citation 143, in which Master Campbell found that where an interpreter's fee fell within the fixed costs regime in CPR, Part 45, it could be recovered by the claimant, because it could properly be described as 'any other disbursement that has arisen due to a particular feature of the dispute' under CPR, r 45.12(2)(c).

- an after-the-event (ATE) insurance premium (or notional premium, as the case may be), but only where there is a suitable pre-commencement funding arrangement.[115]

Where they were necessarily incurred by reason of the claimant being a child or protected party, the court may allow fees payable for instructing counsel (see 50.86) and associated court fees.[116] **50.84**

Where a medical reporting agency has provided a report or a set of medical records, its fees (including the direct cost of obtaining the report or records) may be subject to the Medical Organisation Reporting Agreement, an industry-wide agreement that provides for certain set fees to be paid directly by the defendant's insurer to the agency. This topic is addressed in detail at 52.69–52.71. **50.85**

Counsel's fees There are two ways in which, in theory, counsel's fees may be allowed—although, in practice, only the first is generally encountered. **50.86**

- **Where approval is required** CPR, r 45.12(2)(b)(i), provides that where they were necessarily incurred by reason of the claimant being a child or protected party, the court may allow fees payable for instructing counsel. Patten LJ had this to say on the issue:

  '[F]or counsel's fees for attending a hearing to be recoverable there must, I think, be some complexity in the case which justified their being instructed to appear on the approval hearing. It is not enough to say that counsel would help to remove the stress of the occasion ... Many of these cases ... do not involve difficult issues and can be dealt with shortly on the basis of the written advice on the merits. In such cases the convenience of having counsel attend the hearing has, I think, to be borne by the solicitors as part of their costs just as they would have had to meet the costs of instructing a local agent.'[117]

  Thus the mere fact that the claimant is a child or protected party does not mean that the costs of counsel's attendance will be allowed as 'necessary'; rather, there must be some complexity in the case that would justify the instruction of counsel. An examples of a case in which an allowance was made is a case in which there was scarring.[118] The authors of *Cook on Costs* (both of whom are experienced judges) strongly imply that an allowance may be appropriate in a case in which the court is geographically far removed from the claimant's solicitors' offices.[119] It is worth noting that some solicitors have sought to avoid the need for court approval by settling on the basis of a 'parental indemnity',[120] but Judge Stewart QC has impliedly criticised this practice.[121]

- **Where there is no approval hearing** CPR, r 45.12(2)(c), provides that where there is no need for an approval hearing, counsel's fees will be allowed only if they arose by

115 See the transitional provisions in CPR, r 48.1, which preserve pre-1 April 2013 CPR, r 45.10.

116 See CPR, r 45.12(b).

117 *Tubridy v Sarwar* [2012] EWCA Civ 184, at [54]–[56], heard at the same time as *Dockerill v Tullett* [2012] EWCA Civ 184.

118 See, eg, *Sherred v Carpenter* (unreported), 5 March 2009, Taunton County Court, at [4], *per* Judge O'Malley, in which there is reference to *Miles v London Road Veterinary Clinic* (unreported), 5 December 2007, Norwich County Court, *per* District Judge Sparrow.

119 See *Cook on Costs 2017* (LexisNexis, online), para 26.13.

120 See Ellis, D, 'The Right Price' (2010) 154(17) Solicitors Journal 14.

121 *Coles v Keklik* (unreported), 30 June 2008, Liverpool County Court.

reason of a particular feature of the dispute.[122] It would be difficult to persuade the court that this would include costs that may be the ordinary incident of claim, such as the costs of obtaining counsel's advice on liability.[123]

Multiple claimants

50.87 Where there is more than one potential claimant and two or more claimants instruct the same solicitor or firm of solicitors, the provisions mentioned above apply in respect of each claimant.[124]

Success fees

50.88 Whilst it is not now likely to be relevant, a success fee may also be claimed if the claimant had entered into a pre-commencement funding arrangement of a type specified in CPR, r 48.2. This is recoverable regardless of whether the conditional fee agreement is enforceable.[125] The amount of the success fee is 12.5 per cent, but this should not be paid on the additional amount relating to London claims (see 50.81).

Applications to exceed fixed recoverable costs

50.89 An application may be made for an amount exceeding fixed recoverable costs (excluding any success fee or disbursements), but such applications are fraught with risks and there are penalties for unsuccessful applicants (see 50.94).

50.90 **The two hurdles** It seems that the relevant rules were drafted in such a way as to stack the cards against an application easily succeeding.[126] There are two hurdles that an applicant must clear:

- the applicant must make out 'exceptional circumstances' to justify an award greater than fixed recoverable costs[127] and, if that test is passed, then the court will only 'entertain' making such an award and, even then, only if 'appropriate to do so'[128]—so it is implicit in the way in which the relevant rule has been worded that the court is not obliged to make an award merely because exceptional circumstances have been made out; and

---

[122] CPR, r 45.12.

[123] Whilst nothing more than an example of a first-instance decision, see *Foxewell v Hart* (unreported), 7 March 2014, Liverpool County Court, *per* Deputy District Judge Holligan.

[124] PD 45, para 2.7.

[125] *Nizami v Butt* [2006] EWHC 159 (QB).

[126] To the extent that it might be admissible as an extrinsic aid to interpretation—and that is highly doubtful—it is of note that the industry representatives who negotiated CPR, Part 45, Section II, commented that the criteria for opting out 'should be strict'. This was the view expressed at the Civil Justice Council's Costs Forum II, held 12–14 December 2002.

[127] Whilst it was only an application for permission to appeal and therefore not binding, in respect of a very similarly worded provision, in *Costin v Merron* [2013] EWCA Civ 380, at [6], Leveson LJ had this to say: 'I, for my part, have no difficulty in concluding that the exceptional circumstances to which 45.12 refer must be exceptional in the sense that the case is taken out of the general run of this type of case by reason of some circumstance which means that greater costs are in fact incurred than could reasonably be expected to be incurred.' Put otherwise, the court is permitted (if not required) to look at the amount of costs claimed and the reasons why those costs were incurred. Leveson LJ went on to say this (*ibid*, at [11]): 'In my judgment the phrase "exceptional circumstances" in the context of [CPR, r] 45.12 speaks for itself. It cannot possibly mean anything other than that, for reasons which make it appropriate to order the case to fall outside the fixed costs regime, exceptionally more money has had to be expended on the case by way of costs than would otherwise have been the case.' Thus, if 'exceptionally more money has had to be expended on the case by way of costs' and if this is for reasons that make it appropriate to disapply the fixed costs regime, the test is satisfied.

[128] See CPR, r 45.13.

- if the court allows the application, but then assesses costs at an amount that is less than 20 per cent more than the amount that would have been allowed if only fixed recoverable costs had been awarded, the court will allow the lesser of two amounts.[129]

In view of the above, it should come as no surprise that examples of the court allowing applications are uncommon: one involved a child who may have suffered a severe eating disorder as a result of the index accident;[130] another involved a claim in which the defendant had given the claimant 'the run-around'.[131] Cases in which the court dismissed the application included where a defendant had indicated that it was going to rely on the fact that the accident was a low-velocity impact[132] and another in which the claimant had suffered from a chromosomal disorder, which had led to behavioural problems.[133] **50.91**

Procedural issues Where the claimant wishes to make an application to exceed the amount of the fixed recoverable costs, the claim form must give details of the exceptional circumstances to justify the additional costs.[134] **50.92**

If the court is minded to allow more than fixed recoverable costs, the court will either assess those costs summarily or make an order that they be subject to detailed assessment.[135] If the court does not consider that the application was appropriate, it must make an order for fixed recoverable costs (and any permitted disbursements) only.[136] **50.93**

Costs If the application fails or if the amount allowed does not exceed fixed recoverable costs, the rules expressly provide that the court may deprive the claimant of costs—or may even award costs against the claimant.[137] It is a curious feature of the rules that whilst there is express provision that deals with failure on the part of the claimant, there is silence as to what may happen if the claimant succeeds. This is certainly odd, but the received view is that this does not imply that the court lacks the power to award a successful claimant their costs.[138] **50.94**

Procedure

Fixed recoverable costs will apply only to cases in which no proceedings were issued; as such, cost-only proceedings will be necessary if the parties are unable to come to terms. A claim form should be issued in accordance with CPR, Part 8. Where the claimant is claiming an amount of costs that exceeds the amount of the fixed recoverable costs, the claim form must give details of the exceptional circumstances that justify such an application.[139] If a defendant were to wish to counter this, it would be sensible for them to set out their reasons in their acknowledgement of service. **50.95**

---

[129] CPR, r 45.14.
[130] See *Carlon v Domino's Pizza Group Ltd* (unreported), 27 August 2010, Birmingham County Court, *per* DJ Wyatt.
[131] *Udogaranya v Nwagw* [2010] EWHC 90186 (Costs), at [23], *per* Master Haworth.
[132] See *Briscoe v Tilt* (unreported), 9 February 2012, SCCO, *per* Master O'Hare.
[133] See *Sargeant (by her mother and litigation friend, Kearns) v Fellows* (unreported), 12 October 2012, Dudley County Court, *per* District Judge Lumb.
[134] PD 45, para 2.8.
[135] CPR, r 45.13(2).
[136] CPR, r 45.13(3).
[137] CPR, r 45.15.
[138] This is certainly the view of the authors of *Cook on Costs 2017* (LexisNexis, online), para 26.14.
[139] PD 45, para 2.8.

50.96 Where disbursements are claimed, they must be included on the claim form, as must any details concerning the particular features of the dispute that are going to be relied upon for the purposes of recovering those disbursements.[140] If the parties agree the amount of the fixed recoverable costs and the only dispute is as to the payment or amount of a disbursement, or the amount of any success fee payable, then costs-only proceedings should be brought, but they should not make reference to CPR, Part 45, Section II.[141]

Putative premature issue of claims

50.97 A particular difficulty that has arisen in certain areas is the alleged practice of issuing claims prematurely for the purposes of circumventing the fixed recoverable costs regime. Where that is the case, the court would often assess the costs as if that regime applied, on the basis that CPR, Part 45, Section II, would have applied had the claimant dealt with the matter in a reasonable and sensible way. Prior to 9 April 2009, reliance was placed on the following guidance given in Practice Direction (Protocols), para 2.4: 'The court will exercise its powers ... with the object of placing the innocent party in no worse a position than he would have been in if the protocol had been complied with.'

50.98 Since that date, Practice Direction (Pre-Action Conduct) has applied, which does not contain an express counterpart of the previous guidance—but the spirit of the old guidance is likely to be implied in Practice Direction (Pre-Action Conduct), para 4.5: 'The court will look at the overall effect of non-compliance on the other party when deciding whether to impose sanctions.'

50.99 When faced with such an instance, claimants have argued that the court should not speculate as to what would have happened had proceedings not been issued when they were; in this regard, reliance was often placed on *Straker v Tudor Rose (a firm)*[142] (see 17.103). Whilst not binding, in 2007, Judge Stewart QC found that the court is able to take a view as to what would have happened had proceedings not been issued at the time they were, on the basis of the pre-2009 guidance set out immediately above, that guidance being, in his view, sufficient reason to distinguish *Straker*.[143] Similarly, in a more recent case in which the claimant had been 'slightly premature' in issuing proceedings, Mackay J found that it was open to the costs judge to take a view as to whether the alleged prematurity would have made any difference.[144]

50.100 Arguments concerning alleged premature issue often focus on what is and is not reasonable under the Pre-action Protocol for Personal Injury Claims. In particular, defendants often say that notes of guidance accompanying that Protocol require claimants to afford defendants a reasonable opportunity to negotiate a settlement of the claim. This may be a factor that the court is willing to take into account; thus, if a claim is factually straightforward, the court may find that a decision to remove it from the Protocol was premature if the claimant claims that it was in some way complex.[145]

---

140 PD 45, para 2.9.

141 PD 45, para 2.10.

142 *Straker v Tudor Rose (a firm)* [2007] EWCA 368.

143 *Ellison v Fairclough* (unreported), 13 July 2007, Liverpool County Court.

144 See *Letts v Royal Sun Alliance PLC* [2012] EWHC 875 (QB), at [11]–[13].

145 See, eg, *Kevan v Hamilton* (unreported), 22 March 2013, Liverpool County Court, at [9] and [10], *per* Judge Hornby, in which the only issue was whether or not the claimant had acted improperly in hiring the

The issue of what the court may do if it finds that the claimant did issue the claim prematurely is addressed at 6.107. 50.101

Pre-April 2013 CPR, Part 45, Sections III, IV and V: Fixed Success Fees

The nature of the costs governed by CPR, Part 45, Section III, has changed over the years: Section III now governs 'Portal costs' (which are fixed base costs) (see 50.150), but, prior to 1 April 2013, it governed fixed success fees in road traffic accident claims (the topic addressed below at 50.104–50.149). Similarly, the 'old' Sections IV and V used to govern fixed success fees in employers' liability claims and employers' liability disease claims, respectively (see 50.118 and 50.131, respectively), whereas the 'new' Sections IV and V govern wholly different topics (see 50.312 and 50.342, respectively). 50.102

It is still possible for the 'old' provisions to apply, but this is unlikely because a receiving party would need to have the benefit of a conditional fee agreement that pre-dated 1 April 2013. Notwithstanding this, it is still worth setting out the 'old' law, not only for the sake of completeness, but also to highlight the fact that the courts' approach to certain topics has changed over the years as CPR, Part 45, has grown in scope generally and the court has gained experience of how to manage fixed costs regimes in general. In particular, the way in which the court has approached the issue of what amounts to 'trial' is now very different from what it used to be under the 'old' Sections III, IV and V (see 50.108 and compare this with 50.276), as is the way in which the court deals with conflicts between Part 45 and Part 36 (see 50.114 and compare this with 50.291–50.295). Whilst the courts' approach may have changed in these regards, it ought not to be forgotten that, where the 'old' Sections III, IV and V apply, the law as is set out below; the 'new' approaches apply to other sections. 50.103

What did they cover?

Where the claimant has the benefit of a pre-commencement funding arrangement (see 54.18–54.19), fixed percentage increases (better known as fixed success fees) may be payable. The applicable section will depend on the type of the claim: 50.104

- 'old' CPR, Part 45, Section III, applies to road traffic accident claims (see 50.105);
- 'old' CPR, Part 45, Section IV, applies to employers' liability claims (see 50.118); and
- 'old' CPR, Part 45, Section V, applies to employers' liability disease claims (often known as industrial disease claims) (see 50.131).

'Old' CPR, Part 45, Section III: fixed percentage increases in road traffic accident claims

Scope and application

If a claimant who has brought a claim that arose out of a 'road traffic accident' (see 50.72) has the benefit of a pre-commencement funding arrangement of a type specified in CPR, r 48.2 (see 54.18–54.19), then the amount of any percentage increase payable may continue to be 50.105

vehicle for the period of time that he did and whether there was an opportunity to mitigate those losses, Judge Hornby finding that this was a straightforward issue.

governed by the 'old' CPR, Part 45, Section III (that is, by Section III as it stood immediately before 1 April 2013).[146] Those provisions would not apply to a claim that had been allocated to the small claims track or to an unallocated claim for which the small claims track would have been the normal track.[147] They would also not apply to a claim that was governed by CPR, Part 45, Section II—that is, the section dealing with fixed recoverable costs,[148] which has its own provisions relating to success fees (see 50.88)—and this would be so even if the court were to exercise its discretion to allow a sum that exceeded fixed recoverable costs.[149]

50.106 A fixed success fee would be payable regardless of whether there had been compliance with the indemnity principle.[150]

The amount of the fixed percentage increase: solicitors

50.107 In so far as solicitors were concerned, the fixed percentage increase was 100 per cent where the claim concluded at trial and 12.5 per cent where the claim concluded before trial had commenced or the dispute had settled before the claim was issued.[151] This invites the obvious question of how the court is to gauge whether the claim had concluded at 'trial'.

50.108 **The meaning of 'trial'** What follows applies only to the 'old' CPR, Part 45, Section III; the way in which the court deals with similar provisions in the present incarnation of Part 45 is very different (see 50.276).

50.109 Under the old' CPR, Part 45, Section III, 'trial' was a reference to a final contested hearing or to a contested hearing of any issue ordered to be tried separately; a claim would have concluded at trial if it had concluded by judgment or by settlement after the trial had commenced.[152] Slade J confirmed that a case would have concluded at trial only if it did so after the trial had been opened.[153] This would not be so if the case were merely to settle on the day listed for trial.[154] In another case, Slade J explained that it would be wrong to say that a trial had begun merely because of the commencement of a hearing related to the contested liability hearing (such as an application to adjourn).[155] As a counter-example (albeit not binding), in a case in which the claimant's barrister introduced the parties and then gave way to his opponent, Master Leonard found that a trial had begun.[156]

---

146 See CPR, r 48.1; pre-1 April 2013 CPR, r 45.15(2) and (4)(c). It is assumed that the accident took place on or after 6 October 2003. There were no corresponding provisions in the CPD.

147 See pre-1 April 2013 CPR, r 45.15(4)(a) and (b).

148 See pre-1 April 2013 CPR, r 45.15(3).

149 This is because success fees are expressly excluded from the provisions that give the court discretion: see pre-1 April 2013 CPR, r 45.12(1). The issue is largely academic, however, because a success fee of 12.5 per cent would be allowed in any event; the only practical effect of CPR, Part 45, Section III, not applying is that there is no provision under Section II for the court to allow a higher percentage increase.

150 Although dealing with CPR, Part 45, Section II, see *Nizami v Butt* [2006] EWHC 159 (QB). There can be no serious doubt that the same applies to the 'old' Section III.

151 See pre-1 April 2013 CPR, r 45.16.

152 See pre-1 April 2013 CPR, r 45.15(6).

153 *Amin & Anor v Mullings & Anor* [2011] EWHC 278 (QB).

154 *Ibid.* Whilst not binding, *Sitapuria v Khan* (unreported), 10 December 2007, Liverpool County Court, *per* Judge Stewart QC, is also often cited as authority on the same point; cf *Dahele v Thomas Bates & Son Ltd* [2007] EWHC 90072 (Costs), in which Master Haworth found that a case settling on the day and after the time fixed for trial did conclude at trial. This decision is usually regarded as being correctly decided on its own facts, but confined to its facts: see *Loizou v Gordon & Anor* [2012] EWHC 90221 (Costs), at [12].

155 See *James v Ireland* [2015] EWHC 1259 (QB), at [30] and [40].

156 *Loizou v Gordon & Anor* [2012] EWHC 90221 (Costs), at [41]–[48].

It has been argued that the word 'trial' should not be given its ordinary meaning and that it should be regarded as being fully defined by the words 'final contested hearing'. Wilson LJ disagreed with that proposition,[157] but this was in the context of an application for permission to appeal and, as such, is not a decision that should be cited in court.[158] In any event, Wilson LJ's analysis is not the same as that of many other judges; in particular, whilst his decision is not binding, Judge Stewart QC found that Part 45 was a self-contained code, that the focus ought to be on the words 'final contested hearing' and that the meaning of the word 'trial' in other parts of the CPR was of no assistance.[159] He concluded that the word 'final' included a disposal hearing that had not been listed as being a hearing, which would necessarily have concluded the case.[160] **50.110**

Application for a success fee that is not the same as the fixed amount Where the 'old' CPR, Part 45, Section III, still applies and where the fixed percentage increase is 12.5 per cent, either party may ask the court to exercise its discretion to allow a different amount.[161] That said, one of the following threshold conditions[162] must be met: **50.111**

- damages of more than £500,000 must have been agreed or awarded;[163] or
- if contributory negligence were to be disregarded, it must be the case that such damages would have been awarded or agreed.[164]

Where either of these conditions has been met, then the court must either assess the percentage increase or make an order that it be assessed.[165] Restrictions and disincentives apply, however: if the court is minded to allow less than 7.5 per cent or more than 20 per cent, then the court must instead allow 12.5 per cent and order the applicant to pay the costs of the application.[166] **50.112**

Other than as set out above, the court lacks the power to disallow or reduce the fixed percentage increase. If, for example, a claimant already had alternative means of funding—such as a before-the-event (BTE) policy or legal assistance through their trade union—the court would not be able to reduce or disallow the fixed percentage uplift on the putative basis that it was unreasonable to enter into a conditional fee agreement.[167] **50.113**

Part 36 offers In a similar vein, if acceptance of a Part 36 offer would have avoided a trial and if, at trial, the claimant were to fail to 'beat' that offer, it would not be open to the court to allow 12.5 per cent instead of 100 per cent.[168] Put otherwise, Part 36 did not trump 'old' CPR, Part 45, Section III. This is because (other than as set out above at 50.111–50.113) the court lacks the power to disallow or reduce the fixed percentage **50.114**

---

[157] *Thenga v Quinn* [2009] EWCA Civ 151.

[158] This is as a result of what Lord Woolf MR said in *Clark v University of Lincolnshire and Humberside* [2000] 3 All ER 752, at 762f.

[159] *Watson v Gray* (unreported), 8 February 2005, Liverpool County Court, at [9].

[160] *Ibid*, at [12].

[161] See pre-1 April 2013 CPR, r 45.18(2).

[162] See pre-1 April 2013 CPR, r 45.18(2). This list is condensed; see the rule itself for details.

[163] This figure may include monies awarded by way of periodical payments: see pre-1 April 2013 CPR, r 45.18(3).

[164] See pre-1 April 2013 CPR, r 45.18(3).

[165] See pre-1 April 2013 CPR, r 45.19.

[166] See pre-1 April 2013 CPR, r 45.19.

[167] *Kilby v Gawith* [2008] EWCA Civ 812.

[168] *Lamont v Burton* [2007] EWCA Civ 429.

increase. Again, this is a different approach from that which applies under the present-day provisions. In particular, it is now known that there are circumstances in which Part 36 is capable of taking precedence over certain aspects of the present-day Part 45 (see 50.291–50.295).

The amount of the fixed percentage increase: counsel

50.115 The provisions that related to counsel's percentage increase under the 'old' CPR, Part 45, Section III, were more complex than those that governed solicitors' success fees. Counsel's percentage increased sequentially as the trial approached; the amount of the increase depended on whether the claim proceeded on the fast track or the multitrack. The provisions were found in 'old' CPR, r 45.17:

> '(1) Subject to rule 45.18, the percentage increase which is to be allowed in relation to counsel's fees is—
> (a) 100% where the claim concludes at trial;
> (b) if the claim has been allocated to the fast track—
> (i) 50% if the claim concludes 14 days or less before the date fixed for the commencement of the trial; or
> (ii) 12.5% if the claim concludes more than 14 days before the date fixed for the commencement of the trial or before any such date has been fixed;
> (c) if the claim has been allocated to the multi-track—
> (i) 75% if the claim concludes 21 days or less before the date fixed for the commencement of the trial; or
> (ii) 12.5% if the claim concludes more than 21 days before the date fixed for the commencement of the trial or before any such date has been fixed;
> (d) 12.5% where—
> (i) the claim has been issued but concludes before it has been allocated to a track; or
> (ii) in relation to costs-only proceedings, the dispute is settled before a claim is issued.
> (2) Where a trial period has been fixed, if—
> (a) the claim concludes before the first day of that period; and
> (b) no trial date has been fixed within that period before the claim concludes,
> the first day of that period is treated as the date fixed for the commencement of the trial for the purposes of paragraph (1).
>
> (3) Where a trial period has been fixed, if—
> (a) the claim concludes before the first day of that period; but
> (b) before the claim concludes, a trial date had been fixed within that period, the trial date is the date fixed for the commencement of the trial for the purposes of paragraph (1).
>
> (4) Where a trial period has been fixed and the claim concludes—
> (a) on or after the first day of that period; but
> (b) before commencement of the trial, the percentage increase in paragraph (1)(b)(i) or (1)(c)(i) shall apply as appropriate, whether or not a trial date has been fixed within that period.
>
> (5) For the purposes of this rule, in calculating the periods of time, the day fixed for the commencement of the trial (or the first day of the trial period, where appropriate) is not included.'

50.116 The meaning of the word 'trial' in this context is addressed at 50.108. That said, it should be noted that, for the intermediate stages, the trigger was not the trial itself, but the date fixed for trial. 'Trial period' meant a period of time that had been fixed by the court within which the trial was to take place and, where the court had fixed more than one such period in relation to a claim, it meant the most recent period.[169]

Where the fixed percentage increase would otherwise have been 12.5 per cent, an application could be made for a different percentage increase: the provisions were identical to those set out at 50.111. **50.117**

'Old' CPR, Part 45, Section IV: employers' liability claims and fixed percentage increases

As with road traffic accident claims, where, in an employers' liability claim, the claimant has the benefit of a conditional fee agreement that is a pre-commencement funding arrangement, the success fee continues to be governed by CPR, Part 45, Section IV, as it was immediately before 1 April 2013.[170] There were no corresponding provisions in the Costs Practice Direction (CPD). **50.118**

Scope and application

A fixed percentage increase applied where the following conditions[171] were met: **50.119**

- the dispute was between an employee and their employer,[172] and arose from a bodily injury sustained by the employee in the course of their employment;[173]
- the claimant had entered into a funding arrangement of a type specified in CPR, r 43.2(k)(i),[174] and that conditional fee agreement was made before 1 April 2013;[175]
- the injury did not relate to a disease[176] and the 'old' CPR, Part 45, Section V, did not apply;[177]
- that injury was sustained on or after 1 October 2004;[178]
- the dispute did not arise out of a road traffic accident;[179] and
- the claim had not been allocated to the small claims track[180] or, if the claim was not allocated to a track, the small claims track would not have been the normal track to which it should have been allocated.[181]

As can be seen, claims falling within the 'old' Section V that would otherwise have fallen within the ambit of the 'old' Section IV (that is, industrial diseases) were expressly excluded from Section IV.[182] Put otherwise, the 'old' Sections IV and V were mutually exclusive.[183] **50.120**

---

[169] See pre-1 April 2013 CPR, r 45.15(6)(d).
[170] See CPR, r 48.1.
[171] See pre-1 April 2013 CPR, r 45.20(1) and (2).
[172] See pre-1 April 2013 CPR, r 48.20(1)(a).
[173] See pre-1 April 2013 CPR, r 48.20(1)(a).
[174] See pre-1 April 2013 CPR, r 48.20(1)(b).
[175] See CPR, r 48.1.
[176] See pre-1 April 2013 CPR, r 48.20(2)(a)(i).
[177] See pre-1 April 2013 CPR, r 48.20(2)(a)(iv).
[178] See pre-1 April 2013 CPR, r 48.20(2)(a)(ii).
[179] See pre-1 April 2013 CPR, r 48.20(2)(a)(iii).'Road traffic accident' has the same meaning as that which is defined in pre-1 April 2013 CPR, r 45.7(4)(a) (which is the same as in CPR, r 45.9(4)(a)).
[180] See pre-1 April 2013 CPR, r 48.20(2)(b)(i).
[181] See pre-1 April 2013 CPR, r 48.20(2)(b)(i).
[182] See pre-1 April 2013 CPR, r 48.20(2)(a).
[183] *Patterson v Ministry of Defence* [2012] EWHC 2767 (QB), at [14(2)], *per* Males J.

50.121 **The meaning of 'employee'** The definition of 'employee' was the same as that given in s 2(1) of the Employers' Liability (Compulsory Insurance) Act 1969: '[An] individual who has entered into or works under a contract of service or apprenticeship with an employer whether by way of manual labour, clerical work or otherwise, whether such contract is expressed or implied, oral or in writing.'[184] The same applies to the present-day Pre-Action Protocol for Low Value Personal Injury (Employers' Liability and Public Liability) Claims (the EL/PL Protocol)[185] (and therefore to the present-day CPR, Part 45, Section IIIA).

50.122 The terms of this definition invite the question of what is meant by 'contract of service' and 'contract of apprenticeship'. In view of the fact that the same test continues to apply to the EL/PL Protocol, it is likely to be a question that will occur more often given the rise of the 'gig economy' and zero-hours contracts (see 50.126). Whilst there is no authority to confirm that a costs judge would apply the same test, the modern approach to such issues is to apply a test known as the multiple test. The starting point is to look at the following three issues:

- whether the worker undertook to provide their own work and skill in return for remuneration;
- whether there was a sufficient degree of control over the worker to enable the worker to be called an employee; and
- whether there were any features of the case that were inconsistent with the contract being a contract of employment.[186]

50.123 In considering the terms of the putative contract for employment, it is necessary to look at the surrounding circumstances and the parties' true intentions, including how the contract actually worked in practice.[187] In particular, the question is no longer one of looking primarily at whether the putative employer had control over the putative employee. Indeed, the authors of *Harvey on Industrial Relations and Employment Law* have this to say on the point:

> 'The mixed [ie multiple] test is evidence of a judicial desire to expand the scope of the contract of service beyond the old idea of control. It may be paraphrased by saying that an individual who *could* be an employee *should* be an employee unless there is some good reason for holding otherwise.'[188]

50.124 In a decision that was upheld by the Court of Appeal, Mummery J found that the correct approach to determining whether an individual carried on business on their own account was not to consider the many different aspects of the person's work activity by way of a mechanical exercise of running through items on a checklist to see whether they were present in, or absent from, a given situation; rather, he said: 'The object of the exercise is to paint a picture from the accumulation of detail … It is a matter of evaluation of the overall effect of the detail which is not necessarily the same as the sum of the individual situation.'[189]

---

184 See pre-1 April 2013 CPR, r 45.20(3)(a).
185 See EL/PL Protocol, para 1.1(13).
186 *Ready-Mixed Concrete (South East) Ltd v Minister of Pensions and National Insurance* [1968] 2 QB 497.
187 *Carmichael v National Power plc* [1999] 1 WLR 2042.
188 Napier, B, Smith, I, Eady, J, McMullen, J, and Brennan, T, *Harvey on Industrial Relations and Employment Law* (London: LexisNexis, 1990), para 43, emphasis original.
189 See *Hall (Inspector of Taxes) v Lorimer* [1992] 1 WLR 939 (CA), at 944.

The approach to be taken by a costs judge when deciding whether a person is an 'employee' Whilst he did not expressly reject it, Supperstone J seemed not to be attracted by the notion that it would be inappropriate and impracticable for a costs judge to apply a test that required them to hear evidence on the point.[190] In particular, he made it clear that the phrase 'contract of service' is not to be read purposively and that there is no good reason for giving those words a construction broader than their usual meaning.[191] As is explained at 50.126, this caused Supperstone J to distinguish between employees (to whom Section IV applied) and office holders—namely, police officers (to whom it did not). Some commentators with experience of employment law have criticised this analysis, pointing to the fact that, regardless of the rather esoteric distinction between employees and office holders, the common-law duty to provide a safe system of work is the same for both, so given that they would bring almost identical types of claim, it would be a very curious outcome if they were to be treated differently for the purposes of Section IV. There is obvious force in this argument, but unless and until some higher court says otherwise, Supperstone J's analysis is binding. In any event, one could easily argue that the reason why the outcome is curious is because the drafters of Section IV have (perhaps unwisely) tied that section to the definition in the Employers' Liability (Compulsory Insurance) Act 1969. **50.125**

Specific categories of worker who may be said to be an 'employee' The following categories of worker are worth commenting upon. **50.126**

- **Apprentices** A contract of apprenticeship differs from a contract of employment in that the essential feature of an apprenticeship is that the apprentice contracts to be taught a trade or calling.[192] Although an apprentice has agreed to serve, technically the relationship is not one of employer and employee.[193] That said, it is clear from the wording of Employers' Liability (Compulsory Insurance) Act 1969 that such an arrangement will qualify for the purposes of CPR, Part 45, because the relevant definition includes apprenticeships.
- **Independent contractors** An independent contractor is one who enters a contract for services as opposed to a contract of employment. The parties are not able to change the nature of their contract by giving it the 'wrong' label[194]—a point that becomes more and more important in view of the rise of the 'gig economy' (see below). The courts can and do react against abuse of the law.[195]
- **Persons who work in the 'gig economy'** Whilst, at the time of writing, it was subject to appeal to the Supreme Court, the Court of Appeal has held that—whilst each case will turn on its own facts—it is open to the court to find that a person who works in the 'gig economy' is not an employee, but that their working practices may be such as to meet the definition of 'employment' under s 83(2)(a) of the Equality

[190] See *Broni v Ministry of Defence* [2015] EWHC 66 (QB), at [19] and [26]. That said, the approach would not be the same as was adopted in *Smith v Ministry of Defence* [2013] 1 All ER 778, because that case went to the issue of duty of care, rather than the nature of the putative contract: see *Broni v Ministry of Defence* [2015] EWHC 66 (QB), at [26].

[191] *Broni v Ministry of Defence* [2015] EWHC 66 (QB), at [26].

[192] See *Wiltshire Police Authority v Wynn* [1980] ICR 649, [1981] QB 95, CA.

[193] See *Horan v Hayhoe* [1904] 1 KB 288.

[194] See *Davis v New England College of Arundel* [1977] ICR 6, EAT; *Narich Pty Ltd v Pay-roll Tax Commissioner* [1984] ICR 286, PC.

[195] See, eg, *Young and Woods Ltd v West* [1980] IRLR 201, CA, in which a sheet metalworker deliberately opted for independent status, but was nevertheless declared by the Court of Appeal to be a servant.

Act 2010.[196] The definition of 'employment' in that Act is very different from that which relates to fixed success fees; if the point arises, the reader must conduct their own researches based on the Supreme Court's guidance (which was due to be handed down a few days after this chapter was written).

- **Company directors** Directors of a company are not employees of the company, as such; rather, they are, *prima facie*, office holders. A director may, however, additionally become an employee by entering into a service agreement with the company.
- **Crown servants** For historical reasons, servants of the Crown are treated as a separate category of employee. The principal difference between a servant of the Crown and other employees is that a Crown servant is, in theory, dismissible at any time at the will of the Crown.[197] It is possible that this means that they are not employees for the purposes of CPR, Part 45,[198] but equally the contrary is certainly arguable.
- **Parliamentary staff** The precise status of staff employed in the House of Commons and the House of Lords is obscure, since the common law does not apply within the precincts of the Palace of Westminster. It consequently seems that a servant of either House cannot, technically, be an employee at common law.[199] It is possible that this means that they are not employees for the purposes of CPR, Part 45,[200] but the contrary is arguable.
- **Police officers** Despite the greater size and more regimented organisation of the modern police forces, it remains true that police officers are office holders, rather than employees. This means that (as a matter of long-standing policy[201]) serving police officers and serving members of the Armed Forces should not be regarded as employed under a contract of service. Indeed, Supperstone J has confirmed that this is so in so far as CPR, Part 45, is concerned.[202] As has been mentioned at 50.125, however, some commentators have questioned the correctness of this decision.
- **Members of the Armed Forces** The general points made above about police officers also apply to serving members of the Armed Forces. In particular, it is long-standing policy that members of the Armed Forces have no intention to create legal relations when they entered service.[203]

50.127 **The meaning of 'bodily injury'** There is no definition of what amounts to a 'bodily injury' in the CPR. This is a topic that is relevant not only to the 'old' Part 45, but is also to the present-day CPR, Part 45, Section IIIA (that is, post-Portal fixed costs), because both the RTA Protocol[204] and the EL/PL Protocol[205] refer to 'bodily injury'.

---

[196] *Pimlico Plumbers Ltd & Anor v Smith* [2017] EWCA Civ 51.

[197] Napier, B, *Harvey on Industrial Relations and Employment Law* (LexisNexis, online), para 101.

[198] See *Broni v Ministry of Defence* [2015] EWHC 66 (QB), at [21].

[199] Napier, B, *Harvey on Industrial Relations and Employment Law* (LexisNexis, online), para 102.

[200] See *Broni v Ministry of Defence* [2015] EWHC 66 (QB), at [21].

[201] See *Fisher v Oldham Corpn* [1930] 2 KB 364; more recently, *O'Brien v Ministry of Justice* [2013] 2 All ER 1, at [31], *per* Lord Hope and Lady Hale. See also *Quinn v Ministry of Defence* [1998] PIQR 387, at 396, *per* Swinton Thomas LJ.

[202] See *Broni v Ministry of Defence* [2015] EWHC 66 (QB), at [21].

[203] *Ibid*, at [27], in which Supperstone J applied the *ratio* of *Quinn v Ministry of Defence* [1998] PIQR 387, at 396.

[204] See RTA Protocol, para 1.1(16).

[205] See EL/PL Protocol, para 1.1(14)(a).

Clearly, a corporal injury would be a 'bodily injury', but it is not known whether this definition would include psychiatric injury. Assistance may be drawn from cases dealing with the words 'bodily injury' in Art 17 of the Warsaw Convention.[206] The House of Lords found that the phrase means injury to a person's body, which includes injury to a person's brain or central nervous system, but not shock, anxiety, fear, distress, grief and other emotional disturbances.[207] In practice, the exclusion—if it applies—of psychiatric conditions from the definition of 'bodily injury' would not present too many problems, because most compensable psychiatric conditions would be classified as diseases, so the 'old' CPR, Part 45, Section V, would apply (see 50.133–50.139). In this regard, it is worth noting that (whilst *obiter*) Males J found that psychiatric injuries,[208] work-related upper limb disorders[209] and physical injury alleged to have been caused by exposure to asbestos[210] may be 'bodily injuries'—albeit for the purposes of CPR, Part 45, Section V (see 50.134).[211] **50.128**

The amount of the fixed percentage increase in employers' liability claims

Where the receiving party has the benefit of a conditional fee agreement that was made before 1 April 2013, the provisions that will apply are the same as those used to relate to road traffic accident claims (see 50.115), other than that the minimum success fee (for both counsel and solicitors) is higher—namely, the 12.5 per cent mentioned in those provisions will be replaced by 25 per cent in respect of both solicitors and counsel. If, prior to 1 April 2013, a membership organisation had undertaken to meet the claimant's liabilities for legal costs in accordance with Access to Justice Act 1999, s 30, that figure rises to 27.5 per cent, but only in respect of the solicitors' fees.[212] **50.129**

Likewise, the provisions relating to applications for an alternative percentage increase are the same as those relating to road traffic claims (see 50.111–50.112), other than that, to disapply the percentage increase of 25 per cent (or 27.5 per cent, as the case may be), the court must find that a percentage increase of 40 per cent or more, or 15 per cent or less, would be appropriate.[213] **50.130**

'Old' CPR, Part 45, Section V: employers' liability disease claims and fixed percentage increases

Where a person who has brought a claim arising out of an occupational disease (that is, an industrial disease) has the benefit of a pre-commencement funding arrangement (as defined in CPR, r 48.1), the percentage increases continue to be governed by the 'old' CPR, Part 45, Section V; likewise, now-revoked CPD, art 25B.1, would also continue to apply.[214] **50.131**

206 The Convention for the Unification of Certain Rules Relating to International Carriage by Air, signed at Warsaw on 12 October 1929.
207 *King v Bristow Helicopters Ltd* [2002] UKHL 7.
208 See pre-1 April 2013 CPR, r 45.23(3)(d)(i).
209 See pre-1 April 2013 CPR, r 45.23(3)(d)(ii).
210 See pre-1 April 2013 CPR, r 45.23(3)(c).
211 *Patterson v Ministry of Defence* [2012] EWHC 2767 (QB), at [14(3)].
212 See pre-1 April 2013 CPR, r 45.21.
213 See pre-1 April 2013 CPR, r 45.22.
214 See CPR, r 48.1.

Scope and application

50.132 A fixed percentage increase in an employers' liability disease claim would apply where the following conditions are met:[215]

- the dispute is between an employee (or, if the employee is deceased, the employee's estate or dependants) and the employer (or a person alleged to be liable for the employer's alleged breach of statutory or common-law duties of care);
- the dispute relates to a disease with which the employee is diagnosed that is alleged to have been contracted as a consequence of the employer's alleged breach of statutory or common-law duties of care in the course of the employee's employment;
- the claimant has entered into a funding arrangement of a type specified in CPR, r 43.2(k)(i), and which was made before 1 April 2013;[216]
- the letter of claim was not sent before 1 October 2005; and
- the claim has not been allocated to the small claims track or, if it is a claim not allocated to a track, the small claims track would not be the normal track to which it should be allocated.

50.133 As is set out at 50.120, claims to which Section V applies are excluded from Section VI. Males J has noted that this exclusion applies not only to cases in which the dispute 'relates to a disease',[217] but also where the dispute 'relates to an injury to which Section V of this Part applies',[218] concluding that the CPR therefore contemplate that the terms 'disease' and 'bodily injury' are not mutually exclusive, and that at least some injuries can also be regarded as diseases, in which case they would fall within the ambit of Section V.[219] Put otherwise, a 'bodily injury' that is not a 'disease' would be governed by Section IV, but a 'disease' would be governed by Section V and this would be so regardless of whether it was also a 'bodily injury'.

50.134 **The meaning of 'disease'** Males J has found that the word 'disease' should be given its ordinary meaning.[220] He did not approve any particular definition and, in particular, he did not find dictionary definitions to be of assistance.[221] He noted that psychiatric injuries,[222] work-related upper limb disorders[223] and physical injury alleged to have been caused by exposure to asbestos[224] may be 'bodily injuries' that fall within the ambit of Section V, despite the fact that they would not normally be regarded as being 'diseases'.[225] He went on to find that a non-freezing cold injury (NFCI) to the feet could not be regarded as a 'disease', because the word 'disease' was to be given its natural and ordinary meaning.[226] He had this to say on the point:

> 'NFCI is not caused or contributed to by any virus, bacteria, noxious agent or parasite. It is simply a case where blood fails to reach the cells in the nerves, skin and muscle of the claimant's

---

215 See pre-1 April 2013 CPR, r 45.23(1) and (2).
216 See CPR, r 48.1.
217 See CPR, r 45.20(2)(a)(i).
218 See CPR, r 45.20(2)(a)(iv).
219 *Patterson v Ministry of Defence* [2012] EWHC 2767 (QB), at [14(2)].
220 *Ibid*, at [24].
221 *Ibid*, at [25]–[35].
222 See pre-1 April 2013 CPR, r 45.23(3)(d)(i).
223 See pre-1 April 2013 CPR, r 45.23(3)(d)(ii).
224 See pre-1 April 2013 CPR, r 45.23(3)(c).
225 *Patterson v Ministry of Defence* [2012] EWHC 2767 (QB), at [14(3)].
226 *Ibid*, at [44]–[46].

feet as result of exposure to weather or environmental conditions. Although it involves no trauma in the sense of the direct application of force to the body, the mechanism is essentially the same as occurs in a case of trauma such as when a tourniquet is applied to a limb or a victim is stabbed. The result is damage or injury to the body parts affected, but this cannot be regarded as a "disease". I accept the defendant's submission that if NCFI is a "disease", so too are such conditions as chilblains, hypothermia, frostbite, sunstroke, sunburn and heat blisters which are no more than the result of exposure to weather conditions, and that this would be stretching the meaning of "disease" to surprising lengths which cannot have been intended.'[227]

Whilst the contrary is arguable, many commentators believe that Males J's conclusion was wrong. This, with respect, includes the editor, who is a Member of the Royal College of Physicians, and who, as such, has an instinctive and well-informed understanding of what is and is not a 'disease'. Whilst it is only his opinion, he is perplexed by the suggestion that a non-freezing cold injury is not a 'disease'. The defendant in the case before Males J was the Ministry of Defence and its own literature confirms that non-freezing cold injury is a *chronic* vasculitis of the dermis[228]—which is, without doubt, a disease, albeit a mild and self-limiting one. To physicians—who are the very people who should be most familiar with the ordinary and natural meaning of the medical lexicon—the notion that diseases are limited to conditions that are caused by viruses, bacteria, noxious agents, parasites, etc is simply wrong. **50.135**

In any event, there are other reasons for believing that Males J's decision was incorrect—namely, the fact that not all of the relevant legislative history was drawn to his attention.[229] Had he seen the full history, he would have been told that a disease has consistently been regarded as being something that is not an injury.[230] Phillips J had the following to say about what he believes is the correct analysis: **50.136**

'In my judgment consideration of the legislative history in this case strongly indicates that Parliament intended the term 'disease' in sections IV and V of CPR 45 to include any illness (whether physical or physiological), disorder, ailment, affliction, complaint, malady or derangement other than a physical or physiological injury solely caused by an accident or other similar single event.'[231]

Phillips J had harsh words for an insurer of the paying party when the insurer tried to argue that noise-induced hearing loss was not a 'disease', because he regarded its argument as an attempt to reopen an industry agreement made in 2005 in which it was plain that noise-induced hearing loss was indeed to be treated as a disease.[232] That criticism may well be justified, but it is likely that those in the insurance industry would wish to defend themselves by pointing to the fact that noise-induced hearing claims have spawned an industry of a size that would have been unimaginable in 2005.[233] **50.137**

[227] *Ibid*, at [48].

[228] See Roberts, A, *Synopsis of Causation: Cold Injury* (London: Ministry of Defence, 2008).

[229] See *Dalton v British Telecommunications* [2015] EWHC 616 (QB), at [52], *per* Phillips J. This case was referred to with apparent approval by Coulson LJ in *Williams v The Secretary of State for Business, Energy & Industrial Strategy* [2018] EWCA Civ 852, at [15].

[230] This is discussed at length in *Dalton v British Telecommunications* [2015] EWHC 616 (QB), at [14] *et seq*.

[231] *Ibid*, at [50].

[232] See *ibid*, at [62] *et seq*.

[233] Indeed, speaking in 2014, one ABS declared that it hoped to break the £1 billion barrier as a result of the recent growth of such claims: Rose, N, 'Quindell Targets GBP 1bn Turnover as Deafness Cases Rack up', *Litigation Futures*, 13 October 2014.

50.138 Whilst *obiter*, Phillips J has expressed the hope that paying parties will apply his reasoning to vibration white finger and that they will therefore regard that condition as being a 'disease'.[234]

50.139 Whilst not binding on any court, there are County Court decisions that an exacerbation of a pre-existing condition is not a 'disease'.[235]

50.140 **The meaning of 'employee' and 'letter of claim'** The following points can be made about the words that were used in CPR, Part 45, Section V.

- **'Letter of claim'** This is impliedly defined as a letter containing a summary of the facts on which the claim is based and the main allegations of fault before 1 October 2005.[236]
- **'Employee'** The definition of 'employee' is the same as that given in s 2(1) of the Employers' Liability (Compulsory Insurance) Act 1969: '[An] individual who has entered into or works under a contract of service or apprenticeship with an employer whether by way of manual labour, clerical work or otherwise, whether such contract is expressed or implied, oral or in writing.'[237] This definition has already been addressed at 50.121–50.126.

The amount of the fixed percentage increase: solicitors

50.141 The applicable percentage uplift will depend on the nature of the claim. Claims were categorised into three types, the third of which was a catch-all category that included any claim that did not fall within the first two.[238]

- **'Type A claim'** This was a claim relating to a disease or physical injury alleged to have been caused by exposure to asbestos.
- **'Type B claim'** This was a claim relating to—
  - a psychiatric injury alleged to have been caused by work-related psychological stress; or
  - a work-related upper limb disorder alleged to have been caused by physical stress or strain, excluding hand/arm vibration injuries.
- **'Type C claim'** This was a claim relating to a disease not falling within either Type A or Type B.

50.142 CPD, art 25B.1, comprised a table that continues to be a non-exhaustive list of the conditions that fall within Types A and B. It is reproduced here as Table 50.7.

50.143 If the claim were to conclude at trial, an increase of 100 per cent would be payable; otherwise, the percentage increase depended on the type of case.

- If it was a Type B claim, the percentage increase would have been 100 per cent regardless of when it concluded.
- If it was a Type A claim, the percentage increase would have been 27.5 per cent (or 30 per cent if, prior to 1 April 2013, a membership organisation had undertaken to meet the claimant's liabilities for legal costs in accordance with Access to Justice Act 1999, s 30).
- A Type C claim attracted a 62.5 per cent increase (or 70 per cent if, prior to 1 April 2013, a membership organisation had undertaken to meet the claimant's liabilities for legal costs).[239]

---

[234] See *Dalton v British Telecommunications* [2015] EWHC 616 (QB), at [53].
[235] See, eg, *Bird v Meggitt Aerospace* (unreported), 22 June 2012, Nottingham County Court, *per* DDJ Hales.
[236] See pre-1 April 2013 CPR, r 45.23(2)(a).
[237] See pre-1 April 2013 CPR, r 45.20(3)(a).
[238] See pre-1 April 2013 CPR, r 45.23(3).
[239] See pre-1 April 2013 CPR, r 45.24.

Table 50.7 Categorisation of conditions under the 'old' CPR, Part 45, Section V

Claim type	Description
A	Asbestosis
	Mesothelioma
	Bilateral Pleural Thickening
	Pleural Plaques
B	Repetitive Strain Injury/WRULD
	Carpal Tunnel Syndrome caused by Repetitive Strain Injury
	Occupational Stress

As with the 'old' CPR, Part 45, Sections III and IV, it was possible to apply for an alternative percentage increase, but this could be done only where the fixed percentage uplift would have been 12.5 per cent.[240] Such an application could be made only when one of the following conditions[241] was met: **50.144**

- damages of more than £250,000 (including by way of periodical payments[242]) were agreed or awarded; or
- but for contributory negligence, damages of more than £250,000[243] would have been awarded (including in cases in which the damages had been agreed).

Where one of these conditions was met, the court had to either assess the percentage increase or make an order that it be assessed.[244] There was no need to show 'exceptional circumstances' or any such thing. **50.145**

As with 'old' CPR, Part 45, Sections III and IV, restrictions and disincentives applied; even where the threshold conditions had been met, the dice were loaded against the applicant. This was because of the provisions set out in Table 8, here reproduced as Table 50.8 (which provisions are similar in nature to those that have been described at 50.111–50.112). **50.146**

The amount of the fixed percentage increase: counsel

Where counsel had a pre-commencement funding arrangement, the applicable percentage uplift depended on the nature of the claim—that is, Type A, B or C (see 50.141). Where the claim concluded at trial, the increase would have been 100 per cent.[245] Where the claim had been allocated to the fast track and did not conclude at trial, the percentage increase would have been determined by reference to the table reproduced here as Table 50.9.[246] **50.147**

[240] See pre-1 April 2013 CPR, r 45.26.
[241] See pre-1 April 2013 CPR, r 45.26, which modified the effect of CPR, r 45.18.
[242] See pre-1 April 2013 CPR, r 45.18(3).
[243] See pre-1 April 2013 CPR, r 45.18(3).
[244] See pre-1 April 2013 CPR, r 45.18(4).
[245] See pre-1 April 2013 CPR, r 45.25(1)(a).
[246] See pre-1 April 2013 CPR, r 45.25(2)(a) and Part 45, Table 6.

Table 50.8 Percentage increases for solicitors under the 'old' CPR, Part 45, Section V

Type of claim	Amount allowed	
A	If the percentage increase is assessed as greater than 40% or less than 15%, the percentage increase that is assessed by the court.	If the percentage increase is assessed as no greater than 40% and no less than 15%— (i) 27.5%; and (ii) the costs of the application and assessment shall be paid by the applicant.
B	If the percentage increase is assessed as less than 75%, the percentage increase that is assessed by the court.	If the percentage increase is assessed as no less than 75%— (i) 100%; and (ii) the costs of the application and assessment shall be paid by the applicant.
C	If the percentage increase is assessed as greater than 75% or less than 50%, the percentage increase that is assessed by the court.	If the percentage increase is assessed as no greater than 75% and no less than 50%— (i) 62.5%; and (ii) the costs of the application and assessment shall be paid by the applicant.

Table 50.9 Counsel's percentage increases for claims allocated to the fast track under the 'old' CPR, Part 45, Section V

	If the claim concludes 14 days or less before the date fixed for commencement of the trial	If the claim concludes more than 14 days before the date fixed for commencement of the trial or before any such date has been fixed
Type A claim	50%	27.5%
Type B claim	100%	100%
Type C claim	62.5%	62.5%

50.148 Where the claim had been allocated to the multitrack and did not conclude at trial, the percentage increase would have been determined by reference to the table reproduced here as Table 50.10.[247]

Table 50.10 Counsel's percentage increases for claims allocated to the multitrack under the 'old' CPR, Part 45, Section V

	If the claim concludes 21 days or less before the date fixed for commencement of the trial	If the claim concludes more than 21 days before the date fixed for commencement of the trial or before any such date has been fixed
Type A claim	75%	27.5%
Type B claim	100%	100%
Type C claim	75%	62.5%

[247] See pre-1 April 2013 CPR, r 45.25(2)(a) and Part 45, Table 6.

In calculating the periods of time, the day fixed for the commencement of the trial (or the first day of the trial period) was not included.[248] Where a trial period had been fixed and the claim had concluded on or after the first day of that period, but before the trial had commenced, the figures in the first columns of Table 50.9 or Table 50.10 would have applied, whichever was appropriate.[249] Where, however, a claim had concluded before the first day of a period fixed for trial, but before a new date or period had been given, the first day of that period was treated as the date fixed for the commencement of the trial. If a new date or period had been given, then the first date of that new period was the applicable date.[250] **50.149**

CPR, Part 45, Section III, and the Related Portal: Portal Costs

Terminology

As elsewhere in this chapter, the phrase 'the RTA Protocol' is used to refer to the Pre-Action Protocol for Low Value Personal Injury Claims in Road Traffic Accidents, and the phrase 'the EL/PL Protocol' is used to refer to the Pre-Action Protocol for Low Value Personal Injury (Employers' Liability and Public Liability) Claims. The two are very alike: the term 'the relevant Protocol' is used to refer to them collectively, and the term 'the Portal' is used to refer to the portal that they (along with CPR, Part 45, Section III, and PD 8B) govern. Finally, the term 'Portal costs' is used to refer to costs payable under the Portal. **50.150**

Overview

Some 800,000 claims per year are dealt with under the relevant Protocols.[251] There are three stages through which claims may pass. Stage 1 is designed to ascertain whether, after notification of a claim, the defendant's insurer admits liability. If it does, then Stage 2 is designed to facilitate a settlement of the claim by an agreement between the parties as to quantum. If no settlement is achieved, Stage 3 provides for the dispute as to quantum to be resolved by the court, by a speedy and cost-effective hearing under CPR, Part 8. The details are as follows. **50.151**

- **Stage 1 (liability)** The claimant submits their case via the Portal by submitting a claim notification form (CNF). If the defendant disputes liability or does not respond, the case exits the Portal. If, however, liability is admitted, Stage 1 comes to an end and the Stage 1 fixed costs becomes payable (within ten business days of receipt of the Stage 2 settlement pack).
- **Stage 2 (evidence and negotiations)** The claimant submits a Stage 2 settlement pack, comprising: (a) the Stage 2 settlement pack form (which contains an offer to settle); (b) medical evidence; (c) evidence of pecuniary losses; and (d) evidence of disbursements. If the defendant disputes the claimant's valuation of the claim, they may enter into negotiations and/or put forward their own offer by setting out their proposed figures on the Stage 2 settlement pack form. The settlement pack may go back and forth between the parties as each side puts forward its revised figures. If the matter does not settle, the claimant will send the defendant a court proceedings pack. This pack sets out the claimant's claimed

[248] See pre-1 April 2013 CPR, rr 45.25(3) and 45.17(5).
[249] See pre-1 April 2013 CPR, rr 45.25(3) and 45.17(2)–(5).
[250] See pre-1 April 2013 CPR, rr 45.25(3) and 45.17(2)–(5).
[251] See *Phillips v Willis* [2016] EWCA Civ 401, at [1].

losses, the defendant's responses and the final offers of both sides. It also includes the evidence that each side submitted during Stage 2. The defendant then pays the amount of the defendant's final offer, together with all fixed costs due up to the end of Stage 2. Those costs are payable regardless of whether the matter proceeds to Stage 3.

- **Stage 3 (court proceedings and adjudication)** At the end of Stage 2, the claimant has the right to bring the matter before the court. PD 8B requires the claimant to issue proceedings in the County Court under CPR, Part 8. PD 8B substantially modifies the Part 8 procedure so as to make it suitable for low-value road traffic accident claims in which only quantum is in dispute. The evidence that the parties can rely upon at Stage 3 is limited to that which is contained in the court proceedings pack. The court assesses the items of damages that remain in dispute, either on paper or at a single 'Stage 3 hearing'.

50.152 Different provision may apply if the claimant is a child[252] (see 50.250–50.251) or if the end of the limitation period is approaching (see 50.252).

Jurisdiction and associated rules

50.153 The rules that govern the Portal are a somewhat heterogeneous jurisdiction, which is a well-mannered way of saying that they are a bit of a mess. Even in their original form (namely, the original RTA Protocol), they were fragmented and difficult to follow, but matters were made worse by the fact that the EL/PL Protocol was simply grafted on (see 50.27–50.44 for the relevant history). The end result is that the rules are not easy to follow. That said, Briggs LJ has noted that they are a 'clear, detailed and precise code, negotiated between sophisticated stakeholder groups under the auspices of the Civil Justice Council', and that the court should therefore be slow to imply terms.[253]

50.154 The rules exert their effects by no fewer than three legal mechanisms: the first two stages work via the relevant Protocols themselves; the third operates via a combination of CPR, Part 45, Section III, and PD 8B.

The ambit of the relevant Protocols

50.155 The ambit of Stages 1 and 2 is governed by the relevant Protocols (see 50.193–50.202 and 50.203–50.226, respectively), whereas that of Stage 3 is governed by a combination of CPR, Part 45, Section III, and PD 8B (see 50.227–50.249). CPR, Part 45, Section III, and PD 8B apply to claims that have been,[254] or should have been,[255] started under Part 8 in accordance with PD 8B—better known as the Stage 3 procedure.

50.156 **The ambit of the RTA Protocol** The RTA Protocol applies to claims for damages arising from road traffic accidents occurring on or after 30 April 2010.[256] To fall within the ambit of the RTA Protocol, the claim must:

[252] Briggs LJ has confirmed that this is to allow the court to consider whether to approve a proposed settlement on the child's behalf: *JC and A Solicitors Ltd v Iqbal* [2017] EWCA Civ 355, at [29].

[253] *Ibid*, at [31].

[254] See CPR, r 45.16(1).

[255] See CPR, r 45.16(1). This rule appears to make it unnecessary to rely by analogy on cases such as *Drew v Whitbread* [2010] EWCA 53 because application is a matter of express provision, rather than impliedly as a matter of reasonableness.

[256] See RTA Protocol, para 4.1.

- include a claim for damages for personal injury;[257]
- not be a claim that would normally be allocated to the small claims track; and
- be of a value of no more than the 'upper limit'.[258]

The 'upper limit' is £25,000, where the accident occurred on or after 31 July 2013, or £10,000, where the accident occurred on or after 30 April 2010, but before 31 July 2013.[259] The value of the claim is determined on a full liability basis (including pecuniary losses), but excluding interest.[260] **50.157**

Exclusions from the RTA Protocol The following claims are excluded from the RTA Protocol: **50.158**

- claims in respect of a breach of duty owed to a road user by a person who is not a road user;[261]
- claims made to the Motor Insurer's Bureau (MIB) pursuant to the Untraced Drivers Agreement 2003[262] (although claims under the Uninsured Drivers Agreement are not excluded);
- claims in which one of the parties is deceased or is a protected party;[263]
- claims in which the claimant is bankrupt;[264]
- claims in which the defendant's vehicle is registered outside the UK;[265] and
- claims that were started under the RTA Protocol, but which did not continue under it.[266]

For all practical purposes, the costs-related aspects of the RTA Protocol do not apply where the claimant is a litigant in person.[267] **50.159**

Vehicle-related damages Vehicle-related damages[268] are excluded for the purposes of valuing the claim.[269] Indeed, vehicle-related damages will ordinarily be dealt with peripherally to the RTA Protocol (see 50.222)[270]—although, as a matter of administrative convenience, requests for payment may include those damages. **50.160**

Both RTA and EL/PL aspects to the claim Where a claim is potentially both a road traffic accident and an employers' liability or public liability claim, the RTA Protocol will prevail.[271] **50.161**

---

[257] See RTA Protocol, para 4.2(2). For reasons that are not wholly clear, RTA Protocol, para 1.1(16), defines RTAs according to bodily, not personal, injury.
[258] See RTA Protocol, para 4.1.
[259] See RTA Protocol, para 1.2.
[260] See RTA Protocol, para 1.2.
[261] See RTA Protocol, para 4.5(1).
[262] See RTA Protocol, para 4.5(2).
[263] See RTA Protocol, para 4.5(3) and (4).
[264] See RTA Protocol, para 4.5(5).
[265] See RTA Protocol, para 4.5(6).
[266] See RTA Protocol, para 5.11.
[267] See RTA Protocol, para 4.6.
[268] This includes pre-accident value, vehicle repair charges, insurance excess and vehicle hire charges: see RTA Protocol, para 1.1(18).
[269] See RTA Protocol, para 4.4.
[270] See RTA Protocol, para 6.4.
[271] See EL/PL Protocol, para 4.3(11).

50.162 **The ambit of the EL/PL Protocol** The EL/PL Protocol will apply where:

- the accident in question occurred on or after 31 July 2014, or
- the claim is a disease claim in which no letter of claim was sent before that date;[272]
- the claim includes damages in respect of personal injury;[273]
- the claimant values the claim at a figure that does not exceed the 'upper limit', which is £25,000;[274] and
- the small claims track would not be the normal track for that claim.[275]

50.163 Thus the EL/PL Protocol applies to employers' liability and public liability claims valued between £1,000 and £25,000 in which the accident occurred on or after 31 July 2013, and to employers' liability disease claims in which no letter of claim was sent to the defendant prior to 31 July 2013.

50.164 For the purposes of valuing the claim, it is assumed that damages (including pecuniary losses) are payable on a full liability basis, but interest is excluded.[276]

50.165 *Exclusions from the EL/PL Protocol* The EL/PL Protocol provides[277] that it does not apply to a claim:

- where the claimant or defendant acts as personal representative of a deceased person;[278]
- where the claimant or defendant is a protected party as defined in CPR, r 21.1(2);[279]
- in the case of a public liability claim, where the defendant is an individual;[280]
- where the claimant is bankrupt;[281]
- where the defendant is insolvent and there is no identifiable insurer;[282]
- in the case of a disease claim, where there is more than one employer defendant;[283]
- for personal injury arising from an accident or alleged breach of duty occurring outside England and Wales;[284]
- for damages in relation to harm, abuse or neglect of or by children or vulnerable adults;[285]
- that includes a claim for clinical negligence;[286]

---

272 See EL/PL Protocol, para 4.1(1)(a).
273 See EL/PL Protocol, para 4.1(2).
274 See EL/PL Protocol, para 4.1(3).
275 See EL/PL Protocol, para 4.1(4).
276 See EL/PL Protocol, para 4.1(3).
277 See EL/PL Protocol, para 4.3(1).
278 See EL/PL Protocol, para 4.3(1).
279 See EL/PL Protocol, para 4.3(2).
280 See EL/PL Protocol, para 4.3(3). In this regard, 'individual' does not include a defendant who is sued in their business capacity or in their capacity as an office holder.
281 See EL/PL Protocol, para 4.3(4).
282 See EL/PL Protocol, para 4.3(5).
283 See EL/PL Protocol, para 4.3(6). In *Williams v The Secretary of State for Business, Energy & Industrial Strategy* [2018] EWCA Civ 852, at [32], Coulson LJ explained thus 'This exception is not an accident: all of the new-style Pre-Action Protocols are expressly designed to apply only in cases where there is one defendant. The presence of two or more potential defendants makes it difficult to comply with some of the requirements of the Protocol, and makes the Portal impossible to operate efficiently.'
284 See EL/PL Protocol, para 4.3(7).
285 See EL/PL Protocol, para 4.3(8).
286 See EL/PL Protocol, para 4.3(9).

- for mesothelioma;[287] and
- that was started under the EL/PL Protocol, but which did not continue under it.[288]

Where a claim is potentially both a road traffic accident and an employers' liability or public liability claim, the RTA Protocol will prevail.[289]

Transitional provisions Whilst they will now rarely be relevant, transitional provisions relating to CPR, Part 45, Section III, and the RTA Protocol state that the provisions that were in force before 31 July 2013 shall continue to have effect in respect of any claim in which the claim notification form had already been sent by that date.[290] There are similar provisions governing the changes that were made on 5 April 2015.[291] In so far as they relate to CPR, Part 45, Sections III and IIIA, those latter amendments were largely confined to renumbering and, as such, are of scant practical relevance.[292] **50.166**

How low-value claims are treated There is no provision for a claim to join the relevant Protocol part-way through, so although there may be opportunity to review an approbative decision to engage one of the relevant Protocols, there could never be an opportunity to review a decision not to do so. This means that where there is doubt about whether a claim is substantial enough to qualify, the claimant's representative would be well advised to engage the relevant Protocol and to review the matter at a later stage. If this were to be done, there would be several options that would then be available. **50.167**

- **Claimant** If the choice were between staying within the relevant Protocol and being relegated to the small claims track, few claimants would choose the latter. Fortunately for them, as of 31 July 2013, claimants who leave the relevant Protocol would fall within the ambit of CPR, Part 45, Section IIIA; as such, they would avoid the small claims track cost regime.[293] In any event, unless their opponent arrests engagement of the relevant Protocol (see below), claimants may remain within its ambit if they 'reasonably believe' that their claim is valued at between £1,000 and the Protocol 'upper limit' (see 50.157).[294] Whether that valuation was reasonable would then be a question of fact to be determined on the evidence. The wording of the relevant provisions is such that it can safely be presumed that hindsight will not apply.[295] Moreover, Briggs LJ said that since claims may be pursued within the Protocol only through legal representatives and

[287] See EL/PL Protocol, para 4.3(10).

[288] See EL/PL Protocol, para 5.11.

[289] See EL/PL Protocol, para 4.3(11).

[290] See Civil Procedure (Amendment No 6) Rules 2013 (SI 2013/1695), r 10; 'new' RTA Protocol, para 4.2. Some caution is needed in this regard, because several of the 'new' provisions are relevant to 'old' Protocol claims.

[291] See Civil Procedure (Amendment No 8) Rules 2014 (SI 2014/3299), r 18.

[292] This book uses the new numbers; if any transitional provisions are of practical relevance, they are mentioned in the relevant part of the main text.

[293] See, eg, *Phillips v Willis* [2016] EWCA Civ 401, at [4], *per* Jackson LJ; see also *Singh v Ajaz* (unreported), 27 September 2016, Bristol County Court, *per* Judge Denyer QC.

[294] See RTA Protocol, para 5.9; EL/PL Protocol, para 5.9.

[295] Whilst not binding on any other judge, an example of a case in which the court found that it was reasonable to regard a claim as potentially worth more £1,000 is *Bromley v Hewson* (unreported), 6 September 2012, Medway County Court, in which District Judge Gill found that, in a case involving a child, psychological consequences following accident trauma were common and could well have attracted damages in excess of the threshold.

since the CNF will be supported by a statement of truth, that belief will generally be presumed, in the absence of proof to the contrary.[296]

- **Defendant** Within certain time limits (see 50.242),[297] a defendant has the right to arrest engagement of the relevant Protocol on the grounds that they value the claim as being suitable for the small claims track. If a defendant exercises that right, the claim will no longer continue under the relevant Protocol, but will instead proceed under the Pre-Action Protocol for Personal Injury Claims, starting at para 6.3.[298] Such a step would expose a defendant to the risk that they may ultimately lose the costs protection that the RTA Protocol would otherwise have given them.

50.168 **How high-value claims are treated** As has already been mentioned, the relevant Protocol ceases to apply where, at any stage, a claimant notifies a defendant that the claim has now been revalued at more than the Protocol 'upper limit' (see 50.157).[299] This means that claimants who are in doubt as to whether the value of a claim exceeds the 'upper limit' will have to decide whether to engage the relevant Protocol or to seek to have the claim allocated to the fast track or possibly multitrack. If they unreasonably choose the latter, then CPR, Part 45, Section III, provides that the court may limit the costs to those recoverable under the relevant Protocol.[300] Whilst not binding, Judge Platts has explained that if a claimant manipulates the RTA Protocol procedure to take the claim away from Stage 3 and into Part 7, they will be acting contrary to the spirit, if not the letter, of the Protocol and wholly contrary to the overriding objective.[301] In a case in which that happened, he restricted the costs to those that would have been payable under the RTA Protocol.

Litigants in person and the relevant Protocols

50.169 For all practical purposes, the costs-related aspects of the relevant Protocols do not apply where the claimant is a litigant in person.[302]

Exit from the relevant Protocol

50.170 There are many mechanisms by means of which parties are able to bring the engagement of the relevant Protocol to an end; where this happens, then assuming that the claim notification form was sent after 31 July 2013,[303] CPR, Part 45, Section IIIA, will then be engaged (see 50.267).[304] That said, CPR, Part 45, Section IIIA, will not apply to disease claims that were started under the EL/PL Protocol[305] nor will it apply to claims that have actually been allocated to the multitrack subsequent to leaving the Portal[306]—although it would apply

---

[296] *JC and A Solicitors Ltd v Iqbal* [2017] EWCA Civ 355, at [26].

[297] See RTA Protocol, para 6.15; EL/PL Protocol, para 6.13.

[298] See RTA Protocol, para 6.15(4)(b); EL/PL Protocol, para 6.13(4)(b).

[299] See RTA Protocol, para 4.3; EL/PL Protocol, para 4.2.

[300] CPR, r 45.24(2)(b)(ii).

[301] See *Ilahi v Usman* (unreported), 29 November 2012, Manchester County Court, at [31].

[302] See RTA Protocol, para 4.6; EL/PL Protocol, para 4.4.

[303] See Civil Procedure (Amendment No 6) Rules 2013 (SI 2013/1695), r 10.

[304] CPR, r 36.20, provides that 'this rule applies where a claim no longer continues under the RTA or EL/PL Protocol pursuant to [CPR, r 45.29A(1)]'.

[305] CPR, r 45.29A(2).

[306] The absence of an express exclusion for such cases was the result of a drafting error that has now been rectified: see *Qader v Esure Services Ltd* [2016] EWCA Civ 1109, at [44] *et seq*, *per* Briggs LJ. See also Civil Procedure (Amendment) Rules 2017 (SI 2017/95), r 8, which amended CPR, r 45.29B.

(subject to any escape provisions) to a claim that should have been allocated to the multi-track, but which was not in fact allocated at all.[307]

Exit from the relevant Protocols

Both parties have ample opportunity to bring the relevant Protocol to an end. It should be borne in mind, however, that a party may be penalised in costs for doing so (see 50.254–50.266).[308] In any event, leaving the relevant Protocol will not always be rewarding in terms of cost because the claim is likely to be subject to the provisions of CPR, Part 45, Section IIIA (or, at the very least, the Personal Injuries Pre-Action Protocol). **50.171**

The options for leaving the relevant Protocols include the following. **50.172**

- **At any stage**
  - **Unsuitability** The claimant is, at any stage,[309] able to give notice that the claim is unsuitable for the relevant Protocol, for example because there are complex issues of fact or law or where a claimant is contemplating applying for a group litigation order (GLO). Where this happens, then the claim will no longer continue under the relevant Protocol.[310] Where the court considers that the claimant acted unreasonably in giving such notice, it will award no more than the fixed costs in CPR, r 45.18.[311]
  - **Revaluation** The relevant Protocol will cease to apply if the claimant notifies the defendant that the claim has been revalued at more than the 'upper limit' (see 50.157).[312] That said, the mere resolution of the personal injury element of a claim would not be grounds for the claim automatically exiting the RTA Protocol.[313]
- **During Stage 1**
  - **No CNF response** The claim will no longer continue under the relevant Protocol if, within certain time limits (see 50.242), the defendant does not complete and send their response to the claim notification form.[314]
  - **Non-admission of liability** The same will apply if the defendant does not make an admission of liability within those time limits.[315] It should be noted that, in this context, an admission of liability must include an admission that the defendant's breach of duty caused some loss to the claimant—albeit that the nature and extent of that loss need not be admitted.[316]
  - **Contributory negligence** The same will apply if the defendant makes an admission of liability, but alleges contributory negligence (other than in relation to the claimant's admitted failure to wear a seat belt).[317]

[307] *Qader v Esure Services Ltd* [2016] EWCA Civ 1109, at [54], *per* Briggs LJ.
[308] Whilst not binding, see *Patel v Fortis Insurance Ltd* (unreported), 23 December 2011, Leicester County Court.
[309] The relevant Protocols do not expressly state this, but this is implied by the wording of RTA Protocol, para 7.76, and EL/PL Protocol, para 7.59.
[310] See RTA Protocol, para 7.76; EL/PL Protocol, para 7.59.
[311] See RTA Protocol, para 7.76; EL/PL Protocol, para 7.59.
[312] See RTA Protocol, para 4.3; EL/PL Protocol, para 4.2; Travel Protocol, para 4.2.
[313] See *Phillips v Willis* [2016] EWCA Civ 401, at [33], *per* Jackson LJ.
[314] See RTA Protocol, para 6.15(2); EL/PL Protocol, para 6.14.
[315] See RTA Protocol, para 6.15(3); EL/PL Protocol, para 6.14.
[316] See RTA Protocol, para 1.1(1); EL/PL Protocol, para 1.1(1).
[317] See RTA Protocol, para 6.15(1); EL/PL Protocol, para 6.13(1).

- **Small claims track** The claim will no longer continue under the relevant Protocol if, within certain time limits (see 50.197), the defendant gives notice that if proceedings were started, the small claims track would be the normal track for that claim.[318]
- **Insufficient information** If insufficient information has been provided by the claimant in the claim notification form, the defendant can, within certain time limits (see 50.197), stop the claim from continuing under the relevant Protocol.[319] Where this happens, the court may, when exercising its discretion as to costs, take the claimant's failure into account.[320] Presumably, the court would also take into account the defendant's conduct if the defendant had unreasonably decided that insufficient information had been given.
- **Interim payments** Where the defendant fails to make an interim payment (or makes a payment that the claimant believes is inadequate), the claimant is entitled to give notice that the claim will no longer continue under the relevant Protocol. This must be done within certain time limits, however.[321]

• **During Stage 2**
- **No response during initial consideration period** Where the defendant does not respond within the 'initial consideration period' (see 50.214) in Stage 2, the claim will no longer continue under the relevant Protocol.[322]
- **Small claims track** The claim will no longer continue under the relevant Protocol if, within the 'initial consideration period', the defendant gives notice that if proceedings were started, the small claims track would be the normal track for that claim.[323]
- **Withdrawal of admission of causation** The claim will no longer continue under the relevant Protocol if, within the 'initial consideration period', the defendant withdraws an admission of causation.[324]
- **Withdrawal of offer after consideration period** Where a party withdraws an offer made in the Stage 2 settlement pack form after the 'total consideration period' (or any extension thereof) (see 50.214–50.218) in Stage 2, the claim will no longer continue under the relevant Protocol.[325]
- **Non-payment of costs and damages** The claimant may exit the relevant Protocol if the defendant fails to pay costs in accordance with the provisions in Stage 1. The claimant may do this within ten days of the expiry of the period during which payment ought to have been made[326] (which is during Stage 2[327]). Similar provisions apply to the payment of costs and damages in Stage 2 per se.[328]

---

318 See RTA Protocol, para 6.15(4)(b); EL/PL Protocol, para 6.13(4)(b).

319 See RTA Protocol, para 6.8; EL/PL Protocol, para 6.7.

320 See CPR, r 45.24(2); see also RTA Protocol, para 6.9. There is no corresponding provision in the EL/PL Protocol.

321 See RTA Protocol, para 7.30; EL/PL Protocol, para 7.28.

322 See RTA Protocol, para 7.40; EL/PL Protocol, para 7.28.

323 See RTA Protocol, para 7.39(a); EL/PL Protocol, para 7.36(a).

324 See RTA Protocol, para 7.39(b); EL/PL Protocol, para 7.36(b).

325 See RTA Protocol, para 7.46; EL/PL Protocol, para 7.43.

326 See RTA Protocol, paras 6.18 and 6.19; EL/PL Protocol, para 6.17.

327 See the reference to such costs being payable 'within 10 days after receiving the Stage 2 Settlement Pack' in RTA Protocol, para 6.18; EL/PL Protocol, para 6.17.

328 See RTA Protocol, para 7.75; EL/PL Protocol, para 7.58.

  - **Compensation Recovery Unit (CRU) certificates** Where the defendant fails to comply with certain provision relating to CRU certificates at the end of Stage 2,[329] the claimant may give written notice that the claim will no longer continue under the relevant Protocol and start proceedings under CPR, Part 7.[330]
- **During Stage 3**
  - **Withdrawal of offer after consideration period after proceedings have started** Whilst permission would be required, where an offer is withdrawn after proceedings have begun, the claim will no longer continue under the Stage 3 procedure. That said, the court will give permission only where there is good reason for the claim not to continue under the Stage 3 procedure.[331]
  - **Non-approval** Whilst not something that can be invoked at the behest of either of the parties, where the settlement is not approved at the second settlement hearing, the claim will no longer continue under the Stage 3 procedure.[332]

Claims that no longer continue under the relevant Protocol cannot subsequently re-enter the process.[333]

Fixed costs

The relevant Protocols (in conjunction with CPR, Part 45, Section III, and PD 8B) provide for payments in stages. That scheme is a clear, detailed and precise code,[334] under which the only costs allowed under the present iteration of CPR, Part 45, are: **50.173**

- fixed costs in accordance with CPR, r 45.18 (see 50.174–50.177);
- where applicable, additional fixed costs in accordance with CPR, rr 45.23A or 45.23B (see 50.178–50.180);
- disbursements in accordance with CPR, r 45.19 (see 50.181–50.188);[335] and
- where applicable, additional liabilities (see 50.189–50.190).

Briggs LJ has explained that these payments are not interim payments on account that are conditional on the outcome, but are final payments in their own right.[336]

Types of fixed cost

The types of fixed cost that can be recovered are as follows.[337] **50.174**

- **Type A fixed costs** These are the legal representative's costs.
- **Type B fixed costs** These are the advocate's costs (which may encompass counsel's fees).[338]
- **Type C fixed costs** These are the costs for the advice on the amount of damages where the claimant is a child.

---

329 See RTA Protocol, paras 7.72–7.74; EL/PL Protocol, paras 7.56–7.58.
330 See RTA Protocol, para 7.75; EL/PL Protocol, para 7.58.
331 See PD 8B, para 10.1.
332 See PD 8B, para 12.5.
333 See RTA Protocol, para 5.11; EL/PL Protocol, para 5.11.
334 See *JC and A Solicitors Ltd v Iqbal* [2017] EWCA Civ 355, at [31], *per* Briggs LJ.
335 CPR. r 45.17.
336 See *JC and A Solicitors Ltd v Iqbal* [2017] EWCA Civ 355, at [33]–[37], esp [35], *per* Briggs LJ.
337 See CPR, r 45.18 (1) and (2).
338 See CPR, r 45.18, which refers to the following definition in CPR, r 45.37(2): ' "[A]dvocate" means a person exercising a right of audience as a representative of, or on behalf of, a party.'

50.175 Subject to CPR, r 45.24(2), which concerns conduct (see 50.258), the court will not award more or less than the amounts shown in Tables 6 or 6A.[339] Where appropriate, VAT is payable in addition.[340]

50.176 In so far as the RTA Protocol is concerned, the costs are as set out in Table 50.11.[341]

Table 50.11 Fixed costs in relation to the RTA Protocol (CPR, Part 45, Table 6)

Where the value of the claim for damages is not more than £10,000		Where the value of the claim for damages is more than £10,000, but not more than £25,000	
Stage 1 fixed costs	£200*	Stage 1 fixed costs	£200*
Stage 2 fixed costs	£300*	Stage 2 fixed costs	£600*
Stage 3—Type A fixed costs	£250*	Stage 3—Type A fixed costs	£250*
Stage 3—Type B fixed costs	£250	Stage 3—Type B fixed costs	£250
Stage 3—Type C fixed costs	£150	Stage 3—Type C fixed costs	£150

* These amounts will be increased by 12.5% if the claimant lives and instructs a legal representative who practises in an area set out in PD 45, para 2.6.[343]

50.177 In so far as the EL/PL Protocol is concerned, the fixed costs are as set out in Table 50.12.[342]

Table 50.12 Fixed costs in relation to the EL/PL Protocol (CPR, Part 45, Table 6A)

Where the value of the claim for damages is not more than £10,000		Where the value of the claim for damages is more than £10,000, but not more than £25,000	
Stage 1 fixed costs	£300*	Stage 1 fixed costs	£300*
Stage 2 fixed costs	£600*	Stage 2 fixed costs	£1,300*
Stage 3—Type A fixed costs	£250*	Stage 3—Type A fixed costs	£250*
Stage 3—Type B fixed costs	£250	Stage 3—Type B fixed costs	£250
Stage 3—Type C fixed costs	£150	Stage 3—Type C fixed costs	£150

* These amounts will be increased by 12.5% if the claimant lives and instructs a legal representative who practises in an area set out in PD 45, para 2.6.[344]

Additional fixed costs

50.178 In addition to the provision that govern fixed costs generally, there are two provisions that govern two types of additional fixed cost. They will apply where the claim settled before proceedings are issued under Stage 3 or where additional advice on the value of the claim is reasonably required.

339 See CPR, r 45.18(4).
340 See CPR, r 45.18(6).
341 See CPR, rr 45.18 and 45.19, and Part 45, Table 6.
342 See CPR, rr 45.18 and 45.19, and Part 45, Table 6A.
343 See CPR, r 45.18(5). Those areas are set out in fn 108.
344 See CPR, r 45.18(5). Those areas are set out in fn 108.

Settlement before proceedings are issued under Stage 3 Where there is a settlement after the court proceedings pack has been sent to the defendant, but before proceedings are issued under Stage 3, and the settlement is more than the defendant's relevant Protocol offer, the fixed costs will include an additional amount equivalent to the Stage 3 Type A fixed costs.[345] **50.179**

Additional advice on the value of the claim Where the value of the claim for damages is more than £10,000 additional advice has been obtained from a specialist solicitor or from counsel and that advice is reasonably required to value the claim, the fixed costs may include an additional amount equivalent to the Stage 3 Type C fixed costs.[346] **50.180**

Disbursements

Disbursements in general Subject to the points made at 50.184 about soft-tissue injury claims, the court may allow a claim for a disbursement of a type mentioned below, but 'will not allow a claim for any other type of disbursement'.[347] The strength of this restriction is somewhat diluted by the fact that CPR, r 45.19(2)(e), provides that the court is permitted to allow 'any other disbursement that has arisen due to a particular feature of the dispute'.[348] That said, allowances under this provision are rare. **50.181**

In a claim to which the EL/PL Protocol or the RTA Protocol applies, the disbursements that the court is expressly permitted to allow are: **50.182**

- the costs of obtaining medical records;[349]
- the costs of obtaining a medical report or reports;[350]
- the costs of obtaining any appropriate non-medical expert reports as provided for in the relevant Protocol (which, under the RTA Protocol, includes engineering reports that are reasonably required to value the claim,[351] although this would be the exception rather than the norm);[352]
- the costs of a search of DVLA records;[353]
- the costs of a search of the records of the Motor Insurance Database (MID);[354]
- court fees as a result of CPR, Part 21, being applicable;[355]
- court fees payable where proceedings are started as a result of a limitation period that is about to expire;[356]
- court fees in respect of the Stage 3 procedure;[357] and
- in an appropriate case, an ATE premium (see 50.235).

[345] See CPR, r 45.23A.
[346] See CPR, r 45.23B.
[347] See CPR, r 45.19(1).
[348] See, eg, *Madej v Maciszyn* [2013] Lexis Citation 143, in which Master Campbell allowed the fees of an interpreter.
[349] See CPR, r 45.19(2)(a)(i)
[350] See CPR, r 45.19(2)(a)(ii).
[351] See CPR, r 45.19(2)(a)(ii) and 45.19(3)(1)(a).
[352] See RTA Protocol, para 7.9; EL/PL Protocol, para 7.7.
[353] See CPR, r 45.19(2)(a)(ii)(aa) and 45.19(3)(1)(b)(i).
[354] See CPR, r 45.19(2)(a)(ii)(bb) and 45.19(3)(1)(ii).
[355] See CPR, r 45.19(2)(b).
[356] See CPR, r 45.19(2)(c).
[357] See CPR, r 45.19(2)(d).

50.183 Where a medical reporting agency has provided a report or a set of medical records in a case other than a soft-tissue injury claim, its fees (including the direct cost of obtaining the report or records) may be subject to the Medical Organisation Reporting Agreement, an industry-wide agreement that provides for certain set fees to be paid directly by the defendant's insurer to the agency. This topic is addressed in detail at 52.68–52.71.

50.184 **Disbursements (soft-tissue injuries)** Where the claim is for soft-tissue injury arising out of a road traffic accident, there may be restrictions to the recoverable costs allowed. In particular, in a soft-tissue injury claim in which a claim notification form was submitted under the RTA Protocol on or after 1 October 2014,[358] the following limits and fixed fees[359] will apply:

- for each set of records required,[360] a fee of no more than £30 *plus* the direct cost from the holder of the records, limited to a total of £80 for each set of records required;[361]
- a fee for the first medical report—namely, £180;[362]
- a fee for a further medical report—namely, £420 for a report from an orthopaedic surgeon, £360 from an accident and emergency (A&E) consultant, £180 from a general practitioner (GP) and £180 from a physiotherapist;[363]
- a fee for an addendum report on medical records—namely, £80 for a report from an orthopaedic surgeon and £50 otherwise;[364]
- a fee for answers to Part 35 questions—namely, £80;[365] and
- (arguably) other disbursements or experts' fees, where they can be justified.[366]

Where appropriate, VAT may be recovered in addition to the cost of obtaining a fixed-cost medical report or medical records.[367]

50.185 In a claim to which the RTA Protocol applies, added to the disbursements referred to above are the cost of (a) an engineer's report and (b) a search of the records of the (i) DVLA and (ii) MID.[368]

50.186 CPR, r 45.19, provides as follows:

> (1) Subject to paragraphs (2A) to (2E), the court—
> (a) may allow a claim for a disbursement of a type mentioned in paragraphs (2) or (3); but
> (b) will not allow a claim for any other type of disbursement.

---

358 See Civil Procedure (Amendment No 6) Rules 2014 (SI 2014/2044), r 14.
359 CPR, r 45.19(2A).
360 CPR, r 45.19(2A)(c). That rule confirms that where relevant records are required from more than one holder of records, the fixed fee applies to each set of records required.
361 See CPR, r 45.19(2A)(c).
362 See CPR, r 45.19(2A)(a).
363 See CPR, r 45.19(2A)(b).
364 See CPR, r 45.19(2A)(d).
365 See CPR, r 45.19(2A)(e).
366 This is implied by CPR, r 45.19(2C), which reads: 'The cost of obtaining a further report from an expert not listed in paragraph (2A)(b) is not fixed, but the use of that expert and the cost must be justified.' That said, CPR, r 45.19(2A), is (arguably) an exhaustive list and there is no mention of a right to recover fees for other experts in that list. Perhaps the key lies in the fact that r 45.19(2A) relates to 'fixed cost medical reports'.
367 See CPR, r 45.19(2A) and (2D).
368 See CPR, r 45.19(3).

(2) In a claim to which either the RTA Protocol or EL/PL Protocol applies, the disbursements referred to in paragraph (1) are—

(a) the cost of obtaining—
 (i) medical records;
 (ii) a medical report or reports or non-medical expert reports as provided for in the relevant Protocol;
  (aa) Driver Vehicle Licensing Authority;
  (bb) Motor Insurance Database;

(b) court fees as a result of Part 21 being applicable;

(c) court fees payable where proceedings are started as a result of a limitation period that is about to expire;

(d) court fees in respect of the Stage 3 Procedure; and

(e) any other disbursement that has arisen due to a particular feature of the dispute.

(2A) In a soft tissue injury claim to which the RTA Protocol applies, the only sums (exclusive of VAT) that are recoverable in respect of the cost of obtaining a fixed cost medical report or medical records are as follows—

(a) obtaining the first report from an accredited medical expert selected via the MedCo Portal: £180;

(b) obtaining a further report where justified from an expert from one of the following disciplines—
 (i) Consultant Orthopaedic Surgeon (inclusive of a review of medical records where applicable): £420;
 (ii) Consultant in Accident and Emergency Medicine: £360;
 (iii) General Practitioner registered with the General Medical Council: £180; or
 (iv) Physiotherapist registered with the Health and Care Professions Council: £180;

(c) obtaining medical records: no more than £30 plus the direct cost from the holder of the records, and limited to £80 in total for each set of records required. Where relevant records are required from more than one holder of records, the fixed fee applies to each set of records required;

(d) addendum report on medical records (except by Consultant Orthopaedic Surgeon): £50; and

(e) answer to questions under Part 35: £80.

(2B) Save in exceptional circumstances, no fee may be allowed for the cost of obtaining a report to which paragraph (2A) applies where the medical expert—

(a) has provided treatment to the claimant;

(b) is associated with any person who has provided treatment; or

(c) proposes or recommends that they or an associate then provide.

(2C) The cost of obtaining a further report from an expert not listed in paragraph (2A)(b) is not fixed, but the use of that expert and the cost must be justified.

(2D) Where appropriate, VAT may be recovered in addition to the cost of obtaining a fixed cost medical report or medical records.

(2E) In this rule, "accredited medical expert", "associate", "associated with", "fixed cost medical report" "MedCo" and "soft tissue injury claim" have the same meaning as in paragraph 1.1(A1), (1A), (10A), (12A), and (16A), respectively, of the RTA Protocol.

(3) In a claim to which the RTA Protocol applies, the disbursements referred to in paragraph (1) are also the cost of—

(a) an engineer's report; and

(b) a search of the records of the—
 (i) Driver Vehicle Licensing Authority; and
 (ii) Motor Insurance Database.'

50.187 As can be seen, those provisions do not dictate an amount for each and every type of disbursement; thus claimants are not limited to the medical specialties listed nor to the sums set out in that rule, but they will have to justify the use of any expert not listed and the costs claimed in such circumstances.[369]

50.188 *Disbursements relating to treating clinicians* Other than in exceptional circumstances, no fee may be allowed for the cost of obtaining a report from a medical expert who has provided treatment to the claimant, is associated with any person who has provided treatment, or proposes or recommends that they or an associate provide treatment.[370]

Additional liabilities

50.189 **Success fees** Either party is able to recover a success fee (assuming, of course, that they have a relevant pre-commencement funding agreement).[371]

- **Claimant** The success fee is fixed, with no escape provisions.[372] Only a party who has entered into funding arrangement of the type specified in CPR, r 43.2(1)(k)(i), may recover a success fee and then only if that agreement is a pre-commencement funding arrangement, as defined in CPR, r 48.1. The default percentage uplift is 12.5 per cent.[373] This is the amount that will be payable on claims that settle in Stages 1 or 2. If the end result is determined by the court and if that result is that the claimant has been awarded more than the defendant's RTA Protocol offer, the percentage uplift on the Stage 3 costs will rise to 100 per cent, but only on the fees for that stage.[374]
- **Defendant** If the defendant has the benefit of a pre-commencement funding arrangement as defined in CPR, r 48.1, and the damages awarded at a Stage 3 determination are less than or equal to the defendant's RTA Protocol offer, then the defendant is entitled to a 100 per cent success fee on the relevant Stage 3 fixed costs.[375]

50.190 **ATE and notional premiums** Where the policy in question was taken out before 1 April 2013,[376] an ATE insurance premium will be recoverable as a disbursement.[377] The same applies to an additional amount pursuant to s 30 of the Access to Justice Act 1999, but only where the agreement with the membership organisation was made before 1 April 2013 and where that agreement specifically applied to the claim in question prior to that date.[378]

---

369 See CPR, r 45.19(2C).

370 See CPR, r 45.19(2B). The words 'associate' and 'associated with' have the same meaning as in RTA Protocol, para 1.1(1A) and (10A), respectively: see CPR, r 45n19(2E).

371 See CPR, r 48.1.

372 See pre-1 April 2013 CPR, r 45.31. Uniquely, under the CPR, express provision is made for success fees to be charged by defendants as well as claimants. This is probably a reflection of the fact that many defendant solicitors have, over the years, begun to provide legal services under discounted collective conditional fee agreements.

373 See pre-1 April 2013 CPR, r 45.32(6).

374 That is, different success fees may be payable for costs incurred during different parts of the claim. In cases that are determined at Stage 3 (be that on the papers or at a Stage 3 hearing), the claimant will be entitled to a 12.5 per cent uplift on Stage 1 fixed costs and Stage 2 fixed costs, and will be entitled to a 100 per cent uplift on Stage 3 fixed costs.

375 See pre-1 April 2013 CPR, r 45.31(4).

376 See CPR, r 48.1(1)(a)(i)(bb). It should be noted that additional staged premiums are payable even if the stage (and therefore additional premium) was triggered only after 1 April 2013: see *Plevin v Paragon Personal Finance Ltd* [2017] UKSC 23.

377 CPR, r 45.19.

378 See CPR, r 48.1(1)(a)(iii).

Portal costs stage by stage

What is set out below is only a brief overview of the provisions of the relevant Protocols. In particular, procedural provisions that have no direct consequence in terms of costs may have been omitted. **50.191**

A claimant's decision not to engage the relevant Protocol

Both Protocols specifically state that the claimant is able to give notice that the claim is unsuitable for this Protocol, for example because there are complex issues of fact or law, or because the claimants contemplate applying for a GLO. Where this happens, then the claim will no longer continue under the relevant Protocol.[379] Where the court considers that the claimant acted unreasonably in giving such notice, it will award no more than the fixed costs in CPR, r 45.18.[380] Similar provisions apply in relation to the EL/PL Protocol.[381] **50.192**

Stage 1 (liability)

Stage 1 is the process by which the parties set out their respective cases; it also provides for an interim payment of costs (although Briggs LJ has made it clear that this is a payment that is final, in the sense that it is not merely a payment on account).[382] If the defendant's insurer disputes liability or does not respond, the case exits the Portal. If, however, liability is admitted, Stage 1 comes to an end and the Stage 1 fixed costs become payable (within ten business days of receipt of the Stage 2 settlement pack). **50.193**

Starting claims

The claims notification form Claims are started under the Protocols by the claimant's solicitor completing a claims notification form (CNF).[383] The CNF is an electronic document,[384] which is transmitted to the defendant's insurer. At the same time (or as soon as practicable thereafter) a 'defendant-only CNF' (which is a similar form, but which contains slightly less information) should be sent to the defendant by first-class post.[385] **50.194**

RTA claims In an RTA case, before the CNF is sent to the defendant, the claimant's legal representative must undertake a search of online personal injury inquiry service askCUE PI[386] and must record the unique reference number generated by that search in the CNF.[387] **50.195**

Claims for vehicle-related damages will ordinarily be dealt with outside the provisions of RTA Protocol under industry agreements between relevant organisations and insurers,[388] but where there is a claim for vehicle-related damages, the claimant must explain in the CNF whether the claim is being dealt with by the claimant's legal representatives or whether it is being dealt with by a third party.[389] **50.196**

---

379 See RTA Protocol, para 7.76; EL/PL Protocol, para 7.59.
380 See RTA Protocol, para 7.76; EL/PL Protocol, para 7.59.
381 See RTA Protocol, para 7.58; EL/PL Protocol, para 7.61.
382 See *JC and A Solicitors Ltd v Iqbal* [2017] EWCA Civ 355, at [31].
383 See RTA Protocol, para 6.1; EL/PL Protocol, para 6.1.
384 There are two ways of completing the form: using a standard web browser (http://www.rtapiclaimsprocess.org.uk) or using an application-to-application interface.
385 See RTA Protocol, para 6.1(b); EL/PL Protocol, para 6.1(b).
386 See http://www.askCUE.co.uk
387 See RTA Protocol, para 6.3A(1).
388 See RTA Protocol, para 6.4.
389 See RTA Protocol, para 6.4(1) and (2).

50.197 **Responding to claims and the insurer response** The defendant's insurer must send an electronic acknowledgement the day after receiving the CNF.[390] Subject to what is said immediately below, the insurer will then have a certain amount of time in which to complete the 'insurer response' section of the CNF and to return it to the claimant. This is 15 business days for a road traffic accident claim that is not against the MIB,[391] 30 business days for an employers' liability claim[392] or a claim against the MIB[393] and 40 business days for a public liability claim.[394]

50.198 *Failure to complete the CNF* In a road traffic accident case, if the CNF does not contain the unique reference number referred to at 50.195, the insurer is entitled to require the claimant to resend the CNF with the reference number inserted. If this happens, then the times set out immediately above will not start to run until that request has been satisfied.[395] If the insurer does not make such a request, however, time begins to run immediately[396] and the insurer is debarred from complaining about the putative lack of unique reference number for the purposes of exiting the RTA Protocol.[397] Other than as already noted, where the defendant considers that inadequate mandatory information has been provided in the CNF, that shall be a valid reason for the defendant to decide that the claim should no longer continue under the relevant Protocol.[398] CPR, r 45.24(2) and (2A), sets out the sanctions available to the court where it considers that the claimant provided inadequate information in the CNF.

50.199 *Early exit and integration with other protocols* There are five circumstances in which a claim will automatically exit the relevant Protocol during Stage 1.[399] These are when, within the 15-, 30- or 40-day periods mentioned at 50.197, the defendant:

- makes an admission of liability, but alleges contributory negligence (other than in relation to the claimant's admitted failure to wear a seatbelt);
- does not complete and send the insurer response;
- does not admit liability (in which case reasons must be given);[400]
- notifies the claimant that they consider there to be inadequate mandatory information in the CNF (but see 50.243); or
- notifies the claimant that they consider that if proceedings were to be issued, the small claims track would be the normal track for the claim.

50.200 Where any of these conditions exist, claims will exit the relevant Protocol and proceed under the existing Pre-action Protocol for Personal Injury Claims, starting at para 6.3 (or para 5.1 if the claim exits the Protocol by reason of inadequate information on the CNF).

---

390 See RTA Protocol, para 6.10; EL/PL Protocol, para 6.9.
391 See RTA Protocol, para 6.11; EL/PL Protocol, para 6.11.
392 See EL/PL Protocol, para 6.11(a).
393 See RTA Protocol, para 6.13. This time limit will apply even if the MIB passes the claim to an insurer to act on its behalf: see RTA Protocol, para 6.14.
394 See EL/PL Protocol, para 6.11(b).
395 See RTA Protocol, para 6.3A(2).
396 See RTA Protocol, para 6.3A(3).
397 See RTA Protocol, para 6.8(2).
398 See RTA Protocol, para 6.8(1); EL/PL Protocol, para 6.7.
399 See RTA Protocol, para 6.15; EL/PL Protocol, para 6.13.
400 See RTA Protocol, para 6.16; EL/PL Protocol, para 6.14.

This will provide the defendant with a maximum of three months in which to investigate the claim.

Admissions and early payments Except where the claimant is a child (see 50.266), where liability is admitted (or admitted along with an allegation that the claimant failed to wear a seatbelt[401]), the defendant must pay the Stage 1 fixed costs (see 50.176–50.177) within ten days of receiving the Stage 2 settlement pack.[402] In an RTA case involving a soft-tissue injury, the defendant must also pay the cost of obtaining the fixed-cost medical report and any cost for obtaining medical records.[403] **50.201**

Where a defendant fails to pay in time, the claimant may give written notice that the claim will no longer continue under the relevant Protocol.[404] Any such notice must be given within ten business days of the defendant's failure, in default of which the claim will continue under the relevant Protocol.[405] If the claimant exercises the right to give notice of non-continuance unreasonably, the court is able to take that conduct into account when deciding the issue of costs.[406] **50.202**

Stage 2 (evidence and negotiations)

Stage 2 is the stage during which the parties obtain evidence and try to negotiate. The claimant submits a Stage 2 settlement pack, comprising: (a) the Stage 2 settlement pack form (which contains an offer to settle); (b) a medical report (or reports); (c) evidence of pecuniary losses; and (d) evidence of disbursements (for example the cost of any medical report). If the defendant disputes the claimant's valuation of the claim, they may enter into negotiations and/or put forward their own offer by setting out their proposed figures on the Stage 2 settlement pack form. If the matter does not settle, the claimant sends to the defendant a court proceedings pack. This pack sets out the claimant's claimed losses, the defendant's responses and the final offers of both sides. It also includes the evidence that both sides have submitted during Stage 2. The defendant then pays the amount of the defendant's final offer, together with all fixed costs due up to the end of Stage 2; the costs of the medical report are paid directly. Those costs are payable regardless of whether the matter proceeds to Stage 3. **50.203**

Medical evidence The claimant is required to obtain a medical report[407] and to check its factual accuracy before the same is sent to the defendant.[408] No further opportunity will be afforded to the claimant to do this once the report has been disclosed.[409] Where appropriate, the claimant may obtain a report from more than one medical experts of different disciplines,[410] or a second or subsequent report from the same expert.[411] Where such **50.204**

[401] See RTA Protocol, para 6.18(2).
[402] See RTA Protocol, para 6.18; EL/PL Protocol, para 6.16.
[403] See RTA Protocol, para 6.18. These monies will be payable only if invoices for the cost of obtaining the medical report and any medical records in a soft-tissue injury claim were included in the Stage 2 Settlement Pack: see RTA Protocol, para 6.18(2).
[404] See RTA Protocol, para 6.19; EL/PL Protocol, para 6.17.
[405] See RTA Protocol, para 6.19; EL/PL Protocol, para 6.17.
[406] See CPR, r 45.24.
[407] RTA Protocol, para 7.1; EL/PL Protocol, para 7.1.
[408] RTA Protocol, para 7.3; EL/PL Protocol, para 7.3.
[409] RTA Protocol, para 7.3; EL/PL Protocol, para 7.3.
[410] RTA Protocol, para 7.2; EL/PL Protocol, para 7.2.
[411] RTA Protocol, para 7.8; EL/PL Protocol, para 7.6.

a report is required, the parties should agree to stay the process in the relevant Protocol for a suitable period, in which case the claimant may request an interim payment[412] (see 50.210–50.211).

50.205 In most road traffic accident claims with a value of no more than £10,000, it is expected that the medical expert will not need to see any medical records.[413]

50.206 If a claim is a soft-tissue injury claim in which the CNF was submitted on or after 1 October 2014,[414] then the monies that can be claimed for medical evidence are restricted.[415] In this regard, 'soft-tissue injury claim' means a claim brought by an occupant of a motor vehicle in which the significant physical injury caused is a soft-tissue injury, which includes claims in which there is a minor psychological injury secondary in significance to the physical injury.[416] The restrictions are as follows.

- The first report must be a fixed-cost medical report from an accredited medical expert selected for the claim via the MedCo[417] website.[418]
- It is expected that only one medical report will be required;[419] a further medical report, whether from the first expert instructed or from an expert in another discipline, will be justified only where it is recommended in the first expert's report and that report has first been disclosed to the defendant.[420] Where such a report is required, the parties should agree to stay the process in relevant Protocol for a suitable period, in which case the claimant may request an interim payment[421] (see 50.210–50.211).
- Where the claimant obtains more than one medical report, the first report must be a fixed-cost medical report from an accredited medical expert selected via MedCo and any further report from an expert in any of the following disciplines must also be a fixed-cost medical report:
  - a consultant orthopaedic surgeon;
  - an A&E consultant;
  - a GP registered with the General Medical Council (GMC); or
  - a physiotherapist registered with the Health and Care Professions Council (HCPC).[422]

  The costs of any such report is limited in accordance with CPR, r 45.19(2A) (see 50.184), but the cost of obtaining a further report from an expert not listed above is not subject to those restrictions. That said, the use of the expert and the cost must be justified.[423]

50.207 Where more than one report is obtained, the claimant should explain in the Stage 2 settlement pack why this was so.[424] If relevant, the defendant should, in the Stage 2

412 See RTA Protocol, para 7.12; EL/PL Protocol, para 7.7.
413 RTA Protocol, para 7.5.
414 See Civil Procedure (Amendment No 6) Rules 2014 (SI 2014/2044), r 14.
415 See RTA Protocol, para 4.7.
416 See CPR, r 45.95I(2E); RTA Protocol, para 1.1(16A).
417 See http://www.medco.org.uk
418 See RTA Protocol, para 7.8A(1).
419 See RTA Protocol, para 7.8B(1).
420 See RTA Protocol, para 7.8B(2).
421 See RTA Protocol, para 7.12; EL/PL Protocol, para 7.7.
422 See RTA Protocol, para 7.8B(3); see also PD 8B, para 6.1A(1).
423 See PD 8B, para 6.1A(2).
424 See RTA Protocol, para 7.31; EL/PL Protocol, para 7.29.

settlement pack, identify the report(s) or advice for which they will not pay and explain why.[425]

Non-medical expert reports In most cases, a report from a non-medical expert will not be required, but a report may be obtained where it is reasonably required to value the claim.[426] Where such a report is required, the parties should agree to stay the process in the relevant Protocol for a suitable period, in which case the claimant may request an interim payment[427] (see 50.210–50.211). **50.208**

Specialist legal advice for the purposes of valuation In most cases under this Protocol, it is expected that the claimant's legal representative will be able to value the claim. In some cases with a value of more than £10,000, additional advice from a specialist solicitor or from counsel may be justified where it is reasonably required to value the claim.[428] Where such an advice is obtained, the claimant should explain in the Stage 2 settlement pack why they obtained it.[429] If relevant, the defendant should identify, in the Stage 2 settlement pack, the advice for which they will not pay and explain why.[430] **50.209**

Interim payments A notable feature of the relevant Protocol is the fact that they make provision for early interim payments. Such payments relate primarily to damages, but they are relevant because they may influence the costs. The process begins when the claimant's representative serves an interim settlement pack (ISP), in which the claimant is able to request an interim payment. **50.210**

The request may be for £1,000 or for more, as follows.[431] **50.211**

- **£1,000** If the claimant requests an interim payment of £1,000, the defendant must make such interim payment within ten business days of receiving the interim settlement pack.[432] Failure to do so will result in the claimant being entitled to exit the relevant Protocol. Notice of an intention to quit the relevant Protocol must be given within ten business days of the expiry of the defendant's time to pay; if this is not done, the claim will continue under the relevant Protocol.[433]
- **More than £1,000** If the claimant requests an interim payment of more than £1,000, the claimant must specify the amount requested, the heads of damage that are the subject of the request and the reasons for the request.[434] Once this has been done, the defendant must, within 15 business days of receiving the interim settlement pack, pay:
  - the full amount requested (*less* any deductible benefits);
  - £1,000 and explain why the requested figure has not been agreed; or
  - more than £1,000, but less than the requested sum, and explain why the requested figure has not been agreed.[435]

---

[425] See RTA Protocol, para 7.31; EL/PL Protocol, para 7.29.
[426] See the RTA Protocol, para 7.9; EL/PL Protocol, para 7.7.
[427] See the RTA Protocol, para 7.12; EL/PL Protocol, para 7.7.
[428] See RTA Protocol, para 7.10; EL/PL Protocol, para 7.11.
[429] See RTA Protocol, para 7.31; EL/PL Protocol, para 7.29.
[430] See RTA Protocol, para 7.31; EL/PL Protocol, para 7.29.
[431] There seems to be no provision that allows the claimant to request less than £1,000.
[432] RTA Protocol, paras 7.13 and 7.18; EL/PL Protocol, paras 7.12 and 7.17.
[433] RTA Protocol, paras 7.28–7.30; EL/PL Protocol, paras 7.26–7.28.
[434] RTA Protocol, para 7.16; EL/PL Protocol, para 7.15.
[435] RTA Protocol, para 7.19; EL/PL Protocol, para 7.18.

If anything other than the full amount is paid, the claimant is able to elect to exit the relevant Protocol.[436] If the claimant does this, but is subsequently awarded no more than the amount the defendant had offered, the claimant's costs will be limited to Stages 1 and 2 fixed costs, disbursements and, if appropriate, the success fee.[437]

The above provisions do not apply to child claimants.[438]

50.212 *Submitting the Stage 2 settlement pack to the defendant* Within 15 business days of the claimant approving the final medical report, a Stage 2 settlement pack must be submitted to the defendant.[439] A defendant will not know when the claimant gave their approval, so it is unclear how this aspect of the timetable will be policed. It is implicit that the claimant is required to make an offer when sending the pack to the defendant.[440] The defendant is given a second opportunity to arrest the engagement of the Protocol on the grounds that the claim is a small claims track case.[441]

50.213 Where more than one expert report or an advice from a specialist solicitor or counsel has been obtained, the claimant should explain in the Stage 2 settlement pack why this was needed.[442]

50.214 *Consideration of the claim* The parties are given 35 business days in which to agree settlement (that is, 'the total consideration period'). Within 15 business days of receiving the Stage 2 settlement pack, the defendant must either accept the claimant's offer or make a counter-offer (that is, 'the initial consideration period').[443] Failure to respond within that period results in automatic exit from the RTA Protocol. The parties are explicitly given the ability to agree extensions of time.[444]

50.215 If relevant, the defendant should, in the Stage 2 settlement pack, identify the report(s) or advice for which they will not pay and explain why.[445]

50.216 *The defendant accepts the offer or makes a counter-offer* The defendant's counter-offer must propose an amount for each head of loss and may make a total offer that is more than the sum of the individual parts;[446] thereafter, the parties can use the remaining time to negotiate settlement (that is, 'the negotiation period'). If a party makes an offer five business days or fewer before the end of the consideration period, there will be a further five-day period for the offeree to consider the offer (that is, 'the further consideration period') during which no further offers can be made.[447]

---

436 RTA Protocol, paras 7.28–7.30; EL/PL Protocol, paras 7.26–7.28.

437 CPR, r 45.24(3). In particular, no Stage 3 costs will be payable.

438 RTA Protocol, paras 7.26–17.27; EL/PL Protocol, paras 7.24–7.25. Part 7 proceedings must be commenced and an application made to the court.

439 See RTA Protocol, para 7.33; EL/PL Protocol, para 7.31.

440 See, eg, RTA Protocol, para 7.38; EL/PL Protocol, para 7.35: 'Within the initial consideration period … the defendant must either accept the offer made by the Claimant on the Stage 2 Settlement Pack Form or make a counter-offer using that form.'

441 See RTA Protocol, para 7.39(a); EL/PL Protocol, para 7.36(a).

442 See RTA Protocol, para 7.31; EL/PL Protocol, para 7.29.

443 See RTA Protocol, para 7.35; EL/PL Protocol, para 7.32.

444 Pursuant to RTA Protocol, para 7.36; EL/PL Protocol, para 7.33.

445 See RTA Protocol, para 7.36; EL/PL Protocol, para 7.33.

446 RTA Protocol, para 7.41; EL/PL Protocol, para 7.38.

447 RTA Protocol, para 7.37; EL/PL Protocol, para 7.34.

Where a claimant receives a counter-offer, they will have until the end of the total consideration period to accept or reject the offer.[448] It is theoretically possible for a claimant to postpone rejection of the offer until the last day of the total consideration period, thereby ensuring entry into Stage 3. If the claimant has acted unreasonably in that regard, however, their opponent may be successful in challenging entitlement to Stage 3 costs—although there is no authority on that point. **50.217**

Withdrawal of offer after the consideration period Where, following the expiry of the total consideration period (or further consideration period), a party withdraws an offer made in the Stage 2 settlement pack, the claim automatically exits the relevant Protocol.[449] There is the potential for abuse in this regard.[450] **50.218**

Settlement Where settlement is achieved—except where the claimant is a child (see 50.266)—the defendant must pay: (a) agreed damages, less CRU and interim payments; (b) any unpaid Stage 1 fixed costs; (c) Stage 2 fixed costs; (d) disbursements as applicable; and (e) any success fee, as applicable. This must be done within ten business days of the end of the relevant period during which agreement was reached.[451] **50.219**

Settlement at Stage 2 where the claimant is a child Where the claimant is a child and there is a settlement at Stage 2, then an application will need to be made to the court to approve the settlement. Where this happens, in so far as costs are concerned, then the following rules will apply.[452] **50.220**

- **Approval given** Where the settlement is approved at the settlement hearing, the court will order the costs to be paid in accordance with CPR, r 45.21(2).[453] This means that the court will order the defendant to pay:
  - the Stage 1 and 2 fixed costs;
  - the Stage 3 Type A, B and C fixed costs; and
  - disbursements allowed in accordance with CPR, r 45.19 (see 50.181–50.188).[454]
- **Approval not given at first hearing** Where the court does not approve the settlement at a settlement hearing, it will order the defendant to pay the Stage 1 and 2 fixed costs.[455]
- **Approval not given until second hearing** Where the settlement is not approved at the first settlement hearing and the court orders a second settlement hearing, at which the settlement is approved, the court will order the costs to be paid in accordance

[448] RTA Protocol, para 7.43; EL/PL Protocol, para 7.40.
[449] RTA Protocol, para 7.46; EL/PL Protocol, para 7.43.
[450] There is a risk that less scrupulous claimants will make offers that are unlikely to be accepted by defendants, only to withdraw them following the total consideration period and thus obtain non-Portal costs when Part 7 proceedings are issued. It seems that the new regime offers the defendant very little protection from this potential abuse. It would seem that the only way in which a defendant can protect themselves against this unsatisfactory position is to replicate every offer made within the Stage 2 Settlement Pack and subsequent total consideration period in correspondence as a fully compliant Part 36 offer.
[451] RTA Protocol, para 7.47; EL/PL Protocol, para 7.44. See, however, RTA Protocol, paras 7.73–7.74; EL/PL Protocol, paras 7.46–7.47, under which, at the date of the acceptance of an offer in the Stage 2 Settlement Pack, the defendant does not have a certificate of recoverable benefits that will remain in force for at least ten days.
[452] See CPR, r 45.21(1).
[453] PD 8B, para 12.2.
[454] See CPR, r 45.21(2).
[455] See CPR, r 45.21(3).

with CPR, r 45.21(4)–(6).[456] This means that the court will order the defendant to pay:
- the Stage 3 Type A and C fixed costs for the first settlement hearing;
- disbursements allowed in accordance with CPR, r 45.19 (see 50.181–50.188); and
- the Stage 3 Type B fixed costs for one of the hearings.[457]

The court, in its discretion, may also order:
- the defendant to pay an additional amount of either or both of—
  - the Stage 3 Type A fixed costs;
  - the Stage 3 Type B fixed costs; or
- the claimant to pay an amount equivalent to either or both of—
  - the Stage 3 Type A fixed costs;
  - the Stage 3 Type B fixed costs.[458]

- **Not suitable for Stage 3 procedure** Where the settlement is not approved at the first settlement hearing and the court orders that the claim is not suitable to be determined under the Stage 3 procedure, the court will order costs to be paid in accordance with CPR, r 45.23, and will give directions[459] (see 50.251).
- **No approval, even at second hearing** Where the settlement is not approved at the second settlement hearing, the claim will no longer continue under the Stage 3 procedure and the court will give directions.[460]

50.221 **Costs protection** The offers contained within the Stage 2 settlement pack, and those made during the total and further consideration periods, are not ordinary Part 36 offers because they will not comply with the requirements set out in CPR, r 36.5. This is because the pack does not contain the necessary notices. Moreover, they will not have effect as Part 36 offers until Stage 3 is commenced.[461] It is therefore not wholly clear how a defendant can garner costs protection. One method would be to repeat every offer made within the Stage 2 settlement pack as a separate Part 36 offer, but this would be cumbersome and it would afford protection only if the claim were subsequently to exit the RTA Protocol.[462]

50.222 **Vehicle-related damages** Where they were originally dealt with outside the Protocol, but subsequently brought within it, vehicle-related damages are referred to as 'additional damages'. Once the total consideration period (or the further consideration period) has expired, if both the 'original damages' (that is, those damages set out in the Stage 2 settlement pack) and the additional damages remain outstanding, the claimant must incorporate those losses into the existing claim by amending the Stage 2 settlement pack.[463] If vehicle-related damages were included in the pack from the outset, they remain classified as 'original damages'.

50.223 **Failure to reach agreement: general** Where the parties do not reach an agreement, the claimant must send to the defendant the court proceedings pack form, which must contain:

---

[456] PD 8B, para 12.3.
[457] See CPR, r 45.21(4) and (5).
[458] See CPR, r 45.21(6).
[459] PD 8B, para 12.4.
[460] PD 8B, para 12.5.
[461] See CPR, r 36.26.
[462] See CPR, r 36.28(1) and (2).
[463] RTA Protocol, paras 7.51–7.54.

- in Part A, the final schedule of the claimant's losses and the defendant's responses, together with supporting comments and evidence from both parties on any disputed heads of damage; and
- in Part B, the final offer and counter-offer from the Stage 2 settlement pack form and, where relevant, the offer and any final counter-offer.[464]

Comments in the court proceedings pack (Part A) form must not raise anything that has not been raised in the Stage 2 settlement pack form.[465]

The defendant should check that the court proceedings pack (Part A and Part B) form complies with the relevant requirements. If the defendant considers that the form does not comply, it must be returned to the claimant within five days with an explanation of why.[466] **50.224**

Non-settlement payment by the defendant at the end of Stage 2 Where the claim does not settle at the end of Stage 2, then—except where the claimant is a child—the defendant must pay to the claimant: **50.225**

- the final offer of damages made by the defendant in the court proceedings pack (Part A and Part B) form;
- any unpaid Stage 1 fixed costs;
- the Stage 2 fixed costs; and
- the disbursements that have been agreed (or such amount for the disbursement as the defendant considers reasonable).[467]

The defendant must pay these amounts within 15 days of receiving the court proceedings pack (Part A and Part B) form from the claimant.[468] Where this is not done, the claimant may give written notice that the claim will no longer continue under this Protocol and start proceedings under CPR, Part 7.[469] **50.226**

Stage 3 (court proceedings and adjudication)

Stage 3 is the litigation stage. It is governed by both CPR, Part 45, Section III,[470] and PD 8B. **50.227**

At the end of Stage 2, if agreement has not been reached, the claimant has the right to bring the matter before the court. The claimant must issue proceedings in the County Court under CPR, Part 8, but PD 8B substantially modifies the Part 8 procedure so as to make it suitable for low-value claims in which only quantum is in dispute. The court assesses the items of damages that remain in dispute, either on paper or at a single 'Stage 3 hearing'. **50.228**

Settlement before proceedings are issued under Stage 3 It may happen that the claim settles before proceedings are issued. In particular, where there is a settlement after the court proceedings pack has been sent to the defendant, but before proceedings are issued under Stage 3 and where the settlement is more than the defendant's relevant Protocol **50.229**

[464] RTA Protocol, para 7.64; EL/PL Protocol, para 7.48.
[465] RTA Protocol, para 7.66; EL/PL Protocol, para 7.49.
[466] RTA Protocol, para 7.67; EL/PL Protocol, para 7.50.
[467] RTA Protocol, paras 7.70 and 7.71; EL/PL Protocol, paras 7.53 and 7.54.
[468] RTA Protocol, para 7.72; EL/PL Protocol, para 7.55.
[469] RTA Protocol, para 7.75; EL/PL Protocol, para 7.58.
[470] See CPR, r 45.16(1).

offer, then the fixed costs will include an additional amount equivalent to the Stage 3 Type A fixed costs.[471]

50.230 **Application to the court to determine the amount of damages** Where the claim has not been capable of settlement following the procedure in Stage 2, the claimant should issue proceedings pursuant to PD 8B.[472] An application to the court to determine the amount of damages must be started by a claim form.[473] The claim form must state:

- that the claimant followed the relevant Protocol;
- the date on which the court proceedings pack (Part A) form was sent to the defendant;
- whether the claim should be determined by the court on the papers or at a Stage 3 hearing;
- dates to avoid for the Stage 3 hearing; and
- the value of the claim.[474]

50.231 **Filing and serving written evidence** The claim form must be filed with the following items:

- Part A of the court proceedings pack form;
- Part B of the court proceedings pack form in a sealed envelope;
- copies of medical reports;
- evidence of special damages;
- evidence of disbursements; and
- a notice of funding.[475]

50.232 Service on the defendant of the court proceedings pack form, Parts A and B, remains part of Stage 2. Stage 3 begins when the Part 8 claim form and the documents set out above are filed at court.[476] In particular, the filing of the claim form and documents set out above represent the start of Stage 3 for the purposes of fixed costs.[477]

50.233 **Acknowledgement of service** The defendant must file and serve an acknowledgement of service in Form N210B not more than 14 days after service of the claim form.[478] The acknowledgement of service must state whether the defendant:

- contests the amount of damages claimed;
- contests the making of an order for damages;
- disputes the court's jurisdiction;
- objects to the use of the Stage 3 procedure; or
- wants the claim to be determined by the court on the papers or at a Stage 3 hearing.[479]

Where the defendant objects to the use of the Stage 3 procedure, reasons must be given.[480]

---

[471] See CPR, r 45.23A.
[472] RTA Protocol, para 8.1; EL/PL Protocol, para 8.1. See also PD 8B, para 1.1.
[473] PD 8B, para 5.1.
[474] PD 8B, para 5.2.
[475] PD 8B, para 6.1.
[476] CPR, r 8; PD 8B, para 6.1.
[477] PD 8B, para 6.2.
[478] PD 8B, para 8.1.
[479] PD 8B, para 8.3.
[480] PD 8B, para 8.4.

Dismissal of the claim Where the defendant opposes the claim because the claimant has not followed the procedure set out in the relevant Protocol, or has filed and served additional or new evidence with the claim form that had not been provided under the relevant Protocol, the court will dismiss the claim and the claimant may start proceedings under CPR, Part 7.[481] CPR, r 45.24, sets out the costs consequences of failing to comply with the relevant Protocol (see 50.258). **50.234**

Protocol offers The final Stage 2 settlement pack offer for each side, now contained within Part B of the court proceedings pack form, becomes an effective 'RTA Protocol offer' pursuant to CPR, rr 36.25 and 36.26. The offers are contained in a sealed envelope.[482] **50.235**

RTA Protocol offers must not be communicated to the court during the currency of the claim and other offers must not be communicated to the court at all.[483] Where a claimant achieves a result that is less than or equal to the defendant's RTA Protocol offer, the claimant will pay the fixed costs[484] under CPR, r 45.38 (*plus* interest),[485] but where they achieve a result for more than their own offer, they will be awarded fixed costs *plus* enhanced interest on both the costs and damages.[486] The effect of any Protocol offer will depend on how much the claimant is awarded, as follows. **50.236**

- **Where the claimant beats the defendant's offer** Where a claimant obtains judgment against the defendant for an amount of damages that is more than the defendant's Protocol offer, but less than the claimant's Protocol offer,[487] then the court will order the defendant to pay:
  - where not already paid by the defendant, the Stage 1 and 2 fixed costs (see 50.174–50.177);
  - where the claim is determined—
    - on the papers, Stage 3 Type A fixed costs;
    - at a Stage 3 hearing, Stage 3 Type A and B fixed costs; or
    - at a Stage 3 hearing and the claimant is a child, Type A, B and C fixed costs; and

  disbursements allowed in accordance with CPR, r 45.19 (see 50.181–50.188).[488]
- **Where the claimant beats their own offer** Where a claimant is fortunate enough to obtain judgment against the defendant for an amount of damages that is equal to or more than the claimant's Protocol offer, the following will be payable *in addition to monies set out above*:
  - interest on the whole of the damages awarded at a rate not exceeding 10 per cent above base rate for some or all of the period starting with the date specified in CPR, r 36.26;
  - interest on those fixed costs at a rate not exceeding 10 per cent above base rate; and
  - an additional amount calculated in accordance with CPR, r 36.17(4)(d).[489]

---

[481] PD 8B, para 9.1.
[482] PD 8B, para 6.1(2).
[483] See CPR, r 36.28(1) and (2).
[484] See CPR, r 36.29(2)(a).
[485] See CPR, r 36.29(2)(b). The interest starts to run from the first business day after the deemed date of the RTA Protocol offer under CPR, r 36.26.
[486] See CPR, r 36.29(4). The interest must not exceed 10 per cent above base rate.
[487] See CPR, rr 36.29(3) and 45.20.
[488] See CPR, rr 45.20 and 36.29(1)(b) and (c).
[489] See CPR, rr 36.29(4)(b) and 45.20.

- **Where the claimant fails to beat the defendant's offer** Where the claimant is not so fortunate and where they obtain judgment against the defendant for an amount of damages that is less than or equal to the amount of the defendant's Protocol offer, the court must order the claimant to pay:
  - the fixed costs in CPR, r 45.26, which are:
    - o where the claim is determined—
      on the papers, Stage 3 Type A fixed costs;
      at a hearing, Stage 3 Type A and B fixed costs; or
    - o any Stage 3 disbursements allowed in accordance with CPR, r 45.19 (see 50.181–50.188); and
  - interest on those fixed costs from the first business day after the deemed date of the Protocol offer under CPR, r 36.26.[490]

50.237 A party may withdraw a Protocol offer after proceedings have started only with the court's permission.[491] Where the court gives permission, the claim will no longer continue under the Stage 3 procedure and the court will give directions. The court will give permission only where there is good reason for the claim not to continue under the Stage 3 procedure.[492]

The court's powers regarding case management

50.238 *Allocation* The claim will not be allocated to a track. CPR, Parts 26–29 do not apply.[493]

50.239 *Unsuitable claims* Where the court considers that further evidence must be provided by any party and the claim is not suitable to continue under the Stage 3 procedure, PD 8B, para 7.2, provides that the court may allocate the claim to a track, order that the claim will continue under CPR, Part 7, and give directions.[494] In the event that the court does this, Stage 3 fixed costs will not be payable.[495]

50.240 Whilst *obiter*, Jackson LJ has suggested that such an order may be appropriate if, for example, the claim is for very high car hire charges that involve complex issues of law or fact that are not suitable for resolution at a Stage 3 hearing.[496] That may be so, but it would not be appropriate to allocate a claim to the small claims track merely because the personal injury element of the case had settled. In this regard, Jackson LJ had the following to say:

> 'Once a case is within the RTA protocol, it does not automatically exit when the personal injury claim is settled. On the contrary, the RTA process is carefully designed to whittle down the disputes between the parties as the case passes through the various stages. It is to be expected that the sum in issue between the parties will be much smaller when the case reaches Stage 3 than it was back in Stage 1. The mere fact that the personal injury claim has been resolved is not specified as being a reason to exit from the RTA process.'[497]

50.241 In circumstances in which PD 8B, para 7.2, did not apply, then technically it would also be permissible for the court to exercise its discretion under CPR, r 8.1(3), to disapply the

490 See CPR, r 36.29(3).
491 CPR, r 8; PD 8B, para 10.1.
492 PD 8B, para 10.1.
493 PD 8B, para 17.1.
494 PD 8B, para 7.2.
495 See PD 8B, para 7.3.
496 *Phillips v Willis* [2016] EWCA Civ 401, at [35].
497 *Ibid*, at [33].

relevant Protocol (the provision that allows the court, at any stage, to order the claim to continue as if the claimant had not used the Part 8 procedure). That said, Jackson LJ has explained that the power under CPR, r 8.1(3), should not be used to subvert the Protocol process.[498]

Adjournments Where the court adjourns a settlement hearing or a Stage 3 hearing, it may, in its discretion, order the costs to be paid in accordance with CPR, r 45.27.[499] This means that it may, in its discretion, order a party to pay: **50.242**

- an additional amount of Stage 3 Type B fixed costs; and
- any court fee for that adjournment.[500]

Consideration of the claim Where the claim is to continue, the court will order that damages are to be assessed either on the papers or (if either party so requests or if the court so orders) at a Stage 3 hearing.[501] The court will give the parties at least 21 days' notice of the date of the determination on the papers or the date of the Stage 3 hearing.[502] Where, however, the claim is determined on the papers, the court will give reasons for its decision in the judgment.[503] **50.243**

Costs consequences of a Stage 3 determination Where the claimant obtains a judgment for an amount less than or equal to the defendant's RTA Protocol offer, the claimant will be ordered to pay: **50.244**

- the appropriate type of Stage 3 fixed costs (the claimant having already been paid Stage 1 and Stage 2 fixed costs);
- disbursements; and
- a success fee.[504]

Where the claimant obtains a judgment for an amount more than the defendant's RTA Protocol offer, but less than the claimant's RTA Protocol offer, the defendant will be ordered to pay: **50.245**

- any outstanding Stage 1 or Stage 2 fixed costs;
- the appropriate type of Stage 3 fixed costs;
- disbursements; and
- a success fee.[505]

Where the claimant obtains a judgment for an amount equal to or more than the claimant's own RTA Protocol offer, the court will order the defendant to pay: **50.246**

- any outstanding Stage 1 or Stage 2 fixed costs;
- the appropriate type of Stage 3 fixed costs;
- disbursements;

---

498 *Ibid*, at [36], *per* Jackson LJ.
499 See PD 8B, para 14.1.
500 CPR, r 45.27.
501 See PD 8B, para 11.1.
502 See PD 8B, para 11.2.
503 See PD 8B, para 11.4.
504 CPR, rr 36.29 and 45.26.
505 CPR, rr 36.29 and 45.20.

- a success fee; and
- enhanced interest on damages and costs.[506]

50.247 Whilst not binding, Judge Freedman has found that where a claimant issues proceedings and they merely 'equal' an offer that was made prior to issue, they will, in substance, have lost; as such, it would be illogical and irrational to allow the claimant to recover an issue fee.[507]

50.248 **Where the parties have settled after proceedings have started** Where proceedings have been started under CPR, Part 8, in accordance with PD 8B and the parties have reached written agreement on all issues (including which party is to pay the costs), but they have failed to agree the amount of those costs, then either party may make an application for the court to determine the costs.[508] Where such an application is made, then if the claimant is a child, the provisions set out in CPR, r 45.22, will apply (see 50.250–50.251), but if the claimant is not a child, then the following provisions will apply.[509]

- **Claimant has done better than the defendant's relevant Protocol offer** Where the settlement is more than the defendant's relevant Protocol offer, the court will order the defendant to pay:
  – the Stage 1 and 2 fixed costs where not already paid by the defendant;
  – the Stage 3 Type A fixed costs; and
  – disbursements allowed in accordance with CPR, r 45.19.[510]
- **Claimant has failed to do better than the defendant's relevant Protocol offer** Where the settlement is less than or equal to the defendant's relevant Protocol offer, the court will order the defendant to pay:
  – the Stage 1 and 2 fixed costs where not already paid by the defendant; and
  – disbursements allowed in accordance with CPR, r 45.19.[511]

  The court may, in its discretion, order either party to pay the costs of the application.[512]

50.249 Perhaps rather unnecessarily, CPR, Part 45, Section III, expressly provides that CPR, r 44.5 (namely, the amount of costs where costs are payable pursuant to a contract), does not apply to an application under the foregoing provisions.[513]

50.250 **Approval of child settlements at Stage 3** The relevant Protocol retains the need for court approval of settlements made on behalf of a child claimant.[514] Where the claimant is a child, the claimant must provide to the court the following in relation to a settlement made before or after the start of proceedings:

- the draft consent order;
- the advice by counsel, solicitor or other legal representative on the amount of damages; and

506 CPR, r 36.29.
507 See *Gudgin v Lowe* (unreported), 1 June 2016, Newcastle County Court, at [5].
508 See CPR, r 45.29(1) and (2).
509 See CPR, rr 45.29(3) and 45.25(2).
510 See CPR, r 45.25(2).
511 See CPR, r 45.25(3).
512 See CPR, r 45.25(4).
513 See CPR, r 45.29(4).
514 See, eg, RTA Protocol, paras 7.26 and 7.47; EL/PL Protocol, paras 7.24 and 7.44.

- a statement verified by a statement of truth signed by the litigation friend, which confirms whether the child has recovered in accordance with the prognosis and whether there are any continuing symptoms, which statement will enable the court to decide whether to order the child to attend the settlement hearing.[515]

Where the claimant is a child and there is a settlement, after proceedings are started under the Stage 3 procedure, for more than the defendant's relevant Protocol offer, then when an application is made to the court to approve the settlement, the following will apply.[516] **50.251**

- **Approval given at settlement hearing** Where the settlement is approved at the settlement hearing, the court will order the costs to be paid in accordance with CPR, r 45.22(2).[517] This means that the court will order the defendant to pay:
  - the Stage 1 and 2 fixed costs;
  - the Stage 3 Type A, B and C fixed costs; and
  - disbursements allowed in accordance with CPR, r 45.19 (see 50.181–50.188).[518]
- **Approval not given at settlement hearing** Where the court does not approve the settlement at the settlement hearing, it will order the defendant to pay the Stage 1 and 2 fixed costs.[519] The court will also order the claim to proceed to a Stage 3 hearing.[520]
- **Approval given at Stage 3 hearing** Where the court does not approve the settlement at the first settlement hearing, but does approve the settlement at the Stage 3 hearing, the court will order the defendant to pay:
  - the Stage 3 Type A and C fixed costs for the settlement hearing;
  - disbursements allowed in accordance with CPR, r 45.19 (see 50.181–50.188); and
  - the Stage 3 Type B fixed costs for one of the hearings.[521]
- The court, in its discretion, may also order:
  - the defendant to pay an additional amount of either or both of—
    - the Stage 3 Type A fixed costs;
    - the Stage 3 Type B fixed costs; or
  - the claimant to pay an amount equivalent to either or both of—
    - the Stage 3 Type A fixed costs;
    - the Stage 3 Type B fixed costs.[522]
- **No approval at Stage 3 hearing** Where the settlement is not approved at the Stage 3 hearing, the court will order the defendant to pay the Stage 3 Type A fixed costs.[523]
- **Court orders that the claim is not suitable to be determined under the Stage 3 procedure** Where the claimant is a child and, at a settlement hearing or the Stage 3 hearing, the court orders that the claim is not suitable to be determined under the Stage 3 procedure, the court will order the defendant to pay:
  - the Stage 1 and 2 fixed costs; and
  - the Stage 3 Type A, B and C fixed costs.[524]

---

515 See PD 8B, para 6.5.
516 See CPR, r 45.22(1).
517 See PD 8B, para 13.2.
518 See CPR, r 45.22(2).
519 See CPR, r 45.22(3).
520 See PD 8B, para 13.3.
521 See CPR, r 45.22(4) and (5).
522 See CPR, r 45.22(6).
523 See CPR, r 45.22(7).
524 See CPR, r 45.23.

50.252 **Limitation** Where compliance with the relevant Protocol is not possible before the expiry of a limitation period, the claimant may start proceedings and request a stay so as to comply with the relevant Protocol.[525] Where a stay is granted,[526] most of the provisions in PD 8B are disapplied.[527] Where the claimant subsequently wishes to start the Stage 3 procedure, they must make an application to the court to lift the stay and to request directions.[528] Where such a request is granted, the provisions of PD 8B will apply, and the claimant must amend the claim form accordingly and file all relevant written evidence (see 50.231).[529] If, during Stage 1 or Stage 2, the claimant wishes to start proceedings under CPR, Part 7, the claimant must make an application to the court to lift the stay and to request directions.[530]

50.253 **Defendants' costs and the costs of counterclaims** In addition to fixing claimants' costs, CPR, Part 45, Sections III, caps the costs payable to defendants. The relevant provisions are set out in CPR, Part 45, Section IIIA (see 50.307–50.310).

The consequences of non-compliance

50.254 Where a party has not complied with the relevant Protocol, then—subject to certain qualification (which are discussed below)—CPR, r 45.24, will apply.[531]

The incidence of costs

50.255 As is set out in the following paragraphs, there are specific provisions that restrict the amount of costs that may be paid in certain circumstances in which a party (normally, the claimant) has failed to comply with the relevant Protocol. In most cases, the court will need to look no further than those specific provisions, but in some cases it may be necessary to consider non-compliance with the relevant Protocol for the purposes of making an order as to the incidence of costs.[532] In this regard, it should not be forgotten that CPR, r 44.2(5)(a), defines relevant conduct for the purposes of deciding the incidence of costs as including the extent to which the parties followed any relevant pre-action protocol (see 6.77). It is also worth noting that this general principle is reinforced by the Preamble to each of the relevant Protocols, which specifically states that they describe the conduct that the court would normally expect of the parties.[533]

The consequences of a claimant's non-compliance

50.256 Claimants (or, in reality, their lawyers) may be tempted to leave the relevant Protocol for monetary reasons. The author can do no better than to quote the learned authors of *Cook on Costs* on this point:

> 'There is and always has been a temptation for claimant lawyers to exit their client's case from the Portal in order to make the case more profitable. While that may sound pejorative,

---

[525] See PD 8B, paras 16.1 and 16.2.

[526] There is no express provision in PD 8B that says when the court will or will not grant a stay, but, provided that the claimant has complied with the relevant provisions, it is difficult to imagine a circumstance in which a stay would not be granted.

[527] See PD 8B, para 16.4. All provisions in PD 8B, except paras 1.2, 2.1, 2.2 and 16.1–16.6, are disapplied.

[528] See PD 8B, para 16.5.

[529] See PD 8B, para 16.6. The documents are those listed in PD 8B, para 6.1.

[530] See PD 8B, para 16.7.

[531] CPR, r 45.16(2).

[532] See, eg, *Williams v The Secretary of State for Business, Energy & Industrial Strategy* [2018] EWCA Civ 852.

[533] See RTA Protocol, Preamble, para 2.1; see also EL/PL Protocol, para 2.1.

there is no obvious improvement in the evidence before a court to assess damages between a Stage 3 hearing and a disposal or other assessment of damages hearing so it does not appear to be a question of the client's damages as to why cases exited with alacrity. Consequently, CPR 45.24 spells out the costs consequences if a court considers that the claimant (or his lawyer) has not engaged properly with the Portal ...'[534]

Thus claimants who allow themselves to be lured into leaving the relevant Protocol may find that they are penalised in term of costs pursuant to CPR, r 45.24, which reads as follows: **50.257**

'**Failure to comply or electing not to continue with the relevant Protocol—costs consequences**

45.24 (1) This rule applies where the claimant—
(a) does not comply with the process set out in the relevant Protocol; or
(b) elects not to continue with that process,
and starts proceedings under Part 7.

(2) Where a judgment is given in favour of the claimant but—
(a) the court determines that the defendant did not proceed with the process set out in the relevant Protocol because the claimant provided insufficient information on the Claim Notification Form;
(b) the court considers that the claimant acted unreasonably—
  (i) by discontinuing the process set out in the relevant Protocol and starting proceedings under Part 7;
  (ii) by valuing the claim at more than £25,000, so that the claimant did not need to comply with the relevant Protocol; or
  (iii) except for paragraph (2)(a), in any other way that caused the process in the relevant Protocol to be discontinued; or
(c) the claimant did not comply with the relevant Protocol at all despite the claim falling within the scope of the relevant Protocol,
the court may order the defendant to pay no more than the fixed costs in rule 45.18 together with the disbursements allowed in accordance with rule 45.19.

(2A) Where a judgment is given in favour of the claimant but the claimant did not comply with the process in paragraph 6.3A(2) of the RTA Protocol, the court may not order the defendant to pay the claimant's costs and disbursements save in exceptional circumstances.

(3) Where the claimant starts proceedings under paragraph 7.28 of the RTA Protocol or paragraph 7.26 of the EL/PL Protocol and the court orders the defendant to make an interim payment of no more than the interim payment made under paragraph 7.14(2) or (3) of the RTA Protocol or paragraph 7.17(2) or (3) of the EL/PL Protocol the court will, on the final determination of the proceedings, order the defendant to pay no more than—
(a) the Stage 1 and 2 fixed costs; and
(b) the disbursements allowed in accordance with rule 45.19.'

Costs sanctions for avoidance of or non-compliance with the relevant Protocol CPR, r 45.24, applies where the claimant does not comply with the process set out in the relevant Protocol or elects not to continue with that process and starts proceedings under CPR, Part 7.[535] In particular, it applies where a judgment is given in favour of the claimant, but the court finds that: **50.258**

534 *Cook on Costs 2017* (LexisNexis, online), para 26.21.
535 See CPR, r 45.24(1).

- a claimant has acted unreasonably by:
  - discontinuing the process set out in the relevant Protocol and starting proceedings under Part 7;
  - valuing the claim at more than the 'upper limit', so that the claimant did not need to comply with the relevant Protocol; or
  - causing the process in the relevant Protocol to be discontinued;[536] or
- the claimant did not comply with the relevant Protocol at all, despite the claim falling within the scope of the relevant Protocol,[537]

then the defendant's liability for costs will be limited (not fixed) to the amount that would have been paid had the claim progressed under the relevant Protocol.[538]

50.259 Where a claim has left the relevant Protocol, CPR, Part 45, Section IIIA, will apply (unless it is a disease claim[539]). Nothing in that section, however, will prevent the court from making an order under CPR, r 45.24.[540]

50.260 Coulson LJ has said that the provisions in the Protocol that relate to unreasonable conduct should not be read in such a way as to extend them to situations in which a claimant unreasonably failed to engage with the Protocol at all, but there was no judgment that brought the matter within the ambit of CPR, r 45.24(2)(c).[541] If those were the facts, he went on to say, the court should instead exercise its discretion under CPR, r 44.2, to restrict the costs to those that would have been allowed had the claimant acted reasonably.[542] He said that if a defendant were to wish to take such a point, they should raise that submission as soon as possible (such as in the acknowledgement of service under the Part 8 procedure).[543]

50.261 **Costs sanctions for failures regarding claim notification forms** Where a judgment is given in favour of the claimant, but the court finds that a defendant did not proceed with the process set out in the relevant Protocol because the claimant provided insufficient information on the claim notification form (see 50.171),[544] the defendant's liability for costs will be limited (not fixed) to the amount that would have been paid had the claim progressed under the relevant Protocol.[545]

50.262 As of 5 April 2015, a claimant who does not comply with para 6.3A(2) of the RTA Protocol—a requirement to include the unique reference number on the claim notification as evidence of having undertaken a search of askCUE PI (see 50.195)—will be awarded the costs of their claim only in exceptional circumstances.[546]

---

[536] See CPR, r 45.24(2)(b).
[537] See CPR, r 45.24(2)(c).
[538] See CPR, r 45.24(2).
[539] See CPR, r 45.29A(2).
[540] See CPR, r 45.29A(3).
[541] *Williams v The Secretary of State for Business, Energy & Industrial Strategy* [2018] EWCA Civ 852, at [35]. On the facts of the case before the court, there was no judgment because the matter settled by way of acceptance of a Part 36 offer.
[542] *Ibid*, at [52]–[61], relying, at [57], on *O'Beirne v Hudson* [2010] EWCA Civ 52.
[543] *Williams v The Secretary of State for Business, Energy & Industrial Strategy* [2018] EWCA Civ 852, at [36].
[544] See CPR, r 45.24(2)(a).
[545] See CPR, r 45.24(2).
[546] See CPR, r 45.24(2A).

Costs sanctions regarding interim payments Where the claimant starts proceedings because a defendant has not paid the interim payment that the claimant had requested (see 50.210–50.211)[547] and where the court subsequently orders the defendant to make an interim payment of no more than the interim payment that had been tendered by the defendant,[548] the court will, on the final determination of the proceedings, order the defendant to pay no more than the Stage 1 and 2 fixed costs and the disbursements allowed in accordance with CPR, r 45.19. **50.263**

Costs sanctions and the Stage 3 procedure CPR, r 45.16(1), applies to claims that should have been started under the Stage 3 procedure: 'This Section applies to claims that have been or should have been started under Part 8 in accordance with Practice Direction 8B ("the Stage 3 Procedure").'[549] Thus, in so far as Stage 3 is concerned, the costs regime in CPR, Part 45, Section IIIA (see 50.267), will apply if the court finds that the claim ought to have been managed in accordance with the Stage 3 procedure. It is not known whether this deemed applicability would operate in a mandatory way, but the wording of CPR, Part 45, Section III, suggests that it does.[550] Even before this provision came into force, the court had the power to penalise avoidance of the Stage 3 procedure.[551] **50.264**

For the avoidance of doubt, where CPR, Part 45, Section IIIA, applies, nothing in that section will prevent the court from making an order under CPR, r 45.24.[552] **50.265**

The consequences of a defendant's non-compliance As has already been explained at 50.172, there are many ways in which defendants may leave the relevant Protocol, not least by mere inaction on their part. There are no prescribed costs sanctions for defendants who leave the relevant Protocol because it is assumed that, on the whole, defendants do not need a costs incentive to keep cases in the Portal; it will already be in their interests to do so. (It is worth noting here that, prior to 2013, it was, in some instances, in the interests of defendants to allow cases to default from the RTA Portal into CPR, Part 45, Section II,[553] but this is now no longer the case.) In the event that a defendant acts unreasonably, however, then the powers referred to at 50.255 may be invoked. **50.266**

CPR, Part 45, Section IIIA: Post-Portal Fixed Costs

On 31 July 2013, CPR, Part 45, Section IIIA, was created. It establishes a predictable claimants' costs regime in respect of those claims that exit the RTA and EL/PL Protocols, **50.267**

[547] See RTA Protocol, para 7.28; EL/PL Protocol, para 7.26.

[548] CPR, r 45.24, refers to RTA Protocol, para 7.14(2) or (3), or EL/PL Protocol, para 7.17(2) or (3), but in fact the relevant provisions are RTA Protocol, para 7.19(2) or (3), and EL/PL Protocol, para 7.18(2) or (3).

[549] See CPR, r 45.16(1).

[550] See CPR, r 45.24(2), which appears to impose a limit on the amount that the defendant will be required to pay in certain circumstances, one of which is where the claimant has overvalued the claim.

[551] Whilst not binding, in 2012, Judge Platts explained that if a claimant manipulated the RTA Protocol procedure to take the claim away from Stage 3 and into Part 7, they would be acting contrary to the spirit, if not the letter, of the Protocol and wholly contrary to the overriding objective. In a case in which that happened, he restricted the costs to those that would have been payable under the RTA Protocol: see *Ilahi v Usman* (unreported), 29 November 2012, Manchester County Court, at [31], *per* HHJ Platts.

[552] See CPR, r 45.29A(3).

[553] For a discussion of this point, see Fenn, P, 'Evaluating the Low Value Road Traffic Accident Process', MoJ Research Series 13/12 (July 2012).

and which are either subsequently settled or proceed to judgment. CPR, Part 45, Section IIIA, also imposes certain limits on the amounts that successful defendants may recover. On 7 May 2018, Section IIIA was applied to claims to which the Pre-Action Protocol for the Resolution of Package Travel Claims (the Travel Protocol) applies.

Terminology

50.268 The term 'post-Portal fixed costs' is used to refer to costs payable under CPR, Part 45, Section IIIA. The terms 'predictive costs', 'predictable costs', 'expanded predictable costs' and 'fixed recoverable costs' are best avoided, because they may cause confusion with costs payable under CPR, Part 45, Section II.[554] It should be noted that Section III has not been amended so as to incorporate the Travel Protocol, so a pedant may argue that the term 'post-Portal fixed costs' is inappropriate in those circumstances; that terminology is used notwithstanding this.

The ambit of post-Portal fixed costs

50.269 CPR, Part 45, Section IIIA, will apply only to claims that started in the RTA or EL/PL Protocols after 31 July 2013, but—for whatever reason—have left that Protocol (or the Stage 3 procedure under PD 8B).[555] That said, CPR, Part 45, Section IIIA, does not apply to disease claims that are started under the EL/PL Protocol.[556] It will also apply to claims to which the Travel Protocol applies[557] (but only where the claimant is legally represented).[558] That Protocol will apply to claims that arise from a gastric illness contracted during a package holiday, where no letter of claim has been sent to the defendant before 7 May 2018, the claim includes damages in respect of personal injury and the claimant values the claim at not more than £25,000 on a full liability basis, including pecuniary loss, but excluding interest.[559]

Ambit and track allocation

50.270 CPR, Part 45, Section IIIA, does not apply to claims that, having ceased to continue under the relevant Protocol, have been allocated to the multitrack.[560] Whilst not binding, Judge Denyer QC has found that CPR, Part 45, Section IIIA, does apply where a case leaves the relevant Protocol and is allocated to the small claims track.[561]

Ambit and applications

50.271 CPR, Part 45, Section IIIA, will also apply to applications for pre-action disclosure made pursuant to s 52(2) of the County Courts Act 1984 or s 33 of the Senior Courts Act 1981.[562]

---

554 See the definitions given in Jackson, R, *Review of Civil Litigation Costs: Final Report* (London: HMSO, 2010), Glossary, p x.

555 CPR, r 45.29A(1)(a).

556 CPR, r 45.29A(2).

557 CPR, r 45.29A(1)(b).

558 See Travel Protocol, para 6.3.

559 See Travel Protocol, para 4.1. The Travel Protocol will not apply where the claimant or defendant acts as personal representative of a deceased person, the claimant or defendant is a protected party as defined in CPR, r 21.1(2), the claimant is bankrupt or the defendant is insolvent and there is no identifiable insurer: see Travel Protocol, para 4.3.

560 The absence of an express exclusion for such cases was the result of a drafting error that has now been rectified: see *Qader v Esure Services Ltd* [2016] EWCA Civ 1109, at [44] *et seq*. See also Civil Procedure (Amendment) Rules 2017 (SI 2017/95), r 8, which amended CPR, r 45.29B.

561 See *Singh v Ajaz* (unreported), 27 September 2016, Bristol County Court.

562 See *Sharp v Leeds City Council* [2017] EWCA 33.

Ambit and claims excluded from the relevant Protocols

Post-Portal fixed costs do not apply to all types of claim. If a claim is excluded from the relevant Protocols, they will not apply—although CPR, Part 45, Section II, may if proceedings are not issued. For a list of the types of claims that are excluded, see 50.158 and 50.165. **50.272**

Transitional provisions relating to post-Portal fixed costs

Both the RTA Protocol and CPR, Part 45, Section IIIA, apply to claims for damages arising from road traffic accidents where the claim notification form was submitted on or after 31 July 2013.[563] There are no transitional provisions relating to the EL/PL Protocol. Similarly, in view of the fact that the Travel Protocol applies only to claims in which a letter of claim was sent on or after 7 May 2018, there are no transitional provisions. **50.273**

Whilst very much 'small print', there are transitional provisions that apply to certain changes that were made on 5 April 2015.[564] Because they were largely a matter of renumbering, little turns on them. **50.274**

The quantification of post-Portal fixed costs (road traffic accident claims)

Subject to what is said at 50.297–50.299, where CPR, Part 45, Section IIIA, applies in a road traffic accident claim, the only costs that the court may allow are: **50.275**

- those monies set out in Table 50.13[565] (plus a London enhancement, where appropriate);[566]
- those disbursements[567] allowed in accordance with CPR, r 45.29I; and
- VAT (where appropriate).[568]

Credit will be given for any Stage 1 and Stage 2 Portal costs that have already been paid.[569]

The amounts in Table 50.13 may be increased by 12.5 per cent in cases in which the claimant lives or works in and around London.[570]

The determination of times and damages for the purposes of RTA post-Portal fixed costs

The following points can be made about the wording of and application of Table 50.13. **50.276**

- **The meaning of 'on or after'** The references in Table 50.13 to 'on or after' are to the period beginning on the dates on which the court issues the claim, allocates the claim under Part 26 and lists the claim for trial, respectively.[571]
- **The meaning of 'trial'** Any reference to 'trial' is a reference to the final contested hearing.[572] Briggs LJ has explained that listing a case for a disposal hearing following judgment (pursuant to PD 26, para 12) is listing for trial for the purposes of triggering

[563] See Civil Procedure (Amendment No 6) Rules 2013 (SI 2013/1695), r 10; 'new' RTA Protocol, para 4.2.
[564] See Civil Procedure (Amendment No 8) Rules 2014 (SI 2014/3299), r 18.
[565] See CPR, rr 45.29B(a) and 45.29C(1).
[566] See CPR, r 45.27C(2); PD 45, para 2.6.
[567] See CPR, r 45.29B(b).
[568] See CPR, r 45.29C(3).
[569] See CPR, r 45.28.
[570] See CPR, r 45.27C(2); PD 45, para 2.6. Those areas are set out in fn 108.
[571] See CPR, r 45.29(4)(a).
[572] See CPR, r 45.29C(4)(b) and (c).

Table 50.13 Fixed costs where a claim no longer continues under the RTA Protocol (CPR, Part 45, Table 6B)

Situation	Calculation of fixed costs			
A. If Parties reach a settlement prior to the claimant issuing proceedings under Part 7				
Agreed damages	At least £1,000, but not more than £5,000	More than £5,000, but not more than £10,000	More than £10,000[573]	
Fixed costs	The greater of— (a) £550; or (b) the total of— (i) £100; and (ii) 20% of the damages	The total of— (a) £1,100; and (b) 15% of damages over £5,000	The total of— (a) £1,930; and (b) 10% of damages over £10,000	
B. If proceedings are issued under Part 7, but the case settles before trial				
Stage at which case is settled	On or after the date of issue, but prior to the date of allocation under Part 26	On or after the date of allocation under Part 26, but prior to the date of listing	On or after the date of listing but prior to the date of trial	
Fixed costs	The total of— (a) £1,160; and (b) 20% of the damages	The total of— (a) £1,880; and (b) 20% of the damages	The total of— (a) £2,655; and (b) 20% of the damages	
C. If the claim is disposed of at trial				
Fixed costs	The total of— (a) £2,655; and (b) 20% of the damages agreed or awarded; and (c) the relevant trial advocacy fee			
D. Trial advocacy fees				
Damages agreed or awarded	Not more than £3,000	More than £3,000, but not more than £10,000	More than £10,000, but not more than £15,000	More than £15,000
Trial advocacy fee	£500	£710	£1,070	£1,705

573 Prior to 6 April 2017, this provision was limited to claims with a value of no more than £25,000, but this restriction was lifted by Civil Procedure (Amendment) Rules 2017 (SI 2017/95), r 8.

the third column, where a case settles after listing.[574] Similarly, Coulson J has found that a trial advocacy fee would be payable in a case settled on the day of trial, but before the trial had actually commenced, because such a case would have been disposed of at trial, albeit by way of settlement rather than judgment.[575] It should be noted that this is in contrast to the way in which similar issues under CPR, Part 45, Section III, are treated (see 50.108).
- **The calculation of damages** Other than where the contrary is stated, any reference to 'damages' in Table 50.13 is a reference to agreed damages.[576]

RTA post-Portal fixed costs and disbursements

Other than as set out below, the court may allow any of the following,[577] but will not allow a claim for any other type of disbursement: **50.277**

- the cost of obtaining medical records;[578]
- the cost of obtaining a medical report or reports;[579]
- the cost of obtaining any appropriate non-medical expert reports as provided for in the relevant Protocol (which, under the RTA Protocol, includes engineering reports that are reasonably required to value the claim,[580] although this would be the exception, rather than the norm);[581]
- any expert's fee for attending the trial where the court has given permission for the expert to attend;[582]
- expenses that a party or witness has reasonably incurred in travelling to and from a hearing, or in staying away from home for the purposes of attending a hearing;[583]
- a sum not exceeding £90 (or, where the value of the claim for damages is more than £10,000, £135[584]) for any loss of earnings or loss of leave by a party or witness as a result of attending a hearing or staying away from home for the purpose of attending a hearing;
- the cost of a search of DVLA records;[585]
- the cost of a search of the records of the MID;[586]
- court fees; and
- any other disbursement that has arisen as a result of a particular feature of the dispute.[587]

The restrictions and provisions applying to disbursements payable under CPR, Part 45, Section III, will apply, as set out at 50.181–50.188.[588] In particular, the restrictions relating to soft-tissue injury claims will apply (see 50.184). **50.278**

---

574 See *Bird v Acorn Group Ltd* [2016] EWCA Civ 1096, at [12]. Briggs LJ's reasoning, at [13]–[17], was as follows: (a) that listing a case for disposal means exactly what it says—namely, to dispose of the case at first instance; (b) the fact that a disposal may be uncontested is neither here nor there; (c) in any event, the claimant needs to prepare for a disposal hearing; and (d) finally, there is a useful prehistory to the formulation 'final contested hearing' in CPR, r 45.29E(4)(c), in the sense that, in *Lamont v Burton* [2007] 1WLR 2814, the Court of Appeal worked on the assumption that a disposal was a trial.

575 See *Mendes v Hochtief (UK) Construction Ltd* [2016] EWHC 976 (QB), at [14]–[26].

576 See CPR, r 45.29C(4)(b).

577 See CPR, r 45.29I(1).

578 See CPR, r 45.29I(2)(a)(i).

579 See CPR, r 45.29I(2)(a)(ii).

580 See CPR, rr 45.29I(2)(a)(ii) and 45.19(3)(1)(a); RTA Protocol, para 7.3(a).

581 See RTA Protocol, para 7.9; EL/PL Protocol, para 7.7.

582 CPR, r 45.29I(2)(e).

583 CPR, r 45.29I(2)(f).

584 See PD 45, para 2A.1.

585 See CPR, r 45.29I(2)(a)(ii)(aa) and (3)(1)(b)(i).

586 See CPR, r 45.29I(2)(a)(ii)(bb) and (3)(1)(ii).

587 See CPR, r 45.29I(2)(e).

588 See CPR, r 45.29I(2B)–(2E) and (3). As will be seen, these are virtually indistinguishable from the corresponding provisions in CPR, r 45.19.

Quantification post-Portal fixed costs (employers' liability/public liability claims)

50.279 Subject to what is said at 50.297–50.299, where CPR, Part 45, Section IIIA, applies in an employers' liability claim or a public liability claim or a claim to which the Travel Protocol applies, the only costs that the court may allow are those in Table 50.14 or Table 50.15, whichever is appropriate,[589] and disbursements in accordance with CPR, r 45.29I,[590] *plus* VAT, where appropriate.[591]

50.280 Table 50.14 sets out the post-Portal fixed costs in employers' liability claims.

Table 50.14 Fixed costs where a claim no longer continues under the EL/PL Protocol: employers' liability claims (CPR, Part 45, Table 6C)

Situation	Calculation of fixed costs			
A. If Parties reach a settlement prior to the claimant issuing proceedings under Part 7				
Agreed damages	At least £1,000, but not more than £5,000	More than £5,000, but not more than £10,000	More than £10,000[592]	
Fixed costs	The total of— (a) £950; and (b) 17.5% of the damages	The total of— (a) £1,855; and (b) 12.5% of damages over £5,000	The total of— (a) £2,500; and (b) 10% of damages over £10,000	
B. If proceedings are issued under Part 7, but the case settles before trial				
Stage at which case is settled	On or after the date of issue, but prior to the date of allocation under Part 26	On or after the date of allocation under Part 26, but prior to the date of listing	On or after the date of listing but prior to the date of trial	
Fixed costs	The total of— (a) £2,630; and (b) 20% of the damages	The total of— (a) £3,350; and (b) 25% of the damages	The total of— (a) £4,280; and (b) 30% of the damages	
C. If the claim is disposed of at trial				
Fixed costs	The total of— (a) £4,280; (b) 30% of the damages agreed or awarded; and (c) the relevant trial advocacy fee			
D. Trial advocacy fees				
Damages agreed or awarded	Not more than £3,000	More than £3,000, but not more than £10,000	More than £10,000, but not more than £15,000	More than £15,000
Trial advocacy fee	£500	£710	£1,070	£1,705

589 See CPR, rr 45.29D(a) and 45.29E(1).

590 See CPR, r 45.29D(b).

591 See CPR, r 45.29E(3).

592 Prior to 6 April 2017, this provision was limited to claims with a value of no more than £25,000, but this restriction was lifted by Civil Procedure (Amendment) Rules 2017 (SI 2017/95) r 8.

Table 50.15 Fixed costs where a claim no longer continues under the EL/PL Protocol: public liability claims and travel claims (CPR, Part 45, Table 6D)

Situation	Calculation of fixed costs			
A. If Parties reach a settlement prior to the claimant issuing proceedings under Part 7				
Agreed damages	At least £1,000, but not more than £5,000	More than £5,000, but not more than £10,000	More than £10,000[593]	
Fixed costs	The total of— (a) £950; and (b) 17.5% of the damages	The total of— (a) £1,855; and (b) 10% of damages over £5,000	The total of— (a) £2,370; and (b) 10% of damages over £10,000	
B. If proceedings are issued under Part 7, but the case settles before trial				
Stage at which case is settled	On or after the date of issue, but prior to the date of allocation under Part 26	On or after the date of allocation under Part 26, but prior to the date of listing	On or after the date of listing but prior to the date of trial	
Fixed costs damages	The total of— (a) £2,450; and (b) 17.5% of the damages	The total of— (a) £3,065; and (b) 22.5% of the damages	The total of— (a) £3,790; and (b) 27.5% of the damages	
C. If the claim is disposed of at trial				
Fixed costs	The total of— (a) £3,790; (b) 27.5% of the damages agreed or awarded; and (c) the relevant trial advocacy fee			
D. Trial advocacy fees				
Damages agreed or awarded	Not more than £3,000	More than £3,000, but not more than £10,000	More than £10,000, but not more than £15,000	More than £15,000
Trial advocacy fee	£500	£710	£1,070	£1,705

Table 50.15 sets out the post-Portal fixed costs for public liability claims and those to which the Travel Protocol applies. **50.281**

The amount allowable pursuant to Table 50.14 or Table 50.15 may be enhanced by 12.5 per cent in cases in which the claimant lives or works in and around London.[594] **50.282**

The determination of times and damages for the purposes of EL/PL post-Portal fixed costs

The following points can be made about the wording of and application of Table 50.14 or Table 50.15. **50.283**

[593] Prior to 6 April 2017, this provision was limited to claims with a value of no more than £25,000, but this restriction was lifted by Civil Procedure (Amendment) Rules 2017 (SI 2017/95) r 8.

[594] See CPR, r 45.29E(2); PD 45, para 2.6. Those areas are set out in fn 108.

- **The meaning of 'on or after'** The references in Table 50.14 or Table 50.15 to 'on or after' are to the period beginning on the dates on which the court issues the claim, allocates the claim under Part 26 and lists the claim for trial, respectively.[595]
- **The meaning of 'trial'** The points made in respect of Table 50.13 apply (see 50.276).
- **The calculation of damages** Other than where the contrary is stated, any reference to 'damages' in Table 50.14 or Table 50.15 is a reference to agreed damages.[596]

Post-Portal fixed costs and disbursements

50.284 Other than as set out below, the court may allow any of the following,[597] but will not allow a claim for any other type of disbursement:

- the cost of obtaining medical records and expert medical reports as provided for in the relevant Protocol;[598]
- the cost of obtaining any appropriate non-medical expert reports as provided for in the relevant Protocol;[599]
- the cost of any advice from a specialist solicitor or counsel as provided for in the relevant Protocol;[600]
- any expert's fee for attending the trial where the court has given permission for the expert to attend;[601]
- expenses that a party or witness has reasonably incurred in travelling to and from a hearing or in staying away from home for the purposes of attending a hearing;[602]
- a sum not exceeding £90 (or, where the value of the claim for damages is more than £10,000, £135[603]) for any loss of earnings or loss of leave by a party or witness as a result of attending a hearing or staying away from home for the purpose of attending a hearing;[604]
- court fees;[605] and
- any other disbursement that has arisen as a result of a particular feature of the dispute.[606]

50.285 In a soft-tissue injury claim started under the RTA Protocol, the relevant restrictions and provisions applying to disbursements payable under CPR, Part 45, Section III, will apply, as set out at 50.184–50.186.[607] In a claim started under the RTA Protocol only, the cost of the following may be allowed: an engineer's report and a search of the records of both the Driver Vehicle Licensing Authority (DVLA) and the Motor Insurance Database (MID).[608]

595 See CPR, r 45.29E(4)(a).
596 See CPR, r 45.29E(4)(b) and (c).
597 See CPR, r 45.29I(1).
598 See CPR, r 45.29I(2)(a).
599 See CPR, r 45.29I(2)(b). See also RTA Protocol, para 7.9; EL/PL Protocol, para 7.7.
600 CPR, r 45.29I(2)(c).
601 CPR, r 45.29I(2)(e).
602 CPR, r 45.29I(2)(f).
603 See PD 45, para 2A.1.
604 CPR, r 45.29I(2)(g).
605 CPR, r 45.29I(2)(d).
606 See CPR, r 45.29I(2)(h).
607 See CPR, r 45.29I(2B)–(2E). As will be seen, these are virtually indistinguishable from the corresponding provisions in CPR, r 45.19.
608 See CPR, r 45.29I(3).

Multiple claimants

If there is more than one claimant, then the court may have to determine whether each claimant is entitled to the costs calculated in accordance with the provisions set out above or whether there should be only one amount, shared between them. Whilst not binding, there have been a number of County Court decisions that have suggested the former approach, rather than the latter. Judge Carmel Wall found that, in view of the way in which para 1.1(6) of the RTA Protocol defines a 'claim', the reference to a 'claim started under the RTA Protocol' in CPR, r 45.29B, is a reference to a claim made by a single claimant.[609] Judge Pearce came to much the same conclusion on the basis that the RTA Protocol makes provision for a single person's claim only.[610] These decisions may be correct, but it is anything but clear that CPR, Part 45, Section IIIA, was intended to be as closely coupled to the RTA and EL/PL Protocols as such analyses suggest. Moreover, it should be noted that where other species of fixed costs are intended to be available individually to each of several claimants[611] or where some mechanism is envisaged that deals with multiple parties in some other way,[612] express provision is made. It may also be relevant, albeit only by analogy, that the stage cap in CPR, Part 45, Section IV, applies collectively rather than individually (see 50.330).[613] The editor understands that this is an issue that commonly arises, so no doubt a binding decision will soon be made. **50.286**

Acceptance of Part 36 offers and post-Portal fixed costs

Post-Portal fixed costs and acceptance of Part 36 offers during the 'relevant period'

The instrument that created CPR, Part 45, Section IIIA, also amended CPR, Part 36, so as to accommodate post-Portal fixed costs.[614] If a Part 36 offer is accepted within the 'relevant period'—normally, 21 days—post-Portal fixed costs, including disbursements pursuant to CPR, r 45.29I,[615] will be payable in accordance with the stage at which the notice of acceptance was served.[616] The usual rule that a claimant who accepts such a Part 36 offer is entitled to costs as assessed is disapplied.[617] **50.287**

Where a defendant's Part 36 offer relates to part only of the claim and, at the time of serving notice of acceptance within the 'relevant period', the claimant abandons the balance of the claim, the claimant will be entitled to the same costs as those referred to above[618] (presumably in an attempt to encourage claimants to settle). The value of the claim for the purposes of Tables 50.13–15 will be the amount of the offer that was accepted.[619] **50.288**

---

609 *Mahmud v Saddiq* (unreported), 23 August 2017, Birmingham County Court, at [11].

610 *Neary v Bedspace Resource Ltd* (unreported), 4 December 2015, Chester County Court, at [7]. Judge Rawlings came to much the same conclusion in *Hussain & Ors v Khan* (unreported), 19 January 2016, Stoke on Trent County Court.

611 See, eg, CPR, r 45.40.

612 See, eg, CPR, r 45.40.

613 See *Akhtar v Bhopal Productions (UK) Ltd* [2015] EWHC 154 (IPEC), at [17]–[20], [23]–[26], [31] and [32], *per* Judge Hacon.

614 See Civil Procedure (Amendment No 6) Rules 2013 (SI 2013/1695), r 6.

615 See CPR, r 36.20(13).

616 See CPR, r 36.20 (2).

617 See *Broadhurst v Tan* [2016] EWCA Civ 94, at [8], *per* Dyson MR.

618 See CPR, r 36.20(3).

619 See CPR, r 36.20(10).

Post-Portal fixed costs and acceptance of offers after the 'relevant period' or after exit from the relevant Portal

50.289 The following points may be made about late acceptance of offers.

- **Acceptance of a defendant's Part 36 offer after the 'relevant period'** Subject to what is said below, where a defendant's Part 36 offer is accepted after the 'relevant period', the claimant will be entitled to post-Portal fixed costs (including disbursements pursuant to CPR, r 45.29I[620]) calculated on the basis of the relevant stage as it was when the 'relevant period expired', but there will be a liability for the defendant's costs thereafter.[621]
- **Acceptance of a defendant's Protocol offer after leaving the relevant Protocol** Subject to what is said below, where the claimant accepts the defendant's Protocol offer[622] after the date on which they leave the relevant Protocol, they will be entitled to the applicable Stage 1 and Stage 2 fixed costs in Table 50.11 or Table 50.12, but there will be a liability for the defendant's costs (including disbursements pursuant to CPR, r 45.29I[623]) from the date on which the defendant's Protocol offer is deemed to be made to the date of acceptance.[624]
- **Acceptance of a claimant's Part 36 offer after the 'relevant period'** Whilst not binding, Judge Gosnell has found that, upon the acceptance of a claimant's offer following the expiry of the 'relevant period', the fact that CPR, r 36.13, is not modified by CPR, r 36.20, means it will continue to have full force and effect, and, as such, the claimant will (subject to the injustice test in CPR, r 36.13(5)) be entitled to costs to be assessed.[625] In the absence of reason to do otherwise, that award would be on the standard basis,[626] but there are conflicting authorities on that point.[627] Regardless of whether it is open to the court to allow costs on the standard basis, Judge Grahame Wood QC has found that it would not ordinarily be appropriate to award costs on the indemnity basis merely because an offer has been accepted late.[628]
- **Soft-tissue injury claims** In a soft-tissue injury claim, if the defendant makes a Part 36 offer before the defendant receives a fixed-cost medical report,[629] the provisions referred to above will have effect only if the claimant accepts the offer more than 21 days after the defendant received the report.[630] It is not wholly clear what happens if the claimant

---

620 See CPR, r 36.20(13).

621 See CPR, r 36.20(4)

622 In this regard, a 'defendant's Protocol offer' is either (a) that which is defined at CPR, rr 36.25 and 36.26, or (if the claim left the Protocol before the Court Proceedings Pack Form was sent) or (b) the last offer made by the defendant before the claim left the Protocol (in which case the offer will be deemed to be made on the first business day after the claim leaves the Protocol): see CPR, r 36.20(8). A reference to the 'Court Proceedings Pack Form' is a reference to the form used in the Protocol; a reference to 'business day' is a reference to a business day as defined in CPR, r 6.2: see CPR, r 36.20(9).

623 See CPR, r 36.20(13).

624 See CPR, r 36.20(5).

625 See *Richardson v Wakefield Council* (unreported), 9 June 2017, Wakefield County Court, at [17]–[26].

626 See *ibid*, at [27]–[31], applying *Fitzpatrick Contractors Ltd v Tyco Fire and Integrated Solutions* [2009] EWHC 274.

627 See *McKeown v Venton* (unreported), 12 June 2017, Liverpool County Court, at [48] and [49], *per* Judge Graham Wood QC, in which the court found that there was no power to award costs on the standard basis.

628 See *ibid*, at [43]–[49].

629 'Fixed cost medical report' and 'soft tissue injury claim' have the same meaning as in RTA Protocol. para 1.1(10A) and (16A), respectively: see CPR, r 36.20(7).

630 See CPR, r 36.20(6).

accepts the offer 21 days or less after the defendant received the report; presumably the provisions set out immediately below would apply in default of agreement.

- **Failure to agree the incidence of costs** Where the parties do not agree the liability for costs, the court will make an order as to costs.[631]
- **The value of the claim** The value of the claim for the purposes of the tables will be the amount of the offer that was accepted.[632]
- **The amount of costs in favour of defendants** Where the court makes an order for costs in favour of the defendant, the amount awarded will not exceed the fixed costs in the applicable table, *less* the fixed costs to which the claimant is entitled.[633]
- **Disbursements** Presumably for the avoidance of doubt, CPR, r 36.20(13), provides that the parties are entitled to disbursements allowed in accordance with CPR, r 45.29I, incurred in any period for which costs are payable to them.

Part 36 offers following judgment and post-Portal fixed costs

A claimant's failure to 'beat' a defendant's offer

The following points may be made about the situation in which a claimant fails to 'beat' an offer made by a defendant. **50.290**

- **Claimant's failure to 'beat' defendant's Part 36 offer** Subject to what is said below, where an order for costs is made pursuant to CPR, r 36.17(3), the claimant will be entitled to post-Portal fixed costs (including disbursements pursuant to CPR, r 45.29I[634]) calculated on the basis of the relevant stage as it was when the 'relevant period expired', but there will be a liability for the defendant's costs thereafter.[635]
- **Claimant's failure to 'beat' defendant's Protocol offer** Subject to what is said below, where the claimant accepts the defendant's Protocol offer[636] after the date on which they leave the relevant Protocol, they will be entitled to the applicable Stage 1 and Stage 2 fixed costs in Table 50.11 or Table 50.12, but there will be a liability for the defendant's costs (including disbursements pursuant to CPR, r 45.29I[637]) from the date on which the defendant's Protocol offer is deemed to be made to the date of acceptance.[638] The amount of the judgment is less than the Protocol offer where the judgment is less than the offer once amounts identified in the judgment are deducted.[639]
- **Soft-tissue injury claims** In a soft-tissue injury claim, if the defendant makes a Part 36 offer before the defendant receives a fixed-cost medical report,[640] the provisions referred

---

631 See CPR, r 36.20(11).

632 See CPR, r 36.20(10).

633 See CPR, r 36.20(12).

634 See CPR, r 36.21(10).

635 See CPR, r 36.21(2).

636 In this regard, a 'defendant's Protocol offer' is either (a) that which is defined at CPR, rr 36.25 and 36.26, or (if the claim left the Protocol before the Court Proceedings Pack Form was sent) or (b) the last offer made by the defendant before the claim left the Protocol (in which case the offer will be deemed to be made on the first business day after the claim leaves the Protocol): see CPR, r 36.21(6). A reference to the 'Court Proceedings Pack Form' is a reference to the form used in the Protocol; a reference to 'business day' is a reference to a business day as defined in CPR, r 6.2: see CPR, r 36.21(7).

637 See CPR, r 36.21(10).

638 See CPR, r 36.21(3)(a) and (b).

639 See CPR, r 36.21(3)(c).

640 'Fixed cost medical report' and 'soft tissue injury claim' have the same meaning as in RTA Protocol, para 1.1(10A) and (16A), respectively: see CPR, r 36.21(5).

to in the two paragraphs above will have effect only in respect of costs incurred by either party more than 21 days after the defendant received the report;[641] otherwise, the provisions in CPR, r 36.17, will apply.[642]

- **The amount of costs in favour of the defendant** Where the court makes an order for costs in favour of the defendant, the amount awarded will not exceed the fixed costs in the applicable table, *less* the fixed costs to which the claimant is entitled.[643]
- **Disbursements** Presumably for the avoidance of doubt, CPR, r 36.21(10), provides that the parties are entitled to disbursements allowed in accordance with CPR, r 45.29I, incurred in any period for which costs are payable to them.

A defendant's failure to 'beat' a claimant's offer

50.291 It may be that a claimant makes a Part 36 offer—either during the period when the claim is in the relevant Portal or otherwise. If so, it is possible that, once the claim has exited the relevant Protocol, the claimant may obtain judgment that is more advantageous than that offer. Put otherwise, the claimant may 'beat' that offer in circumstances in which CPR, Part 45, Section IIIA, ostensibly applies. If this happens, then this will give rise to the question of whether the claimant is, for the period after expiry of the 'relevant period', entitled to indemnity basis costs (that is, assessed costs) or to post-Portal fixed costs.

50.292 In contrast to the specific provisions referred to above, there is nothing in the CPR that expressly deals with that topic. Indeed, there is a tension between CPR, rr 45.29B and 36.21. The former says that the only costs to be awarded in Section IIIA cases are post-Portal fixed costs, whereas the latter says that, in such cases, CPR, r 36.17, will apply subject only to the modifications stated in CPR, r 36.21, none of which affect CPR, r 36.17(3).

50.293 Dyson MR resolved this tension by finding that, in claims governed by CPR, Part 45, Section IIIA, costs were payable on the indemnity basis as a result of a claimant having made a Part 36 offer that they subsequently 'beat', because CPR, r 36.17(3), has not been modified by the provisions in CPR, r 36.21, and, as such, it continues to have full force and effect.[644] Post-Portal fixed costs are not to be equated with indemnity costs and any tension between CPR, rr 45.29B and 36.21, had to be resolved in favour of the latter. This is so regardless of whether the offer was made under Part 36 as it was before 6 April 2015 or after.[645]

50.294 For the avoidance of doubt, where a claimant 'beats' their own Part 36 offer in this way, they will not be entitled to double recovery of costs (that is, the claimant will not be entitled to both fixed costs and costs on the indemnity basis following expiry of the 'relevant period'), because there is a distinction between fixed costs and indemnity costs, and the latter do not include the former.[646] Instead, where a claimant makes a successful Part 36 offer in a CPR, Part 45, Section IIIA case, they will be awarded post-Portal fixed costs to the last staging point provided in the relevant table; they will then be awarded costs to be

641 See CPR, r 36.21(4).
642 This is the effect of CPR, r 36.21(1).
643 See CPR, r 36.21(9).
644 *Broadhurst v Tan* [2016] EWCA Civ 94, at [22]–[28].
645 See *ibid*, at [1].
646 This was made clear by Dyson MR *ibid*, at [33].

assessed on the indemnity basis in addition from the date on which the offer became effective.[647] This does not require any apportionment. It may lead to a generous outcome for the claimant, but this is not a reason to depart from the method.[648]

It has been suggested that Dyson MR's analysis represents a blow to the defendant industry, which had fought hard for a regime that limited claimants to fixed costs on fast-track cases, as *quid pro quo* for the benefits of qualified one-way costs shifting (QOCS). This may be so, but perhaps the better analysis is that of Mukesh Kainth, vice president of the Forum of Insurance Lawyers, who had this to say: **50.295**

> 'It remains to be seen if parliament will intervene, but surely it is preferable to have a position where the parties are scrutinising the part 36 offers thoroughly, together with the associated risks. If *Broadhurst*[649] results in claimants actively making more offers and defendants paying greater heed, this should result in quicker settlements and less use of court resources, which is beneficial to the legal system as a whole.'[650]

A procedural point regarding claimants' Part 36 offers Most claims that leave the relevant Protocol will be allocated to the fast track. PD 44, para 9.5(4)(a), requires that a statement of costs is filed and served for a fast-track trial. As such, in light of the above, where a claimant has made an offer upon which they intend to rely, it will be necessary to prepare a statement of costs for work after the expiry of the offer's 'relevant period'. **50.296**

The discretion to allow more than post-Portal fixed costs

The court has the power to allow a receiving party to escape the constraints of post-Portal fixed costs, but only where certain thresholds have been met, as follows. **50.297**

- **The first threshold (exceptionally)** If there are 'exceptional circumstances making it appropriate to do so',[651] the court has the power to find that it should 'consider a claim for an amount of costs' (excluding disbursements) that is greater than the applicable post-Portal fixed costs payable under CPR, Part 45, Section IIIA.[652] It is implicit in the rule that even if that threshold is met, the court is not obliged to allow the application; hence the points made at 50.90 apply by analogy. Where the court finds that it is appropriate to 'consider [such] a claim' and where the court allows that claim, it will either summarily assess the costs or it will make an order for the costs to be subject to detailed assessment.[653] Where, however, that threshold is not met, the court will allow the applicable post-Portal fixed costs (or, if the receiving party is a defendant, the lower of those costs and costs as assessed).[654] Whilst not binding, Recorder Hancock QC found that the mere fact that a trial had been listed over two days did not satisfy the requirement of exceptionality[655] and again, whilst not binding, Judge Tindall found

[647] See *ibid*, at [31].
[648] *Ibid*, at [31].
[649] *Broadhurst v Tan* [2016] EWCA Civ 94.
[650] Kainth, M, 'Is *Broadhurst v Tan* a Step Backwards?', *Solicitors Journal*, 31 May 2016.
[651] As to the test to be applied, see (by way of analogy) fn 127, which refers to *Costin v Merron* [2013] EWCA Civ 380, at [6] and [11]. Whilst not binding, Judge Tindall accepted this to be the correct test in *Parsa v DS Smith plc* (unreported), 8 September 2017, Birmingham County Court, at [28].
[652] CPR, r 45.29J(1).
[653] CPR, r 45.29J(2).
[654] CPR, r 45.29J(3).
[655] *Barker v Stonehouse* (unreported), 18 August 2015, Chelmsford County Court, at [11].

that a degree of legal complexity did not satisfy that requirement.[656] In the editor's experience, however, successful applications are becoming relatively common, especially where it is demonstrably the case that the costs reasonably claimed are in the order of 50 per cent or more of the post-Portal fixed costs[657] (although it has to be stressed that each case will turn on its own facts and there is certainly no benchmark figure).

- **The second threshold (one-fifth more)** The fact that a receiving party persuades the court to 'consider a claim' for costs that exceed post-Portal fixed costs will not guarantee that they will actually succeed in that claim. This is because the 'exceptional circumstances' test is only the first of two threshold tests; the second is that the applicant must persuade the court to allow at least 20 per cent more than expanded recoverable costs (exclusive of VAT). If they fail to do this, they will be paid either the fixed costs or the assessed costs, whichever is the lesser.[658]

50.298 It is not wholly clear what the procedure for making an application to escape post-Portal fixed costs is. Unlike the similar provisions in CPR, r 45.13 (see 50.92), there is no express requirement in this regard.[659] Whilst no more than the editor's opinion, it seems that it would generally be sensible to make a formal application, but—at the very least—the reasons for making the claim that exceptional circumstances exist ought to be set out in clear terms (such as at the very start of the narrative to the bill of costs). Again, whilst it is only the editor's view, any application should be accompanied by a bill of costs (or at least a detailed statement of what the costs are), because one of the most important factors that the court is likely to take into account is disparity between the costs that are claimed and the amount of the post-Portal fixed costs.[660]

50.299 If the application fails (by virtue of the applicant failing either the first threshold or the second), the applicant will be at risk on costs. In particular, not only does the court have the power to deprive the applicant of the costs of the costs-only proceedings or detailed assessment, but it may also condemn that party to pay their opponent's costs.[661]

The discretion to restrict costs to post-Portal fixed costs

50.300 The power of the court to restrict claimants to Portal costs remains and CPR, Part 45, Section IIIA, confirms that nothing in the Section prevents the court from exercising that power.[662] Whilst an obvious point, a claimant would be poorly advised to exit from or ignore the relevant Protocol solely in an attempt to avoid Portal costs.

---

656 *Parsa v DS Smith plc* (unreported), 8 September 2017, Birmingham County Court, at [29].

657 By way of example, in *Lloyd v 2 Sisters Poultry Ltd* (unreported), 22 May 2018, Caernarfon County Court, Deputy District Judge Owen Weldon Williams (a retired full-time district judge) allowed an application in a case in which the reasonable costs (which he had provisionally assessed) were about 65 per cent more than post-Portal fixed costs, where the severity of the claimant's injuries were not fully appreciated at the time his claim was entered into the Portal.

658 CPR, r 45.29K(1).

659 That requirement may be found at PD 45, para 2.8.

660 Whilst not binding (because it was only an application for permission to appeal), see *Costin v Merron* [2013] EWCA Civ 380, at [6] and [11], *per* Leveson LJ.

661 CPR, r 45.29L.

662 See CPR, r 45.29A(3), which expressly confirms that CPR, r 45.24, will, where appropriate, apply.

Claimants' costs of interim applications

Where the court makes an order for costs of an interim application to be paid by a defendant, the order shall be for a sum equivalent to half of the applicable Type A and Type B costs in Table 50.14 or Table 50.15.[663] Disbursements are payable in accordance with CPR, r 45.29I,[664] as is VAT.[665] London weighting may also apply (see 50.275 for details).[666] **50.301**

It has been said that this rule has been drafted in such a way (that is, with potentially heavy costs penalties) in an effort to discourage parties from making unnecessary applications.[667] **50.302**

Post-Portal fixed costs in favour of defendants

Subject to what is said below, where the court makes an order in favour of the defendant in any case to which CPR, Part 45, Sections III or IIIA,[668] apply, the amount payable must not exceed that which would have been payable had the defendant been ordered to pay costs at the same stage of the proceedings.[669] This means that costs will be limited to those in the appropriate table (that is, Table 50.14 and Table 50.15),[670] *plus* disbursements payable in accordance with CPR, r 45.29I[671] *plus* VAT, where appropriate.[672] **50.303**

This rule will not apply, however, if a Part 36 offer is accepted or if the claimant fails to 'beat' a defendant's Part 36 offer. In those circumstances, CPR, rr 36.20 or 36.21, respectively, will apply instead of CPR, r 45.29F.[673] Similarly, this rule will not apply if any of the exceptions to QOCS in CPR, rr 44.15 and 44.16 is established.[674] **50.304**

CPR, r 45.29F(3), reads as follows: **50.305**

> 'For the purpose of assessing the costs payable to the defendant by reference to the fixed costs in Table 6 [Table 50.11], Table 6A [Table 50.12], Table 6B [Table 50.13], Table 6C [Table 50.14] and Table 6D [Table 50.15], "value of the claim for damages" and "damages" shall be treated as references to the value of the claim.'

It is not entirely clear what this seemingly otiose provision means. It may simply be intended to clarify that the value of the claim for the purpose of using Tables 50.11–15 is the amount claimed and not some discounted or adjusted amount. In any event, that value is ascertained in the following way. **50.306**

- Where the value of the claim is stated on the claim form, that figure will be used, excluding any amount not in dispute, any interest or costs, and any deduction for

663 See CPR, r 45.29H(1).
664 See CPR, r 45.29H(3).
665 See CPR, r 45.29H(4).
666 See CPR, r 45.29H(2).
667 See, eg, Hoe, M, 'The Expanded Portal and Predictable Costs Regimes', *PI Brief Update*, 17 July 2013.
668 CPR, r 45.29F(2), refers to 'this Section', which almost certainly means CPR, Part 45, Section III and Section IIIA, because CPR, r 45.29(3), refers to provisions in both of those sections.
669 CPR, rr 45.29(1)(c) and 45.29F(2).
670 CPR, r 45.29F(3).
671 CPR, r 45.29F(6).
672 CPR, r 45.29F(7).
673 See CPR, r 45.29F(1)(a) and (8) and (9).
674 See CPR, r 45.29F(1)(b) and (10).

contributory negligence.[675] Where the claim is a road traffic accident claim, any claim for vehicle-related damages will also be excluded.[676]

- If no amount is specified in the claim form, the value of the claim is the maximum amount that the claimant reasonably expected to recover according to the statement of value included in the claim form.[677]
- If the claim form states that the claimant cannot reasonably say how much is likely to be recovered, the value of the claim will be £25,000.[678]

The amounts derived from the tables may be enhanced by 12.5 per cent in cases in which the defendant lives or works in and around London.[679]

Counterclaims and post-Portal fixed costs

50.307 In any claim in which a defendant brings a counterclaim for personal injuries that falls within the ambit of the RTA Protocol, CPR, rr 45.29B, 45.29C and 45.29I–45.29L, will apply to any order for costs of the counterclaim that may be made in the defendant's favour.[680] Disbursements in accordance with CPR, r 45.27I, will be payable in addition.[681] This means that a counterclaimant who claims for personal injury will be treated much the same as a claimant.

50.308 Where, however, a successful counterclaim does not include a claim for personal injuries, the order for costs of the counterclaim will be for a sum equivalent to half of the applicable Type A and Type B costs in Table 50.11.[682] The defendant will also be entitled to disbursements in accordance with CPR, r 45.29I.[683]

50.309 There are provisions for VAT (see 50.275)[684] and an enhancement of post-Portal fixed costs where the defendant lives or works in and around London.[685] At first glance, it seems from the numbering of those provisions that they will apply only where the defendant makes a claim that does not include a personal injuries claim, but this is because the provisions that apply to counterclaims that include personal injuries incorporate other provisions that provide for the London enhancement and VAT.[686]

50.310 There are no corresponding provisions for employers' liability or public liability claims, presumably because counterclaims are inherently unlikely in such matters.

Defendants' post-Portal fixed costs of interim applications

50.311 Where the court makes an order for costs of an interim application to be paid by a claimant, the order shall be for a sum equivalent to half of the applicable Type A and Type B costs

[675] CPR, r 45.29F(4)(a).
[676] CPR, r 45.29F(4)(a).
[677] CPR, r 45.29F(4)(b).
[678] CPR, r 45.29F(4)(c).
[679] See CPR, r 45.27E(2); PD 45, para 2.6. Those areas are set out in fn 108.
[680] CPR, r 45.29G(1).
[681] See the list of tables in CPR, r 45.2.
[682] CPR, r 45.29G(2).
[683] CPR, r 45.29G(2)
[684] CPR, r 45.29G(2)(d).
[685] See CPR, r 45.27E(2); PD 45, para 2.6.
[686] See CPR, r 45.29C(2)(b) and (c).

in Table 50.11 or Table 50.12.[687] Disbursements are payable in accordance with CPR, r 45.29I,[688] as is VAT.[689] London weighting may also apply (see 50.275 for details).[690]

CPR, Part 45, Section IV: Scale Costs for Claims in the Intellectual Property Enterprise Court

This section deals with scale costs in the Intellectual Property Enterprise Court (IPEC), previously known as the Patents County Court (PCC). It also deals with the incidence of costs in the IPEC (see 50.336), but only in so far as the incidence of costs is relevant to the application of CPR, Part 45, Section IV. **50.312**

The renaming of the court took place on 1 October 2013, at which time it became a specialist list established within the Chancery Division of the High Court.[691] Lord Younger, then Minister for Intellectual Property, explained that the changes reflected the fact that the court's jurisdiction covers not only patents, but also a wide range of intellectual property matters, including trade marks, designs and copyright.[692] It is worth noting that the PCC had already been reformed in 2010 to make it more accessible;[693] the new reforms were an extension of the old. The combined effect of those reforms is that the IPEC is widely regarded as being a forum for resolving intellectual property disputes without a party having to fear it will be financially ruined if it loses the claim. Whilst nothing more than the editor's opinion, it would be fair to say that the IPEC is a shining example of how a carefully crafted costs regime can be of genuine benefit to court users. **50.313**

Jurisdiction in the Intellectual Property Enterprise Court

The relevant provisions are set out in CPR, Parts 63 (procedure), 30 (transfers) and 45 (costs), and in their respective practice directions. **50.314**

The ambit of CPR, Part 45, Section IV

CPR, r 63.26(3), provides as follows: 'Where the court makes a summary assessment of costs, it will do so in accordance with Section IV of Part 45.' **50.315**

For the reasons set out at 50.337, it will almost always be the case that costs in the IPEC are assessed summarily and, as such, CPR, Part 45, Section IV, will apply by default. Subject **50.316**

---

687 See CPR, r 45.29H(1).

688 See CPR, r 45.29H(3).

689 See CPR, r 45.29H(4).

690 See CPR, r 45.29H(2).

691 See Civil Procedure (Amendment No 7) Rules 2013 (SI 2013/1974); CPR, r 65.1(1)(g). Transitional provisions apply: see Civil Procedure (Amendment No 7) Rules 2013 (SI 2013/1974), r 30. Proceedings that were already in the PCC as at 1 October 2013 will continue in the IPEC afterwards as if they had been started in that court (r 30(a)). Anything done in accordance with the rules that applied in the PCC before reconstitution will be treated as being done in accordance with the corresponding rules of the IPEC (r 30(b)) and any judgment or order of the PCC has the same effect as if it had been a judgment or order of the IPEC (r 30(c)).

692 See Department for Business, Innovation & Skills, 'Sweeping Reforms to IP Court Save Businesses Time and Money', Press Release, 1 October 2013.

693 This followed the publication of Intellectual Property Court Users' Committee, *Final Report of the Working Group on Proposals for Reform of the Patents County Court* (London: HMSO, 2010), §5.

to what is said below, the only significant exception to this is where the claim proceeds on the small claims track.[694]

50.317 CPR, r 45.30, provides as follows:

> '(1) Subject to paragraph (2), this Section applies to proceedings in the Intellectual Property Enterprise Court.
>
> (2) This Section does not apply where—
> (a) the court considers that a party has behaved in a manner which amounts to an abuse of the court's process; or
> (b) the claim concerns the infringement or revocation of a patent or registered design or registered trade mark the validity of which has been certified by a court or by the Comptroller-General of Patents, Designs and Trade Marks in earlier proceedings.'

50.318 Thus, unless the court considers that a party has behaved in a manner that amounts to an abuse of the court's process (see 50.331), or unless the claim concerns the infringement or revocation of certain patents, designs or trade marks that have previously been certified as being valid, then the provisions in CPR, Part 45, Section IV, will apply. This will be the case, however, only if the claim proceeds in the IPEC—in particular, CPR, Part 45, Section IV, will not apply to claims in the Chancery Division of the High Court.

50.319 Whether a case is suitable for the IPEC is addressed by CPR, r 63,17A, which reads as follows:

> '(1) In proceedings in the Intellectual Property Enterprise Court in which a claim is made for damages or an account of profits, the amount or value of that claim shall not exceed £500,000.
>
> (2) In determining the amount or value of a claim for the purpose of paragraph (1), a claim for—
> (a) interest, other than interest payable under an agreement; or
> (b) costs,
> shall be disregarded.
>
> (3) Paragraph (1) shall not apply if the parties agree that the Intellectual Property Enterprise Court shall have jurisdiction to award damages or profits in excess of £500,000.'

50.320 Further guidance is given in PD 30, para 9.1, which (by the operation of CPR, r 63.1) governs the issue of whether a claim should be transferred to or from the IPEC:

> '9.1 When deciding whether to order a transfer of proceedings to or from the Intellectual Property Enterprise Court the court will consider whether—
> (1) a party can only afford to bring or defend the claim in the Intellectual Property Enterprise Court; and
> (2) the claim is appropriate to be determined by the Intellectual Property Enterprise Court having regard in particular to—
>   (a) the value of the claim (including the value of an injunction);
>   (b) the complexity of the issues; and
>   (c) the estimated length of the trial.'

50.321 Thus, should a party want CPR, Part 45, Section IV, to apply (or not to apply), it would be open to that party to seek to have the case transferred to (or from) the IPEC in accordance

[694] See CPR, r 63.28(2), which makes no mention of CPR, r 63.26(3), applying to claims on the small claims track.

with the guidance given in PD 30, para 9.1. The court would have regard to whether the party would be able to afford to bring or defend the claim in courts other than the IPEC; it would also have particular regard to the value of the claim, the complexity of the issues and the estimated length of the trial. If, in a claim worth more than £500,000, the party in question were to want the benefit of CPR, Part 45, Section IV, it would also be open to that party to persuade their opponent to consent to this in accordance with CPR, r 63.17A(3).

Terminology of costs in the Intellectual Property Enterprise Court

The costs allowable in the IPEC are usually referred to as 'scale costs', which are defined as 'the costs set out in Table A and Table B of the Practice Direction supplementing this Part'[695]—a relatively narrow definition. Judge Hacon has said that he tends to avoid the term 'scale costs' because that term is used in a way that leads to ambiguity[696] (that is, that it is not always clear whether that term refers to the costs in total or only the monies set out in the tables). He prefers the terms 'stage costs' to mean the costs set out in the tables and 'total costs' to mean the costs of the proceedings as a whole.[697] **50.322**

It should be noted that, notwithstanding the fact that they are often called scale costs, the relevant figures (see Tables 50.16 and 50.17) are upper limits rather than fixed amounts. Judge Birss QC had this to say on the point: **50.323**

> 'Although CPR Part 45, in which the relevant rules are found, is entitled "Fixed Costs", the costs ... are not fixed. The various sums provided for by the rules and practice direction in this system are maxima. The costs spent or awarded for any particular stage may not be as high as the maximum for a particular stage. By rule 45.41(3) the court will make a summary assessment of the costs of the party in whose favour any costs order is made.'[698]

Caps in the Intellectual Property Enterprise Court

Scale costs are governed by CPR, r 45.31, which reads as follows: **50.324**

> '(1) Subject to rule 45.32, the court will not order a party to pay total costs of more than—
> (a) £50,000 on the final determination of a claim in relation to liability; and
> (b) £25,000 on an inquiry as to damages or account of profits.
>
> (2) The amounts in paragraph (1) apply after the court has applied the provision on set off in accordance with rule 44.12(a).[[699]]
>
> (3) The maximum amount of scale costs that the court will award for each stage of the claim is set out in Practice Direction 45.
>
> (4) The amount of the scale costs awarded by the court in accordance with paragraph (3) will depend on the nature and complexity of the claim.
>
> (4A) Subject to assessment where appropriate, the following may be recovered in addition to the amount of the scale costs set out in Practice Direction 45—Fixed Costs—
> (a) court fees;

---

695 CPR, r 45.30(4).

696 *Akhtar v Bhopal Productions (UK) Ltd* [2015] EWHC 154 (IPEC), at [13].

697 *Ibid.*

698 *Indigo Furniture Ltd v Futurelook Ltd* [2011] EWPCC 013, at [11], which refers to the principles set out in *Westwood v Knight* [2011] EWPCC 011.

699 The reference to CPR, r 44.12(a), contains a typographical error in that it should be a reference to CPR, r 44.12(1)(a): see *Global Flood Defence Systems Ltd v Johann Van Den Noort Beheer BV* [2016] EWHC 189 (IPEC), at [6], *per* Judge Hacon.

(b) costs relating to the enforcement of any court order; and
(c) wasted costs.

(5) Where appropriate, VAT may be recovered in addition to the amount of the scale costs and any reference in this Section to scale costs is a reference to those costs net of any such VAT.'

50.325 Judge Hacon has explained the effect of these provisions in the following way:

> 'Rule 45.31 does five things. First, it imposes the overall caps on costs, to be applied after any set off (paragraphs (1) and (2)). Those paragraphs are expressly stated to be concerned only with the "total costs". Secondly, it provides for maximum costs to be applied to each stage of the proceedings: those set out in Tables A and B in Practice Direction 45 (paragraph (3)). Thirdly, it provides that the award of costs for each stage should be calibrated to the nature and complexity of the claim (paragraph (4)). Fourthly, it allows certain costs to be awarded in addition to the "scale costs" (paragraph (5)). Fifthly, rule 45.31 provides that "scale costs" are net of VAT. Where, unusually, the VAT on such costs may be claimed by a party, VAT is added without regard to the relevant caps.'[700]

The global cap

50.326 In every case, the amount of the scale costs awarded by the court will depend on the nature and complexity of the claim.[701] There is a global cap on costs of £50,000 on the final determination of a claim in relation to liability (or £25,000 on an inquiry as to damages or account of profits).[702]

Stage costs (stage caps) where proceedings were started on or after 1 October 2013

50.327 In addition to the global cap, there are caps at various stages in the proceedings—that is, the costs that Judge Hacon refers to as 'stage costs'. Stage costs are to be applied in a broad way that is not limited by the fact that the stages appear to be chronologically ordered.[703] The costs applicable to each stage are set out in Tables A and B of PD 45, Section IV. Table A is reproduced here as Table 50.16 and Table B, as Table 50.17.

Stage costs (stage caps) where proceedings were started before 1 October 2013

50.328 Table 50.16 and Table 50.17 apply only to proceedings started on or after 1 October 2013. Where proceedings were started earlier than that date, the lower scale costs set out in Tables A (reproduced here as Table 50.18) and B (reproduced here as Table 50.19) of PD 45, Section 25C, will continue to apply—and this will be so even in relation to matters occurring after that date.[704]

50.329 In addition, CPR, r 45.43, makes the following provisions: 'Costs awarded to a party under rule 63.26(2) are in addition to the total costs that may be awarded to that party under rule 45.31.' This means that where a party has behaved unreasonably and the court has (pursuant to CPR, r 63.26(2)) made an order for costs at the conclusion of a hearing, those costs will be payable in addition (that is, they will not be subject to the global cap).[705]

---

700 *Akhtar v Bhopal Productions (UK) Ltd* [2015] EWHC 154 (IPEC), at [17].
701 See CPR, r 45.31(4).
702 CPR, r 45.31(1).
703 *Westwood v Knight* [2011] EWPCC 011, at [30], *per* Judge Birss QC.
704 See *Phonographic Performance Ltd v Hamilton Entertainment Ltd (No 2)* [2013] EWHC 3801 (IPEC), *per* Birss J.
705 They will, however, be subject to the stage caps: see *Akhtar v Bhopal Productions (UK) Ltd* [2015] EWHC 154 (IPEC), at [17], *per* Judge Hacon.

Table 50.16 Scale costs for each stage of a claim up to determination of liability (PD 45, Table A)

Stage of a claim	Maximum amount of costs
Particulars of claim	£7,000
Defence and counterclaim	£7,000
Reply and defence to counterclaim	£7,000
Reply to defence to counterclaim	£3,500
Attendance at a case management conference	£3,000
Making or responding to an application	£3,000
Providing or inspecting disclosure or product/process description	£6,000
Performing or inspecting experiments	£3,000
Preparing witness statements	£6,000
Preparing experts' report	£8,000
Preparing for and attending trial and judgment	£16,000
Preparing for determination on the papers	£5,500

Table 50.17 Scale costs for each stage of an inquiry as to damages or account of profits (PD 45, Table B)

Stage of a claim	Maximum amount of costs
Points of claim	£3,000
Points of defence	£3,000
Attendance at a case management conference	£3,000
Making or responding to an application	£3,000
Providing or inspecting disclosure	£3,000
Preparing witness statements	£6,000
Preparing experts' report	£6,000
Preparing for and attending trial and judgment	£8,000
Preparing for determination on the papers	£3,000

Miscellaneous points regarding the caps

The following miscellaneous points may be made about the operation of the caps. It should be noted that many of the points made about the incidence of costs in the IPEC may also be relevant (see 50.336). **50.330**

- **VAT** The limits are net of VAT.[706]
- **Set-off** The global cap applies after any set-off.[707]
- **Additional liabilities** Where a party has the benefit of a pre-commencement funding arrangement, they will be entitled to additional liabilities in principle, but in practice

[706] See CPR, r 45.31(5).
[707] See CPR, r 45.31(2).

Table 50.18 Scale costs for each stage of a claim up to determination of liability (PD 45, Table A—old provisions)

Stage of a claim	Maximum amount of costs
Particulars of claim	£6,125
Defence and counterclaim	£6,125
Reply and defence to counterclaim	£6,125
Reply to defence to counterclaim	£3,000
Attendance at a case management conference	£2,500
Making or responding to an application	£2,500
Providing or inspecting disclosure or product/process description	£5,000
Performing or inspecting experiments	£2,500
Preparing witness statements	£5,000
Preparing experts' report	£7,500
Preparing for and attending trial and judgment	£15,000
Preparing for determination on the papers	£5,000

Table 50.19 Scale costs for each stage of an inquiry as to damages or account of profits (PD 45, Table B—old provisions)

Stage of a claim	Maximum amount of costs
Points of claim	£2,500
Points of defence	£2,500
Attendance at a case management conference	£2,500
Making or responding to an application	£2,500
Providing or inspecting disclosure	£2,500
Preparing witness statements	£5,000
Preparing experts' report	£5,000
Preparing for and attending trial and judgment	£7,500
Preparing for determination on the papers	£2,500

they will rarely benefit from this because those liabilities would, in general, be regarded as being included in the cap.[708]

- **Proceedings begun before 1 October 2013** Where proceedings were started on or after 1 October 2013, court fees, costs relating to enforcement of an order and wasted costs are excluded from those caps.[709]

---

708 *Henderson v All Around the World Recordings Ltd* [2013] EWPCC 19, at [3], [4], [12] and [38]–[41], *per* Judge Birss QC. See also *Crocuer Enterprises v Giordano Poultry* [2013] EWHC 2491 (Ch), in which Mann J referred to *Henderson* and declined to transfer a claim from the High Court, because (on the facts of the case before him) such a transfer would have unfairly deprived the claimant of the legitimate benefit of a (pre-April 2013) conditional fee agreement.

709 See CPR, r 45.31(4A).

- **Costs incurred in other courts** Scale costs do not apply to costs incurred in circumstances in which the rest of the IPEC measures did not apply;[710] hence costs incurred in the High Court before transfer to the IPEC will be assessed without reference to scale costs.[711]
- **More than one receiving party** Judge Hacon has found that where there was more than one receiving party, the stage costs cap had to be shared between them and did not apply to them individually.[712] Similarly, it is not open to a claimant to aggregate two costs caps when its case was conducted as a single claim that was case managed as a single set of proceedings; hence it would not be open to a claimant to say that they should have the benefit of one figure for liability and another for quantum.[713] Judge Birss QC commented that if a party argues at the case management conference that its claims on liability and damages should be separated, that could have been taken into account in deciding whether to order a single trial.[714]
- **More than one defendant** Where there is more than one defendant, the parties should consider the likely effect of the costs capping provisions, because the cap may act as a global limit, in respect of the costs a claimant may claim[715] *and* the costs that successful defendants might claim.[716] Judge Birss QC explained that this was because certainty was to be preferred over compensation:

> 'The procedures applicable in the Patents County Court are to facilitate access to justice for small and medium sized enterprises in intellectual property disputes. The costs cap has an important role in facilitating access to justice in that it allows a litigant to be confident about its possible costs exposure if it loses the case.'[717]

- **Preliminary issues** Whilst his comments were *obiter* and Judge Hacon has declined to follow,[718] Judge Birss QC suggested that where a case proceeds by way of a trial on a preliminary issue, that trial will be a 'trial' for the purposes of stage costs, and the stages that apply to and include a trial will apply.[719] In view of what is said below, however, even if Judge Birss's comments were to be applied, they would relate only to stage costs (that is, they would not relate to the global cap).
- **Meaning of 'claim'** Judge Birss QC had the following to say about the meaning of the word 'claim' in what is now CPR, r 45.31(1)(a) (the provision that imposes the global cap):

> 'It is true that in some places in the CPR the word claim is used to refer to different claims in a single proceeding which was started by a single claim form, with a "claim" against one defendant and a separate "claim" against another defendant. But the expression is also used in a similar

---

[710] *Westwood v Knight* [2011] EWPCC 011, at [13], *per* Judge Birss QC; *Technical Fibre Products & Anor v David Walton Bell & Ors* [2010] EWPCC 011, at [8]. See also *Caljan Rite-Hite Ltd v Sovex Ltd* [2010] EWHC 669 (Ch), *per* Kitchin J.

[711] *Westwood v Knight* [2011] EWPCC 011, at [13] and [38], *per* Judge Birss QC.

[712] *Akhtar v Bhopal Productions (UK) Ltd* [2015] EWHC 154 (IPEC), at [17]–[20], [23]–[26], [31] and [32], *per* Judge Hacon.

[713] *Azzurrin Communications Ltd v International Telecommunications Equipment Ltd* [2013] EWPCC 22, at [7].

[714] *Ibid*, at [8].

[715] See *Gimex v Chillbag* [2012] EW PCC 34.

[716] See *Liversidge v Owen Mumford (Costs)* [2012] EWPCC 40.

[717] See *Gimex v Chillbag* [2012] EW PCC 34, at [18].

[718] See *Global Flood Defence Systems Ltd v Johann Van Den Noort Beheer BV* [2016] EWHC 189 (IPEC), at [11].

[719] See *Destra Software Ltd v Comada (UK) LLP* [2012] EWPCC Civ 39.

way to refer to separate claims brought against the same defendant. If [counsel's] submission were right then a claimant with two claims against a single defendant would be entitled to two cost caps. I do not believe that is correct and I reject this submission. Moreover if one took a formalistic approach to the rule then a normal case for infringement of a registered right like a registered design or patent, which consists of a claim for infringement and a counterclaim for revocation, could be regarded as two claims for the purposes of the rule. I do not think that is right. In my judgment the claim referred to in [what is now CPR, r 45.31(1)(a)] means a single set of proceedings. ... I conclude that [CPR, r 45.31(1)] protects the paying party and means that the court cannot award total costs of more than £50,000 in the Patents County Court.'[720]

Judge Hacon agreed with this analysis and found that, as such, the assessment of costs in the IPEC is something that must wait until all issues have been resolved.[721]

- **Small claims** Whilst the rules regarding summary assessment will apply to a claim allocated to the small claims track, the caps will not.[722]
- **Part 20 claims** A Part 20 claim gives rise to a separate overall costs cap and, within it, separate stage caps.[723]
- **When in doubt** Finally, it is worth noting that the Intellectual Property Enterprise Court Guide helpfully suggests that when there is doubt about the likely effect of the cap, the parties should raise the matter at the case management conference.[724]

Discretion regarding the caps

50.331 The court has the power to disapply the caps. There are two mechanisms by which this can be done.[725] The first will come into play if the court considers that a party has behaved in a manner that amounts to an abuse of the court's process; where the court makes such a finding, the limits in CPR, Part 45, Section IV, do not apply.[726] The second mechanism will apply where a party has behaved unreasonably, in which case the court may make an order for costs at the conclusion of the hearing[727] and those costs are in addition to those that are subject to the global cap.[728] This would be an exercise of the court's ordinary jurisdiction regarding costs (that is, the jurisdiction under CPR, r 44.2).

Unreasonable conduct and the disapplication of the caps

50.332 Judge Birss QC had this to say about the exercise of discretion in a case in which the paying party was accused of poor conduct:

'The discretion [to set the global cap aside] exists but to exercise it to depart from the cap in anything other than a truly exceptional case would undermine the point of the costs capping

[720] *Liversidge v Owen Mumford Ltd* [2012] EWPCC Civ 40, at [13] and [19].

[721] See *Global Flood Defence Systems Ltd v Johann Van Den Noort Beheer BV* [2016] EWHC 189 (IPEC), at [15].

[722] See CPR, r 63.28(2), which makes no mention of CPR, r 63.26(3), applying to the claim, but does apply CPR, r 63.26(1) and (2).

[723] See *Martin v Kogan* [2017] EWHC 3266 (IPEC), at [49], *per* Judge Hacon.

[724] See HM Courts & Tribunals Service, Intellectual Property Enterprise Court Guide (London: HMSO, 2016), para 2.12.

[725] See CPR, rr 63.26(2) and 45.32.

[726] See CPR, r 45.30(2)(a).

[727] See CPR, r 63.26(2).

[728] See CPR, r 45.32. It should be noted that costs payable pursuant to CPR, r 63.26(2), are themselves still subject to the stage cap. So, eg, unreasonable behaviour in an application will lead to a costs order, payable following that hearing, of up to £3,000, but no more; if all other costs at the end of the case exceed the global cap, the relevant party will be awarded £50,000. The £3,000 already paid will be ignored for the purpose of the global cap.

> system. ... the point of the PCC costs rules are to favour certainty as opposed to a fully compensatory approach to costs.'[729]

Thus a global cap will be lifted only if the case is 'truly exceptional'.

Judge Hacon has found that the stage caps may be lifted in less than truly exceptional circumstances, saying this on the point: **50.333**

> 'I [take] the view that the general discretion could be exercised to lift one or more of the caps on stage costs in less than truly exceptional circumstances if the result was that the overall cap on total costs was left undisturbed.'[730]

Thus, in a 'truly exceptional' case, the court is able, as a matter of discretion, to lift the global cap. In a case that was not truly exceptional, however, the court could lift the stage caps, but only if the global cap remained in place.[731] Judge Hacon had this to say about the standard of conduct that would justify the stage caps being lifted: 'There can be no question of a further sanction in the form of the lifting of the stage cap on costs of the application without unusually bad behaviour on the part of the offending party.'[732] **50.334**

It is worth noting that applications to lift the caps are allowed only infrequently. One reason for this is that the IPEC is very much aware of the fact that a party's perception of the apparent fairness of the caps is often influenced by whether that party has won. This much is clear from the following observations of Judge Birss QC, which are often quoted when a successful partly complains about the putative injustice of the caps: **50.335**

> 'I believe what is really happening ... is an example of a psychological phenomenon I have become familiar with in the PCC. When the risk was in the future, the claimant wished to litigate in the Patents County Court to protect herself against the risk of an adverse costs award. That is why proceedings were brought and pursued in this court with this costs regime. The impact of the PCC cap on the claimant's actual costs if she won was predictable. If the claimant had lost, the costs cap would have been strongly relied on. The claimant was able to enforce her intellectual property rights in this case because of the predictability of the costs cap remaining in place. She was relying on it. Now that the claimant has won, the uncertainty has evaporated. The balance of risk and reward is now entirely different. [It] now seems to the claimant quite unfair that the cap prevents her from recovering a higher share of her costs. But that is because the position after judgment is very different.'[733]

---

[729] In *Henderson v All Around The World Recordings Ltd* [2013] EWPC 19, at [12]. By way of example, in *Skyscape Cloud Services Ltd v Sky plc* [2016] EWHC 1340 (IPEC), Judge Hacon found that a lack of clarity in a party's case was not 'truly exceptional' and, as such, he declined to lift the overall cap (but see below for his decision on stage caps).

[730] *Akhtar v Bhopal Productions (UK) Ltd* [2015] EWHC 154 (IPEC), at [20], in which Judge Hacon cited his own judgment in *FH Brundle v Perry* [2014] EWHC 979 (IPEC), at [16].

[731] See *FH Brundle v Perry* [2014] EWHC 979 (IPEC), at [14]–[17], *per* Judge Hacon.

[732] See *ibid.* By way of example, in *Skyscape Cloud Services Ltd v Sky plc* [2016] EWHC 1340 (IPEC), Judge Hacon did decide to raise one of the individual caps from £3,000 to £8,000, which still left the overall costs with the overarching cap, and he noted that the claimant's conduct was 'not ideal', which was presumably an understatement, given his comments in *FH Brundle*.

[733] *Henderson v All Around The World Recordings Ltd* [2013] EWPC 19, at [40]. See, eg, *Global Flood Defence Systems Ltd v Johann Van Den Noort Beheer BV* [2016] EWHC 189 (IPEC), at [16], *per* Judge Hacon.

A note on costs orders (that is, the incidence of costs) in the Intellectual Property Enterprise Court

50.336 Because costs in the IPEC are summarily assessed,[734] there tends to be a degree of overlap between decisions on the incidence of costs (CPR, Part 44) and the amounts of costs. In view of this, it is worth making the following points regarding the way in which the IPEC makes decisions regarding the incidence of costs.

- **Issues-based orders in general** In the normal course, at the end of a trial, the court will decide which party is the overall winner. The winner may have lost in relation to some issues. That does not necessarily mean that the winner's costs will be subject to a discount or that there will be a set-off, but in appropriate cases this will be done.[735] Where this is so, this will invite the question as to whether the caps should be applied before or after the issues-based adjustment. The answer is that the caps will apply after the issue-based adjustment has been made, rather than before.[736] Put otherwise, the cap comes last. Judge Hacon has summarised the steps the court would ordinarily take in this regard:

  '(1) Identify the party who is the winner overall.

  Assuming there is an overall winner,

  (2) identify any sufficiently circumscribed issues in relation to which the winner should be deprived of his costs, having lost on those issues;
  (3) identify any other issues sufficiently exceptional such that the winner should pay the loser's costs of those issues;
  (4) taking into account (2) and (3), assess an overall discount to be applied to the award of costs to the winner (any issues falling under (3) will usually count double so that, for instance, if an issue accounts for 10% of the total costs, the net effect of the winner paying the loser is to reduce the award to the winner by 20%);
  (5) make a summary assessment of the costs that would be awarded for each stage identified in Table A of PD 45 Section IV without taking into account the cost caps for each stage;
  (6) apply the overall discount to each of those summary assessments;
  (7) compare the result in each case with the corresponding cost cap in Table A ... ;
  (8) make an award for each stage by reference to that comparison;
  (9) add together those stage awards to reach a final total.

  This final total will be the award in costs, subject to the overall cap of £50,000.'[737]

  Thus each of the stage costs incurred by the winner will be subjected to summary assessment and then, if appropriate, a discount or a set-off will be applied to each of the assessed costs. The total of all of the assessed stage costs after discount or set-off will be awarded, subject to the overall cap.[738]
- **Set-off** CPR, r 45.31(2), expressly requires that, where it arises, a set-off must be applied before the overall cap is to be taken into account.

---

[734] See CPR, r 45.30(3).

[735] See *Global Flood Defence Systems Ltd v Johann Van Den Noort Beheer BV* [2016] EWHC 189 (IPEC), at [7], *per* Judge Hacon.

[736] *BOS GmbH & Co KG v Cobra UK Automotive Products Division Ltd (in administration)* [2012] EWPCC 44, *per* Judge Birss QC. See also *Global Flood Defence Systems Ltd v Johann Van Den Noort Beheer BV* [2016] EWHC 189 (IPEC), *per* Judge Hacon.

[737] See *The National Guild of Removers and Storers Ltd v Milner* [2014] EWHC 1117 (IPEC), at [5].

[738] See *BOS GmbH & Co KG v Cobra UK Automotive Products Division Ltd* [2012] EWPCC 44, at [23] and [24], *per* Judge Birss QC; see also *Global Flood Defence Systems Ltd v Johann Van Den Noort Beheer BV* [2016] EWHC 189 (IPEC), at [7], *per* Judge Hacon.

- **Percentage orders in patent cases** After having reviewed a number of (general) costs authorities relating to issues-based costs awards, Birss J has concluded that percentage orders can usually be made in patent cases and should be made if they can be.[739] This case was decided in the High Court, rather than in the IPEC, but there is no particular reason to believe that different principles would apply in the IPEC.
- **Poor conduct** In addition to the discretion to disapply the caps where the poorly behaved party is the paying party (see 50.331), poor conduct may result in a diminution of the costs that a party may receive when they would otherwise be the receiving party. In a case in which a claimant had failed to send a letter of claim, for example, Judge Hacon reduced certain costs by 50 per cent.[740]
- **Offers in general** The IPEC is able to take offers into account when deciding the incidence of costs.[741] Mr Daniel Alexander QC (sitting as an Enterprise judge) has explained that it is important for the IPEC to be careful not to encourage disputes to continue that are, in essence, only about costs and that one of the ways in which the court can achieve this aim is to take account of reasonable admissible offers made to settle a case at an early stage of proceedings in determining what costs should be paid if an action is pressed to trial in the face of such offers.[742] It seems that where the court reduces costs to take account of an offer, the reduction may, in an appropriate case, be applied to the capped amounts (that is, the reduction may be imposed after the cap rather than merely subject to the cap, which is what generally happens if the court makes an issues-based costs order or if the court allows costs to be set-off against costs).[743]
- **Claimants' Part 36 offers** Where a claimant is entitled to the benefit of having made and 'beaten' a Part 36 offer, there is a tension between the provision of CPR, r 36.17(4), and the caps on costs in the IPEC. Judge Hacon has considered *Broadhurst v Tan*,[744] in which Dyson MR considered the putatively analogous tension between CPR, r 36.17(4), and CPR, Part 45, Section IIIA (see 50.293). Whilst Judge Hacon did not find all of Dyson MR's observations to be relevant, on balance he found that CPR, r 36.17(4), takes precedence over the caps on costs in IPEC and that, as such, if a claimant is fortunate enough to 'beat' their own Part 36 offer, neither the stage costs nor the overall cap will apply to any costs awarded on the indemnity basis as a result.[745] That said, in a subsequent case, Judge Hacon explained that costs remain in the discretion of the court and that, in the absence of serious misconduct by the defendant, the costs are likely to be restricted to the caps for each stage *plus* 25 per cent.[746]

---

739 *Unwired Planet International Ltd v Huawei Technologies Co Ltd* [2016] EWHC 410 (Pat), at [10].

740 See *Baxter Healthcare UK Ltd v Fresenius Kabi* [2014] EWHC 3021 (IPEC).

741 See, eg, *Wilkinson v London Strategic Health Authority* [2012] EWPCC 55, at [49], in which Judge Birss QC took account of offers made to resolve the case at an early stage of proceedings, which, overall, resulted in percentage reductions in costs, even though the offers made were not for all of the relief claimed including costs.

742 See *Bocacina Ltd v Boca Cafes Ltd* [2014] EWHC 26 (IPEC), at [12] and [13].

743 See, eg, *ibid*, at [55].

744 *Broadhurst v Tan* [2016] EWCA Civ 94.

745 *Phonographic Performance Ltd v Hagan* [2016] EWHC 3076 (IPEC), at [39].

746 *Martin v Kogan* [2017] EWHC 3266 (IPEC), at [29]–[33]. In this regard, Judge Hacon took into account what was said in Jackson, R, *Review of Civil Litigation Costs: Supplemental Report* (London: HMSO, 2017), Annex 15, para 3.15.

- **Defendants' Part 36 offers** Where a defendant is entitled to the benefit of having made and 'beaten' a Part 36 offer, it will be entitled to costs from the date of the expiry of the relevant period, but that entitlement will be subject to the cap.[747]

Procedure in the Intellectual Property Enterprise Court

Summary assessments only

50.337 CPR, r 45.30(3), provides as follows: 'The court will make a summary assessment of the costs of the party in whose favour any order for costs is made. Rules 44.2(8), 44.7(b) and Part 47 do not apply to this Section.'

50.338 Thus, in the IPEC, all costs are assessed summarily[748]—a feature that the IPEC regards as being of particular importance.[749] This rule applies whether the trial has taken a single day or has taken more time. Presumably as a consequence, rules as to interim payments and detailed assessment proceedings are specifically disapplied.[750]

Interim hearings

50.339 At the interim stage, costs of an application in the IPEC will be reserved to the conclusion of the trial.[751] Moreover, Judge Hacon has said that the assessment of costs in the IPEC is something that must wait until after all of the issues in the claim have been resolved.[752]

Statements of costs

50.340 Notwithstanding the fact that scale costs may apply, statements of costs should be in the standard form and should include, in particular, information as to time spent.[753] In preparing their statement of costs, parties should bear in mind that they will need to explain which costs relate to which stages of the claim.[754] In a case in which the receiving party provided a breakdown of costs by stage together with a summary schedule setting out totals for each stage, Judge Birss QC commented that the schedule was a useful document and commended it to other litigants in the future.[755]

50.341 In a case in which the receiving party was unable to explain which costs related to which stage, Mr Recorder Douglas Campbell made the following observations:

> 'I am not prepared either to make assumptions in the defendant's favour about matters which the defendant could have proved, or to award some arbitrary sum, since to do so would be unfair to the claimant. I therefore make no award for the defendant's costs relating to disclosure over this period.'[756]

---

[747] See *Martin v Kogan* [2017] EWHC 3266 (IPEC), at [39], *per* Judge Hacon.

[748] CPR, r 45.30(3). The general approach to the summary assessment process is explained in *Westwood v Knight* [2011] EWPCC 11.

[749] *Westwood v Knight* [2011] EWPCC 011, *per* Judge Birss QC.

[750] See CPR, r 45.30(3).

[751] See CPR, r 63.26(1).

[752] See *Global Flood Defence Systems Ltd v Johann Van Den Noort Beheer BV* [2016] EWHC 189 (IPEC), at [15], *per* Judge Hacon.

[753] *Indigo Furniture Ltd v Futurelook Ltd* [2011] EWPCC 013, at [18].

[754] See HM Courts & Tribunals Service, Intellectual Property Enterprise Court Guide (London: HMSO, 2014).

[755] *Westwood v Knight* [2011] EWPCC 011.

[756] See *Lumos Skincare Ltd v Sweet Squared Ltd* [2012] EWPCC 28, at [23].

CPR, Part 45, Section V: Fixed Costs—HM Revenue & Customs

Fixed costs relating to HM Revenue & Customs (HMRC) are governed by CPR, Part 45, Section V (previously Section VIII). That Section applies where the only claim is conducted by an HMRC officer[757] in the County Court and its hearing centres for recovery of a debt[758] and the officer obtains judgment on the claim. The costs, known as HMRC charges, are not the costs in the traditional sense, but are monies payable for the work carried out by an HMRC officer; as such, they are a species of litigant-in-person costs. They are nonetheless treated as if they were solicitors' profit fees.[759] They are 'fixed' only in the sense that they are default figures; the court is able to 'order otherwise',[760] which presumably means that the court is able to exercise its discretion according to CPR, rr 44.2 and 44.4. **50.342**

Court fees and fixed commencement costs may be claimed.[761] The latter, however, comprise the HMRC charges and are calculated on the basis of Table 50.20 in accordance with the value of the claim as stated on the claim form.[762] **50.343**

Where judgment is entered, 'fixed costs on entry of judgment' are added, which are £15 if the value of the claim does not exceed £5,000 and £20 if it does.[763] If, however, the full **50.344**

Table 50.20 Fixed costs on commencement of a County Court claim conducted by an HMRC officer (CPR, Part 44, Table 7)

Value of claim	Cost
Where the value of the claim exceeds £25 but does not exceed £500	£33
Where the value of the claim exceeds £500 but does not exceed £1,000	£47
Where the value of the claim exceeds £1,000 but does not exceed £5,000	£53
Where the value of the claim exceeds £5,000 but does not exceed £15,000	£67
Where the value of the claim exceeds £15,000 but does not exceed £50,000	£90
Where the value of the claim exceeds £50,000 but does not exceed £100,000	£113
Where the value of the claim exceeds £100,000 but does not exceed £150,000	£127
Where the value of the claim exceeds £150,000 but does not exceed £200,000	£140
Where the value of the claim exceeds £200,000 but does not exceed £250,000	£153
Where the value of the claim exceeds £250,000 but does not exceed £300,000	£167
Where the value of the claim exceeds £300,000	£180

[757] 'HMRC Officer' means a person appointed by the Commissioners under Commissioners for Revenue and Customs Act 2005, s 2, and authorised to conduct County Court proceedings for recovery of debt under s 25(1A) of that Act: see CPR, r 45.33(2).

[758] 'Debt' means any sum payable to the Commissioners under or by virtue of an enactment or under a contract settlement: see CPR, r 45.33(2).

[759] CPR, r 45.33(3), provides that HMRC charges shall, for the purpose of CPR, Part 45, Section VIII, be claimed as 'solicitor costs' on relevant court forms.

[760] CPR, r 45.33(1).

[761] See CPR, r 45.33(5) and (6), respectively.

[762] See CPR, r 45.34.

[763] See CPR, r 45.35, and Pt 45, Table 8.

amount of the claim and the fixed costs on commencement are paid within 14 days of service of the particulars of claim, nothing else is payable unless the court orders otherwise.[764]

CPR, Part 45, Section VI: Fast-Track Trial Costs

Scope and application

50.345 CPR, Part 45, Section VI, deals with the amount of costs that the court may award for an advocate who prepares for and appears at a fast-track trial.[765] Fast-track trial costs under CPR, Part 45, Section VI, apply only where CPR, Part 45, Section IIIA, does not apply. The following general points can be made about allocation to the fast track.

- **Allocation criteria** Whilst the court may order otherwise if the claim cannot be dealt with justly on the fast track,[766] the fast track is the normal track for any claim for which the small claims track is not the normal track and which has a value of not more than £25,000 (or £15,000, if the proceedings were issued before 6 April 2009).[767] This will not be the case, however, if the trial is likely to last for longer than one day[768] (based on a 5-hour day[769]) or oral expert evidence is needed of experts in more than two expert fields (or more than one expert per party in any one field).[770]
- **Value of the claim for allocation purposes** It is for the court to assess the financial value of a claim and, in doing so, it will disregard any amount not in dispute, any claim for interest, costs and any contributory negligence[771] (see 50.352–50.355). Where two or more claimants have started a claim against the same defendant using the same claim form and each claimant has a claim against the defendant separate from that of the other claimant(s), the court will consider the claim of each claimant separately when it assesses financial value.[772] The topic of valuation for the purposes of calculating the amount of the fixed fee is addressed at 50.352–50.355.
- **Factors other than the value of the claim** In considering whether to allocate a claim to a track that is not the normal track according to the value of the claim, the test the court applies is whether the case could be dealt with justly on the fast track.[773] The court will have regard to:[774]
  - the nature of the remedy sought;[775]

[764] See CPR, r 45.36.

[765] CPR, r 45.37(1); PD 45, para 4.1.

[766] This is implied by CPR, r 26.7, and PD 26, para 9.1. The latter provides as follows: 'Where the court is to decide whether to allocate to the fast track or the multi-track a claim for which the normal track is the fast track, it will allocate the claim to the fast track unless it believes that it cannot be dealt with justly on that track.'

[767] See CPR, r 26.6(4).

[768] See CPR, r 26.6(5). PD 26, para 9.1(3)(c), provides as follows: 'The possibility that a trial might last longer than one day is not necessarily a conclusive reason for the court to allocate or to re-allocate a claim to the multi-track.'

[769] See PD 26, para 9.2(3)(a).

[770] See CPR, r 26.6(5).

[771] See CPR, r 26.8(2).

[772] See CPR, r 26.8(3).

[773] See PD 26, para 9.1(1).

[774] See CPR, r 26.7(1).

[775] See CPR, r 26.8(1)(b).

- the likely complexity of the facts, law or evidence;[776]
- the number of parties or likely parties;[777]
- the value of any counterclaim or other Part 20 claim and the complexity of any matters relating to it;[778]
- the amount of oral evidence that may be required;[779]
- the importance of the claim to persons who are not parties to the proceedings;[780]
- the views expressed by the parties;[781] and
- the circumstances of the parties.[782]

- **Counterclaims and other Part 20 claims** A claim and a counterclaim will not be relegated to the small claims track merely because the court makes an award after set-off for a net amount that is below the small claims limit; rather, the court will look at the matter in the round.[783] Where the case involves a counterclaim or other Part 20 claim that will be tried with the claim and, as a result, the trial will last more than a day, the court may not allocate it to the fast track.[784]
- **Split trials** A claim may be allocated to the fast track or ordered to remain on that track even though there is to be a split trial.[785]
- **Misallocation** The topic of misallocation (that is, where a claim has been allocated to the wrong track because of exaggeration or mistake) is addressed at 50.396, albeit in the context of the small claims track. It should be borne in mind that there is a practice direction that provides that CPR, Part 45, Section VI, applies only where, at the date of the trial, the claim is allocated to the fast track; it goes on to say that Section VI does not apply in any other case, irrespective of the final value of the claim.[786]
- **Reallocation** The topic of reallocation is addressed at 50.388 (albeit in the context of the small claims track). Reallocation is, however, not generally problematic in the context of fast-track trial fees, because it will be the final allocation that is relevant.

[776] See CPR, r 26.8(1)(c). Moreover, PD 26, para 9.2, provides that 'the court will, in particular, take into account the limits likely to be placed on disclosure, the extent to which expert evidence may be necessary and whether the trial is likely to last more than a day'.

[777] See CPR, r 26.8(1)(d).

[778] See CPR, r 26.8(1)(e). Furthermore, PD 26, para 7.7, provides as follows: 'Where the case involves more than one money claim (for example where there is a Part 20 claim or there is more than one claimant each making separate claims) the court will not generally aggregate the claims. Instead it will generally regard the largest of them as determining the financial value of the claims.'

[779] See CPR, r 26.8(1)(f).

[780] See CPR, r 26.8(1)(g).

[781] See CPR, r 26.8(1)(h). In addition, PD 26, para 7.1, provides as follows: 'The court will treat these views as an important factor, but the allocation decision is one for the court, to be taken in the light of all the circumstances, and the court will not be bound by any agreement or common view of the parties.'

[782] See CPR, r 26.8(1)(i).

[783] *Boynton v Willers* [2003] EWCA Civ 904, at [41].

[784] See PD 26, para 9.1(3)(e).

[785] See PD 26, para 9.1(3)(d).

[786] See PD 45, para 4.2.

50.346 These provisions apply only where, at the date of the trial, the claim is allocated to the fast track. They do not apply in any other case, irrespective of the final value of the claim.[787] In particular, they do not apply to any disposal hearing at which the amount to be paid under a judgment or order is decided by the court.[788]

50.347 'Fast-track trial costs' means the costs of a party's advocate for preparing for and appearing at the trial, but does not include any other disbursements or VAT.[789]

50.348 'Advocate' means a person exercising a right of audience as a representative of, or on behalf of, a party, which definition is not limited to counsel.[790]

50.349 'Trial' includes a hearing at which the court decides an amount of money or the value of goods following a judgment under CPR, Part 12 ('Default judgment'), or CPR, Part 14 ('Admissions'), but does not include the following:

- the hearing of an application for summary judgment (under CPR, Part 24); or
- the court's approval of a settlement (under CPR, r 21.1).[791]

The amount of fast-track trial costs

50.350 Where the receiving party is a litigant in person, the costs will be assessed in the usual way.[792] Otherwise, the amount of costs depends on the value of the claim in accordance with Table 50.21.[793]

50.351 For costs incurred on or after 1 October 2007, the appropriate amounts are as set out in Table 50.21.

Table 50.21 Amount of fast-track trial costs (CPR, Part 45, Table 9)

Value of the claim	Amount of fast-track trial costs that the court may award
No more than £3,000	£485
More than £3,000 but not more than £10,000	£690
More than £10,000 but not more than £15,000	£1,035
For proceedings issued on or after 6 April 2009, more than £15,000	£1,650

787 PD 45, para 4.2.
788 PD 45, para 4.3; see also PD 26, para 12.8. The same used to be true of a claim that has been allocated to the small claims track with the consent of the parties given under CPR, r 26.7(3), but that provision no longer exists.
789 CPR, r 45.37(2).
790 CPR, r 45.37(2).
791 CPR, r 45.37(2).
792 CPR, r 45.39(5).
793 CPR, r 45.38(1).

The measure of the value of the claim varies, depending on whether the claim is a money claim and on whether the receiving party is the claimant or the defendant.[794] **50.352**

- **Money only (claimant)** For the purposes of evaluating a money-only claim in which costs are payable to a claimant, the figure is the amount of the judgment, but interest and costs are disregarded, as is any reduction made for contributory negligence.[795]
- **Money only (defendant)** For the purposes of evaluating a money-only claim in which costs are payable to a defendant, the figure is the amount specified in the claim form, but interest and costs are disregarded.[796] If no amount is stated in the claim form, then the figure is the maximum amount the claimant reasonably expected to recover according to the statement of value included in the claim form under CPR, r 16.3.[797] If the claim form states that the claimant cannot reasonably say how much they expect to recover, then the amount is £15,000.[798]
- **Non-money only (claimant/defendant)** Where the claim is only for a remedy other than the payment of money, then, unless the court orders otherwise, the value of the claim is deemed to be more than £3,000, but not more than £10,000.[799]
- **Both money and non-money (claimant/defendant)** Where the claim includes both a claim for the payment of money and for a remedy other than the payment of money, the value of the claim is deemed to be the higher of:
  – the value of the money claim (decided as above); or
  – the deemed value of the other remedy (decided as above).[800]
  The court may order otherwise, however.[801]

Where the court assesses the costs of a claim that has been allocated to the fast track, but which has settled before the start of the trial, it may not allow, in respect of the advocate's costs, an amount that exceeds the amount of fast-track trial costs that would have been payable had the trial taken place.[802] When deciding the amount to be allowed in respect of the advocate's costs, the court shall have regard to when the claim was settled and when the court was notified that the claim had settled.[803] **50.353**

As to valuation where there is more than one claimant or defendant, see 50.362–50.367. **50.354**

Where a defendant has made a counterclaim against the claimant that has a higher value than the claim, and where the claimant succeeds at trial on both their claim and the counterclaim, the value of the claim is the value of the defendant's counterclaim calculated in accordance with the provisions set out above.[804] **50.355**

[794] CPR, r 45.38(3), (4) and (5).
[795] CPR, r 45.38(3)(a).
[796] CPR, r 45.38(3)(b)(i).
[797] CPR, r 45.38(3)(b)(ii).
[798] CPR, r 45.38(3)(b)(iii).
[799] CPR, r 45.38(4).
[800] CPR, r 45.38(5).
[801] CPR, r 45.38(5).
[802] See CPR, r 46.12(1).
[803] CPR, r 46.12(2).
[804] CPR, r 45.38(6).

The power to award more or less than fast-track trial costs

50.356 The court may not award more or less than the amount shown in Table 50.21 except where:

- it decides not to award any fast-track trial costs; or
- one of the circumstances set out below applies.

The court may, however, apportion the amount awarded between the parties to reflect their respective degrees of success on the issues at trial.[805]

Unreasonable conduct

50.357 Where the court considers that the party to whom fast-track trial costs are to be awarded has behaved unreasonably or improperly during the trial, it may award that party an amount less than would otherwise be payable for that claim, as it considers appropriate.[806]

Improper conduct

50.358 Where the court considers that the party who is to pay the fast-track trial costs has behaved improperly during the trial, the court may award such additional amount to the other party as it considers appropriate.[807]

Multiple trials

50.359 Where there is more than one trial (for example a trial on limitation, followed by a trial generally), the court may award an additional amount in respect of the additional trial, but the amount must not exceed two-thirds of the amount payable for that claim, subject to a minimum award of £485.[808]

Cross-orders as to costs

50.360 Where a defendant has made a counterclaim against the claimant, and the claimant has succeeded on their claim *and* the defendant has succeeded on their counterclaim, the court will quantify the amount of the award of fast-track trial costs to which:

- but for the counterclaim, the claimant would be entitled for succeeding on their claim; and
- but for the claim, the defendant would be entitled for succeeding on their counterclaim.

It will then make one award of the difference, if any, to the party entitled to the higher award of costs.[809]

Necessary to be attended

50.361 If the court believes that it was 'necessary' for another legal representative to attend the trial to assist the advocate, the court may award an additional £345 in respect of that person's attendance.[810]

Fast-track trial costs where there is more than one claimant or defendant

50.362 Where one advocate is acting for more than one claimant and where each claimant has a separate claim against the defendant, the value of the claim is as follows.[811]

---

805 CPR, r 45.38(2).
806 CPR, r 45.39(7).
807 CPR, r 45.39(8).
808 CPR, r 45.39(3) and (4).
809 CPR, r 45.39(6).
810 CPR, r 45.39(2).
811 CPR, r 45.40(3) and (6).

Money-only (claimant)

50.363 Where the only claim of each claimant is for the payment of money, if the award of costs is in favour of the claimants, the value of the claim is the total amount of the judgment made in favour of all of the claimants jointly represented.

Money-only (defendant)

50.364 Where the award is in favour of the defendant, the value of the claim is the total amount claimed by the claimants, quantified, in either case, in accordance with the principles set out at 50.352.

Non-money-only (claimant and defendant)

50.365 Where the only claim of each claimant is for a remedy other than the payment of money, the value of the claim is deemed to be more than £3,000, but not more than £10,000.

Both money and non-money (claimant and defendant)

50.366 Where the claims of the claimants include a claim for both the payment of money and a remedy other than the payment of money, the value of the claim will be deemed to be more than £3,000, but not more than £10,000. If greater, the value of the money claims will be calculated in accordance with the provisions above.

50.367 Once the value of the claim has been gauged, the costs will be awarded on the following basis.

- Where the same advocate is acting for more than one party, the court may make only one award in respect of fast-track trial costs payable to that advocate. The parties for whom the advocate is acting are jointly entitled to any fast-track trial costs awarded by the court.[812]
- Where there is more than one defendant and any or all of the defendants are separately represented, the court may award fast-track trial costs to each party who is separately represented.[813]
- Where there is more than one claimant, but only one defendant, the court may make only one award to the defendant of fast-track trial costs, for which the claimants are jointly and severally liable.[814]

CPR, Part 45, Section VII: Costs Limits in Aarhus Convention Claims

50.368 Many environmental cases are in a different class from other claims. This is because there is a treaty known as the Aarhus Convention[815] that imposes an obligation on public authorities to ensure that certain claims (known as Aarhus Convention claims) are not 'prohibitively expensive'. If a claim is an Aarhus Convention claim, then the parties may be able to claim the benefit of CPR, Part 45, Section VII, in which case the amounts that either of the parties may be ordered to pay are significantly restricted. This is dealt with at 13.78–13.99.

---

812 CPR, r 45.40(1).
813 CPR, r 45.40(4).
814 CPR, r 45.40(5).
815 The UNECE Convention on Access to Information, Public Participation in Decision-Making and Access to Justice in Environmental Matters, 25 June 1998, Aarhus, Denmark.

Costs on the Small Claims Track

General provisions

50.369 As a rule, the court's power to award costs on the small claims track is significantly restricted. The relevant provisions may be found in CPR, r 27.14(2):

> '(1) This rule applies to any case which has been allocated to the small claims track unless paragraph (5) applies.
>
> (Rules 46.11 and 46.13 make provision in relation to orders for costs made before a claim has been allocated to the small claims track.)
>
> (2) The court may not order a party to pay a sum to another party in respect of that other party's costs, fees and expenses, including those relating to an appeal, except—
>
> (a) the fixed costs attributable to issuing the claim which—
>   (i) are payable under Part 45; or
>   (ii) would be payable under Part 45 if that Part applied to the claim;
>
> (b) in proceedings which included a claim for an injunction or an order for specific performance a sum not exceeding the amount specified in Practice Direction 27 for legal advice and assistance relating to that claim;
>
> (c) any court fees paid by that other party;
>
> (d) expenses which a party or witness has reasonably incurred in travelling to and from a hearing or in staying away from home for the purposes of attending a hearing;
>
> (e) a sum not exceeding the amount specified in Practice Direction 27 for any loss of earnings or loss of leave by a party or witness due to attending a hearing or to staying away from home for the purposes of attending a hearing;
>
> (f) a sum not exceeding the amount specified in Practice Direction 27 for an expert's fees;
>
> (g) such further costs as the court may assess by the summary procedure and order to be paid by a party who has behaved unreasonably;
>
> (h) the Stage 1 and, where relevant, the Stage 2 fixed costs in rule 45.18 where—
>   (i) the claim was within the scope of the Pre-Action Protocol for Low Value Personal Injury Claims in Road Traffic Accidents ('the RTA Protocol') or the Pre-action Protocol for Low Value Personal Injury (Employers' Liability and Public Liability) Claims ('the EL/PL Protocol');
>   (ii) the claimant reasonably believed that the claim was valued at more than the small claims track limit in accordance with paragraph 4.1(4) of the relevant Protocol; and
>   (iii) the defendant admitted liability under the process set out in the relevant Protocol; but
>   (iv) the defendant did not pay those Stage 1 and, where relevant, Stage 2 fixed costs; and
>
> (i) in an appeal, the cost of any approved transcript reasonably incurred.
>
> (3) A party's rejection of an offer in settlement will not of itself constitute unreasonable behaviour under paragraph (2)(g) but the court may take it into consideration when it is applying the unreasonableness test.
>
> (4) The limits on costs imposed by this rule also apply to any fee or reward for acting on behalf of a party to the proceedings charged by a person exercising a right of audience by virtue of an order under section 11 of the Courts and Legal Services Act 19901 (a lay representative).'

As can be seen, these limits apply not only to 'costs' in the general sense of that word, but also to fees rendered by a lay representative for acting on behalf of a party to the proceedings (see CPR, r 27.14(4)).

Certain sums may be payable, notwithstanding these general provisions, as follows. 50.370

- Experts' fees may be recoverable in principle, but they are limited to £750 for each report.[816]
- Where a party seeks an injunction or specific performance, they may be entitled to a contribution towards their costs of obtaining legal advice and assistance, but the amount must not exceed £260.[817]
- A party or its witnesses may be entitled to a payment of loss of earnings or compensation for loss of an entitlement to leave, but the amount payable (per party or per witness) is to be no more than £95 in any one day.[818]

The applicability of the small claims restriction

The provisions that govern allocation are set out in CPR, r 26.8: 50.371

> '(1) When deciding the track for a claim, the matters to which the court shall have regard include—
> (a) the financial value, if any, of the claim;
> (b) the nature of the remedy sought;
> (c) the likely complexity of the facts, law or evidence;
> (d) the number of parties or likely parties;
> (e) the value of any counterclaim or other Part 20 claim and the complexity of any matters relating to it;
> (f) the amount of oral evidence which may be required;
> (g) the importance of the claim to persons who are not parties to the proceedings;
> (h) the views expressed by the parties; and
> (i) the circumstances of the parties.
>
> (2) It is for the court to assess the financial value of a claim and in doing so it will disregard—
> (a) any amount not in dispute;
> (b) any claim for interest;
> (c) costs; and
> (d) any contributory negligence.
>
> (3) Where—
> (a) two or more claimants have started a claim against the same defendant using the same claim form; and
> (b) each claimant has a claim against the defendant separate from the other claimants,
> the court will consider the claim of each claimant separately when it assesses financial value under paragraph (1).'

Guidance on the interpretation of these provisions may be found in PD 26, para 7. That guidance stresses that whilst the court will regard the parties' own views as a factor to take into account, the final decision is a matter for the court itself.[819] Thus the fact that the parties' estimates show a high degree of commonality would no doubt help the court and possibly give it reassurance, but would not in any way bind the court or prevent it from coming to a different conclusion. 50.372

816 PD 27, para 7.3(2).
817 CPR, r 27.14(2)(b); PD 27, para 7.2.
818 See PD 27, para 7.3(1).
819 PD 26, paras 7.3 and 7.4.

50.373 PD 26, para 7.4, is particularly relevant:

> '7.4 In deciding, for the purposes of rule 26.8(2), whether an amount is in dispute the court will apply the following general principles:
> (1) Any amount for which the defendant does not admit liability is in dispute,
> (2) Any sum in respect of an item forming part of the claim for which judgment has been entered (for example a summary judgment) is not in dispute,
> (3) Any specific sum claimed as a distinct item and which the defendant admits he is liable to pay is not in dispute,
> (4) Any sum offered by the defendant which has been accepted by the claimant in satisfaction of any item which forms a distinct part of the claim is not in dispute.
> It follows from these provisions that if, in relation to a claim the value of which is above the small claims track limit of £10,000, the defendant makes, before allocation, an admission that reduces the amount in dispute to a figure below £10,000 (see CPR, Part 14), the normal track for the claim will be the small claims track. As to recovery of pre-allocation costs, the claimant can, before allocation, apply for judgment with costs on the amount of the claim that has been admitted (see CPR rule 14.3 but see also paragraph 7.1(3) of Practice Direction 46 under which the court has a discretion to allow pre-allocation costs).'

50.374 Where the case involves more than one money claim (for example where there is a Part 20 claim or there is more than one claimant each making separate claims), the court will, in general, not aggregate the claims; instead, it will regard the largest of them as the relevant figure.[820]

50.375 Whilst *obiter*, Patten LJ has said that he sees no reason in principle why a modest damages claim by an infant should be taken out of the small claims track merely because of the age of the claimant.[821]

Very modest claims requiring the court's approval

50.376 Where a claim for approval is brought under CPR, r 21.10(2), the claim will automatically be allocated to the multi-track (see CPR, r 8.9(c)). If that claim would otherwise have been allocated to the small claims track, this would create a tension between its actual allocation and its natural allocation. Patten LJ resolved that tension by finding that the court is able to exercise its discretion as to what is reasonable and proportionate:

> '[T]he costs judge is entitled to take into account the size and complexity of the claim ... What he is required to do is to look realistically at the underlying claim for damages which has been settled and consider whether the costs claimed in the Part 21.10(2) proceedings are proportionate to the issues involved. In practice the issues raised in the approval proceedings are unlikely to be any more or less complex than those which would have existed had the damages claim been issued and tried. Although the claimants are children, I accept [the paying party's] submission that in a simple and straightforward case (which these are) not involving serious injuries and with no real issues about liability or quantum the court is likely to have allocated the claim to its normal track and to have been able to deal with the case on that basis. This will obviously be highly material to a consideration of whether it was proportionate

---

[820] PD 26, para 7.7.
[821] *Dockerill v Tullett* [2012] EWCA Civ 184, at [18].

for the claimant to have employed solicitors to handle the approval proceedings beyond providing a written advice on the merits of the settlement in accordance with the Practice Direction.'[822]

Put otherwise, the court is entitled to look at the matter in the round and if the court is satisfied that the matter would have been allocated to the small claims track, the court is permitted to allow costs by reference to that track, but as a matter of discretion, rather than as a matter of the direct operation of CPR, r 27.14. **50.377**

Appeals

The small claims provisions apply to the costs of an appeal brought against a decision in a small claim.[823] This is also true of second appeals.[824] Sir Stanley Burnton has added that whilst CPR, r 52.9A, confers power to limit costs of an appeal, it does not confer power to award costs where there is a provision of the CPR precluding a costs order.[825] The costs of obtaining any approved transcript reasonably incurred may be recovered.[826] The provisions at CPR, r 52.14, do not detract from the protection afforded by the small claims track costs regime.[827] **50.378**

Pre-allocation

Where a claim has yet to be allocated, no special restrictions will apply. This is made clear by PD 47, para 7.1(1), which provides: 'Before a claim is allocated to either the small claims track or the fast track the court is not restricted by any of the special rules that apply to that track but see paragraph 8.2 below.' The reference to PD 47, para 8.2, is to the power to restrict costs to those that apply to the track that would have applied had the claim been allocated (see 50.393–50.395). **50.379**

Thus whilst the court should not regard itself as being fettered by the rules that would have applied upon allocation, it is open to the court to take those rules into account (or not), whichever is appropriate. In a case that was decided before PD 47, para 7.1, put the matter beyond doubt, Hughes LJ confirmed that it is open to the court to take into account the value of the claim at the time the letter of claim was sent rather than its value at the time proceedings were issued.[828] This may be relevant if, for example, a defendant has taken steps to diminish the value of the claim in an attempt to limit their liability for costs.[829] **50.380**

---

822 *Ibid*, at [37]–[42].

823 See CPR, r 27.14(2), which reads: 'The court may not order a party to pay a sum to another party in respect of that other party's costs, fees and expenses, including those relating to an appeal, except [those allowed under the small claims regime].'

824 See *Akhtar v Boland (Costs)* [2014] EWCA Civ 943, at [7], *per* Sir Stanley Burnton; *Conlon v Royal Sun Alliance Insurance plc* [2015] EWCA Civ 92, at [15], *per* Kitchin LJ. See also *Dammermann v Lanyon Bowdler LLP* [2017] EWCA Civ 269, at [15] and [35].

825 *Akhtar v Boland (Costs)* [2014] EWCA Civ 94, at [7].

826 See CPR, r 27.14(2)(i).

827 *Akhtar v Boland* [2014] EWCA Civ 943.

828 *BCC v Lee* [2008] EWCA Civ 891, at [36].

829 The example that was before Hughes LJ was where a claim for disrepair initially included a claim for specific performance, but the repairs were carried out on a certain date prior to the claim being made. Hughes LJ found that the appropriate order in that instance was that the costs should be determined on the fast track up to that date and that the small claims regime would apply thereafter.

Upon allocation

50.381 Allocation to the small claims track results in the small claims costs restriction applying. This is now the case in all claims that have been allocated to the small claims track. It used to be the case that CPR, r 27.14(1), provided that the small claims costs regime would not apply where (a) the financial value of a claim exceeded the limit for the small claims track and (b) the parties had agreed not only that the matter should be allocated to the small claim track, but also that fast-track costs provisions should continue to apply. That exception was struck from the rule on 1 April 2015. This ought not to cause any difficulties, however, because the provision in CPR, r 26.7(3), that gave the court the power to allocate a claim to the small claims track despite the amount being claimed being greater than the small claims limit was also struck from the CPR. As such, it should now never be the case that a claim for an amount greater than the small claims limit will be allocated to the small claims track.

50.382 Generally speaking, other than where a costs order had already been made,[830] the effect of allocation (as opposed to reallocation) will be retrospective. This is made clear by CPR, r 46.11, which provides as follows:

> '(1) Part 27 (small claims) and Part 45 Section VI (fast track trial costs) contain special rules about—
> (a) liability for costs;
> (b) the amount of costs which the court may award; and
> (c) the procedure for assessing costs.
>
> (2) Once a claim is allocated to a particular track, those special rules shall apply to the period before, as well as after, allocation except where the court or a practice direction provides otherwise.'

50.383 There are no practice directions that 'provide otherwise'. Whilst (as far as the author is aware) no court has ever made such an order, it would appear that CPR, r 46.11(2), gives the power to disapply the small claims limit for that period that pre-dated allocation. That power may exist in theory, but it could be exercised only by flouting PD 46, para 7.1(2), which reads:

> '(2) Where a claim has been so allocated, the special rules which relate to that track will apply to work done before as well as after allocation save to the extent (if any) that an order for costs in respect of that work was made before allocation.'

50.384 PD 46, para 7.1(3), makes the following provisions about claims that are allocated to the small claims track solely as a result of a defendant making a partial admission:

> '(3) Where a claim, issued for a sum in excess of the normal financial scope of the small claims track, is allocated to that track only because an admission of part of the claim by the defendant reduces the amount in dispute to a sum within the normal scope of that track; on entering judgment for the admitted part before allocation of the balance of the claim the court may allow costs in respect of the proceedings down to that date.'

50.385 Clearly, something has gone wrong with the drafting of this provision. Whilst not binding, District Judge Brett has found that it provides that the court may allow costs to the date of the entry of judgment—that is, that the reference to 'that date' is a reference to the date on which judgment was entered.[831]

---

[830] See CPR, r 46.13(1).

[831] See *Cameron v Office Depot UK Ltd* (unreported), 13 July 2016, Bromley County Court, at [4].

Costs orders made prior to allocation will still stand. This is made clear by CPR, r 46.13(1): 'Any costs orders made before a claim is allocated will not be affected by allocation.' **50.386**

Thus, other than to the extent that orders for costs have already been made, the effect of allocation is generally retrospective. **50.387**

Reallocation

The effect of reallocation is, in general, not retrospective. This is made clear by CPR, r 46.13(2), which provides as follows: **50.388**

> '(2) Where—
> (a) claim is allocated to a track; and
> (b) the court subsequently re-allocates that claim to a different track,
> then unless the court orders otherwise, any special rules about costs applying—
> (i) to the first track, will apply to the claim up to the date of re-allocation; and
> (ii) to the second track, will apply from the date of re-allocation.'

CPR, r 27.15, makes a very similar provision relating to claims that are reallocated upwards from the small claims track to another track: **50.389**

> 'Where a claim is allocated to the small claims track and subsequently re-allocated to another track, rule 27.14 (costs on the small claims track) will cease to apply after the claim has been re-allocated and the fast track or multi-track costs rules will apply from the date of re-allocation.'

Where this happens (that is, where a claim is reallocated from the small claims track to another track), the court must decide whether any party should pay costs already incurred in accordance with the rules about costs contained in CPR, Part 27. This is made clear by PD 46, para 8.1: **50.390**

> 'Before reallocating a claim from the small claims track to another track, the court must decide whether any party is to pay costs to the date of the order to re-allocate in accordance with the rules about costs contained in Part 27. If it decides to make such an order the court will make a summary assessment of those costs in accordance with that Part.'

Kitchin LJ has commented that if a court does reallocate a claim, CPR, r 46.13, implies that the court has the power to order 'backdate the re-allocation for costs purposes'—but he went on to say that any court contemplating making such an order would need to be satisfied that there were good reasons for doing so.[832] **50.391**

Discretionary application of the small costs limit

Where the natural home of a claim was the small claims track, there are two circumstances in which the court may be asked to apply the small claims costs limit: where the claim was not ever allocated; and where the claim was misallocated to either the fast track or the multitrack. **50.392**

No allocation Where a claim has not been allocated, the absence of allocation is anything but conclusive of the issue. It used to be the case that whilst the small claims regime ought not to be *applied* where a party has an order for assessment in their favour, the court was able to take that regime into account and, by that route, to assess the costs at a level that **50.393**

[832] *Conlon v Royal Sun Alliance Insurance plc* [2015] EWCA Civ 92, at [19].

was commensurate with the small claims regime.[833] The fine distinction between applying the small claims restrictions and allowing costs that are commensurate with those restrictions was difficult to understand and even more difficult to apply, so it is fortunate that the CPR now expressly provides that the court may restrict costs to those that would have applied had the claim been allocated.

50.394 Where a claim has not been allocated, the court has the power to treat it as if it had been allocated, but only if the award of costs is not on the indemnity basis. This is made clear by CPR, r 46.13(3):

> '(3) Where the court is assessing costs on the standard basis of a claim which concluded without being allocated to a track, it may restrict those costs to costs that would have been allowed on the track to which the claim would have been allocated if allocation had taken place.'

50.395 PD 46, para 8.2, says much the same thing:

> 'Where a settlement is reached or a Part 36 offer accepted in a case which has not been allocated but would, if allocated, have been suitable for allocation to the small claims track, rule 46.13 enables the court to allow only small claims track costs in accordance with rule 27.14. This power is not exercisable if the costs are to be paid on the indemnity basis.'

50.396 **Misallocation** The usual circumstances in which the small claims restrictions will apply as a matter of discretion are where a claim has been exaggerated and, but for that exaggeration, would have been allocated to the small claims track. In particular, if it can be shown that the claim was pleaded at a level above the small claims limit because of exaggeration, then the court will usually have no difficulty in imposing the small claims costs regime.[834] It might well do likewise if it can be shown that the claim was pleaded above the small claims limit because of mistake, oversight or carelessness. Both culpable and innocent exaggeration are discussed at 6.144–6.155.

50.397 Waller LJ has explained that whilst, in the absence of a 'special order', it would not be permissible for a costs judge to *apply* a fixed costs regime upon an assessment, it would be permissible for a costs judge to carry out an item-by-item assessment on the basis that, properly managed, a fixed costs regime *would* have applied—although he accepted that the difference between these two approaches may be very fine.[835]

- **Exaggeration prevented the claim from being allocated to the small claims track** The court is permitted to take into account the fact that the claim ought to have been

[833] *O'Beirne v Hudson* [2010] EWCA Civ 52, at [19], *per* Waller LJ, and at [22], *per* Hooper LJ. Similarly, in *Voice and Script International Ltd v Ashraf Alghafar* [2003] EWCA Civ 736, at [21], Judge LJ said that, '[in] the absence of any specific factors suggesting otherwise, in a case like this where, if sought, an allocation would have been made to small claims track the normal rule should be that small claims costs regime for costs should apply'. See also, in a different context, *Lahey v Pirelli* [2007] 1 WLR 998, at [19]–[22], *per* Dyson LJ.

[834] This was true even under the old regime: see *Devine v Franklin* [2002] EWHC 1846 (QB), *per* Gray J; *E Ivor Hughes Educational Foundation v Leach* [2005] EWHC 1317 (Ch).

[835] See *Drew v Whitbread* [2010] EWCA 53, at [41], in which Waller LJ said: 'I say to some extent this is what she did because in my view the costs judge was not entitled simply to rule that she was going to assess the costs of trial as if the case were on the fast track. To so rule does seem to me to rescind the Recorder's order. I cannot accept that in ruling as she did it can be said she was simply "assessing costs on the standard basis taking into account that the case should have been allocated to the fast track" which in my view is the permissible approach. It may in some cases be a distinction without a major difference.'

litigated on the small claims track. Whilst the small claims regime ought not to be directly applied in those circumstances, the costs judge would be able to take the existence of that regime into account when assessing the reasonableness of the costs and, by that route, the costs judge would, in appropriate case, be entitled to assess the profit costs at nil, or close to nil.[836]

- **Exaggeration prevented the claim from being allocated to the fast track** Whilst this section focuses on claims whose natural environment is the small claims track, it is worth mentioning that PD 45, para 4.2, provides that CPR, Part 45, Section VI, applies only where, at the date of the trial, the claim is allocated to the fast track and that it does not apply in any other case, irrespective of the final value of the claim.
- **Exaggeration prevented compromise** Where there has been exaggeration that has resulted in misallocation, it does not necessarily follow that the exaggerator will be awarded the costs that would have been allowed had it been correctly allocated. In particular, if the defendant is able to show that had the claim not been exaggerated, it would not have been settled on commercial grounds, the claimant may be required to pay costs.[837]
- **Exaggeration by a counterclaimant** Where a claim was misallocated to the multi-track as a result of the defendant keeping in play a counterclaim that ought never to have been brought and where the claim would have been allocated to the small claims track if the counterclaim had not been brought, Goldring LJ found that this was conduct that should be given weight when the court was exercising its discretion under what is now CPR, r 44.2.[838] In this regard, it should be noted that a claim and a counterclaim will not be relegated to the small claims track merely because set-off would give rise to a net amount that is below the small claims limit.[839]

When deciding whether a claim has been exaggerated, there is authority to suggest that a settlement figure may be a factor that can be taken into account. An example of such an approach is *E Ivor Hughes Educational Foundation v Leach*,[840] in which Peter Smith J said: **50.398**

> 'It is appropriate that the costs which the claimant recovers ... should be measured by its recovery. They have recovered £5,000. Once again, they chose to take the £5,000. If they were not happy with that or they wanted to protect their costs position further, they could have proceeded to trial to ... to establish liability beyond that. They have chosen not to do so.'[841]

It is trite costs law that costs should not be assessed with the benefit of hindsight, so presumably the settlement figure can be taken into account only where it can fairly be said **50.399**

---

836 *O'Beirne v Hudson* [2010] EWCA 52, at [19], *per* Waller, and at [22], *per* Hooper LJ. See also, in a different context, *Lahey v Pirelli* [2007] 1 WLR 998, at [19]–[22], *per* Dyson LJ; in the context of Part 45, *Dockerill v Tullett* [2012] EWCA Civ 184. See also *E Ivor Hughes Educational Foundation v Leach* [2005] EWHC 1317 (Ch), in which Peter Smith J restricted the exaggerator's costs in a multitrack matter.

837 Whilst not binding, an oft-cited example of this is *Khan v Metainy Maintenance Ltd* (unreported), 21 January 2013, Aldershot & Farnham County Court, in which Judge Iain Hughes QC ordered a claimant to pay 80 per cent of the defendant's costs on the grounds that if the claim had been made without exaggeration, it would have been for such a small sum (£150) that it would certainly have settled on commercial grounds.

838 *Peackman v Linbrooke Services Ltd* [2008] EWCA Civ 1239; see also *Singh v Aqua Descaling Ltd* (unreported), 12 June 2008, Walsall County Court, *per* Judge Oliver-Jones QC.

839 *Boynton v Willers* [2003] EWCA Civ 904, at [41].

840 *E Ivor Hughes Educational Foundation v Leach* [2005] EWHC 1317 (Ch).

841 *Ibid*, at [25].

to indicate the true value of the claim as it ought to have been perceived at the time of allocation.

Unreasonable behaviour

The test to be applied

50.400 Longmore and McFarlane LJJ (giving judgment of the court) had the following to say about the approach when considering whether there has been unreasonable behaviour:

> 'We doubt if we can usefully give general guidance in relation to the circumstances in which it will be appropriate for a court to decide whether a party "has behaved unreasonably" since all such cases must be highly fact-sensitive. In the somewhat different context of the jurisdiction to order a party's legal (or other) representative to meet what are called "wasted costs" ... defined as costs incurred "as a result of any improper, unreasonable or negligent act or omission" of such representative), the court speaking through Sir Thomas Bingham MR said:—
>
> > "... conduct cannot be described as unreasonable simply because it leads in the event to an unsuccessful result or because other more cautious legal representatives would have acted differently. The acid test is whether the conduct permits of a reasonable explanation. If so, the course adopted may be regarded as optimistic and as reflecting in a practitioner's judgment, but it is not unreasonable," see *Ridehalgh v Horsefield* [1994] Ch 205, 232F.
>
> While we would not wish to incorporate all the learning about wasted costs orders into decisions under CPR Part 27.14 (2)(g), we think that the above dictum should give sufficient guidance on the word "unreasonably" to district judges and circuit judges dealing with cases allocated to the Small Claims Track. *Ridehalgh* was, of course, dealing with acts or omissions of legal representatives but the meaning of "unreasonably" cannot be different when applied to litigants in person in Small Claims cases. Litigants in person should not be in a better position than legal representatives but neither should they be in any worse position than such representatives.'[842]

Thus the test is whether the conduct permits of a reasonable explanation; if so, then whilst the course adopted may be regarded as optimistic and as reflecting in a party's judgment, it will not be unreasonable for the purposes of CPR, r 27.14 (2)(g).

50.401 Each case will turn on its own facts, but it is worth making the following points.

- **Offers** CPR, r 27.14(3), provides: 'A party's rejection of an offer in settlement will not of itself constitute unreasonable behaviour under paragraph (2)(g) but the court may take it into consideration when it is applying the unreasonableness test.' This rule is particularly relevant because CPR, Part 36, does not apply to claims allocated to the small claims track.[843] Whilst a rejection of an offer would not, of itself, be sufficient to justify a finding of unreasonable behaviour, there can be no doubt that such behaviour can be taken into account.[844]
- **Legal complexity** The fact that a legal point of some complexity was involved is a factor that would militate against a finding that it was unreasonable to argue that point.[845]

---

842 *Dammermann v Lanyon Bowdler LLP* [2017] EWCA Civ 269, at [30] and [31], *per curium*.

843 See CPR, r 27.2(1)(g).

844 *Dammermann v Lanyon Bowdler LLP* [2017] EWCA Civ 269, at [28], *per curium* (Longmore and McFarlane LJJ).

845 *Ibid*, at [24]–[26].

- **Pre-action protocols** Whilst allowances would almost certainly be made in cases in which litigants are unrepresented, non-compliance with the relevant pre-action protocol may be a factor to be taken into account.[846]
- **Defending a claim** There can be no doubt that the mere fact that a defendant defended a claim is not, of itself, unreasonable behaviour. In the context of a claim in which the defendant had capitulated, but only at the second appeal, Kitchin LJ had this to say:

> 'I see nothing unreasonable about [the defendant's] behaviour. The claim was properly allocated to the small claims track and [the defendant] defended it as it was entitled to do. The deputy district judge had a wide discretion as to how he dealt with the hearing and, in accordance with the rules, conducted it in a relatively informal way, no doubt in an attempt to arrive at a just decision but at proportionate cost.'[847]

- **Failure to settle** Hughes LJ has confirmed that a failure to settle will not usually amount to unreasonable behaviour, for two reasons: first, because to categorise a failure to settle on particular terms as unreasonable conduct would open up wide questions with ramifications for other forms of litigation; and secondly, because the investigation of whether an offer of settlement was reasonable or not would require the trial of the case, which would be inconsistent with the objectives of the CPR.[848]

Anecdotally, costs are said to be awarded in circumstances such as the following: **50.402**

- failing to comply with orders for directions (such as orders to give disclosure or to serve evidence);
- wilfully exaggerating a claim;
- defending a claim that has no defence;
- failing to respond to correspondence;
- obstructing attempts to settle the claim; and
- lack of objectivity on the part of professional advisers.

Unreasonable behaviour and appeals

As to the exercise of discretion in relation to the costs of appeals, Longmore and McFarlane LJJ (giving judgment of the court) had this to say: **50.403**

> '[It] would be unfortunate if litigants were too easily deterred from using the Small Claims Track by the risk of being held to have behaved unreasonably and thus rendering themselves liable for costs. The rules could have provided that on appeal the normal rules as to costs should prevail, but Part 27.14(2) applies in terms to costs relating to an appeal; an appellate court should therefore be wary of ordering costs on appeal to be paid if they were not ordered below, unless circumstances on appeal are truly different.'[849]

In so far as appeals are concerned, the fact that permission was given to the losing party is a relevant factor.[850]

---

[846] See, eg, *BCC v Lee* [2008] EWCA Civ 891, at [33].
[847] *Conlon v Royal Sun Alliance Insurance plc* [2015] EWCA Civ 92, at [15].
[848] *BCC v Lee* [2008] EWCA Civ 891, at [32].
[849] *Dammermann v Lanyon Bowdler LLP* [2017] EWCA Civ 269, at [32], *per curium*.
[850] *Ibid*, at [26].

51

HOURLY RATES

51.01 The topics addressed in this chapter are as follows:

- the history of time-based charging (51.03);
- the relevance of 'guideline rates' (51.15);
- pre-CPR terminology (51.24) and its place under the CPR (51.38):
  - the A factor (51.26);
  - the B factor (51.32);
- the modern approach (51.44):
  - time—the time when the work was done (51.45);
  - status—the status of the person who did the work (usually referred to as the 'grade of fee earner') (51.46);
  - place—the place where the work was done (51.52);
  - other factors—such as the complexity of the work, the value of the matter, etc (51.78);
- the use of comparators and precedents (51.84); and
- composite and hybrid rates (51.87).

51.02 The issues this chapter examines are hourly rates and their assessment between opposing parties. Whilst this Part of the book focuses on the quantum of costs between opposing parties, the indemnity principle will (with certain rare exceptions) apply, so the amount that is recoverable may turn on what is allowable between solicitor and client. That topic is addressed in Chapter 38.

The History of Time-based Charging

51.03 It may come as a surprise to the modern reader to learn that books such as Sayer's *The Law of Costs* (1768), Tidd's *The Law of Costs in Civil Actions* (1793), Q Le Riche's *Handy Book on the Taxation of Common Law Costs* (1859) make no mention of hourly rates. Indeed, in so far as the costs of litigation were concerned, neither of the editions of Hullock's masterly *The Law of Costs* (1796 and 1810) mentions time-based charging even as a factor to be taken into account. Thus it seems that the near-hegemonic influence of the hourly rate is comparatively new.

51.04 It may come as a further surprise to find out just *how* new: the routine use of hourly rates in England and Wales began to emerge no earlier than the late 1960s—perhaps as a result of cross-pollination from secondary legislation relating to family law and legal aid.[1]

[1] Such as the Matrimonial Causes (Costs) Rates 1968.

The rise of the hourly rate in the United States

The story may begin in the United States in 1940, when a lawyer named Reginald Heber Smith began to advocate the use of hourly billing: **51.05**

> 'The service lawyers render is their professional knowledge and skill, but the commodity they sell is time, and each lawyer has only a limited amount of that. Efficiency and economy are a race against time. The great aim of all organizations is to get a given legal job properly done with the expenditure of the fewest possible hours.'[2]

Heber Smith was referring to the use of time-based charging as a practice management tool. He said that a timesheet should be used to enable the job to be done in the fewest possible hours and that this should be seen as being a vehicle to manage the cost of work. **51.06**

As with many things in the law of costs, practice deviated from theory. In his critique of hourly billing, Ronald Baker (a US advocate of value-pricing) had this to say: **51.07**

> '[As Heber Smith made] clear, the timesheet was introduced mainly to perform cost accounting. It was a way to manage and cost the inventory, but after lawyers became acclimated to completing a daily timesheet, it became the inventory lawyers sold.'[3]

Thus hourly billing in the United States came about because a time and cost-management tool became the template for billing. Speaking extrajudicially, Lord Neuberger has commented that this resulted in the total price becoming a function of hourly cost of each element of the job—and he went on to say that the obvious consequence of this is that rather than acting as a brake on litigation costs, hourly billing became a vehicle for the expansion of those costs.[4]

The rise of the hourly rate in the United Kingdom

Much the same happened in this jurisdiction. In 1967, the Law Society published a booklet entitled *Know What It Costs You* that contained an early version of what would become the 'Expense of Time' calculation (see 51.27). That calculation was merely a practice management tool, but, as is explained below, it gradually inveigled its way into the process of assessment. **51.08**

By the mid-1970s, charging by time had become established in matrimonial cases (although scale costs also existed for many types of civil claim).[5] By the late 1970s, hourly rates began to appear in civil cases, but they were not even remotely regarded as being 'the' way in which costs were assessed. In *Treasury Solicitor v Regester & Anor*,[6] for example, Donaldson J commented that hourly rates were 'only one of a number of cross-checks on the fairness and reasonableness of the final figure'.[7] **51.09**

[2] Heber Smith, R, 'Law Office Organization' (1940) 26 ABA Journal 393, at 393.

[3] Baker, R, *Implementing Value Pricing: A Radical Business Model for Professional Firms* (Chichester: John Wiley & Sons, 2010), pp 116 *et seq.*

[4] See Lord Neuberger, 'Keynote Address: Fourteenth Lecture in the Implementation Programme', Association of Costs Lawyers' Annual Conference, 11 May 2012, para 16.

[5] See, eg, *Castillejo v Castillejo* (1974) The Times, 12 December; see also *Dwyer v Dwyer* [1976] 2 All ER 1.

[6] *Treasury Solicitor v Regester & Anor* [1978] 1 WLR 446.

[7] *Ibid*, at 451.

51.10 Donaldson J returned to the topic of hourly rates in *R v Wilkinson*[8] (a criminal case). The solicitor relied on the 'Expense of Time' calculation in preparing his bill. Donaldson J made a number of comments about that calculation that led, in 1988, to the Law Society issuing revised guidance regarding the calculation, so that it contained more explicit guidance as to the appropriate methodology. The widespread use of hourly rates took off from there—despite the fact that the revised publication, *The Expense of Time*, expressly stated that the 'Expense of Time' calculation was intended to be a tool for management purposes rather than for the ascertainment of costs (see 51.28).[9]

51.11 It is worth pausing here to note that, up until as recently as 1990, the various incarnations of the Solicitors Acts stated that remuneration would be by 'gross sum, or by commission or percentage, or by salary or otherwise' as the appropriate measures.[10] There was no mention of payment by hourly rates.

The (possible) decline of the hourly rate

51.12 By the mid-1990s, hourly rates had become a commonly used method of calculating fees. In the 2000s, the usage of hourly rates had become ubiquitous, but so had the problem of excessive and disproportionate costs—a problem exacerbated by the fact that, at that time, additional liabilities were recoverable between opposing parties.

51.13 In 2005, the Civil Justice Council proposed that a costs council should oversee the introduction, implementation and monitoring of (amongst other things) hourly rates.[11] This recommendation gained the support of both practitioners and senior judges. Indeed, in 2006, Senior Costs Judge Hurst wrote a paper in support of such a proposal.[12] In the event, the proposals were not implemented. In 2007, the Master of the Rolls took on responsibility for publishing guideline hourly rates.[13] In 2008, he directed that a committee be formed—the Advisory Committee on Civil Costs (ACCC)—for the purposes of advising as to what the rates would be.[14] As is explained at 51.17, the ACCC failed to obtain satisfactory evidence, with the result that guideline hourly rates were not updated; indeed, they were last updated as long ago as 2010.

51.14 It is perhaps no coincidence that this was in the context of the senior judiciary starting to question the routine usage of time-based charging. In 2010, Sir Rupert Jackson commented that 'the recoverable hourly rates of lawyers [were] not satisfactorily controlled'.[15] Speaking in 2012, Lord Neuberger (then Master of the Rolls) went much further, saying that 'hourly billing fails to reward the diligent, the efficient and the able: its focus on the cost of time, a truly movable feast, simply does not reflect the value of work', and imploring

[8] *R v Wilkinson* [1980] 1 WLR 396.

[9] The current edition warns that 'the procedure used in this booklet will enable you [ie the solicitor] to calculate what each matter has cost you ... It is not a means of calculating the charge to be made to the client'.

[10] In 1990, the words 'hourly rates' were inserted by Courts and Legal Services Act 1990, s 98(5).

[11] Civil Justice Council, *Improved Access to Justice: Funding Options and Proportionate Costs—Report and Recommendations* (London: HMSO, 2005).

[12] Hurst, P, 'Costs Council Recommendation', 27 March 2006.

[13] See Master of the Rolls, 'Guideline Hourly Rates', 28 July 2014, available online at https://www.judiciary.gov.uk/wp-content/uploads/2014/07/ghr-mor-decision-july2104.pdf

[14] See Civil Justice Council Costs Committee, *Report to the Master of the Rolls: Recommendations on Guideline Hourly Rates for 2014*, May 2014, available online at https://www.judiciary.gov.uk/wp-content/uploads/2014/07/ghr-final-report.pdf, para 1.6.

[15] Jackson, R, *Review of Civil Litigation Costs: Final Report* (London: HMSO, 2010), ch 4, para 3.1(vi).

the legal profession to find new ways of charging for its services.[16] This is a topic that is addressed in more detail in Chapter 42.

The Relevance of Guideline Rates

Guideline rates come in the form of tables that are published from time to time for localities, those localities being collected into 'bands'.[17] Rates are then given for each 'grade' of fee earner (from Grade A to Grade D).[18] The overall effect is that rates are classified according to time, place and grade. **51.15**

There are three national bands (Bands 2 and 3 have effectively been the same since the rates were revised in 2009) and three London bands (City of London, Central London and Outer London). Rates for Outer London, Bands A and B are presented as ranges to reflect the wide variety of work transacted in these areas. The reason for regional differences is to reflect the differing costs of various locations, such as salaries and commercial accommodation costs. **51.16**

The formulation of guideline rates

Prior to 2010, guideline rates tended to be published either annually or biannually. It had been intended that guideline rates should reflect market rates, but this could be achieved only if there was evidence of what the market is charging. Four attempts have been made to set up a system for obtaining that information, but (as is set out below) only the first gained any real traction. **51.17**

- **Local judges and practitioners pre-banding** Prior to 2000 and up to 2003, the figures for each locality were determined by local judges and practitioners. They would often have the benefit of expense rate surveys carried out by the local law society (see 51.31).[19] Once satisfied that they were appropriate, the designated civil judge for each area would then approve the local rates and inform the Senior Courts Costs Office (SCCO) accordingly.[20] The SCCO, acting under the oversight of the Deputy Head of Civil Justice,[21] would then prepare a table of guideline rates for publication as an Annex to the *SCCO Guide to Summary Assessment*. Up to 2003, the rates were published for each area in circuit order; thus each town and city had its own rate. This may be why local law societies were so willing to carry out expense rate surveys—namely, the fact that their efforts would have a real influence on the rates that would be allowed. Approval by a designated civil judge meant that they carried some weight. The only real drawback with this system

[16] Lord Neuberger, 'Keynote Address: Fourteenth Lecture in the Implementation Programme', Association of Costs Lawyers' Annual Conference, 11 May 2012.

[17] The most recent incarnation of the Guidelines does not use the word 'bands', but the old terminology persists.

[18] Rather confusingly, the most recent incarnation of guideline rates refers to the grades of fee earner as bands, but that terminology is rarely used.

[19] See Civil Justice Council Costs Committee, *Report to the Master of the Rolls: Recommendations on Guideline Hourly Rates for 2014*, May 2014, available online at https://www.judiciary.gov.uk/wp-content/uploads/2014/07/ghr-final-report.pdf, para1.4.

[20] See Underwood, K, 'Guideline Hourly Rates: Their Use and Misuse', 5 March 2013, p 3.

[21] See Master of the Rolls, 'Guideline Hourly Rates', 28 July 2014, available online at https://www.judiciary.gov.uk/wp-content/uploads/2014/07/ghr-mor-decision-july2104.pdf

was that there were dozens of published guideline rates and this made the SCCO's summary of rates a somewhat difficult document to navigate.

- **Local judges and practitioners post-banding** In 2003, a banding system was introduced, presumably in an attempt to simplify the SCCO's summary of rates. This meant that truly local rates would no longer be published and that designated civil judges would no longer be able to approve the rates; instead, the rates would be set centrally. In view of this, there was scant incentive to provide detailed, highly localised information, because it was unlikely that it would have any impact. This may have been the cause of what happened next, which is that local practitioners and judges fell out of the habit of carrying out surveys and submitting detailed data. There was a lack of evidence, which explains, at least in part, why the rates for 2005 and 2007 were based on little more than an inflationary uplift.[22]
- **The Advisory Committee on Civil Costs (ACCC)** In 2007, the Master of the Rolls took on responsibility for publishing the guideline rates.[23] In 2008, he directed that a committee be formed—the ACCC—for the purposes of advising on the rates.[24] The ACCC failed to obtain satisfactory evidence, however. In 2008, for example, it attempted to match the guideline rates to market rates, but this was thwarted by a survey response rate of less than 8 per cent.[25] Moreover, what little evidence the ACCC did have was not representative of market.[26] Previous editions of this book pointed to methodological errors on the part of the ACCC, such as selection bias or the absence of random selection, as well as the absence of any attempt to calculate confidence intervals.[27] The 2010 rates were based on a simple inflationary uplift of those 2009 figures, which were accepted by the then Master of the Rolls as an interim measure; a year later, in 2011, he did not feel able to set new rates on the same basis (that is, a further recommendation from the ACCC for another purely inflationary index-linked calculation), without a broader base of evidence having been sought from practitioners.
- **The Civil Justice Council's Costs Committee** In October 2012, the ACCC was abolished by way of a written ministerial statement[28] and responsibility for making recommendations passed to the Civil Justice Council's new Costs Committee.[29] That

[22] See Civil Justice Council Costs Committee, *Report to the Master of the Rolls: Recommendations on Guideline Hourly Rates for 2014*, May 2014, available online at https://www.judiciary.gov.uk/wp-content/uploads/2014/07/ghr-final-report.pdf, para 1.6.

[23] See Master of the Rolls, 'Guideline Hourly Rates', 28 July 2014, available online at https://www.judiciary.gov.uk/wp-content/uploads/2014/07/ghr-mor-decision-july2104.pdf

[24] See Civil Justice Council Costs Committee, *Report to the Master of the Rolls: Recommendations on Guideline Hourly Rates for 2014*, May 2014, available online at https://www.judiciary.gov.uk/wp-content/uploads/2014/07/ghr-final-report.pdf, para 1.6.

[25] See Advisory Committee on Civil Costs, 'The Derivation of New Guideline Hourly Rates', 9 December 2008.

[26] See Advisory Committee on Civil Costs, 'Guideline Hourly Rates: Conclusions', March 2010, para 2. There is no mention of any evidence that the firms referred to therein were representative. See also the 2008 report, to which one firm submitted separate responses from each of its offices.

[27] See the second edition of this book, at para 28.3.

[28] Commons Hansard, 30 October 2012, Vol 552, the Parliamentary Under-Secretary of State for Justice (Mrs Helen Grant).

[29] See Civil Justice Council Costs Committee, *Report to the Master of the Rolls: Recommendations on Guideline Hourly Rates for 2014*, May 2014, available online at https://www.judiciary.gov.uk/wp-content/uploads/2014/07/ghr-final-report.pdf, para 1.6.

Committee, chaired by Foskett J, attempted an 'Expense of Time', evidence-based approach to the issue,[30] but it ran into the same problem as the ACCC—namely, a lack of data. In early 2014, the Costs Committee recommended new rates, but the then Master of Rolls (Lord Dyson) rejected those recommendations because they were 'not based on sufficiently robust evidence'.[31] In a statement released in April 2015, he affirmed that the existing rates will therefore remain in force for the foreseeable future, observing that guideline hourly rates are becoming 'less and less relevant' for several reasons, including advances in technology, changing business practices and models, the ever-increasing sub-specialisation of the law, which is seeing the market increasingly dictate rates in some fields (particularly commercial law), the judiciary's use of proportionality as a driving principle in assessing costs, and the greater application of costs budgeting and fixed costs.[32] That said, in recognition of the fact that rates are still relevant, he went on to say this:

> 'Less relevance is not the same as no relevance, and I am conscious that there are still many uses to which [guideline hourly rates] are put. They remain an integral part of the process of judges making summary assessments of costs in proceedings. They also form a part, even if only a starting reference point, in the preparation of detailed assessments. They also provide a yardstick for comparison purposes in costs budgeting.'[33]

There are those who say that the reasons why the last three attempts to match guideline rates to market rates failed are that, first, it is not possible (or, for that matter, desirable) to do so, and secondly, evidence is too hard to collect because local practitioners do not derive any benefit (because no local rates are publishable under the banding system). They would say that there is a difficulty in accurately matching guideline rates to market rates because the latter is a function of the former. In this regard, for example, they would point towards the fact that many personal injury firms charge only those rates that they are confident will be recovered from opponents; they therefore tend to apply the guideline rates.[34] **51.18**

There is force in these points: the mere fact that broad-brush guideline rates are published at all means that the market cannot be what economists call 'the perfect market'; rather, any measurement of putative market rates will—at least to an extent—be influenced not by market forces, but by the guideline rates themselves. Whilst market forces and 'Expense of Time' surveys should no doubt be taken into account, it might also be said that it is not desirable to set guideline rates that strive to mimic market rates, because the assessment of costs is about costs, not charges.[35] Those who hold **51.19**

---

[30] See *ibid*, para 634.

[31] See Master of the Rolls, 'Guideline Hourly Rates', 28 July 2014, available online at https://www.judiciary.gov.uk/wp-content/uploads/2014/07/ghr-mor-decision-july2104.pdf

[32] See Master of the Rolls, 'Guideline Hourly Rates', April 2015, available online at https://www.judiciary.uk/wp-content/uploads/2015/04/mr-ghr-decision-april-2015.pdf, p 1.

[33] *Ibid.*

[34] This is not limited to conditional fee agreements; many private retainers will refer to the allowable rate as being the guideline rate in their local County Court hearing centre.

[35] See, eg, Evans J in *Johnson v Reed Corrugated Cases Ltd* [1992] 1 All ER 169; see also *KMT & Ors (Children) v Kent County Council* [2012] EWHC 2088 (QB), at [13], *per* Eady J.

that view would point towards the first of the systems above and say that the reason that system worked was because it was not hide-bound by statistical analysis; instead, it was merely *informed* by statistical analysis and, at the end of the day, the rates were set by designated civil judges who would use their discretion and local knowledge to set rates that were appropriate.

The use of guideline rates

51.20 Decided cases are replete with exhortations that guideline rates are not binding.[36] It is certainly true to say that they are intended to be guidelines only, and cannot be taken to have supplanted the experience and knowledge of the court.[37] Some, however, go so far as to say that they are of no use at all in the context of detailed assessments. Respected commentator Kerry Underwood has this to say on the point:

> 'Quite simply they have no application at all in relation to anything other than summary assessment, and even in summary assessments they are guidelines and not tramlines, and are not supposed to replace the experience and knowledge of those familiar with the local area and field and the field of law generally.'[38]

51.21 Not everyone would agree with those comments. In practice, a court will almost invariably be referred to, and will consider, guideline rates in determining an hourly rate.[39] The Civil Justice Council had this to say on the topic:

> 'They have ... become the widely-accepted guideline for the recoverable hourly rate for different grades of fee earner in different regions of England and Wales. [Guideline hourly rates] may also be used as a reference point for the purposes of costs budgeting and management.'[40]

51.22 One would have hoped that, so long after the introduction of the Civil Procedure Rules (CPR), the legal principles involved in setting hourly rates would be established and precise. Regrettably, this is far from being the case and, in practice, a court has a wide ambit of discretion. Perhaps the very existence of that wide discretion has allowed a multiplicity of different methods to flourish and has discouraged dissatisfied parties from seeking to clarify the law.

51.23 One notable feature of the topic is the frequent use that is made of pre-CPR methodology. Some commentators say that this is a reflection of the lack of any forensic structure under the CPR for setting hourly rates. Others might argue that the pre-CPR law has been supplanted by a new approach. Be that as it may, it is necessary to say something of the relevant pre-CPR terminology and methodology.

---

[36] See, eg, cites *KMT v Kent County Council* [2012] EWHC 2088 (QB), at [13], *per* Eady J. See also *Higgs v Camden & Islington Health Authority* [2003] EWHC 15 (QB).

[37] See, eg, *Cox & Anor v MGN Ltd & Ors* [2006] EWHC 1235 (QB), at [66].

[38] See Underwood, K, 'Guideline Hourly Rates', 25 November 2013.

[39] See *G (by her mother and litigation friend M) v Kingston upon Hull City Council* (unreported), 18 September 2013, Kingston upon Hull County Court, at [40].

[40] Civil Justice Council, 'FAQ: Guideline for Hourly Rates Survey', 2013, available online at *https://www.judiciary.gov.uk/related-offices-and-bodies/advisory-bodies/cjc/guideline-hourly-rates/ghrsurveyfaq/*, para 1.

Pre-CPR Terminology

The pre-CPR approach to the ascertainment of hourly rates involved the combination of two components: the 'A factor' and the 'B factor'. The A and the B factors were combined to make the hourly charging rate. Thus the pre-CPR method was referred to as the 'A plus B' approach. The A factor was an approximation of the expense of carrying out the work in question (such as the costs of employing staff, providing premises, administration, etc), whilst the B factor represented the solicitor's remuneration (that is, profit and hence the term 'profit costs'). The A and the B factors were combined by multiplying the A factor by the B factor and then adding this figure back to the A factor to give an 'hourly charging rate'. For example, an A factor of £100 per hour, when combined with a B factor of 85 per cent, would have given an hourly charging rate of £185 per hour.[41] **51.24**

For the remainder of this discussion, the following terminology will be used: 'hourly charging rate'; 'A factor'; 'B factor'; and (when referring to modern day rates) 'guideline rates'. Where appropriate, the phrase 'hourly rate' refers to the rate that would be allowed in an assessment under the CPR. **51.25**

The A factor

In essence, the A factor was the hourly cost of running the relevant aspects of the solicitor's practice, calculated by reference to the fee earner in respect of whom costs were claimed. Brightman J put it this way: **51.26**

> '[The A factor is] the proper cost per hour of the time so spent having regard to a reasonable estimate of the overhead expenses of the solicitors' firm including (if the time spent is that of

---

[41] The 'A plus B' approach was first described by Brightman J in *In re Eastwood, dec'd; Lloyds Bank Ltd v Eastwood* [1975] Ch 112, at 119: 'The [receiving party's solicitor] submits (A) what is the proper cost per hour of the time so spent having regard to a reasonable estimate of the overhead expenses of the solicitors' firm including (if the time spent is that of an employee) the reasonable salary of the employee or (if the time spent is that of a partner) a notional salary. The firm will also submit … (B) what is a proper additional sum to be allowed over and above (A) by way of further profit costs.'

Shortly after the introduction of the terms 'A factor' and 'B factor', the terminology grew and became more refined (and also more confusing). In *Leopold Lazarus Ltd v Secretary of State for Trade and Industry* (1976) Costs LR Core vol 62, at 62, Kerr J explained that the 'A factor' was the 'direct cost' to the firm of carrying out the work, and should be sufficient 'to cover the salary and the appropriate share of the general overheads' of the person doing the work; thus (for a short while) the 'A factor' became known as the direct costs. It also became known as the hourly expense rate (which should not be confused with the hourly charging rate).

In about 1980, the phrase 'broad average direct costs' became the preferred term: *R v Wilkinson* [1980] 1 All ER 597, at 604, *per* Goff J. The intention was to reflect the fact that the A factor should be based on a broad range of the costs of running a firm in a particular area, rather than the actual costs applicable to the individual firm whose fees were the subject of the assessment. In 1996, however, the Court of Appeal said that the term 'comparable direct costs' was to be preferred: *L v L* [1997] 1 Costs LR 9, at 13. This was because it was felt that the word 'average' was capable of misunderstanding in that it might lead to assessments being made by an arithmetical calculation, rather than by the exercise of judicial assessment.

Like the A factor, the B factor has also had a number of labels over the years, the most commonly used of which is 'care and conduct'. Other terms include 'care and attention', 'care, skill and attention', 'mark-up', 'profit element', 'service increment' or just 'uplift'. Where the work is non-contentious work, the phrase 'value element' is often used, which is not entirely the same as 'care and conduct', but is sufficiently similar to be thought of as the non-contentious equivalent.

an employee) the reasonable salary of the employee or (if the time spent is that of a partner) a notional salary.'[42]

'Expense of Time' calculations

51.27 The A factor differed from fee earner to fee earner. It was a calculation that had its roots in the Law Society's 1967 booklet entitled *Know What It Costs You* (see 51.08). That booklet had been written to help solicitors to assess what it cost to carry out work; as such, it was intended to be a practice management tool rather than an aid to assessing costs. In due course, it evolved into the booklet entitled *The Expense of Time* and the resulting 'Expense of Time' calculation.[43]

51.28 The results of the 'Expense of Time' calculation are highly influenced by figures that must be assumed rather than measured. It is, for example, possible to derive extravagant or frugal rates from the same data simply by altering the figure that is assumed for the number of hours billed per year.[44] This presents no difficulty when using the calculation for its original intended purpose (that is, practice management) because appropriate assumptions can be made across the whole practice, but the same is not true when it is used for assessing costs. This is because different firms will—for entirely legitimate reasons—make different assumptions. It is primarily for this reason that *The Expense of Time* booklet cautioned against using the calculation as a means of calculating costs.

51.29 Notwithstanding this, the figures derived from the 'Expense of Time' calculation became almost synonymous with the A factor. Indeed, there was a time when the court tolerated solicitors submitting their own 'Expense of Time' calculations on a case-by-case basis. That practice soon fell by the wayside,[45] but, in essence, the task of ascertaining the A factor ceased to be based on the facts of the case in hand and became instead a

---

42 *In re Eastwood, dec'd; Lloyds Bank Ltd v Eastwood* [1975] Ch 112, at 119.

43 Broadly speaking, the 'Expense of Time' calculation involved ascertaining the expenses of a practice and then apportioning those expenses amongst the fee earners within that firm in accordance with their actual (or, in the case of non-salaried partners, notional) salaries. The result was that it was possible to estimate how much it cost to employ and support an individual fee earner over any given period of time. If that cost was then divided by the number of hours for which that fee earner had been able to render fees, their cost per hour could be calculated. For the purposes of calculating costs, a notional figure was used (because otherwise a hard-working fee earner would be rewarded with an artificially low rate). Thus a number of factors had to be assumed, including the notional salary and the number of hours for which a full-time fee earner could have been expected to raise a fee.

44 This figure is often taken as being 1,100 hours, but (more realistically) it might be 1,500 hours. It would be rare for a fee earner to bill more than 1,800 hours per year.

45 In *Leopold Lazarus Ltd v Secretary of State for Trade and Industry* (1976) Costs LR Core vol 62, at 62, Kerr J emphasised that the assessment of the expense rate ('the A factor') was a task for the costs judge and that the assessment 'would be based on the [costs judge's] knowledge and experience of the average solicitor or executive employed by the average firm in the area concerned'. In *R v Wilkinson* [1980] 1 All ER 598, at 608, Goff J cast doubt on the suitability of the 'Expense of Time' calculation as a basis for calculating costs: 'I have come to the conclusion that The Expense of Time, laudable though it is in many ways, does not in its present form provide a reliable basis for the taxation of costs; and I also conclude that it will be difficult in practice for any such system to form such a basis without some prior monitoring by an appropriate body.' The need to look at the average, rather than the specific, was reaffirmed by Hirst J in *Stubbs v Board of Governors of the Royal National Orthopaedic Hospital* [1997] Costs LR (Core Vol) 117, QBD, at 122, in the following terms: 'It is ... a matter which is properly approached by reference to averages since it is unlikely that there will be a very wide divergence between comparable firms of solicitors operating in similar fields or work in similar geographical areas.'

task to be carried out generically by the court using its own knowledge of local solicitors' charges. There were exceptions to this,[46] some of which remain relevant today.[47] In times gone by, the main concern was that the court tended to allow rates that were too low; in response, guidance was given that the A factor was to be ascertained in a realistic way—and attempts to inflate the B factor for the purpose of compensating for an unreasonably low A factor were to be discouraged.[48]

The fact that the use of individual 'Expense of Time' calculations was discouraged continues to have resonance even today, because it highlights the difference between costs and charges. Evans J had this to say on the topic: **51.30**

> 'There remains the question ... of what weight, if any, the [costs judge] should give to *Expense of Time* calculations, if they are produced in a particular case. The answer, in my judgment, is that, if the figures for an individual solicitor, or firm, are produced for the purposes of the assessment in that case, then they should be given very little weight ... The "market" is for charges, not for costs.'[49]

Expense rates surveys

Partly as a result of Evans J's comments and partly as a result of the realisation that A factors were being allowed at rates that were artificially low (see 51.29), the practice of local law societies carrying out 'expense rate surveys' began to flourish. This was a practice in which data would be collected from a number of representative firms in a locality. Up to 2003, that data would be published on a town-by-town basis, but from 2003 onwards, the banding system was introduced (51.17). Up until 2003, the use of local expense rate surveys became part of the process of assessing the hourly rate.[50] The present-day relevance of this is that that data no longer exists—or, more accurately, very rarely exists (again, see 51.17)[51]—which means that a strict adherence to the A-plus-B approach is not only undesirable, but also usually not even possible. **51.31**

The B factor

The exercise of ascertaining the B factor was not a fact-finding exercise, but a matter of judgement and discretion. The B factor was usually expressed as a percentage of the A factor.[52] Broadly speaking, in a run-of-the-mill claim, it would be 50 per cent, rising to 100 per cent and beyond in exceptional claims (see 51.35). Contrary to present-day practices, differential B factors (and therefore different hourly charging rates) would **51.32**

---

[46] *Finley v Glaxo Laboratories Ltd* (1989) Costs LR Core vol 106, at 110, in which Hobhouse J took account of an 'Expense of Time' calculation in calculating the appropriate hourly rate.

[47] See *Jones v Secretary of State for Wales* [1997] 1 WLR 1008.

[48] See *Loveday v Renton (No 2)* [1992] 3 All ER 184.

[49] *Johnson v Reed Corrugated Cases Ltd* [1992] 1 All ER 169, at 180.

[50] Those surveys were only a factor to be taken into account by the costs judge: *L v L* [1997] 1 Costs LR 9, at 13, *per* Neill LJ.

[51] Some local law societies still publish data. There are those who seek to derive an A factor from the guideline rates by subtracting a third (which equates to a B factor of 50 per cent), but whether this is legitimate is debatable, because the guideline rates are not based on local data. There are, however, examples of this approach being adopted: see *Higgs v Camden and Islington Health Authority* [2003] EWHC 15 (QB).

[52] The percentage was not the percentage of the hourly charging rate, but of the A factor. Thus, if, in a run-of-the-mill claim, the B factor is 50 per cent and the hourly charging rate is £150 per hour, the A factor would be £100 per hour rather than £75 per hour.

routinely be applied to certain types of work within the same bill.[53] The reference to 'the B factor' generally was a reference to the figure that applied to that work which attracted the highest percentage increment.

Relevant factors

51.33 On a between-the-parties basis, the B factor was based on the first seven of those factors that are now listed in CPR, r 44.3(3), known as 'the seven pillars of wisdom':

- the conduct of all of the parties;
- the amount or value of any money or property involved;
- the importance of the matter to all of the parties;
- the particular complexity of the matter or the difficulty or novelty of the questions raised;
- the skill, effort, specialised knowledge and responsibility involved;
- the time spent on the case; and
- the place where and the circumstances in which work or any part of it was done.[54]

The level of the uplift

51.34 Evans J explained the appropriate method in the following way:

> 'I approach the assessment on the following basis. I am advised that the range for normal, ie nonexceptional, cases starts at 50%, which the [costs judge] regarded, rightly in my view, as an appropriate figure for "run-of-the-mill" cases.'[55]

It is worth pausing here to note that the reference to the uplift being 50 per cent is entirely in keeping with other business activities, this being because a profit of about a third of income is in no way unusual. It should be noted, however, that recent surveys had indicated that the amount of profit made by middle-sized firms is only 21.28 per cent of income.[56] If that is correct, then the 'normal' B factor ought to be in the region of 27 per cent. The Civil Justice Council Costs Committee has gone even further by saying that the industry norm is to make a profit that is 16 per cent of income (which is an uplift of 20 per cent).[57] In any event, Evans J went on to say this about uplifts in general:

> 'The figure increases above 50% so as to reflect a number of possible factors ... but only a small percentage of accident cases results in an allowance over 70%. To justify a figure of 100% or even one closely approaching 100% there must be some factor or combination of factors which mean that the case approaches the exceptional. A figure above 100% would seem to be appropriate only when the individual case, or cases of the particular kind, can properly be regarded as exceptional, and such cases will be rare.'[58]

---

[53] Pre-CPR B factors, usually of less than 50 per cent, applied to some aspects of a solicitor's work. Thus travelling tended not to attract any B factor at all and sitting behind counsel or attending upon counsel would attract a lower B factor than other work.

[54] Pre-CPR, the relevant factors were marginally different—in particular, the conduct of the parties was not a factor specifically to be taken into account.

[55] *Johnson v Reed Corrugated Cases Ltd* [1992] 1 All ER 169, at 183.

[56] See the Law Society's Research Unit Law Management Section Survey 2013, as cited at Civil Justice Council Costs Committee, *Report to the Master of the Rolls: Recommendations on Guideline Hourly Rates for 2014*, May 2014, available online at https://www.judiciary.gov.uk/wp-content/uploads/2014/07/ghr-final-report.pdf, para 4.5.

[57] Civil Justice Council Costs Committee, *Report to the Master of the Rolls: Recommendations on Guideline Hourly Rates for 2014*, May 2014, available online at https://www.judiciary.gov.uk/wp-content/uploads/2014/07/ghr-final-report.pdf, para 5.29.

[58] *Johnson v Reed Corrugated Cases Ltd* [1992] 1 All ER 169, at 183.

A B factor in excess of 100 per cent has always been a level of uplift that required justification, as explained by Hobhouse J: **51.35**

> 'To justify an uplift of 100 percent it is necessary ... to demonstrate that the case is exceptional. There has been a tendency among some firms of solicitors to put forward grossly inflated percentages by way of uplift and a failure to appreciate that to justify an uplift even as high as 100 percent requires the demonstration that the case is exceptional.'[59]

B factors of significantly higher than 100 per cent are correspondingly difficult to justify, as Cazalet J explained: 'In my view to justify a percentage uplift of 150 percent a case would not have to be not just exceptional but extraordinary. To achieve an uplift of 100 percent a case would indeed have to be exceptional.'[60] **51.36**

The following are case examples (albeit ones that involved an exceptional degree of responsibility being taken by the solicitors). **51.37**

- Hobhouse J allowed an uplift of 75 per cent in a clinical negligence case involving alleged vaccine damage.[61]
- Hobhouse J allowed an uplift of 125 per cent in a group litigation case concerning the damage done by whooping cough vaccine and which involved 'technical evidence which differed in degree, though not in kind, from that experienced in other cases involving scientific or medical disputes' and in which 'the volume of documentation was very large indeed'.[62]

The Relevance of Pre-CPR Law Under the CPR

It is undoubtedly the case that, under the CPR, both practitioners and the courts are encouraged to express hourly charging rates as a single figure (for example £150 per hour, rather than £100 per hour *plus* a B factor of 50 per cent). For example, in a consultation paper by the Lord Chancellor's Department in which it was explained that solicitors would be required, in the interests of transparency, to provide an inclusive charging basis, it was said that such an approach would 'thereby [abolish] the uplift for care and conduct element claimed in a bill of costs'.[63] **51.38**

There are, however, those who argue that the A-plus-B approach (or something very similar to it) is not only permissible under the CPR, but necessary. There is support for this view in that the A-plus-B approach is little more than an expression of the fact that professional charges—all professional charges—will contain an element of cost and an element of profit. Those who advocate that view would say that whilst the CPR might have abolished the practice of *describing* these two components separately, they still exist and, in the absence of a better analytical tool for dealing with hourly rates, it will be appropriate, from **51.39**

---

[59] *Loveday v Renton (No 2)* [1992] 3 All ER 184 at 189.

[60] *Foroughi v Foroughi* (unreported), 30 July 1993, Fam, *per* Cazalet J, but recited by Cazalet J in *Re Children Act 1989 (Taxation of Costs)* [1994] 2 FLR 934, at 953.

[61] *Finley v Glaxo Laboratories Ltd* (1989) Costs LR Core vol 106, at 112.

[62] *Loveday v Renton (No 2)* [1992] 3 All ER 184 at 188.

[63] Lord Chancellor's Department, *Controlling Costs: A Consultation Paper* (London: HMSO, 1999), para 82.

time to time, to consider rates from the A-plus-B perspective. Eady J had the following to say on this matter:

> 'It is important to have in mind the observation in *Cook* [*on Costs*[64]]: "Whether or not the A and B factors are identified or concealed in a charging rate, they will still be there. Any commercial enterprise must base its prices and charges on costs plus profit and it is naive to think that the legal profession could operate in some other way".'[65]

51.40 Fulford J did not object to an A-plus-B analysis being applied to costs incurred under the CPR (albeit in 2003, in the early days of the CPR). The case before him was a clinical negligence claim in which the claimant suffered a quadriplegic cerebral palsy with dyskinetic features.[66] Liability was in dispute until only three weeks before trial. It settled for £3.5 million. The claimant's solicitors were based in the City of London (an EC1 postcode).[67] The costs were incurred between 1999 and 2001 by a fee earner of more than 20 years' experience. An hourly rate of £300 per hour was claimed. The costs judge carried out an A-plus-B analysis by deriving an A factor from the guideline rates; he accepted the rate as claimed as representing an A factor of £150 per hour plus a B factor of 100 per cent.

51.41 The paying party (the defendant) argued that this was not a legitimate way of dealing with the hourly rate. The defendant argued that a single (composite) rate was appropriate because this is what was encouraged by the Lord Chancellor's consultation paper.[68] Fulford J disagreed with these submissions, reminding himself that the rates set out in the *Guide to the Summary Assessment of Costs* were only guideline rates and going on to make the following findings concerning the A-plus-B analysis:

> 'The CPR and the Costs Practice Direction discourage the use of the A plus B calculation, and commend the claiming of costs on the basis of a single charging rate. I fully accept the advantages that the single hourly rate has for both the paying and the receiving party. However I am not persuaded that the learned judge did more than use the A plus B method as one of the measures and indicators to ensure that he was able to gauge the propriety or otherwise of a figure of £300 per hour ... I am unable to accept the submission that the learned judge misdirected himself in considering the A plus B basis. It may well be that reliance on that method of calculation will rapidly diminish, but in this case I consider the learned judge did not misdirect himself when he took it into consideration.'[69]

51.42 As to Fulford J's prediction that reliance on the A-plus-B approach would diminish over time, Master Gordon-Saker made the following observations in 2008:

> 'I suspect that now ... may be time to bury concepts such as expense rates, mark-ups, A figures and B figures, for we must by now have sufficient experience of the single hourly rates that have been claimed and allowed since 1999.'[70]

51.43 That view is not universally held. In particular, many judges still use the A-plus-B approach (or rather, aspects of it) as a cross-check. Where such an approach is used, Table 51.1 may

---

64 See Cook, M, *Cook on Costs 2005* (London: Butterworths Law, 2004).
65 *Cox v MGN* [2006] EWHC 1235, QB, at [67].
66 *Higgs v Camden and Islington Health Authority* [2003] EWHC 15 (QB).
67 Some of these details are not in the judgment; they have been kindly provided by Anne Winyard, a partner of the firm involved.
68 Lord Chancellor's Department, *Controlling Costs: A Consultation Paper* (London: HMSO, 1999).
69 *Higgs v Camden and Islington Health Authority* [2003] EWHC 15 (QB), at [51].
70 *Holliday v EC Realisations Ltd* [2008] EWHC 90103 (Costs), at [22].

Table 51.1 Hourly rate converter[71]

To convert Guideline to 'A plus B'		To convert 'A plus B' to Guideline	
% above Guideline	Intended 'B' factor	Intended 'B' factor	Required increase in Guideline rate
0%	50%	50%	0%
2%	53%	60%	7%
5%	58%	65%	10%
7½%	61%	70%	13%
10%	65%	75%	17%
15%	73%	80%	20%
20%	80%	85%	23%
25%	88%	90%	27%
30%	95%	95%	30%
33%	100%	100%	33%
40%	110%	105%	37%
45%	118%	110%	40%
50%	125%	115%	43%
55%	133%	125%	50%
60%	140%	130%	53%
67%	151%	135%	57%
80%	170%	140%	60%
85%	178%	145%	63%
90%	185%	150%	67%

assist with calculations as may Tables 68.3–68.10. This table above is based on the assumption that the relevant guideline rate includes a B factor of 50 per cent. This assumption could well be wrong; it is impossible to say because there is no reliable data by which the A factor can be discovered. This means that the role of the A-plus-B analysis is limited to being a cross-check or a tool for comparing rates;[72] it should not be used as a means of calculating rates *de novo*.

The Modern Approach

Eady J has summarised the modern approach in this way: **51.44**

> 'The court is required to take into account all the circumstances including, in particular, the factors listed at [CPR, r 44.4(3)], which are sometimes referred to as the "Seven Pillars of

[71] Reproduced with the kind permission of Master Colum Leonard.

[72] Comparison of rates by the A-plus-B method is unobjectionable. In particular, if a judge is in the habit of allowing a particular rate for run-of-the-mill work for solicitors in their locality, it would be difficult to object to them using the A-plus-B analysis for the purposes of adjusting that rate for more difficult cases. Indeed, such a method could be commended on the basis that it brings structure and consistency to a process that otherwise may lack these attributes.

> Wisdom". It is necessary to have regard to the solicitor's particular skill, effort, specialised knowledge and responsibility. Obviously, also, the case in hand must be assessed for importance, complexity, difficulty or novelty. All the while the court will apply the test of proportionality.'[73]

Thus there are certain factors that the court is required to take into account—that is, the seven (now eight) pillars of wisdom (see 51.33). To this extent, the court's discretion is exercised in a structured way, but it would be wrong to believe that the court will explicitly and individually take each factor into account. Most experienced costs judges prefer to focus only on the factors that are relevant to the case in hand rather than to work through each factor in turn. The resultant rate will, of course, be limited to the amount allowed for in the retainer.[74]

The time when the work was done

51.45 The costs must be assessed as at the time the work was done,[75] with no allowance being made for the passing of the years.[76] There will usually be no factual dispute as to when the work was carried out; if there is, the court would have to determine the issue sitting as a tribunal of fact (and, in doing so, it would give due weight to the presumption afforded by the certificate to the bill). It would rarely be the case that the court would have to determine the reasonableness of when the work was done;[77] timing is therefore usually an uncomplicated point of fact.

The grade of person who did the work

51.46 Fee earners are graded according to their qualifications and experience—a system originally devised jointly by the SCCO, the Association of District Judges and the Law Society. Whilst, originally, only two grades of fee earner existed, in 1999 a third was added, and a fourth in 2001.[78] A call for a fifth grade was rejected in 2014.[79] Certain revisions were made on 1 October 2014[80] and if those revisions are taken into account, then the grading system seems to be as follows (although minor variations are encountered).[81]

---

[73] *Cox v MGN* [2006] EWHC 1235 (QB), at [55].

[74] See *The General of Berne Insurance Co v Jardine Reinsurance Management Ltd* [1998] 2 All ER 301.

[75] See, eg, *Finley v Glaxo Laboratories Ltd* (1989) Costs LR Core vol 106, at 111.

[76] Whilst the matter would depend on the wording of the retainer, it could be argued that the correct measure is not when the work was done, but the date upon which the invoice for the work was rendered, or could have been rendered. With conditional fee agreements, that would be long after the work was done.

[77] It usually arises in the context of long-standing group litigation in which the court has set out a detailed roadmap of what should be done and when.

[78] See Civil Justice Council Costs Committee, *Report to the Master of the Rolls: Recommendations on Guideline Hourly Rates for 2014*, May 2014, available online at https://www.judiciary.gov.uk/wp-content/uploads/2014/07/ghr-final-report.pdf, para 2.1.

[79] See Master of the Rolls, 'Guideline Hourly Rates', 28 July 2014, available online at https://www.judiciary.gov.uk/wp-content/uploads/2014/07/ghr-mor-decision-july2104.pdf

[80] These being a revision that allowed costs lawyers to qualify for Grade B or C and a revision that allowed legal executives with more than eight years' post-qualified experience to claim Grade A. These changes were made in Master of the Rolls, 'Guideline Hourly Rates', 28 July 2014, available online at https://www.judiciary.gov.uk/wp-content/uploads/2014/07/ghr-mor-decision-july2104.pdf

[81] The wording of the revised grading system has not been published for many years; what is set out is the editor's interpretation of how the changes in fn 80 apply to the provisions set out in the HM Courts & Tribunals Service, *Supreme Court Costs Office Guide to Summary Assessment* (London: HMSO, 2006).

- **Grade A** Solicitors or legal executives with more than eight years' post-qualification experience (PQE), including at least eight years' litigation experience
- **Grade B** Solicitors and legal executives with more than four years' PQE, including at least four years' litigation experience; costs lawyers conducting advocacy and litigation work (where justified by the complexity of the work)
- **Grade C** Other solicitors and legal executives, and fee earners of equivalent experience; costs lawyers with more than one year's experience[82]
- **Grade D** Trainee solicitors, paralegals and other fee earners

'Legal executive' means a Fellow of the Chartered Institute of Legal Executives.[83]

Table 51.2 sets out the percentages of the legal workforce in solicitors' firms in 2014 who fell into each grade.[84] **51.47**

Table 51.2 Distribution of fee earners (2014)

	A	B	C	D
In London	29.53%	9.08%	28.39%	33.00%
Nationally	35.26%	11.08%	20.65%	33.00%

Factual issues

There may be a dispute as to which fee earner actually carried out the work, but such disputes should be rare because Practice Direction (PD) 47, para 5.11(2), provides that the background information included in the bill should set out the relevant details, including 'a statement of the status of the legal representatives' employee in respect of whom costs are claimed and (if those costs are calculated on the basis of hourly rates) the hourly rates claimed for each such person'. **51.48**

If there is a dispute as to who actually carried out the work, the court would have to resolve that issue sitting as a tribunal of fact (and, in doing so, it would give due weight to the presumption afforded by the certificate to the bill). By far the more common dispute, however, is whether it was *reasonable* for the work in question to have been carried out by the person who did it or whether the work should acting reasonably have been delegated to junior fee earners.[85] These are matters of discretion to be decided on the basis of all of the circumstances, including the fee earner's expertise. The circumstances and factors that the court may take into account are addressed below. **51.49**

A frequently encountered argument is that the work should have been allocated to a lower grade of fee earner, but the contrary argument may arise from time to time—namely, that a junior fee earner was punching above their weight and that this should be reflected in the hourly rate. That type of argument may cross over to become an argument about a **51.50**

---

[82] This seems to have been what the CJC Costs Committee recommended: see Civil Justice Council Costs Committee, *Report to the Master of the Rolls: Recommendations on Guideline Hourly Rates for 2014*, May 2014, available online at https://www.judiciary.gov.uk/wp-content/uploads/2014/07/ghr-final-report.pdf, Annex 8.

[83] This was made clear by now-revoked CPD, art 4.5.

[84] See Civil Justice Council Costs Committee, *Report to the Master of the Rolls: Recommendations on Guideline Hourly Rates for 2014*, May 2014, available online at https://www.judiciary.gov.uk/wp-content/uploads/2014/07/ghr-final-report.pdf, para 7.7.

[85] See, eg, *Dawe v Idg Communications Ltd* [2013] EWPCC 33, at [19]–[25] and [31], *per* Richard Meade QC.

fee earner having special expertise (see 51.73 and 51.79). These issues will be decided on a case-by-case basis, having regard to the factors in CPR, r 44.4(3), and (on the standard basis) to proportionality.

51.51 Whilst not binding, Judge Jeremy Richardson QC noted that the definitions of grade of fee earner make express reference to post-qualification experience rather than experience in general.[86] He went on to explain that other experience may be relevant to the question of whether the fee earner in question ought to be awarded a higher rate than that which normally attaches to their grade.

The place where work was done

51.52 There are three London bands (London 1, 2 and 3) and three national bands (National 1, 2 and 3). The Civil Justice Council Costs Committee has explained that these bands are intended to apply as follows.[87]

- **London 1 ('City')** This applies to postcodes EC1, EC2, EC3 and EC4.
- **London 2 ('Central London')** This applies to postcodes W1, WC1, WC2 and SW1.
- **London 3 ('Outer London')** This applies to all other London postcodes (SW, NW, N, E, SE and W other than W1), Bromley, Croydon, Dartford, Gravesend and Uxbridge.
- **National 1** This applies to major cities and legal centres (for example Birmingham, Manchester, Cardiff), the south east (for example Cambridge, Guildford) and other wealthy areas (for example Chester).
- **National 2** This applies to other cities (for example Coventry, Nottingham and Sheffield) and outer city areas (for example Outer Leeds, Outer Newcastle).
- **National 3** This applies to smaller cities (for example Leicester, Stoke, Preston), larger towns and rural areas (for example Grimsby, Blackburn, Hereford and Shrewsbury).[88]

The bandings are simply guidance and indicative of the appropriate rate. A court may take into account local knowledge.

Is National Band 3 still relevant?

51.53 The Civil Justice Council Costs Committee has said that, in practice, no distinction is made between National 2 and National 3, because there are few differences in the overheads of running practices in (say) small cities as compared to large towns.[89] The 2010 guideline rates make no mention of National 3; indeed, historically, the difference between National 2 and National 3 has been modest (that is, between £15 and £20 per hour for a Grade A fee earner). The court may, however, take into account the fact that, in some areas, overheads are lower (or higher) than in others.

---

[86] *G (by her mother and litigation friend M) v Kingston upon Hull city Council* (unreported), 18 September 2013, Kingston upon Hull County Court, at [41] and [42].

[87] See Civil Justice Council Costs Committee, *Report to the Master of the Rolls: Recommendations on Guideline Hourly Rates for 2014*, May 2014, available online at https://www.judiciary.gov.uk/wp-content/uploads/2014/07/ghr-final-report.pdf, para 2.2.

[88] See *ibid*, para 2.2.

[89] See *ibid*, para 2.2.

Arguments about locus *raised by receiving parties*

Occasionally, a receiving party will say that a rate higher than the local norm would be appropriate because the nature of the case was such that they could have instructed solicitors in a costlier area and still have remained within the bounds of that which was reasonable. That argument will usually fail.[90] That said, if the local firm needed to bear higher overheads to maintain a specialism (see 51.79), this may justify an increase in the rate. That said, it is occasionally the case that rates higher than the local norm will be allowed if the fee earners in question were part of a practice that was based in a more expensive area. An example of this is a case in which a London firm that provided commercial litigation services had offices in Guilford from which much of its London work was done; it was held that this justified an increase in the rates that might otherwise apply.[91] **51.54**

Arguments about locus *raised by paying parties*

It is not infrequently the case that a paying party will argue that the hourly rates are too high because solicitors could have been instructed locally at a lesser rate. Each case will turn on its own facts, but there is a degree of guidance available from the authorities (some of which are pre-CPR, but still relevant). In so far as the pre-CPR authorities give guidance on issues unrelated to the A-plus-B analysis, they are usually regarded as still being good law. The principles are broadly the same regardless of whether the receiving party brought or defended the claim.[92] **51.55**

The issue was addressed in two appeals that were heard at the same time: *Wraith v Sheffield Forgemasters Ltd* and *Truscott v Truscott*.[93] It is worth dealing with the facts of both *Wraith* and *Truscott* in some detail because those facts are often referred to in practice. **51.56**

The facts of *Wraith* and *Truscott* were as follows: **51.57**

- ***Wraith*** Mr Wraith was injured in an accident at his workplace in Sheffield. He brought a claim funded by his union. As was its habit, the union instructed specialist personal injury solicitors in London. Proceedings were commenced in London, but transferred to Sheffield. Mr Wraith was awarded substantial damages and costs. The defendant argued that it was not reasonable of Mr Wraith to have instructed London solicitors. Whilst that argument failed in the courts below, the Court of Appeal agreed with it, and consequently Mr Wraith was restricted to local rates.
- ***Truscott*** Mr Truscott was pursued by his former wife for maintenance payments. He lived in Tunbridge Wells and had previously instructed solicitors in East Grinstead (also in Kent). Although the order was enforceable only in the magistrates' court, his former wife's solicitors obtained an order for sale of his house. Acting on a recommendation made by a friend, he instructed a firm of solicitors in central London. His new solicitors

[90] See *Re Ajanaku* (unreported), 28 October 1991, QBD, *per* Eastham J. This is a pre-CPR authority, but it is usually accepted as still being good law. See also *Devon County Council v Celtic Bioenergy Ltd* [2014] EWHC 309 (TCC), at [16], in which Stuart-Smith J relied on *NAP Anglia Ltd v Sun-Land Development Co Ltd (No 2)* [2012] EWHC 51 (TCC), at [24], *per* Edwards-Stuart J, and *Devon County Council v Celtic Bioenergy Ltd* [2014] EWHC 309 (TCC), at [16], *per* Stuart Smith J.

[91] See *Accenuate Ltd v Asigra Inc* [2013] EWHC 889 (QB), at [25]–[29], *per* Tugendhat J. This case, perhaps, ought to be treated with some caution because the paying party was a litigant in person.

[92] See *Walbrook Properties Ltd v Severn Trent Water Ltd & Ors* [2002] EWHC 9016 (Costs), in which a defendant's hourly rate was reduced from London rates to Birmingham rates.

[93] *Truscott v Truscott; Wraith v Sheffield Forgemasters Ltd* [1998] 1 WLR 132, CA.

obtained an order striking out the order for sale; Mr Truscott was awarded costs. Again, the defendant said that London solicitors ought not to have been instructed. That argument had a degree of success in the courts below, but the Court of Appeal ultimately rejected it and awarded Mr Truscott London rates.

51.58 Both *Wraith* and *Truscott* demonstrate that the touchstone is a test of reasonableness. Kennedy LJ said:

> '[The] focus is primarily upon the reasonable interests of the [claimant] in the litigation so that, in relation to broad categories of costs, such as those generated by the decision of a [claimant] to employ a particular status or type of solicitor or counsel, or one located in a particular area, one looks to see whether, having regard to the extent and importance of the litigation to a reasonably minded [claimant], a reasonable choice or decision has been made.'[94]

51.59 Kennedy LJ found that a paying party could object to a receiving party's choice of lawyer if that choice had been a 'luxury':

> '[Costs may be disallowed if they have] not been "reasonably incurred" to the extent that they had been augmented by employment of a solicitor who, by reason of his calibre, normal area of practice, status or location, amounts to an unsuitable or "luxury" choice, made on grounds other than grounds which would be taken into account by an ordinary reasonable litigant concerned to obtain skilful competent and efficient representation in the type of litigation concerned.'[95]

51.60 Kennedy LJ identified a number of factors that were relevant when considering the issue of whether it was reasonable to instruct a town firm in preference to a local firm.[96] Whilst the test is not a subjective test (see 51.63), he emphasised the need to deal with the matter within the context of the particular circumstances of the particular litigants with whom the court is concerned. Kennedy LJ's list is as follows.

- **Importance** The importance of the matter to the client
- **Complexities** The legal and factual complexities involved (in so far as the client could reasonably be expected to understand them)
- **Location** The location of the client's home, their place of work and the location of the court
- **History** The client's previous experience of local solicitors

---

[94] *Ibid*, at 142.

[95] *Ibid*, at 142.

[96] *Ibid*, at 141: 'The following are matters which, as it seems to me, the judge should have regarded as relevant when considering the reasonableness of Mr Truscott's decision to instruct ATC [his solicitors]. (1) The importance of the matter to him. It was obviously of great importance. It threatened his home. (2) The legal and factual complexities, in so far as he might reasonably be expected to understand them. Due to the incompetence of MFC the matter had taken on an appearance of some complexity. (3) The location of his home, his place of work and the location of the court in which the relevant proceedings had been commenced. (4) Mr Truscott's possibly well-founded dissatisfaction with the solicitors he had originally instructed, which may well have resulted in a natural desire to instruct solicitors further afield, who would not be inhibited in representing his interests. (5) The fact that he had sought advice as to whom to consult, and had been recommended to consult ATC. (6) The location of ATC, including their accessibility to him, and their readiness to attend at the relevant court. (7) What, if anything, he might reasonably be expected to know of the fees likely to be charged by ATC as compared with the fees of other solicitors whom he might reasonably be expected to have considered.'

- **Advice** Any advice that the client might have received (including, presumably, recommendations)
- **Accessibility** The location of the town solicitors, their accessibility and their readiness to attend at the relevant court
- **Knowledge of rates** What, if anything, the client could be expected to know of the difference in rates charged by town and local solicitors

Both Moses J and Tugendhat J have commented that this list must not be read as a comprehensive or exclusive list applicable to all cases.[97] Factors not on this list, for example, might include the age of the client and the urgency with which the instructions must be placed.[98] In short, each case is to be decided on its own facts. **51.61**

Subjective or imputed knowledge about difference in rates

Whilst the court will take into account the client's actual knowledge, Kennedy LJ has confirmed that knowledge may be imputed.[99] Thus, whilst, as a matter of fact, the client may not have had the information that they needed to allow them to make a reasoned decision, they may be taken to have had that information if it was reasonably available to them and if they reasonably could have been expected to find it. The client's degree of sophistication may be relevant: in a case in which the client was an intelligent and experienced professional woman who earned £120,000 as a national sales manager, Jeremy Baker J found that she would have been aware that solicitors in various locations in and out of London would charge differing hourly rates.[100] This demonstrates the objectivity of the appropriate test. **51.62**

The need to examine the matter from an objective viewpoint, rather than from a subjective viewpoint, had also been emphasised by May LJ in *Sullivan v Co-operative Insurance Society*.[101] Litigants are entitled to engage any lawyer they choose and, from a subjective point of view, the choice may be entirely reasonable, but the question is to be judged objectively.[102] The test is not an entirely objective one, however, as Latham LJ made clear in a different case: **51.63**

> 'It seems to me that the conclusion that one can properly reach from the judgment of Kennedy LJ [in *Wraith*] is that, whereas it is clear that the test must involve an objective element when determining the reasonableness or otherwise of instructing the particular legal advisers in question, nonetheless that must always be a question which is answered within the context of the particular circumstances of the particular litigants with whom the court is concerned.'[103]

The relevant factors are to be considered from the perspective of the reasonable litigant without regard to the fact that they may be legally aided and have no interest in the costs. Teare J said this on the matter: **51.64**

> 'In assessing whether the reasonable litigant might reasonably have been expected to be aware of the comparative level of fees it seems to me that one must put to one side the

[97] *Higgins v Ministry of Defence* [2010] EWHC 654 (QB), at [14] and [24], *per* Tugendhat J, and esp at [22], where Tugendhat J refers to Moses J's comments in the unreported case of *Rana v Harrar*, as cited by Master Campbell in *Wicks v MoD* (unreported), 30 July 2003, SCCO.

[98] *Higgins v Ministry of Defence* [2010] EWHC 654 (QB), at [24].

[99] *Truscott v Truscott; Wraith v Sheffield Forgemasters Ltd* [1998] 1 WLR 132, CA, at 142.

[100] See *Kelly v Hays plc* [2015] EWHC 735 (QB), at [26] and [10].

[101] *Sullivan v Co-operative Insurance Society Ltd* [1999] 2 Costs LR 158.

[102] *Ibid*, at 165 *et seq*.

[103] *Griffiths v Solutia UK Ltd* [2001] EWCA Civ 736, at [16].

fact that this particular claimant was legally aided and assume that the reasonable litigant is funding his legal representation himself. Otherwise the question of cost would not feature in the analysis of what a reasonable litigant would have done. Such a litigant would clearly inquire into the level of fees charged by Bhatt Murphy before instructing that firm. He would also compare that level of fees with the level of fees charged by a Sheffield firm with experience of bringing actions against the police. Indeed, the attendance notes manifest the claimant's concern with the comparable charges because he was anxious to know how much his contribution to his legal expenses would be. The reasonable litigant would make himself aware of the comparative charges by consulting the Sheffield firm and the London firm. He would have appreciated that there was a substantial difference in rates. . . .'[104]

51.65 Hooper J has explained that the question to be asked is whether the solicitor chosen was the sort of solicitor that a person would have instructed with a view to the proper conduct of their case in minimising the costs of litigation.[105] These comments are still often cited today.[106] A more recent view was expressed by Jeremy Baker J, who explained that the question was what type of firm should have been retained, not what type of firm it would have been reasonable for the claimant to instruct.[107]

51.66 **The relevance of geographical differences in rates** The differential between distant solicitors and local rates not only may be a factor, but also, in an appropriate case, may be a factor that *must* be taken into account. This was explained by Sir Christopher Staughton:

> 'It does not appear that the costs judge or the deputy judge on appeal were told what the difference was between the costs of London solicitors and Manchester solicitors. But how can one answer the question whether it was reasonable to engage a London solicitor unless one at least takes into account the answer to that question? In this case we did ask and we were told ... This ... is a matter of some importance.'[108]

These comments were made in the context of group litigation in which the rising costs were a particular concern.

51.67 Tugendhat J has said that a reasonable litigant will normally be expected to investigate the hourly rates of solicitors whom they might instruct and to take advice thereupon before choosing whom to instruct, adding that other relevant factors that the client would be expected to take into account would include the time and costs associated with geographical location.[109] Notwithstanding those high expectations, Tugendhat J found that the other factors in the case before him (namely, the urgency of the matter and the age of the client) justified the decision of the receiving party to instruct distant solicitors—but he was at pains to point out that each case must be decided on its own facts rather than in a formulaic way.[110]

---

104 *A v Chief Constable of South Yorkshire* [2008] EWHC 1658 (QB), at [34].
105 See *A v F Co Ltd* (unreported), c 1995, QBD; *S v F Co Ltd* (1996) SCTO Digest 13.
106 See, eg, The White Book 2017, para 47.14.9.
107 *Kelly v Hays Plc* [2015] EWHC 735 (QB), at [20].
108 *Griffiths v Solutia UK Ltd* [2001] EWCA Civ 736, at [24].
109 *Higgins v Ministry of Defence* [2010] EWHC 654 (QB), at [26].
110 *Ibid*, at [14] and [24].

The relevance of instructions arising out of habit Both May LJ and Kennedy LJ have confirmed that the fact that a union or other organisation habitually instructs a particular firm of solicitors is a relevant factor, but of limited relevance on assessment in an individual case.[111] Notwithstanding this guidance, there are many first-instance decisions in which the court has found that the firm's familiarity with the organisation's working practices had resulted in savings in the time spent and that this justified the use of distant solicitors (see, on a related point, 51.71 and 51.73). **51.68**

The relevance of *locus*, geographical convenience, etc May LJ has explained that the fact that a case has no obvious connection with the area in which solicitors were instructed is a relevant factor—the more so if the case did not require expertise only to be found there.[112] **51.69**

It may be that a claim is so well rooted in a particular location that it can be said to be, for example, 'a Manchester case'. May LJ has confirmed that this would be a relevant factor.[113] Judge LJ added: **51.70**

> 'In reality this was a Manchester case. The cause of action arose from the plaintiff's employment by the defendants in Manchester and his consequent fault exposure to asbestos which caused him serious personal injury. Even as the case developed through the identification of witnesses and the selection of experts and discovery, the case remained a Manchester case with no, or no relevant, connection at all with London.'[114]

The matter is not limited to geographical convenience because the court must take into account all of the circumstances, including those that do not pertain to geography. In a case in which London solicitors had been instructed to carry out a search-and-seize order in Manchester, Judge Hegarty QC (sitting as a High Court judge) found that this was reasonable, given the urgency of the situation, the fact that the client was based outside the UK, and the fact that the solicitors who were instructed were familiar with the claimants' business and needs.[115] In a similar vein, Latham LJ has found that the absence of a connection with the town in question is not, of itself, sufficient to make the decision to instruct solicitors there an unreasonable decision; in the case before him, Latham LJ took into account all of the facts, rather than only those relating to geography.[116] **51.71**

Distant solicitor rates may be uplifted to take into account the complexities of the case,[117] but Jeremy Baker J held that it would be wrong to uplift rates such that they were indistinguishable from rates that the court had previously said should not apply.[118] **51.72**

---

[111] *Sullivan v Co-operative Insurance Society Ltd* [1999] 2 Costs LR 158, at 167, *per* May LJ; *Truscott v Truscott; Wraith v Sheffield Forgemasters Ltd* [1998] 1 WLR 132, CA, at 142, *per* Kennedy LJ.

[112] *Sullivan v Co-operative Insurance Society Ltd* [1999] 2 Costs LR 158, at 167. Whilst *obiter*, see also *Higgins v Ministry of Defence* [2010] EWHC 654 (QB), at [26].

[113] The facts were that the claim was a case involving asbestos exposure without extraordinary legal complication or special features. The claimant lived in Manchester, the cause of action arose in Manchester, the lay witnesses lived in or around Manchester, one of the claimant's experts practised close to Manchester, the defendant was based in Manchester and there were many firms of solicitors in the Manchester area who were capable of handling the claim. May LJ found that it was 'pre-eminently a Manchester case with no obvious connection with London': *Sullivan v Co-operative Insurance Society Ltd* [1999] 2 Costs LR 158, at 167.

[114] *Ibid*, at 167.

[115] *Fisher Price Inc & Mattel UK Ltd v RSW Group plc* [2004] EWHC 1610 (Ch).

[116] *Griffiths v Solutia UK Ltd* [2001] EWCA Civ 736, at [20].

[117] *KMT v Kent County Council* [2012] EWHC 2088 (QB), at [16].

[118] See *Kelly v Hays plc* [2015] EWHC 735 (QB), at [23], *per* Jeremy Baker J.

51.73 **Geographical variations in specialist expertise** Whilst an obvious point, if a solicitor has specialist expertise that is not available elsewhere, that would be a factor to be taken into account in deciding whether it was reasonable to instruct them. (For a discussion of the relevance of specialist experts in general, see 51.79.) A solicitor's expertise would be a relevant factor even where it has been gained as a result of prior experience of the case in question.[119]

51.74 **The paying party's conduct concerning *locus* and geography** Mance LJ has commented that if a paying party remained silent about the fact that the receiving party had instructed distant solicitors, then that would be a factor that the court could take into account.[120] In practice, however, most claimants will have already instructed solicitors before their opponents are given any opportunity to comment.

51.75 **Proportionality and distant solicitors** In giving judgment in an appeal in which the test of proportionality did not apply, Sir Christopher Staughton made it clear that his decision might have been different if it had.[121] The clear implication is that it is possible for a decision to instruct distant solicitors to be reasonable, but disproportionate.

51.76 The following miscellaneous points may be made about the *Wraith* argument generally.

- **Experience of local solicitors** The fact that the client's experience of local solicitors may be relevant was commented upon in *Wraith* (see 51.60). In *Ryan v Tretol Group Ltd*,[122] Wright J found[123] that it was reasonable for a claimant with an asbestos-related claim to disinstruct local solicitors in favour of London solicitors; a client who is dissatisfied with their first choice of solicitors is not always required to 'shop around' for suitable specialist local solicitors. Similarly, in a claim in which the receiving party instructed London solicitors because her previous solicitors had said that the claim had no merit, Cranston J found that London rates should apply.[124]
- **Enquiries in respect of local solicitors** Teare J has found that, in an appropriate case, a litigant can be expected to make reasonable enquiries as to the availability of local specialist expertise.[125]
- **Recommendations and support groups and professional bodies** Cranston J has held that where the client had been told by local solicitors that her claim would not be successful, it was reasonable for her to consult her professional body, which agreed to support her by obtaining a second opinion from distant solicitors; as such, their

[119] *Griffiths v Solutia UK Ltd* [2001] EWCA Civ 736, at [33], *per* Mance LJ.

[120] *Ibid*, at [33].

[121] *Ibid*, at [27]. This case was decided before *Lownds v Home Office* [2002] EWCA 365, but there is nothing in *Lownds* that undermines Sir Christopher Staughton's reasoning.

[122] *Ryan v Tretol Group Ltd* [2002] All ER (D) 156.

[123] It should be noted that, to a large extent, the appeal was allowed by consent, in that it was conceded that if it was reasonable for the receiving party to disinstruct his solicitor in Nottingham, it would have been reasonable for him to instruct solicitors in London; hence Wright J did not have to consider the issue of whether Mr Ryan had acted reasonably in instructing solicitors in London, as opposed to Sheffield, or Manchester, or Leeds.

[124] *Royal Devon & Exeter NHS Foundation Trust v Acres* [2013] EWHC 652 (QB), at [19]–[27].

[125] *A v Chief Constable of South Yorkshire* [2008] EWHC 1658 (QB), at [27].

rates were recoverable.[126] In a similar vein, any advice given by support groups may be relevant.[127]

- **Geographical availability of a specialist bar** A factor that might be relevant is the availability of a specialist bar. *Gazley v Wade*[128] concerned a man who was wrongly identified as a paedophile by a national newspaper. He initially instructed local solicitors, but after he grew dissatisfied with their services, he instructed specialist solicitors in London. Eady J said this:

 'It is important to recognise that in order to have the necessary or the proportionate expertise available one does not always need to instruct London specialist solicitors. An important factor is that any competent litigation solicitor in the country can call upon specialist members of the bar at very short notice. Indeed, as I have already said, [the claimant's solicitors] themselves took advice from counsel.'[129]

- **Travelling as a factor** Whilst she was dealing with a costs-capping application, rather than an assessment, Hallett J has implied that the court may take the costs of travelling into account.[130] Judge Behrens (sitting as a judge of the High Court) has commented that where a complex case involves a great deal of travelling (which, he observed, is an activity that does not involve difficult work), then either the travelling ought to be reflected in a generally lower rate for all of the work or a differential hourly rate for travel.[131] In the case before him, he allowed those rates published in the *Guide to the Summary Assessment of Costs* for travel costs.

City rates

Master Hurst has had this to say about City rates (that is, rates applicable to the City of London): **51.77**

> 'City rates for City solicitors are recoverable where the City solicitor is undertaking City work, which is normally heavy commercial or corporate work. Defamation is not in that category, and, particularly given the reduction in damages awards for libel, is never likely to be. A City firm which undertakes work, which could be competently handled by a number of Central London solicitors, is acting unreasonably and disproportionately if it seeks to charge City rates.'[132]

---

126 *Acres v Royal Devon and Exeter NHS Foundation Trust* [2013] EWHC 652 (QB).

127 Astill J, for example, allowed town rates in an asbestos-related disease case in which one of the main reasons for instructing town solicitors was because a local support group had recommended those solicitors: *Patterson v Cape Darlington & Ors* [2001] EWHC 9005 (Costs).

128 *Gazley v Wade* [2004] EWHC 2675 (QB).

129 *Ibid*, at [40].

130 *Ledward v Kent & Medway Health Authority* [2003] EWHC 2551 (QB), at [22]. On the facts of that case, the town solicitors were actually cheaper than the local solicitor and the issue was whether those savings justified the travelling time.

131 *Thornley (a child) v Ministry of Defence* [2010] EWHC 2584 (QB), at [67]–[76].

132 *King v Telegraph Group plc* [2005] EWHC 90015 (Costs), at [92]. (These comments are not binding, but given the fact that hourly rates and other issues of quantum are matters that are particularly within Master Hurst's realm of expertise, they must be regarded as being highly persuasive.) See, however, *KPMG Peat Marwick McLintock v HLT Group Ltd* [1995] 2 All ER 180, in which Auld J allowed City rates in a case that was not a commercial case, but which 'had commercial undertones'. This case was, however, decided before the jurisdiction established by the line of cases following *Truscott v Truscott; Wraith v Sheffield Forgemasters Ltd* [1998] 1 WLR 132, CA, had matured; it was also pre-CPR.

Other factors

Complexity

51.78 Complexity is a factor to be taken into account; indeed, it is one of the factors listed in CPR, r 44.4(3). The following miscellaneous points can be made.

- **Factual complexity** Both Hallett J and Lewison J have implied (albeit briefly) that factual complexity will not necessarily merit the high rates claimed by specialist lawyers; rather, something more is usually required.[133]
- **Legal complexity** Legal complexity is a factor to be taken into account. It is open to the court to take into account a note prepared by counsel explaining the difficulties that were encountered.[134]
- **Emotional complexity** Hallett J has said (*obiter*) that it is doubtful that the difficulty and unpleasantness of formulating allegations in an emotionally charged case would merit an unusually high hourly rate.[135] Similarly, in a case that involved the anal and vaginal rape of an autistic child, Judge Jeremy Richardson QC said that the court 'must place all feelings of sympathy for the claimant to one side when determining the arid territory of [the hourly rate]'.[136]
- **Group litigation** Where work is being carried out on individual (non-lead) claims that form part of group litigation, it might be appropriate to award a lower rate for that work than would be allowed for the generic work.[137] Lord Neuberger MR has implied that the costs of obtaining clients and getting business may be a factor that could be reflected in the hourly rate in group litigation.[138]

Specialist expertise

51.79 The following miscellaneous points may be made about specialist expertise.

- **Higher overheads arising out of specialism** It may be that a receiving party seeks a higher hourly rate on the basis that a specialist firm was instructed that had higher overheads than other less specialists firms, for example if it has to pay its assistant solicitors and other staff higher salaries, or it has to provide extra facilities for demanding clients.[139] Such an argument may, in principle, be accepted, but increased overheads generally have to be proved by evidence. In *Jones v Secretary of State for Wales*,[140] the receiving party's claim for a higher rate failed because that evidence was not put before the court. Eady J has impliedly confirmed that the requirement for evidence has survived the

[133] *Ledward v Kent & Medway Health Authority* [2003] EWHC 2551 (QB), at [42], *per* Hallett J; *Ross v Stonewood Securities Ltd* [2004] EWHC 2235 (Ch), at [31], *per* Lewison J.

[134] *A v Chief Constable of South Yorkshire* [2008] EWHC 1658 (QB), at [22]–[23]. Teare J found that such a note is admissible notwithstanding the fact that it may partly be opinion. He went on to say that the court is not obliged to accept the opinion of counsel, because the court must decide matters in dispute for itself.

[135] *Ledward v Kent & Medway Health Authority* [2003] EWHC 2551 (QB), at [42].

[136] *G (by her mother and litigation friend M) v Kingston upon Hull city Council* (unreported), 18 September 2013, Kingston upon Hull County Court, at [1].

[137] *Giambrone v JMC Holidays Ltd* [2002] EWHC 495 (QB), at [22]–[26], *per* Nelson J.

[138] *Motto & Ors v Trafigura Ltd & Anor* [2011] EWCA Civ 1150, at [110].

[139] A hypothetical example that is often cited is a firm that specialises in representing foreign commercial clients. One would expect such a firm's overheads to be higher as a result of the need to keep the office open to take calls from clients in different time zones. Indeed, this is mentioned in *Kelly v Hays plc* [2015] EWHC 735 (QB), at [10], where Jeremy Baker J recited the judgment of Master Campbell in the court below.

[140] *Jones v Secretary of State for Wales* [1997] 1 WLR 1008.

introduction of the CPR. In a case in which a lawyer sought to justify a very high rate on the basis of his supposedly fearsome reputation, Eady J made the following remarks:

> '[The paying party] argued as follows: "If you wish to take yourself out of the norm you have to provide the court with evidence to enable you to do so. You may have a niche practice, and you may be able to persuade celebrities that you are the solicitor to go to at whatever rate you choose to charge them, but without evidence that your overheads are out of the ordinary there is no basis for holding that a *Jones* increase should apply". I find his reasoning persuasive.'[141]

- **Discretionary enhancement for specialist expertise** A receiving party may seek a discretionary enhancement (which under the A-plus-B model would be an increase in B, rather than A). If the argument is limited in this way—that is, if it is not based on an assertion that there are increased overheads—then evidence would not usually be required. The justification for a discretionary enhancement would usually be based on the premise that a specialist lawyer would complete the task in hand with greater frugality of time than a generalist. There are examples of the court accepting such an argument,[142] but the expertise has to be relevant in the sense that it may assist in disposing of the claim.[143]
- **Teams and distribution of responsibility** Where work is being carried out by a team that is made up of senior members who bear a greater burden of responsibility than the junior members, the level of responsibility borne by each member may be an important factor.[144] This means that it may be appropriate to allow differential enhancements above the rates that would have been allowed to generalists.[145] Jeremy Baker J put it like this: '[A]lthough some degree of uplift may be appropriate for the main decision taker, which is normally the grade A fee earner ... this is less likely to apply the further down the pecking order of fee grades.'[146] Nelson J has commented that if a single enhancement is contemplated, it ought to reflect the average level of responsibility borne rather than the highest.[147]
- **Counsel's specialisation** The availability of a specialist bar has already been mentioned at 51.76. Whilst speaking in the context of whether it was reasonable to instruct solicitors in a particular locality, Eady J commented that any solicitor is able to call upon the services of specialist counsel;[148] therefore the availability of a local specialist bar (or lack thereof) may be relevant.

---

141 *Cox and Carter v MGN Ltd* [2006] EWHC 1235 (QB), at [61].

142 Although dealing with legal aid enhancement, Sullivan J allowed an enhanced rate to take account of a fee earner's expertise gained outside his legal practice (in that case, as a dentist), on the basis that the fee earner's expertise saved time: see *Diacou v Staden* [2000] EWHC 9003 (Costs).

143 In a case that involved psychiatric issues, issues concerning ethnicity and claims against the police, Teare J found that although counsel would have been assisted by the fact that his instructing solicitors were specialists in these areas, experienced personal injury counsel could have been expected to bring the claim to a successful conclusion without that additional assistance: *A v Chief Constable of South Yorkshire Police* [2008] EWHC 1658 (QB), at [23].

144 Supervision may be relevant in this regard. Whilst not binding, see *G (by her mother and litigation friend M) v Kingston upon Hull city Council* (unreported), 18 September 2013, Kingston upon Hull County Court, at [56], *per* Judge Jeremy Richardson QC.

145 *Giambrone v JMC Holidays Ltd* [2002] EWHC 495 (QB), at [22]–[26], *per* Nelson J.

146 *Kelly v Hays plc* [2015] EWHC 735 (QB), at [30].

147 *Giambrone v JMC Holidays Ltd* [2002] EWHC 495 (QB), at [21], *per* Nelson J.

148 *Gazley v Wade* [2004] EWHC 2675 (QB), at [53].

Unusually low overheads, in-house solicitors and government departments

51.80 It may be that the paying party seeks a reduction in the hourly rates because of unusually *low* overheads. In a case in which this was so, Arden J referred to *London Scottish Benefit Society v Chorley*[149] and, in particular, to the following extract from Brett MR's judgment: 'The unsuccessful adversary of a solicitor appearing in person cannot be charged for what does not exist'.[150] Arden J found that the costs judge had been correct to assess the hourly rate on the basis that no allowance should be made for overheads that did not exist. The case before Arden J involved a solicitor-litigant; it is not known whether the same analysis would apply to the assessment of costs where the receiving party was separately represented. There is some authority to suggest that it would, albeit in a context other than hourly rates.[151]

51.81 **In-house solicitors** It may be argued that the fact that the receiving party was represented by an in-house solicitor is a factor to be taken into account because such solicitors do not have the same overheads of a firm of solicitors nor do they have to pay for marketing and professional indemnity insurance. In a case in which that argument was raised, Martin Roger QC (sitting in the Upper Tribunal (Lands Chamber)) rejected the contention that evidence of overheads should be adduced.[152] He explained that this was because it would be impractical and contrary to authority to require a landlord to justify the costs claimed for legal works undertaken by an employed solicitor by apportioning the overheads of its business to a particular transaction. The general principles that Mr Roger QC relied upon are described at 18.107–18.113. The rule is not, however, an absolute one and can take an in-house solicitor's overheads into account if the case is a 'special' case (see 18.110).

51.82 **Government departments** Government departments may have accounting arrangements such that one department may pay a certain rate for legal services provided by another. Where this is so, the points made above about in-house solicitors will usually apply. Lord Morris had the following points to make on the topic.

(1) The receiving party, although nominally the Secretary of State for the Home Department is, in truth, the government, or 'the Crown'.
(2) The Government Legal Department, under the Treasury Solicitor, is part of the same one and indivisible entity.
(3) The costs that can properly be claimed by the receiving party are therefore to be based on the costs to which the government (not merely the Secretary of State or their department) is put to in defending the claim.
(4) Internal payments, for example between the Secretary of State and the Government Legal Department, cannot be relied upon as demonstrating the cost to the receiving party, because neither of them is 'the government' or 'the Crown'.
(5) Whatever accounting arrangements may be imposed between the Government Legal Department and any other department or agency, the Treasury Solicitor and the Government Legal Department remain part of the executive process of

---

149 *London Scottish Benefit Society v Chorley* (1884) 13 QBD 872.

150 *Stubblefield v Kemp* [2001] 1 Costs LR 30, at 37.

151 *Henderson v Merthyr Tydfil Urban District Council* [1900] 1 QB 434, at 437.

152 See *Re Alka Arora*, sub nom *68b Maud Road, London, E13 0JU* [2013] UKUT 362 (LC). This decision relied heavily on *Re Eastwood (dec'd)* [1975] Ch 112.

government—that is, part of 'the Crown'. They are the government's in-house solicitor and the payment arrangements do not separate them or give any reason to treat them like a solicitor in private practice engaged by a client.[153]

Thus, for all practical purposes, the principles in *Eastwood*[154] (see 18.114) will apply.

Urgency and pressure of time

The need for the urgent supply of legal services may justify a higher hourly rate. Peter Smith J, for example, allowed £400 per hour as against a guideline rate of £317 per hour, because 'given the nature of the application and the urgency a figure higher than the guideline figure [was] justified; the application was to commit a party to prison for failure to comply with the terms of a freezing order'.[155] **51.83**

The use of Comparators and Precedents

The amounts charged by a party's previous solicitors might be an appropriate comparator,[156] as may rates charged by an opponent.[157] Where a party seeks to rely on the rates charged by other local firms, they must prove that point by way of evidence (which might include expert evidence).[158] A comparison with rates paid by those who regularly instruct firms to represent defendants may not be a helpful comparator. Hallett J explained that this is because 'their "clout" in the market place is such that they can drive down lawyers' fees and still benefit from the assistance of experienced solicitors'.[159] The ACCC came to much the same conclusion following a survey that referred to costs incurred in 2007: **51.84**

> '[The researchers found] a large gap between the rates charged by claimants' solicitors and those charged by defendants' solicitors for Personal Injury (PI) or Clinical Negligence (CN) cases. No such gap exists for Chancery (CH) or Employment Tribunal (ET) cases. In PI/CN cases the rates charged by claimants' solicitors were around the [guideline hourly rates], those charged by defendants' solicitors were 20–35 percent lower.'[160]

An expert commentator has suggested that the difference between claimants' rates and defendants' rates can be accounted for by the irrecoverable costs of case screening, the need to maintain cash flow, the need to pay for marketing and the need to pay referral fees (before they were banned).[161] Further, now that it is clear that the costs of funding are **51.85**

---

[153] *Town Investments Ltd & Ors v Department of the Environment* [1978] AC 359, at 399–401. See also *R (on the application of Bakhtiyar) v Secretary of State for the Home Department* [2015] UKUT 519 (IAC), at [31], *per* Mr C M G Ockelton.

[154] *In re Eastwood, dec'd; Lloyds Bank Ltd v Eastwood* [1975] Ch 112.

[155] *Global Marine Drillships Ltd v La Bella* [2010] EWHC 2498 (Ch), at [8].

[156] *Ross v Stonewood Securities Ltd* [2004] EWHC 2235 (Ch), at [31], *per* Lewison J.

[157] See, eg, *Intergraph (UK) Ltd v Wolfson Microelectronics plc* [2012] EWHC 1862 (Ch), at [3] and [4], *per* Mr Snowdon QC.

[158] Whilst he was dealing with a judicial review concerning criminal costs, see *Watson v HM Courts & Tribunals Service National Taxing Team* [2012] EWHC 2865 (Admin), in which Silber J said that there must be cogent and convincing expert evidence.

[159] *Ledward v Kent & Medway Health Authority* [2003] EWHC 2551 (QB), at [32]; see also *Mainwaring v Goldtech Investments Ltd* [1997] 1 All ER 467.

[160] See Advisory Committee on Civil Costs, 'The Derivation of New Guideline Hourly Rates', 9 December 2008, p 2. These figures should be read in the context of the criticism made at 44.03, however, because they are derived from the same data, which is questionable, to say the least.

[161] Gibbs, S, 'Pay Gap' (2011) 155(45) Solicitors Journal 19.

not recoverable, it has been suggested that the work of setting up a retainer and arranging funding should also be taken into account.[162]

51.86 As to the rates allowed in other cases, the court has repeatedly stressed that each case is to be decided on its own facts. In the context of the court below having declined to give weight to a decision recently decided by another judge, Lewison J said:

> 'He was rightly unimpressed with the attempt to use [that case] as a comparator. [That case] was a decision on its own facts, and did not establish any general rule about the appropriate level of charging rates, even in specialised cases.'[163]

Composite and Hybrid Rates

51.87 Composite rates are a blend of unequal hourly rates (usually applicable to different time periods). If, for example, a bill claims relatively modest sums in the period 2009–11, it might be seen as proportionate and sensible to apply a single composite rate throughout rather than three or four different rates, each applicable to a different time period. The composite rate may be based on an arithmetical mean or it may be based on mid-point (that is, the 2010 rate in the example above). Weighted averages may be appropriate in some circumstances.[164]

51.88 Evans J has confirmed the legality of such an approach in principle, saying the following:

> 'Whether he [the costs judge] takes an average figure covering a number of years or an annual figure which he applies to the work done in each particular year is a matter of convenience and entirely a question for him, in the particular circumstances of the individual case.'[165]

51.89 It should be noted that Evans J was referring to what the *costs judge* was able to do, not to what the parties were able to do. Whilst an assessment based on a composite rate is nothing more than a judicial shortcut, the same may not be true if a composite rate is claimed in the bill of costs. This is because of the 'principle of individual application' (see 18.11–18.14), which means that the indemnity principle applies to each and every item, rather than as a cap.

51.90 In a similar vein, it is open to the court to allow a hybrid hourly rate that aggregates the rates of more than one grade of fee earner. If the court is concerned, for instance, that much of the work subject to assessment should have been delegated, it may award a single rate reflecting the lower rates of more junior fee earners.

---

162 Stark, I, 'Reality Check on Costs' (2011) 76 Litigation Funding 12.

163 *Ross v Stonewood Securities Ltd* [2004] EWHC 2235 (Ch), at [30].

164 A weighted average would be particularly appropriate where the work was not spread out evenly over the periods in question. Thus, if twice as much work was done in 2001 than in the other years, that year may be afforded a double share when the average is calculated.

165 *Johnson v Reed Corrugated Cases Ltd* [1992] 1 All ER 169, at 178. These comments were made prior to the introduction of the CPR.

52

DISBURSEMENTS AND EXPENSES

This chapter deals with the following topics: **52.01**

- introduction and types of disbursement (52.02):
  - actual disbursements (52.04);
  - services disbursements (52.06);
  - true expenses (52.07);
  - client disbursements (52.08);
  - office disbursements (52.09);
- expert witnesses and advisory experts (52.10):
  - instructing experts and the recoverability of experts' fees in principle (52.11);
  - whether it was reasonable to instruct the expert (52.22);
  - experts instructed without the court's permission (52.29);
  - measure of experts' fees (52.33);
  - jointly instructed experts and questions to experts (52.43);
- fixed-cost medical reports and the Medical Reporting Organisation Agreement (52.46);
- factual witnesses (52.47):
  - conduct money (52.49);
  - miscellaneous matters concerning factual witnesses (52.56);
  - witness and receiving party the same person (52.57);
  - professional witnesses of fact (52.58);
- medical records (52.60);
- other types of personal records (52.62);
- medical agencies (52.63);
- copying charges (52.73);
- couriers, postage, etc (52.77);
- legal representatives' hotel expenses (52.79);
- legal representatives' travelling expenses (52.81);
- disbursement funding loans (52.85);
- court fees (52.87);
- foreign lawyers (52.98); and
- interpreters (52.100).

Introduction and Types of Disbursement

52.02 'Disbursements are money paid on behalf of the client', according to Vaughan Williams LJ.[1] This is true of most disbursements, but it is not a fully inclusive definition; perhaps a more workable definition is that, as between solicitor and client, disbursements are those monies that are not profit costs[2] or taxes, but which can properly be included within a statute bill.[3] As between opposing parties, this definition would need to be expanded to include recoverable monies paid by the client to persons other than their legal representative (these often being referred to as client disbursements or expenses).[4] That said, there are exceptions, such that expenses do not include after-the-event (ATE) insurance premiums, because these are in a category of their own as between opposing parties.[5] For present purposes, the following types of disbursements and expenses can be identified.

- **Actual disbursements** These are monies paid by legal representatives (usually solicitors) for goods or services that they are, by law or by custom, required to disburse. They are also known as professional disbursements.
- **Services disbursements** These are fees charged for services rendered or to be rendered by persons who are not legal representatives (such as experts).
- **True expenses** These are legal representatives' rechargeable expenses (such as the costs of photocopying carried out by a bureau).
- **Client disbursements (otherwise known as expenses)** These are expenses of a similar nature to any of those mentioned above, but incurred by the client (such as where a client pays an expert directly).
- **Office disbursements** These are expenses charged by legal representatives for administrative services (such as for photocopying carried out in-house).

52.03 This categorisation does not exist in law, but is merely the editor's invention for the purposes of describing the law. There is considerable overlap between these categories—in particular, the first category (actual disbursements) includes both services disbursements and true expenses (see Figure 52.1). Each category is considered in turn.

Actual disbursements

52.04 Actual disbursements may be identified as those payments that a legal representative (usually a solicitor) is bound, either by law or by custom, to make.[6] Where a solicitor is not bound by law or custom to make it, a payment made on behalf of the client would not be an actual disbursement and would not appear in the solicitor's statute bill; instead, it would appear as an entry in the client account. Other than experts' fees, counsel's fees and the like (see 52.06), actual disbursements mostly relate to non-contentious work, so they are not commonly encountered in costs practice. They include stamp

[1] *Browne v Barber* [1913] 2 KB 553, at 573.
[2] This would have to include success fees, where appropriate.
[3] See *Joel v Barnato* (1929) 45 TLR 167.
[4] This is what is meant by this term in CPR, r 1.1(1).
[5] *BNM v MGN Ltd* [2017] EWCA Civ 1767, at [73], *per* Sir Terence Etherton MR.
[6] See, eg, *Re Remnant* (1849) 11 Beav 603, at 611. Monies described as being actual disbursements may, according to some authorities, also include monies that would not be regarded as being costs, such as debt or damages: see *Re Fletcher and Dyson* [1903] 2 Ch 688; *Prothero v Thomas* (1815) 6 Taunt 196.

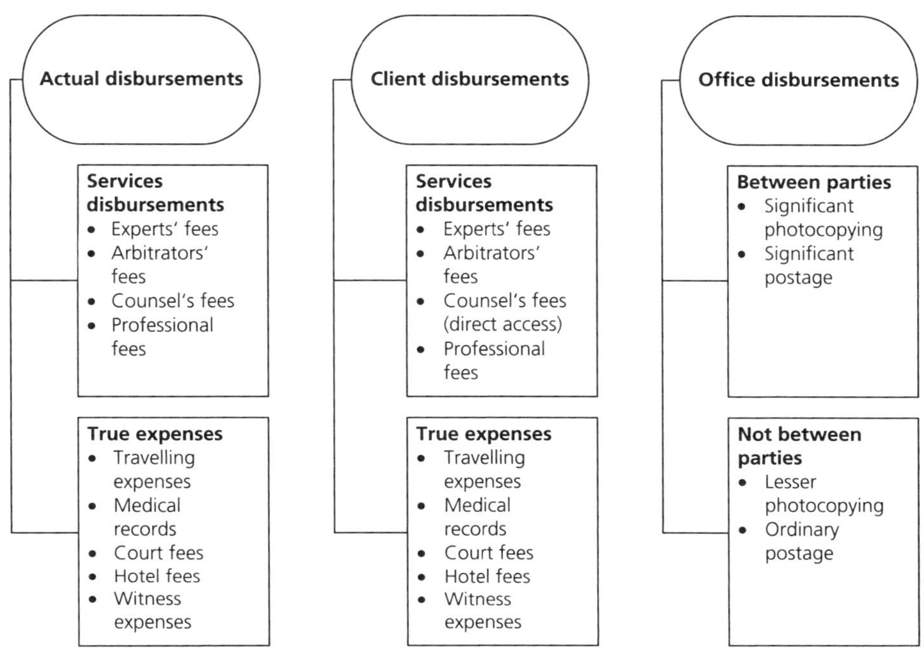

Figure 52.1 Types of disbursement

duties,[7] purchase monies,[8] estate duties[9] and deposits.[10] The distinction between what is and is not an actual disbursement was explained by Langdale MR:

> 'It appears to me, that it is the practice of solicitors, who may have to pay or advance money on behalf of their clients, carefully to distinguish such professional disbursements as ought to be entered in their bill of costs, from such other advances or payments, as ought to be entered only in their cash accounts, as cash payments or advances. And it seems to me a very reasonable and proper rule, that those payments only, which are made in pursuance of the professional duty undertaken by the solicitor, and which he is bound to perform, or which are sanctioned as professional payments, by the general and established custom and practice of the profession, ought to be entered or allowed as professional disbursements in the bill of costs.'[11]

Thus a payment made by a solicitor on behalf of a client will not become a disbursement merely by reason of it being made by the legal representative rather than by the client.[12]

Whilst, at the time of writing his decision was subject to appeal, Soole J has said that as between solicitor and client an after-the-event (ATE) premium may be an actual **52.05**

[7] *Re Blair and Girling* [1906] 2 KB 131.
[8] *Re Remnant* (1849) 11 Beav 603.
[9] *Re Kingdon and Wilson* [1902] 2 Ch 242.
[10] *Re Buckwell and Berkeley* [1902] 2 Ch 596.
[11] *Re Remnant* (1849) 11 Beav 603, at 613. This decision was endorsed by the Court of Appeal in *Buckwill v Berkley* [1902] 2 Ch D 596.
[12] The act of giving express authority will not make a disbursement into an actual disbursement: *Re Page (No 3)* (1863) 32 Beav 487; *Re Blair & Girling* [1906] 2 KB 131, at 137–8; *Re Fletcher and Dyson* [1903] 2 Ch 688, at 693; *Re Porter Amphlett and Jones* [1912] 2 Ch 98.

disbursement not only because premiums have customarily been included in bills as such,[13] but also (on the facts of the case before him) by reason of 'the purchase of ATE insurance cover [being] an inextricable part of the package which the solicitor provides to the client'.[14] Soole J went on to say that the 'fact that there was a contract between client (insured) and insurer is not decisive',[15] and he concluded by saying that he did 'not accept that the sum was paid as mere agent for the client, independent of [the solicitor's] duty as her solicitor'.[16] Whilst no more than the editor's own observation, it is possible that—if Soole J's analysis survives appeal—a similar analysis may apply to fees payable under litigation funding agreements if those fees can properly be said to be a part of a package of funding offered to a client.

Services disbursements

52.06 Services disbursements are monies (other than profit costs) payable to third parties for services rendered or to be rendered. Examples of services disbursements are experts' fees, accountancy fees, counsel's fees, etc. There is a degree of overlap with the other types of disbursement: where a legal representative pays for services as a matter of custom or professional etiquette, for example, that payment will be both a services disbursement and an actual disbursement (see 52.04 and Figure 52.1);[17] and where a client pays a service provider directly, then the payment will be both a services disbursement and a client disbursement (see 52.08 and Figure 52.1). Services disbursements must be distinguished from those monies paid by legal representatives to agents for the procurement of services that are then accounted for as if they had been provided by the legal representative themselves (see Chapter 22), which monies will be absorbed by the legal representative's own practice as practice expenses and paid out of the office account. A legal representative may be able to make a profit by accounting for services in this way, because they may be able to charge notional profit costs that exceed the fee paid.[18] Similarly, in a case in which a conditional fee agreement was made before 1 April 2013, the legal representative may also be able to claim a success fee between opposing parties.[19] Whether a legal representative is entitled to account for services in this way (or is required to do so) will depend on the nature of the services—in particular, they must be legal services that the legal representative could have provided themselves. There must also be a degree of supervision, as was explained by May LJ: '[A] characteristic of such work [ie work which may be recharged as profit costs] is whether the solicitor remains responsible to the client for its proper conduct.'[20] This is a topic that is explored in more detail in Chapter 22 (see especially 22.13–22.20).

13 See *Herbert v HH Law Ltd* [2018] EWHC 580 (QB), at [73].

14 *Ibid*, at [69].

15 *Ibid*, at [69].

16 *Ibid*, at [73].

17 This is not an immutable category. It has been held, for example, that fees for shorthand notes are monies that have become payable by the solicitor who requests them and that, as such, they are actual disbursements: *Cocks v Bruce Searl & Good* (1904) 21 TLR 62.

18 *Smith Graham v Lord Chancellor's Department* [1999] 2 Costs LR 1, a legal aid assessment in which Hallett J allowed recovery for the time spent by an enquiry agent at the instructing solicitor's hourly rate; cf *Re UIC Insurance Co Ltd* [2006] EWHC 2717 (Ch).

19 *Crane v Cannons Leisure Centre* [2007] EWCA Civ 1352.

20 *Ibid*, at [14] (Maurice Kay LJ dissenting).

True expenses

The label 'true expenses' is self-explanatory: it is a category that includes a legal representative's out-of-pocket expenses, such as hotel bills, parking fees, tolls, etc. Where the sums involved are modest, true expenses may be challenged on the basis that, given the hourly rate, the legal representative can be expected to bear the costs themselves.[21] Practice Direction (PD) 47 makes provision for this in respect of local travelling expenses, postage and copying fees.[22] PD 47 does not govern the position between legal representative and client, however; that is governed by the terms of the retainer. Thus it is entirely plausible that an expense may be categorised as a true expense as between legal representative and client, but not between opposing parties. **52.07**

Client disbursements

A client disbursement (which, when paid via the agency of a legal representative, is known as a non-professional disbursement[23]) is a sum of money paid by the client (either personally, or by some other person acting on the client's behalf) for services or provisions pertaining to the litigation. An example would be where the client had agreed to pay an expert directly, or where they agreed to bear a witness's travel expenses. Client disbursements are recoverable from an opponent regardless of whether there is an enforceable retainer.[24] They may be paid through the agency of the legal representative; where this is done, they may be distinguished from an actual disbursement by virtue of the fact that the legal representative will have no duty to disburse the monies.[25] If there is a dispute as to whether an item included within a statute bill is an actual disbursement or a client disbursement, then the burden will lie with the solicitor to prove that it is properly chargeable as an actual disbursement.[26] Client disbursements will, where appropriate, appear in the cash account, but the cash account itself does not have a bearing on whether a disbursement is an actual disbursement or a client disbursement.[27] In particular, the fact that a client has put their solicitor in funds for a disbursement (such as counsel's fees) will not generally have a bearing on whether that disbursement is or is not an actual disbursement.[28] **52.08**

Office disbursements

Office disbursements are notional sums charged by the legal representative for the supply of goods or services that are ancillary to the supply of professional legal services. Office disbursements include charges for in-house photocopying, in-house binding, etc. There is a degree of overlap with true expenses and the points made at 52.05 also apply to office disbursements. Indeed, some charges may be placed in either category (such as mileage or rounded-up postal charges). **52.09**

---

[21] This is often referred to as 'absorbing the expenses within the overhead'.

[22] Local travelling expenses (PD 47, para 5.22(3)), postage and courier's fee (PD 47, para 5.22(4)), and copying charges (PD 47, para 5.22(5)).

[23] See, eg, *Quick on Costs* (Thomson Reuters, online), para 2.930.

[24] *Hollins v Russell* [2003] EWCA Civ 718, at [114]–[115].

[25] See *Re Remnant* (1849) 11 Beav 603, at 613; *Re Buckwell and Berkley* [1902] 2 Ch 596.

[26] *Re Blair and Girling* [1906] 2 KB 131, at 139, *per* Fletcher Moulton LJ. If a disbursement has been included in bills that have been assessed, then that will be compelling evidence that the disbursement is an actual disbursement: *Re Blair and Girling* [1906] 2 KB 131, at 138.

[27] *Re Remnant* (1849) 11 Beav 603, at 612.

[28] *Re Seal, ex p Crickett* (1893) 37 SJ 685, at 842; *Devereux v White* (1896) 13 TLR 52.

Expert Witnesses and Advisory Experts

52.10 An expert is a person who has expertise beyond that which is possessed by a layman. An expert may be an expert witness or an advisory expert. An expert witness will generally prepare a report that may be used as evidence and will be relied upon by the party instructing them (or, if they are a joint expert, by both parties). An advisory expert will advise the party by whom they are instructed about matters such as the merits of the claim, cross-examination, etc, but they will not give evidence.

Instructing experts and the recoverability of experts' fees in principle

52.11 Expert witnesses' fees are recoverable in principle as disbursements;[29] the costs of attending upon expert witnesses are recoverable as profit costs.[30] The following issues relating to experts' instructions are dealt with in this section:

- the issue of estimates of fees and restrictions made by way of a court order (see 52.12);
- area of expertise (see 52.14);
- no need to prove that there is a contract of retainer with the expert (see 52.15);
- the position of in-house experts (see 52.17);
- the conditional and contingency funding of experts (see 52.18);
- agreements to limit fees (see 52.20); and
- medical and reporting agencies (see 52.20 and 52.62–52.73).

Estimates of fees and restrictions by way of order

52.12 As of 1 April 2013, a party seeking to rely on an expert witness's evidence has had to provide an estimate of the proposed expert's fees.[31] The court may impose a restriction on the recoverability of an expert's fees at the time the costs order is made. In particular, the court has the power to limit the extent to which the fees of a party's expert may be recovered from any other party.[32] Such orders apply between opposing parties only and, in view of this, it would be sensible for the party whose costs have been limited to liaise with the expert to ask if they are content to provide their services on the terms as ordered, because otherwise the expert may seek a greater amount. If fees were incurred at a time when permission to rely on an expert's evidence was lacking, then the court may disallow those fees[33] (especially if no permission was subsequently granted). Disallowances of this nature are a relatively common occurrence in relation to advisory experts.

52.13 In cases in which costs management applies, expert witnesses' fees will be subject to budgeting in the same manner as profit costs and counsel's fees. Costs budgeting is dealt with in Chapter 12.

---

29 *Crane v Cannons Leisure Centre* [2007] EWCA Civ 1352, at [7]; *Re Remnant* (1849) 11 Beav 603, at 613.

30 PD 47, para 5.12(3), specifically provides that time is allowed for attending upon experts.

31 See CPR, r 35.4(2).

32 See CPR, r 35.4(4), Moreover, where the expert fails to answer CPR Part 35 questions, the court is permitted to disallow those fees altogether: see CPR, r 35.6(4).

33 See, eg, *LPI (Hotels) Ltd v Technical & General Guarantee Co SA* [2010] EWHC 2049 (TCC), in which Akenhead J found that the fees had been speculatively incurred.

Area of expertise

It is trite law that an expert must confine their evidence to matters within the area of their expertise.[34] If they fail to do this, it will be open to the court to disallow the fees on the basis of relevance and reasonableness. **52.14**

Experts' contracts of retainer

Where the expert has been instructed by a solicitor, there is, in general, no need for the receiving party to prove the existence of a contract of retainer with the expert, because a solicitor is personally liable as a matter of professional good practice and etiquette to discharge the fees of any expert that it has engaged.[35] That said, the Civil Justice Council advises that terms of appointment are agreed and, in particular, that the following should be addressed: **52.15**

> '17. Terms of appointment should be agreed at the outset and should normally include:
> a. the capacity in which the expert is to be appointed (e.g. party appointed expert or single joint expert);
> b. the services required of the expert (e.g. provision of an expert's report, answering questions in writing, attendance at meetings and attendance at court);
> c. time for delivery of the report;
> d. the basis of the expert's charges (e.g. daily or hourly rates and an estimate of the time likely to be required, or a fixed fee for the services). Parties must provide an estimate to the court of the costs of the proposed expert evidence and for each stage of the proceedings (CPR.35.4(2));
> e. travelling expenses and disbursements;
> f. cancellation charges;
> g. any fees for attending court;
> h. time for making the payment;
> i. whether fees are to be paid by a third party;
> j. if a party is publicly funded, whether the expert's charges will be subject to assessment; and
> k. guidance that the expert's fees and expenses may be limited by the court.'[36]

There are further recommendations relating to experts who are jointly instructed: **52.16**

> '40. Where experts are instructed by two or more parties, the terms of appointment should, unless the court has directed otherwise, or the parties have agreed otherwise, include:
> (a) a statement that all the instructing parties are jointly and severally liable to pay the experts' fees and, accordingly, that experts' invoices should be sent simultaneously to all instructing parties or their solicitors (as appropriate); and
> (b) a copy of any order limiting experts' fees and expenses (CPR 35.8(4)(a)).'[37]

[34] *Whitehouse v Jordan* [1981] 1 WLR 246, at 256. See also *National Justice Compania Naviera SA v Prudential Assurance Co Ltd, The Ikarian Reefer* [1993] 2 Lloyd's Rep 68, at 81–2, *per* Cresswell J; Civil Justice Council, *Guidance for the Instruction of Experts in Civil Claims* (August 2014), available online at https://www.judiciary.gov.uk/wp-content/uploads/2014/08/experts-guidance-cjc-aug-2014-amended-dec-8.pdf, para 24. There may be a qualification that it is not always possible for an expert to strictly confine themselves to their own area of expertise; when assessing the significance of certain evidence, they may be entitled to make use of the skills of other experts or draw on their general specialist knowledge: *The Ikarian Reefer* [1995] 1 Lloyd's Rep 455, at 496, *per* Stuart-Smith LJ.

[35] *Young v Leighton* (unreported), c 1969, QBD, *per* Mocatta J.

[36] See Civil Justice Council, *Guidance for the Instruction of Experts in Civil Claims* (August 2014), available online at https://www.judiciary.gov.uk/wp-content/uploads/2014/08/experts-guidance-cjc-aug-2014-amended-dec-8.pdf, para 17. The Guidance came into force on 1 December 2014 and replaced the earlier Civil Justice Council, *Protocol for the Instruction of Experts to give Evidence in Civil Claims* (June 2005, amended October 2009).

[37] See Civil Justice Council, *Guidance for the Instruction of Experts in Civil Claims* (August 2014), available online at https://www.judiciary.gov.uk/wp-content/uploads/2014/08/experts-guidance-cjc-aug-2014-amended-dec-8.pdf, para 40.

In-house experts

52.17 Ordinarily, a receiving party may not recover, by way of costs, any payment for the time of its employees. Where, however, the assistance of an expert witness is required, it may well be that the party's own specialist employees are the most suitable or convenient persons to engage. In such circumstances, the fact that an expert may be in-house would not necessarily preclude recovery of the resultant costs (assuming, of course, that the work done was not merely marshalling the facts).[38] Whether the work of the company's employees qualifies for inclusion in an order for costs depends on whether the employees are truly experts and on the nature of the work carried out.[39] It is unlikely that costs will be recovered where the putative expert is merely marshalling existing factual evidence[40] (see 49.104–49.110). Where the expenses of engaging the putative expert are not recoverable as costs, then there would be scope (albeit limited) to recover those monies as damages.[41]

Conditional or contingency funding of experts

52.18 Lord Phillips MR has explained that it would be a 'very rare case indeed' for the court to permit an expert witness to be remunerated in such a way that their fees would be dependent on their client's success (because such an arrangement would generally be at risk of being champertous).[42] The Civil Justice Council has echoed Lord Phillips MR's guidance.[43] Advisory experts are in a different position, however: where a professional's role is limited to their client, then—whilst each case would have to be decided on its own facts—it would not necessarily be unlawful for that person to be paid on a conditional basis. Indeed, it may even be permissible for the amount of the expert's remuneration to vary depending on the degree of the success[44] (that is, in a way that is analogous to the way in which contingency fees are paid). Such an arrangement was upheld as lawful by the Court of Appeal in *Factortame (No 8)*.[45]

---

38 *Re Nossen's Patent* [1969] 1 WLR 638, at 643, *per* Lloyd-Jacob J, applied in *Admiral Management Services Ltd v Para-Protect Europe Ltd* [2002] EWHC 233 (Ch). See also *Richards & Wallington (Plant Hire) Ltd v Monk & Co* (1984) Costs LR Core vol 79, at 83, in which the costs were found to be irrecoverable by reason of the work being marshalling factual evidence.

39 *Admiral Management Services Ltd v Para-Protect Europe Ltd* [2002] EWHC 233 (Ch).

40 *Re Nossen's Patent* [1969] 1 WLR 638.

41 This is a matter that is largely beyond the ambit of this book, but see Chapter 3 for a general discussion of the topic. See also *Admiral Management Services Ltd v Para-Protect Europe Ltd* [2002] EWHC 233 (Ch); *R+V Versicherung AG v Risk Insurance and Reinsurance Solutions SA (No 3)* [2006] EWHC 42 (Comm); *Aerospace Publishing Ltd v Thames Water Utilities Ltd* [2007] EWCA Civ 3.

42 *R (on the application of Factortame) v Secretary of State for Transport (No 2)* [2002] EWCA Civ 932, at [73].

43 See Civil Justice Council, *Protocol for the Instruction of Experts to give Evidence in Civil Claims* (June 2005, amended October 2009), para 7.6.

44 *R (on the application of Factortame) v Secretary of State for Transport (No 2)* [2002] EWCA Civ 932.

45 *Ibid.* In *Factortame*, the claimants—whose funds were nearly exhausted after ten years of litigation against the respondent Secretary of State—entered into agreements with a firm of chartered accountants whereby the accountants would provide services ancillary to the conduct of the remaining litigation, including preparing the claims for loss and damage, for a share of 8 per cent of the damages recovered. The firm also advised the claimants on settlement offers. An independent expert was appointed to give expert evidence, who was paid in the usual way. The court held that the agreements were not champertous and the claimants were entitled to recover the 8 per cent paid from the Secretary of State. Factors that influenced the court included: the care the accountants had taken in engaging independent expert witnesses, the modest percentage that had been agreed (see *ibid*, at [84]) and the fact that the litigation was conducted by experienced solicitors who had retained overall control (see *ibid*, at [90]). See also *Papera Traders Co Ltd & Ors v Hyundai Merchant*

Agreements to delay payment of experts' fees until after the conclusion of cases are not regarded as being champertous as long as the amount of the fee does not depend on the outcome of the case.[46] **52.19**

Agreements to limit experts' fees

Whilst he was giving judgment prior to the coming into force of the CPR, Phillips J has accepted as being desirable an agreement that an expert would limit their fees to those that are assessed by the court; although the point was not argued before him, this would, in an appropriate case, need to be on the basis that the expert would be paid regardless of whether the case was won or lost, because otherwise the law of champerty would make that agreement unlawful (see 52.18).[47] **52.20**

Medical and reporting agencies

This topic is addressed at 52.63–52.72. **52.21**

Whether it was reasonable to instruct the expert

The court has an affirmative duty to restrict expert evidence to that which is reasonably required to resolve the proceedings.[48] Alternatives to the traditional order that both parties have their own experts who prepare on the basis that they will enter the witness box sequentially include the following: **52.22**

- a single joint expert;[49]
- one expert who will answer written questions;[50]
- experts who meet and prepare a joint statement;[51]
- experts who give evidence concurrently[52] in compliance with a concurrent expert evidence direction (CEED);[53] or
- no experts, with the court relying on assessors instead.[54]

Whether it was reasonable of a receiving party to instruct (or reinstruct) an expert will turn on the facts of each case, but one factor that would be particularly relevant is whether that

Marine Co Ltd, The Keihin Co Ltd [2002] EWHC 2130 (Comm), in which a salvage agent's fee of 5 per cent of the recovery in a salvage operation was allowed as costs in marine litigation.

46 See Civil Justice Council, *Protocol for the Instruction of Experts to give Evidence in Civil Claims* (June 2005, amended October 2009) at para 7.7. This advice was not repeated in Civil Justice Council, *Guidance for the Instruction of Experts in Civil Claims* (August 2014), available online at https://www.judiciary.gov.uk/wp-content/uploads/2014/08/experts-guidance-cjc-aug-2014-amended-dec-8.pdf, but because para 17 of the Guidance recommends that parties agree a date for making payment, it is suggested that the position remains the same.

47 *Cementation Construction Ltd v Keaveney* (1988) The Independent, 12 July.

48 CPR, r 35.1.

49 CPR, r 35.7. See also the parenthetic note in CPR, r 35.4; PD 35, para 7.

50 CPR, r 35.6.

51 CPR, r 35.12.

52 This means that experts are examined at the same time, known colloquially as hot tubbing. See Ames, J, 'Hot-tubbing: Cutting Costs and Time—Will Experts Appearing Together in the Witness Box Help to Simplify Complex Trials?', *The Times*, 10 March 2011.

53 For details of procedure, see Genn, H, *Manchester Concurrent Evidence Pilot: Interim Report* (January 2012), available online at https://www.judiciary.gov.uk/wp-content/uploads/JCO/Documents/Reports/concurrent-evidence-interim-report.pdf; PD 35, para 11.

54 CPR, r 35.15.

party had permission to rely on the expert and, if so, in what capacity (see 52.29). In this regard, CPR, r 35.4, may be relevant:

> '(1) No party may call an expert or put in evidence an expert's report without the court's permission.
>
> (2) When parties apply for permission they must provide an estimate of the costs of the proposed expert evidence and identify—
> (a) the field in which expert evidence is required and the issues which the expert evidence will address; and
> (b) where practicable, the name of the proposed expert.
>
> (3) If permission is granted it shall be in relation only to the expert named or the field identified under paragraph (2). The order granting permission may specify the issues which the expert evidence should address.
>
> [...]
>
> (4) The court may limit the amount of a party's expert's fees and expenses that may be recovered from any other party.'

52.23 CPR, r 35.4, was amended on 1 April 2013 to incorporate the requirements to identify the issues and to provide an estimate of the cost of the proposed expert. The estimate will no doubt be one of the factors that the court will take into account when assessing the costs. Thus the assessment of an expert's costs may need to take into account not only the fact of their instruction, but also their identity (see 52.32), the field that their evidence covered, the nature and complexity of the issues covered, and whether the costs were limited under CPR, r 35.4(4).

The small claims track and claims on the fast track

52.24 CPR, r 35.4(3A), provides as follows: 'Where a claim has been allocated to the small claims track or the fast track, if permission is given for expert evidence, it will normally be given for evidence from only one expert on a particular issue.' On the small claims track, experts' fees are recoverable, but are limited to £750 for each expert report[55] (see 50.369–50.370).

The relevance of pre-action protocols and portals

52.25 Where a pre-action protocol anticipates the use of an expert, the court may take that guidance into account when deciding whether it was reasonable to instruct an expert. Hughes LJ has commented that each case must be decided on its own facts and that guidance contained in a protocol would not be determinative of the matter.[56] The amounts that are allowed under any given protocol or portal are set out in Chapter 50.

Replacing experts and obtaining further expert evidence

52.26 A party may be dissatisfied with their expert's evidence (or with the evidence of an expert they have jointly instructed). Where this is so, that party may wish to instruct a different expert. Whilst he was dealing with substantive litigation rather than costs, Neuberger J identified the following factors as relevant to whether it would be reasonable to seek further expert evidence:

- the nature of the issue(s);
- the number of issues between the parties;

---

55 PD 27, para 7.3(2).
56 *Birmingham City Council v Lee* [2008] EWCA Civ 891, at [37(iii)].

- the reason for requiring the new expert;
- the amount at stake or the nature of the issues at stake and their importance;
- the effect of permitting one party to call further expert evidence on the conduct of the trial;
- any delay caused in the proceedings;
- any other special features; and
- the overall justice to the parties in the context of the litigation.[57]

Multiple experts

Even before the introduction of the CPR, the use of multiple experts in a single discipline was frowned upon. As long ago as the 1920s, for example, it was noted that the costs of three experts in one discipline could be justified only in exceptional cases.[58] Under the CPR, the court has an affirmative duty to restrict expert evidence to that which is reasonably required to resolve the proceedings.[59] Further provisions apply where a claim has been allocated to the small claims track or the fast track (see 52.24). **52.27**

The fact that a witness's evidence is not used is a factor that may be taken into account, but that fact of itself does not preclude the recovery of fees.[60] Although it related to the incidence, rather than the ascertainment, of costs, Smith LJ found that the costs of medical reports that had been abandoned because the expert had been 'outclassed and outgunned' by an opponent's expert ought not to be recoverable.[61] Peter Smith J declined to interfere with reductions made where an expert was repeatedly asked to redraft reports by the lawyers who instructed him; indeed, the judge was critical of such conduct.[62] **52.28**

Experts instructed without the court's permission

Where permission is required to rely on a witness (expert or otherwise) and where the receiving party incurs costs without having obtained permission, it is open to the court to find that those costs were not reasonably incurred.[63] This means that the provisions relating to permission are relevant to the issue of costs. **52.29**

Permission is required to rely on expert evidence[64] and the CPR provide that expert evidence should be restricted to that which is reasonably required to resolve the proceedings.[65] **52.30**

[57] *Cosgrove v Pattison* (2001) The Times, 13 February, in the context of an application to rely upon a unilaterally instructed expert where a joint expert had been instructed.

[58] *Graigola Merthyr Co Ltd v Swansea Corpn* [1927] WN 30, *per* Tomlin J. Lord Hanworth MR made it clear that Tomlin J's comments should not be taken to be setting a tariff, but he reaffirmed the court's desire to restrict the use of experts to those who are necessary: *Frankenburg v Famous Lasky Film Service Ltd* [1931] 1 Ch 428.

[59] CPR, r 35.1.

[60] *Fulham Leisure Holdings Ltd v Nicholson Graham & Jones* [2006] EWHC 2428 (Ch), at [15]; see also *London Chatham and Dover Rly Co v South Eastern Rly Co* (1889) 60 LT 753.

[61] *Hall v Stone* [2007] EWCA Civ 1354, at [47] and [79].

[62] *Sibley & Co v Reachbyte Ltd* [2008] EWHC 2665 (Ch), at [57]–[59].

[63] See, by way of analogy with factual witnesses, *Leeds Forge Co Ltd v Deighton's Patent Flue and Tube Co Ltd* [1903] 1 Ch 475.

[64] CPR, r 35.4(1).

[65] CPR, r 35.1.

52.31 Where a party instructs an expert prior to the court having ruled on whether permission should be granted, the starting point would be that, unless there is reason to do otherwise, permission ought to be granted for a single joint expert.[66] Thus jumping the gun would put a party at risk as to the expert's fees if the court were subsequently to decide that a joint expert should be instructed.[67]

52.32 Where permission is granted to instruct an expert identified by name, that permission will not extend to another expert in the same discipline.[68] Where a receiving party has instructed an expert who is not the expert named in the order, then that is a factor that the court will be able to take into account.

The measure of experts' fees

52.33 The court will allow fees that were reasonably incurred and which are reasonable in amount (or, on the standard basis, reasonable and proportionate in amount). The following topics are now addressed:

- breach of the duties of expert witnesses (see 52.34);
- reading-in time (see 52.35);
- 'qualifying fees' (see 52.36);
- cancellation fees (see 52.37);
- non-expert professional services (see 52.38);
- travelling expenses (see 52.39);
- stand-by expert reports (see 52.40); and
- experts' hourly rates (see 52.42).

The duties of expert witnesses

52.34 In assessing the correct figure, the court may have regard to the duties of the expert. If the expert has been instructed for the purposes of giving evidence, then those duties can be summarised in the following way.[69]

- Expert evidence presented to the court should be, and should be seen to be, the independent product of the expert uninfluenced by the exigencies of litigation.
- An expert witness should provide independent assistance to the court by way of objective and unbiased opinion on matters within their expertise.
- An expert witness should never assume the role of an advocate.
- An expert witness should state the facts or assumptions on which their opinion is based.
- An expert witness should not omit to consider material facts that could detract from their concluded opinion.
- An expert witness should make it clear when a particular question or issue falls outside their expertise.
- If an expert's opinion is not properly researched because they consider that insufficient data are available, then this must be stated.

---

[66] See CPR, r 35.7; *Peet v Mid Kent Healthcare NHS Trust* [2001] EWCA Civ 1703, *per* Woolf CJ. See also *Daniels v Walker* [2000] 1 WLR 1382.

[67] *Thomas Johnson Ciker v Barkkand Clearing Co* (1999) The Times, 6 December, CA.

[68] *Hajigeorgeiou v Vasiliou* [2005] EWCA Civ 236.

[69] *National Justice Compania Naviera SA v Prudential Life Assurance Co Ltd (No 1)* [1995] 1 Lloyd's Rep 455.

- If, after exchange of reports, an expert changes their view on a material matter, having read the other side's expert's report or for any other reason, such change of view should be communicated to the other side without delay and, when appropriate, to the court.

Whilst there is no authority on the point, it is likely that the court would be entitled to take any infringement of the duties into account when assessing an expert's fees. Alternatively, the court could make a non-party costs order against the offending expert (see 9.73).

Reading-in time for experts

It has long been held that experts are allowed an allowance for reading in and for familiarising themselves with the factual material.[70] Occasionally, the costs of such work will be claimed as a separate fee. **52.35**

Experts' 'qualifying fees'

A 'qualifying fee' is a type of booking fee that, in principle, is allowable,[71] even if it was paid before the issue of proceedings.[72] A qualifying fee differs from the allowance for reading in, in that it is not necessarily paid for reading factual material, but may be paid simply to retain the expert. Qualifying fees are rarely encountered nowadays and therefore may be difficult to justify. **52.36**

Experts' cancellation fees

A cancellation fee is payable in the event of a witness's attendance being cancelled at short notice. In a pre-CPR case, Bingham J opined that parties who leave it to the last minute to settle must expect to pay for that privilege.[73] This continues to be true under the CPR. Holland J has stressed the desirability of good experts being able to commit themselves to attending hearings for the purposes of assisting the court.[74] He had this to say on the point: **52.37**

> 'The essential point is that it is the busy person who is the expert that one wants to have in court. Even at the Bar I was always impressed by the expert who wanted to get away because there was a lot to do somewhere else. I was always worried by those who were content to sit around waiting to hear the judgment.'[75]

Cancellation fees are also often justified on the basis that the expert had to book annual or exceptional leave from a salaried position to be available to attend court.

Non-expert professional services

An expert's fees must not include the fees of providing ordinary professional services to their client. By way of example, in a case concerning a company's finances, an accountant's fee was reduced because part of the work carried out by the expert was merely putting his client's books in order.[76] In cases to which the Pre-Action Protocol for Low Value Personal Injury Claims in Road Traffic Accidents (the RTA Protocol) **52.38**

---

[70] See, eg, *Smith v Buller* (1875) LR 19 Eq 473.
[71] See, eg, *A-G v Birmingham Drainage Board* (1908) 52 Sol Jo 855.
[72] *Jones v D Davies & Sons Ltd* [1914] 3 KB 549.
[73] *Reynolds v Meston* (unreported), 24 February 1986, QBD.
[74] *Martin v Holland & Barrett Ltd* [2002] 3 Costs LR 530.
[75] *Ibid*, at [23].
[76] *Great Western Rly Co v Carpalla United China Clay Co Ltd (No 2)* [1909] 2 Ch 471.

or Pre-Action Protocol for Low Value Personal Injury (Employers' Liability and Public Liability) Claims (the EL/PL Protocol) apply, there is a specific prohibition against experts providing such services.[77]

Experts' expenses

52.39 Experts' travelling expenses are, in principle, allowable.[78] Although of only persuasive value at most,[79] the guidance in the Crown Court is that first-class travel may be allowed, but in practice is by no means automatic. Whilst the court may take into account 'cheap fares', the court should be realistic.[80] By analogy with factual witnesses, the travelling expenses of an overseas expert could, in principle, be allowed.[81] To the extent that it is relevant (if at all), Crown Court guidance says that where an expert has travelled by air, the court may take into account the time saved.[82]

Stand-by expert reports

52.40 Whilst each case will turn on its own facts, Mann J has indicated that he did not believe it was reasonable to have a stand-by report that had been prepared in anticipation of the possibility that the litigation might change direction.[83]

Experts' hourly rates

52.41 Most experts will charge on a time basis. In a heavy case (that is, a case in which the expert's fees are considerable), evidence as to market rate may be admissible; indeed, the expert themselves may be permitted to give evidence on the point.[84]

52.42 **The status and standing of experts** Even before the CPR, the expert's status was a factor to be taken into account.[85] CPR, r 44.4(3), will apply (that is, the court may take into account the skill, effort, specialised knowledge and responsibility involved). The following points may be made.

- **Experts' overhead costs** Where a technical or scientific expert is instructed to give evidence that necessitates investigatory work, the court is entitled to take into account the fact that the expert would have overhead expenses in running a laboratory, employing staff, etc. A reasonable allowance should be made in that regard, as well as a profit element on such expenditure.[86]

---

77 See CPR, rr 45.19(2B) and 45.29I(2B).

78 They are, for example, an item that must be included within Precedent H and, as such, are a budgeted item.

79 The link between the civil courts and the Crown Court is not as tenuous as it may first appear, because the CPR make occasional reference to the sums allowable in the Crown Court: see PD 34A, para 3.3. That said, those references relate to conduct money, rather than the assessment of expenses: see 52.49–52.55.

80 Carter, D, *Guide to Allowances under Part V of the Costs in Criminal Cases (General) Regulations 1986* (London: HMSO, 2007), para 8.2.

81 *Picasso v Maryport Harbour Trustees* (1884) WN 85.

82 Carter, D, *Guide to Allowances under Part V of the Costs in Criminal Cases (General) Regulations 1986* (London: HMSO, 2007), paras 8.3 and 8.4.

83 *Fulham Leisure Holdings Ltd v Nicholson Graham & Jones* [2006] EWHC 2428 (Ch), at [19].

84 *Cementation Construction Ltd v Keaveney* (1988) The Independent, 12 July.

85 *Railways Commissioner v O'Rourke* [1896] AC 594.

86 *Nossen's Letter Patent* [1969] 1 WLR 638, at 643, *per* Lloyd-Jacob J. This is to be distinguished from an 'in-house' expert, in which case only the 'actual and direct costs of the work undertaken' would be allowed, excluding overheads. Whilst this is a pre-CPR case, it is often still relied upon.

- **More than one role for the expert** Where an expert has more than one role to play in the litigation, it may be appropriate to allow different rates for each role.[87]
- **The availability of other forms of professional assistance** Where the expert's involvement is for the purposes of assisting the receiving party, rather than giving evidence (that is, where the expert is an advisory expert), the court is entitled to look at whether the work done by the expert could have been carried out by a person of lower status.[88]
- **Trade conventions and statements** Conventions concerning expert's fees are not binding on the court and are merely factors to be taken into account.[89] Presumably, the same would apply if guidance as to fees had been published by the expert's professional body or union.

Jointly instructed experts and questions to experts

The CPR makes provision for experts to be jointly instructed by the parties.[90] Where the court gives permission for a joint expert, it has the power to give directions about their fees[91] and may limit the amount thereof.[92] Unless there is reason to do otherwise, the parties will be jointly and severally liable for the expert's fees[93]—although the principle of equal apportionment would ordinarily apply where there was a need to determine the 'shares' of each party (see Chapter 20). **52.43**

By analogy with factual witnesses, where an expert is jointly instructed in such a way that their fees are shared, the receiving party would be entitled to recover its 'share' in the bill of costs upon conclusion of the claim.[94] **52.44**

Unless the court orders otherwise, where CPR, Part 35, questions are put to an expert, the party instructing the expert must pay the expert's fee. That rule does not in any way tie the court's hands over the issue of who should ultimately pay those costs.[95] If an expert fails to respond to Part 35 questions, the court is able to order that their fees will not be recoverable.[96] **52.45**

Fixed-Cost Medical Reports and the Medical Reporting Organisation Agreement

The topic of fixed-cost disbursements (including medical reports) in the context of the RTA and EL/PL Protocols is addressed at 50.182–50.188, 50.204–50.208, 50.277 and 50.284. It is worth noting that CPR, Part 35, contains provisions that regulate expert evidence in such a way as to complement the allowances for costs made in those Protocols **52.46**

[87] Whilst not binding, see *McCann v Department for Social Development* (unreported), 30 October 2007, Land Tribunal (NI).
[88] See, eg, *BCC v Avril Lee* [2008] EWCA Civ 891, at [37(iii)], in which Hughes LJ noted that the task of preparing a schedule of repairs in a housing disrepair claim could have been lower if a builder had been used, rather than a surveyor.
[89] *Morgan v Hinton Organics (Wessex Ltd)* [2009] EWCA Civ 107.
[90] CPR, r 35.7; *Kranidiotes v Paschali* [2001] EWCA Civ 357.
[91] CPR, r 35.8(3)(a).
[92] See CPR, r 35.8(4)(a).
[93] See CPR, r 35.8(5).
[94] *Allen v Yoxall* (1844) 1 Car & Kir 315.
[95] PD 35, para 6.2.
[96] CPR, r 35.6(4).

(see CPR, r 35.4(3B)). The Protocols do not go so far as to prescribe the level of fees for all medical reports; in this regard, where a medical reporting agency has been used, the Medical Reporting Organisation (MRO) Agreement would be relevant (see 52.68–52.71). Where it applies, it provides for the payment directly by the defendant's insurer to the medical reporting agency of certain agreed and fixed fees. The details of the payable fees are at Table 52.4.

Factual Witnesses

52.47 There is a long-established principle that witnesses' expenses are recoverable as costs between opposing parties.[97] One or both of the following may be claimed.

- **Conduct money** These are monies that are paid to a witness in anticipation of their expenses of attending court. Where a party wishes to compel a witness to give evidence, conduct monies must be paid in advance, either by paying the money to the court and asking the court to serve the summons or by paying the monies directly to the witness.[98]
- **The witness's actual expenses** These are the expenses actually incurred by a witness.

52.48 It is commonly the case that a receiving party will claim only conduct money; where this is so, then the rules and regulations relating to conduct monies may apply (see 52.49–52.55). In any event, the receiving party will bear the burden of proving that it was reasonable to pay conduct money—and, if the case settled before the witness gave evidence, that it was reasonable not to seek a refund (see 52.56). Where both conduct money and expenses are claimed, care should be taken to ensure that there is no duplication of allowances; in many cases, this will mean that the conduct money should be disregarded altogether because it is akin to a payment on account of the witness's expenses. Compliance with the indemnity principle is almost never a problem.[99]

Conduct money

52.49 A witness may be compelled to attend court by way of a witness summons, but only if they have been paid conduct money (which is an advance payment of expenses paid for the purposes of securing attendance). Although the CPR do not refer to 'conduct money' by that name,[100] they make provision for it at CPR, r 34.7:

> 'At the time of service of a witness summons the witness must be offered or paid—
> (a) a sum reasonably sufficient to cover his expenses in travelling to and from the court; and

[97] Although a pre-CPR case, see *Atkins v Johnson Matthey & Co Ltd* (unreported), 12 November 1970, QBD.

[98] See CPR, r 34.7; PD 34A, para 3.1.

[99] Compliance with the indemnity principle can usually be demonstrated by one or both of the two following mechanisms. The *legal representative's liability*, ie the communications that take place for the purposes of securing the witness's attendance at trial, will readily give rise to an implied contract that the legal representative will discharge the witness's expenses: see, eg, *Miller v Appleton* (1906) 50 Sol Jo 192, in which the court found that the solicitors' conduct created an implied contract. That said, the mere act of serving a witness summons would not always be sufficient for that purpose: see *Robins v Bridge* (1837) 3 M & W 114. The *client's liability* refers to the fact that a party allows a witness to attend to give evidence is ordinarily sufficient to demonstrate a promise by the receiving party to pay their expenses: see *Pell v Daubeny* (1850) 5 Exch 955; *Hallet v Mears* (1810) 13 East 15.

[100] It seems to be a term of ancient origin. It did not appear in the RSC or the CCR, but did last appear in *Practice Direction (Costs: Taxation: Procedure) (No 2 of 1992)* [1993] 1 All ER 263.

(b) such sum by way of compensation for loss of time as may be specified in Practice Direction 34A.'

CPR, r 34.7(a), is nothing new in that rules of court have always made an allowance for the witness's out-of-pocket expenses. CPR, r 34.7(b), however, is novel, in the sense that it affords the witness a right to claim something for which rules of court have not previously made any express provision—namely, a right to recover compensation for loss of a witness's time.[101] For the reasons set out below, it would seem that those monies are not intended to compensate the witness for the loss of time per se, but for financial losses suffered as a result of the loss of time.[102] This would be in keeping with the small claims provisions, which provide that a witness may claim a sum not exceeding the amount specified in PD 27 (that is, £95)[103] for any loss of earnings or loss of leave arising out of their attendance at a hearing.[104]

PD 34A, para 3, makes the following provisions: **52.50**

'3.1 When a witness is served with a witness summons he must be offered a sum to cover his travelling expenses to and from the court and compensation for his loss of time.

3.2 If the witness summons is to be served by the court, the party issuing the summons must deposit with the court:
(1) a sum sufficient to pay for the witness's expenses in travelling to the court and in returning to his home or place of work, and
(2) a sum in respect of the period during which earnings or benefit are lost, or such lesser sum as it may be proved that the witness will lose as a result of his attendance at court in answer to the witness summons.

3.3 The sum referred to in 3.2(2) is to be based on the sums payable to witnesses attending the Crown Court.

3.4 Where the party issuing the witness summons wishes to serve it himself, he must:
(1) notify the court in writing that he wishes to do so, and
(2) at the time of service offer the witness the sums mentioned in paragraph 3.2 above.'

Thus there is a link with the method of assessment in the Crown Court. That link is anything but helpful, however, because it focuses attention on the conduct monies, when in fact the focus ought to be on the actual expenses incurred.

The Crown Court method of calculating conduct money

For the reasons set out above, there is a link between the expenses in the Crown Court and conduct money in the civil courts. The Crown Court provisions go to the amount of conduct money that may be claimed, but they do not go to the assessment of expenses in general. Conduct monies are supposed to be an approximation of the witness's likely expense and so, in theory, they should not be regarded as *limiting* the amount that the receiving **52.51**

---

[101] See, eg, The White Book, vol 1, para 34.7.1.

[102] See Carter, D, *Guide to Allowances under Part V of the Costs in Criminal Cases (General) Regulations 1986* (London: HMSO, 2007), para 2.2 (to which PD 34A indirectly refers—see below), which reads: 'A financial loss allowance is payable to an ordinary witness to compensate for any expenditure (other than travelling, lodging or subsistence) to which the witness would not otherwise have been subject, or for any loss of earnings or benefit under the enactments relating to National Insurance.'

[103] PD 27, para 7.3.

[104] See CPR, r 27.14(2)(e).

party is entitled to recover[105] nor should they be taken as being the measure of a witness's *actual* expenses.[106] In practice, however, they are often taken as being one or other of these things. In particular, mileage allowances are more often than not calculated on the basis of the Crown Court method (often without the parties realising that that is what they are doing).

52.52 There are two sets of regulations governing witnesses in the Crown Court: one for witnesses in general;[107] another for the Crown Prosecution Service (CPS).[108] Established custom favours the former.[109] The sums allowable are revised from time to time and are, at time of writing, as laid out in Table 52.1.[110]

Table 52.1 Allowances in criminal cases (conduct money)

Item	Allowance
Financial loss allowance for period of absence not exceeding 4 hours	A maximum of £33.50
Financial loss allowance for period of absence exceeding 4 hours	A maximum of £67.00
Subsistence allowance for period of absence not exceeding 5 hours	A maximum of £2.25
Subsistence allowance for period of absence exceeding 5 hours, but not exceeding 10 hours	A maximum of £4.50
Subsistence allowance for period of absence exceeding 10 hours	A maximum of £9.75
Hotel (London, Birmingham, Manchester, Leeds, Liverpool or Newcastle upon Tyne city centres)	A maximum of £95.00
Hotel (elsewhere)	A maximum of £65.00
Overnight stay with family or friends	A maximum of £25.00
Public transport rate (motor cycles and cars)	25 pence per mile
Standard rate (motor cycles and cars)[[111]]	45 pence per mile
Parking fees	Amount reasonably incurred
Pedal cycle	20 pence per mile

[105] *JH Shannon v Country Casuals Holdings plc* (1997) The Times, 16 June, *per* Garland J (this is because conduct money is an estimate of expenditure and it may not ultimately prove to be accurate). In the context of family law, see *M v M* [2006] All ER (D) 58 (Jun).

[106] Whilst a family case, see *M v M* [2006] All ER (D) 58 (Jun), in which Peter Hughes QC (sitting as a deputy judge of the High Court) found that a witness who attended in response to a subpoena was entitled to their costs in complying with the subpoena, in addition to conduct money—although it is not clear whether Peter Hughes QC was asked to decide this point following argument.

[107] See the Costs in Criminal Cases (General) Regulations 1986 (SI 1986/1335) (as amended)—esp Pt V. Those Regulations are made under the Prosecution of Offences Act 1985.

[108] See Crown Prosecution Service (Witnesses' etc Allowances) Regulations 1988 (SI 1988/1862) (as amended).

[109] See, eg, the appropriate entry in The White Book, vol 1.

[110] See Carter, D, *Guide to Allowances under Part V of the Costs in Criminal Cases (General) Regulations 1986* (London: HMSO, 2007).

[111] There are two exceptions to the general rules governing payment of travelling expenses: where, in the opinion of the court, a person is suffering from a serious illness; and where heavy exhibits have to be carried to court. Where either of these are the circumstances, an amount in excess of the normal allowances may be paid: see *ibid*, para 8.12.

The 'standard rate' applies where the use of a private motor vehicle would be necessary (for example because no public transport was available) or where a considerable saving of time would be made.[112] An alternative to the travelling allowances is to allow the amount that would actually be spent on public transport. Where a rail fare is claimed, it will—in contrast to expert witnesses (see 52.39)—ordinarily be limited to the standard fare.[113] **52.53**

Table 52.2 will apply to a loss of professional witnesses' time. **52.54**

Table 52.2 Allowances in criminal cases (professional witnesses)

Item	Allowance (no locum engaged)	Allowance (locum engaged)
Professional witness allowance for period of absence not exceeding 2 hours	A maximum of £83.50	A maximum of £89.00
Professional witness allowance for period of absence exceeding 2 hours, but not exceeding 4 hours	A maximum of £117.00	A maximum of £125.00
Professional witness allowance for period of absence exceeding 4 hours, but not exceeding 6 hours	A maximum of £174.00	A maximum of £250.00
Professional witness allowance for period of absence exceeding 6 hours	A maximum of £234.00	A maximum of £250.00
Other expenses	As per factual witnesses *plus* £21.00 'Night Subsistence Allowance' and £5.00 'Personal Incidental Allowance' if at a hotel, with effect from 1 June 2005	As opposite

Thus, where a party claims conduct monies, the amount of those monies may be gauged by reference to Tables 52.1 and 52.2. What is often not fully appreciated, however, is the fact that the tables would be of marginal relevance if the court were to be asked to assess the witness's actual expenses, because the conduct monies would then be regarded as akin to a payment on account to the witness of their actual expenses. It is commonly the case, however, that only conduct monies are claimed;[114] perhaps this is because it is often easier to rely on the tables than to incur the costs of adducing evidence. **52.55**

Miscellaneous matters concerning factual witnesses

The following miscellaneous points may be made about factual witnesses. **52.56**

- **Permission** Where permission is required to rely on a person as witness and where the receiving party incurs costs without having obtained that permission, it

[112] See *ibid*, paras 8.7–8.9.

[113] See *ibid*, para 8.2.

[114] Whilst it is no more than the author's observations, the decision to claim conduct monies instead of actual expenses often seems to arise as a result of the receiving party electing not to make detailed enquiries of the witness as to what the expenses actually were. This is understandable because the sums involved are often so modest that the costs of writing to the witness to ask for details of expenditure would exceed the difference between actual expenditure and conduct monies.

would be open to the court to find that that person's expenses were not reasonably incurred.[115]

- **Non-attendance of factual witness** Where the receiving party chooses not to call a witness or use their evidence, that may be a factor to be taken into account.[116]
- **Non-attendance and conduct money** Where a witness has been stood down after having been paid conduct money, then, to recover those monies from an opponent, the receiving party must show that a reasonable effort had been made to obtain a refund.[117] In practice, however, the costs of seeking a refund would often exceed the conduct monies themselves (especially if a success fee were payable), which would mean that the receiving party is likely to be able to justify the monies claimed on the grounds that the expense of requesting and enforcing repayment of the expenses would often be more than that anticipated refund.
- **Travelling expenses of factual witnesses** The measure of travelling expenses is, in general, the monies actually and reasonably expended in travelling. Whilst, strictly speaking, they are not relevant, mileage is often allowed on the 'public transport rate' (25 pence per mile) or 'standard rate' (45 pence per mile), as set out under the Crown Court method (see Table 52.1). Indeed, those two rates have become the *de facto* guideline rates. The 'standard rate' will apply only where the use of a private motor vehicle was necessary (for example because no public transport was available) or where a considerable saving of time would be made by not using public transport.[118] An alternative to the travelling allowances is to allow the amount that would actually have been spent on public transport had the witness travelled in that way. Where a rail fare is claimed, it will—in contrast to expert witnesses (see 52.39)—ordinarily be limited to the standard fare.[119] In an appropriate case, a witness may be allowed expenses for travelling from overseas.[120] If the travelling was for purposes other than attendance at a hearing, then the monies may be apportioned.[121]
- **Overnight expenses of factual witnesses** Where a witness seeks overnight expenses, the court may take into account the nature of their evidence and the probability that they will be recalled.[122]
- **Factual witnesses and the costs of legal advice** Where a witness has been summonsed to attend court and where they need to take advice on the summons, then the costs of taking advice are, in principle, recoverable.[123]

Where the witness and receiving party are the same person

52.57 Where the witness is also the receiving party, they are, in theory, treated in a similar manner to any other witness.[124] This is subject to the important qualification that they may not

[115] See *Leeds Forge Co Ltd v Deighton's Patent Flue and Tube Co Ltd* [1903] 1 Ch 475.
[116] *London Chatham and Dover Rly Co v South Eastern Rly Co* (1889) 60 LT 753.
[117] *Martin v Andrews* (1856) 7 E&B 1.
[118] See Carter, D, *Guide to Allowances under Part V of the Costs in Criminal Cases (General) Regulations 1986* (London: HMSO, 2007), paras 8.7–8.9.
[119] See *ibid*, para 8.2.
[120] *Picasso v Maryport Harbour Trustees* (1884) WN 85.
[121] *Griffin v Hoskyns* (1856) 1 H & N 95.
[122] *Railways Commissioner v O'Rourke* [1896] AC 594.
[123] *J H Shannon v Country Casual Holdings plc* (1997) The Times, 16 June, *per* Garland J.
[124] *Davey v Durrant* (1858) 24 Beav 493.

recover the costs of being a litigant[125] and, in particular, may not recover travelling expenses.[126] In many cases, the costs of being a litigant and the costs of being a witness will be one and the same, in which case the received teaching is that no monies will be recoverable because the expenses would have been incurred regardless of whether the receiving party had to attend to present themselves for cross-examination. This received teaching may be incorrect, however.[127] On the small claims track, these monies are to compensate the receiving party for loss of earnings or loss of leave arising out of their attendance at a hearing,[128] but, in the absence of a finding of unreasonable behaviour, the amount that can be claimed is limited to a sum that does not exceed the amount specified in PD 27 (that is, £95).[129]

Professional witnesses of fact

A professional witness is a witness of fact, but one whose evidence is given in a professional capacity, rather than in a personal capacity.[130] This is relevant because a professional witness is likely to incur expenses (such as loss of earnings, locum's fees, etc) arising out of their involvement in the litigation. **52.58**

The court's approach will depend on what is claimed. **52.59**

- **Fees for loss of time and out-of-pocket expenses** These will be assessed and a reasonable amount will be allowed. The court will often allow a professional witness their ordinary professional rates (an example being a solicitor witness, who is entitled to expenses as if they were profit costs).[131] The distinction between professional and expert witnesses is not always easy to make, however, and there are instances of the court treating professional witnesses as if they were expert witnesses.[132]
- **Conduct monies** Where conduct monies are claimed, then the Crown Court method may be relevant, in which case Table 52.1 would apply.

Medical Records

The Data Protection Act 1998 creates a qualified right of access to medical records. Delegated legislation made under that Act limits the fee that can be charged for providing **52.60**

[125] *London Scottish Benefit Society v Chorley* (1884) 13 QBD 872.

[126] See *R v Legal Aid Board (Merseyside) Area Office, ex p Eccleston* [1998] 1 WLR 1279. This is based on the same principles as those by which the costs of attending a legal or medical adviser are not recoverable: *Atkins v Johnson Matthew & Co* (unreported), c 1970, QBD, *per* Donaldson J.

[127] Whilst there is no authority on the point, the following observations are likely to be relevant: (a) the CPR do not carve out an exception for witnesses who are also parties; and (b), in the small claims track, there is express provision that the receiving party's own expenses and loss of time are allowed as if they were a witness (see CPR, r 27.14(2)(d) and (e)) and it would be very curious if those monies were allowable on the small claims track, but not on the fast track or multitrack.

[128] See CPR, r 27.14(2)(e).

[129] PD 27, para 7.3.

[130] The existence of professional witnesses as a category that is distinct from other factual witnesses is necessarily implied by the fact that it is a category that is referred to in the provisions that govern expenses in the Crown Court—something that is relevant under the CPR: see PD 34A, para 3.3.

[131] See *Hamilton v Colhoun* [1906] 2 IR 104; *Butler v Hobson* (1838) 5 Bing NC 128.

[132] See, eg, *Aktieselskabet de Danske Sukkerfabriker v Bajamar Cia Naviera SA, The Torenia* [1983] 2 Lloyd's Rep 210, at 233, in which Hobhouse J found that a professional witness is a species of expert witness.

Table 52.3 Subject access fees for copying

No of pages of information comprising the copy	Maximum fee	No of pages of information comprising the copy	Maximum fee
Fewer than 20	£1	100–149	£10
20–29	£2	150–199	£15
30–39	£3	200–249	£20
40–49	£4	250–299	£25
50–59	£5	300–349	£30
60–69	£6	350–399	£35
70–79	£7	400–449	£40
80–89	£8	450–499	£45
90–99	£9	500 or more	£50

medical records, which fee is referred to as a 'subject access fee'. It is that fee which is usually claimed as the cost of obtaining medical records, although an additional agency fee may also be charged (see 52.63–52.72).

52.61 The maximum subject access fee for accessing computerised records is £10. The maximum subject access fee is £50 for paper records, but there is a sliding scale based on the number of pages copied,[133] as laid out in Table 52.3. It should be noted that now that the General Data Protection Regulation (GDPR)[134] has come into force (that having been on 25 May 2018), certain information must be supplied free of charge.

Other Types of Personal Records

52.62 Credit records and educational records are treated in a similar way to medical records (see 52.60 and 52.61). Other records containing personal data must be supplied to the person to whom they relate for a subject access fee of no more than £10.[135]

Medical Agencies

52.63 Legal representatives often instruct medical agencies to carry out the administrative tasks of obtaining medical reports and medical records. Medical agencies are unregulated, but a non-statutory association exists, the Association of Medical Reporting Organisations (AMRO), which encourages membership and publishes a code of conduct.

[133] See Data Protection (Subject Access) (Fees and Miscellaneous Provisions) Regulations 2000 (SI 2000/191) (as amended), reg 6(2) and Sch.

[134] Regulation (EU) 2016/679 of the European Parliament and of the Council of 27 April 2016 on the protection of natural persons with regard to the processing of personal data and on the free movement of such data . . . , OJ L 119/1, 4 May 2016.

[135] Data Protection (Subject Access) (Fees and Miscellaneous Provisions) Regulations 2000 (SI 2000/191) (as amended), reg 3; Data Protection Act 1998, s 7(1).

Agency fees

Where an agency is used, the fee charged is often a single, composite fee that includes both the agency's fee and the fee paid to the expert, clinic or practice. **52.64**

There is no binding authority as to the recoverability of the agency element of the fee, but the following comments of Judge Cook are persuasive: **52.65**

> 'I am satisfied that there is no principle which precludes the fees of a medical agency being recoverable between the parties, provided it is demonstrated that their charges do not exceed the reasonable and proportionate costs of the work if it had been done by the solicitors.'[136]

A pedant would say that the agency element ought to be claimed as profit costs, rather than as a disbursement.[137] The pedant would be correct in many instances, but in practice such fees are often presented as disbursements. **52.66**

Receiving parties are often reluctant to reveal details concerning the agency element. Judge Cook deprecated that attitude: **52.67**

> 'To demonstrate the point by taking an extreme, if the doctor's fee was only £75 and [the agency] charges £300, the total of £375 would undoubtedly be unreasonable and disproportionate. It does therefore seem to be important that, whilst there is much to commend the use of medical agencies, it is important that their invoices (or "fee notes") should distinguish between the medical fee and their own charges, the latter being sufficiently particularised to enable the costs officer to be satisfied they do not exceed the reasonable and proportionate costs of the solicitors doing the work.'[138]

Agency fees and fixed costs

An issue that commonly used to arise was the interaction between agency fees and fixed costs. Where fixed costs were payable and where work that could have been carried out by the legal representative had, in fact, been delegated to an agency, the court often used to be vexed by the issue of whether the agency element could be recovered or whether the fixed costs regimes precluded its recovery. For the reasons set out below, this point now arises only rarely. **52.68**

Whilst there is no binding authority on this issue, there is an informal and seemingly durable industry consensus that (whilst now partly superseded by CPR, Part 45) is so rarely disregarded as to be almost a rule of practice. That consensus arose out of an appeal from a decision of Master Hurst,[139] which appeal was disposed of by way of a mediated agreement that initially was known as the Woollard Agreement, but came to be better known as the MRO Agreement.[140] The MRO Agreement permits a participating reporting agency to **52.69**

---

[136] *Stringer v Copley* (unreported), 17 May 2002, Kingston on Thames County Court, at 7, to which May LJ referred with apparent approval in *Crane v Cannons Leisure Centre* [2007] EWCA Civ 1352, at [7]. The proposition was accepted as accurate by Master Hurst in *Claims Direct Test Cases Tranche 2 Issues* [2003] EWHC 9005 (Costs), at [114].

[137] Although see *Claims Direct Test Cases Tranche 2 Issues* [2003] EWHC 9905 (Costs), at [115], in which Master Hurst took the view that the fees of the medical support agencies should be treated as a disbursement.

[138] *Stringer v Copley* (unreported), 17 May 2002, Kingston on Thames County Court, at 8.

[139] *Woollard & Anor v Fowler* [2005] EWHC 90051 (Costs). Despite its neutral citation reference, this case was heard in 2006.

[140] This was originally dated 11 May 2007, and was updated on 2 April 2009, 2 April 2011 and 2 April 2012.

Table 52.4 MRO Agreement (amounts)

	Rate A: payable if paid within 90 days	Rate B: payable if not paid within 90 days
General practitioner report—no medical records	£200	£225
Review of medical records by general practitioner	£50	£55
Orthopaedic report—including review of medical records	£425	£465
Accident and emergency report—including review of medical records	£375	£410
Addendum	Cost *plus* £25	Cost *plus* £30
Costs of obtaining each set of medical records	Cost *plus* £25	Cost *plus* £30

send an invoice directly to the defendant's insurer. Many defendant insurers[141] and medical agencies[142] are content to abide by that Agreement.

52.70 The amounts payable under the MRO Agreement depend on the length of the period during which the agency's fees remain unpaid. The sums payable, exclusive of value added tax (VAT), are set out in Table 52.4. (For the sake of completeness, the fees for the reports are listed, as well as the fees for medical records.)

52.71 The MRO Agreement applies to the following types of case:

> 'Any claim for damages for personal injury alleged to have arisen as a result of a road traffic accident or an employer's or public liability claim where the level of general damages anticipated by the Claimant at the time the Report was commissioned did not exceed £15,000.'[143]

It would ordinarily be incorrect to rely on these figures as comparators in other types of case. To a large extent, the MRO Agreement has been superseded by the fact that, in a soft-tissue injury claim in which a claim notification form was submitted under the RTA Protocol on or after 1 October 2014,[144] specific limits and fixed fees will apply[145] (see Chapter 50, and in particular, 50.184).

Value added tax and agency fees

52.72 Although it is now unusual for there to be a dispute about the fees for medical records themselves, there is occasionally dispute about the amount of VAT to be paid on those fees. This is because the VAT provisions relating to the agency element may be different from those relating to the rest of the costs. Where the fees were incurred before 1 May 2007, VAT would usually be payable only on the agency element; the agency (or the legal

[141] Which originally were Zurich, Aviva, Allianz, Fortis, HSBC, AXA, Churchill, Direct Line, National Insurance and UK Insurance, but now include many more.

[142] Which originally were Doctors Chambers Ltd, e-Reporting Group Ltd, Mobile Doctors Ltd, Medical-Legal Reporting, Premex Services Ltd, Premier Medical Ltd, Speed Medical Examination Services Ltd and UK Independent Medical Services Ltd, but now include Aman Health-care Ltd, Aslam Mohammed Ltd, First Legal Support, Inquiry QED Ltd, Insurance Medial Reporting Ltd and others.

[143] Medical Reporting Organisation Agreement, 2 April 2012, Definitions.

[144] See Civil Procedure (Amendment No 6) Rules 2014 (SI 2014/2044), r 14.

[145] CPR, r 45.19(2A).

representative) could elect whether to pay VAT on the balance. Whilst not binding, there have been instances of the court disallowing VAT where the legal representative had elected to claim VAT in circumstances in which they were not obliged so to do.[146] The issue of whether VAT is payable on the agency fee for obtaining medical records or the fee paid for release of the records is covered at 55.25.

Copying Charges

PD 47, para 5.22(5), provides as follows: **52.73**

> 'The cost of making copies of documents will not in general be allowed but the court may exceptionally in its discretion make an allowance for copying in unusual circumstances or where the documents copied are unusually numerous in relation to the nature of the case. Where this discretion is invoked the number of copies made, their purpose and the costs claimed for them must be set out in the bill.'

Whilst not binding, Master Gordon-Saker has confirmed that the court is able to take into account the overall costs claimed; hence, if the overall costs are small, it would be open to the court to find that even relatively small amounts of copying fall into the category of being exceptional.[147]

Evans J had the following to say (in a pre-CPR case): **52.74**

> '[Counsel for the receiving party] submitted that the maximum number of pages which might require copying in a personal injury case of a normal kind would be 1,000, and that therefore this case did involve an unusual number. I sympathise with this submission, but I am troubled that neither the plaintiffs nor the registrar have made an allowance for the number which in the normal case would form part of the solicitor's general overheads.'[148]

Therefore, where the threshold is reached where charges are recoverable, it is only the excess beyond that threshold (or some other suitable figure) that is recoverable, rather than the total.

Copying charges in the Court of Appeal

Copying charges for appeals in the Court of Appeal are often treated differently from copying charges in other arenas, because the allowance for copying that is included in the hourly rate will have been used up in the lower court. The *Guide to the Summary Assessment of Costs* has this to say on the point: **52.75**

> '(9) In most appeals it will be appropriate to make an allowance for copy documents. The allowance for copying which is included in the solicitor's hourly rates will have already been used up or exceeded in the lower court. An hourly rate charge is appropriate for selecting and collating documents and dictating the indices. If the paperwork is voluminous much of this should be delegated to a trainee. Note that:

[146] See, eg, *Sutton v Selwyns Travel* (unreported), 8 August 2008, Birkenhead County Court (Regional Costs), *per* District Judge Smedley.

[147] *Ahmed v Aventis Pharma Ltd (Rev 1)* [2009] EWHC 90152 (Costs), at [19].

[148] *Johnson v Reed Corrugated Cases Ltd* (1990) Costs LR Core vol 180, at 185.

(a) For the copying itself, a fair allowance is 10p per page, ie £100 per 1,000 sheets. This includes an allowance for checking the accuracy of the copying.
(b) Time spent standing at the photocopier and time spent taking the papers to a local photocopy shop is not recoverable. Such work is not fee earner work; it is secretarial.'[149]

Amounts of copying charges

52.76 Hallett J has commented (with reference to criminal costs, rather than civil costs) that where the court is inclined to allow a commercial rate for photocopying, that rate should take into account the fact that a legal representative who regularly uses the services of commercial copying bureau ought to be able to negotiate a commercial rate.[150] The implication is that a realistic rate ought to be allowed for copying carried out in-house.

Couriers, Postage, etc

52.77 PD 47, para 5.22(4), stipulates that the cost of postage and couriers will, in general, not be allowed, but the court may exceptionally, in its discretion, allow such expenses in unusual circumstances or where the cost is unusually heavy.

52.78 Presumably, Evans J's comments referred to at 52.74 also apply to courier charges and postage (that is, it is probable that, once the threshold has been reached, it is only the excess beyond the threshold that is payable).

Legal Representatives' Hotel Expenses

52.79 Hotel expenses are recoverable as disbursements. If a room is paid for, but not used, the test will be whether it was likely to have been required.[151]

52.80 Whilst only persuasive, the Privy Council has held that where expenses are claimed for a period longer than is necessary, the hotel expenses may be apportioned accordingly.[152] Although its applicability is limited to factual witnesses, guidance exists for assessing hotel expenses in the Crown Court. That guidance is described at 52.51–52.55 and it can be seen that it is arguable whether it is binding, persuasive or merely a factor to be taken into account.

Legal Representatives' Travelling Expenses

52.81 Local travelling expenses are not recoverable under the CPR, but the court has discretion as to what is meant by 'local'. PD 47, para 5.22(3), makes the following provisions:

---

[149] HM Courts & Tribunals Service, *Guide to the Summary Assessment of Costs* (London: HMSO, 2011), para 65(9).
[150] *Landau & Cohen v Lord Chancellor's Department* [1999] 2 Costs LR 5, in which Hallett J noted that the commercial rate may be as low as 4 pence per page.
[151] See, by way of analogy with witness expenses, *Railways Commissioner v O'Rourke* [1896] AC 594.
[152] *Horsford v Bird* [2006] UKPC 55.

> 'Local travelling expenses incurred by legal representatives will not be allowed. The definition of "local" is a matter for the discretion of the court. As a matter of guidance, "local" will, in general, be taken to mean within a radius of 10 miles from the court dealing with the case at the relevant time. Where travelling and waiting time is claimed, this should be allowed at the rate agreed with the client unless this is more than the hourly rate on the assessment.'

Hallett J has stated that unless the client is housebound or in hospital, it is normal for them to visit the legal representative rather than the other way around.[153] It would be reasonable to infer from this that the expenses of travelling to see a client who is not housebound or in hospital would, absent justification, be irrecoverable. **52.82**

In considering the reasonableness of the expenses claimed, the court is entitled to examine the whole costs—in particular, the savings that may have been made by reason of the travelling. Thus, where travelling has resulted in savings elsewhere (such as by avoiding the need to instruct agents or a saving in the hourly rate[154]), the court may take those savings into account. **52.83**

Whilst its applicability is limited to factual witnesses, guidance exists for assessing travelling expenses in the Crown Court (see 52.51–51.55). One particular aspect on which that guidance focuses is whether public transport was reasonably available for use by the witness; where it was, it would be open to the court to find that the costs of travelling by private car were not allowable unless this resulted in a saving in costs.[155] **52.84**

Disbursement Funding Loans

Disbursement funding loans—or, more accurately, the interest on, and the costs of setting up and managing, the loan—are not directly recoverable between opposing parties. They are mentioned in this context primarily to make the point that they are irrecoverable because they are not properly characterised as legal costs.[156] The existence of a disbursement funding and of the rate charged under it may, however, be taken into account where the court exercises its discretion as to the rate of interest payable to a receiving party.[157] **52.85**

From a legal representative and client perspective, compliance with the relevant consumer protection regulations is usually a prerequisite for enforceability.[158] Whilst there is no authority on the point, some commentators have suggested that loans that are *de facto* funded by the fruits of the claim may be champertous.[159] **52.86**

---

153 *Ledward v Kent & Medway Health Authority* [2003] EWHC 2551 (QB), at [24].

154 *Ibid*, at [17].

155 Although a criminal case, see *R v Slessor* (1984) Taxing Masters Compendium, App 7.

156 *Hunt v RM Douglas (Roofing) Ltd* (1987) The Times, 23 November, CAT.

157 See, eg, *Jones v Secretary of State for Energy and Climate Change* [2013] EWHC 1023 (QB) affirmed at [2014] EWCA Civ 363.

158 See Consumer Credit Act 1974, as amended by the Consumer Credit Act 2006, and the relevant delegated legislation.

159 Capper, D, 'Litigation Funding for "Big Money" Divorces: An Assessment of Legal Risk' (2007) 26 CJQ 447. It may be that a disgruntled client would be able to take that point if successful in the litigation, but wishing to avoid repaying the loan.

Court Fees

The fee for starting proceedings (usually known as the issue fee)

52.87 Court fees have increased dramatically over recent years, for reasons discussed at 1.187. The fee for starting proceedings is payable on a sliding scale, increasing with the value of the claim.[160] The order that creates it refers to it as 'the fee for starting proceedings', but it is usually referred to colloquially as 'the issue fee'. Whilst there is no authority on the point, it is the author's experience that if a claimant recovers damages that are less than were claimed, the court can often be persuaded to allow the fee that would have been levied had the claim been made for the amount actually allowed. From 9 March 2015,[161] the fees for money claims worth £10,000 are set at 5 per cent of the value of the claim, capped at a maximum fee of £10,000.[162] Table 52.5 sets out the changes.[163] Court users who submit their claim through secure data transfer or Money Claim Online[164] will receive a 10 per cent discount.

Allocation/directions questionnaire fees

52.88 Before 1 July 2013, this fee used to be payable when the allocation questionnaire was filed.[165] From 1 July 2013 to 21 April 2014, this fee was known as a directions questionnaire fee.[166] That fee ceased to be separately charged on 22 April 2014, because a single composite fee has been payable in place of both the issue fee and the allocation

Table 52.5 Fees for starting proceedings (comparison table)

Value of claim	Fee now (paper)	New fee	Increase in fee	% increase
£20,000	£610	£1,000	£390	64%
£40,000	£610	£2,000	£1,390	228%
£90,000	£910	£4,500	£3,590	395%
£150,000	£1,315	£7,500	£6,185	470%
£190,000	£1,315	£9,500	£8,185	622%
£200,000	£1,515	£10,000	£8,725	576%
£250,000	£1,720	£10,000	£8,280	481%

160 See Civil Proceedings Fees Order 2008 (SI 2008/1053), Sch 1, para 1.1.

161 Civil Proceedings and Family Proceedings Fees (Amendment) Order 2015 (SI 2015/576), art 1. There are no transitional provisions, but the Ministry of Justice has explained, in a press release, that if a claim was received on or before 6 March 2015 in a fit state to issue, the old fee structure continued to apply even if the claim is issued after 9 March 2015. That said, the Ministry warned that applications received prior to 6 March 2015, but returned because of an error on the claim form, would attract the new fee if they were subsequently resubmitted after the fee change.

162 See Civil Proceedings Fees Order 2008 (SI 2008/1053), Sch 1, para 1.1, as amended by Civil Proceedings and Family Proceedings Fees (Amendment) Order 2015 (SI 2015/576), art 2.

163 This is based on a table in Law Society, 'Court Fees Increase from Monday 9 March', 5 March 2015, formerly available online.

164 See https://www.moneyclaim.gov.uk/

165 See Civil Proceedings Fees Order 2008 (SI 2008/1053), Sch 1, para 1.1, as amended from time to time.

166 See Civil Proceedings Fees Order 2008 (SI 2008/1053), Sch 1, para 1.1, as amended by the Civil Proceedings Fees (Amendment No 2) Order 2013 (SI 2013/1410).

questionnaire fee.[167] This change was made following a policy decision to reduce administrative processes for the courts and the court users; the cost of the allocation process has now been included in the issue fees.[168]

Pre-trial checklist (listing questionnaire)

Where it was paid before 1 May 2008, the court is able to disallow the listing fee if the case **52.89** settled more than 14 days before trial, because the claimant could have reclaimed the fee.[169] After that date, different provisions applied (see below).

Hearing fee

Refunds of hearing fees for cases on all tracks in the County Court and High Court have **52.90** now been abolished for all cases in which notice of the trial date was given after 6 March 2017, by operation of the Civil Proceedings Fees (Amendment) Order 2017.[170] This approach has been adopted in accordance with the government's stated intention to recover the full cost of the civil court system through fees, excluding the cost of remissions.[171]

Where the fee was paid after 1 May 2008, but before 22 April 2014, the listing fee could **52.91** not be refunded, but the much larger hearing fee could, depending on how long before trial the matter settled. Where the court receives notice in writing from the party who paid the hearing fee that the case has been settled or discontinued and if the case was on the multitrack or fast track, the following percentages of the hearing fee will be refunded:

- 100 per cent, if the court is notified more than 28 days before the hearing;
- 75 per cent, if the court is notified between 15 and 28 days before the hearing; and
- 50 per cent, if the court is notified between 7 and 14 days before the hearing.[172]

From 22 April 2014 onwards, a single fee has been payable in place of the listing question- **52.92** naire fee and the hearing fee. This change has been made following a policy decision that a fee will no longer be charged when listing the trial, in an attempt to reduce administrative processes for the courts and the court users.[173] The cost of the listing process has now been included in the hearing fees.[174]

Where a case was on the multitrack or fast track and notice of the trial date was given be- **52.93** fore 6 March 2017 (see 52.90), then the percentage reductions stated at 52.91 continue to apply.[175] If a refund has gone unclaimed, then it is the editor's experience that the court

[167] See Civil Proceedings Fees Order 2008 (SI 2008/1053), Sch 1, para 1.1, as amended by the Civil Proceedings Fees (Amendment) Order 2014 (SI 2014/874).

[168] See the Explanatory Memorandum to the Civil Proceedings Fees (Amendment) Order 2014 (SI 2014/874).

[169] Civil Proceedings Fees Order 2004 (SI 2004/3121), Sch 1, para 2.3.

[170] Civil Proceedings Fees (Amendment) Order 2016 (SI 2016/1191), art 2.

[171] Ministry of Justice, *Impact Assessment: Court Fees—Cost Recovery*, IA No MoJ221 (2 December 2013), available online at https://consult.justice.gov.uk/digital-communications/court-fees-proposals-for-reform/supporting_documents/costrecoveryia.pdf

[172] See Civil Proceedings Fees Order 2008 (SI 2008/1053), Sch 1, para 2.3.

[173] See the Explanatory Memorandum to the Civil Proceedings Fees (Amendment) Order 2014 (SI 2014/874).

[174] *Ibid.*

[175] See Civil Proceedings Fees Order 2008 (SI 2008/1053), Sch 1, para 1.1, as amended by the Civil Proceedings Fees (Amendment) Order 2014 (SI 2014/874).

would rarely require the paying party to bear that part of the fee which could have been refunded. There is, however, no authority on that point.

Group litigation

52.94 Directions questionnaire fees and pre-trial checklist (that is, listing questionnaire) fees were, up to 22 April 2014,[176] not payable on individual claims listed after a group litigation order (GLO) has been made.[177] On or after that date, those fees ceased to be payable (see above).

Detailed assessments

52.95 The bill of costs must not contain any court fees that relate solely to the detailed assessment proceedings[178] (unless, of course, the costs are those of a detailed assessment). When filing a request for detailed assessment where the bill contains a claim for costs payable by an opponent only, the fee will be payable in accordance with the sliding scale laid out in Table 52.6.[179] The same fees apply to solicitor-and-client assessments.[180] If the assessment is of legal aid costs only, or of costs payable by the Legal Services Commission (LSC) or the Lord Chancellor, the fee will be a flat fee of £220.[181] Where the assessment is of both legal aid costs and costs payable between opposing parties, by the LSC or by the Lord Chancellor, the fee will be attributed proportionately to the two parties, legal aid, LSC or Lord Chancellor (as the case may be) portions of the bill on the basis of the amount *allowed*.[182]

Table 52.6 Fees for detailed assessments

Where the amount of costs claimed:	the fee will be
(a) does not exceed £15,000;	£369
(b) exceeds £15,000 but does not exceed £50,000;	£643
(c) exceeds £50,000 but does not exceed £100,000;	£1,106
(d) exceeds £100,000 but does not exceed £150,000;	£1,480
(e) exceeds £150,000 but does not exceed £200,000;	£1,848
(f) exceeds £200,000 but does not exceed £300,000;	£2,772
(g) exceeds £300,000 but does not exceed £500,000; and	£4,620
(h) exceeds £500,000.	£6,160

[176] The Civil Proceedings Fees (Amendment) Order 2014 (SI 2014/874) amended the 2008 provision in such a way as to remove any mention of GLOs.

[177] Civil Proceedings Fees Order 2008 (SI 2008/1053), Sch 1, para 2.2, as amended by the Civil Proceedings, First-tier Tribunal, Upper Tribunal and Employment Tribunals Fees (Amendment) Order (SI 2016/807).

[178] PD 47, para 5.19.

[179] See Civil Proceedings Fees Order 2008 (SI 2008/1053), Sch 1, para 5.2, as amended by the Civil Proceedings, First-tier Tribunal, Upper Tribunal and Employment Tribunals Fees (Amendment) Order 2016 (SI 2016/807).

[180] Civil Proceedings Fees Order 2008 (SI 2008/1053), Sch 1, para 5.2, as amended.

[181] See the Civil Proceedings Fees Order 2008 (SI 2008/1053), Sch 1, para 5.1, as amended.

[182] See the Civil Proceedings Fees Order 2008 (SI 2008/1053), Sch 1, para 5.2, as amended.

A request for the issue of a default costs certificate will attract a fee of £66 and an application to set it aside will cost £121.[183] On commencing an appeal against a decision made in detailed assessment proceedings, the fee will be £231.[184] **52.96**

Benefits

Receiving parties who were on state benefits at the material time may not have been required to pay court fees.[185] If that was the case, the court may disallow the fee on the grounds that it was not reasonably incurred. **52.97**

Foreign Lawyers

The following points can be made about engaging lawyers in jurisdictions other than England and Wales. It should be noted that the position of litigants in person may be different from that set out below (see 59.30 and 59.35). **52.98**

- **Engaging foreign lawyers in proceedings in other jurisdictions** Where they were incurred in proceedings in other jurisdictions, the costs and expenses of foreign lawyers may be recoverable as damages (3.38).[186]
- **Engaging foreign lawyers in proceedings in England and Wales** Where foreign lawyers are engaged for the purposes of proceedings in England and Wales (such as where a lawyer gives expert evidence as to foreign law or where a foreign lawyer gives advice about foreign law), then their fees and expenses will, in principle, be recoverable as costs under the CPR. Whilst not binding, Master Gordon-Saker's test is generally regarded as the appropriate forensic method:

  > '[The] amount of the [foreign] lawyers' fees must be assessed according to the rules and in the way in which they would have been assessed in [the lawyer's home court]. But that does not prevent the paying party from contending on detailed assessment that the fees are disproportionate and unnecessary or were unreasonably incurred and so should not be allowed at all.'[187]

  Provided that it was reasonable to engage the lawyer in question and provided that the costs claimed are not disproportionate, the correct measure of fees would be the measure used in that lawyer's home jurisdiction.[188] This would be the case even where costs were payable according to a scale.[189] The fact that a foreign lawyer has been engaged does not absolve the lawyers in this jurisdiction from all responsibility. In particular, a failure to instruct an appropriate expert may lead to costs sanctions.[190]

---

[183] See Civil Proceedings Fees Order 2008 (SI 2008/1053), Sch 1, paras 5.3 and 5.5, as amended.

[184] See Civil Proceedings Fees Order 2008 (SI 2008/1053), Sch 1, para 5.5, as amended.

[185] For details, see the Civil Proceedings Fees Order 2004 (SI 2004/3121).

[186] See, eg, *Starlight Shipping Co v Allianz Marine & Aviation Versicherungs AG* [2014] EWCA Civ 1010, at [21] *per* Longmore LJ, in which insurers obtained damages for costs incurred by reason of proceedings commenced in Greece by shipowners in breach of English jurisdiction and settlement agreements. See also *Seavision Investment SA v Norman Thomas Evennett, The Tiburon* [1992] 2 Lloyd's Rep 26.

[187] See *Societa Finanziaria Industrie Turistiche SpA v Manfredi Lefebvre D'Ovidio De Clunieres Di Balsorano & Anor* [2006] EWHC 90068 (Costs), at [42].

[188] Whilst it is not binding, see Master Gordon-Saker's analysis of the authorities on this point *ibid.*

[189] See *Slingsby v Attorney-General* [1918] P 236 (a pre-CPR case).

[190] See, eg, *Mengiste v Endowment Fund for the Rehabilitation of Tigray* [2013] EWHC 1087 (Ch), in which Peter Smith J found that the first stage in the procedure to grant a wasted costs order had been satisfied

- **Engaging lawyers in other jurisdictions within the British Isles and Eire** It should not be forgotten that several jurisdictions exist within the British Isles[191] and Eire.[192] In theory, any such costs ought to be assessed by the rules that apply in the lawyer's home jurisdiction, but (whilst unable to cite authority on the point), it is the editor's experience that, in practice, such fees are often added to a bill of costs and assessed in much the same way as any other costs.[193]
- **Engaging foreign lawyers for reasons of geographical convenience** It may be that the most practicable option is to instruct local lawyers to carry out work, such as obtaining evidence[194] or examining witnesses,[195] overseas. Where this is so, the costs of carrying out the work will be recoverable as costs, regardless of whether the foreign lawyers are in a common-law or civil jurisdiction.[196] There is authority for the proposition that the costs of foreign lawyers may be claimed only as disbursements.[197] Where the work that is being done is the same as the work that would have been done had the receiving party's solicitors travelled to carry out the work themselves, it is questionable whether that authority is still good law.[198]
- **Ambiguity as to whether the monies are costs or damages** Where the fees and expenses of engaging a foreign lawyer are properly and unambiguously regarded as costs, then they would not be recoverable as damages; hence a party cannot claim damages from a party if, in truth, those monies would be or have been disallowed as costs against the same party (see 3.38–3.41).[199] Sometimes, however, the distinction between costs and damages is extremely narrow. Sir Mark Waller, for example, acknowledged this when he explained that a claim for costs incurred by an owner of an arrested ship for the purposes of obtaining bail was truly a damages claim, but the costs of putting up a guarantee to avoid an arrest can properly be said to be costs.[200]

52.99 In so far as procedure is concerned, Diplock J has commented that where the bill of costs contains a foreign lawyer's fees, it ought to include a detailed statement of the circumstances

where a firm of solicitors had allowed a purported expert witness on the Ethiopian legal code to serve reports and give oral evidence, although the court had found his evidence to be tendentious and inappropriate.

191 They include: Scotland, the Act of Sederunt (Rules of the Court of Session 1994) 1994 (SI 1994/1443); Northern Ireland, the Rules of the Court of Judicature (Northern Ireland) 1980 (SR 1080/346); and the Isle of Man, Rules of the High Court of Justice 2009 (SD 352/09).

192 See Rules of the Superior Courts 1986 (SI 1986/15).

193 This is not likely to be objectionable because the measures of costs in those jurisdictions is often very similar to the measure of costs under CPR, Part 44.

194 See *Slingsby v Attorney General* [1918] P 236, at 243, in which Swinfen Eady LJ cited, with apparent approval, the judgment of a registrar in allowing the fees of American lawyers for obtaining evidence in the United States.

195 See *Wentworth v Lloyd (No 2)* (1865) 34 Beav 455, at 457, in which Romily MR allowed fees for examining witnesses in Australia.

196 See, eg, *Earl Nelson v Lord Bridport* (1845) 8 Beav 527, at 547, and 10 Beav 305, in which Langdale MR allowed evidence to be obtained in Sicily; *Lord v Colvin* (1859) 4 Drew 366, in which Kindersly allowed evidence to be obtained in France.

197 *McCullie v Butler* [1962] 2 QB 309, at 314, *per* Diplock J.

198 This is because *McCullie v Butler* [1962] 2 QB 309 turned on whether work fell within the ambit of a legal aid certificate and, in any event, the law seems to have moved on since the 1960s: see *Smith Graham v Lord Chancellor's Department* [1999] 2 Costs LR 1; *Crane v Canons Leisure Centre* [2007] EWCA Civ 1352.

199 See *Carroll v Kynaston* [2010] EWCA Civ 1404, at [23] *per* Ward LJ.

200 *Ene 1 Kos Ltd v Petroleo Brasileiro SA* [2010] EWCA Civ 772, at [39]–[57].

that required their services.[201] Presumably, if the court were to find that the involvement of a foreign lawyer was not justified, the court would make an allowance based on the costs that would have been incurred had the work been carried out domestically. Diplock J also commented that it is the receiving party's responsibility to provide a sufficiently detailed breakdown within the bill to allow the local costs regime to be applied.[202] Whilst there is no modern example of such an approach being taken, there is authority for the proposition that where it would be difficult to assess a foreign lawyer's fees, it may be appropriate to refer the matter to the home court of the lawyer in question.[203]

Interpreters

Where a party or a witness needs the assistance of an interpreter, those costs are recoverable **52.100**
in principle.[204]

Whilst not binding, Master Campbell has found that where an interpreter's fee fell within **52.101**
the fixed-costs regime in CPR, Part 45, it could be recovered by the claimant, because it could properly be described as 'any other disbursement that has arisen due to a particular feature of the dispute' under CPR, r 45.12(2)(c).[205]

201 *McCullie v Butler* [1962] 2 QB 309, at 313, *per* Diplock J.
202 *Ibid.*
203 See *Wentworth v Lloyd (No 2)* (1865) 34 Beav 455, at 457, *per* Romily MR.
204 *Thomas v Parry* (1880) WN 184.
205 *Madej v Maciszyn* [2013] Lexis Citation 143.

53

COUNSEL'S FEES

53.01 This chapter focuses on those aspects of counsel's practice and remuneration that are relevant to the law of costs, both between opposing parties and, to a lesser extent, between counsel and their clients. Practising barristers may like to note that the Bar Council publishes guidance that deals with the conundrums of life at the Bar.[1] This chapter covers the following topics:

- the nature of counsel's right to payment (53.04);
- fee agreements in default (53.08);
- non-contractual agreements with professional clients (53.09);
- contractual agreements with professional clients (53.16);
- contractual agreements with licensed access clients (53.19);
- contractual agreements with lay clients (53.24);
- liability for fees as between counsel and their instructing solicitor (53.27);
- counsel not in independent practice (53.29);
- counsel's fees between opposing parties (53.32);
- the basis of charging (53.40);
- the scope of instructions (53.42);
- evidencing counsel's fees (53.45);
- the quantum of counsel's fees (53.51);
- delivery, going short and abatement (53.67);
- the relevance of time (53.87) and the use of comparators (53.91);
- other factors relevant to quantum (53.97);
- refreshers (53.103);
- hourly charging (advices, skeleton arguments, etc) (53.107);
- fees per item (53.114);
- retainers (or commitment fees) (53.116);
- booking fees (53.118);
- leading counsel (53.119);
- two counsel (53.124);
- informal arrangements between counsel (devilling) (53.130);
- more than two counsel (53.131); and
- the new terms of work (53.135).

53.02 For the purposes of this chapter, a distinction is drawn between professional clients (which generally means lawyers authorised by approved regulators),[2] licensed access clients (such

[1] See Bar Council, *Guidance for Barristers and Clerks Relating to Privately Funded Civil Litigation* (December 2013) available online at http://www.barcouncil.org.uk/media/201555/guidance_for_barristers_and_clerks_relating_to_privately_funded_civil_litigation.pdf

[2] The definition given in the Bar Standards Board (BSB) Handbook, Part 6, para 157, is as follows: '... (a) any *person* authorised by another *approved regulator* or *licensing authority*; (b) an *employed barrister*

as architects and accountants)[3] and lay clients. Unless the contrary is obvious from the context, what is set out in this chapter relates to professional clients. Similarly, unless otherwise indicated, what is set out in this chapter relates to barristers in independent practice (that is, barristers who hold themselves out as practising barristers and who are not employed barristers acting in the course of their employment[4]) rather than employed barristers.[5]

On 6 January 2014, the first edition of the Bar Standards Board (BSB) Handbook came into force as a replacement for the Code of Conduct of the Bar of England and Wales 2004 (8th edn) (to be referred to as the 'old' Code of Conduct).[6] Like the Solicitors Code of Conduct 2011 (see 4.14), the BSB Handbook marks a move towards outcomes-focused regulation. This chapter uses the BSB Handbook as its touchstone. The BSB Handbook sets out a number of 'Core Duties' (for example CD1, CD2, etc),[7] which are supplemented by 'guidance' (for example gCD1, gCD2, etc) and mandatory 'rules' (for example rCD1, rCD2, etc). Transitional provisions exist.[8] **53.03**

The Nature of Counsel's Right to Payment

Whilst now superseded by statute, common law provides that counsel is not able to enter into an enforceable contract for the supply of professional services as a barrister.[9] **53.04**

---

or registered European lawyer; (c) any *practising barrister* or registered European lawyer acting on their own behalf; (d) any *BSB authorised person* who is authorised to conduct litigation; (e) a *foreign lawyer*; (f) a Scottish or Northern Irish *Solicitor*; or (g) the representative of any body (such as a Legal Advice Centre or Pro Bono or Free Representation Unit) which arranges for the supply of legal services to the public without a fee, and which has been and remains designated by the *Bar Standards Board* (subject to such conditions as may be imposed by the *Bar Council* or *Bar Standards Board* in relation to insurance or any other matter whatsoever) as suitable for the instruction of *barristers*, and which instructs a *barrister* to supply legal services without a fee ...'

[3] BSB Handbook, Part 6, para 120, defines a 'licensed access client' as 'a *person* or organisation approved as such by the *Bar Standards Board* in accordance with the Licensed Access Recognition Regulations ...'.

[4] See BSB Handbook, rB.S9.

[5] Employed barristers are best regarded as a species of fee earner, ie as subject to the principles set out in Chapters 28 and 29.

[6] For more detail about the old Code of Conduct, see the second edition of this book.

[7] The Core Duties are as follows: 'CD1 You must observe your duty to the court in the administration of justice [CD1]. CD2 You must act in the best interests of each client [CD2]. CD3 You must act with honesty and integrity [CD3]. CD4 You must maintain your independence [CD4]. CD5 You must not behave in a way which is likely to diminish the trust and confidence which the public places in you or in the profession [CD5]. CD6 You must keep the affairs of each client confidential [CD6]. CD7 You must provide a competent standard of work and service to each client [CD7]. CD8 You must not discriminate unlawfully against any person [CD8]. CD9 You must be open and co-operative with your regulators [CD9]. CD10 You must take reasonable steps to manage your practice, or carry out your role within your practice, competently and in such a way as to achieve compliance with your legal and regulatory obligations [CD10]'.

[8] In essence, 'anything done or omitted to be done or otherwise arising before 6 January 2014' will be dealt with under the Code of Conduct 2004: see BSB Handbook, rC.13, for further details.

[9] The (now abolished) position at common law was described by Swinfen Eady LJ in *Wells v Wells* [1914] 1 P 157, at 162: 'It is settled beyond all question that counsel's fee is not a debt but an honorarium, the fees are payable as a matter of honour and not of legal obligation.' In *Re Le Brasseur and Oakley* [1896] 2 Ch 487, at 496, Lopes LJ said this: '[*Kennedy v Broun* (1862) 32 LJ (CP) 137] establishes the unqualified doctrine that the relation of counsel and solicitor renders the parties mutually incapable of making any legal contract

In particular, prior to the intervention of statute, barristers were not able to recover their fees as debts[10] and they were not permitted to sue on the basis of representations that they would be paid.[11] This was true even if counsel's instructing solicitor had been placed in funds for counsel's fees.[12] The type of fee that barristers sought was an honorarium; it is commonly said that this arrangement was based on the courteous understanding that counsel could neither sue nor be sued, but Plucknett (an Oxford legal historian) has said that the rule originated in the 17th century and was born of a desire on the part of barristers to assert social superiority over those who instructed them by declining to sue for their fees.[13] On 1 January 1991, statute intervened in the form of s 61 of the Courts and Legal Services Act 1990:

> '**61. Right of barrister to enter into contract for the provision of his services**
>
> (1) Any rule of law which prevents a barrister from entering into a contract for the provision of his services as a barrister is hereby abolished.
>
> (2) Nothing in subsection (1) prevents the General Council of the Bar from making rules (however described) which prohibit barristers from entering into contracts or restrict their right to do so.'

Rather than seizing upon this statutory provision as their financial salvation, most barristers continued with the tradition of not entering into contractual arrangements. It was not until 31 January 2013 that that state of affairs changed.

53.05 Prior to 31 January 2013, the default position was that unless some other arrangement had been made, where a barrister was instructed by a solicitor, the Terms of Work on Which Barristers Offer Their Services to Solicitors (the 'old' Terms of Work) would apply.[14] Those terms were not contractual; rather, they were published by the Bar Council[15] as part of the Withdrawal of Credit Scheme 1998 (see 53.13–53.15) and, as such, counsel's response to non-payment was not to sue their instructing solicitor, but to invoke that Scheme. That Scheme applied only to solicitors. On 31 January 2013, however, things changed. The Bar Council implemented new terms of engagement—namely, the Standard Contractual Terms for the Supply of Legal Services by Barristers to Authorised Persons 2012 (the 'new' Terms of Work)—and these new terms were capable of applying to any professional client rather than only solicitors. The old Terms of Work were abolished, as was the Withdrawal of Credit List, the latter being replaced by a new list—namely, the List of Defaulting Solicitors and Other Authorised Persons. The Withdrawal of Credit Scheme 1998 ceased to apply to new agreements and was gradually wound down.

---

of hiring and service in regard to litigation. That rule has existed for a long time, and, speaking for myself, I should be very sorry to see it in any way impugned.' See also *Re Sandiford (No 2)* [1935] Ch 681. The law can be traced back to *Moor v Row* (1629) 1 Rep Ch 38 and then again to Roman law: see Lex Cincia c 204 BC. The non-contractual nature of the retainer used to exist even if the services were provided in a different jurisdiction: *R v Doutre* (1884) 9 App Cas 745, PC, at 752.

10 *Wells v Wells* [1914] P 157; *Re Sandiford (No 2)* [1935] Ch 681.

11 *Hobart v Butler* (1859) 9 ICLR 157.

12 *Re Sandiford (No 2)* [1935] Ch 681.

13 See Plucknett, T, *A Concise History of the Common Law* (Indianapolis, IN: Liberty Fund Inc, 2010), ch 12.

14 See old Terms of Work, para 2.

15 They could be found in Bar Code of Conduct, Annex G1 and G2.

The new Terms of Work are capable of applying where instructions are received from any professional client. They are not mandatory[16] and are not terms that apply by default.[17] The Bar Council says that default terms are not needed because the Provision of Services Regulations 2009[18] require barristers to publish their own standard terms.[19] This is relevant because, on 31 January 2013, the ambit of the cab-rank rule was enlarged such that it applied not only where the professional client sought to instruct counsel on the new Terms of Work, but also where the instructions were offered on counsel's own standard terms (if any).[20] Moreover, the cab-rank rule was changed such that barristers were permitted (if they wished) to take instructions on credit from solicitors who had been named as bad debtors.[21] This means that the List of Defaulting Solicitors and Other Authorised Persons differs from its predecessor in that it is an advisory list, rather than a list of persons to whom credit must not be offered. **53.06**

Counsel's ability to enter into a contract for the supply of legal services is subject to the rules made by the General Council of the Bar. Broadly speaking, those rules permit (or have permitted in the past) counsel to enter into the following types of fee agreement: **53.07**

- non-contractual agreements with professional clients (see 53.09);
- contractual agreements with professional clients (see 53.16);
- contractual agreements with licensed access clients (see 53.19); and
- contractual agreements with lay clients (see 53.24).

Each of these arrangements is considered in turn, but the default position—that is, where counsel lawfully accepts instructions without having entered into an express agreement regarding fees—is addressed first.

Fee Agreements in Default

Mishaps occur and it may happen that counsel accepts instructions without having come to any express agreement regarding fees. There can be little doubt that the fact that counsel has lawfully carried out work will create *some* form of right to payment, but it is far from certain that the right would necessarily be enforceable in law. Much depends on the nature of the client (that is, whether they are a professional client, a licensed access client or a lay client) and when the instructions were given. **53.08**

- **Professional clients (prior to 31 January 2013)** Prior to 31 January 2013, where instructions came from a solicitor, a failure to expressly agree terms would not have caused

[16] BSB Handbook, rC9.7, reads: '[Y]ou must only propose, or accept, fee arrangements which are legal.' Prior to 6 January 2014, the position was governed by Code of Conduct, para 405. See also Bar Council, *Implementation of New Terms of Engagement for Barristers*, 17 October 2013, para 5, which read: 'Barristers will continue to be free to agree any terms, no terms, or to amend the new Contractual Terms.'

[17] See Bar Council, *Implementation of New Terms of Engagement for Barristers*, 17 October 2013, para 4.

[18] SI 2009/2999.

[19] The Bar Council says that this obligation arises under the Provision of Services Regulations 2009 (SI 2009/2999): see Bar Council, *Implementation of New Terms of Engagement for Barristers*, 17 October 2013, para 4.

[20] See BSB Handbook, rrC29 and C30, esp rC30.9(c).

[21] The current rules are in BSB Handbook, r 28.7(c). See also Bar Council, *Implementation of New Terms of Engagement for Barristers*, 17 October 2013, para 4.

any major problems, because there were 'deeming' provisions in the old Terms of Work that made the position tolerably clear.[22] Moreover, the precise nature of the fee agreement was usually only of academic interest, because solicitors were inured to having to pay counsel as a matter of custom[23] and, in any event, considerable pressure was exerted on them by virtue of counsel's ability to invoke the Withdrawal of Credit Scheme 1988.

- **Professional clients (after 31 January 2013)** The position is now less clear and potentially more problematic. This is not only because of the noticeable absence of any deeming provisions,[24] but also because of the lack of any effective mechanism for applying pressure on professional clients to pay (other, of course, than suing them). Whilst it is unlikely that the court would find that the new Terms of Work apply by default as a matter of general principle, there is no reason why the court, in an appropriate case, could not find that those terms were incorporated into the fee agreement by implication. If, for example, a barrister had not published their own standard terms (see 53.05 and 53.06), it would be open to the court to find that, by not publishing bespoke terms, the barrister impliedly offered their services under the new Terms of Work. Similarly, if the barrister had published their own standard terms, it would (facts permitting) be open to the court to find that those terms had been incorporated. There is, however, no authority on these points. Presumably, the issues addressed in relation to 'implied retainers' at 27.190–27.206 would be relevant.
- **Licensed access clients (at any time)** Where instructions have been received from a licensed access client, then, by implication, the Licensed Access Terms of Work would apply by default,[25] regardless of whether instructions were received before or after

[22] See old Terms of Work, paras 2 ('Any solicitor who sends a brief or instructions to a barrister will be deemed to instruct that barrister on these Terms unless and to the extent that the barrister and the solicitor have agreed in writing in relation to the particular matter or generally (a) that the Contractual Terms on which Barristers Offer their Services to Solicitors 2000 shall apply, or (b) to exclude or vary these Terms'), 25 ('Neither the General Council of the Bar in authorising these Terms nor a barrister in offering his services to a solicitor on these Terms has any intention to create legal relations or to enter into any contract or other obligation binding in law') and 26 ('Neither the sending by a solicitor of a brief or instructions to a barrister nor the acceptance by a barrister of a brief or instructions nor anything done in connection therewith nor the arrangements relating thereto (whether mentioned in these Terms or in the Bar Code of Conduct or to be implied) nor these Terms or any agreement or transaction entered into or payment made by or under them shall be attended by or give rise to any contractual relationship rights duties or consequences whatsoever or be legally enforceable by or against or be the subject of litigation with either the barrister or the General Council of the Bar')

[23] See *Hobart v Butler* (1859) 9 ICLR 157; see also *Re Seal, ex p Crickett* (1893) 37 Sol Jo 685. The professional rules governing solicitors used to provide that non-payment of fees was a disciplinary offence, but that express provision did not appear in the Solicitors Code of Conduct 2007 nor does it appear in the Solicitors Regulation Authority (SRA) Code of Conduct 2011.

[24] The Bar Council has been at pains to point out that there are no deeming provisions: see Bar Council, *Implementation of New Terms of Engagement for Barristers*, 17 October 2013, para 4. It could be argued that whilst Courts and Legal Services Act 1990, s 61, abolishes '[a]ny rule of law which prevents a barrister from entering into a contract', it does not go so far as to provide that any agreement as to counsel's fees is to be regarded as a contract. In the absence of a deeming provision, it could easily be argued that the type of agreement that is created by default is not an enforceable contract, but the more familiar non-contractual type of arrangement that has existed for centuries and which continued to be adopted by the Bar for more than 20 years after the 1990 Act had come into force.

[25] See para 6 of the Licence Access Rules prior to 31 January 2014 and rC136 after that date, both of which, by necessary implication, provide that the default position is that the Licenced Access Terms of Work apply by default. See also para 1 of the Licensed Access Terms of Work, which provides: 'They apply save to the extent that they have been varied or excluded by written agreement ...'

the BSB Handbook became operative (that is, 6 January 2014). The Licensed Access Terms of Work provide that if no fee has been agreed, then a reasonable fee will be payable.[26] The agreement would be an enforceable contract.[27]

- **Public access clients (at any time)** Both before[28] and after 6 January 2014,[29] barristers who have accepted instruction under the BSB Public Access Rules have been required by those rules to deal with the issue of fees in writing. There are no default provisions. The nearest there is to default provisions is a model client care letter published by the Bar Council. The BSB Handbook states that:

  '[S]ave in exceptional circumstances, a barrister will have complied with [the requirement to deal with the issue of fees in writing] if he has written promptly to the public access client in the terms of the model letter provided on the Bar Standards Board website.'[30]

  In view of the express requirement to create a written record of the fee agreement, it is possible that where there is no written record, there is no enforceable contract (especially in view of the consumer protection provisions addressed at in Chapter 28). The factors discussed in relation to 'implied retainers' at 27.190–27.206 would—with appropriate modifications—also be relevant.

Non-contractual Agreements with Professional Clients

Non-contractual agreements made after 31 January 2013 should now be a rarity, but where counsel was instructed prior to 31 January 2013, non-contractual agreements with solicitors would have been the norm, rather than the exception (see 53.05). As such, non-contractual agreements are likely to be encountered for many years to come. **53.09**

Prior to 31 January 2013, counsel was able to enter into any type of agreement they wanted, but it was rare for counsel to stray from the old Terms of Work. Clause (3) of those terms relied heavily on professional customs, providing as follows: 'By the established custom of the profession a barrister looks for payment of his fees to the solicitor who instructs him and not to his lay client.' **53.10**

With one or two exceptions,[31] counsel's instructions did not create any form of enforceable agreement between counsel and their lay client.[32] Thus, subject to those exceptions, counsel was (and still is) not able to sue their lay client for their fees. Similarly, **53.11**

[26] Licensed Access Terms of Work, para 10(1).
[27] See Licensed Access Terms of Work, para 6(1).
[28] See Public Access Rules, para 6(g).
[29] See BSB Handbook, rC125.7.
[30] See BSB Handbook, rC126.
[31] See paras 48.19–48.25. There is ancient authority that where counsel has communicated directly with the lay client, a promise that counsel would be paid was a promise that could be enforced at law: *Marsh and Rainsford's Case* (1687) Leon 111. It is, however, very doubtful whether this authority is still good law, not least because it would cut across modern consumer protection provisions.
[32] Support for the first of these analyses is gained from authority suggesting that a solicitor does not act as its lay client's agent when it instructs counsel: *Mostyn v Mostyn* (1870) LR 5 Ch App 457.

counsel's clerk was (and still is) also unable to sue the lay client for fees.[33] If counsel was not paid, their only remedy was to invoke the Withdrawal of Credit Scheme 1988 (see 53.13–53.15).

53.12 For the sake of completeness, it is worth mentioning that whilst counsel was not able to sue for their fees as if they were a debtor, the court is able to order a solicitor to pay counsel's fees in the exercise of its administrative jurisdiction to supervise solicitors as officers of the court. The circumstances in which the court would make such an order would be few and far between.[34] It is most unlikely that the court would make such an order where counsel had brought a claim specifically in respect of their own fee.[35]

The old Terms of Work

53.13 The following points can be made about fees payable under the now-revoked Withdrawal of Credit Scheme 1988.

- **Default position and allowable fees arrangements** The old Terms of Work provided that counsel was able to agree either a fee or a charging rate before commencing work, but that, in default of agreement, a reasonable professional rate would be payable.[36]
- **Payment of fees** The old Terms of Work terms also provided that fees should be paid within one month of receipt of the fee note, regardless of whether the case is ongoing.[37]
- **Interest** If counsel's fees go unpaid, interest would be payable, but only where the principle of payment of interest had been agreed.

Disputes and enforcement of payment under the old Terms of Work

53.14 Where fees remain unpaid, counsel's remedy used to be to invoke the procedure set out in the Withdrawal of Credit Scheme 1988 (which is now in run-off and which now will not accept new referrals other than in exceptional circumstances). In essence, if there was a dispute about counsel's fees or if fees went unpaid, the matter would (subject to certain time limits) be referred to an expert tribunal known as the Joint Tribunal. The referral could be made by either the professional client or counsel.

- **Professional client** If there was a dispute about the amount claimed, the professional client had to complain in writing by no later than three months after receipt of the fee note.[38] Morland J has found that if this was not done, the professional client would be taken to have assented to and accepted the fee as claimed as payable.[39]
- **Counsel** If the fee went unpaid, then the barrister was able to refer the matter to the Joint Tribunal. In principle, this was for the purposes of determining whether the

---

[33] This is a reference to the clerk's own fees (which are often a percentage of counsel's fee). Whilst an ancient authority, *Ex p Cotton* (1846) 9 Beav 107 probably remains good law. Counsel's clerk can, however, sue counsel: *Lyster v Spearman* (1882) 72 LT Jo 391.

[34] An example would be where a trustee in bankruptcy is paid counsel's fees, but refuses to pass them on to counsel: see *Ex p James* (1874) LR 9 Ch 609; *In re Carnac, ex p Simmonds* (1885) 16 QBD 308. See also *Re Farman* (1883) 18 L Jo 352; *Re a Solicitor, ex p Incorporated Law Society* (1894) 63 LJQB 397, DC.

[35] See, eg, *Re a Solicitor, ex p Incorporated Law Society* (1909) The Times, 27 January.

[36] Old Terms of Work, para 10(1).

[37] Old Terms of Work, paras 8 and 13.

[38] Old Terms of Work, para 14(1) and (2).

[39] *Spath Holmes Ltd v Chairman of the Greater Manchester and Lancashire Rent Assessment Committee* [1998] 1 Costs LR 40, at 46.

professional client should be included in the Withdrawal of Credit List; in practice, it was for the purposes of enforcing payment. Other than in exceptional circumstances, the Joint Tribunal would accept referrals only if the fee had not been outstanding for more than two years.[40]

Further details of that Scheme and further references can be found in the second edition of this book at paras 32.17–32.20.

Morland J has found that if a solicitor files a signed bill of costs (that is, a between-the-parties bill of costs) in which counsel's fees are claimed, the solicitor must be taken to have assented in principle to payment of those monies.[41] This finding was made in a case that related to the Withdrawal of Credit Scheme 1988, but it did not heavily rely on the wording of that scheme; in view of this, it is easily arguable that Morland J's observations continue to apply. **53.15**

Contractual Agreements with Professional Clients

Given the changes referred to at 53.05, contractual agreements entered into after 31 January 2013 have been the norm, rather than the exception. Contractual agreements made before that date will also be encountered, but not commonly. Both the old and the new regimes are addressed in this section. **53.16**

Where a barrister is instructed by a solicitor and where they have agreed in writing that the agreement between them shall be contractually binding, a contract enforceable at law will be created; this was true under the old regime and continues to be true under the new. The following points can be made about the ambit and terms of any such agreement. **53.17**

- **Terms and ambit under the old regime** Prior to 31 January 2013, unless some other terms had been agreed, the Contractual Terms of Work on Which Barristers Offer Their Services to Solicitors 2001 (the 'old' Contractual Terms) would have applied.[42] The way in which the old Contractual Terms operated was that they disapplied certain provisions in the old Terms of Work and, in so doing, they created a retainer that would continue to exist for the purposes of the Withdrawal of Credit Scheme 1988, but which was also an enforceable contract. The old Contractual Terms provided that counsel was able to agree either a fee or a charging rate before commencing work, but that, in default of agreement, a reasonable professional rate would be payable.[43]
- **Terms and ambit under the new regime** In most instances, there will be an express agreement that the new Terms of Work will apply. Where this is so (or where they apply by implication), the new Terms of Work will define the ambit and terms of counsel's retainer. The new Terms of Work provide that if no charging rate was agreed, a reasonable

[40] Bar Council, *Fees Collection Committee Guidelines*, available online at http://www.barcouncil.org.uk/media/9019/12_5_guidance_for_report_forms.pdf, para 7.

[41] *Spath Holmes Ltd v Chairman of the Greater Manchester and Lancashire Rent Assessment Committee* [1998] 1 Costs LR 40, at 47.

[42] These terms apply only to agreements made on or after 24 March 2001 (see Contractual Terms, para 28); agreements made before that date are probably unenforceable.

[43] See old Contractual Terms, para 9(1).

rate should apply.[44] Fees had to be paid within one month of receipt of the fee note, in default of which simple interest (which usually stipulated to be 2 per cent above base rate) would be payable. The new Terms of Work contain the following provision regarding payment:

> 'The Authorised Person must pay the Invoice within 30 days of delivery, time being of the essence, whether or not the Authorised Person has been put in funds by the Lay Client. The Invoice must be paid without any set-off (whether by reason of a complaint made or dispute with the Barrister or otherwise), and without any deduction or withholding on account of any taxes or other charges.'[45]

The new Terms of Work also provide that interest will be payable on any unpaid fees, in accordance with the Late Payment of Commercial Debts (Interest) Act 1998.[46]

53.18 Not everyone is happy about the new Terms of Work—not least because they were published without having been agreed with the Law Society, which has this to say:

> 'The new standard contractual terms have been adopted by the Bar unilaterally. The Law Society is concerned that, under the terms, the balance of obligations is weighted strongly in favour of barristers. It is our view that the relationship between solicitors and barristers is a commercial one, the terms of which ought to be agreed between themselves. It is, however, open to solicitors to negotiate alternative terms.'[47]

At the end of this chapter (see 53.135) is a draft of the new Terms of Work that has been annotated to include most of the specific points that the Law Society has made about it.

Contractual Agreements with Licensed Access Clients

53.19 A scheme exists, known as the licensed access scheme, which permits barristers to accept instructions from professionals other than professional clients (but only if to do so would be in the lay client's best interests).[48] That scheme seeks to maximise client access to the legal profession whilst ensuring that the Bar retains its identity as a referral profession.[49] Licensed access is subject to the Licensed Access Rules (which now form part of the BSB Handbook at rC132–rC141) and the Licensed Access Recognition Regulations (which are published by the BSB on its website).

---

[44] See new Terms of Work, para 11.

[45] See new Terms of Work, para 12.4.

[46] See new Terms of Work, para 12.6.1.

[47] See Law Society, *Practice Note: Instructing a Barrister—New Standard Contractual Terms* (24 January 2013), para 2.1.

[48] There are other circumstances in which counsel might be instructed by someone other than a solicitor. Pursuant to Courts and Legal Services Act 1990 (as amended), s 28, the General Council of the Bar is authorised to grant the right to conduct litigation and it has done so in respect of employed barristers where they are acting for their employer or, if their employer is a solicitor, for a client of their employer. Patents Act 1977, s 104(2), permits patent agents to instruct counsel for the purpose of conducting patent appeals; indeed, some patent agents are allowed the right to conduct any kind of litigation involving intellectual property. Criminal Justice and Court Services Act 2000, s 15, permits officers of the Children and Family Court Advisory and Support Service to instruct counsel in certain circumstances.

[49] See Bar Council, Licensed Access Guidance Handbooks for Barristers and Chambers and Licensed Access Clients, para 2.1.

Before they can instruct counsel directly, a professional who is not a professional client (that is, who is not a regulated lawyer) must obtain a licence from the BSB.[50] Provided that they are members of an appropriate professional body,[51] the following professionals are entitled to apply for a licence: accountants and taxation advisers; insolvency practitioners; architects, surveyors and town planners; engineers; valuers; actuaries; chartered secretaries and administrators; and insurers. **53.20**

The agreement between the barrister and the licensed access client is contractual.[52] Paragraph 6 of the Licensed Access Terms of Work provide as follows: **53.21**

> '6 **Liability for the fees:** The licensed access client is liable for a barrister's fee due in respect of work carried out by the barrister under any instructions. In a case where the matter concerns a lay client, the licensed access client is solely and exclusively liable to the barrister for the fees. In this regard:
> (1) The relationship between the barrister and the licensed access client is a contractual one.
> (2) Any individual giving or purporting to give the instructions on behalf of any partnership firm, company, individual or other person warrants to the barrister that he is authorised by the latter to do so.
> (3) If the licensed access client is a partnership or a firm or unincorporated association, the liability of the partners or members and on death that of their estates for the barrister's fees is joint and several.'

Thus the licensed access client is solely and exclusively liable for counsel's fees. Paragraph 10(1) of the Licensed Access Terms of Work goes on to say that, in default of an agreement as to the amount of fees, counsel will be entitled to a reasonable professional rate. Fees must be paid within 30 days of receipt of a fee note,[53] failing which interest will be payable.[54] **53.22**

The Withdrawal of Credit Scheme 1988 never applied to work accepted under the licensed access scheme. Counsel's ultimate remedy is (and always has been) to sue for their fees. **53.23**

Contractual Agreements with Lay Clients

Provided that it is in the best interests of the client, an appropriately qualified barrister may accept instructions directly from a lay client rather than through a solicitor or a licensed access client. This is known as public access. **53.24**

Not all barristers are eligible to undertake public access work. To qualify, a barrister must have been in practice for a period of not less than three years from the completion of pupillage, must have complied with certain training requirements and must have registered with the Bar Council the fact that they intend to do public access work.[55] **53.25**

---

[50] See BSB, Licensed Access Recognition Regulations, regs 1–6.
[51] These are listed in BSB, Licensed Access Recognition Regulations, Sch One.
[52] See BSB, Licensed Access Rules and Recognition Regulations, reg 6; Licensed Access Guidance Handbooks for Barristers and Chambers and Licensed Access Clients, para 3.22.
[53] See Licensed Access Terms of Work, para 10(3).
[54] See Licensed Access Terms of Work, para 10(4).
[55] See BSB Handbook, rC120.

53.26 The arrangement between the client and the barrister will be by way of written agreement in which the barrister must set out the fees they propose to charge or the basis on which their fee will be calculated.[56] The agreement will be a contract enforceable at law. A model client care letter is published on the Bar Council's website. Care should be taken to comply with the Consumer Contracts (Information, Cancellation and Additional Charges) Regulations 2013[57] (see 28.67 *et seq*). If necessary, any model agreement that does not comply with those regulations should be redrafted.

Liability for Fees as between Counsel and their Instructing Solicitor

Set-off

53.27 Unless there has been agreement to the contrary or unless the solicitor has formally challenged the fees, a client is not entitled to set off counsel's fee. The Contractual Terms provide that counsel's fees will be payable without any deductions or set-off whatsoever[58] and the old Terms of Work make similar provision.[59] That said, the Law Society has recommended that solicitors give thought to amending these stock provisions[60] and, as such, the issue will turn on the contract in question, rather than on what was provided for in the Contractual Terms.

Agents

53.28 Many fee agreements will deal with the issue expressly, but where counsel is instructed by an agent and there is no reason to believe otherwise, the agent is responsible for discharging counsel's fees.[61] Where the putative agent is an intermediary who has instructed counsel on behalf of a lay client, counsel is required to inform the lay client in writing of the fact that the intermediary is the agent of the lay client and not the agent of the barrister.[62]

Counsel not in Independent Practice

53.29 In general, this chapter assumes that where a barrister seeks payment, it will be as a barrister in independent practice. That said, there are two other circumstances that merit mention.

Not practising as a barrister

53.30 A person qualified as a barrister may provide legal services in a capacity other than as a barrister in independent practice.[63] Examples might include an employed barrister or a barrister who holds themselves out as a non-practising barrister providing legal services in another capacity (such as a costs consultant). In these circumstances, that person's

---

56 Prior to 6 January 2014, see the Public Access Rules, para 6(g); after 6 January 2014, see BSB Handbook, rC125.

57 SI 2013/3134.

58 Contractual Terms, para 12(4).

59 Old Terms of Work, para 14(4).

60 Law Society, *Practice Note: Instructing a Barrister—New Standard Contractual Terms* (24 January 2013), para 3.2.2.

61 *Re Nelson, Son and Hastings* (1885) 30 Ch D 1, at 10.

62 See BSB Handbook, rC125.5.

63 Code of Conduct, para 201.

remuneration will usually be dependent on a contract and their fees will be assessed by reference to the capacity in which the legal services are supplied. A barrister who is employed ought not to hold themselves out as a barrister in independent practice.[64]

Not supplying legal services

A barrister in independent practice may supply services that are not legal services, in which case counsel would usually be able to sue the recipient of those services for any unpaid fees. Examples include acting as an arbitrator,[65] a returning officer,[66] a lecturer, an umpire or a judge. The modern position is dealt with in the BSB Handbook, which defines 'legal services' as follows: **53.31**

> ' "Legal services" includes legal advice representation and drafting or settling any statement of case witness statement affidavit or other legal document but does not include:
> a) sitting as a judge or arbitrator or acting as a mediator;
> b) lecturing in or teaching law or writing or editing law books articles or reports;
> c) examining newspapers, periodicals, books, scripts and other publications for libel, breach of copyright, contempt of court and the like;
> d) communicating to or in the press or other media;
> e) giving advice on legal matters free to a friend or relative or acting as unpaid or honorary legal adviser to any charitable benevolent or philanthropic institution;
> f) in relation to a barrister who is a non-executive director of a company or a trustee or governor of a charitable benevolent or philanthropic institution or a trustee of any private trust, giving to the other directors trustees or governors the benefit of his learning and experience on matters of general legal principle applicable to the affairs of the company institution or trust;
> g) early neutral evaluation, expert determination and adjudications.'[67]

For obvious reasons, it will generally be the case that fees for providing services other than legal services will not be the subject of assessment.

Counsel's Fees between Opposing Parties

A number of points can be made about the way in which counsel's fees are assessed between opposing parties—but some of the conclusions that have been reached are not easy to reconcile. **53.32**

The nature of fees

Counsel's fees are recoverable as disbursements, and this is true regardless of the fact that the solicitor could have instructed someone other than counsel to carry out the work and could have charged for that work as if they had carried it out themselves.[68] **53.33**

[64] This was made clear by Maurice Kay LJ in *Kingstons Solicitors v Reiss Solicitors* [2014] EWCA Civ 172, at [48] and [49]; indeed, Maurice Kay LJ felt so strongly about the issue that he referred the matter to the barristers' regulatory body.

[65] See *Norjarl K/S A/S v Hyundai Heavy Industries Co Ltd* [1991] 3 All ER 211; *Virany v Warne* (1801–04) 4 Esp 47; *Hoggins v Gordon* (1842) 3 QB 466; *Sinclair v Great Eastern Railway Co* (1870) 21 LT 752.

[66] *Egan v Kensington Union Guardians* (1841) 3 QB 935.

[67] See the definitions schedule at the end of the BSB Handbook. The current definition differs from its predecessor in that it does not include the activity of exercising the powers of a commissioner for oaths.

[68] *Crane v Cannons Leisure Centre* [2007] EWCA Civ 1352 at [28], *per* Maurice Kay LJ.

The indemnity principle

53.34 In so far as privately payable fees are concerned, the fact that counsel cannot enforce their fees against the solicitor does not present the paying party with an opportunity to say that there has been a breach of the indemnity principle.[69] This is because it is the liability between the solicitor and the client that is relevant, not the liability between counsel and solicitor; once counsel has been paid, the solicitor is able to enforce the debt against the client irrespective of whether its agreement with counsel is one that the latter can enforce.

Unpaid counsel's fees

53.35 Where counsel's fees are unpaid at the time a solicitor-and-client bill is assessed, those fees will not be allowed.[70] This is a procedural impediment, however, and does not have a bearing on the right to payment. It is questionable whether a paying party would ever be able to rely on non-payment of counsel's fees in a modern-day assessment. This is because there would be no breach of the indemnity principle unless the court were satisfied that the receiving party would not be liable for the legal representative's fees in any circumstances.[71] It could be argued, however, that this could never be the case because the receiving party's solicitor would be able to enforce the debt immediately upon disbursing counsel's fees.[72]

Conditional fee agreements

53.36 The law set out in Chapter 9 applies to counsel's fees. There are two additional points that merit attention.

Unintended conditional fee agreements

53.37 Where, as commonly happens, counsel naively makes an oral agreement to accept one fee if the case is won, but a lower fee (or no fee) if the case is lost, the agreement will be unenforceable for the reasons set out at 27.214–27.215.

Success fees where the solicitors were instructed before 1 April 2013 and counsel was instructed after that date

53.38 In view of the fact that many solicitors' firms rushed to sign clients up to conditional fee agreements before 1 April 2013, it is commonly the case that counsel's professional client has the benefit of a pre-1 April 2013 conditional fee agreement (that is, an agreement under which the success fee will be recoverable from the other side), whilst counsel has no such benefit. The question that often arises is whether anything can be done to allow counsel to recover a success fee. There have been several attempts to create relations that would supposedly allow this, but there is no authority to confirm that any of them have been successful.

Apportioning fees

53.39 Where a paying party is responsible for paying only part of counsel's fee, then the court will have to decide how that part is to be quantified. Where the fee is a simple unstaged

---

69 *Morris v Hunt* (1819) 1 Chit 544.

70 *Re Taxation of Costs, Re a Solicitor* [1936] 1 KB 523.

71 *R v Miller* [1983] 1 WLR 1056, esp at 1061.

72 See *Morris v Hunt* (1819) 1 Chit 544, which confirms that the solicitor can enforce counsel's fees once they have been disbursed.

fee, Hallett J found that the correct measure is to decide what proportion of the brief fee is payable and that it was permissible to take into account not only the work done during the period for which fees were payable, but also the fact that, during that period, counsel would have committed themselves to carrying out further work.[73] Patten J has found that where a brief fee is payable in stages, the stage payments became costs incurred as and when they were paid, and, unless the court decided otherwise, they would be apportioned on that basis.[74]

The Basis of Charging

Many years ago, it used to be the case that counsel was required to charge a separate fee for each discrete item of work,[75] but this is no longer so because there is now no rule to prescribe the method by which counsel may charge.[76] Prior to 6 January 2014, there was a prohibition against payment by a wage or salary, but even that prohibition has now been withdrawn.[77] There used to be an affirmative rule that permitted counsel to charge in any way that was lawful;[78] that express affirmation no longer exists,[79] but it is extremely doubtful that this has narrowed the scope of fee arrangements open to counsel in any way. **53.40**

The following bases of charging are encountered in practice: **53.41**

- brief fees (see 53.51);
- refreshers (see 53.103);
- hourly charging (see 53.107);
- fees per item (see 53.114); and
- retainers (or commitment fees) (see 53.116).

Each of these is addressed in turn, but two points of principle are addressed first: the scope of counsel's instructions; and the evidence by which counsel's fees may be proved.

The Scope of Instructions

Counsel carries out work on instructions. Regardless of the nature of the work, counsel is entitled to be paid only for that work which they have been instructed to do. Any work that goes beyond these instructions will go unremunerated. This principle has survived the introduction of the Civil Procedure Rules (CPR) and may, on occasion, result in significant reductions in counsel's fees.[80] **53.42**

---

[73] *Bowcott v Walding* [2003] EWHC 9042 (Costs).

[74] *Cantor Fitzgerald International v Tradition (UK) Ltd* [2003] EWHC 1907 (Ch).

[75] As to the 'item by item' approach, see the old Code of Conduct. This rule has now been withdrawn.

[76] See BSB Handbook, rC9.7.

[77] See old Code of Conduct, para 405. That prohibition does not appear in the BSB Handbook: see BSB Handbook, rC9.7.

[78] Prior to 6 January 2014, the position was governed by old Code of Conduct, para 405, which read as follows: 'Subject to paragraph 307 a self-employed barrister may charge for any work undertaken by him (whether or not it involves an appearance in Court) on any basis or by any method he thinks fit provided that such basis or method: (a) is permitted by law; [and] (b) does not involve the payment of a wage or salary.'

[79] See BSB Handbook, rC9.7, which reads 'you must only propose, or accept, fee arrangements which are legal'.

[80] See, eg, *Sibley & Co v Reachbyte Ltd* [2008] EWHC 2665, *per* Peter Smith J.

53.43 Hobhouse J explained that this rule does not mean that counsel must carry out work for no pay; rather, it means that counsel must negotiate a fee that is sufficient to cover any work that needs to be done.[81] Hobhouse J also explained that where this has not been done, counsel must either make some other arrangement for the delivery of supplementary instructions or must agree an additional fee (or both). In a similar vein, Brooke J explained that if, after having discussed the matter with their clients, counsel realises that they need to carry out work that is not covered within the four corners of their present instructions, counsel must seek additional instructions.[82] Brooke J made it clear that this would not be a rule to be applied inflexibly and, in practice, it is not uncommon for the court to find that the requirement for instructions has been met by, for example, a brief exchange of emails.

53.44 It will occasionally happen that counsel not only strays from the four corners of their instructions, but also disobeys those instructions altogether. Where this is the case, counsel's entire fees may be at risk, including those for work done before the disobedience.[83]

Evidencing Counsel's fees

53.45 The points made about evidence in detailed assessment generally apply to counsel's fees; the issues addressed in this discussion are limited to those that pertain to counsel. Other than their instructions, etc, there are three types of evidence that are commonly put before the court in support of counsel's fees: contemporaneous records; notes from counsel; and counsel's written work.

Contemporaneous records in support of counsel's fees

53.46 Since July 2000, barristers in independent practice have been required to make and retain 'adequate' and 'proper' records supporting their fees.[84] Special provisions apply where counsel has been instructed under the public access scheme.[85]

[81] *Loveday v Renton (No 2)* [1992] 3 All ER 184 at 191, in which Hobhouse J disallowed charges made by counsel for work at the weekend on the basis that they had not been instructed to carry out that work.

[82] *Brush v Bower Cotton & Bower (a firm)* [1993] 4 All ER 741, at 765.

[83] *Re Harrison* [1908] 1 Ch 282.

[84] BSB Handbook, rC87, is a provision that merely provides that proper records of counsel's practice must be kept. BSB Handbook, rC88, however, provides as follows: 'You must: [1] ensure that adequate records supporting the fees charged or claimed in a case are kept at least until the later of the following: [a] your fees have been paid; and [b] any determination or assessment of costs in the case has been completed and the time for lodging an appeal against that assessment or determination has expired without any such appeal being lodged, or any such appeal has been finally determined.' For work carried out prior to 6 January 2014, see old Code of Conduct, para 701(f), which reads: '[The barrister] must ensure that adequate records supporting the fees charged or claimed in a case are kept at least until the last of the following: his fees have been paid, any taxation or determination or assessment of costs in the case has been completed, or the time for lodging an appeal against assessment or the determination of that appeal, has expired.'

[85] BSB Handbook, rC129, imposes the following obligations: 'A barrister who accepts public access instructions must either himself retain or take reasonable steps to ensure that the lay client will retain for at least seven years after the date of the last item of work done: 1 copies of all instructions (including supplemental instructions); 2 copies of all advices given and documents drafted or approved; 3 the originals, copies or a list of all documents enclosed with any instructions; [and] 4 notes of all conferences and of all advice given on the telephone.'

The Bar Council has issued detailed guidance as to how counsel should keep records.[86] There is no requirement that these are to be produced on a detailed assessment, but there is a requirement that counsel makes the records available to their client,[87] who may then choose whether to put them before the court. The admissibility of such evidence has been confirmed by Fulford J.[88] **53.47**

[86] That guidance is contained in Professional Practice Committee, *Fee Notes and Records* (February 2014): '1. All clients are entitled to know the basis on which fees are charged, not least so that they can protect their interests in respect of any assessments of costs. 2. You are reminded that rC88 requires you to "ensure that adequate records supporting the fees charged or claimed in a case are kept" and that you "must provide your client with such records or details of the work you have done as may reasonably be required for the purposes of verifying your charges". Accordingly, in order to assist lay and professional clients, Judges, Costs Judges and, in the event of opposed assessments of costs, lay and professional clients justifying your fees to opposing parties, you should keep careful records of the time taken on each individual item of work done, such as: (a) Pleadings, indictments, or other procedural documents[;] (b) Witness statements[;] (c) Experts' reports[;] (d) Schedules[;] (e) Written Advices and Opinions[;] (f) Letters[;] (g) Skeleton arguments[;] (h) Written submissions[;] (i) Preparation of Briefs[;] (j) Conferences and telephone conferences and the preparation for such conferences. 3. You are also reminded that paragraph rC88 requires such records to be kept at least until the later of the following: your fees have been paid, any determination or assessment of costs in the case has been completed and the time for lodging an appeal against that assessment or determination has expired without any such appeal being lodged, or any such appeal has been finally determined. 4. The following further steps are also advised as a matter of good practice: 4.1 When you are instructed orally, including by telephone, you should make a note of the nature of the instructions and of the response given[;] 4.2 When you ask orally for further information, you should make a note of the nature of the request, and of the answer if the answer is given orally[;] 4.3 When any particularly novel or complex issue of fact or law arises in the course of the conduct of a case, you should (unless the subject is dealt with in a written advice or opinion) make a note summarising the relevant issue or issues and the research undertaken in like manner as is required by (i) above[;] 4.4 When a consultation or conference takes place, unless the professional client makes an attendance note which is sent to you for approval or amendment, you should make a note of the topics covered and the general nature of the advice given[;] 4.5 When you are involved in negotiations, either between Counsel or by way of leading, assisting or supporting the professional client in the conduct of negotiations, you should make a note of the general nature of the involvement[;] 4.6 Notes made pursuant to subparagraphs (i) to (v) above should be kept by you unless they are returned to an instructing solicitor. 5. In cases where there is not an instructing solicitor, it may be advisable to keep more detailed records. 6. When a brief fee has not been agreed and is claimed by you in a sum greater than the product of an hourly rate and the number of hours actually worked in preparation of the brief, this should be recorded in a note to be submitted with the fee note. Details in the supplementary note should include, but are not limited to: (i) The seniority, reputation and relevant expertise of Counsel[;] (ii) The complexity of the case[;] (iii) The amount of preparation required in advance of the hearing[;] (iv) Counsel's commitment to a fixed hearing date, if any[;] (v) The expected length of the case and, therefore, the time reserved for it in Counsel's diary[;] (vi) The urgency of the matter when Counsel was briefed[;] (vii) The amount of work required out of Court and in the preparation of any kind of written submission during the hearing[;] (viii) The importance of the case to the parties or any of them, or to the public interest[;] (ix) Details of any expenses incurred by Counsel. 7. When a brief fee has been agreed you or your Clerk should keep a written record of the date upon which such agreement was reached, the method by which such agreement was reached and by whom, and of the precise terms of such agreement together with such records as will enable a note containing the details set out at paragraph 4(i)–(ix) above to be produced on request. 8. Clients in cases where you fail to keep proper records to support claimed fees may find the fees reduced. You may then find that a complaint of inadequate professional service may be upheld, in which circumstance you can be ordered to reduce or waive fees and/or to pay compensation. 9. In any case in which you appear properly in a privately paid case at a hearing without a brief fee having been agreed (for example on an interim application) you should make and keep a record of the time spent at Court before the start of the hearing, and of the length of the hearing.'

[87] See BSB Handbook, rC88.2, which provides that counsel must 'provide your client with such records or details of the work you have done as may reasonably be required for the purposes of verifying your charges'. Similar provisions existed prior to 6 January 2014: see old Code of Conduct, para 701(f).

[88] *Edwards & Ors v Roche Products Ltd* [2003] EWHC 9022 (Costs).

Notes from counsel in support of their fees

53.48 Counsel may seek to place a note before the court in support of their fees.[89] The admissibility and relevance of material such as that was confirmed by Lloyd J, who had this to say in the context of an assessment of substantial fees:

> 'It would certainly be helpful to the court and wise from the point of view of counsel to furnish at least some substantial additional material at the stage of the detailed assessment as to why the substantial fees ought to be regarded as proper. It may, for example, be a useful practice for counsel to prepare a short note in the course of, or at the conclusion of the case, to be submitted to the solicitors with fee notes for the purposes of the legal aid assessment.'[90]

Lewison J has pointed out that Lloyd J's comments were not intended to create a legal duty to supply a note; instead, Lloyd J was merely highlighting the fact that if counsel does not supply a note, their fees may be at risk.[91]

53.49 There is no prescribed format, but, according to guidance issued many years ago by the General Council of the Bar, the contents of the note may usefully address:

- the seniority, reputation and relevant expertise of counsel;
- the complexity of the case;
- the amount of preparation required in advance of the hearing;
- counsel's commitment to a fixed hearing date, if any;
- the expected length of the case and therefore the time reserved for it in counsel's diary;
- the urgency of the matter when counsel was briefed;
- the amount of work required out of court and in the preparation of any kind of written submission during the hearing; and
- the importance of the case to the parties or any one of them, or to the public interest.[92]

Counsel's written work as evidence in support of their fees

53.50 The admissibility of counsel's written work in support of their fees for that work is beyond doubt; indeed, if it were not produced on cue, the court would probably be concerned about its absence. It is not essential that counsel's written work is produced, however, and even an extreme lack of documentation will not automatically preclude recovery. Where, for example, counsel failed to give disclosure of the written work that he had been specifically ordered to produce, Evans-Lombe J found that the court was still entitled to find as a matter of fact that the work had been done.[93]

---

[89] This is something that is often formally encouraged: see, eg, para 26.7 of the House of Lords, *Practice Directions Applicable to Judicial Taxations in the House of Lords* (26 March 2007), para 26.7.

[90] *Armitage v Nurse* [2000] 2 Costs LR 231, at 234.

[91] *Ross v Stonewood Securities Ltd* [2004] EWHC 2235 (Ch), at [39]. A serious failure to assist in the recovery of their fees could result in a finding of inadequate professional services against the barrister: Guidance of the Professional Standards and Remuneration Committee of the Bar Council, 22 March 2000, para 6.

[92] Guidance of the Professional Standards and Remuneration Committee of the Bar Council, 22 March 2000.

[93] *Melvin v England Palmer (a firm)* [2004] EWHC 90019 (Costs).

The Quantum of Counsel's fees

Brief fees

A brief is a document drawn up for the purposes of instructing counsel who is to conduct the matter in court; a brief fee is the fee paid for the appearance. It may be a single fee or (as is often the case with larger trials) it may be a fee payable in stages, each stage payment becoming payable at a set juncture in the litigation. **53.51**

The 'hypothetical counsel' test

The starting point for the assessment of any brief fee (and, arguably, for the assessment of any fee charged by counsel) is the 'hypothetical counsel' test, originally articulated by Pennycuick J thus: **53.52**

> 'One must envisage a hypothetical counsel capable of conducting the particular case effectively but unable or unwilling to insist on the particularly high fee sometimes demanded by counsel of pre-eminent reputation. Then one must estimate what fee this hypothetical character would be content to take on the brief . . . There is, in the nature of things, no precise standard of measurement. The taxing master, employing his knowledge and experience, determines what he considers the right figure.'[94]

This test remains the correct approach under the CPR.[95] Although Hobhouse J did not expressly refer to the hypothetical counsel test, he made the following comments, which sit alongside that test without any disharmony: **53.53**

> 'In assessing the brief fee one also has to take into account what will be earned by way of refreshers and what will be the totality of the work that will be required from counsel in the proper discharge of their obligations to protect the interests of their client and the extent to which that work will not be separately remunerated.'[96]

It is, accordingly, permissible to look at the totality of counsel's fees associated with the hearing rather than at only the brief fee. Jackson J built on this approach by saying that where a brief fee includes a skeleton argument, the correct method is to look at the fees that have been provisionally allowed for the hearing and the skeleton argument, and then (as a cross-check) to consider the total amount.[97] The context in which Jackson J was speaking was in respect of costs in the Court of Appeal, but there is no reason to believe that his approach would not be appropriate for any hearing in which a brief fee includes a specific item of written work, such as a skeleton argument. Jackson J had the following to say: **53.54**

> 'Stage 1: The fee for the skeleton argument should be assessed. In the ordinary run of cases, this can be done largely by reference to the amount of time which counsel has reasonably and proportionately devoted to reading the documents, researching the law and drafting the skeleton argument.
>
> Stage 2: The brief fee should be assessed. This exercise involves considering both the amount of time properly spent and many other factors . . . In relation to a brief fee in the Court of

---

[94] *Simpsons Motor Sales (London) v Hendon Borough Council* [1965] 1 WLR 112, at 117.

[95] See, eg, *Orwin v British Coal Corpn* [2003] EWHC 757 (Ch), at [12]; *Higgs v Camden and Islington Health Authority* [2003] EWHC 15 (QB), at [56].

[96] *Loveday v Renton (No 2)* [1992] 3 All ER 184, at 194.

[97] *Hornsby v Clark Kenneth Leventhal (a firm)* [2000] 4 All ER 567.

Appeal [where skeleton arguments are required] it is important to avoid double payment. Insofar as counsel prepared himself/herself whilst drafting the skeleton argument, that preparation time should not be paid for in the brief fee.

Stage 3: Having arrived at an appropriate skeleton argument fee and brief fee, a cross check should then be done. The two figures should be aggregated to see whether the total appears too large or too small for the overall conduct of the case in the Court of Appeal. If the total figure seems to be disproportionately large or disproportionately small, then an appropriate adjustment should be made to the brief fee or the skeleton fee.'[98]

53.55 In summary, the test is an objective test that assumes that counsel is unable or unwilling to insist on the particularly high fees sometimes demanded by counsel of pre-eminent reputation. In applying this test, the court is entitled to take into account all of the facts, including the fees for work other than the hearing itself, but associated with it.[99]

The scope of the brief fee

53.56 The ambit of the brief fee is a central issue for two reasons: first, both counsel and their instructing solicitor must, for the purposes of negotiating it, be aware of what the fee is intended to include; and secondly, the ambit of the fee may be relevant in the assessment of costs if it is said that a fee other than the brief fee ought to be disallowed because the work to which it relates has been included within the brief fee.

53.57 The effect of the principles set out at 53.40 is that (subject to one or two constraints) counsel may negotiate whatever form of remuneration they like. This was not the case when many of the older authorities on the topic were decided.[100] Where counsel has negotiated a different form of remuneration, it would be open the court to look at the total amount claimed in respect of a hearing and then to assess that total as if it were a brief fee. The following points are made on the assumption that either the fee in question is a traditional brief fee or the court has decided to assess the total claimed as if it were a traditional brief fee.

53.58 Hobhouse J has explained that a brief fee covers work done by way of preparation for representation at the hearing and attendance on the first day of the hearing.[101] In addition, Practice Direction (PD) 52, para 14, gives further guidance:

'Advocates' brief (or, where appropriate, refresher) fee includes:
(1) remuneration for taking a note of the judgment of the court;
(2) having the note transcribed accurately;
(3) attempting to agree the note with the other side if represented;
(4) submitting the note to the judge for approval where appropriate;
(5) revising it if so requested by the judge;
(6) providing any copies required for the appeal court, instructing solicitors and lay client; and
(7) providing a copy of his note to an unrepresented appellant.'[102]

---

[98] *Ibid*, at 572.
[99] *Ibid.*
[100] This is because many of those cases were decided under regulations that, for all practical purposes, limited counsel to charging a traditional brief fee.
[101] *Loveday v Renton (No 2)* [1992] 3 All ER 184, at 190.
[102] These provision follow *Practice Note (Barrister: Fees)* [1994] 1 WLR 74, which in turn was based on *Practice Direction of 9 May (Barrister: Fees)* [1989] 1 WLR 605.

The following additional points relate only to the scope of the brief fee; factors relevant to quantum are discussed at 53.67–53.102. **53.59**

Conferences

Cooke J has found that, unless there are exceptional circumstances that change the whole nature of the dispute, the brief fee includes conferences after delivery of the brief.[103] **53.60**

Skeleton arguments

Unless the case is an exceptional one of considerable complexity,[104] a brief fee will include the fee for a skeleton argument.[105] This analysis assumes, of course, that the skeleton argument is for the purposes of the hearing. Regardless of how it was originally formulated, where the skeleton argument relates to an appeal, the statement of costs must show the amount claimed for the skeleton argument separately.[106] **53.61**

Judgment

A brief fee does not include attending at a later date when judgment is given.[107] **53.62**

After-care

Where appropriate, a brief fee includes an allowance for explaining the outcome of the case; Jackson J has referred to that type of work as 'after-care'.[108] It seems that Jackson J was not referred to the principle stated immediately above, however, and there is a tension between these two principles that will have to be resolved on a case-by-case basis. **53.63**

Additional material

There is ancient authority that if additional material is sent to counsel such that counsel has to carry out work that was not envisaged when the brief fee was negotiated, then an additional fee may be allowable.[109] In practice, the additional work would usually be addressed by counsel renegotiating their fee or by the court assessing the totality of the costs as if counsel had renegotiated their fee. **53.64**

Work occasioned by a material change in the case

On a related point, if there is a material change in the case such that counsel has to carry out work that was not envisaged when the brief fee was negotiated, then an additional fee may be allowable, where appropriate. An example would be where a hearing was unexpectedly opposed when it was previously believed to be unopposed.[110] **53.65**

These last two points (at 53.64 and 53.65) are based on old authority and, in the light of the guidance of the more modern authorities mentioned at 53.60 and 53.61, the events that prompted the additional or renegotiated fee would probably have to be unusual, or possibly even exceptional, before the court would regard the extra fees as recoverable. **53.66**

103 *XYZ v Schering Health Care: Oral Contraceptive Litigation* [2004] All ER (D) 577 (Mar), *per* Cooke J.
104 *Chohan v Times Newspapers Ltd* (unreported), 7 September 1998, QBD, *per* Nelson J.
105 *Loveday v Renton (No 2)* [1992] 3 All ER 184, at 191.
106 See PD 52A, para 5.3.
107 *Practice Note (Barristers' Fees)* [1994] 1 WLR 74, at [2]; see also *Practice Note: Brief Fees* [1989] 1 WLR 605, CA.
108 *Hornsby v Clark Kenneth Leventhal (a firm)* [2000] 4 All ER 567, at 572.
109 *Wakefield v Brown* (1874) LR 9 CP 410.
110 *Stephens v Lord Newborough* (1848) 11 Beav 403.

Delivery, Going Short and Abatement

The stage at which it can be said that counsel's brief was delivered

53.67 As between counsel and their instructing solicitor, there are no fetters capable of limiting the stage at which a brief will be said to be delivered. Bespoke, commercially minded arrangements are commonplace, such as staged fees (where counsel's fee will be incurred, and usually paid, at certain predefined stages in the litigation) or escalating fees (where counsel's brief fee will sequentially increase up to the full amount if the matter does not settle). Thus it may be difficult (or impossible) to define 'the' stage at which the brief was said to be delivered.

53.68 The fact that a brief may have been delivered as between counsel and their instructing solicitor does not mean that the court will necessarily find that that was reasonable. In particular, Danckwerts J considered a case in which it was said that counsel's brief had been delivered prematurely (that is, during ongoing negotiations); on the facts of that case, he rejected this submission (placing reliance on the fact that counsel was conducting those negotiations and the brief fee was his only means of remuneration),[111] but it was implicit from his judgment that premature delivery is, in principle, possible.

53.69 A finding that a brief has or has not been delivered in no way ties the court's hands, because the court has significant freedom to allow a reasonable fee regardless of delivery. In particular, the following points may be made.

Where the court finds that there has been delivery

53.70 Jack J has found that 'the old, the very old, rule' that brief fees were payable immediately upon delivery does not fetter the court and had the following to say about the modern approach: 'In short it is today appropriate to take a realistic and practical approach rather than to apply rigidly the old rule that a brief fee becomes payable on delivery of the brief.'[112]

Where the court finds that there has been no delivery

53.71 Although there is no authority specifically on the point, where the court has disallowed the brief fee for want of delivery, the court would be able to rely on counsel's fee agreement for the purposes of allowing a reasonable fee for the work done.[113]

53.72 While the court has considerable freedom to assess the fee without being fettered by any finding of fact as to the date of delivery, that finding is a background fact that may be taken into account in ascertaining the proper fee. An example would be where delivery meant that counsel had to set aside time and rearrange their diary. Whether the brief has been delivered may also be relevant in the sense that it may have a bearing on the liability as between counsel and their instructing solicitor; it may therefore determine the maximum amount payable between opposing parties.

---

[111] *Re Holberton's Settlement Trusts* [1953] 2 All ER 506, at 507.

[112] *Miller v Hales* [2006] EWHC 1717, at [7].

[113] If, eg, the instructions were given before 31 January 2013, the court would be able to rely on Withdrawal of Credit Scheme 1988, para 10, which provides that counsel will be entitled to a reasonable professional rate for work not covered by an agreed fee.

The approach where the brief was delivered at a late stage

The fact that the brief was delivered late is irrelevant to the ascertainment of counsel's fee. Hobhouse J had this to say on the topic: 53.73

> 'It is not uncommon ... that the actual brief is delivered late and the barrister has to start his preparation for his appearance at the trial on the faith of the solicitor's statement that he will deliver a brief; this does not prejudice the assessment of the proper brief fee when the brief is later delivered.'[114]

The effect of carrying out the work before a brief fee has been agreed

On a related point, it may be that the brief was delivered, but there has been a failure to agree a fee before the work was carried out. A paying party might argue that this precludes recovery of any fee that is subsequently claimed in the bill. This would go against the provisions of both the Withdrawal of Credit Scheme 1988 and the new Terms of Work, both of which specifically provide that counsel is entitled to a reasonable fee.[115] 53.74

Morland J has found that a brief fee can be impliedly and retrospectively agreed—in particular, that a solicitor is to be taken to have agreed a fee if it includes that brief fee in a signed bill of costs.[116] Morland J did not have to address the argument that agreements going to quantum cannot be made after the receiving party has become entitled to costs, but that argument could be met by saying that there was no new agreement, but merely discovery of the level of fees that were payable under a pre-existing agreement. 53.75

There is a further mechanism by means of which the court may find that there has been an implied agreement: the solicitor will lose the right to object to the fee if it chooses not to raise an objection during the three-month period after receipt of the fee note (see 53.14).[117] 53.76

Finally, there is no requirement that the fee be marked on the brief. There is no basis under the CPR, the Withdrawal of Credit Scheme 1988 or the new Terms of Work for arguing that the absence of the fee on the brief precludes recovery. 53.77

The effect of adjournments

It may be that counsel is denied a fee because a hearing has been adjourned. Although counsel would be entitled to a fee for the work actually done and thrown away by the adjournment, the fact that they have lost the opportunity to earn the full fee is only a background fact, as Hobhouse J explained: 53.78

> 'The brief fee [relating to the vacated hearing] can only remunerate counsel for the work done on the brief delivered and lost opportunities can only be taken into account as a general background fact to the level of barristers' fees overall in the same way as their overhead expenses and lost time. It is however legitimate for counsel to point to the commitment of time that it involves both for preparation and in the reservation of time for the trial.'[118]

---

[114] *Loveday v Renton (No 2)* [1992] 3 All ER 184, at 192.

[115] See old Terms of Work, para 10(1); new Terms of Work, para 11.

[116] *Spath Holmes Ltd v Chairman of the Greater Manchester and Lancashire Rent Assessment Committee* [1998] 1 Costs LR 40, at 46 and 47.

[117] See 32.16–32.24.

[118] *Loveday v Renton (No 2)* [1992] 3 All ER 184, at 194. It should be noted that (*obiter*) comments made by Leggatt LJ in *Norjarl K/S A/S v Hyundai Heavy Industries Co Ltd* [1991] 3 All ER 211, at 222, have suggested that loss of opportunity is something that can be taken into account.

53.79 It is not wholly clear what weight should be given to that type of background fact. In some cases, the loss of opportunity would be very relevant, even if it were relegated to the status of background fact. Nonetheless, with smaller cases, the practice is to give only marginal weight to loss of opportunity, focusing instead on the work actually done and thrown away. In cases in which adjournment was foreseeable, it is open to the court to find that a fee should have been agreed in advance for the contingency of the matter being adjourned.[119]

The effect of late compromise

53.80 On a related point, it may be that a hearing is vacated because the claim, or part of it, has settled. The starting point is that if a brief has been delivered, the full brief fee is payable.[120] This is only the starting point, because an abatement may be appropriate.

Abatement between counsel and their instructing solicitor

53.81 The Bar Council encourages counsel to renegotiate fees in cases in which it would be appropriate. The renegotiated fee would take into account both the work done and (between counsel and their instructing solicitor) loss of opportunity.

Abatement between opposing parties

53.82 If the matter settles before trial, the court is able to abate counsel's fee to reflect the fact that they did not attend the hearing to which the fee relates. In a matter analogous to late compromise,[121] Hallett J found that the correct measure is not whether counsel had carried out the work, but what proportion of the brief fee is payable, and that it was reasonable to take into account the fact that counsel had to commit time to the hearing and that a commitment fee (as Hallett J called it) was payable.[122] Likewise, Mitting J has confirmed that the brief fee for a full trial or an aborted trial covered the commitment for that trial plus preparation and any negotiations before the trial.[123] He commented that it is irrelevant whether or not counsel was able to take on other work and that it would be wrong to assume that counsel would be able to do so.[124] Whilst *obiter*, Leggatt LJ has explained that, in a case set down for a lengthy hearing, an abated brief fee would normally include an element of compensation for possible loss of refreshers.[125] The following examples illustrate the approach in practice.

53.83 **One to two weeks before the hearing** In a matter that settled 13 days before a three-day trial, Holland J allowed just under a third of the full brief fee,[126] in addition to a conference fee. Holland J commented that the two ought to be considered together; if this approach is taken, he allowed just over a third of the total of the brief fee and the conference fee. It should be noted that Holland J did not state the amount of the unabated brief fee and, as such, the reduction may include an element that is not abatement.

---

119 *Sibley & Co v Reachbyte Ltd* [2008] EWHC 2665 (Ch), at [64]–[66], *per* Peter Smith J.

120 See *Re Holberton's Settlements Trusts* [1953] 1 WLR 1080.

121 A Part 36 offer had been made, which meant that the paying party was liable for costs up to a point shortly before trial, but the matter did not settle until after the trial had started.

122 *Bowcott v Walding* [2003] EWHC 9042 (Costs).

123 *Lewis v The Royal Shrewsbury Hospital* (unreported) 20 May 2005, QBD (summarised as SCCO Summary No 15 of 2005).

124 *Ibid.*

125 *K/S Norjarl A/S v Hyundai Heavy Industries Co Ltd* [1991] 3 All ER 211, at 222.

126 *Martin v Holland & Barrett Ltd* [2002] 3 Costs LR 530.

Two to three weeks before the hearing In a matter set down for a longer period of time than three days,[127] which (for present purposes[128]) can be taken to have settled about 18 days before trial, Hallett J allowed half of the full brief fee. In a clinical negligence claim that settled three weeks before trial[129] and at a stage when little preparation had been carried out, Mitting J found that half the brief fee should be allowed.[130] **53.84**

There is nothing in any of these cases to suggest that they were intended to set a tariff or to establish any points of principle. Indeed, if anything, they demonstrate that each case must be decided on its own facts. **53.85**

The effect of hearings going short

It may be that a hearing goes short (either because the matter is settled at the doors of the court or for some other reason). Where this is the case, counsel would ordinarily be entitled to their full brief fee.[131] This can be justified as a payment based on the principle of swings and roundabouts (that is, some hearings go short, but some last longer than was originally envisaged). **53.86**

The Relevance of Time

It is often said that counsel's fees are not based on an arithmetical analysis of the time spent; indeed, some commentators have put that point with vigour.[132] It is undoubtedly the case that brief fees are not assessed in the same way as solicitors' fees (that is, by mathematically applying a reasonable hourly rate to a reasonable allowance of time) and it is also undoubtedly the case that there is 'no precise standard of measurement' of brief fees, to use Pennycuick J's words.[133] Thus time is not a factor that should determine the fee and, to that extent, those commentators are correct. **53.87**

It is, however, a moot point whether time is as unimportant as it was a decade or so ago. In a relatively recent case, Cooke J confirmed that whilst it was not appropriate to determine a brief fee by having regard solely to an hourly rate, time was a factor to be taken into account when determining the appropriate fee.[134] Indeed, there are recent examples of the court determining in a *quantitative* way the time that would have been reasonably spent in preparation and then using that figure to ascertain the appropriate fee[135]—an approach that was rarely seen a decade or so ago. **53.88**

---

[127] *Bowcott v Walding* [2003] EWHC 9042 (Costs). The case report does not state the exact length.

[128] *Ibid.* The matter was more complex than a straightforward settlement, but those complexities are not relevant to the topic in hand.

[129] Unfortunately, the case summary does not state the length of the trial.

[130] *Lewis v The Royal Shrewsbury Hospital* (unreported), 20 May 2005, QBD (summarised as SCCO Summary No 15 of 2005).

[131] See, eg, *Re a Company (No 004081 of 1989)* [1995] 2 All ER 155; see also *Charman v Brandon* (1900) 82 LT 369.

[132] See *Butterworths Costs Service*, J:III:202, in which HHJ Peter Birts QC explains the benefits of charging by the item, rather than by the hour.

[133] *Simpsons Motor Sales (London) v Hendon Borough Council* [1965] 1 WLR 112, at 118.

[134] *XYZ v Schering Health Care: Oral Contraceptive Litigation* [2004] All ER (D) 577 (Mar); see also *Global Marine Drillships Ltd v La Bella* [2010] EWHC 2498 (Ch), at [13], *per* Peter Smith J.

[135] *Orwin v British Coal Corpn* [2003] EWHC 757 (Ch), at [11]–[14]; see also *Hornsby v Clark Kenneth Leventhal (a firm)* [2000] 4 All ER 567, at 573.

53.89 Even if time is a factor that is becoming increasingly important, care must be taken not to give disproportionate weight to the time reasonably spent. Although it did not deal specifically with counsel, art 11.3 of the Costs Practice Direction (CPD) used to give the following guidance:

> 'Where a trial takes place, the time taken by the court in dealing with a particular issue may not be an accurate guide to the amount of time properly spent by the legal or other representatives in preparation for the trial of that issue.'

53.90 In summary, time is a factor to be taken into account, but it would be wrong to afford it greater weight than it deserves.

The Use of Comparators

53.91 Many other comparisons may be made, but three types of comparator are often relied upon in practice:

- the amount charged by opposing counsel;
- the amount charged by other lawyers on the same side; and
- the amount previously charged by the barrister whose fees are being assessed.

Comparators (opponents)

53.92 The fee charged by opposing counsel is relevant, but it should not be given disproportionate weight, as Pennycuick J emphasised:

> '[The fee charged by an opponent] is certainly a factor of weight but not, I think, by any means conclusive. In the ordinary course of events it often happens that the clerks to counsel of comparable degree ask for rather different fees, but I do not think that in these circumstances one is justified without more ado in saying that one counsel has asked too much. It can equally be said that the other has asked too little. The truth is that there is no exact figure which can be said to represent the proper fee.'[136]

53.93 As with any comparator, like should be compared with like. It may be necessary to consider the appropriateness of the comparator, as well as the weight that it should be afforded. Care should be taken where the comparator counsel has had the benefit of being able to read their opponent's submissions before beginning their own preparation.[137] Sir Charles Gray has warned that where comparators are taken into account, it is necessary to consider them carefully to exclude those that are inappropriate or misleading.[138]

53.94 It would be wrong to give disproportionate weight to an opponent's fees; nevertheless, this does not mean that comparators will be only a minor factor. In a pre-CPR case, Romer J found that there were circumstances in which it could be implied that counsel whose fees were being assessed had done at least as much work as their opponent and that the first counsel's fee should therefore not be lower.[139] Where inexplicable differences exist

136 *Simpsons Motor Sales (London) v Hendon Borough Council* [1965] 1 WLR 112, at 119.

137 See *Hornsby v Clark Kenneth Leventhal (a firm)* [2000] 4 All ER 567, at 573 (relating to fees of counsel on the same side).

138 See, eg, *Lord Chancellor v Rees* [2008] EWHC 3168 (QB), at [63], in which Sir Charles Gray found that it was not appropriate to use privately payable fees as comparators for publically funded work.

139 *Re Bennett (Viscount), Barclays Bank Ltd* [1950] 1 All ER 435.

between the fees in question and the comparator's fees, that is a factor that may be afforded weight.[140] Commenting on the changes brought about by the CPR, Lawrence Collins J indicated that summary assessment has led to comparison being a more important factor than it was in the past and that this was also true of detailed assessments.[141]

Comparators (same side)

Where leading and junior counsel are both instructed, it is often the case that the junior counsel's fee is allowed as a fixed proportion of that of the leading counsel. This topic is addressed in more detail at 53.119–53.123. Occasionally, it will be appropriate to take into account the fees charged by counsel's instructing solicitors (but usually only in a way that affords them very little weight). The Guide to the Summary Assessment of Costs makes the following observations about counsel's fees in the Court of Appeal: 'Where both Counsel and solicitors have been instructed, the reasonable fees of Counsel are likely to exceed the reasonable fees of the solicitor.'[142] Presumably, if counsel's fees were lower than those of their instructing solicitors, the court might take this into account as an indicator that counsel's fees were reasonable. **53.95**

Comparators (fees previously charged)

There used to be a custom that brief fees in the Court of Appeal were to be the same as those in the court below,[143] but that custom seems to have fallen by the wayside (although it stills seems to be relevant in so far as refreshers are concerned).[144] The fee claimed previously is now merely a factor that the court may take into account in appropriate circumstances. The Guide to the Summary Assessment of Costs makes the following observations about counsel's fees in the Court of Appeal: **53.96**

> '(3) The fact that the same Counsel appeared in the lower court does not greatly reduce the reasonable fee unless, for example, the lower court dealt with a great many more issues than are raised on the appeal. It is reasonable for Counsel to spend as much time preparing issues for the Court of Appeal hearing as he spent preparing those issues for the lower court hearing.'[145]

Other Factors Relevant to Quantum

'Going rate'

Whilst it is a difficult factor to identify and describe, both judicial[146] and extrajudicial[147] comments support the notion that the court takes into account a 'going rate'. This, presumably, is a way of referring to the judge's own experience. **53.97**

---

[140] *Lord Chancellor v Wright* [1993] 1 WLR 1561.

[141] *Orwin v British Coal Corpn* [2003] EWHC 757 (Ch), at [12].

[142] HM Courts & Tribunals Service, *Guide to the Summary Assessment of Costs* (London: HMSO, 2011), para 65.

[143] *Sunnucks v Smith* [1950] 1 All ER 550.

[144] *Hornsby v Clark Kenneth Leventhal (a firm)* [2000] 4 All ER 567, at 574.

[145] See HM Courts & Tribunals Service, *Guide to the Summary Assessment of Costs* (London: HMSO, 2011), para 65.

[146] See, eg, the comments of Cazalet J in *H v H (Financial Relief: Costs)* [1995] 1 FCR 718, sub nom *Re H (a minor)* [1995] 2 FCR 733; see also *F v F (Ancillary Relief: Costs)* [1995] 2 FLR 702, at 710.

[147] See *Butterworths Costs Service*, J:III:266, in which HHJ Birts QC has indicated that this is a factor that is habitually taken into account.

London counsel and local bar

53.98 The availability of a local bar may be a factor to be taken into account,[148] but there is authority to show that where the local bar is able to offer only a small number of suitable counsel, the instruction of London counsel can be justified.[149]

Work outside business hours

53.99 There is authority for the proposition that counsel is expected to work at unsociable hours from time to time and that no extra remuneration is to be allowed for this.[150] That said, the urgency of the work may be a factor to be taken into account and where urgent work needs to be done in the long vacation of the courts, a higher fee may be appropriate to take account of the fact that counsel may be kept waiting for a judge.[151]

Researching the law

53.100 This is a topic that is addressed in detail at 49.117–49.120; the principles for solicitor and counsel are broadly the same. Common sense dictates that counsel who is instructed as a specialist will be deemed to know a greater part of the relevant law than those who instruct them.

Travelling

53.101 Although the context was public funding, Sachs J has confirmed that an allowance may be made if counsel is required to travel to attend court.[152] That said, Mitting J has commented that counsel could ordinarily be expected to work whilst on a train journey and that no time ought ordinarily to be allowed for travelling—although he accepted that there will be occasions on which travelling times could not be usefully spent.[153] In practice, Sachs J's approach seems generally to be preferred (not least because counsel is able to decline instructions if the fee is insufficient to cover the expenses they will incur).[154] There are limits to what counsel can claim, however—in particular, there is no legal basis for counsel being allowed a 'special fee' to compensate them for inconvenient travel.[155]

Overlap between cases

53.102 There is old authority that if counsel has more than one case in the same court, their fee would be assessed on the basis that the only case they had was the case in question.[156] Each case must be decided on its own facts, however, and there would be no reason why the court could not take into account the factual background created by counsel's involvement in the other case(s).

---

[148] See, eg, Wallington J's *obiter* comment in *Young v Young and Kohler* [1955] 1 All ER 796; see also *Eaves v Eaves and Powell* [1956] P 154.

[149] *Self v Self* [1954] 2 All ER 550, at 551; *Raybould v Raybould* [1968] 1 All ER 608.

[150] *R v Mills and Morris* [1997] 1 Costs LR 49.

[151] *Global Marine Drillships Ltd v La Bella* [2010] EWHC 2498 (Ch), at [8] and [14], *per* Peter Smith J.

[152] *Self v Self* [1954] 2 All ER 550, at 551.

[153] *Lewis v The Royal Shrewsbury Hospital* (unreported), 20 May 2005, QBD (summarised as SCCO Summary No 15 of 2005).

[154] See BSB Handbook, gC90 and rC30.8. Prior to 6 January 2014, see old Code of Conduct, para 604(b)(iii).

[155] *The Warkworth* (1885) 1 TLR 659, CA. Such fees used to be required by circuit rules: see *Payne v Schmidt* [1949] 2 All ER 741 for a discussion of this.

[156] *Isaacs v Isaacs* [1955] 2 All ER 811, at 812.

Refreshers

According to dramatist Reynolds, 'barristers . . . can only be kept alive by refreshers'.[157] The word 'refresher' used to refer to a fee paid on an adjournment, but its use is now limited to a fee payable for appearing on the second or subsequent days of a hearing. To an extent, the points made about brief fees apply to refreshers; the following additional points may be made. **53.103**

Abated refresher

It has long been established that it is open to the court to find that a refresher should be reduced if a case lasts only a short part of a day. Where the court does this, the allowance should be based on a fair fee and should not be a mere mechanical calculation based on the number of hours actually spent in court.[158] **53.104**

Comparators (fees previously charged)

Jackson J has commented that the refreshers charged in the lower court may be relevant to the refresher claimed in an appeal court.[159] This may be a particularly helpful comparator because the level and intensity of the work would usually be directly comparable, especially in a second appeal. **53.105**

Obsolete authorities

Refreshers used to be determined by the application of the 'five-hour rule'.[160] That rule has no counterpart under the CPR, but it is worth being aware of it for two reasons: first, because obsolete authorities ought to be recognised as such; and secondly, because it has given rise to a number of decisions about what is and is not time spent 'in court'. Denning MR, for example, found that the lunch hour is not time spent in court;[161] another example is that the time with the judge in chambers is equivalent to time in court.[162] The relevance of these cases under the CPR is peripheral at best, but they may occasionally be encountered when the court assesses the appropriate refresher on the basis of the time spent in court.[163] **53.106**

Hourly Charging

Much of counsel's working day is spent carrying out work that will be charged by the hour. In particular, drafting pleadings, drafting advices, advising in conference, etc, will usually be charged on this basis. Even if they have not been charged on this basis, it would be open to the court to assess the reasonable costs by reference to the time spent—but only as one factor amongst others (see 53.87–53.90). **53.107**

---

157 Reynolds, F, *A Playwright's Adventures* (London: Longman, Rees, Orme, Brown, & Green, 1831), p 108.

158 Although decided under the 'five-hour rule', the analysis set out in *Re Mercury Model Aircraft Supplies Ltd* [1956] 1 WLR 1153 still has resonance under the CPR.

159 *Hornsby v Clark Kenneth Leventhal (a firm)* [2000] 4 All ER 567, at 574.

160 RSC Ord 65, r 27(48).

161 *Wright v Bennett* [1947] KB 828.

162 *Lawson v Tiger* [1953] 1 WLR 503.

163 See, eg, *Sibley & Co v Reachbyte Ltd* [2008] EWHC 2665 (Ch), at [67], *per* Peter Smith J.

Advices

53.108 The distinction between preliminary opinions and advices[164] is obsolete, and ought not to be made under the CPR. In particular, there is no rule that preliminary opinions will, in general, not be allowed.

Conferences and consultations

53.109 Conferences are usually charged at an hourly rate,[165] but conferences that take place after delivery of the brief may be covered by the brief fee.[166] The same is true of consultations with leading counsel.

Counsel's view

53.110 A counsel's 'view' is a site visit. Unless it is part and parcel of the brief fee, a reasonable fee may be charged on the basis of time spent.[167]

Skeleton arguments

53.111 Skeleton arguments may be charged by the hour or on an item-by-item basis; they may also be charged as part of a brief fee (see 53.54). Regardless of how it was originally formulated, where the skeleton argument relates to an appeal, the statement of costs must show the amount claimed for the skeleton argument separately.[168] Toulson LJ has noted that there is a tendency towards prolixity, describing the 132-page document before him as 'a grotesque example of a tendency to burden the court with documents of grossly disproportionate quantity and length'.[169] The full costs of such documents are not likely to be recoverable. In a similar vein, Mummery LJ said this:

> 'We remind practitioners that skeleton arguments should not be prepared as verbatim scripts to be read out in public or as footnoted theses to be read in private. Good skeleton arguments are tools with practical uses: an agenda for the hearing, a summary of the main points, propositions and arguments to be developed orally, a useful way of noting citations and references, a convenient place for making cross references, a time-saving means of avoiding unnecessary dictation to the court and laborious and pointless note-taking by the court.'[170]

53.112 Specific provisions apply where the skeleton argument is for an appeal. The cost of preparing a skeleton argument that does not comply with those requirements will not be allowed on assessment except to the extent that the court directs otherwise.[171] Similarly, if a skeleton argument for an appeal was not filed within the time limits provided by PD 52A (or any further time granted by the court), then the costs will be disallowed save to the extent that the court orders otherwise.[172]

---

164 See *Practice Direction (Counsel's Fees)* [1957] 1 WLR 839.

165 If authority were needed on the point, it can be found in *Re Cosedge* (1885) 29 SJ.

166 *XYZ v Schering Health Care: Oral Contraceptive Litigation* [2004] All ER (D) 577 (Mar), *per* Cooke J.

167 If authority were needed on the point, it can be found at *Leeds Forge Company Ltd v Deighton's Patent Flue and Tube Co Ltd* [1903] 1 Ch 475.

168 See PD 52A, para 5.3.

169 *Midgulf International Ltd v Groupe Chimiche Tunisien* (2010) EWCA Civ 66, at [71] *et seq.*

170 *Tombstone Ltd v Raja* [2008] EWCA Civ 1444, at [125].

171 See PD 52A, para 5.1(5)(a).

172 See PD 52A, para 5.1(5)(b).

Other documents

Not all work carried out by counsel will be capable of being neatly compartmentalised into a category such as those mentioned above. The fact that work is of an unusual nature will not, of itself, prevent a fee being charged.[173] **53.113**

Fees Per Item

Another method of ascertaining counsel's costs is on an item-by-item basis. The time spent is often a major factor in determining the appropriate fee, but there will be occasions on which this is not the predominant factor. An example would be where a skeleton argument has been prepared for a hearing, but has been prepared so far in advance of the hearing that a separate fee has been charged, in which case a simple hourly rate would not be appropriate because of the possibility of overlap between the work done in preparing the skeleton argument and the work done in preparing for the hearing. Jackson J explained this thus: **53.114**

> 'The process of drafting a skeleton argument has the effect of at least partially preparing an advocate to argue his case in court. Thus, there is an overlap between the work which is covered by a skeleton argument fee and the work which is covered by a brief fee. If the skeleton argument is drafted shortly before the hearing, then the overlap is greater than it would be if the skeleton argument is drafted far in advance of the hearing.'[174]

While he did not purport to lay down any point of principle, Jackson J's approach to assessing a fee for a skeleton argument prepared in advance of the hearing was as follows.[175] **53.115**

(1) He found, as a matter of fact, the number of hours spent in preparing it.
(2) He reduced that figure to a reasonable and proportionate figure.
(3) He allowed a figure that was based on all of the factors, including the figure mentioned above and the fee that was claimed.
(4) He carried out a 'cross-check', in that he ensured that when the brief fee and the skeleton argument were combined, they did not exceed a sum that was reasonable and disproportionate.

As can be seen, although Jackson J's approach was not limited to ascertaining a reasonable time, the time reasonably spent was a significant factor in his adjudication.

Retainers (or Commitment Fees)

A retainer is an obsolete arrangement in which a client pays a fee for the right to call upon counsel generally in the future to provide advice or advocacy services. The phrase 'commitment fee' may also be used to refer to such an arrangement. They are to be distinguished from booking fees (see 53.118), which are fees for specific professional services to be supplied and are payable in anticipation of counsel carrying out specific work or being available for a specific period of time. A retainer differs from a booking fee in that it lacks the **53.116**

---

[173] See, eg, *D v D* [2002] EWHC 2511 (Fam), in which counsel was allowed a fee for drafting an accountancy schedule.
[174] *Hornsby v Clark Kenneth Leventhal (a firm)* [2000] 4 All ER 567, at 572.
[175] *Ibid*, at 573 and 574.

specificity of a booking fee. 'General retainers' used to exist, which debarred counsel from acting against that client in any matter; not only are such arrangements now antediluvian, but also they are regarded as professionally impermissible (because, in the absence of a true conflict, such an arrangement would be an affront to the cab-rank rule and the free availability of legal services).[176] 'Special retainers' (or 'common retainers') relate only to a specified matters and their effect is to debar counsel from accepting instructions from other parties; these too are likely to be impermissible, at least up to the point at which specific instructions are given.[177] In any event, whilst there is no authority on the point, it is likely that, in an appropriate case, it would be open to the court to disallow a retainer fee on the basis that it was a solicitor-and-client expense.

53.117 While speaking in the context of retainers for arbitrators, rather than counsel, Stuart-Smith LJ has made it clear that once a retainer has been agreed and paid, a further retainer would be justified only if there were a change of circumstances.[178] In the same case, Leggatt LJ made the following comments about a proposal to charge a retainer of 100 per cent for a period of 60 days:

> 'The arbitrators' original requirement of a 100% commitment fee was more than was required to protect them against loss. In those circumstances to refer to the commitment fee as "earned" by the instalments demanded was an abuse of language. A fee is only earned if and in so far as a hearing takes place. Yet payment was demanded for being available to conduct it, irrespective of whether the arbitrators did any work or not, or ... as protection against the risk of *not* working ... The notion that, if the arbitration were settled before it started, these particular arbitrators would find themselves unemployed for the whole of the period set aside (assuming that they then held themselves out as available to accept instructions) seems little short of absurd.'[179]

It is clear from what Leggatt LJ had to say that retainers must be reasonable and that it would not be reasonable to treat retainers as brief fees.

Booking fees

53.118 A booking fee is a fee paid to counsel for the purposes of counsel carrying out specific work in the future or of counsel being available to carry out work at a specific time. Booking fees, unlike retainers, are professionally permissible.[180] The question of whether the arrangement is permissible will depend on whether the fee can be said to be incurred for identifiable professional services supplied or to be supplied.[181] For example, where a barrister agrees to keep themselves free to undertake a particular piece of work, they are at liberty to charge a non-refundable fee, but only if that fee is genuinely a payment in respect of the work it is

176 See Bar Council's Professional Practice Committee, *Retainers and other Fee Arrangements* (December 2014), available online at http://www.barcouncil.org.uk/media/321222/retainers_and_novel_fee_arrangements.pdf

177 See *ibid.*

178 *Norjarl K/S A/S v Hyundai Heavy Industries Co Ltd* [1991] 3 All ER 211.

179 *Ibid*, at 222, emphasis original.

180 See Bar Council's Professional Practice Committee, *Retainers and other Fee Arrangements* (December 2014), available online at http://www.barcouncil.org.uk/media/321222/retainers_and_novel_fee_arrangements.pdf

181 See *ibid.* See also BSB Handbook, gC18.3.

anticipated will be carried out. It does not matter that counsel may ultimately be relieved of the burden of actually doing the work. Similarly, it is permissible for counsel to be paid a fee for blocking out a defined period of time in their diary for a specific case.[182] If, however, the fee is merely for counsel 'agreeing to act' in respect of a particular matter (but not for undertaking any further obligation), the fee would probably be regarded as an impermissible specific retainer.[183]

Leading Counsel

Giving judgment in the Divisional Court, Woolf LJ explained that the appropriate test is whether the receiving party acted reasonably in instructing its choice of counsel and not whether more junior counsel could have dealt adequately with the case.[184] **53.119**

The following relevant factors were listed by Evans J (albeit in the context of whether both leading and junior counsel were required): **53.120**

'(a) the nature of the case;
(b) its importance for the client;[[185]]
(c) the amount of damages likely to be recovered;
(d) the general importance of the case, eg as affecting other cases;
(e) any particular requirements of the case, eg the need for legal advice, or for special expertise, eg witnesses; and
(f) other claims why experienced and senior advocate may be required.'[186]

Evans J went on to say that, in personal injury claims, the following may be relevant: **53.121**

'(1) The nature and severity of the plaintiff's injury.
(2) The likely duration of the trial.
(3) Difficult questions regarding the quantum of damages including medical evidence and questions of law.
(4) Difficult questions of fact, including expert engineering evidence, or issues as to causation.'[187]

Whether the other side has instructed a leader is relevant, but not conclusive.[188] **53.122**

Each case will turn on its own facts, but there are some circumstances in which leading counsel's involvement would be hard to justify. In particular, Lindsay J has commented that it could not be said to be necessary, or even usual, for leading counsel to attend a hearing when all that was required was a simple assent on their client's behalf to terms already agreed.[189] In a case in which leading counsel had been instructed to represent a **53.123**

[182] Bar Council's Professional Practice Committee, *Retainers and other Fee Arrangements* (December 2014), available online at http://www.barcouncil.org.uk/media/321222/retainers_and_novel_fee_arrangements.pdf
[183] *Ibid.*
[184] *R v Dudley Magistrates' Court, ex p Power City Stores Ltd* (1990) 154 JP 654.
[185] As an example of a higher fee being allowed on the basis of importance (amongst other factors), see *Global Marine Drillships Ltd v La Bella* [2010] EWHC 2498 (Ch), at [13], in which Peter Smith J allowed a high fee on the basis that whilst the application was short, it concerned a person's liberty.
[186] *Juby v LFCDA and Saunders v Essex County Council* (unreported), 24 April 1990, QBD, at the third paragraph after the heading 'Was it reasonable to instruct a leader?'.
[187] *Ibid*, at the fourth paragraph after the same heading.
[188] *British Metal Corpn Ltd v Ludlow Bros* [1938] Ch 987.
[189] *Re a Company (No 004081 of 1989)* [1995] 2 All ER 155, at 157.

client at a permission-to-appeal hearing before the Court of Appeal, Bean J found that it was reasonable to instruct leading counsel, largely because it was potentially the last opportunity that the client would have to put his case and also because the issues were of some public importance.[190] As to the quantum of leading counsel's fees, counsel who has recently taken silk would often charge as though still a junior, but there is no rule that would compel that counsel to do this, either during the first year after taking silk or otherwise.

Two Counsel

53.124 There is no prohibition against two juniors being instructed,[191] but it is usual that where two counsel are instructed, at least one of them will be leading counsel. Where this is so, the points made immediately above would be relevant. After having set out the questions mentioned at 53.120 and 53.121, Evans J went on to explain that there may be many reasons why a junior would be necessary for proper conduct of the case, such as to provide the following types of assistance:

> '(a) to assist the court proceedings either by taking an active part (examining or cross-examining some witnesses or dealing with a discreet part of the case, eg expert evidence, damage, etc) or by keeping a full note of the evidence, editing transcripts, etc;
> (b) dealing with documents generally, particularly when the junior counsel has taken part in discovery;
> (c) to carry out legal and other research, eg on matters on which expert evidence is given;
> (d) to assist leading counsel in negotiations with the other party, particularly when, as in many accident cases, junior counsel has already advised the litigant in person and has become known to him. The lay client might well fail to understand why the junior who has dealt with the case up to the trial should no longer be present when his claim is settled by negotiation or dealt with by judgment.'[192]

53.125 It may be relevant to the issue of reasonableness that where more than one counsel is instructed, they have a duty to consider whether it would be in the best interest of their lay client for fewer of them to be instructed.[193] For obvious reasons, counsel's conclusion would not bind the court, but where there was evidence that counsel had considered this issue and concluded that more than one counsel was required, it would be open to the court to take that fact into account. Where there are co-parties and where there is no conflict between them, then the costs of separate representation may not be justified[194]—particularly in the context of appeals, because the issues will be well defined. Lord Keith has commented that, where appropriate, it is the duty of counsel to consider this issue carefully.[195]

---

190 *McCrea v Herefordshire Council* (unreported), 18 June 2014, QBD.

191 *Douglas v Associated Newspapers* (1922) 67 Sol Jo 48.

192 *Juby v LFCDA and Saunders v Essex County Council* (unreported), 24 April 1990, QBD, at the sixth paragraph after the heading 'If a leader is instructed, should a junior be instructed also?'.

193 Whilst now superseded, see the old Code of Conduct (as it was prior to 6 January 2014), para 606.2.

194 *Birmingham City Council v H (a minor)* [1994] 2 WLR 31, at 33, *per* Lord Keith. More recently, see *Commission for Equality & Human Rights v Griffin* [2011] EWHC 675 (Admin), at [16], *per* Moore-Bick LJ.

195 *Birmingham City Council v H (a minor)* [1994] 2 WLR 31, at 33.

In contrast to criminal costs,[196] there is no rule in civil cases setting any ratio determining the amount of leading and junior counsel's fees.[197] There used to be a convention in civil litigation that the junior's fee should be either a half or two-thirds that of their leader,[198] but this was merely a custom, rather than a rule of law. **53.126**

Nonetheless, whilst it is not a rule of law, that ratio is often used as a rule of thumb. Where the court does apply it, a ratio of between a half and two-thirds would usually be taken as the appropriate measure. Nonetheless, Garland J has explained that the court should look at the time spent and the work actually carried out.[199] In a similar vein, Cazalet J explained that each case must be decided on its own facts: **53.127**

> 'In a normal case I would expect 50% broadly to reflect the division of responsibility, effort and the other factors ... There will be cases, however, where the burden of the preparation and argument is borne by leading counsel and where junior counsel has performed little more than a noting function. In these cases 50% of leading counsel's fee will be well beyond the remuneration for junior counsel ... Moving to the other extreme there will be cases in which junior counsel may carry out the vast proportion of the preparation for trial and make a most substantial input to the case. In such circumstances 50% would be unlikely to reflect his contribution and a fee of or approaching two-thirds of leading counsel's fee could well be appropriate.'[200]

The Guide to the Summary Assessment of Costs 2005, for example, gives the following guidance about summary assessments in the Court of Appeal: **53.128**

> '(4) If the case merits leading Counsel it may merit also the instruction of a junior to assist him. The junior's fees should be allowed at one half of the leader's fees unless:
> - the junior is a senior junior and the case merited both a leader and a senior junior.
> - The junior took a responsibility which was equal to or larger than that taken by the leader.
> - The junior undertook work not covered by the brief.'[201]

Although it would be uncommon, it is not unknown for the junior's fee to equal, or even exceed, that of their leader.[202]

Whilst each case will turn on its own facts, the following points can be made about the use of two counsel. **53.129**

- **Arbitration** It is unusual for more than one counsel to be allowed on a reference for arbitration.[203]
- **Unopposed claims** Whilst it would be a factor to take into account, the fact that a claim is unopposed would not necessarily result in disallowance of the fee of second counsel.[204]

---

[196] See, eg, Crown Prosecution Service, *Fees Guidance* (1 April 1995), para 5.

[197] There is, however, some authority that 50 per cent is the starting point: see *Perloff v Gordon Dadds & Co* (1989) The Independent, 20 November, *per* Webster J.

[198] See, eg, *Practice Direction (Refresher Fees to Counsel)* [1959] 1 WLR 350.

[199] *Matthews v Dorkin* [2000] All ER (D) 1584.

[200] *F v F (Ancillary Relief: Costs)* [1995] 2 FLR 702, at 710.

[201] HM Courts & Tribunals Service, *Guide to the Summary Assessment of Costs* (London: HMSO, 2011), para 65.

[202] See, eg, *Matthews v Dorkin* [2000] All ER (D) 351, *per* Garland J.

[203] *Drew v Josolyne* (1888) 4 TLR 717, DC.

[204] *Friend v Solly* (1847) 10 Beav 329.

Informal Arrangements between Counsel (devilling)

53.130 It will occasionally be the case that counsel will seek assistance from another barrister (often a pupil or very junior barrister) for the purposes of examining factual material, carrying out legal research, etc. This practice is called devilling. Where counsel devils work to another barrister, counsel is entitled to charge the other barrister's fee as if they were counsel's own (although they will be responsible for paying the other barrister).[205] This means that the devil's fee would usually be subsumed; it would rarely be the case that a devil's fee would appear as a separate item, either in counsel's fee note or in the bill of costs.

More than two Counsel

53.131 In general, the court will be reluctant to allow the fees of more than two counsel at any one hearing.[206] Indeed, even on a solicitor-and-client basis, the costs of instructing more than two counsel would require justification and, in particular, it would often be regarded as 'unusual' for the purposes of CPR, r 48.8(2).[207]

53.132 The decision will ultimately be for the costs judge, but where three counsel have been instructed, the trial judge will often express a view as to whether that was reasonable.[208]

53.133 Whether it was reasonable to instruct three or more counsel is a topic that is particularly fact-sensitive. The following are examples of the types of case in which three counsel may be justified:

- ongoing group litigation lasting many years;[209]
- cases requiring significant legal research;[210]
- cases involving extremely lengthy and detailed pleadings;[211] and
- ongoing cases involving significant examination of scientific experts.[212]

53.134 The following would *not* generally be regarded as justifying the employment of three counsel:

- concerns about counsel's availability;[213]
- junior counsel originally instructed taking silk;[214] and

---

205 Whilst now superseded, see the old Code of Conduct (as it was prior to 6 January 2014), para 406.

206 See, eg, *Mercedes Daimler Motor Co Ltd v FIAT Motor Cab Co Ltd* (1913) 31 RPC 8.

207 See *Re Broad and Broad* (1885) 15 QBD 252, DC.

208 This was the guidance of the Court of Appeal in *Fluflon Ltd v William Frost & Sons Ltd* [1965] RPC 574. As an example of this, see *Mahme Trust Reg & Ors v Lloyds TSB Bank plc* [2006] EWHC 1782 (Ch), at [30], *per* Evans-Lombe J.

209 *AB & Ors v British Coal Corpn* [2006] EWCA Civ 987, in which the litigation (or, more accurately, a court-managed compensation scheme) lasted for over a decade.

210 See, eg, *Carl Zeiss Stiftung v Rayner & Keeler Ltd (No 2)* [1965] Ch 596, [1965] 1 All ER 300, CA, in which the issues involved wasted costs and conflict of law.

211 See, eg, *Mahme Trust Reg & Ors v Lloyds TSB Bank plc* [2006] EWHC 1782 (Ch), at [30], *per* Evans-Lombe J—although it should be noted that costs in that case were payable on the indemnity basis.

212 See, eg, *Great Western Rly Co v Carpalla United China Clay Co Ltd (No 2)* [1909] 2 Ch 471, in which counsel had to prepare 'examination of varied scientific theories and investigations'.

213 *Perry & Co Ltd v Hessin & Co* (1913) 108 LT 332.

214 *Betts v Cleaver* (1872) 20 WR 732.

- as a result of a professional rule or custom.[215]

Evans-Lombe J has implied that the use of three counsel should be kept under review, especially as the issues are narrowed and the intensity of the work is reduced.[216]

The New Terms of Work

The contract set out below is the Bar Council's draft contract, published in 2012. It was not agreed with the Law Society prior to publication. The Law Society has made a number of comments about it.[217] Where relevant, these are noted. The Law Society has also said that solicitors should give thought to including the following paragraphs in the agreements: **53.135**

> '4.6 The Barrister shall not be entitled under any circumstances to exercise any lien over all or part of his Instructions.
>
> 11.5 Where a charging rate and an estimated time for the work have been agreed, the Barrister shall notify the Authorised Person promptly if more work than had been estimated is required, and shall give the firm a reasonable opportunity, taking into account the urgency of the matter, to accept or refuse the performance of such additional work.
>
> 12.7 If a fee note or part of it is the subject of a challenge, the Authorised Person shall be under no obligation to pay to the Barrister all or any of the fees specified (save for those fees not the subject of the challenge) or all of any interest on such fees until payment is ordered by a tribunal or the challenge is withdrawn, abandoned or compromised by the Authorised Person.
>
> 12.8 Where the Lay Client has made a complaint to the Legal Ombudsman or any other regulatory body or has indicated that he will be issuing proceedings against the Barrister in respect of all or part of the service that is the subject of this Agreement, the fees charged in the fee note in respect of that service shall not be payable to the Barrister until the complaint, proceedings or pre-action process have been resolved by agreement, disciplinary proceedings, arbitration award, or court order, have been withdrawn or confirmed by the Authorised Person to have been abandoned, or, following the giving of a formal written notice, the pre-action process, complaint, or proceedings have not been brought or commenced within 4 (four) months after the date of such notice, whichever is the earlier.'[218]

THE (NEW) STANDARD CONTRACTUAL TERMS FOR THE SUPPLY OF LEGAL SERVICES BY BARRISTERS TO AUTHORISED PERSONS 2012—
STANDARD CONDITIONS OF CONTRACT FOR THE SUPPLY OF LEGAL SERVICES BY BARRISTERS TO AUTHORISED PERSONS 2012

1. DEFINITIONS AND INTERPRETATION

1.1 In these Conditions of Contract for the Supply of Services by Barristers to Authorised Persons (as defined below) ("the Conditions"):

1.1.1 reference to a clause is to the relevant clause of these Conditions;

1.1.2 headings are included for convenience only and do not affect the interpretation of these Conditions;

1.1.3 references to "parties" or a "party" are references to the parties or a party to the Agreement;

---

215 *Payne v Schmidt* [1949] 2 All ER 741.

216 *Mahme Trust Reg & Ors v Lloyds TSB Bank plc* [2006] EWHC 1782 (Ch), at [30], *per* Evans-Lombe J.

217 See Law Society, *Practice Note: Instructing a Barrister—New Standard Contractual Terms* (24 January 2013).

218 See *ibid*. Note that the numbering is the editor's own suggestion.

1.1.4 references to the masculine include the feminine and references to the singular include the plural and vice versa in each case;

1.1.5 references to a person include bodies corporate (including limited liability partnerships) and partnerships, in each case whether or not having a separate legal personality, except where the context requires otherwise;

1.1.6 references to an Act of Parliament, statutory provision or statutory instrument include a reference to that Act of Parliament, statutory provision or statutory instrument as amended, extended or re-enacted from time to time and to any regulations made under it;

1.1.7 references to any provision of the Code include references to that provision as amended replaced or renumbered from time to time; and

1.1.8 references to a person or body include references to its successor.

1.2 In these Conditions, the following words have the following meanings, except where the context requires otherwise:

"the Agreement"

the agreement between the Barrister and the Authorised Person for the Barrister to provide the Services on the terms set out in these Conditions;

"the Authorised Person"

the person who is an authorised person for the purposes of s. 18(1)(a) of the Legal Services Act 2007 and whose approved regulator under that Act is the Law Society and/or the SRA, and all successors and assignees;

"the Barrister"

the barrister, practising as a member of the Bar of England & Wales, who is willing and able in that capacity to provide the Services in connection with the Case and in accordance with the Instructions from the Authorised Person on behalf of the Lay Client;

"the Case"

the particular legal dispute or matter, whether contentious or non-contentious, in respect of which the Barrister is Instructed to provide the Services;

"the Code"

the Code of Conduct of the Bar of England and Wales, as amended from time to time;

"Conditional Fee Agreement"

the meaning ascribed to those words by section 58 of the Courts and Legal Services Act 1990;

"the Instructions"

the briefs, instructions and requests for work to be done (and all accompanying materials) given by the Authorised Person to the Barrister in whatever manner to enable him to supply the Services, and "Instruct" and "Instructing" shall have corresponding meanings;

"Invoice"

includes a fee note not amounting to a VAT invoice

"the Law Society"

the Law Society of England and Wales

"the Lay Client"

the person for whose benefit or on behalf of whom the Barrister is Instructed by the Authorised Person to provide the Services (who may be the Authorised Person where the Case concerns the affairs of the Authorised Person)

"the Services"

the legal services provided by the Barrister in connection with the Case pursuant to the Instructions provided by the Authorised Person;

"the SRA"

the Solicitors Regulation Authority; and

"the SRA Code"
the part of the SRA Handbook published by the SRA on 16 September 2011 referred to as the "SRA Code of Conduct 2011" as amended from time to time.

2. APPLICATION OF THESE CONDITIONS

2.1 The Barrister provides the Services requested by the Authorised Person on the terms set out in these Conditions and subject to his professional obligations under the Code.

2.2 These Conditions (other than this clause 2.2) may be varied if, but only if, expressly agreed by the Parties in writing (including by exchange of emails).

2.3 By instructing the Barrister to provide further Services in relation to the Case, the Authorised Person accepts these Conditions in relation to those further Services, as well as in relation to the Services which the Barrister is initially instructed to provide.

2.4 These Conditions do not apply in the following circumstances:

2.4.1 the Barrister is paid directly (a) by the Legal Services Commission, through the Community Legal Service or the Criminal Defence Service or (b) by the Crown Prosecution Service; or

2.4.2 the Barrister has entered into a Conditional Fee Agreement in relation to the Case that does not specifically incorporate these Conditions.

2.5 Nothing in these Conditions nor any variation referred to in clause 2.2 shall operate so as to conflict with the Barrister's duty under the Code or with the Authorised Person's duty under the SRA Code.

3. THE INSTRUCTIONS TO THE BARRISTER

3.1 The Authorised Person must ensure the Instructions delivered to the Barrister are adequate to supply him with the information and documents reasonably required and in reasonably sufficient time for him to provide the Services requested.

3.2 The Authorised Person must respond promptly to any requests for further information or instructions made by the Barrister.

3.3 The Authorised Person must inform the Barrister immediately if there is reason to believe that any information or document provided to the Barrister is not true and accurate.

3.4 Where the Authorised Person requires the Barrister to perform all or any part of the Services urgently the Authorised Person must ensure that:

3.4.1 all relevant Instructions are clearly marked "Urgent"; and

3.4.2 at the time the Instructions are delivered the Barrister is informed in clear and unambiguous terms of the timescale within which the Services are required and the reason for the urgency.

3.5 The Authorised Person must inform the Barrister within a reasonable time if the Case is settled or otherwise concluded.

4. RECEIPT AND ACCEPTANCE OF THE INSTRUCTIONS

4.1 Upon receipt of the Instructions, the Barrister will within a reasonable time review the Instructions and inform the Authorised Person whether or not he accepts the Instructions.

4.2 The Barrister may accept or refuse the Instructions in the circumstances and for the reasons set out in the Code and the Barrister incurs no liability if he refuses any Instructions in accordance with the Code.

4.3 Notwithstanding acceptance of Instructions in accordance with Clause 4.1 above, the Barrister shall be entitled to carry out any customer due diligence required by the Money Laundering Regulations 2007. The Authorised Person will provide the Barrister with all reasonable assistance to carry out any necessary customer due diligence including (if required to do so) consenting to the Barrister relying upon the Authorised Person under Regulation 17 of the Money Laundering Regulations 2007.[219]

4.4 In the event that the Barrister reasonably considers that the requirements of the Money Laundering Regulations have not been satisfied he may within a reasonable period after receipt of the Instructions withdraw any acceptance of those Instructions without incurring any liability

4.5 Subject to the preceding provisions of this Clause 4, the Agreement comes into effect upon the Barrister accepting the Instructions.

5. CONFIDENTIAL INFORMATION AND PUBLICITY

5.1 The Barrister will keep confidential all information provided to him in connection with the Case unless:

5.1.1 he is authorised by the Authorised Person or the Lay Client to disclose it;

5.1.2 the information is in or comes into the public domain without any breach of confidentiality on the part of the Barrister; or

5.1.3 he is required or permitted to disclose it by law, or by any regulatory or fiscal authorities, in which case, to the extent that he is permitted to do so, he will endeavour to give the Authorised Person and/or the Lay Client as much advance notice as possible and permitted of any such required disclosure.

5.2 The Barrister owes the same duty of confidentiality to other lay clients, and will therefore not disclose or make use of any information that might be given to him in confidence in relation to any other matter without the consent of his other lay client, even if it is material to providing the Services.

5.3 Unless the Authorised Person expressly informs the Barrister to the contrary in advance in writing, the Barrister may allow the Instructions to be reviewed by another barrister or by a pupil (including a vacation pupil or mini-pupil) in chambers, on terms that that other barrister or pupil complies with clause 5.1.

5.4 Subject to his obligation under clause 5.1, the Barrister may make and retain copies of the Instructions and any written material produced by him.

5.5 To the extent such information is already in the public domain, the Barrister may disclose in his marketing and similar materials, and to prospective clients and publishers of legal directories that he is or has been instructed by the Authorised Person and/or for the Lay Client and the nature of the Case. To the extent any such information is not already in the public domain, the Barrister may only refer to it for marketing purposes in a form which sufficiently preserves the Lay Client's privilege and confidentiality and (where the law so requires) with the Lay Client's consent.

6. ELECTRONIC COMMUNICATION

6.1 Unless otherwise directed by the Authorised Person, the Barrister may correspond by means of electronic mail, the parties agreeing hereby:

6.1.1 to accept the risks of using electronic mail, including but not limited to the risks of viruses, interception and unauthorised access; and

6.1.2 to use commercially reasonable procedures to maintain security of electronic mail and to check for commonly known viruses in information sent and received electronically.

[219] *Ibid*, para 3.1.1, the Law Society gives the following advice to solicitors: 'You should consider how far you are willing to provide this comfort to barristers. In practice, much of this work may well have been undertaken by the firm in any case, but the firm may wish to consult its insurers and consider how appropriate this is in individual cases before agreeing to it.'

7. DATA PROTECTION

7.1 The Barrister is a data controller for the purposes of the Data Protection Act and is bound by the Act amongst other things, to take appropriate technical and organisational measures against unauthorised processing of personal data and against accidental loss or destruction of, or damage to, personal data. He is entitled to process (which includes obtaining, consulting, holding, using and disclosing) personal data of the Lay Client, the Authorised Person and others to enable him to provide the Services, to liaise with the Authorised Person in respect of the Lay Client's case or on the Lay Client's behalf, to maintain and update client records, to produce management data, to prevent crime, to publicise his activities as set out in clause 5.5 above, to comply with regulatory requirements and as permitted or required by law. The Lay Client and the Authorised Person each have a right of access and a right of correction in respect of their personal data which the Barrister holds about them, in accordance with data protection legislation.

8. PROVIDING THE SERVICES

8.1 The Barrister will exercise reasonable skill and care in providing the Services. The Barrister acknowledges the existence of a duty of care owed to the Lay Client at common law, subject to his professional obligations to the Court and under the Code.

8.2 The Barrister will provide the Services by such date as may be agreed between the parties, and in any event will do so within a reasonable time having regard to the nature of the Instructions and his other pre-existing professional obligations as referred to in paragraph 701 of the Code.

8.3 The Barrister may delegate the provision of any part of the Services but will remain responsible for the acts, omissions, defaults or negligence of any delegate as if they were the acts, omissions, defaults or negligence of the Barrister.

8.4 The Barrister will, in addition, provide all information reasonably required to enable the Lay Client and/or Authorised Person to assess what costs have been incurred and to obtain and enforce any order or agreement to pay costs against any third party.

9. INTELLECTUAL PROPERTY RIGHTS[220]

9.1 All copyright and other intellectual property rights of whatever nature in or attaching to the Barrister's work product, including all documents, reports, written advice or other materials provided by the Barrister to the Authorised Person or the Lay Client belong to and remain with the Barrister. The Authorised Person and the Lay Client have the right and licence to use the Barrister's work product for the particular Case and the particular purpose for which it is prepared. If the Authorised Person or the Lay Client wishes to use copies of the Barrister's work product for purposes other than those for which it is prepared, this will require the express written permission of the Barrister. The moral rights of the Barrister in respect of his work product are asserted.

10. LIABILITY[221]

10.1 Subject to Clause 10.2 below, the Barrister is not liable:

10.1.1 For any loss or damage, however suffered, by any person other than the Lay Client;

---

220 *Ibid*, para 3.1.2, the Law Society gives the following advice to solicitors: 'You may wish to consider how far this clause may affect your firm's knowledge management systems and how it works with the existing general law with regard to intellectual property. You may wish to agree reasonable rights with the barrister to contain advice in your firm's knowledge management systems for internal guidance only. In addition, you should discuss this clause with the client and your insurers before agreeing to it.'

221 *Ibid*, para 3.1.3, the Law Society gives the following advice to solicitors: 'This clause excludes liability for loss or damage caused to any person other than the lay client and would appear to prevent solicitors suing for loss caused to themselves. In practice, this may be of relatively little significance. However, you may wish to negotiate with the barrister for this clause to be deleted or to add the words "or solicitor" at the end of clause 10.1.1. In addition, the contract seeks to exclude liability for loss or damages arising out of inaccurate, incomplete or late instructions. This provision appears to be unnecessary since the existing law will establish whether or not it is appropriate for liability to be found in such circumstances and it is hard to see how such a provision can be in the client's interests.'

10.1.2 for any loss or damage, however suffered, which is caused by inaccurate, incomplete or late Instructions;
10.1.3 for any indirect or consequential loss however suffered.

10.2 Nothing in Clause 10.1 shall operate so as to exclude liability where such exclusion is prohibited by law.

11. FEES[222]

11.1 The fee for the Services shall in all cases comply with paragraph 405 of the Code and will be calculated as agreed between the Barrister (or his clerk on his behalf) and the Authorised Person, whether prospectively or retrospectively.

11.2 The Barrister may agree to provide the Services for a fixed fee or may agree to provide the Services on the basis of an agreed hourly rate or on such other basis as may from time to time be agreed. If an hourly rate is agreed:
11.2.1 the agreed hourly rate will be subject to reasonable periodic review by the Barrister, and in addition may be reviewed by the Barrister to reflect any reasonably significant changes in his status or seniority;
11.2.2 any variation of the agreed hourly rate and the date on which it shall take effect shall be agreed with the Authorised Person, and in default of agreement the Barrister shall be entitled to treat the Agreement as having been terminated by the Authorised Person, subject to the Barrister's obligations under paragraph 610 of the Code.

11.3 If no fee or hourly rate is agreed, then the Barrister is entitled to charge a reasonable fee for the Services having regard to all relevant circumstances.

11.4 The fee for the Barrister's Services is exclusive of any applicable Value Added Tax (or any tax of a similar nature), which shall be added to the fee at the appropriate rate.

12. BILLING, PAYMENT AND INTEREST[223]

12.1 The Barrister shall be entitled to deliver an Invoice to the Authorised Person in respect of the Services or any completed part thereof and any disbursements at any time after supplying the Services or the relevant part thereof.

12.2 The Barrister shall deliver an Invoice to the Authorised Person in respect of the Services or any part thereof and any disbursements as soon as reasonably practicable after and not more than 3 months from the earliest of: (a) a request by the Authorised Person; (b) notification by the Authorised Person that the Case has settled or otherwise concluded; or (c) termination of the Agreement.

12.3 The Invoice must set out an itemised description of:
12.3.1 the Services provided by the Barrister and the fees charged;
12.3.2 any disbursements incurred and the cost thereof; and
12.3.3 VAT (or any tax of a similar nature), if any.

12.4 The Authorised Person must pay the Invoice within 30 days of delivery, time being of the essence, whether or not the Authorised Person has been put in funds by the Lay Client. The Invoice must be paid without any set-off (whether by reason of a complaint made or

222 *Ibid*, having noted that the draft agreement permits counsel to revise the hourly rate, the Law Society says that a solicitor should discuss the issue with the lay client and ask whether they are content for this to be agreed.

223 *Ibid*, para 3.1.4, the Law Society gives the following advice to solicitors: 'You should consider how far this will affect your existing procedures for dealing with bills from suppliers and sub-contractors and whether you wish to propose changes.'

dispute with the Barrister or otherwise), and without any deduction or withholding on account of any taxes or other charges.[224]

12.5 Where the Barrister has delivered a fee note, on request by the Authorised Person the Barrister will deliver a VAT invoice following receipt of payment.

12.6 If the Invoice remains outstanding more than 30 days from the date of delivery, the Barrister is entitled:

12.6.1 to the fixed sum and interest in accordance with the Late Payment of Commercial Debts (Interest) Act 1998;

12.6.2 to sue the Authorised Person for payment; and

12.6.3 subject to the Barrister's obligations to the Court and under paragraph 610 of the Code, to refrain from doing any further work on the Case unless payment for that further work is made in advance.

13. TERMINATION

13.1 The Authorised Person may terminate the Agreement by giving notice to the Barrister in writing at any time.

13.2 The Agreement will terminate automatically as soon as the Barrister is under an obligation pursuant to Part VI of the Code or otherwise to withdraw from the Case or to cease to act and has complied with any requirements of the Code in so doing.

13.3 The Barrister may terminate the Agreement by written notice when he is entitled pursuant to Paragraphs 608 to 610 of the Code or otherwise to withdraw from the Case or cease to act and has complied with any requirements of the Code in so doing.

13.4 For the avoidance of doubt, termination of the Agreement, whether under this clause 13 or otherwise, does not affect or prejudice any accrued liabilities, rights or remedies of the parties under the Agreement.

14. WAIVER

14.1 Except where expressly stated, nothing done or not done by the Barrister or the Authorised Person constitutes a waiver of that party's rights under the Agreement.

15. SEVERABILITY

15.1 If any provision of these Conditions is found by a competent court or administrative body of competent jurisdiction to be invalid or unenforceable for any reason, such invalidity or unenforceability shall not affect the other provisions of these Conditions which will remain in full force and effect.

15.2 If any provision of these Conditions is found to be invalid or unenforceable but would be valid or enforceable if some part of the provision were deleted, the provision in question will apply with such deletions as may be necessary to make it valid and enforceable.

[224] *Ibid*, para 3.2.2, the Law Society gives the following advice to solicitors: '[I[t is open to you to agree that the barrister should not be paid until the solicitor has been paid by the client. Any such agreement should be recorded in writing and you should include the following passage in the contract: "If the Barrister and the Authorised Person expressly agree in writing that the Authorised Person shall not be liable for the Barrister's fees until the Authorised Person has been put in funds by the Lay Client, the payment provisions of the Agreement shall apply only from the date upon which the Authorised Person has been put in funds by the Lay Client in respect of the Barrister's fees." Clause 12.4 also refers to time being of the essence as regards payment and excludes any set off, for example as a result of a complaint by the client or dispute over the fees charged, and any deduction or withholding on account of any taxes or other charges. If you do agree to that clause, you should seek agreement to delete those references.'

16. EXCLUSION OF RIGHTS OF THIRD PARTIES

16.1 This Agreement governs the rights and obligations of the Barrister and the Authorised Person towards each other and confers no benefit upon any third party (including the Lay Client). The ability of third parties to enforce any rights under the Contracts (Rights of Third Parties) Act 1999 is hereby excluded.

17. ENTIRE AGREEMENT

17.1 Subject to clauses 2.2 and 11.1, the Agreement, incorporating these Conditions, comprises the entire agreement between the parties to the exclusion of all other terms and conditions and prior or collateral agreements, negotiations, notices of intention and representations and the parties agree that they have not been induced to enter into the Agreement on the basis of any representation.

18. NOTICES AND DELIVERY

18.1 Any notice or other written communication to be given or delivered under this Agreement may be despatched in hard copy or in electronic form (including fax and email) and shall in the case of a notice to be given to the Barrister be given to him at his last known Chambers' address, fax number or email address and shall in the case of a notice to be given to the Authorised Person be given to him at his last known place of business, fax number or email address.

18.2 Notices and other written communications under this Agreement shall be deemed to have been received:-

18.2.1 In the case of hard copy documents despatched by first class post, on the second working day next following the day of posting;

18.2.2 In the case of documents despatched by second class post, on the fourth working day next following the day of posting;

18.2.3 In the case of documents in electronic form, on the working day next following the date of despatch.

19. GOVERNING LAW, JURISDICTION AND DISPUTE RESOLUTION

19.1 The Agreement and these Conditions shall be governed by and construed in accordance with the law of England and Wales.

19.2 Unless any alternative dispute resolution procedure is agreed between the parties, the parties agree to submit to the exclusive jurisdiction of the Courts of England and Wales in respect of any dispute which arises out of or under this Agreement.[†]

19.3 Without prejudice to Clause 19.2, the parties may agree to alternative methods of dispute resolution, including submission of any dispute regarding fees to the Voluntary Joint Tribunal on Barristers' Fees where the Authorised Person is a solicitor.[†]

[†] The parties are reminded that if a judgment or a Voluntary Joint Tribunal's award is not fully paid within 30 days, the Barrister may request the Chairman of the General Council of the Bar to include the solicitor on the List of Defaulting Solicitors.

54

ADDITIONAL LIABILITIES

This chapter deals with the following topics: **54.01**

- jurisdiction (54.04):
  - jurisdiction relating to success fees (54.05);
  - jurisdiction relating to ATE premiums (54.11);
  - transitional and savings provisions governing the CPR (54.15);
  - savings provisions relating to specific types of case (54.21);
  - human rights and additional liabilities (54.42);
- points of principle regarding success fees (54.43):
  - recovery of success fees retrospectively (54.44);
  - differential rates for different periods (54.47);
  - the position of costs draftspersons and costs lawyers (54.48);
  - budgets and success fee (54.49);
  - fixed success fees (54.50);
  - solicitor-and-client issues (54.51);
- the assessment of the amount of success fees (54.54):
  - types of success fee (54.56);
  - prematurity and early risk assessments (54.64);
  - risk and success fees (54.67);
  - factors other than risk and success fees (54.100);
- notice of funding and failure to serve (54.108);
- statement of reasons and failure to serve (54.124);
- the assessment of the amount of ATE premiums (54.127);
  - the components and language of premiums (54.128);
  - the role of rules of court in relation to premiums (54.130);
  - the assessment of premiums (54.131);
  - evidence relating to premiums (54.163);
  - the deconstruction of premiums (54.172);
- miscellaneous points regarding ATE premiums;
  - more than one set of proceedings (54.175);
  - extension of ATE policies and top-up policies (54.176);
  - budgets and ATE premiums (54.178);
- membership organisations and notional premiums (54.179):
  - the statutory framework relating to notional premiums (54.181);
  - notional premiums (54.188); and
- alternative means of funding and alternatives to litigation (54.191):
  - the relevance of legal advice regarding funding (54.195);
  - inquiries relating to funding (54.197).

54.02 This chapter deals with additional liability as between opposing parties. This is a topic that, for the reasons set out below (see 54.07), is now far less important than it used to be. In view of this, this chapter deals with the topic in less detail than did previous editions of this book. If a difficult point arises, Chapter 30 in the second edition ought to be consulted; specific reference to the second edition is made, where appropriate.

54.03 The funding aspects of after-the-event (ATE) insurance are addressed in Chapter 34. Contractual issues relating to success fees are addressed in Chapter 29. Unless otherwise stated, it is assumed that the funding arrangement in question is enforceable; if this is in doubt, then those two chapters should be consulted.

Jurisdiction

54.04 The jurisdiction that governs the recoverability of additional liabilities is complex because it is now governed almost entirely by transitional provisions.

Jurisdiction relating to success fees

54.05 The Privy Council has confirmed that success fees are not recoverable in the absence of specific statutory authority.[1]

54.06 The Courts and Legal Services Act 1990 provides that certain conditions must be met before a conditional fee agreement may lawfully provide for a success fee (see 29.19–29.23).[2] Generally speaking, material non-compliance with the requirements of the 1990 Act will result in the entire agreement being unenforceable (see 29.14). This topic is addressed in Chapter 29. For present purposes, it is assumed that the agreement in question is compliant with those provisions and is enforceable. What follows deals with the recoverability of success fees between opposing parties, which is governed by separate provisions from those that govern the enforceability of conditional fee agreements themselves.

Jurisdiction concerning success fees

54.07 The starting point is Courts and Legal Services Act 1990, s 58A(6), which deals with the recoverability—or, rather, what is now the *ir*recoverability—of success fees in principle. It reads as follows: 'A costs order made in proceedings may not include provision requiring the payment by one party of all or part of a success fee payable by another party under a conditional fee agreement.'[3] Thus, whilst a success fee may exist and may be payable between legal services provider and client, it may not be recovered between opposing parties (subject to the matters discussed below). This is precisely the opposite of what this subsection said prior to 1 April 2013—a change that has come about as the

[1] The Privy Council came to this decision on the basis that the addition of a success fee to a fee that was reasonable and proportionate would almost certainly render the resultant fee unreasonable and disproportionate: *Seaga v Harper* [2009] UKPC 26.

[2] Courts and Legal Services Act 1990, s 58(4) (as amended).

[3] It is worth stating that Jackson LJ (speaking extrajudicially) has recommended the abrogation of the recovery of success fees between the parties: Jackson, R, *Review of Civil Litigation Costs: Final Report* (London: HMSO, 2009), ch 10.

result of an amendment made by Legal Aid, Sentencing and Punishment of Offenders Act 2012, s 44(4).

That said, the 2012 Act contains savings provisions. In particular, the Legal Aid, Sentencing and Punishment of Offenders Act 2012, s 44(6), provides as follows: **54.08**

> '44 (6) The amendment made by subsection (4) does not prevent a costs order including provision in relation to a success fee payable by a person ("P") under a conditional fee agreement entered into before the day on which that subsection comes into force ("the commencement day") if—
> (a) the agreement was entered into specifically for the purposes of the provision to P of advocacy or litigation services in connection with the matter that is the subject of the proceedings in which the costs order is made, or
> (b) advocacy or litigation services were provided to P under the agreement in connection with that matter before the commencement day.'

Thus a success fee will be recoverable from an opponent if the conditional fee agreement was entered into before 1 April 2013 *and*:

- it was entered into specifically for the purposes of the provision of advocacy or litigation services in connection with the proceedings in which the costs order was made; or
- advocacy or litigation services had been provided under that agreement before 1 April 2013.[4]

The first of these conditions refers to conditional fee agreements, and the second to collective conditional fee agreements.

The savings provisions referred to immediately above are referred to in this chapter as the 'general savings provisions'. There are corresponding general savings provisions governing ATE premiums (see 54.11–54.20) and notional premiums (see 54.182–54.186). There are, however, three other circumstances in which a success fee may continue to be recoverable between opposing parties—namely, in: **54.09**

- mesothelioma claims (see 54.22–54.30);
- certain older insolvency-related proceedings (see 54.31–54.34); and
- publication and privacy proceedings (see 54.35–54.37).

The provisions preserving recoverability in these circumstances are referred to in this chapter as 'special savings provisions'. As will be explained below, there are corresponding special savings provisions in relation to ATE premiums (for mesothelioma claims only) and notional premiums.

Criminal, quasi-criminal and family matters

Where the general savings provisions apply, then a success fee may be recovered in almost any type of claim. That said, there are certain restrictions. In particular, conditional fee agreements are proscribed entirely in criminal or family matters (see 29.18), and success fees are proscribed in certain other types of litigation (see 29.20). In particular, proceedings **54.10**

[4] The aim was to ensure that the transitional provisions applied to claims funded by way of collective conditional fee agreements. This is made clear by PD 48, para 1.2. Moreover, this was explained in a letter from Lord McNally to Lord Bach, dated 20 March 2012.

under s 82 of the Environmental Protection Act 1990 may be funded by way of a conditional fee agreement, but they may not be funded by an agreement that provides for a success fee.[5]

Jurisdiction relating to ATE premiums

54.11 Under the common law, an ATE premium is not recoverable between opposing parties.[6]

54.12 As of 1 April 2013, Courts and Legal Services Act 1990, s 58C(1) (as amended), has read as follows:

> '(1) A costs order made in favour of a party to proceedings who has taken out a costs insurance policy may not include provision requiring the payment of an amount in respect of all or part of the premium of the policy, unless such provision is permitted by regulations under subsection (2).'

Thus, whilst a premium may be payable between client and ATE insurer, it may not be recovered between opposing parties (subject to the provisions discussed below). The section that used to permit the recovery of premiums prior to 1 April 2013—namely, s 29 of the Access to Justice Act 1999—has been revoked.[7]

54.13 As with success fees, however, there are general savings provisions. They may be found in s 46(3) of the 2012 Act, which reads as follows:

> '(3) The amendments made by this section do not apply in relation to a costs order made in favour of a party to proceedings who took out a costs insurance policy in relation to the proceedings before the day on which this section comes into force.'

Thus, if the policy in question was incepted before 1 April 2013, the premium payable under it may still be recovered.

54.14 As will be explained below, in addition to the general savings provisions there are special savings provisions relating to the following types of claim:

- mesothelioma claims (see 54.22–54.30);
- certain older insolvency-related proceedings (see 54.31–54.34);
- publication and privacy proceedings (see 54.35–54.37); and
- clinical negligence claims (see 54.38–54.41).

It should be noted that the special savings provisions in relation to clinical negligence claims are only partial.

Transitional and savings provisions governing the CPR

54.15 The CPR contain provisions that correspond with both the general and the special savings provisions referred to above. Those that relate to the special savings provisions are addressed in turn (see 54.22–54.41); what is set out immediately below relates to the general savings provisions.

---

[5] See Courts and Legal Services Act 1990, s 58A(1)(a); Conditional Fee Agreements Order 2013 (SI 2013/689), art 2.

[6] See *Seaga v Harper* [2009] UKPC 26 (Jamaica) for an indication of the position under the common law. On a similar point, see *McGraddie v McGraddie & Anor* [2015] UKSC 1.

[7] See Legal Aid, Sentencing and Punishment of Offenders Act 2012, s 46.

Whilst arguably otiose, Courts and Legal Services Act 1990, s 58A(7), reads as follows: 'Rules of court may make provision with respect to the assessment of any costs which include fees payable under a conditional fee agreement (including one which provides for a success fee).' Thus the recoverability of success fees is subject to the applicable rules of court. **54.16**

On 1 April 2013, the existing provisions in the CPR relating to additional liabilities were revoked,[8] as was the Costs Practice Direction (CPD). That said, where the conditional fee agreement or ATE policy is a 'pre-commencement funding arrangement' (see 54.18), then the CPR as they were immediately before 1 April 2013 will still apply. This is made clear by CPR, r 48.1, which provides as follows: **54.17**

> '(1) The provisions of CPR Parts 43 to 48 relating to funding arrangements, and the attendant provisions of the Costs Practice Direction, will apply in relation to a pre-commencement funding arrangement as they were in force immediately before 1 April 2013, with such modifications (if any) as may be made by a practice direction on or after that date.
>
> (2) A reference in rule 48.2 to a rule is to that rule as it was in force immediately before 1 April 2013.'

This means that there continues to be a framework that governs the way in which additional liabilities are assessed—namely, the 'old' CPR and CPD. Whether that framework will apply will turn on whether the arrangement in question falls within the ambit of the definition of pre-commencement funding arrangement.

In so far as the general savings provisions are concerned, CPR, r 48.1(1)(a)(i) and (ii), reads as follows: **54.18**

> '(1) A pre-commencement funding arrangement is—
> (a) in relation to proceedings other than insolvency-related proceedings, publication and privacy proceedings or a mesothelioma claim—
> (i) a funding arrangement as defined by rule 43.2(1)(k)(i) where—
> (aa) the agreement was entered into before 1 April 2013 specifically for the purposes of the provision to the person by whom the success fee is payable of advocacy or litigation services in relation to the matter that is the subject of the proceedings in which the costs order is to be made; or
> (bb) the agreement was entered into before 1 April 2013 and advocacy or litigation services were provided to that person under the agreement in connection with that matter before 1 April 2013 ...
> (ii) a funding arrangement as defined by rule 43.2(1)(k)(ii) where the party seeking to recover the insurance premium took out the insurance policy in relation to the proceedings before 1 April 2013; ...'

Thus the following will fall into the category of pre-commencement funding arrangement for the purposes of the general savings provisions: **54.19**

- a conditional fee agreement that was entered into before 1 April 2013;
- a collective conditional fee agreement under which litigation services were provided before 1 April 2013; and
- an ATE policy that was taken out before 1 April 2013.

There is also a corresponding provision relating to notional premiums (see 54.184–54.186).

[8] See Civil Procedure (Amendment) Rules 2013 (SI 2013/262), r 15.

54.20 Rather confusingly, the provisions in the CPR that correspond with the special savings provisions (see 54.21–54.41) are also governed by whether the arrangement in question is a pre-commencement funding arrangement, and this will be so notwithstanding the fact that such an arrangement will have been made on or after 1 April 2013. In this regard, the phrase 'pre-commencement funding arrangement' should be regarded as a term of art that does not necessarily imply that the arrangement in question was made prior to 2013.

Savings provisions relating to specific types of case

54.21 Each of the special savings provisions is dealt with in turn. For each, the savings provision in relation to the primary legislation is discussed first, followed by the corresponding provision in the CPR.

Savings relating to mesothelioma claims

54.22 The Legal Aid, Sentencing and Punishment of Offenders Act 2012, s 48, delays the coming into force of the provisions that would otherwise abrogate the recoverability of certain additional liabilities in mesothelioma claims:

> '(1) Sections 44 and 46 may not be brought into force in relation to proceedings relating to a claim for damages in respect of diffuse mesothelioma until the Lord Chancellor has—
> (a) carried out a review of the likely effect of those sections in relation to such proceedings, and
> (b) published a report of the conclusions of the review.
>
> (2) In this section "diffuse mesothelioma" has the same meaning as in the Pneumoconiosis etc (Workers' Compensation) Act 1979.'

It should be noted that these provisions relate only to success fees and ATE premiums. There is no such provision in relation to notional premiums. This is reflected in the relevant commencement provisions,[9] which create savings only for success fees and ATE premiums.

54.23 As with all of the other savings provisions (both general and special), there are corresponding provisions in the CPR. In so far as they are relevant, they can be found at CPR, r 48.2(1)(b) and (2):

> '48.2 (1) A pre-commencement funding arrangement is—
> [...]
> (b) in relation to ... a mesothelioma claim—
> (i) a funding arrangement as defined by rule 43.2(1)(k)(i) where—
> (aa) the agreement was entered into before the relevant date specifically for the purposes of the provision to the person by whom the success fee is payable of advocacy or litigation services in relation to the matter that is the subject of the proceedings in which the costs order is to be made; or
> (bb) the agreement was entered into before the relevant date and advocacy or litigation services were provided to that person under the agreement in connection with that matter before the relevant date;

[9] Legal Aid, Sentencing and Punishment of Offenders Act 2012 (Commencement No 5 and Saving Provisions) Order 2013 (SI 2013/77), art 4(a).

(ii) a funding arrangement as defined by rule 43.2(1)(k)(ii) where the party seeking to recover the insurance premium took out the insurance policy in relation to the proceedings before the relevant date.

(2) In paragraph (1)—...

[...]

(d) "a mesothelioma claim" is a claim for damages in respect of diffuse mesothelioma (within the meaning of the Pneumoconiosis etc. (Workers' Compensation) Act 1979; and

(e) "the relevant date" is the date on which sections 44 and 46 of the Legal Aid, Sentencing and Punishment of Offenders Act 2012 came into force in relation to proceedings of the sort in question.'

Strictly speaking, the above provisions are transitional provisions rather than savings provisions because they contemplate some date—'the relevant date'—on which the Legal Aid, Sentencing and Punishment of Offenders Act 2012, ss 44 and 46, will come into force and additional liabilities will cease to be recoverable. That said, no 'relevant date' had been set at the time of writing and, consequently, additional liabilities continue to be recoverable between opposing parties (see 54.28–54.30). **54.24**

Matters are further explained by Practice Direction (PD) 48, para 2, which reads as follows: **54.25**

'2.1 By virtue of section 48 of the 2012 Act, the changes relating to recoverable success fees and insurance premiums which are made by sections 44 and 46 of the Act may not be commenced, and accordingly will not apply, in relation to mesothelioma claims (defined by section 48(2) of the Act as having the same meaning as in the Pneumoconiosis etc. (Workers' Compensation) Act 1979) until such time as a review has been carried out and the conclusions of that review published. It will accordingly remain possible for a costs order in favour of a party to such proceedings to include provision requiring the payment of success fees and premiums under after the event costs insurance policies, and so the provisions of the CPR relating to funding arrangements as in force immediately prior to 1 April 2013 will continue to apply in relation to such proceedings, whether commenced before or after 1 April 2013. This will include the provision for fixed recoverable success fees in respect of employers' liability disease claims in Section V of Part 45 (CPR 45.23 to 45.26), which will otherwise cease to apply other than to claims in which a CFA was entered into or a costs insurance policy taken out before 1 April 2013).

2.2 On the later date when sections 44 and 46 are brought into force in relation to mesothelioma claims, the saving provisions of sections 44(6) and 44(3) will have effect in relation to funding arrangements in such claims as they do more generally, save that the operative date for the saving provisions will not be 1 April 2013 but the later date.'

It is worth pausing here to note that para 6(2)(a) of the Conditional Fee Agreements Order 2013[10] means that the limits on success fees that apply to personal injury claims (that is, as between legal services provider and client) do not apply to mesothelioma claims. Fixed recoverable success fees in respect of employers' liability disease claims will apply instead (see 50.113–50.149). This is why PD 48, para 2, refers to CPR, Part 45, Section V. **54.26**

The compromise that led to the savings provisions in mesothelioma claims In its passage through Parliament, the House of Lords sought to amend the Legal Aid, Sentencing and Punishment of Offenders Bill in such a way as to exempt claims arising from occupationally **54.27**

[10] SI 2013/689.

related respiratory illness or disease from the provisions that would make additional liabilities irrecoverable.[11] This amendment was initially rejected by the House of Commons,[12] but a compromise was reached whereby there would be an exemption for mesothelioma claims until a review of the likely effect of ss 44 and 46 on mesothelioma proceedings had been undertaken and published by the government.[13]

54.28 **The future of the provisions relating to mesothelioma** The Lord Chancellor is obliged to carry out a review of the likely effect this would have and to publish a report of the conclusions of the review.[14] On 18 December 2012, Parliamentary Under-Secretary of State for Justice Helen Grant announced a consultation on proposals to reform the way in which mesothelioma cases were dealt with generally, saying that 'as part of that consultation we will carry out the review required under Section 48'. The intention was to conclude the review by 24 July 2013. In the event, there was slippage of the timetable and the consultation document was not issued until autumn 2013.[15]

54.29 In a written statement dated 4 December 2013, the government announced that it had decided that, with effect from July 2014, ss 44 and 46 of the Act would apply to mesothelioma cases.[16] In its formal response to the consultation, published on 6 March 2014, the government confirmed this position.[17] However, that decision was challenged by judicial review and, on 2 October 2013, William Davies J quashed it.[18]

54.30 Independently of the judicial review, a parliamentary select committee examined the issue. In a scathing report, that committee found that the government had rushed through the review prematurely because it 'was not reconciled to the concession it was forced to make', and that, as a result, the review was 'not prepared in a thorough and even-handed manner'.[19] The committee's inquiry brought to light controversial documents drawn up between insurers and the government. One such document, styled as heads of agreement[20]—but which the claimant lobby have called 'a secret deal'[21]—prompted the following comments by the committee:

> 'We are concerned that the Government has not been transparent or open, either with us or with other interested parties, about the fact that its overall policy in relation to mesothelioma has been shaped in accordance with an "agreement", however informal and elastic, which it had reached with employers' liability insurers. It is hard to see how a balanced and informed public debate can take place when a prior agreement has been reached between

[11] HL Deb, 14 March 2012, cols 309–33.
[12] HC Deb, 17 April 2012, cols 264–85.
[13] HC Deb, 24 April 2012, cols 830–54.
[14] Legal Aid, Sentencing and Punishment of Offenders Act 2012, s 48.
[15] The document was Ministry of Justice, *Reforming Mesothelioma Claims: A Consultation on Proposals to Speed up the Settlement of Mesothelioma Claims in England and Wales* (London: HMSO, 2013).
[16] HC Deb, 4 December 2013, cols 55–56 WS.
[17] Ministry of Justice, *Reforming Mesothelioma Claims: The Government Response to Consultation on Proposals to Speed up the Settlement of Mesothelioma Claims in England and Wales* (London: HMSO, 2014).
[18] *R (on the application of Whitston) (Asbestos Victims Support Groups Forum UK) v Secretary of State for Justice* [2014] EWHC 3044 (Admin).
[19] House of Commons Justice Committee, *Mesothelioma Claims: Third Report of the Session 2014–15*, HC 308 (London: HMSO, 2014), p 4.
[20] *Ibid*, pp 26–9.
[21] Hyde, H, 'High Court Deals LASPO Blow to Grayling', *Law Society Gazette*, 2 October 2014.

two of the principal parties to that debate, and that agreement is not known to others participating in the debate, including victims.'[22]

James Dalton, head of motor and liability at the Association of British Insurers (ABI), said that he was 'frustrated' by the development 'which delays long overdue reform of the legal system for mesothelioma sufferers'.[23] Be that as it may, at the time of writing, no 'relevant date' (see 54.24) had been set.

Savings relating to certain older insolvency-related proceedings

Insolvency litigation has often been treated differently from other types of litigation.[24] There are many reasons for this, but perhaps the most compelling—from the government's point of view—is that not only is HM Revenue & Customs (HMRC) the claimant in many such claims, but also because even where they are not claimants, public-sector creditors tend to benefit as a by-product of litigation brought by private-sector creditors.[25] **54.31**

It is perhaps because of this that, prior to 6 April 2016 (but not thereafter),[26] there were special savings provisions in insolvency-related proceedings for success fees and ATE premiums (but not notional premiums).[27] This was achieved by art 4 of the Legal Aid, Sentencing and Punishment of Offenders Act 2012 (Commencement No 5 and Saving Provisions) Order 2013,[28] which reads as follows: **54.32**

> '4. Articles 2(1)(a) and (c) and article 3(a) and (c) do not apply to—
>
> [...]
>
> (c) proceedings in England and Wales brought by a person acting in the capacity of—
> (i) a liquidator of a company which is being wound up in England and Wales or Scotland under Parts IV or V of the 1986 Act; or
> (ii) a trustee of a bankrupt's estate under Part IX of the 1986 Act;
> (d) proceedings brought by a person acting in the capacity of an administrator appointed pursuant to the provisions of Part II of the 1986 Act;
> (e) proceedings in England and Wales brought by a company which is being wound up in England and Wales or Scotland under Parts IV or V of the 1986 Act; or
> (f) proceedings brought by a company which has entered administration under Part II of the 1986 Act.'

22 House of Commons Justice Committee, *Mesothelioma Claims: Third Report of the Session 2014–15*, HC 308 (London: HMSO, 2014), p 29.

23 Hyde, H, 'High Court Deals LASPO Blow to Grayling', *Law Society Gazette*, 2 October 2014.

24 In the 19th century, for example, insolvency practitioners were permitted to assign causes of action vested in insolvent estates: see *Seear v Lawson* (1880) 15 Ch D 426. When conditional fee agreements were first made lawful, insolvency litigation was one of only three types of litigation that were permitted to use them: see the Conditional Fee Agreements Order 1995 (SI 1995/1674).

25 Walton, P, *The Likely Effect of the Jackson Reforms on Insolvency Litigation: An Empirical Investigation* (April 2014), available online at https://www.r3.org.uk/media/documents/policy/Jackson_Campaign/Jackson_Reforms_Insolvency_Litigation_April_2014.pdf

26 See Legal Aid, Sentencing and Punishment of Offenders Act 2012 (Commencement No 12) Order 2016 (SI 2016/345).

27 See Legal Aid, Sentencing and Punishment of Offenders Act 2012 (Commencement No 5 and Saving Provision) Order 2013 (SI 2013/77), art 3(c).

28 SI 2013/77. Conditional Fee Agreements Order 2013 (SI 2013/689), art 6(2), made almost identical provisions to those in Legal Aid, Sentencing and Punishment of Offenders Act 2012 (Commencement No 5 and Saving Provision) Order 2013 (SI 2013/77), art 4. This was somewhat curious because those limits apply only to personal injury cases. Indeed, one could be forgiven for wondering if they were unthinkingly copied and pasted from one Order into the other.

54.33 There are corresponding provisions in the CPR. In so far as it is relevant, CPR, r 48.2, reads as follows:

> '48.2 (1) A pre-commencement funding arrangement is—
> [...]
> (b) in relation to insolvency-related proceedings, publication and privacy proceedings ...—
> (i) a funding arrangement as defined by rule 43.2(1)(k)(i) where—
> (aa) the agreement was entered into before the relevant date specifically for the purposes of the provision to the person by whom the success fee is payable of advocacy or litigation services in relation to the matter that is the subject of the proceedings in which the costs order is to be made; or
> (bb) the agreement was entered into before the relevant date and advocacy or litigation services were provided to that person under the agreement in connection with that matter before the relevant date;
> (ii) a funding arrangement as defined by rule 43.2(1)(k)(ii) where the party seeking to recover the insurance premium took out the insurance policy in relation to the proceedings before the relevant date.
> (2) In paragraph (1)—
> (a) "insolvency-related proceedings" means any proceedings—
> (i) in England and Wales brought by a person acting in the capacity of—
> (aa) a liquidator of a company which is being wound up in England and Wales or Scotland under Parts IV or V of the Insolvency Act 1986; or
> (bb) a trustee of a bankrupt's estate under Part IX of the Insolvency Act 1986;
> (ii) brought by a person acting in the capacity of an administrator appointed pursuant to the provisions of Part II of the Insolvency Act 1986;
> (iii) in England and Wales brought by a company which is being wound up in England and Wales or Scotland under Parts IV or V of the Insolvency Act 1986; or
> (iv) brought by a company which has entered administration under Part II of the Insolvency Act 1986;
> [...]
> (e) "the relevant date" is the date on which sections 44 and 46 of the Legal Aid, Sentencing and Punishment of Offenders Act 2012 came into force in relation to proceedings of the sort in question.'

Where the old provisions still apply, funding arrangements continue to be pre-commencement funding arrangements. Vos C has explained that if a query arises as to whether a funding arrangement will or will not apply to any given claim, the matter is best determined at the end of the claim rather than part of the way through.[29]

54.34 In so far as the position after 6 April 2016 is concerned, the transitional provisions in ss 44(6) and 46(3) of the Legal Aid, Sentencing and Punishment of Offenders Act 2012—that is, the general savings provisions—have effect.[30] Put otherwise, the matters set out in 54.08–54.09 and 54.13 will apply, but with the applicable date being 6 April 2016, rather than 1 April 2013.

[29] See *Mawer v Moore* [2017] EWHC 1242 (Comp).

[30] See the Explanatory Note to Legal Aid Sentencing and Punishment of Offenders Act 2012 (Commencement No 12) Order 2016 (SI 2016/345).

Savings relating to publication and privacy claims

Publication and privacy claims were excluded from the provisions that abrogated the recoverability of success fees and ATE premiums (but not notional premiums).[31] This was achieved by art 4 of the Legal Aid, Sentencing and Punishment of Offenders Act 2012 (Commencement No 5 and Saving Provision) Order 2013,[32] which reads as follows: 'Articles 2(1)(a) and (c) and article 3(a) and (c) do not apply to ... (b) publication and privacy proceedings.' **54.35**

PD 48, para 3, adds the following commentary: **54.36**

> '3.2 ... sections 44 and 46 of the 2012 Act are not being commenced immediately in respect of publication and privacy proceedings, which will accordingly be in a similar position as regards funding arrangements to mesothelioma claims and insolvency-related proceedings until such time as those sections are commenced in relation to them.'

Again, there are corresponding provisions in the CPR. In so far as it is relevant, CPR, r 48.2, reads as follows: **54.37**

> '48.2 (1) A pre-commencement funding arrangement is—
> [...]
> (b) in relation to ... publication and privacy proceedings ...—
> (i) a funding arrangement as defined by rule 43.2(1)(k)(i) where—
> (aa) the agreement was entered into before the relevant date specifically for the purposes of the provision to the person by whom the success fee is payable of advocacy or litigation services in relation to the matter that is the subject of the proceedings in which the costs order is to be made; or
> (bb) the agreement was entered into before the relevant date and advocacy or litigation services were provided to that person under the agreement in connection with that matter before the relevant date;
> (ii) a funding arrangement as defined by rule 43.2(1)(k)(ii) where the party seeking to recover the insurance premium took out the insurance policy in relation to the proceedings before the relevant date.
> (2) In paragraph (1)—[[33]]
> [...]
> (b) "news publisher" means a person who publishes a newspaper, magazine or website containing news or information about or comment on current affairs;
> (c) "publication and privacy proceedings" means proceedings for—
> (i) defamation;
> (ii) malicious falsehood;
> (iii) breach of confidence involving publication to the general public;
> (iv) misuse of private information; or
> (v) harassment, where the defendant is a news publisher.
> [...]
> (e) "the relevant date" is the date on which sections 44 and 46 of the Legal Aid, Sentencing and Punishment of Offenders Act 2012 came into force in relation to proceedings of the sort in question.'

[31] See Legal Aid, Sentencing and Punishment of Offenders Act 2012 (Commencement No 5 and Saving Provision) Order 2013 (SI 2013/77), art 3(c).

[32] SI 2013/77.

[33] This wording is used despite the fact that CPR, r 48.2(1), does not use the words 'news publisher'.

Savings relating to clinical negligence claims

54.38 In the same way as there were concerns about the effect that the abrogation of the recovery of additional liabilities may have on those who brought claims for damages for having contracted mesothelioma (see 54.22–54.30), there were concerns about access to justice for claimants with clinical negligence claims. In view of this, Legal Aid, Sentencing and Punishment of Offenders Act 2012, s 46(1), created a new s 58C of the Courts and Legal Services Act 1990. It reads as follows:

> '(1) A costs order made in favour of a party to proceedings who has taken out a costs insurance policy may not include provision requiring the payment of an amount in respect of all or part of the premium of the policy, unless such provision is permitted by regulations under subsection (2).
>
> (2) The Lord Chancellor may by regulations provide that a costs order may include provision requiring the payment of such an amount where—
> (a) the order is made in favour of a party to clinical negligence proceedings of a prescribed description,
> (b) the party has taken out a costs insurance policy insuring against the risk of incurring a liability to pay for one or more expert reports in respect of clinical negligence in connection with the proceedings (or against that risk and other risks),
> (c) the policy is of a prescribed description,
> (d) the policy states how much of the premium relates to the liability to pay for an expert report or reports in respect of clinical negligence ("the relevant part of the premium"), and
> (e) the amount is to be paid in respect of the relevant part of the premium.
>
> (3) Regulations under subsection (2) may include provision about the amount that may be required to be paid by the costs order, including provision that the amount must not exceed a prescribed maximum amount.
>
> (4) The regulations may prescribe a maximum amount, in particular, by specifying—
> (a) a percentage of the relevant part of the premium;
> (b) an amount calculated in a prescribed manner.
>
> (5) In this section—
> "clinical negligence" means breach of a duty of care or trespass to the person committed in the course of the provision of clinical or medical services (including dental or nursing services);
> "clinical negligence proceedings" means proceedings which include a claim for damages in respect of clinical negligence;
> "costs insurance policy", in relation to a party to proceedings, means a policy insuring against the risk of the party incurring a liability in those proceedings;
> "expert report" means a report by a person qualified to give expert advice on all or most of the matters that are the subject of the report;
> "proceedings" includes any sort of proceedings for resolving disputes (and not just proceedings in court), whether commenced or contemplated.'

54.39 The relevant secondary legislation, the Recovery of Costs Insurance Premiums in Clinical Negligence Proceedings (No 2) Regulations 2013,[34] came into force on 1 April 2013. The applicable provisions are in reg 3, which reads as follows:

[34] SI 2013/739. These were preceded by the Recovery of Costs Insurance Premiums in Clinical Negligence Proceedings Regulations 2013 (SI 2013/92), but they were revoked before they came into force.

'3. (1) A costs order made in favour of a party to clinical negligence proceedings who has taken out a costs insurance policy may include provision requiring the payment of an amount in respect of all or part of the premium of that policy if—

(a) the financial value of the claim for damages in respect of clinical negligence is more than £1,000; and

(b) the costs insurance policy insures against the risk of incurring a liability to pay for an expert report or reports relating to liability or causation in respect of clinical negligence (or against that risk and other risks).

(2) The amount of the premium that may be required to be paid under the costs order shall not exceed that part of the premium which relates to the risk of incurring liability to pay for an expert report or reports relating to liability or causation in respect of clinical negligence in connection with the proceedings.'

When s 58C of the Courts and Legal Services Act 1990 (as amended) is read in conjunction with those Regulations, it can be seen that ATE premiums are recoverable in clinical negligence proceedings if:

- the financial value of the claim for damages in respect of clinical negligence is more than £1,000;
- the party has taken out a policy insuring against the risk of incurring a liability to pay for one or more expert reports in respect of clinical negligence in connection with the proceedings (or against that risk and other risks);
- the risk insured is of incurring liability to pay for an expert relating to liability or causation; and
- the policy states how much of the premium relates to the liability to pay for an expert report or reports in respect of clinical negligence.

Recoverability is limited to that part of the premium relating to the 'risk of incurring liability to pay for an expert or reports relating to liability or causation in respect of clinical negligence in connection with the proceedings'.[35] **54.40**

PD 48, para 4, adds the following: **54.41**

'4.1 Section 46 of the 2012 Act enables the Lord Chancellor by regulations to provide that a costs order may include provision requiring the payment of an amount in respect of all or part of the premium of a costs insurance policy, where—

(a) the order is made in favour of a party to clinical negligence proceedings of a prescribed description;

(b) the party has taken out a costs insurance policy insuring against the risk of incurring a liability to pay for one or more expert reports in respect of clinical negligence in connection with the proceedings (or against that risk and other risks);

(c) the policy is of a prescribed description;

(d) the policy states how much of the premium relates to the liability to pay for such an expert report or reports, and the amount to be paid is in respect of that part of the premium.

4.2 The regulations made under the power are the Recovery of Costs Insurance Premiums in Clinical Negligence Proceedings Regulations 2013 (S.I. 2013/92).[[36]] The regulations

[35] See Recovery of Costs Insurance Premiums in Clinical Negligence Proceedings (No 2) Regulations 2013 (SI 2013/739), reg 3(2).

[36] This appears not to have been updated to take account of the fact that the 2013 Regulations were revoked before they came into force.

relate only to clinical negligence cases where a costs insurance policy is taken out on or after 1 April 2013, so the provisions in force in the CPR prior to 1 April 2013 relating to funding arrangements will not apply.'

Human rights and additional liabilities

54.42 This topic is addressed at 24.43–24.53.

Points of Principle Regarding Success Fees

54.43 The following points of principle regarding success fees are addressed:

- recovery of success fees retrospectively (see 54.44–54.46);
- different rates for different periods (see 54.47);
- the position of costs draftspersons and costs lawyers (see 54.48–54.49);
- fixed success fees (see 54.50); and
- solicitor-and-client issues (see 54.51–54.53).

Recovery of success fees retrospectively

54.44 Provided that it falls within the statutory scheme created by Courts and Legal Services Act 1990, s 58(1), legal services providers and clients may agree whatever arrangement they like. This may include a retrospective success fee. That said, Christopher Clarke J has confirmed that the court is permitted take into account the interests of the paying party for the purposes of assessment.[37]

54.45 The argument against recovery of retrospective success fees between opposing parties is that the CPR require that notice of funding be given[38] (see 54.108–54.123). The argument is that it would run contrary to the spirit of that requirement if a success fee could be recovered for work done prior to a conditional fee agreement being made.[39]

54.46 A receiving party may seek to recover a success fee retrospectively in a number of circumstances, depending on the nature of the pre-existing retainer (if any) and the period in respect of which the success fee is sought. The three circumstances most often encountered are as follows.

- **Transfer of liabilities from a private retainer to a conditional fee agreement** A client's existing liability for fees incurred under a private retainer may, by agreement with their legal service providers, be transferred such that they are payable conditionally under a conditional fee agreement. Christopher Clarke J found that there was nothing objectionable about such a transfer, largely because the court has the ability to disallow unreasonably incurred success fees.[40] He also explained that the appropriate standpoint for

[37] See *Forde v Birmingham City Council* [2009] EWHC 12 (QB), at [134].

[38] See CPR, r 44.15(1) and (2); CPD, art 19; Practice Direction (Protocols), para 4A.

[39] Indeed, whilst only persuasive, CPD, art 57.9(3), provides: 'Nothing in the legislation referred to above [ie Courts and Legal Services Act 1990 (as amended), etc] makes provision for a party who has entered into a funding arrangement to recover from another party any amount of an additional liability which relates to anything done or any costs incurred before the arrangement was entered into.'

[40] *Forde v Birmingham City Council* [2009] EWHC 12 (QB), at [150]. Some commentators have pointed out that Christopher Clarke J's attention seems not to have been drawn to the encouragement given by the

gauging the success fee would not be the time when instructions were received, but the time when the agreement was made. Both Rix LJ[41] and Edis J[42] have stressed the importance of the paying party being given notice of the correct date on which the conditional fee agreement was made (as opposed merely to the date on which it became retrospectively effective). The fact that retrospective success fees may be recoverable in principle does not, however, mean that they will always be allowed in practice.[43]

- **Revision of a percentage increase** Where a new percentage increase is agreed that retrospectively replaces that which was originally agreed, the success fee may be said to have been revised.[44] Christopher Clarke J implied that such a success fee is recoverable in principle, but that the court would be able to disallow it on the grounds of reasonableness, in appropriate circumstances.[45] The receiving party may face arguments arising out the interpretation of the agreements and, in an extreme instances, they may face an argument that the success fee should be disallowed by reason of presumed undue influence. The second of these arguments would be unlikely to succeed (see 32.52).
- **Retrospective claim where a costs entitlement has already materialised** It will rarely be the case that the court will allow costs that have come into being as the result of the receiving party voluntarily accepting a liability after they have become entitled to costs. Whilst he was discussing contentious business agreements rather than conditional fee agreements, Irwin J said:

  > 'I would be hesitant to conclude that any CBA entered into by a Claimant, after an adverse Costs Order had been made . . . could be held to alter retrospectively the rights and obligations as between claimant and solicitor. The reason is obvious. To uphold a retrospective re-arrangement in circumstances like that, would be to uphold the retrospective revision of—or even creation of—the defendant's costs liability.'[46]

  Other cases have pointed in much the same direction.[47]

Differential rates for different periods

It used to be the case that CPD, art 11.8(2), permitted the court to allow different percentage uplifts for different items of costs and for different periods during which costs were incurred. That provision was found to be *ultra vires*. Brooke LJ explained why: **54.47**

> 'The approach [of allowing different rates for different periods] negates the whole purpose of assessing at the outset the risks involved in pursuing a claim. The solicitor did not have

then Practice Direction (Protocols) to give notice of funding pre-issue; however, his judgment seems not to have turned on the issue of when notice was given.

[41] *Hawksford Trustees Jersey Ltd (Trustee of The Bald Eagle Trust) v Stella Global UK Ltd* [2012] EWCA Civ 987, at [53].

[42] *O'Brien v Shorrock and MIB* [2015] EWHC 1630 (QB), at [44] and [47].

[43] In a case, for example, in which he stressed that each case should be decided on its merits, Master Gordon-Saker declined to allow a retrospective success fee in a case in which he believed that it had been incurred unreasonably: *JN Dairies Ltd v Johal Dairies Ltd & Anor* [2011] EWHC 90211 (Costs), at [28].

[44] If, for example, a legal services provider was entitled to terminate an agreement because of the risks of the litigation changing adversely, but if it were then to agree to enter into a new agreement that provides for a higher success fee, then that would be an example of a success fee being revised.

[45] *Forde v Birmingham City Council* [2009] EWHC 12 (QB), at [150] and [151].

[46] *Crook v Birmingham City Council* [2007] EWHC 1415 (QB), at [36].

[47] See, eg, *Kellar v Williams* [2004] UKPC 30; *Oyston v Royal Bank of Scotland* [2006] EWHC 90053 (Costs).

> the contractual power or the professional duty to do what [was] suggested, namely to re-negotiate the success fee once it became clear that the risks were now very small and that there was no longer any need to fear a "worst case scenario" such as might have been in the solicitor's mind when the CFA was initially agreed.'[48]

This principle—that differential rates should not be imposed—applies to the fees of a costs draftsperson engaged as agent for the purposes of a detailed assessment (see 54.48).

The position of costs draftspersons and costs lawyers

54.48 Although Maurice Kay LJ dissented, May LJ and Hallett LJ have found that costs draftsperson's fees are profit costs, rather than disbursements (see 22.22–22.24), with the effect that a success fee is payable on those fees[49] (assuming, of course, that the work is covered by a pre-commencement funding arrangement). There is no reason to believe that the same logic does not apply to agents in general, including costs lawyers (but only where they are engaged as agents, not where they are instructed by the client directly). For the reasons set out at 54.47, where a costs draftsperson or costs lawyer carries out work as agent, the same percentage increase will be payable on their work as is payable by their instructing solicitor for the work on the claim itself.[50] In principle, the success fee is not only recoverable when a costs draftsperson is engaged to deal with the costs at the conclusion of a claim, but also when costs-only proceedings are brought under CPR, Part 8.[51]

Budgets and success fees

54.49 Mann J has confirmed that budgets should not include success fees.[52] As such, if—for whatever reason—additional liabilities arise in the context of a costs-managed case, they will be assessed without reference to the budget (other than, of course, to the extent that the underlying base costs may themselves be subject to a costs management order).

Fixed success fees

54.50 Fixed success fees may apply in the following types of claim:

- road traffic accidents;
- employers' liability claims; and
- industrial disease claims.

These are issues that are discussed at length in Chapter 50 (see 50.150 *et seq*).

Solicitor-and-client issues

54.51 There was once a regulatory requirement that conditional fee agreements must provide that (unless the court were to order otherwise[53]) no client would have to pay a percentage increase if and to the extent that it had been reduced on assessment on the grounds of

[48] *U v Liverpool City Council (Practice Note)* [2005] EWCA Civ 475, at [36], as well as [42] and [49].
[49] *Crane v Canons Leisure Centre* [2007] EWCA Civ 1352.
[50] *Ibid.*
[51] *Halloran v Delaney* [2003] 1 WLR 28.
[52] See *Various Claimants v MGN Ltd* [2016] EWHC 1894 (Ch), *per* Mann J.
[53] Pre-1 April 2013 CPR, r 44.16.

reasonableness.[54] There was a similar requirement that limited the monies clients had to pay if success fees were agreed.[55] Those regulatory requirements ceased to exist in 2005, but the industry had become used to them and, right up until 31 March 2013, it was almost always the case that conditional fee agreements would contain some such provision (especially where the legal services provider was a solicitor). Indeed, it was so common that it would be arguable that they were terms that could be implied. Where a legal services provider seeks to charge its client more than was assessed, it must make an application; the procedure will depend on whether the costs between opposing parties were going to be assessed by way of summary assessment[56] or detailed assessment. The procedure was set out in CPD, arts 20.5 and 20.6 (which will still apply if the agreement is a pre-commencement funding arrangement), which read as follows:

> '20.5 Where the paying party serves points of dispute seeking a reduction in any percentage increase charged by a legal representative acting for the receiving party, and that legal representative intends, if necessary, to apply for an order that any amount of the percentage disallowed as against the paying party shall continue to be payable by his client, the solicitor acting for the receiving party must, within 14 days of service of the points of dispute, give to his client a clear written explanation of the nature of the relevant point of dispute and the effect it will have if it is upheld in whole or in part by the court, and of the client's right to attend any subsequent hearings at court when the matter is raised.
>
> 20.6 Where the solicitor acting for a receiving party files a request for a detailed assessment hearing it must if appropriate, be accompanied by a certificate signed by him stating:
>
> (1) that the amount of the percentage increase in respect of counsel's fees or solicitor's charges is disputed;
> (2) whether an application will be made for an order that any amount of that increase which is disallowed should continue to be payable by his client;
> (3) that he has given his client an explanation in accordance with paragraph 20.5; and,
> (4) whether his client wishes to attend court when the amount of any relevant percentage increase may be decided.'

Within seven days of receiving notice of the date of the assessment hearing, the legal services provider had to notify its client and, if appropriate, counsel of the date, time and place of the hearing (CPD, art 20.7(1)). CPD, art 20.8, would then apply: **54.52**

> '(1) At the detailed assessment hearing, the court will deal with the assessment of the costs payable by one party to another, including the amount of the percentage increase, and give a certificate accordingly.

[54] See Conditional Fee Agreements Regulations 2000 (SI 2000/692), reg 3(2)(b); Collective Conditional Fee Agreements Regulations 2000 (SI 2000/2988), reg 5(2)(b).

[55] See Conditional Fee Agreements Regulations 2000 (SI 2000/692), reg 3(2)(c); Collective Conditional Fee Agreements Regulations 2000 (SI 2000/2988), reg 5(2)(c).

[56] Where the issue arises at the conclusion of a summary assessment, the court may choose between dealing with the matter then and there or remitting it to a costs judge for a determination. In this regard, CPD, art 20.3, still applies (assuming, of course, that the agreement is a pre-commencement funding arrangement): '(1) If the court disallows any amount of a legal representative's percentage increase, the court will, unless sub-paragraph (2) applies, give directions to enable an application to be made by the legal representative for the disallowed amount to be payable by his client, including, if appropriate, a direction that the application will be determined by a costs judge or district judge of the court dealing with the case. (2) The court that has made the summary assessment may then and there decide the issue whether the disallowed amount should continue to be payable, if: (a) the receiving party and all parties to the relevant agreement consent to the court doing so; (b) the receiving party (or, if corporate, an officer) is present in court; and (c) the court is satisfied that the issue can be fairly decided then and there.'

(2) The court may decide the issue whether the disallowed amount should continue to be payable under the relevant conditional fee agreement without an adjournment if:

(a) the receiving party and all parties to the relevant agreement consent to the court deciding the issue without an adjournment,

(b) the receiving party (or, if corporate, an officer or employee who has authority to consent on behalf of the receiving party) is present in court, and

(c) the court is satisfied that the issue can be fairly decided without an adjournment.

(3) In any other case the court will give directions and fix a date for the hearing of the application.'

54.53 Further provisions applied where counsel's success fees were challenged. CPD, art 20.4 (which still applies where the agreement is a pre-commencement funding arrangement), reads as follows:

'(1) Where detailed assessment proceedings have been commenced, and the paying party serves points of dispute (as to which see Section 34 of this Practice Direction), which show that he is seeking a reduction in any percentage increase charged by counsel on his fees, the solicitor acting for the receiving party must within 3 days of service deliver to counsel a copy of the relevant points of dispute and the bill of costs or the relevant parts of the bill.

(2) Counsel must within 10 days thereafter inform the solicitor in writing whether or not he will accept the reduction sought or some other reduction. Counsel may state any points he wishes to have made in a reply to the points of dispute, and the solicitor must serve them on the paying party as or as part of a reply.

(3) Counsel who fails to inform the solicitor within the time limits set out above will be taken to accept the reduction unless the court otherwise orders.'

Counsel should be told of the date and time of the detailed assessment hearing (see CPD, art 20.7). Counsel does not need to attend in person and instead may make their representations in writing (CPD, art 20.7(1)).

The Assessment of the Amount of Success Fees

54.54 Unless it is otherwise stated, this section deals with success fees payable between opposing parties, which means that it concerns only those cases in which the receiving party has a conditional fee agreement that is a pre-commencement funding arrangement, as defined in CPR, r 48.2(1). It is also assumed that fixed success fees do not apply, which topic is addressed in Chapter 50.

54.55 In formal usage, a success fee is a sum of money.[57] This differs from the ordinary usage of that term, which is that 'success fee' means both the sum of money *and* the percentage that is used to calculate it. That percentage is properly called a 'percentage increase'.[58]

---

57 See Courts and Legal Services Act 1990 (as amended), s 58(2)(c).

58 See the pre-2013 iteration of CPR, 43.2(1)(l). It is 'the percentage by which the amount of a legal representative's fee can be increased in accordance with a conditional fee agreement which provides for a success fee'.

Types of success fee

Single-stage success fees

A single-stage success fee is the conventional type of success fee where the same percentage increase will, regardless of what happens during the claim, apply throughout (including the detailed assessment). **54.56**

There is a well-recognised method for assessing single-stage fees that has at its heart a mathematical formula (see 54.67–54.99 and 54.82–54.83 in particular). In general, a single-stage success fee will be assessed by identifying the entire risk in the claim (including, where appropriate, the risks relating to quantum and the risk posed by the costs proceedings that might follow the claim), and then by gauging the appropriate percentage increase that best suits that overall risk. **54.57**

The court lacks the power to order that the percentage increase be adjusted so that different percentage increases apply to different periods[59] (see 54.47). Likewise, it is not permissible simply to adopt and apply the relevant allowances in pre-1 April 2013 CPR, Part 45,[60] although examples do exist of the court taking those allowances into account, presumably as a cross-check.[61] **54.58**

Two- or multi-stage success fees

A two- or multi-stage success fee is based on a percentage increase that will change (with retrospective effect throughout the claim) at certain predefined stages in the litigation. At the end of the claim, the success fee will be based on a single percentage increase throughout, but that figure will depend on what happened at the predetermined stages. The percentage increase will usually rise as the claim progresses, but there is no reason in principle why it should not decrease, such as where the percentage increase would be abated with retrospective effect if liability were to be admitted within a certain period. **54.59**

The rationale for two-stage or multi-stage success fees was explained by Woolf CJ thus: 'It can properly be assumed that if, notwithstanding the compliance with the protocol, the other party is not prepared to settle, or not prepared to settle upon reasonable terms, there is a serious defence.'[62] Brooke LJ has repeatedly supported this approach,[63] pointing in particular to another advantage of two- and multi-stage success fees (from legal service providers' point of view)—namely, that if the case does not settle, a high success fee will be more readily defensible than otherwise might have been the case.[64] , where a single-stage success fee is used, a high percentage increase will need to be justified.[65] **54.60**

---

59 *U v Liverpool City Council* [2005] EWCA Civ 475, at [49].

60 *Atack v Lee* [2004] EWCA Civ 1712, at [52], *per* Brooke LJ. Similarly, Edis J has confirmed that it would be an error to believe that, because fixed success fees payable under CPR, Part 45, tend to be higher if the case reaches trial, the same ought to apply where a single-stage success fee is to be assessed rather than fixed: see *O'Brien v Shorrock and MIB* [2015] EWHC 1630 (QB), at [24], citing *Atack v Lee* [2004] EWCA Civ 1712, at [12].

61 See, eg, *Thornley (a child) v Ministry of Defence* [2010] EWHC 2584 (QB), at [50], *per* HHJ Behrens (sitting as a judge of the High Court).

62 *Callery v Gray* [2001] EWCA Civ 1117, at [108].

63 See, eg, *Atack v Lee* [2004] EWCA Civ 1712, at [7]–[11]; *Halloran v Delaney* [2002] EWCA Civ 1258, as clarified in *Claims Direct Test Cases* [2003] EWCA Civ 136, at [101].

64 *U v Liverpool City Council* [2005] EWCA Civ 475, at [21].

65 See *O'Brien v Shorrock and MIB* [2015] EWHC 1630 (QB), at [30].

54.61 It will not always be the case that two- or multi-stage success will stand up to judicial scrutiny, however. In a case in which the agreement put the solicitors at risk of Part 36 offers, for example, Sir Robert Nelson found that a second-stage success fee of 100 per cent could not be justified because an admission of liability had removed a large part of the risk.[66] He held that the first stage (claimed at 25 per cent) was itself not justified and that it was not an appropriate platform for the second-stage fee.

54.62 There is no special method for calculating two- or multi-stage success fees (see 54.63), but Woolf CJ has explained that even if the matter settles at an early stage, a success fee will still be payable (that is, it would not be nil). This is because:

- the legal services providers would be entitled to be compensated for accepting a retainer on a 'no win, no fee' basis, with the inevitable risk that that would involve; and
- an appropriate success fee would contribute towards those cases in which no fees are payable because they end unsuccessfully.[67]

54.63 Whilst there is no authority on the point, there is no conceptual difficulty with adapting the method of assessment of single-stage success fees (see 54.67–54.99) so that it may be used to assess two- or multi-stage success fees. This can be done by recognising that, by setting stages, separate risk profiles are created. If, for example, a two-stage success fee is determined by whether liability will be admitted by the time proceedings are issued, then—in effect—this creates a low-risk profile (where liability is admitted within that profile) and a high-risk profile (where liability is not). The fact that it is not known which profile will ultimately apply will in no way prevent the risks in each profile being assessed in the usual way (albeit based on hypothetical facts relevant to each); the percentage increase for each profile may then be set according to the methods described in 54.67–54.99. This causes no difficulties because the profiles are separately determinable and the risks can be gauged in advance at the time that the conditional fee agreement is made.

Prematurity and early risk assessments

54.64 It is well established that a legal services provider is able to enter into a conditional fee agreement and set its success fee at an early stage of the litigation. Speaking at a time when success fees were still generally recoverable between opposing parties, Woolf CJ had the following to say on the topic:

> 'We do not consider [that it is] mandatory for the claimant to delay entering into a CFA or taking out ATE insurance in order to enable his legal representative to acquire a greater knowledge of the circumstances of the case than that provided to him by the claimant. In the type of claim with which these appeals are concerned, the circumstances of the case will often lead the legal representative to assess the risk of failure, not only on the basis of particular features of the case, but on his general experience that claims which appear to have every prospect of success none the less occasionally founder as a result of matters which are unforeseen.'[68]

Woolf CJ explained that one of the reasons why he had arrived at this conclusion was because that would make it less likely that the burden of paying for unsuccessful claims

---

[66] *Fortune v Roe* [2011] EWHC 2953 (QB), at [18], [36]–[37], [46] and [51]–[53].
[67] *Callery v Gray* [2001] EWCA Civ 1117, at [110].
[68] *Callery v Gray* [2001] EWCA Civ 1117, at [96]–[97].

would fall on the few with strong defences, rather than on the many with defences of varying strength. He said that it would be more equitable if success fees were borne in relatively small amounts by many unsuccessful defendants, rather than borne in much larger amounts by those unsuccessful defendants who persist in contesting liability.[69]

There are those who have argued that the right to set a success fee at an early stage is limited to modest road traffic claims (because such claims are often, as a class, much the same, so that they 'do not turn on the peculiar features of the claim itself').[70] There is a divergence of judicial opinion as to how a success fee set at an early stage ought to be assessed. There can be no little doubt that a success fee based on an assessment of risk on enquiry will be easier to justify than an initial assessment based on the absence of information,[71] but there have been differing approaches as to how the latter should be addressed. In the context of a clinical negligence case decided when success fees were still generally recoverable, Jack J said this: **54.65**

> '[Some may say] that a solicitor should not enter an agreement at an early stage. However, as I have said, he is entitled to do so. It follows inevitably from that entitlement that he will be in a position of ignorance compared with that when he has the medical records and expert advice. But he is likely to be experienced in the field and he will have some knowledge of the claim. His "ignorance" is relative. He may have taken on a winner: he does not know. But equally he may have taken on a case where greater knowledge would show the chances were well below 50 percent.'[72]

Thus Jack J was influenced by the risk of *not* yet knowing what the evidence, upon enquiry, would hold. Whilst he too was influenced by this factor (albeit to a lesser degree), Mackay J—in a case that was very similar on the facts—refused to follow Jack J's analysis in full; instead, he concluded that if a success fee is set at a stage that was too early for a full assessment of risk to be made, then weight ought to be given to the facts that, first, it would have been open to the legal services provider to have set a two- or multi-stage success fee,[73] and secondly, it would usually be possible to terminate the agreement if subsequent enquiries were to show the case to be laden with risk.[74]

Regardless of which analysis is correct, it is likely that no legal services provider can shut its eyes to evidence that would easily be available at the time the risk assessment was carried out. In this regard, it is relevant that Brooke LJ found that, on the facts of the case before him, a solicitor ought to have made a telephone call to ascertain certain facts.[75] Some judges have gone further and disallowed success fees entirely (albeit not on the basis of prematurity per se, but on the basis that excessive haste can result in a failure to try to **54.66**

[69] *Ibid*, at [99].

[70] *Ibid*, at [84].

[71] Whilst not binding, see *Barhan v Athreya and (2) Barking, Havering & Redbridge NHS Trust* (unreported), 16 June 2007, Central London County Court, at [53], *per* HHJ Dean QC.

[72] *Oliver v Whipps Cross University NHS Trust* [2009] EWHC 1104 (QB), at [17]. It is perhaps worth noting that Jack J had before him data that had been prepared by the receiving party's solicitors, which showed that about half of the clinical negligence cases that were initially investigated ultimately failed. Therefore, by assessing risks at a very early stage, the solicitor was not merely having a stab in the dark, but was purposively placing the case in a category about which data existed and in respect of which risks could be ascertained.

[73] *McCarthy v Essex Rivers Healthcare NHS Trust* (unreported), 13 November 2009, QBD, at [18].

[74] *Ibid*, at [8], ie this was the analysis in the court below and Mackay J did not interfere with it.

[75] *Ellerton v Harris* [2004] EWCA Civ 1712, at [49].

resolve the dispute). In a case in which the receiving party had acted hastily in the sense that it did not trouble itself with the pre-action protocol, Akenhead J found that no success fee should be recoverable.[76] There were several grounds for that finding,[77] but one of them was that compliance with the protocol might have resolved the dispute. Undoubtedly, that conclusion was correct on the facts, but it is rare for the court to deal with the issue of success fees in that way.

Risk and success fees

54.67 What follows is very much a summary of the relevant law and principles. A more detailed discussion of the topic of risk and success fees may be found Chapter 30 of the second edition of this book. If a difficult topic arises, it may be necessary to read both this chapter and that older edition.

54.68 The editor is grateful to Professor Paul Sweeting (University of Kent at Canterbury) for his assistance with the equations that are described in the following paragraphs.

54.69 The relevant factors may be divided into those going to risk and those not going to risk. The latter include the 'postponement charge' and the 'disbursement charge', and are dealt with at 54.101–54.105 and 54.105–54.107, respectively. Those going to risk are addressed below (at 54.70–54.99).

54.70 Risks may be categorised according to the nature of the event to which they relate; hence a risk of the case being lost entirely may be called a liability risk, the risk of failing to achieve a better result than an opponent's Part 36 offer may be called a quantum risk, etc. This categorisation is useful for the purposes of *describing* the various types of risk that might pertain in any given case, but the percentage uplift is usually based on the aggregate risk (see 54.89). Put otherwise, a single percentage increase is set by reference to the entirety of risk, rather than based on component parts, with each set by reference to its own component risk.

Risk in general

54.71 Where the conditional fee agreement is a pre-commencement funding arrangement, the (now-revoked) CPD will continue to apply. It provided as follows:

> 'In deciding whether a percentage increase is reasonable relevant factors to be taken into account may include:
> (a) the risk that the circumstances in which the costs, fees or expenses would be payable might or might not occur ...'[78]

54.72 Thus it is necessary to identify the circumstances in which the legal services provider may fail to recover its fees. This will turn on how 'win' or 'success' is defined in the conditional fee agreement and, in this regard, it may be necessary to look at the circumstances in which the agreement was made, as well as the agreement itself.[79]

---

[76] *Buildability Ltd v O'Donnell Developments Ltd* [2009] EWHC 3196 (TCC), at [27]. For a discussion of the difference between disallowing a success fee and assessing it at nil, see para 30.43 of the second edition of this book.

[77] The other reasons were lack of risk, lack of evidence as to whether there had been a success and a need to amend the claim.

[78] CPD, art 11.8(1).

[79] In *Manning v Kings College Hospital NHS Trust* [2011] EWHC 2954 (QB), for example, Spencer J found that an agreement that stated that 'win' would include any award of damages did not mean that the

54.73 The CPD went on to provide the following guidance:

> 'Subject to paragraph 17.8(2),[[80]] when the court is considering the factors to be taken into account in assessing an additional liability, it will have regard to the facts and circumstances as they reasonably appeared to the solicitor or counsel when the funding arrangement was entered into and at the time of any variation of the arrangement.'[81]

54.74 In a similar vein, Moore-Bick LJ has explained that the court should deal with risk in the following way: 'The success fee must reflect a reasonable and rational assessment of the risks facing the solicitor at the time when the agreement was entered into.'[82] Often, the court will have the benefit of a contemporaneous risk assessment (see 54.76–54.77), but Brooke LJ has confirmed that, where the risk assessment is inadequate, the court must substitute its own assessment from the standpoint of a reasonably careful legal services provider assessing the risk on the basis of what was known at the time.[83]

54.75 Where a success fee is recoverable between opposing parties, there are no significant rules limiting the factors that the court may take into account when assessing the nature and level of the relevant risk (or risks). The court may not take hindsight into account[84]—although the outcome of the litigation is, from time to time, used as a cross-check in the sense that it is evidence of what the parties believed the merits to be.[85]

54.76 As mentioned above, it may be that there is a contemporaneous risk assessment. Such assessments are often generic and of little—if any—use, but even where it is a bespoke risk assessment that is based on the facts of the case in hand, the court will scrutinise it with care, and this will be especially so if it was prepared only for the purpose of setting the percentage increase. The reasons for this were explained by Neuberger MR:

> 'I believe that there may be a regrettable, if understandable, tendency to charge the maximum success fee of 100% in every case. The client with whom the fee is negotiated by the lawyer has no interest in the level of success fee (at least in a case such as this, where he has to pay no more than he is entitled to recover from the paying party), and the lawyer has an obvious and strong interest in the success fee being as high as possible. In many cases, it is easy for a lawyer, acting in complete good faith, to persuade himself that the prospects of his client's case succeeding are no better than 50% when it is in his interest to do so, and when he has no negotiations with the party who will or may have to pay the success fee. The court has a particular duty, therefore, to be vigilant in considering the reasonableness of the level of success fee agreed, but, as I have said, this does not mean that the court can invoke the wisdom of hindsight or should adopt an unduly harsh approach.'[86]

---

case had already been won by reason of certain admissions that had already been made at the time the agreement was made.

[80] The reference to 'paragraph 17.8(2)' is a reference to a provision that applies only to costs-only proceedings, which provision is possibly *ultra vires*, but in any event can be disregarded for present purposes.

[81] CPD, art 11.7.

[82] *C (a patient acting by her litigation friend Jocelyn Fox) v W* [2008] EWCA Civ 1459, at [8].

[83] *Atack v Lee* [2004] EWCA Civ 1712, at [37].

[84] See *O'Brien v Shorrock and MIB* [2015] EWHC 1630 (QB), at [23], *per* Edis J.

[85] Whilst not binding, see *Designers Guild Ltd v Russell Williams (Textiles) Ltd (t/a Washington DC) (No 2)* [2003] EWHC 9024 (Costs), in which Master Hurst had the following to say: 'There is an argument for saying that in any case which reached trial a success fee of 100% is easily justified because both sides presumably believed that they had an arguable and winnable case. In this case we have no doubt at all that the matter was finely balanced and that the appropriate success fee is therefore 100%.' See also paras 30.48 and 30.49 of the second edition of this book.

[86] *Drake v Fripp* [2011] EWCA Civ 1282, at [21].

54.77 It may, however, be that the court is presented with a risk assessment that has been carried out both for the purposes of setting a success fee and for the purposes of obtaining ATE insurance. Such assessments are generally afforded more weight. Edis J had this to say on the topic:

> 'In undertaking this exercise the profession had to balance competing considerations. The ATE insurers wanted the prospects to be good and loaded the premium or refused cover if they were not. The solicitors wanted the prospects to be bad because that would justify a higher success fee if the case succeeded. With these considerations pulling in opposite directions there was some incentive to assess the prospects as accurately as possible. Having done that, there is little room for further adjustment at the conversion stage which is, and rationally should be, a matter of arithmetic.'[87]

In any event, all relevant factual material ought to be taken into account; a failure to do so may amount to a procedural irregularity.[88] In practice, many judges will give weight to what is said in correspondence to the receiving party, what was said to and by counsel, and what is recorded in file notes in general.

54.78 Once risk has been quantified, it needs to be converted into a percentage increase. The theory underlying that process was explained by Jack J in these terms:

> 'The rationale behind the percentage mark up as it is applied in our courts is that the successful cases should pay for the unsuccessful ones. The theory runs as follows. If a solicitor acts in two cases with 50% chances of success, he will win one and lose one, and so he needs a success fee, or mark up, on the costs in the successful action of 100% to recover the costs of both. If he acts in three cases each with a one third chance of success, he will win one and lose two. So in the winning case he needs a mark up of 200%. But the maximum allowed in law is 100%. If he acts in three cases each with a two thirds chance of success, he will win two and lose one. So in each winning case he needs a mark up of 50%. If he acts in five cases with a 60% chance of success, he should win three and lose two, so he needs a mark up of two thirds (or 67% as Master Campbell took it) on each of the three to pay for the two. It can be seen that a small decrease in the chances of success, results in a comparatively large increase in the mark up required.'[89]

Whilst the calculation of success fees is a matter of justice rather than mere calculation, the essence of Jack J's analysis can be expressed in terms of a formula (see 54.82).

54.79 In an appropriate case, the court might be assisted by statistical data,[90] but Mackay J had this to say on that topic:

> '[A] complex statistical analysis of the cases dealt with by these [the firms in question] will not help me resolve this appeal and nor should such evidence need to be put before costs

87 See *O'Brien v Shorrock and MIB* [2015] EWHC 1630 (QB), at [29]. *Ibid*, at [30], Edis J said this: '[If] the risk assessment is adequate it is a matter or arithmetic to convert it into a success fee. … There is nothing wrong with [the costs judge's] decision not to conduct a thorough re-assessment of the risks by reference to the original evidence. This would be practically impossible in many cases. Where, however the court has not done this it is difficult to discern a proper basis for departing from the assessment conducted by the solicitors at the time.'

88 See *Tucker v Hampshire Hospitals NHS Foundation Trust* [2017] EWHC 3650 (QB).

89 *Oliver v Whipps Cross University NHS Trust* [2009] EWHC 1104 (QB), at [2].

90 See, eg, *ibid*, at [17].

judges every time they have to assess such cases. I agree with her that that would be an undesirable and onerous task and should not be encouraged.'[91]

In practice, it is fleetingly rare for statistical data to be relied upon. Retrospective experience of other cases may, however, occasionally be relevant.[92]

The fact that risks may be capable of being managed may have a bearing on the success fee. Where, for example, a conditional fee agreement relates to a preliminary issue only (such as liability, but not quantum), this will generally mean that the risks of any subsequent stages will be capable of being managed[93] and this militates against a high percentage increase. **54.80**

Liability risk

There is much more detail on this topic in the second edition of this book. In particular, the following topics are covered in the following paragraphs in that edition (with updating as set out below): **54.81**

- admissions, denials and the risk of withdrawals (para 30.40)—since when Singh J has found that the fact that an offer was made shortly prior to the making of a conditional fee agreement justified the lowering of the percentage increase;[94]
- complexity (para 30.42);
- low-risk litigation (para 30.43);[95]
- the possibility of withdrawal of instructions (para 30.44);
- the relevance of a client's solvency (para 30.45);
- the relevance of the size of the claim (para 30.46);
- the relevance of the size of the firm (para 30.47);
- costs-only proceedings (para 30.48);
- rear-end shunts (para 30.50);
- passenger claims (para 30.51);
- risk arising out of costs litigation (para 30.52);
- risk of suing the wrong defendant and risks arising out of insurance issues (para 30.53);
- the relevance of contributory negligence (para 30.54);
- the relevance of uncertainty in the law and of technical points (para 30.55);
- the relevance of acceptance of responsibility for disbursements (para 30.56);
- the relevance of advice given to the client and counsel's advices (para 30.57); and
- adverse selection (para 30.58).

---

[91] *McCarthy v Essex Rivers Healthcare NHS Trust* (unreported), 13 November 2009, QBD, at [19].

[92] See *Motto & Ors v Trafigura Ltd & Anor* [2011] EWCA Civ 1150, at [128], *per* Lord Neuberger MR.

[93] See *O'Brien v Shorrock and MIB* [2015] EWHC 1630 (QB), at [26], *per* Edis J.

[94] See *Briggs v First Choice Holidays & Flights Ltd* [2017] EWHC 2012 (QB), at [53], *per* Singh J.

[95] Judge Wood QC (sitting a judge of the High Court) found that if a driver were to lose control when no other car was involved and passengers were injured, then that fact by itself might be capable of giving rise to a rebuttable inference that the driver was to blame (ie *res ipsa loquitur*). However, as soon as a possible explanatory cause was provided, such as black ice, the inference ceased to carry weight and other factors such as speed became important: see *Dronsfield v Street* (unreported), 25 June 2013, Manchester District Registry, *per* Judge Wood QC.

54.82 If the only risk in question is the liability risk (that is, the risk of losing), then it is generally accepted that the following formula[96] is appropriate for converting risk into a percentage uplift:

$$s = \frac{f}{1-f}$$

Where

s is the percentage increase expressed as a fraction
f is the risk of failure expressed as a fraction

This is the formula that is used to calculate the well-known 'ready reckoner' that is often found in publications on success fees and textbooks on costs. Just such a ready reckoner may be found at Table 68.12 (or, in abbreviated form, on the inside front cover of this book).

54.83 This formula is nothing more than an algebraic way of expressing the notion that the success fee is (a) that proportion of the total base costs which, on average, will go unpaid as a result of the risk in question divided by (b) that proportion of the base costs which will be paid. This is a manifestation of the 'neutrality principle'—namely, that the success fee compensates for lost income.

54.84 It may be that there is a need to work backwards to derive the risks from the success fee (or, more accurately, from the percentage increase). Assuming that the only risk in question is the risk of losing, the following formula allows this to be done:

$$s_{\%} = \frac{100 - p_{\%}}{p_{\%}}$$

Where

$s\%$ and $p\%$ are the percentage increases and prospects of success, expressed in percentages

54.85 This analysis assumes that it is possible to estimate risks in a quantitative way. It may be, however, that there is so little information that it is difficult even to assess the risk. In those circumstances, the case may be categorised as having 'uncertain prospects', to use Jack J's phrase.[97] Where this is the case, a high success fee may or may not be justified, depending on the facts.[98] Moore-Bick LJ has suggested that if the risks are very difficult to assess, it may be appropriate to enter into a variant of a two-stage agreement in which the risks are to be reassessed if an offer is made.[99] Mackay J has confirmed that if the solicitor has the opportunity to abandon the claim if the prospects of success become too bleak, then that is something that can be reflected in the success fee (see 54.65).[100]

[96] This formula is only an approximation, because most conditional fee agreements will deprive the legal services provider of its success fee in the event of its client failing to beat a Part 36 offer. It would be possible to include that factor in the calculation, but there is no authority to suggest that this should be done.

[97] *Oliver v Whipps Cross University NHS Trust* [2009] EWHC 1104 (QB), at [17]. See, however, *McCarthy v Essex Rivers Healthcare NHS Trust* (unreported), 13 November 2009, QBD, at [17]–[21], in which Mackay J questions the correctness of Jack J's analysis.

[98] On the facts of the case before him, Jack J allowed a success fee of 100 per cent, but he did not intend to create any precedent in that regard. It is perhaps worth noting that although Jack J said that the risk was uncertain, on the facts of the case before him, this finding immediately put the case into a larger category of similar cases in respect of which there was data that quantified the risk; hence one could argue that the 'uncertain' risks could perhaps better be described as 'less certain than would ideally be the case'.

[99] *C (a patient acting by her litigation friend Jocelyn Fox) v W* [2008] EWCA Civ 1459, at [24].

[100] *McCarthy v Essex Rivers Healthcare NHS Trust* (unreported), 13 November 2009, QBD, at [18].

Discounted agreements (liability risk)

Where a success fee is payable pursuant to a discounted conditional fee agreement (see 29.03), the fact that discounted fees are payable in the absence of success needs to be taken into account. Whilst it has never been approved by any court,[101] the following formula is generally regarded as being of assistance: **54.86**

$$s = \frac{f(1-d)}{1-f}$$

Where

s is the percentage increase expressed as a fraction
f is the risk of failure expressed as a fraction
d is the fraction of costs payable in the event of the claim not succeeding

Quantum risk

Quantum risk is the risk of costs being disallowed as a result of the party in question—usually a claimant—failing to 'beat' a Part 36 offer or other offer. It will apply only where the conditional fee agreement puts the legal services provider at risk on quantum (see 29.02–29.03). Where there is an allegation of contributory negligence in a personal injury claim, quantum risk may be a significant factor to be taken into account.[102] **54.87**

Whether a conditional fee agreement puts the legal services provider at risk on quantum is a matter of contractual interpretation. If the agreement says that the legal services provider will not be paid base costs in the event that its client fails to beat a Part 36 offer, then the agreement can be said to provide for a quantum risk. If there is no such provision, then this will generally not be the case,[103] but such a provision may be implied by the circumstances.[104] **54.88**

Whilst quantum risk will often simply be subsumed within the percentage increase without any need to give thought to it as a separate entity,[105] Moore-Bick LJ has given guidance as to how quantum risk should be analysed in cases in which it justifies specific attention: **54.89**

> 'The task facing [the legal services providers] was to assess, as best they could, the risk of losing part of their fees for reasons of that kind, and then expressing that as a percentage of the total fees likely to be earned to trial. Only by doing so could they calculate a success fee expressed as a percentage uplift on the whole of their profit costs.'[106]

Thus the quantum risk is expressed in terms of a percentage of the total fees likely to be earned to trial (see 54.90). Moore-Bick LJ went on to refer to the overall risk as a risk 'equivalent to failure overall'.[107]

---

[101] Whilst he did not expressly refer to the formula, Master Gordon-Saker applied it in *Commissioners for HMRC v Blue Sphere Global Ltd* [2011] EWHC 90217 (Costs).

[102] See, eg, *Bright v Motor Insurers' Bureau* [2014] EWHC 1557 (QB).

[103] *Atack v Lee* [2004] EWCA Civ 1712, at [38].

[104] See *Manning v Kings College Hospital NHS Trust* [2011] EWHC 2954 (QB), at [97]–[147], *per* Spencer J, applying *Investors Compensation Scheme Ltd v West Bromwich Building Society (No 1)* [1998] 1 WLR 896.

[105] See, eg, *Ellerton v Harris* [2004] EWCA Civ 1712, at [49], in which Brooke LJ found that 'the only significant risk related to the possibility of the Claimant accepting her solicitor's advice and then not beating a payment in' and that 'this [was] just one of the rare risks which justified a success fee set as high as 20% in the simplest of claims'.

[106] *C (a patient acting by her litigation friend Jocelyn Fox) v W* [2008] EWCA Civ 1459, at [17].

[107] *Ibid*, at [24].

54.90 The following is an example of how a quantum risk may be reflected in a percentage increase. If Part 36 offers were to pose a 30 per cent risk that half of the fees would be disallowed, it would be fair to say that 15 per cent of the costs were at risk in this way. If the prospects of success generally were 80 per cent, then a single, global figure for risk (or an 'equivalent' figure, to use Moore-Bick LJ's terminology) would be 85 per cent of 80 per cent—that is, 68 per cent (rounded up to 70 per cent for ease of calculation). If the formula at 54.82 is then applied to that risk, the appropriate percentage increase would be 42 per cent. This contrasts with 25 per cent, which is what the percentage increase would have been had the conditional fee agreement not provided for a quantum risk.

54.91 It can be seen that all of these risks are somewhat nebulous and, at the very least, difficult to assess, which means that there is little point in aiming for spurious accuracy. In view of this, the ready reckoner at Table 68.12 includes three columns marked 'high', 'medium' and 'low', which represent an entirely arbitrary assumption that these categories of risk can be assessed as putting 30 per cent, 20 per cent and 10 per cent of the costs at risk of non-recovery by reason of Part 36 offers. The formula that has been used to create that ready reckoner is as follows—and recall that *p%* represents the prospect of success expressed as a percentage and *s%* represents the percentage uplift expressed as a percentage (see 54.82–54.83):

$$s = \frac{1 - pq}{pq}$$

Where

s is the percentage increase expressed as a fraction
p is the prospects of success expressed as a fraction
q is the fraction of costs to trial at risk as a result of offers

For the avoidance of doubt, q does not represent the fraction that would be disallowed in a case in which an offer *had* been beaten, but the fraction that would be disallowed as a result of quantum risk on average.

54.92 The fact that a quantum risk may exist in principle does not mean that it will exist as a matter of course, as Moore-Bick LJ remarked:

> 'The chance that [the legal services providers] would advise [the claimant] to reject an offer which she subsequently failed to beat at trial is difficult to assess, but one would not expect highly experienced solicitors practising in this field to differ very widely in their assessment of the bracket in which an award would be likely to fall, provided they had access to the same information.'[108]

54.93 It should also be borne in mind that, for a quantum risk to eventuate, the offer has to be made *and then beaten*. This makes that risk relatively remote (which tends to drive the size of the success fee down). This is why the effect of a quantum risk is usually relatively modest. It is possible, however, for a quantum risk to have a dramatic influence on the percentage increase. Crane J, for example, refused to interfere with a percentage increase of 87 per cent in a case that he described as 'very far from straightforward'— a case in which the only significant risk was a quantum risk.[109]

---

108 *Ibid*, at [17].
109 *Smiths Dock Ltd v Edwards* [2004] EWHC 116 (QB), at [35].

Recovery risk

Recovery risk is the risk that costs will be disallowed notwithstanding the fact that the case has been won and the traps posed by offers have been successfully negotiated. The risk will be relevant only if the conditional fee agreement in question provides that the legal services provider, rather than the client, will bear the risk that costs may not be awarded. Whether this is so will be a matter of contractual interpretation. A recovery risk will usually arise in the context of an agreement whereby the legal services provider's full entitlement to fees is that which the paying party is ordered to pay—that is, a CFA Lite (see 29.03)—but this will not always be the case. **54.94**

Indeed, there are many different types of recovery risk. At the most conservative end of the spectrum, the legal services provider may agree to forgo any costs in respect of which an order is not made (such as where the costs of an issue are disallowed or where a percentage award is made); at the other end of the spectrum, the entitlement is limited to the actual figures awarded by the court (which would mean that the legal services provider would be at risk not only by reason of an unfavourable decision on the incidence of costs, but also by reason of costs being reduced by way of assessment). **54.95**

Regardless of at which end of the spectrum the case lies, subject to the point made immediately below, there is no reason to believe that the method described as quantum risk at 54.87 would not apply—that is, the task is to arrive at a single, global figure for risk and then to convert that into a percentage uplift. **54.96**

The exception is the fact that a case might be at risk of being non-costs-bearing by reason of it being a small claim, as Brooke LJ explained: **54.97**

> 'In a claim as small as this, it is not reasonable that the defendant should have to pay the claimant's solicitor a higher success fee against the risk that the value of the claim was so low that legal costs would not be recoverable at all: this is a risk the solicitor must bear himself if he is willing to act at all.'[110]

It is possible that other exceptions exist, such as the risk of non-recovery arising out of factors that were wholly within the receiving party's control.

Enforcement risk

An enforcement risk will exist where, in addition to bearing a recovery risk (see 54.94–54.97), the legal services provider bears the risk of not being able to enforce the award against the paying party. This is the most risk-laden type of conditional fee agreement there is. Although there is no authority on the point, the principles of ascertainment are likely to be as set out under quantum risk and recovery risk. **54.98**

Risk premium

A risk premium is a premium payable to compensate the risk-taker for having borne the risk. It is rarely relied upon for the purposes of calculating success fees. A discussion of this topic may, however, be found at para 30.159 of the second edition of this book. **54.99**

Factors other than risk and success fees

There are two issues other than risk that are worth mentioning: delay (54.101–54.104 and Table 54.1); and liability for disbursements (54.105–54.107). It should be borne in mind that it is relatively rare for either of these factors to be reflected in a success fee. **54.100**

[110] *U v Liverpool City Council* [2005] EWCA Civ 475, at [24].

Delay

54.101 A success fee may contain an element that relates to the cost to the legal services provider of the postponement of the payment of its fees and expenses.[111] That element is commonly referred to as a postponement charge.

54.102 Prior to 1 October 2009, the postponement charges were not recoverable between the parties, but the court has, on the face of it, now been given the power to order otherwise.[112] That said, it is arguable that those provisions did nothing to override the principle that the costs of financing a claim are not recoverable between opposing parties and that therefore the court ought not to exercise its discretion in favour of allowing a postponement charge. For what it is worth, the editor's view is that the postponement charge may not be taken into account for the purposes of assessing costs as between parties. What follows therefore arguably applies only as between legal services provider and client.

54.103 There is no authority establishing the correct principle of quantifying the postponement charge. If it were to be assumed that the correct measure is the amount of interest that would have been paid had the relevant monies been borrowed, then calculating it is merely a matter of arithmetic. That said, it is very difficult to know in advance what the period of any such borrowing should be.

54.104 Various methods have been proposed for estimating the postponement charge,[113] but it is also possible to accurately calculate the interest that would have been paid by using standard actuarial methods. The calculation itself is too complex to be applied on a case-by-case basis. If the total fee receivable is F, the annual rate of interest rate expressed as a fraction is i and the case lasts for n years (where n can be anything from 0 upwards, including fractions of years), then the adjusted fee allowing for interest can be set out[114] as:

$$\left(\frac{F}{n}\right)\frac{(1+i)^n-1}{\log(1+i)}$$

Subtracting F gives the amount of the increase over the fee F and dividing by F gives a standardised increase. The appropriate formula is:

$$\left(\frac{\left((1+i^n)-1\right)}{n log\left(1+i\right)}\right)-1$$

The results of the calculation can be summarised in a table. Whilst it must be stressed that there is no authority for this method, Table 54.1 summarises those results. These figures are appropriate only where the accumulation of fees will, in general, be constant

111 See, eg, Conditional Fee Agreements Regulations 2000 (SI 2000/692), reg 3(1)(b), which makes specific reference to such an element.

112 CPR, r 44.3B(1)(a). The changes that were made on 1 October 2009 were to insert the words 'unless the court orders otherwise'.

113 A plausible method is to use standard actuarial tables to discount the fees for an estimated term certain and then to work out the percentage uplift required to negate that discount. It would be entirely logical to apply that discount to only half of the fees, (by analogy to special damages) to take account of the fact that the fees will accrue steadily as the case progresses.

114 The editor is grateful to Professor Paul Sweeting for his assistance in formulating this equation.

Table 54.1 Enhancements for delay

Estimated duration of claim (yrs)	Interest rate (% per yr)				
	2%	4%	6%	8%	10%
1	1.0%	2.0%	3.0%	3.9%	4.9%
2	2.0%	4.0%	6.1%	8.1%	10.2%
3	3.0%	6.1%	9.3%	12.5%	15.8%
4	4.1%	8.3%	12.6%	17.1%	21.7%
5	5.1%	10.5%	16.1%	22.0%	28.1%
6	6.2%	12.7%	19.7%	27.1%	34.9%
7	7.3%	15.1%	23.5%	32.5%	42.2%
8	8.4%	17.5%	27.4%	38.2%	50.0%
9	9.5%	19.9%	31.5%	44.2%	58.3%
10	10.6%	22.4%	35.7%	50.6%	67.2%

throughout the duration of the claim. Where this condition is not met, adjustments will need to be made.

Liability for disbursements

If the legal services provider is bearing the risk of paying for the disbursements, the percentage increase may be enhanced to take account of this. Where the agreement is a pre-commencement funding arrangement, (now-revoked) CPD, art 11.8(1), continues to apply, which read as follows: **54.105**

> 'In deciding whether a percentage increase is reasonable relevant factors to be taken into account may include—
> [...]
> (b) the legal representative's liability for any disbursements.'

There was no guidance in either the pre-1 April 2013 CPR or the CPD as to how the appropriate percentage increase ought to be calculated, but one method is to estimate the disbursements as a percentage of base profit costs and then to adjust the percentage increase so that the success fee covers not only the profit costs of unsuccessful cases, but also the disbursements. This is an easy calculation: **54.106**

$$p_{(disb)\%} = \frac{((100 + b_{\%})p_{\%})}{100}$$

Where

p% the starting percentage increase expressed as a percentage
b% is the proportion of disbursements to base profit costs expressed as a percentage
p(disb)% is the percentage increase adjusted to take account of disbursements

Eady J has noted a point that might have a bearing on the issue, albeit that it is a point with which many receiving parties would vehemently disagree.[115] He has said that where a **54.107**

115 See para 30.56 of the second edition of this book.

firm has accepted the risk of disbursements, this is a factor that is capable of cutting both ways, because whilst funding disbursements increases the potential liability, it can be taken as being an indicator that the legal services provider was sufficiently confident as to the prospects of success that it was prepared to accept that additional burden.[116] For obvious reasons, each case would have to be decided on its own facts, but this might be a factor to take into account in appropriate cases. Equally, the facts might demonstrate that the decision to fund disbursements had nothing to do with the merits of the claim, but was merely the funding policy of the firm in question.

Notice of Funding and Failure to Serve

54.108 The next few paragraphs focus primarily on success fees. That said, the principles apply equally to any other type of additional liability.

Default provisions where notice of funding has not been given

54.109 Where the conditional fee agreement in question is a pre-commencement funding agreement, the following restrictions—which can be found in pre-1 April 2013 CPR, r 44.3B—will apply:

> '(1) Unless the court orders otherwise, a party may not recover as an additional liability—
> [...]
> (c) any additional liability for any period in the proceedings during which that party failed to provide information about a funding arrangement in accordance with a rule, practice direction or court order
> [...]
>
> (Paragraph 9.3 of the Practice Direction (Pre-action Conduct) provides that a party must inform any other party as soon as possible about a funding arrangement entered into before the start of proceedings.)
>
> (Rule 3.9 sets out the circumstances the court will consider on an application for relief from a sanction for failure to comply with any rule, practice direction or court order.)'

Spencer J has explained that this provision does not impose a blanket penalty rendering irrecoverable each and every additional liability for the period during which notice was not served, but that it applies only to the specific additional liability that was the subject of the default.[117]

When notice of funding has to be given

54.110 CPR, r 44.15 (as it was prior to 1 April 2013), will apply.[118] It sets out the need not only to give initial notice of funding, but also to renew notice of funding in the event of a change that renders the initial notice inaccurate:

> '(1) A party who seeks to recover an additional liability must provide information about the funding arrangement to the court and to other parties as required by a rule, practice direction or court order.
>
> (2) Where the funding arrangement has changed, and the information a party has previously provided in accordance with paragraph (1) is no longer accurate, that party must file notice of the change and serve it on all other parties within 7 days.

---

116 *Cox v MGM* [2006] EWHC 1235 (QB), at [34] and [41].

117 *Manning v Kings College Hospital NHS Trust* [2011] EWHC 2954 (QB), at [93]. See also *Springer v University of Leicester NHS Trust* [2018] EWCA Civ 436.

118 See PD 48, para 1.4(b).

(3) Where paragraph (2) applies, and a party has already filed—
(a) an allocation questionnaire; or
(b) a pre-trial check list (listing questionnaire)
he must file and serve a new estimate of costs with the notice.

(The costs practice direction sets out—
- the information to be provided when a party issues or responds to a claim form, files an allocation questionnaire, a pre-trial check list, and a claim for costs;
- the meaning of estimate of costs and the information required in it)

(Rule 44.3B sets out situations where a party will not recover a sum representing any additional liability.)'

In so far as success fees are concerned, the information that needed to be given (and, where appropriate, still needs to be given) was defined by now-revoked CPD, art 19.4(1) and (2), which read as follows: **54.111**

'(1) Unless the court otherwise orders, a party who is required to supply information about a funding arrangement must state whether he has—
- entered into a conditional fee agreement which provides for a success fee within the meaning of section 58(2) of the Courts and Legal Services Act 1990;
- taken out an insurance policy to which section 29 of the Access to Justice Act 1999 applies;
- made an arrangement with a body which is prescribed for the purpose of section 30 of that Act;

or more than one of these.

(2) Where the funding arrangement is a conditional fee agreement, the party must state the date of the agreement and identify the claim or claims to which it relates (including Part 20 claims if any).'

There is no requirement to state the amount of additional liability.[119] (The corresponding requirements relating to ATE premium may be found at 54.130 (in footnote 163).)

The points at which notice of funding must be given are: **54.112**

- upon the court ordering that notice be given;[120]
- 'as soon as possible' after entering into a funding arrangement,[121] which Hickenbottom LJ has confirmed 'unambiguously means "as soon as possible", no more and no less';[122]

[119] CPD, art 19.1(1), used to read as follows: 'A party who wishes to claim an additional liability in respect of a funding arrangement must give any other party information about that claim if he is to recover the additional liability. There is no requirement to specify the amount of the additional liability separately nor to state how it is calculated until it falls to be assessed. That principle is reflected in rules 44.3A and 44.15, in the following paragraphs and in Sections 6, 13, 14 and 31 of this Practice Direction. Section 6 deals with estimates of costs, Sections 13 and 14 deal with summary assessment and Section 31 deals with detailed assessment.'

[120] See pre-1 April 2013 CPR, r 45.15(1).

[121] See Practice Direction (Pre-Action Protocols), para 9.3 (as amended), which reads: 'Where a party enters into a funding arrangement within the meaning of rule 43.2(1)(k), that party must inform the other parties about this arrangement as soon as possible and in any event either within 7 days of entering into the funding arrangement concerned or, where a claimant enters into a funding arrangement before sending a letter before claim, in the letter before claim.' In 2009, the provisions were amended to make it clear that the requirement is mandatory, not directory; the details can be found in the second edition of this book. See also *Springer v University of Leicester NHS Trust* [2018] EWCA Civ 436, at [3]–[14], for a recital of the relevant history.

[122] *Ibid*, at [47]. He went on to say that it may be that in some cases this could not be done because the correct defendant could not be identified: see *ibid*, at [63].

- when the letter of claim is sent[123]—although specific provisions applied to personal injury[124] and disease and illness claims;[125]
- when a claimant serves the claim form or a defendant serves their 'first document', such as an acknowledgement of service; and
- where the information previously provided is no longer accurate.[126]

There is no reason to believe that these requirements do not apply to claims in which savings provisions preserve the recoverability of the success fee.

54.113 There is no need to give notice of an agreement with an additional legal representative.[127] Spencer J has held that there was a requirement to give notice of funding where the legal representative makes an agreement in the same claim, but with a new client.[128]

54.114 It may be that the receiving party seeks to recover a success fee for a period before the conditional fee agreement was made. Edis J has said that there was nothing in the rules to prevent such a party from giving notice of funding that stated both the date on which the agreement was made and the date on which it became effective.[129] On the facts of the case before him (in which only the latter had been given), Edis J found that there had been a failure to give notice of funding in accordance with CPD, art 19.4, and that the breach was significant, meaning that the receiving party needed to apply for relief from sanctions.

Notices of funding and applications for relief from sanctions

54.115 If a party who seeks to recover an additional liability has failed to serve notice of funding (or fails to serve it timeously), then they may have to make an application for relief from sanctions. In this regard, now-revoked CPD, art 10, reads as follows:

> '10.1 In a case to which rule 44.3B(1)(c) or (d) applies the party in default may apply for relief from the sanction. He should do so as quickly as possible after he becomes aware of

---

[123] See Practice Direction (Pre-Action Protocols), art 9.3.

[124] From 1 April 2005, Pre-Action Protocol for Personal Injury Claims, para 3.2, has made the following provision in relation to the letter of claim: 'Where the case is funded by a conditional fee agreement (or collective conditional fee agreement), notification should be given of the existence of the agreement and where appropriate, that there is a success fee and/or insurance premium, although not the level of the success fee or premium.'

[125] Pre-Action Protocol for Disease and Illness Claims, para 6.2, has made the following provision in relation to the letter of claim: 'Where the case is funded by a conditional fee agreement, notification should be given of the existence of the agreement and where appropriate, that there is a success fee and insurance premium, although not the level of the success fee or premium.'

[126] See CPD, art 19.3, which reads: '(1) Rule 44.15 imposes a duty on a party to give notice of change if the information he has previously provided is no longer accurate. To comply he must file and serve notice containing the information set out in Form N251. Rule 44.15(3) may impose other duties in relation to new estimates of costs. (2) Further notification need not be provided where a party has already given notice: (a) that he has entered into a conditional fee agreement with a legal representative and during the currency of that agreement either of them enters into another such agreement with an additional legal representative; or (b) of some insurance cover, unless that cover is cancelled or unless new cover is taken out with a different insurer. (3) Part 6 applies to the service of notices. (4) The notice must be signed by the party or by his legal representative.'

[127] See now-revoked CPD, art 19.3(2)(a).

[128] *Manning v Kings College Hospital NHS Trust* [2011] EWHC 2954 (QB), at [81]. In the case before Spencer J, the new agreement was with the personal representative of the original claimant, who had died part-way through the claim.

[129] *O'Brien v Shorrock and MIB* [2015] EWHC 1630 (QB), at [53]. In the event, he allowed relief from sanctions, but he restricted this to allowing only half of the success fee for that period between the effective date and the date on which the agreement had been made.

the default. An application, supported by evidence, should be made under Part 23 to a costs judge or district judge of the court which is dealing with the case. (Attention is drawn to rules 3.8 and 3.9 which deal with sanctions and relief from sanctions.)

10.2 Where the amount of any percentage increase recoverable by counsel may be affected by the outcome of the application, the solicitor issuing the application must serve on counsel a copy of the application notice and notice of the hearing as soon as practicable and in any event at least 2 days before the hearing. Counsel may make written submissions or may attend and make oral submissions at the hearing. (Paragraph 1.4 contains definitions of the terms "counsel" and "solicitor".)'

The test that will be applied is post-2013 CPR, r 3.9, in accordance with the three-stage approach in *Denton* (see 26.60–26.70):[130] **54.116**

> 'The first stage is to identify and assess the seriousness and significance of the "failure to comply with any rule, practice direction or court order" which engages rule 3.9(1). If the breach is neither serious nor significant, the court is unlikely to need to spend much time on the second and third stages. The second stage is to consider why the default occurred. The third stage is to evaluate "all the circumstances of the case, so as to enable [the court] to deal justly with the application including [factors CPR, r 3.9(1)(a) and (b)]".'[131]

CPR, r 3.9, itself reads as follows: **54.117**

> '(1) On an application for relief from any sanction imposed for a failure to comply with any rule, practice direction or court order, the court will consider all the circumstances of the case, so as to enable it to deal justly with the application, including the need—
> (a) for litigation to be conducted efficiently and at proportionate cost; and
> (b) to enforce compliance with rules, practice directions and orders.
>
> (2) An application for relief must be supported by evidence.'

Thus there are three stages to the *Denton* test, as follows. **54.118**

- **Stage one** The court should identify and assess the seriousness and significance of the failure to give notice in accordance with the provisions referred to above.
- **Stage two** The court should consider why the default occurred.
- **Stage three** The court should evaluate all of the circumstances of the case to enable it to deal justly with the application, including the need:
  (a) for litigation to be conducted efficiently and at proportionate cost; and
  (b) to enforce compliance with rules, practice directions and orders.

If the breach is neither serious nor significant, the court is unlikely to need to spend much time on the second and third stages. The *Denton* test is discussed in more detail in Chapter 26 (at 26.55–26.70).

***Denton* stage one: seriousness and significance** A failure to give notice will generally be a serious and significant failure. Hildyard J (in a judgment affirmed by Gloster LJ) has explained that the court does not take into account the seriousness and significance arising out of the fact that the defaulting party has a pre-commencement funding arrangement in place, but instead takes into account the seriousness and significance for the opponents and other court users of the fact that they were late in receiving their **54.119**

[130] *Denton v TH White Ltd* [2014] EWCA Civ 906.
[131] *Ibid*, at [24].

notification.[132] He went on to say that the fact that the rules provide automatic sanctions for failing to give notice of funding probably reflects the fact that funding arrangements are, by their nature, of considerable significance.

54.120 It is possible to envisage failures that would not be serious and significant, however. The points made about informal notice of funding at 54.123 may be relevant in that regard.

54.121 ***Denton* stage two: the reasons for the breach** This will be a question of fact. In this regard, it is relevant that an application for relief must be supported by evidence.[133] As to the relevance of the reason for the breach, see 54.123.

54.122 ***Denton* stage three: all of the circumstances and discretion** The question of whether relief for sanctions will be given is a matter of judicial discretion[134] and each case must necessarily be determined on its own facts.[135]

54.123 The following miscellaneous points may be made.

- **The effect of granting relief** Under the pre-2013 checklist at CPR, r 3.9, one of the factors that the court was require to take into account was the prejudice that would be suffered if relief were to be granted; this no longer appears in that checklist. Gloster LJ has explained that whilst this may still be a factor to be taken into account, it has now been relegated to become a subsidiary factor.[136] In a similar vein, Gloster LJ has explained that the focus of CPR, r 3.9(1)(a), is on the effect of the breach on the conduct of the litigation at proportionate cost, not on the effect of granting relief.[137]
- **The relevance of the 2013 changes to recoverability of additional liabilities** The fact that the regime has changed such that additional liabilities are no longer generally recoverable between opposing parties and that a party seeking relief is trying to 'take advantage' of the old regime is not a factor that should be afforded much weight.[138] The fact that the overriding objective seeks to achieve a level playing field does not change this.[139]
- **The relevance of there being no good reason for the breach** Giving judgment under the pre-2013 version of CPR, r 3.9, Floyd J had this to say:

  > 'Relief from sanctions should not be granted lightly and any party who fails to comply with the CPR runs a significant risk that he will be refused relief. Thus if a party does not have a good explanation, or the other side is prejudiced by his failure, relief from sanctions will usually be refused. It is vitally important to the administration of justice that the rules of procedure are observed.'[140]

  Thus weight is to be given to the reason for the breach in the sense that relief is not granted lightly. This undoubtedly remains true, but it does not imply that the absence of

---

[132] *Caliendo v Mishcon De Reya (a firm)* [2014] EWHC 3414 (Ch), at [38], aff'd at [2015] EWCA Civ 1029.

[133] See CPR, r 3.9(2).

[134] See *Fred Perry (Holdings) Ltd v Brands Plaza Trading Ltd & Anor* [2012] EWCA Civ 224, at [18], cited with approval by Gloster LJ in *Caliendo v Mishcon De Reya (a firm)* [2015] EWCA Civ 1029, at [10].

[135] *Caliendo v Mishcon De Reya (a firm)* [2015] EWCA Civ 1029, at [17(i)].

[136] *Ibid*, at [24(ii)].

[137] *Ibid*, at [29].

[138] *Ibid*, at [24(iii) and (iv)].

[139] *Ibid*, at [24(v)].

[140] *Supperstone v Hurst* [2008] EWHC 735 (Ch), at [39].

a good reason will automatically mean that relief will be refused.[141] Indeed, this is very far from the case: the fact that there is no good reason (even if the failure to give notice was potentially negligent[142]) is not something that will necessarily weigh heavily against granting relief; the weight to be given is a matter for a judge's own exercise of their discretion, taking into account all of the circumstances.[143]

- **Prejudice** Where prejudice can be shown, it may play a significant role in a decision not to grant relief.[144] Whilst not binding, Judge Hamilton QC has said that an absence of prejudice on the part of the paying party would not, of itself, be sufficient to justify relief from sanctions.[145] This would certainly continue to be true under post-1 April 2013 CPR, r 3.9. That said, in a claim in which the claimant was three-and-a-half months late in giving notice of funding, Hildyard J gave considerable weight to the fact that there was a *complete* absence of prejudice.[146] Indeed, this seems to have been the primary reason he granted relief in the case before him.
- **Evidential issues regarding prejudice** Gloster LJ has explained that where a non-defaulting party wishes to assert prejudice, it would be open to that party to adduce evidence that the failure to give notice prevented them from giving serious consideration to making an offer, with consequent substantial prejudice; there would be no need for that party to waive privilege by giving details of the offer that may have been made.[147] Gloster LJ went on to imply that a failure to adduce such evidence may work against a party who wishes to assert prejudice, however.
- **The relevance of prior negotiations** The fact that the parties have already engaged in extensive negotiations without reaching a settlement may be relevant to the issue of prejudice.[148]
- **Informal notice of funding** It used often to be (and probably still is) the case that if formal notice of funding (that is, as Form N251) was not given, but informal notice of the existence of a funding arrangement had been given in correspondence (usually the letter of claim), then that was a factor that could be taken into account. In 2004, Langley J had the following to say about the court's approach to those circumstances:

> '[I]n my judgment, [the paying party] has from the outset had the information to which it was entitled and I cannot see any conceivable prejudice to [the paying party] from the breaches of the practice directions ... In those circumstances I think [the receiving parties] are entitled to relief from the sanction provided for by Rule 44.3(B)(i)(c) and so are not to be deprived of the opportunity in principle to recover the agreed success fee.'[149]

---

141 See *Denton v TH White Ltd* [2014] EWCA Civ 906, at [31], [35] and [36], *per* Dyson LJ, referred to in the context of notice of funding by Gloster LJ in *Caliendo v Mishcon De Reya (a firm)* [2015] EWCA Civ 1029, at [20].

142 Indeed, the court is entitled to take into account the fact that granting relief may prevent satellite litigation in the form of a claim in professional negligence: see *Caliendo v Mishcon De Reya (a firm)* [2015] EWCA Civ 1029, at [32], *per* Gloster LJ.

143 *Ibid*, at [19].

144 See, eg, *Springer v University of Leicester NHS Trust* [2018] EWCA Civ 436 (failure to inform an NHS trust that led to a denial of opportunity to investigate and resolve dispute).

145 *Connor v Birmingham City Council* (unreported), 16 March 2005, Birmingham County Court.

146 *Caliendo v Mishcon De Reya (a firm)* [2014] EWHC 3414 (Ch), at [42]–[54], aff'd at [2015] EWCA Civ 1029.

147 *Caliendo v Mishcon De Reya (a firm)* [2015] EWCA Civ 1029, at [17(ii)].

148 *Ibid*, at [17(iii)].

149 *Montlake & Ors v Lambert Smith Hampton Group Ltd* [2004] EWHC 1503 (Comm), at [15].

It is likely that if a receiving party is able to show that informal notice of funding was given, this will be a factor that the court would be able to take into account under the *Denton* test.

- **Constructive knowledge** In a similar vein, Spencer J (in a case decided under the pre-2013 provisions) found that a costs judge had been entitled to grant relief from sanctions in respect of a claimant's failure to serve notice, because he had correctly identified that the crucial matter in exercising his discretion was that the defendant had known all along that he was in litigation with a claimant who was funded by a conditional fee agreement.[150]
- **Late notice** Where notice is given late in a case in which a success fee is claimed, one option available to the court is to grant relief, but only for a period of time. Akenhead J has explained that the notification requirements relating to funding arrangements are important, because an opponent might wish to make its dispositions as soon as it had formal notice of what costs risk it faced; those dispositions might include simply admitting liability or making an offer.[151] Unless there is a good reason for non-notification in accordance with the CPR, the default set out in CPR, r 44.3B(1), should apply. Thus, generally, the successful party should not recover its success fee for the period during which notice ought to have been given, but had not been given.
- **The relevance of a party's response to being given late notice** When notification is given late, a party's response may be relevant to the issue of any prejudice (especially if an offer to settle was made at the same time).[152]

Statement of Reasons and Failure to Serve

54.124 If an additional liability is claimed in a bill of costs, then the receiving party must serve on the paying party the 'relevant details'.[153] In so far as conditional fee agreements are concerned, those details were set out at CPD, art 32.5(1), as follows:

> '(1) In the case of a conditional fee agreement with a success fee:
> (a) a statement showing the amount of costs which have been summarily assessed or agreed, and the percentage increase which has been claimed in respect of those costs;
> (b) a statement of the reasons for the percentage increase given in accordance with Regulation 3(1)(a) of the Conditional Fee Agreements Regulations or Regulation 5(1)(c) of the Collective Conditional Fee Agreements Regulations 2000. [Both sets of regulations were revoked by the Conditional Fee Agreements (Revocation) Regulations 2005,[154] but continue to have effect in relation to conditional fee agreements and collective conditional fee agreements entered into before 1 November 2005.]'

Barling J has found that the time to serve this information is at the commencement of the detailed assessment proceedings.[155]

---

150 See *Scott v Duncan* [2012] EWHC 1792 (QB). See also *Haydon v Strudwick* [2010] EWHC 90164 (Costs); *Forstater v Python (Monty) Pictures Ltd* [2013] EWHC 3759 (Ch), at [50], *per* Norris J (relief granted where there was no prejudice and informal notice was given, albeit late).

151 *Redwing Construction Ltd v Wishart* [2011] EWHC 19 (TCC), at [15(f)].

152 *Caliendo v Mishcon De Reya (a firm)* [2015] EWCA Civ 1029, at [17(iv)], *per* Gloster LJ.

153 CPD, arts 32.4 and 32.7.

154 SI 2005/2305.

155 *Long v Value Properties Ltd* [2014] EWHC 2981 (Ch), at [31], [37] and [39].

54.125 Pre-1 April 2013 CPR, r 44.3B(1), continues to impose a restriction on recovery of an additional liability where the statement of reasons (that is, CPD, art 32.5(1)(b), above) has not been served:

> 'Unless the court orders otherwise, a party may not recover as an additional liability—
> [...]
> (d) any percentage increase where that party has failed to comply with—
> (i) a requirement in the costs practice direction; or
> (ii) a court order,
> to disclose in any assessment proceedings the reasons for setting the percentage increase at the level stated in the conditional fee agreement.'

Barling J has found that this sanction will be engaged only if there has been a complete failure to serve the reasons, not if they were merely served late, saying that if the reasons were merely late, the sanction in CPR, r 44.3B(1)(c), would apply.[156] Similarly, service of redacted details may suffice.[157]

54.126 Relief from sanctions may be sought (see 54.115–54.123 and 26.55–26.70). Under the pre-2013 provisions, it was common for relief from sanctions to be granted, but even then this was not invariably the case. Whilst not binding, Judge Rubery found that where a receiving party failed without good reason to serve a statement of reasons in support of an additional liability, it was (on the facts of that case, in which there had been opportunity to remedy matters) wrong to afford relief from sanctions.[158]

The Assessment of the Amount of ATE Premiums

54.127 The topic of after-the-event (ATE) insurance in general is addressed in Chapter 34. This chapter deals only with those aspects of the matter that go to the recoverability of ATE premiums as between opposing parties. Most of what is said in this chapter will apply only where the receiving party has insurance that is a pre-commencement funding arrangement (see 54.17–54.18).

The components and language of premiums

54.128 The components of an ATE insurance premium (and the applicable terminology) are described at 34.37. As can be seen, an ATE insurance premium will comprise burning costs, risk/profit costs, administrative costs and distribution commission.

54.129 That may be so, but the court does not seek to be its own actuarial adviser. Indeed, Buxton LJ has emphasised the breadth of the discretion conferred on the costs judge by what is now CPR, r 44.4, and that it is a discretion that cannot be exercised with mathematical nicety.[159] Unless a specific case merits expert evidence—which would be extremely rare—there is no need for the court to decide issues of reasonableness by reference to actuarial principles and the components of a premium. Nonetheless, there is no harm in knowing the language of

---

156 *Ibid*, at [54].
157 See *Light on Line Ltd v Zumtobel Lighting Ltd* [2012] EWHC 3376 (QB), *per* Slade J.
158 *Szfranski v Twyfords Ltd* (unreported), 2 October 2008, Stoke-on-Trent County Court.
159 *Sharratt v London Central Bus Co & Ors (No 2) The Accident Group Test Cases* [2004] EWCA Civ 575, at [37].

insurance nor is there any harm in knowing the fundamentals of how premiums are calculated, which topics are covered in detail in the second edition of this book at para 30.156.

The role of rules of court in relation to premiums

54.130 Premiums continue to be subject to assessment under the CPR notwithstanding the changes to the law made on 1 April 2013.[160] Where the receiving party has a pre-commencement funding arrangement, the relevant parts of the pre-1 April 2013 CPR will continue to apply. There are, however, only two rules of any relevance, as follows.

- **Publication cases** CPR, r 44.12B, imposes a specific restriction in 'publication cases' (that is, defamation, malicious falsehood, etc) (see 54.139).
- **Notice of funding** CPR, r 44.3B(1)(e), provided as follows:

> 'Unless the court orders otherwise, a party may not recover as an additional liability … any insurance premium where that party has failed to provide information about the insurance policy in question by the time required by a rule, practice direction or court order.'[161]

Thus, even when they have a pre-commencement funding arrangement, a party will not be able to recover a premium where they have failed to give their opponent notice of funding, the principles of which are broadly the same as those relating to success fee (see 54.108–54.123).[162] There was also a requirement to serve a copy of the certificate at the time the bill of costs is served.[163] The very similar issue of failure to supply a statement of reasons in respect of the success fee has already been dealt with at 54.124–54.126 and those principles are not repeated here.

The assessment of premiums

54.131 This topic is addressed in three parts:

- the issue of whether it was reasonable to incept a policy (see 54.133–54.141);
- the reasonableness of premiums in general (see 54.142–54.171); and
- deconstruction—that is, a process whereby the premium is broken down into its constituent parts (see 54.172–54.174).

The topic of proportionality is addressed at 25.84–25.89.

54.132 It has to be stressed that deconstruction is mentioned largely for the sake of completeness: it would rarely, if ever, be permissible to deconstruct a premium simply for the purpose of gauging its reasonableness (see 54.148–54.149). Indeed, the court will rarely entertain a

---

[160] See *Peterborough v Stamford Hospitals NHS Trust* [2017] EWCA 1941 (Civ), at [55], *per* Lewison LJ.

[161] This was from 1 October 2009 only. Prior to that date, there was no CPR, r 44.3B(1)(e). This led to confusion because the other provision in CPR, r 44.3B(1), related to percentage increases and periods; as such, it was not well suited to governing premiums.

[162] See CPD, art 19.4(3), which provides: 'Where the funding arrangement is an insurance policy, the party must—(a) state the name and address of the insurer, the policy number and the date of the policy and identify the claim or claims to which it relates (including Part 20 claims if any); (b) state the level of cover provided by the insurance; and (c) state whether the insurance premiums are staged and, if so, the points at which an increased premium is payable.'

[163] CPD, art 32.5(2), which provides: 'If the additional liability is an insurance premium: a copy of the insurance certificate showing whether the policy covers the receiving party's own costs; his opponents costs; or his own costs and his opponent's costs; and the maximum extent of that cover, and the amount of the premium paid or payable.'

challenge beyond considering whether it was reasonable to take out the particular policy that was incepted, checking that it is not grossly out of line with the market norm,[164] and taking a view as to whether it is proportionate. Simon J has explained that challenges to premiums must be resolved on the basis of evidence and analysis, rather than by assertion and counter-assertion, adding that the issues should be identified promptly and, where necessary, there should be directions for the proper determination of specific issues.[165] That is undoubtedly right, but, in practice, the court relies very heavily on the insurer to rate the premium in a reasonable and equitable way, and it would be rare for the court to delve into such matters.

The inception of ATE policies and reasonableness

Whether it was reasonable to take out a policy will depend on the facts of each case, but, for the reasons expanded upon at 54.136–54.137, those facts may extend beyond the individual case to include the wider context of the ATE market itself (although see 25.87). That wider context has been referred to as 'insurance macroeconomics'. Whilst premiums are—like all costs—assessed under CPR, r 44.4, the method of assessment is unique to costs law in that premiums may be allowed on assessment notwithstanding the fact that they may not have been incurred solely for the purposes of funding the case in in hand. **54.133**

There are five topics that merit discussion regarding whether it was reasonable to take out a policy: **54.134**

- alternative means of funding (a substantial topic that is addressed at 54.191–54.206);
- the supposed absence of risk (see 54.135);
- adverse selection (see 54.136);
- timing (see 54.138); and
- agreements not to seek costs (see 54.141).

Absence of risk and ATE premiums The lower the risk that an adverse costs order may be made, the less pressing the need for insurance. There are examples of the court finding that the risk was so low that no insurance was required at all,[166] but it would not often be the case that the level of risk would be the sole determining factor. In particular, it may be that the receiving party's solicitor is obliged to recommend a policy as a condition of its delegated authority (known as obligatory recommendation). Many delegated authority schemes impose an obligation of this type in an effort to avoid adverse selection (see 54.136–54.137). In a pre-2013 case, Akenhead J explained that it is important that claimants do not use insurance as a commercial threat to defendants; where the risks are low, it is legitimate for the court to ask itself whether, in any particular case, it was reasonable and proportionate to take out insurance.[167] The implication in Akenhead J's logic is that if the **54.135**

---

164 See, eg, *Hahn v NHS England* (unreported), 3 August 2015, Liverpool County Court, *per* Judge Wood QC.

165 *Kris Motor Spares Ltd v Fox Williams LLP* [2010] EWHC 1008 (QB), at [46].

166 As an illustration, see *Dhanoia v Mehmi* (unreported), 17 October 2007, Bristol County Court, in which a district judge found that so little was in dispute that it was unreasonable to take out ATE insurance, notwithstanding the modest size of the premium.

167 *Redwing Construction Ltd v Wishart* [2011] EWHC 19 (TCC), at [16].

court believes the policy to have been taken out for the purposes of gaining a tactical advantage, the premium may be disallowed. Such findings are permissible, but rare.

54.136 **Adverse selection, macroeconomics and premiums** Adverse selection is a form of cherry-picking—more accurately, it is what is left on the tree after the best cherries have been picked. It results from the solicitor or other legal services provider electing not to recommend insurance in those cases in which the risks are very low (or, conversely, seeking cover only if the risks are perceived to be high). If the insurer's underwriting assumptions have been based on data where there has been no adverse selection, then those assumptions will be undermined by the fact that the risk will be much greater, on average, than envisaged. This can lead to a failure to charge an adequate premium and—in extreme cases—can even lead to gross/net premium income (that is, the monies received as premiums) being less than the burning risk (that is, the monies that are paid out: see 34.37).

54.137 These considerations do not relate to the individual litigant or to the case in question, but to the insurer and *its* economic needs. Whilst his was a dissenting judgment, Lord Scott has used the word 'macroeconomics' to describe that topic.[168] Notwithstanding Lord Scott's powerful dissent, there can now be no doubt that it is reasonable and legitimate for an insurer to have concerns about the macroeconomic position of the insurance book in question. Indeed, Woolf CJ has even gone so far as to say that delegated authority schemes will not work unless there are safeguards against adverse selection.[169] He has explained that if a solicitor is—without restraint—permitted to choose which cases merit ATE insurance and which do not, then the principle that the many will pay for the few will become distorted. He went on to find that the need to avoid adverse selection might amount to reasonable justification of a decision to take a policy. This was a significant development in the law of costs because it meant that costs could be recovered notwithstanding the fact that the case itself (taken in isolation) did not justify those costs being incurred. In a recent judgment, Lewison LJ had this to say on the point:

> 'It is ... clear that the departure from the usual case-by-case assessment of costs was deliberate on the part of this court and upheld by the House of Lords, despite serious reservations by Lord Hoffmann and a powerful dissent by Lord Scott. In effect, therefore, the question was settled at a macro level by reference to the general run of cases and the macro economics of the ATE insurance market, and not by reference to the facts of any specific case.'[170]

54.138 **Timing (prematurity and late application) and premiums** The next issue is whether it would be appropriate to object to a premium on the basis that the policy was taken out too early (early inception) or too late (late application). It could never be the case that a policy had been taken out so prematurely that it fell beyond the jurisdiction of the Access to Justice Act 1999. This is because the Act permits recovery of the premium even where the policy was taken out only in contemplation of proceedings and before they were commenced.[171] Assuming that the policy in question is a pre-commencement funding agreement, the issue is therefore not a jurisdictional one, but a question of reasonableness.

---

168 *Callery v Gray* [2002] UKHL 28, at [114].

169 *Callery v Gray* [2001] EWCA Civ 1117, at [67].

170 See *Peterborough v Stamford Hospitals NHS Trust* [2017] EWCA 1941 (Civ) at [26], *per* Lewison LJ.

171 *Ibid*, at [54], *per* Woolf CJ.

In most cases, a paying party would find it difficult to persuade the court that a policy was taken out too early. Woolf CJ has given the following reasons why it may have been reasonable to have taken out ATE insurance at an early stage.[172] 54.139

- Premiums would produce cover that would benefit defendants in the sense that there would be a means by which costs awarded in their favour would be paid.
- The interests of defendants could, with the assistance of the court, be preserved by restricting premiums to amounts that are reasonable, having regard to the overall requirements of the scheme created by the Access to Justice Act 1999.
- Claimants would be able to know at the outset that a satisfactory arrangement had been made to provide cover for an adverse costs order.
- Access to justice would be enhanced by legal services providers being about to offer claimants a service that includes all of these benefits.
- There is a risk that unless a policy is taken out before it is known whether liability is going to be contested, the premium might rise substantially, or no policy might be available at all.

Woolf CJ's comments were made in the context of modest road traffic accident cases; the relevance of this is that it is not necessarily the case that the same logic would apply to less quotidian types of claim. Indeed, the fact that the CPR deals with one type of claim (publication claims) in such a way as to discourage early inception suggests that different considerations apply to other types of claim.[173]

At the other end of the spectrum is where it is said that the receiving party left it so late to apply for insurance that they have made it difficult to obtain insurance at modest cost. Simon J has explained that late inception may (in some cases) indicate that a contractual premium was an unreasonable cost, but that there is no principle that the premium on a late-incepting policy is irrecoverable as an unreasonable cost.[174] He explained that each case is likely to depend on its facts.[175] Where the deferral was for good reason (such as an 54.140

[172] *Ibid*, at [99].

[173] Publication claims include claims in defamation and malicious falsehood. They are notoriously expensive. Where a publication claim settles prior to the issue of proceedings, the CPR impose significant restrictions on the recoverability of premiums. Those restrictions were recommended by the Civil Justice Council following consultation resulting in the 'Theobalds Park Plus Agreement' (see CP 16/07). Although those restrictions are not phrased in the language of prematurity and reasonableness, it must be the case that they have a bearing on that issue, because they can only be a strong disincentive to litigants taking out ATE insurance at a stage earlier than the expiry of the prescribed periods. Those restrictions are set out in CPR, r 44.12B, as follows: '(1) If in proceedings to which rule 44.12A applies it appears to the court that—(a) if proceedings had been started, they would have been publication proceedings; (b) one party admitted liability and made an offer of settlement on the basis of that admission; (c) agreement was reached after that admission of liability and offer of settlement; and (d) either—(i) the party making the admission of liability and offer of settlement was not provided by the other party with the information about an insurance policy as required by the Practice Direction (Pre-Action Conduct); or (ii) that party made the admission of liability and offer of settlement before, or within 42 days of, being provided by the other party with that information, no costs may be recovered by the other party in respect of the insurance premium. (2) In this rule, "publication proceedings" means proceedings for—(a) defamation; (b) malicious falsehood; or (c) breach of confidence involving publication to the public at large.' To a certain extent, these provisions place the issue of liability for premiums in the hands of the paying party.

[174] *Kris Motor Spares Ltd v Fox Williams LLP* [2010] EWHC 1008 (QB), at [41].

[175] *Ibid.* It is worth noting that the points made about macroeconomics at 54.143 would not apply in these circumstances. Whilst the point was not mentioned by Simon J, this is likely to be one of the reasons why cases of late inception turn on their own facts.

attempt to limit costs until they became unavoidable), it is not likely that the court would find fault.[176] This will particularly be the case if the premium is for 'top-up' insurance because it would be difficult to identify the 'right' time to take out such cover.[177]

54.141 **Agreements not to seek adverse costs** It will occasionally be the case that the need for ATE insurance will be diminished or negated by agreement between the parties as to how the litigation should be managed. It is, for example, not unknown for defendants in clinical negligence disputes to agree not to seek costs, in return for the claimant's agreement not to incept insurance in respect of those costs. Such agreements would now be otiose in the context of qualified one-way costs shifting (QOCS)—and would generally be irrelevant anyway post-1 April 2013—but they may still be encountered in longer-running cases.[178]

Quantum of premiums (other than deconstruction)

54.142 **Measure and judicial approach relating to premiums** There are two ways in which the reasonableness of a premium may be gauged: it may be measured in terms of its overall reasonableness; or it may be broken down into its constituent parts. The latter is called deconstruction and is considered at 54.172–54.174.

54.143 It is trite costs law that the court will not allow costs that are unreasonable, which means that the court is able to take a robust view and to reduce a premium if it is unreasonable.[179] For the reason set out below, however, reductions will not be common without case-specific evidence. That said, they are not unknown.[180] The topic of proportionality is addressed at 25.85–25.88.

54.144 On the whole, reductions will be made on the basis of case-specific or macroeconomic evidence (which will usually mean expert evidence). In this regard, CPD, art 11.10, used to give the following guidance about the appropriate factors to be taken into account:

> 'In deciding whether the cost of insurance cover is reasonable, relevant factors to be taken into account include:
> (1) where the insurance cover is not purchased in support of a conditional fee agreement with a success fee, how its cost compares with the likely cost of funding the case with a conditional fee agreement with a success fee and supporting insurance cover;
> (2) the level and extent of the cover provided;
> (3) the availability of any pre-existing insurance cover;
> (4) whether any part of the premium would be rebated in the event of early settlement; [and]
> (5) the amount of commission payable to the receiving party or his legal representatives or other agents.'

---

[176] See, eg, *Re RSA Pursuit Test Cases* [2005] EWHC 90003 (Costs), at [365]–[374]. In *Kris Motor Spares Ltd v Fox Williams LLP* [2010] EWHC 1008 (QB), for example, Simon J found that the decision to take out insurance at a very late stage was reasonable because the insured's opponent had instructed leading counsel, thereby increasing the risk in terms of costs.

[177] See, eg, *Percy v Anderson-Young* [2017] EWHC 2712 (QB), at [75], *per* Martin Spencer J.

[178] Such arrangements may apply to more than one case and may even be properly described as being protocols. An example of this is a consultant urogynaecologist who caused some 400 cases to be brought against his former employer. A formal protocol was agreed that may ultimately have had the effect of reducing the burden of additional liabilities by as much as £8 million: see Locke, D, 'New Lease of Life' (2010) 160(7418) NLJ 717. The figures were provided by Mr Locke in a personal communication with the editor in January 2011.

[179] *Callery v Gray (No 2)* [2001] EWCA Civ 1246, at [11].

[180] See, eg, *Smith v Interlink Express Parcels Ltd* [2007] EWHC 90095 (Costs).

A conspicuous omission from this list is risk (see 54.155–54.161). Simon J has explained that there is no presumption that the premium is reasonable unless the contrary is shown.[181] He went on to explain that, notwithstanding this, it is for the paying party to raise the contention that the premium is unreasonable and the evidential burden is on the paying party to advance at least some material in support of that contention.[182] Simon J said that this is not to reverse the burden on assessment, because if—having heard the evidence and the argument—there is still a doubt about the reasonableness of the premium, that doubt must be resolved in favour of the paying party.[183] **54.145**

Comparing ATE insurance with conditional funding A comparison with conditional funding[184] will be relevant in certain older cases in which no success fee is claimed. The task is to compare the premium with the additional liability that would have been charged had the receiving party's legal services provider acted under a conditional fee agreement that provided for a success fee. Presumably, this means that the court should form a view about the level of success fee that would have been charged if a conditional fee agreement had been made at the time the policy was incepted. Like must be compared with like (namely, this method of assessment would be appropriate only where policy was for the receiving party's own costs) and, in any event, it would be a mistake to try to deal with the comparison with any degree of mathematical nicety.[185] **54.146**

The level of cover afforded by ATE policies The level of cover is a factor that may be taken into account. There are two ways in which it may be relevant: **54.147**

- it may be said that the level of cover was excessive and that a less expensive policy with a lower level of cover ought to have been used;[186] and
- it may be said that the premium was excessive, given the level of cover (that is, that the premium was overrated by the insurer).

Martin Spencer J has explained that there is an 'important distinction' to be drawn between these two scenarios and that whilst the court would generally be able to apply a broad-brush adjustment in the former, this would not generally be appropriate in the latter.[187] He did not entirely rule out the possibility of the court substituting its own figure in the second of the two scenarios, but he said—on the facts of the case before him, in which the premium was very substantial—that this could have been done only with the benefit of expert evidence.[188]

Martin Spencer J's comments are a reflection of the fact that the point at which the court abjures any notion of its own actuarial competence is quickly reached and it would **54.148**

[181] *Kris Motor Spares Ltd v Fox Williams LLP* [2010] EWHC 1008 (QB), at [35].

[182] *Ibid*, at [44].

[183] *Ibid*, at [44]. There is, of course, a fundamental difference between the burden of proof and the provisions concerning resolution of doubt, but presumably Simon J was merely illustrating his point by reference to the latter, rather than suggesting that that is the mechanism that avoids reversal of the evidential burden.

[184] See CPD, art 11.10(1).

[185] *Sharratt v London Central Bus Co & Ors (No 2) The Accident Group Test Cases* [2004] EWCA Civ 575, at [33]–[37].

[186] Whilst *obiter* and whilst overturned on appeal on a different point, see *Kai Surrey v Barnet & Chase Farm Hospitals NHS Trust* [2016] EWHC 1589, at [116]–[120], *per* Foskett J.

[187] See *Percy v Anderson-Young* [2017] EWHC 2712 (QB) at [68], Martin Spencer J.

[188] *Ibid*, at [68].

generally be only in cases of gross overrating of the premium that the court would claim the ability to intervene. Brooke LJ had the following to say:

> '[The court does not have] the expertise to judge the reasonableness of a premium except in very broad brush terms, and the viability of the ATE market will be imperilled if they regard themselves (without the assistance of expert evidence) as better qualified than the underwriter to rate the financial risk the insurer faces.'[189]

Thus the court will tend to rely on the expertise and skill of the insurer, and will rarely question the way in which a policy has been rated.

54.149 That said, a 'back of the envelope' calculation may be used as a screening test in some cases and as a cross-check in others. Where there is no suitable factual or expert evidence, it may also be a judicial method of last resort.[190] It is possible to estimate the burning costs by looking at the level of cover and the risks in the litigation generally; once the burning costs have been estimated, an allowance may then be made for the costs of administration, etc. It is possible to arrive at a rough approximation of what the premium should be, based on the assumptions that led to the relevant figures being selected.

54.150 **The availability of alternative means of funding and premiums** This topic is addressed at 54.191–54.206. Whilst it usually goes to recoverability in principle, the availability of pre-existing insurance cover is capable of going to the issue of quantum. This is because BTE cover may have been available up to a certain limit. If the costs exceed the limit of a pre-existing policy and if it was not fully utilised, then it could be argued that the premium ought to be reduced accordingly.

54.151 **Staged/rebated premiums** The term 'staged premium' is discussed at 34.25. The underlying rationale is that riskier cases are selected by virtue of the fact that they do not settle and that it is therefore appropriate to levy higher premiums in those cases to take account of the higher-than-average risk.

54.152 Common sense dictates that the fact that a rebate was available during the early part of the proceedings would be a factor the court could take into account when assessing the reasonableness of the premium. The receiving party would argue that, under a staged-premium model, the source of the gross/net premium income shifts from those claims that settle early to those claims that do not. This shift is between claims, rather than within claims, which means that it would not be legitimate to compare final-stage premiums with the premium that would apply under a single-premium model (referred to as 'the unrebated premium').[191] Notwithstanding this, there are examples of the court looking at the reasonableness of the individual stages,[192] albeit with palpable reluctance.

54.153 There is no guidance in the CPR or elsewhere as to how stage premiums should be assessed. It can, however, be demonstrated by elementary actuarial calculations that the final-stage premium can be surprisingly high when compared with the unrebated premium. If, for example, the first-stage premium is 75 per cent of the unrebated premium and if only 5 per cent of cases reach trial, the final-stage premium must be 5.75 times higher than the

[189] *Rogers v Merthyr Tydfil County Borough Council* [2006] EWCA Civ 1134, at [111] and [117].
[190] See, eg, *Smith v Interlink Express Parcels Ltd* [2007] EWHC 90095 (Costs).
[191] *Rogers v Merthyr Tydfil County Borough Council* [2006] EWCA Civ 1134, at [111].
[192] See, eg, *Smith v Interlink Express Parcels Ltd* [2007] EWHC 90095 (Costs).

unrebated premium (and this assumes that those cases that go to trial will be no more likely to lose than the average case). If the insurer wishes to reduce the lower premium to 50 per cent of the unrebated premium, the higher premium must rise 10.5 times higher than the unrebated premium to preserve gross/net premium income. Thus small changes can have *very* large effects. The relevance of this is that it can be difficult to form a view as to the reasonableness of staged premiums. Again, the court tends to rely on the skill and expertise of the insurer to rate the premium in a reasonable and equitable way (see 54.148).

Commission and premiums Commission is money that the insurer pays to a third party for the purposes of obtaining business. The CPD does not refer to commission in general, but only to commission payable to the receiving party or their legal services providers or other agents.[193] This type of commission is dealt with separately because, in general, it is not payable by the paying party. By way of example, if, out of a premium of £450, a commission of £50 is payable to the receiving party's solicitor, the maximum indemnity that the paying party could be asked to provide would be £400, because the receiving party would be able to ask their solicitor to account to them for the commission of £50 (see 34.45 and 34.48). **54.154**

Risk and premiums A noticeable omission from the CPD's list of relevant factors (see 54.142) is the risk that a claim may be made on the policy. Brooke LJ has confirmed, however, that it is a relevant factor.[194] Risk may be taken into account for the purposes of making a rough estimate of the burning costs, but this is generally used only as a cross-check for confirming (or refuting) the reasonableness of the premium[195]—although there have been instances of it being used to calculate premiums.[196] **54.155**

Where the premium is block-rated, then the risk in the individual case will be an irrelevance because the premium would have been calculated without reference to that risk, but where the premium has been individually rated, it may be a relevant factor. The relevance of risk, and the many and complex ways in which it may be measured, has been addressed at 54.67–54.99 (albeit in the context of success fees). It can be seen that it would be naive and occasionally plainly wrong to say that a risky case justifies a high premium. Where, however, there is evidence that it is relevant to the way in which the premium has been calculated, then it will be a factor to be taken into account. Akenhead J has said (in the context of an individually rated premium) that it had to be a reasonable presumption that premiums were linked to an assessment of risks. He opined that the allowable premium can be adjusted downwards to reflect the fact that, at the time when the insurance was entered into, the prospects of success were good or high.[197] Such downwards adjustments are, however, rare—if not extremely rare. In general, where risk is taken into account, it is **54.156**

---

[193] CPD, art 11.10(5).

[194] *Rogers v Merthyr Tydfil County Borough Council* [2006] EWCA Civ 1134, at [108].

[195] See, eg, *Tyndall v Battersea Dogs Home* [2005] EWHC 90011 (Costs), at [80]–[98] (in the context of a block-rated premium); *Rogers v Merthyr Tydfil County Borough Council* [2006] EWCA Civ 1134 (in the context of an individually rated premium).

[196] Whilst not binding, see *Larner v University Hospital Birmingham NHS Foundation Trust* (unreported), 6 May 2015, Worcester County Court, *per* Judge Pearce-Higgins QC.

[197] *Redwing Construction Ltd v Wishart* [2011] EWHC 19 (TCC), at [15(d)]. Notwithstanding the fact that such an approach would afford the court a good deal of freedom, it has to be said that this method of assessment has been widely adopted. Indeed, there are those who suggest that Akenhead J's judgment on this point should be regarded as being restricted to its own facts.

because the court is referring to it for the purposes of illustrating why the insurer was entitled to rate the premium in the way that it did.[198] The points made at 54.148 are relevant in this regard.

54.157 The risk includes any risk that may be covered by insurance falling within the ambit of Access to Justice Act 1999, s 29. In particular, there is no objection in principle to a premium being based on a risk that the insured may fail to beat a Part 36 offer and may be required to pay costs as a result.[199]

54.158 Risk is difficult to measure and therefore premiums based on an estimate of risk are difficult to monitor. This means that there is the potential for profiteering. That potential ought to be limited by the concept of equity (that is, the professional goal of rating a premium at a level that is fair), but—in insurance generally—the ultimate moderating influence is the market. In the ATE insurance business (in relation to pre-commencement funding arrangements) the market is skewed by the fact that the insurer will very often look to a stranger for payment of its premium rather than to its own client. This potential for abuse was noted by Lord Bingham in the following terms:

> 'A . . . possible abuse [of the system of funding by way of CFAs and ATE] was that claimants, although able to obtain after the event insurance, would be able to do so only at an unreasonably high price, the after the event insurers having no incentive to moderate a premium which would be paid by the defendant or his insurers and which might be grossly disproportionate to the risk which the insurer was underwriting.'[200]

54.159 Brooke LJ seems to have placed greater faith in the ability of the market to regulate premiums, but he had this to say:

> 'Although the claimant very often does not have to pay the premium himself, this does not mean that there are no competitive or other pressures at all in the market. As the evidence before this court shows, it is not in an insurer's interest to fix a premium at a level which will attract frequent challenges.'[201]

54.160 Brooke LJ's analysis is entirely in keeping with the principle of equity. There are, however, those who say that it is hard to reconcile Brooke LJ's analysis with the following comments of Lord Nicholls:

> 'ATE insurers do not compete for claimants, still less do they compete on premiums charged. They compete for solicitors who will sell or recommend their product. And they compete by offering solicitors the most profitable arrangements to enable them to attract profitable work. There is only one restraining force on the premium charged and that is how much the costs judge will allow on an assessment against the liability insurer.'[202]

---

198 See, eg, *Percy v Anderson-Young* [2017] EWHC 2712 (QB), at [72], *per* Martin Spencer J.

199 *Callery v Gray* [2001] EWCA 1246, at [31]. See also *Percy v Anderson-Young* [2017] EWHC 2712 (QB), at [70]–[73], *per* Martin Spencer J (a case in which a 'top-up' premium had been obtained after a Part 36 offer had been made), in which the risk posed by the offer was reasonably equated with a risk of losing at trial.

200 *Callery v Gray (No 2)* [2001] EWCA Civ 1246, at [31].

201 *Rogers v Merthyr Tydfil County Borough Council* [2006] EWCA Civ 1134, at [105]. See also *Kris Motor Spares Ltd v Fox Williams LLP* [2010] EWHC 1008 (QB), at [44], in which Simon J impliedly confirms that the same principles have continued to apply even after the passage of some years.

202 *Callery v Gray* [2002] UKHL 28, at [43].

Although the two analyses may at first appear to be directly contradictory, on closer analysis, this proves not to be so. This is because Lord Nicholls was speaking about a general, theoretical concern about policies that fund themselves wholly from the monies recovered as costs, whilst Brooke LJ was giving judgment on the basis of evidence going to the state of a particular market at a particular time. Put another way, the extent to which the court can rely on the market as a moderating influence will depend on the circumstances of the market in question. As has been explained above, however, it is rare for the court to entertain a submission that a premium has been overrated. **54.161**

Proportionality and premiums This topic is addressed at 25.85–25.88. As can be seen, with very limited exceptions, the pre-2013 method applies. That said, it is possible for premiums to be reduced solely on the grounds of proportionality. **54.162**

Evidence and comparators relating to premiums

Judicial notice and judges' personal knowledge relating to premiums Phillips MR has confirmed that a judge is permitted to take personal knowledge into account when assessing a premium: **54.163**

> 'When considering whether a premium is reasonable, the Court must have regard to such evidence as there is, or knowledge that experience has provided, of the relationship between the premium and the risk and also of the cost of alternative cover available.'[203]

It is likely that Phillips MR was referring to personal knowledge of the market in general, rather than to knowledge of specific types of insurance. Put otherwise, if a judge is aware of the fact that a premium is grossly out of line with the market norm, the premium may be reduced on that basis. That said, there have been instances of the court drawing upon its knowledge of specific types of policy to fill in gaps in the evidence.[204] The basis upon which the court does this is not entirely clear. It certainly cannot be said that knowledge of the ATE insurance market could fall within either of the categories of judicial notice (that is, notice upon enquiry, and notice of notorious and commonly known facts). That said, Lord Buckmaster has held that, 'properly applied, and within reasonable limits', the court is entitled to use its own knowledge of matters that were commonly known within the locality[205] and it is only a small step to expand this principle so that a court with a particular specialism is entitled to take into account that which is commonly known within that specialism. Even if this is wrong, it is well established that as long as the judge does not give evidence to themselves that contradicts the evidence adduced, a judge is entitled to draw on specialised knowledge when evaluating evidence.[206]

Comparators relating to premiums A paying party will often seek to challenge a premium on the basis that an apparently cheaper alternative was available at the material time.[207] **54.164**

[203] *Callery v Gray (No 2)* [2001] EWCA Civ 1246, at [69].

[204] See *Sharratt v London Central Bus Co & Ors (No 2) The Accident Group Test Cases* [2004] EWCA Civ 575, at [30].

[205] See *Keane v Mount Vernon Colliery Co Ltd* [1933] AC 309, at 317; *Reynolds v Llanelly Associated Tinplate Co Ltd* [1948] 1 All ER 140, CA. These cases were decided under the Workmen's Compensation Acts, but the principles were confirmed, in *Mullen v Hackney London Borough Council* [1997] 1 WLR 1103, to be of general applicability.

[206] Whilst it related to criminal evidence rather than civil costs, see *Wetherall v Harrison* [1976] QB 773, *per* Widgery CJ.

[207] See, eg, *Hahn v NHS England* (unreported), 3 August 2015, Liverpool County Court, Judge Wood QC.

While each case will turn on its own facts and whilst global comparisons may prove persuasive from time to time,[208] such challenges tend to be fraught with difficulties. This is not only because of problems in adducing relevant and sufficiently persuasive evidence (see below), but also because the court recognises that receiving parties' solicitors will not always be able to select from a variety of products and offer different policies to different clients. Brooke LJ had this to say on the point:

> 'For block rating to work the insurer needs to be sure that it is receiving a full and fair selection of cases, ranging from those where liability is unlikely to be in doubt to those where it is contested. In order to avoid adverse selection it is standard practice for ATE insurers to require solicitors to insure all available cases with the ATE provider. In practice, therefore, claimants' solicitors cannot simply pick and choose from a variety of products and offer different policies to different clients. This approach is, in any event, incompatible with block rating.'[209]

54.165 Unlike most issues concerning the assessment of costs, the court will, as a rule, insist on an exacting standard of evidence if it is to entertain a challenge to the reasonableness of a premium and whilst there are no specific exclusory rules, there tends to be only a narrow range of evidence that the court will regard as being probative of a challenge.

54.166 *Evidence relation to the market* Experience or evidence of the market are factors that can be taken into account.[210] Evidence must be case-specific. This means that (unless the evidence is for a purpose such as showing the general state of the market or for making a point about macroeconomics), it must show not what was available in the market generally, but what was available to the receiving party on the facts of the particular claim in question.[211] A case-specific report would often be required, usually from an expert broker. Such reports are extremely difficult to obtain, however.

54.167 *Efficiency and premiums* Evidence of extravagant expenditure may prove that a policy is uncompetitive, with the result that the premium is not recoverable in full.[212] Evidence that the insurer lost money on the transaction is irrelevant to the issue of whether the premium was reasonable.[213]

54.168 *Actuarial method relating to premiums* Phillips MR has confirmed that it is open to an insurer to adduce evidence as to the reasonableness of the premium sought, but he emphasised that it was not the court's task to carry out an audit of the insurer's business.[214]

54.169 *Evidence relating to the amount of premiums* The points made above about the need to adduce evidence in support of a challenge to the quantum of a premium do not mean that evidence must be adduced in support of an unchallenged premium; compliance with the

---

208 See, eg, *Sharratt v London Central Bus Co & Ors (No 2) The Accident Group Test Cases* [2004] EWCA Civ 575, at [34].

209 *Rogers v Merthyr Tydfil County Borough Council* [2006] EWCA Civ 1134, at [33].

210 *Callery v Gray (No 2)* [2001] EWCA Civ 1246, at [13].

211 *Rogers v Merthyr Tydfil County Borough Council* [2006] EWCA Civ 1134, at [108]–[112], approving of *Re RSA Pursuit Test Cases* [2005] EWHC 90003 (Costs), at [235].

212 *Callery v Gray (No 2)* [2001] EWCA Civ 1246, at [13].

213 *Sharratt v London Central Bus Co & Ors (No 2) The Accident Group Test Cases* [2004] EWCA Civ 575, at [33].

214 *Callery v Gray (No 2)* [2001] EWCA Civ 1246, at [16].

CPD is generally regarded as being sufficient. Service of the bill of costs ought to be accompanied by a copy of the insurance certificate showing:

- whether the policy covers the receiving party's own costs, its opponent's costs, or its own costs and its opponent's costs;
- the maximum extent of that cover; and
- the amount of the premium paid or payable.[215]

If a receiving party wishes to go further, however, it may; if it anticipates a challenge to the premium, evidence may be adduced as reasonableness. If this is done and if the evidence is detailed, however, the receiving party would create a risk of impliedly accepting a deconstructive approach, and it is for this reason that there is often reluctance on the part of such parties to adduce detailed evidence.

Nonetheless, the receiving party may wish to prove that, after having made reasonably diligent enquiries, the policy was the most appropriate that it could find. Alternatively, it may wish to prove that extensive enquiries would have been disproportionate in the particular circumstances of the claim. Such evidence need not be elaborate, as was explained by Brooke LJ: **54.170**

> '[If] an issue arises about the size of a ... premium, it will ordinarily be sufficient for a claimant's solicitor to write a brief note for the purposes of the costs assessment explaining how he came to choose the particular ATE product for his client, and the basis upon which the premium is rated—whether block rated or individually rated.'[216]

Brooke LJ went on to imply that expert evidence might be required in some circumstances. In a different case, Simon J has said that where a real issue was raised, the court envisaged the hearing of expert evidence as to the reasonableness of the premium.[217] Akenhead J has implied much the same thing, but he went on to say that, on a summary assessment, such evidence would be disproportionate.[218] It is fair to say, however, that expert evidence on any assessment—even the most involved of detailed assessments—is a considerable rarity.

The policy Gray J has indicated (*obiter*) that policies ought not to be privileged and that they ought to be disclosed 'as a matter of course'.[219] Whilst his comments can be read in other ways, it seems likely that what he meant was that if it is foreseeable that an opponent will reasonably wish to see it, a policy ought to be drafted in such a way that the issue of privilege does not arise. Notwithstanding this, it is probably the case that the court lacks the power to require a party to disclose its policy (unless, of course, there are grounds on which the court can find that it is not privileged).[220] In a detailed assessment, however, the court can put the receiving party to their election. Indeed, in some circumstances, the court may even impose a condition of disclosure (which is not an order to disclose, but an **54.171**

---

215 CPD, art 32.5(2).

216 *Rogers v Merthyr Tydfil County Borough Council* [2006] EWCA Civ 1134, at [117].

217 *Kris Motor Spares Ltd v Fox Williams LLP* [2010] EWHC 1008 (QB), at [44]. See also *Percy v Anderson-Young* [2017] EWHC 2712 (QB), at [68], *per* Martin Spencer J.

218 *Redwing Construction Ltd v Wishart* [2011] EWHC 19 (TCC), at [15].

219 *Henry v British Broadcasting Corpn* [2005] EWHC 2503 (QB), at [26].

220 Although a non-costs case, see *West London Pipeline & Storage Ltd v Total UK Ltd* [2008] EWHC 1296 (Comm).

order to choose whether to disclose or to bear the consequences of not disclosing) during the substantive case itself.[221]

The deconstruction of premiums

54.172 Deconstruction is the process of dismantling a premium for the purposes of examining its constituent parts.[222] It would be possible to deconstruct a premium simply for the purposes of examining the reasonableness of each component, but that is not usually its intended purpose (or, for that matter, generally permissible); rather, deconstruction is usually—albeit infrequently—carried out for the purposes of isolating and excluding monies that are not true premium monies, and which are to be subtracted from the amount claimed.[223]

54.173 To know what is to be excluded, it is necessary to know what is to be included, which means that it is necessary to have a definition of what a premium *is*. The following definition is generally received as being appropriate in the context of ATE insurance: 'The consideration required of the assured in return for which the insurer undertakes [its] obligation under the contract of insurance.'[224] Thus a premium is a sum paid to the insurer and does not include monies paid to an intermediary (unless, of course, it is received by the intermediary on behalf of the insurer). An intermediary cannot make its fee into a premium by the mere expedient of calling it a premium.[225]

54.174 The following are examples of monies that might be disallowed upon deconstruction, depending on the circumstances:

- money paid for the right to be included within a claims management scheme;[226]
- referral fees;[227]
- the costs of 'ring-fencing' damages;[228] and
- voluntary payments made by claims management companies to an underwriter for the purposes of securing extra capacity.

Monies that are not true premium monies may be irrecoverable for reasons unconnected with, or additional to, those mentioned above. Where, for example, a fee is an *unlawful* referral fee, it would become irrecoverable by reason of implied statutory prohibition against the enforceability of that fee, which would be an additional reason for its disallowance.[229]

---

[221] Such as a condition for the continuance of group litigation: see *Barr v Biffa Waste Services Ltd* [2009] EWHC 1033 (TCC).

[222] *Sharratt v London Central Bus Co & Ors (No 2) The Accident Group Test Cases* [2004] EWCA Civ 575, at [17].

[223] *Callery v Gray (No 2)* [2001] EWCA Civ 1246, at [12].

[224] This definition is taken from *MacGillivray on Insurance Law* (9th edn, London: Sweet & Maxwell, 1998), and was approved of in both *Claims Direct Litigation* [2003] EWCA Civ 136, at [25], and *Sharratt v London Central Bus Co & Ors (No 2) The Accident Group Test Cases* [2004] EWCA Civ 575, at [17].

[225] *Sharratt v London Central Bus Co & Ors (No 2) The Accident Group Test Cases* [2004] EWCA Civ 575, at [17]; see also *Re Claims Direct Test Cases* [2003] EWCA Civ 136, at [35]–[46].

[226] See, eg, *Re Claims Direct Test Cases* [2003] EWCA Civ 136.

[227] See, eg, *Sharratt v London Central Bus Co & Ors (No 2) The Accident Group Test Cases* [2004] EWCA Civ 575, at [39]–[42].

[228] Although not binding, see, eg, *Re Claims Direct Test Cases* [2002] All ER (D) 76, at [214], *per* Master Hurst, aff'd at [2003] EWCA Civ 136, but not on this specific point.

[229] See, eg, *Sharratt v London Central Bus Co & Ors (No 2) The Accident Group Test Cases* [2004] EWCA Civ 575, at [39]–[42].

Miscellaneous Points Regarding ATE Premiums

More than one set of proceedings

It may be that a party takes out ATE insurance that is, as between insurer and insured, in respect of more than one set of proceedings (such as where it is taken on an appeal with the intention of covering the costs of the trial). In an appeal in which this was so, Rix and Etherton LJJ (Patten LJ dissenting) have explained that the premium or part thereof that relates to the proceedings other than the instant proceedings would not be recoverable; if it were otherwise, costs of trial could, in effect, be increased retrospectively, to the prejudice of the losing party.[230] They reached this conclusion on the basis that the reference to 'proceedings' in Access to Justice Act 1999, s 29, ought be read as relating only to the proceedings in hand. **54.175**

Extension of ATE policies and top-up policies

It may be that a party needs a higher level of cover than was provided for by an ATE policy that they took out prior to 1 April 2013. Where this is so, the options would be (a) to obtain a new top-up policy or (where possible) (b) to extend the cover under the existing policy (see 34.38–34.40). Lord Sumption has confirmed that the cost of extended cover falls within the ambit of Legal Aid, Sentencing and Punishment of Offenders Act 2012, s 46(3), saying this on the topic: **54.176**

> 'The purpose of the transitional provisions of [the Legal Aid, Sentencing and Punishment of Offenders Act 2012], in relation to both success fees and ATE premiums, is to preserve vested rights and expectations arising from the previous law. That purpose would be defeated by a rigid distinction between different stages of the same litigation. It may or may not be reasonable to expect an insured party who fails at trial to abandon the fight for want of funding. That will depend mainly on the merits of the appeal. But an insured claimant who succeeds at trial and becomes the respondent to an appeal is locked into the litigation. Unless he is prepared to forego the fruits of his judgment, which by definition represents his rights unless and until it is set aside, he has no option but to defend the appeal. The topping-up of his ATE policy to cover the appeal is in reality part of the cost of defending what he has won by virtue of being funded under the original policy. The effect, if the top-up premium is not recoverable, would be retrospectively to alter the balance of risks on the basis of which the litigation was begun.'[231]

Thus the costs of an extension to an ATE policy are recoverable between opposing parties.

Whilst there is no authority on the point, it is also arguable that the costs of a new top-up policy are recoverable. This is because s 46(3) of the 2012 Act confers the advantage of recoverability on the 'party ... who took out a costs insurance policy in relation to the **54.177**

[230] *Hawksford Trustees Jersey Ltd (as Trustee of the Bald Eagle Trust) v Stella Global UK Ltd* [2012] EWCA Civ, at [58]–[60]. See also *Gabriel v BPE Solicitors* [2015] AC 1663, at [16]. It should be noted that, in *Plevin v Paragon Personal Finance Ltd* [2017] UKSC 23, at [18]–[19], Lord Sumption had the opportunity to comment adversely on *Hawksford*, but despite coming to a different conclusion as to what the word 'proceedings' meant in a different part of the CPR, he did not do so. As such, it seems unlikely that his decision in *Plevin* casts doubt on the decision in *Hawksford*.

[231] *Plevin v Paragon Personal Finance Ltd* [2017] UKSC 23, at [21].

proceedings', which, on the face of it, is a broad definition that does not limit itself to a policy taken out before 1 April 2013.

Budgets and ATE premiums

54.178 Mann J has confirmed that budgets should not include ATE premiums.[232] As such, if—for whatever reason—additional liabilities arise in the context of a costs-managed case, they will be assessed without reference to the budget.

Membership Organisations and Notional Premiums

54.179 Whilst now becoming a rarity, a notional premium[233] is an amount charged by a membership organisation as compensation for bearing the responsibility for meeting adverse costs orders made against its members. It is akin to an ATE premium, but is payable to a membership organisation instead of an insurer. This means that there is no market capable of directly exerting any moderating influence on the amount claimed.

54.180 For the reasons set out below, to be able to recover a notional premium, the membership organisation in question must have given an undertaking relating to the specific case in question before 1 April 2013 (see 54.181–54.187). This is why such cases are now becoming a rarity.

The statutory framework relating to notional premiums

54.181 Whilst it will now apply only to the extent that its effect is preserved by saving provisions (see 54.184–54.186), Access to Justice Act 1999, s 30 (as amended), reads as follows:

> '**30. Recovery where body undertakes to meet costs liabilities**
>
> (1) This section applies where a body of a prescribed description undertakes to meet (in accordance with arrangements satisfying prescribed conditions) liabilities which members of the body or other persons who are parties to proceedings may incur to pay the costs of other parties to the proceedings.
>
> (2) If in any of the proceedings a costs order is made in favour of any of the members or other persons, the costs payable to him may, subject to subsection (3) and (in the case of court proceedings) to rules of court, include an additional amount in respect of any provision made by or on behalf of the body in connection with the proceedings against the risk of having to meet such liabilities.
>
> (3) But the additional amount shall not exceed a sum determined in a prescribed manner; and there may, in particular, be prescribed as a manner of determination one which takes into account the likely cost to the member or other person of the premium of an insurance policy against the risk of incurring a liability to pay the costs of other parties to the proceedings.
>
> (4) In this section "prescribed" means prescribed by regulations made by the Lord Chancellor by statutory instrument; and a statutory instrument containing such regulations shall be subject to annulment in pursuance of a resolution of either House of Parliament.
>
> (5) Regulations under subsection (1) may, in particular, prescribe as a description of body one which is for the time being approved by the Lord Chancellor or by a prescribed person.'

[232] See *Various Claimants v MGN Ltd* [2016] EWHC 1894 (Ch).

[233] The term 'self-insurance premium' is also often used, but this ought not to be confused with self-insur*ing* policies, which fund themselves by recovery of enhanced premiums payable only in the event of success.

The regulations referred to obliquely in s 30(1) are the Access to Justice (Membership Organisation) Regulations 2005,[234] the relevant parts of which read as follows: 54.182

> '**Bodies of a prescribed description**
>
> 3. The bodies which are prescribed for the purpose of section 30 (recovery where body undertakes to meet costs liabilities) are those bodies which are for the time being approved by the Secretary of State for that purpose.
>
> **Requirements for arrangements to meet costs liabilities**
>
> 4. (1) Section 30(1) applies to arrangements which satisfy the following conditions.
>
> (2) The arrangements must be in writing.
>
> (3) The arrangements must contain a statement specifying the circumstances in which the member may be liable to pay costs of the proceedings.
>
> **Recovery of additional amount for insurance costs**
>
> 5. (1) Where an additional amount is included in costs by virtue of section 30(2) (costs payable to a member of a body or other person party to the proceedings to include an additional amount in respect of provision made by the body against the risk of having to meet the member's or other person's liabilities to pay other parties' costs), that additional amount must not exceed the following sum.
>
> (2) That sum is the likely cost to the member of the body or, as the case may be, the other person who is a party to the proceedings in which the costs order is made of the premium of an insurance policy against the risk of incurring a liability to pay the costs of other parties to the proceedings.'

Neither the Access to Justice Act 1999 nor the Regulations made under s 30 of that Act state what should happen in the event of non-compliance with those Regulations. It is perhaps for this reason that there has been little litigation on the issue of regulatory compliance. Non-compliance may mean that the receiving party is precluded from recovering its notional premium, but there is no authority to support this contention. 54.183

Transitional provisions relating to notional premiums

Access to Justice Act 1999, s 30, was repealed on 1 April 2013 by Legal Aid, Sentencing and Punishment of Offenders Act 2012, s 47(1). Savings provision apply, however, in that s 47(2) of the 2012 Act reads as follows: 54.184

> '(2) The repeal made by subsection (1)[[235]] does not apply in relation to a costs order made in favour of a person to whom a body gave an undertaking before the day on which this section comes into force if the undertaking was given specifically in respect of the costs of other parties to proceedings relating to the matter which is the subject of the proceedings in which the costs order is made.'

Thus a notional premium will continue to be recoverable if the body (that is, the union, association or other such body) gave the relevant undertaking before 1 April 2013, but only if this was in respect of the specific case in question.

[234] SI 2005/2306. This was so only if the arrangements were made on or after 1 November 2005; prior to this date, the Access to Justice (Membership Organisations) Regulations 2000 (SI 2000/693) applied. The transitional provisions are at reg 2(2) of the 2005 Regulations; the 2000 Regulations are addressed in detail in the second edition of this book, at para 49.130.

[235] This subsection omitted Access to Justice Act 1999, s 30.

54.185 In so far as the CPR are concerned, CPR, r 48.2(1)(a)(iii), reads as follows:

> '(1) A pre-commencement funding arrangement is—
> (a) in relation to proceedings other than insolvency-related proceedings, publication and privacy proceedings or a mesothelioma claim—
> [...]
> (iii) a funding arrangement as defined by rule 43.2(1)(k)(iii) where the agreement with the membership organisation to meet the costs was made before 1 April 2013 specifically in respect of the costs of other parties to proceedings relating to the matter which is the subject of the proceedings in which the costs order is to be made; ...'

54.186 It should be noted that there are no special savings provisions relating to notional premiums. Put otherwise, the exceptions that apply to ATE premiums as listed at 54.14 do not apply to notional premiums.

Membership organisations

54.187 An organisation has to be approved before it is able to hold itself out as a membership organisation. A certification officer (a civil servant) keeps a record of those organisations. All unions listed by the certification officer are automatically approved; in addition, some 13 other organisations were approved, including a number of professional organisations and cycling organisations.[236] The approval criteria are discussed in the second edition of this book (at 30.234).

Notional premiums

54.188 Notice had to be given of an intention to claim a notional premium.[237] Whilst there is no authority on the point, the principles already discussed pertaining to notice of funding in other circumstances are likely to apply (see 54.108–54.123). As explained above, reg 5 of the Access to Justice (Membership Organisation) Regulations 2005[238] provides that the amount payable by an opponent must not exceed the likely cost of 'an insurance policy against the risk of incurring a liability to pay the costs of other parties to the proceedings'. This means that a notional premium ought not to exceed the sum the market would bear for an ATE policy.[239] This restriction used to be echoed in the Access to Justice Act 1999 itself[240] and in the CPD.[241]

---

[236] They are: AA Legal Service; British Cycling Federation; Defence Police Federation; Durham Colliery Overmen Deputies and Shotfirers Retired Members Group; Engineering Employers' Federation; Police Federation of England and Wales; RAC Motoring Services; the Cyclist Touring Club; the London Cycling Campaign; British Triathlon Federation; the Co-operative Group; the National Union of Students; and the British Association of Social Workers (I Akhtar, Ministry of Justice, Personal communication with the author, 20 July 2009).

[237] See CPD, art 32.5(3), which reads: 'If the receiving party claims an additional amount under Section 30 of the Access of Justice Act 1999: a statement setting out the basis upon which the receiving party's liability for the additional amount is calculated.'

[238] SI 2005/2306.

[239] Historically, ATE premiums have tended to be higher than notional premiums, which, unfortunately, can lead to somewhat circular arguments about what the appropriate measure should be.

[240] Access to Justice Act 1999, s 30(3), provides that the notional premium shall not exceed a sum determined in a prescribed manner and that 'there may, in particular, be prescribed as a manner of determination one which takes into account the likely cost to the member or other person of the premium of an insurance policy against the risk of incurring a liability to pay the costs of other parties to the proceedings'.

[241] CPD, arts 32.6 and 11.11.

As to the factors to be taken into account, CPD, art 11.11, gave the following guidance: **54.189**

> 'Where the court is considering a provision made by a membership organisation ... the court will, when assessing the additional liability, have regard to the factors set out in paragraph 11.10 above, in addition to the factors set out in rule 44.5.'

Thus not only were notional premiums limited to the amount of equivalent ATE premiums, but also they were to be assessed by reference to the same criteria. The court would not have the benefit of an actual premium as to the starting point, so presumably—unless there was evidence as to the 'going rate'—the court would have to draw upon its own experience of the ATE market (see 54.163). That said, Judge Behrens was persuaded to carry out an assessment by way of hypothetical deconstruction in a case in which there was no evidence of comparators.[242]

Not all membership organisations charged notional premiums. Some took the view that it was in their interests (or those of their members) to take out ATE insurance instead. This was often on the basis that a premium would allow recovery for own-disbursement cover, whereas notional premiums did not.[243] **54.190**

Alternative Means of Funding

The following discussion addresses alternative means of funding and, in particular, BTE insurance. The topic of BTE insurance in general is addressed in Chapter 34. **54.191**

In the present context, 'alternative' means any type of funding that does not give rise to additional liabilities. This would include before-the-event (BTE) insurance (see 34.04), trades union funding and legal aid. **54.192**

If a receiving party unreasonably eschews an alternative means of funding in favour of incurring additional liabilities, then it would be open to the court to make an evaluative judgment to disallow those liabilities on the basis that they had been unreasonably incurred.[244] **54.193**

The fact that an alternative means of funding was available would not necessarily mean that it would be unreasonable not to use it. All of the circumstances of the individual case in hand need to be taken into account. This is in contrast to the 'macroeconomic' approach that may be taken when alternative means of funding are not available, in which factors that go beyond the individual case may be taken into account and given significant weight (see 54.136–54.137).[245] Lewison LJ has explained that the court may—and, in practical **54.194**

[242] See *Evans v Arriva Yorkshire Ltd* (unreported), 28 November 2013, Leeds County Court.

[243] Paying parties usually argue that own-disbursement cover is something that can be taken into account when setting the success fee.

[244] See CPR, r 44.4. See also now-revoked CPD, art 11.8, which gave the following guidance: '(1) In deciding whether a percentage increase is reasonable relevant factors to be taken into account may include: (c) what other methods of financing the costs were available to the receiving party.' In a similar vein, CPD, art 11.10, reads as follows: 'In deciding whether the cost of insurance cover is reasonable, relevant factors to be taken into account include: ... (3) the availability of any pre-existing insurance cover.'

[245] See *Surrey v Barnet & Chase Farm Hospitals NHS Trust & Ors* [2018] EWCA Civ 451, at [30], *per* Lewison LJ.

terms, often must—examine the reasons why the receiving party incurred the costs that they did.[246]

The relevance of legal advice regarding funding

54.195 Where a receiving party was faced with seemingly similar funding options from their point of view and where they choose an option that is more burdensome for the paying party, the receiving party will have to justify that choice.[247] Following legal advice will not, of itself, be sufficient to justify that choice.[248] If the advice is wrong in law, then that may militate against recoverability of additional liabilities,[249] as will advice that is based on misjudged or fanciful risks.[250] If advice was given that was incomplete, the burden will be on the receiving party to show that they would still have made the same choice if they had been given complete advice.[251]

54.196 The court may take into account the extent to which the receiving party was counselled about the options available. There can be no doubt that if a solicitor is minded to advise a client to choose a method of funding that is beneficial to the solicitor yet adverse to the client's rational self-interests, the client must be fully informed. In this regard, Lewison LJ approved of District Judge Besford's comments: 'Where one of two or more options available to a client is more financially beneficial to the solicitor, the need for transparency becomes ever greater.'[252] Lewison LJ went on to say:

> 'This a reflection of the fundamental principle of equity that where a person stands in a fiduciary relationship to another, the fiduciary is not permitted to retain a profit derived from that fiduciary relationship without the fully informed consent of the other'.[253]

This may be relevant where, for example, a solicitor is considering giving advice that a client should give up legal aid and enter into a conditional fee agreement instead.[254]

Inquiries relating to funding

54.197 Speaking extrajudicially, Jackson LJ made the following comments about the importance of funding inquiries:

> 'The first question which any litigation solicitor should, and would, ask of a client with a claim in the categories mention [34.11, these being cases in which BTE cover is likely to be available] is whether the client has household insurance and, if so, what are its terms. Indeed

---

246 See *ibid*, at [17]. In this regard, he emphasised that there may be a range of reasonable options available to a receiving party, drawing assistance from the way in which *Wraith v Sheffield Forgemasters Ltd* [1998] 1 WLR 133 dealt with hourly rates: see *Surrey v Barnet & Chase Farm Hospitals NHS Trust & Ors* [2018] EWCA Civ 451, [15].

247 See *ibid*, at [30].

248 See *ibid*, at [32].

249 In, eg, *ibid*, at [15], the receiving party's solicitor incorrectly advised that a client, who already had the benefit of legal aid, may be at risk of having to 'top up' fees—something that would have been unlawful: see Access to Justice Act 1999 ss 10(1) and 22(2).

250 See, eg, *Surrey v Barnet & Chase Farm Hospitals NHS Trust & Ors* [2018] EWCA Civ 451, at [43].

251 See *ibid*, at [51] and [53]. The advice that was not properly given in the cases before the court was that the clients were not told that, by electing to enter into pre-2013 CFA Lites, they would lose the right to an uplift on general damages as in *Simmons v Castle* [2012] EWCA Civ 1039.

252 See *Surrey v Barnet & Chase Farm Hospitals NHS Trust & Ors* [2018] EWCA Civ 451, at [60].

253 See *ibid*, at [61].

254 See, eg, *ibid*.

solicitors are required, as a matter of professional conduct, to discuss with their clients at the outset whether the client's costs are covered by insurance.'[255]

These comments were made before 1 April 2013, but even now, solicitors are obliged to carry out funding inquiries so that they can give advice about the best method of funding. A sobering reminder of this is a case in which Hickenbottom J found that a master had been entitled to assess a solicitor's bill of costs at nil where the solicitor had failed to ascertain that the client was entitled to free legal representation as a benefit of her trade union membership.[256]

The extent of funding inquiries

The extent to which a solicitor is expected to conduct funding enquiries will depend on the facts and, in particular, will depend on the amount at stake.[257] Solicitors are not obliged to conduct treasure hunts.[258] As to what is required, Phillips MR had this to say: **54.198**

> '[P]roper modern practice dictates that a solicitor should normally invite a client to bring to the first interview any relevant motor insurance policy, any household insurance policy and any stand-alone BTE insurance policy belonging to the client and/or any spouse or partner living in the same household as the client.'[259]

This guidance is limited to unremarkable, modest road traffic accident cases.[260] Dyson LJ explained that Phillips MR's guidance would have no application in high-volume, low-value work of the type typically referred by claims management companies.[261]

Funding inquiries and credit cards In so far as credit cards are concerned, Phillips MR gave the following advice: **54.199**

> 'So far as credit cards and charge cards are concerned ... [we] are inclined to think that the time taken by a solicitor in assisting a client to identify and pursue such cover would at present be likely to result in this course proving more expensive than an ATE premium in this class of case.'[262]

Whilst he indicated that the financial landscape might change at some point so as to justify such enquiries, there is nothing to suggest that this has yet happened.

Funding enquiries and the Solicitors Regulation Authority (SRA) Code of Conduct 2011 The standard of the requisite enquiries is not the same as the standard applicable to claims in negligence.[263] Whilst it is arguable that it is irrelevant, the SRA Code of Conduct 2011 requires solicitors to discuss 'how the client will pay, including whether **54.200**

---

[255] Jackson, R, *Review of Civil Litigation Costs: Final Report* (London: HMSO, 2010), para 8.5.5. The reference to professional obligations was a reference to Solicitors Code of Conduct 2007, para 2.03(1)(d)(ii).

[256] *McDaniel & Co v Clarke* [2014] EWHC 3826 (QB).

[257] *Sarwar v Alam* [2001] EWCA Civ 1401, at [46]. While the test being addressed was itself not the same as the present test, *Garrett v Halton Borough Council; Myatt v National Coal Board* [2006] Civ 1017, at [73]–[76], gives some guidance as to factors that may be relevant, such as the nature of the circumstances in which the solicitor was instructed, the nature of the claim and the cost of the alternative (ie ATE insurance).

[258] *Sarwar v Alam* [2001] EWCA Civ 1401, at [46].

[259] *Ibid*, at [45].

[260] *Ibid*, at [50].

[261] *Garrett v Halton Borough Council; Myatt v National Coal Board* [2006] EWCA Civ 1017, at [70].

[262] *Sarwar v Alam* [2001] EWCA Civ 1401, at [49].

[263] *Ibid*, at [51]. This is of practical relevance because it means that a client who failed to recover their ATE premium by reason of inadequate BTE inquiries might be able to bring a claim against their solicitor.

public funding may be available, whether the client has insurance that might cover the fees, and whether the fees may be paid by someone else such as a trade union'.[264]

54.201 **Funding enquiries and opponents** Enquiries should not be curtailed or avoided merely because the person of whom they are made is also an opposing party (such as where the claimant was injured in a car being driven by the defendant). Phillips MR explained that each case must turn on its own facts:

> 'Now that motor insurance often contains provision for BTE cover for a claim brought by a passenger, the solicitor should ordinarily ask the client passenger to obtain a copy of the driver's insurance policy, if reasonably practicable. Whether it is reasonably practicable to comply with the solicitor's request is likely to be fact-sensitive.'[265]

The suitability of BTE insurance

54.202 This is addressed at 34.18–34.20.

The relevance of private means

54.203 The fact that a receiving party had means to fund litigation privately would not be a justification for disallowing additional liabilities and this would be so regardless of whether the receiving party was a commercial concern[266] or an individual.[267] Likewise, the fact that a person who brings a subrogated claim had the benefit of liability insurance would not be a reason to disallow additional liabilities.[268]

The relevance of legal aid

54.204 Whilst is an issue that will rarely now arise, if a party has the option to use legal aid, but unreasonably eschews it, that is a factor that may justify additional liabilities being disallowed.[269] It may be the case that a party who had legal aid prior to 1 April 2013 entered into a conditional fee agreement or took out an ATE policy to ensure that any additional liabilities were recoverable; this may be for perfectly sound reasons, such as there being some form of limit on the extent to which legal aid could have been used. Where this happens, a factor that the court may take into account is whether the client was advised about whether the change in funding method would have a bearing on the uplift in damages, as in *Simmons v Castle*.[270] If appropriate advice was not given, then this may militate against recovery of additional liabilities (see 54.194–54.195).

Trade union funding

54.205 Trades unions and professional organisations often provide, as a benefit of membership, legal assistance for their members and families of their members. In most cases of trade union funding in which the funding began before 1 April 2013, the union is likely to seek

264 SRA Code of Conduct 2011, IB(1.16).
265 *Sarwar v Alam* [2001] EWCA Civ 1401, at [47].
266 *Sandvik Intellectual Property AB v Kennametal UK Ltd* [2012] EWHC 245 (Pat), *per* Arnold J.
267 *Campbell v MGN Ltd (No 2)* [2005] UKHL 61, at [27].
268 *Sousa v Waltham Forest London Borough Council* [2011] EWCA Civ 194, at [28]–[39].
269 See *Surrey v Barnet & Chase Farm Hospitals NHS Trust & Ors* [2018] EWCA Civ 451.
270 *Simmons v Castle* [2012] EWCA Civ 1288. This is an uplift that the court has no discretion but to award to persons who are legally aided: see *Summers v Bundy* [2016] EWCA Civ 126.

both a success fee and a notional premium under Access to Justice Act 1999, s 30. The relevance of this is that it does not follow that a receiving party who eschewed trade union funding should be denied additional liabilities on the grounds that they were unreasonably incurred.

Employer funding

Employers may provide legal expenses funding as a perquisite, but that benefit is usually **54.206** provided in the form of BTE insurance. The fact that the employee has to pay tax on the benefit received has made employer funding a relative rarity.

55

VALUE ADDED TAX

55.01 This chapter deals with the following topics:

- introduction (55.02);
- output tax and liability for value added tax (VAT) (55.04):
  - whether VAT is chargeable by the receiving party's legal representatives (55.05);
  - the time when VAT falls due—tax points (55.06);
  - rates of VAT (55.10);
  - tax on disbursements—qualifying disbursements (55.15);
- expert reports and records:
  - non-medical and non-dental experts (55.22);
  - medical and dental experts (55.23);
  - medical and dental records (55.24);
  - medical agencies (55.25);
- VAT between opposing parties:
  - general principles and input tax (55.26);
  - reasonableness (55.29);
- changes of the rate of VAT (55.33); and
- the wording of relevant provisions (55.45).

Introduction

55.02 Value added tax (VAT) is a form of consumption tax that all member states of the European Union must charge.[1] This chapter addresses VAT between solicitor and client (see 55.04–55.21), and its recoverability between opposing parties (see 55.26–55.44).[2] It will examine the following topics, which will determine the extent to which VAT is payable (or recoverable).

- **Output tax** The first topic (output tax) relates to profit costs and counsel's fees. It is whether the legal representatives who carried out the work are obliged to charge VAT as 'output tax' and, if so, how much. The issues that may arise in this regard are:
  - whether the legal representatives are registered for VAT (see 55.04);
  - the points at which tax becomes payable—a matter that will depend on whether they are solicitors (see 55.05–55.07) or barristers (see 55.08); and

---

[1] Council Directive 2006/112/EC of 28 November 1006 on the common system of value added tax, OJ L 347/1, 11 December 2006 (the Principal VAT Directive).

[2] The author is not an accountant, so if any accountancy issues arise, readers must either take their own advice or must discuss the matter directly with HM Revenue & Customs (HMRC).

  - the rate of VAT that they must claim (see 55.10–55.12).
- **Tax on disbursements** The next topic is whether tax is payable on disbursements. Disbursements may attract VAT when they are first disbursed or as a result of being recharged to the client via the legal party's legal representatives (see 55.15–55.21). The following issues often arise in practice:
  - the amount of VAT payable for medical or dental reports (see 55.23) or records (see 55.24); and
  - the amount payable for reports and records that have been obtained by medical agencies (see 55.25).
- **Input tax** The third topic is whether VAT, or any part thereof, can be recovered by the receiving party as 'input tax' (see 55.26–55.28). This is relevant because if the receiving party is able to reclaim input tax, the paying party will not have to pay it (see 55.26).
- **Reasonableness** The fourth and final topic is whether it is reasonable for the receiving party to claim VAT from the paying party (see 55.29–55.32). In particular, a problem that often arises in practice is whether a paying party should pay VAT at the full rate claimed if the receiving party's legal representative had the right to elect to charge a lower rate (see 55.29).

Many people find VAT confusing in the context of the law of costs. Figure 55.1 is a forensic sieve (in the form of a flowchart) that may assist in understanding the way in which VAT is to be determined. **55.03**

Output Tax and Liability for VAT

In the present context, 'output tax' means VAT on supplies made by a 'taxable person'[3]—that is, a person who is or who ought to be registered for VAT.[4] 'Input tax' is the VAT on the supply to a taxable person of any goods or services.[5] Thus, from the point of view of the legal representative supplying legal services, output tax is the VAT on work done and services provided, whereas input tax is the VAT that the legal representative pays on supplies. The former must be paid to HM Revenue & Customs (HMRC), whereas the latter may be claimed, reclaimed or deducted.[6] **55.04**

Whether VAT is chargeable by the receiving party's legal representatives

Most legal representatives will be registered for VAT and will claim output tax on the legal services supplied. There may be occasions, however, on which liability for VAT does not arise. The issues that are often encountered in practice are as follows. **55.05**

- **Legal representative not registered for VAT** A handful of lawyers will not be VAT-registered, the most common examples being recently called counsel[7] and mediators. If a legal representative lawfully instructs counsel who is not registered for VAT,

[3] See Value Added Tax Act 1994, s 24(2).
[4] See Value Added Tax Act 1994, s 3(1).
[5] See Value Added Tax Act 1994, s 24(1).
[6] See Value Added Tax Regulations 1995 (SI 1995/2518), reg 29.
[7] Since April 2011, the threshold for compulsory registration has been £73,000.

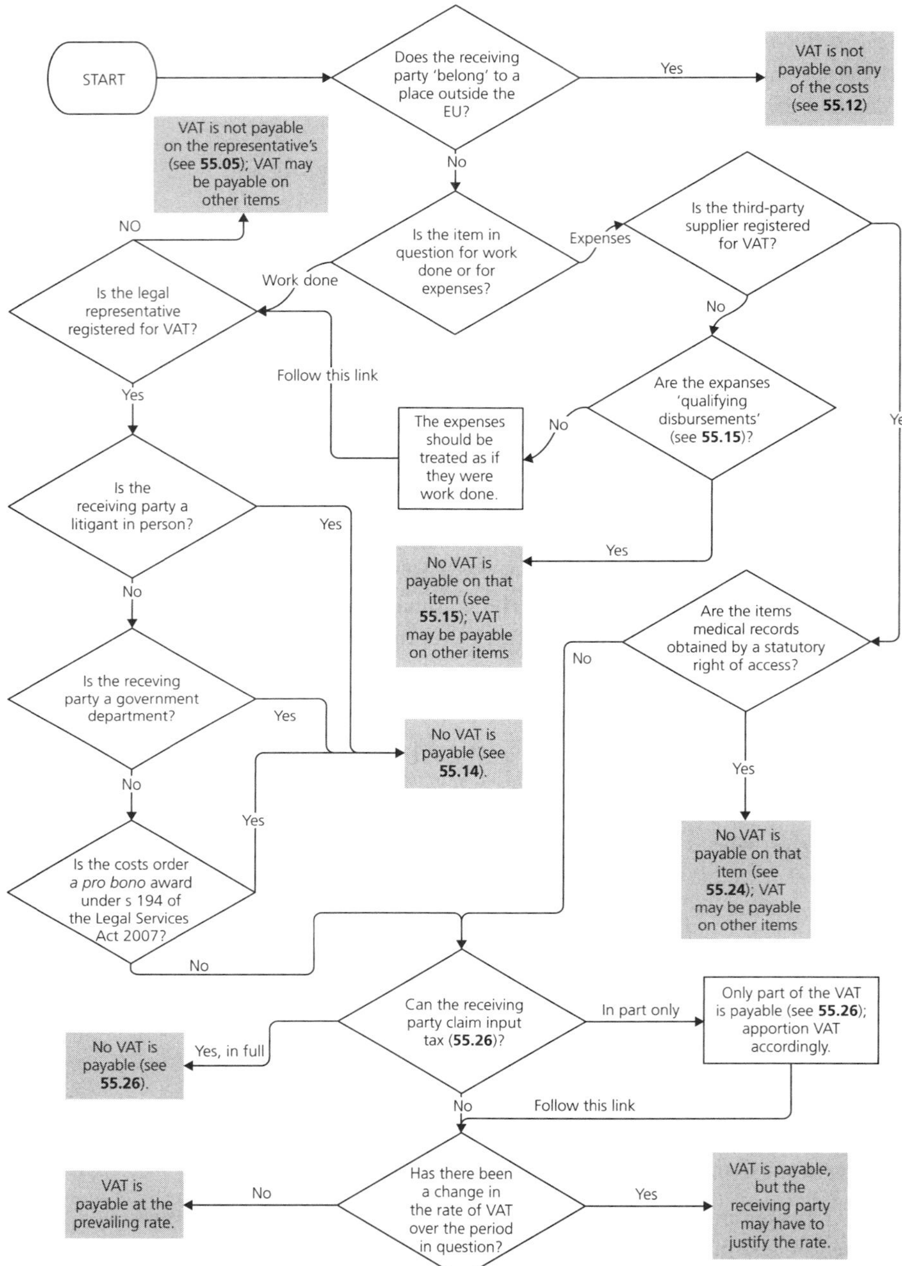

Figure 55.1 Forensic sieve for deciding whether, and at what rate, VAT is payable between opposing parties

their services will be deemed to be part of the services provided by that legal representative[8] and, as a result, VAT will be payable in principle. In practice, however, HMRC will permit the legal representative to 'readdress' counsel's fee note,[9] with the effect of making it payable directly by the lay client as a 'qualifying disbursement' (see 55.15). Thus the liability for VAT can be avoided reasonably easily. This is why a receiving party will not normally be able to recover VAT on the fees of counsel who is not registered for VAT.

- **No supply of legal services** Even where a legal representative is VAT-registered, it is not always the case that VAT has to be charged on the work they have done. An example would be where work is carried out by legal representatives who are employed in-house:[10] if those are the facts, then—in general (see 55.14)—there would be no supply of services and hence no VAT. Likewise, if a legal representative is acting on their own behalf, they are not treated as having supplied a service, so no VAT would be chargeable (see 55.14).

The time when VAT falls due: tax points

Basic and actual tax points

As between legal representative and client, VAT will become payable only once a liability for output tax has arisen. Such a liability will arise only upon the creation of either a 'basic tax point' or an 'actual tax point'. **55.06**

- **Basic tax points** A basic tax point[11] is generally created on completion of the work.[12] HMRC gives the following advice about basic tax points:

> 'The majority of supplies by a solicitor are single supplies, albeit the supply may involve work undertaken over an extended period of time. A good example of this is litigation. The basic tax point occurs when the services have been fully completed. But it can be difficult sometimes to establish precisely when this might be, especially where the matter has taken a number of years to be resolved.
>
> Some solicitors make supplies on a regular basis to an individual client. In most cases this will represent a series of separate supplies, each of which will be subject to its own basic tax point ... Only in exceptional circumstances, such as where a solicitor is retained and remunerated as a permanent legal adviser or to act as the client's legal office, might this kind of relationship represent a continuous supply of services.'[13]

Thus a basic tax point is the date on which the supply of all of the services (except the invoicing[14]) has been fully completed. In so far as solicitors are concerned, this is addressed at 55.07 below.

[8] This is a matter of accountancy, rather than costs law. It is an entirely different issue from those matters discussed in Chapter 22.

[9] This agreement was first published in the *Law Society Gazette* on 4 April 1973; it is now recorded in Revenue Law Committee, *The Law Society's VAT Guide* (London: Law Society, 1996), para 1.2.2.

[10] See Revenue Law Committee, *The Law Society's VAT Guide* (London: Law Society, 1996), para 1.9.3.

[11] See Value Added Tax Act 1994, s 6(3).

[12] VATTOS8540 draws a distinction between contentious and non-contentious work; non-contentious work will give rise to a basic tax point when it is complete and any subsequent solicitor-and-client assessment will be accounted for by an adjustment, but where the fees are to be paid by a paying party, the basic tax point will arise upon conclusion of the assessment. See also Revenue Law Committee, *The Law Society's VAT Guide* (London: Law Society, 1996), para 2.1.9.

[13] See VATTOS8520 (Tax points for specific categories of supplier: solicitors: basic tax point).

[14] VATTOS4310 (Basic tax points: performance of services: introduction).

- **Actual tax points** A basic tax point may be overridden by an 'actual tax point', be that before or after the basic tax point. An actual tax point may be created upon payment or upon issue of a VAT invoice, whichever is the earlier.[15] HMRC has issued further guidance on legally aided work.[16]

Solicitors

55.07 As a matter of general principle, the supply of services will, subject to certain exceptions,[17] be treated as taking place at the time when the services are performed.[18] This has traditionally been regarded as being the date on which all of the work, except the invoicing, has been completed.[19] Special provisions relate to solicitors, however, and in this regard, HMRC draws a distinction between contentious and non-contentious work:

> '**Contentious work (non-Legal Aid)**: The losing party to the legal action may be ordered to pay costs. Where this is the case, the solicitor for the successful party prepares a bill which is then either agreed with the solicitor for the loser, or is referred to the Court for scrutiny under the taxation procedures. Settling of the costs in these circumstances is part and parcel of the solicitor's overall supply to the client. A basic tax point does not therefore occur until either the costs have been agreed between the solicitors or the taxation procedure is complete.
>
> **Non-contentious (non-Legal Aid)**: By law a client may ask the Law Society to scrutinise a solicitor's bill to ensure that it is fair and reasonable. Under this procedure the Law Society can reduce the amount payable by the client. None of this action forms part of the supply by the solicitor to the client and the basic tax point will have occurred when all the work, except the invoicing, was completed. Where this has resulted in tax being accounted for in advance of a reduction to the bill, the solicitor may subsequently adjust the amount accounted for subject to the normal rules regarding credits.'[20]

If a solicitor's fees are not known at or before the time when the services were supplied, the supply may be treated as taking place at the time of the issue of the VAT invoice, rather than upon completion of the work to which the fees relate. There is a long-stop of three months after the date of performance of the services. The supply of services does not include the time spent preparing the invoice to the client.[21]

Barristers

55.08 Barristers are often paid months, or even years, after they carried out the work and, to take account of this, they are permitted to defer liability for output tax until receipt of payment.[22] Thus the tax point will normally be the date on which fee notes are

---

[15] See Law Society, 'VAT Change: Reversion of the Standard Rate to 17.5 Per Cent', 15 December 2009, para 2.2.

[16] See VATTOS8560 (Tax points for specific categories of supplier: solicitors: legal aid work (contracting arrangements)).

[17] See Value Added Tax Act 1994, s 6(4)–(14). Section 6(4) provides that a person making the supply may elect whether, in certain circumstances, the supply shall—to the extent covered by the invoice or payment—be treated as taking place at the time the invoice is issued or the payment is received.

[18] See Value Added Tax Act 1994, s 6(3).

[19] VATTOS4310 (Basic tax points: performance of services: introduction).

[20] See VATTOS8540 (Tax points for specific categories of supplier: solicitors: adjustments to fees).

[21] See VATTOS8540; Law Society, 'VAT Change: Reversion of the Standard Rate to 17.5 Per Cent', 15 December 2009, para 2.1.

[22] The power derives from Value Added Tax Regulations 1995 (SI 1995/2518), reg 92.

receipted. In this regard, reg 92 of the Value Added Tax Regulations 1995[23] reads as follows:

> '92 Services supplied by a barrister ... acting in that capacity, shall be treated as taking place at whichever is the earliest of the following times—
> (a) when the fee in respect of those services is received by the barrister or advocate,
> (b) when the barrister or advocate issues a VAT invoice in respect of them, or
> (c) the day when the barrister or advocate ceases to practise as such.'

Other legal representatives

There are no special provisions that relate to legal representatives who are neither solicitors nor barristers and, as such, they would be treated according to general principles. The question of whether a basic tax point has arisen is a question of determining when the relevant services have been performed. This is often a matter of fact and law; in particular, it is a question that will turn on the contract for services (that is, the legal representative's contract of retainer), as well as the work done. Where (as will often be the case) the legal representative is to be paid one consideration for the services as a whole—that is, where there is a contract entire (see 27.07–27.28)—no basic tax point will arise until all of the work (other than the invoicing[24]) has been completed.[25] Periods of work may be severable, however, in that a job of work may contain shorter tasks, each of which may have its own point of conclusion and its own basic tax point.[26] This would probably apply if, for example, a costs lawyer were to draft a bill of costs, then draft replies to points of dispute and then appear for the receiving party at a hearing: each of those items of work could well attract its own basic tax point, depending on the facts and what was said in the contract of retainer. **55.09**

Rates of VAT

The issue of changes to the rate of VAT is addressed later in this chapter (see 55.33–55.44). **55.10**

Standard, reduced, zero and exempt rating

Not all services provided by legal representatives will attract a standard rate of VAT. Table 55.1 summarises the position. **55.11**

Place where persons 'belong'

Services provided to persons 'belonging'[27] to a place outside the European Union will be zero-rated[28] (other than where those services relate to UK land[29]), as will services provided **55.12**

---

[23] SI 1995/2518.

[24] By custom, invoicing is usually disregarded: see VATTOS4310 (Basic tax points: performance of services: introduction).

[25] See, by analogy, *Trustees for the Greater World Association Trust v Customs and Excise Commissioners* [1989] VATTR 91.

[26] See, eg, *Mercantile Contracts Ltd v Customs and Excise Commissioners* (1990) VAT Decisions 4357, 5266, [1990] STI 90, 918. This was a case in which a contract with a builder provided that he should be paid five years after having converted a number of flats; it also provided that he was obliged to maintain those flats over that five-year period. The VAT and Duties Tribunal found that the services should be regarded as being divisible such that a basic tax point would arise upon the completion of conversion works and then again upon the expiry of the five-year maintenance period.

[27] Value Added Tax (Place of Supply of Services) Order 1992 (SI 1992/3121), art 7(11).

[28] Value Added Tax Act 1994, s 4(1).

[29] For a discussion of the law, see *W H Payne & Co* (1995) VAT Decision 13668. For a description of the effect of the law, see Revenue Law Committee, *The Law Society's VAT Guide* (London: Law Society, 1996), Appx.

Table 55.1 Measures and exemptions

Rate	Example
Standard rate	Supply of legal services to persons in the UK (other than relating to land outside the UK) and to private (ie non-business) clients in the EU
	Disbursements that are not 'qualifying disbursements' or zero-rated or exempt, such as taxi fares, tolls (privately operated), hotel bills, etc
Reduced rate	There are no legal supplies within this category
Zero rate	Disbursements relating to public transport, such as rail fares
Exempt	Some disbursements, such as postal services and (prior to about 1 May 2007) medical experts' fees
Outside scheme	Services supplied outside the EU
	Services supplied by non-taxable person
	Tolls (publically operated) and the congestion charge
	Statutory fees, such as court fees

for business purposes to persons belonging outside the UK.[30] An individual receiving the services for non-business purposes belongs where they have their usual place of residence.[31] Otherwise, the person will belong

- where they have their only place of business or other fixed establishment;
- if they have no such place or establishment, where they have their usual place of residence;[32] or
- if they have business or fixed establishments in more than one country, where the establishment at which, or for the purposes of which, the services are to be used is located.

A person carrying on a business through a branch or agency in any country shall be treated as having a business establishment there.[33]

The resolution of disputes regarding rating

55.13 If there is a dispute as to whether a service is zero-rated or exempt, Practice Direction (PD) 44, para 5.6, provides that the receiving party is to obtain the view of HMRC and that that view should be made available to the court at the hearing at which the costs are assessed. Unlike the corresponding provision in the old Costs Practice Direction (CPD), PD 44, para 5.6, makes it clear that the receiving party must make the appropriate enquiries prior to the assessment hearing.

Self-supply of legal services and pro bono *awards*

55.14 VAT-registered litigants in person may receive the benefit of their legal work, but whether this will amount to supply of a taxable service will depend on the circumstances.

---

[30] Value Added Tax Act 1994, s 9. See also Revenue Law Committee, *The Law Society's VAT Guide* (London: Law Society, 1996), para 1.7.

[31] See Value Added Tax Act 1994, s 9.

[32] This will be the place where it is legally constituted if the person is a corporation: see Value Added Tax Act 1994, s 9(5)(b).

[33] Value Added Tax Act 1994, s 9(5)(a).

- **Corporate persons** No VAT is chargeable on the costs of employed in-house solicitors nor is VAT chargeable where a firm carries out work for itself (see 55.05). PD 44 specifically provides that government departments which use their own staff to provide legal services (such as the Treasury Solicitor) are not able to claim VAT relating to those legal services.[34] That said, VAT may be charged where one entity within a group of companies supplies services to another discrete entity.
- **Natural persons** Where a litigant acts in person, that litigant is not treated for the purposes of VAT as having supplied services and therefore no VAT is chargeable (even where, for example, that litigant is a solicitor or other legal representative).[35] PD 44, para 2.12, says that where the receiving party is a litigant in person, the 'bill of costs should not claim any VAT', but this is unlikely to be a correct statement of the law because even a litigant in person is entitled to claim VAT that has been charged by third-party suppliers.

Another circumstance in which legal work will not count as the supply of services for the purposes of VAT is where an order is made under s 194(3) of the Legal Services Act 2007—that is, a *pro bono* award of the type discussed at 18.121. PD 44 provides that any bill presented for agreement or assessment pursuant to that type of order must not include a claim for VAT,[36] but—once again—it is arguable that this is not a correct statement of the law because any litigant is entitled to claim VAT that has been charged by third-party suppliers.

Tax on disbursements: qualifying disbursements

Legal representatives often make payments to third parties for the supply of goods or services where no VAT was chargeable on the supply by the third party.[37] This may give rise to the question of whether legal representatives should include VAT in respect of these payments when invoicing their clients.[38] This turns on whether the payment was a 'disbursement' in the accountancy sense of that word, which is a narrower meaning than its legal sense. To avoid confusion, the term 'qualifying disbursement' will be used to mean a disbursement in the accountancy sense, in contrast to 'non-qualifying expenses' or 'petty disbursements'.[39] The relevance of the classification is that if an expense is classified as a qualifying disbursement, then no VAT will be payable as a result of the fact that it has been handled by the legal representative—although, of course, VAT may be payable if it was charged by the third-party supplier (see 55.21).[40] If the payment is a non-qualifying expense, then it is treated as being part of the supply of legal services **55.15**

[34] See PD 44, para 2.13.
[35] See PD 44, para 2.12.
[36] See PD 44, para 2.14.
[37] PD 44, para 2.11(1), gives the examples of meals taken and travel costs.
[38] See PD 44, para 2.11(1).
[39] See PD 44, para 2.11.
[40] The starting point in this regard is Art 73 of the Principal VAT Directive (Directive 2006/112/EC), which provides that 'the taxable amount shall include everything which constitutes consideration obtained or to be obtained by the supplier, in return for the supply, from the customer or a third party'. Article 79 provides: 'The taxable amount shall not include the following factors: ... (c) amounts received by a taxable person from the customer, as repayment of expenditure incurred in the name and on behalf of the customer, and entered into his books in a suspense account. The taxable person must furnish proof of the actual amount of the expenditure referred to in point (c) of the first paragraph and may not deduct any VAT which may have been charged.'

and VAT is added in the ordinary way.[41] One of the key issues is whether the third-party supply (a) was made to the legal representative (and therefore subsumed in the onward supply of legal services), or (b) was made directly to the receiving party (the third party having no right to demand payment from the legal representative, who makes the payment only as agent for the receiving party).[42] Thus, if the payment has been made to allow a legal representative to provide a service to its client, then (for VAT purposes) those monies are not regarded as being a qualifying disbursement and the legal representative must claim VAT.[43]

The test of what is and is not a qualifying disbursement

55.16 The Law Society has commented that 'this is not an easy area of VAT law', which is certainly true.[44] In general terms, the distinction is relatively easy to state.[45]

- **Non-qualifying expenses** These are expenses paid to a third party that have been incurred by the legal representatives in the course of making their own supply of services to their client and which were part of the whole of the services rendered by them to their client.
- **Qualifying disbursements** These are expenses for specific services that have been supplied by the third party to the legal representative's client, and they have merely acted as their client's known and authorised representatives in paying the third party.

55.17 Difficulties arise, however, when an attempt is made to formulate a definitive test. Whilst neither of them are sources of law, both PD 44 and HMRC's *Notice 700: The VAT Guide* refer to a test under which the legal representative may treat a payment to a third party as a qualifying disbursement if all of the following conditions are met:

- the legal representative was acting as the agent of the client (which condition will almost always be met);
- the client actually received and used the goods or services provided by the third party (which condition usually prevents the legal representative's own travelling and subsistence expenses, telephone bills, postage and other costs being treated as disbursements for VAT purposes);
- the client[46] was responsible for paying the third party (examples might include estate duty and stamp duty payable by the client on a contract to be made by the client);
- the client authorised the legal representative to make the payment on their behalf and the client knew that the goods or services would be provided by a third party;

[41] That is, the supply is treated as having been made by the solicitor under Value Added Tax Act 1994, s 47(3). See PD 44, para 2.11 for a discussion of the practical effect of the law discussed in this section.

[42] See PD 44, para 2.11(4). Where the legal representative makes a payment on behalf of the client, the client's account must be debited for precisely the same amount as was paid to the third party: Principal VAT Directive, Art 79(c).

[43] See PD 44, para 2.11.

[44] See Law Society, 'Practice Notes on VAT on Disbursements', 10 March 2011, para 3.2.2.

[45] This test is paraphrased from *Nell Gwynn House Maintenance Fund Trustees v C& E Commissioners* [1999] STC 79.

[46] Whilst not binding on any court, Master Pollard found that the fact that monies would be payable out of public funds, rather than directly by the client, does not mean that this condition is not met: *R v Findlay and MacGregor* [2002] 2 Costs LR 322.

- the legal representative's outlay is separately itemised when the client is invoiced;
- the legal representative recovers only the exact amount that it paid to the third party; and
- the goods or services are clearly additional to the supplies that the legal representative makes to its client on its own account.[47]

The Law Society, however, has pointed to a more purposive approach.[48] Whilst, at the time of writing, it was in the process of reviewing its advice,[49] it has previously said that an expense will be a qualifying disbursement only if the supply is made by the relevant third party to the client and not to the legal representative. It said that, to qualify as a disbursement, the expense must meet the following conditions: **55.18**

'a) Your client should have either requested that you obtain the service on their behalf or authorised you to do so.
b) In the case of a report or a search result, the final report should be sent to your client either by you or the supplier. You can retain a copy.[50]
c) The amount you charge your client should be exactly the same as the amount charged to you by the supplier.
d) The expense should be separately itemised on the invoice you send to your client.
e) The supplier should be aware that the service is being provided to a third party,[51] i.e. your client.'[52]

Examples of qualifying disbursements

Examples of what are and are not qualifying disbursements are given in Table 55.2. (The examples are necessarily very general and the classification may vary from case to case; moreover, there is doubt about some of the finer distinctions.) **55.19**

It can be seen that the classification of monies as qualifying disbursements or non-qualifying expenses is not wholly intuitive. For example, if a company search is made personally by a solicitor, it is the solicitor, rather than the client, who receives the supply and the fee cannot properly be regarded as a qualifying disbursement. If, however, exactly the same search is requested via post and the results are then passed on to the client for their own use, then the fee can properly be regarded as being a qualifying **55.20**

[47] See HMRC, *Notice 700: The VAT Guide* (London: HMSO, 2002), para 25.1.1; see also PD 44, para 2.11(4).

[48] In doing so, they refer to *De Danske Bilimportører v Skatteministeriet, Told- og Skattestyrelsen* [2006] ECR I-4945, in which the European Court of Justice agreed that an expense was incurred 'in the interests' of the person identified as the recipient of the supply: see Law Society, 'Practice Notes on VAT on Disbursements', 10 March 2011, para 3.2.

[49] The Law Society's interim guidance may be found online at http://www.lawsociety.org.uk/news/stories/vat-on-electronic-property-searches--interim-guidance-to-firms

[50] The Law Society goes on to add the following, *ibid*: 'To comply with (b) you should give the original report to your client. Where this is not possible, for example the original search report must be provided to a mortgage provider or an original medical report must be made available to the court in a personal injury action, you must give a copy of the report to your client.'

[51] The Law Society goes on to add the following, *ibid*: 'To comply with (e) you should tell the supplier the identity of your client. Where your client does not wish their identity to be revealed or the process involved (such as electronic form submission) does not enable your client's identity to be communicated to the supplier, you should provide the supplier with some identifying feature such as a client and/or file reference number.'

[52] See *ibid*, para 3.2.1.

Table 55.2 Qualifying disbursements and non-qualifying expenses

	Qualifying disbursements *VAT is not chargeable (unless VAT is charged by the third party)*	Non-qualifying expenses *VAT is chargeable*
Services purchased from other professionals, such as counsel, experts, agents and interpreters	Some experts' fees (see 55.21 and 55.22)	Some experts' fees (see 55.21 and 55.22)
	Counsel's fees (but only where the fee note is readdressed)[53]	Counsel's fees (where the fee note is not readdressed)
	Mediators' fees[54]	Agent's fees;[55] process servers' fees[56]
	Oath fees paid to a solicitor or commissioner for oaths[57]	
	Interpretation and translation fees where the purpose of the service is to allow the client to communicate with the legal representative or to understand court proceedings[58]	Interpretation and translation fees where the purpose is to allow the legal representative to understand what is being said[59]
Reports	Fees for medical reports[60]	Fees for police reports[61] and specialist video production services (such as CCTV imaging)[62]
Research	Local authority search fees relating to searches carried out by post and supplied directly to the client[63]	Local authority search fees relating to searches carried out electronically or personally[64]
	Company search fees (but not where the purpose of the search is to allow the legal representative to give advice)[65]	Mining search fees[66]
		Lexis (and similar) charges (again, these would usually be absorbed within the solicitors' overheads)

(continued)

[53] See 50.05.

[54] See Law Society, 'Practice Notes on VAT on Disbursements', 10 March 2011, para 4.20.

[55] *Ibid*, para 4.7.

[56] *Ibid*, para 4.8.

[57] See Revenue Law Committee, *The Law Society's VAT Guide* (London: Law Society, 1996), para 1.1.2.4.2; for fees for oaths administered, see para 3.2.3.1 of that guide.

[58] Law Society, 'Practice Notes on VAT on Disbursements', 10 March 2011, para 4.15.

[59] *Ibid*, para 4.16.

[60] See Revenue Law Committee, *The Law Society's VAT Guide* (London: Law Society, 1996), para 1.1.2.4.2.

[61] See Law Society, 'Practice Notes on VAT on Disbursements', 10 March 2011, para 4.18. It is worth noting that the Law Society used to advise that fees for police reports were qualifying disbursements: see Revenue Law Committee, *The Law Society's VAT Guide* (London: Law Society, 1996), para 1.1.2.4.2.

[62] See Law Society, 'Practice Notes on VAT on Disbursements', 10 March 2011, para 4.19.

[63] See *ibid*, para 4.1.2. See also *David John Curtis* (2007) VAT Decision 20330, in which the VAT and Duties Tribunal found that adding a surcharge of £10 to each fee suggested that it was not a qualifying disbursement.

[64] Law Society, 'Practice Notes on VAT on Disbursements', 10 March 2011, para 4.1.2(b), has this to say on the point: 'HMRC's view is that fees for local authority searches are subject to VAT when you charge them to your client. However, historically by concession, they are prepared to allow solicitors to treat postal search fees as disbursements so that VAT will not be payable on the amount of the fee which should thus be shown separately on your bill. At present HMRC contend that this concession does not apply to local authority searches that are requested and received electronically.' See also *Brabners LLP v Commissioners for HM Revenue & Customs* [2017] UKFTT 0666 (TC).

[65] See *ibid*, para 4.10.

[66] See *ibid*, para 4.1.2(d).

Table 55.2 Continued

	Qualifying disbursements *VAT is not chargeable (unless VAT is charged by the third party)*	Non-qualifying expenses *VAT is chargeable*
Court and statutory fees	Court fees and witness fees[67] Company registration fees[68]	
Financial services	Insurance premiums (IPT is, however, payable)	CHAPS/TT fees,[69] bank charges for supplying a bankers' draft, administration charges,[70] and debit and credit card fees[71]
	Courier charges (but only where the service is provided to or for the benefit of the client)	All other courier charges
Sundry office charges	Photocopying bureau charges (unless the copying is done to allow the solicitor to provide a service)[72]	Photocopies made in the office Telephone call charges and postage (these would usually be absorbed within the solicitors' overheads in any event)[73] Telephone conference fees
Travelling, etc	Travel tickets purchased for client[74]	Travelling expenses,[75] car parking fees,[76] hotel and accommodation expenses[77]

disbursement. Fortunately, the advice of practising accountants is that there is a certain amount of flexibility in this regard.[78]

For the avoidance of doubt, if the third party charges VAT, this can properly be passed on to the client and will, in principle, be payable by the paying party. Thus, if an accountant prepares an expert report, the VAT charged by the accountant will, in principle, **55.21**

[67] See PD 44, para 2.11(2); see also Law Society, 'Practice Notes on VAT on Disbursements', 10 March 2011, para 4.14.

[68] Law Society, 'Practice Notes on VAT on Disbursements', 10 March 2011, para 4.9.

[69] *Shuttleworth & Co v Commissioners of Customs and Excise* (LON/94/986A).

[70] See *National Transit Insurance Co Ltd v Customs and Excise Commissioners* [1975] STC 35.

[71] Law Society, 'Practice Notes on VAT on Disbursements', 10 March 2011, para 4.6.

[72] See *ibid*, para 4.2.

[73] See PD 44, para 2.11(2) and (6); see also Law Society, 'Practice Notes on VAT on Disbursements', 10 March 2011, para 4.5.

[74] See *Rowe & Maw v Customs and Excise Commissioners* [1975] STC 340, at 345, *per* Bridge J.

[75] See *ibid*; see also PD 44, para 2.11(5).

[76] Law Society, 'Practice Notes on VAT on Disbursements', 10 March 2011, para 4.3, gives the following advice: 'Where car parking charges are incurred, these should be treated in the same way as other travelling expenses as subject to VAT at the standard rate. Some charges are paid to VAT registered businesses, eg NCP car parks, whereas others are not, eg council car parks. Given that these sums are likely to be only a few pounds, it would be administratively burdensome for you to have to check the VAT position of the car park provider and ascertain the VAT element of the car parking charges for input tax purposes. To reduce administration you may therefore charge your client the full fee and then charge VAT at the standard rate.'

[77] PD 44, 2.11(5).

[78] It is said that where the invoice is not in the client's name, then HMRC does not object to the agent recovering the input tax, issuing a tax invoice to the client and accounting for the corresponding output tax, because this has the same overall effect as if the expense had been treated as a disbursement, but provides the client with a VAT invoice in their name to enable recovery of the VAT: see Lovewell Blake, 'VAT Treatment of Disbursements', Spring 2009.

be recoverable from the paying party irrespective of whether the accountant's fees are to be regarded as a qualifying disbursement.

Expert Reports and Records

Non-medical and non-dental experts

55.22 In deciding whether expenditure on experts' services can be treated as a qualifying disbursement, it is necessary to consider who received the supply of the services provided. Where an expert's report has been obtained by a legal representative as part of the evidence in support of its client's case, then it is likely (but by no means certain) that payment for the report can be treated as being a qualifying disbursement.[79] That said, this will often make no practical difference because most experts will charge VAT on their services anyway.

Medical and dental experts

55.23 The VAT status of medical and dental experts has changed over recent years. In general, the services of medical and dental experts are exempt from VAT if:

- the services consist of care, diagnosis, treatment or assessment of a patient;
- the services are within the discipline in which the expert is registered to practice; and
- performance of those services requires the application of knowledge, skills and judgment acquired in the course of the expert's professional training.[80]

Until about 1 May 2007, the provision of medical or dental reports was regarded as fulfilling these criteria; only work that was predominantly the supply of legal services (such as arbitration, mediation, negotiation, etc) would have attracted VAT. In 2003, the European Court of Justice (ECJ) ruled that the first of the above requirements related to medical care that had a therapeutic aim and thus was given for the purpose of protecting, maintaining or restoring human health. Accordingly, a medical service whose principal purpose was not therapy, but the provision advice for legal purposes, was not exempt.[81] Following consultation, HMRC amended the relevant schedule of the Value Added Tax Act 1994,[82] so as to fall in line with that decision. Therefore, since 1 May 2007, medical or dental reports prepared for legal purposes have been subject to VAT.[83] The same is true of fees for attending court (unless, of course, the doctor or dentist is attending court as an ordinary witness).[84] Where, exceptionally, the doctor or dentist has not charged VAT (perhaps because they are not registered for VAT), then, provided that the report was obtained for the client's use, it

---

[79] See Law Society, 'Practice Notes on VAT on Disbursements', 10 March 2011, para 4.12, referring to *Barratt, Goff and Tomlinson v Revenue and Customs Commissioners (Law Society intervening)* [2011] UKFTT 71 (TC). The reason that there is uncertainty about this is because it is difficult to reconcile the decision in *Barratt* with that in *Brabners LLP v Commissioners for HM Revenue & Customs* [2017] UKFTT 0666 (TC).

[80] See VAT Notice 701/57, para 2.2.

[81] *Peter d'Ambrumenil and Dispute Resolution Services Ltd v Commissioners of Customs & Excise* [2003] EWECJ C307/01, at [53], [55] and [58]–[61]. See also HMRC 'Reference Notice 701/57', 28 July 2014, para 2.5, which says that 'services not aimed at the prevention, diagnosis, treatment or cure of a disease or health disorder' are not exempt from VAT.

[82] That is, Group 7 (Health and Welfare) of Sch 9 (Exemptions) to the Value Added Tax Act 1994, item 1(a).

[83] Value Added Tax (Health and Welfare) Order 2007 (SI 2007/206).

[84] Law Society, 'Practice Notes on VAT on Disbursements', 10 March 2011, para 4.13.1.

will (arguably) be treated as a qualifying disbursement,[85] which means that no VAT will be payable on that report (see 55.15). This, in any event, is very much the exception, rather than the rule.

Medical and dental records

The situation with medical and dental records is similar—although it is now less clear since the coming into force of the General Data Protection Regulation (GDPR).[86] Two issues arise: first, whether the supply of such records is exempt for VAT purposes at the point of supply to the legal representative; and secondly, whether the legal representative is required to charge VAT as a result of the records being part and parcel of its supply of legal services. This second point turns on whether or not records are qualifying disbursements (see 55.15). **55.24**

- **Whether exempt** The supply of medical and dental records has generally been regarded as exempt from VAT. Where the request is made under the Data Protection Act 1998, the Access to Medical Reports Act 1988 or the Access to Health Records Act 1990, then that activity is beyond the scope of VAT.[87] Where a copy of a health record is provided in circumstances that do not fall within one of these statutory obligations, that is a taxable supply.[88] The relevant HMRC Reference Note has not been updated to take account of the fact that requests may now be made under the GDPR; given the wording of the present Note, it is arguable that this means that any such request will not be exempt. On any sensible analysis, however, this must be seen as merely an oversight on the part of HMRC.
- **Qualifying disbursements** Judge David Demack (sitting in the First-Tier Tribunal Tax Chamber) has found that it was merely administrative convenience that led to solicitors paying for the medical records and that, when those sums were recharged to the client, they were qualifying disbursements.[89] He found that the records were obtained for the interest of the client, not the lawyer—in particular, that the client needed the records to establish his claim. In arriving at his conclusion, Judge David Demack preferred a purposive interpretation of what is and is not a qualifying disbursement.[90] There is doubt, however, as to whether that analysis is correct.[91]

The effect of the above is that, in general, VAT tends not to be charged on medical or dental records obtained for the purpose of personal injury and clinical negligence claims. There must be a doubt as to whether that is correct, however.

---

[85] *Barratt, Goff and Tomlinson v Revenue and Customs Commissioners (Law Society intervening)* [2011] UKFTT 71 (TC), at [40] and [52]–[58].

[86] Regulation (EU) 2016/679 of the European Parliament and of the Council of 27 April 2016 on the protection of natural persons with regard to the processing of personal data and on the free movement of such data, and repealing Directive 95/46/EC, 4 May 2016, OJ L 119/1.

[87] HMRC, 'Reference Notice 701/57', January 2007, para 3.1.

[88] *Ibid.*

[89] *Barratt, Goff and Tomlinson v Revenue and Customs Commissioners (Law Society intervening)* [2011] UKFTT 71 (TC), at [40] and [52]–[58].

[90] In particular, he referred to *De Danske Bilimportører v Skatteministeriet, Told- og Skattestyrelsen* [2006] ECR I-4945: see *Barratt, Goff and Tomlinson v Revenue and Customs Commissioners (Law Society intervening)* [2011] UKFTT 71 (TC), at [51]–[56].

[91] This is because it is difficult to reconcile with *Brabners LLP v Commissioners for HM Revenue & Customs* [2017] UKFTT 0666 (TC).

Medical agencies

55.25 Whilst it may or may not be the case that VAT attaches directly to the costs of obtaining medical or dental records (see 55.24), it may be that VAT will, in any event, attach when the legal representative uses a medical agency to obtain medical or dental records or reports. There can be little doubt that VAT is payable on that part of the fee which relates to medical agency's work in obtaining the medical or dental reports[92] or records, but what is less clear is whether VAT is payable on the remainder of the fee—because it is arguable that VAT is not payable on that part of the fee which relates to the records themselves (assuming that no VAT is payable thereupon). The Law Society seems to take the view that, where a medical agency is used, the items supplied are not provided directly to the client and that, as such, the fee is not a qualifying disbursement; in so doing, the Law Society seems to make no distinction between that part of the fee which is attributable to the report or records and that which is not.[93] If the Law Society's analysis is correct, then VAT will be payable on the whole of the fee, regardless of whether the doctor or dentist charged VAT for supplying the records. This analysis has been challenged:[94] whilst not binding, Judge Platts has found that if a VAT-registered agency obtains a report from an expert who is not VAT-registered, it would not be reasonable for the agency to add VAT to the cost of the report.[95] There is, however, a lack of binding authority on the point.

VAT between Opposing Parties

General principles and input tax

55.26 Whilst not expressly included within the definition of 'costs' within the Civil Procedure Rules (CPR),[96] VAT is recoverable between opposing parties.[97] If VAT can be recovered by the receiving party as input tax, it ought not to be claimed from the paying party as costs,[98] because the receiving party would have suffered no net loss in respect of that VAT.[99] Where the receiving party is able to obtain credit from HMRC for a proportion of the VAT as input tax, only that proportion which is not eligible for credit should be included in the claim for costs.[100] PD 44 makes it clear that it is the receiving party who is responsible for ensuring that VAT is claimed only in so far as the receiving party is unable to recover VAT as input tax.[101] The irrecoverable VAT therefore ought to be excluded from the bill. Where

---

[92] In so far as reports are concerned, this is put beyond doubt by HMRC 'Reference Notice 701/57', 28 July 2014, para 4.9, which reads: 'Medical evidence services which are outsourced administrative services, such as arranging the provision of expert witnesses and obtaining medical reports, are also liable to VAT at the standard rate.'

[93] Law Society, 'Practice Notes on VAT on Disbursements', 10 March 2011, para 4.13.3.

[94] See, eg, *Evans v Wakefield Metropolitan District Council* (unreported), c 2012. Leeds County Court, *per* His Honour Judge Cockroft, as reported in *BLM Costs Review*, October 2012.

[95] See *Kellett (a Protected Party by her Litigation Friend, Alison McMahon) v Wigan & District Community Transport* (unreported), 16 September 2015, Manchester County Court, at [25]–[29]. See also *Evans v Wakefield Metropolitan District Council* (unreported), c 2012. Leeds County Court, *per* His Honour Judge Cockroft, as reported in *BLM Costs Review*, October 2012.

[96] See CPR, r 44n.1.

[97] This is implied by PD 44, paras 2.3–2.9.

[98] See PD 44, para 2.3.

[99] See Revenue Law Committee, *The Law Society's VAT Guide* (London: Law Society, 1996), para 1.9.1.2.2.

[100] See PD 44, para 2.3.

[101] See PD 44, para 2.3.

VAT is properly claimed, in general it cannot be recovered by the paying party as input tax (not least because no services would have been supplied to the paying party).[102] There are exceptions to this, but they will rarely arise in the context of disputes about costs.[103]

The resolution of disputes regarding input tax

Where there is a dispute as to whether (or to what extent) VAT can be recovered as input tax, PD 44, para 2.5, provides that the receiving party must provide a certificate as to recovery of VAT. This must be signed either by the receiving party's legal representatives or by the receiving party's auditors, who must certify the extent to which the receiving party is able to recover VAT as input tax. Although PD 44 lays down no hard-and-fast rules in this regard, it is clear from Precedent F of the model certificates attached to the Schedule of Costs Precedents annexed to PD 47 that the receiving party's legal representatives or auditors are expected to base their opinion on the receiving party's most recent VAT return. **55.27**

Subrogated claims, indemnities and insurers

It is the ability of the receiving party themselves to recover VAT as input tax that is relevant, not the ability of any insurer or funder that may be funding the litigation. In particular, the fact that an insurer has conducted a subrogated claim in the name of an insured or that it provided an indemnity is irrelevant for the purposes of assessing the paying party's liability for VAT.[104] If the insured is unable to claim input tax for any reason, the legal representative's invoice may be sent directly to the insurer, but this must not be treated as a VAT invoice that gives rise to a right on the part of the insurer to claim input tax. Put otherwise, input tax cannot be claimed by the back door.[105] Where, however, the insured is able to claim input tax, then a VAT invoice may be sent directly to the insured, with the insurer paying the non-VAT element.[106] Where the insurer is itself the litigant, then it is commonly the case that it is able to claim only a tiny fraction of the VAT as input tax, which may mean that VAT between opposing parties will be reclaimed at a rate that is different from the prevailing standard rate. **55.28**

Reasonableness

It will rarely be the case that a receiving party has the option of avoiding VAT, so the issue of reasonableness will arise only infrequently. That said, an opportunity to make an election may arise if there is a change of rate (see 55.33–55.44): if VAT is charged **55.29**

[102] See *Saheid v Revenue & Customs Commissioners* [2013] UKFTT 38 (TC), at [39]; see also *N O Turner (t/a Turner Agricultural) v Commissioners of Customs & Excise* [1992] STC 621.

[103] VATSC92100 (Direction of supplies: Payment of another party's legal costs: Agreement with the Law Society's Revenue Law Committee on VAT in respect of third-party cost payments) makes it clear that no input tax will be claimable where, (a) following completion of litigation (or arbitration), one party is ordered to pay the other party's costs or (b) a party to a transaction undertakes to pay the other party's costs and the matter does not proceed to completion, so the costs are 'abortive'. Where, however, a transaction obliges one party to be responsible for the costs of the other relating to that transaction, then the payment of costs will be part of the consideration for the supply (provided that the transaction proceeds to completion). In those circumstances, then the VAT would be capable of being reclaimed as input tax. These facts are unlikely to arise in practice, but it is possible that they may arise if, in compromise of a claim, one party agreed to fund a transaction for the other party.

[104] See Revenue Law Committee, *The Law Society's VAT Guide* (London: Law Society, 1996), para 1.9.4.

[105] See *ibid*, para 1.9.4.5.

[106] See *ibid*, para 1.9.4.8.

at a higher rate than is reasonably required, the court will order the paying party to pay that rate only if the receiving party is able to justify the decision not to elect to charge at the lower rate.[107]

55.30 In practice, where a decision has been taken to charge at a higher rate, this is often for sound accountancy reasons pertaining to the receiving party's legal representatives and, in those circumstances, the court may be satisfied that the election to charge that rate was reasonable, because the alternative would have been to incur the costs of instructing new legal representatives. Examples do exist, however, of VAT being disallowed as a result of it being incurred voluntarily.[108]

Proportionality

55.31 Generally speaking, VAT ought to be disregarded for the purpose of considering whether the costs are proportionate (see 25.82).

Part 36 offers relating to costs and Part 47 offers

55.32 Both offers under 'new' CPR, Part 36, relating to costs and offers under 'old' CPR, Part 47 (that is, made under the pre-April 2013 CPR), will be deemed to be inclusive of VAT unless the contrary is stated.[109] If recoverability of VAT is in dispute, it would be sensible for parties to make it clear beyond doubt whether their offers include or exclude VAT.

Changes to the Rate of VAT

55.33 The rates of VAT that have applied over recent years are set out in Table 55.3.

55.34 This invites the obvious question of how such changes in rate are to be dealt with between opposing parties. This is largely a matter of examining the options that are or were available to the receiving party's legal representative and then deciding which was the most reasonable course of action. If VAT is charged at a higher rate than is reasonably

Table 55.3 Rates of VAT

Period	Rate (%)
Prior to 1 December 2008	17.5%
Between 1 December 2008 and 31 December 2009[110]	15%
Between 1 December 2010 and 4 January 2011	17.5%
After 3 January 2011	20%

[107] PD 44, para 2.8.

[108] See, eg, *Sutton v Selwyns Travel* (unreported), 8 August 2008, Birkenhead County Court, *per* Regional Costs Judge Smedley.

[109] See PD 47, para 19, and CPD, art 46.2, respectively.

[110] Value Added Tax (Change of Rate) Order 2008 (SI 2008/3020). This Order reduced the rate of VAT by $^{142}/_{7}$ per cent to effect a reduction from 17.5 per cent to 15 per cent and makes a consequential change to the Value Added Tax Act 1994. This Order had effect from 1 December 2008 to 30 November 2009.

required, the court will order the paying party to pay that rate only if the receiving party is able to justify the decision not to elect to charge at the lower rate.[111]

Changes of rate before the assessment

Whilst an oversimplification, legal representatives are permitted to elect to use either the rate of VAT in force at the time of the basic tax point—that is, at the time the services were completed (see 55.06)—or the prevailing rate at the time of the actual tax point—that is, the date of issue of the bill (see 55.06–55.07). PD 44, paras 2.7 and 2.8, like the CPD that preceded it, summarise the position in this way: **55.35**

> '**Form of bill of costs where VAT rate changes**
>
> 2.7 Where there is a change in the rate of VAT, suppliers of goods and services are entitled by ss. 88 (1) and 88(2) of the VAT Act 1994 in most circumstances to elect whether the new or the old rate of VAT should apply to a supply where the basic and actual tax points span a period during which there has been a change in VAT rates.
>
> 2.8 It will be assumed, unless a contrary indication is given in writing, that an election to take advantage of the provisions mentioned in paragraph 2.7 above and to charge VAT at the lower rate has been made. In any case in which an election to charge at the lower rate is not made, such a decision must be justified to the court assessing the costs.'

Legislative provisions

In so far as it is relevant, s 88 of the Value Added Tax Act 1994 provides as follows: **55.36**

> '**88 Supplies spanning change of rate etc.**
>
> (1) This section applies where there is a change in the rate of VAT in force under section 2 or 29A or in the descriptions of exempt, zero-rated or reduced-rate supplies or exempt, zero-rated or reduced-rate acquisitions.
>
> (2) Where—
>
> (a) a supply affected by the change would, apart from section 6(4), (5), (6) or (10), be treated under section 6(2) or (3) as made wholly or partly at a time when it would not have been affected by the change; or
>
> (b) a supply not so affected would apart from section 6(4), (5), (6) or (10) be treated under section 6(2) or (3) as made wholly or partly at a time when it would have been so affected,
>
> the rate at which VAT is chargeable on the supply, or any question whether it is zero-rated or exempt or a reduced-rate supply], shall if the person making it so elects be determined without regard to section 6(4), (5), (6) or (10).
>
> (3) Any power to make regulations under this Act with respect to the time when a supply is to be treated as taking place shall include power to provide for this section to apply as if the references in subsection (2) above to section 6(4), (5), (6) or (10) included references to specified provisions of the regulations. ...
>
> [...]
>
> (6) No election may be made under this section in respect of a supply to which section 6(9) or paragraph 7 of Schedule 4 applies. ...
>
> [...]
>
> (8) References in this section—
>
> (a) to a supply being a reduced-rate supply, or
>
> (b) to an acquisition being a reduced-rate acquisition,
>
> are references to a supply, or (as the case may be) an acquisition, being one on which VAT is charged at the rate in force under section 29A.'

[111] PD 44, para 2.8.

55.37 The reference to s 6(4), (5), (6) or (10) of the Value Added Tax Act 1994 is a reference to the following:

> '**6 Time of supply**
>
> [...]
>
> (4) If, before the time applicable under subsection (2) or (3) above, the person making the supply issues a VAT invoice in respect of it or if, before the time applicable under subsection (2) (a) or (b) or (3) above, he receives a payment in respect of it, the supply shall, to the extent covered by the invoice or payment, be treated as taking place at the time the invoice is issued or the payment is received.
>
> (5) If, within 14 days after the time applicable under subsection (2) or (3) above, the person making the supply issues a VAT invoice in respect of it, then, unless he has notified the Commissioners in writing that he elects not to avail himself of this subsection, the supply shall (to the extent that it is not treated as taking place at the time mentioned in subsection (4) above) be treated as taking place at the time the invoice is issued.
>
> (6) The Commissioners may, at the request of a taxable person, direct that subsection (5) above shall apply in relation to supplies made by him (or such supplies made by him as may be specified in the direction) as if for the period of 14 days there were substituted such longer period as may be specified in the direction. ...
>
> [...]
>
> (10) The Commissioners may, at the request of a taxable person, by direction alter the time at which supplies made by him (or such supplies made by him as may be specified in the direction) are to be treated as taking place, either—
>
> (a) by directing those supplies to be treated as taking place—
> (i) at times or on dates determined by or by reference to the occurrence of some event described in the direction; or
> (ii) at times or on dates determined by or by reference to the time when some event so described would in the ordinary course of events occur,
>
> the resulting times or dates being in every case earlier than would otherwise apply; or
>
> (b) by directing that, notwithstanding subsections (5) and (6) above, those supplies shall (to the extent that they are not treated as taking place at the time mentioned in subsection (4) above) be treated as taking place—
> (i) at the beginning of the relevant working period (as defined in his case in and for the purposes of the direction); or
> (ii) at the end of the relevant working period (as so defined).'

55.38 Thus there is a right of election such that the legal representative can choose whether to apply the rate that was in force at the time the work was completed (but see below about work done over a period of time) or that which was in force at the time invoice was raised, subject to a long-stop of three months from the date of completion of the work.

55.39 This invites the obvious question of what is to happen in cases in which the prevailing rate at the time the work was done was different from that which applied at the conclusion of the claim. In this regard, the Law Society has given the following guidance:

> '**3. Special change of rate rules**
>
> Under the normal rules, standard rated supplies with tax points created by payments received or VAT invoices issued on or after 04 January 2011 will be liable to the 20 per cent rate. However, there are optional change of rate rules that you may wish to apply:
>
> - Where you issue a VAT invoice or receive a payment on or after 04 January 2011 for work that was completed before 04 January 2011 you may account for VAT at 17.5 per cent.

- Where work commenced after 01 January 2010 and before 04 January 2011 but will not be completed until on or after 04 January you can apportion the supply between that liable to 17.5 per cent and that liable to 20 per cent.

You can apply the rules selectively to different clients and you can adopt them without notifying HMRC. If your client is VAT registered and able to recover the VAT charged in full, the use of the special rules will not save them any tax.'[112]

Thus, should the legal representative so choose, the applicable rate is that which pertained at the time the work was done. PD 44 goes on to give further guidance (see 55.45). In essence, the costs for which VAT is claimed must be set out in separate parts of the bill of costs, so as to show work done before, on and after the date(s) from which any change in the rate of VAT takes effect. Lump sums may be apportioned.[113] Should there be a change in the rate between the conclusion of a detailed assessment and the issue of the final costs certificate, then the court is able to vary the assessment accordingly. Once the final costs certificate has been issued, however, no such variation can be made.[114] **55.40**

Disbursements

The relevant date in respect of disbursement will be the date on which the invoice is issued, regardless of when the disbursement was incurred.[115] **55.41**

Counsel

As to counsel's fees, the Law Society has given the following advice: **55.42**

'Normally, the tax point for Counsel's services will be determined by payment and not delivery of a fee note. On payment, Counsel's clerk will add the VAT number of Counsel and other particulars required under Regulation 13 of the VAT Regulations 1995 to constitute a document as a VAT invoice so that the receipted fee note is a VAT invoice.

Fees received on or after 01 January 2010 will be liable to VAT at 17.5 per cent. However, if you pay fees after 01 January for cases completed before that, these can still be subject to VAT at 15 per cent. Similarly, if you pay a fee after 01 January 2010 which covers services partly performed while the 15 per cent VAT rate applied, these the fees may be apportioned so that the rate of 15 per cent applies to those fees accrued before 01 January 2010. You should clarify the VAT treatment of the fees with Counsel's clerk before payment.'[116]

The Bar Council's advice is similar: **55.43**

'17. In general, barristers can choose to charge and account for VAT at either the rate in force when the work was done or the rate in force when the fee is received. Assuming barristers will wish to charge the lowest rate (and ignoring prepayments and flat-rate scheme), this means:

(a) Work before 1st December 2008 can be charged with VAT at 17.5%;
(b) Work between 1st December 2008 and 1st January 2010 can be charged with VAT at 15%.
(c) Work done on or after 1st January 2010 and 3rd January 2011 can be charged with VAT at 17.5%.

---

[112] See Law Society, 'VAT change: Increase in the Standard Rate to 20 Per Cent', 24 November 2010.
[113] PD 44, para 2.9.
[114] PD 44, para 2.10.
[115] See Law Society, 'VAT Change: Reversion of the Standard Rate to 17.5 *Per* Cent', 15 December 2009, para 3.5.
[116] See *ibid*, para 3.6.

(d) Work done on or after 4th January 2011 must be charged at 20%.
(e) Where work on a single matter spans a change in rate, the fee can be apportioned.'[117]

Changes of rate after the assessment

55.44 Should there be a change in the rate between the conclusion of a detailed assessment and the issue of the final costs certificate, any interested party may apply for the detailed assessment to be varied so as to take account of any increase or reduction in the amount of tax payable. Once the final costs certificate has been issued, no such variation will be permitted.[118]

The Wording of Relevant Provisions

55.45 The wording of the relevant part of PD 44 is as follows:

> '2.1 This section deals with claims for value added tax (VAT) which are made in respect of costs being dealt with by way of summary assessment or detailed assessment.
>
> **VAT Registration Number**
>
> 2.2 The number allocated by HMRC to every person registered under the Value Added Tax Act 1983 (except a Government Department) must appear in a prominent place at the head of every statement, bill of costs, fee sheet, account or voucher on which VAT is being included as part of a claim for costs.
>
> **Entitlement to VAT on Costs**
>
> 2.3 VAT should not be included in a claim for costs if the receiving party is able to recover the VAT as input tax. Where the receiving party is able to obtain credit from HMRC for a proportion of the VAT as input tax, only that proportion which is not eligible for credit should be included in the claim for costs.
>
> 2.4 The receiving party has responsibility for ensuring that VAT is claimed only when the receiving party is unable to recover the VAT or a proportion thereof as input tax.
>
> 2.5 Where there is a dispute as to whether VAT is properly claimed the receiving party must provide a certificate signed by the legal representatives or the auditors of the receiving party substantially in the form illustrated in Precedent F in the Schedule of Costs Precedents annexed to Practice Direction 47. Where the receiving party is a litigant in person who is claiming VAT, evidence to support the claim (such as a letter from HMRC) must be produced at the hearing at which the costs are assessed.
>
> 2.6 Where there is a dispute as to whether any service in respect of which a charge is proposed to be made in the bill is zero rated or exempt from VAT, reference should be made to HMRC and its view obtained and made known at the hearing at which the costs are assessed. Such enquiry should be made by the receiving party. In the case of a bill from a solicitor to his own client, such enquiry should be made by the client.
>
> **Form of bill of costs where VAT rate changes**
>
> 2.7 Where there is a change in the rate of VAT, suppliers of goods and services are entitled by ss 88(1) and 88(2) of the VAT Act 1994 in most circumstances to elect whether the new or the old rate of VAT should apply to a supply where the basic and actual tax points span a period during which the rate changed.

[117] Bar Council, 'Bar Council Guide: Standard Rate VAT Increase', 4 January 2011.
[118] PD 44, para 2.10.

2.8 It will be assumed, unless a contrary indication is given in writing, that an election to take advantage of the provisions mentioned in paragraph 2.7 above and to charge VAT at the lower rate has been made. In any case in which an election to charge at the lower rate is not made, such a decision must be justified to the court assessing the costs.

Apportionment

2.9 Subject to 2.7 and 2.8, all bills of costs, fees and disbursements on which VAT is included must be divided into separate parts so as to show work done before, on and after the date or dates from which any change in the rate of VAT takes effect. Where, however, a lump sum charge is made for work which spans a period during which there has been a change in VAT rates, and paragraphs 2.7 and 2.8 above do not apply, reference should be made to paragraphs 30.7 and 30.8 of the VAT Guide (Notice 700)(or any revised edition of that notice) published by HMRC. If necessary, the lump sum should be apportioned. The totals of profit costs and disbursements in each part must be carried separately to the summary.

Change in VAT rate between the conclusion of a detailed settlement and the issue of a final certificate

2.10 Should there be a change in the rate between the conclusion of a detailed assessment and the issue of the final costs certificate, any interested party may apply for the detailed assessment to be varied so as to take account of any increase or reduction in the amount of tax payable. Once the final costs certificate has been issued, no variation under this paragraph will be permitted.

Disbursements not classified as such for VAT purposes

2.11 (1) Legal representatives often make payments to third parties for the supply of goods or services where no VAT was chargeable on the supply by the third party: for example, the cost of meals taken and travel costs. The question whether legal representatives should include VAT in respect of these payments when invoicing their clients or in claims for costs between litigants should be decided in accordance with this Practice Direction and with the criteria set out in the VAT Guide (Notice 700).

(2) Payments to third parties which are normally treated as part of the legal representative's overheads (for example, postage costs and telephone costs) will not be treated as disbursements. The third party supply should be included as part of the costs of the legal representatives' legal services and VAT must be added to the total bill charged to the client.

(3) Disputes may arise in respect of payments made to a third party which the legal representative shows as disbursements in the invoice delivered to the receiving party. Some payments, although correctly described as disbursements for some purposes, are not classified as disbursements for VAT purposes. Items not classified as disbursements for VAT purposes must be shown as part of the services provided by the legal representative and, therefore, VAT must be added in respect of them whether or not VAT was chargeable on the supply by the third party.

(4) Guidance as to the circumstances in which disbursements may or may not be classified as disbursements for VAT purposes is given in the VAT Guide (Notice 700, paragraph 25.1). One of the key issues is whether the third party supply—

(a) was made to the legal representative (and therefore subsumed in the onward supply of legal services); or

(b) was made direct to the receiving party (the third party having no right to demand payment from the legal representative, who makes the payment only as agent for the receiving party).

(5) Examples of payments under subparagraph (4)(a) are: travelling expenses, such as an airline ticket, and subsistence expenses, such as the cost of meals, where the person travelling and receiving the meals is the legal representative. The supplies by the airline and the restaurant are supplies to the legal representative, not to the client

(6) Payments under subparagraph (4)(b) are classified as disbursements for VAT purposes and, therefore, the legal representative need not add VAT in respect of them. Simple examples are payments by a legal representative of court fees and payment of fees to an expert witness.

2.12 Reference is made to the criteria set out in the VAT Guide (Customs and Excise Notice 700 – 1 August 1991 edition paragraph 83, or any revised edition of that Notice), as to expenses which are not subject to VAT. Charges for the cost of travel by public transport, postage, telephone calls and telegraphic transfers where these form part of the service rendered by the solicitor to his client are examples of charges which do not satisfy these criteria and are thus liable to VAT at the standard rate.

Litigants acting in person

2.12 Where a litigant acts in person, that litigant is not treated for the purposes of VAT as having supplied services and therefore no VAT is chargeable in respect of work done by that litigant (even where, for example, that litigant is a solicitor or other legal representative). Consequently in such circumstances a bill of costs should not claim any VAT.

Government Departments

2.13 On an assessment between parties, where costs are being paid to a Government Department in respect of services rendered by its legal staff, VAT should not be added.

Payment Pursuant to an order under section 194(3) of the Legal Services Act 2007

2.14 Where an order is made under section 194(3) of the Legal Services Act 2007 any bill presented for agreement or assessment pursuant to that order must not include a claim for VAT.'

56

INTEREST BETWEEN OPPOSING PARTIES

This chapter deals with the following topics: **56.01**

- terminology (56.02);
- overview (56.04);
- prescribed rate interest (PRI) (56.08):
  - jurisdiction and principles (56.10);
  - the date upon which interest begins to run (56.22);
  - the rate of interest (56.41);
  - discounts and adjustments (56.49);
- compensatory rate interest (CRI):
  - jurisdiction and principles (56.55);
  - the date upon which interest begins to run (56.66);
  - the rate of interest and discretion generally (56.69);
- enhanced rate interest (ERI) pursuant to CPR, Part 36:
  - jurisdiction and principles (56.83);
  - the date upon which interest begins to run (56.88);
  - the rate of interest (56.90);
- special situations:
  - deemed costs orders (56.101);
  - appeals and interest on costs (56.103);
  - interest on costs that have been overpaid (56.105);
  - advance and multiple orders for costs (56.108);
  - interest payable out of a fund (56.112);
  - interest on the costs of assessment (56.114);
  - pursuant to contract or as damages (56.116);
  - pursuant to the equitable jurisdiction of the court (56.123);
  - in arbitrations (56.125); and
  - compound interest (56.126).

Terminology

There is no satisfactory system of taxonomy for interest on costs. The following terminology—which is no more than the editor's own invention and is far from perfect—is used in this chapter. **56.02**

- **Prescribed rate interest (PRI)** This is interest that is allowed at the rate that has been prescribed by the Judgment Debts (Rate of Interest) Order 1993.[1] At the time of writing, that rate was 8 per cent per annum.

[1] SI 1993/564.

- **Compensatory rate interest (CRI)** This is interest set by the court pursuant to its discretion to allow compensatory interest in the period (or any part thereof) prior to the PRI date.
- **Enhanced rate interest (ERI)** This is interest that is allowed pursuant to r 36.14(3)(c) of the Civil Procedure Rules (CPR)—that is, when a claimant has 'beaten' their own Part 36 offer. It is a discretionary rate of up to 10 per cent per annum above base rate.

56.03 In addition, the following terminology applies to dates.

- **Accrual date** This is the date (or dates) on which the receiving party became liable to pay incurred costs as between legal services provider and client. This may or may not be the same as the CRI date (see below).
- **Payment date** This is the date (or dates) on which the receiving party paid costs as between legal services provider and client. This may or may not be the same as the CRI date.
- **Judgment date** This is the date on which the order that has given rise to the costs in question was made. It may or may not be the same as the PRI date.
- **CRI date** This is the date (or, less commonly, dates) on which compensatory rate interest starts to run (assuming it to be payable). It may be the same as the accrual date(s) or the payment date(s), or it may be some other date entirely.
- **PRI date** This is the date on which PRI starts to run. By default, it is the same as the judgment date, but may be some other date.

Figure 56.1 illustrates the relationship between these dates.

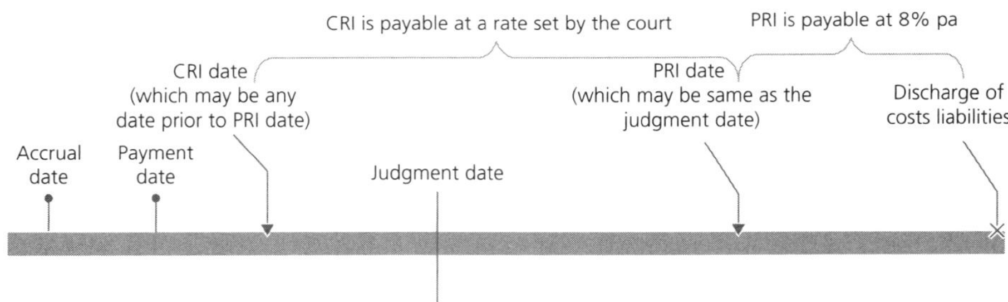

Figure 56.1 Relationship between dates

Overview

56.04 The provisions that relate to interest are complex. Lord Goff had this to say on the point:

> 'One would expect to find, in any developed system of law, a comprehensive and reasonably simple set of principles by virtue of which the courts have power to award interest ... Sadly, however, that is not the position in English law.'[2]

[2] *Westdeutsche Landesbank Girozentrale v Islington London Borough Council* [1996] AC 669, at 684.

Interest is not recoverable between opposing parties under the common law.[3] This means that—subject to certain rare exceptions (see 56.106 and 56.124)—the court has no power to award interest on costs beyond that which is granted by statute or secondary legislation.[4] The following statutory powers are relevant: **56.05**

- Judgments Act 1838, s 17 (as amended); and
- County Court Act 1984, s 74 (as amended).

In addition, the following secondary legislation may have a bearing on the way in which the court allows interest: **56.06**

- CPR, r 40.8(2), gives the court the general power to set the PRI date and/or the CRI date;
- CPR, r 44.2(6)(g), provides a very similar power, but it relates specifically to orders for costs;
- CPR, r 36.14(3)(c), is the provision that gives rise to the power to award ERI;
- CPR, rr 47.8(3), 47.20(6), 47.14(4) and 36.49(4), relate to detailed assessments only;
- CPR, r 44.9(4), relates to deemed costs orders; and
- CPR, r 52.10(2)(d), relates to appeals.

The first three provisions are by far the most important. In very general terms, they work in the following way. **56.07**

- The default position is that PRI will be payable from the judgment date; there is no default position as regards CRI.
- The court has the power to set the PRI date. In theory, the court may choose any date (before or after the judgment date); in practice, it usually chooses the judgment date or a later date.
- The court also has the power to award CRI and to set a CRI date (or dates).
- The rate of PRI is fixed, whereas the rate of CRI is discretionary (to be ascertained on compensatory principles).
- If the receiving party is a claimant who has 'beaten' their own offer under CPR, Part 36, then ERI may be payable instead.

Prescribed Rate Interest

When judges and practitioners talk of 'interest on costs', they are usually referring to PRI. This is by far the most common form of interest on costs encountered in practice. **56.08**

Prescribed rate interest is, in practice, payable only on undischarged judgment debt. It therefore tends to relate only to post-judgment interest (that is, to interest that has accrued after the applicable order for costs has been made). This is not always the case, however. In particular, powers originally created for the purposes of allowing the court **56.09**

---

[3] *Nykredit Mortgage Bank plc v Edward Erdman Group Ltd (No 2)* [1997] 1 WLR 1627, at 1635. Compare this with the position in relation to interest on damages in relation to which a restricted power has existed at certain times, eg, *Page v Newman* (1829) 9 B&C 378; cf *London, Chatham and Dover Railway Co v South Eastern Railway Co* [1893] AC 429. Compare also with the equitable jurisdiction to award interest in certain courts: see *The Northumbria* (1869) LR 3 A&E 6; *Black v Davies* [2005] EWCA Civ 531.

[4] *Nykredit Mortgage Bank plc v Edward Erdman Group Ltd (No 2)* [1997] 1 WLR 1627, at 1635. See also *London, Chatham and Dover Railway Co v South Eastern Railway Co* [1893] AC 429.

to make an award of interest following the judgment date are now understood to have a wider role (see 56.29–56.30).

Jurisdiction and principles

56.10 An order for payment of costs ranks as a judgment[5] and it is for this reason that PRI applies to orders for costs.[6] The starting point is that PRI is payable from the date on which a party became entitled to costs[7]—what is often referred to as the *incipitur* date.

56.11 The applicable provisions differ from court to court, and there is, in particular, a need to draw a distinction between the High Court and the County Court.

Prescribed rate interest in the High Court

56.12 Prescribed rate interest in the High Court is governed by s 17 of the Judgments Act 1838 (as amended):

> '17 **Judgment debts to carry interest**
>
> (1) ... Every judgment debt shall carry interest at the rate of [8 per cent per annum] from such time as shall be prescribed by rules of court ... until the same shall be satisfied, and such interest may be levied under a writ of execution on such judgment.
>
> (2) Rules of court may provide for the court to disallow all or part of any interest otherwise payable under subsection (1).'

56.13 The starting point is that PRI in the High Court begins to run from the date on which a party becomes entitled to costs (56.23–56.26), this principle being the *incipitur* rule.

Prescribed rate interest in the County Court

56.14 The equivalent legislation in the County Court is s 74 of the County Court Act 1984 (as amended):

> '74 **Interest on judgment debts etc**
>
> (1) The Lord Chancellor may by order made with the concurrence of the Treasury provide that any sums to which this subsection applies shall carry interest at such rate and between such times as may be prescribed by the order.
>
> (2) The sums to which subsection (1) applies are—
> (a) sums payable under judgments or orders given or made in the County Court, including sums payable by instalments; and
> (b) sums which by virtue of any enactment are, if the County Court so orders, recoverable as if payable under an order of that court, and in respect of which the County Court has so ordered.
>
> (3) The payment of interest due under subsection (1) shall be enforceable as a sum payable under the judgment or order.
>
> (4) The power conferred by subsection (1) includes power—
> (a) to specify the descriptions of judgment or order in respect of which interest shall be payable;
> (b) to provide that interest shall be payable only on sums exceeding a specified amount;

[5] *Nykredit Mortgage Bank plc v Edward Erdman Group Ltd (No 2)* [1997] 1 WLR 1627, at 1635.

[6] Likewise, it is for this reason that an agreement to pay costs that is contained within the schedule of a Tomlin order will not bear interest: see, by analogy, *Horizon Technologies International v Lucky Wealth Consultants Ltd* [1992] 1 WLR 24.

[7] *Simcoe v Jacuzzi UK Group Plc* [2012] EWCA Civ 137, at [35]–[48], *per* Lord Neuberger MR.

(c) to make provision for the manner in which and the periods by reference to which the interest is to be calculated and paid;
(d) to provide that any enactment shall or shall not apply in relation to interest payable under subsection (1) or shall apply to it with such modifications as may be specified in the order; and
(e) to make such incidental or supplementary provisions as the Lord Chancellor considers appropriate.

(5) Without prejudice to the generality of subsection (4), an order under subsection (1) may provide that the rate of interest shall be the rate specified in section 17 of the Judgments Act 1838 as that enactment has effect from time to time.

(5A) The power conferred by subsection (1) includes power to make provision enabling the County Court to order that the rate of interest applicable to a sum expressed in a currency other than sterling shall be such rate as the court thinks fit (instead of the rate otherwise applicable).

[...]

(6) The power to make an order under subsection (1) shall be exercisable by statutory instrument subject to annulment in pursuance of a resolution of either House of Parliament.'

The Order to which s 74(1) refers (that is, the order that sets the rate of interest) is the County Court (Interest on Judgment Debts) Order 1991 (as amended).[8] The combined effect of that Order and the County Courts Act 1984 is that the rate of interest will be the same as that specified in s 17 of the Judgments Act 1838.[9] There are, however, three ways in which interest on costs in the County Court and its hearing centres may differ from that in the High Court: **56.15**

- certain parts of the CPR could well be *ultra vires* in the County Court (see 56.16–56.17);
- in the County Court, interest is not payable on amounts less than £5,000 (see 56.18–56.19); and
- in the County Court, the accrual of interest is suspended during enforcement proceedings (see 56.20–56.21).

CPR provisions conferring the power to alter the date on which interest begins to run are ultra vires Article 2(2) of the County Court (Interest on Judgment Debts) Order 1991 (as amended)[10] provides that interest runs from the judgment date—that is, the *incipitur* date (see 56.10). In 2012, Lord Neuberger MR explained that, to the extent that it provides otherwise, CPR, r 40.8, is *ultra vires*.[11] This means that the County Court lacks the power to award interest on costs that begins on any other date. Surprisingly, at the time of writing, no delegated legislation had been made to rectify matters. As such, CPR, r 40.8, seems still to be *ultra vires*.[12] **56.16**

---

[8] SI 1991/1184, as amended by the County Courts (Interest on Judgment Debts) (Amendment) Order 1996 (SI 1996/2516).

[9] See County Court (Interest on Judgment Debts) Order 1991 (SI 1991/1184), art 5.

[10] SI 1991/1184, as amended by the County Courts (Interest on Judgment Debts) (Amendment) Order 1996 (SI 1996/2516).

[11] *Simcoe v Jacuzzi UK Group Plc* [2012] EWCA Civ 137, at [23]–[31]. The reason for this is that the only delegated legislation that is capable of modifying the County Court (Interest on Judgment Debts) Order 1991 (SI 1991/1184) is that which is made with the concurrence of the Treasury (see County Court Act 1984, s 74(1)) and the CPR were not made in that way.

[12] The author has raised this point with HM Treasury. At the time of writing, HM Treasury was actively in the process of considering the issue.

56.17 Whilst there is no authority on the point, there is no particular reason to believe that the position is any different in so far as the other provisions in the CPR that relate to interest are concerned. In particular, it is easily arguable that the provisions referred to at 56.06 are *ultra vires* in the County Court. If that argument is correct, then very little of what follows in this chapter applies in the County Court.

56.18 **No interest on small debts in the County Court** Interest in the County Court is generally not payable on sums of money of less than £5,000. Article 2(1) of the County Court (Interest on Judgment Debts) Order 1991 (as amended)[13] provides that interest will be payable only in respect of a 'relevant judgment', whilst art 1(2) of that Order defines a relevant judgment in the following way:

> ' "[R]elevant judgment" means a judgment or order of a County Court for the payment of a sum of money (a) of not less than £5,000 or (b) in respect of a debt which is a qualifying debt for the purposes of the Late Payment of Commercial Debts (Interest) Act 1998 and, in relation to a judgment debt, means the judgment or order which gives rise to the judgment debt.'

56.19 Whilst the contrary is arguable, the received view is that the measure of the sums of money involved is the aggregate of the costs and the damages; hence, if a claimant recovers £3,000 in damages and £3,000 in costs, they will be entitled to PRI on the costs (and the damages), notwithstanding the fact that, individually, both the damages and the costs are below £5,000.[14] This restriction on the recovery of interest will not apply to judgments below £5,000 where the judgment is either due to or from the Crown, however.[15] If a costs creditor wishes to recover interest where the sums involved are less than £5,000, then, provided that the outstanding debt (including court costs) was £600 or above, they would be able to apply to have the matter transferred to the High Court for enforcement by a High Court enforcement officer.[16] Prescribed rate interest would then be payable from the date of the certificate of transfer.

56.20 **Suspension of interest during enforcement proceedings** In the County Court, the accrual of interest will be suspended whilst enforcement proceedings are being brought, but only if those proceedings are successful. Article 4(1) of the County Court (Interest on Judgment Debts) Order 1991 (as amended)[17] provides:

> 'Where a judgment creditor takes proceedings in a county court to enforce payment under a relevant judgment, the judgment debt shall cease to carry interest thereafter, except where those proceedings fail to produce any payment from the debtor in which case interest shall accrue as if those proceedings had never been taken.'

This, presumably, is to avoid the possibility of enforcement proceedings being brought in respect of a moving target.

---

[13] SI 1991/1184, as amended by the County Courts (Interest on Judgment Debts) (Amendment) Order 1996 (SI 1996/2516).

[14] *Twigg Farnell v Wildblood* (unreported) CA, 26 September 1997, this appeal having been decided on the same day as that which was reported as (1998) PNLR 211. It should be noted that the issue was not argued before the Court of Appeal, but was based on a concession.

[15] See Crown Proceedings Act 1947, s 24.

[16] The relevant provisions can be found at CPR, r 70.3, and PD 70, para 2.

[17] SI 1991/1184, as amended by the County Courts (Interest on Judgment Debts) (Amendment) Order 1996 (SI 1996/2516).

In a similar vein, where an administration order or an attachment of earnings order is made, interest will not accrue during the time the order is in force.[18] **56.21**

The date upon which interest begins to run

CPR, r 40.8 (which is a general provision relating to any type of monetary award the court makes, rather than a provision relating solely to costs), provides as follows: **56.22**

> '(1) Where interest is payable on a judgment pursuant to section 17 of the Judgments Act 1838 or section 74 of the County Courts Act 1984, the interest shall begin to run from the date that judgment is given unless—
> (a) a rule in another Part or a practice direction makes different provision; or
> (b) the court orders otherwise.
>
> (2) The court may order that interest shall begin to run from a date before the date that judgment is given.'

Lord Neuberger MR has found that CPR, r 40.8, is *ultra vires* in the County Court (see 56.16–56.17); as such, the matters set out at 56.29–56.38 may not apply in that court.[19]

The incipitur *and the* allocatur *rules*

In ancient times, practices differed between common law[20] and the courts of Chancery.[21] In particular, the rule relating to common-law cases—often referred to as the *incipitur* rule—was that interest ran from the date on which judgment was pronounced;[22] hence *incipitur*, meaning 'it begins'. In Chancery, a different rule applied, the *allocatur* rule, under which interest ran from the date of the costs certificate; hence *allocatur*, meaning 'it is allowed'.[23] Lord Ackner explained the difference in this way: **56.23**

> 'In the first place, this deeming of the ascertainment of quantum, which in fact may have taken place months or years later, to have occurred on the date of judgment is the origin of the Latin name of the Common Law Rule, the *incipitur* rule. This Latin word has a connotation of reference back to the beginning or origin of the entitlement. The alternative Chancery Rule was known as the *allocatur* rule, which has connotations of the date on which a precise quantification or allocation of money to the previously unquantified sum occurs.'[24]

The Judicature Acts of 1873[25] and 1875[26] fused the hitherto split system of courts. The then rules of court were drafted in such a way as to lead to uncertainty as to the correct law,[27]

---

[18] See County Court (Interest on Judgment Debts) Order 1991 (SI 1991/1184), art 4(3).

[19] *Simcoe v Jacuzzi UK Group Plc* [2012] EWCA Civ 137, at [23]–[31].

[20] Those being the Court of the Queen's Bench and the Court of Common Pleas.

[21] Those being the Court of Chancery and the Court of Exchequer.

[22] See *Fisher v Dudding* 9 Dowl 872, at 874, *per* Tindal CJ ('the legal meaning of those words must be taken to be the time of signing judgment, or making the entry of the *incipitur* in the Master's book'); see also *Newton v Grand Junction Railway Co* (1846) 153 ER 1133.

[23] See the practice referred to in *Boswell v Coaks* (1888) 57 LJ Ch 101, at 105, where Lindley LJ referred to the Chancery Courts having issued forms of writ of *fieri facias* providing for interest to run from the date of the taxing master's certificate.

[24] *Thomas v Bunn* [1991] 1 AC 362, at 376.

[25] Supreme Court of Judicature Act 1873, 36 & 37 Vict c 66.

[26] Supreme Court of Judicature Act 1875, 38 and 39 Vict c 77.

[27] This arose out of the fact that the relevant provision appeared to be contained in something as insubstantial as a footnote to a precedent: see *Schroder v Clough* (1877) 35 LT 850. The fact that the footnote was amended without explanation did not assist.

but after those rules were amended, the general consensus was that the *incipitur* rule was to be preferred.[28]

56.24 Chitty J noted that, by the late 19th century, it had become settled practice generally to apply the *incipitur* rule.[29] The Rules of the Supreme Court were revised in 1965, however—and, in particular, a footnote that had been pivotal to the interpretation in favour of the *incipitur* rule ceased to exist. Lord Denning MR said that 'a little common sense' was required and that the *allocatur* rule should apply.[30] Stephenson LJ agreed, noting that he was 'free to choose the better rule'.[31]

56.25 In 1990, the House of Lords came to the opposite conclusion, for the following reasons:

> 'It is the unsuccessful party to the litigation who, *ex hypothesi*, has caused the costs unnecessarily to be incurred. Hence the order made against him. Since interest is not awarded on costs incurred and paid by the successful party before judgment, why should he suffer the added loss of interest on costs incurred and paid after judgment but before the taxing master gives his certificate? Since ... payments of costs are likely nowadays to be made to lawyers prior to taxation, then the application of the *allocatur* rule would generally speaking do greater injustice than the operation of the *incipitur* rule. Moreover, the *incipitur* rule provides a further necessary stimulus for payments to be made on account of costs and disbursements prior to taxation, for costs to be more readily agreed, and for taxation, when necessary, to be expedited, all of which are desirable developments. Barristers, solicitors and expert witnesses should not be expected to finance their clients' litigation until it is completed and the taxing master's certificate obtained.'[32]

56.26 Thus the *incipitur* rule prevails[33]—although this is not the case in many other common-law jurisdictions.[34] The *incipitur* rule prevails even where the receiving party's contract of retainer is a conditional fee agreement.[35] The position relating to costs should be contrasted with the situation in respect of interest on damages, where the *allocatur* rule is to be preferred.[36]

56.27 **Discretionary disapplication of the *incipitur* rule** Whilst *obiter*, Leggatt J has noted that if that is what justice requires, there is no reason why the court should not order that PRI should run from the date on which the amount of costs payable has been assessed (this being pursuant to the powers set out at 56.29).[37] He went on to say this:

> '*Hunt's case* decides that an order for payment of costs to be assessed is a judgment for the purpose of section 17 of the Judgments Act. It also decided that, as the law stood before the

---

[28] See *Pyman & Co v Burt, Boulton & Anor* [1884] WN 100, *per* Field J. This was followed in the High Court in *Landowners' West of England and South Wales Land Drainage and Inclosure Co v Ashford* [1884] 33 WR 41 and, subsequently, in the Court of Appeal in *Boswell v Coaks* (1888) 57 LJ Ch 101, at 105.

[29] *In re London Wharfing Co* (1885) 54 LJ Ch 1137, at 1138. Contrary findings were made, however: see, eg, *Schroeder v Cleugh* (1877) 46 LJQB 365.

[30] *K v K (Divorce Costs: Interest)* (1977) Fam 39, at 48 and 49. This decision was followed in *Erven Warnink BV v J Townend & Sons (Hull) Ltd* [1979] AC 731.

[31] *K v K (Divorce Costs: Interest)* (1977) Fam 39, at 53–6.

[32] *Hunt v RM Douglas* [1990] 1 AC 398, at 451, *per* Lord Ackner (with whom Lords Brandon, Jauncey and Griffiths agreed).

[33] Not only is the *incipitur* rule the default position under the CPR, but also, in the County Court, it is the default position by reason of other delegated legislation: see County Court (Interest on Judgment Debts) Order 1991 (SI 1991/1184), art 2(2) (as amended).

[34] See, eg, *Hamdan v Widodo (No 2)* [2010] WASC 6 S.

[35] *Simcoe v Jacuzzi UK Group Plc* [2012] EWCA Civ 137.

[36] *Thomas v Bunn* [1991] 1 AC 362.

[37] *Involnert Management Inc v Aprilgrange Ltd & Ors* [2015] EWHC 2834 (Comm).

> Civil Procedure Rules were introduced, the balance of justice favoured a rule that interest automatically ran from the date of the costs order over a rule that interest automatically ran from the date of assessment. The House of Lords did not decide that, if the court were in future to be given a discretion to set the date from which interest under the Judgments Act is to run and a separate power to award interest for periods prior to that date, it would not be just to exercise the court's discretion by ordering Judgments Act interest to run from the date of assessment. I do, however, recognise that in none of the cases mentioned above has it been thought appropriate to make such an order.'[38]

This, at first blush, appears to make significant inroads into the notion that the *incipitur* rule prevails over the *allocatur* rule, but it should be borne in mind that Leggatt J was merely hypothesising. As far as the editor is aware, no court has subsequently made such an order.

In any event, clear language would be required to disapply the *incipitur* rule in preference **56.28**
for the *allocatur* rule; a phrase such as 'costs when taxed or agreed shall be paid' would not be sufficient to do so.[39]

Discretion as to the date on which PRI begins to run

As has been noted at 56.22, CPR, r 40.8(2), affords the court the power to vary the date **56.29**
on which PRI starts to run—at least in so far as the High Court is concerned (see 56.16). CPR, r 44.2(6)(g), creates similar provisions that relate specifically to costs:

> 'The orders which the court may make under this rule include an order that a party must pay—
> [. . .]
> (g) interest on costs from or until a certain date, including a date before judgment.'

Lord Neuberger MR has confirmed that the starting point is that interest is payable from **56.30**
the judgment date (that is, the *incipitur* date).[40] Put otherwise, the default position is that the PRI date is the same as the judgment date. It is, however, open to the court to make some other order. This may be achieved by ordering that PRI should run from a date after (see 56.31–56.40) or before the judgment date (although, in practice, if the court is going to award interest during the period prior to the judgment date, this would be by setting a CRI date and awarding CRI between that date and the PRI date).

Orders that interest should run from a date after judgment In 2009, Christopher Clarke **56.31**
J explained that the ability of the High Court to depart from the *incipitur* rule (see 56.29) was, in part, to enable the court to take account of the fact that money would often be expended before any judgment.[41] He went on to say, conversely, that where money had not been expended prior to judgment—such as where the bulk of the costs had been paid at a date long after the relevant judgment—justice may require the PRI date to be postponed. He added the following points (which were subsequently cited with approval by Lord Neuberger MR).[42]

- The general rule is that PRI runs from the judgment date.
- A departure from that general rule is justified if it is 'what justice requires'.
- The notion that a departure can be justified only in 'exceptional' cases is an unhelpful guide.

---

[38] *Ibid*, at [22].
[39] *Electricity Supply Nominees Ltd v Farrell* [1997] 2 All ER 498, at 504, *per* Kennedy LJ.
[40] *Simcoe v Jacuzzi UK Group Plc* [2012] EWCA Civ 137, at [35]–[48].
[41] *Fattal v Walbrook Trustees (Jersey) Ltd* [2009] EWHC 1674 (Ch), at [26] and [27].
[42] *Simcoe v Jacuzzi UK Group Plc* [2012] EWCA Civ 137, at [47]–[48].

- The primary purpose of an award of interest is 'to compensate the recipient for [having] been precluded from obtaining a return on [his] money'.[43]
- 'Since the payment of solicitors' costs involves the payment of money which could otherwise have been profitably employed, the overwhelming likelihood is that justice requires some recompense in the form of interest.'[44]

It should be noted that many of these points appear to regard interest on costs as compensatory, which highlights the fact that there is a certain amount of overlap between the decisions that the court takes regarding PRI and those that go to any award of compensatory rate interest.

56.32 Some years later in 2015—a time when base rates were noticeably low—Christopher Clarke LJ noted the fact that the character of PRI of 8 per cent per annum was penal—although not prescribed by way of a penalty (see 56.44)—and he went on to say this: 'In that context a number of judges have regarded it as unjust that the 8 per cent rate should begin the moment that a judgment for costs has been given.'[45] As will be explained at 56.39, there have been many cases in which other judges have come to a similar view. Many of those cases illustrate the fact that the court will often consider the issue of postponement of the PRI date as intimately bound up with the issue of whether CRI should be paid (that is, whether a lower rate of interest should be paid prior to the date on which PRI begins to accrue).

56.33 *No requirement that the case must be unusual before the court orders postponement* Whilst his approach has been qualified (see 56.34–56.35), Andrew Smith J has explained that, to make good a case for deferment of PRI date, a paying party would have to point to something that justified a departure from that rate:

> 'Typically the Applicant would have to show that particular features of the case mean that the application of the general rule would be so unfair to him that justice requires departure from it. This might be because a large amount of costs is likely to be outstanding for a particularly long period and the Applicant cannot be expected to avoid this by assessing what costs he will have to pay and making (or tendering) a substantial payment on account. I agree with the Claimants that, if such unfairness is shown, the fact that the Judgments Act interest rate encourages the paying party to reach a compromise would not be a proper reason to refuse an order.'[46]

56.34 Thus, according to Andrew Smith J, there must be a 'proper reason' to depart from the *incipitur* rule. This may be right, but it does not mean that the case must be exceptional.[47] Leggatt J had this to say on the point:

> 'There is nothing in the Judgments Act or the Civil Procedure Rules which expressly or impliedly restricts the power of the court under CPR 40.8(1) to order the interest payable under section 17 of the Judgments Act to run from a different date, or which requires exceptional circumstances to be shown before that power is exercised. To the

[43] *Ibid.*
[44] *Ibid.*
[45] *Excalibur Ventures LLC v Texas Keystone Inc & Ors* [2015] EWHC 566 (Comm), at [7].
[46] *Fiona Trust v Privalov* [2011] EWHC 1312 (Comm), at [4]. This paragraph was cited with approval by Mann J in *Sycamore Bidco Ltd v Breslin* [2013] EWHC 583 (Ch), at [76].
[47] See *Simcoe v Jacuzzi UK Group Plc* [2012] EWCA Civ 137, at [47]–[48].

> contrary, the power to "order otherwise" is to be exercised in accordance with the overriding objective of dealing with cases justly, and the essential question is therefore what justice requires.'[48]

Thus, according to Leggatt J, the approach is unfettered as merely a matter of 'what justice requires'. He went on to say that in so far as the remarks of Andrew Smith J might be taken to suggest that it is necessary to show that a case has unusual features to justify departure from the default rule, he did not concur, adding that '[t]here is no necessity for the default position to be the usual position'.[49]

Leggatt J went on to say, however, that he did agree with Andrew Smith J—and, for that matter, with Mann J (see 56.40)—that the PRI date should not be deferred simply because PRI is payable at a considerably higher rate than CRI. He said that the rate at which interest should be payable under the Judgments Act 1838 is a matter for the Secretary of State to decide, and that the court's concern is to identify the date from which it is appropriate that such interest should run.[50] **56.35**

The approach in commercial cases Leggatt J had this to say about the PRI date (in the context of a commercial case in which CRI was payable up to the date on which PRI became payable): **56.36**

> 'I do not think it just to make an order under which interest begins to run at the rate appropriate for unpaid judgment debts before the paying party could reasonably be expected to pay the debt; and, in a case where the court has ordered a suitable interim payment to be made on account of costs, I do not think it reasonable to expect the party liable for costs to pay the balance of the debt until it knows exactly what sums are being claimed by the party awarded costs and has had a fair opportunity to decide what sums it accepts are properly payable.'[51]

Thus, where the receiving party is already receiving compensatory interest, Leggatt J believes that it would be unjust to condemn the paying party to pay PRI (at the full 8 per cent per annum) until such time as that party could reasonably be expected to pay the debt. Leggatt J went on to say that this principle should not be 'confined to cases where a particularly large amount of costs is likely to be outstanding for a particularly long period, albeit that it is clearly more acute in such cases'.[52]

A new benchmark in commercial cases? Having made these points (see 56.36), Leggatt J went on to make the following points of practice (in the context of a commercial case in which CRI was payable up to the PRI date): **56.37**

> 'I think it desirable to set a date from which Judgments Act interest will run which is based, if possible, on some objective benchmark and does not depend simply on the judge's general feeling of what length of postponement is fair. I agree with Andrew Smith J that certainty and clarity are important in this context. It will do no favours to litigants—particularly as the amount of money at stake, while not negligible, is never likely to be

48 *Involnert Management Inc v Aprilgrange Ltd & Ors* [2015] EWHC 2834 (Comm), at [20].
49 *Ibid*, at [20].
50 *Ibid*, at [21].
51 *Ibid*, at [23].
52 *Ibid*, at [23].

large—if the date from which Judgments Act interest will be ordered to run is unpredictable, thus encouraging argument on the issue in every case. With this in mind, it seems to me that a reasonable objective benchmark to take is the period prescribed by the rules of court for commencing detailed assessment proceedings. Pursuant to CPR 47.7, where an order is made for payment of costs which are to be the subject of a detailed assessment if not agreed, the time by which detailed assessment proceedings must be commenced (unless otherwise agreed or ordered) is three months after the date of the costs order. In order to commence such proceedings, the receiving party must serve on the paying party a bill of costs giving particulars of the costs claimed. It is then for the paying party to decide which items in the bill of costs it wishes to dispute. Postponing the date from which Judgments Act interest begins to run by three months will therefore generally serve to ensure that the party liable for costs has received the information needed to make a realistic assessment of the amount of its liability before it begins to incur interest at the rate applicable to judgment debts for failing to pay that amount.'[53]

56.38 Respected commentators have criticised Leggatt J's analysis. In particular, the authors of *Cook on Costs 2017* had this to say:

'The suggested benchmark seems odd because:
(i) in most multi-track cases the paying party will have a clear idea of the receiving party's costs from the last agreed or approved budget;
(ii) in many other cases a schedule of costs is often produced for the purpose of negotiation prior to a formal bill;
(iii) in those cases where CPR 44.3(2)(a) applies, there is nothing to stop the paying party making its own realistic assessment of what is a proportionate sum by reference to the factors at CPR 44.3(5) and paying that sum on account;
(iv) CPR 44.2(8) encourages the court to award sums on account of costs and ... there is nothing to prevent a court making such an order even in the absence of a statement of costs (*Astonleigh Residential v Goldfarb* [2014] EWHC 4100 (Ch)). It might be thought that what is sauce for the court is also sauce for the paying party.'[54]

These are certainly valid points, but it should be borne in mind that Leggatt J was not dealing with a situation in which he was ordering postponement *simpliciter*; rather, he was ordering postponement in the context of a commercial rate of interest being allowed from the date on which the costs were paid to the date of postponement. Against this backdrop, Leggatt J's 'benchmark' seems pragmatic and sensible (especially in the context of historically low base rates). That said, it would seem that (at the time of writing) there were no reported cases in which any other judge had adopted Leggatt J's new benchmark.

56.39 *Case examples regarding postponement* As might be expected, given the discretionary nature of the power of postponement (be that of PRI or interest generally), there has been a divergence of judicial opinion on the topic. A number of cases can be identified in which a postponement was awarded, along with several in which it was not (see 56.40). The following types of case can be identified, but it should be noted that the issue of postponement is highly fact-sensitive and that, in nearly all of the cases listed, there were several factors at play.

[53] *Ibid*, at [24].
[54] See *Cook on Costs 2017* (LexisNexis, online), para 32.5.

- **Real issues as to the amount of costs that are claimed** Both Hamblen J[55] and Roth J[56] have explained that deferment may be appropriate in cases in which there were likely to be real issues of proportionality and reasonableness on assessment, particularly if large amounts of costs are in issue.
- **Conspicuously low base rate** Akenhead J awarded interest for a period during which the prevailing base rate was low, finding that the interests of justice would best be met by making an order that interest did not begin to run until six months after the costs order had been made.[57]
- **'Sizeable windfall'** In a case in which he regarded it as unjust for interest to accrue at that rate immediately after the costs order was made, David Steel J postponed the accrual of that rate for six months.[58] He noted that any other order would have represented a very sizeable windfall for the receiving party. He also noted that postponement would increase the pressure on the receiving party to deal with the costs promptly.[59]
- **Further information required** The court may postpone interest for the purposes of enabling the receiving party to provide further information as to its bill and the paying party to appreciate more clearly what the receiving party was likely to obtain on assessment. This may be done in the hope that it would encourage the parties to reach some kind of compromise.[60]

Similarly, there have been cases in which the court declined to order postponement. **56.40**

- Mann J rejected an argument that the court should use its power under CPR, r 40.8(1), to postpone the date from which interest became payable until the date on which the costs were quantified on a detailed assessment, because he did not accept that the differential between the judgment rate and a commercial rate of interest provided a good reason to order such a postponement in circumstances in which fixing the judgment rate is a matter for Parliament.[61] He also did not consider that it would be proper to use that power to address the anomaly that an order for costs to be assessed is treated as a judgment for the purpose of the Judgments Act 1938, in circumstances in which that rule has been fixed by a higher court.
- Lewison J came to a similar conclusion in a different case.[62]

The rate of interest

The rate applicable to CRI is addressed at 56.69–56.82; the next few paragraphs deal solely with PRI. **56.41**

[55] *Standard Chartered Bank v Ceylon Petroleum Corpn* [2011] EWHC 2094 (Comm), at [27].
[56] *London Tara Hotel Ltd v Kensington Close Hotel Ltd* [2011] EWHC 29 (Ch), at [28].
[57] *Multiple Claimants v Corby District Council (Corby Group Litigation)* [2009] EWHC 2109 (TCC), at [43].
[58] *Colour Quest Ltd v Total Downstream (UK) Ltd* [2009] EWHC 823 (Comm).
[59] *Ibid*, at [40]–[43]. See also *D Pride and Partners v Institute for Animal Health* [2009] EWHC 1617 (QB), at [77] and [78], in which Tugendhat J came to much the same conclusion (four months' postponement to avoid giving receiving party an incentive not to deal with costs promptly).
[60] See, eg, *Generics (UK) Ltd v Yeda Research & Development Co Ltd* [2012] EWHC 2283 (Ch), at [2]–[4], *per* Arnold J (four-month postponement to allow for negotiations). This case was appealed, but on a different point.
[61] *Schlumberger Holdings Ltd v Electromagnetic Geoservices AS* [2009] EWHC 773 (Pat).
[62] *Cranway Ltd v Playtech Ltd* [2009] EWHC 823.

The rate of PRI on judgments in sterling

56.42 In both the High Court and the County Court,[63] PRI is set at the rate specified by order[64] and—other than where judgment is given in a currency other than pounds sterling[65] (see 56.46–56.48)—may not be varied.[66] Mann J has confirmed that this applies to interest on costs.[67]

56.43 Only the Secretary of State has the power to vary the rate.[68] At times, it has been as high as 15 per cent per annum;[69] at the time of writing, it is 'only' 8 per cent per annum and it has been at that level since 1 April 1993.[70] In theory, the rate could change at any time. In view of this, Christopher Clarke LJ has said that references to the rate ought to be to 'the rate prescribed' rather than to a specific percentage per annum,[71] but this is—perhaps—a counsel of perfection.

56.44 **Is PRI penal?** Christopher Clarke LJ had this to say about the nature of the applicable rate:

> 'Eight per cent is very significantly above current commercial rates. Although the rate prescribed under the Act is not prescribed by way of penalty, in circumstances where the commercial rate taken is 1.5 per cent, its commercial character is penal. ... The 8 per cent rate is something of an anomaly. It is prescribed by regulation but it has remained at that rate for a long time despite changes in current interest rates. In principle it is difficult to justify other than by treating it as an inducement to paying parties to agree costs or to proceed swiftly to an assessment.'[72]

56.45 **Miscellaneous points regarding the rate of PRI** The following miscellaneous points can be made.

- **Prescribed rate interest and Part 36** Whilst it is arguable that it is no longer good law, PRI (that is, at 8 per cent per annum at time of writing) will apply from the PRI date onwards even where a claimant has 'beaten' their own offer and has become entitled to ERI prior to that date.[73]
- **Detailed assessments** It is possible to disallow interest pursuant to CPR, rr 47.8(3) and 47.14(4), thereby achieving a result similar to a lowering of the rate, but Mann J

---

63 See County Court (Interest on Judgment Debts) Order 1991 (SI 1991/1184), art 5.

64 The parent provision is Judgments Act 1838, s 17(1).

65 See Administration of Justice Act 1970, s 44A; in the County Court, see County Courts Act 1984, s 74(5A) (as amended).

66 *Thomas v Bunn* [1991] 1 AC 362, HL; *Rocco Guiseppe & Figli v Tradex Export SA* [1984] 1 WLR 742. The same is true in many other common-law jurisdictions: see, eg, *Hartley Poynton Ltd v Ali* [2005] VSCA 53. Whilst now based on old authority, it probably remains the case that where a contract provides for payment of interest on costs at a rate higher than judgment debt rate, the court cannot award interest at that higher rate: *Economic Life Assurance Society v Usborne* [1902] AC 152.

67 *Schlumberger Holdings Ltd v Electromagnetic Geoservices AS* [2009] EWHC 773 (Pat). It has to be said that there are instances of the court awarding post-judgment interest at rates other than that prescribed in statute; it is likely that those are instances of the correct law not being drawn to the court's attention.

68 In the High Court, see Administration of Justice Act 1970, s 44; in the County Court, see County Court Act 1984, s 74(1).

69 See, eg, the Judgment Debts (Rate of Interest) Order 1985 (SI 1985/437).

70 The Judgment Debts (Rate of Interest) Order 1993 (SI 1993/564). Previously, the rate had been 15 per cent since 16 April 1985.

71 See *Excalibur Ventures LLC v Texas Keystone Inc & Ors* [2015] EWHC 566 (Comm), at [3].

72 See *ibid*, at [6] and [7].

73 Whilst it related to the 'old' Part 36, see *McPhilemy v Times Newspapers Ltd & Ors (No 2)* [2001] EWCA Civ 933, at [24], *per* Chadwick LJ.

has expressed disapproval of this, explaining that a fixed rate affords a degree of certainty and clarity, and is capable of providing an incentive for paying sooner, rather than later.[74] Coulson J came to a similar conclusion, but he commented that it may be best to defer the application of the statutory rate until after the amount of costs is known.[75] This would have the effect of allowing a lower rate for that period during which the paying party was ignorant of the precise figure that it had to pay.

Interest on costs in foreign currencies

Where judgment has been given for costs in a currency other than sterling, the court may order that the rate of interest shall be such rate as it thinks fit.[76] The fact that a contract between parties includes an English jurisdiction clause would not be sufficient to displace that power.[77] **56.46**

The fact that the prescribed rate for sterling (see 56.42–56.43) has departed from commercial rates by such a marked amount in recent years should not be taken as implying that there is a legislative policy of providing more than ordinary financial compensation by the award of interest on a judgment in a foreign currency.[78] This means that interest on foreign currencies tends to be compensatory and lower than the prescribed rate. For example (albeit one that related to damages rather than costs), Christopher Clarke J found that an appropriate rate was the US dollar London inter-bank offered rate (LIBOR) *plus* 2.5 per cent.[79] In a case in which the damages were in US dollars and the costs in sterling, Jefford J allowed a rate on the former that was based on the applicable US prime rate (that is, 4 per cent above) and a rate on the latter that was based on UK base rates (that is, 2 per cent above).[80] **56.47**

Although it related to costs that had been allowed on an indemnity basis, Arnold J allowed a lump sum to compensate the receiving party for losses arising out of the movement of the relevant exchange rate.[81] It seems that Arnold J allowed this as an alternative to a higher rate of interest. **56.48**

Discounts and adjustments

The interests of justice may require an adjustment to be made to the amount of interest payable, but there are only very limited circumstances in which this is possible. Christopher Clarke J has (in the context of deciding the date from which interest should run) stated that the most important criterion is that any award should reflect what justice requires.[82] **56.49**

---

[74] *Schlumberger Holdings Ltd v Electromagnetic Geoservices AS* [2009] EWHC 773 (Pat).

[75] *London Tara Hotel Ltd v Kensington Close Hotel Ltd* [2011] EWHC 29 (Ch), at [34] *et seq*. This was not dissimilar to the pre-CPR practice of adjusting the period during which interest was payable so as to give rise to equitable overall amount of interest: see *Kuwait Airways Corpn v Iraqi Airways Co (No 2)* [1995] 1 All ER 790. This is a practice that was limited to only a very small class of cases, however—namely, successful appeals in which there was a need to change and to backdate the original costs order.

[76] See Administration of Justice Act 1970, s 44A; County Courts (Interest on Judgment Debts) Order 1991 (SI 1991/1184), art 5(2); in the County Court, County Courts Act 1984 (as amended), s 74(5A).

[77] See *Standard Chartered Bank v Ceylon Petroleum Corpn* [2011] EWHC 2094 (Comm).

[78] *Novoship (UK) Ltd v Mikhaylyuk* [2014] EWCA Civ 908; see also *Barnett v Creggy* [2015] EWHC 1316 (Ch).

[79] *Novoship (UK) Ltd v Mikhaylyuk* [2013] EWHC 89 (Comm), at [47]–[64].

[80] *Triple Point Technology Inc v PTT Public Co Ltd* [2018] EWHC (TCC).

[81] *Elkamet Kunststofftechnik GmbH v Saint-Gobain Glass France SA* [2016] EWHC 3321 (Pat), at [13].

[82] *Fattal v Walbrook Trustees (Jersey) Ltd* [2009] EWHC 1674 (Ch), at [26], cited with approval in *Lake v Hunt Kid Law Firm LLP (in administration)* [2011] EWHC 766 (QB), at [34] and [35], *per* Wyn Williams J.

He noted that the primary purpose of an award of interest is to compensate the recipient for the fact that they have been precluded from obtaining a return on the money in question.[83] Whilst *obiter* that dealt with interest between solicitor and client, Wyn Williams J has explained that the fact that the paying party may, for whatever reason, also have been deprived of the use of that money would not generally be sufficient reason to justify a reduction in the interest properly payable.[84]

Delay in detailed assessment proceedings

56.50 Interest may be disallowed as a result of delay in the detailed assessment. CPR, r 47.8(3), makes the following provisions:

> 'If—
> (a) the paying party has not made an application in accordance with paragraph (1); and
> (b) the receiving party commences the proceedings later than the period specified in rule 47.7,
>
> the court may disallow all or part of the interest otherwise payable to the receiving party under—
> (i) section 17 of the Judgments Act 1838; or
> (ii) section 74 of the County Courts Act 1984,
>
> but must not impose any other sanction except in accordance with rule 44.11 (powers in relation to misconduct).'

Thus delay in commencing detailed assessment proceedings may result in interest being disallowed. It is possible, however, that this provision is *ultra vires* in the County Court (see 56.16).

56.51 Likewise, CPR, r 47.14(4), makes almost identical provision concerning delay in applying for an assessment hearing. The court is probably not permitted to exercise this power if the paying party has made an application for an order requiring the receiving party to commence detailed assessment proceedings (see 43.105–43.107). As with the provisions at CPR, r 47.8(3), it is possible that this provision is *ultra vires* in the County Court (see 56.16–56.17).

56.52 Longmore LJ has described the disallowance of interest as 'the normal sanction for penalising delay', commenting that 'the prescribed sanction of the disallowance of interest is likely to be both comparatively uncontroversial and also calculable without unnecessary dispute'.[85]

56.53 Where delay amounts to misconduct, the sanction may extend beyond the mere disallowance of interest.[86] This topic is addressed at 23.57–23.82.

Funders

56.54 It may be that a litigation funder has become liable for costs. Where this is so, it does not follow that the funder will automatically follow the fortunes of the party whom it was

83 *Fattal v Walbrook Trustees (Jersey) Ltd* [2009] EWHC 1674 (Ch), at [26], referred to *London Chatham & Dover Railway Co v South Eastern Railways Co* [1893] AC 429, at 437, and *Earl of Malmesbury, James Carleton Seventh v Strutt and Parker (a partnership)* [2008] EWHC 424 (QB).

84 *Lake v Hunt Kid Law Firm LLP (in administration)* [2011] EWHC 766 (QB), at [34] and [35].

85 *Haji-Ioannou v Frangos* [2006] EWCA Civ 1663, at [17]–[18].

86 CPR, r 44.14(2)(a); *Haji-Ioannou v Frangos* [2006] EWCA Civ 1663.

funding in the sense that the funder will have to pay PRI for the same period of time as its client.[87]

Compensatory Rate Interest

Jurisdiction and underlying policy

The origin of the power to award CRI

Compensatory rate interest is allowed pursuant to CPR, r 44.2(6)(g). This raises more questions than it answers, however, because it is far from certain whether that provision creates a self-contained power regarding interest. In particular, it is possible that such awards are—ultimately—made pursuant to s 17 of the Judgments Act 1838 in the High Court. If so, then this would give rise to the problems referred to at 56.70—namely, the possibility that the court does not have the power to award anything other than PRI. For the reasons set out at 56.70, however, it is unlikely that the court would entertain any such argument. In particular, the fact that CRI has a somewhat unclear jurisdictional basis has been known for years,[88] yet—as far as the editor is aware—it is not a point that has ever prevented the court from making such an award. **56.55**

The points made previously about the County Court may apply to CPR, r 44.2(6)(g) (see 56.16–56.17). If this is so, then it is possible that there is no power at all to allow CRI in the County Court. **56.56**

Compensatory rate interest in general

Waller LJ has had this to say of the power to award CRI: **56.57**

> '[I]n principle there seems no reason why the Court should not do so [ie make an award of compensatory rate interest] where a party has had to put up money paying its solicitors and been out of the use of that money in the meanwhile.'[89]

It is therefore surprising that, other than in the Commercial Court (see 56.60–56.61), the power to award CRI is a power that is not commonly exercised.[90]

In a similar vein to the comments made by Waller LJ, Laddie J had this to say: **56.58**

> 'The purpose of a costs order is to compensate the winning party for the real cost of having conducted the litigation and the real cost is not measured simply by adding up mathematically the bills that it has paid to or agreed to pay to its lawyers. A pound paid in 1980 may be the same coin that is paid in 2005, but it is not the same in value. What the award of interest on costs allows the court to do is to ensure that the receiving party is compensated properly for the real cost to it of having conducted the litigation successfully. In my view, the discretion to award interest on costs is a broad

---

[87] *Excalibur Ventures LLC v Texas Keystone Inc & Ors* [2015] EWHC 566 (Comm), at [8]–[11], *per* Christopher Clarke LJ.

[88] It was raised in oral argument in *Simcoe v Jacuzzi UK Group Plc* [2012] EWCA Civ 137.

[89] *Earl of Malmesbury, James Carleton Seventh v Strutt and Parker (a partnership)* [2008] EWHC 424 (QB).

[90] Examples of such orders being made include: *Earl of Malmesbury v Strytt & Parker (Interest on Costs)* [2008] EWHC 616 (QB); *Lloyd v Svenby* [2006] EWHC 576 (QB); *Douglas v Hello! Ltd* [2004] EWHC 63 (Ch).

one. Courts can take into account all the circumstances in coming to a conclusion as to what to do.'[91]

56.59 Thus the Court has a discretion to allow the receiving party interest on costs prior to the date of the costs order to compensate it for being out of pocket when it has paid costs as the case ran along.

Compensatory rate interest in commercial cases

56.60 Unlike the practice in other courts, such awards are common in commercial cases. If anything, it is the rule, rather than the exception that interest is awarded on costs from the date(s) on which they were paid (or on which payment became due). As long ago as 2002, Langley J had this to say on the topic:

> 'For my part, I think it may well be appropriate, at least in substantial proceedings involving commercial interests of significant importance both in balance sheet and reputational terms, that the court should award interest on costs under the rule where substantial sums have inevitably been expended perhaps a year or more before an award of costs is made . . .'[92]

56.61 More recently, Leggatt J had this to say:

> 'Since *Hunt's case* was decided, the Civil Procedure Rules have given the court power to order interest to be paid on costs from a date before judgment: see CPR 44.2(6)(g). This power is now routinely exercised when an order for costs is made following a trial to award interest at a commercial rate from the dates when the costs were incurred until the date when interest becomes payable under the Judgments Act.'[93]

Leggatt J went on to find that the fact that CRI may be allowed prior to the judgment date was a factor that was capable of militating against the court allowing the *incipitur* rule to apply in so far as PRI was concerned (see 56.36).

No requirement of exceptionality

56.62 There is no requirement that exceptional circumstances must be made out before the court can make such an award. In this regard, Kitchen J said this:

> '[I]t seems to me that the court has a broad discretion when deciding whether to award interest on costs from a date before judgment. That discretion must be exercised in accordance with the principles set out in CPR 44.3 and the court must take into account all the circumstances of the case, including such matters as the conduct of the parties and the degree to which a party has succeeded. Further, the discretion must be exercised in accordance with the overriding objective of dealing with the case justly. I am unable to accept the submission that interest on costs should only be awarded in a case which is in some way out of the norm . . .'[94]

Presumably, the points made at 56.33–56.35 would apply (with appropriate modifications).

---

91 *IPC Media v Highbury Leisure Publishing Ltd* [2005] EWHC 283 (Ch), at [12] and [13].

92 *UK Exploration Co v British American Offshore Ltd* [2002] BLR 135, at [10].

93 *Involnert Management Inc v Aprilgrange Ltd & Ors* [2015] EWHC 2834 (Comm), at [7].

94 *Nova Productions v Mazooma Games* [2006] EWHC 189 (Ch), at [16]; see also *Fattal v Walbrook Trustees (Jersey) Ltd* [2009] EWHC 1674 (Ch).

Avoiding complexity

The making of an award of CRI will tend to add complexity to the process of ascertaining the total amount payable to the receiving party. Dingemans J found that this was a factor that counted against making such an award: 56.63

> '[The] making of such an order will introduce an unnecessary level of sophistication into the process for assessing costs, with parties being required to show not only when bills were rendered, but how and when they were paid. This is likely to generate further costs for both parties in preparing such schedules of information, and in checking them. The generation of further costs creates barriers for parties litigating in the Courts.'[95]

Dingemans J went on to mention another factor that may be relevant—namely, the fact that summary assessments of the costs of interim hearings may have led to timely defrayment of the receiving party's expenditure.[96]

Dingemans J's comments were no doubt appropriate for the case before him, but they seem not to have been followed with any real frequency. In any event, rather than not making an award of CRI at all, a different approach to avoiding complexity of calculation is to allow interest from a single date, rather than from the date on which multiple invoices were paid—an approach adopted by Warren J.[97] 56.64

Referring to Christopher Clarke J's observations, as set out at 56.31, Lord Neuberger MR added the following points: 56.65

> 'I would discourage too detailed an approach into the facts of the particular case in hand for the purpose of determining the date from which interest should run. ... Prolonged argument, let alone detailed evidence, on the issue must be avoided. There will often be no perfect date, and the decision inevitably will, indeed should, be broad brush. Further, if interest was to run from different dates on different components of the costs, it would, in many cases, lead to arguments which would do the legal system no credit.'[98]

As such, simplicity is the watchword.

The date on which interest begins to run

Compensatory rate interest may be awarded from the accrual date,[99] from the payment date[100] or from some other date. There seems to be no judicial consensus as to which of these should be used by default; rather, it seems that each case is to be decided on its own facts. Once a date has been chosen, however, it will become the CRI date (see 56.02 and Figure 56.1). 56.66

The award may be influenced by factors other than when invoices were rendered and when they were paid. In the context of a claim funded by a conditional fee agreement,[101] 56.67

---

95 *Schumann v Veale Wasbrough* [2013] EWHC 4070 (QB), at [4].
96 *Ibid*, at [5].
97 See, eg, *Re Southern Counties Fresh Foods Ltd, Cobden Investments Ltd v Romford Wholesale Meats Ltd* [2011] EWHC 1370 (Ch), at [112].
98 *Simcoe v Jacuzzi UK Group Plc* [2012] EWCA Civ 137, at [48].
99 See, eg, *Bim Kemi AB v Blackburn Chemicals Ltd* [2003] EWCA Civ 889.
100 See, eg, *Douglas & Ors v Hello! Ltd & Ors* [2004] EWHC 63 (Ch), at [24], *per* Lindsy LJ.
101 This related to the 'old' CPR Part 36. It is arguable that the case is wrongly decided in so far as the analysis of Part 36 is concerned, but even if there was an error, the comments about interest were still instructive.

Ramsay J allowed interest from the date on which the work was done, rather than from some later date, this counterbalancing the fact that there would be a delay in paying the success fee.[102]

56.68 Whilst an obvious point, if CRI is awarded, it should not be calculated in such a way as to cover the same period as an award of PRI.[103]

The rate of interest and discretion generally

56.69 In so far as CRI is concerned, the appropriate rate will depend on the circumstances. It is therefore convenient to consider the rate of interest and the issue of discretion together. It should be borne in mind that other considerations may apply, however—in particular, that the court may wish to set a single rate both for interest on costs and interest on damages.[104]

Compensatory rate interest is discretionary

56.70 The generally received view is that the rate that applies when CRI is awarded pursuant to CPR, r 44.2(6)(g), is a discretionary matter. It is—just about—arguable that this is wrong, because it is possible that such awards are made pursuant to s 17 of the Judgments Act 1838 (as amended), or the corresponding County Court provision (see 56.55), and the court's discretion in this regard is fettered (see 56.42–56.43). The notion of CRI being discretionary is now so deeply ingrained, however, that it is unlikely that the court would entertain any contrary argument.

56.71 Sharp LJ has explained that the court has to conduct a general appraisal of the position having regard to what would be reasonable for both the paying and receiving parties.[105] Waller LJ has noted that the practice of the Commercial Court is to award interest at a rate that broadly represents that which the successful party would have had to pay had the money been borrowed commercially.[106] Albeit in a slightly different context, Pollock CB said that account should be taken of the fact that the monies had been 'fructifying in the wrong pocket'.[107]

56.72 **Commercial cases in general** In commercial cases, the rate is usually set by reference to the short-term cost of unsecured borrowing for the relevant class of litigant.[108] Davies LJ has explained that the court should carry out 'a general appraisal, having regard to what is fair, reasonable and proportionate as between both paying party and

---

102 *Eiles v Southwark London Borough Council* [2006] EWHC 2014 (TCC), at [75].

103 If authority were needed on the point, it can be found in *Douglas & Ors v Hello! Ltd & Ors* [2004] EWHC 63 (Ch).

104 In a case in which the court had already made a decision regarding the rate that should apply to interest on damages, Mann J said that, in the absence of any reason to depart from it, that rate should apply to the costs: *Sycamore Bidco Ltd v Breslin* [2013] EWHC 583 (Ch), at [71].

105 *Jones v Secretary of State for Energy and Climate Change* [2014] EWCA Civ 363, at [17].

106 *Bim Kemi AB v Blackburn Chemicals Ltd* [2003] EWCA Civ 889, at [18]. This case mostly concerned an overpayment of costs, but it also dealt with interest payable to a receiving party.

107 *Newton v Grand Junction Railway Co* (1846) 153 ER 1133, at 1134. This was a phrase that previously had been used in Parliament by Sir Robert Peel in the context of national debts: see HC Deb, 6 February 1832, vol 9, cols 1285–351.

108 *Jones v Secretary of State for Energy and Climate Change* [2014] EWCA Civ 363, at [18], *per* Sharp LJ.

receiving party'.[109] The rate might differ depending on whether the borrower was classed as a 'first-class borrower', a small-to-medium-sized enterprise (SME) or a private individual.[110] In particular, SMEs and private individuals tend to recover interest at a higher rate to reflect the real cost of borrowing to that class of litigant.[111] In practice, whilst it would be wrong to think that such rules of thumb give rise to an immutable tariff,[112] rates under CPR, r 44.2(6)(g), tend to be between 1 per cent and 3 per cent above base rate.[113] It is always possible for a party to displace the 'rule of thumb' by adducing evidence and the rate charged to a receiving party who has actually borrowed money may be relevant, but is not determinative.[114]

No 'eggshell skull' principle There is a limit to the extent to which the court will take into account the receiving party's circumstances, at least in so far as commercial claims are concerned. In this regard, Davies LJ has explained that the 'eggshell skull' principle[115] ought not to apply.[116] There are several cases that illustrate this point. The first is a commercial case in which the litigation had been funded by loans in which—in contrast to the way in which Sharpe LJ had dealt with disbursement funding loans in a non-commercial setting (see 56.79)[117]—Davis LJ found that it was not right to pass on the loan rate to the paying party, not least because this would come close to allowing costs that are irrecoverable on principle (that is, the costs of funding by way of bridging loans).[118] The second example is a case in which the receiving party's *business* was financed through loans with heavy interest in which, unsurprisingly, Floyd J found that it would be unfair to pass that rate on to the paying party.[119] In a third and final example, Mann J commented that paying parties should not be required to pay rates that are based on related-party lending.[120] **56.73**

[109] See *F & C Alternative Investments (Holdings) Ltd & Ors v Barthelemy* [2012] EWCA Civ 843, at [98(4)].

[110] *Jones v Secretary of State for Energy and Climate Change* [2014] EWCA Civ 363, at [18], *per* Sharp LJ. See also *Mehjoo v Harben Barker (a firm) & Anor* [2013] EWHC 1669 (QB), at [83], in which Silber J allowed 2 per cent above base rate to a receiving party who was a businessman, but who was suing on his own account (ie not on behalf of a large company).

[111] *Jones v Secretary of State for Energy and Climate Change* [2014] EWCA Civ 363, at [18], *per* Sharp LJ. In a case in which the receiving party was a medium-sized enterprise, for example, Mann J allowed 3 per cent above base rate until February 2009 and 2.5 per cent from that date: *Sycamore Bidco Ltd v Breslin* [2013] EWHC 583 (Ch), at [72].

[112] See Tomlinson LJ's comments in *F & C Alternative Investments (Holdings) Ltd & Ors v Barthelemy* [2012] EWCA Civ 843, at [105].

[113] See, eg, *Ahmed v Jura* [2002] EWCA Civ 210, in which a rate of 3 per cent above base rate was allowed. Waller LJ has said that the practice of the Commercial Court is to allow a rate of 1 per cent above base, but that the rate can be varied up or even down to meet the justice of the situation: see *Bim Kemi AB v Blackburn Chemicals Ltd* [2003] EWCA Civ 889, at [18].

[114] *Jones v Secretary of State for Energy and Climate Change* [2014] EWCA Civ 363, at [17], *per* Sharp LJ.

[115] This is the principle that unexpected frailty of a person who is entitled to damages is not a valid defence to the seriousness of any injury caused to them.

[116] See *F & C Alternative Investments (Holdings) Ltd & Ors v Barthelemy* [2012] EWCA Civ 843, at [98(4)], *per* Davis LJ.

[117] *Jones v Secretary of State for Energy and Climate Change* [2014] EWCA Civ 363, at [25].

[118] See *F & C Alternative Investments (Holdings) Ltd & Ors v Barthelemy* [2012] EWCA Civ 843, at [98(3)].

[119] See *Research in Motion UK Ltd v Visto Corpn* [2008] EWHC 819 (Pat), at [68]–[72], in which Floyd J relied upon *Tate & Lyle Industries Ltd v Greater London Council* [1982] 1 WLR 149.

[120] *Sycamore Bidco Ltd v Breslin* [2013] EWHC 583 (Ch), at [72].

Specific types of receiving party

56.74 *Large businesses* Unless it would be unfair to make such an award, 'first-class borrowers' generally recover interest at base rate *plus* 1 per cent.[121] The same is usually true for any business that could be expected to have access to capital markets.[122] If no evidence is offered on the point, an allowance of 1 per cent above base rate is likely to be made.[123]

56.75 *Government bodies* Unless there is evidence to show the contrary, government bodies tend to be treated as if they were large businesses.[124]

56.76 *Small-to-medium-sized enterprises and ordinary commercial concerns* A rate of 2 per cent above base rate is often allowed for ordinary commercial concerns.[125] In a case in which the receiving party was a medium-sized business, for example, Mann J allowed 3 per cent above base rate until February 2009 and 2.5 per cent thereafter.[126]

56.77 *Small businesses* A higher rate might be appropriate is where the receiving party is a small business. In this regard, Waller LJ cited with approval the following judgment of Rix LJ:

> 'It is right that the defendants who have kept small businessmen out of money to which a court ultimately judges them to be entitled should pay a rate which properly reflects the cost of borrowing by such a class of businessmen. The law should be prepared to recognise, as I suspect the evidence might well reveal, that the borrowing costs generally incurred by them are well removed from the conventional rate of 1% above base, (and sometimes even less) available to first class borrowers.'[127]

56.78 Waller LJ went on to imply that evidence of actual (rather than hypothetical) expenditure would be required if a significantly higher rate were to be sought—that it would be insufficient for a receiving party merely to adduce evidence of what *might* have been charged if they had borrowed to fund the litigation. He had this to say:

> 'The question is whether the evidence in this case demonstrates that a rate greater than 1% above base rate should be applied. Evidence of what a bank might have charged *if* money had been borrowed is not we think sufficient. It is not clear to us what takes [the receiving party] outside the norm to which the 1% above base rate presumption applies.'[128]

---

[121] Whilst *obiter*, see *Jones v Secretary of State for Energy and Climate Change* [2014] EWCA Civ 363, at [18], *per* Sharp LJ.

[122] That said, see HM Courts & Tribunals Service, *Commercial Court Guide* (London: HMSO, 2014), para J14.1, cited with approval by Sharp LJ in *Jones v Secretary of State for Energy and Climate Change* [2014] EWCA Civ 363, at [18].

[123] See, eg, *D Pride and Partners v Institute for Animal Health* [2009] EWHC 1617 (QB), at [76], *per* Tugendhat J.

[124] See, eg, *ibid*, at [75] and [76].

[125] See, eg, *Mehjoo v Harben Barker (a firm)* [2013] EWHC 1669 (QB), at [81]–[83], in which Silber J found that a rate of 2 per cent above base rate was a suitable mid-point considering the rates allowed by other judges in other cases. Silber J referred to and relied upon *Brown v KMR Services* [1995] 2 Lloyd's Rep 513 and *Eron Park Ltd v Secretary of State for Environment* [2001] 3 ELR 133, both of which were cases in which an allowance of 2 per cent above base rate was allowed.

[126] *Sycamore Bidco Ltd v Breslin* [2013] EWHC 583 (Ch), at [72].

[127] *Bim Kemi AB v Blackburn Chemicals Ltd* [2003] EWCA Civ 889, at [18], quoting from *Jaura v Ahmed* [2002] EWCA Civ 210, at [26]. *Jaura* was a case concerning damages, but Waller LJ obviously thought that it was analogous on this point.

[128] *Bim Kemi AB v Blackburn Chemicals Ltd* [2003] EWCA Civ 889, at [18], emphasis original.

A rate of 3 per cent above base rate is often awarded if the receiving party is a small business.[129]

Private individuals Sharp LJ has confirmed that where the receiving party is an individual who has made use of a disbursement funding loan, the court is at liberty to take into account and, if appropriate, allow the rate as chargeable under the loan agreement (which, on the facts of the case before her, was 4 per cent above base rate).[130] Some commentators have criticised the decision at first instance on the basis that it putatively places the burden of funding on paying parties;[131] they point to other cases in which the court was careful not to allow the full amount of incurred interest, as that would come perilously close to allowing the costs of funding.[132] Perhaps the correct analysis is that CRI is an adjectival remedy rather than a substantive right, and that whilst the court is not able to *allow* costs (that is, items of expenditure) that go solely to funding, there is no reason why, in an appropriate case, that expenditure cannot be taken into account for the purposes of dealing with interest. The amount actually expended would, presumably, act as a cap. **56.79**

Persons who have entered into conditional fee agreements Warren J has confirmed that the power to award CRI may be exercised even if the receiving party has entered into a conditional fee agreement, in the sense that interest may be awarded by reference to costs actually paid in the period before such an agreement was entered into.[133] **56.80**

Funding by a person other than the receiving party personally Akenhead J has confirmed that it is open to the court to allow interest notwithstanding the fact that the costs were incurred by a successful party's insurers rather than by that party themselves.[134] It does not necessarily follow that this will apply in all instances of funding by third parties: both Akenhead J[135] and Christopher Clarke J[136] have commented (*obiter*) that a party could be denied interest if they were funded on a voluntary or favourable basis. Moreover, the prohibition against the recovery of costs of funding may apply. Conventional wisdom is that it is within the court's discretion to set an appropriate rate, but this may not be correct (see 56.70). **56.81**

Doomed persons It may be appropriate to award CRI in cases in which the paying party was doomed to be condemned in costs as a result of some event or decision.[137] **56.82**

---

129 See, eg, *F & C Alternative Investments (Holdings) Ltd & Ors v Barthelemy* [2012] EWCA Civ 843, at [82], *per* Davis LJ.

130 See *Jones v Secretary of State for Energy and Climate Change* [2014] EWCA Civ 363, at [25]; cf the approach in commercial claims such as *F & C Alternative Investments (Holdings) Ltd & Ors v Barthelemy* [2012] EWCA Civ 843, at [98(3)], *per* Davis LJ.

131 See Anon, 'High Court Ruling Passes Cost of Disbursement Funding to Defendant', *Litigation Futures*, 15 May 2013.

132 See, in particular, *F & C Alternative Investments (Holdings) Ltd & Ors v Barthelemy* [2012] EWCA Civ 843, at [98(3)], in which Davis LJ said this: 'Further … costs of funding litigation by way of bridging loans are not ordinarily recoverable in themselves as costs of litigation: but the judge's approach comes near to having that consequence.'

133 *Re Southern Counties Fresh Foods Ltd, Cobden Investments Ltd v Romford Wholesale Meats Ltd* [2011] EWHC 1370 (Ch), at [112].

134 *Fosse Motor Engineers Ltd v Conde Nast and National Magazine Distributors Ltd* [2008] EWHC 2527 (QB), at [10].

135 *Ibid.*

136 *Fattal v Walbrook Trustees (Jersey) Ltd* [2009] EWHC 1674 (Ch), at [28]–[30].

137 See, eg, *Dupont Nutrition Biosciences ApS V Novozymes A/S* [2013] EWHC 483 (Pat), at [28]–[29] and [33]–[34], *per* Floyd J.

Enhanced Rate Interest

Jurisdiction

56.83 Where judgment is entered against the defendant that is at least as advantageous to the claimant as the proposals contained in that claimant's Part 36 offer, the court may make an award of ERI on the claimant's costs from the date on which the relevant period expired. The rate must not exceed 10 per cent above base rate. This topic is discussed further at 56.90–56.100; claimants' Part 36 offers, in general, are addressed in Chapter 17. The court will make such an award unless it considers it to be unjust to do so (see 17.118–17.161).[138]

56.84 In practical terms, this is one of the most important powers relating to interest on costs, but it is also the most difficult to pin down in terms of its jurisdictional origin. It seems likely that such an award has at its jurisdictional core the same provisions that relate to PRI (see 56.08–56.54), but this analysis gives rise to tensions because the CPR prescribe a rate that is not the same as that which is allowable under those provisions.[139]

56.85 It has been argued that ERI is awarded under a different *vires* (such as under the general powers conferred by s 51 of the Senior Courts Act 1981 or the CPR generally, or both), but—in the analogous context of CRI payable under CPR, r 44.2(6)(g)—Lord Neuberger MR rejected that argument, saying:

> 'The defendant contends the [the Civil Procedure Act 1997] Act represented a wholly new source of authority for making rules for the County Court, including rules with regard to the payment of interest on sums of money awarded by the court, including costs. I cannot accept that. Section 1 of the 1997 Act states that the CPR should govern the "practice and procedure" in the English civil courts. This does not suggest that they were intended to empower those courts to have the substantive power to award interest ... My view is supported by CPR 40.8(1) itself, which states in terms that the powers which it confers derive not from the 1997 Act, but from the 1838 Act in the High Court and from the 1984 Act in the County Court.'[140]

Thus it seems, by analogy, that the power to award ERI is a species of the power to award PRI (see 56.08–56.54), but it is not clear how this can be reconciled with the fact that the court will routinely allow an enhanced rate that is different from the prescribed rate.

56.86 These points may be of academic interest, but in practice they are of little relevance. This is because the notion of ERI is so ingrained that it is close to inconceivable that the court would find that it lacked the power to make such an award. That said, the points made previously about the County Court do need to be made again (see 56.16–56.17).

---

[138] CPR, r 36.14(3).

[139] See, eg, *McPhilemy v Times Newspapers Ltd & Ors (No 2)* [2001] EWCA Civ 933, at [24], in which Chadwick LJ refused to allow the then provisions concerning interest payable, where a claimant had beaten his own Part 36 offer, to interfere with the rate prescribed for judgment debt interest.

[140] *Simcoe v Jacuzzi UK Group Plc* [2012] EWCA Civ 137, at [24].

No ERI arising out of Part 36 offers made by defendants

Coulson J has explained that there is no corresponding express power to award ERI to a defendant who has 'beaten' their own offer.[141] 56.87

The date on which interest begins to run

Where ERI is awarded[142] pursuant to CPR, r 36.14(3)(c), it is awarded from the date of the expiry of the 'relevant period', as defined in CPR, r 36.3(c).[143] The court will not be bound to make such an order if it considers it would be unjust to do so, which means that the court is able to defer the effect of a claimant's Part 36 offer.[144] 56.88

In considering whether it would be unjust to make such an order, the court will take into account all of the circumstances of the case, including: 56.89

- the terms of any Part 36 offer;
- the stage in the proceedings at which any Part 36 offer was made—in particular, how long before the trial started the offer was made;
- the information available to the parties at the time when the Part 36 offer was made; and
- the conduct of the parties with regard to giving, or refusing to give, information for the purposes of enabling the offer to be made or evaluated.[145]

A claimant will not necessarily be deprived of ERI merely because their conduct can be criticised.[146]

The rate of interest and discretion as to rate generally

The decision as to whether to make an award of ERI and the decision as to what rate to allow are separate stages. 56.90

The enhancement is limited such that the rate must not exceed 10 per cent above base rate.[147] Where the court awards ERI and also awards interest on the same sum and for the same period under any other power, the total rate of interest must not exceed 10 per cent above base rate.[148] 56.91

Vos C had the following points to make (here paraphrased). 56.92

- The specified rate of 10 per cent is not a starting point, but the maximum possible enhancement.[149]

---

141 *J Murphy & Sons Ltd v Johnson Precast Ltd (No 2) (Costs)* [2008] EWHC 3104 (TCC), at [38]–[40], citing (in relation to the 'old' Part 36) *Excelsior Commercial Industrial Holdings Ltd v Salisbury Hammer Aspden and Johnston* [2002] EWCA Civ 879, at [18], *per* Lord Woolf.

142 It is worth noting here that it is arguable that the power to make an award under CPR, r 36.14(3)(c), does not exist in the County Court and its hearing centres (see 51.11).

143 This is the effect of CPR, r 36.15(3)(b) and (c).

144 As an example of this, see *Epsom College v Pierse Contracting Southern Ltd (formerly Biseley Construction Ltd) (in liquidation)* [2011] EWCA Civ 1449, at [67], *per* Rix LJ.

145 CPR, r 36.14(4).

146 See, eg, *Crema v Cenkos Securities plc* [2011] EWCA Civ 10, in which the claimant had taken a number of time-wasting points and was awarded only 75 per cent of his costs. Notwithstanding this, he was still entitled to enhanced interest.

147 See CPR, r 36.14(3)(a) and (3)(c).

148 See CPR, r 36.14(5).

149 See *OMV Petrom SA v Glencore International AG* [2017] EWCA Civ 195, at [31].

- The objective of the rule has always been, in large measure, to encourage good practice and hence a party who has behaved unreasonably forfeits the opportunity of achieving a reduction in the rate of enhanced interest.[150]
- The whole thrust of the CPR after the Jackson reforms is 'to use both the carrot and the stick'.[151]

56.93 Vos C has explained that the court will take into account all of the relevant circumstances at both the stage of deciding whether to make an award of ERI and at the stage of deciding what that rate should be.[152] He went on to make the following comments:

> 'I accept that those circumstances may include, for example, (a) the length of time that elapsed between the deadline for accepting the offer and judgment, (b) whether the defendant took entirely bad points or whether it had behaved reasonably in continuing the litigation, despite the offer, to pursue its defence, and (c) what general level of disruption can be seen, without a detailed inquiry, to have been caused to the claimant as a result of the refusal to negotiate or to accept the Part 36 offer.'[153]

56.94 Vos C made these points in the context of deciding the rate to be payable on damages. He made the point that different factors may be relevant in so far as the rate payable on costs is concerned—in particular, that account may need to be taken of how the costs were incurred.[154] On the facts of the case before him, he ultimately treated the two species of interest as the same, but it should be borne in mind that this will by no means always be appropriate. In the context of a case in which the costs claimed were so high as to cause him to refer to the funding arrangements as 'grotesque', Jackson LJ implied that the court would be able to look at the total effect of the interest and to disallow or reduce the same if that total would give rise to an unjust burden falling upon the paying party.[155]

56.95 Whilst Vos C stressed that it would by no means be automatic that the maximum award of ERI would be appropriate, on the (unusual) facts of the case before him, he allowed that maximum award, in which regard the following factors were relevant:

- the defendant's refusal to engage in settlement discussions or to respond to the Part 36 offer;
- the fact that the eventual award was very significantly greater than the Part 36 offer itself; and
- the defendant's 'deplorable, if not outrageous' conduct of the litigation (it being a case in which the defendant aggressively, and unsuccessfully, resisted allegations of fraud and was found to have lied).[156]

56.96 It remains to be seen whether such awards will become commonplace. Prior to Vos C's guidance, a rate of about 4–5 per cent above base rate was not an unusual rate[157] and

---

150 See *ibid*, at [32].
151 See *ibid*, at [34].
152 See *ibid*, at [38].
153 *Ibid*.
154 See *ibid*, at [43].
155 *Pankhurst v (1) White and (2) Motor Insurers Bureau* [2010] EWCA Civ 1445, at [54].
156 See *OMV Petrom SA v Glencore International AG* [2017] EWCA Civ 195, at [41].
157 See, eg, *McPhilemy v Times Newspapers (No 4)* [2001] EWCA Civ 933, at [23]. See also *Linklaters Business Services v Sir Robert Mcalpine Ltd & Ors* [2010] EWHC 3123 (TCC), at [30], in which Akenhead J allowed 5 per cent above base rate almost as a matter of course; *Crema v Cenkos Securities plc* [2011] EWCA Civ 10, at [11], *per* Aikens LJ.

perhaps this will continue to be so in cases in which there is no suggestion of bad faith or poor conduct. In a case in which only post-judgment interest was sought, Warby J allowed a rate of 10 per cent, on the basis that it was 2 per cent higher than the rate of interest that would have been payable had the offer not been made.[158]

Is ERI penal?

In *McPhilemy v Times Newspapers (No 4)*,[159] Chadwick LJ expressed certain views about the policies underpinning CPR, Part 36. Whilst those comments were often quoted in the past, Vos C has made it clear both that certain powers were not drawn to Chadwick LJ's attention and that, in any event, the culture of litigation has changed since those early days of the CPR.[160] Vos C went on to explain that whilst awards of ERI were perhaps not best described as penal, they were not limited to mere compensatory awards. In this regard, he had the following to say: **56.97**

> '[The] use of the word "penal" to describe the award of enhanced rate interest under CPR Part 36.14(3)(a) is probably unhelpful. The court undoubtedly has a discretion to include a non-compensatory element to the award . . ., but the level of interest awarded must be proportionate to the circumstances of the case.'[161]

In addition, Vos C went on to say this: **56.98**

> 'But there will be many factors that may be relevant. All cases will be different. Just as the court is required to have regard to "all the circumstances of the case" in deciding whether it would be unjust to make all or any of the four possible orders in the first place, it must have regard to all the circumstances of the case in deciding what rate of interest to award . . . [The] power is one intended to achieve a fairer result for the claimant. That does not, however, imply that the rate of interest can only be compensatory. In some cases, a proportionate rate will have to be greater than purely compensatory to provide the appropriate incentive to defendants to engage in reasonable settlement discussions and mediation aimed at achieving a compromise, to settle litigation at a reasonable level and at a reasonable time, and to mark the court's disapproval of any unreasonable or improper conduct, as Briggs LJ put the matter, *pour encourager les autres*.'[162]

Vos C also said that if the rulemakers had intended to say that all or any of the awards were to be made only if they represented compensation for litigation inconvenience, it would have been very easy for them to do so.[163] He also said that if it were right to say that the provision for additional interest was entirely compensatory, the 10 per cent cap would only rarely be engaged and that, in any event, such an approach would lead to undesirable satellite litigation.[164] He went on to note the fact that the Jackson reforms undoubtedly introduced a penal award of up to £75,000 as an additional amount (see 17.81), and that the Final Report expressly stated that Part 36 was to be 'backed up by a scheme of penalties and rewards in order to encourage the making of reasonable settlement offers and the acceptance of such offers'.[165] **56.99**

---

158 *Barkhuysen v Hamilton* [2016] EWHC 3371 (QB), at [19].
159 *McPhilemy v Times Newspapers (No 4)* [2001] EWCA Civ 933, at [23].
160 See *OMV Petrom SA v Glencore International AG* [2017] EWCA Civ 195, at [39].
161 See *ibid*, at [38].
162 See *ibid*, at [38].
163 See *ibid*, at [33].
164 See *ibid*, at [36].
165 See *ibid*, at [37], in which Vos C referred to Jackson, R, *Review of Civil Litigation Costs: Final Report* (London: HMSO, 2010), ch 41, para 1.1.

56.100 For all of these reasons, it is now clear that awards of ERI are not limited purely to compensatory awards. Cases decided before Vos C's guidance (in May 2017) may therefore need to be viewed with some caution, because they may have been made on an incorrect footing.

Special Situations

Deemed costs orders

56.101 Deemed costs orders will arise on acceptance of a Part 36 offer, on discontinuance of a claim and where a claim is struck out for non-payment of fees (see 7.103–7.140).[166]

56.102 CPR, r 44.9(4), provides:

> 'Interest payable under section 17 of the Judgments Act 1838 or section 74 of the County Courts Act 1984 on the costs deemed to have been ordered under paragraph (1) will begin to run from the date on which the event which gave rise to the entitlement to costs occurred.'

Thus interest will run from the date of acceptance, discontinuance or striking out. This provision reverses the effect of a ruling in the House of Lords in which their Lordships rejected the notion that interest should be payable upon acceptance of monies paid into court notwithstanding the absence of an order entitling the offeree to costs.[167] It should be noted that CPR, r 44.9(1)(b)—upon which CPR, r 44.9(4), relies—refers to acceptance of Part 36 offer under CPR, r 36.13, only; it makes no mention of acceptance under CPR, rr 36.20 or 36.21. One could argue that it was an intentional omission to ensure that no more than fixed costs were paid, but this would mean that a party who was bound to pay costs would not pay interest on delayed payment of such costs, which would be a curious outcome. Perhaps the better interpretation is that the failure to refer to CPR, rr 36.20 or 36.21, was merely an oversight.

Appeals and interest on costs

56.103 In a claim in which there had been a successful appeal that had reversed the costs order made in the court below, Waller LJ held that interest on the costs of the ultimately successful party should ordinarily run from the date of the original costs order, rather than from the date of the order on appeal.[168] In addition to having all of the powers of the lower court,[169] a court hearing an appeal has an express and specific power to make an order for interest.[170] It is possible that this power goes more to interest on damages than to interest on costs, but, notwithstanding this, it is easily arguable that its wording captures interest on both damages and costs.

56.104 Likewise, where a party is entitled to recoup costs that have been overpaid, they may be entitled to interest (see below).

---

166 CPR, r 44.9(2).
167 *Legal Aid Board v Russell* [1991] 2 AC 317.
168 *Bim Kemi AB v Blackburn Chemicals Ltd* [2003] EWCA Civ 889.
169 See CPR, r 52.10(1).
170 See CPR, r 52.10(2)(d), which reads: 'The appeal court has power to make orders for the payment of interest.'

Interest on overpaid costs

Where a party is found to have overpaid costs to an opponent, the court has the jurisdiction to award interest on that overpayment.[171] 56.105

This jurisdiction to make such an award is found in CPR, r 44.2(6)(g). It is, however, worth mentioning the pre-CPR position, because this was an example of one of the very limited exceptions to the general rule that interest on costs—or, more accurately, monies very similar to interest—are payable only pursuant to statute. Lord Nicholls dealt with the issue in this way: 56.106

> 'This has given rise to the question whether, when ordering repayment, the House has jurisdiction to award interest on the money ordered to be repaid. I am in no doubt that the answer to this question is "Yes". The court has no general, inherent power to order the payment of interest. But the situation now under consideration is not directed at requiring a defendant against whom the plaintiff has a cause of action to pay interest on money to which the plaintiff's cause of action entitles him. Nor is it directed at requiring him to pay interest on unpaid costs. Rather, when ordering repayment the House is unravelling the practical consequences of orders made by the courts below and duly carried out by the unsuccessful party. The result of the appeal to this House was that, to the extent indicated, orders made in the courts below should not have been made. This result could, in some cases, be an idle exercise unless the House were able to make consequential orders which achieve, as nearly as is reasonably practicable, the restitution which this result requires. This requires that the House should have power to order repayment of money paid over pursuant to an order which is subsequently set aside. It also requires that in suitable cases the House should have power to award interest on amounts ordered to be repaid. Otherwise the unravelling would be partial only.'[172]

It is possible that this jurisdiction continues to exist. That said, given the powers under CPR, r 44.2(6)(g), there would never be any need to rely upon it; that said, Lord Nicholls' guidance would continue to be relevant to the issue of discretion.

Awards are usually made on the basis of simple interest.[173] 56.107

Advance and multiple orders for costs

It is not uncommon for orders for costs to be made at different times. An example would be where there has been a split trial on liability and quantum, and separate costs orders have been made in respect of each. Less commonly, a party might become entitled to costs before those costs have been incurred, such as where a party is given permission to appeal on a point of general principle, but on the condition that the party would bear the costs of the appeal in any event. 56.108

Difficulties can arise in such circumstances: not only may there be a dispute about which order should be the subject of the *incipitur* rule, but also a strict application of the *incipitur* rule can lead to injustice. The solution lies in CPR, r 44.2(6)(g), which affords the court the flexibility to make an order that meets the justice of the situation. 56.109

---

[171] *Bim Kemi AB v Blackburn Chemicals Ltd* [2003] EWCA Civ 889, at [18].

[172] *Nykredit Mortgage Bank plc v Edward Erdman Group Ltd (No 2)* [1997] 1 WLR 1627, at 1636.

[173] If the jurisdiction mentioned at 56.106 continues to exist, it would be possible to construct an argument that compound interest should apply (see 56.126). There is no authority for this, however.

56.110 An example of the problems that may arise can be found in *Powell v Herefordshire Health Authority*,[174] a claim in tort in which liability had been agreed (together with an entitlement to costs) in 1994. The case did not settle until 2001. If interest had been permitted to run from 1994, not only would the claim for interest have been almost as great as the principal costs, but also interest would have been payable on costs that had yet to be incurred. The costs judge's attention had not been drawn to CPR, r 44.2(6)(g), and he consequently felt constrained to allow interest in full (that is, from 1994); the Court of Appeal found this to be unjust. In allowing the appeal, Kay LJ made the following comments:

> 'There was ... no need in law for [the costs judge] to find himself in the legal straightjacket that the parties had suggested. He had a discretion which enabled him to look at the dates when the costs had been incurred, and to come to a conclusion in relation to the payments of interest that fitted the justice of the circumstances of the particular case.'[175]

56.111 Practice Direction (PD) 47 provides that where the bill of costs includes costs payable under an order or orders in respect of which the receiving party wishes to claim interest from different dates, the bill of costs should be divided to enable such interest to be calculated.[176]

Interest payable out of a fund

56.112 In *Wills v Crown Estate Commissioners*,[177] Peter Smith J considered the issue of whether the court should make an award of interest where costs were payable out of a fund (as opposed to where costs were payable as a result of an adversarial order).

56.113 Peter Smith J confirmed that the 19th-century cases of *A-G v Nethercote*[178] and *Re Marsdens Estate*[179] remained good law, and that it would be wrong to interpret the former as limited to the administration of estates. This means that interest is not normally payable on costs to be paid out of a fund:

> 'It is quite clear that whenever there are funds, out of which costs are paid, there is not an order which attracts interest. The reason for that is that there is not an order of the court in adversarial litigation.'[180]

Thus interest is not generally payable on such costs.

Interest on the costs of assessment

56.114 The pre-CPR position was that interest on the costs of assessment was payable from the date on which the receiving party was awarded the costs that are the subject of the assessment.[181] This is no longer the case, however, because CPR, r 47.20(6), makes the following provisions: 'Unless the court otherwise orders, interest on the costs of detailed assessment proceedings will run from the date of default, interim or final costs certificate, as the case

[174] *Powell v Herefordshire Health Authority* [2002] EWCA Civ 1786.
[175] *Ibid*, at [13].
[176] See PD 47, para 5.8(6).
[177] *Wills v Crown Estate Commissioners* [2003] EWHC 1718 (Ch).
[178] *A-G v Nethercote* (1841) 11 SIM 529.
[179] *Re Marsdens Estate* (1889) 40 Ch D 475.
[180] *Wills v Crown Estate Commissioners* [2003] EWHC 1718 (Ch), at [19], *per* Peter Smith J.
[181] *Ross v Bowbelle (Owners)* [1997] 1 WLR 1159.

may be.' Interest on the costs of the detailed assessment will therefore tend to run from the date of the relevant default, interim or final costs certificate.

Enhanced rate interest may apply if a receiving party 'beats' their own Part 36 offer, be that an offer made during the substantive litigation[182] or an offer made in the assessment.[183] The principles set out at 43.345 will be relevant. **56.115**

Interest Payable Pursuant to Contract, as Damages, etc

The issue of costs (that is, expenses incurred in paying lawyers, experts, court fees, etc) payable as damages is addressed at 3.38–3.47. Similarly, the issue of costs payable under a contract is addressed at 66.02–66.34. Where costs are payable as damages or as debt, interest may also be payable. **56.116**

It is not always obvious whether legal fees should be regarded as costs or damages. This is a question that will depend on the circumstances (see 3.38–3.47). The relevance of this seemingly arcane point is that it may (albeit rarely) determine the basis upon which interest is calculated. Interest payable on costs as damages or a costs debt differs from the other types of interest referred to in this chapter, in that it is possible for interest to be recoverable *as* damages or debt, as opposed to *on* costs as damages or a costs debt, which means that—in theory—compound interest may be payable (see 56.126). Three situations are worth examining: **56.117**

- where costs are payable as a contractual debt (see 56.118);
- where costs are payable as damages arising out of breach of contract (see 56.119–56.120); and
- where costs are payable as damages arising out of some tortious act or omission (see 56.121).

Costs payable under contract as a debt

It may be that a party is contractually obliged to pay costs. This may be a requirement to pay another person's lawyer directly for legal services,[184] but, more often than not, it is a requirement to provide an indemnity for costs. That contract may or may not make provision for interest to be payable in the event of late payment. Where such provision exists, then the court will usually determine the incidence and rate of interest in accordance with the terms of the contract (see 66.04–66.07).[185] That interest will be payable as a debt. Where both of the parties are businesses and where there is no other enactment that provides for the payment of interest, then the Late Payments of Commercial Debts (Interest) Act 1998 (as amended on 16 March 2013 by the Late Payment of Commercial Debts Regulations 2013) may apply (see 38.97–38.102). Where the contract contains no provisions for late payment and where the 1998 Act does not apply (which will always be the case if one or more of the parties was not acting as a 'business'), then, in the absence of some specific provision relating to the type of contract in question, no interest will be **56.118**

[182] See CPR, r 36.49(4)(c).
[183] See CPR, r 36.49(4)(a).
[184] An example of this is the government compensation schemes relating to miners, most of which provide for fixed payments to certain nominated solicitors.
[185] *Gomba Holdings Ltd v Minories Finance Ltd (No 2)* [1993] Ch 171.

payable as of right. Discretionary interest may, however, be payable under s 35A(1) of the Senior Courts Act 1981 or, in the County Court, under s 69(1) of the County Courts Act 1984.[186] Where the contract in question is a contract of retainer between a solicitor and a client, then special rules may apply (see 38.86–38.102).

Costs payable as damages for breach of contract

56.119 It may be that, by reason of a counterparty's failure to perform its obligations under a contract, it has put the other counterparty to the expense of incurring legal fees and associated expenses (see 3.42–3.43).[187] An example would be where a contract concerning development of a property provided that party A was obtaining certain consents; if party A were to fail to discharge that obligation, then party B would be forced to engage solicitors to obtain those consents. The fees and expenses that party B would have to pay would not be costs of the claim (not least because they would be non-contentious), but it is possible that they would be damages (see 3.42–3.43). There are limits to what can be recovered, however: the losses must 'fairly and reasonably be considered [to arise] naturally'—that is, according to the usual course of things'[188]—or they must 'reasonably be supposed to have been in the contemplation of both parties at the time they made the contract'.[189] It used to be thought that the first of these mechanisms (that is, 'arising naturally') would not extend to include recovery of interest as damages,[190] but this is no longer the case (see 56.126–56.128). Thus, in the example above, if the developer had to take out a funding loan for the purposes of obtaining consents, then interest may well be recoverable as damages.

56.120 It may be that, for whatever reason, costs are recoverable as damages, but interest is not. In the example above, this might be the case if party B funded the solicitors itself rather than by means of a funding load. If so, then s 35A(1) of the Senior Courts Act 1981 (or, in the County Court, s 69(1) of the County Courts Act 1984) would apply, in which case the court would have discretion to make an award of interest on the damages (as opposed to awarding interest as damages). For practical purposes, the difference between recovery of interest *as* damages and recovery of interest *on* damages is that the former may, in certain circumstances, be compound, whereas the latter is always simple (see 56.126).

Tort

56.121 Similar situations may arise where a tort has been committed. That said, other than the recovery of costs of mitigation in professional negligence claims and recovery of costs incurred in other jurisdictions, recovery of costs as damages in tortious claims is a rarity. The recovery of interest will be under s 35A(1) of the Senior Courts Act 1981 (or, in the County Court, s 69(1) of the County Courts Act 1984).

---

[186] Law Reform (Miscellaneous Provisions) Act 1934, s 3, continues to apply to other courts of record.

[187] An example would be where costs in foreign proceedings are claimed as damages or where non-contentious costs are claimed as damages. Whilst not all of the following relate to breach of contract, see, eg, *Berry v British Transport Commission* [1961] 3 All ER 65; *Seavision Investment SA v Norman Thomas Evennett, The Tiburon* [1992] 2 Lloyd's Rep 26; *British Racing Drivers' Club Ltd v Hextall Erskine & Co (a firm)* [1996] 3 All ER 667; *Union Discount Co Ltd v Zoller (Costs)* [2001] EWCA Civ 1755.

[188] See *Hadley v Baxendale* [1843–60] All ER Rep 461, at 465, *per* Alderson B. See also *Peak Construction (Liverpool) Ltd v McKinney Foundation* (1970) 1 Build LR 111; *Hutchinson v Harris* [1978] 10 BLR 19, at 39.

[189] See *Hadley v Baxendale* [1843–60] All ER Rep 461, at 465, *per* Alderson B.

[190] *London, Chatham and Dover Railway Co v South Eastern Railway Co* [1893] AC 429.

The Late Payment of Commercial Debts (Interest) Act 1998

From the point of view of costs between opposing parties, it will almost never be the case that the Late Payment of Commercial Debts (Interest) Act 1998 will apply, because it will apply only to a contract for the supply of goods or services under which the purchaser and the supplier are each acting in the course of a business.[191] **56.122**

Pursuant to the equitable jurisdiction of the court

Interest may be awarded in respect of equitable remedies such as the taking of an account. Interest may also be awarded where money has been obtained by fraud or misapplication by someone in a fiduciary position. **56.123**

The practical relevance of this jurisdiction is that, in cases of fraud or misapplication by someone in a fiduciary position, it is commonly the case that the court will make an award of compound interest.[192] Whilst there is no authority on the point, there is no reason why the same should not apply where a party pays interest because it has obtained costs (or avoided paying them) fraudulently. **56.124**

Interest in arbitrations

Section 49 of the Arbitration Act 1996 specifically permits the award of compound interest. The London Maritime Arbitrators Association reported to the Law Commission that (in respect of damages) it was 'the general practice' to award compound interest 'quite simply because it seems commercially just to do so'.[193] Whether the same applies to awards of costs is not known. **56.125**

Compound interest

It used to be thought that there was no power to make an award of compound interest other than in cases of fraud or misapplication (see 56.124).[194] This was because there was no statutory provision for interest to be compounded. The law has now been clarified in such a way that there is the possibility of awards being made of compound interest (albeit not in respect of awards made under statute). **56.126**

Lord Nicholls explained the reasoning behind that line of thinking in the following way: **56.127**

> 'Legal rules which are not soundly based resemble proverbial bad pennies: they turn up again and again. The unsound rule returning once more for consideration by your Lordships' House concerns the negative attitude of English law to awards of compound interest on claims for debts paid late.'[195]

---

[191] Late Payment of Commercial Debts (Interest) Act 1998, s 2(1). Furthermore, a debt does not carry (and shall be treated as never having carried) statutory interest if, or to the extent that, a right to demand interest on it, which exists by virtue of any rule of law, is exercised: see Late Payment of Commercial Debts (Interest) Act 1998, s 3(2) and (3).

[192] See *Black v Davies* [2005] EWCA Civ 531, at [87]; *Westdeutsche Landesbank Girozentrale v Islington London Borough Council* [1996] AC 669. That said, compound interest may be awarded in situations that do not involve fraud or misapplication: see *Sempra Metals Ltd (formerly Metallgesellschaft Ltd) v Inland Revenue Commissioners & Anor* [2007] UKHL 34.

[193] Law Commission, *Pre-judgment Interest of Debts and Damages*, Law Com No 287 (23 February 2004), fn 51.

[194] This is not the case in arbitrations: see Arbitration Act 1996, s 49.

[195] *Sempra Metals Ltd (formerly Metallgesellschaft Ltd) v Inland Revenue Commissioners & Anor* [2007] UKHL 34, at [51].

He added:

> 'We live in a world where interest payments for the use of money are calculated on a compound basis. Money is not available commercially on simple interest terms. This is the daily experience of everyone, whether borrowing money on overdrafts or credit cards or mortgages or shopping around for the best rates when depositing savings with banks or building societies. If the law is to achieve a fair and just outcome when assessing financial loss it must recognise and give effect to this reality.'[196]

56.128 It remains to be seen whether these sentiments will result in changes being made to statute.

[196] *Ibid*, at [52].

57

CONDUCT AND MISCONDUCT, AND THE QUANTUM OF COSTS

This chapter deals with the following topics: **57.01**

- conduct as one of the 'seven pillars' (57.02);
- conduct in general (57.05);
- pre-issue conduct and pre-action protocols (57.08);
- exaggeration and the amount of costs (57.18);
- misconduct (57.37):
  - under CPR, r 44.11(1)(a) (57.38);
  - under CPR, r 44.11(1)(b) (57.42); and
  - procedural matters relating to misconduct (57.61).

It should be noted that this chapter does not deal with conduct in the context of the incidence of costs. That topic is addressed at 6.76 *et seq*.

Conduct as One of the 'Seven Pillars'

Even the most quotidian of assessments will, in some way or another, take into account the conduct of the parties. Their behaviour—and how it bore the burden of being litigants—will be a relevant factor, even if unremarkable. Indeed, this is one of the factors that distinguishes an assessment from a mere exercise of accounting. **57.02**

The Civil Procedure Rules (CPR) afford conduct the status of being first among the 'seven pillars'—of which there are now eight (see 25.26). Indeed, CPR, r 44.4(3)(a), bolsters that first pillar in the following way: **57.03**

> 'The court will ... have regard to—
> (a) the conduct of all the parties, including in particular—
> (i) conduct before, as well as during, the proceedings; and
> (ii) the efforts made, if any, before and during the proceedings in order to try to resolve the dispute.'

The ways in which conduct may be taken into account are as diverse as the ways in which parties may choose to conduct themselves, but four topics merit special attention: **57.04**

- the principles applying to conduct in general (see 57.05–57.07);
- conduct prior to the issue of the claim (known as anterior conduct) (see 57.08–57.16);
- exaggeration in the context of the assessment of costs (see 57.17–57.36); and
- misconduct (see 57.37–57.64).

It should be noted that whilst this chapter deals only with the assessment of costs, there is a certain degree of overlap with the way in which the court takes conduct into account when determining the incidence of costs (see 6.77–6.155). In particular, the matters set out at 6.87–6.92 regarding s 57 of the Criminal Justice and Courts Act 2015 may be relevant to both.

Conduct in General

The restraining effect of the order

57.05 For the foregoing reasons, consideration of the parties' conduct will be a central part of any detailed assessment. This is not to say, however, that the costs judge will always be permitted to take into account all aspects of the parties' behaviour, without fetter. This is because a costs order is capable of restraining a costs judge from considering certain issues. This may be so where the order expressly or impliedly imposes a constraint, where issues of double jeopardy arise or where the court concludes that the topic in question ought to have been raised at the time the order was made. These matters are addressed at 57.19 and at 57.24. It should be borne in mind that such restraints are rare: the vast majority of assessments are conducted on the basis that the costs judge is entitled to—indeed, for that matter, required to—take into account *all* relevant aspects of the parties' behaviour, without favour or constraint.

No hindsight for the purposes of considering conduct

57.06 It is trite costs law that costs should not be assessed with hindsight.[1] In particular, it would be wrong to assess the costs on the basis of the outcome of the claim in question. Thus, where a party was awarded the costs of a preliminary issue, it would be wrong in principle to assess those costs at nil solely because subsequent proceedings showed that the claim itself was misconceived.[2] This is not only because the parties would have been unaware of the outcome of the litigation at the time the costs were incurred, but also because they might not have had a clear view of the facts. Although speaking in a context other than civil litigation (namely, costs in an employment tribunal), Sir Hugh Griffiths had this to say: 'Ordinary experience of life frequently teaches us that which is plain for all to see once the dust of battle has subsided was far from clear to the combatants once they took up arms.'[3]

Which parties' conduct may be taken into account?

57.07 Whilst an obvious point, the appropriate test is the conduct of *all* of the parties, not only the paying party. It is worth bearing in mind, however, that, for the purposes of deciding whether the costs are disproportionate, CPR, r 44.3(5), refers only to 'additional work generated by the conduct of the paying party' (see 25.29). For the reasons given at 25.32, it would rarely be the case that the court would take the receiving party's conduct into account for the purposes of determining whether the costs were

---

1 *Francis v Francis and Dickerson* [1956] P 87, at 91.

2 Although it was not phrased in terms of hindsight, see Mann J's analysis in *Business Environment Bow Lane v Deanwater Estates Ltd* [2009] EWHC 2014 (Ch).

3 *E T Marler v Robertson* [1974] ICR 72, NIRC, at 77.

affirmatively proportionate, but the court is likely to be able to take it into account for the purposes of finding that the costs are disproportionate. This is similar to what happens when the court makes decisions about the incidence of costs, in which regard the fact that a receiving party has litigated unreasonably or extravagantly may well be relevant.[4]

Pre-issue Conduct and Pre-action Protocols

For reasons set out at 49.147–49.150, pre-issue costs are recoverable, but only to the extent that they are attributable to the paying party's actions or omissions. Authorities on that point often speak of 'conduct', rather than 'actions' and 'omissions', but the meaning is the same. **57.08**

The CPR specifically refer to the court having a mandatory duty to have regard both to the parties' conduct before the proceedings and to the efforts that were made to try to resolve the dispute[5] (see 57.03). This is in keeping with the emphasis on 'front-loading' costs and, in particular, is consistent with the notion that the pre-issue management of disputes will, in many cases, be governed by pre-action protocols. **57.09**

In principle, costs incurred for the purposes of complying with a pre-action protocol will be recoverable as costs of the claim.[6] Conversely, non-compliance with a pre-action protocol may result in the disallowance of costs. The following four general points can be made: **57.10**

- litigation should be seen as the option of last resort (see 57.11–57.12);
- the parties are under a duty to seek to narrow the issues (see 57.13);
- there must be cooperation in relation to certain types of disclosure (see 57.14–57.15); and
- obstructive behaviour may lead to sanctions being imposed (see 57.16–57.17).

Litigation is supposed to be the 'last resort'

Most pre-action protocols contain provisions similar to the following (which has, by way of an example, been taken from the Pre-action Protocol for Defamation): **57.11**

> 'The parties should consider whether some form of alternative dispute resolution procedure would be more suitable than litigation, and if so, endeavour to agree which form to adopt. Both the Claimant and Defendant may be required by the Court to provide evidence that alternative means of resolving their dispute were considered. The Courts take the view that litigation should be a last resort, and that claims should not be issued prematurely when a settlement is still actively being explored. Parties are warned that if the protocol is not followed (including this paragraph) then the Court must have regard to such conduct when determining costs.'[7]

Thus a failure to consider alternative dispute resolution (ADR) could result in a disallowance of costs. The protocols that contain similar provisions are those relating **57.12**

---

[4] As an example (albeit a family case), see *J v J* [2014] EWHC 3654 (Fam), in which Mostyn J limited the costs payable to an applicant because she had litigated almost as disproportionately as her opponent.

[5] CPR, r 44.4(3)(a).

[6] See the *obiter* comment of Woolf CJ in *Callery v Gray* [2001] EWCA Civ 1117, at [54(ii)].

[7] Pre-Action Protocol for Defamation, para 3.7.

to personal injury,[8] disease and illness claims,[9] clinical negligence,[10] professional negligence,[11] judicial reviews[12] and package travel claims.[13]

Pre-action conduct and narrowing the issues

57.13 One particular aspect of claims conducted under a pre-action protocol is that they afford the parties a chance to narrow the issues.[14] If the conduct of one of the parties prevents this, then that would be a factor to be taken into account.

Unreasonable delay in providing medical records

57.14 The pre-action protocols relating to clinical negligence,[15] industrial disease[16] and (by implication) package travel[17] claims provide that the court may take into account any unreasonable delay in providing medical records.

57.15 While non-compliance with the relevant pre-action protocol might lead to adverse costs consequences, so may overly rigid compliance—especially where it is used as a tactic for generating costs. The Practice Direction (Pre-Action Conduct) provides: 'The parties must not use this Practice Direction as a tactical device to secure an unfair advantage for one party or to generate unnecessary costs.'[18] That said, reasonable and proper compliance with a pre-action protocol will generally be a factor in favour of the recovery of the costs. Indeed, such compliance may even bring costs within the ambit of the costs order where otherwise they would have been beyond it.[19]

The effect of obstructive behaviour

57.16 Obstructive behaviour may be taken into account either generally (that is, as one of the 'seven pillars') or as misconduct (see 57.51). In this regard, Practice Direction (PD) 44, para 11.2, reads as follows: 'Conduct which is unreasonable or improper includes steps which are calculated to prevent or inhibit the court from furthering the overriding objective.'[20] Thus intentional non-compliance with a pre-action protocol may lead to a finding of misconduct (see 57.37–57.64).

57.17 In general, where a defendant successfully resists a claim such that a different claim is pursued when proceedings are eventually issued, the court will lack the power to award the

8 Pre-Action Protocol for Personal Injury Claims, para 2.16.

9 Pre-Action Protocol for Disease and Illness Claims, para 2A.1.

10 Pre-Action Protocol for the Resolution of Clinical Disputes, para 5.1.

11 Pre-Action Protocol for Professional Negligence, para B1.6.

12 Pre-Action Protocol for Judicial Review, para 3.1.

13 Pre-Action Protocol for the Resolution of Package Travel Claims, para 14.3.

14 See Practice Direction (Pre-Action Conduct), Annex A, para 6.1, which states: 'At the very least, it should be possible to establish what issues remain outstanding so as to narrow the scope of the proceedings and therefore limit potential costs.'

15 Pre-Action Protocol for the Resolution of Clinical Disputes, para 3.12.

16 Pre-Action Protocol for Disease and Illness Claims, para 4.5.

17 Pre-Action Protocol for the Resolution of Package Travel Claims, paras 2.2 and 7.1.

18 Practice Direction (Pre-Action Conduct), Annex A, para 6.2.

19 See *Lobster Group Ltd v Heidelberg Graphic Equipment Ltd* [2008] EWHC 1431 (TCC). This related to the costs of a failed mediation that, in an earlier judgment ([2008] EWHC 413 (TCC)), Coulson J had found were not costs that would ordinarily be costs of the proceedings.

20 CPD, art 18.3, used to refer to 'conduct before or during the proceedings'. Nothing turns on this, however, because CPR, r 44.11(1)(b), expressly refers to conduct before the proceedings as being relevant.

defendant costs in respect of the claim that was not pursued.[21] Whilst *obiter*, Coulson J has implied that where 'exceptional circumstances' exist—which, presumably, would include poor conduct—it would be possible for an award of costs to cover such a claim.[22] Whether this is so would be a matter of interpretation of the order in question.

Exaggeration and the Amount of Costs

The topic of exaggeration has already been addressed at 6.144–6.155, albeit in the context of the incidence of costs. Much of what is said there also applies to the assessment of costs. The following discussion builds on what is said in Chapter 7, but it addresses only those topics that are peculiar to the assessment of costs. In particular, it examines the mechanisms by which a costs judge may take exaggeration into account (see 57.24–57.36). It should be noted that most of what follows will apply only where the exaggeration was 'culpable exaggeration' (see 6.144–6.153), as opposed to 'innocent exaggeration' (see 6.154–6.155). Indeed, innocent exaggeration would generally have no bearing on the assessment of costs. **57.18**

Factual findings and double jeopardy

A receiving party must not be subjected to double jeopardy. In particular, if exaggeration has already been reflected in the costs order, that fact should be taken into account when assessing the costs. Whether the court will allow or disallow the costs of pursuing the exaggerated claim will be a matter of interpretation of the order (see, by analogy, 6.197–6.204). This does not mean, however, that a costs judge would necessarily disregard exaggeration that had already been reflected in the costs order. Each case will turn on its own facts and on the terms of the order for costs in question. Waller LJ, for example, has explained that where there has been dishonesty on the part of the receiving party and where that has been reflected in a percentage reduction, the natural construction of the costs order would be that the costs judge would *not* allow the costs of advancing a dishonest claim.[23] **57.19**

Much will depend on whether the costs judge is able to identify the costs that have been incurred as a result of the putative exaggeration and this may depend on what findings of fact were made by the trial judge. Gloster LJ has said that it would be unrealistic to suppose that a costs judge would be able to make disallowances if the trial judge had not made any findings of fact regarding the exaggeration.[24] She also stressed that care should be taken not to re-litigate issues that were fairly and squarely before the trial judge, and within their knowledge.[25] That said, it may be that the costs judge has access to papers that were not available to the trial judge; if those papers were to justify such a step, it would be difficult to think of a principled reason why the costs judge would not be able to make findings of fact that went further than those of the trial judge. **57.20**

Misallocation as a consequence of exaggeration

Where, through exaggeration, a claim has been allocated to a track and where, absent that exaggeration, it would have been allocated to a lesser track, the judge assessing the costs **57.21**

[21] This is because they are not incidental to the proceedings and therefore do not fall within the ambit of Senior Courts Act 1981, s 51.
[22] See *McGlinn v Waltham Contractors Ltd* [2005] EWHC 1419 (TCC), at [11].
[23] *Northstar Systems v Fielding* [2006] EWCA Civ 1660, at [33].
[24] *Walker Construction (UK) Ltd v Quayside Homes Ltd* [2014] EWCA Civ 93, at [96].
[25] *Ibid.*

may, in practice, confine the claimant to those costs to which they would have been entitled had there been no exaggeration.[26] No special order would be required in this regard. Indeed, this may even lead to costs being restricted to those that are allowed under the small claims track regime.[27] That said, in none of those situations should the costs judge directly *apply* the costs regime of the lesser track; rather, the judge would merely be entitled to take that regime into account when determining the reasonableness of the costs incurred (see 50.396–50.399).[28] The distinction between these two approaches may be very fine.

Exaggeration in the context of an opponent's non-disclosure

57.22 Where a receiving party is accused of exaggeration, it may be the case that the paying party had within its powers the means to put an end to the receiving party's deception by, for example, disclosing surveillance evidence. Jonathan Parker LJ said that, in the absence of special circumstances (which he did not define), a receiving party could not be heard to complain about the paying party's decision not to put an end to the receiving party's own deception.[29]

The effect of offers on exaggeration

57.23 For the reasons set out at 6.152, an exaggerator may afford themselves a degree of protection from the costs consequences of their exaggeration if they make an offer that is more realistic than their claim. Whilst this is plainly a factor to be taken into account, it is of less relevance to the assessment of costs than it is to the incidence of costs. This is because the offer will, in general, neither prove nor disprove the reasonableness of the costs incurred in pursuing the exaggerated claim.

The means by which exaggeration is reflected in the amounts allowed

57.24 What follows focuses on exaggeration, but much of what is said would also apply in other situations, such as where a party had been obstructive or dishonest. Where the court finds that the receiving party's conduct is such that it ought to be reflected in the amount of costs allowed, the court must decide which powers it will invoke. Exaggeration will always be relevant to the 'seven pillars' and this may have a number of consequences, the most wide-ranging of which (in the absence of misconduct) would be that the costs are found to be generally disproportionate. This topic is dealt with in Chapter 25.

57.25 Whilst there is no recognised nomenclature for the ways in which the court may disallow an exaggerator's costs, the following list is as good as any (although 'substitution' is of doubtful legality):

- individual disallowance (see 57.27);
- collective deletion (that is, deleting a part of the costs, such as the costs from a certain date) (see 57.28–57.30);
- substitution (that is, allowing those costs that ought to have been incurred, rather than those that were incurred) (see 57.31–57.32); and

---

[26] *Devine v Frankilin* [2002] EWHC 1846 (QB), *per* Gray J. See also *Drew v Whitbread* [2010] EWCA Civ 53, at [41]; *E Ivor Hughes Educational Foundation v Leach* [2005] EWHC 1317 (Ch); *Peakman v Linbrooke Services Ltd* [2008] EWCA Civ 1239.

[27] *O'Beirne v Hudson* [2010] EWCA Civ 52, at [19], *per* Waller LJ.

[28] *Ibid*, at [19], *per* Waller LJ, and at [22], *per* Hooper LJ.

[29] *Booth v Britannia Hotels Ltd* [2002] EWCA Civ 579, at [32].

- disallowance for fundamental dishonesty in personal injuries claims (see 57.33 and 6.87–6.92).

In addition, CPR, r 44.11 (misconduct), may be invoked (see 57.37–57.64).

There are two methods of dealing with exaggeration that are unlawful (unless, of course, there is a special order that permits such a method or there is some other legal mechanism at play, such as CPR, r 44.11): **57.26**

- complete disallowance as a matter of principle (see 57.34); and
- advance abatement (that is, allowing only a percentage or a proportion of the costs) (see 57.35–57.36).

Individual disallowance

The term 'individual disallowance' refers to the item-by-item disallowance of costs on the basis that they were unreasonably or disproportionately incurred. Put otherwise, it is the ordinary process of assessment. It is unquestionably lawful. **57.27**

Collective deletion

For the reasons set out at 57.35, advance abatement of costs by a costs judge (that is, reducing the amount at the outset by a fixed amount) is generally not permitted, but much the same effect may be achieved by methods that are permissible. In particular, a costs judge is entitled to delete costs collectively. 'Deletion' refers to the disallowing of whole parts of the bill of cost or groups of items on a reasoned, but common, basis, such as where, on the grounds of reasonableness, a court disallows the costs of issuing proceedings. Dyson LJ had the following to say on the topic: **57.28**

> '[The receiving party] concedes (rightly) that in an appropriate case, the costs judge can disallow entire sections of a bill of costs. If the costs judge considers that the claimant acted unreasonably in refusing an offer to settle made before proceedings were issued, he is entitled to disallow all the costs post-issue on the footing that they were costs "unreasonably incurred": rule [44.3(1)]. Similarly, where he decides that a party was unreasonable to raise and pursue an issue, the costs judge is entitled to disallow the costs relating to that issue on the grounds that they were unreasonably incurred.'[30]

In an appropriate case, the whole of the bill may be deleted,[31] but this would be lawful only if it were on the grounds of reasonableness or proportionality (or both)—and such an approach may easily tip over into something that is impermissible, as is explained at 57.34.

As has been explained at 49.03–49.05, a costs judge is required to stay within the four corners of the order that governs the costs being assessed and, in this regard, they are required not to contradict that order. The extent to which a costs judge is able to embark on a process of collective deletion will be a matter of interpretation of the order. In this regard, Kennedy LJ had this to say: **57.29**

> 'I accept of course that the district judge must work within the ambit of the order made in relation to costs, whether it be a consent order or an order made after a contested hearing. But such an order does not in any way deprive the district judge of the powers expressly granted to her by [the pre-CPR equivalent of CPR, r 44.3(2)].'[32]

---

30 *Lahey v Pirelli Tyres Ltd* [2007] EWCA Civ 91, at [23].
31 See, eg, *O'Beirne v Hudson* [2010] EWCA Civ 52, at [19].
32 *Lahey v Pirelli Tyres Ltd* [2007] EWCA Civ 91, at [23].

In a similar vein, Chadwick LJ has explained that a costs judge may disallow the costs of an issue that was not pursued at trial.[33] There is no reason to believe that a similar approach would not be permissible where a costs judge wishes to disallow the costs of an issue for other reasons, such as where a discrete issue was pursued solely as a result of exaggeration.

57.30 The power to reduce a bill of costs by collective deletion may be tempered by estoppel (see 23.07–23.27).

Substitution

57.31 A costs judge may conclude that the receiving party ought to have adopted a different management plan from that which was actually implemented. It may be, for example, that, absent exaggeration, different experts would have been instructed. Where the court believes this to be the case, the court may find itself having to choose between assessing the costs on the basis of the work that *was* done, and assessing the costs on the basis of the work that *would have been* done had the claim been managed reasonably and proportionately. The latter may lead to the court considering whether to substitute the costs.

57.32 There is ample authority to confirm that the court is at liberty to *restrict* costs to those that would have been incurred had the claim been managed properly. If, for example, the claim has been misallocated as a result of the claimant's exaggeration, then the costs may be limited accordingly (see 57.21). In contrast, it is trite costs law that the court is not permitted simply to make a stock 'one size fits all' allowance for managing the claim.[34] What is less clear is the extent to which the court is able to substitute costs that have been disallowed with costs which would have been incurred had the claim been appropriately managed. This is an issue that could be argued either way. It is difficult to see why there should be any sensible objection to the court allowing, for example, the costs of a video conference (a disbursement) in lieu of the profit costs of travelling to a face-to-face conference. There is, however, no authority to confirm that this would be lawful. Indeed, there is authority that would support the argument that it would be a breach of the indemnity principle (see 18.11–18.14; also see 3.09). In practice, however, minor substitutions are frequently made.

Fundamental dishonesty in personal injuries claims

57.33 The matters set out at 6.87–6.92 regarding Criminal Justice and Courts Act 2015, s 57, may be relevant to the assessment of costs in a personal injuries claim in which the trial judge has made an order under that section that a claim was exaggerated in the context of the claimant's fundamental dishonesty.

Complete disallowance as a matter of principle

57.34 Complete disallowance as a matter of principle refers to the situation in which a costs judge, rather than carrying out an item-by-item assessment, disallows some or all of the costs on the grounds of a finding of fact relating to the conduct of the parties (as opposed to the operation of law). Such a step would usually be contrary to the true interpretation of the costs order[35] or would be seen to give excessive weight to certain factors at the expense

---

[33] *Shirley v Caswell* [2000] Lloyds Rep PN 955, CA, at [60]. Dyson LJ has explained that this is nothing more than an example of the costs judge disallowing costs that have been unreasonably incurred: see *Lahey v Pirelli Tyres Ltd* [2007] EWCA Civ 91, at [21].

[34] See *1-800 Flowers Inc v Phonenames Ltd* [2001] EWCA Civ 712, at [114].

[35] Although on a slightly different point, see *Business Environment Bow Lane v Deanwater Estates Ltd* [2009] EWHC 2014 (Ch). If the receiving party's conduct was such that complete disallowance would meet

of taking others into account.[36] That said, complete disallowance (in part or in whole) as a matter of reasonableness following item-by-item scrutiny of the bill of costs is a species of individual disallowance and is permitted (see 57.28). Waller LJ had this to say on that point:

> 'There is a real distinction between directing at the outset that nothing but small claims costs will be awarded and giving items on a bill very anxious scrutiny to see whether costs were necessarily or reasonably incurred, and thus whether it is reasonable for the paying party to pay more than would have been recoverable in a case that should have been allocated to the small claims track. Was it for example necessary to have had lawyers and is it reasonable for the paying party to have to pay for lawyers are questions that should arise where a claim should have been allocated to the small claims track.'[37]

This topic will generally arise in the context of a party having failed to take advantage of a no-costs or low-costs regime. Where this is so, it would be permissible to make substantial, or possibly even complete, reductions, but this must be on the basis of an item-by-item assessment that takes into account all of the relevant circumstances.

Advance abatement

Advance abatement is similar to complete disallowance as a matter of principle (see 57.34) **57.35**
in that costs are reduced globally (such as by a percentage or a fraction) at the outset of the assessment, as opposed to as a consequence or as part of an item-by-item assessment (see 57.28). Abatement in advance would, in theory, be permissible if there were a special order that gave the costs judge that power, such as where a trial judge has delegated the task of apportionment to the costs judge (see 20.66), but this would be rare, if not very rare. A costs judge exercising their ordinary jurisdiction in the absence of a special order would lack the power to abate costs in advance. Dyson LJ had the following to say on this topic:

> 'There is a real distinction between (a) carrying out an assessment and deciding as part of the assessment to reduce the bill by a percentage and (b) deciding in advance of the assessment that the receiving party will only receive a percentage of the assessed costs. The figure that results from (a) represents 100% of the assessed costs. In deciding as part of the assessment to reduce the bill by a percentage, the costs judge is giving effect to an order that the successful party is entitled to his costs, to be assessed if not agreed. The figure that results from (b) represents less than 100% of the assessed costs. In deciding in advance of the assessment that the receiving party will only receive a percentage of the assessed costs, the costs judge is not giving effect to an order that the successful party is entitled to his costs, to be assessed if not agreed.'[38]

The Supreme Court considered these comments and came to much the same conclusion. Lord **57.36**
Hope had this to say, in the context of an EU directive that imposed an obligation on member states to ensure that certain costs were not 'prohibitively expensive' (see 13.84–13.85):

> 'The test of reasonableness which [judges carrying out an assessment] must apply is directed to their assessment of the costs incurred by the receiving party: see CPR 44.5 as

the justice of the situation, then there are two ways in which that could be achieved: the paying party could bring an appeal against the costs order; or the paying party could make an application to the original court to have the costs order varied or set aside (see *ibid*, at [40]).

[36] See, eg, *Briggs v First Choice Holidays* [2017] EWHC 2012 (QB), at [45], *per* Singh J.
[37] *O'Beirne v Hudson* [2010] EWCA Civ 52, at [19].
[38] *Lahey v Pirelli Tyres Ltd* [2007] EWCA Civ 91, at [19].

to the factors to be taken into account by the costs judge when exercising his discretion as to costs. It is not directed to the entirely different question of whether the cost to the paying party would be prohibitively expensive, which is what the Aarhus test is concerned with.'[39]

Misconduct

57.37 The court has always had the power to disallow costs in recognition of poor conduct. In Victorian times, for example, costs might have been 'expunged for scandal and impertinency'.[40] The language may now be less elegant, but the court's powers relating to misconduct remain. The modern-day provisions may be found in CPR, r 44.11, which is worded in the following way:

'(1) The court may make an order under this rule where—
(a) a party or his legal representative, in connection with a summary or detailed assessment, fails to comply with a rule, practice direction or court order; or
(b) it appears to the court that the conduct of a party or that party's legal representative, before or during the proceedings or in the assessment proceedings, was unreasonable or improper.

(2) Where paragraph (1) applies, the court may—
(a) disallow all or part of the costs which are being assessed; or
(b) order the party at fault or that party's legal representatives to pay costs which that party or legal representative has caused any other party to incur.

(3) Where—
(a) the court makes an order under paragraph (2) against a legally represented party; and
(b) the party is not present when the order is made,

the party's legal representative must notify his client in writing of the order no later than 7 days after the legal representative receives notice of the order.'

Thus there are two types of misconduct.[41] The first is governed by CPR, r 44.11(1)(a), and concerns failure to comply with rules, practice directions or court orders in connection with the assessment; the second is governed by CPR, r 44.11(1)(b), which concerns unreasonable or improper conduct. It should be noted that, since 1 April 2013, the second has applied to unreasonable conduct during the assessment itself.[42] Before that date, only misconduct during the substantive litigation that gave rise to the costs in question would have engaged the provision in CPR, r 44.11(1)(b).

CPR, r 44.11(1)(a): failure to comply with rules, practice directions or court orders

57.38 The threshold test under CPR, r 44.11(1)(a), is whether a party or their legal representative has failed, in connection with either a summary or detailed assessment, to comply with a rule, practice direction or court order. It is therefore a narrower test than CPR, r 44.11(1)(b),

39 *R (on the application of Edwards & Anor) v Environment Agency & Ors* [2010] UKSC 57, at [25].
40 (1884) Law Times LXXVIII 115/2.
41 These two limbs should not be confused with the other aspects of CPR, r 44.11, ie the powers concerning the incidence of costs under CPR, r 44.11(2)(b)—a topic addressed at 9.100–9.102. The two topics are not the same.
42 See Civil Procedure (Amendment) Rules 2013 (SI 2013/262).

which is whether there has been unreasonable or improper conduct. The conduct of a solicitor will encompass the conduct of any agent who may have been engaged by the solicitor (such as a costs draftsperson).[43]

Once the threshold criteria have been met, the matter becomes one of discretion (see 57.40–57.41 and 57.49) and the burden of proof will lie with the person alleging misconduct.[44] Longmore LJ has made it clear that there does not need to be a causative link between the defaulting party's conduct and the costs that are ordered to be paid.[45] This, of course, is entirely as one would expect: any misconduct during the assessment would, by definition, have taken place after the costs had been incurred, so it would generally be impossible to show a causal link (unless, of course, the misconduct was claiming costs that ought not to have been claimed). **57.39**

Discretion

As to discretion, Longmore LJ had this to say: **57.40**

> 'The important point is that, while a non-compliance with a rule, practice direction or court order is the only jurisdictional requirement for the exercise of the power contained in Rule [44.11], it will usually be appropriate as a matter of discretion to consider the extent of any misconduct which has occurred in the course of such non-compliance.'[46]

Although he expressly declined to give any general guidance, it is clear from Longmore LJ's method that prejudice is a factor to be taken into account in the exercise of the court's discretion.

Speaking of CPR, r 44.11, generally (albeit in a case in which the focus of the case was on CPR, r 44.11(1)(b)), Hickinbottom LJ has said this: **57.41**

> 'The jurisdiction is not compensatory: it is not necessary to show that the applicant has suffered any loss as a result of the misconduct. It is a jurisdiction intended to mark the court's disapproval of the failure of a party or of a legal representative to comply with his duty to the court by way of an appropriate and proportionate sanction.'[47]

The points made at 57.49 are likely to apply. In particular, any sanction must be proportionate to the misconduct, in all of the circumstances.

CPR, r 44.11(1)(b): unreasonable or improper conduct

A finding of misconduct under CPR, r 44.11(1)(b), is a two-stage procedure: first, the court must determine whether the relevant threshold criteria have been met (that is, whether there has been improper or unreasonable behaviour); and secondly, the court must consider whether it would be just to impose a discretionary sanction.[48] The conduct of a solicitor will encompass the conduct of any agent who may have been engaged **57.42**

[43] *Gempride v Bamrah* [2018] EWCA Civ 1367, at [26(i)].
[44] *Ibid*, at [26(v)].
[45] *Haji-Ioannou v Frangos* [2006] EWCA Civ 1663, at [8], approving the decision of Lindsay J in the court below ([2005] EWHC 279 (Ch), at [14]).
[46] *Haji-Ioannou v Frangos* [2006] EWCA Civ 1663, at [10].
[47] *Gempride v Bamrah* [2018] EWCA Civ 1367, at [14].
[48] *Haji-Ioannou v Frangos* [2006] EWCA Civ 1663, at [10]. Longmore LJ's comments related to CPR, r 44.11(1)(a) (ie misconduct during the assessment) rather than r 44n.11(1)(b), but there is no reason to believe that different principles apply.

by the solicitor (such as a costs draftsperson).[49] Hickinbottom LJ had this to say on the point:

> '[The] following propositions ... can be made.
> i) A solicitor as a legal representative owes a duty to the court, and remains responsible for the conduct of anyone to whom he subcontracts work that he (the solicitor) is retained to do. That is particularly so where the subcontractor is not a legal representative and so does not himself owe an independent duty to the court.
> ii) Whilst "unreasonable" and "improper" conduct are not self-contained concepts, "unreasonable" is essentially conduct which permits of no reasonable explanation, whilst "improper" has the hallmark of conduct which the consensus of professional opinion would regard as improper.
> iii) Mistake or error of judgment or negligence, without more, will be insufficient to amount to "unreasonable or improper" conduct.
> iv) Although the conduct of the relevant legal representative must amount to a breach of duty owed by the representative to the court to perform his duty to the court, the conduct does not have be in breach of any formal professional rule nor dishonest.
> v) Where an application under CPR rule 44.11 is made, the burden of proof lies on the applicant in the sense that the court cannot make an order unless it is satisfied that the conduct was "unreasonable or improper".
> vi) Even where the threshold criteria are satisfied, the court still has a discretion as to whether to make an order.
> vii) If the court determines to make an order, any order made (or "sanction") must be proportionate to the misconduct as found, in all the circumstances.'[50]

57.43 It should be noted that mistakes or errors of judgement or negligence, without more, will be insufficient to amount to unreasonable or improper conduct.[51] Hickinbottom LJ has explained that although the conduct of the relevant legal representative must amount to a breach of duty owed by representatives to the court to perform their duty to the court, the conduct does not have to be in breach of any formal professional rule nor dishonest.[52] He went on to say that even where the threshold criteria are satisfied, the court still has discretion whether to make an order.[53]

Unreasonable behaviour

57.44 Hickinbottom LJ has explained that ' "unreasonable" is essentially conduct which permits of no reasonable explanation'.[54] Longmore LJ has found that although the then-equivalent of CPR, r 44.11(1)(b), did not itself contain the word 'misconduct', that word was contained in the title and that title points to the nature of the court's discretion.[55] Dyson LJ has commented (*obiter*) that the word 'unreasonable' in CPR, r 44.11(1)(b), is to be construed 'quite narrowly' in much the same way as it is construed in the context of wasted costs.[56]

[49] *Gempride v Bamrah* [2018] EWCA Civ 1367, at [26(i)].
[50] *Ibid*, at [14].
[51] *Ibid*, at [26(iii)].
[52] *Ibid*, at [26(iv)]; see also *ibid*, at [105]–[115], in respect of dishonesty.
[53] *Ibid*, at [26(vi)].
[54] *Ibid*, at [26(ii)].
[55] See *ibid*, at [10], referred to with approval in *Lahey v Pirelli Tyres Ltd* [2007] EWCA Civ 91, at [28]. Dyson LJ noted that there was some tension between comments made by Lord Woolf MR under the corresponding pre-CPR provisions in *Burrows v Vauxhall Motors Ltd* [1998] PIQR P48, CA, which dealt with RSC Ord 62, r 10(1), but Longmore LJ's analysis was to be preferred.
[56] *Lahey v Pirelli Tyres Ltd* [2007] EWCA Civ 91, at [29]. He commented that it was unlikely that the drafter intended that a legal representative could be ordered to pay costs under CPR, r 44n.11, in

He concluded that the meaning of the word should not vary depending on whether it is the client or the legal representative whose conduct is under consideration.[57]

Improper behaviour

Hickinbottom LJ has explained that ' "improper" has the hallmark of conduct which the consensus of professional opinion would regard as improper'.[58] In this regard, guidance can be gleaned from authorities concerning wasted costs.[59] This may create its own difficulties because that definition focuses solely on professional obligations,[60] which, of course, parties themselves would not bear. In practice, however, most parties are legally represented, so conduct that was said to be improper could usually be measured against that standard. **57.45**

Sanctions

To address the topic of sanctions, it is necessary to know something the history of the relevant law. The power to impose sanctions arising out of unreasonable or improper conduct is a continuation of a long-standing power[61] that, three decades ago, vested only in the judge who made the entitling costs order. Contrary to the wishes of the Law Society, that power was delegated in the first instance to masters[62] and then to all costs judges[63] (other than authorised court officers[64]). The relevance of this is that the power to impose a sanction derives from a power that was originally vested in the trial judge. It is also worth pausing to note that the power to impose a sanction was just that: as Michael Cook said in 1995, it was a power to impose something that was 'not just compensatory ... but [also] punishment'.[65] This was something that was entirely in keeping with the fact that the power originally vested in the trial judge. Where a penalty was made, it commonly took the form of a percentage discount or flat reduction.[66] **57.46**

Thus the pre-CPR law was that misconduct could lead to sanctions in the form of a disallowance of part or all of the costs. Given the fact that the CPR have preserved the power to impose sanctions (and that the CPR expressly refer to a power to 'disallow all or part of the costs which are being assessed'), it would be curious if the court's powers to impose a sanction were any less liberal. In view of this, the following comments of Dyson LJ (which were made in 2007) may come as a surprise: **57.47**

> 'The short answer to the defendant's submission [that the cost should be reduced by a percentage] is that the costs judge has no power to vary the costs order that is deemed to have

circumstances under which a wasted costs order could not be made. See also *Gempride v Bamrah* [2018] EWCA Civ 1367, at [17].

[57] *Ibid.*

[58] *Gempride v Bamrah* [2018] EWCA Civ 1367, at [26(ii)].

[59] *Ibid*, at [17], in which Hickinbottom LJ referred to *Lahey v Pirelli Tyres Ltd* [2007] EWCA Civ 91, at [29].

[60] See *Ridehalgh v Horsefield* [1994] Ch 205, at 232, in which Lord Bingham MR said that improper 'covers ... conduct which would ordinarily be held to justify disbarment, striking off, suspension from practice or other serious professional penalty'.

[61] See RSC Ord 62, r 28.

[62] This was as a result of comments made by Megarry V-C in *Re Solicitors* [1982] 2 All ER 683, at 688.

[63] See Cook, M, *Cook on Costs* (2nd edn, London: Butterworths, 1995), p 239, for a discussion of this topic.

[64] See CPR, r 47.3.

[65] See Cook, M, *Cook on Costs* (2nd edn, London: Butterworths, 1995), p 240.

[66] See, eg, *Chapman v Chapman* [1985] 1 WLR 599; *Morrow v Naddeem (No 2)* (1990) The Times, 23 March, QB.

been made. In our judgment, this is a complete answer to [the paying party's] submissions, whether based on [the then equivalents of CPR, rr 44.3 and 44.4 or 44.11]. It follows that the costs judge has no jurisdiction to make an order of the kind contended for by the defendant in this case.'[67]

57.48 At first blush, it seems as if Dyson LJ had ruled out the exact form of penalty that one would expect to be imposed as a result of misconduct (that is, a reduction in the receiving party's entitlement to costs). This, however, was at a time when the power under what is now CPR, r 44.11(1)(b), was limited to misconduct during the claim itself. It is likely that Dyson LJ's comments continue to apply where the misconduct took place in those circumstances. Indeed, Longmore LJ (giving judgment in a different case) has made it clear that the power to disallow costs by reason of unreasonable or improper conduct during the claim is limited to those costs that were incurred as a result of that conduct.[68] This, arguably, adds little to the power that the costs judge would have under CPR, r 44.5, generally.

57.49 Unreasonable or improper conduct during the assessment seems to be treated in a different way, however. It used to not be wholly clear how the court was to exercise its discretion once the threshold criteria had been met in respect of such misconduct, but it is now known that a less restrictive approach is required. Newey LJ, for example, made no adverse comment about a decision to disallow costs entirely in a case in which the unreasonable or improper conduct (namely, miscertification) took place during the assessment.[69] It seems that the approach under the post-2013 Rules is that the court will impose a sanction (such as a percentage reduction) that marks the court's disapproval of the misconduct[70] and which is, in all of the circumstances, proportionate to that misconduct.[71] In practice, this tends to mean that the court exercises it discretion so that the sanction is sufficient to mark the court's disapproval, but not so severe as to be disproportionate in all of the circumstances.

Case examples of misconduct during the claim

57.50 The following are examples of the type of conduct that may (or may not) be said to amount to misconduct.

57.51 **Obstructive behaviour** PD 44, para 11.2, confirms that where a party takes steps that are calculated to prevent or inhibit the court from furthering the overriding objective, that party would be engaging in conduct that may be said to be unreasonable or improper.

57.52 **Withholding information** In a case in which relevant information capable of leading to resolution of the claim had been withheld, Lord Woolf MR commented that the court had the power, on an assessment, to disallow all or part of the claimant's costs.[72] That decision was based on the predecessor to CPR, r 44.11,[73] and should therefore be viewed with caution, but it is still cited from time to time as an enlightening example.

---

67 *Lahey v Pirelli Tyres Ltd* [2007] EWCA Civ 91, at [22].

68 *Haji-Ioannou v Frangos* [2006] EWCA Civ 1663, at [8].

69 See *GSD Law Ltd v Wardman & Ors* [2017] EWCA Civ 2144, at [38], where, it should be noted, Newey LJ referred to this being the result of the exercise of a power under CPR, r 44.11(2)(a), but he almost certainly meant to refer to CPR, r 44.11(2)(b), because he referred to the conduct in question as being 'unreasonable and improper'.

70 *Gempride v Bamrah* [2018] EWCA Civ 1367, at [14].

71 *Ibid*, at [26(vii)].

72 *Burrows v Vauxhall Motors Ltd* [1998] PIQR P48, CA. The continuing relevance of this case has been doubted: see the *obiter* postscript to *Haji-Ioannou v Frangos* [2006] EWCA Civ 1663.

73 That is, it dealt with RSC Ord 62, rr 10(1) and 28(1).

Failure to comply with practice directions Although he was dealing with the incidence provisions of CPR, r 44.11, rather than the assessment provisions (see 9.100–9.102), Wall J has found that a complete and unexplained failure to comply with a practice direction is capable of amounting to unreasonable conduct.[74] Lesser failures may not justify such a finding: for example, Arden LJ declined to find that a failure to comply properly with certain practice directions concerning costs estimates was insufficient to amount to misconduct.[75] 57.53

Failure to comply with rules of professional conduct Arden LJ's case[76] also touched upon rules of professional conduct—namely, the receiving party's lawyer was, technically, in breach of his professional obligations. The fact that there was no misconduct found demonstrates that a breach of the rules of professional conduct will not necessarily amount to misconduct. 57.54

Criminality Although he did not have to decide the issue, Phillips MR raised no objection to the suggestion that an act of criminal conduct would be capable of amounting to misconduct.[77] 57.55

Case examples of misconduct during the assessment

Delay The most frequently encountered allegation of misconduct during the assessment is perhaps the most minor—namely, delay. This topic is addressed in detail at 23.50–23.82. 57.56

Negotiation on a false basis Towards the end of the last decade, the courts in certain areas of the country noted a number of cases in which without-prejudice schedules for costs were submitted that were for significantly greater amounts that those that were ultimately claimed (or claimable) in the bill of costs.[78] Whilst there were also other factors in play, just such a case had recently resulted in a series of bills of costs being disallowed in their entirety.[79] It should be noted, however, that whilst a paying party will often try to prove dishonesty as a particularly serious form of improper behaviour, it is not necessary under CPR, r 44.11. Where the court is asked to make a finding of dishonesty, it is no longer appropriate to apply the *Ghosh* test.[80] 57.57

Miscertification of a bill of costs The court will generally regard miscertification as a serious matter, especially where it happens systematically or if opportunities were missed to correct a misleading certificate. Whilst it is a pre-CPR case, the starting point in respect of any such matter continues to be the following extract from a 1998 judgment given by Henry LJ: 57.58

> '[The rule that governed certificates] requires the solicitor who brings proceedings for taxation to sign the bill of costs. In so signing he certifies that the contents of the bill are correct.

---

[74] *Re CH (a minor)* (2000) The Times, 6 June. The failure to comply meant that Wall J was forced to conduct a trial in a family matter with virtually no papers.
[75] *Garbutt v Edwards* [2005] EWCA Civ 1206, at [47].
[76] *Ibid.*
[77] *Earl of Portsmouth v Hamilton* (2000) The Independent, 27 October. In that instance, the alleged criminality was using papers stolen from an opponent's lawyers.
[78] See Duerden, J, 'The Costs-Only Minefield' (2009) 62 Litigation Funding 12.
[79] *GSD Law Ltd v Wardman & Ors* [2017] EWCA Civ 2144.
[80] See *Ivey (Appellant) v Genting Casinos (UK) Ltd t/a Crockfords* [2017] UKSC 67, referring to the test established in *R v Ghosh* [1982] EWCA Crim 2.

That signature is no empty formality. The bill specifies the hourly rates applied, and the care and attention uplift claimed. If an agreement between the receiving solicitor and his client ... restricted (say) the hourly rate payable by the client, that hourly rate is the most that can be claimed or recovered on taxation ... The signature of the bill of costs under the rules is effectively the certificate by an officer of the court that the receiving party's solicitors are not seeking to recover in relation to any item more than they have agreed to charge their client under a contentious business agreement ... The court can (and should unless there is evidence to the contrary) assume that his signature to the bill of costs shows that the indemnity principle has not been offended ... And the other side of a presumption of trust afforded to the signature of an officer of the court must be that breach of that trust should be treated as a most serious disciplinary offence.'[81]

57.59 The matter with which Henry LJ was dealing concerned the indemnity principle, but there is no reason to believe that a certificate relating to any other aspect of the matter (such as accuracy) should be treated any differently. Indeed, Judge Gosnell had the following to say (in a judgment that was subsequently confirmed by Newey LJ):

> 'The signing of a certificate on the bill of costs certifying its accuracy is very important. If paying parties lost confidence in the *bona fides* of solicitors signing these certificates the consequences for civil litigation as a whole would be significant. Paying parties would be reluctant to negotiate informal settlement of costs ...'[82]

In the case with which Judge Gosnell and Newey LJ were dealing, the solicitor was found to have dishonestly (and systematically) miscertified certain documents; the entire costs were disallowed as a consequence.

57.60 Whilst not binding, in a case in which there had been a 'cockup and not [a] conspiracy', Master Whalan visited a 50 per cent reduction on the receiving party in response to her solicitors having repeatedly certified a bill of costs as accurately claiming a success fee where, in truth, no success fee could ever have been payable.[83] Likewise, in a case in which the solicitor had, in the absence of dishonesty, miscertified the bill as to rate properly claimable, Hickenbottom LJ disallowed half of the relevant profit costs (although there were also other factors at play).[84]

Procedure

57.61 Where the court makes an order under CPR, r 44.11(2), it must observe certain procedural requirements. In particular, before making an order under CPR, r 44.11(2), the court must give the party or legal representative in question a reasonable opportunity to attend a hearing to give reasons why the court should not make such an order.[85]

57.62 The extent to which the court will permit a detailed enquiry into the misconduct alleged will depend on the nature of the issues and the sanctions that are sought. There is a spectrum of allegations that may fall to be considered under the CPR, r 44.11. At one end of the spectrum are cases in which the conduct complained of is failings on the part of the receiving party's legal representatives and the sanctions sought are similar to those that

---

[81] *Bailey v IBC Vehicles Ltd* [1998] 3 All ER 570, at 575–6.
[82] *GSD Law Ltd v Wardman & Ors* [2017] EWCA Civ 2144, at [24].
[83] *Jago v Whitbread Group plc* (unreported), 15 October 2016, SCCO.
[84] *Gempride v Bamrah* [2018] EWCA Civ 1367.
[85] See PD 44, para 11.1.

would be made under the wasted costs provisions. Where this is so, it may be appropriate to adopt the summary procedure akin to that which is used for dealing with wasted costs orders (see 9.123–9.126). Where, however, the allegations are more serious and where the sanctions that are sought are greater (such as where the paying party seeks disallowance of the costs that are being assessed), a non-summary procedure may be appropriate.[86] Indeed, in serious cases, a full trial of the issues may be necessary, albeit as part of the assessment.

After having referred to the passages quoted at 57.58 and 57.59, Newey LJ had this to say on the topic: **57.63**

> '[Where] it is suggested that costs "which are being assessed" should be disallowed (under CPR 44.11(2)(a)) because of "unreasonable or improper" conduct in connection with the assessment of costs, it appears to me that the guidance found in *Ridehalgh v Horsefield* and *Medcalf v Mardell* is much less relevant. Doubtless, the Court should still have in mind the overriding objective and, specifically, proportionality, but there will not be the same risk of satellite litigation. It may well be possible and appropriate to deal with the application in the course of pending assessment proceedings and conduct put forward as justifying the disallowance of costs may also be relevant to how costs should be assessed if not disallowed ... It is also relevant that, as can be seen from what was said in *Bailey v IBC Vehicles Ltd*, ... there is a strong public interest in ensuring that solicitors do not certify costs figures dishonestly: as Judge Gosnell noted, there would be unfortunate consequences if paying parties "lost confidence in the *bona fides* of solicitors signing these certificates". Having regard both to seriousness of the allegations and to the sums potentially at stake, I do not think it was disproportionate to have a three-day hearing.'[87]

Where the court makes an order under CPR, r 44.11(2), against a legally represented party and the party is not present when the order is made, the party's legal representative must notify that party in writing of the order no later than seven days after the legal representative receives notice of the order.[88] Although the rules do not specify any sanction for breach of that obligation, the court may—either in the order under CPR, r 44.11(2), or in a subsequent order—require the legal representative to produce to the court evidence that the legal representative took reasonable steps to comply with the obligation.[89] Presumably, this power stops short of requiring the solicitor to produce privileged material.[90] **57.64**

86 See *GSD Law Ltd v Wardman & Ors* [2017] EWCA Civ 2144, at [38] and [39], *per* Newey LJ.
87 *Ibid*, at [39].
88 See CPR, r 44.11(3).
89 See PD 44, para 11.3.
90 See, on a related topic, *General Mediterranean Holdings SA v Patel* [2000] 1 WLR 272, which confirms that secondary legislation and practice directions do not have the *vires* to require a party to waive privilege.

58

LEGISLATIVE FETTERS ON THE RECOVERY OF COSTS

58.01 This chapter deals with the following topics:

- the slander of women (58.03); and
- patent claims (58.04).

58.02 Whilst they tend to relate only to certain types of litigation, there is a small number of legislative restrictions that are capable of having a bearing on the quantum of costs.[1] They tend to be specific and, as such, they are apt to take precedence over more general statutory provisions.[2] The only commonly encountered example is 'the County Court restriction', which has already been described at 37.18–37.23. For the reasons set out therein, it is not likely to give rise to any limit on the recovery of costs beyond those that would apply for other reasons.

The Slander of Women

58.03 The Slander of Women Act 1891[3] used to make specific provision for the recovery of damages where a statement was made that conveyed the imputation that a woman had a contagious or infectious disease as a result of her unchastity or adultery. Section 1 of that Act used to limit the amount of costs to the amount of damages. That Act was, however, repealed (without transitional provisions) on 1 January 2014.[4] As such, that limit no longer applies. This brought to an end a line of legislation that could be traced back directly to 1601 (see 1.44–1.46).

Patent Claims

58.04 Subject to what is said below, if a patents claim was commenced in the High Court and it could have been brought in what is now the Intellectual Property Enterprise Court (IPEC)—formerly the Patents County Court (PCC)—the costs may be restricted to those

---

[1] The restriction on the recovery costs in the CPR (such as the small claims regime and fixed costs) are not included because they have been made by delegated legislation, rather than statute.

[2] *Hasker v Wood* (1885) 54 LJQB 419, CA; *Reeve v Gibson* [1891] 1 QB 652, CA; *Re Butler's Will, ex p Metropolitan Board of Works* (1912) 106 LT 673.

[3] The Slander of Women Act 1891 (54 & 55 Vict. c51).

[4] See Defamation Act 2013, s 14(1); Defamation Act 2013 (Commencement) (England and Wales) Order 2013 (SI 2013/3027), art 2.

allowable in the IPEC. This is as a result of s 290 of the Copyright, Designs and Patents Act 1988, which provides:

> '(1) Where an action is commenced in the High Court which could have been commenced in a patents county court and in which a claim for a pecuniary remedy is made, then, subject to the provisions of this section, if the plaintiff recovers less than the prescribed amount, he is not entitled to recover any more costs than those to which he would have been entitled if the action had been brought in the county court.
>
> (2) For this purpose a plaintiff shall be treated as recovering the full amount recoverable in respect of his claim without regard to any deduction made in respect of matters not falling to be taken into account in determining whether the action could have been commenced in a patents county court.
>
> (3) This section does not affect any question as to costs if it appears to the High Court that there was reasonable ground for supposing the amount recoverable in respect of the plaintiff's claim to be in excess of the prescribed amount.
>
> (4) The High Court, if satisfied that there was sufficient reason for bringing the action in the High Court, may make an order allowing the costs or any part of the costs on the High Court scale or on such one of the county court scales as it may direct.
>
> (5) This section does not apply to proceedings brought by the Crown.
>
> (6) In this section "the prescribed amount"[5] means such amount as may be prescribed by Her Majesty for the purposes of this section by Order in Council.
>
> (7) No recommendation shall be made to Her Majesty to make an Order under this section unless a draft of the Order has been laid before and approved by a resolution of each House of Parliament.'

It is not wholly clear whether this provision still operates. It came into force on 1 August 1989[6] and it has remained remarkably unscathed since. It has, however, been prospectively repealed, albeit from a date of appointment that has not yet been set.[7] As such, it seems that s 290 of the 1988 Act continues to exist, but with a sword of Damocles hanging over its head. This is somewhat confusing, not only because of the archaic language it uses, but also because the PCC has now been replaced by the IPEC, which is part of the Chancery Division.[8] It is also worth noting that the Intellectual Property Enterprise Court Guide[9] makes no mention s 290 of Copyright, Designs and Patents Act 1988.

---

[5] See High Court and County Courts Jurisdiction Order 1991 (SI 1991/724), art 2(5).

[6] Copyright, Designs and Patents Act 1988 (Commencement No 1) Order 1989 (SI 1989/816), art 2.

[7] See Courts and Legal Services Act 1990, s 125(7) and Sch 20, this being from a date yet to be appointed under s 124(3) of that Act.

[8] See HM Courts & Tribunals Service, *Intellectual Property Enterprise Court Guide* (London: HMSO, 2014).

[9] Ibid.

Part XIV

PARTICULAR PERSONS

59

LITIGANTS IN PERSON AND LAWYERS WHO ACT IN THEIR OWN CAUSE

This chapter addresses the (surprisingly difficult) topic of the recovery of costs by litigants in person. In particular, it deals with the following topics: **59.01**

- jurisdiction to allow costs to litigants in person (59.02);
- quantum of costs that may be allowed to litigants who represent themselves (59.08):
  - general principles of quantification (59.10);
  - allowances for time spent (where there has been financial loss) (59.13);
  - allowances for time spent (where there has been no financial loss) (59.23);
  - disbursements and witness allowances (59.28);
  - payments for legal services actually purchased (59.35);
  - expert assistance in respect of costs (59.36);
- lawyers acting for themselves and on behalf of their firms (59.38):
  - solicitors and the *Chorley* principle (59.39);
  - counsel (59.47);
  - other lawyers (59.50); and
- corporate litigants (59.54).

Jurisdiction to Allow Costs to Litigants in Person

Under the common law, a litigant in person (other than a solicitor[1] or possibly a barrister[2]) is not entitled to claim costs in respect of their time;[3] only out-of-pocket expenses are recoverable.[4] Statute has intervened to allow the recovery of costs for time spent by a **59.02**

---

[1] Under the common law, a solicitor who appeared as a litigant in person was entitled to costs as a solicitor, but only if they would have been able to charge a fee as a solicitor in the court in question had they been representing a client: see, eg, *H Tolputt & Co Ltd v Mole* [1911] 1 KB 87; *R v Sharpe* (unreported), 10 November 1995, QBD, *per* Dyson J.

[2] See *R (on the application of Sivanandan) v Disciplinary Tribunal of the Council of the Inns of Court* [2014] EWHC 1570 (Admin), at [24], *per* Moses LJ, aff'd at [2016] EWCA Civ 478.

[3] *Buckland v Watts* [1970] 1 QB 27; see also *London Scottish Benefit Society v Chorley, Crawford and Chester* (1884) 12 QBD 452. Whilst not binding on any court, the VAT Tribunal has found that the principle of equality in European law did not have a bearing on the principle against the recovery of a litigant in person's costs under common law: *Serpes v Revenue & Customs Commissioners* (unreported), 22 December 2008.

[4] The effect of the common law was demonstrated in a case that was decided in the days when a company was not able to be treated as a litigant in person. The receiving party was represented in court by a director, but his costs were not recoverable, despite the fact that he had been given a right of audience to represent the company at a trial: *Jonathan Alexander Ltd v Proctor* [1996] 1 WLR 518.

litigant in person, in the form of the Litigants in Person (Costs and Expenses) Act 1975 (as amended), s 1(1), of which reads as follows:

> 'Where, in any proceedings to which this subsection applies, any costs of a litigant in person are ordered to be paid by any other party to the proceedings or in any other way, there may, subject to rules of court, be allowed on the taxation or other determination of those costs sums in respect of any work done, and any expenses and losses incurred, by the litigant in or in connection with the proceedings to which the order relates.'

The relevant rules of court are the Civil Procedure Rules (CPR)—in particular, CPR, rr 46.5 and 45.39(5). These have largely eclipsed the common law—although the latter may still be relevant in tribunals in which the CPR do not apply and the litigant in person is someone to whom 'the *Chorley* principle'[5] applies (see 59.39).[6]

59.03 The 1975 Act will not apply in all instances, which means that costs for time spent and work done will not be recoverable by all litigants in person, but this will rarely be an issue in most courts and tribunals.[7]

The definition and status of litigants in person

59.04 There is no definition of a litigant in person in the Litigants in Person (Costs and Expenses) Act 1975 (as amended) or the CPR.[8] Peter Gibson LJ has explained that if a person is represented at all (even by an agent), then they may lose their status as a litigant in person,[9] although there are some exceptions to this, as follows.

(1) A person may receive legal advice in the conduct of their claim and still be classified as a litigant in person for those aspects of the claim that they conducted themselves.[10]
(2) A litigant in person may, without losing their status, receive help in respect of an assessment from a costs practitioner.[11]
(3) A person may continue to be a litigant in person notwithstanding the fact that they have instructed counsel under the Licensed Access Scheme.[12]

59.05 The first and third of these exceptions are a reflection of the fact that the right of representation is separate from the right to conduct litigation and that, in any event, a person's status will not necessarily be the same throughout the claim.[13]

59.06 Although it stops short of providing a definition of the phrase 'litigant in person', CPR, r 46.5(6), has the effect of widening the ambit of that phrase:

---

5 After *London Scottish Benefit Society v Chorley, Crawford and Chester* (1884) 12 QBD 452.

6 See, eg, *R (on the application of Sivanandan) v Disciplinary Tribunal of the Council of the Inns of Court* [2014] EWHC 1570 (Admin) (aff'd at [2016] EWCA Civ 478), in which Moses LJ found that the CPR did not apply in the Disciplinary Tribunal of the Council of the Inns of Court, with the result that counsel was entitled to charge for expenditure of her own professional skill.

7 The Litigants in Person (Costs and Expenses) Act 1975 applies only to those tribunals in respect of which it is applied by s 1(2) of that Act or by Order. It applies in most costs-bearing tribunals, including all civil courts, the Land Tribunal, the First-tier Tribunal and the Upper Tribunal; where it does not apply, only out-of-pocket disbursements are recoverable: *Customs and Excise Commissioners v Ross* [1990] 2 All ER 65.

8 Other than some qualifying remarks at CPR, r 46.5(6).

9 *Jonathan Alexander Ltd v Proctor* [1996] 1 WLR 518, at 525G.

10 CPR, r 46.5(3)(b).

11 CPR, r 46.5(3)(c).

12 *Agassi v Robinson (HM Inspector of Taxes)* [2005] EWCA Civ 1507, at [25].

13 See the discussion of this topic *ibid*.

'(6) For the purposes of this rule, a litigant in person includes—
(a) a company or other corporation which is acting without a legal representative; and
(b) any of the following who acts in person (except where any such person is represented by a firm in which that person is a partner)—
  (i) a barrister;
  (ii) a solicitor;
  (iii) a solicitor's employee;
  (iv) a manager of a body recognised under section 9 of the Administration of Justice Act 1985; or
  (v) a person who, for the purposes of the 2007 Act, is an authorised person in relation to an activity which constitutes the conduct of litigation (within the meaning of that Act).'

Thus companies and certain legal representatives are capable of being litigants in person, which topics are addressed in detail at 59.54 and 59.38, respectively. Where certain types of lawyer or legal firm fall outside the ambit of litigants in person, the *Chorley* principle may apply (see 59.39), in which case they would be able to recover their fees unhindered by the restrictions set out in this chapter.

The Crown is not able to be a litigant in person.[14] **59.07**

Quantum of Costs that may be Allowed to Litigants who Represent Themselves

In general, there are two tiers at which a litigant in person's costs may be assessed: an upper tier, where the litigant can prove financial loss; and a lower tier, where no loss can be proven. These two tiers are separate and mutually exclusive. **59.08**

- Where a litigant in person is able to prove financial loss, then—subject to certain restrictions—they would be entitled to compensation for that loss (see 59.13–59.22).
- Where they are not able to show financial loss, then the litigant in person would able to recover costs on the basis of a fixed, but relatively prescribed low, hourly rate (see 59.23–59.27).

Neither of these tiers will apply if the *Chorley* principle applies (see 59.39–59.46), although this would be so only if a lawyer were carrying out work in circumstances in which they were *not* acting as a litigant in person. That situation should not be confused with the upper tier, even though it may superficially appear similar.

With one or two exceptions (see 59.29–59.34), disbursements will be treated in a like manner to disbursements in any other context. In that regard, there is no difference in principle between the two tiers mentioned above. **59.09**

The general principles of quantification

The two tiers are created and fashioned by CPR, r 46.5: **59.10**

'[...]

(2) The costs allowed under this rule must not exceed, except in the case of a disbursement, two-thirds of the amount which would have been allowed if the litigant in person had been represented by a legal representative.

---

[14] Although the Crown is unable to recover monies as a litigant in person, statutory office holders (such as the official receiver or registrars of births, deaths and marriages) can: *Official Receiver v Brunt,* sub nom *In re Minotaur Data Systems Ltd* [1999] 1 WLR 1129.

(3) The litigant in person shall be allowed—
(a) costs for the same categories of—
    (i) work; and
    (ii) disbursements,
    which would have been allowed if the work had been done or the disbursements had been made by a legal representative on the litigant in person's behalf;
(b) the payments reasonably made by him for legal services relating to the conduct of the proceedings; and
(c) the costs of obtaining expert assistance in assessing the costs claim.

(4) The amount of costs to be allowed to the litigant in person for any item of work claimed shall be—
(a) where the litigant can prove financial loss, the amount that he can prove he has lost for time reasonably spent on doing the work; or
(b) where the litigant cannot prove financial loss, an amount for the time reasonably spent on doing the work at the rate set out in the practice direction.'

59.11 Thus, in so far as costs for time spent are concerned, there is a cap of two-thirds of the amount that would have been allowed had the work been carried out by a legal representative. The policy underlying that restriction has its origins in the fundamental tenet that litigants must not profit from litigation.[15] There is then a further limit if the litigant in person is unable to show financial loss.[16] It is therefore convenient to consider the law both where there is financial loss (see 59.13–59.22) and where there is no such loss (see 59.23–59.27).

59.12 A litigant is entitled to know how their application for costs had been determined so that they may challenge that decision, if appropriate.[17]

Allowances for time spent (where there has been financial loss)

59.13 There are two issues that the court must address when quantifying costs for time spent where it is said that there has been financial loss: the first is the issue of whether there has, in truth, been financial loss; the second is the amount to be allowed.

Proof of financial loss

59.14 The issue of whether there has been pecuniary loss is a question of mixed fact and law.[18] The burden of proof rests with the receiving party[19] and is to be proved on evidence,[20] but the requisite standard of evidence will vary from case to case, depending on the occupational

---

15 *Hart v Aga Khan Foundation (UK)* [1984] 1 WLR 994, at 997, *per* Lloyd J, ie it is that part of a solicitor's profit costs which represents the costs of running the practice, with the profit element discounted.

16 CPR, r 46.5(4).

17 Whilst a criminal case, see *R (on the application of JBOL LTD) v City of Westminster Magistrates' Court* [2013] EWHC 1010 (Admin).

18 *Official Receiver v Brunt,* sub nom *In re Minotaur Data Systems Ltd* [1999] 1 WLR 1129, at 1137.

19 Pecuniary loss must be proved by evidence. The litigants in person in both *Mainwaring v Goldtech Investments Ltd* [1997] 1 All ER 467 and *Mealing-McLeod v Common Professional Examination Board* [2000] Costs LR 223 failed to do this.

20 Where a litigant in person commences detailed assessment proceedings, they should serve copies of written evidence of financial loss (if they intend to prove loss) with the notice of commencement: PD 46, para 3.3. They should also serve a copy of that evidence on any party against whom they seek costs at least 24 hours before the hearing at which the question may be decided: PD 46, para 3.2.

circumstances in which the work was done. Robert Walker J described the two ends of the spectrum of possible circumstances:

> '[A]t one extreme ... a self-employed tradesman in a small but profitable way of business who has more customers than he can cope with and can fill every working hour to advantage; at the other extreme, a retired civil servant with an index-linked pension who finds the conduct of litigation a more interesting pastime than bowls or crossword puzzles.'[21]

Evidence does not need to be highly specific. Whilst no more than persuasive, Gillen J (a High Court judge in Northern Ireland) has explained that Parliament did not intend to require litigants in person to prove precisely what they might otherwise have been doing when each item on a bill of costs came to be addressed.[22]

Loss of time has long been regarded as capable of equating to loss of income. Mainstay J had this to say (of a solicitor litigant in person to whom the common law applied): **59.15**

> 'Time is money to a solicitor; and why should he not be as much entitled to his proper costs, if he affords the time and skill which he brings to bear upon the business where he is a party to the action as he is where he is not a party.'[23]

Professional persons

In more recent times, Douglas Brown J has found (albeit by implication) that loss of a professional's time is capable of amounting to a loss of earnings.[24] The fact that a loss of time is capable of giving rise to financial loss will not shift the evidential burden, however, because proof of actual loss is required, rather than mere proof of status. Patten J gave the following guidance: **59.16**

> 'It is not ... enough for the solicitor merely to establish that he or she was in practice during the relevant period. The solicitor must show that he could have charged for the time which he expended on his personal litigation. This does not ... mean that the solicitor in that position will have to prove that for all of the time expended on the litigation he could otherwise have been engaged on other clients' business, nor will it be necessary for the Court to examine in detail how successful or otherwise the solicitor's practice was at the relevant time. The rule is, for purely practical reasons, more broad-brush than that. The Court will assume that it was possible for the solicitor to have hired out his services to clients during the relevant period. But for his time to be regarded as valuable, the solicitor does, I believe, have to demonstrate that he has used up time in litigation during which he would otherwise have been able to pursue his practice as a solicitor for reward.'[25]

Thus it is necessary both to show that loss of time was capable of causing financial loss and that this in fact did happen.

Patten J was referring to a solicitor litigant in person, but there is no reason to believe that the same would not be the case with any other profession or trade in which fees are ordinarily calculated on a time basis. Not all losses of such a person's time would equate to a loss **59.17**

---

21 *Mainwaring v Goldtech Investments Ltd* [1997] 1 All ER 467, at 467–8.

22 See *N&R Devine Ltd v McAteer* [2013] NEQB 102, at [24].

23 *London Scottish Benefit Society v Chorley, Crawford and Chester* (1884) 12 QBD 452, at 457; see also *Malkinson v Trim* [2002] EWCA Civ 1273.

24 *Stockinger v Highdorn Co Ltd* [2001] All ER (D) 62 (Apr) (QBD), at [20], *per* Douglas Brown J.

25 *Joseph v Boyd & Hutchinson* [2003] EWHC 413 (Ch), at [19].

of income: a distinction may be drawn between work carried out in such a way as to reduce a professional's working day and work done during that person's leisure time. Lloyd J has explained that the latter would not be regarded as giving rise to a financial loss.[26]

Determinants other than direct loss of fees

59.18 Loss of a professional's time that otherwise would have been billed to a client is not the only way in which financial loss can be determined; losses can also be incurred in a variety of ways other than a direct loss of fees (such as where a person is employed or where they have to employ a *locum tenens*). The fact that a holder of statutory office is salaried and that their salary would have been paid in any event will not prevent the court from finding that there has been pecuniary loss.[27] One method of gauging whether there has been loss is to ascribe notional fees to the work done;[28] another would be to look at the detrimental effect that the litigation has had on the litigant in person's business accounts. The relevant determinant will depend on the facts of the case.[29]

Quantification in cases of financial loss

59.19 In the early days of the CPR,[30] there was concern that if a litigant in person could show loss, they would be entitled to an amount of two-thirds of the reasonable fee of a notional lawyer regardless of whether their losses justified such an allowance.[31] Given the common-sense way in which the CPR were interpreted,[32] there is some doubt as to whether these concerns were justified, but, on 2 December 2002, the CPR were amended[33] so as to put the issue beyond doubt. The appropriate measure is the amount that the litigant in person can prove they have lost for time reasonably spent on doing the work[34] (subject, of course, to the maximum of two-thirds the reasonable fees of a notional lawyer).

59.20 There are two layers to the court's discretion: the first is the hourly rate; the second is the time to be allowed. The first layer is a process of making a finding of fact as to the litigant's losses expressed as an hourly rate and then limiting that rate to two-thirds of the reasonable rate of a notional lawyer. The first of these steps will not always be a matter of looking at the litigant's usual charging rate, because their losses may not be the same as would ordinarily be charged. An example is a case in which Arden J found that where a professional person had avoided his usual overheads, the allowable rate could reflect the fact that there was no loss relating to those overheads.[35]

---

[26] *Hart v Aga Khan Foundation (UK)* [1984] 1 WLR 994, at 998; cf *Malkinson v Trim* [2002] EWCA Civ 1273, at [21], in which it was held that work done in the firm's time is recoverable in full.

[27] *Official Receiver v Brunt*, sub nom *In re Minotaur Data Systems Ltd* [1999] 1 WLR 1129, at 1138, by analogy with *In re Eastwood, dec'd* [1975] Ch 112.

[28] See *Crown & Stafford Stone v Eccleshall Magistrates' Court* [1988] 1 All ER 430, in which a solicitor was allowed his notional fees for appearing in his own case in a magistrates' court; *R v Boswell, R v Halliwell* [1987] 2 All ER 513, in which a barrister was allowed a notional fee for attending an appeal in respect of his own fees.

[29] Whilst no more than persuasive because it was a decision in Northern Ireland, Gillen J took this approach in a case in which an accountant had been deprived of the opportunity to carry out new business: see *N&R Devine Ltd v McAteer* [2013] NEQB 102, at [23].

[30] The method of quantification was restated on 2 December 2002.

[31] Curiously, the provisions relating to fast-track trial costs (CPR, r 45.39(5)) have not been amended so as to be in line with CPR, r 46.5.

[32] See, in particular, *HM Customs & Excise v Chitolie* [2000] BPIR 275 (CA), in which Robert Walker LJ made it clear that the amount to be allowed was the lower of the actual losses and the notional lawyer's fees.

[33] Civil Procedure (Amendment) Rules 2002 (SI 2002/2058), r 19.

[34] CPR, r 46.5(4).

[35] *Stubblefield v Kemp* [2001] 1 Costs LR 30.

Although there is no authority on the point, common sense dictates that if the costs are to be assessed on the basis of a notional lawyer's rate, the appropriate measure of time is the time that would have been spent by that notional lawyer; the fact that the work has not been carried out by a lawyer does not expand the categories of work for which costs may be allowed. This would be entirely in keeping with the way in which time is assessed where there has been no financial loss (see 59.23–59.27) and with the express terms of CPR, r 46.5(3). **59.21**

It may be that a litigant in person is able to prove financial loss, but that loss is less than the prescribed rate of £19 per hour. Whilst there is no authority on the point, it is likely that the litigant in person would be treated as having been unable to prove financial loss—that is, it is likely that the phrase 'cannot prove financial loss' in CPR, r 46.5(4)(b), ought to be read as meaning 'cannot prove financial loss that exceeds the prescribed rate'. **59.22**

Allowances for time spent (where there has been no financial loss)

The amount that may be allowed where the litigant in person has suffered no financial loss is £19 per hour.[36] It is possible that this is an upper limit,[37] but, in practice, there would be no reason to allow a lower rate. For all practical purposes, the assessment of a litigant in person's costs where they cannot show financial loss focuses only on the time spent, rather than the hourly rate. **59.23**

Lloyd J (sitting in the Court of Appeal) has explained that the measure of time is that which would have been spent by a solicitor.[38] Buckley J acknowledged that approach, but explained that it was a test that must be applied sensibly: **59.24**

> 'We wondered whether [Lloyd J] had kept in mind that it is appropriate, in a proper case, to allow a litigant in person more time for a particular task that would be allowed to a solicitor. A solicitor's charging rate includes or takes account of the fact that he has support staff, secretaries, messengers and so forth. A litigant in person, for example, must himself post letters, take files to court and photocopy documents. "The time spent reasonably doing the work ..." mentioned in [CPR, r 46.56(4)] permits a reasonable assessment of the time spent by the litigant in person and should reflect those matters.'[39]

Some commentators have implied that Buckley J's comments should be treated with caution,[40] but even if this is correct, the extent of that caution need not be great, because Buckley J was merely explaining that whilst the measure is the time spent by a solicitor, that measure must be applied in the factual circumstances in which the litigant found **59.25**

[36] PD 46, para 3.4. On 1 October 2011 this increased from £9.25 per hour, which had been the rate since 1995.

[37] In *Morris v Wiltshire and Woodspring District Council* (unreported), 16 January 1998, QBD, Jacob J has explained the correct method, which is as follows: 'Find out in respect of the item what, at the litigant in person's charging rate, the total is. Compare that with two thirds of the notional solicitor rate. Give the lower of the two items.' That said, the wording of the CPR does not suggest that the court would contemplate allowing a rate lower than the prescribed rate. There is no surviving transcript of Jacob J's decision, but it is referred to in *Stockinger v Highdorn Co Ltd* [2001] All ER (D) 62 (Apr) (QBD), at [13].

[38] *Hart v Aga Khan Foundation (UK)* [1984] 1 WLR 994, at 998 and 1005. More recently, see *R v LSC, ex p Wulfsohn* [2002] EWCA Civ 250, in which Rix J impliedly accepted this principle as being correct; see also *Greville v Sprake* [2001] EWCA Civ 234.

[39] *Mealing-McLeod v Common Professional Examinations Board* [2000] 2 Costs LR 223, at 225.

[40] See, eg, Civil Bench Book, para 8.75, published by the Judicial Studies Board (JSB) c 2010.

themselves. There can be no objection to that. In particular, Buckley J did not say anything that runs contrary to what is now CPR, r 46.5(3)(a):

> '(3) The litigant in person shall be allowed—
> (a) costs for the same categories of—
> (i) work; and
> (ii) disbursements,
> which would have been allowed if the work had been done or the disbursements had been made by a legal representative on the litigant in person's behalf.'

59.26 These provisions mean that it would be wrong to make an allowance for work that would not be recoverable if carried out by a solicitor; Buckley J's comments went to the amount of time to be allowed, rather than the types of work to which it relates, so there is no conflict. A pragmatic approach is generally adopted. Whilst a solicitor would be hard pressed to persuade a court to allow time claimed for research into procedure, for example, Rimer LJ has confirmed that such work *is* allowable in principle to a litigant in person.[41]

59.27 Costs that are not recoverable generally will not become recoverable solely by reason of the work having been carried out by the litigant personally. A litigant in person is, for example, not able to recover costs for time spent carrying out expert work beyond their own sphere of expertise.[42]

Disbursements and witness allowances

59.28 The right to payment in respect of disbursements is defined by CPR, r 46.5(3)(a). It is the right to be allowed costs for the same categories of disbursements that would have been allowed if the disbursements had been made by a legal representative on the litigant in person's behalf. Disbursements are allowable without the two-thirds restriction (reflecting the fact that there is no profit in recovering an outlay). For the reasons set out below, only disbursements actually incurred as real disbursements can be recovered; disbursements cannot be recovered if they were incurred in lieu of work that would have been done by the notional legal representative (see 59.30).

Notional disbursements

59.29 A litigant in person is not entitled to notional disbursements (also see 3.09). This was explained by Lloyd J in the context of a claim for a notional counsel's fee:

> 'There is a clear contrast between work and disbursements. Disbursements are allowed in full, just as they were before the Litigants in Person (Costs and Expenses) Act 1975, provided they would have been allowed if incurred by a solicitor, and provided they are actually incurred by the litigant in person. Work, on the other hand, is treated as if it had been done by a solicitor, and is then allowed up to two-thirds of the appropriate rate. What a solicitor would have been allowed is, of course, notional; but there is no room for a notional disbursement. Otherwise one would get the absurd position that the litigant in person would be allowed 100 per cent of counsel's notional brief fee as a "disbursement", but only two-thirds of the solicitor's notional fee for attendance.'[43]

---

41 *Grand v Gill* [2011] EWCA Civ 902, at [14], citing *R v Legal Services Commission, ex p Wulfsohn* [2002] EWCA Civ 250.

42 *Sisu Capital Fund Ltd v Tucker* [2005] EWHC 2321 (Ch). This case is useful for illustrating this point, but not all of it remains good law, so it should be treated with caution.

43 *Hart v Aga Khan Foundation (UK)* [1984] 1 WLR 994, at 997.

Professional fees in lieu of legal representatives' work

Dyson LJ has explained that if the expenditure is a fee for work that the notional legal representative would normally have done itself, it is not a disbursement within the meaning of what is now CPR, r 46.5(3)(a)(ii), primarily because it is not a disbursement that the legal representative would have incurred (see 3.97–3.99).[44] This, of course, applies only where the disbursement is the fee levied by a person who is not a legal representative (such as where the assistance is provided by an accountant or a surveyor); the fees of legal representatives can, in principle, be recovered.[45] Where, however, the fees relate to services provided by lawyers in another jurisdiction (in lieu of work that would otherwise have been carried out by lawyers in this jurisdiction), those fees would generally not be recoverable (see 59.35). In this regard, Newey LJ said that the true policy consideration in the interpretation of these rules is that those who provide advice and assistance in connection with litigation in this jurisdiction should be properly qualified, regulated and insured in this jurisdiction.[46] **59.30**

It would be wrong to believe that the fees of claims consultants (or other consultants who give advice and support in litigation) would always be irrecoverable Jefford J had this to say on the point: **59.31**

> 'In my judgment, *Agassi*[47] is not ... authority for a general proposition that costs of claims consultants or other consultants who give advice and support in litigation can never be recovered. The principles I derive from that decision are these:
> (i) Where a litigant-in-person seeks to recover the costs of a consultant's assistance, the relevant question is whether, in the particular instance, the consultant's costs are recoverable as a disbursement.
> (ii) That question is answered by posing and answering the question whether those costs would have been recoverable as a disbursement if it had been made by a solicitor.
> (iii) Costs would be recoverable as a disbursement by solicitors if the work is such as would not normally be done by solicitors.
> (iv) But there nonetheless may be specialist assistance the cost of which would be recoverable.'[48]

Jefford J went on to say this: **59.32**

> 'It is in [the] area of specialist assistance where there is a difficult dividing line between what is and is not recoverable. Although Dyson LJ [in *Agassi*] characterised the kind of specialist assistance that he had in mind as "work that would not normally be done by the solicitor instructed", it is equally clear that he had in mind matters such as briefing counsel which, on the face of it, is very much the work normally carried out by a solicitor. These two potentially conflicting approaches can be reconciled, if it is recognised that, in particular circumstances, a solicitor might well normally not carry out work himself but rely on a specialist, even though the work in its broad description might be "solicitors' work".'[49]

---

44 See *Agassi v HM Inspector of Taxes* [2005] EWCA Civ 1507, at [73]–[76]; see also *United Building and Plumbing Contractors v Kajila* [2002] EWCA Civ 628.
45 CPR, r 46.5(3)(b).
46 *Campbell v Campbell* [2018] EWCA Civ 80, at [12].
47 *Agassi v Robinson (HM Inspector of Taxes)* [2005] EWCA Civ 1507.
48 *Octoesse LLP v Trak Special Projects Ltd* [2016] EWHC 3180 (TCC), at [29].
49 *Ibid*, at [30].

Jefford J added that what amounts to normal solicitors' disbursements may vary according to the nature of the case or the type of case, and may reflect differing norms in different areas of practice and, indeed, changes in practice.

Disbursements in lieu of legal representatives' work

59.33 The same principle applies where the disbursement is for expenditure other than a fee. Pre-CPR authorities on that issue are no longer good law: prior to the introduction of the CPR, the disbursements incurred in lieu of a legal representative's fees would, in principle, have been recoverable,[50] but the test under the CPR now limits the allowable disbursements to those that would have been allowed if the disbursements had been made by a legal representative on the litigant in person's behalf.[51] Thus the points made at 59.30 would apply.

Witness allowances

59.34 A litigant who is allowed costs for attending court to conduct their case is not also entitled to a witness allowance in respect of that attendance.[52]

Payments for legal services actually purchased

59.35 A litigant in person is entitled to payments reasonably made by them for legal services relating to the conduct of the proceedings.[53] Those monies may or may not be disbursements, depending on the status of the legal representative. Fees of lawyers outside the jurisdiction would generally not be recoverable in this way.[54]

Expert assistance in respect of costs

59.36 Where a litigant in person requires expert assistance with the assessment of costs, they will be entitled to the reasonable fees of a costs practitioner (known as an expert assistant).[55]

59.37 To qualify as an expert assistant, the person in question must be a barrister, a solicitor, a Fellow of the Chartered Institute of Legal Executives (CILEx), a Fellow of the Association of Costs Lawyers (ACL),[56] a law costs draftsperson who is a member of the Academy of Experts or a law costs draftsperson who is a member of the Expert Witness Institute (see 3.95–3.96).[57]

Lawyers Acting for Themselves and on Behalf of their Firms

59.38 Where a lawyer acts for themselves or on behalf of their firm, they may wish to avoid being categorised as a litigant in person in an attempt to avoid their fees being restricted as per the regime outlined thus far.

---

50 See, eg, *Law Society v Persaud* (1990) Costs LR Core vol 114, *per* Hobhouse J.
51 See *United Building and Plumbing Contractors v Malkit Singh Kajila* [2002] EWCA Civ 628, at [14].
52 CPR, r 46.5(5).
53 CPR, r 46.5(3)(b).
54 *Campbell v Campbell* [2016] EWHC 1828 (Ch), at [15]–[17], *per* David Foxton QC, aff'd at [2018] EWCA Civ 80.
55 See CPR, r 46.5(3)(c).
56 The reference to 'Fellow' is probably an error because the ACL confers no such rank; it is almost certainly intended to refer simply to costs lawyers.
57 See PD 46, para 3.1.

Solicitors (and the *Chorley* principle)

The starting point is the position under the common law. In *Chorley*,[58] the Court of Appeal held that, at common law, solicitors who successfully defended proceedings in person were entitled to the same costs as if they had employed a solicitor and were not restricted to out-of-pocket expenses or such other costs as would ordinarily be allowed to other litigants. Sir Terence Etherton MR summarised this principle—which he called 'the *Chorley* principle'—in the following way: **59.39**

> 'The common law principle established by the *Chorley* case ("the *Chorley* principle") may be summarised as being that: (1) a solicitor who acts for himself as a party to litigation can recover not only his out of pocket expenses but also his profit costs, but he cannot recover for anything which his acting in person has made unnecessary; (2) the reason is not because of some special privilege but on the purely pragmatic grounds that (a) there has actually been an expenditure of professional skill and labour by the solicitor party, (b) that expenditure is measurable, (c) the solicitor party would otherwise employ another solicitor and, if successful, would be entitled to recover the costs of that other solicitor, and (d) since he cannot recover for anything which his acting in person has made unnecessary, the unsuccessful party will have the benefit of that disallowance and so would pay less than if the solicitor party had instructed another solicitor.'[59]

Thus the *Chorley* principle allows solicitors to recover their costs—albeit with certain restrictions (see 59.46). The *Chorley* principle, however, is now subject to rules of court.

In particular, the *Chorley* principle used to be subject to the original incarnation of what is now CPR, r 46.6(6). The rules as originally made were supplemented by art 52.5 of the (now-revoked) Costs Practice Direction (CPD), which used to provide that 'a solicitor who, instead of acting for himself, is represented in the proceedings by his firm or by himself in his firm name, is not, for the purposes of the CPR, a litigant in person'. In *Malkinson v Trim*,[60] Chadwick LJ interpreted the CPR/CPD as meaning that the *Chorley* principle continued to apply where a solicitor was represented by their firm in its name.[61] Thus, under the CPR/CPD as they were originally made, a solicitor who was represented by their firm would be able to recover costs unhindered by the provisions that apply to litigants in person. This meant that when a solicitor claimed costs for having acted in their own cause (or that of a colleague in the same firm), the first question was whether the solicitor should be regarded as **59.40**

[58] *London Scottish Benefit Society v Chorley, Crawford and Chester* (1884) 13 QBD 872.

[59] See *EMW Law LLP v Halborg* [2017] EWCA Civ 793, at [19]. The *Chorley* principle explains why, at common law, a successful solicitor litigant in person was entitled to recover his costs in *H Tolputt & Co Ltd v Mole* [1911] 1 KB 87, *per* Phillimore and Avory JJ, and on appeal at [1911] 1 KB 836, CA, but the successful solicitor litigant in person in *In the Matter of the Prosecution of Offences Act 1985 and the Costs in Criminal Cases (General) Regulations 1986; In the Matter of an application of Timothy Sharpe* (unreported), 20 November 1995, QBD was not entitled to recover a fee for advocacy where he had no right of audience as a solicitor. That was a criminal case in which the argument proceeded on the assumption that the *Chorley* principle applied to a defendant's costs in favour of a solicitor defendant who was acquitted. See also *Buckland v Watts* [1970] 1 QB 27, at 35G–H and 37F.

[60] *Malkinson v Trim* [2002] EWCA Civ 1273. That was a case in which a solicitor defendant, who was represented on the record by the firm of solicitors of which he was a partner, successfully defended the proceedings; the Court of Appeal upheld the decision of the costs judge that the solicitor defendant's costs were recoverable under the *Chorley* principle even though the defendant did not personally expend his own time and skill in defending the claim, which was handled by one of his partners or others within the firm.

[61] Chadwick LJ said that support for that view could be found in the decision of Stirling J in *Bidder v Bridges* [1887] WN 208 and in *obiter* views expressed by Simon Brown J in *R v Stafford, Stone and Eccleshall Justices, ex p Robinson* [1988] 1 WLR 369, at 372.

a litigant in person: if so, then the two-thirds limit would apply; if not, the solicitor would be entitled to full remuneration for 'expenditure of his own professional skill'.[62]

59.41 The reasoning behind that distinction was explained by Chadwick LJ in the following terms:

> '[T]here is now more clearly recognised a distinction between the solicitor litigant who provides, in connection with his own litigation, professional skill and knowledge in the course of his practice as a solicitor—that is to say, who "is represented by himself in his firm name"—and the solicitor litigant who provides skill and in what might be described as "his own time"—that is to say, outside the course of his practice as a solicitor and (typically) outside the office. The latter is treated as a litigant in person for the purposes of [the then] CPR 48.6; and so is subject to the restrictions imposed by that rule, including the two-thirds restriction imposed by sub-rule (2). The former is not.'[63]

59.42 The relevant provisions have now been changed (see 59.06), such that CPR, r 46.6(6)(b), refers to authorised persons (including solicitors) being litigants in person 'except where any such person is represented by a firm in which that person is a partner'. Whilst this new provision is wider than the old provision in the sense that its scope is no longer limited to solicitors (see 59.47 and 59.50), it is—at first blush—narrower in the sense that it will include only a solicitor litigant who is represented by a firm 'in which he is a partner'. This invites the question of whether this has changed the way in which the *Chorley* principle is applied.

59.43 The answer, in short, is that the new wording of the CPR has not changed matters to any significant extent. Sir Terence Etherton MR had this to say about the operation of CPR, r 46.6(6):

> 'It is not in identical terms to the former CPR 48.6 which was the subject of the *Malkinson* case, but its derivation from that earlier rule and paragraph 52.5 of the then Costs Practice Direction is clear, as is the intention to continue to apply the *Chorley* principle as applied in the *Malkinson* case. The latter is achieved by the exclusion of the persons mentioned in CPR 46.5(6) from the litigant in person provisions in CPR 46.5(1)–(5).'[64]

Thus it would appear that the law continues to be as it was under *Malkinson* (that is, as originally formulated under the CPR).

59.44 It has been said that the wording of CPR, r 46.6(6), prevents solicitor sole practitioners from recovering their costs unhindered by the rules relating to litigants in person. Sir Terence Etherton MR had this to say about that:

> 'That is a slavishly literal interpretation which would produce an absurd and plainly unintended result. [Counsel] offered no policy rationale for such a distinction between, on

[62] See *R (on the application of Sivanandan) v Disciplinary Tribunal of the Council of the Inns of Court* [2014] EWHC 1570 (Admin), at [19], *per* Moses LJ, aff'd at [2016] EWCA Civ 478.

[63] *Malkinson v Trim* [2002] EWCA Civ 1273, at [22].

[64] See *EMW Law LLP v Halborg* [2017] EWCA Civ 793, at [19]. The *Chorley* principle explains why, at common law, a successful solicitor litigant in person was entitled to recover his costs in *H Tolputt & Co Ltd v Mole* [1911] 1 KB 87, *per* Phillimore and Avory JJ, and on appeal at [1911] 1 KB 836, CA, but the successful solicitor litigant in person in *In the Matter of the Prosecution of Offences Act 1985 and the Costs in Criminal Cases (General) Regulations 1986; In the Matter of an application of Timothy Sharpe* (unreported), 20 November 1995, QBD, was not entitled to recover a fee for advocacy where he had no right of audience as a solicitor (in a criminal case in which the argument proceeded on the assumption that the *Chorley* principle applied to a defendant's costs in favour of a solicitor defendant who was acquitted). See also *Buckland v Watts* [1970] 1 QB 27, at 35G–H and 37F.

> the one hand, a solicitor litigant in sole practice who represents himself and, on the other hand, a solicitor litigant who is represented by the firm of which he is one of a number of partners ... Nothing has been shown to us to indicate that a conscious decision was taken by the Civil Procedure Rule Committee or the Government, in bringing into effect CPR 46.5, to create what, on the face of it, would be an irrational and indeed absurd distinction.'[65]

Etherton MR went on to say that the words in parenthesis at the beginning of CPR 46.5(6)(b)—namely, 'except where any such person is represented by a firm in which that person is a partner'—should be given a purposive interpretation in the light of *Malkinson* and the history of the *Chorley* principle, explaining that the word 'firm' includes a solicitor in sole practice and 'partner' includes a case in which there is only one principal in the firm.[66] Etherton MR went on to explain that a limited liability partnership (LLP) should be treated in the same way.

For the reasons set out above, where a solicitor litigant avoids being classed as a litigant in person, they are entitled to recover costs as though they had instructed a solicitor to act on their behalf.[67] This principle applies regardless of whether the solicitor acts through themselves, or through a partner or firm,[68] or through their employee.[69] It is a principle that is based not on contract, but on compensation for the expenditure of time. Chadwick LJ described it in this way: **59.45**

> '[A] partner who is represented in legal proceedings by his firm incurs no liability to the firm; but he suffers loss for which under the indemnity principle he ought to be compensated, because the firm of which he is a member expends time and resources which would otherwise be devoted to other clients. The only sensible way in which effect can be given to the indemnity principle is by allowing those costs.'[70]

Even where a solicitor avoids being classed as a litigant in person, there are certain types of cost that cannot be recovered as a matter of principle (see 3.14). In particular, a solicitor litigant is not entitled to recover those costs that the fact of their acting has directly rendered unnecessary (such as costs of taking instructions from themselves, etc).[71] In view of the fact that the recovery of a litigant in person's costs operates independently of contract, it is unlikely that a success fee would be recoverable even if the case pre-dated 2013.[72] **59.46**

Counsel

At the time of writing, the way in which barristers work was regulated was in a process of change—in particular, provisions were being formulated that would allow barristers to enter into partnerships. It is possibly in anticipation of this change that the CPR have been amended so as to state that a barrister who is represented by a firm in which that person **59.47**

65 See *EMW Law LLP v Halborg* [2017] EWCA Civ 793, at [34].
66 See *ibid*, at [35].
67 *London Scottish Benefit Society v Chorley* (1884) 13 QBD 872.
68 *Bidder v Bridges* (1887) WN 208, at 209, *per* Stirling J.
69 *R v Stafford Stone and Eccleshall Magistrate's Court, ex p Robinson* [1988] 1 All ER 430, at 432, *per* Simon Brown J.
70 *Malkinson v Trim* [2002] EWCA Civ 1273, at [24].
71 *London Scottish Benefit Society v Chorley* (1884) 13 QBD 872.
72 *Malkinson v Trim* [2002] EWCA Civ 1273, esp [23]–[26].

is a partner is not to be regarded as a litigant in person[73] (this being the same provision as referred to at 59.39 in the context of solicitors). Where counsel is not in a partnership, however, they will be classed as a litigant in person;[74] for the foreseeable future, this will almost always be the case if counsel is in independent practice. It should be noted that a barristers' chambers should not be equated with a firm (because they are not in any sense partnerships).

59.48 Whilst a criminal case and therefore only persuasive in the context of the CPR, Mitchell J has found that counsel may recover professional remuneration for work done where that work required the application of their training, skills and professional experience. What counsel cannot do, however, is recover professional remuneration by reason of their 'attendance' at any hearing or at any conference, or by reason of any 'work' they performed that could have been performed by any intelligent lay client.[75] Mitchell J's analysis is, in essence, an extension of the principles relating to solicitors, as referred to at 59.45. That analysis would no doubt be of relevance if a barrister were able to show that they were not a litigant in person (because it would allow a barrister to recover their usual hourly rate), but it is doubtful whether it goes much further than this under the CPR. In particular, if a barrister was acting as a litigant in person, the court would probably quantify the barrister's costs by making a finding of fact as to whether they had suffered financial loss (59.16–59.17) and, as such, there would be no need to invoke Mitchell J's analysis.

59.49 Whilst it will rarely be of any practical application, Moses LJ (sitting in the Administrative Court) found that the *Chorley* principle may, as a matter of common law, apply to counsel, but this would be so only where CPR, r 46.5(6), does not apply,[76] such as where the CPR does not apply at all (such as in certain disciplinary tribunals).

Other lawyers

59.50 In addition to applying to barristers and solicitors, the provisions referred to at 59.46—namely, that where an authorised person is represented by a firm in which that person is a partner that person will not be a litigant in person for the purposes of the CPR—also applies to:

- the manager of a body recognised under s 9 of the Administration of Justice Act 1985; and
- a person who, for the purposes of the Legal Services Act 2007, is an authorised person in relation to an activity that constitutes the conduct of litigation (within the meaning of that Act).[77]

59.51 It is not easy to think of circumstances in which the first of these categories could be relevant, but the second would be capable of applying to costs lawyers (amongst others). A costs lawyer would want to rely on this provision only if the activity for which they sought costs was one in respect of which they were an authorised person.

---

[73] See CPR, r 48.6(6)(b).

[74] See CPR, r 48.6(6)(b).

[75] *Khan v Lord Chancellor* [2003] EWHC 12 (QB), at [78], Mitchell J's analysis was based on the civil law and was thorough, so must be highly persuasive.

[76] See *R (on the application of Sivanandan) v Disciplinary Tribunal of the Council of the Inns of Court* [2014] EWHC 1570 (Admin), at [19], aff'd at [2016] EWCA Civ 478.

[77] See CPR, r 48.6(6)(b).

Mitchell J made the following comments that appear to be of general application (albeit in the context of a case concerning counsel): **59.52**

> 'In this special class of case, work involving the time and skills of a practising lawyer for the purposes of legal proceedings to which he is a party is to be treated as an expense properly incurred because, in the event of a successful outcome, not only will he have mitigated his costs, but he is entitled to be indemnified in respect of that professional time and skill.'[78]

These comments, which are *ratio*, are very wide in the sense that they allowed Mitchell J to decide the case before him not on some narrow point relating specifically to counsel, but on first principles. Therefore, it may well be that they would apply equally to other species of authorised litigator, such as costs lawyers. For the reasons set out at 59.48, however, Mitchell J's analysis would usually be of relevance only if the authorised person were found not to be acting as a litigant in person. **59.53**

Corporate Litigants

Where a corporate entity acts on its own without legal representation, then it will, without question, be a litigant in person.[79] Etherton MR has explained, however, that where that corporate entity acts through an in-house legal representative who is in possession of a practising certificate or equivalent authorisation, it will not be treated as a litigant in person and the legal representative will be able to recover costs in the normal way on behalf of the company.[80] For the avoidance of doubt, the same will apply where the corporate entity is a solicitors' LLP, which acts through its members or their employees.[81] **59.54**

In a similar vein, the reference to 'authorised persons' in CPR, r 46.5(6)(b)(v), should be read as though it applied only to individuals.[82] As such, the fact that a corporate litigant was an 'authorised person' for the purposes of the Legal Services Act 2007 would not mean that it would be necessarily be a litigant in person. **59.55**

---

78 *Khan v Lord Chancellor* [2003] EWHC 12 (QB), at [76].

79 See CPR, r 46.5(6).

80 See *EMW Law LLP v Halborg* [2017] EWCA Civ 793, at [45], *per* Etherton MR.

81 *Ibid*, at [45].

82 See *ibid*, at [50].

60

CHILDREN AND PROTECTED PERSONS

60.01 This chapter focuses on the way in which the court safeguards the rights of vulnerable parties, such as children and protected persons.[1] It deals with the following topics:

- children and costs (60.03):
  - costs orders (60.04);
  - the position as between solicitor and child (60.09);
  - the position of a paying party and the indemnity principle (60.20);
  - the position between solicitor and litigation friend (60.28);
  - procedural issues (60.31);
  - a litigation friend's expenses (children) (60.40);
- protected persons and costs (60.49):
  - the Mental Capacity Act 2005 (60.52);
  - the common law (60.57);
  - the effect of incapacity (60.58);
  - the steps necessary to deal with mental incapacity (60.64); and
  - a litigation friend's expenses (protected parties) (60.68).

60.02 The topic of capacity is addressed solely from the viewpoint of costs. The analysis is necessarily rudimentary; if a thorny issue arises, other texts dealing specifically with capacity ought to be consulted.

Children and Costs

60.03 A person becomes an adult on attaining the age of 18.[2] Prior to this, in the eyes of the law, a person is a child[3] and therefore lacking in capacity. This means that unless the court permits the child to conduct their own proceedings, a child must litigate through a litigation friend,[4] who is an officer of the court appointed to look after the child's interests[5] and bound to do so until released from that role.[6] In the ordinary run of things, a litigation

---

[1] This chapter does not deal with all aspects of capacity. In particular, it does not deal with the issue of capacity and corporations nor does it deal with insolvency. Again, other texts should be consulted for guidance on that type of issue.

[2] Family Law Reform Act 1969, s 1(1).

[3] This is the term used in the Children Act 1989 and the CPR (see CPR, r 21.2); the terms 'minor' and 'infant' are used in statutes prior to 1989.

[4] CPR, r 21.2 (3).

[5] *Rhodes v Swithenbank* (1889) 22 QBD 577, CA, at 579.

[6] *Re E (mental health patient)* [1985] 1 All ER 609, at 616.

friend is not a party to the proceedings[7] and has no rights to be heard as a party in their own right.[8]

Costs orders

In view of the child's lack of capacity, the issue of liability for costs generally focuses on the liability of the litigation friend, rather than that of the child personally.[9] Other than this, the modern approach to making orders for costs in litigation involving children is the same as in any other form of litigation. There are ancient authorities on the exercise of the court's discretion, but care must be exercised when seeking guidance from those cases because many of them deal with the position between the child and their litigation friend, rather than between opposing parties.[10] This may not always be apparent from what is said in older reported cases. **60.04**

Timing and procedure

Although it pre-dates the Civil Procedure Rules (CPR), there is authority that where an order is sought against a litigation friend, it must be sought at the time the costs order is made.[11] If the receiving party wishes the court to address the point at some future time, that aspect of the matter ought to be reserved.[12] Regardless of whether these principles have survived the introduction of the CPR, they are undoubtedly guidelines for good practice. **60.05**

Principles concerning litigation friends

A child may be *awarded* costs in just the same way as may any other litigant. In so far as the indemnity principle is concerned, a child is able to recover costs from an opponent by the mechanisms described at 60.09–60.15. Where the court is minded to make an order *against* a child, it generally would be effective against the litigation friend,[13] who may then be able to claim those costs from the child as expenses[14] (see 60.40–60.47). Indeed, it is implicit in CPR, r 21.4(3)(c), that a litigation friend acting on behalf of a claimant **60.06**

[7] *Dyke v Stephens* (1885) 30 Ch D 189, at 190.

[8] *Rhodes v Swithenbank* (1889) 22 QBD 577, CA, at 579.

[9] Other than in cases of fraud, a child would not usually be ordered to pay costs personally: *Lemprière v Lange* (1879) 12 Ch D 675, at 679; *Elsey v Cox* (1858) 26 Beav 95. This is a reflection of the principle that a child could not personally make themselves liable for an opponent's costs: *Turner v Turner* (1726) 2 Stra 708. There are numerous exceptions to this rule—see, eg, *Brockelbank v Brockelbank and Borlase* (1911) 27 TLR 569—but, with the modern facility for the court to ensure that a litigation friend is able to meet a costs order, it would rarely be the case that the court would have to consider those exceptions.

[10] There is ancient authority establishing a principle that a litigation friend will not be required personally to pay the costs of an unsuccessful defence unless they have been guilty of gross misconduct: *Vivian v Kennelly* (1890) 63 LT 778. The modern equivalent of that principle would be that the court would make the order against the litigation friend as if they were any other litigant, but then deal with misconduct in the exercise of its discretion in terms of the litigant friend's expenses.

[11] *Re Picton, Picton v Picton* [1931] WN 254.

[12] *Caley v Caley* (1877) 25 WR 528.

[13] It has long been the case that where a defendant successfully defends a claim brought by a child, the court has been able to order the litigation friend to pay the costs; there is no reason to believe that the situation is any different under the CPR: see, eg, *Huxley v Wootton* (1912) 29 TLR 132; *Slaughter v Talbott* (1739) Willes 190; *Catt v Wood* [1908] 2 KB 458, CA, at 473.

[14] The litigation friend may bring a claim against the child for an indemnity in respect of those costs: *Steeden v Walden* [1910] 2 Ch 393. Those monies may not be recoverable if the litigation was not brought for the child's benefit—see, eg, *Re Fish, Bennett v Bennett* [1893] 2 Ch 413, CA—or if it was improper litigation: *Re Hicks, Lindon v Hemery* [1893] WN 138.

undertakes to meet any adverse costs order that may be made in the proceedings. In so far as it is relevant, CPR, r 21.4(3)(c) provides as follows:

> 'If nobody has been appointed by the court ... a person may act as a litigation friend if he ... undertakes to pay any costs which the child or protected party may be ordered to pay in relation to the proceedings, subject to any right he may have to be repaid from the assets of the child or protected party.'

60.07 A similar, but more explicit, provision is made in Practice Direction (PD) 21, para 2.2(e), which makes provision for the litigation friend to file a written undertaking.[15] A litigation friend may be required to prove compliance with the undertaking upon evidence.[16]

60.08 A litigation friend's liability is not without end, however. In this regard, CPR, r 21.9(6), makes the following provisions:

> 'The liability of a litigation friend for costs continues until—
> (a) the person in respect of whom his appointment to act has ceased serves the notice referred to in paragraph (4); or
> (b) the litigation friend serves notice on the parties that his appointment to act has ceased.'

The position as between solicitor and child

60.09 In the following discussion, it should be borne in mind that the topic of the retainer between the solicitor and child would often be little more than a distraction because there would usually be a retainer with the litigation friend who would recover their outlay from the child as expenses. There would, in those circumstances, be no need for a retainer with the child directly because those expenses would be recovered under the CPR, rather than under a retainer (see 27.36 and 60.40–60.47).

60.10 Where the retainer is with the litigation friend, the child's rights would be preserved not only by the court's supervision of the expenses (see 60.40–60.47), but also by the child's right to apply for an assessment pursuant to s 71 of the Solicitors Act 1974 (although, for the reasons set out in 36.82, the latter confers few practical benefits).

60.11 Retainers with children are not entirely unknown. With certain exceptions—most notably, contracts for 'necessaries'—a contract with a child is, in general, voidable rather than void.[17] For the reasons set out at 60.16, it is entirely possible that contracts for legal services are—or, more accurately, are capable of being—contracts for necessaries; where this is so, the difficulties described immediately below would tend not to arise.

The meaning of voidable

60.12 What follows will be relevant only in the comparatively rare situation in which the contract of retainer is with the child. If, as is nearly always the case, there is a contract of retainer

[15] PD 21, para 2.2(e), reads as follows: 'A person who wishes to become a litigation friend without a court order pursuant to r 21.5(3) must file a certificate of suitability in Practice Form N235 ... where the child or protected party is a claimant, undertaking to pay any costs which the child or protected party may be ordered to pay in relation to the proceedings, subject to any right he may have to be repaid from the assets of the child or protected party.'

[16] See PD 21, para 3.3(4).

[17] *Bruce v Warwick* (1815) 6 Taunt 118; *Nash v Inman* [1908] 2 KB 1.

with the litigation friend, then, for the reasons set out at 60.09, it would usually be appropriate to focus on that contract instead (see 60.21–60.22 and 60.28–60.30).

Where there is a contract with a child, it will be voidable rather than void (see 60.11). In **60.13**
this context, 'voidable' means one of two things: that the contract is not enforceable against the child unless and until they ratify it upon reaching majority; or that the contract may be repudiated by the child while they remain a child and for a reasonable period of time thereafter. Surprisingly, there is no authority as to whether contracts of retainer would fall into the former or the latter category, but in view of the fact that the latter usually pertains to contracts for land, property, etc,[18] it is likely that the former would apply. This means that unless the contract of retainer is for the provision of services that are 'necessaries' (see 60.16), it will probably be unenforceable against the child unless and until it is ratified upon the child reaching majority. The contrary is arguable, however (see 60.27).

If the above analysis is right, then a contract with a child will become enforceable against **60.14**
that child if ratified (see 60.24–60.25) when they reach majority.[19] In a similar vein, a child may, within a reasonable period of time after reaching maturity, elect to become liable under the contract of retainer and they can do so even if they have previously avoided the contract.[20] Beyond these things, there is—in the present context—no power of election that would result in the contract being enforceable against the child. (This does not mean that the contract is of no effect, however, because, in most instances, the child would be able to elect to enforce the contract of retainer against their solicitors,[21] but that is irrelevant for the purposes of costs because it would give no power of enforcement against the child.)

The effect of payment under a contract of retainer with a child is a moot point. If the con- **60.15**
tract is of the second type of contract mentioned at 60.13, the child may be debarred from recouping monies they have paid out,[22] but, for the reasons set out above, it is not likely that contracts of retainer would fall within that category. It is therefore likely that if a contract of retainer is unenforceable by reason of the client being a child, the unenforceability would have a similar effect to unenforceability of any other origin.

Necessaries

It should not be forgotten that a contract of retainer with the child is often merely a dis- **60.16**
traction (see 60.09). Where this is not the case, however, and where the receiving party (or the legal representative) is forced to rely on the existence of an enforceable contract, it may be necessary to look at the law of necessaries. A contract for necessaries would generally be enforceable against the child.[23]

[18] See the discussion of this topic in *North Western Rly Co v M'Michael* (1850) 5 Exch 114, at 123.
[19] *Williams v Moor* (1843) 11 M & W 256.
[20] *North Western Rly Co v M'Michael* (1850) 5 Exch 114, at 127.
[21] *Ibid; Re Smith's Trusts* (1890) 25 LR Ir 439.
[22] *Steinberg v Scala (Leeds) Ltd* [1923] 2 Ch 452, CA, at 461. In those circumstances, the question will not be whether the child got value for money, but whether there was a total failure of consideration.
[23] *Chapple v Cooper* (1844) 13 M & W 252, at 258, *per* Alderson B. A child who is so young as to be incapable of consent would not be bound by a contract, even if it were for necessaries: *R v Oldham Metropolitan Borough Council, ex p G* [1993] 1 FLR 645.

60.17 Whether services can be said to be necessaries is a question of mixed fact and law.[24] Broadly speaking, necessaries are—as the name implies—things without which an individual cannot reasonably function. Although authority on the point is lacking,[25] there is no reason to believe that, in appropriate circumstances, a contract for the supply of legal services could not be a contract for necessaries.[26] An argument in support of that contention would be particularly persuasive if the legal services related to a claim for an injury that resulted in the lack of capacity. It has been held that the supply of money to purchase necessaries is itself necessary;[27] it may be that the same logic applies where the purpose of the claim is to provide necessaries such as care, accommodation, etc.

60.18 There is, however, a potential problem with relying on the doctrine of necessaries in a case in which the retainer is a conditional fee agreement. This is because it is possible that the basis of the liability created by the supply of necessaries is restitutionary, rather than contractual.[28] If this is correct, then a paying party would, with some justification, argue that there can be no such thing as a conditional restitutionary remedy in circumstances in which Parliament has expressly reserved to itself all control over conditional fee agreements.[29]

Prejudicial contracts

60.19 It is worth making one or two further points about children and contracts. Contracts that are prejudicial to a child are wholly void (as opposed to being merely voidable).[30] In the context of costs, such contracts will rarely arise, but some contracts for disbursement funding loans may conceivably fall within such a category.[31] Whether a contract is prejudicial is a matter of balancing the prejudicial aspects against the general benefit that the contract confers upon the child.[32] Likewise, contracts (even for the supply of necessaries) that contain provisions that are harsh or onerous upon the child may be adjudged void.[33] Again, such contracts will be rare in the context of costs litigation, but an example might be a post-2013 conditional fee agreement that provides for a particularly sizeable success fee or a private retainer that provides for an outlandishly high hourly rate.

The position of a paying party and the indemnity principle

60.20 Where a paying party is ordered to pay a child's costs, the fact that the child lacks capacity to enter into a contract of retainer may lead to uncertainty as to whether there has been compliance with the indemnity principle.

---

24 *Ryder v Wombwell* (1868) LR 4 Exch 32, at 38, *per* Willes J.

25 The nearest authority is *De Stacpoole v De Stacpoole* (1887) 37 Ch D 139, which confirms that legal advice for certain non-contentious services (drawing a marriage settlement) were necessaries.

26 In *Helps v Clayton* (1864) 17 CB (NS) 553, for example, a father acting for his daughter was described as acting in the role of agent in respect of the preparation of a marriage settlement and the daughter's minority was held not to be a defence to an action against her by solicitors to recover the costs of the marriage settlement. This was in circumstances in which the preparation of the settlement was considered to be a 'necessary' suitable to her condition.

27 *Beavan, Davies, Banks & Co v Beavan* [1912] 1 Ch 196.

28 See the competing analyses of Fletcher Moulton LJ and Buckley LJ in *Nash v Inman* [1908] 2 KB 1.

29 See Courts and Legal Services Act 1990, s 58 (as amended).

30 *Slator v Brady* (1863) 14 ICLR 61.

31 See, in relation to loans in general, *Martin v Gale* (1876) 4 Ch D 428.

32 *Chaplin v Leslie Frewin (Publishers) Ltd* [1966] Ch 71.

33 *Roberts v Gray* [1913] 1 KB 520.

Where there is a contract of retainer with the litigation friend

In the ordinary run of things, the child's litigation friend will have entered into a retainer (often in the form of a contract of retainer under which they and the child are jointly liable for the solicitor's fees: see 60.30). Where this is the case, compliance with the indemnity principle can usually be proved by reason of the litigation friend's right to seek expenses from the child.[34] That is not a contractual obligation, so issues of the child's capacity do not arise. There is a cap of between 25–50 per cent in cases in which the amount awarded is £5,000 or less (see 60.40–60.47),[35] but—whilst there is no authority on the point—it is unlikely that CPR, r 21.12, would be interpreted as having an adverse bearing on the indemnity principle, not least because the restriction will apply 'unless the court directs otherwise'.[36] **60.21**

The effect of substitution of a litigation friend It may be that a contract of retainer made by a litigation friend is challenged on the basis that the litigation friend was subsequently substituted. Whilst not binding, Master Brown found that the principles in *Blankley v Central Manchester and Manchester Children's University Hospitals NHS Trust*[37] (see 27.79–27.81) would apply by analogy and that, as such, the original retainer would be capable of continuing to have effect.[38] This may be relevant where, as in the case before Master Brown, the original contract of retainer was a pre-1 April 2013 conditional fee agreement, but the substitution took place after that date. **60.22**

Where there is no contract of retainer with the litigation friend

What follows (in 60.24–60.27) will be relevant only in the comparatively rare situation in which the contract of retainer is with the child and not with the litigation friend. If, as is nearly always the case, there is a contract of retainer with the litigation friend, then, for the reasons set out at 60.09, it would usually be appropriate to focus on that contract instead. **60.23**

Ratification on reaching majority Ratification is an aspect of the law of agency: a principal may ratify the unauthorised acts of a person who has purported to act for them whilst having no actual authority.[39] If a child, upon reaching majority, were to ratify the retainer, then the retainer would become enforceable against the child-turned-adult. If such ratification were to be accepted by the court, this would result in compliance with the indemnity principle. **60.24**

A paying party could argue that it was unreasonable for the child to ratify the retainer, but it is not likely that the court would accept such an argument. A better argument (albeit a highly unattractive one) would be that ratification after the costs order was made ought to be of no effect, but there is no authority to confirm or counter that argument. **60.25**

Necessaries If the child were able to show that the legal services were 'necessaries', then the legal services provider might be able to rely on that doctrine to establish a liability **60.26**

---

[34] See CPR, r 21.4(3)(c); PD 21, paras 2.2(e) and 3.3(4). See also *Re Fish, Bennett v Bennett* [1893] 2 Ch 413; Practice Direction (Children and Protected Parties), paras 2.2(e) and 3.3(4).

[35] CPR, r 22.12(6).

[36] CPR, r 22.12(6).

[37] *Blankley v Central Manchester and Manchester Children's University Hospitals NHS Trust* [2015] EWCA Civ 18.

[38] See *CM (a protected person by his litigation friend, The Official Solicitor) v Parkdean Holiday Parks Ltd* (unreported), 29 March 2017, SCCO, at [17]–[22], *per* Master Brown.

[39] Watts, P, *Bowstead and Reynolds on Agency* (21st edn, London: Sweet & Maxwell, 2017), para 2-004.

on the part of the child. This would not present any problems in the case of a private retainer, but it might give rise to difficulties if the retainer were a conditional retainer, for the reasons mentioned at 60.18.

60.27 **Public policy** As mentioned at 60.12–60.15, a category of contracts exists in which a contract would be regarded as enforceable unless and until the child took steps to avoid it. Whether a contract falls within that category seems to be a matter of public policy. The public policy underlying the rules regarding children and their contracts is there to protect children against their immaturity and inexperience.[40] It is—to say the least—doubtful that policy would be advanced by allowing it to be used as a vehicle for establishing breaches of the indemnity principle. It is therefore arguable that retainers are within that special group of contracts and that they are enforceable until the child takes steps to avoid them. There is, however, no authority to support that contention. In any event, for the reasons set out at 60.21, the point ought not to arise in modern litigation.

The position between solicitor and litigation friend

60.28 Where a litigation friend instructs solicitors, in the absence of an express retainer there will ordinarily be an implied term that the litigation friend will be liable for the solicitors' fees.[41] Where the litigation was properly conducted for the child's benefit, the litigation friend would then be able to recover the monies from the child as expenses.[42] This would be so regardless of whether the child is a claimant or a defendant.[43] Thus the child would indirectly be responsible for the solicitor's fees (subject, of course, to the litigation friend's expenses being appropriate (see 60.40–60.47)).

60.29 If the court declines to allow expenses that are their own solicitors' fees and disbursements, the litigation friend may or may not continue to be liable for the monies that have been disallowed. This will depend on the terms of the contract of retainer. It would, of course, always be open to the litigation friend to challenge any such monies in a solicitor-and-client assessment.

Joint contracts of retainer

60.30 The litigation friend and the child may be (and very often are) jointly liable under the same retainer. Where this is so, the former is not bound by the contract if it can be performed only jointly.[44] If, however, it can be performed by the litigation friend acting alone, then they would remain liable under it.[45] This would be the situation with most—if not nearly all—contracts of retainer. Put otherwise, the rules pertaining to contractual joint liability will rarely result in a breach of the indemnity principle, so it usually creates no problems if the child and the litigation friend are counterparties to the same retainer.

---

[40] Latey, J, *Report of the Committee on the Age of Majority*, Cmnd 3342 (London: HMSO, 1967), para 289.

[41] *Re Payne, Randle v Payne* (1883) 23 Ch D 288, CA, at 289.

[42] See CPR, r 21.4(3)(c); PD 21, paras 2.2(e) and 3.3(4). See also *Re Fish, Bennett v Bennett* [1893] 2 Ch 413; Practice Direction (Children and Protected Parties), paras 2.2(e) and 3.3(4).

[43] *Earl of Orford v Churchill* (1814) 3 Ves & B 59, at 71.

[44] *Gill v Russell* (1673) Freem KB 62.

[45] *Chaplin v Leslie Frewin (Publishers) Ltd* [1966] Ch 71.

Procedural issues

In general, the procedure relating to children is similar to that relating to adults, but a number of additional provisions apply. In so far as litigation friends, orders, etc, are concerned, the relevant procedure is governed by CPR, Part 21, and its associated Practice Direction. In addition, CPR, Part 46, contains a number of relevant provisions. **60.31**

Statement of interest

If a person who has an interest in the outcome of an assessment of costs is a child, then a statement to that effect must accompany a request for a detailed assessment hearing.[46] **60.32**

Assessment of costs payable to or by a child

The 'general rule'—which is not an absolute rule by any means—is that where costs are payable either to or by a child, those costs will be assessed by way of detailed assessment. CPR, r 46.4, makes the following provisions: **60.33**

> '(1) This rule applies to any proceedings where a party is a child or protected party and—
> (a) money is ordered or agreed to be paid to, or for the benefit of, that party; or
> (b) money is ordered to be paid by him or on his behalf.
>
> ("Child" and "protected party" have the same meaning as in rule 21.1(2).)
> (2) The general rule is that—
> (a) the court must order a detailed assessment of the costs payable by, or out of money belonging to, any party who is a child or protected party; and
> (b) on an assessment under paragraph (a), the court must also assess any costs payable to that party in the proceedings, unless—
> (i) the court has issued a default costs certificate in relation to those costs under rule 47.11; or
> (ii) the costs are payable in proceedings to which Section II or Section III of Part 45 applies.
>
> (3) The court need not order detailed assessment of costs in the circumstances set out Practice Direction 46.
>
> (4) Where—
> (a) a claimant is a child or protected party; and
> (b) a detailed assessment has taken place under paragraph (2)(a),
>
> the only amount payable by the child or protected party is the amount which the court certifies as payable.
>
> (5) Where the costs payable comprise only the success fee claimed by the child's or protected party's legal representative under a conditional fee agreement or the balance of any payment under a damages based agreement, the court may direct that—
> (a) the assessment procedure referred to in rule 46.10 and paragraph 6 of Practice Direction 46 shall not apply; and
> (b) such costs be assessed summarily.
>
> (This rule applies to a counterclaim by or on behalf of a child or protected party by virtue of rule 20.3.)'

Thus this general rule will not apply to the assessment of certain success fees or fees payable under damages-based agreements (see CPR, r 46.4(5)) nor will it apply in 'the **60.34**

[46] PD 46, para 18.3(c).

circumstances set out in Practice Direction 46', which circumstances are listed in PD 46, para 2.1:

> '(a) where there is no need to do so to protect the interests of the child or protected party or their estate;
> (b) where another party has agreed to pay a specified sum in respect of the costs of the child or protected party and the legal representative acting for the child or protected party has waived the right to claim further costs;
> (c) where the court has decided the costs payable to the child or protected party by way of summary assessment and the legal representative acting for the child or protected party has waived the right to claim further costs;
> (d) where an insurer or other person is liable to discharge the costs which the child or protected party would otherwise be liable to pay to the legal representative and the court is satisfied that the insurer or other person is financially able to discharge those costs; and
> (e) where the court has given a direction for summary assessment pursuant to rule 46.4(5).'

Fixed costs

60.35 In proceedings to which CPR, Part 45, Section II, applies—that is, where predictable costs are payable—or where CPR, Part 45, Section III, applies—that is, where the Pre-Action Protocol for Low Value Personal Injury Claims in Road Traffic Accidents (the RTA Protocol) or the Pre-Action Protocol for Low Value Personal Injury (Employers' Liability and Public Liability) Claims (the EL/PL Protocol) apply—the court will not make an order for detailed assessment of the costs payable to the child, but will assess the costs in the manner set out in the relevant section (see 50.86 and 50.250–50.251).[47]

Summary assessment of costs payable to or by a child

60.36 Corresponding provisions exist in relation to summary assessment. Where costs are payable by a child, the court may carry out a summary assessment,[48] but where the costs are payable to a child, the court will not make a summary assessment of the costs unless the solicitor acting for the child has waived the right to further costs.[49]

Contentious business agreements

60.37 Where the costs are payable by a child pursuant to a contentious business agreement that has been entered into by the child's guardian acting in a representative capacity, the agreement must be laid before the court for the court's approval before payment. Failure to do this can result in the guardian being ordered to account to the child.[50] This is dealt with in detail at 27.178–27.181.

Compromise by a child

60.38 Compromises involving children have to be approved.[51] The purpose of this is to protect children from themselves and their legal advisers by imposing a framework within which the court checks on the propriety of any settlement.[52]

---

47 CPR, r 21.10(3).
48 PD 44, para 9.9(2).
49 PD 44, para 9.9(1). CPR, r 21.10(3), disapplies this for those claims under CPR, Part 45, Sections II and III; this provision appears still to apply to those claims under CPR, Part 45, Section IIIA.
50 See Solicitors Act 1974, s 62.
51 See CPR, r 21.10.
52 *Dunhill v Burgin* [2014] UKSC 18.

That said, Clarke MR has confirmed (*obiter*) that the approval of the court is not required if the terms of the compromise were such that the child would have no interest in the matter.[53] Thus it would not be necessary to seek the court's approval of a compromise of costs under a CFA Lite; likewise, it would not be necessary to seek approval in circumstances in which the solicitor was willing to waive any monies not recovered from the paying party. **60.39**

A litigation friend's expenses (children)

Where a litigation friend enters into a contract of retainer to pursue a claim on behalf of the child, the costs incurred in that claim will be recoverable from the child, but only to the extent that they are reasonable. Express provision for this is made at CPR, r 21.12. It should be noted that, on 6 April 2015,[54] CPR, r 21.12(1A), was inserted in such a way as to ensure that recoverable costs are subject to assessment, but that certain success fees may be assessed summarily: **60.40**

> '(1) Subject to paragraph (1A), in proceedings to which rule 21.11 applies, a litigation friend who incurs costs or expenses on behalf of a child or protected party in any proceedings is entitled on application to recover the amount paid or payable out of any money recovered or paid into court to the extent that it—
> (a) has been reasonably incurred; and
> (b) is reasonable in amount.
>
> (1A) Costs recoverable under this rule are limited to—
> (a) costs incurred by or on behalf of a child and which have been assessed by way of detailed assessment pursuant to rule 46.4(2); or
> (b) costs incurred by or on behalf of a child by way of success fee under a conditional fee agreement or sum payable under a damages based agreement in a claim for damages for personal injury where the damages agreed or ordered to be paid do not exceed £25,000, where such costs have been assessed summarily pursuant to rule 46.4(5).
>
> (2) Expenses may include all or part of—
> (a) a premium in respect of a costs insurance policy (as defined by section 58C(5) of the Courts and Legal Services Act 1990); or
> (b) interest on a loan taken out to pay a premium in respect of a costs insurance policy or other recoverable disbursement.'

The effect of CPR, r 21.12(1A)(b) (in combination of CPR r 46.4(5)(b), and PD 21, para 11), is that where the claim is a personal injury claim in which the damages are £25,000 or less, a proposed deduction of a success fee or sum payable under a damages-based agreement may be dealt with by summary, rather than detailed, assessment. It should be noted that this applies only to children; it does not apply to protected parties. Moreover, it does not allow assessment of any other costs and, as such, is (arguably) not as useful a provision as it may first appear. **60.41**

It used to be the case that these provisions used the words 'costs' and 'expenses' in a way that invited all manner of problems. Fortunately, CPR, r 21.12, has now been amended, but there is still ambiguity as to what those two words mean.[55] It may be that references **60.42**

53 *Tankard v John Fredricks Plastics Ltd* [2008] EWCA Civ 1375, at [7].
54 See Civil Procedure (Amendment No 2) Rules 2015 (SI 2015/670), r 11, Civil Procedure (Amendment No 8) Rules 2014 (SI 2014/3299), r 5, and the associated practice direction.
55 See, eg, *Cook on Costs 2017* (LexisNexis, online), para 34.3.

to 'costs' are to those monies (which may include disbursements) that are capable of assessment between opposing parties, whereas 'expenses' means (or at least includes) other outlays that a litigant friend may have to make, such as (irrecoverable) insurance premiums and interest on loans (not to mention out-of-pocket expenses).

Discouragement of multiple assessments

60.43 If costs have already been assessed, the court discourages a further assessment by placing a bar on the recovery of costs that have been disallowed on the prior assessment. CPR, r 21.12(3), makes the following provisions:

> '(3) No application may be made under this rule for costs or expenses that—
> (a) are of a type that may be recoverable on an assessment of costs payable by or out of money belonging to a child or protected party; but
> (b) are disallowed in whole or in part on such an assessment.
>
> (Costs and expenses which are also "costs" as defined in rule 44.1(1) are subject to rule 46.4(2) and (3).)'

Basis of assessment

60.44 The CPR do not state a basis on which the expenses will be assessed, but they lay the foundation for an assessment that would be very similar to an assessment of costs. CPR, r 22.12(4) and (5), provides as follows:

> '(4) In deciding whether the costs or expenses were reasonably incurred and reasonable in amount, the court will have regard to all the circumstances of the case including the factors set out in rule 44.4(3) and 46.9.
>
> (5) When the court is considering the factors to be taken into account in assessing the reasonableness of the costs or expenses, it will have regard to the facts and circumstances as they reasonably appeared to the litigation friend or to the child's or protected party's legal representative when the cost or expense was incurred.'

Low-value claims

60.45 Where judgment is given on terms that the amount awarded does not exceed £5,000, the sums that may be recovered in expenses are limited to no higher than 25 per cent of the sums awarded (or, if the court gives permission, up to 50 per cent). CPR, r 22.12(6) and (7), makes the following provision:

> '(6) Subject to paragraph (7), where the claim is settled or compromised, or judgment is given, on terms that an amount not exceeding £5,000 is paid to the child or protected party, the total amount the litigation friend may recover under paragraph (1) must not exceed 25% of the sum so agreed or awarded, unless the court directs otherwise. Such total amount must not exceed 50% of the sum so agreed or awarded.
>
> (7) The amount which the litigation friend may recover under paragraph (1) in respect of costs must not (in proceedings at first instance) exceed 25% of the amount of the sum agreed or awarded in respect of—
> (a) general damages for pain, suffering and loss of amenity; and
> (b) damages for pecuniary loss other than future pecuniary loss,
>
> net of any sums recoverable by the Compensation Recovery Unit of the Department for Work and Pensions.'

It is arguable that this limit would, in some circumstances, operate as a cap between opposing parties, but this would be unlikely to be as a result of the operation of the indemnity principle because the restriction applies 'unless the court directs otherwise'. In any event, the point would not commonly arise because such small claims would often be relegated to the small claims track, where, of course, the issue of costs would be unlikely to arise.

Additional liabilities payable out of damages

Whilst not binding, District Judge Lumb (an experienced regional costs judge) has noted that, since the abrogation of the recoverability of additional liabilities in 2013, more applications are being made for approval for the payment of additional liabilities payable by children. In a case in which an after-the-event (ATE) premium was claimed in a modest claim that was anything but laden with risk, he declined to make an allowance, because he believed that qualified one-way costs shifting (QOCS) would have afforded sufficient protection.[56] **60.46**

Procedure

From the procedural point of view, PD 21, para 11, makes the following provisions: **60.47**

> '11.1 A litigation friend may make a claim for expenses under rule 21.12(1)—
> (1) where the court has ordered an assessment of costs under rule 46.4(2), at the detailed assessment hearing;
> (2) where the litigation friend's expenses are not of a type which would be recoverable as costs on an assessment of costs between the parties, to the Master or district judge at the hearing to approve the settlement or compromise under Part 21 (the Master or district judge may adjourn the matter to the costs judge); or
> (3) where an assessment of costs under Part 46.4(2) is not required, and no approval under Part 21 is necessary, by a Part 23 application supported by a witness statement to a costs judge or district judge as appropriate.
>
> 11.2 In all circumstances, the litigation friend must support a claim for expenses by filing a witness statement setting out—
> (1) the nature and amount of the expense; and
> (2) the reason the expense was incurred.'

Where a success fee or fee under a damages-based agreement is claimed, PD 21, para 11.3, adds the following provisions: **60.48**

> '11.3 Where the application is for payment out of the damages in respect of costs pursuant to rule 21.12 (1A) the witness statement must also include (or be accompanied by)—
> (1) a copy of the conditional fee agreement or damages based agreement;
> (2) the risk assessment by reference to which the success fee was determined;
> (3) the reasons why the particular funding model was selected;
> (4) the advice given to the litigation friend in relation to funding arrangements;
> (5) details of any costs agreed, recovered or fixed costs recoverable by the child; and
> (6) confirmation of the amount of the sum agreed or awarded in respect of—
> (a) general damages for pain, suffering and loss of amenity; and
> (b) damages for pecuniary loss other than future pecuniary loss, net of any sums recoverable by the Compensation Recovery Unit of the Department for Work and Pensions.'

[56] *A & Anor v Royal Mail Groupat* [2015] EW Misc B24 (CC).

Protected Persons and Costs

60.49 Persons who lack mental capacity have, in the past, been referred to as 'lunatics', 'mental patients' and the 'mentally disordered'; some of these terms are still encountered from time to time in older authorities, but the terms 'persons who lack mental capacity' and 'protected party' seem, at present, to be most well received. The latter is used in this book, not least because it is the term that is used in the CPR.[57]

60.50 There are three sources of the law relevant to costs: the common law; statute; and codes of practice. The common law establishes a test of capacity and acts in such a way as to protect persons who have entered into contracts that they were unable to understand. Statute gives guidance and, in particular, it lays down five principles that affect the test of capacity. Statute also creates mechanisms by which a person's affairs may be managed for them if they lack capacity. Much of the guidance in the Mental Capacity Act 2005 is all-encompassing and non-specific, and the need for detailed guidance (if only by analogy) is likely to be met by existing common-law authorities.

60.51 The topic is addressed in four parts: first is a summary of the Mental Capacity Act 2005 (see 60.52) and, in particular, of the five presumptions mentioned above (see 60.54); secondly, there is an outline of the common law (see 60.57); thirdly, there is a brief overview of the effect that a person's incapacity would have on their ability to enter into a contract of retainer (see 60.58); and finally, there is a brief account of the steps that must be taken where a person is found to lack capacity, or it is thought that they might lack capacity (see 60.64).

The Mental Capacity Act 2005

60.52 The Mental Capacity Act 2005 came into force in 2007.[58] It is supplemented by a Code of Practice issued by the Lord Chancellor.[59] The Code of Practice acknowledges that the 2005 Act's new definition of 'capacity' is in line with the existing common-law authorities and it goes on to say that judges are at liberty to adopt the new definitions if they think it is appropriate.[60] Thus there is plasticity in the law, which is necessary because the issue of capacity is largely a factual exercise and the relevant factors will differ from one area of law to another. Mental Capacity Act 2005, s 2(1), provides the following general definition of 'incapacity':

> '(1) For the purposes of this Act, a person lacks capacity in relation to a matter if at the material time he is unable to make a decision for himself in relation to the matter because of an impairment of, or a disturbance in the functioning of, the mind or brain.'

60.53 What amounts to impairment or disturbance of the functioning of the mind or brain will depend on the circumstances, and on the nature and extent of the impairment.

---

57 See CPR, r 21.1(2)(d).

58 The provisions relevant to the law of costs came into force on 1 October 2007. Transitional provisions apply: see Mental Capacity Act 2005 (Transitional and Consequential Provisions) Order 2007 (SI 2007/1898).

59 Which was issued by the Lord Chancellor on 23 April 2007, in accordance with Mental Capacity Act 2005, ss 42 and 43. At the time of writing, it had last been updated on 12 January 2016.

60 Mental Capacity Act 2005 Code of Practice, para 4.32.

To that extent, some guidance may be obtained from the common law. Notwithstanding the occasional need to refer to the common law, both the Mental Capacity Act 2005 and its Code of Practice give guidance and it would be rare for further guidance to be necessary in a detailed assessment or other matter relating to costs.

The Mental Capacity Act 2005 establishes five key principles that empower and protect people who are thought to lack capacity: **60.54**

- a person must be assumed to have capacity unless it is established that they lack capacity;
- a person is not to be treated as unable to make a decision unless all practicable steps to help them to do so have been taken without success;
- a person is not to be treated as unable to make a decision merely because they make an unwise decision;
- an act done, or decision made, under this Act for or on behalf of a person who lacks capacity must be done, or made, in their best interests; and
- before any such act is done or any such decision is made, regard must be had to whether the purpose for which it is needed can be as effectively achieved in a way that is less restrictive of the person's rights and freedom of action.[61]

In addition, the Mental Capacity Act 2005 stipulates that it does not matter whether the impairment or disturbance is permanent or temporary.[62] A lack of capacity cannot be established merely by reference to a person's age or appearance, or a condition of theirs, or an aspect of their behaviour that might lead others to make unjustified assumptions about their capacity.[63] Any question of whether a person lacks capacity within the meaning of the Mental Capacity Act 2005 must be decided on the balance of probabilities.[64] **60.55**

The Act goes on to provide that a person lacks capacity in respect of a decision if they are unable to: **60.56**

- understand the information relevant to the decision;
- retain that information;
- use or weigh that information as part of the process of making the decision; or
- communicate their decision (whether by talking, using sign language or any other means).[65]

The common law

The common-law test of capacity is whether or not the person was capable of understanding the nature of the contract into which they were entering.[66] It is the person's capacity to understand the actual contract under consideration that is relevant, rather than their capacity in general.[67] The nature of the contract is therefore a relevant factor. Although there is no authority on the point, it is possible that a client may have capacity to understand **60.57**

---

[61] Mental Capacity Act 2005, s 1.
[62] Mental Capacity Act 2005, s 2(2).
[63] Mental Capacity Act 2005, s 2(3).
[64] Mental Capacity Act 2005, s 2.
[65] Mental Capacity Act 2005, s 3.
[66] *Boughton v Knight* (1873) LR 3 P & D 64.
[67] *Ibid*, at 72.

a simple contract of retainer (such as a CFA Lite), but at the same time lack capacity to understand a more complex retainer (such as a retainer that provides for an hourly rate and a value element).[68] Capacity is also time-specific—that is, capacity may be regained, albeit temporarily, during lucid intervals.[69]

The effect of incapacity

60.58 A contract is binding upon the person who lacks capacity unless it can be shown that the other contracting party knew,[70] or ought to have known,[71] of the person's lack of capacity. It is not clear whether a paying party would be in a position to prove these things (or, for that matter, to challenge the receiving party's capacity) in circumstances in which an allegedly incapable receiving party wishes to rely upon the contract of retainer to recover their costs.[72] The following points can be made, none of which make heartening reading for a paying party who wishes to rely on an opponent's incapacity. The topic of what happens if a client loses capacity after having previously had capacity is addressed at 27.79–27.81.

Enforceable until proven otherwise

60.59 There is no reason to believe that the *Bailey* presumption[73] (see 18.30) is to be afforded any less weight simply because one of the issues implicitly covered by the certificate to the bill is the factual issue of capacity. The court is likely to say that capacity is, on the whole, a factual issue and an issue of professional judgement, and that weight therefore ought to be afforded to the certificate. The paying party would be hampered by the fact that, under the Mental Capacity Act 2005, there are presumptions that require cogent evidence before the court could make a finding of incapacity. Whilst there is no authority on the point, there is scope for the court to go further than this and to say that a person who is thought to be incapacitated ought to have been given help to avoid that finding (see the second presumption at 60.54), and that it would be undesirable to impose a retrospective finding of incapacity in circumstances in which the receiving party had not received the assistance that Parliament has said that they ought to have had.

Putative termination of contracts of retainer by loss of capacity

60.60 The issue of whether a contract of retainer is terminated by loss of capacity is dealt with in detail at 27.79–27.81.

Adoption in the context of loss of capacity

60.61 If the incapacity is temporary or if the contract of retainer is validated by a person with capacity who lawfully acts on behalf of the person who lacks capacity, the court has the power to find that a contract has been adopted and thus validated *ab initio*.[74]

---

[68] See, by way of analogy, *Manches v Trimborn* (1946) 174 LT 344, in which a person was found capable of understanding what a cheque was and what it did, but was found not to be capable of understanding the transaction for which a cheque was given in payment.

[69] *Drew v Nunn* (1879) 4 QBD 661.

[70] *Imperial Loan Co Ltd v Stone* [1892] 1 QB 599, CA.

[71] *York Glass Co Ltd v Jubb* (1925) 134 LT 36, CA, at 41.

[72] Whilst not directly on point, the reasoning of the Court of Appeal in *Garbutt v Edwards* [2005] 1 All ER 553 may apply in this regard.

[73] After *Bailey v IBC Vehicles Ltd* [1998] 3 All ER 570.

[74] *Baldwyn v Smith* [1900] 1 Ch 588. As to the position of creditors once a person's property and affairs have become subject to the court's jurisdiction, see *ibid*, at 682, 686 and 699.

Necessaries (common law)

Under common law,[75] where a contract for 'necessaries' was entered into by a person who did not have capacity to enter into that contract, that person would nonetheless be required to pay a reasonable price for the services rendered (but only if the circumstances suggest that this would be just).[76] The law relating to necessaries extends to the supply of necessary services.[77] The law of necessaries has already been addressed in the context of children (see 60.16–60.18). **60.62**

Necessary services (statute)

The Mental Capacity Act 2005 provides that if necessary services are supplied to a person who lacked capacity to contract for the supply of those services, that person must pay a reasonable price for those services. The Act stipulates that 'necessary' means suitable to a person's condition in life and to their actual requirements at the time when the services are supplied.[78] To an extent, this provision reflects the common law (see 60.16). There is no reason why a contract for the supply of legal services could not fall within this category. Whilst technically *obiter*, Phillips J has confirmed that this principle may apply even where a deputy has been appointed: **60.63**

> '[Section 7 of the Mental Capacity Act 2005] is designed to protect persons who provide necessary goods and services directly to persons lacking capacity, including day to day matters which a deputy may well not be able to deal with on a patient's behalf.'[79]

That said, s 7 of the Mental Capacity Act 2005 will have no application if the instructions were to be given directly by the deputy.[80]

The steps necessary to deal with mental incapacity

Thought will need to be given to the issues both where a new client is thought to lack capacity and where an existing client is thought to have lost capacity. The Solicitors Regulation Authority (SRA) Code of Conduct 2011 does not say a great deal on the point. The Guidance to the Solicitors' Code of Conduct 2007 used to state that a retainer will automatically terminate if a client loses mental capacity.[81] Whilst this advice was probably not correct (see 27.80–27.81), it is worth bearing in mind as at least as a possibility. **60.64**

If a solicitor is concerned that a client may lack capacity to enter into a contract of retainer, the Code of Practice under the 2005 Act states that it is the solicitor's responsibility to assess the client[82] and to record this fact in the file.[83] The Code of Practice **60.65**

---

[75] Where the 'necessaries' are goods, rather than services (as may be the case in respect of some disbursements), Sale of Goods Act 1954, s 3, made a very similar provision; in so far as mental capacity is concerned, that section has been repealed so as not to conflict with Mental Capacity Act 2005, s 7.

[76] *Re Rhodes, Rhodes v Rhodes* (1890) 44 Ch D 94, CA.

[77] *Ibid; Re Beavan, Davies, Banks & Co v Beavan* [1912] 1 Ch 196 (in the context of the law of costs, it is worth noting that the Court of Appeal found that necessaries may include rent audit expenses, which would seem to be analogous to legal costs).

[78] Mental Capacity Act 2005, s 7.

[79] See *Blankley v Central Manchester and Manchester Children's University Hospitals NHS Trust* [2014] EWHC 168 (QB), at [56], which finding was left undisturbed on appeal at [2015] EWCA Civ 18.

[80] See *ibid*, at [57], which was left undisturbed on appeal at [2015] EWCA Civ 18.

[81] See para 6(a)(iii) of the Guidance to Solicitors' Code of Conduct 2007, r 2.01.

[82] Mental Capacity Act 2005 Code of Practice, para 4.41.

[83] Mental Capacity Act 2005 Code of Practice, para 4.61.

recommends that, in cases of doubt, an opinion from a doctor or other professional expert should be obtained.[84] Where a person's capacity to enter into a contract could be challenged later, the Code of Practice recommends that a formal assessment be carried out.[85] This may be required in any event to establish whether a person needs the assistance of the Official Solicitor or some other litigation friend.

Donees and deputies

60.66 If a person lacks capacity, it is possible for other persons to be given authority to act on their behalf. There are two mechanisms by which this may be done, as follows.

- **Donee** A person who does not have capacity may (while they still have capacity) appoint another person to exercise lasting powers of attorney, which person is referred to as a 'donee'. Such an arrangement must comply with certain formalities and must be registered.[86]
- **Deputy** Where the court finds that a person lacks capacity, the court has the authority to make decisions on that person's behalf or to appoint another person to make decisions on their behalf,[87] which person is referred to as a 'deputy'.

Unless there is reason to suggest otherwise, a donee or a deputy may enter into a contract of retainer on behalf of the person who lacks capacity.

Contentious business agreements

60.67 Where the costs are payable by a person who lacks capacity pursuant to a contentious business agreement that has been entered into by a person acting in a representative capacity, the agreement must be laid before the court for the court's approval before payment. Failure to do this may result in the representative person being ordered to account to the protected person.[88] This is dealt with in detail at 27.179–27.180. It should be borne in mind that a written agreement may easily be a contentious business agreement and that this may be so even if this was not the intention of the counterparties.

A litigation friend's expenses (protected parties)

60.68 In general, the points made at 60.40–60.48 apply where the litigant friend has been appointed for a protected party. That said, CPR, r 21.12(1A)(b) (see 60.40), mentions only children; on the face of it, it does not apply to protected parties. If this is right, then this means that a request for approval of deduction of a success fee or sum payable under a damages-based agreement falls to be dealt with under CPR, r 46.4 (see 60.33), and, as such, the general rule is that the court must order a detailed assessment (CPR, r 46.4(2)(a)) unless permitted to order otherwise (see 60.33 and 60.34). This would be entirely logical, however, because protected parties are far less numerous than litigants who are children, so perhaps the Civil Procedure Rule Committee wanted to restrict the use of summary assessment to only those classes of litigant for whom steps needed to be taken to ensure that court time was used efficiently.

---

84 Mental Capacity Act 2005 Code of Practice, para 4.41.
85 Mental Capacity Act 2005 Code of Practice, para 4.54.
86 Mental Capacity Act 2005, s 9(2).
87 Mental Capacity Act 2005, s 16.
88 Solicitors Act 1974, s 62.

There is a more fundamental problem with CPR, r 21.12(1A), however: on a strict reading, it appears to prevent the court from making any allowances under CPR, r 21.12, of 'costs' at all in cases involving protected parties. This would be a strange result; perhaps the more sensible interpretation would be to read the references to children in CPR, r 21.12(1A), as though they restricted the application of that rule only to cases that involve children. It is possible that this would require a purposive interpretation, but one could easily argue that such an approach is justified. **60.69**

61

PUBLIC BODIES AND THE CROWN

61.01 This short chapter deals with the following topics:

- orders against the Crown (61.03); and
- public bodies discharging an administrative function (61.07).

61.02 In most instances, there will be little difference between costs litigation brought by or against public bodies or the Crown and those brought by or against other persons. There are, however, a number of distinct principles that may arise from time to time. What follows is, in general, a discussion relating to civil litigation under the Civil Procedure Rules (CPR) in the civil courts; in other tribunals, the CPR may apply only by analogy or possibly not at all, in which case specific statutory or tribunal-made principles may apply. In particular, it is common for the 'general rule' that the loser pays (CPR, r 44.2(2)(a)) to apply only in the indirect sense that success is taken into account as a factor relevant to the incidence of costs.[1] Whilst one or two such tribunals are referred to for the purposes of illustration, such issues are generally beyond the scope of this book.

Orders Against the Crown

61.03 Since 1 January 1948, civil proceedings to which the Crown is a party[2] have been procedurally similar to those brought against any other party.[3] Unless CPR, Part 66, a practice direction or any enactment provides otherwise, the CPR apply to civil proceedings by or against the Crown and to other civil proceedings to which the Crown is a party.[4] In this regard, s 7 of the Administration of Justice (Miscellaneous Provisions) Act 1933 makes the following provisions:

> '7 (1) In any civil proceedings to which the Crown is a party in any court having power to award costs in cases between subjects, and in any arbitration to which the Crown is a party, the costs of and incidental to the proceedings shall be in the discretion of the court or arbitrator to be exercised in the same manner and on the same principles as in cases between

[1] See, eg, *The Racecourse Association v The Respondent et al* [2006] CAT 1, at [8], *per* Rimer J (sitting in the Competition Appeals Tribunal).

[2] In the context of the CPR, 'civil proceedings by the Crown' are those described in Crown Proceedings Act 1947, s 23(1), but excluding the proceedings described in s 23(3), 'civil proceedings against the Crown' means those proceedings described in s 23(2) of that Act, but excluding the proceedings described in s 23(3), and 'civil proceedings to which the Crown is a party' has the same meaning as it has for the purposes of Parts III and IV of that Act by virtue of s 38(4): see CPR, r 66.1(2).

[3] Crown Proceedings Act 1947.

[4] CPR, r 66.2.

subjects, and the court or arbitrator shall have power to make an order for the payment of costs by or to the Crown accordingly:

Provided that—

(a) in the case of proceedings to which by reason of any enactment or otherwise the Attorney-General, a Government department or any officer of the Crown as such is required to be made a party, the court or arbitrator shall have regard to the nature of the proceedings and the character and circumstances in which the Attorney-General, the department or officer of the Crown appears, and may in the exercise of its or his discretion order any other party to the proceedings to pay the costs of the Attorney-General, department or officer, whatever may be the result of the proceedings; and

(b) nothing in this section shall affect the power of the court or arbitrator to order, or any enactment providing for, the payment of costs out of any particular fund or property, or any enactment expressly relieving any department or officer of the Crown of the liability to pay costs.

(2) In this section the expression "civil proceedings" includes ... proceedings by the Crown in the High Court or the county court for the recovery of fines or penalties, and references to proceedings to which the Crown is a party include references to proceedings to which the Attorney-General or any Government department or any officer of the Crown as such is a party, so, however, that the Crown shall not be deemed to be a party to any proceedings by reason only that the proceedings are proceedings by the Attorney-General on the relation of some other person.'

Thus the main difference between the Crown and other litigants is that, in certain circumstances, there is an express statutory requirement that the court shall have regard to the nature of the proceedings, and the character and circumstances, in which the Crown appears. In practice, this adds little because these factors would be taken into account in any event under CPR, r 44.3. This, however, is markedly different from the preceding common law, which was that the Crown neither paid nor received costs.[5]

In so far as the exercise of discretion is concerned, there is no reason to believe that the principles set out at 61.07–61.10—namely, that, in civil litigation, public bodies will not be afforded special protection solely by virtue of their being public bodies—will not apply; indeed, this much seems to be expressly provided for in the legislation set out above. It may also be relevant that many government departments have, where possible, committed themselves to alternative dispute resolution (ADR) (see 6.129). The culture of making no order for costs where one party was publicly funded and the other was a public body, on the ground that it would simply amount to transferring funds from one public body to another, was no longer acceptable.[6] The fact that a public body may be overworked is not a factor that can properly be taken into account.[7] **61.04**

Where any costs are awarded to or against the Crown in the High Court, interest shall be payable upon those costs unless the court otherwise orders and any interest so payable shall **61.05**

[5] It has been suggested that this rule came about by reason of the fact that the Statute of Gloucester did not name the Crown, thereby impliedly excluding it from the regime of costs between opposing parties: see *Blackstone's Commentaries on the Laws of England* (a facsimile of the 1st edn of 1765–69, reprinted by the University of Chicago Press, 1979), vol 3, p 400. See also *Swift & Co v Board of Trade* [1926] 2 KB 131 at 137.

[6] *R (on the application of Bahta & Ors) v Secretary of State for the Home Department & Ors* [2011] EWCA Civ 895, at [61], *per* Pill LJ.

[7] *Ibid*, at [60].

be at the same rate as that at which interest is payable upon judgment debts due from or to the Crown.[8]

61.06 Other than these points, the differences between costs litigation involving the Crown and that involving only other persons are largely procedural.

- **Place of proceedings** CPR, r 30.3(2)(h), provides that, in the case of civil proceedings by or against the Crown, the court must have regard to the location of the relevant government department or officers of the Crown and, where appropriate, any relevant public interest in the matter, and that, where appropriate, the matter should be tried in London. It is not clear whether this provision applies to detailed assessments.
- **Payment** Final and interim costs certificates and orders for costs summarily assessed are not enforced against the Crown in the usual way; instead, a certificate is issued in the relevant amount, which is then paid by the department in question. The Crown Proceedings Act 1947 makes specific provision for costs where the order provides for the payment of costs and the costs are required to be assessed: a proper officer may issue the certificate at any time after the costs have been assessed or within 21 days of the order, whichever is the later.[9] An application for such a certificate may be made without notice.[10]

Public Bodies Discharging an Administrative Function

61.07 Where a public body (which may include the Crown) is a litigant by reason of the exercise of some statutory or other public duty, it may be argued that it ought to be afforded a degree of protection against costs that arise out of that state of affairs. In civil litigation, the court tends to reject such a suggestion (see 61.08–61.10); in other tribunals, that argument may find favour (see 61.12). It should be noted that in none of those cases cited in the latter category (that is, other tribunals) was the tribunal exercising any powers under s 51 of the Senior Courts Act 1981 (as amended); as such, it is safe to work on the basis that, in civil litigation, the position is governed by the principles set out at 61.08–61.10, rather than that set out at 61.12.

61.08 Perhaps the starting point is to state the law as it is now known *not* to be. The incorrect law was stated by Harman J in the following terms:

> 'I think I can properly say that there has grown up something of a practice in the court not to visit upon the department costs incurred by a director who has been proceeded against in a case where there is cause to investigate ... but, more than that, cause to believe that there is a *prima facie* case of unfitness to be a director, which *prima facie* case is then rebutted by the evidence that comes in. So had evidence, being credible evidence and unlikely to be destroyed by cross-examination, shows that the appearance of unfitness was, indeed, no more than an appearance.'[11]

[8] Crown Proceedings Act 1947, s 24(2).

[9] See Crown Proceedings Act 1947, s 25(1).

[10] CPR, r 66.6(3).

[11] *Re Southbourne Sheet Metal Co Ltd* [1993] 1 WLR 244, in which there is an extract taken from the court below, which is reported at [1992] BCLC 361, at 363.

In a scathing judgment with which McCowan and Beldam LJJ agreed, Nourse LJ found that the supposed practice was unlawful.[12] In a different case, Sedley LJ commented that the public body in question—namely, the Crown Prosecution Service (CPS)—had no 'special litigation position or status'.[13] Dyson J came to a similar conclusion in an administrative matter.[14] Lord Neuberger MR had this to say (in the context of the public law claim): **61.09**

> '[I]t may be said that government and public bodies should be encouraged to settle, and should not therefore be penalised in costs if they do so after proceedings have been issued. There are four answers to that. First, if it is a good point, it should apply to any litigation, whether in private law or public law, and in very few, if any, private law cases would such an argument carry any weight. The implication that public authority Defendants should be in a more privileged position than other Defendants in this connection is not, in my view, maintainable. Secondly, it is simply unfair on the Claimant or his lawyers if, at least in the absence of special factors, he does not recover his costs of bringing wholly successful proceedings, provided that they have been properly brought and conducted. Thirdly, while Defendants may be more ready to concede a claim rather than fight it if they know that they will not thereby be liable for the Claimant's costs, it can forcefully be said that the fact that, if Defendants know they will have to pay the Claimant's costs, it would be a powerful incentive to concede the claim sooner rather than later. Fourthly, if the Defendants wish to settle, the time to do so is before proceedings are issued: that is one of the main reasons for the introduction of the Protocol.'[15]

On the whole, first-instance tribunals exercising a civil (that is, non-regulatory) function have taken a similar view, as have most appellate tribunals.[16] This is discussed in more detail at 61.12 and 61.13.

Brooke LJ has explained that public bodies need to engage in the process of dispute resolution in the same way as does any other litigant. He had this to say: **61.10**

> 'But that does not, in my judgment, mean that the CPS were entitled to behave, as litigants far too often behaved before the CPR came in, by simply standing back and saying:
>
> "We will make no offer at all for the court to consider when it decides what order as to costs is a reasonable one to make. We will simply see you in court." '[17]

Brooke LJ went on to criticise the CPS for having made no offers.

In a different case, Brooke LJ explained that the fact that the public authority may have incurred costs to clarify a point of law of particular contemporary concern did not mean that it should be relieved of the burden of paying its opponent's costs if unsuccessful.[18] Likewise, Moses LJ has explained that a public body will not be immune from being **61.11**

[12] *Re Southbourne Sheet Metal Co Ltd* [1993] 1 WLR 244, at 245. To the extent that other judges may have adopted the supposed practice, they were wrong to do so and, in that regard, the costs relating to *Re Austinsuite Furniture Ltd* [1992] BCLC 1047, *per* Vinelott J, were wrongly decided.

[13] *Grimes v Crown Prosecution Service* [2003] EWCA Civ 1814, at [30]; see also *R (on the application of Bahta & Ors) v Secretary of State for the Home Department & Ors* [2011] EWCA Civ 895, at [60], *per* Pill LJ.

[14] Dyson J (as he then was) in *R v Lord Chancellor, ex p Child Poverty Action Group* [1999] 1 WLR 347. See also *R (on the application of AK & Ors) v Secretary of State for the Home Department & Ors* [2011] EWCA Civ 895.

[15] *M v Mayor and Burgesses of the London Borough of Croydon* [2012] EWCA Civ 595, at [53].

[16] See, eg, in respect of non-penalty cases in the Competition Appeals Tribunal, *Racecourse Association v OFT et al* [2006] CAT 1, at [9], *per* Rimer J.

[17] *Grimes v Crown Prosecution Service* [2003] EWCA Civ 1814, at [21] and [22].

[18] *Bradford Metropolitan District Council v Yorkshire Water Services Ltd* [2001] EWHC 803 (Admin).

ordered to pay costs on the indemnity basis solely by reason of a putative need to protect the public purse:

> '[If] anyone should suffer as a result of HMRC's laudable persistence, it is the taxpayer at large, on whose behalf HMRC fought this particular appeal. It lost, and it is difficult to see why, in those circumstances, a particular trader which vindicated its rights ... should be deprived of the effect of its Part 36 offer. If the Crown wishes its particular position to be acknowledged in the Rules, then they should seek amendment.'[19]

61.12 In a similar vein, Lord Neuberger MR has said that it would 'not be good enough for [a public authority] to say that [it] had not got round to dealing with the Claimant's claim because of [its] "heavy workload" or "constraints upon [its] resources" '.[20]

61.13 Public bodies will not always be denied special status, however, and this will be particularly so where the public body in question is taking an essentially administrative decision (to use the phraseology of Neuberger MR).[21] In the context of licensing appeals,[22] Bingham CJ has said that where a complainant has successfully challenged an administrative decision by a regulatory authority acting honestly, reasonably, properly and on grounds that reasonably appeared to be sound, in exercise of its public duty, the court should consider, in addition to any other relevant fact or circumstances, both (a) the financial prejudice to the particular complainant in the particular circumstances if an order for costs is not made in its favour, and (b) the need to encourage public authorities to make and stand by honest, reasonable and apparently sound administrative decisions, in the public interest, without fear of exposure to undue financial prejudice if the decision is successfully challenged.[23] In a similar vein, Lord Neuberger MR has explained that this approach may be appropriate where the body in question was performing one of its regulatory functions.[24] He went on to explain that the approach also applied where the body in question was carrying out its functions of seeking a sanction.[25]

61.14 This approach—usually known as the *Booth* principle[26]—has been applied in one guise or another in several regulatory contexts. Examples include disciplinary proceedings against accountants,[27] disciplinary proceedings against solicitors,[28] proceedings under the Dangerous Dogs Act 1871,[29] vehicle licensing proceedings,[30] proceedings under s 80 of

---

[19] *Commissioners for HM Revenue and Customs v Blue Sphere Global Ltd* [2010] EWCA Civ 1448, at [11].

[20] *M v Mayor and Burgesses of the London Borough of Croydon* [2012] EWCA Civ 595, at [54], quoting with approval *R (on the application of Bahta & Ors) v Secretary of State for the Home Department & Ors* [2011] EWCA Civ 895, at [63].

[21] See, eg, *R (on the application of Perinpanathan) v City of Westminster Magistrates' Court & Anor* [2010] EWCA Civ 40, at [64].

[22] Which are not conducted under the CPR.

[23] *Bradford Metropolitan District Council v Booth* (2000) 164 JP 485, at 488; see also *R (on the application of Telford and Wrekin Borough Council) v Crown Court at Shrewsbury* [2003] EWHC 230 (Admin), *per* Moses J.

[24] *R (on the application of Perinpanathan) v City of Westminster Magistrates' Court & Anor* [2010] EWCA Civ 40, at [65].

[25] *Ibid*, at [71]. Whilst not binding, see also *Eden Brown v Office of Fair Trading* [2011] CAT 29, at [15], *per* Roth J.

[26] After *Bradford Metropolitan District Council v Booth* (2000) 164 JP 485.

[27] *R (on the application of Gorlov) v Institute of Chartered Accountants in England and Wales* [2001] EWHC 220 (Admin), *per* Jackson J. This, of course, will be subject to any tribunal-specific rules.

[28] *Baxendale-Walker v Law Society* [2006] EWHC 643 (Admin). This, of course, will be subject to any tribunal-specific rules.

[29] *Swale Borough Council v Boulter* [2002] All ER (D) 378 (Oct), *per* Maurice Kay J.

[30] *Milton Keynes Council v Edwards* [2004] EWHC 267 (Admin), *per* Harrison J.

the Environmental Protection Act 1990,[31] proceedings concerning antisocial behaviour orders[32] and forfeiture proceedings.[33] The *Booth* principle has its limits, however: whilst not binding, Roth J has explained that where there is an appeal from an administrative or regulatory decision, the *Booth* principle will not apply.[34] Examples of that type of tribunal would include the Competition Appeals Tribunal[35] and the Asylum and Immigration Tribunal.[36]

It is important to note that none of these examples relates to the exercise of the court's discretion under CPR, r 44.2; as such, they are of very limited application in the context of civil litigation. **61.15**

31 *Waveney District Council v Lowestoft (North East Suffolk) Magistrates' Court* [2008] EWHC 3295 (Admin), *per* Charles J.

32 *Manchester City Council v Manchester Crown Court & Ors* [2009] EWHC 1866 (Admin), *per* Burton J.

33 *R (on the application of Perinpanathan) v City of Westminster Magistrates' Court & Anor* [2010] EWCA Civ 40, *per* Lord Neuberger MR.

34 *Eden Brown v Office of Fair Trading* [2011] CAT 29, at [15], citing *Walker v Royal College of Veterinary Surgeons* [2007] UKPC 20.

35 See *Eden Brown v Office of Fair Trading* [2011] CAT 29, at [16], *per* Roth J.

36 *R (on the application of Bahta & Ors) v Secretary of State for the Home Department & Ors* [2011] EWCA Civ 895, at [60], *per* Pill LJ.

62

COSTS AGAINST LEGALLY AIDED PERSONS

62.01 This chapter deals with the following topics:

- costs protection (62.04);
- transfer from the Legal Services Commission to the Lord Chancellor (62.07);
- s 26 of the Legal Aid, Sentencing and Punishment of Offenders Act 2012 (62.10); and
- the wording of the relevant provisions (62.43).

62.02 There are two methods by which a receiving party may obtain costs that have been incurred in litigation against a publicly funded opponent: costs may be sought against the legally aided party personally; or they may be sought against the Lord Chancellor. In addition, where costs are payable by a legally aided party who is also the recipient of costs or damages, those costs may be the subject of set-off, which issue is dealt with in detail at 21.20–21.42.

62.03 This edition of this book deals primarily with the regime under the Legal Aid, Sentencing and Punishment of Offenders Act 2012, which came into force on 1 April 2013. That regime is so similar to the regime that preceded it (under s 11 of the Access to Justice Act 1999[1]) that, for all practical purposes, they can be regarded as one and the same. Different (but not wholly dissimilar) rules applied where the publicly funded person was awarded funding under the Legal Aid Act 1988. That old regime is still referred to from time to time, and is described in the second edition of this book at paragraphs 7.343–7.377.

Costs Protection

62.04 Where a legally aided party has cost protection and where they are unable to afford to pay costs, that party will not be required to pay any costs. This is called costs protection.[2] With limited exceptions (see 62.05), cost protection applies in respect of costs incurred by the receiving party during the period in which civil legal services were provided, whether before or after the commencement of proceedings.[3] Where a certificate is limited by reference to specified steps or stages, rather than by reference to issues, it will apply to the whole of the claim up to the point at which those steps have been taken or

[1] This was revoked on 1 April 2013 by Legal Aid Sentencing and Punishment of Offenders Act 2012, s 51.

[2] Costs protection applies only to costs incurred by a receiving party in relation to proceedings that are, as regards the legally aided party, 'relevant proceedings': see Civil Legal Aid (Costs) Regulations 2013 (SI 2013/611), reg 5. This means civil proceedings or contemplated proceedings before a court: see Civil Legal Aid (Costs) Regulations 2013 (SI 2013/611), reg 2.

[3] Civil Legal Aid (Costs) Regulations 2013 (SI 2013/611), reg 8(1).

stages reached.[4] Once those steps are complete or the stages are reached, the certificate will become spent.[5]

In so far as civil costs are concerned, costs protection does not apply to costs incurred: **62.05**

- before the date of issue of a certificate;[6]
- after the date on which a determination that the legally aided party qualified for civil legal services has been withdrawn;[7] and
- before, at the time of or after the date of revocation of a determination.[8]

Moreover, cost protection does not apply to parts of proceedings for which civil legal services are provided in the form of help at court or legal help.[9]

If a certificate is withdrawn, cost protection will shield the legally aided party up to the date **62.06** on which legal aid ceased to be provided, which will not necessarily be the same date as that on which the certificate was formally discharged.[10] Moreover, a decision not to make use of a certificate will negate costs protection for the period of non-use; hence a putatively legally aided party who has given notice of the fact that they intend to act in person will not enjoy cost protection for the period of self-representation.[11]

Transfer from the Legal Services Commission to the Lord Chancellor

On 1 April 2013, the Legal Aid Sentencing and Punishment of Offenders Act 2012 trans- **62.07** ferred responsibility for managing legal aid from the Legal Services Commission (LSC) to the Lord Chancellor.[12] Since that date, the Lord Chancellor has managed legal aid through the Legal Aid Agency (LAA), an executive agency of the Ministry of Justice.

---

[4] Whilst a very old case based on long-since-revoked legislation, the authority that is usually quoted on this point is *Boorman & Anor v Godfrey* [1981] 2 All ER 1012.

[5] Whilst decided under an old regime, see *Turner v Plasplugs Ltd* [1996] 2 All ER 939, CA, referred to with apparent approval in *Murphy v Rayner* [2013] EWHC 3878 (Ch), at [58], *per* Nicholas Strauss QC. The same conclusion had been reached in *Littaur v Steggles Palmer* [1986] 1 WLR 287, in which it was decided that the legal representative was entitled to his normal fees, for all of his work, when the client had been a legally assisted person only in respect of one discrete issue.

[6] See Civil Legal Aid (Costs) Regulations 2013 (SI 2013/611), reg 8(2)(a). This will not apply in certain family cases: see Civil Legal Aid (Costs) Regulations 2013 (SI 2013/611), regs 7 and 8(3).

[7] See Civil Legal Aid (Costs) Regulations 2013 (SI 2013/611), reg 8(2)(b).

[8] See Civil Legal Aid (Costs) Regulations 2013 (SI 2013/611), reg 8(2)(c).

[9] See Civil Legal Aid (Costs) Regulations 2013 (SI 2013/611), reg 6.

[10] *Burridge v Stafford; Khan v Ali* [2000] 1 WLR 927. In *Burridge*, the issue was whether the defendant, who had been granted legal aid, but whose solicitors had ceased to act for her, remained a legally assisted person. The court found that she ceased to be a legally assisted person when her solicitors had ceased to act for her and had informed the claimant's solicitors of this: see *ibid*, at [14] and [30]. In *Khan*, the issue was whether the non-funded party could recover against the Legal Aid Board in respect of an unsuccessful appeal pursued by the legally aided party after his solicitors had ceased to act for him. Again, the certificate ceased to apply when the solicitors for the non-funded party were told that Mr Khan had decided to act in person: see *ibid*, at [24] and [33]. See also *Re H (minors) (No 2) (abduction: custody rights)* [1992] 2 AC 303, HL.

[11] Whilst decided under a now-redundant regime, see *Mohamadi v Shellpoint Trustees Ltd* [2009] EWHC 1098 (Ch), *per* Briggs J.

[12] See Legal Aid, Sentencing and Punishment of Offenders Act 2012, ss 1, 2 and 8.

62.08 The LSC ceased to exist on 1 April 2013.[13] Moreover, the statutory framework that governed legal aid prior to that date was revoked without any saving provisions[14] and, as a result, this impliedly revoked the delegated legislation made under it.[15] This included the much-criticised Community Legal Services (Costs) Regulations 2000[16] and the Community Legal Services (Costs Protection) Regulations 2000.[17] According to the Minister for Policing and Criminal Justice, the new provisions 'substantially reproduce' the provisions that existed before that date, but, in doing so, they bring together the rules on costs into a single set of regulations.[18] Those regulations are the Civil Legal Aid (Costs) Regulations 2013.[19]

62.09 The property, rights, powers, duties and liabilities of the LSC were transferred to the Lord Chancellor.[20] Anything done (or having effect as if done) before 1 April 2013 by or in relation to the LSC is to have effect as if done by or in relation to the Lord Chancellor.[21] Moreover, any reference to the LSC in a document, including an enactment is to have effect as a reference to the Lord Chancellor.[22]

Section 26 of the Legal Aid, Sentencing and Punishment of Offenders Act 2012

62.10 The current regime requires the costs judge not only to quantify costs, but also to decide whether the Lord Chancellor is to pay those costs. It was introduced on 1 April 2013, when s 26 of the Legal Aid, Sentencing and Punishment of Offenders Act 2012 came into force, but that regime is so similar to the regime that preceded it (under s 11 of the Access to Justice Act 1999[23]) that, for all practical purposes, they can be regarded as one and the same.

62.11 This edition of this book deals only with the law relating to comparatively recent orders. In the unlikely event that the reader needs to know about the law relating to orders made before 1 April 2000, then the second edition of this book should be consulted (at paragraphs 7.337–7.339). Complex transitional provisions apply.[24]

62.12 The relevant statutory provisions are contained in s 26 of the 2012 Act (which is set out in full at 62.34). The detail is contained in delegated legislation made under that Act—namely,

---

13 See Legal Aid, Sentencing and Punishment of Offenders Act 2012, s 38(1).

14 See Legal Aid, Sentencing and Punishment of Offenders Act 2012, Sch 5, para 51.

15 See Office of Public Sector Information, *Statutory Instrument Practice* (4th edn, London: HMSO, 2006), para 1.2.11, which reads as follows: 'If an enabling Act, or the enabling section of it, is repealed, instruments made under it will lapse unless they are saved, i.e. continued in effect.'

16 SI 2000/441.

17 SI 2000/824.

18 HC Deb, 6 March 2013, col 5 (Damien Green before the Seventh Delegated Legislation Committee).

19 SI 2013/611, made under Legal Aid, Sentencing and Punishment of Offenders Act 2012, ss 5(2), 26(3)–(5), and (6)(a)–(g), (7) and (9).

20 See Legal Aid, Sentencing and Punishment of Offenders Act 2012, Sch 4, para 7(1).

21 See Legal Aid, Sentencing and Punishment of Offenders Act 2012, Sch 4, para 7(3).

22 See Legal Aid, Sentencing and Punishment of Offenders Act 2012, Sch 4, para 7(5).

23 This was revoked on 1 April 2013 by Legal Aid Sentencing and Punishment of Offenders Act 2012, s 51.

24 See Access to Justice Act 1999 (Commencement No 3, Transitional Provisions and Savings Order) 2000 (SI 2000/774), art 8(3); see also CPD, art 22.3.

the Civil Legal Aid (Costs) Regulations 2013.[25] Those Regulations (which are reproduced at 62.35) are best regarded as a consolidation of the provisions they replaced under the Access to Justice Act 1999—namely, the Community Legal Service (Costs) Regulations 2000[26] and the Community Legal Service (Cost Protection) Regulations 2000[27] (as amended).[28]

Procedural issues

Lord Philips MR has described the procedure as a two-stage affair in which the trial judge is responsible for stage one and the costs judge discharges the court's duties under stage two.[29] Lord Phillips MR noted that whilst it is arguable that the trial court has the power to discharge the duties under both stages, it should restrict its function to stage one only.[30] When applying that regime, it is the position of the parties to the litigation that is relevant, not the position of third parties who may be affected by the litigation.[31] **62.13**

Stage one

In the first stage, the trial judge has the following tasks to perform. **62.14**

(1) They must decide whether to make an order for costs against a legally aided party.[32]
(2) They must decide whether they are in a position to specify the amount, if any, to be paid by the legally aided party.[33]
(3) They must make a costs order against the legally aided party that either:
   (a) specifies the amount, if any, to be paid by the legally aided party and states the amount of the full costs; or
   (b) does not specify the amount to be paid by the legally aided party.[34]
(4) Where the order does not specify the amount to be paid by the legally aided party, they must make, if they see fit, findings of fact as to the parties' conduct, in the proceedings or otherwise, which are relevant to the determination of that amount.[35]

Stage two

Stage two is the province of the costs judge. The procedure is as follows. **62.15**

(1) The receiving party may, within three months of the making of the costs order, request a hearing to determine the costs payable to them.[36] That time limit may be disregarded only if there is good reason for the delay,[37] or (for requests relating solely to the legally aided party) if there has been a significant change in the legally aided

[25] SI 2013/611. They are made under Legal Aid, Sentencing and Punishment of Offenders Act 2012, ss 5(2), 26(3)–(5), and (6)(a)–(g), (7) and (9).
[26] SI 2000/441.
[27] SI 2000/824.
[28] The Minister for Policing and Criminal Justice (Damian Green) has said that the new provisions 'substantially reproduce' the old provisions with the aim of bringing together the rules into a single set of regulations: HC Deb, 6 March 2013, col 5.
[29] *R v Secretary of State for the Home Department, ex p Gunn* [2001] EWCA Civ 891.
[30] *Ibid*, at [29].
[31] *Aehmed v Legal Services Commission* [2009] EWCA Civ 572.
[32] Civil Legal Aid (Costs) Regulations 2013 (SI 2013/611), reg 15(1).
[33] Civil Legal Aid (Costs) Regulations 2013 (SI 2013/611), reg 15(2).
[34] Civil Legal Aid (Costs) Regulations 2013 (SI 2013/611), reg 15(3) and (4).
[35] Civil Legal Aid (Costs) Regulations 2013 (SI 2013/611), reg 15(7).
[36] Civil Legal Aid (Costs) Regulations 2013 (SI 2013/611), regs 10(3)(b)(i) and 16(2).
[37] See Civil Legal Aid (Costs) Regulations 2013 (SI 2013/611), regs 10(3)(b)(ii) and 16(2).

party's circumstances[38] or material additional information as to the legally aided party's resources has come to light.[39] The request may be made formally (by means of Form N244, in respect of which a court fee is payable) or informally (by way of a letter to the court).[40]

(2) The receiving party may, at the same time, seek a costs order against the Lord Chancellor.[41]

(3) The receiving party must, when making the request, file the following items with the court:[42]

 (a) a bill of costs (which must be compliant with any requirements of relevant rules of court relating to the form and content of a bill of costs);[43]

 (b) a statement of resources[44] (but not if the court is determining an application for a costs order against the Lord Chancellor and the costs were not incurred in a court of first instance);[45] and

 (c) a written notice that a costs order is sought against the Lord Chancellor.[46]

 The receiving party must, in addition to filing these items, serve them on the legally aided party.[47] If an order is sought against them, these items must also be served on the Lord Chancellor.[48]

(4) The publicly funded person must, within 21 days of the date of receipt of a copy of the receiving party's statement of resources, file a statement of resources, and serve this on the receiving party and the Lord Chancellor (where a claim is made on them).[49] Where appropriate, points of dispute may also be served.[50]

---

[38] See Civil Legal Aid (Costs) Regulations 2013 (SI 2013/611), reg 19(4)(b).

[39] See Civil Legal Aid (Costs) Regulations 2013 (SI 2013/611), reg 19(4)(b).

[40] This is not a regulatory requirement, but guidance given in HM Courts & Tribunals Service, *Senior Court Costs Office Guide* (London: HMSO, 2013), para 25.5.

[41] Civil Legal Aid (Costs) Regulations 2013 (SI 2013/611), reg 16(3)(c).

[42] Civil Legal Aid (Costs) Regulations 2013 (SI 2013/611), reg 16(5). The CPD used to give guidance as to which was the appropriate court; that guidance is not replicated in the current rules. In so far as it is still of relevance, CPD, arts 23.2 and 23.2A, gave detailed directions as to what is the appropriate court: in essence, the appropriate court is that which made the stage one order unless the court is in or around London, in which case it is the SCCO.

[43] See Civil Legal Aid (Costs) Regulations 2013 (SI 2013/611), reg 16(3)(a).

[44] See Civil Legal Aid (Costs) Regulations 2013 (SI 2013/611), reg 16(3)(b). Civil Legal Aid (Costs) Regulations 2013 (SI 2013/611), reg 14(1), gives the following guidance about statements or resources: 'For the purposes of this Part, a statement of resources is a statement, verified by a statement of truth—(a) made by a party to proceedings, other than a legally aided party who is a legal person, setting out—(i) the party's income and capital and financial commitments during the previous year and, if applicable, those of the party's partner; (ii) the party's estimated future financial resources and expectations and, if applicable, those of the party's partner; and (iii) a declaration stating whether the party, and, if applicable, the party's partner, have deliberately forgone or deprived themselves of any resources or expectations, together (if applicable and as far as is practical) with details of those resources or expectations and the manner in which they have been forgone or the party or partner deprived of them; (iv) particulars of any application for legal aid made by the party in connection with the proceedings; and (v) any other facts relevant to the determination of the party's resources; or (b) made by a legally aided party—(i) setting out the information previously provided by that party in order to determine that the party's financial resources were such that the party was eligible for civil legal services; and (ii) either stating that there has been no significant change in the party's financial circumstances since the date on which the information was provided or, as the case may be, providing details of any such change.'

[45] See Civil Legal Aid (Costs) Regulations 2013 (SI 2013/611), reg 16(3)(b) and (4).

[46] Civil Legal Aid (Costs) Regulations 2013 (SI 2013/611), reg 16(3)(c).

[47] Civil Legal Aid (Costs) Regulations 2013 (SI 2013/611), reg 16(5)(a).

[48] Civil Legal Aid (Costs) Regulations 2013 (SI 2013/611), reg 16(5)(a).

[49] Civil Legal Aid (Costs) Regulations 2013 (SI 2013/611), reg 16(6) and (7).

[50] Civil Legal Aid (Costs) Regulations 2013 (SI 2013/611), reg 16(8).

(5) The court sets a date for the hearing[51] (but the court does not have to do this if the legally aided party, without good reason, fails to file a statement of resources[52]).
(6) The court conducts the hearing, assesses the costs (if any) to be paid by the legally aided party and, where appropriate, makes a costs order against the Lord Chancellor.[53]

In an *obiter* comment Walls LJ has made it clear that where the real dispute is about whether the Lord Chancellor should pay the costs rather than whether a costs order under the then-equivalent of s 26 of the Legal Aid, Sentencing and Punishment of Offenders Act 2012 should be made, the parties should act sensibly and agree an order that allows those arguments to be put to the costs judge.[54] **62.16**

As to the interplay between the trial judge and the costs judge, Phillips MR has commented that it was open to the trial judge to make any findings in relation to the conduct of the parties or facts that have emerged in the course of the proceedings that have relevance to the task to be performed by the costs judge or district judge—but the trial court should not go beyond this, because to do so would be to usurp the functions of the costs judge.[55] **62.17**

Timing

Two issues concerning timing merit particular mention: the first is whether the court can make a s 26(1) order in circumstances in which aspects of the litigation remain to be decided; the second is the three-month time limit during which an application for an order against the Lord Chancellor must be made. **62.18**

'Finally decided'

Regulation 10(1) of the Civil Legal Aid (Costs) Regulations 2013[56] provides that the foregoing regime will apply when 'proceedings are finally decided in favour of a non-legally aided party'. It is not, however, always obvious whether the proceedings have been finally decided, such as where a court has allowed an appeal, but remitted the matter for a further determination. Such situations can cause difficulties because the court could, in theory, make a s 26(1) order in circumstances in which the costs judge would have no jurisdiction to make an order against the Lord Chancellor until the conclusion of the entire proceedings. The receiving party could therefore be placed in the invidious position of both having to wait until the conclusion of the proceedings and having to comply with the three-month time limit during which an application must be made for the court to decide whether an order should be made against the Lord Chancellor (see below). Chadwick LJ found that, in those circumstances, it would not usually be appropriate for the trial judge to adjourn making the then-equivalent of a s 26(1) costs order until the conclusion of the litigation; rather, the trial judge should make the order immediately on the basis that, if necessary, the costs judge could adjourn stage two, as appropriate.[57] In any event, Chadwick LJ approved **62.19**

---

[51] Civil Legal Aid (Costs) Regulations 2013 (SI 2013/611), reg 10(10).
[52] Civil Legal Aid (Costs) Regulations 2013 (SI 2013/611), reg 10(9).
[53] *R v Secretary of State for the Home Department, ex p Gunn* [2001] EWCA Civ 891, at [38].
[54] *Wyatt v Portsmouth Hospitals NHS Trust* [2006] EWCA Civ 529, at [62].
[55] *R v Secretary of State for the Home Department, ex p Gunn* [2001] EWCA Civ 891, at [33]–[34].
[56] SI 2013/611.
[57] *Masterman-Lister v Brutton & Co (No 2)* [2003] EWCA Civ 70; see also *Wyatt v Portsmouth Hospitals NHS Trust* [2006] EWCA Civ 529, at [25].

a definition of proceedings that, for the purposes of orders out of public funds, defined them in such a way as to be limited to the proceedings immediately to hand (which, in the case before him, was the appeal itself).[58]

The three-month time limit

62.20 If they seek costs against the Lord Chancellor, the receiving party must, within three months of the making of the s 26(1) costs order, request a hearing to determine the costs payable to them.[59] That time limit may be disregarded only if there is good reason for the delay.[60] (There are provisions that allow an application to be made at a later stage if the legally aided person's fortunes change or if new material comes to light, but they apply only to costs orders against the legally funded person; they do not apply to requests for costs against the Lord Chancellor.[61]) Under the last regime—that is, under Access to Justice Act 1999, s 11(1), prior to 3 December 2001—the court had no discretion to extend or disapply that time limit.[62] Practitioners came to refer to it as 'the ten-two trap', after reg 10(2) of Community Legal Service (Costs) Regulations 2000.[63] After that date, the relevant regulations were amended in such a way as to allow the court to extend that period if there is 'good reason for the delay'.[64] It is the editor's experience that the court will not generally accept ignorance of the rules as good reason. If the application is made in the wrong court, it is open to the judge to find that the application has thereby been made out of time.[65] Cox J has found that it is not open to a judge to extend time generally under CPR, r 3.1, as a means by which to avoid the need to find that there is a good reason for the delay.[66]

Government departments

62.21 The nature of public funding is that the litigation is often against government departments (or other publicly funded bodies). Where those are the circumstances, it could be argued that the court should not make an order against the Lord Chancellor, because that would be merely to order that money is moved from one government coffer to another. Whilst the court has expressed some sympathy for that argument,[67] it has consistently and repeatedly rejected it.[68] In particular, the fact that the non-legally aided party is a government department does not remove jurisdiction to make an order against the Lord

[58] *Masterman-Lister v Brutton & Co (No 2)* [2003] EWCA Civ 70, approving *General Accident Car and Life Assurance Corpn Ltd v Foster* [1972] 3 All ER 877. Chadwick LJ's analysis was applied by Wall LJ in *Wyatt v Portsmouth Hospitals NHS Trust* [2006] EWCA Civ 529.

[59] Civil Legal Aid (Costs) Regulations 2013 (SI 2013/611), regs 10(3)(b)(i) and 16(2).

[60] See Civil Legal Aid (Costs) Regulations 2013 (SI 2013/611), regs 10(3)(b)(ii) and 16(2).

[61] See Civil Legal Aid (Costs) Regulations 2013 (SI 2013/611), reg 19(4)(b).

[62] *R v Secretary of State for the Home Department, ex p Gunn* [2001] EWCA Civ 891, at [27] *et seq*; see also CPD, art 23.4.

[63] SI 2000/441.

[64] This was originally effected by the Community Legal Service (Cost Protection) (Amendment No 2) Regulations 2001 (SI 2001/3812). As an example of this in practice, see *Floyd & Anor v Legal Services Commission* [2010] EWHC 906 (QB).

[65] *Liverpool Freeport Electronics Ltd v Habib Bank Ltd & Legal Services Commission* [2009] EWHC 861 (QB).

[66] *Floyd v S Floyd v Legal Services Commission* [2010] EWHC 906 (QB), at [21].

[67] *R v Secretary of State for the Home Department, ex p Gunn* [2001] EWCA Civ 891, at [51].

[68] Historically, see *R v Greenwich LBC, ex p Lovelace (No 2)* [1992] QB 155; *In re O (Costs: Liability of Legal Aid Board)* [1997] 1 FLR 465.

Chancellor in its favour[69] nor does it affect the procedure to be adopted when the court is exercising its discretion.[70]

Discretion

Discretion at stage one

This section deals with the trial judge's discretion to make an order under s 26(1) of the Legal Aid, Sentencing and Punishment of Offenders Act 2012. Prior to 1 April 2013, the matter would have been governed by s 11(1) of the Access to Justice Act 1999, but the principles were the same. There are three components to the decision: **62.22**

- whether to make an order (see 62.23–62.28);
- whether to state the amount (see 62.29–62.30); and
- whether to make any comments that would assist the costs judge in stage two (see 62.31–62.34).

Whether to make an order Where the court is considering whether to make a s 26(1) costs order, it shall consider whether, but for cost protection, it would have made a costs order against the legally aided party and, if so, whether it would, on making the costs order, have specified the amount to be paid under that order.[71] **62.23**

There is nothing in the regime set out above that should be taken as requiring the court to make a costs order where it would not otherwise have made one[72] nor is there anything that affects the court's power to make a wasted costs order.[73] **62.24**

Wall LJ has confirmed that the provisions in the then-equivalent of CPR, r 44.2, still apply and that the court may therefore take the matters set out in that rule into account.[74] **62.25**

Whilst the guidance was given in the context of litigation that had the flavour of family litigation, Wall LJ firmly rejected the notion that, to justify an order being made against a legally aided party, that person's conduct must have been unreasonable or in some way discreditable; likewise, he rejected the idea that there must be 'exceptional circumstances'.[75] **62.26**

Wall LJ has emphasised the need to separate the first and the second stages, and has commented that the first stage is a threshold test: **62.27**

> 'In our judgment, it is of crucial importance to remember throughout that we are not being asked to make an order for costs against the [Lord Chancellor], nor are we deciding the extent to which, if at all, the [Lord Chancellor] should underwrite the Trust's costs. Those are matters for the costs judge at stage two of the regulatory procedure. It is for the costs judge to decide whether or not it is just and equitable to make an order against the [Lord Chancellor]. What Parliament has done is to set a hypothetical threshold criterion without which the costs judge cannot entertain an application against the [Lord Chancellor]. In our judgment, this case easily crosses that threshold.'[76]

[69] *R v Secretary of State for the Home Department, ex p Gunn* [2001] EWCA Civ 891, at [38].
[70] *Ibid*, at [50].
[71] See Civil Legal Aid (Costs) Regulations 2013 (SI 2013/611), reg 15(1).
[72] Civil Legal Aid (Costs) Regulations 2013 (SI 2013/611), reg 3(a).
[73] Civil Legal Aid (Costs) Regulations 2013 (SI 2013/611), reg 3(b).
[74] *Wyatt v Portsmouth Hospitals NHS Trust* [2006] EWCA Civ 529, at [29].
[75] *Ibid*, at [43].
[76] *Ibid*, at [51].

62.28 Wall LJ has implicitly made it clear that one factor the court can take into account is the effect that any order would have on the parties and their subsequent relationship.[77] This may be a particularly relevant factor where the litigation is a public interest case.

62.29 **Whether to state the amount** When exercising its discretion to make a s 26(1) costs order, there are two factors that will govern the way in which the court deals with the matter: the first is whether, had cost protection not applied, the court would have assessed the full amount of costs payable; and the second is whether the court is to specify the amount (if any) that the legally aided party is to pay under that order. The options that the court has are as follows.[78]

- **If, in the absence of cost protection, the court would not have assessed the costs** If the court considers that, had cost protection applied, it would have made a costs order against the legally aided party, but it would not have assessed those costs, then the court shall, when making the s 26(1) costs order, specify the amount (if any) that the legally aided person is to pay under that order if—but only if—it:
  - considers that it has sufficient information before it to decide what amount is, in that case, a reasonable amount for the legally aided person to pay, in accordance with s 26(1) of the Legal Aid, Sentencing and Punishment of Offenders Act 2012 (see 62.12); and
  - is satisfied that if it were to determine the full costs at that time, they would exceed the amount referred to immediately above.[79]

  Otherwise, the court shall not specify the amount the legally aided party is to pay under the costs order,[80] in which case (a) the 'stage two' procedure (see 62.15) will apply,[81] and (b) the court may make findings of fact as to the parties' conduct in the proceedings or otherwise relevant to the determination of that amount and those findings shall be taken into consideration in that determination.[82] The legally aided party may be ordered to make a payment on account of costs.[83] Upon the conclusion of the stage two procedure, the court will state the full amount of costs.[84]
- **If, in the absence of cost protection, the court would have assessed the costs** If the court considers that, had cost protection applied, it would have made a costs order against the legally aided person and that it would have specified the amount to be paid under it, when making the s 26(1) costs order the court will:
  - state the amount of the full costs;[85] and
  - specify the amount (if any) that the legally aided party is to pay under that order if—but only if—it considers that it has sufficient information before it to decide what

[77] *Ibid*, at [60].

[78] See Civil Legal Aid (Costs) Regulations 2013 (SI 2013/611), reg 16(2)–(7). Those provisions are almost the same as those under Community Legal Service (Costs) Regulations 2000 (SI 2000/441), reg 9, which were discussed in *Wyatt v Portsmouth Hospitals NHS Trust* [2006] EWCA Civ 529, at [54].

[79] See Civil Legal Aid (Costs) Regulations 2013 (SI 2013/611), reg 16(2).

[80] See Civil Legal Aid (Costs) Regulations 2013 (SI 2013/611), reg 16(2)(b).

[81] See Civil Legal Aid (Costs) Regulations 2013 (SI 2013/611), reg 16(5).

[82] See Civil Legal Aid (Costs) Regulations 2013 (SI 2013/611), reg 16(7).

[83] See Civil Legal Aid (Costs) Regulations 2013 (SI 2013/611), reg 17. The payment on account is actually a payment into court. Details as to the procedure are set out in Civil Legal Aid (Costs) Regulations 2013 (SI 2013/611), reg 17.

[84] See Civil Legal Aid (Costs) Regulations 2013 (SI 2013/611), reg 16(6).

[85] See Civil Legal Aid (Costs) Regulations 2013 (SI 2013/611), reg 16(4).

amount is, in that case, a reasonable amount for the legally aided party to pay, in accordance with s 26(1) of the 2012 Act (see 62.12).[86]

Otherwise, the court will not specify the amount the legally aided party is to pay under the costs order,[87] in which case (a) the 'stage two' procedure (see 62.15) will apply,[88] and (b) the court may make findings of fact as to the parties' conduct in the proceedings or otherwise relevant to the determination of that amount and those findings shall be taken into consideration in that determination.[89] The legally aided party may be ordered to make a payment on account of costs.[90]

The wording of the relevant provisions can be found at 62.35.

Discretion at stage two

There are two aspects to the court's discretion pertaining to stage two (that is, the discretion exercised by the costs judge): the extent to which the funded person should bear the costs themselves (see 62.31–62.34); and whether, and to what extent, the Lord Chancellor should bear the costs (see 62.35–62.40). **62.30**

Personal liability Section 26(1) of the Legal Aid, Sentencing and Punishment of Offenders Act 2012 provides that costs ordered against an individual who is a legally aided party must not exceed the amount (if any) that it is reasonable for that party to pay, having regard to all of the circumstances, including: **62.31**

- the financial resources of all of the parties to the proceedings; and
- their conduct in connection with the dispute to which the proceedings relate.

Wall LJ has found that the trial court is entitled to accept assertions that the legally aided party is impecunious and is therefore entitled to make a finding that the sum the legally aided party should personally pay is nil.[91] **62.32**

The first £100,000 of the value of the legally aided party's interest in the main or only dwelling in which the legally aided party resides must not be taken into account in having regard to that party's resources for the purposes of s 26(1) of the 2012 Act.[92] Moreover, the court may not take into account the legally aided party's clothes or household furniture, or the implements of that party's trade, unless—and, if so, only to the extent that—the court considers the circumstances of the case to be exceptional, having regard in particular to the quantity or value of the items concerned.[93] The resources of the party's partner are to be treated as the resources of the party to the proceedings (but not if the partner has a contrary interest in the proceedings).[94] **62.33**

---

86 See Civil Legal Aid (Costs) Regulations 2013 (SI 2013/611), reg 16(3).
87 See Civil Legal Aid (Costs) Regulations 2013 (SI 2013/611), reg 16(3)(b).
88 See Civil Legal Aid (Costs) Regulations 2013 (SI 2013/611), reg 16(5).
89 See Civil Legal Aid (Costs) Regulations 2013 (SI 2013/611), reg 16(7).
90 See Civil Legal Aid (Costs) Regulations 2013 (SI 2013/611), reg 17. The payment on account is actually a payment into court. Details as to the procedure are set out in Civil Legal Aid (Costs) Regulations 2013 (SI 2013/611), reg 17.
91 *Wyatt v Portsmouth Hospitals NHS Trust* [2006] EWCA Civ 529, at [58].
92 See Civil Legal Aid (Costs) Regulations 2013 (SI 2013/611), reg 13(1).
93 See Civil Legal Aid (Costs) Regulations 2013 (SI 2013/611), reg 13(2).
94 See Civil Legal Aid (Costs) Regulations 2013 (SI 2013/611), reg 13(3) and (4).

62.34 For the purposes of s 26(1) of the 2012 Act, where a party is acting in a representative, fiduciary or official capacity, the court (a) must not (other than as implied by (c)) take the personal resources of the party acting in such a capacity into account, (b) must have regard to the value of any property or estate, or the amount of any fund, out of which that party is entitled to be indemnified, and (c) may also have regard to the resources of any person who has a beneficial interest in that property, estate or fund, including, if applicable, that party.[95]

62.35 **The liability of the Lord Chancellor** The court may make an order against the Lord Chancellor only where:

- the amount (if any) that the legally aided party is required to pay personally under that costs order is less than the amount of the full costs due under the s 26(1) order (that is, there is a shortfall that the non-legally aided party can look to the Lord Chancellor to pay);[96]
- unless there is a good reason for the delay, the non-legally aided party has made a request for a determination of the Lord Chancellor's liability within three months of the making of the s 26(1) order;
- as regards costs incurred in a court of first instance, the proceedings were instituted by the legally aided party, the non-legally aided party is an individual and the court is satisfied that the non-legally aided party will suffer financial hardship unless the order is made; and
- in any case, the court is satisfied that it is just and equitable in the circumstances that provision for the costs should be made out of public funds.[97]

Wall LJ explained that the difference between first-instance hearings and appeals is that a hearing at first instance is a necessary thing that is required to make findings of fact and to establish the parties' rights, but an appeal is a matter of choice.[98]

62.36 In considering these matters, the costs judge is expressly required to consider the financial resources of the non-funded person and their partner (but not if that latter person has a contrary interest in the matter).[99] Where the non-legally aided party is acting in a representative, fiduciary or official capacity, the court will have regard to the value of the property, estate or fund and the resources of the beneficiaries, if any.[100]

62.37 Where a court decides any proceedings in favour of a non-legally aided party and an appeal lies (with or without permission) against that decision, any order for costs against the Lord Chancellor must not take effect where:

- permission to appeal is required, unless the time limit for an application for permission to appeal expires without such an application being made;

[95] See Civil Legal Aid (Costs) Regulations 2013 (SI 2013/611), reg 13(5) of the Civil Legal Aid (Costs) Regulations 2013 (SI 2013/611).

[96] Where the legally aided party receives civil legal services in connection with only part of the proceedings, the costs that the Lord Chancellor can be ordered to pay are limited to so much of those costs as is attributable to the part of the proceedings for which civil legal services are provided: Community Legal Service (Cost Protection) Regulations 2000 (SI 2000/824), reg 10(4).

[97] See Civil Legal Aid (Costs) Regulations 2013 (SI 2013/611), reg 10(3).

[98] *Wyatt v Portsmouth Hospitals NHS Trust* [2006] EWCA Civ 529, at [36]–[42].

[99] See Civil Legal Aid (Costs) Regulations 2013 (SI 2013/611), reg 10(6) and (7).

[100] Civil Legal Aid (Costs) Regulations 2013 (SI 2013/611), reg 10(8).

- an application for permission is made within the time limit, unless the application is refused; or
- permission to appeal is granted or is not required, unless the time limit for appeal expires without an appeal being brought.[101]

Where the costs judge is deciding whether to exercise their discretion in a case involving costs in the Court of Appeal, Phillips MR has confirmed that the following comments of Lord Woolf MR (which were made under a now-revoked regime) remain good law: **62.38**

> 'If the court comes to a conclusion that in those circumstances it would make the hypothetical order for costs, [ie a s 11(1) order] then in the case of an appeal the court will usually conclude in the absence of some special circumstance that for the purposes of section 18(4)(c) [of the Legal Aid Act 1988] it is just and equitable to make an order. Contrary to [counsel's] submission a local authority, because it is a public body, is not at a disadvantage as compared with any other litigant in seeking an order against the board.'[102]

Lord Phillips MR went on to say that:

> 'Costs judges should proceed on the premise that it is just and equitable that the commission should stand behind their "client", by definition under the Regulations the individual who receives funded services, unless they are aware of facts which render that result unjust or inequitable.'[103]

In courts at first instance, it will be necessary for the non-legally aided party to show financial hardship.[104] Sharp J has commented that the question of whether the non-legally aided party would suffer financial hardship if their costs were not paid was a question of fact and degree—a question that must take into account the impact or the likely consequences to the non-funded person if their costs were not paid.[105] Sharp J found that the removal of the word 'severe' means that the wording of the regulations represented a deliberate and significant relaxation of the formerly stringent regime.[106] **62.39**

Where the legally aided party receives civil legal services in connection with only part of the proceedings, the costs that the Lord Chancellor can be ordered to pay are limited to so much of those costs as is attributable to the part of the proceedings for which civil legal services are provided.[107] Giving judgment in a case in which the duration of the certificate covered only part of the proceedings, Nicholas Strauss QC (sitting as a deputy judge of the High Court) explained that this does not restrict the party seeking their costs to recover costs only during those periods in which the claimant had been in receipt of funding; instead, the party seeking their costs would be entitled to recover those costs caused by the funding of the earlier stages of the proceedings.[108] **62.40**

---

[101] See Civil Legal Aid (Costs) Regulations 2013 (SI 2013/611), reg 10(5).
[102] *R v Secretary of State for the Home Department, ex p Gunn* [2001] EWCA Civ 891, at [46], approving *In re O (Costs: Liability of Legal Aid Board)* [1997] 1 FLR 465.
[103] *R v Secretary of State for the Home Department, ex p Gunn* [2001] EWCA Civ 891, at [50].
[104] Civil Legal Aid (Costs) Regulations 2013 (SI 2013/611), reg 10(3)(c).
[105] *Legal Services Commission v F, A, & V* [2011] EWHC 899 (QB), at [49].
[106] *Ibid*, at [48].
[107] Civil Legal Aid (Costs) Regulations 2013 (SI 2013/611), reg 10(4).
[108] *Murphy v Rayner* [2013] EWHC 3878 (Ch), at [9], [96], [99]–[101], [103] and [108]. Nicholas Strauss QC noted that the Court of Appeal in *Burridge v Stafford; Khan v Ali* [2000] 1 WLR 927 appears to

Put otherwise, the word 'attributable' in what is now reg 10(4) of the Civil Legal Aid (Costs) Regulations 2013[109] denotes a simple causal link between the services funded and the defence costs of the non-funded party.

62.41 **Changes in circumstances and variation** The receiving party may apply to the court for a variation of the amount that the legally aided party is required to pay on the ground that there has been a significant change in that party's circumstances since the date of the order.[110] Similarly, an application may be made if material additional information as to the legally aided party's resources becomes available and that information could not, with reasonable diligence, have been obtained by the receiving party previously.[111] There is a long-stop of six years from the date on which the s 26(1) order was made.[112]

62.42 **Revocation of the certificate** Where a legally aided opponent has had their legal aid certificate revoked, it is open to the court to give effect to that revocation by varying any costs order that had been made against them in such a way as to remove the bar against immediate enforcement.[113]

The Wording of the Provisions

62.43 Section 26 of Legal Aid, Sentencing and Punishment of Offenders Act 2012 provides as follows:

> '26 **Costs in civil proceedings**
>
> (1) Costs ordered against an individual in relevant civil proceedings must not exceed the amount (if any) which it is reasonable for the individual to pay having regard to all the circumstances, including—
> (a) the financial resources of all of the parties to the proceedings, and
> (b) their conduct in connection with the dispute to which the proceedings relate.
>
> (2) In subsection (1) "relevant civil proceedings", in relation to an individual, means—
> (a) proceedings for the purposes of which civil legal services are made available to the individual under this Part, or
> (b) if such services are made available to the individual under this Part for the purposes of only part of proceedings, that part of the proceedings.
>
> (3) Regulations may make provision for exceptions from subsection (1).
>
> (4) In assessing for the purposes of subsection (1) the financial resources of an individual to whom civil legal services are made available, the following must not be taken into account, except so far as prescribed—
> (a) the individual's clothes and household furniture, and
> (b) the implements of the individual's trade.

have found otherwise, but he found that this was based on an assumption in respect of which the court had not heard much argument.

109 SI 2013/611.
110 Civil Legal Aid (Costs) Regulations 2013 (SI 2013/611), reg 19.
111 Civil Legal Aid (Costs) Regulations 2013 (SI 2013/611), reg 19.
112 See Civil Legal Aid (Costs) Regulations 2013 (SI 2013/611), reg 19(5).
113 *Deg-Deutsche Investitions und Entwicklungsgesellschaft mbH v Koshy* [2001] EWCA Civ 79.

(5) Subject to subsections (1) to (4), regulations may make provision about costs in relation to proceedings for the purposes of which civil legal services are made available under this Part.

(6) Regulations under subsection (5) may, in particular, make provision—

(a) specifying the principles to be applied in determining the amount of any costs which may be awarded against a party to whom civil legal services are made available under this Part,

(b) limiting the circumstances in which, or the extent to which, an order for costs may be enforced against such a party,

(c) as to the cases in which, and the extent to which, such a party may be required to give security for costs and the manner in which it is to be given,

(d) requiring the payment by the Lord Chancellor of the whole or part of any costs incurred by a party to whom civil legal services are not made available under this Part,

(e) specifying the principles to be applied in determining the amount of costs which may be awarded to a party to whom civil legal services are made available under this Part,

(f) as to the court, tribunal or other person by whom the amount of any costs is to be determined, and

(g) as to the extent to which any determination of that amount is to be final.

(7) Regulations may provide that an individual is to be treated, for the purposes of subsection (1) or regulations under subsection (3) or (5), as having or not having financial resources of a prescribed description (but such regulations have effect subject to subsection (4)).

(8) Regulations under subsection (7) may, in particular, provide that the individual is to be treated as having prescribed financial resources of a person of a prescribed description.

(9) Regulations under this section may include provision requiring information and documents to be provided.'

The relevant parts of the Civil Legal Aid (Costs) Regulations 2013[114] read as follows: **62.44**

'[...]

Effect of this Part

9. (1) This Part applies where cost protection applies.

(2) The court may not, except in accordance with this Part, make an order requiring the Lord Chancellor to pay the whole or part of any costs incurred by a non-legally aided party because the proceedings are relevant proceedings as regards another party.

Costs order against the Lord Chancellor

10. (1) This regulation applies where relevant proceedings are finally decided in favour of a non-legally aided party.

(2) Subject to paragraphs (3) to (8), the court may make an order for the payment by the Lord Chancellor to the non-legally aided party of the whole or any part of the costs incurred by that party in the proceedings (other than the costs that the legally aided party is required to pay under a section 26(1) costs order).

(3) An order under paragraph (2) may only be made if the following conditions are satisfied—

(a) a section 26(1) costs order is made against the legally aided party in the proceedings, and the amount (if any) which the legally aided party is required to pay under that costs order is less than the amount of the full costs;

(b) the non-legally aided party makes a request—

[114] SI 2013/611.

(i) under regulation 16(2), within three months of the date on which the section 26(1) costs order is made; or
(ii) after the expiry of the time limit under regulation 16(2), where there is a good reason for the delay in the request being made;

(c) as regards costs incurred in a court of first instance, the following conditions are met—
(i) the proceedings were instituted by the legally aided party;
(ii) the non-legally aided party is an individual; and
(iii) the court is satisfied that the non-legally aided party will suffer financial hardship unless the order is made; and

(d) in any case, the court is satisfied that it is just and equitable in the circumstances that provision for the costs should be made out of public funds.

(4) Where the legally aided party receives civil legal services in connection with only part of the proceedings, the reference in paragraph (2) to the costs incurred by the non-legally aided party in the proceedings is to be construed as a reference to so much of those costs as is attributable to the part of the proceedings for which civil legal services are provided.

(5) Where a court decides any proceedings in favour of a non-legally aided party and an appeal lies (with or without permission) against that decision, any order made under this regulation must not take effect—

(a) where permission to appeal is required, unless the time limit for an application for permission to appeal expires without such an application being made;
(b) where an application for permission is made within the time limit, unless the application is refused; or
(c) where permission to appeal is granted or is not required, unless the time limit for appeal expires without an appeal being brought.

(6) Subject to paragraph (7), in determining whether the conditions in paragraph (3)(c)(iii) and (d) are satisfied, the court must have regard to the resources of the non-legally aided party and of that party's partner.

(7) The court must not have regard to the resources of the partner of the non-legally aided party if the partner has a contrary interest in the proceedings.

(8) Where the non-legally aided party is acting in a representative, fiduciary or official capacity and is entitled to be indemnified in respect of costs from any property, estate or fund, the court must, for the purposes of determining whether the conditions in paragraph (3)(c)(iii) and (d) are satisfied, have regard to the value of the property, estate or fund and the resources of any person who has a beneficial interest in that property, estate or fund.

Enforcement of costs order against a legally aided party

11. Where, for the purpose of enforcing a costs order against a legally aided party who is not a legal person, a charging order is made under section 1 of the Charging Orders Act 1979(a) (alone or together with any other judgment or order) in respect of that party's interest in the main or only dwelling in which that party resides—

(a) that charging order must operate to secure the amount payable under the costs order (including, without limitation, any interest) only to the extent of the amount (if any) by which the proceeds of sale of the legally aided party's interest in the dwelling (having deducted any mortgage debts) exceed £100,000; and
(b) an order for the sale of the dwelling must not be made in favour of the person in whose favour the charging order is made.

[...]

Assessment of resources

13. (1) The first £100,000 of the value of the legally aided party's interest in the main or only dwelling in which the legally aided party resides must not be taken into account in having regard to that party's resources for the purposes of section 26(1) of the Act.

(2) In having regard to the legally aided party's resources for the purposes of section 26(1) of the Act, the court may not take into account the legally aided party's clothes or household furniture, or the implements of that party's trade, unless, and if so only to the extent that, the court considers the circumstances of the case are exceptional, having regard in particular to the quantity or value of the items concerned.

(3) Subject to paragraph (4), in having regard to the resources of a party to the proceedings for the purposes of section 26(1) of the Act, the resources of the party's partner are to be treated as the resources of the party to the proceedings.

(4) The resources of a party's partner are not to be treated as that party's resources if the partner has a contrary interest in the proceedings.

(5) For the purposes of section 26(1) of the Act, where a party is acting in a representative, fiduciary or official capacity, the court—

(a) subject to sub-paragraph (c), must not take the personal resources of the party acting in such a capacity into account;

(b) must have regard to the value of any property or estate, or the amount of any fund, out of which that party is entitled to be indemnified; and

(c) may also have regard to the resources of any person who has a beneficial interest in that property, estate or fund, including, if applicable, that party.

(6) For the purposes of section 26(1) of the Act, where a party is acting as a litigation friend to a legally aided party, the court must not take the personal resources of the litigation friend into account in assessing the resources of the legally aided party.

(7) This regulation does not apply in respect of a legally aided party who is a legal person.

Statements of resources

14. (1) For the purposes of this Part, a statement of resources is a statement, verified by a statement of truth—

(a) made by a party to proceedings, other than a legally aided party who is a legal person, setting out—

   (i) the party's income and capital and financial commitments during the previous year and, if applicable, those of the party's partner;

   (ii) the party's estimated future financial resources and expectations and, if applicable, those of the party's partner; and

   (iii) a declaration stating whether the party, and, if applicable, the party's partner, have deliberately forgone or deprived themselves of any resources or expectations, together (if applicable and as far as is practical) with details of those resources or expectations and the manner in which they have been forgone or the party or partner deprived of them;

   (iv) particulars of any application for legal aid made by the party in connection with the proceedings; and

   (v) any other facts relevant to the determination of the party's resources; or

(b) made by a legally aided party—

   (i) setting out the information previously provided by that party in order to determine that the party's financial resources were such that the party was eligible for civil legal services; and

   (ii) either stating that there has been no significant change in the party's financial circumstances since the date on which the information was provided or, as the case may be, providing details of any such change.

(2) Any party to proceedings in which another party is a legally aided party may make a statement of resources, and file it with the court.

(3) A person making and filing a statement of resources under paragraph (2) must serve a copy of it on the legally aided party.

(4) If the copy of a statement of resources served under paragraph (3) has been served not less than seven days before the date fixed for a hearing at which the amount to be paid under a section 26(1) costs order falls, or may fall, to be decided, the legally aided party must also make a statement of resources, and must produce it at that hearing.

Determination of costs

15. (1) Where the court is considering whether to make a section 26(1) costs order, it must consider whether—
(a) but for cost protection, it would have made a costs order against the legally aided party; and
(b) if so, whether, on making the costs order, it would have specified the amount to be paid under that order.

(2) If the court considers that it would have made a costs order against the legally aided party, but that it would not have specified the amount to be paid under it, the court must, when making the section 26(1) costs order—
(a) specify the amount (if any) that the legally aided party is to pay under that order if—
(i) it considers that it has sufficient information before it to decide what amount is, in that case, a reasonable amount for the legally aided party to pay, in accordance with section 26(1) of the Act; and
(ii) it is satisfied that, if it were to determine the full costs at that time, they would exceed the amount referred to in (i) above; or
(b) not otherwise specify the amount that the legally aided party is to pay under that order.

(3) If the court considers that it would have made a costs order against the legally aided party, and that it would have specified the amount to be paid under it, the court must, when making the section 26(1) costs order—
(a) specify the amount (if any) that the legally aided party is to pay under that order if it considers that it has sufficient information before it to decide what amount is, in that case, a reasonable amount for the legally aided party to pay, in accordance with section 26(1) of the Act; or
(b) not otherwise specify the amount the legally aided party is to pay under that order.

(4) Any order made under paragraph (3) must state the amount of the full costs.

(5) Regulation 16 applies to the determination of—
(a) the amount (if any) to be paid by the legally aided party where paragraph (2)(b) or paragraph (3)(b) applies; and
(b) any application for a costs order against the Lord Chancellor.

(6) Where a determination under regulation 16 follows an order to which paragraph (2)(b) applies, the amount of the full costs must also be assessed.

(7) Where the court makes a section 26(1) costs order that does not specify the amount which the legally aided party is to pay under it, it may also make findings of fact (as to the parties' conduct in connection with the dispute to which the proceedings relate or otherwise) relevant to the determination of that amount, and those findings must be taken into consideration in that determination.

Determination of costs where no amount specified

16. (1) Paragraphs (2) to (12) apply where the amount to be paid under a section 26(1) costs order, or an application for a costs order against the Lord Chancellor, is to be determined under this regulation in accordance with regulation 15(5).

(2) Subject to regulations 10(3)(b)(ii) and 19(3), the receiving party may, within three months of the date on which a section 26(1) costs order is made, request a hearing to determine the amount to be paid to that party.

(3) A request under paragraph (2) must be accompanied by—
(a) if the section 26(1) costs order does not state the full costs, the receiving party's bill of costs, which must comply with any requirements of relevant rules of court relating to the form and content of a bill of costs where the court is assessing a party's costs;
(b) unless the conditions set out in paragraph (4) are satisfied, a statement of resources; and
(c) if the receiving party is seeking a costs order against the Lord Chancellor or may seek such an order subject to the determination of the amount to be paid under the section 26(1) costs order, written notice to that effect.

(4) The conditions referred to in paragraph (3)(b) are that—
(a) the court is determining an application for a costs order against the Lord Chancellor; and
(b) the costs were not incurred in a court of first instance.

(5) The receiving party must file the documents referred to in paragraph (3) with the court and at the same time serve copies of them—
(a) on the legally aided party, if a determination of costs payable under section 26(1) of the Act is sought; and
(b) on the Lord Chancellor, if notice has been given under paragraph (3)(c).

(6) Where documents are served on the legally aided party under paragraph (5)(a), that party must make a statement of resources.

(7) The legally aided party must, within 21 days of the date of receipt of a copy of the receiving party's statement of resources—
(a) file with the court the statement of resources made under paragraph (6);
(b) serve a copy of that statement on the receiving party; and
(c) if notice has been given under paragraph (3)(c), serve a copy of that statement on the Lord Chancellor.

(8) The legally aided party may, at the same time as filing and serving a statement of resources under paragraph (7), file, and serve on the same persons, a statement setting out any points of dispute in relation to the bill of costs referred to in paragraph (3)(a).

(9) If the legally aided party, without good reason, fails to file a statement of resources in accordance with paragraph (7), the court—
(a) must determine the amount which that party is to be required to pay under the section 26(1) costs order (and, if relevant, the full costs), having regard to the statement made by the receiving party; and
(b) may do so without an oral hearing.

(10) Subject to paragraph (9)(b), the court must set a date for the hearing if—
(a) the legally aided party files a statement of resources in accordance with paragraph (7);
(b) the period for filing the statement under paragraph (7) expires; or
(c) the costs payable by the legally aided party have already been determined.

(11) The court must, at least 14 days before the hearing date, serve notice of the date on—
(a) the receiving party;
(b) the legally aided party (unless the costs payable by that party have already been determined); and
(c) if a costs order against the Lord Chancellor is or may be sought, the Lord Chancellor.

(12) The amount of costs to be determined under this regulation may include the costs incurred in relation to a request under paragraph (2).

Payment on account of costs

17. (1) Where the court—
(a) makes a section 26(1) costs order but does not specify the amount which the legally aided party is to pay under it; and

(b) has sufficient information before it to decide the minimum amount which the legally aided party is likely to be ordered to pay on a determination under regulation 16, the court may order the legally aided party to pay an amount on account of the costs which are the subject of the order.

(2) The amount of any payment on account of costs must not exceed the minimum amount which the court decides that the legally aided party is likely to be ordered to pay on a determination under regulation 16.

(3) Where the court orders a legally aided party to make a payment on account of costs—
(a) it must order the legally aided party to make the payment into court; and
(b) the payment must remain in court unless and until the court—
 (i) makes a determination under regulation 16 of the amount which the legally aided party should pay to the receiving party under the section 26(1) costs order, and orders the payment on account or part of it to be paid to the receiving party in satisfaction or part satisfaction of the legally aided party's liability under that order; or
 (ii) makes an order under paragraph (4)(b) or (c) that the payment on account or part of it be repaid to the legally aided party.

(4) Where a legally aided party has made a payment on account of costs pursuant to an order under paragraph (1)—
(a) the receiving party must request a hearing under regulation 16;
(b) if the receiving party fails to request such a hearing within the time permitted by regulation 16(2), the payment on account must be repaid to the legally aided party;
(c) if upon the hearing under regulation 16 the amount of costs which it is determined that the legally aided party should pay is less than the amount of the payment on account, the difference must be repaid to the legally aided party.

Appeals, etc.

18. (1) Subject to this regulation and regulation 19, any determination under regulation 15 or regulation 16 is final.

(2) Any party with a financial interest in an assessment of the full costs may appeal against that assessment if, and to the extent that, the party would but for this Part be entitled to appeal against an assessment of costs by the court in which the relevant proceedings are taking place.

(3) Where the court has under regulation 15(2)(a) specified an amount which a legally aided party is required to pay under a section 26(1) costs order, the legally aided party may apply to the court for a determination of the full costs.

(4) If, on a determination under paragraph (3), the amount of the full costs is less than the amount which the court previously specified under regulation 15(2)(a), the legally aided party must instead be required to pay the amount of the full costs.

(5) The receiving party or the Lord Chancellor may appeal, on a point of law, against the making of a costs order against the Lord Chancellor (including the amount of costs which the Lord Chancellor is required to pay under the order), or, in the case of the receiving party, against the court's refusal to make such an order.

Variation and late determination of amount of costs

19. (1) This regulation applies where the court makes a section 26(1) costs order.

(2) Where the amount (if any) which the legally aided party is required to pay under the section 26(1) costs order, together with the amount which the Lord Chancellor is required to pay under any costs order against the Lord Chancellor, is less than the full costs, the receiving party may, on the ground set out in paragraph (4)(a), apply to the court for an order varying the amount which the legally aided party is required to pay under the section 26(1) costs order.

(3) The receiving party may, on any of the grounds set out in paragraph (4), apply for a determination of the amount that the legally aided party is required to pay where—

(a) the receiving party has not, within the time limit in regulation 16(2), applied to have that amount determined in accordance with regulation 16; and

(b) the court has not specified the amount to be paid under the section 26(1) costs order.

(4) The grounds referred to in paragraphs (2) and (3) are that—

(a) there has been a significant change in the legally aided party's circumstances since the date of the order;

(b) material additional information as to the legally aided party's resources is available, and that information could not with reasonable diligence have been obtained by the receiving party in time to make an application in accordance with regulation 16; or

(c) there is a good reason for the receiving party's delay in making the request within the time limit under regulation 16(2).

(5) Any application under paragraph (2) or (3) must be made by the receiving party within six years from the date on which the section 26(1) costs order is first made.

(6) On any application under paragraph (2), the amount that the legally aided party is required to pay under the section 26(1) costs order may be varied as the court thinks fit, but the amount of costs ordered (excluding any costs ordered to be paid under paragraph (9)) must not exceed the amount of the full costs.

(7) When the amount which the legally aided party is required to pay under the section 26(1) costs order has been determined under regulation 15(2)(a), and the receiving party applies under paragraph (2) for an order varying that amount—

(a) the receiving party must file with the application under paragraph (2) that party's bill of costs, which must comply with any requirements of relevant rules of court relating to the form and content of a bill of costs where the court is assessing a party's costs; and

(b) the court must, when determining the application, assess the full costs.

(8) Where civil legal services have been provided to the receiving party in relation to the proceedings, the Lord Chancellor may make an application under paragraph (2) or (3), and—

(a) when making the application the Lord Chancellor must file with the court a statement of the receiving party's costs or, if those costs have not been assessed, the receiving party's bill of costs; and

(b) paragraphs (4) and (5) apply to that application as if "the Lord Chancellor" were substituted for "the receiving party" in those paragraphs.

(9) The amount of costs to be determined under this regulation may include the costs incurred in relation to an application made under this regulation.

[...]'

63

ROAD TRAFFIC INSURERS AND LIABILITY FOR COSTS

63.01 This short chapter deals with the liability of road traffic insurers for orders for costs made against their insureds and other tortfeasors. It is very much an overview; if a point of complexity arises, then the reader is referred to specialist texts dealing with road traffic insurance.

63.02 The insurance industry maintains a structure that is designed to ensure that victims of road traffic accidents (RTAs) are able to recover compensation (including costs). Part of that structure is governed by statute, but much of it is a creation of the industry itself. It has been created so as to comply with a consolidating EU directive made in 2009.[1] Whilst some commentators say that the structure is not being applied in a way that is consistent with the directive,[2] it is unlikely that any such issue would arise in the context of a dispute about costs.

63.03 The structure has been called a liability tree,[3] in reference to the fact if a victim drops down a 'branch', there is generally another branch that will catch them. It is only if the victim cascades to the very bottom that they will need to look to the funder of last resort—namely, the Motor Insurance Bureau (MIB). The tree can be illustrated as in Figure 63.1.

63.04 In order of priority, the branches of the tree are as follows.[4]

- **Contractual liability** First and foremost, where a valid policy of motor insurance has been delivered to the tortfeasor and where there is no reason to avoid the policy, there is the contractual liability of the motor insurer providing compulsory third-party indemnity cover.[5] The vast majority of RTA claims are met by insurers in this way.
- **Modified contractual liability** The next branch is created by s 148 of the Road Traffic Act 1988, which provides that certain matters are to be 'of no effect' in so far as a third

[1] See Directive 2009/103/EC of the European Parliament and of the Council of 16 September 2009 relating to insurance against civil liability in respect of the use of motor vehicles, and the enforcement of the obligation to insure against such liability, OJ L 263/11, 7 October 2009.

[2] Bevan, N, 'Trial and Error', *New Law Journal*, 20 April 2012.

[3] See Worthington, S, 'Motor Insurance: Contractual, Section 151, Article 75, MIB Central Fund—Who Pays?', 12 King's Bench Walk Chambers in-house release, 8 May 2013.

[4] The following summary of the law is based on Bevan, N, 'Trial and Error', *New Law Journal*, 20 April 2012, and Worthington, S, 'Motor Insurance: Contractual, Section 151, Article 75, MIB Central Fund—Who Pays?', 12 King's Bench Walk Chambers in-house release, 8 May 2013.

[5] See Road Traffic Act 1988, s 143 and s 145.

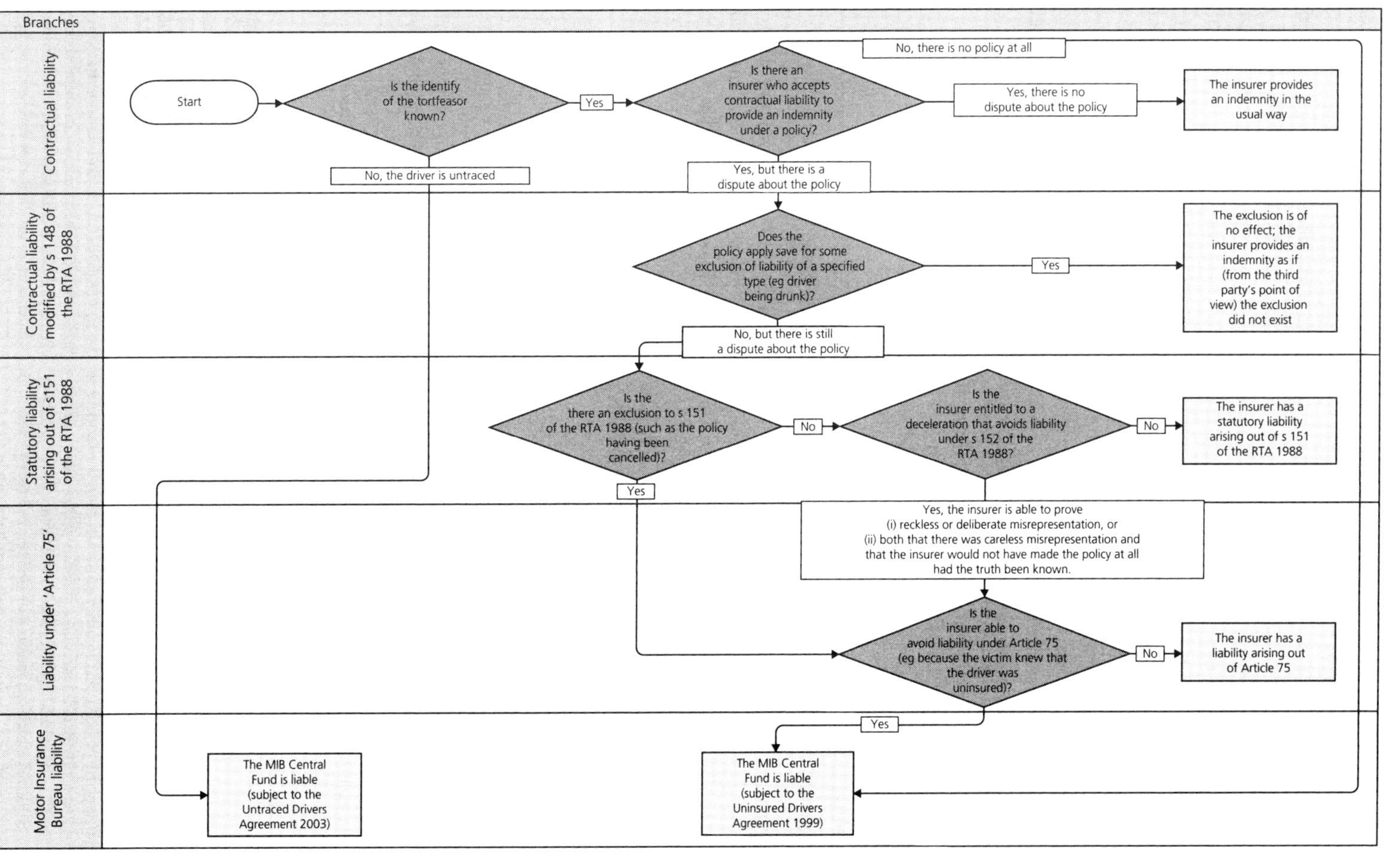
Branches
Contractual liability
Contractual liability modified by s 148 of the RTA 1988
Statutory liability arising out of s151 of the RTA 1988
Liability under 'Article 75'
Motor Insurance Bureau liability
Start
Is the identify of the tortfeasor known?
Yes
No, the driver is untraced
Is there an insurer who accepts contractual liability to provide an indemnity under a policy?
No, there is no policy at all
Yes, there is no dispute about the policy
The insurer provides an indemnity in the usual way
Yes, but there is a dispute about the policy
Does the policy apply save for some exclusion of liability of a specified type (eg driver being drunk)?
Yes
The exclusion is of no effect; the insurer provides an indemnity as if (from the third party's point of view) the exclusion did not exist
No, but there is still a dispute about the policy
Is the there an exclusion to s 151 of the RTA 1988 (such as the policy having been cancelled)?
No
Is the insurer entitled to a deceleration that avoids liability under s 152 of the RTA 1988?
No
The insurer has a statutory liability arising out of s 151 of the RTA 1988
Yes
Yes, the insurer is able to prove
(i) reckless or deliberate misrepresentation, or
(ii) both that there was careless misrepresentation and that the insurer would not have made the policy at all had the truth been known.
Is the insurer able to avoid liability under Article 75 (eg because the victim knew that the driver was uninsured)?
No
The insurer has a liability arising out of Article 75
Yes
The MIB Central Fund is liable (subject to the Untraced Drivers Agreement 2003)
The MIB Central Fund is liable (subject to the Uninsured Drivers Agreement 1999)

Figure 63.1 The liability tree

party is concerned.[6] For example, if the policy seeks to exclude liability for an accident that occurred whilst the driver was drunk or because the car was carrying too many passengers, that provision would be of no effect in so far as the third party is concerned.[7] There are many such provisions that the Act negates[8]—in particular, an attempt to avoid liability for late notification of the claim will be of no effect as against a third party.[9]

- **Statutory RTA liability** The next branch down is a secondary level of protection that applies where a policy would have covered the accident,[10] but, for some reason, the insurer is entitled to avoid or cancel it. An example would be where a policy covers the tortfeasor, but where there has been non-disclosure or misrepresentation that has abrogated that cover from inception. Where this happens, the starting point is that the insurer is converted by statute into a non-contractual compensatory agency.[11] Subject to certain exceptions[12] and subject to a 'section 151 notice' having been given,[13] s 151 of Road Traffic Act 1988 creates a statutory liability notwithstanding the fact that the insurer is entitled to avoid or cancel the contract. In so far as costs are concerned, it reads as follows:

  '(5) Notwithstanding that the insurer may be entitled to avoid or cancel, or may have avoided or cancelled, the policy or security, he must, subject to the provisions of this section, pay to the persons entitled to the benefit of the judgment ... (c) any amount payable in respect of costs.'

  Section 151(8) of the Road Traffic Act 1988 then permits the insurer to seek recompense from the person who caused or permitted the use of the vehicle that gave rise to the liability.[14]

  Alternatively, where appropriate, the insurer is able to seek a declaration that it is entitled to avoid the policy on the ground that it was obtained (a) by the non-disclosure of a material fact, or (b) by a representation of fact that was false in some material particular.[15] Where the insurer obtains such a declaration, the third party will drop down to the next branch. The test that is applied for the purpose of obtaining a declaration has, in respect of all policies made or renewed on or after 6 April 2013, been made more rigorous from the insurer's point of view.[16]

---

[6] The exclusion or limit may, however, still be effective as against the insured tortfeasor.

[7] See Road Traffic Act 1988, s 148(5).

[8] See Road Traffic Act 1988, s 148(5).

[9] See Road Traffic Act 1988, s 148(5).

[10] The insurer is liable only in respect of the use which is covered by the policy: see *Keely v Pashen* [2004] EWCA Civ 1491. See also *Bristol Alliance Ltd v Williams* [2012] EWCA Civ 1267.

[11] See Road Traffic Act 1988, s 151.

[12] For example, Road Traffic Act 1988, s 151(4), excludes liability under s 151 where the passenger was allowing themselves to be carried in or upon the vehicle and knew or had reason to believe that the vehicle had been stolen.

[13] Road Traffic Act 1988, s 152(1)(a), imposes, as a condition precedent of liability under s 151, the requirement that the person making the claim must give notice of proceedings to the insurer before or within seven days of their commencement, ie the 'Section 151 notice' that tends to be served in almost every motor claim. This is of little practical relevance, however, because there is nothing to stop a third party from discontinuing the claim, serving a Section 151 notice and bringing new proceedings: *Horton v Sadler* [2008] UKHL 27.

[14] If the tortfeasor is also the victim, then see *Churchill Insurance Co Ltd v Fitzgerald & Wilkinson & Ors* [2012] EWCA Civ 1166.

[15] See Road Traffic Act 1988, s 152(2).

[16] Where the policy is a consumer contract, then the Consumer Insurance (Disclosure and Representations) Act 2012 amends Road Traffic Act 1988, s 152, so as to create a distinction between careless misrepresentations, on the one hand, and reckless or deliberate misrepresentation, on the other. The legal burden is on the insurer to prove either (a) reckless or deliberate misrepresentation, or (b) both that there was careless misrepresentation and that the insurer would not have made the policy at all had the truth been known.

- **'Article 75' liability** That next branch is the creation of art 75 of the MIB's memorandum and articles of association.[17] It creates a liability that is a counterpart to statutory RTA liability and best thought of as also being a secondary level of protection. In very general terms, it will apply where the insurer has successfully obtained a declaration in respect of statutory RTA liability (see above) but still has some connection with the tortfeasor in the sense that it 'was providing any insurance in respect of the vehicle from the use of which the liability of the judgment debtor arose'.[18] Article 75 provides (with some exceptions[19]) that the insurer will provide an indemnity in respect of the third party's costs. The benefits to an insurer in seeking a declaration and falling within the ambit of art 75 are that (a) the insurer will have the benefit of the Uninsured Drivers Agreement 1999, which provides that no liability will attach where the defendant knew, or ought to have known, that the driver had no insurance,[20] and (b) it is possible that the insurer may fall lower down the tree than another insurer, in which case the insurer higher up the tree will bear responsibility for the third party's claim.[21]
- **The liability of the MIB** This tertiary level of protection is managed by the MIB, as the funder of last resort. The MIB's role is governed by two private law agreements with the Secretary of State for Transport:
  - the Uninsured Drivers Agreement 1999, which applies when the tortfeasor had no insurance at all; and
  - the Untraced Drivers Agreement 2003, which applies where the tortfeasor cannot be identified.

  Damages and costs are paid out of the MIB's central fund, to which all motor insurers contribute.

In practical terms, the existence of the secondary layer of protection—the statutory RTA liability/art 75 liability—means that a person who has been injured in an RTA is usually able to look directly to the tortfeasor's insurer (if they have one) for payment of costs, regardless of whether there is a contractual liability under the policy. It is important to note that the exclusions and restrictions relating to any given branch are irrelevant for the purposes of the branches above it. It would therefore be wrong to point to a failure to deliver a section 151 notice (that is, a notice that is a condition precedent for statutory RTA liability) in a case in which there is a contractual liability. **63.05**

[17] Memorandum and Articles of Association of the Motor Insurers Bureau, as amended on 3 July 2008.
[18] See *ibid*, art 75(2)(a).
[19] See *ibid*, art 75(2). Examples include the policy having been cancelled, having been declared void prior to the accident or having expired.
[20] See Uninsured Drivers Agreement 1999, para 6(1)(a)(iii).
[21] See Worthington, S, 'Motor Insurance: Contractual, Section 151, Article 75, MIB Central Fund—Who Pays?', 12 King's Bench Walk Chambers in-house release, 8 May 2013.

64

COSTS AGAINST THE COURTS SERVICE

64.01 This chapter deals with the following topics:

- the power to make payments (64.03);
- the exercise of discretion (64.09):
  - the Principles of Good Administration (64.11);
  - the Principles for Remedy (64.12);
  - the Principles of Good Complaint Handling (64.13);
- quantum (64.15); and
- procedure (64.18).

64.02 Her Majesty's Courts and Tribunals Service (HMCTS, or the Courts Service) is able to make *ex gratia* compensation payments for costs thrown away by its error. Such payments are not costs, but compensation; in particular, the Courts Service will rarely agree to an order that it pays costs to be assessed.

The Power to Make Payments

64.03 Although a litigant would have a theoretical right to apply for a non-party costs order against the Courts Service, in practice this is never done because of the availability of *ex gratia* payments.

64.04 Prior to the coming into force of the Human Rights Act 1998, the House of Lords had ruled that s 51 of the Senior Courts Act 1981 did not impliedly confer a power on the court to make an order out of central funds to compensate a litigant for costs thrown away as a result of court maladministration.[1] In a case in which the first-instance judge was found to have been biased, a disgruntled litigant challenged that position on the grounds that Art 6(1) of the European Convention on Human Rights (ECHR) required the court, as an emanation of the state, to provide an impartial tribunal; that point was not decided, however, because Phillips MR (with whom Brooke and Walker LJJ agreed) found that, on the facts of that particular case, the litigant was not a 'victim' for the purposes of making a claim under s 7(1) of the Human Rights Act 1998.[2] In most instances of maladministration, however, the issue of Art 6(1) ECHR will be irrelevant, because most instances of

[1] *Steele Ford & Newton v Crown Prosecution Service* [1994] 1 AC 22, overruling *Re Central Independent Television plc & Ors* [1991] 1 All ER 347 and *R v Bow Street Metropolitan Stipendiary Magistrate, ex p Mirror Group Newspapers Ltd* [1992] 2 All ER 638 (QBD).

[2] *Director General of Fair Trading v Proprietary Association of Great Britain, In re Medicaments & Related Classes of Goods (No 4)* [2002] 1 WLR 269.

costs being thrown away are the result of mundane clerical errors rather than the lack of an unbiased tribunal.

Subject to the above points, the power to make payments does not arise from s 51 of the Senior Courts Act 1981 (or, for that matter, from any other similar Act); it is probably an instance of the Crown exercising its prerogative power. There is, however, no authority on this point. **64.05**

There are no published rules that govern of the Courts Service's powers to make an *ex gratia* payment.[3] That said, there is a well-established principle that payments will be made only in respect of costs thrown away by maladministration. The principles underlying such payments are as follows: **64.06**

> 'Where a public body has failed to get it right and this has led to injustice or hardship, it should take steps to put things right. That means, if possible, returning complainants and, where appropriate, others who have suffered the same injustice or hardship as a result of the same maladministration or poor service, to the position they were in before this took place. If that is not possible, it means compensating complainants and such others appropriately.'[4]

Thus it would seem that there are three requirements that must be satisfied before a payment can be made: **64.07**

- there must have been maladministration or poor services;
- there must be injustice or hardship; and
- there must be a causal link between the two.

Although *ex gratia* payments are limited to recompensing complainants for costs thrown away, the Courts Service has a discretion to make payments relating to other errors and events, which, in appropriate circumstances, may include the following: 'Financial compensation for direct or indirect financial loss, loss of opportunity, inconvenience, distress, or any combination of these.'[5] This may be relevant in the sense that a litigant may not be entitled to only their own costs thrown away by maladministration (that is, direct financial loss), but also to any costs that they might be ordered to pay as a result of that maladministration (that is, indirect financial loss). **64.08**

The Exercise of Discretion

It is not always easy to distinguish between maladministration and judicial error. One might think that the issue turns on whether the complainant had a right to apply for permission to appeal, but that cannot be right because maladministration may be the cause of subsequent judicial error (and indeed often is). Moreover, budgetary constraints mean that **64.09**

[3] HM Courts & Tribunals Service, 'I Want to Complain: What Do I Do?'. EX343, available online at https://assets.publishing.service.gov.uk/government/uploads/system/uploads/attachment_data/file/223545/contact-director-wales-hmcts-annex-a.pdf, states that the complaints procedure cannot be used for complaining about a judicial decision, but it makes no mention of maladministration.

[4] Parliamentary and Health Service Ombudsman, 'Ombudsman's Principles: Principles of Good Complaint Handling', 13 February 2009, available online at https://www.ombudsman.org.uk/about-us/our-principles/principles-good-complaint-handling

[5] *Ibid.*

judges are increasingly having to do work that, in years gone by, would have been carried out by court staff, which means that the opportunity for maladministration by judges is very real. There is no authority on the topic of whether such an error would be regarded as compensable or not, but it would be difficult to justify a state of affairs in which a court user was denied compensation solely because the person who made the error was a judge, rather than a member of staff. It would be much easier to justify an approach that focuses on the nature of the error, rather than on the status of the person who made it. There is, however, no authority on that point.

64.10 An application for costs will be determined in accordance with the Ombudsman's Principles, as published from time to time by the Parliamentary Commissioner for Administration—a statutory role that combines with the Health Service Commissioner to form the office of the Parliamentary and Health Service Ombudsman (sometimes referred to simply as the 'Parliamentary Ombudsman').[6] There are three sets of principles governing the matter: the Principles of Good Administration; the Principles for Remedy; and the Principles of Good Complaint Handling. All three of these are based on a common six-part framework that comprises:

- getting it right;
- being customer-focused;
- being open and accountable;
- acting fairly and proportionately;
- putting things right; and
- seeking continuous improvement.

The Principles of Good Administration

64.11 The Principles of Good Administration were first published on 27 March 2007, following a consultation that took place at the end of 2006.[7] They include a range of guiding principles grouped under the above six headings. The details are published on the website of the Parliamentary and Health Service Ombudsman.[8]

The Principles for Remedy

64.12 The Principles for Remedy were first published on 11 October 2007, following a consultation that took place in early 2007.[9] They are as follows:

> '1 **Getting it right**
> - Quickly acknowledging and putting right cases of maladministration or poor service that have led to injustice or hardship.
> - Considering all relevant factors when deciding the appropriate remedy, ensuring fairness for the complainant and, where appropriate, for others who have suffered injustice or hardship as a result of the same maladministration or poor service.

[6] See HM Courts & Tribunals Service, 'I Want to Complain: What Do I Do?'. EX343, available online at https://assets.publishing.service.gov.uk/government/uploads/system/uploads/attachment_data/file/223545/contact-director-wales-hmcts-annex-a.pdf

[7] Parliamentary and Health Service Ombudsman, *Principles of Good Administration: Response to Consultation* (London: HMSO, 2009).

[8] See https://www.ombudsman.org.uk/about-us/our-principles

[9] Parliamentary and Health Service Ombudsman, *Report on the Consultation on Principles for Remedy* (London: HMSO, 2007).

2 **Being customer focused**
- Apologising for and explaining the maladministration or poor service.
- Understanding and managing people's expectations and needs.
- Dealing with people professionally and sensitively.
- Providing remedies that take account of people's individual circumstances.

3 **Being open and accountable**
- Being open and clear about how public bodies decide remedies.
- Operating a proper system of accountability and delegation in providing remedies.
- Keeping a clear record of what public bodies have decided on remedies and why.

4 **Acting fairly and proportionately**
- Offering remedies that are fair and proportionate to the complainant's injustice or hardship.
- Providing remedies to others who have suffered injustice or hardship as a result of the same maladministration or poor service, where appropriate.
- Treating people without bias, unlawful discrimination or prejudice.

5 **Putting things right**
- If possible, returning the complainant and, where appropriate, others who have suffered similar injustice or hardship, to the position they would have been in if the maladministration or poor service had not occurred.
- If that is not possible, compensating the complainant and such others appropriately.
- Considering fully and seriously all forms of remedy (such as an apology, an explanation, remedial action, or financial compensation).
- Providing the appropriate remedy in each case.

6 **Seeking continuous improvement**
- Using the lessons learned from complaints to ensure that maladministration or poor service is not repeated.
- Recording and using information on the outcome of complaints to improve services.'

The Principles of Good Complaint Handling

The Principles of Good Complaint Handling should be read in conjunction with the other principles. They are as follows: **64.13**

'1 **Getting it right**
- Acting in accordance with the law and relevant guidance, and with regard for the rights of those concerned.
- Ensuring that those at the top of the public body provide leadership to support good complaint management and develop an organisational culture that values complaints.
- Having clear governance arrangements, which set out roles and responsibilities, and ensure lessons are learnt from complaints.
- Including complaint management as an integral part of service design.
- Ensuring that staff are equipped and empowered to act decisively to resolve complaints.
- Focusing on the outcomes for the complainant and the public body.
- Signposting to the next stage of the complaints procedure, in the right way and at the right time.

2 **Being customer focused**
- Having clear and simple procedures.
- Ensuring that complainants can easily access the service dealing with complaints, and informing them about advice and advocacy services where appropriate.
- Dealing with complainants promptly and sensitively, bearing in mind their individual circumstances.

- Listening to complainants to understand the complaint and the outcome they are seeking.
- Responding flexibly, including co-ordinating responses with any other bodies involved in the same complaint, where appropriate.

3 **Being open and accountable**
- Publishing clear, accurate and complete information about how to complain, and how and when to take complaints further.
- Publishing service standards for handling complaints.
- Providing honest, evidence-based explanations and giving reasons for decisions.
- Keeping full and accurate records.

4 **Acting fairly and proportionately**
- Treating the complainant impartially, and without unlawful discrimination or prejudice.
- Ensuring that complaints are investigated thoroughly and fairly to establish the facts of the case.
- Ensuring that decisions are proportionate, appropriate and fair.
- Ensuring that complaints are reviewed by someone not involved in the events leading to the complaint.
- Acting fairly towards staff complained about as well as towards complainants.

5 **Putting things right**
- Acknowledging mistakes and apologising where appropriate.
- Providing prompt, appropriate and proportionate remedies.
- Considering all the relevant factors of the case when offering remedies.
- Taking account of any injustice or hardship that results from pursuing the complaint as well as from the original dispute.

6 **Seeking continuous improvement**
- Using all feedback and the lessons learnt from complaints to improve service design and delivery.
- Having systems in place to record, analyse and report on the learning from complaints.
- Regularly reviewing the lessons to be learnt from complaints.
- Where appropriate, telling the complainant about the lessons learnt and changes made to services, guidance or policy.'

64.14 Further details are given in the Ombudsman's Principles.[10] Most of the guidance contained in that document is not relevant for present purposes, but it does make clear that the Courts Service must act in accordance with its own policy and guidance. In this regard, it may be relevant that the Courts Service's own guidance is that processes and procedures will be designed to suit the user, rather than the administrator.[11]

Quantum

64.15 The Courts Service is not required to take the 'seven pillars' outlined under r 44.5(3) of the Civil Procedure Rules (CPR) into account. Instead, it may take into account:

- the nature of the complaint;
- the impact on the complainant;

[10] Parliamentary and Health Service Ombudsman, 'Ombudsman's Principles: Principles of Good Complaint Handling', 13 February 2009, available online at https://www.ombudsman.org.uk/about-us/our-principles/principles-good-complaint-handling

[11] HM Courts Service, *Business Strategy* (February 2006), p 4.

- how long it took to resolve the complaint; and
- the trouble the complainant was put to in pursuing it.[12]

Compensation may include the costs of making the claim itself, in which regard the following guidance is given: 'Remedies may also need to take account of any injustice or hardship that has resulted from pursuing the complaint as well as from the original dispute.'[13] **64.16**

None of the guidance specifically mentions interest, but there is no reason to suppose that this would not be an indirect financial loss. The complainant may need to prove loss in this regard (that is, they may need to prove either that they have had to pay interest or that they would have earned interest on monies they have had to pay out). **64.17**

Procedure

It would be a mistake to make a claim for compensation within litigation. In particular, it ought not to be made upon application or by way of a claim under CPR, Part 8; rather, a claim should be made to the relevant court in writing.[14] It used to be the case that complaints could be sent to the Complaints Correspondence and Litigation Team (CCLT) in Westminster,[15] but it would seem that this is no longer the correct thing to do.[16] **64.18**

A standard form exists for making complaints (namely, EX343A) and although it is not well suited to making a claim for costs, it would probably be best to use it nonetheless. Whilst there is no prescribed procedure, it would be sensible for a complainant to focus on the three requirements identified at 40.06—that is, whether there has been maladministration/poor services, whether there has been injustice or hardship and whether there is a causal link between the two. **64.19**

A reply should be received within ten working days of receipt of the complaint. If a complainant is dissatisfied by the response, they may ask for an internal review by a senior manager; again, the court will aim to complete such a review within ten working days.[17] If they are not satisfied with the senior manager's reply, the complainant can appeal in writing to: **64.20**

Customer Service Unit
Post Point 4.01
4th Floor
102 Petty France
London SW1H 9AJ
DX 152380 Westminster 8

[12] Parliamentary and Health Service Ombudsman, 'Ombudsman's Principles: Principles of Good Complaint Handling', 13 February 2009, available online at https://www.ombudsman.org.uk/about-us/our-principles/principles-good-complaint-handling

[13] *Ibid.*

[14] See HM Courts & Tribunals Service, 'I Want to Complain: What Do I Do?'. EX343, available online at https://assets.publishing.service.gov.uk/government/uploads/system/uploads/attachment_data/file/223545/contact-director-wales-hmcts-annex-a.pdf, p 1.

[15] See EX343 as it was in 2012.

[16] There is no mention of this in the most recent edition of EX343.

[17] See HM Courts & Tribunals Service, 'I Want to Complain: What Do I Do?'. EX343, available online at https://assets.publishing.service.gov.uk/government/uploads/system/uploads/attachment_data/file/223545/contact-director-wales-hmcts-annex-a.pdf

The Customer Service Unit will look at the matter *de novo* and aims to reply within 15 working days.[18]

64.21 If a complainant is dissatisfied by a response to a claim, then they may make an application to the Parliamentary Commissioner for Administration via the Parliamentary and Health Service Ombudsman. They may do this, however, only if the complainant's member of Parliament (MP) has agreed to make the referral.[19]

64.22 The exercise of discretion is justiciable notwithstanding the fact that it is a non-statutory power;[20] hence a refusal to pay compensation may, in theory, be amenable to judicial review. Such things are the preserve of specialists, however, and advice ought to be taken from a person specialising in administrative law. Strict time limits apply. In any event, the court may dismiss an application on the basis that the complainant has an alternative remedy—that is, to apply for a non-party costs order and/or to complain to the Ombudsman.

---

[18] See *ibid.*

[19] *Ibid.*

[20] See *Council of Civil Service Unions v Minister of State for Civil Service* [1985] AC 374 for a general discussion of this.

Part XV

PARTICULAR CIRCUMSTANCES

65

GROUP LITIGATION, DERIVATIVE CLAIMS AND REPRESENTATIVE CLAIMS

This chapter addresses the costs of group litigation, derivative claims and representative claims. It deals with the following topics: **65.01**

- group litigation:
  - terminology (65.04);
  - jurisdiction (65.09);
  - the history of the jurisdiction (65.12);
  - case and costs management in group litigation (65.16);
  - the incidence of costs in group litigation (65.46);
  - the distribution of costs in group litigation:
    - how group co-litigants bear their own costs (65.55);
    - how group co-litigants bear adverse costs (65.70);
  - the quantum of costs in group litigation (65.90);
  - procedural issues relating to group litigation (65.104);
  - forensic sieve relating to group litigation (65.115);
- representative claims (65.116); and
- derivative claims (65.123).

Group Litigation

Broadly speaking, this section addresses litigation that is governed by group litigation orders (GLOs). There are, however, other ways in which litigation involving groups of disputants can be managed, such as by case consolidation and by way of bringing representative claims (see 65.116). Those other methods of management have a great deal in common with group litigation, so much of what is said below would apply even if there were no GLO. **65.02**

It is assumed that the reader is familiar with the principles of distribution of costs (see Chapter 20)—particularly the doctrine of equal apportionment (see 20.16–20.33). **65.03**

Terminology

Terminology under the CPR

The CPR define a number of relevant terms, as follows.[1] **65.04**

[1] See CPR, r 46.6(2) and Part 19, Section III; PD 19B.

- **Group litigation order (GLO) and GLO issues** A GLO is an order to provide for the case management of claims that give rise to common or related issues of fact or law—that is, the GLO issues.[2]
- **Group litigant** A group litigant is a claimant or defendant whose claim is entered onto a group register[3]—although, to make matters clearer in this chapter, the terms 'group co-litigant' and 'opponents' are used instead (see 65.05).
- **Group register** A group register is a register on which the claims managed under the GLO will be entered.[4] The register is kept either by the court or by one of the parties' solicitors (usually the claimants').[5]
- **Test claim** A test claim is a claim of a person on the group register litigated for the purpose of resolving GLO issues.[6] A test claim will often—but not always[7]—be representative of the other claims.
- **Management court and managing judge** The management court is that court which has been appointed to manage the claims on the group register.[8] If a judge is appointed to oversee the GLO, that judge is the managing judge.[9]
- **Individual costs** Individual costs are those costs incurred in relation to an individual claim on the group register.[10]
- **Common costs (including GLO costs, test claim costs and administration costs)** Common costs are those costs incurred in relation to the GLO issues,[11] including the costs of individual claims that are proceeding as test claims.[12] Common costs will include costs incurred by the lead solicitor in administering the group litigation,[13] such as the costs of keeping the group register. These three species of common costs are often referred to as 'GLO costs', 'test claim costs' and 'administration costs', respectively.

Other terminology used in this chapter

65.05 Non-standard terminology may be encountered from time to time. This book uses the following phrases, largely to avoid lengthy repetition.

- **Group co-litigants** This phrase is used to refer to those persons who form the (or a) group that is the focus of the GLO and which pursues a common cause. This will usually be a group of claimants or counterclaimants, but this is not always the case.[14]

[2] CPR, r 19.10.
[3] CPR, r 46.6(2).
[4] CPR, r 19.11(2)(a).
[5] See PD 19B, para 6.5.
[6] There is no express definition of test claim in the CPR, but this definition is implied by CPR, r 46.6.
[7] That is, where a claimant's claim is the only one of its type and there are no other similar cases in the litigation, that case can (and probably must) proceed as a test case: *Nash v Eli Lilly* [1993] 4 All ER 383, at 414.
[8] CPR, r 19.11(2)(c).
[9] See PD 19B, para 8.
[10] CPR, r 46.6(2).
[11] CPR, r 46.6(2)(i).
[12] CPR, r 46.6(2)(ii).
[13] CPR, r 46.6(2)(iii).
[14] See, eg, *Nationwide Building Society v Various Solicitors (No 4)* (1999) The Independent, 25 October, in which a single claimant issued hundreds of claims against various firms of solicitors.

- **Opponents** This term is used to refer to those persons who are the opponents of the group co-litigants and against whom the group co-litigants' common cause is directed. These will nearly always be defendants (or defendants to a counterclaim).

Other non-standard terms that may be encountered include 'lead costs', which may be used to refer to test claim costs, and 'generic costs', which should be treated with caution because it will often have a specific meaning ascribed to it by the GLO. Where this is not so, it is usually—but not always—used to refer to common costs. **65.06**

The terminology of costs sharing agreements

Although not defined in the CPR, there are two species of costs sharing agreement, as follows. **65.07**

- **Funding costs sharing agreement (FCSA)** This is a costs sharing agreement that determines group co-litigants' relative or absolute contributions towards their own costs.
- **Liability costs sharing agreement (LCSA)** This is a costs sharing agreement that determines group co-litigants' relative or absolute liability for their opponents' costs.

Many agreements contain both an FCSA and LCSA within the same written instrument. That document often contains other provisions as to how the litigation is to be managed, in which case it may be called a litigation management agreement.

Contractual issues concerning costs sharing agreements are addressed at 27.315–27.318. Where there is no cost sharing agreement, then a costs sharing order may be made in lieu. Moreover, a costs sharing agreement may be replaced, varied or affirmed by a costs sharing order. Indeed, many such agreements expressly record the fact that they are subject to any costs sharing order that the court may make (see 20.41). **65.08**

Jurisdiction

In addition to Parts 1 and 3 of the Civil Procedure Rules (CPR), the adjectival provisions that govern group litigation are: **65.09**

- CPR, Part 19, Section III; and
- Practice Direction (PD) 19B (but only where the group co-litigants are claimants).[15]

These provisions establish a framework for the management of 'claims which give rise to common or related issues of fact or law' (see CPR, r 19.10). The editors of the White Book say that those provisions are intended to provide flexibility for the court to deal with the particular problems created by these cases.[16] **65.10**

Neither CPR, Part 19, Section III, nor PD 19B say a great deal about costs, partly because the costs aspects of group litigation are addressed by provisions in CPR, r 46.6. That said, even those provisions are remarkable for their brevity—something that is made all the more noticeable by reason of the absence of any corresponding practice direction. **65.11**

---

[15] See PD 16B, para 1. Where the group co-litigants are defendants, then the court will give whatever directions are appropriate.

[16] See The White Book 2018, para 19.10.0.

The history of the jurisdiction

65.12 Prior to the coming into force of the CPR, litigation that bore a resemblance to group actions was not unknown.[17] Indeed, by the end of the 1980s, active case management had led to a relatively flexible approach to multiparty litigation[18] and the courts had even developed a nascent jurisdiction over costs sharing.[19] That said, the only ways in which disputants could pursue or defend claims that gave rise to common or related issues of fact or law were by way of representative actions under Rules of the Supreme Court (RSC) Order 15, r 4, by way of consolidated claims under RSC Ord 15, r 4 or by way of joinder. As Lord Woolf pointed out in his Final Report, these were costly and unwieldy means of managing multiparty litigation.[20]

65.13 Lord Woolf recommended that new procedures be created for dealing with multiparty claims. He recommended that those procedures should:

- provide access to justice where numbers of people have been affected by another's wrongdoing, but where individual loss is so small that it makes an individual action economically unviable;
- create expeditious, effective and proportionate means of resolving cases, where individual damages are large enough to justify individual action, but where the number of claimants and the nature of the issues involved mean that the cases cannot be managed satisfactorily in accordance with normal procedure; and
- achieve a balance between the normal rights of claimants and defendants to pursue and defend cases individually, and the interests of a group of parties to litigate the action as a whole in an effective manner.[21]

65.14 Thus what Lord Woolf suggested was the creation of an adjectival framework that would act as an aggregation device to allow the pursuit of claims that could otherwise not be brought because of the high costs relative to the anticipated recovery. This, in turn, led to the creation of CPR, Part 19, Section III, and its associated practice direction.

Case and costs management in group litigation

Group litigation orders

65.15 This section deals with the following topics:

- GLOs in general (see 65.16);
- the procedural aspects of applying for GLOs (see 65.20);
- the circumstances in which the court will make a GLO (see 65.22);

---

17 See, eg, *Connelly v RTZ Corp Plc (No 2)* [1998] AC 584; *Lubbe v Cape Plc* [2000] 1 WLR 1545.

18 See *Horrocks v Ford Motor Co Ltd* (1990) The Times, 15 February, CA.

19 See, eg, *Davies v Eli Lilly & Co* [1987] 1 WLR 1136, in which a costs sharing order was made. That type of order was refined in *Ward v Guinness Mahon Plc* [1996] 1 WLR 894, in which the concept of several liability on the part of a group of claimants was confirmed and applied to the liability that they might have for costs of defendants. In addition, May J had developed a system of quarterly rests for dealing with apportionment: see *Foster v Roussel Laboratories* (unreported), 29 October 1997, QBD. There is no surviving transcript of this decision, but May J's comments are recorded in *Sayers v Merck SmithKline Beecham plc; X v Schering Healthcare Ltd; Afrika v Cape plc* [2001] EWCA Civ 2017, at [11]. The relevant text is set out in full at 65.85.

20 See Lord Woolf, *Access to Justice: Final Report* (London: HMSO, 1996), ch 17 (multiparty actions).

21 *Ibid.*

- variation of GLOs (see 65.25);
- the effect of GLOs (see 65.26); and
- alternatives to GLOs—claims handling agreements (see 65.27).

GLOs in general A GLO is an order made under CPR, r 19.11, to provide for the case management of claims that give rise to 'common or related issues of fact or law' (the GLO issues).[22] It should be noted that GLO issues merely have to be common or related, in contrast to representative claims, in which the issues have to be the same (see 65.116–65.117). There must be common issues, however, for claims to be subject to a GLO; it is not sufficient that the claims arise in similar circumstances against the same opponents.[23] **65.16**

CPR, r 19.11, gives the following guidance about the form and content of a GLO: **65.17**

> '**19.11 Group Litigation Order**
>
> (1) The court may make a GLO where there are or are likely to be a number of claims giving rise to the GLO issues.
>
> (The practice direction provides the procedure for applying for a GLO.)
>
> (2) A GLO must—
> (a) contain directions about the establishment of a register (the "group register") on which the claims managed under the GLO will be entered;
> (b) specify the GLO issues which will identify the claims to be managed as a group under the GLO; and
> (c) specify the court (the "management court") which will manage the claims on the group register.
>
> (3) A GLO may—
> (a) in relation to claims which raise one or more of the GLO issues—
> (i) direct their transfer to the management court;
> (ii) order their stay until further order; and
> (iii) direct their entry on the group register;
> (b) direct that from a specified date claims which raise one or more of the GLO issues should be started in the management court and entered on the group register; and
> (c) give directions for publicising the GLO.'

A GLO may not be made (a) in the Queen's Bench Division, without the consent of the President of the Queen's Bench Division, (b) in the Chancery Division, without the consent of the Chancellor of the High Court, or (c) in the County Court, without the consent of the Head of Civil Justice.[24] **65.18**

Subject to these consents, the court may make a GLO of its own initiative.[25] **65.19**

Applications for GLOs (procedure) An application for a GLO must be made in accordance with CPR, Part 23, may be made at any time before or after any relevant claims have been issued, and may be made either by a claimant or by a defendant.[26] The following **65.20**

---

22 See CPR, r 19.10.

23 See, eg, *Schmitt v Depuy International Ltd* [2016] EWHC 638 (QB), in which the proposed lead claimant's claims were not thought to be sufficiently representative of other claims to justify a GLO.

24 See PD 19B, para 3.3.

25 See PD 19B, para 4.

26 See PD 19B, para 3.1.

information should be included in the application notice or in written evidence filed in support of the application:

- a summary of the nature of the litigation;
- the number and nature of claims already issued;
- the number of parties likely to be involved;
- the common issues of fact or law (that is, the GLO issues) that are likely to arise in the litigation; and
- whether there are any matters that distinguish smaller groups of claims within the wider group.[27]

65.21 The procedure for applying for GLO will depend on whether the claim is in the High Court or the County Court.

- **High Court** In the High Court in London, the application for the GLO should be made to the senior master in the Queen's Bench Division or the chief master in the Chancery Division; for claims that are proceeding or are likely to proceed in a specialist list, the application should be made to the senior judge of that list.[28] Outside London, the application should be made to a presiding judge or a Chancery supervising judge of the circuit in which the district registry that has issued the application notice is situated.[29]
- **County Court** Where the application notice is issued in the County Court, the application should be made to the Designated Civil Judge for the area in which the application notice has been issued.[30] The applicant for a GLO should request the relevant County Court hearing centre to refer the application notice to the judge by whom the application will be heard as soon as possible after the application notice has been issued.[31]

65.22 **Whether the court will make a GLO** The number of group co-litigants that are required to justify a GLO is not stated in the CPR, but Jackson LJ has noted that 'far more than two claimants are necessary to constitute a viable group action'.[32]

65.23 Issues regarding funding may be relevant to whether a GLO is made. In a case in which there was only sparse evidence before the court as to how a group of claimants intended to fund their proposed group claim, Jackson LJ declined to interfere with a decision not to make a GLO.[33]

65.24 The decision as to whether to make a GLO is an exercise in case management discretion that will not be interfered with lightly on appeal.[34]

65.25 **Variation of GLOs** Any application to vary the terms of the GLO must be made to the management court.[35]

---

27 See PD 19B, para 3.2.
28 See PD 19B, para 3.5.
29 See PD 19B, para 3.6.
30 See PD 19B, para 3.7.
31 See PD 19B, para 3.8.
32 *Austin & Ors v Miller Argent (South Wales) Ltd* [2011] EWCA Civ 928, at [38].
33 See *Alyson Austin v Miller Argent (South Wales) Ltd* [2011] EWCA Civ 928, at [33]–[44].
34 See *ibid.*
35 See PD 19B, para 12.2.

The effect of GLOs CPR, r 19.12, gives the following guidance about the effect of a GLO: 65.26

> **'19.12 Effect of the GLO**
>
> (1) Where a judgment or order is given or made in a claim on the group register in relation to one or more GLO issues—
> (a) that judgment or order is binding on the parties to all other claims that are on the group register at the time the judgment is given or the order is made unless the court orders otherwise; and
> (b) the court may give directions as to the extent to which that judgment or order is binding on the parties to any claim which is subsequently entered on the group register.
>
> (2) Unless paragraph (3) applies, any party who is adversely affected by a judgment or order which is binding on him may seek permission to appeal the order.
>
> (3) A party to a claim which was entered on the group register after a judgment or order which is binding on him was given or made may not—
> (a) apply for the judgment or order to be set aside, varied or stayed; or
> (b) appeal the judgment or order,
> but may apply to the court for an order that the judgment or order is not binding on him.
>
> (4) Unless the court orders otherwise, disclosure of any document relating to the GLO issues by a party to a claim on the group register is disclosure of that document to all parties to claims—
> (a) on the group register; and
> (b) which are subsequently entered on the group register.'

Alternatives to GLOs: claims handling agreements It may be that, instead of a formal GLO, the parties have agreed a contractual mechanism for managing large numbers of claims known as a claims handling agreement. This tends to happen in disputes involving massive numbers of claimants (such as the *British Coal Respiratory Disease Litigation*[36] or the *British Coal Vibration White Finger Litigation*[37]). Where this is so, the fact that there is no GLO will not prevent the court from ensuring that claims were processed fairly and efficiently, and promoting the just disposal of cases, applied as if it were group litigation (see 5.21). 65.27

Group registers

PD 19B, para 6, gives details about the group register. Once a GLO has been made, a group register will be established on which will be entered such details as the court may direct of the cases that are to be subject to the GLO.[38] A claim must be issued before it can be entered on a group register.[39] An application for details of a case to be entered on a group register may be made by any party to the case.[40] 65.28

An order for details of the case to be entered on the group register will not be made unless the case gives rise to at least one of the GLO issues.[41] 65.29

---

[36] *Griffiths & Ors v British Coal Corpn* [2007] EWHC 672 (QB).
[37] See *AB v British Coal Corpn (Department of Trade and Industry)* [2006] EWCA Civ 1357.
[38] See PD 19B, para 6.1.
[39] See PD 19B, para 6.1A. This follows comments made by Lord Woolf in *Boake Allen Ltd v Revenue and Customs Commissioners* [2007] UKHL 25.
[40] See PD 19B, para 6.2.
[41] See PD 19B, para 6.3.

65.30 The court, if it is not satisfied that a case can be conveniently case managed with the other cases on the group register or if it is satisfied that the entry of the case on the group register would adversely affect the case management of the other cases, may refuse to allow details of the case to be entered on the group register or order removal of such details from the register if already entered, even though the case gives rise to one or more of the group issues.[42]

65.31 The group register will normally be maintained by and kept at the court, but the court may direct this to be done by the solicitor for one of the parties to a case entered on the register.[43]

65.32 **Removal from the group register** CPR, r 19.14, gives the following guidance about removal from the register:

> '**19.14 Removal from the register**
>
> (1) A party to a claim entered on the group register may apply to the management court for the claim to be removed from the register.
>
> (2) If the management court orders the claim to be removed from the register it may give directions about the future management of the claim.'

65.33 **Test claims and the group register** The management court may direct that one (or more) of the claims is to proceed as a test claim.[44]

65.34 CPR, r 19.15, gives the following guidance about test claims and the register:

> '**19.15 Test claims**
>
> (1) Where a direction has been given for a claim on the group register to proceed as a test claim and that claim is settled, the management court may order that another claim on the group register be substituted as the test claim.
>
> (2) Where an order is made under paragraph (1), any order made in the test claim before the date of substitution is binding on the substituted claim unless the court orders otherwise.'
>
> [...]'

65.35 **Cut-off dates for the group register** The management court may specify a date after which no claim may be added to the group register unless the court gives permission. An early cut-off date may be appropriate in the case of 'instant disasters' (such as transport accidents). In the case of consumer claims—particularly pharmaceutical claims—it may be necessary to delay the ordering of a cut-off date.[45] Turner J has noted that the use of cut-off dates (and their observation) are essential to maintaining good case management of claims within the ambit of a GLO.[46]

65.36 A cut-off date will have no bearing on limitation and would not prevent an individual from issuing their own proceedings or from seeking the court's permission to join the register at a later stage.[47] That said, a failure to abide by a cut-off date will be treated as default from which relief from sanctions may be required.[48]

---

42 See PD 19B, para 6.4.
43 See PD 19B, para 6.5.
44 See PD 19B, para 12.3.
45 See PD 19B, para 13.
46 *Pearce v Secretary of State for Energy and Climate Change* [2015] EWHC 3775 (QB).
47 See *T (formerly H) v Nugent Care Society (formerly Catholic Social Services)* [2004] EWCA Civ 51.
48 See *Holloway v Transport Medical Group (CS) Ltd* [2014] EWHC 1641 (QB); see also *Pearce v Secretary of State for Energy and Climate Change* [2015] EWHC 3775 (QB).

Case management of group litigation in general

The management court may give case management directions at the time the GLO is made or subsequently. Directions given at a case management hearing will generally be binding on all claims that are subsequently entered on the group register.[49] **65.37**

CPR, r 19.13, gives the following guidance about case management in group litigation: **65.38**

> '**19.13 Case management**
>
> Directions given by the management court may include directions—
> (a) varying the GLO issues;
> (b) providing for one or more claims on the group register to proceed as test claims;
> (c) appointing the solicitor of one or more parties to be the lead solicitor for the claimants or defendants;
> (d) specifying the details to be included in a statement of case in order to show that the criteria for entry of the claim on the group register have been met;
> (e) specifying a date after which no claim may be added to the group register unless the court gives permission; and
> (f) for the entry of any particular claim which meets one or more of the GLO issues on the group register.
>
> (Part 3 contains general provisions about the case management powers of the court.)'

Costs judge assessors in group litigation Costs issues in group litigation can become complex and challenging, and this is particularly likely if the costs issues are not actively managed during the litigation itself. The CPR make express provision for the managing judge to appoint a costs judge to assist them as an assessor and to attend case management hearings (which presumably includes costs management hearings), where this is appropriate.[50] **65.39**

Managing judge and appointed master or district judge in group litigation A judge (the managing judge) will be appointed for the purpose of the GLO as soon as possible. They will assume overall responsibility for the management of the claims and will generally hear the GLO issues.[51] A master or a district judge may be appointed to deal with procedural matters, which they will do in accordance with any directions given by the managing judge.[52] **65.40**

Lead solicitors PD 19B, para 2.2, recommends that where more than one firm is involved in group litigation, a solicitors' group should be formed and one of their number should be nominated to take the lead role. Indeed, this invariably happens. The solicitor's role should be defined in writing.[53] In very complex claims, different lead roles may need to be allocated to different firms. There may be other reasons for there to be more than one lead solicitor, but Turner J has cautioned against there being too many, because an excessive number may lead to duplication of effort, delay and misunderstandings.[54] **65.41**

49 See CPR, r 19.12(1); PD 19B, para 12.1.
50 PD 19B, para 8.
51 PD 19B, para 8.
52 PD 19B, para 8.
53 See also CPR, r 19.13(c).
54 See *Hutson v Tata Steel UK Ltd* [2017] EWHC 2647 (QB).

65.42 **Disclosure of funding in group litigation** Thirlwall J has explained that the court has the power, pursuant to CPR, r 3.1(2)(m), to order a defendant to provide a witness statement setting out whether that party has adequate insurance to fund its participation in the litigation.[55] That said, in a subsequent application in the same case for further information, Thirlwall J declined the request on the basis that it was an attempt to establish in advance how much money was available from the defendant.[56] Claimants may be required to disclose details of funding too.[57] This is a topic that is addressed in more detail in Chapter 33 (see 33.85–33.90).

65.43 Costs conditions relating to disclosure of funding may be imposed, such as the condition concerning disclosure of an after-the-event (ATE) policy where there is one.[58]

65.44 **Notice of funding in group litigation** As to notice of funding, now-revoked Costs Practice Direction (CPD), art 19.5, used to provide as follows: 'Where the court makes a Group Litigation Order, the court may give directions as to the extent to which individual parties should provide information in accordance with rule 44.15. (Part 19 deals with Group Litigation Orders.)'

Orders regarding distribution by the judge awarding costs of mixed hearings or applications

65.45 It may be that the court makes an order about costs in relation to a mixed hearing or application (that is, a hearing or application that touches upon both GLO issues and issues relevant only to individual claims). Where this is so, CPR, r 46.6(5), will apply:

> '(5) Where the court makes an order about costs in relation to any application or hearing which involved—
> (a) one or more GLO issues; and
> (b) issues relevant only to individual claims,
>
> the court will direct the proportion of the costs that is to relate to common costs and the proportion that is to relate to individual costs.'

Thus, where the court makes an order about costs in relation to a mixed hearing or application, it 'will direct' the proportion that relates to the GLO issues and the issues relevant only to the individual claim. Put otherwise, the court will make an order as to the distribution of those costs. Notwithstanding the seemingly mandatory wording of this rule, it should be noted that PD 19B, para 16, creates a mechanism for a costs judge to carry out the task of distribution in the event that that task has not been performed by the judge who made the costs order (see 65.114).

The incidence of costs in group litigation

65.46 This section deals with the incidence of costs in general in group litigation. That said, there is a great deal of overlap with the topic of 'Group co-litigants' liability for adverse costs' (see 65.71). Indeed, the two sections ought to be read in conjunction. For obvious reasons, the matters set out in Chapter 6 may be relevant in addition to what is set out below.

---

[55] *In re PIP Breast Implant Litigation* [2013] EWHC 3643 (QB); see also *XYZ v Various (Including Transform Medical Group (CS) Ltd and Spire Healthcare Ltd) & Ors* [2014] EWHC 4056 (QB).

[56] *XYZ v Various (Including Transform Medical Group (CS) Ltd and Spire Healthcare Ltd) & Ors* [2014] EWHC 4056 (QB), at [31].

[57] See, eg, *Wall v The Royal Bank of Scotland plc* [2016] EWHC 2460 (Comm); cf *Re The RBS Rights Issue Litigation* [2017] EWHC 1217 (Ch).

[58] *Barr v Biffa Waste Services Ltd* [2009] EWHC 1033 (TCC).

In essence, the incidence of costs in group litigation is dealt with according to the principles that apply to any other type of litigation. That said, it is worth examining the following topics: **65.47**

- issues-based orders and group litigation (see 65.48);
- whether it was reasonable for a party to raise, pursue or contest a point in the context of group litigation (see 65.51);
- the relevance of offers to settle (see 65.53); and
- the position where there is one claimant and many defendants (see 65.54).

Issues-based orders and group litigation

In the *Phurnacite Litigation*,[59] the lead claimants had succeeded in showing causation in respect of lung cancer and respiratory diseases, but not bladder cancer or basal cell carcinoma. This gave rise to the question of how the court should deal with the costs as between the claimants and the defendants. Swift J agreed with the parties that it would be inappropriate to make issues-based orders because this would present 'extremely complex problems for the judge carrying out the detailed assessment of costs and would in all probability add significantly to the costs of the assessment process'.[60] **65.48**

As to the approach to be taken in respect of issues where some had been lost at trial, Swift J had this to say: **65.49**

> 'I accept the claimants' submission that it would be inappropriate, when considering whether there should be any reduction in the claimants' entitlement to costs, and if so how much, for me to look only at what happened at trial. A good deal of the work of investigation, the assembling of documents and the collection of lay and expert evidence took place before the trial and the work spent on each of the generic issues at that stage was not necessarily proportionate to the time spent on the issue at trial. It seems to me that I must consider the work done on the litigation as a whole.'[61]

Abandoned issues David Steel J has commented that where the costs of abandoned issues are to be taken into account in the context of group litigation, a broad-brush approach would be appropriate.[62] **65.50**

CPR, r 44.2(5)(b) (whether it was reasonable for a party to raise, pursue or contest a point), and the incidence of costs

CPR, r 44.2(5)(b), requires the court, when exercising its discretion as to the incidence of costs, to consider whether it was reasonable for a party to raise, pursue or contest a particular allegation or issue. Clearly, if a point was unreasonably raised, pursued or contested, this will be a relevant factor, but it may be that one side or the other says that the court should take into account the fact that it was reasonable to argue a point, even if ultimately unsuccessfully, because of the number of group co-litigants who stood to be affected by it. **65.51**

There can be little doubt that this is a factor that the court can take into account, but, in the *Phurnacite Litigation*[63] (see 65.48), Swift J rejected the notion that it would be appropriate **65.52**

[59] *Jones v Secretary of State for Energy and Climate Change* [2012] EWHC 3647 (QB).
[60] *Ibid*, at [8].
[61] *Ibid*, at [53].
[62] *Colour Quest Ltd v Total Downstream UK plc* [2009] EWHC 823 (Comm).
[63] *Jones v Secretary of State for Energy and Climate Change* [2012] EWHC 3647 (QB).

to deal with the incidence of costs on the basis of what was reasonable (as opposed to on the basis of who had won the issues in question). She had this to say on the point:

> 'The difficulty with that [approach] ... is that it could be applied to every case where the unsuccessful party has not acted unreasonably in pursuing an issue and even, in a closely fought case, to both parties to the same action. Its application would involve a minute examination of the reasonableness or otherwise of decisions taken by both parties at different times in the proceedings and would in practice be wholly unworkable. Moreover, if the reasonableness of proceeding were to be the determining factor, the outcome of such an examination would often run counter to the general principle that costs follow the event.'[64]

Swift J went on to award the claimants 80 per cent of their common costs.

Offers to settle

65.53 Neither the CPR nor PD 19B gives any guidance regarding settlements and offers. The editors of the White Book highlight the following problems that may arise in group litigation:

- what should happen when an 'acceptable' offer to settle a lead or test case is made (beyond giving the court the discretion to order that another case might be substituted); and
- what the court might do when a 'global' offer to settle the entire action is made, without the offeree specifying how the sum might be divided between the individual recipients (a situation that can lead to disputes between the claimants, which are far from easy for their legal representatives to resolve).[65]

The editors of the White Book go on to say that introduction of Part 36 offers may further highlight this latter problem.

One claimant and many defendants

65.54 In litigation in which there was a single claimant and many defendants, and in which the claimant was successful in about 78 per cent of its claims but the defendants were successful in about 11 per cent (the remainder falling by the wayside), Blackburne J ordered the defendants to pay 60 per cent of the claimant's common costs.[66]

How group co-litigants bear their own costs

65.55 As between group co-litigants, the following issues regarding their own costs may arise.

- **Individual costs** This concerns the extent to which any given group co-litigant is to bear the individual costs incurred in respect of the other group co-litigant's cases (see 65.56).
- **GLO costs and administration costs** This concerns the extent to which any given group co-litigant is to bear the GLO costs and administration costs incurred on behalf of the group co-litigants generally (see 65.57–65.61).
- **Test claim costs** This concerns the extent to which the group co-litigants in general—and those who bring or defend test claims in particular—are each to bear the test claim costs as between themselves (see 65.62–65.69).

---

64 *Ibid*, at [60].
65 See The White Book 2018, para 19.15.1.
66 *Nationwide Building Society v Various Solicitors (No 4)* (1999) The Independent, 25 October.

How individual costs are treated as between group co-litigants

Unless there is an FCSA (or order) that makes provision to the contrary (see 20.40–20.48), any given group co-litigant will be responsible for the costs attributable to their own claim,[67] but they will not be responsible for the costs incurred solely in pursuing someone else's claim, unless that claim is a test claim (see 65.62). These issues are dealt with more fully at 20.13–20.15 and 20.37, but, in essence, any costs relating solely to the claim of one client should be charged to that client only and to the exclusion of the other clients.[68] As is explained at 65.58, where any given group co-litigant is a paying party, CPR, r 46.6(4), will impose a general rule that that party will be liable for their individual costs. A similar rule applies as a result of the common law (see 65.59). **65.56**

How GLO costs and administration costs are treated as between group co-litigants

The issues concerning liability for the costs of GLO issues and administration costs are addressed at 20.16–20.19, 20.26–20.27 and 20.37–20.39. In essence, unless there is an order or contractual provision that says otherwise, the principle of equal apportionment will apply.[69] Where there is an agreement dealing with the issue of apportionment (such as an FCSA), the court would not be bound by that agreement, but would rarely depart from its terms (see 20.42–20.47).[70] **65.57**

The default position under the CPR In addition to the points made in Chapter 20, there is a default provision that will apply to any paying party in group litigation even where there is no express provision within an FCSA or an order dealing with the liability for common costs. This is as a result of CPR, r 46.6(4), which reads as follows: **65.58**

> '(4) The general rule is that where a group litigant is the paying party, he will, in addition to any costs he is liable to pay to the receiving party, be liable for—
> (a) the individual costs of his claim; and
> (b) an equal proportion, together with all the other group litigants, of the common costs.'

Thus there is a 'general rule' that when a group litigant is a paying party, they will be liable not only for the costs of their own claim, but also for their share of the common costs. To this extent, the CPR mirror the common law (that is, the principle of equal apportionment).

The default position under the common law A very similar position exists by reason of the common law. Smith LJ has explained that even where there is no FCSA relating to common costs, a group co-litigant would be liable to their solicitors for their share of the common costs properly incurred for their benefit: **65.59**

> 'I am satisfied that there is no requirement for [a costs sharing] agreement relating to generic costs [ie common costs]. The client's entitlement is to recover the costs for which he would have been liable to his solicitor. He would be liable for all costs properly

[67] See CPR, r 46.6(4); *Bayliss v Kelly & Ors* [1997] 2 Costs LR 54; *AB v Liverpool City Council* [2003] EWHC 1539 (QB).

[68] *Bayliss v Kelly & Ors* [1997] 2 Costs LR 54.

[69] *In re Colquhoun* (1854) 5 DM & G 35; *Ellingsen v Det Skandinaviske Compani* [1919] 2 KB 567; more recently, *Bayliss v Kelly & Ors* [1997] 2 Costs LR 54. See also CPR, r 46.6(4)(b).

[70] *Bank of Credit and Commerce International SA (in liquidation) v Ali (No 5)* [2000] 2 Costs LR 243; by analogy, *Gomba Holdings Ltd v Minories Finance Ltd (No 2)* [1993] Ch 171.

> incurred whether they were incurred solely on his behalf or whether they were incurred for the benefit of a large group and he had only to pay an appropriate proportion. There is nothing fundamentally different or special about generic costs; they are simply costs that have been shared for the sensible purpose of keeping the costs of each claim down. I can see no merit in the suggestion that some special rule applies to the generic element of a bill of costs.'[71]

Park J came to much the same conclusion in a matter in which there was no written costs sharing agreement, but he did so by finding what, in effect, was an implied FCSA[72] (see 20.43–20.47).

65.60 **Late joiners, settlers and discontinuers** Even a principle as straightforward as that of equal apportionment can become unwieldy if group co-litigants drift in and out of the litigation. CPR, r 46.6(6), makes the following provision about late joiners (that is, those who become group co-litigants at a stage after that group has already been established and after common costs have already been incurred): 'Where common costs have been incurred before a claim is entered on the group register, the court may order the group litigant to be liable for a proportion of those costs.' The court *may* (not must) order a late joiner to bear a part of the costs that had already been incurred before they joined and the court has a discretion to depart from the principle of equal apportionment should the circumstances permit.

65.61 CPR, r 46.6(7), makes similar provision for settlers and discontinuers. This is dealt with at 65.87–65.89. The notion of 'rests' may also be relevant (see 65.85).

How test claim costs are treated as between group co-litigants

65.62 The management court may give directions about how the costs of resolving common issues or the costs of claims proceeding as test claims are to be borne or shared as between group co-litigants.[73]

65.63 Unless there is an agreement or order to the contrary, the doctrine of equal apportionment will apply (see 20.16 *et seq*). This is illustrated by *Davies v Eli Lilly & Co*,[74] which was one of the first group action cases in which the issue of costs sharing arose,[75] in which some 1,500 claimants claimed damages arising out of the use of a drug. The managing judge ordered that the claimants would bear the costs of the test claims on a *per capita* basis (which is equal apportionment based on the number of group co-litigants); this was on the advice of an *amicus* appointed by the court.

65.64 In a different case some years later, Longmore LJ approved of that approach:

> 'This resolved an important practical difficulty that, if there was to be one or more legal actions, the claimants in those lead actions would otherwise have had to bear all the costs themselves. Even if such claimants won, the burden of irrecoverable costs would be too

---

[71] *Russell Young & Co v Brown & Ors* [2007] EWCA Civ 43, at [31].
[72] *Bank of Credit and Commerce International SA (in liquidation) v Ali (No 5)* [2000] 2 Costs LR 243.
[73] See PD 19B, para 12.4.
[74] *Davies v Eli Lilly & Co* [1987] 1 WLR 1136.
[75] See *Aiden Shipping Co Ltd v Interbulk Ltd* [1986] AC 965. Group litigation orders did not exist before the mid-1980s; moreover, it was not until 1986 that it was realised that costs orders could be made in respect of non-parties.

great for any claimant, who did not have legal aid, to bear them; moreover, even any legally aided claimant would be liable to find his damages wiped out by the Law Society's charge for costs.'[76]

Donaldson MR also commented favourably on *per capita* apportionment: 'Those who have practised in the Commercial Court . . . will recognise the age old respectability of such an order, based as it clearly is upon the Rhodian Law, the Rolls of Oleron and the maritime law of general average.'[77] **65.65**

Test claim costs are common costs and therefore the 'general rule' in CPR, r 46.6(4), applies (see 65.58). Likewise, the rules concerning late joiners[78] and early leavers[79] will also apply (see 65.60–65.61). **65.66**

The relevance of methods of funding In general, the methods by which the group co-litigants are funded will be irrelevant.[80] **65.67**

The personal position of test claim litigants for group co-litigants' costs Test claim costs should not concurrently be categorised as individual costs, which means that the individual group co-litigant to whom the costs relate would generally not be personally liable for the whole of the costs incurred while their claim was proceeding as a test claim. This seems to reflect the position vis-à-vis the test claim litigant's liability for adverse costs (see 65.78). This would usually be true even if the other group co-litigants were to object to paying those costs on the grounds of some perceived impropriety on the part of the test claim litigant, one reason for which is to avoid discouraging those who would otherwise put themselves forward as test claim litigants (also see 20.31).[81] **65.68**

The existence of a fee sharing agreement will not deprive a successful test claim litigant of the benefit of their success—that is, by being awarded only part of their costs.[82] **65.69**

How group co-litigants bear adverse costs

As between opposing parties where a costs order has been made, the following issues may arise. **65.70**

- **Group co-litigants' liability for adverse costs** This concerns the extent to which any given group co-litigant is to bear the opponents' costs if ordered to pay those costs (see 65.71–65.79).
- **Opponents' liability for some, but not all, of the costs** This concerns the extent to which the opponents are to bear the group co-litigants' costs if ordered to pay the costs of some, but not all, of those costs (see 65.80–65.84).

[76] *Sayers v Merck SmithKline Beecham plc; X v Schering Healthcare Ltd; Afrika v Cape plc* [2001] EWCA Civ 2017, at [10]. See also *AB v Liverpool City Council* [2003] EWHC 1539 (QB).

[77] *Davies v Eli Lilly & Co* [1987] 1 WLR 1136, at 1141.

[78] CPR, r 46.6(6).

[79] CPR, r 46.6(7).

[80] See, eg, *Davies v Eli Lilly & Co* [1987] 1 WLR 1136, in which the court found that no distinction should be made between parties who are legally aided and those who are privately funded.

[81] *Bank of Credit and Commerce International SA (in liquidation) v Ali (No 5)* [2000] 2 Costs LR 243.

[82] *Nash v Eli Lilly & Co* [1993] 4 All ER 383, at 415. In practice, in many cases the amount that a successful test claim claimant is ultimately awarded may be restricted by the operation of the indemnity principle.

- **Liability for adverse costs for late joiners, settles and discontinuers** This concerns the extent to which persons who join or leave the group register may be liable for (or entitled to) costs between opposing parties (see 65.85–65.89).

Group co-litigants' liability for adverse costs

65.71 The issue here is the extent to which group co-litigants are each to bear their opponents' costs in the event of an adverse costs order being made against them.

65.72 **Preliminary rulings in relation to distribution of the burden of adverse costs** The court may be asked to make a preliminary ruling at the outset of the litigation dealing with the potential individual liabilities of the group co-litigants in the event of an adverse costs order being made (see 65.77). Such an order is not a pre-emptive order in the sense that it determines the incidence of costs, but it is pre-emptive in the sense that it legislates for how costs should be apportioned if and when the incidence of costs is determined against the group co-litigants.[83] The power to make such orders was discovered prior to the introduction of the CPR,[84] but undoubtedly continues to exist.

65.73 In a combined judgment of the court, Mummery, Buxton and Longmore LJJ said that, in so far as settlers were concerned, they do not usually need any presumptive order as to the incidence of costs, since costs will be part of the discussion leading to settlement in any event.[85]

65.74 **Several liability and apportionment in relation to adverse costs** Group co-litigants often need to know their potential liability before the litigation is commenced. This is why CPR, r 46.6(3), creates the following default rule: 'Unless the court orders otherwise, any order for common costs against group litigants imposes on each group litigant several liability for an equal proportion of those common costs.' Thus, unless the court orders otherwise, if they are condemned to pay the opponents' costs, any given group co-litigant will be liable for only an equal proportion of the relevant common costs.

65.75 This rule may be otiose because the same conclusion is reached under common law. In *Ward v Guinness Mahon plc*,[86] a large number of investors claimed damages against the sponsor of a business venture that ultimately failed. Lord Bingham MR commented that the order in *Davies v Eli Lilly & Co*[87] (see 65.63) was directed to the position of the claimants amongst themselves (that is, funding costs), rather than to the position of the co-claimants vis-à-vis the defendant (that is, adverse costs). He went on to consider whether he had a jurisdiction to make an order that could 'bite on the defendants', as he put it, and he found that he did.[88]

[83] *Sayers v Merck SmithKline Beecham plc; X v Schering Healthcare Ltd; Afrika v Cape plc* [2001] EWCA Civ 2017, at [15].

[84] One of the first instances was *In re Westdock Realisations Ltd* [1988] BCLC 354, albeit not in group litigation. The first instance of the jurisdiction being exercised in group litigation was *Ward v Guinness Mahon plc* [1996] 1 WLR 894.

[85] *Sayers v Merck SmithKline Beecham plc; X v Schering Healthcare Ltd; Afrika v Cape plc* [2001] EWCA Civ 2017, at [16].

[86] *Ward v Guinness Mahon plc* [1996] 1 WLR 894.

[87] *Davies v Eli Lilly & Co* [1987] 1 WLR 1136.

[88] *Ward v Guinness Mahon plc* [1996] 1 WLR 894, at 898.

The defendants argued that each co-claimant (including each test claim claimant) should be jointly liable. The claimants argued that their liability should be restricted (that is, several) to a proportionate share of the common costs (which would include the costs of the test claims). Without such an order, they argued, there would be reluctance on the part of individual claimants to be selected as test claimants. **65.76**

Lord Bingham MR preferred the claimants' arguments. He took account of a report published in 1995 by a Law Society working party in which the following recommendation was made: **65.77**

> 'One point on which there is general agreement is that if defendants win on common issues and costs are ordered against the plaintiffs, the liability of plaintiffs should be several rather than joint. Thus, if a defendant incurs £1m costs defending the common issues of claims brought by 1,000 plaintiffs, the maximum common costs liability of any individual plaintiff will be £1,000 (subject to costs protection for legally-aided claimants). Any other arrangement would make the risk inherent in group actions so great as to limit access to justice solely to those plaintiffs with nothing at all to lose. Regardless of the number of plaintiffs sharing costs, no individual plaintiff could hope to satisfy the private client test. Whilst several liability will make it much harder for defendants to recover their costs when they are successful, we see no real alternative to such a rule.'[89]

Lord Bingham MR rejected the submission that it would be best to wait until the end of the litigation before making any order, saying that that approach would run counter to the need to allow co-claimants to know—before they start—where they stand.[90]

The personal position of test claim litigants for adverse costs In group litigation in which the claimants had failed to prove causation in their claim for professional negligence against their former solicitors, the trial judge awarded the defendants 75 per cent of their costs, 75 per cent of which was to be paid by the two hapless lead claimants and the remainder, by the other claimants.[91] In allowing a cross-appeal in respect of the apportionment, Swinton Thomas LJ made the following comments: **65.78**

> '[U]nless preliminary issues can be identified, it is usually agreed that all the claimants will share the costs of the lead action *pro rata* between them. The issue as to common costs was a matter for the Judge's discretion. ... Now that we have all the material before us, some of which was not before the Judge, I can discern no proper basis for making a distinction between the Lead Claimants and the other Common Claimants. To do so, would be unjust to the defendants and also, at least theoretically, to the [lead] claimants ... I would order that all the claimants pay 75% of the defendant's costs.'[92]

Part of Swinton Thomas LJ's thinking was the fact that there was nothing to suggest that the claimants and their advisers had not intended that the costs of the lead actions should be borne proportionately by all claimants; hence there was no proper basis for making a distinction between the lead claimant and the other claimants. This seems to reflect the position vis-à-vis the test claim litigant's liability for own-side costs (see 65.68).

[89] Law Society, *Group Litigation Working Party Report* (London: Law Society, 1995), para 7.4.2.
[90] *Ward v Guinness Mahon plc* [1996] 1 WLR 894, at 900.
[91] *Ochwat v Watson Burton (a firm)* [1999] All ER (D) 1407.
[92] *Ibid*, at the final paragraph.

65.79 **Late joiners, settlers and discontinuers** A liability costs sharing order may include a period during which a number of group co-litigants are taken off the register. There is usually no need for that factor to be specifically taken into account at the time the order is made, because the opponents' bill of costs can be split into parts in such a way as to enable the costs to be assessed by reference only to those periods during which any given litigant was on the group register. The same is not true of late joiners, however: the court will need to consider whether to make an order that the late joiner is to bear a part of the common costs already incurred.[93] Thus specific provision will usually have to be made for late joiners, both in the order and in the bill of costs.

Opponents' liability for costs

65.80 The issue here is the extent to which opponents are to bear the group co-litigants' costs if ordered to pay the costs of some, but not all, of the group co-litigants.

65.81 **Failed claims** The opponents' liability will usually be obvious from the context in which the order was made—in particular, the fact that the court has limited the beneficiaries of the order to some, but not all, of the group co-litigants will usually make it palpably clear that the opponents are not to be liable for the costs of the failed claims. However, the successful group co-litigants may argue that they should be fully indemnified in respect of their costs and that that indemnity embraces all common costs, rather than merely a proportionate share thereof.

65.82 In most cases, such an argument would be defeated by the principle of equal apportionment, because the indemnity principle would restrict the opponents' liability (see Figure 20.1 and 20.16–20.17). Moreover, even if the successful group co-litigants were able to show that the costs were not restricted as a result of the operation of the indemnity principle, they would still have to demonstrate that the principle of equal apportionment should not apply to the interpretation of the costs order—and that would be a difficult to thing to do in circumstances in which the court has made an order that some, but not all, of the group co-litigants be awarded their costs.

65.83 **Set-off** As to set-off of individual costs in circumstances in which a claimant has succeeded individually, but is liable for common costs, see 21.37.

65.84 **No costs sharing agreement** It may be that the opponents say that common costs are not recoverable for want of an FCSA. That would be a difficult argument to make good. In particular, Smith LJ has found that where there is no formal GLO and no costs sharing agreement, a group co-litigant would still have a liability for their share of the common costs properly incurred for their benefit.[94]

Liability for adverse costs for late joiners, settlers and discontinuers

65.85 Where a group co-litigant joins or leaves the group register, their potential liability for or entitlement to costs may need to be adjusted accordingly. In view of this, May J created the concept of the cost sharing order that provides for quarterly rests, for the purpose of calculating the costs of settlers and discontinuers. He had this to say on the topic:

> 'In principle the plaintiffs, individually and as a group, and the defendants need to know the basis upon which costs liabilities would be spread if an order for costs were made or came into

[93] CPR, r 46.6(6).
[94] *Russell Young & Co v Brown & Ors* [2007] EWCA Civ 43; see 65.59 for Smith LJ's judgment.

force. The underlying principle should be that costs which it is appropriate to apportion between or for the benefit of plaintiffs should be divided by the total number of relevant plaintiffs. Costs which it is appropriate to apportion could include (a) the defendants' costs, if one or more of the plaintiffs becomes liable to pay them, and (b) plaintiffs' central administration costs and other plaintiffs' costs which are incurred for the benefit of plaintiffs as a whole, rather than for individual plaintiffs. Any plaintiff who joins the group in the future will acquire the benefit of work done in the past and should become potentially liable for apportionable costs liabilities going back to the beginning. Thus the defendant should be potentially liable to each individual plaintiff for that plaintiff's proper individual costs and for a fraction of the plaintiffs' central costs whose denominator is the number of plaintiffs in the group. Each plaintiff should be potentially liable for a fraction of the defendants' costs whose denominator is the number of plaintiffs in the group. If plaintiffs leave the group by settlement or discontinuance before the conclusion of the litigation when a general costs order is made, a calculation should be made to withdraw from the plaintiffs' central costs and from the defendants' costs a fraction of each of the then totals whose denominator is the number of plaintiffs then in the group before the departing plaintiff leaves. If the departing plaintiff is to pay the defendants' costs, the amount will be the amount of the defendants' costs so withdrawn. If the defendant is to pay the departing plaintiff's costs, the amount will be the amount withdrawn from the plaintiffs' central costs plus the departing plaintiff's proper individual costs. All this would be subject to taxation. This means that costs calculations will need to be made on a quarterly basis, and both the plaintiffs centrally and the defendants need to keep records appropriately.'[95]

Late joiners For the reasons set out at 65.79, it may be necessary to consider the position of late joiners. In particular, if a group co-litigant joined the litigation part-way through the proceedings, then, if the group co-litigants were to be awarded costs, the court may need to make an order stating whether the opponents should pay anything towards that person's share (if any) of the common costs incurred before their name was entered on the group register. The notion of 'rests' may be relevant in that regard (see 65.85). **65.86**

Settlers and discontinuers In the same way as provision is made for late joiners, CPR, r 46.6(7), makes the following provision for settlers and discontinuers: **65.87**

'Where a claim is removed from the group register, the court may make an order for costs in that claim which includes a proportion of the common costs incurred up to the date on which the claim is removed from the group register. (Part 19 sets out rules about group litigation.)'

Thus, where a group co-litigant leaves the litigation early, that person's liability for common costs may be reduced accordingly. Again, the notion of 'rests' may be relevant (see 65.85).

Longmore LJ has commented that there are many reasons why a claimant might discontinue a claim in group litigation other than their claim being without merit, such that a *prima facie* rule that a discontinuer should pay costs would be too blunt an instrument that would give an inappropriate advantage to defendants.[96] He made the following comments about how best to manage discontinuers: **65.88**

'A *prima facie* rule tends to become the accepted rule, especially if it is necessary to incur the expense of going to the judge and asking, against opposition, for a different order. It is

[95] *Foster v Roussel Laboratories* (unreported), 29 October 1997, QBD. There is no surviving transcript of this decision, but May J's comments are recorded in *Sayers v Merck SmithKline Beecham plc; X v Schering Healthcare Ltd; Afrika v Cape plc* [2001] EWCA Civ 2017, at [11].

[96] *Sayers v Merck SmithKline Beecham plc; X v Schering Healthcare Ltd; Afrika v Cape plc* [2001] EWCA Civ 2017, at [18].

therefore not merely more sensible but also more consonant with justice that both the recoverability of common costs and the liability (if any) of discontinuing claimants for costs of common issues should be determined at the same time as orders for common costs are made in respect of those common issues. The court then has a full picture and can make whatever order is just in all the circumstances.'[97]

65.89 If the *prima facie* rule—that is, at CPR, r 38.6(1) (see 7.112–7.114)—is to be set aside, an order will have to be made to the effect (preferably in the GLO).

Quantum of costs in group litigation and costs management

65.90 Costs of group litigation are assessed in the same way as any other costs, but the following miscellaneous issues may merit special attention. They are addressed in no particular order.

Proportionality

65.91 Whilst it would be wrong to say that very small claims should result in very small costs, there should be economies of scale, even when each claim requires individual attention (see 25.100).[98] Whilst he was addressing the pre-April 2013 test of proportionality, Moreland J has confirmed that proportionality applies to all costs assessed on the standard basis, including those that are awarded prior to the conclusion of the group litigation.[99] As to proportionality in general, Sir Christopher Staughton had this to say:

> 'It would seem that particular care should be paid to the costs likely to be incurred in group litigation cases if they may, in the course of the proceedings, be likely to become disproportionate to the amount at stake. Such actions, as we have been told, may involve a considerable amount of administrative management which do not perhaps require any particular legal skill. That in itself could give rise to disproportionate expense unless controlled.'[100]

Where there is a need to look at the overall costs claimed, it would not generally be appropriate to disaggregate costs into segments or parts (see 25.41–25.42).

65.92 **Proportionality in consumer claims** Whilst her decision was not binding—and was the subject of a successful appeal on a different point (see 65.103)—Master James has outlined those factors that the court is likely to regard as relevant when deciding whether costs in group litigation involving consumers are proportionate.[101] The test that she applied was the pre-April 2013 test, but the following general principles are likely to be more widely relevant in group litigation involving claimants who are consumers.[102]

- The average award per claimant was low (less than £3,000) and the proceedings comprised many straightforward, low-value claims (although there were also a small number of higher-value claims).
- There should have been costs savings on overlapping work, but no such economies could be discerned.

---

[97] *Ibid*, at [19].

[98] *Giambrone v JMC Holidays Ltd (formerly Sunworld Holidays Ltd)* [2002] EWHC 2932 (QB), at [52], *per* Moreland J.

[99] *Ibid*, at [48].

[100] *Griffiths v Solutia UK Ltd* [2001] EWCA Civ 736, at [30].

[101] See *Briggs v First Choice Holidays and Flights Ltd* (unreported), 23 September 2016, SCCO.

[102] *Ibid*, at [61] and [67]–[97].

- The time spent on the case carried little weight, as did the fact that the claim was defended—in particular, the defendant's robust defence did not constitute poor conduct.
- The large number of claims (just under 600) did not make them complex.
- Although it took expertise to process that number of claims, the hourly rate that the court would allow came with the expectation that the matter would be dealt with expeditiously and cost-effectively.

Master James concluded that the costs were disproportionate. She allowed the rate as claimed, but took this very much into account in so far as the time was concerned.

Estimates, budgeting and capping

Budgeting is addressed in detail Chapter 12 (see, in particular, 12.29 and 12.80). **65.93**

Unless the court orders otherwise, every claim managed under a GLO is automatically allocated to the multitrack,[103] so, in theory, every individual claim could be the subject of an individual costs budget. In practice, however, this tends not to occur. There will often be two (or more) budgets, one of which will relate to common costs and the rest, to the individual costs. The individual budget will often be based on a representative 'worst case' claim (see 12.29), but where there are several categories of claim, it may be necessary to have one for each category. Respected practitioners have commented on the need to ensure that there is a rigorous approach to dealing with assumptions and contingencies, even to the point of not being afraid to state the obvious.[104] Where this is done, however, it is often difficult to take into account the fact that there may be economies of scale. Put otherwise, whilst it might be entirely reasonable that, in any individual claim, a certain amount of time is spent taking witness statements, it does not necessarily follow that it would take 12 times as long to prepare 12 such statements. One way of dealing with this is to combine costs capping with costs budgeting—that is, to budget the costs of each claim in the usual way, but impose an additional overarching cap collectively. **65.94**

In cases that are not budgeted, costs caps have, in the past, often been imposed by consent (at least in so far as the principle of capping is concerned).[105] **65.95**

Hourly rates

Differential rates are commonplace: common costs usually merit a higher hourly rate than individual costs, but administration costs do not always merit a high hourly rate. As to geography, an individual litigant may have had little choice but to instruct geographically distant solicitors (because they would have little choice but to instruct the solicitors who had conduct of the matter on behalf of the other group litigants). **65.96**

Wrong court, registers, etc

Group litigation orders usually provide that claims should be commenced in the management court.[106] Where a claim has been commenced in breach of such an order, then **65.97**

---

[103] PD 19B, para 7(1).

[104] See Hogan, A, 'Group Litigation, Costs Budgeting and Costs Capping', *Costs Barrister Blog*, 1 November 2013, available online at http://costsbarrister.co.uk/uncategorized/group-litigation-costs-budgeting-and-costs-capping/

[105] See, eg, *Various Claimants v Corby Borough Council* [2008] EWHC 619 (TCC).

[106] See CPR, r 19.11(3)(b); PD 19B, para 9.1.

the paying party can legitimately object to the additional costs incurred as a consequence. Occasionally, a claim will be litigated in circumstances in which it could have been entered onto a group register, but was not. If those are the circumstances, the paying party may wish to argue that a claim ought to have been litigated within the GLO and that, if this had happened, the costs would have been lower. Where the paying party is unsure of the terms of the GLO to which they wish to refer, assistance can be obtained from the Law Society's Multi Party Action Information Service.[107] In any event, care should be taken to ensure that the claim was not commenced after a cut-off date for entry of claims onto the group register[108]—another regard in which the Law Society is often able to assist.

'Failure' to comply with directions

65.98 Pre-existing directions will be set aside automatically when a claim is entered onto a group register;[109] hence it would be wrong to object to costs arising from the apparent 'failure' to comply with those directions.

Circular letters

65.99 It is common to find time claimed for printing and dispatching circular letters. The receiving party may not be entitled to the full 6-minute unit for each letter.[110]

Media and promotion

65.100 The costs of dealing with the media may be a recoverable cost in group litigation.[111] This is dealt with in more detail in discussion of the media at 49.127–49.129, which describes the applicable three-factor test—that is, use and service, relevance and attributability. It should be borne in mind that the court may have given directions for publicising the GLO.[112] The costs of publicity will not, however, extend to the costs of promoting the interests of the solicitors. In this regard, Lord Neuberger MR had this to say:

> 'It seems to me that the expenses of getting business, whether advertising to the public as potential clients, making a presentation to a potential client, or discussing a possible instruction with a potential client, should not normally be treated as attributable to, and payable by, the ultimate client or clients. Rather, such expenses should generally be treated as part of a solicitor's general overheads or expenses, which can be taken into account when assessing appropriate levels of charging, such as hourly rates.'[113]

Travelling

65.101 Although common issues are normally tried at the management court, individual issues may be directed to be tried at other courts whose locality is convenient for the parties.[114]

---

107 See https://www.lawsociety.org.uk/support-services/help-for-solicitors/practice-advice-service/multi-party-action-information-service/

108 See CPR, r 19.13(e); PD 19B, para 13.

109 PD 19B, para 7(2).

110 See *Giambrone v JMC Holidays Ltd* [2002] EWHC 495 (QB), at [7]–[13], *per* Nelson J, as discussed at 49.102.

111 *Ross v Owners of the Bowbelle (Review of Taxation under Ord 62 r 35)* (1997) 2 Lloyd's Rep 196 (Note), QBD (Admlty).

112 CPR, r 19.11(3)(c).

113 *Motto & Ors v Trafigura Ltd & Anor* [2011] EWCA Civ 1150, at [110].

114 PD 19B, para 15.2.

Costs of funding

The costs of funding are irrecoverable. This extends to the costs of giving advice about ATE insurance[115] (see 49.112–49.116). Whether this exclusory principle extends to the costs of giving advice about costs sharing agreements is a moot point. **65.102**

Alternative means of dispute resolution

It may be the case that group co-litigants had a means of resolving disputes that, if utilised, would have avoided litigation entirely. This is relatively common where the group co-litigants are bringing claims as consumers. Whilst each case will turn on its own facts, in a case in which holidaymakers' breaks had been spoiled by illness, Singh J found that a costs judge had gone too far by finding that it had been inherently unreasonable for those persons to enter into conditional fee agreements rather than to make use of a voluntary arbitration scheme.[116] **65.103**

Procedural issues relating to costs litigation

Procedurally, a detailed assessment of group litigation costs will be similar to other detailed assessments. The following issues may, however, arise from time to time. **65.104**

The bill of costs

Group litigants may be added to and removed from the group register at different stages of the litigation.[117] The bill of costs may need to be split into parts appropriately (see 43.36 and 65.85). **65.105**

The categorisation of costs

Costs will usually need to be categorised as common costs or individual costs and they may need to be further categorised as GLO costs, administration costs, test claim costs, etc.[118] The categorisation will be a question of mixed fact and law. If there is dispute about categorisation, that dispute can often be resolved by referring to the GLO, which will usually specify the GLO issues and thereby impliedly define the GLO costs. The GLO will also often define the other subcategories of costs—or at least give an indication as to what they are.[119] Categorisation is sometimes too challenging to be resolved by proportionate means, in which case it may be necessary to create a catch-all category (for example 'other costs') or to define a default position whereby, if there is doubt, the costs are to be attributed to a particular category. **65.106**

Preliminary issues hearings

Where appropriate, the court may order that certain issues are to be determined as preliminary issues. An example is the issue of distribution between common costs and individual costs, which PD 19B refers to as suitable for determination before the assessment itself (see 65.114).[120] Such preliminary issues must be clearly defined and reduced into writing.[121] **65.107**

[115] *Motto & Ors v Trafigura Ltd & Anor* [2011] EWCA Civ 1150, at [104]–[114].
[116] *Briggs and Ors v First Choice Holidays & Flights Ltd* (unreported), 8 February 2017, QBD.
[117] CPR, r 19.14.
[118] This is often necessary because different rates are often allowed for these different types of work: see 65.96.
[119] CPR, r 19.11(2)(b).
[120] PD 19B, para 16.2.
[121] *Lahey v Pirelli Tyres Ltd* [2007] EWCA Civ 91, at [4].

Case management

65.108 It will occasionally be the case that there will be such a large number of claims that the detailed assessment of those claims will themselves give rise to GLO issues (see 43.25). Where this is the case, then those issues may be managed by an appointed costs judge or by the managing judge. Examples exist of the task being shared between both judges.[122]

Appointed costs judge (or appointed costs court)

65.109 It is not unusual for all of the costs (including the individual costs) to be allocated to a particular court (which may or may not be the management court), or even a particular judge.[123] This was the practice well before the CPR.[124] Where this happens, the court may order that some of the assessments are to proceed as test claims.[125]

Forthwith orders

65.110 Group litigation can create difficulties in that it can tie up the parties' resources for many years (see 7.92–7.93). That said, this would not generally be a reason to make a 'forthwith' order in respect of costs awarded prior to the conclusion of the proceedings, as Morland J explained:

> 'In . . . almost all group litigation cases there should be no need for any detailed assessment of costs until the conclusion of the group litigation. Solicitors engaged in group litigation will be specialists and experienced in the field. Solicitors for claimants are fully entitled to an adequate cash flow from the defendants once the general issue of liability has been admitted or determined in the claimants' favour, similarly on determination of generic issues in the claimants' favour and on the assessment or settlement of awards of damages to individual or batches of claimants.'[126]

Interim payments

65.111 As Morland J implied (see above), whilst it would not be usual for a forthwith order to be made prior to the conclusion of group litigation, the court is able to make an order that a payment be made on account or an interim payment be made. Applications should be made to the nominated trial judge, where at all possible (see 14.06):

> 'It is to be hoped that in most cases defendants' solicitors would agree to pay at various stages in the group litigation a realistic interim amount on account of a final detailed assessment of costs if necessary. If agreement cannot be reached as to an interim payment of costs, it should be dealt with cheaply and shortly by the nominated trial Judge who will be familiar with the general issues in the case and the realistic overall size of the claim under his powers under CPR 44.3(8).'[127]

65.112 It is not clear whether the court has a jurisdiction to make an order, other than by consent, that a payment on account of costs be made in costs-only proceedings in group litigation.[128]

---

122 See, eg, *AB and Ors v British Coal Corpn* [2006] EWCA Civ 987.
123 PD 19B, para 8.
124 *In re Salaman* [1894] 2 Ch 201.
125 PD 19B, para 12.3.
126 *Giambrone v JMC Holidays Ltd (formerly Sunworld Holidays Ltd)* [2002] EWHC 2932 (QB), at [10].
127 *Ibid*, at [11]–[12].
128 *Banchio v Lai* [2003] EWHC 9038 (Costs).

Disclosure

Where disclosure is given by one person (either in the assessment or in the claim itself), this may cause a dispute about whether that document can be relied upon for the purposes of dealing with costs claimed by or against another person. Where that document relates to a GLO issue, it can be taken to have been disclosed to all parties, unless the court orders otherwise.[129] **65.113**

Distribution of undistributed costs of mixed hearings or applications

It will be recalled that where the court makes an order about costs in relation to a mixed hearing or application, it will—pursuant to CPR, r 46.6(5)—direct that proportion which relates to the GLO issues and the issues relevant only to the individual claim (see 65.45). If this does not happen, then PD 19B, para 16.2, may be relevant: **65.114**

> '16.1 CPR 46 contains rules about costs where a GLO has been made.
>
> 16.2 Where the court has made an order about costs in relation to any application or hearing which involved both—
> (1) one or more of the GLO issues; and
> (2) an issue or issues relevant only to individual claims;
>
> and the court has not directed the proportion of the costs that is to relate to common costs and the proportion that is to relate to individual costs in accordance with rule 46.6(5), the costs judge will make a decision as to the relevant proportions at or before the commencement of the detailed assessment of costs.'

Thus, where the court has made an order about the costs of an application or hearing that involved both GLO issues and issues relevant only to individual claims, the costs judge may have to make a decision as to the relevant proportions.[130] That would not be an exercise dictated by equal apportionment or any legal principles; rather, it would be a straightforward matter of fact.

A forensic sieve relating to group litigation

It is often appropriate to consider the issue of costs at an early stage in the litigation. The following issues may merit attention. **65.115**

- **Cost sharing agreements** Whether a costs sharing agreement (or order in lieu) should be made
- **Test claims** Whether any orders or agreements are required concerning how the costs of test claims are to be borne[131]
- **Estimates** Whether estimates of costs are required and, if so, whether those estimates should relate to common costs, individual costs, or both
- **Budgeting and capping** Whether a costs capping order should be made and what, if anything, should be done with respect to budgeting
- **Rests** Whether there should be quarterly rests for discontinuers and settlers (see 65.85–65.89)
- **Discontinuers, settlers and late joiners** Whether the GLO should make other provisions for discontinuers and settlers, and whether it should make provision for late joiners[132]

[129] CPR, r 19.12(4).
[130] CPR, r 46.6(5); PD 19B, para 16.2.
[131] PD 19B, para 12.4.
[132] In particular, whether any special provisions should apply in relation to discontinuers.

- **Other categories of costs** Whether there is a need for any category of costs to be accounted for separately, such as administration costs, GLO costs, etc
- **Forthwith assessments** Whether the parties who are awarded costs before the conclusion of the litigation should be permitted to have their costs assessed forthwith
- **ATE insurance** Whether ATE insurance provision (if any) is appropriate and adequate
- **Litigation funding** Whether litigation funding (that is, third-party funding) should be considered

This list is not, by any means, exhaustive.

Representative Claims

65.116 A representative claim that is brought in the context of group litigation is properly characterised as a test claim, so the matters discussed above will, to that extent, be relevant.

65.117 A representative claim may be brought outside of group litigation. The relevant procedure is found in CPR, Part 19, Section II. It is a claim that is brought by a person who acts as a representative of other persons who have an interest shared by the representative claimant.[133]

65.118 Generally speaking, an order made in a representative claim is binding on all persons represented in the claim, but it may be enforced by or against a person who is not a party to the claim only with the permission of the court.[134] That provision invites the question of whether an order for costs made against a representative claimant or defendant is binding on the persons who were represented.

65.119 This issue was addressed by Cox J in a representative claim brought by two members on behalf of an unincorporated association.[135] The claim was dismissed with costs. The costs order was against 'the claimants'; no application had been made for a non-party order against the other members. Cox J rejected the submission that the order bound the other members, commenting that if the receiving party wanted to enforce against the other members, they should have made an application for a non-party costs order.[136]

65.120 Where an application for a non-party costs order is brought, it is far from being a foregone conclusion that it will be made. Each case will turn on its own facts, such as the extent to which the non-parties funded the matter, the extent to which they directed the litigation, the extent to which they had a financial interest in the matter, etc. Whilst *obiter*, Denning LJ has emphasised the fact that no automatic liability will arise:

> 'In a representative action, the one who is named as a Plaintiff is, of course, a full party to the action. The others who are not named, but whom she represents are also parties to the action. They are all bound by the eventual decision in the case. They are not full parties because they are not liable individually for costs.'[137]

65.121 Where the representative party is acting autonomously, the non-parties may well not be held liable for costs. Vaughan Williams LJ had the following to say on the topic: 'The

[133] CPR, r 19.6(1).
[134] CPR, r 19.6(4).
[135] *Howells v Dominion Insurance Co Ltd* [2005] EWHC 552 (QB).
[136] *Ibid*, at [38].
[137] *Moon v Atherton* [1972] 2 QB 435, at [44].

Plaintiff is the self-elected representative of the others. He has not to obtain their consent. It is true that consequently they are not liable for costs, but they will be bound by the estoppel created by the decision.'[138]

The issue of non-party costs orders is dealt with in detail in Chapter 9. Where an application for a non-party costs order is made, certain procedural rules may apply, depending on the nature of the claim, as set out in CPR, r 19.8A. **65.122**

Derivative Claims

A derivative claim is a claim in which a company, other body corporate or trade union is said to be entitled to a remedy and the claim for that remedy is made by a member of that company, body or union. The definition does not include petitions for protection of members of a company against unfair prejudice made under s 996 of the Companies Act 2006.[139] Where it relates to a company, a derivative claim is a claim in respect of a cause of action arising from an actual or proposed act or omission involving negligence, default, breach of duty or breach of trust by a director of the company.[140] **65.123**

The court may order the company, body corporate or union to indemnify the claimant against liability for costs incurred in the permission application or in the derivative claim (or both).[141] Where a claimant seeks such a pre-emptive costs order from the court, this should be stated in the permission application or claim form (or both), as the case requires.[142] It is incumbent on a claimant who seeks such an order to establish that such an order is genuinely needed.[143] An order may be refused if, for example, it is not genuinely needed because the claimant already is able to claim lien and an indemnity out of the assets.[144] **65.124**

The claimant usually has to make out a *prima facie* case—something that must be done at the start of the litigation.[145] The decision whether the claimant's evidence comprises such a case will normally be made without submissions from, or attendance by, the company, body corporate or union. If, without invitation from the court, the company, body corporate or union volunteers a submission or attendance, it will not normally be allowed any costs of that submission or attendance.[146] **65.125**

---

138 *Markt & Co Ltd v Knight Steamship Co Ltd* [1910] 2 KB 1201, at 1039.

139 CPR, r 19.9(1).

140 Companies Act 2006, s 260(3).

141 CPR, r 19.9E. This is a codification of the type of order that originally was made in *Wallersteiner v Moir (No 2)* [1975] QB 373, at 389, 391, 392 and 403–5, which is still occasionally referred to as a '*Wallersteiner and Moir* order' even now: see The White Book, vol 1, para 19.9E.1. See also *Smith v Croft* [1986] 1 WLR 580, CA.

142 PD 19C, para 2(2).

143 Whilst a pre-CPR authority, see *Smith v Croft* [1986] 1 WLR 580, CA.

144 *Mumbray v Lapper* [2005] EWHC 1152.

145 See Companies Act 2006, ss 261, 262 and 264.

146 PD 19C, para 5.

66

CONTRACTS AND TRUSTS

66.01 This chapter deals with the following topics:

- costs payable pursuant to contract or powers conferred by contract (66.02):
  - the general principle in *Gomba* (66.04);
  - interpretation and the ambit of contractual rights to costs (66.17);
  - the basis of assessment of costs payable under a contract (66.18);
  - orders made in ignorance of, or without prejudice to, contractual provisions for costs (66.21);
  - mortgages and costs (66.23);
  - leases and costs (66.29);
  - trust deeds and costs (66.31);
- the costs relating to trusts (other than as a matter of contract) (66.35):
  - costs incurred by trustees (66.36);
  - controlling costs in disputes regarding trusts (66.43);
  - costs incurred by beneficiaries (66.45);
  - costs of proceedings as between trustee and beneficiary (and others) (66.46);
  - pre-emptive orders and applications for directions (66.56);
  - the principles of assessment of trustees' costs (66.75); and
  - costs payable out of a fund (66.80).

Costs Payable Pursuant to Contract or Powers Conferred by Contract

66.02 It is commonly the case that contracts (particularly mortgage contracts and leasehold agreements) impose an obligation on one of the counterparties (usually the mortgagor or lessee) to indemnify the other for costs incurred. Other contracts (such as some forms of legal expenses insurance) impose a contractual obligation to pay costs, either to another counterparty or to a third party. Yet others (such as trust deeds) grant the power for costs to be paid under a contract.

66.03 This chapter deals not only with the question of how costs payable under such contracts are assessed, but also with the more challenging issue of what the court should do when a party to litigation asserts a contractual right to some or all of their costs.

The general principle in *Gomba*

The general principle in *Gomba*[1] is that, where there is a contractual right to the costs, discretion should ordinarily be exercised so as to reflect that contractual right. This principle applies where a person involved in litigation asserts a putative right to costs arising out of a contract. This principle is well established as setting out the law; it has been cited with apparent approval in the House of Lords[2] and the Privy Council,[3] and has been adopted in many other common-law jurisdictions.[4] **66.04**

The facts of *Gomba*,[5] in essence, are that the receiving party (a mortgagee) became entitled to costs via two means: under a between-the-parties order for costs on the standard basis and by means of a contractual entitlement to costs on the indemnity basis. The question was whether the court should deal with the costs on the standard or the indemnity basis. As is set out below, the court's conclusion was that where there is a contractual right to the costs, discretion should ordinarily be exercised so as to reflect that contractual right. This is usually what is meant when a reference is made to 'the general principle in *Gomba*'. **66.05**

In *Gomba*, Scott LJ identified certain principles that are to be applied in a mortgage case—although some of those principles are, by analogy, of wider application than that (see 66.07). They can be paraphrased in the following way.[6] **66.06**

(1) An order for the payment of costs of proceedings is always a discretionary order (see Senior Courts Act 1981, s 51, but also see 66.10).
(2) Where there is a contractual right to the costs, discretion should ordinarily be exercised so as to reflect that contractual right.
(3) The power of the court to disallow costs that a mortgagee seeks to add to the mortgage security is a power that does not derive from s 51 of the 1981 Act, but from the power of courts of equity to fix the terms on which redemption will be allowed.
(4) A decision by a court to refuse costs, in whole or in part, to a mortgage litigant may be a decision:
   – in the exercise of the s 51 discretion;
   – in the exercise of the power to fix the terms on which redemption will be allowed;

[1] *Gomba Holdings Ltd v Minories Finance Ltd (No 2)* [1993] Ch 171.

[2] It was cited favourably by the House of Lords in *Callery v Gray (Nos 1 and 2)* [2002] UKHL 28.

[3] See *Cukurova Finance International Ltd v Alfa Telecom Turkey Ltd* [2013] UKPC 20, at [41], *per* Lord Mance.

[4] See, eg, *Re Red Sail Frozen Foods Ltd (in receivership)* [2007] 2 IR 361; *Bula Ltd v Crowley* [2003] IESC 10 (in the Republic of Ireland); *Elders Trustee & Executor Co Ltd v EG Reeves Pty Ltd* (1988) 20 FCR 164 (Federal Court of Australia); *Macquarie International Health Clinic Pty Ltd v Sydney South West Area Health Service (No 2)* [2011] NSWCA 171 (New South Wales); *Carey v Korda* [2012] WASCA 228 (Western Australia); *Bunting v Buchanan* [2013] NZHC 1921 (New Zealand).

[5] In more detail, the case concerned a dispute between a borrower and a mortgagee. After default on the part of the borrower, receivers were appointed. The borrower commenced redemption proceedings and raised sufficient money to satisfy its liabilities, thereby allowing the receivers to be discharged. The borrower disputed the amount of the mortgagee's costs (which were payable on the indemnity basis under a term in the mortgage). A further issue arose out of the fact that, during the course of proceedings, the mortgagor had been awarded costs, but on the standard basis.

[6] *Gomba Holdings Ltd v Minories Finance Ltd (No 2)* [1993] Ch 171, at 194A.

– as to the extent of a mortgagee's contractual right to add their costs to the security; or
– a combination of two or more of the above.

The pleadings in the case and the submissions made to the judge may indicate the nature of the decision that is made.

(5) A mortgagee is not to be deprived of a contractual or equitable right to add costs to the security merely by reason of an order for payment of costs made without reference to the mortgagee's contractual or equitable rights and without any adjudication as to whether or not the mortgagee should be deprived of those costs.

66.07 As can be seen, (3)–(4) would apply only where the contract is a mortgage agreement (or other agreement relating to a security). However, (1) and (2) apply whenever a party seeks to rely on putative right to costs arising out of any agreement or contract.[7] The principle in (2) is what is meant when reference is made to the 'general principle in *Gomba*'. Warren J (sitting in the Court of Appeal) has made it clear that it is principle, rather than a rule of law, and that it may well be that in a particular case—or even in a class of case—the court's discretion should be used to override the contractual right[8]—although see the points made at 66.11.

The exercise of discretion and Gomba

66.08 Whilst there are two distinct mechanisms[9] by which a party who enjoys a contractual right to costs may be entitled to costs—the first, via the court's discretion under r 44.2 of the Civil Procedure Rules (CPR); the second, by relying on the contract—and whilst an order under the former does not detract from the rights under the latter,[10] as a matter of principle the court should exercise its discretion under CPR, r 44.2, so as to reflect the entitlement under the contract.[11] Put otherwise, whilst those mechanisms are distinct, in practice there is such a degree of overlap that, in most instances, the two converge so as to accord with the contractual right.

66.09 By this means, any award under CPR, r 44.2, is kept consistent with what would be allowed if the costs payable under contract were to be assessed under CPR, r 44.5 (see 66.18).[12]

66.10 In practical terms, the general principle in *Gomba* means that, when exercising its discretion under CPR, r 44.2, to award costs to a party who claims to have an entitlement to costs as a matter of contract, the court needs to have regard to the costs that would be allowed under that contract. The aim, in general, would then be to make an award that reflects that entitlement. This does not mean, however, that the court will necessarily award everything that falls within the ambit of the contract without reference to any other factor; indeed, quite the opposite is true in that all of the relevant facts ought to be

[7] In this regard, Roch LJ is reported to have said 'the statements of principle in the *Gomba Holdings* case are not confined to mortgage cases and have a wider application': see *Church Commissioners for England v Ibrahim* [1997] 1 EGLR 13, at 14.

[8] *Forcelux Ltd v Binnie (Costs)* [2009] EWCA Civ 1077, at [12].

[9] The fact that they are distinct was confirmed by Ramsey J in *Astrazeneca UK Ltd v International Business Machines Corpn* [2011] EWHC 3373 (TCC), at [41].

[10] *John v Price Waterhouse* [2002] 1 WLR 953, at [22]–[23], *per* Ferris J; see also *Astrazeneca UK Ltd v International Business Machines Corpn* [2011] EWHC 3373 (TCC), at [41].

[11] *Gomba Holdings Ltd v Minories Finance Ltd (No 2)* [1993] Ch 171, at 194A; see also *Venture Finance plc v Mead* [2005] EWCA Civ 325, at [22].

[12] *Venture Finance plc v Mead* [2005] EWCA Civ 325, at [22]; see also *Astrazeneca UK Ltd v International Business Machines Corpn* [2011] EWHC 3373 (TCC), at [44].

taken into account.[13] Nor does it mean that the court will be fettered by the terms of the contract: even an express contractual provision regarding costs will yield to the exercise of the court's ultimate discretion to determine what costs ought reasonably to be met.[14]

The elements of discretion under *Gomba* For the reasons set out above, the court is able to allow or disallow costs as a matter of discretion. The elements of discretion can be identified thus.[15] **66.11**

- **The basis of costs** It may be that the basis upon which costs are to be paid is not expressly stated in the relevant contract. Where this is so, the court will have to decide whether the indemnity basis or standard basis would best suit the circumstances. In a case in which the contract—a lease—provided that the lessee would 'pay to the Lessor all costs and expenses ... which may be incurred', Briggs LJ found that whilst such phraseology did not refer expressly to costs being payable on the indemnity basis, it corresponded more closely with assessment upon the indemnity basis than upon the standard basis[16] (see also 66.17 and 66.18).
- **Reasonableness** Costs unreasonably incurred would not be recoverable even where there is a contractual right to costs[17] (unless, of course, there was an express contractual term to the contrary, which would be unlikely). This principle may apply both at the stage of deciding the incidence of costs and at the stage of the ascertainment of costs. Where circumstances so required, significant reductions may be made.[18] The power to make such reductions does not mean that the judge making the order for costs is required to delve into the detail, however; in particular, if the party who is to be ordered to pay costs is merely concerned that the costs are excessive in amount, then their remedy would be to ask for an assessment, at which stage the court would be permitted to disallow costs as having been unreasonably incurred.[19]
- **Equity, 'good reasons' and 'special orders'** As with any contractual right, equity may intervene if it would be inequitable and unconscionable to allow a party the benefit—or the entirety of the benefit—of its rights under the contract in question.[20] In this regard, the provisions of a contract will not be allowed to prevail if that would lead to an unjust outcome.[21] Lord Mance has emphasised that equity does not recognise a general or open-ended discretion.[22] That said, in a suitably exceptional case, the court is able to

[13] *Venture Finance plc v Mead* [2005] EWCA Civ 325, at [22], *per* Chadwick LJ.

[14] *Cukurova Finance International Ltd v Alfa Telecom Turkey Ltd* [2013] UKPC 20, at [57], *per* Lord Mance. See also *Bank of Baroda v Panessar* [1987] Ch 335, at 355 D–F, *per* Walton J; *Gomba Holdings Ltd v Minories Finance Ltd (No 2)* [1993] Ch 171, at 186H–187A.

[15] This categorisation is the editor's own invention and it should not be afforded more weight than it deserves.

[16] *Littlestone & Ors v Macleish* [2016] EWCA Civ 127, at [41].

[17] See *Fairview Investments Ltd v Sharma* (unreported), 14 October 1999, CA, at 12 of the approved transcript.

[18] As an example of the court making a significant adjustment to an indemnified party's entitlement on the grounds that the costs claimed were unreasonable, see *Cooperative Bank plc v Phillips* [2014] EWHC 2862, *per* Morgan J.

[19] *Mortgage Funding Corpn plc v Kashef-Hamadani* (unreported), 26 April 1993, CA.

[20] See, eg, *Cukurova Finance International Ltd v Alfa Telecom Turkey Ltd* [2013] UKPC 20, at [42] and [44], *per* Lord Mance.

[21] See, eg, *Forcelux Ltd v Binnie (Costs)* [2009] EWCA Civ 1077, at [12] *et seq*, in which the court found that there was good reason to deprive the mortgagee of costs by virtue of the fact that the mortgagor had won.

[22] *Cukurova Finance International Ltd v Alfa Telecom Turkey Ltd* [2013] UKPC 20, at [42] and [44].

make what Lord Mance called 'a special order' by which it would deny a party the benefit of a contractual right to costs.[23] Roch LJ has explained that a party which is entitled to costs under a contract must not be deprived of that right unless there is 'good reason' to do so—and that applies both to the making of a costs order in that party's favour and to the extent that costs are to be paid to that party.[24] As to what would amount to 'good reason', Roch LJ had this to say:

> 'A good reason for depriving a successful litigant to part of the costs to which the contractual term would entitle him would be that that part of the costs came within the definition of wasted costs in section 51(7), that is to say they were costs incurred by him as a result of improper, unreasonable or negligent conduct on his part or that of his legal or other representatives. There may well be other sufficient reasons for interfering with the basis of taxation.'[25]

- **General discretion** Whilst the editor has qualms about whether it exists as a separate element of discretion, it is arguable that the court has a discretion to make an award for a lesser amount than that which would reasonably be allowed under a contract that does not derive from equity.[26] If that is so, it would be a wider-reaching element than the others (namely, basis, reasonableness and equity). Warren J (sitting in the Court of Appeal) had this to say:

> 'For example, if a lessor loses a piece of litigation at first instance which it was reasonable for him to fight, it might be wrong to deprive him of a contractual right to costs. But if he goes on to appeal the decision against him and loses the appeal, then it is not obvious to me that the general rule should be that the discretion should be exercised in accordance with the contractual right; or if it is the general rule, then the court should be willing to depart from it quite readily.'[27]

Warren J seems to be describing the exercise of a jurisdiction that is not dependent on a finding of unreasonable or inequitable conduct. If this is correct, then it is getting perilously close to being the type of 'general or open-ended discretion' that Lord Mance said does not exist.[28] Similarly, it would not sit well with the fact that Balcome LJ has said that a contractual right to costs may be lost or curtailed only where there has been a 'violation or culpable neglect of ... duty under the contract'[29] nor does it sit well with the fact that Lord Selbourn LC has said that it may be lost only where there has been 'improper defence or other misconduct'.[30] In view of these things, perhaps the best analysis is that Warren J was simply exercising an unarticulated equitable jurisdiction and that the factors to which he pointed (such as losing an appeal) amounted to a 'good reason' to disallow costs, albeit tacitly.

---

23 *Ibid.*

24 See *Church Commissioners for England v Ibrahim* [1997] 1 EGLR 13.

25 *Ibid*, at 14.

26 See, eg, *Cotterell v Stratton* (1872) LR 8 Ch App 295, at 295.

27 *Forcelux Ltd v Binnie (Costs)* [2009] EWCA Civ 1077, at [13].

28 *Cukurova Finance International Ltd v Alfa Telecom Turkey Ltd* [2013] UKPC 20, at [42] and [44]; cf Blair J in *The Law Debenture Trust Corpn plc v Ukraine* [2017] EWHC 1902 (Comm), at [30(iii)], in which the costs of certain 'very contentious issues' were disallowed.

29 *Mortgage Funding Corpn plc v Kashef-Hamadani* ([1993] Lexis Citation 1542, 26 April 1993, CA, at the 12th paragraph of the transcript.

30 *Cotterell v Stratton* (1872) LR 8 Ch App 295, at 295.

In any event, it is clear from Warren J's analysis that a party who has an entitlement to costs is more likely to lose that entitlement if they were to suffer defeat on their appeal than would be the case if they had lost at first instance. **66.12**

Misconduct and exceptionally poor conduct Misconduct[31] or exceptionally poor conduct on the part of the indemnified party may result in an award that not only deprives the putatively indemnified party of the benefit of the indemnity,[32] but also requires that party to pay the other party's costs.[33] In an appropriate case, the court may deprive an indemnified party of the right to costs on the indemnity basis and award costs on the standard basis instead.[34] An issues-based approach may be taken[35] and this may lead to a party being awarded only a percentage of the costs it claimed as its contractual entitlement.[36] **66.13**

As to conduct and factors that will *not* justify the court making such an order, Roch LJ had this to say: **66.14**

> 'In my opinion, it is not a proper exercise of a judge's discretion to refuse to allow a successful litigant to recover his contractual entitlement to costs because the judge considers that [that party] has an unfairly strong bargaining position or it is desirable that the courts keep a careful control of costs in undefended possession claims.'[37]

Roch LJ was speaking nearly 20 years ago, however, and it may be that the law has moved on since then (see below). **66.15**

Consumer issues It has been suggested, in the context of mortgages being given by consumers, that imposing a blanket contractual obligation on a consumer to pay a mortgagee's costs is contrary to modern-day consumer protection legislation (see 28.40–28.44 and 28.149–28.155).[38] It would seem that there is no authority on that specific point, but it is difficult to see why the matters set out in Chapter 28 would not apply to contracts that imposed costs obligations on consumers. In particular, the points made at 28.41–28.44 would seem to be potentially relevant. **66.16**

---

[31] See *Webb v Crosse* [1912] 1 Ch 323, at 330, *per* Parker J, cited with apparent approval by Lord Mance in *Cukurova Finance International Ltd v Alfa Telecom Turkey Ltd* [2013] UKPC 20, at [32]. See also *Snell's Equity* (32nd edn, London: Sweet & Maxwell, 2010), para 38-040.

[32] See, eg, *Rourke v Robinson* [1911] 1 Ch 480 (in which, without good reason, the mortgagee's solicitor declined to execute a reconveyance when the mortgagor attended to redeem). Whilst it relates to interest rather than costs, see *Midleton v Eliot* (1847) 15 Sim 531 (when redemption would have occurred on time had it not been for the fact that the mortgagee had lost some of the deeds).

[33] As an example of this, see *Edmondson v Copland* [1911] 2 Ch 301, cited with apparent approval by Lord Mance in *Cukurova Finance International Ltd v Alfa Telecom Turkey Ltd* [2013] UKPC 20, at [39].

[34] See, eg, *Cukurova Finance International Ltd v Alfa Telecom Turkey Ltd* [2013] UKPC 20, at [59].

[35] See *Cotterell v Stratton* (1872) LR 8 Ch App 295, at 302, in which Lord Selbourne said that 'a mortgagee who denies the mortgagor's right to redeem may be deprived of costs, or may even be ordered to pay them' and held that 'justice will be done if I disallow the Plaintiffs of such of the costs as are fairly attributable to their having put forward a case which has failed'. Those comments were cited with approval by Lord Mance in *Cukurova Finance International Ltd v Alfa Telecom Turkey Ltd* [2013] UKPC 20, at [40].

[36] In *Astrazeneca UK Ltd v International Business Machines Corpn* [2011] EWHC 3373 (TCC), for example, both parties had a contractual right to an indemnity; Ramsey J made a percentage award that took into account the competing rights.

[37] See *Church Commissioners for England v Ibrahim* [1997] 1 EGLR 13, at 14.

[38] See Bates, J, 'Costs in Mortgage Possession Proceedings: An Unfair Contract Term?' (2005) 8(3) Journal of Housing Law 31.

Interpretation and the ambit of contractual rights to costs

66.17 Whether the costs that are claimed fall within the ambit of the contract in question will be a matter of contractual interpretation; as will the terms upon which costs are to be paid. The following points can be made.

- **'All of their costs' or 'fully for any costs'** Where a contract provides that a party is entitled to 'all of their costs', the word 'all' does not enable or entitle the party entitled to costs to recover costs that were *un*reasonably incurred or which are *un*reasonable in amount;[39] rather, it means that the appropriate basis of assessment is the indemnity basis—that is, the basis set out in CPR, r 44.5 (see 66.18).[40] The same applies where the contract provides that one party must indemnify the other 'fully for any costs'.[41]
- **'Solicitor and own-client costs'** Where a contract provides that a party will pay another party's 'solicitor and own-client costs', the appropriate basis of assessment is the indemnity basis—that is, the basis set out in CPR, r 44.5 (see 66.18).[42]
- **'Recoverable legal costs'** In a matter concerning a guarantee for arbitration costs, Popplewell J has found that the term 'recoverable legal costs' should not be read so narrowly as to exclude the fees of the arbitrator.[43]
- **'Reasonable attorneys' fees'** This has been interpreted (in the context of litigation) as meaning costs on the standard basis.[44]
- **'In contemplation of proceedings'** Where a lease provides that a tenant should pay all reasonable costs incurred in contemplation of proceedings, costs would fall into that category only if, at the time the expenditure was incurred, the landlord actually had the proceedings in mind as part of the reason for their expenditure.[45]
- **'Defence costs'** The use of the term 'defence costs' would, where the definition of that term made no distinction between bringing a claim and defending it, include the costs of bringing a claim.[46]
- **Law of Property Act 1925, s 146** Chadwick LJ has said that a right to costs of proceedings under s 146 of the 1925 Act falls into three distinct phases:
  (1) the lessor's costs in relation to the preparation and service of a s 146 notice;
  (2) the costs incurred by the lessor after notice and in contemplation of proceedings to enforce the right of re-entry (that is, contemplated possession proceedings); and

[39] *Fairview Investments Ltd v Sharma* (unreported), 14 October 1999, CA, at 12 of the approved transcript.

[40] *Deutsche Bank (Suisse) SA v Gulzar Ahmed Khan & Ors* [2013] EWHC 1020 (Comm), at [19] and [23]–[24], *per* Hamblen J. See also *Littlestone & Ors v Macleish* [2016] EWCA Civ 127, at [41], *per* Briggs LJ.

[41] See *Church Commissioners for England v Ibrahim* [1997] 1 EGLR 13, at 14, *per* Roch LJ.

[42] See *Astrazeneca UK Ltd v International Business Machines Corpn* [2011] EWHC 3373 (TCC), at [39]–[41], in which Ramsey J made it clear that the presumptions in what is now CPR, r 46.9(3), do not apply. Whilst a pre-CPR case, this point was also made by Robert Megarry VC in *EMI Records Ltd v Ian Cameron Wallace Ltd* [1983] Ch 59, at 74G.

[43] *Wealcan Enterprises Inc v Banque Algerienne Du Commerce Exterieur SA* [2012] EWHC 4151 (Comm).

[44] See *Euro Asian Oil SA v Credit Suisse AG & Ors* [2016] EWHC 3340 (Comm), at [7], *per* Cranston J.

[45] Whilst not binding, see *Barrett v Anne Robinson* [2014] UKUT 322 (LC), at [47]–[52], *per* Martin Rodger QC.

[46] *Astrazeneca UK Ltd v International Business Machines Corpn* [2011] EWHC 3373 (TCC), at [34], *per* Ramsey J.

(3) the costs of proceedings actually commenced (that is, actual possession proceedings).[47]

A provision for costs of steps taken 'in or in contemplation of, or in relation to, any proceedings under the Law of Property Act 1925, s 146', would not include the costs of correspondence sent to the tenant trying to enforce an obligation to undertake repairs.[48] Where a lease provides that the tenant should pay all costs 'incurred by the lessor in or in contemplation ... of any steps or proceedings under Section 146 of the Landlord and Tenant Act 1925', then possession proceedings brought to enforce a right of re-entry following service of a notice under s 146(1) of that Act would fall within the limits of the indemnity.[49]

- **Other enactments** Chadwick LJ has qualified the first of the five statements of principle in *Gomba* (see 66.06), on the basis that Senior Courts Act 1981, s 51(1), is expressly made subject to the provisions of any other enactment.[50] Chadwick LJ took the view that s 146(3) of the Law of Property Act 1925[51] applied and took precedence. Having made this point, Chadwick LJ went on to say that it is enough to rely on the second statement of principle in *Gomba*: where there is a contractual right to costs, the discretion should ordinarily be exercised so as to reflect that contractual right.

The basis of assessment of costs payable under a contract

Ultimately, the basis of assessment will be heavily dependent on the interpretation of the contract in question (see 66.11 and 66.19), but, unless the contrary has been agreed, the CPR imposes an adjectival presumption that the costs will be assessed on a basis that is very similar to the indemnity basis. In this regard, CPR, r 44.5, reads as follows: **66.18**

> '(1) Subject to paragraphs (2) to (3), where the court assesses (whether by the summary or detailed procedure) costs which are payable by the paying party to the receiving party under the terms of a contract, the costs payable under those terms are, unless the contract expressly provides otherwise, to be presumed to be costs which—
> (a) have been reasonably incurred; and
> (b) are reasonable in amount,
> and the court will assess them accordingly.
>
> (2) The presumptions in paragraph (1) are rebuttable. Practice Direction 44—General rules about costs sets out circumstances where the court may order otherwise.
>
> (3) Paragraph (1) does not apply where the contract is between a solicitor and his client.'

[47] *Fairview Investments Ltd v Sharma* (unreported), 14 October 1999, CA; see also *Forcelux Ltd v Binnie (Costs)* [2009] EWCA Civ 1077, at [6].

[48] *Agricullo Ltd v Yorkshire Housing Ltd (formerly Yorkshire Community Housing Ltd)* (2010) EWCA Civ 229.

[49] *Forcelux Ltd v Binnie (Costs)* [2009] EWCA Civ 1077, at [6], *per* Warren J (sitting in the Court of Appeal).

[50] *Fairview Investments Ltd v Sharma* (unreported), 14 October 1999, CA, at 8 of the official transcript.

[51] Law of Property Act 1925, s 146(3), provides that: 'A lessor shall be entitled to recover as a debt due to him from a lessee, and in addition to damages (if any), all reasonable costs and expenses properly incurred by the lessor in the employment of a solicitor and surveyor or valuer, or otherwise, in reference to any breach giving rise to a right of re-entry or forfeiture which, at the request of the lessee, is waived by the lessor, or from which the lessee is relieved, under the provisions of this Act.'

Whilst a different interpretation is arguable,[52] it seems that costs payable under a contract will be presumed to have been both reasonably incurred and to be reasonable in amount. This will not always be the case, however, because the presumptions are expressly stated to be rebuttable.[53]

66.19 What is actually payable will, by and large, be a matter of contractual interpretation. Where a contract provides that a party is entitled to claim for 'all of their costs,'[54] 'fully for any costs'[55] or for 'solicitor and own-client' costs,[56] the appropriate basis of assessment is the indemnity basis (that is, the basis set out in CPR, r 44.5). The word 'all' does not, however, enable or entitle the lessor to recover costs and expenses that are *un*reasonably incurred or which are *un*reasonable in amount[57] (see 66.17).

66.20 The now-revoked CPD used to make specific provision that costs unreasonably incurred or costs that were unreasonable in amount could be disallowed.[58] That provision has not been carried over into PD 44, but this is probably of no importance given the fact that CPR, r 44.5(2), now expressly states that presumptions in CPR, r 44.5(1), are rebuttable.

Orders made in ignorance of, or without prejudice to, contractual provisions for costs

66.21 A perfected order made in ignorance of—or, presumably, without prejudice to—a contractual right to costs will not be set aside solely for that reason nor will it detract from any contractual right to costs enforceable by other means.[59] This is in contrast to the orders referred to at 66.06, in which the order for costs is intended to match or contradict the contractual entitlement to costs.

---

[52] The reference in CPR, r 44.5(2), to the court being able to 'order otherwise' is ambiguous in that it is not clear whether the objects of the phrase 'where the court may order otherwise' are the presumptions (ie where 'otherwise' would mean that the presumptions do not apply) or the power to rebut them (ie where 'otherwise' would mean not exercising the power to rebut the presumptions). This could be an important point because, despite the fact that there is a reference to PD 44 setting out the circumstances in which the court may 'order otherwise', PD 44 is silent on that topic. As such, it is arguable that the true meaning of CPR, r 44.5(2), is that PD 44 sets out those circumstances in which the presumptions in r 44.5(1) may not be rebutted and, in view of the fact that PD 44 is silent on the matter, the presumptions are *always* rebutted. This would be a very strange outcome, but it is certainly arguable. The more attractive interpretation, however, is that the reference to 'ordering otherwise' is a reference to the court disapplying the presumptions in r 44.5(1). The legislative history is relevant in this regard, because CPR, r 44.5, evolved from old CPR, r 48.3, the main difference between the two being the fact that the latter did not include the words 'The presumptions in paragraph (1) are rebuttable'. If those words are disregarded for a moment, the meaning of CPR, r 44.5(2), becomes clear.

[53] See CPR, r 44.5(2).

[54] *Deutsche Bank (Suisse) SA v Gulzar Ahmed Khan & Ors* [2013] EWHC 1020 (Comm), at [19] and [23]–[24], *per* Hamblen J.

[55] See *Church Commissioners for England v Ibrahim* [1997] 1 EGLR 13, at 14, *per* Roch LJ.

[56] See *Astrazeneca UK Ltd v International Business Machines Corpn* [2011] EWHC 3373 (TCC), at [39]–[41], in which Ramsey J made it clear that the presumptions in what is now CPR, r 46.9(3), do not apply. Whilst a pre-CPR case, this point was also made by Robert Megarry VC in *EMI Records Ltd v Ian Cameron Wallace Ltd* [1983] Ch 59, at 74G.

[57] *Fairview Investments Ltd v Sharma* (unreported), 14 October 1999, CA, at 12 of the approved transcript.

[58] See CPD, art 50.1, which reads: 'Where the court is assessing costs payable under a contract, it may make an order that all or part of the costs payable under the contract shall be disallowed if it is satisfied by the paying party that costs have been unreasonably incurred or are unreasonable in amount.'

[59] *Elton John v Price Waterhouse* [2002] 1 WLR 953.

In a case in which a costs order was made on the standard basis before the parties realised that the receiving party already had a contractual right to costs on the indemnity basis, Ferris J refused to interfere with the original order because the court's jurisdiction under Senior Courts Act 1981, s 51, had been exhausted.[60] He accepted that the fact that he had made an order for the standard basis did not detract from any contractual right of the defendants to indemnity costs under the terms of the articles of association of the claimants. Ferris J commented that, under the CPR, there probably is a jurisdiction to reopen the issue (because this might save the costs of a fresh claim being brought), but he would have been inclined to exercise that jurisdiction only if it were clear that there could be no defence to a contractual claim for indemnity costs, so that if a fresh claim were commenced, summary judgment would be given in favour of the defendant. That was not so in the claim before him. Thus, if they wanted to pursue the full extent of the indemnity, the defendants would have to bring a fresh claim. **66.22**

Mortgages and costs

Echoing the guidance that Scott LJ gave in *Gomba* (see 66.06), PD 44, para 7.2, gives the following guidance about mortgages: **66.23**

> '(1) The following principles apply to costs relating to a mortgage.
>
> (2) An order for the payment of costs of proceedings by one party to another is always a discretionary order: section 51 of the Senior Courts Act 1981 ("the section 51 discretion").
>
> (3) Where there is a contractual right to the costs, the discretion should ordinarily be exercised so as to reflect that contractual right.
>
> (4) The power of the court to disallow a mortgagee's costs sought to be added to the mortgage security is a power that does not derive from section 51, but from the power of the courts of equity to fix the terms on which redemption will be allowed.
>
> (5) A decision by a court to refuse costs in whole or in part to a mortgagee may be—
> (a) a decision in the exercise of the section 51 discretion;
> (b) a decision in the exercise of the power to fix the terms on which redemption will be allowed;
> (c) a decision as to the extent of a mortgagee's contractual right to add the mortgagee's costs to the security; or
> (d) a combination of two or more of these things.
>
> (6) A mortgagee is not to be deprived of a contractual or equitable right to add costs to the security merely by reason of an order for payment of costs made without reference to the mortgagee's contractual or equitable rights, and without any adjudication as to whether or not the mortgagee should be deprived of those costs.'

PD 44, para 7.3, makes provision for the mortgagor to seek an account, in appropriate cases. It reads as follows: **66.24**

> '(1) Where the contract entitles a mortgagee to—
> (a) add the costs of litigation relating to the mortgage to the sum secured by it; or
> (b) require a mortgagor to pay those costs,

[60] See *ibid*, the facts of which were as follows. The defendants, who were the claimant's auditors, successfully defended a claim brought against them. The defendants initially expressly said that they did not seek costs on the indemnity basis; an order for costs on the standard basis was drawn up and perfected. At a subsequent hearing, the defendants sought to reopen the issue of costs because they had discovered that, under the articles of association of the claimant, they were contractually entitled to costs on the indemnity costs.

the mortgagor may make an application for the court to direct that an account of the mortgagee's costs be taken.

(Rule 25.1(1)(n) provides that the court may direct that a party file an account.)

(2) The mortgagor may then dispute an amount in the mortgagee's account on the basis that it has been unreasonably incurred or is unreasonable in amount.

(3) Where a mortgagor disputes an amount, the court may make an order that the disputed costs are assessed under rule 44.5.'

Adding monies to the mortgage debt

66.25 Citing a line of authority that stretches back more than a century,[61] Nourse LJ had the following to say about what can and cannot be added to the mortgage debt:

> 'A mortgagee is allowed to reimburse himself out of the mortgaged property for all costs, charges and expenses reasonably and properly incurred in enforcing or preserving his security. Often the process of enforcement or preservation makes it necessary for him to take or defend proceedings. In regard to such proceedings three propositions may be stated.
> (1) The mortgagee's costs, reasonably and properly incurred, of proceedings between himself and the mortgagor or his surety are allowable. The classical examples are proceedings for payment, sale, foreclosure or redemption, but nowadays the most common are those for possession of the mortgaged property preliminary to an exercise of the mortgagee's statutory power of sale out of court.
> (2) Allowable also are the mortgagee's costs, reasonably and properly incurred, of proceedings between himself and a third party where what is impugned is the title to the estate. In such a case the mortgagee acts for the benefit of the equity of redemption as much as for that of the security.
> (3) But where a third party impugns the title to the mortgage, or the enforcement or exercise of some right or power accruing to the mortgagee thereunder, the mortgagee's costs of the proceedings, even though they be reasonably and properly incurred, are not allowable.'[62]

The points made at points (1) and (2) comprise a general rule, and point (3) is the exception to it. Both the general rule[63] and the exception[64] have long-standing pedigrees.

66.26 Thus, where the litigation involves a third party and it is the title to the *mortgage* that is challenged (as opposed to the title to the property), then those monies are not, as a rule, to be added to the mortgage debt. Where the litigation falls largely in category (3)—where a third party impugns the title to the mortgage—it may be that some of the costs are recoverable as being incurred in the ordinary course of enforcing the mortgage contract.[65]

Relief against forfeiture

66.27 Lord Mance has explained that relief against forfeiture will, as a general rule, be made conditional upon payment on an indemnity basis of costs incurred by the party against whom

[61] See *Owen v Church* (1857) 5 WR 545; *Parker v Watkins* (1859) John 133; *In re Smith's Mortgage* (1931) 2 Ch 168.

[62] *Parker-Tweedale v Dunbar Bank plc (No 2)* [1991] Ch 26, at 33. See also *Re Red Sail Frozen Foods Ltd (in receivership)* [2006] IEHC 328; *Re Leighton's Conveyance* [1936] 3 All ER 1033.

[63] See, eg, *Detillin v Gale* [1802] 7 Ves 583; *Dryden v Frost* (1838) 3 My & C 670; *National Provincial Bank of England v Games* (1886) LR 31 Ch D 582.

[64] See, eg, *Owen v Crouch* [1857] 5 WR 545; *Parker v Watkins* [1859] 70 ER 369; *Re Smith's Mortgage* [1931] 2 Ch 168.

[65] *Credit & Mercantile plc v Kaymuu Ltd* [2014] EWHC 1746 (Ch), at [196]–[214], *per* Tim Kerr QC.

relief is claimed, other than to the extent that it is shown that such costs were unreasonably incurred or unreasonable in amount.[66]

No automatic summary assessment

As to the type of assessment that will follow litigation involving mortgages, PD 44, para 9.3, reads as follows: **66.28**

> 'The general rule in paragraph 9.2 [that the court should make a summary assessment of the costs] does not apply to a mortgagee's costs incurred in mortgage possession proceedings or other proceedings relating to a mortgage unless the mortgagee asks the court to make an order for the mortgagee's costs to be paid by another party.'

Thus, if they are condemned in costs, the mortgagor is entitled to a detailed assessment. Commentators have said that this is an attempt to level the playing field between mortgagor and mortgagee.[67]

Leases and costs

With appropriate modifications, similar principles to those that apply to mortgages will tend to apply to leases. **66.29**

If a lease provides for payment of costs in certain circumstances, this may override the restriction on costs between opposing parties in the small claims track (see 49.164).[68] **66.30**

Trust deeds and costs

It may be that a trust deed specifically grants trustees either an indemnity for their own costs (or any liability for costs) out of the fund or the power to authorise the grant of the payment of another person's costs of an application under CPR, r 64.2(a), out of the fund. Where such a power exists and is exercised, then an order is not required and the trustees are entitled to recover out of the fund any costs that they pay pursuant to the agreement made in the exercise of such power.[69] (If such a power exists, but the trustees choose not to exercise it, then the procedure set out at 66.68 would apply instead.[70]) The trustees' power to recover those monies from the fund would be a contractual right and, as such, would be governed by CPR, r 44.5. **66.31**

The trustees' entitlement to reimbursement of those costs would be limited to those that are 'properly incurred', which means 'not improperly incurred', the burden of proof being on the party challenging the expenses.[71] Blair J had this to say about what was meant by 'properly incurred': **66.32**

> 'The court's view is that in the context of a financial transaction of this kind, this means commercial reasonableness (*UBS AG, London Branch v Glas Trust Corp Ltd* [2017] EWHC

---

[66] See *Cukurova Finance International Ltd v Alfa Telecom Turkey Ltd* [2013] UKPC 20, at [57], *per* Lord Mance. See also *Bank of New South Wales v O'Connor* (1889) 14 PC 273, at 278; *Patel v K & J Restaurants Ltd* [2010] EWCA Civ 1211, at [104].

[67] See, eg, *Cook on Costs 2017* (LexisNexis, online), para 36.2.

[68] *Chaplair Ltd v Kumari* [2015] EWCA Civ 798, at [19]–[26].

[69] See PD 64A, para 6.2.

[70] See PD 64A, para 6.3.

[71] See *The Law Debenture Trust Corpn plc v Ukraine* [2017] EWHC 1902 (Comm), at [21], *per* Blair J, citing *Re Beddoe* [1893] 1 Ch 547.

> 1788 (Comm) at [48]), and that effect must be given to the parties' agreement that costs properly incurred are to be paid on a full indemnity basis. A trustee could not safely take on this kind of responsibility if when acting properly it risked ending up out of pocket.'[72]

Where such a right to costs exists, it is open to the court to order that they be awarded by way of summary judgment.[73] That said, it will, in general, be appropriate to send costs for assessment where they are disputed on cogent grounds, where the details regarding the costs are sparse or where they are unusually sizeable. Indeed, Morgan J has said that sending the costs for assessment is 'the most convenient course'.[74]

66.33 Where costs 'properly incurred' are to be assessed, this will be on the indemnity basis.[75]

Procedure where a party claims a contractual right to costs

66.34 The following miscellaneous procedural points can be made.

- **Contractual right not pleaded** Where a party wishes to rely on a putative contractual right to receive an indemnity for the costs of proceedings, the fact that that right was not pleaded will not automatically mean that the point cannot be pursued.[76]
- **Co-assessment of contractual costs** Where an assessment of the costs as between solicitor and client needs to be carried out, there is no reason why that assessment may not take place at the same time as the assessment of the contractual liability.[77]
- **Assessment not mandatory** CPR, r 44.5, applies only if the court is assessing costs payable under a contract. It does not (a) require the court to make an assessment of such costs or (b) require a mortgagee to apply for an order for those costs where there is a contractual right to recover out of the mortgage funds.[78]
- **Litigation involving mortgages** For the reasons set out at 66.24, if a mortgagee is ordered to pay costs, they are entitled to a detailed assessment.

Costs Relating to Trusts and Trustees

66.35 It may be that a trust deed specifically grants trustees either an indemnity for their own costs (or any liability for costs) out of the fund or the power to authorise the grant of the payment of another person's costs of an application under CPR, r 64.2(a), out of the fund. Where that is so and where the trustees wish to avail themselves of those powers, then the matters set out at 66.31–66.33 will apply. In all other circumstances, the matters set out below will apply.

---

72 See *The Law Debenture Trust Corpn plc v Ukraine* [2017] EWHC 1902 (Comm), at [22].

73 See *The Law Debenture Trust Corpn plc v Elektrim Finance BV* [2005] EWHC 1999, at [71], in which Hart J relied on the detailed narrative and the fact that no 'plausible reason' or 'clear case' had been advanced as to unreasonableness in relation to any particular item.

74 See *Renewable Power & Light Ltd v McCarthy Tetrault* [2014] EWHC 3848 (Ch), at [40].

75 See *The Law Debenture Trust Corpn plc v Ukraine* [2017] EWHC 1902 (Comm), at [30(i)], *per* Blair J.

76 See *Cukurova Finance International Ltd v Alfa Telecom Turkey Ltd* [2013] UKPC 20. See also the Hong Kong case of *Abani Trading Pte Ltd v BNP Paribas* [2014] SGHC 111.

77 *Tim Martin Interiors Ltd v Akin Gump LLP* [2010] EWHC 2951 (Ch), at [42], *per* Lewison J, upheld on appeal at [2011] EWCA Civ 1574.

78 See PD 44, para 7.1.

Costs incurred by trustees

In general, a trustee is entitled to reimbursement from the trust funds[79] of their costs properly incurred[80] in administering the trust,[81] including remuneration paid to agents.[82] That right has existed since well before the fusion of the administration of the common law and equity by the Judicature Acts, and was expressly preserved by those Acts.[83] A trustee may assert lien over trust property in respect of funds that they have applied to preserve the trust.[84] A trustee will also be entitled to the costs of litigation brought on behalf of the trust, but only to the extent that those costs are not recovered or paid by any other person. In this regard, CPR, r 46.3, makes the following provisions: **66.36**

> '(1) This rule applies where—
> (a) a person is or has been a party to any proceedings in the capacity of trustee or personal representative; and
> (b) rule 44.5 does not apply.[[85]]
>
> (2) The general rule is that he is entitled to be paid the costs of those proceedings, insofar as they are not recovered from or paid by any other person, out of the relevant trust fund or estate.
>
> (3) Where he is entitled to be paid any of those costs out of the fund or estate, those costs will be assessed on the indemnity basis.'

Thus, whilst the court has the power to order otherwise,[86] the general rule is that a trustee will be allowed their costs. The now-revoked CPD used to confirm that the trustee's costs may include costs awarded against the trustee in favour of another party;[87] PD 46 does not contain that provision,[88] but, in view of the fact that the CPD never had the status of a source of law (see 4.50), it is doubtful whether anything turns on this.

Contracts of retainer with trustees

The topic of the contract of retainer between a trustee and their solicitor is addressed at 27.323. **66.37**

Denial of the costs of proceedings

This section deals primarily with whether a trustee should be denied their costs out of the fund. The principles as to awards of costs between trustee and beneficiary—including 'the *Buckton* categories'[89]—are addressed at 66.46–66.55, as are other issues of entitlement. **66.38**

---

[79] 'Trust funds' means income or capital funds of the trust: see Trustee Act 2000, s 39(1).

[80] This requirement is ancient and implied: see, eg, *Re Grimthorpe* [1958] Ch 615, at 623. See 66.32 for a discussion of what is meant by 'properly incurred'.

[81] Trustee Act 2000, s 31(1).

[82] Trustee Act 2000, s 32(1).

[83] See Order 55 of the Rules annexed as a Schedule to the 1875 Act.

[84] *Clack v Holland* (1854) 19 Beav 262, at 273.

[85] CPR, r 44.5, will apply if the costs are payable pursuant to a contract: see 66.18.

[86] This power was created to negate the old practice of the Court of Chancery of allowing the trustee their costs as a matter of course. The discretion was originally governed by Order 65 of the General Order 1883: see *Re Beddoe, Downs v Cottam* [1893] 1 Ch 547, at 554.

[87] See CPD, art 50A.1, which used to read: 'A trustee or personal representative is entitled to an indemnity out of the relevant trust fund or estate for costs properly incurred, which may include costs awarded against the trustee or personal representative in favour of another party.'

[88] See PD 46, para 1.1.

[89] After *In re Buckton* [1907] 2 Ch 406.

66.39 Each case will be decided on its own facts, but misconduct on the part of the trustee may result not only in the trustee being denied their costs, but also in them being condemned in costs (see 66.46–66.55).[90] Where the trustee was acting unreasonably in bringing or defending a claim, the putative trustee may be deprived of their costs from the fund.[91] This may extend to the costs of entire proceedings if they were brought unnecessarily.[92] Where the proceedings were not brought or defended in the capacity of trustee, the trustee may or may not be denied their costs, depending on the circumstances (see 66.40–66.41). Where the proceedings are brought for their own private benefit, the trustee may be deprived of their costs, or part of them, and may be required to pay costs[93] (see 66.46–66.58).

Errors as to status and disputed trusts

66.40 Where a person reasonably pursues a claim believing themselves to be a trustee, they may still be entitled to their costs out of the fund (or part of them) even if it is ultimately shown that they were not a trustee.[94]

66.41 Likewise, where there is a disputed trust that is set aside, it will not automatically be the case that the person who was acting as trustee will be deprived of costs.[95] Given the facts that the would-be trustee would usually be the loser and that there may be no fund upon which to draw, it is not surprising that Kekewich J described the discretion as being difficult to exercise.[96] That said, the modern law is that the would-be trustee would often be penalised in costs as a result of having acted unreasonably.[97] This may be on the grounds that they incurred expenditure and liabilities in an unsuccessful effort to prefer one class of beneficiaries (for example the express beneficiaries specified in the trust instrument) over another (for example the trustees in bankruptcy or creditors), thereby acting otherwise than for the benefit of the trust. Each case will, however, be decided on its own facts.

Costs of appeals

66.42 A distinction is made between the costs of appeals brought by the trustee and the costs of appeals brought by others. In general, the principle that costs should be paid from the trust regardless of the outcome will apply only at first instance and not on appeal. Where a trustee brings an appeal concerning the law or administration of the trust, the trustee may be at risk of bearing those costs personally.[98] The trustee who appealed will

---

90 See, eg, *Re Knox's Trusts* [1895] 2 Ch 483, CA. A trustee cannot easily avoid liability by pointing to a specific provision within the trust instrument providing that the beneficiary must bear their share of proceedings instituted by them: see *Re Williams, Williams v Williams* [1912] 1 Ch 399.

91 See, eg, *Holding Ltd v Property Trust plc* [1989] 1 WLR 1313 (trustee of a maintenance fund for a block of flats sought to increase expenditure in a way that was adverse to the tenants' interests and was not supported by either the tenants or the landlord).

92 See, eg, *Horner v Wheelwright* (1857) 2 Jur NS 367.

93 See, eg, *Re Dargie, Miller v Thornton-Jones* [1954] Ch 16, at 20–1; historically, see *Henley v Philips* (1740) 2 Atk 48.

94 *In re Preston's Estate* [1951] 1 Ch 878.

95 *Ideal Bedding Co Ltd v Holland* [1907] 2 Ch 157.

96 *In re Buckton* [1907] 2 Ch 406.

97 *Alsop Wilkinson (a firm) v Neary* [1996] 1 WLR 1220, at 1225.

98 *Re Earl of Radnor's Will Trust* (1890) 45 Ch D 402, CA.

need to show exceptional circumstances to recover those costs from the fund; exceptional circumstances may exist where the appeal was in the interests of other persons (such as those yet to be born). Where the appeal is brought by others, a trustee will often be allowed costs[99]—especially in the Court of Appeal[100] and especially where the trustee is supporting a previously made order concerning the administration of the trust.[101] The *Buckton* categories (see 66.46 *et seq*) will not, in general, apply to the costs of appeals.[102] The difference between appeals and litigation at first instance was described by Carnwath J in the following way:

> 'So one sees that where there is a genuine difficulty, trustees, and by analogy beneficiaries, may be able to seek authoritative guidance of the High Court at the expense of the fund, but once such guidance has been obtained from the High Court's decision, then in the absence of some special circumstances, such for example as difficulties arising from that decision itself, the parties have the authoritative guidance they need. The fact that they do not like it is not a reason for litigating further at the expense of the fund. That principle would apply equally in this case. The judgment provides the sort of clear guidance which is required under the *Buckton* approach, and the fact that some of the parties do not like it would not justify the costs of the appeal.'[103]

Thus pre-emptive orders are unlikely to be made in respect of the costs of appeals.[104]

Controlling costs in disputes regarding trusts

Special provisions apply to costs incurred in proceedings in relation to trust funds, which provisions are intended to make it easier for the court to make a costs capping order. Those provisions are found in PD 3F, para 5, which reads as follows: **66.43**

> **'Section II – Costs Capping Orders In Relation To Trust Funds**
>
> 5.1 In this Section "trust fund" means property which is the subject of a trust, and includes the estate of a deceased person.
>
> 5.2 This Section contains additional provisions to enable—
> (a) the parties to consider whether to apply for; and
> (b) the court to consider whether to make of its own initiative,
> a costs capping order in proceedings relating to trust funds.
>
> 5.3 This Section supplements rules 3.19 to 3.21 and Section I of this Practice Direction.
>
> 5.4 Any party to such proceedings who intends to apply for an order for the payment of costs out of the trust fund must file and serve on all other parties written notice of that intention together with an estimate of the costs likely to be incurred by that party.
>
> 5.5 The documents mentioned in paragraph 5.4 must be filed and served—
> (a) in a Part 7 claim, with the first statement of case; and

---

99 Each case will be determined on its own facts. One factor that might be relevant is whether the trustee was put on notice that there may be an objection to paying their costs: see *Re Stuart, Johnson v Williams* [1940] 4 All ER 80, at 82, *per* Clauson LJ.

100 *Ibid.*

101 See, eg, *Chettiar v Chettiar (No 2)* [1962] 2 All ER 238, at 245.

102 See, eg, *Chessels v British Telecommunications plc* [2002] Pens LR 141; *HR Trustees Ltd v German & IMG (UK) Ltd* [2010] EWHC 3467 (Ch).

103 *Laws v National Grid Plc* [1998] PLR 295, at 314.

104 *Chessels v British Telecommunications plc* [2002] Pens LR 141, *per* Laddie J.

(b) in a Part 8 claim, with the evidence (or, if a defendant does not intend to serve and file evidence, with the acknowledgement of service).

5.6 When proceedings first come before the court for directions the court may make a costs capping order of its own initiative whether or not any party has applied for such an order.'

66.44 Unless the court so orders, the provisions regarding budgeting do not apply to claims begun under CPR, Part 8 (see CPR, r 3.12). As such, if any party believes that a budget needs to be set, an application will have to be made accordingly.

Costs incurred by beneficiaries

66.45 A beneficiary would normally be entitled to payment of their costs from the estate in accordance with the terms of the trust. Any beneficiary may be entitled to their costs, regardless of their status.[105] Where a beneficiary brings a claim for the administration of the estate, they may be entitled to costs from the trustee personally if the trustee is found to have brought the claim upon themselves by reason of their own default or neglect.[106] The same is true if the claim is for an account that the trustee has brought upon themselves.[107] Where, however, the beneficiary is found to have commenced the claim too hastily or without good reason, they may be ordered to bear the costs personally.[108]

Costs of proceedings as between trustee and beneficiary (and others)

66.46 Disputes may be 'friendly'[109] or 'hostile'.[110] Lightman J has identified three types of dispute in which costs may be sought against a trustee—as opposed to where a trustee may be denied their costs from the fund (see 66.38–66.42).[111] This classification can be combined with the better known taxonomy identified by Kekewich J—known as the *Buckton* categories[112]—to produce the following.

- **Trust disputes** In general, these are proceedings for the construction of a trust instrument or guidance on some other question of law concerning the administration of the trust. They may include the following.[113]
  - ***Buckton* category (1)** Friendly (or amicable) claims brought by the trustee (see 66.48)
  - ***Buckton* category (2)** Friendly claims brought by a person other than the trustee, usually a beneficiary (see 66.49)
  - ***Buckton* category (3)** Hostile (or adverse) claims brought by person other than the trustee, usually a beneficiary (see 66.50)

---

105 Where the Attorney-General, acting under a certificate issued to him under Charitable Trusts Act 1853, s 20, takes out an originating summons for the determination of a question of construction relating to charitable bequests under a will, as representing the objects of a charity, he is in the same position as any other beneficiary and is entitled to costs out of the estate: *In re Cardwell, A-G v Day* [1912] 1 Ch 779.

106 See, eg, *Re Skinner, Cooper v Skinner* [1904] 1 Ch 289.

107 See, eg, *Re Holton's Settlement Trusts, Holton v Holton* (1918) 88 LJ Ch 444.

108 See, eg, *Re Dartnall, Sawyer v Goddard* [1895] 1 Ch 474, CA.

109 Such as a dispute as to the true construction of the trust instrument.

110 Such as a challenge to the validity of the trust.

111 *Alsop Wilkinson (a firm) v Neary* [1996] 1 WLR 1220.

112 After *In re Buckton* [1907] 2 Ch 406.

113 *Ibid.*

- **Beneficiaries' disputes** These, in general, are hostile disputes in which the trustee's actions or inactions are challenged. Such disputes may, for example, take the form of proceedings for breach of trust and/or an order removing the trustees.
- **Third-party disputes** These are disputes with persons other than beneficiaries. An example would be a dispute with a contractor about payment under a contract for services provided to the trust.

There may be overlap between these categories; moreover, not every case of construction or dispute about the administration of the trust will fall within the *Buckton* categories.[114] Arden LJ has explained that the *Buckton* categories are not closed and that a further category may exist where the issue of construction is being pursued not only by a beneficiary in a way that is analogous to category (2) (see 66.49), but also by a third party for its own separate interests.[115] She implied that more categories may exist. Where a case falls outside the classic *Buckton* categories, it may be necessary to consider novel ways of meeting the justice of the situation. Moreover, the guidance in *Buckton* is not mandatory. In this regard, Warren J had this to say: **66.47**

> 'There is always room ... for an exceptional case to be dealt with on its own facts; and, indeed, when a case does not fall neatly within any of the *Buckton* categories, the court must exercise its statutory jurisdiction in the way it considers best to achieve fairness and justice.'[116]

Buckton *category (1): amicable claim brought by the trustee*

Buckton category (1) claims are brought for the benefit of both the trustee and the beneficiaries. Regardless of the outcome, the costs of the parties are generally treated as necessarily incurred for the benefit of the trust. An example might be where the parties ask the court to construe the instrument of trust. Kekewich J regarded the costs of the parties in such cases as necessarily incurred for the benefit of the trust; hence, provided that the claim was reasonable and was brought in good faith, the usual order would be that costs were to be paid out of the fund. **66.48**

Buckton *category (2): amicable claim brought by a person other than the trustee*

Claims in *Buckton* category (2) differ in form, not in substance, from claims in the first category. They are claims that would have fallen into category (1) if they had been brought by the trustee, but—for one reason or another—they have in fact been brought by someone other than the trustee (usually a beneficiary). Costs are dealt with as per *Buckton* category (1). **66.49**

Buckton *category (3): adverse claim brought by a beneficiary*

Claims in *Buckton* category (3) differ in substance from those in the other two categories. They are often also referred to as 'hostile claims' or 'adverse claims'. Such claims are usually made by a beneficiary and may be adverse to other beneficiaries. Kekewich J had this to say: **66.50**

---

[114] See, eg, *Green (as administratrix of the Estate of Peter Maclean Maitland, dec'd) v Astor* [2013] EWHC 1857 (Ch), at [54]–[58], *per* Roth LJ.

[115] *Singapore Airlines Ltd & Anor v Buck Consultants Ltd* [2011] EWCA Civ 1542, at [75].

[116] See *IBM United Kingdom Pensions Trust Ltd v Metcalfe* [2012] EWHC 125 (Ch), at [20]; see also *Green (as administratrix of the Estate of Peter Maclean Maitland, dec'd) v Astor* [2013] EWHC 1857 (Ch), at [48], *per* Roth LJ.

'It is often difficult to discriminate between cases of the second and third classes, but when [a claim falls in the third category] I apply the rule which ought, I think, to be rigidly enforced in adverse litigation, and order the unsuccessful party to pay the costs. Whether he ought to be ordered to pay the costs of the trustees, who are, of course, respondents, or not, is sometimes open to question, but with this possible exception the unsuccessful party bears the costs of all whom he has brought before the Court.'[117]

Thus, where a claim falls within *Buckton* category (3), the general rule applies (that is, the loser pays costs to the winner[118]), but the court is able, in an appropriate case, to order the loser to pay the trustee's costs. It seems that Kekewich J particularly had in mind the situation in which two or more beneficiaries raise mutually antagonistic arguments.

66.51 Where a beneficiary argues for one particular construction against the interests of another beneficiary and where this has a bearing on the beneficiaries' respective shares of the fund, it would usually be the case that the costs would be borne by the losing beneficiary. This is because it would be unjust to impose upon the successful beneficiary the burden of paying for the litigation out of funds successfully obtained.[119] This would particularly be so if the losing beneficiary were litigating for personal gain.[120]

66.52 Where a trustee pursues a hopeless case, they will do so on the basis that they are at risk on costs.[121] The same will apply if they adopt a role that is not neutral.[122] Similarly, where a trustee behaves unreasonably, they will be at risk.[123]

66.53 Issues-based orders may be made—in particular, if, in a *Buckton* category (1) or (2) claim, a party uses the litigation as an opportunity to raise issues not germane to the issues before the court, they may be condemned to pay the costs that were incurred as a result.[124] Similarly, if a party behaves unreasonably (such as where a trustee fails to provide information that ought to have been provided[125]), they may be condemned to pay costs.

66.54 Whilst a more robust attitude to costs is appropriate under the CPR than that discussed in *Buckton*, Kekewich J's guidelines remain relevant and have not been superseded.[126] Other pre-CPR authorities must be treated with due caution, however. Appeals are in a class of their own (see 66.42), and where a trustee brings an appeal concerning the law or administration of the trust, as well as being at risk of bearing their own costs personally (see above), they may also be at risk of having to personally bear the other side's costs.

---

117 *In re Buckton* [1907] 2 Ch 406, at 041500.

118 See, eg, *Williams v Jones* (1886) 34 Ch D 120. For a recent affirmation of the principle that the normal costs rules apply, see *Davies v Watkins* [2012] EWCA Civ 1570, at [23], *per* Lloyd LJ.

119 *In re Halson* [1912] 1 Ch 439.

120 See, eg, *Pell Frischmann Consultants Ltd v Prabhu* [2013] EWHC 2203 (Ch), at [59] and [60], *per* Penelope Reed QC.

121 *In re Preston's Estate* [1951] 1 Ch 878.

122 See, eg, *Breadner v Granville-Grossman (Costs)* [2001] WTLR 377, *per* Park J.

123 See, eg, *In the Matter of the Administration of the Estate of Jimmy Savile* [2014] EWHC 1683 (Ch), in which an award was made against a trustee who had withheld their arguments until trial.

124 See, eg, *Grender v Dresden* [2009] EWHC 500 (Ch), in which Norris J made an order on the indemnity basis against such a party.

125 See, eg, *Curtis v Pulbrook* [2009] EWHC 1370 (Ch), *per* Richard Sheldon QC.

126 *D'Abo v Paget (No 2)* (2000) The Times, 10 August, *per* Lawrence Collins QC.

Where a defaulting trustee is ordered to pay costs, it will usually be on the standard basis.[127] Arden LJ has explained that there is a close analogy between the position of a trustee and a director in this regard[128]—although there are exceptions to the standard basis in the case of a defaulting trustee, such as where the trustee has acted wholly unreasonably. **66.55**

Pre-emptive orders and applications for directions

The court has an exceptional jurisdiction,[129] which must be exercised in accordance with the rules of court and established principles,[130] to make a pre-emptive order (sometimes also called a prospective costs order) as to whether costs should be paid out of the fund.[131] The jurisdiction to make such an order is modern—that is, found in Senior Courts Act 1981, s 51(3), and probably CPR, r 3.1(2)(m)—but it is based on principles that have a long lineage.[132] Laddie J described the discretion in this way: **66.56**

> 'For most purposes a trust is treated like any other litigant. If it brings or is embroiled in civil litigation with others, the basic rule that costs follow the event applies. However, whatever the relationship may be between the trust and opponents, special provisions as to costs need to be put in place as between the trust and the trustees. ... The trust is operated by the trustees for the beneficiaries' benefit. It may be appropriate for the trustees to seek the assistance of the court in determining how the trust instrument should be construed or as to the proper administration of the trust so as to enable them to execute their duties properly. They can then act in accordance with that guidance without fear that they are in breach of their duties to the beneficiaries.'[133]

Laddie J went on to explain that there are two types of case in which such a pre-emptive order might be appropriate: **66.57**

> 'First the trustees may need to advance claims against, or defend against claims brought by, third parties which could affect the estate. If they bring the proceedings or defend them properly for the benefit of the estate, they will be entitled to be reimbursed for their costs from the estate, even if they lose in the litigation. However waiting until the end of the litigation for an order for indemnification to be made could place an unreasonable burden on the trustees. Therefore it is open to them, and prudent, to make an application to the court for permission to bring or defend the proceedings on the basis of a pre-emptive indemnity out of the estate for the costs of doing so: see *re Beddoe* [1893] 1 Ch 547. It does not matter what the outcome of the litigation is. Because they will be acting for the benefit of the trust estate, they are protected.
>
> ... There is a second group of cases in which the trustees can seek an order for costs out of the estate. These are cases in which the trustees want guidance from the court as to their powers or duties. There may not be opponents as such. The trustees' actions are to ensure proper administration of the trust and are therefore for the benefit of the trust as a whole.

[127] *Bartlett v Barclays Bank Trust Co Ltd* [1980] Ch 515, referred to with apparent approval by Arden LJ in *Carlisle & Cumbria United Independent Supports' Society Ltd v CUFC Holding Ltd* [2010] EWCA Civ 463, at [23].

[128] *Carlisle & Cumbria United Independent Supports' Society Ltd v CUFC Holding Ltd* [2010] EWCA Civ 463, at [23].

[129] See *Alsop Wilkinson (a firm) v Neary* [1996] 1 WLR 1220.

[130] See *Machin v National Power* [1998] OPLR 187.

[131] See PD 64A, para 6.3.

[132] *Re Beddoe* [1893] 1 Ch 457; see also *Re Buckton* [1907] 2 Ch 406, at 414.

[133] *Chessels v British Telecommunications plc* [2002] Pens LR 141, at [45]–[46].

For that reason, in such cases the trustees are indemnified out of the estate for the cost of seeking help from the court.'[134]

66.58 Where a trustee does not have, or decides not to exercise, a power to enter or pay costs, the trustee or any other party concerned may apply to the court at any stage of proceedings for an order that the costs of any party (including the costs of the trustees) shall be paid out of the fund.[135] (If, however, the trustee has the power to make the payment out of the fund, then they may do so without obtaining an order[136] and, where this is so, CPR, r 44.5, will apply.[137]) When an application is made, the orders that the court may make are set out in PD 64A, para 6.4:

'6.4 The court, on an application for a prospective costs order, may—
(a) in the case of the trustees' costs, authorise the trustees to raise and meet such costs out of the fund;
(b) in the case of the costs of any other party, authorise or direct the trustees to pay such costs (or any part of them, or the costs incurred up to a particular time) out of the trust fund to be assessed, if not agreed by the trustees, on the indemnity basis or, if the court directs, on the standard basis, and to make payments from time to time on account of such costs. A model form of order is annexed to this Practice Direction.'

66.59 Where a pre-emptive order is made for the benefit of a trustee in a claim brought by or against a third party, it is often referred to as a '*Beddoe* order'.[138] The most common type of pre-emptive order is also that which affords the greatest protection: it is an order by which the trustee is awarded costs out of the fund in any event (that is, regardless of whether they win or lose).[139] There is pre-CPR authority to suggest that an application for a pre-emptive order can be made even where proceedings have been begun and the trustees are already parties.[140] Lloyd LJ has explained that this is only a particular example of the sort of application that trustees can make to the court for guidance if they are in doubt as to what course to take in the execution of the relevant trusts.[141] In addition to applications regarding litigation, such applications may seek directions such as to whether to accept an offer to purchase a trust asset or whether to take particular steps to sell such an asset.

66.60 Pre-emptive orders may be made for the benefit of persons other than the trustee, such as a representative beneficiary.[142] This might be appropriate where a beneficiary with a limited interest seeks to vindicate the right of others or where a beneficiary brings proceedings to determine an administrative issue for the purposes of ensuring the proper running of the trust.[143] A pre-emptive order may be made in respect of a representative notwithstanding the fact that they have not been formally appointed as a representative under CPR,

---

134 *Ibid*, at [46]–[48].
135 See PD 64A, para 6.3.
136 See PD 64A, para 6.2.
137 See PD 64A, para 6.2.
138 After *Re Beddoe* [1893] 1 Ch 457.
139 *Re Dallaway (dec'd)* [1982] 1 WLR 756.
140 *Westdock Realisations Ltd* [1988] BCLC 354.
141 *Davies v Watkins* [2012] EWCA Civ 1570, at [23].
142 See, eg, *In re AXA Equity & Law Life Assurance Society plc (No 1)* (2001) 2 BCLC 447; *Wallerstiener v Moir* [1975] QB 373. See also 66.66 and, in so far as derivative claims are concerned, 65.124.
143 For example, minority shareholder's actions were treated like *Beddoe* cases in *Wallersteiner v Moir (No 2)* [1975] QB 373.

r 19.7(2).[144] Where more than one class of beneficiary can be identified, it may be appropriate to make a pre-emptive order that allows for the costs of separate representation for each of those classes.[145]

The mere fact that a trustee chooses not to apply for a pre-emptive order should not be taken as indicative of wilful wrongdoing and would not constitute a breach of trust.[146] That said, a trustee who defends proceedings brought by a representative without obtaining their own pre-emptive order will be at risk on costs and this may be so even if the trustee was advised by counsel that they had a good defence to the claim.[147] **66.61**

The exercise of the court's discretion will depend on the facts of each case.[148] Four elements of discretion are particularly relevant to the issue of whether a pre-emptive costs order should be made: **66.62**

- the merits of the claim (see 66.63);
- the likely order as to costs (see 66.64);
- the justice of the matter (see 66.65); and
- other factors (see 66.66).[149]

Pre-emptive orders and the merits of the proposed litigation

The merits of the claim or defence in question are of importance when considering whether that claim or defence are to be financed out of the fund.[150] A pre-emptive order should not be used to require a fund (or any person) to pay unconditionally for a claim that is not brought on reasonable grounds or is brought in bad faith.[151] Where a *Beddoe* order is sought, the trustee is required to make full disclosure of the strengths and weaknesses of their case.[152] The court then assesses whether to give permission and, in so doing, it does not determine whether the trustee will win or lose, but only whether the decision to litigate it is a proper exercise of the trustee's duties to the trust.[153] **66.63**

Pre-emptive orders and the likely order to be made as to costs

In general,[154] a pre-emptive order should be made only if the court is satisfied that, at the end of the proceedings, no other order regarding costs could properly be made.[155] In this **66.64**

144 *IBM United Kingdom Pensions Trust Ltd v Metcalfe* [2012] EWHC 125 (Ch).
145 See, eg, *Re British Airways Pension Schemes* [2000] Pens LR 311, *per* Park J.
146 See *Bonham v Blake Lapthorne Linell and Fishwick* [2006] EWHC 2513 (Ch), *per* Kitchin J.
147 *Singh v Bhasin* [2000] WTLR 275, *per* Mr Alan Boyle QC.
148 *Re Evans (dec'd)* [1986] 1 WLR 101.
149 *Re Biddencare Ltd* [1994] 2 BCLC 160; *Alsop Wilkinson (a firm) v Neary* [1996] 1 WLR 1220.
150 *Re Evans (dec'd)* [1986] 1 WLR 101.
151 *Re Wedstock Realisations Ltd* [1988] BCLC 354. For an example of a claim that failed the merits test, see *Trustee Corpn Ltd v Nadir* (2001) The Independent, 29 January.
152 See *McDonald v Horn* [1995] 1 All ER 961, at 970, *per* Hoffmann LJ; *Chessels v British Telecommunications plc* [2002] Pens LR 141, at [47], *per* Laddie J.
153 *Chessels v British Telecommunications plc* [2002] Pens LR 141, at [47], *per* Laddie J.
154 To an extent, by analogy with derivative claims, pension fund cases are an exception: see 66.66.
155 *Chessels v British Telecommunications plc* [2002] Pens LR 141, at [54] (but see fn 174); see also *Re Wedstock Realisations Ltd* [1988] BCLC 354. In *McDonald v Horn* [1995] 1 All ER 961, at 972, Hoffmann LJ said: 'I think that before granting a pre-emptive application in ordinary trust litigation or proceedings concerning the ownership of a fund held by a trustee or other fiduciary, the judge must be satisfied that the judge at the trial could properly exercise his discretion only by ordering the applicant's costs to be paid out of the fund. Otherwise the order may indeed fetter the judge's discretion.'

regard, the nature of the litigation is relevant: if the litigation is a 'trust dispute' or a 'third-party dispute'—that is, *Buckton* categories (1) and (2) (see 66.48)—then it is likely that the trustee will recover their costs from the fund in any event, but if it is a 'beneficiaries dispute' (*Buckton* category (3)), then costs will probably follow the event. In particular, where it is a hostile beneficiaries dispute (that is, where it is adverse to the trustee), the court should make a pre-emptive order only if satisfied that the trustee could not properly be deprived of their costs from the fund.[156] Hoffmann LJ has explained that the court may sometimes be sufficiently confident that the claim is within *Buckton* categories (1) or (2) to be able to make a pre-emptive order that parties other than the trustees are to have their costs in any event.[157] The fact that no other order could be made at the end of the proceedings is close to being a condition prerequisite. In particular, Hoffmann LJ has explained that, in cases in which it is not clear that the trial judge would be bound to make an order in favour of the applicant, the court would be 'very reluctant to make a prospective order'.[158]

Pre-emptive orders and the justice of the matter

66.65 The order should not be one that will defeat the justice of the situation. For example, if a beneficiary brings a claim that, if successful, would result in their winning the property in the trust, it might be unfair to burden the trust pre-emptively with the costs of the trustee if the reality is that this would mean that the successful beneficiary might be indirectly condemned to pay the unsuccessful trustee's costs.[159]

Other factors relating to pre-emptive orders and applications for directions

66.66 The following miscellaneous points can be made.

- **Disputed trusts** If the existence of the trust is in dispute or if there is a dispute as to whether a litigant is a trustee, then it would usually be inappropriate to make a pre-emptive order.[160]
- **Appeals** For the reasons set out at 66.42, a litigant is not generally able to rely on the *Buckton* categories on appeal. In particular, proceedings that would, at first instance, have been in either of *Buckton* categories (1) or (2) would, on appeal, generally cease to be regarded as being brought for the purposes of seeking guidance as to the construction or administration of the trust (see 66.42).[161] It is possible, however, for alternative grounds for a pre-emptive order to be made out. For example, if the applicant beneficiaries are not volunteers, such as where they are beneficiaries to a pension fund (see below), special principles may apply.[162] This may apply both in hostile litigation and in cases that, at first instance, would be in one or other of *Buckton* categories (1) and (2).[163]

---

156 *Chessels v British Telecommunications plc* [2002] Pens LR 141.

157 See *McDonald v Horn* [1995] 1 All ER 961, at 971, *per* Hoffmann LJ. Such orders have been made at the request of, or with the support of, the trustee or other fiduciary bringing the proceedings: see *Re Exchange Securities and Commodities Ltd (No 2)* [1985] BCLC 392, at 395.

158 *McDonald v Horn* [1995] 1 All ER 961, at 971. As an example of a case in which an order was not made, see *Re Charge Card Services Ltd* [1987] Ch 150.

159 See, eg, *Re Evans (dec'd)* [1986] 1 WLR 101.

160 See, eg, *R v National Anti-Vivisection Society Ltd v Duddington* (1989) The Times, 23 November, *per* Mummery J.

161 See also *Chessels v British Telecommunications plc* [2002] Pens LR 141; *HR Trustees Ltd v German & IMG (UK) Ltd* [2010] EWHC 3467 (Ch), at [40].

162 *McDonald v Horn* [1995] 1 All ER 961, at 973–5.

163 *HR Trustees Ltd v German & IMG (UK) Ltd* [2010] EWHC 3467 (Ch), at [41]–[52], *per* Arnold J.

- **Representative trustees** If litigation is necessary to resolve a large number of similar disputes or to resolve a representative dispute that might affect a large number of persons, then the interests of justice might require that a party who is to be a representative trustee is properly funded.[164] An example of this would be where funding is necessary for the purposes of testing the arguments of other parties.[165] In this regard, the applicant's access to other means of funding is a relevant factor.[166] The jurisdiction to make a pre-emptive order benefiting a representative trustee was held not to be dependent upon their appointment as a representative under CPR, r 19.7(2).[167] Pension funds held in trust are often regarded as comparable[168] (see below).
- **Trustees who sought the role** If a person becomes a trustee not by having that role thrust upon them, but as a result of having sought it out, then that may be a factor that the court can take into account—especially where the motive for doing so is self-interest.[169]
- **Poor conduct by beneficiaries** Where a beneficiary's unreasonable conduct had caused substantial costs to be incurred by forcing a trustee to apply to court for directions (such as approving a settlement), then the beneficiary should ordinarily bear those costs rather than the estate.[170]
- **Pension funds** The leading authority on the principles to be applied to applications for prospective costs orders in pension fund cases is the decision of the Court of Appeal in *McDonald v Horn*.[171] After he had noted that the general principles that apply to trustees and beneficiaries apply to cases involving pensions funds, Hoffmann LJ found that, in principle, the ability of the court to make a pre-emptive order that a company should indemnify a claimant against liability for costs incurred in a derivative claim (see 65.123–65.125)—which, at the time, was known as a '*Wallersteiner and Moir* order',[172] but which is now governed by CPR, r 19.9—may extend by analogy to pension fund members.[173] Hoffmann LJ went on to say that the power to make such an order should be exercised with caution as a result of 'the dangers of too easily making orders which allow minority shareholders to litigate at the cost of the company', but that this did not mean undertaking a close examination of the merits of the dispute.[174] It is not a pre-requisite to a pre-emptive order being made that it be shown that the trial judge could properly exercise their discretion only by ordering that costs be paid out of the trust estate.[175]

---

[164] See, eg, *IBM Pensions Trust Ltd v Metcalfe* [2012] EWHC 125 (Ch).

[165] See, eg, *In re AXA Equity & Law Life Assurance Society plc (No 1)* (2001) 2 BCLC 447.

[166] *Trustee Corpn Ltd v Nadir* (2001) The Independent, 29 January.

[167] *IBM Pensions Trust Ltd v Metcalfe* [2012] EWHC 125 (Ch), at [23]–[25], *per* Warren J.

[168] See, eg, *Spencer v Fielder* [2014] EWHC 2768 (Ch).

[169] See, eg, *Vallee v Birchwook* [2013] EWHC 1449 (Ch), at [44]–[56], *per* Jonathan Gaunt QC.

[170] See *Green (as administratrix of the Estate of Peter Maclean Maitland, dec'd) v Astor* [2013] EWHC 1857 (Ch), at [54]–[58], *per* Roth LJ.

[171] *McDonald v Horn* [1995] 1 All ER 961.

[172] After *Wallersteiner v Moir (No 2)* [1975] QB 373.

[173] See *McDonald v Horn* [1995] 1 All ER 961, at 972j–973e.

[174] See *ibid*, at 974e.

[175] See *Alsop Wilkinson v Neary* [1995] 1 All ER 431, at 437; *HR Trustees Ltd v German & IMG (UK) Ltd* [2010] EWHC 3467 (Ch), at [43], *per* Arnold J. In this regard, Arnold J doubted Laddie J's reasoning in *Chessels v British Telecommunications plc* [2002] Pens LR 141, at [55]–[58]: see *HR Trustees Ltd v German & IMG (UK) Ltd* [2010] EWHC 3467 (Ch), [44]–[52]. See also *Re British Airways Pension Schemes* [2000] Pens LR 311, *per* Park J; *Stevens v Bell (Costs)* [2001] OPLR 123, *per* Park J.

The costs of the application for a pre-emptive order

66.67 As regards the costs of the application for directions and a pre-emptive order, the normal rule is that, absent improper conduct, the costs of the trustee and of the beneficiary defendants will be paid out of the trust fund.[176]

The procedure regarding applications for pre-emptive orders

66.68 Applications for pre-emptive orders are made under CPR, r 64.2, and must be made by issuing a Part 8 claim form where no claim is already in existence.[177] A model form of order can be found at the end of PD 64A.[178] The following is only a brief summary of the applicable procedure; reference ought to be made to PD 64B and PD 64A, para 6,[179] for further guidance.

66.69 All of the trustees must be parties and any trustee who does not consent to being a claimant must be made a defendant.[180] The trustees' evidence should be given by witness statement. To ensure that, if directions are given, the trustees are properly protected by the order, they must ensure full disclosure of relevant matters, even if the case is to proceed with the participation of beneficiaries as defendants.[181] PD 64A, para 6.7, makes the following provisions:

> '6.7 The evidence in support of an application for a prospective costs order should be given by witness statement. The trustees and the applicant (if different) must ensure full disclosure of the relevant matters to show that the case is one which falls within the category of case where a prospective costs order can properly be made.'

66.70 Whilst, in some cases, it would not be appropriate to include all of the items,[182] applications for directions whether or not to take or defend or pursue litigation should be supported by evidence of:

- the advice of an appropriately qualified lawyer as to the prospects of success;
- an estimate in summary form of:
  - the value or other significance to the trust estate of the issues in the proceedings;
  - the costs likely to be incurred by the trustees in the proceedings, by reference to the principal stages in the proceedings; and
  - the costs of other parties to the proceedings for which, if unsuccessful, the trustees may be exposed to liability;
- any known facts concerning the means of other parties to the proceedings;
- any other factors relevant to the court's decision whether to give the directions sought;[183]

---

176 See *Davies v Watkins* [2012] EWCA Civ 1570, at [26], *per* Lloyd LJ.

177 See CPR, r 64.3.

178 PD 64A, para 6.8, provides that the model form of order 'is designed for use in the more straightforward cases, where a question needs to be determined which has arisen in the administration of the trust, whether the claimants are the trustees or a beneficiary. The form may be adapted for use in less straightforward cases, in particular where the proceedings are hostile, but special factors may also have to be reflected in the terms of the order in such a case.'

179 Or, in the Chancery Division, to HM Courts & Tribunals Service, *Chancery Guide* (London: HMSO, 2016), paras 29.18–29.19.

180 CPR, r 64.4.

181 See PD 64B, para 7.1. See also PD 64B, para 7.2, which provides that where an application is made for directions whether to take or defend or pursue litigation, it should be supported by evidence that includes details relating to costs.

182 See *Davies v Watkins* [2012] EWCA Civ 1570, at [45], *per* Lloyd LJ.

183 See PD 64B, para 7.5.

- a statement as to whether the Practice Direction (Pre-Action Conduct) or any relevant pre-action protocol has been complied with;[184] and
- a statement as to whether the trustees have proposed or undertaken, or intend to propose, alternative dispute resolution (ADR) and (in each case) if not, why not.[185]

The qualifications of the lawyer should be stated. If the advice is given on formal instructions, the instructions should always be put in evidence as well, so that the court can see the basis on which the advice was given. If it is not given on instructions, the advice must state fully the basis on which it is given.[186] If confidentiality of the directions sought is important (for example where the directions relate to actual or proposed litigation with a third party who could find out what directions the trustees are seeking through access to the claim form under CPR, r 5.4), the statement of the remedy sought may be expressed in general terms. The trustees must, in that case, state specifically in the evidence what it is that they seek to be allowed to do.[187] **66.71**

PD 64A, paras 6.5 and 6.6, make the following provisions regarding hearings: **66.72**

> '6.5 The court will always consider whether it is possible to deal with the application for a prospective costs order on paper without a hearing and in an ordinary case would expect to be able to do so. The trustees must consider whether a hearing is needed for any reason. If they consider that it is they should say so and explain why in their evidence. If any party to the application referred to in paragraph 6.1 above (or any other person interested in the trust fund) considers that a hearing is necessary (for instance because he wishes to oppose the making of a prospective costs order) this should be stated, and the reasons explained, in his evidence, if any, or otherwise in a letter to the court.
>
> 6.6 If the court would be minded to refuse the application on a consideration of the papers alone, the parties will be notified and given the opportunity, within a stated time, to ask for a hearing.'

As of 1 October 2011, PD 64B, para 6.1, has provided that the court will dispose of the application without a hearing, if it considers that to do so will save time or expense and that a hearing is not necessary. As such, applicants must consider whether a hearing is necessary and, if so, explain why in their evidence. Where the court deals with an application without a hearing, it will give the parties an opportunity, within a stated time, to apply to vary or discharge the order at an oral hearing.[188] **66.73**

As of 6 April 2015, masters now have the same jurisdiction as judges to deal with applications.[189] The application must be made to a master other than the assigned master dealing with the main litigation. The application will normally be heard by a master, unless the master refers it to a judge. District judges, however, may deal with such applications only with the consent of their supervising judge.[190] **66.74**

---

[184] In this regard, it may be relevant that Practice Direction (Pre-action Conduct), para 2.2, does not apply to 'most applications for directions by a trustee or other fiduciary'.
[185] See PD 64B, para 7.2.
[186] PD 64B, para 7.3.
[187] See PD 64B, para 2.
[188] See PD 64B, para 6.2.
[189] See PD 2B.
[190] PD 2B, para 7B.2(c).

The principles of assessment of trustees' costs

66.75 It will often be the case that the dispute as to what is and is not payable will be dealt with item by item on the assessment, rather than as a matter of principle at the time a costs order is made. As mentioned above, costs are assessed on the indemnity basis.

66.76 Costs improperly[191] or unnecessarily[192] incurred will not be payable.[193] Under the Rules of the Supreme Court (RSC), costs were presumed to have been unreasonably incurred if they were incurred contrary to the duty of the trustee.[194] This rule is not expressly preserved in the CPR, but that is not likely to mean that such costs would be recoverable. Where the cost are payable directly out of a fund, special procedural provisions apply (see 66.**80**–66.84).

66.77 In so far as proceedings are concerned, PD 46, paras 1.1 and 1.2, give the following additional guidance:

> '1.1 A trustee or personal representative is entitled to an indemnity out of the relevant trust fund or estate for costs properly incurred. Whether costs were properly incurred depends on all the circumstances of the case including whether the trustee or personal representative ("the trustee")—
> (a) obtained directions from the court before bringing or defending the proceedings;[[195]]
> (b) acted in the interests of the fund or estate or in substance for a benefit other than that of the estate, including the trustee's own; and
> (c) acted in some way unreasonably in bringing or defending, or in the conduct of, the proceedings.
>
> 1.2 The trustee is not to be taken to have acted for a benefit other than that of the fund by reason only that the trustee has defended a claim in which relief is sought against the trustee personally.'

Monies disbursed prior to appointment

66.78 Where, prior to their appointment, a trustee has incurred funds setting up the trust or obtaining a statement of trust property, they will be entitled to be reimbursed those monies out of the estate notwithstanding the fact that they were not appointed at the time those monies were disbursed.[196]

More than one trustee

66.79 There is a long-standing practice that, where there is more than one trustee, the costs of only one of them will be allowed[197] unless separate representation was necessary, such as where one of them is subject to a hostile attack[198] or where one of them is a beneficiary,[199] etc.

---

191 *Hosegood v Pedler* (1896) 66 LJQB 18.

192 *Malcolm v O'Callaghan* (1837) 3 My & Cr 52, CA, at 62.

193 Care ought to be exercised when considering what is meant by 'necessary' in pre-CPR cases: that word tends to be used to mean 'required', rather than necessary, in the sense that it used to be used in the second stage of the *Lownds* test (after *Lownds v Home Office* [2002] EWCA Civ 365).

194 RCS Ord 62, r 14.

195 This is a reference to a *Beddoe* application (after *Re Beddoe, Downes v Cottam* [1893] 1 Ch 547), which is an application in which a trustee seeks a pre-emptive order: see para 66.59.

196 *Harvey v Olliver* (1887) WN 149.

197 See, eg, *Nicholson v Falkiner* (1830) 1 Mol 555.

198 *Bruty v Edmundson* [1918] 1 Ch 112, CA.

199 *Re Love, Hill v Spurgeon* (1885) 29 Ch D 348, CA.

Costs payable out of a fund

Procedural issues

Contrary to the general provision at CPR, r 44.10(1)(a), that where an order is silent as to costs, no party is entitled to costs in relation to that order, an order that is silent as to costs will not affect any entitlement of a party to recover costs out of a fund held by them as trustee or personal representative, or pursuant to any lease, mortgage or other security.[200] **66.80**

Special provisions apply to assessment of costs payable out of a fund. They are contained in CPR, r 47.19: **66.81**

> '(1) Where the court is to assess costs which are payable out of a fund other than the Community Legal Service Fund, the receiving party may commence detailed assessment proceedings by filing a request in the relevant practice form.
> (2) A request under paragraph (1) must be filed within 3 months after the date when the right to detailed assessment arose.
> (3) The court may direct that the party seeking assessment serve a copy of the request on any person who has a financial interest in the outcome of the assessment.
> (4) The court will, on receipt of the request for assessment, provisionally assess the costs without the attendance of the receiving party, unless it considers that a hearing is necessary.
> (5) After the court has provisionally assessed the bill, it will return the bill to the receiving party.
> (6) The court will fix a date for an assessment hearing if the party informs the court, within 14 days after he receives the provisionally assessed bill, that he wants the court to hold such a hearing.'

Thus the costs will usually be provisionally assessed without the benefit of points of dispute or replies—in much the same way as Community Legal Service (CLS)-only costs are, other than that the costs will be on the indemnity, rather than the standard, basis. The court may direct that a person—usually a beneficiary—who has a financial interest in the outcome of the assessment may be served with a copy of the request for a detailed assessment.

PD 47, para 18, provides additional guidance: **66.82**

> '18.1 Rule 47.19 enables the court to direct under rule 47.19(3) that the receiving party must serve a copy of the request for assessment and copies of the documents which accompany it, on any person who has a financial interest in the outcome of the assessment.
>
> 18.2 A person has a financial interest in the outcome of the assessment if the assessment will or may affect the amount of money or property to which that person is or may become entitled out of the fund. Where an interest in the fund is itself held by a trustee for the benefit of some other person, that trustee will be treated as the person having such a financial interest unless it is not appropriate to do so. "Trustee" includes a personal representative, receiver or any other person acting in a fiduciary capacity.
>
> 18.3 The request for a detailed assessment of costs out of the fund should be in Form N258B, be accompanied by the documents set out at paragraph 17.2(1) (a) to (e) and the following—
> (a) a statement signed by the receiving party giving his name, address for service, reference, telephone number,
> (b) a statement of the postal address of any person who has a financial interest in the outcome of the assessment; and

[200] CPR, r 44.10(1)(b).

(c) if a person having a financial interest is a child or protected party, a statement to that effect.

18.4 The court will decide, having regard to the amount of the bill, the size of the fund and the number of persons who have a financial interest, which of those persons should be served and may give directions about service and about the hearing. The court may dispense with service on all or some of those persons.

18.5 Where the court makes an order dispensing with service on all such persons it may proceed at once to make a provisional assessment, or, if it decides that a hearing is necessary, give appropriate directions. Before deciding whether a hearing is necessary, the court may require the receiving party to provide further information relating to the bill.

18.6

(1) The court will send the provisionally assessed bill to the receiving party with a notice in Form N253. If the receiving party is legally represented the legal representative should, if the provisional assessment is to be accepted, then complete the bill.

(2) The court will fix a date for a detailed assessment hearing, if the receiving party informs the court within 14 days after receiving the notice in Form N253, that the receiving party wants the court to hold such a hearing.

18.7 The court will give at least 14 days' notice of the time and place of the hearing to the receiving party and to any person who has a financial interest and who has been served with a copy of the request for assessment.

18.8 If any party or any person who has a financial interest wishes to make an application in the detailed assessment proceedings, the provisions of Part 23 (General Rules about Applications for Court Orders) apply.

18.9 If the receiving party is legally represented the legal representative must complete the bill by inserting the correct figures in respect of each item and must recalculate the summary of the bill.'

66.83 If the items listed in PD 47, para 17.2(1), are taken into account, the request for a detailed assessment hearing must be accompanied by:

- a copy of the bill;
- the document giving rise to the right to detailed assessment;
- copies of all orders made by the court relating to the costs that are to be assessed;
- fee notes of both counsel and experts;
- written evidence as to any other disbursement that is claimed and which exceeds £500;
- a statement signed by the receiving party giving their name, address for service, reference, telephone number and fax number (if any);
- a statement of the postal address of any person who has a financial interest in the outcome of the assessment; and
- in respect of each person stated to have such an interest, if such person is a child or protected party, a statement to that effect.

66.84 In deciding whether notice should be given to any person with a financial interest in the outcome of the assessment, the court will take into account the size of the fund and the number of persons who have a financial interest. If notice is to be given, the court may (and usually will) give directions about service and the hearing.

67

PUBLIC LAW AND JUDICIAL REVIEW

67.01 This chapter deals with the following topics:

- application for permission for judicial review (67.03);
- acknowledgement of service of judicial review proceedings (67.08);
- discretion relating to the costs of judicial review proceedings (67.10); and
- interested parties and interveners in judicial review proceedings (67.15).

Judicial review costs capping is addressed at 13.46–13.77. The limits relating to the costs of Aarhus Convention claims are addressed at 13.78–13.99 and 13.108.

67.02 This chapter is the briefest of overviews. Rather than describing the law in full, it seeks to identify the key factors that distinguish public law costs from private law costs. Notwithstanding those differences, it should be borne in mind there is nothing in Part 54 of the Civil Procedure Rules (CPR) that removes the discretionary powers conferred by s 51 of the Senior Courts Act 1981.[1] Thus the similarities far outweigh the differences and nearly all of what is said in Part III of this book will apply to judicial review proceedings.

Application for Permission for Judicial Review

67.03 A grant of permission to bring a claim for judicial review will, if silent on the issue of costs or unless the court orders otherwise, be taken to contain an order that the applicant's costs be costs in the claim.[2] Where an order for costs made on an application for permission to seek judicial review is challenged or where the quantum of such an order is challenged, written submissions should be made.[3]

The costs of the application and hearing

67.04 A defendant who chooses to attend and oppose an oral application for permission cannot ordinarily expect to recover its costs of doing so even if permission is refused, but it may be awarded costs in exceptional circumstances (see below).[4] This principle is confirmed in Practice Direction (PD) 54A, paras 8.5 and 8.6, which read as follows:

> '8.5 Neither the defendant nor any other interested party need attend a hearing on the question of permission unless the court directs otherwise.

---

[1] *R (on the application of Mount Cook Land Ltd) v Westminster City Council* [2003] EWCA Civ 1346, at [67].

[2] *Practice Statement (Judicial Review: Costs)* [2004] 1 WLR 1760; see also CPR, r 44.10(2).

[3] See *R (on the application of Loucif) v Secretary of State for the Home Department* [2011] EWHC 3640 (Admin), citing *Ewing v ODPM* [2005] All ER (D) 315.

[4] *R (on the application of Mount Cook Land Ltd) v Westminster City Council* [2003] EWCA Civ 1346, at [76]; aff'd in *Davey v Aylesbury Vale DC* (2007) EWCA Civ 1166.

8.6 Where the defendant or any party does attend a hearing, the court will not generally make an order for costs against the claimant.'

67.05 Some observers have commented adversely on PD 54A, saying that it appears to be at odds with established practices and the CPR themselves.[5] Auld LJ gave the following guidance, which, amongst other things, explained how the Practice Direction should be applied in practice:

'(1) ... a successful defendant or other party at the permission stage who has filed an acknowledgment of service, pursuant to CPR 54.8, should generally recover the costs of doing so from the claimant, whether or not he attends any permission hearing.
(2) The effect of para 8.6, when read with para 8.5, of the practice direction, in conformity with the long-established practice of the courts in judicial review ... is that a defendant who attends and successfully resists the grant of permission at a renewal hearing should not generally recover from the claimant his costs of, and occasioned by, doing so.
(3) A court, in considering an award against an unsuccessful claimant of the defendant's and/or any other interested party's costs at a permission hearing, should depart from the general guidance in the practice direction only if he considers that there are exceptional circumstances for doing so.
(4) A court considering costs at the permission stage should be allowed a broad discretion as to whether, on the facts of the case, there are exceptional circumstances justifying the award of costs against an unsuccessful claimant.
(5) Exceptional circumstances may consist in the presence of one or more of the features in the following non-exhaustive list:
  (a) the hopelessness of the claim;
  (b) the persistence in it by the claimant after having been alerted to facts and/or of the law demonstrating its hopelessness;
  (c) the extent to which the court considers that the claimant, in the pursuit of his application, has sought to abuse the process of judicial review for collateral ends—a relevant consideration as to costs at the permission stage, as well as when considering discretionary refusal of relief at the stage of substantive hearing, if there is one; and
  (d) whether, as a result of the deployment of full argument and documentary evidence by both sides at the hearing of a contested application, the unsuccessful claimant has had, in effect, the advantage of an early substantive hearing of the claim.
(6) A relevant factor for a court, when considering the exercise of its discretion on the grounds of exceptional circumstances, may be the extent to which the unsuccessful claimant has substantial resources that it has used to pursue the unfounded claim, and that are available to meet an order for costs.'[6]

Acquiescence

67.06 It will occasionally be the case that the defendant will acquiesce to the claimant's claim in such a way that proceedings become otiose either before or shortly after the application for permission. Where this is the case, then the claimant would ordinarily be entitled to their costs.[7]

[5] See *Halsbury's Laws of England* (London: Butterworths, 2010), vol 1, para 178, fn 5.
[6] *R (on the application of Mount Cook Land Ltd) v Westminster City Council* [2003] EWCA Civ 1346, at [76].
[7] The principles are much the same as they are in a private law setting (see 7.156–7.168). As an example in a public law setting, see *R v Kensington and Chelsea Royal London Borough Council, ex p Ghebregiogis* [1994]

Judicial review costs capping

Where the application is defended, the claimant may, where appropriate, be able to apply at the permission stage for a judicial review costs capping order. This is addressed at 13.46–13.77. **67.07**

Acknowledgement of Service of Judicial Review Proceedings

An unsuccessful claimant must expect to pay the defendant's costs of filing an acknowledgement of service.[8] **67.08**

Errors, omissions and excessive detail

Errors concerning acknowledgements of service may be taken into account. Where a person who has been served with proceedings takes part in a hearing without having taken appropriate steps in relation to the acknowledgement of service, they may suffer in terms of costs.[9] An overly detailed acknowledgement may also result in costs sanctions; the allowable costs would usually be limited to those that would have been incurred had only a summary of the grounds been drafted.[10] **67.09**

Discretion Relating to the Costs of Judicial Review Proceedings

Unless the court orders otherwise, where a defendant incurs costs in opposing a claim, those costs would be recoverable only if the claimant obtains permission and ultimately loses.[11] Put otherwise, costs follow the event. The principles set out in Chapter 6 apply. The following miscellaneous points may be made: **67.10**

- **Success and reconsideration of impugned decisions** Securing a reconsideration of an impugned decision would generally be considered to amount to success for the purposes of CPR, r 44.2(2)(a).[12]
- **Issues-aware awards** If a claimant achieves a partial success (such as winning on only some of the issues brought), it is open to the court to take that into account in just the same way as such factors would be taken into account in private law claims,[13] but the mere fact that an unconvincing argument is advanced will not necessarily lead to an issues-aware order (especially if both sides advance such arguments).[14]

COD 502. Late concessions will usually not impress the court: see *R v Islington London Borough Council, ex p Hooper* [1995] COD 76. Equally, if discontinuance is required, there must be no delay on the part of the claimant: see *R v Warley Justices, ex p Callis* [1994] COD 240.

[8] *R (Leach) v Commissioner for Local Administration* [2001] EWHC 455 (Admin), at [50]; see also *R (on the application of Mount Cook Land Ltd) v Westminster City Council* [2003] EWCA Civ 1346, at [54].

[9] See CPR, r 54.9(2).

[10] *Ewing v ODPM* [2005] All ER (D) 315.

[11] *R (on the application of Thurman) v Lewisham LBC* (unreported), 1 January 2007, QBD (Admin), approved of in *Davey v Aylesbury Vale DC* (2007) EWCA Civ 1166.

[12] *R (on the application of Tesfay) v Secretary of State for the Home Department* [2016] EWCA Civ 415.

[13] See, eg, *R (on the application of Srinivasans Solicitors) v Croydon County Court* [2013] EWCA Civ 249, in which the claimant was found to have abandoned issues and reshaped points.

[14] See, eg, *R (on the application of Whistl UK Ltd (formerly TNT Post UK Ltd)) v Revenue and Customs Commissioners* [2014] EWHC 4118 (Admin), at [5], *per* Kenneth Parker J.

- **Public interest** Where a claim raises an issue of public interest, that may be a factor upon which a claimant may rely.[15]

Sedley-Clarke principles

67.11 Sedley LJ has given guidance, which is often referred to as the 'Sedley-Clarke principles',[16] as follows:

> '(1) On the conclusion of full judicial review proceedings in a defendant's favour, the nature and purpose of the particular claim is relevant to the exercise of the judge's discretion as to costs. In contrast to a judicial review claim brought wholly or mainly for commercial or proprietary reasons, a claim brought partly or wholly in the public interest, albeit unsuccessful, may properly result in a restricted or no order for costs.
> (2) If awarding costs against the claimant, the judge should consider whether they are to include preparation costs in addition to acknowledgement costs. It will be for the defendant to justify these. There may be no sufficient reason why such costs, if incurred, should be recoverable.
> (3) It is highly desirable that these questions should be dealt with by the trial judge and left to the costs judge only in relation to the reasonableness of individual items.
> (4) If at the conclusion of such proceedings the judge makes an undifferentiated order for costs in a defendant's favour:
> (a) the order has to be regarded as including any reasonably incurred preparation costs; but
> (b) the 2004 Practice Statement should be read so as to exclude any costs of opposing the grant of permission in open court, which should be dealt with on the *Mount Cook* principles.'[17]

Principle (3) has subsequently been emphasised by other members of the Court of Appeal.[18]

67.12 Clarke MR commented upon these principles by adding the following note of caution:

> 'It does seem to me that costs should ordinarily follow the event and that it is for the claimant who has lost to show that some different approach should be adopted on the facts of a particular case ... That said, I agree with Sedley LJ's second proposition ... that it will be for the successful defendant to justify preparation costs. That is, however, because (as stated above) he must show that it was reasonable and proportionate to incur such costs. If the claimant wishes to submit that any or all the costs which would be otherwise recoverable should not be recovered, however reasonable and proportionate they were, it is, as I see it, for him to persuade the court to that effect.'[19]

Thus, if the claimant wishes to avoid paying costs that are reasonable and proportionate in amount, the burden of persuading the court lies with the claimant, rather than the defendant.

---

[15] See, eg, *R (on the application of Valentines Homes & Construction Ltd) v Revenue and Customs Commissioners* [2010] EWCA Civ 345.

[16] This is because they were approved of by Clarke MR: *R (Roudham & Larling Parish Council) v Breckland Council* [2008] EWCA Civ 714.

[17] *Davey v Aylesbury Vale DC* [2007] EWCA Civ 1166, at [21].

[18] This was further emphasised in *R (Roudham & Larling Parish Council) v Breckland Council* [2008] EWCA Civ 714.

[19] *Davey v Aylesbury Vale DC* [2007] EWCA Civ 1166, at [29]–[30].

Review of decisions of inferior courts or tribunals

Where the judicial review relates to the decision of an inferior court or tribunal, special rules may apply.[20] In particular, the court would generally make no order for costs against an inferior court or tribunal if it chose not to appear to resist the claim,[21] unless there had been a flagrant instance of improper conduct or it unreasonably declined to sign a consent order disposing of the proceedings.[22] If the inferior court appeared merely to assist the court in a neutral fashion, this would not count against it. There have, however, been departures from the above principles in cases in which the applicant has no source of funding. **67.13**

Settled claims and supervening events

The topic of claims that settle leaving only the incidence of costs at large is addressed at 7.141–7.168. **67.14**

Interested Parties and Interveners in Judicial Review Proceedings

It has long been the case that an unsuccessful claimant would not generally be required to pay the costs of more than one of the other parties.[23] This would not always be the case, however, in that, in the past, the claimant may be asked to meet the costs of an interested party who had to address issues that were discrete from those addressed by the defendant.[24] Other than where the claim form was filed before 13 April 2015,[25] the matter is now governed by the provision referred to below. **67.15**

CPR, r 46.15, provides as follows: **67.16**

> '(1) In this rule the terms "intervener" and "relevant party" have the same meaning as in section 87 of the Criminal Justice and Courts Act 2015 ("the 2015 Act").
>
> (2) A relevant party may apply to the court for an order for an intervener to pay costs in accordance with section 87 of the 2015 Act.
>
> (Section 87 of the 2015 Act applies to judicial review proceedings in the High Court and Court of Appeal.)
>
> (Rule 54.17 makes provision for any person to be able to apply for permission to file evidence or make representations at the hearing of a judicial review.)'

This is merely a signpost to the provisions in the Criminal Justice and Courts Act 2015, as s 87: **67.17**

> '87 **Interveners and costs**
>
> (1) This section applies where—
> (a) a person is granted permission to file evidence or make representations in judicial review proceedings, and
> (b) at that time, the person is not a relevant party to the proceedings.

---

[20] See the review of authorities in *R (on the application of Davies) v Birmingham Deputy Coroner* [2004] EWCA Civ 207.

[21] See, eg, *T v Cardiff City and County Council* [2007] EWHC 2568 (Admin). For a case in which an order was made, see *R (on the application of Tull) v Camberwell Green Magistrates' Court* [2004] EWHC 2780 (Admin).

[22] See, eg, *R (on the application of Varma) v Redbridge Magistrates' Court* [2009] EWHC 836 (Admin).

[23] *Bolton Metropolitan District Council v Secretary of State for the Environment* [1996] 1 All ER 184. As to the pedigree of that principle, see *R v Industrial Disputes Tribunal, ex p American Express Co Inc* [1954] 2 All ER 764.

[24] See, eg, *R v Panel on Take-overs and Mergers, ex p Datafin plc* [1987] QB 815.

[25] See Criminal Justice and Courts Act 2015 (Commencement No. 1, Saving and Transitional Provisions) Order 2015 (SI 2015/778), Sch 2, para 6.

(2) That person is referred to in this section as an "intervener".

(3) A relevant party to the proceedings may not be ordered by the High Court or the Court of Appeal to pay the intervener's costs in connection with the proceedings.

(4) Subsection (3) does not prevent the court making an order if it considers that there are exceptional circumstances that make it appropriate to do so.

(5) On an application to the High Court or the Court of Appeal by a relevant party to the proceedings, if the court is satisfied that a condition described in subsection (6) is met in a stage of the proceedings that the court deals with, the court must order the intervener to pay any costs specified in the application that the court considers have been incurred by the relevant party as a result of the intervener's involvement in that stage of the proceedings.

(6) Those conditions are that—
(a) the intervener has acted, in substance, as the sole or principal applicant, defendant, appellant or respondent;
(b) the intervener's evidence and representations, taken as a whole, have not been of significant assistance to the court;
(c) a significant part of the intervener's evidence and representations relates to matters that it is not necessary for the court to consider in order to resolve the issues that are the subject of the stage in the proceedings;
(d) the intervener has behaved unreasonably.

(7) Subsection (5) does not require the court to make an order if it considers that there are exceptional circumstances that make it inappropriate to do so.

(8) In determining whether there are exceptional circumstances that are relevant for the purposes of subsection (4) or (7), the court must have regard to criteria specified in rules of court.

(9) In this section, "judicial review proceedings" means—
(a) proceedings on an application for leave to apply for judicial review,
(b) proceedings on an application for judicial review,
(c) any proceedings on an application for leave to appeal from a decision in proceedings described in paragraph (a) or (b), and
(d) proceedings on an appeal from such a decision,
and the proceedings described in paragraphs (a) to (d) are "stages" of judicial review proceedings.

(10) For the purposes of this section, "a relevant party" to judicial review proceedings means any of the following—
(a) a person who is or has been an applicant or defendant in the proceedings described in subsection (9)(a), (b) or (c);
(b) a person who is or has been an appellant or respondent in the proceedings described in subsection (9)(d);
(c) any other person who is or has been directly affected by the proceedings and on whom the application for judicial review, or for leave to apply for judicial review, has been served.

(11) If a person who is an intervener in judicial review proceedings becomes a relevant party to the proceedings, the person is to be treated for the purposes of subsections (3) and (5) as having been a relevant party, rather than an intervener, at all times when involved in the proceedings.'

Part XVI

MATERIALS

68

TABLES

Table 68.1 Senior Courts Costs Office

(a) Masters in the Senior Courts Costs Office

Chief Master Gordon-Saker (Senior Costs Judge)	Court 101
Master Brown	Court 97
Master Haworth	Court 94
Master James	Court 95
Master Leonard	Court 96
Master Nagalingam	Court 99
Master Rowley	Court 100
Master Whalan	Court 93

(b) Contact details for the Senior Courts Costs Office

Address	Thomas More Building Royal Courts of Justice Strand LONDON WC2A 2LL
Document exchange	DX 44454 Strand
General enquiries	scco@hmcts.gsi.gov.uk
eBills	sccoebills@hmcts.gsi.gov.uk
Group listing	sccogrouplisting@hmcts.gsi.gov.uk
Telephone (clerks to the Masters)	020 7947 7124
	020 7947 6468
Telephone (issue team and certificates)	020 7947 6406
	020 7947 6334
Telephone (costs officers)	020 7947 7330
	020 7947 6996
Fax	None

Table 68.2 Regional costs judges

(a) North Eastern Circuit

District Judge Barraclough	Huddersfield
District Judge Batchelor	Sheffield
District Judge Besford	Kingston Upon Hull
District Judge Corkhill	Barnsley
District Judge Keating	Teesside
District Judge Neaves	Scarborough
District Judge Searle	Newcastle and Sunderland

(b) North Western Circuit

District Judge Baldwin	Liverpool
District Judge Clarke	Burnley
District Judge Dodd	Carlisle
District Judge Jenkinson	Liverpool
District Judge Moss	Manchester
District Judge Wallace	Macclesfield
District Judge Woosnam	Blackpool

(c) Midlands Circuit

District Judge Gibson	Worcester
District Judge Griffith	Birmingham
District Judge Hale	Nottingham
District Judge Lumb	Birmingham
District Judge McIlwaine	Lincoln
District Judge Rouine	Birmingham

(d) Wales

District Judge Lloyd-Davies	Carmarthen and Llanelli
District Judge Phillips	Cardiff
District Judge Thomas	Prestatyn
District Judge Sandercock	South East Wales

(e) South Eastern Circuit

District Judge Bosman	Cambridge
District Judge W Jackson	Canterbury
District Judge Matthews	Oxford
District Judge Reeves	Norwich
District Judge White	Luton

(f) South Western Circuit

District Judge Cope	Bristol
District Judge James	Aldershot & Farnham
District Judge Middleton	Bodmin & Truro
District Judge Woodburn	Gloucester & Cheltenham

Table 68.3 Guideline hourly rates and CPI adjusted guideline rates (with no uplift)

		2007	2008	2009	2010	2011	2012	2013	2014	2015	2016	2017	2018
National Band 1	Grade A	£180	£203	£213	£217	£218	£223	£228	£237	£242	£251	£255	£261
	Grade B	£173	£180	£189	£192	£193	£198	£201	£210	£214	£222	£226	£231
	Grade C	£145	£151	£158	£161	£162	£166	£169	£176	£179	£186	£189	£193
	Grade D	£106	£110	£116	£118	£118	£121	£124	£129	£131	£136	£139	£142
National Band 2	Grade A	£183	£191	£198	£201	£202	£207	£211	£219	£224	£232	£236	£242
	Grade B	£161	£168	£174	£177	£178	£182	£186	£193	£197	£204	£208	£213
	Grade C	£133	£139	£144	£146	£147	£150	£153	£159	£162	£168	£171	£175
	Grade D	£101	£105	£109	£111	£111	£114	£116	£121	£123	£128	£130	£133
National Band 3	Grade A	£167	£174	£198	£201	£202	£207	£211	£219	£224	£232	£236	£242
	Grade B	£150	£156	£174	£177	£178	£182	£186	£193	£197	£204	£208	£213
	Grade C	£128	£133	£144	£146	£147	£150	£153	£159	£162	£168	£171	£175
	Grade D	£95	£99	£109	£111	£111	£114	£116	£121	£123	£128	£130	£133
City of London (EC1–EC4)	Grade A	£380	£396	£402	£409	£412	£422	£430	£447	£456	£473	£481	£492
	Grade B	£274	£285	£291	£296	£298	£305	£311	£323	£330	£342	£348	£356
	Grade C	£210	£219	£222	£226	£227	£233	£237	£247	£252	£261	£266	£272
	Grade D	£129	£134	£136	£138	£139	£142	£145	£150	£154	£159	£162	£166
Central London (W1, WC1, WC2 and SW1)	Grade A	£292	£304	£312	£317	£319	£327	£333	£346	£353	£366	£373	£381
	Grade B	£222	£231	£238	£242	£243	£249	£254	£264	£270	£279	£285	£291
	Grade C	£181	£189	£193	£196	£197	£202	£206	£214	£218	£226	£230	£235
	Grade D	£116	£121	£124	£126	£127	£130	£132	£137	£140	£145	£148	£151

Outer London (all other London postcodes)	Grade A	£246	£256	£263	£267	£269	£275	£280	£292	£297	£308	£314	£321
	Grade A/B	£210	£219	£225	£229	£230	£236	£240	£250	£255	£264	£269	£275
	Grade B	£158	£165	£169	£172	£173	£177	£180	£188	£191	£199	£202	£207
	Grade C	£152	£158	£162	£165	£166	£170	£173	£180	£184	£190	£194	£198
	Grade D	£111	£116	£119	£121	£121	£124	£127	£132	£135	£139	£142	£145

Notes The table includes rates that, from 2010 onwards, have been derived from the 2010 rates by adjusting them for inflation (these being the figures in the shaded part of the table). The fact that they are included in this book should not be regarded as being an endorsement of any judicial method that uses them. That said, the Consumer Price Index now includes a category that deals specifically with legal services (or, from 2015 onwards, with legal services and accountancy): that category is 'SPPI: 6910000000: Legal Services'. As such, it is possible to make a principled adjustment that is based on the amounts that legal services providers are actually charging their clients (albeit only consumer clients).

National Band 1 = Aldershot, Farnham, Bournemouth (incl Poole), Birmingham Inner, Bristol, Cambridge City, Harlow, Canterbury, Maidstone, Medway, Tunbridge Wells, Cardiff (Inner), Chelmsford South, Essex, East Suffolk, Fareham, Winchester, Hampshire, Dorset, Wiltshire, Isle of Wight, Kingston, Guildford, Reigate, Epsom, Leeds Inner (within 2 km of City Art Gallery), Lewes, Liverpool, Birkenhead, Manchester Central, Newcastle—City Centre (within 2m of St Nicholas Cathedral), Norwich City, Nottingham City, Oxford, Thames Valley, Southampton, Portsmouth, Swindon, Basingstoke, Watford

National Band 2 = Bath, Cheltenham, Gloucester, Taunton, Yeovil, Bury, Chelmsford North, Cambridge County, Peterborough, Bury St Edmunds, Norfolk, Lowestoft, Chester, North Wales, Coventry, Rugby, Nuneaton, Stratford, Warwick, Exeter, Plymouth, Hull (City), Leeds Outer, Wakefield, Pontefract, Leigh, Lincoln, Luton, Bedford, St Albans, Hitchin, Hertford, Manchester Outer, Oldham, Bolton, Tameside, Newcastle (other than City Centre), Nottingham, Derbyshire, Sheffield, Doncaster, South Yorkshire, Southport, St Helens, Stockport, Altrincham, Salford, Swansea, Newport, Cardiff (Outer), Wigan, Wolverhampton, Walsall, Dudley, Stourbridge, York, Harrogate

National Band 3 = Birmingham Outer, Bradford, Dewsbury, Halifax, Huddersfield, Keighley, Skipton, Cumbria, Devon, Cornwall, Grimsby, Skegness, Hull Outer, Kidderminster, Northampton, Leicester, Preston, Lancaster, Blackpool, Chorley, Accrington, Burnley, Blackburn, Rawenstall, Nelson, Scarborough, Ripon, Stafford, Stoke, Tamworth, Teesside, Worcester, Hereford, Evesham, Redditch, Shrewsbury, Telford, Ludlow, Oswestry, South Wales, West Wales

Table 68.4 Guideline hourly rates and CPI adjusted guideline rates (uplifted by 7.5%—roughly a B factor of 60%)

		2007	2008	2009	2010	2011	2012	2013	2014	2015	2016	2017	2018
National Band 1	Grade A	£189	£213	£224	£228	£229	£234	£239	£249	£254	£264	£268	£274
	Grade B	£182	£189	£198	£202	£203	£208	£211	£221	£225	£233	£237	£243
	Grade C	£152	£159	£166	£169	£170	£174	£177	£185	£188	£195	£198	£203
	Grade D	£111	£116	£122	£124	£124	£127	£130	£135	£138	£143	£146	£149
National Band 2	Grade A	£192	£201	£208	£211	£212	£217	£222	£230	£235	£244	£248	£254
	Grade B	£169	£176	£183	£186	£187	£191	£195	£203	£207	£214	£218	£224
	Grade C	£140	£146	£151	£153	£154	£158	£161	£167	£170	£176	£180	£184
	Grade D	£106	£110	£114	£117	£117	£120	£122	£127	£129	£134	£137	£140
National Band 3	Grade A	£175	£183	£208	£211	£212	£217	£222	£230	£235	£244	£248	£254
	Grade B	£158	£164	£183	£186	£187	£191	£195	£203	£207	£214	£218	£224
	Grade C	£134	£140	£151	£153	£154	£158	£161	£167	£170	£176	£180	£184
	Grade D	£100	£104	£114	£117	£117	£120	£122	£127	£129	£134	£137	£140
City of London (EC1–EC4)	Grade A	£399	£416	£422	£429	£433	£443	£452	£469	£479	£497	£505	£517
	Grade B	£288	£299	£306	£311	£313	£320	£327	£339	£347	£359	£365	£374
	Grade C	£221	£230	£233	£237	£238	£245	£249	£259	£265	£274	£279	£286
	Grade D	£135	£141	£143	£145	£146	£149	£152	£158	£162	£167	£170	£174
Central London (W1, WC1, WC2 and SW1)	Grade A	£307	£319	£328	£333	£335	£343	£350	£363	£371	£384	£392	£400
	Grade B	£233	£243	£250	£254	£255	£261	£267	£277	£284	£293	£299	£306
	Grade C	£190	£198	£203	£206	£207	£212	£216	£225	£229	£237	£242	£247
	Grade D	£122	£127	£130	£132	£133	£137	£139	£144	£147	£152	£155	£159
Outer London (all other London postcodes)	Grade A	£258	£269	£276	£280	£282	£289	£294	£307	£312	£323	£330	£337
	Grade A/B	£221	£230	£236	£240	£242	£248	£252	£263	£268	£277	£282	£289
	Grade B	£166	£173	£177	£181	£182	£186	£189	£197	£201	£209	£212	£217
	Grade C	£160	£166	£170	£173	£174	£179	£182	£189	£193	£200	£204	£208
	Grade D	£117	£122	£125	£127	£127	£130	£133	£139	£142	£146	£149	£152

Note Rates in the shaded part of the table have been derived from the 2010 rates; they should be used with caution, if at all. For more on this and details of the national bands, see the notes to Table 68.3.

Table 68.5 Guideline hourly rates and CPI adjusted guideline rates (uplifted by 10%—roughly a B factor of 65%)

		2007	2008	2009	2010	2011	2012	2013	2014	2015	2016	2017	2018
National Band 1	Grade A	£198	£223	£234	£239	£240	£245	£251	£261	£266	£276	£281	£287
	Grade B	£190	£198	£208	£211	£212	£218	£221	£231	£235	£244	£249	£254
	Grade C	£160	£166	£174	£177	£178	£183	£186	£194	£197	£205	£208	£212
	Grade D	£117	£121	£128	£130	£130	£133	£136	£142	£144	£150	£153	£156
National Band 2	Grade A	£201	£210	£218	£221	£222	£228	£232	£241	£246	£255	£260	£266
	Grade B	£177	£185	£191	£195	£196	£200	£205	£212	£217	£224	£229	£234
	Grade C	£146	£153	£158	£161	£162	£165	£168	£175	£178	£185	£188	£193
	Grade D	£111	£116	£120	£122	£122	£125	£128	£133	£135	£141	£143	£146
National Band 3	Grade A	£184	£191	£218	£221	£222	£228	£232	£241	£246	£255	£260	£266
	Grade B	£165	£172	£191	£195	£196	£200	£205	£212	£217	£224	£229	£234
	Grade C	£141	£146	£158	£161	£162	£165	£168	£175	£178	£185	£188	£193
	Grade D	£105	£109	£120	£122	£122	£125	£128	£133	£135	£141	£143	£146
City of London	Grade A	£418	£436	£442	£450	£453	£464	£473	£492	£502	£520	£529	£541
	Grade B	£301	£314	£320	£326	£328	£336	£342	£355	£363	£376	£383	£392
	Grade C	£231	£241	£244	£249	£250	£256	£261	£272	£277	£287	£293	£299
	Grade D	£142	£147	£150	£152	£153	£156	£160	£165	£169	£175	£178	£183
Central London	Grade A	£321	£334	£343	£349	£351	£360	£366	£381	£388	£403	£410	£419
	Grade B	£244	£254	£262	£266	£267	£274	£279	£290	£297	£307	£314	£320
	Grade C	£199	£208	£212	£216	£217	£222	£227	£235	£240	£249	£253	£259
	Grade D	£128	£133	£136	£139	£140	£143	£145	£151	£154	£160	£163	£166
Outer London	Grade A	£271	£282	£289	£294	£296	£303	£308	£321	£327	£339	£345	£353
	Grade A/B	£231	£241	£248	£252	£253	£260	£264	£275	£281	£290	£296	£303
	Grade B	£174	£182	£186	£189	£190	£195	£198	£207	£210	£219	£222	£228
	Grade C	£167	£174	£178	£182	£183	£187	£190	£198	£202	£209	£213	£218
	Grade D	£122	£128	£131	£133	£133	£136	£140	£145	£149	£153	£156	£160

Note Rates in the shaded part of the table have been derived from the 2010 rates; they should be used with caution, if at all. For more on this and details of the national bands, see the notes to Table 68.3.

Table 68.6 Guideline hourly rates and CPI adjusted guideline rates (uplifted by 17.5%—roughly a B factor of 75%)

		2007	2008	2009	2010	2011	2012	2013	2014	2015	2016	2017	2018
National Band 1	Grade A	£212	£239	£250	£255	£256	£262	£268	£278	£284	£295	£300	£307
	Grade B	£203	£212	£222	£226	£227	£233	£236	£247	£251	£261	£266	£271
	Grade C	£170	£177	£186	£189	£190	£195	£199	£207	£210	£219	£222	£227
	Grade D	£125	£129	£136	£139	£139	£142	£146	£152	£154	£160	£163	£167
National Band 2	Grade A	£215	£224	£233	£236	£237	£243	£248	£257	£263	£273	£277	£284
	Grade B	£189	£197	£204	£208	£209	£214	£219	£227	£231	£240	£244	£250
	Grade C	£156	£163	£169	£172	£173	£176	£180	£187	£190	£197	£201	£206
	Grade D	£119	£123	£128	£130	£130	£134	£136	£142	£145	£150	£153	£156
National Band 3	Grade A	£196	£204	£233	£236	£237	£243	£248	£257	£263	£273	£277	£284
	Grade B	£176	£183	£204	£208	£209	£214	£219	£227	£231	£240	£244	£250
	Grade C	£150	£156	£169	£172	£173	£176	£180	£187	£190	£197	£201	£206
	Grade D	£112	£116	£128	£130	£130	£134	£136	£142	£145	£150	£153	£156
City of London	Grade A	£447	£465	£472	£481	£484	£496	£505	£525	£536	£556	£565	£578
	Grade B	£322	£335	£342	£348	£350	£358	£365	£380	£388	£402	£409	£418
	Grade C	£247	£257	£261	£266	£267	£274	£278	£290	£296	£307	£313	£320
	Grade D	£152	£157	£160	£162	£163	£167	£170	£176	£181	£187	£190	£195
Central London	Grade A	£343	£357	£367	£372	£375	£384	£391	£407	£415	£430	£438	£448
	Grade B	£261	£271	£280	£284	£286	£293	£298	£310	£317	£328	£335	£342
	Grade C	£213	£222	£227	£230	£231	£237	£242	£251	£256	£266	£270	£276
	Grade D	£136	£142	£146	£148	£149	£153	£155	£161	£165	£170	£174	£177
Outer London	Grade A	£289	£301	£309	£314	£316	£323	£329	£343	£349	£362	£369	£377
	Grade A/B	£247	£257	£264	£269	£270	£277	£282	£294	£300	£310	£316	£323
	Grade B	£186	£194	£199	£202	£203	£208	£212	£221	£224	£234	£237	£243
	Grade C	£179	£186	£190	£194	£195	£200	£203	£212	£216	£223	£228	£233
	Grade D	£130	£136	£140	£142	£142	£146	£149	£155	£159	£163	£167	£170

Note Rates in the shaded part of the table have been derived from the 2010 rates; they should be used with caution, if at all. For more on this and details of the national bands, see the notes to Table 68.3.

Table 68.7 Guideline hourly rates and CPI adjusted guideline rates (uplifted by 20%—roughly a B factor of 80%)

		2007	2008	2009	2010	2011	2012	2013	2014	2015	2016	2017	2018
National Band 1	Grade A	£216	£244	£256	£260	£262	£268	£274	£284	£290	£301	£306	£313
	Grade B	£208	£216	£227	£230	£232	£238	£241	£252	£257	£266	£271	£277
	Grade C	£174	£181	£190	£193	£194	£199	£203	£211	£215	£223	£227	£232
	Grade D	£127	£132	£139	£142	£142	£145	£149	£155	£157	£163	£167	£170
National Band 2	Grade A	£220	£229	£238	£241	£242	£248	£253	£263	£269	£278	£283	£290
	Grade B	£193	£202	£209	£212	£214	£218	£223	£232	£236	£245	£250	£256
	Grade C	£160	£167	£173	£175	£176	£180	£184	£191	£194	£202	£205	£210
	Grade D	£121	£126	£131	£133	£133	£137	£139	£145	£148	£154	£156	£160
National Band 3	Grade A	£200	£209	£238	£241	£242	£248	£253	£263	£269	£278	£283	£290
	Grade B	£180	£187	£209	£212	£214	£218	£223	£232	£236	£245	£250	£256
	Grade C	£154	£160	£173	£175	£176	£180	£184	£191	£194	£202	£205	£210
	Grade D	£114	£119	£131	£133	£133	£137	£139	£145	£148	£154	£156	£160
City of London	Grade A	£456	£475	£482	£491	£494	£506	£516	£536	£547	£568	£577	£590
	Grade B	£329	£342	£349	£355	£358	£366	£373	£388	£396	£410	£418	£427
	Grade C	£252	£263	£266	£271	£272	£280	£284	£296	£302	£313	£319	£326
	Grade D	£155	£161	£163	£166	£167	£170	£174	£180	£185	£191	£194	£199
Central London	Grade A	£350	£365	£374	£380	£383	£392	£400	£415	£424	£439	£448	£457
	Grade B	£266	£277	£286	£290	£292	£299	£305	£317	£324	£335	£342	£349
	Grade C	£217	£227	£232	£235	£236	£242	£247	£257	£262	£271	£276	£282
	Grade D	£139	£145	£149	£151	£152	£156	£158	£164	£168	£174	£178	£181
Outer London	Grade A	£295	£307	£316	£320	£323	£330	£336	£350	£356	£370	£377	£385
	Grade A/B	£252	£263	£270	£275	£276	£283	£288	£300	£306	£317	£323	£330
	Grade B	£190	£198	£203	£206	£208	£212	£216	£226	£229	£239	£242	£248
	Grade C	£182	£190	£194	£198	£199	£204	£208	£216	£221	£228	£233	£238
	Grade D	£133	£139	£143	£145	£145	£149	£152	£158	£162	£167	£170	£174

Note Rates in the shaded part of the table have been derived from the 2010 rates; they should be used with caution, if at all. For more on this and details of the national bands, see the notes to Table 68.3.

Table 68.8 Guideline hourly rates and CPI adjusted guideline rates (uplifted by 27.5%—roughly a B factor of 90%)

		2007	2008	2009	2010	2011	2012	2013	2014	2015	2016	2017	2018
National Band 1	Grade A	£230	£259	£272	£277	£278	£284	£291	£302	£309	£320	£325	£333
	Grade B	£221	£230	£241	£245	£246	£252	£256	£268	£273	£283	£288	£295
	Grade C	£185	£193	£201	£205	£207	£212	£215	£224	£228	£237	£241	£246
	Grade D	£135	£140	£148	£150	£150	£154	£158	£164	£167	£173	£177	£181
National Band 2	Grade A	£233	£244	£252	£256	£258	£264	£269	£279	£286	£296	£301	£309
	Grade B	£205	£214	£222	£226	£227	£232	£237	£246	£251	£260	£265	£272
	Grade C	£170	£177	£184	£186	£187	£191	£195	£203	£207	£214	£218	£223
	Grade D	£129	£134	£139	£142	£142	£145	£148	£154	£157	£163	£166	£170
National Band 3	Grade A	£213	£222	£252	£256	£258	£264	£269	£279	£286	£296	£301	£309
	Grade B	£191	£199	£222	£226	£227	£232	£237	£246	£251	£260	£265	£272
	Grade C	£163	£170	£184	£186	£187	£191	£195	£203	£207	£214	£218	£223
	Grade D	£121	£126	£139	£142	£142	£145	£148	£154	£157	£163	£166	£170
City of London	Grade A	£485	£505	£513	£521	£525	£538	£548	£570	£581	£603	£613	£627
	Grade B	£349	£363	£371	£377	£380	£389	£397	£412	£421	£436	£444	£454
	Grade C	£268	£279	£283	£288	£289	£297	£302	£315	£321	£333	£339	£347
	Grade D	£164	£171	£173	£176	£177	£181	£185	£191	£196	£203	£207	£212
Central London	Grade A	£372	£388	£398	£404	£407	£417	£425	£441	£450	£467	£476	£486
	Grade B	£283	£295	£303	£309	£310	£317	£324	£337	£344	£356	£363	£371
	Grade C	£231	£241	£246	£250	£251	£258	£263	£273	£278	£288	£293	£300
	Grade D	£148	£154	£158	£161	£162	£166	£168	£175	£179	£185	£189	£193
Outer London	Grade A	£314	£326	£335	£340	£343	£351	£357	£372	£379	£393	£400	£409
	Grade A/B	£268	£279	£287	£292	£293	£301	£306	£319	£325	£337	£343	£351
	Grade B	£201	£210	£215	£219	£221	£226	£230	£240	£244	£254	£258	£264
	Grade C	£194	£201	£207	£210	£212	£217	£221	£230	£235	£242	£247	£252
	Grade D	£142	£148	£152	£154	£154	£158	£162	£168	£172	£177	£181	£185

Note Rates in the shaded part of the table have been derived from the 2010 rates; they should be used with caution, if at all. For more on this and details of the national bands, see the notes to Table 68.3.

Table 68.9 Guideline hourly rates and CPI adjusted guideline rates (uplifted by 33%—roughly a B factor of 100%)

		2007	2008	2009	2010	2011	2012	2013	2014	2015	2016	2017	2018
National Band 1	Grade A	£240	£271	£284	£289	£291	£297	£304	£316	£323	£335	£340	£348
	Grade B	£231	£240	£252	£256	£257	£264	£268	£280	£285	£296	£301	£308
	Grade C	£193	£201	£211	£215	£216	£221	£225	£235	£239	£248	£252	£257
	Grade D	£141	£147	£155	£157	£157	£161	£165	£172	£175	£181	£185	£189
National Band 2	Grade A	£244	£255	£264	£268	£269	£276	£281	£292	£299	£309	£315	£323
	Grade B	£215	£224	£232	£236	£237	£243	£248	£257	£263	£272	£277	£284
	Grade C	£177	£185	£192	£195	£196	£200	£204	£212	£216	£224	£228	£233
	Grade D	£135	£140	£145	£148	£148	£152	£155	£161	£164	£171	£173	£177
National Band 3	Grade A	£223	£232	£264	£268	£269	£276	£281	£292	£299	£309	£315	£323
	Grade B	£200	£208	£232	£236	£237	£243	£248	£257	£263	£272	£277	£284
	Grade C	£171	£177	£192	£195	£196	£200	£204	£212	£216	£224	£228	£233
	Grade D	£127	£132	£145	£148	£148	£152	£155	£161	£164	£171	£173	£177
City of London	Grade A	£507	£528	£536	£545	£549	£563	£573	£596	£608	£631	£641	£656
	Grade B	£365	£380	£388	£395	£397	£407	£415	£431	£440	£456	£464	£475
	Grade C	£280	£292	£296	£301	£303	£311	£316	£329	£336	£348	£355	£363
	Grade D	£172	£179	£181	£184	£185	£189	£193	£200	£205	£212	£216	£221
Central London	Grade A	£389	£405	£416	£423	£425	£436	£444	£461	£471	£488	£497	£508
	Grade B	£296	£308	£317	£323	£324	£332	£339	£352	£360	£372	£380	£388
	Grade C	£241	£252	£257	£261	£263	£269	£275	£285	£291	£301	£307	£313
	Grade D	£155	£161	£165	£168	£169	£173	£176	£183	£187	£193	£197	£201
Outer London	Grade A	£328	£341	£351	£356	£359	£367	£373	£389	£396	£411	£419	£428
	Grade A/B	£280	£292	£300	£305	£307	£315	£320	£333	£340	£352	£359	£367
	Grade B	£211	£220	£225	£229	£231	£236	£240	£251	£255	£265	£269	£276
	Grade C	£203	£211	£216	£220	£221	£227	£231	£240	£245	£253	£259	£264
	Grade D	£148	£155	£159	£161	£161	£165	£169	£176	£180	£185	£189	£193

Note Rates in the shaded part of the table have been derived from the 2010 rates; they should be used with caution, if at all. For more on this and details of the national bands, see the notes to Table 68.3.

Table 68.10 **Guideline hourly rates and CPI adjusted guideline rates (uplifted by 40%—roughly a B factor of 110%)**

		2007	2008	2009	2010	2011	2012	2013	2014	2015	2016	2017	2018
National Band 1	Grade A	£252	£284	£298	£304	£305	£312	£319	£332	£339	£351	£357	£365
	Grade B	£242	£252	£265	£269	£270	£277	£281	£294	£300	£311	£316	£323
	Grade C	£203	£211	£221	£225	£227	£232	£237	£246	£251	£260	£265	£270
	Grade D	£148	£154	£162	£165	£165	£169	£174	£181	£183	£190	£195	£199
National Band 2	Grade A	£256	£267	£277	£281	£283	£290	£295	£307	£314	£325	£330	£339
	Grade B	£225	£235	£244	£248	£249	£255	£260	£270	£276	£286	£291	£298
	Grade C	£186	£195	£202	£204	£206	£210	£214	£223	£227	£235	£239	£245
	Grade D	£141	£147	£153	£155	£155	£160	£162	£169	£172	£179	£182	£186
National Band 3	Grade A	£234	£244	£277	£281	£283	£290	£295	£307	£314	£325	£330	£339
	Grade B	£210	£218	£244	£248	£249	£255	£260	£270	£276	£286	£291	£298
	Grade C	£179	£186	£202	£204	£206	£210	£214	£223	£227	£235	£239	£245
	Grade D	£133	£139	£153	£155	£155	£160	£162	£169	£172	£179	£182	£186
City of London	Grade A	£532	£554	£563	£573	£577	£591	£602	£626	£638	£662	£673	£689
	Grade B	£384	£399	£407	£414	£417	£427	£435	£452	£462	£479	£487	£498
	Grade C	£294	£307	£311	£316	£318	£326	£332	£346	£353	£365	£372	£381
	Grade D	£181	£188	£190	£193	£195	£199	£203	£210	£216	£223	£227	£232
Central London	Grade A	£409	£426	£437	£444	£447	£458	£466	£484	£494	£512	£522	£533
	Grade B	£311	£323	£333	£339	£340	£349	£356	£370	£378	£391	£399	£407
	Grade C	£253	£265	£270	£274	£276	£283	£288	£300	£305	£316	£322	£329
	Grade D	£162	£169	£174	£176	£178	£182	£185	£192	£196	£203	£207	£211
Outer London	Grade A	£344	£358	£368	£374	£377	£385	£392	£409	£416	£431	£440	£449
	Grade A/B	£294	£307	£315	£321	£322	£330	£336	£350	£357	£370	£377	£385
	Grade B	£221	£231	£237	£241	£242	£248	£252	£263	£267	£279	£283	£290
	Grade C	£213	£221	£227	£231	£232	£238	£242	£252	£258	£266	£272	£277
	Grade D	£155	£162	£167	£169	£169	£174	£178	£185	£189	£195	£199	£203

Note Rates in the shaded part of the table have been derived from the 2010 rates; they should be used with caution, if at all. For more on this and details of the national bands, see the notes to Table 68.3.

Table 68.11 Jim Diamond's hourly rate survey, 2003–15

	2003	2005	2007	2009 (Great Recession)	2010	2013	2015
City of London 'Magic Circle' firms	P: £375–450	P: £425–525	P: £625–700	P: £450	P: £450–500	P: £700–850	P: £775–850
	(G: £342)	(G3: £370)	(G: £380)	(G: £402)	(G: £409)	(G: £430)	(G: £456)
	A: £245–280	A: £250–300	A: £375–450	A: £375	A: £450–550	A: £450–550	A: £500–575
	(G: £247)	(G: £259)	(G: £274)	(G: £291)	(G: £296)	(G: £311)	(G: £330)
	S: £175–185	S: £180–215	S: £235–250	S: £250	S: £300–350	S: £350–£425	S: £350–500
	(G: £189)	(G: £198)	(G: £210)	(G: £222)	(G: £226)	(G: £237)	(G: £252)
US leading firms			P: £450–500	P: £400	P: £550–600	P: £550–700	P: £700–900
			A: £325–360	A: £300–375	A: £450–550	A: £450–550	A: £500–595
			S: £215–225	S: £225	S: £250–300	S: £275–235	S: £375–525
City of London	P: 325–375	P: £350–475	P: £400–495	P: £375	P: £375–640	P: £450–800	P: £550–800
Top firms other than above	(G: £342)	(G: £370)	(G: £380)	(G: £402)	(G: £409)	(G: £430)	(G: £456)
	A: £215–225	A: £225–300	A: £285–315	A: £250	A: £285–535	A: £325–475	A: £350–495
	(G: £247)	(G: £259)	(G: £274)	(G: £291)	(G: £296)	(G: £311)	(G: £330)
	S: £150–155	S: £170–195	S: £185–225	S: £180	S: £180–345	S: £225–300	S: £250–350
	(G: £189)	(G: £198)	(G: £210)	(G: £222)	(G: £226)	(G: £237)	(G: £252)
National firms with regional offices	P: £185–250	P: £190–315	P: £350–375	P: £325	P: £325–450	P: £400–500	P: £400–500
	(G: £175)	(G: £184)	(G: £195)	(G: £213)	(G: £217)	(G: £228	(G: £242)
	A: £135–195	A: £150–225	A: £225–275	A: £250	A: £250–300	A: £300–350	A: £300–350
	(G: £155)	(G: £163)	(G: £173)	(G: £189)	(G: £192)	(G: £201	(G: £214)
	S: £100–140	S: £125–160	S: £185–210	S: £175	S: £175–210	S: £195–275	S: £195–295
	(G: £130)	(G: £137)	(G: £145)	(G: £158)	(G: £161)	(G: £169	(G: £179)
Jersey (high end)	P: £300–350	P: £325–400	P: £400–450	P: £475–525	P: £475–575	P: £475–550	P: £495–625
	A: £225.235	A: £235–275	A: £260–295	A: £300	A: £300–375	A: £300–375	A: £325–395
	S: £150–160	S: £175–215	S: £195–225	S: £275	S: £285–325	S: £285–325	S: £285–350

Note Figures based on an ongoing and enduring survey carried out by Jim Diamond, a costs lawyer. Whilst the survey has not been carried out in a way that would survive peer review, it is generally regarded as a good indicator of the rates that are *charged* to clients (as opposed to those that are allowed between opposing parties). Indeed, the survey has been published or referred to by The Law Society, The Legal 500, *Financial Times*, *Legal Week* and *The Guardian*.

Abbreviations P = a partner; A = a solicitor of five years' or more post-qualification experience (PQE); S = a newly qualified solicitor; G = guideline (for comparison)

Table 68.12 Success fees

Chances of winning	(1) Percentage increase where the agreement does not put the legal services provider at risk from Part 36 offers	(2) Percentage increase where up to 10 per cent of the costs are at risk by reason of Part 36 offers	(3) Percentage increase where up to 20 per cent of the costs are at risk by reason of Part 36 offers	(4) Percentage increase where up to 30 per cent of the costs are at risk by reason of Part 36 offers
Less than 50%	Limited to 100%	Limited to 100%	Limited to 100%	Limited to 100%
50%	100%[a]	Limited to 100%	Limited to 100%	Limited to 100%
55%	82%[b]	82%–100%	82%–100%	82%–100%[c]
60%	67%	67%–85%	67%–100%[d]	67%–100%
65%	54%[e]	54%–71%	54%–92%	54%–100%
67.7%	50%[f]	50%–66%	50%–86%	50%–100%
70%	43%	43%–58%	43%–78%	43%–100%
75%	33%[g]	33%–48%	33%–67%	33%–90%
80%	25%	25%–38%	25%–50%	25%–78%
85%	18%[h]	18%–30%	18%–47%	18%–38%
90%	11%[i]	11%–23%[j]	11%–39%	11%–58%
95%	5%[k]	5%–16%	5%–31%	5%–50%

Notes

[a] See, eg, *Oliver v Whipps Cross University NHS Trust* [2009] EWHC 1104 (QB) (a clinical negligence claim in which the facts were not clear at the time the agreement was made); *King v Telegraph Group Ltd* [2005] EWHC 90015 (Costs) (a fully contested defamation claim).

[b] See, eg, *Hanley v Smith* [2009] EWHC 90144 (Costs) (a complex road traffic accident claim).

[c] See, eg, *Smiths Docks v Edwards* [2004] EWHC 116 (QB) (considerable risk posed by Part 36 offers).

[d] See, eg, *Sprialstream Ltd v Marks & Spencer plc* [2007] EWHC 90084 (Costs) (modest risk posed by Part 36 offers).

[e] See, eg, *Woolley v Haden Building Services Ltd (No 2)* [2008] EWHC 90111 (Costs) (a complex mesothelioma claim).

[f] See, eg, *Atack v Lee* [2004] EWCA Civ 1712 (a fully contested road traffic accident claim in which 50% was allowed, but up to 67% would have been permissible on the facts); *Abrew v Tesco plc* [2003] EWHC 9003 (Costs) (slipping and tripping); *U v Liverpool City Council* [2005] EWCA Civ 475 (occupiers' liability).

[g] See, eg, *Holliday v E C Realisations Ltd* [2008] EWHC 90103 (Costs) (an unremarkable mesothelioma claim).

[h] See, eg, *Bensusan v Freedman* [2001] EWHC 9001 (Costs) (a case of very straightforward dental negligence in which 20% was allowed); *Ellerton v Harris* [2004] EWCA Civ 1712 (a straightforward slipping claim in which 20% was allowed).

[i] See, eg, *Callery v Gray (No 2)* [2001] EWCA Civ 1246 (a straightforward road traffic accident claim).

[j] See, eg, *C (a patient acting by her litigation friend Jocelyn Fox) v W* [2008] EWCA Civ 1459 (small risk on quantum).

[k] See, eg, *Halloran v Delaney* [2002] EWCA Civ 1258 (liability conceded); *Haines v Sarner* [2005] EWHC 90009 (Costs) (judgment entered for the claimant).

Column (1) (unshaded) refers to ordinary conditional fee agreements under which the legal services provider is not put at risk by Part 36 offers (or under which that risk is very low) and where the agreement is not a CFA Lite. It is based on the formula referred to at 54.82.

Columns (2)–(4) (shaded) relate to conditional fee agreements under which the legal services providers' right to payment is, in part, put at risk by reason of Part 36 offers. The rationale for the figures given is given at 54.87–54.93. The fact that there is a range of figures reflects: (a) the fact that the amount of costs put at risk by a Part 36 offer may vary, depending on when an offer is—or is likely to be—made; and (b) the fact that the risk posed by any such offer may vary, depending on its level. In any ordinary case in which the risk posed by Part 36 offers is unremarkable, the appropriate figure will tend to be towards the lower end of the range given in column (2). It should be noted that the figures in columns (2)–(4) are based on arbitrary figures and that, in an appropriate case, a higher percentage increase may be appropriate. If, for example, a Part 36 offer were to be made before the conditional fee agreement was made in a case that was all about quantum, then that may justify a higher figure than is set out in column (4).

Where the conditional fee agreement is a CFA Lite, then a rough approximation of the applicable percentage increase may be made by using the figures towards the higher end of the range in the appropriate shaded column (see 54.94–54.97). In the editor's experience, in an unremarkable case, the figures tend to be towards the higher end of the range in column (1).

Where the agreement is a discounted conditional fee agreement, then the percentage increase should be discounted to take account of this (see 54.86). If, for example, the agreement provides for a third of the fees to be payable in any event, the percentage increase should be reduced by a third.

INDEX

Aarhus Convention
costs capping in cases under (appeals) 13.108
costs capping in cases under (first instance) 13.79–13.99
indemnity basis 16.67
Abatement
by costs judge (advance abatement) 57.35
of counsel's fees 53.80–53.82
shoddy work, in the context of 38.36–38.37
Abuse of process
Aaron v Shelton, rule in 23.43–23.46
costs proceedings, within 23.28–23.30
generally 23.31–23.32
Henderson v Henderson, rule in 23.33–23.42
meaning 23.28–23.30
nominal damages 6.70
proportionality distinguished 23.47–23.48
res judicata distinguished 23.29
scope 23.28–23.30
special orders 23.49
suing for recovery of costs 40.24
wasted costs (including hopeless cases) 9.154–9.157, 9.170
Accord and satisfaction
costs debtors 19.26–19.27
meaning 39.17
partial payments distinguished 36.23
Acting as solicitor 3.54–3.74
meaning 2.09
non-party costs orders where acting without authority 9.61–9.71
Activity codes
see also **Phase codes**; **Task codes**
activity codes under the CPR
appear for/attend (A1) 49.51–49.55
billable travel time (A9) 49.76–49.80
communicate with client (A3) 49.58–49.59
communicate with counsel (A2) 49.56–49.57
communicate with experts (A5) 49.61
communicate with external parties (A7) 49.63–49.64
communicate internally (A8) 49.65–49.75
communicate with other parties (A6) 49.62
communicate with witnesses (A4) 49.60
plan, prepare, draft, review (A10) 49.89–49.95
background 49.22
EW-UTBMS (J-Code) task codes 49.178
generally 49.21–49.23
list of 49.50
Additional liabilities
alternative means of funding, and *see* **Alternative means of funding** 54.150, 54.191–54.206
ATE premiums *see* **ATE insurance**; **ATE premiums**
budgets, and 54.49
costs lawyers and costs draftspersons, and 54.48, 22.22–22.24
human rights, and 24.43–24.53
meaning 2.09
membership organisations 54.179–54.190
notice of funding *see* **Notice of funding**
notional premiums *see* **Notional premiums**
solicitor and client issues 54.51–54.53
specific types of claim
clinical negligence claims 54.38–54.41
employers' liability claims (fixed costs) 50.118–50.130
employers' liability (industrial) disease claims (fixed costs) 50.131–50.149
insolvency-related proceedings 54.31–54.34
mesothelioma claims 54.22–54.30
publication claims 54.35–54.37
road traffic accidents (fixed costs) 50.105–50.117
statement of reasons *see* **Statements of reasons**
success fees *see* **Success fees**
summary assessment, and 44.37–44.42
Additional party orders (where there are several parties)
cut-through orders 7.28–7.31
meaning 7.03, Figure 7.2
passing-up-the-line orders 7.26–7.27
strings of contracts 7.27
Admiralty collision claims
Part 61 offers 6.244–6.245
Admissible offers
admissibility in principle 6.210
admissibility of withdrawn offers, etc 6.219
admissibility of offers to mediate 6.220
exceptions to inadmissibility of without prejudice offers 6.218
without prejudice offers and negotiations 6.207, 6.213–6.217
basis of costs, relevance to 16.34–16.37
Calderbank offers 6.06, 6.207
effect of a refusal to waive privilege 6.223
effect of admissible offers on the incidence of costs 6.224–6.244
absence of offers 6.238
all-inclusive offers 6.229–6.231, 43.358
alternative cases 6.238
conditional offers 6.241–6.243
defendant's refusal to come to a commercial settlement 6.233–6.234
detailed assessments, effect on costs of 43.296–43.298, 43.358
discontinuance 7.124
'drop hands' offers 6.227–6.228
exaggeration, in cases of 6.152, 6.155, 6.238
fraud, suspected 6.232

Admissible offers (*cont.*)
effect of admissible offers on the incidence of costs (*cont.*)
Intellectual Property and Enterprise Court 50.336
markedly divergent offers 6.235–6.236
'near misses', and 6.73
non-monetary offers 6.237
non-statutory assessments (solicitor and client) 39.07
offers on the small claims track 6.221–6.222
unrealistic offers 6.235
very late offers 6.239
withdrawn Part 36 offers 6.212, 6.240, 17.60–17.63, 17.214–17.217
generally 6.17, 6.76, 6.207
meaning 2.09, 6.06
negotiations, distinguished from 6.208
Part 36 offers, distinguished from 6.207, 6.212, 6.340, 17.25
when to consider an admissible offer 6.209
Advocacy services
meaning 2.09
After the event insurance *see* **ATE insurance**
Agency
authority, relevance of 22.19–22.20
bills of costs and agents' fees 43.40
generally 22.02–22.05
non-solicitor agents, fees of 22.08–22.20
retainer, relevance of 22.16–22.18
solicitor agents, fees of 22.06–22.07
supervision, relevance of 22.13–22.15
specific relationships 22.21–22.27
costs lawyers and costs draftspersons, fees of 22.22–22.24
counsel, no relationship of agency 22.24
experts 22.26
medical agencies, in general 22.27, 52.63–52.71
medical agencies, VAT 52.72, 55.25
union funding 18.63
Alternative dispute resolution (ADR)
see also **Arbitration of costs; Early neutral evaluation; Mediation**
assessment of costs of ADR 49.40
benefits of ADR 48.06–48.07
code-sets and ADR 49.40
costs arbitration *see* **Arbitration of costs**
costs mediation *see* **Mediation**
costs early neutral evaluation *see* **Early neutral evaluation**
definition of ADR 48.04
flexibility of costs ADR 48.07
generally 48.01–48.03
initiating ADR 48.11–48.12
pendulum arbitration *see* **Arbitration of costs**
policy and the CPR 48.08–48.09
refusal to engage in ADR and the incidence of costs *see* **Refusal to engage in ADR**
types of costs ADR 48.05
Alternative means of funding 34.18–34.20, 54.150, 54.191–54.206
BTE insurance, relevance of 54.191–54.201
employer funding, relevance of 54.206
funding enquiries in general 54.197–54.201
funding enquiries and credit cards 54.199
funding enquiries and opponents 54.201
funding enquiries and the SRA Code of Conduct 2011 54.200
legal advice regarding funding, relevance of 54.195–54.196
legal aid, relevance of 54.204
private means, relevance of 54.203
suitability of BTE insurance 34.18–34.20
trades union funding, relevance of 54.205
Alternatives to solicitor and client statutory assessments
generally 39.01
Legal Ombudsman 39.22–39.34
non-statutory assessments 39.03–39.07
remuneration certificates (obsolete) 39.02
Appeals
amount of costs, appeals concerning 45.23–45.24
appeal court, meaning of 45.04
appeal notice, meaning of 45.04
appellant, meaning of 45.04
assessors 45.66–45.69
authorised court officers *see* **Appeals from authorised court officers**
case management decisions, appeal concerning 45.28
conditional permission to appeal 45.52
costs of (and in court below) 7.184–7.185, 45.57–45.59
failure to give reasons in court below 45.25–45.26
findings of fact 45.64
forthwith orders, and 7.87–7.90
fresh evidence 45.60–45.63
generally 45.01–45.03, 45.55
material not referred to in judgment 45.65
new evidence, at 45.61–45.63
incidence of costs, appeals concerning 45.21–45.22
interest on overpaid costs 45.57–45.59, 56.103–56.104
interim decisions, appeals concerning 45.29
judicial review 45.02, 45.73–45.76
Ladd v Marshall 45.60–45.63
legal aid assessments 45.56
litigants in person 45.12–45.13
lower court, meaning of 45.04
material not referred to in judgment 45.65
new evidence 45.60–45.63
Part 36 offers, and 17.31
permission to appeal 45.49–45.53
procedure 45.32–45.56
appellant's notice 45.44
bundles 45.55
conditional permission to appeal 45.52
destination courts 45.39–45.42
documents to be filed 45.46
filing 45.33–45.35
grounds for appeal 45.45

hearings 45.55
leapfrog procedure 45.39–45.42
legal aid assessments 45.56
permission to appeal 45.49–45.53
refusal of permission to appeal 45.54
respondent's notice 45.45
service 45.36
skeleton arguments 45.47–45.48
stay of proceedings 45.37–45.38
timing 45.33–45.35
venue 45.43
publicly funded appellants and legal aid assessments 45.56
reasons, failure to give 45.25–45.26
refusal of permission to appeal 45.54
respondent, meaning of 45.04
retainers, relating to 27.22
second appeals 45.70–45.72
security for costs 15.12
substantive claim not heard by lower court, appeals concerning 45.30–45.31
summary assessment, appeals concerning 45.27
terminology 45.04
tests and general approach 45.16–45.20
amount of costs, appeals concerning 45.23–45.24
case management decisions, appeal concerning 45.28
failure of court below to give reasons 45.25–45.26
general approach 45.17–45.19
incidence of costs, appeals concerning 45.21–45.22
interim decisions, appeals concerning 45.29
review rather than rehearing 45.16
substantive claim not heard by lower court, appeals concerning 45.30–45.31
summary assessment, appeals concerning 45.27
timing 45.08–45.09, 45.33–45.35
trustees, and 66.42
types of 45.02

Appeals from authorised court officers
generally 45.02
governing provisions 45.05
litigants in person, and 45.12–45.13
procedure 45.06–45.07
record of the hearing below 45.10–45.11
timing 45.08–45.09

Apportionment
see also **Distribution; Division**
costs sharing agreements, role *see also* **Costs sharing agreements** 20.40–20.49
counsel's fees 53.39
discretionary matters 34.146–34.150
doctrine 20.16–20.39
equal apportionment 20.03, 20.16–20.33
deviation from equal apportionment 20.26–20.33
history of equal apportionment 20.20–20.25
meaning 20.03
retainers involving more than one client (apportionment between clients) 20.34–20.39
disclosure of contact of retainer 20.39
flexibility of approach 20.37–20.38
special orders 20.66

Appropriate authorised body
meaning 2.09

Arbitration of costs
see also **Alternative dispute resolution**
advantages 48.67
arbitration agreements 48.76–48.77
arbitration awards
costs awards 48.93
effect 48.94
generally 48.93
interim awards 49.93
main awards 48.93
types 48.93
benefits of 48.67
confidentiality 48.85–48.86
costs 48.97–48.104
disadvantages 48.68
funding 48.95–48.96
issue-by-issue final-offer arbitration 48.91
jurisdiction 48.69–48.72
procedural law 48.72
proper law 48.71
sources of arbitral law 48.69–48.70
meaning of 48.65
nature of costs arbitration 48.66–48.68
principles of arbitration 48.73–48.75
procedure 48.78–48.84
commencement of 48.79
hearing 48.84
pre-hearing conference 48.83
preliminary meeting 48.80–48.82
written submissions 48.67
variants
double-offer arbitration 48.91
'night baseball' arbitration 48.91
pendulum arbitration 48.87–48.92

Assessment of costs
absence of attendance/file notes 49.14
activities not defined in CPR 49.103–49.146
activity codes *see* **Activity codes**
adequate examination of material 49.10
administration of an estate 49.161–49.162
administrative work 49.130–49.131
alternative dispute resolution 49.40
attendance notes 49.12–49.14
bill of costs, costs of preparing and checking 49.140–49.146
budgeting 49.45
case management 49.29
circular letters 49.102
code-sets
activity codes *see* **Activity codes** 49.21
background to CPR code-set 49.22
EW-UTBMS codes 49.13, 49.22, 49.165–49.189
J-Codes 49.13, 49.22, 49.165–49.189
levels 49.21

Assessment of costs (*cont.*)
code-sets (*cont.*)
phase codes *see* **Phase codes** 49.21
phases 49.21, 49.23–49.49
task codes *see* **Task codes** 49.21
tasks 49.21
types 49.21
use 49.20
computerised recording of time 49.12–49.14
costs incurred after an order costs 49.151
costs management 49.06
costs of preparing material not used 49.125–49.126
counterclaim, costs of 49.124
damages, costs as 49.163–49.164
deemed orders 49.05
delegation 49.68–49.73
disclosure 49.30–49.31
duty to examine material 49.09–49.11
emails 49.97
estimated time
assessment 49.19
long attendances 49.19
meaning 49.15
'padding' of the bill 49.19
recoverability 49.17–49.18
repeated failure to record time 49.19
short attendances 49.19
stating in bill 49.16
extrapolation 49.11
funding, costs of 49.112–49.116
generally 49.01–49.02
Gibson principles 49.07
incoming correspondence 49.100
inconsistency with entitling order 49.03–49.05
inquests 49.154–49.162
inquiries 49.154–49.159
interim matters 49.05
interlocutory applications 49.41
interpretation of order 49.05
issue of proceedings 49.27, 49.28
J-Codes 49.13, 49.22, 49.165, 49.165–49.189
legal research, costs of 49.117–49.120
marshalling facts, costs of 49.104–49.111
media, costs of dealing with 49.127–49.129
mediation 49.40, 49.133–49.139
negotiation 49.132
perfunctory letters 49.101
phase codes *see* **Phase codes**
practice management systems 49.13
pre-action protocols 49.24–49.25
pre-issue costs 49.147–49.150
pre-trial review 49.36
preparation for trial 49.37
principles 49.06–49.11
proportionality *see* **Proportionality** 49.06
routine communications 49.97
Sachs's sensible solicitor 49.08
samples 49.11
settlements 49.40
SMS texts 49.99
solicitor and client work 49.121–49.123
special orders 49.05
statements of case 49.27, 49.28
statutory demands 49.160
stay of proceedings, costs incurred during 49.152–49.153
supervision and delegation 49.74–49.75
task codes *see* **Task codes**
time recording 49.12–49.14
timed communications 49.98
trial 49.38–49.39
trustees' costs and trusts 49.161–49.162, 66.75–66.77
witness statements 49.32–49.33
Assessors 45.66–45.69
Assignment
assignment generally 32.08, 32.28–32.33
assignment in law 32.29
absolute assignment, need for 32.29
consideration, relevance of 32.39
date, effective from 32.30
intention, requirement for 32.29
writing, need for 32.29
assignment, mechanisms of 32.28
causes of action, assignment of 30.10, 30.38–30.43
contractual bars to assignment 32.33
champerty and assignment 30.10, 30.22, 30.38–30.43
debts, assignment of 30.10, 32.08
equitable assignment 32.31
novation, distinguished from 32.11, 32.36
privity, relevance of 32.09–32.11
Part 36 offers, and 17.171
security for costs
asset sequestration 15.47
evasion 15.52–15.53
nominal claimants 15.44
set-off 21.35
subrogation, distinguished from 18.73
transfer of contracts of retainer *see* **Transfer of contracts of retainer**
Assisted person
meaning 2.09
ATE insurance 34.27, 54.31–54.34
see also **ATE premiums; Legal expenses insurance**
accessing the market 34.34–34.36
brokers 34.34
delegated authority 34.36
merits requirement 34.32
stage at which to apply for insurance 34.35
anti-avoidance clauses 15.39, 34.31
challenges to premiums (by insured) 34.41, 52.04
formalities 34.42–34.59
Conduct of Business Rules 34.51–34.58
demands and needs statements 34.59
disclosure requirements 34.55–34.57
general prohibition 34.43–34.46
Scope Rules 34.47–34.50
suitability requirements 34.58
generally 34.21
litigation funding, and 33.30, 33.71
market in ATE insurance 34.22–34.24
availability 34.28–34.33
history and origins 34.22–34.23
types of claim covered post-2013 34.24

meaning 2.09
security for costs and ATE insurance 15.37–15.39
anti-avoidance clauses 15.39, 34.31
direct deeds of indemnity 15.39
types of cover and types of claim covered 34.26–34.27
adverse-only cover 34.26
both sides' costs cover 34.26
clinical negligence 34.24, 54.38–54.41
cover for defendants 34.31
insolvency-related claims 34.27, 54.31–54.34
mesothelioma claims 34.24, 54.22–54.30
own-costs cover (for solicitors' fees) 34.31
own-disbursements cover 34.26
own-premium cover 34.26
personal injury claims 34.27
publication and privacy claims 34.24, 54.35–54.37
top-up insurance 34.38–34.40

ATE premiums
alternative means of funding, and *see* **Alternative means of funding** 54.150, 54.191–54.206, 34.18–34.20
budgets and ATE premiums 54.178
challenges to premiums (by insured) 34.41, 52.04
clinical negligence, and 54.38–54.41
components of the premium 34.37, 54.128–54.129
administrative costs 34.37
burning costs 34.37, 54.149, 54.155
distribution commission 34.37
risk/profit costs 34.37
human rights and premiums 24.43–24.53
meaning 2.09
more than one set of proceedings 54.175
quantum of premiums (generally) 54.127–54.174
actuarial method and evidence 54.168
comparators in general 54.163–54.165
comparison with conditional funding 54.146
evidence generally 54.169–54.170
evidence relating to the market 54.166
judicial approach in general 54.131–54.132, 54.142–54.145
judicial notice of comparators 54.163
level of cover, relevance of 54.147–54.149
policies and disclosure 54.171
proportionality 54.162, 25.84–25.89
rebated (staged) premiums 54.151–54.153
risk, relevance of 54.155–54.161
uncompetitive premiums 54.167
quantum of premiums (deconstruction)
commission, relevance of 54.154
deconstruction of premiums 54.132, 54.148–54.149, 54.172–54.174
reasonableness to incept policy *see also* **Alternative means of funding**
absence of risk, relevance of 54.135
adverse selection 54.136–54.137
agreements not to seek costs 54.141
macroeconomics 54.136–54.137
overview 54.133–54.134
timing (prematurity and late application) 54.138–54.140
rules of court, role of 54.130
need to serve certificate 54.130
notice of funding *see also* **Notice of funding** 54.130
publication claims 54.130, 54.139
types of premium 54.25
deferred premiums 34.25
deposit premium 34.25
single premiums 34.25
staged premiums 34.25, 54.151–54.153
top-up policies 54.176–54.177

Attendance notes
assessment of costs 49.12–49.14

Authorised court officers
allocation of assessments to 43.19–43.24
appeals
governing provisions 45.05
litigants in person 45.12–45.13
procedure 45.06–45.07
records 45.10–45.11
timing 45.08–45.09
meaning 2.09
powers 5.17–5.19, 43.23–43.24
provisional assessments 43.205–43.206

Authorised litigator 59.38
conditional fee agreements, and 29.198
meaning 2.09
work carried out by 3.48, 3.57, 3.60–3.61, 3.66
work carried out by person other than 3.94, 29.199–29.202

Authorised person
meaning 2.09
work carried out by 3.48–3.51, 3.67, 3.77–3.82
work carried out by person other than 3.92–3.100

Bankruptcy
solicitors' rights and remedies 40.130–40.132
statutory demands 35.113
statutory demands and solicitors' fees 43.414
wasted costs 9.185

Base costs
meaning 2.09, 29.02

Bases of assessment
see also **Indemnity basis; Standard basis**
as between solicitor and client
contentious costs 37.04
generally 37.02–37.05
informed approval 37.10–37.13
non-contentious costs 37.24–37.29
percentage increases 37.30–37.31
solicitor and client presumptions 37.06–37.09
unreasonable costs 16.04, 37.03
unusual nature or amount 37.14–37.16
consumer protection (as between solicitor and client), modification of 37.05
discounts 37.36
price reductions 37.37
representations 37.33
unfair terms 37.34–37.35
contracts, costs payable under 66.02–66.34
see also **Contract, costs payable under**
deemed orders 7.104, 7.134–7.135
default position under CPR 16.03

Bases of assessment (*cont.*)
difference between bases 16.10–16.12
doubtful factual issues, relevance of basis to 16.08
generally 16.01, 37.02–37.05
proportionality 16.06–16.07, 16.12
tests 16.04–16.05
trusts *see* **Trusts and trustees**
Before-the-event insurance *see* **BTE insurance**
Bills *see* **Bills of costs (between opposing parties); Interim statute bills; Statute bills**
Bills of costs (between opposing parties)
choice between old style bill and new style bill 43.30
costs of preparing and checking, 49.140–49.146
discontinuance 43.394–43.406
final filing 43.384–43.387
form 43.29–43.37
new-style electronic bills
budgets 43.50
columns 43.50
content 43.35–43.42
data 43.50
division of the bill into parts 43.36, 43.37
editing 43.50
filing 43.48
filters 43.50
hourly rates 43.50
isolating entries 43.50
layout 43.49
meaning 43.29
model bill 43.45
navigation 43.50
old-style bills, applicable provisions 43.47
Precedent S 43.45, 43.49, 43.50
preservation of data 43.50
service 43.48
sorting and reordering 43.50
use 43.31
worksheets 43.49
old-style written bills
content 43.35–43.42
division of the bill into parts 43.36, 43.37
format 43.33–43.34
layout 43.35
meaning 43.29
provisions applicable to new-style bills 43.47
privilege 46.14–46.15
time of delivery 36.15–36.16
transitional provisions 43.32
Brexit, impact of 24.02
BTE insurance
see also **Legal expenses insurance**
contents of policies (including contractual provisions) 34.11–34.13
appointed representatives provisions 34.12
basis of payment provisions 34.12
cooperation requirements 34.12
disclosure requirements 34.12
exclusions 34.12
limits of cover 34.12
merits requirements 34.12
mitigation requirements 34.12
notification requirements 34.12
own-side costs cover 34.13
persons covered 34.12
generally 34.04
history of 34.05–34.06
meaning 2.09
prevalence and availability 34.07–34.10
restrictions on use of 34.14–34.17
suitability 34.18–34.20
adverse conditions 34.20
cover provided by opponent's policy 34.20
legitimate restrictions 34.20
limit of cover 34.20
size of claim 34.20
top-up insurance 34.38–34.40
Budget discussion report
meaning 2.09
Budgets
see also **Costs budgeting**
assessment of costs 49.45–49.46
ATE premiums 54.178
legal project management 41.41–41.45
meaning 2.09
success fees 54.49
Bullock **order**
generally *see* **Co-defendant orders**
meaning 2.09
Businesses
purchasers, protection as
generally 28.215
misleading marketing 28.216
remedies 28.217–28.218
Business agreements
see also **Contentious business agreements; Non-contentious business agreements**
categories 27.107–27.108
other agreements distinguished 27.109–27.110
purported compromises 27.111–27.114

Case management
alternative dispute resolution 48.08
assessment of costs 49.29
code-set 49.27
costs capping orders 13.43–13.45
detailed assessment
costs management 43.26
debarring orders 43.28
generally 43.25
stay 43.27
CCFA *see* **Collective conditional fee agreements**
CFA Lite
children, approval 60.39
collective CFA Lites 29.113, 29.119
Conditional Fee Agreement Regulations 2000 29.37–29.39, 29.67–29.76
costs sharing agreements, and 27.317
documents other than agreement, effect of 29.41
history 1.161
indemnity principle 18.20, 18.86–18.90
insurance, effect of 29.42–29.43
meaning 2.09, 29.03
percentage increase, assessment of 54.94, Table 68.12

Champerty 29.199, 29.200
access to justice 30.20–30.21
administration of justice 30.20
case examples 30.32–30.54
development of law 30.19
generally 30.02
history 30.19
maintenance, relationship to 30.18, 30.04–30.17
modern approach 30.26–30.31
public policy 30.25, 33.04
relevance 30.02
retainers 30.02
wanton and officious intermeddling 30.22–30.24
Changes in the law (incidence of costs) 6.246
Charging orders 40.89–40.99, 43.414
Charging Orders Act 1979 40.99
enforcement of costs order
charging orders generally 43.413–43.414
fixed assets 43.409
Solicitors Act 1974, s 73 40.89–40.98
'any court', meaning of 40.91
assignment 40.96
'been employed', meaning of 40.91
cases where no money recovered 40.92
children 40.96
competing securities 40.96
diminution in value of property 40.93
discretion 40.94–40.95
injunctions 40.96
insolvency 40.96
limitation 23.99
monies paid into court 15.121
no need for assessment 40.96
procedure 40.97–40.98
'property', meaning of 40.91
security for costs 40.93
set-off 40.96
statutory provisions 40.90
timing 40.96
Chief value officer (CVO)
value-based pricing 42.37–42.38
Children
compromise 60.38–60.39
contentious business agreement 60.37
costs orders 60.03–60.08
definition 60.03
fixed costs 60.35
generally 60.01–60.02
indemnity principle 60.20–60.21
limitation 23.133
litigation friend 60.06–60.08
expenses of, 60.40–60.42
no contract of retainer 60.23
position between solicitor and 60.28–60.30
majority, reaching 60.24–60.25
necessaries 60.16–60.18, 60.26
paying party, position of 60.20–60.21
position between solicitor and child 60.09–60.19
prejudicial contracts 60.19
procedural issues 60.31–60.39
public policy 60.27
ratification on reaching majority 60.24–60.25
retainers 27.325
security for costs 15.96
summary assessment 44.12, 60.36
Citation of authorities
costs judgments 2.07
neutral citation 2.06
reported citations 2.08
Civil Procedure Rules (CPR)
CCR 4.42
directions 4.41
discretion of court 4.40
evidential rules 4.43
Henry VIII clauses 4.36
interpretation 4.37–4.40
jurisdiction 4.33–4.35
legal representative, under 2.09
new approach to justice 26.15–26.16
open-textured nature 4.40
overriding objective 4.39, 26.02–26.08
previous rules 4.42
RSC 4.42
status 4.32
Claim and counterclaim *see* **Counterclaims**
Clarification of orders 10.04
Clinical negligence
ATE insurance 34.24, 54.38–54.41
Co-defendant orders
availability 7.04–7.07
Bullock orders 7.04–7.25
choice between orders 7.22–7.23
conduct 7.21
consideration of order 7.08–7.09
discretion 7.07
doubts as to true law 7.24
legal aid 7.25
meaning 7.03
not mandatory orders 7.11
policy 7.04
requirements
alternative, claims are in the 7.17–7.20
nexus between claims 7.15–7.16
success against one defendant 7.12–7.14
Sanderson orders 7.04–7.25
types of order 7.05–7.06
Collective conditional fee agreements (CCFA)
CCFA Regulations 2000 29.117–29.128
generally 29.111
meaning 2.09, 29.03
present day use 29.129–29.131
regulatory control 29.116
structure 29.112–29.115
Collective proportionality
collective proportionality under the CPR 26.31–26.44
general principles 26.40–26.41
individual cases 26.42–26.44
tempering of justice 26.35–26.39
Cropper v Smith 26.31
history 26.28–26.31
interplay with individual proportionality 26.45

Collective proportionality (*cont.*)
other jurisdictions 26.46–26.47
overriding objective 26.02–26.08
Common interest privilege 46.10
Compromise
accord and satisfaction 39.17–39.18
between solicitor and client 39.08–39.21
disputed compromise and contested agreements 39.08–39.21
summary assessment 44.13
Computer printouts
assessment of costs 49.12–49.14
Conditional fee agreements
additional liabilities *see* **Additional liabilities; Success fees**
ambit, work carried out beyond 27.36
amended agreements 29.104–29.105
Bailey presumption, and 18.38–18.39, 29.44–29.52
basic requirements for
generally 29.14–29.16
prohibited agreements 29.18
success fees, further requirements 29.19–29.23
writing 29.17
CFA Lite *see* **CFA Lite**
circumstances in which client may be liable 29.79
clarity, relevance of 29.31
common law
contentious business 29.192–29.197
generally 29.179–29.184
non-contentious business 29.185–29.190
persons other than lawyers 29.198–29.202
Conditional Fee Agreements Regulations 2000 29.24–29.110, 29.217–29.218
see also below 'older agreements (2000–2005)'
consumer protection 28.177, 29.29–29.30
contentious business agreements, and 27.163–27.164
contractual interpretation 29.09–29.13
counsel's conditional fee agreements 53.36–53.38
damages-based agreements *see also* **Damages-based agreements** 29.141–29.178
meaning 2.09, 29.03
definitions
language of conditional fee agreements 2.09, 29.02
statutory definition of conditional fee agreement 29.04–29.08
types of conditional fee agreements 29.03
discounted conditional fee agreements *see* **Discounted conditional fee agreements**
entire contracts, and 27.21
generally 29.01
genuine issues, and 18.38–18.39, 29.44–29.52
history 1.132, 1.143, 1.148, 1.155, 1.157–1.162, 1.167, 1.173, 29.203–29.216
language of 29.02–29.03
materiality 29.53–29.71
meaning 2.09, 29.33–29.36
older agreements (2000–2005) 29.24–29.110
see also **CFA Lites**
alternative means of funding, advice 29.86–29.87
availability of insurance, advice 29.81–29.85
ambit and effect, to be stated 29.56–29.60
circumstances in which clients must pay, advice 29.79
clients' right to assessment, advice 29.80
effect as between opposing parties 29.109–29.110
effect as between solicitor and client 29.106–29.108
explanation, requirement for 29.97–29.101
further information, requirements for 29.88–29.90
materiality 29.53–29.71
panel membership, relevance of 29.91–29.96
postponement charge, requirements 29.62–29.64
pre-contract counselling, requirements for 29.77–29.78
reasons for level of percentage increase, requirements 29.61
reductions in success fee, requirements 29.65–29.66
signature, requirement for 29.102–29.103
statement of compliance, requirement for 29.59–29.60
variation of 29.104–29.105
oral and implied conditional fee agreements 27.214–27.216
prohibited conditional fee agreements 29.18
redaction 29.51
retainers 27.22
retrospectivity
backdating 29.140
parties, between 29.137–29.139
solicitor and client 29.132–29.136
statutory definition of 29.04–29.08
success fee *see also* **Success fees** 29.02, 29.19–29.23
summary assessment, and 44.22
termination of 27.86, 28.152
terminology 29.02–29.03
transfer of *see* **Transfer of contracts of retainer**
types, list of 29.03
unintended conditional fee agreements 29.09–29.13
unlawful retainers 27.259
unwritten conditional fee agreements 27.214–27.216
Conditional offers
admissible offers 6.241–6.243
Conduct and misconduct
conduct and the assessment of costs 57.07
costs capping orders 13.38
deemed orders 7.125–7.128
delay 23.58–23.73
exaggeration 57.18–57.36
admissions 6.153
culpable exaggeration 6.149–6.153
double jeopardy 57.19–57.20
effect of offers 57.23
general approach 6.151
innocent exaggeration 6.154–6.155
meaning 6.147–6.148
means by which reflected in amounts allowed 57.24–57.36
misallocation and exaggeration 57.21

non-disclosure by opponent 57.22
offers 6.152
Part 36 offers 6.152
personal injury claims 6.151
terminology 6.147–6.148
failing to respond to offers 6.141–6.143
generally 6.03, 6.78–6.79
improper conduct and fast track trial costs 50.358
incidence of costs and conduct
non-parties 9.28
Intellectual Property Enterprise Court 50.336
misconduct 57.37
criminality 57.55
delay 57.56
discretion 57.40–57.41
failure to comply with rules, practice directions or court orders 57.38–57.39
false basis of negotiations 57.57
improper behaviour 57.45
miscertification of bill 57.58–57.60
misconduct during the assessment 57.56–57.64
misconduct during the claim 57.37–57.55
non-compliance with practice directions 57.53
obstructive behaviour 57.51
procedure 57.61–57.64
rules of professional conduct 57.54
sanctions 57.46–57.49
unreasonable behaviour 57.42–57.44
withholding information 57.52
one of the seven pillars, as 57.02–57.04
order, effect of 57.05
personal injury claims 6.87–6.92
pre-action protocols 57.08–57.17
duty to narrow the issues 57.13
litigation as the 'last resort' 57.11–57.12
obstructive behaviour 57.16–57.17
unreasonable conduct and fast track trial costs 50.357
unreasonable delay providing medical records 57.14–57.15
pre-proceedings conduct 6.78, 6.79
commercial court 6.83–6.84
non-procedural conduct 6.82
other courts 6.85–6.86
personal injury claims 6.87–6.92
procedural and non-procedural conduct 6.79
restraining effect of order 57.05
rule against hindsight 57.06
Confidentiality
arbitration 48.85–48.86
mediation 48.43–48.47
Consent orders
see also **Tomlin orders**
draft orders 7.65
formalities 7.67–7.69
providing for irrecoverable costs 3.18
setting aside 10.27
uses 7.65
Consumer protection
baseline protection for businesses 28.11
bases of assessment between solicitor and client
discounts 37.36
price reductions 37.37
representations 37.33
unfair terms 37.34–37.35
businesses
baseline protection 28.11
current legislation 28.12, 28.13
remedies 28.14–28.15
cancellation of contracts made in consumer's home/place of work 28.163–28.200
Consumer Contracts (Information, Cancellation and Additional Charges) Regulations 2013
ambit 28.63–28.64
background 28.59–28.61
cancellation rights 28.89–28.96
distance contracts of retainer 28.81–28.88
durable medium 28.66
evidence 28.100
non-compliance 28.97–28.99
off-premises contracts of retainer 28.74–28.80
on-premises contracts of retainer 28.69–28.73
overview 28.58
pre-contract information 28.67–28.68
terms used 28.65
types of consumer contract 28.65
vires 28.62
Consumer Protection from Unfair Trading Regulations 2008
aggressive commercial practices 28.124–28.125
average customer 28.108–28.110
codes of conduct 28.117
consumer 28.107
discounts 28.140–28.142
enforcing terms 28.143–28.144
factors to be taken into account 28.120
infringing actions 28.113
invitation to purchase 28.121
misleading actions 28.114–28.118
misleading omissions 28.119, 28.122–28.123
non-compliance with regulations 28.131–28.133
overview 28.101–28.103
price reductions 28.146–28.148
professional diligence 28.111–28.112, 28.120
proscribed unfair practices 28.129–28.130
remedies 28.134–28.136
repeat performance 28.145
terminology 28.106–28.110
trade marks 28.116
trader 28.107
unwind, right to 28.137–28.139
vires 28.104–28.105
Consumer Rights Act 2015
consumer 28.26
contracting out, no 28.36
definitions 28.26–28.27
existing rights 28.28
information given by legal services provider 28.30–28.34
legislative history 28.23–28.25
no diminution of existing rights 28.28
overview 28.22
performance of services within a reasonable time 28.38–28.39

Consumer protection (*cont.*)
Consumer Rights Act 2015 (*cont.*)
reasonable price for a reasonable service 28.37
remedies 28.35
revisions to information 28.34
trader 28.27
unfair terms 28.40–28.44
contract, costs payable pursuant to 66.16
current legislation 28.06–28.07
development, history and legislative background 1.10
discounts 37.36
distance selling 28.201–28.212
doorstep selling 28.163–28.200
EU legislation 28.17–28.21
older legislation 28.10
overview 28.02–28.05
price reductions 37.37
Provision of Services Regulations 2009
ambit 28.46
consumer 28.54
consumer information by traders 28.55–28.57
contact details 28.50
declaring non-judicial dispute resolution procedures 28.51
definitions 28.54
general information 28.47
generally 28.45
information that must be given 28.52
means of providing information 28.48–28.49
traders 28.54
remedies 28.08
revoked legislation 28.09
Supply of Goods and Services Act 1982 28.156–28.158
Unfair Contract Terms Act 1977 28.159–28.162
unfair terms
Consumer Rights Act 2015 28.40–28.44
effect of unfair term/notice 28.42
greylist 28.43–28.44
test of unfairness 28.41
Unfair Terms in Consumer Contracts Regulations 1999 28.149–28.155
Contentious business
assessment of costs 3.21, 37.04
county court, jurisdiction of 36.43
definition and meaning 2.09, 3.25–3.30
examples of 3.31
non-contentious business distinguished 3.23–3.30
solicitors' security for costs 40.100–40.105
suing for payment of fees 40.18–40.19
Contentious business agreements
approval 27.189
change of solicitor 27.182–27.184
children 60.37
conditional fee agreements, and 27.163–27.164
death 27.182–27.184
effect of 27.156–27.159
enforcement and examination 27.166–27.167
fair and reasonable 27.175–27.177
form and content 27.142–27.143
notice, need for 27.154–27.155
signature, no need for 27.151–27.153
specificity, need for 27.148–27.150
terms as to costs 27.145–27.147
writing, requirement to be in 27.144
generally 27.135–27.138
hourly rate, agreements providing for 27.174
inadvertent contentious business agreements 39.11–39.12
incapacity 27.182–27.184, 60.67
meaning 2.09
other retainers compared 27.160–27.165
partial performance 27.182–27.184
procedural issues
enforcement 27.186–27.188
seeking approval 27.189
reasonableness 27.175–27.177
re-opening agreement 27.168, 27.185
representative capacity, client acting on 27.178–27.181
setting aside 27.173
Solicitors Act 1974 27.135–27.141
Contingency fee agreements
meaning 2.09, 29.03
Contra proferentum
interpretation of retainer 31.40
Contract, costs payable under
costs payable pursuant to
basis of assessment 66.18–66.20
consumer protection 66.16
generally 66.01
Gomba principles 66.04–66.11
interpretation 66.17
misconduct 66.13–66.14
orders made in ignorance of provisions 66.21–66.22
procedure 66.34
Contract of retainer *see* **Retainers**
Contributions
costs debtors, between 19.34–19.44
limitation 23.107–23.110
orders for costs
irrelevant factors 6.257–6.259
Contributory negligence
Part 36 offers 17.31
Copying charges
disbursements 52.73–52.76
Correction of orders
slip rule 10.05–10.07
Costs
damages compared 3.37–3.41
general characteristics 3.03–3.05
actually incurred 3.09
arise from litigation 3.06
calculable 3.10–3.11
costs not charges 3.07–3.08
'loss-of-opportunity' costs 3.12
neither punishment nor reward 3.16
not costs of being a litigant 3.13, 3.14
relevant factors 3.05, 3.19
remoteness, no test for 3.15
informal guidance, relevance of 4.63–4.67
meaning 2.09, 3.02, 3.04
regulated person 2.09
relevant lawyer 2.09
requests for payment on account 2.09
reserved instrument activities 2.09

reserved legal activities 2.09
unqualified person 2.09
Costs budgeting
see also **Costs capping; Costs management; Costs management orders**
additional information for budget 12.45–12.47
agreed budgets 12.48–12.50
amendments 12.107–12.129
approval, meaning of 12.03
assessment of costs
developments at trial 12.164
early settlement 12.157
failure to revise the budget 12.158
generally 12.137
hourly rates 12.161–12.163
incurred costs 12.138–12.139
indemnity basis 12.154–12.156, 12.166–12.168
no costs management order made, where 12.169–12.171
proportionality 12.159
standard basis 12.140–12.153
surveillance evidence 12.165
very large cases 12.160
assumptions 12.35
budget discussion reports 12.51–12.55
budget, meaning 12.03
budgeting, meaning 12.03
case management 12.63–12.64
client knowledge of budget 12.42
code-sets 49.45–49.46
content of budget 12.30
content of phases 12.31
contingencies 12.36–12.41
costs of the exercise 12.130–12.136
exchanging budgets 12.43–12.50
excluded costs 12.32–12.33
failure to file a budget 12.56–12.60
filing budget 12.43–12.50
form H 12.21–12.42
format of the budget 12.21–12.42
group litigation 12.29
history 1.172, 12.04–12.13
jurisdiction
costs lite 12.18
discretionary jurisdiction 12.19
generally 12.14
limited life expectancy, claimants with 12.18
litigants in person 12.18
local practices 12.18
older cases 12.18
Part 8 claims 12.18
prescribed jurisdiction 12.15–12.18
smaller claims 12.18
large cases 12.29
litigants in person 12.18
meaning 12.02
precedent H 12.21–12.42
purpose 12.02
replying to budgets 12.51–12.55
revisions 12.107–12.129
smaller cases 12.28
terminology 12.03
types of hearing 12.03
verification of budget 12.34
Costs capping
Aarhus convention claims 13.79–13.99, 13.108
access to justice 13.25
appeals
Aarhus Convention claims 13.108
non-Aarhus Convention claims 13.101–13.107
'arms race' 13.25
case management 13.43–13.45
circumstances in which order made 13.24–13.25
closed-material cases 13.44–13.45
comparators 13.38
conditions for order
exceptionality 13.22–13.23
generally 13.17
inadequate control of risk 13.18–13.21
conduct and misconduct 13.38
costs of application 13.38
costs of capping exercise 13.42
defamation claims 13.39–13.40
environmental claims 13.79–13.99
group litigation 13.26
history of the jurisdiction 13.07–13.13
judicial review
appeals 13.69
conditions for order 13.53–13.61
costs of applications 13.77
costs capping 13.62–13.65
crowdfunding 13.68
directions 13.72
discretion 13.62–13.65
evidence 13.72
exceptionality 13.60
financial resources 13.66–13.68
form of application 13.72
generally 13.46
history 13.47
impecuniosity 13.68
LSC conditions 13.68
origins of power 13.50–13.52
procedure 13.72
public interest proceedings 13.54–13.57
scope 13.50–13.52
service 13.72
terminology 13.48
transitional provisions 13.49
unilateral cap 13.63
variation 13.73–13.76
withdrawal of application 13.58–13.59
jurisdiction 13.04, 13.07–13.15
meaning 13.03
parties 13.16
postponement of payment 13.38
procedure for making order
contents of application 13.27
effect of order 13.31–13.34
evidence of costs lawyer/ draftsperson 13.29
exercise of jurisdiction 13.30
mandatory requirements 13.27
Precedent H 13.28

Costs capping (*cont.*)
procedure for making order (*cont.*)
quantum of cap 13.35–13.38
scope of order 13.31–13.34
proceedings relating to trusts 66.43
quantum of cap 13.35–13.38
satellite litigation 13.25
scope 13.16
source of the jurisdiction 13.14–13.15
stage of proceedings 13.16
success fees 13.38
terminology 13.06
value of claim 13.38
variation of order 13.41
Costs debtors
accord and satisfaction 19.26–19.27
full payment by one or more debtors 19.23
joint liability 19.21–19.29
joint and several liability 19.31–19.33
partial payment 19.24–19.25
Costs of detailed assessment
factors to be taken into account
amount of reduction 43.336–43.338
conduct 43.334–43.335
generally 43.331–43.333
reasonable to claim items 43.339–43.341
reasonable to dispute 43.339–43.341
generally 43.327–43.328
incidence of costs 43.329–43.335
interest 56.114–56.115
liability 43.327–43.375
presumptions 43.330
regimes governing 43.238
relevant factors
Part 36 offers (*see* **Part 36 offers**) 43.254–43.279
Part 47 offers (*see* **Part 47 offers**) 43.356–43.375
Costs judge
detailed assessment 43.12–43.15
meaning 2.09
Costs management
see also **Costs budgeting; Costs management order**
hearings 12.61–12.62
historical background 12.04–12.13
meaning 2.09
Costs management orders
comparison of budgets 12.93–12.94
disapplication because no order required 12.75
disapplication in part 12.78
disapproval of agreed budget 12.77
disapproval of unagreed budget 12.76
discretion to make order 12.69–12.74, 12.82–12.83
grossly excessive budgets 12.103
group litigation 12.80
hourly rates 12.95–12.98
interim applications 12.106
jurisdiction 12.67
level of budget 12.87–12.91
limited life expectancy 12.79
meaning 2.09, 12.03
personal injury cases 12.81
post-approval procedure 12.104–12.105
powers 12.66
proportionality 12.99–12.102
purpose 12.65
timing of futurity 12.92
treatment of costs already incurred 12.84–12.86
Costs mediation *see* **Mediation**
Costs protection (legal aid)
amount, whether to state 62.29
changes in circumstances 62.41
discretion 62.30
exclusions 62.05
governing provisions 62.10–62.12, 62.43–62.44
government departments 62.21
liability of Lord Chancellor 62.35–62.40
Lord Chancellor, payment of costs by 62.10–62.20
meaning 62.04
personal liability of legally aided party 62.31–62.34
pro bono funding 18.130
procedure 62.13–62.17
responsibility 62.07–62.09
revocation of certificate 62.42
timing 62.18–62.20
variation of amount 62.41
whether to make an order 62.23–62.28
withdrawal of certificate 62.06
Costs sharing agreements
absence of (default position) 65.58–65.59, 65.84
contractual issues 27.315–27.318
effect as between co-litigants 20.42–20.47
effect as between opposing parties 20.49
relevance of forms of funding, and 20.48
test claimants, and 65.59
types and forms 20.40–20.41, 65.07–65.08
variation of effect by order 65.08
Costs-only proceedings
alternatives and putative alternatives to 11.12
see also **Everything agreed save for costs**
restriction on use of alternatives 11.06, 11.12
where claimant claims costs and costs-only proceedings unavailable 7.170–7.175
where defendant claims costs and costs-only proceedings unavailable 7.176–7.182
assessment of costs 11.25
availability of 11.06
basis on which costs are assessed 11.23–11.24, 16.03
costs of the proceedings 11.26–11.28
default costs certificates 11.28, 43.148
failure to comply with procedure 11.28
fixed costs 50.299
Part 36 offers 11.28
Part 47 offers 11.28, 43.293
provisional assessments 11.28, 43.232, 43.359
small claims 11.28
description of 11.02
fixed costs 11.14–11.15, 50.96
historical background and policy 11.03–11.05
jurisdiction 11.05
Part 36 offers, pre-action acceptance 7.109, 7.173, 17.27
payments on account 14.05, 65.112
procedure
allocation 11.20

claim form (and content thereof) 11.09–11.11
consent orders 11.19
contested claims 11.17–11.18
disposal 11.21–11.22
fixed costs 11.14–11.15
generally 11.07
persons who may bring a claim 11.08
representative claims 11.10
small claims 11.20
uncontested claims 11.16
venue 11.13
Counsel's fees
agents 53.28
Bar Standards Board Handbook 53.03
basis of charging 53.40–53.41
cab-rank rule 53.06
code of conduct 53.03
commitment fees 53.116–53.117
contractual agreements
lay clients 53.33–53.39
licensed access client 53.19–53.32
professional clients 53.16–53.18
contractual arrangements with persons not entitled to conduct litigation 3.100
default, fee agreements in 53.08
devilling 53.130
evidencing counsel's fees and procedure
between solicitor and client 36.100
contemporaneous records 53.46–53.47
general rule 53.45
notes from counsel 53.48–53.49
written work 53.50
express agreement, acceptance of instructions without 53.07, 53.08
fast track 50.350–50.352
fees between opposing parties
conditional fee agreements 53.36–53.38
general principle 53.32
indemnity principle 53.34
nature of fees 53.33
unpaid fees 53.35
fees per item 53.114–53.115
generally 53.01
honorarium, nature of 53.04
hourly charging
advices 53.107
conferences 53.109
consultations 53.109
counsel's view 53.110
meaning 53.107
skeleton arguments 53.111
indemnity principle 53.34
informal arrangements for two counsel 53.130
leading counsel 53.119–53.123
licensed access client, contractual agreements with 53.19–53.23
methods of charging
booking fees 53.118
brief fees 53.51–53.102
fees per item 53.114–53.115
hourly charging 53.107–53.113
refreshers 53.103–53.106
retainers 53.116–53.117
more than two counsel 53.131–53.134
nature of right to payment 22.24, 53.04–53.07
new Terms of Work 53.05, 53.06, 53.135
non-contractual agreements with professional clients 53.09–53.15
not practising as a barrister in independent practice 53.30
not supplying legal services 53.31
old Terms of Work 53.05, 53.14–53.15
publication of standard terms 53.06
quantum
additional material 53.64
after-care 53.63
brief fees 53.51
comparators 53.91–53.96, 53.105
conferences 53.60
'going rate' 53.97
hypothetical counsel test 53.52–53.55
judgment 53.62
London counsel and the provincial bar 53.98
material changes in the case 53.65–53.66
overlap between cases 53.102
relevance of time 53.87–53.90
researching the law 53.100
scope of brief fee 53.56–53.66
skeleton arguments 53.61
travelling 53.101
work outside business hours 53.99
refreshers
abated refresher 53.104
comparators 53.105
meaning 53.103
obsolete authorities 53.106
retainers 53.116
scope of instructions 53.42–53.44
set-off 53.27
two counsel 53.124–53.129
types of client 53.02
types of fee agreement 53.07
VAT 55.3, 55.08
Withdrawal of Credit List 53.05
Counterclaims
see **Distribution**, *Medway Oil*, etc assessment of costs 49.124
distribution of costs (and *Medway Oil*) 20.50–20.63
fast track trial costs 50.345
fixed costs 50.253, 50.307–50.310, 50.345, 50.355, 50.360
incidence of costs 6.63–6.64, 7.34–7.37
Part 36 offers 17.31, 17.34–17.40, 17.190
portal costs 50.253
qualified one-way costs shifting 8.14
security for costs 15.10, 15.65–15.70, 15.118
Set-off 21.31
County Court Rules 26.09–26.14
County court, jurisdiction of
local practices 4.48
London and SCCO 43.03
solicitor and client claims and assessments 36.43, 37.18–37.23, 40.19

Couriers
disbursements 52.77–52.78
Court
definition 3.34–3.36
meaning 2.09
Court fees
disbursements 52.87–52.97
non-payment of and deemed orders 7.105–7.107
remission 52.90–52.93
Court guides
admissibility 4.64
Courts Service
discretion
exercise of 64.09–64.14
principles governing 64.11–64.14
ex gratia payments by 64.02
generally 64.01–64.02
power to make payments 64.03–64.08
procedure 64.18–64.22
quantum 64.15–64.17
Criminality
misconduct 57.55
pre-proceedings conduct 6.103
Cross-examination
detailed assessment hearing 43.321–43.323
Crown
orders against 61.03–61.06
Custom or usage
implied retainers 27.198–27.199
implied terms 31.63–31.68

Damages
costs compared 3.37–3.41
fees for professional advisors 3.42–3.43
misclassification 3.44–3.47
Damages-based agreements
conditions 29.143, 29.145
Damages-Based Agreements Regulations 2013 (DBA Regulations 2013) 29.149–29.175, 29.219
generally 29.141–29.146
indemnity principle 29.176–29.178
meaning 2.09, 29.03, 29.144
non-contentious business agreement 29.147–29.148
opt-out collective proceedings 29.146
unlawful retainers 27.260–27.286
use 29.142
Deemed orders 7.100–7.140
bases of assessment 7.104, 7.134–7.135
conduct 7.125–7.128
CPR Part 36
acceptance of offer 7.109–7.111
discontinuance 7.112–7.124, 7.137
constructive discontinuance 7.119
discretion 7.120–7.124
enforcement 7.140
group litigation 7.137–7.138, 7.138
indemnity basis, costs on the 7.134, 7.135
jurisdiction 7.114
part of claim discontinued 7.119
premature issue 7.128
qualified one-way costs shifting 7.139
service of notice 7.118
small claims 7.136
supervening events 7.129–7.133
discretion 7.101
dishonoured cheques 7.108
interest 56.101–56.102
meaning 2.09
non-payment of court fees 7.105–7.107
starting point 7.103
Defamation
costs capping orders 13.39–13.40
Default costs certificate
conditions 43.161–43.164
costs of issue 43.148
effectiveness 43.141
errors 43.157–43.164
estoppel by convention 43.156
form of application 43.146–43.147
issue 43.142–43.148
meaning 2.09
pro bono work 43.165
procedural irregularities 43.164
procrastination by paying party 43.163
promptness 43.162
purpose 43.140
setting aside 43.149–43.155, 43.157–43.164
solicitor and client assessments, absence of provision for 36.115
timing of applications 43.144–43.145
Defective retainers
generally 32.42
management 32.42–32.74
remedial steps where there is an entitlement to costs 32.65–32.66
interpretation 32.66
quantum meruit 32.66
rectification 32.67–32.74
remedial steps where there is no entitlement to costs 32.56–32.64
deeds 32.59–32.63
practice points 32.64
rectification 32.58–32.63
undue influence and remedial steps *see also* **Undue influence** 32.43–32.55
Delay
see also **Detailed assessment**, 'commencement of process', and 'requesting hearing' admissible offers 6.239
conduct 23.58–23.73
detailed assessment, sanctions for delay in misconduct 57.56
generally 23.50–23.56
incidence of costs generally and 9.189
delay in giving disclosure 57.14–57.15
intention 23.75
interest 23.57
loss of interest as sanction 23.77–23.78
procedure 23.81–23.82
solicitor and client assessment, application for 36.04–36.06
unless orders 23.74
wasted costs 9.189

Dental records
VAT 55.23–55.24
Derivative claims 65.123–65.125
Detailed assessment
see also **Bills of costs (between opposing parties); Final costs certificates; Interim costs certificates; Part 36 offers; Part 47 offers**
additional liabilities, assessment of 43.55, 43.83–43.84
agreed costs
discontinuance 43.247–43.249
final costs certificates 43.243–43.245
general rule 43.239
Tomlin orders 43.246
uncontested agreements 43.240–43.242
withdrawal 43.247–43.249
allocation
authorised court officers 43.19–43.24
costs judges 43.12–43.15
generally 43.10–43.11
regional costs judges 43.16–43.18
appeals and forthwith orders 43.74–43.82
appeals from 45.1
appropriate office 43.02–43.03
Calderbank offers 43.298
case management
costs management 43.26
debarring orders 43.28
generally 43.25
stay 43.27
commencement of process
additional liabilities 43.55
application for permission 43.62–43.68
breakdown of costs for each phase 43.52
'concluded' 43.69–43.73
counting days 43.87
delay 43.85–43.88
extending period by application 43.89
finality 43.59
generally 43.51
late commencement 43.85–43.88
multiple bills 43.59
notice of commencement 43.51–43.54
period of time allowed 43.85–43.86
prescribed form 43.51
sanctions for delay 43.94–43.95
service of notices 43.57–43.58
standard form 43.53
status of persons served 43.56
variation of time limits 43.88
commercial offers 43.299–43.300
consensual extension of time 43.90, 43.91–43.93
contested agreements 43.250–43.251
costs of proceedings, *see* **Costs of detailed assessment**
amount of reduction 43.336–43.338
conduct 43.334–43.335
factors to be taken into account 43.331–43.332
generally 43.327–43.328
incidence of costs 43.329–43.333
Part 36 offers 43.342–43.355
presumption 43.330
reasonableness 43.339–43.341
County Court hearings 43.03
default costs certificates, *see* **Default costs certificates**
discontinuance 43.394–43.406
final costs certificates, *see* **Final costs certificates**
forthwith orders 43.61, 43.74–43.82
generally 43.01
hearing
accompanying documents 43.181–43.185
additional liabilities 43.305
cross-examination 43.321–43.323
determination of issues of fact 43.230–43.325
disclosure 43.315–43.316
electronic filing 43.310–43.311
fees 43.186–43.189
filing papers 43.307–43.308
fixing date 43.302–43.304
hearsay 43.325
issues between legal services provider and client 43.326
judgments 43.317–43.319
listing 43.302–43.304
misconduct 43.305
new evidence coming to light during hearing 23.27
notices 43.305
preparation 43.305–43.308
reasons 43.317–43.319
referral to trial judge 43.324
request 43.176–43.195
statements of costs 43.309
submissions 43.312–43.314
venue 43.306
hybrid offers 43.301
interim costs certificates, *see* **Interim costs certificates**
offers to settle
Calderbank offers 43.298
Part 36 offers *see also* **Part 36 offers** 43.254–43.279
Part 47 offers 43.280–43.301
types of offer 43.253
Part 36 offers 17.31, 43.254–43.279
Part 47 offers 43.280–43.301
points of dispute
additional liabilities 43.123–43.124
brevity 43.113–43.114
budgets 43.122
content 43.111–43.117
estimates 43.122
format 43.109–43.110
individual offers 43.116–43.117
open global offers 43.118–43.121
prolixity 43.115
purpose 43.108
service 43.135–43.139
time limits 43.126–43.134
variation 43.125
replies 43.166–43.175
requesting hearing
delay 43.190–43.193
disallowing interest 43.193
documents 43.181–43.185
fees 43.186–43.189

Detailed assessment (*cont.*)
requesting hearing (*cont.*)
form of request 43.178–43.180
general rule 43.176
orders vs interest 43.194–43.195
time limits 43.177
unless orders 43.191–43.192
security for costs 15.23
Senior Courts Costs Office (SCCO)
referral to 43.04–43.05
venue 43.03
specialist lists 43.03
time limits 43.85–43.86
application to extend 43.89
consensual extension of time 43.91–43.93
counting days 43.87
period of time allowed 43.85–43.86
retrospective extension of time 43.90
sanctions for delay 43.94–43.95
variation 43.88
transfer between courts 43.06–43.09
unless orders 43.96–43.107, 43.191–43.192
wasted costs 9.100–9.101
Detailed bill
generally 35.99–35.108
meaning 2.09, 35.99
Detailed breakdown
generally 35.89, 36.64, 36.99
meaning 2.09, 35.89, 35.101
Devilling
counsel's fees 53.130
Disbursements
actual disbursements
examples 52.04
meaning 52.02
scope 52.04
agents, non-solicitor 22.08–22.20
agents, solicitor 22.06–22.07
categorisation 52.02–52.03
client disbursements 52.02, 52.08
conduct money 52.49–52.55
copying charges 52.73–52.76
couriers 52.77–52.78
court fees 52.87–52.97
benefits, effect of 52.97
group litigation 52.94
hearing fee 52.90–52.93
issue fee 52.87
listing questionnaire 52.89
definition 52.02
detailed assessments 43.302, 52.95–52.96
expert witnesses
cancellation fees 52.37
duties 52.34
expenses of expert 52.39
hourly rates 52.41
instructed without court's permission 52.29–52.32
joint instructions 52.43–52.45
meaning of expert 52.10
measure of fees 52.33–52.41
medical agencies 52.63–52.72
multiple experts 52.27–52.28
non-expert professional services 52.38
overheads 52.42
qualifying fees 52.36
reading-in time 52.35
recoverability of fees in principle 52.11–52.21
stand-by reports 52.40
status of expert 52.42
unused reports 52.28
whether reasonable to instruct 52.22–52.28
factual witnesses
conduct money 52.49–52.55
Crown Court method, by analogy with 52.51
expenses 52.56
general principle 52.47
legal advice 52.56
non-attendance 52.56
permission 520.56
professional witnesses 52.58–52.59
travelling expenses 52.56
witness and receiving party same person 52.57
fixed costs 50.83, 50.96, 50.181–50.188, 50.277, 50.284
foreign lawyers 52.98–52.99
funding loans 52.85–52.86
generally 52.01
hotel expenses 52.79–52.80
interpreters 52.100–52.101
litigants in person 59.09, 59.28–59.34
meaning 2.09, 52.02
medical agencies 52.63–52.72
medical records 52.60–52.61
MRO agreement (Woollard agreement) 52.69–52.71
notional 59.29
office disbursements 52.02, 52.09
personal records other than medical records 52.62
portal costs
generally 50.181–50.183
soft-tissue injuries 50.184–50.187
treating clinicians 50.188
postage 52.77–52.78
professional witnesses 52.58–52.59
services
examples 52.06
meaning 52.02, 52.06
solicitor-and-client assessments 35.116–35.119, 36.62, 36.69, 36.100
travelling expenses 52.81–52.84
true expenses 52.02, 52.07
types 52.02
VAT 55.02, 55.15–55.21
vouchers 36.100, 43.51, 43.183
Disclosure
adverse inferences 46.73
adverse material 46.31–46.37
assessment of costs 49.30–49.31
assumptions 46.74
ATE insurance 34.55–34.57

BTE insurance 34.12
burden of proof 46.72
code-sets 49.30
consequences of disclosure 46.69–46.71
defective retainer 32.64
election 46.69–46.71
fraud 46.75
group litigation 65.113
implied waiver 46.60–46.66
litigation funding agreements 46.19
non-party costs orders 9.89–9.92
non-privileged documents
administrative records 46.17
communications with other persons 46.22–46.24
non-privileged material 46.76
Part 36 offers 17.57–17.59
privileged documents
advice privilege 46.08–46.09
bills 46.14–46.15
client care letters 46.16
communications made prior to litigation 46.23
counsel's papers 46.20
documents 46.14–46.27
expert reports 46.21
litigation privilege 46.10
types of privilege 46.06
redaction 29.51
security for costs 15.127–15.130
wasted costs 9.181
Discontinuance *see* **Deemed orders**
costs proceedings 43.394–43.406
group litigation 65.79, 65.85–65.88
Discounted conditional fee agreements
ATE insurance, and 34.26, 34.33
entire contracts, and 27.22
percentage increase, gauging level of 29.22
percentage increase, assessing 54.86, Table 68.12
litigation funding, and 33.67
meaning 2.09, 29.03
Discretion
co-defendant orders 7.07
deemed orders 7.120–7.124
everything agreed save for costs 7.142–7.152
judicial review
costs capping 13.62–13.65
payments on account 14.09–14.10
wasted costs 9.117–9.119
Dishonoured cheques
deemed orders 7.108
Disputed compromise 39.08–39.21
accord and satisfaction 39.17–39.18
agreements 39.11–39.12
authorities 39.09
bills 39.15–39.16
business agreements, inadvertent 39.11–39.12
meaning 39.08
oral agreements 39.13–39.14
promissory estoppel 39.19
sources of compromise 39.10
subsequent promise 39.20–39.21
waiver 39.20–39.21
Distance selling
consumer protection 28.201–28.212
electronic commerce 28.213
Distribution
see also **Apportionment**; **Division**
apportionment 20.16–20.39
division 20.03, 20.13–20.15
group litigation 65.57–65.65, 65.74–65.84, 65.114
issues orders, and 20.64–20.65
Medway Oil principle 20.04, 20.50–20.63, 20.59
overview 20.06–20.10 and Figure 20.1
reciprocal entitlements 20.50–20.63
cross-orders 20.52
Medway Oil: background and facts 20.52–20.58
Medway Oil: principle 20.59–20.60
no formal counterclaim 20.61
other than claim and counterclaim 20.63
Part 36 offers 20.62
relevance of distribution to the incidence of costs 20.11–20.12
special orders 20.66
stages of distribution 20.27
terminology 20.03
types 20.05
Division
see also **Apportionment**; **Distribution**
broad-brush division 20.14–20.15
distinguished from apportionment 2.03
nature of division 20.13

Early neutral evaluation
see also **Alternative dispute resolution (ADR)**
combined with other forms of ADR 48.61
funding 48.64
generally 48.58–48.61
meaning 48.58
nature of 48.59
procedure 48.62–48.63
Election 46.40–46.74
blanket election 46.55
consequences 46.69–46.71
disclosure compared 46.40
discretion 46.45–46.54
formal approach 46.48–46.54
human rights 46.44
informal approach 46.45–46.47
Pamplin procedure 46.42
principles 46.40–46.44
procedure 46.45–46.54, 46.77–46.79
proportionality 46.57–46.59
purpose 46.41
waiver
assessments, limited to 46.56
implied waiver 46.60–46.66
limited waiver 46.67
withdrawal of waiver 46.68
Employees
meaning of 50.121–50.128
representation by 47.32
retainers 27.324
work carried out by 3.83–3.90, 18.105–18.120

Enforcement
costs debt 43.407–43.414
Entire contracts 27.06, 27.07–27.28
conditional fee agreements, and 27.22
effect of 27.08–27.12, 27.23
general retainers, and 27.22
historical perspective 27.13–27.20
modern approach 27.21
options and stages 27.22
relating to appeals 27.22
right to payment where no full performance
acceptance of partial performance 27.25
frustration 27.27
partial performance 27.26
repudiation 27.28
substantial performance 27.24
Estimated time
assessment 49.19
long attendances 49.19
meaning 49.15
'padding' of the bill 49.19
recoverability 49.17–49.18
repeated failure to record time 49.19
short attendances 49.19
stating in bill 49.16
Estimates
code-sets 49.44
Consumer Contracts (Information, Cancellation and Additional Charges) Regulations 2013 28.71–28.72, 28.77
Consumer Rights Act 2015 28.33–28.34, 38.68–38.73
contractual duties 38.54
duty to give an estimate 38.44–38.75
experts 52.12–52.13
group litigation 65.93–65.95
history 12.05–12.08
incomplete estimates 38.79
instructions 38.55
listing questionnaire 4.60
non-binding nature 38.60
'old-style' estimates 12.169–12.171
poor estimates 38.79
practice directions 38.56
Provision of Services Regulations 2009 28.52
qualifies estimates 38.76–38.78
relevance as between solicitor and client 38.60–38.79
revised estimates 38.74–38.75
where no costs management order 12.169–12.171
Estoppel
cause of action estoppel 23.08–23.18
default costs certificates 43.156
disputed compromise 39.19
indemnity principle 18.100–18.104
issue estoppel 23.19–23.27
limitation 23.134
Part 36 offers 17.66
promissory estoppel 39.19
European Convention for the Protection of Human Rights and Fundamental Freedoms 1950
benefits under 24.08
generally 24.03
Everything agreed save for costs
compromise 7.156, 7.164
concessions 7.156
concessions on appeal 7.163
discontinuance 7.155
jurisdiction and discretion 7.142–7.154
evidence 7.153
fact-finding, etc 7.152–7.154
general approach 7.144–7.147
need to avoid litigation solely about costs 7.148–7.151
'trial lite' 7.154
whether to make an order 7.143
where there is a clear winner, examples 7.159–7.164
where there is no clear winner, examples 7.165–7.168
Evidence
see also **Election; Legal professional privilege**
burden of proof in detailed assessments 46.72
filing, meaning 46.03
generally 46.01–46.03
hearsay evidence 43.325
oral evidence 43.321–43.322
overview 46.03
procedure 46.77–46.79
retainers 27.95–27.101
security for costs 15.127–15.130
wasted costs 9.128–9.140
Exaggeration
see also **Conduct and misconduct**
admissible offers 6.238
admissions 6.153
conduct and misconduct 57.18–57.36
culpable 6.149–6.153
general approach 6.151
innocent 6.154–6.155
meaning 6.148
offers 6.152
Part 36 offers 6.152
personal injury claims 6.151
terminology 6.147
Executors
retainers 27.323
Expenses
see also **Disbursements**
true expenses 52.02, 52.07
Expert assistance
litigants in person 59.36–59.37
Expert reports
assessment of costs 49.34–49.35
code-sets 49.34–49.35
Expert witnesses
see also **Disbursements**
hourly rates 52.41
reports 46.21

Failure to respond to offer
conduct 6.141–6.143
Fast-track trial costs
advocates 50.348
allocation criteria 50.345

amount of costs 50.350–50.355
application of provisions 50.346
counterclaims 50.345
cross-orders 50.360
factors affecting allocation 50.345
generally 50.345
improper conduct 50.358
meaning 50.347
misallocation to track 50.345
more than one claimant/defendant 50.362–50.367
multiple trials 50.359
power to award more or less 50.356–50.361
reallocation 50.345
scope 50.345
split trials 50.345
trials 50.349
unreasonable conduct 50.357
value of the claim 50.345

Fee sharing agreements
see **Costs sharing agreements**

Filing of papers
additional liabilities 46.29
adverse material 46.31, 46.32–46.37
detailed assessment hearing 43.310
error, documents filed in 46.38–46.39
governing provisions 46.28
material mistakenly filed 46.38–46.39
meaning 46.03
order of filing 46.29
retainer documentation 46.05

Final costs certificates
calculations 43.385
completed bills 43.392
delay 43.386
enforcement 43.391
final filing 43.384–43.386
generally 43.383
instalments 43.391
interest 43.391
meaning 2.09
outstanding payments 43.391
payments already made 43.391
pro bono work 43.387
stay 43.391
VAT rate changes 43.391
wording of relevant provisions 43.392–43.393

Finality of litigation 23.03–23.06

Fixed costs
children 60.35
circumstances in which will apply 50.49–50.54
definition 50.04
discretion of court 50.52–50.54
fixed commencement costs
amount 50.57–50.60
scope 50.55
specified sum, claim for 50.56
fixed enforcement costs 50.66
fixed judgment costs 50.62–50.65
fixed percentage increases
employers' liability claims 50.118–50.130
employers' liability disease claims 50.131–50.149
road traffic accident claims 50.105–50.117
fixed recoverable costs
ambit 50.68–50.71
amount 50.79–50.85
application to exceed 50.89–50.91
costs 50.94
counsel's fees 50.86
definitions 50.72–50.78
disbursements 50.83–50.84
generally 50.67
importance of provisions 50.67
multiple claimants 50.87
older cases 50.71
Part 36 offers 50.70
procedure 50.92–50.93, 50.95–50.96
profit costs 50.80–50.82
putative premature issue of claims 50.97–50.101
success fees 50.88
generally 50.01–50.03
governing provisions 50.02
historical background
fixed recoverable costs 50.19–50.20
fixed success fees 50.19–50.20
generally 50.07
hourly rates 50.08–50.09
Jackson reforms 50.21–50.25
Ministry of Justice reforms 50.26
pre-Woolf history 50.10–50.14
RTA Protocol 50.27–50.47
Woolf reforms 50.15–50.18
HM Revenue & Customs
calculation 50.243–50.244
governing provisions 50.342
meaning 2.09, 50.48
miscellaneous fixed costs 50.61
post-Portal fixed costs
ambit 50.269–50.274
counterclaims 50.307–50.310
defendants, costs in favour of 50.303–50.306
discretion to allow more than fixed cost 50.297–50.299
discretion to restrict costs 50.300
EL/PL claims 50.279–50.285
generally 50.267
interim applications 50.301–50.302, 50.311
meaning 50.268
multiple claimants 50.286
Part 36 offers 50.287–50.296
road traffic accident claims 50.275–50.278
scale costs 50.04
scope 50.49–50.54
terminology 50.04–50.06, 50.07

Foreign lawyers
disbursements 52.98–52.99

Forthwith orders
additional liabilities 7.91
appeals 7.87–7.90
appropriate uses 7.82–7.84
case examples 7.94–7.99
costs judges 7.86
group litigation 7.92–7.93, 65.110

Forthwith orders (*cont.*)
legal aid 7.85
meaning 2.09
procedure 7.81
stay of proceedings 7.87–7.90
uses 7.80
Fraud
admissible offers 6.232
disclosure 46.75
equitable remedies 40.114
indemnity basis 16.50–16.52
limitation 23.135–23.136
Freedom of expression
incidence of costs, relevance of status to 6.261
Fund
costs payable out of 66.80–66.84
interest payable out of 56.112–56.113
meaning 2.09
Funding
code-sets 49.43–49.44
third-party *see* **Litigation funding** 33.03

General retainer
meaning 2.09
Gross sum bill
meaning 2.09
narrative 35.52
statutory provisions 35.99
requests for bills containing detailed items 35.99–35.108
effect of making request 35.88, 35.100
distinguished from request from clarification 35.102–35.103
doubt as to nature of request 35.105
where there was no request 35.89, 35.108
where available 35.58, 35.98–35.98
Group litigation
abandoned issues 65.50
adverse costs 65.71–65.79
apportionment 65.03
bearing own costs 65.55
case management 65.37–65.44
claims handling agreements 65.27
common costs 65.04
costs capping 13.26
costs judge assessors 65.39
disclosure of funding 65.42, 65.43
discontinuance 7.137–7.138, 65.61, 65.79, 65.87–65.89
district judge 65.40
forensic sieve 65.115
generally 65.01
incidence of costs 65.46–65.47
individual costs treated as group costs 65.56
issues-based orders 65.48–65.55
jurisdiction 65.09–65.14
late joiners 65.60, 65.79, 65.85, 65.86
lead solicitors 65.41
liability for costs 65.57–65.61
managing judge 65.40
mixed hearings 65.45
non-party costs orders 9.76
notice of funding 65.44
offers to settle 65.53
one claimant and many defendants 65.54
opponent's liability
failed claims 65.81–65.82
generally 65.80
no costs sharing agreement 65.84
set-off 65.83
orders
alternatives 65.27
applications 65.20–65.24
consent 65.18, 65.19
content 65.17
decision to make order 65.22–65.24
effect 65.26
form 65.17
generally 65.02, 65.15
group registers 65.28–65.36
meaning 65.16
procedure 65.20–65.24
variation 65.25
procedure 65.104–65.114
bill of costs 65.105
case management 65.108
categorisation of costs 65.106
disclosure 65.113
forthwith orders 65.110
interim payments 65.111–65.112
mixed hearings 65.114
preliminary issues 65.107
quantum
alternative dispute resolution 65.103
circular letters 49.102, 65.99
costs of funding 65.102
court fees 52.94
estimates 65.93–65.95
failure to comply with directions 65.98
generally 65.90
hourly rates 65.96
media 65.100
proportionality 65.91–65.92
travelling 65.101
wrong court 65.97
register
case management 65.30
cut-off dates 65.35–65.36
details of case 65.29, 65.30
establishment 65.28
removal 65.32
test claims 65.33–65.34
security for costs 15.56
settlements 65.61, 65.79, 65.87–65.89
solicitor and client assessments 36.10
terminology 65.04–65.08
test cases 65.56
test claims 65.62–65.70

Hansard
sources of law 4.73–4.76
Hearings
non-attendance
wasted costs 9.191
Hearsay
detailed assessment hearing 43.325

History of costs
Anglo-Saxon period 1.06–1.07
Edwardian period 1.106–1.109
First World War 1.110–1.111
generally 1.03–1.05
Georgian period
George II 1.61–1.68
George III 1.69–1.72
interwar period 1.112–1.118
new millennium
first decade 1.157–1.170
modern times 1.171–1.189
Norman period 1.08–1.10
Plantagenet period
Angevin kings 1.12–1.14
generally 1.11
House of Lancaster 1.30
House of York 1.31
main line 1.15–1.29
post-war times
1950s 1.126–1.130
1960s 1.131–1.132
1970s 1.133–1.135
1980s 1.136–1.144
1990s 1.145–1.156
Second World War 1.119–1.125
Stuart period
Carolean period 1.54–1.56
generally 1.45–1.49
Glorious Revolution 1.60
Jacobean period 1.50–1.53
Restoration 1.57–1.59
terminology 1.02
Tudor period
Elizabeth I 1.40–1.44
Henry VII 1.32–1.34
Henry VIII 1.35–1.39
Victorian times
post-Judicature Acts 1.92–1.102
pre-Judicature Acts 1.73–1.91
Hourly rates
A factor 51.26–51.31
A-plus-B analysis (pre-CPR) 51.24–51.43
B factor 51.32–51.37
City rates 51.77
comparators, use of 51.84–51.86
complexity of case 51.78
composite rates 51.87–51.90
conduct concerning *locus* 51.74
expert witnesses 52.41
generally 51.01–51.02
geographical convenience 51.69–51.72
geographical differences in rates 51.66–51.67
government departments 51.82
grade of person who did work 51.46–51.51
guideline rates
form 51.15
formulation 51.17–51.19
grades 51.15
national bands 51.16
relevance 51.15–51.23
habitual instructions 51.68
historical background 50.08–50.09
history of time-based charging
decline of the hourly rate 51.12–51.14
generally 51.03–51.04
United Kingdom 51.08–51.11
United States 51.05–51.07
implied terms 31.70
in-house solicitors 51.81
indemnity principle 51.02
low overheads 51.80
meaning 51.25
modern approach 51.44–51.83
place where work done 51.52–51.65
pre-CPR terminology 51.24–51.37
proportionality and distance 51.75–51.76
solicitor and client, between 38.06–38.07, 38.09–38.14
specialist expertise 51.73, 51.79
time pressure 51.83
time when work done 51.45
urgent cases 51.83
use 51.20–51.23
Human rights
access to justice 24.34–24.42
acts prescribed by law 24.24–24.25
additional liabilities 24.43–24.53
Brexit, impact of 24.02
costs-specific issues 24.34–24.42
Courts Service 24.54
declarations of incompatibility 24.19–24.22
determining incompatibility 24.23–24.31
ECHR, benefits of 24.08
ECtHR 24.04–24.07
HRA 1998 24.09–24.11
conflict with ECtHR 24.12
inequality of arms 24.40
jurisdiction 24.03
margin of appreciation 24.30–24.31
necessity 24.27–24.29
permissible aim 24.26
proportionality 24.27–24.29
remedies 24.13–24.22
right to privacy 24.56–24.57
security for costs 15.04–15.05, 24.58
wasted costs 24.59

Impecuniosity
admissible offers 6.248
plural liability and entitlement 19.19
security for costs 15.96
Implied retainers
consumer contracts 27.195–27.197
disputed existence 27.200–27.206
generally 27.190–27.206
modes of implication
see also **Implied terms**
custom or usage 27.198–27.199
presumption in favour of payment 18.28, 27.191–27.194
presumption that reasonable price will be paid 27.195–27.197
necessary inference 27.195–27.197

Implied retainers (*cont.*)
terms 27.206
work carried out beyond ambit of written retainer 27.36
Implied terms
contracts entire 27.08
custom or usage 27.198–27.199, 31.63–31.68
fairness 31.62
general law 31.57
intention 31.62
legal expenses insurance 34.66
modern approach 31.62
necessity 31.62
reasonableness 31.62
specific implied terms and situations
consumer clients 27.195–27.197
business clients 28.156–28.158, 31.73
deemed terms 31.72
estimates, duty to provide 38.54
hourly rates 27.206, 31.70
interim payments 27.56–27.59, 31.71
interim statute bills 27.60–27.61
litigation friends 60.28
rebuttable presumptions 31.69
types of implication 31.58–31.61
Indemnity basis
budgets, and 12.166–12.168
causation 16.30
circumstances in which ordered 16.13–16.14
contracts, costs payable under 66.04, 66.11, 66.17
costs of issues 16.29
costs-only proceedings 11.23–11.24
culpability, relevance of 16.21–16.27
exercise of jurisdiction 16.18–16.30
funders, position of 9.44, 16.28
general forensic method 16.19–16.20
jurisdiction 16.15, 16.15–16.30, 16.16
legally aided persons, restrictions 16.16
meaning 2.09
origins and history 1.49, 1.64, 1.86, 1.98, 1.144, 16.15
Part 36 offers, and 17.80–17.81, 17.85, 17.88–17.91, 17.96
detailed assessments 43.345
Enterprise and Intellectual Property Court 50.336
injustice test 17.147, 17.151,
late acceptance 17.182–17.183
Part 36 offers and fixed costs 17.163, 50.293–50.294
persons at fault 16.28
retainers, restrictions in 16.16
standard basis distinguished from 16.10–16.12
solicitor and client, as between 37.02, 37.06, 37.24, 37.27
test 16.09
two bases 16.02
trustees, costs payable to 66.36
specific circumstances
Aarhus Convention 13.189, 16.67
abandonment of a case 16.43–16.45
ADR, refusal to engage in 6.118, 6.133, 16.33
ADR, refusal to engage in (detailed assessments) 48.54–48.57
aggressive correspondence 6.107
anti-suit provisions 16.65
arbitration 16.65
breach of fiduciary duty 16.62
changing case to fit the circumstances 16.53
contempt of court 16.49
contractual entitlements 16.64, 66.04, 66.11, 66.17
courting publicity 16.63
discontinuance 7.134
dishonesty 16.47, 16.48
enquiries, failure to make 16.55
exaggeration 6.151, 6.238, 16.50–16.52
experts 16.60–16.61
failure to cooperate 16.32
fraud 6.232, 16.50–16.52
inflammatory behaviour 16.49
judicial encouragement, failure to act on 16.33
jurisdiction clauses 16.65
letter of claim, failure to send 6.106
litigation solely about costs 16.66
mediation 16.33
misleading conduct 16.47–16.48
offers 6.212, 16.34–16.37
offers, failure to respond to 6.142
overenthusiastic pursuance of a case 16.46
pre-action protocols 16.56
procedural requirements, failure to comply with 16.57–16.59
qualified one-way costs shifting 8.22
relief from sanctions 16.41–16.42
weak cases 16.38–16.40
Indemnity principle
agreement by solicitor not to enforce against client 18.83
bad debt, effect of declaring costs debt as 18.84
Bailey presumption 18.30–18.34
CFA Lites, effect of 18.86–18.90
children and 59.6
client liable for fees 18.28–18.29
conditional fee agreements 18.38–18.39
counsel's fees 53.34
credit, solicitor acting on 18.85
cross-examination 18.54
disapplication 18.23
dual liability for costs 18.59–18.72
employers 18.70
insurers 18.67–18.68
motoring organisations 18.69
principle 18.59–18.62
state funding 18.72
subrogation 18.73–18.77
unions 18.63–18.66
estoppel 18.100–18.104
ethos of the CPR 18.51–18.52
evidence of payment 18.56
evidencing the indemnity principle 18.24–18.57
exceptions to 18.15–18.23
generally 18.01, 18.02
genuine issue 18.35–18.37
historical perspective 18.03–18.05
individual application, the principle of 18.11–18.14

legal staff, costs of 18.105–18.114
litigants in person 18.16
no profit 18.10
non-legal staff, costs of 18.115–18.120
notice of challenges 18.55
policy 18.06–18.09
presumptions 18.26–18.37
privilege 18.57
pro bono funding 18.121–18.136
procedure 18.46–18.50
public funding 18.17–18.18
quantum meruit 18.91–18.99
'top-up' fees 18.79–18.81
waiver of fees 18.82
Inquests
assessment of costs 49.154–49.159
Inquiries
assessment of costs 49.154–49.159
Insolvency
payments on account 14.14
Instructions
wasted costs 9.186, 9.187
Insurance
privilege 46.18
unlawful retainers 27.272–27.301
Intellectual Property Enterprise Court
conduct 50.336
costs orders 50.336
interim hearings 50.339
issues-based orders 50.336
jurisdiction 50.314
offers 50.336
Part 36 offers 50.336
percentage orders 50.336
procedure 50.337–50.341
renaming of court 50.313
scale costs
ambit of Part 45 50.315–50.321
caps 50.324–50.335
definition 50.322
generally 50.312–50.313
terminology 50.322–50.333
upper limits 50.323
set-off 50.336
statements of costs 50.340–50.341
summary assessment 44.05, 50.337–50.338
Interest
accrual date 56.03
advance orders 56.108
appeals 56.103–56.104
arbitration 56.125
compensatory rate interest
commercial cases 56.60–56.61, 56.72
complexity, avoidance of 56.63–56.65
conditional fee agreements 56.80
date 56.03
date in which interest begins to run 56.66–56.68
discretion 56.69–56.71
doomed persons 56.82
eggshell skull principle, no 56.73
generally 56.57–56.59
government bodies 56.75
insurers 56.81
large businesses 56.74
meaning 56.02
no exceptionality requirement 56.62
origins of power to award 56.55–56.56
private individuals 56.79
rate of interest 56.69–56.71
receiving party 56.74–56.82
small businesses 56.77–56.78
small-to-medium sized enterprises 56.76
compound interest 56.126–56.128
contractual 56.116–56.120
costs of assessment 56.114–56.115
deemed costs orders 7.103, 56.101–56.102
enhanced rate interest
date on which interest begins to run 56.88–56.89
jurisdiction 56.83–56.87
meaning 56.02
Part 36 offers 56.87
policies 56.97–56.99
rate of interest 56.90–56.96
equitable jurisdiction 56.123–56.124
funds 56.112–56.113
generally 56.01
governing provisions 56.04–56.07
judgment date 56.03
late payment of commercial debt 56.122
multiple orders 56.109–56.111
overpaid costs 56.105–56.107
overview 56.04–56.07
payment date 56.03
prescribed rate of interest
adjustments 56.49
alteration of date on which interest begins to run 56.16–56.17
common form of interest, as 56.08
County Court 56.14–56.15
date 56.03
date upon which interest begins to run 56.22–56.40
delay in detailed assessment 56.50–56.53
detailed assessments 56.45
discounts 56.49
foreign currencies 56.46–56.47
funders 56.54
jurisdiction 56.10–56.13
meaning 56.02
nature of applicable rate 56.44
Part 36 56.45
payable, circumstances in which 56.09
principles 56.10–56.13
rate of interest 56.42–56.48
small debts 56.18–56.19
sterling, judgments in 56.42–56.43
suspension of interest during enforcement 56.20–56.21
reversal of costs orders on appeal, overpayments 45.57–45.59
solicitor and client, between 27.328
contentious costs 38.92
discretion 38.93–38.94

Interest (*cont.*)
solicitor and client, between (*cont.*)
generally 38.86–38.88
judgment debt interest 38.93–38.94
late payment of commercial debts 38.97–38.102
non-contentious costs 38.89–38.91
terminology 56.02–56.03
tort 56.121
unless orders 43.105–43.107
Interim costs certificates
discretion 43.378
enforcement 43.380
jurisdiction 43.377
meaning 2.09, 43.376
non-compliance 43.382
payment on account distinguished 43.376
pro bono work 43.381
procedure 43.379–43.382
stays 43.380
Interim costs orders
available orders 6.266
costs reserved 6.266
discretion 6.267–6.269
effect of order 6.270–6.273
generally 6.03, 6.266
Interim injunctions
orders for costs 6.274
Interim invoices
distinguishing types 35.15–35.27
balance, carrying forward 35.27
conduct 35.24–35.25
form of invoice 35.23
information given 35.19–35.21
natural breaks 27.64–27.65, 35.28–35.26
natural breaks, absence of 35.22
retainer 35.17–35.18
subject matter 35.26
written notification 35.23
requests for payment on account 35.10–35.14
statute bills 35.06–35.09
Interim statute bill
see also **Interim invoices; Statute bills**
distinguishing from bills for payment on account *see* **Interim invoices** 35.15–35.27
distinguishing from internal invoices 35.38–35.39
generally 35.06–35.09
meaning 2.09, 35.06–35.09
natural breaks 27.64–27.65, 35.28–35.26
Interpretation of contracts of retainer
ambiguous terms 31.38–31.40, 35.20
asymmetry of information 27.51
conditional fee agreements 29.64
consumers 27.51, 27.130, 35.21
contra proferentum 31.40
interim statute bills, provision for 27.50–27.55
non-contentious business agreements 27.130
background facts 31.05–31.08
evidence 31.12
hindsight 31.09–31.10
law as fact 31.11
matrix of fact 31.05–31.08
prior negotiations 31.13
commercial common sense 31.14–31.33
ineffective, avoidance of such an interpretation 31.26–31.28
meaning of words and business common sense 31.16–31.20
mistakes 31.30–31.33, 31.41–31.47
model contracts, relevance of 31.32–32.33
place of business common sense 31.21–31.23
rewriting contract, no 31.24–31.25
standard wording, relevance of 31.32–32.33
uncommercial outcomes 31.15
unenforceability, avoidance of such an interpretation 31.29
implied terms 31.57–31.73
see also **Implied terms**
inconsistent terms 31.34–31.37
bespoke terms 31.36
case examples 31.37
conditional fee agreements 29.64, 29.100
inconsistent terms included by mistake 31.45–31.46
incorporation of documents 31.36
quantum, terms as to 31.36
repugnant clauses 31.36
joinder 31.52–31.55
missing terms 31.48–31.51
submission 31.50, 31.51
waiver 31.50
mistakes 31.41–31.47
inconsistent terms included by mistake 31.45–31.46
time pressure on drafting 31.47
overview 31.02–31.04
severance 31.56
Interpreters
disbursements 52.100–52.101
Invoices
see also **Interim invoices; Statute bills**
disputes as to status 35.05
internal invoices 35.37–35.39
statute bills distinguished *see* **Interim invoices** 35.02–35.05
Irrelevant factors, concerning the incidence of costs
additional liabilities 6.256
amount of costs 6.254
availability of private funding 6.250
contributions 6.257–6.259
financial inequality 6.249
freedom of expression 6.261
generally 6.247
impecuniosity 6.248
late payment in other applications 6.260
litigant in person 6.253
proportionality 6.255
Issue-aware costs orders
abandoned issues 6.195–6.206, 6.202–6.206
adjustment stage 6.174
apportionment 20.64–20.65
both parties entitled to costs, where 7.34
contributory negligence 6.189–6.190
'costs building' 6.191–6.193
CPR, effect of 6.161–6.163

depriving party of costs of unsuccessful issue 6.177
discretion 6.170
Dooley v Parker 6.200–6.201
double jeopardy 6.197
formulation stage 6.172
group litigation 6.206, 65.48–65.55
historical perspective 6.158–6.160
Intellectual Property Enterprise Court 50.336
meaning of 'issue' 6.164–6.168
need to consider approach 6.169
Part 36 offers 6.176
personal injury claims 6.188
preliminary issues hearings 6.194
requiring party to pay costs of unsuccessful issue 6.178–6.190
set-off 21.11
Shirley v Caswell 6.198–6.199
successful issues taken unreasonably 6.191–6.193
terminology 6.157
two-stage process 6.171–6.175

J-Codes 49.22, 49.165, 49.165–49.189
Joinder
interpretation of retainer 31.52–31.55
Joint liability
costs debtors 19.21–19.29
meaning 19.05–19.07
Joint orders
uses 7.03, 7.32–7.33
Joint and several liability
costs debtors 19.31–19.33
meaning 19.09
Joint and several orders
uses 7.03, 7.32–7.33
Journals
reliance on 4.65
Judicial review 45.73–45.76
acknowledgment of service 67.08–67.09
acquiescence 67.06
application for permission 67.03–67.05
costs capping 67.07
amount of the cap 13.70–13.71
appeals 13.69
conditions for order 13.53–13.61
costs of applications 13.77
directions 13.72
discretion 13.62–13.65
evidence 13.72
exceptionality 13.60
financial resources 13.66–13.68
form of application 13.72
generally 13.46
history 13.47
origins of power 13.50–13.52
procedure 13.72
public interest proceedings 13.54–13.57
scope 13.50–13.52
service 13.72
terminology 13.48
unilateral cap 13.63
variation 13.73–13.76
withdrawal of application 13.58–13.59
discretion 67.10–67.14
generally 67.01–67.02
interested parties 67.15–67.16
review of decision of inferior courts/tribunals 67.13
settled claims 67.14

Lawyers, work of 3.48–3.91, 3.91
agents 3.83–3.90
authorised litigators 3.51
conduct of litigation 3.78–3.79
employees 3.83–3.90
employers 3.83–3.90
fees 3.52
reserved instrument activities 3.81–3.82
rights of audience 3.80
Leases
costs 66.29–66.30
Legal advice privilege
basic rule 46.08
disclosed information 46.09
lawyers 46.07
meaning 46.06
nature of advice 46.09
other jurisdictions 46.09
prerequisites 46.09
public domain, information in 46.09
Legal aid
co-defendant orders 7.25
costs protection 62.04–62.06
forthwith orders 7.85
meaning 2.09
Legal expenses insurance
see also **ATE insurance**; **BTE insurance**
nature of legal expenses insurance 34.02–34.03
rights against insurers
Contracts (Rights of Third Parties) Act 1999 34.65
declarations 34.66
generally 34.60
implied contract 34.66
implied terms 34.66
road traffic accident cases 34.66
Third Parties (Rights against Insurers) Acts 34.61–34.64
trusts 34.66
set-off 21.36
top-up insurance 34.38–34.40, 54.176–54.177
types of legal expenses insurance 34.03
Legal Ombudsman
complainants 39.24
complaints to 38.40
costs orders 39.33
delay 39.24
determinations 39.34
employees 39.24
fees 39.26
generally 39.22
jurisdiction 39.24
legal proceedings 39.24
nature of the complaint 39.24
powers 39.27–39.32

Legal Ombudsman (*cont.*)
publications 39.25
respondents 39.24
time limits 39.24
Legal professional privilege
absolute nature 46.05
administrative records 46.17
bills 46.14–46.15
client care letters 46.16
communications with employees of clients of corporate clients 46.24
communications prior to litigation 46.23
documents 46.14–46.27
expert reports 46.21
insurance policies 46.18
internal documents 46.25
invoices 46.14–46.15
legal advice privilege
basic rule 46.08
disclosed information 46.09
lawyers 46.07
meaning 46.06
nature of advice 46.09
other jurisdictions 46.09
prerequisites 46.09
public domain, information in 46.09
third party information 46.09
litigation privilege
communications prior to litigation 46.23
lawyers 46.07
marshalled documents 46.27
meaning 46.06
scope 46.10
marshalled documents 46.27
meaning 2.09, 46.04
mediation 48.43
non-lawyer advisers 46.22
non-party costs orders 9.89–9.92
public interest 46.05
third-party agreements 46.19
Legal project management
activities 41.03
actual expenditure 41.03
actual progress 41.03
aims 41.07
baseline 41.03
budgets 41.41–41.45
change requests 41.55–41.59
communication plans 41.46–41.47
completion of project 41.60
contract breakdown structures 41.39
control of project 41.48–41.50
costs breakdown structures 41.41–41.45
deliverables 41.03
earned value analysis 41.51–41.54
execution of project 41.48–41.50
forecast expenditure 41.03
funding 41.03
history 41.05–41.06
initiation 41.15–41.21
legal practice management distinguished 41.11
non-traditional project management 41.61–41.63
objectives 41.03
organisational breakdown structures 41.35–41.38
phases 41.03, 41.13–41.60
planning 41.22–41.23
plans 41.28–41.29
pricing distinguished 41.12
product breakdown structures 41.30–41.32
products 41.03
project 41.03
quality 41.03
relevance to costs 41.08–41.09
risk breakdown structures 41.40
scope of project 41.03
stakeholders 41.03, 41.46–41.47
terminology 41.03–41.04
tools 41.50
triangle, project management 41.24–41.27
value of project 41.03
value-based pricing 42.24, 42.31–42.34
work breakdown structures 41.33–41.34
Legal representative
meaning 2.09
Legal Services Commission
abolition 62.08
transfer of legal aid responsibility to Lord Chancellor 62.07–62.09
Lien
bad debts 40.84
client terminating retainer 40.67–40.68
constructive discharge 40.60
delivery up 40.69–40.72
dissolution of solicitor's firm 40.60
duty of holder to take care of property 40.43
effluxion of time 40.84
equitable lien 40.39–40.42
generally 40.36
limitation 23.97
loss of lien 40.73–40.83
abandonment 40.76
alternative securities 40.77–40.78
bankruptcy 40.79
discharge 40.74–40.75
liquidation 40.79
parting possession 40.80–40.81
preservation of property 40.82
receivership 40.79
silence when proving costs debt 40.83
tender 40.74–40.75
waiver 40.76
particular lien
acquisition 40.58
effect 40.46–40.47
extent 40.58
meaning 40.38
relief from lien 40.59–40.60
retaining, effect of 40.44
retaining lien
client accounts 40.55
companies 40.56
effect 40.36, 40.44–40.45
escrow accounts 40.54
extent 40.48–40.50

monies held for a purpose 40.52–40.53
not acting as a solicitor 40.51
privilege 40.57
property held for a purpose 40.52–40.53
registration and companies 40.56
right to claim 40.37
trusts 40.52–40.53
solicitor still acting, where 40.66
specific costs 40.84
taking consistent securities 40.84
termination of retainer, by client 40.67–40.68
termination of retainer, by solicitor 40.61–40.65
undertakings to hold to order 40.85–40.88
want of payment 40.60
winding up 40.79

Limitation
acknowledgment 23.123–23.130
assessing costs 23.111–23.115
children 23.133
contractual retainers 23.85
defence, as, denial 23.131–23.136
discretion 23.88
effect of successful defence 23.96
estoppel 23.134
fraud 23.135–23.136
generally 23.50–23.56, 23.83–23.84
incidental work 23.94
interest 23.57
lack of capacity 23.132
late request for assessment of paid costs 23.100–23.102
lien 23.98
more than one type of costs debt 23.95
non-contractual retainers 23.86–23.87
part payment 23.123–23.130
seeking action for order for costs 23.103–23.110, 23.116–23.122
solicitor and client 23.85–23.102
trusts 23.97
when time begins to run 23.89–23.93

Limited liability partnerships
retainers 27.321

Liquidators
retainers 27.323

Litigants in person
consent orders 7.65, 7.67–7.69
corporate litigants in person
generally 59.54–59.55
in-house legal departments 59.54
managerial time 3.100
costs of being a litigant 3.13
costs management, and 12.18, 12.44
disbursements and professional fees
claims consultants 59.31–59.32
counsel not properly instructed 3.100
disbursements in lieu of legal representatives' work 59.33
expert assistance in respect of costs 3.95–3.96, 59.36–59.37
generally 59.09, 59.58
McKenzie friends, fees of 3.100
notional disbursements 59.29
payments for legal services actually purchased 59.35
professional fees in lieu of legal representatives' work 3.97–3.99, 59.30–59.32
witness allowances 59.34
fast track 50.350
fixed costs 50.68, 50.159, 50.169
incidence of costs, relevance of status to 6.110, 6.253
indemnity basis 16.40
indemnity principle 18.16
jurisdiction to allow costs 59.02–59.07
the Crown 59.07
definition and status of litigant in person 59.04–59.06
lawyers acting for themselves and on behalf of their firms 59.38–59.53
authorised litigators 59.50–59.52
Chorley principle 3.14, 59.08, 59.39–59.46
costs lawyers 59.51
counsel 59.47–59.49
other lawyers 59.50–59.53
solicitors 59.39–59.46
Part 36 offers 17.161
quantum where there has been financial loss
proof of financial loss 59.14–59.15
professional persons 59.16–59.18
quantification 59.18–59.22
quantum where there has been no financial loss
assessment of time 59.24–59.26
irrecoverable work 59.27
prescribed rate 59.23
small claims track 3.100
solicitor and client assessments 36.52, 36.76
summary assessment 44.23
VAT 55.14, 55.45
wasted costs, sought by 9.152

Litigation friend
children 60.06–60.08
expenses 60.40–60.42
substitution of litigation friend 60.22
persons who lack mental capacity 60.68
retainers involving 27.36
security for costs 15.96

Litigation funding
acceptance of cases 33.67–33.68
adverse event provision 33.84
agreement 2.09
alternative business structures 33.31
ATE insurance, need for 33.30
availability and practice 33.59–33.63
champerty 33.04
Code of Conduct for Litigation Funders 2018 33.28–33.29
Consumer Credit Act 1974 33.51–33.58
consumers, provision to 33.34–33.57
contractual provisions 33.74–33.84
control of litigation 33.73
definition 33.03
disclosure of agreements 46.19
disclosure of funding 33.85–33.90

Litigation funding (*cont.*)
disputes resolution procedure 33.83
Financial Services and Markets Act 2000 33.36–33.50
future developments and regulation 33.27
historical background 33.04–33.26
independent legal advice 33.72
legality 33.05
management provision 33.78
minimum values 33.65–33.66
precedence condition 33.75
present legislative control 33.32–33.33
priorities provision 33.82
public policy 33.04
remuneration 33.69–33.70
remuneration and terms 33.24
reporting provision 33.76–33.77
representations as to truth 33.76–33.77
security for costs 33.84
termination provision 33.79–33.81
terminology 33.03
types of claim 33.64
Litigation privilege
lawyers 46.07
marshalled documents 46.27
meaning 46.06
scope 46.10
Litigation services
meaning 2.09
Lord Chancellor
transfer of legal aid responsibility to Lord Chancellor 62.07–62.09
***Lownds* test**
see **Proportionality**
LSC-funded client
meaning 2.09

***McKenzie* friends**
representation 47.05, 47.10–47.11
Maintenance
analogous statutes 30.16
assignment of causes of action 30.10
case examples 30.32–30.54
champerty, relationship to 30.18
collateral interests 30.11–30.12
fact, question of 30.16
historic aspects 30.04–30.05
modern law 30.06–30.09
public policy 30.13–30.15
Media
costs of dealing with 49.127–49.129
group litigation 65.100
Mediation
see also **Alternative dispute resolution**
advantages of 48.15
code-sets 49.40
funding of mediation and costs 48.50–48.57
assessment of costs of 49.133–49.139
costs of 48.51–48.52
funding and mediators' fees 48.50
unreasonable refusal to mediate costs disputes *see also* **Refusal to engage in ADR** 48.53–48.57
mediation agreements 48.26–48.27
mediation agreements and contents thereof 48.26
mediators and mediation providers
Civil Mediation Council 48.17
conflict of interest 48.23
neutrality of mediator 48.22
regulation 48.17
specialist costs mediators 48.18–48.20
nature of costs mediation 48.13–48.14
benefits 48.15
disadvantages 48.16
procedure during mediation 48.17–48.28, 48.36–48.39
caucuses (closed sessions) 48.36
conclusion of mediation 48.28
disclosure 48.40–48.42
enforcement of settlements 48.27
legal professional privilege 48.43
plenary (joint) sessions 48.36
preparation for facultative mediation 48.31–48.35
position statements 48.34
procedure during evaluative mediation 48.48–48.49
privacy and confidentiality 48.43–48.37
stages of facultative mediation 48.38–48.39
timing 48.24–48.25
'without prejudice' communications 48.43
types of mediation
evaluative mediation 48.48–48.49
facilitative mediation 48.29–48.47
Medical agencies
see also **Disbursements**
agency 22.27
code of conduct 52.63
disbursements 52.63–52.72
fixed costs 52.68–52.71
purpose 52.63
VAT 52.72
Medical records
see also **Disbursements**
disbursements 52.60–52.61
unreasonable delay in providing 57.14–57.15
VAT 55.23–55.25
***Medway Oil* principle** 20.04, 20.59
Membership organisations 54.179–54.190
meaning 2.09
Mesothelioma proceedings 34.24, 54.22–54.30
Misallocation
exaggeration 57.21
Mistake
interpretation of retainer 31.30–31.33, 31.41–31.47
Mortgages
costs 66.23–66.28
summary assessment and 44.12
Motor Insurance Bureau (MIB)
road traffic insurers 63.03, 63.04
Multiple parties
additional party orders
cut-through orders 7.28–7.31
meaning 7.03
passing-up-the-line orders 7.26–7.27
strings of contracts 7.27
co-defendant orders

alternative, claims are in the 7.17–7.20
choice between orders 7.22–7.23
conduct 7.21
consideration of order 7.08–7.09
doubts as to true law 7.24
legal aid 7.25
meaning 7.03
nexus between claims 7.15–7.16
not mandatory orders 7.10–7.11
policy 7.04
requirements 7.12–7.20
success against one defendant 7.12–7.14
types of order 7.05–7.06
generally 7.02
joint orders 7.03, 7.32–7.33
joint and several orders 7.03, 7.32–7.33

Natural breaks
contractual issues 27.64–27.65
invoices 35.28–35.26
Necessaries
children 60.16–60.18
protected persons 60.62
No hearing on substantive issues, costs orders where there has been 7.169–7.182
No order as to costs 6.262–6.264
Non-contentious business agreements
assessment of costs 3.21
compromise 39.11–39.12
conditional fee agreements 27.214–27.216
contentious business distinguished 3.23–3.30
effect of agreement 27.128–27.129
examples of 3.32
generally 27.115–27.118
interpretation 27.130–27.131
meaning 2.09
oral, effect of 27.210–27.213
requirements 27.119
security for fees 27.127
signature 27.122
solicitors' security for costs 40.104
statement of terms 27.123–27.125
termination 27.132
unfairness 27.133–27.134
unintended agreements 27.126
unreasonableness 27.133–27.134
writing requirement 27.119, 27.120–27.121
Non-party costs orders
administrators 9.31
analogous orders 9.09
availability of alternative securities or remedies 9.29
categories of non-party
active shareholders 9.31
administrators 9.31
causative persons 9.72–9.75
controllers 9.21–9.27
funders 9.32–9.59
commercial funders 9.37–9.59
pure funders 9.34–9.36
generally 9.20
group actions and representative claims 9.76, 65.116–65.122
insurers 9.31
legal representatives 9.60–9.71
receivers 9.31
related claims 9.75
secured creditors 9.31
tribunals 9.77
causation 9.15–9.19
causative persons 9.72–9.75
champerty and maintenance, relevance of 30.02
conduct 9.28
controllers
active shareholders 9.31
alternative securities or remedies 9.29
conduct 9.28
examples 9.22–9.27
funding 9.30
meaning 9.21
evidence 9.84–9.88
exceptionality 9.11–9.14
funders
Arkin case 9.39–9.42
categories 9.32, 9.33
commercial funders 9.37
legal expenses insurers 9.54–9.55
legal representatives 9.47–9.52
lenders 9.46
liability insurers 9.56, 9.56–9.57
litigation funders 9.38–9.44
meaning 9.32
non-commercial funders 9.45
peripherally interested persons 9.53
pure funders 9.34–9.36
trade unions 9.58, 9.58–9.59
funding 9.30
group litigation 9.76
jurisdiction 9.03–9.10
legal representatives 9.60–9.71
meaning 2.09, 9.02
non-statutory powers 9.10
privilege 9.89–9.92
procedure 9.78–9.83
qualified one-way costs shifting 9.08
related claims 9.75
statutory powers 9.03–9.07
tribunals 9.77
Non-statutory assessments between solicitor and client
Palomo assessment 39.03–39.07
Notice of funding
ATE premiums 54.130
constructive knowledge 54.123
default provisions where notice has not been given 54.109, 54.130, 54.188
generally 54.109–54.123
informal notice 54.123
notional premiums 54.188
relief from sanctions 54.115–54.123
Denton test on relief from sanctions 54.118–54.123
effect of granting relief 54.123
evidential issues 54.123
late notice 54.123
prejudice, relevance of 54.123

Notice of funding (*cont.*)
relief from sanctions (*cont.*)
prior negotiations, relevance of 54.123
response to late notice, relevance of 54.123
requirement to give notice 54.110–54.114
Notional premiums
approved membership organisations 54.187
limited among 54.189
meaning 2.09
notice of intention to claim 54.188
organisations not charging 54.190
requirements for recovery 54.180
statutory framework 54.181–54.183
transitional provisions 54.184–54.186
Novation
see also **Transfer of contract of retainer**
assignment, distinguished from 32.11, 32.36
instructions, effect of giving 32.25–32.27
generally 32.34–32.41
meaning 32.34
pre-2013 conditional fee agreements 32.38
types 32.35

Oral retainers
business agreements 27.210–27.213
conditional fee agreements 27.214–27.216
generally 27.207
issues of fact 27.208
issues of law 27.209–27.216
Orders for costs
see also **Conduct and misconduct**
appeals 7.184–7.185
available orders 6.29–6.41
checklists 6.26–6.28
clarification of order 10.04
conduct
generally 6.03
consent orders 7.65–7.69
deemed orders 7.100–7.140
default orders 7.102
discretion of court 6.17
equitable jurisdiction of court 6.14
factors to be taken into account 6.24
additional liabilities 6.256
freedom of expression 6.264
irrelevant factors 6.247–6.261
contributions 6.257–6.259
late payment in other applications 6.260
proportionality 6.255
form of order 6.16–6.17
formulation of the award 6.03
general rule
departure from 6.03, 7.39–7.49
meaning 6.03
pre-action disclosure 7.47–7.49
importance and meaning of order
meaning of success 6.45
measure of success 6.46
inherent jurisdiction of court 6.14
interim injunctions 6.274
irrelevant factors
amount of costs 6.254
ATE insurance 6.252
financial inequality 6.249
funding 6.251
impecuniosity 6.248
litigants in person 6.253
private funding 6.250
public funding 6.250
issue-aware costs orders 6.03, 6.156–6.206
Johnsey Estates guidance 6.26, 6.27
judicial approach 6.22–6.23
jurisdiction to award costs
formalities 6.15
non-statutory powers 6.13–6.14
statutory powers 6.09–6.12
mathematical exercise, not 6.25
Multiplex guidance 6.26, 6.28
no hearing on substantive issues 7.169–7.182
no order as to costs 6.262–6.264
non-statutory powers 6.13
orders where proceedings are not issued 7.169–7.182
overall justice of the case 6.16
partnerships 7.50–7.51
percentage orders 6.32–6.37, 6.32–6.41
issues-based orders compared 6.37
method of making order 6.39–6.41
reciprocal orders compared 6.38
probate 7.52–7.64
range of orders available 6.29–6.41
reasoned awards 6.22–6.23
recusal by judge 7.188
rules are essential working tool 6.20–6.21
sealed orders 10.03
statutory powers 6.09–6.12
success and the general rule 6.42–6.75
summary of law 6.03
taking all relevant circumstances into account 6.18–6.19
technical approach, avoiding 6.20–6.21
terminology 6.05–6.06, 10.03
terms of art 6.07–6.08
transfer between courts 7.187
'whole battlefield' approach 6.03
wills 7.52–7.64
wrong venue, commencement of proceedings in 7.186
Orders where proceedings not issued
claimant refuses to pay 7.176–7.182
defendant refusing to pay 7.170–7.175
Overriding objective
alternative dispute resolution 48.08
Civil Procedure Rules 4.39, 26.02–26.08, 26.15–26.16
interpretation 26.17–26.26

Part 36 offers
see also **Enhanced rate interest**
absence, effect of 6.238
acceptance of Part 36 offers 17.164–17.194
see also 'just out of time jurisdiction' below
after the 'relevant period', incidence of costs 17.177–17.181
after the 'relevant period', basis of costs 17.182–17.187

before the 'relevant period' 17.166–17.172
circumstances in which adjudication is required 17.176
counterclaims, and 17.190
deemed orders, and 7.103, 7.109
detailed assessments, in 43.276–43.277
effect of, generally 7.103, 7.109, 17.167
effect of, pre-issue 7.173
effect of, where CPR Part 45, applies, *see* 'Part 45, interaction with' below
less than 21 days before trial 17.184
no discretion to disapply deemed order 7.111, 10.24
part of claim, offers in respect of 17.185–17.187
procedure 17.192–17.194
simple acceptance, costs 17.167–17.171
simple acceptance, in general 17.166
simple acceptance of second or subsequent offers 17.172
split trials, and 17.188
struck out, where claim has been 17.189
where permission is required 17.176–17.187
admissible offers, distinguished from 6.207, 6.212, 6.225
ambit of 17.40
amount offered, gauging
deductible benefits 17.111–17.112
generally 17.106–7.112
interest 17.106–17.108
non-monetary claims 17.109
when to gauge 17.110
appeals 17.31, 17.113–17.114
battle of offers 17.145
beating an offer, claimant 17.81–17.85, 17.88–17.91
beating offer, defendant 17.98–17.105
budgeted cases
detailed assessments, offers in 43.272–43.275
failure to file a budget, and 12.58, 17.115–17.117
children 17.161
clarity of offers, relevance of 17.55–17.56
conditional offers, relevance of 43.271
conduct, relevance of 17.132–17.135
confusing offers 17.136
costs, relevance of 17.97, 17.158–17.160
costs-only proceedings, and 11.28
counterclaims, and 17.31, 17.34, 17.40, 17.190, 20.62
deemed costs orders, and 7.102, 7.109–7.111
detailed assessments and Part 36 offers 17.31
acceptance of offers 43.276–43.277
budgeted cases, offers in 43.272–43.275
early offers 43.259, 43.351
disclosure to the court 43.315
'failed' Part 36 offers 43.296
form of 43.255–43.257
injustice test 43.348–43.349
interest, treatment of 43.261–43.268
jurisdiction 43.254
late offers 43.260, 43.352
measure of offers 43.350
partial offer 43.271
paying parties beating their own offers, effect of 43.343–43.344
procedure generally 43.278–43.279
provisional assessments, and 43.185, 43.208, 43.231, 43.233
receiving parties beating their own offers, effect of 43.345–43.347
sealed envelopes 43.185, 43.208, 43.233
unclear offers 43.349, 43.355
VAT, treatment of 43.269, 55.32
when to make offer 43.258–43.260
withdrawn Part 36 offers 43.353
discretion, *see* 'injustice test' below
disclosure of offers to court 17.57–17.59
split trials 17.58
where disclosure is given 17.59
downgraded Part 36 offers, *see* 'withdrawal of Part 36 offers' below
effect of beating offer, claimant 17.81–17.85, 17.88–17.97
costs, relevance of 17.97
equalling an offer by judgment 17.92
generally 17.81–17.85
more than one defendant 17.94
subrogated claims 17.95
summary judgment 17.93
effect of beating offer, defendant 17.98–17.105
'near misses' 17.100–17.104
effect of 'equalling' an offer 17.92
enhanced interest 17.96
'equivalent awards' 17.62–17.64
evidential developments, relevance of 17.142
factual issues, offers in respect of 17.156
'failed' Part 36 offers, effect of 6.207, 6.212, 6.240, 17.62–17.64
fixed costs, *see* 'Part 45, interaction with' below
forgo costs, offers to 17.96
Form N242A 17.39
formalities 17.40–17.42, 17.49–17.50
in detailed assessments 43.255–43.257
history of Part 36 offers 1.59, 17.06–17.17
improved Part 36 offers 17.200–17.203
procedure 17.203
relation with original offers 17.202
when may be made 17.201
inadequate information
injustice test, relevance to 17.137–17.141
status of offer, relevance to 17.54
injustice test 17.118–17.161
apologies, relevance of refusing to make 17.157
battles of offers 17.145
conduct, relevance of 17.132–17.135
confusing offers, relevance of 17.136
costs, relevance of 17.158–17.160
detailed assessments and 43.348–43.349
developments extraneous to parties, relevance of 17.143
discretion once threshold met 17.126–17.128
evidential developments, relevance of 17.142
experience of legal advisors, relevance of 17.144
factual issues, relevance of offers in respect of 17.156
factors to be taken into account
generally 17.129–17.131

Part 36 offers (*cont.*)
injustice test (*cont.*)
failed issues, relevance of 17.146
generally 17.118–17.119
inadequate information, relevance of 17.137–17.141
'just' and 'fair' 17.120–17.123
modest discounts, relevance of offers to accept 17.149–17.155
not all or nothing 17.124–17.125
partial success 17.145
specific types of person 17.161
Intellectual Property Enterprise Court 50.336
Interpretation, of 17.20–17.21, 17.67–17.77
issue-aware costs orders, and 6.176
jurisdictional issues
contract law distinguished 17.22–17.23
CPR, Part 3 distinguished 17.24
CPR, Part 44 distinguished 17.25
self-contained code, Part 36 as 17.20–17.21
'just-out-of-time' jurisdiction 7.111, 17.173
more than one offer, and 17.175
risks 17.174
litigants in person 17.161
modest discounts, offers to accept 17.149–17.155
more than one set of proceedings 17.31
nature of Part 36 17.20–17.21
near misses 6.73, 17.86
non-acceptance 17.80
non-compliant offers, *see* 'technically deficient offers' below
non-monetary offers 17.31
Part 20 defendants 17.161
Part 45, interaction with
CPR, Part 45, Section II 50.70
'old' CPR, Part 45, Section III 50.114
CPR, Part 45, Section IIIA 17.163, 50.287–50.296, 50.304
CPR, Part 45, Section IV 17.163, 50.336
partial success 17.146
parties, status of 17.33–17.38
patients 17.161
payments on account, relevance of 17.87
personal injury claims 17.32, 17.48–17.52
post-Portal fixed costs 17.32, 50.287–50.296
pre-issue Part 36 offers 7.163, 17.27
procedure 43.278–43.279, 43.355
punitive outcomes 17.147–17.148
rejection of Part 36 offers 17.195–17.196
'relevant period' 17.40, 17.46–17.47
requirements of Part 36 offers
see also 'technically deficient offers' below
claimants 17.41
defendants 17.42
generally 17.40
incompatible provisions 17.45
personal injury claims 17.48–17.52
'relevant period', requirement to state 17.40, 17.46–17.47
service of 17.43–17.44
restrictions on payment 43.270
self-contained code, as 17.20–17.21
service 17.31, 17.43–17.44
set-off, and 21.12
small claims track
generally 50.401
misallocation 50.395
solicitor-and-client assessments 36.77
split trials 17.58
status of the parties 17.33–17.34, 17.33–17.38, 17.161
detailed assessment proceedings 43.255, 43.374
determining status 17.37–17.38
injustice test 17.161
need to determine status 17.35–17.36
where there is a counterclaim generally 17.34
summary judgment 17.93
technically deficient offers
effect of 6.207, 6.212, 6.240, 17.62–17.64
estoppel 17.66
generally 17.60–17.79
interpretation 17.67–17.77
status of 17.77–17.79
substantial compliance 17.65
waiver 17.66
terminology 17.03–17.05
time
time, when begins to run 17.28–17.29
time, when offers may be made 17.26–17.27
time, when to gauge value 17.110
time-limited offers 17.219–17.220
timing of offers in detailed assessments 43.258–43.260
Tomlin orders, and 17.45
transitional provisions 17.18
types of claim to which offers may apply 17.30–17.32
appeals and cross-appeals 17.31
counterclaims 17.31
contributory negligence 17.31
detailed assessment 17.31
future performance 17.31
non-monetary offers 17.31
more than one set of proceedings 17.31
Protocol claims 17.32
unjust to allow benefits, *see* 'injustice test' above
value of offers 17.106–17.117
when an offer may be made 17.26–17.27
withdrawal of Part 36 offers 4.353–4.354, 17.197–17.199, 17.204–17.220
effect of withdrawn offers 6.207, 6.212, 6.240, 16.37, 17.214–17.217
no implied withdrawal 17.218
notices 17.206
procedure 17.207–17.213
time-limited offers 17.219–17.220
writing, requirement to be in 17.40
Part 47 offers
acceptance 43.291–43.294
content 43.284–43.285
directions 43.374–43.375
early offers 43.360
effect of acceptance 43.293–43.294
expiry of offers 43.287

form of offer 43.281
fully inclusive offers 43.358
funded offers 43.364
generally 43.280
interest 43.370–43.372
late acceptance 43.292
late offers 43.361
limited by time, offers 43.288
measure of offers 43.357
pre-offer costs 43.367–43.369
procedure 43.295, 43.373
receiving parties, offers made by 43.366
rejection 43.290
rules 43.374–43.375
set-off 43.365
technically deficient offers 43.363
timing of offer 46.282–46.283
variation 43.289
VAT 43.285
withdrawal 43.286, 43.362

Part 61 offers 6.244–6.245

Partnerships
dissolution of accounts 7.50–7.51

Patents
scale costs *see* **Intellectual Property Enterprise Court**
restriction of costs 58.04

Payments
charges 36.27
compromise 36.28
deductions 36.22
delivery after payment 36.25–36.26
meaning 36.18–36.28
mortgages 36.27
negotiable instruments 36.24
partial payment 36.23
putative payments 36.19–36.21

Payments on account (as between solicitor and client)
meaning 2.09, 6.03
overpayment 40.32
solicitors' rights and remedies 40.31–40.32
subsequent effect of voluntary payment 40.32

Payments on account of cost
amount
additional liabilities 14.31
budgeted costs 14.27–14.28
comparators 14.36
general principles 14.21–14.28
information 14.32–14.33
irreducible minimum 14.21
modern approach 14.22–14.24
multiple receiving parties 14.37
observations of court 14.35
proportionality 14.29
reasonable sum 14.21
solvency of receiving party 14.34
costs judges 14.08
costs-only proceedings 14.05
discretion 14.09–14.11
failure to make payment 14.19–14.20
financial resources 14.14
generally 14.01–14.02
insolvency 14.14
instalments 14.13
interim statute bills distinguished 35.15–35.27
judges other than trial judges 14.07
jurisdiction 14.03–14.05
meaning 14.02
natural breaks 35.28–35.36
Part 36 offers 17.87
prerequisites 14.04
presumptions 14.09
proportionality 14.29
retainers 14.30
set-off 14.12
status 14.15–14.18
trial judges 14.06

Pendulum arbitration 48.87–48.92

Percentage increase
meaning 2.09

Percentage orders 6.32–6.41
both parties entitled to costs, where 7.34
issues-based orders compared 6.37
meaning 6.32
method of making order 6.39–6.41
preferred option 6.33–6.36
reciprocal orders compared 6.38

Perfected orders
meaning 10.03

Personal injury claims
ATE insurance 34.27
BTE insurance, suitability 34.19–34.20
conduct and misconduct 6.87–6.92
costs management 12.81
exaggeration 6.151
fundamental dishonesty 6.87–6.92
issue-aware costs orders 6.188
leading counsel, use of 53.121
Part 36 offers 17.48–17.52
qualified one-way costs shifting *see* **Qualified one-way costs shifting (QOCS)**

Personal records
disbursements 52.62

Phase codes
see also **Activity codes; Task codes**
background 49.22
EW-UTBMS (J-Code) task codes 49.178, 49.180
generally 49.21–49.23
phases codes under the CPR
alternative dispute resolution/settlement (P10) 49.40
budgeting (P13) 49.45–49.46
case management conference (P3) 49.29
costs assessment 49.48–49.49
costs management conference (P14) 49.47
disclosure (P4) 49.30
expert reports (P6) 49.34–49.35
funding (P12) 49.43–49.44
initial and pre-action protocol work (P1) 49.24–49.26
interim applications (P11) 49.41–49.42
issue/statements of case (P2) 49.27–49.28
Phase Code 1 (P1) 49.24–49.26
Phase Code 2 (P2) 49.27–49.28

Phase codes (*cont.*)
generally (*cont.*)
Phase Code 3 (P3) 49.29
Phase Code 4 (P4) 49.30–49.31
Phase Code 5 (P5) 49.32–49.33
Phase Code 6 (P6) 49.34–49.35
Phase Code 7 (P7) 49.36
Phase Code 8 (P8) 49.37
Phase Code 9 (P9) 49.38–49.39
Phase Code 10 (P10) 49.40
Phase Code 11 (P11) 49.41–49.42
Phase Code 12 (P12) 49.43–49.44
Phase Code 13 (P13) 49.45–49.46
Phase Code 14 (P14) 49.47
Phase Code 15 (P15) 49.48–49.49
pre-trial review (P7) 49.36
trial (P9) 49.38–49.39
trial preparation (P8) 49.37
witness statements (P5) 49.32–49.33
Precedent H, and 12.26
Plural liability and entitlement
costs debtors 19.21–19.44
fast-track trial costs 19.20
interpretation of awards 19.11–19.15
liability of firms 19.18
meaning 19.03
silence as to severance 19.17
types 19.05
joint liability or entitlement 19.05–19.07
joint and several liability 19.09
several liability or entitlement 19.08
Points of dispute
brevity 43.113–43.114
content 43.111–43.112, 43.111–43.115
failure to serve 43.139
format 43.109–43.110
generally 43.108
Precedent G 43.110
prolixity 43.115
purpose 43.108
replies to
content 43.171–43.175
format 43.167
generally 43.166
procedure 43.168–43.170
service 43.135–43.139
time limits 43.126–43.134
variation 43.125
Portal costs
admissions 50.201–50.202
ATE and notional premiums 50.190
child claimants 50.152
claims notification form
completion 50.194
failure to complete 50.198
court proceedings and adjudication (Stage 3)
acknowledgment of service 50.233
adjournments 50.242
application to court to determine damages 50.230
case management 50.238–50.241
child settlements 50.250–50.251
consideration of the claim 50.243
costs consequences of determination 50.244–50.247
counterclaims 50.253
defendants' costs 50.253
dismissal of the claim 50.234
filing written evidence 50.231–50.232
generally 50.227
limitation 50.252
protocol offers 50.235–50.237
service of written evidence 50.231–50.232
settlement after commencement of proceedings 50.248–50.249
settlement before proceedings are issued 50.229
decision not to use protocol 50.192
disbursements
generally 50.181–50.183
soft-tissue injuries 50.184–50.187
treating clinicians 50.188
early exit from protocol 50.199–50.200
early payments 50.201–50.202
evidence and negotiations (Stage 2)
acceptance of offer 50.216–50.217
consideration of the claim 50.214–50.215
counter-offers 50.216–50.217
interim payments 50.210–50.211
meaning 50.203
medical evidence 50.204–50.207
non-medical expert reports 50.208
settlement 50.219–50.226
settlement pack submitted to defendant 50.212–50.213
specialist legal advice for valuation purposes 50.209
withdrawal of offer 50.218
exit from the relevant protocol 50.170–50.172
failure to complete claims notification form 50.198
fixed costs
additional advice on value of the claim 50.180
additional fixed costs 50.178
generally 50.173
settlement before proceedings issues 50.179
types 50.174–50.177
governing provisions 50.153–50.154
jurisdiction 50.153–50.155
liability (Stage 1) 50.193–50.202
admissions 50.201–50.202
early payments 50.201–50.202
responding to claims 50.197–50.200
starting claims 50.194–50.196
liability stage 50.193
limitation periods 50.152
non-compliance with protocol
claimant 50.256–50.257
costs sanctions 50.258–50.260
defendants 50.266
failure to file claim notification forms 50.261–50.262
general rule 50.254
incidence of costs 50.255
interim payments 50.263
Stage 3 procedure 50.264–50.265
overview 50.151–50.152
payments in stages 50.173

responding to claims 50.197–50.200
scope of protocols
EL/PL Protocol 50.162–50.169
generally 50.155
RTA Protocol 50.156–50.161
stages 50.151
starting claims 50.194–50.196
success fees 50.189
terminology 50.150

Postage
disbursements 52.77–52.78

Postponement charge
Conditional Fee Agreement Regulations 2000 29.62–29.64
generally 54.101–54.104, Table 54.1
meaning 2.09, 29.02

Practice directions
application of 4.53–4.55
CPR 4.39
failure to comply 57.53
local practice directions 4.48
not a source of law 4.50
power to make 4.47–4.49
status of 4.46–4.55
ultra vires directions 4.51–4.55

Pre-action disclosure
departure from the general rule 7.47–7.49
indemnity principle 7.47–7.49

Pre-action protocols
see also **Portal costs**
assessment of costs 4 9.24–49.25
code-sets
phase code 49.24
tasks 49.25
costs sanctions 4.61
list 4.57
meaning 2.09, 4.56
pre-action conduct 4.57
pre-issue conduct 57.08–57.17
relevance of 4.58–4.59
stages 50.151
substance of 4.60

Pre-emptive orders
see **Trusts and Trustees**

Pre-proceedings conduct 6.77–6.78
allowing opponent to proceed on incorrect footing 6.110
amendments 6.116
budget failings 6.114
Commercial Court 6.83–6.84
cooperation 6.117
criminality 6.103
departing from industry practice 6.109
exaggerated claims 6.108
fabricating evidence 6.108
failure to disclose evidence 6.113
good conduct 6.117
grandstanding 6.115
late amendments 6.116
non-procedural 6.82
case examples, list of 6.102–6.117
collateral purposes 6.105
mitigation of costs 6.104
taking advantage of opponent's oversights 6.112
oppression 6.107
other courts 6.85–6.86
overly-elaborate evidence 6.115
prematurity and aggression 6.107
procedural 6.93–6.101
case examples, list of 6.102–6.117
departing from industry practice 6.109
failure to send letter of claim 6.106
prolixity 6.115
refusal to engage in ADR 6.118–6.140
refusal to pay costs properly incurred 6.111
right to silence 6.113
wrong court, commencing proceedings in 6.114

Pre-trial review
assessment of costs 49.36
code-sets 49.36

Predictable costs
meaning 50.06

Predictive costs
meaning 50.06

Prejudicial contacts
children 60.19

Pricing
see also **Value-based pricing**
costs-plus pricing 42.09–42.15
legal project management distinguished 41.12

Privacy, right to 24.56–24.57

Privilege
see also **Legal professional privilege**
common interest privilege 46.10
types 46.06, 46.12
without prejudice offers 6.207, 6.213–6.218, 46.06

***Pro bono* funding and work**
assessment of monies payable
costs of assessment 43.330, 43.374
default costs certificate 43.165
deferred issue 43.389
final costs certificate 43.387, 390
interim costs certificates 43.381
issue 43.388
quantification of awards 18.131
costs capping 13.65, 13.71
costs protection 18.130
deemed orders 7.103
discretion to make award 18.126–18.129
history 1.107, 18.121
jurisdiction 18.123–18.125
meaning 2.09, 18.121
monies payable in lieu of costs 18.122
payments 18.136
procedure 18.132–18.135
set-off 21.14
VAT 55.14

Probate
contentious business 3.31
fees for probate work 38.31, Table 38.2, 42.07–42.10
non-contentious business 3.23, 3.32
orders for costs 7.52–7.64
Court of Appeal 7.64

Probate (*cont.*)
orders for costs (*cont.*)
probate rule 7.56–6.72
testator or beneficiaries at fault 7.53–7.55
will and third parties 7.63
reserved legal activities 3.49, 3.77
Professional conduct rules 4.29
failure to comply 57.54
Profit costs
agents 22.06–22.07, 22.14, 22.23, 35.116, 52.66
assessment of, solicitor and client 36.54
codification 49.179–49.189
costs draftspersons' fee 22.22–22.24
meaning 2.09
medical agencies 22.27
Project management *see* **Legal project management**
Promissory notes
payment by 36.24
suing for recovery of costs 40.09–40.12, 35.115
Proportionality
additional liabilities
after-the-event insurance 25.84–25.88, 54.162
success fees 25.83
bases of assessment 16.06–16.07, 16.10, 16.12, 16.54
budgeted costs 12.159, 12.170
collective proportionality *see* **Collective proportionality** 26.26–26.47
group litigation 65.91–65.92, 25.100–25.101
consumer claims 65.101
history 1.129, 1.156, 1.190, 25.04–25.14
incidence of costs, irrelevance to 6.255
management of assessments, election and 46.57–46.59
management of claims 25.20–25.24
budgeting (costs management) 12.62, 12.99–12.103, 25.22
collective proportionality *see* **Collective proportionality**
legal project management 25.23–25.24, 41.03, 41.18, 41.24, 41.45
planning 25.23–25.24
pre-action protocols 6.99
meaning 25.15–25.16
miscellaneous points (both pre-2013 and post-2013 methods)
alternative dispute resolution 25.92
appeals 25.103
appropriate use of court time 25.72
budgets 25.89
capped costs 25.90
case plan 25.96
chains of Part 20 claims 25.102
counsel's notes 25.99
discussion and correspondence between fee earners 25.98
dishonesty 25.91
financial position of the parties 25.73–25.74
high-value litigation 25.80
judicial discretion 25.70–25.71
low-value litigation 25.78–25.79
non-local solicitors 51.75
non-monetary factors 25.81
pre-action protocols 25.97
settlements 25.93–25.95
success fees 25.83
test 25.28–25.69
transitional provisions 25.17–25.19
value of the claim 25.75–25.77
VAT 25.82, 55.31
payments on account of costs 14.29
post-2013 method
District Judge Middleton's guidance 25.57–25.58, Table 25.1
factor-drive approach 25.57
factors to be taken into account 25.26–25.27, 25.29–25.30, 25.32–25.36
guidance, need for 25.59–25.62
measure of what is a proportionate amount 25.47–25.62
necessity, precedence over 25.49–25.50
test of whether costs are proportionate 25.29–25.36
pre-2013 method (*Lownds* test)
doubt, resolution of 25.43
factors to be taken into account 25.26
measure of value 25.41–25.42
measure of what is a proportionate amount 25.63–25.68
necessity, test of 25.64–25.68
test of whether costs are proportionate 25.37–25.44
preclusion by proportionality 23.47–23.48
terminology 25.02–25.03
transitional provisions 25.17–25.19
where both pre-2013 and post-2013 methods apply 25.45
value-based pricing 42.11
Protected persons
common law 60.57
enforceable until proven otherwise 60.59
generally 60.49–60.51
incapacity
contentious business agreements 60.67
deputy, authority to act 60.66
donee, authority to act 60.66
steps to deal with 60.64–60.67
incapacity, effect of 60.58–60.63
litigation friends 60.68–60.69
meaning 60.49
Mental Capacity Act 2005 60.52–60.56
necessaries 60.62
necessary services 60.63
putative termination of contract 60.60
sources of law 60.50
temporary 60.61
Provisional assessments
costs of assessment 43.229–43.238
future of 43.199
generally 43.198
jurisdiction 43.200–43.206
origins 43.198
procedure 43.207–43.228
selected courts, at 43.199

Public bodies
Booth principle 61.14
discharge of administrative function 61.07–61.15
Public law *see* **Judicial review**

QOCS *see* **Qualified one-way costs shifting (QOCS)**
Qualified one-way costs shifting (QOCS) 8.01–8.55
background 8.05–8.09
effect 8.22–8.26
exceptions
generally 8.27
mixed claims 8.52–8.55
permission not required 8.28–8.31
permission required 8.32–8.47
proceedings for financial benefit of another person 8.48–8.51
jurisdiction 8.04
meaning 2.09, 8.02
policies underpinning 8.05–8.09
retrospective effect 8.16
scope
additional claims 8.14
appeals 8.15
counterclaims 8.14
definition 8.10
mixed claims 8.12
pre-action disclosure 8.13
types of proceeding 8.11–8.15
terminology 8.03
transitional provisions 8.17–8.21
Quantum of costs between opposing parties *see* **Assessment of costs; Hourly rates**
Quantum of costs between solicitor and client
assurances about provision of services 38.81–38.85
comparators 38.08
estimates 38.43–38.79
Consumer Rights Act 2015 38.68–38.73
contractual duties 38.54
duty to provide estimates 38.44–38.75
guidance 38.49–38.52
incomplete estimates 38.79
instructions 38.55
poor estimates 38.79
practice directions 38.56
qualified estimates 38.76–38.78
revised estimates 38.74–38.75
unrealistic estimates 38.57
factors to be taken into account
adrenalin factor 38.14, 38.23–38.24
'bath-time' factor 38.14, 38.25–38.26
factors other than value 38.22–38.27
hourly rates 38.12
value charge 38.10–38.11
generally 38.01–38.03
hourly rates 38.06–38.07, 38.09–38.14
interest between solicitor and client
contentious costs 38.92
discretion 38.95–38.96
generally 38.85–38.88
judgment debts 38.93–38.94
late payment of commercial debts 38.97–38.102
non-contentious costs 38.89–38.91
methods 38.04
putative waiver of fees 38.80
shoddy work
abatement 38.36–38.37
change of solicitor 38.38–38.39
consumer protection 38.35
general rule 38.35
ombudsman 38.40
terminology 38.05
value charge 38.05
challenges to 38.17
focusing on all aspects 38.19–38.21
generally 38.15
Law Society guidance 38.18
meaning 38.05
purpose 38.16
value element
conveyancing 38.32
duplication 38.07
estates 38.31
general regressive scale 38.29
hourly rates 38.06–38.07
leasehold work 38.33
meaning 38.05
mortgage work 38.34
probate 38.31
weight to be given to value 38.28–38.34
waiver of fees 38.80
Quantum meruit 27.10
cancellation of consumer contracts 28.212
champertous agreements 30.29
defective retainers 32.66, 18.94–48.98
indemnity principle 18.91–18.99
limitation 23.87
no written retainer 18.93
repudiated retainer 18.99
retainer fails to specify basis of payment 18.93
work carried out beyond ambit of retainer 27.36
wrongful termination of retainer 27.88

Reciprocal costs orders
both parties entitled to costs 7.34–7.37
percentage orders compared 6.38
Rectification
defective contract of retainer 32.66, 32.67–32.74
Recusal of judge
documents filed in error 46.38–46.39
orders for costs 7.188
Part 36 offer 46.233, 43.316
wasted costs 9.200
Refusal to engage in ADR
early case law 6.119–6.121
generally 6.118
guidance 6.122–6.123
Halsey guidance 6.122–6.123
specific circumstances
aggressive insistence on ADR 6.140
attempts to settle, other methods 6.133
bare refusal 6.128
costs of ADR 6.134, 48.53–48.57
delay 6.136

Refusal to engage in ADR (*cont.*)
specific circumstances (*cont.*)
dispute between neighbours 6.128
failure to attend 6.128
failure to respond 6.128
lip service 6.128
merits of the case 6.130–6.132
nature of the dispute 6.129
reasonable and justifiable 6.122–6.123
reasonable prospect of success 6.137–6.139
relevance of party's response 6.126–6.128
Regional costs judge
detailed assessment, allocation 43.16–43.18
list of Table 68.2
meaning 2.09, 43.16
procedure 43.18
referral to 43.17
Relief from sanctions
indemnity basis 16.41–16.42
jurisdiction 26.50–26.52
notice of funding, failure to serve *see* **Notice of funding** 54.108–54.123, 54.130, 54.188
proportionality 26.48–26.70
purpose 26.48–26.49
statement of reasons, failure to serve *see* **Statement of reasons** 54.124–54.126, 54.130
Remuneration certificates
meaning 2.09
past use 39.02
Representation
advocates wishing to be heard on own fees 47.18–47.22
authorised persons
barristers 47.12
costs lawyers 47.13–47.16
discretion not to hear 47.17
solicitors 47.12
authority of costs practitioners 47.23–47.29
bankrupt persons 47.30–47.31
companies 47.32
expert assistants 47.10–47.11
generally 47.01–47.03
independent costs draftspersons 47.07–47.08
McKenzie friends 47.05, 47.10–47.11
notification 47.04
persons who are not authorised persons 47.05–47.11
employed costs draftspersons 47.09
general approach 47.06
independent costs draftspersons 47.07–47.08
McKenzie friends 47.05, 47.10–47.11
reserved legal activities 47.02, 47.03
Representative claims 65.116–65.122
Res judicata
cause of action estoppel 23.08–23.18
claim preclusion 23.08–23.18
issue estoppel 23.19–23.27
issue preclusion 23.19–23.27
meaning 23.07
Reserved legal activity
meaning 2.09
offences 47.03
representation 47.02
Retainers
ambit of retainer 27.8, 27.29–27.36
assignment *see* **Assignment**; **Transfer of contracts of retainer**
champerty 30.02
children 27.325
codes of conduct 27.97–27.101
companies 27.319–27.320
conditional fee agreements 27.22
defective retainers *see* **Defective retainers**
desirable provisions
ADR clause 27.337
costs recovered 27.329
deemed increase clause 27.335, 27.337
deemed signature clause 27.334
destination of interest clause 27.328
FCA declaration 27.338
force majeure 27.332
forum provision 27.330
generally 27.326
notices 27.339
severability clause 27.331
unusual costs provision 27.327
disambiguation 27.03
documentation 27.05
employees 27.324
entire contracts *see* **Entire contracts** 27.06, 27.07–27.28
executors 27.323
factual disputes 27.92–27.101
frustration 27.27–27.28
general retainers 27.21
generally 27.01–27.02
implied 27.190–27.206
implied terms *see* **Implied terms**
interim payments 27.38–27.43
interpretation of *see* **Interpretation of contracts of retainer**
joint obligations
costs sharing agreements 27.315–27.318
express 27.302
implied 27.302
plurality of debtors 27.303
limited liability partnerships 27.321
liquidators 27.323
meaning 2.09, 27.03–27.04
non-legal representatives 30.02
novation *see* **Novation**; **Transfer of contracts of retainer**
oral 27.207–27.227
partial performance 27.25, 27.26
plurality of debtors
generally 27.303, 27.304
joint instructions in joint matters 27.313–27.314
joint instructions in separate matters 27.310–27.312
nature of obligations 27.305–27.314
separate instructions in joint matters 27.309
separate instructions in separate matters 27.308
private 27.102–27.106
quantum meruit see also ***Quantum meruit*** 27.36
rectification 32.66, 32.67–32.74

sham retainers 27.217–27.227
Solicitors Code of Conduct 2007 27.62
Solicitors Code of Conduct 2011 27.63–27.66
substantial performance 27.27
suspension 27.89
termination *see* **Termination of retainers**
transfer of contracts
see also **Transfer of contracts of retainer**
generally 32.02–32.04
methods of transfer 32.05–32.41
trustees 27.323
undue influence 27.91
unincorporated associations 27.322
unlawful 27.228–27.301
codes of conduct, breaches of 27.267–27.269
conditional fee agreements 27.259
Conduct of Business Rules 27.297–27.299
consumer protection 27.271
contingency fee agreements 27.260–27.266
contracts to commit a legal wrong 27.235–27.237
damages-based agreements 27.260–27.286
discretion 27.258
insurance 27.272–27.301
morality 27.252–27.256
performance 27.246–27.251
prohibited contracts 27.238–27.245
Solicitors' Code of Conduct 2007 27.296
SRA Code of Conduct 27.295
SRA Financial Services (Scope) Rules 2001 27.291–27.293
statutory prohibition 27.229–27.234
value-based pricing, and 42.24, 42.28–42.30
waiver of rights 27.90
Revision of orders 10.08–10.26
Right to conduct litigation 3.60–3.64, 3.73, 3.74
definition 3.78
meaning 2.09
serving proceedings 3.79
Rights of audience
meaning 2.09, 3.75, 3.80
Road traffic insurers
article 75 liability 63.04, 63.05
generally 63.01–63.03
liability tree 63.03–63.04
Motor Insurance Bureau (MIB) 63.03, 63.04
statutory liability 63.04

***Sanderson* order**
generally *see* **Co-defendant orders**
meaning 2.09
Security for costs 40.100–40.105
administrators 15.96
appeals 15.12
available remedies 15.03
children 15.96
claimants 15.96
conditions
ability to pay 15.34–15.39
access to funding 15.80
address 15.40–15.42
appeals 15.50–15.51
asset sequestration 15.46–15.49
counterclaims 15.65–15.70
cross-undertakings as to damages 15.90
discretion 15.57–15.63
evasion 15.52–15.53
financial position of parties 15.76–15.79
group litigation 15.56
nominal claimants 15.43–15.45
plural litigants 15.71
primary jurisdiction 15.26–15.57
residence 15.30–15.33, 15.72–15.75
stifling the claim, possibility of 15.82–15.89
third parties 15.54–15.56
wealth as factor 15.81
counterclaims 15.10
cross liabilities 15.95
detailed assessments 15.23
disclosure 15.127–15.130
discretion 15.24, 15.25, 15.97–15.101
evidence 15.127–15.130
form of the security 15.121–15.123
generally 15.01
group litigation 15.56
human rights 15.04–15.05
interpleaders 15.14
jurisdiction 15.02–15.23
late applications 15.91–15.93
legal representatives 15.96
liquidators 15.96
litigation friends 15.96
nature of the costs 15.94
primary 15.06–15.14
procedure 15.124–15.126
quantum 15.110–15.120
reapplication for order 15.102–15.106
receivers 15.96
secondary 15.15–15.23
third parties 15.13
unless orders 15.107–15.109
unsuitable cases 15.22
variation of order 15.102–15.106
Service
appeals 45.36
meaning 2.09
methods 43.135–43.138
Part 36 offers 17.31, 17.43–17.44
Set-off
assignment 21.35
Civil Procedure Rules 21.09–21.10
contract 21.13
counsel's fees 53.27
discretion 21.21–21.42
effect of order 21.28–21.29
exercise of discretion 21.30–21.32
factors to be taken into account 21.33–21.42
form of order 21.28–21.29
scope of discretion 21.22–21.27
effect of order 21.21–21.42
foreign currency claims 21.38
funding methods 21.14–21.15
Hanak requirements 21.08
inchoate claims 21.38

Set-off (*cont.*)
insolvency 21.34
Intellectual Property Enterprise Court 50.336
interests of justice 21.37
issues-based orders 21.11
jurisdictional basis
common law 21.05
equity 21.05
inherent jurisdiction 21.06
statutory basis 21.05–21.06
lack of mutuality 21.37
legal expenses insurance 21.36
overview 21.03–21.04
Part 36 offers 21.12
Part 47 offers 43.365
payments on account 14.12
procedure 21.16–21.20
third parties 21.40
time-barred claims 21.39
unpaid solicitors 21.41–21.42
unquantified claims 21.38
Setting aside
consent orders 10.27
contentious business agreement 27.173
default costs certificate 43.157–43.164
Settlements
assessment of costs 49.40
code-sets 49.40
Several liability
costs debtors 19.30
meaning 2.09, 19.08
Severance
interpretation of retainer 31.56
Skeleton arguments
appeals 45.47–45.48
bills of costs 49.28, 49.39, 49.41
counsel's fees 53.54, 53.61, 53.111–53.112, 53.114
statements of costs 44.27
Slip rule
correct of orders 10.05–10.07
Small claims track
admissible offers 6.221–6.226
applicability of restriction 50.371–50.392
discretionary application of limit 50.392–50.399
generally 50.369, 50.370
unreasonable behaviour 50.400–50.403
Solicitor-and-client assessments
assessment hearing 36.96–36.112
attendance 36.104
breakdown of costs 36.99
cash account 36.99
client papers and privilege 36.107–36.108
court order 36.98
detailed breakdown of costs 36.99
directions 36.97
disputes 36.101
fee notes 36.100
filing of papers 36.106
guidance 36.96
Precedent L 36.98
private hearings 36.109–36.110
privilege 36.107–36.108
procedure after hearing 36.111–36.112
request for hearing 36.102–36.103
right to be heard 36.104
bringing a claim/application 36.39–36.41
challenging contentious business agreements 36.43
disputed retainers 36.42–36.45
formalities 36.46
informal means, applications by 36.46
interpretation of retainers 36.42–36.45
venue 36.47–36.50
costs of detailed assessment
costs already assessed and paid 36.69
discounted bills 36.62
excluded items 36.66–36.67
generally 36.57–36.58
gross sum bills 36.64
more than one solicitor's costs 36.68
multiple bills 36.65
one-fifth rule, generally 36.59–36.70
Part 36 offers 36.77
special circumstances 36.71–36.76
VAT 36.70
disbursements 36.62
discretion of court 36.31
final costs certificates 36.113–36.116
generally 36.01–36.02
hearing of application 36.52
interim payment and interim costs certificates 36.113–36.116
one month, meaning of 36.29
order for an assessment 36.51
party chargeable, on application of 36.03
as of right 36.30
discretion of court 36.31
effluxion of time, effect of 36.04
one month and 12 months 36.29
'party chargeable with bill'
payments, meaning *see* **Statute bills** 36.18–36.28
right to assessment 36.30
special circumstances 36.32–36.38
statutory provisions 36.03
time barred 36.05–36.06
time of delivery *see* **Statute bills** 36.14–36.17, 36.29
'party chargeable', meaning 36.07–36.13
group litigation 36.10
joint representatives 36.12
joint retainers 36.11
professional clients 36.09
quantification of claim against assets 36.13
trustees 36.09, 36.12
procedural issues, other 36.39–36.41
filing of papers 36.107–36.108
hearing 36.96–36.112
non-attendance 36.78
points of dispute 36.101
post-hearing procedure 36.111–36.112
private hearings 36.109–36.110
request for hearing 36.102–36.103

stay of detailed assessment 36.53
variation of documents 36.105
right to assessment 36.30
scope of assessment 36.54–36.56
solicitor, on application of 36.03
special circumstances 36.33–36.37
appeals in respect of 36.38
case examples (application for assessment) 36.36
case examples (costs of assessment) 36.76
generally (application for assessment) 36.32–36.38
generally (costs of assessment) 36.71–36.76
third parties, on application of 36.79–36.95
administrators 36.79
any person interested in the property 36.95
applications 36.86–36.90
claims for account 36.84
declarations 36.85
disallowed items 36.85
effect of order 36.85
executors 36.79
generally 36.35
liability disputed 36.79
overpayments 36.85
person other than the party chargeable with the bill 36.91–36.94
reasonableness of costs 36.79
refunds 36.85
relevant law 36.81–36.83
trustees 36.79
time limits 36.04–36.06
trustees 36.09, 36.12
12 months, meaning of 36.29
winding up 16.17

Solicitors' charging orders
see **Charging orders**

Solicitors' Code of Conduct 2007 4.14

Solicitors' Code of Conduct
see also **SRA Code of Conduct 2011**

Solicitors Regulation Authority
generally 39.22
governance 39.23

Solicitors' rights and remedies
see also **Charging orders; Lien**
bankruptcy 40.130–40.132
equitable interference
bona fide negotiations 40.119
discretion 40.111–40.113
fraud by client 40.114
generally 40.106–40.107
jurisdiction 40.108–40.110
notice given to paying party 40.115–40.118
procedure 40.120
generally 40.01
payments on account 40.31–40.32
security for costs 40.100–40.105
statutory demands 40.121–40.129
suing for recovery of costs 40.02–40.30
abuse of process 40.24
claim for assessment by client 40.07–40.08
contentious work 40.18–40.19
declarations 40.16
default judgment 40.24–40.26
disclosure 40.14
dishonoured cheques 40.09–40.12
evidence 40.14
general principles 40.04
non-contentious work 40.17
one-month period after delivery, need for 40.05–40.06
procedure 40.15
promissory notes 40.09–40.12
striking out 40.27–40.30
summary judgment 40.20–40.23
venue 40.013
withdrawal of services 40.33–40.35

Sources of legal information and law
books 4.66–4.67
case law 4.03–4.05
costs law 4.02–4.13
court guides 4.64
dictionaries 4.67
Hansard 4.73–4.76
learned journals 4.65
Parliamentary/Government papers
business papers 4.70–4.72
Command papers 4.78–4.80
consultation papers 4.81
Hansard 4.73–4.76
meaning 4.69
papers presented to Parliament 4.77–4.81
usefulness 4.68
precedents 4.06
statutory interpretation 4.08–4.13

SRA Code of Conduct 2011
accounting rules 4.29–4.30
breach 4.18–4.28
discretion 4.22, 4.22–4.23, 4.23
effect 4.15
factors affecting breach decisions 4.26–4.28
financial rules 4.29–4.30
guidance notes 4.31
history of rules 4.14
implied statutory prohibition 4.19–4.21
indicative behaviours 4.16
jurisdiction 4.15
motive for breach 4.26
'outcomes-focused regulation' 4.16, 4.17
power to make codes 4.15
present code 4.14
prohibition 4.19
public policy 4.18, 4.21, 4.25
timing 4.24
vires 4.15

Standard basis
see also **Bases of assessment**
indemnity basis distinguished 16.10–16.12
test 16.05

Statements of case
assessment of costs 49.27, 49.28

Statement of reasons
failure to serve and relief from sanctions 54.126, 54.130
requirements 54.12–54.125

Statute bills
Chamberlain bills 36.15–36.16
completeness, specific circumstances
client's own knowledge 35.70
computer printouts 35.65
fairness, client able to judge 35.63
'for professional services' 35.67
intended purpose 35.69
numerous errors 35.64
omission of narrative by implied agreement 35.66
several courts 35.68
superfluous information 35.71
delivery of 35.85–35.86
delivery, specific circumstances
agents, employees, etc 35.86
Chamberlain bills 35.86
more than one client 35.86
new solicitors 35.86
qualified bills 35.86
series of invoices 35.86
unintended delivery 35.86
delivery, time of
generally 36.14–36.17
series of invoices 36.15–36.16
winding up 36.17
detailed bills
meaning 35.40
disbursements, and 35.116–35.119
distinguished from other types of invoice *see* **Interim invoices**
errors in 35.87–35.98
failure to comply with requirements of
loss of client's protection 35.115
payment 35.112
set-off 35.114
statutory demand 35.113
unable to bring proceedings 35.109–35.111
gross sum bills *see* **Gross sum bills**
interim invoices on account *see* **Interim invoices** 35.06–35.09
interim statute bills *see* **Interim statute bills** 2.09
meaning 35.06–35.09
invoices, as 35.04
meaning 2.09
party chargeable with 36.07–36.13
payment 36.18–36.28
charges and mortgages 36.27
client unaware 36.22
conditions for 36.18
deduction 36.22
defective bill 35.112, 36.19–36.21
negotiable instruments 36.24
no bill 36.19–36.21
partial payment 36.23
prior to delivery 36.25–36.26
putative compromise 36.28
power to order delivery 35.120–35.129
request for detailed breakdown 35.99–35.108
requirements 35.42–35.62
delivery 35.85–35.86
reasonably complete 35.47–35.51
signature 35.72–35.84
sufficiency of narrative 35.52–35.62
series of bills 36.15–36.16
signature, specific circumstances 35.72–35.84
accompanying correspondence 35.82–35.83
conduct 35.84
electronic signatures 35.76–35.75
printed signatures 35.80–35.81
rubber stamps 35.80–35.81
substitution 35.87–35.98
variation 36.105
vary, power to 35.87–35.98
withdrawal of bills 35.90–35.98
by consent 35.91
reservation of right 35.90
with permission of court 35.90–35.98
Statutory demands 43.414
solicitors' rights and remedies 40.121–40.129
Statutory fetters on costs 34.160–34.163
Success and the incidence of costs
cases with more than one issue 6.47
commercial litigation 6.65–6.67
effect of costs on 6.73
effect on costs 6.71
equal degrees of success 6.68
general rule 6.42–6.75
many issues 6.50–6.51
meaning 6.45
measure of 6.46
nominal damages 6.69–6.71
one predominant issue 6.48–6.49
partial 6.74
preservation of success 6.72
primary and secondary cases 6.52
starting points 6.54–6.61
Welamson doctrine 6.75
Success fees
alternative means of funding *see* **Alternative means of funding** 54.150, 54.191–54.206
assessment of amount *see also below* 'factors other than risk, relevance of' and 'risk, relevance and types of'
delay in payment, relevance of 54.101–54.104
disbursements, relevance of 54.105–54.107
multi-stage success fees 54.59–54.63
prematurity, relevance of 54.64–54.66
'ready reckoner' Table 68.12
single-stage success fee (ordinary success fees) 54.56–54.58
two-stage success fees (adaptive success fees) 54.59–54.63
types of success fee 54.56–54.63
budgets and success fees 54.49
costs capping orders 13.38
costs lawyers and costs draftspersons 54.48
differential rates 54.47
factors other than risk, relevance of
carrying disbursements (liability for disbursements) 54.105-54.108
delay in payment 54.101–54.104, Table 54.1
fixed success fees

employers' liability claims 50.118–50.130
employers' liability disease claims 50.131–50.149
generally 50.102–50.149
history 50.19–50.20
road traffic accident claims 50.105–50.117
generally 54.43
jurisdiction
criminal matters 54.10
enforceable agreement 54.06
family matters 54.10
generally 54.05
irrecoverability 54.07
quasi-criminal matters 54.10
recoverability 54.08
saving provisions 54.08–54.10
meaning 2.09
notice of funding *see* **Notice of funding**
percentage increase 2.09, 54.55
retrospective recovery 54.44–54.46
revision of percentage increase 54.46
risk, relevance and types of
categorisation of risk 54.70
CFA Lites 54.94–54.98
discounted conditional fee agreements 54.86
enforcement risk 54.98
general risk 54.71–54.80
liability risk 54.81–54.86
overview 54.67–54.70
quantum risk 54.87–54.93
recovery risk 54.94–54.97
'risk premiums' 54.99
solicitor-and-client issues 54.51–54.53
statement of reasons *see* **Statement of reasons**
transfer of liabilities from private retainer 54.46
Suing for recovery of costs
abuse of process 40.24
claim for assessment by client 40.07–40.08
contentious costs 40.18–40.19
declarations 40.16
default judgment 40.24–40.26
disclosure 40.14
dishonoured cheques 40.09–40.12
evidence 40.14
general principles 40.04
non-contentious work 40.17
one-month period after delivery 40.05–40.06
procedure 40.15
promissory notes 40.09–40.12
striking out 40.27–40.30
venue 40.13
Summary assessment
additional liabilities 44.37–44.42
appeals 45.27
children, costs payable by or to 60.36, 60.68
compromise 44.13
discretion not to carry out assessment
challenge to indemnity principle 44.21
complex objections 44.20
conditional fee agreements 44.22
delay 44.15–44.16
fetter, no 44.24
generally 44.14
lack of time 44.15–44.16
litigants in person 44.23
substantial costs 44.18
substantial objections 44.19
entitlement to a summary assessment 44.03–44.13
children 44.12
discretion to carry out assessment 44.08–44.11
exceptions to the general rule 44.12
general rule 44.04–44.05
legally aided party 44.12
mortgagees 44.12, 66.28
protected persons 44.12
summary of specific provisions 44.06–44.07
generally 44.01–44.02
Intellectual Property Enterprise Court 44.05, 50.315, 50.336–50.338
meaning 44.02
power to carry out assessment 44.03
procedure
additional liabilities 44.37–44.42
children 50.39–50.48
failure by party to serve statement of costs 44.28–44.32
generally 44.25–44.27
remittal of assessments 44.33–44.36

Task codes
see also **Activity codes; Phase codes**
background 49.22
EW-UTBMS (J-Code) task codes 49.178, 49.182
generally 49.21–49.23
tasks codes under the CPR
advocacy (T21) 49.39
amendment of statement of case (T7) 49.28
budgeting (T34–T36) 49.46
case management conference (T8) 49.29
costs assessment (T38–T41) 49.49
costs management conference (T37) 49.47
factual investigation (T1) 49.25, 49.26
funding (T33) 49.43
general work regarding preparation for trial (T20) 49.37
inspection of other side's disclosure (T12) 49.31
interim applications (T26–T32) 49.42
issue and service (T4) 49.28
joint expert evidence (T17) 49.35
judgment and post-trial activity (T23) 49.39
legal investigation (T2) 49.25
mediation (T24) 49.40
obtaining and reviewing documents (T10) 49.31
other party(s) expert evidence (T16) 49.35
other settlement matters (T25) 49.40
own expert evidence (T15) 49.35
pre-action protocol work (T3) 49.25, 49.26
pre-trial review (T18) 49.36
preparation of disclosure report and proposal (T9) 49.31
preparation of trial bundle (T19) 49.37
preparing and serving disclosure lists (T11) 49.31
requests for further information (T6) 49.28

Task codes (*cont.*)
tasks codes under the CPR (*cont.*)
review of statement of case (T5) 49.28
reviewing other party(s) witness statements (T14) 49.33
statements of case (T4) 49.28
support of advocated (T22) 49.39
taking, preparing and finalising witness statements (T13) 49.33
Termination of retainers
circumstances 27.68
client, by 27.69
death 27.77–27.78
effect 27.84–27.86
generally 27.67
insolvency 27.82–27.83
legal services provider, by 27.70–27.75
loss of capacity 27.79–27.81
superseding retainer 27.76
wrongful termination 27.87–27.88
Third-party funding *see* **Litigation funding**
Tomlin orders 7.70–7.79
costs of drafting Table 12.1
detailed assessments 43.246
effect of order 7.75–7.79
form of order 7.71–7.74
formalities 6.15
meaning 7.70
Part 36 offers 17.45
wasted costs 9.166
Top-up insurance 34.38–34.40, 54.140, 54.176–54.177
Transfer of contracts of retainer
assignment (generally) *see* **Assignment**
benefits and rights already accrued 32.12
future property and conditional fee agreements 32.13–32.15
personal contracts, relevance of 32.17–32.18
right to be paid for work already carried out 32.12, 32.16
contractual bars to assignment (in retainers) 32.33–32.37
generally 32.02–32.04
Jenkins assignments 32.06, 32.20–32.23, 32.41
meaning 32.08
methods of 32.05
need for 32.02–32.03
novation 32.34–32.41
instructions, effect of giving 32.25–32.27
meaning 32.34
pre-2013 conditional fee agreements 32.38
types 32.35
privity 32.09–32.11
right to be paid for work yet to be done 32.19
conditional benefit principle, non-availability of 32.24
instructions, effect of giving 32.25–32.27
putative assignment of obligations and burdens 32.20–32.23
summary 32.41
Travelling expenses
activity code 49.76–49.80
attend on client, travelling to 49.77
counsel, travelling expenses of 53.104
disbursements 3.17, 52.81–52.84
expert witnesses 52.39
factual witnesses 52.56
group litigation 65.101
private car 49.80
public transport 49.80
saving other costs 49.78
technology rendering travel unnecessary 49.79
Trusts and trustees
assessment of trustees' costs 66.75–66.77
basis 16.14, 66.36, 66.75
monies disbursed prior to appointment 66.78
more than one trustee 66.79
upon application by beneficiaries *see* **Solicitor-and client-assessments,** 'third parties'
beneficiaries, costs incurred by 66.45
champerty 30.42–30.43
costs against trustees 66.46–66.55
beneficiary, adverse claim brought by 66.50–66.55
beneficiary, amicable claim brought by 66.49
trustee, amicable claim brought by 66.48
costs capping 66.43
costs incurred by trustees 66.31, 66.36–66.42
appeals 66.42
denial of costs 66.38–66.39
disputed trusts 66.40–66.41
errors as to status 66.40–66.41
generally 66.35
properly incurred costs 66.32–66.33
trust deeds and entitlement to costs 66.31—66.33
costs management (budgeting) 66.44
costs payable out of fund 66.80–66.84
procedure 66.80–66.84
statute barred 23.97, 23.111
under a trust deed 66.31—66.33
fund, definition 2.09
lien 40.52–50.43
pre-emptive orders 66.56–66.74
appeals 66.66
conduct 66.66
costs of application 66.67
disputed trusts 66.66
justice of the matter 66.65
likely costs order 66.64
merits of legislation 66.63
pensions funds 66.66
principles of assessment 66.75–66.77
procedure 66.68–66.74
representative trustees 66.66
trustees seeking the role 66.66
retainers with trustees 27.82, 27.323, 32.04, 66.37
security for costs 15.96
trust disputes, types of 66.46–66.55
Buckton category (1): amicable by trustee 66.48
Buckton category (2): amicable by other 66.49
Buckton category (3): adverse 66.50
Turner & Co v Palomo **qualifications (non-statutory assessments)** 39.03–39.07

Undue influence
aggressive commercial practices 28.124–28.126
assessment of costs 37.44
defective retainers 32.43–32.55
generally
actual undue influence 32.46–32.48
effect 32.50–32.51
presumed undue influence 32.46–32.48
probate rule 7.62
retainers
custom and prior dealings 31.66
ordinary motives in changing a retainer 32.49
payment of fees, request for 32.52
success fees, and 32.53, 32.57, 54.46
withholding information 27.91
solicitors security for costs 40.102
without prejudice privilege 6.218
Unfair terms
Consumer Rights Act 2015, Part 2 28.40–28.44, 37.34–37.35
assessment of fees, and 37.34
effect of unfair term/notice 28.42
greylist 28.43–28.44
legislative background 28.23
test of unfairness 28.41
interpretation of contracts of retainer 27.130
mandatory ADR, and 27.337, 28.152
Unfair Contract Terms Act 1977 28.159–28.162
Unfair Terms in Consumer Contracts Regulations 1999 28.149–28.155
effect of a term being unfair 28.154
mandatory arbitration 28.152
request for payment of fee, mere request 32.52
small print 28.152
termination at will 28.152
transfer of control 28.152
unfair accounting 28.152
Unless orders
commencement of detailed assessment, delay 43.96–43.102
CLS funded cases 43.99
discretion 43.100–43.102
interest, interaction with 43.105–43.107
jurisdiction 43.96
Lord Chancellor funded cases 43.99
relief 43.103–43.104
without notice applications 43.98
delay amounting to misconduct, and 23.74
discretion generally 43.100
payments on account of costs, delay in making 14.20
relief from sanctions 26.49, 26.64, 43.103–43.104
requests for assessment, delay 43.191–43.192
security for costs, and 15.107–15.109

Value added tax (VAT)
chargeable by receiving party's lawyers, whether 55.05
complexity of law 55.03
dental records 55.23–55.24
disbursements 55.02, 55.15–55.21
dispute resolution 55.27
expenses 55.15–55.21
generally 55.01
indemnities 55.28
input tax 55.02
medical agencies 55.25
medical records 55.23–55.25
medical records and agency fees 52.72
opposing parties 55.26–55.32
output tax
liability 55.04–55.21
meaning 55.02
pro bono work 55.14
proportionality 55.31
rate changes 43.391
rates
changes to the rate of VAT 55.33–55.44
exempt rating 55.11
overview 55.12
place where person belongs 55.12
pro bono work 55.14
reduced rate 55.11
resolution of ratings disputes 55.13
standard rates 55.11
zero rating 55.11
reasonableness 55.02, 55.29–55.30
relevant CPR provisions 55.45
subrogation 55.28
tax points
actual tax points 55.06
basic tax points 55.06
time when due
actual tax points 55.06
barristers 55.08
basic tax points 55.06
other legal representatives 55.09
solicitors 55.07
Value-based pricing
advantages 42.19–42.23
alternative fee agreements 42.28
analytics 42.39–42.42
chief value officer (CVO) 42.37–42.38
client discussions 42.24
client perspective 42.25
costs-plus pricing, distinguished from 42.09–42.15
disadvantages 42.19–42.23
fee structures 42.28–42.30
generally 42.02–42.03
legal project management 42.24, 42.31–42.34
meaning 42.16–42.18
method 42.24
options, pricing 42.24
post-project reviews 42.35–42.36
price-led costing 42.24
reporting 42.39–42.42
retainers 42.24, 42.28–42.30
service levels 42.26–42.27
state of the market 42.05–42.08
strategies for pricing 42.39–42.42
theories of value
labour theory of value 42.04
subjective theory of value 42.04
value element, distinguished from 38.13, 38.31

Waiver
fees, conditional waiver of 29.09–29.13
fees, putative waiver of 18.82, 38.80, 39.21
interpretation of retainer, omitted terms 31.50
lien, waiver of 40.76–40.78, 40.96
Part 36 offers, waiver of defects 17.66
privilege, waiver of 36.107–36.108, 46.56, 46.60–46.69
retainers, waiver or rights under 27.90
Warrant of execution 43.414
Wasted costs
causation 9.164–9.168
costs of application 9.221
discretion 9.119–9.127
enquiry, costs of 9.120–9.122
generally 9.119
proportionality 9.120–9.122
public funding, relevance of 9.127
status of persons involved 9.125–9.126
summary nature of jurisdiction 9.123–9.124
evidential issues 9.128–9.140
admissibility of judicial findings 9.139, 9.140
burden of proof 9.129–9.131
fact finding 9.139
inferences 9.132–9.138
privilege 9.132–9.138
generally 9.93–9.94
jurisdiction 9.95–9.140
applicant, need to be a party 9.106–9.107
compromised proceedings 9.116
general costs orders, and 9.115
issued proceedings, requirement for 9.111
own legal representative, application against 9.105
pre-proceedings work 9.112–9.114
relationship with other powers 9.98
rules of court (detailed assessments) 9.100–9.102
rules of court (substantive litigation) 9.99
status of person against whom order sought 9.108–9.110
meaning 2.09
overrunning trial 9.193
procedure 9.197–9.221
ancillary proceedings 9.217
detail of costs claims 9.220
initiation of enquiry 9.103–9.104
notice, need to give adequate 9.218
particulars, need to give adequate 9.213–9.216
settled applications 9.219
timing 9.205–9.212
two stages 9.201–9.204
quantum 9.194–9.196
standard of conduct 9.141, 9.142
impropriety 9.141–9.145
negligence 9.149–9.158
unreasonableness 9.146–9.148
types of conduct and specific circumstances 9.169–9.193
abusive proceedings 9.170
advice, failure to take 9.163
counsel, sheltering behind 9.159–9.161
court, failure to liaise with 9.175
delay, unacceptable 9.189
disclosure, failure to give 9.181
evidence, advancing incorrect 9.180
experts, failure to liaise with 9.176
experts, relevance of reliance on 9.162
frivolous proceedings 9.171
hearings, non-attendance 9.191
hopeless cases 9.153–9.157
incapacity, failure to realise client's 9.185
issues drawn to party's attention, failure to heed 9.179
instructions, absence of, etc 9.186, 9.187
new points raised at late stage 9.192
notices, failure to serve 9.190
opponents, failure to assist 9.178
opponents, failure to liaise with 9.177
pointless proceedings 9.173
preparation, failure to carry out 9.174
specialist proceedings 9.183
time limits, failure to observe 9.188
vexatious proceedings 9.172
witnesses, incredible 9.182
wrong proceedings 9.184
***Welamson* doctrine**
meaning 6.75
Without prejudice
admissible offers 6.207, 6.213–6.218
meaning 2.09
mediation 48.43
Witness expenses
conduct money 52.49–52.55
factual witnesses 52.47–52.59
litigants in person 59.34
professional witnesses 52.58–52.59
Witness statements
assessment of costs 49.32–49.33
code-sets 49.32–49.33
Women
slander of, costs 58.03
Work done by non-lawyers 3.92–3.100
agents acting on instruction 22.08–22.20
conditional fee agreements, and 29.198–29.202
counsel 3.100
experts on the law of costs 3.95–3.96
experts other than on the law of costs 3.98, 52.10–52.54
counsel acting without proper instructions 3.100
litigants in person *see* **Litigants in person**
McKenzie friends 3.100
managerial time 3.100
non-legal staff, employed by litigant 18.115–18.120
small claims track 3.100
Written notifications
see also **Interim invoices**
generally 35.12, 35.23, 35.37–35.38
payment, and 35.112

Phases, tasks and activities for purposes of the electronic bill of costs

P	Phases	T	Tasks
1	*Initial and Pre-Action Protocol Work*	1	Factual investigation
		2	Legal investigation
		3	Pre-action protocol (or similar) work
2	*Issue / Statements of Case*	4	Issue and Serve Proceedings and Preparation of Statement(s) of Case
		5	Review of Other Party(s)' Statements of Case
		6	Requests for Further Information
		7	Amendment of Statements of Case
3	*Case Management Conference*	8	Case Management Conference
4	*Disclosure*	9	Preparation of the disclosure report and the disclosure proposal
		10	Obtaining and reviewing documents
		11	Preparing and serving disclosure lists
		12	Inspection and review of the other side's disclosure for work undertaken after exchange of disclosure lists.
5	*Witness statements*	13	Taking, preparing and finalising witness statement(s)
		14	Reviewing Other Party(s)' witness statement(s)
6	*Expert reports*	15	Own expert evidence
		16	Other Party(s)' expert evidence
		17	Joint expert evidence
7	*Pre-Trial Review*	18	Pre-Trial Review
8	*Trial preparation*	19	Preparation of trial bundles
		20	General work regarding preparation for trial
9	*Trial*	21	Advocacy
		22	Support of advocates
		23	Judgment and post-trial activity
10	*ADR / Settlement*	24	Mediation
		25	Other Settlement Matters
11	*Interim Applications and Hearings (Interlocutory Applications)*	26	Applications relating to originating process or Statement of Case or for default or summary judgment
		27	Applications for an injunction or committal
		28	Applications for disclosure or Further Information
		29	Applications concerning evidence
		30	Applications relating to Costs alone
		31	Permission applications
		32	Other applications
12	*Funding*	33	Funding
13	*Budgeting incl. costs estimates*	34	Budgeting—own side's costs
		35	Budgeting—Precedent H
		36	Budgeting—between the parties
14	*Costs Management Hearing*	37	Costs Management Hearing
15	*Costs Assessment*	38	Preparing costs claim
		39	Points of dispute, Replies and Negotiations
		40	Hearings
		41	Post Assessment Work (excluding Hearings)